A Regency Reference Library Book

The NIV Exhaustive Concordance

Edward W. Goodrick &
John R. Kohlenberger III
Donald L. Potts & James A. Swanson,
Associate Editors

Zondervan Publishing House
A Subsidiary of HarperCollinsPublishers
Grand Rapids, Michigan

THE NIV EXHAUSTIVE CONCORDANCE
Copyright © 1990 by The Zondervan Corporation

Requests for information should be addressed to:
Zondervan Publishing House
Grand Rapids, Michigan 49530

Zondervan Publishing House is a subsidiary of Harper Collins Publishers

Library of Congress Cataloging in Publication Data
Goodrick, Edward W., 1913–
   The NIV exhaustive concordance / Edward W. Goodrick,
John R. Kohlenberger III.
     p. cm.
   ISBN 0-310-43690-7
   1. Bible—Concordances, English—New International. 2. Hebrew language—
Dictionaries—English. 3. Aramaic language—Dictionaries—English. 4. Greek
language. Biblical—Dictionaries—English.
I. Kohlenberger, John R. II. Title.
BS425.G62 1990
220.5'208—dc20
                               90-41517
                                CIP

Printed in the United States of America

96 97 98 99 00 / DW / 15 14 13 12 11 10 9 8 7 6

This edition is printed on acid-free paper and meets the American National Standards
Institute Z39.48 standard.

CONTENTS

PREFACE

A Brief History of the NIV Concordance Project

The King James Version was published in 1611. Its first multilingual concordance, Robert Young's *Analytical Concordance to the Bible*, appeared 268 years later. It took forty years of manual labor—including three years of typesetting! In 1894, James Strong's *Exhaustive Concordance to the Bible* joined Young's. It too involved nearly three decades of labor. The Revised Standard Version was completed in 1952, and its first multilingual concordance was issued in 1988: *Eerdmans' Analytical Concordance to the Revised Standard Version*, edited by Richard E. Whitaker. The New American Standard was published in 1971. *The New American Standard Exhaustive Concordance of the Bible* (Holman) appeared in 1981, a project that involved more than ten years and seventy contributors under the general editorship of Robert L. Thomas. *The NIV Exhaustive Concordance* now joins these multilingual concordances after seven years of labor on the part of two full-time editors, two part-time associate editors, and two consulting computer analysts.

The NIV Exhaustive Concordance is in fact the fourth to be produced by The NIV Concordance Project. Within two years of its inception in October of 1979, and just three years after the release of the New International Version itself, the Project created *The NIV Complete Concordance* (Zondervan, 1981). The following year, 1982, saw the release of *The NIV Handy Concordance*, which is also printed in millions of NIV Bibles as the NIV "Mini" or "Standard" Concordance. (Anglicized Editions of these two *Concordances* were prepared and published by Hodder and Stoughton in 1983 and 1985, respectively.) A further abridgement, known in-house as the NIV "Micro" Concordance, was also made in 1982 and is published only in NIV Bibles.

Work on *The NIV Exhaustive Concordance* began in 1983, pairing editors Edward W. Goodrick and John R. Kohlenberger III with computer analysts Dennis B. Thomas and Barbara Perz. Proofreaders James Swanson and Donald Potts put in so many hours on the project that they were named associate editors. The analysts developed software that would assist the editors to manually interrelate or "match up" the NIV to the Hebrew, Aramaic, and Greek originals. The primary focus of this "match-up" process was on the identification of the lexical or root form of each Hebrew, Aramaic, and Greek word and describing the interrelation of each word of the original with each word of the NIV. The "match-up" process and its several levels of proofreading took six years—from 1983 through 1989.

The database that resulted from this process contains nearly 900,000 lines, each of which has five fields of data. Thus, the database contains nearly 4,500,000 items of information that required at least 10 million editorial decisions. This database, dubbed the "Portland Index" after its place of origin, can be read in either the order of the NIV or the order of the original languages. It serves as the basis for this concordance, for the computer program the **NIV**^{PC} (Zondervan Electronic Publishing, 1989), and for all future concordances and indexes to the NIV planned by Zondervan and The NIV Concordance Project.

The *Concordance* was typeset by John R. Kohlenberger III, using Xerox Ventura Publisher 2.0 and WordPerfect 5.0, and is perhaps the largest and most complex book yet produced by desktop publishing technology. The typesetting process, from first proofs to camera-ready copy, took only ten weeks.

ACKNOWLEDGMENTS

So many people have encouraged us by word and with prayer over the past decade that we cannot possibly begin to thank you all. But the authors do want to specially acknowledge those who have had direct involvement in the planning, shaping and production of this concordance.

Bob De Vries, former publisher of Zondervan, entrusted this project to two unknown educators from Oregon and never wavered in his support. Paul Hillman, former president of Zondervan Publishing House, was also supportive and sensitive to our needs.

Stan Gundry, General Manager, Zondervan Publishing House, and Publisher, Academic and Professional Books, was directly in charge of this project throughout its history. He was always there to make decisions and to provide encouragement and support. Editor Ed van der Maas was close to the project for its last three years and personally worked through its final marathon typesetting sessions. The corporate management at Zondervan, especially Jim Buick and Bruce Ryskamp, showed great interest and support.

John Van Diest, publisher of Multnomah Press, saw the value of the project from the beginning and encouraged us to pursue it.

Bob Lind and Dennis Thomas, formerly of Control Data, were introduced to us by Dale Benoit and helped get the project underway. Rolf Engelbrecht provided creative input for the design of the original software. Dennis Thomas and Barbara Perz developed original software for all phases of the concordance project.

Jim Swanson began as a proofreader for both the New and Old Testament materials but developed into an associate editor greatly responsible for the integrity of the concordance database. He also did the lion's share of the work on the KJV cross-references and on the indexes to Strong's numbering system. Don Potts, also an associate editor, spent many long hours helping to correct the New Testament data and was instrumental in the design of the concordance.

Drs. Ronald Youngblood and Walter Wessel of Bethel Seminary West interacted with our text-critical questions. However, we assume full responsibility for the text represented in the concordance.

Jan Goodrick graciously tolerated the invasion of her home by the disruptive activities of the concordance gang.

Rex Koivisto of Multnomah School of the Bible helped significantly with the Greek vocabulary lists. Hodder and Stoughton provided preliminary materials comparing the North American and Anglicized editions of the NIV. Carolyn Kohlenberger compared the two editions in their entirety to develop the exhaustive lists of spelling and word differences. She also helped complete the NIV related-word list and the KJV cross-references.

Ed Smith provided technical proofreading and helped complete the Hebrew transliterations. Laura Weller read every heading and context line of the main concordance and with amazingly good humor found many intentional and unintentional errors.

Larry and Cyndi Stone and Aaron Jarrard of OmniTek Computers in Portland, Oregon provided invaluable technical assistance and allowed us to experiment endlessly with their hardware and software. Bob Palioca, chief executive officer of Kethiv Technologies, also of Portland, provided counsel and the use of equipment without reserve.

Mark Hunt, John J. Hughes, and Jeffrey William Gillette of Zondervan Electronic Publishing supplied us with an early release of their Scripture Fonts software, designed by Ronald Allen Simkins, which was used to produce the Hebrew, Aramaic, and Greek characters in the biblical-language index-lexicons.

The staff of Multnomah Graphics, particularly its director Eric Weber and typesetter Brian Davis, provided us 24-hour access to their offices and equipment for two long weeks in June.

DEDICATION

This concordance is dedicated to our wives and children
who for so many years endured so much with love, patience, and support.

To the memory of Gwen Goodrick.
To Janet Goodrick, John Goodrick, Cynthia Goodrick Parkhurst,
Lynda Goodrick Bock, and James Goodrick.

To Carolyn Kohlenberger.
To Sarah Kohlenberger and Joshua Kohlenberger.

INTRODUCTION

A concordance is an index to a book. It is usually arranged in alphabetical order and shows the location of each word in the book. In addition, it often supplies several words of the context in which each word is found.

There are two kinds of Bible concordances for the nonspecialist: those that deal only with the English text of the Bible version on which they are based, and those that also deal with the Hebrew, Aramaic, and Greek texts from which the Bible version was translated.

Examples of English-only concordances are *Cruden's Complete Concordance* for the King James Version and the *NIV Complete Concordance*. The best-known examples of multilingual concordances are Young's *Analytical Concordance* and Strong's *Exhaustive Concordance*, both based on the King James Version.

An *analytical* concordance is organized in English alphabetical order and shows a complete index of all the different words of a given translation (with the exception of the most common articles, conjunctions, prepositions, and pronouns, such as *a, and, to,* and *he*). Each entry is subdivided according to the Hebrew, Aramaic, or Greek words that underlie the English. Each reference in these subdivisions is listed with a brief context. The analytical concordance also contains index-lexicons of biblical-language vocabulary, showing the various English words that translate them.

An *exhaustive* concordance by definition should contain every reference to every word of the Bible version on which it is based. This is true of Strong's *Exhaustive Concordance to the Bible* (but not of Thomas's *New American Standard Exhaustive Concordance of the Bible*, which did not index the most common articles, conjunctions, prepositions, and pronouns). An exhaustive concordance is organized in English alphabetical order, indexes every word of the Bible, and lists every single biblical reference in which that word appears. For all but the most common words, a context is also given

with each reference. (In Strong's work, the more common words are exhaustively indexed but without contexts.) Unlike the analytical concordance, an exhaustive concordance lists the references for each English word in biblical order, from Genesis to Revelation.

In Strong's *Concordance* and the NAS *Concordance*, the relationship of the English to the originals is indicated by a numbering system that was originally devised for Strong's concordance. Strong made a list of the Hebrew and "Chaldee" (Aramaic) words used in the Old Testament and of the Greek words used in the New. To each word he assigned a number. This number appears at the end of each context line to indicate the word the English translates. By consulting the dictionaries in the back of these exhaustive concordances, the user can match numbers in order to identify the biblical word, to see its "root" definition, and to find its range of translation in the English Bible.

The *NIVEC* adopts the simple format of the exhaustive concordance for the main concordance. Like Strong's, it is truly exhaustive, indexing even the most frequent articles, conjunctions, prepositions, and pronouns in their own special section. Like Strong's, the *NIVEC* uses a numbering system but, for reasons explained below (p. xvi), it is an entirely new system. Two indexes cross-reference Strong's numbers to the new numbers and vice versa. For its biblical-language indexes, the *NIVEC* adopts the format of the analytical concordance. It has three separate indexes—Hebrew, Aramaic, and Greek—that list every word in the original-language texts and every word and phrase used to translate them in the NIV. Thus the *NIVEC* combines the best features of Young's and Strong's concordances.

FEATURES OF THE
NIV EXHAUSTIVE CONCORDANCE

The *NIVEC* is divided into four major sections: (1) the Main Concordance, (2) the Index of Articles, Conjunctions,

Particles, Prepositions, and Pronouns, (3) the Biblical Language Indexes, and (4) the Numbering System Indexes.

THE MAIN CONCORDANCE

Below is a typical entry from the Main Concordance:

AARON (318) [AARON'S, AARONIC]
Ex 4:14 "What about your brother, **A** the Levite?   195
   4:27 The LORD said to **A,** "Go into the desert   195

The heading consists of:
(1) the indexed word (AARON);
(2) the frequency count in parentheses (318);
(3) the list of related words (AARON'S, AARONIC).

The context lines consist of:
(1) the book-chapter-verse reference;
(2) the context for the indexed word;
(3) the number key to the index-lexicon.

Headings

There are four kinds of headings: (1) NIV word headings, (2) NIV "See" references, (3) NIV Anglicized "See" references, and (4) KJV "See" references.

NIV Word Headings

The North American Edition of the NIV contains 726,109 total words, with a unique vocabulary of 14,462. The *NIVEC* is an exhaustive alphabetic index to every word and numeral of the NIV.

The simplest heading is composed of the NIV word and its frequency count, for example:

ABBA (3)

The frequency count lists the total number of times the word appears in the NIV, which is also the number of contexts listed in the concordance. The *NIVEC* is the first exhaustive concordance to provide this information.

The headings show the indexed words exactly as they are spelled in the NIV. If the word occurs in other forms or spellings, these words appear in square brackets following the frequency count:

ABANDON (13) [ABANDONED, ABANDONS]

ABANDONED (36) [ABANDON]

ABANDONS (1) [ABANDON]

Rather than listing all related words after each indexed word, the editors chose one indexed word to act as the "group heading." All related words are listed after the group heading, and each of the related word headings points back to the group heading. In the example above, ABANDON serves as the group heading for ABANDONED and ABANDONS.

The headings also group together words that share common elements. For example:

ABLE (133) [ABILITY, ABLE-BODIED, DISABLED, ENABLE, ENABLED, ENABLES, ENABLING]

Place names composed of more than one word have a single, multiple-word heading:

BAAL GAD (3) [BAAL, GAD]

If the second or third term of a multiple-word place name is not indexed as an NIV word in its own right, it still appears in the Main Concordance as a heading that refers to the multiple-word heading:

AMMONI See KEPHAR AMMONI

(Multiple-word headings appear only for place names generated by transliteration. They are not used for place names that combine a geographic term and a proper noun, such as the Jordan River, the Sea of Galilee, or Mount Sinai.)

NIV "See" References

78 words occur a total of 364,004 times—more than half the bulk of the NIV! These words are exhaustively indexed in their own section: the Index of Articles, Conjunctions, Particles, Prepositions, and Pronouns (see p. xiv). These words are also represented by headings in the Main Concordance, with a message referring to this special index:

A (9144) [AN] See Index of Articles Etc.

Eight of these 78 words have a selected listing of contexts in the Main Concordance.

HAD, HAS, and HAVE are usually used as auxiliary verbs to indicate the English perfect tense, as in the clause "everything I **have** commanded you." As auxiliary verbs, these words are not indexed in the Main Concordance. But these words also occur as verbs in their own right, expressing the idea of ownership, "He **had** so many flocks," or causing action, "God **had** me wander." In these latter cases, the words are indexed in the Main Concordance: HAD 533 of 2791 occurrences, HAS 266 of 2407, HAVE 827 of 4313.

Neither I nor AM is indexed in the Main Concordance, but many important passages containing the self-revelation of

God contain the phrase I AM, such as Exodus 3:14, "**I AM WHO I AM**," and John 8:58, "before Abraham was born, **I am!**" 61 highly significant verses have been selected from the 1036 occurrences of the phrase I AM for the Main Concordance.

When ON is used as a proper name (4 of 4658 occurrences), it is indexed in the Main Concordance, as is SO (1 of 3003). When WILL is used in the sense of volition, as in the will of God or will of man (166 of 10,192 occurrences), it is indexed in the Main Concordance.

NIV Anglicized "See" References

The Anglicized Edition of the NIV was published in the United Kingdom in 1979. Anglicization "in Bible translation has come to mean the adoption of the English spelling, vocabulary, and usages common to British, as distinct from American, readers" (*The NIV: The Making of a Contemporary Translation*, p. 137 [Zondervan, 1986]).

Most of the differences between the North American and Anglicized editions are matters of spelling. At the end of this introduction is a list of the 288 words that are consistently spelled differently between the two editions, words such as "centre" and "center," "honour" and "honor," "pasture-land" and "pastureland."

In 227 verses, however, the differences between the two editions go beyond spelling. These more major differences are handled in two ways. First, at the end of the introduction, there is a complete, alphabetical listing of verbal differences involving indexed words. Second, "See" references for 65 key word differences have been included in the Main Concordance. They appear in headings such as:

EARS OF CORN (Anglicized) See HEADS OF GRAIN

The editors hope that these features will make the *NIVEC* fully useful to readers of both the North American and Anglicized editions of the NIV.

KJV "See" References

The King James or Authorized Version has been the dominant English Bible translation from the early seventeenth century to the latter half of the twentieth century. Because of this, the KJV has had profound impact on the language of both the Church and English-speaking society. To help users familiar with KJV vocabulary find the proper NIV terms, more than 2000 KJV words appear in 1600 KJV "See" references. These include such headings as:

COMFORTER (KJV) See COUNSELOR

[GIVE UP THE] GHOST (KJV) See BREATHED HIS LAST, DIE, DIED, DYING GASP, GAVE UP HIS SPIRIT, PERISHED

[HOLY] GHOST (KJV) See [HOLY] SPIRIT

Context Lines

Concordances are word indexes. At the very least, they index the book, chapter, and verse in which these words are located. Most concordances also show each word within a brief phrase or clause: a context. This gives the user a better idea of the use of the word and helps to locate a specific verse that contains that word.

Most concordances limit their contexts to a single line. This is generally true of the *NIVEC*; however, it has many two-line and several three-line contexts. These longer contexts help give a better glimpse into a word's function within the English text and give a better idea of the relationship of the English to the original languages.

The purpose of context lines in a concordance is merely to help the reader recognize or find a specific verse in the Bible. For word study—or any kind of Bible study—the context offered by a concordance is rarely enough to go on. Nevertheless, sometimes a short sentence or a whole verse fits on one line, as in the case of John 11:35: "Jesus wept." Under the heading PRAISE, the *NIVEC* was able to present the entirety of Psalm 150 on thirteen consecutive lines!

Taken by themselves, context lines can and do misrepresent the teaching of Scripture by omitting key words. "There is no God" is a context taken straight from Psalm 14:1. Of course the Bible does not teach this; it is what "the fool says in his heart"! Similarly, a context for Leviticus 24:16 might read "the LORD must be put to death" while the text actually says "anyone who blasphemes the name of the LORD must be put to death."

Great care has been taken by the editors, programmers, and proofreaders of the *NIVEC* to create contexts that are informative and accurate. But the reader should always check word contexts by looking them up in the NIV itself. "The Wicked Bible," a KJV edition of 1631, accidentally omitted the word "not" from the seventh commandment, for which the printers were fined 300 pounds sterling! Though there are no such fines for misleading contexts, the editors are still deeply concerned that the *NIVEC* be used discerningly.

Bible Translating and Concordance Making

Traduttore traditore, "the translator is a traitor," is an ancient proverb oft quoted in books about Bible translations. To a degree this proverb is true, for no translation can perfectly bring over all the meaning and nuances of one language into another. Because no two languages share identical grammar and an identical range of word meanings, not even the best-intentioned word-for-word translation can claim to perfectly represent the original.

If the translator is a traitor, the concordance maker must be his partner in crime. For no multilingual concordance can perfectly represent both the English and biblical-language texts it indexes. It can perfectly represent the vocabulary of the English text, for it needs only to list the location of each of its words. In this respect a concordance is either absolutely right or absolutely wrong. But when a concordance attempts to display the relationship between the English text and the biblical languages, it falls heir to the same difficulties that face the Bible translator.

Much of Bible translation involves one-to-one relationships. More often than not, אֱלֹהִים is translated "God," Ἰησοῦς "Jesus," and ἀγαπάω "love." This part of translating and concordance making is easy.

Often, however, more than one word is needed in English to render a word in the originals. For example, the Greek word τεκνίον is regularly translated "little children" in the KJV and NAS and "dear children" in the NIV. Conversely, one English word can translate several words from the originals. Thus the infamous number "666" of Revelation 13:18 translates three Greek words.

Sometimes, because of differences in idiom, it takes several English words to translate two or more words from the original languages. This is called "dynamic equivalence" or "functional equivalence." For example, the famous KJV expletive "God forbid!" translates one word in Hebrew and two words in Greek—neither of which has either "God" or "forbid" as part of its "literal" meaning! Nevertheless, "God forbid!" is the *functional* equivalent of the Greek and Hebrew phrases.

Multilingual concordances of the past have tended to display the relationship between English and the original languages as if it were almost always one-to-one. Scan a few columns of Strong's *Concordance*, and you see context after context presenting one indexed word followed by one number. Over the years, this has lent support to the misconception that the KJV is an absolutely "literal," word-for-word translation. However, the original preface to the KJV stated, "We have not tied our selves to an uniformity of phrasing, or to an identity of words, as some peradventure would wish that we had done. . . ." Young's *Analytical Concordance*, and more so *Eerdmans' Analytical Concordance to the RSV* that followed it, attempt to show multiple-word translation by means of multiple-word headings. However, nothing within the context itself shows how the indexed word relates to the original Greek or Hebrew.

The *NIVEC*, by means of three different typefaces in the context line and a more nuanced use of its entirely new numbering system, shows more fully than any previous concordance the interrelation of the English text and the biblical languages.

Context Lines: Word-for-Word Translation

The simplest context line presents four items of information. First, the location of the indexed word by book, chapter, and verse. Second, the context line. Third, within the context line, the indexed word is abbreviated by its first letter and is *usually* in bold type. Fourth, a number at the right margin indicates the Hebrew, Aramaic, or Greek word the indexed word translates. For example, under the heading AARON on page 1:

> Ex 4:14 "What about your brother, **A** the Levite?   195
>   4:27 The LORD said to **A**, "Go into the desert   195

Note that the book abbreviation is not repeated in the second reference. Book abbreviations are repeated at the top of new columns (see columns 2 and 3, page 1). A complete list of NIV book abbreviations appears at the beginning of the Main Concordance.

The numbering system indicates which biblical language is translated. Hebrew words are represented by numbers in normal "roman" type, from 1 through 9597. Aramaic word numbers are also in roman type, from 10001 through 10779. Greek word numbers are in italics, from *1* through *6068*. This "Goodrick/Kohlenberger numbering system," named after its editors, is hereafter referred to as "G/K numbers."

Context Lines: Multiple-Word Translation

One English Word—Multiple Original Words. When the indexed word translates more than one word from the original, this is indicated by an appropriate number of G/K numbers at the end of the line. This is especially true of numerals, for example:

> Rev 7:5 From the tribe of Judah **12,000**   *1577+5942*

> Nu 1:46 The total number was **603,550.**
>   *547+547+2256+2256+2256*
>   *+2822+2822+4395+4395+8993+9252*

The second example is a very rare occurrence of a string of G/K numbers too long to fit on one line. In this case, the string of numbers is broken to fit on two lines; the second line begins with a plus (+) to show that it is a continuation of the previous line. Strings of G/K numbers are always organized in numerical order.

In some cases, multiple English words are needed to define a Hebrew, Aramaic, or Greek word or phrase. We will refer to this as "multiple-word translation." In other cases, multiple English words are needed to translate the inflection of the original, to express, for example, the tense of a verb or the number and gender of a noun. We will refer to this as "assisting in translation." These two concepts are explained below.

Multiple-word Translation. As mentioned above, the Greek word τεκνίον is regularly translated "little children" in the KJV and NAS and "dear children" in the NIV. If you were to look up the word "little" in either Strong's or the NAS *Concordance* and look at the context for 1 John 2:1, you would find the word abbreviated by its first letter with the number *5040* at the end of the line. However, if you looked up the word "children" you would find the same thing:

1Jo 2: 1 My *l* children, these things write   *5040*

1Jo 2: 1 My little *c*, these things write I   *5040*

In these examples (reproduced from Strong's *Concordance*), it would appear that the Greek word number *5040* meant only "little" or "children," depending on which entry you looked up first. Nothing in the context line would inform you that Greek word *5040* actually means "little children." Young's *Concordance*, on the other hand, does not list 1 John 2:1 under the word "little," but has a heading "CHILD or children, little—" under which our verse is indexed.

The *NIVEC* has solved the problem of indicating such multiple-word translations by putting *all* the words in bold type. Using the same example of 1 John 2:1, under the headings "dear" and "children":

1Jn 2: 1 My **d children,** I write this to you so   *5448*

1Jn 2: 1 My **dear c,** I write this to you so   *5448*

If more than one English word is used to render several words from the original, the typefaces and the G/K numbers show all the words involved in this multiple-word translation. Such is the case with "have children" in Mark 12:19, as indexed under both words:

Mk 12:19 must marry the widow and **have c**   *1985+5065*

Mk 12:19 widow and **h children** for his brother.   *1985+5065*

This unique convention shows at a glance all the words involved in a multiple-word translation, the English words as well as the original-language words.

Assist in Translation. The biblical languages use spelling or "inflection" to indicate such things as the subject and tense of a verb, or the number and gender of a noun. Such inflections are not part of the definition of a word, but are necessary to reflect in translation.

English does not inflect to the same degree as the biblical languages. Thus translators have to use auxiliary or "assisting" words to render these inflections. Common assisting words are pronouns such as "he" and "she," auxiliary verbs such as "shall" and "will," and quantifying words such as "many," "some," and even "two."

If you were to look up the word "will" in either Strong's or the NAS *Concordance*, you would notice that for most of the several thousand references to the word, there is no number at the end of the context line. Some might take this to mean that the word does not represent any word in the original but was simply supplied by the translators. But for the most part this is not true. The word "will" was used to translate the inflection of a Hebrew, Aramaic, or Greek verb, not the verb itself. But the editors did not put the number of that verb at the end of the context line lest the user misinterpret "will" as the *definition* of that number.

The *NIVEC* has solved this problem by means of different typefaces and a code. If an indexed word is a word that "assists in translation," the context line displays it in three ways, as shown in the following example, found under the heading LET:

Ge 1:26 God said, *"L us* **make** man in our image,   AIT

First, the abbreviation of the indexed word is in italics, because it is not the main word but a word that assists in the translation of "make." Second, the word it assists ("make") is in bold. Third, the code AIT ("Assisting In Translation") appears at the end of the line in the place of a G/K number.

On the other hand, if the indexed word is assisted by other NIV words, the indexed word is abbreviated and in bold type, but the assisting words are in italics. Using the same example, but looking now under the heading MAKE:

Ge 1:26 God said, *"Let us* **m** man in our image,   6913

In both examples, the auxiliary verb "Let" and the pronoun "us" are marked as assisting words by the italic typeface. In both contexts, the verb "make" is shown to be the main, "defining" word by the bold typeface. Under their own headings, the code AIT also marks the assisting word, while the G/K number identifies the defining word.

By using these conventions to identify multiple-word translations and to distinguish between defining words and assisting words, the *NIVEC* more thoroughly displays the relationship between the English and the biblical languages than any concordance that has preceded it.

Context Lines: "Substitution" Translation _____

For stylistic reasons, Bible translators often substitute nouns for pronouns and pronouns for nouns. For example, John 8:1 in the KJV reads "Jesus went unto the mount of Olives." Strong tells us that here "Jesus" translates Greek word *846*, which is not the proper name Ἰησοῦς (Strong's word *2424*), but the pronoun αὐτός, "he." Such "substitutionary" translations are common and acceptable in Bible translations, but other concordances treat them as if they were one-to-one translations.

The *NIVEC* indicates substitutionary translation by attaching a raised "S" to the G/K number or numbers at the end of the context line. For example, under AARON:

Ex 30:21 This is to be a lasting ordinance for **A**   2257[S]

Ex 10:11 Then **Moses and A** were driven out   4392[S]

In the first example, "Aaron" substitutes for the masculine singular pronominal suffix וֹ, normally translated "he," "him," or "his." In the second example, the phrase "Moses and Aaron" substitutes for the masculine plural pronominal suffix ם, normally translated "they," "their," or "them."

Similarly, the NIV often uses forms of the verb "do" to substitute for a more specific verb repeated in the context. For example, Deuteronomy 6:16 reads "Do not test the LORD your God as you **did** at Massah" rather than "Do not test the LORD your God as you **tested** him at Massah." This substitutionary translation is indicated under DID:

Dt 6:16 Do not test the LORD your God as *you* **d**   5814[S]

The NIV is not unique in using substitutionary translation. The *NIVEC* is unique in displaying it.

Context Lines: "Not in Hebrew" and "Not in Greek" —

Because modern English and ancient Hebrew, Aramaic, and Greek do not have identical rules of grammar and style, translators must often add words for the sake of clarity. For example, Mark 16:9 in the KJV begins "Now when Jesus was risen early. . . ." Strong has no number at the end of this context line because there is no Greek word for "Jesus" in this verse; it was supplied by the translators to give a subject to the verb.

The *NIVEC* follows this practice of indicating NIV words that are not in the originals by using the code NIH, "Not In Hebrew," for both the Hebrew and Aramaic of the Old Testament and *NIG*, "Not In Greek," for the New. Under the heading ABRAHAM, for example, we find:

Ge 21:33 **A** planted a tamarisk tree in Beersheba,   NIH

Heb 6:15 **A** received what was promised.   *NIG*

As in the case of the KJV in Mark 16:9, these proper names were supplied for clarity, for the benefit of the reader.

A Note on NIV Typefaces

In the NIV text itself, italics are used when a Hebrew, Aramaic, or Greek word is not translated, but merely spelled out in English letters. These "transliterated" words include *Selah* in the Psalms and *"Eloi, eloi, lama sabachthani?"* in Matthew 27:46 and Mark 15:34. However, the NIV italic typeface could be confused with the italics used in the

concordance for words that assist in translation (AIT). Therefore, all italics used in the NIV text are printed as normal "roman" type in context lines.

The NIV uses half brackets (⌊ ⌋) to indicate words supplied for clarity. The KJV, NAS and other translations use italics for the same purpose. (Compare 1 Samuel 13:1 in the NIV, KJV, and NAS.) The *NIVEC* uses regular brackets ([ ]) instead.

The NIV uses a typographical convention to distinguish between two different Hebrew words, both of which are usually translated "Lord" in English versions. For the proper name of God, יהוה ("Yahweh"), the NIV uses "LORD." For the title אֲדֹנָי, it uses "Lord." The *NIVEC* also distinguishes these two words under two separate headings. "Lord" and its possessive form "Lord's" are indexed under the headings *LORD and *LORD'S (pages 683-86). "LORD" and "LORD's" are indexed under the headings †LORD and †LORD'S (pages 686-708). In context lines, these words appear as in the NIV text.

THE INDEX OF ARTICLES, CONJUNCTIONS, PARTICLES, PREPOSITIONS, AND PRONOUNS

The Main Concordance indexes 363,965 references to 14,452 NIV words, numerals, and compound proper names. The Index of Articles, Conjunctions, Particles, Prepositions, and Pronouns indexes 364,004 references to 78 NIV words. These include 55 words that appear more than 1000 times each, such as "I," "me," and "my," and 23 less frequent words that are related to them, such as "myself," "I'll," and "I'm." This index makes the *NIVEC* the first truly exhaustive concordance since Strong's.

The format of the Index of Articles Etc. is very simple. Each of the 78 words has its own heading, followed by a frequency count. For example:

A (9144)

The eight words that are partially indexed in the Main Concordance (AM, HAD, HAS, HAVE, I, ON, SO, and WILL, see above pages x-xi) also have the message "See also selected list in the Main Concordance."

The 78 words of this section are indexed without contexts, since providing contexts would be of little benefit to the reader and would double the size of the *NIVEC*! Book, chapter, and verse references appear in biblical order. Books and chapters are set in bold print for easy location. If the indexed word occurs more than once in a verse, the total number of occurrences is indicated by a raised number:

Lev 1:3[2], 9, 10[2], 13, 14[3], 17; **2:**1, 2[2], 3, 4, 5, 6, 7,

This example from the indefinite article "A" shows that the article appears twice in Leviticus 1:3, 1:10, and 2:2, and three times in 1:14. Note too that book and chapter references appear just once. Verses within the same chapter are set off by commas. The final verse of the chapter is followed by a semicolon. The final verse of the entry is followed by a period.

THE BIBLICAL-LANGUAGE INDEX-LEXICONS

At the end of each context line in the Main Concordance is a code or a G/K number, describing the relationship of the NIV to the original languages. The three Biblical-Language Index-Lexicons list all of the words that are found in the Hebrew, Aramaic, and Greek texts from which the NIV was translated. These lists are in the alphabetical order of each of the three languages, which is also the order of the G/K numbering system.

The Index-Lexicon follows the pattern of Young's *Analytical Concordance* rather than that of Strong's dictionaries. This system more accurately interrelates the original languages to the NIV and is easier to read. The entry for Greek word *27* can serve as an example for most features of all three Index-Lexicons:

27 ἀγάπη *agapē* (116)
   love (109)
   love (2) +26
   love (2) +2400
   it^s (1) +3836
   love feasts (1)
   loves (1)

The heading begins with the G/K number, in bold type for easy location. Next is the lexical form or dictionary form of the word, followed by its transliteration, and the total number of occurrences in the biblical text. (The transliteration follows the system used in Zondervan's *Expositor's Bible Commentary*. A complete transliteration and pronunciation guide appears before each index.)

The heading is followed by a list of all the ways in which the word is translated in the NIV, in descending order of frequency. If two words (or phrases) have the same frequency, they are listed in alphabetical order. Following the NIV word is its frequency count, in parentheses.

One-to-one translations are indicated by one NIV word, as in the case of the first and last NIV words in the example above. Multiple-word translations are indicated in two ways: by multiple NIV words and/or multiple G/K numbers. The next-to-the-last line, "love feasts (1)," indicates a multiple-word NIV translation. If you look up "love" and "feasts" in the Main Concordance, you will find the following contexts under Jude 1:12:

Jude 1:12 These men are blemishes at your l **feasts,**   27

Jude 1:12 These men are blemishes at your **love f,**   27

Under both headings, the phrase "love feasts" is shown to be the definition of Greek word *27*. (Multiple-word translation is described above on page xiii.)

When an NIV word or phrase translates more than one word of the original, the G/K number of the additional word (or words) follows the frequency count. That is why there are three separate lines for "love" in the example above. The first is a one-to-one translation. The second shows that in two cases "love" translates two Greek words: *27* and *26*. Similarly, the third shows that "love" translates Greek words *27* and *2400*.

Words that "assist in translation" (see above, page xiii) do not appear in the Index-Lexicons. This is because they do not *define* words. Rather, they assist words in translating tense, number, gender, and mood.

"Substitution" translation (see above, pages xiii-xiv) is noted with a raised "S," as in the Main Concordance. The fourth indexed word in the example above indicates that "it" is a substitution translation for Greek words *27+3836*. Because "it" is not indexed in the Main Concordance, you cannot locate this reference. (No other multilingual concordance allows the user to do this either.) By reading through the rest of the index, however, you see that the normal translation of the word is "love."

Untranslated Words

There is one other category of words in the Index-Lexicons that cannot be looked up in the Main Concordance. If a word in the originals is not translated in the NIV, either directly or in multiple-word translation, this is noted by the word "untranslated." This word is always last in the index list and includes a frequency count.

For example, the Hebrew word שָׁנָה (G/K 9102, Strong 8141) is normally translated "year(s)" in English versions. But its use with numbers is so repetitious in the Hebrew text that no English version translates it every time it appears. A word-for-word translation of Genesis 23:1 would be: "And the life of Sarah was one hundred **year** and twenty **year** and seven **years**—the **years** of the life of Sarah." Though שָׁנָה appears four times in this verse, "year(s)" appears only twice in the KJV and NAS, and once in the NIV.

According to the Hebrew Index-Lexicon to Young's *Analytical Concordance*, שָׁנָה is translated 805 times in the KJV. The Hebrew-Aramaic Dictionary of the NAS *Concordance* has a total of 789 occurrences. Actually, the word appears 880 times in the Hebrew text. The Hebrew Index-Lexicon of the *NIVEC* lists this word (9102) as translated 780 times and untranslated 100 times. Although all Bible translations leave words untranslated, the *NIVEC* is the first multilingual concordance to indicate this.

"Variant; not used"

The Index-Lexicons of the *NIVEC* list several hundred words that are alternate spellings of Hebrew, Aramaic, and Greek words, or words not found in the original-language texts translated by the NIV. The three word lists were compiled from several standard lexicons and grammars in the hope that the G/K numbering system could be used in a multitude of reference works, describing the textual base of most of the Bible translations currently in print.

Because these words are not translated by the NIV, they have no NIV words to index. Rather, on the line following the heading is the message "Variant; not used." The first word in each of the three Index-Lexicons (each of which is the first letter of its respective alphabet) is an example of this convention.

The Index-Lexicons to the *NIVEC* have three features not found in the indexes or dictionaries of any other concordance. First, the *NIVEC* provides frequency statistics of both the biblical languages and the English, including untranslated words. Second, each entry lists exhaustively all the NIV words and phrases that translate each word of the original, showing multiple-word translation and substitution translation. Third, the NIV words and phrases indexed are in their exact textual spelling, so the user can locate its heading in the Main Concordance without any further cross-referencing.

Index-Lexicon Versus Dictionary Format

The index-lexicon format was chosen over the dictionary format used in Strong's *Concordance* and the NAS *Concordance* for two reasons. First, it is the best and most readable format to show the relationship between the English text and the biblical languages. Second, it avoids a major problem inherent in the traditional dictionary format.

The dictionaries in Strong's *Concordance* and the NAS *Concordance* usually give a single "root" definition for each word. This is often misunderstood as the *only* definition or the "literal" meaning of the word and can be misused to criticize other valid translations of the word—even in the KJV and NAS themselves! For example, Young's Index-Lexicon to the New Testament lists 57 different KJV translations of the Greek word ποιέω (POIEŌ). Strong's dictionary defines this word as "to *make* or *do*." Either the KJV translators were wrong in 96% of their definitions or there is more to the meaning of ποιέω than "to *make* or *do*"!

The lists of NIV translations in the Index-Lexicons do in fact constitute a dictionary. The best definition of a biblical word is its range of meaning throughout the Bible.

THE NUMBERING SYSTEM INDEXES

You may have noticed in the examples above that the "Goodrick/Kohlenberger" numbering system differs from that of Strong. Advances in biblical scholarship have made it difficult, if not impossible, to use Strong's century-old system. In the first place, Strong's system indexes only the vocabulary of the original-language texts that underlie the KJV. Second, modern analysis of the biblical languages divides many words of identical spelling into two or three or more unique "homographs"—words with the same spelling but different meanings (such as the English word "bow"). This is especially true of biblical Hebrew. Third, Strong mixed the Hebrew and Aramaic ("Chaldee") vocabularies together into one numbering scheme, whereas all modern lexicons and grammars treat them as different languages. Fourth, even after a century and dozens of corrected editions, Strong's system still suffers from numerous typographical and factual errors. These factors demand both expansion and revision of Strong's system.

The general editor of the NAS *Concordance* opted to retain Strong's numbers. Typographical and factual errors were corrected while indexing the dictionaries to the NAS. To overcome the need for additional words and numbers, letters of the alphabet were added to Strong's existing numbers. For example, to number a word not included in Strong's original list that should be alphabetized between words 112 and 113, the NAS altered Strong's numbers to 112a, 112b, and 113.

Rather than attempt to similarly patch up Strong's well-worn system, the editors of the *NIVEC* decided to make a clean break and develop a new standard for use in up-to-date biblical-language reference works. But for the benefit of those who want to cross-reference to Strong's system, the editors also created two sets of indexes to show the relationship of these two numbering schemes.

Index of Strong to Goodrick/Kohlenberger Numbers

The first index is organized according to Strong's numbering system. It first indexes Strong's Hebrew and Aramaic ("Chaldee") numbers, then his Greek numbers.

Most of the index involves a one-to-one correspondence:

Strong	G/K
1	3
2	10003
3	4
4	10004

The first four words of Strong's Hebrew/Aramaic numbering system consist of two Hebrew and two Aramaic words. This is immediately apparent by the five-digit (Aramaic) G/K numbers.

Sometimes a single Strong's number corresponds to more than one G/K number, due to spelling variations. In this case, each corresponding G/K number is listed on its own line, but Strong's is replaced by a ditto mark (").

11 10
" 11

Sometimes Strong assigned a number to a compound name that the NIV treats as two separate words. The plus sign (+) marks this relationship:

25 . . . . 3+1500

Index of Goodrick/Kohlenberger to Strong Numbers

This set of indexes has one for each of the biblical languages: Hebrew, Aramaic, and Greek. Each index is organized according to the G/K numbering system.

As in the case of the previous set, most relationships are one-to-one:

G/K . . . . Strong
1 1
2 2
3 3
4 4

Sometimes a G/K number corresponds to more than one

Strong number. In this case, each corresponding Strong number is listed on its own line, but the G/K number is replaced by a ditto mark (").

41 39
" 40

Sometimes a G/K number is assigned to a compound word that Strong treated only as two separate words. The plus sign (+) marks this relationship:

15 . . 18 + 2041

In many cases, a G/K number has no corresponding Strong number. In this case, the G/K number is simply followed by blank space, as is the case with Greek numbers 122 and 207.

In Conclusion

To Ralph Waldo Emerson, "A foolish consistency is the hobgoblin of little minds." To the editors of the *NIVEC*, there is no such thing as a foolish consistency in a biblical reference book. Every effort has been made by the editors, programmers, and proofreaders to make the *NIVEC* consistent and error-free. Strong's and Young's *Concordances* have each been through more than two dozen revisions, and we realize that our work has not been perfect either.

If you find anything that appears to be an error, write to The NIV Concordance Project, c/o Zondervan Publishing House, 1415 Lake Drive, S.E., Grand Rapids, MI 49506.

List of Spelling Differences between the Anglicized and North American Editions

Anglicized	North American
Abel Karamim	Abel Keramim
afterwards	afterward
ageing	aging
almug-wood	almugwood
any more	anymore
armour-bearer	armor-bearer
armour-bearers	armor-bearers
armour	armor
armoury	armory
authorisation	authorization
authorised	authorized
axe	ax
axe-head	axhead
backwards	backward
baptise	baptize
baptised	baptized
baptising	baptizing
battering-rams	battering rams
battle-bow	battle bow
behaviour	behavior
Berakiah	Berekiah
birth-pains	birth pains
blood-relative	blood relative
blood-relatives	blood relatives
broken-hearted	brokenhearted
burnt-out	burned-out
cauldron	caldron
cauldrons	caldrons
cancelled	canceled
cancelling	canceling
centre	center
centres	centers
channelled	channeled
chiselled	chiseled
chiselling	chiseling
clamour	clamor
coloured	colored
colourful	colorful
colours	colors
commander-in-chief	commander in chief
conies	coneys
counselled	counseled
counsellor	counselor
counsellors	counselors
criticised	criticized
Chuza	Cuza
defence	defense
defences	defenses
dishonour	dishonor
dishonoured	dishonored
dishonours	dishonors
distil	distill
door-frame	doorframe
door-frames	doorframes
door-keeper	doorkeeper
door-post	doorpost
drag-net	dragnet
dwelling-place	dwelling place
dwelling-places	dwelling places
ear-rings	earrings
enquire	inquire
enquiring	inquiring
enrol	enroll
enrolment	enrollment
equalled	equaled
ever-flowing	ever flowing
eye-witnesses	eyewitnesses
face down	facedown
faint-hearted	fainthearted
fault-finders	faultfinders

favour	favor	market-place	marketplace	rumour	rumor
favourable	favorable	market-places	marketplaces	rumours	rumors
favourably	favorably	marshalled	marshaled	sandalled	sandaled
favoured	favored	marvelled	marveled	sand-bar	sandbar
favouritism	favoritism	marvelling	marveling	sand-bars	sandbars
favours	favors	marvellous	marvelous	Saviour	Savior
fellow-citizens	fellow citizens	Michmash	Micmash	sawn	sawed
fellow-elder	fellow elder	mid-air	midair	sceptre	scepter
fellow-man	fellowman	misdemeanour	misdemeanor	sceptres	scepters
fellow-men	fellow men	mobilised	mobilized	Shammau	Shammua
fellow-prisoner	fellow prisoner	moulded	molded	sheep-shearers	sheepshearers
fellow-prisoners	fellow prisoners	moulding	molding	shield-bearer	shield bearer
fellow-servant	fellow servant	moulds	molds	shrine-prostitute	shrine prostitute
fellow-servants	fellow servants	mouldy	moldy	shrine-prostitutes	shrine prostitutes
fellow-soldier	fellow soldier	money-lender	moneylender	shrivelled	shriveled
fellow-worker	fellow worker	multicoloured	multicolored	sick-bed	sickbed
fellow-workers	fellow workers	moustache	mustache	side walls	sidewalls
fertilise	fertilize	naiive	naive	signalled	signaled
fervour	fervor	near by	nearby	signalling	signaling
fig-tree	fig tree	near-sighted	nearsighted	simple-hearted	simplehearted
fig-trees	fig trees	neighbour	neighbor	skilful	skillful
fish-hooks	fishhooks	neighbour's	neighbor's	skilfully	skillfully
flavour	flavor	neighbouring	neighboring	smoulder	smolder
for ever	forever	neighbours	neighbors	smouldering	smoldering
for evermore	forevermore	neighbours'	neighbors'	smoulders	smolders
fulfil	fulfill	newly-built	newly built	sombre	somber
fulfilment	fulfillment	night-time	nighttime	south-east	southeast
fulfils	fulfills	no-one	no one	south-west	southwest
fulness	fullness	north-easter	northeaster	splendour	splendor
good-bye	good-by	north-west	northwest	storey	story
grape-pickers	grape pickers	odour	odor	stout-hearted	stouthearted
grey	gray	offence	offense	stumbling-block	stumbling block
grey-haired	gray-haired	offences	offenses	stumbling-stone	stumbling stone
half-dead	half dead	open-handed	openhanded	sub-division	subdivision
half-tribe	half tribe	over-righteous	overrighteous	sub-divisions	subdivisions
hand mill	handmill	panelled	paneled	sulphur	sulfur
harbour	harbor	panelling	paneling	symbolises	symbolizes
harboured	harbored	paralysed	paralyzed	sympathise	sympathize
harbours	harbors	parcelled	parceled	sympathised	sympathized
hard-hearted	hardhearted	pasture-land	pastureland	thank-offering	thank offering
head-dresses	headdresses	pasture-lands	pasturelands	thank-offerings	thank offerings
heavenwards	heavenward	plough	plow	theatre	theater
hiding-place	hiding place	ploughed	plowed	threshing-cart	threshing cart
hiding-places	hiding places	ploughing	plowing	threshing-floor	threshing floor
home town	hometown	ploughman	plowman	threshing-floors	threshing floors
honour	honor	ploughs	plows	threshing-sledge	threshing sledge
honourable	honorable	ploughshares	plowshares	threshing-sledges	threshing sledges
honourably	honorably	plumb-line	plumb line	tight-fisted	tightfisted
honoured	honored	practise	practice	totalled	totaled
honouring	honoring	practised	practiced	towards	toward
jaw-bone	jawbone	practises	practices	travelled	traveled
Joash	Jehoash	pre-eminent	preeminent	traveller	traveler
jewellery	jewelry	pretence	pretense	travellers	travelers
Joshbakashah	Joshbekashah	quarrelled	quarreled	travelling	traveling
kind-hearted	kindhearted	quarrelling	quarreling	treasure-house	treasure house
labour	labor	realise	realize	tumble-weed	tumbleweed
laboured	labored	realised	realized	tumours	tumors
labourer	laborer	realising	realizing	unauthorised	unauthorized
labourer's	laborer's	recognise	recognize	unequalled	unequaled
labourers	laborers	recognised	recognized	unfavourable	unfavorable
labouring	laboring	recognises	recognizes	unploughed	unplowed
labours	labors	recognising	recognizing	unsandalled	unsandaled
laughing-stock	laughingstock	re-entered	reentered	untravelled	untraveled
law-breaker	lawbreaker	re-established	reestablished	upside-down	upside down
law-breakers	lawbreakers	resting-place	resting place	upwards	upward
levelled	leveled	revelled	reveled	vapour	vapor
licence	license	revellers	revelers	vigour	vigor
life-time	lifetime	revelling	reveling	water-carrier	water carrier
lustre	luster	river bed	riverbed	water-carriers	water carriers

wilful	willful	woollen	woolen	worshipping	worshiping
wilfully	willfully	worshipped	worshiped	worth while	worthwhile
wind-blown	windblown	worshipper	worshiper	yoke-fellow	yokefellow
wing-span	wingspan	worshippers	worshipers		

Index of Word Differences Between the Anglicized and North American Editions

Anglicized . . . . *North American* . . . *Verse Reference*

Anglicized	North American	Verse Reference
360	three hundred and sixty	2Sa 2:31
a man	anyone	Jn 7:51
ankles do not turn over	ankles do not turn	2Sa 22:37
ankles do not turn over	ankles do not turn	Ps 18:36
assistant	aide	Ex 24:13
assistant	aide	Ex 33:11
assistant	aide	Nu 11:28
assistant	aide	Jos 1:1
assistant	aide	Ne 6:5
become	be	1Ki 1:17
bind	obligate	Nu 30:2
binds	obligates	Nu 30:3
binds	obligates	Nu 30:6
binds	obligates	Nu 30:8
binds	obligates	Nu 30:8
binds	obligates	Nu 30:10
bitumen	tar	Ge 11:3
bound	obligated	Nu 30:4
bound	obligated	Nu 30:5
bound	obligated	Nu 30:7
bound	obligated	Nu 30:11
bound	obligated	Ro 1:14
brazier	fire pot	Ge 15:17
brazier	fire pot	Jer 36:22
brazier	fire pot	Jer 36:23
brazier	fire pot	Zec 12:6
bring up	rear	Hos 9:12
bringing them up	rearing them	2Ki 10:6
brought	took	Lk 10:34
brought up	reared	Isa 51:18
bruises	welts	Isa 1:6
burnt-out	burned-out	Jer 51:25
call	get	Nu 20:25
camp	encamp	Ex 14:2 [twice]
caused	raised	Ac 9:21
Chuza	Cuza	Lk 8:3
cock	rooster	Pr 30:31
cock	rooster	Mt 26:34
cock	rooster	Mt 26:74
cock	rooster	Mt 26:75
cock	rooster	Mk 13:35
cock	rooster	Mk 14:30
cock	rooster	Lk 22:34
cock	rooster	Lk 22:60
cock	rooster	Lk 22:61
cock	rooster	Jn 13:38
cock	rooster	Jn 18:27
corn	grain	Ge 37:7
corn	grain	Ex 22:6
corn	grain	Dt 16:9
corn	grain	Dt 23:25
corn	grain	Jdg 15:5 [twice]
corn	grain	2Ki 4:42
corn	grain	Ps 65:13
corn	grain	Ps 65:9
corn	grain	Ps 72:16
corn	grain	Isa 17:5
corn	grain	Isa 36:17
corn	grain	Jer 50:11
corn	grain	Jer 9:22
corn	grain	Eze 36:29
corn	grain	Hos 14:7
corn	grain	Mk 4:28
corn in the ear	kernel in the head	Mk 4:28
cornfield	grainfield	Dt 23:25
cornfields	grainfields	Mt 12:1
cornfields	grainfields	Mk 2:23
cornfields	grainfields	Lk 6:1
dishes	basins	1Ki 7:50
ears	kernels	Dt 23:25
ears	heads	Mt 13:26
ears of corn	heads of grain	Ge 41:5
ears of corn	heads of grain	Ge 41:6
ears of corn	heads of grain	Ge 41:7
ears of corn	heads of grain	Ge 41:22
ears of corn	heads of grain	Ge 41:24
ears of corn	heads of grain	Ge 41:26
ears of corn	heads of grain	Ge 41:27
ears of corn	heads of grain	Job 24:24
ears of corn	heads of grain	Isa 17:5
ears of corn	heads of grain	Mt 12:1
ears of corn	heads of grain	Mk 2:23
ears of corn	heads of grain	Lk 6:1
edge	ledge	Eze 43:14
elder	older	1Sa 18:17
eldest	oldest	1Ch 24:31
entrance	entryway	2Ki 16:18
entrance	entryway	Mk 14:68
expend	spend	Dt 32:23
feigned insanity	pretended to be insane	1Sa 21:13
fishing nets	fishnets	Eze 26:14
fourth	quarter	2Ki 6:25
further	farther	Lk 24:28
gave	delivered	1Sa 24:10
gave	delivered	1Sa 24:18
gave	delivered	1Sa 26:23
give	turn	Nu 27:7
give	turn	Nu 27:8
given	delivered	1Sa 26:8
go	get away	1Sa 20:29
grain	kernels	Lk 6:1
grain	kernel	Jn 12:24
grains	kernels	Dt 32:14
hand	turn	Ps 27:12
handcrafted	crafted	Nu 31:51
handed	turned	Jer 39:14
have just seen	just saw	2Sa 18:10
heap	pile	Lk 14:35
I am	I'm	2Sa 18:14
ill-treat	mistreat	Ge 31:50
ill-treat	mistreat	Ex 22:21
ill-treat	mistreat	Lev 19:33
ill-treat	mistreat	1Sa 25:7
ill-treat	mistreat	1Sa 25:15
ill-treat	mistreat	Jer 38:19
ill-treat	mistreated	Eze 22:7
ill-treat	mistreat	Eze 22:29
ill-treat	mistreat	Lk 6:28
ill-treat	mistreat	Ac 14:5
ill-treated	mistreated	Ge 15:13

ill-treated	mistreated	Ge 16:6
ill-treated	mistreated	Nu 20:15
ill-treated	mistreated	Dt 26:6
ill-treated	mistreated	Jer 13:22
ill-treated	mistreated	Mt 22:6
ill-treated	mistreated	Ac 7:6
ill-treated	mistreated	Ac 7:24
ill-treated	mistreated	Heb 11:25
ill-treated	mistreated	Heb 11:37
ill-treated	mistreated	Heb 13:3
ill-treating	mistreating	Ac 7:27
in back	behind	Rev 4:6
in flood	at flood stage	Jos 3:15
in flood	at flood stage	Jos 4:18
legally made over	deeded	Ge 23:17
legally made over	deeded	Ge 23:20
let	have	Ex 10:11
light to the other	light to the other side	Ex 14:20
made	had	Ge 24:11
made	had	Lev 23:43
made	had	Nu 5:18
made	had	Nu 11:24
made	had	Nu 27:22
made	had	1Sa 16:8
made	had	1Sa 16:9
made	had	1Sa 16:10
made	had	1Sa 20:17
made	had	2Ch 34:32
made	had	2Ch 34:33
make	have	Ge 45:1
make	have	Ex 19:10
make	have	Ex 28:5
make	have	Nu 5:16
make	have	Nu 5:24
make	have	Nu 5:26
make	have	Nu 5:30
make	have	Nu 8:7
make	have	Nu 8:8
make	have	Nu 8:13
make	have	Nu 9:2
make	have	Nu 11:16
make	have	Nu 27:19
make	have	Dt 21:12
make	have	Dt 31:19
make	have	Jos 6:4
make	have	Jos 6:5
make	have	Jos 6:6
make	have	2Ki 5:8
make	have	2Ki 7:13
make	have	2Ki 17:27
make	have	2Ki 22:4
make	have	2Ki 22:5
make	have	2Ki 22:6
make	have	Ne 7:3
make	have	Lk 9:14
make	have	Jn 6:10
nowhere	no place	Lk 9:58
nowhere	no place	Mt 8:20
offence	stench	1Sa 13:4
offence	stench	2Sa 10:6
offence	stench	1Ch 19:6
on fire	afire	Dt 32:22
onto	on	2Ki 4:35
pushes	shoves	Nu 35:20
pushes	shoves	Nu 35:22
put...on bail	made...post bond	Ac 17:9
quietened	quieted	Ps 131:2
quietened	quieted	Ac 19:35
raped	violated	Ge 34:2
receives	gets	2Sa 15:4
required	obligated	Gal 5:3
round	around	Ge 37:7
round	around	Lev 25:31
round	around	Eph 6:14
sank	melted	Jos 2:11
sawn	sawed	Heb 11:37
scrawny	rawboned	Ge 49:14
shall	will	Nu 17:12
short-sighted	nearsighted	2Pe 1:9
sink	melt with fear	Jos 14:8
slaughtered	butchered	1Sa 28:24
slaughtered	butchered	Mt 22:4
spat	spit	Nu 12:14
spat	spit	Mt 26:67
spat	spit	Mt 27:30
spat	spit	Mk 7:33
spat	spit	Mk 15:19
spat	spit	Jn 9:6
standing corn	standing grain	Isa 17:5
stones from the field	fieldstones	Dt 27:6
supple	limber	Ge 49:24
tidy up	take care of	Ac 9:34
timber	lumber	2Ch 2:9
to and fro	back and forth	Est 2:11
to and fro	back and forth	Job 1:7
to and fro	back and forth	Job 2:2
to and fro	back and forth	Eze 37:2
to hand	on hand	1Sa 21:3
to hand	on hand	1Sa 21:4
turn him over	hand him over	Mk 15:1
turned over	handed over	Lk 18:32
two thousand seven hundred	twenty-seven hundred	1Ch 26:32
two thousand six hundred	twenty-six hundred	2Ch 35:8
until	through	Ex 12:15
warder	warden	Ge 39:21
was in the ear	headed	Ex 9:31
young plant	sprout	Isa 61:11

THE NIV
EXHAUSTIVE CONCORDANCE

FEATURES OF THE MAIN CONCORDANCE

NIV WORD HEADING
The indexed word as spelled in the NIV (see the introduction, pages x, xi).

FREQUENCY COUNT
Total number of occurrences in the NIV (see the introduction, page x).

RELATED WORD LIST
Other spellings and related words in the NIV (see the introduction, page x).

ABLE   (133)   [ABILITY, ABLE-BODIED, DISABLED, ENABLE, ENABLED, ENABLES, ENABLING]

Ge 13: 6   that *they were* **not a** to stay together.   3523

G/K NUMBER
Refers to the biblical-language index-lexicons; one- to four-digit "roman" type is Hebrew; five-digit is Aramaic; *italic* is Greek (see the introduction, pages xii, xv, xvi). For the explanation of a superscript "S" after a G/K number (for example, 3523^S), see the introduction, pages xiii, xiv.

INDEXED WORD
Abbreviated by its first letter, usually in **bold** type.

BIBLICAL REFERENCE
See the abbreviations table below.

ITALIC TYPEFACE
Indicates words that "assist in translation" (see the introduction, page xiii).

1Ch 9: 13   They were **a men,**   1475+2657

ADDITIONAL G/K NUMBER(S)
Indicates more than one Hebrew, Aramaic, or Greek word is represented by the NIV translation (introduction, page xiii).

BOLD TYPEFACE
In addition to the indexed word, indicates multiple-word translation (intro., p. xiii).

2Ch 1: 10   for who *is a to* **govern** this great people   AIT

AIT
Indicates the indexed word "assists in translation"; the indexed word abbreviation in *italics*, the word it assists is in **bold** (see the introduction, page xiii).

Rev 5: 5   He is **a** to open the scroll   *NIG*

***NIG* or NIH**
"Not in Greek" and "Not in Hebrew/Aramaic" indicates the indexed word was supplied for clarity in translation (see the introduction, page xiv).

A   (9144)   [AN] See Index of Articles Etc.

NIV "See" REFERENCES
Refers to an index in another location (see the introduction, page x).

ABATED   (KJV)   See RECEDED, GONE

KJV "See" REFERENCES
Cross-references key words to NIV vocabulary (introduction, p. xi).

ASSISTANT   (Anglicized)   See also AIDE

ANGLICIZED "See" REFERENCES
Cross-references Anglicized and North American editions of the NIV (see the introduction, page xi, and word lists, pages xvii-xx).

ABBREVIATIONS FOR THE BOOKS OF THE BIBLE

Genesis . . . . Ge	2 Kings 2Ki	Isaiah . . . . Isa	Nahum . . . . Na	Romans . . . . Ro	Titus . . . . Tit
Exodus . . . . Ex	1 Chronicles 1Ch	Jeremiah . . . . Jer	Habakkuk . . . . . Hab	1 Corinthians . . . 1Co	Philemon . . . . . . Phm
Leviticus . . . . . . Lev	2 Chronicles 2Ch	Lamentations . . . . La	Zephaniah . . . . . Zep	2 Corinthians . . . 2Co	Hebrews . . . . . . Heb
Numbers . . . . . . Nu	Ezra . . . . Ezr	Ezekiel . . . . Eze	Haggai . . . . Hag	Galatians . . . . . . Gal	James . . . . Jas
Deuteronomy . . . Dt	Nehemiah . . . . . . Ne	Daniel . . . . Da	Zechariah . . . . . Zec	Ephesians . . . . . Eph	1 Peter 1Pe
Joshua . . . . Jos	Esther . . . . Est	Hosea . . . . Hos	Malachi . . . . . . Mal	Philippians . . . . Php	2 Peter 2Pe
Judges . . . . Jdg	Job . . . . Job	Joel . . . . Joel	Matthew . . . . . . Mt	Colossians . . . . . Col	1 John 1Jn
Ruth . . . . Ru	Psalms . . . . Ps	Amos . . . . Am	Mark . . . . Mk	1 Thessalonians . 1Th	2 John 2Jn
1 Samuel 1Sa	Proverbs . . . . Pr	Obadiah . . . . . . Ob	Luke . . . . Lk	2 Thessalonians . 2Th	3 John 3Jn
2 Samuel 2Sa	Ecclesiastes . . . . Ecc	Jonah . . . . Jnh	John . . . . Jn	1 Timothy 1Ti	Jude . . . . Jude
1 Kings 1Ki	Song of Songs . . . SS	Micah . . . . Mic	Acts . . . . Ac	2 Timothy 2Ti	Revelation . . . . Rev

NIV EXHAUSTIVE CONCORDANCE

A

A (9144) [AN] See Index of Articles Etc.

AARON (318) [AARON'S, AARONIC]

Ex	4:14	"What about your brother, A the Levite?	195
	4:27	The LORD said to A, "Go into the desert	195
	4:28	Then Moses told A everything	195
	4:29	Moses and A brought together all the elders	195
	4:30	and A told them everything	195
	5: 1	Afterward Moses and A went to Pharaoh	195
	5: 4	But the king of Egypt said, "Moses and A,	195
	5:20	they found Moses and A waiting	195
	6:13	and A about the Israelites and Pharaoh king	195
	6:20	who bore him A and Moses.	195
	6:23	A married Elisheba, daughter	195
	6:25	of A married one of the daughters of Putiel,	195
	6:26	It was this same A and Moses to whom	195
	6:27	It was the same Moses and A.	195
	7: 1	your brother A will be your prophet.	195
	7: 2	and your brother A is to tell Pharaoh to let	195
	7: 6	Moses and A did just as the LORD commanded them.	195
	7: 7	and A eighty-three when they spoke	195
	7: 8	The LORD said to Moses and A,	195
	7: 9	'Perform a miracle,' then say to A,	195
	7:10	and A went to Pharaoh and did just as	195
	7:10	A threw his staff down in front of Pharaoh	195
	7:19	The LORD said to Moses, "Tell A,	195
	7:20	Moses and A did just as the LORD had commanded.	195
	7:22	he would not listen to **Moses and A,**	2157S
	8: 5	Then the LORD said to Moses, "Tell A,	195
	8: 6	So A stretched out his hand over the waters	195
	8: 8	Pharaoh summoned Moses and A and said,	195
	8:12	After Moses and A left Pharaoh,	195
	8:15	and would not listen to **Moses and A,**	2157S
	8:16	Then the LORD said to Moses, "Tell A,	195
	8:17	and when A stretched out his hand and	195
	8:25	Pharaoh summoned Moses and A and said,	195
	9: 8	Then the LORD said to Moses and A,	195
	9:12	and he would not listen to **Moses and A,**	2157S
	9:27	Then Pharaoh summoned Moses and A.	195
	10: 3	So Moses and A went to Pharaoh and said	195
	10: 8	Then Moses and A were brought back	195
	10:11	Then **Moses and** A were driven out	4392S
	10:16	Pharaoh quickly summoned Moses and A	195
	11:10	Moses and A performed all these wonders	195
	12: 1	The LORD said to Moses and A in Egypt,	195
	12:28	the LORD commanded Moses and A.	195
	12:31	the night Pharaoh summoned Moses and A	195
	12:43	The LORD said to Moses and A,	195
	12:50	the LORD had commanded Moses and A.	195
	16: 2	community grumbled against Moses and A.	195
	16: 6	So Moses and A said to all the Israelites,	195
	16: 9	Then Moses told A,	195
	16:10	While A was speaking to the whole Israelite	195
	16:33	So Moses said to A,	195
	16:34	A put the manna in front of the Testimony,	195
	17:10	and Hur went to the top of the hill.	195
	17:12	A and Hur held his hands up—	195
	18:12	and A came with all the elders of Israel	195
	19:24	"Go down and bring A up with you.	195

Ex	24: 1	"Come up to the LORD, you and A,	195
	24: 9	Moses and A, Nadab and Abihu,	195
	24:14	A and Hur are with you,"	195
	27:21	A and his sons are to keep	195
	28: 1	"Have A your brother brought to you from	195
	28: 2	Make sacred garments for your brother A,	195
	28: 3	that they are to make garments for A,	195
	28: 4	for your brother A and his sons,	195
	28:12	A is to bear the names on his shoulders as	195
	28:29	"Whenever A enters the Holy Place,	195
	28:30	Thus A will always bear the means	195
	28:35	A must wear it when he ministers.	195
	28:41	on your brother A and his sons,	195
	28:43	A and his sons must wear them	195
	28:43	"This is to be a lasting ordinance for A	2257S
	29: 4	Then bring A and his sons to the entrance	195
	29: 5	the garments and dress A with the tunic,	195
	29: 9	Then tie sashes on A and his sons.	195
	29: 9	In this way you shall ordain A and his sons.	195
	29:10	and A and his sons shall lay their hands	195
	29:15	and A and his sons shall lay their hands	195
	29:19	and A and his sons shall lay their hands	195
	29:20	the lobes of the right ears of A and his sons,	195
	29:21	and sprinkle it on A and his garments and	195
	29:24	the hands of A and his sons and wave them	195
	29:27	of the ordination ram that belong to A	195
	29:28	the regular share from the Israelites for A	195
	29:32	A and his sons are to eat the meat of	195
	29:35	"Do for A and his sons everything I have commanded you,	195
	29:44	the altar and will consecrate A and his sons	195
	30: 7	"A must burn fragrant incense on	195
	30:10	a year A shall make atonement on its horns.	195
	30:19	A and his sons are to wash their hands	195
	30:21	This is to be a lasting ordinance for A	2257S
	30:30	"Anoint A and his sons	195
	31:10	both the sacred garments for A the priest	195
	32: 1	they gathered around A and said, "Come,	195
	32: 2	A answered them, "Take off the gold earrings	195
	32: 3	and brought them to A.	195
	32: 5	When A saw this, he built an altar	195
	32:21	He said to A, "What did these people do	195
	32:22	"Do not be angry, my lord," A answered.	195
	32:25	that A had let them get out of control and	195
	32:35	of what they did with the calf A had made.	195
	34:30	When A and all the Israelites saw Moses,	195
	34:31	so A and all the leaders of the community	195
	35:19	both the sacred garments for A the priest	195
	38:21	under the direction of Ithamar son of A,	195
	39: 1	They also made sacred garments for A,	195
	39:27	For A and his sons,	195
	39:41	both the sacred garments for A the priest	195
	40:12	"Bring A and his sons to the entrance to	195
	40:13	Then dress A in the sacred garments,	195
	40:31	and Moses and A and his sons used it	195
Lev	1: 7	The sons of A the priest are to put fire on	195
	2: 3	The rest of the grain offering belongs to A	195
	2:10	The rest of the grain offering belongs to A	195
	6: 9	"Give A and his sons this command:	195
	6:16	A and his sons shall eat the rest of it,	195
	6:18	Any male descendant of A may eat it.	195
	6:20	the offering A and his sons are to bring to	195
	6:25	"Say to A and his sons:	195
	7:10	belongs equally to all the sons of A.	195
	7:31	but the breast belongs to A and his sons.	195
	7:33	of A who offers the blood and the fat of	195
	7:34	that is presented and have given them to A	195
	7:35	by fire that were allotted to A and his sons	195
	8: 2	"Bring A and his sons,	195
	8: 6	Then Moses brought A	195
	8: 7	He put the tunic on A,	2257S

Lev	8:14	A and his sons laid their hands on its head.	195
	8:18	A and his sons laid their hands on its head.	195
	8:22	A and his sons laid their hands on its head.	195
	8:27	of A and his sons and waved them before	195
	8:30	and sprinkled them on A and his garments	195
	8:30	So he consecrated A and his garments	195
	8:31	Moses then said to A and his sons,	195
	8:31	saying, 'A and his sons are to eat it.'	195
	8:36	So A and his sons did everything	195
	9: 1	On the eighth day Moses summoned A	195
	9: 2	He said to A, "Take a bull calf	195
	9: 7	Moses said to A, "Come to the altar	195
	9: 8	So A came to the altar and slaughtered	195
	9:15	A then brought the offering that was for	NIH
	9:20	and then A burned the fat on the altar.	NIH
	9:21	A waved the breasts and the right thigh	195
	9:22	Then A lifted his hands toward the people	195
	9:23	and A then went into the Tent of Meeting.	195
	10: 3	Moses then said to A,	195
	10: 3	A remained silent.	195
	10: 6	Then Moses said to A and his sons Eleazar	195
	10: 8	Then the LORD said to A,	195
	10:12	Moses said to A and his remaining sons,	195
	10:19	A replied to Moses,	195
	11: 1	The LORD said to Moses and A,	195
	13: 1	The LORD said to Moses and A,	195
	13: 2	he must be brought to A the priest or to one	195
	14:33	The LORD said to Moses and A,	195
	15: 1	The LORD said to Moses and A,	195
	16: 1	the death of the two sons of A who died	195
	16: 2	"Tell your brother A not to come	195
	16: 3	how A is to enter the sanctuary area:	195
	16: 6	"A is to offer the bull	195
	16: 9	A shall bring the goat whose lot falls to	195
	16:11	"A shall bring the bull	195
	16:17	from the time A goes in to make atonement	2257S
	16:20	"When A has finished making atonement	NIH
	16:23	"Then A is to go into the Tent of Meeting.	195
	17: 2	to A and his sons and to all the Israelites	195
	21: 1	"Speak to the priests, the sons of A,	195
	21:17	"Say to A: 'For the generations to come	195
	21:21	of A the priest who has any defect is	195
	21:24	to A and his sons and to all the Israelites.	195
	22: 2	"Tell A and his sons to treat with respect	195
	22: 4	of A has an infectious skin disease or	195
	22:18	to A and his sons and to all the Israelites	195
	24: 3	A is to tend the lamps before the LORD	195
	24: 9	It belongs to A and his sons,	195
Nu	1: 3	and A are to number by their divisions all	195
	1:17	A took these men whose names had been given,	195
	1:44	by Moses and A and the twelve leaders	195
	2: 1	The LORD said to Moses and A:	195
	3: 1	the account of the family of A and Moses at	195
	3: 2	of A were Nadab the firstborn and Abihu,	195
	3: 4	during the lifetime of their father A.	195
	3: 6	of Levi and present them to A the priest	195
	3: 9	Give the Levites to A and his sons;	195
	3:10	Appoint A and his sons to serve as priests;	195
	3:32	of the Levites was Eleazar son of A,	195
	3:38	and A and his sons to camp to the east	195
	3:39	at the LORD's command by Moses and A	195
	3:48	the additional Israelites to A and his sons."	195
	3:51	the redemption money to A and his sons,	195
	4: 1	The LORD said to Moses and A:	195
	4: 5	A and his sons are to go in and take down	195
	4:15	"After A and his sons have finished	195
	4:16	"Eleazar son of A, the priest,	195
	4:17	The LORD said to Moses and A,	195
	4:19	A and his sons are to go into the sanctuary	195
	4:27	under the direction of A and his sons.	195
	4:28	be under the direction of Ithamar son of A,	195

Nu	4:33	under the direction of Ithamar son of A,	195
	4:34	A and the leaders of the community	195
	4:37	Moses and A counted them according to	195
	4:41	Moses and A counted them according to	195
	4:45	Moses and A counted them according to	195
	4:46	and A and the leaders of Israel counted all	195
	6:23	"Tell A and his sons,	195
	7:8	under the direction of Ithamar son of A,	195
	8:2	"Speak to A and say to him,	195
	8:3	A did so; he set up the lamps	195
	8:11	A is to present the Levites before	195
	8:13	the Levites stand in front of A and his sons	195
	8:19	to A and his sons to do the work at the Tent	195
	8:20	A and the whole Israelite community did	195
	8:21	Then A presented them as a wave offering	195
	8:22	under the supervision of A and his sons.	195
	9:6	they came to Moses and A that same day	195
	10:8	"The sons of A, the priests,	195
	12:1	and A began to talk against Moses because	195
	12:4	the LORD said to Moses, A and Miriam,	195
	12:5	to the Tent and summoned A and Miriam.	195
	12:10	A turned toward her and saw	195
	13:26	and A and the whole Israelite community	195
	14:2	Israelites grumbled against Moses and A,	195
	14:5	Then Moses and A fell facedown in front of	195
	14:26	The LORD said to Moses and A:	195
	15:33	to Moses and A and the whole assembly,	195
	16:3	as a group to oppose Moses and A and said	195
	16:11	Who is A that you should grumble	195
	16:16	you and they and A.	195
	16:17	and A are to present your censers also."	195
	16:18	and stood with Moses and A at the entrance	195
	16:20	The LORD said to Moses and A,	195
	16:22	Moses and A fell facedown and cried out,	NIH
	16:37	of A, the priest, to take the censers out of	195
	16:40	of A should come to burn incense before	195
	16:41	community grumbled against Moses and A.	195
	16:42	to Moses and A and turned toward the Tent	195
	16:43	Then Moses and A went to the front	195
	16:46	Then Moses said to A,	195
	16:47	So A did as Moses said,	195
	16:47	but A offered the incense	NIH
	16:50	Then A returned to Moses at the entrance to	195
	18:1	The LORD said to A,	195
	18:8	Then the LORD said to A,	195
	18:20	The LORD said to A,	195
	18:28	the LORD's portion to A the priest.	195
	19:1	The LORD said to Moses and A:	195
	20:2	in opposition to Moses and A.	195
	20:6	Moses and A went from the assembly to	195
	20:8	and you and your brother A gather	195
	20:10	He and A gathered the assembly together	195
	20:12	But the LORD said to Moses and A,	195
	20:23	the LORD said to Moses and A,	195
	20:24	"A will be gathered to his people.	195
	20:25	Get A and his son Eleazar and take them	195
	20:26	for A will be gathered to his people;	195
	20:28	And A died there on top of the mountain.	195
	20:29	whole community learned that A had died,	195
	25:7	Phinehas son of Eleazar, the son of A,	195
	25:11	the son of A, the priest,	195
	26:1	to Moses and Eleazar son of A,	195
	26:9	and A and were among Korah's followers	195
	26:59	To Amram she bore A,	195
	26:60	A was the father of Nadab and Abihu.	195
	26:64	among those counted by Moses and A	195
	27:13	as your brother A was,	195
	33:1	under the leadership of Moses and A.	195
	33:38	the LORD's command A the priest went	195
	33:39	A was a hundred and twenty-three years old	195
Dt	9:20	And the LORD was angry enough with A	195
	9:20	but at that time I prayed for A too.	195
	10:6	There A died and was buried,	195
	32:50	just as your brother A died on Mount Hor	195
Jos	21:4	of A the priest were allotted thirteen towns	195
	21:10	of A who were from the Kohathite clans of	195
	21:13	of A the priest they gave Hebron (a city	195
	21:19	the descendants of A, were thirteen,	195
	24:5	" 'Then I sent Moses and A,	195
	24:33	And Eleazar son of A died and was buried	195
Jdg	20:28	the son of A, ministering before it.)	195
1Sa	12:6	and A and brought your forefathers up out	195
	12:8	and the LORD sent Moses and A,	195
1Ch	6:3	A, Moses and Miriam.	195
	6:3	The sons of A: Nadab, Abihu, Eleazar and	195
	6:49	But A and his descendants were	195
	6:50	These were the descendants of A:	195
	6:54	of A who were from the Kohathite clan,	195
	6:57	So the descendants of A were given Hebron	195
	12:27	leader of the family of A, with 3,700 men,	195
	15:4	He called together the descendants of A	195
	23:13	The sons of Amram: A and Moses.	195
	23:13	A was set apart,	195
	23:32	under their brothers the descendants of A,	195
	24:1	These were the divisions of the sons of A:	195
	24:1	The sons of A were Nadab, Abihu,	195
	24:19	for them by their forefather A,	195
	24:31	as their brothers the descendants of A did,	195
	27:17	Hashabiah son of Kemuel; over A:	195
2Ch	13:9	the sons of A, and the Levites,	195
	13:10	the LORD are sons of A,	195
	26:18	the descendants of A,	195
	29:21	the descendants of A,	195
	31:19	As for the priests, the descendants of A,	195
	35:14	because the priests, the descendants of A,	195
Ezr	7:5	the son of A the chief priest is—	195
Ne	10:38	A priest descended from A is to accompany	195
Ne	12:47	the portion for the descendants of A.	195
Ps	77:20	like a flock by the hand of Moses and A.	195
	99:6	Moses and A were among his priests,	195
	105:26	He sent Moses his servant, and A,	195
	106:16	grew envious of Moses and of A,	195
	115:10	O house of A, trust in the LORD—	195
	115:12	he will bless the house of A,	195
	118:3	Let the house of A say:	195
	135:19	O house of A, praise the LORD;	195
Mic	6:4	also A and Miriam.	195
Lk	1:5	also a descendant of A.	2
Ac	7:40	They told A, 'Make us gods who will go	2
Heb	5:4	he must be called by God, just as A was.	2
	7:11	not in the order of A?	2

AARON'S (35) [AARON]

Ex	7:12	But A staff swallowed up their staffs.	195
	15:20	Then Miriam the prophetess, A sister,	195
	28:30	be over A heart whenever he enters	195
	28:38	It will be on A forehead.	195
	28:38	on A forehead continually so that they will	2257S
	28:40	sashes and headbands for A sons,	195
	29:26	the breast of the ram for A ordination,	195
	29:29	"A sacred garments will belong	195+4200
Lev	1:5	then A sons the priests shall bring the blood	195
	1:8	& A sons the priests shall arrange the pieces,	195
	1:11	of the altar before the LORD, and A sons	195
	2:2	and take it to A sons the priests.	195
	3:2	A sons the priests shall sprinkle	195
	3:5	Then A sons are to burn it on the altar	195
	3:8	Then A sons shall sprinkle its blood against	195
	3:13	Then A sons shall sprinkle its blood against	195
	6:14	A sons are to bring it before the LORD,	195
	8:9	the turban on A head and set the gold plate,	2257S
	8:12	of the anointing oil on A head	195
	8:13	Then he brought A sons forward,	195
	8:23	and put it on the lobe of A right ear,	195
	8:24	also brought A sons forward and put some	195
	10:1	A sons Nadab and Abihu took their censers,	195
	10:6	sons of A uncle Uzziel, and said to them,	195
	10:16	A remaining sons, and asked,	195
Nu	3:3	Those were the names of A sons,	195
	17:3	On the staff of Levi write A name,	195
	17:6	and A staff was among them.	195
	17:8	of the Testimony and saw that A staff,	195
	17:10	"Put back A staff in front of the Testimony,	195
	20:26	Remove A garments and put them	195
	20:28	Moses removed A garments and put them	195
1Ch	23:28	of the Levites was to help A descendants in	195
Ps	133:2	running down on A beard,	195
Heb	9:4	A staff that had budded,	2

AARONIC (1) [AARON]

2Ch	35:14	for themselves and for the A priests.	195+1201

AARONITES (KJV) See AARON

ABADDON (1)

Rev	9:11	whose name in Hebrew is A, and in Greek,	3

ABAGTHA (1)

Est	1:10	Mehuman, Biztha, Harbona, Bigtha, A,	5

ABANA (1)

2Ki	5:12	Are not A and Pharpar,	76

ABANDON (13) [ABANDONED, ABANDONS]

Dt	4:31	not a or destroy you or forget the covenant	8332
Jos	10:6	"Do not a your servants.	3338+4946+8332
1Ki	6:13	and will not a my people Israel."	6440
2Ch	12:5	therefore, I now a you to Shishak.' "	6440
Ne	9:19	not a them in the desert.	6440
	9:31	not put an end to them or a them,	6440
Ps	16:10	because you will not a me to the grave,	6440
	138:8	do not a the works of your hands,	8332
Jer	12:7	"I will forsake my house, a my inheritance;	5759
	48:28	A your towns and dwell among the rocks,	6440
Eze	27:29	All who handle the oars will a their ships;	3718+4946
Ac	2:27	because you will not a me to the grave,	1593
1Ti	4:1	that in later times some will a the faith	923

ABANDONED (36) [ABANDON]

Ge	24:27	who has not a his kindness and faithfulness	6440
Dt	29:25	"It is because this people a the covenant of	6440
	32:15	He a the God who made him and rejected	5759
Jdg	4:15	and Sisera with his chariot and fled on foot.	3718
	5:6	in the days of Jael, the roads were a;	2532
	6:13	now the LORD has a us and put us into	5759
1Sa	30:13	My master a me	6440
	31:7	they a their towns and fled.	6440
2Sa	5:21	The Philistines a their idols there,	6440
1Ki	18:18	You have a the LORD's commands	6440
2Ki	7:7	the dusk and a their tents and their horses	6440
1Ch	10:7	they a their towns and fled.	6440
	14:12	The Philistines had a their gods there,	6440
2Ch	11:14	even a their pasturelands and property,	6440
	12:1	he and all Israel with him a the law of	6440
	12:5	'You have a me;	6440
	16:5	he stopped building Ramah and a his work.	8697
2Ch	24:18	They a the temple of the LORD,	6440
Ne	9:28	Then you a them to the hand	6440
Job	18:4	is the earth to be a for your sake?	6440
Ps	78:60	He a the tabernacle of Shiloh,	5759
Isa	2:6	You have a your people, the house of Jacob.	5759
	10:14	as men gather a eggs,	6440
	17:9	like places a to thickets and undergrowth.	6440
	27:10	an settlement, forsaken like the desert;	8938
	32:14	The fortress will be a,	5759
	54:7	"For a brief moment I a you,	6440
Jer	7:29	and a this generation that is	5759
	49:25	Why has the city of renown not been a,	6440
La	2:7	and a his sanctuary.	5545
Mic	2:7	Therefore Israel will be a until the time	5989
Zep	2:4	Gaza will be a and Ashkelon left in ruins.	6440
Ac	2:31	that he was not a to the grave,	1593
Ro	1:27	also a natural relations with women	918
2Co	4:9	but not a; struck down, but not destroyed,	1593
Jude	1:6	of authority but a their own home—	657

ABANDONS (1) [ABANDON]

Jn	10:12	he a the sheep and runs away.	918

ABARIM (5) [IYE ABARIM]

Nu	27:12	in the A range and see the land I have given	6305
	33:47	and camped in the mountains of A,	6305
	33:48	of A and camped on the plains of Moab by	6305
Dt	32:49	into the A Range to Mount Nebo in Moab,	6305
Jer	22:20	cry out from A,	6305

ABASE, ABASED, ABASING (KJV) See FRIGHTENED, LOW, LOWER, HUMBLE, IN NEED

ABASHED (1)

Isa	24:23	The moon will be a, the sun ashamed;	2917

ABATED (KJV) See RECEDED, GONE

ABBA (3)

Mk	14:36	"A, Father," he said, "everything is possible	5
Ro	8:15	And by him we cry, "A, Father."	5
Gal	4:6	the Spirit who calls out, "A, Father."	5

ABDA (2)

1Ki	4:6	Adoniram son of A—	6272
Ne	11:17	and A son of Shammua, the son of Galal,	6272

ABDEEL (1)

Jer	36:26	and Shelemiah son of A to arrest Baruch	6274

ABDI (3)

1Ch	6:44	Ethan son of Kishi, the son of A,	6279
2Ch	29:12	of A and Azariah son of Jehallelel;	6279
Ezr	10:26	Mattaniah, Zechariah, Jehiel, A,	6279

ABDIEL (1)

1Ch	5:15	Ahi son of A, the son of Guni,	6280

ABDOMEN (3)

Nu	5:21	to waste away and your a to swell.	1061
	5:22	so that your a swells	1061
	5:27	her a will swell and her thigh waste away,	1061

ABDON (9)

Jos	19:28	It went to A, Rehob, Hammon and Kanah,	6278
	21:30	from the tribe of Asher, Mishal, A,	6278
Jdg	12:13	After him, A son of Hillel, from Pirathon,	6277
	12:15	Then A son of Hillel died,	6277
1Ch	6:74	the tribe of Asher they received Mashal, A,	6278
	8:23	A, Zicri, Hanan,	6277
	8:30	and his firstborn son was A,	6277
	9:36	and his firstborn son was A,	6277
2Ch	34:20	Ahikam son of Shaphan, A son of Micah,	6277

ABEDNEGO (14)

Da	1:7	and to Azariah, A.	6284
	2:49	and A administrators over the province	10524
	3:12	Shadrach, Meshach and A—	10524
	3:13	Nebuchadnezzar summoned Shadrach, Meshach and A.	10524
	3:14	"Is it true, Shadrach, Meshach and A,	10524
	3:16	Meshach and A replied to the king,	10524
	3:19	Meshach and A, and his attitude	10524
	3:20	Meshach and A and throw them into	10524
	3:22	up Shadrach, Meshach and A,	10524
	3:26	"Shadrach, Meshach and A,	10524
	3:26	Meshach and A came out of the fire,	10524
	3:28	be to the God of Shadrach, Meshach and A,	10524
	3:29	and A be cut into pieces and their houses	10524
	3:30	Meshach and A in the province of Babylon.	10524

ABEL (13)

Ge	4:2	Later she gave birth to his brother A.	2040
	4:2	A kept flocks, and Cain worked the soil.	2040
	4:4	But A brought fat portions from some of	2040
	4:4	The LORD looked with favor on A	2040

Ge   4: 8   Now Cain said to his brother A,   2040
     4: 8   Cain attacked his brother A and killed him.   2040
     4: 9   "Where is your brother A?"   2040
     4:25   another child in place of A,   2040
2Sa 20:18   'Get your answer at A,' and that settled it.   64
Mt 23:35   from the blood of righteous A to the blood   6
Lk 11:51   the blood of A to the blood of Zechariah,   6
Heb 11: 4   By faith A offered God   6
    12:24   a better word than the blood of A.   6

ABEL BETH MAACAH (4)

2Sa 20:14   the tribes of Israel to A and   68
    20:15   and besieged Sheba in A.   68
1Ki 15:20   A and all Kinnereth   68
2Ki 15:29   Assyria came and took Ijon, A, Janoah,   68

ABEL KERAMIM (1)

Jdg 11:33   vicinity of Minnith, as far as A.   70

ABEL MAIM (1)

2Ch 16: 4   A and all the store cities of Naphtali.   72

ABEL MEHOLAH (3) [MEHOLAH]

Jdg 7:22   as the border of A near Tabbath.   71
1Ki 4:12   from Beth Shan to A across   71
    19:16   from A to succeed you as prophet.   71

ABEL MIZRAIM (1) [MIZRAIM]

Ge 50:11   near the Jordan is called A.   73

ABEL SHITTIM (1) [SHITTIM]

Nu 33:49   from Beth Jeshimoth to A.   69

ABEZ (KJV) See EBEZ

ABHOR (12) [ABHORRED, ABHORRENT, ABHORS]

Lev 26:11   and I will not a you.   1718
    26:15   and if you reject my decrees and a my laws   1718
    26:30   I will a you.   1718
    26:44   or a them so as to destroy them completely,   1718
Dt   7:26   Utterly a and detest it,   9210+9210
    23: 7   Do not a an Edomite, for he is your brother.   9493
    23: 7   Do not a an Egyptian,   9493
Ps 26: 5   I a the assembly of evildoers and refuse   8533
   119:163 I hate and a falsehood but I love your law.   9493
   139:21   and a those who rise up against you?   7752
Am   6: 8   "I a the pride of Jacob   9290
Ro   2:22   You who a idols, do you rob temples?   1009

ABHORRED (4) [ABHOR]

Lev 20:23   they did all these things, I a them.   7762
    26:43   and a my decrees.   1718
Ps 106:40   with his people and a his inheritance.   9493
Isa 49: 7   and a by the nation, to the servant of rulers: 9493

ABHORRENT (4) [ABHOR]

Jer 15: 4   I will make them a to all the kingdoms of   2317
    24: 9   I will make them a and an offense to all   2317
    29:18   and will make them a to all the kingdoms   2317
    34:17   and will make you a to all the kingdoms of   2317

ABHORS (2) [ABHOR]

Ps   5: 6   and deceitful men the LORD a.   9493
Pr 11: 1   The LORD a dishonest scales,   9359

ABI-ALBON (1)

2Sa 23:31   A the Arbathite, Azmaveth the Barhumite,   50

ABIA, ABIAH (KJV) See ABIJAH

ABIASAPH (1)

Ex   6:24   of Korah were Assir, Elkanah and A.   25

ABIATHAR (30)

1Sa 22:20   But A, a son of Ahimelech son of Ahitub,   59
    22:22   Then David said to A: 59
    23: 6   (Now A son of Ahimelech had brought   59
    23: 9   he said to A the priest, "Bring the ephod."   59
    30: 7   Then David said to A the priest,   59
    30: 7   A brought it to him,   59
2Sa 8:17   and Ahimelech son of A were priests;   59
    15:24   and A offered sacrifices until all   59
    15:27   and Jonathan son of A.   59
    15:27   You and I take your two sons with you.   NIH
    15:29   So Zadok and A took the ark of God back   59
    15:35   the priests Zadok and A be there with you?   59
    15:36   of Zadok and Jonathan son of A,   59
    17:15   Hushai told Zadok and A, the priests,   59
    19:11   to Zadok and A, the priests: 59
    20:25   Zadok and A were priests;   59
1Ki 1: 7   with Joab son of Zeruiah and with A   59
     1:19   A the priest and Joab the commander of   59
     1:25   the commanders of the army and A   59
     1:42   Jonathan son of A the priest arrived.   59
     2:22   for A the priest and Joab son of Zeruiah!"   59
     2:26   To A the priest the king said,   59

1Ki 2:27   So Solomon removed A from   59
     2:35   the army in Joab's position and replaced A   59
     4: 4   Zadok and A—priests;   59
1Ch 15:11   David summoned Zadok and A the priests,   59
    18:16   and Ahimelech son of A were priests;   59
    24: 6   of A and the heads of families of the priests   59
    27:34   by Jehoiada son of Benaiah and by A.   59
Mk   2:26   In the days of A the high priest,   8

ABIB (5)

Ex 13: 4   Today, in the month of A, you are leaving.   26
    23:15   at the appointed time in the month of A,   26
    34:18   at the appointed time in the month of A,   26
Dt 16: 1   the month of A and celebrate the Passover   26
    16: 1   of A he brought you out of Egypt by night.   26

ABIDA (2)

Ge 25: 4   Epher, Hanoch, A and Eldaah.   30
1Ch 1:33   Ephah, Epher, Hanoch, A and Eldaah.   30

ABIDAH (KJV) See ABIDA

ABIDAN (5)

Nu   1:11   from Benjamin, A son of Gideoni;   29
     2:22   of the people of Benjamin is A son   29
     7:60   On the ninth day A son of Gideoni,   29
     7:65   This was the offering of A son of Gideoni.   29
    10:24   and A son of Gideoni was over the division   29

ABIDE, ABIDETH, ABIDING (KJV) See LIVE, REMAIN, SURVIVE

ABIEL (3)

1Sa 9: 1   whose name was Kish son of A,   24
    14:51   and Abner's father Ner were sons of A.   24
1Ch 11:32   from the ravines of Gaash, A the Arbathite,   24

ABIEZER (6) [ABIEZRITE, ABIEZRITES]

Jos 17: 2   the clans of A, Helek, Asriel, Shechem,   48
Jdg 8: 2   the full grape harvest of A?   48
2Sa 23:27   A from Anathoth, Mebunnai   48
1Ch 7:18   to Ishhod, A and Mahlah.   48
    11:28   of Ikkesh from Tekoa, A from Anathoth,   48
    27:12   for the ninth month, was A the Anathothite,   48

ABIEZRITE (1) [ABIEZER]

Jdg 6:11   in Ophrah that belonged to Joash the A,   49

ABIEZRITES (3) [ABIEZER]

Jdg 6:24   To this day it stands in Ophrah of the A.   49
     6:34   summoning the A to follow him.   48
     8:32   of his father Joash in Ophrah of the A.   49

ABIGAIL (17)

1Sa 25: 3   and his wife's name was A.   28
    25:14   One of the servants told Nabal's wife A: 28
    25:18   A lost no time.   28
    25:23   When A saw David, she quickly got off   28
    25:32   David said to A, "Praise be to the LORD,   28
    25:36   When A went to Nabal,   28
    25:39   Then David sent word to A,   28
    25:40   His servants went to Carmel and said to A,   28
    25:42   A quickly got on a donkey and,   28
    27: 3   Ahinoam of Jezreel and A of Carmel,   28
    30: 5   Ahinoam of Jezreel and A,   28
2Sa 2: 2   Ahinoam of Jezreel and A,   28
     3: 3   Kileab the son of A the widow of Nabal   28
    17:25   an Israelite who had married A,   28
1Ch 2:16   Their sisters were Zeruiah and A.   28
     2:17   A was the mother of Amasa,   28
     3: 1   the second, Daniel the son of A of Carmel;   28

ABIHAIL (6)

Nu   3:35   of the Merarite clans was Zuriel son of A;   38
1Ch 2:29   Abishur's wife was named A.   35
     5:14   These were the sons of A son of Huri,   38
2Ch 11:18   of David's son Jerimoth and of A,   35
Est 2:15   the daughter of his uncle A) to go to   38
     9:29   So Queen Esther, daughter of A,   38

ABIHU (12)

Ex   6:23   and she bore him Nadab and A,   33
    24: 1   you and Aaron, Nadab and A,   33
    24: 9   Moses and Aaron, Nadab and A,   33
    28: 1   along with his sons Nadab and A,   33
Lev 10: 1   and A took their censers, put fire in them   33
Nu   3: 2   of Aaron were Nadab the firstborn and A,   33
     3: 4   Nadab and A, however, fell dead before   33
    26:60   Aaron was the father of Nadab and A,   33
    26:61   And A died when they made an offering   33
1Ch 6: 3   Nadab, A, Eleazar and Ithamar.   33
    24: 1   The sons of Aaron were Nadab, A,   33
    24: 2   Nadab and A died before their father did,   33

ABIHUD (1)

1Ch 8: 3   The sons of Bela were: Addar, Gera, A,   34

ABIJAH (31) [ABIJAH'S]

1Sa 8: 2   and the name of his second was A,   31
1Ki 14: 1   At that time A son of Jeroboam became ill,   31
    14:31   And A his son succeeded him as king.   31
    15: 1   A became king of Judah.   31
    15: 7   There was war between A and Jeroboam.   31
    15: 8   And A rested with his fathers   31
2Ki 18: 2   His mother's name was A daughter   23
1Ch 2:24   A the wife of Hezron bore him Ashhur   31
     3:10   Solomon's son was Rehoboam, A his son,   31
     6:28   Joel the firstborn and A the second son.   31
     7: 8   Omri, Jeremoth, A, Anathoth and Alemeth.   31
    24:10   the seventh to Hakkoz, the eighth to A,   31
2Ch 11:20   who bore him A, Attai,   31
    11:22   Rehoboam appointed A son of Maacah to   31
    12:16   And A his son succeeded him as king.   31
    13: 1   A became king of Judah,   31
    13: 2   There was war between A and Jeroboam.   31
    13: 3   A went into battle with a force   31
    13: 4   A stood on Mount Zemaraim,   31
    13:15   and all Israel before A and Judah.   31
    13:17   and his men inflicted heavy losses   31
    13:19   A pursued Jeroboam and took from him   31
    13:20   not regain power during the time of A.   32
    13:21   But A grew in strength.   32
    14: 1   And A rested with his fathers   31
    29: 1   His mother's name was A daughter   31
Ne 10: 7   Meshullam, A, Mijamin,   31
    12: 4   Iddo, Ginnethon, A,   31
Mt   1: 7   Rehoboam the father of A,   7
     1: 7   A the father of Asa,   7
Lk   1: 5   to the priestly division of A;   7

ABIJAH'S (4) [ABIJAH]

1Ki 15: 6   and Jeroboam throughout [A] lifetime.   2257S
    15: 7   As for the other events of A reign,   31
2Ch 13:22   The other events of A reign,   31
Ne 12:17   of A, Zicri; of Miniamin's   31

ABILENE (1)

Lk   3: 1   and Lysanias tetrarch of A—   9

ABILITY (14) [ABLE]

Ge 47: 6   of any among them with special a,   2657
Ex 31: 3   a and knowledge in all kinds of crafts—   9312
    35:31   a and knowledge in all kinds of crafts—   9312
    35:34   of the tribe of Dan, the a to teach others.   4213
    36: 1   to whom the LORD has given skill and a   9312
    36: 2   to whom the LORD had given a   928+2683+4213
Dt   8:18   for it is he who gives you the a   3946
Ezr 2:69   to their a they gave to the treasury   3946
Da   5:12   and also the a to interpret dreams,   AIT
Mt 25:15   each according to his a.   1539
Ac   8:19   "Give me also this a so that everyone   2026
    11:29   The disciples, each according to his a,   2344
2Co 1: 8   far beyond our a to endure,   1539
     8: 3   and even beyond their a.   1539

ABIMAEL (2)

Ge 10:28   Obal, A, Sheba,   42
1Ch 1:22   Obal, A, Sheba,   42

ABIMELECH (61) [ABIMELECH'S]

Ge 20: 2   Then A king of Gerar sent for Sarah   43
    20: 3   to A in a dream one night and said to him,   43
    20: 4   Now A had not gone near her, so he said,   43
    20: 8   next morning A summoned all his officials,   43
    20: 9   Then A called Abraham in and said,   43
    20:10   And A asked Abraham,   43
    20:14   Then A brought sheep and cattle and male   43
    20:15   And A said, "My land is before you;   43
    20:17   and God healed A,   43
    21:22   At that time A and Phicol the commander   43
    21:25   Then Abraham complained to A about   43
    21:26   A said, "I don't know who has done this.   43
    21:27   and cattle and gave them to A,   43
    21:29   and A asked Abraham,   43
    21:32   A and Phicol the commander   43
    26: 1   and Isaac went to A king of the Philistines   43
    26: 8   A king of the Philistines looked down from   43
    26: 9   So A summoned Isaac and said,   43
    26:10   A said, "What is this you have done to us?   43
    26:11   So A gave orders to all the people: 43
    26:16   Then A said to Isaac, "Move away from us;   43
    26:26   A had come to him from Gerar,   43
Jdg 8:31   also bore him a son, whom he named A.   43
     9: 1   A son of Jerub-Baal went   43
     9: 3   they were inclined to follow A,   43
     9: 4   and A used it to hire reckless adventurers,   43
     9: 6   at the pillar in Shechem to crown A king.   43
     9:18   and made A, the son of his slave girl,   43
     9:19   may A be your joy, and may you be his,   43
     9:20   let fire come out from A and consume you,   43
     9:20   and Beth Millo, and consume A!"   43
     9:21   because he was afraid of his brother A.   43
     9:22   After A had governed Israel three years,   43
     9:23   an evil spirit between A and the citizens   43
     9:23   who acted treacherously against A.   43
     9:24   might be avenged on their brother A and on   43
     9:24   and this was reported to A.   43
     9:27   and drinking, they cursed A.   43
     9:28   Then Gaal son of Ebed said, "Who is A,   43

Jdg	9:28	Why should we serve A?	5647S
	9:29	I would say to A, 'Call out your whole army	43
	9:31	Under cover he sent messengers to A,	43
	9:34	So A and all his troops set out by night	43
	9:35	at the entrance to the city gate just as A	43
	9:38	'Who is A that we should be subject	43
	9:39	the citizens of Shechem and fought A.	43
	9:40	A chased him, and many fell wounded	43
	9:41	A stayed in Arumah,	43
	9:42	and this was reported to A.	43
	9:44	A and the companies with him rushed	43
	9:45	All that day A pressed his attack against	43
	9:47	A heard that they had assembled there,	43
	9:49	all the men cut branches and followed A.	43
	9:50	Next A went to Thebez and besieged it	43
	9:52	A went to the tower and stormed it,	43
	9:55	When the Israelites saw that A was dead,	43
	9:56	the wickedness that A had done	43
	10: 1	After the time of A a man of Issachar,	43
2Sa	11:21	Who killed A son of Jerub-Besheth?	43
Ps	34: T	When he pretended to be insane before A,	43

ABIMELECH'S (2) [ABIMELECH]

Ge	20:18	closed up every womb in A household	43
	21:25	a well of water that A servants had seized.	43

ABINADAB (9) [ABINADAB'S]

1Sa	16: 8	Then Jesse called A and had him pass	44
	17:13	the second, A; and the third, Shammah.	44
	31: 2	and they killed his sons Jonathan, A	44
2Sa	6: 3	and brought it from the house of A,	44
	6: 3	Uzzah and Ahio, sons of A,	44
1Ch	2:13	the second son was A, the third Shimea,	44
	8:33	Malki-Shua, A and Esh-Baal.	44
	9:39	Malki-Shua, A and Esh-Baal.	44
	10: 2	and they killed his sons Jonathan, A	44

ABINADAB'S (2) [ABINADAB]

1Sa	7: 1	They took it to A house on the hill	44
1Ch	13: 7	the ark of God from A house on a new cart,	44

ABINOAM (4)

Jdg	4: 6	She sent for Barak son of A from Kedesh	45
	4:12	of A had gone up to Mount Tabor,	45
	5: 1	and Barak son of A sang this song:	45
	5:12	Take captive your captives, O son of A.'	45

ABIRAM (11)

Nu	16: 1	Dathan and A, sons of Eliab,	53
	16:12	Then Moses summoned Dathan and A,	53
	16:24	from the tents of Korah, Dathan and A.' "	53
	16:25	Moses got up and went to Dathan and A,	53
	16:27	from the tents of Korah, Dathan and A.	53
	16:27	and A had come out and were standing	53
	26: 9	of Eliab were Nemuel, Dathan and A.	53
	26: 9	The same Dathan and A	53
Dt	11: 6	and what he did to Dathan and A,	53
1Ki	16:34	at the cost of his firstborn son A,	53
Ps	106:17	it buried the company of A.	53

ABISHAG (5)

1Ki	1: 3	for a beautiful girl and found A,	54
	1:15	to see the aged king in the room, where A	54
	2:17	to give me A the Shunammite as my wife."	54
	2:21	"Let A the Shunammite be given in marriage	54
	2:22	"Why do you request A the Shunammite	54

ABISHAI (26)

1Sa	26: 6	then asked Ahimelech the Hittite and A son	57
	26: 6	"I'll go with you," said A.	57
	26: 7	So David and A went to the army by night,	57
	26: 8	A said to David,	57
	26: 9	But David said to A, "Don't destroy him!	57
2Sa	2:18	Joab, A and Asahel.	57
	2:24	But Joab and A pursued Abner,	57
	3:30	(Joab and his brother A murdered Abner	57
	10:10	of A his brother and deployed them against	93
	10:14	they fled before A and went inside the city.	57
	16: 9	Then A son of Zeruiah said to the king,	57
	16:11	David then said to A and all his officials,	57
	18: 2	of Joab, a third under Joab's brother A son	57
	18: 5	The king commanded Joab, A and Ittai,	57
	18:12	the king commanded you and A and Ittai,	57
	19:21	Then A son of Zeruiah said,	57
	20: 6	David said to A,	57
	20: 7	under the command of A.	2257S
	20:10	and his brother A pursued Sheba son	57
	21:17	A son of Zeruiah came to David's rescue;	57
	23:18	A the brother of Joab son	57
1Ch	2:16	Zeruiah's three sons were A,	93
	11:20	A the brother of Joab was chief of	93
	18:12	A son of Zeruiah struck	93
	19:11	under the command of A his brother,	93
	19:15	they too fled before his brother A and went	93

ABISHALOM (2)

1Ki	15: 2	mother's name was Maacah daughter of A.	58
	15:10	His grandmother's name was Maacah daughter of A.	58

ABISHUA (5)

1Ch	6: 4	Phinehas the father of A,	55
	6: 5	A the father of Bukki,	55
	6:50	Phinehas his son, A his son,	55
	8: 4	A, Naaman, Ahoah,	55
Ezr	7: 5	the son of A, the son of Phinehas, the son	55

ABISHUR (1) [ABISHUR'S]

1Ch	2:28	The sons of Shammai: Nadab and A.	56

ABISHUR'S (1) [ABISHUR]

1Ch	2:29	A wife was named Abihail,	56

ABITAL (2)

2Sa	3: 4	the fifth, Shephatiah the son of A;	40
1Ch	3: 3	Shephatiah the son of A;	40

ABITUB (1)

1Ch	8:11	By Hushim he had A and Elpaal.	39

ABIUD (2)

Mt	1:13	Zerubbabel the father of A,	10
	1:13	A the father of Eliakim,	10

ABJECTS (KJV) See ATTACKERS

ABLAZE (12)

Dt	5:23	while the mountain was a with fire,	1277
	9:15	from the mountain while it was a with fire.	1277
Job	41:21	His breath sets coals a,	4265
Ps	83:14	the forest or a flame sets the mountains a,	4265
Isa	9:18	sets the forest thickets a,	3675
	30:33	like a stream of burning sulfur, sets it a,	1277
	33:12	like cut thornbushes they will be set a."	836+928+2021+3675
	43: 2	the flames will not set you a.	1277
	50:11	and of the torches you have set a.	1277
	64: 2	fire sets twigs a and causes water to boil,	7706
Da	7: 9	and its wheels were all a.	10178+10471
Rev	8: 8	all a, was thrown into the sea.	2794+4786

ABLE (133) [ABILITY, ABLE-BODIED, DISABLED, ENABLE, ENABLED, ENABLES, ENABLING]

Ge	13: 6	that they were not a to stay together.	3523
	14:23	so that you will never be a to say,	AIT
	45: 3	But his brothers were not a to answer him,	3523
Ex	7:18	the Egyptians will not be a to drink	4206
	18:23	you will be a to stand the strain,	3523
Lev	26:26	ten women will be a to bake your bread	AIT
	26:37	not be a to stand before your enemies.	9538
Nu	1: 3	or more who are a to serve in the army.	AIT
	1:20	or more who were a to serve in the army	AIT
	1:22	or more who were a to serve in the army	AIT
	1:24	or more who were a to serve in the army	AIT
	1:26	or more who were a to serve in the army	AIT
	1:28	or more who were a to serve in the army	AIT
	1:30	or more who were a to serve in the army	AIT
	1:32	or more who were a to serve in the army	AIT
	1:34	or more who were a to serve in the army	AIT
	1:36	or more who were a to serve in the army	AIT
	1:38	or more who were a to serve in the army	AIT
	1:40	or more who were a to serve in the army	AIT
	1:42	or more who were a to serve in the army	AIT
	1:45	or more who were a to serve in Israel's army	AIT
	5:28	be a to have children.	2445+2446
	14:16	not a to bring these people into	3523
	22: 6	be a to defeat them and drive them out of	3523
	22:11	be a to fight them and drive them away.' "	3523
	22:37	Am I really not a to reward you?"	3523
	26: 2	or more who are a to serve in the army	AIT
Dt	7:24	No one will be a to stand against you;	3523
	9:28	the LORD was not a to take them into	3523
	11:25	No man will be a to stand against you.	AIT
	31: 2	and twenty years old and I am no longer a	3523
Jos	1: 5	be a to stand up against you all the days	AIT
	10: 8	one of them will be a to withstand you."	AIT
	17:12	the Manassites were not a to occupy	3523
	22:27	not be a to say to ours,	AIT
	23: 9	this day no one has been a to withstand you.	AIT
	24:19	"You are not a to serve the LORD.	3523
Jdg	2:14	whom they were no longer a to resist.	3523
	8: 3	What was I a to do compared to you?"	3523
1Sa	17: 9	If he is a to fight and kill me,	3523
	17:33	not a to go out against this Philistine	3523
1Ki	3: 9	For who is a to govern this great people	3523
2Ki	2:16	"we your servants have fifty a men.	1201+2657
	9:37	so that no one will be a to say,	AIT
	18:35	gods of these countries has been a to save his land	AIT
1Ch	9:13	They were a men,	1475+2657
	12: 2	with bows and were a to shoot arrows or	NIH
	12: 8	ready for battle and a to handle the shield	AIT
	26: 7	and Semakiah were also a men.	1201+2657
	26: 9	who were a men— 18 in all.	1201+2657
	26:30	seventeen hundred a men—	1201+2657
	26:32	were a men and heads of families,	1201+2657
	29:14	we should be a to give as generously	3946+6806
2Ch	1:10	for who is a to govern this great people	AIT
	2: 6	But who is a to build a temple for him,	3946+6806

2Ch	13: 3	of four hundred thousand a fighting men,	1033
	13: 3	with eight hundred thousand a troops.	1033
	13:17	among Israel's a men.	1033
	20:37	The ships were wrecked and were not a	6806
	25: 5	a to handle the spear and shield.	AIT
	30: 3	not been a to celebrate it at the regular time	3523
	32:13	the gods of those nations ever a to deliver their land	3523+3523
	32:14	that my fathers destroyed has been a	3523
	32:15	or kingdom has been a to deliver his people	3523
Ne	8: 2	up of men and women and all who were a	1067
	10:28	and all their sons and daughters who are a	3359
	11: 6	in Jerusalem totaled 468 a men.	2657
	11:14	who were a men—128.	1475+2657
Job	41:10	Who then is a to stand against me?	AIT
Ps	36:12	thrown down, not a to rise!	3523
Isa	36:20	gods of these countries has been a to save his land	3523
Eze	7:19	and gold will not be a to save them in	AIT
Da	2:26	"Are you a to tell me what I saw	3523
	2:47	for you were a to reveal this mystery."	10346
	3:15	Then what god will be a to rescue you	10321
	3:17	the God we serve is a to save us from it,	AIT
	4:37	those who walk in pride he is a to humble.	10321
	5:16	that you are a to give interpretations and	10321
	6:20	been a to rescue you from the lions?"	10321
	11:16	no one will be a to stand against him.	AIT
	11:25	be a to stand because of the plots devised	AIT
Hos	5:13	But he is not a to cure you,	3523
	5:13	not a to heal your sores.	NIH
Zep	1:18	Neither their silver nor their gold will be a	3523
Mt	9:28	"Do you believe that I am a to do this?"	1538
	18:25	Since he was not a to pay,	2400
	26:61	'I am a to destroy the temple of God	1538
Mk	3:20	he and his disciples were not even a to eat.	1538
	6:19	But she was not a to,	1538
Lk	1:20	now you will be silent and not a to speak	1538
	8:19	but they were not a to get near him because	1538
	13:24	will try to enter and will not be a to.	2710
	14:29	For if he lays the foundation and is not a	2710
	14:30	'This fellow began to build and was not a	2710
	14:31	down and consider whether he is a	1543
	14:32	If he is not a,	NIG
	21:15	that none of your adversaries will be a	1538
	21:36	that you may be a to escape all that is about	2996
	21:36	that you may be a to stand before the Son	AIT
Jn	18:28	they wanted to be a to eat the Passover.	AIT
Ac	5:39	you will not be a to stop these men;	1538
	15:10	that neither we nor our fathers have been a	2710
	19:40	In that case we would not be a to account	1538
	22:13	And at that very moment I was a to see him.	329
	24: 8	By examining him yourself you will be a	1538
	27:16	we were hardly a to make the lifeboat	2710
Ro	8:39	be a to separate us from the love of God	1538
	11:23	for God is a to graft them in again.	1543
	12: 2	Then you will be a to test and	1650+3836
	14: 4	for the Lord is a to make him stand.	1542
1Co	12:28	those a to help others,	516
2Co	8: 3	they gave as much as they were a,	1539+2848
	9: 8	God is a to make all grace abound to you,	1542
Eph	3: 4	you will be a to understand my insight	1538
	3:20	Now to him who is a to do immeasurably	1538
	6:13	you may be a to stand your ground,	1538
Php	1:10	so that you may be a to discern what is best	AIT
1Ti	3: 2	respectable, hospitable, a to teach,	1434
2Ti	1:12	that he is a to guard what I have entrusted	1543
	2:24	he must be kind to everyone, a to teach,	1434
	3: 7	but never able to acknowledge the truth.	1538
	3:15	which are a to make you wise for salvation	1538
Heb	2:18	when he was tempted, he is a	1538
	3:19	So we see that they were not a to enter,	1538
	5: 2	He is a to deal gently with those who are ignorant	1538
	7:25	Therefore he is a to save completely	1538
	9: 9	and sacrifices being offered were not a	1538
Jas	3: 2	a to keep his whole body in check.	1543
	4:12	the one who is a to save and destroy.	1538
2Pe	1:15	after my departure you will always be a	2400
Jude	1:24	To him who is a to keep you from falling	1538
Rev	5: 5	He is a to open the scroll	NIG

ABLE-BODIED (3) [ABLE]

Dt	3:18	But all your a men, armed for battle,	2657
2Sa	24: 9	In Israel there were eight hundred thousand a men who could handle	2657
1Ch	5:18	a men who could handle shield and sword,	1201+2657

ABNER (56) [ABNER'S]

1Sa	14:50	the commander of Saul's army was A son	46
	17:55	he said to A, commander of the army,	79
	17:55	"A, whose son is that young man?"	79
	17:55	A replied, "As surely as you live, O king,	79
	17:57	A took him and brought him before Saul,	79
	20:25	opposite Jonathan, and A sat next to Saul,	79
	26: 5	He saw where Saul and A son of Ner,	79
	26: 7	A and the soldiers were lying around him.	79
	26:14	He called out to the army and to A son	79
	26:14	"Aren't you going to answer me, A?"	79
	26:14	A replied, "Who are you who calls to	79
2Sa	2: 8	Meanwhile, A son of Ner, the commander	79
	2:12	A son of Ner, together with the men	79
	2:14	Then A said to Joab,	79
	2:17	and A and the men of Israel were defeated	79

2Sa	2:19	He chased A, turning neither to the right	79
	2:20	A looked behind him and asked,	79
	2:21	Then A said to him,	79
	2:22	Again A warned Asahel, "Stop chasing me!	79
	2:23	so A thrust the butt of his spear	79
	2:24	But Joab and Abishai pursued A,	79
	2:25	the men of Benjamin rallied behind A.	79
	2:26	A called out to Joab,	79
	2:29	that night A and his men marched through	79
	2:30	Then Joab returned from pursuing A	79
	2:31	and sixty Benjamites who were with A.	79
	3: 6	A had been strengthening his own position	79
	3: 7	and Ish-Bosheth said to A,	79
	3: 8	A was very angry because	79
	3: 9	May God deal with A,	79
	3:11	not dare to say another word to A,	79
	3:12	Then A sent messengers on his behalf	79
	3:16	Then A said to him, "Go back home!"	79
	3:17	A conferred with the elders of Israel	79
	3:19	A also spoke to the Benjamites in person.	79
	3:20	When A, who had twenty men with him,	79
	3:21	Then A said to David,	79
	3:21	David sent A away, and he went in peace.	79
	3:22	But A was no longer with David in Hebron,	79
	3:23	that A son of Ner had come to the king and	79
	3:24	Look, A came to you.	79
	3:25	You know A son of Ner;	79
	3:26	and sent messengers after A,	79
	3:27	Now when A returned to Hebron,	79
	3:28	the Lord concerning the blood of A son	79
	3:30	(Joab and his brother Abishai murdered A	79
	3:31	and walk in mourning in front of A."	79
	3:32	They buried A in Hebron.	79
	3:33	The king sang this lament for A:	79
	3:33	"Should A have died as the lawless die?	79
	3:37	the king had no part in the murder of A son	79
	4: 1	of Saul heard that A had died in Hebron,	79
1Ki	2: 5	A son of Ner and Amasa son of Jether.	79
	2:32	A son of Ner, commander of Israel's army,	79
1Ch	26:28	A son of Ner and Joab son of Zeruiah,	79
	27:21	Jaasiel son of A;	79

ABNER'S (3) [ABNER]

1Sa	14:51	and A father Ner were sons of Abiel.	79
2Sa	3:32	and the king wept aloud at A tomb.	79
	4:12	of Ish-Bosheth and buried it in A tomb	79

ABNORMALLY (1) [NORMALLY]

1Co	15: 8	he appeared to me also, as to one a born.	1765

ABOARD (7) [BOARD]

Eze	27: 8	O Tyre, were a as your seamen.	928
Jnh	1: 3	he went a and sailed for Tarshish to flee	928+3718
Jn	21:11	Simon Peter climbed a and dragged	326
Ac	20:13	where we were going to take Paul a.	377
	20:14	we took him a and went on to Mitylene.	377
	21: 6	we went a the ship,	1650
	27:17	When the men had hoisted it a,	149

ABODE (2)

Job	38:19	"What is the way to the a of light?	8905
Isa	33:20	your eyes will see Jerusalem, a peaceful a,	5659

ABODEST (KJV) See STAY

ABOLISH (4) [ABOLISHED, ABOLISHING]

Da	11:31	and will a the daily sacrifice.	6073
Hos	2:18	Bow and sword and battle I will a from	8689
Mt	5:17	not think that I have come to a the Law or	2907
	5:17	not come to a them but to fulfill them.	2907

ABOLISHED (2) [ABOLISH]

Da	12:11	the daily sacrifice is a and the abomination	6073
Gal	5:11	the offense of the cross has been a.	2934

ABOLISHING (1) [ABOLISH]

Eph	2:15	by a in his flesh the law	2934

ABOMINABLE (3) [ABOMINATION]

Isa	66:17	the flesh of pigs and rats and other a things—	9211
Jer	32:34	They set up their a idols in the house	9199
Rev	17: 4	with a things and the filth of her adulteries.	1007

ABOMINATION (5) [ABOMINABLE, ABOMINATIONS]

Da	9:27	a wing [of the temple] he will set up an a	9199
	11:31	up the a that causes desolation.	9199
	12:11	and the a that causes desolation is set up,	9199
Mt	24:15	'the a that causes desolation,' spoken of	1007
Mk	13:14	'the a that causes desolation' standing	1007

ABOMINATIONS (3) [ABOMINATION]

Pr	26:25	for seven a fill his heart.	9359
Isa	66: 3	and their souls delight in their a;	9199
Rev	17: 5	BABYLON THE GREAT THE MOTHER OF PROSTITUTES AND OF THE A OF THE EARTH.	1007

ABOUND (7) [ABOUNDING, ABOUNDS]

2Ki	9:22	all the idolatry and witchcraft of your mother Jezebel a?"	8041
Ps	4: 7	when their grain and new wine a.	8045
	72: 7	prosperity will a till the moon is no more.	8044
	72:16	Let grain a throughout the land;	2118+7172
2Co	9: 8	And God is able to make all grace a to you,	4355
	9: 8	you will a in every good work.	4355
Php	1: 9	that your love may a more and more	4355

ABOUNDED, ABOUNDETH (KJV) See also ENHANCE, INCREASE, OVERFLOW

ABOUNDING (10) [ABOUND]

Ex	34: 6	slow to anger, a in love and faithfulness,	8041
Nu	14:18	a in love and forgiving sin and rebellion.	8041
Dt	33:23	Naphtali is a with the favor of the Lord	8428
Ne	9:17	slow to anger and a in love.	8041
Ps	86: 5	O Lord, a in love to all who call to you.	8041
	86:15	slow to anger, a in love and faithfulness.	8041
	103: 8	slow to anger, a in love.	8041
Pr	8:24	when there were no springs a with water;	3877
Joel	2:13	slow to anger and a in love,	8041
Jnh	4: 2	slow to anger and a in love,	8041

ABOUNDS (1) [ABOUND]

Hab	1: 3	there is strife, and conflict a.	5951

ABOUT (873)

Ge	3:17	from the tree a which I commanded you,	AIT
	12:11	As he was a to enter Egypt,	7928
	12:20	Pharaoh gave orders a Abram to his men,	6584
	13: 5	Now Lot, who was moving a with Abram,	2143
	18:10	surely return to you a this time next year,	3869
	18:17	from Abraham what I am a to do?	AIT
	18:19	so that the Lord will bring a	995
	19:14	the Lord is a to destroy the city!"	AIT
	21: 6	and everyone who hears a this will laugh	AIT
	21:12	"Do not be so distressed a the boy	6584
	21:16	a a bowshot away, for she thought,	3869
	21:25	Abraham complained to Abimelech a	128+6584
	21:26	and I heard a it only today."	6584
	22: 2	of the mountains I will tell you a."	AIT
	22: 3	for the place God had told him a.	AIT
	22: 9	they reached the place God had told him a,	AIT
	24:28	and told her mother's household a	3869
	24:57	"Let's call the girl and ask her a it."	AIT
	25:32	"Look, I am a to die," Esau said.	2143
	26: 7	the men of that place asked him a his wife,	AIT
	26:32	and told him a the well they had dug.	128+6584
	29:13	As soon as Laban heard the news a Jacob,	AIT
	31:43	Yet what can I do today a these daughters	4200
	31:43	or a the children they have borne?	4200
	34: 5	so he kept quiet a it until they came home.	AIT
	37: 2	he brought their father a bad report a them.	3869
	38:24	Three months later Judah was told,	3869
	41:25	to Pharaoh what he is a to do.	AIT
	41:28	God has shown Pharaoh what he is a to do.	AIT
	42: 9	Then he remembered his dreams a them	4200
	43: 7	"The man questioned us closely a	4200
	43:27	"How is your aged father you told me a?	AIT
	43:29	he looked a and saw his brother Benjamin,	5951+6524
	43:39	the one you told me a?"	AIT
	45: 2	and Pharaoh's household heard a it.	AIT
	45:13	Tell my father a all	AIT
	45:13	in Egypt and a everything you have seen.	NIH
	45:20	Never mind a your belongings,	6584
	48:21	Then Israel said to Joseph, "I am a to die,	AIT
	49:29	"I am a to be gathered to my people.	AIT
	50: 5	'I am a to die;	AIT
	50:24	Joseph said to his brothers, "I am a to die.	AIT
Ex	1: 8	a new king, who did not know a Joseph,	3359
	2:25	on the Israelites and was concerned a them.	3359
	3: 7	and I am concerned a their suffering.	3359
	4:14	"What a your brother, Aaron the Levite?	2022+4202
	4:24	the Lord met [Moses] and was a to	1335
	4:28	told Aaron everything the Lord had sent him to say, and also a	AIT
	4:31	that the Lord was concerned a them	7212
	6:13	and Aaron a the Israelites and Pharaoh king	448
	6:27	spoke to Pharaoh king of Egypt a	AIT
	8:12	to the Lord a the frogs he had brought	1821+6584
	11: 4	'A midnight I will go throughout Egypt.	3869
	12:37	There were a six hundred thousand men	3869
	14: 5	and his officials changed their minds a	448
	18: 8	told his father-in-law a	AIT
	18: 8	and the Egyptians for Israel's sake and a all	NIH
	18: 9	Jethro was delighted to hear a all	6584
	22: 9	other lost property a which somebody says,	AIT
	32:28	and that day a three thousand of	3869
Lev	5: 1	something he has seen or learned a,	3359
	5: 4	any matter one might carelessly swear a—	NIH
	6: 2	to the Lord by deceiving his neighbor a	928
	6: 3	or if he finds lost property and lies a it, or	928
	6: 5	or whatever it was he swore falsely a.	6584
	10:16	When Moses inquired a the goat of	2011+2011
	11:29	the animals that move a on the ground,	9237
	11:41	that moves a on the ground is detestable;	9237
	11:42	not to eat any creature that moves a	9237
	11:44	by any creature that moves a on the ground.	8253
	11:46	in the water and every creature that moves a	9237
Lev	15: 3	This is how his discharge will bring a	928+2118
	19:16	" 'Do not go a spreading slander	2143
Nu	11: 1	"We are setting out for the place a which	AIT
	11: 1	the people complained a their hardships in	AIT
	11:31	the camp to a three feet above the ground,	3869
	13:32	a bad report a the land they had explored.	AIT
	14:10	the whole assembly talked a stoning them.	AIT
	14:13	"Then the Egyptians will hear a it!	AIT
	14:14	tell the inhabitants of this land a	AIT
	14:15	the nations who have heard this report a	AIT
	14:36	against him by spreading a bad report a	6584
	14:37	spreading the bad report a the land	AIT
	16:30	the Lord brings a something totally new,	1343
	20:14	You know a all the hardships	3359
	21:17	O well! Sing a it,	4200
	21:18	a the well that the princes dug, that	NIH
	30: 4	and her father hears a her vow or pledge	AIT
	30: 5	if her father forbids her when he hears a it,	AIT
	30: 7	and her husband hears a it but says nothing	AIT
	30: 8	her husband forbids her when he hears a it,	AIT
	30:11	and her husband hears a it but says nothing	AIT
	30:12	when he hears a them,	AIT
	30:14	says nothing to her a	AIT
	30:14	by saying nothing to her when he hears a	AIT
	30:15	he nullifies them some time after he hears a	AIT
	32:28	Then Moses gave orders a them to Eleazar	4200
Dt	1:22	and bring back a report a the route we are	AIT
	2: 4	'You are a to pass through the territory	AIT
	3:26	"Do not speak to me anymore a this matter.	928
	4: 1	the decrees and laws I am a to teach you.	AIT
	4: 6	who will hear a all these decrees and say,	AIT
	4:22	but you are a to cross over	AIT
	4:32	Ask now a the former days,	4200
	6: 7	Talk a them when you sit at home and	928
	9: 1	You are now a to cross the Jordan to go in	AIT
	9: 2	You know a them and have heard it said:	3359
	11:19	talking a them when you sit at home and	928
	11:31	You are a to cross the Jordan to enter	AIT
	12:29	before you the nations you are a to invade	AIT
	12:30	be careful not to be ensnared by inquiring a	4200
	13:12	If you hear it said a one of the towns	928
	20: 2	When you are a to go into battle,	AIT
	23:14	the Lord your God moves a in your camp	2143
	24: 1	because he finds something indecent a her,	928
	28:29	At midday you will grope a like	5491
	33: 7	And this he said a Judah:	4200
	33: 8	A Levi he said:	4200
	33:12	A Benjamin he said:	4200
	33:13	A Joseph he said:	4200
	33:18	A Zebulun he said:	4200
	33:20	A Gad he said:	4200
	33:22	A Dan he said:	4200
	33:23	A Naphtali he said:	4200
	33:24	A Asher he said:	4200
Jos	1: 2	into the land I am a to give to them—	AIT
	3: 4	But keep a distance of a a thousand yards	3869
	4:13	A forty thousand armed for battle crossed	3869
	5: 6	The Israelites had moved a in	2143
	6:18	bring a your own destruction	3049
	7: 4	So a three thousand men went up;	3869
	7: 5	who killed a thirty-six of them.	3869
	7: 9	the other people of the country will hear a	AIT
	8:12	Joshua had taken a five thousand men	3869
	9: 1	of the Jordan heard a these things—	AIT
	10:13	and delayed going down a a full day.	3869
	14: 6	the man of God at Kadesh Barnea a you	128+6584
	14:10	while Israel moved a in the desert.	2143
	22:33	And they talked no more a going to war	AIT
	23:14	"Now I am a to go the way of all the earth.	AIT
Jdg	3:16	sword a a foot and a half long,	1688
	3:29	down a ten thousand Moabites, all vigorous	3869
	4: 9	because of the way you are going a this,	2143
	6:13	that our fathers told us a when they said,	AIT
	8:10	of a fifteen thousand men, all that were left	3869
	8:15	a whom you taunted me by saying,	AIT
	9: 7	When Jotham was told a this,	AIT
	9:49	a a thousand men and women, also died.	3869
	16:27	and on the roof were a three thousand men	3869
	17: 2	of silver that were taken from you and a	NIH
	19:30	Think a it!	6584
	20:12	"What a this awful crime	AIT
	20:31	that a thirty men fell in the open field and	3869
	20:39	casualties on the men of Israel (a thirty).	3869
Ru	1: 4	After they had lived there a ten years,	3869
	2:11	"I've been told a what you have done	5583+5583
	2:17	and it amounted to a an ephah.	3869
	2:19	told her mother-in-law a	AIT
1Sa	2:22	heard a everything his sons were doing	AIT
	2:23	hear from all the people a	AIT
	3:11	"See, I am a to do something in Israel	AIT
	3:13	because of the sin he knew a;	3359
	4: 2	who killed a four thousand of them on	3869
	9: 5	or my father will stop thinking a	4946
	9: 5	about the donkeys and start worrying a us."	3869
	9:13	you should find him a this time."	3869
	9:16	"A this time tomorrow I will send you	3869
	9:17	"This is the man I spoke to you a;	AIT
	9:20	do not worry a them; they have been found.	4200
	9:22	invited—a thirty in number.	3869
	9:23	They rose a daybreak and Samuel called	3869
	10: 2	your father has stopped thinking a them	AIT
	10: 2	about them and is worried a you.	4200
	10: 2	He is asking, "What shall I do a my son?"	4200
	10:16	not tell his uncle what Samuel had said a	AIT
	12:16	the Lord is a to do before your eyes!	AIT
	13: 3	and the Philistines heard a it.	AIT

1Sa 13:15	They numbered **a** six hundred.	3869
14: 2	With him were **a** six hundred men,	3869
14:14	in an area of **a** half an acre.	3869
14:45	he who has **brought a** this great deliverance	6913
16: 2	Saul *will* **hear** *a* it and kill me."	AIT
18:20	and when *they* told Saul *a* it,"	AIT
19: 3	I'll speak to him **a** you	928
19:21	Saul *was* **told** *a* it, and he sent more men,	AIT
20:23	And **a** the matter you and I discussed—	NIH
21: 2	*to* **know** anything **a** your mission	3359
21:11	Isn't he the one they sing in their dances:	4200
22: 1	and his father's household **heard** *a* it,	AIT
22: 2	A four hundred men were with him.	3869
22: 8	None of you is concerned **a** me or tells me	6584
22:15	for your servant knows nothing at all **a**	928
23:13	**a** six hundred in number,	3869
23:23	Find out **a** all the hiding places he uses	4946
23:25	and when David *was* **told** *a* it,	AIT
25:13	A four hundred men went up with David,	3869
25:38	A ten days later,	3869
26:12	No one saw or **knew** *a* it,	3359
28: 9	a trap for my life to **bring a** my **death?"**	4637
29: 3	"**What a** these **Hebrews?"**	4537
29: 5	the David they sang in their dances:	4200
2Sa 3:28	Later, when David **heard** *a* this, he said,	AIT
4: 4	He was five years old when the **news** *a* Saul	AIT
5:17	but David **heard** *a* it and went down to	AIT
7:19	also spoken **a** the future of the house	4200
10: 5	When David *was* **told** *a* this,	AIT
11: 3	and David sent someone to find out **a** her.	4200
13:13	**What a** me?	2256
13:13	And **what a** you?	2256
13:33	not *be* **concerned a** the report that all	448+4213+8492
15:11	**knowing** nothing **a** the matter.	3359
15:20	today *shall I* **make** you **wander a** with us,	5675
17: 9	whoever **hears** *a* it will say,	AIT
17:19	No *one* **knew** anything **a** it.	3359
18: 3	*they* won't **care a** us.	448+4213+8492
18:29	"I saw great confusion just as Joab was **a**	NIH
19:10	So why *do you* **say nothing** *a* bringing	AIT
19:42	Why are you angry **a** it?	6584
22: 5	"The waves of death **swirled a** me;	705
23:10	The LORD **brought a** a great victory.	6913
23:12	and the LORD **brought a** a great victory.	6913
1Ki 1:18	and *you*, my lord the king, *do not* **know a** it.	3359
2: 2	"I *am a* to **go** the way of all the earth,"	AIT
2:27	the LORD had spoken at Shiloh **a**	6584
4:33	He also taught **a** animals and birds,	6584
8: 5	of Israel that had gathered **a** him were	6584
10: 1	When the queen of Sheba **heard** *a* the fame	AIT
10: 2	and **talked** with him *a* all that she had	AIT
10: 6	"The **report** I heard in my own country **a**	6584
11: 2	from nations *a* **which** the LORD had told	AIT
11:29	A that time Jeroboam was going out	928
14: 5	"Jeroboam's wife is coming to ask you **a**	448
16: 3	So I *am a* to **consume** Baasha and his house,	AIT
19:11	for the LORD *is a* to **pass by."**	AIT
20: 6	But **a** this time tomorrow I am going	3869
22: 6	**a** four hundred men—	3869
22: 8	he never prophesies anything good **a**	6584
22:18	that he never prophesies anything good **a**	6584
2Ki 2: 1	**a** *to* **take** Elijah **up**	AIT
3:20	**a** the time for offering the sacrifice,	3869
4:16	"A this time next year," Elisha said,	4200
4:17	and the next year **a** that same time	4200
7: 1	A this time tomorrow,	3869
7:18	"A this time tomorrow,	3869
8: 4	"**Tell** me *a* all the great things Elisha	AIT
8: 6	The king **asked** the woman *a* it,	AIT
9:23	Joram **turned** *a* and fled,	2200+3338
9:25	when the LORD made this prophecy **a**	6584
9:30	When Jezebel **heard** *a* it,	AIT
11: 2	who were *a* to **be murdered.**	AIT
12:17	**A this time** Hazael king of Aram went up	255
14:13	a section **a six hundred feet** long.	564+752+4395
22:13	for all Judah **a** what is written in this book	6584
23:27	*a* **which** I said, 'There shall my Name be.'"	AIT
1Ch 11:14	the LORD **brought a** a great victory.	3828+9591
14: 8	David **heard** *a* it and went out to meet them.	AIT
15:13	*We did* not **inquire of** him *a* how to do it in	AIT
17:17	you have spoken **a** the future of the house	4200
19: 5	someone came and told David **a** the men,	6584
2Ch 2: 4	Now I *am a* to **build** a temple for the Name	AIT
5: 6	of Israel that had gathered **a** him were	6584
9: 1	to Solomon and **talked** with him *a*	AIT
9: 5	"The **report** I heard in my own country **a**	6584
15: 5	In those days it was not safe to **travel a,**	995+2256+3655
15:15	All Judah rejoiced **a** the oath	6584
18: 7	he never prophesies anything good **a**	6584
18:17	that he never prophesies anything good **a**	6584
21:14	now the LORD *is a* to **strike** your people,	AIT
22:14	God **brought a** Ahaziah's downfall.	2118+4946
22:11	royal princes *who were a* to **be murdered**	AIT
24:27	the many prophecies **a** him,	6584
25: 9	"But **what a** the hundred talents I paid	6584
25:23	a section **a six hundred feet** long.	564+752+4395
29:36	at what God *had* **brought a** for his people,	3922
31: 9	Hezekiah asked the priests and Levites **a**	6584
32: 3	and military staff **a** blocking off the water	4200
32:19	They spoke **a** the God of Jerusalem	448
32:19	the God of Jerusalem as they did **a** the gods	6584
32:20	of Amoz cried out in prayer to heaven **a**	6584
32:31	of Babylon to ask him **a** the miraculous sign	AIT
34:21	and for the remnant in Israel and Judah **a**	6584
35: 3	It is not to be **carried a** on your shoulders.	5362
Ezr 7:14	the king and his seven advisers to inquire **a**	10542
8:23	So we fasted and petitioned our God **a** this,	6584
Ne 1: 2	and I questioned them **a** the Jewish remnant	6584
1: 2	and also **a** Jerusalem.	6584
2:10	and Tobiah the Ammonite official **heard** *a*	AIT
2:18	I also told them **a** the gracious hand	AIT
2:19	and Geshem the Arab **heard** *a* it,	AIT
6: 6	reports *you are a* to **become** their king	6584
6: 7	to make this proclamation **a** you	6584
6:16	When all our enemies **heard** *a* this,	AIT
13: 7	Here I learned **a** the evil thing	928
Est 1:18	of the nobility who have **heard** *a*	AIT
2: 1	and what he had decreed **a** her.	6584
2:22	But Mordecai **found out** *a* the plot	AIT
3: 4	Therefore *they* **told** Haman *a* it	AIT
4: 4	and eunuchs came and **told** her *a*	AIT
5:11	Haman **boasted** to them *a* his vast wealth,	AIT
6: 4	**speak** to the king *a* hanging Mordecai	AIT
9:32	Esther's decree confirmed these **regulations a**	AIT
Job 2:11	**heard** *a* all the troubles that had come	AIT
3: 4	*may* God above not **care a** it;	2011
11:18	*you will* **look** *a* and take your rest	2916
15:23	He **wanders a**—food for vultures;	5610
21: 6	When *I* **think** *a* this, I am terrified;	2349
21:11	their little ones **dance a.**	8376
21:21	For what does he **care a**	928
22:14	as *he goes a* in the vaulted heavens.'	2143
24: 5	the poor **go a** their labor of foraging food;	3655
24:10	Lacking clothes, *they* **go a** naked;	2143
27:11	"I will teach you **a** the power of God;	928
30:22	*you* **toss** me *a* in the storm.	4570
30:28	*I* **go a** blackened, but not by the sun;	2143
33: 2	*I am a* to **open** my mouth;	AIT
36:30	See how he scatters his lightning **a** him,	6584
38:41	its young cry out to God and **wander a**	9494
41:14	**ringed** *a* with his fearsome teeth?	6017
Ps 12: 8	The wicked freely strut **a**	6017
22:30	future generations will be told **a** the Lord.	4200
26: 6	and **go a** your altar, O LORD,	6015
35:11	on things *I* **know** nothing **a.**	3359
35:14	*I* **went** *a* mourning as though for my friend	2143
38: 6	all day long *I* **go a** mourning.	2143
38:17	*I am a* to **fall**, and my pain is ever with me.	3922
39: 6	He **bustles a**, but only in vain;	2159
40: 7	it is written **a** me in the scroll.	6584
42: 9	Why *must I* **go a** mourning,	2143
43: 2	Why *must I* **go a** mourning,	2143
48:12	**Walk a** Zion, go around her,	6015
55:10	Day and night *they* **prowl a** on its walls;	6015
59: 6	snarling like dogs, and **prowl a** the city.	6015
59:11	In your might **make** them **wander a,**	5675
59:14	snarling like dogs, and **prowl a** the city.	6015
59:15	They **wander a** for food and howl if	5675
64: 5	*they* **talk** *a* hiding their snares;	AIT
69:26	and **talk a** the pain of those you hurt.	448
77: 5	*I* **thought** *a* the former days,	AIT
82: 5	They **walk a** in darkness;	2143
109:19	May it be like a cloak wrapped **a** him,	4200
118:13	I was pushed back and *a* to **fall,**	AIT
119:45	*I will* **walk a** in freedom,	2143
142: 7	the righteous *will* **gather a** me because	4193
Pr 6:12	who **goes a** with a corrupt mouth,	2143
20:14	then off he goes and **boasts a** his purchase.	AIT
23: 7	of man who is always thinking **a** the cost.	928
24: 2	and their lips **talk a** making trouble.	AIT
24:12	If you say, "But *we* **knew** nothing **a** this,"	3359
27: 1	Do not **boast a** tomorrow,	928
29: 7	The righteous **care a** justice for the poor,	3359
31:17	*She* **sets a** her **work** vigorously;	2520+5516
Ecc 7:14	a man cannot **discover** anything *a*	AIT
12: 5	to his eternal home and mourners **go a**	6015
SS 3: 2	I will get up now and **go a** the city,	6015
Isa 3: 1	*is a* to **take** from Jerusalem and Judah	AIT
5: 1	for the one I love a song **a** his vineyard:	4200
8: 7	the Lord *is a* to **bring** against them	AIT
13:21	and there the wild goats *will* **leap a.**	8376
22:17	*a* to **take firm hold**	AIT
26:17	and as she gives birth writhes and cries out	7928
27: 2	In that day—"Sing **a** a fruitful vineyard:	4200
35: 8	wicked fools *will* not **go a** on it.	9494
38:19	fathers tell their children **a**	448
45:11	do you question me **a** my children,	6584
45:11	or give me orders **a** the work of my hands?	6584
45:20	Ignorant are those *who* **carry a** idols	5951
46: 1	images that are **carried a**	5953
46:11	What I have said, that *will I* **bring a;**	995
60: 4	"Lift up your eyes and **look a** you:	6017
66:18	*am a* to **come** and gather all nations	AIT
Jer 1:15	I *am a* to **summon** all the peoples of	AIT
2:36	Why *do you* **go a** so much,	261
5:12	They have **lied a** the LORD;	928
6:20	**What do I care a**	2296+3276+4200+4200+4537
6:24	We have heard **reports a** them,	AIT
6:28	**going a** to slander.	2143
7:22	I did not just give them commands **a**	1821+6584
9:24	but let him who boasts **boast a** this;	928
11:21	"Therefore this is what the LORD **says a**	6584
12: 1	Yet I would speak with you **a** your justice;	NIH
12: 3	you see me and test my thoughts **a** you.	907
14:10	This is what the LORD **says a** this people:	4200
14:15	this is what the LORD **says a**	6584
16: 3	For this is what the LORD **says a** the sons	6584
16: 3	and **a** the women who are their mothers	6584
21: 4	I *am a* to **turn against** you the weapons	AIT
22: 6	the LORD **says a** the palace of the king	6584
22:11	the LORD **says a** Shallum son of Josiah,	448
Jer 22:18	Therefore this is what the LORD **says a**	448
26:10	the officials of Judah **heard** *a* these things,	AIT
26:19	We *are a* to **bring** a terrible disaster	AIT
27:19	the LORD Almighty says **a** the pillars,	448
27:21	says **a** the things that are left in the house	6584
28:16	'I *am a* to **remove** you from the face of	AIT
29:16	the LORD says **a** the king who sits	448
29:21	says **a** Ahab son of Kolaiah	448
29:31	'This is what the LORD says **a** Shemaiah	448
31:24	and *those who* **move** *a* with their flocks.	5825
32: 3	*a* to **hand** this city **over**	AIT
32:28	*a* to **hand** this city **over**	AIT
32:36	"You are saying **a** this city, 'By the sword,	448
33: 4	says **a** the houses in this city and	6584
33:10	'You say **a** this place,	928
34: 2	*a* to **hand** this city **over**	AIT
36: 3	Perhaps *when* the people of Judah **hear a**	AIT
36:30	the LORD **says a** Jehoiakim king	6584
37: 5	the **report a** them,	AIT
38:24	not let anyone know **a** this conversation.	928
39:11	of Babylon had given these orders **a**	6584
39:16	I *am a* to **fulfill** my words	AIT
40: 3	And now the LORD *has* **brought** it **a;**	995
40:16	What you are saying **a** Ishmael is not true."	448
41: 4	before anyone **knew** *a* it,	3359
41:11	with him **heard** *a* all the crimes Ishmael son	AIT
44:21	and **think a** the incense burned in the towns	4213+6584+6590
46:13	**spoke** to Jeremiah the prophet *a*	AIT
46:25	"I *am a* to **bring punishment** on Amon god	AIT
47: 4	The LORD *is a* to **destroy** the Philistines,	AIT
50:43	king of Babylon has heard **reports** *a* them,	AIT
51:60	**written** on a scroll *a*	AIT
La 3:54	*a* to **be cut off.**	AIT
4:15	When they flee and **wander a,**	5675
Eze 1:17	wheels *did* not **turn a** as the creatures went.	6015
6: 3	I *am a* to **bring** a sword against you,	AIT
7: 8	I *am a* to **pour out** my wrath on you	4946+6964+7940
8:16	were **a** twenty-five men.	3869
10:11	not **turn a** as the cherubim went.	6015
12:19	'This is what the Sovereign LORD **says a**	4200
12:27	and he prophesies **a** the distant future.'	4200
16: 6	"Then I passed by and saw you **kicking a**	1008
16:22	**kicking a** in your blood.	1008
16:44	"'Everyone who quotes proverbs will quote this proverb **a**	6584
18: 2	by quoting this proverb **a** the land of Israel:	6584
19: 4	The nations heard **a** him,	448
19: 8	those from regions **round a.**	6017
20:47	I *am a* to **set fire** to you,	AIT
21:28	'This is what the Sovereign LORD **says a**	448
21:29	concerning you and lying divinations **a**	4200
23:28	*a* to **hand** you **over**	AIT
23:43	Then I said **a** the one worn out by adultery,	4200
24:16	with one blow I *am a* to **take away** from you	AIT
24:21	I *am a* to **desecrate** my sanctuary—	AIT
25:16	I *am a* to **stretch out** my hand against	AIT
32: 2	in the seas **thrashing a** in your streams,	1631
32: 9	the hearts of many peoples when I **bring a**	995
33:30	your countrymen are talking together **a** you	928
38: 7	you and all the hordes gathered **a** you,	6584
Da 1:20	of wisdom and understanding **a** which	AIT
2:27	to the king the mystery he *has* **asked** *a,*	AIT
4: 2	to **tell** you *a* the miraculous signs	AIT
4:33	Immediately what had been said **a**	10542
6:12	and spoke to him **a** his royal decree:	10542
7: 8	"While I was thinking **a** the horns,	10089
7:20	to know the ten horns on its head and	10542
7:20	on its head and **a** the other horn that came	NIH
8: 5	As I was thinking **a** this,	NIH
8:27	I got up and **went a** the king's business.	6913
9:21	came to me in swift flight **a** the time **a**	3869
10:11	consider carefully the words I *am a* to **speak**	AIT
Hos 3: 2	for fifteen shekels of silver and **a** a homer	NIH
5: 3	I **know all a** Ephraim;	3359
Joel 1:18	The herds **mill a**	1003
Am 4: 5	and **brag a** your freewill offerings—	AIT
4: 5	**boast a** them, you Israelites,	AIT
Ob 1: 1	This is what the Sovereign LORD **says a**	4200
Jnh 2: 3	and the currents **swirled a** me;	6015
4: 6	and Jonah was very happy **a** the vine.	6584
4: 9	"Do you have a right to be angry **a**	6584
4:10	"You have been concerned **a** this vine,	6584
4:11	not be concerned **a** that great city?"	6584
Mic 1: 8	*I will* **go a** barefoot and naked.	2143
2: 6	"Do not prophesy **a** these things;	4200
Na 2: 4	*they* **dart a** like lightning.	8132
3:19	the **news a** you claps his hands at your fall,	AIT
Hab 1:13	though *a* to **devour** the wretched who were	NIH
Zec 8:10	No one *could* **go a** his **business** safely	995+2256+3655
Mal 3:14	and **going a** like mourners before	2143
Mt 1:18	how the birth of Jesus Christ **came a:**	1639
4:24	**News** *a* him spread all over Syria,	*AIT*
6:25	I tell you, *do not* **worry a** your life,	*3534*
6:25	or **a** your body, what you will wear.	*NIG*
6:28	"And why do you **worry a** clothes?	*4309*
6:34	Therefore do not **worry a** tomorrow,	*1650*
6:34	for tomorrow *will* **worry a** itself.	*3534*
9:30	"See that no one **knows a** this."	*1182*
9:31	But they went out and **spread the news a**	*1424*
10:19	*do not* **worry a** what to say or how to say it.	*3534*
11: 7	Jesus began to speak to the crowd **a** John:	*4309*
11:10	This is the one **a** whom it is written:	*4309*
13:19	the message **a** the kingdom and does	*AIT*
13:52	law who has been instructed **a** the kingdom	*AIT*

Mt	14: 1	the tetrarch heard the reports a **Jesus,**	AIT
	14:21	of those who ate was a five thousand men,	6059
	15: 7	Isaiah was right when he prophesied a you:	4309
	16: 8	why are you talking among yourselves a	4022
	16:11	that I was not talking to you a bread?	4309
	16:15	"But what a you?"	NIG
	17:13	that he was talking to them a John	4309
	18:13	he is happier a that one sheep than about	2093
	18:13	about that one sheep than a the ninety-nine	2093
	18:19	I tell you that if two of you on earth agree a	4309
	19:17	"Why do you ask me a what is good?"	4309
	20: 3	"A the third hour he went out	4309
	20: 5	"He went out again a the sixth hour and	4309
	20: 6	A the eleventh hour he went out	4309
	20: 9	"The workers who were hired a the eleventh	4309
	20:24	*When* the ten **heard** a this,	201
	21:45	they knew he was talking a them.	4309
	22:31	But a the resurrection of the dead—	4309
	22:42	"What do you think a the Christ?	4309
	24:36	"No one knows a that day or hour,	4309
	24:39	and they knew nothing a what would happen	1182
	26:24	of Man will go just as it is written a him.	4309
	26:70	"I don't know what *you're* **talking a,"**	3306
	27:46	A the ninth hour Jesus cried out in	4309
Mk	1: 1	the gospel a **Jesus Christ,** the **Son** of God	AIT
	1:28	News a **him** spread quickly over	AIT
	1:30	and they told Jesus a her.	4309
	3:21	*When* his family **heard** a this,	201
	4:10	others around him asked him a the **parables.**	AIT
	5:13	The herd, a two thousand in number,	6055
	5:16	and told the pigs as well.	4309
	5:27	When she heard a Jesus,	4309
	5:43	not to let anyone **know** a this,	1182
	6:14	King Herod **heard** a this,	201
	6:48	A the fourth watch of the night he went out	4309
	6:48	He was a to pass by them,	NIG
	6:52	for they had not understood a the loaves;	2093
	7: 6	"Isaiah was right when he prophesied a	4309
	7:17	his disciples **asked** him a this parable.	2089
	7:25	In fact, as soon as she heard a him,	4309
	7:36	the more they *kept* **talking** a it.	3062
	8: 9	A four thousand men were present.	6055
	8:17	"Why *are you* **talking** a having no bread?	1368
	8:29	"But what a you?"	NIG
	8:30	Jesus warned them not to tell anyone a	4309
	8:32	*He* **spoke** plainly a this,	3281
	9:13	just as it is written a him."	2093
	9:16	**arguing** with them a?"	5184
	9:32	and were afraid *to* **ask** him a it.	2089
	9:33	"*What were you* **arguing** a on the road?"	1368
	9:34	on the way *they had* **argued** a who was	1363
	9:39	in the next moment say anything *bad* a me,	2800
	10:10	the disciples asked Jesus a this.	4309
	10:41	*When* the ten **heard** a this,	201
	12:26	Now a the dead rising—	4309
	13: 4	the sign that they *are* all **a to** be fulfilled?"	3516
	13:11	*do* not **worry beforehand** a what to say.	4628
	13:32	"No one knows a that day or hour,	4309
	14:21	of Man will go just as it is written a him.	4309
	14:68	or understand what you're **talking a,"**	4309
	14:71	"I don't know this man *you're* **talking a."**	3306
Lk	1:56	for a three months and then returned home.	6055
	1:65	of Judea *people were* **talking** a	1362
	1:66	Everyone who heard this **wondered** a it,	1877+2840+3836+5502
	2:15	which the Lord *has* **told** us a."	1192
	2:17	concerning what had been told them a	4309
	2:33	and mother marveled at what was said a	4309
	2:38	she gave thanks to God and spoke a	4309
	3:23	Now Jesus himself was a thirty years old	6059
	4:14	and news a him spread through	4309
	4:37	And the news a him spread throughout	4309
	5:15	Yet the news a him spread all the more,	4309
	7: 2	was sick and a **to** die.	3516
	7:17	This news a Jesus spread throughout Judea	4309
	7:18	John's disciples told him a all these things.	4309
	7:24	Jesus began to speak to the crowd a John:	4309
	7:27	This is the one a whom it is written:	4309
	8: 1	Jesus **traveled** a from one town	1476
	8:42	a girl of a twelve, was dying.	6055
	9: 7	the tetrarch **heard** a all that was going on.	201
	9: 9	Who, then, is this I hear such things a?	4005+4309
	9:11	the crowds **learned** a it and followed him.	1182
	9:11	and spoke to them a the kingdom of God,	4309
	9:14	(A five thousand men were there.)	6059
	9:14	"Have them sit down in groups of a fifty	6059
	9:20	"But what a you?"	NIG
	9:28	A eight days after Jesus said this,	6059
	9:31	*They* **spoke** a his departure,	3306
	9:31	which *he was* **a to** bring to fulfillment	3516
	9:44	to what I **am a to** tell *you:*	3364+3836+4047
	9:45	and they were afraid to ask him a it.	4309
	10: 1	to every town and place where he *was* **a to**	3516
	10:41	"you are worried and upset a many things,	4309
	12:22	not **worry** a how you will defend yourselves	3534
	12:22	*do* not **worry** a your life, what you will eat;	3534
	12:22	or a your body, what you will wear.	NIG
	12:26	why do you worry a the rest?	4309
	12:29	*do* not **worry** a it.	3577
	13: 1	at that time who told Jesus a	4309
	14:31	"Or suppose a king *is* a to go to war	4513
	16: 2	'What is this I hear a you?	4309
	18: 2	a judge who neither feared God nor **cared** a	1956
	18: 4	though I don't fear God or **care** a men,	1956
	18: 7	not God **bring** a justice for his chosen ones,	4472
	18:11	Pharisee stood up and prayed a himself:	4639
	18:31	a the **Son** *of* **Man** will be fulfilled.	AIT

Lk	18:34	they did not know what *he was* **talking a.**	3306
	21: 5	Some of his disciples were remarking a	4309
	21: 7	And what will be the sign that they *are* **a to**	3516
	21:36	be able to escape all that *is* **a to** happen,	3516
	22:37	what is written a me	4309
	22:41	He withdrew a a stone's throw	6059
	22:59	A an hour later another asserted,	6059
	22:60	"I don't know what *you're* **talking a!"**	3306
	23: 8	From what he had heard a him,	4309
	23:44	It was now a the sixth hour,	6059
	23:54	and the Sabbath was **a to begin.**	2216
	24: 4	While they were wondering a this,	4309
	24:13	a seven miles **from** Jerusalem.	600
	24:14	They were talking with each other a	4309
	24:19	"A Jesus of Nazareth," they replied.	4309
	24:36	*While* they were *still* **talking** a this,	3281
	24:44	be fulfilled that is written a me in the Law	4309
Jn	1:22	What do you say a yourself?"	4309
	1:39	It was the tenth hour.	6055
	1:45	"We have found the one Moses **wrote a** in	1211
	1:45	and a whom the prophets also wrote—	NIG
	2:25	He did not need man's testimony a man,	4309
	3:26	the one you **testified a**—	3455
	4: 6	It was a the sixth hour.	6055
	4:32	to eat that you know nothing **a."**	NIG
	5:31	"If I testify a myself,	4309
	5:32	and I know that his testimony a me is valid.	4309
	5:39	These are the Scriptures that testify a me,	4309
	5:46	you would believe me, for he wrote a me.	4309
	6:10	a five thousand of them.	6055
	6:41	At this the Jews began to grumble a him	4309
	6:61	Aware that his disciples were grumbling a	4309
	7:12	crowds there was widespread whispering a	4309
	7:13	But no one would say anything publicly a	4309
	7:18	there is nothing false a him.	1877
	7:32	the crowd whispering such things a him	4309
	8:27	not understand that *he was* **telling** them a	3306
	9:17	"What have you to say a him?	4309
	10:36	what a the one whom the Father set apart	NIG
	10:41	all that John said a this man was true."	4309
	11:54	Therefore Jesus no longer **moved** a publicly	4344
	12: 3	Then Mary took a a **pint** of pure nard,	3354
	12: 6	not say this because he cared a the poor but	4309
	12:16	that these things had been written a him	2093
	12:41	because he saw Jesus' glory and spoke a	4309
	13:27	"What *you are a to* **do,** do quickly,"	AIT
	15:26	he will testify a me.	4309
	16:19	Jesus saw that they wanted to ask him a	NIG
	16:25	of language but will tell you plainly a	4309
	16:19	the high priest questioned Jesus a	4309
	18:34	"or did others talk to you a me?"	4309
	19:14	Passover Week, a the sixth hour.	6055
	19:39	a seventy-five pounds.	6055
	21: 8	a a hundred yards.	6055
	21:21	he asked, "Lord, what a him?"	NIG
Ac	1: 1	I wrote a all that Jesus began to do and	4309
	1: 3	over a period of forty days and spoke a	4309
	1: 4	which you have heard me speak a.	NIG
	1:15	group **numbering** a a hundred and twenty)	6059
	1:19	Everyone in Jerusalem **heard** a this,	1181+1196
	2:25	David said a him:	1650
	2:41	and a three thousand were added	6059
	3: 3	When he saw Peter and John a to enter,	3516
	4: 4	the number of men grew to a five thousand.	6055
	4:20	For we cannot **help speaking** a	3281+3590
	5: 7	A three hours later his wife came in,	6055
	5:11	the whole church and all who **heard** a	201
	5:36	and a four hundred men rallied to him.	6055
	7:13	Pharaoh **learned** a Joseph's family.	1181+5745
	7:18	another king, who **knew** nothing a Joseph,	3857
	8:34	please, who is the prophet talking a,	4309
	8:35	**told** him **the good news a**	2294
	8:40	appeared at Azotus and **traveled a,**	1451
	9:13	"I have heard many reports a this man	4309
	9:28	**moved** a freely in Jerusalem,	1660+1744+2779
	9:32	**Traveled** a the country,	1328+1451+4246
	9:37	A that time she became sick and died,	1877
	10: 3	at a three in the afternoon he had a vision.	4309+6059
	10: 9	A noon the following day as they were	4309
	10:17	While Peter *was* **wondering** a the meaning	1389
	10:19	While Peter was still thinking a the vision,	4309
	10:43	All the prophets testify *a* him	AIT
	11:12	The Spirit told me to have no hesitation a	NIG
	11:20	**telling** them **the good news a**	2294
	12: 1	It was a this time	2848
	12:17	"**Tell** James and the brothers a	550
	13:11	darkness came over him, and he **groped a,**	4310
	13:12	he was amazed at the teaching a the **Lord.**	AIT
	13:18	he endured their conduct for a forty years	6055
	13:20	All this took a 450 years.	6055
	13:29	that was written a him,	4309
	13:42	the people invited them *to* **speak** further a	3281
	14: 6	But *they* **found out** a it and fled to	5328
	15: 2	see the apostles and elders a	4309
	15:12	and Paul **telling** a the miraculous signs	2007
	16:25	A midnight Paul and Silas were praying	2848
	16:27	he drew his sword and *was* **a to** kill himself	3516
	17:18	the good news a **Jesus** and the resurrection.	AIT
	17:21	but **talking** and listening a	3306
	17:32	*When* they **heard** a the resurrection of	201
	18:14	Just as Paul *was* **a to** speak,	3516
	18:14	"If you Jews were **making a complaint** a	1639S
	18:15	But since it involves questions a words	4309
	18:25	and he spoke with great fervor and taught a	4309
	19: 7	There were a twelve men in all.	6059
	19: 8	arguing persuasively a the kingdom	4309

Ac	19:15	and *I* **know** a Paul, but who are you?"	2179
	19:23	A that time there arose a great disturbance	2848
	19:23	that time there arose a great disturbance a	4309
	19:34	they all shouted in unison for a two hours:	6055
	20: 3	a plot against him just *as he was* **a to** sail	3516
	20:25	among whom *I have* **gone** a preaching	1451
	21:24	in these reports a you,	4309
	21:37	*As* the soldiers *were* **a to** take Paul into	3516
	22: 6	"A noon as I came near Damascus,	4309
	22:18	they will not accept your testimony a me.'	4309
	22:29	Those who *were* **a to** question him	3516
	23: 5	not **speak** evil a the ruler of your people.' "	3306
	23:11	As you have **testified** a me in Jerusalem,	4309
	23:15	of wanting more accurate information a	4309
	23:20	of wanting more accurate information a	4309
	23:27	by the Jews and they *were* **a to** kill him,	3516
	23:29	to do with questions *a* their **law,**	AIT
	24: 2	and your foresight *has* **brought** a reforms	1181
	24: 8	the truth a all these charges we are bringing	4309
	24:24	for Paul and listened to him as he spoke a	4309
	25:19	they had some points of dispute with him a	4309
	25:19	with him about their own religion and a	4309
	25:24	Jewish community has petitioned me a	4309
	25:26	to write to His Majesty a him.	4309
	26:13	A noon, O king, as I was on the road,	NIG
	27: 2	a ship from Adramyttium **a to** sail for ports	3516
	27:27	across the Adriatic Sea, when a midnight	2848
	28:21	or said anything bad a you.	4309
	28:23	of God and tried to convince them a Jesus	4309
	28:31	of God and taught a the Lord Jesus Christ.	4309
Ro	1:19	what may be known *a* God is plain to them,	AIT
	2:17	on the law and **brag** a your relationship	3016
	2:23	You who **brag** a the law,	1877
	4: 2	he had **something to boast** a—	3017
	4:19	since he was a hundred years old—	4543
	10: 2	I can testify *a* them that they are zealous	AIT
	11: 2	the Scripture says in the passage a Elijah—	NIG
	13:14	*do* not **think** a how to gratify the desires of the sinful nature.	4472+4630
	14:22	So whatever you believe a	NIG
	15:21	"Those who were not told a him will see,	4309
	16:19	Everyone *has* **heard** a your obedience,	919
	16:19	but I want you to be wise a what is good,	1650
	16:19	and innocent a what is evil.	1650
1Co	1: 6	our testimony *a* **Christ** was confirmed	AIT
	2: 1	as I proclaimed to you the testimony *a* God.	AIT
	2:15	The spiritual man **makes judgments** a	373
	3:21	So then, no more boasting a men!	1877
	6: 4	if you have disputes a such matters,	NIG
	7: 1	Now for the matters you wrote **a:**	4309
	7:25	Now a virgins: I have no command from the	4309
	7:32	An unmarried man *is* **concerned** a	3534
	7:33	a married man *is* **concerned** a the affairs	3534
	7:34	or virgin *is* **concerned** a the Lord's affairs:	3534
	7:34	a married woman *is* **concerned** a the affairs	3534
	8: 1	Now a food sacrificed to **idols:**	4309
	8: 4	So then, a eating food sacrificed to idols:	4309
	9: 9	Is it *a* oxen that God is concerned?	AIT
	11:16	If anyone wants to be contentious a this,	NIG
	12: 1	Now a spiritual gifts, brothers,	4309
	14:35	If they want *to* **inquire** a something,	3443
	15:15	we are then found to be false witnesses a	NIG
	15:15	for we have testified a God	2848
	16: 1	Now a the collection for God's people:	4309
	16:12	Now a our brother Apollos:	4309
2Co	7: 7	He told us a your longing for me,	NIG
	7:14	I had boasted to him a you,	5642
	7:14	so our **boasting** a you to Titus has proved	3018
	8:10	And here is my advice a what is best	NIG
	9: 1	to write to you a this service to the saints.	4309
	9: 2	and *I have been* **boasting** a it to	3016
	9: 3	the brothers in order that our boasting a	5642
	9: 4	not *to* **say** anything a you—	3306
	10: 8	if I boast somewhat freely a the authority	4309
	10:16	not *want to* **boast** a work already done	3016
	11:12	with us in the things *they* **boast a.**	3016
	11:21	What anyone else dares to boast a—	NIG
	11:21	I also dare to boast a.	NIG
	12: 5	I will boast a a man like that,	5642
	12: 5	but I will not boast a myself,	5642
	12: 5	except a my weaknesses.	1877
	12: 9	Therefore I will boast all the more gladly a	1877
Gal	4:20	because I am perplexed a you!	1877
	6:13	to be circumcised that they may boast a	1877
Eph	1:15	*since* I **heard** a your faith in the Lord Jesus	201
	3: 2	Surely *you have* **heard** a the administration	201
	5:32	but I am talking a Christ and the church.	1650
Php	1: 7	It is right for me to feel this way a all	5642
	1:27	whether I come and see you or only hear a	4309
	2:19	also may be cheered when I receive news a	4309
	4: 6	*Do* not **be anxious** a anything,	3534
	4: 8	**think** a such things.	3357
Col	1: 5	that *you have* **already heard** a in the word	4578
	1: 9	since the day we **heard** a you,	201
	2:18	**goes into great detail** a what he has seen,	1836
	4: 7	Tychicus will tell you all the news a me,	2848
	4: 8	the express purpose that you may know a	4309
	4:10	(You have received instructions a him;	4309
1Th	1: 8	we do not need to **say** anything a it,	3281
	3: 5	I sent to **find out** a your faith.	1182
	3: 6	*has* **brought good news** a your faith	2294
	3: 7	and persecution we were encouraged a you	2093
	4: 9	Now a brotherly love we do not need	4309
	4:13	to be ignorant a those who fall asleep,	4309
	5: 1	a times and dates we do not need to write	4309

2Th	1:4	among God's churches we boast **a**	5642
1Ti	1:7	not know what *they are* **talking a**	3306
	1:18	with the prophecies once made **a** you,	2093
	5:13	into the habit of being idle and **going a**	4320
	6:4	and **quarrels a** words that result in envy,	3363
	6:15	which God *will* **bring a** in his own time—	1259
2Ti	1:8	do not be ashamed to testify *a* our **Lord,**	AIT
	2:14	before God against **quarreling a** words;	3362
	3:10	You, however, **know all a** my teaching,	4158
Tit	2:8	because they have nothing bad to say *a* us.	4309
	2:10	the teaching *a* God our **Savior** attractive.	AIT
	3:9	and arguments and quarrels *a* the **law,**	3788
Phm	1:7	because I hear *a* your **faith** in the Lord	AIT
Heb	1:8	But *a* the Son he says, "Your throne,	4639
	2:5	*a* which we are speaking.	4309
	4:4	For somewhere he has spoken *a*	4309
	4:8	not have spoken later *a* another day.	4309
	5:11	We have much to say *a* this,	4309
	5:13	with the teaching *a* **righteousness.**	AIT
	6:1	the elementary teachings *a* **Christ** and go on	AIT
	6:2	instruction *a* **baptisms,**	AIT
	7:14	in regard to that tribe Moses said nothing *a*	4309
	8:5	*when he was a* to build the tabernacle—	3516
	10:7	it is written *a* me in the scroll—	4309
	10:15	The Holy Spirit also **testifies** to us *a* this.	3455
	11:7	when warned *a* things not yet seen,	4309
	11:17	the promises *was a* to **sacrifice** his one	AIT
	11:22	spoke *a* the exodus of the Israelites	4309
	11:22	from Egypt and gave instructions *a*	4309
	11:32	I do not have time to tell *a* Gideon, Barak,	4309
	11:37	*They* **went** *a* in sheepskins and goatskins,	4320
	12:17	*He could* **bring** *a* no change of mind,	2351
Jas	1:11	even while he **goes** *a* his business.	4512
	1:20	for man's anger *does* not **bring** *a*	2237
	2:16	but does nothing *a* his physical needs,	AIT
	3:14	do not boast *a* it or deny the truth.	NIG
	5:11	the Lord finally brought *a.*	NIG
2Pe	1:16	when *we* told you *a* the power	1192
	1:20	that no prophecy of Scripture **came** *a* by	1181
	3:12	That day will **bring** *a* the destruction of	1328
1Jn	2:26	I am writing these things to you *a*	4309
	2:27	as his anointing teaches you *a* all things	4309
	5:9	which he has given *a* his Son.	4309
	5:10	not believed the testimony God has given *a*	4309
	5:16	I am not saying that he should pray *a* that.	4309
3Jn	1:3	and **tell** *a* your faithfulness to the truth	3455
	1:6	They *have* **told** the church *a* your love.	3455
	1:10	gossiping maliciously *a* about us.	5826
Jude	1:3	although I was very eager to write to you *a*	4309
	1:4	men whose condemnation **was written** *a*	4592
	1:9	when he was disputing with the devil *a*	4309
	1:14	prophesied *a* these *men:*	AIT
	1:16	they boast *a* themselves and flatter others	NIG
Rev	2:10	not be afraid of what *you are* *a* to suffer.	3516
	3:2	Strengthen what remains and *is a* to die,	3516
	3:16	*I am a* to spit you out of my mouth.	3516
	8:1	there was silence in heaven for a half	6055
	8:13	of the trumpet blasts *about* to be sounded by	3516
	10:4	the seven thunders spoke, *I was a* to write;	3516
	10:11	in the days when the seventh angel *is a* to	3516
	10:11	"You must prophesy again *a* many peoples,	2093
	12:2	in pain *as she was a* to **give birth.**	AIT
	12:4	of the woman *from was a* to give birth,	3516
	16:21	From the sky huge hailstones of *a*	6055

ABOVE (147)

Ge	1:7	under the expanse from the water *a* it.	4946+6584
	1:20	and let birds fly *a* the earth across	6584
	3:14	"Cursed are you *a* all the livestock and all	4946
	7:17	the ark high *a* the earth.	4946+6584
	27:39	away from the dew of heaven *a.*	4946+6584
	28:13	There *a* it stood the LORD, and he said:	6584
	32:31	The sun rose *a* him as he passed Peniel,	4200
	49:25	with blessings of the heavens *a,*	4946+6584
Ex	20:4	an idol in the form of anything in heaven *a*	4946+5087
	25:22	*a* the cover between the two cherubim	4946+6584
	28:27	close to the seam **just** *a* the waistband	4946+6584
	39:20	close to the seam **just** *a* the waistband	4946+5087
	40:36	from *a* the tabernacle, they would set out;	6584
Lev	16:13	the atonement cover *a* the Testimony,	6584
	26:19	and make the **sky** *a* you like iron and	AIT
Nu	7:89	two cherubim *a* the atonement cover	4946+6584
	9:15	the cloud *a* the tabernacle looked like fire.	6584
	9:17	Whenever the cloud lifted from *a* the Tent,	6584
	10:11	the cloud lifted from *a* the tabernacle of	6584
	11:31	camp to about three feet *a* the ground,	6584+7156
	12:10	When the cloud lifted from *a* the Tent,	6584
	16:3	Why then do you set yourselves *a*	6584
Dt	4:39	the LORD is God in heaven *a* and on	4946+5087
	5:8	an idol in the form of anything in heaven *a*	4946+5087
	10:15	their descendants, *a* all the nations,	4946
	11:21	as the days that the heavens are *a* the earth.	6584
	26:19	fame and honor high *a* all	6584
	28:1	the LORD your God will set you high *a*	6584
	28:43	The alien who lives among you will rise *a*	6584
	33:13	the precious dew **from** heaven *a* and with	AIT
Jos	2:11	the LORD your God is God in heaven *a*	4946+6584
2Sa	22:49	You exalted me *a* my foes;	4946
1Ki	7:3	with cedar *a* the beams that rested on	4946+5087+6584
	7:11	A were high-grade stones, cut to size,	2025+4200+4946+5087
	7:20	*a* the bowl-shaped part next to the network,	4200+4946+4946+5087+6645

1Ki	7:29	A and below the lions	4946+5087
	8:23	like you in heaven *a* or on earth below	4946+5087
2Ki	19:30	and bear fruit *a.*	2025+4200+5087
1Ch	4:38	The men listed *a* by name were leaders	NIH
	11:21	He was doubly honored than the Three	4946
	16:25	he is to be feared *a* all gods.	6584
	29:3	**over and** *a* everything I have provided	2025+4200+5087
2Ch	7:3	and the glory of the LORD *a* temple,	6584
	34:4	to pieces the incense altars that were *a*	2025+4200+5087
Ne	3:28	A the Horse Gate, the priests made repairs,	4946+6584
	3:31	and as far as the **room** *a* the corner;	6608
	3:32	the **room** *a* the corner and the Sheep Gate	6608
	8:5	because he was standing *a* them;	4946+6584
	9:5	may it be exalted *a* all blessing and praise.	6584
	12:37	and passed *a* the house of David to	4946+6584
Est	5:11	how he had elevated him *a* the other nobles	6584
Job	3:4	may God *a* not care about it;	4946+5087
	18:16	up below and his branches wither *a.*	4946+5087
	19:5	If indeed you would exalt yourselves *a* me	6584
	31:2	For what is man's lot from God *a,*	4946+5087
	35:5	gaze at the clouds so high *a* you.	4946
Ps	8:1	You have set your glory *a* the heavens.	6584
	18:48	You exalted me *a* my foes;	4946
	27:6	be exalted *a* the enemies who surround me;	6584
	45:7	therefore God, your God, has set you *a*	4946
	50:4	He summons the heavens *a,*	4946+6584
	57:5	Be exalted, O God, *a* the heavens;	6584
	57:11	Be exalted, O God, *a* the heavens;	6584
	68:33	to him who rides the ancient **skies** *a,*	9028+9028
	78:23	Yet he gave a command to the skies *a*	4946+5087
	89:6	in the **skies** *a* can compare with the LORD?	8836
	95:3	the great King *a* all gods.	6584
	96:4	he is to be feared *a* all gods.	6584
	97:9	you are exalted far *a* all gods.	6584
	103:11	For as high as the heavens are *a* the earth,	6584
	104:6	the waters stood *a* the mountains.	6584
	108:5	Be exalted, O God, *a* the heavens;	6584
	113:4	his glory *a* the heavens.	6584
	138:2	for you have exalted *a* all things your name	6584
	148:1	praise him in the **heights a.**	5294
	148:4	you highest heavens and you waters *a*	4946+5087
	148:13	his splendor is *a* the earth and the heavens.	6584
Pr	4:23	A all else, guard your heart,	4946
	8:28	when he established the clouds *a*	4946+5087
Isa	2:2	it will be raised *a* the hills,	4946
	6:2	A him were seraphs, each with six wings:	4946+5087
	10:15	the ax raise itself *a* him who swings it,	6584
	14:13	I will raise my throne *a* the stars of God;	4946+5087
	14:14	I will ascend *a* the tops of the clouds,	6584
	24:21	the powers in the heavens *a*	928+2021+5294
	37:31	and bear fruit *a.*	2025+4200+5087
	40:22	He sits enthroned *a* the circle of the earth,	6584
	45:8	"You heavens *a,* rain down righteousness;	4946+5087
Jer	4:28	the earth will mourn and the heavens *a*	4946+5087
	17:9	The heart is deceitful *a* all things and	4946
	21:13	you *who* **live** *a* this valley *on*	AIT
	31:37	"Only if the heavens *a* can be measured	2025+4200+4946+5087
	43:10	he will spread his royal canopy *a* them.	6584
	52:23	the total number of pomegranates *a*	6584
Eze	1:22	Spread out *a* the heads of	6584
	1:25	a voice from the expanse over their heads	6584
	1:26	A the expanse over their	4946+5087
	1:26	and **high** *a* on the throne was a figure like	2025+4200+4946+5087
	9:3	of Israel went up from *a* the cherubim,	6584
	10:1	a throne of sapphire the expanse that was	448
	10:4	Then the glory of the LORD rose from *a*	6584
	10:18	of the temple and stopped *a* the cherubim.	6584
	10:19	the glory of the God of Israel was *a* them.	2025+4200+4946+5087
	11:22	the glory of the God of Israel was *a* them.	2025+4200+4946+5087
	11:23	the city and stopped *a* the mountain east	6584
	19:11	It towered high *a* the thick foliage,	1068+6584
	29:15	and will never again exalt itself *a*	6584
	31:3	its top *a* the thick foliage,	1068
	31:10	lifting its top *a* the thick foliage,	448+1068
	31:14	lifting their tops *a* the thick foliage,	448+1068
	41:6	one *a* another, thirty on each level.	448
	41:17	In the space *a* the outside of the entrance	4946+6584
	41:20	the floor to the area *a* the entrance,	4946+6584
Da	11:36	He will exalt and magnify himself *a*	6584
	11:37	but will exalt himself *a* them all.	6584
	12:6	who was *a* the waters of the river,	4946+5087
	12:7	who was *a* the waters of the river,	4946+5087
Am	2:9	I destroyed his fruit *a* and his roots below.	4946+5087
Mic	4:1	it will be raised *a* the hills,	4946
Mt	10:24	"A student is not *a* his teacher,	5642
	10:24	nor a servant *a* his master.	5642
	27:37	A his head they placed the written charge	2062
Mk	2:4	made an opening in the roof *a* Jesus	3963
Lk	6:40	A student is not *a* his teacher,	5642
	23:38	There was a written notice *a* him,	2093
Jn	3:31	"The one who comes **from** *a* is above all;	540
	3:31	"The one who comes from above is *a* all;	2062
	3:31	"The one who comes from heaven is *a* all.	2062
	8:23	"You are from below; I am from *a.*	539
	19:11	over me if it were not given to you **from** *a.*	540

Ac	2:19	the heaven *a* and signs on the earth below,	539
Ro	12:10	Honor one another *a* yourselves.	4605
Gal	4:26	But the Jerusalem that is *a* is free,	539
Eph	1:21	**far** *a* all rule and authority,	5645
Php	2:9	and gave him the name that is *a*	5642
Col	3:1	set your hearts on things *a,*	539
	3:2	Set your minds on things *a,*	539
1Ti	3:2	Now the overseer must be *a* **reproach,**	455
Heb	1:9	therefore God, your God, has set you *a*	4123
	4:5	And again in **the passage** *a* he says,	4047
	7:26	**exalted** *a* the heavens.	5734
	9:5	A the ark were the cherubim of the Glory,	5645
Jas	1:17	Every good and perfect gift is **from a,**	540
	5:12	A all, my brothers, do not swear—	4574
1Pe	4:8	A all, love each other deeply,	4574
2Pe	1:20	A all, you must understand	4047+4754
Rev	10:1	with a rainbow *a* his head;	2093

ABRAHAM (230) [ABRAHAM'S, ABRAM, ABRAM'S]

Ge	17:5	your name will be A,	90
	17:9	Then God said to A, "As for you,	90
	17:15	God also said to A,	90
	17:17	A fell facedown; he laughed	90
	17:18	And A said to God,	90
	17:22	When he had finished speaking with A,	90
	17:23	On that very day A took his son Ishmael	90
	17:24	A was ninety-nine years old	90
	17:26	A and his son Ishmael were both circumcised	90
	18:1	to A near the great trees of Mamre	2257S
	18:2	A looked up and saw three men	2257S
	18:6	So A hurried into the tent to Sarah.	90
	18:11	A and Sarah were already old	90
	18:13	Then the LORD said to A,	90
	18:16	and A walked along with them to see them	90
	18:17	"Shall I hide from A what I am about	90
	18:18	A will surely become a great	90
	18:19	about for A what he has promised him."	90
	18:22	A remained standing before the LORD.	90
	18:23	Then A approached him and said:	90
	18:27	Then A spoke up again:	90
	18:31	A said, "Now that I have been so bold as	NIH
	18:33	the LORD had finished speaking with A,	90
	18:33	he left, and A returned home.	90
	19:27	the next morning A got up and returned to	90
	19:29	he remembered A, and he brought Lot out	90
	20:1	Now A moved on from there into	90
	20:2	and there A said of his wife Sarah,	90
	20:9	Then Abimelech called A in and said,	90
	20:10	And Abimelech asked A,	90
	20:11	A replied, "I said to myself,	90
	20:14	and female slaves and gave them to A,	90
	20:17	Then A prayed to God,	90
	21:2	Sarah became pregnant and bore a son to A	90
	21:3	A gave the name Isaac to the son	90
	21:4	When his son Isaac was eight days old, A	90
	21:4	circumcised him,	90
	21:5	A was a hundred years old	90
	21:7	to A that Sarah would nurse children?	90
	21:8	and on the day Isaac was weaned A held	90
	21:9	the Egyptian had borne to A was mocking,	90
	21:10	and she said to A,	90
	21:11	The matter distressed A greatly	90
	21:14	Early the next morning A took some food	90
	21:22	the commander of his forces said to A,	90
	21:24	A said, "I swear it."	90
	21:25	Then A complained to Abimelech about	90
	21:27	So A brought sheep and cattle	90
	21:28	A set apart seven ewe lambs from the flock,	90
	21:29	and Abimelech asked A,	90
	21:33	A planted a tamarisk tree in Beersheba,	NIH
	21:34	And A stayed in the land of the Philistines	90
	22:1	Some time later God tested A.	90
	22:1	He said to him, "A!"	90
	22:3	Early the next morning A got up	90
	22:4	the third day A looked up and saw the place	90
	22:6	A took the wood for the burnt offering	90
	22:7	Isaac spoke up and said to his father A,	90
	22:7	"Yes, my son?" A replied.	NIH
	22:8	A answered, "God himself will provide	90
	22:9	A built an altar there and arranged	90
	22:11	to him from heaven, "A! Abraham!"	90
	22:11	to him from heaven, "Abraham! A!"	90
	22:13	A looked up and there in a thicket he saw	90
	22:14	A called that place The LORD Will Provide.	90
	22:15	of the LORD called to A from heaven	90
	22:19	Then A returned to his servants,	90
	22:19	And A stayed in Beersheba.	90
	22:20	Some time later A was told,	90
	23:2	and A went to mourn for Sarah and to weep	90
	23:3	Then A rose from beside his dead wife	90
	23:5	The Hittites replied to A,	90
	23:7	A rose and bowed down before the	90
	23:10	among his people and he replied to A in	90
	23:12	Again A bowed down before the people of	90
	23:14	Ephron answered A,	90
	23:16	A agreed to Ephron's terms	90
	23:18	to A as his property in the presence of all	90
	23:19	Afterward A buried his wife Sarah in	90
	23:20	in it were deeded to A by the Hittites as	90
	24:1	A was now old and well advanced in years,	90
	24:6	not take my son back there," A said.	90
	24:9	the thigh of his master A and swore an oath	90
	24:12	"O LORD, God of my master A,	90
	24:12	and show kindness to my master A.	90
	24:27	the God of my master A,	90

Ge	24:42	I said, 'O LORD, God of my master A,	90
	24:48	the God of my master A,	90
	25: 1	A took another wife,	90
	25: 5	A left everything he owned to Isaac.	90
	25: 7	A lived a hundred and seventy-five years.	90
	25: 8	Then A breathed his last and died at	90
	25:10	the field A had bought from the Hittites.	90
	25:10	There A was buried with his wife Sarah.	90
	25:12	Hagar the Egyptian, bore to A.	90
	25:19	A became the father of Isaac,	90
	26: 3	the oath I swore to your father A.	90
	26: 5	A obeyed me and kept my requirements,	90
	26:15	in the time of his father A,	90
	26:18	in the time of his father A,	90
	26:18	the Philistines had stopped up after A died,	90
	26:24	"I am the God of your father A.	90
	26:24	for the sake of my servant A."	90
	28: 4	the blessing given to A,	90
	28: 4	the land God gave to A."	90
	28: 9	and daughter of Ishmael son of A,	90
	28:13	God of your father A and the God of Isaac.	90
	31:42	the God of A and the Fear of Isaac,	90
	31:53	May the God of A and the God of Nahor,	90
	32: 9	Jacob prayed, "O God of my father A,	90
	35:12	The land I gave to A and Isaac I also give	90
	35:27	Hebron), where A and Isaac had stayed.	90
	48:15	"May the God before whom my fathers A	90
	48:16	by my name and the names of my fathers A	90
	49:30	which A bought as a burial place	90
	49:31	There A and his wife Sarah were buried,	90
	50:13	which A had bought as a burial place	90
	50:24	to the land he promised on oath to A,	90
Ex	2:24	and he remembered his covenant with A,	90
	3: 6	"I am the God of A, the God of A,	90
	3:15	the God of A, the God of Isaac and the God	90
	3:16	the God of A, Isaac and Jacob—	90
	4: 5	the God of A, the God of Isaac and the God	90
	6: 3	I appeared to A, to Isaac and to Jacob	90
	6: 8	with uplifted hand to give to A,	90
	32:13	Remember your servants A,	90
	33: 1	go up to the land I promised on oath to A,	90
Lev	26:42	with Isaac and my covenant with A,	90
Nu	32:11	the land I promised on oath to A, Isaac	90
Dt	1: 8	to A, Isaac and Jacob—	90
	6:10	to A, Isaac and Jacob, to give you—	90
	9: 5	to A, Isaac and Jacob.	90
	9:27	Remember your servants A,	90
	29:13	and as he swore to your fathers, A, Isaac	90
	30:20	to give to your fathers, A, Isaac	90
	34: 4	"This is the land I promised on oath to A,	90
Jos	24: 2	including Terah the father of A and Nahor,	90
	24: 3	But I took your father A from the land	90
1Ki	18:36	"O LORD, God of A, Isaac and Israel,	90
2Ki	13:23	for them because of his covenant with A,	90
1Ch	1:27	and Abram (that is, A).	90
	1:28	The sons of A: Isaac and Ishmael.	90
	1:34	A was the father of Isaac.	90
	16:16	the covenant he made with A,	90
	29:18	O LORD, God of our fathers A,	90
2Ch	20: 7	to the descendants of A your friend?	90
	30: 6	return to the LORD, the God of A,	90
Ne	9: 7	of Ur of the Chaldeans and named him A.	90
Ps	47: 9	the people of the God of A, for the kings of	90
	105: 6	O descendants of A his servant,	90
	105: 9	the covenant he made with A,	90
	105:42	holy promise given to his servant A.	90
Isa	29:22	who redeemed A, says to the house	90
	41: 8	you descendants of A my friend,	90
	51: 2	look to A, your father, and	90
	63:16	though A does not know us	90
Jer	33:26	to rule over the descendants of A,	90
Eze	33:24	'A was only one man,	90
Mic	7:20	and show mercy to A,	90
Mt	1: 1	Jesus Christ the son of David, the son of A:	11
	1: 2	A was the father of Isaac,	11
	1:17	in all from A to David,	11
	3: 9	'We have A as our father.'	11
	3: 9	God can raise up children for A.	11
	8:11	will take their places at the feast with A,	11
	22:32	'I am the God of A,	11
Mk	12:26	how God said to him, 'I am the God of A,	11
Lk	1:55	to A and his descendants forever,	11
	1:73	the oath he swore to our father A:	11
	3: 8	'We have A as our father.'	11
	3: 8	God can raise up children for A.	11
	3:34	the son of A, the son of Terah,	11
	13:16	should not this woman, a daughter of A,	11
	13:28	and gnashing of teeth, when you see A,	11
	16:23	he looked up and saw A far away,	11
	16:24	So he called to him, 'Father A,	11
	16:25	"But A replied, 'Son, remember that	11
	16:29	"A replied, 'They have Moses and	11
	16:30	" 'No, father A,' he said,	11
	19: 9	because this man, too, is a son of A.	11
	20:37	for he calls the Lord 'the God of A,	11
Jn	8:39	"A is our father," they answered.	11
	8:39	"then you would do the things A did.	11
	8:40	A did not do such things.	11
	8:52	A died and so did the prophets,	11
	8:53	Are you greater than our father A?	11
	8:56	Your father A rejoiced at the thought	11
	8:57	"and you have seen A!"	11
	8:58	Jesus answered, "before A was born, I am!"	11
Ac	3:13	The God of A, Isaac and Jacob,	11
	3:25	He said to A, 'Through your offspring	11
	7: 2	The God of glory appeared to our father A	11
	7: 5	even though at that time A had no child.	899S

Ac	7: 8	he gave A the covenant of circumcision.	899S
	7: 8	And A became the father of Isaac	NIG
	7:16	that A had bought from the sons of Hamor	11
	7:17	near for God to fulfill his promise to A,	11
	7:32	the god of A, Isaac and Jacob.'	11
	13:26	"Brothers, children of A,	11
Ro	4: 1	What then shall we say that A,	11
	4: 2	If, in fact, A was justified by works,	11
	4: 3	"A believed God, and it was credited	11
	4:12	of the faith that our father A had	11
	4:13	that A and his offspring received	11
	4:16	but also to those who are of the faith of A.	11
	4:18	A in hope believed and so became	4005S
	11: 1	I am an Israelite myself, a descendant of A,	11
Gal	3: 6	Consider A: "He believed God,	11
	3: 7	that those who believe are children of A.	11
	3: 8	and announced the gospel in advance to A:	11
	3: 9	along with A, the man of faith.	11
	3:14	that the blessing given to A might come to	11
	3:16	The promises were spoken to A and	11
	3:18	in his grace gave it to A through a promise.	11
	4:22	For it is written that A had two sons,	11
Heb	6:13	When God made his promise to A,	11
	6:15	A received what was promised.	NIG
	7: 1	He met A returning from the defeat of	11
	7: 2	and A gave him a tenth of everything.	11
	7: 4	patriarch A gave him a tenth of the plunder!	11
	7: 5	their brothers are descended from A.	11
	7: 6	a tenth from A and blessed him who had	11
	7: 9	paid the tenth through A,	11
	7:10	because when Melchizedek met A,	899S
	11: 8	By faith A, when called to go to	11
	11:11	By faith A, even though he was past age—	NIG
	11:17	By faith A, when God tested him,	11
	11:19	A reasoned that God could raise the dead,	NIG
Jas	2:21	not our ancestor A considered righteous	11
	2:23	"A believed God, and it was credited	11
1Pe	3: 6	who obeyed A and called him her master.	11

ABRAHAM'S (23) [ABRAHAM]

Ge	17:27	And every male in A household,	2257S
	20:18	because of A wife Sarah.	90
	22:23	to A brother Nahor.	90
	24:15	who was the wife of A brother Nahor.	90
	24:34	So he said, "I am A servant.	90
	24:52	When A servant heard what they said,	90
	24:59	with her nurse and A servant and his men.	90
	25:11	After A death, God blessed his son Isaac,	90
	25:12	This is the account of A son Ishmael,	90
	25:19	This is the account of A son Isaac.	90
	26: 1	besides the earlier famine of A time—	90
1Ch	1:32	The sons born to Keturah, A concubine:	90
Lk	16:22	and the angels carried him to A side.	11
Jn	8:33	"We are A descendants	11
	8:37	I know you are A descendants.	11
	8:39	"If you were A children," said Jesus,	11
Ro	4:12	that A faith was credited to him	11
	4:16	and may be guaranteed to all A offspring—	NIG
	9: 7	Nor because they are his descendants are they all A children.	11
	9: 8	children of the promise who are regarded as A offspring.	NIG
2Co	11:22	Are they A descendants?	11
Gal	3:29	then you are A seed,	11
Heb	2:16	it is not angels he helps, but A descendants.	11

ABRAM (60) [ABRAHAM]

Ge	11:26	he became the father of A,	92
	11:27	Terah became the father of A,	92
	11:29	A and Nahor both married,	92
	11:31	Terah took his son A,	92
	11:31	Sarai, the wife of his son A,	92
	12: 1	The LORD had said to A,	92
	12: 4	So A left, as the LORD had told him;	92
	12: 4	A was seventy-five years old	92
	12: 6	A traveled through the land as far as	92
	12: 7	The LORD appeared to A and said,	92
	12: 9	A set out and continued toward the Negev.	92
	12:10	and A went down to Egypt to live there for	92
	12:14	When A came to Egypt,	92
	12:16	He treated A well for her sake,	92
	12:16	and A acquired sheep and cattle,	2257S
	12:18	So Pharaoh summoned A.	92
	12:20	Pharaoh gave orders about A to his men,	2257S
	13: 1	So A went up from Egypt to the Negev,	92
	13: 2	A had become very wealthy in livestock	92
	13: 4	There A called on the name of the LORD.	92
	13: 5	Now Lot, who was moving about with A,	92
	13: 8	So A said to Lot,	92
	13:12	A lived in the land of Canaan,	92
	13:14	The LORD said to A after Lot had parted	92
	13:18	So A moved his tents and went to live near	92
	14:13	and reported this to A the Hebrew.	92
	14:13	Now A was living near the great trees	2085S
	14:13	all of whom were allied with A.	92
	14:14	When A heard that his relative had been taken captive,	92
	14:15	the night A divided his men to attack them	2085S
	14:17	After A returned from defeating	2257S
	14:19	and he blessed A,	2084S
	14:19	saying, "Blessed be A by God Most High,	92
	14:20	Then A gave him a tenth of everything.	NIH
	14:21	The king of Sodom said to A,	92
	14:22	But A said to the king of Sodom,	92
	14:23	'I made A rich.'	92

Ge	15: 1	the word of the LORD came to A in	92
	15: 1	"Do not be afraid, A.	92
	15: 2	But A said, "O Sovereign LORD,	92
	15: 3	A said, "You have given me no children;	92
	15: 6	A believed the LORD, and he credited it	NIH
	15: 8	But A said, "O Sovereign LORD,	NIH
	15:10	A brought all these to him,	NIH
	15:11	but A drove them away.	92
	15:12	A fell into a deep sleep,	92
	15:18	the LORD made a covenant with A	92
	16: 2	so she said to A,	92
	16: 2	A agreed to what Sarai said.	92
	16: 3	after A had been living in Canaan ten years,	92
	16: 5	Then Sarai said to A,	92
	16: 6	"Your servant is in your hands," A said.	92
	16: 6	So Hagar bore A a son,	92
	16:15	and A gave the name Ishmael to	92
	16:16	A was eighty-six years old	92
	17: 1	When A was ninety-nine years old,	92
	17: 3	A fell facedown, and God said to him,	92
	17: 5	No longer will you be called A;	92
1Ch	1: 27	and A (that is, Abraham).	92
Ne	9: 7	who chose A and brought him out of Ur of	92

ABRAM'S (5) [ABRAHAM]

Ge	11:29	The name of A wife was Sarai,	92
	12:17	and his household because of A wife Sarai.	92
	13: 7	And quarreling arose between A herdsmen	92
	14:12	They also carried off A nephew Lot	92
	16: 1	Sarai, A wife, had borne him no children.	92

ABROAD (4)

Ps	41: 6	he goes out and spreads it a.	2021+2575+4200
	112: 9	He has scattered a his gifts to the poor,	7061
SS	1: 3	that its fragrance may spread a.	5688
2Co	9: 9	"He has scattered a his gifts to the poor;	5025

ABRONAH (2)

Nu	33:34	They left Jotbathah and camped at A.	6307
	33:35	They left A and camped at Ezion Geber.	6307

ABSALOM (92) [ABSALOM'S]

2Sa	3: 3	the third, A the son of Maacah daughter	94
	13: 1	the beautiful sister of A son of David.	94
	13:20	Her brother A said to her,	94
	13:22	A never said a word to Amnon,	94
	13:24	A went to the king and said,	94
	13:25	Although A urged him,	NIH
	13:26	Then A said, "If not,	94
	13:27	But A urged him,	94
	13:28	A ordered his men, "Listen!	94
	13:29	to Amnon what A had ordered.	94
	13:30	"A has struck down all the king's sons,	94
	13:34	Meanwhile, A had fled.	94
	13:37	A fled and went to Talmai son	94
	13:38	After A fled and went to Geshur,	94
	13:39	the spirit of the king longed to go to A,	94
	14: 1	that the king's heart longed for A.	94
	14:21	Go, bring back the young man A."	94
	14:23	and brought A back to Jerusalem.	94
	14:24	So A went to his own house and did not see	94
	14:25	for his handsome appearance as A.	94
	14:27	Three sons and a daughter were born to A.	94
	14:28	A lived two years in Jerusalem	94
	14:29	Then A sent for Joab in order to send him	94
	14:32	A said to Joab, "Look,	94
	14:33	Then the king summoned A,	94
	14:33	And the king kissed A.	94
	15: 1	A provided himself with a chariot	94
	15: 2	A would call out to him,	94
	15: 3	Then A would say to him, "Look,	94
	15: 4	And A would add,	94
	15: 5	A would reach out his hand,	NIH
	15: 6	A behaved in this way toward all	94
	15: 7	At the end of four years, A said to the king,	94
	15:10	Then A sent secret messengers throughout	94
	15:10	then say, 'A is king in Hebron.' "	94
	15:11	from Jerusalem had accompanied A.	94
	15:12	While A was offering sacrifices,	94
	15:13	"The hearts of the men of Israel are with A."	94
	15:14	or none of us will escape from A.	94
	15:19	Go back and stay with King A.	NIH
	15:31	among the conspirators with A."	94
	15:34	But if you return to the city and say to A,	94
	15:37	at Jerusalem as A was entering the city.	94
	16: 8	the kingdom over to your son A.	94
	16:15	A and all the men of Israel came	94
	16:16	David's friend, went to A and said to him,	94
	16:17	A asked Hushai, "Is this the love you show	94
	16:18	Hushai said to A, "No,	94
	16:20	A said to Ahithophel, "Give us your advice.	94
	16:22	So they pitched a tent for A on the roof,	94
	16:23	and A regarded all of Ahithophel's advice.	94
	17: 1	Ahithophel said to A,	94
	17: 4	This plan seemed good to A and to all	94
	17: 5	But A said, "Summon also Hushai	94
	17: 6	When Hushai came to him, A said,	94
	17: 7	Hushai replied to A,	94
	17: 9	among the troops who follow A.'	94
	17:14	A and all the men of Israel said,	94
	17:14	in order to bring disaster on A.	94
	17:15	"Ahithophel has advised A and the elders	94
	17:18	But a young man saw them and told A.	94
	17:24	and A crossed the Jordan with all the men	94

2Sa	17:25	A had appointed Amasa over the army	94
	17:26	The Israelites and A camped in the land	94
	18:5	with the young man A for my sake."	94
	18:5	the king giving orders concerning A to each	94
	18:9	Now A happened to meet David's men.	94
	18:10	"I just saw A hanging in an oak tree."	94
	18:12	'Protect the young man A for my sake.'	94
	18:14	into Absalom's heart while A was still alive	5647S
	18:15	ten of Joab's armor-bearers surrounded A,	94
	18:17	They took A, threw him into a big pit in	94
	18:18	During his lifetime A had taken a pillar	94
	18:29	"Is the young man A safe?"	94
	18:32	"Is the young man A safe?"	94
	18:33	As he went, he said: "O my son A!	94
	18:33	My son, my son A!	94
	18:33	O A, my son, my son!"	94
	19:1	"The king is weeping and mourning for A."	94
	19:4	"O my son A!	94
	19:4	O A, my son, my son!"	94
	19:6	be pleased if A were alive today and all	94
	19:9	now he has fled the country because of A;	94
	19:10	and A, whom we anointed to rule	94
	20:6	of Bicri will do us more harm than A did.	94
1Ki	1:6	and was born next after A.)	94
	2:7	by me when I fled from your brother A.	94
	2:28	with Adonijah though not with A,	94
1Ch	3:2	A the son of Maacah daughter	94
2Ch	11:20	Then he married Maacah daughter of A,	94
	11:21	A more than any of his other wives	94
Ps	3:T	When he fled from his son A.	94

ABSALOM'S (12) [ABSALOM]
2Sa	13:4	Tamar, my brother A sister."	94
	13:20	And Tamar lived in her brother A house,	94
	13:23	sheepshearers were at Baal Hazor	94+4200
	13:29	So A men did	94
	13:32	This has been A expressed intention ever	94
	14:30	So A servants set the field on fire.	94
	14:31	Joab did go to A house and he said to him,	94
	15:12	and A following kept on increasing.	94
	17:20	A men came to the woman at the house,	94
	18:9	A head got caught in the tree.	2257S
	18:14	into A heart while Absalom was still alive	94
	18:18	and it is called A Monument to this day.	94

ABSENCE (3) [ABSENT]
Ac	24:17	"After an A of several years,	NIG
Php	1:27	and see you or only hear about you in my a,	582
	2:12	but now much more in my a—	707

ABSENT (5) [ABSENCE]
Pr	10:19	When words are many, sin is not a,	2532
2Co	10:11	in our letters when we are a,	582
	13:2	I now repeat it while a:	582
	13:10	when I am a, that when I come I may	582
Col	2:5	For though I am a from you in body,	582

ABSOLUTE (1) [ABSOLUTELY]
1Ti	5:2	as sisters, with a purity.	4246

ABSOLUTELY (3) [ABSOLUTE]
Ex	22:17	her father a refuses to give her to him,	4412+4412
Gal	2:17	that Christ promotes sin? A not!	1181+3590
	3:21	opposed to the promises of God? A not!	1181+3590

ABSTAIN (7) [ABSTAINED, ABSTAINS]
Ex	19:15	A from sexual relations."	440+448+851+5602
Nu	6:3	he must a from wine	5693
Ac	15:20	telling them to a from food polluted	600
	15:29	You are to a from food sacrificed to idols,	600
	21:25	that they should a from food sacrificed	5875
1Ti	4:3	and order them to a from certain foods,	600
1Pe	2:11	to a from sinful desires,	600

ABSTAINED (1) [ABSTAIN]
Ex	31:17	and on the seventh day he a from work	8697

ABSTAINS (1) [ABSTAIN]
Ro	14:6	and he who a, does so to the Lord	2266+3590

ABSTINENCE (KJV) See FAST, FASTING

ABUNDANCE (33) [ABUNDANT]
Ge	27:28	an a of grain and new wine.	8044
	41:29	of great a are coming throughout the land	8426
	41:30	Then all the a in Egypt will be forgotten,	8426
	41:31	The a in the land will not be remembered,	8426
	41:34	of Egypt during the seven years of a.	8426
	41:47	of a the land produced plentifully.	8426
	41:48	The food produced in those seven years of a	NIH
	41:53	The seven years of a in Egypt came to	8426
Dt	33:19	they will feast on the a of the seas,	9179
1Ch	29:16	as for all this a that we have provided	2162
	29:21	and other sacrifices in a for all Israel.	4200+8044
2Ch	29:35	There were burnt offerings in a,	4200+8044
Ne	9:25	olive groves and fruit trees in a.	4200+8044
Job	36:31	the nations and provides food in a.	3892
	38:6	They feast on the a of your house;	2016
Ps	65:11	and your carts overflow with a.	2016

Ps	66:12	but you brought us to a place of a.	8122
	73:10	to them and drink up waters in a.	4849
Pr	20:15	Gold there is, and rubies in a,	8044
Ecc	5:12	the a of a rich man permits him no sleep.	8426
Isa	7:22	the a of the milk they give,	8044
	30:33	with an a of fire and wood;	2221
	33:23	Then an a of spoils will be divided and	5269
	66:11	and delight in her overflowing a."	3883
Jer	2:22	with soda and use an a of soap,	8049
	31:14	I will satisfy the priests with a,	2016
	40:12	And they harvested an a of wine	2221+4394
Mt	13:12	and he will have an a.	4355
	25:29	and he will have an a.	4355
Lk	12:15	not consist in the a of his possessions."	4355
1Pe	1:2	Grace and peace be yours in a.	4437
2Pe	1:2	in a through the knowledge of God and	4437
Jude	1:2	Mercy, peace and love be yours in a.	4437

ABUNDANT (31) [ABUNDANCE, ABUNDANTLY]
Nu	24:7	their seed will have a water.	8041
Dt	28:11	The LORD will grant you a prosperity—	3855
	32:2	like a rain on tender plants.	8053
2Ch	11:23	He gave them a provisions	4200+8044
Ne	5:18	and every ten days an a supply of wine	2221
	9:37	its a harvest goes to	8049
Est	1:7	and the royal wine was a,	8041
Job	36:28	down their moisture and a showers fall	8041
Ps	68:9	You gave a showers, O God;	5607
	78:15	in the desert and gave them water as a as	8041
	132:15	I will bless her with a provisions;	1385+1385
	145:7	They will celebrate your a goodness	8041
Pr	12:11	He who works his land will have a food,	8425
	13:23	A poor man's field may produce a food,	8044
	14:4	the strength of an ox comes an a harvest.	8044
	28:19	He who works his land will have a food,	8425
Isa	23:18	for a food and fine clothes.	8429
Jer	33:6	and will let them enjoy a peace	6988
	33:9	the prosperity and peace I provide for it.'	3972
Eze	17:5	He planted it like a willow by a water,	8041
	17:8	It had been planted in good soil by a water	8041
	19:10	and full of branches because of a water.	8041
	31:5	spreading because of a waters.	8041
	31:7	for its roots went down to a waters.	8041
	31:9	I made it beautiful with a branches,	8044
	31:15	and its waters were restrained.	8041
	32:13	from beside a waters no longer to be stirred	8041
Da	4:12	Its leaves were beautiful, its fruit a,	10678
	4:21	with beautiful leaves and a fruit,	10678
Joel	2:23	He sends you a showers,	1773
Ro	5:17	much more will those who receive God's a provision	4353

ABUNDANTLY (5) [ABUNDANT]
Ge	24:35	The LORD has blessed my master a,	4394
Jos	17:14	and the LORD has blessed us a."	889+3907+6330+6330
Ps	65:9	you enrich it a.	8041
	78:20	water gushed out, and streams flowed a.	8851
1Ti	1:14	poured out on me a,	5670

ABUSE (5) [ABUSED, ABUSIVE, ABUSIVELY]
1Sa	31:4	and run me through and a me."	6618
1Ch	10:4	uncircumcised fellows will come and a me."	6618
Ps	55:10	malice and a are within it.	6662
Pr	9:7	whoever rebukes a wicked man incurs a.	4583
1Pe	4:4	and they heap a on you.	1059

ABUSED (1) [ABUSE]
Jdg	19:25	and they raped her and a her throughout	6618

ABUSIVE (2) [ABUSE]
Ac	18:6	when the Jews opposed Paul and became a,	1059
2Ti	3:2	a, disobedient to their parents, ungrateful,	1061

ABUSIVELY (2) [ABUSE]
Ac	13:45	and talked a against what Paul was saying.	1059
Jude	1:10	Yet these men speak a against	1059

ABUTTED (1)
Eze	40:18	It a the sides of the gateways and was	448

ABYSS (9)
Lk	8:31	not to order them to go into the A.	12
Rev	9:1	star was given the key to the shaft of the A.	12
	9:2	When he opened the A,	12
	9:2	by the smoke from the A.	5853
	9:11	as king over them the angel of the A.	12
	11:7	that comes up from the A will attack them,	12
	17:8	up out of the A and go to his destruction.	12
	20:1	the A and holding in his hand a great chain.	12
	20:3	He threw him into the A,	12

ACACIA (28) [ACACIAS]
Ex	25:5	of sea cows; a wood;	8847
	25:10	"Have them make a chest of a wood—	8847
	25:13	of a wood and overlay them with gold.	8847
	25:23	"Make a table of a wood—	8847
	25:28	Make the poles of a wood,	8847

Ex	26:15	"Make upright frames of a wood for	8847
	26:26	"Also make crossbars of a wood:	8847
	26:32	on four posts of a wood overlaid with gold	8847
	26:37	and five posts of a wood overlaid with gold.	8847
	27:1	"Build an altar of a wood,	8847
	27:6	of a wood for the altar and overlay them	8847
	30:1	an altar of a wood for burning incense.	8847
	30:5	of a wood and overlay with gold.	8847
	35:7	of sea cows; a wood;	8847
	35:24	and everyone who had a wood for any part	8847
	36:20	They made upright frames of a wood for	8847
	36:31	They also made crossbars of a wood:	8847
	36:36	They made four posts of a wood for it	8847
	37:1	Bezalel made the ark of a wood—	8847
	37:4	of a wood and overlaid them with gold.	8847
	37:10	They made the table of a wood—	8847
	37:15	for carrying the table were made of a wood	8847
	37:25	the altar of incense out of a wood.	8847
	37:28	of a wood and overlaid them with gold.	8847
	38:1	the altar of burnt offering of a wood,	8847
	38:6	of a wood and overlaid them with bronze.	8847
Dt	10:3	So I made the ark out of a wood	8847
Isa	41:19	I will put in the desert the cedar and the a,	8847

ACACIAS (1) [ACACIA]
Joel	3:18	and will water the valley of a.	8847

ACBOR (7)
Ge	36:38	Baal-Hanan son of A succeeded him	6570
	36:39	When Baal-Hanan son of A died,	6570
2Ki	22:12	Ahikam son of Shaphan, A son of Micaiah,	6570
	22:14	Hilkiah the priest, Ahikam, A,	6570
1Ch	1:49	Baal-Hanan son of A succeeded him	6570
Jer	26:22	however, sent Elnathan son of A to Egypt,	6570
	36:12	of Shemaiah, Elnathan son of A,	6570

ACCAD (KJV) See AKKAD

ACCENT (1)
Mt	26:73	for your a gives you away."	3282

ACCEPT (77) [ACCEPTABLE, ACCEPTABLY, ACCEPTANCE, ACCEPTED, ACCEPTING, ACCEPTS]
Ge	14:23	that I will a nothing belonging to you,	4374
	14:24	I will a nothing but what my men have eaten	NIH
	21:30	"A these seven lambs from my hand as	4374
	23:13	A it from me so I can bury my dead there."	4374
	33:10	a this gift from me.	4374
	33:11	Please a the present that was brought	4374
Ex	22:11	The owner is to a this,	4374
	23:8	"Do not a a bribe,	4374
Lev	22:25	and you must not a such animals from	NIH
	26:23	of these things you do not a my correction	3579
Nu	7:5	"A these from them,	4374
	16:15	"Do not a their offering.	7155
	32:30	they must a their possession with you	296
	35:31	not a a ransom for the life of a murderer,	4374
	35:31	not a a ransom for anyone who has fled to	4374
Dt	16:19	Do not a a bribe,	4374
	20:11	If they a and open their gates,	6699
	21:8	A this atonement for your people Israel,	4105
1Sa	2:15	he won't a boiled meat from you,	4374
	10:4	which you will a from them.	4374
	26:19	then may he a an offering.	8193
2Sa	24:23	"May the LORD your God a you."	8354
2Ki	5:15	Please a now a gift from your servant,"	4374
	5:16	whom I serve, I will not a a thing."	4374
	5:23	He urged Gehazi to a them,	NIH
	5:26	or to a clothes, olive groves, vineyards,	4374
Est	4:4	but he would not a them.	7691
Job	2:10	Shall we a good from God,	7691
	22:22	A instruction from his mouth and lay	4374
	42:8	and I will a his prayer and not deal	5951+7156
Ps	15:5	and does not a a bribe against the innocent.	4374
	20:3	and a your burnt offerings.	2014
	119:108	A, O LORD, the willing praise	8354
Pr	1:25	and would not a my rebuke,	14
	1:30	not a my advice and spurned my rebuke,	14
	2:1	if you a my words and store	4374
	4:10	Listen, my son, a what I say,	4374
	6:35	He will not a any compensation;	5951+7156
	10:8	The wise in heart a commands,	4374
	19:20	Listen to advice and a instruction,	7691
Ecc	5:19	to a his lot and be happy in his work—	5951
Isa	29:24	those who complain will a instruction,	4340
Jer	14:10	So the LORD does not a them;	8354
	14:12	I will not a them.	8354
Eze	20:40	and there I will a them.	8354
	20:41	I will a you as fragrant incense	8354
	22:12	In you men a bribes to shed blood;	4374
	43:27	Then I will a you,	8354
Da	4:27	O king, be pleased to a my advice:	NIH
Am	5:22	I will not a them.	8354
Zep	3:7	'Surely you will fear me and a correction!'	4374
Mal	1:8	Would he a you?	5951+7156
	1:9	will he a you?"—	5951+7156
	1:10	I will a no offering from your hands.	8354
	1:13	should I a them from your hands?"	8354
Mt	11:14	And if you are willing to a it,	1312
	19:11	"Not everyone can a this word,	6003
	19:12	The one who can a this should accept it."	6003
	19:12	The one who can accept this should a it."	6003

Mk	4:20	hear the word, **a** it, and produce a crop—	4138
Jn	3:11	but still *you people do* not **a** our testimony.	3284
	5:34	Not that I **a** human testimony;	3284
	5:41	"*I do* not **a** praise from men,	3284
	5:43	and *you do* not **a** me;	3284
	5:43	in his own name, *you will* **a** him.	3284
	5:44	How can you believe *if you* **a** praise	3284
	6:60	Who can **a** it?"	201
	12:48	and *does* not **a** my words;	3284
	14:17	The world cannot **a** him,	3284
Ac	16:21	for us Romans *to* **a** or practice."	4138
	22:18	*they will* not **a** your testimony about me.'	4138
Ro	14: 1	A him whose faith is weak,	4689
	15: 7	A one another, then, just	4689
1Co	2:14	not **a** the things that come from the Spirit	1312
	16:11	No one, then, *should* **refuse to a** him.	2024
Jas	1:21	the evil that is so prevalent and humbly **a**	1312
1Jn	5: 9	*We* **a** man's testimony,	3284

ACCEPTABLE (17) [ACCEPT]

Ex	28:38	so that they will be **a** to the LORD.	8356
Lev	1: 3	to the Tent of Meeting so that it will be **a** to	8356
	22:21	be without defect or blemish to be **a.**	8356
	22:27	*it will* **be a** as an offering made to	8354
	27: 9	" 'If what he vowed is an animal that *is* **a**	7928
	27:11	not **a** as an offering to the LORD—	7928
Jdg	14: 3	an **a** woman among your relatives or	NIH
Pr	21: 3	To do what is right and just *is* more **a** to	1047
Isa	58: 5	a day **a** to the LORD?	8356
Jer	6:20	Your burnt offerings are not **a;**	8356
Mal	1:14	an **a** male in his flock and vows to give it,	NIH
	3: 4	and Jerusalem *will be* **a** to the LORD,	6844
Ro	15:16	the Gentiles might become an offering **a**	2347
	15:31	and that my service in Jerusalem may be **a**	2347
2Co	8:12	the gift is **a** according to what one has,	2347
Php	4:18	They are a fragrant offering, an **a** sacrifice,	1283
1Pe	2: 5	offering spiritual sacrifices **a** to God	2347

ACCEPTABLY (1) [ACCEPT]

Heb	12:28	so worship God **a** with reverence and awe,	2299

ACCEPTANCE (3) [ACCEPT]

Ro	11:15	what will their **a** be but life from the dead?	4691
1Ti	1:15	a trustworthy saying that deserves full **a:**	628
	4: 9	a trustworthy saying that deserves full **a**	628

ACCEPTED (34) [ACCEPT]

Ge	4: 7	If you do what is right, will you not be **a?**	8420
	33:11	And because Jacob insisted, Esau **a** it.	4374
Lev	1: 4	and *it will* **be a** on his behalf	8354
	7:18	*it will* not **be a**	8354
	19: 5	sacrifice it in such a way that it will be **a**	8356
	19: 7	it is impure and *will* not **be a.**	8354
	22:19	in order that it may be **a** *on your behalf.*	8356
	22:20	because it will not **be a** on your behalf.	8356
	22:23	*it will* not **be a** in fulfillment of a vow.	8354
	22:25	*They will* not **be a** on your behalf,	8354
	22:29	sacrifice it in such a way that it will be **a**	8356
	23:11	the LORD so it will be **a** *on your behalf;*	8356
Nu	31:51	Moses and Eleazar the priest **a** from them	4374
	31:54	the priest **a** the gold from the commanders	4374
Jdg	13:23	he would not have **a** a burnt offering	4374
1Sa	8: 3	and **a** bribes and perverted justice.	4374
	12: 3	From whose hand *have I* **a** a bribe?	4374
	25:35	Then David **a** from her hand	4374
Job	42: 9	and the LORD **a** Job's prayer.	906+5951+4374
Isa	56: 7	and sacrifices *will be* **a** on my altar;	8356
	60: 7	they will be **a** as offerings on my altar,	8356
Lk	4:24	"no prophet is **a** in his hometown.	1283
Jn	3:33	The man who *has* **a** it has certified	3284
	17: 8	the words you gave me and they **a** them.	3284
Ac	2:41	Those who **a** his message were baptized,	622
	8:14	in Jerusalem heard that Samaria *had* **a**	1312
	15: 8	that he **a** them by giving the Holy Spirit	NIG
Ro	10:16	But not all the Israelites **a** the good news.	5634
	14: 3	for God *has* **a** him.	4689
	15: 7	then, just as Christ **a** you,	4689
2Co	11: 4	or a different gospel from the one *you* **a,**	1312
Gal	1: 9	to you a gospel other than what *you* **a,**	4161
1Th	2:13	*you* **a** it not as the word of men,	1312
Heb	10:34	in prison and joyfully **a** the confiscation	4657

ACCEPTING (2) [ACCEPT]

2Ki	5:20	by not **a** from him what he brought.	4374
Isa	33:15	and keeps his hand from **a** bribes,	9461

ACCEPTS (15) [ACCEPT]

Dt	10:17	who shows no partiality and **a** no bribes.	4374
	27:25	"Cursed is the man *who* **a** a bribe to kill	4374
Ps	6: 9	the LORD **a** my prayer.	4374
Pr	17:23	A wicked man **a** a bribe in secret to pervert	4374
Mic	7: 3	the ruler demands gifts, the judge **a** bribes,	NIH
Zep	3: 2	She obeys no one, *she* **a** no correction.	4374
Mal	2:13	or **a** them with pleasure from your hands.	4374
Jn	3:32	but no one **a** his testimony.	3284
	13:20	whoever **a** anyone I send accepts me;	3284
	13:20	whoever accepts anyone I send **a** me;	3284
	13:20	and whoever **a** me accepts	3284
	13:20	and whoever accepts me **a**	3284
Ac	10:35	a men from every nation who fear him	1283+1639
Heb	12: 6	and he punishes everyone he **a** as a son."	4138
Jas	1:27	Religion that God our Father **a** as pure	NIG

ACCESS (3)

Est	1:14	Persia and Media *who* **had special a** to	7156+8011
Ro	5: 2	through whom we have gained **a** by faith	4643
Eph	2:18	through him we both have **a** to the Father	4643

ACCESSORIES (7)

Ex	25:39	be used for the lampstand and all these **a.**	3998
	30:27	the lampstand and its **a,**	3998
	31: 8	the pure gold lampstand and all its **a,**	3998
	35:14	that is for light with its **a,** lamps and oil for	3998
	37:24	the lampstand and all its **a** from one talent	3998
	39:37	with its row of lamps and all its **a,** and	3998
Nu	4:10	Then they are to wrap it and all its **a** in	3998

ACCHO (KJV) See ACCO

ACCIDENTALLY (4)

Nu	35:11	who has killed someone **a** may flee.	928+8705
	35:15	who has killed another **a** can flee there.	928+8705
Jos	20: 3	so that anyone who kills a person **a**	928+8705
	20: 9	who killed someone **a** could flee	928+8705

ACCLAIM (2) [ACCLAMATION]

Ps	89:15	to **a** you, who walk in the light	9558
Isa	24:14	from the west *they* **a** the LORD's majesty.	7412

ACCLAMATION (1) [ACCLAIM]

2Ch	15:14	an oath to the LORD with loud **a,**	7754

ACCO (1)

Jdg	1:31	in **A** or Sidon or Ahlab or Aczib or Helbah	6573

ACCOMPANIED (25) [ACCOMPANY]

Ge	50: 7	All Pharaoh's officials **a** him—	907+6590
Ru	1:22	So Naomi returned from Moab **a** by Ruth	6640
1Sa	10:26	also went to his home in Gibeah, **a** by	2143+6640
2Sa	15:11	from Jerusalem *had* **a** Absalom.	907+2143
	15:18	the six hundred Gittites who *had* **a** him	995+8079
1Ki	20: 1	A thirty-two kings with their horses	907
1Ch	15:16	**a** by musical instruments:	928
	25: 1	**a** by harps, lyres and cymbals.	928
2Ch	5:12	They were **a** by 120 priests	6640
	5:13	A by trumpets, cymbals	928
	29:27	**a** by trumpets and the instruments	3338+6584
	29:35	and the drink offerings that **a**	4200
	30:21	**a** by the LORD's instruments of praise.	928
Jer	17:25	**a** by the men of Judah and those living	NIH
	22: 4	**a** by their officials and their people.	2256
Mk	6: 1	**a** by his disciples.	199
	16:20	by the signs that **a** it.	2051
Jn	19:39	*He was* **a** by Nicodemus,	2262+2779
Ac	18:18	**a** by Priscilla and Aquila.	5250
	20: 4	He *was* **a** by Sopater son of Pyrrhus	5299
	20:38	and *they* **a** him to the ship.	4636
	21: 5	and their wives and children **a** us out of	1636
	21:16	Some of the disciples from Caesarea **a** us	5250+5302
1Co	10: 4	from the spiritual rock *that* **a** them,	199
Jas	2:17	faith by itself, if *it is* not **a** by action,	2400

ACCOMPANIES (3) [ACCOMPANY]

Isa	40:10	and his recompense **a** him.	4200+7156
	62:11	and his recompense **a** him.' "	4200+7156
2Co	9:13	for the obedience that **a** your **confession** of	AIT

ACCOMPANY (10) [ACCOMPANIED, ACCOMPANIES, ACCOMPANYING]

Ge	33:12	on our way; I'll **a** you."	2143+4200+5584
Dt	28: 2	upon you and **a** you if you obey	5952
1Sa	28: 1	your men *will* **a** me in the army."	907+3655
Ne	10:38	A priest descended from Aaron is to **a**	6640
Est	5:12	the only person Queen Esther invited to **a**	6640
Ecc	8:15	Then joy *will* **a** him in his work all	4277
Mk	16:17	And these signs *will* **a** those who believe:	4158
1Co	16: 4	*they will* **a** me.	4513+5250
2Co	9: 4	he was chosen by the churches to **a** us	5292
Heb	6: 9	things that **a** salvation.	2400

ACCOMPANYING (1) [ACCOMPANY]

Nu	28: 7	The **a** drink offering is to be a quarter of	NIH

ACCOMPLICE (1)

Pr	29:24	The **a** *of* a thief is his own enemy;	2745+6640

ACCOMPLISH (11) [ACCOMPLISHED, ACCOMPLISHES, ACCOMPLISHING]

Ge	50:20	but God intended it for good to **a** what is	6913
Dt	9: 5	to **a** what he swore to your fathers,	7756
2Ki	8:13	a mere dog, **a** such a feat?"	6913
	19:31	zeal of the LORD Almighty *will* **a** this.	6913
Ecc	2: 2	And what *does* pleasure **a?**"	6913
Isa	9: 7	zeal of the LORD Almighty *will* **a** this.	6913
	37:32	zeal of the LORD Almighty *will* **a** this.	6913
	44:28	'He is my shepherd and *will* **a** all	8966
	55:11	my word, but *will* **a** what I desire	6913
Jer	48:30	"and her boasts **a** nothing.	6913
Rev	17:17	*to* **a** his purpose by agreeing to give	4472

ACCOMPLISHED (7) [ACCOMPLISH]

Jdg	8: 2	"What *have I* **a** compared to you?	6913
Isa	26:12	all *that* we have **a** you have done for us.	5126
Mt	5:18	from the Law until everything *is* **a.**	1181
Lk	1:45	what the Lord has said to her will be **a!**"	5459
Ro	15:18	of anything except what Christ *has* **a**	2981
Eph	3:11	according to his eternal purpose which *he* **a**	4472
Rev	10: 7	the mystery of God *will be* **a,**	5464

ACCOMPLISHES (2) [ACCOMPLISH]

Jer	23:20	until he **fully a** the purposes of his heart.	2256+6913+7756
	30:24	until he **fully a** the purposes of his heart.	2256+6913+7756

ACCOMPLISHING (2) [ACCOMPLISH]

2Ki	10:30	in **a** what is right in my eyes and have done	6913
Jn	11:47	"What *are we* **a?**"	4472

ACCORD (6) [ACCORDED, ACCORDANCE, ACCORDING, ACCORDINGLY]

Nu	24:13	I could not do anything of my own **a,**	4213
2Ki	10:15	"Are you in **a** with me, as I am with you?"	3838+4222
Jer	5: 5	But **with one a** they too had broken off	3481
Jn	10:18	but I lay it down of **my own a,**	1831
	12:49	For I did not speak of **my own a,**	1831
Tit	2: 1	You must teach what *is* in **a**	4560

ACCORDANCE (59) [ACCORD]

Ex	12: 4	the amount of lamb needed in **a** with	4200+7023
	24: 8	the LORD has made with you in **a** with	6584
	34:27	for in **a** with these words I have made	6584+7023
Nu	6:21	to the LORD in **a** with his separation,	6584
	9: 3	in **a** with all its rules and regulations."	6584
	9:14	the LORD's Passover must do so in **a** with	3869
	9:23	in **a** with his command through Moses.	6584
	14:19	In **a** with your great love,	3869
Dt	2:37	But in **a** with the command of	889+3972
Jos	6:22	in **a** with your oath to her."	889+3869
	15:13	In **a** with the LORD's command to him,	448
	19: 9	which they had acquired in **a** with	6584
1Ki	16:12	in **a** with the word of the LORD spoken	3869
	16:34	in **a** with the word of the LORD spoken	3869
2Ki	9:26	in **a** with the word of the LORD.	3869
	14: 6	in **a** with what is written in the Book of	3869
	14:25	in **a** with the word of the LORD,	3869
	16:11	So Uriah the priest built an altar in **a** with	3869
	17:13	in **a** with the entire Law	3869
	17:33	also served their own gods in **a** with	3869
	22:13	not acted in **a** with all that is written there	3869
	23:16	in **a** with the word of	3869
	23:25	in **a** with all the Law of Moses.	3869
	24: 2	in **a** with the word of	3869
1Ch	5: 1	in the genealogical record in **a** with	4200
	6:49	in **a** with all that Moses the servant	3869
	15:15	as Moses had commanded in **a** with	3869
	28:19	in **a** with everything written in the Law of	4200
2Ch	25: 4	but acted in **a** with what is written in	3869
	34:21	not acted in **a** with all that is written	3869
	34:32	of Jerusalem did this in **a** with the covenant	3869
Ezr	3: 2	in **a** with what is written in the Law	3869
	3: 4	Then in **a** with what is written,	3869
	7:18	in **a** with the will of your God.	10341
	7:25	Ezra, in **a** with the wisdom of your God,	10341
	10: 3	in **a** with the counsel of my lord and	928
	10: 8	in **a** with the decision of the officials	3869
Ne	8:18	in **a** with the regulation,	3869
Ps	109:26	save me in **a** with your love.	3869
	119:149	Hear my voice in **a** with your love;	3869
Jer	42: 5	if we do not act in **a** with everything	3869+4027
Eze	7: 9	I will repay you in **a** with your conduct and	3869
	25:14	and they will deal with Edom in **a** with	3869
	35:11	I will treat you in **a** with the anger	3869
Da	1:13	treat your servants in **a** with what you see."	3869
	6: 8	in **a** with the laws of the Medes	10341
	6:12	in **a** with the laws of the Medes	10341
Mt	2:16	in **a** with the time he had learned from	2848
	22:16	and that you teach the way of God in **a** with	1877
Mk	12:14	but you teach the way of God in **a** with	2093
Lk	20:21	teach the way of God in **a** with the truth.	2093
Jn	19:40	This was in **a** with Jewish burial customs.	2777
Ro	8: 5	but those who live in **a** with	2848
	8:27	the Spirit intercedes for the saints in **a** with	2848
	12: 3	with sober judgment, in **a** with the measure	6055
Eph	1: 5	in **a** with his pleasure and will—	2848
	1: 7	in **a** with the riches of God's grace	2848
	4:21	and were taught in him in **a** with the truth	2777
2Th	2: 9	the lawless one will be in **a** with the work	2848

ACCORDED (1) [ACCORD]

Ge	45:13	Tell my father about all the **honor** *a* me	AIT

ACCORDING (297) [ACCORD]

Ge	1:11	**a** to their various kinds."	4200
	1:12	plants bearing seed **a** to their kinds,	4200
	1:12	and trees bearing fruit with seed in it **a** to	4200
	1:21	**a** to their kinds,	4200
	1:21	and every winged bird **a** to its kind.	4200
	1:24	"Let the land produce living creatures **a** to	4200
	1:24	and wild animals, each **a** to its kind."	4200

Ge 1:25 the wild animals **a** to their kinds, 4200
1:25 the livestock **a** to their kinds, 4200
1:25 along the ground **a** to their kinds. 4200
7:14 They had with them every wild animal **a** to 4200
7:14 all livestock **a** to their kinds, 4200
7:14 that moves along the ground **a** to its kind 4200
7:14 and every bird **a** to its kind, 4200
10:32 **a** to their lines of descent, 4200
23:16 **a** to the **weight current** among merchants, 6296
25:16 the names of the twelve tribal rulers **a** to 928
36:30 **a** to their divisions, in the land of Seir. 4200
36:40 by name, **a** to their clans and regions: 4200
36:43 **a** to their settlements in 4200
47:12 **a** to the number of their children. 4200
Ex 6:16 of the sons of Levi **a** to their records: 4200
6:19 the clans of Levi **a** to their records. 4200
25:40 See that you make them **a** to 928
26:30 the tabernacle **a** to the plan shown you on 3869
30:13 all **a** to the sanctuary shekel— 928
30:24 **a** to the sanctuary shekel. 928
38:24 **a** to the sanctuary shekel. 928
38:25 shekels, **a** to the sanctuary shekel— 928
38:26 half a shekel, **a** to the sanctuary shekel, 928
Lev 5:15 **a** to the sanctuary shekel. 928
20:23 You must not live **a** to the customs of 928
27: 3 **a** to the sanctuary shekel; 928
27: 8 will set the value for him **a** to what 6584+7023
27:16 to be set **a** to the amount of seed required 928
27:18 the priest will determine the value **a** to 6584
27:25 to be set **a** to the sanctuary shekel, 928
Nu 1:20 **a** to the records of their clans and families. 4200
1:22 **a** to the records of their clans and families. 4200
1:24 **a** to the records of their clans and families. 4200
1:26 **a** to the records of their clans and families. 4200
1:28 **a** to the records of their clans and families. 4200
1:30 **a** to the records of their clans and families. 4200
1:32 **a** to the records of their clans and families. 4200
1:34 **a** to the records of their clans and families. 4200
1:36 **a** to the records of their clans and families. 4200
1:38 **a** to the records of their clans and families. 4200
1:40 **a** to the records of their clans and families. 4200
1:42 **a** to the records of their clans and families. 4200
1:45 to serve in Israel's army were counted **a** to 4200
2: 9 **a** to their divisions, number 186,400. 4200
2:16 **a** to their divisions, number 151,450. 4200
2:24 **a** to their divisions, number 108,100. 4200
2:32 counted **a** to their families. 4200
3:20 **a** to their families. 4200
3:39 by Moses and Aaron **a** to their clans, 4200
3:47 **a** to the sanctuary shekel. 928
3:50 shekels, **a** to the sanctuary shekel. 928
4:37 Moses and Aaron counted them **a** to 6584
4:41 Moses and Aaron counted them **a** to 6584
4:45 Moses and Aaron counted them **a** to 6584
6:21 **a** to the law of the Nazirite.' " 6584
7:13 both **a** to the sanctuary shekel, 928
7:19 both **a** to the sanctuary shekel, 928
7:25 both **a** to the sanctuary shekel, 928
7:31 both **a** to the sanctuary shekel, 928
7:37 both **a** to the sanctuary shekel, 928
7:43 both **a** to the sanctuary shekel, 928
7:49 both **a** to the sanctuary shekel, 928
7:55 both **a** to the sanctuary shekel, 928
7:61 both **a** to the sanctuary shekel, 928
7:67 both **a** to the sanctuary shekel, 928
7:73 both **a** to the sanctuary shekel, 928
7:79 both **a** to the sanctuary shekel, 928
7:85 **a** to the sanctuary shekel. 928
7:86 **a** to the sanctuary shekel. 928
18:16 **a** to the sanctuary shekel. 928
26:54 to receive its inheritance **a** to the number 4200
26:55 be **a** to the names for its ancestral tribe. 4200
29:18 and drink offerings **a** to 928
29:21 and drink offerings **a** to 928
29:24 and drink offerings **a** to 928
29:27 and drink offerings **a** to 928
29:30 and drink offerings **a** to 928
29:33 and drink offerings **a** to 928
29:37 and drink offerings **a** to 928
33:54 Distribute the land by lot, **a** to your clans. 4200
33:54 Distribute it **a** to your ancestral tribes. 4200
35:24 the avenger of blood **a** to these regulations. 6584
Dt 12:15 **a** to the blessing the LORD your God gives 3869
17:10 You must act **a** to the decisions 6584+7023
17:11 Act **a** to the law they teach you and 6584+7023
26:13 **a** to all you commanded. 3869
29:21 **a** to all the curses of the covenant written 3869
30: 2 and with all your soul **a** to 3869
32: 8 for the peoples **a** to the number of the sons 4200
Jos 4: 5 **a** to the number of the tribes of 4200
4: 8 **a** to the number of the tribes of 4200
8:31 He built it **a** to what is written in the Book 3869
11:23 to Israel **a** to their tribal divisions. 3869
12: 7 as an inheritance to the tribes of Israel **a** to 3869
14: 7 And I brought him back a report **a** to 889+3869
17: 4 **a** to the LORD's command. 448
18: 4 **a** to the inheritance of each. 4200+7023
18:10 to the Israelites **a** to their tribal divisions. 3869
1Sa 2:35 who will do **a** to what is in my heart 3869
6: 4 **a** to the number of the Philistine rulers, NIH
6:18 And the gold rats was **a** to NIH
2Sa 3:39 May the LORD repay the evildoer **a** to 3869
7:21 the sake of your word and **a** to your will, 3869
22:21 "The LORD has dealt with me **a** to 3869
22:21 **a** to the cleanness of my hands 3869
22:25 The LORD has rewarded me **a** to 3869
22:25 **a** to my cleanness in his sight. 3869

1Ki 2: 6 Deal with him **a** to your wisdom, 3869
3: 3 for the LORD by walking **a** to the statutes 928
6:38 in all its details **a** to its specifications. 4200
8:39 deal with each man **a** to all he does, 3869
8:59 of his people Israel **a** to each day's need, 928
13: 5 and its ashes poured out **a** to the sign given 3869
15:29 **a** to the word of the LORD given 3869
2Ki 1:17 **a** to the word of the LORD 3869
2:22 **a** to the word Elisha had spoken. 3869
4:44 **a** to the word of the LORD 3869
10:17 **a** to the word of the LORD spoken 3869
22:16 and its people, **a** to everything written in 907
23:35 and gold from the people of the land **a** to 3869
24: 3 Surely these things happened to Judah **a** to 6584
1Ch 5: 7 listed **a** to their genealogical records: 4200
6:19 of the Levites listed **a** to their fathers: 4200
6:32 They performed their duties **a** to 3869
7: 4 **A** to their family genealogy, 4200
15:20 and Benaiah were to play the lyres **a** to 6584
15:21 directing **a** to sheminith. 6584
16:37 **a** to each day's requirements. 4200
17:19 the sake of your servant and **a** to your will, 3869
23:27 **A** to the last instructions of David, 928
24:19 **a** to the regulations prescribed for them 3869
24:30 These were the Levites **a** to their families. 4200
26:13 **a** to their families, young and old alike. 4200
26:31 Jeriah was their chief **a** to 4200
28:15 **a** to the use of each lampstand; 3869
2Ch 4: 7 He made ten gold lampstands **a** to 3869
6:16 in all they do to walk before me **a** to 928
6:30 and deal with each man **a** to all he does, 3869
8:13 **a** to the daily requirement 928
8:14 the priests **a** to each day's requirement. 4200
24:13 the temple of God **a** to its original design 6584
25: 5 of Judah together and assigned them **a** to 4200
26:11 to go out by divisions **a** to their numbers 928
30: 5 not been celebrated in large numbers **a** to 3869
30:19 not clean **a** to the rules of the sanctuary." 3869
31: 2 them **a** to their divisions as priests 3869+7023
31:15 to their fellow priests **a** to their divisions, 928
31:16 the daily duties of their various tasks, **a** to 928
31:17 **a** to their responsibilities 928
35: 4 **a** to the directions written by David king 928
35:26 what is written in the Law of 3869
Ezr 2:69 **A** to their ability they gave to the treasury 3869
6:14 the temple **a** to the command of the God 10427
6:18 **a** to what is written in the Book of Moses. 10341
10: 3 Let it be done **a** to the Law. 3869
Ne 6: 6 **a** to these reports you are about 3869
12:45 **a** to the commands of David 3869
13:22 show mercy to me **a** to your great love. 3869
Est 8: 6 "**A** to law, what must be done 3869
Job 42: 8 and not deal with you **a** to your folly. NIH
Ps 6: T **A** to sheminith. 6584
7: 8 O LORD, **a** to my righteousness, 3869
7: 8 **a** to my integrity, O Most High. 3869
8: T **A** to gittith. 6584
12: T **A** to sheminith. 6584
18:20 The LORD has dealt with me **a** to 3869
18:20 **a** to the cleanness of my hands 3869
18:24 The LORD has rewarded me **a** to 3869
18:24 **a** to the cleanness of my hands in his sight. 3869
25: 7 **a** to your love remember me, 3869
46: T **A** to alamoth. 6584
51: 1 O God, **a** to your unfailing love; 3869
51: 1 **a** to your great compassion blot out my
transgressions. 3869
53: T **A** to mahalath. 6584
62:12 Surely you will reward each person **a** to 3869
81: T **A** to gittith. 6584
84: T **A** to gittith. 6584
88: T **A** to mahalath leannoth. 6584
103:10 as our sins deserve or repay us **a** to 3869
119: 1 who walk **a** to the law of the LORD. 928
119: 9 By living **a** to your word. 3869
119:25 preserve my life **a** to your word. 3869
119:28 strengthen me **a** to your word. 3869
119:37 preserve my life **a** to your word. 928
119:41 your salvation **a** to your promise; 3869
119:58 be gracious to me **a** to your promise. 3869
119:65 Do good to your servant **a** to your word, 3869
119:76 **a** to your promise to your servant. 3869
119:88 Preserve my life **a** to your love, 3869
119:107 O LORD, **a** to your word. 3869
119:116 Sustain me **a** to your promise, 3869
119:124 Deal with your servant **a** to your love 3869
119:133 Direct my footsteps **a** to your word; 928
119:154 preserve my life **a** to your promise. 4200
119:156 preserve my life **a** to your laws. 3869
119:159 O LORD, **a** to your love. 3869
119:169 give me understanding **a** to your word. 3869
119:170 deliver me **a** to your promise. 3869
122: T the LORD **a** to the statute given to Israel. NIH
Pr 12: 8 A man is praised **a** to his wisdom, 4200+7023
24:12 Will he not repay each person **a** to 3869
26: 4 Do not answer a fool **a** to his folly, 3869
26: 5 Answer a fool **a** to his folly, 3869
Isa 8:20 If they do not speak **a** to this word, 3869
59:18 **A** to what they have done, 3869+6584
63: 7 **a** to all the LORD has done for us— 3869+6584
63: 7 **a** to his compassion and many kindnesses, 3869
Jer 17:10 to reward a man **a** to his conduct, 3869
17:10 **a** to what his deeds deserve." 3869
25:14 I will repay them **a** to their deeds and 3869
32:19 you reward everyone **a** to his conduct and 3869
Eze 7: 3 I will judge you **a** to your conduct 3869

Eze 7: 8 I will judge you **a** to your conduct 3869
7:27 I will deal with them **a** to their conduct, 4946
18:30 I will judge you, each one **a** to his ways, 3869
20:44 with you for my name's sake and not **a** to 3869
23:24 they will punish you **a** to their standards. 928
24:14 You will be judged **a** to your conduct 3869
31:11 for him to deal with **a** to its wickedness. 3869
33:20 But I will judge each of you **a** to 3869
36:19 I judged them **a** to their conduct 3869
39:24 I dealt with them **a** to their uncleanness 3869
44:24 as judges and decide it **a** to my ordinances. 928
45: 8 the house of Israel to possess the land **a** to 4200
47:21 among yourselves **a** to the tribes of Israel. 4200
Da 6:15 that **a** to the law of the Medes NIH
9: 2 **a** to the word of the LORD given 889
Hos 12: 2 he will punish Jacob **a** to his ways 3869
12: 2 to his ways and repay him **a** to his deeds. 3869
Zec 5: 3 for **a** to what it says on one side, 4017
5: 3 and **a** to what it says on the other, 4017
Mt 9:29 "**A** to your faith will it be done to you"; 2848
16:27 and then he will reward each person **a** to 2848
25:15 each **a** to his ability. 2848
Mk 7: 5 "Why don't your disciples live **a** to 2848
Lk 1: 9 **a** to the custom of the priesthood, 2848
2:22 the time of their purification **a** to the Law 2848
2:42 they went up to the Feast, **a** to the custom. 2848
Jn 19: 7 and **a** to that law he must die, 2848
Ac 7:44 **a** to the pattern he had seen. 2848
11:29 The disciples, each **a** to his ability, 2777
15: 1 *a* to the custom taught by Moses, AIT
21:21 or live *a* to our customs. AIT
23: 3 You sit there to judge me **a** to the law, 2848
26: 5 that **a** to the strictest sect of our religion, 2848
Ro 2: 6 to each person **a** to what he has done." 2848
8: 4 not live **a** to the sinful nature but according 2848
8: 4 to the sinful nature but **a** to the Spirit. 2848
8: 5 Those who live **a** to the sinful nature 2848
8:12 not to the sinful nature, to live **a** to it. 2848
8:13 For if you live **a** to the sinful nature, 2848
8:28 who have been called **a** to his purpose. 2848
12: 6 **a** to the grace given us. 2848
16:25 **a** to the revelation of the mystery hidden 2848
1Co 3: 8 each will be rewarded **a** to his own labor. 2848
15: 3 Christ died for our sins **a** to the Scriptures, 2848
15: 4 that he was raised on the third day **a** to 2848
2Co 1:12 We have done so not **a** to worldly wisdom 1877
1:12 not according to worldly wisdom but **a** to 1877
8:11 **a** to *your* means. 1666+2400+3836
8:12 the gift is acceptable **a** to what one has, 2848
8:12 not **a** to what he does not have. 2848
Gal 1: 4 **a** to the will of our God and Father, 2848
and heirs **a** to the promise. 2848
Eph 1: 9 of his will **a** to his good pleasure, 2848
1:11 having been predestined **a** to the plan 2848
3:11 **a** to his eternal purpose which he
accomplished 2848
3:20 **a** to his power that is at work within us, 2848
4:29 for building others up **a** to their needs, NIG
Php 2:13 to will and to act **a** to his good purpose. 5642
3:17 and take note of those who live **a** to 4048
4:19 And my God will meet all your needs **a** to 2848
Col 1:11 with all power **a** to his glorious might so 2848
1Th 4:15 **A** to the Lord's own word, 1877
2Th 1:12 **a** to the grace of our God and 2848
3: 6 not live **a** to the teaching you received 2848
2Ti 1: 1 **a** to the promise of life that is 2848
2: 5 unless he competes **a** to **the rules.** 3789
Heb 2: 4 and gifts of the Holy Spirit distributed **a** to 2848
8: 5 "See to it that you make everything **a** to 2848
1Pe 1: 2 who have been chosen **a** to 2848
4: 6 be judged **a** to men in regard to the body, 2848
4: 6 but live **a** to God in regard to the spirit. 2848
4:19 those who suffer **a** to 2848
1Jn 5:14 we ask anything **a** to his will, he hears us. 2848
Rev 2:23 I will repay each of you **a** to your deeds. 2848
20:12 The dead were judged **a** to 2848
20:13 and each person was judged **a** to 2848
22:12 to everyone **a** to what he has done. 6055

ACCORDINGLY (3) [ACCORD]

Lev 25:52 that and pay for his redemption **a**. 3869+7023
1Ki 20:25 He agreed with them and acted **a**. 4027
1Ch 24: 4 and they *were* **divided** *a*: AIT

ACCOUNT (75) [ACCOUNTABLE, ACCOUNTED, ACCOUNTING, ACCOUNTS]

Ge 2: 4 This is the **a** of the heavens and the earth 9352
5: 1 This is the written **a** of Adam's **line**. 9352
6: 9 This is the **a** of Noah. 9352
10: 1 This is the **a** of Shem, Ham and Japheth, 9352
11:10 This is the **a** of Shem. 9352
11:27 This is the **a** of Terah. 9352
25:12 This is the **a** of Abraham's son Ishmael, 9352
25:19 This is the **a** of Abraham's son Isaac. 9352
26: 7 of this place might kill me **on a of** 6584
26: 9 I thought I might lose my life **on a of** her." 6584
36: 1 This is the **a** of Esau (that is, Edom). 9352
36: 9 the **a** of Esau the father of the Edomites in 9352
37: 2 This is the **a** of Jacob. 9352
Ex 12: 4 having **taken into a** the number 928
Nu 3: 1 the **a of the family** *of* Aaron and Moses at 9352
6: 7 make himself ceremonially unclean **on a of** 4200
9: 6 they were ceremonially unclean **on a of** 4200
13:27 *They gave Moses this* **a**: 6218

Dt	9: 4	it is on a of the wickedness	928
	9: 5	on a of the wickedness of these nations,	928
	18:19	I myself will call him to a.	2011+4946+6640
Jos	22:23	may the LORD himself call us to a.	1335
1Sa	17:32	"Let no one lose heart on a of	6584
	20:16	call David's enemies to a."	1335+3338+4946
	23:10	to Keilah and destroy the town on a of me.	6288
2Sa	11:18	Joab sent David a full a of the battle.	1821
	11:19	the king this a of the battle,	1821
	13: 2	of illness on a of his sister Tamar,	6288
	21: 1	"It is on a of Saul	448
1Ki	9:15	Here is the a of the forced labor	1821
	11:27	the a of how he rebelled against the king:	1821
2Ki	22: 7	not a for the money entrusted to them,	907+3108
1Ch	27:24	on Israel on a of this numbering,	928
2Ch	24:22	the LORD see this and call you to a."	2011
	24:27	The a of his sons,	NIH
Est	10: 2	together with a full a of the greatness	7308
Job	31:14	What will I answer when called to a?	7212
	31:37	I would give him an a of my every step;	5031
Ps	10:13	"He won't call me to a"?	2011
	10:15	call him to a for his wickedness	2011
	56: 7	On no a let them escape;	224+6584
Ecc	3:15	call the past to a.	1335
Isa	2:22	Of what a is he?	3108
	23:13	this people that is now of no a!	4202
Eze	16:14	among the nations on a of your beauty,	928
	28:17	Your heart became proud on a of	928
Mt	10:18	On my a you will be brought	1915
	11: 6	the man who does not fall away on a of	1877
	12:36	give a on the day of judgment for	625
	26:31	you will all fall away on a of me,	1877
	26:33	"Even if all fall away on a of you,	1877
Mk	12:26	in the a of the bush,	2093
	13: 9	On a of me you will stand before governors	1915
Lk	1: 1	Many have undertaken to draw up an a of	1456
	1: 3	also to me to write an orderly a for you,	1211
	7:23	the man who does not fall away on a of	1877
	16: 2	Give an a of your management,	3364
	20:37	But in the a of the bush,	2093
	21:12	and all on a of my name.	1915
Jn	12:11	for on a of him many of	1328
Ac	4: 9	If we are being called to a today for	373
	19:40	In that case we would not be able to a	625+4946
Ro	5:13	not taken into a when there is no law.	1824
	11:28	they are enemies on your a;	1328
	11:28	they are loved on a of the patriarchs,	1328
	14:12	each of us will give an a of himself to God.	3364
1Co	6: 4	appoint as judges even men of little a!	2024
2Co	7:12	not on a of the one who did the wrong or	1915
Php	1:26	in Christ Jesus will overflow on a of me.	1877
	4:17	for what may be credited to your a.	3364
Heb	4:13	the eyes of him to whom we must give a.	3364
	13:17	over you as men who must give an a.	3364
1Pe	4: 5	to give an a to him who is ready to judge	3364
1Jn	2:12	your sins have been forgiven on a of	1328
Rev	16:21	they cursed God on a of the plague of hail,	1666

ACCOUNTABLE (8) [ACCOUNT]

Eze	3:18	I will hold you a for his blood.	1335+3338+4946
	3:20	I will hold you a for his blood.	1335+3338+4946
	33: 6	I will hold the watchman a	2011+3338+4946
	33: 8	I will hold you a for his blood.	1335+3338+4946
	34:10	shepherds and will hold them a	2011+3338+4946
Da	6: 2	The satraps were made a to them so that	10302
Jnh	1:14	not hold us a for killing an innocent man,	5989+6584
Ro	3:19	silenced and the whole world held a	1181+5688

ACCOUNTED (1) [ACCOUNT]

Ezr	8:34	Everything was a for by number	NIH

ACCOUNTING (5) [ACCOUNT]

Ge	9: 5	your lifeblood I will surely demand an a.	2011
	9: 5	I will demand an a from every animal.	2011
	9: 5	I will demand an a for the life	2011
	42:22	Now we must give an a for his blood."	2011
2Ki	12:15	They did not require an a from those	3108

ACCOUNTS (3) [ACCOUNT]

Job	21:29	Have you paid no regard to their a—	253
Mt	18:23	like a king who wanted to settle a	3364
	25:19	those servants returned and settled a	3364+5256

ACCREDITED (1) [CREDIT]

Ac	2:22	of Nazareth was a man a by God to you	617

ACCUMULATE (1) [ACCUMULATED]

Dt	17:17	not a large amounts of silver and gold	4394+8049

ACCUMULATED (4) [ACCUMULATE]

Ge	12: 5	all the possessions they had a and	8223
	31:18	with all the goods he had a in Paddan Aram,	8223
1Ki	10:26	Solomon a chariots and horses;	665
2Ch	1:14	Solomon a chariots and horses;	665

ACCURATE (7) [ACCURATELY]

Dt	25:15	You must have a and honest weights	8969
Pr	11: 1	but a weights are his delight.	8969
Eze	45:10	You are to use a scales,	7406
	45:10	an ephah and an accurate bath.	7406
	45:10	an accurate ephah and an a bath.	7406

Ac	23:15	the pretext of wanting more a information	209
	23:20	of wanting more a information about him.	209

ACCURATELY (1) [ACCURATE]

Ac	18:25	with great fervor and taught about Jesus a,	209

ACCURSED (5) [CURSE]

Nu	5:27	and she will become a among her people.	460
2Ki	22:19	that they would become a and laid waste,	7839
Isa	65:20	to reach a hundred will be considered a.	7837
Mic	6:10	and the short ephah, which is a?	2404
2Pe	2:14	in greed—an a brood!	2932

ACCUSATION (7) [ACCUSE]

Ezr	4: 6	they lodged an a against the people	8478
Mic	6: 2	Hear, O mountains, the LORD's a;	8190
Ac	23:29	I found that the a had to do with questions	1592
	24: 9	The Jews joined in the a,	5298
Col	1:22	without blemish and free from a—	441
1Ti	5:19	an a against an elder unless it is brought	2990
Jude	9	to bring a slanderous a against him,	3213

ACCUSATIONS (3) [ACCUSE]

Ps	35:20	but devise false a against those who live	1821
Ac	26: 2	as I make my defense against all the a of	1592
2Pe	2:11	not bring slanderous a against such beings	3213

ACCUSE (18) [ACCUSATION, ACCUSATIONS, ACCUSED, ACCUSER, ACCUSERS, ACCUSES, ACCUSING]

Dt	19:16	If a malicious witness takes the stand to a	6699
1Sa	22:15	Let not the king a your servant	928+1821+8492
2Sa	3: 8	Yet now you a me of an offense	6584+7212
Ps	50:21	I will rebuke you and a you to your face.	6885
	103: 9	He will not always a,	8189
	109: 4	In return for my friendship they a me,	8476
Pr	3:30	Do not a a man for no reason—	8189
Isa	57:16	I will not a forever,	8189
Hos	4: 4	let no man a another,	3519
Zec	3: 1	Satan standing at his right side to a him.	8476
Mt	12:10	Looking for a reason to a Jesus,	2989
Mk	3: 2	for a reason to a Jesus,	2989
Lk	3:14	and don't a people falsely—	5193
	6: 7	for a reason to a Jesus,	2989
	23: 2	And they began to a him, saying,	2989
Jn	5:45	do not think I will a you before the Father.	2989
	10:36	Why then do you a me of blasphemy	3306
1Pe	2:12	though they a you of doing wrong,	2895

ACCUSED (18) [ACCUSE]

Nu	35:12	so that a person a of murder may not die	8357
	35:25	the one a of murder from the avenger	8357
	35:26	the a ever goes outside the limits of the city	8357
	35:27	of blood may kill the a without being guilty	8357
	35:28	The a must stay in his city of refuge until	NIH
Dt	19:15	not enough to convict a man a of	4200
Jos	20: 5	they must not surrender the one a,	8357
	21:13	(a city of refuge for one a of murder),	8357
	21:21	(a city of refuge for one a of murder),	8357
	21:27	(a city of refuge for one a of murder),	8357
	21:32	(a city of refuge for one a of murder),	8357
	21:38	(a city of refuge for one a of murder),	8357
Ne	5: 7	I pondered them in my mind and then a	8189
Da	6:24	the men who had falsely a Daniel were brought	10030+10642
Mt	27:12	When he was a by the chief priests and	2989
Mk	15: 3	The chief priests a him of many things.	2989
Lk	16: 1	a rich man whose manager was a	1330
Ac	22:30	to find out exactly why Paul was being a by	2989

ACCUSER (5) [ACCUSE]

Job	31:35	let my a put his indictment in writing.	408+8190
Ps	109: 6	let an a stand at his right hand.	8477
Isa	50: 8	Who is my a?	1251+5477
Jn	5:45	Your a is Moses,	2989
Rev	12:10	For the a of our brothers,	2992

ACCUSERS (10) [ACCUSE]

Ps	71:13	May my a perish in shame;	8476
	109:20	be the LORD's payment to my a,	8476
	109:25	I am an object of scorn to my a;	2157S
	109:29	My a will be clothed with disgrace	8476
Jer	18:19	hear what my a are saying!	3742
Ac	23:30	I also ordered his a to present	2991
	23:35	when your a get here."	2991
	24:12	My a did not find me arguing with anyone	NIG
	25:16	any man before he has faced his a	2400+2991
	25:18	When his a got up to speak,	2991

ACCUSES (3) [ACCUSE]

Job	40: 2	Let him who a God answer him!"	3519
Isa	54:17	you will refute every tongue that a you.	2021+4200+5477+7756
Rev	12:10	who a them before our God day and night,	2989

ACCUSING (7) [ACCUSE]

Ps	31:20	you keep them safe from a tongues.	8190
Mk	15: 4	See how many things they are a you of."	2989
Lk	23:10	standing there, vehemently a him.	2989
Jn	8: 6	in order to have a basis for a him.	2989

Ac	23:28	I wanted to know why they were a him,	1592
	26: 7	of this hope that the Jews are a me.	1592
Ro	2:15	and their thoughts now a,	2989

ACCUSTOMED (3) [CUSTOM]

Jer	2:24	a wild donkey a to the desert, sniffing	4341
	13:23	Neither can you do good who are a to	4341
1Co	8: 7	Some people are still so a to idols that	5311

ACELDAMA (KJV) See AKELDAMA

ACHAIA (10)

Ac	18:12	While Gallio was proconsul of A,	938
	18:27	When Apollos wanted to go to A,	938
	19:21	passing through Macedonia and A.	938
Ro	15:26	and A were pleased to make a contribution	938
1Co	16:15	of Stephanas were the first converts in A,	938
2Co	1: 1	together with all the saints throughout A:	938
	9: 2	since last year you in A were ready to give;	938
	11:10	in the regions of A will stop this boasting	938
1Th	1: 7	to all the believers in Macedonia and A	938
	1: 8	from you not only in Macedonia and A—	938

ACHAICUS (1)

1Co	16:17	Fortunatus and A arrived,	939

ACHAN (7)

Jos	7: 1	A son of Carmi, the son of Zimri,	6575
	7:18	and A son of Carmi, the son of Zimri,	6575
	7:19	Then Joshua said to A, "My son,	6575
	7:20	A replied, "It is true!	6575
	7:24	took A son of Zerah, the silver, the robe,	6575
	7:26	Over A they heaped up a large pile	2257S
	22:20	When A son of Zerah	6575

ACHAR (1)

1Ch	2: 7	The son of Carmi: A,	6580

ACHAZ (KJV) See AHAZ

ACHBOR (KJV) See ACBOR

ACHE (1)

Pr	14:13	Even in laughter the heart may a,	3872

ACHIEVE (4) [ACHIEVED, ACHIEVEMENT, ACHIEVEMENTS, ACHIEVING]

Job	5:12	so that their hands a no success.	6913
Ecc	2:11	to a, everything was meaningless,	6913
Isa	55:11	and a the purpose for which I sent it.	7503
Da	11:24	and will a what neither his fathers	6913

ACHIEVED (3) [ACHIEVE]

1Ki	9: 1	and had a all he had desired to do,	NIH
	16:27	what he did and the things he a,	6913
	22:45	the things he a and his military exploits,	6913

ACHIEVEMENT (1) [ACHIEVE]

Ecc	4: 4	I saw that all labor and all a spring	4179+5126

ACHIEVEMENTS (10) [ACHIEVE]

1Ki	10: 6	about your a and your wisdom is true.	1821
	15:23	all the other events of Asa's reign, all his a,	1476
	16: 5	what he did and his a,	1476
2Ki	10:34	all he did, and all his a,	1476
	13: 8	all he did and his a,	1476
	13:12	all he did and his a,	1476
	14:15	what he did and his a,	1476
	14:28	all his a and his military a,	1476
	20:20	all his a and how he made the pool and	1476
2Ch	9: 5	about your a and your wisdom is true.	1821

ACHIEVING (1) [ACHIEVE]

2Co	4:17	For our light and momentary troubles are a	2981

ACHIM (KJV) See AKIM

ACHISH (19)

1Sa	21:10	from Saul and went to A king of Gath.	429
	21:11	But the servants of A said to him,	429
	21:12	and was very much afraid of A king	429
	21:14	A said to his servants, "Look at the man!	429
	27: 2	and went over to A son of Maoch king	429
	27: 3	David and his men settled in Gath with A.	429
	27: 5	Then David said to A,	429
	27: 6	So on that day A gave him Ziklag,	429
	27: 9	Then he returned to A.	429
	27:10	When A asked,	429
	27:12	A trusted David and said to himself,	429
	28: 1	A said to David,	429
	28: 2	A replied, "Very well,	429
	29: 2	at the rear with A.	429
	29: 3	A replied, "Is this not David,	429
	29: 6	So A called David and said to him,	429
	29: 9	A answered, "I know that you have been	429
1Ki	2:39	two of Shimei's slaves ran off to A son	429

1Ki	2:40	he saddled his donkey and went to A	429

ACHMETHA (KJV) See ECBATANA

ACHOR (5)
Jos	7:24	to the Valley of A.	6574
	7:26	the Valley of A ever since.	6574
	15: 7	then went up to Debir from the Valley of A	6574
Isa	65:10	the Valley of A a resting place for herds,	6574
Hos	2:15	will make the Valley of A a door of hope.	6574

ACHSA, ACHSAH (KJV) See ACSAH

ACHSHAPH (KJV) See ACSAPH

ACHZIB (KJV) See ACZIB

ACKNOWLEDGE (40)
[ACKNOWLEDGED, ACKNOWLEDGES, ACKNOWLEDGMENT]
Dt	4:39	A and take to heart this day that	3359
	21:17	He must a the son of his unloved wife as	5795
	33: 9	or a his own children,	3359
1Ch	28: 9	my son Solomon, a the God of your father,	3359
Ps	79: 6	not a you, on the kingdoms that do not call	3359
	87: 4	and Babylon among those who a me—	3359
Pr	3: 6	in all your ways a him,	3359
Isa	19:21	and in that day they will a the LORD.	3359
	29:23	they will a the holiness of the Holy One	7727
	33:13	you who are near, a my power!	3359
	45: 4	though you do not a me.	3359
	59:12	and we a our iniquities;	3359
	61: 9	All who see them will a that they are	5795
	63:16	Abraham does not know us or Israel a us;	5795
Jer	3:13	Only a your guilt.	3359
	9: 3	they do not a me," declares the LORD.	3359
	9: 6	in their deceit they refuse to a me,"	3359
	10:25	on the nations that do not a you,	3359
	14:20	we a our wickedness and the guilt	3359
Eze	12:16	they may a all their detestable practices.	6218
Da	4:25	until you a that the Most High is sovereign	10313
	4:26	to you when you a that Heaven rules.	10313
	4:32	until you a that the Most High is sovereign	10313
	11:39	and will greatly honor those who a him.	5795
Hos	2:20	and you will a the LORD.	3359
	5: 4	they do not a the LORD.	3359
	6: 3	Let us a the LORD;	3359
	6: 3	let us press on to a him.	3359
	8: 2	'O our God, we a you!'	3359
	13: 4	You shall a no God but me,	3359
Mt	10:32	also a him before my Father in heaven.	3933
Lk	12: 8	of Man will also a him before the angels	3933
Ac	23: 8	but the Pharisees a them all.)	3933
	24: 3	we a this with profound gratitude.	622
1Co	14:37	let him a that what I am writing to you is	2106+2262
2Ti	3: 7	always learning but never able to a	2106+2262
1Jn	4: 3	but every spirit that does not a Jesus is not	3933
2Jn	1: 7	not a Jesus Christ as coming in the flesh,	3933
Rev	3: 5	but will a his name before my Father	3933
	3: 9	at your feet and a that I have loved you.	1182

ACKNOWLEDGED (8) [ACKNOWLEDGE]
Lev	22:32	I must be a as holy by the Israelites.	7727
1Ch	29:22	a Solomon son of David as king	4887
Ps	32: 5	Then I a my sin to you and did not cover	3359
Isa	45: 5	though you have not a me,	3359
Da	5:21	with the dew of heaven, until he a that	10313
Hos	11: 3	not a that I was the one who gave her	3359
Lk	7:29	a that God's way was right,	1467
Jn	9:22	that anyone who a that Jesus was	3933

ACKNOWLEDGES (6) [ACKNOWLEDGE]
Ps	91:14	I will protect him, for he a my name.	3359
Mt	10:32	"Whoever a me before men,	3933
Lk	12: 8	"I tell you, whoever a me before men,	3933
1Jn	2:23	whoever a the Son has the Father also.	3933
	4: 2	that a that Jesus Christ has come in	3933
	4:15	If anyone a that Jesus is the Son of God,	3933

ACKNOWLEDGMENT (2)
[ACKNOWLEDGE]
Hos	4: 1	no love, no a of God in the land.	1981
	6: 6	and a of God rather than burnt offerings.	1981

ACQUAINTANCE (1) [ACQUAINTANCES, ACQUAINTED]
Php	4:15	in the early days of your a with the gospel,	NIG

ACQUAINTANCES (1) [ACQUAINTANCE]
Job	19:13	my a are completely estranged from me.	3359

ACQUAINTED (4) [ACQUAINTANCE]
Ac	24:22	Then Felix, who was well a with the Way,	3857
	26: 3	so because you are well a with all	1195
Gal	1:18	to Jerusalem to get a with Peter and stayed	2707
Heb	5:13	is not a with the teaching	586

ACQUIRE (5) [ACQUIRED, ACQUIRES, ACQUIRING]
Ge	34:10	Live in it, trade in it, and a property in it."	296
Lev	25:28	if he does not a the means to repay him,	5162
Dt	17:16	not a great numbers of horses for himself	8049
Ru	4: 5	you a the dead man's widow,	7864
Ne	5:16	we did not a any land.	7864

ACQUIRED (13) [ACQUIRE]
Ge	12: 5	and the people they had a in Haran,	6913
	12:16	and Abram a sheep and cattle,	2118+4200
	36: 6	and all the goods he had a in Canaan,	8223
	46: 6	and the possessions they had a in Canaan,	8223
	47:27	They a property there and were fruitful	296
Nu	31:50	to the LORD the gold articles each of us a—	5162
Jos	22: 9	which they had a in accordance with	296
Ru	4:10	I have also a Ruth the Moabitess,	7864
2Ch	32:29	and a great numbers of flocks and herds,	5238
Ecc	2: 8	I a men and women singers,	6913
Isa	15: 7	So the wealth they have a and stored	6913
Jer	48:36	The wealth they a is gone.	6913
Rev	3:17	I have a wealth and do not need a thing.'	4456

ACQUIRES (2) [ACQUIRE]
Lev	25:26	and a sufficient means to redeem it,	5162
Pr	18:15	The heart of the discerning a knowledge;	7864

ACQUIRING (1) [ACQUIRE]
Pr	1: 3	for a a disciplined and prudent life,	4374

ACQUIT (3) [ACQUITTED, ACQUITTING]
Ex	23: 7	for I will not a the guilty.	7405
Isa	5:23	who a the guilty for a bribe,	7405
Mic	6:11	Shall I a a man with dishonest scales,	2342

ACQUITTED (1) [ACQUIT]
Mt	12:37	For by your words you will be a,	1467

ACQUITTING (2) [ACQUIT]
Dt	25: 1	a the innocent and condemning the guilty.	7405
Pr	17:15	A the guilty and condemning	7405

ACRE (1) [TEN-ACRE]
1Sa	14:14	in an area of about half an a.	5103+7538

ACROSS (52) [CROSS]
Ge	1:20	above the earth a the expanse of the sky."	6584+7156
	9:23	and Japheth took a garment and laid it a	6584
	32:23	After he had sent them a the stream,	6296
Ex	10:13	and the LORD made an east wind blow a	928
	23: 4	"If you come a your enemy's ox	7003
Nu	22: 1	and camped along the Jordan a from	4946+6298
	26: 3	So on the plains of Moab by the Jordan a	AIT
	26:63	of Moab by the Jordan a from Jericho.	AIT
	31:12	by the Jordan a from Jericho.	AIT
	33:48	of Moab by the Jordan a from Jericho.	AIT
	33:50	The Jordan a from Jericho the LORD said	AIT
	35: 1	On the plains of Moab by the Jordan a	AIT
	36:13	of Moab by the Jordan a from Jericho.	AIT
Dt	3:20	the LORD your God is giving them, a	928+6298
	3:28	for he will lead this people a	4200+6296+7156
	9: 3	the LORD your God is the one who goes a	6296
	11:30	these mountains are a the Jordan,	928+6298
	22: 6	If you come a a bird's nest beside the road,	4200+7156+7925
	32:49	a from Jericho, and view Canaan,	6584+7156
	34: 1	of Moab to the top of Pisgah, a from	6584+7156
Jos	7: 7	why did you ever bring this people a	6296+6296
	13:32	in the plains of Moab a the Jordan east	4946+6298
Jdg	20:48	All the towns they came a they set on fire.	5162
1Sa	31: 7	and those the Jordan saw	928+6298
2Sa	19:15	the king and bring him a the Jordan.	6296
	19:41	bring him and his household a	6296
1Ki	4:12	from Beth Shan to Abel Meholah a	4946+6298
	6:21	and he extended gold chains a the front of	4200
	7:38	and measuring four cubits a,	NIH
2Ki	3:22	To the Moabites a the way,	4946+5584
1Ch	6:78	from the tribe of Reuben a the Jordan	4946+6298
2Ch	3: 4	of the temple was twenty cubits long a	6584+7156
Job	38: 5	Who stretched a measuring line a it?	6584
SS	2: 8	Here he comes, leaping a the mountains,	6584
Isa	9: 4	the bar a their shoulders,	AIT
	16: 1	from Sela, a the desert,	2025
	16:22	the kings of the coastlands a the sea;	928+6298
Eze	41: 4	and its width was twenty cubits a the end	448
Joel	2: 2	Like dawn spreading a the mountains	6584
Hab	1: 6	who sweep a the whole earth	4200
Mt	4:25	and the region a the Jordan followed him.	4305
	16: 5	When they went a the lake,	1650+3836+4305
Mk	3: 8	the regions a the Jordan and around Tyre	4305
	5: 1	They went a the lake to the region of	4305
	10: 1	into the region of Judea and a the Jordan.	4305
Lk	8:26	which is a the lake from Galilee.	527
Jn	6:17	a boat and set off a the lake for Capernaum.	4305
	10:40	Then Jesus went back a the Jordan to	4305
	11:38	a cave with a stone laid a the entrance.	2130
Ac	27: 5	When we had sailed a the open sea off	1386
	27:27	fourteenth night we were still being driven a	1877
Rev	20: 9	They marched a the breadth of the earth	2093

ACSAH (5)
Jos	15:16	"I will give my daughter A in marriage to	6578
	15:17	so Caleb gave his daughter A to him	6578
Jdg	1:12	"I will give my daughter A in marriage to	6578
	1:13	so Caleb gave his daughter A to him	6578
1Ch	2:49	Caleb's daughter was A.	6578

ACSAPH (3)
Jos	11: 1	to the kings of Shimron and A,	439
	12:20	the king of A one	439
	19:25	Helkath, Hali, Beten, A,	439

ACT (41) [ACTED, ACTING, ACTION, ACTIONS, ACTIVE, ACTIVITY, ACTS]
Ex	8:29	not a deceitfully again by not letting	9438
Lev	20:21	it is an a of impurity;	5614
Nu	5:13	been caught in the a),	9530
	23:19	Does he speak and then not a?	6913
Dt	17:10	You must a according to	6913
	17:11	A according to the law they teach you and	6913
	24:13	be regarded as a righteous a in the sight of	7407
Jdg	20: 6	lewd and disgraceful a	2365
1Sa	14: 6	Perhaps the LORD will a in our behalf.	6913
2Sa	6: 7	against Uzzah because of his irreverent a;	8915
	14: 2	A like a woman who has spent many days grieving	2118
1Ki	8:32	then hear from heaven and a.	6913
	8:39	your dwelling place. Forgive and a;	6913
	8:39	"Is this how you a as king of Israel?"	6913
2Ch	6:23	then hear from heaven and a.	6913
	19:11	A with courage, and may the LORD be	6913
	24: 5	But the Levites did not a at once.	4554
Ezr	10:14	Let our officials a for the whole assembly.	6641
Ne	5:15	of reverence for God I did not a like that.	6913
Ps	119:126	It is time for you to a, O LORD;	6913
Pr	3:27	when it is in your power to a.	6913
Isa	43:13	When I a, who can reverse it?"	7188
	52:13	See, my servant will a wisely;	8505
Jer	6:28	they all a corruptly.	8845
	42: 5	against us if we do not a in accordance	6913
Eze	24:14	The time has come for me to a.	6913
Da	9:19	O Lord, hear and a!	6913
	11:23	he will a deceitfully,	6913
Mic	6: 8	To a justly and to love mercy and	6913
Zep	3: 7	But they were still eager to a corruptly	8845
Jn	8: 4	this woman was caught in the a of adultery.	900+2093+2898
Ac	4: 9	a of kindness shown to a cripple	2307
Ro	5:18	of one a of righteousness was justification	1468
	12: 1	this is your spiritual a of worship.	3301
2Co	8: 6	to completion this a of grace on your part.	5921
	10: 6	be ready to punish every a of disobedience,	4157
	12:18	Did we not a in the same spirit and follow	4344
Php	2:13	and to a according to his good purpose.	1919
Col	4: 5	in the way you a toward outsiders;	4344
2Th	1:11	and every a prompted by your faith.	2240
Jas	2:12	and a as those who are going to be judged	4472

ACTED (29) [ACT]
Dt	32: 5	They have a corruptly toward him;	8845
Jos	7: 1	Israelites a unfaithfully in regard to	5085+5086
	22:20	of Zerah a unfaithfully regarding	5085+5086
	22:31	not a unfaithfully toward the LORD.	5085
Jdg	9:16	if you have a honorably and in good faith	6913
	9:19	if then you have a honorably and	6913
	9:23	who a treacherously against Abimelech.	953
1Sa	13:13	"You a foolishly," Samuel said.	6118
	21:13	he was in their hands he a like a madman,	2147
	26:21	Surely I have a like a fool,	6118
1Ki	8:47	we have done wrong, we have a wickedly';	8399
	20:25	He agreed with them and a accordingly.	6913
2Ki	12:15	because they a with complete honesty.	6913
	22:13	they have not a in accordance with all	6913
2Ch	6:37	we have done wrong and a wickedly';	8399
	11:23	He a wisely, dispersing some of his sons	1067
	25: 4	but a in accordance with what is written in	NIH
	34:21	not a in accordance with all that is written	6913
Ne	1: 7	We have a very wickedly toward you.	2472+2472
	9:33	you have a faithfully, while we did wrong.	6913
Ps	106: 6	we have done wrong and a wickedly.	8399
Isa	48: 3	then suddenly I a, and they came to pass.	6913
Jer	38: 9	these men have a wickedly	8317
Eze	25:15	'Because the Philistines a in vengeance	6913
Lk	16: 8	because he had a shrewdly.	4472
	24:28	Jesus a as if he were going farther.	4701
Ac	3:17	brothers, I know that you a in ignorance,	4556
1Ti	1:13	because I a in ignorance and unbelief.	4472

ACTING (9) [ACT]
2Sa	12:21	"Why are you a this way?	6913
2Ki	10:19	But Jehu was a deceptively in order	6913
	22: 7	because they are a faithfully."	6913
Eze	16:30	a like a brazen prostitute.	5126
Mal	2:14	the LORD is a as the witness between you	6386
Ro	14:15	you are no longer a in love.	4344
1Co	7:36	Are you not a like mere men?	4344
	7:36	If anyone thinks he is acting improperly toward	858
Gal	2:14	that they were not a in line with the truth	3980

ACTION (7) [ACT]
Jer	32:39	I will give them singleness of heart and a,	2006
Da	11:28	He will take a against it and then return	6913

Lk	23:51	not consented *to* their decision and a.	4552
Ac	7:22	and was powerful in speech and a.	2240
2Co	9: 2	**stirred** most of them to a.	2241
Jas	2:17	if it is not accompanied by a, is dead.	2240
1Pe	1:13	**prepare** your minds for a;	350+3836+4019

ACTIONS (24) [ACT]

Pr	20:11	Even a child is known by his a,	5095
Isa	66:18	I, because of their a and their imaginations,	5126
Jer	4:18	"Your own conduct and a have brought this	5095
	7: 3	Reform your ways and your a,	5095
	7: 5	and your a and deal with each other justly,	5095
	18:11	and reform your ways and your a.'	5095
	26:13	and your a and obey the LORD your God.	5095
	35:15	from your wicked ways and reform your a;	5095
	44:22	LORD could no longer endure your wicked a	5095
	44:25	by your a what you promised	3338
Eze	14:22	and when you see their conduct and their a,	6613
	14:23	when you see their conduct and their a,	6613
	20:43	and all the a by which you have defiled	6613
	24:14	according to your conduct and your a,	6613
	36:17	they defiled it by their conduct and their a.	6613
	36:19	according to their conduct and their a.	6613
Mt	11:19	But wisdom is proved right by her a."	2240
2Co	10:11	we will be *in our* a when we are present.	2240
	11:15	Their end will be *what* their a **deserve**	2240+2848
Gal	6: 4	Each one should test his own a.	2240
Tit	1:16	but *by* their a they deny him.	2240
Jas	2:22	and his a were working together,	2240
1Jn	3:12	Because his own a were evil	2240
	3:18	not love with words or tongue but with a	2240

ACTIVE (2) [ACT]

Phm	1: 6	that you may be a in sharing your faith,	1921
Heb	4:12	For the word of God is living and a.	1921

ACTIVITY (5) [ACT]

Ne	11:23	which regulated their daily a.	1821
Ecc	3: 1	and a season for every a under heaven:	2914
	3:17	for there will be a time for every a,	2914
Ac	5:38	For if their purpose or a is of human origin,	2240
2Co	10:15	our **area** of a among you	2834

ACTS (36) [ACT]

Ex	6: 6	and with mighty a **of judgment.**	9150
	7: 4	with mighty a **of judgment** I will bring out my divisions,	9150
Jdg	5:11	They recite the **righteous** a *of* the LORD,	7407
	5:11	the **righteous** a *of* his warriors in Israel.	7407
1Sa	12: 7	the **righteous** a performed by the LORD	7407
1Ch	16: 9	tell of all his **wonderful** a.	AIT
2Ch	32:32	and his a **of devotion** are written in	2876
	35:26	of Josiah's reign and his a **of devotion,**	2876
Est	10: 2	And all his a *of* power and might,	5126
Ps	71:16	I will come and proclaim your **mighty** a,	1476
	71:24	of your **righteous** a all day long,	7407
	105: 2	tell of all his **wonderful** a.	AIT
	106: 2	Who can proclaim the **mighty** a *of*	1476
	145: 4	they will tell of your **mighty** a.	1476
	145:12	that all men may know of your **mighty** a	1476
	150: 2	Praise him for his a **of power;**	1476
Pr	12:10	but the **kindest** a *of* the wicked are cruel.	8171
	13:16	Every prudent man a *out* of knowledge,	6913
Isa	59: 6	and a *of* violence are in their hands.	7189
	64: 6	*who* a on behalf of those who wait for him.	6913
	64: 6	and all our **righteous** a are like filthy rags;	7407
Jer	13:27	I have seen your **detestable** a on the hills	9199
	29:26	you should put any madman *who* a **like a prophet** into the stocks	5547
Eze	22: 9	the mountain shrines and commit **lewd** a.	2365
Da	9:16	in keeping with all your **righteous** a,	7407
Mic	6: 5	that you may know the **righteous** a *of*	7407
Mt	6: 1	to do your **'a of righteousness'** before men,	1466
Jn	7: 4	to become a public figure a in secret.	4472
Ro	1:27	Men committed **indecent** a with other men,	859
Gal	5:19	The a of the sinful nature are obvious:	2240
Heb	6: 1	of repentance from a that lead to death,	2240
	9:14	cleanse our consciences from a that lead	2240
	10:17	and **lawless** a I will remember no more."	490
Jude	1:15	of all the ungodly a they have done in	2240
Rev	15: 4	for your **righteous** a have been revealed."	1468
	19: 8	(Fine linen stands for the **righteous** a of	1468

ACTUAL (1) [ACTUALLY]

Dt	21:16	in preference to his a firstborn,	NIH

ACTUALLY (8) [ACTUAL]

Ge	37: 8	*Will you* a **rule** us?"	5440+5440
	37:10	your brothers a **come** and bow down to	995+995
Jos	9:22	while you a live near us?	NIH
Jer	8: 8	when a the lying pen of	434
Jn	7:22	because Moses gave you circumcision (**though** a it did not come from Moses,	4022
Ro	7:10	to bring life a brought death.	NIG
1Co	5: 1	is a reported that there is sexual immorality	3914
1Th	2:13	but as it is, the word of God,	242

ACZIB (4)

Jos	15:44	Keilah, A and Mareshah—	424
		and came out at the sea in the region of A,	424
Jdg	1:31	or Sidon or Ahlab or A or Helbah or Aphek	424
Mic	1:14	The town of A will prove deceptive to	424

ADADAH (1)

Jos	15:22	Kinah, Dimonah, A,	6368

ADAH (8)

Ge	4:19	one named A and the other Zillah.	6336
	4:20	A gave birth to Jabal;	6336
	4:23	Lamech said to his wives, "A and Zillah,	6336
	36: 2	A daughter of Elon the Hittite,	6336
	36: 4	A bore Eliphaz to Esau,	6336
	36:10	Eliphaz, the son of Esau's wife A,	6336
	36:12	These were grandsons of Esau's wife A.	6336
	36:16	they were grandsons of A.	6336

ADAIAH (9)

2Ki	22: 1	mother's name was Jedidah daughter of A;	6347
1Ch	6:41	the son of Zerah, the son of A,	6347
	8:21	A, Beraiah and Shimrath were the sons	6347
	9:12	A son of Jeroham, the son of Pashhur,	6347
2Ch	23: 1	Azariah son of Obed, Maaseiah son of A,	6348
Ezr	10:29	Meshullam, Malluch, A, Jashub,	6347
	10:39	Shelemiah, Nathan, A,	6347
Ne	11: 5	the son of Hazaiah, the son of A,	6347
	11:12	A son of Jeroham, the son of Pelaliah,	6347

ADALIA (1)

Est	9: 8	Poratha, A, Aridatha,	130

ADAM (21) [ADAM'S]

Ge	2:20	But for A no suitable helper was found.	134
	3:17	To A he said, "Because you listened	134
	3:20	A named his wife Eve,	134
	3:21	for A and his wife and clothed them.	134
	4: 1	A lay with his wife Eve,	134
	4:25	A lay with his wife again,	134
	5: 3	When A had lived 130 years,	134
	5: 4	A lived 800 years and had other sons	134
	5: 5	Altogether, A lived 930 years,	134
Jos	3:16	a town called A in the vicinity of Zarethan,	136
1Ch	1: 1	A, Seth, Enosh,	134
Hos	6: 7	Like A, they have broken the covenant—	134
Lk	3:38	the son of Seth, the son *of* A,	77
Ro	5:14	from the time of A to the time of Moses,	77
	5:14	by breaking a command, as did A, who was	77
1Co	15:22	For as in A all die,	77
	15:45	"The first man A became a living being";	77
	15:45	the last A, a life-giving spirit.	77
1Ti	2:13	For A was formed first, then Eve.	77
	2:14	And A was not the one deceived;	77
Jude	1:14	Enoch, the seventh from A,	77

ADAM'S (1) [ADAM]

Ge	5: 1	This is the written account of A line.	134

ADAMAH (1)

Jos	19:36	A, Ramah, Hazor,	142

ADAMANT (KJV) See FLINT

ADAMI NEKEB (1)

Jos	19:33	passing A and Jabneel to Lakkum	146

ADAR (9)

Ezr	6:15	on the third day of the month A,	10009
Est	3: 7	the month of A.	160
	3:13	the month of A, and to plunder their goods.	160
	8:12	the month of A,	160
	9: 1	the month of A,	160
	9:15	on the fourteenth day of the month of A,	160
	9:17	on the thirteenth day of the month of A,	160
	9:19	the month of A as a day of joy and feasting,	160
	9:21	and fifteenth days of the month of A	160

ADBEEL (2)

Ge	25:13	the firstborn of Ishmael, Kedar, A,	118
1Ch	1:29	the firstborn of Ishmael, Kedar, A,	118

ADD (32) [ADDED, ADDING, ADDITION, ADDITIONAL, ADDS]

Ge	30:24	"May the LORD a to me another son."	3578
Lev	2:13	a salt to all your offerings.	7928
	5:16	a a fifth of the value to that and give it all	3578
	6: 5	a a fifth of the value to it and give it all to	3578
	6:12	Every morning the priest *is to* a firewood	6584
	22:14	to the priest for the offering and a a fifth of	3578
	27:13	*he must* a a fifth to its value.	3578
	27:15	*he must* a a fifth to its value,	3578
	27:19	*he must* a a fifth to its value,	3578
	27:31	*he must* a a fifth of the value to it.	3578
Nu	5: 7	a one fifth to it and give it all to	3578
Dt	4: 2	*Do* not a to what I command you and do	3578
	12:32	*do* not a to it or take away from it.	3578
	20: 8	Then the officers *shall* a,	3578
2Sa	15: 4	And Absalom *would* a,	606
2Ki	20: 6	I *will* a fifteen years to your life.	3578
1Ch	22:14	And *you may* a to them.	3578
2Ch	28:13	Do you intend to a to our sin and guilt?	3578
Pr	1: 5	let the wise listen and a to their learning,	3578
	9: 9	teach a righteous man and *he will* a	3578
	30: 6	*Do* not a to his words,	3578

ACTIONS – ADDITION columns continue

Isa	5: 8	to you *who* a house to house and join field	5595
	29: 1	A year to year and let your cycle	3578
	38: 5	I *will* a fifteen years to your life.	3578
Jer	7:21	*Go ahead,* a your burnt offerings	3578
	30:19	*I will* a to their **numbers,**	8049
Eze	16:43	*Did you* not a lewdness	6913
Mt	6:27	by worrying can a a single hour to his life?	4707
Lk	12:25	by worrying can a a single hour to his life?	4707
Gal	3:15	Just as no one can set aside or a to	2112
2Pe	1: 5	*to* a to your faith goodness;	2220
Rev	22:18	God *will* a to him the plagues described	2202

ADDAN (KJV) See ADDON

ADDAR (2) [HAZAR ADDAR, ATAROTH ADDAR]

Jos	15: 3	Then it ran past Hezron up to A and curved	162
1Ch	8: 3	The sons of Bela were: A, Gera, Abihud,	161

ADDED (39) [ADD]

Ge	16:10	The angel a, "I will so increase	606
	21: 7	And *she* a, "Who would have said	606
	24:25	And *she* a, "We have plenty of straw	606
	30:28	*He* a, "Name your wages,	606
	38:25	she said. And *she* a, "See	606
Ex	12:34	before *the* yeast *was* a,	2806
Lev	10: 1	put fire in them and a incense;	8492
Nu	36: 3	from our ancestral inheritance and a to that	3578
	36: 4	their inheritance *will be* a to that of	3578
Dt	5:22	and *he* a nothing more.	3578
Jdg	19:13	*He* a, "Come, let's try to reach Gibeah	606
Ru	2:20	She a, "That man is our close relative;	606
	3:17	and a, "He gave me these six measures	606
1Sa	12:19	for *we have* a to all our other sins the evil	3578
	26:18	*he* a, "Why is my lord pursuing his servant?	606
2Sa	19:35	Why should your servant be an a burden	6388
1Ki	2:14	*he* a, "I have something to say to you."	606
	22:28	*he* a, "Mark my words, all you people!"	606
2Ch	2:12	And Hiram a: "Praise be to	606
	18:27	*he* a, "Mark my words, all you people!"	606
Est	5:14	"And that's not all," Haman a.	606
Pr	9:11	and years *will be* a to your life.	3578
Ecc	3:14	nothing *can be* a to it and nothing taken	3578
Jer	36:32	many similar words were a to them.	3578+6388
	40: 5	Jeremiah turned to go, Nebuzaradan a,	NIH
	44:19	The women a, "When we burned incense	NIH
	45: 3	The LORD *has* a sorrow to my pain;	3578
Zec	1:15	but they a to the calamity.'	6468
	5: 6	And *he* a, "This is the iniquity of the people	606
Lk	3:20	Herod a this to them all:	4707
Jn	1:51	*He* then a, "I tell you the truth,	3306
Ac	1:26	so *he* was a to the eleven apostles.	5164
	2:41	about three thousand *were* a to their number	4707
	2:47	And the Lord a to their number daily	4707
	5:14	in the Lord and *were* a to their number.	4707
Ro	5:20	The law *was* a so that	4209
Gal	2: 6	those men a nothing to my message.	4707
	3:19	*It was* a because of transgressions until	4707
Rev	19: 9	*he* a, "These are the true words of God."	3306

ADDER (2) [ADDERS]

Job	20:16	the fangs of an a will kill him.	704
Isa	59: 5	and when one is broken, an a is hatched.	704

ADDERS (1) [ADDER]

Isa	30: 6	of a and darting snakes,	704

ADDERS (KJV) See also VIPER

ADDI (1)

Lk	3:28	the son *of* A, the son of Cosam,	79

ADDICTED (1)

Tit	2: 3	not to be slanderers or a to much wine,	1530

ADDING (5) [ADD]

Lev	27:27	a a fifth of the value to it.	3578
2Sa	14:11	to prevent the avenger of blood from a to	8049
1Ki	11:25	a to the trouble caused by Hadad.	907+2256
Ezr	10:10	you have married foreign women, a	3578
Ecc	7:27	"A one thing to another to discover	NIH

ADDITION (38) [ADD]

Ge	28: 9	in a to the wives he already had.	6584
Lev	9:17	burned on the altar in a to	963+4200+4946
	23:38	These offerings are in a to those	963+4200+4946
	23:38	and in a to your gifts	963+4200+4946
Nu	6:21	in a to whatever else he can afford.	963+4200+4946
	16:49	in a to those who had died	963+4200+4946
	28:10	in a to the regular daily offering	6584
	28:23	Prepare these in a to	963+4200+4946
	28:24	it is to be prepared in a to	6584
	28:31	in a to the regular burnt offering	963+4200+4946
	29: 6	These are in a to the monthly	963+4200+4946
	29:11	in a to the sin offering	963+4200+4946
	29:16	in a to the regular burnt offering	963+4200+4946
	29:19	in a to the regular burnt offering	963+4200+4946
	29:22	in a to the regular burnt offering	963+4200+4946
	29:25	in a to the regular burnt offering	963+4200+4946

Nu	29:28	in a to the regular burnt offering	963+4200+4946
	29:31	in a to the regular burnt offering	963+4200+4946
	29:34	in a to the regular burnt offering	963+4200+4946
	29:38	in a to the regular burnt offering	963+4200+4946
	29:39	" 'In a to what you vow	963+4200
	35: 6	In a, give them forty-two other towns.	2256
Dt	29: 1	in a to the covenant he had made	963+4200+4946
Jos	13:22	In a to those slain in battle,	448
Jdg	20:15	in a to seven hundred chosen men	963+4200
1Ki	5:11	in a to twenty thousand baths	2256
	15:20	and all Kinnereth in a to Naphtali.	6584
2Ch	31:16	In a, they distributed to	963+4200+4946
Ezr	1: 6	In a to all the freewill offerings.	963+4200
Ne	5:15	of silver from them in a to food and wine.	339
Ecc	12:12	my son, of anything in a to them.	3463
Eze	16:23	In a to all your other wickedness,	339
	39:14	in a to them,	907
	44: 7	In a to all your other detestable practices,	448
Lk	24:22	In a, some of our women amazed us.	247+2779
2Co	7:13	In a to our own encouragement,	1254+2093
	8:22	In a, we are sending	1254
Eph	6:16	In a to all this, take up the shield of faith,	NIG

ADDITIONAL (3) [ADD]
Ge	43:22	also brought a silver with us to buy food.	337
Ex	26:12	As for the a length of the tent curtains,	6369
Nu	3:48	the redemption of the a Israelites to Aaron	6369

ADDON (2)
Ezr	2:59	Tel Harsha, Kerub, A and Immer,	150
Ne	7:61	Tel Harsha, Kerub, A and Immer,	124

ADDRESS (3) [ADDRESSED, ADDRESSES]
Dt	20: 2	the priest shall come forward and a	1819
Ac	12:21	delivered a public a to his people.	1319
1Co	3: 1	not a you as spiritual but as worldly—	3281

ADDRESSED (3) [ADDRESS]
Ac	2:14	raised his voice and a the crowd:	710
	5:35	Then he a them:	3306
	15: 7	Peter got up and a them:	3306+4639

ADDRESSES (1) [ADDRESS]
Heb	12: 5	that word of encouragement that a you	1363

ADDS (5) [ADD]
Job	34:37	To his sin he a rebellion;	3578
Pr	10:22	and he a no trouble to it.	3578
	10:27	The fear of the LORD a length to life,	3578
Heb	10:17	Then he a: "Their sins	3306
Rev	22:18	If anyone a anything to them,	2202

ADEQUATELY (1)
Ac	18:26	to him the way of God more a.	209

ADER (KJV) See EDER

ADHERE (1)
2Ki	17:34	neither worship the LORD nor a to	3869+6913

ADIEL (3)
1Ch	4:36	Jaakobah, Jeshohaiah, Asaiah, A, Jesimiel,	6346
	9:12	and Maasai son of A, the son of Jahzerah,	6346
	27:25	of A was in charge of the royal storehouses.	6346

ADIN (4)
Ezr	2:15	of A 454	6350
	8: 6	of the descendants of A, Ebed son	6350
Ne	7:20	of A 655	6350
	10:16	Adonijah, Bigvai, A,	6350

ADINA (1)
1Ch	11:42	A son of Shiza the Reubenite,	6351

ADITHAIM (1)
Jos	15:36	A and Gederah (or Gederothaim)—	6353

ADJOINING (5) [JOIN]
Ne	3: 2	The men of Jericho built the a section,	3338+6584
	3:10	A this, Jedaiah son of Harumaph	3338+6584
Eze	41:11	and the base a the open area	AIT
	42:10	a the temple courtyard and opposite	448+7156
	45: 6	cubits long, a the sacred portion;	4200+6645

ADJOURNED (1)
Ac	24:22	with the Way, a the proceedings.	327

ADJURE (KJV) See CHARGE, COMMAND, SWEAR

ADLAI (1)
1Ch	27:29	Shaphat son of A was in charge of	6354

ADMAH (5)
Ge	10:19	Gomorrah, A and Zeboiim, as far as Lasha.	144
	14: 2	Shinab king of A,	144
	14: 8	the king of Gomorrah, the king of A,	144
Dt	29:23	the destruction of Sodom and Gomorrah, A	144
Hos	11: 8	How can I treat you like A?	144

ADMATHA (1)
Est	1:14	Carshena, Shethar, A, Tarshish, Meres,	148

ADMINISTER (7) [ADMINISTERED, ADMINISTERING, ADMINISTRATION, ADMINISTRATOR, ADMINISTRATORS]
1Ki	3:28	that he had wisdom from God to a justice.	6913
2Ch	19: 8	and heads of Israelite families to a the law	NIH
Ezr	7:25	appoint magistrates and judges to a justice	10169
Jer	21:12	" 'A justice every morning;	1906
Zec	7: 9	This is what the LORD Almighty says: 'A true justice;	9149
2Co	8:19	which we a in order to honor	1354
	8:20	of the way we a this liberal gift.	1354

ADMINISTERED (1) [ADMINISTER]
Heb	11:33	a justice, and gained what was promised;	2237

ADMINISTERING (2) [ADMINISTER]
1Ki	3:11	but for discernment in a justice,	9048
1Pe	4:10	faithfully a God's grace	3874

ADMINISTRATION (3) [ADMINISTER]
1Co	12:28	those with gifts of a,	3236
Eph	3: 2	the a of God's grace that was given to me	3873
	3: 9	and to make plain to everyone the a	3873

ADMINISTRATOR (7) [ADMINISTER]
2Ki	10: 5	So the palace a, the city governor,	889+6584S
	18:18	Eliakim son of Hilkiah the palace a,	889+6584S
	18:37	Eliakim son of Hilkiah the palace a,	889+6584S
	19: 2	He sent Eliakim the palace a,	889+6584S
Isa	36: 3	Eliakim son of Hilkiah the palace a,	889+6584S
	36:22	Eliakim son of Hilkiah the palace a,	889+6584S
	37: 2	He sent Eliakim the palace a,	889+6584S

ADMINISTRATORS (8) [ADMINISTER]
2Ch	35: 8	the a of God's temple,	5592
Est	9: 3	the governors and the king's a helped	4856+6913
Da	2:49	and Abednego a over the province	10525
	6: 2	with three a over them,	10518
	6: 3	so distinguished himself among the a and	10518
	6: 4	the a and the satraps tried to find grounds	10518
	6: 6	So the a and the satraps went as a group to	10518
	6: 7	The royal a, prefects, satraps,	10518

ADMIRABLE (1)
Php	4: 8	whatever is lovely, whatever is a—	2368

ADMIT (7) [ADMITTED]
Jos	20: 4	Then they are to a him into their city	665
Job	27: 5	a you are in the right;	7405
	40:14	Then I myself will a to you	3344
Isa	48: 6	Will you not a them?	5583
Hos	5:15	to my place until they a their guilt.	870
Ac	24:14	I a that I worship the God of our fathers as	3933
2Co	11:21	To my shame I a that we were too weak	3306

ADMITTED (2) [ADMIT]
Ne	13: 1	or Moabite should ever be a into	995
Heb	11:13	And they a that they were aliens	3933

ADMONISH (2) [ADMONISHED, ADMONISHING, ADMONITION]
Col	3:16	and a one another with all wisdom,	3805
1Th	5:12	over you in the Lord and who a you.	3805

ADMONISHED (2) [ADMONISH]
Ne	9:26	who had a them in order to turn them back	6386
	9:30	By your Spirit you a them	6386

ADMONISHING (1) [ADMONISH]
Col	1:28	a and teaching everyone with all wisdom,	3805

ADMONITION (2) [ADMONISH]
Mal	2: 1	"And now this a is for you, O priests.	5184
	2: 4	that I have sent you this a so	5184

ADNA (2)
Ezr	10:30	From the descendants of Pahath-Moab: A,	6363
Ne	12:15	of Harim's, A; of Meremoth's, Helkai;	6363

ADNAH (2)
1Ch	12:20	A, Jozabad, Jediael, Michael, Jozabad,	6367
2Ch	17:14	A the commander, with 300,000	6365

ADO (KJV) See COMMOTION

ADONI-BEZEK (3) [BEZEK]
Jdg	1: 5	that they found A and fought against him,	152
	1: 6	A fled, but they chased him	152
	1: 7	Then A said, "Seventy kings	152

ADONI-ZEDEK (2)
Jos	10: 1	Now A king of Jerusalem heard	155
	10: 3	So A king of Jerusalem appealed	155

ADONIJAH (26) [ADONIJAH'S]
2Sa	3: 4	A the son of Haggith;	153
1Ki	1: 5	Now A, whose mother was Haggith,	153
	1: 7	A conferred with Joab son of Zeruiah and	153
	1: 8	and David's special guard did not join A.	154
	1: 9	A then sacrificed sheep,	154
	1:11	"Have you not heard that A,	154
	1:13	Why then has A become king?'	154
	1:18	But now A has become king, and you,	153
	1:24	declared that A shall be king after you,	154
	1:25	"Long live King A!'	154
	1:41	A and all the guests who were	154
	1:42	A said, "Come in.	154
	1:50	But A, in fear of Solomon,	154
	1:51	"A is afraid of King Solomon	154
	1:53	A came and bowed down to King Solomon,	NIH
	2:13	Now A, the son of Haggith,	154
	2:19	to King Solomon to speak to him for A,	154
	2:21	be given in marriage to your brother A."	154
	2:22	the Shunammite for A?	154
	2:23	so severely, if A does not pay with his life	154
	2:24	A shall be put to death today!"	154
	2:25	and he struck down A and he died.	2257S
	2:28	who had conspired with A though not	153
1Ch	3: 2	the fourth, A the son of Haggith;	153
2Ch	17: 8	Asahel, Shemiramoth, Jehonathan, A,	154
Ne	10:16	A, Bigvai, Adin,	153

ADONIJAH'S (1) [ADONIJAH]
1Ki	1:49	all A guests rose in alarm and dispersed.	154+4200

ADONIKAM (3)
Ezr	2:13	of A 666	156
	8:13	of the descendants of A,	156
Ne	7:18	of A 667	156

ADONIRAM (5)
2Sa	20:24	A was in charge of forced labor;	157
1Ki	4: 6	A son of Abda—in charge of forced labor.	157
	5:14	A was in charge of the forced labor.	157
	12:18	King Rehoboam sent out A,	157
2Ch	10:18	King Rehoboam sent out A,	2067

ADOPT (1) [ADOPTED, ADOPTION]
Job	15: 5	you a the tongue of the crafty.	1047

ADOPTED (3) [ADOPT]
Est	2:15	Esther (the girl Mordecai had a,	1426+4200+4374
Ps	106:35	with the nations and a their customs.	4340
Eph	1: 5	to be a as his sons through Jesus Christ,	5625

ADOPTION (2) [ADOPT]
Ro	8:23	as we wait eagerly for our a as sons,	5625
	9: 4	Theirs is the a as sons;	5625

ADORAIM (1)
2Ch	11: 9	A, Lachish, Azekah,	126

ADORE (1)
SS	1: 4	How right they are to a you!	170

ADORN (7) [ADORNED, ADORNMENT, ADORNS]
Job	40:10	Then yourself with glory and splendor,	6335
Ps	144:12	be like pillars carved to a a palace.	9322
Pr	1: 9	and a chain to a your neck.	NIH
Isa	60: 7	and I will a my glorious temple.	6995
	60:13	to a the place of my sanctuary.	6995
Jer	4:30	You a yourself in vain.	3636
	10: 4	They a it with silver and gold;	3636

ADORNED (9) [ADORN]
2Sa	1:24	who a your garments with ornaments	6584+6590
2Ch	3: 6	He a the temple with precious stones.	4200+7596+9514
Ps	45: 8	from palaces a with ivory the music of	AIT
Eze	16:11	I a you with jewelry:	6335
	16:13	So you were a with gold and silver;	6335
	28:13	every precious stone a you:	5010
Hos	10: 1	his land prospered, he a his sacred stones.	3512
Am	3:15	the houses a with ivory will be destroyed	AIT
Lk	21: 5	how the temple was a with beautiful stones	3175

ADORNMENT (1) [ADORN]
1Pe	3: 3	not come from outward a,	3180

ADORNS (3) [ADORN]
Ps	93: 5	holiness **a** your house for endless days,	5533
Isa	61:10	as a bridegroom **a** his **head** like a priest,	6996
	61:10	and as a bride *herself with* her jewels.	6335

ADRAMMELECH (3)
2Ki	17:31	the fire as sacrifices to **A** and Anammelech,	165
	19:37	his sons **A** and Sharezer cut him down with	166
Isa	37:38	his sons **A** and Sharezer cut him down with	166

ADRAMYTTIUM (1)
Ac	27: 2	a ship **from A** about to sail for ports along	101

ADRIATIC (1)
Ac	27:27	across the **A Sea,**	102

ADRIEL (2)
1Sa	18:19	she was given in marriage to **A** of Meholah.	6377
2Sa	21: 8	whom she had borne to **A** son of Barzillai	6377

ADULLAM (9) [ADULLAMITE]
Ge	38: 1	to stay with a man **of A** named Hirah.	6356
Jos	12:15	the king of **A** one	6355
	15:35	Jarmuth, **A,** Socoh, Azekah,	6355
1Sa	22: 1	and escaped to the cave of **A.**	6355
2Sa	23:13	down to David at the cave of **A,**	6355
1Ch	11:15	down to David to the rock at the cave of **A,**	6355
2Ch	11: 7	Beth Zur, Soco, **A,**	6355
Ne	11:30	**A** and their villages,	6355
Mic	1:15	the glory of Israel will come to **A.**	6355

ADULLAMITE (2) [ADULLAM]
Ge	38:12	and his friend Hirah the **A** went with him.	6356
	38:20	the young goat by his friend the **A** in order	6356

ADULTERER (3) [ADULTERY]
Lev	20:10	**a** and the adulteress must be put to death.	5537
Job	24:15	The eye of the **a** watches for dusk;	5537
Heb	13: 4	the **a** and all the sexually immoral.	3659

ADULTERERS (9) [ADULTERY]
Ps	50:18	you throw in your lot with **a.**	5537
Isa	57: 3	you offspring of **a** and prostitutes!	5537
Jer	9: 2	they *are* all **a,** a crowd of unfaithful people.	5537
	23:10	The land is full of **a;**	5537
Hos	7: 4	They *are* all **a,**	5537
Mal	3: 5	to testify against sorcerers, **a** and perjurers,	5537
Lk	18:11	evildoers, **a**—or even like this tax collector.	3659
1Co	6: 9	the sexually immoral nor idolaters nor **a**	3659
1Ti	1:10	*for* **a** and perverts, for slave traders	4521

ADULTERESS (12) [ADULTERY]
Lev	20:10	adulterer and the **a** must be put to death.	5537
Pr	2:16	It will save you also from the **a,**	851+2424
	5: 3	For the lips of an **a** drip honey,	2424
	5:20	Why be captivated, my son, by an **a?**	2424
	6:26	and the **a** preys upon your very life.	408+851
	7: 5	they will keep you from the **a,**	851+2424
	22:14	The mouth of an **a** is a deep pit;	2424
	30:20	"This is the way of an **a:**	5537
Hos	3: 1	though she is loved by another and *is an* **a.**	5537
Mt	5:32	causes her *to* **become an a,**	3658
Ro	7: 3	she is called an **a.**	3655
	7: 3	from that law and is not an **a,**	3655

ADULTERESSES (KJV) See WOMEN
WHO COMMIT ADULTERY

ADULTERIES (7) [ADULTERY]
Jer	3: 8	and sent her away because of all *her* **a.**	5537
	13:27	your **a** and lustful neighings,	5539
Rev	14: 8	the maddening wine *of* her **a."**	4518
	17: 2	intoxicated with the wine *of* her **a."**	4518
	17: 4	and the filth of her **a.**	4518
	18: 3	the maddening wine *of* her **a.**	4518
	19: 2	corrupted the earth by her **a.**	4518

ADULTEROUS (9) [ADULTERY]
Eze	6: 9	how I have been grieved by their **a** hearts,	2388
	16:32	" 'You **a** wife!	5537
	23:45	they *are* **a** and blood is on their hands.	5537
Hos	1: 2	an **a** wife and children of unfaithfulness,	2393
	2: 2	Let her remove the **a look** from her face	2393
Mt	12:39	"A wicked and **a** generation asks for	3655
	16: 4	A wicked and **a** generation looks for	3655
Mk	8:38	in this **a** and sinful generation,	3655
Jas	4: 4	*You* **a** people, don't you know	3655

ADULTERY (48) [ADULTERER,
ADULTERERS, ADULTERESS,
ADULTERIES, ADULTEROUS]
Ex	20:14	"You shall not commit **a.**	5537
Lev	20:10	a man **commits a** with another man's wife	5537
Dt	5:18	"You shall not commit **a.**	5537
Ps	51: T	David *had* **committed a** with Bathsheba.	448+995
Pr	6:32	But *a man who* **commits a** lacks judgment;	5537
Jer	3: 6	and has **committed a** there.	2388

Jer	3: 8	she also went out and **committed a.**	2388
	3: 9	and **committed a** with stone and wood.	5537
	5: 7	yet *they* **committed a** and thronged to	5537
	7: 9	**commit a** and perjury,	5537
	23:14	They **commit a** and live a lie.	5537
	29:23	*they* have **committed a**	5537
Eze	16:38	*women who* **commit a** and who shed blood;	5537
	23:37	for *they* have **committed a** and blood is	5537
	23:37	They **committed a** with their idols;	5537
	23:43	Then I said about the one out by **a,**	5539
	23:45	to the punishment of *women who* **commit a**	5537
Hos	1: 2	**guilty of the vilest a**	2388+2388
	2: 4	because they are the children of **a.**	2393
	4: 2	lying and murder, stealing and **a;**	5537
	4:13	and your daughters-in-law *to* **a.**	5537
	4:14	your daughters-in-law when *they* **commit a,**	5537
	4:15	"Though you **commit a,** O Israel,	2388
Mt	5:27	'Do not **commit a.'**	3658
	5:28	who looks at a woman lustfully *has* already **committed a** with her	3658
	5:32	the divorced woman **commits a.**	3656
	15:19	**a,** sexual immorality, theft, false testimony,	3657
	19: 9	and marries another woman **commits a."**	3656
	19:18	" 'Do not murder, *do* not **commit a,**	3658
Mk	7:21	sexual immorality, theft, murder, **a,**	3657
	10:11	and marries another woman **commits a**	3656
	10:12	and marries another man, *she* **commits a."**	3656
	10:19	'Do not murder, *do* not **commit a,**	3658
Lk	16:18	and marries another woman **commits a,**	3658
	16:18	a divorced woman **commits a.**	3658
	18:20	'Do not **commit a,** do not murder,	3658
Jn	8: 3	in a woman caught in **a.**	3657
	8: 4	this woman was caught in the act *of* **a.**	3658
Ro	2:22	that people *should* not **commit a,**	3658
	2:22	*do you* **commit a?**	3658
	13: 9	The commandments, *"Do* not **commit a,"**	3658
Jas	2:11	For he who said, *"Do* not **commit a,"**	3658
	2:11	not **commit a** but do commit murder,	3658
2Pe	2:14	With eyes full of **a,**	3655
Rev	2:22	and I will make those who **commit a**	3658
	17: 2	the earth **committed a** and the inhabitants	4519
	18: 3	The kings of the earth **committed a**	4519
	18: 9	the kings of the earth who **committed a**	4519

ADULTS (1)
1Co	14:20	but in your thinking be **a.**	5455

ADUMMIM (2)
Jos	15: 7	which faces the Pass of **A** south of	147
	18:17	which faces the Pass of **A,**	147

ADVANCE (20) [ADVANCED, ADVANCES,
ADVANCING]
Dt	1: 7	Break camp and **a** *into* the hill country of	5825
Jos	6: 7	And he ordered the people, **"A!**	6296
	8: 5	I and all those with me *will* **a** on the city,	7928
Jdg	4:15	At Barak's **a,** the LORD routed Sisera	4200+7156
	9:33	**a** against the city.	7320
2Sa	22:30	With your help *I can* **a** *against* a troop;	8132
Job	19:12	His troops **a** in force;	995
	30:14	They **a** *as through* a gaping breach;	910
Ps	18:29	With your help *I can* **a** *against* a troop;	8132
	27: 2	evil men **a** against me to devour my flesh,	7928
Pr	30:27	yet *they* **a** together in ranks;	3655
Eze	38:16	*You will* **a** against my people Israel like	6590
Da	11:13	*he will* **a** with a huge army fully equipped.	995
Joel	3:12	let them **a** into the Valley of Jehoshaphat,	6590
Hab	1: 9	Their hordes **a** like a desert wind	2025+7156
Ro	9:23	whom *he* **prepared** in **a** for glory—	4602
2Co	9: 5	to urge the brothers to **visit** you in **a**	1650+4616
Gal	3: 8	**announced** the gospel in **a**	4603
Eph	2:10	which God **prepared** in **a** for us to do.	4602
Php	1:12	to me has really served to **a** the gospel.	4620

ADVANCED (18) [ADVANCE]
Ge	18:11	and Sarah were already old and **well a**	995
	24: 1	Abraham was now old and **well a**	995
Jos	13: 1	When Joshua was old and **well a** in years,	995
	23: 1	Joshua, by then old and **well a** in years,	995
	23: 2	"I am old and **well a** in years.	995
Jdg	1:10	They **a** against the Canaanites living	2143
	1:11	From there they **a** against the people living	2143
	1:29	From there *he* **a** *against* the Ammonites.	6296
1Sa	17:12	and in Saul's time he was old and **well a**	995
2Sa	10:13	Then Joab and the troops with him **a**	5602
1Ki	1: 1	King David was old and **well a** in years,	995
	20:21	of Israel **a** and overpowered the horses	3655
2Ki	24:10	of Babylon **a** *on* Jerusalem and laid siege	6590
1Ch	19:14	Then Joab and the troops with him **a**	5602
	19:17	*he* **a** against them	995
Job	32: 7	'a years should teach wisdom.'	8044
Ps	18:12	of the brightness of his presence clouds **a,**	6296
	48: 4	when *they* **a** together,	6296

ADVANCES (3) [ADVANCE]
Jer	4:13	*He* **a** like the clouds,	6590
	46:22	a fleeing serpent as the enemy **a** in force;	2143
Na	2: 1	An attacker **a** against you, [Nineveh]	6590

ADVANCING (4) [ADVANCE]
1Ki	20:17	who reported, "Men *are* **a** from Samaria."	3655
Eze	38: 9	**a** like a storm;	995
Mt	11:12	of heaven *has been* **forcefully a,**	1041

ADVANTAGE (13)
Ex	22:22	"Do not **take a** of a widow or an orphan.	6700
Lev	25:14	*do* not **take a** of each other.	3561
	25:17	*Do* not **take a** of each other,	3561
Dt	24:14	Do not **take a** of a hired man who is poor	6943
Ecc	3:19	man has no **a** over the animal.	4639
	6: 8	What **a** has a wise man over a fool?	3463
	7:12	but the **a** of knowledge is this:	3862
Isa	30: 5	who bring neither help nor **a,**	3603
Ro	3: 1	What **a,** then, is there in being a Jew,	4356
2Co	11:20	or **takes a** of you or pushes himself forward	3284
1Th	4: 6	or **take a** of him.	4430
Heb	13:17	for that would be of **no a** to you.	269
Jude	1:16	and flatter others for their own **a.**	6066

ADVENTURERS (2)
Jdg	9: 4	and Abimelech used it to hire reckless **a,**	7069
	11: 3	where a group of **a** gathered around him	8199

ADVERSARIES (14) [ADVERSARY]
Dt	32:41	on my **a** and repay those who hate me.	7640
2Sa	19:22	This day you have become my **a!**	8477
	22:40	you made my **a** bow at my feet.	7756
Job	27: 7	my **a** like the unjust!	7756
Ps	18:39	you made my **a** bow at my feet.	7756
	44: 7	you put our **a** to shame.	8533
	44:10	and our **a** have plundered us.	8533
	74:23	Do not ignore the clamor of your **a,**	7675
	89:23	before him and strike down his **a.**	8533
	92:11	My eyes have seen the defeat of my **a;**	8806
	106:11	The waters covered their **a;**	7640
	139:20	your **a** misuse your name.	6839
Da	4:19	to your enemies and its meaning to your **a!**	10568
Lk	21:15	that none of your **a** will be able to resist	512

ADVERSARY (9) [ADVERSARIES,
ADVERSITY]
Dt	32:27	lest the **a** misunderstand and say,	7640
1Ki	5: 4	and there is no **a** or disaster.	8477
	11:14	LORD raised up against Solomon an **a,**	8477
	11:23	God raised up against Solomon another **a,**	8477
	11:25	Rezon was Israel's **a** as long	8477
Est	7: 6	"The **a** and enemy is this vile Haman."	7640
Mt	5:25	**a** who is taking you **to court.**	508
Lk	12:58	As you are going with your **a** to	508
	18: 3	'Grant me justice against my **a.'**	508

ADVERSITIES (KJV) See ANXIETY,
CALAMITY, TROUBLE

ADVERSITY (2) [ADVERSARY]
Pr	17:17	and a brother is born for **a.**	7650
Isa	30:20	Although the Lord gives you the bread of **a**	7639

ADVERTISE (KJV) See WARN, BRING TO
ATTENTION

ADVICE (37) [ADVISE]
Ex	18:19	now to me and *I will* **give** you *some* **a,**	3619
Nu	31:16	the ones who followed Balaam's **a**	1821
2Sa	15:34	by frustrating Ahithophel's **a.**	6783
	16:20	"Give us your **a.**	6783
	16:23	in those days the **a** Ahithophel **gave**	3619+6783
	16:23	and Absalom regarded all of Ahithophel's **a.**	6783
	17: 6	"Ahithophel has given this **a.**	1821
	17: 7	**a** Ahithophel *has given*	3619+6783
	17:14	"The **a** *of* Hushai the Arkite is better than	6783
	17:14	to frustrate the good **a** *of* Ahithophel	6783
	17:23	When Ahithophel saw that his **a** had	6783
	20:22	to all the people with her **wise a,**	2683
1Ki	12: 8	rejected the **a** the elders **gave**	3619+6783
	12: 9	He asked them, "What *is* your **a?**	3619
	12:13	Rejecting the **a** **given** him by the elders,	3619+6783
	12:14	he followed the **a** *of* the young men	6783
	12:14	**seeking a,** the king made two golden calves.	3619
2Ch	10: 8	rejected the **a** the elders **gave** him	3619+6783
	10: 9	He asked them, "What *is* your **a?**	3619
	10:13	Rejecting the **a** *of* the elders,	6783
	10:14	he followed the **a** *of* the young men	6783
Est	1:21	and his nobles were pleased with this **a,**	1821
	2: 4	This **a** appealed to the king.	1821
Job	26: 3	What **a** *you* have **offered** to one	3619
Pr	1:25	since you ignored all my **a** and would	6783
	1:30	not accept my **a** and spurned my rebuke,	6783
	12: 5	but the **a** of the wicked is deceitful.	9374
	12:15	but a wise man listens to **a.**	6783
	13:10	but wisdom is found in *those who* **take a.**	3619
	19:20	Listen to **a** and accept instruction,	6783
	20:18	Make plans by seeking **a;**	6783
Isa	19:11	of Pharaoh give senseless **a.**	6783
Eze	11: 2	and **giving** wicked **a** in this city.	3619+6783
Da	4:27	O king, be pleased to accept my **a:**	10422
Ac	27:11	followed the **a** of the pilot and of the owner	NIG
	27:21	"Men, you should *have* **taken** my **a** not	4272
2Co	8:10	And here is my **a** about what is best for you	1191

ADVISABLE (1) [ADVISE]

1Co	16: 4	If *it seems* a for me to go also,	545+1639

ADVISE (5) [ADVICE, ADVISABLE, ADVISED, ADVISER, ADVISERS]

2Sa	17:11	"So *I* a you: Let all Israel,	3619
1Ki	1:12	let me a you how you can save	3619+6783
	12: 6	*would* you a me to answer these people?"	3619
2Ch	10: 6	"How *would* you a me	3619
Ac	5:38	Therefore, in the present case *I* a you:	3306

ADVISED (5) [ADVISE]

2Sa	17:15	"Ahithophel *has* a Absalom and the elders	3619
	17:15	but I *have* a them to do so and so.	3619
	17:21	Ahithophel *has* a such and such	3619
1Ki	20:23	the officials of the king of Aram a him,	606
Jn	18:14	Caiaphas was the one who *had* a the Jews	5205

ADVISER (3) [ADVISE]

Ge	26:26	with Ahuzzath his **personal** a and Phicol	5335
1Ki	4: 5	a priest and **personal** a *to* the king;	8291
2Ch	25:16	"Have we appointed you an a to the king?	3446

ADVISERS (20) [ADVISE]

2Sa	8:18	and David's sons were **royal** a.	3913
2Ki	25:19	of the fighting men and five royal a.	7156+8011
2Ch		after his father's death they became his a,	3446
	25:17	Amaziah king of Judah **consulted** his a,	3619
Ezr	7:14	You are sent by the king and his seven a	10325
	7:15	that the king and his a have freely given to	10325
	7:28	to me before the king and his a and all	3446
	8:25	the articles that the king, his a, his officials	3446
Est	6:13	His a and his wife Zeresh said to him,	2682
Job	12:20	the lips of **trusted** a and takes away	586
Pr	11:14	but many a make victory sure.	3446
	15:22	but with many a they succeed.	3446
	24: 6	and for victory many a.	3446
Jer	52:25	and seven royal a.	7156+8011
Da	3: 2	prefects, governors, a, treasurers, judges,	10011
	3: 3	So the satraps, prefects, governors, a,	10011
	3:24	to his feet in amazement and asked his a,	10196
	3:27	and royal a crowded around them.	10196
	4:36	My a and nobles sought me out,	10196
	6: 7	a and governors have all agreed that	10196

ADVOCATE (1) [ADVOCATING]

Job	16:19	my witness is in heaven; my a is on high.	8446

ADVOCATING (2) [ADVOCATE]

Ac	16:21	by a customs unlawful for us Romans	2859
	17:18	"He seems to be a foreign gods."	2858

AENEAS (3)

Ac	9:33	There he found a man named A,	138
	9:34	"A," Peter said to him,	138
	9:34	Immediately A got up.	NIG

AENON (1)

Jn	3:23	John also was baptizing at A near Salim,	143

AFAR (16) [FAR]

Job	36: 3	I get my knowledge from a;	8158
	36:25	men gaze on it from a.	8158
	39:25	He catches the scent of battle from a,	8158
	39:29	his eyes detect it from a.	8158
Ps	138: 6	but the proud he knows from a.	5305
	139: 2	you perceive my thoughts from a.	8158
Pr	31:14	bringing her food from a.	5305
Isa	10: 3	when disaster comes from a?	5305
	30:27	the Name of the LORD comes from a,	5305
	33:17	and view a land that **stretches** a.	5305
	43: 6	from a and my daughters from the ends of	8158
	49:12	See, they will come from a—	8158
	60: 4	your sons come from a,	8158
	60: 9	bringing your sons from a,	8158
Jer	50:26	Come against her from a.	7891
Hab	1: 8	their horsemen come from a.	8158

AFFAIR (2) [AFFAIRS]

Nu	25:18	when they deceived you in the a *of* Peor	1821
1Sa	22:15	at all about this whole a."	1821

AFFAIRS (12) [AFFAIR]

1Ch	26:32	to God and for the a *of* the king.	1821
Ne	11:24	was the king's agent in all a relating to	1821
Ps	112: 5	who conducts his a with justice.	1821
Pr	31:27	She watches over the a *of* her household	2142
Da	3:12	over the a *of* the province of Babylon—	10525
	6: 4	in his conduct of **government** a,	10424
1Co	7:32	concerned about the Lord's a—	3836
	7:33	But a married man is concerned about **the** a	3836
	7:34	or virgin is concerned about the Lord's a:	3836
	7:34	a married woman is concerned about **the** a	3836
1Ti	5:17	the a of the church well are worthy	NIG
2Ti	2: 4	as a soldier gets involved in **civilian** a	1050+4548

AFFECT (1) [AFFECTED, AFFECTS]

Job	35: 6	If you sin, how *does* that a him?	7188

AFFECTED (3) [AFFECT]

Lev	13:50	and isolate the **a article** for seven days.	5596
	13:55	After the **a article** has been washed,	5596
	13:55	the mildew has a one side or the other.	928

AFFECTION (6)

Dt	7: 7	The LORD *did* not **set** his a on you	3137
	10:15	the LORD **set** his a on your forefathers	3137
Eze	24:21	delight of your eyes, the object of your a.	5883
2Co	6:12	We are not withholding our a from you,	5073
	7:15	And his a for you is all the greater	5073
Php	1: 8	for all of you with the a of Christ Jesus.	5073

AFFECTS (1) [AFFECT]

Job	35: 8	Your wickedness a only a man	4200

AFFINITY (KJV) See ALLIANCE, ALLIED BY MARRIAGE, INTERMARRY

AFFIRM (1) [REAFFIRM]

1Ti	1: 7	about or what *they* so **confidently** a.	1331

AFFIXING (1) [FIX]

Ne	9:38	our Levites and our priests *are* a their **seals**	3159

AFFLICT (6) [AFFLICTED, AFFLICTING, AFFLICTION, AFFLICTIONS]

Lev	26:24	be hostile toward you and *will* a you	5782
Dt	28:27	The LORD *will* a you with the boils	5782
	28:28	The LORD *will* a you with madness,	5782
	28:35	The LORD *will* a your knees and legs	5782
Ps	55:19	will hear them and a them—	6700
Na	1:12	[O Judah,] *I will* a you no more.	6700

AFFLICTED (45) [AFFLICT]

Dt	29:22	with which the LORD *has* a it.	2703
Jos	24: 5	and *I* a the Egyptians by what I did there,	5597
Jdg	2:18	under those who oppressed and a them.	1895
Ru	1:21	The LORD *has* a me;	6700
1Sa	5: 6	upon them and a them with tumors.	5782
	5: 9	*He* a the people of the city,	5782
	5:12	Those who did not die *were* a with tumors,	5782
1Ki	8:35	from their sin because *you have* a them,	6700
2Ki	15: 5	The LORD a the king *with* leprosy until	5595
	17:20	*he* a them and gave them into the hands	6700
2Ch	6:26	from their sin because *you have* a them,	6700
	16:12	of his reign Asa *was* a with a disease	2688
	21:18	the LORD a Jehoram with	5597
	26:20	because the LORD *had* a him.	5595
Job	2: 7	and a Job with painful sores from the soles	5782
	30:11	that God has unstrung my bow and a me,	6700
	36: 6	the wicked alive but gives the a their rights.	6714
Ps	9:12	he does not ignore the cry of the a.	6705
	9:18	nor the hope of the a ever perish.	6705+6714
	10:17	You hear, O LORD, the desire of the a;	6705
	22:24	or disdained the suffering of the a *one*;	6714
	25:16	for I am lonely and a.	6714
	34: 2	let the a hear and rejoice.	6705
	72: 2	your a *ones* with justice.	6714
	72: 4	He will defend the a *among* the people	6714
	72:12	the a who have no one to help.	6714
	74:19	the lives of your a *people* forever.	6714
	76: 9	to save all the a *of* the land.	6705
	88:15	From my youth I have been a and close	6714
	90:15	for as many days as you have a us,	6700
	102: T	A prayer of an a *man*.	6714
	116:10	I believed; therefore I said, "I *am* greatly a."	6700
	119:67	Before *I was* a I went astray,	6700
	119:71	*to be* a so that I might learn your decrees.	6700
	119:75	and in faithfulness *you have* a me.	6700
Isa	1: 5	your whole heart. a	1868
	14:32	and in her his a people will find refuge."	6714
	49:13	and will have compassion on his a *ones*.	6714
	51:21	Therefore hear this, you a *one*,	6714
	53: 4	smitten by him, and a.	6700
	53: 7	He was oppressed and a,	6700
	54:11	"O a city, lashed by storms and	6714
Jer	14:19	Why *have you* a us so that we cannot	5782
Na	1:12	Although *I have* a you, [O Judah,]	6700
Zec	11:11	and so the a *of* the flock	6714

AFFLICTING (1) [AFFLICT]

2Sa	24:16	and said to the angel who *was* a the people,	8845

AFFLICTION (21) [AFFLICT]

Dt	16: 3	of a, because you left Egypt in haste—	6715
Job	10:15	I am full of shame and drowned in my a.	6715
	36: 8	held fast by cords of a,	6715
	36:15	he speaks to them in their a.	4316
	36:21	which you seem to prefer to a.	6715
Ps	25:18	Look upon my a and my distress	6715
	31: 7	for you saw my a and knew the anguish	6715
	31:10	my strength fails because of my a,	6411
	107:17	and **suffered** a because of their iniquities.	6700
	107:41	of their a and increased their families	6715
	119:92	I would have perished in my a.	6715
Ecc	5:17	with great frustration, a and anger.	2716
Isa	30:20	of a, your teachers will be hidden no more;	4316
	48:10	I have tested you in the furnace of a.	6715
La	1: 3	After a and harsh labor,	6715

La	1: 7	In the days of her a	6715
	1: 9	"Look, O LORD, on my a,	6715
	3: 1	I am the man who has seen a by the rod	6715
	3:19	I remember my a and my wandering,	6715
	3:33	not willingly **bring** a or grief to the children	6700
Ro	12:12	Be joyful in hope, patient *in* a,	2568

AFFLICTIONS (5) [AFFLICT]

Lev	26:21	I will multiply your a seven times over,	4804
1Ki	8:38	each one aware of the a *of* his own heart,	5596
2Ch	6:29	each one aware of his a and pains,	5596
Col	1:24	in regard to Christ's a,	2568
Rev	2: 9	I know your a and your poverty—	2568

AFFORD (9) [AFFORDED]

Lev	5: 7	" 'If he cannot a a lamb,	1896+3338+5595
	5:11	he cannot a two doves	3338+5952
	12: 8	If she cannot a a lamb,	1896+3338+5162
	14:21	"If, however, he is poor and cannot a these,	3338+5952
	14:22	which he can a,	3338+5952
	14:30	which the person can a,	3338+5952
	14:32	an infectious skin disease and who cannot a	3338+5952
	27: 8	what the man making the vow can a.	3338+5952
Nu	6:21	in addition to whatever else he can a.	3338+5952

AFFORDED (2) [AFFORD]

Ro	7: 8	the opportunity a by the commandment,	1328
	7:11	the opportunity a by the commandment,	1328

AFFRIGHT (KJV) See TERRIFY

AFIRE (1) [FIRE]

Dt	32:22	and its harvests and **set** a the foundations of	4265

AFLAME (1) [FLAME]

Isa	13: 8	at each other, their faces a.	4258

AFOOT (1) [FOOT]

Ac	14: 5	There was a **plot** a among the Gentiles	3995

AFOREHAND (KJV) See BEFOREHAND

AFORETHOUGHT (5) [THINK]

Nu	35:20	If anyone with **malice** a shoves another	8534
Dt	4:42	if he had unintentionally killed his neighbor without **malice** a.	4946+8533+8997+9453
	19: 4	one who kills his neighbor unintentionally, without **malice** a.	4946+8533+8997+9453
	19: 6	he did it to his neighbor without **malice** a.	4946+8533+8997+9453
Jos	20: 5	and without **malice** a.	4946+8533+8997+9453

AFRAID (211) [FEAR]

Ge	3:10	and *I was* a because I was naked; so I hid."	3707
	15: 1	"Do not be a, Abram.	3707
	18:15	Sarah *was* a, so she lied and said,	3707
	19:30	for he was a to stay in Zoar.	3707
	20: 8	they *were* very much a.	3707
	21:17	*Do* not *be* a,	3707
	26: 7	"She is my sister," because *he was* a to say,	3707
	26:24	*Do* not *be* a, for I am with you;	3707
	28:17	*He was* a and said,	3707
	31:31	Jacob answered Laban, "*I was* a,	3707
	32:11	for *I am* a he will come and attack me,	3707
	35:17	"Don't *be* a, for you have another son."	3707
	42: 4	he was a that harm might come to him.	606S
	43:23	"Don't *be* a.	3707
	46: 3	"*Do* not *be* a to go down to Egypt,	3707
	50:19	But Joseph said to them, "Don't *be* a.	3707
	50:21	So then, don't *be* a.	3707
Ex	2:14	Then Moses *was* a and thought,	3707
	3: 6	because *he was* a to look at God.	3707
	14:13	Moses answered the people, "*Do* not *be* a.	3707
	20:20	Moses said to the people, "*Do* not *be* a.	3707
	34:30	and *they were* a to come near him.	3707
Lev	26: 6	down and no *one* will **make** you a.	3006
Nu	12: 8	not a to speak against my servant Moses?"	3707
	14: 9	And *do* not *be* a *of* the people of the land,	3707
	14: 9	*Do* not *be* a of them."	3707
	21:34	"*Do* not *be* a of him,	3707
Dt	1:17	*Do* not *be* a of any man,	1593
	1:21	*Do* not *be* a; do not be discouraged."	3707
	1:29	*do* not *be* a of them.	3707
	2: 4	*They* will *be* a of you, but be very careful.	3707
	3: 2	"*Do* not *be* a of him,	3707
	3:22	*Do* not *be* a of them,	3707
	5: 5	because *you were* a of the fire and did	3707
	7:18	But *do* not *be* a of them;	3707
	13:11	Then all Israel will hear and *be* a,	3707
	17:13	All the people will hear and *be* a,	3707
	18:22	*Do* not *be* a of him.	1593
	19:20	of the people will hear of this and *be* a,	3707
	20: 1	*do* not *be* a of them,	3707
	20: 3	*Do* not *be* fainthearted or a;	3707
	20: 8	"Is any man a or fainthearted?"	3710
	21:21	All Israel will hear of it and *be* a.	3707
	31: 6	*Do* not *be* a or terrified because of them,	3707
	31: 8	*Do* not *be* a; do not be discouraged."	3707

Ref		Text	Strong's
Jos	8:1	the LORD said to Joshua, "Do not be a;	3707
	10:8	"Do not be a of them;	3707
	10:25	Joshua said to them, "Do not be a;	3707
	11:6	"Do not be a of them,	3707
Jdg	4:18	Don't be a."	3707
	6:23	Do not be a.	3707
	6:27	because he was a of his family and the men	3707
	7:10	If you are a to attack,	3710
	8:20	because he was only a boy and was a.	3707
	9:21	because he was a of his brother Abimelech.	NIH
Ru	3:11	And now, my daughter, don't be a.	3707
1Sa	3:15	He was a to tell Eli the vision,	3707
	4:7	the Philistines were a.	3707
	7:7	they were a because of the Philistines.	3707
	12:20	"Do not be a," Samuel replied.	3707
	15:24	I was a of the people and so I gave in	3707
	18:12	Saul was a of David,	3707
	18:15	he was a of him.	1593
	18:29	Saul became still more a of him,	3707
	21:12	and was very much a of Achish king	3707
	22:23	Stay with me; don't be a;	3707
	23:3	"Here in Judah we are a.	3710
	23:17	"Don't be a," he said.	3707
	28:5	Saul saw the Philistine army, he was a;	3707
	28:13	The king said to her, "Don't be a.	3707
2Sa	1:14	"Why were you not a to lift your hand	3707
	3:11	because he was a of him.	3707
	6:9	David was a of the LORD that day	3707
	9:7	"Don't be a," David said to him,	3707
	10:19	So the Arameans were a to help	3707
	12:18	David's servants were a to tell him that	3707
	13:28	Don't be a.	3707
	14:15	because the people have made me a.	3707
1Ki	1:51	"Adonijah is a of King Solomon	3707
	17:13	Elijah said to her, "Don't be a.	3707
	19:3	Elijah was a and ran for his life.	3707
2Ki	1:15	do not be a of him."	3707
	6:16	"Don't be a," the prophet answered.	3707
	19:6	Do not be a of what you have heard—	3707
	25:24	"Do not be a of the Babylonian officials,"	3707
1Ch	13:12	David was a of God that day and asked,	1286
	21:30	because he was a of the sword of the angel	1286
	22:13	Do not be a or discouraged.	3707
	28:20	Do not be a or discouraged,	3707
2Ch	20:15	'Do not be a or discouraged because	3707
	20:17	Do not be a; do not be discouraged.	3707
	32:7	not be a or discouraged because of the king	3707
	32:18	make them in order to capture the city.	987
Ezr	4:4	and make them to go on building.	987
Ne	2:2	I was very much a,	3707
	4:14	"Don't be a of them.	3707
	6:16	all the surrounding nations were a	3707
Est	9:2	of all the other nationalities were a of them.	5877+6584+7065
Job	6:21	you see something dreadful and are a.	3707
	11:19	with no one to make you a,	3006
	39:22	He laughs at fear, a of nothing;	3169
Ps	27:1	of whom shall I be a?	7064
	56:3	When I am a, I will trust in you.	3707
	56:4	I will not be a.	3707
	56:11	I will not be a.	3707
	118:6	The LORD is with me; I will not be a.	7064
Pr	3:24	you will not be a;	7064
Ecc	9:2	so with those who are a to take them.	3707
	12:5	when men are a of heights and of dangers in	3707
Isa	7:4	'Be careful, keep calm and don't be a.	3707
	10:24	do not be a of the Assyrians,	3707
	12:2	I will trust and not be a.	7064
	17:2	with no one to make them a.	3006
	20:5	in Cush and boasted in Egypt will be a	3169
	37:6	Do not be a of what you have heard—	3707
	40:9	lift it up, do not be a;	3707
	41:14	Do not be a, O worm Jacob, O little Israel,	3707
	43:5	Do not be a, for I am with you;	3707
	44:2	Do not be a, O Jacob, my servant,	3707
	44:8	Do not tremble, do not be a.	3724
	54:4	"Do not be a; you will not suffer shame.	3707
Jer	1:8	Do not be a of them,	3707
	23:4	and they will no longer be a or terrified,	3707
	30:10	and no one will make him a.	3006
	38:19	I am a of the Jews who have gone over to	1793
	40:9	"Do not be a to serve the Babylonians,"	3707
	41:18	They were a of them because Ishmael son	3707
	42:11	Do not be a of the king of Babylon,	3707
	42:11	Do not be a of him, declares the LORD,	3707
	46:27	and no one will make him a.	3006
	51:46	or be a when rumors are heard in the land;	3707
Eze	2:6	do not be a of them or their words.	3707
	2:6	Do not be a,	3707
	2:6	be a of what they say or terrified by them,	3707
	3:9	Do not be a or terrified by them,	3707
	34:28	and no one will make them a.	3006
	39:26	in their land with no one to make them a.	3006
Da	1:10	"I am a of my lord the king,	3710
	4:5	I had a dream that made me a.	10167
	10:12	Then he continued, "Do not be a, Daniel.	3707
	10:19	"Do not be a, O man highly esteemed,"	3707
Joel	2:21	Be not a, O land; be glad and rejoice.	3707
	2:22	Be not a, O wild animals,	3707
Jnh	1:5	All the sailors were a and each cried out	3707
Mic	4:4	and no one will make them a,	3006
	7:17	the LORD our God and will be a of you.	3707
Zep	3:13	lie down and no one will make them a."	3006
Zec	8:13	Do not be a, but let your hands be strong.	3707
	8:15	Do not be a.	3707
Mt	1:20	not be a to take Mary home as your wife,	5828
	2:22	he was a to go there.	5828
Mt	8:26	"You of little faith, why are you so a?"	1264
	10:26	"So do not be a of them.	5828
	10:28	Do not be a of those who kill the body	5828
	10:28	be a of the One who can destroy both soul	5828
	10:31	So don't be a;	5828
	14:5	but he was a of the people,	5828
	14:27	Don't be a."	5828
	14:30	But when he saw the wind, he was a and,	5828
	17:7	"Don't be a."	5828
	21:26	we are a of the people,	5828
	21:46	but they were a of the crowd because	5828
	25:25	I was a and went out	5828
	28:4	so a of him that they shook and became	5832
	28:5	The angel said to the women, "Do not be a,	5828
	28:8	a yet filled with joy,	3552+5832
	28:10	Then Jesus said to them, "Do not be a.	5828
Mk	4:40	"Why are you so a?	1264
	5:15	and they were a.	5828
	5:36	Don't be a; just believe."	5828
	6:50	Don't be a."	5828
	9:32	not understand what he meant and were a	5828
	10:32	while those who followed were a.	5828
	12:12	But they were a of the crowd;	5828
	16:8	because they were a.	5828
Lk	1:13	"Do not be a, Zechariah;	5828
	1:30	But the angel said to her, "Do not be a,	5828
	2:10	But the angel said to them, "Do not be a,	5828
	5:10	Then Jesus said to Simon, "Don't be a;	5828
	8:35	and they were a.	5828
	8:50	Jesus said to Jairus, "Don't be a;	5828
	9:34	and they were a as they entered the cloud.	5828
	9:45	and they were a to ask him about it.	5828
	12:4	do not be a of those who kill the body and	5828
	12:7	of your head are all numbered. Don't be a;	5828
	12:32	"Do not be a, little flock,	5828
	19:21	I was a of you,	5828
	20:19	But they were a of the people.	5828
	22:2	for they were a of the people,	5828
Jn	6:20	But he said to them, "It is I; don't be a."	5828
	9:22	His parents said this because they were a of	5828
	12:15	"Do not be a, O Daughter of Zion;	5828
	14:27	be troubled and do not be a.	1262
	19:8	he was even more a,	5828
Ac	9:26	but they were all a of him,	5828
	18:9	"Do not be a;	5828
	23:10	the commander was a Paul would be torn	5828
	24:25	Felix was a and said,	1873
	27:24	'Do not be a, Paul.	5828
Ro	11:20	Do not be arrogant, but be a.	5828
	13:4	But if you do wrong, be a,	5828
2Co	11:3	But I am a that just as Eve was deceived	5828
	12:20	For I am a that when I come I may	5828
	12:21	I am a that when I come again	NIG
Gal	2:12	because he was a of those who belonged	5828
1Th	3:5	I was a that in some way	NIG
Heb	11:23	and they were not a of the king's edict.	5828
	13:6	I will not be a.	5828
2Pe	2:10	not a to slander celestial beings;	5554
Rev	1:17	"Do not be a.	5828
	2:10	not be a of what you are about to suffer.	5828

AFRESH (KJV) See ALL OVER AGAIN

AFTER (723) [AFTERWARD]

Ref		Text	Strong's
Ge	3:24	A he drove the man out,	2256
	4:17	and he named it a his son Enoch.	3869
	5:4	A Seth was born,	339
	5:7	And a he became the father of Enosh,	339
	5:10	And a he became the father of Kenan,	339
	5:13	And a he became the father of Mahalalel,	339
	5:16	And a he became the father of Jared,	339
	5:19	And a he became the father of Enoch,	339
	5:22	And a he became the father of Methuselah,	339
	5:26	And a he became the father of Lamech,	339
	5:30	A Noah was born,	339
	5:32	A Noah was 500 years old,	2256
	7:10	And a the seven days the floodwaters came	4200
	8:6	a forty days Noah opened	4946+7891
	8:19	came out of the ark, one kind a another.	2157+4200+5476
	9:9	with you and with your descendants a you	339
	9:28	A the flood Noah lived 350 years.	339
	10:1	who themselves had sons a the flood.	339
	10:32	the nations spread out over the earth a	339
	11:10	Two years a the flood,	339
	11:11	And a he became the father of Arphaxad,	339
	11:13	And a he became the father of Shelah,	339
	11:15	And a he became the father of Eber,	339
	11:17	And a he became the father of Peleg,	339
	11:19	And a he became the father of Reu,	339
	11:21	And a he became the father of Serug,	339
	11:23	And a he became the father of Nahor,	339
	11:25	And a he became the father of Terah,	339
	11:32	A Terah had lived 70 years,	2256
	13:14	to Abram a Lot had parted from him,	339
	14:17	A Abram returned from defeating	339
	15:1	A this, the word of the LORD came	339
	16:3	So a Abram had been living	4946+7891
	17:7	and you and your descendants a you for	339
	17:7	and the God of your descendants a you.	339
	17:8	to you and your descendants a you;	339
	17:9	you and your descendants a you for	339
	17:10	with you and your descendants a you,	339
	17:19	for his descendants a him.	339
	18:12	"A I am worn out and my master is old,	339
Ge	18:19	and his household a him to keep the way of	339
	21:32	A the treaty had been made at Beersheba,	2256
	24:19	A she had given him a drink, she said,	3983
	24:67	Isaac was comforted a his mother's death.	339
	25:11	A Abraham's death, God blessed his son	339
	25:26	A this, his brother came out,	339
	26:18	which the Philistines had stopped up a	339
	27:30	A Isaac finished blessing him	889+3869
	29:14	A Jacob had stayed with him for	2256
	30:25	A Rachel gave birth to Joseph,	889+3869
	31:33	A he came out of Leah's tent,	2256
	31:54	A they had eaten,	2256
	32:23	A he had sent them across the stream,	2256
	33:18	A Jacob came from Paddan Aram,	928
	35:9	A Jacob returned from Paddan Aram,	928
	35:12	to your descendants a you."	339
	37:17	So Joseph went a his brothers	339
	37:27	A all, he is our brother,	3954
	38:12	A a long time Judah's wife,	2256
	38:19	A she left, she took off her veil and put	2256
	38:23	A all, I did send her this young goat,	2180
	39:7	and a a while his master's wife took notice	339+465+1821+2021+2021
	39:10	And though she spoke to Joseph day a day,	AIT
	40:4	A they had been in custody for some time,	2256
	41:3	A them, seven other cows, ugly and gaunt,	339
	41:6	A them, seven other heads	339
	41:19	A them, seven other cows came up—	339
	41:21	But even a they ate them,	2256
	41:23	A them, seven other heads sprouted—	339
	42:25	A this was done for them,	2256
	43:31	A he had washed his face, he came out and,	2256
	44:4	"Go a those men at once,	339
	47:7	A Jacob blessed Pharaoh,	2256
	48:4	to your descendants a you.'	339
	48:6	Any children born to you a them will	339
	50:14	A burying his father,	339
	50:26	And a they embalmed him,	2256
Ex	2:11	One day, a Moses had grown up,	2256
	3:20	A that, he will let you go.	339
	7:25	Seven days passed a the LORD struck	339
	8:12	A Moses and Aaron left Pharaoh,	2256
	10:5	They will devour that little you have left a	4946
	10:15	They devoured all that was left a the hail—	NIH
	11:1	A that, he will let you go from here,	339
	11:8	A that I will leave."	339
	12:44	Any slave you have bought may eat of it a	255
	13:10	at the appointed time year a year.	2025
	13:11	"A the LORD brings you into the land of	3954
	13:20	A leaving Succoth they camped at Etham	2256
	14:10	and there were the Egyptians, marching a	339
	14:17	of the Egyptians so that they will go in a	339
	16:1	on the fifteenth day of the second month a	NIH
	18:2	A Moses had sent away his wife Zipporah,	2256
	19:1	the third month a the Israelites left Egypt—	NIH
	19:2	A they set out from Rephidim,	2256
	19:14	A Moses had gone down the mountain to	2256
	21:21	to be punished if the slave gets up a a day	NIH
	22:3	but if it happens a sunrise,	AIT
	28:41	A you put these clothes	2256
	29:26	A you take the breast of the ram	2256
	36:3	to bring freewill offerings morning a	928
Lev	13:7	But if the rash does spread in his skin a	339
	13:35	But if the itch does spread in the skin a	339
	13:55	A the affected article has been washed,	339
	13:56	the mildew has faded a	339
	14:8	A this he may come into the camp,	339
	14:19	A that, the priest shall slaughter	339
	14:36	A this the priest is to go in and inspect	339
	14:43	in the house a the stones have been torn out	339
	14:48	not spread a the house has been plastered,	339
	15:28	and a that she will be ceremonially clean.	339
	16:1	The LORD spoke to Moses a the death of	339
	22:7	and a that he may eat the sacred offerings,	339
	23:11	to wave it on the day a the Sabbath.	4740
	23:15	" 'From the day a the Sabbath,	4740
	23:16	up to the day a the seventh Sabbath,	4740
	23:39	a you have gathered the crops of the land,	928
	24:8	the LORD regularly, Sabbath a Sabbath,	928+928+2021+2021+3427+3427+8701+8701
	25:29	the right of redemption a full year a	6330
	25:48	of redemption a he has sold himself.	339
	26:18	" 'If a all this you will not listen to me,	6330
	27:18	But if he dedicates his field a the Jubilee,	339
Nu	1:1	of the second year a the Israelites came out	4200
	4:15	"A Aaron and his sons have finished	339+4027
	5:18	A the priest has had the woman stand	2256
	5:26	a that, he is to have the woman drink	339
	6:19	" 'A the Nazirite has shaved off the hair	339
	6:20	A that, the Nazirite may drink wine.	339
	7:88	the dedication of the altar a it was anointed.	339
	8:12	"A the Levites lay their hands on the heads	2256
	8:15	"A you have purified the Levites	339+4027
	8:22	A that, the Levites came to do their work at	339
	9:1	the second year a they came out of Egypt.	4200
	12:14	a that she can be brought back."	339
	12:16	A that, the people left Hazeroth	339
	15:2	'A you enter the land I am giving you as	3954
	15:39	and not prostitute yourselves by going a	339
	19:7	A that, the priest must wash his clothes	2256
	21:32	A Moses had sent spies to Jazer,	2256
	26:1	A the plague the LORD said to Moses	339
	27:13	A you have seen it,	2256
	30:6	"If she marries a she makes a vow or	2256
	30:6	"If she marries after she makes a vow or a	NIH
	30:15	he nullifies them some time a he hears	339
	31:2	A that, you will be gathered	339

Ref	Text	No.
Nu 32: 9	A they went up to the Valley of Eshcol	2256
32:42	and called it Nobah a himself.	928
33: 3	the **day** a the Passover.	4740
33:38	of the fortieth year a the Israelites came out	4200
35:28	only a the death of the high priest	339
Dt 1: 4	This was a he had defeated Sihon king of	339
1: 8	and to their descendants a them."	339
3:14	it was named a him,	6584
3:20	A **that,** each of you may go back to	2256
4: 9	to your children and to their children a	NIH
4:25	A you have had children and grandchildren	3954
4:37	and chose their descendants a them,	339
4:40	with you and your children a you and	339
6: 2	and their children a them may fear	NIH
9: 4	a the LORD your God has driven them out	928
12:25	with you and your children a you,	339
12:28	with you and your children a you,	339
12:30	and a they have been destroyed before you,	339
16:13	the Feast of Tabernacles for seven days a	928
21:13	a she has lived in your house	339+4027
22:13	If a man takes a wife and, a lying with her,	2256
24: 2	**and** if a she leaves his house she becomes	2256
24: 4	to marry her again a she has been defiled.	339
24: 9	to Miriam along the way a you came out	928
28:29	**day** a **day** you will be oppressed	2021+3427+3972
28:32	watching for them **day** a **day,**	2021+3427+3972
31:24	A Moses finished writing in a book	3869
31:27	how much more will you rebel a I die!	339
31:29	For I know that a my death you are sure	339
Jos 1: 1	A the death of Moses the servant of	339
1:15	A **that,** you may go back	2256
2: 5	Go a them quickly.	339
3: 2	A three days the officers went	4946+7895
5: 4	in the desert on the way a leaving Egypt.	928
5: 8	a the whole nation had been circumcised,	889+3869
5:11	The **day** a the Passover, that very day,	4740
5:12	the **day** a they ate this food from the land;	4740
7:25	and a they had stoned the rest,	2256
8:17	in Ai or Bethel who did not go a Israel.	339
9:16	Three days a they made the treaty with	339
10: 9	A an all-night march from Gilgal,	2256
14:15	(Hebron used to be called Kiriath Arba a	NIH
18: 6	A you have written descriptions of	2256
19:47	settled in Leshem and named it Dan a	3869+9005
23: 1	A a long time had passed and	339
24:20	a he has been good to you."	339
24:29	A these things, Joshua son of Nun,	339
Jdg 1: 1	A the death of Joshua,	339
1: 9	A **that,** the men of Judah went down	339
2: 6	A Joshua had dismissed the Israelites,	2256
2:10	A that whole generation had been gathered	1685+2256
3:18	A Ehud had presented the tribute,	889+3869
3:22	Even the handle sank in a the blade,	339
3:24	A he had gone,	2256
3:31	A Ehud came Shamgar son of Anath,	339
4: 1	A Ehud died, the Israelites once again did evil in the eyes of the LORD.	339
5:15	rushing a him into the valley.	928+8079
7:19	**just** a they had changed the guard.	421
9:22	A Abimelech had governed Israel three years,	2256
9:27	A they had gone out into the fields	2256
10: 1	A **the time of** Abimelech a man of Issachar,	339
11:39	A the two months,	4946+7891
12: 8	A him, Ibzan of Bethlehem led Israel.	339
12:11	A him, Elon the Zebulunite led Israel	339
12:13	A him, Abdon son of Hillel, from Pirathon,	339
16:16	With such nagging she prodded him **day** a **day**	2021+3427+3972
16:22	the hair on his head began to grow again a it had been shaved.	889+3869
18:23	As they shouted a them,	448
18:29	named it Dan a their forefather Dan,	928+9005
19: 2	A she had been there four months,	2256
19:21	A they had washed their feet,	2256
20: 5	During the night the men of Gibeah came a	6584
20:45	They kept pressing a the Benjamites as far	339
Ru 1: 4	A they had lived there about ten years,	2256
2: 9	and follow along a the girls.	339
2:18	and gave her what she had left over a	4946
3:10	You have not run a the younger men,	339
1Sa 1: 3	Year a year this man went up	2025
1: 7	This went on year a year.	928
1:22	"A the boy is weaned,	6330
1:24	A he was weaned,	889+3869
5: 1	A the Philistines had captured the ark	2256
5: 9	But a they had moved it,	339
7: 2	of Israel mourned and sought a the LORD.	339
8: 3	They turned aside a dishonest gain	339
9:25	A they came down from the high place to	2256
10: 5	"A that you will go to Gibeah of God,	339
10:13	A Saul stopped prophesying,	2256
12: 8	"A Jacob entered Egypt,	889+3869
12:21	Do not turn away a useless idols.	339
13:14	the LORD has sought out a man a	3869
14:12	"Climb up a me;	339
14:31	a the Israelites had struck down	2256
14:36	"Let us go down a the Philistines by night	339
14:37	"Shall I go down a the Philistines?	339
14:47	A Saul had assumed rule over Israel,	2256
17:35	I went a it, struck it and rescued the sheep	339
17:51	A he killed him,	2256
18: 1	A David had finished talking with Saul,	3869
18: 6	When the men were returning home a	928
20: 5	until the evening of the **day** a **tomorrow.**	8958

Ref	Text	No.
1Sa 20:12	by this time the **day** a tomorrow!	8958
20:19	The **day** a **tomorrow,** toward evening,	8992
20:37	Jonathan called out a him,	339
20:41	the boy a him,	NIH
23:14	**Day** a **day** Saul searched for him,	2021+3427+3972
24: 1	A Saul returned from pursuing	889+3869
31: 2	The Philistines **pressed hard** a Saul	1815
2Sa 1: 1	A the death of Saul, David returned	339
1:10	that a he had fallen he could not survive.	339
3:26	Joab then left David and sent messengers a	339
4: 7	A they stabbed and killed him,	2256
5:13	A he left Hebron,	339
6:18	A he had finished sacrificing	2256
7: 1	A the king was settled in his palace and	3954
8:13	And David became famous a he returned	928
10:15	A the Arameans saw	2256
11: 8	and a gift from the king was sent a him.	339
12:15	A Nathan had gone home,	2256
12:20	A he had washed,	2256
12:28	and it will be named a me."	6584
13: 4	look so haggard morning a morning?	928
13:17	of here and bolt the door a her.	339
13:18	and bolted the door a her.	339
13:38	A Absalom fled and went to Geshur,	2256
17:21	A the men had gone,	339
18:18	He named the pillar a himself,	6584
20:13	A Amasa had been removed from the road,	889+3869
21:12	where the Philistines had hung them a	928+3427
21:14	A **that,** God answered prayer in behalf of	339
23: 4	the brightness a rain that brings the grass	4946
24: 5	A crossing the Jordan,	2256
24: 8	A they had gone through the entire land,	2256
24:10	David was conscience-stricken a	339+4027
1Ki 1: 6	also very handsome and was born **next** a	339
1:13	"Surely Solomon your son shall be king a	339
1:17	'Solomon your son shall be king a me,	339
1:20	on the throne of my lord the king a him.	339
1:24	declared that Adonijah shall be king a you,	339
1:27	on the throne of my lord the king a him?"	339
1:30	Solomon your son shall be king a me,	339
1:40	And all the people went up a him,	339
2:22	a all, he is my older brother—	3954
3:18	The third day a my child was born,	4200
5:11	to do this for Hiram year a year.	928
6: 1	In the four hundred and eightieth year a	4200
8: 9	the Israelites a they came out of Egypt.	928
9:24	A Pharaoh's daughter had come up from	421
10:25	Year a year, everyone who came	928+1821
11: 2	because they will surely turn your hearts a	339
11: 4	his wives turned his heart a other gods,	339
12:16	**Look** a your own house, O David!"	8011
12:28	A seeking advice, the king made two golden calves.	2256
13:14	and rode a the man of God.	339
13:31	A burying him, he said to his sons,	339
13:33	Even a this, Jeroboam did	339
16:24	calling it Samaria, a Shemer,	6584
18: 1	A a long time, in the third year,	2256
19:11	A the wind there was an earthquake,	339
19:12	A the earthquake came a fire,	339
19:12	A the fire came a gentle whisper.	339
19:20	Elisha then left his oxen and ran a Elijah.	339
20:36	**And** a the man went away,	2256
21:26	He behaved in the vilest manner by going a	339
22:46	male shrine prostitutes who remained there **even** a the reign of his father Asa.	928
2Ki 1: 1	A Ahab's death, Moab rebelled	339
3: 5	But a Ahab died, the king of Moab rebelled	3869
3: 9	A a roundabout march of seven days,	2256
4:20	A the servant had lifted him up	2256
5:19	A Naaman had traveled some distance,	2256
5:20	I will run a him and get something	339
5:21	So Gehazi hurried a Naaman.	339
6: 8	A conferring with his officers, he said,	2256
6:20	A they entered the city, Elisha said,	3869
6:23	**and** a they had finished eating	2256
7:14	the king sent them a the Aramean army.	339
10:15	A he left there,	2256
14: 5	A the kingdom was firmly in his grasp,	889+3869
14:17	for fifteen years a the death of Jehoash son	339
14:19	but they sent men a him to Lachish	339
14:22	to Judah a Amaziah rested with his fathers.	339
18: 5	either before him or a him.	339
23:25	Neither before nor a Josiah was there	339
1Ch 2:24	A Hezron died in Caleb Ephrathah,	339
6:31	of the LORD a the ark came to rest there.	4946
8: 8	Sons were born to Shaharaim in Moab a	4946
10: 2	The Philistines **pressed hard** a Saul	339
12:19	a consultation, their rulers sent him away.	928
12:22	**Day** a day men came to help David,	928
15: 1	A David had constructed buildings	2256
16: 2	A David had finished sacrificing	2256
16:23	proclaim his salvation day a day.	448
17: 1	A David was settled in his palace,	889+3869
19:16	A the Arameans saw that they had been	2256
2Ch 1:12	before you ever had and none a	339
2:17	a the census his father David had taken;	339
5:10	the Israelites a they came out of Egypt.	928
9:24	Year a year, everyone who came	928+1821
10:16	**Look** a your own house, O David!"	8011
12: 1	A Rehoboam's position	3869
20: 1	A this, the Moabites and Ammonites	339
20:21	A consulting the people,	2256
20:23	A they finished slaughtering the men	3869

Ref	Text	No.
2Ch 20:36	A these were built at Ezion Geber,	2256
21:18	A all this, the LORD afflicted Jehoram	339
22: 4	as the house of Ahab had done, for a	339
24:17	A the death of Jehoiada,	339
25: 3	A the kingdom was firmly in his control	889+3869
25:17	A Amaziah king of Judah	2256
25:25	for fifteen years a the death of Jehoash son	339
25:27	but they sent men a him to Lachish	339
26: 2	to Judah a Amaziah rested with his fathers.	339
26:16	But a Uzziah became powerful,	3869
31: 1	A they had destroyed all of them,	6330
32: 1	A all that Hezekiah had so faithfully done,	339
35:14	**A this,** they made preparations	339
35:20	A all this, when Josiah had set the temple	339
Ezr 3: 5	A that, they presented the regular burnt offerings,	339
3: 8	the second year a their arrival at the house	4200
7: 1	A these things, during the reign	339
9: 1	A these things had been done,	3869
9:10	now, O our God, what can we say a this?	339
Ne 2:11	**and** a staying there three days	2256
4:14	A I looked things over,	339
7: 1	A the wall had been rebuilt	889+3869
8:18	**Day** a **day,** from the first day to the last,	928
9:28	in your compassion you delivered them **time** a **time.**	6961+8041
Est 3: 1	A these events, King Xerxes honored Haman son of Hammedatha,	339
3: 4	**Day** a **day** they spoke to him but he refused	2256
Job 3: 1	A this, Job opened his mouth and cursed	339
5: 5	and the thirsty **pant** a his wealth.	AIT
10: 6	and probe a my sin—	4200
13:25	*Will you **chase** a dry chaff?*	8103
19:26	And a my skin has been destroyed,	339
21: 3	and a I have spoken, mock on.	339
21:33	all men follow a him,	339
29:22	A I had spoken, they spoke no more;	339
31: 5	in falsehood or my foot has hurried a	6584
37: 4	A that comes the sound of his roar;	339
37:21	the skies a the wind has swept them clean.	2256
42: 7	A the LORD had said these things to Job,	339
42:10	A Job had prayed for his friends,	928
42:16	A this, Job lived a hundred and forty years;	339
Ps 16: 4	of those will increase *who* **run** a other gods.	4554
19: 2	**Day** a day they pour forth speech;	4200
19: 2	night a night they display knowledge.	4200
49:11	though they had named lands a themselves.	928
51: T	the prophet Nathan came to him a	889+3869
61: 8	to your name and fulfill my vows **day** a	AIT
68:25	a them the musicians;	339
78:38	**Time** a **time** he restrained his anger and did	8049
96: 2	proclaim his salvation day a day.	4200
Pr 1:19	all who **go** a ill-gotten gain;	1298+1299
6:25	**lust** in your heart a	2773
8:30	I was filled with delight **day** a day,	AIT
20: 7	blessed are his children a him.	339
24:27	A **that,** build your house.	339
27:18	*he who* **looks** a his master will be honored.	9068
29: 1	A man who remains stiff-necked a	NIH
Ecc 1:14	a chasing the wind.	8296
1:17	too, is a **chasing** a the wind.	8301
2:11	a **chasing** a the wind.	8296
2:17	a **chasing** a the wind.	8296
2:18	to the one who comes a me.	339
2:26	a **chasing** a the wind.	8296
3:22	to see what will happen a him?	339
4: 4	a **chasing** a the wind.	8296
4: 6	with toil and **chasing** a the wind.	8296
4:16	a **chasing** a the wind.	8301
6: 9	a **chasing** a the wind.	8296
6:12	under the sun a he is gone?	339
10:14	can tell him what will happen a him?	339+4200
11: 1	for a many days you will find it again.	928
12: 2	and the clouds return a the rain;	339
Isa 1:23	they all love bribes and **chase** a gifts.	8103
5:11	in the morning *to* **run** a their drinks,	8103
21: 8	And the lookout shouted, "**Day** a day,	3429+9458
24:13	gleanings are left a the grape harvest.	561+3983
24:22	up in prison and be punished a many days.	4946
28:19	morning a morning, by day and by night,	928
38: 9	of Hezekiah king of Judah a his illness	928
43:10	nor will there be one a me.	339
53:11	A the suffering of his soul,	4946
58: 2	For **day** a day they seek me out;	AIT
62:12	and you will be called **Sought A,**	2011
64:12	A all this, O LORD,	6584
Jer 2:23	I have not run a the Baals'?	339
2:25	I love foreign gods, and I must go a them.'	339
3: 7	I thought that a she had done all this	339
3:15	I will give you shepherds a my own heart,	3869
7:25	until now, **day** a **day,** again	3427
12:15	But a I uproot them,	339
13:10	of their hearts and go a other gods to serve	339
16:16	A that I will send for many hunters,	339
21: 7	A that, declares the LORD,	339
25:26	near and far, one a the other—	448
25:26	And a all of them,	339
28:12	**Shortly** a the prophet Hananiah had broken the yoke off the neck of the prophet	339
29: 2	(This was a King Jehoiachin and	339
31:19	A I strayed, I repented.	339
31:19	A I came to understand, I beat my breast.	339
31:33	with the house of Israel a that time,"	339
32:16	"A I had given the deed of purchase	339
32:18	into the laps of their children a them.	339
32:39	and the good of their children a them.	339

Jer	34: 8	the LORD a King Zedekiah had made	339
	34:14	A he has served you six years,	2256
	36:13	A Micaiah told them everything he had heard	2256
	36:20	A they put the scroll in the room	2256
	36:27	A the king burned the scroll containing	339
	37:11	A the Babylonian army had withdrawn	928
	39:12	"Take him and look a him;	6524+6584+8492
	40: 1	the LORD a Nebuzaradan commander of	339
	40: 4	if you like, and I will look a you	6524+6584+8492
	41: 4	The day a Gedaliah's assassination,	9108
	41:16	from Ishmael son of Nethaniah a	339
	45: 1	a Baruch had written on a scroll	339
La	1: 3	A affliction and harsh labor,	4946
Eze	4: 6	"A you have finished this, lie down again,	2256
	6: 9	which have lusted a their idols.	339+2388
	15: 4	And a it is thrown on the fire as fuel and	NIH
	16:28	A even a that, you still were not satisfied.	2256
	16:34	runs a you for your favors.	339+2388
	20:24	and their eyes [lusted] a their fathers' idols.	339
	20:30	the way your fathers did and lust a	339+2388
	23: 5	she lusted a her lovers, the Assyrians	6311+6584
	23: 7	with all the idols of everyone she lusted a.	6311
	23:12	She too lusted a the Assyrians—	448+6311
	23:16	she lusted a them and sent messengers	6311+6584
	23:17	A she had been defiled by them,	2256
	23:20	There she lusted a her lovers,	6311+6584
	23:30	because you lusted a the nations	339+2388
	34:11	for my sheep and look a them.	1329
	34:12	As a shepherd looks a his scattered flock	1333
	34:12	so will I look a my sheep.	1329
	38: 8	A many days you will be called to arms.	4946
	40: 1	the fourteenth year A the fall of the city—	339
	44:10	from me a their idols must bear	339
	44:26	A he is cleansed, he must wait seven days.	339
	46:12	he shall go out, and a he has gone out,	339
	48:31	the city will be named a the tribes of Israel.	6584
Da	1: 5	a that they were to enter the king's service.	4946+7921
	2:39	"A you, another kingdom will rise,	10092
	4: 8	a the name of my god,	10341
	7: 6	"A that, I looked, and there	10092
	7: 7	"A that, in my vision at night I looked,	10092
	7:24	A them another king will arise,	10021
	8: 1	a the one that had already appeared to me.	339
	9:26	A the sixty-two 'sevens,'	339
	11: 4	A he has appeared,	3869
	11: 6	A some years, they will become allies.	4200+7891
	11:13	and a several years,	4200+7891
	11:19	A this, he will turn back toward	2256
	11:23	A coming to an agreement with him,	4946
Hos	1: 8	A she had weaned Lo-Ruhamah,	2256
	2: 5	She said, 'I will go a my lovers,	339
	2: 7	She will chase a her lovers but	8103
	2:13	and went a her lovers, but me she forgot,"	339
	6: 2	A two days he will revive us;	4946
Am	7: 1	He was preparing swarms of locusts a	339
Jnh	1: 3	A paying the fare,	2256
Zec	2: 8	"A he has honored me and has sent me	339
	14:16	go up year a year to worship the King,	928+1896+4946
Mt	1:12	A the exile to Babylon:	3552
	1:20	But a he had considered this,	AIT
	2: 1	A Jesus was born in Bethlehem in Judea,	AIT
	2: 9	A they had heard the king,	AIT
	2:19	A Herod died, an angel of	AIT
	3:11	a me will come one who is more powerful	3958
	4: 2	A fasting forty days and forty nights,	AIT
	6:32	For the pagans run a all these things,	2118
	9:25	A the crowd had been put outside,	4021
	11: 1	A Jesus had finished instructing his twelve disciples,	4021
	14:23	A he had dismissed them,	AIT
	15:23	for she keeps crying out a us."	3957
	15:39	A Jesus had sent the crowd away,	AIT
	16:24	"If anyone would come a me,	3958
	17: 1	A six days Jesus took with him Peter,	3552
	17:24	A Jesus and his disciples arrived	AIT
	21:32	And even a you saw this,	AIT
	24:29	"Immediately a the distress of those days	3552
	25:19	"A a long time the master	3552
	25:36	I was sick and you looked a me,	2170
	25:43	and in prison and you did not look a me."	2170
	26:22	began to say to him one a the other,	1651+1667
	26:32	But a I have risen, I will go ahead of you	3552
	26:73	A a little while, those standing there went	3552
	27:31	A they had mocked him,	4021
	27:34	but a tasting it, he refused to drink it.	AIT
	27:53	and a Jesus' resurrection they went into	3552
	27:62	The next day, the one a Preparation Day,	3552
	27:63	'A three days I will rise again.'	3552
	28: 1	A the Sabbath, at dawn on the first day of the week,	4067+4879
Mk	1: 7	"A me will come one more powerful than I,	3958
	1:14	A John was put in prison,	3552
	1:32	That evening a sunset the people brought	4021
	2: 4	a digging through it,	AIT
	5:40	A he put them all out,	AIT
	6:46	A leaving them, he went up on	AIT
	7:17	A he had left the crowd and entered	4021
	7:33	A he took him aside, away from	AIT
	8:31	be killed and a three days rise again.	3552
	8:34	"If anyone would come a me,	3958
	9: 2	A six days Jesus took Peter,	3552
	9:28	A Jesus had gone indoors,	AIT
	9:31	and a three days he will rise."	3552
	14:28	But a I have risen, I will go ahead of you	3552
	14:70	A a little while, those standing near said	3552

Mk	16: 2	on the first day of the week, just a sunrise,	422+2463+3836
	16:14	those who had seen him a he had risen.	AIT
	16:19	A the Lord Jesus had spoken to them,	3552
Lk	1:24	A this his wife Elizabeth became pregnant	3552
	1:59	to name him a his father Zechariah,	2093
	2:36	with her husband seven years a	608
	2:43	A the Feast was over,	AIT
	2:46	A three days they found him in	3552
	5:27	A this, Jesus went out and saw	3552
	5:39	no one a drinking old wine wants the new,	AIT
	7:24	A John's messengers left,	AIT
	8: 1	A this, Jesus traveled about	1877+2759+3836
	8: 4	to Jesus from town a town,	2848
	9:23	"If anyone would come a me,	3958
	9:28	About eight days a Jesus said this,	3552
	10: 1	A this the Lord appointed seventy-two	3552
	10:35	'Look a him,' he said, 'and when I return,	2150
	12: 4	be afraid of those who kill the body and a	3552
	12: 5	Fear him who, a the killing of the body,	3552
	12:30	For the pagan world runs a all such things,	2118
	15: 4	in the open country and go a the lost sheep	2093
	15:13	"Not long a that, the younger son	3552
	15:14	A he had spent everything,	AIT
	17: 7	a servant plowing or looking a the sheep.	4477
	17: 8	a that you may eat and drink'?	3552
	17:23	Do not go running off a them.	599+1503+3593
	19:14	and sent a delegation a him to say,	3958
	19:28	A Jesus had said this, he went on ahead,	AIT
	22:17	A taking the cup, he gave thanks and said,	AIT
	22:20	a the supper he took the cup, saying,	3552
Jn	1:15	'He who comes a me has surpassed me	3958
	1:16	of his grace we have all received one blessing a another.	505
	1:27	He is the one who comes a me,	3958
	1:30	'A man who comes a me has surpassed me	3958
	2:10	and then the cheaper wine a	4020
	2:12	A this he went down to Capernaum	3552
	2:22	A he was raised from the dead,	4021
	3:22	A this, Jesus and his disciples went out into	3552
	4:43	the two days he left for Galilee.	3552
	6: 1	Some time a this, Jesus crossed to	3552
	6:14	the people saw the miraculous sign	AIT
	6:23	a the Lord had given thanks.	AIT
	7: 1	A this, Jesus went around in Galilee,	3552
	7:10	a his brothers had left for the Feast,	6055
	11:11	A he had said this, he went on to tell them,	3552
	11:28	And a she had said this,	AIT
	12:16	Only a Jesus was glorified did they realize	4021+5538
	12:19	how the whole world has gone a him!"	3958
	12:37	a Jesus had done all these miraculous signs	AIT
	13: 5	A that, he poured water into a basin	1663
	13:21	A he had said this, Jesus was troubled	AIT
	14: 9	a I have been among you such a long time?	NIG
	16:16	and then a little while you will see me,"	4099
	16:17	and then a little while you will see me,'	4099
	16:19	and then a a little while you will see me"?	4099
	17: 1	A Jesus said this, he looked toward heaven	NIG
	20:20	A he said this, he showed them his hands	AIT
	21:14	to his disciples a he was raised from	AIT
Ac	1: 2	a giving instructions through	AIT
	1: 3	A his suffering, he showed himself	3552
	1: 9	A he said this, he was taken up	AIT
	4:21	A further threats they let them go.	AIT
	4:31	A they prayed, the place	AIT
	5: 4	And a it was sold,	AIT
	5:37	A him, Judas the Galilean appeared in	3552
	5:42	Day a day, in the temple courts and	2465+4246
	7: 4	A the death of his father,	3552
	7: 5	and his descendants a him would possess	3552
	7: 8	and circumcised him eight days a his birth.	NIG
	7:14	A this, Joseph sent for his father Jacob	1254
	7:30	"A forty years had passed,	4444
	9:19	and a taking some food,	AIT
	9:23	A many days had gone by,	6055
	10:37	beginning in Galilee a the baptism	3552
	10:41	by us who ate and drank with him a he rose	3552
	12: 4	A arresting him, he put him in prison,	AIT
	12: 4	to bring him out for public trial a	3552
	12:19	A Herod had a thorough search made for	AIT
	13: 3	a they had fasted and prayed,	AIT
	13:15	A the reading from the Law and	3552
	13:20	"A this, God gave them judges until	3552
	13:22	A removing Saul, he made David their king.	AIT
	13:22	'I have found David son of Jesse a man a	2848
	13:25	No, but he is coming a me,	3552
	14:20	a the disciples had gathered around	AIT
	14:24	A going through Pisidia,	AIT
	15: 7	A much discussion, Peter got up	NIG
	15:16	" 'A this I will return	3552
	15:33	A spending some time there,	AIT
	16:10	A Paul had seen the vision,	6055
	16:23	A they had been severely flogged,	AIT
	16:40	A Paul and Silas came out	AIT
	18: 1	A this, Paul left Athens and went	3552
	18:23	A spending some time in Antioch,	AIT
	19: 4	the people to believe in the one coming a	3552
	19:21	A all this had happened,	6055
	19:21	"A I have been there," he said,	3552
	19:41	A he had said this,	AIT
	20: 1	for the disciples and, a encouraging them,	AIT
	20: 6	But we sailed from Philippi a the Feast	3552
	20:11	A talking until daylight, he left.	AIT
	20:15	The day a that we crossed over to Samos,	2283
	20:29	I know that a I leave,	3552
	20:30	the truth in order to draw away disciples a	3958

Ac	21: 1	A we had torn ourselves away	AIT
	21: 3	A sighting Cyprus and passing to the south	AIT
	21: 6	A saying good-by to each other,	AIT
	21:10	A we had been there a number of days	AIT
	21:15	A this, we got ready and went up	3552
	24:17	"A an absence of several years,	1328
	25: 1	Three days a arriving in the province,	3552
	25: 6	A spending eight or ten days with them,	AIT
	25:12	A Festus had conferred with	AIT
	27: 9	because by now it was a the Fast.	4216
	27:21	A the men had gone	AIT
	27:35	A he said this, he took some bread	AIT
	28: 6	but a waiting a long time	AIT
	28: 8	Paul went in to see him and, a prayer,	AIT
	28:11	A three months we put out to sea in a ship	3552
	28:25	a Paul had made this final statement:	AIT
Ro	4:10	Was it a he was circumcised,	1639+1877+4364
	4:10	It was not a, but before!	NIG
	11:24	A all, if you were cut out of an olive tree	1142
	15:24	I have enjoyed your company for a while.	4754
	15:28	So a I have completed this task	AIT
1Co	3: 5	What, a all, is Apollos?	4036
	9:27	so that a I have preached to others,	AIT
	11:25	same way, a supper he took the cup,	3552+3836
	15: 6	A that, he appeared to more	2083
	15:24	the Father a he has destroyed all dominion,	4020
	15:46	but the natural, and a that the spiritual.	2083
	16: 5	A I go through Macedonia,	4020
2Co	12:14	A all, children should not have to save	1142
Gal	1:18	Then a three years, I went up to Jerusalem	3552
	3: 3	A beginning with the Spirit,	AIT
Eph	5:29	A all, no one ever hated his own body,	1142
	6:13	and a you have done everything, to stand.	AIT
Col	4:16	A this letter has been read to you,	4020
1Th	4:17	A that, we who are still alive	2083
Tit	3:10	A that, have nothing to do with him.	3552
Heb	1: 3	A he had provided purification for sins,	AIT
	6:15	A waiting patiently,	AIT
	7:27	not need to offer sacrifices day a day,	2465+2848
	7:28	but the oath, which came a the law,	3552
	8:10	with the house of Israel a that time,	3552
	9:27	and a that to face judgment,	3552
	10: 1	same sacrifices repeated endlessly year a year,	1929+2848
	10:11	Day a day every priest stands	2465+2848
	10:16	the covenant I will make with them a	3552
	10:26	If we deliberately keep on sinning a	3552+3836
	10:32	a you had received the light,	AIT
	11:23	for three months a he was born,	AIT
	11:30	a the people had marched around	AIT
Jas	1:15	A desire has conceived, it gives birth to sin;	AIT
	1:24	a looking at himself, goes away	AIT
	1:27	to look a orphans and widows	2170
1Pe	5:10	a you have suffered a little while,	AIT
2Pe	1:15	that a my departure you will always be able	3552
	2: 8	living among them day a day,	1666
Rev	1:19	A this I looked, and there before me	3552
	4: 1	and I will show you what must take place a	3552
	7: 1	A this I saw four angels standing at	3552
	7: 9	A this I looked and there before me was	3552
	11:11	But a the three and a half days a breath	3552
	15: 5	A this I looked and in heaven the temple,	3552
	18: 1	A this I saw another angel coming down	3552
	19: 1	A this I heard what sounded like the roar of	3552
	20: 3	A that, he must be set free for a short time.	3552

AFTERBIRTH (1)

Dt	28:57	the a from her womb and	8953

AFTERNOON (5)

Jdg	19: 8	Wait till a!"	2021+3427+5742
Lk	9:12	Late in the a the Twelve came	806+2465+3111
Ac	3: 1	the time of prayer—at three in the a.	1888
	10: 3	at about three in the a he had a vision.	1888+2465+3836+6052
	10:30	at three in the a.	1888

AFTERWARD (36) [AFTER]

Ge	6: 4	in those days—and also a—	339+4027
	15:14	and a they will come out	339+4027
	23:19	A Abraham buried his wife Sarah in	339+4027
	41:27	ugly cows that came up a are seven years,	339
	45:15	A his brothers talked with him.	339+4027
Ex	5: 1	A Moses and Aaron went to Pharaoh	339
	32: 6	A they sat down to eat and drink and got up	2256
	34:32	A all the Israelites came near him,	339+4027
Lev	16:26	a he may come into the camp.	339+4027
	16:28	a he may come into the camp.	339+4026
Jos	8:34	A, Joshua read all the words of the law	339+4027
Jdg	7:11	A, you will be encouraged to attack	339
	19: 6	A the girl's father said,	2256
1Sa	9:13	a, those who are invited will eat.	339+4027
	24: 5	A, David was conscience-stricken	339+4027
1Ki	17: 1	and a they returned them to the guardroom.	2256
	20:22	A, the prophet came to the king of Israel	2256
2Ki	4: 5	She left him and a shut the door behind her	2256
2Ch	12:11	and a they returned them to the guardroom.	2256
	33:14	A he rebuilt the outer wall of the City	339+4027
Est	2: 1	A Mordecai returned to the king's gate.	2256
Ps	73:24	and a you will take me into glory.	339
Ecc	9: 3	and a they join the dead.	339
Isa	1:26	a you will be called the City	339+4027
Jer	34:11	But a they changed their minds	339+4027
	49: 6	"Yet a, I will restore the fortunes of	339+4027
Eze	20:39	But a you will surely listen to me	339

Hos	3: 5	A the Israelites will return and seek	339
Joel	2:28	a, I will pour out my Spirit on all people.	339+4027
Mt	15:37	A the disciples picked up seven basketfuls	2779
Mk	8: 8	A the disciples picked up seven basketfuls	2779
	16:12	A Jesus appeared in a different form to two	3552+4047
Lk	7:11	Soon a, Jesus went to a town called Nain,	1877+2009+3836
Jn	21: 1	A Jesus appeared again to his disciples	3552+4047
Ac	7: 7	a they will come out of that country	3552+4047
Heb	12:17	A, as you know, when he wanted	3575

AGABUS (2)

| Ac | 11:28 | One of them, named A, | 13 |
| | 21:10 | a prophet named A came down from Judea. | 13 |

AGAG (7) [AGAGITE]

Nu	24: 7	"Their king will be greater than A;	97
1Sa	15: 8	He took A king of the Amalekites alive,	97
	15: 9	the army spared A and the best of the sheep	97
	15:20	and brought back A their king.	97
	15:32	"Bring me A king of the Amalekites."	97
	15:32	A came to him confidently, thinking,	97
	15:33	And Samuel put A to death before	97

AGAGITE (5) [AGAG]

Est	3: 1	the A, elevating him and giving him a seat	98
	3:10	the A, the enemy of the Jews.	98
	8: 3	an end to the evil plan of Haman the A,	98
	8: 5	of Hammedatha, the A, devised and wrote	98
	9:24	For Haman son of Hammedatha, the A,	98

AGAIN (459)

Ge	4:25	Adam lay with his wife a,	6388
	8:10	He waited seven more days and a sent out	3578
	8:12	and sent the dove out a,	6388
	8:21	"Never a will I curse the ground	3578+6388
	8:21	And never a will I destroy all living creatures,	3578+6388
	9:11	Never a will all life be cut off by the waters	6388
	9:11	never a will there be a flood to destroy	6388
	9:15	Never a will the waters become a flood	6388
	18:27	Then Abraham spoke up:	NIH
	18:29	Once a he spoke to him,	3578+6388
	19:34	Let's get him to drink wine a tonight,	1685
	19:35	A he was not aware of it when she lay	2256
	20:17	so they could have children a,	NIH
	23:12	A Abraham bowed down before the people	2256
	24:16	filled her jar and came up a.	AIT
	29:33	She conceived a, and when she gave birth	6388
	29:34	A she conceived, and when she gave birth	6388
	29:35	She conceived a, and when she gave birth	6388
	30: 7	Rachel's servant Bilhah conceived a	6388
	30:19	Leah conceived a and bore Jacob	6388
	35: 9	God appeared to him a and blessed him.	6388
	35:21	Israel moved on a and pitched his tent	2256
	38: 4	She conceived a and gave birth to a son	6388
	38:19	and put on her widow's clothes a.	2256
	38:26	And he did not sleep with her a.	3578+6388
	40:21	he once a put the cup into Pharaoh's hand,	AIT
	41: 5	He fell asleep a and had a second dream:	2256
	42:24	but then turned back and spoke to them a.	NIH
	43: 3	not see my face a unless your brother is	NIH
	43: 5	not see my face a unless your brother is	NIH
	44:23	you will not see my face a.'	3578
	46: 4	And I will surely bring you back a.	1685
	48:11	"I never expected to see your face a,	NIH
Ex	8:29	that Pharaoh does not act deceitfully a by	3578
	9:34	and thunder had stopped, he sinned a;	3578
	10:14	nor will there ever be a.	339
	10:28	Make sure you do not appear before me a!	3578
	10:29	"I will never appear before you a."	3578+6388
	11: 6	has ever been or ever will be a.	3578
	14:13	The Egyptians you see today you will never see a.	3578+6388
	30: 8	He must burn incense a when he lights	2256
Lev	13: 6	to examine him a, and if the sore has faded	9108
	13: 7	he must appear before the priest a,	9108
	13:58	must be washed a, and it will be clean."	9108
	27:15	and the house will a become his.	AIT
	27:19	and the field will a become his.	AIT
Nu	11: 4	and a the Israelites started wailing and said,	8740
	11:25	they prophesied, but they did not do so a.	3578
	18: 5	that wrath will not fall on the Israelites a.	6388
	20:20	A they answered: "You may	2256
	22:25	So he beat her a.	3578
	32:15	he will a leave all this people in	3578+6388
Dt	9:18	once a I fell prostrate before	2021+3869+8037
	9:19	But a the LORD listened to me.	928+1685+2021+2021+2085+7193
	13:11	among you will do such an evil thing a.	3578
	17:13	and will not be contemptuous a.	6388
	17:16	"You are not to go back that way a."	3578+6388
	19:20	and never a will such an evil thing be done	3578+6388
	24: 4	to marry her a after she has been defiled.	8740
	24:21	go over the vines a.	339+6618
	28:68	a journey I said you a from all the nations	3578+6388
	30: 3	and gather you a from all the nations	8740
	30: 8	You will a obey the LORD	8740
	30: 9	The LORD will a delight in you	8740
Jos	5: 2	and circumcise the Israelites a."	8740+9108

Jos	24:10	blessed you a and again,	1385+1385
	24:10	blessed you again and a,	1385+1385
Jdg	3:12	Once a the Israelites did evil in the eyes of	3578
	3:15	the Israelites cried out to the LORD,	2256
	4: 1	the Israelites once a did evil in the eyes of	3578
	6: 1	A the Israelites did evil in the eyes of	2256
	8:28	the Israelites and did not raise its head a.	3578
	8:33	the Israelites a prostituted themselves to	8740
	9:37	But Gaal spoke up a:	3578+6388
	10: 6	A the Israelites did evil in the eyes of	3578
	13: 1	A the Israelites did evil in the eyes of	3578
	13: 8	let the man of God you sent to us come a	6388
	13: 9	and the angel of God came a to the woman	6388
	13:21	of the LORD did not show himself a	3578+6388
	16:14	A she called to him, "Samson,	2256
	16:22	But the hair on his head began to grow a	AIT
	20:22	and took up their positions	3578
	20:23	up a to battle against the Benjamites,	3578
	20:28	a to battle with Benjamin our brother,	3578+6388
Ru	1:14	At this they wept a.	6388
1Sa	3: 6	A the LORD called, "Samuel!"	3578+6388
	7:13	and did not invade Israelite territory a.	3578+6388
	9: 8	The servant answered him a.	3578
	15:35	he did not go to see Saul a,	3578
	20:27	David's place was empty a.	2256
	23: 4	Once a David inquired of the LORD,	3578+6388
	23:12	A David asked, "Will the citizens	2256
	26:21	I will not try to harm you a.	6388
2Sa	2:22	A Abner warned Asahel, "Stop chasing me!	3578+6388
	3:34	And all the people wept over him a.	3578
	6: 1	David brought together out	3578
	12:23	Can I bring him back a?	6388
	14:10	and he will not bother you a."	3578+6388
	15:25	and let me see it and his dwelling place a.	NIH
	18:22	Ahimaaz son of Zadok a said to Joab,	3578+6388
	20:10	Without being stabbed a, Amasa died.	9101
	21:15	Once a there was a battle between	6388
	21:17	"Never a will you go out with us to battle,	6388
	24: 1	A the anger of the LORD burned	3578
1Ki	10:10	Never a so many spices brought in	6388
	12:24	the word of the LORD and went home a,	8740
	12:27	a will a give their allegiance	4213+8740
	18:34	"Do it a," he said, and they did it again.	9101
	18:34	"Do it again," he said, and they did it a.	9101
	18:37	that you are turning their hearts back a."	NIH
	19: 6	He ate and drank and then lay down a.	8740
	20: 5	The messengers came a and said,	8740
	20:22	the king of Aram will attack you a."	NIH
2Ki	2:21	Never a will it cause death or make	6388
	5:17	servant will never a make burnt offerings	6388
	6:10	Time and a Elisha warned the king,	285+2256+4202+4202+9109
	19: 9	So he a sent messengers to Hezekiah	8740
	21: 8	not a make the feet of the Israelites wander	3578
	24: 7	not march out from his own country a,	3578+6388
1Ch	7:23	Then he lay with his wife a,	NIH
	14:14	so David inquired of God a,	6388
2Ch	19: 4	and he went out among the people	8740
	28:17	The Edomites had a come	6388
	33: 8	not a make the feet of the Israelites leave	3578
	36:15	through his messengers again and a,	2256+8899+8938
	36:15	through his messengers again and a,	2256+8899+8938
Ezr	9:14	Shall we a break your commands	8740
Ne	9:28	they a did what was evil in your sight.	8740
	9:28	And when they cried out to you a,	8740
	13:21	If you do this a, I will lay hands on you."	9101
Est	1:19	that Vashti is never a to enter the presence	NIH
	5: 6	the king a asked Esther,	2256
	7: 2	the king a asked, "Queen Esther,	1685
	8: 3	Esther a pleaded with the king,	3578
Job	7: 7	my eyes will never see happiness a.	8740
	7:10	He will never come to his house a.	6388
	10: 9	turn me to dust a?	8740
	10:16	a lion and a display your awesome power	8740
	14: 7	If it is cut down, it will sprout a,	6388
	14:14	If a man dies, will he live a?	2649
	16:14	A and again he bursts upon me	7287+7288+7288
	16:14	Again and a he bursts upon me	7287+7288+7288
	17:10	"But come on, all of you, try a!	8740
	20: 9	The eye that saw him will not see him a;	3578
	34:32	if I have done wrong, I will not do so a.'	3578
	41: 8	the struggle and never do it a!	3578
Ps	3: 5	the LORD made him prosperous a	8654+8740
	3: 5	I wake a, because the LORD sustains me.	NIH
	28: 5	down and never build them up a.	AIT
	39:13	that I may rejoice a before I depart	AIT
	71:20	many and bitter, you will restore my life a;	8740
	71:20	of the earth you will a bring me up.	8740
	71:21	and comfort me once a.	6015
	77: 7	Will he never show his favor a?	3578+6388
	78:34	they eagerly turned to him a.	8740
	78:41	A and again they put God to the test;	8740
	78:41	Again and a they put God to the test;	8740
	85: 4	Restore us a, O God our Savior,	8740
	85: 6	Will you not revive us a,	8740
	94:15	Judgment will a be founded	8740
	104: 9	never a will they cover the earth.	8740
Pr	19:19	you will have to do it a.	3578+6388
	24:16	he rises a, but the wicked are brought	2256
Ecc	1: 7	there they return a.	8740
	1: 9	What has been will be a,	AIT
	1: 9	what has been done will be done a;	AIT
	4: 1	A I looked and saw all the oppression	8740
	4: 7	A I saw something meaningless under	8740

Ecc	9: 6	never a will they have a part in anything	6388
	11: 1	for after many days you will find it a.	AIT
SS	5: 3	must I put it on a?	NIH
	5: 3	must I soil them a?	NIH
Isa	6:13	it will a be laid waste.	8740
	7:10	A the LORD spoke to Ahaz,	3578
	8: 5	The LORD spoke to me a:	3578+6388
	14: 1	once a he will choose Israel	6388
	14:20	wicked will never be mentioned a.	4200+6409
	21:12	and come back yet a."	8740
	24:20	never to rise a.	3578
	34:10	ever pass through it a.	4200+5905+5905
	38:11	I said, "I will not a see the LORD,	NIH
	43:17	and they lay there, never to rise a,	AIT
	51:22	you will never drink a.	6388
	52: 1	and defiled will not enter you a.	3578+6388
	54: 9	the waters of Noah would never a cover	6388
	54: 9	never to rebuke you a.	NIH
	60:20	Your sun will never set a,	6388
	62: 8	"Never a will I give your grain as food	6388
	62: 8	and never a will foreigners drink	NIH
	65:20	"Never a will there be in it	6388
Jer	1:13	The word of the LORD came to me a:	9108
	2: 9	"Therefore I bring charges against you a,"	6388
	3: 1	should he return to her a?	6388
	6: 9	pass your hand over the branches a,	8740
	7:13	I spoke to you a and again,	8899
	7:13	I spoke to you again and a,	8899
	7:25	a and again I sent you my servants	8899
	7:25	again and a I sent you my servants	8899
	11: 7	I warned them a and again, saying,	8899
	11: 7	I warned them again and a, saying,	8899
	12:15	I will a have compassion	8740
	22:10	nor see his native land a."	NIH
	22:12	he will not see this land a."	6388
	23:36	not mention 'the oracle of the LORD' a,	6388
	25: 3	and I have spoken to you a and again,	8899
	25: 3	and I have spoken to you again and a,	8899
	25: 4	the prophets to you a and again,	8899
	25: 4	the prophets to you again and a,	8899
	26: 5	whom I have sent to you a and again	8899
	26: 5	whom I have sent to you again and a	8899
	29:19	"words that I sent to them a and again	8899
	29:19	"words that I sent to them again and a	8899
	30:10	Jacob will a have peace and security,	8740
	31: 4	I will build you up a and you will	6388
	31: 4	A you will take up your tambourines	6388
	31: 5	A you will plant vineyards on the hills	6388
	31:23	in its towns they will once a use these words:	6388
	31:40	The city will never a be uprooted	6388
	32:15	fields and vineyards will a be bought	6388
	32:33	though I taught them a and again,	8899
	32:33	though I taught them again and a,	8899
	33:12	in all its towns there will a be pastures	6388
	33:13	flocks will a pass under the hand of	6388
	34:11	and enslaved them a.	NIH
	34:16	to become your slaves a.	NIH
	35:14	But I have spoken to you a and again,	8899
	35:14	But I have spoken to you again and a,	8899
	35:15	A and again I sent all my servants	8899
	35:15	Again and a I sent all my servants	8899
	42:18	you will never see this place a.'	6388
	44: 4	A and again I sent my servants	8899
	44: 4	Again and a I sent my servants	8899
	44:26	in Egypt will ever a invoke my name	6388
	46:27	Jacob will a have peace and security,	8740
	50:39	It will never a be inhabited or lived in	8740
La	3: 3	against me a and again,	8740
	3: 3	against me again and a,	8740
Eze	3:19	"A, when a righteous man turns	2256
	4: 6	"After you have finished this, lie down a,	2256
	5: 4	A, take a few of these and throw them into	6388
	5: 9	before and will never do a.	6388
	8:13	A, he said, "You will see them doing things	2256
	11:17	the land of Israel a.'	NIH
	16:63	be ashamed and never a open your mouth	6388
	17:14	brought low, unable to rise a,	5951
	21: 5	it will not return a."	6388
	22:23	A the word of the LORD came to me:	2256
	24:13	you will not be clean a until my wrath	6388
	26:21	but you will never a be found,	6388
	29:15	of kingdoms and will never a exalt itself	6388
	29:15	that it will never a rule over the nations.	AIT
	36:12	you will never a deprive them	3578+6388
	36:16	A the word of the LORD came to me:	2256
	36:37	Once a I will yield to the plea of the house	6388
	37:22	and they will never a be two nations or	6388
	43: 7	of Israel will never a defile my holy name—	6388
Da	10:18	A the one who looked like	3578
	11:29	the South a, but this time the outcome will	8740
Hos	3: 1	Gomer conceived a and gave birth to	6388
	3: 1	"Go, show your love to your wife a,	6388
	12: 9	I will make you live in tents a,	6388
	14: 3	We will never a say 'Our gods'	6388
	14: 7	Men will dwell a in his shade.	8740
Joel	2:19	never a will I make you an object of scorn	6388
	2:26	never a will my people be shamed.	4200+4202+6409
	2:27	never a will my people be shamed.	4200+4202+6409
	3:17	never a will foreigners invade her.	3578
Am	5: 2	never to rise a, deserted in her own land,	3578
	8:14	they will fall, never to rise a."	6388
	8:14	never a to be uprooted from	3578
Jnh	2: 4	I will look a toward your holy temple.'	3578
Mic	1: 7	of prostitutes they will a be used."	8740
	7:19	You will a have compassion on us;	8740

Zep	3:11	Never **a** will you be haughty	3578+6388
	3:15	never **a** will you fear any harm.	6388
Zec	1:17	'My towns will **a** overflow with prosperity,	6388
	1:17	and the LORD will **a** comfort Zion	6388
	2:12	the holy land and will **a** choose Jerusalem.	6388
	4:12	**A** I asked him,	9108
	5: 1	I looked **a**—and there before me	8740
	6: 1	I looked up **a**—and there before me	8740
	7: 8	word of the LORD came **a** to Zechariah:	NIH
	8: 1	**A** the word of the LORD Almighty came	2256
	8: 4	"Once **a** men and women	6388
	8:15	"so now I have determined to do good **a**	8740
	8:18	**A** the word of the LORD Almighty came	2256
	9: 8	Never **a** will an oppressor overrun my people,	6388
	11:15	Take **a** the equipment of a foolish shepherd.	6388
	14:11	never **a** will it be destroyed.	6388
Mal	3:18	And you will **a** see the distinction between	8740
Mt	4: 8	**A**, the devil took him to	4099
	5:13	how can it be made salty **a**?	4099
	5:22	**A**, anyone who says to his brother, 'Raca,'	1254
	5:33	"**A**, you have heard that it was said to	4099
	12:29	"Or **a**, how can anyone enter	NIG
	13:44	When a man found it, he hid it **a**,	NIG
	13:45	"**A**, the kingdom of heaven is like	4099
	13:47	"Once **a**, the kingdom of heaven is like	4099
	18:19	"**A**, I tell you that if two of you	4099
	19:24	**A** I tell you, it is easier for a camel to go	4099
	20: 5	"He went out **a** about the sixth hour and	4099
	21:19	"May you never bear fruit **a**!"	172+1650+3836
	22: 1	Jesus spoke to them **a** in parables, saying,	4099
	23:39	you will not see me **a** until you say,	608+785
	24:21	never to be equaled **a**.	3590+4024
	25:14	"**A**, it will be like a man going on	NIG
	26:43	he **a** found them sleeping,	4099
	26:72	He denied it **a**, with an oath:	4099
	27:30	and struck him on the head **a** and again.	NIG
	27:30	and struck him on the head **again and a**.	NIG
	27:50	when Jesus had cried out **a** in a loud voice,	4099
	27:63	'After three days *I will* rise **a**.'	1586
Mk	2: 1	when Jesus **a** entered Capernaum,	4099
	2:13	Once **a** Jesus went out beside the lake.	4099
	3:20	and **a** crowd gathered,	4099
	4: 1	**A** Jesus began to teach by the lake.	4099
	4:30	**A** he said, "What shall we say the kingdom	2779
	5:10	And he begged Jesus **a** and again not	4498
	5:10	And he begged Jesus **again and a** not	4498
	5:21	When Jesus had **a** crossed over by boat to	4099
	7:14	**A** Jesus called the crowd to him and said,	4099
	8:31	he must be killed and after three days **rise a**.	482
	9:25	come out of him and **never** enter him **a**."	3600
	9:50	how can you make it salty **a**?	NIG
	10: 1	**A** crowds of people came to him,	4099
	10:10	When they were in the house **a**,	4099
	10:24	But Jesus said, "Children,	4099
	10:32	**A** he took the Twelve aside	4099
	11:14	"May no one ever eat fruit from you **a**."	3600
	11:27	They arrived **a** in Jerusalem,	4099
	13:19	and never to be equaled **a**.	NIG
	14:25	I will not drink **a** of the fruit of the vine	4033
	14:40	he **a** found them sleeping,	4099
	14:61	**A** the high priest asked him,	4099
	14:69	she said **a** to those standing around,	4099
	14:70	**A** he denied it.	4099
	15: 4	So **a** Pilate asked him,	4099
	15:19	*A and again they* **struck** him **on** the head	AIT
	15:19	*a they* **struck** him **on** the head with a staff	AIT
Lk	13:20	**A** he asked, "What shall I compare	4099
	13:35	you will not see me **a** until you say,	NIG
	14:34	how can it be made salty **a**?	NIG
	15:24	this son of mine was dead and *is* **alive a**;	348
	15:32	of yours was dead and *is* **alive a**;	348
	18:33	On the third day *he will* **raised a**."	482
	22:16	I will not eat it **a** until it finds fulfillment in	NIG
	22:18	For I tell you I will not drink **a** of the fruit	608+3814+3836
	23:20	Pilate appealed to them **a**.	4099
	24: 7	and on the third day **be raised a**.' "	482
Jn	1:35	The next day John was there **a** with two	4099
	2:19	and *I will* **raise** it **a** in three days."	1586
	3: 3	the kingdom of God unless he is born **a**."	540
	3: 7	'You must be born **a**.'	540
	4:13	"Everyone who drinks this water will be thirsty **a**,	4099
	5:14	"See, you are well **a**.	NIG
	6:15	withdrew **a** to a mountain by himself.	4099
	8: 2	At dawn he appeared **a** in	4099
	8: 8	**A** he stooped down and wrote on	4099
	8:12	When Jesus spoke **a** to the people, he said,	4099
	9:17	Finally they turned **a** to the blind man,	4099
	9:27	Why do you want to hear it **a**?	4099
	10: 7	Therefore Jesus said **a**, "I tell you the truth,	4099
	10:17	only to take it up **a**.	4099
	10:18	to lay it down and authority to take it up **a**.	4099
	10:19	At these words the Jews were **a** divided.	4099
	10:31	**A** the Jews picked up stones to stone him,	4099
	10:39	**A** they tried to seize him,	4099
	11:23	Jesus said to her, "Your brother *will* **rise a**."	482
	11:24	"I know *he will* **rise a** in the resurrection at	482
	12:28	"I have glorified it, and will glorify it **a**."	4099
	16:22	but I will see you **a** and you will rejoice,	4099
	18: 7	he asked them, "Who is it you want?"	4099
	18:27	**A** Peter denied it,	4099
	18:38	With this he went out **a** to the Jews	4099
	19: 3	**went** up to him *a and again*,	AIT
	19: 3	**went** up to him *again and a*,	AIT
	20:21	**A** Jesus said, "Peace be with you!	4099

Jn	20:26	his disciples were in the house **a**,	4099
	21: 1	Afterward Jesus appeared **a** to his disciples,	4099
	21:16	**A** Jesus said, "Simon son of John,	1309+4099
Ac	4:18	in **a** and commanded them not to speak	NIG
	8:39	and the eunuch did not see him **a**,	4033
	9:17	so that *you may* **see a** and be filled with	329
	9:18	and *he could* **see a**.	329
	11:10	and then it was all pulled up to heaven **a**.	4099
	17:32	"We want to hear you **a** on this subject."	4099
	20:11	he went upstairs **a** and broke bread and ate.	NIG
	20:25	the kingdom will **ever** see me **a**.	4033
	20:38	**never** see his face **a**.	4033
	27: 4	From there we put out to sea **a** and passed	NIG
	27:28	A short time later they took soundings **a**	4099
Ro	5:16	**A**, the gift of God is not like the result of	2779
	6: 9	he **cannot** die **a**;	4033
	8:15	not receive a spirit that makes you a slave **a**	4099
	10:19	**A** I ask: Did Israel not understand?	247
	11:11	**A** I ask: Did they stumble	4036
	11:23	for God is able to graft them in **a**.	4099
	15:10	**A**, it says, "Rejoice, O Gentiles,	4099
	15:11	And **a**, "Praise the Lord, all you Gentiles,	4099
	15:12	And **a**, Isaiah says, "The Root	4099
	15:15	**remind** you of them **a**,	2057
1Co	3:20	and **a**, "The Lord knows that the thoughts	4099
	7: 5	Then come together **a** so that Satan will	4099
	8:13	I will **never** eat meat **a**,	172+1650+3590+3836+4024
	14: 8	**A**, if the trumpet does not sound	2779
2Co	3: 1	to commend ourselves **a**?	4099
	5:12	not trying to commend ourselves to you **a**,	4099
	5:15	him who died for them and *was* **raised a**.	1586
	10: 7	he should consider **a** that we belong	4099
	11:23	and been exposed to death **a and again**.	4490
	11:23	and been exposed to death **again and a**.	4490
	12:21	when I come **a** my God will humble me	4099
Gal	1: 9	As we have already said, so now I say **a**:	4099
	2: 1	Fourteen years later I went up **a**.	4099
	4: 9	to be enslaved by them **all over a**?	540+4099
	4:19	for whom I am **a** in the pains of childbirth	4099
	5: 1	and do not let yourselves be burdened **a** by	4099
	5: 3	**A** I declare to every man who lets himself	4099
Php	1:26	that through my being with you **a** your joy	4099
	2:28	that when you see him **a** you may be glad	4099
	3: 1	for me to write the same things to you **a**,	NIG
	3:18	before and now say **a** even with tears,	NIG
	4: 4	I will say it **a**: Rejoice!	4099
	4:16	you sent me aid **a** and again when I was	562
	4:16	you sent me aid **again and a** when I was	1489
1Th	2:18	certainly I, Paul, did, **a** and again—	562
	2:18	certainly I, Paul, did, again and **a**—	1489
	3:10	that we may see you **a**	NIG
	4:14	that Jesus died and **rose a** and so we believe	482
Heb	1: 5	Or **a**, "I will be his Father,	4099
	1: 6	And **a**, when God brings his firstborn into	4099
	2:13	And **a**, "I will put my trust in him."	4099
	2:13	And he says, "Here am I,	4099
	4: 5	And **a** in the passage above he says,	4099
	4: 7	Therefore God **a** set a certain day,	4099
	5:12	of God's word all over **a**.	4099
	6: 1	not laying **a** the foundation of repentance	4099
	6: 6	**crucifying** the Son of God **all over a**	416
	9:25	to offer himself **a and again**,	4490
	9:25	to offer himself **again and a**,	4490
	10:11	**a and again** he offers the same sacrifices.	4490
	10:11	**again and a** he offers the same sacrifices.	4490
	10:30	"I will repay," and **a**,	4099
	11:35	received back their dead, **raised to life a**.	414
Jas	5:18	**A** he prayed, and the heavens gave rain,	4099
1Pe	1:23	*For you have been* **born a**,	335
2Pe	2:20	and Savior Jesus Christ and are **a** entangled	4099
Rev	2: 8	who died and came to life **a**.	NIG
	3:12	Never **a** will he leave it.	2285
	7:16	**Never a** will they hunger;	2285+4024
	7:16	**never a** will they thirst.	2285+4028
	10:11	"You must prophesy **a** about many peoples,	4099
	18:21	never to be found **a**.	2285
	18:22	will never be heard in you **a**.	2285
	18:22	of any trade will ever be found in you **a**.	2285
	18:22	of a millstone will never be heard in you **a**.	2285
	18:23	of a lamp will never shine in you **a**.	2285
	18:23	and bride will never be heard in you **a**.	2285
	19: 3	And **a** they shouted: "Hallelujah!	1309

AGAINST (1303)

Ge	13:13	and were sinning greatly **a** the LORD.	4200
	14: 2	**went to war** *a* Bera king of Sodom,	AIT
	14: 9	**a** Kedorlaomer king of Elam, Tidal king	907
	14: 9	four kings **a** five.	907
	16:12	be **a** everyone and everyone's hand	928
	16:12	be against everyone and everyone's hand **a**	928
	18:20	"The **outcry** *a* Sodom and Gomorrah is	AIT
	19:13	**outcry** to the LORD *a*	AIT
	20: 6	and so I have kept you from sinning **a** me.	4200
	20:16	the offense **a** you before all who are	4200
	27:41	Esau **held a grudge** *a* Jacob because of	8475
	34:30	and if they join forces **a** me and attack me,	6584
	39: 9	a wicked thing and sin **a** God?"	4200
	42:22	"Didn't I tell you not to sin **a** the boy?	928
	42:36	Everything is **a** me!"	6584
	50:15	"What if Joseph **holds a grudge** *a* us	8475
Ex	1:10	fight **a** us and leave the country."	928
	4:14	then the LORD's anger burned **a** Moses	928
	7: 5	the LORD when I stretch out my hand **a**	6584
	9:14	the full force of my plagues **a** you and	448
	9:14	and **a** your officials and your people,	928

Ex	9:17	You still set yourself **a** my people and will	928
	10:16	"I have sinned **a** the LORD your God and	4200
	10:16	against the LORD your God and **a** you.	4200
	14:25	The LORD is fighting for them **a** Egypt."	928
	14:31	the great power the LORD displayed **a**	928
	15:24	So the people grumbled **a** Moses, saying,	6584
	16: 2	the whole community grumbled **a** Moses	6584
	16: 7	he has heard your grumbling **a** him.	6584
	16: 7	that you should grumble **a** us?"	6584
	16: 8	he has heard your grumbling **a** him.	6584
	16: 8	You are not grumbling **a** us,	6584
	16: 8	but **a** the LORD."	6584
	17: 3	and they grumbled **a** Moses.	6584
	17:16	be at war **a** the Amalekites from generation	928
	19:22	or the LORD will break out **a** them."	928
	19:24	or he will break out **a** them."	928
	20:16	or give false testimony **a** your neighbor.	928
	23:21	Do not rebel **a** him;	928
	23:33	or they will cause you to sin **a** me,	4200
	24:11	not raise his hand **a** these leaders of	448
	29:16	and sprinkle it **a** the altar on all sides.	6584
	29:20	Then sprinkle blood **a** the altar on all sides.	6584
	32:10	so that my anger may burn **a** them and	928
	32:11	"why should your anger burn **a**	928
	32:29	for you were **a** your own sons and brothers,	4200
	32:33	"Whoever has sinned **a** me I will blot out	4200
Lev	1: 5	and sprinkle it **a** the altar on all sides at	6584
	1:11	the priests shall sprinkle its blood **a**	6584
	3: 2	the priests shall sprinkle the blood **a**	6584
	3: 8	Aaron's sons shall sprinkle its blood **a**	6584
	3:13	Aaron's sons shall sprinkle its blood **a**	6584
	5: 9	of the blood of the sin offering **a** the side of	6584
	5:19	he has been guilty of wrongdoing **a**	4200
	7: 2	and its blood is to be sprinkled **a** the altar	6584
	8:19	the ram and sprinkled the blood **a** the altar	6584
	8:24	he sprinkled blood **a** the altar on all sides.	6584
	9:12	and he sprinkled it **a** the altar on all sides.	6584
	9:18	and he sprinkled it **a** the altar on all sides.	6584
	17: 6	the blood **a** the altar of the LORD at	6584
	17:10	I will set my face **a** that person	928
	19:18	" 'Do not seek revenge or **bear a grudge** *a*	5757
	20: 3	I will set my face **a** that man	928
	20: 5	I will set my face **a** that man and his family	928
	20: 6	" I will set my face **a** the person who turns	928
	26:17	I will set my face **a** you so that you will	928
	26:22	I will send wild animals **a** you,	928
	26:40	their treachery **a** me and their hostility	928
Nu	5:13	(since there is no witness **a** her and she has	928
	10: 9	When you go into battle in your own land **a**	6584
	11:33	of the LORD burned **a** the people,	928
	12: 1	and Aaron began to talk **a** Moses because	928
	12: 8	not afraid to speak **a** my servant Moses?"	928
	12: 9	The anger of the LORD burned **a** them,	928
	12:11	do not hold **a** us the sin we have	6584
	14: 2	the Israelites grumbled **a** Moses and Aaron,	6584
	14: 9	Only do not rebel **a** the LORD.	928
	14:27	"How long will this wicked community grumble **a** me?	6584
	14:29	in the census and who has grumbled **a** me.	6584
	14:34	and know what it is like to have me **a** you.'	9481
	14:35	which has banded together **a** me.	6584
	14:36	and made the whole community grumble **a**	6584
	16: 2	and rose up **a** Moses.	4200+7156
	16:11	It is **a** the LORD that you	6584
	16:11	Who is Aaron that you should grumble **a**	6584
	16:41	the whole Israelite community grumbled **a**	6584
	17: 5	of this constant grumbling **a** you by	6584
	17:10	will put an end to their grumbling **a**	4946+6584
	18: 1	**responsibility for offenses** *a*	AIT
	18: 1	**responsibility for offenses** *a*	AIT
	18:23	**responsibility for offenses** *a* it.	AIT
	20:20	Then Edom came out **a** them with a large	7925
	20:24	both of you rebelled **a** my command at	907
	21: 5	they spoke **a** God and against Moses,	928
	21: 5	they spoke **a** God and a Moses,	928
	21: 7	"We sinned when we spoke **a** the LORD	928
	21: 7	when we spoke against the LORD and **a**	928
	21:23	and marched out into the desert **a** Israel.	7925
	21:26	who had fought **a** the former king of Moab	928
	22:25	crushing Balaam's foot **a** it.	448
	23:23	There is no sorcery **a** Jacob,	928
	23:23	no divination **a** Israel.	928
	24:10	Then Balak's anger burned **a** Balaam.	448
	25: 3	And the LORD's anger burned **a** them.	928
	25: 8	the plague **a** the Israelites was stopped	4946+6584
	26: 9	the community officials who rebelled **a**	6584
	26: 9	when they rebelled **a** the LORD.	6584
	27: 3	who banded together **a** the LORD,	6584
	31: 3	of your men to go to war **a** the Midianites	6584
	31: 7	They fought **a** Midian,	6584
	32:13	The LORD's anger burned **a** Israel	6584
	32:23	you will be sinning **a** the LORD;	4200
Dt	1:26	you rebelled **a** the command of	907
	1:41	"We have sinned **a** the LORD.	4200
	1:43	You rebelled **a** the LORD's command and	907
	1:44	in those hills came out **a** you;	7925
	2:15	The LORD's hand was **a** them	928
	4:26	I call heaven and earth as witnesses **a**	928
	5:20	nor give false testimony **a** your neighbor.	928
	6:15	is a jealous God and his anger will burn **a**	928
	7: 4	and the LORD's anger will burn **a** you	928
	7:24	No one will be able to stand up **a** you;	928+7156
	8:19	I testify **a** you today that you will surely	928
	9: 2	"Who can stand up **a** the Anakites?"	4200+7156
	9: 7	you have been rebellious **a** the LORD.	6640
	9:16	I saw that you had sinned **a** the LORD	4200
	9:23	But you rebelled **a** the command of	907

Dt		
9:24	You have been rebellious a the LORD	6640
11:17	Then the LORD's anger will burn a you,	928
11:25	No man will be able to stand a you.	928+7156
13: 5	because he preached rebellion a the LORD	6584
15: 9	He may then appeal to the LORD a you,	6584
19:18	giving false testimony a his brother,	928
20: 1	to war a your enemies and see horses	6584
20: 3	today you are going into battle a	6584
20: 4	with you to fight for you a your enemies	6640
20:18	and you will sin a the LORD your God.	4200
20:19	fighting a it to capture it,	6584
21:10	When you go to war a your enemies and	6584
23: 9	When you are encamped a your enemies,	6584
24:15	Otherwise he may cry to the LORD a you,	6584
28: 7	that the enemies who rise up a you will	6584
28:48	the enemies the LORD sends a you.	928
28:49	The LORD will bring a nation a you	928
29: 7	and Og king of Bashan came out to fight a	7925
29:20	his wrath and zeal will burn a that man.	928
29:27	the LORD's anger burned a this land,	928
30:19	and earth as witnesses a you that I have set	928
31:19	so that it may be a witness for me a them.	4200+7156
31:21	this song will testify a them,	4200+7156
31:26	There it will remain as a witness a you.	928
31:27	If you have been rebellious a the LORD	6640
31:28	and call heaven and earth to testify a them,	928
32:23	upon them and spend my arrows a them.	928
32:24	I will send wasting famine a them,	928
32:24	I will send a them the fangs of wild beasts,	NIH
33: 7	Oh, be his help a his foes!"	4946
33:11	Smite the loins of those who rise up a him;	AIT
Jos		
1: 5	stand up a you all the days of your life.	4200+7156
1:18	Whoever rebels a your word and does	907
7: 1	So the LORD's anger burned a Israel.	928
7: 3	"Not all the people will have to go up a	AIT
7:12	Israelites cannot stand a their enemies	4200+7156
7:13	You cannot stand a your enemies	4200+7156
7:20	I have sinned a the LORD	4200
8: 5	and when the men come out a us,	7925
8:14	that an ambush had been set a him behind	4200
8:20	and saw the smoke of the city rising	2025
8:20	the desert had turned back a their pursuers.	448
8:22	of the ambush also came out of the city a	7925
9: 2	they came together to make war a Joshua	6640
9:18	The whole assembly grumbled a the leaders	6584
10: 5	with all their troops and took up positions a	6584
10: 6	from the hill country have joined forces a	448
10:21	and no one uttered a word a the Israelites.	4200
10:31	he took up positions a it and attacked it.	6584
10:34	they took up positions a it and attacked it.	6584
11: 5	to fight a Israel.	6640
11: 7	and his whole army came a them suddenly	6584
11:18	Joshua waged war a all these kings for	907
11:20	to wage war a Israel,	AIT
15:15	From there he marched a the people living	448
22:12	of Israel gathered at Shiloh to go to war a	6584
22:16	and build yourselves an altar in rebellion a	928
22:18	" 'If you rebel a the LORD today,	928
22:19	But do not rebel a the LORD or against us	928
22:19	But do not rebel against the LORD or a us	907
22:29	"Far be it from us to rebel a the LORD	928
22:33	about going to war a them to devastate	6584
23:16	the LORD's anger will burn a you,	928
24: 8	They fought a you,	907
24: 9	prepared to fight a Israel,	928
24:11	The citizens of Jericho fought a you,	928
24:22	"You are witnesses a yourselves	928
24:27	"This stone will be a witness a us.	928
24:27	It will be a witness a you if you are untrue	928
Jdg		
1: 1	to go up and fight for us a the Canaanites?"	448
1: 3	to fight the Canaanites.	928
1: 5	that they found Adoni-Bezek and fought a	928
1: 9	down to fight a the Canaanites living in	928
1:10	They advanced a the Canaanites living	448
1:11	From there they advanced a the people	448
2:14	In his anger a Israel the LORD handed them	928
2:15	of the LORD was a them to defeat them,	928
3: 8	The anger of the LORD burned a Israel so	928
4:24	the Israelites grew stronger and stronger a	6584
5:20	from their courses they fought a Sisera.	6640
5:23	to help the LORD a the mighty.'	928
7: 2	In order that Israel may not boast a me	6584
7: 9	"Get up, go down a the camp,	928
7:24	down a the Midianites and seize the waters	7925
8: 3	their resentment a him subsided.	4946+6584
9:18	(but today you have revolted a	6584
9:23	who acted treacherously a Abimelech.	928
9:24	that the crime a Jerub-Baal's seventy sons,	AIT
9:31	to Shechem and are stirring up the city a	6584
9:33	advance a the city.	6584
9:33	When Gaal and his men come out a you,	448
9:45	All that day Abimelech pressed his attack a	928
9:49	They piled them a the stronghold and set it	6584
10: 9	the Jordan to fight a Judah, Benjamin and	928
10:10	"We have sinned a you,	4200
10:18	the attack a the Ammonites will be	928
11:12	"What do you have a us	4200
11:27	by waging war a me.	928
11:29	from there he advanced a the Ammonites.	AIT
12: 4	the men of Gilead and fought a Ephraim.	907
16:26	so that I may lean a them."	6584
16:29	Bracing himself a them,	6584
18:27	a a peaceful and unsuspecting people.	6584
20: 9	We'll go up a it as the lot directs.	448
20:11	and united as one man a the city.	448
20:14	at Gibeah to fight a the Israelites.	6640
20:18	"Who of us shall go first to fight a	6640

Jdg		
20:20	up battle positions a them at Gibeah.	907
20:23	up again to battle a the Benjamites,	6640
20:23	The LORD answered, "Go up a them."	448
20:30	up a the Benjamites on the third day	448
20:30	on the third day and took up positions a	448
Ru		
1:13	the LORD's hand has gone out a me!"	928
1Sa		
2:10	He will thunder a them from heaven;	6584
2:25	If a man sins a another man,	4200
2:25	but if a man sins a the LORD,	4200
3:12	At that time I will carry out a	448
3:12	against Eli everything I spoke a	448
4: 1	Israelites went out to fight a the Philistines.	7925
5: 9	the LORD's hand was a that city,	928
7: 6	"We have sinned a the LORD."	4200
7:10	the LORD thundered with loud thunder a	6584
7:13	hand of the LORD was a the Philistines.	928
12: 3	Testify a me in the presence of the LORD	928
12: 5	"The LORD is witness a you,	928
12: 9	and the king of Moab, who fought a them.	448
12:12	of the Ammonites was moving a you,	6584
12:14	and serve and obey him and do not rebel a	907
12:15	and if you rebel a his commands,	907
12:15	his hand will be a you,	928
12:15	as it was a your fathers.	928
12:23	that I should sin a the LORD by failing	4200
13:12	Philistines will come down a me at Gilgal,	448
14:33	the men are sinning a the LORD	4200
14:34	Do not sin a the LORD by eating meat	4200
14:47	he fought a their enemies on every side:	928
17:19	fighting a the Philistines."	6640
17:33	"You are not able to go out a this Philistine	448
17:45	"You come a me with sword and spear	448
17:45	but I come a you in the name of	448
18:17	"I will not raise a hand a him.	928
18:21	so that the hand of the Philistines may be a	928
22: 8	Is that why you have all conspired a me?	6584
22:13	"Why have you conspired a me,	6584
22:13	so that he has rebelled a me and lies in wait	448
23: 1	the Philistines are fighting a Keilah	928
23: 3	if we go to Keilah a the Philistine forces!"	448
23: 9	David learned that Saul was plotting a him,	6584
24: 6	or lift my hand a him;	928
24:10	I said, 'I will not lift my hand a my master,	928
24:14	"A whom has the king of Israel come out?	339
25:39	who has upheld my cause a Nabal	3338+4946
26:19	If the LORD has incited you a me,	928
27:10	"A the Negev of Judah" or "Against	6584
27:10	of Judah" or "A the Negev of Jerahmeel" or	6584
27:10	or "Against the Negev of Jerahmeel" or "A	448
28: 1	to fight a Israel.	928
28:15	"The Philistines are fighting a me,	928
28:18	the LORD or carry out his fierce wrath a	928
29: 4	or he will turn a us during the fighting.	2118+4200+8477
29: 8	"What have you found a your servant from	928
29: 8	Why can't I go and fight a the enemies	928
30:23	over to us the forces that came a us.	448
31: 1	Now the Philistines fought a Israel;	928
2Sa		
1:16	Your own mouth testified a you	928
4: 8	the LORD has avenged my lord the king a	4946
5:20	the LORD has broken out a my enemies	AIT
6: 7	The LORD's anger burned a Uzzah	928
6: 8	the LORD's wrath had broken out a	928
10: 9	and deployed them a the Arameans.	7925
10:10	of Abishai his brother and deployed them a	7925
10:17	to meet David and fought a him.	6640
11:17	the city came out and fought a Joab, some	907
11:23	"The men overpowered us and came out a	448
11:25	Press the attack a the city and destroy it.'	448
12: 5	with anger a the man and said to Nathan,	928
12:13	"I have sinned a the LORD."	4200
12:26	Meanwhile Joab fought a Rabbah of	928
12:27	"I have fought a Rabbah	928
14: 7	the whole clan has risen up a your servant;	6584
14:13	then have you devised a thing like this a	6584
17:21	Ahithophel has advised such and such a	6584
18:12	I would not lift my hand a the king's son.	448
18:28	the men who lifted their hands a my lord	928
18:31	from all who rose up a you."	6584
20:10	Amasa was not on his guard a the dagger	928
20:15	and it stood at the outer fortifications,	928
20:21	has lifted up his hand a the king,	928
20:21	up his hand against the king, a David.	928
21: 5	for the man who destroyed us and plotted a	4200
21:15	David went down with his men to fight a	AIT
22:30	With your help I can advance a a troop;	AIT
23: 8	he raised his spear a eight hundred men,	6584
23:18	He raised his spear a three hundred men,	6584
23:21	Benaiah went a him with a club.	448
24: 1	the anger of the LORD burned a Israel,	928
24: 1	and he incited David a them, saying,	928
24:12	Choose one of them for me to carry out a	4200
1Ki		
5: 3	waged a my father David from all sides,	6015
6: 5	A the walls of the main hall	6584
8:33	an enemy because they have sinned a you,	4200
8:35	because your people have sinned a you,	4200
8:44	your people go to war a their enemies	6584
8:46	"When they sin a you—	4200
8:50	who have sinned a you;	4200
8:50	the offenses they have committed a you,	928
11:14	Lord raised up a Solomon an adversary,	7854
11:23	up a Solomon another adversary,	4200
11:26	Jeroboam son of Nebat rebelled a the king.	928
11:27	the account of how he rebelled a the king:	928
12:19	So Israel has been in rebellion a the house	928
12:21	to make war a the house of Israel and	6640
12:24	Do not go up to fight a your brothers,	6640

1Ki		
13: 2	He cried out a the altar by the word of	6584
13: 4	of God cried out a the altar at Bethel,	6584
13:32	of the LORD a the altar in Bethel and	6584
13:32	the LORD against the altar in Bethel and a	6584
15:17	Baasha king of Israel went up a Judah	6584
15:20	the commanders of his forces a the towns	6584
15:27	Abijah of the house of Issachar plotted a	6584
16: 1	the LORD came to Jehu son of Hanani a	6584
16: 9	of half his chariots, conspired a him.	6584
16:12	the word of the LORD spoken a Baasha	448
16:16	in the camp heard that Zimri had plotted a	AIT
17:18	"What do you have a me, man of God?	4200
20:26	and went up to Aphek to fight a Israel.	6640
21:13	sat opposite him and brought charges a	6386
22: 4	with me to fight a Ramoth Gilead?"	NIH
22: 6	"Shall I go to war a Ramoth Gilead,	6584
22:15	shall we go to war a Ramoth Gilead,	448
2Ki		
1: 1	After Ahab's death, Moab rebelled a Israel.	928
3: 5	of Moab rebelled a the king of Israel.	928
3: 7	"The king of Moab has rebelled a me.	928
3: 7	Will you go with me to fight a Moab?"	448
3:21	that the kings had come to fight a them;	928
3:26	of Moab saw that the battle had gone a	4946
3:27	The fury a Israel was great;	6584
6:32	shut the door and hold it shut a him.	AIT
8:20	Edom rebelled a Judah and set	3338+4946+9393
8:22	To this day Edom has been in rebellion a Judah.	3338+4946+9393
8:28	of Ahab to war a Hazael king of Aram	6640
9:14	the son of Nimshi, conspired a Joram.	448
9:14	all Israel had been defending Ramoth Gilead a Hazael	4946+7156
10: 9	It was I who conspired a my master	6584
10:10	a word the LORD has spoken a the house	6584
12:20	His officials conspired a him	AIT
13: 3	So the LORD's anger burned a Israel,	928
13:12	including his war a Amaziah king of Judah,	6640
14:15	including his war a Amaziah king of Judah,	6640
14:19	They conspired a him in Jerusalem,	6584
15:10	Shallum son of Jabesh conspired a	6584
15:25	Pekah son of Remaliah, conspired a him.	6584
15:30	Then Hoshea son of Elah conspired a	6584
15:37	of Aram and Pekah son of Remaliah a	928
16: 5	**marched up** to fight a Jerusalem	AIT
17: 5	**marched** a Samaria and laid siege to it	AIT
17: 7	because the Israelites had sinned a	4200
17: 9	The Israelites secretly did things a	6584
18: 7	He rebelled a the king of Assyria and did	928
18: 9	Shalmaneser king of Assyria marched a	6584
18:20	that you rebel a me?	928
18:25	to march a this country and destroy it.' "	6584
19: 8	he withdrew and found the king fighting a	6584
19: 9	was marching out to fight a him.	907
19:21	the word that the LORD has spoken a	6584
19:22	A whom have you raised your voice	6584
19:22	A the Holy One of Israel!	6584
19:27	when you come and go and how you rage a	448
19:28	Because you rage a me	448
19:28	before it with shield or build a siege ramp a	6584
21:13	**measuring line** used a	AIT
21:13	the **plumb line** used a the house of Ahab.	AIT
21:23	Amon's officials conspired a him	6584
21:24	of the land killed all who had plotted a	6584
22:13	Great is the LORD's anger that burns a us	928
22:17	my anger will burn a this place and will not	928
22:19	when you heard what I have spoken a	6584
23:17	from Judah and pronounced a the altar	6584
23:26	which burned a Judah because of all	928
24: 1	then he changed his mind and rebelled a	928
24: 2	Moabite and Ammonite raiders a him.	928
24:20	Zedekiah rebelled a the king of Babylon.	928
25: 1	of Babylon marched a Jerusalem	6584
1Ch		
5:10	During Saul's reign they waged war a	6640
5:19	They waged war a the Hagrites, Jetur,	6640
10: 1	Now the Philistines fought a Israel;	928
11:11	he raised his spear a three hundred men,	6584
11:20	He raised his spear a three hundred men,	6584
11:23	Benaiah went a him with a club.	448
12:19	when he went with the Philistines to fight a	6584
12:21	They helped David a a raiding bands,	6584
13:10	The LORD's anger burned a Uzzah,	928
13:11	the LORD's wrath had broken out a	928
14:11	God has **broken out** a my enemies	AIT
15:13	the LORD our God broke out in anger a	928
19:10	and deployed them a the Arameans.	7925
19:11	and they were deployed a the Ammonites.	7925
19:17	he advanced a them	448
19:17	and they fought a him.	6640
21: 1	Satan rose up a Israel and incited David	6584
21:10	Choose one of them for me to carry out a	4200
2Ch		
6:24	an enemy because they have sinned a you,	4200
6:26	because your people have sinned a you,	4200
6:34	your people go to war a their enemies	6584
6:36	"When they sin a you—	4200
6:39	who have sinned a you.	4200
10:19	So Israel has been in rebellion a the house	928
11: 1	to make war a Israel and to regain	6640
11: 4	Do not go up to fight a your brothers.	6640
11: 4	turned back from marching a	448
13: 3	and Jeroboam drew up a battle line a him	6640
13: 6	rebelled a his master.	6584
13:12	the battle cry a you.	6584
13:12	Men of Israel, do not fight a the LORD,	6640
14: 9	Zerah the Cushite marched out a them with	
14:11	like you to help the powerless a the mighty.	1068
14:11	and in your name we have come a	6584
14:11	do not let man prevail a you."	6640

2Ch	16: 1	went up a Judah and fortified Ramah	6584
	16: 4	the commanders of his forces a the towns	448
	17: 1	as king and strengthened himself a Israel.	6584
	18: 3	"Will you go with me a Ramoth Gilead?"	AIT
	18: 5	"Shall we go to war a Ramoth Gilead,	448
	18:14	shall we go to war a Ramoth Gilead,	448
	19:10	to warn them not to sin a the LORD;	4200
	20: 2	"A vast army is coming a you from Edom,	6584
	20:16	Tomorrow march down a them.	6584
	20:22	the LORD set ambushes a the men	6584
	20:23	up a the men from Mount Seir to destroy	6584
	20:29	how the LORD had fought a the enemies	6640
	20:37	of Dodavahu of Mareshah prophesied a	6584
	21: 8	Edom rebelled a Judah and set	3338+4946+9393
	21:10	To this day Edom has been in rebellion a Judah.	3338+4946+9393
	21:16	The LORD aroused a Jehoram	6584
	22: 5	of Ahab king of Israel to war a Hazael king	6584
	24:19	and though they testified a them,	928
	24:21	But they plotted a him,	6584
	24:23	the army of Aram marched a Joash;	6584
	24:25	His officials conspired a him for murdering	6584
	24:26	Those who conspired a him were Zabad,	6584
	25:15	The anger of the LORD burned a	928
	25:27	they conspired a him in Jerusalem	6584
	26: 6	He went to war a the Philistines and broke	928
	26: 7	God helped him a the Philistines and	6584
	26: 7	and a the Arabs who lived in Gur Baal and	6584
	26: 7	the Arabs who lived in Gur Baal and a	NIH
	26:13	a powerful force to support the king a	6584
	28:10	also guilty of sins a the LORD your God?	4200
	32:16	Sennacherib's officers spoke further a	6584
	32:16	against the LORD God and a	6584
	32:17	the God of Israel, and saying this a him:	6584
	33:11	So the LORD brought a them	6584
	33:24	Amon's officials conspired a him	6584
	33:25	of the land killed all who had plotted a	6584
	34:27	when you heard what he spoke a this place	6584
	36: 8	and all that was found a him,	6584
	36:13	He also rebelled a King Nebuchadnezzar,	928
	36:16	of the LORD was aroused a his people	928
	36:17	up a them the king of the Babylonians,	6584
Ezr	4: 5	to work a them and frustrate their plans	6584
	4: 6	they lodged an accusation a the people	6584
	4: 8	and Shimshai the secretary wrote a letter a	10542
	4:19	that this city has a long history of revolt a	10542
	7:23	Why should there be wrath a the realm of	10542
	8:22	his great anger is a all who forsake him."	6584
Ne	1: 6	have committed a you.	4200
	2:19	"Are you rebelling a the king?"	6584
	4: 8	and fight a Jerusalem and stir up trouble	928
	4: 8	against Jerusalem and stir up trouble a it.	4200
	5: 1	and their wives raised a great outcry a	448
	6:12	but that he had prophesied a me	6584
	9:10	You sent miraculous signs and wonders a	928
	9:10	a all his officials and all the people	928
	9:26	they were disobedient and rebelled a you;	928
	9:29	They sinned a your ordinances.	928
	13:15	I warned them a selling food on that day.	AIT
	13:18	Now you are stirring up more wrath a	6584
Est	1:16	not only a the king but also against all	6584
	1:16	also a all the nobles and the peoples of all	6584
	4:16	even though it is a the law.	3869+4202
	5: 9	he was filled with rage a Mordecai.	6584
	6:13	you cannot stand a him—	4200
	8: 3	which he had devised a the Jews.	6584
	9: 2	No one could stand a them,	4200+7156
	9:24	had plotted a the Jews to destroy them	6584
	9:25	that the evil scheme Haman had devised a	6584
Job	2: 3	though you incited me a him to ruin him	928
	6: 4	God's terrors are marshaled a me.	AIT
	8: 4	When your children sinned a him,	4200
	10: 2	but tell me what charges you have a me.	AIT
	10:16	and again display your awesome power a	928
	10:17	You bring new witnesses a me	5584
	10:17	your forces come a me wave upon wave.	6640
	11: 5	that he would open his lips a you	6640
	13:19	Can anyone bring charges a me?	6643
	13:26	For you write down bitter things a me	6584
	15: 6	your own lips testify a you.	928
	15:13	so that you vent your rage a God	448
	15:25	at God and vaunts himself a the Almighty,	448
	15:26	defiantly charging a him with a thick,	448
	16: 4	I could make fine speeches a you	6584
	16: 8	my gauntness rises up and testifies a me	928+7156
	16:10	in scorn and unite together a me.	6584
	17: 8	the innocent are aroused a the ungodly.	6584
	19: 5	above me and use my humiliation a me,	6584
	19:11	His anger burns a me;	6584
	19:12	they build a siege ramp a me and encamp	6584
	19:19	those I love have turned a me.	928
	20:23	God will vent his burning anger a him	928
	20:27	the earth will rise up a him.	4200
	22: 4	that he rebukes you and brings charges a	6640
	23: 6	No, he would not press charges a me.	928
	23:14	He carries out his decree a me,	AIT
	24:13	"There are those who rebel a the light,	AIT
	27:22	It hurls itself a him without mercy	6584
	30:12	they build their siege ramps a me.	6584
	31:13	when they had a grievance a me,	6643
	31:21	if I have raised my hand a the fatherless,	448
	31:30	to sin by invoking a curse a his life—	AIT
	31:38	"if my land cries out a me	6584
	32:14	But Job has not marshaled his words a me,	448
	34:37	among us and multiplies his words a God."	4200
	39:23	The quiver rattles a his side,	6584
	40:23	the Jordan should surge a his mouth.	448
Job	41:10	Who then is able to stand a me?	4200+7156
	41:11	Who has a claim a me that I must pay?	7709
Ps	2: 2	the rulers gather together a the LORD and	6584
	2: 2	the LORD a his Anointed One.	6584
	3: 1	How many rise up a me!	6584
	3: 6	of thousands drawn up a me on every side.	6584
	5:10	rise up a the rage of my enemies.	928
	7: 6	rise up a the rage of my enemies.	928
	11: 2	they set their arrows a the strings to shoot	6584
	15: 5	without usury and does not accept a bribe a	6584
	18:29	With your help I can advance a a troop;	AIT
	21:11	Though they plot evil a you	6584
	22:13	Roaring lions tearing their prey open their mouths wide a me.	6584
	27: 2	evil men advance a me to devour my flesh,	6584
	27: 3	though war break out a me,	6584
	27:12	for false witnesses rise up a me,	928
	31:13	they conspire a me and plot to take my life.	6584
	31:18	and contempt they speak arrogantly a	6584
	32: 2	the LORD does not count a him	4200
	34:16	face of the LORD is a those who do evil,	928
	35: 1	fight a those who fight against me.	907
	35: 1	fight against those who fight a me.	AIT
	35: 3	and javelin a those who pursue me.	7925
	35:15	attackers gathered a me	6584
	35:20	but devise false accusations a	6584
	36:11	May the foot of the proud not come a me,	AIT
	37:12	The wicked plot a the righteous	4200
	41: 4	heal me, for I have sinned a you."	4200
	41: 7	All my enemies whisper together a me;	6584
	41: 9	has lifted up his heel a me.	6584
	43: 1	and plead my cause a an ungodly nation;	4946
	50: 7	O Israel, and I will testify a you:	928
	50:20	You speak continually a your brother	928
	51: 4	A you, you only, have I sinned	4200
	55:12	if a foe were raising himself a me,	6584
	55:18	from the battle waged a me,	4200
	59: 1	protect me from those who rise up a me.	AIT
	59: 3	Fierce men conspire a me for no offense	6584
	60: 4	a banner to be unfurled a the bow.	4946+7156
	60:11	Give us aid a the enemy,	4946
	61: 3	a strong tower a the foe.	4946+7156
	64: 8	He will turn their own tongues a them	6584
	66: 7	let not the rebellious rise up a him.	4200
	71:10	For my enemies speak a me;	4200
	74: 1	Why does your anger smolder a the sheep	928
	75: 5	Do not lift your horns a heaven;	4200
	76:10	Surely your wrath a men brings you praise,	AIT
	78:17	But they continued to sin a him,	4200
	78:17	rebelling in the desert a the Most High.	AIT
	78:19	They spoke a God, saying,	928
	78:21	his fire broke out a Jacob,	928
	78:21	and his wrath rose a Israel,	928
	78:31	God's anger rose a them;	928
	78:40	How often they rebelled a him in	AIT
	78:49	He unleashed a them his hot anger,	928
	78:56	But they put God to the test and rebelled a	907
	79: 8	Do not hold a us the sins of the fathers;	4200
	80: 4	how long will your anger smolder a	928
	81: 5	statute for Joseph when he went out a Egypt	6584
	81:14	and turn my hand a their foes!	6584
	83: 3	With cunning they conspire a your people;	6584
	83: 3	they plot a those you cherish.	4200
	83: 5	they form an alliance a you—	6584
	91:12	that you will not strike your foot a a stone.	928
	94:16	Who will rise up for me a the wicked?	6640
	94:16	Who will take a stand for me a evildoers?	6640
	94:21	They band together a the righteous	6584
	102: 8	those who rail a me use my name as	AIT
	105:25	to conspire a his servants.	928
	105:28	for had they not rebelled a his words?	907
	106:33	for they rebelled a the Spirit of God,	907
	107:11	for they had rebelled a the words of God	AIT
	108:12	Give us aid a the enemy,	4946
	109: 2	deceitful men have opened their mouths a	6584
	109: 2	they have spoken a me with lying tongues.	907
	119:11	in my heart that I might not sin a you.	4200
	124: 3	when their anger flared a us,	928
	135: 9	O Egypt, a Pharaoh and all his servants.	928
	137: 9	and dashes them a the rocks.	928
	138: 7	you stretch out your hand a the anger	6584
	139:21	and abhor those who rise up a you?	AIT
	141: 5	my prayer is ever a the deeds of evildoers;	928
	149: 9	to carry out the sentence written a them.	928
Pr	3:29	Do not plot harm a your neighbor.	6584
	17:11	a merciless official will be sent a him.	6584
	19: 3	yet his heart rages a the LORD.	6584
	21:30	no plan that can succeed a the LORD.	4200+5584
	23:11	he will take up their case a you.	907
	24:15	like an outlaw a a righteous man's house,	4200
	24:28	not testify a your neighbor without cause,	928
	25:18	the man who gives false testimony a	928
Ecc	9:14	And a powerful king came a it,	448
	9:14	surrounded it and built huge siegeworks a	6584
	10: 4	If a ruler's anger rises a you,	6584
Isa	1: 2	but they have rebelled a me.	6586
	1:25	I will turn my hand a you;	6584
	2: 4	Nation will not take up sword a nation,	448
	3: 5	man a man, neighbor against neighbor.	928
	3: 5	man against man, neighbor a neighbor.	928
	3: 8	their words and deeds are a the LORD,	448
	3: 9	The look on their faces testifies a them;	928
	3:14	into judgment a the elders and leaders	6640
	5:25	the LORD's anger burns a his people;	928
	7: 1	of Israel marched up to fight a Jerusalem,	6584
Isa	8: 7	therefore the Lord is about to bring a them	6584
	9: 8	The Lord has sent a message a Jacob;	928
	9:11	the LORD has strengthened Rezin's foes a	6584
	9:21	together they will turn a Judah.	6584
	10: 6	I send him a a godless nation,	928
	10: 6	I dispatch him a a people who anger me,	6584
	10:12	When the Lord has finished all his work a	928
	10:15	or the saw boast a him who uses it?	6584
	10:24	who beat you with a rod and lift up a club a	6584
	10:25	Very soon my anger a you will end	NIH
	13:17	See, I will stir up a them the Medes,	6584
	14: 4	you will take up this taunt a the king	6584
	14:22	"I will rise up a them,	6584
	19: 2	"I will stir up Egyptian a Egyptian—	928
	19: 2	brother will fight a brother,	928
	19: 2	neighbor a neighbor, city against city,	928
	19: 2	city a city, kingdom against kingdom.	928
	19: 2	city against city, kingdom a kingdom.	928
	19:12	the LORD Almighty has planned a Egypt.	6584
	19:16	that the LORD Almighty raises a them.	6584
	19:17	of what the LORD Almighty is planning a	6584
	20: 3	as a sign and portent a Egypt and Cush,	6584
	23: 8	Who planned this a Tyre,	6584
	25: 4	the ruthless is like a storm driving a a wall	AIT
	27: 4	I would march a them in battle;	928
	28:22	of the destruction decreed a the whole land.	6584
	29: 3	I will encamp a you all around;	6584
	29: 3	with towers and set up my siege works a	6584
	29: 7	hordes of all the nations that fight a Ariel,	6584
	29: 8	of all the nations that fight a Mount Zion.	6584
	31: 2	He will rise up a the house of the wicked,	6584
	31: 2	a those who help evildoers.	6584
	31: 4	of shepherds is called together a him, he is	6584
	31: 6	to him you have so greatly revolted a,	6240
	33:15	who stops his ears a plots of murder	4946
	33:15	against plots of murder and shuts his eyes a	4946
	36: 5	that you rebel a me?	928
	36:10	to march a this country and destroy it.' "	448
	37: 8	he withdrew and found the king fighting a	6584
	37: 9	was marching out to fight a him.	907
	37:22	this is the word the LORD has spoken a	6584
	37:23	A whom have you raised your voice	6584
	37:23	A the Holy One of Israel!	448
	37:28	when you come and go and how you rage a	448
	37:29	Because you rage a me and	448
	37:33	before it with shield or build a siege ramp a	6584
	41:11	"All who rage a you will surely	928
	41:12	Those who wage war a you will be	AIT
	42:24	a whom we have sinned?	4200
	43:27	your spokesmen rebelled a me.	928
	45:24	All who have raged a him will come to him	928
	48:14	LORD's chosen ally will carry out his purpose a Babylon;	928
	48:14	his arm will be a the Babylonians.	NIH
	50: 8	Who then will bring charges a me?	907
	54:17	no weapon forged a you will prevail,	6584
	59:12	and our sins testify a us.	928
	59:13	rebellion and treachery a the LORD,	928
	63:10	and he himself fought a them.	928
	64: 5	But when we continued to sin a them,	928
	66:24	the dead bodies of those who rebelled a	928
Jer	1:15	they will come a all her surrounding walls	6584
	1:15	against all her surrounding walls and a all	6584
	1:18	a bronze wall to stand a the whole land—	6584
	1:18	a the kings of Judah, its officials,	4200
	1:19	They will fight a you but will	448
	2: 8	the leaders rebelled a me.	928
	2: 9	"Therefore I bring charges a you again,"	907
	2: 9	"And I will bring charges a	907
	2:21	did you turn a me into a corrupt, wild vine?	4200
	2:29	"Why do you bring charges a me?	448
	2:29	You have all rebelled a me,"	928
	3:13	you have rebelled a the LORD your God,	4200
	3:25	We have sinned a the LORD our God,	4200
	4:12	Now I pronounce my judgments a them."	907
	4:16	raising a war cry a the cities of Judah.	6584
	4:17	because she has rebelled a me,' "	907
	5:15	"I am bringing a distant nation a you—	6584
	6: 3	Shepherds with their flocks will come a	448
	6: 4	"Prepare for battle a her!	6584
	6: 6	down the trees and build siege ramps a	6584
	6:12	when I stretch out my hand a	6584
	8:14	because we have sinned a him.	4200
	11:19	I did not realize that they had plotted a me,	6584
	12: 6	they have raised a loud cry a you.	339
	13:14	I will smash them one a the other,	448
	14: 7	Although our sins testify a us, O LORD,	928
	14: 7	we have sinned a you.	4200
	14:20	we have indeed sinned a you.	4200
	15: 3	"I will send four kinds of destroyers a	6584
	15: 8	At midday I will bring a destroyer a	6584
	15:14	a fire that will burn a you.	6584
	15:20	they will fight a you but will	448
	16:10	the LORD decreed such a great disaster a	6584
	16:10	What sin have we committed a	4200
	18:11	a disaster for you and devising a plan a	6584
	18:18	"Come, let's make plans a Jeremiah,"	6584
	18:22	when you suddenly bring invaders a them,	6584
	19:15	around it every disaster I pronounced a	6584
	21: 4	to turn a you the weapons of war that are	6015
	21: 5	I myself will fight a you with	907
	21:13	I am a you, [Jerusalem,]	448
	21:13	you who say, "Who can come a us?	6584
	22: 7	I will send destroyers a you,	6584
	23:30	"I am a the prophets who steal	6584
	23:31	the LORD, "I am a the prophets who wag	6584
	23:32	I am a those who prophesy false dreams,"	6584

Jer	24:10	and plague a them until they are destroyed	928
	25: 9	"and I will bring them a this land	6584
	25: 9	against this land and its inhabitants and a	6584
	25:13	that land all the things I have spoken a it,	6584
	25:13	in this book and prophesied by Jeremiah a	6584
	25:30	"Now prophesy all these words a them	448
	25:30	from his holy dwelling and roar mightily a	6584
	25:30	shout a all who live on the earth.	448
	25:31	for the LORD will bring charges a	928
	26:11	because he has prophesied a this city.	448
	26:12	to prophesy a this house and this city all	448
	26:13	not bring the disaster he has pronounced a	6584
	26:19	not bring the disaster he pronounced a?	6584
	26:20	he prophesied the same things a this city	6584
	28: 8	disaster and plague a many countries	448
	28:16	because you have preached rebellion a	448
	29:17	"I will send the sword, famine and plague a	448
	29:32	because he has preached rebellion a me.'"	6584
	31:20	I often speak a him, I still remember him.	928
	32: 5	If you fight a the Babylonians,	907
	33: 4	to be used a the siege ramps and the sword	448
	33: 8	from all the sin they have committed a me	4200
	33: 8	and will forgive all their sins of rebellion a	928
	34: 1	in the empire he ruled were fighting a	6584
	34: 7	of Babylon was fighting a Jerusalem and	6584
	34:22	They will fight a it,	6584
	35:17	in Jerusalem every disaster I pronounced a	6584
	36: 7	and wrath pronounced a this people by	448
	36:31	of Judah every disaster I pronounced a	448
	37:18	"What crime have I committed a you	4200
	39: 1	of Babylon marched a Jerusalem	448
	39:16	I am about to fulfill my words a this city	448
	40: 3	because you people sinned a the LORD	4200
	41: 9	of his **defense** a Baasha king of Israel.	4946+7156
	42: 5	the LORD be a true and faithful witness a	928
	43: 3	But Baruch son of Neriah is inciting you a	6584
	44: 6	it raged a the towns of Judah and the streets	928
	44:23	and have sinned a the LORD and have	4200
	44:29	that my threats of harm a you will	6584
	46: 2	This is the message a the army	6584
	46:20	but a gadfly is coming a her from the north.	928
	46:22	they will come a her with axes,	4200
	48: 8	The destroyer will come a every town,	448
	48:18	for he who destroys Moab will come up a	928
	49: 2	"when I will sound the battle cry a Rabbah	448
	49:19	And what shepherd can stand a me?"	4200+7156
	49:20	hear what the LORD has planned a Edom,	448
	49:20	what he has purposed a those who live	448
	49:30	of Babylon has plotted a you;	6584
	49:30	he has devised a plan a you.	6584
	49:36	I will bring a Elam the four winds from	448
	50: 7	for they sinned a the LORD,	4200
	50: 9	For I will stir up and bring a Babylon	6584
	50: 9	They will take up their positions a her,	4200
	50:14	for she has sinned a the LORD.	4200
	50:15	Shout a her on every side!	6584
	50:26	Come a her from afar.	4200
	50:29	"Summon archers a Babylon,	448
	50:31	"See, I am a you, O arrogant one,"	448
	50:35	"A sword a the Babylonians!"	6584
	50:35	"a those who live in Babylon and	448
	50:35	"against those who live in Babylon and a	448
	50:36	A sword a her false prophets!	448
	50:36	A sword a her warriors!	448
	50:37	A sword a her horses and chariots and all	448
	50:37	A sword a her treasures!	448
	50:44	And what shepherd can stand a me?"	4200+7156
	50:45	hear what the LORD has planned a	448
	50:45	what he has purposed a the land of	448
	51: 1	up the spirit of a destroyer a Babylon and	6584
	51:12	Lift up a banner a the walls of Babylon!	448
	51:12	his decree a the people of Babylon.	448
	51:25	"I am a you, O destroying mountain,	448
	51:25	"I will stretch out my hand a you,	6584
	51:27	Prepare the nations for battle a her;	6584
	51:27	summon a her these kingdoms:	6584
	51:27	Appoint a commander a her;	6584
	51:28	Prepare the nations for battle a her—	6584
	51:29	the LORD's purposes a Babylon stand—	6584
	51:46	of violence in the land and of ruler a ruler.	6584
	51:53	I will send destroyers a her,"	4200
	51:56	A destroyer will come a Babylon;	6584
	52: 3	Zedekiah rebelled a the king of Babylon.	928
	52: 4	of Babylon marched a Jerusalem	6584
La	1:15	an army a me to crush my young men.	6584
	1:18	yet I **rebelled** a his command.	AIT
	2:16	All your enemies open their mouths wide a	6584
	2:22	you summoned a me **terrors** on every side.	AIT
	3: 3	he has turned his hand a me again	928
	3:46	"All our enemies have opened their mouths	
		wide a us.	6584
	3:60	all their plots a me.	4200
	3:61	all their plots a me—	6584
	3:62	what my enemies whisper and mutter a	6584
Eze	2: 3	a rebellious nation that has rebelled a me;	928
	2: 3	they and their fathers have been in revolt a	928
	3:13	the wings of the living creatures brushing a	448
	4: 2	Then lay siege to it: Erect siege works a it,	6584
	4: 2	set up camps a it and put battering rams	6584
	4: 7	and with bared arm prophesy a her.	6584
	5: 6	Yet in her wickedness she has rebelled a	907
	5: 8	I myself am a you, Jerusalem,	6584
	5:13	"Then my anger will cease and my wrath a	928
	5:17	I will send famine and wild beasts a you,	6584
	5:17	and I will bring the sword a you.	6584
	6: 2	set your face a the mountains of Israel;	448
	6: 2	mountains of Israel; prophesy a them	448

Eze	6: 3	I am about to bring a sword a you,	6584
	6:14	And I will stretch out my hand a them	6584
	7: 3	upon you and I will unleash my anger a	928
	7: 6	It has roused itself a you.	448
	7: 8	on you and spend my anger a you;	928
	11: 4	Therefore prophesy a them;	6584
	11: 8	and the sword is what I will bring a you,	6584
	13: 2	prophesy a the prophets of Israel who are	448
	13: 8	I am a you, declares the Sovereign LORD.	448
	13: 9	be a the prophets who see false visions	448
	13:15	So I will spend my wrath a the wall and	928
	13:15	against the wall and a those who covered it	928
	13:17	set your face a the daughters	448
	13:17	their own imagination. Prophesy a them	6584
	13:20	I am a your magic charms	448
	14: 8	I will set my face a that man and make him	928
	14: 9	and I will stretch out my hand a him	6584
	14:13	if a country sins a me by being unfaithful	4200
	14:13	and I stretch out my hand a it	6584
	14:17	if I bring a sword a that country and say,	6584
	14:21	How much worse will it be when I send a	448
	15: 7	I will set my face a them.	928
	15: 7	And when I set my face a them,	928
	16:27	So I stretched out my hand a you	6584
	16:37	I will gather them a you from all around	6584
	16:40	They will bring a mob a you,	6584
	16:42	my wrath a you will subside	928
	17:15	But the king rebelled a him	6584
	18:20	of the wicked will be **charged** a him.	6584
	18:22	be remembered a him.	4200
	19: 8	Then the nations came a him,	6584
	20: 8	" 'But they rebelled a me and would	928
	20: 8	and spend my anger a them in Egypt.	928
	20:13	people of Israel rebelled a me in the desert.	928
	20:21	" 'But the children rebelled a me:	928
	20:21	and spend my anger a them in the desert.	928
	20:38	of those who revolt and rebel a me.	928
	20:46	preach a the south and prophesy against	448
	20:46	against the south and prophesy a the forest	448
	21: 2	set your face a Jerusalem and preach	448
	21: 2	and preach a the sanctuary.	448
	21: 2	Prophesy a the land of Israel	448
	21: 3	I am a you,	448
	21: 4	my sword will be unsheathed a everyone	448
	21:12	son of man, for it is a my people;	6584
	21:12	it is a all the princes of Israel.	928
	21:20	Mark out one road for the sword to come a	907
	21:20	of the Ammonites and another a Judah	907
	21:22	to set battering rams a the gates,	6584
	21:31	upon you and breathe out my fiery anger a	6584
	23:22	I will stir up your lovers a you,	6584
	23:22	from in disgust, and I will bring them a you	6584
	23:24	They will come a you with weapons,	6584
	23:24	up positions a you on every side with large	6584
	23:25	I will direct my jealous anger a you,	928
	23:46	a mob a them and give them over to terror	6584
	24:13	not be clean again until my wrath a	928
	25: 2	set your face a the Ammonites	448
	25: 2	against the Ammonites and prophesy a	448
	25: 6	the malice of your heart a the land of Israel,	448
	25: 7	therefore I will stretch out my hand a you	6584
	25:13	I will stretch out my hand a Edom	6584
	25:16	to stretch out my hand a the Philistines,	6584
	26: 3	I am a you, O Tyre,	6584
	26: 3	and I will bring many nations a you,	6584
	26: 7	to bring a Tyre Nebuchadnezzar king	448
	26: 8	he will set up siege works a you,	6584
	26: 8	up to your walls and raise his shields a you.	6584
	26: 9	of his battering rams a your walls	928
	28: 7	to bring foreigners a you, the most ruthless	6584
	28: 7	they will draw their swords a your beauty	6584
	28:21	set your face a Sidon;	448
	28:21	face against Sidon; prophesy a her	6584
	28:22	" 'I am a you, O Sidon,	6584
	28:23	with the sword a her on every side.	928
	29: 2	set your face a Pharaoh king of Egypt.	6584
	29: 2	and prophesy a him and against all Egypt.	6584
	29: 2	and prophesy against him and a all Egypt.	6584
	29: 3	" 'I am a you, Pharaoh king of Egypt,	6584
	29: 8	a sword a you and kill your men	6584
	29:10	therefore I am a you and	448
	29:10	therefore I am against you and a	448
	29:18	in a hard campaign a Tyre;	448
	29:18	from the campaign he led a Tyre.	6584
	30: 4	A sword will come a Egypt,	928
	30:11	They will draw their swords a Egypt	6584
	30:22	I am a Pharaoh king of Egypt.	448
	30:25	the king of Babylon and he brandishes it a	448
	32:11	of the king of Babylon *will* **come** a you.	AIT
	33: 2	'When I bring the sword a a land,	6584
	33: 3	and he sees the sword coming a the land	6584
	33:16	be remembered a him.	4200
	34: 2	prophesy a the shepherds of Israel;	6584
	34:10	I am a the shepherds	448
	35: 2	set your face a Mount Seir;	6584
	35: 2	against Mount Seir; prophesy a it	6584
	35: 3	I am a you, Mount Seir,	448
	35: 3	and I will stretch out my hand a you	6584
	35:12	the contemptible things you have said a	6584
	35:13	You boasted a me and spoke against me	6584
	35:13	You boasted against me and spoke a me	6584
	36: 5	In my burning zeal I have spoken a the rest	6584
	36: 5	the rest of the nations, and a all Edom,	6584
	38: 2	set your face a Gog, of the land of Magog,	448
	38: 2	Meshech and Tubal; prophesy a him	6584
	38: 3	I am a you, O Gog,	448
	38:12	I will plunder and loot and turn my hand a	6584

Eze	38:16	You will advance a my people Israel like	6584
	38:16	O Gog, I will bring you a my land,	6584
	38:17	for years that I would bring you a them.	6584
	38:21	a sword a Gog on all my mountains,	6584
	38:21	Every man's sword will be a his brother.	928
	39: 1	"Son of man, prophesy a Gog and say:	6584
	39: 1	I am a you, O Gog,	448
	39: 2	the far north and send you a the mountains	6584
Da	3:29	or language who say anything a the God	10542
	4:24	the decree the Most High has issued a	10542
	5:23	you have set yourself up a the Lord	10542
	6: 4	to find grounds for charges a Daniel	10378
	6: 5	"We will never find any basis for charges a	10378
	7:21	this horn was waging war a the saints	10554
	7:25	He will speak a the Most High	10378+10608
	8: 4	No animal could stand a him,	4200+7156
	8: 7	The ram was powerless to stand a him;	4200+7156
	8:25	and take his stand a the Prince of princes.	6584
	9: 8	with shame because we have sinned a you.	4200
	9: 9	even though we have rebelled a him;	928
	9:11	because we have sinned a you.	4200
	9:12	You have fulfilled the words spoken a us	6584
	9:12	against us and a our rulers by bringing	6584
	10:20	Soon I will return to fight a the prince	6640
	10:21	(No one supports me a them except Michael	6584
	11: 2	he will stir up everyone a the kingdom	907
	11: 7	he will fight a them and be victorious.	928
	11:11	in a rage and fight a the king of the North,	6640
	11:14	"In those times many will rise a the king of	6584
	11:16	no one will be able to stand a him.	4200+7156
	11:25	up his strength and courage a the king of	6584
	11:25	to stand because of the plots devised a him.	6584
	11:28	his heart will be **set** a the holy covenant.	6584
	11:28	He will take action a it and then return	NIH
	11:30	Then he will turn back and vent his fury a	6584
	11:36	and will say unheard-of things a the God	6584
	11:40	the king of the North will storm out a him	6584
Hos	4: 1	because the LORD has a charge to bring a	6640
	4: 4	like *those who* **bring charges** a a priest.	AIT
	4: 7	the more they sinned a me;	4200
	5: 1	This judgment is a you:	4200
	5: 5	Israel's arrogance testifies a them;	928+7156
	5: 7	Israel's arrogance testifies a him,	928+7156
	7:13	because they have rebelled a me!	928
	7:13	I long to redeem them but they speak lies a	6584
	7:15	but they plot evil a me.	448
	8: 1	and rebelled a my law.	6584
	8: 5	My anger burns a them.	928+6330
	10:10	nations will be gathered a them to put them	4200
	10:14	the roar of battle will rise a your people, so	928
	11:12	And Judah is unruly a God,	6640
	11:12	even a the faithful Holy One.	6640
	12: 2	The LORD has a charge to bring a Judah;	6640
	13: 9	because you are a me, against your helper.	928
	13: 9	because you are against me, a your helper.	928
	13:16	because they have rebelled a their God.	928
Joel	3: 2	There I will enter into judgment a them	6640
	3: 4	"Now what have you a me,	4200
Am	1: 8	I will turn my hand a Ekron,	6584
	3: 1	Hear this word the LORD has spoken a	6584
	3: 1	a the whole family I brought up out	6584
	3:13	"Hear this and testify a the house	928
	6:14	"I will stir up a nation a you,	6584
	7: 9	with my sword I will rise a the house	6584
	7:10	"Amos is raising a conspiracy a you in	6584
	7:16	You say, " 'Do not prophesy a Israel,	6584
	7:16	and stop preaching a the house of Isaac.'	6584
Ob	1: 1	"Rise, and let us go a her for battle"—	6584
	1:10	of the **violence** a your brother Jacob,	AIT
Jnh	1: 2	to the great city of Nineveh and preach a it,	6584
Mic	1: 2	the Sovereign LORD may witness a you,	928
	1:15	a conqueror a you who live in Mareshah.	4200
	2: 3	"I am planning disaster a this people,	6584
	3: 5	they prepare to wage war a him.	6584
	4: 3	Nation will not take up sword a nation,	448
	4:11	But now many nations are gathered a you.	6584
	5: 1	O city of troops, for a siege is laid a us.	6584
	5: 5	we will raise a him seven shepherds,	6584
	6: 2	For the LORD has a case a his people;	6640
	6: 2	he is lodging a charge a Israel.	6640
	7: 6	a daughter rises up a her mother,	928
	7: 6	a daughter-in-law a her mother-in-law—	928
	7: 9	Because I have sinned a him,	6640
Na	1: 2	and maintains his wrath a his enemies.	4200
	1: 9	Whatever they plot a	448
	1:11	has come forth who plots evil a	448
	2: 1	attacker advances a you, [Nineveh].	6584+7156
	2:13	"I am a you,"	448
	3: 5	"I am a you,"	448
Hab	3: 8	Was your wrath a the streams?	928
	3: 8	Did you rage a the sea when you rode	928
Zep	1: 4	"I will stretch out my hand a Judah and	6584
	1: 4	against Judah and a all who live	6584
	1:16	and battle cry a the fortified cities and	6584
	1:16	the fortified cities and a the corner towers.	6584
	1:17	because they have sinned a the LORD.	4200
	2: 5	the word of the LORD is a you,	6584
	2: 8	who insulted my people and made threats a	6584
	2: 8	He will stretch out his hand a the north	6584
Zec	1:21	of the nations who lifted up their horns a	448
	2: 8	and has sent me a the nations	448
	2: 9	I will surely raise my hand a them so	6584
	8:10	for I had turned every man a his neighbor.	928
	8:17	*do* not **plot** evil a your neighbor,	928+3108+4222
	9: 1	The word of the LORD is a the land of	928
	9: 8	I will defend my house a marauding forces.	4946
	9:13	I will rouse your sons, O Zion, a your sons,	6584

```
Zec 10: 3   "My anger burns a the shepherds,                          6584
    12: 3   the nations of the earth are gathered a her,             6584
    13: 7   "Awake, O sword, a my shepherd,                          6584
    13: 7   a the man who is close to me!"                           6584
    13: 7   and I will turn my hand a the little ones.               6584
    14: 2   the nations to Jerusalem to fight a it;                   NIH
    14: 3   Then the LORD will go out and fight a                     928
    14:12   the nations that fought a Jerusalem:                     6584
Mal  3: 5   I will be quick to testify a sorcerers,                   928
     3: 5   a those who defraud laborers                              928
     3:13   "You have said harsh things a me,"                       6584
     3:13   "Yet you ask, 'What have we said a you?'                 6584
Mt   4: 6   you will not strike your foot a a stone.' "              4639
     5:11   and falsely say all kinds of evil a you,                 2848
     5:23   that your brother has something a you,                   2848
     6:14   if you forgive men when they sin a you,                  4183
     7:25   and the winds blew and beat a that house;                4700
     7:27   and the winds blew and beat a that house,                4684
    10:17   "Be on your guard a men;                                  608
    10:21   children will rebel a their parents                      2060
    10:35   I have come to turn " 'a man a his father,               2848
    10:35   a daughter a her mother,                                 2848
    10:35   a daughter-in-law a her mother-in-law—                   2848
    12:25   "Every kingdom divided a itself will                     2848
    12:25   or household divided a itself will not stand.            2848
    12:26   he is divided a himself.                                 2093
    12:30   "He who is not with me is a me,                          2848
    12:31   blasphemy a the Spirit will not be forgiven.             1060
    12:32   a word a the Son of Man will be forgiven,                2848
    12:32   but anyone who speaks a the Holy Spirit                  2848
    14:24   by the waves because the wind was a it.                  1885
    16: 6   on your guard a the yeast of the Pharisees                608
    16:11   on your guard a the yeast of the Pharisees                608
    16:12   not telling them to guard a the yeast used                608
    16:12   but a the teaching of the Pharisees                       608
    18:15   "If your brother sins a you,                             1650
    18:21   when he sins a me?                                       1650
    20:11   they began to grumble a the landowner.                   2848
    23:31   So you testify a yourselves that you are                  AIT
    24: 7   Nation will rise a nation,                               2093
    24: 7   and kingdom a kingdom.                                   2093
    26:59   for false evidence a Jesus so                            2848
    26:62   testimony that these men are bringing a                  2909
    27: 6   "It is a the law to put this into the treasury,          4024
    27:13   testimony they are bringing a                            2909
    27:37   the written charge a him:                                 162
Mk   3:24   If a kingdom is divided a itself,                       2093
     3:25   If a house is divided a itself,                         2093
     3:29   But whoever blasphemes a                                1650
     5:31   "You see the people crowding a you,"                    5315
     6:11   as a testimony a them."                                  AIT
     6:19   So Herodias nursed a grudge a John                      1923
     6:48   because the wind was a them.                            1885
     9:40   for whoever is not a us is for us.                      2848
    10:11   marries another woman commits adultery a                2093
    11:25   if you hold anything a anyone, forgive him,             2848
    12:12   the parable a them.                                     4639
    13: 8   Nation will rise a nation,                              2093
    13: 8   and kingdom a kingdom.                                  2093
    13:12   Children will rebel a their parents                     2060
    14:55   for evidence a Jesus so                                 2848
    14:56   Many testified falsely a him,                          2848
    14:57   up and gave this false testimony a him:                2848
    14:60   What is this testimony that these men are
            bringing a you?"                                        2909
    15:26   The written notice of the charge a him read:            AIT
    15:46   Then he rolled a stone a the entrance of                2093
Lk   2:34   and to be a sign that will be spoken a,                 515
     4:11   you will not strike your foot a a stone.' "             4639
     8:45   crowding and pressing a                                 5309
     9: 5   as a testimony a them."                                 2093
     9:50   "for whoever is not a you is for you."                  2848
    10:11   that sticks to our feet we wipe off a you.               669
    11: 4   for we also forgive everyone who sins a us.              AIT
    11:17   "Any kingdom divided a itself will                      2093
    11:17   and a house divided a itself will fall.                 2093
    11:18   If Satan is divided a himself,                          2093
    11:23   "He who is not with me is a me,                         2848
    12: 1   on your guard a the yeast of the Pharisees,              608
    12:10   a word a the Son of Man will be forgiven,               1650
    12:10   but anyone who blasphemes a                             1650
    12:15   Be on your guard a all kinds of greed;                   608
    12:52   be five in one family divided a each other,              NIG
    12:52   three a two and two against three.                      2093
    12:52   three against two and two a three.                      2093
    12:53   father a son and son against father,                   2093
    12:53   father against son and son a father,                   2093
    12:53   mother a daughter and daughter a mother,               2093
    12:53   against daughter and daughter a mother,                2093
    12:53   mother-in-law a daughter-in-law                        2093
    12:53   and daughter-in-law a mother-in-law."                  2093
    14:31   a king is about to go war a another king.               AIT
    14:31   to oppose the one coming a him                         2093
    15:18   I have sinned a heaven and against you.                1650
    15:18   I have sinned against heaven and a you.                1967
    15:21   I have sinned a heaven and against you,                1650
    15:21   I have sinned against heaven and a you.                1967
    17: 4   If he sins a you seven times in a day,                 1650
    18: 3   'Grant me justice a my adversary.'                      608
    19:43   an embankment a you and encircle you                    AIT
    20:19   they knew he had spoken this parable a                 4639
    21:10   "Nation will rise a nation,                            2093
    21:10   and kingdom a kingdom.                                 2093
    21:23   in the land and wrath a this people.                    AIT
    23: 4   "I find no basis for a charge a this man."             1877
    23:14   and have found no basis for your charges a             2848
Jn  13:18   has lifted up his heel a me.'                          2093

Jn  13:25   Leaning back a Jesus, he asked him, "Lord,             2093
    18:29   "What charges are you bringing a                       2848
    18:38   "I find no basis for a charge a him.                   1877
    19: 4   that I find no basis for a charge a him."              1877
    19: 6   I find no basis for a charge a him."                   1877
    21:20   (This was the one who had leaned back a                2093
Ac   4:26   the rulers gather together a the Lord and              2848
     4:26   against the Lord and a his Anointed One.'              2848
     4:27   to conspire a your holy servant Jesus,                 2093
     5:39   you will only find yourselves fighting a
            God."                                                  2534
     6: 1   among them complained a                                4639
     6:10   but they could not stand up a his wisdom                468
     6:11   of blasphemy a Moses and against God."                 1650
     6:11   of blasphemy against Moses and a God."                  NIG
     6:13   "This fellow never stops speaking a                    2848
     6:13   against this holy place and a the law.                  NIG
     7:60   "Lord, do not hold this sin a them."                    AIT
     8: 1   On that day a great persecution broke out a            2093
     9: 1   Saul was still breathing out murderous
            threats a the Lord's disciples.                        1650
    10:28   "You are well aware that it is a our law for            116
    13:11   Now the hand of the Lord is a you.                     2093
    13:45   with jealousy and talked abusively a                    515
    13:50   stirred up persecution a Paul and Barnabbas            2074
    13:51   from their feet in protest a them and went             2093
    14: 2   up the Gentiles and poisoned their minds a             2848
    16:22   The crowd joined in the attack a Paul                  2848
    19:38   a grievance a anybody,                                 4639
    20: 3   the Jews made a plot a him just as he was               AIT
    21:28   the man who teaches all men everywhere a               2848
    23:29   but there was no charge a him                           NIG
    23:30   of a plot to be carried out a the man,                 1650
    23:30   to present to you their case a him.                    4639
    24: 1   and they brought their charges a Paul                  2848
    24: 8   charges we are bringing a him."                        2989
    24:13   charges they are now making a me.                      2989
    24:19   bring charges if they have anything a me.              4639
    25: 2   and presented the charges a Paul.                      2848
    25: 5   with me and press charges a the man there,             2989
    25: 7   bringing many serious charges a him,                   2965
    25: 7   "I have done nothing wrong a the law of                1650
    25: 8   the Jews or a the temple or against Caesar."           1650
    25: 8   the Jews or against the temple or a Caesar."           1650
    25:11   the charges brought a me by these Jews                 2989
    25:15   the Jews brought charges a him and asked               2848
    25:16   an opportunity to defend himself a                     4309
    25:27   a prisoner without specifying the charges a            2848
    26: 2   as I make my defense a all the accusations             4309
    26:10   I cast my vote a them.                                 2965
    26:11   In my obsession a them,                                 NIG
    26:14   It is hard for you to kick a the goads.'               4639
    27: 4   the lee of Cyprus because the winds were a             1885
    27:29   that we would be dashed a the rocks,                   2848
    28:17   although I have done nothing a our people              1883
    28:17   against our people or a the customs                     NIG
    28:19   had any charge to bring a my own people.               2989
    28:22   that people everywhere are talking a                   515
Ro   1:18   of God is being revealed from heaven a all             2093
     2: 2   Now we know that God's judgment a                     2093
     2: 5   you are storing up wrath a yourself for                2848
     2:21   You who preach a stealing, do you steal?               3590
     4: 8   the Lord will never count a him."                       NIG
     4:18   All hope, Abraham in hope believed a                   4123
     7:23   waging war a the law of my mind                        529
     8:31   If God is for us, who can be a us?                     2848
     8:33   Who will bring any charge a                            2848
    11: 2   how he appealed to God a Israel:                      2848
    13: 2   he who rebels a the authority is rebelling             530
    13: 2   against the authority is rebelling a                   468
1Co  4: 6   not take pride in one man over a another.              2848
     6: 6   one brother goes to law a another—                    3552
     6:18   he who sins sexually sins a his own body.              1650
     8:12   When you sin a your brothers in this way               1650
     8:12   you sin a Christ.                                      1650
    11:27   be guilty of sinning a the body and blood              1944
2Co  2:11   not counting men's sins a them.                        AIT
    10: 5   that sets itself up a the knowledge of God,            2848
    13: 8   For we cannot do anything a the truth,                2848
Gal  5:23   A such things there is a no law.                      2848
Eph  6:11   of God so that you can take your stand a               4639
     6:12   For our struggle is not a flesh and blood,             4639
     6:12   but a the rulers, against the authorities,             4639
     6:12   but against the rulers, a the authorities,             4639
     6:12   a the powers of this dark world and against            4639
     6:12   against the powers of this dark world and a            4639
Col  2:14   that was a us and that stood opposed to us;            2848
     3:13   forgive whatever grievances you may have
            a one another.                                         4639
1Ti  3:10   and then if there is nothing a them,                   441
     5:19   an accusation against an elder unless it is brought    2848
2Ti  2:14   before God a quarreling about words;                   3590
     4:15   You too should be on your guard a him,                 5875
     4:16   May it not be held a them.                              AIT
Heb 12: 4   In your struggle a sin,                               4639
Jas  4:11   Anyone who speaks a his brother                       2895
     4:11   judges him speaks a the law and judges it.            2895
     5: 3   Their corrosion will testify a you                     AIT
     5: 4   workmen who mowed your fields are
            crying out a you.                                      608
     5: 9   Don't grumble a each other, brothers,                 2848
1Pe  2:11   which war a your soul.                                2093
     3:12   face of the Lord is a those who do evil."             2093
     3:16   so that those who speak maliciously a                 2092
2Pe  2:11   do not bring slanderous accusations a                 2848
Jude 1: 9   bring a slanderous accusation a                       2214
     1:10   Yet these men speak abusively a                       1059

Jude 1:15   harsh words ungodly sinners have spoken a             2848
Rev  2: 4   Yet I hold this a you:                                2848
     2:14   Nevertheless, I have a few things a you:              2848
     2:16   to you and will fight a them with the sword           3552
     2:20   Nevertheless, I have this a you:                      2848
    12: 7   and his angels fought a the dragon,                   3552
    12:17   at the woman and went off to make war a               3552
    13: 4   Who can make war a him?"                              3552
    13: 7   He was given power to make war a                      3552
    17:14   They will make war a the Lamb,                        3552
    19:19   to make war a the rider on the horse                  3552
```

AGAR (KJV) See HAGAR

AGATE (2)
```
Ex  28:19   an a and an amethyst;                                 8648
    39:12   an a and an amethyst;                                 8648
```

AGATES (KJV) See RUBY

AGE (67) [AGE-OLD, AGED, AGES, AGING]
```
Ge  15:15   in peace and be buried at a good old a.               8484
    17:17   Will Sarah bear a child at the a of ninety?"       1426+9102
    18:11   and Sarah was past the a of childbearing.
                                            784+851+2021+3869
    21: 2   and bore a son to Abraham in his old a,              2421
    21: 7   Yet I have borne him a son in his old a."            2421
    24:36   a son in her old a,                                  2420
    25: 8   a good old a, an old man and full of years;          8484
    37: 3   he had been born to him in his old a;                2421
    44:20   a young son born to him in his old a.                2421
    48:10   because of old a,                                    2419
    50:26   Joseph died at the a of a hundred and ten.
                                                       1201+9102
Nu   4: 3   from thirty to fifty years of a who come             1201
     4:23   from thirty to fifty years of a who come             1201
     4:30   from thirty to fifty years of a who come             1201
     4:35   from thirty to fifty years of a who came             1201
     4:39   from thirty to fifty years of a who came             1201
     4:43   from thirty to fifty years of a who came             1201
     4:47   to fifty years of a who came to do the work          1201
     8:25   but at the a of fifty,                               1201
Jos  5: 4   all the men of military a—                           4878
     5: 6   until all the men who were of military a             4878
    24:29   died at the a of a hundred and ten.          1201+9102
Jdg  2: 8   died at the a of a hundred and ten.          1201+9102
     8:32   at a good old a and was buried in the tomb           8484
Ru   4:15   and sustain you in your old a.                       8484
2Sa 19:32   a very old man, eighty years of a.                   1201
1Ki 14: 4   his sight was gone because of his a.                 8483
    15:23   In his old a, however,                               2420
1Ch 29:28   He died at a good old a,                             8484
2Ch 24:15   he died at the a of a hundred and thirty    1201+9102
Ezr  3: 8   Levites twenty years of a and older                 1201
Job 32: 7   I thought, 'A should speak,                          3427
Ps  92:14   They will still bear fruit in old a,                 8484
Isa 46: 4   Even to your old a and gray hairs I am he,           2420
Da   1:10   the other young men your a?                          1636
     5:31   at the a of sixty-two.                      10120+10732
Zec  8: 4   and women of ripe old a will sit in                  2418
     8: 4   with cane in hand because of his a.          3427+8044
Mt  12:32   either in this a or in the age to come.              172
    12:32   either in this age or in the a to come.              NIG
    13:39   The harvest is the end of the a,                     172
    13:40   so it will be at the end of the a.                   172
    13:49   This is how it will be at the end of the a.          172
    24: 3   of your coming and of the end of the a?"             172
    28:20   to the very end of the a."                           172
Mk  10:30   a hundred times as much in this present             2789
    10:30   and in the a to come, eternal life.                  172
Lk   1:36   to have a child in her old a,                       1179
    18:30   to receive many times as much in this a             2789
    18:30   in the a to come, eternal life."                     172
    20:34   "The people of this a marry and are given            172
    20:35   in that a and in the resurrection from               172
Jn   9:21   He is of a; he will speak for himself."             2461
     9:23   "He is of a; ask him."                              2461
1Co  1:20   Where is the philosopher of this a?                  172
     2: 6   not the wisdom of this a or of the rulers            172
     2: 6   of this age or of the rulers of this a,              172
     2: 8   None of the rulers of this a understood it,          172
     3:18   by the standards of this a,                          172
2Co  4: 4   The god of this a has blinded the minds             172
Gal  1: 4   to rescue us from the present evil a,                172
     1:14   in Judaism beyond many Jews of my own a             5312
Eph  1:21   in the present a but also in the one to come.        172
1Ti  6:19   as a firm foundation for the coming a,               NIG
Tit  2:12   upright and godly lives in this present a,           172
Heb  6: 5   of God and the powers of the coming a,               172
    11:11   Abraham, even though he was past a—                 2461
```

AGE-OLD (4) [AGE]
```
Ge  49:26   than the bounty of the a hills.                      6409
Jdg  5:21   river Kishon swept them away, the a river,           7704
Isa 58:12   will raise up the a foundations;      1887+1887+2256
Hab  3: 6   and the a hills collapsed.                           6409
```

AGED (11) [AGE]
```
Ge  43:27   "How is your father you told me about?               2418
    44:20   And we answered, 'We have an a father,               2418
Lev 19:32   " 'Rise in the presence of the a,                    8484
1Ki  1:15   So Bathsheba went to see the a king          2416+4394
```

2Ch 36:17 nor young woman, old man or **a.** 3844
Job 12:12 Is not wisdom found among the **a?** 3813
   15:10 The gray-haired and the **a** are on our side, 3813
   32: 9 the **a** who understand what is right. 2418
Pr 17: 6 Children's children are a crown to the **a,** 2418
Isa 25: 6 a banquet of **a** wine— 9069
   47: 6 Even on the **a** you laid a very heavy yoke. 2418

AGEE (1)
2Sa 23:11 to him was Shammah son of **A** the Hararite. 96

AGENT (2)
Ne 11:24 the king's **a** in all affairs relating to 3338+4200
Ro 13: 4 **a** of wrath **to bring punishment** 1690

AGES (14) [AGE]
Ge 43:33 order of their **a,** from the firstborn to 1148+7584
Lev 27: 3 between the **a** *of* twenty and sixty 1201+9102
   27: 5 between the **a** of five and twenty, 1201+9102
Isa 45:17 to shame or disgraced, to **a** everlasting. 6409
Joel 2: 2 as never was of old nor ever will be in **a** 9102
Ac 15:18 that have been known for **a.** 172
Ro 16:25 of the mystery hidden *for* long **a** past, 173
1Co 10:11 on whom the fulfillment *of* the **a** has come. 172
Eph 2: 7 in order that in the coming **a** he might show 172
   3: 9 which *for* **a** past was kept hidden in God, 172
Col 1:26 the mystery that has been kept hidden for **a** 172
Heb 9:26 at the end *of* the **a** to do away with sin by 172
Jude 1:25 through Jesus Christ our Lord, before all **a,** 172
Rev 15: 3 Just and true are your ways, King *of* the **a.** 172

AGGRESSION (1) [AGGRESSIVE, AGGRESSOR]
Isa 14: 6 in fury subdued nations with relentless **a.** 5284

AGGRESSIVE (2) [AGGRESSION]
Isa 18: 2 an **a** nation of strange speech, 4431
   18: 7 an **a** nation of strange speech, 4431

AGGRESSOR (1) [AGGRESSION]
Isa 16: 4 the **a** will vanish from the land. 8252

AGHAST (2)
Job 26:11 pillars of the heavens quake, **a** at his rebuke. 9449
Isa 13: 8 *They will* **look** at each other, 9449

AGING (1) [AGE]
Heb 8:13 what is obsolete and **a** will soon disappear. 1180

AGITATING (1) [AGITATORS]
Ac 17:13 **a** the crowds and stirring them up. 4888

AGITATORS (1) [AGITATING]
Gal 5:12 As for those **a,** 415

AGO (48)
Jos 24: 2 'Long **a** your forefathers, 4946+6409
1Sa 9:20 the donkeys you lost three days **a,** 2021+3427
   30:13 when I became ill three days **a.** AIT
2Sa 20:18 "Long **a** they used to say, 928+2021+8037
2Ki 19:25 Long **a** I ordained it. 4200+4946+8158
Ezr 5:11 the temple that was built many years **a,** 10180+10427+10622
Ne 12:46 For long **a,** in the days of David 4946+7710
Ps 44: 1 in their days, in days long **a.** 7710
   77: 5 the years of long **a;** 6409
   77:11 I will remember your miracles of long **a.** 7710
   93: 2 Your throne was established long **a;** 255+4946
   119:152 Long **a** I learned from your statutes 7710
   143: 5 I remember the days of long **a.** 7710
Ecc 1:10 It was here already, long **a;** 4200+6409
Isa 22:11 for the One who planned it long **a.** 4946+8158
   25: 1 things planned long **a.** 4946+8158
   37:26 Long **a** I ordained it. 4200+4946+8158
   44: 8 not proclaim this and foretell it long **a?** 255+4946
   45:21 Who foretold this long **a,** 4946+7710
   46: 9 the former things, those of long **a,** 6409
   48: 3 I foretold the former things long **a,** 255+4946
   48: 5 I told you these things long **a;** 255+4946
   48: 7 They are created now, and not long **a;** 255+4946
Jer 2:20 "Long **a** you broke off your yoke 4946+6409
La 2:17 which he decreed long **a.** 3427+4946+7710
Eze 26:20 go down to the pit, to the people of long **a.** 6409
Mic 7:14 in Bashan and Gilead as in days long **a.** 6409
   7:20 on oath to our fathers in days long **a.** 7710
Mt 5:21 that it was said *to* the **people** long **a,** 792
   5:33 that it was said *to* the **people** long **a,** 792
   11:21 they would have repented long **a** 4093
Mk 6:15 like one of the prophets of long **a."** NIG
Lk 1:70 through his holy prophets of long **a,** 172
   9: 8 of the prophets *of* long **a** had come back 792
   9:19 of the prophets *of* long **a** has come back 792
   10:13 they would have repented long **a.** 4093
Jn 11: 8 "a short while **a** the Jews tried to stone you, 3814
Ac 1:16 the Holy Spirit **spoke** long **a** through 4625
   3:21 as he promised long **a.** 172+608
   5:36 **Some time a** Theudas appeared, 2465+3836+4047+4574

Ac 10:30 "Four days **a** I was in my house praying NIG
   15: 7 **some time a** God made a choice 608+792+2465
   21:38 the desert **some time a?"** 2465+3836+4047+4574
   24:11 no more than twelve days **a** I went up 608+4005
2Co 12: 2 in Christ who fourteen years **a** was caught 4574
1Pe 3:20 who disobeyed long **a** when God waited 4537
2Pe 3: 5 But they deliberately forget that **long a** 1732
Jude 1: 4 about **long a** have secretly slipped in 4093

AGONE (KJV) See AGO

AGONY (11)
Ps 6: 2 O LORD, heal me, for my bones *are* **in a.** 987
   42:10 My bones suffer **mortal a.** 8358
Jer 4:19 Oh, the **a** of my heart! 7815
Eze 30:16 Pelusium *will* **writhe in a.** 2655+2655
Mic 4:10 Writhe **in a,** O Daughter of Zion, 1631
Zec 9: 5 Gaza *will* **writhe in a,** and Ekron too, 2655+4394
Lk 16:24 because *I am* **in a** in this fire.' 3849
   16:25 now he is comforted here and you *are* **in a.** 3849
Ac 2:24 freeing him from the **a** of death, 6047
Rev 9: 5 the **a** they suffered was like that of the sting 990
   16:10 Men gnawed their tongues in **a** 4506

AGREE (14) [AGREED, AGREEING, AGREEMENT, AGREEMENTS, AGREES, DISAGREE, DISAGREEMENT]
Ge 34:17 But if *you will* not **a** to be circumcised, 9048
2Sa 14:16 the king *will* **a** to deliver his servant from 9048
1Ki 20: 8 "Don't listen to him or **a** to his **demands."** 14
   22:13 *Let* your word **a** with theirs, 285+2118+3869
2Ch 18:12 *Let* your word **a** with theirs, 285+2118+3869
Mt 18:19 of you on earth **a** about anything you ask 5244
   20:13 Didn't *you* **a** to work for a denarius? 5244
Mk 14:56 but their statements did not **a.** 2698
   14:59 Yet even then their testimony did not **a.** 2698
Ac 5: 9 *could you* **a** to test the Spirit of the Lord? 5244
Ro 7:16 *I* **a** that the law is good. 5238
1Co 1:10 that all of *you* **a** with one another 899+3306+3836
Php 4: 2 with Syntyche to **a** with each other in 5858
1Ti 6: 3 and *does* not **a** to the sound instruction 4665

AGREED (27) [AGREE]
Ge 16: 2 Abram **a** to what Sarai said. 9048
   23:16 Abraham **a** to Ephron's *terms* 9048
   30:34 "**A,**" said Laban. 2176
   34:24 All the men who went out of the city gate **a** 9048
   37:27 His brothers **a.** 9048
Ex 2:21 Moses **a** to stay with the man, 3283
Jos 2:21 "**A,**" she replied. 4026
Jdg 15:13 "**A,**" they answered. 4202
   17:11 So the Levite **a** to live with him, 3283
1Ki 15:20 Ben-Hadad **a** with King Asa and sent 9048
   20:25 He **a** with them and acted accordingly. 4200+7754+9048
2Ki 12: 8 The priests **a** that they would 252
1Ch 13: 4 The whole assembly **a** to do this, 606
2Ch 16: 4 Ben-Hadad **a** with King Asa and sent 9048
   20:36 He **a** with him to construct a fleet 2489
   30:23 The whole assembly then **a** to celebrate 3619
Est 9:23 So the Jews **a** to continue 7691
Jer 34:10 into this covenant **a** 9048
   34:10 They **a,** and set them free. 9048
Da 1:14 So he **a** to this and tested them for ten days. 9048
   6: 7 advisers and governors *have* all **a** that 10324
Am 3: 3 Do two walk together unless *they have* **a** 3359
Mt 20: 2 He **a** to pay them a denarius for the day 5244
Lk 22: 5 They were delighted and **a** 5338
Ac 15:25 So we all **a** to choose some men 1181+3924
   23:20 "The Jews *have* **a** to ask you to bring Paul 5338
Gal 2: 9 They **a** that we should go to the Gentiles, NIG

AGREEING (1) [AGREE]
Rev 17:17 *by* **a** to give the beast their power to rule, 1191+1651+4472

AGREEMENT (12) [AGREE]
Ge 26:28 'There ought to be **a sworn a** between us'— 460
2Sa 3:12 Make an **a** with me, 1382
   3:13 "I will make an **a** with you. 1382
Ne 9:38 we are making a **binding a,** 591
Job 2:11 and **met** together by **a** to go and sympathize 3585
   41: 4 Will he make an **a** with you for you 1382
Isa 28:15 with the grave we have made an **a.** 2603
   28:18 your **a** with the grave will not stand. 2607
Da 11:23 After **coming** to an **a,** 2489
Ac 15:15 words of the prophets *are* **in a** with this, 5244
2Co 6:16 What **a** is there between the temple of God 5161
1Jn 5: 8 and the three are **in a.** 1650+1651+3836

AGREEMENTS (1) [AGREE]
Hos 10: 4 take false oaths and make **a;** 1382

AGREES (3) [AGREE]
Ac 7:42 **This a** with what is written in the book of 2777
   24:14 I believe everything that **a** with the Law and 2848
1Co 4:17 **which a** with what I teach everywhere 2777

AGRIPPA (11)
Ac 25:13 A few days later King **A** and Bernice 68

Ac 25:22 Then **A** said to Festus, "I would like to hear 68
   25:23 The next day **A** and Bernice came 68
   25:24 "King **A,** and all who are present with us, 68
   25:26 and especially before you, King **A,** 68
   26: 1 Then **A** said to Paul, "You have permission 68
   26: 2 "King **A,** I consider myself fortunate 68
   26:19 King **A,** I was not disobedient to the vision 68
   26:27 King **A,** do you believe the prophets? 68
   26:28 Then **A** said to Paul, "Do you think 68
   26:32 **A** said to Festus, "This man could have been 68

AGROUND (4) [GROUND]
Ac 27:17 that *they* would **run a** on the sandbars 1738
   27:26 we must **run a** on some island." 1738
   27:39 where they decided *to* **run** the ship **a** 2034
   27:41 But the ship struck a sandbar and **ran a.** 2131

AGUE (KJV) See FEVER

AGUR (1)
Pr 30: 1 The sayings of **A** son of Jakeh— 101

AH (15) [AHA]
Ge 27:27 he blessed him and said, "**A,** 8011
Nu 24:23 "**A,** who can live when God does this? 208
Jos 7: 7 And Joshua said, "**A,** Sovereign LORD, 177
Jdg 6:22 he exclaimed, "**A,** Sovereign LORD! 177
Isa 1: 4 **A,** sinful nation, a people loaded with guilt, 2098
   1:24 "**A,** I will get relief from my foes 2098
   44:16 He also warms himself and says, "**A!** 2027
Jer 1: 6 "**A,** Sovereign LORD," I said, 177
   4:10 Then I said, "**A,** Sovereign LORD, 177
   14:13 But I said, "**A,** Sovereign LORD, 177
   32:17 "**A,** Sovereign LORD, you have made 177
   47: 6 " '**A,** sword of the LORD,' [you cry,] 2098
Eze 9: 8 crying out, "**A,** Sovereign LORD! 177
   11:13 "**A,** Sovereign LORD! 177
   20:49 Then I said, "**A,** Sovereign LORD! 177

AHA (11) [AH]
Job 39:25 At the blast of the trumpet he snorts, '**A!**' 2027
Ps 35:21 They gape at me and say, "**A!** 2027
   35:21 at me and say, "Aha! **A!** 2027
   35:25 Do not let them think, "**A,** 2027
   40:15 May those who say to me, "**A!** 2027
   40:15 May those who say to me, "Aha! **A!"** 2027
   70: 3 May those who say to me, "**A!** 2027
   70: 3 May those who say to me, "Aha! **A!"** 2027
Eze 25: 3 Because you said "**A!"** 2027
   26: 2 because Tyre has said of Jerusalem, '**A!** 2027
   36: 2 The enemy said of you, "**A!** 2027

AHAB (85) [AHAB'S]
1Ki 16:28 And **A** his son succeeded him as king. 281
   16:29 **A** son of Omri became king of Israel, 281
   16:30 **A** son of Omri did more evil in the eyes of 281
   16:33 **A** also made an Asherah pole and did more 281
   17: 1 from Tishbe in Gilead, said to **A,** 281
   18: 1 "Go and present yourself to **A,** 281
   18: 2 So Elijah went to present himself to **A.** 281
   18: 3 and **A** had summoned Obadiah, 281
   18: 5 **A** had said to Obadiah, 281
   18: 6 **A** going in one direction and Obadiah 281
   18: 9 over to **A** to be put to death? 281
   18:12 If I go and tell **A** and he doesn't find you, 281
   18:15 I will surely present myself to **A** today." 2257S
   18:16 So Obadiah went to meet **A** and told him, 281
   18:16 and **A** went to meet Elijah. 281
   18:20 So **A** sent word throughout all Israel 281
   18:41 And Elijah said to **A,** "Go, eat and drink, 281
   18:42 So **A** went off to eat and drink, 281
   18:44 So Elijah said, "Go and tell **A,** 281
   18:45 a heavy rain came on and **A** rode off 281
   18:46 he ran ahead of **A** all the way to Jezreel. 281
   19: 1 **A** told Jezebel everything Elijah had done 281
   20: 2 He sent messengers into the city to **A** king 281
   20:10 Ben-Hadad sent another message to **A:** 2257S
   20:13 Meanwhile a prophet came to **A** king 281
   20:14 "But who will do this?" asked **A.** 281
   20:15 So **A** summoned the young officers of NIH
   20:33 **A** had him come up into his chariot. 281
   20:34 [**A** said,] "On the basis of NIH
   21: 1 close to the palace of **A** king of Samaria. 281
   21: 2 **A** said to Naboth, "Let me have your vineyard 281
   21: 4 So **A** went home, sullen and angry 281
   21:15 she said to **A,** "Get up and take possession 281
   21:16 When **A** heard that Naboth was dead, 281
   21:18 "Go down to meet **A** king of Israel, 281
   21:20 **A** said to Elijah, "So you have found me, 281
   21:21 and cut off from **A** every last male 281
   21:24 to **A** who die in the country. 281
   21:25 (There was never a man like **A,** 281
   21:27 When **A** heard these words, 281
   21:29 how **A** has humbled himself before me? 281
   22:20 'Who will entice **A** into attacking 281
   22:40 **A** rested with his fathers. 281
   22:41 in the fourth year of **A** king of Israel. 281
   22:49 At that time Ahaziah son of **A** said 281
   22:51 of **A** became king of Israel in Samaria in 281
2Ki 3: 1 of **A** became king of Israel in Samaria in 281
   3: 5 But after **A** died, the king of Moab rebelled 281
   8:16 In the fifth year of Joram son of **A** king 281

2Ki	8:18	as the house of A had done,	281
	8:18	for he married a daughter of A.	281
	8:25	In the twelfth year of Joram son of A king	281
	8:27	of the house of A and did evil in the eyes of	281
	8:27	as the house of A had done,	281
	8:28	Ahaziah went with Joram son of A to war	281
	8:29	down to Jezreel to see Joram son of A	281
	9: 7	to destroy the house of A your master,	281
	9: 8	The whole house of A will perish.	281
	9: 8	I will cut off from A every last male	281
	9: 9	I will make the house of A like the house	281
	9:25	in chariots behind A his father when	281
	9:29	(In the eleventh year of Joram son of A,	281
	10: 1	in Samaria seventy sons of the house of A.	281
	10:10	against the house of A will fail.	281
	10:11	in Jezreel who remained of the house of A,	281
	10:18	"A served Baal a little;	281
	10:30	and have done to the house of A all I had	281
	21: 3	as A king of Israel had done.	281
	21:13	the plumb line used against the house of A.	281
2Ch	18: 1	and he allied himself with A by marriage.	281
	18: 2	Some years later he went down to visit A.	281
	18: 2	A slaughtered many sheep and cattle	281
	18: 3	A king of Israel asked Jehoshaphat king	281
	18:19	'Who will entice A king of Israel	281
	21: 6	as the house of A had done,	281
	21: 6	for he married a daughter of A.	281
	21:13	just as the house of A did.	281
	22: 3	in the ways of the house of A,	281
	22: 4	as the house of A had done,	281
	22: 5	with Joram son of A king of Israel to war	281
	22: 6	down to Jezreel to see Joram son of A	281
	22: 7	to destroy the house of A.	281
	22: 8	executing judgment on the house of A,	281
Jer	29:21	about a son of Kolaiah and Zedekiah son	281
	29:22	like Zedekiah and A,	282

AHAB'S (8) [AHAB]

1Ki	16:34	In A time, Hiel of Bethel rebuilt Jericho.	2257S
	21: 8	So she wrote letters in A name,	281
	22:39	As for the other events of A reign,	281
2Ki	1: 1	After A death, Moab rebelled against Israel.	281
	8:27	for he was related by marriage to A family.	281
	10: 1	and to the guardians of A children.	281
	10:17	killed all who were left there of A family;	281
Mic	6:16	of Omri and all the practices of A house,	281

AHARAH (1)

1Ch	8: 1	Ashbel the second son, A the third,	341

AHARHEL (1)

1Ch	4: 8	and Hazzobebah and of the clans of A son	342

AHASAI (KJV) See AHZAI

AHASBAI (1)

2Sa	23:34	Eliphelet son of A the Maacathite,	335

AHASUERUS' (KJV) See XERXES

AHAVA (3)

Ezr	8:15	at the canal that flows toward A,	178
	8:21	There, by the A Canal, I proclaimed a fast,	178
	8:31	the first month we set out from the A Canal	178

AHAZ (44)

2Ki	15:38	And A his son succeeded him as king.	298
	16: 1	A son of Jotham king of Judah began	298
	16: 2	A was twenty years old	298
	16: 5	to fight against Jerusalem and besieged A,	298
	16: 7	A sent messengers to say	298
	16: 8	And A took the silver and gold found in	298
	16:10	Then King A went to Damascus	298
	16:11	with all the plans that King A had sent	298
	16:11	and finished it before King A returned.	298
	16:15	King A then gave these orders to Uriah	298
	16:16	the priest did just as King A had ordered.	298
	16:17	King A took away the side panels	298
	16:19	As for the other events of the reign of A,	298
	16:20	A rested with his fathers and was buried	298
	17: 1	In the twelfth year of A king of Judah,	298
	18: 1	Hezekiah son of A king of Judah began	298
	20:11	down on the stairway of A.	298
	23:12	on the roof near the upper room of A,	298
1Ch	3:13	A his son, Hezekiah his son,	298
	8:35	Pithon, Melech, Tarea and A.	298
	8:36	A was the father of Jehoaddah,	298
	9:41	Pithon, Melech, Tahrea and A.	298
	9:42	A was the father of Jadah,	298
2Ch	27: 9	And A his son succeeded him as king.	298
	28: 1	A was twenty years old	298
	28:16	that time King A sent to the king of Assyria	298
	28:19	because of A king of Israel,	298
	28:21	A took some of the things from the temple	298
	28:22	In his time of trouble King A became	298
	28:24	A gathered together the furnishings from	298
	28:27	A rested with his fathers and was buried in	298
	29:19	that King A removed in his unfaithfulness	298
Isa	1: 1	Jotham, A and Hezekiah, kings of Judah.	298
	7: 1	When A son of Jotham, the son of Uzziah,	298
	7: 2	the hearts of A and his people were shaken,	2257S
	7: 3	to meet A at the end of the aqueduct of	298

Isa	7:10	Again the LORD spoke to A,	298
	7:12	But A said, "I will not ask;	298
	14:28	This oracle came in the year King A died:	298
	38: 8	down on the stairway of A.' "	298
Hos	1: 1	Jotham, A and Hezekiah, kings of Judah.	298
Mic	1: 1	A and Hezekiah, kings of Judah—	298
Mt	1: 9	Jotham the father of A,	937
	1: 9	A the father of Hezekiah,	937

AHAZIAH (39) [AHAZIAH'S]

1Ki	22:40	And A his son succeeded him as king.	302
	22:49	At that time A son of Ahab said	302
	22:51	A son of Ahab became king of Israel	302
2Ki	1: 2	Now A had fallen through the lattice	301
	1:17	Because A had no son,	2257S
	8:24	And A his son succeeded him as king.	302
	8:25	A son of Jehoram king of Judah began	302
	8:26	A was twenty-two years old	302
	8:28	A went with Joram son of Ahab to war	NIH
	8:29	Then A son of Jehoram king of Judah went	302
	9:16	because Joram was resting there and A king	301
	9:21	of Israel and A king of Judah rode out,	302
	9:23	calling out to A, "Treachery, Ahaziah!"	302
	9:23	calling out to Ahaziah, "Treachery, A!"	301
	9:27	A king of Judah saw what had happened,	302
	9:29	A had become king of Judah.	301
	10:13	he met some relatives of A king of Judah	302
	10:13	They said, "We are relatives of A,	302
	11: 1	the mother of A saw that her son was dead,	302
	11: 2	daughter of King Jehoram and sister of A,	302
	11: 2	took Joash son of A and stole him away	301
	12:18	Jehoshaphat, Jehoram and A,	302
	13: 1	of Joash son of A king of Judah,	302
	14:13	the son of A, at Beth Shemesh.	302
1Ch	3:11	Jehoram his son, A his son, Joash his son,	302
2Ch	20:35	of Judah made an alliance with A king	301
	20:37	you have made an alliance with A,	302
	21:17	Not a son was left to him except A,	3370
	22: 1	The people of Jerusalem made A,	302
	22: 1	So A son of Jehoram king of Judah began	302
	22: 2	A was twenty-two years old	302
	22: 6	Then A son of Jehoram king of Judah went	302
	22: 7	When A arrived, he went out with Joram	2257S
	22: 8	who had been attending A,	302
	22: 9	He then went in search of A,	302
	22: 9	in the house of A powerful enough to retain	302
	22:10	the mother of A saw that her son was dead,	302
	22:11	took Joash son of A and stole him away	302
	25:23	the son of A, at Beth Shemesh.	3370

AHAZIAH'S (5) [AHAZIAH]

2Ki	1:18	As for all the other events of A reign,	302
2Ch	22: 7	Through A visit to Joram,	NIH
	22: 7	God brought about A downfall.	302
	22: 8	of Judah and the sons of A relatives,	302
	22:11	of the priest Jehoiada, was A sister, she hid	302

AHBAN (1)

1Ch	2:29	who bore him A and Molid.	283

AHEAD (97) [HEAD]

Ge	31:18	drove all his livestock a	5627
	32: 3	Jacob sent messengers a of him	4200+7156
	32:16	and said to his servants, "Go a of me,	4200+7156
	32:20	with these gifts I am sending on a;	4200+7156
	32:21	So Jacob's gifts went on a of him,	6584+7156
	33: 3	He himself went on a and bowed down	4200+7156
	33:14	So let my lord go on a of his servant,	4200+7156
	45: 5	to save lives that God sent me a of you	4200+7156
	45: 7	But God sent me a of you to preserve	4200+7156
	46:28	Jacob sent Judah a of him to Joseph	4200+7156
	48:20	So he put Ephraim a of Manasseh.	4200+7156
Ex	13:21	By day the LORD went a of them in	4200+7156
	17: 5	"Walk on a of the people.	4200+7156
	23:20	an angel of you to guard you along	4200+7156
	23:23	My angel will go a of you and bring	4200+7156
	23:27	"I will send my terror a of you	4200+7156
	23:28	hornet a of you to drive the Hivites,	4200+7156
Nu	22:26	Then the angel of the LORD moved on a	6296
	32:17	we are ready to arm ourselves and go a	4200+7156
Dt	1:22	"Let us send men a to spy out the land	4200+7156
	1:33	who went a of you on your journey,	4200+7156
	3:18	over a of your brother Israelites.	4200+7156
	9: 3	the one who goes across a of you like	4200+7156
	31: 3	God himself will cross over a of you,	4200+7156
	31: 3	Joshua also will cross over a of you,	4200+7156
Jos	1:14	must cross over a of your brothers.	4200+7156
	3: 6	ark of the covenant and pass on a of	4200+7156
	3: 6	So they took it up and went a of them.	4200+7156
	3:11	will go into the Jordan a of you.	4200+7156
	3:14	the ark of the covenant went a of them	4200+7156
	6: 7	the armed guard going a of the ark	4200+7156
	6: 9	The armed guard marched a of	4200+7156
	6:13	The armed men went a of them and	4200+7156
Jdg	24:12	I sent the hornet a of you,	4200+7156
	4:14	Has not the LORD gone a of you?"	4200+7156
	7:24	the Jordan a of them as far as Beth Barah."	4200
Ru	2: 2	Naomi said to her, "Go a, my daughter."	2143
1Sa	9:12	"He's a of you.	4200+7156
	9:19	"Go up a of me to the high place,	4200+7156
	9:27	"Tell the servant to go a of us"—	4200+7156
	10: 8	"Go down a of me to Gilgal.	4200+7156
	14: 7	"Go a; I am with you heart and soul."	5742
	17: 7	His shield bearer went a of him.	4200+7156

1Sa	23:24	set out and went to Ziph a of Saul.	4200+7156
	25:19	Then she told her servants, "Go on a;	4200+7156
	30:20	and his men drove them a of	4200+7156
2Sa	7: 3	go a and do it, for the LORD is with you."	2143
	15: 1	and horses and with fifty men to run a	4200+7156
	15:22	David said to Ittai, "Go a, march on."	2143
1Ki	1: 5	with fifty men to run a of him.	4200+7156
	18:46	he ran a of Ahab all the way to Jezreel.	4200+7156
2Ki	4:31	went on a and laid the staff on the boy's face,	4200+7156
	5:23	and they carried them a of Gehazi.	4200+7156
	6:32	The king sent a messenger a,	4200+4946+7156
Ne	4: 7	the repairs to Jerusalem's walls had gone a	6590
Pr	4:25	Let your eyes look straight a,	4200+5790
Jer	7:21	Go a, add your burnt offerings	AIT
	44:25	"Go a then, do what you promised!	AIT
Eze	1: 9	Each one went straight a;	448+6298+7156
	1:12	Each one went straight a.	448+6298+7156
	10:22	Each one went straight a.	448+6298+7156
Joel	2: 8	each marches straight a.	5019
Mt	2: 9	the star they had seen in the east went a of	4575
	11:10	" 'I will send my messenger a of you,	4574+4725
	14:22	and go on a of him to the other side,	4575
	21: 2	"Go to the village a of you,	2978
	21: 9	The crowds that went a of him and those	4575
	21:31	entering the kingdom of God a of you.	4575
	24:25	See, I have told you a of time.	4625
	26:32	I will go a of you into Galilee."	4575
	28: 7	from the dead and is going a of you	4575
Mk	1: 2	"I will send my messenger a of you,	4574+4725
	6:33	from all the towns and got there a of them.	4601
	6:45	the boat and go on a of him to Bethsaida.	4575
	11: 2	"Go to the village a of you,	2978
	11: 9	Those who went a and those who followed	4575
	13:23	told you everything a of time.	4625
	14:28	I will go a of you into Galilee."	4575
	16: 7	'He is going a of you into Galilee.	4575
Lk	7:27	" 'I will send my messenger a of you,	4574+4725
	9:52	And he sent messengers on a,	4574+4725
	10: 1	two by two a of him to every town	4574+4725
	19: 4	So he ran a and climbed	1869
	19:28	After Jesus had said this, he went on a,	1869
	19:30	"Go to the village a of you,	2978
	19:32	Those who were sent a went	NIG
Jn	3:28	'I am not the Christ but am sent a of him.'	1869
	3:28	someone else goes down a of me."	4574
	10: 4	he goes on a of them,	1869
Ac	2:31	Seeing what was a, he spoke	4632
	20: 5	These men went on a and waited for us	4601
	20:13	We went on a to the ship and sailed	4601
1Co	11:21	each of you goes a without waiting	4624
Php	3:13	behind and straining toward what is a,	1869
1Ti	5:24	reaching the place of judgment a of them;	4575
Heb	11:26	because he was looking a to his reward.	611
2Jn	1: 9	Anyone who runs a and does not continue	4575

AHER (1)

1Ch	7:12	and the Hushites the descendants of A.	338

AHI (2)

1Ch	5:15	A son of Abdiel, the son of Guni,	306
	7:34	A, Rohgah, Hubbah and Aram.	306

AHIAH (1)

Ne	10:26	A, Hanan, Anan,	308

AHIAM (2)

2Sa	23:33	A son of Sharar the Hararite,	307
1Ch	11:35	A son of Sacar the Hararite,	307

AHIAN (1)

1Ch	7:19	A, Shechem, Likhi and Aniam.	319

AHIEZER (6)

Nu	1:12	from Dan, A son of Ammishaddai;	323
	2:25	The leader of the people of Dan is A son	323
	7:66	On the tenth day A son of Ammishaddai,	323
	7:71	the offering of A son of Ammishaddai.	323
	10:25	A son of Ammishaddai was in command.	323
1Ch	12: 3	A their chief and Joash the sons	323

AHIHUD (2)

Nu	34:27	A son of Shelomi, the leader from the tribe	310
1Ch	8: 7	and who was the father of Uzza and A.	312

AHIJAH (21) [AHIJAH'S]

1Sa	14: 3	among whom was A,	308
	14:18	Saul said to A, "Bring the ark of God."	308
1Ki	4: 3	Elihoreph and A, sons of Shisha—	308
	11:29	and A the prophet of Shiloh met him on	308
	11:30	and A took hold of the new cloak	308
	12:15	to Jeroboam son of Nebat through A	308
	14: 2	A the prophet is there—	308
	14: 4	Now A could not see;	308
	14: 5	But the LORD had told A,	309
	14: 6	So when A heard the sound of her footsteps	309
	14:18	through his servant the prophet A.	309
	15:27	of A of the house of Issachar plotted	308
	15:29	of the LORD given through his servant A	308
	15:33	Baasha son of A became king of all Israel	308
	21:22	of Nebat and that of Baasha son of A,	308
2Ki	9: 9	and like the house of Baasha son of A.	308

1Ch	2:25	Bunah, Oren, Ozem and **A**.	308
	8: 7	**A**, and Gera, who deported them	308
	11:36	Hepher the Mekerathite, **A** the Pelonite,	308
2Ch	9:29	of **A** the Shilonite and in the visions of Iddo	308
	10:15	to Jeroboam son of Nebat through **A**	309

AHIJAH'S (1) [AHIJAH]

1Ki	14: 4	and went to **A** house in Shiloh.	308

AHIKAM (20)

2Ki	22:12	**A** son of Shaphan, Acbor son of Micaiah,	324
	22:14	Hilkiah the priest, **A**, Acbor,	324
	25:22	of Babylon appointed Gedaliah son of **A**,	324
2Ch	34:20	**A** son of Shaphan, Abdon son of Micah,	324
Jer	26:24	**A** son of Shaphan supported Jeremiah,	324
	39:14	over to Gedaliah son of **A**,	324
	40: 5	"Go back to Gedaliah son of **A**,	324
	40: 6	of **A** at Mizpah and stayed with him among	324
	40: 7	of **A** as governor over the land	324
	40: 9	Gedaliah son of **A**, the son of Shaphan,	324
	40:11	and had appointed Gedaliah son of **A**,	324
	40:14	Gedaliah son of **A** did not believe them.	324
	40:16	But Gedaliah son of **A** said to Johanan son	324
	41: 1	came with ten men to Gedaliah son of **A**	324
	41: 2	up and struck down Gedaliah son of **A**,	324
	41: 6	he said, "Come to Gedaliah son of **A**."	324
	41:10	of the imperial guard had appointed Gedaliah son of **A**,	324
	41:16	after he had assassinated Gedaliah son of **A**:	324
	41:18	of Nethaniah had killed Gedaliah son of **A**,	324
	43: 6	with Gedaliah son of **A**,	324

AHILUD (5)

2Sa	8:16	Jehoshaphat son of **A** was recorder;	314
	20:24	Jehoshaphat son of **A** was recorder;	314
1Ki	4: 3	Jehoshaphat son of **A**—	314
	4:12	Baana son of **A**—	314
1Ch	18:15	Jehoshaphat son of **A** was recorder;	314

AHIMAAZ (15)

1Sa	14:50	wife's name was Ahinoam daughter of **A**.	318
2Sa	15:27	with your son **A** and Jonathan son	318
	15:36	**A** son of Zadok and Jonathan son	318
	17:17	Jonathan and **A** were staying at En Rogel.	318
	17:20	they asked, "Where are **A** and Jonathan?"	318
	18:19	Now **A** son of Zadok said,	318
	18:22	**A** son of Zadok again said to Joab,	318
	18:23	Then **A** ran by way of the plain and outran	318
	18:27	that the first one runs like **A** son of Zadok."	318
	18:28	**A** called out to the king, "All is well!"	318
	18:29	**A** answered, "I saw great confusion just	318
1Ki	4:15	**A**—in Naphtali (he had married Basemath	318
1Ch	6: 8	Zadok the father of **A**,	318
	6: 9	**A** the father of Azariah,	318
	6:53	Zadok his son and **A** his son.	318

AHIMAN (4)

Nu	13:22	where **A**, Sheshai and Talmai,	317
Jos	15:14	Sheshai, **A** and Talmai—	317
Jdg	1:10	and defeated Sheshai, **A** and Talmai.	317
1Ch	9:17	Akkub, Talmon, **A** and their brothers,	317

AHIMELECH (19)

1Sa	21: 1	David went to Nob, to **A** the priest.	316
	21: 1	**A** trembled when he met him, and asked,	316
	21: 2	David answered **A** the priest,	316
	21: 8	David asked **A**, "Don't you have a spear or	316
	22: 9	of Jesse come to **A** son of Ahitub at Nob.	316
	22:10	**A** inquired of the LORD for him;	NIH
	22:11	the king sent for the priest **A** son of Ahitub	316
	22:14	**A** answered the king, "Who of all	316
	22:16	But the king said, "You will surely die, **A**,	316
	22:20	But Abiathar, a son of **A** son of Ahitub,	316
	23: 6	of **A** had brought the ephod down with him	316
	26: 6	then asked **A** the Hittite and Abishai son	316
	30: 7	the son of **A**, "Bring me the ephod."	316
2Sa	8:17	and **A** son of Abiathar were priests;	316
1Ch	18:16	and **A** son of Abiathar were priests;	316
	24: 3	a descendant of Eleazar and **A** a descendant	316
	24: 6	**A** son of Abiathar and the heads of families	316
	24:31	and of Zadok, **A**, and the heads of families	316
Ps	52: T	"David has gone to the house of **A**."	316

AHIMOTH (1)

1Ch	6:25	The descendants of Elkanah: Amasai, **A**,	315

AHINADAB (1)

1Ki	4:14	**A** son of Iddo—in Mahanaim;	320

AHINOAM (7)

1Sa	14:50	His wife's name was **A** daughter	321
	25:43	David had also married **A** of Jezreel,	321
	27: 3	**A** of Jezreel and Abigail of Carmel,	321
	30: 5	**A** of Jezreel and Abigail,	321
2Sa	2: 2	**A** of Jezreel and Abigail,	321
	3: 2	His firstborn was Amnon the son of **A**	321
1Ch	3: 1	The firstborn was Amnon the son of **A**	321

AHIO (6)

2Sa	6: 3	Uzzah and **A**, sons of Abinadab,	311

2Sa	6: 4	and **A** was walking in front of it.	311
1Ch	8:14	**A**, Shashak, Jeremoth,	311
	8:31	Gedor, **A**, Zeker	311
	9:37	Gedor, **A**, Zechariah and Mikloth.	311
	13: 7	with Uzzah and **A** guiding it.	311

AHIRA (5)

Nu	1:15	from Naphtali, **A** son of Enan."	327
	2:29	of the people of Naphtali is **A** son of Enan.	327
	7:78	On the twelfth day **A** son of Enan,	327
	7:83	This was the offering of **A** son of Enan.	327
	10:27	and **A** son of Enan was over the division of	327

AHIRAM (1) [AHIRAMITE]

Nu	26:38	through **A**, the Ahiramite clan;	325

AHIRAMITE (1) [AHIRAM]

Nu	26:38	through Ahiram, the **A** clan;	326

AHISAMACH (3)

Ex	31: 6	I have appointed Oholiab son of **A**,	322
	35:34	both him and Oholiab son of **A**,	322
	38:23	with him was Oholiab son of **A**, of the tribe	322

AHISHAHAR (1)

1Ch	7:10	Ehud, Kenaanah, Zethan, Tarshish and **A**.	328

AHISHAR (1)

1Ki	4: 6	**A**—in charge of the palace;	329

AHITHOPHEL (17) [AHITHOPHEL'S]

2Sa	15:12	he also sent for **A** the Gilonite,	330
	15:31	"**A** is among the conspirators	330
	16:15	and **A** was with him.	330
	16:20	Absalom said to **A**, "Give us your advice.	330
	16:21	**A** answered, "Lie with your father's	330
	16:23	Now in those days the advice **A** gave was	330
	17: 1	**A** said to Absalom, "I would choose	330
	17: 6	Absalom said, "**A** has given this advice.	330
	17: 7	advice **A** has given is not good this time.	330
	17:14	the Arkite is better than that of **A**."	330
	17:14	of **A** in order to bring disaster on Absalom.	330
	17:15	"**A** has advised Absalom and the elders	330
	17:21	**A** has advised such and such against you."	330
	17:23	When **A** saw that his advice had	330
	23:34	Eliam son of **A** the Gilonite,	330
1Ch	27:33	**A** was the king's counselor.	330
	27:34	**A** was succeeded by Jehoiada son	330

AHITHOPHEL'S (3) [AHITHOPHEL]

2Sa	15:31	turn **A** counsel into foolishness."	330
	15:34	you can help me by frustrating **A** advice.	330
	16:23	and Absalom regarded all of **A** advice.	330

AHITUB (15)

1Sa	14: 3	He was a son of Ichabod's brother **A** son	313
	22: 9	of Jesse come to Ahimelech son of **A**	313
	22:11	of **A** and his father's whole family,	313
	22:12	Saul said, "Listen now, son of **A**."	313
	22:20	But Abiathar, a son of Ahimelech son of **A**,	313
2Sa	8:17	Zadok son of **A** and Ahimelech son	313
1Ch	6: 7	Amariah the father of **A**,	313
	6: 8	**A** the father of Zadok,	313
	6:11	Amariah the father of **A**,	313
	6:12	**A** the father of Zadok,	313
	6:52	Amariah his son, **A** his son,	313
	9:11	the son of Meraioth, the son of **A**,	313
	18:16	Zadok son of **A** and Ahimelech son	313
Ezr	7: 2	the son of Zadok, the son of **A**,	313
Ne	11:11	the son of Meraioth, the son of **A**,	313

AHLAB (1)

Jdg	1:31	or Sidon or **A** or Aczib or Helbah or Aphek	331

AHLAI (2)

1Ch	2:31	Sheshan was the father of **A**.	333
	11:41	Uriah the Hittite, Zabad son of **A**,	333

AHOAH (1)

1Ch	8: 4	Abishua, Naaman, **A**,	291

AHOHITE (5)

2Sa	23: 9	to him was Eleazar son of Dodai the **A**.	292+1201
	23:28	Zalmon the **A**, Maharai the Netophathite,	292
1Ch	11:12	to him was Eleazar son of Dodai the **A**,	292
	11:29	Sibbecai the Hushathite, Ilai the **A**,	292
	27: 4	for the second month was Dodai the **A**;	292

AHOLAH (KJV) See OHOLAH

AHOLIAB (KJV) See OHOLIAB

AHOLIBAH (KJV) See OHOLAH

AHOLIBAMAH (KJV) See OHOLIBAMAH

AHUMAI (1)

1Ch	4: 2	and Jahath the father of **A** and Lahad.	293

AHUZZAM (1)

1Ch	4: 6	Naarah bore him **A**, Hepher,	303

AHUZZATH (1)

Ge	26:26	with **A** his personal adviser and Phicol	304

AHZAI (1)

Ne	11:13	Amashsai son of Azarel, the son of **A**,	300

AI (37)

Ge	12: 8	with Bethel on the west and **A** on the east.	6504
	13: 3	and **A** where his tent had been earlier	6504
Jos	7: 2	Now Joshua sent men from Jericho to **A**,	6504
	7: 2	So the men went up and spied out **A**.	6504
	7: 3	the people will have to go up against **A**.	6504
	7: 4	but they were routed by the men of **A**,	6504
	8: 1	and go up and attack **A**.	6504
	8: 1	into your hands the king of **A**,	6504
	8: 2	You shall do to **A** and its king as you did	6504
	8: 3	and the whole army moved out to attack **A**.	6504
	8: 9	between Bethel and **A**, to the west of Ai—	6504
	8: 9	between Bethel and Ai, to the west of **A**—	6504
	8:10	of Israel marched before them to **A**.	6504
	8:11	They set up camp north of **A**,	6504
	8:12	in ambush between Bethel and **A**,	6504
	8:14	When the king of **A** saw this,	6504
	8:16	the men of **A** were called to pursue them,	6504
	8:17	Not a man remained in **A** or Bethel who did	6504
	8:18	toward the javelin that is in your hand,	6504
	8:18	Joshua held out his javelin toward **A**.	2021+6551S
	8:20	of **A** looked back and saw the smoke of	6504
	8:21	around and attacked the men of **A**.	6504
	8:23	of **A** alive and brought him to Joshua.	6504
	8:24	the men of **A** in the fields and in the desert	6504
	8:24	to **A** and killed those who were in it.	6504
	8:25	fell that day—all the people of **A**.	6504
	8:26	until he had destroyed all who lived in **A**.	6504
	8:28	So Joshua burned **A** and made it	6504
	8:29	the king of **A** on a tree and left him there	6504
	9: 3	to Jericho and **A**,	6504
	10: 1	of Jerusalem heard that Joshua had taken **A**	6504
	10: 1	to **A** and its king as he had done to Jericho	6504
	10: 2	it was larger than **A**,	6504
	12: 9	the king of Jericho one the king of **A**	6504
Ezr	2:28	of Bethel and **A** 223	6504
Ne	7:32	of Bethel and **A** 123	6504
Jer	49: 3	"Wail, O Heshbon, for **A** is destroyed!	6504

AIAH (4) [AIAH'S]

Ge	36:24	The sons of Zibeon: **A** and Anah.	371
2Sa	3: 7	a concubine named Rizpah daughter of **A**.	371
	21:10	of **A** took sackcloth and spread it out	371
1Ch	1:40	The sons of Zibeon: **A** and Anah.	371

AIAH'S (2) [AIAH]

2Sa	21: 8	the two sons of **A** daughter Rizpah,	371
	21:11	David was told what **A** daughter Rizpah,	371

AIATH (1)

Isa	10:28	They enter **A**; they pass	6569

AID (10) [AIDE]

Ge	50:24	But God will **surely come to** your **a**	7212+7212
	50:25	"God will **surely come to** your **a**,	7212+7212
Ex	13:19	"God will **surely come to** your **a**,	7212+7212
Ru	1: 6	the LORD had **come to the a** of his people	7212
Ps	35: 2	arise and come to my **a**.	6476
	60:11	Give us **a** against the enemy,	6476
	106: 4	**come to** my **a** when you save them,	7212
	108:12	Give us **a** against the enemy,	6476
Isa	38:14	I am troubled; O Lord, **come to** my **a**!"	6842
Php	4:16	you sent me **a** again and again when I was	NIG

AIDE (5) [AID]

Ex	24:13	Then Moses set out with Joshua his **a**,	9250
	33:11	but his young **a** Joshua son of Nun did	9250
Nu	11:28	*who had been* Moses' **a** since youth,	9250
Jos	1: 1	to Joshua son of Nun, Moses' **a**:	9250
Ne	6: 5	Sanballat sent his **a** to me with	5853

AIJA (1)

Ne	11:31	**A**, Bethel and its settlements,	6509

AIJALON (10)

Jos	10:12	O moon, over the Valley of **A**."	389
	19:42	Shaalabbin, **A**, Ithlah,	389

Jos	21:24	A and Gath Rimmon, together	389
Jdg	1:35	in Mount Heres, A and Shaalbim, but when	389
	12:12	and was buried in A in the land of Zebulun.	389
1Sa	14:31	down the Philistines from Micmash to A,	389
1Ch	6:69	A and Gath Rimmon,	389
	8:13	in A and who drove out the inhabitants	389
2Ch	11:10	Zorah, A and Hebron. These were fortified	
		cities in Judah	389
	28:18	A and Gederoth, as well as Soco,	389

AILS (1)

Job	16: 3	What a you that you keep on arguing?	5344

AIM (4) [AIMLESSLY]

Ps	21:12	when *you* a at them with drawn bow.	3922
	64: 3	and a their words like deadly arrows.	2005
1Co	7:34	Her a is to be devoted to the Lord in	2671
2Co	13:11	A for perfection, listen to my appeal,	2936

AIMLESSLY (1) [AIM]

1Co	9:26	I do not run like a man running a;	85

AIN (5)

Nu	34:11	to Riblah on the east side of A and continue	6526
Jos	15:32	Shilhim, A and Rimmon—	6526
	19: 7	A, Rimmon, Ether and Ashan—	6526
	21:16	A, Juttah and Beth Shemesh, together	6526
1Ch	4:32	Their surrounding villages were Etam, A,	6526

AIR (59) [AIRING, MIDAIR]

Ge	1:26	the fish of the sea and the birds of the a	9028
	1:28	the fish of the sea and the birds of the a and	9028
	1:30	of the earth and all the birds of the a and all	9028
	2:19	of the field and all the birds of the a.	9028
	2:20	of the a and all the beasts of the field.	9028
	6: 7	and birds of the a—	9028
	7:23	and the birds of the a were wiped from	9028
	9: 2	of the a, upon every creature that moves	9028
Ex	9: 8	a furnace and have Moses toss it into the a	9028
	9:10	Moses tossed it into the a,	9028
Dt	4:17	on earth or any bird that flies in the a,	9028
	4:17	for all the birds of the a and the beasts of	9028
1Sa	17:44	to the birds of the a and the beasts of	9028
	17:46	the Philistine army to the birds of the a and	9028
2Sa	21:10	she did not let the birds of the a touch them	9028
1Ki	14:11	of the a will feed on those who die in	9028
	16: 4	of the a will feed on those who die in	9028
	21:24	of the a will feed on those who die in	9028
Job	12: 7	or the birds of the a, and they will tell you;	9028
	28:21	concealed even from the birds of the a.	9028
	35:11	the birds of the a?"	9028
	41:16	to the next that no a can pass between.	8120
Ps	8: 8	the birds of the a,	9028
	79: 2	as food to the birds of the a,	9028
	104:12	The birds of the a nest by the waters;	9028
Ecc	10:20	a bird of the a may carry your words,	9028
Jer	7:33	for the birds of the a and the beasts of	9028
	9:10	the a have fled and the animals are gone.	9028
	15: 3	the dogs to drag away and the birds of the a	9028
	16: 4	for the birds of the a and the beasts of	9028
	19: 7	as food for the birds of the a and the beasts	9028
	34:20	for the birds of the a and the beasts of	9028
Eze	29: 5	of the earth and the birds of the a.	9028
	31: 6	All the birds of the a nested in its boughs,	9028
	31:13	the birds of the a settled on the fallen tree,	9028
	32: 4	I will let all the birds of the a settle on you	9028
	38:20	The fish of the sea, the birds of the a,	9028
Da	2:38	of the field and the birds of the a	10723
	4:12	and the birds of the a lived in its branches;	10723
	4:21	in its branches for the birds of the a—	10723
Hos	2:18	the beasts of the field and the birds of the a	9028
	4: 3	the beasts of the field and the birds of the a	9028
	7:12	I will pull them down like birds of the a.	9028
Zep	1: 3	the birds of the a and the fish of the sea.	9028
Mt	6:26	Look at the birds *of* the a;	4041
	8:20	and birds *of* the a have nests,	4041
	13:32	*of* the a come and perch in its branches."	4041
Mk	4:32	the birds *of* the a can perch in its shade."	4041
Lk	8: 5	and birds *of* the a ate it up.	4041
	9:58	and birds *of* the a have nests,	4041
	13:19	the birds *of* the a perched in its branches."	4041
Ac	10:12	as reptiles of the earth and birds *of* the a.	4041
	11: 6	wild beasts, reptiles, and birds *of* the a.	4041
	22:23	and flinging dust into the a,	113
1Co	9:26	I do not fight like a man beating the a.	113
	14: 9	You will just be speaking into the a.	113
Eph	2: 2	and of the ruler of the kingdom of the a,	113
1Th	4:17	in the clouds to meet the Lord in the a.	113
Rev	16:17	into the a, and out of the temple came	113

AIRING (1) [AIR]

Pr	18: 2	but delights in a his own opinions.	1655

AJAH (KJV) See AIAH

AJALON (KJV) See AIJALON

AKAN (2)

Ge	36:27	The sons of Ezer: Bilhan, Zaavan and A.	6826
1Ch	1:42	The sons of Ezer: Bilhan, Zaavan and A.	6826

AKELDAMA (1) [BLOOD, FIELD]

Ac	1:19	they called that field in their language A,	192

AKIM (2)

Mt	1:14	Zadok the father of A,	943
	1:14	A the father of Eliud,	943

AKKAD (1)

Ge	10:10	Erech, A and Calneh, in Shinar.	422

AKKUB (8)

1Ch	3:24	Hodaviah, Eliashib, Pelaiah, A, Johanan,	6822
Ezr	2:42	The gatekeepers: Shallum, Ater, Talmon, A,	6822
	2:45	descendants of Shallum, Ater, Talmon, A,	6822
Ne	7:45	Lebanah, Hagabah, A,	6822
	8: 7	descendants of Shallum, Ater, Talmon, A,	6822
	11:19	Jeshua, Bani, Sherebiah, Jamin, A,	6822
	12:25	A, Talmon and their associates,	6822
		and A were gatekeepers who guarded	6822

ALABASTER (3)

Mt	26: 7	with a **jar** of very expensive perfume,	223
Mk	14: 3	with an a **jar** of very expensive perfume,	223
Lk	7:37	she brought an a **jar** of perfume,	223

ALAMETH (KJV) See ALEMETH

ALAMMELECH (KJV) See ALLAMMELECH

ALAMOTH (2)

1Ch	15:20	to play the lyres according to a,	6628
Ps	46: T	According to a.	6628

ALARM (7) [ALARMED]

1Ki	1:49	all Adonijah's guests rose *in* a	3006
Job	33: 7	No fear of me *should* a you,	1286
Ps	31:22	In my a I said,	2905
Da	4:19	*do not let* the dream or its meaning a you."	10097
	11:44	from the east and the north *will* a him,	987
Joel	2: 1	**sound** the a on my holy hill.	8131
2Co	7:11	what indignation, what a, what longing,	5832

ALARMED (13) [ALARM]

Jos	10: 2	*He and his people were* very much a at this,	3707
2Sa	4: 1	he lost courage, and all Israel *became* a.	987
2Ch	20: 3	A, Jehoshaphat resolved to inquire of	3707
Job	40:23	When the river rages, *he is* not a;	2905
Da	5:10	"Don't *be* a,	10097
Mt	24: 6	but see to it that *you are* not a.	2583
Mk	13: 7	*do* not *be* a.	2583
	16: 5	and they were a.	1701
	16: 6	"Don't *be* a," he said.	1701
Ac	16:38	and Silas were Roman citizens, *they were* a.	5828
	20:10	"Don't *be* a," he said.	2572
	22:29	The commander himself *was* a	5828
2Th	2: 2	not to become easily unsettled or a	2583

ALAS (11)

Jer	4:31	stretching out her hands and saying, "A!	208
	6: 4	But, a, the daylight is fading,	208
	15:10	A, my mother, that you gave me birth,	208
	22:18	not mourn for him: 'A,	2098
	22:18	A, my sister!'	2098
	22:18	They will not mourn for him: 'A,	2098
	22:18	A, his splendor!'	2098
	34: 5	a fire in your honor and lament, "A,	2098
Eze	6:11	and stamp your feet and cry out "A!"	277
	30: 2	" 'Wail and say, "A for that day!"	2081
Joel	1:15	A for that day!	177

ALCOVE (2) [ALCOVES]

Eze	40:12	of each a was a wall one cubit high,	9288
	40:13	the top of the rear wall of one a to the top	9288

ALCOVES (9) [ALCOVE]

Eze	40: 7	The a for the guards were one rod long	9288
	40: 7	between the a were five cubits thick.	9288
	40:10	the east gate were three a on each side;	9288
	40:12	and the a were six cubits square.	9288
	40:16	The a and the projecting walls inside	9288
	40:21	Its a—three on each	9288
	40:29	Its a, its projecting walls	9288
	40:33	Its a, its projecting walls	9288
	40:36	as did its a, its projecting walls	9288

ALEMETH (4)

1Ch	6:60	Geba, A and Anathoth,	6630
	7: 8	Omri, Jeremoth, Abijah, Anathoth and A.	6631
	8:36	Jehoaddah was the father of A,	6631
	9:42	Jadah was the father of A,	6631

ALERT (8)

Jos	8: 4	All of you be **on the** a.	3922
Ps	17:11	with eyes a, to throw me to the ground.	8883
Isa	21: 7	*let him be* a, fully alert."	7992+7993
	21: 7	let him be alert, fully a."	7993
Mk	13:33	on guard! Be a! You do not know	1063
Eph	6:18	be a and always keep on praying for all	70

1Th	5: 6	but *let us be* a and self-controlled.	1213
1Pe	5: 8	Be self-controlled and a.	1213

ALEXANDER (5)

Mk	15:21	Simon, the father *of* A and Rufus,	235
Ac	4: 6	A and the other men of	235
	19:33	The Jews pushed A to the front,	235
1Ti	1:20	Among them are Hymenaeus and A,	235
2Ti	4:14	A the metalworker did me a great deal	235

ALEXANDRIA (2) [ALEXANDRIAN]

Ac	6: 9	of Cyrene and A as well as the provinces	233
	18:24	a native **of** A, came to Ephesus.	233

ALEXANDRIAN (2) [ALEXANDRIA]

Ac	27: 6	There the centurion found an A ship sailing	234
	28:11	It was an A ship with the figurehead of	234

ALGUM (1) [ALGUMWOOD, ALMUGWOOD]

2Ch	2: 8	pine and a logs from Lebanon,	454

ALGUMWOOD (2) [ALGUM]

2Ch	9:10	they also brought a and precious stones.	454+6770
	9:11	The king used the a to make steps for	454+6770

ALIAH (KJV) See ALVAH

ALIEN (73) [ALIEN'S, ALIENATE, ALIENATED, ALIENS]

Ge	17: 8	where you are now an a,	4472
	19: 9	they said, "This fellow came here *as an* a,	1591
	21:23	the country where *you are* living as an a	1591
	23: 4	"I am an a and a stranger among you.	1591
	28: 4	of the land where you now **live as an** a,	4472
Ex	2:22	"I have become an a in a foreign land."	1731
	12:19	whether he is an a or native-born.	1731
	12:48	"An a living among you who wants	1731
	12:49	to the native-born and to the a living	1731
	18: 3	"I have become an a in a foreign land";	1731
	20:10	nor the a within your gates.	1731
	22:21	"Do not mistreat an a or oppress him,	1731
	23: 9	"Do not oppress an a;	1731
	23:12	and the a as well, may be refreshed.	1731
Lev	16:29	whether native-born or an a living	1731
	17: 8	or any a living among them who offers	1731
	17:10	" 'Any Israelite or any a living	1731
	17:12	nor may an a living among you eat blood."	1731
	17:13	" 'Any Israelite or any a living	1731
	17:15	" 'Anyone, whether native-born or a,	1731
	19:10	Leave them for the poor and the a.	1731
	19:33	" 'When an a lives with you in your land,	1731
	19:34	The a living with you must be treated	1731
	20: 2	or any a living in Israel who gives any	1731
	22:18	either an Israelite or an a living in Israel—	1731
	23:22	Leave them for the poor and the a.	1731
	24:16	Whether an a or native-born,	1731
	24:22	You are to have the same law for the a and	1731
	25:35	as you would an a or a temporary resident,	1731
	25:47	" 'If an a or a temporary resident	1731
	25:47	and sells himself to an a living among you	1731
Nu	9:14	" 'An a living among you who wants	1731
	9:14	the same regulations for the a and	1731
	15:14	whenever an a or anyone else living	1731
	15:15	the same rules for you and for the a living	1731
	15:15	the a shall be the same before the LORD;	1731
	15:16	to you and to the a living among you.' "	1731
	15:29	a native-born Israelite or an a.	1731
	15:30	whether native-born or a,	1731
Dt	1:16	or between one of them and an a.	1731
	5:14	nor the a within your gates,	1731
	10:18	and loves the a, giving him food	1731
	14:21	You may give it to an a living in any	1731
	23: 7	because you lived as an a in his country.	1731
	24:14	a brother Israelite or an a living in one	1731
	24:17	Do not deprive the a or the fatherless	1731
	24:19	Leave it for the a,	1731
	24:20	Leave what remains for the a,	1731
	24:21	Leave what remains for the a,	1731
	26:12	you shall give it to the Levite, the a,	1731
	26:13	the a, the fatherless and the widow,	1731
	27:19	the man who withholds justice from the a,	1731
	28:43	The a who lives among you will rise	1731
Jos	20: 9	Any of the Israelites or any a living	1731
Jdg	19:12	We won't go into an a city,	5799
2Sa	1:13	"I am the son of an a, an Amalekite,"	1731
Job	19:15	the land was given when no a passed	2424
	19:15	they look upon me as an a.	5799
Ps	39:12	For I dwell with you as an a, a stranger,	1731
	69: 8	an a to my own mother's sons;	5799
	81: 9	you shall not bow down to an a god.	5797
	94: 6	They slay the widow and the a;	1731
	105:23	Jacob **lived as an** a in the land of Ham.	1591
	146: 9	over the a and sustains the fatherless and	1731
Isa	28:21	and perform his task, his a task.	5799
Jer	7: 6	if you do not oppress the a,	1731
	22: 3	Do no wrong or violence to the a,	1731
Eze	14: 7	or any a living in Israel separates himself	1731
	22: 7	the a and mistreated the fatherless and	1731
	22:29	the poor and needy and mistreat the a,	1731
	47:23	In whatever tribe the a settles,	1731
Hos	8:12	but they regarded them as *something* a.	2424
Zec	7:10	the fatherless, the a or the poor.	1731

ALIEN'S (1) [ALIEN]
Lev 25:47 among you or to a member of the **a** clan,   1731

ALIENATE (1) [ALIEN]
Gal 4:17 What they want is *to* **a** you [from us],   *1710*

ALIENATED (3) [ALIEN]
Job 19:13 *"He has* **a** my brothers from me;   8178
Gal 5: 4 to be justified by law *have been* **a**   2934
Col 1:21 Once you were **a** **from** God   558

ALIENS (33) [ALIEN]
Ex 6: 4 where they lived *as* **a**.   1591
22:21 for you were **a** in Egypt.   1731
23: 9 you yourselves know how it feels to be **a**,   1731
23: 9 because you were **a** in Egypt.   1731
Lev 18:26 the **a** living among you must not do any   1731
19:34 for you were **a** in Egypt.   1731
25:23 because the land is mine and you are but **a**   1731
Nu 15:26 the **a** living among them will be forgiven,   1731
19:10 both for the Israelites and for the **a** living   1731
35:15 **a** and any other people living among them,   1731
Dt 10:19 And you are to love those who are **a**,   1731
10:19 for you yourselves were **a** in Egypt.   1731
14:29 or inheritance of their own) and the **a**,   1731
16:11 the Levites in your towns, and the **a**,   1731
16:14 and the Levites, the **a**,   1731
26:11 and the **a** among you shall rejoice in all   1731
29:11 and the **a** living   1731
31:12 and the **a** living in your towns—   1731
Jos 8:33 All Israel, **a** and citizens alike,   1731
8:35 and the **a** who lived among them.   1731
2Sa 4: 3 and have lived there *as* **a** to this day.   1591
1Ch 22: 2 to assemble the **a** living in Israel,   1731
29:15 We are **a** and strangers in your sight,   1731
2Ch 2:17 a census of all the **a** who were in Israel,   1731
30:25 including the **a** who had come from Israel   1731
Isa 14: 1 A will join them and unite with the house   1731
61: 5 A will shepherd your flocks.   2424
La 5: 2 Our inheritance has been turned over to **a**,   2424
Eze 47:22 and for the **a** who have settled among you   1731
Mal 3: 5 and deprive **a** of justice,   1731
Eph 2:19 you are no longer foreigners and **a**,   *4230*
Heb 11:13 that they were **a** and strangers on earth.   *3828*
1Pe 2:11 I urge you, as **a** and strangers in the world,   *4230*

ALIKE (26) [LIKE]
Ge 18:25 treating the righteous and the wicked **a**.   3869
Ex 11: 2 Tell the people that men **and** women **a** are   2256
35:22 All who were willing, men **and** women **a**,   6584
36:29 both were made **a**.   4027
Nu 5: 3 Send away male **and** female **a**;   6330
Dt 1:17 **both** small *and* great **a**.   3869
Jos 8:33 All Israel, aliens **and** citizens **a**,   3869
1Sa 30:24 All will share **a**."   3481
1Ch 25: 8 Young and old **a**,   4200+6645
26:13 young and old **a**.   3869
2Ch 31:15 old and young **a**.   3869
Job 34:29 Yet he is over man and nation **a**,   3480
Ps 49: 2 both low and high, rich and poor **a**:   3480
49:10 the foolish and the senseless **a** perish   3480
115:13 small **and** great **a**.   6640
Jer 6:13 prophets **and** priests **a**, all practice deceit.   6330
6:21 Fathers and sons **a** will stumble over them;   3481
8:10 prophets **and** priests **a**, all practice deceit.   6330
13:14 fathers and sons **a**, declares the LORD.   3481
Eze 1:18 and all four looked **a**.   285
10:10 the four of them looked **a**;   285
18: 4 **both** **a** belong to me.   AIT
Lk 14:18 "But they all **a** began to make excuses.   608+1651
Ac 26:22 and testify to small and great **a**.   *NIG*
Ro 3: 9 the charge that Jews **and** Gentiles **a** are all under sin.   2779+5445
14: 5 another man considers every day **a**.   *NIG*

ALIVE (85) [LIVE]
Ge 6:19 male and female, to **keep** them **a** with you.   2649
6:20 the ground will come to you *be* kept **a**.   2649
7: 3 **keep** their various kinds **a**   2649
11:28 **While** his father Terah was **still** **a**,   6584+7156
43:28 "Your servant our father is still **a**   2645
45:26 They told him, "Joseph is still **a**!   2645
45:28 My son Joseph is still **a**.   2645
46:30 I have seen for myself that you are still **a**."   2645
Ex 4:18 in Egypt to see if any of them are still **a**."   2645
22: 4 "If the stolen animal is found **a**   2645
Lev 16:10 as the scapegoat shall be presented **a** before   2645
Nu 16:30 and they go down **a** into the grave,   2645
16:33 They went down **a** into the grave,   2645
Dt 4: 4 to the LORD your God are still **a** today.   2645
5: 3 with all of us who are **a** here today.   2645
6:24 we might always prosper and be **kept a**,   2649
20:16 *do* not **leave** **a** anything that breathes.   2649
31:27 the LORD while I am still **a** and with you,   2645
Jos 6:23 the king of Ai **a** and brought him to Joshua.   2645
14:10 he has **kept** me **a** for forty-five years since   2649
1Sa 15: 8 The LORD brings death and **makes a**;   8636
14:36 **leave** one of them **a**."   8636
15: 8 He took Agag king of the Amalekites **a**,   2645
25:22 if by morning *I* **leave a** one male   8636
25:34 to Nabal *would have* been **left a**   3855
27: 9 **leave** a man or woman **a**,   2649
27:11 **leave** a man or woman **a**   2649

2Sa 1: 9 in the throes of death, but I'm still **a**.'   928+5883
12:21 While the child was **a**,   2645
12:22 He answered, "While the child was still **a**,   2645
17:12 nor any of his men *will* be left **a**.   3855
18:14 while Absalom was still **a** in the oak tree.   2645
19: 6 be pleased if Absalom were **a** today and all   2645
1Ki 3:23 'My son is **a** and your son is dead,'   2645
3:23 Your son is dead and mine is **a**.' "   2645
3:26 The woman whose son was **a** was filled   2645
17:23 "Look, your son is **a**!"   2645
18: 5 **keep** the horses and mules **a**   2649
20:18 for peace, take them **a**;   2645
20:18 if they have come out for war, take them **a**."   2645
20:32 The king answered, "Is he still **a**?   2645
21:15 He is no longer **a**, but dead."   2645
2Ki 7:12 and then we will take them **a** and get into   2645
10:14 "Take them **a**!"   2645
10:14 So they took them **a** and slaughtered them   2645
2Ch 25:12 of Judah also captured ten thousand *men* **a**,   2645
Ne 5: 2 in order for us to eat and **stay a**.   2649
Job 36: 6 *He does* not **keep** the wicked **a** but gives   2649
Ps 22:29 *those who* cannot **keep** themselves **a**.   2649
33:19 to deliver them from death and **keep** them **a**   2649
55:15 let them go down **a** to the grave,   2645
124: 3 they would have swallowed us **a**;   2645
Pr 1:12 let's swallow them **a**, like the grave,   2645
Ecc 4: 2 are happier than the living, who are still **a**.   2645
Isa 7:21 a man *will* **keep** **a** a young cow   2649
La 1:11 for food to **keep themselves a**.   5883+8740
1:19 for food to **keep themselves a**.   906+4392+5883+8740
Mt 27:63 that while *he was* still **a** that deceiver said,   2409
Mk 16:11 that Jesus *was* **a** and that she had seen him,   2409
Lk 15:24 this son of mine was dead and *is* **a again**;   *348*
15:32 of yours was dead and *is* **a again**,   *348*
20:38 but of the living, for to him *all are* **a**."   2409
24:23 who said he *was* **a**.   2409
Jn 21:22 "If I want him to remain **a** until I return,   *NIG*
21:23 "If I want him to remain **a** until I return,   *NIG*
Ac 2: that he was **a**.   2409
9:41 the widows and presented her to them **a**.   2409
20:10 be alarmed," he said. "He's **a**!"   899+1877
20:12 The people took the young man home **a**   2409
25:19 dead man named Jesus who Paul claimed *was* **a**.   2409
Ro 6:11 count yourselves dead to sin but **a** to God   2409
7: 2 to her husband *as long as he is* **a**,   2409
7: 3 *while* her husband *is still* **a**,   2409
7: 9 Once *I was* **a** apart from law;   2409
8:10 your spirit is **a** because of righteousness.   2437
1Co 15:22 so in Christ all *will* be **made a**.   2443
2Co 4:11 For we who *are* **a** are always being given   2409
Eph 2: 5 **made** us **a** **with** Christ even   5188
Col 2:13 God **made** you **a** **with** Christ.   5188
1Th 4:15 we tell you that we who *are still* **a**,   2409
4:17 we who *are still* **a** and are left will   2409
1Pe 3:18 He was put to death in the body but **made a**   2443
Rev 1:18 and behold I am **a** for ever and ever!   2409
3: 1 you have a reputation of *being* **a**,   2409
19:20 of them were thrown **a** into the fiery lake   2409

ALL (4660)
Ge 1:25 and **a** the creatures that move along   3972
1:26 over the livestock, over **a** the earth,   3972
1:26 and over **a** the creatures that move along   3972
1:30 to **a** the beasts of the earth and all the birds   3972
1:30 of the earth and **a** the birds of the air and all   3972
1:30 of the earth and all the birds of the air and **a**   3972
1:31 God saw **a** that he had made,   3972
2: 1 in **a** their vast array.   3972
2: 2 the seventh day he rested from **a** his work.   3972
2: 3 on it he rested from **a** the work of creating   3972
2: 9 And the LORD God made **a** *kinds*   3972
2:19 the ground the beasts of the field and all   3972
2:19 the ground all the beasts of the field and **a**   3972
2:20 So the man gave names to **a** the livestock,   3972
2:20 of the air and **a** the beasts of the field.   3972
3:14 "Cursed are you above **a** the livestock   3972
3:14 the livestock and **a** the wild animals!   3972
3:14 on your belly and you will eat dust **a**   3972
3:17 through painful toil you will eat of it **a**   3972
3:20 because she would become the mother of **a**   3972
4:21 the father of **a** who play the harp and flute.   3972
4:22 who forged **a** *kinds of* tools out of bronze   3972
6: 5 of the thoughts of his heart was only evil **a**   3972
6:12 for **a** the people on earth had corrupted   3972
6:13 "I am going to put an end to **a** people,   3972
6:17 to destroy **a** life under the heavens,   3972
6:19 into the ark two of **a** living creatures,   3972
7: 5 And Noah did **a** that the LORD commanded   3972
7: 8 of birds and of **a** creatures that move along   3972
7:11 on that day **a** the springs of   3972
7:14 livestock according to their kinds,   3972
7:15 of **a** creatures that have the breath of life   3972
7:19 and **a** the high mountains under   3972
7:21 **a** the creatures that swarm over the earth,   3972
7:21 that swarm over the earth, and **a** mankind.   3972
8: 1 and the wild animals and the livestock   3972
8: 9 because there was water over **a** the surface   3972
8:17 the animals, and **a** the creatures that move   3972
8:19 A the animals and all the creatures   3972
8:19 the animals and **a** the creatures that move   3972
8:19 along the ground and **a** the birds—   3972
8:20 of **a** the clean animals and clean birds,   3972
8:21 never again will I destroy **a** living creatures,   3972
9: 2 and dread of you will fall upon **a** the beasts   3972

Ge 9: 2 the beasts of the earth and **a** the birds of   3972
9: 2 and upon **a** the fish of the sea;   3972
9:10 the livestock and **a** the wild animals,   3972
9:10 **a** those that came out of the ark with you—   3972
9:11 Never again will **a** life be cut off by   3972
9:12 a covenant for **a** generations to come: NIH
9:15 between me and you and **a** living creatures   3972
9:15 the waters become a flood to destroy **a** life.   3972
9:16 and **a** living creatures of every kind on   3972
9:17 between me and **a** life on the earth."   3972
10:21 Shem was the ancestor of **a** the sons   3972
10:29 A these were sons of Joktan.   3972
11: 8 from there over **a** the earth,   3972
12: 3 and **a** peoples on earth will be blessed   3972
12: 5 **a** the possessions they had accumulated   3972
13:15 A the land that you see I will give to you   3972
14: 3 A these latter kings joined forces in   3972
14:11 The four kings seized **a** the goods   3972
14:11 of Sodom and Gomorrah and **a** their food;   3972
14:13 **a** *of whom* were allied with Abram.   2156S
14:16 He recovered **a** the goods   3972
15:10 Abram brought **a** these to him,   3972
16:12 in hostility toward **a** his brothers."   3972
17:23 and **a** those born in his household   3972
18: 4 and then *you may* **a** **wash** your feet and rest   AIT
18:18 and **a** nations on earth will be blessed   3972
18:25 Will not the Judge of **a** the earth do right?"   3972
19: 4 **a** the men from every part of the city   3972
19:25 including **a** those living in the cities—   3972
19:28 toward **a** the land of the plain,   3972
19:31 as is the custom **a** *over* the earth.   3972
20: 7 be sure that you and **a** yours will die."   3972
20: 8 next morning Abimelech summoned **a** his officials,   3972
20: 8 when he told them **a** that had happened,   3972
20:16 the offense against you before **a** who are   3972
22:18 and through your offspring **a** nations   3972
23:10 the hearing of **a** the Hittites who had come   3972
23:17 **a** the trees within the borders of the field—   3972
23:18 the presence of **a** the Hittites who had come   3972
24: 2 the one in charge of **a** that he had,   3972
24:10 taking with him **a** *kinds of* good things   3972
24:20 and drew enough for **a** his camels.   3972
24:66 Then the servant told Isaac **a** he had done.   3972
25: 4 A these were descendants of Keturah.   3972
25:18 in hostility toward **a** their brothers.   3972
26: 3 your descendants I will give **a** these lands   3972
26: 4 in the sky and will give them **a** these lands,   3972
26: 4 and through your offspring **a** nations   3972
26:11 So Abimelech gave orders to **a** the people: 3972
26:15 the wells that his father's servants had dug   3972
27:37 and have made **a** his relatives his servants,   3972
28:14 A peoples on earth will be blessed   3972
28:22 and of **a** that you give me I will give you   3972
29: 3 When **a** the flocks were gathered there,   3972
29: 8 "until **a** the flocks are gathered and   3972
29:13 and there Jacob told him **a** these things.   3972
29:22 So Laban brought together **a** the people of   3972
30:32 through **a** your flocks today and remove   3972
30:35 That same day he removed the male goats   NIH
30:35 and **a** the speckled or spotted female goats   3972
30:35 or spotted female goats (**a** that had white   3972
30:35 on them) and **a** the dark-colored lambs,   3972
30:38 Then he placed the peeled branches in **a**   NIH
31: 1 and has gained **a** this wealth   3972
31: 6 for your father with **a** my strength,   3972
31: 8 the flocks gave birth to speckled young;   3972
31: 8 then the flocks bore streaked young.   3972
31:12 and see that **a** the male goats mating with   3972
31:12 for I have seen **a** that Laban has been doing   3972
31:16 Surely **a** the wealth that God took away   3972
31:18 and he drove **a** his livestock ahead of him,   3972
31:18 along with **a** the goods he had accumulated   3972
31:21 So he fled with **a** he had,   3972
31:37 you have searched through **a** my goods,   3972
31:43 A you see is mine.   3972
32:10 I am unworthy of **a** the kindness   3972
32:17 who owns **a** these animals in front of you?'   NIH
32:19 and **a** the others who followed the herds: 3972
32:23 he sent over **a** his possessions.   NIH
33: 7 **Last** of **a** came Joseph and Rachel,   339
33: 8 by **a** these droves I met?"   3972
33:11 to me and I have **a** *I* **need**."   3972
33:13 **a** the animals will die.   3972
34:15 like us by circumcising **a** your males.   3972
34:19 of **a** his father's household,   3972
34:23 and their other animals become ours?   3972
34:24 The men who went out of   3972
34:25 while **a** of them were still in pain,   NIH
34:29 They carried off **a** their wealth   3972
34:29 and **a** their women and children,   3972
35: 2 to his household and to **a** who were   3972
35: 4 So they gave Jacob the foreign gods   3972
35: 5 of God fell upon the towns **a** **around** them   6017
35: 6 and **a** the people with him came to Luz   3972
36: 6 and sons and daughters and **a** the members   3972
36: 6 as his livestock and **a** his other animals   3972
36: 6 and **a** the goods he had acquired in Canaan,   3972
37: 5 they hated him **a** the more.   3578+6388
37: 8 they hated him **a** the more because   3578+6388
37:14 "Go and see if **a** is well with your brothers   NIH
37:27 **after** **a**, he is our brother,   3954
37:35 A his sons and daughters came   3972
38:23 **After** **a**, I did send this young goat,   2180
39: 5 of his household and of **a** that he owned,   3972
39:22 in charge of **a** those held in the prison,   3972
39:22 and he was made responsible for **a**   3972

Ge	40:14	But when *a* goes well with you,	AIT
	40:17	In the top basket were **a kinds** of baked goods	3972+4946
	40:20	and he gave a feast for *a* his officials.	3972
	41: 8	for *a* the magicians and wise men of Egypt.	3972
	41:19	I had never seen such ugly cows in *a*	3972
	41:30	*a* the abundance in Egypt will be forgotten,	3972
	41:35	They should collect *a* the food	3972
	41:37	to Pharaoh and to *a* his officials.	3972
	41:39	"Since God has made *a* this known to you,	3972
	41:40	*a* my people are to submit to your orders.	3972
	41:44	or foot in *a* Egypt."	3972
	41:48	Joseph collected *a* the food produced	3972
	41:51	God has made me forget *a* my trouble	3972
	41:51	and *a* my father's household."	3972
	41:54	There was famine in *a* the other lands,	3972
	41:55	When *a* Egypt began to feel the famine,	3972
	41:55	Then Pharaoh told *a* the Egyptians,	3972
	41:57	And *a* the countries came to Egypt	3972
	41:57	the famine was severe in *a* the world.	3972
	42: 6	the one who sold grain to *a* its people.	3972
	42:11	We are *a* the sons of one man.	3972
	42:17	And he put **them** *a* in custody for three days.	AIT
	42:29	they told him *a* that had happened to them.	3972
	43: 2	So when they had eaten *a*	3983
	43: 9	I will bear the blame before you *a* my life.	3972
	43:23	"It's *a* **right**," he said.	8934
	44:13	Then they *a* loaded their donkeys	408
	44:32	before you, my father, *a* my life!'	3972
	45: 1	before *a* his attendants,	3972
	45: 8	and ruler of *a* Egypt.	3972
	45: 9	God has made me lord of *a* Egypt.	3972
	45:10	your flocks and herds, and *a* you have.	3972
	45:11	and your household and *a* who belong	3972
	45:13	about *a* the honor accorded me in Egypt	3972
	45:15	And he kissed *a* his brothers and wept	3972
	45:16	Pharaoh and *a* his officials were pleased.	NIH
	45:20	the best of *a* Egypt will be yours.' "	3972
	45:26	In fact, he is ruler of *a* Egypt."	3972
	46: 1	So Israel set out with *a* that was his,	3972
	46: 6	Jacob and *a* his offspring went to Egypt.	3972
	46: 7	and granddaughters—*a* his offspring.	3972
	46:15	and daughters of his were thirty-three in *a*.	3972
	46:18	to his daughter Leah—sixteen in *a*.	5883
	46:22	born to Jacob—fourteen in *a*.	3972
	46:25	to his daughter Rachel—seven in *a*.	3972
	46:26	*A* those who went to Egypt with Jacob—	3972
	46:27	which went to Egypt, were seventy in *a*.	3972
	46:34	for *a* shepherds are detestable to	3972
	47:12	and *a* his father's household with food,	3972
	47:14	Joseph collected *a* the money that was to	3972
	47:15	*a* Egypt came to Joseph and said,	3972
	47:17	with food in exchange for *a* their livestock.	3972
	47:20	So Joseph bought *a* the land in Egypt	3972
	47:20	The Egyptians, **one and a**, sold their fields,	408
	48:15	God who has been my shepherd *a* my **life**	4946+6388
	48:16	Angel who has delivered me from *a* harm	3972
	49:26	Let *a* these **rest** on the head of Joseph,	AIT
	49:28	*a* these are the twelve tribes of Israel,	3972
	50: 7	*A* Pharaoh's officials accompanied him—	3972
	50: 7	the dignitaries of his court and *a*	3972
	50: 8	besides *a* the members	3972
	50:14	and *a* the others who had gone with him	3972
	50:15	*a* grudge against us and pays us back for *a*	3972
	50:22	along with *a* his father's family.	NIH
Ex	1: 5	of Jacob numbered seventy in *a*;	3972
	1: 6	Now Joseph and *a* his brothers and all	3972
	1: 6	Now Joseph and all his brothers and *a*	3972
	1:14	and mortar and with *a* **kinds** of work in	3972
	1:14	in *a* their hard labor	3972
	1:22	Pharaoh gave this order to *a* his people:	3972
	3:20	and strike the Egyptians with *a* the wonders	3972
	4:19	for *a* the men who wanted	3972
	4:21	see that you perform before Pharaoh *a*	3972
	4:28	and also about *a*	3972
	4:29	and Aaron brought together *a* the elders of	3972
	5:11	but your work will not be reduced at *a*.' "	1821
	5:12	So the people scattered *a* over Egypt	3972
	5:23	**rescued** your people at *a*."	5911+5911
	7:19	over the ponds and *a* the reservoirs'—	3972
	7:20	and *a* the water was changed into blood.	3972
	7:24	And *a* the Egyptians dug along the Nile	3972
	8: 4	and your people and *a* your officials.' "	3972
	8:17	*A* the dust throughout the land	3972
	9: 6	*A* the livestock of the Egyptians died,	3972
	9:11	that were on them and on *a* the Egyptians.	3972
	9:14	that there is no one like me in *a* the earth.	3972
	9:16	and that my name might be proclaimed in *a*	3972
	9:22	the sky so that hail will fall *a* over Egypt—	3972
	9:24	in *a* the land of Egypt since it had become	3972
	10: 6	of *a* your officials and all the Egyptians—	3972
	10: 6	of all your officials and *a* the Egyptians—	3972
	10:13	across the land *a* day and all that night.	3972
	10:13	across the land all that day and *a* that night.	3972
	10:14	they invaded *a* Egypt and settled down	3972
	10:15	They covered *a* the ground	3972
	10:15	They devoured *a* that was left after	3972
	10:15	on tree or plant in *a* the land of Egypt.	3972
	10:22	and total darkness covered *a* Egypt	3972
	10:23	Yet *a* the Israelites had light in the places	3972
	11: 5	and *a* the firstborn of the cattle as well.	3972
	11: 8	*A* these officials of yours will come to me,	3972
	11: 8	you and *a* the people who follow you!'	3972
	11:10	and Aaron performed *a* these wonders	3972
	12: 6	when *a* the people of the community	3972
	12:12	and I will bring judgment on *a* the gods	3972

Ex	12:16	Do no work **at** *a* on these days,	3972
	12:16	that is *a* you may do.	963+4200
	12:21	Then Moses summoned *a* the elders	3972
	12:29	the LORD struck down *a* the firstborn	3972
	12:29	and the firstborn of *a* the livestock as well.	3972
	12:30	and *a* his officials and all the Egyptians got	3972
	12:30	and all his officials and *a* the Egyptians got	3972
	12:33	"For otherwise," they said, "we will *a* die!"	3972
	12:41	*a* the LORD's divisions left Egypt.	3972
	12:42	on this night *a* the Israelites are	3972
	12:48	the LORD's Passover must have *a*	3972
	12:50	*A* the Israelites did just what	3972
	13:12	*A* the firstborn males	3972
	14: 4	for myself through Pharaoh and *a* his army,	3972
	14: 7	along with *a* the other chariots of Egypt,	3972
	14: 7	with officers over *a* of them.	3972
	14: 9	*a* Pharaoh's horses and chariots,	3972
	14:17	through Pharaoh and *a* his army,	3972
	14:20	so neither went near the other *a* night *long*.	3972
	14:21	and *a* that night the LORD drove	3972
	14:23	and *a* Pharaoh's horses and chariots	3972
	15:20	and *a* the women followed her,	3972
	15:26	to his commands and keep *a* his decrees,	3972
	16: 3	and ate *a* the food we **wanted,**	8427
	16: 6	Moses and Aaron said to *a* the Israelites,	3972
	16: 8	*a* the bread you **want** in the morning,	8425
	18: 8	the Egyptians for Israel's sake and about *a*	3972
	18: 9	Jethro was delighted to hear about *a*	3972
	18:11	the LORD is greater than *a* other gods,	3972
	18:12	and Aaron came with *a* the elders of Israel	3972
	18:14	When his father-in-law saw *a*	3972
	18:14	while *a* these people stand around you	3972
	18:21	select capable men from *a* the people—	3972
	18:22	as judges for the people at *a* times,	3972
	18:23	and *a* these people will go home satisfied."	3972
	18:25	from *a* Israel and made them leaders of	3972
	18:26	as judges for the people at *a* times.	3972
	19: 5	then out of *a* nations you will	3972
	19: 7	the people and set before them *a* the words	3972
	19: 8	The people *a* responded together,	3972
	19:11	on Mount Sinai in the sight of *a* the people.	3972
	20: 1	And God spoke *a* these words:	3972
	20: 9	and do *a* your work,	3972
	20:11	the sea, and *a* that is in them,	3972
	22: 9	In *a* cases of illegal possession of an ox,	3972
	23:17	"Three times *a* year *a* the men are to appear	3972
	23:22	to what he says and do *a* that I say,	3972
	23:27	I will make *a* your enemies turn their backs	3972
	24: 3	the people *a* the LORD's words and laws,	3972
	24: 8	in accordance with *a* these words."	3972
	25: 9	and *a* its furnishings exactly like	3972
	25:22	with you and give you *a* my commands for	3972
	25:30	on this table to be before me **at a times.**	9458
	25:33	the same for *a* six branches extending from	NIH
	25:35	six branches in *a*.	NIH
	25:36	and branches shall *a* be of one piece with	3972
	25:39	for the lampstand and *a* these accessories.	3972
	26: 2	*A* the curtains are to be the same size—	3972
	26: 8	*A* eleven curtains are to be the same size—	NIH
	26:17	Make the frames of the tabernacle	3972
	26:24	the bottom **a the way to** the top, and fitted	6584
	27: 3	Make *a* its utensils of bronze—	3972
	27:17	*A* the posts around the courtyard are	3972
	27:19	*A* the other articles used in the service of	3972
	27:19	including *a* the tent pegs for it and those for	3972
	28: 3	Tell *a* the skilled men	3972
	29:13	Then take *a* the fat around the inner parts,	3972
	29:16	and sprinkle it against the altar **on a sides.**	6017
	29:20	sprinkle blood against the altar **on a sides.**	6017
	29:24	Put *a* these in the hands of Aaron	3972
	30: 3	the top and *a* the sides and the horns	6017
	30:14	*A* who cross over, those twenty years old or	3972
	30:24	*a* according to the sanctuary shekel—	NIH
	30:27	the table and *a* its articles,	3972
	30:28	the altar of burnt offering and *a* its utensils,	3972
	30:34	and pure frankincense, *a* in equal amounts,	NIH
	31: 3	and knowledge in *a* **kinds** of crafts—	3972
	31: 5	to engage in *a* **kinds** of craftsmanship.	3972
	31: 6	Also I have given skill to *a* the craftsmen	3972
	31: 7	and *a* the other furnishings of the tent—	3972
	31: 8	pure gold lampstand and *a* its accessories,	3972
	31: 9	and *a* its utensils, the basin with its stand—	3972
	32: 3	So *a* the people took off their earrings	3972
	32:13	I will give your descendants *a* this land I promised them,	3972
	32:26	And *a* the Levites rallied to him.	3972
	33: 8	*a* the people rose and stood at the entrances	3972
	33:10	they *a* stood and worshiped,	3972
	33:16	and your people from the other people on	3972
	33:19	"I will cause *a* my goodness to pass in front	3972
	34:10	*a* your people I will do wonders never	3972
	34:10	before done in any nation in *a* the world.	3972
	34:19	including *a* the firstborn males	3972
	34:20	Redeem *a* your firstborn sons.	3972
	34:23	a year *a* your men are to appear before	3972
	34:30	Aaron and *a* the Israelites saw Moses,	3972
	34:31	so Aaron and *a* the leaders of	3972
	34:32	Afterward *a* the Israelites came near him,	3972
	34:32	and he gave them *a* the commands	3972
	35:10	"*A* who are skilled among you are to come	3972
	35:13	the table with its poles and *a* its articles and	3972
	35:16	its poles and *a* its utensils;	3972
	35:21	Tent of Meeting, for *a* its service,	3972
	35:22	*A* who were willing, men and women alike,	3972
	35:22	and brought gold jewelry of *a* **kinds:**	3972
	35:22	They *a* presented their gold as	3972
	35:26	And *a* the women who were willing	3972

Ex	35:29	*A* the Israelite men and women	3972
	35:29	to the LORD freewill offerings for *a*	3972
	35:31	and knowledge in *a* **kinds** of crafts—	3972
	35:33	to work in wood and to engage in *a* kinds	3972
	35:35	He has filled them with skill to do *a* **kinds**	3972
	35:35	*a* of them master craftsmen and designers.	3972
	36: 1	how to carry out *a* the work of constructing	3972
	36: 3	They received from Moses *a* the offerings	3972
	36: 4	So *a* the skilled craftsmen who were doing	3972
	36: 4	craftsmen who were doing the work	3972
	36: 7	more than enough to do *a* the work.	3972
	36: 8	*A* the skilled men among	3972
	36: 9	*A* the curtains were the same size—	285
	36:15	*A* eleven curtains were the same size—	285
	36:22	They made *a* the frames of the tabernacle	3972
	36:29	the bottom **a the way to** the top and fitted	448
	37:19	the same for *a* six branches extending from	NIH
	37:21	six branches in *a*.	NIH
	37:22	and the branches were *a* of one piece with	3972
	37:24	and *a* its accessories from one talent	3972
	37:26	They overlaid the top and *a* the sides and	6017
	38: 3	They made *a* its utensils of bronze—	3972
	38:16	*A* the curtains around the courtyard were	3972
	38:17	so *a* the posts of the courtyard	3972
	38:20	*A* the tent pegs of the tabernacle and of	3972
	38:24	from the wave offering used for *a* the work	3972
	38:30	with its bronze grating and *a* its utensils,	3972
	38:31	for its entrance and *a* the tent pegs for	3972
	39:32	So *a* the work on the tabernacle,	3972
	39:33	the tent and *a* its furnishings, its clasps,	3972
	39:36	the table with *a* its articles and the bread of	3972
	39:37	with its row of lamps and *a* its accessories,	3972
	39:39	its poles and *a* its utensils;	3972
	39:40	*a* the furnishings for the tabernacle,	3972
	39:42	The Israelites had done *a* the work just as	3972
	40: 9	consecrate it and *a* its furnishings,	3972
	40:10	the altar of burnt offering and *a* its utensils;	3972
	40:15	that will continue for *a* generations	4392S
	40:36	In *a* the travels of the Israelites,	3972
	40:38	in the sight of *a* the house of Israel	3972
	40:38	the house of Israel during *a* their travels.	3972
Lev	1: 5	against the altar **on a sides** at the entrance to	6017
	1: 9	and the priest is to burn *a* of it on the altar.	3972
	1:11	against the altar **on a sides.**	6017
	1:13	and the priest is to bring *a* of it and burn it	3972
	2: 2	together with the incense,	3972
	2:13	Season *a* your grain offerings with salt.	3972
	2:13	add salt to *a* your offerings.	3972
	3: 2	together with the incense,	3972
	3: 2	the blood against the altar **on a sides.**	6017
	3: 3	*a* the fat that covers the inner parts	3972
	3: 8	against the altar **on a sides.**	6017
	3: 9	to the backbone, *a* the fat that covers	3972
	3:13	against the altar **on a sides.**	6017
	3:14	*a* the fat that covers the inner parts	3972
	3:16	*A* the fat is the LORD's.	3972
	4: 8	He shall remove *a* the fat from the bull of	3972
	4:11	But the hide of the bull and *a* its flesh,	3972
	4:12	*a* *the rest* of the bull—	3972
	4:19	He shall remove *a* the fat from it	3972
	4:26	He shall burn *a* the fat on the altar	3972
	4:31	He shall remove *a* the fat,	3972
	4:35	He shall remove *a* the fat,	3972
	5:16	add a fifth of the value to that and give it *a*	NIH
	6: 5	the value to it and give it *a* to the owner on	NIH
	6:15	with the incense on the grain offering,	3972
	7: 2	to be sprinkled against the altar **on a sides.**	6017
	7: 3	*A* its fat shall be offered:	3972
	7:10	belongs equally to *a* the sons of Aaron.	3972
	8:11	anointing the altar and *a* its utensils and	3972
	8:15	and with his finger he put it on the horns	6017
	8:16	also took *a* the fat around the inner parts,	3972
	8:19	the blood against the altar **on a sides.**	6017
	8:24	against the altar **on a sides.**	6017
	8:25	the fat tail, *a* the fat around the inner parts,	3972
	8:27	He put *a* these in the hands of Aaron	3972
	9:12	he sprinkled it against the altar **on a sides.**	6017
	9:18	he sprinkled it against the altar **on a sides.**	6017
	9:23	and the glory of the LORD appeared to *a*	3972
	9:24	And when *a* the people saw it,	3972
	10: 3	of *a* the people I will be honored.' "	3972
	10: 6	But your relatives, *a* the house of Israel,	3972
	10:11	and you must teach the Israelites *a*	3972
	11: 2	'Of *a* the animals that live on land,	3972
	11: 9	" 'Of *a* the creatures living in the water of	3972
	11:10	But *a* creatures in the seas or streams	3972
	11:10	among the swarming things or among all	3972
	11:10	among all the swarming things or among *a*	3972
	11:20	"*A* flying insects that walk	3972
	11:20	that walk on *a* **fours** are to be detestable	752
	11:21	some winged creatures that walk on **fours**	752
	11:23	But *a* other winged creatures	3972
	11:27	Of *a* the animals that walk on all fours,	3972
	11:27	Of all the animals that walk on *a* **fours,**	752
	11:31	Of *a* those that move along the ground,	3972
	11:42	or walks on *a* **fours** or on many feet;	752
	13:12	the disease **breaks out a over** his skin	7255+7255
	13:12	it covers *a* the skin of the infected person	3972
	13:13	Since it has *a* turned white, he is clean.	3972
	14: 8	shave off *a* his hair and bathe with water;	3972
	14: 9	seventh day he must shave off *a* his hair;	3972
	14:41	He must have the inside walls of	6017
	14:45	its stones, timbers and *a* the plaster—	3972
	16:18	the goat's blood and put it on the horns of	6017
	16:21	over it the wickedness and rebellion of	3972
	16:21	rebellion of the Israelites—*a* their sins—	3972
	16:22	The goat will carry on itself *a* their sins to	3972

Lev	16:30	you will be clean from a your sins.	3972
	16:33	and for the priests and a the people of	3972
	16:34	Atonement is to be made once a year for a	3972
	17: 2	to Aaron and his sons and to a the Israelites	3972
	18:27	for a these things were done by	3972
	19:24	In the fourth year a its fruit will be holy,	3972
	19:37	" 'Keep a my decrees and all my laws	3972
	19:37	" 'Keep all my decrees and a my laws	3972
	20: 5	both him and a who follow him	3972
	20:22	" 'Keep a my decrees and laws	3972
	20:23	they did a these things, I abhorred them.	3972
	21:24	and his sons and to a the Israelites.	3972
	22:18	to Aaron and his sons and to a the Israelites	3972
	23:31	You shall do no work at a.	3972
	23:38	and a the freewill offerings you give to	3972
	23:42	A native-born Israelites are to live	3972
	24:14	A those who heard him are	3972
	25:10	throughout the land to a its inhabitants.	3972
	26: 5	a the food you **want**	8427
	26:14	to me and carry out a these commands,	3972
	26:15	and fail to carry out a my commands and	3972
	26:18	" 'If after a **this** you will not listen to me,	465
	26:34	Then the land will enjoy its sabbath years a	3972
	26:35	a the time that it lies desolate,	3972
Nu	1: 3	to number by their divisions a the men	3972
	1:20	A the men twenty years old	3972
	1:22	A the men twenty years old	3972
	1:24	A the men twenty years old	3972
	1:26	A the men twenty years old	NIH
	1:28	A the men twenty years old	3972
	1:30	A the men twenty years old	3972
	1:32	A the men twenty years old	3972
	1:34	A the men twenty years old	3972
	1:36	A the men twenty years old	3972
	1:38	A the men twenty years old	3972
	1:40	A the men twenty years old	3972
	1:42	A the men twenty years old	3972
	1:45	A the Israelites twenty years old	3972
	1:50	over a its furnishings	3972
	1:50	the tabernacle and a its furnishings;	3972
	1:54	The Israelites did a this just as	3972
	2: 9	A the men assigned to the camp of Judah,	3972
	2:16	A the men assigned to the camp of Reuben,	3972
	2:24	A the men assigned to the camp of Ephraim,	3972
	2:31	A the men assigned to the camp of Dan	3972
	2:32	A those in the camps, by their divisions,	3972
	3: 8	They are to take care of a the furnishings of	3972
	3:13	for a the firstborn are mine.	3972
	3:13	I struck down a the firstborn in Egypt,	3972
	3:22	The number of a the males a month old	3972
	3:28	The number of a the males a month old	3972
	3:34	The number of a the males a month old	3972
	3:36	its crossbars, posts, bases, a its equipment,	3972
	3:40	The LORD said to Moses, "Count a	3972
	3:41	in place of a the firstborn of the Israelites,	3972
	3:41	of the Levites in place of a the firstborn of	3972
	3:42	So Moses counted a the firstborn	3972
	3:45	"Take the Levites in place of a the firstborn	3972
	4: 3	Count a the men from thirty to fifty years	3972
	4: 9	and a its jars for the oil used to supply it.	3972
	4:10	and a its accessories in a covering of hides	3972
	4:12	to take a the articles used for ministering in	3972
	4:14	on it a the utensils used for ministering at	3972
	4:15	the holy furnishings and a the holy articles,	3972
	4:23	Count a the men from thirty to fifty years	3972
	4:26	and a the equipment used in its service.	3972
	4:26	The Gershonites are to do a that needs to	3972
	4:27	A their service, whether carrying	3972
	4:27	as their responsibility a they are to carry.	3972
	4:30	Count a the men from thirty to fifty years	3972
	4:32	a their equipment and everything related	3972
	4:35	A the men from thirty to fifty years	3972
	4:37	This was the total of a those in	3972
	4:39	A the men from thirty to fifty years	3972
	4:43	A the men from thirty to fifty years	3972
	4:46	the leaders of Israel counted a the Levites	3972
	4:47	A the men from thirty to fifty years	3972
	5: 7	and give it a to the person he has wronged.	NIH
	5: 9	A the sacred contributions	3972
	7: 1	and consecrated it and a its furnishings.	3972
	7: 1	and consecrated the altar and a its utensils.	3972
	7: 8	They were a under the direction	NIH
	8:17	I struck down a the firstborn in Egypt,	3972
	8:18	the Levites in place of a the firstborn sons	3972
	8:19	**Of** a the Israelites,	4946+9348
	9: 3	with a its rules and regulations."	3972
	9:12	they must follow a the regulations.	3972
	10:25	Finally, as the rear guard for a the units,	3972
	11:11	that you put the burden of a these people	3972
	11:12	Did I conceive a these people?	3972
	11:13	Where can I get meat for a these people?	3972
	11:14	I cannot carry a these people by myself;	3972
	11:22	Would they have enough if a the fish in	3972
	11:29	that a the LORD's people were prophets	3972
	11:31	It brought them down a **around** the camp to	6017
	11:32	A that day and night and all the next day	3972
	11:32	All that day and night and a the next day	3972
	11:32	they spread them out a **around** the camp.	6017
	12: 4	a **three** of you."	AIT
	12: 7	he is faithful in a my house.	3972
	13: 3	A of them were leaders of the Israelites.	3972
	13:32	A the people we saw there are of great size.	3972
	14: 1	That night a the people of	
	14: 2	the Israelites grumbled against Moses	3972
	14:10	at the Tent of Meeting to a the Israelites.	3972
	14:11	of a the miraculous signs I have performed	3972
	14:15	you put these people to death a at one time,	408

Nu	14:39	Moses reported this to a the Israelites,	3972
	14:45	and beat them down a **the way to** Hormah.	6330
	15:26	because a the people were involved in	3972
	15:39	and so you will remember a the commands	3972
	15:40	to obey a my commands and will	3972
	16: 5	Then he said to Korah and a his followers:	3972
	16: 6	Korah, and a your followers are to do this:	3972
	16:10	and a your fellow Levites near himself,	3972
	16:11	and a your followers have banded together.	3972
	16:16	and a your followers are to appear before	3972
	16:17	250 censers in a—	NIH
	16:19	When Korah had gathered a his followers	3972
	16:22	"O God, God of the spirits of a mankind,	3972
	16:26	be swept away because of a their sins."	3972
	16:28	the LORD has sent me to do a these things	3972
	16:31	As soon as he finished saying a this,	3972
	16:32	with their households and a Korah's men	3972
	16:32	and a their possessions.	3972
	16:34	the Israelites around them fled, shouting,	3972
	17: 9	Then Moses brought out a the staffs from	3972
	17: 9	the staffs from the LORD's presence to a	3972
	17:12	We are lost, we are a lost!	3972
	17:13	Are we a going to die?"	9462
	18: 3	and are to perform a the duties of the Tent,	3972
	18: 4	a the work at the Tent—	3972
	18: 8	a the holy offerings the Israelites give me	3972
	18: 9	From a the gifts they bring me	3972
	18:11	from the gifts of a the wave offerings of	3972
	18:12	"I give you a the finest olive oil and all	3972
	18:12	"I give you all the finest olive oil and a	3972
	18:13	A the land's firstfruits that they bring to	3972
	18:21	"I give to the Levites a the tithes in Israel	3972
	18:28	to the LORD from a the tithes you receive	3972
	19:18	and sprinkle the tent and a the furnishings	3972
	20:14	about a the hardships that have come	3972
	21:25	Israel captured a the cities of the Amorites	3972
	21:25	and a its surrounding settlements.	3972
	21:26	of Moab and had taken from him a his land	3972
	21:30	Heshbon is destroyed a **the way to** Dibon.	6330
	22: 2	of Zippor saw a that Israel had done to	3972
	23: 6	with a the princes of Moab.	3972
	23:13	you will see only a part but not a of them.	3972
	23:25	"Neither **curse** them at a nor bless	7686+7686
	23:25	at all nor **bless** them at a!"	1385+1385
	24:17	the skulls of a the sons of Sheth.	3972
	25: 4	"Take a the leaders of these people,	3972
	26: 2	a those twenty years old	3972
	26:43	A of them were Shuhamite clans;	3972
	26:62	the male Levites a month old	3972
	27:16	the God of the spirits of a mankind,	3972
	28:11	a year old, a **without defect.**	AIT
	28:19	a year old, a **without defect.**	AIT
	29: 2	a year old, a **without defect.**	AIT
	29: 8	a year old, a **without defect.**	AIT
	29:13	a year old, a **without defect.**	AIT
	29:17	a year old, a **without defect.**	AIT
	29:20	a year old, a **without defect.**	AIT
	29:23	a year old, a **without defect.**	AIT
	29:26	a year old, a **without defect.**	AIT
	29:29	a year old, a **without defect.**	AIT
	29:32	a year old, a **without defect.**	AIT
	29:36	a year old, a **without defect.**	AIT
	29:40	Moses told the Israelites a that	3972
	30: 4	then a her vows and every pledge	3972
	30:11	then a her vows or the pledges	3972
	30:14	then he confirms a her vows or	3972
	31: 9	and took a the Midianite herds.	3972
	31:10	They burned a the towns where	3972
	31:10	as well as a their camps.	3972
	31:11	They took a the plunder and spoils,	3972
	31:13	and a the leaders of the community went	3972
	31:15	"Have you allowed a the women to live?"	3972
	31:17	Now kill a the boys.	3972
	31:19	"A of you who have killed anyone	3972
	31:26	of the community are to count a the people	4917S
	31:51	a the crafted articles.	3972
	31:52	A the gold from the commanders	3972
	32:15	he will again leave a this people in	3972
	32:21	if a of you will go armed over the Jordan	3972
	33: 3	They marched out boldly in full view of a	3972
	33: 4	who were burying a their firstborn, whom	3972
	33:52	drive out a the inhabitants of the land	3972
	33:52	Destroy a their carved images	3972
	33:52	and demolish a their high places.	3972
	35: 3	flocks and a their other livestock.	3972
	35: 7	In a you must give	3972
Dt	1: 1	to a Israel in the desert east of the Jordan—	3972
	1: 3	Moses proclaimed to the Israelites a that	3972
	1: 7	to a the neighboring peoples in the Arabah,	3972
	1:12	and your disputes a **by myself?**	963+3276+4200
	1:19	the hill country of the Amorites through a	3972
	1:22	Then a of you came to me and said,	3972
	1:31	a the way you went until you reached this	3972
	1:44	and beat you down from Seir a **the way to**	6330
	1:46	a the time you spent there.	3869
	2: 7	The LORD your God has blessed you in a	3972
	2:25	the terror and fear of you on a the nations	3972
	2:32	When Sihon and a his army came out	3972
	2:34	At that time we took a his towns	3972
	2:36	The LORD our God gave us a of them.	3972
	3: 3	of Bashan and a his army.	3972
	3: 4	At that time we took a his cities.	3972
	3: 5	A these cities were fortified with high walls	3972
	3: 7	But a the livestock and the plunder	3972
	3:10	We took a the towns on the plateau,	3972
	3:10	the plateau, and a Gilead, and all Bashan	3972
	3:10	and a Bashan as far as Salecah and Edrei,	3972

Dt	3:13	The rest of Gilead and also a of Bashan,	3972
	3:18	But a your able-bodied men,	3972
	3:21	"You have seen with your own eyes a that	3972
	3:21	the same to a the kingdoms over there	3972
	4: 4	but a of you who held fast to	3972
	4: 6	who will hear about a these decrees	3972
	4:19	a the heavenly array—	3972
	4:19	the LORD your God has apportioned to a	3972
	4:29	if you look for him with a your heart and	3972
	4:29	with all your heart and with a your soul.	3972
	4:30	and a these things have happened to you,	3972
	4:34	like a the things the LORD your God did	3972
	4:40	the LORD your God gives you for a time.	3972
	4:49	included a the Arabah east of the Jordan,	3972
	5: 1	Moses summoned a Israel and said:	3972
	5: 3	with a of us who are alive here today.	3972
	5:13	and do a your work,	3972
	5:23	a the leading men of your tribes	3972
	5:27	to a that the LORD our God says.	3972
	5:29	and keep a my commands always,	3972
	5:31	so that I may give you a the commands,	3972
	5:33	Walk in a the way that the LORD your God	3972
	6: 2	as long as you live by keeping a his decrees	3972
	6: 5	with a your heart and with all your soul and	3972
	6: 5	with all your heart and with a your soul and	3972
	6: 5	with all your soul and with a your strength.	3972
	6:11	with a **kinds of** good things you did	3972
	6:19	thrusting out a your enemies before you,	3972
	6:24	to obey a these decrees and to fear	3972
	6:25	if we are careful to obey a this law before	3972
	7: 6	of a the peoples on the face of the earth to	3972
	7: 7	for you were the fewest of a peoples.	3972
	7:15	but he will inflict them on a who hate you.	3972
	7:16	You must destroy a the peoples	3972
	7:18	to Pharaoh and to a Egypt.	3972
	7:19	the same to a the peoples you now fear.	3972
	7:22	be allowed to eliminate them a **at once,**	4554
	8: 2	the LORD your God led you a the way in	3972
	8:13	and a you have is multiplied,	3972
	9:10	On them were a the commandments	3972
	9:18	because of a the sin you had committed,	3972
	10:12	to walk in a his ways, to love him,	3972
	10:12	the LORD your God with a your heart and	3972
	10:12	with all your heart and with a your soul,	3972
	10:15	their descendants, above a the nations,	3972
	10:22	down into Egypt were seventy in a,	5883S
	11: 6	the middle of a Israel and swallowed them	3972
	11: 7	that saw a these great things	3972
	11: 8	Observe therefore a the commands I am giving you today,	3972
	11:13	with a your heart and with all your soul—	3972
	11:13	with all your heart and with a your soul—	3972
	11:22	If you carefully observe a these commands	3972
	11:22	walk in a his ways and to hold fast to him—	3972
	11:23	the LORD will drive out a these nations	3972
	11:32	be sure that you obey a the decrees	3972
	12: 2	Destroy completely a the places on	3972
	12: 5	among a your tribes to put his Name there	3972
	12:10	from a your enemies around you so	3972
	12:11	special gifts, and a the choice possessions	3972
	12:28	to obey a these regulations I am giving you,	3972
	12:31	they do a **kinds of** detestable things	3972
	12:32	See that you do a I command you;	3972
	13: 3	with a your heart and with all your soul.	3972
	13: 3	with all your heart and with a your soul.	3972
	13: 9	and then the hands of a the people.	3972
	13:11	Then a Israel will hear and be afraid,	3972
	13:15	to the sword a who live in that town.	NIH
	13:16	Gather a the plunder of the town into	3972
	13:16	and a its plunder as a whole burnt offering	3972
	13:18	keeping a his commands	3972
	14: 2	of a the peoples on the face of the earth,	3972
	14: 9	Of a the creatures living in the water,	3972
	14:19	A flying insects that swarm are unclean	3972
	14:22	of a that your fields produce each year.	3972
	14:28	bring a the tithes of that year's produce	3972
	14:29	the LORD your God may bless you in a	3972
	15: 5	to follow a these commands I am giving you today.	3972
	15:10	your God will bless you in a your work	3972
	16: 3	so that a the days	3972
	16: 4	be found in your possession in a your land	3972
	16:15	in your harvest and in all the work	3972
	16:15	in all your harvest and in a the work	3972
	16:16	Three times a year a your men must appear	3972
	17: 7	and then the hands of a the people.	3972
	17:13	A the people will hear and be afraid,	3972
	17:14	"Let us set a king over us like a the nations	3972
	17:19	and he is to read it a the days of his life so	3972
	17:19	and follow carefully a the words of this law	3972
	18: 5	and their descendants out of a your tribes	3972
	18: 6	and comes in a earnestness to the place	3972
	18: 7	like a his fellow Levites who serve there in	3972
	19: 9	because you carefully follow a these laws	3972
	20:11	a the people in it shall be subject	3972
	20:13	put to the sword a the men in it.	3972
	20:15	how you are to treat a the cities that are at	3972
	20:18	to follow a the detestable things they do	3972
	21: 5	the LORD and to decide a cases of dispute	3972
	21: 6	Then a the elders of the town nearest	3972
	21:17	by giving him a double share of a he has.	3972
	21:21	Then a the men of his town shall stone him	3972
	21:21	A Israel will hear of it and be afraid.	3972
	23:24	a the grapes you **want,**	8427
	24:19	the LORD your God may bless you in a	3972
	25:18	and cut off a who were lagging behind;	3972
	25:19	the LORD your God gives you rest from a	3972

Dt	26: 2	of the firstfruits of a that you produce from	3972
	26:11	and the aliens among you shall rejoice in a	3972
	26:12	a tenth of a your produce in the third year,	3972
	26:13	according to a you commanded.	3972
	26:16	carefully observe them with a your heart	3972
	26:16	with all your heart and with a your soul.	3972
	26:18	and that you are to keep a his commands.	3972
	26:19	above a the nations he has made and	3972
	27: 1	"Keep a these commands	3972
	27: 3	Write on them a the words of this law	3972
	27: 8	And you shall write very clearly a	3972
	27: 9	who are Levites, said to Israel, "Be silent,	3972
	27:14	to a the people of Israel in a loud voice:	3972
	27:15	Then a the people shall say, "Amen!"	3972
	27:16	Then a the people shall say, "Amen!"	3972
	27:17	Then a the people shall say, "Amen!"	3972
	27:18	Then a the people shall say, "Amen!"	3972
	27:19	Then a the people shall say, "Amen!"	3972
	27:20	Then a the people shall say, "Amen!"	3972
	27:21	Then a the people shall say, "Amen!"	3972
	27:22	Then a the people shall say, "Amen!"	3972
	27:23	Then a the people shall say, "Amen!"	3972
	27:24	Then a the people shall say, "Amen!"	3972
	27:25	Then a the people shall say, "Amen!"	3972
	27:26	Then a the people shall say, "Amen!"	3972
	28: 1	carefully follow a his commands I give you	3972
	28: 1	above a the nations on earth.	3972
	28: 2	A these blessings will come upon you	3972
	28:10	Then a the peoples on earth will see	3972
	28:12	and to bless a the work of your hands.	3972
	28:15	not carefully follow a his commands	3972
	28:15	a these curses will come upon you	3972
	28:25	and you will become a thing of horror to a	3972
	28:26	Your carcasses will be food for a the birds	3972
	28:33	but cruel oppression a your days.	3972
	28:37	of scorn and ridicule to a the nations where	3972
	28:42	of locusts will take over a your trees and	3972
	28:45	A these curses will come upon you.	3972
	28:52	to a the cities throughout your land until	3972
	28:52	They will besiege a the cities throughout	3972
	28:55	It will be a he has left because of	3972
	28:55	on you during the siege of a your cities.	3972
	28:58	If you do not carefully follow a the words	3972
	28:60	He will bring upon you a the diseases	3972
	28:64	LORD will scatter you among a nations,	3972
	29: 2	Moses summoned a the Israelites and said	3972
	29: 2	Your eyes have seen a that the LORD did	3972
	29: 2	to a his officials and to all his land.	3972
	29: 2	to all his officials and to a his land.	3972
	29:10	A of you are standing today in the presence	3972
	29:10	and a the other men of Israel,	3972
	29:20	A the curses written in this book will fall	3972
	29:21	The LORD will single him out from a	3972
	29:21	to a the curses of the covenant written	3972
	29:24	A the nations will ask:	3972
	29:27	so that he brought on it a the curses written	3972
	29:29	that we may follow a the words of this law.	3972
	30: 1	When a these blessings	3972
	30: 2	with a your heart and with all your soul	3972
	30: 2	with all your heart and with a your soul,	3972
	30: 3	from the nations where he scattered you.	3972
	30: 6	so that you may love him with a your heart	3972
	30: 6	with all your heart and with a your soul,	3972
	30: 7	The LORD your God will put a these curses	3972
	30: 8	follow a his commands I am giving you	3972
	30: 9	in a the work of your hands and in the fruit	3972
	30:10	the LORD your God with a your heart and	3972
	30:10	with all your heart and with a your soul.	3972
	31: 1	and spoke these words to a Israel:	3972
	31: 5	to them a that I have commanded you.	3972
	31: 7	and said to him in the presence of a Israel,	3972
	31: 9	to a the elders of Israel.	3972
	31:11	when a Israel comes to appear before	3972
	31:12	and follow carefully a the words	3972
	31:18	on that day because of a their wickedness	3972
	31:28	before me a the elders of your tribes	3972
	31:28	of your tribes and a your officials,	NIH
	32: 4	and a his ways are just.	3972
	32: 8	when he divided a mankind,	NIH
	32:27	the LORD has not done a this.' "	3972
	32:44	of Nun and spoke a the words of this song	3972
	32:45	Moses finished reciting a these words	3972
	32:45	When Moses finished reciting all these words to a Israel,	3972
	32:46	"Take to heart a the words	3972
	32:46	to obey carefully a the words of this law.	3972
	33: 3	a the holy ones are in your hand.	3972
	33: 3	At your feet they a bow down,	NIH
	33:11	Bless a his skills, O LORD,	NIH
	33:12	for he shields him a day long,	3972
	33:16	Let a these rest on the head of Joseph,	AIT
	34: 2	a of Naphtali, the territory of Ephraim	3972
	34: 2	a the land of Judah as far as	3972
	34:11	who did a those miraculous signs	3972
	34:11	and to a his officials and to his whole land.	3972
	34:12	that Moses did in the sight of a Israel.	3972
Jos	1: 2	Now then, you and a these people,	3972
	1: 4	a the Hittite country—	3972
	1: 5	be able to stand up against you a the days	3972
	1: 7	Be careful to obey a the law	3972
	1:14	but a your fighting men, fully armed,	3972
	2: 9	that a who live in this country are melting	3972
	2:13	and a who belong to them,	3972
	2:18	and a your family into your house.	3972
	2:22	the pursuers had searched a along the road	3972
	2:24	the people are melting in fear because of	3972
	3: 1	and a the Israelites set out from Shittim	3972

Jos	3: 7	to exalt you in the eyes of a Israel,	3972
	3:11	of a the earth will go into the Jordan ahead	3972
	3:13	the Lord of a the earth—	3972
	3:15	Jordan is at flood stage a during harvest.	3972
	3:17	while a Israel passed by until	3972
	4:11	and as soon as a of them had crossed,	3972
	4:14	in the sight of a Israel;	3972
	4:14	and they revered him a the days of his life,	3972
	4:24	that a the peoples of the earth might know	3972
	5: 1	Now when a the Amorite kings west of	3972
	5: 1	the Amorite kings west of the Jordan and a	3972
	5: 4	A those who came out of Egypt—	3972
	5: 4	a the men of military age—	3972
	5: 5	A the people that came out had been circumcised,	3972
	5: 5	but a the people born in the desert during	3972
	5: 6	until a the men who were of military age	3972
	6: 3	around the city once with a the armed men.	3972
	6: 5	have a the people give a loud shout;	3972
	6: 9	A this time the trumpets were sounding.	2143
	6:17	The city and a that is in it are to be devoted	3972
	6:17	and a who are with her in her house shall	3972
	6:19	A the silver and gold and the articles	3972
	6:22	and bring her out and a who belong to her,	3972
	6:23	and brothers and a who belonged to her.	3972
	6:25	with her family and a who belonged to her,	3972
	7: 3	"Not a the people will have to go up	3972
	7: 3	to take it and do not weary a the people,	3972
	7:15	along with a that belongs to him.	3972
	7:24	brought them to Joshua and a the Israelites	3972
	7:24	Then Joshua, together with a Israel,	3972
	7:24	his tent and a that he had,	3972
	7:25	Then a Israel stoned him,	3972
	8: 4	A of you be on the alert.	3972
	8: 5	I and a those with me will advance on	3972
	8:13	a those in the camp to the north of the city	3972
	8:14	and a the men of the city hurried out early	3972
	8:15	and a Israel let themselves be driven back	3972
	8:16	A the men of Ai were called	3972
	8:21	and a Israel saw that the ambush had taken	3972
	8:24	When Israel had finished killing a the men	3972
	8:24	the Israelites returned to Ai	3972
	8:25	fell that day—a the people of Ai.	3972
	8:26	until he had destroyed a who lived in Ai.	3972
	8:33	A Israel, aliens and citizens alike,	3972
	8:34	Joshua read a the words of the law—	3972
	8:35	a word of a that Moses had commanded	3972
	9: 1	when a the kings west of the Jordan heard	3972
	9: 5	A the bread of their food supply was dry	3972
	9: 9	a that he did in Egypt,	3972
	9:10	and a that he did to the two kings of	3972
	9:11	and a those living in our country said to us,	3972
	9:19	but a the leaders answered,	3972
	9:24	and to wipe out a its inhabitants from	3972
	10: 2	and a its men were good fighters.	3972
	10: 5	up with a their troops and took up positions	3972
	10: 6	because a the Amorite kings from	3972
	10: 7	including a the best fighting men.	3972
	10:10	down a the way to Azekah and Makkedah.	6330
	10:15	Then Joshua returned with a Israel to	3972
	10:24	he summoned a of Israel and said	3972
	10:25	to a the enemies you are going to fight."	3972
	10:29	Then Joshua and a Israel with him moved	3972
	10:31	Then Joshua and a Israel with him moved	3972
	10:34	Then Joshua and a Israel with him moved	3972
	10:36	Then Joshua and a Israel with him went up	3972
	10:38	Then Joshua and a Israel with him turned	3972
	10:40	together with a their kings.	3972
	10:40	He totally destroyed a who breathed,	3972
	10:42	A these kings and their lands Joshua conquered in one campaign,	3972
	10:43	Then Joshua returned with a Israel to	3972
	11: 4	with a their troops and a large number	3972
	11: 5	A these kings joined forces	3972
	11: 6	by this time tomorrow I will hand a	3972
	11: 8	and pursued them a the way to	6330
	11:10	the head of a these kingdoms.)	3972
	11:12	Joshua took a these royal cities	3972
	11:14	for themselves a the plunder and livestock	3972
	11:14	but a the people they put to the sword	3972
	11:15	of a that the LORD commanded Moses.	3972
	11:16	the hill country, a the Negev,	3972
	11:17	He captured a their kings and struck them	3972
	11:18	Joshua waged war against a these kings for	3972
	11:19	who took them a in battle.	3972
	11:21	from a the hill country of Judah,	3972
	11:21	and from a the hill country of Israel.	3972
	12: 1	including a the eastern side of the Arabah:	3972
	12: 5	a of Bashan to the border of the people	3972
	12:24	king of Tirzah one thirty-one kings in a.	3972
	13: 2	a the regions of the Philistines	3972
	13: 3	a of it counted as Canaanite (the territory of	NIH
	13: 4	a the land of the Canaanites,	3972
	13: 5	and a Lebanon to the east,	3972
	13: 6	"As for a the inhabitants of	3972
	13: 6	that is, a the Sidonians,	3972
	13:10	a the towns of Sihon king of the Amorites,	3972
	13:11	a of Mount Hermon and all Bashan as far	3972
	13:11	all of Mount Hermon and a Bashan as far	3972
	13:17	to Heshbon and a its towns on the plateau,	3972
	13:21	—a the towns on the plateau and	3972
	13:25	a the towns of Gilead and half	3972
	13:30	and including a of Bashan, the entire realm	3972
	13:30	a the settlements of Jair in Bashan,	3972
	15:46	a that were in the vicinity of Ashdod,	3972
	16: 9	also included a the towns and their villages	3972
	17:16	and a the Canaanites who live in	3972

Jos	18:20	of the clans of Benjamin on a sides.	6017
	19: 8	and a the villages around these towns as far	3972
	21:19	A the towns for the priests,	3972
	21:26	A these ten towns	3972
	21:33	A the towns of the Gershonite clans	3972
	21:39	four towns in a.	3972
	21:40	A the towns allotted to the Merarite clans,	3972
	21:41	by the Israelites were forty-eight in a,	3972
	21:42	this was true for a these towns.	3972
	21:43	So the LORD gave Israel a the land	3972
	21:44	the LORD handed a their enemies over	3972
	21:45	Not one of a the LORD's good promises	3972
	22: 2	"You have done a that Moses the servant	3972
	22: 5	to walk in a his ways,	3972
	22: 5	to him and to serve him with a your heart	3972
	22: 5	with all your heart and a your soul."	3972
	23: 1	from a their enemies around them,	3972
	23: 2	summoned a Israel—their elders,	3972
	23: 3	to a these nations for your sake;	3972
	23: 4	an inheritance for your tribes a the land of	3972
	23: 6	to obey a that is written in the Book of	3972
	23:14	"Now I am about to go the way of a	3972
	23:14	You know with a your heart and soul that	3972
	23:14	that not one of a the good promises	3972
	23:15	on you a the evil he has threatened,	3972
	24: 1	Then Joshua assembled a the tribes	3972
	24: 2	Joshua said to a the people,	3972
	24:14	and serve him with a faithfulness.	9459
	24:17	on our entire journey and among a	3972
	24:18	LORD drove out before us a the nations,	3972
	24:27	he said to a the people.	3972
	24:27	It has heard a the words	3972
Jdg	2: 4	of the LORD had spoken these things to a	3972
	2: 7	and who had seen a the great things	3972
	2:14	sold them to their enemies a around,	4946+6017
	3: 1	to test a those Israelites who had	3972
	3: 3	a the Canaanites, the Sidonians,	3972
	3:19	And a his attendants left him.	3972
	3:29	a vigorous and strong; not a man escaped.	3972
	4:13	and a the men with him,	3972
	4:15	the LORD routed Sisera and a his chariots	3972
	4:16	A the troops of Sisera fell by the sword;	3972
	5:30	a this as plunder?'	NIH
	5:31	"So may a your enemies perish, O LORD!	3972
	6: 4	the land and ruined the crops a the way to	6330
	6: 9	and from the hand of a your oppressors.	3972
	6:13	why has a this happened to us?	3972
	6:13	Where are a his wonders	3972
	6:16	a the Midianites together."	285+408+3869
	6:33	Now a the Midianites,	3972
	6:37	If there is dew only on the fleece and a	3972
	6:40	a the ground was covered with dew.	3972
	7: 1	and a his men camped at the spring	3972
	7: 6	A the rest got down on their knees to drink.	3972
	7: 7	Let a the other men go,	3972
	7:12	and a the other eastern peoples had settled	3972
	7:16	and empty jars in the hands of a of them,	3972
	7:18	and a who are with me blow our trumpets,	3972
	7:18	then from a around the camp blow yours	3972
	7:21	a the Midianites ran,	3972
	7:23	Asher and a Manasseh were called out,	3972
	7:24	So a the men of Ephraim were called out	3972
	8:10	a that were left of the armies of	3972
	8:27	A Israel prostituted themselves	3972
	8:34	the hands of a their enemies on every side.	3972
	8:35	for a the good things he had done for them.	3972
	9: 1	and said to them and to a his mother's clan,	3972
	9: 2	"Ask a the citizens of Shechem,	3972
	9: 2	to have a seventy of Jerub-Baal's sons rule	3972
	9: 3	the brothers repeated a this to the citizens	3972
	9: 6	Then a the citizens of Shechem	3972
	9:14	"Finally a the trees said to the thornbush,	3972
	9:34	and a his troops set out by night and took	3972
	9:40	a the way to the entrance to the gate.	6330
	9:45	A that day Abimelech pressed his attack	3972
	9:48	he and a his men went up Mount Zalmon.	3972
	9:49	So a the men cut branches	3972
	9:49	So a the people in the tower of Shechem,	3972
	9:51	to which a the men and women—	3972
	9:51	a the people of the city—fled.	3972
	9:57	of Shechem pay for a their wickedness.	3972
	10: 8	For eighteen years they oppressed a	3972
	10:18	be the head of a those living in Gilead."	3972
	11: 8	and you will be our head over a who live	3972
	11:11	And he repeated a his words before	3972
	11:13	a the way to the Jordan.	6330
	11:20	He mustered a his men and encamped	3972
	11:21	and a his men into Israel's hands,	3972
	11:21	over a the land of the Amorites who lived	3972
	11:22	capturing a of it from the Arnon to	3972
	11:26	the surrounding settlements and a	3972
	12: 6	"A right, say 'Shibboleth.' "	5528
	13:13	"Your wife must do a that I have told her.	3972
	13:23	nor shown us a these things or	3972
	14: 3	or among a our people?	3972
	16: 2	the place and lay in wait for him a night at	3972
	16: 3	and tore them loose, bar and a.	6640
	16:27	the rulers of the Philistines were there,	3972
	16:30	Then he pushed with a his might,	NIH
	16:30	down came the temple on the rulers and a	3972
	18: 2	These men represented a their clans.	7896
	18:31	a the time the house of God was in Shiloh.	3972
	19:29	and sent them into a the areas of Israel.	3972
	20: 1	Then a the Israelites from Dan	3972
	20: 2	The leaders of a the people of the tribes	3972
	20: 7	Now, a you Israelites, speak up	3972
	20: 8	A the people rose as one man, saying,	3972

Jdg	20:10	of every hundred from a the tribes of Israel,	3972
	20:10	for a this vileness done in Israel."	3972
	20:11	So a the men of Israel got together	3972
	20:16	Among a these soldiers there were	3972
	20:17	a of them fighting men.	3972
	20:25	a of them armed with swords.	3972
	20:26	Then the Israelites, a the people,	3972
	20:33	A the men of Israel moved	3972
	20:35	Benjamites, a armed with swords.	3972
	20:44	a of them valiant fighters.	3972
	20:46	a of them valiant fighters.	3972
	20:48	went back to Benjamin and put a the towns	5507
	20:48	A the towns they came across they set	3972
	21: 5	"Who from a the tribes of Israel has failed	3972
	21:14	But there were not enough for a of them.	NIH
Ru	2:11	"I've been told a about what you have done	3972
	2:14	She ate a she wanted	8425
	2:21	until they finish harvesting a my grain.' "	3972
	3:11	I will do for you a you ask.	3972
	3:11	A my fellow townsmen know that you are	3972
	4: 9	Then Boaz announced to the elders and a	3972
	4: 9	from Naomi a the property of Elimelech.	3972
	4:11	Then the elders and a those at the gate said,	3972
1Sa	2:13	to his wife Peninnah and to a her sons	3972
	1:11	then I will give him to the LORD for a	3972
	1:21	the man Elkanah went up with a his family	3972
	2:14	how they treated a the Israelites who came	3972
	2:22	to a Israel and how they slept with	3972
	2:23	from a the people about these wicked deeds	3972
	2:28	of a the tribes of Israel to be my priest,	3972
	2:28	I also gave your father's house a	3972
	2:33	and a your descendants will die in	3972
	3:20	And a Israel from Dan	3972
	4: 1	And Samuel's word came to a Israel.	3972
	4: 5	a Israel raised such a great shout that	3972
	4: 6	"What's a this shouting in	1524
	4: 8	the Egyptians with a kinds of plagues in	3972
	5: 8	So they called together a the rulers of	3972
	5:11	So they called together a the rulers of	3972
	6: 3	but by a means send a guilt offering to him.	
			8740+8740
	6:12	keeping on the road and lowing a the way;	
			2143+2143
	6:16	the Philistines saw a this and then returned	NIH
	7: 2	It was a long time, twenty years in a,	NIH
	7: 2	and a the people of Israel mourned	3972
	7: 3	to the LORD with a your hearts,	3972
	7: 5	"Assemble a Israel at Mizpah	3972
	7:15	as judge over Israel a the days of his life.	3972
	7:16	judging Israel in a those places.	3972
	8: 4	So the elders of Israel gathered together	3972
	8: 5	such as a the other nations have."	3972
	8: 7	"Listen to a that the people are saying	3972
	8:10	Samuel told a the words of the LORD to	3972
	8:20	Then we will be like a the other nations,	3972
	8:21	When Samuel heard a that the people said,	3972
	9:19	and will tell you a that is in your heart.	3972
	9:20	to whom is the desire of Israel turned,	3972
	9:20	if not to you and a your father's family?"	3972
	9:21	and is not my clan the least of a the clans	3972
	10: 9	and a these signs were fulfilled that day.	3972
	10:11	When a those who had formerly known	
		him saw him prophesying	3972
	10:18	and the kingdoms that oppressed you.'	3972
	10:19	who saves you out of a your calamities	3972
	10:20	Samuel brought a the tribes of Israel near,	3972
	10:24	Samuel said to a the people,	3972
	10:24	There is no one like him among a	3972
	11: 1	And a the men of Jabesh said to him,	3972
	11: 2	of you and so bring disgrace on a Israel."	3972
	11: 4	they a wept aloud.	3972
	11:15	So a the people went to Gilgal	3972
	11:15	and a the Israelites held a great celebration.	3972
	12: 1	Samuel said to a Israel,	3972
	12: 7	with evidence before the LORD as to a	3972
	12:18	So a the people stood in awe of the LORD	3972
	12:19	The people a said to Samuel,	3972
	12:19	to a our other sins the evil of asking for	3972
	12:20	"You have done a this evil;	3972
	12:20	but serve the LORD with a your heart.	3972
	12:24	and serve him faithfully with a your heart;	3972
	13: 4	So a Israel heard the news:	3972
	13: 7	and a the troops with him were quaking	3972
	13:13	over Israel for a time.	6409
	13:20	So a Israel went down to the Philistines	3972
	14: 7	"Do a that you have in mind,"	3972
	14:16	the army melting away in a directions.	2151
	14:20	and a his men assembled and went to	3972
	14:22	When a the Israelites who had hidden in	3972
	14:38	a you who are leaders of the army,	3972
	14:40	Saul then said to a the Israelites,	3972
	14:52	A the days of Saul there was bitter war with	3972
	15: 6	for you showed kindness to a the Israelites	3972
	15: 7	a the way from Havilah to Shur,	995
	15: 8	and a his people he totally destroyed with	3972
	15:11	and he cried out to the LORD a that night.	3972
	16:11	"Are these a the sons you have?"	9462
	17:11	Saul and a the Israelites were dismayed	3972
	17:19	They are with Saul and a the men of Israel	3972
	17:24	they a ran from him in great fear.	3972
	17:47	A those gathered here will know that it is	3972
	17:47	and he will give a of you into our hands."	NIH
	18: 5	This pleased a the people,	3972
	18: 6	the women came out from a the towns	3972
	18:16	But a Israel and Judah loved David,	3972
	18:22	and his attendants a like you;	3972
	19: 1	and a the attendants to kill David.	3972

1Sa	19: 5	a great victory for a Israel,	3972
	19:18	at Ramah and told him a that Saul had done	3972
	19:24	He lay that way a that day and night.	3972
	20: 6	If your father misses me at a, tell him,	7212+7212
	20:39	(The boy knew nothing of a this;	4399
	22: 2	A those who were in distress or in debt	3972
	22: 6	with a his officials standing around him.	3972
	22: 7	Will the son of Jesse give a of you fields	3972
	22: 7	Will he make a a of you commanders	3972
	22: 8	that why you have a conspired against me?	3972
	22:11	and they a came to the king.	3972
	22:14	of a your servants is as loyal as David,	3972
	22:15	your servant knows nothing at a	196+1524+7785
	23: 8	And Saul called up a his forces for battle,	3972
	23:23	Find out about a the hiding places he uses	3972
	23:23	in the area, I will track him down among a	3972
	24: 2	from a Israel and set out to look for David	3972
	25: 1	a Israel assembled and mourned for him;	3972
	25: 6	And good health to a that is yours!	3972
	25:16	Night and day they were a wall around us a	3972
	25:21	a my watching over this fellow's property	3972
	25:22	of a who belong to him!"	3972
	25:26	and a who intend to harm my master be	NIH
	25:37	his wife told him a these things,	NIH
	26:12	They were a sleeping,	3972
	26:24	and deliver me from a trouble."	3972
	28: 3	and a Israel had mourned for him	3972
	28: 4	while Saul gathered the Israelites and set	3972
	28:20	for he had eaten nothing a that day	3972
	29: 1	The Philistines gathered a their forces	3972
	30: 2	the women and a who were in it,	NIH
	30:20	He took a the flocks and herds,	3972
	30:22	But a the evil men and troublemakers	3972
	30:24	A will share alike."	AIT
	30:31	to those in a the other places where David	3972
	31: 6	and a his men died together that same day.	3972
	31:12	a their valiant men journeyed through	3972
2Sa	1:11	and the men with him took hold	3972
	2: 9	Benjamin and a Israel.	3972
	2:14	"A right, let them do it,"	7756[s]
	2:28	and the men came to a halt;	3972
	2:29	A that night Abner and his men marched	3972
	2:30	and assembled a his men. .	3972
	3:12	I will help you bring a Israel over to you."	3972
	3:16	weeping behind her a the way to Bahurim.	2143
	3:18	and from the hand of a their enemies.' "	3972
	3:21	and assemble a Israel for my lord the king,	3972
	3:21	over a that your heart desires."	3972
	3:23	Joab and a the soldiers with him arrived,	3972
	3:29	of Joab and upon a his father's house!	3972
	3:31	Then David said to Joab and a the people	3972
	3:32	A the people wept also.	3972
	3:34	And a the people wept over him again.	3972
	3:35	Then they a came and urged David	3972
	3:36	A the people took note and were pleased;	3972
	3:37	on that day a the people and all Israel knew	3972
	3:37	on that day all the people and a Israel knew	3972
	4: 1	and a Israel became alarmed.	3972
	4: 7	they traveled a night by way of the Arabah.	3972
	4: 9	who has delivered me out of a trouble,	3972
	5: 1	A the tribes of Israel came to David	3972
	5: 3	When a the elders of Israel had come	3972
	5: 5	over a Israel and Judah thirty-three years.	3972
	5:25	a the way from Gibeon to Gezer.	995+6330
	6: 1	thirty thousand in a.	3972
	6: 2	and a his men set out from Baalah of Judah	3972
	6: 5	with a their might before the LORD,	3972
	6:14	danced before the LORD with a his might,	3972
	6:19	And a the people went to their homes.	3972
	7: 1	from a his enemies around him,	3972
	7: 7	Wherever I have moved with a	3972
	7: 9	and I have cut off a your enemies from	3972
	7:11	also give you rest from a your enemies.	3972
	7:17	Nathan reported to David a the words	3972
	8: 4	He hamstrung a but a hundred of	3972
	8:11	from a the nations he had subdued;	3972
	8:14	and a the Edomites became subject	3972
	8:15	David reigned over a Israel,	3972
	8:15	and right for a his people.	3972
	9: 7	to you a the land that belonged	3972
	9:12	and a the members	3972
	10:17	David was told of this, he gathered a Israel,	3972
	10:19	When a the kings who were vassals	3972
	11: 9	with a his master's servants and did not go	3972
	12: 8	And if a this had been too little,	NIH
	12:12	in broad daylight before a Israel.' "	3972
	12:31	He did this to a the Ammonite towns.	3972
	13:21	King David heard a this, he was furious.	3972
	13:23	he invited a the king's sons to come there.	3972
	13:25	"A of us should not go;	3972
	13:29	Then a the king's sons got up,	3972
	13:30	"Absalom has struck down a	3972
	13:31	and a his servants stood by	3972
	13:32	"My lord should not think that they killed a	3972
	13:33	the report that a the king's sons are dead.	3972
	13:36	too, and a his servants wept very bitterly.	3972
	14:19	"Isn't the hand of Joab with you in a this?"	3972
	14:19	and who put a these words into the mouth	3972
	14:25	In a Israel there was not a man	3972
	15: 6	Absalom behaved in this way toward a	3972
	15:14	Then David said to a his officials who were	3972
	15:17	with a the people following him,	3972
	15:18	A his men marched past him,	3972
	15:18	along with a the Kerethites and Pelethites;	3972
	15:18	with all the Kerethites and Pelethites; and a	3972
	15:22	the Gittite marched on with a his men and	3972

2Sa	15:23	The whole countryside wept aloud as a	3972
	15:23	a the people moved on toward the desert.	3972
	15:24	and a the Levites who were	3972
	15:24	until the people had finished leaving	3972
	15:30	A the people with him covered their heads	3972
	16: 4	"A that belonged to Mephibosheth is	3972
	16: 6	He pelted David and a the king's officials	3972
	16: 6	though a the troops and	3972
	16: 8	for a the blood you shed in the household	3972
	16:11	then said to Abishai and a his officials,	3972
	16:14	The king and a the people with him arrived	3972
	16:15	and a the men of Israel came to Jerusalem,	3972
	16:18	and by a the men of Israel—	3972
	16:21	Then a Israel will hear	3972
	16:22	in the sight of a Israel.	3972
	16:23	how both David and Absalom regarded a	3972
	17: 2	and then a the people with him will flee.	3972
	17: 3	and bring a the people back to you.	3972
	17: 3	will mean the return of a;	3972
	17: 3	a the people will be unharmed."	3972
	17: 4	to Absalom and to a the elders of Israel.	3972
	17:10	for a Israel knows that your father is	3972
	17:11	Let a Israel, from Dan to Beersheba—	3972
	17:13	then a Israel will bring ropes to that city,	3972
	17:14	Absalom and a the men of Israel said,	3972
	17:16	or the king and a the people with him will	3972
	17:22	So David and a the people with him set out	3972
	17:24	and Absalom crossed the Jordan with a	3972
	18: 4	So the king stood beside the gate while a	3972
	18: 5	And a the troops heard the king	3972
	18:17	a the Israelites fled to their homes.	3972
	18:28	to the king, "A is well!"	8934
	18:31	from a who rose up against you."	3972
	18:32	the king and a who rise up to harm you be	3972
	19: 5	"Today you have humiliated a your men,	3972
	19: 6	if Absalom were alive today and a	3972
	19: 7	be worse for you than a the calamities	3972
	19: 8	they a came before him.	3972
	19: 9	the people were a arguing with each other,	3972
	19:14	over the hearts of a the men of Judah as	3972
	19:14	"Return, you and a your men."	3972
	19:28	A my grandfather's descendants deserved	
		nothing	3972
	19:39	So a the people crossed the Jordan,	3972
	19:40	A the troops of Judah and half the troops	3972
	19:41	Soon a the men of Israel were coming to	3972
	19:41	together with a his men?"	3972
	19:42	The men of Judah answered the men	3972
	20: 2	So a the men of Israel deserted David	3972
	20: 2	stayed by their king a the way from the	
		Jordan	4946
	20: 7	and a the mighty warriors went out under	3972
	20:12	and the man saw that a the troops came to	3972
	20:13	a the men went on with Joab	3972
	20:14	Sheba passed through a the tribes of Israel	3972
	20:15	A the troops with Joab came	3972
	20:22	Then the woman went to a the people	3972
	21: 9	A seven of them fell together;	AIT
	21:20	on each foot—twenty-four in a.	5031
	22: 1	of a his enemies and from the hand of Saul.	3972
	22:23	A his laws are before me;	3972
	22:31	He is a shield for a who take refuge in him.	3972
	22:46	They a lose heart;	AIT
	23: 6	evil men are a to be cast aside like thorns,	3972
	23:39	There were thirty-seven in a.	3972
	24: 7	toward the fortress of Tyre and a the towns	3972
	24:23	O king, Araunah gives a this to the king."	3972
1Ki	1: 9	He invited a his brothers, the king's sons,	3972
	1: 9	and a the men	3972
	1:19	and has invited the king's sons,	3972
	1:20	the eyes of a Israel are on you,	3972
	1:25	He has invited the king's sons,	3972
	1:39	the trumpet and a the people shouted,	3972
	1:40	And a the people went up after him,	3972
	1:41	Adonijah and a the guests who were	3972
	1:41	the meaning of a the noise in the city?"	NIH
	1:43	"Not at a!" Jonathan answered.	66
	1:49	a Adonijah's guests rose in alarm	3972
	2: 2	"I am about to go the way of a the earth,"	3972
	2: 3	so that you may prosper in a you do	3972
	2: 4	before me with a their heart and soul,	3972
	2:15	A Israel looked to me as their king.	3972
	2:22	after a, he is my older brother—	3954
	2:26	and shared a my father's hardships."	3972
	2:44	in your heart a the wrong you did	3972
	3:15	Then he gave a feast for a his court.	3972
	3:28	When a Israel heard the verdict	3972
	4: 1	So King Solomon ruled over a Israel.	3972
	4: 7	over a Israel, who supplied provisions for	3972
	4:10	and a the land of Hepher were his);	3972
	4:12	and Megiddo, and in a of Beth Shan next	3972
	4:21	And Solomon ruled over a the kingdoms	3972
	4:21	and were Solomon's subjects a his life.	3972
	4:24	For he ruled over a the kingdoms west of	3972
	4:24	and had peace on a sides.	3972
	4:27	for King Solomon and a who came to	3972
	4:30	the wisdom of a the men of the East,	3972
	4:30	and greater than a the wisdom of Egypt.	3972
	4:31	to a the surrounding nations.	3972
	4:34	Men of a nations came to listen	3972
	4:34	sent by a the kings of the world,	3972
	5: 3	waged against my father David from a	
		sides,	6015
	5: 8	and will do a you want in providing	3972
	5:10	with a the cedar and pine logs he wanted,	3972
	5:13	King Solomon conscripted laborers from a	
		Israel—	3972

1Ki	6:10	he built the side rooms a along the temple.	3972
	6:12	and keep a my commands and obey them,	3972
	6:29	On the walls a around the temple,	3972
	6:38	the temple was finished in a its details	3972
	7: 5	A the doorways had rectangular frames;	3972
	7: 9	A these structures, from the outside to	3972
	7:14	experienced in a kinds of bronze work.	3972
	7:14	He came to King Solomon and did a	3972
	7:20	pomegranates in rows a around.	6017
	7:33	spokes and hubs were a of cast metal.	3972
	7:36	with wreaths a around.	6017
	7:37	They were a cast in the same molds	3972
	7:40	So Huram finished a	3972
	7:45	A these objects that Huram made	3972
	7:47	Solomon left a these things unweighed,	3972
	7:48	also made a the furnishings that were in	3972
	7:51	When a the work King Solomon had done	3972
	8: 1	a the heads of the tribes and the chiefs of	3972
	8: 2	A the men of Israel came together	3972
	8: 3	When a the elders of Israel had arrived,	3972
	8: 4	the LORD and the Tent of Meeting and a	3972
	8:25	if only your sons are careful in a they do	2006
	8:39	deal with each man according to a he does,	3972
	8:39	(for you alone know the hearts of a men),	3972
	8:40	that they will fear you a the time they live	3972
	8:43	so that a the peoples of the earth may know	3972
	8:48	if they turn back to you with a their heart	3972
	8:50	forgive the offenses they have committed	3972
	8:53	from a the nations of the world to	3972
	8:54	When Solomon had finished a these prayers	3972
	8:56	of a the good promises he gave	3972
	8:58	in a his ways and to keep the commands,	3972
	8:60	so that a the peoples of the earth may know	3972
	8:62	and a Israel with him offered sacrifices	3972
	8:63	and a the Israelites dedicated the temple of	3972
	8:65	and a Israel with him—	3972
	8:65	fourteen days in a.	NIH
	8:66	for a the good things the LORD had done	3972
	9: 1	and had achieved a he had desired to do,	3972
	9: 4	and do a I command	3972
	9: 7	and an object of ridicule among a peoples.	3972
	9: 8	a who pass by will be appalled	3972
	9: 9	the LORD brought a this disaster	3972
	9:11	because Hiram had supplied him with a	3972
	9:19	as well as a his store cities and the towns	3972
	9:19	in Jerusalem, in Lebanon and throughout a	3972
	9:20	A the people left from the Amorites,	3972
	10: 2	with him about a that she had on her mind.	3972
	10: 3	Solomon answered a her questions;	3972
	10: 4	of Sheba saw a the wisdom of Solomon	3972
	10:13	the queen of Sheba a she desired and asked	3972
	10:15	from the Arabian kings and the governors	3972
	10:21	A King Solomon's goblets were gold,	3972
	10:21	and a the household articles in the Palace	3972
	10:23	in riches and wisdom than a the other kings	3972
	10:29	They also exported them to a the kings of	3972
	11: 8	He did the same for a his foreign wives,	3972
	11:15	had struck down a the men in Edom.	3972
	11:16	Joab and the Israelites stayed there	3972
	11:16	until they had destroyed a the men	3972
	11:32	which I have chosen out of a the tribes	3972
	11:34	I have made him ruler a the days of his life	3972
	11:37	you will rule over a that your heart desires;	3972
	11:41	a he did and the wisdom he displayed—	3972
	11:42	in Jerusalem over a Israel forty years.	3972
	12: 1	for a the Israelites had gone there	3972
	12:12	and a the people returned to Rehoboam,	3972
	12:16	When a Israel saw that the king refused	3972
	12:18	but a Israel stoned him to death.	3972
	12:20	When a the Israelites heard	3972
	12:20	and made him king over a Israel.	3972
	12:31	and appointed priests from a sorts	7896
	13:11	whose sons came and told him a that	3972
	13:32	and against a the shrines on the high places	3972
	13:33	for the high places from a sorts of people.	7896
	14: 8	and followed me with a his heart,	3972
	14: 9	You have done more evil than a who lived	3972
	14:10	until it is a gone.	9462
	14:13	A Israel will mourn for him and bury him.	3972
	14:18	and a Israel mourned for him,	3972
	14:21	the LORD had chosen out of a the tribes	3972
	14:24	in a the detestable practices of the nations	3972
	14:26	He took everything, including a	3972
	14:29	and a he did,	3972
	15: 3	He committed a the sins his father had done	3972
	15: 5	to keep any of the LORD's commands a	3972
	15: 7	and a he did,	3972
	15:12	of a the idols his fathers had made.	3972
	15:14	to the LORD a his life.	3972
	15:18	then took a the silver and gold that was left	3972
	15:20	and a Kinnereth in addition to Naphtali.	3972
	15:22	King Asa issued an order to a Judah—	3972
	15:23	As for a the other events of Asa's reign,	3972
	15:23	of Asa's reign, a his achievements,	3972
	15:23	a he did and the cities he built,	3972
	15:27	while Nadab and a Israel were besieging it.	3972
	15:29	but destroyed them a, according to	NIH
	15:31	other events of Nadab's reign, and a he did,	3972
	15:33	of Ahijah became king of a Israel	3972
	16: 7	of a the evil he had done in the eyes of	3972
	16:13	because of a the sins Baasha	3972
	16:14	other events of Elah's reign, and a he did,	3972
	16:17	and a the Israelites with him withdrew	3972
	16:25	and sinned more than a those before him.	3972
	16:26	He walked in a the ways of Jeroboam son	3972
	16:33	anger than did a the kings of Israel	3972
	18: 5	"Go through the land to a the springs	3972

1Ki	18:19	the people from a over Israel to meet me	3972
	18:20	So Ahab sent word throughout a Israel	3972
	18:24	a the people said, "What you say is good."	3972
	18:30	Then Elijah said to a the people,	3972
	18:36	and have done a these things	3972
	18:39	When a the people saw this,	3972
	18:46	he ran ahead of Ahab a the way to Jezreel.	995+3870+6330
	19: 1	and how he had killed a the prophets with	3972
	19: 5	A at once an angel touched him and said,	2180+2296
	19:18	a whose knees have not bowed down	3972
	19:18	and a whose mouths have not kissed him."	3972
	20: 1	I and a I are yours."	3972
	20: 7	of Israel summoned a the elders of the land	3972
	20: 8	The elders and the people a answered,	3972
	20: 9	'Your servant will do a you demanded	3972
	20:15	the rest of the Israelites, 7,000 in a.	3972
	20:24	Remove a the kings from their commands	408
	22:10	with a the prophets prophesying	3972
	22:12	A the other prophets were prophesying	3972
	22:17	"I saw a Israel scattered on the hills	3972
	22:19	the LORD sitting on his throne with a	3972
	22:22	in the mouths of a his prophets,'	3972
	22:23	in the mouths of a these prophets of yours.	3972
	22:28	he added, "Mark my words, a you people!"	3972
	22:35	A day long the battle raged,	928+2021+2021+2085+3427
	22:39	including a the	3972
2Ki	1:14	the first two captains and a their men.	AIT
	1:18	for a the other events of Ahaziah's reign,	AIT
	3: 6	from Samaria and mobilized a Israel.	3972
	3:19	stop up a the springs.	3972
	3:21	Now a the Moabites had heard that	3972
	3:25	They stopped up a the springs and cut	3972
	4: 2	"Your servant has nothing there at a,"	3972
	4: 3	and ask a your neighbors for empty jars.	3972
	4: 4	Pour oil into a the jars,	3972
	4: 6	When a the jars were full,	NIH
	4:13	'You have gone to a this trouble for us.	3972
	4:23	"It's a right," she said.	8934
	4:26	'Are you a right?	8934
	4:26	Is your husband a right?	8934
	4:26	Is your child a right?'"	8934
	4:26	"Everything is a right," she said.	8934
	5: 5	"By a means, go," the king of Aram replied.	995+2143
	5:15	and a his attendants went back to the man	3972
	5:15	that there is no God in a the world except	3972
	5:21	"Is everything a right?"	8934
	5:22	"Everything is a right," Gehazi answered.	8934
	5:23	"By a means, take two talents,"	3283
	6:17	of horses and chariots of fire a around	6017
	7:13	like that of a the Israelites left here—	2162+3972
	7:13	like a these Israelites who are doomed.	2162+3972
	8: 4	about a the great things Elisha has done."	3972
	8: 6	including a the income from her land from	3972
	8: 7	"The man of God has come a the way up	6330
	8: 9	with him as a gift forty camel-loads of a	3972
	8:21	Jehoram went to Zair with a his chariots.	3972
	8:23	Jehoram's reign, and a he did,	3972
	9: 7	of a the LORD's servants shed by Jezebel.	3972
	9:11	"Is everything a right?	8934
	9:14	a Israel had been defending Ramoth Gilead	3972
	9:22	a the idolatry and witchcraft of your mother Jezebel abound?"	8041
	10: 7	the princes and slaughtered a seventy	NIH
	10: 9	He stood before a the people and said,	3972
	10: 9	but who killed a these?	3972
	10:11	as well as a his chief men,	3972
	10:17	he killed a who were left there	3972
	10:18	Then Jehu brought a the people together	3972
	10:19	Now summon a the prophets of Baal,	3972
	10:19	a his ministers and all his priests.	3972
	10:19	all his ministers and a his priests.	3972
	10:21	and a the ministers of Baal came;	3972
	10:22	"Bring robes for a the ministers of Baal."	3972
	10:30	and have done to the house of Ahab a I had	3972
	10:31	the God of Israel, with a his heart.	3972
	10:33	in a the land of Gilead (the region of Gad,	3972
	10:34	the other events of Jehu's reign, a he did,	3972
	10:34	a he did, and a his achievements,	3972
	11: 7	that normally go off Sabbath duty are a	3972
	11:14	and a the people of the land were rejoicing	3972
	11:18	A the people of the land went to the temple	3972
	11:19	the guards and a the people of the land,	3972
	11:20	and a the people of the land rejoiced.	3972
	12: 2	the eyes of the LORD a the years Jehoiada	3972
	12: 4	"Collect a the money that is brought	3972
	12: 9	into the chest a the money that was brought	3972
	12:12	and met a the other expenses of restoring	3972
	12:18	But Joash king of Judah took a	3972
	12:18	and a the gold found in the treasuries of	3972
	12:19	reign of Joash, and a he did,	3972
	13: 8	a he did and his achievements,	3972
	13:12	a he did and his achievements,	3972
	14:14	He took a the gold and silver and all	3972
	14:14	the gold and silver and a the articles found	3972
	14:21	Then a the people of Judah took Azariah,	3972
	14:28	other events of Jeroboam's reign, a he did,	3972
	15: 6	Azariah's reign, and a he did,	3972
	15:16	and ripped open a the pregnant women.	3972
	15:21	Menahem's reign, and a he did,	3972
	15:26	Pekahiah's reign, and a he did,	3972
	15:29	including a the land of Naphtali.	3972
	15:31	other events of Pekah's reign, and a he did,	3972
	16:11	the priest built an altar in accordance with a	3972

2Ki	16:15	burnt offering of a the people of the land,	3972
	16:15	the altar a the blood of the burnt offerings	3972
	17: 7	A this took place because	AIT
	17: 9	high places in a their towns.	3972
	17:13	and Judah through a his prophets and seers:	3972
	17:16	They forsook a the commands of	3972
	17:16	They bowed down to a the starry hosts,	3972
	17:20	the LORD rejected a the people of Israel;	3972
	17:22	The Israelites persisted in a the sins	3972
	17:23	as he had warned through a his servants	3972
	17:32	appointed a sorts of their own people	4946+7896
	17:39	from the hand of a your enemies."	3972
	18: 5	like him among a the kings of Judah,	3972
	18:12	a that Moses the servant of	3972
	18:13	of Assyria attacked a the fortified cities	3972
	18:15	So Hezekiah gave him a the silver	3972
	18:21	of Egypt to a who depend on him.	3972
	18:35	Who of a the gods of these countries	3972
	19: 2	the leading priests, a wearing sackcloth,	AIT
	19: 4	the LORD your God will hear a the words	3972
	19:11	of Assyria have done to a the countries,	3972
	19:15	you alone are God over a the kingdoms of	3972
	19:19	so that a kingdoms on earth may know	3972
	19:24	With the soles of my feet I have dried up a	3972
	19:35	there were a the dead bodies!	3972
	20:13	the messengers and showed them a	3972
	20:13	or in a his kingdom that Hezekiah did	3972
	20:17	and a that your fathers have stored up	NIH
	20:20	a his achievements and how he made	3972
	21: 3	to a the starry hosts and worshiped them.	3972
	21: 5	he built altars to a the starry hosts.	3972
	21: 7	which I have chosen out of a the tribes	3972
	21:14	be looted and plundered by a their foes,	3972
	21:17	Manasseh's reign, and a he did,	3972
	21:21	He walked in a the ways of his father;	3972
	21:24	of the land killed a who had plotted	3972
	22: 2	in the eyes of the LORD and walked in a	3972
	22:13	for me and for the people and for a Judah	3972
	22:13	with a that is written there concerning us."	3972
	22:17	by a the idols their hands have made,	3972
	22:20	not see a the disaster I am going to bring	3972
	23: 1	Then the king called together a the elders	3972
	23: 2	a the people from the least to the greatest.	3972
	23: 2	in their hearing a the words of the Book of	3972
	23: 3	regulations and decrees with a his heart	3972
	23: 3	with all his heart and a his soul,	3972
	23: 3	Then a the people pledged themselves to	3972
	23: 4	to remove from the temple of the LORD a	3972
	23: 4	for Baal and Asherah and a the starry hosts.	3972
	23: 5	the constellations and to a the starry hosts.	3972
	23: 8	Josiah brought a the priests from the towns	3972
	23:19	Josiah removed and defiled a the shrines at	3972
	23:20	Josiah slaughtered a the priests	3972
	23:21	The king gave this order to a the people:	3972
	23:24	and a the other detestable things seen	3972
	23:25	with a his heart and with all his soul and	3972
	23:25	with all his heart and with a his soul and	3972
	23:25	with all his soul and with a his strength,	3972
	23:25	in accordance with a the Law of Moses.	3972
	23:26	which burned against Judah because of a	3972
	23:28	other events of Josiah's reign, and a he did,	3972
	24: 3	of the sins of Manasseh and a he had done,	3972
	24: 5	Jehoiakim's reign, and a he did,	3972
	24: 7	of Babylon had taken a his territory,	3972
	24:12	his nobles and his officials a surrendered	AIT
	24:13	Nebuchadnezzar removed a the treasures	3972
	24:13	and took away a the gold articles	3972
	24:14	He carried into exile a Jerusalem:	3972
	24:14	a the officers and fighting men,	3972
	24:14	and a the craftsmen and artisans—	3972
	24:20	of the LORD's anger that a this happened	AIT
	25: 1	the city and built siege works a around it.	6017
	25: 5	A his soldiers were separated from him	3972
	25: 9	the royal palace and a the houses	3972
	25:14	dishes and a the bronze articles used in	3972
	25:15	a that were made of pure gold or silver.	NIH
	25:17	and pomegranates of bronze a around.	3972
	25:20	Nebuzaradan the commander took them a	AIT
	25:23	When a the army officers	3972
	25:26	a the people from the least to the greatest,	3972
1Ch	1:23	A these were sons of Joktan.	3972
	1:33	A these were descendants of Keturah.	3972
	2: 4	Judah had five sons in a.	3972
	2: 6	and Darda—five in a.	3972
	2:23	A these were descendants of Makir	3972
	3: 8	Elishama, Eliada and Eliphelet—nine in a.	NIH
	3: 9	A these were the sons of David,	3972
	3:22	and Shaphat—six in a.	NIH
	3:23	and Azrikam—three in a.	NIH
	3:24	and Anani—seven in a.	NIH
	4:33	and a the villages around these towns as far	3972
	5:13	and Eber—seven in a.	NIH
	5:16	and on a the pasturelands of Sharon as far	3972
	5:17	A these were entered in	3972
	5:20	the Hagrites and a their allies over to them,	3972
	6:48	Their fellow Levites were assigned to a	3972
	6:49	on the altar of incense in connection with a	3972
	6:49	in accordance with a that Moses the servant	3972
	6:60	were thirteen in a.	3972
	7: 1	and Shimron—four in a.	NIH
	7: 3	A five of them were chiefs.	3972
	7: 5	to a the clans of Issachar,	3972
	7: 5	in their genealogy, were 87,000 in a.	3972
	7: 7	of families—five in a.	NIH
	7: 8	A these were the sons of Beker.	3972
	7:11	A these sons of Jediael were heads	3972
	7:28	and Shechem and its villages a the way to	6330

Ref	Text	Num
1Ch 7:40	A these were descendants of Asher—	3972
8:28	A these were heads of families,	AIT
8:38	A these were the sons of Azel.	3972
8:40	and grandsons—150 in a.	NIH
8:40	A these were the descendants of Benjamin.	3972
9: 1	A Israel was listed in	3972
9: 9	A these men were heads of their families.	3972
9:29	of the furnishings and a the other articles of	3972
9:34	A these were heads of Levite families,	AIT
10: 6	and a his house died together.	3972
10: 7	When a the Israelites in the valley saw that	3972
10:11	When a the inhabitants of Jabesh Gilead	3972
10:12	a their valiant men went and took	3972
11: 1	A Israel came together to David at Hebron	3972
11: 3	When a the elders of Israel had come	3972
11: 4	and a the Israelites marched to Jerusalem	3972
11:10	they, together with a Israel,	3972
12:15	when it was overflowing a its banks,	3972
12:21	for a of them were brave warriors,	3972
12:32	with a their relatives under their command;	3972
12:38	A these were fighting men who volunteered	3972
12:38	to make David king over a Israel.	3972
12:38	A the rest of the Israelites were also	3972
13: 4	because it seemed right to a the people.	3972
13: 5	So David assembled a the Israelites,	3972
13: 6	David and a the Israelites with him went	3972
13: 8	David and a the Israelites were celebrating	3972
13: 8	with a their might before God,	3972
14: 8	over a Israel, they went up in full force	3972
14:16	a the way from Gibeon to Gezer.	6330
14:17	the LORD made a the nations fear him.	3972
15: 3	David assembled a Israel in Jerusalem	3972
15:27	as were a the Levites who were carrying	3972
15:28	So a Israel brought up the ark of	3972
16: 9	tell of a his wonderful acts.	3972
16:14	his judgments are in a the earth.	3972
16:23	Sing to the LORD, a the earth;	3972
16:24	his marvelous deeds among a peoples.	3972
16:25	he is to be feared above a gods.	3972
16:26	For a the gods of the nations are idols,	3972
16:30	Tremble before him, a the earth!	3972
16:32	Let the sea resound, and a that is in it;	4850
16:36	Then a the people said "Amen" and "Praise	3972
16:43	Then a the people left,	3972
17: 6	Wherever I have moved with a	3972
17: 8	and I have cut off a your enemies from	3972
17:10	I will also subdue a your enemies.	3972
17:15	Nathan reported to David a the words	3972
17:19	and made known a these great promises.	3972
18: 4	He hamstrung a but a hundred of	3972
18:10	Hadoram brought a kinds of articles	3972
18:11	and gold he had taken from a these nations:	3972
18:13	a the Edomites became subject to David.	3972
18:14	David reigned over a Israel,	3972
18:14	and right for a his people.	3972
19:17	he gathered a Israel and crossed the Jordan;	3972
20: 3	David did this to a the Ammonite towns.	3972
20: 6	on each foot—twenty-four in a.	NIH
21: 3	are they not a my lord's subjects?	3972
21: 5	In a Israel there were one million one	
	hundred thousand men who could handle	3972
21:23	I will give a this."	3972
22: 5	and splendor in the sight of a the nations.	3972
22: 9	and I will give him rest from a his enemies	3972
22:17	Then David ordered a the leaders of Israel	3972
23: 2	He also gathered together a the leaders	3972
23: 8	and Joel—three in a.	NIH
23: 9	and Haran—three in a.	NIH
23:10	These were the sons of Shimei—four in a.	NIH
23:12	and Uzziel—four in a.	NIH
23:23	and Jerimoth—three in a.	NIH
23:28	of a sacred things and the performance	3972
23:29	and a measurements of quantity and size.	3972
25: 3	Shimei, Hashabiah and Mattithiah, six in a,	NIH
25: 5	A these were sons of Heman	3972
25: 6	A these were under the supervision	3972
25: 7	a of them trained and skilled in music for	3972
26: 8	A these were descendants of Obed-Edom;	3972
26: 8	descendants of Obed-Edom, 62 in a.	NIH
26: 9	who were able men—18 in a.	NIH
26:11	sons and relatives of Hosah were 13 in a.	3972
26:26	of a the treasuries for the things dedicated	3972
26:28	and a the other dedicated things were in	3972
26:30	of the Jordan for a the work of the LORD	3972
27: 1	and their officers, who served the king in a	3972
27: 3	of a the army officers for the first month.	3972
27:31	A these were the officials in charge	3972
28: 1	David summoned a the officials of Israel	3972
28: 1	of a the property and livestock belonging to	3972
28: 1	the mighty men and a the brave warriors.	3972
28: 4	to make me king over a Israel.	3972
28: 5	Of a my sons—	3972
28: 8	the sight of a Israel and of the assembly of	3972
28: 8	Be careful to follow a the commands of	3972
28:12	of a that the Spirit had put in his mind for	3972
28:12	the LORD and a the surrounding rooms,	3972
28:13	and for a the work of serving in the temple	3972
28:13	as for a the articles to be used in its service.	3972
28:14	the weight of gold for a the gold articles to	3972
28:14	the weight of silver for a the silver articles	3972
28:19	"A this," David said, "I have in writing	3972
28:19	and he gave me understanding in a	3972
28:20	not fail you or forsake you until a the work	3972
28:21	of the priests and Levites are ready for a	3972
28:21	in any craft will help you in a the work.	3972
28:21	The officials and a the people will obey	3972
29: 2	With a my resources I have provided for	3972

Ref	Text	Num
1Ch 29: 2	and a kinds of fine stone and marble—	3972
29: 2	a of these in large quantities.	NIH
29: 5	for a the work to be done by the craftsmen.	3972
29:11	you are exalted as head over a.	3972
29:12	you are the ruler of a things.	3972
29:12	and power to exalt and give strength to a.	3972
29:15	as were a our forefathers.	3972
29:16	for a this abundance that we have provided	3972
29:16	and a of it belongs to you.	3972
29:17	A these things have I given willingly and	3972
29:20	So they a praised the LORD,	3972
29:21	other sacrifices in abundance for a Israel.	3972
29:23	He prospered and a Israel obeyed him.	3972
29:24	A the officers and mighty men,	3972
29:24	as well as a of King David's sons,	3972
29:25	in the sight of a Israel and bestowed	3972
29:26	David son of Jesse was king over a Israel.	3972
29:30	and the kingdoms of a the other lands.	3972
2Ch 1: 2	Then Solomon spoke to a Israel—	3972
1: 2	to the judges and to a the leaders in Israel,	3972
1:17	They also exported them to a the kings of	3972
2: 5	our God is greater than a other gods.	3972
2:14	He is experienced in a kinds of engraving	3972
2:16	and we will cut a the logs from Lebanon	3972
2:17	a census of a the aliens who were in Israel,	3972
4:16	shovels, meat forks and a related articles.	3972
4:16	the objects that Huram-Abi made	NIH
4:18	A these things that Solomon made	3972
4:19	also made a the furnishings that were	3972
5: 1	When a the work Solomon had done for	3972
5: 1	the silver and gold and a the furnishings—	3972
5: 2	a the heads of the tribes and the chiefs of	3972
5: 3	And a the men of Israel came together to	3972
5: 4	When a the elders of Israel had arrived,	3972
5: 5	up the ark and the Tent of Meeting and a	3972
5:11	A the priests who were there had	
	consecrated themselves,	3972
5:12	A the Levites who were musicians—	3972
6:16	in a they do to walk before me according	2006
6:30	deal with each man according to a he does,	3972
6:31	and walk in your ways a the time they live	3972
6:33	so that a the peoples of	3972
6:38	if they turn back to you with a their heart	3972
7: 3	When a the Israelites saw the fire coming	3972
7: 4	the king and a the people offered sacrifices	3972
7: 5	So the king and a the people dedicated	3972
7: 6	and a the Israelites were standing.	3972
7: 8	and a Israel with him—	3972
7:11	and had succeeded in carrying out a he had	
	in mind	3972
7:17	and do a I command,	3972
7:20	and an object of ridicule among a peoples.	3972
7:21	a who pass by will be appalled and say,	3972
7:22	that is why he brought a this disaster	3972
8: 4	He also built up Tadmor in the desert and a	3972
8: 6	as well as Baalath and a his store cities,	3972
8: 6	and a the cities for his chariots and	3972
8: 6	in Jerusalem, in Lebanon and throughout a	3972
8: 7	A the people left from the Hittites,	3972
8:16	A Solomon's work was carried out,	3972
9: 1	with him about a she had on her mind.	3972
9: 2	Solomon answered a her questions;	3972
9:12	of Sheba a she desired and asked for;	3972
9:14	Also a the kings of Arabia and	3972
9:20	A King Solomon's goblets were gold,	3972
9:20	and a the household articles in the Palace	3972
9:22	in riches and wisdom than a the other kings	3972
9:23	A the kings of the earth sought audience	3972
9:26	He ruled over a the kings from the River to	3972
9:28	from Egypt and from a other countries.	3972
9:30	in Jerusalem over a Israel forty years.	3972
10: 1	for a the Israelites had gone there	3972
10: 3	and a Israel went to Rehoboam and said	3972
10:12	and a the people returned to Rehoboam,	3972
10:16	When a Israel saw that the king refused	3972
10:16	So a the Israelites went home.	3972
11: 3	to a the Israelites in Judah and Benjamin,	3972
11:12	He put shields and spears in a the cities,	3972
11:13	and Levites from a their districts	3972
11:21	In a, he had eighteen wives	3954
11:23	and to a the fortified cities.	3972
12: 1	he and a Israel with him abandoned the law	3972
12:13	the LORD had chosen out of a the tribes	3972
13: 4	"Jeroboam and a Israel, listen to me!	3972
13:15	and a Israel before Abijah and Judah.	3972
14: 8	A these were brave fighting men.	3972
14:14	They destroyed a the villages,	3972
14:14	They plundered a these villages,	3972
15: 2	Asa and a Judah and Benjamin.	3972
15: 5	for a the inhabitants of the lands were	3972
15: 9	Then he assembled a Judah and Benjamin	3972
15:12	with a their heart and soul.	3972
15:13	A who would not seek the LORD,	3972
15:15	A Judah rejoiced about the oath	3972
15:17	fully committed [to the LORD] a his life.	3972
16: 4	and a the store cities of Naphtali.	3972
16: 6	King Asa brought a the men of Judah,	3972
17: 2	He stationed troops in a the fortified cities	3972
17: 5	and a Judah brought gifts to Jehoshaphat,	3972
17: 9	around to a the towns of Judah and taught	3972
17:10	of the LORD fell on a the kingdoms of	3972
18: 9	with a the prophets prophesying	3972
18:11	A the other prophets were prophesying	3972
18:16	"I saw a Israel scattered on the hills	3972
18:18	the LORD sitting on his throne with a	3972
18:21	in the mouths of a his prophets,"	3972
18:27	he added, "Mark my words, a you people!"	3972

Ref	Text	Num
2Ch 18:34	A day long the battle raged,	
		928+2021+2021+2085+3427
20: 3	and he proclaimed a fast for a Judah.	3972
20: 6	over a the kingdoms of the nations.	3972
20:13	A the men of Judah,	3972
20:15	King Jehoshaphat and a who live in Judah	3972
20:18	and a the people of Judah	3972
20:27	a the men of Judah	3972
20:29	The fear of God came upon a the kingdoms	3972
21: 2	A these were sons of Jehoshaphat king	3972
21: 4	he put a his brothers to the sword along	3972
21: 9	with his officers and a his chariots.	3972
21:17	and carried off a the goods found in	3972
21:18	After a this, the LORD afflicted Jehoram	3972
22: 1	had killed a the older sons.	3972
22: 9	who sought the LORD with a his heart."	3972
23: 2	and the heads of Israelite families from a	3972
23: 5	and a the other men are to be in	3972
23: 6	but a the other men are to guard what	3972
23: 8	The Levites and a the men of Judah did just	3972
23:10	He stationed a the men,	3972
23:13	and a the people of the land were rejoicing	3972
23:17	A the people went to the temple of Baal	3972
23:20	the rulers of the people and a the people of	3972
23:21	and a the people of the land rejoiced.	3972
24: 2	of the LORD a the years of Jehoiada	3972
24: 5	the money due annually from a Israel,	3972
24:10	A the officials and all the people	3972
24:10	All the officials and a the people	3972
24:23	it invaded Judah and Jerusalem and killed a	3972
24:23	They sent a the plunder to their king	3972
25: 5	and commanders of hundreds for a Judah	3972
25:12	down so that a were dashed to pieces.	3972
25:24	He took a the gold and silver and all	3972
25:24	the gold and silver and a the articles found	3972
26: 1	Then a the people of Judah took Uzziah,	3972
26:20	and a the other priests looked at him,	3972
27: 7	including a his wars and	3972
28:14	in the presence of the officials and a	3972
28:15	the plunder they clothed a who were naked.	3972
28:15	A those who were weak they put	3972
28:23	and the downfall of a Israel.	3972
28:26	of his reign and a his ways,	3972
29: 5	Remove a defilement from the sanctuary.	AIT
29:18	of burnt offering with a its utensils,	3972
29:18	the consecrated bread, with a its articles.	3972
29:19	We have prepared and consecrated a	3972
29:24	for a sin offering to atone for a Israel,	3972
29:24	and the sin offering for a Israel.	3972
29:28	A this continued until the sacrifice of	3972
29:31	a whose hearts were willing brought burnt	
	offerings.	3972
29:32	a of them for burnt offerings to	3972
29:34	were too few to skin a the burnt offerings;	3972
29:36	Hezekiah and a the people rejoiced	3972
30: 1	to a Israel and Judah and also wrote letters	3972
30:17	the Passover lambs for a those who were	3972
30:22	Hezekiah spoke encouragingly to a	3972
30:25	and a who had assembled from Israel,	3972
31: 1	When a this had ended,	3972
31: 1	After they had destroyed a of them,	NIH
31: 5	and honey and a that the fields produced.	3972
31:16	a who would enter the temple of	3972
31:18	They included a the little ones, the wives,	3972
31:19	among them and to a who were recorded in	3972
32: 1	a that Hezekiah had so faithfully done,	AIT
32: 4	and they blocked a the springs and	3972
32: 5	Then he worked hard repairing a	3972
32: 9	and a his forces were laying siege	3972
32: 9	for a the people of Judah who were there:	3972
32:13	and my fathers have done to a the peoples	3972
32:14	Who of a the gods of these nations	3972
32:21	who annihilated a the fighting men and	3972
32:22	of Assyria and from the hand of a others.	3972
32:23	on he was highly regarded by a the nations.	3972
32:27	spices, shields and a kinds of valuables.	3972
32:33	A Judah and the people	3972
33: 3	to a the starry hosts and worshiped them.	3972
33: 5	he built altars to a the starry hosts.	3972
33: 7	which I have chosen out of a the tribes	3972
33: 8	concerning a the laws,	3972
33:14	He stationed military commanders in a	3972
33:15	as well as a the altars he had built on	3972
33:19	as well as a his sins and unfaithfulness,	3972
33:19	a are written in the records of the seers.	4392S
33:22	Amon worshiped and offered sacrifices to a	3972
33:25	of the land killed a who had plotted	3972
34: 7	the idols to powder and cut to pieces a	3972
34: 9	and the entire remnant of Israel and from a	3972
34: 9	a who were skilled	3972
34:13	had charge of the laborers and supervised a	3972
34:21	they have not acted in accordance with a	3972
34:24	a the curses written in the book	3972
34:25	to anger by a that their hands have made,	3972
34:28	not see a the disaster I am going to bring	3972
34:29	Then the king called together a the elders	3972
34:30	a the people from the least to the greatest.	3972
34:30	in their hearing a the words of the Book of	3972
34:31	regulations and decrees with a his heart	3972
34:31	with all his heart and a his soul,	3972
34:33	Josiah removed a the detestable idols	3972
34:33	from a the territory belonging to	3972
34:33	and he had a who were present	3972
35: 3	who instructed a Israel	3972
35: 7	for a the lay people who were there a total	3972
35: 7	a from the king's own possessions.	465S
35:13	and served them quickly to a the people.	3972

2Ch	35:18	and a Judah and Israel who were there with	3972
	35:20	After a this, when Josiah had set the temple	3972
	35:24	a Judah and Jerusalem mourned for him.	3972
	35:25	and to this day a the men	3972
	35:27	a the events, from beginning	NIH
	36: 8	and a that was found against him,	NIH
	36:14	a the leaders of the priests and	3972
	36:14	a the detestable practices of	3972
	36:17	God handed a of them over	3972
	36:18	to Babylon the articles from the temple	3972
	36:19	they burned a the palaces	3972
	36:21	a the time of its desolation it rested,	3972
	36:23	of heaven, has given me a the kingdoms of	3972
Ezr	1: 2	of heaven, has given me a the kingdoms of	3972
	1: 6	a their neighbors assisted them	3972
	1: 6	in addition to a the freewill offerings.	3972
	1:11	In a, there were 5,400 articles of gold and	3972
	1:11	Sheshbazzar brought a these along when	3972
	3: 5	for a the appointed sacred feasts of	3972
	3: 8	and a who had returned from the captivity	3972
	3: 9	and brothers—a Levites—	NIH
	3:11	And a the people gave a great shout	3972
	6:17	as a sin offering for a Israel,	10353
	6:20	and were a ceremonially clean.	3972
	6:20	the Passover lamb for a the exiles,	3972
	6:21	with a who had separated themselves from	3972
	7:16	with the silver and gold you may obtain	10353
	7:19	of Jerusalem the articles entrusted	AIT
	7:21	order the treasurers of Trans-Euphrates—	10353
	7:25	to a the people of Trans-Euphrates—	10353
	7:25	a who know the laws of your God.	10353
	7:28	before the king and his advisers and a	3972
	8:20	A were registered by name.	3972
	8:21	with a our possessions.	3972
	8:22	against a who forsake him."	3972
	8:25	and a Israel present there had donated for	3972
	8:35	twelve bulls for a Israel, ninety-six rams,	3972
	8:35	A this was a burnt offering to the LORD.	3972
	10: 3	to send away a these women	3972
	10: 5	the leading priests and Levites and a Israel	3972
	10: 7	and Jerusalem for a the exiles to assemble	3972
	10: 8	failed to appear within three days would forfeit a his property,	3972
	10: 9	the men of Judah	3972
	10: 9	a the people were sitting in the square	3972
	10:16	and a of them designated by name.	3972
	10:17	the first month they finished dealing with a	3972
	10:19	a gave their hands **in pledge**	AIT
	10:44	A these had married foreign women,	3972
Ne	4: 6	the wall till a of it reached half its height,	3972
	4: 6	for the people worked with a their **heart.**	AIT
	4: 8	They a plotted together to come and fight	3972
	4:15	we a returned to the wall,	3972
	4:16	The officers posted themselves behind a	3972
	5:16	A my men were assembled there for	3972
	5:18	an abundant supply of wine of a kinds.	3972
	5:18	In spite of this,	NIH
	5:19	for a I have done for these people.	3972
	6: 9	They were a trying to frighten us, thinking,	3972
	6:16	When our enemies heard about this,	3972
	6:16	a the surrounding nations were afraid	3972
	8: 1	a the people assembled as one man in	3972
	8: 2	up of men and women and a who were able	3972
	8: 3	And a the people listened attentively to	3972
	8: 5	A the people could see him	3972
	8: 5	and as he opened it, the people a stood up.	3972
	8: 6	and a the people lifted their hands	3972
	8: 9	the people said to them **a,**	3972
	8: 9	For a the people had been weeping	3972
	8:11	The Levites calmed a the people, saying,	3972
	8:12	a the people went away to eat and drink,	3972
	8:13	the heads of a the families,	3972
	9: 2	Those of Israelite descent had separated themselves from a foreigners.	3972
	9: 5	be exalted above a blessing and praise.	3972
	9: 6	and a their starry host,	3972
	9: 6	the earth and a that is on it,	3972
	9: 6	the seas and a that is in them.	3972
	9:10	against a his officials and all the people	3972
	9:10	against all his officials and a the people	3972
	9:25	with a kinds of good things.	3972
	9:32	do not let a this hardship seem trifling	3972
	9:32	upon our fathers and a your people,	3972
	9:33	In a that has happened to us,	3972
	9:38	"In view of a this,	3972
	10:28	and a who separated themselves from	3972
	10:28	and a their sons and daughters who are able	3972
	10:29	a these now join their brothers the nobles,	NIH
	10:29	the servant of God and to obey carefully a	3972
	10:31	the land and will cancel a debts.	3972
	10:33	for a the duties of the house of our God.	3972
	10:37	the fruit of a our trees and of our new wine	3972
	10:37	the tithes in a the towns where we work.	3972
	11: 2	The people commended a the men	3972
	11:20	were in a the towns of Judah,	3972
	11:24	was the king's agent in a affairs relating to	3972
	11:30	a the way from Beersheba **to**	6330
	12:47	a Israel contributed the daily portions for	3972
	13: 3	from Israel a who were of foreign descent.	3972
	13: 6	But while a this was going on,	3972
	13: 8	and threw a Tobiah's household goods out	3972
	13:10	that a the Levites and singers responsible	408
	13:12	A Judah brought the tithes of grain,	3972
	13:15	grapes, figs and a other kinds of loads.	3972
	13:15	And they were bringing a this	NIH
	13:16	in fish and a kinds of merchandise	3972
	13:18	so that our God brought a this calamity	3972

Ne	13:20	and sellers of a kinds of goods spent	3972
	13:26	and God made him king over a Israel,	3972
	13:27	you too are doing a this terrible wickedness	3972
Est	1: 3	a banquet for a his nobles and officials.	3972
	1: 5	a the people from the least to the greatest,	3972
	1: 8	for the king instructed a the wine stewards	3972
	1:16	not only against the king but also against a	3972
	1:16	against all the nobles and the peoples of a	3972
	1:17	to a the women,	3972
	1:18	about the queen's conduct will respond to a	3972
	1:20	throughout a his vast realm,	3972
	1:20	a the women will respect their husbands,	3972
	1:22	He sent dispatches to a parts of	3972
	2: 3	of his realm to bring a these beautiful girls	3972
	2:18	for a his nobles and officials.	3972
	2:23	A this was recorded in the book of	AIT
	3: 1	a seat of honor higher than that of a	3972
	3: 2	the royal officials at the king's gate knelt	3972
	3: 6	for a way to destroy a Mordecai's people,	3972
	3: 8	among the peoples in a the provinces	3972
	3: 8	from those of a other people and who do	3972
	3:12	of each people a Haman's orders to	3972
	3:13	by couriers to a the king's provinces with	3972
	3:13	kill and annihilate a the Jews—	3972
	4: 1	Mordecai learned of a that had been done,	3972
	4:11	"A the king's officials and the people of	3972
	4:13	in the king's house you alone of a	3972
	4:16	gather together a the Jews who are in Susa,	3972
	4:17	and carried out a of Esther's instructions.	3972
	5:11	and a the ways the king had honored him	3972
	5:12	"And that's not a," Haman added.	677
	5:13	But a this gives me no satisfaction as long	3972
	5:14	His wife Zeresh and a his friends said	3972
	6:13	and a his friends everything	3972
	8: 5	devised and wrote to destroy the Jews in a	3972
	8: 9	They wrote out a Mordecai's orders to	3972
	8:12	for the Jews to do this in a the provinces	3972
	9: 2	The Jews assembled in their cities in a	3972
	9: 2	of a the other nationalities were afraid	3972
	9: 3	And a the nobles of the provinces,	3972
	9: 5	The Jews struck down a their enemies with	3972
	9:20	and he sent letters to a the Jews throughout	3972
	9:24	the Agagite, the enemy of a the Jews,	3972
	9:27	and a who join them should without fail	3972
	9:30	And Mordecai sent letters to a the Jews in	3972
	10: 2	And a his acts of power and might,	3972
	10: 3	and spoke up for the welfare of a the Jews.	3972
Job	1: 3	the greatest man among a the people of	3972
	1:22	In a this, Job did not sin by charging God	3972
	2: 4	"A man will give a he has for his own life.	3972
	2:10	In a this, Job did not sin in what he said.	3972
	2:11	heard about a the troubles that had come	3972
	4:14	and made a my bones shake.	8044
	6: 2	be weighed and a my misery be placed on	3480
	8:13	Such is the destiny of a who forget God;	3972
	9:22	It is a **the same;**	285
	9:28	I still dread a my sufferings,	3972
	11: 2	"Are a these words to go unanswered?	8044
	12: 3	Who does not know a these things?	4017
	12: 9	of a these does not know that the hand of	3972
	12:10	and the breath of a mankind.	3972
	13: 1	"My eyes have seen a this,	3972
	13: 4	you are worthless physicians, a of you!	3972
	13:27	you keep close watch on a my paths	3972
	14:14	A the days of my hard service I will wait	3972
	14:20	You overpower him once for a,	4200+5905
	15:20	A his days the wicked man suffers torment,	3972
	15:20	the ruthless through a the years stored up	5031
	15:21	when a seems well, marauders attack him.	NIH
	16: 2	miserable comforters are you **a!**	3972
	16:12	A was **well** with me, but he shattered me;	AIT
	17:10	"But come on, a of you, try again!	3972
	19:19	A my intimate friends detest me;	3972
	21:33	a men follow after him,	3972
	22:10	That is why snares are a around you,	6017
	23:15	when I think of a this, I fear him.	NIH
	24: 4	and force a the poor of the land into hiding.	3480
	24:17	For a them	3481
	24:24	and gathered up like a others;	3972
	26: 5	those beneath the waters and a that live in	AIT
	27:10	Will he call upon God at a times?	3972
	27:12	You have a seen this yourselves.	3972
	27:19	when he opens his eyes, a is gone.	5647ˢ
	28:10	his eyes see a its treasures.	3972
	29:19	the dew will lie a night on my branches.	4328
	30:23	to the place appointed for a the living.	3972
	31:38	against me and a its furrows are wet	3480
	33:11	he keeps close watch on a my paths.'	3972
	33:29	"God does a these things to a man—	3972
	34:15	a mankind would perish together	3972
	34:19	for they are a the work of his hands?	3972
	36:19	or even a your mighty efforts sustain you	3972
	36:25	A mankind has seen it;	3972
	37: 7	a men he has made may know his work,	3972
	37:24	for does he not have regard for a the wise	3972
	38: 7	and a the angels shouted for joy?	3972
	38:18	Tell me, if you know a this.	3972
	40:13	Bury **them** a in the dust together;	AIT
	40:20	and a the wild animals play nearby.	3972
	41:34	He looks down on a that are haughty;	3972
	41:34	he is king over a that are proud."	3972
	42: 2	"I know that you can do a things;	3972
	42:11	A his brothers and sisters	3972
	42:11	over a the trouble the LORD had brought	3972
	42:15	in a the land were there found women	3972
Ps	2:12	Blessed are a who take refuge in him.	3972
	3: 7	Strike a my enemies on the jaw;	3972

Ps	5: 5	you hate a who do wrong.	3972
	5:11	But let a who take refuge in you be glad;	3972
	6: 6	a night long I flood my bed with weeping	3972
	6: 7	they fail because of a my foes.	3972
	6: 8	Away from me, a you who do evil,	3972
	6:10	A my enemies will be ashamed	3972
	7: 1	save and deliver me from a who pursue me,	3972
	8: 1	how majestic is your name in a the earth!	3972
	8: 7	a flocks and herds,	3972
	8: 8	a that swim the paths of the seas.	NIH
	8: 9	how majestic is your name in a the earth!	3972
	9: 1	O LORD, with a my heart;	3972
	9: 1	I will tell of a your wonders.	3972
	9:17	a the nations that forget God.	3972
	10: 4	in a his thoughts there is no room for God.	3972
	10: 5	he sneers at a his enemies.	3972
	12: 3	May the LORD cut off a flattering lips	3972
	14: 3	A have turned aside,	3972
	16: 3	the glorious ones in whom is a my delight.	3972
	18: T	of a his enemies and from the hand of Saul.	3972
	18:22	A his laws are before me;	3972
	18:30	He is a shield for a who take refuge in him.	3972
	18:45	They a lose heart;	AIT
	19: 4	Their voice goes out into a the earth,	3972
	20: 3	May he remember a your sacrifices	3972
	20: 4	and make a your plans succeed.	3972
	20: 5	May the LORD grant a your requests.	3972
	21: 8	Your hand will lay hold on a your enemies;	3972
	22: 7	A who see me mock me;	3972
	22:14	and a my bones are out of joint.	3972
	22:17	I can count a my bones;	3972
	22:23	A you descendants of Jacob, honor him!	3972
	22:23	Revere him, a you descendants of Israel!	3972
	22:27	A the ends of the earth will remember	3972
	22:27	and a the families of the nations will bow	3972
	22:29	A the rich of the earth will feast	3972
	22:29	a who go down to the dust will kneel	3972
	23: 6	Surely goodness and love will follow me a	3972
	24: 1	the world, and a who live in it;	AIT
	25: 5	and my hope is in you a day long.	3972
	25: 5	A the ways of the LORD are loving	3972
	25:18	and my distress and take away a my sins.	3972
	25:22	O God, from a their troubles!	3972
	26: 7	and telling of a your wonderful deeds.	3972
	27: 4	in the house of the LORD a the days	3972
	29: 9	And in his temple a cry, "Glory!"	3972
	31:11	Because of a my enemies,	3972
	31:23	Love the LORD, a his saints!	3972
	31:24	a you who hope in the LORD.	3972
	32: 3	through my groaning a day long.	3972
	32:11	sing, a you who are upright in heart!	3972
	33: 4	he is faithful in a he does.	3972
	33: 6	Let a the earth fear the LORD;	3972
	33: 8	let a the people of the world revere him.	3972
	33:11	his heart through a generations.	1887+1887+2256
	33:13	down and sees a mankind;	3972
	33:14	from his dwelling place he watches a who live	3972
	33:15	he who forms the hearts of a,	3480
	33:17	despite a its **great** strength it cannot save.	AIT
	34: 1	I will extol the LORD at a times;	3972
	34: 4	he delivered me from a my fears.	3972
	34: 6	he saved him out of a his troubles.	3972
	34:17	he delivers them from a their troubles.	3972
	34:19	but the LORD delivers him from them a;	3972
	34:20	he protects a his bones,	3972
	35:26	May a who gloat over my distress be put	3481
	35:26	may a who **exalt** themselves over me	AIT
	35:28	and of your praises a day long.	3972
	37:38	But a sinners will be destroyed;	3481
	38: 6	a day long I go about mourning.	3972
	38: 9	A my longings lie open before you,	3972
	38:12	a day long they plot deception.	3972
	39: 8	Save me from a my transgressions;	3972
	39:12	a stranger, as a my fathers were.	3972
	40:14	May a who seek to take my life be put	3480
	40:14	may a who **desire** my ruin be turned back	AIT
	41: 3	But may a who seek you rejoice and	3972
	41: 7	A my enemies whisper together against me;	3972
	42: 3	while men say to me a day long,	3972
	42: 7	a your waves and breakers have swept	3972
	42:10	saying to me a day long,	3972
	44: 8	In God we make our boast a day long,	3972
	44:15	My disgrace is before me a day long,	3972
	44:17	A this happened to us,	3972
	44:22	Yet for your sake we face death a day long;	3972
	45: 8	A your robes are fragrant with myrrh	3972
	45:13	A glorious is the princess	3972
	45:17	through a generations;	3972
	47: 1	Clap your hands, a you nations;	3972
	47: 2	the great King over a the earth!	3972
	47: 7	For God is the King of a the earth;	3972
	49: 1	Hear this, a you peoples;	3972
	49: 1	listen, a who live in this world,	3972
	49:10	For a can see that wise men die;	AIT
	50:12	for the world is mine, and a that is in it.	4850
	51: 2	Wash away a my iniquity and cleanse me	2221
	51: 9	from my sins and blot out a my iniquity.	3972
	52: 1	Why do you boast a day long,	3972
	54: 7	he has delivered me from a my troubles,	3972
	56: 1	a day long they press their attack.	3972
	56: 2	My slanderers pursue me a day long;	3972
	56: 5	A day long they twist my words;	3972
	57: 5	let your glory be over a the earth.	3972
	57:11	let your glory be over a the earth.	3972
	59: 5	rouse yourself to punish a the nations;	3972
	59: 8	you scoff at a those nations.	3972

Ps 62: 3 Would a of you throw him down— 3972
62: 8 Trust in him at a times, O people; 3972
63:11 a who swear by God's name will praise him, 3972
64: 8 a who see them will shake their heads 3972
64: 9 A mankind will fear; 3972
64:10 let the upright in heart praise him! 3972
65: 2 to you a men will come. 3972
65: 5 the hope of a the ends of the earth and of 3972
66: 1 Shout with joy to God, a the earth! 3972
66: 4 A the earth bows down to you; 3972
66:16 a you who fear God; 3972
67: 2 your salvation among a nations. 3972
67: 3 may a the peoples praise you. 3972
67: 5 may a the peoples praise you. 3972
67: 7 and a the ends of the earth will fear him. 3972
69:19 a my enemies are before you. 3972
69:34 the seas and a that move in them, 3972
70: 2 may a who desire my ruin be turned back AIT
70: 4 But may a who seek you rejoice and 3972
71: 8 declaring your splendor a day long. 3972
71:15 of your salvation a day long, 3972
71:18 your might to a who are to come. 3972
71:24 of your righteous acts a day long, 3972
72: 5 through a generations. 1887+1887
72:11 A kings will bow down to him 3972
72:11 down to him and a nations will serve him. 3972
72:15 for him and bless him a day long. 3972
72:17 A nations will be blessed through him, 3972
73:14 A day long I have been plagued; 3972
73:16 When I tried to understand a this, AIT
73:27 you destroy a who are unfaithful to you. 3972
73:28 I will tell of a your deeds. 3972
74: 3 a this destruction the enemy has brought on 3972
74: 6 They smashed a the carved paneling 3480
74:17 It was you who set a the boundaries of 3972
74:22 remember how fools mock you a day long. 3972
75: 3 When the earth and a its people quake, 3972
75: 8 and a the wicked of the earth drink it down 3972
75:10 I will cut off the horns of a the wicked, 3972
76: 9 to save a the afflicted of the land. 3972
76:11 let the neighboring lands bring gifts to 3972
77: 8 his promise failed for a time? 1887+1887+2256
77:12 I will meditate on a your works 3972
77:12 and consider a your mighty deeds. NIH
78:14 by day and with light from the fire a night. 3972
78:25 a the food they could eat. 8427
78:28 a around their tents. 6017
78:32 In spite of a this, they kept on sinning; 3972
78:51 He struck down a the firstborn of Egypt, 3972
79: 3 like water a around Jerusalem, 6017
80:12 so that a who pass by pick its grapes? 3972
82: 5 a the foundations of the earth are shaken. 3972
82: 6 you are a sons of the Most High.' 3972
82: 8 for a the nations are your inheritance. 3972
83:11 a their princes like Zebah and Zalmunna, 3972
83:18 that you alone are the Most High over a 3972
85: 2 of your people and covered a their sins. 3972
85: 3 You set aside a your wrath and turned 3972
85: 5 through a generations? 1887+1887+2256
86: 3 O Lord, for I call to you a day long. 3972
86: 5 abounding in love to a who call to you. 3972
86: 9 A the nations you have made will come 3972
86:12 O Lord my God, with a my heart; 3972
87: 2 of Zion more than a the dwellings of Jacob. 3972
87: 7 "A my fountains are in you." 3972
88: 7 with a your waves. 3972
88:17 A day long they surround me like a flood; 3972
89: 1 through a generations. 1887+1887+2256
89: 4 through a generations.' " 1887+1887+2256
89: 7 he is more awesome than a who surround him. 3972
89:11 you founded the world and a that is in it. 4850
89:16 They rejoice in your name a day long; 3972
89:35 Once for a, I have sworn by my holiness— 285
89:40 You have broken through a his walls 3972
89:41 A who pass by have plundered him; 3972
89:42 you have made a his enemies rejoice. 3972
89:47 For what futility you have created a men! 3972
89:50 in my heart the taunts of a the nations, 3972
90: 1 throughout a generations. 1887+1887+2256
90: 9 A our days pass away under your wrath; 3972
90:14 we may sing for joy and be glad a our days. 3972
91:11 to guard you in a your ways; 3972
92: 7 up like grass and a evildoers flourish, 3972
92: 9 a evildoers will be scattered. 3972
93: 2 you are from a eternity. 6409
94: 4 the evildoers are full of boasting. 3972
94:15 and the upright in heart will follow it. 3972
95: 3 the great King above a gods. 3972
96: 1 sing to the LORD, a the earth. 3972
96: 3 his marvelous deeds among a peoples. 3972
96: 4 he is to be feared above a gods. 3972
96: 5 For the gods of the nations are idols, 3972
96: 9 tremble before him, a the earth. 3972
96:11 let the sea resound, and a that is in it; 4850
96:12 a the trees of the forest will sing for joy, 3972
97: 5 before the Lord of a the earth. 3972
97: 6 and a the peoples see his glory. 3972
97: 7 A who worship images are put to shame, 3972
97: 7 worship him, a you gods! 3972
97: 9 are the Most High over a the earth; 3972
97: 9 you are exalted far above a gods. 3972
98: 3 a the ends of the earth have seen 3972
98: 4 Shout for joy to the LORD, a the earth, 3972
98: 7 the world, and a who live in it. AIT
99: 2 he is exalted over a the nations. 3972

Ps 100: 1 Shout for joy to the LORD, a the earth. 3972
100: 5 through a generations. 1887+1887+2256
101: 8 Every morning I will put to silence a 3972
102: 8 A day long my enemies taunt me; 3972
102:12 through a generations. 1887+1887+2256
102:15 a the kings of 3972
102:24 years go on through a generations. 1887+1887
102:26 they will a wear out like a garment. 3972
103: 1 a my inmost being, praise his holy name. 3972
103: 2 O my soul, and forget not a his benefits— 3972
103: 3 who forgives a your sins 3972
103: 3 and heals a your diseases, 3972
103: 6 and justice for a the oppressed. 3972
103:19 and his kingdom rules over a. 3972
103:21 Praise the LORD, a his heavenly hosts, 3972
103:22 a his works everywhere in his dominion. 3972
104:11 They give water to a the beasts of the field; 3972
104:20 and a the beasts of the forest prowl. 3972
104:24 In wisdom you made them a; 3972
104:27 These a look to you to give them their food 3972
104:33 I will sing to the LORD a my life; 928
105: 2 tell of a his wonderful acts. 3972
105: 7 his judgments are in a the earth. 3972
105:16 on the land and destroyed a their supplies 3972
105:21 ruler over a he possessed, 3972
105:36 He struck down a the firstborn in their land, 3972
105:36 the firstfruits of a their manhood. 3972
106:46 to be pitied by a who held them captive. 3972
106:48 Let a the people say, "Amen!" 3972
107:18 They loathed a food and drew near 3972
107:42 but a the wicked shut their mouths. 3972
108: 1 I will sing and make music with a my soul. 677
108: 5 and let your glory be over a the earth. 3972
109:11 May a creditor seize a he has; 3972
111: 1 the LORD with a my heart in the council 3972
111: 2 they are pondered by a who delight 3972
111: 7 a his precepts are trustworthy. 3972
111:10 a who follow his precepts have good understanding. 3972
113: 4 The LORD is exalted over a the nations, 3972
115: 8 and so will a who trust in them. 3972
116:11 in my dismay I said, "A men are liars." 3972
116:12 the LORD for a his goodness to me? 3972
116:14 the LORD in the presence of a his people. 3972
116:18 the LORD in the presence of a his people, 3972
117: 1 Praise the LORD, a you nations; 3972
117: 1 extol him, a you peoples. 3972
118:10 A the nations surrounded me; 3972
119: 2 and seek him with a their heart. 3972
119: 6 when I consider a your commands. 3972
119:10 I seek you with a my heart; 3972
119:13 With my lips I recount a the laws that come 3972
119:20 with longing for your laws at a times. 3972
119:34 and obey it with a my heart. 3972
119:58 I have sought your face with a my heart; 3972
119:63 I am a friend to a who fear you, 3972
119:63 to a who follow your precepts. AIT
119:69 I keep your precepts with a my heart. 3972
119:86 A your commands are trustworthy; 3972
119:90 through a generations; 1887+1887+2256
119:91 for a things serve you. 3972
119:96 To a perfection I see a limit; 3972
119:97 I meditate on it a day long. 3972
119:99 I have more insight than a my teachers, 3972
119:118 You reject a who stray from your decrees, 3972
119:119 A the wicked of the earth you discard 3972
119:128 because I consider a your precepts right, 3972
119:145 I call with a my heart; 3972
119:151 O LORD, and a your commands are true. 3972
119:160 A your words are true; 8031
119:160 a your righteous laws are eternal. 3972
119:168 for a my ways are known to you. 3972
119:172 for a your commands are righteous. 3972
121: 7 The LORD will keep you from a harm— 3972
128: 1 Blessed are a who fear the LORD, 3972
128: 5 the LORD bless you from Zion a the days 3972
129: 5 May a who hate Zion be turned back 3972
130: 8 from a their sins. 3972
132: 1 and a the hardships he endured. 3972
134: 1 a you servants of the LORD who minister 3972
135: 5 that our Lord is greater than a gods. 3972
135: 6 in the seas and a their depths. 3972
135: 9 against Pharaoh and a his servants. 3972
135:11 of Bashan and a the kings of Canaan— 3972
135:13 O LORD, through a generations. 1887+1887+2256
135:18 and so will a who trust in them. 3972
138: 1 O LORD, with a my heart; 3972
138: 2 above a things your name and your word. 3972
138: 4 May a the kings of the earth praise you, 3972
139: 3 you are familiar with a my ways. 3972
139:16 A the days ordained for me were written 3972
143: 5 I meditate on a your works 3972
143:12 destroy a my foes, for I am your servant. 3972
145: 9 The LORD is good to a; 3972
145: 9 he has compassion on a he has made. 3972
145:10 A you have made will praise you, 3972
145:13 so that a men may know of your mighty acts 132+1201+2021
145:13 through a generations. 3972
145:13 The LORD is faithful to a his promises 3972
145:13 and loving toward a he has made. 3972
145:14 The LORD upholds a those who fall 3972
145:14 and lifts up a who are bowed down. 3972
145:17 The eyes of a look to you, 3972
145:17 The LORD is righteous in a his ways 3972
145:17 and loving toward a he has made. 3972
145:18 The LORD is near to a who call on him, 3972

Ps 145:18 to a who call on him in truth. 3972
145:20 The LORD watches over a who love him, 3972
145:20 but a the wicked he will destroy. 3972
146: 2 I will praise the LORD a my life; 928
146:10 reigns forever, your God, O Zion, for a generations. 1887+1887+2256
148: 2 Praise him, a his angels, praise him, 3972
148: 2 praise him, a his heavenly hosts. 3972
148: 3 praise him, a you shining stars. 3972
148: 7 you great sea creatures and a ocean depths, 3972
148: 9 you mountains and a hills, 3972
148: 9 fruit trees and a cedars, 3972
148:10 wild animals and a cattle, 3972
148:11 kings of the earth and a nations, 3972
148:11 you princes and a rulers on earth, 3972
148:14 the praise of a his saints, of Israel, 3972
149: 9 This is the glory of a his saints. 3972
Pr 1:13 we will get a sorts of valuable things 3972
1:17 to spread a net in full view of a the birds! 3972
1:19 the end of a who go after ill-gotten gain; 3972
1:25 since you ignored a my advice and would 3972
3: 5 the LORD with a your heart and lean not 3972
3: 6 in a your ways acknowledge him, 3972
3: 9 with the firstfruits of a your crops; 3972
3:17 and a her paths are peace. 3972
4: 4 "Lay hold of my words with a your heart; NIH
4: 7 it cost a you have, get understanding. 3972
4:23 Above a else, guard your heart, 3972
5:21 and he examines a his paths. 3972
6:31 it costs him a the wealth of his house. 3972
7:22 A at once he followed her like an ox going 7328
8: 4 I raise my voice to a mankind. 132+1201
8: 8 A the words of my mouth are just; 3972
8: 9 To the discerning a of them are right; 3972
8:16 and a nobles who rule on earth. 3972
8:36 a who hate me love death." 3972
9: 4 a who are simple come in AIT
9:16 a who are simple come in AIT
10:12 but love covers over a wrongs. 3972
11: 7 a he expected from his power comes AIT
14:23 A hard work brings a profit, 3972
15:15 A the days of the oppressed are wretched, 3972
16: 2 A a man's ways seem innocent to him, 3972
16: 5 The LORD detests a the proud of heart. 3972
16:11 a the weights in the bag are of his making. 3972
17:17 A friend loves at a times, 3972
18: 1 he defies a sound judgment. 3972
19: 7 A poor man is shunned by a his relatives— 3972
20: 8 he winnows out a evil with his eyes. 3972
21: 2 A a man's ways seem right to him, 3972
21:20 but a foolish man devours a he has. 5647S
21:26 A day long he craves for more, 3972
22: 2 The LORD is the Maker of them a. 3972
22:18 in your heart and have a of them ready 3481
27:24 and a crown is not secure for a generations. 1887+1887+2256
29:12 a his officials become wicked. 3972
30: 4 Who has established a the ends of 3972
31: 5 and deprive a the oppressed of their rights. 3972
31: 8 for the rights of a who are destitute. 3972
31:12 not harm, a the days of her life. 3972
31:21 for a of them are clothed in scarlet. 3972
31:29 but you surpass them a." 3972
Ecc 1: 3 from a his labor at which he toils under 3972
1: 7 A streams flow into the sea, 3972
1: 8 A things are wearisome, 3972
1:13 and to explore by wisdom a that is done 3972
1:14 I have seen a the things that are done under 3972
1:14 a of them are meaningless, 3972
2: 5 and planted a kinds of fruit trees in them. 3972
2: 9 In a this my wisdom stayed with me. 677
2:10 My heart took delight in a my work, 3972
2:10 and this was the reward for a my labor. 3972
2:11 when I surveyed a that my hands had done 3972
2:17 A of it is meaningless, 3972
2:18 I hated a the things I had toiled for under 3972
2:19 Yet he will have control over a the work 3972
2:20 to despair over a my toilsome labor under 3972
2:21 and then he must leave a he owns AIT
2:22 a man get for a the toil and anxious striving 3972
2:23 A his days his work is pain and grief; 3972
3:13 and find satisfaction in a his toil— 3972
3:19 A have the same breath; 3972
3:20 A go to the same place; 3972
3:20 a come from dust, and to dust all return. 3972
3:20 all come from dust, and to dust a return. 3972
4: 1 Again I looked and saw a the oppression 3972
4: 4 that a labor and all achievement spring 3972
4: 4 a achievement spring from man's envy 3972
4: 8 There was a man a alone; 401+9108
4:15 I saw that a who lived and walked under 3972
4:16 There was no end to a the people who were 3972
5: 9 The increase from the land is taken by a; 3972
5:17 A his days he eats in darkness, 3972
6: 6 Do not a go to the same place? 3972
6: 7 A man's efforts are for his mouth, 3972
7:18 man who fears God will avoid a [extremes]. 3972
7:23 A this I tested by wisdom and I said, 3972
7:28 not one [upright] woman among them a. 3972
8: 9 A this I saw, 3972
8:15 Then joy will accompany him in his work a NIH
8:17 then I saw a that God has done. 3972
8:17 Despite a his efforts to search it out, AIT
9: 1 So I reflected on a this and concluded that 3972
9: 2 A share a common destiny— 3972
9: 3 The same destiny overtakes a. 3972
9: 9 a the days of this meaningless life 3972

Ecc	9: 9	a your meaningless days.	3972
	9:10	do it with a your might, for in the grave,	NIH
	9:11	but time and chance happen to them a.	3972
	11: 5	the Maker of a things.	3972
	11: 8	let him enjoy them a.	3972
	11: 9	that for a these things God will bring you	3972
	12: 4	but a their songs grow faint;	3972
	12:13	Now a has been heard;	3972
SS	3: 1	A night long on my bed I looked for	928+2021+4326
	3: 6	and incense made from a the spices of	3972
	3: 8	a of them wearing the sword,	3972
	3: 8	a experienced in battle,	NIH
	4: 4	a of them shields of warriors.	3972
	4: 7	A beautiful you are, my darling;	3972
	4:14	and aloes and a the finest spices.	3972
	8: 7	to give a the wealth of his house for love,	3972
Isa	1:23	they a love bribes and chase after gifts.	3972
	1:25	and remove a your impurities.	3972
	2: 2	and a nations will stream to it.	3972
	2:12	a day in store for a the proud and lofty,	3972
	2:12	for a that is exalted (and they will	3972
	2:13	for a the cedars of Lebanon,	3972
	2:13	tall and lofty, and a the oaks of Bashan,	3972
	2:14	for a the towering mountains and all	3972
	2:14	for all the towering mountains and a	3972
	3: 1	a supplies of food and all supplies of water,	3972
	3: 1	all supplies of food and a supplies of water,	3972
	4: 3	a who are recorded among the living	3972
	4: 5	Then the LORD will create over a	3972
	4: 5	over a the glory will be a canopy.	3972
	5:14	with a their brawlers and revelers.	NIH
	5:25	Yet for a this, his anger is not turned away,	3972
	5:28	a their bows are strung;	3972
	7: 9	you will not stand at a.' "	3954
	7:19	They will a come and settle in	3972
	7:19	on a the thornbushes and at all	3972
	7:19	the thornbushes and at a the water holes.	3972
	7:22	A who remain in the land will eat curds	3972
	7:25	for a the hills once cultivated by the hoe,	3972
	8: 7	the king of Assyria with a his pomp.	3972
	8: 7	It will overflow a its channels,	3972
	8: 7	run over a its banks	3972
	8: 9	Listen, a you distant lands.	3972
	9: 9	A the people will know it—	3972
	9:12	Yet for a this, his anger is not turned away,	3972
	9:17	Yet for a this, his anger is not turned away,	3972
	9:21	Yet for a this, his anger is not turned away,	3972
	10: 4	Yet for a this, his anger is not turned away,	3972
	10: 8	'Are not my commanders a kings?'	3481
	10:12	When the Lord has finished a his work	3972
	10:14	so I gathered a the countries;	3972
	11: 9	nor destroy on a my holy mountain,	3972
	12: 5	let this be known to a the world.	3972
	13: 7	Because of this, a hands will go limp,	3972
	13:15	a who are caught will fall by the sword.	3972
	13:20	lived in through a generations;	1887+1887+2256
	14: 7	A the lands are at rest and at peace;	3972
	14: 9	The grave below is a astir to meet you	8074
	14: 9	a those who were leaders in the world;	3972
	14: 9	a those who were kings over the nations.	3972
	14:10	They will a respond, they will say to you,	3972
	14:11	A your pomp has been brought down to	NIH
	14:18	A the kings of the nations lie in state,	3972
	14:26	the hand stretched out over a nations.	3972
	14:29	a you Philistines, that the rod	3972
	14:31	Melt away, a you Philistines!	3972
	15: 3	and in the public squares they a wail,	3972
	15: 4	their voices are heard a the way to Jahaz.	6330
	16:14	and a her many people will be despised,	3972
	17: 9	And a will be desolation.	AIT
	18: 3	A you people of the world,	3972
	18: 6	They will a be left to the mountain birds	3481
	18: 6	the birds will feed on them a summer,	7810
	18: 6	the wild animals a winter.	3069
	19: 8	a who cast hooks into the Nile;	3972
	19:10	and a the wage earners will be sick at heart.	3972
	19:14	they make Egypt stagger in a that she does,	3972
	21: 2	to an end the groaning she caused.	3972
	21: 9	A the images of its gods lie shattered on	3972
	21:16	a the pomp of Kedar will come to an end.	3972
	22: 1	that you have a gone up on the roofs,	3972
	22: 3	A your leaders have fled together;	3972
	22: 3	A you who were caught were taken prisoner together,	3972
	22:24	A the glory of his family will hang on him:	3972
	22:24	a its lesser vessels,	3972
	22:24	from the bowls to a the jars.	3972
	23: 9	to bring low the pride of a glory and	3972
	23: 9	and to humble a who are renowned on	3972
	23:17	as a prostitute and will ply her trade with a	3972
	24: 7	a the merrymakers groan.	3972
	24:11	a joy turns to gloom,	3972
	24:11	all gaiety is banished from the earth.	NIH
	25: 6	a feast of rich food for a peoples, a banquet	3972
	25: 7	the shroud that enfolds a peoples, the sheet	3972
	25: 7	the sheet that covers a nations;	3972
	25: 8	the tears from a faces;	3972
	25: 8	the disgrace of his people from a the earth.	3972
	26:12	a that we have accomplished you have done for	3972
	26:14	you wiped out a memory of them.	3972
	26:15	you have extended a the borders of	3972
	27: 4	I would set them a on fire.	3480
	27: 6	and blossom and fill a the world with fruit.	7156
	27: 9	When he makes a the altar stones to be	3972
	28: 8	A the tables are covered with vomit	3972

Isa	28:29	A this also comes from the LORD	AIT
	29: 3	I will encamp against you a around;	1885+2021+3869
	29: 7	Then the hordes of a the nations that fight	3972
	29: 8	with the hordes of a the nations that fight	3972
	29:20	and a who have an eye for evil will	3972
	30:17	at the threat of five you will a flee away,	AIT
	30:18	Blessed are a who wait for him!	3972
	32:13	for a houses of merriment and for this city	3972
	34: 1	Let the earth hear, and a that is in it,	4850
	34: 1	the world, and a that comes out of it!	3972
	34: 2	The LORD is angry with a nations;	3972
	34: 2	his wrath is upon a their armies.	3972
	34: 4	A the stars of the heavens will be dissolved	3972
	34: 4	a the starry host will fall	3972
	34:12	a her princes will vanish away.	3972
	36: 1	of Assyria attacked a the fortified cities	3972
	36: 6	of Egypt to a who depend on him.	3972
	36:20	Who of a the gods of these countries	3972
	37: 2	the leading priests, a wearing sackcloth,	AIT
	37:11	of Assyria have done to a the countries,	3972
	37:16	you alone are God over a the kingdoms of	3972
	37:17	listen to a the words Sennacherib has sent	3972
	37:18	Assyrian kings have laid waste a these peoples	3972
	37:20	so that a kingdoms on earth may know	3972
	37:25	With the soles of my feet I have dried up a	3972
	37:36	there were a the dead bodies!	3972
	38:13	but like a lion he broke a my bones;	3972
	38:15	I will walk humbly a my years because	3972
	38:17	you have put a my sins behind your back.	3972
	38:20	with stringed instruments a the days	3972
	39: 2	or in a his kingdom that Hezekiah did	3972
	39: 6	and a that your fathers have stored up	NIH
	40: 2	the LORD's hand double for a her sins.	3972
	40: 5	and a mankind together will see it.	3972
	40: 6	"A men are like grass,	3972
	40: 6	a their glory is like the flowers of the field.	3972
	40:17	Before him a the nations are as nothing;	3972
	40:26	Who created a these?	AIT
	41:11	"A who rage against you will surely	3972
	41:12	who wage war against you will be as nothing at a.	401+700+2256
	41:29	See, they are a false!	3972
	42: 5	the earth and a that comes out of it,	7368
	42:10	and a that is in it, you islands,	4850
	42:10	you islands, and a who live in them.	AIT
	42:15	and hills and dry up a their vegetation;	3972
	42:22	a of them trapped in pits or hidden away	3972
	43: 9	A the nations gather together and	3972
	43:14	to Babylon and bring down a as fugitives a	3972
	44: 9	A who make idols are nothing,	3972
	44:11	Let them a come together	3972
	44:13	of man in a his glory,	NIH
	44:23	you forests and a your trees,	3972
	44:24	I am the LORD, who has made a things,	3972
	44:28	'He is my shepherd and will accomplish a	3972
	45: 7	I, the LORD, do a these things.	3972
	45:13	I will make a his ways straight.	3972
	45:16	A the makers of idols will be put to shame	3972
	45:22	a you ends of the earth;	3972
	45:23	my mouth has uttered in a integrity	AIT
	45:24	A who have raged against him will come	3972
	45:25	the LORD a the descendants of Israel will	3972
	46: 3	a you who remain of the house of Israel,	3972
	46:10	and I will do a that I please.	3972
	47: 9	and a your potent spells.	4394
	47:13	A the counsel you have received has only worn you out!	8044
	47:15	That is a they can do for you—	AIT
	48: 6	look at them a.	3972
	48:13	I summon them, they a stand up together.	AIT
	48:14	"Come together, a of you, and listen:	3972
	49:11	I will turn a my mountains into roads,	3972
	49:18	a your sons gather and come to you.	3972
	49:18	"you will wear them a as ornaments;	3972
	49:21	I was left a alone, but these—	963+4200
	49:26	Then a mankind will know that I,	3972
	50: 9	They will a wear out like a garment;	3972
	50:11	a you who light fires	3972
	51: 3	with compassion on a her ruins;	3972
	51: 8	my salvation through a generations."	1887+1887
	51:18	Of a the sons she bore there was none	3972
	51:18	of a the sons she reared there was none	3972
	52: 5	a day long my name is constantly blasphemed.	3972
	52:10	in the sight of a the nations,	3972
	52:10	and a the ends of the earth will see	3972
	53: 6	We a, like sheep, have gone astray,	3972
	53: 6	on him the iniquity of us a.	3972
	54: 5	he is called the God of a the earth.	3972
	54:12	and a your walls of precious stones.	3972
	54:13	A your sons will be taught by the LORD,	3972
	55: 1	"Come, a you who are thirsty,	3972
	55:12	a the trees of the field will clap their hands.	3972
	56: 6	a who keep the Sabbath	3972
	56: 7	be called a house of prayer for a nations."	3972
	56: 9	Come, a you beasts of the field,	3972
	56: 9	a you beasts of the forest!	3972
	56:10	they a lack knowledge;	3972
	56:10	they are a mute dogs, they cannot bark;	3972
	56:11	they a turn to their own way,	3972
	57:10	You were wearied by a your ways,	8044
	57:13	The wind will carry a your workers.	3972
	58: 3	as you please and exploit a your workers.	3972
	59: 9	We look for light, but a is darkness;	NIH
	59:11	We a growl like bears;	3972

Isa	60: 4	A assemble and come to you;	3972
	60: 6	And a from Sheba will come,	3972
	60: 7	A Kedar's flocks will be gathered to you,	3972
	60:14	a who despise you will bow down	3972
	60:15	and the joy of a generations.	1887+1887+2256
	60:21	Then will a your people be righteous	3972
	61: 2	to comfort a who mourn,	3972
	61: 9	A who see them will acknowledge	3972
	61:11	and praise spring up before a nations.	3972
	62: 2	a kings your glory;	3972
	63: 3	and I stained a my clothing.	3972
	63: 7	according to a the LORD has done	3972
	63: 9	In a their distress he too was distressed,	3972
	63: 9	up and carried them a the days of old.	3972
	64: 6	A of us have become like one who is unclean,	3972
	64: 6	and a our righteous acts are like filthy rags;	3972
	64: 6	we a shrivel up like a leaf,	3972
	64: 8	we are a the work of your hand.	3972
	64: 9	we pray, for we are a your people.	3972
	64:11	and a that we treasured lies in ruins.	3972
	64:12	After a this, O LORD,	AIT
	65: 2	A day long I have held out my hands to	3972
	65: 5	a fire that keeps burning a day.	3972
	65: 8	I will not destroy them a.	3972
	65:12	and you will a bend down for the slaughter;	3972
	65:25	nor destroy on a my holy mountain,"	3972
	66: 2	Has not my hand made a these things,	3972
	66: 6	LORD repaying his enemies a they deserve.	AIT
	66:10	a you who love her;	3972
	66:10	a you who mourn over her.	3972
	66:16	upon a men, and many will be those slain	3972
	66:18	to come and gather a nations and tongues,	3972
	66:20	And they will bring a your brothers,	3972
	66:20	from a the nations, to my holy mountain	3972
	66:23	a mankind will come and bow down	3972
	66:24	and they will be loathsome to a mankind."	3972
Jer	1:14	be poured out on a who live in the land.	3972
	1:15	I am about to summon the peoples of	3972
	1:15	against a her surrounding walls and	3972
	1:15	and against a the towns of Judah.	3972
	2: 3	a who devoured her were held guilty,	3972
	2: 4	a you clans of the house of Israel.	3972
	2:11	(Yet they are not gods at a.)	AIT
	2:29	You have a rebelled against me,"	3972
	2:34	Yet in spite of a this	3972
	3: 5	but you do a the evil you can."	AIT
	3: 7	after she had done a this she would return	3972
	3: 8	because of a her adulteries.	3972
	3:10	In spite of a this,	3972
	3:10	not return to me with a her heart,	3972
	3:17	and a nations will gather in Jerusalem	3972
	4:24	a the hills were swaying.	3972
	4:26	a its towns lay in ruins before the LORD,	3972
	4:29	A the towns are deserted;	3972
	5: 7	supplied a their needs,	8425
	5:16	a of them are mighty warriors.	3972
	5:19	'Why has the LORD our God done a this	3972
	6:13	a are greedy for gain;	3972
	6:13	prophets and priests alike, a practice deceit.	3972
	6:15	have no shame at a;	1017+1017
	6:28	They are a hardened rebels,	3972
	6:28	they a act corruptly.	3972
	7: 2	the word of the LORD, a you people	3972
	7:10	safe to do a these detestable things?	3972
	7:13	While you were doing a these things,	3972
	7:15	just as I did a your brothers,	3972
	7:23	Walk in a the ways I command you,	3972
	7:27	"When you tell them a this,	3972
	8: 2	be exposed to the sun and the moon and a	3972
	8: 3	Wherever I banish them, a the survivors	3972
	8:10	a are greedy for gain;	3972
	8:10	prophets and priests alike, a practice deceit.	3972
	8:12	they have no shame at a;	1017+1017
	8:16	the city and a who live there."	AIT
	9: 2	for they are a adulterers,	3972
	9:25	I will punish a who are circumcised only	3972
	9:26	Moab and a who live in the desert	3972
	9:26	a these nations are really uncircumcised,	3972
	10: 7	Among a the wise men of the nations and	3972
	10: 7	of the nations and in a their kingdoms,	3972
	10: 8	They are a senseless and foolish;	285+928
	10: 9	a made by skilled workers.	3972
	10:16	for he is the Maker of a things,	3972
	10:20	a its ropes are snapped.	3972
	10:21	not prosper and a their flock is scattered.	3972
	11: 6	"Proclaim a these words in the towns	3972
	11: 8	So I brought on them a the curses of	3972
	11:12	they will not help them at a when disaster strikes.	3828+3828
	12: 1	Why do a the faithless live at ease?	3972
	12: 9	Go and gather a the wild beasts;	3972
	12:12	Over a the barren heights in	3972
	12:14	"As for a my wicked neighbors who seize	3972
	13:13	with drunkenness a who live in this land,	3972
	13:13	the priests, the prophets and a those living	3972
	13:19	A Judah will be carried into exile,	3972
	14:22	for you are the one who does a this.	3972
	15: 4	to a the kingdoms of the earth because	3972
	15:13	of a your sins throughout your country.	3972
	16:10	"When you tell these people a this	3972
	16:15	up out of the land of the north and out of a	3972
	16:17	My eyes are on a their ways;	3972
	17: 3	and a your treasures I will give away	3972
	17: 9	The heart is deceitful above a things and	3972
	17:13	a who forsake you will be put to shame.	3972
	17:19	stand also at a the other gates of Jerusalem.	3972

Jer 17:20 and a people of Judah and everyone living 3972
18:16 a who pass by will be appalled 3972
18:23 O LORD, a their plots to kill me. 3972
19: 8 a who pass by will be appalled 3972
19: 8 and will scoff because of a its wounds. 3972
19:13 a the houses where they burned incense on 3972
19:13 where they burned incense on the roofs to a 3972
19:14 of the LORD's temple and said to a 3972
20: 4 a terror to yourself and to a your friends; 3972
20: 4 I will hand a Judah over to the king 3972
20: 5 to their enemies a the wealth of this city— 3972
20: 5 a its products, all its valuables and all 3972
20: 5 all its products, a its valuables and all 3972
20: 5 and a the treasures of the kings of Judah. 3972
20: 6 and a who live in your house will go 3972
20: 6 you and a your friends 3972
20: 7 I am ridiculed a day long; 3972
20: 8 and reproach a day long. 3972
20:10 My friends are waiting for me to slip, 3972
22:15 so a went well with him. NIH
22:16 and so a went well. NIH
22:20 for a your allies are crushed. 3972
22:22 wind will drive a your shepherds away, 3972
22:22 because of a your wickedness. 3972
23: 3 of a the countries where I have driven them 3972
23: 8 up out of the land of the north and out of a 3972
23: 9 a my bones tremble. 3972
23:14 They are a like Sodom to me; 3972
23:17 And to a who follow the stubbornness 3972
24: 7 for they will return to me with a their heart. 3972
24: 9 an offense to a the kingdoms of the earth, 3972
25: 1 The word came to Jeremiah concerning a 3972
25: 2 the prophet said to a the people of Judah 3972
25: 2 of Judah and to a those living in Jerusalem: 3972
25: 4 though the LORD has sent a his servants 3972
25: 9 I will summon a the peoples of the north 3972
25: 9 and against a the surrounding nations. 3972
25:13 upon that land a the things I have spoken 3972
25:13 a that are written in this book 3972
25:13 and prophesied by Jeremiah against a 3972
25:15 with the wine of my wrath and make a 3972
25:17 the LORD's hand and made a the nations 3972
25:19 his officials and a his people, 3972
25:20 and a the foreign people there; 3972
25:20 a the kings of Uz; 3972
25:20 a the kings of the Philistines (those 3972
25:22 a the kings of Tyre and Sidon; 3972
25:23 Tema, Buz and a who are in distant places; 3972
25:24 a the kings of Arabia and all the kings of 3972
25:24 all the kings of Arabia and a the kings of 3972
25:25 a the kings of Zimri, Elam and Media; 3972
25:26 and a the kings of the north, near 3972
25:26 a the kingdoms on the face of the earth. 3972
25:26 And after a of them, NIH
25:29 a sword upon a who live on the earth, 3972
25:30 "Now prophesy a these words against them 3972
25:30 shout against a who live on the earth. 3972
25:31 he will bring judgment on a mankind 3972
26: 2 and speak to a the people of the towns 3972
26: 6 an object of cursing among a the nations of 3972
26: 7 the prophets and a the people heard 3972
26: 8 But as soon as Jeremiah finished telling a 3972
26: 8 the prophets and a the people seized him 3972
26: 9 And a the people crowded around Jeremiah 3972
26:11 and the prophets said to the officials and a 3972
26:12 Then Jeremiah said to a the officials and all 3972
26:12 Then Jeremiah said to all the officials and a 3972
26:12 and this city a the things you have heard. 3972
26:15 to speak a these words in your hearing." 3972
26:16 Then the officials and a the people said to 3972
26:18 He told a the people of Judah, 3972
26:21 When King Jehoiakim and a his officers 3972
27: 6 Now I will hand a your countries over 3972
27: 7 A nations will serve him and his son 3972
27:16 I said to the priests and a these people, 3972
27:20 with a the nobles of Judah and Jerusalem— 3972
28: 1 the presence of the priests and a the people: 3972
28: 3 to this place a the articles of 3972
28: 4 and a the other exiles from Judah who went 3972
28: 5 and a the people who were standing in 3972
28: 6 the LORD's house and a the exiles back 3972
28: 7 in your hearing and in the hearing of a 3972
28:11 before a the people, "This is what 3972
28:11 of Babylon off the neck of a the nations 3972
28:14 an iron yoke on the necks of a these nations 3972
29: 1 the prophets and a 3972
29: 4 says to a those I carried into exile 3972
29:13 when you seek me with a your heart. 3972
29:14 I will gather you from a the nations 3972
29:16 the king who sits on David's throne and a 3972
29:18 and will make them abhorrent to a 3972
29:18 among a the nations where I drive them. 3972
29:20 a you exiles whom I have sent away 3972
29:22 a the exiles from Judah who are 3972
29:25 You sent letters in your own name to a 3972
29:25 and to a the other priests. 3972
29:31 "Send this message to a the exiles: 3972
30: 2 in a book a the words I have spoken to you. 3972
30:11 'Though I completely destroy a the nations 3972
30:14 A your allies have forgotten you; 3972
30:16 " 'But a who devour you will be devoured; 3972
30:16 a your enemies will go into exile. 3972
30:16 a who make spoil of you I will despoil. 3972
30:20 I will punish a who oppress them. 3972
31: 1 "I will be the God of a the clans of Israel, 3972
31:24 in Judah and a its towns— 3972
31:34 because they will a know me, 3972

Jer 31:37 be searched out will I reject a 3972
31:37 of Israel because of a they have done," 3972
31:40 and a the terraces out to the Kidron Valley 3972
32:12 and of a the Jews sitting in the courtyard of 3972
32:19 Your eyes are open to a the ways of men; 3972
32:20 both in Israel and among a mankind, NIH
32:23 So you brought a this disaster upon them. 3972
32:27 the God of a mankind. 3972
32:32 of Israel and Judah have provoked me by a 3972
32:37 I will surely gather them from a the lands 3972
32:41 in this land with a my heart and soul. 3972
32:42 As I have brought a this great calamity 3972
32:42 on this people, so I will give them a 3972
33: 5 from this city because of a its wickedness. 3972
33: 8 from the sin they have committed 3972
33: 8 and will forgive a their sins of rebellion 3972
33: 9 praise and honor before a nations on earth 3972
33: 9 on earth that hear of a the good things I do 3972
33:12 in a its towns there will again be pastures 3972
34: 1 and a his army and all the kingdoms 3972
34: 1 and all his army and a the kingdoms 3972
34: 1 and a its surrounding towns. 3972
34: 6 the prophet told a this to Zedekiah king 3972
34: 8 a covenant with the people in Jerusalem 3972
34:10 So a the officials and people who entered 3972
34:17 to a the kingdoms of the earth. 3972
34:19 and a the people of the land who walked 3972
35: 3 and his brothers and a his sons— 3972
35:15 and again I sent a my servants the prophets 3972
35:18 and have followed a his instructions 3972
36: 2 and write on it a the words I have spoken 3972
36: 2 Judah and a the other nations from 3972
36: 4 and while Jeremiah dictated a the words 3972
36: 6 to a the people of Judah who come in 3972
36: 9 before the LORD was proclaimed for a 3972
36:10 to a the people at the LORD's temple 3972
36:11 heard a the words of the LORD from 3972
36:12 where a the officials were sitting: 3972
36:12 and a the other officials. 3972
36:14 the officials sent Jehudi son 3972
36:16 When they heard a these words, 3972
36:16 "We must report a these words to 3972
36:17 "Tell us, how did you come to write a this? 3972
36:18 "he dictated a these words to me, 3972
36:21 the secretary and read it to the king and a 3972
36:24 a his attendants who heard all these words 3972
36:24 who heard a these words showed no fear, 3972
36:28 and write on it a the words that were on 3972
36:32 Baruch wrote on it a the words of the scroll 3972
37:21 of the bakers each day until a the bread in 3972
38: 1 heard what Jeremiah was telling a the people 3972
38: 4 as well as a the people, 3972
38: 9 in a they have done to Jeremiah 3972
38:22 A the women left in the palace of the king 3972
38:23 "A your wives and children will 3972
38:27 A the officials did come to Jeremiah 3972
39: 3 Then a the officials of the king 3972
39: 3 a high official and a the other officials of 3972
39: 4 and a the soldiers saw them, they fled; 3972
39: 6 before his eyes and also killed a the nobles 3972
39:13 a high official and a the other officers of 3972
40: 1 among a the captives from Jerusalem 3972
40: 3 A this happened because you people sinned AIT
40: 7 When a the army officers 3972
40:11 When a the Jews in Moab, Ammon, 3972
40:11 Edom and a the other countries heard that 3972
40:12 they a came back to the land of Judah, 3972
40:12 from a the countries 3972
40:13 of Kareah and a the army officers still in 3972
40:15 Why should he take your life and cause a 3972
41: 3 Ishmael also killed a the Jews who were 3972
41: 9 the cistern where he threw a the bodies of 3972
41:10 Ishmael made captives of a the rest of 3972
41:10 along with a the others who were left there, 3972
41:11 When Johanan son of Kareah and a 3972
41:11 about the crimes Ishmael son 3972
41:12 they took a their men and went 3972
41:13 When a the people Ishmael had 3972
41:14 A the people Ishmael had taken captive 3972
41:16 Then Johanan son of Kareah and a 3972
41:16 with him led away a the survivors 3972
42: 1 Then a the army officers, 3972
42: 1 and a the people from the least to 3972
42: 8 and a the army officers who were with him 3972
42: 8 the army officers who were with him and a 3972
42:17 a who are determined to go to Egypt 3972
42:21 the LORD your God in a he sent me 3972
43: 1 the people a the words of the LORD 3972
43: 2 and a the arrogant men said to Jeremiah, 3972
43: 4 of Kareah and a the army officers and all 3972
43: 4 of Kareah and all the army officers and a 3972
43: 5 and a the army officers led away all 3972
43: 5 the army officers led away the remnant 3972
43: 5 in the land of Judah from a the nations 3972
43: 6 They also led away a the men, 3972
44: 1 This word came to Jeremiah concerning a 3972
44: 2 on Jerusalem and on a the towns of Judah. 3972
44: 8 and reproach among a the nations on earth 3972
44:11 on you and to destroy a Judah. 3972
44:12 They will a perish in Egypt; 3972
44:15 Then a the men who knew 3972
44:15 with a the women who were present— 3972
44:15 and a the people living in Lower 3972
44:20 Then Jeremiah said to a the people, 3972
44:24 Then Jeremiah said to a the people, 3972
44:24 a you people of Judah in Egypt. 3972
44:26 a Jews living in Egypt: 3972

Jer 44:27 and famine until they are a destroyed. 3972
45: 5 For I will bring disaster on a people, 3972
46:28 "Though I completely destroy a the nations 3972
47: 2 a who dwell in the land will wail 3972
47: 4 For the day has come to destroy a 3972
47: 4 to cut off a survivors who could help Tyre 3972
48:17 Mourn for her, a who live around her, 3972
48:17 a who know her fame; 3972
48:24 to a the towns of Moab, far and near. 3972
48:31 for a Moab I cry out, 3972
48:38 On a the roofs in Moab and in 3972
48:39 an object of horror to a those around her." 3972
49: 5 I will bring terror on you from a those 3972
49:13 and a its towns will be in ruins forever." 3972
49:17 a who pass by will be appalled 3972
49:17 and will scoff because of a its wounds. 3972
49:26 a her soldiers will be silenced in that day," 3972
49:29 be carried off with a their goods 3972
50:10 a who plunder her will have their fill," 3972
50:13 A who pass Babylon will be horrified 3972
50:13 and scoff because of a her wounds. 3972
50:14 a you who draw the bow. 3972
50:27 Kill a her young bulls; 3972
50:29 a those who draw the bow. 3972
50:29 Encamp a around her; let no one escape. 6017
50:30 a her soldiers will be silenced in that day," 3972
50:32 that will consume a who are around her." 3972
50:33 A their captors hold them fast, 3972
50:37 against her horses and chariots and a 3972
51:19 for he is the Maker of a things, 3972
51:24 and a who live in Babylonia for all 3972
51:24 for a the wrong they have done in Zion," 3972
51:28 their governors and a their officials, 3972
51:28 and a the countries they rule. 3972
51:38 Her people a roar like young lions, 3481
51:47 be disgraced and her slain will a lie fallen 3972
51:48 and earth and a that is in them will shout 3972
51:49 the slain in a the earth have fallen because 3972
51:60 Jeremiah had written on a scroll about a 3972
51:60 a that had been recorded 3972
51:61 see that you read a these words aloud. 3972
52: 3 of the LORD's anger that a this happened AIT
52: 4 the city and built siege works a around it. 6017
52: 8 A his soldiers were separated from him 3972
52:10 he also killed a the officials of Judah. 3972
52:13 the royal palace and a the houses 3972
52:14 the imperial guard broke down a the walls 3972
52:17 the temple of the LORD and they carried a 3972
52:19 dishes and a the bronze articles used in 3972
52:19 a that were made of pure gold or silver. AIT
52:22 and pomegranates of bronze a around. 3972
52:26 Nebuzaradan the commander took them a AIT
52:30 There were 4,600 people in a. 3972
La 1: 2 Among a her lovers there is none 3972
1: 2 A her friends have betrayed her; 3972
1: 3 A who pursue her have overtaken her in 3972
1: 4 A her gateways are desolate, 3972
1: 6 A the splendor has departed from 3972
1: 7 and wandering Jerusalem remembers a 3972
1: 8 A who honored her despise her, 3972
1:10 The enemy laid hands on a her treasures; 3972
1:11 A her people groan as they search 3972
1:12 "Is it nothing to you, a you who pass by? 3972
1:13 He made me desolate, faint a the day long. 3972
1:15 "The Lord has rejected a the warriors 3972
1:18 Listen, a you peoples; 3972
1:21 A my enemies have heard of my distress; 3972
1:22 "Let a their wickedness come before you; 3972
1:22 with me because of a my sins. 3972
2: 2 the Lord has swallowed up a the dwellings 3972
2: 4 Like a foe he has slain a who were pleasing 3972
2: 5 He has swallowed up a her palaces 3972
2:15 A who pass your way clap their hands 3972
2:16 A your enemies open their mouths wide 3972
3: 3 against me again and again, a day long. 3972
3:14 I became the laughingstock of a my people; 3972
3:14 they mock me in song a day long. 3972
3:18 a that I had hoped AIT
3:34 To crush underfoot a prisoners in the land, 3972
3:46 "A our enemies have opened their mouths 3972
3:51 because of a the women of my city. 3972
3:60 a their plots against me. 3972
3:61 a their plots against me— 3972
3:62 and mutter against me a day long. 3972
Eze 1: 8 A four of them had faces and wings, AIT
1:16 and a four looked alike. AIT
1:18 and a four rims were full AIT
1:18 of eyes a around. 6017
2: 6 though briers and thorns are a around you 907
3:10 and take to heart a the words I speak 3972
5: 2 and strike it with the sword a around 6017
5: 5 with countries a around her. 6017
5: 9 Because of a your detestable idols, 3972
5:10 on you and will scatter a your survivors to 3972
5:11 with a your vile images 3972
5:14 in the sight of a who pass by. 3972
6: 9 and for a their detestable practices. 3972
6:11 of the wicked and detestable practices of 3972
6:13 and on a the mountaintops, 3972
6:13 to a their idols. 3972
7: 3 for a your detestable practices. 3972
7: 8 for a your detestable practices. 3972
7:16 A who survive and escape will be in 3972
7:21 I will hand it a over as plunder AIT
8:10 and I saw portrayed a over 6017+6017+6584
8:10 over the walls a kinds of crawling things 3972
8:10 and detestable animals and a the idols 3972

Ref	Text	Num
Eze 9: 4	over a the detestable things that are done	3972
11:18	to it and remove a its vile images	3972
12:14	to the winds a those around him—	3972
12:14	his staff and a his troops—	3972
12:16	they go they may acknowledge a their detestable practices.	3972
12:19	because of the violence of a who live there.	3972
13:18	on a their wrists and make veils	3972
14: 3	let them **inquire** of *me* at a?	2011+2011+4200
14: 5	who have a deserted me for their idols.'	3972
14: 6	and renounce a your detestable practices!	3972
14:11	with a their sins.	3972
16:22	In a your detestable practices	3972
16:23	In addition to a your other wickedness,	3972
16:30	when you do a these things,	3972
16:33	but you give gifts to a your lovers,	3972
16:36	and because of a your detestable idols,	3972
16:37	to gather a your lovers,	3972
16:37	from a **around** and will strip you in front	6017
16:37	and they will see a your nakedness.	3972
16:43	but enraged me with a these things,	3972
16:43	to a your other detestable practices?	3972
16:47	in a your ways you soon became more depraved than they.	3972
16:51	by a these things you have done.	3972
16:54	of a you have done in giving them comfort.	3972
16:57	the daughters of Edom and a her neighbors	3972
16:57	a those around you who despise you.	NIH
16:63	for you for a you have done,	3972
17: 9	A its new growth will wither.	3972
17:18	in pledge and yet did a these things,	3972
17:21	A his fleeing troops will fall by the sword,	3972
17:24	A the trees of the field will know that I	3972
18:13	he has done a these detestable things,	3972
18:14	"But suppose this son has a son who sees a	3972
18:19	and has been careful to keep a my decrees,	3972
18:21	"But if a wicked man turns away from a	3972
18:21	and keeps a my decrees	3972
18:28	Because he considers a the offenses	3972
18:30	Turn away from a your offenses;	3972
18:31	of a the offenses he have committed,	3972
19: 7	The land and a **who were in** it were terrified	4850
20: 6	the most beautiful of a lands.	3972
20:15	most beautiful of a lands—	3972
20:31	to defile yourselves with a your idols.	3972
20:40	along with a your holy sacrifices.	3972
20:43	your conduct and a the actions	3972
20:43	and you will loathe yourselves for a	3972
20:47	and it will consume a your trees,	3972
21: 5	Then a people will know that I	3972
21:12	it is against a the princes of Israel.	3972
21:15	the sword for slaughter at a their gates.	3972
21:24	revealing your sins in a that you do—	3972
22: 2	confront her with a her detestable practices	3972
22: 4	to the nations and a laughingstock to a	3972
22:18	a of them are the copper, tin,	3972
22:19	'Because you have a become dross,	3972
22:31	down on their own heads *a* they have **done,**	AIT
23: 6	a of them handsome young men,	3972
23: 7	as a prostitute to a the elite of the Assyrians	3972
23: 7	of the Assyrians and defiled herself with a	3972
23:12	a handsome young men.	3972
23:15	a of them looked like Babylonian	3972
23:23	the Babylonians and a the Chaldeans,	3972
23:23	and a the Assyrians with them,	3972
23:23	a of them governors and commanders,	3972
23:23	a mounted on horses.	3972
23:43	for that is a she is.'	NIH
23:48	that a women may take warning and	3972
24: 4	a the choice pieces—	3972
24:12	It has frustrated *a* **efforts;**	AIT
25: 6	rejoicing with a the malice of your heart	3972
25: 8	the house of Judah has become like a	3972
26:11	of his horses will trample a your streets;	3972
26:16	Then a the princes of the coast will step	3972
26:17	you put your terror on a who lived there.	3972
27: 5	They made a your timbers of pine trees	3972
27: 9	A the ships of the sea	3972
27:21	" 'Arabia and a the princes	3972
27:22	of a *kinds of* spices and precious stones,	3972
27:27	your merchants and a your soldiers,	3972
27:29	A who handle the oars will abandon their ships;	3972
27:29	and a the seamen will stand on the shore.	3972
27:34	your wares and a your company have gone	3972
27:35	A who live in the coastlands are appalled	3972
28:18	in the sight of a who were watching.	3972
28:19	A the nations who knew you are appalled	3972
28:26	on a their neighbors who maligned them.	3972
29: 2	against him and against a Egypt.	3972
29: 4	with a the fish sticking to your scales.	3972
29: 5	you and a the fish of your streams.	3972
29: 6	Then a who live in Egypt will know	3972
30: 5	Cush and Put, Lydia and a Arabia,	3972
30: 8	to Egypt and a her helpers are crushed.	3972
31: 4	their streams flowed a **around** its base	6017
31: 4	around its base and sent their channels to a	3972
31: 5	So it towered higher than a the trees of	3972
31: 6	A the birds of the air nested in its boughs,	3972
31: 6	a the beasts of the field gave birth	3972
31: 6	the great nations lived in its shade.	3972
31: 9	of a the trees of Eden in the garden of God.	3972
31:12	Its boughs fell on the mountains and in a	3972
31:12	its branches lay broken in a the ravines of	3972
31:12	A the nations of the earth came out from	3972
31:13	A the birds of the air settled on	3972
31:13	and a the beasts of the field were	3972

Ref	Text	Num
Eze 31:14	they are a destined for death,	3972
31:15	and a the trees of the field withered away.	3972
31:16	Then a the trees of Eden,	3972
31:16	a the trees that were well-watered,	3972
31:18	" 'This is Pharaoh and a his hordes,	3972
32: 4	I will let a the birds of the air settle on you	3972
32: 4	of the air settle on you and a the beasts of	3972
32: 6	with your flowing blood a **the way to**	448
32: 8	A the shining lights in the heavens	3972
32:12	the most ruthless of a nations.	3972
32:12	and a her hordes will be overthrown.	3972
32:13	I will destroy a her cattle from	3972
32:15	when I strike down a who live there,	3972
32:16	Egypt and a her hordes they will chant it,	3972
32:20	let her be dragged off with a her hordes.	3972
32:22	by the graves of a her slain,	3972
32:22	a who have fallen by the sword.	NIH
32:23	A who had spread terror in the land of	3972
32:24	with a her hordes around her grave.	3972
32:24	A of them are slain, fallen by the sword.	3972
32:24	A who had spread terror in the land of	NIH
32:25	with a her hordes around her grave.	3972
32:25	A of them are uncircumcised.	3972
32:26	with a their hordes around their graves.	3972
32:26	A of them are uncircumcised.	3972
32:29	her kings and a her princes;	3972
32:30	"A the princes of the north and all	3972
32:30	of the north and a the Sidonians are there;	3972
32:31	"Pharaoh—he and a his army—	3972
32:31	and he will be consoled for a his hordes	3972
32:32	Pharaoh and a his hordes will be laid	3972
33:29	of a the detestable things they have done.'	3972
33:33	"When a **this** comes true—	2023S
34: 5	for a the wild animals.	3972
34: 6	My sheep wandered over a the mountains	3972
34: 8	and has become food for a	3972
34:12	I will rescue them from a the places	3972
34:13	in the ravines and in a the settlements in	3972
34:21	butting the weak sheep with your horns	3972
35: 7	and cut off from it *a* who **come** and go.	AIT
35: 8	and in your valleys and in a your ravines.	3972
35:12	that I the LORD have heard a	3972
35:15	O Mount Seir, you and a of Edom.	3972
36: 5	the rest of the nations, and against a Edom,	3972
36:24	from a the countries and bring you back	3972
36:25	I will cleanse you from a your impurities	3972
36:25	and from a your idols.	3972
36:29	I will save you from a your uncleanness.	3972
36:33	On the day I cleanse you from a your sins,	3972
36:34	of lying desolate in the sight of a who pass	3972
37:16	belonging to Joseph and a the house	3972
37:21	from a **around** and bring them back	6017
37:22	over a *of* them and they will never again	3972
37:23	from a their sinful backsliding,	3972
37:24	and they will a have one shepherd.	3972
38: 4	a *of* them brandishing their swords.	3972
38: 5	a with shields and helmets,	3972
38: 6	with a its troops, and Beth Togarmah from	3972
38: 6	from the far north with a its troops—	3972
38: 7	you and a the hordes gathered about you,	3972
38: 8	and now a *of* them live in safety.	3972
38: 9	and a your troops and the many nations	3972
38:11	a *of* them living without walls and	3972
38:13	of Tarshish and a her villages will say	3972
38:15	a *of* them riding on horses, a great horde,	3972
38:20	and a the people on the face of	3972
38:21	a sword against Gog on a my mountains,	3972
39: 4	and a your troops and the nations with you.	3972
39: 4	as food to a kinds of carrion birds and to	3972
39:11	Gog and a his hordes will be buried there.	3972
39:13	A the people of the land will bury them,	3972
39:17	Call out to every kind of bird and a	3972
39:17	and come together from a **around** to	6017
39:18	a *of* them fattened animals from Bashan.	3972
39:21	and a the nations will see	3972
39:23	and they a fell by the sword.	3972
39:25	and will have compassion on a the people	3972
39:26	and the unfaithfulness they showed	3972
40:14	projecting walls a **around** the inside	6017+6017
40:16	by narrow parapet openings a **around,**	6017+6017
40:16	the openings a **around** faced inward.	6017+6017
40:17	that had been constructed a **around**	6017+6017
40:25	portico had narrow openings a **around**	6017+6017
40:29	and its portico had openings a **around.**	6017+6017
40:33	and its portico had openings a **around.**	6017+6017
40:36	and it had openings a **around.**	6017+6017
40:41	eight tables in a—	NIH
40:43	were attached to the wall a **around,**	6017+6017
41: 6	There were ledges a **around** the wall	6017+6017
41: 7	The side rooms a **around**	6015
41: 8	the temple had a raised base a **around**	6017+6017
41:10	was twenty cubits wide a **around**	6017+6017
41:11	area was five cubits wide a **around.**	6017+6017
41:12	was five cubits thick a **around,**	6017+6017
41:17	walls at regular intervals a **around**	6017+6017
41:19	They were carved a **around**	6017+6017
42:15	and measured the area a **around:**	6017+6017
42:20	So he measured the area on *a* **four** sides.	AIT
43:11	of a they have done, make known to them	3972
43:11	its whole design and a its regulations	3972
43:11	to its design and follow a its regulations.	3972
43:12	A the surrounding area on top of	3972
43:17	a cubit and a gutter of a cubit a **around.**	6017
43:20	of the upper ledge and a **around** the rim,	6017
44: 5	concerning a the regulations regarding	3972
44: 5	the entrance of the temple and a the exits of	3972
44: 7	to a your other detestable practices,	3972

Ref	Text	Num
Eze 44:14	the temple and a the work that is to be done	3972
44:24	and my decrees for a my appointed feasts,	3972
44:30	The best of a the firstfruits and	3972
44:30	and of a your special gifts will belong to	3972
45:16	A the people of the land will participate	3972
45:17	at a the appointed feasts of the house	3972
45:22	for himself and for a the people of the land.	3972
46: 4	and a ram, *a* **without defect.**	AIT
46: 6	six lambs and a ram, *a* **without defect.**	AIT
46:23	with places for fire built a **around** under	6017
47:12	of a *kinds* will grow on both banks of	3972
48:19	from the city who farm it will come from a	3972
48:35	distance a **around** will be 18,000 cubits.	6017
Da 1:17	and understanding of a *kinds of* literature	3972
1:17	and dreams of a *kinds.*	3972
1:20	he found them ten times better than a	3972
2:12	that he ordered the execution of a	10353
2:38	he has made you ruler over them a.	10353
2:40	so it will crush and break a the others.	10353
2:44	It will crush a those kingdoms	10353
2:48	and placed him in charge of a its wise men.	10353
3: 2	and a the other provincial officials to come	10353
3: 3	judges, magistrates and a the other	10353
3: 5	lyre, harp, pipes and a kinds of music,	10353
3: 7	harp and a kinds of music, all the peoples,	10353
3: 7	harp and all kinds of music, a the peoples,	10353
3:10	pipes and a kinds of music must fall down	10353
3:15	lyre, harp, pipes and a kinds of music,	10353
4: 1	who live in a the world:	10353
4: 6	that a the wise men of Babylon be brought	10353
4:12	its fruit abundant, and on it was food for a.	10353
4:21	providing food for a, giving shelter to	10353
4:28	A this happened to King Nebuchadnezzar.	10353
4:35	A the peoples of the earth are regarded	10353
4:37	and a his ways are just.	NIH
5: 8	Then a the king's wise men came in,	10353
5:19	a the peoples and nations and men	10353
5:22	though you knew a this.	10353
5:23	in his hand your life and a your ways.	10353
6: 7	advisers and governors have a agreed that	10353
6:24	and crushed a their bones.	10353
6:25	Then King Darius wrote to a the peoples,	10353
7: 7	It was different from a the former beasts,	10353
7: 9	and its wheels were a **ablaze.**	10178+10471
7:14	a peoples, nations and men	10353
7:16	and asked him the true meaning of a this.	10353
7:19	which was different from a the others	10353
7:23	from a the other kingdoms and will devour	10353
7:27	and a rulers will worship and obey him.'	10353
9: 4	of love with *a* who **love** him	AIT
9: 6	and to a the people of the land.	3972
9: 7	and people of Jerusalem and a Israel,	3972
9: 7	and all Israel, both near and far, in a	3972
9:11	A Israel has transgressed your law	3972
9:13	a this disaster has come upon us,	3972
9:16	in keeping with a your righteous acts,	3972
9:16	an object of scorn to a those around us.	3972
10: 3	used no lotions at a	6057+6057
11: 2	who will be far richer than a *the others.*	3972
11:37	but will exalt himself above *them* a.	3972
11:43	of the treasures of gold and silver and a	3972
12: 7	a these things will be completed."	3972
12: 8	what will the outcome of *a* **this** be?"	AIT
Hos 1: 6	that *I should* at a **forgive** them.	5951+5951
2:11	I will stop a her celebrations;	3972
2:11	a her appointed feasts.	3972
2:18	so that a may lie down in safety.	4392S
4: 2	*they* **break** a **bounds,**	7287
4: 3	and a who live in it waste away;	3972
5: 2	I will discipline a of them.	3972
5: 3	I **know** a **about** Ephraim;	3359
7: 2	that I remember a their evil deeds.	3972
7: 4	They are a adulterers,	3972
7: 6	Their passion smolders a night;	3972
7: 7	A their are hot as an oven;	3972
7: 7	A their kings fall,	3972
7:10	but despite a this he does not return to	3972
9: 4	a who eat them will be unclean.	3972
9: 8	yet snares await him on a his paths,	3972
9:15	"Because of a their wickedness in Gilgal,	3972
9:15	a their leaders are rebellious.	3972
10:14	that a your fortresses will be devastated—	3972
11: 8	a my compassion is aroused.	3480
12: 1	the east wind a day and multiplies lies	3972
12: 8	With a my wealth they will not find	3972
13: 2	a *of* them the work of craftsmen.	3972
13:10	Where are your rulers in a your towns,	3972
13:15	be plundered of a its treasures.	3972
14: 2	"Forgive a our sins	3972
Joel 1: 2	listen, a who live in the land.	3972
1: 5	Wail, a you drinkers of wine;	3972
1:12	a the trees of the field—are dried up.	3972
1:14	and a who live in the land to the house of	3972
1:19	and flames have burned up a the trees of	3972
2: 1	Let a who live in the land tremble,	3972
2: 7	They *a* march in line,	AIT
2:12	"return to me with a your heart,	3972
2:28	I will pour out my Spirit on a people.	3972
3: 2	I will gather a nations and bring them	3972
3: 4	and Sidon and a you regions of Philistia?	3972
3: 9	Let a the fighting men draw near	3972
3:11	a you nations from every side,	3972
3:12	for there I will sit to judge a the nations	3972
3:18	a the ravines of Judah will run with water.	3972
3:20	and Jerusalem through a **generations.**	1887+1887+2256
Am 1:11	with a sword, stifling *a* **compassion,**	AIT

Am	2: 3	and kill a her officials with him,"	3972
	3: 2	"You only have I chosen of the families	3972
	3: 2	therefore I will punish you for a your sins."	3972
	5:16	"There will be wailing in a the streets	3972
	5:17	There will be wailing in a the vineyards,	3972
	6:14	that will oppress you a the way	NIH
	7:10	The land cannot bear a his words.	3972
	8: 8	and a who live in it mourn?	3972
	8:10	into mourning and a your singing	3972
	8:10	I will make a of you wear sackcloth	3972
	9: 1	Bring them down on the heads of a	3972
	9: 5	and a who live in it mourn—	3972
	9: 9	among the nations as grain is shaken in	3972
	9:10	A the sinners among my people will die by	3972
	9:10	will die by the sword, a those who say,	NIH
	9:12	the remnant of Edom and a the nations	3972
		the mountains and flow from a the hills.	3972
Ob	1: 7	A your allies will force you to the border;	3972
	1:15	of the LORD is near for a nations.	3972
	1:16	so a the nations will drink continually;	3972
Jnh	1: 5	A the sailors were afraid and each cried out	NIH
	1: 8	for making a this trouble for us?"	NIH
	2: 3	a your waves and breakers swept over me.	3972
	3: 5	They declared a fast, and a of them,	NIH
Mic	1: 2	Hear, O peoples, a of you, listen,	3972
	1: 2	listen, O earth and a who are in it,	4850
	1: 5	A this is because of Jacob's transgression,	3972
	1: 7	Her idols will be broken to pieces;	3972
	1: 7	a her temple gifts will be burned with fire;	3972
	1: 7	I will destroy a her images.	3972
	1:10	Tell it not in Gath; weep not at a.	1134+1134
	2:10	it is ruined, beyond a remedy.	5344
	2:12	"I will surely gather a of you, O Jacob;	3972
	3: 7	They will a cover their faces	3972
	3: 9	who despise justice and distort a	3972
	4: 5	A the nations may walk in the name	3972
	4:13	their wealth to the Lord of a the earth.	3972
	5: 9	and a your foes will be destroyed.	3972
	5:11	and tear down a your strongholds.	3972
	6:16	the statutes of Omri and a the practices	3972
	7: 2	A men lie in wait to shed blood;	3972
	7: 3	they a conspire together.	AIT
	7:16	deprived of a their power.	3972
	7:19	and hurl a our iniquities into the depths of	3972
Na	1: 4	he makes a the rivers run dry.	3972
	1: 5	the world and a who live in it.	3972
	2: 1	brace yourselves, marshal a your strength!	4394
	2: 9	the wealth from a its treasures!	3972
	3: 4	a because of the wanton lust of a harlot,	8044
	3: 7	A who see you will flee from you and say,	3972
	3:10	and a her great men were put in chains.	3972
	3:12	A your fortresses are like fig trees	3972
	3:13	Look at your troops—they are a women!	NIH
Hab	1: 9	they a come bent on violence.	3972
	1:10	They laugh at a fortified cities;	3972
	1:15	wicked foe pulls a of them up with hooks,	3972
	2: 5	he gathers to himself a the nations	3972
	2: 5	the nations and takes captive a the peoples.	3972
	2: 6	"Will not a of them taunt him with ridicule	3972
	2:20	let a the earth be silent before him."	3972
Zep	1: 4	against Judah and against a who live	3972
	1: 8	and the king's sons and a those clad	3972
	1: 9	that day I will punish a who avoid stepping	3972
	1:11	a your merchants will be wiped out,	3972
	1:11	a who trade with silver will be ruined.	3972
	1:18	a sudden end of a who live in the earth."	3972
	2: 3	Seek the LORD, a you humble of the land,	3972
	2:11	be awesome to them when he destroys a	3972
	2:15	A who pass by her scoff	3972
	3: 6	no one will be left—no one at a.	NIH
	3: 7	nor a my punishments come upon her.	3972
	3: 7	to act corruptly in a they did.	3972
	3: 8	a my fierce anger.	3972
	3: 9	that a of them may call on the name of	3972
	3:11	that day you will not be put to shame for a	3972
	3:14	Be glad and rejoice with a your heart,	3972
	3:19	with a who oppressed you;	3972
	3:20	and praise among the peoples of the earth	3972
Hag	2: 4	Be strong, a you people of the land,'	3972
	2: 7	I will shake a nations,	3972
	2: 7	and the desired of a nations will come,	3972
	2:17	I struck a the work of your hands	3972
Zec	2:13	Be still before the LORD, a mankind,	3972
	4:14	to serve the Lord of a the earth."	3972
	6: 3	a of them powerful.	AIT
	7: 5	"Ask a the people of the land and	3972
	7:14	'I scattered them with a whirlwind among a	3972
	8:12	I will give a these things as an inheritance	3972
	8:17	I hate a this," declares the LORD.	3972
	8:23	"In those days ten men from a languages	3972
	9: 1	of men and a the tribes of Israel are on	3972
	10:11	and a the depths of the Nile will dry up.	3972
	11:10	the covenant I had made with a the nations.	3972
	12: 2	to make Jerusalem a cup that sends a	3972
	12: 3	when a the nations of the earth are gathered	3972
	12: 3	an immovable rock for a the nations.	3972
	12: 3	A who try to move it will injure themselves.	3972
	12: 4	but I will blind a the horses of the nations.	3972
	12: 6	and left a the surrounding peoples,	3972
	12: 9	On that day I will set out to destroy a	3972
	12:14	and the rest of the clans and their wives.	3972
	14: 2	I will gather a the nations to Jerusalem	3972
	14: 5	and a the holy ones with him.	3972
	14:12	with which the LORD will strike a	3972
	14:14	of the surrounding nations will	3972
	14:15	and a the animals in those camps.	3972
	14:16	Then the survivors from a the nations	3972

Zec	14:19	and the punishment of a the nations that do	3972
	14:21	and a who come to sacrifice will take some	3972
Mal	2: 9	to be despised and humiliated before a	3972
	2:10	Have we not a one Father?	3972
	2:17	"A who do evil are good in the eyes of	3972
	3:12	"Then a the nations will call you blessed,	3972
	4: 1	A the arrogant and every evildoer will	3972
	4: 4	and laws I gave him at Horeb for a Israel.	3972
Mt	1:17	Thus there were fourteen generations in a	4246
	1:22	A this took place to fulfill what	3910
	2: 3	and a Jerusalem with him.	4246
	2: 4	When he had called together a	4246
	2:16	and he gave orders to kill a the boys	4246
	3: 5	to him from Jerusalem and a Judea and	4246
	3:15	for us to do this to fulfill a righteousness."	4246
	4: 8	to a very high mountain and showed him a	4246
	4: 9	"A this I will give you," he said,	4246
	4:24	News about him spread a over Syria,	1650+3910
	4:24	and people brought to him a who were ill	4246
	5:11	and falsely say a kinds of evil against you	4246
	5:34	But I tell you, Do not swear at a:	3914
	6:29	in a his splendor was dressed like one	4246
	6:32	For the pagans run after a these things,	4246
	6:33	a these things will be given to you as well.	4246
	7: 4	when a the time there is a plank	NIG
	8:16	the spirits with a word and healed a	4246
	8:33	went into the town and reported a this,	4246
	9:26	News of this spread through a that region.	3910
	9:31	the news about him a over that region.	3910
	9:35	through a the towns and villages,	4246
	10:22	A men will hate you because of me,	4246
	10:30	the very hairs of your head are a numbered.	4246
	11:13	For a the Prophets and the Law prophesied	4246
	11:27	"A things have been committed to me	4246
	11:28	a you who are weary and burdened,	4246
	12:15	and he healed a their sick,	4246
	12:23	A the people were astonished and said,	4246
	13: 2	while a the people stood on the shore.	4246
	13:32	Though it is the smallest of a your seeds,	4246
	13:33	a large amount of flour until it worked a	3910
	13:34	Jesus spoke a these things to the crowd	4246
	13:41	that causes sin and a who do evil.	NIG
	13:44	then in his joy went and sold a he had	4012+4246
	13:47	into the lake and caught a kinds of fish.	4246
	13:51	"Have you understood a these things?"	4246
	13:56	Aren't a his sisters with us?	4246
	13:56	then did this man get a these things?"	4246
	14:20	They a ate and were satisfied,	4246
	14:35	to a the surrounding country.	3910
	14:35	People brought a their sick to him	4246
	14:36	and a who touched him were healed.	4012
	15:37	They a ate and were satisfied.	4246
	17:11	Elijah comes and will restore a things.	4246
	18:25	and a that he had be sold to repay the debt.	4012+4246
	18:32	'I canceled a that debt of yours	4246
	18:34	until he should pay back a he owed.	4246
	19:20	"A these I have kept," the young man said.	4246
	19:26	but with God a things are possible."	4246
	19:28	at the renewal of a things,	NIG
	20: 6	'Why have you been standing here a day long doing nothing?'	3910
	20:31	but they shouted a the louder, "Lord,	3505
	21:12	and drove out a who were buying	4246
	21:26	for they a hold that John was a prophet."	4246
	21:37	Last of a, he sent his son to them.	5731
	22:10	and gathered a the people they could find,	4246
	22:28	since a of them were married to her?"	4246
	22:37	with a your heart and with all your soul and	3910
	22:37	with all your heart and with a your soul and	3910
	22:37	with all your soul and with a your mind.'	3910
	22:40	A the Law and the Prophets hang	3910
	23: 8	and you are a brothers.	4246
	23:35	upon you will come a the righteous blood	4246
	23:36	a this will come upon this generation.	4246
	24: 2	"Do you see a these things?"	4246
	24: 8	A these are the beginning of birth pains.	4246
	24: 9	and you will be hated by a nations because	4246
	24:14	as a testimony to a nations,	4246
	24:30	and a the nations of the earth will mourn.	4246
	24:33	Even so, when you see a these things,	4246
	24:34	until a these things have happened.	4246
	24:39	until the flood came and took them a away.	570
	24:47	in charge of a his possessions.	4246
	25: 5	and they a became drowsy and fell asleep.	4246
	25: 7	"Then a the virgins woke up	4246
	25:31	and a the angels with him,	4246
	25:32	A the nations will be gathered before him,	4246
	26: 1	Jesus had finished saying a these things,	4246
	26:27	saying, "Drink from it, a of you.	4246
	26:31	"This very night you will a fall away	4246
	26:33	"Even if a fall away on account of you,	4246
	26:35	And a the other disciples said the same.	4246
	26:52	"for a who draw the sword will die by	4246
	26:56	But this has a taken place that the writings	3910
	26:56	Then a the disciples deserted him and fled.	4246
	26:64	"But I say to a to a you:	NIG
	26:70	But he denied it before them a.	4246
	27: 1	a the chief priests and the elders of	4246
	27:22	They a answered, "Crucify him!"	4246
	27:23	But they shouted a the louder,	4360
	27:25	A the people answered,	4246
	27:45	until the ninth hour darkness came over a	4246
	27:54	the earthquake and a that had happened,	NIG
	28:18	"A authority in heaven and on earth	4246
	28:19	go and make disciples of a nations,	4246
Mk	1: 5	and a the people of Jerusalem went out	4246

Mk	1:27	The people were a so amazed	570
	1:32	after sunset the people brought to Jesus a	4246
	2:12	and walked out in full view of them a.	4246
	3: 8	When they heard a he was doing,	4012
	3:28	a the sins and blasphemies of men will	4246
	4: 1	while a the people were along the shore at	4246
	4:28	A by itself the soil produces grain—	897
	4:32	and becomes the largest of a garden plants,	4246
	5:20	And a the people were amazed.	4246
	5:26	of many doctors and had spent a she had,	4246
	5:39	"Why a this commotion and wailing?	NIG
	5:40	After he put them a out,	4246
	6:30	and reported to him a they had done,	4246
	6:33	on foot from a the towns and got there	4246
	6:39	to have a the people sit down in groups on	4246
	6:41	He also divided the two fish among them a.	4246
	6:42	They a ate and were satisfied,	4246
	6:50	because they saw him and were terrified.	4246
	6:56	and a who touched him were healed.	323+4012
	7: 3	(The Pharisees and the Jews do not eat	4246
	7:19	Jesus declared a foods "clean.")	4246
	7:23	A these evils come from inside and make	4246
	7:27	"First let the children eat a they want,"	5963
	9: 2	where they were a alone.	3668
	9:12	and restores a things.	4246
	9:15	As soon as a the people saw Jesus,	4246
	9:35	and the servant of a."	4246
	10:20	"a these I have kept since I was a boy."	4246
	10:27	a things are possible with God."	4246
	10:44	to be first must be slave of a.	4246
	10:48	but he shouted a the more, "Son of David,	3189+3437+4498
	11:17	be called a house of prayer for a nations'?	4246
	12: 6	He sent him last of a, saying,	2274
	12:22	Last of a, the woman died too.	4246
	12:28	he asked him, "Of a the commandments,	4246
	12:30	with a your heart and with all your soul and	3910
	12:30	with all your heart and with a your soul and	3910
	12:30	with all your soul and with a your mind	3910
	12:30	and with a your strength.'	3910
	12:33	To love him with a your heart,	4246
	12:33	with a your understanding and	3910
	12:33	and with a your strength,	3910
	12:33	is more important than a burnt offerings	4246
	12:43	into the treasury than a the others.	4246
	12:44	They a gave out of their wealth;	4246
	12:44	a she had to live on."	3910+4012
	13: 2	"Do you see a these great buildings?"	NIG
	13: 4	And what will be the sign that they are a	4246
	13:10	gospel must first be preached to a nations.	4246
	13:13	A men will hate you because of me,	4246
	13:30	until a these things have happened.	4246
	14:23	and they a drank from it.	4246
	14:27	"You will a fall away," Jesus told them,	4246
	14:29	Peter declared, "Even if a fall away,	4246
	14:31	And a the others said the same.	4246
	14:53	and a the chief priests,	4246
	14:64	They a condemned him as worthy of death.	4360
	15:14	But they shouted a the louder,	4360
	16:15	into the world and preach the good news	570
	16:15	and preach the good news to a creation.	4246
	16:18	it will not hurt them at a;	3590+4024
Lk	1: 6	observing a the Lord's commandments	4246
	1:10	the time for the burning of incense came, a	4246
	1:48	now on a generations will call me blessed,	4246
	1:65	The neighbors were a filled with awe,	4246
	1:65	about a these things.	4246
	1:71	and from the hand of a who hate us—	4246
	1:75	and righteousness before him a our days.	4246
	2:10	of great joy that will be for a the people.	4246
	2:18	and a who heard it were amazed at what	4246
	2:19	But Mary treasured up a these things	4246
	2:20	for a the things they had heard and seen,	4246
	2:31	in the sight of a people,	4246
	2:38	the child to a who were looking forward to	4246
	2:51	But his mother treasured a these things	4246
	3: 3	into a the country around the Jordan,	4246
	3: 6	And a mankind will see God's salvation.' "	4246
	3:15	and were a wondering in their hearts	4246
	3:16	John answered them a,	4246
	3:19	and a the other evil things he had done,	4246
	3:20	Herod added this to them a:	4246
	3:21	When a the people were being baptized,	570
	4: 5	a high place and showed him in an instant a	4246
	4: 6	"I will give you a their authority	570
	4: 7	So if you worship me, it will a be yours."	4246
	4:13	the devil had finished a this tempting,	4246
	4:22	A spoke well of him and were amazed at	4246
	4:28	A the people in the synagogue were furious	4246
	4:35	the man down before them a and came out	NIG
	4:36	A the people were amazed and said	4246
	4:40	to Jesus a who had various kinds	570
	5: 5	we've worked hard a night	3910
	5: 9	and a his companions were astonished at a	4246
	5:15	Yet the news about him spread a the more,	3437
	6:10	He looked around at them a,	4246
	6:17	and a great number of people from a over	4246
	6:19	and the people a tried to touch him,	4246
	6:19	from him and healing them a.	4246
	6:26	Woe to you when a men speak well of you,	4246
	7: 1	When Jesus had finished saying a this in	4246
	7:16	They were a filled with awe	4246
	7:18	about a these things.	4246
	7:29	(A the people, even the tax collectors,	4246
	7:35	wisdom is proved right by a her children."	4246
	8:24	the storm subsided, and a was calm.	NIG
	8:37	Then a the people of the region of	570

Lk	8:39	man went away and told a over town	2848+3910
	8:40	for they were a expecting him.	4246
	8:45	When they a denied it, Peter said, "Master,	4246
	8:47	In the presence of a the people,	4246
	8:52	a the people were wailing and mourning	4246
	9: 1	to drive out a demons and to cure diseases,	4246
	9: 7	Now Herod the tetrarch heard about a	4246
	9:13	we go and buy food for a this crowd."	4246
	9:17	They a ate and were satisfied,	4246
	9:23	Then he said to them a:	4246
	9:43	And they were a amazed at the greatness	4246
	9:43	While everyone was marveling at a	4246
	9:48	For he who is least among you a—	4246
	10:19	and scorpions and to overcome a the power	4246
	10:22	"A things have been committed to me	4246
	10:27	with a your heart and with all your soul and	3910
	10:27	with all your heart and with a your soul and	3910
	10:27	with all your soul and with a your strength	3910
	10:27	and with a your mind';	3910
	10:40	by a the preparations that had to be made.	4498
	11:42	rue and a other kinds of garden herbs,	4246
	11:50	of a the prophets that has been shed since	4246
	11:51	be held responsible for it a.	NIG
	12: 7	the very hairs of your head are a numbered.	4246
	12:15	Be on your guard against a kinds of greed;	4246
	12:18	there I will store a my grain and my goods.	4246
	12:27	in a his splendor was dressed like one	4246
	12:30	the pagan world runs after a such things,	4246
	12:44	in charge of a his possessions.	4246
	13: 2	these Galileans were worse sinners than a	4246
	13: 3	unless you repent, you too will a perish.	4246
	13: 4	do you think they were more guilty than a	4246
	13: 5	unless you repent, you too will a perish."	4246
	13:11	could not straighten up at a.	1650+3836+4117
	13:17	a his opponents were humiliated,	4246
	13:17	with a the wonderful things he was doing.	4246
	13:21	a large amount of flour until it worked a	3910
	13:27	Away from me, a you evildoers!'	4246
	13:28	and a the prophets in the kingdom of God,	4246
	14:10	in the presence of a your fellow guests.	4246
	14:18	"But they a alike began to make excuses.	4246
	15: 1	and "sinners" were a gathering around	4246
	15:13	the younger son got together a he had,	4246
	15:29	A these years I've been slaving for you	AIT
	16:14	heard a this and were sneering at Jesus.	4246
	16:26	And besides a this, between us and you	4246
	17:17	Jesus asked, "Were not a ten cleansed?	3836
	17:27	Then the flood came and destroyed them a.	4246
	17:29	down from heaven and destroyed them a.	4246
	18:12	a week and give a tenth of a I get.'	4012+4246
	18:21	"A these I have kept since I was a boy,"	4246
	18:28	We have left a we had to follow you!"	2625+3836
	18:39	but he shouted a the more, "Son of David,	3437+4498
	18:43	a the people saw it, they also praised God.	4246
	19: 7	A the people saw this and began to mutter,	4246
	19:37	to praise God in loud voices for a	4246
	19:48	because the a people hung on his words.	570
	20: 6	'From men,' a the people will stone us,	570
	20:38	but of the living, for to him a are alive."	4246
	20:45	While a the people were listening,	4246
	21: 3	"this poor widow has put in more than a	4246
	21: 4	A these people gave their gifts out	4246
	21: 4	of her poverty put in a she had to live on."	4246
	21:12	But before a this, they will lay hands on you	4246
	21:12	and a on account of my name.	NIG
	21:17	A men will hate you because of me.	4246
	21:22	the time of punishment in fulfillment of a	4246
	21:24	be taken as prisoners to a the nations.	4246
	21:29	"Look at the fig tree and a the trees.	4246
	21:32	until a these things have happened.	4246
	21:35	For it will come upon a those who live on	4246
	21:36	be able to escape a that is about to happen,	4246
	21:38	and a the people came early in the morning	4246
	22:12	a large upper room, a furnished.	NIG
	22:70	They a asked, "Are you then the Son	4246
	23: 5	up the people a over Judea by his teaching.	3910
	23: 5	in Galilee and has come a the way here."	NIG
	23:48	When a the people who had gathered	4246
	23:49	But a those who knew him,	4246
	24: 9	they told a these things to the Eleven and	4246
	24: 9	to the Eleven and to a the others.	4246
	24:19	and deed before God and a the people.	4246
	24:21	it is the third day since a this took place.	NIG
	24:25	to believe a that the prophets have spoken!	4246
	24:27	beginning with Moses and a the Prophets,	4246
	24:27	to them what was said in a the Scriptures	4246
	24:47	be preached in his name to a nations,	4246
Jn	1: 3	Through him a things were made;	4246
	1: 7	so that through him a men might believe.	4246
	1:12	Yet to a who received him,	4012
	1:16	of his grace we have a received one blessing	4246
	1:28	This a happened at Bethany on	NIG
	2:15	and drove a from the temple area,	4246
	2:18	to prove your authority to do a this?"	NIG
	2:24	for he knew a men.	4246
	3:31	one who comes from above is above a;	4246
	3:31	one who comes from heaven is above a.	4246
	4:45	They had seen a that he had done	4246
	4:53	So he and a his household believed.	3910
	5:18	For this reason the Jews tried a the harder	3437
	5:20	the Son and shows him a he does.	4246
	5:22	but has entrusted a judgment to the Son,	4246
	5:23	that a may honor the Son just as they honor	4246
	5:28	for a time is coming when a who are	4246
	6:12	When they had a had enough to eat,	NIG
	6:37	A that the Father gives me will come to me,	4246

Jn	6:39	I shall lose none of a that he has given me,	4246
	6:45	'They will a be taught by God.'	4246
	7:21	and you are a astonished.	4246
	8: 2	where a the people gathered around him,	4246
	8:25	Just what I have been claiming a along	794+3836
	10: 4	When he has brought out a his own,	4246
	10: 8	A who ever came before me were thieves	4246
	10:29	is greater than a;	4246
	10:41	a that John said about this man was true."	4246
	11:49	spoke up, "You know nothing at a!	4024+4029
	11:56	Isn't he coming to the Feast at a?"	3590+4024
	12:16	not understand a this.	AIT
	12:32	will draw a men to myself."	4246
	12:37	Jesus had done a these miraculous signs	5537
	13: 3	Jesus knew that the Father had put a things	4246
	13:18	"I am not referring to a of you;	4246
	13:35	By this a men will know	4246
	14:25	"A this I have spoken while still with you.	AIT
	14:26	will teach you a things	4246
	16: 1	"A this I have told you so that you will	AIT
	16:13	comes, he will guide you into a truth.	4246
	16:15	A that belongs to the Father is mine.	4246
	16:30	that you know a things and that you do not	4246
	16:32	You will leave me a alone.	3667
	17: 2	over a people that he might give eternal life	4246
	17: 2	to a those you have given him.	4246
	17:10	A I have is yours, and all you have is mine.	4246
	17:10	All I have is yours, and a you have is mine.	NIG
	17:21	that a of them may be one,	4246
	18: 4	knowing a that was going to happen	4246
	18:20	where a the Jews come together.	4246
	19:28	Later, knowing that a was now completed,	4246
	21:17	He said, "Lord, you know a things;	4246
Ac	1: 1	about a that Jesus began to do and to teach	4246
	1: 8	and in a Judea and Samaria,	4246
	1:14	They a joined together constantly in prayer,	4246
	1:18	and a his intestines spilled out.	4246
	2: 1	they were a together in one place.	4246
	2: 4	A of them were filled with the Holy Spirit	4246
	2: 7	a these men who are speaking Galileans?	570
	2:14	"Fellow Jews and a of you who live	4246
	2:17	I will pour out my Spirit on a people.	4246
	2:32	and we are a witnesses of the fact.	4246
	2:36	"Therefore let a Israel be assured of this:	4246
	2:39	and for a who are far off—	4246
	2:39	for a whom the Lord our God will call.	323+4012
	2:44	A the believers were together	4246
	2:47	praising God and enjoying the favor of a	3910
	3: 9	When a the people saw him walking	4246
	3:11	a the people were astonished	4246
	3:16	as you can a see.	4246
	3:18	through a the prophets,	4246
	3:24	"Indeed, a the prophets from Samuel on,	4246
	3:25	'Through your offspring a peoples	4246
	4:10	you and a the people of Israel:	4246
	4:18	to speak or teach at a in the name of Jesus.	2773
	4:21	because a the people were praising God	570
	4:23	to their own people and reported a that	4012
	4:31	And they were a filled with the Holy Spirit	570
	4:32	A the believers were one in heart and mind.	4436
	4:33	and much grace was upon them a.	4246
	5: 5	great fear seized a who heard what had happened.	4246
	5:11	and a who heard about these events.	4246
	5:12	And a the believers used to meet together	570
	5:16	and a of them were healed.	570
	5:17	Then the high priest and a his associates,	4246
	5:34	who was honored by a the people,	4246
	5:36	a his followers were dispersed,	4246
	5:36	and it came to nothing.	NIG
	5:37	and a his followers were scattered.	4246
	6: 2	So the Twelve gathered a the disciples together	4436
	6:15	A who were sitting in the Sanhedrin	4246
	7:10	and rescued him from a his troubles.	4246
	7:10	over Egypt and a his palace.	3910
	7:11	"Then a famine struck a Egypt and Canaan,	3910
	7:14	and his whole family, seventy-five in a.	6034
	7:22	Moses was educated in a the wisdom of	4246
	7:50	Has not my hand made a these things?'	4246
	7:57	they a rushed at him,	3924
	8: 1	and a except the apostles were scattered	4246
	8: 6	they a paid close attention to what he said.	3924
	8: 9	and amazed a the people of Samaria.	NIG
	8:10	and a the people,	4246
	8:27	in charge of a the treasury of Candace,	4246
	8:40	in a the towns until he reached Caesarea.	4246
	9:13	about this man and a the harm he has done	4012
	9:14	from the chief priests to arrest a who call	4246
	9:21	A those who heard him were astonished	4246
	9:26	but they were a afraid of him,	4246
	9:35	A those who lived in Lydda	4246
	9:39	A the widows stood around him,	4246
	9:40	Peter sent them a out of the room;	4246
	9:42	This became known a over Joppa,	3910
	10: 2	He and a his family were devout	4246
	10:12	It contained a kinds	4246
	10:22	who is respected by a the Jewish people.	3910
	10:33	Now we are a here in the presence of God	4246
	10:36	who is Lord of a.	4246
	10:38	and healing a who were under the power of	4246
	10:41	He was not seen by a the people,	4246
	10:43	A the prophets testify about him	4246
	10:44	the Holy Spirit came on a who heard	4246
	11:10	then it was a pulled up to heaven again.	570
	11:14	and a your household will be saved.'	4246
	11:23	and encouraged them a to remain true to	4246

Ac	11:23	to the Lord with a their hearts.	NIG
	13:10	of a kinds of deceit and trickery.	4246
	13:20	A this took about 450 years.	NIG
	13:24	John preached repentance and baptism to a	4246
	13:29	When they had carried out a	4246
	13:48	and a who were appointed	4012
	14:16	he let a nations go their own way.	4246
	14:27	the church together and reported a that	4012
	15: 3	This news made a the brothers very glad.	4246
	15:17	and a the Gentiles who bear my name,	4246
	15:25	So we a agreed to choose some men	NIG
	15:36	in a the towns where we preached the word	4246
	16: 3	for they a knew that his father was a Greek.	570
	16:26	At once a the prison doors flew open,	4246
	16:28	We are a here!"	570
	16:32	to him and to a the others in his house.	4246
	16:33	and a his family were baptized.	4246
	17: 6	"These men who have caused trouble a	NIG
	17: 7	They are a defying Caesar's decrees,	4246
	17:21	(A the Athenians	4246
	17:25	because he himself gives a men life	4246
	17:30	now he commands a people everywhere	4246
	17:31	to a men by raising him from the dead."	4246
	18: 2	because Claudius had ordered a the Jews	4246
	18:17	Then they a turned on Sosthenes	4246
	18:23	strengthening a the disciples.	4246
	19: 7	There were about twelve men in a.	4246
	19:10	so that a the Jews and Greeks who lived in	4246
	19:16	on them and overpowered them a.	317
	19:17	they were a seized with fear,	4246
	19:21	After a this had happened,	NIG
	19:26	that man-made gods are no gods at a.	4024
	19:34	they a shouted in unison for	4246
	19:35	doesn't a the world know that the city	476+1639+4005+5515
	20:26	that I am innocent of the blood of a men.	4246
	20:28	Keep watch over yourselves and a the flock	4246
	20:32	among a those who are sanctified.	4246
	20:36	he knelt down with a of them and prayed.	4246
	20:37	They a wept as they embraced him	4246
	21: 5	A the disciples and their wives	4246
	21:18	and a the elders were present.	4246
	21:20	and a of them are zealous for the law.	4246
	21:21	They have been informed that you teach a	4246
	21:28	the man who teaches a men everywhere	4246
	21:30	the people came running from a directions.	NIG
	21:40	When they were a silent,	4498+4968
	22: 5	high priest and a the Council can testify.	4246
	22:10	be told a that you have been assigned	4246
	22:12	of the law and highly respected by a	4246
	22:15	to a men of what you have seen and heard.	4246
	22:30	the chief priests and a the Sanhedrin	4246
	23: 1	to God in a good conscience to this day."	4246
	23: 8	but the Pharisees acknowledge them a.)	317
	24: 5	up riots among the Jews a over the world.	4246
	24: 8	about a these charges we are bringing	4246
	25:24	and a who are present with us,	4246
	25:26	I have brought him before a of you,	NIG
	26: 2	against a the accusations of the Jews,	4246
	26: 3	so because you are well acquainted with a	4246
	26: 4	"The Jews a know	4246
	26: 9	"I too was convinced that I ought to do a	4498
	26:14	We a fell to the ground,	4246
	26:20	then to those in Jerusalem and in a Judea,	4246
	26:29	that not only you but a who are listening	4246
	27:20	we finally gave up a hope of being saved.	4246
	27:24	the lives of a who sail with you.'	4246
	27:33	Just before dawn Paul urged them a to eat.	570
	27:35	and gave thanks to God in front of them a.	4246
	27:36	They were a encouraged	4246
	28: 2	and welcomed us a because it was raining	4246
	28:30	and welcomed a who came to see him.	4246
Ro	1: 5	from among a the Gentiles to the obedience	4246
	1: 7	To a in Rome who are loved by God	4246
	1: 8	I thank my God through Jesus Christ for a	4246
	1: 8	because your faith is being reported a over	3910
	1:10	in my prayers at a times;	4121
	1:18	against a the godlessness and wickedness	4246
	2:12	A who sin apart from the law will	4012
	2:12	and a who sin under the law will be judged	4012
	3: 2	First of a, they have been entrusted with	4754
	3: 4	Not at a! Let God be true,	1181+3590
	3: 9	Are we any better? Not at a!	4122
	3: 9	and Gentiles alike are a under sin.	4246
	3:12	A have turned away,	4246
	3:22	in Jesus Christ to a who believe.	4246
	3:23	for a have sinned and fall short of the glory	4246
	3:31	nullify the law by this faith? Not at a!	1181+3590
	4:11	he is the father of a who believe but have	4246
	4:16	be guaranteed to a Abraham's offspring—	4246
	4:16	He is the father of us a.	4246
	4:18	Against a hope, Abraham in hope believed	1828
	5:12	and in this way death came to a men,	4246
	5:12	to all men, because a sinned—	4246
	5:18	for a men, so also the result of one act	4246
	5:18	that brings life for a men.	4246
	5:20	sin increased, grace increased a the more,	5668
	6: 3	that a of us who were baptized	4012
	6:10	he died to sin once for a;	2384
	8:24	But hope that is seen is no hope at a.	NIG
	8:28	And we know that in a things God works	4246
	8:32	but gave him up for us a—	4246
	8:32	graciously give us a things?	4246
	8:36	"For your sake we face death a day long;	3910
	8:37	in a these things we are more than conquerors	4246
	8:39	nor anything else in a creation,	NIG

Ro	9: 5	who is God over **a**, forever praised!	4246
	9: 6	a who are descended from Israel are Israel.	4246
	9: 7	they are his descendants are they **a**	
		Abraham's children.	4246
	9:14	Is God unjust? **Not at a!**	1181+3590
	9:17	and that my name might be proclaimed in a	4246
	10:12	of **a** and richly blesses all who call on him,	4246
	10:12	of all and richly blesses a who call on him,	4246
	10:16	not **a** the Israelites accepted the good news.	4246
	10:18	"Their voice has gone out into the earth,	4246
	10:21	"A day **long** I have held out my hands to	3910
	11:11	to fall beyond recovery? **Not at a!**	1181+3590
	11:24	**After a**, if you were cut out of an olive tree	1142
	11:26	so a Israel will be saved, as it is written:	4246
	11:32	For God has bound a **men** over	4246
	11:32	so that he may have mercy on them **a**.	4246
	11:36	through him and to him are a **things**.	3836+4246
	12: 4	and these members do not a have	4246
	12: 5	and each member belongs to **a the others.**	253
	14:10	we will a stand before God's judgment seat	4246
	14:20	A food is clean,	4246
	15:11	again, "Praise the Lord, a you Gentiles,	4246
	15:11	and sing praises to him, a you peoples."	4246
	15:13	*with* a joy and peace as you trust in him,	4246
	15:19	a the way around to	3588
	15:33	The God of peace be with you **a**. Amen.	4246
	16: 4	Not only I but **a** the churches of	4246
	16:15	and Olympas and **a** the saints with them.	4246
	16:16	A the churches of Christ send greetings.	4246
	16:26	a nations might believe and obey him—	4246
1Co	1: 2	together with **a** those everywhere who call	4246
	1: 5	in **a** your speaking and	4246
	1: 5	and in a your knowledge—	4246
	1:10	that **a** of you agree with one another so	4246
	2:10	The Spirit searches **a** *things*,	4246
	2:15	about a *things*, but he himself is not subject	4246
	3: 5	What, **after a**, is Apollos?	4036
	3:21	A *things* are yours,	4246
	3:22	or the future—a are yours,	4246
	4: 8	Already *you* **have a** you want!	1639+3170
	5:10	not at **a** meaning the people	4122
	6:18	A other sins a man commits are outside his	
		body,	4246
	7: 7	I wish that **a** men were as I am.	4246
	7:17	the rule I lay down in a the churches.	4246
	8: 1	We know that we a possess knowledge.	4246
	8: 4	that an idol is nothing at **a** in the world and	NIG
	8: 6	from whom **a things** came and	3836+4246
	8: 6	through whom **a** things came and	4246
	9:12	shouldn't we have it **a the more?**	3437
	9:22	I have become a *things* to all men so that	4246
	9:22	I have become all things *to* a men so that	4246
	9:22	that **by a possible means** I might save	
		some.	4122
	9:23	I do **a** this for the sake of the gospel,	4246
	9:24	not know that in a race the runners run,	4246
	10: 1	that our forefathers were **a** under the cloud	4246
	10: 1	the cloud and that they a passed through	4246
	10: 2	They were **a** baptized into Moses in	4246
	10: 3	They **a** ate the same spiritual food	4246
	10:17	for we a partake of the one loaf.	4246
	10:31	do it a for the glory of God.	4246
	12: 6	the same God works a *of them* in all men.	4246
	12: 6	the same God works all of them in a *men*.	4246
	12:11	A these are the work of one and	4246
	12:12	a its parts are many, they form one body.	4246
	12:13	For we were **a** baptized by one Spirit	4246
	12:13	we were a given the one Spirit to drink.	4246
	12:19	If they were **a** one part,	4246
	12:28	God has appointed **first of a** apostles,	4754
	12:29	Are **a** apostles?	4246
	12:29	Are a prophets?	4246
	12:29	Are a teachers?	4246
	12:29	Do a work miracles?	4246
	12:30	Do a have gifts of healing?	4246
	12:30	Do a speak in tongues?	4246
	12:30	Do a interpret?	4246
	13: 2	of prophecy and can fathom a mysteries	4246
	13: 2	and a knowledge, and if I have a faith	4246
	13: 3	If I give a I possess to the poor	4246
	14:10	Undoubtedly there are a sorts of languages	5537
	14:18	that I speak in tongues more than a of you.	4246
	14:24	by a that he is a sinner and will be judged	4246
	14:24	that he is a sinner and will be judged by a,	4246
	14:26	A *of these* must be done for	4246
	14:31	For you can a prophesy in turn so	4246
	14:33	As in a the congregations of the saints,	4246
	15: 7	then *to* **a** the apostles,	4246
	15: 8	and last *of* a he appeared to me also,	4246
	15:10	No, I worked harder than a of them—	4246
	15:19	we are to be pitied more than a men.	4246
	15:22	For as in Adam a die,	4246
	15:22	so in Christ a will be made alive.	4246
	15:24	after he has destroyed a dominion,	4246
	15:25	until he has put a his enemies	4246
	15:28	so that God may be in a all.	4246
	15:28	so that God may be all in **a**.	4246
	15:29	If the dead are not raised **at a**,	3914
	15:39	A flesh is not the same:	4246
	15:51	We will not a sleep,	4246
	15:51	but we will a be changed—	4246
	16:20	A the brothers here send you greetings.	4246
	16:24	My love to **a** of you in Christ Jesus. Amen.	4246
2Co	1: 1	with a the saints throughout Achaia,	4246
	1: 3	of compassion and the God of **a** comfort,	4246
	1: 4	who comforts us in a our troubles,	4246
	2: 3	I had confidence in **a** of you,	4246

2Co	2: 3	that you would **a** share my joy.	4246
	2: 5	not so much grieved me as he has grieved **a**	4246
	3:18	who with unveiled faces **a** reflect	4246
	4:15	A this is for your benefit,	4246
	4:17	glory **that far outweighs them a.**	
			983+1650+2848+5651+5651
	5:10	For we must **a** appear before	4246
	5:14	we are convinced that one died for **a**,	4246
	5:14	and therefore a died.	4246
	5:15	And he died for **a**,	4246
	5:18	A *this* is from God,	4246
	7: 4	in a our troubles my joy knows no bounds.	4246
	7:13	**By a this** we are encouraged.	1328+4047
	7:13	his spirit has been refreshed by **a** of you.	4246
	7:15	for you is the greater when he remembers	NIG
	7:15	that you were **a** obedient,	4246
	8:18	with him the brother who is praised by **a**	4246
	9: 8	God is able to make **a** grace abound to you,	4246
	9: 8	so that in **a** *things* at all times,	4246
	9: 8	so that in all things **at a** *times*,	4121
	9: 8	having **a** that you need,	4246
	11:28	my concern for **a** the churches.	4246
	12: 9	Therefore I will boast **a the more** gladly	3437
	12:14	**After a**, children should not have to save	1142
	12:19	Have you been thinking **a** along	4093
	13:13	A the saints send their greetings.	4246
	13:14	fellowship of the Holy Spirit be with you **a**.	4246
Gal	1: 2	and **a** the brothers with me, To	4246
	1: 7	which is really **no** gospel **at a**.	4024
	2:10	**A they asked was** that we should continue	3667
	2:14	I said to Peter in front of *them* **a**,	4246
	3: 8	"A nations will be blessed through you."	4246
	3:10	A who rely on observing the law are under	4012
	3:26	You are **a** sons of God through faith	4246
	3:27	for a *of you* **who** were baptized	4012
	3:28	for you are **a** one in Christ Jesus.	4246
	4: 9	to be enslaved by them **a over again?**	540+4099
	4:15	What has happened to **a** your joy?	NIG
	5: 2	**no** value to you **at a**.	4029
	6: 6	in the word must share **a** good things	4246
	6:10	let us do good to **a** *people*,	4246
	6:16	Peace and mercy to **a** who follow this rule,	4012
Eph	1: 8	on us with **a** wisdom and understanding.	4246
	1:10	to bring **a things** in heaven and	3836+4246
	1:15	in the Lord Jesus and your love for **a**	4246
	1:21	far above a rule and authority,	4246
	1:22	And God placed **a** *things* under his feet	4246
	2: 3	A of us also lived among them at one time,	4246
	3: 8	I am less than the least of **a** God's people,	4246
	3: 9	who created **a** *things*.	3836+4246
	3:18	together with **a** the saints,	4246
	3:19	that you may be filled to the measure of **a**	4246
	3:20	to do immeasurably more than **a** we ask	4246
	3:21	in Christ Jesus throughout **a** generations,	4246
	4: 6	one God and Father of **a**,	4246
	4: 6	who is over **a** and through all and in all.	4246
	4: 6	who is over all and through **a** and in all.	4246
	4: 6	who is over all and through all and in **a**.	4246
	4:10	the very one who ascended higher *than* **a**	4246
	4:13	until we **a** reach unity in the faith and in	4246
	4:15	in **a** *things* grow up into him who is	4246
	4:19	**Having lost a sensitivity,**	556
	4:25	for we are a members of one body.	NIG
	4:31	Get rid of a bitterness, rage and anger,	4246
	5: 9	the fruit of the light consists in a goodness,	4246
	5:29	**After a**, no one ever hated his own body,	1142
	6:16	In addition to a *this*,	4246
	6:16	with which you can extinguish **a**	4246
	6:18	in the Spirit on **a** occasions with all kinds	4246
	6:18	in the Spirit on all occasions with all **kinds**	4246
	6:18	be alert and always keep on praying for **a**	4246
	6:24	Grace to **a** who love our Lord Jesus Christ	4246
Php	1: 1	To **a** the saints in Christ Jesus at Philippi,	4246
	1: 4	In **a** my prayers for all of you,	4246
	1: 4	In all my prayers for **a** of you,	4246
	1: 7	It is right for me to feel this way about **a**	4246
	1: 7	a of you share in God's grace with me.	4246
	1: 8	how I long for **a** of you with the affection	4246
	1:25	with **a** of you for your progress and joy in	4246
	2:17	I am glad and rejoice with **a** of you.	4246
	2:26	For he longs for **a** of you and is distressed	4246
	2:28	I am **the more eager** to send him,	5081
	3: 8	for whose sake I have lost **a** *things*.	4246
	3:12	Not that I have already obtained **a** this,	NIG
	3:15	A of us who are mature should take such	4012
	4: 5	Let your gentleness be evident to **a**.	476+4246
	4: 7	which transcends **a** understanding,	4246
	4:19	And my God will meet **a** your needs	4246
	4:21	Greet **a** the saints in Christ Jesus.	4246
	4:22	A the saints send you greetings,	4246
Col	1: 4	and of the love you have for **a** the saints—	4246
	1: 6	**A over** the world this gospel is bearing fruit	4246
	1: 6	and understood God's grace in **a** its truth.	NIG
	1: 9	of his will through **a** spiritual wisdom	4246
	1:11	being strengthened with **a** power according	4246
	1:15	the firstborn *over* **a** creation.	4246
	1:16	For by him **a things** were created:	3836+4246
	1:16	a *things* were created by him and for him.	4246
	1:17	He is before **a** *things*,	4246
	1:17	and in him **a things** hold together.	3836+4246
	1:19	to have **a** his fullness dwell in him,	4246
	1:20	him to reconcile to himself **a** *things*,	3836+4246
	1:28	and teaching everyone with **a** wisdom,	4246
	1:29	struggling with **a** his energy,	NIG
	2: 1	and for **a** who have not met me personally,	4012
	2: 3	in whom are hidden **a** the treasures	4246
	2: 9	in Christ **a** the fullness of the Deity lives	4246

Col	2:13	He forgave us **a** our sins,	4246
	2:22	These are a destined to perish with use,	4246
	3: 8	of **a** such *things* as these:	4246
	3:11	slave or free, but Christ is **a**, and is in all.	4246
	3:11	slave or free, but Christ is all, and is in **a**.	4246
	3:14	And over **a** these virtues put on love,	4246
	3:14	which binds them **a** together	NIG
	3:16	and admonish one another with **a** wisdom,	4246
	3:17	do it **a** in the name of the Lord Jesus,	4246
	3:23	work at it with **a** your heart,	NIG
	4: 7	Tychicus will tell you **a** the news about me.	4246
	4:12	you may stand firm in **a** the will of God,	4246
1Th	1: 2	We always thank God for **a** of you,	4246
	1: 7	so you became a model *to* **a** the believers	4246
	2:15	and are hostile *to* **a** men	4246
	3: 7	in **a** our distress and persecution	4246
	3: 9	for you in return for **a** the joy we have in	4246
	3:13	with **a** his holy ones.	4246
	4: 6	The Lord will punish men for **a** such sins,	4246
	4:10	you do love **a** the brothers	4246
	5: 5	You are **a** sons of the light and sons of	4246
	5:18	give thanks in **a** *circumstances*,	4246
	5:26	Greet **a** the brothers with a holy kiss.	4246
	5:27	before the Lord to have this letter read *to* **a**	4246
2Th	1: 4	about your perseverance and faith in **a**	4246
	1: 5	A this is evidence	NIG
	1:10	at among **a** those who have believed.	4246
	2: 9	the work of Satan displayed in **a** *kinds*	4246
	2:12	and so that **a** will be condemned who have	4246
	3:16	of peace himself give you peace at **a** *times*	4246
	3:16	The Lord be with **a** of you.	4246
	3:17	the distinguishing mark in **a** my letters.	4246
	3:18	of our Lord Jesus Christ be with you **a**.	4246
1Ti	2: 1	I urge, then, first *of* **a**, that requests,	4246
	2: 2	for kings and **a** those in authority,	4246
	2: 2	and quiet lives in **a** godliness and holiness.	4246
	2: 4	who wants **a** men to be saved and to come	4246
	2: 6	who gave himself as a ransom for **a** *men*—	4246
	3:16	**Beyond a question**, the mystery	3935
	4: 8	but godliness has value for **a** *things*,	4246
	4:10	who is the Savior of **a** men,	4246
	5: 4	these should learn **first of a**	4754
	5: 5	in need and **left a alone** puts her hope	3670
	5:10	in trouble and devoting herself *to* **a** kinds	4246
	6: 1	**A** who are under the yoke	4012
	6:10	love of money is a root of **a** kinds of evil.	4246
	6:11	But you, man of God, flee from **a** *this*,	AIT
2Ti	2: 7	the Lord will give you insight into **a** this.	4246
	3: 6	and are swayed by **a kinds of** evil desires,	4476
	3:10	You, however, **know a about** my teaching,	4158
	3:11	Yet the Lord rescued me from **a** *of them*.	4246
	3:16	A Scripture is God-breathed and is useful	4246
	4: 5	But you, keep your head in **a** *situations*,	4246
	4: 5	**discharge a** the duties of your ministry.	4442
	4: 8	*to* **a** who have longed for his appearing.	4246
	4:17	and **a** the Gentiles might hear it.	4246
	4:21	Linus, Claudia and **a** the brothers.	4246
Tit	1:15	To the pure, **a** *things* are pure,	4246
	2:11	that brings salvation has appeared *to* **a** men.	4246
	2:14	for us to redeem us from **a** wickedness and	4246
	2:15	Encourage and rebuke with **a** authority.	4246
	3: 2	and to show true humility toward **a** men.	4246
	3: 3	by **a kinds** of passions and pleasures.	4476
	3:15	Grace be with you **a**.	4246
Phm	1: 5	in the Lord Jesus and your love for **a**	4246
Heb	1: 2	whom he appointed heir *of* **a** *things*,	4246
	1: 3	sustaining **a things** by his powerful word.	
			3836+4246
	1: 6	he says, "Let **a** God's angels worship him."	4246
	1:11	they will **a** wear out like a garment.	4246
	1:14	Are not **a** angels ministering spirits sent	4246
	2:15	and free those who **a** their lives were held	4246
	3: 2	as Moses was faithful in **a** God's house.	3910
	3: 5	as a servant in **a** God's house,	3910
	3:16	Were they not **a** those Moses led out	4246
	4: 4	God rested from **a** his work."	4246
	4:13	Nothing in **a** creation is hidden	NIG
	5: 9	of eternal salvation *for* **a** who obey him	4246
	5:12	the elementary truths of God's word **a**	NIG
	6: 6	**crucifying** the Son of God **a over again**	416
	6:16	and puts an end to **a** argument.	4246
	7:27	He sacrificed for their sins **once for a**	2384
	8:11	because they will **a** know me,	4246
	9:12	the Most Holy Place **once for a**	2384
	9:19	of the law *to* **a** the people,	4246
	9:19	and sprinkled the scroll and **a** the people,	4246
	9:26	now he has appeared **once for a** at the end	562
	10: 2	worshipers would have been cleansed **once**	
		for a,	562
	10:10	of the body of Jesus Christ **once for a**.	2384
	10:12	this priest had offered **for a time** one	
		sacrifice	1457+1650+3836
	10:25	**a the more** as you see the Day approaching.	
			3437+5537
	11:13	A these people were still living by faith	4246
	11:39	These were **a** commended for their faith,	4246
	12: 9	we have a had human fathers who	
		disciplined us	NIG
	12:14	to live in peace with **a** *men* and to be holy;	4246
	12:23	You have come to God, the judge of **a** *men*,	4246
	13: 4	Marriage should be honored by **a**,	4246
	13: 4	the adulterer and **a** the sexually immoral.	NIG
	13: 9	Do not be carried away *by* **a kinds of**	4476
	13:24	Greet **a** your leaders and all God's people.	4246
	13:24	Greet all your leaders and **a** God's people.	4246
	13:25	Grace be with you **a**.	4246
Jas	1: 5	who gives generously *to* **a**	4246

Jas 1: 8 unstable in a he does. 4246
1:18 be a kind of firstfruits of a he created. NIG
1:21 get rid of a moral filth and the evil that is 4246
2:10 at just one point is guilty of breaking a 4246
3: 2 We a stumble in many ways. 570
3: 7 A kinds of animals, birds, 4246
3:17 that comes from heaven is **first of a** pure; 4754
4:16 A such boasting is evil. 4246
5:12 Above a, my brothers, do not swear— 4246
1Pe 1: 6 to suffer grief in a **kinds** of trials. 4476
1:15 so be holy in a you do; 4246
1:24 For, "A men are like grass, 4246
1:24 a their glory is like the flowers of the field; 4246
2: 1 rid yourselves of a malice and all deceit, 4246
2: 1 rid yourselves of all malice and a deceit, 4246
2:18 to your masters with a respect, 4246
3: 8 a of you, live in harmony with one another; 4246
3:18 For Christ died for sins **once for a**, 562
3:20 In it only a few people, eight in a, NIG
4: 7 The end of a things is near. 4246
4: 8 Above a, love each other deeply, 4246
4:11 so that in a things God may be praised 4246
5: 5 A of you, clothe yourselves with humility 4246
5: 7 Cast a your anxiety on him 4246
5:10 And the God of a grace, 4246
5:14 Peace to a of you who are in Christ. 4246
2Pe 1:10 be a **the more** eager to make your calling 3437
1:20 **Above a**, you must understand 4047+4754
3: 3 **First of a**, you must understand that in 4047+4754
3:16 He writes the same way in a his letters, 4246
1Jn 1: 5 in him there is no darkness **at a**. 4029
1: 7 his Son, purifies us from a sin. 4246
1: 9 and purify us from a unrighteousness. 4246
2:20 and a of you know the truth. 4246
2:27 as his anointing teaches you about a *things* 4246
5:17 A wrongdoing is sin, 4246
2Jn 1: 1 not I only, but also a who know the truth— 4246
3Jn 1: 2 and that a may go well with you, 4246
Jude 1: 3 that was **once for a** entrusted to the saints. 562
1: 5 Though you already know a *this*, 4246
1:15 and to convict a the ungodly of all 4246
1:15 of a the ungodly acts they have done in 4246
1:15 in the ungodly way, and of a 4246
1:25 before a ages, now and forevermore! 4246
Rev 1: 7 and a the peoples of the earth will mourn 4246
1:16 like the sun shining in a its brilliance. NIG
2:11 **not** be hurt **at a** 3590+4024
2:23 Then a the churches will know 4246
4: 8 and was covered with eyes a **around**, 3239
4:11 for you created a **things**, 3836+4246
5: 6 the seven spirits of God sent out into a 4246
5:13 and a that is in them, singing: 4246
7: 4 144,000 from a the tribes of Israel. 4246
7:11 A the angels were standing around 4246
8: 3 with the prayers *of* a the saints, 4246
8: 7 and a the green grass was burned up. 4246
8: 8 a ablaze, was thrown into the sea. 2794+4786
10: 6 who created the heavens and a that is NIG
10: 6 the earth and a that is in it, NIG
10: 6 and the sea and a that is in it, and said, NIG
12: 5 who will rule a the nations with 4246
13: 8 A inhabitants of the earth will worship 4246
13: 8 a whose names have not been written in NIG
13:12 He exercised the authority of 4246
13:15 and cause a who refused to worship 1569+4012
14: 8 which made a the nations drink 4246
15: 4 A nations will come and worship 4246
18: 3 For a the nations have drunk 4246
18:14 A your riches and splendor have vanished, 4246
18:17 and a who travel by ship, the sailors, 4246
18:17 and a **who** earn their living from the sea, 4012
18:19 where a who had ships on the sea 4246
18:23 By your magic spell a the nations 4246
18:24 *of* a who have been killed on the earth." 4246
19: 5 "Praise our God, a you his servants, 4246
19:17 a loud voice *to* a the birds flying in midair, 4246
19:18 and the flesh *of* a *people*, free and slave, 4246
19:21 and a the birds gorged themselves 4246
21: 7 He who overcomes will inherit a this, NIG
21: 8 the idolaters and a liars— 4246
22: 9 and *of* a **who** keep the words of this book. 3836

ALL-NIGHT (1) [NIGHT]
Jos 10: 9 After an a march from Gilgal, 2021+3972+4326

ALL-SURPASSING (1) [SURPASS]
2Co 4: 7 to show that this a power is from God and 5651

ALLAMMELECH (1)
Jos 19:26 A, Amad and Mishal. On the 526

ALLEGIANCE (3) [ALLY]
1Ki 12:27 they *will* **again give** their a to their lord, 4213+8740
Isa 19:18 and **swear a** to the LORD Almighty. 8678
Eze 21:23 like a false omen to those *who* have **sworn a** 8652+8678

ALLEGING (KJV) See PROVING

ALLEGORY (1)
Eze 17: 2 an a and tell the house of Israel a parable. 2648

ALLELUIA (KJV) See HALLELUIA

ALLEYS (1)
Lk 14:21 into the streets and a of the town and bring 4860

ALLIANCE (8) [ALLY]
1Ki 3: 1 Solomon **made an a** with Pharaoh king 3161
2Ch 20:35 of Judah **made an a** with Ahaziah king 2489
20:37 Because you *have* **made an a** with Ahaziah, 2489
Ps 83: 5 they form an a against you— 1382
Isa 30: 1 **forming an a**, but not by my Spirit, 5011+5818
Jer 50: 9 against Babylon an a *of* great nations from 7736
Da 11: 6 to the king of the North to make an a, 4797
11:17 of his entire kingdom and will make an a 3838

ALLIED (8) [ALLY]
Ge 14: 5 the kings a **with** him went out and defeated 907
14:13 all of whom were a *with* Abram. 1251+1382
14:17 and the kings a **with** him, 907
Jos 13:21 **princes** a with Sihon— AIT
1Ki 20:16 while Ben-Hadad and the 32 kings a **with** 6468
2Ch 18: 1 a himself with Ahab **by marriage**. 3161
Ps 94:20 *Can* a corrupt throne *be* a with you— 2489
Isa 7: 2 "Aram *has* a *itself* with Ephraim"; 5663

ALLIES (13) [ALLY]
1Ch 5:20 handed the Hagrites and all their a 6640+8611ˢ
Jer 13:21 as your special a? 476
22:20 for all your a are crushed. 170
22:22 and your a will go into exile. 170
30:14 All your a have forgotten you; 170
La 1:19 "I called to my a but they betrayed me. 170
Eze 30: 6 " 'The a *of* Egypt will fall 6164
31:17 its a among the nations, 2432
32:21 of Egypt and her a, 6468
Da 11: 6 After some years, *they* will become a. 2489
Ob 1: 7 All your a will force you to the border; 408+1382
Na 1:12 "Although *they* have a are numerous, 8969
3: 9 Put and Libya were among her a. 6476

ALLOCATE (1)
Jos 13: 6 *to* a this land to Israel for an inheritance, 5877

ALLON (1)
1Ch 4:37 the son of A, the son of Jedaiah, 474

ALLON BACUTH (1)
Ge 35: 8 So it was named A. 475

ALLOT (3) [ALLOTMENT, ALLOTS, ALLOTTED, ALLOTTING]
Eze 45: 1 " 'When you a the land as an inheritance, 5877
47:22 *to* a it as an inheritance for yourselves and 5877
48:29 *to* a as an inheritance to the tribes of Israel, 5877

ALLOTMENT (13) [ALLOT]
Ge 47:22 because they received a **regular** a 2976
47:22 from the a Pharaoh gave them. 2976
Dt 12:12 who have no a or inheritance of their own. 2750
14:27 they have no a or inheritance of their own. 2750
14:29 the Levites (who have no a or inheritance 2750
18: 1 are to have no a or inheritance with Israel. 2750
Jos 15: 1 The a for the tribe of Judah, clan by clan, 1598
16: 1 The a for Joseph began at the Jordan 1598
17: 1 This was the a for the tribe of Manasseh 1598
17: 2 So this a was for the rest of the people NIH
17:14 "Why have you given us only one a 1598
17:17 You will have not only one a 1598
Eze 48:13 the Levites will have an a 25,000 NIH

ALLOTS (4) [ALLOT]
Job 20:29 Such is the fate God a the wicked, 4946
21:17 the fate God a in his anger? 2745
27:13 "Here is the fate God a to the wicked, 6640
Isa 34:17 He a their portions, 5877

ALLOTTED (32) [ALLOT]
Lev 7:35 **portion** of the offerings made to the LORD by fire that were a AIT
Nu 26:53 *to* **be** a to them as an inheritance based on 2745
34: 2 the land that *will be* a to you as 5877
36: 3 the inheritance a to us will be taken away. 1598
Dt 32: 9 Jacob his a inheritance. 2475
Jos 14: 1 and the heads of the tribal clans of Israel a 5706
18:11 Their a territory lay between the tribes 1598
19:49 the land into its a **portions**, 1473
21: 4 of Aaron the priest *were* a thirteen towns 928+1598+2021+2118
21: 5 of Kohath's descendants were a ten towns 928+1598+2021
21: 6 of Gershon were a thirteen towns from the tribe 928+1598+2021
21: 8 the Israelites a to the Levites these towns 928+1598+2021+5989
21: 9 From the tribes of Judah and Simeon *they* a 5989
21:20 Levites *were* a towns from the tribe 1598+2118
21:40 All the towns a to the Merarite clans, 1598+2118
23: 4 Remember how *I* have a as an inheritance 5877
24:33 which *had* been a to his son Phinehas in 5989

Jdg 1: 3 "Come up with us into the **territory** a 1598
1Sa 18:26 So before the a **time** elapsed, 3427
1Ch 6:54 of their settlements a as their **territory** 1473
6:61 of Kohath's descendants were a ten towns 928+1598+2021
6:62 were a thirteen towns from the tribes 4200
6:63 were a twelve towns from the tribes 928+1598+2021
6:65 Simeon and Benjamin *they* a 928+1598+2021+5989
Ne 5:14 neither I nor my brothers ate the **food** a to AIT
5:18 I never demanded the **food** a to AIT
Job 7: 3 so I *have* been a months of futility, 5706
21:21 behind when his a months come to an end? 5031
Ps 78:55 and a their lands *to* them as an inheritance; 5877
125: 3 not remain over the *land* a *to* the righteous, 1598
Eze 47:22 with you *they are to be* a an inheritance 5877
Da 12:13 to receive your a **inheritance."** 1598

ALLOTTING (1) [ALLOT]
Ne 9:22 a *to* them even the remotest frontiers. 2745

ALLOW (19) [ALLOWANCE, ALLOWED, ALLOWING, ALLOWS]
Ex 10:25 "You *must* a us to have sacrifices 5989
22:18 "*Do* not a a sorceress **to live**. 2649
Nu 33:55 those *you* a **to remain** will become barbs 3855
35:32 a him *to* **go back** AIT
Jdg 6:39 A me one more **test** AIT
1Sa 16:22 saying, "A David *to* **remain** in my service, AIT
24: 7 and *did* not a them to attack Saul. 5989
2Ch 20:10 whose territory *you would* not a Israel 5989
Job 11:14 and a no evil **to dwell** 8905
Ps 132: 4 *I will* a no sleep to my eyes, 5989
Pr 6: 4 A no sleep to your eyes, 5989
Jer 13:14 *I will* a no **pity** or mercy or compassion 2798
Eze 45: 8 a the house of Israel **to possess** 5989
Mk 5:12 a us to go into them." NIG
11:16 not a anyone to carry merchandise through 918
Lk 4:41 But *he* rebuked them and *would* not a them 1572
Ac 16: 7 but the Spirit of Jesus *would* not a them to. 1572
27: 7 a us **to hold** our **course**, 4661
Ro 14:16 Do *not* a what you consider good *to be* **spoken of as evil.** AIT

ALLOWANCE (3) [ALLOW]
2Ki 25:30 by day the king gave Jehoiachin a regular a 786
Jer 52:34 of Babylon gave Jehoiachin a regular a 786
Lk 12:42 of his servants to give them their **food** a at 4991

ALLOWED (25) [ALLOW]
Ge 3:22 He must **not** be a to reach out his hand 7153
31: 7 However, God *has* not a him to harm me. 5989
46:34 *be* a *to* **settle** in the region of Goshen, AIT
48:11 God *has* a me **to see** your children too." 8011
Lev 11:39 " 'If an animal that you are a to eat dies, 4200
Nu 31:15 a all the women **to live?"** 2649
Dt 7:22 *You will* not *be* a to eliminate them all 3523
24: 4 is not a to marry her again 3523
Jdg 2:23 a those nations **to remain**; 5663
3:28 *they* a no one to cross over. 5989
2Sa 8: 2 and the third length *was* a to live. 2649
1Ki 1:48 who *has* a my eyes to see a successor 5989
1Ch 16:21 He a no man to oppress them; 5663
2Ch 25:13 and *had* not a *to* **take part** in AIT
34:11 had a **to fall into ruin.** 8845
Est 1: 8 By the king's command each guest *was* a 401+646
4: 2 because no one clothed in sackcloth was a NIH
Job 31:30 not a my mouth to sin by invoking a curse 5989
Ps 105:14 *He* a no one to oppress them; 5663
Eze 33:12 *will* not *be* a to live because 3523
Da 7:12 but *were* a *to* live for a period of time.) 10314
Ac 27: 3 and Julius, in kindness to Paul, a him to go 2205
28: 4 Justice *has* not a him **to live."** 1572
28:16 Paul *was* a to live by himself, 2205
1Co 14:34 They *are* not a to speak, 2205

ALLOWING (2) [ALLOW]
Lev 22:16 by a them *to* **eat** the sacred offerings and AIT
Jdg 1:34 not a them to come down into the plain. 5989

ALLOWS (2) [ALLOW]
Ex 21:22 woman's husband demands and the court a. 5989
Ro 14: 2 One man's faith a him to eat everything, NIG

ALLURE (1) [ALLURING]
Hos 2:14 "Therefore I *am* now *going to* a her; 7331

ALLURING (1) [ALLURE]
Na 3: 4 a, the mistress of sorceries, 2834+3202

ALLY (2) [ALLEGIANCE, ALLIANCE, ALLIED, ALLIES]
Jos 23:12 "But if you turn away and a *yourselves* 1815
Isa 48:14 LORD's **chosen** a will carry out his purpose 170

ALMIGHTY (345) [MIGHT]
Ge 17: 1 "I am God A; 8724
28: 3 May God A bless you 8724
35:11 And God said to him, "I am God A; 8724

Ge 43:14 And may God A grant you mercy before 8724
48: 3 "God A appeared to me at Luz in the land 8724
49:25 who helps you, because of the A, 8724
Ex 6: 3 to Isaac and to Jacob as God A, 8724
Nu 24: 4 who sees a vision from the A, 8724
24:16 who sees a vision from the A, 8724
Ru 1:20 because the A has made my life very bitter. 8724
1:21 the A has brought misfortune upon me." 8724
1Sa 1: 3 to worship and sacrifice to the LORD A 7372
1:11 she made a vow, saying, "O LORD A, 7372
4: 4 the ark of the covenant of the LORD A, 7372
15: 2 This is what the LORD A says: 7372
17:45 against you in the name of the LORD A, 7372
2Sa 5:10 because the LORD God A was with him. 7372
6: 2 the name of the LORD A, 7372
6:18 the people in the name of the LORD A. 7372
7: 8 'This is what the LORD A says: 7372
7:26 'The LORD A is God over Israel!' 7372
7:27 "O LORD A, God of Israel, 7372
1Ki 18:15 Elijah said, "As the LORD A lives, 7372
19:10 very zealous for the LORD God A. 7372
19:14 very zealous for the LORD God A. 7372
2Ki 3:14 "As surely as the LORD A lives, 7372
19:31 zeal of the LORD A will accomplish this. 7372
1Ch 11: 9 because the LORD A was with him. 7372
17: 7 'This is what the LORD A says: 7372
17:24 Then men will say, 'The LORD A, 7372
Job 5:17 so do not despise the discipline of the A. 8724
6: 4 The arrows of the A are in me, 8724
6:14 even though he forsakes the fear of the A. 8724
8: 3 Does the A pervert what is right? 8724
8: 5 you will look to God and plead with the A, 8724
11: 7 Can you probe the limits of the A? 8724
13: 3 to the A and to argue my case with God. 8724
15:25 at God and vaunts himself against the A, 8724
21:15 Who is the A, that we should serve him? 8724
21:20 let him drink of the wrath of the A. 8724
22: 3 What pleasure would it give the A 8724
22:17 What can the A do to us?' 8724
22:23 If you return to the A, you will be restored: 8724
22:25 then the A will be your gold, 8724
22:26 in the A and will lift up your face to God. 8724
23:16 the A has terrified me. 8724
24: 1 the A not set times for judgment? 8724
27: 2 who has denied me justice, the A, 8724
27:10 Will he find delight in the A? 8724
27:11 the ways of the A I will not conceal. 8724
27:13 a ruthless man receives from the A: 8724
29: 5 when the A was still with me 8724
31: 2 his heritage from the A on high? 8724
31:35 let the A answer me; 8724
32: 8 it is the spirit in a man, the breath of the A, 8724
33: 4 the breath of the A gives me life. 8724
34:10 from the A to do wrong. 8724
34:12 that the A would pervert justice. 8724
35:13 the A pays no attention to it. 8724
37:23 The A is beyond our reach and exalted 8724
40: 2 with the A correct him? 8724
Ps 24:10 The LORD A— he is the King of glory. 7372
46: 7 The LORD A is with us; 7372
46:11 The LORD A is with us; 7372
48: 8 have we seen in the city of the LORD A, 7372
59: 5 O LORD God A, the God of Israel, 7372
68:14 When the A scattered the kings in the land, 8724
69: 6 O Lord, the LORD A; 7372
80: 4 O LORD God A, 7372
80: 7 Restore us, O God A; 7372
80:14 Return to us, O God A! 7372
80:19 Restore us, O LORD God A; 7372
84: 1 lovely is your dwelling place, O LORD A! 7372
84: 3 a place near your altar, O LORD A, 7372
84: 8 Hear my prayer, O LORD God A; 7372
84:12 O LORD A, blessed is the man who trusts 7372
89: 8 O LORD God A, who is like you? 7372
91: 1 in the shadow of the A. 8724
Isa 1: 9 the LORD A had left us some survivors, 7372
1:24 Therefore the Lord, the LORD A, 7372
2:12 The LORD A has a day in store for all 7372
3: 1 See now, the Lord, the LORD A, 7372
3:15 declares the Lord, the LORD A. 7372
5: 7 The vineyard of the LORD A is the house 7372
5: 9 The LORD A has declared in my hearing: 7372
5:16 the LORD A will be exalted in his justice, 7372
5:24 of the LORD A and spurned the word of 7372
6: 3 "Holy, holy, holy is the LORD A; 7372
6: 5 the King, the LORD A." 7372
8:13 The LORD A is the one you are to regard 7372
8:18 and symbols in Israel from the LORD A, 7372
9: 7 zeal of the LORD A will accomplish this. 7372
9:13 nor have they sought the LORD A. 7372
9:19 the LORD A the land will be scorched and 7372
10:16 Therefore, the Lord, the LORD A, 7372
10:23 The Lord, the LORD A, 7372
10:24 this is what the Lord, the LORD A, says: 7372
10:26 The LORD A will lash them with a whip, 7372
10:33 See, the Lord, the LORD A, 7372
13: 4 LORD A is mustering an army for war. 7372
13: 6 it will come like destruction from the A. 8724
13:13 at the wrath of the LORD A, 7372
14:22 declares the LORD A. 7372
14:23 declares the LORD A. 7372
14:24 The LORD A has sworn, "Surely, 7372
14:27 For the LORD A has purposed, 7372
17: 3 declares the LORD A. 7372
18: 7 to the LORD A from a people tall 7372
18: 7 the place of the Name of the LORD A. 7372
19: 4 declares the Lord, the LORD A. 7372

Isa 19:12 the LORD A has planned against Egypt. 7372
19:16 the uplifted hand that the LORD A raises 7372
19:17 because of what the LORD A is planning 7372
19:18 and swear allegiance to the LORD A. 7372
19:20 be a sign and witness to the LORD A in 7372
19:25 The LORD A will bless them, saying, 7372
21:10 what I have heard from the LORD A, 7372
22: 5 The Lord, the LORD A, 7372
22:12 The Lord, the LORD A, 7372
22:14 The LORD A has revealed this 7372
22:14 says the Lord, the LORD A. 7372
22:15 This is what the Lord, the LORD A, says: 7372
22:25 "In that day," declares the LORD A, 7372
23: 9 The LORD A planned it, 7372
24:23 for the LORD A will reign on Mount Zion 7372
25: 6 the LORD A will prepare a feast 7372
28: 5 the LORD A will be a glorious crown, 7372
28:22 the Lord, the LORD A, 7372
28:29 All this also comes from the LORD A, 7372
29: 6 the LORD A will come with thunder 7372
31: 4 the LORD A will come down to do battle 7372
31: 5 the LORD A will shield Jerusalem; 7372
37:16 "O LORD A, God of Israel, enthroned 7372
37:32 zeal of the LORD A will accomplish this. 7372
39: 5 "Hear the word of the LORD A: 7372
44: 6 Israel's King and Redeemer, the LORD A: 7372
45:13 says the LORD A." 7372
47: 4 the LORD A is his name— 7372
48: 2 the LORD A is his name: 7372
51:15 the LORD A is his name. 7372
54: 5 the LORD A is his name— 7372
Jer 2:19 declares the Lord, the LORD A. 7372
5:14 the LORD God A says: 7372
6: 6 This is what the LORD A says: 7372
6: 9 This is what the LORD A says: 7372
7: 3 This is what the LORD A, 7372
7:21 " 'This is what the LORD A, 7372
8: 3 declares the LORD A.' 7372
9: 7 Therefore this is what the LORD A says: 7372
9:15 Therefore, this is what the LORD A, 7372
9:17 This is what the LORD A says: 7372
10:16 the LORD A is his name. 7372
11:17 The LORD A, who planted you, 7372
11:20 O LORD A, you who judge righteously 7372
11:22 therefore this is what the LORD A says: 7372
15:16 for I bear your name, O LORD God A. 7372
16: 9 For this is what the LORD A, 7372
19: 3 This is what the LORD A says: 7372
19:11 'This is what the LORD A says: 7372
19:15 the LORD A, the God of Israel, says: 7372
20:12 O LORD A, you who examine 7372
23:15 this is what the LORD A says concerning 7372
23:16 This is what the LORD A says: 7372
23:36 the LORD A, our God. 7372
25: 8 Therefore the LORD A says this: 7372
25:27 tell them, 'This is what the LORD A, 7372
25:28 tell them, 'This is what the LORD A says: 7372
25:29 declares the LORD A.' 7372
25:32 This is what the LORD A says: "Look! 7372
26:18 'This is what the LORD A says: 7372
27: 4 'This is what the LORD A says: 7372
27:18 let them plead with the LORD A that 7372
27:19 For this is what the LORD A says about 7372
27:21 this is what the LORD A, 7372
28: 2 the LORD A, the God of Israel, says: 7372
28:14 This is what the LORD A, 7372
29: 4 the LORD A, the God of Israel, says 7372
29: 8 Yes, this is what the LORD A, 7372
29:17 this is what the LORD A says: 7372
29:21 This is what the LORD A, 7372
29:25 the LORD A, the God of Israel, says: 7372
30: 8 " 'In that day,' declares the LORD A, 7372
31:23 This is what the LORD A, 7372
31:35 the LORD A is his name: 7372
32:14 the LORD A, the God of Israel, says: 7372
32:15 For this is what the LORD A, 7372
32:18 whose name is the LORD A, 7372
33:11 saying, "Give thanks to the LORD A, 7372
33:12 "This is what the LORD A says: 7372
33:13 the LORD A, the God of Israel, says: 7372
35:17 "Therefore, this is what the LORD God A, 7372
35:18 "This is what the LORD A, 7372
35:19 Therefore, this is what the LORD A, 7372
38:17 This is what the LORD God A, 7372
39:16 'This is what the LORD A, 7372
42:15 This is what the LORD A, 7372
42:18 This is what the LORD A, 7372
43:10 say to them, 'This is what the LORD A, 7372
44: 2 the LORD A, the God of Israel, says: 7372
44: 7 "Now this is what the LORD God A, 7372
44:11 "Therefore, this is what the LORD A, 7372
44:25 This is what the LORD A, 7372
46:10 that day belongs to the Lord, the LORD A— 7372
46:10 For the Lord, the LORD A, 7372
46:18 whose name is the LORD A, 7372
46:25 The LORD A, the God of Israel, says: 7372
48: 1 This is what the LORD A, 7372
48:15 whose name is the LORD A, 7372
49: 5 declares the Lord, the LORD A. 7372
49: 7 This is what the LORD A says: 7372
49:26 declares the LORD A. 7372
49:35 This is what the LORD A says: 7372
50:18 Therefore this is what the LORD A, 7372
50:25 for the Sovereign LORD A has work to do 7372
50:31 the LORD A, "for your day has come, 7372
50:33 This is what the LORD A says: 7372
50:34 the LORD A is his name. 7372

Jer 51: 5 the LORD A, though their land is full 7372
51:14 The LORD A has sworn by himself: 7372
51:19 the LORD A is his name. 7372
51:33 This is what the LORD A says: 7372
51:57 whose name is the LORD A. 7372
51:58 This is what the LORD A says: 7372
Eze 1:24 like the voice of the A, 7372
10: 5 like the voice of God A when he speaks. 8724
Hos 12: 5 the LORD God A, 7372
Joel 1:15 it will come like destruction from the A. 8724
Am 3:13 declares the Lord, the LORD God A. 7372
4:13 the LORD God A is his name. 7372
5:14 Then the LORD God A will be with you, 7372
5:15 the LORD God A will have mercy on 7372
5:16 the LORD God A, says: 7372
5:27 says the LORD, whose name is God A. 7372
6: 8 the LORD God A declares, 7372
6:14 For the LORD God A declares, 7372
9: 5 The Lord, the LORD A, 7372
Mic 4: 4 for the LORD A has spoken. 7372
Na 2:13 "I am against you," declares the LORD A. 7372
3: 5 "I am against you," declares the LORD A. 7372
Hab 2:13 Has not the LORD A determined that 7372
Zep 2: 9 as surely as I live," declares the LORD A, 7372
2:10 and mocking the people of the LORD A. 7372
Hag 1: 2 This is what the LORD A says: 7372
1: 5 Now this is what the LORD A says: 7372
1: 7 This is what the LORD A says: 7372
1: 9 declares the LORD A. 7372
1:14 to work on the house of the LORD A, 7372
2: 4 For I am with you,' declares the LORD A. 7372
2: 6 "This is what the LORD A says: 7372
2: 7 says the LORD A. 7372
2: 8 declares the LORD A. 7372
2: 9 says the LORD A. 7372
2: 9 declares the LORD A." 7372
2:11 "This is what the LORD A says: 7372
2:23 " 'On that day,' declares the LORD A, 7372
2:23 declares the LORD A." 7372
Zec 1: 3 This is what the LORD A says: 7372
1: 3 'Return to me,' declares the LORD A, 7372
1: 3 to you,' says the LORD A. 7372
1: 4 This is what the LORD A says: 7372
1: 6 'The LORD A has done 7372
1:12 the angel of the LORD said, "LORD A, 7372
1:14 This is what the LORD A says: 7372
1:16 declares the LORD A. 7372
1:17 This is what the LORD A says: 7372
2: 8 For this is what the LORD A says: 7372
2: 9 that the LORD A has sent me. 7372
2:11 that the LORD A has sent me to you. 7372
3: 7 "This is what the LORD A says: 7372
3: 9 says the LORD A, 7372
3:10 declares the LORD A." 7372
4: 6 but by my Spirit,' says the LORD A. 7372
4: 9 that the LORD A has sent me to you. 7372
5: 4 The LORD A declares, 'I will send it out, 7372
6:12 Tell him this is what the LORD A says: 7372
6:15 that the LORD A has sent me to you. 7372
7: 3 the priests of the house of the LORD A 7372
7: 4 the word of the LORD A came to me: 7372
7: 9 "This is what the LORD A says: 7372
7:12 the LORD A had sent by his Spirit through 7372
7:12 So the LORD A was very angry. 7372
7:13 I would not listen,' says the LORD A. 7372
8: 1 the word of the LORD A came to me. 7372
8: 2 This is what the LORD A says: 7372
8: 3 and the mountain of the LORD A will 7372
8: 4 This is what the LORD A says: 7372
8: 6 This is what the LORD A says: 7372
8: 6 declares the LORD A. 7372
8: 7 This is what the LORD A says: 7372
8: 9 This is what the LORD A says: 7372
8: 9 for the house of the LORD A, 7372
8:11 declares the LORD A. 7372
8:14 This is what the LORD A says: 7372
8:14 says the LORD A, 7372
8:18 the word of the LORD A came to me. 7372
8:19 This is what the LORD A says: 7372
8:20 This is what the LORD A says: 7372
8:21 the LORD and seek the LORD A. 7372
8:22 to seek the LORD A and to entreat him." 7372
8:23 This is what the LORD A says: 7372
9:15 and the LORD A will shield them. 7372
10: 3 for the LORD A will care for his flock, 7372
12: 5 because the LORD A is their God.' 7372
13: 2 declares the LORD A. 7372
13: 7 declares the LORD A. 7372
14:16 the King, the LORD A, and to celebrate 7372
14:17 the LORD A, they will have no rain. 7372
14:21 and Judah will be holy to the LORD A, 7372
14:21 a Canaanite in the house of the LORD A. 7372
Mal 1: 4 But this is what the LORD A says: 7372
1: 6 says the LORD A. 7372
1: 8 says the LORD A. 7372
1: 9 says the LORD A. 7372
1:10 says the LORD A. 7372
1:11 says the LORD A. 7372
1:13 says the LORD A. 7372
1:14 For I am a great king," says the LORD A, 7372
2: 2 says the LORD A. 7372
2: 4 says the LORD A. 7372
2: 7 he is the messenger of the LORD A. 7372
2: 8 with Levi," says the LORD A. 7372
2:12 he brings offerings to the LORD A. 7372
2:16 says the LORD A. 7372
3: 1 will come," says the LORD A. 7372

Mal 3: 5 but do not fear me," says the LORD A. 7372
3: 7 says the LORD A. 7372
3:10 Test me in this," says the LORD A, 7372
3:11 says the LORD A. 7372
3:12 says the LORD A. 7372
3:14 about like mourners before the LORD A? 7372
3:17 "They will be mine," says the LORD A, 7372
4: 1 says the LORD A. 7372
4: 3 says the LORD A. 7372
Ro 9:29 "Unless the Lord A had left us descendants, 4877
2Co 6:18 says the Lord A." 4120
Jas 5: 4 the ears of the Lord A. 4877
Rev 1: 8 and who was, and who is to come, the A." 4120
4: 8 "Holy, holy, holy is the Lord God A, 4120
11:17 "We give thanks to you, Lord God A, 4120
15: 3 and marvelous are your deeds, Lord God A. 4120
16: 7 "Yes, Lord God A, 4120
16:14 for the battle on the great day of God A. 4120
19: 6 For our Lord God A reigns. 4120
19:15 of the fury of the wrath of God A. 4120
21:22 Lord God A and the Lamb are its temple. 4120

ALMODAD (2)
Ge 10:26 Joktan was the father of A, Sheleph, 525
1Ch 1:20 Joktan was the father of A, Sheleph, 525

ALMON (1)
Jos 21:18 and A, together with their pasturelands— 6626

ALMON DIBLATHAIM (2) [BETH DIBLATHAIM]
Nu 33:46 and camped at A. 6627
33:47 They left A and camped in 6627

ALMOND (7) [ALMONDS]
Ge 30:37 a and plane trees and made white stripes 4280
Ex 25:33 Three cups shaped like a flowers with buds 5481
25:34 to be four cups shaped like a flowers 5481
37:19 Three cups shaped like a flowers with buds 5481
37:20 lampstand were four cups shaped like a flowers 5481
Ecc 12: 5 when the a tree blossoms and 9196
Jer 1:11 "I see the branch of an a tree," I replied. 9196

ALMONDS (2) [ALMOND]
Ge 43:11 some pistachio nuts and a. 9196
Nu 17: 8 blossomed and produced a. 9196

ALMOST (16)
Ex 17: 4 They are a ready to stone me." 5071+6388
Jos 10:20 a to a man— 4392+6330+9462
Jdg 19: 9 said, "Now look, it's a evening. 8332
19:11 near Jebus and the day was a gone, 4394
2Sa 1: 6 with the chariots and riders a upon him. 1815
Job 10:20 Are not my few days a over? AIT
Ps 73: 2 But as for me, my feet had a slipped; 3869+5071
119:87 They a wiped me from the earth, 3869+5071
Lk 8:42 the crowds a crushed him. AIT
24:29 the day is a over." 3111
Jn 2:13 it was a time for the Jewish Passover, 1584
11:55 When it was a time for the Jewish Passover, 1584
Ac 13:44 the next Sabbath a the whole city gathered 5385
Ro 13:12 The night is nearly over; the day is a here. 1581
Php 2:27 Indeed he was ill, and a died. 4180
2:30 because he a died for the work of Christ, 1581

ALMS (KJV) See ACTS OF RIGHTEOUSNESS, GIVE TO NEEDY, TO THE POOR

ALMSDEEDS (KJV) See HELPING THE POOR

ALMUGWOOD (3) [ALGUM]
1Ki 10:11 they brought great cargoes of a 523+6770
10:12 The king used the a to make supports 523+6770
10:12 So much a has never been imported 523+6770

ALOES (5)
Nu 24: 6 like a planted by the LORD, 193
Ps 45: 8 with myrrh and a and cassia; 189
Pr 7:17 with myrrh, a and cinnamon. 193
SS 4:14 with myrrh and a and all the finest spices. 189
Jn 19:39 a mixture of myrrh and a, 264

ALONE (123) [LONELY]
Ge 2:18 "It is not good for the man to be a. 963+4200
32:24 So Jacob was left a, 963+4200
Ex 4:26 So the LORD let him a. 8332
14:12 Leave us a; let us serve the Egyptians 2532+4946
18:14 Why do you a sit as judge, 963+4200
18:18 you cannot handle it a. 963+4200
21: 3 If he comes a, he is to go free alone; 928+1727+2257
21: 3 If he comes alone, he is to go free a; 928+1727+2257
24: 2 but Moses a is to approach the LORD; 963+4200
32:10 Now leave me a so that my anger may burn 5663

Lev 13:46 He must live a; 970
Nu 11:17 so that you will not have to carry it a. 963+4200
18: 1 and you and your sons a are to bear NIH
Dt 1: 9 a burden for me to carry a. 963+4200
8: 3 not live on bread a but on every word 963+4200
9:14 Let me a, so that I may destroy them 8332
16:20 Follow justice and justice a, AIT
32:12 The LORD a led him; 970
33:28 So Israel will live in safety a; 970
Jdg 3:20 approached him while he was sitting a 963+4200
1Sa 21: 1 and asked, "Why are you a? 963+4200
25:24 "My lord, let the blame be on me a. 638+3276
2Sa 16:11 this Benjamite! Leave him a; 5663
18:24 he looked out, he saw a man running a. 963+4200
18:25 The king said, "If he is a, 963+4200
18:26 "Look, another man running a!" 963+4200
1Ki 3:18 also had a baby. We were a; 3481
8:39 you know his heart (for you a know 963+4200
11:29 two of them were a out in the country, 963+4200
2Ki 4:27 but the man of God said, "Leave her a! 8332
19:15 you a are God over all the kingdoms of 963+4200
19:19 on earth may know that you a, 963+4200
23:18 "Leave it a," he said. 5663
2Ch 6:30 you know his heart (for you a know 963+4200
Ezr 4: 3 We a will build it for the LORD, 3480
Ne 9: 6 You a are the LORD. 963+4200
Est 4:13 because you are in the king's house you a NIH
Job 7:16 Let me a; my days have no meaning. 2532
7:19 or let me a even for an instant? 8332
9: 8 He a stretches out the heavens 963+4200
14: 6 So look away from him and let him a, 2532
15:19 (to whom a the land was given 963+4200
19: 4 my error remains my concern a. AIT
21:14 Yet they say to God, 'Leave us a! 4946+6073
22:17 They said to God, 'Leave us a! 4946+6073
23:13 he stands a, and who can oppose him? 285+928
28:23 to it and he a knows where it dwells, 2085
Ps 4: 8 for you a, O LORD, 970+4200
62: 1 My soul finds rest in God a; 421
62: 2 He a is my rock and my salvation; 421
62: 5 in God a; my hope comes from him. 421
62: 6 He a is my rock and my salvation; 421
71:16 I will proclaim your righteousness, yours a. 963+4200
72:18 who a does marvelous deeds. 963+4200
76: 7 You a are to be feared. 911+911
83:18 you a are the Most High over all the earth. 963+4200
86:10 you a are God. 963+4200
102: 7 I have become like a bird a on a roof. 969
136: 4 to him who a does great wonders, 963+4200
148:13 for his name a is exalted; 963+4200
Pr 5:17 Let them be yours a, 963+4200
9:12 if you are a mocker, you a will suffer." 963+4200
Ecc 4: 8 There was a man all a; 401+9108
4:11 But how can one keep warm a? AIT
SS 6: 6 Each has its twin; not one of them is a. 8891
6: 6 Each has its twin, not one of them is a. 8891
Isa 2:11 the LORD a will be exalted in that day, 963+4200
2:17 the LORD a will be exalted in that day, 963+4200
5: 8 till no space is left and you live a in 963+4200
26:13 but your name a do we honor. 963+4200
37:16 you a are God over all the kingdoms of 963+4200
37:20 on earth may know that you a, 963+4200
44:24 who a stretched out the heavens 963+4200
45:24 'In the LORD a are righteousness NIH
49:21 I was left all a, but these— 963+4200
63: 3 "I have trodden the winepress a; 963+4200
Jer 15:17 I sat a because your hand was on me 970
41: 8 So he let them a and did not kill them 2532
49:31 its people live a. 970
La 3:28 Let him sit a in silence, 970
Eze 14:16 While they were killing and I was left a, 8636
14:16 They a would be saved, 963+4200
14:18 They a would be saved. 963+4200
37: 3 I said, "O Sovereign LORD, you a know." AIT
44:16 They a are to enter my sanctuary; AIT
44:16 they a are to come near my table to minister AIT
Da 10: 8 I was left a, gazing at this great vision; 963+4200
11: 8 leave the king of the North a. 4946+6641
Hos 4:17 Ephraim is joined to idols; leave him a! 5663
8: 9 to Assyria like a wild donkey wandering a. 969
Mt 4: 4 'Man does not live on bread a, 3668
14:23 When evening came, he was there a, 3668
27:49 The rest said, "Now leave him a. 918
Mk 2: 7 Who can forgive sins but God a?" 1651
4:10 When he was a, 2848+3668
4:34 when he was a with his own disciples, 2625+2848
6:47 and he was a on land. 3668
9: 2 where they were all a. 2625
10:18 "No one is good—except God a. 1651
14: 6 "Leave her a," said Jesus. 918
15:36 "Now leave him a. 918
Lk 4: 4 'Man does not live on bread a.' " 3668
5:21 Who can forgive sins but God a?" 3668
9:36 they found that Jesus was a. 3668
13: 8 'leave it a for one more year, 918
18:19 "No one is good—except God a. 1651
Jn 6:22 but that they had gone away a. 3668
8:16 my decisions are right, because I am not a. 3668
8:29 he has not left me a, 3667
12: 7 "Leave her a," Jesus replied. 918
16:32 You will leave me all a. 3667
16:32 Yet I am not a, for my Father is with me. 3668
17:20 "My prayer is not for them a. 3667
Ac 5:38 Leave these men a! 923
Ro 4:23 credited to him" were written not for him a, 3668

Ro 14: 7 of us lives to himself a and none of us dies NIG
14: 7 and none of us dies to himself a. NIG
1Co 7: 4 not belong to her but also to her husband. NIG
7: 4 not belong to him a but also to his wife. NIG
1Ti 5: 5 in need and left all a puts her hope 3670
6:16 who a is immortal and who lives 3668
Jas 2:24 by what he does and not by faith a. 3667
Rev 15: 4 For you a are holy. 3668

ALONG (307) [ALONGSIDE]
Ge 1:24 livestock, creatures that move a the ground, NIH
1:25 the creatures that move a the ground AIT
1:26 the creatures that move a the ground." 6584
2:14 it runs a the east side of Asshur. 2143
6: 7 creatures that move a the ground, 8254
6:20 and of every kind of creature that moves a AIT
7: 8 and of all creatures that move a the ground, 6584
7:14 every creature that moves a the ground 6584
7:23 and animals and the creatures that move a NIH
8:17 all the creatures that move a the ground— 6584
8:19 that move a the ground and all the birds— NIH
9: 2 that moves a the ground, and upon all 8253
15: 9 a with a dove and a young pigeon." 2256
18:16 and Abraham walked a with them 2143
24:59 a with her nurse and Abraham's servant 2256
31:18 a with all the goods he had accumulated 2256
33:14 while I move a slowly at the pace of 5633
43: 4 If you will send our brother a with us, 907
43: 8 the boy a with me and we will go at once, 907
44: 2 a with the silver for his grain." 2256
46:32 tend livestock, and they have brought a AIT
48: 1 and Ephraim a with him. 6640
49:17 a viper a the path, 6584
49:30 a with the field. NIH
50:13 a with the field. 907
50:22 a with all his father's family. 2256
Ex 2: 3 the child in it and put it among the reeds a 6584
2: 5 and her attendants were walking a 6584
2:17 Some shepherds came a 995
7:24 And all the Egyptians dug a the Nile 6017
10:10 a with your women and children! 2256
12: 8 a with bitter herbs, 6584
14: 7 a with all the other chariots of Egypt, 2256
18: 8 and about all the hardships they had met a 928
23:18 to me a with anything containing yeast. 6584
23:20 to guard you a the way and to bring you to 928
26: 4 Make loops of blue material a the edge of 6584
26:10 Make fifty loops a the edge of 6584
26:10 and also a edge of the end curtain in 6584
28: 1 a with his sons Nadab and Abihu, 907
29: 3 a with the bull and the two rams. 2256
29:25 on the altar a with the burnt offering for 6584
34:25 to me a with anything containing yeast, 6584
36:11 Then they made loops of blue material a 6584
36:17 Then they made fifty loops a the edge of 6584
36:17 and also a the edge of the end curtain in 6584
Lev 5: 2 creatures that move a the ground— 9238
7:12 then a with this thank offering he is 6584
7:13 A with his fellowship offering 6584
11:31 Of all those that move a the ground, 9238
14:10 a with three-tenths of an ephah 2256
14:12 a with the log of oil; 2256
20:25 or anything that moves a the ground— 8253
24: 7 A each row put some pure incense as 6584
Nu 1:47 were not counted a with the others. 928+9348
2:33 were not counted a with the other Israelites, 928+9348
5: 8 to the priest, a with the ram 963+4200+4946
13:23 a with some pomegranates and figs. 6584
13:29 Canaanites live near the sea and the a 3338+6584
14:25 and set out toward the desert a the route to AIT
15:24 a with its prescribed grain offering 2256
16:46 a with fire from the altar, 2256
20:17 We will travel a the king's highway and 2143
20:19 "We will go a the main road, 928
21: 1 heard that Israel was coming a the road AIT
21: 4 traveled from Mount Hor a AIT
21:15 of Ar and lie a the border of Moab." 4200
21:22 We will travel a the king's highway 928
21:33 Then they turned and went up a the road AIT
22: 1 of Moab and camped a the Jordan across 4200
26:10 and swallowed them a with Korah, 2256
26:62 not counted a with the other Israelites 928+9348
28: 8 a with the same kind of grain offering NIH
31: 6 a with Phinehas son of Eleazar, the priest, 2256
33:49 There on the plains of Moab they camped a 6584
34: 3 of the Desert of Zin a the border of Edom. 6584
34:11 and continue a the slopes east of the Sea 6584
34:12 down a the Jordan and end at the Salt Sea. 2025
Dt 1: 7 in the Negev and a the coast, 928
1:40 set out toward the desert a the route AIT
2: 1 set out toward the desert a the route AIT
2: 8 and traveled a the desert road of Moab. 6296
2:37 the land a the course of the Jabbok nor that 3338
3: 1 and went up a the road toward Bashan, AIT
4:18 like any creature that moves a the ground 928
6: 7 when you sit at home and when you walk a 928
11:19 when you sit at home and when you walk a 928
24: 9 to Miriam a the way after you came out 928
25:17 to you a the way when you came out 928
31: 4 whom he destroyed a with their land. 2256
33: 5 a with the tribes of Israel. 3480
Jos 2:22 the pursuers had searched all a the road 928
5:22 of the Jordan and all the Canaanite kings a 6584
6: 2 a with its king and its fighting men. 2256
7:15 a with all that belongs to him. 2256

Jos	9: 1	the western foothills, and a the entire coast	928
	10:10	Israel **pursued** them a the road going up	AIT
	15: 4	*It* then **passed** a to Azmon and joined	6296
	15: 7	It **continued** a to the waters of En Shemesh	6296
	15: 8	Then it ran up the Valley of Ben Hinnom a	448
	15:10	ran a the northern slope of Mount Jearim	448
	15:11	**passed** a to Mount Baalah	6296
	17: 4	Joshua gave them an inheritance a with	928+9348
	18:14	on the south the boundary turned south a	4200
	18:16	the Hinnom Valley a the southern slope of	448
Jdg	5:10	and you who walk a the road,	6584
	11:18	passed the eastern side of the country	4946
	11:26	and all the towns a the Arnon.	3338+6584
	14: 9	with his hands and ate as *he* went a.	2143+2143
	18:20	and the carved image and went a with	928+7931
	20:45	the Israelites cut down five thousand men a	928
Ru	2: 9	and **follow** a after the girls.	2143
	4: 1	the kinsman-redeemer he had mentioned came a,	6296
1Sa	1:24	a with a three-year-old bull,	928
	6:11	the cart and a with it the chest containing	NIH
	7:11	slaughtering them a the way to	NIH
	15: 6	so that I do not destroy you a with them;	6640
	17:18	**Take** a these ten cheeses to the commander	995
	17:52	Their dead were strewn a	928
	18: 4	a with his tunic, and even his sword,	2256
	19:23	and *he* **walked** a prophesying until	2143+2143
	23:26	Saul was going a one side of the mountain,	4946
	24: 3	He came to the sheep pens a the way;	6584
	29:10	Now get up early, a with	2256
	31: 7	Israelites a the valley and those across	928+6298
2Sa	5:11	a with cedar logs and carpenters	2256
	8: 3	to restore his control a the Euphrates River.	928
	15:18	a with all the Kerethites and Pelethites;	2256
	15:19	"Why should you come a with us?	907
	16:13	So David and his men continued a the road	928
	16:13	along the road while Shimei was going a	6584
	19:17	a thousand Benjamites, a with Ziba,	2256
1Ki	6:10	he built the side rooms all a the temple.	6584
	9:25	burning incense before the LORD a with	907
	10:22	of trading ships at sea a with the ships	6640
	18: 7	Obadiah was **walking** a, Elijah met him.	928+2006+2021
2Ki	2:11	were **walking** a and talking *together*,	2143+2143
	2:23	As he was **walking** a,	928
	4:42	a with some heads of new grain.	2256
	6:30	As he went a the wall, the people looked,	6584
	10:16	Then *he* had him **ride** a in his chariot.	8206
	14: 9	Then a wild beast in Lebanon came a	6296
	15:25	a with Argob and Arieh,	907
	25:11	a with the rest of the populace	2256
1Ch	7:29	A the borders of Manasseh were Beth Shan,	6584
	14: 1	a with cedar logs,	2256
	18: 3	when he went to establish his control a	928
	25: 7	A with their relatives—	6640
2Ch	21: 4	put all his brothers to the sword a with	1685+2256
	25:18	Then a wild beast in Lebanon came a	6296
	30:25	a with the priests and Levites	2256
	35: 9	Conaniah a with Shemaiah and Nethanel,	2256
Ezr	1:11	Sheshbazzar **brought** all these a when	6590
	2:70	a with some of the other people,	2256
	8:31	from enemies and bandits a the way.	6584
	10:14	a with the elders and judges of each town,	6640
Ne	4:19	from each other a the way.	6584
	7: 2	a with Hananiah the commander of	2256
	7:73	a with certain of the people and the rest of	2256
	8:13	a with the priests and the Levites,	NIH
	9:24	to them, a with their kings and the peoples	2256
	12:33	a with Azariah, Ezra, Meshullam,	2256
Est	5:12	And she has invited me a with	6640
	9:29	a with Mordecai the Jew,	2256
Job	1:10	"If *he* **comes** a and confines you in prison	2736
	39:23	a with the flashing spear and lance.	NIH
	40:15	which I made a with you and which feeds	5973
	42:15	an inheritance a with their brothers.	928+9348
Ps	26: 9	Do not take away my soul a with sinners,	6640
	58: 8	Like a slug melting away *as it* **moves** a,	2143
	87: 4	Philistia too, and Tyre, a with Cush—	6640
	140: 5	of their net and have set traps for me a	3338+4200
Pr	1:11	If they say, "Come a with us;	907
	1:15	do not go a with them,	907
	4:11	of wisdom and lead you a straight paths.	928
	7: 8	**walking** a *in* the direction of her house	7575
	8: 2	On the heights a the way,	6584
	8:20	a the paths of justice,	928+9348
	12:28	a that path is immortality.	2006
	28:10	the upright a an evil path will fall	928
Ecc	10: 3	Even as he **walks** a the road,	928
	12: 5	and the grasshopper **drags** himself a	6022
Isa	3:16	**walking** a with outstretched necks,	2143
	3:16	**tripping** a with mincing steps,	2143+2256+3262
	5:18	*those who* **draw** sin a with cords of deceit,	5432
	9: 1	by the way of the sea, a the Jordan—	6298
	14:11	a with the noise of your harps;	NIH
	15: 8	Their outcry **echoes** a the border of Moab;	5938
	18: 1	the land of whirring wings a the rivers	4946+6298
	19: 7	also the plants a the Nile,	6584
	19: 7	Every **sown field** *a* the Nile,	AIT
	19:24	a with Egypt and Assyria,	4200
	23:10	Till your land as a the Nile,	NIH
	42:16	a unfamiliar paths I will guide them;	928
	59:10	Like the blind *we* **grope** a the wall,	1779
	59:19	that the breath of the LORD **drives** a.	5674
	60: 8	"Who are these *that* **fly** a like clouds,	6414
Jer	19: 1	Take a some of the elders of the people and	NIH
	23:39	of my presence a the city I gave to you	2256
	26:22	a with some other men.	907

Jer	27:20	a with all the nobles of Judah	2256
	32:29	they will burn it down, a with the houses	2256
	39: 9	a with those who had gone over to him,	2256
	41: 9	the men he had killed a with Gedaliah	928+3338
	41:10	the king's daughters a with all	2256
	44:15	a with all the women who were present—	2256
	49:18	a with their neighboring towns,"	2256
	50:40	and Gomorrah a with	2256
	52:15	a with the rest of the craftsmen	2256
Eze	1:20	the wheels would rise a with them,	4200+6645
	1:21	the wheels rose a with them,	4200+6645
	16:53	and your fortunes a with them,	928+9348
	20:40	a all your holy sacrifices.	928
	21:12	They are thrown to the sword a with	907
	23:42	from the desert a with men from the rabble,	448
	25:10	I will give Moab a with the Ammonites to	6584
	25:16	and destroy those **remaining** *a* the coast.	AIT
	30: 5	by the sword a with Egypt.	907
	38:20	every creature that moves a the ground	6584
	39: 2	I will turn you around and **drag** you a.	9255
	40:14	He **measured** *a* the faces of	AIT
	40:17	there were thirty rooms a the pavement.	448
	42:10	On the south side a the length of the wall	928
	45:24	a with a hin of oil for each ephah.	2256
	46: 5	a with a hin of oil for each ephah.	2256
	46: 7	a with a hin of oil with each ephah.	2256
	46:11	a with a hin of oil for each ephah.	2256
	47:10	Fishermen will stand a the shore;	6584
	47:17	a the northern border of Damascus,	NIH
	47:18	a the Jordan between Gilead and the land	NIH
	47:19	then a the Wadi [of Egypt] to	NIH
	47:22	a with you they are to divide	907
	48:20	a with the property of the city.	448
	48:28	then a the Wadi [of Egypt] to	NIH
Da	1: 2	a with some of the articles from the temple	2256
	6:24	a with their wives and children.	NIH
Hos	2:18	and the **creatures that move** *a* the ground.	AIT
	9: 8	The prophet, a with my God,	6640
Joel	2: 4	*they* **gallop** a like cavalry.	8132
	2: 9	they run a the wall.	928
Am	3:15	the winter house a with the summer house;	6584
	4:10	a with your captured horses.	6640
Mt	4:15	a the Jordan, Galilee of the Gentiles—	4305
	10: 9	*Do* not **take** a any gold or silver or copper	3227
	13: 4	some fell a the path,	4123
	13:19	This is the seed sown a the path.	4123
	15:29	Jesus left there and went a the Sea	4123
	18:16	he will not listen, take one or two others a,	3552
	22:16	They sent their disciples to him a with	3552
	25: 4	however, took oil in jars a with their lamps.	3552
	26:37	**took** Peter and the two sons of Zebedee a	4161
Mk	2:14	*As he* **walked** a,	4135
	2:23	and as his disciples **walked** a,	3847+4472
	4: 1	while all the people were a the shore at	2093
	4: 4	some fell a the path,	4123
	4:15	Some people are like seed a the path,	4123
	4:36	*they* **took** him a, just as he was, in the boat.	4161
	8:34	Then he called the crowd to him a with	5250
	10:52	and followed Jesus a the road.	1877
	11:20	In the morning, *as they* **went** a,	4182
	14:33	He took Peter, James and John a with him,	3552
Lk	1: 7	and they were both **well** a in years.	4581
	1:18	I am an old man and my wife is **well** a	4581
	5:12	a man came a who was covered	NIG
	7:11	and a large crowd **went** a with him.	5233
	8: 5	some fell a the path;	4123
	8:12	Those a the path are the ones who hear,	4123
	9:57	As they were **walking** a the road,	1877
	17: 7	'Come a now and sit down to eat'?	4216
	17:11	Jesus **traveled** a the border	1451
	19:36	*As* he **went** a,	4513
	23:33	a with the criminals—	2779
	24:15	Jesus himself came up and **walked** a with	5233
	24:17	*as you* **walk** a?"	4344
Jn	8:25	"Just what I have been claiming **all** a,"	794+3836
	9: 1	*As* he **went** a, he saw a man blind from birth	4135
	11:33	Jews who *had* **come** a with her also weeping,	5302
Ac	1:14	a with the women and Mary the mother	5250
	8:36	As they traveled a the road,	2848
	10:23	some of the brothers from Joppa **went** a.	5302
	15: 2	a with some other believers,	2779
	16: 3	Paul wanted to take him a on the journey,	899+5250
	19:25	a with the workmen in related trades,	2779
	21:26	the men and purified himself a with them.	5250
	25: 3	an ambush to kill him a the way.	2848
	27: 2	from Adramyttium about to sail for ports a	2848
	27: 8	We **moved** a the coast with difficulty	4162
	27:13	and sailed a **the shore** of Crete.	839
	27:15	so *we* gave way to it and *were* **driven** a.	5770
	27:17	let the ship *be* **driven** a.	5770
Ro	8:32	how will he not also, a with him,	5250
1Co	7:36	and if she is **getting** a **in years**	5644
	9: 5	**take** a believing wife a	4310
	16:11	I am expecting him a with the brothers.	3552
2Co	8:18	And we are sending a with him	3552
	12:19	Have you been thinking **all** a	4093
Gal	2: 1	*I* **took** Titus a also.	5221
	3: 9	So those who have faith are blessed a with	5250
Eph	4:31	a with every form of malice.	5250
Php	4: 3	a with Clement and the rest	3552
1Ti	5:14	with the faith and love that are	3552
2Ti	2:22	a with those who call on the Lord out of	3552
Heb	11:25	He chose *to be* **mistreated** a with the people	5156
2Pe	1:21	*as they were* **carried** *a* by the Holy Spirit.	AIT

3Jn	1: 2	even as your soul **is getting** a **well.**	2338
Jude	1:12	**blown** a by the wind;	4195
Rev	17:12	as kings a with the beast.	3552

ALONGSIDE (5) [ALONG]

Ex	20:23	Do not make any gods to be a me;	907
Nu	21:13	They set out from there and camped a	4946+6298
1Ch	26:16	Guard was a of guard;	4200+6645
Eze	27: 9	the ships of the sea and their sailors came a	928
	48:13	"A the territory of the priests,	4200+6645

ALOOF (3)

Job	21:16	I **stand** a from the counsel of the wicked.	8178
	22:18	I **stand** a from the counsel of the wicked.	8178
Ob	1:11	On the day you stood a	4946+5584

ALOTH (1)

1Ki	4:16	Baana son of Hushai—in Asher and in A;	6599

ALOUD (33) [LOUD]

Ge	27:38	Then Esau wept a.	5951+7754
	29:11	Jacob kissed Rachel and began to weep a.	906+5951+7754
Nu	14: 1	community raised their voices and **wept** a.	1134
Jdg	2: 4	the people wept a,	906+5951+7754
Ru	1: 9	Then she kissed them and they wept a	5951+7754
1Sa	11: 4	they all wept a.	906+5951+7754
	24:16	And he wept **a.**	5951+7754
	30: 4	So David and his men wept a	906+5951+7754
2Sa	3:32	the king wept a at Abner's tomb.	906+5951+7754
	13:19	**weeping** a as she went.	2410
	15:23	The whole countryside wept a as all	1524+7754
	19: 4	The king covered his face and cried a,	1524+7754
Ezr	3:12	wept a when they saw the foundation	928+1524+7754
Ne	8: 3	*He* read it from daybreak till noon	7924
	13: 1	Book of Moses was **read** a in the hearing	7924
Job	2:12	they began to weep a,	5951+7754
Ps	3: 4	To the LORD I cry a,	7754
	26: 7	proclaiming a your praise and telling	928+7754
	81: 1	**shout** a to the God of Jacob!	8131
	95: 1	*let us* **shout** a to the Rock	8131
	142: 1	I cry a to the LORD;	7754
Pr	1:20	Wisdom **calls** a in the street,	8264
	2: 3	for insight and **cry** a for understanding,	5989+7754
	8: 3	at the entrances, *she* **cries** a:	8264
Isa	12: 6	**Shout** a and sing for joy, people of Zion,	7412
	33: 7	Look, their brave men **cry** a in the streets;	7590
	44:23	**shout** a, O earth beneath.	8131
	58: 1	"**Shout** it a, do not hold back.	928+1744+7924
Jer	4: 5	Cry a and say: 'Gather together!	4848
	51:61	**read** all these words **a.**	7924
Mic	4: 9	Why *do you* now **cry** a—	8131+8275
Zep	3:14	Sing, O Daughter of Zion; **shout** a,	8131
Gal	4:27	break forth and **cry** a,	1066

ALPHA (3)

Rev	1: 8	"I am the A and the Omega,"	270
	21: 6	I am the A and the Omega,	270
	22:13	I am the A and the Omega,	270

ALPHAEUS (5)

Mt	10: 3	James *of* A, and Thaddaeus;	271
Mk	2:14	*of* A sitting at the tax collector's booth.	271
	3:18	Thomas, James son *of* A, Thaddaeus,	271
Lk	6:15	Thomas, James son *of* A,	271
Ac	1:13	James *son of* A and Simon the Zealot,	271

ALREADY (89) [READY]

Ge	18:11	and Sarah were a old and well advanced	NIH
	28: 9	in addition to the wives *he* a had.	AIT
	33: 9	But Esau said, "I *a* **have** plenty, my brother.	AIT
Ex	1: 5	Joseph was *a* in Egypt.	AIT
	4:14	He is a on his way to meet you,	2180
	30:13	to those *a* **counted** is to give a half shekel,	AIT
	36: 7	what *they* *a* **had** was more than enough	AIT
Lev	13:11	because he is a unclean.	NIH
	27:26	since the firstborn *a* **belongs** to the LORD;	NIH
Nu	14:14	*They have a* **heard** that you, O LORD,	AIT
	16:47	The plague *had a* **started** among the people,	AIT
Dt	14:21	Do not eat anything you find a **dead.**	5577
Jos	18: 7	Manasseh *have a* **received** their inheritance	AIT
Jdg	8: 6	"Do you *a* have the hands of Zebah	6964
	8:15	'Do you *a* have the hands of Zebah	6964
1Sa	29: 3	He *has a* **been** with me for over a year,	AIT
2Sa	13:16	a greater wrong than what *you have a* **done**	AIT
2Ch	20: 2	It is a in Hazazon Tamar" (that is, En Gedi).	2180
	28:13	For our guilt is a great,	NIH
Ne	5: 5	of our daughters *have a* **been enslaved,**	AIT
	9:25	wells *a* **dug,** vineyards,	AIT
Est	7: 7	realizing that the king *had a* **decided** his fate,	AIT
Job	9:29	Since I *am a* **found** guilty,	AIT
	38:21	Surely you know, for you were *a* born!	255
Ecc	1:10	It was here *a*, long ago;	3893
	2:12	What more can the king's successor do than what has *a* been done?	3893
	3:15	Whatever is has *a* been,	3893
	4: 2	I declared that the dead, who had *a* died,	3893
	6:10	Whatever exists has *a* been named,	3893
Isa	16:13	the LORD has *a* **spoken** concerning Moab.	255+4946

Isa	56: 8	to them besides *those a* gathered."	AIT
Da	8: 1	after the one that had *a* appeared to me.	928+2021+9378
Jnh	1:10	because *he had a* told them so.)	AIT
Mal	2: 2	Yes, *I have a* **cursed** them,	AIT
Mt	3:10	The ax is *a* at the root of the trees,	2453
	5:28	woman lustfully has *a* committed adultery	2453
	14:15	and it's getting late.	2453
	14:24	but the boat was *a a* considerable distance	2453
	15:32	they have *a* been with me three days	2453
	17:12	But I tell you, Elijah has *a* come,	2453
Mk	6:35	they said, "and it's a very late.	2453
	8: 2	they have *a* been with me three days	2453
	11:11	but since it was *a* late,	2453
	15:44	to hear that he was *a* dead.	2453
	15:44	he asked him if Jesus had *a* died.	4093
Lk	3: 9	The ax is *a* at the root of the trees,	2453
	6:24	for *you have a* **received** your comfort.	AIT
	11: 7	The door is *a* locked,	2453
	12:49	and how I wish it were *a* kindled!	2453
	19:25	" 'Sir,' they said, *'he a* has ten!'	AIT
Jn	3:18	not believe stands condemned *a*	2453
	6: 6	*he a had in* mind what he was going to do.	AIT
	9:22	for *a* the Jews had decided	2453
	9:27	"I have told you *a* and you did not listen.	2453
	11:17	Jesus found that Lazarus had *a* been in	2453
	13: 2	the devil had *a* prompted Judas Iscariot,	2453
	15: 3	You are *a* clean because of	2453
	19:33	to Jesus and found that he was *a* dead,	2453
Ac	10:41	*by* witnesses whom God *had a* **chosen**—	4742
	27: 9	and sailing had *a* become dangerous	2453
Ro	3: 9	*We have a* **made the charge** that Jews	4577
	8:24	Who hopes for what *he a* has?	AIT
1Co	3:11	the one *a* laid,	AIT
	4: 8	*A* you have all you want!	2453
	4: 8	*A* you have become rich!	2453
	5: 3	And I have *a* passed judgment on	2453
	6: 7	you have been completely defeated *a.*	2453
	7:18	a man *a* **circumcised** when he was called?	AIT
2Co	10:16	not want to boast about **work** *a* **done**	2289
	11: 1	but *you are a* **doing that.**	AIT
	13: 2	I *a* gave you a **warning**	4625
Gal	1: 9	As *we have a* **said,** so now I say again:	4625
Eph	1: 8	as *I have a* **written** briefly.	4592
Php	3:12	Not that I have *a* obtained all this,	2453
	3:12	or have *a* been made perfect,	2453
	3:16	up to what *we have a* **attained.**	AIT
Col	1: 5	in heaven and that *you have a* **heard about**	4578
1Th	4: 6	as *we have a* **told** you and warned you.	4625
2Th	2: 2	saying that the day of the Lord *has a* **come.**	AIT
	2: 7	secret power of lawlessness is *a* at work;	2453
1Ti	5:15	in fact a turned away to follow Satan.	2453
2Ti	2:18	that the resurrection has *a* taken place,	2453
Heb	4: 6	*for there are a* **men** who offer	AIT
	9:11	*of* the good things **that are** *a* here,	AIT
2Pe	3:17	dear friends, *since you a* **know** this,	4589
1Jn	2: 8	and the true light is *a* shining.	2453
	4: 3	and even now is *a* in the world.	2453
Jude	1: 5	Though you *a* know all this,	562

ALSO (813)

Ge	1:16	He *a* made the stars.	2256
	2:12	aromatic resin and onyx are *a* there.)	NIH
	3: 6	*and a* desirable for gaining wisdom,	2256
	3: 6	She *a* gave some to her husband,	1685
	3:22	be allowed to reach out his hand and take *a*	1685
	4:22	Zillah *a* had a son, Tubal-Cain,	1685
	4:26	Seth *a* had a son, and he named him Enosh.	1685
	6: 4	in those days—and *a* afterward—	1685
	7: 3	*and a* seven of every kind of bird,	1685
	9:26	He *a* said, "Blessed be the Lord,	2256
	10:21	Sons were *a* born to Shem,	1685
	13: 5	*a* had flocks and herds and tents.	1685
	13: 7	The Canaanites and Perizzites were *a* living	1685
	14:12	They *a* carried off Abram's nephew Lot	2256
	15: 7	He *a* said to him, "I am the Lord,	1685
	16:11	The angel of the Lord *a* said to her:	2256
	17:15	God *a* said to Abraham,	2256
	19:25	*and a* the vegetation in the land.	2256
	19:35	to drink wine that night *a,*	1685
	19:38	The younger daughter *a* had a son,	1685
	20: 5	and didn't she *a* say, 'He is my brother'?	1685
	21:13	son of the maidservant into a nation *a,*	1685+2256
	22:20	"Milcah is *a* a mother:	1685
	22:24	whose name was Reumah, *a* had sons:	1685
	24:46	So I drank, and she watered the camels *a.*	1685
	24:53	he *a* gave costly gifts to her brother and	2256
	24:64	Rebekah *a* looked up and saw Isaac.	2256
	25:30	(That is why he was *a* called Edom.)	NIH
	26:21	but they quarreled over that one *a;*	1685
	26:34	*and a* Basemath daughter of Elon	2256
	27:16	She *a* covered his hands and	2256
	29:27	then we will give you the younger one *a,*	1685
	29:30	Jacob lay with Rachel *a,*	1685
	31:49	It was *a* called Mizpah, because he said,	2256
	31:51	Laban *a* said to Jacob, "Here is this heap,	2256
	32: 1	Jacob *a* went on his way,	2256
	32:11	and the mothers with their children.	NIH
	32:19	He *a* instructed the second,	1685
	35:12	The land I gave to Abraham and Isaac I *a*	NIH
	35:14	he *a* poured oil on it.	2256
	36: 3	*a* Basemath daughter of Ishmael and sister	2256
	36:12	Esau's son Eliphaz *a* had	2256
	38:10	so he put him to death *a.*	1685
	41:22	"In my dreams I *a* saw seven heads	2256

Ge	42: 5	for the famine was in the land of Canaan *a.*	NIH
	43:13	Take your brother *a* and go back to the man	2256
	43:15	the amount of silver, *and* Benjamin *a.*	2256
	43:22	We have *a* brought additional silver with us	2256
	44: 5	the cup my master drinks from *and a* uses	2256
	45:19	"You are *a* directed to tell them, 'Do this:	2256
	45:21	*and he a* gave them provisions	2256
	46: 6	They *a* took with them their livestock and	2256
	47: 4	They *a* said to him,	2256
	47:12	Joseph *a* provided his father	2256
	50: 9	Chariots and horsemen *a* went up with him.	1685
	50:23	*A* the children of Makir son	1685
Ex	3:15	God *a* said to Moses, "Say to the Israelites,	6388
	4:28	*and a* about all	2256
	4:30	He *a* performed the signs before the people,	2256
	6: 2	God *a* said to Moses, "I am the Lord.	2256
	6: 4	I *a* established my covenant with them	1685+2256
	7:11	and the Egyptian magicians *a* did	1685
	8: 7	they *a* made frogs come up on the land	2256
	8:32	But this time *a* Pharaoh hardened his heart	1685
	12:32	And *a* bless me."	1685
	14:19	The pillar of cloud *a* moved from front	2256
	16: 8	Moses *a* said, "You will know that it was	2256
	21:29	the bull must be stoned and the owner *a*	1685
	21:31	This law *a* applies if the bull gores a son	NIH
	25:25	*A* make around it a rim a handbreadth wide	2256
	26:10	the edge of the end curtain in one set *and a*	2256
	26:26	"A make crossbars of acacia wood:	2256
	26:29	*A* overlay the crossbars with gold.	2256
	27:11	The north side shall *a* be	4027
	27:13	the courtyard shall *a* be fifty cubits wide.	2256
	28:30	*A* put the Urim and the Thummim in	2256
	29:43	there *a* I will meet with the Israelites,	2256
	30:20	*A,* when they approach the altar to minister	196
	31: 6	*A* I have given skill to all the craftsmen	2256
	31:10	*and a* the woven garments,	2256
	35:28	They *a* brought spices and olive oil for	2256
	36:12	They *a* made fifty loops on one curtain	NIH
	36:17	the edge of the end curtain in one set *and a*	2256
	36:31	They *a* made crossbars of acacia wood:	2256
	36:34	They *a* overlaid the crossbars with gold.	2256
	37:12	They *a* made around it a rim	2256
	37:29	They *a* made the sacred anointing oil and	2256
	38:11	The north side was *a* a hundred cubits long	2256
	38:13	toward the sunrise, was *a* fifty cubits wide.	2256
	39: 1	They *a* made sacred garments for Aaron,	2256
Lev	6:19	The Lord *a* said to Moses,	2256
	8: 7	He *a* tied the ephod to him	2256
	8:16	Moses *a* took all the fat around	2256
	8:24	Moses *a* brought Aaron's sons forward	2256
	8:29	He *a* took the breast—	2256
	9: 17	He *a* brought the grain offering,	2256
	16:25	He shall *a* burn the fat of the sin offering	2256
	20:18	*and* she has *a* uncovered it.	2256
	22: 4	He will *a* be unclean	2256
	23:39	*and* the eighth day *a*	2256
	25:45	You may *a* buy some of	1685+2256
	26:39	*a* because of their fathers' sins will waste away.	677+2256
Nu	3:11	The Lord *a* said to Moses,	2256
	3:44	The Lord *a* said to Moses,	2256
	4:22	"Take a census *a* of the Gershonites	1685
	5:15	He must *a* take an offering of a tenth of	2256
	7: 1	He *a* anointed and consecrated the altar	2256
	10:10	*A* at your times of rejoicing—	2256
	11: 5	*a* the cucumbers, melons, leeks,	NIH
	11: 9	the manna *a* came down.	NIH
	11:26	Yet the Spirit *a* rested on them,	2256
	12: 2	"Hasn't *he a* spoken through us?"	1685
	15:10	*A* bring half a hin of wine as	2256
	16: 8	Moses *a* said to Korah, "Now listen,	2256
	16:13	And now you *a* want to lord it over us?	1685
	16:17	and Aaron are to present your censers *a.*"	2256
	18:11	"This *a* is yours:	2256
	18:28	In this way you *a* will present an offering	1685
	19: 8	The man who burns it must *a*	2256
	19:10	of the heifer must *a* wash his clothes,	2256
	19:18	must *a* sprinkle anyone who has touched	2256
	19:21	of cleansing must *a* wash his clothes,	2256
	26:58	These *a* were Levite clans:	NIH
	31: 8	They *a* killed Balaam son of Beor with	2256
	31:23	But it must *a* be purified with the water	421
Dt	1:37	of you the Lord became angry with me *a*	1685
	3: 3	So the Lord our God *a* gave	1685
	3: 5	and there were *a* a great many	963+4200
	3:13	The rest of Gilead *and a* all of Bashan,	2256
	9:21	*A* I took that sinful thing of yours,	2256
	9:22	You *a* made the Lord angry at Taberah,	2256
	10: 1	*A* make a wooden chest.	2256
	10:10	the Lord listened to me at this time *a.*	1685
	14: 8	The pig is *a* unclean.	2256
	22: 9	not only the crops you plant **but** *a* the fruit	2256
	28:61	The Lord will *a* bring on you every kind	1685
	29:15	the presence of the Lord our God **but** *a*	2256
	31: 3	Joshua *a* will cross over ahead of you,	NIH
Jos	8:22	The men of the ambush *a* came out of	2256
	10:30	The Lord *a* gave that city and its king	1685
	12: 3	He *a* ruled over the eastern Arabah from	2256
	13:11	It *a* included Gilead, the territory of	2256
	15:19	give me *a* springs of water."	1685
	16: 9	It *a* included all the towns	2256
	17:11	Manasseh *a* had Beth Shan,	2256
	21:23	*A* from the tribe of Dan	2256
	24:11	as did the Amorites, Perizzites,	2256
	24:12	*a* the two Amorite kings.	NIH
Jdg	1: 8	of Judah attacked Jerusalem *a* and took it.	2256
	1:15	give me *a* springs of water."	2256

Jdg	1:18	The men of Judah *a* took Gaza,	2256
	1:35	**And** the Amorites were determined *a*	2256
	4:10	*a* and Deborah *a* went with him.	2256
	6:35	and *a* into Asher, Zebulun and Naphtali,	1685
	7:25	They *a* captured two of	2256
	8:17	He *a* pulled down the tower of Peniel	2256
	8:31	who lived in Shechem, *a* bore him a son,	1685
	8:35	They *a* failed to show kindness to	2256
	9:49	about a thousand men and women, *a* died.	1685
	9:57	God *a* made the men of Shechem pay	2256
	10: 9	The Ammonites *a* crossed the Jordan	1685
	11: 2	Gilead's wife *a* bore him sons,	2256
	11:17	They sent *a* to the king of Moab,	1685
	18: 7	*A,* they lived a long way from	2256
Ru	1: 5	both Mahlon and Kilion *a* died,	1685
	2:18	Ruth *a* brought out	2256
	3:15	He *a* said, "Bring me	2256
	4:10	I have *a* acquired Ruth the Moabitess,	1685
1Sa	2:28	I *a* gave your father's house all	2256
	4:17	A your two sons, Hophni and Phinehas,	1685+2256
	7:17	*and* there he *a* judged Israel.	2256
	10:11	Is Saul *a* among the prophets?"	1685
	10:12	"Is Saul *a* among the prophets?"	1685
	10:26	Saul *a* went to his home in Gibeah,	1685
	12: 5	*and a* his anointed is witness this day,	1685
	17:25	He will *a* give him his daughter in marriage	2256
	19:20	of God came upon Saul's men and they *a*	1685
	19:21	and they *a* prophesied.	1685
	19:24	He stripped off his robes and *a* prophesied	1685
	19:24	"Is Saul *a* among the prophets?"	1685
	22:10	he *a* gave him provisions and the sword	2256
	22:19	He *a* put to the sword Nob,	2256
	22:23	the man who is seeking your life is seeking mine *a.*	NIH
	25:43	David had *a* married Ahinoam of Jezreel,	2256
	28:19	The Lord will *a* hand over the army	1685
2Sa	2: 3	David *a* took the men who were with him,	2256
	2: 9	Ashuri and Jezreel, *and a* over Ephraim,	2256
	3:19	Abner *a* spoke to the Benjamites in person.	1685
	3:32	All the people wept *a.*	2256
	7:11	I will *a* give you rest	2256
	7:19	you have *a* spoken about the future of	1685
	8: 2	David *a* defeated the Moabites.	2256
	8:12	He *a* dedicated the plunder taken	2256
	10: 6	*and a* twelve thousand men from Tob.	2256
	10:18	He *a* struck down Shobach the commander	2256
	11:21	If he asks you this, then say to him, 'A,	1685
	15: 5	*A,* whenever anyone approached him	2256
	15:12	he *a* sent for Ahithophel the Gilonite,	2256
	15:23	The king *a* crossed the Kidron Valley,	2256
	15:27	The king *a* said to Zadok the priest,	2256
	17: 5	"Summon *a* Hushai the Arkite,	1685
	17:28	They *a* brought wheat and barley,	2256
	19:24	*a* went down to meet the king.	2256
	19:31	the Gileadite *a* came down from Rogelim	2256
	21:20	He *a* was descended from Rapha.	1685
	23:20	He *a* went down into a pit on a snowy day	2256
	24:23	Araunah *a* said to him,	2256
1Ki	1: 6	He was a very handsome	1685
	1:47	*A,* the royal officials have come	1685+2256
	2:44	The king *a* said to Shimei,	2256
	3:18	this woman *a* had a baby.	1685
	4: 7	Solomon *a* had twelve district governors	2256
	4:28	They *a* brought to	2256
	4:33	He *a* taught about animals and birds,	2256
	6:20	*and* he *a* overlaid the altar of cedar.	2256
	6:22	He *a* overlaid with gold the altar	2256
	6:25	The second cherub *a* measured ten cubits,	2256
	6:30	He *a* covered the floors of both the inner	2256
	6:34	He *a* made two pine doors,	2256
	7: 8	Solomon *a* made a palace like this hall	2256
	7:16	He *a* made two capitals of cast bronze	2256
	7:27	He *a* made ten movable stands of bronze;	2256
	7:40	He *a* made the basins and shovels	2256
	7:48	Solomon *a* made all the furnishings	2256
	7:50	the Most Holy Place, and *a* for the doors of	NIH
	9:23	They were *a* chief officials in charge	NIH
	9:26	King Solomon *a* built ships at Ezion Geber,	2256
	10:17	He *a* made three hundred small shields	2256
	10:26	which he kept in the chariot cities *and a*	2256
	10:29	They *a* exported them to all the kings of	2256
	11:21	*and* that Joab the commander of the army was *a* dead.	2256
	11:26	*A,* Jeroboam son of Nebat rebelled against	2256
	12:32	**And** at Bethel he *a*	2256
	13: 5	*A,* the altar was split apart	2256
	13:11	They *a* told their father what he had said to	2256
	14:23	They *a* set up for themselves high places,	1685
	15:22	up Geba in Benjamin, *and a* Mizpah.	2256
	16: 7	*and a* because he destroyed it.	2256
	16:31	**but** he married Jezebel daughter	2256
	16:33	Ahab *a* made an Asherah pole	2256
	17:20	have you brought tragedy *a*	1685
	18:38	*and a* licked up the water in the trench.	2256
	19:16	*A,* anoint Jehu son of Nimshi king	2256
	20:25	You must *a* raise an army like	2256
	20:27	**When** the Israelites *a* set	2256
	21:23	*a* concerning Jezebel the Lord says:	1685
	22: 5	**But** Jehoshaphat *a* said to the king	2256
	22:44	Jehoshaphat was *a* at peace with the king	2256
2Ki	3: 7	He *a* sent this message to Jehoshaphat king	2256
	3:18	he will *a* hand Moab over to you.	2256
	5:18	*and* I bow there *a*—	2256
	5:18	*a* from it and hid them *a.*	2256
	11:17	He *a* made a covenant between the king	2256
	13: 6	*A,* the Asherah pole remained standing	1685+2256
	14:10	and that of Judah *a?*"	6640

Ref	Text	Number
2Ki 14:14	He a took hostages and returned	2256
17:32	**but** they a appointed all sorts	2256
17:33	**but** they a served their own gods	2256
21: 3	he a erected altars to Baal and made	2256
21:16	Manasseh a shed so much innocent blood	2256
22: 6	A have them purchase timber	2256
23: 7	He a tore down the quarters of	2256
23:13	The king a desecrated the high places	2256
23:15	and burned the Asherah pole **a.**	2256
23:27	"I will remove Judah a from my presence	1685
24:15	He a took from Jerusalem to Babylon	2256
24:16	The king of Babylon a deported to Babylon	2256
25:14	They a took away the pots, shovels,	2256
25:19	He a took the secretary who was chief	2256
25:25	and assassinated Gedaliah **and a** the men	2256
1Ch 1:51	Hadad a died.	2256
2:49	She a gave birth to Shaaph the father	2256
3: 6	There were a Ibhar, Elishua, Eliphelet,	2256
3:20	There were a five others:	2256
4:36	a Elioenai, Jaakobah, Jeshohaiah,	2256
4:41	the Hamites in their dwellings **and a**	2256
5:21	a took one hundred thousand people captive	2256
6:71	in Bashan **and a** Ashtaroth, together	2256
11:22	He went down into a pit on a snowy day	2256
12:16	and some men from Judah a came to David	2256
12:38	the rest of the Israelites were a of one mind	1685
12:40	A, their neighbors from as far away	1685+2256
13: 2	**and a** to the priests and Levites who are	2256
15:24	and Jehiah were a to be doorkeepers for	2256
15:27	David a wore a linen ephod.	2256
16:38	He a left Obed-Edom	2256
16:38	Obed-Edom son of Jeduthun, **and a** Hosah,	2256
17:10	I will a subdue all your enemies.	2256
18: 2	David a defeated the Moabites,	2256
19:18	He a killed Shophach the commander	2256
20: 6	He a was descended from Rapha.	1685
21: 7	This command was a evil in the sight	2256
22: 1	**and a** the altar of burnt offering for Israel."	2256
22: 4	He a provided more cedar logs than could	2256
23: 2	He a gathered together all the leaders	2256
23:30	They were a to stand every morning	2256
24:31	They a cast lots,	1685
26: 4	Obed-Edom a had sons:	2256
26: 6	His son Shemaiah a had sons,	2256
26: 7	his relatives Elihu and Semakiah were a	NIH
28:18	He a gave him the plan for the chariot,	2256
28:20	David a said to Solomon his son,	2256
29: 9	David the king a rejoiced greatly.	1685+2256
2Ch 1:12	And I will a give you wealth,	2256
1:14	which he kept in the chariot cities **and a**	2256
1:17	They a exported them to all the kings of	2256
2: 8	"Send me a cedar,	2256
3: 9	He a overlaid the upper parts with gold.	2256
3:11	while its other wing, a five cubits long,	NIH
3:12	and its other wing, a five cubits long,	NIH
3:16	He a made a hundred pomegranates	2256
4: 8	a made a hundred gold sprinkling bowls.	2256
4:11	He a made the pots and shovels	2256
4:19	Solomon a made all the furnishings	2256
8: 4	He a built up Tadmor in the desert and all	2256
8:10	They were a King Solomon's chief officials	2256
8:14	He a appointed the gatekeepers	2256
9:10	they a brought algumwood	1685+2256
9:14	A all the kings of Arabia and the governors	2256
9:16	He a made three hundred small shields	2256
9:25	which he kept in the chariot cities **and a**	2256
14:15	They a attacked the camps of the herdsmen	1685+2256
15:16	King Asa a deposed his grandmother	1685+2256
17:13	He a kept experienced fighting men	2256
18: 4	**But** Jehoshaphat a said to the king	2256
19: 8	In Jerusalem a, Jehoshaphat appointed	1685+2256
20:25	of equipment and clothing **and a** articles	2256
21:11	He had a built high places on the hills	1685
21:13	have a murdered your own brothers,	1685+2256
22: 5	He a followed their counsel when he went	1685
23:19	He a stationed doorkeepers at the gates of	2256
24:12	and a workers in iron and bronze to repair	1685
24:14	and for the burnt offerings, **and a** dishes	2256
25: 6	He a hired a hundred thousand fighting men from Israel	2256
25:12	The army of Judah a	2256
25:19	and that of Judah a?"	6640
26:10	He a built towers in the desert	2256
27: 5	the same amount a in the second	2256
28: 2	of the kings of Israel and a made cast idols	2256
28: 5	was a given into the hands of the king	1685+2256
28: 8	They a took a great deal of plunder,	1685+2256
28:10	**But** aren't you a guilty of sins against	8370
29: 7	They a shut the doors of the portico	1685
29:27	singing to the LORD began **a,**	2256
30: 1	to all Israel and Judah and a wrote letters	1685
30:12	A in Judah the hand of God was on	1685
31: 6	of Judah a brought a tithe of their herds	1685
31:14	the contributions made to the LORD **and a**	2256
32: 5	He a made large numbers of weapons	2256
32:17	king a wrote letters insulting the LORD,	2256
32:28	He a made buildings to store the harvest	2256
33: 3	he a erected altars to the Baals	2256
33:14	he a made it much higher.	2256
34:11	They a gave money to the carpenters	2256
35: 7	**and a** three thousand cattle—	2256
35: 8	His officials a contributed voluntarily to	2256
35: 9	A Conaniah along with Shemaiah	2256
36: 7	Nebuchadnezzar a took to Babylon articles	2256
36:13	He a rebelled against King Nebuchadnezzar,	1685+2256
Ezr 2:65	and they a had 200 men	2256
5: 4	They a asked, "What are the names	10008+10358
5:10	We a asked them their names,	10059+10221
6: 5	A, the gold and silver articles	10059+10221
7: 7	a came up to Jerusalem in the seventh year	2256
7:24	You are a to know	10221
8:20	They a brought 220 of	2256
8:36	They a delivered the king's orders to	2256
Ne 1: 2	**and a** about Jerusalem.	2256
2: 7	I a said to him, "If it pleases the king,	1685
2: 9	The king had a sent army officers	2256
2:18	I a told them about the gracious hand	2256
3: 4	**and** next to him Zadok son of Baana a	2256
3:13	They a repaired five hundred yards of	2256
3:15	He a repaired the wall of the Pool	2256
4:11	A our enemies said,	2256
4:22	At that time I a said to the people,	1685
5:10	my brothers and my men are a lending	1685+2256
5:11	and a the usury you are charging them—	2256
5:13	I a shook out the folds of my robe and said,	1685
5:15	Their assistants a lorded it over the people.	1685
6:14	remember a the prophetess Noadiah	1685+2256
6:17	A, in those days the nobles	1685
7: 3	A appoint residents of Jerusalem as guards,	2256
7:67	**and they** a had 245 men	2256
10:35	"We a assume responsibility for bringing	2256
10:36	"As it is a written in the Law,	2256
12: 8	Sherebiah, Judah, and a Mattaniah, who,	NIH
12:28	The singers a were brought together from	2256
12:31	I a assigned two large choirs	2256
12:35	and a Zechariah son of Jonathan,	NIH
12:42	and a Maaseiah, Shemaiah,	2256
12:43	The women and children a rejoiced.	1685+2256
12:45	as did a the singers and gatekeepers,	2256
12:47	They a set aside the portion for	2256
13: 5	**and a** the tithes of grain,	2256
13:10	I a learned that the portions assigned to	2256
13:22	Remember me for this **a,** O my God,	1685
13:31	I a made provision for contributions	2256
Est 1: 9	Queen Vashti a gave a banquet for	1685
1:16	against the king but a against all the nobles	NIH
1:19	A let the king give her royal position	2256
2: 7	This girl, who was a known as Esther,	NIH
2: 8	Esther a was taken to the king's palace	2256
4: 8	He a gave him a copy of the text of	2256
8: 9	and the language of each people **and a** to	2256
8:14	**And** the edict was a	2256
9: 7	They a killed Parshandatha, Dalphon,	2256
9:12	It will be granted."	6388
9:13	to carry out this day's edict tomorrow a,	1685
9:16	in the king's provinces a assembled	2256
Job 1: 6	and Satan a came with them.	1685
2: 1	and Satan a came with them	1685
3:18	Captives a enjoy their ease;	3480
5:18	For he wounds, but he a binds up;	2256
5:18	he injures, **but** his hands a heal.	2256
13: 2	What you know, I a know;	1685
16: 4	I a could speak like you,	1685
31:28	then these a would be sins to be judged,	1685
32: 3	He was a angry with the three friends,	2256
42:13	And he a had seven sons	2256
Ps 16: 9	my body a will rest secure,	677
19:13	Keep your servant a from willful sins;	1685
74:16	The day is yours, **and** yours a the night;	677
78:20	**But** can he a give us food?	1685
84: 6	the autumn rains a cover it with pools.	1685
89:11	heavens are yours, **and** yours a the earth;	677
89:27	I will a appoint him my firstborn,	677
Pr 2:16	It will save you a from the adulteress,	NIH
9: 2	she has a set her table.	677
24:14	a that wisdom is **sweet**	4027S
24:23	These a are sayings of the wise:	1685
31:28	her husband a, and he praises her:	NIH
Ecc 1:17	and a of madness and folly,	2256
2: 1	But that a proved to be meaningless.	1685
2: 7	I a owned more herds	1685
2:12	and a madness and folly.	2256
2:15	"The fate of the fool will overtake me **a.**	1685
3:11	He has a set eternity in the hearts of men;	1685
3:18	I thought, "As for men,	NIH
4:11	A, if two lie down together,	1685
9:13	I a saw under the sun this example	1685
12: 9	**but a** he imparted knowledge to the people.	6388
Isa 7:13	Will you try the patience of my God a?	1685
7:20	and to take off your beards a.	1685
14:10	"You a have become weak, as we are;	1685
16: 8	the vines of Sibmah a.	NIH
19: 7	a the plants along the Nile,	NIH
21:12	"Morning is coming, but a the night.	1685
28: 7	And these a stagger from wine and reel	1685
28:29	All this a comes from	1685
30:23	He will a send you rain for	2256
34:14	the night creatures a repose and find	421
34:15	there a the falcons will gather,	421
44:15	**But** he a fashions a god and worships it;	677
44:16	He a warms himself and says, "Ah!	677
49:11	I will a make you a light for the Gentiles,	2256
57:15	**but** a with him who is contrite and lowly	1685
66: 4	so I will a choose harsh treatment for them	1685
66:21	of them a to be priests and Levites,"	1685
Jer 2:16	A, the men of Memphis	1685
2:37	You will a leave that place with your hands	1685
3: 8	she a went out and committed adultery.	1685
17:19	stand a at all the other gates of Jerusalem.	2256
28: 4	I will a bring back	2256
29: 7	A, seek the peace and prosperity of the city	2256
35: 7	A you must never build houses,	2256
Jer 36:29	A tell Jehoiakim king of Judah,	2256
39: 6	of Zedekiah before his eyes **and** a killed all	2256
41: 3	Ishmael a killed all the Jews who were	2256
43: 6	They a led away all the men,	2256
46:14	proclaim it in Memphis and Tahpanhes:	2256
52:10	he a killed all the officials of Judah.	1685+2256
52:18	They a took away the pots, shovels,	2256
52:25	He a took the secretary who was chief	2256
La 4:21	**But** to you a the cup will be passed;	1685
Eze 1:10	each had the face of an eagle.	2256
1:19	from the ground, the wheels a rose.	NIH
1:21	When the creatures moved, they a moved;	NIH
1:21	the creatures stood still, they a stood still;	NIH
4:11	A measure out a sixth of a hin of water	2256
8:17	Must they a fill the land with violence	NIH
10:17	the cherubim stood still, they a stood still;	NIH
16:17	You a took the fine jewelry I gave you,	2256
16: 7	A the food I provided for you—	2256
17:13	He a carried away the leading men of	2256
20:12	A I gave them my Sabbaths as a sign	1685+2256
20:15	A with uplifted hand I swore to them	1685+2256
20:23	A with uplifted hand I swore to them	1685
20:25	I a gave them over to statutes that were	1685+2256
20:27	In this a your fathers blasphemed me	6388
23:26	They will a strip you of your clothes	2256
23:38	They have a done this to me:	6388
31:17	had a gone down to the grave with it,	1685
34:18	Must you a trample the rest of your pasture	2256
34:18	Must you a muddy the rest with your feet?	2256
36: 7	the nations around you will a suffer scorn.	NIH
38: 6	a Gomer with all its troops,	NIH
39:16	(A a town called Hamonah will be	1685+2256
40:27	The inner court a had a gate facing south,	2256
40:42	There were a four tables of dressed stone	2256
41: 2	He a measured the outer sanctuary;	2256
41:13	with its walls were a hundred cubits long.	NIH
41:16	The side rooms of the temple a	2256
43:17	The upper ledge a is square,	2256
45:15	you are a to provide a young bull and a ram	2256
45:15	A one sheep is to be taken from every flock	2256
46:14	You are a to provide with it morning	2256
46:16	it will a belong to his descendants;	NIH
Da 2:26	king asked Daniel (a called Belteshazzar)	NIH
4:19	Then Daniel (a called Belteshazzar)	NIH
5:12	and a the ability to interpret dreams,	NIH
7:20	I a wanted to know about the ten horns	10221
11: 8	He will a seize their gods,	1685+2256
11:41	He will a invade the Beautiful Land.	2256
Hos 4: 6	I a reject you as my priests;	2256
4: 6	I a will ignore your children.	1685
5: 5	Judah a stumbles with them.	1685
6:11	"A for you, Judah, a harvest is appointed.	1685
Am 2:11	I a raised up prophets from	2256
4: 7	"I a withheld rain from you when	1685+2256
7:14	**and** I a took care of sycamore-fig trees.	2256
Mic 6: 4	a Aaron and Miriam.	NIH
Zep 1: 5	and swear by the LORD **and** who a swear	2256
Zec 4: 3	A there are two olive trees by it,	2256
4: 9	his hands will a complete it.	2256
Mt 4: 7	Jesus answered him, "It is a written:	4099
5:39	turn to him the other a.	2779
6:12	as we a have forgiven our debtors.	2779
6:14	your heavenly Father will a forgive you.	2779
6:21	your treasure is, there your heart will be **a.**	2779
10:32	I will a acknowledge him before my Father	2779
13:26	then the weeds a appeared.	2779
19:28	you who have followed me will a sit	2779
20: 4	'You a go and work in my vineyard,	2779
20: 7	'You a go and work in my vineyard.'	2779
20:10	But each one of them a received a denarius.	2779
21:21	but a you can say to this mountain, 'Go,	2779
21:24	"I will a ask you one question.	2779
23:18	You a say, 'If anyone swears by the altar,	2779
23:26	and then the outside a will be clean.	2779
24:44	So you a must be ready,	2779
25:11	"Later the others a came.	2779
25:17	**So a,** the one with	6058
25:22	"The man with the two talents a came.	2779
25:44	"They a will answer, 'Lord,	2779
26:13	what she has done will a be told,	2779
26:69	"You a were with Jesus of Galilee,"	2779
27:44	the robbers who were crucified with him a	2779
Mk 1:34	He a drove out many demons,	2779
1:38	so I can preach there a.	2779
2:26	And he a gave some to his companions."	2779
4:26	He a said, "This is what the kingdom	2779
4:36	There were a other boats with him.	2779
6:41	He a divided the two fish among them all.	2779
8: 7	he gave thanks for them a and told	NIG
12:21	but he a died, leaving no child.	2779
14: 9	what she has done will a be told,	2779
14:67	"You a were with that Nazarene, Jesus,"	2779
15:32	Those crucified with him a heaped insults	2779
15:41	up with him to Jerusalem were a there.	NIG
Lk 1: 3	it seemed good a to me to write	2779
1: 5	his wife Elizabeth was a a descendant	NIG
2: 4	So Joseph a went up from the town	2779
2:36	There was a a prophetess, Anna,	2779
3:12	Tax collectors a came to be baptized.	2779
6: 4	the kingdom of God to the other towns a,	2779
6: 4	And he a gave some to his companions."	2779
6:13	whom he a designated apostles:	2779
6:29	turn to him the other a.	2779
6:39	He a told them this parable:	2779
11: 4	**and** a we forgive everyone who sins against us.	2779
11:30	a will the Son of Man be to this generation.	2779

Lk
11:34	your whole body a is full of light.	2779
11:34	your body a is full of darkness.	2779
11:40	the outside make the inside a?	2779
11:45	when you say these things, you insult us a."	2779
12: 8	the Son of Man will a acknowledge him	2779
12:34	your treasure is, there your heart will be a.	2779
12:40	You a must be ready,	2779
16:10	with very little can a be trusted with much,	2779
16:10	with very little will a be dishonest	2779
16:22	The rich man a died and was buried.	2779
16:28	so that they will not a come to this place	2779
17:10	So you a, when you have done everything you were told to do,	2779
17:26	a will it be in the days of the Son of Man.	2779
18:15	People were a bringing babies to Jesus	2779
18:43	all the people saw it, they a praised God.	2779
20: 3	He replied, "I will a ask you a question.	2779
20:11	but that one they beat	2779
21: 2	He a saw a poor widow put	1254
22:24	A a dispute arose among them as to which	2779
22:36	take it, and a a bag;	3931
22:58	"You a are one of them."	2779
23: 7	who was a in Jerusalem at that time.	2779
23:32	were a led out with him to be executed.	2779
23:36	The soldiers a came up and mocked him.	2779

Jn
1:45	and about whom the prophets a wrote—	NIG
2: 2	and his disciples had a been invited to	2779
3:23	John was baptizing at Aenon near Salim,	2779
4:12	as did a his sons and his flocks and herds?"	2779
4:45	for they a had been there.	2779
5:19	whatever the Father does the Son a does.	2779
7:10	he went a, not publicly, but in secret.	2779
7:47	"You mean he has deceived you a?"	2779
8:19	you would know my Father a."	2779
9:15	Therefore the Pharisees a asked him	2779
10:16	I must bring them a.	2779
11:16	"Let us a go, that we may die with him."	2779
11:33	the Jews who had come along with her a	NIG
11:52	that nation but a for the scattered children	2779
12: 9	only because of him but a to see Lazarus	2779
12:26	and where I am, my servant a will be.	2779
13:14	you a should wash one another's feet.	2779
14: 1	Trust in God; trust a in me.	2779
14: 3	and take you to be with me that you a may	2779
14:19	Because I live, you a will live.	2779
15:20	they will persecute you a.	2779
15:20	they will obey yours a.	2779
15:27	And you a must testify,	2779
17:20	I pray a for those who will believe in me	2779
17:21	May they a be in us so that	2779
18:18	Peter a was standing with them,	2779
19:35	and he testifies so that you a may believe.	2779
20: 8	the tomb first, a went inside.	2779

Ac
1:23	Joseph called Barsabbas (a known	4005
2:26	my body a will live in hope,	2779
5: 1	a sold a piece of property.	NIG
5: 9	and they will carry you out a."	NIG
5:16	Crowds gathered a from the towns	2779
6: 5	a Philip, Procorus, Nicanor, Timon,	2779
8:19	"Give me a this ability so that everyone	2779
11: 1	throughout Judea heard that the Gentiles a	2779
11:12	These six brothers a went with me,	2779
11:20	to Antioch and began to speak to Greeks a,	2779
12: 3	he proceeded to seize Peter a.	2779
12:12	of Mary the mother of John, a called Mark,	NIG
12:25	taking with them John, a called Mark.	NIG
13: 9	Then Saul, who was a called Paul,	2779
15:37	a called Mark, with them,	2779
17:12	as did a a number	2779
17:34	a woman named Damaris,	2779
19:21	he said, "I must visit Rome a."	2779
19:27	but a that the temple of	2779
20: 4	Gaius from Derbe, Timothy a,	2779
21:13	but a to die in Jerusalem for the name of	2779
22: 5	as a the high priest and all	2779
23:11	so you must a testify in Rome."	2779
23:30	I a ordered his accusers to present	2779
26: 4	and a in Jerusalem.	5445
26:20	and to the Gentiles a,	2779
27:10	and to our own lives a."	2779

Ro
1: 6	And you a are among those who are called	2779
1:15	to preach the gospel a to you who are	2779
1:27	the men a abandoned natural relations	2779
1:32	but a approve of those who practice them.	2779
2:12	the law will a perish apart from the law,	2779
2:15	their consciences a bearing witness,	2779
4: 9	or a for the uncircumcised?	2779
4:12	And he is the father of	2779
4:12	not only circumcised but who a walk in	2779
4:16	not only to those who are of the law but a	2779
4:19	and that Sarah's womb was a dead.	NIG
4:24	but a for us,	2779
5: 3	but we a rejoice in our sufferings,	2779
5:11	but we a rejoice in God	2779
5:18	so a the result of one act	2779
5:19	so a through the obedience of the one man	2779
5:21	so a grace might reign	2779
6: 5	we will certainly a be united with him	2779
6: 8	we believe that we will a live with him.	2779
7: 4	you a died to the law through the body	2779
8:11	he who raised Christ from the dead will a	2779
8:17	in order that we may a share in his glory.	2779
8:29	For those God foreknew he a predestined	2779
8:30	And those he predestined, he a called;	2779
8:30	those he called, he a justified;	2779
8:30	those he justified, he a glorified.	2779
8:32	how will he not a, along with him,	2779

Ro
8:34	the right hand of God and is a interceding	2779
9:24	whom he a called,	2779
9:24	from the Jews but a from the Gentiles?	2779
11:22	Otherwise, you a will be cut off.	2779
13: 5	of possible punishment but a because	2779
13: 6	This is a why you pay taxes,	2779
16: 5	Greet a the church that meets	2779

1Co
1:16	I a baptized the household of Stephanas;	2779
6:14	and he will raise us a.	2779
7: 4	to her alone but a to her husband.	NIG
7: 4	not belong to him alone but a to his wife.	NIG
7:37	this man a does the right thing.	NIG
10:13	he will a provide a way out so	2779
11:12	so a man is born of woman.	2779
11:23	from the Lord what I a passed on to you:	2779
12:28	a those having gifts of healing,	2083
14:15	but I will a pray with my mind;	2779
14:15	but I will a sing with my mind.	2779
15: 8	and last of all he appeared to me a,	2779
15:18	Then those a who have fallen asleep	2779
15:21	the resurrection of the dead comes a	2779
15:40	There are a heavenly bodies	2779
15:44	there is a a spiritual body.	2779
15:48	so a are those who are of heaven.	2779
16: 4	If it seems advisable for me to go a,	2779
16:18	For they refreshed my spirit and yours a.	2779

2Co
1: 5	so a through Christ our comfort overflows.	2779
1: 7	so a you share in our comfort.	2779
2:10	If you forgive anyone, I a forgive.	2779
4:10	life of Jesus may a be revealed in our body.	2779
4:13	With that same spirit of faith we a believe	2779
4:14	the Lord Jesus from the dead will a raise us	2779
5:11	and I hope it is a plain to your conscience.	2779
6:13	open wide your hearts a.	2779
7: 7	but a by the comfort you had given him.	2779
8: 6	to bring a to completion this act of grace	2779
8: 7	see that you a excel in this grace of giving.	2779
8:10	to give but a to have the desire to do so.	2779
8:21	not only in the eyes of the Lord but a	2779
9: 6	Whoever sows sparingly will a	2779
9: 6	and whoever sows generously will a	2779
9:10	the sower and bread for food will a supply	NIG
9:12	but is a overflowing in many expressions	2779
11:21	I a dare to boast about.	2779

Gal
2: 1	I took Titus along a.	2779
2: 8	was a at work in my ministry as an apostle	2779
4: 3	So a, when we were children,	2779
4: 7	you are a son, God has made you a an heir.	2779
6: 1	watch yourself, or you a may be tempted.	2779

Eph
1:11	In him we were a chosen,	2779
1:13	And you a were included in Christ	NIG
1:18	I pray a that the eyes of your heart may	NIG
1:21	in the present age but a in the one to come.	2779
2: 3	All of us a lived among them at one time,	2779
4: 9	that he a descended to the lower,	2779
5:24	so a wives should submit to their husbands	2779
5:33	each one of you a must love his wife	2779
6:19	Pray a for me,	2779
6:21	so that you a may know how I am	2779

Php
1:29	but a to suffer for him,	2779
2: 4	but a to the interests of others.	2779
2:19	that I may be cheered	2779
2:25	who is a your messenger,	1254
2:27	and not on him only but a on me,	2779

Col
1: 8	and who told us of your love in the Spirit.	2779
2:11	In him you were a circumcised,	2779
3: 4	then you a will appear with him in glory.	2779
4: 1	because you know that you a have a Master	2779
4:11	who is called Justus, a sends greetings.	NIG
4:16	see that it is a read in the church of	2779

1Th
1: 5	but a with power,	2779
2:13	And we a thank God continually because,	2779
2:15	the Lord Jesus and the prophets and a	2779
3: 6	just as we a long to see you.	2779

1Ti
1: 9	We a know that law is made not for	NIG
2: 9	I a want women to dress modestly,	6058
3: 7	He must a have a good reputation	2779
5:13	but a gossips and busybodies,	2779

2Ti
1: 5	I am persuaded, now lives in you a.	2779
2: 2	to reliable men who will a be qualified	2779
2:11	we will a live with him;	2779
2:12	we will a reign with him.	2779
2:12	If we disown him, he will a disown us;	2779
2:20	but a of wood and clay;	2779
3: 8	so a these men oppose the truth—	2779
4: 8	a to all who have longed for his appearing.	2779

Phm
1: 9	and now a prisoner of Christ Jesus—	2779

Heb
1:10	He says, "In the beginning, O Lord,	2779
2: 4	God a testified to it by signs,	5296
4: 2	we a have had the gospel preached to us,	2779
4:10	for anyone who enters God's rest a rests	2779
5: 5	So Christ a did not take upon himself	2779
7: 2	then a, "king of Salem" means "king	2779
7:12	there must a be a change of the law.	2779
8: 3	for this one a to have something to offer.	2779
9: 1	for worship and a an earthly sanctuary.	5445
10:15	The Holy Spirit a testifies to us about this.	2779
12:26	not only the earth but a the heavens."	2779
13:12	so Jesus a suffered outside the city gate	2779

Jas
2: 2	a poor man in shabby clothes a comes in.	2779
2:11	"Do not commit adultery," a said,	2779
3: 6	The tongue a is a fire,	2779

1Pe
2: 5	you a, like living stones, are being built	2779
2: 5	which is a what they are destined for.	2779
2:18	but a to those who are harsh.	2779
3:19	through whom a he went and preached to	2779
3:21	that now saves you a—	2779

1Pe
4: 1	arm yourselves a with the same attitude,	2779
5: 1	of Christ's sufferings and one who a	2779

2Pe
2: 1	But there were a false prophets among	2779
3: 6	By these waters a the world of	NIG
3:15	as our dear brother Paul a wrote you with	NIG

1Jn
1: 3	so that you a may have fellowship with us.	2779
2: 2	and not only for ours but a for the sins of	2779
2:23	the Son has the Father a.	2779
2:24	you a will remain in the Son and in	2779
4:11	we a ought to love one another.	2779
4:21	Whoever loves God must a	2779
5:20	We know a that the Son of God has come	1254

2Jn
1: 1	not I only, but a all who know the truth—	2779

3Jn
1:10	He a stops those who want to do so	2779
1:	We a speak well of him,	2779

Rev
2: 6	the practices of the Nicolaitans, which I a	2779
2:15	Likewise you a have those who hold to	2779
2:17	I will give him a white stone with	2779
2:28	I will give him the morning star.	2779
3:10	I will a keep you from the hour of trial	2779
3:12	and I will a write on him my new name.	2779
4: 6	A before the throne there was what looked	2779
8:12	and a a third of the night.	3931
11: 8	where a their Lord was crucified.	2779
13: 4	and they a worshiped the beast and asked,	2779
13:16	He a forced everyone, small and great,	2779
17:10	They are a seven kings.	2779

ALTAR (381) [ALTARS]

Ge
8:20	Then Noah built an a to the LORD and,	4640
12: 7	So he built an a there to the LORD,	4640
12: 8	an a to the LORD and called on the name	4640
13: 4	and where he had first built an a.	4640
13:18	where he built an a to the LORD.	4640
22: 9	an a there and arranged the wood on it.	4640
22: 9	and laid him on the a,	4640
26:25	an a there and called on the name of	4640
33:20	up an a and called it El Elohe Israel.	4640
35: 1	and build an a there to God,	4640
35: 3	where I will build an a to God,	4640
35: 7	There he built an a,	4640

Ex
17:15	Moses built an a and called it	4640
20:24	"'Make an a of earth for me and sacrifice	4640
20:25	If you make an a of stones for me,	4640
20:26	And do not go up to my a on steps,	4640
21:14	take him away from my a and put him	4640
24: 4	up early the next morning and built an a at	4640
24: 6	and the other half he sprinkled on the a.	4640
27: 1	"Build an a of acacia wood,	4640
27: 2	so that the horns and the a are of one piece,	5647S
27: 2	and overlay the a with bronze.	2257S
27: 5	the ledge of the a so that it is halfway up	4640
27: 5	of the altar so that it is halfway up the a.	4640
27: 6	of acacia wood for the a and overlay them	4640
27: 7	be on two sides of the a when it is carried.	4640
27: 8	Make the a hollow, out of boards.	2257S
28:43	of Meeting or approach the a to minister in	4640
29:12	on the horns of the a with your finger,	4640
29:12	pour out the rest of it at the base of the a.	4640
29:13	and burn them on the a.	4640
29:16	and sprinkle it against the a on all sides.	4640
29:18	Then burn the entire ram on the a.	4640
29:20	sprinkle blood against the a on all sides.	4640
29:21	on the a and some of the anointing oil	4640
29:25	on the a along with the burnt offering for	4640
29:36	Purify the a by making atonement for it,	4640
29:37	For seven days make atonement for the a	4640
29:37	Then the a will be most holy,	4640
29:38	to offer on the a regularly each day:	4640
29:44	and the a and will consecrate Aaron	4640
30: 1	an a of acacia wood for burning incense.	4640
30: 4	Make two gold rings for the a below	2257S
30: 6	Put the a in front of the curtain that is	4640
30: 7	on the a every morning when he tends	2257S
30: 9	Do not offer on this a any other incense	2257S
30:18	between the Tent of Meeting and the a,	4640
30:20	when they approach the a to minister	4640
30:27	the a of incense,	4640
30:28	the a of burnt offering and all its utensils,	4640
31: 8	the a of incense,	4640
31: 9	the a of burnt offering and all its utensils,	4640
32: 5	an a in front of the calf and announced,	4640
35:15	the a of incense with its poles,	4640
35:16	the a of burnt offering	4640
37:25	the a of incense out of acacia wood.	4640
38: 1	the a of burnt offering of acacia wood,	4640
38: 2	that the horns and the a were of one piece,	5647S
38: 2	and they overlaid the a with bronze.	2257S
38: 4	They made a grating for the a,	4640
38: 4	to be under its ledge, halfway up the a.	2257S
38: 7	be on the sides of the a for carrying it.	4640
38:30	the bronze a with its bronze grating	4640
39:38	the gold a, the anointing oil,	4640
39:39	the bronze a with its bronze grating,	4640
40: 5	the gold a of incense in front of the ark of	4640
40: 6	"Place the a of burnt offering in front of	4640
40: 7	of Meeting and the a and put water in it.	4640
40:10	the a of burnt offering and all its utensils;	4640
40:10	consecrate the a, and it will be most holy.	4640
40:26	the gold a in the Tent of Meeting in front	4640
40:29	the a of burnt offering near the entrance to	4640
40:30	and the a and put water in it for washing,	4640
40:32	the Tent of Meeting or approached the a,	4640
40:33	and a and put up the curtain at the entrance	4640

Lev
1: 5	the a on all sides at the entrance to the Tent	4640
1: 7	of Aaron the priest are to put fire on the a	4640

Lev	1: 8	on the burning wood that is on the a.	4640
	1: 9	and the priest is to burn all of it on the a.	4640
	1:11	the north side of the a before the LORD,	4640
	1:11	against the a on all sides.	4640
	1:12	on the burning wood that is on the a.	4640
	1:13	to bring all of it and burn it on the a.	4640
	1:15	The priest shall bring it to the a,	4640
	1:15	wring off the head and burn it on the a;	4640
	1:15	be drained out on the side of the a.	4640
	1:16	and throw it to the east side of the a,	4640
	1:17	on the wood that is on the fire on the a.	4640
	2: 2	burn this as a memorial portion on the a,	4640
	2: 8	who shall take it to the a.	4640
	2: 9	from the grain offering and burn it on the a	4640
	2:12	to be offered on the a as a pleasing aroma.	4640
	3: 2	the blood against the a on all sides.	4640
	3: 5	the a on top of the burnt offering that is on	4640
	3: 8	against the a on all sides.	4640
	3:11	The priest shall burn them on the a as food,	4640
	3:13	against the a on all sides.	4640
	3:16	The priest shall burn them on the a as food,	4640
	4: 7	of the a of fragrant incense that is before	4640
	4: 7	of the a of burnt offering at the entrance to	4640
	4:10	Then the priest shall burn them on the a	4640
	4:18	the horns of the a that is before the LORD	4640
	4:18	of the a of burnt offering at the entrance to	4640
	4:19	the fat from it and burn it on the a,	4640
	4:25	the a of burnt offering and pour out the rest	4640
	4:25	the rest of the blood at the base of the a.	4640
	4:26	on the a as he burned the fat of	4640
	4:30	the a of burnt offering and pour out the rest	4640
	4:30	the rest of the blood at the base of the a.	4640
	4:31	the a as an aroma pleasing to the LORD.	4640
	4:34	the a of burnt offering and pour out the rest	4640
	4:34	the rest of the blood at the base of the a.	4640
	4:35	and the priest shall burn it on the a on top	4640
	5: 9	of the sin offering against the side of the a;	4640
	5: 9	be drained out at the base of the a.	4640
	5:12	as a memorial portion and burn it on the a	4640
	6: 9	to remain on the a hearth throughout	4640
	6: 9	and the fire must be kept burning on the a.	4640
	6:10	on the a and place them beside the altar.	4640
	6:10	on the altar and place them beside the altar.	4640
	6:12	The fire on the a must be kept burning;	4640
	6:13	be kept burning on the a continuously;	4640
	6:14	in front of the a.	4640
	6:15	and burn the memorial portion on the a as	4640
	7: 2	to be sprinkled against the a on all sides.	4640
	7: 5	on the a as an offering made to the LORD	4640
	7:31	The priest shall burn the fat on the a,	4640
	8:11	of the oil on the a seven times,	4640
	8:11	anointing the a and all its utensils and	4640
	8:15	on all the horns of the a to purify the altar.	4640
	8:15	on all the horns of the altar to purify the a.	4640
	8:15	the rest of the blood at the base of the a.	4640
	8:16	and burned it on the a.	4640
	8:19	and sprinkled the blood against the a	4640
	8:21	the whole ram on the a as a burnt offering,	4640
	8:24	Then he sprinkled blood against the a	4640
	8:28	from their hands and burned them on the a	4640
	8:30	of the blood from the a and sprinkled them	4640
	9: 7	to the a and sacrifice your sin offering	4640
	9: 8	So Aaron came to the a and slaughtered	4640
	9: 9	the blood and put it on the horns of the a;	4640
	9: 9	at the base of the a.	4640
	9:10	On the a he burned the fat,	4640
	9:12	he sprinkled it against the a on all sides.	4640
	9:13	and he burned them on the a.	4640
	9:14	on top of the burnt offering on the a.	4640
	9:17	took a handful of it and burned it on the a	4640
	9:18	he sprinkled it against the a on all sides.	4640
	9:20	and then Aaron burned the fat on the a.	4640
	9:24	and the fat portion on the a,	4640
	10:12	and offer it on the a,	4640
	14:20	the a before the LORD and two handfuls	4640
	16:12	"Then he shall come out to the a that is	4640
	16:18	and put it on all the horns of the a.	4640
	16:20	the Tent of Meeting and the a,	4640
	16:25	the fat of the sin offering on the a.	4640
	16:33	for the Tent of Meeting and the a,	4640
	17: 6	against the a of the LORD at the entrance	4640
	17:11	for yourselves on the a;	4640
	21:23	not go near the curtain or approach the a,	4640
	22:22	on the a as an offering made to the LORD	4640
Nu	3:26	the tabernacle and a, and the ropes—	4640
	4:11	the gold a they are to spread a blue cloth	4640
	4:13	from the bronze a and spread a purple cloth	4640
	4:14	the utensils used for ministering at the a,	2257S
	4:26	the tabernacle and a,	4640
	5:25	before the LORD and bring it to the a.	4640
	5:26	a memorial offering and burn it on the a;	4640
	7: 1	and consecrated the a and all its utensils.	4640
	7:10	When the a was anointed,	4640
	7:10	and presented them before the a.	4640
	7:11	for the dedication of the a."	4640
	7:84	of the a when it was anointed;	4640
	7:88	the offerings for the dedication of the a	4640
	16:38	the censers into sheets to overlay the a,	4640
	16:39	to overlay the a,	4640
	16:46	along with fire from the a,	4640
	18: 3	the furnishings of the sanctuary or the a,	4640
	18: 5	for the care of the sanctuary and the a,	4640
	18: 7	in connection with everything at the a and	4640
	18:17	the a and burn their fat as an offering made	4640
	23: 2	of them offered a bull and a ram on each a.	4640
	23: 4	on each I have offered a bull and a ram."	4640

Nu	23:14	and offered a bull and a ram on each a.	4640
	23:30	and offered a bull and a ram on each a.	4640
Dt	12:27	Present your burnt offerings on the a of	4640
	12:27	beside the a of the LORD your God,	4640
	16:21	the a you build to the LORD your God,	4640
	26: 4	in front of the a of the LORD your God.	4640
	27: 5	to the a of the LORD your God, an a of stones.	4640
	27: 5	to the LORD your God, an a of stones.	4640
	27: 6	Build the a of the LORD your God	4640
	33:10	and whole burnt offerings on your a.	4640
Jos	8:30	Then Joshua built on Mount Ebal an a to	4640
	8:31	an a of uncut stones,	4640
	9:27	the community and for the a of the LORD	4640
	22:10	of Manasseh built an imposing a there by	4640
	22:11	the Israelites heard that they had built the a	4640
	22:16	from the LORD and build yourselves an a	4640
	22:19	against us by building an a for yourselves,	4640
	22:19	other than the a of the LORD our God.	4640
	22:23	If we have built our own a to turn away	4640
	22:26	'Let us get ready and build an a—	4640
	22:28	Look at the replica of the LORD's a,	4640
	22:29	by building an a for burnt offerings,	4640
	22:29	the a of the LORD our God that stands	4640
	22:34	and the Gadites gave the a this name:	4640
Jdg	6:24	So Gideon built an a to the LORD there	4640
	6:25	down your father's a to Baal and cut down	4640
	6:26	a proper kind of a to the LORD your God	4640
	6:28	there was Baal's a, demolished,	4640
	6:28	on the newly built a!	4640
	6:30	because he has broken down Baal's a	4640
	6:31	when someone breaks down his a."	4640
	6:32	because he broke down Baal's a.	4640
	13:20	As the flame blazed up from the a	4640
	21: 4	Early the next day the people built an a	4640
1Sa	2:28	to go up to my a, to burn incense,	4640
	2:33	of you that I do not cut off from my a will	4640
	7:17	And he built an a there to the LORD.	4640
	14:35	Then Saul built an a to the LORD.	4640
2Sa	24:18	an a to the LORD on the threshing floor	4640
	24:21	"so I can build an a to the LORD,	4640
	24:25	David built an a to the LORD there	4640
1Ki	1:50	went and took hold of the horns of the a.	4640
	1:51	and is clinging to the horns of the a.	4640
	1:53	and they brought him down from the a.	4640
	2:28	and took hold of the horns of the a.	4640
	2:29	of the LORD and was beside the a.	4640
	3: 4	a thousand burnt offerings on that a.	4640
	6:20	and he also overlaid the a of cedar.	4640
	6:22	also overlaid with gold the a that belonged	4640
	7:48	in the LORD's temple: the golden a;	4640
	8:22	before the a of the LORD in front of	4640
	8:31	the oath before your a in this temple,	4640
	8:54	he rose from before the a of the LORD,	4640
	8:64	because the bronze a before	4640
	9:25	on the a he had built for the LORD,	4640
	12:32	and offered sacrifices on the a.	4640
	12:33	he offered sacrifices on the a he had built	4640
	12:33	and went up to the a to make offerings.	4640
	13: 1	as Jeroboam was standing by the a to make	4640
	13: 2	He cried out against the a by the word of	4640
	13: 2	of the LORD: "O a, altar!	4640
	13: 2	of the LORD: "O altar, a!	4640
	13: 3	The a will be split apart and the ashes	4640
	13: 4	of God cried out against the a at Bethel,	4640
	13: 4	he stretched out his hand from the a	4640
	13: 5	the a was split apart,	4640
	13:32	of the LORD against the a in Bethel and	4640
	16:32	up an a for Baal in the temple of Baal	4640
	18:26	they danced around the a they had made.	4640
	18:30	and he repaired the a of the LORD	4640
	18:32	With the stones he built an a in the name of	4640
	18:35	around the a and even filled the trench.	4640
2Ki	11:11	near the a and the temple,	4640
	12: 9	He placed it beside the a,	4640
	16:10	He saw an a in Damascus and sent to Uriah	4640
	16:10	to Uriah the priest a sketch of the a,	4640
	16:11	So Uriah the priest built an a in accordance	4640
	16:12	from Damascus and saw the a,	4640
	16:13	of his fellowship offerings on the a.	4640
	16:14	The bronze a that stood before	4640
	16:14	the new a and the temple of the LORD—	4640
	16:14	and put it on the north side of the new a.	4640
	16:15	"On the large new a,	4640
	16:15	on the a all the blood of the burnt offerings	2257S
	16:15	the bronze a for seeking guidance."	4640
	18:22	"You must worship before this a"	4640
	23: 9	of the high places did not serve at the a of	4640
	23:15	Even the a at Bethel,	4640
	23:15	even that a and high place he demolished.	4640
	23:16	from them and burned on the a to defile it,	4640
	23:17	from Judah and pronounced against the a	4640
1Ch	6:49	on the a of burnt offering and on the altar	4640
	6:49	on the a of incense in connection with all	4640
	16:40	on the a of burnt offering regularly,	4640
	21:18	an a to the LORD on the threshing floor	4640
	21:22	of your threshing floor so I can build an a	4640
	21:26	David built an a to the LORD there	4640
	21:26	from heaven on the a of burnt offering.	4640
	21:29	of the a of burnt offering were at that time on	4640
	22: 1	and also the a of burnt offering for Israel."	4640
	28:18	and the weight of the refined gold for the a	4640
2Ch	1: 5	But the bronze a that Bezalel son of Uri,	4640
	1: 6	the bronze a before the LORD in the Tent	4640
	4: 1	He made a bronze a twenty cubits long,	4640
	4:19	in God's temple: the golden a;	4640
	5:12	stood on the east side of the a,	4640
	6:12	before the a of the LORD in front of	4640

2Ch	6:22	the oath before your a in this temple,	4640
	7: 7	the bronze a he had made could not hold	4640
	7: 9	the dedication of the a for seven days and	4640
	8:12	On the a of the LORD that he had built	4640
	15: 8	He repaired the a of the LORD that was	4640
	23:10	near the a and the temple,	4640
	26:16	of the LORD to burn incense on the a	4640
	26:19	in their presence before the incense a in	4640
	29:18	the a of burnt offering with all its utensils,	4640
	29:19	They are now in front of the LORD's a."	4640
	29:21	to offer these on the a of the LORD.	4640
	29:22	the blood and sprinkled it on the a;	4640
	29:22	and sprinkled their blood on the a;	4640
	29:22	and sprinkled their blood on the a.	4640
	29:24	the goats and presented their blood on the a	4640
	29:27	to sacrifice the burnt offering on the a.	4640
	32:12	before one a and burn sacrifices on it'?	4640
	33:16	Then he restored the a of the LORD	4640
	35:16	and the offering of burnt offerings on the a	4640
Ezr	3: 2	and his associates began to build the a of	4640
	3: 3	they built the a on its foundation	4640
	7:17	and sacrifice them on the a of the temple	10401
Ne	10:34	a contribution of wood to burn on the a of	4640
Ps	26: 6	and go about your a, O LORD,	4640
	43: 4	Then will I go to the a of God, to God,	4640
	51:19	then bulls will be offered on your a.	4640
	84: 3	a place near your a, O LORD Almighty,	4640
	118:27	up to the horns of the a.	4640
Isa	6: 6	which he had taken with tongs from the a.	4640
	19:19	be an a to the LORD in the heart of Egypt,	4640
	27: 9	the stones to be like chalk stones crushed	4640
	29: 2	she will be to me like an a hearth.	789
	36: 7	"You must worship before this a"?	4640
	40:16	Lebanon is not sufficient for a fires,	AIT
	56: 7	and sacrifices will be accepted on my a;	4640
	60: 7	they will be accepted as offerings on my a,	4640
La	2: 7	The Lord has rejected his a	4640
Eze	8: 5	the gate of the a I saw this idol of jealousy.	4640
	8:16	between the portico and the a.	4640
	9: 2	in and stood beside the bronze a.	4640
	40:46	for the priests who have charge of the a.	4640
	40:47	And the a was in front of the temple.	4640
	41:22	There was a wooden a three cubits high	4640
	43:13	the a in long cubits, that cubit being a cubit	4640
	43:13	And this is the height of the a:	4640
	43:15	The a hearth is four cubits high,	2219
	43:16	The a hearth is square,	789
	43:17	The steps of the a face east."	2084S
	43:18	and sprinkling blood upon the a	4640
	43:20	and put it on the four horns of the a and on	2257S
	43:20	so purify the a and make atonement for it.	2257S
	43:22	and the a is to be purified as it was purified	4640
	43:26	to make atonement for the a and cleanse it;	4640
	43:27	and fellowship offerings on the a.	4640
	45:19	the four corners of the upper ledge of the a	4640
	47: 1	south of the a.	4640
Joel	1:13	wail, you who minister before the a.	4640
	2:17	weep between the temple porch and the a.	4640
Am	2: 8	down beside every a on garments taken	4640
	3:14	the horns of the a will be cut off and fall to	4640
	9: 1	I saw the Lord standing by the a,	4640
Zec	9:15	for sprinkling the corners of the a.	4640
	14:20	be like the sacred bowls in front of the a.	4640
Mal	1: 7	"You place defiled food on my a.	4640
	1:10	you would not light useless fires on my a!	4640
	2:13	You flood the LORD's a with tears.	4640
Mt	5:23	if you are offering your gift at the a	2603
	5:24	leave your gift there in front of the a.	2603
	23:18	You also say, 'If anyone swears by the a,	2603
	23:19	the gift, or the a that makes the gift sacred?	2603
	23:20	the a swears by it and by everything on it.	2603
	23:35	between the temple and the a.	2603
Lk	1:11	at the right side of the a of incense.	2603
	11:51	who was killed between the a and	2603
Ac	17:23	I even found an a with this inscription:	1117
1Co	9:13	the a share in what is offered on the altar?	2603
	9:13	the altar share in what is offered on the a?	2603
	10:18	the sacrifices participate in the a.	2603
Heb	7:13	from that tribe has ever served at the a.	2603
	9: 4	which had the golden a of incense and	2593
	13:10	an a from which those who minister at	2603
Jas	2:21	when he offered his son Isaac on the a?	2603
Rev	6: 9	the a the souls of those who had been slain	2603
	8: 3	came and stood at the a.	2603
	8: 3	on the golden a before the throne.	2603
	8: 5	filled it with fire from the a,	2603
	9:13	from the horns of the golden a that is	2603
	11: 1	and measure the temple of God and the a,	2603
	14:18	came from the a and called in a loud voice	2603
	16: 7	And I heard the a respond:	2603

ALTARS (61) [ALTAR]

Ex	34:13	Break down their a,	4640
Lev	26:30	cut down your incense a,	2802
Nu	3:31	the table, the lampstand, the a,	4640
	23: 1	Balaam said, "Build me seven a here,	4640
	23: 4	and Balaam said, "I have prepared seven a,	4640
	23:14	and there he built seven a and offered	4640
	23:29	Balaam said, "Build me seven a here,	4640
Dt	7: 5	Break down their a,	4640
	12: 3	down their a, smash their sacred stones	4640
Jdg	2: 2	but you shall break down their a.'	4640
1Ki	19:10	broken down your a,	4640
	19:14	broken down your a,	4640
2Ki	11:18	the a and idols to pieces and killed Mattan	4640
	11:18	the priest of Baal in front of the a.	4640

2Ki 18:22	high places and a Hezekiah removed,	4640
21: 3	he also erected a to Baal and made	4640
21: 4	He built a in the temple of the LORD,	4640
21: 5	he built a to all the starry hosts.	4640
23:12	down the a the kings of Judah had erected	4640
23:12	the a Manasseh had built in the two courts	4640
23:20	on the a and burned human bones on them.	4640
2Ch 14: 3	the foreign a and the high places,	4640
14: 5	the high places and incense a in every town	2802
23:17	the a and idols and killed Mattan the priest	4640
23:17	the priest of Baal in front of the a.	4640
28:24	up a at every street corner in Jerusalem.	4640
30:14	the a in Jerusalem and cleared away	4640
30:14	in Jerusalem and cleared away the incense a	5232
31: 1	the high places and the a throughout Judah	4640
32:12	and a, saying to Judah	4640
33: 3	he also erected a to the Baals	4640
33: 4	He built a in the temple of the LORD,	4640
33: 5	he built a to all the starry hosts.	4640
33:15	as all the a he had built on the temple hill	4640
34: 4	the a of the Baals were torn down;	4640
34: 4	he cut to pieces the incense a that were	2802
34: 5	the bones of the priests on their a,	4640
34: 7	he tore down the a and the Asherah poles	4640
34: 7	to powder and cut to pieces all the incense a	2802
Isa 17: 8	They will not look to the a,	4640
17: 8	and the incense a their fingers have made.	2802
27: 9	no Asherah poles or incense a will	2802
36: 7	and a Hezekiah removed,	4640
65: 3	and burning incense on a of brick;	4246
Jer 11:13	and the a you have set up to burn incense	4640
17: 1	of their hearts and on the horns of their a.	4640
17: 2	Even their children remember their a	4640
Eze 6: 4	Your a will be demolished	4640
6: 4	be demolished and your incense a will	2802
6: 5	and I will scatter your bones around your a.	4640
6: 6	your a will be laid waste and devastated,	4640
6: 6	your incense a broken down,	2802
6:13	around their a, on every high hill and on all	4640
Hos 8:11	Ephraim built many a for sin offerings,	4640
8:11	these have become a for sinning.	4640
10: 1	As his fruit increased, he built more a;	4640
10: 2	The LORD will demolish their a	4640
10: 8	and thistles will grow up and cover their a.	4640
12:11	Their a will be like piles of stones on	4640
Am 3:14	I will destroy the a of Bethel;	4640
Ro 11: 3	and torn down your a;	2603

ALTER (1) [ALTERED]
Ps 89:34	or a what my lips have uttered.	9101

ALTERED (1) [ALTER]
Da 6: 8	and put it in writing so that it cannot be a—	10731

ALTERNATE (1) [ALTERNATED]
Ex 28:34	the pomegranates are to a around the hem	2256+2298+7194+8232S

ALTERNATED (2) [ALTERNATE]
Ex 39:26	and pomegranates a around the hem of	2256+7194+8232S
Eze 41:18	Palm trees a with cherubim.	1068

ALTHOUGH (65) [THOUGH]
Ge 42: 8	A Joseph recognized his brothers,	2256
Ex 19: 5	A the whole earth is mine,	3954
34: 9	A this is a stiff-necked people,	3954
Dt 14: 7	A they chew the cud,	3954
14: 8	a it has a split hoof,	3954
Jdg 12: 2	and a I called,	AIT
Ru 3:12	A it is true that I am near of kin,	3954
1Sa 2:32	A good will be done to Israel,	889+928+3972
15:17	"A you were once small in your own eyes,	561
2Sa 13:25	A Absalom urged him,	2256
23:21	A the Egyptian had a spear in his hand,	2256
1Ki 11:10	A he had forbidden Solomon	2256
15:14	A he did not remove the high places,	2256
2Ki 17:15	They imitated the nations around them a	889
23: 9	A the priests of the high places did	421
1Ch 11:23	A the Egyptian had a spear like	2256
26:10	Shimri the first (a he was not the firstborn,	3954
2Ch 15:17	A he did not remove the high places	8370
24:19	A the LORD sent prophets to the people	2256
24:24	A the Aramean army had come with only	3954
30:18	A most of the many people who came	3954
Ne 5: 5	A we are of the same flesh and blood	6964
Job 9:21	"A I am blameless, I have no concern	NIH
34: 6	A I am right, I am considered a liar;	6584
34: 6	A I am guiltless,	NIH
Ecc 8:12	A a wicked man commits a hundred crimes	889
Isa 12: 1	A you were angry with me,	3954
17:13	A the peoples roar like the roar	NIH
30:20	A the Lord gives you the bread of adversity	2256
60:15	"A you have been forsaken and hated,	9393
Jer 2:22	A you wash yourself with soda and use	561+3954
5: 2	A they say, 'As surely as the LORD lives,'	561
14:11	A they cry out to me,	2256
14: 7	A our sins testify against us, O LORD,	561
14:12	A they fast, I will not listen to their cry;	3954
23:38	A you claim, 'This is the oracle of	561
48:33	A there are shouts,	NIH
Eze 8:18	A I shout in my ears,	2256
11:16	A I sent them far away among the nations	3954
15: 7	A they have come out of the fire,	NIH
Eze 20:13	a the man who obeys them will live	NIH
20:21	a the man who obeys them will live	NIH
20:38	A I will bring them out of the land	NIH
32:32	A I had him spread terror in the land of	3954
Hos 8:10	A they have sold themselves among	1685+3954
Na 1:12	"A they have allies and are numerous,	561
1:12	A I have afflicted you, [O Judah,]	2256
Lk 14:14	A they cannot repay you,	4022
Jn 4: 2	a in fact it was not Jesus who baptized,	2793
Ac 20:19	a I was severely tested	AIT
28:17	a I have done nothing against our people or	AIT
Ro 1:21	For a they knew God,	AIT
1:22	A they claimed to be wise,	AIT
1:32	A they know God's righteous decree	AIT
1Co 7:21	a if you can gain your freedom, do so.	247
2Co 12: 1	A there is nothing to be gained,	AIT
Gal 4: 1	a he owns the whole estate.	AIT
Eph 3: 8	A I am less than the least of all God's people	NIG
1Ti 3:14	A I hope to come to you soon,	AIT
Phm 1: 8	a in Christ I could be bold	AIT
Heb 5: 8	A he was a son, he learned obedience	2788
10: 8	(a the law required them to be made).	NIG
Jas 3: 4	A they are so large and are driven	AIT
2Pe 2:11	a they are stronger and more powerful,	AIT
Jude 1: 3	a I was very eager to write to you about	NIG

ALTOGETHER (22) [TOGETHER]
Ge 5: 5	A, Adam lived 930 years, and then he died.	3972
5: 8	A, Seth lived 912 years, and then he died.	3972
5:11	A, Enosh lived 905 years, and then he died.	3972
5:14	A, Kenan lived 910 years,	3972
5:17	A, Mahalalel lived 895 years,	3972
5:20	A, Jared lived 962 years, and then he died.	3972
5:23	A, Enoch lived 365 years,	3972
5:27	A, Methuselah lived 969 years,	3972
5:31	A, Lamech lived 777 years,	3972
9:29	A, Noah lived 950 years, and then he died.	3972
25: 7	A, Abraham lived a hundred	465+2256
25:17	A, Ishmael lived a hundred	465+2256
Ex 26: 7	over the tabernacle—eleven a.	NIH
36:14	over the tabernacle—eleven a.	NIH
Nu 7:85	the silver dishes weighed two thousand	3972
7:86	A, the gold dishes weighed a hundred	3972
1Ch 9:22	A, those chosen to be gatekeepers at	3972
Job 13: 5	If only you would be silent!	3087+3087
Ps 19: 9	of the LORD are sure and a righteous.	3481
50:21	you thought I was a like you.	2118+2118
SS 5:16	he is a lovely,	3972
Ac 27:37	A there were 276 of us on board.	3836+4246

ALUSH (2)
Nu 33:13	They left Dophkah and camped at A.	478
33:14	They left A and camped at Rephidim,	478

ALVAH (2)
Ge 36:40	and regions: Timna, A,	6595
1Ch 1:51	The chiefs of Edom were: Timna, A,	6595

ALVAN (2)
Ge 36:23	A, Manahath, Ebal, Shepho and Onam.	6597
1Ch 1:40	A, Manahath, Ebal, Shepho and Onam.	6597

ALWAYS (135)
Ge 26:29	but a treated you well and sent you away	8370
Ex 19: 9	and will a put their trust in you."	4200+6409
28:30	Thus Aaron will a bear the means	9458
29:28	This is a to be the regular share from	6409
Lev 25:32	" The Levites a have the right	6409
Nu 22:30	which you have a ridden, to this day?	4946+6388
Dt 5:29	and keep all my commands a,	2021+3427+3972
6:24	that we might a prosper and be kept alive,	2021+3427+3972
11: 1	his laws and his commands a,	2021+3427+3972
12:28	so that it may a go well with you	6330+6409
14:23	to revere the LORD your God a.	2021+3427+3972
15:11	There will a be poor people in the land	2532+4202
18: 5	minister in the LORD's name a.	2021+3427+3972
19: 9	to love the LORD your God and to walk a in	
	his ways—	2021+3427+3972
28:13	you will a be at the top,	8370
Jos 4:24	and so that you might a fear	2021+3427+3972
1Sa 1:22	and he will live there a."	6330+6409
2:35	he will minister before my anointed one a.	2021+3427+3972
7:17	But he a went back to Ramah,	NIH
2Sa 9: 7	and you will a eat at my table."	9458
9:10	will a eat at my table."	9458
9:13	because he a ate at the king's table,	9458
1Ki 5: 1	because he had a been on friendly terms	2021+3427+3972
9: 3	My eyes and my heart will a be there.	2021+3427+3972
11:36	that David my servant may a have a lamp	2021+3427+3972
12: 7	they will a be your servants."	2021+3427+3972
22: 8	about me, but a bad.	NIH
2Ki 17:37	You must a be careful to keep the decrees	2021+3427+3972
1Ch 16:11	seek his face a.	9458
2Ch 7:16	My eyes and my heart will a be there.	2021+3427+3972
10: 7	they will a be your servants."	2021+3427+3972
18: 7	about me, but a bad.	3427+3972
Job 31:32	for my door was a open to the traveler—	AIT

Ps 9:18	But the needy will not a be forgotten,	4200+5905
10: 5	His ways are a prosperous;	928+3972+6961
10: 6	I'll a be happy and never have trouble."	1887+1887+2256+4200
16: 8	I have set the LORD a before me.	9458
34: 1	his praise will a be on my lips.	9458
35:27	may they a say, "The LORD be exalted,	9458
37:26	They are a generous and lend freely;	2021+3427+3972
40:11	may your love and your truth a protect me.	9458
40:16	may those who love your salvation a say,	9458
51: 3	and my sin is a before me.	9458
56: 7	they are a plotting to harm me.	3972
70: 4	may those who love your salvation a say,	9458
71: 3	Be my rock of refuge, to which I can a go;	9458
71:14	But as for me, I will a have hope;	6409
73:12	a carefree, they increase in wealth.	6409
73:23	Yet I am a with you;	9458
103: 9	He will not a accuse,	4200+5905
105: 4	seek his face a.	9458
109:15	May their sins a remain before the LORD,	9458
119:44	I will a obey your law, for ever and ever.	9458
119:117	I will a have regard for your decrees.	9458
119:132	as you a do to those who love your name.	5477
Pr 5:19	may her breasts satisfy you a,	928+3972+6961
6:14	he a stirs up dissension.	928+3972+6961
8:30	rejoicing a in his presence,	928+3972+6961
23: 7	for he is the kind of man who is a thinking	AIT
23:17	but a be zealous for the fear of the LORD.	2021+3427+3972
28:14	Blessed is the man who a fears the LORD,	4200+6329
29:14	his throne will a be secure.	4200+6329
Ecc 9: 8	A be clothed in white,	928+3972+6961
9: 8	and a anoint your head with oil.	440+2893
Isa 57:16	nor will I a be angry,	4200+5905
58:11	The LORD will guide you a;	9458
60:11	Your gates will a stand open,	9458
Jer 3: 5	will you a be angry?	4200+6409
8: 5	Why does Jerusalem a turn away?	5904
12: 1	You are a righteous, O LORD,	NIH
12: 2	You are a on their lips but far	7940
17: 8	its leaves are a green.	AIT
32:39	that they will a fear me for their own good	2021+3427+3972
La 5:20	Why do you a forget us?	4200+5905
Hos 5:20	they are a before me.	6964
12: 6	and wait for your God a.	9458
Mal 1: 4	people a under the wrath of the LORD.	6330+6409
Mt 18:10	their angels in heaven a see the face	1328+4246
26:11	The poor you will a have with you,	4121
26:11	but you will not a have me.	4121
28:20	And surely I am with you a,	2465+3836+4246
Mk 14: 7	The poor you will a have with you,	4121
14: 7	But you will not a have me.	4121
Lk 15:31	the father said, 'you are a with me,	4121
18: 1	to show them that they should a pray and	4121
21:36	Be a on the watch,	1877+2789+4246
Jn 5:17	a at his work to this	AIT
8:29	for I do what pleases him."	4121
11:42	I knew that you a hear me,	4121
12: 8	You will a have the poor among you,	4121
12: 8	but you will not a have me."	4121
18:20	"I a taught in synagogues or at the temple,	4121
Ac 2:25	" 'I saw the Lord a before me.	1328+4246
7:51	You a resist the Holy Spirit!	107
9:36	who was a doing good and helping	4441
24:16	So I strive to a keep my conscience clear	1328+4246
Ro 15:20	It has a been my ambition to preach	AIT
1Co 1: 4	I a thank God for you because	4121
13: 7	It a protects, always trusts, always hopes,	4246
13: 7	It always protects, a trusts, always hopes,	4246
13: 7	It always protects, always trusts, a hopes,	4246
13: 7	always trusts, always hopes, a perseveres.	4246
15:58	A give yourselves fully to the work of	4121
2Co 1:19	but in him it has a been "Yes."	AIT
2:14	who a leads us in triumphal procession	4121
4:10	We a carry around in our body the death	4121
4:11	For we who are alive are a being given	107
5: 6	Therefore we are a confident and know that	4121
6:10	sorrowful, yet a rejoicing;	107
Gal 4:18	to be so a and not just when I am with you.	4121
Eph 5:20	a giving thanks to God the Father	4121
6:18	and a keep on praying for all the saints.	4246
Php 1: 4	I a pray with joy	4121
1:20	now as a Christ will be exalted in my body,	4121
2:12	my dear friends, as you have a obeyed—	4121
4: 4	Rejoice in the Lord a.	4121
Col 4: 2	We a thank God,	4121
4: 6	Let your conversation be a full of grace,	4121
4:12	He is a wrestling in prayer for you,	4121
1Th 1: 2	We a thank God for all of you,	4121
2:16	In this way they a heap up their sins to	4121
3: 6	that you have pleasant memories of us a	4121
5:15	but a try to be kind to each other and	4246
5:16	Be joyful a;	4121
2Th 1: 3	We ought a to thank God for you, brothers,	4121
2:13	But we ought a to thank God for you,	4121
2Ti 3: 7	a learning but never able to acknowledge	4121
Tit 1:12	"Cretans are a liars, evil brutes,	107
Phm 1: 4	I a thank my God as I remember you	4121
Heb 3:10	and I said, 'Their hearts are a going astray,	107
7:25	because he a lives to intercede for them.	4121
1Pe 3:15	A be prepared to give an answer	107
2Pe 1:12	So I will a remind you of these things,	107
1:15	that after my departure you will a be able	1668

AM (1125) [BE] See Index of Articles Etc.—
See also selected listing under I AM

AMAD (1)
Jos 19:26   Allammelech, A and Mishal.   6675

AMAL (1)
1Ch 7:35   Zophah, Imna, Shelesh and A.   6663

AMALEK (12) [AMALEKITE, AMALEKITES]
Ge	36:12	Timna, who bore him A.	6667
	36:16	Korah, Gatam and A. These were the chiefs descended from Eliphaz	6667
Ex	17:14	the memory of A from under heaven."	6667
Nu	24:20	Then Balaam saw A and uttered his oracle:	6667
	24:20	"A was first among the nations,	6667
Dt	25:19	you shall blot out the memory of A from	6667
Jdg	5:14	whose roots were in A;	6667
1Sa	15: 5	of A and set an ambush in the ravine.	6667
2Sa	8:12	the Ammonites and the Philistines, and A.	6667
1Ch	1:36	and Kenaz; by Timna: A.	6667
	18:11	the Ammonites and the Philistines, and A.	6667
Ps	83: 7	Ammon and A, Philistia,	6667

AMALEKITE (4) [AMALEK]
Ex	17:13	So Joshua overcame the A army with	6667
1Sa	30:13	"I am an Egyptian, the slave of an A.	6668
2Sa	1: 8	" 'An A,' I answered.	6668
	1:13	"I am the son of an alien, an A,"	6668

AMALEKITES (34) [AMALEK]
Ge	14: 7	the whole territory of the A,	6668
Ex	17: 8	The A came and attacked the Israelites	6667
	17: 9	of our men and go out to fight the A.	6667
	17:10	Joshua fought the A as Moses had ordered,	6667
	17:11	the A were winning.	6667
	17:16	The LORD will be at war against the A	6667
Nu	13:29	The A live in the Negev;	6667
	14:25	A and Canaanites are living in the valleys,	6668
	14:43	the A and Canaanites will face you there.	6668
	14:45	Then the A and Canaanites who lived in	6668
Dt	25:17	Remember what the A did to you along	6667
Jdg	3:13	Getting the Ammonites and A to join him,	6667
	6: 3	A and other eastern peoples invaded	6667
	6:33	A and other eastern peoples joined forces	6667
	7:12	the A and all the other eastern peoples	6667
	10:12	the A and the Maonites oppressed you	6667
	12:15	in the hill country of the A.	6668
1Sa	14:48	He fought valiantly and defeated the A,	6667
	15: 2	'I will punish the A for what they did	6667
	15: 3	attack the A and totally destroy everything	6667
	15: 6	the A so that I do not destroy you along	6668
	15: 6	So the Kenites moved away from the A.	6667
	15: 7	the A all the way from Havilah to Shur,	6667
	15: 8	He took Agag king of the A alive,	6667
	15:15	"The soldiers brought them from the A;	6668
	15:18	and completely destroy those wicked people, the A;	6667
	15:20	the A and brought back Agag their king.	6667
	15:32	"Bring me Agag king of the A."	6667
	27: 8	the Girzites and the A.	6668
	28:18	or carry out his fierce wrath against the A,	6667
	30: 1	the A had raided the Negev and Ziklag.	6668
	30:18	David recovered everything the A had taken	6667
2Sa	1: 1	the A and stayed in Ziklag two days.	6667
1Ch	4:43	the remaining A who had escaped,	6667

AMAM (1)
Jos 15:26   A, Shema, Moladah,   585

AMANA (1)
SS 4: 8   Descend from the crest of A,   592

AMARIAH (15) [AMARIAH'S]
1Ch	6: 7	Meraioth the father of A,	618
	6: 7	A the father of Ahitub,	618
	6:11	Azariah the father of A,	618
	6:11	A the father of Ahitub,	618
	6:52	Meraioth his son, A his son, Ahitub his son,	618
	23:19	Jeriah the first, A the second,	618
	24:23	Jeriah the first, A the second,	619
2Ch	19:11	"A the chief priest will be over you	619
	31:15	A and Shecaniah assisted him faithfully in	619
Ezr	7: 3	the son of A, the son of Azariah,	618
	10:42	Shallum, A and Joseph.	618
Ne	10: 3	Pashhur, A, Malkijah,	618
	11: 4	the son of A, the son of Shephatiah,	618
	12: 2	A, Malluch, Hattush,	618
Zep	1: 1	the son of A, the son of Hezekiah,	618

AMARIAH'S (1) [AMARIAH]
Ne 12:13   of Ezra's, Meshullam; of A, Jehohanan;   618

AMASA (18)
2Sa	17:25	Absalom had appointed A over the army	6690
	17:25	A was the son of a man named Jether,	6690
	19:13	And say to A,	6690
	20: 4	Then the king said to A,	6690
	20: 5	But when A went to summon Judah,	6690
	20: 8	A came to meet them.	6690

2Sa	20: 9	Joab said to A, "How are you,	6690
	20: 9	Then Joab took A by the beard	6690
	20:10	A was not on his guard against the dagger	6690
	20:10	Without being stabbed again, A died.	6690
	20:11	One of Joab's men stood beside A and said,	2257S
	20:12	A lay wallowing in his blood in the middle	6690
	20:12	that everyone who came up to A stopped,	6690
	20:13	After A had been removed from the road,	NIH
1Ki	2: 5	Abner son of Ner and A son of Jether.	6690
	2:32	and A son of Jether,	6690
1Ch	2:17	Abigail was the mother of A,	6690
2Ch	28:12	and A son of Hadlai—	6690

AMASAI (5)
1Ch	6:25	The descendants of Elkanah: A, Ahimoth,	6691
	6:35	the son of Mahath, the son of A,	6691
	12:18	Then the Spirit came upon A,	6691
	15:24	Shebaniah, Joshaphat, Nethanel, A,	6691
2Ch	29:12	Mahath son of A and Joel son of Azariah;	6691

AMASHSAI (1)
Ne 11:13   A son of Azarel, the son of Ahzai,   6692

AMASIAH (1)
2Ch 17:16   A son of Zicri,   6674

AMASSED (2) [AMASSES]
Ecc 2: 8   I a silver and gold for myself,   4043
Eze 28: 4   and a gold and silver in your treasuries.   6913

AMASSES (1) [AMASSED]
Pr 28: 8   by exorbitant interest a it for another,   7695

AMAZED (39) [AMAZEMENT]
Isa	29: 9	and a, blind yourselves and be sightless;	9449
Hab	1: 5	and be utterly a.	9449+9449
Mt	7:28	the crowds were a at his teaching,	1742
	8:27	The men were a and asked,	2513
	9:33	The crowd was a and said,	2513
	13:54	and they were a.	1742
	15:31	The people were a when they saw	2513
	21:20	When the disciples saw this, they were a.	2513
	22:22	When they heard this, they were a.	2513
Mk	1:22	The people were a at his teaching,	1742
	1:27	so a that they asked each other,	2501
	2:12	This a everyone and they praised God,	2014
	5:20	And all the people were a.	2513
	6: 2	and many who heard him were a.	1742
	6: 6	And he was a at their lack of faith.	2513
	6:51	They were completely a,	2014
	10:24	The disciples were a at his words.	2501
	10:26	The disciples were even more a,	1742
	11:18	the whole crowd was a at his teaching,	1742
	12:17	And they were a at him.	1703
	15: 5	Jesus still made no reply, and Pilate was a.	2513
Lk	2:18	and all who heard it were a at what	2513
	2:47	Everyone who heard him was a	2014
	4:22	and were a at the gracious words that came	2513
	4:32	They were a at his teaching,	1742
	4:36	the people were a and said to each other,	2502
	5:26	Everyone was a and gave praise to God. 1749+3284
	7: 9	When Jesus heard this, he was a at him,	2513
	9:43	And they were all a at the greatness of God.	1742
	11:14	and the crowd was a.	2513
	24:22	In addition, some of our women a us.	2014
Jn	5:28	"Do not be a at this,	2513
	7:15	The Jews were a and asked,	2513
Ac	2: 7	Utterly a, they asked:	2014+2513
	2:12	A and perplexed, they asked one another,	2014
	7:31	When he saw this, he was a at the sight.	2513
	8: 9	in the city and a all the people of Samaria.	2014
	8:11	They followed him because he had a them	2014
	13:12	for he was a at the teaching about the Lord.	1742

AMAZEMENT (7) [AMAZED, AMAZING]
Da	3:24	leaped to his feet in a and asked	10097+10755
Mt	27:14	to the great a of the governor.	2513
Mk	7:37	People were overwhelmed with a.	1742+5669
Lk	8:25	In fear and a they asked one another,	2513
	24:41	not believe it because of joy and a,	2513
Jn	5:20	to your a he will show him	2513
Ac	3:10	with wonder and a at what had happened	1749

AMAZIAH (40) [AMAZIAH'S]
2Ki	12:21	And A his son succeeded him as king.	604
	13:12	including his war against A king of Judah.	604
	14: 1	A son of Joash king of Judah began	605
	14: 8	Then A sent messengers to Jehoash son	605
	14: 9	But Jehoash king of Israel replied to A king	605
	14:11	A, however, would not listen.	605
	14:11	He and A king of Judah faced each other	605
	14:13	Jehoash king of Israel captured A king	605
	14:15	including his war against A king of Judah,	605
	14:17	A son of Joash king of Judah lived	605
	14:21	and made him king in place of his father A.	605
	14:22	after A rested with his fathers.	2021+4889S
	14:23	In the fifteenth year of A son of Joash king	605
	15: 1	Azariah son of A king of Judah began	604
	15: 3	just as his father A had done.	605
1Ch	3:12	A his son, Azariah his son, Jotham his son,	605
	4:34	Meshobab, Jamlech, Joshah son of A,	604

1Ch	6:45	the son of A, the son of Hilkiah,	604
2Ch	24:27	And A his son succeeded him as king.	605
	25: 1	A was twenty-five years old	605
	25: 5	A called the people of Judah together	605
	25: 9	A asked the man of God,	605
	25:10	So A dismissed the troops who had come	605
	25:11	A then marshaled his strength	605
	25:13	Meanwhile the troops that A had sent back	605
	25:14	When A returned from slaughtering	605
	25:14	The anger of the LORD burned against A,	605
	25:17	A king of Judah consulted his advisers,	605
	25:18	But Jehoash king of Israel replied to A king	605
	25:20	A, however, would not listen.	605
	25:21	He and A king of Judah faced each other	605
	25:23	Jehoash king of Israel captured A king	605
	25:25	A son of Joash king of Judah lived	605
	25:27	the time that A turned away from following	605
	26: 1	and made him king in place of his father A.	605
	26: 2	after A rested with his fathers.	2021+4889S
	26: 4	just as his father A had done.	605
Am	7:10	Then A the priest of Bethel sent a message	604
	7:12	Then A said to Amos, "Get out, you seer!	604
	7:14	Amos answered A, "I was neither a prophet	604

AMAZIAH'S (2) [AMAZIAH]
2Ki 14:18   As for the other events of A reign,   605
2Ch 25:26   As for the other events of A reign,   605

AMAZING (3) [AMAZEMENT]
Jos 3: 5   for tomorrow the LORD will do a things   7098
Jdg 13:19   the LORD did an a thing while Manoah   7098
Pr 30:18   "There are three things that are too a   7098

AMBASSADOR (1) [AMBASSADORS]
Eph 6:20   for which I am an a in chains.   4563

AMBASSADORS (2) [AMBASSADOR]
Isa 57: 9   You sent your a far away;   7495
2Co 5:20   We are therefore Christ's a,   4563

AMBASSAGE (KJV) See DELEGATION

AMBER (KJV) See GLOWING METAL

AMBITION (7)
Ro	15:20	It has always been my a to preach	5818
Gal	5:20	jealousy, fits of rage, selfish a, dissensions,	2249
Php	1:17	The former preach Christ out of selfish a,	2249
	2: 3	Do nothing out of selfish a or vain conceit,	2249
1Th	4:11	Make it your a to lead a quiet life,	5818
Jas	3:14	But if you harbor bitter envy and selfish a	2249
	3:16	For where you have envy and selfish a,	2249

AMBUSH (25) [AMBUSHES]
Jos	8: 2	Set an a behind the city."	741
	8: 4	You are to set an a behind the city.	741
	8: 7	you are to rise up from a and take the city.	741
	8: 9	and they went to the place of a and lay	4422
	8:12	about five thousand men and set them in a	741
	8:13	to the north of the city and the a to the west	6811
	8:14	not know that an a had been set against him	741
	8:19	the men in the a rose quickly	741
	8:21	and all Israel saw that the a had taken	741
	8:22	The men of the a also came out	465S
Jdg	9:25	of Shechem set men on the hilltops to a	741
	9:43	into three companies and set an a in	741
	20:29	Then Israel set an a around Gibeah.	741
	20:33	and the Israelite a charged out of its place	741
	20:36	because they relied on the a they had set	741
	20:37	been in a made a sudden dash into Gibeah	741
	20:38	the a that they should send up a great cloud	741
1Sa	15: 5	of Amalek and set an a in the ravine.	741
2Ch	13:13	in front of Judah the a was behind them.	4422
Ps	10: 8	from a he murders the innocent,	5041
	64: 4	They shoot from a at the innocent man;	5041
Jer	51:12	station the watchmen, prepare an a!	741
Hos	6: 9	As marauders lie in a for a man,	2675
Ac	23:21	of them are waiting in a for him.	1910
	25: 3	for they were preparing an a to kill him	1909

AMBUSHES (1) [AMBUSH]
2Ch 20:22   the LORD set a against the men   741

AMEN (57)
Nu	5:22	Then the woman is to say, "A. So be it."	589+589
Dt	27:15	Then all the people shall say, "A!"	589
	27:16	Then all the people shall say, "A!"	589
	27:17	Then all the people shall say, "A!"	589
	27:18	Then all the people shall say, "A!"	589
	27:19	Then all the people shall say, "A!"	589
	27:20	Then all the people shall say, "A!"	589
	27:21	Then all the people shall say, "A!"	589
	27:22	Then all the people shall say, "A!"	589
	27:23	Then all the people shall say, "A!"	589
	27:24	Then all the people shall say, "A!"	589
	27:25	Then all the people shall say, "A!"	589
	27:26	Then all the people shall say, "A!"	589
1Ki	1:36	of Jehoiada answered the king, "A!	589
1Ch	16:36	Then all the people said "A" and "Praise	589
Ne	5:13	At this the whole assembly said, "A,"	589

Ne	8: 6	people lifted their hands and responded, "A!	589
	8: 6	and responded, "Amen! A!"	589
Ps	41:13	A and Amen.	589
	41:13	Amen and A.	589
	72:19	A and Amen.	589
	72:19	Amen and A.	589
	89:52	A and Amen.	589
	89:52	Amen and A.	589
	106:48	Let all the people say, "A!"	589
Jer	11: 5	I answered, "A, LORD."	589
	28: 6	He said, "A!	589
Ro	1:25	who is forever praised. A.	297
	9: 5	over all, forever praised! A.	297
	11:36	be the glory forever! A.	297
	15:33	The God of peace be with you all. A.	297
	16:27	through Jesus Christ! A.	297
1Co	14:16	those who do not understand say "A"	297
	16:24	My love to all of you in Christ Jesus. A.	297
2Co	1:20	And so through him the "A" is spoken by us	297
Gal	1: 5	to whom be glory for ever and ever. A.	297
	6:18	with your spirit, brothers. A.	297
Eph	3:21	for ever and ever! A.	297
Php	4:20	for ever and ever. A.	297
	4:23	the Lord Jesus Christ be with your spirit. A.	297
1Ti	1:17	for ever and ever. A.	297
	6:16	be honor and might forever. A.	297
2Ti	4:18	for ever and ever. A.	297
Heb	13:21	for ever and ever. A.	297
1Pe	4:11	for ever and ever. A.	297
	5:11	To him be the power for ever and ever. A.	297
2Pe	3:18	both now and forever! A.	297
Jude	1:25	now and forevermore! A.	297
Rev	1: 6	for ever and ever! A.	297
	1: 7	So shall it be! A.	297
	3:14	These are the words of the A,	297
	5:14	The four living creatures said, "A,"	297
	7:12	"A! Praise and glory	297
	7:12	for ever and ever! A."	297
	19: 4	And they cried: "A, Hallelujah!"	297
	22:20	I am coming soon." A.	297
	22:21	grace of Lord Jesus be with God's people. A.	297

AMENDS (3)

2Sa	21: 3	How *shall I* **make a** so that you will bless	4105
Job	20:10	His children *must* **make a** *to* the poor;	8355
Pr	14: 9	Fools mock at **making a for sin,**	871

AMERCE (KJV) See FINE

AMETHYST (3)

Ex	28:19	an agate and an **a**;	334
	39:12	an agate and an **a**;	334
Rev	21:20	the eleventh jacinth, and the twelfth **a.**	287

AMI (1)

Ezr	2:57	Pokereth-Hazzebaim and A	577

AMIABLE (KJV) See LOVELY

AMID (7) [MIDDLE]

Job	4:13	A disquieting dreams in the night,	928
	30:14	**a** the ruins they come rolling in.	9393
Ps	47: 5	God has ascended **a** shouts of joy,	928
	47: 5	the LORD **a** the sounding of trumpets.	928
Am	1:14	that will consume her fortresses **a** war cries	928
	1:14	a violent winds on a stormy day.	928
	2: 2	in great tumult **a** war cries and the blast of	928

AMINADAB (KJV) See AMMINADAB

AMISS (KJV) See WRONG

AMITTAI (2)

2Ki	14:25	spoken through his servant Jonah son of A,	624
Jnh	1: 1	of the LORD came to Jonah son of A:	624

AMMAH (1) [METHEG AMMAH]

2Sa	2:24	they came to the hill of A,	565

AMMI (KJV) See MY PEOPLE

AMMINADIB (KJV) See PEOPLE

AMMIEL (6)

Nu	13:12	from the tribe of Dan, A son of Gemalli;	6653
2Sa	9: 4	the house of Makir son of A in Lo Debar."	6653
	9: 5	from the house of Makir son of A.	6653
	17:27	and Makir son of A from Lo Debar,	6653
1Ch	3: 5	by Bathsheba daughter of A.	6653
	26: 5	A the sixth, Issachar the seventh	6653

AMMIHUD (10)

Nu	1:10	from Ephraim, Elishama son of A;	6654
	2:18	of Ephraim is Elishama son of A.	6654
	7:48	On the seventh day Elishama son of A,	6654
	7:53	This was the offering of Elishama son of A.	6654
	10:22	Elishama son of A was in command.	6654
	34:20	Shemuel son of A, from the tribe	6654
	34:28	Pedahel son of A,	6654
2Sa	13:37	Absalom fled and went to Talmai son of A,	6654
1Ch	7:26	Ladan his son, A his son, Elishama his son,	6654
	9: 4	Uthai son of A,	6654

AMMINADAB (16)

Ex	6:23	daughter of A and sister of Nahshon,	6657
Nu	1: 7	from Judah, Nahshon son of A;	6657
	2: 3	of the people of Judah is Nahshon son of A.	6657
	7:12	on the first day was Nahshon son of A	6657
	7:17	This was the offering of Nahshon son of A.	6657
	10:14	Nahshon son of A was in command.	6657
Ru	4:19	Ram the father of A,	6657
	4:20	A the father of Nahshon,	6657
1Ch	2:10	Ram was the father of A,	6657
	2:10	and A the father of Nahshon,	6657
	6:22	A his son, Korah his son, Assir his son,	6657
	15:10	A the leader and 112 relatives.	6657
	15:11	Joel, Shemaiah, Eliel and A the Levites.	6657
Mt	1: 4	Ram the father of A,	300
	1: 4	A the father of Nahshon,	300
Lk	3:33	the son *of* A,	300

AMMISHADDAI (5)

Nu	1:12	from Dan, Ahiezer son of A;	6659
	2:25	of the people of Dan is Ahiezer son of A.	6659
	7:66	On the tenth day Ahiezer son of A,	6659
	7:71	This was the offering of Ahiezer son of A.	6659
	10:25	Ahiezer son of A was in command.	6659

AMMIZABAD (1)

1Ch	27: 6	His son A was in charge of his division.	6655

AMMON (15) [AMMONITE, AMMONITES]

Jdg	11:28	The king of A, however,	1201+6648
	11:33	Thus Israel subdued A.	1201+6648
2Ki	23:13	the detestable god of the people of A.	6648
2Ch	20:10	"But now here are men from A,	6648
	20:22	against the men of A and Moab	6648
	20:23	The men of A and Moab rose up against	6648
Ne	13:23	from Ashdod, A and Moab.	6649
Ps	83: 7	A and Amalek, Philistia,	6648
Jer	9:26	A, Moab and all who live in the desert	1201+6648
	25:21	Edom, Moab and A;	1201+6648
	27: 3	word to the kings of Edom, Moab, A,	1201+6648
	40:11	When all the Jews in Moab, A,	1201+6648
Eze	25: 5	for camels and A into a resting place	1201+6648
Da	11:41	the leaders of A will be delivered	1201+6648
Am	1:13	"For three sins of A, even for four,	1201+6648

AMMONI   See KEPHAR AMMONI

AMMONITE (21) [AMMON]

Dt	23: 3	No A or Moabite or any	6649
Jos	13:25	the A country as far as Aroer,	1201+6648
Jdg	11:12	to the A king with the question:	1201+6648
	11:14	messengers to the A king,	1201+6648
1Sa	11: 1	the A went up and besieged Jabesh Gilead.	6649
	11: 2	But Nahash the A replied,	6649
2Sa	10: 3	the A nobles said to Hanun their lord,	1201+6648
	12:31	He did this to all the A towns.	1201+6648
	23:37	Zelek the A, Naharai the Beerothite,	6649
1Ki	14:21	Naamah; she was an A.	6649
	14:31	Naamah; she was an A.	6649
2Ki	24: 2	Moabite and A raiders against him.	1201+6648
1Ch	11:39	Zelek the A, Naharai the Berothite,	6649
	19: 3	the A nobles said to Hanun,	1201+6648
	20: 3	David did this to all the A towns.	1201+6648
2Ch	12:13	Naamah; she was an A.	6649
	24:26	son of Shimeath an A *woman,*	6649
Ne	2:10	and Tobiah the A official heard about this,	6649
	2:19	the A official and Geshem the Arab heard	6649
	4: 3	Tobiah the A, who was at his side, said,	6649
	13: 1	and there it was found written that no A	6649

AMMONITES (88) [AMMON]

Ge	19:38	he is the father of the A of today.	1201+6648
Nu	21:24	but only as far as the A,	1201+6648
Dt	2:19	When you come to the A,	1201+6648
	2:19	of any land belonging to the A.	1201+6648
	2:20	but the A called them Zamzummites.	6649
	2:21	from before **the A,**	2157S
	2:37	not encroach on any of the land of the A,	1201+6648
	3:11	It is still in Rabbah of the A.)	1201+6648
	3:16	which is the border of the A.	1201+6648
Jos	12: 2	which is the border of the A.	1201+6648
	13:10	out to the border of the A.	1201+6648
Jdg	3:13	Getting the A and Amalekites to join him,	1201+6648
	10: 6	the A and the gods of the Philistines.	1201+6648
	10: 7	the hands of the Philistines and the A,	1201+6648
	10: 9	The A also crossed the Jordan to fight	1201+6648
	10:11	the Egyptians, the Amorites, the A,	1201+6648
	10:17	the A were called to arms and camped	1201+6648
	10:18	the A will be the head of all those	1201+6648
	11: 4	when the A made war on Israel,	1201+6648
	11: 6	"be our commander, so we can fight the A."	1201+6648
	11: 8	come with us to fight the A,	1201+6648
	11: 9	the A and the LORD gives them to me	1201+6648
	11:13	the A answered Jephthah's messengers	1201+6648
Jdg	11:15	the land of Moab or the land of the A.	1201+6648
	11:27	between the Israelites and the A."	1201+6648
	11:29	from there he advanced against the A.	1201+6648
	11:30	"If you give the A into my hands,	1201+6648
	11:31	when I return in triumph from the A	1201+6648
	11:32	Jephthah went over to fight the A,	1201+6648
	11:36	of your enemies, the A.	1201+6648
	12: 1	go to fight the A without calling us	1201+6648
	12: 2	in a great struggle with the A,	1201+6648
	12: 3	and crossed over to fight the A,	1201+6648
1Sa	11:10	They said to the A,	NIH
	11:11	the A and slaughtered them until the heat of	6648
	12:12	of the A was moving against you,	1201+6648
	14:47	the A, Edom, the kings of Zobah,	1201+6648
2Sa	8:12	the A and the Philistines, and Amalek.	1201+6648
	10: 1	the king of the A died,	1201+6648
	10: 2	David's men came to the land of the A	1201+6648
	10: 6	the A realized that they had become	1201+6648
	10: 8	The A came out and drew up	1201+6648
	10:10	and deployed them against the A.	1201+6648
	10:11	but if the A are too strong for you,	1201+6648
	10:14	A saw that the Arameans were fleeing,	1201+6648
	10:14	from fighting the A and came	1201+6648
	10:19	to help the A anymore.	1201+6648
	11: 1	the A and besieged Rabbah.	1201+6648
	12: 9	killed him with the sword of the A.	1201+6648
	12:26	of the A and captured the royal citadel.	1201+6648
	17:27	of Nahash from Rabbah of the A,	1201+6648
1Ki	11: 1	Moabites, A, Edomites,	6649
	11: 5	and Molech the detestable god of the A.	6649
	11: 7	Molech the detestable god of the A.	1201+6648
	11:33	and Molech the god of the A,	1201+6648
1Ch	18:11	Moab, the A and the Philistines,	1201+6648
	19: 1	Nahash king of the A died,	1201+6648
	19: 2	the land of the A to express sympathy	1201+6648
	19: 6	the A realized that they had become	1201+6648
	19: 6	the A sent a thousand talents of silver	1201+6648
	19: 7	the A were mustered from their towns	1201+6648
	19: 9	The A came out and drew up	1201+6648
	19:11	and they were deployed against the A.	1201+6648
	19:12	but if the A are too strong for you,	1201+6648
	19:15	A saw that the Arameans were fleeing,	1201+6648
	19:19	not willing to help the A anymore.	1201+6648
	20: 1	the A and went to Rabbah and besieged it,	1201+6648
2Ch	20: 1	A with some of the Meunites came	1201+6648
	26: 8	The A brought tribute to Uzziah.	6649
	27: 5	the king of the A and conquered them.	1201+6648
	27: 5	the A paid him a hundred talents	1201+6648
	27: 5	The A brought him the same amount	1201+6648
Ezr	9: 1	Hittites, Perizzites, Jebusites, A, Moabites,	6648
Ne	4: 7	the A and the men of Ashdod heard that	6649
Isa	11:14	and the A will be subject to them.	1201+6648
Jer	40:14	Baalis king of the A has sent Ishmael	1201+6648
	41:10	and set out to cross over to the A.	1201+6648
	41:15	from Johanan and fled to the A.	1201+6648
	49: 1	Concerning the A: This is what the LORD says:	1201+6648
	49: 2	the battle cry against Rabbah of the A;	1201+6648
	49: 6	I will restore the fortunes of the A,"	1201+6648
Eze	21:20	the sword to come against Rabbah of the A	1201+6648
	21:28	the Sovereign LORD says about the A	1201+6648
	25: 2	the A and prophesy against them.	1201+6648
	25:10	with the A to the people of the East	1201+6648
	25:10	the A will not be remembered among	1201+6648
Zep	2: 8	insults of Moab and the taunts of the A	1201+6648
	2: 9	the A like Gomorrah—	1201+6648

AMNON (28) [AMNON'S]

2Sa	3: 2	His firstborn was A the son of Ahinoam	596
	13: 1	A son of David fell in love with Tamar,	596
	13: 2	A became frustrated to the point of illness	596
	13: 3	Now A had a friend named Jonadab son	596
	13: 4	He asked A, "Why do you, the king's son,	2257S
	13: 4	A said to him, "I'm in love with Tamar,	596
	13: 6	So A lay down and pretended to be ill.	596
	13: 6	the king came to see him, A said to him,	596
	13: 7	of your brother A and prepare some food	596
	13: 8	Tamar went to the house of her brother A,	596
	13: 9	"Send everyone out of here," A said.	596
	13:10	Then A said to Tamar,	596
	13:10	to her brother A in his bedroom.	596
	13:15	Then A hated her with intense hatred.	596
	13:15	A said to her, "Get up and get out!"	596
	13:20	"Has that A, your brother, been with you?	578
	13:22	Absalom never said a word to A,	596
	13:22	he hated A because he had disgraced his sister	596
	13:26	please let my brother A come with us."	596
	13:27	with him A and the rest of the king's sons.	596
	13:28	When A is in high spirits	596
	13:28	'Strike A down,' then kill him.	596
	13:29	to A what Absalom had ordered.	596
	13:32	only A is dead.	596
	13:32	since the day A raped his sister Tamar.	2257S
	13:33	Only A is dead."	596
1Ch	3: 1	The firstborn was A the son of Ahinoam	596
	4:20	A, Rinnah, Ben-Hanan and Tilon.	596

AMNON'S (1) [AMNON]

2Sa	13:39	for he was consoled concerning A death.	596

AMOK (1) [AMOK'S]

Ne	12: 7	A, Hilkiah and Jedaiah.	6651

AMOK'S (1) [AMOK]

| Ne | 12:20 | of Sallu's, Kallai; of A, Eber; | 6651 |

AMON (18) [AMON'S]

1Ki	22:26	and send him back to A the ruler of the city	571
2Ki	21:18	And A his son succeeded him as king.	571
	21:19	A was twenty-two years old	571
	21:24	of the land killed all who had plotted	
		against King A,	571
1Ch	3:14	A his son, Josiah his son.	571
2Ch	18:25	and send him back to A the ruler of the city	571
	33:20	And A his son succeeded him as king.	571
	33:21	A was twenty-two years old	571
	33:22	A worshiped and offered sacrifices to all	571
	33:23	A increased his guilt.	571
	33:25	of the land killed all who had plotted	
		against King A,	571
Ne	7:59	Pokereth-Hazzebaim and A	571
Jer	1: 2	the reign of Josiah son of A king of Judah,	571
	25: 3	the thirteenth year of Josiah son of A king	571
	46:25	"I am about to bring punishment on A god	572
Zep	1: 1	the reign of Josiah son of A king of Judah:	571
Mt	1:10	Manasseh the father of A,	321
	1:10	A the father of Josiah,	321

AMON'S (3) [AMON]

2Ki	21:23	A officials conspired against him	571
	21:25	As for the other events of A reign,	571
2Ch	33:24	A officials conspired against him	2257S

AMONG (812)

Ge	3: 8	the LORD God a the trees of the garden.	928+9348
	6: 9	blameless a the people of his time,	928
	13:12	while Lot lived a the cities of the plain	928
	17:10	Every male a you shall be circumcised.	4200
	17:12	For the generations to come every male a	4200
	23: 4	"I am an alien and a stranger a you.	6640
	23: 6	You are a mighty prince a us.	928+9348
	23: 9	to me for the full price as a burial site a	928+9348
	23:10	Ephron the Hittite was sitting a his people	
			928+9348
	23:16	the weight current a the merchants.	4200
	24: 3	a whom I am living,	928+7931
	25:27	staying a the tents.	AIT
	27:46	If Jacob takes a wife from a the women	4946
	28: 2	from a the daughters of Laban,	4946
	33: 1	so he divided the children a Leah,	6584
	34:10	You can settle a us; the land is open to you.	907
	34:16	We'll settle a you and become one people	907
	34:23	and they will settle a us.	907
	36:15	These were the chiefs a Esau's descendants:	AIT
	41: 2	sleek and fat, and they grazed a the reeds.	928
	41:18	fat and sleek, and they grazed a the reeds.	928
	42: 5	So Israel's sons were a those who went	928+9348
	47: 6	of any a them with special ability,	928
	49:26	on the brow of the prince a his brothers.	AIT
Ex	2: 3	in it and put it a the reeds along the bank of	928
	2: 5	She saw the basket a the reeds	928+9348
	3:20	all the wonders that I will perform a	928+7931
	10: 1	miraculous signs of mine a them	928+7931
	10: 2	and how I performed my signs a them,	928
	11: 7	But a the Israelites not a dog will bark	3972+4200
	12:48	"An alien living a you who wants	907
	12:49	the native-born and to the alien living a	928+9348
	13: 2	of every womb a the Israelites belongs	928
	13: 7	nothing with yeast in it is to be seen a you,	4200
	13:13	Redeem every firstborn a your sons.	928
	15:11	"Who a the gods is like you, O LORD?	928
	17: 7	"Is the LORD a us or not?"	928
	22:25	of my people a you who is needy, do not be	6640
	23:11	Then the poor a your people may get food	AIT
	23:25	I will take away sickness from a you,	7931
	25: 8	and I will dwell a them.	928+9348
	27:21	a lasting ordinance a the Israelites	907+4946
	28: 1	to you from a the Israelites,	9348
	29:45	Then I will dwell a the Israelites and	928+9348
	29:46	of Egypt so that I might dwell a them.	928+9348
	34:10	The people you live a will see	928+7931
	34:12	or they will be a snare a you.	928+7931
	35:10	"All who are skilled a you are to come	928
	36: 8	All the skilled men a the workmen made	928
Lev	10: 3	"'A those who approach me I will show	
		myself holy;	928
	11:10	whether a all the swarming things or	4946
	11:10	among all the swarming things or a all	928+9348
	15:31	which is a them.'"	928+9348
	16:16	which is a them in the midst	907+8905
	16:29	whether native-born or an alien living a	928+9348
	17: 8	or any alien living a them who offers	928+9348
	17:10	"'Any Israelite or any alien living a	928+9348
	17:12	nor may an alien living a you eat blood."	928+9348
	17:13	"'Any Israelite or any alien living a	928+9348
	18:26	the aliens living a you must not do any	928+9348
	19:16	"'Do not go about spreading slander a	928
	20:14	so that no wickedness will be a you.	928+9348
	20:27	or woman who is a medium or spiritist a	928
	21:10	the one a his brothers who has had	4946
	21:15	he will not defile his offspring a his people.	928
	23:30	I will destroy from a his people anyone who	7931
	24:10	father went out a the Israelites,	928+9348
	25: 6	and temporary resident who live a you,	6640
	25:33	towns of the Levites are their property a	928+9348
	25:35	and is unable to support himself a you,	6640
	25:35	so he can continue to live a you.	6640

Lev	25:36	to live a you.	6640
	25:39	of your countrymen becomes poor a you	6640
	25:40	as a hired worker or a temporary resident a	6640
	25:45	of the temporary residents living a you	6640
	25:47	or a temporary resident a you becomes rich	6640
	25:47	to the alien living a you or to a member of	6640
	26:11	I will put my dwelling place a you,	928+9348
	26:12	I will walk a you and be your God,	928+9348
	26:25	I will send a plague a you,	928+9348
	26:33	I will scatter you a the nations	928
	26:38	You will perish a the nations;	928
Nu	3:12	the Levites from a the Israelites in place of	9348
	5: 3	where I dwell a them."	928+9348
	5:27	she will become accursed a her people.	928+7931
	8: 6	the Levites from a the other Israelites	9348
	9:14	"'An alien living a you who wants	907
	11: 1	Then fire from the LORD burned a them	928
	11: 1	fire from the LORD had burned a them.	928
	11:16	as leaders and officials a the people.	AIT
	11:20	who is a you, and have wailed before him,	
			928+7931
	11:21	"Here I am a six hundred thousand men	928+7931
	11:26	They were listed a the elders,	928
	12: 6	prophet of the LORD is a	AIT
	13:32	And they spread a the Israelites	448
	14: 6	who were a those who had explored	4946
	14:11	miraculous signs I have performed a	928+7931
	14:13	brought these people up from a them,	7931
	15:14	whenever an alien or anyone else living a	907
	15:15	for you and for the alien living a you;	NIH
	15:16	both to you and to the alien living a you.'"	907
	15:26	aliens living a them will be forgiven,	928+9348
	16:47	The plague had already started a	928
	17: 6	and Aaron's staff was a them.	928+9348
	18: 6	from a the Israelites as a gift to you.	9348
	18:20	nor will you have any share a them;	928+9348
	18:20	I am your share and your inheritance a	928+9348
	18:23	They will receive no inheritance a	928+9348
	18:24	'They will have no inheritance a	928+9348
	19:10	the Israelites and for the alien living a	928+9348
	20:13	and where he showed himself holy a them.	928
	21: 6	the LORD sent venomous snakes a them;	928
	23:21	the shout of the King is a them.	928
	24:20	"Amalek was first a the nations,	AIT
	25:11	as zealous as I am for my honor a them,	928+9348
	26: 9	and Aaron were a Korah's followers	928
	26:56	by lot a the larger and smaller groups."	1068
	26:62	because they received no inheritance a	928+9348
	26:64	of them was a those counted by Moses	4946
	27: 3	He was not a Korah's followers,	928+9348
	27: 4	Give us property a our father's relatives	928+9348
	27: 7	an inheritance a their father's relatives	928+9348
	31: 8	A their victims were Evi, Rekem, Zur,	6584
	33: 4	whom the LORD had struck down a them;	928
	35:15	and any other people living a them,	928+9348
	35:34	for I, the LORD, dwell a the Israelites.'	928+9348
Dt	2:16	when the last of these fighting men a	4946+7931
	4: 3	The LORD your God destroyed from a	7931
	4:27	The LORD will scatter you a the peoples,	928
	4:27	of you will survive a the nations to which	928
	6:15	the LORD your God, who is a you,	928+7931
	7:20	the LORD your God will send the hornet a	928
	7:21	is a you, is a great and awesome God.	928+7931
	10: 9	the Levites have no share or inheritance a	6640
	12: 5	the LORD your God will choose from a	4946
	13: 1	appears a you and announces to you	928+7931
	13: 5	You must purge the evil from a you.	7931
	13:11	and no one a you will do such	7931
	13:13	that wicked men have arisen a you	4946+7931
	13:14	this detestable thing has been done a	928+7931
	15: 4	However, there should be no poor a you,	928
	15: 7	If there is a poor man a your brothers	928
	16:11	fatherless and the widows living a you	928+7931
	17: 2	woman living a you in one of the towns	928+7931
	17: 7	You must purge the evil from a you.	7931
	17:15	He must be from a your own brothers.	7931
	18: 2	They shall have no inheritance a	928+7931
	18:10	be found a you who sacrifices his son	7931
	18:15	up for you a prophet like me from a	7931
	18:18	a prophet like you from a their brothers;	7931
	19:19	You must purge the evil from a you.	7931
	19:20	an evil thing be done a you.	928+7931
	21:11	if you notice a the captives	928
	21:21	You must purge the evil from a you.	7931
	22:21	You must purge the evil from a you.	7931
	22:24	You must purge the evil from a you.	7931
	23:14	that he will not see a you anything indecent	928
	23:16	Let him live a you wherever he likes	928
	24: 7	You must purge the evil from a you.	7931
	26:11	you and the Levites and the aliens a	928+7931
	28:43	The alien who lives a you will rise	928+7931
	28:54	Even the most gentle and sensitive man a	928
	28:56	most gentle and sensitive woman a you—	928
	28:64	the LORD will scatter you a all nations,	928
	28:65	A those nations you will find no repose,	928
	29:17	You saw a them their detestable images	6640
	29:18	clan or tribe a you today	928
	29:18	make sure there is no root a you	928
	30: 1	the LORD your God disperses you a	928
	31: 7	divide it a them as their inheritance.	AIT
	32:51	you did not uphold my holiness a	928+7931
	33:16	on the brow of the prince a his brothers.	AIT
Jos	3: 5	the LORD will do amazing things a you.	928+7931
	3:10	you will know that the living God is a	928+7931
	4: 2	"Choose twelve men from a the people,	4946
	4: 6	to serve as a sign a you.	928+7931
	6:25	and she lives a the Israelites to this day.	928+7931

Jos	7:12	unless you destroy whatever a	4946+7931
	7:13	which is devoted is a you, O Israel.	928+7931
	8:35	and the aliens who lived a them.	928+7931
	13: 7	an inheritance a the nine tribes and half of	928
	13:13	so they continue to live a the Israelites	928+7931
	14: 3	not granted the Levites an inheritance a	928+9348
	14:15	who was the greatest man a the Anakites.)	928
	16:10	Canaanites live a the people of Ephraim	928+7931
	17: 4	to give us an inheritance a our brothers	928+9348
	17: 6	of Manasseh received an inheritance a	928+9348
	17: 9	Ephraim lying a the towns of Manasseh	928+7931
	18: 7	however, do not get a portion a you,	928+7931
	19:49	of Nun an inheritance a them,	928+7931
	20: 9	of the Israelites or any alien living a	928+9348
	22:14	of a family division a the Israelite clans.	4200
	23: 7	with these nations that remain a you;	907
	23:12	the survivors of these nations that remain a	907
	24:17	He protected us on our entire journey and a	928
	24:23	"throw away the foreign gods that are a	928+7931
Jdg	1:16	with the men of Judah to live a the people	907
	1:29	Canaanites continued to live there a them.	
			928+7931
	1:30	who remained a them;	928+7931
	1:32	the people of Asher lived a	928+7931
	1:33	but the Naphtalites too lived a	928+7931
	3: 5	The Israelites lived a the Canaanites,	928+7931
	5: 8	a shield or spear was seen a forty thousand	928
	5: 9	with the willing volunteers a the people.	928
	5:16	Why did you stay a the campfires to hear	1068
	10:16	Then they got rid of the foreign gods a	4946+7931
	14: 3	an acceptable woman a your relatives or	928
	14: 3	among your relatives or a all our people?	928
	16:25	When they stood him a the pillars,	1068
	18: 1	yet come into an inheritance a the tribes	928+9348
	20:12	that was committed a you?	928
	20:16	A all these soldiers there were seven	4946
	21:12	They found a the people living	4946
Ru	2: 7	'Please let me glean and gather a	928
	2:15	"Even if she gathers a the sheaves,	1068
	4:10	from a his family or from the town records.	6640
1Sa	2:24	not a good report that I hear spreading a	6296
	9: 2	an impressive young man without equal a	4946
	10:11	Is Saul also a the prophets?"	928
	10:12	"Is Saul also a the prophets?"	928
	10:22	he has hidden himself a the baggage."	448
	10:23	and as he stood a the people he was	928+9348
	10:24	There is no one like him a all the people."	928
	13: 6	they hid in caves and thickets, a the rocks,	928
	14: 3	a whom was Ahijah,	NIH
	14:34	he said, "Go out a the men and tell them,	928
	15:33	so will your mother be childless a women."	4946
	19:24	"Is Saul also a the prophets?"	928
	23:19	"Is not David hiding a us in the strongholds	6640
	23:23	if he is in the area, I will track him down a	928
	30:22	But all the evil men and troublemakers a	4946
	31: 9	the temple of their idols and a their people.	907
2Sa	11:13	to sleep on his mat a his master's servants;	6640
	12:19	servants were whispering a themselves	4317
	15:31	"Ahithophel is a the conspirators	928
	17: 9	'There has been a slaughter a	928
	19:28	a place a those who sat at your table.	928
	22:50	O LORD, a the nations;	928
	23:19	even though he was not included a them.	6330
	23:23	but he was not included a the Three.	448
	23:24	A the Thirty were:	928
1Ki	2: 7	of Gilead and let them be a those who eat	928
	3: 8	Your servant is here a	928+9348
	3:13	in your lifetime you will have no equal a	928
	6:13	And I will live a the Israelites and will	928+9348
	9: 7	and an object of ridicule a all peoples.	928
	14: 7	from a the people and made you a leader	9348
	21: 9	and seat Naboth in a prominent place a	AIT
	21:12	and seated Naboth in a prominent place a	AIT
2Ki	4:13	"I have a home a my own people."	928+9348
	11: 2	of Ahaziah and stole him away from a	9348
	17:25	so he sent lions a them	928
	17:26	He has sent lions a them,	928
	18: 5	There was no one like him a all the kings	928
	20:13	and everything found a his treasures.	928
	20:15	"There is nothing a my treasures that I did	928
1Ch	6:60	which were distributed a	928
	7:15	a wife from a the Huppites and Shuppites.	4200
	10: 9	of the Philistines to proclaim the news a	AIT
	11:21	even though he was not included a them.	6330
	11:25	but he was not included a the Three.	448
	12: 1	of Saul son of Kish (they were a	928
	12: 4	a mighty man a the Thirty,	928
	16: 8	known a the nations what he has done.	928
	16:24	Declare his glory a the nations,	928
	16:24	his marvelous deeds a all peoples.	928
	16:31	let them say a the nations,	928
	22: 2	and from a them he appointed stonecutters	NIH
	24: 4	A larger number of leaders were found a	AIT
	24: 4	among Eleazar's descendants than a	NIH
	24: 5	of God a the descendants of both Eleazar	4946
	26:31	and capable men a the Hebronites	928
	27: 6	a mighty man a the Thirty and was over	AIT
2Ch	7:13	the land or send a plague a my people,	928
	7:20	and an object of ridicule a all peoples.	928
	11:22	to be the chief prince a his brothers,	928
	13:17	five hundred thousand casualties a Israel's	928
	15: 5	Manasseh and Simeon who had settled a	6640
	19: 4	and he went out again a the people	928
	20:25	and they found a them a great amount	928
	22:11	from a the royal princes who were about to	9348
	26: 6	and elsewhere a the Philistines.	928
	31:19	to distribute portions to every male a them	928

2Ch	36:23	Anyone of his people a you—	928
Ezr	1: 3	Anyone of his people a you—	928
	2:61	And from a the priests:	4946
	8:15	I checked the people and the priests,	928
	10:18	A the descendants of the priests,	4946
	10:23	A the Levites: Jozabad,	4946
	10:25	And a the other Israelites:	4946
Ne	1: 8	I will scatter you a the nations,	928
	4:11	be right there a them and will kill them	448+9348
	6: 6	"It is reported a the nations—	928
	7:63	And from a the priests:	4946
	9:17	to remember the miracles you performed a	6640
	11:17	Bakbukiah, second a his associates;	4946
	12:23	The family heads a the descendants of Levi	NIH
	13:26	A the many nations there was no king	928
Est	2: 6	a those taken captive with Jehoiachin king	6640
	3: 8	a certain people dispersed and scattered a	1068
	4: 3	there was great mourning a the Jews,	4200
	8:17	there was joy and gladness a the Jews,	4200
	9:28	nor should the memory of them die out a	4946
	10: 3	preeminent a the Jews,	4200
Job	1: 3	He was the greatest man a all the people of	4946
	2: 8	and scraped himself with it as he sat a	928+9348
	3: 6	not be included a the days of the year nor	928
	5: 5	taking it even from a thorns,	448
	8:17	of rocks and looks for a place a the stones.	1075
	12:12	Is not wisdom found a the aged?	4946
	15:19	land was given when no alien passed a	928+9348
	17:10	I will not find a wise man a you.	928
	18:19	He has no offspring or descendants a	3869
	19:11	he counts me a his enemies.	3869
	24:11	They crush olives a the terraces;	1068
	29:25	I dwelt as a king a his troops;	928
	30: 6	a the rocks and in holes in the ground.	NIH
	30: 7	They brayed a the bushes and huddled in	1068
	30: 9	I have become a byword a them,	4200
	34:37	scornfully he claps his hands a us	1068
	36:14	a male prostitutes of the shrines.	928
	40:19	He ranks first a the works of God,	AIT
	40:21	hidden a the reeds in the marsh.	AIT
	41: 6	Will they divide him up a the merchants?	1068
Ps	9:11	proclaim a the nations what he has done.	928
	12: 1	the faithful have vanished from a men.	4946
	12: 8	about when what is vile is honored a men.	4200
	18:49	Therefore I will praise you a the nations,	928
	22:18	They divide my garments a them	4200
	35:18	a throngs of people I will praise you.	928
	36: 7	low a men find refuge in the shadow	132+1201
	42: 4	and thanksgiving a the festive throng.	NIH
	44:11	and have scattered us a the nations.	928
	44:14	You have made us a byword a the nations;	928
	45: 9	of kings are a your honored women;	928
	46:10	I will be exalted a the nations,	928
	54: T	"Is not David hiding a us?"	6640
	55:15	for evil finds lodging a them.	928+7931
	57: 4	I lie a ravenous beasts—	NIH
	57: 9	I will praise you, O Lord, a the nations;	928
	57: 9	I will sing of you a the peoples.	928
	58: 1	Do you judge uprightly a men?	NIH
	67: 2	your salvation a all nations.	928
	68:13	Even while you sleep a the campfires,	1068
	68:30	Rebuke the beast a the reeds,	AIT
	68:30	the herd of bulls a the calves of the nations.	928
	72: 4	He will defend the afflicted a the people	AIT
	77:14	you display your power a the peoples.	928
	78:31	he put to death the sturdiest a them,	928
	78:60	the tent he had set up a men.	928
	79:10	make known a the nations that you avenge	928
	81: 9	You shall have no foreign god a you;	928
	82: 1	he gives judgment a the "gods":	928+7931
	86: 8	A the gods there is none like you, O Lord;	928
	87: 4	"I will record Rahab and Babylon a	4200
	88: 4	I am counted a those who go down to	6640
	89: 6	like the Lord a the heavenly beings?	928
	89:19	I have exalted a young man from a	4946
	94: 8	you senseless ones a the people;	928
	96: 3	Declare his glory a the nations,	928
	96: 3	his marvelous deeds a all peoples.	928
	96:10	Say a the nations, "The Lord reigns."	928
	99: 6	Moses and Aaron were a his priests,	928
	99: 6	Samuel was a those who called	928
	102: 6	like an owl a the ruins.	AIT
	104:12	they sing a the branches.	1068+4946
	105: 1	known a the nations what he has done.	928
	105:27	They performed his miraculous signs a	928
	105:37	and from a their tribes no one faltered.	928
	106:18	Fire blazed a their followers;	928
	106:27	make their descendants fall a the nations	928
	106:29	and a plague broke out a them.	928
	108: 3	I will praise you, O Lord, a the nations;	928
	108: 3	I will sing of you a the peoples.	928
	120: 5	that I live a the tents of Kedar!	6640
	120: 6	Too long have I lived a	6640
	126: 2	Then it was said a the nations,	928
	136:11	from a them His love endures forever.	9348
Pr	6:19	a man who stirs up dissension a brothers.	1068
	7: 7	I saw a the simple,	928
	7: 7	I noticed a the young men,	928
	14: 9	but goodwill is found a the upright.	1068
	14:33	even a fools she lets herself be known.	928+7931
	15:31	a life-giving rebuke will be at home a	928+7931
	16:19	be lowly in spirit and a the oppressed than	907
	23:28	and multiplies the unfaithful a men.	928
	25: 6	and do not claim a place a great men;	928
	30:14	the needy from a mankind.	4946
	30:30	mighty a beasts, who retreats	928
	31:23	he takes his seat a the elders of the land.	6640
Ecc	7:28	I found one [upright] man a a thousand,	4946
	7:28	but not one [upright] woman a them all.	928
	9: 4	Anyone who is a the living has hope—	2489
SS	2: 2	Like a lily a thorns is my darling among	1068
	2: 2	among thorns is my darling a the maidens.	1068
	2: 3	Like an apple tree a the trees of	928
	2: 3	among the trees of the forest is my lover a	1068
	2:16	he browses a the lilies.	928
	4: 5	like twin fawns of a gazelle that browse a	928
	5:10	outstanding a ten thousand.	4946
	6: 3	he browses a the lilies.	928
	6:12	my desire set me a the royal chariots	AIT
Isa	2: 2	be established as chief a the mountains;	AIT
	4: 3	all who are recorded a the living	4200
	5:17	lambs will feed a the ruins of the rich.	AIT
	6: 5	and I live a a people of unclean lips,	928+9348
	7: 6	let us tear it apart and divide it a ourselves,	448
	8:16	Bind up the testimony and seal up the law a	928
	10: 4	but to cringe a the captives or fall among	9393
	10: 4	but to cringe among the captives or fall a	9393
	12: 4	known a the nations what he has done,	928
	12: 6	great is the Holy One of Israel a you."	928+7931
	13: 4	Listen, an uproar a the kingdoms,	AIT
	24:13	will it be on the earth and a the nations,	928+9348
	29:23	When they see a them their children,	928+7931
	30:14	shattered so mercilessly that a its pieces not	928
	39: 2	his entire armory and everything found a	928
	39: 4	"There is nothing a my treasures that I did	928
	41:28	no one a them to give counsel,	4946
	43:12	I, and not some foreign god a you.	928
	44:14	He let it grow a the trees of the forest,	928
	45: 9	a potsherd a the potsherds on the ground.	907
	50:10	Who a you fears the Lord and obeys	928
	53:12	Therefore I will give him a portion a	928
	57: 5	You burn with lust a the oaks and	928
	57: 6	[The idols] a the smooth stones of	928
	59:10	a the strong, we are like the dead.	928
	61: 9	be known a the nations and their offspring	928
	61: 9	among the nations and their offspring a	928+9348
	63:11	he who set his Holy One a them,	928+7931
	65: 4	who sit a the graves	928
	66:19	"I will set a sign a them,	928
	66:19	They will proclaim my glory a the nations.	928
Jer	4: 3	up your unplowed ground and do not sow a	448
	4:29	some climb up a the rocks.	928
	5:26	"A my people are wicked men who lie	928
	6:15	So they will fall a the fallen;	928
	8:12	So they will fall a the fallen;	928
	8:17	"See, I will send venomous snakes a you,	928
	9:16	I will scatter them a nations	928
	10: 7	A all the wise men of the nations and	928
	11: 9	"There is a conspiracy a the people	928
	12:14	and I will uproot the house of Judah from a	9348
	12:16	they will be established a my people.	928+9348
	14: 9	You are a us, O Lord,	928+7931
	18:13	"Inquire a the nations:	928
	23:13	"A the prophets of Samaria	928
	23:14	And a the prophets	928
	25:16	because of the sword I will send a them."	1068
	25:27	because of the sword I will send a you.'	1068
	26: 6	of cursing a all the nations of the earth.' "	4200
	29: 1	to the surviving elders a the exiles and to	AIT
	29: 8	"Do not let the prophets and diviners a	928+7931
	29:18	a all the nations where I drive them.	928
	29:27	who poses as a prophet a you?	4200
	29:32	He will have no one left a this people,	928+9348
	30:11	the nations a which I scatter you,	9004S
	30:21	their ruler will arise from a them.	7931
	31: 8	A them will be the blind and the lame,	928
	32:20	both in Israel and a all mankind,	928
	37: 4	Jeremiah was free to come and go a	928+9348
	37:12	of the property a the people there.	928+9348
	39:14	So he remained a his own people.	928+9348
	40: 1	in chains a all the captives from Jerusalem	928+9348
	40: 5	and live with him a the people,	928+9348
	40: 6	him a the people who were left behind	928+9348
	44: 8	of cursing and reproach a all the nations	928
	46:18	"one will come who is like Tabor a	928
	46:28	the nations a which I scatter you,	2025
	48:27	Was she caught a thieves,	928
	48:28	Abandon your towns and dwell a the rocks,	928
	49:15	"Now I will make you small a the nations,	928
	49:15	among the nations, despised a men.	928
	50: 2	and proclaim a the nations, lift up a banner	928
	50:23	How desolate is Babylon a the nations!	928
	50:46	its cry will resound a the nations.	928
	51:27	Blow the trumpet a the nations!	928
	51:41	a horror Babylon will be a the nations!	928
La	1: 1	who once was great a the nations!	928
	1: 1	She who was queen a the provinces has	928
	1: 2	A all her lovers there is none	4946
	1: 3	She dwells a the nations;	928
	1:17	Jerusalem has become an unclean thing a	1068
	2: 9	and her princes are exiled a the nations,	928
	3:45	You have made us scum and refuse a	928+7931
	4:15	people a the nations say,	928
	4:20	that under his shadow we would live a	928
Eze	1: 1	I was a the exiles by the Kebar River,	928+9348
	1:13	Fire moved back and forth a the creatures;	1068
	2: 5	will know that a prophet has been a	928+9348
	2: 6	around you and you live a scorpions.	448
	3:15	I sat a them for seven days—	928+9348
	3:25	so that you cannot go out a the people.	928+9348
	4:13	of Israel will eat defiled food a the nations	928
	5:14	and a reproach a the nations around you,	928
	6: 7	Your people will fall slain a you,	928+9348
Eze	6: 8	the sword when you are scattered a	928
	6:13	when their people lie slain a their idols	928+9348
	7: 4	and the detestable practices a you.	928+9348
	7: 9	and the detestable practices a you.	928+9348
	8:11	of Shaphan was standing a them.	928+9348
	10: 2	"Go in a the wheels beneath the cherubim.	1068
	10: 2	from a the cherubim and scatter them over	1068
	10: 6	"Take fire from a the wheels,	1068
	10: 6	from a the cherubim,"	1068
	10: 7	to the fire that was a them.	1068
	11: 1	I saw a them Jaazaniah son of Azzur	928+9348
	11:16	Although I sent them far away a	928
	11:16	among the nations and scattered them a	928
	12: 2	you are living a a rebellious people.	928+9348
	12:12	"The prince a them will put his things	928+9348
	12:15	when I disperse them a the nations	928
	12:24	or flattering divinations a the people	928+9348
	13: 4	O Israel, are like jackals a ruins.	928
	13:19	You have profaned me a my people for	448
	14: 9	and destroy him from a my people Israel.	9348
	15: 6	the vine a the trees of the forest as fuel for	928
	16:14	And your fame spread a the nations	928
	18:18	and did what was wrong a his people.	928+9348
	19: 2	a lioness was your mother a the lions!	1068
	19: 2	She lay down a the young lions	928+9348
	19: 6	He prowled a the lions,	928+9348
	20: 9	in the eyes of the nations they lived a	928+9348
	20:23	in the desert that I would disperse them a	928
	20:41	and I will show myself holy a you in	928
	22:15	I will disperse you a the nations	928
	22:26	so that I am profaned a them.	928+9348
	22:30	a man a them who would build up the wall	4946
	23:10	She became a byword a women,	4200
	24:23	your sins and groan a yourselves.	278+408+448
	25: 4	up their camps and pitch their tents a you;	928
	25:10	the Ammonites will not be remembered a	928
	27:36	The merchants a the nations hiss at you;	928
	28:14	you walked a the fiery stones.	928+9348
	28:16	O guardian cherub, from a the fiery stones.	9348
	28:25	I will show myself holy a them in the sight	928
	29: 3	you great monster lying a your streams.	928+9348
	29: 4	I will pull you out from a your streams,	9348
	29:12	I will make the land of Egypt desolate a	928+9348
	29:12	her cities will lie desolate forty years a	928+9348
	29:12	And I will disperse the Egyptians a	928
	29:21	and I will open your mouth a them.	928+9348
	30: 7	'They will be desolate a desolate lands,	928+9348
	30: 7	and their cities will lie a ruined cities.	928+9348
	30:23	I will disperse the Egyptians a the nations	928
	30:26	I will disperse the Egyptians a the nations	928
	31:13	the beasts of the field were a its branches.	448
	31:14	for the earth below, a mortal men,	928+9348
	31:17	its allies a the nations,	928+9348
	31:18	you will lie a the uncircumcised,	928+9348
	32: 2	" 'You are like a lion a the nations;	AIT
	32: 9	when I bring about your destruction a	928
	32: 9	a lands you have not known.	6584
	32:19	Go down and be laid a the uncircumcised.'	907
	32:20	will fall a those killed by the sword.	928+9348
	32:25	A bed is made for her a the slain,	928+9348
	32:25	they are laid a the slain.	928+9348
	32:28	broken and will lie a the uncircumcised	928+9348
	32:32	Pharaoh and all his hordes will be laid a	928+9348
	33:33	that a prophet has been a them."	928+9348
	34:24	my servant David will be prince a them	928+9348
	35:11	of them and I will make myself known a	928
	36:19	I dispersed them a the nations,	928
	36:20	And wherever they went a	448
	36:21	the house of Israel profaned a the nations	928
	36:22	which you have profaned a the nations	928
	36:23	which has been profaned a the nations,	928
	36:23	the name you have profaned a them.	928+9348
	36:30	so that you will no longer suffer disgrace a	928
	37: 2	He led me back and forth a them,	6584
	37:26	I will put my sanctuary a them forever.	928+9348
	37:28	when my sanctuary is a them forever.'	928+9348
	39: 7	" 'I will make known my holy name a	928+9348
	39:21	"I will display my glory a the nations,	928
	39:28	though I sent them into exile a the nations,	448
	43: 7	where I will live a the Israelites forever.	928+9348
	43: 9	and I will live a them forever.	928+9348
	44: 9	the foreigners who live a the Israelites.	928+9348
	46:10	The prince is to be a them,	928+9348
	47:13	an inheritance a the twelve tribes of Israel,	4200
	47:14	You are to divide it equally a.	278+408+2257+3869
	47:21	to distribute this land a yourselves	4200
	47:22	for the aliens who have settled a you	928+9348
	47:22	to be allotted an inheritance a the tribes	928+9348
Da	1: 6	A these were some from Judah:	928
	2:11	and they do not live a men."	10554
	2:25	a man a the exiles from Judah who can tell	10427
	4:15	with the animals a the plants of the earth.	10089
	6: 3	Now Daniel so distinguished himself a	10542
	7: 8	a little one, which came up a them;	10099
	11:14	The violent men a your own people	AIT
	11:24	loot and wealth a his followers.	4200
Hos	5: 9	A the tribes of Israel I proclaim what is certain.	928
	8: 8	she is a the nations like a worthless thing.	928
	8:10	Although they have sold themselves a	928
	9:17	they will be wanderers a the nations.	928
	11: 9	the Holy One a you.	928+7931
	13:15	even though he thrives a his brothers.	1068
Joel	2:17	a byword a the nations.	928
	2:17	Why should they say a the peoples,	928
	2:25	my great army that I sent a you.	928

Joel	2:32	a the survivors whom the LORD calls.	928
	3: 2	for they scattered my people a the nations	928
	3: 9	Proclaim this a the nations:	928
Am	2:11	up prophets **from** a your sons and Nazirites	4946
	2:11	from among your sons and Nazirites **from** a	4946
	3: 9	and the oppression a her people."	928+7931
	4:10	"I sent plagues a you as I did to Egypt.	928
	6: 7	Therefore you will be a the first to go	928
	7: 8	a plumb line a my people Israel;	928+7931
	9: 9	of Israel a all the nations as grain is shaken	928
	9:10	All the **sinners** a my people will die by	AIT
Ob	1: 2	I will make you small a the nations;	928
	1: 4	the eagle and make your nest a the stars,	1068
Mic	3:11	"Is not the LORD a us?"	928+7931
	4: 1	be established as **chief** a the mountains;	AIT
	5: 2	though you are small a the clans of Judah,	928
	5: 8	The remnant of Jacob will be a the nations,	928
	5: 8	like a lion a the beasts of the forest,	928
	5: 8	like a young lion a flocks of sheep,	928
	5:10	from a you and demolish your chariots.	7931
	5:13	and your sacred stones from a you;	7931
	5:14	from a you your Asherah poles	7931
Na	1:10	They will be entangled a thorns and drunk	6330
	1:12	Put and Libya were a her allies.	928
Zep	3:20	and praise a all the peoples of the earth	928
Hag	2: 5	And my Spirit remains a you.	928+9348
Zec	1: 8	He was standing a the myrtle trees in	1068
	1:10	man standing a the myrtle trees explained,	1068
	1:11	who was standing a the myrtle trees,	1068
	2:10	For I am coming, and I will live a you,"	928+9348
	2:11	I will live a you and you will know that	928+9348
	3: 7	of my courts, and I will give you a place a	1068
	7:14	'I scattered them with a whirlwind a all	6584
	8:13	As you have been an object of cursing a	928
	10: 9	Though I scatter them a the peoples,	928
	12: 6	like a flaming torch a sheaves.	928
	12: 8	that the feeblest a them will be like David,	928
	14: 1	your plunder will be divided a you.	928+7931
Mal	1:11	My name will be great a the nations,	928
	1:11	my name will be great a the nations,"	928
	1:14	"and my name is to be feared a the nations.	928
Mt	2: 6	are by no means least a the rulers of Judah;	1877
	4:23	and healing every disease and sickness a	1877
	10: 5	"Do not go a the Gentiles or enter any town	1650
	10:16	sending you out like sheep a wolves.	1877+3545
	11:11	A those born of women there has	1877
	13: 7	Other seed fell a thorns,	2093
	13:22	that fell a the thorns is the man who hears	324+3545
	13:25	his enemy came and sowed weeds a	1877
	16: 7	They discussed this a themselves and said,	1877
	16: 8	why are you talking a yourselves	1877
	18: 2	little child and had him stand a them.	1877+3545
	20:26	whoever wants to become great a you must	1877
	21:25	They discussed it a themselves and said,	1877
	22:25	Now there were seven brothers a us.	4123
	23:11	The greatest a you will be your servant.	AIT
	26: 5	"or there may be a riot a the people."	1877
	27:56	A them were Mary Magdalene,	1877
	28:15	And this story has been widely circulated a	4123
Mk	4: 7	Other seed fell a thorns,	1650
	4:18	Still others, like seed sown a thorns,	1650
	5: 5	Night and day the tombs and in	1877
	5:12	"Send us a the pigs;	1650
	6: 4	a his relatives and in his own house is	1877
	6:41	He also divided the two fish a them all.	NIG
	9:36	took a little child and had him stand a	1877+3545
	10:43	whoever wants to become great a you must	1877
	11:31	They discussed it a themselves and said,	4639
	15:31	and the teachers of the law mocked him a	4639
	15:40	A them were Mary Magdalene,	1877
Lk	1: 1	of the things that have been fulfilled a us,	1877
	1:25	and taken away my disgrace a the people."	1877
	1:42	"Blessed are you a women,	1877
	1:61	"There is no one a your relatives who has	1666
	2:44	for him a their relatives and friends.	1877
	2:46	sitting a the teachers,	1877+3545
	7:16	"A great prophet has appeared a us,"	1877
	7:28	I tell you, a those born	1877
	7:49	The other guests began to say a	1877
	8: 7	Other seed fell a thorns,	1877+3545
	8:14	that fell a thorns stands for those who hear,	1650
	9:46	An argument started a the disciples as	1877
	9:48	For he who is least a you all—	1877
	10: 3	I am sending you out like lambs a wolves.	1877+3545
	16:15	What is highly valued a men is detestable	1877
	19:47	and the leaders a **the people** were trying	AIT
	20: 5	They discussed it a themselves and said,	4639
	22:17	"Take this and divide it a you.	1650
	22:23	They began to question a themselves which	4639
	22:24	Also a dispute arose a them as to which	1877
	22:26	greatest a you should be like the youngest,	1877
	22:27	But I am a you as one who serves.	1877+3545
	24: 5	"Why do you look for the living a	3552
	24:36	Jesus himself stood a them and said	1877+3545
Jn	1:14	and made his dwelling a us.	1877
	1:26	"but a you stands one you do not know.	3545
	6: 9	but how far will they go a so many?"	1650
	6:43	"Stop grumbling a yourselves,"	3552
	6:52	Jews began to argue sharply a themselves,	4639
	7:12	A the crowds there was widespread	1877
		whispering about him.	
	7:35	**people live scattered** a the Greeks,	1402+3836
	11:54	about publicly a the Jews.	1877
	12: 2	while Lazarus was a those reclining at	1651+1666
	12: 8	You will always have the poor a you,	3552
	12:20	Now there were some Greeks a	1666

Jn	12:42	even a the leaders believed in him.	1666
	14: 9	after I have been a you such a long time?	3552
	15:24	I had not done a them what no one else did,	1877
	19:24	**divided** my garments a	1374
	20:19	Jesus came and stood a them	1650+3545+3836
	20:26	Jesus came and stood a them	1650+3545+3836
	21:23	the rumor spread a the brothers	1650
Ac	1:15	Peter stood up a the believers	1877+3545
	1:21	the Lord Jesus went in and out a us,	2093
	2:22	which God did a you through him,	1877+3545
	3:22	a prophet like me **from** a your own people;	1666
	3:23	be completely cut off from a his people.'	NIG
	4:17	from spreading any further a the people,	1650
	4:34	There were no needy persons a them.	1877
	5:12	and wonders a the people.	1877
	6: 1	the Grecian Jews a them complained	NIG
	6: 3	choose seven men **from** a	1666
	6: 8	did great wonders and miraculous signs a	1877
	9:21	the man who raised havoc in Jerusalem a	NIG
	12:18	there was no small commotion a	1877
	14: 5	a **the Gentiles** and **Jews**,	AIT
	15: 7	a choice a you that the Gentiles might hear	1666
	15:12	and wonders God had done a the Gentiles	1877
	15:22	two men who were leaders a the brothers.	1877
	17:34	A them was Dionysius,	1877
	20:25	that none of you a whom I have gone	1877
	20:29	savage wolves **will come in** a you and will	1656
	20:32	up and give you an inheritance a	1877
	21:19	and reported in detail what God had done a	1877
	21:21	that you teach all the Jews who live a	2848
	24: 5	up riots a **the Jews all** over the world.	AIT
	26:18	a place a those who are sanctified by faith	1877
	28:25	They disagreed a themselves and began	4639
Ro	1: 5	and apostleship to call people **from** a all	1877
	1: 6	also are a those who are called to belong	1877
	1:13	now) in order that I might have a harvest a	1877
	1:13	just as I have had a the other Gentiles.	1877
	2:24	"God's name is blasphemed a the Gentiles	1877
	8:29	be the firstborn a many brothers.	1877
	11:17	have been **grafted** a the others and	1596
	15: 5	a spirit of unity a yourselves	1877
	15: 9	"Therefore I will praise you a the Gentiles;	1877
	15:26	a contribution for the poor a **the saints**	AIT
	16: 7	They are outstanding a the apostles,	1877
1Co	1:10	so that there may be no divisions a you and	1877
	1:11	that there are quarrels a you.	1877
	2: 6	speak a message of wisdom a the mature,	1877
	2:11	For who a **men** knows the thoughts of	AIT
	3: 3	there is jealousy and quarreling a you,	1877
	5: 1	that there is sexual immorality a you, and	1877
	5: 1	a kind that does not occur even a pagans:	1877
	5:13	"Expel the wicked man **from** a you."	1666
	6: 5	that there is nobody a you wise enough	1877
	6: 7	The very fact that you have lawsuits a	3552
	9:11	If we have sown spiritual seed a you,	AIT
	11:18	there are divisions a you,	1877
	11:19	No doubt there have to be differences a you	1877
	11:30	That is why many a you are weak and sick,	1877
	14:16	how can one who finds himself a	5536
	14:25	exclaiming, "God is really a you!"	1877
2Co	1:19	who was preached a you by me and Silas	1877
	2:17	For we are to God the aroma of Christ a	1877
	6:16	"I will live with them and **walk** a them,	1853
	8:23	he is my partner and fellow worker a you;	1650
	10:15	of activity a you will greatly expand,	1877
	12:12	were done a you with great perseverance.	1877
	13: 3	but is powerful a you.	1877
Gal	1:16	so that I might preach him a the Gentiles,	1877
	2: 2	the gospel that I preach a the Gentiles.	1877
	3: 5	and **work** miracles a you	1919
Eph	2: 3	All of us also lived a them at one time,	1877
	5: 3	But a you there must not be even a hint	1877
Col	1: 6	just as it has been doing a you since	1877
	1:18	he is the beginning and the firstborn **from** a	1666
	1:27	To them God has chosen to make known a	NIG
	4:11	the only Jews a my fellow workers for	NIG
1Th	1: 5	how we lived a you for your sake.	1877
	2: 7	but we were gentle a you,	1877+3545
	2:10	and blameless we were a you who believed.	AIT
	5:12	to respect those who work hard a you,	1877
2Th	1: 4	a God's churches we boast	1877
	1:10	in his holy people and to be marveled at a	1877
	3:11	We hear that some a you are idle.	1877
1Ti	1:20	A them are Hymenaeus and Alexander,	AIT
	3:16	was preached a the nations,	1877
2Ti	2:17	A them are Hymenaeus and Philetus,	AIT
Heb	5: 1	Every high priest is selected **from** a men	1666
Jas	1: 1	To the twelve tribes scattered a the nations:	1877
	2: 4	have you not discriminated a yourselves	1877
	3: 6	a world of evil a the parts of the body.	1877
	3:13	Who is wise and understanding a you?	1877
	4: 1	What causes fights and quarrels a you?	1877
1Pe	2:12	Live such good lives a the pagans that,	1877
	2:13	to every authority instituted a **men:**	474
	5: 1	To the elders a you,	1877
2Pe	2: 1	there were also false prophets a the people,	1877
	2: 1	just as there will be false teachers a you.	1877
	2: 8	**living** a them day after day,	1594
1Jn	4: 9	This is how God showed his love a us:	1877
	4:17	love is made complete a us so	3552
Jude	1: 4	about long ago have secretly slipped in a	NIG
Rev	1:13	and a the lampstands was someone "like a	
		son of man,"	1877+3545
	2: 1	walks the seven golden lampstands:	1877+3545
	6: 6	I heard what sounded like a voice a	1877+3545
	6:15	in caves and a the rocks of the mountains.	1650
	14: 4	They were purchased **from** a men	608

AMORITE (10) [AMORITES]

Ge	14:13	near the great trees of Mamre the A,	616
Nu	21:13	in the desert extending into A territory.	616
Dt	2:24	I have given into your hand Sihon the A,	616
	4:47	the two A kings east of the Jordan.	616
Jos	5: 1	when all the A kings west of the Jordan	616
	10: 6	because all the A kings from	616
	24:12	also the two A kings.	616
Eze	16: 3	your father was an A and your mother	616
	16:45	a Hittite and your father an A.	616
Am	2: 9	"I destroyed the A before them,	616

AMORITES (76) [AMORITE]

Ge	10:16	Jebusites, A, Girgashites,	616
	14: 7	the A who were living in Hazazon Tamar.	616
	15:16	the A has not yet reached its full measure."	616
	15:21	A, Canaanites, Girgashites and Jebusites."	616
	48:22	from the A with my sword and my bow."	616
Ex	3: 8	the home of the Canaanites, Hittites, A,	616
	3:17	A, Perizzites, Hivites and Jebusites—	616
	13: 5	Hittites, A, Hivites and Jebusites—	616
	23:23	of you and bring you into the land of the A,	616
	33: 2	A, Hittites, Perizzites,	616
	34:11	I will drive out before you the A,	616
Nu	13:29	Jebusites and A live in the hill country;	616
	21:13	between Moab and the A.	616
	21:13	to say to Sihon king of the A:	616
	21:25	the cities of the A and occupied them,	616
	21:26	the city of Sihon king of the A,	616
	21:29	as captives to Sihon king of the A.	616
	21:31	So Israel settled in the land of the A.	616
	21:32	and drove out the A who were there.	616
	21:34	to him what you did to Sihon king of the A,	616
	22: 2	that Israel had done to the A,	616
	32:33	of Sihon king of the A and the kingdom	616
	32:39	and drove out the A who were there.	616
Dt	1: 4	after he had defeated Sihon king of the A,	616
	1: 7	and advance into the hill country of the A;	616
	1:19	toward the hill country of the A through all	616
	1:20	the hill country of the A,	616
	1:27	into the hands of the A to destroy us.	616
	1:44	The A who lived in those hills came out	616
	3: 2	to him what you did to Sihon king of the A,	616
	3: 8	of the A the territory east of the Jordan,	616
	3: 9	the A call it Senir.)	616
	4:46	in the land of Sihon king of the A,	616
	7: 1	the Hittites, Girgashites, A, Canaanites,	616
	20:17	Completely destroy them—the Hittites, A,	616
	31: 4	the kings of the A,	616
Jos	2:10	the two kings of the A east of the Jordan,	616
	3:10	Perizzites, Girgashites, A and Jebusites.	616
	7: 7	into the hands of the A to destroy us?	616
	9: 1	A, Canaanites, Perizzites,	616
	9:10	that he did to the two kings of the A east of	616
	10: 5	Then the five kings of the A—	616
	10:12	On the day the LORD gave the A over	616
	11: 3	to the A, Hittites, Perizzites and Jebusites	616
	12: 2	Sihon king of the A,	616
	12: 8	the lands of the Hittites, A, Canaanites,	616
	13: 4	the region of the A,	616
	13:10	and all the towns of Sihon king of the A,	616
	13:21	and the entire realm of Sihon king of the A,	616
	24: 8	of the A who lived east of the Jordan.	616
	24:11	as did also the A, Perizzites, Canaanites,	616
	24:15	or the gods of the A,	616
	24:18	including the A, who lived in the land.	616
Jdg	1:34	The A confined the Danites to	616
	1:35	And the A were determined also to hold out	616
	1:36	of the A was from Scorpion Pass to Sela	616
	3: 5	A, Perizzites, Hivites and Jebusites.	616
	6:10	do not worship the gods of the A,	616
	10: 8	the land of the A.	616
	10:11	the A, the Ammonites, the Philistines,	616
	11:19	to Sihon king of the A,	616
	11:21	the land of the A who lived in that country,	616
	11:23	the A out before his people Israel,	616
1Sa	7:14	there was peace between Israel and the A.	616
2Sa	21: 2	a part of Israel but were survivors of the A;	616
1Ki	4:19	(the country of Sihon king of the A and	616
	9:20	All the people left from the A, Hittites,	616
	21:26	the A the LORD drove out before Israel.)	616
2Ki	21:11	the A who preceded him and has led Judah	616
1Ch	1:14	Jebusites, A, Girgashites,	616
2Ch	8: 7	All the people left from the Hittites, A,	616
Ezr	9: 1	Ammonites, Moabites, Egyptians and A.	616
Ne	9: 8	A, Perizzites, Jebusites and Girgashites.	616
Ps	135:11	the A, Og king of Bashan and all the kings	616
	136:19	of the A His love endures forever.	616
Am	2:10	in the desert to give you the land of the A.	616

AMOS (8)

Am	1: 1	of A, one of the shepherds of Tekoa—	6650
	7: 8	LORD asked me, "What do you see, A?"	6650
	7:10	"A is raising a conspiracy against you in	6650
	7:11	For this is what A is saying:	6650
	7:12	Amaziah said to A, "Get out, you seer!	6650
	7:14	A answered Amaziah,	6650
	8: 2	"What do you see, A?"	6650
Lk	3:25	the son of A, the son of Nahum,	322

AMOUNT (24) [AMOUNTED, AMOUNTS]

Ge	43:12	Take **double** the a of silver with you,	AIT
	43:15	So the men took the gifts and **double** the a	AIT
Ex	12: 4	**determine** the a of lamb **needed**	4082

Ex	38:24	The **total** *a* of the gold from	AIT
Lev	25: 8	of years **a to** a period of forty-nine years.	2118
	27: 8	the vow is too poor to pay the **specified a,**	6886
	27:16	according to the *a* of seed required for it—	7023
1Sa	30:16	the **great** *a* of plunder they had taken from	1524
2Ki	12:10	that there was a **large** *a* of money in	8041
	12:11	When the **a** had **been determined,**	9419
1Ch	22: 3	a **large** *a* of iron to make nails for	4200+8044
2Ch	14:13	Judah carried off a **large** *a* of plunder.	2221+4394
	20:25	a **great** *a* of equipment and clothing	4200+8044
	24:11	and they saw that there was a **large** *a*	8041
	24:11	and collected a **great** *a* of money.	4200+8044
	27: 5	The Ammonites brought him the **same** *a*	2296ˢ
	31: 5	They brought a **great** *a*,	4200+8044
	31:10	and this **great** *a* is left over."	2162
Est	4: 7	including the **exact** *a*	7308
Isa	41:29	Their deeds **a to nothing;**	700
Da	1: 5	The king assigned them a daily *a* of food	1821
Mt	13:33	a **large** *a* of flour until it worked all through	4929
Lk	13:21	mixed into a **large** *a* of flour	236+4929+5552
	19: 8	I will pay back four times the **a.**"	NIG

AMOUNTED (3) [AMOUNT]

Ru	2:17	and **it** *a* to about an ephah.	2118
2Ch	4:18	All these things that Solomon made **a** to	NIH
	29:33	The animals consecrated as sacrifices **a**	NIH

AMOUNTS (5) [AMOUNT]

Ex	30:34	pure frankincense, all **in equal a,**	928+963+963
	38:21	These are the *a* of the materials used for	7217
Dt	17:17	*He must* not **accumulate large a** of silver	4394+8049
Mk	12:41	Many rich people threw in **large** *a.*	AIT
2Co	10:10	and his speaking **a to nothing.**"	2024

AMOZ (13)

2Ki	19: 2	to the prophet Isaiah son of A.	576
	19:20	Isaiah son of A sent a message to Hezekiah:	576
	20: 1	of A went to him and said, "This is what	576
2Ch	26:22	are recorded by the prophet Isaiah son of A.	576
	32:20	and the prophet Isaiah son of A cried out	576
	32:32	the vision of the prophet Isaiah son of A in	576
Isa	1: 1	that Isaiah son of A saw during the reigns	576
	2: 1	of A saw concerning Judah and Jerusalem.	576
	13: 1	that Isaiah son of A saw:	576
	20: 2	the LORD spoke through Isaiah son of A.	576
	37: 2	to the prophet Isaiah son of A.	576
	37:21	Isaiah son of A sent a message to Hezekiah:	576
	38: 1	of A went to him and said, "This is what	576

AMPHIPOLIS (1)

Ac	17: 1	When they had passed through A	315

AMPLIATUS (1)

Ro	16: 8	Greet A, whom I love in the Lord.	309

AMPLY (1)

Php	4:18	*I am* **a supplied,**	4444

AMRAM (13) [AMRAM'S, AMRAMITES]

Ex	6:18	The sons of Kohath were A, Izhar,	6688
	6:20	A married his father's sister Jochebed,	6688
	6:20	A lived 137 years.	6688
Nu	3:19	A, Izhar, Hebron and Uzziel.	6688
	26:58	(Kohath was the forefather of A;	6688
	26:59	To A she bore Aaron,	6688
1Ch	6: 2	A, Izhar, Hebron and Uzziel.	6688
	6: 3	The children of A:	6688
	6:18	A, Izhar, Hebron and Uzziel.	6688
	23:12	A, Izhar, Hebron and Uzziel—four in all.	6688
	23:13	The sons of A: Aaron and Moses.	6688
	24:20	from the sons of A:	6688
Ezr	10:34	From the descendants of Bani: Maadai, A,	6688

AMRAM'S (1) [AMRAM]

Nu	26:59	the name of A wife was Jochebed,	6688

AMRAMITES (2) [AMRAM]

Nu	3:27	To Kohath belonged the clans of the A,	6689
1Ch	26:23	From the A, the Izharites,	6689

AMRAPHEL (2)

Ge	14: 1	At this time A king of Shinar,	620
	14: 9	A king of Shinar and Arioch king	620

AMZI (2)

1Ch	6:46	the son of A,	603
Ne	11:12	the son of A, the son of Zechariah,	603

AN (1185) [A] See Index of Articles Etc.

ANAB (2)

Jos	11:21	from Hebron, Debir and A,	6693
	15:50	A, Eshtemoh, Anim,	6693

ANAH (12)

Ge	36: 2	the Hittite, and Oholibamah daughter of A	6704
	36:14	of Esau's wife Oholibamah daughter of A	6704
	36:18	Esau's wife Oholibamah daughter of A.	6704
	36:20	Lotan, Shobal, Zibeon, A,	6704
	36:24	The sons of Zibeon: Aiah and A.	6704
	36:24	the A who discovered the hot springs in	6704
	36:25	The children of A:	6704
	36:25	Dishon and Oholibamah daughter of A.	6704
	36:29	Lotan, Shobal, Zibeon, A,	6704
1Ch	1:38	The sons of Seir: Lotan, Shobal, Zibeon, A,	6704
	1:40	The sons of Zibeon: Aiah and A.	6704
	1:41	The son of A: Dishon.	6704

ANAHARATH (1)

Jos	19:19	Hapharaim, Shion, A,	637

ANAIAH (2)

Ne	8: 4	Shema, A, Uriah, Hilkiah and Maaseiah;	6717
	10:22	Pelatiah, Hanan, A,	6717

ANAK (7) [ANAKITES]

Nu	13:22	Sheshai and Talmai, the descendants of A,	6737
	13:28	We even saw descendants of A there.	6737
	13:33	(the descendants of A come from	6737
Jos	15:13	(Arba was the forefather of A.)	6737
	15:14	and Talmai—descendants of A.	6737
	21:11	(Arba was the forefather of A.)	6710
Jdg	1:20	who drove from it the three sons of A.	6737

ANAKIMS (KJV) See ANAKITE

ANAKITES (11) [ANAK]

Dt	1:28	We even saw the A there.' "	1201+6737
	2:10	and as tall as the A.	6737
	2:11	the A, they too were considered Rephaites,	6737
	2:21	and as tall as the A.	6737
	9: 2	The people are strong and tall—A!	1201+6737
	9: 2	"Who can stand up against the A?"	1201+6737
Jos	11:21	that time Joshua went and destroyed the A	6737
	11:22	No A were left in Israelite territory;	6737
	14:12	the A were there and their cities were large	6737
	14:15	who was the greatest man among the A.)	6737
	15:14	Hebron Caleb drove out the three A—	1201+6737

ANAMIM (KJV) See ANAMITES

ANAMITES (2)

Ge	10:13	Mizraim was the father of the Ludites, A,	6723
1Ch	1:11	Mizraim was the father of the Ludites, A,	6723

ANAMMELECH (1)

2Ki	17:31	as sacrifices to Adrammelech and A,	6724

ANAN (1)

Ne	10:26	Ahiah, Hanan, A,	6728

ANANI (1)

1Ch	3:24	Pelaiah, Akkub, Johanan, Delaiah and A—	6730

ANANIAH (2)

Ne	3:23	Azariah son of Maaseiah, the son of A,	6731
	11:32	in Anathoth, Nob and A,	6732

ANANIAS (13)

Ac	5: 1	Now a man named A,	393
	5: 3	Then Peter said, "A, how is it	393
	5: 5	When A heard this, he fell down and died.	393
	5: 8	the property and A got for the land?"	NIG
	9:10	In Damascus there was a disciple named A.	393
	9:10	The Lord called to him in a vision, "A!"	393
	9:12	a vision he has seen a man named A come	393
	9:13	A answered, "I have heard many reports	393
	9:15	But the Lord said to A, "Go!	899ˢ
	9:17	Then A went to the house and entered it.	393
	22:12	"A man named A came to see me.	393
	23: 2	the high priest A ordered those standing	393
	24: 1	Five days later the high priest A went down	393

ANATH (2)

Jdg	3:31	After Ehud came Shamgar son of A,	6742
	5: 6	"In the days of Shamgar son of A,	6742

ANATHEMA (KJV) See CURSE

ANATHOTH (18) [ANATHOTHITE]

Jos	21:18	A and Almon, together	6743
2Sa	23:27	Abiezer **from** A, Mebunnai the Hushathite,	6745
1Ki	2:26	"Go back to your fields in A.	6743
1Ch	6:60	Geba, Alemeth and A,	6743
	7: 8	Omri, Jeremoth, Abijah, A and Alemeth.	6744
	11:28	of Ikkesh from Tekoa, Abiezer **from** A,	6745
Ezr	2:23	of A 128	6743
Ne	7:27	of A 128	6743
	10:19	Hariph, A, Nebai,	6744
	11:32	in A, Nob and Ananiah,	6743
Isa	10:30	Listen, O Laishah! Poor A!	6743
Jer	1: 1	the priests at A in the territory of Benjamin.	6743
	11:21	of A who are seeking your life and saying,	6743
	11:23	of A in the year of their punishment.' "	6743
	29:27	not reprimanded Jeremiah **from** A,	6745
	32: 7	'Buy my field at A,	6743
	32: 8	'Buy my field at A in the territory	6743
	32: 9	the field at A from my cousin Hanamel	6743

ANATHOTHITE (2) [ANATHOTH]

1Ch	12: 3	Beracah, Jehu the A,	6745
	27:12	for the ninth month, was Abiezer the A,	6745

ANCESTOR (4) [ANCESTORS, ANCESTRAL, ANCESTRY]

Ge	10:21	Shem was the *a* of all the sons of Eber.	3
Jos	17: 1	Makir was the *a* of the Gileadites,	3
Heb	7:10	Levi was still in the body of his *a.*	4252
Jas	2:21	not our *a* Abraham considered righteous	4252

ANCESTORS (4) [ANCESTOR]

Lev	26:45	with their *a* whom I brought out of Egypt	8037
1Ki	19: 4	"Take my life; I am no better than my *a.*"	3
Am	2: 4	the gods their *a* followed,	3
Ac	28:17	or against the customs of our *a,*	4262

ANCESTRAL (10) [ANCESTOR]

Nu	1:16	the leaders of their *a* tribes.	3
	13: 2	From each *a* tribe send one of its leaders."	3
	17: 2	from the leader of each of their *a* tribes.	3
	17: 3	be one staff for the head of each *a* tribe.	3
	17: 6	one for the leader of each of their *a* tribes,	3
	18: 2	Bring your fellow Levites from your *a* tribe	3
	26:55	be according to the names for its *a* tribe.	3
	33:54	Distribute it according to your *a* tribes.	7110
	36: 3	from our *a* inheritance and added to that of	3
Ne	11:20	each on his *a* **property.**	5709

ANCESTRY (6) [ANCESTOR]

Nu	1:18	The people **indicated** *their* **a** by their clans	3528
Eze	16: 3	Your *a* and birth were in the land of	4808
	21:30	in the land of your *a,* I will judge you.	4808
	29:14	the land of their *a.*	4808
Ro	9: 5	from them is traced the **human** *a* of Christ,	4922
Heb	7:16	as to his *a* but on the basis of the power of	4921

ANCHOR (3) [ANCHORED, ANCHORS]

Ac	27:13	they **weighed** *a* and sailed along the shore	149
	27:17	the **sea** *a* and let the ship be driven along.	5007
Heb	6:19	We have this hope as an *a* for the soul,	46

ANCHORED (1) [ANCHOR]

Mk	6:53	they landed at Gennesaret and *a* there.	4694

ANCHORS (3) [ANCHOR]

Ac	27:29	they dropped four *a* from the stern	46
	27:30	to lower some *a* from the bow.	46
	27:40	Cutting loose the *a,*	46

ANCIENT (33) [ANCIENTS]

Ge	49:26	the blessings of the *a* mountains,	6329
Dt	33:15	with the choicest gifts of the *a* mountains	7710
1Sa	27: 8	(From a **times** these peoples had lived in	6409
1Ch	4:22	(These records are **from a times.**)	6972
Ezr	4:15	a place of rebellion from *a* times.	10550
Ps	24: 7	be lifted up, you *a* doors,	6409
	24: 9	lift them up, you *a* doors,	6409
	68:33	to him who rides the *a* skies above,	7710
	119:52	I remember your *a* laws, O LORD,	4946+6409
Pr	22:28	Do not move an *a* boundary stone set up	6409
	23:10	not move an *a* boundary stone or encroach	6409
Isa	19:11	a disciple of the *a* kings"?	7710
	43:13	Yes, and from a **days** I am he.	NIH
	44: 7	since I established my *a* people,	6409
	46:10	from a **times,** what is still to come.	7710
	58:12	Your people will rebuild the *a* ruins	6409
	61: 4	They will rebuild the *a* ruins and restore	6409
	64: 4	Since *a* **times** no one has heard,	6409
Jer	5:15	an *a* and enduring nation,	4946+6409
	6:16	ask for the *a* paths,	6409
	18:15	in their ways and in the *a* paths.	6409
Eze	25:15	with *a* hostility sought to destroy Judah,	6409
	26:20	as in a **ruins,**	4946+6409
	35: 5	with *a* hostility and delivered the Israelites	6409
	36: 2	The *a* heights have become our **possession.**" '	6409
Da	7: 9	and the A *of* Days took his seat.	10578
	7:13	He approached the A *of* Days and was led	10578
	7:22	until the A *of* Days came	10578
Mic	5: 2	from *a* old, from a **times.**"	6409
Hab	3: 6	The *a* mountains crumbled and	6329
2Pe	2: 5	not spare the *a* world when he brought	792
Rev	12: 9	that a serpent called the devil, or Satan,	792
	20: 2	He seized the dragon, that *a* serpent,	792

ANCIENTS (1) [ANCIENT]

Heb	11: 2	This is what the *a* were commended for.	4565

ANCLE (KJV) See ANKLE, ANKLES

AND (29600) See Index of Articles Etc.

ANDREW (14)

Mt	4:18	Simon called Peter and his brother A.	436
	10: 2	and his brother A;	436
Mk	1:16	he saw Simon and his brother A casting	436
	1:29	and John to the home of Simon and A.	436
	3:18	A, Philip, Bartholomew,	436
	13: 3	James, John and A asked him privately,	436
Lk	6:14	his brother A, James, John, Philip,	436
Jn	1:40	A, Simon Peter's brother,	436
	1:41	The first thing A did was	4047S
	1:44	Philip, like A and Peter,	436
	6: 8	Another of his disciples, A,	436
	12:22	Philip went to tell A;	436
	12:22	A and Philip in turn told Jesus.	436
Ac	1:13	present were Peter, John, James and A;	436

ANDRONICUS (1)

Ro	16: 7	Greet A and Junias,	438

ANEM (1)

1Ch	6:73	and A, together with their pasturelands;	6722

ANER (3)

Ge	14:13	a brother of Eshcol and A,	6738
	14:24	to A, Eshcol and Mamre.	6738
1Ch	6:70	the tribe of Manasseh the Israelites gave A	6739

ANETHOTHITE, ANETOTHITE (KJV)
See ANATHOTH, ANATHOTHITE

ANEW (2) [NEW]

Mt	26:29	on until that day when I drink it a with you	2785
Mk	14:25	when I drink it a in the kingdom of God."	2785

ANGEL (207) [ANGEL'S, ANGELS, ARCHANGEL]

Ge	16: 7	The a of the LORD found Hagar near	4855
	16: 9	Then the a of the LORD told her,	4855
	16:10	The a added, "I will	3378+4855
	16:11	The a of the LORD also said to her:	4855
	21:17	the a of God called to Hagar from heaven	4855
	22:11	But the a of the LORD called out to him	4855
	22:15	The a of the LORD called to Abraham	4855
	24: 7	he will send his a before you so	4855
	24:40	will send his a with you	4855
	31:11	The a of God said to me in the dream,	4855
	48:16	A who has delivered me from all harm—	4855
Ex	3: 2	There the a of the LORD appeared to him	4855
	14:19	Then the a of God,	4855
	23:20	an a ahead of you to guard you along	4855
	23:23	My a will go ahead of you and bring you	4855
	32:34	and my a will go before you.	4855
	33: 2	I will send an a before you and drive out	4855
Nu	20:16	and sent an a and brought us out of Egypt.	4855
	22:22	and the a of the LORD stood in the road	4855
	22:23	the a of the LORD standing in the road	4855
	22:24	the a of the LORD stood in a narrow path	4855
	22:25	When the donkey saw the a of the LORD,	4855
	22:26	Then the a of the LORD moved on ahead	4855
	22:27	When the donkey saw the a of the LORD,	4855
	22:31	and he saw the a of the LORD standing in	4855
	22:32	The a of the LORD asked him,	4855
	22:34	Balaam said to the a of the LORD,	4855
	22:35	The a of the LORD said to Balaam,	4855
Jdg	2: 1	The a of the LORD went up from Gilgal	4855
	2: 4	When the a of the LORD had spoken these	4855
	5:23	'Curse Meroz,' said the a of the LORD.	4855
	6:11	The a of the LORD came and sat down	4855
	6:12	the a of the LORD appeared to Gideon,	4855
	6:20	The a of God said to him,	4855
	6:21	the a of the LORD touched the meat and	4855
	6:21	And the a of the LORD disappeared.	4855
	6:22	When Gideon realized that it was the a of	4855
	6:22	I have seen the a of the LORD face	4855
	13: 3	The a of the LORD appeared to her	4855
	13: 6	He looked like an a of God,	4855
	13: 9	and the a of God came again to the woman	4855
	13:13	The a of the LORD answered,	4855
	13:15	Manoah said to the a of the LORD,	4855
	13:16	The a of the LORD replied,	4855
	13:16	not realize that it was the a of the LORD.)	4855
	13:17	Manoah inquired of the a of the LORD,	4855
	13:20	the a of the LORD ascended in the flame.	4855
	13:21	When the a of the LORD did	4855
	13:21	Manoah realized that it was the a of	4855
1Sa	29: 9	as pleasing in my eyes as an a of God.	4855
2Sa	14:17	an a of God in discerning good and evil.	4855
	14:20	My lord has wisdom like that of an a	4855
	19:27	My lord the king is like an a of God;	4855
	24:16	When the a stretched out his hand	4855
	24:16	to the a who was afflicting the people,	4855
	24:16	The a of the LORD was then at	4855
	24:17	When David saw the a who was striking	4855
1Ki	13:18	an a said to me by the word of the LORD:	4855
	19: 5	All at once an a touched him and said,	4855
	19: 7	The a of the LORD came back	4855

2Ki	1: 3	a of the LORD said to Elijah the Tishbite,	4855
	1:15	The a of the LORD said to Elijah,	4855
	19:35	That night the a of the LORD went out	4855
1Ch	21:12	the a of the LORD ravaging every part	4855
	21:15	And God sent an a to destroy Jerusalem.	4855
	21:15	But as the a was doing so,	NIH
	21:15	to the a who was destroying the people,	4855
	21:15	The seventh is about to sound his trumpet,	4855
	21:16	up and saw the a of the LORD standing	4855
	21:18	Then the a of the LORD ordered Gad	4855
	21:20	he turned and saw the a;	4855
	21:27	Then the LORD spoke to the a,	4855
	21:30	because he was afraid of the sword of the a	4855
2Ch	32:21	And the LORD sent an a,	4855
Job	33:23	if there is an a on his side as a mediator,	4855
Ps	34: 7	The a of the LORD encamps	4855
	35: 5	the a of the LORD driving them away;	4855
	35: 6	with the a of the LORD pursuing them.	4855
Isa	37:36	Then the a of the LORD went out and put	4855
	63: 9	and the a of his presence saved them.	4855
Da	3:28	who has sent his a	10417
	6:22	My God sent his a,	10417
Hos	12: 4	He struggled with the a and overcame him;	4855
Zec	1: 9	The a who was talking with me answered,	4855
	1:11	And they reported to the a of the LORD,	4855
	1:12	Then the a of the LORD said,	4855
	1:13	and comforting words to the a who talked	4855
	1:14	Then the a who was speaking to me said,	4855
	1:19	I asked the a who was speaking to me,	4855
	2: 3	Then the a who was speaking to me left,	4855
	2: 3	and another a came to meet him	4855
	3: 1	the high priest standing before the a of	4855
	3: 3	in filthy clothes as he stood before the a.	4855
	3: 4	The a said to those who were standing	NIH
	3: 5	while the a of the LORD stood by.	4855
	3: 6	The a of the LORD gave this charge	4855
	4: 1	Then the a who talked with me returned	4855
	4: 4	I asked the a who talked with me,	4855
	4:11	Then I asked the a,	2257S
	5: 5	Then the a who was speaking	4855
	5:10	I asked the a who was speaking to me.	4855
	6: 4	I asked the a who was speaking to me,	4855
	6: 5	The a answered me,	4855
	12: 8	the A of the LORD going before them.	4855
Mt	1:20	an a of the Lord appeared to him in	34
	1:24	the a the Lord had commanded him	34
	2:13	an a of the Lord appeared to Joseph in	34
	2:19	an a of the Lord appeared in a dream	34
	28: 2	a of the Lord came down from heaven and,	34
	28: 5	The a said to the women,	34
Lk	1:11	Then an a of the Lord appeared to him,	34
	1:13	But the a said to him:	34
	1:18	Zechariah asked the a,	34
	1:19	The a answered, "I am Gabriel.	34
	1:26	God sent the a Gabriel to Nazareth,	34
	1:28	The a went to her and said, "Greetings,	34
	1:30	But the a said to her, "Do not be afraid,	34
	1:34	"How will this be," Mary asked the a,	34
	1:35	The a answered, "The Holy Spirit will come upon you,	34
	1:38	Then the a left her.	34
	2: 9	An a of the Lord appeared to them,	34
	2:10	But the a said to them, "Do not be afraid.	34
	2:13	of the heavenly host appeared with the a,	34
	2:21	the name the a had given him	34
	22:43	An a from heaven appeared to him	34
Jn	12:29	others said an a had spoken to him.	34
Ac	5:19	the night an a of the Lord opened the doors	34
	6:15	that his face was like the face of an a.	34
	7:30	an a appeared to Moses in the flames of	34
	7:35	the a who appeared to him in the bush.	34
	7:38	the a who spoke to him on Mount Sinai,	34
	8:26	Now an a of the Lord said to Philip,	34
	10: 3	He distinctly saw an a of God,	34
	10: 4	The a answered, "Your prayers and gifts to	NIG
	10: 7	When the a who spoke to him had gone,	34
	10:22	A holy a told him to have you come	34
	11:13	how he had seen an a appear in his house	34
	12: 7	an a of the Lord appeared and a light shone	34
	12: 8	Then the a said to him,	34
	12: 8	the a told him.	NIG
	12: 9	the a was doing was really happening;	34
	12:10	suddenly the a left him.	34
	12:11	without a doubt that the Lord sent his a	34
	12:15	they said, "It must be his a."	34
	12:23	an a of the Lord struck him down,	34
	23: 9	if a spirit or an a has spoken to him?"	34
	27:23	Last night an a of the God whose I am	34
1Co	10:10	and were killed by the destroying a.	NIG
2Co	11:14	Satan himself masquerades as an a of light.	34
Gal	1: 8	if we or an a from heaven should preach	34
	4:14	you welcomed me as if I were an a of God,	34
Rev	1: 1	by sending his a to his servant John,	34
	2: 1	"To the a of the church in Ephesus write:	34
	2: 8	"To the a of the church in Smyrna write:	34
	2:12	"To the a of the church in Pergamum write:	34
	2:18	"To the a of the church in Thyatira write:	34
	3: 1	"To the a of the church in Sardis write:	34
	3: 7	the a of the church in Philadelphia write:	34
	3:14	"To the a of the church in Laodicea write:	34
	5: 2	a mighty a proclaiming in a loud voice,	34
	7: 2	I saw another a coming up from the east,	34
	8: 3	Another a, who had a golden censer,	34
	8: 5	Then the a took the censer,	34
	8: 7	The first a sounded his trumpet,	NIG
	8: 8	The second a sounded his trumpet,	34
	8:10	The third a sounded his trumpet,	34

Rev	8:12	The fourth a sounded his trumpet,	34
	9: 1	The fifth a sounded his trumpet,	34
	9:11	as king over them the a of the Abyss,	34
	9:13	The sixth a sounded his trumpet,	34
	9:14	It said to the sixth a who had the trumpet,	34
	10: 1	Then I saw another mighty a coming down	34
	10: 5	the a I had seen standing on the sea and on	34
	10: 7	the seventh a is about to sound his trumpet,	34
	10: 8	of the a who is standing on the sea and on	34
	10: 9	to the a and asked him to give me	34
	11:15	The seventh a sounded his trumpet,	34
	14: 6	Then I saw another a flying in midair,	34
	14: 8	A second a followed and said, "Fallen!	34
	14: 9	A third a followed them and said in	34
	14:15	Then another a came out of the temple	34
	14:17	Another a came out of the temple	34
	14:18	Still another a, who had charge of the fire,	34
	14:19	The a swung his sickle on the earth,	34
	16: 2	The first a went and poured out his bowl on	NIG
	16: 3	The second a poured out his bowl on	NIG
	16: 4	The third a poured out his bowl on	NIG
	16: 5	I heard the a in charge of the waters say:	34
	16: 8	The fourth a poured out his bowl on	NIG
	16:10	The fifth a poured out his bowl on	NIG
	16:12	The sixth a poured out his bowl on	34
	16:17	The seventh a poured out his bowl into	NIG
	17: 3	Then the a carried me away in the Spirit	NIG
	17: 7	the a said to me: "Why are you astonished?	34
	17:15	Then the a said to me,	NIG
	18: 1	After this I saw another a coming down	34
	18:21	a mighty a picked up a boulder the size of	34
	19: 9	Then the a said to me, "Write:	NIG
	19:17	And I saw an a standing in the sun,	34
	20: 1	I saw an a coming down out of heaven,	34
	21:15	The a who talked with me had	NIG
	21:17	which the a was using.	34
	22: 1	showed me the river of the water of life,	NIG
	22: 6	The a said to me,	NIG
	22: 6	sent his a to show his servants the things	34
	22: 8	the a who had been showing them to me.	34
	22:16	have sent my a to give you this testimony	34

ANGEL'S (2) [ANGEL]

Rev	8: 4	went up before God from the a hand.	34
	10:10	the little scroll from the a hand and ate it.	34

ANGELS (96) [ANGEL]

Ge	19: 1	The two a arrived at Sodom in the evening,	4855
	19:15	With the coming of dawn, the a urged Lot,	4855
	28:12	and the a of God were ascending	4855
	32: 1	and the a of God met him.	4855
Job	1: 6	One day the a came to present themselves	466+1201+2021
	2: 1	the a came to present themselves before	466+1201+2021
	4:18	if he charges his a with error,	4855
	38: 7	and all the a shouted for joy?	466+1201
Ps	78:25	Men ate the bread of a;	52
	78:49	a band of destroying a.	4855
	91:11	For he will command his a concerning you	4855
	103:20	Praise the LORD, you his a,	4855
	148: 2	Praise him, all his a, praise him,	4855
Mt	4: 6	" 'He will command his a concerning you,	34
	4:11	and a came and attended him.	34
	13:39	and the harvesters are a.	34
	13:41	The Son of Man will send out his a,	34
	13:49	The a will come and separate the wicked	34
	16:27	to come in his Father's glory with his a,	34
	18:10	that their a in heaven always see the face	34
	22:30	they will be like the a in heaven.	34
	24:31	he will send his a with a loud trumpet call,	34
	24:36	not even the a in heaven, nor the Son,	34
	25:31	and all the a with him,	34
	25:41	for the devil and his a.	34
	26:53	put at my disposal more than twelve legions of a?	34
Mk	1:13	and a attended him.	34
	8:38	in his Father's glory with the holy a."	34
	12:25	they will be like the a in heaven.	34
	13:27	And he will send his a and gather his elect	34
	13:32	not even the a in heaven, nor the Son,	34
Lk	2:15	the a had left them and gone into heaven,	34
	4:10	" 'He will command his a concerning you	34
	9:26	in the glory of the Father and of the holy a.	34
	12: 8	also acknowledge him before the a of God.	34
	12: 9	before men will be disowned before the a	34
	15:10	the a of God over one sinner who repents."	34
	16:22	when the beggar died and the a carried him	34
	20:36	for they are like the a.	2694
	24:23	that they had seen a vision of a,	34
Jn	1:51	and the a of God ascending and descending	34
	20:12	and saw two a in white,	34
Ac	7:53	that was put into effect through a but have	34
	23: 8	and that there are neither a nor spirits,	34
Ro	8:38	neither a nor demons,	34
1Co	4: 9	to a as well as to men.	34
	6: 3	Do you not know that we will judge a?	34
	11:10	For this reason, and because of the a,	34
	13: 1	If I speak in the tongues of men and of a,	34
Gal	3:19	The law was put into effect through a by	34
Col	2:18	and the worship of a disqualify you for	34
2Th	1: 7	in blazing fire with his powerful a.	34
1Ti	3:16	by the Spirit, was seen by a,	34
	5:21	of God and Christ Jesus and the elect a,	34
Heb	1: 4	So he became as much superior to the a as	34

Heb	1:5	For to which *of* the a did God ever say,	34
	1:6	he says, "Let all God's a worship him."	34
	1:7	In speaking *of* the a he says,	34
	1:7	"He makes his a winds,	34
	1:13	To which *of* the a did God ever say,	34
	1:14	Are not all a ministering spirits sent	NIG
	2:2	if the message spoken by a was binding,	34
	2:5	not *to* a that he has subjected the world	34
	2:7	You made him a little lower than the a;	34
	2:9	who was made a little lower than the a,	34
	2:16	For surely it is not a he helps,	34
	12:22	upon thousands *of* a in joyful assembly,	34
	13:2	by so doing some people have entertained a	34
1Pe	1:12	Even a long to look into these things.	34
	3:22	with a, authorities and powers	34
2Pe	2:4	if God did not spare a when they sinned,	34
	2:11	yet even a, although they are stronger	34
Jude	1:6	And the a who did not keep their positions	34
Rev	1:20	seven stars are the a of the seven churches,	34
	1:20	before my Father and his a.	34
	5:11	I looked and heard the voice *of* many a,	34
	7:1	After this I saw four a standing at	34
	7:2	*to* the four a who had been given power	34
	7:11	the a were standing around the throne and	34
	8:2	I saw the seven a who stand before God,	34
	8:6	Then the seven a who had	34
	8:13	about to be sounded by the other three a!"	34
	9:14	"Release the four a who are bound at	34
	9:15	And the four a who had been kept ready	34
	12:7	and his a fought against the dragon,	34
	12:7	and the dragon and his a fought back.	34
	12:9	and his a with him.	34
	14:10	the presence of the holy a and of the Lamb.	34
	15:1	seven a with the seven last plagues—	34
	15:6	Out of the temple came the seven a with	34
	15:7	the seven a seven golden bowls filled with	34
	15:8	*of* the seven a were completed.	34
	16:1	from the temple saying *to* the seven a,	34
	17:1	the seven a who had the seven bowls came	34
	21:9	the seven a who had the seven bowls full of	34
	21:12	and with twelve a at the gates.	34

ANGER (262) [ANGERED, ANGERS, ANGRY]

Ge	39:19	he burned with a.	678
	49:6	for they have killed men in their a	678
	49:7	Cursed be their a, so fierce, and their fury,	678
Ex	4:14	Then the LORD's a burned against Moses	678
	11:8	Then Moses, hot with a, left Pharaoh.	678
	15:7	You unleashed your **burning a**;	3019
	22:24	My a will be aroused,	678
	32:10	Now leave me alone so that my a may burn	678
	32:11	"why should your a burn	678
	32:12	Turn from your fierce a;	678
	32:19	his a burned and he threw the tablets out	678
	34:6	and gracious God, slow to a, abounding	678
Lev	26:28	then in my a I will be hostile toward you,	2779
Nu	11:1	and when he heard them his a was aroused.	678
	11:33	the a of the LORD burned against	678
	12:9	The a of the LORD burned against them,	678
	14:18	'The LORD is slow to a,	678
	24:10	Then Balak's a burned against Balaam.	678
	25:3	And the LORD's a burned against them.	678
	25:4	that the LORD's fierce a may turn away	678
	25:11	has turned my a away from the Israelites;	2779
	32:10	The LORD's a was aroused that day	678
	32:13	The LORD's a burned against Israel	678
Dt	4:25	and **provoking** him to a,	4087
	6:15	is a jealous God and his a will burn	678
	7:4	and the LORD's a will burn against you	678
	9:7	**provoked** the LORD your God to a	7911
	9:18	and so **provoking** him to a.	4087
	9:19	I feared the a and wrath of the LORD,	678
	11:17	Then the LORD's a will burn against you,	678
	13:17	that the LORD will turn from his fierce a;	678
	29:23	which the LORD overthrew in fierce a.	678
	29:24	Why this fierce, burning a?"	678
	29:27	the LORD's a burned against this land,	678
	29:28	In furious and in great wrath	678
	31:29	of the LORD and **provoke** him to a	4087
Jos	7:1	So the LORD's a burned against Israel.	678
	7:26	Then the LORD turned from his fierce a.	678
	23:16	the LORD's a will burn against you,	678
Jdg	2:12	**provoked** the LORD to a	4087
	2:14	*In His* a against Israel	678+3013
	3:8	The a of the LORD burned against Israel	678
	4:19	Burning with a, he went up	678
1Sa	11:6	and he burned with a.	678
	17:28	he burned with a at him and asked,	678
	20:30	Saul's a flared up at Jonathan and he said	678
	20:34	Jonathan got up from the table in fierce a;	678
2Sa	6:7	The LORD's a burned against Uzzah	678
	11:20	the king's a may flare up,	2779
	12:5	with a against the man and said to Nathan,	678
	24:1	the a of the LORD burned against Israel,	678
1Ki	14:9	you *have* **provoked** me to a and thrust me	4087
	14:15	**provoked** the LORD to a	4087
	14:22	**stirred up** his **jealous** a	7861
	15:30	**provoked** the LORD, the God of Israel, **to a**.	4087+4088
	16:2	to sin and to **provoke** me **to a** by their sins,	4087
	16:7	**provoking** him **to a** by the things he did,	4087
	16:13	**provoked** the LORD, the God of Israel, **to a**	4087
	16:26	**provoked** the LORD, the God of Israel, **to a**	4087
	16:33	**provoke** the LORD, the God of Israel, **to a**	4087
	21:22	because *you have* **provoked** me to a	4087+4088

1Ki	22:53	**provoked** the LORD, the God of Israel, **to a**,	4087
2Ki	13:3	So the LORD's a burned against Israel,	678
	17:11	**provoked** the LORD **to a**.	4087
	17:17	**provoking** him **to a**.	4087
	21:6	**provoking** him **to a**.	4087
	21:15	in my eyes and have **provoked** me **to a**	4087
	22:13	the LORD's a that burns against us	2779
	22:17	to other gods and **provoked** me **to a** by all	4087
	22:17	my a will burn against this place and will	2779
	23:19	**provoked** the LORD **to a**.	4087
	23:26	not turn away from the heat of his fierce a,	678
	23:26	to **provoke** him **to a**	4087+4088
	24:20	of the LORD's a that all this happened	678
1Ch	13:10	The LORD's a burned against Uzzah,	678
	15:13	that the LORD our God **broke out in a**	7287
2Ch	12:12	the LORD's a turned from him,	678
	24:18	God's a came upon Judah and Jerusalem.	7912
	25:15	The a of the LORD burned	678
	28:11	for the LORD's fierce a rests on you."	678
	28:13	and his fierce a rests on Israel."	678
	28:25	**provoked** the LORD, the God of his fathers, **to a**.	4087
	29:8	the a *of* the LORD has fallen on Judah	7912
	29:10	so that his fierce a will turn away from us.	678
	30:8	that his fierce a will turn away from you.	678
	33:6	**provoking** him **to a**.	4087
	34:21	Great is the LORD's a that is poured out	2779
	34:25	to other gods and **provoked** me **to a** by all	4087
	34:25	my a will be poured out on this place	2779
Ezr	8:22	his great a is against all who forsake him."	678
	10:14	until the fierce a *of* our God	678
Ne	9:17	slow to a and abounding in love.	678
Est	1:12	the king became furious and burned with a.	2779
	2:1	when the a *of* King Xerxes had subsided,	2779
Job	4:9	at the blast of his a they perish.	678
	9:5	and overturns them in his a.	678
	9:13	God does not restrain his a;	678
	10:17	against me and increase your a toward me;	4089
	14:13	and conceal me till your a has passed!	678
	16:9	and tears me in his a and gnashes his teeth	678
	18:4	You who tear yourself to pieces in your a,	678
	19:11	His a burns against me;	678
	20:23	God will vent his burning a against him	678
	21:17	the fate God allots in his a?	678
	32:5	his a was aroused.	678
	35:15	that his a never punishes and he does	678
Ps	2:5	in his a and terrifies them in his wrath,	678
	4:4	*In your* a do not sin;	8074
	6:1	do not rebuke me in your a or discipline me	678
	7:6	O LORD, in your a;	678
	27:9	do not turn your servant away in a;	678
	30:5	For his a lasts only a moment,	678
	37:8	Refrain from a and turn from wrath;	678
	38:1	do not rebuke me in your a or discipline me	7912
	55:3	upon me and revile me in their a.	678
	56:7	in your a, O God, bring down the nations.	678
	69:24	let your fierce a overtake them.	678
	74:1	Why does your a smolder against the sheep	678
	77:9	Has he in a withheld his compassion?"	678
	78:31	God's a rose against them;	678
	78:38	Time after time he restrained his a and did	678
	78:49	He unleashed against them his hot a,	678
	78:50	He prepared a path for his a;	678
	80:4	how long *will your* a **smolder** against	6939
	85:3	and turned from your fierce a.	678
	85:5	Will you prolong your a	678
	86:15	and gracious God, slow to a, abounding	678
	90:7	by your a and terrified by your indignation.	678
	90:11	Who knows the power of your a?	678
	95:11	So I declared on oath in my a,	678
	103:8	slow to a, abounding in love.	678
	103:9	nor *will he* **harbor** *his* a forever;	5757
	106:29	**provoked** the LORD **to a**	4087
	124:3	when their a flared against us,	678
	138:7	you stretch out your hand against the a	678
	145:8	slow to a and rich in love.	678
Pr	15:1	but a harsh word stirs up a.	678
	21:14	A gift given in secret soothes a,	678
	27:4	A is cruel and fury overwhelming,	2779
	29:8	but wise men turn away a.	678
	29:11	A fool gives full vent to his a,	8120
	30:33	so stirring up a produces strife."	678
Ecc	5:17	with great frustration, affliction and a.	7912
	7:9	for a resides in the lap of fools.	4088
	10:4	If a ruler's a rises against you,	8120
Isa	5:25	the LORD's a burns against his people;	678
	5:25	Yet for all this, his a *is not* turned away,	678
	7:4	because of the fierce a *of* Rezin and Aram	678
	9:12	Yet for all this, his a is not turned away,	678
	9:17	Yet for all this, his a is not turned away,	678
	9:21	Yet for all this, his a is not turned away,	678
	10:4	Yet for all this, his a is not turned away,	678
	10:5	"Woe to the Assyrian, the rod of my a,	678
	10:6	I dispatch him against a people who a me,	6301
	10:25	Very soon my a against you will end	2405
	12:1	your a has turned away	678
	13:9	a cruel day, with wrath and fierce a—	678
	13:13	in the day of his burning a.	678
	14:6	which in a struck down peoples	6301
	30:27	with burning a and dense clouds of smoke;	678
	30:30	down with raging a and consuming fire,	678
	42:25	So he poured out on them his burning a,	678
	54:8	of a I hid my face from you for a moment,	7912
	57:17	I punished him, and hid my face in a,	7911
	60:10	Though in a I struck you,	7912
	63:3	in my a and trod them down in my wrath;	678
	63:6	I trampled the nations in my a;	678

Isa	66:15	he will bring down his a with fury,	678
Jer	4:8	for the fierce a *of* the LORD has	678
	4:26	before the LORD, before his fierce a.	678
	7:18	to other gods to **provoke** me to a.	4087
	7:20	My a and my wrath will be poured out	678
	8:19	"Why *have they* **provoked** me to a	4087
	10:24	in your a, lest you reduce me to nothing.	678
	11:17	and **provoked** me to a by burning incense	4087
	12:13	because of the LORD's fierce a."	678
	15:14	for my a will kindle a fire that will burn	678
	17:4	for you have kindled my a,	678
	18:23	deal with them in the time of your a.	678
	21:5	a mighty arm in a and fury and great wrath.	678
	23:20	The a *of* the LORD will not turn back	678
	25:6	*do not* **provoke** me to a	4087
	25:37	be laid waste because of the fierce a *of*	678
	25:38	and because of the LORD's fierce a.	678
	30:24	The fierce a *of* the LORD will	678
	32:29	where *the people* **provoked** me to a	4087
	32:31	this city has so aroused my a and wrath	678
	32:37	where I banish them in my furious a	678
	33:5	of the men I will slay in my a and wrath.	678
	36:7	for the a and wrath pronounced	678
	42:18	'As my a and wrath have been poured out	678
	44:3	They **provoked** me to a by burning incense	4087
	44:6	Therefore, my fierce a was poured out;	678
	44:8	Why **provoke** me to a	4087
	49:37	even my fierce a," declares the LORD.	678
	50:13	of the LORD's a she will not be inhabited	7912
	51:45	Run from the fierce a of the LORD.	678
	52:3	of the LORD's a that all this happened	678
La	1:12	on me in the day of his fierce a?	678
	2:1	of Zion with the cloud of his a!	678
	2:1	in the day of his a.	678
	2:3	In fierce a he has cut off every horn	678
	2:6	in his fierce a he has spurned both king	678
	2:21	You have slain them in the day of your a;	678
	2:22	the day of the LORD's a no one escaped	678
	3:43	"You have covered yourself with a	678
	3:66	Pursue them in a and destroy them from	678
	4:11	he has poured out his fierce a.	678
Eze	3:14	in bitterness and in the a of my spirit,	2779
	5:13	"Then my a will cease and my wrath	678
	5:15	in a and in wrath and with stinging rebuke.	678
	7:3	now upon you and I will unleash my a	678
	7:8	on you and spend my a against you;	678
	8:17	and continually **provoke** me to a?	4087
	8:18	Therefore I will deal with them in a;	2779
	13:13	a violent wind, and in my a hailstones	678
	16:26	and **provoked** me to a	4087
	16:38	of my wrath and **jealous** a.	7863
	16:42	and my **jealous** a will turn away	7863
	20:8	and spend my a against them in Egypt.	678
	20:21	and spend my a against them in the desert.	678
	20:28	made offerings that **provoked** me to a,	4088
	21:31	and breathe out my fiery a against you;	6301
	22:20	so will I gather you in my a and my wrath	678
	22:31	and consume them with my fiery a,	6301
	23:25	I will direct my **jealous** a against you,	7863
	25:14	in accordance with my a and my wrath;	678
	35:11	I will treat you in accordance with the a	678
	38:18	my hot a will be aroused,	678
	43:8	So I destroyed them in my a.	678
Da	9:16	turn away your a and your wrath	678
	11:20	yet not in a or in battle.	678
Hos	8:5	My a burns against them.	678
	11:9	I will not carry out my fierce a,	678
	12:14	Ephraim *has* bitterly **provoked** him to a;	4087
	13:11	So in my a I gave you a king,	678
	14:4	for my a has turned away from them.	678
Joel	2:13	slow to a and abounding in love,	678
Am	1:11	because his a raged continually	678
Jnh	3:9	and with compassion turn from his fierce a	678
	4:2	slow to a and abounding in love,	678
Mic	5:15	I will take vengeance in a and wrath upon	678
Na	1:3	LORD is slow to a and great in power;	678
	1:6	Who can endure his fierce a?	678
Hab	3:12	the earth and in a you threshed the nations.	678
Zep	2:2	before the fierce a *of* the LORD comes	678
	2:3	be sheltered on the day of the LORD's a.	678
	3:8	all my fierce a.	678
	3:8	be consumed by the fire of my **jealous** a.	7863
Zec	10:3	"My a burns against the shepherds,	678
Mt	18:34	*In* his a his master turned him over to	3974
Mk	3:5	He looked around at them in a and,	3973
Ro	8:8	there will be wrath and a.	2596
2Co	12:20	jealousy, **outbursts of** a, factions, slander,	2596
Eph	4:26	"In *your* a do not sin":	3974
	4:31	Get rid of all bitterness, rage and a,	3973
Col	3:8	a, rage, malice, slander,	3973
1Ti	2:8	without a or disputing.	3973
Heb	3:11	So I declared on oath in my a,	3973
	4:3	"So I declared on oath in my a,	3973
	11:27	not fearing the king's a;	2596
Jas	1:20	for man's a does not bring about	3973

ANGERED (9) [ANGER]

Dt	32:16	and a him with their detestable idols.	4087
	32:19	and rejected them because he was a	4088
	32:21	and a me with their worthless idols.	4087
Ezr	5:12	because our fathers a the God of heaven,	10653
Ps	78:58	*They* a him with their high places;	4087
	106:32	the waters of Meribah a the LORD,	7911
Pr	22:24	do not associate with one **easily** a,	2779
Zec	8:14	when your fathers a me,"	7911
1Co	13:5	it is not self-seeking, *it is* not **easily** a,	4236

ANGERS (1) [ANGER]
Pr 20: 2 *he who* a him forfeits his life. 6297

ANGLE (5)
2Ch 26: 9 the Valley Gate and at the **a of the wall,** 5243
Ne 3:19 the ascent to the armory as far as the **a.** 5243
3:20 from the **a** to the entrance of the house 5243
3:24 from Azariah's house to the **a** and 5243
3:25 the **a** and the tower projecting from 5243

ANGRY (118) [ANGER]
Ge 4: 5 So Cain *was* very **a,** 3013
4: 6 the LORD said to Cain, "Why *are* you **a?** 3013
18:30 Then he said, "*May* the Lord not *be* **a,** 3013
18:32 Then he said, "*May* the Lord not *be* **a,** 3013
27:45 When your brother is no longer **a** with you 678
30: 2 Jacob *became* **a** with her and said, 678+3013
31:35 Rachel said to her father, "Don't *be* **a,** 928+3013+6524
31:36 Jacob *was* **a** and took Laban to task. 3013
40: 2 Pharaoh *was* **a** with his two officials, 7911
41:10 Pharaoh *was once* **a** with his servants, 7911
44:18 *Do not be* **a** with your servant, 678+3013
45: 5 *be* **a** with yourselves for selling me here, 3013
Ex 16:20 So Moses *was* **a** with them. 7911
32:22 "*Do not be* **a,** my lord," Aaron answered. 678+3013
Lev 10: 6 or you will die and the LORD *will be* **a** 7911
10:16 *he was* **a** with Eleazar and Ithamar, 7911
Nu 11:10 The LORD *became* exceedingly **a,** 678+3013
16:15 Then Moses *became* very **a** and said to 3013
16:22 *will* you *be* **a** with the entire assembly 7911
22:22 But God *was* **a** when he went, 678+3013
22:27 he *was* **a** and beat her with his staff. 678+3013
31:14 Moses *was* **a** with the officers of 678+3013
32:14 and making the LORD even more **a** 678+3019
Dt 1:34 he *was* **a** and solemnly swore: 7911
1:37 of you the LORD *became* **a** with me also 647
3:26 because of you the LORD *was* **a** with me 6297
4:21 The LORD *was* **a** with me because of you, 647
9: 8 the LORD's wrath so that he *was* **a** *enough* 647
9:19 he *was* **a** *enough* with you to destroy you. 7911
9:20 And the LORD *was* **a** enough with Aaron 647
9:22 *You* also made the LORD **a** at Taberah, 2118+7911
31:17 On that day I *will become* **a** with them 678+3013
32:21 I *will* make them **a** by a nation 4087
Jos 22:18 *be* **a** with the whole community of Israel. 7911
Jdg 2:20 the LORD *was* very **a** with Israel 678+3013
6:39 Gideon said to God, "*Do not be* **a** with me. 678+3013
9:30 he *was* very **a.** 678+3013
10: 7 he *became* **a** with them. 678+3013
1Sa 18: 8 Saul *was* very **a;** this refrain galled him. 3013
29: 4 the Philistine commanders *were* **a** with him 7911
2Sa 3: 8 Abner *was* very **a** because 3013
6: 8 Then David *was* **a** because 3013
19:42 Why *are* you **a** about it? 3013
22: 8 they trembled because he *was* **a.** 3013
1Ki 8:46 and *you become* **a** with them and give them 647
11: 9 The LORD *became* **a** with Solomon 647
20:43 and **a,** the king of Israel went to his palace 2409
21: 4 sullen and **a** because Naboth 2409
2Ki 5:11 But Naaman went away and said, 7911
13:19 The man of God *was* **a** with him and said, 7911
17:18 So the LORD *was* very **a** with Israel 647
1Ch 13:11 Then David *was* **a** because 3013
2Ch 6:36 and *you become* **a** with them and give them 647
16:10 Asa *was* **a** with the seer because of this; 4087
26:19 to burn incense, *became* **a.** 2406
28: 9 the God of your fathers, *was* **a** with Judah, 2779
Ezr 9:14 not *be* **a** enough with us to destroy us, 647
Ne 4: 1 he *became* **a** and was greatly incensed. 3013
4: 7 they *were* very **a.** 3013
5: 6 I *was* very **a.** 3013
Est 2:21 *became* **a** and conspired 7911
Job 32: 2 *became* very **a** with Job 678+3013
32: 3 He *was* also **a** with the three friends, 678+3013
42: 7 "I *am* **a** with you and your two friends, 678+3013
Ps 2:12 *be* **a** and you be destroyed in your way, 647
18: 7 they trembled because he *was* **a.** 3013
60: 1 *you have been* **a**— now restore us! 647
76: 7 before you when you are **a?** 678
78:21 *he was* very **a;** 6297
78:59 When God heard them, *he was* very **a;** 6297
78:62 *he was* very **a** with his inheritance. 6297
79: 5 *Will* you *be* **a** 647
85: 5 *Will* you *be* **a** with us forever? 647
89:38 *you have been* very **a** 6297
95:10 forty years I *was* **a** with that generation; 7752
106:40 the LORD *was* **a** with his people 678+3013
Pr 25:23 so a sly tongue brings **a** looks. 2404
29:22 An **a** man stirs up dissension, 678
Ecc 5: 6 *be* **a** at what you say and destroy the work 7911
SS 1: 6 My mother's sons *were* **a** with me 5723
Isa 12: 1 Although *you were* **a** with me, 647
27: 4 I am not **a.** 2779
34: 2 The LORD is **a** with all nations; 7912
47: 6 I *was* **a** with my people 7911
54: 9 So now I have sworn not *to be* **a** with you, 7911
57:16 nor *will* I always *be* **a,** 7911
64: 5 to sin against them, you *were* **a.** 7911
64: 9 *Do not be* **a** beyond measure, O LORD; 7911
Jer 2:35 he is not **a** with me.' 678+8740
3: 5 *will* you always *be* **a?** 5757
3:12 'I *will* not *be* **a** forever. 5757

Jer 10:10 When he is **a,** the earth trembles; 7912
37:15 They *were* **a** with Jeremiah 7911
La 5:22 and *are* **a** with us beyond measure. 7911
Eze 16:42 I will be calm and no longer **a.** 4087
Da 2:12 the king so **a** and furious that he ordered 10113
Jnh 4: 1 Jonah was greatly displeased and *became* **a.** 3013
4: 4 "Have you any right *to be* **a?"** 3013
4: 9 "Do you have a right *to be* **a** about 3013
4: 9 "I *am* **a** enough to die." 3013
Mic 2: 7 "*Is* the Spirit of the LORD **a?** 7918
7:18 You do not stay **a** forever but delight 678
Hab 3: 8 *Were you* **a** with the rivers, O LORD? 3013
Zec 1: 2 LORD *was* very **a** with your forefathers 7911+7912
1:12 which *you have been* **a** 2404
1:15 I *am* very **a** with the nations that feel secure. 7911+7912
1:15 I *was* only a little **a,** 7911
7:12 So the LORD Almighty was very **a.** 7912
Mt 5:22 that anyone who *is* **a** with his brother will 3974
Lk 14:21 *became* **a** and ordered his servant, 3974
15:28 "The older brother *became* **a** and refused 3974
Jn 7:23 why *are* you **a** with me for healing 5957
Ro 10:19 I *will* make you **a** by a nation 4239
Eph 4:26 the sun go down while you are still **a,** 4240
Heb 3:10 That is why I *was* **a** with that generation, 4696
3:17 And with whom *was he* **a** for forty years? 4696
Jas 1:19 slow to speak and slow to become **a,** 3973
Rev 11:18 The nations *were* **a;** 3974

ANGUISH (42) [ANGUISHED]
Ex 15:14 **a** will grip the people of Philistia. 2659
Dt 2:25 of you and will tremble and *be* in **a** because 2655
1Sa 1:16 I have been praying here out of my great **a** 8490
Job 6: 2 "If only my **a** could be weighed 4089
7:11 I will speak out in the **a** *of* my spirit, 7639
15:24 Distress and **a** fill him with terror; 5188
26: 5 "The dead *are* in deep **a,** 2655
Ps 6: 3 My soul is in **a.** 987+4394
25:17 free me from my **a.** 5188
31: 7 for you saw my affliction and knew the **a** 7650
31:10 My life is consumed by **a** and my years 3326
38: 8 I groan in **a** *of* heart. 5639
39: 2 even saying anything good, my **a** increased. 3873
55: 4 My heart is in **a** within me; 2655
116: 3 the **a** *of* the grave came upon me; 5210
118: 5 In my **a** I cried to the LORD, 5210
Pr 31: 6 wine to *those who* are in **a;** 5253+5883
Isa 13: 8 pain and **a** will grip them; 2477
23: 5 *they* will be in **a** at the report from Tyre. 2655
38:15 because of this **a** *of* my soul. 5253
38:17 it was for my benefit that I suffered *such* **a.** 5253
65:14 from **a** *of* heart and wail in brokenness 3873
Jer 4:19 Oh, my **a,** my anguish! 5055
4:19 Oh, my anguish, my **a!** 5055
6:24 **A** has gripped us, 7650
15: 8 suddenly I will bring down on them **a** 6552
49:24 **a** and pain have seized her, 7650
50:43 **A** has gripped him, 7650
La 1: 4 her maidens grieve, and she is in bitter **a.** 5253
Eze 27:31 with **a** *of* soul and with bitter mourning. 5253
30: 4 and **a** will come upon Cush. 2714
30: 9 **A** will take hold of them on the day 2714
Da 10:16 "I am overcome with **a** *because* of 7496
Joel 2: 6 At the sight of them, nations *are* in **a;** 2655
Am 5:16 wailing in all the streets and cries of **a** 2082+2082
Hab 3: 7 the dwellings of Midian in **a.** 8074
Zep 1:15 a day of distress and **a,** 5188
Lk 21:25 nations will be in **a** and perplexity at 5330
22:44 And being in **a,** he prayed more earnestly, 75
Jn 16:21 but when her baby is born she forgets the **a** 2568
Ro 9: 2 I have great sorrow and unceasing **a** 3850
2Co 2: 4 For I wrote you out of great distress and **a** 5330

ANGUISHED (2) [ANGUISH]
Jer 48: 5 on the road down to Horonaim **a** cries over 7639
Da 6:20 he called to Daniel in an **a** voice, "Daniel, 10565

ANIAM (1)
1Ch 7:19 Ahian, Shechem, Likhi and **A.** 642

ANIM (1)
Jos 15:50 Anab, Eshtemoh, **A,** 6719

ANIMAL (85) [ANIMALS]
Ge 6:20 of every kind of **a** and of every kind 989
7: 2 with you seven of every kind of clean **a,** 989
7: 2 and two of every kind of unclean **a,** 989
7:14 with them every wild **a** according 2651
9: 5 I will demand an accounting from every **a.** 2651
37:20 and say that a ferocious **a** devoured him. 2651
37:33 Some ferocious **a** has devoured him. 2651
43:16 slaughter an **a** and prepare dinner; 3181
Ex 9: 4 no **a** belonging to the Israelites will die.' " 1821S
9: 6 not one **a** belonging to the Israelites died. 5238
9:19 the hail will fall on every man and **a** 989
11: 7 not a dog will bark at any man or **a.'** 989
13: 2 whether man or **a."** 989
13:15 both man and **a,** 989
19:13 Whether man or **a,** 989
21:34 and the dead **a** will be his. AIT
21:35 both the money and the dead **a** equally. AIT
21:36 the owner must pay, **a** for animal, 8802
21:36 the owner must pay, animal for **a,** 8802
21:36 and the dead **a** will be his. AIT

Ex 22: 4 stolen **a** is found alive in his possession— AIT
22:10 a sheep or any other **a** to his neighbor 989
22:12 But if the **a** was stolen from the neighbor, NIH
22:13 was torn to pieces by a wild **a,** 3271+3271
22:13 not be required to pay for the torn **a.** NIH
22:14 "If a man borrows an **a** from his neighbor 989
22:15 But if the owner is with the **a,** 2257S
22:15 If the **a** was hired, 2085S
22:19 with an **a** must be put to death. 989
22:31 **a** torn by wild beasts; 3274
Lev 1: 2 to the LORD, bring as your offering an **a** 989
3: 1 and he offers an **a** from the herd, NIH
3: 1 he is to present before the LORD an **a** 5647S
3: 6 an **a** from the flock as a fellowship offering NIH
7:21 or an unclean **a** or any unclean, 989
7:24 The fat of an **a** found dead or torn 5577
7:25 of an **a** from which an offering by fire may 989
7:26 you must not eat the blood of any bird or **a.** 989
11: 3 You may eat any **a** that has 989
11:26 " 'Every **a** that has a split hoof 989
11:39 " 'If an **a** that you are allowed to eat dies, 989
17:13 among you who hunts any **a** or bird 2651+7473
18:23 " 'Do not have sexual relations with an **a** 989
18:23 A woman must not present herself to an **a** 989
20:15 " 'If a man has sexual relations with an **a,** 989
20:15 and you must kill the **a.** 989
20:16 an **a** to have sexual relations with it, 989
20:16 kill both the woman and the **a.** 989
20:25 Do not defile yourselves by any **a** or bird 989
22:24 an **a** whose testicles are bruised, NIH
24:18 of someone's **a** must make restitution— 989
24:18 Whoever kills an **a** must make restitution, 989
27: 9 an **a** that is acceptable as an offering to 989
27: 9 an **a** given to the LORD becomes holy. 5647S
27:10 if he should substitute *one* **a** for another, 989
27:11 a ceremonially unclean **a**— 989
27:11 the **a** must be presented to the priest, 989
27:13 If the owner wishes to redeem the **a,** 5626S
27:26 may dedicate the firstborn of an **a,** 989
27:28 whether man or **a** or family land— 989
27:32 every tenth **a** that passes under NIH
27:33 both the **a** and its substitute become holy 2085S
Nu 3:13 whether man or **a.** 989
8:17 whether man or **a,** is mine. 989
18:15 both man and **a,** 989
Dt 4:17 or like any **a** on earth or any bird that flies 989
14: 6 You may eat any **a** that has 989
15:21 If an **a** has a defect, is lame or blind, 2257S
16: 2 an **a** from your flock or herd at the place 7366
27:21 "Cursed is the man who has sexual relations with any **a.**" 989
Job 39:15 that some wild **a** may trample them. 2651
Ps 50:10 for every **a** *of* the forest is mine, 2651
Pr 12:10 righteous man cares for the needs of his **a,** 989
Ecc 3:19 man has no advantage over the **a.** 989
3:21 and if the spirit of the **a** goes down into 989
Jer 51:62 so that neither man nor **a** will live in it; 989
Eze 29:11 No foot of man or **a** will pass through it; 989
44:31 priests must not eat anything, bird or **a,** 989
Da 4:16 and let him be given the mind of an **a,** 10263
5:21 from people and given the mind of an **a;** 10263
8: 4 No **a** could stand against him, 2651
Hos 13: 8 a wild **a** will tear them apart. 2651
Mal 1:14 then sacrifices a **blemished** *a* to the Lord. AIT
Heb 12:20 "If even an **a** touches the mountain, 2563
Jas 3: 3 we can turn the whole **a.** NIG

ANIMALS (145) [ANIMAL]
Ge 1:24 and wild **a,** each according to its kind." 2651
1:25 the wild **a** according to their kinds, 2651
3: 1 of the wild **a** the LORD God had made. 2651
3:14 above all the livestock and all the wild **a!** 2651
6: 7 men and **a,** and creatures that move along 989
7: 8 Pairs of clean and unclean **a,** 989
7:16 The **a** going in were male and female AIT
7:21 birds, livestock, wild **a,** 2651
7:23 and **a** and the creatures that move along 989
8: 1 the wild **a** and the livestock that were 2651
8:17 the **a,** and all the creatures that move along 989
8:19 the **a** and all the creatures that move along 2651
8:20 of all the clean **a** and clean birds, 989
9:10 the birds, the livestock and all the wild **a,** 2651
30:40 and dark-colored **a** *that belonged* 7366
30:40 and did not put them with Laban's **a.** 7366
30:41 the **a** so they would mate near the branches, 7366
30:42 but if the **a** were weak, 7366
30:42 So the weak **a** went to Laban and NIH
31:39 **a** torn by wild beasts; 3274
32:17 and who owns all these **a** in front of you?' NIH
33:13 all the **a** will die. 7366
34:23 and all their *other* **a** become ours? 989
36: 6 as well as his livestock and all his *other* **a** 989
45:17 Load your **a** and return to the land 1248
Ex 8:17 gnats came upon men and **a.** 989
8:18 And the gnats were on men and **a.** 989
9: 7 even one of the **a** *of* the Israelites had died. 5238
9: 9 on men and **a** throughout the land." 989
9:10 and festering boils broke out on men and **a.** 989
9:22 on men and **a** and on everything growing in 989
9:25 both men and **a;** 989
12: 5 The **a** you choose must be year-old males 8445
12:12 both men and **a**— 989
12:21 at once and select the **a** for your families 7366
20:10 nor your **a,** nor the alien within your gates. 989
23:11 and the wild **a** may eat what they leave. 2651
23:29 and the wild **a** too numerous for you. 2651

Lev	5: 2	whether the carcasses of unclean **wild a** or	2651
	7:24	or torn by wild **a** may be used	3274
	11: 2	'Of all the **a** that live on land,	989
	11:27	Of all the **a** that walk on all fours,	2651
	11:29	" 'Of the **a** that move about on the ground,	9238
	11:46	" 'These are the regulations concerning **a,**	989
	17:15	or torn by wild **a** must wash his clothes	3274
	19:19	" 'Do not mate different kinds of **a.**	989
	20:25	a distinction between clean and unclean **a**	989
	22: 8	or torn by wild **a,**	3274
	22:25	and you must not accept such from	465ˢ
	25: 7	as well as for your livestock and the **wild a**	2651
	26:22	I will send wild **a** against you,	2651
	27:27	If it is one of the unclean **a,**	989
Nu	7:87	of **a** for the burnt offering came	1330
	7:88	The total number of **a** for the sacrifice of	1330
	18:15	and every firstborn male of unclean **a.**	989
	28:31	Be sure the **a** are without defect.	NIH
	31:11	including the people and **a,**	989
	31:26	the people and **a** that were captured.	989
	31:30	cattle, donkeys, sheep, goats or other **a.**	989
	31:47	of every fifty persons and **a,**	989
Dt	5:14	nor your ox, your donkey or any of your **a,**	989
	7:22	or the wild **a** will multiply around you.	2651
	12:15	you may slaughter your **a** in any	NIH
	12:21	you may slaughter **a** from the herds	NIH
	14: 4	These are the **a** you may eat:	989
Jdg	20:48	the **a** and everything else they found.	989
2Sa	21:10	of the air touch them by day or the wild **a**	2651
1Ki	4:33	He also taught about **a** and birds,	989
	18: 5	so we will not have to kill any of our **a."**	989
2Ki	3: 9	for themselves or for the **a** with them.	989
	3:17	your cattle and your other **a** will drink.	989
2Ch	29:33	The **a** consecrated as sacrifices amounted	AIT
	35:11	while the Levites skinned the **a.**	NIH
	35:13	the **Passover a** over the fire as prescribed,	7175
Job	5:23	and the wild **a** will be at peace with you.	2651
	12: 7	"But ask the **a,** and they will teach you,	989
	37: 8	The **a** take cover; they remain in their dens.	2651
	40:20	and all the wild **a** play nearby.	2651
Ps	66:15	I will sacrifice **fat a** to you and an offering	4671
	135: 8	the firstborn of men and **a.**	989
	148:10	**wild a** and all cattle,	2651
Ecc	3:18	that they may see that they are like the **a.**	989
	3:19	Man's fate is like that of the **a;**	989
Isa	1:11	of rams and the fat of **fattened a;**	5309
	18: 6	of prey and to the wild **a;**	989
	18: 6	the wild **a** all winter.	989
	30: 6	An oracle concerning the **a** of the Negev:	989
	40:16	nor its **a** enough for burnt offerings.	2651
	43:20	The wild **a** honor me,	2651
Jer	9:10	of the air have fled and the **a** are gone.	989
	12: 4	the **a** and birds have perished.	989
	21: 6	both men and **a—**	989
	27: 5	the earth and its people and the **a** that are	989
	27: 6	I will make even the wild **a** subject to him.	2651
	28:14	even give him control over the wild **a.' "**	2651
	31:27	with the offspring of men and of **a.**	989
	32:43	'It is a desolate waste, without men or **a,**	989
	33:10	"It is a desolate waste, without men or **a."**	989
	33:10	inhabited by neither men nor **a,**	989
	33:12	desolate and without men or **a—**	989
	36:29	and cut off both men and **a** from it?"	989
	50: 3	both men and **a** will flee away.	989
Eze	4:14	or torn by wild **a.**	3274
	8:10	of crawling things and detestable and all	989
	14:13	upon it and kill its men and their **a,**	989
	14:17	and I kill its men and their **a,**	989
	14:19	killing its men and their **a,**	989
	14:21	to kill its men and their **a!**	989
	25:13	against Edom and kill its men and their **a.**	989
	29: 8	against you and kill your men and their **a.**	989
	33:27	in the country I will give to the **wild a** to	2651
	34: 3	with the wool and slaughter the **choice a,**	AIT
	34: 5	for all the wild **a,**	2651
	34: 8	and has become food for all the wild **a,**	2651
	34:28	nor will wild **a** devour them.	2651
	36:11	I will increase the number of men and **a**	989
	39: 4	of carrion birds and to the wild **a.**	2651
	39:17	to every kind of bird and all the wild **a:**	2651
	39:18	all of them **fattened a** from Bashan.	5309
	44:31	found dead or **torn by wild a.**	3274
Da	4:14	Let the **a** flee from under it and the birds	10263
	4:15	with the **a** among the plants of the earth.	10263
	4:23	let him live like the wild **a,**	10263
	4:25	from people and will live with the wild **a;**	10263
	4:32	from people and will live with the wild **a;**	10263
Hos	2:12	and wild **a** will devour them.	2651
Joel	1:20	Even the wild **a** pant for you;	989
	2:22	Be not afraid, O wild **a,**	989
Hab	2:17	and your destruction of **a** will terrify you.	989
Zep	1: 3	"I will sweep away both men and **a;**	989
Zec	14:15	and all the **a** in those camps.	989
Mal	1: 8	When you bring **blind a** for sacrifice,	AIT
	1: 8	When you sacrifice crippled or **diseased a,**	AIT
	1:13	or **diseased a** and offer them as sacrifices,	AIT
Mk	1:13	He was with the wild **a,**	2563
Ac	10:12	It contained all kinds of **four-footed a,**	5488
	11: 6	into it and saw **four-footed a** of the earth,	5488
	15:20	the **meat of strangled a** and from blood.	4465
	15:29	the **meat of strangled a**	4465
	21:25	from the **meat of strangled a** and	4465
Ro	1:23	to look like mortal man and birds and **a**	5488
1Co	15:39	of flesh, **a** have another,	3229
Heb	13:11	the blood of **a** into the Most Holy Place as	2442
Jas	3: 7	All kinds of **a,** birds,	2563
Jude	1:10	by instinct, like unreasoning **a—**	2442

ANISE (KJV) See DILL

ANKLE (1) [ANKLE-DEEP, ANKLES]

Isa	3:20	the headdresses and **a** chains and sashes,	7578

ANKLE-DEEP (1) [ANKLE, DEEP]

Eze	47: 3	and then led me through water that was **a.**	701

ANKLES (4) [ANKLE]

2Sa	22:37	so that my **a** do not turn.	7972
Ps	18:36	so that my **a** do not turn.	7972
Isa	3:16	with ornaments jingling on their **a.**	8079
Ac	3: 7	the man's feet and **a** became strong.	5383

ANNA (1)

Lk	2:36	There was also a prophetess, **A,**	483

ANNALS (40)

1Ki	11:41	are they not written in the book of the **a**	1821
	14:19	in the book of the **a** of the kings	1821+3427
	14:29	in the book of the **a** of the kings	1821+3427
	15: 7	in the book of the **a** of the kings	1821+3427
	15:23	in the book of the **a** of the kings	1821+3427
	15:31	in the book of the **a** of the kings	1821+3427
	16: 5	in the book of the **a** of the kings	1821+3427
	16:14	in the book of the **a** of the kings	1821+3427
	16:20	in the book of the **a** of the kings	1821+3427
	16:27	in the book of the **a** of the kings	1821+3427
	22:39	in the book of the **a** of the kings	1821+3427
	22:45	in the book of the **a** of the kings	1821+3427
2Ki	1:18	in the book of the **a** of the kings	1821+3427
	8:23	in the book of the **a** of the kings	1821+3427
	10:34	in the book of the **a** of the kings	1821+3427
	12:19	in the book of the **a** of the kings	1821+3427
	13: 8	in the book of the **a** of the kings	1821+3427
	13:12	in the book of the **a** of the kings	1821+3427
	14:15	in the book of the **a** of the kings	1821+3427
	14:18	in the book of the **a** of the kings	1821+3427
	14:28	in the book of the **a** of the kings	1821+3427
	15: 6	in the book of the **a** of the kings	1821+3427
	15:11	in the book of the **a** of the kings	1821+3427
	15:15	in the book of the **a** of the kings	1821+3427
	15:21	in the book of the **a** of the kings	1821+3427
	15:26	in the book of the **a** of the kings	1821+3427
	15:31	in the book of the **a** of the kings	1821+3427
	15:36	in the book of the **a** of the kings	1821+3427
	16:19	in the book of the **a** of the kings	1821+3427
	20:20	in the book of the **a** of the kings	1821+3427
	21:17	in the book of the **a** of the kings	1821+3427
	21:25	in the book of the **a** of the kings	1821+3427
	23:28	in the book of the **a** of the kings	1821+3427
	24: 5	in the book of the **a** of the kings	1821+3427
1Ch	27:24	in the book of the **a** of King David.	1821+3427
2Ch	20:34	are written in the **a** of Jehu son of Hanani,	1821
	33:18	are written in the **a** of the kings of Israel.	1821
Ne	12:23	in the book of the **a.**	1821+3427
Est	2:23	All this was recorded in the book of the **a**	1821+3427
	10: 2	in the book of the **a** of the kings	1821+3427

ANNAS (4)

Lk	3: 2	the high priesthood of **A** and Caiaphas,	483
Jn	18:13	and brought him first to **A,**	484
	18:24	Then **A** sent him, still bound,	484
Ac	4: 6	**A** the high priest was there,	484

ANNIHILATE (6) [ANNIHILATED, ANNIHILATION]

Dt	9: 3	and **a** them quickly,	6
2Sa	21: 2	for Israel and Judah had tried to **a** them.)	5782
2Ch	20:23	from Mount Seir to destroy and **a** them.	9012
Est	3:13	kill and **a** all the Jews—	6
	8:11	and **a** any armed force of any nationality	6
Da	11:44	in a great rage to destroy and **a** many.	3049

ANNIHILATED (1) [ANNIHILATE]

2Ch	32:21	who **a** all the fighting men and the leaders	3948

ANNIHILATION (2) [ANNIHILATE]

Est	4: 8	a copy of the text of the edict for their **a,**	9012
	7: 4	for destruction and slaughter and **a.**	6

ANNIVERSARY (1)

Dt	16: 6	on the **a** of your departure from Egypt.	4595

ANNOTATIONS (2) [NOTE]

2Ch	13:22	are written in the **a** of the prophet Iddo.	4535
	24:27	of the temple of God are written in the **a** on	4535

ANNOUNCE (13) [ANNOUNCED, ANNOUNCEMENT, ANNOUNCES, ANNOUNCING]

Jdg	7: 3	**a** now to the people,	7924
Isa	42: 9	before they spring into being **I a** them	9048
	48:20	**A** this with shouts of joy and proclaim it.	5583
Jer	4: 5	"**A** in Judah and proclaim in Jerusalem	5583
	5:20	"**A** this to the house of Jacob	5583
	18: 7	at any time **I a** that a nation or kingdom is	1819
	18: 9	And if at another time **I a** that a nation	1819
	46:14	"**A** this in Egypt, and proclaim it in Migdol;	5583
	48:20	**A** by the Arnon that Moab is destroyed.	5583
	50: 2	"**A** and proclaim among the nations, lift up	5583
	51:31	and messenger follows messenger to **a** to	5583
Zec		**A** I that I will restore twice as much	5583
Mt	6: 2	do not **a** it **with trumpets,**	4895

ANNOUNCED (13) [ANNOUNCE]

Ex	32: 5	he built an altar in front of the calf and **a,**	7924
Lev	23:44	So Moses **a** to the Israelites	1819
Ru	4: 9	Boaz **a** to the elders and all the people,	606
1Ki	20:13	to Ahab king of Israel and **a,** "This is what	606
Ps	68:11	The Lord **a** the word,	5989
Isa	48: 3	my mouth **a** them and I made them known;	3655
	48: 5	before they happened **I a** them **to** you so	9048
La	1:21	the day **you have a** so they may become	7924
Da	4:17	" 'The decision is **a** by messengers,	10141
Lk	23: 4	Pilate **a** to the chief priests and the crowd,	3306
Gal	3: 8	**a the gospel in advance**	4603
Heb	2: 3	which **was** first **a** by the Lord,	3281
Rev	10: 7	just as **he a** to his servants the prophets."	2294

ANNOUNCEMENT (1) [ANNOUNCE]

Isa	48:16	the first **a** I have not spoken in secret;	NIH

ANNOUNCES (2) [ANNOUNCE]

Dt	13: 1	among you and **a** to you a miraculous sign	5989
Job	36:33	His thunder **a** the coming storm;	5583

ANNOUNCING (1) [ANNOUNCE]

Jer	4:15	A voice **is a** from Dan,	5583

ANNOYANCE (1)

Pr	12:16	A fool shows his **a** at once,	4088

ANNUAL (7) [ANNUALLY]

Ex	30:10	This **a** atonement must be made	285+928+2021+9102
Jdg	21:19	the festival of the LORD in Shiloh,	2025+3427+3427+4946
1Sa	1:21	with all his family to offer the **a** sacrifice to	3427
	2:19	up with her husband to offer the **a** sacrifice.	3427
	20: 6	because an **a** sacrifice is being made there	3427
2Ch	8:13	New Moons and the three **a** feasts—	928+2021+7193+9102
Heb	10: 3	those sacrifices are an **a** reminder of sins,	1929+2848

ANNUALLY (2) [ANNUAL]

2Ch	24: 5	and collect the money **due a** from all Israel,	928+1896+4946+9102+9102
Est	9:21	to have them celebrate **a** the fourteenth	928+2256+3972+9102+9102

ANNULLED (1) [NULLIFY]

Isa	28:18	Your covenant with death **will be a;**	4105

ANOINT (28) [ANOINTED, ANOINTING]

Ex	28:41	**a** and ordain them.	5417
	29: 7	the anointing oil and **a** him by pouring it	5417
	29:36	and **a** it to consecrate it.	5417
	30:26	Then use it **to a** the Tent of Meeting,	5417
	30:30	"**A** Aaron and his sons and consecrate them	5417
	40: 9	"Take the anointing oil and **a** the tabernacle	5417
	40:10	Then **a** the altar of burnt offering	5417
	40:11	**A** the basin and its stand	5417
	40:13	**a** him and consecrate him	5417
	40:15	**a** them just as you anointed their father,	5417
Jdg	9: 8	One day the trees went out to **a** a king	5417
	9:15	'If you really **want to a** me king over you,	5417
1Sa	9:16	**A** him leader over my people Israel;	5417
	15: 1	the one the LORD sent to **a** you king	5417
	16: 3	**You are to a** for me the one I indicate."	5417
	16:12	Then the LORD said, "Rise and **a** him;	5417
1Ki	1:34	and Nathan the prophet **a** him king	5417
	19:15	you get there, **a** Hazael king over Aram.	5417
	19:16	**a** Jehu son of Nimshi king over Israel,	5417
	19:16	and **a** Elisha son of Shaphat	5417
2Ki	9: 3	**I a** you king over Israel.'	5417
	9: 6	'**I a** you king over the LORD's people	5417
	9:12	**I a** you king over Israel.'	5417
Ps	23: 5	**You a** my head with oil; my cup overflows.	2014
Ecc	9: 8	and always **a** your head **with** oil.	6584
Da	9:24	to seal up vision and prophecy and to **a**	5417
Mk	16: 1	so that **they might go to a** Jesus' body.	230
Jas	5:14	and **a** him with oil in the name of the Lord.	230

ANOINTED (83) [ANOINT]

Ge	31:13	where **you a** a pillar and where you made	5417
Ex	29:29	so that they **can be a** and ordained in them.	5417
	40:15	Anoint them just as **you a** their father,	5417
Lev	4: 3	" 'If the **a** priest sins,	5431
	4: 5	Then the **a** priest shall take some of	5431
	4:16	Then the **a** priest is to take some of	5431
	6:20	to bring to the LORD on the day he **is a:**	5417
	6:22	to succeed him as **a** priest shall prepare it.	5431
	7:36	On the day they **were a,**	5417
	8:10	and the tabernacle and everything in it,	5417
	8:12	and **a** him to consecrate him.	5417

Lev	16:32	The priest who *is* a and ordained	5417
Nu	3: 3	the a priests, who were ordained to serve	5417
	7: 1	he a it and consecrated it	5417
	7: 1	He also a and consecrated the altar	5417
	7:10	When the altar *was* a,	5417
	7:84	for the dedication of the altar when it *was* a:	5417
	7:88	for the dedication of the altar after it **was** a.	5417
	35:25	who *was* a with the holy oil.	5417
1Sa	2:10	to his king and exalt the horn of his a."	5431
	2:35	he will minister before my a one always.	5431
	10: 1	"*Has* not the LORD a you leader	5417
	12: 3	in the presence of the LORD and his a.	5431
	12: 5	and also his a is witness this day,	5431
	15:17	The LORD a you king over Israel.	5417
	16: 6	"Surely the LORD's a stands here before	5431
	16:13	So Samuel took the horn of oil and a him	5417
	24: 6	the LORD's a, or lift my hand	5431
	24: 6	for he is the a *of* the LORD.	5431
	24:10	because he is the LORD's a.'	5431
	26: 9	Who can lay a hand on the LORD's a and	5431
	26:11	that I should lay a hand on the LORD's a?	5431
	26:16	not guard your master, the LORD's a.	5431
	26:23	I would not lay a hand on the LORD's a."	5431
2Sa	1:14	to destroy the LORD's a?"	5431
	1:16	'I killed the LORD's a.' "	5431
	2: 4	to Hebron and there *they* a David king over	5417
	2: 7	and the house of Judah *has* a me king	5417
	3:39	And today, though I *am* the a king,	5417
	5: 3	and *they* a David king over Israel,	5417
	5:17	that David *had been* a king over Israel,	5417
	12: 7	'I a you king over Israel,	5417
	19:10	whom *we* a to rule over us,	5417
	19:21	He cursed the LORD's a,"	5431
	22:51	he shows unfailing kindness to his a,	5431
	23: 1	the man a *by* the God of Jacob,	5431
1Ki	1:39	of oil from the sacred tent and a Solomon.	5417
	1:45	and Nathan the prophet *have* a him king	5417
	5: 1	of Tyre heard that Solomon *had been* a king	5417
2Ki	11:12	*They* a him, and the people clapped their hands	5417
	23:30	of Josiah and a him and made him king	5417
1Ch	11: 3	and *they* a David king over Israel,	5417
	14: 8	that David *had* **been** a king over all Israel,	5417
	16:22	"Do not touch my a ones;	5431
2Ch	6:42	O LORD God, do not reject your a one.	5431
	22: 7	the LORD *had* a to destroy the house	5417
	23:11	*They* a him and shouted,	5417
Ps	2: 2	against the LORD and against his A *One.*	5431
	18:50	he shows unfailing kindness to his a,	5431
	20: 6	Now I know that the LORD saves his a;	5431
	28: 8	a fortress of salvation for his a one.	5431
	45: 2	and your lips *have* **been** a *with* grace,	3668
	84: 9	look with favor on your a one.	5431
	89:20	with my sacred oil *I* have a him.	5417
	89:38	you have been very angry with your a one.	5431
	89:51	of your a one.	5431
	105:15	"Do not touch my a ones;	5431
	132:10	do not reject your a one.	5431
	132:17	for David and set up a lamp for my a one.	5431
Isa	45: 1	"This is what the LORD says to his a,	5431
	61: 1	the LORD *has* a me to preach good news	5417
La	4:20	The LORD's a, our very life breath,	5431
Eze	28:14	You were a as a guardian cherub,	4937
Da	9:25	and rebuild Jerusalem until the A *One,*	5431
	9:26	the A *One* will be cut off	5431
Hab	3:13	to save your a *one.*	5431
Zec	4:14	the two *who are* a to serve the Lord of all the earth."	1201+2021+3658
Mk	6:13	and a many sick people with oil	230
Lk	4:18	because *he has* a me to preach good news to	5987
Ac	4:26	against the LORD and against his A *One.*'	5986
	4:27	against your holy servant Jesus, whom *you* a	5987
	10:38	how God a Jesus of Nazareth with	5987
2Co	1:21	you stand firm in Christ. *He* a us,	5987

ANOINTING (30) [ANOINT]

Ex	25: 6	for the a oil and for the fragrant incense;	5418
	29: 7	Take the a oil and anoint him by pouring it	5418
	29:21	the blood on the a and some of the a oil	5418
	30:25	Make these into a sacred a oil,	5418
	30:25	It will be the sacred a oil.	5418
	30:31	to be my sacred a oil for the generations	5418
	31:11	and the a oil and fragrant incense for	5418
	35: 8	for the a oil and for the fragrant incense;	5418
	35:15	the a oil and the fragrant incense;	5418
	35:28	and olive oil for the light and for the a oil	5418
	37:29	also made the sacred a oil and the pure,	5418
	39:38	the a oil, the fragrant incense,	5418
	40: 9	"Take the a oil and anoint the tabernacle	5418
	40:15	Their a will be to a priesthood.	5420
Lev	8: 2	the a oil, the bull for the sin offering,	5418
	8:10	Then Moses took the a oil and anointed	5418
	8:11	a the altar and all its utensils and the basin	5417
	8:12	the a oil on Aaron's head and anointed him	5418
	8:30	of the a oil and some of the blood from	5418
	10: 7	because the LORD's a oil is on you."	5418
	21:10	the a oil poured on his head	5418
	21:12	because he has been dedicated by the a oil	5418
Nu	4:16	the regular grain offering and the a oil.	5418
1Ch	29:22	a him before the LORD to be ruler	5417
Ps	45: 7	above your companions by a you with	5417
Heb	1: 9	above your companions by a you with	5987
1Jn	2:20	But you have an a from the Holy One,	5984
	2:27	a you received from him remains in you,	5984
	2:27	as his a teaches you about all things and as	5984
	2:27	and as that is real, not counterfeit—	NIG

ANON (KJV) See AT ONCE

ANOTH See BETH ANOTH

ANOTHER (359) [ANOTHER'S]

Ge	4:25	"God has granted me a child in place	337
	8:19	came out of the ark, **one kind after** a.	2157+4200+5476
	25: 1	Abraham took a wife,	3578
	26:21	Then they dug a well,	337
	26:22	He moved on from there and dug a well,	337
	29:27	in return for a seven years of work."	337+6388
	29:30	And he worked for Laban a seven years.	337+6388
	30:24	"May the LORD add to me a son."	337
	35:17	"Don't be afraid, for you have a son."	1685
	37: 9	Then he had a dream,	337+6388
	37: 9	"Listen," he said, "I had a dream,	6388
	38: 5	to **still** a son and named him Shelah.	3578+6388
	42:21	They said to one a,	278S
	43: 6	by telling the man you had a brother?"	6388
	43: 7	'Do you have a brother?'	NIH
Ex	1:21	and a one on the seventh day.	5246+7731S
	21:10	If he marries a *woman,*	337
	21:14	a man schemes and kills a man deliberately,	8276S
	21:16	"Anyone who kidnaps a and	408S
	21:35	"If a man's bull injures the bull of a	8276S
	22: 5	and they graze in a *man's* field,	337
	26: 9	into one and the other six **into** a set.	963+4200
	36:16	into one set and the other six into *a* set.	AIT
Lev	13: 5	he is to keep him in isolation a seven days.	9108
	13:33	to keep him in isolation a seven days.	9108
	13:54	Then he is to isolate it for a seven days.	9108
	19:11	" 'Do not deceive one a.	6660S
	19:20	a slave girl promised to a man but who has	NIH
	20:10	man commits adultery with a man's wife—	NIH
	26:37	over one a as though fleeing from	278S
	27:10	if he should substitute one animal for a,	989S
Nu	5: 6	a man or woman wrongs a in any way	132+2021S
	5:13	by sleeping with a man,	NIH
	23:13	with me to a place where you can see them;	337
	23:27	"Come, let me take you to a place.	337
	35:15	anyone who has killed a accidentally can flee there.	5883S
	35:20	with malice aforethought shoves a	5647S
	35:22	'But if without hostility someone suddenly shoves a	2257S
Dt	4:34	for himself one nation out of a nation,	NIH
	19: 4	the rule concerning the *man who* kills a	8357
	22:22	a man is found sleeping with a man's wife,	NIH
	22:24	the man because he violated a **man's** wife.	8276
	24: 2	she becomes the wife of a man,	337
	28:30	but a will take her and ravish her.	337
	28:32	and daughters will be given to a nation,	337
	29:28	from their land and thrust them into a land,	337
Jdg	2:10	a generation grew up,	337
	11: 2	"because you are the son of a woman."	337
	19:10	But, unwilling to stay a night,	NIH
	20:22	the men of Israel encouraged **one** a	2021+6639
	20:25	down a eighteen thousand Israelites,	6388
Ru	1: 9	in the home of a husband."	2023S
	1:12	I am too old to have a husband.	NIH
	2: 8	in a field and don't go away from here.	337
1Sa	2:25	If a man sins against a man,	NIH
	10: 3	a three loaves of bread,	285S
	10: 3	and a skin of wine.	285S
	13:18	a toward Beth Horon,	285S
	17: 3	and the Israelites a,	2021+2215+2296+4946S
2Sa	3:11	Ish-Bosheth did not dare to say a word	6388
	11:25	the sword devours one as well as a.	2296S
	18:20	"You may take the news a time,	337
	18:26	Then the watchman saw a man running,	337
	18:26	"Look, a man running alone!"	NIH
	21:18	there was a battle with the Philistines,	6388
	21:19	In a battle with the Philistines at Gob,	6388
	21:20	In **still** a battle, which took place	6388
1Ki	11:23	up against Solomon a adversary,	NIH
	13:10	So he took a road and did not return by	337
	18: 6	in one direction and Obadiah in a	285S
	20:10	Then Ben-Hadad sent a message to Ahab:	NIH
	20:37	The prophet found a man and said,	337
	21: 6	I will give you a vineyard in its place.'	NIH
	22:20	"One suggested this, and a that.	2296S
2Ki	1:11	At this the king sent to Elijah a captain	337
	4: 6	she said to her son, "Bring me a one."	6388
	7: 6	so that they said to one a, "Look,	278S
	7: 8	and entered a tent and took some things	337
1Ch	2:26	Jerahmeel had a wife,	337
	7:15	A descendant was named Zelophehad,	9108
	16:20	from one kingdom to a,	337
	17: 5	I have moved from one tent site to a,	185S
	17: 5	from one dwelling place to a.	NIH
	20: 5	In a battle with the Philistines,	6388
	20: 6	In **still** a battle, which took place	6388
2Ch	5: 6	One nation was being crushed by a	1580S
	15: 6	by another and one city by a,	6551S
	18:19	"One suggested this, and a that.	2296S
	20:23	they helped to destroy one a.	8276S
	30:23	for a seven days they celebrated joyfully.	NIH
	32: 5	He built a wall outside that one	337
Ne	3:11	of Pahath-Moab repaired a section,	9108
	3:19	ruler of Mizpah, repaired a section,	9108
	3:20	of Zabbai zealously repaired a section,	9108
	3:21	the son of Hakkoz, repaired a section,	9108
	3:24	Binnui son of Henadad repaired a section,	9108
	3:27	the men of Tekoa repaired a section,	9108

Ne	3:30	the sixth son of Zalaph, repaired a section.	9108
	9: 3	and spent a quarter in confession and	NIH
Est	2:14	the morning return to a part *of* the harem	9108
	4:14	for the Jews will arise from a place,	337
	8: 8	Now write a decree in the king's name	NIH
	9:22	of food to one a and gifts to the poor.	8276S
Job	1:16	a **messenger** came and said,	2296S
	1:17	a **messenger** came and said,	2296
	1:18	yet a **messenger** came and said,	2296S
	2: 1	On a day the angels came	2021S
	19:27	I, and not a.	2424
	21:25	A man dies in bitterness of soul,	AIT
	31:10	then may my wife grind a *man's* grain,	337
	33:14	God does speak—now one way, now a—	9109
	41:17	They are joined fast to one a;	278S
Ps	49: 7	No man can redeem the life of a or give	278S
	75: 7	He brings one down, he exalts a.	2296S
	105:13	from one kingdom to a.	337
	109: 8	may a take his place of leadership.	337
	145: 4	One generation will commend your works to a;	1887S
Pr	5:10	and your toil enrich a **man's** house.	5799
	5:20	Why embrace the bosom of a *man's wife?*	5799
	6: 1	if you have struck hands in pledge for a,	2424
	6:29	So is he who sleeps with a **man's** wife;	8276
	11:15	up security for a will surely suffer,	2424
	11:24	a **withholds** unduly, but comes to poverty.	AIT
	13: 7	a **pretends** to be poor,	AIT
	18:17	till a comes forward and questions him.	8276S
	23:35	will I wake up so I can find a drink?"	3578+6388
	25: 9	do not betray a *man's* confidence,	337
	27: 2	Let a praise you, and not your own mouth;	2424
	27:17	iron sharpens iron, so one man sharpens a.	8276S
	28: 8	a, who will be kind	AIT
Ecc	6: 1	I have seen a evil under the sun,	NIH
	7:27	to a to discover the scheme of things—	285S
Isa	6: 3	And they were calling to one a:	2296S
	42: 8	I will not give my glory to a or my praise	337
	44: 5	a will call himself by the name of Jacob;	2296S
	44: 5	still a will write on his hand,	2296S
	48:11	I will not yield my glory to a.	337
	65:15	but to his servants he will give a name.	337
	66:23	to a and from one Sabbath to another,	2544S
	66:23	to another and from one Sabbath to a,	8701S
Jer	3: 1	and she leaves him and marries a man,	337
	3:16	nor will a one be made.	6388
	5: 8	each neighing for a *man's* wife.	8276S
	9: 3	They go from one sin to a;	8288S
	9:20	teach one a a lament.	8295S
	18: 4	so the potter formed it into a pot,	337
	18: 9	And if **at a time** I announce that a nation	8092
	22: 8	by this city and will ask one a,	8276S
	22:26	into a country, where neither	337
	23:27	dreams they tell one a will make my people forget my name,	8276S
	23:30	from one a words supposedly from me.	8276S
	26:20	from Kiriath Jearim was a man who prophesied	1685
	36:28	"Take a scroll and write on it all the words	337
	36:32	So Jeremiah took a scroll and gave it to	337
	46:12	One warrior will stumble over a;	1475S
	48:11	not poured from one jar to a—	3998S
	51:31	One courier follows a	8132S
	51:46	one rumor comes this year, a the next	2021+9019S
Eze	1: 9	and their wings touched one a.	295S
	1:11	one touching the wing of a **creature** on	408S
	12: 3	and go from where you are to a place.	337
	17: 7	" 'But there was a great eagle	285
	19: 5	she took a of her cubs and made him	285S
	21:20	against Rabbah of the Ammonites and a	NIH
	22:11	a shamefully defiles his daughter-in-law,	408S
	22:11	and a violates his sister,	408S
	34:17	I will judge between one sheep and a,	8445S
	34:22	I will judge between one sheep and a,	8445S
	37:16	Then take a stick of wood, and write on it,	285S
	40:44	and a at the side of the south gate	NIH
	41: 6	one above a, thirty on each level.	7521S
	41:11	one on the north and a on the south;	285S
	46:21	and I saw in each corner a court.	NIH
	47: 3	He measured off a thousand cubits	NIH
	47: 4	He measured off a thousand and led me	NIH
	47: 5	He measured off a thousand,	NIH
Da	2:39	"After you, a kingdom will rise,	10023
	2:44	nor will it be left to a people.	10023
	7: 6	I looked, and there before me was a beast,	10023
	7: 8	there before me was a horn, a little one,	10023
	7:24	After them a king will arise,	10025
	8: 9	Out of one of them came a horn,	285S
	8:13	and a holy one said to him,	285S
	11:13	the king of the North will muster a army,	8740
Hos	1: 8	Gomer had a son.	NIH
	3: 1	she is loved by a and is an adulteress.	8276S
Am	4: 7	let no man accuse a,	NIH
	4: 7	but withheld it from a.	285S
	4: 7	a had none and dried up.	2754S
Hag	2:15	before one stone was laid on a in	74S
Zec	2: 3	and a angel came to meet him	337
	7: 9	show mercy and compassion to one a.	278S
	8:21	inhabitants of one city will go to a and say,	285S
	14:13	Each man will seize the hand of a,	8276S
Mal	2:10	by breaking faith with one a?	278S
	2:13	A thing you do: You flood the LORD's	9108
	2:12	they returned to their country by a route.	257
Mt	8:21	A disciple said to him, "Lord,	2283
	10:23	in one place, flee to a.	2283
	13:24	Jesus told them a parable:	257
	13:31	He told them a parable:	257

Mt	13:33	He told them **still** a parable: 257
	19: 9	and marries a *woman* commits adultery." 257
	21:33	"Listen to a parable: 257
	21:35	they beat one, killed **a**, and stoned a third. 4005
	22: 5	one to his field, a to his business. 1254+4005
	24: 2	not *one* stone here will be left on a; 3345S
	25:15	*to* a two talents, and to another one 1254+4005
	25:15	two talents, and *to* a one talent, 1254+4005
	25:32	and he will separate the people one from a 253
	26:71	a *girl* saw him and said to the people there, 257
Mk	3: 1	**A** time he went into the synagogue, 4099
	8: 1	During those days a large crowd gathered. 4099
	8:16	They discussed this with **one** a and said, 253
	10:11	and marries a *woman* commits adultery 257
	10:12	and marries a *man*, 257
	12: 4	Then he sent **still** a servant to them; 257
	12: 5	He sent **still** a, and that one they killed. 257
	12: 7	the tenants said to **one** a, 'This is the heir. 1571
	13: 2	"Not one stone here will be left on a; 3345S
	14: 4	to **one** a, "Why this waste 1571
	14:58	and in three days will build a, 257
Lk	2:15	the shepherds said to **one** a, 253
	6: 6	On a Sabbath he went into the synagogue 2283
	6:11	to discuss with **one** a what they might do 253
	8: 1	**from** one town and village to a, 2848
	8:25	In fear and amazement they asked **one** a, 253
	9:56	and they went to a village. 2283
	9:59	He said to a *man*, "Follow me." 2283
	9:61	Still a said, "I will follow you, Lord; 2283
	12: 1	so that they were trampling on **one** a, 253
	14:19	"A said, 'I have just bought five yoke 2283
	14:20	"Still a said, 'I just got married, 2283
	14:31	a king is about to go to war *against* a king. 2283
	18:18	and marries a *woman* commits adultery, 2283
	19:20	"Then a servant came and said, 'Sir, 2283
	19:44	They will not leave one stone on **a**, 3345S
	20:11	He sent a servant, 2283
	21: 6	when not one stone will be left on a; 3345S
	22:59	About an hour later a asserted, 257+5516
Jn	1:16	of his grace we have all received one blessing after **a**. 5921S
	4:37	the saying 'One sows and a reaps' is true. 257
	5:32	There is **a** who testifies in my favor, 257
	5:44	if you accept praise from **one** a, 253
	6: 8	**A** of his disciples, Andrew, 1651
	7:35	The Jews said to **one** a, 1571
	11:56	in the temple area they asked **one** a, 253
	12:19	So the Pharisees said to **one** a, "See, 1571
	13:22	His disciples stared at **one** a. 253
	13:34	"A new command I give you: Love one a. 253
	13:34	I have loved you, so you must love **one** a. 253
	13:35	you are my disciples, if you love **one** a." 253
	14:16	and he will give you a Counselor to be 257
	16:17	Some of his disciples said to **one** a, 253
	16:19	"Are you asking **one** a what I meant 253
	18:15	and a disciple were following Jesus. 257
	18:36	But now my kingdom is **from** a place." 1949
	19:24	"Let's not tear it," they said to **one** a. 253
	19:37	as a scripture says, 2283
Ac	1:20	and, " 'May a take his place of leadership.' 2283
	2:12	Amazed and perplexed, they asked **one** a, 257+257+4639
	7:18	Then **a** king, who knew nothing 2283
	12:17	he said, and then he left for **a** place. 2283
	17: 7	saying that there is a king, 2283
	19:32	Some were shouting one thing, some **a**. 257
	21:34	in the crowd shouted one thing and some **a**, 257
	22:19	**from** one synagogue to **a** 2848
	26:11	**from** one synagogue to **a** 2848+4246+5252
	26:31	and while talking with one **a**, they said, 253
Ro	1:24	the degrading of their bodies with **one** a. 899
	1:27	and were inflamed with lust for **one** a. 253
	7: 3	if she marries a *man* 2283
	7: 3	even though she marries a *man*. 2283
	7: 4	that you might belong to **a**, 2283
	7:23	but I see a law at work in the members 2283
	12:10	Be devoted to **one** a in brotherly love. 253
	12:10	Honor **one** a above yourselves. 253
	12:16	Live in harmony with **one** a. 253
	13: 8	except the continuing debt to love **one** a, 253
	14: 5	but a man, whose faith is weak, NIG
	14: 5	One man considers one day more sacred than **a**; 2465S
	14: 5	**a** man considers every day alike. 1254+4005
	14:13	let us stop passing judgment on **one** a. 253
	15: 7	Accept **one** a, then, just 253
	15:14	and competent to instruct **one** a. 253
	16:12	**a** *woman* who has worked very hard in 4015
	16:16	Greet **one** a with a holy kiss. 253
1Co	1:10	of you agree with one a so that there may NIG
	1:12	a, "I follow Apollos"; 1254
	1:12	a, "I follow Cephas"; 1254
	1:12	**still** a, "I follow Christ." 1254
	3: 4	For when one says, "I follow Paul," and a, 2283
	4: 6	you will not take pride in one man over against **a**. 2283+3836
	6: 1	If any of you has a dispute with **a**, 253
	6: 6	instead, one brother goes to law against a— 81S
	7: 7	one has this gift, a has that. 1254+3836
	11:21	One remains hungry, a gets drunk. 1254+4005
	12: 8	*to* a the message of knowledge by means 257
	12: 9	*to* a faith by the same Spirit, 2283
	12: 9	*to* a gifts of healing by that one Spirit, 257
	12:10	*to* a miraculous powers, 257
	12:10	*to* a prophecy, to another distinguishing 257
	12:10	*to* a distinguishing between spirits, 257
	12:10	*to* a speaking in different kinds of tongues, 2283

1Co	12:10	and *to* still a the interpretation of tongues. 257
	15:39	of flesh, animals have **a**, 257
	15:39	birds and fish another. 257
	15:39	birds another and fish **a**. 257
	15:40	and the splendor of the earthly bodies is **a**. 2283
	15:41	the moon a and the stars another; 257
	15:41	the moon another and a **a**. 257
	16:20	Greet **one** a with a holy kiss. 253
2Co	2: 1	that I would not make a painful visit 4099
	10:16	in a *man's* territory. 259
	13:12	Greet **one** a with a holy kiss. 253
Gal	5:13	rather, serve **one** a in love. 253
Eph	4: 2	be patient, bearing with **one** a in love. 253
	4:32	Be kind and compassionate to **one** a, 253
	5:19	Speak *to* **one** a with psalms, 4932
	5:21	*to* **one** a out of reverence for Christ. 253
Col	3:13	forgive whatever grievances you may have against one a. NIG
	3:16	and admonish **one** a with all wisdom, 4932
1Th	5:11	encourage **one** a and build each other up, 253
Tit	3: 3	being hated and hating **one** a. 253
Heb	3:13	But encourage **one** a daily, 4932
	4: 8	not have spoken later about a day. 257
	5: 6	And he says in a *place*, 2283
	7:11	why was there still need for a priest 2283
	7:15	if a priest like Melchizedek appears, 2283
	8: 7	no place would have been sought for **a**. 1311
	10:24	And let us consider how we may spur **one** a 253
	10:25	but let us encourage one a— NIG
Jas	4:11	Brothers, do not slander **one** a. 253
1Pe	1:22	love **one** a deeply, from the heart. 253
	3: 8	all of you, live in harmony with **one** a; NIG
	4: 9	to **one** a without grumbling. 253
	5: 5	with humility *toward* **one** a, 253
	5:14	Greet **one** a with a kiss of love. 253
1Jn	1: 7	we have fellowship with **one** a, 253
	3:11	We should love **one** a. 253
	3:23	and to love **one** a as he commanded us. 253
	4: 7	Dear friends, let us love **one** a, 253
	4:11	we also ought to love **one** a. 253
	4:12	but if we love **one** a, God lives in us 253
2Jn	1: 5	I ask that we love **one** a. 253
Rev	6: 4	Then a horse came out, a fiery red one. 257
	7: 2	I saw a angel coming up from the east, 257
	8: 3	A angel, who had a golden censer, 257
	10: 1	Then I saw a mighty angel coming down 257
	12: 3	Then a sign appeared in heaven: 257
	13:11	I saw a beast, coming out of the earth. 257
	14: 6	Then I saw a angel flying in midair, 257
	14:15	Then a angel came out of the temple 257
	14:17	A angel came out of the temple in heaven, 257
	14:18	Still a angel, who had charge of the fire, 257
	15: 1	in heaven a great and marvelous sign: 257
	18: 1	After this I saw a angel coming down 257
	18: 4	Then I heard a voice from heaven say: 257
	20:12	A book was opened, 257

ANOTHER'S (4) [ANOTHER]

Jer	19: 9	and they will eat one another's flesh during 8276S
Zec	11: 9	Let those who are left eat one another's flesh." 8295S
Jn	13:14	you also should wash **one** a feet. 253
1Co	10:29	be judged by a conscience? 257

ANSWER (158) [ANSWERABLE, ANSWERED, ANSWERING, ANSWERS]

Ge	41:16	but God *will* give Pharaoh *the* a he desires." 6699
	45: 3	But his brothers were not able to a him, 6699
	46:34	*you should* **a**, 'Your servants have tended 606
Ex	19: 8	Moses brought their a back to the LORD. 1821
Nu	22: 8	"and I will bring you back the **a** 1821
Dt	29:25	And *the* a will be: 606
Jos	22:28	or to our descendants, *we will* **a**: 606
Jdg	5:29	The wisest of her ladies a her; 6699
	14:12	"If *you can give* me the a within 5583+5583
	14:13	If you can't *tell* me the **a**, 5583
	14:14	For three days they could not give the **a**. 2648
	14:16	but you haven't *told* me *the* **a**." 5583
	19:28	But there was no **a**. 6699
1Sa	2:16	the servant *would* then **a**, "No, 606
	8:18	the LORD *will* not a you in that day." 6699
	14:37	But God *did* not a him that day. 6699
	14:41	the God of Israel, "Give me the **right a**." 9459
	26:14	"Aren't *you going to* a me, Abner?" 6699
	28: 6	not a him by dreams or Urim or prophets. 6699
2Sa	14:18	not keep from me the a to what I am going 1821
	15: 2	*He would* **a**, "Your servant is from one of 606
	20:18	**Get** *your* a at Abel,' and that settled it. 8626+8626
	22:42	to the LORD, but *he did* not **a**. 6699
	24:13	think it over and decide how *I should* a 1821+8740
1Ki	9: 9	*People will* a, 'Because they have forsaken 606
	12: 6	you advise me to a these people?" 1821+8740
	12: 7	**give** them a favorable **a**, 1819+1821
	12: 9	How *should* we a these people 1821+8740
	14: 5	**give** her such and such **an a**. 1819
	18:26	"O Baal, a us!" 6699
	18:37	A me, O LORD, answer me, 6699
	18:37	Answer me, O LORD, a me, 6699
	20: 9	and took the a back to Ben-Hadad. 1821
2Ki	4:29	and if anyone greets you, *do not* **a**. 6699
	18:36	"*Do not* a him." 6699
	22:20	So they took her a back to the king. 1821
1Ch	21:12	how *I should* a the one who sent me." 1821+8740
2Ch	7:22	*People will* a, 'Because they have forsaken 606
	10: 6	to a these people?" 1821+8740
	10: 7	**give** them a favorable **a**, 1819+1821

2Ch	10: 9	How *should we* a these people 1821+8740
	34:28	So they took her a back to the king. 1821
Ezr	5:11	This is the a they gave us: 10601
Ne	6: 4	and each time I gave them the same **a**. 1821
Est	4:13	he sent back *this* a: 606
	5: 8	Then *I will* a the king's question." 6913
Job	5: 1	"Call if you will, but *who will* a you? 6699
	9: 3	not a him one time out of a thousand. 6699
	9:15	*I could* not a him; 6699
	9:32	not a man like me that *I might* a him, 6699
	13:22	Then summon me and I will **a**, 6699
	14:15	You will call and I *will* a you; 6699
	15: 2	"*Would* a wise man a *with* empty notions 6699
	19:16	I summon my servant, but *he does* not **a**, 6699
	20: 2	"My troubled thoughts **prompt** me to **a** 8740
	23: 5	I would find out what *he would* a me, 6699
	30:20	"I cry out to you, O God, but *you do* not **a**; 6699
	31:14	What *will I* a when called to account? 8740
	31:35	*let* the Almighty a me; 6699
	32:14	and *I will* not a him with your arguments. 8740
	33: 5	A me then, if you can; 8740
	33:32	If you have anything to say, a me; 8740
	35:12	*He does* not a when men cry out because of 6699
	38: 3	I will question you, and *you shall* a me. 3359
	40: 2	*Let him* who accuses God a him!" 6699
	40: 5	I spoke once, but *I have* no a— 6699
	40: 7	I will question you, and *you shall* a me. 3359
	42: 4	I will question you, and *you shall* a me.' 3359
Ps	4: 1	A me when I call to you, 6699
	13: 3	Look on me and a, O LORD my God. 6699
	17: 6	I call on you, O God, for *you will* a me; 6699
	18:41	to the LORD, but *he did* not **a**. 6699
	20: 1	the LORD a you when you are in distress; 6699
	20: 9	A us when we call! 6699
	22: 2	I cry out by day, but *you do* not **a**, 6699
	27: 7	be merciful to me and a me, 6699
	38:15	you *will* **a**, O Lord my God. 6699
	55: 2	hear me and a me. 6699
	65: 5	*You* a us with awesome deeds 6699
	69:13	O God, a me with your sure salvation. 6699
	69:16	A me, O LORD, out of the goodness 6699
	69:17	a me quickly, for I am in trouble. 6699
	86: 1	Hear, O LORD, and a me, 6699
	86: 7	for *you will* a me. 6699
	91:15	He will call upon me, and *I will* a him; 6699
	102: 2	when I call, a me quickly. 6699
	119:42	then *I will* a the one who taunts me, 1821+6699
	119:145	I call with all my heart; a me, O LORD, 6699
	143: 7	A me quickly, O LORD; 6699
Pr	1:28	they will call to me but *I will* not **a**. 6699
	15: 1	A gentle a turns away wrath, 5101
	24:26	An honest a is like a kiss on the lips. 1821+8740
	26: 4	*Do not* a a fool according to his folly, 6699
	26: 5	A a fool according to his folly, 6699
	26:16	than seven *men who* a discreetly. 8740
	27:11	then *I can* a anyone who treats me 1821+8740
Ecc	10:19	but money is the **a** for everything. 6699
SS	5: 6	I called him but *he did* not **a**. 6699
Isa	14:32	What *shall be* given to the envoys of 6699
	21: 9	And *he gives back* the **a**: 6699
	29:11	please," *he will* a, "I can't; it is sealed." 606
	29:12	and say, "Read this, please," *he will* **a**, 606
	30:19	As soon as *he hears, he will* a you. 6699
	36:21	"*Do not* a him." 6699
	41:17	But the LORD *will* a them; 6699
	41:28	no one to give a when I ask them. 1821
	46: 7	Though one cries out to it, *it does* not **a**; 6699
	49: 8	"In the time of my favor *I will* a you, 6699
	50: 2	I called, why was there no *one to* a? 6699
	58: 9	you will call, and the LORD *will* **a**; 6699
	65:12	for I called but *you did* not **a**, 6699
	65:24	Before they call *I will* **a**; 6699
Jer	7:13	I called you, but *you did* not **a**. 6699
	7:27	when you call to them, *they will* not **a**. 6699
	22: 9	And *the* a will be: 'Because they have 606
	23:35	'*What is the* LORD's **a**? 6699
	23:37	'*What is the* LORD's a *to you*?' 6699
	33: 3	to me and *I will* a you and tell you great 6699
	35:17	I called to them, but *they did* not **a**.' " 6699
	38:15	"If *I give* you an **a**, will you not kill me? 5583
Eze	14: 4	I the LORD *will* a him myself in keeping 6699
	14: 7	I the LORD *will* a him myself. 6699
Da	9:23	soon as you began to pray, an a was given, 1821
Hos	14: 8	I *will* a him and care for him. 6699
Mic	3: 4	but *he will* not a them. 6699
	3: 7	because there is no a *from* God." 5101
Hab	2: 1	How have I burdened you? A me. 6699
	2: 1	a *I am to give* 8740
Zec	10: 6	the LORD their God and *I will* **a** them. 6699
	13: 6	*he will* a, 'The wounds I was given at 606
	13: 9	on my name and *I will* a them; 6699
Mt	15:23	Jesus *did* not a a word. 646
	21:24	If *you a* me, 3306
	25:37	"Then the righteous *will* a him, 'Lord, 646
	25:44	"They also *will* a, 'Lord, 646
	26:62	"*Are you* not going to **a**? 646
	27:12	*he gave* no **a**. 646
Mk	11:29	A me, and I will tell you 646
	12:28	*given* them a good **a**, 646
	14:60	"*Are you* not going to **a**? 646
	14:61	But Jesus remained silent and **gave** no **a**. 646
	15: 4	"*Aren't you* going to **a**? 646
Lk	13:25	"But *he will* **a**, 646
	20:26	astonished by his **a**, they became silent. 647
	22:68	and if I asked you, *you would* not **a**. 646
	23: 9	but Jesus **gave** him no **a**. 646
Jn	1:22	an a to take back to those who sent us. 647

Jn	5:19	Jesus gave them this a: 646
	18:22	"Is this the way you a the high priest?" 646
	19:9	he asked Jesus, but Jesus gave him no a. 647
Ac	12:13	and a servant girl named Rhoda came to a 5634
Ro	11:4	And what was God's a to him? 3306
1Co	4:13	when we are slandered, we a kindly. 4151
2Co	1:11	for the gracious favor granted us in a to 1666
	5:12	so that you can a those who take pride NIG
Col	4:6	so that you may know how to a everyone 646
Phm	1:22	because I hope to be restored to you in a to 1328
1Pe	3:15	an a to everyone who asks you to give 665

ANSWERABLE (1) [ANSWER]

Mt	5:22	'Raca,' is a to the Sanhedrin. 1944

ANSWERED (397) [ANSWER]

Ge	3:10	He a, "I heard you in the garden, 606
	16:8	from my mistress Sarai," she a. 606
	18:5	"Very well," they a, "do as you say." 606
	18:30	He a, "I will not do it if I find thirty there." 606
	18:32	He a, "For the sake of ten, 606
	19:2	they a, "we will spend the night in 606
	22:8	Abraham, "God himself will provide 606
	23:14	Ephron a Abraham, 6699
	24:24	She a him, "I am the daughter of Bethuel, 606
	24:50	and Bethuel a, "This is from the LORD; 6699
	24:65	"He is my master," the servant a. 606
	25:21	The LORD a his prayer, 6983
	26:9	"She is my sister'?" Isaac a him, 606
	26:28	They a, "We saw clearly that 606
	27:1	"Here I am," he a. 606
	27:18	"Yes, my son," he a. 606
	27:32	"I am your son," he a, "your firstborn, 606
	27:37	Isaac a Esau, "I have made him lord 6699
	27:39	His father Isaac a him, 6699
	29:5	"Yes, we know him," they a. 606
	31:11	I a, 'Here I am.' 606
	31:31	Jacob a Laban, "I was afraid, 6699
	31:43	Laban a Jacob, "The women are my daughters, 6699
	32:27	"Jacob," he a. 606
	33:5	Jacob a, "They are the children God has graciously given your servant." 606
	35:3	who a me in the day of my distress 6699
	37:17	on from here," the man a. 606
	38:18	and the staff in your hand," she a. 606
	40:8	"We both had dreams," they a, 606
	42:10	"No, my lord," they a. 606
	43:7	We simply a his questions. 5583
	44:20	And we a, 'We have an aged father, 606
Ex	1:19	The midwives a Pharaoh, 606
	2:8	"Yes, go," she a. 606
	2:19	They a, "An Egyptian rescued us from 606
	4:1	Moses a, "What if they do not believe me 6699
	8:29	Moses a, "As soon as I leave you, 606
	10:9	Moses a, "We will go with our young 606
	14:13	Moses a the people, "Do not be afraid. 606
	17:5	The LORD a Moses, 606
	18:15	Moses a him, "Because the people come 606
	19:19	and the voice of God a him. 6699
	32:2	Aaron a them, "Take off the gold earrings 606
	32:22	"Do not be angry, my lord," Aaron a. 606
Nu	9:8	Moses a them, "Wait until I find out what 606
	10:30	He a, "No, I will not go 606
	11:23	The LORD a Moses, 606
	20:18	But Edom a: "You may 606
	20:20	Again they a: "You may not pass through." 606
	22:18	But Balaam a them, 6699
	22:29	Balaam a the donkey, 606
	23:12	He a, "Must I not speak what 606
	23:26	Balaam a, "Did I not tell you 6699
	24:12	Balaam a Balak, "Did I not tell 606
	32:31	The Gadites and Reubenites a, 6699
Dt	1:14	You a me, "What you propose 6699
Jos	1:16	Then they a Joshua, 6699
	9:9	They a: "Your servants have come from a 606
	9:11	but all the leaders a, 606
	9:24	They a Joshua, "Your servants were clearly 6699
	17:15	"If you are so numerous," Joshua a, 606
	24:16	Then the people a, 6699
Jdg	1:2	The LORD a, "Judah is to go; 606
	6:16	The LORD a, "I will be with you, 606
	8:2	But he a them, 606
	8:8	but they a as the men of Succoth had. 6699
	8:18	"Men like you," they a, 606
	8:25	They a, "We'll be glad to give them." 606
	9:9	"But the olive tree a, 606
	9:13	"But the vine a, 606
	11:9	Jephthah a, "Suppose you take me back 606
	11:13	the Ammonites a Jephthah's messengers, 606
	12:2	Jephthah a, "I and my people were engaged 606
	13:13	The angel of the LORD a, 606
	13:23	But his wife a, 606
	15:10	they a, "to do to him as he did to us." 606
	15:11	"I merely did to them what they did 606
	15:13	"Agreed," they a. 606
	16:7	Samson a her, "If anyone ties me 606
	18:6	The priest a them, "Go in peace. 606
	18:9	They a, "Come on, let's attack them! 606
	18:19	They a him, "Be quiet! 606
	18:25	The Danites a, "Don't argue with us, 606
	19:18	He a, "We are on our way from Bethlehem 606
	20:23	The LORD a, "Go up against them." 606
Ru	3:5	"I will do whatever you say," Ruth a. 606
1Sa	1:17	Eli a, "Go in peace, 6699
1Sa	3:4	Samuel a, "Here I am." 606
	3:16	Samuel a, "Here I am." 606
	5:8	They a, "Have the ark of the god 606
	6:3	They a, "If you return the ark of the god 606
	7:9	and the LORD a him. 6699
	8:22	The LORD a, "Listen to them 606
	9:8	The servant a him again. 6699
	9:12	"He is," they a. 6699
	9:21	Saul a, "But am I not a Benjamite, 6699
	10:12	A man who lived there a, 6699
	15:15	Saul a, "The soldiers brought them from 606
	16:11	"There is still the youngest," Jesse a, 606
	16:18	One of the servants a, 6699
	17:30	and the men a him as before. 1821+8740
	20:28	Jonathan a, "David earnestly asked me 6699
	21:2	David a Ahimelech the priest, 606
	21:4	But the priest a David, 606
	22:12	"Yes, my lord," he a. 606
	22:14	Ahimelech a the king, 6699
	23:2	The LORD a him, "Go, 606
	23:4	and the LORD a him, "Go down to Keilah, 6699
	25:10	Nabal a David's servants, 606
	26:22	"Here is the king's spear," David a. 6699
	29:9	Achish a, "I know that you have been 6699
	30:8	"Pursue them," he a. 606
	30:15	He a, "Swear to me before God 606
2Sa	1:3	He a, "I have escaped from 606
	1:8	" 'An Amalekite,' I a. 606
	1:13	the son of an alien, an Amalekite," he a. 606
	2:1	"To Hebron," the LORD a. 606
	2:20	"It is," he a. 606
	2:27	Joab a, "As surely as God lives, 606
	3:8	because of what Ish-Bosheth said and he a, 606
	4:9	David a Recab and his brother Baanah, 6699
	5:19	The LORD a him, "Go, 606
	5:23	and he a, "Do not go straight up, 606
	9:3	Ziba a the king, "There is still a son 606
	9:4	a, "He is at the house of Makir son 606
	12:22	He a, "While the child was still alive, 606
	14:19	The woman a, "As surely as you live, 6699
	15:15	The king's officials a him, 606
	16:2	Ziba a, "The donkeys are for 606
	16:21	Ahithophel a, "Lie with 606
	17:20	The woman a them, 606
	18:4	The king a, "I will do whatever seems best 606
	18:29	Ahimaaz a, "I saw great confusion just 606
	19:34	But Barzillai a the king, 606
	19:42	All the men of Judah a the men of Israel, 6699
	19:43	Then the men of Israel a the men of Judah, 6699
	20:17	"I am," he a. 606
	21:4	The Gibeonites a him, 606
	21:5	They a the king, 606
	21:14	God a prayer in behalf of the land. 6983
	24:21	"To buy your threshing floor," David a, 606
	24:25	the LORD a prayer in behalf of the land. 6983
1Ki	1:36	Benaiah son of Jehoiada a the king, 6699
	1:43	"Not at all!" Jonathan a. 606
	2:13	He a, "Yes, peacefully." 606
	2:22	King Solomon a his mother, 6699
	2:30	But he a, "No, I will die here." 606
	2:30	"This is how Joab a me." 6699
	2:38	Shimei a the king, "What you say is good. 606
	3:6	Solomon a, "You have shown great kindness 606
	10:3	Solomon a all her questions; 5583
	12:5	Rehoboam a, "Go away for three days and 606
	12:13	The king a the people harshly. 6699
	12:16	they a the king: 1821+8740
	13:8	But the man of God a the king, 606
	13:18	The old prophet a, "I too am a prophet, 606
	18:26	But there was no response; no one a. 6699
	18:29	But there was no response, no one a, 6699
	20:4	The king of Israel a, "Just as you say, 6699
	20:8	The elders and the people all a, 606
	20:11	The king of Israel a, "Tell him: 6699
	20:14	The prophet a, "You will." 606
	20:32	The king a, "Is he still alive? 606
	21:6	He a her, "Because I said to Naboth 1819
	21:20	"I have found you," he a, 606
	22:6	they a, "for the Lord will give it into 606
	22:8	The king of Israel a Jehoshaphat, 606
	22:15	"Attack and be victorious," he a, 606
	22:17	Then Micaiah a, "I saw all Israel scattered 606
2Ki	1:10	Elijah a the captain, "If I am a man of God, 6699
	3:8	"Through the Desert of Edom," he a. 606
	3:11	An officer of the king of Israel a, 6699
	3:13	"No," the king of Israel a, 606
	4:43	But Elisha a, "Give it to the people to eat. 606
	5:16	The prophet a, "As surely as 606
	5:25	"Everything is all right," Gehazi a. 606
	5:25	Your servant didn't go anywhere," Gehazi a. 606
	6:16	"Don't be afraid," the prophet a. 606
	6:22	"Do not kill them," he a. 606
	6:28	She a, "This woman said to me, 606
	7:2	a Elisha, "but you will not eat any of it!" 606
	7:13	One of his officers a, 6699
	8:10	Elisha a, "Go and say to him, 606
	8:12	the harm you will do to the Israelites," he a. 606
	8:13	you will become king of Aram," a Elisha. 606
	10:15	"I am," Jehonadab a. 606
	20:9	Isaiah a, "This is the LORD's sign to you 606
1Ch	5:20	He a their prayers, 6983
	14:10	The LORD a him, "Go, 606
	14:14	and God a him, "Do not go straight up, 606
	21:26	the LORD a him with fire from heaven on 6699
	21:28	the LORD had a him on the threshing floor 6699
2Ch	1:8	Solomon a God, "You have shown great kindness to David 606
2Ch	9:2	Solomon a all her questions; 5583
	10:5	Rehoboam a, "Come back to me 606
	10:13	The king a them harshly. 6699
	10:16	the king a: 8740
	18:5	they a, "for God will give it into 606
	18:7	The king of Israel a Jehoshaphat, 606
	18:14	"Attack and be victorious," he a, 606
	18:16	Then Micaiah a, "I saw all Israel scattered 606
	31:10	from the family of Zadok, a, 606
	32:24	who a him and gave him a miraculous sign. 606
Ezr	4:3	of the heads of the families of Israel a, 606
	8:23	and he a our prayer. 6983
Ne	2:5	and I a the king, 606
	2:20	I a them by saying, 1821+8740
Est	5:6	for him," his attendants a. 606
	6:5	His attendants a, "Haman is standing in 606
	6:7	So he a the king, 606
	7:3	Then Queen Esther a, 606
	9:13	"If it pleases the king," Esther a, 606
Job	1:7	Satan a the LORD, 6699
	2:2	Satan a the LORD, 6699
	12:4	though I called upon God and he a— 6699
	32:12	none of you has a his arguments. 6699
	38:1	Then the LORD a Job out of the storm. 6699
	40:3	Then Job a the LORD: 6699
Ps	34:4	I sought the LORD, and he a me; 6699
	81:7	I a you out of a thundercloud; 6699
	99:6	they called on the LORD and he a them. 6699
	99:8	O LORD our God, you a them; 6699
	118:5	and he a by setting me free. 6699
	118:21	I will give you thanks, for you a me; 6699
	119:26	I recounted my ways and you a me; 6699
	138:3	When I called, you a me; 6699
Pr	21:13	he too will cry out and not be a. 6699
Isa	6:11	O Lord?" And he a: 606
	66:4	For when I called, no one a, when I spoke, 6699
Jer	1:13	tilting away from the north," I a. 606
	11:5	I a, "Amen, LORD." 6699
	21:3	But Jeremiah a them, "Tell Zedekiah, 606
	24:3	"Figs," I a. 606
	38:5	"He is in your hands," King Zedekiah a. 606
Eze	9:9	He a me, "The sin of the house of Israel 606
Da	2:4	Then the astrologers a the king in Aramaic, 1819
	2:8	the king a, "I am certain that you are trying 10558
	2:10	The astrologers a the king, 10558
	4:19	Belteshazzar a, "My lord, 10558
	5:17	Then Daniel a the king, 10558
	6:12	The king a, "The decree stands— 10558
	6:21	Daniel a, "O king, live forever! 10425
Hos	4:12	a wooden idol and are a by a stick of wood. 5583
Am	7:14	Amos a Amaziah, "I was neither a prophet 6699
	8:2	"A basket of ripe fruit," I a. 606
Jnh	1:9	He a, "I am a Hebrew and I worship 606
	2:2	to the LORD, and he a me. 6699
Mic	6:5	and what Balaam son of Beor a. 6699
Hag	2:12	The priests a, "No." 6699
Zec	1:9	The angel who was talking with me a, 606
	1:19	He a me, "These are the horns 606
	1:21	He a, "These are the horns 606
	2:2	He a me, "To measure Jerusalem, 606
	4:2	I a, "I see a solid gold lampstand with 606
	4:5	He a, "Do you not know what these are?" 6699
	5:2	I a, "I see a flying scroll, 606
	6:5	The angel a me, 6699
Mt	4:4	Jesus a, "It is written: 646
	4:7	Jesus a him, "It is also written: 5774
	9:15	Jesus a, "How can the guests of 3306
	12:3	He a, "Haven't you read what David did 646
	12:39	He a, "A wicked and adulterous 646
	13:29	he a, 'because while you are pulling 5774
	13:37	He a, "The one who sowed 646
	14:17	of bread and two fish," they a. 646
	15:24	He a, "I was sent only to the lost sheep 646
	15:28	Jesus a, "Woman, you have great faith! 646
	15:33	His disciples a, "Where could we get 3306
	16:16	Simon Peter a, "You are the Christ, 646
	17:26	"From others," Peter a. 3306
	18:22	Jesus a, "I tell you, not seven times, 3306
	19:21	Jesus a, "If you want to be perfect, go, 5774
	19:27	Peter a him, "We have left everything 646
	20:7	" 'Because no one has hired us,' they a. 3306
	20:13	"But he a one of them, 'Friend, 646
	20:22	"We can," they a. 3306
	20:33	"Lord," they a, "we want our sight." 3306
	21:11	The crowds a, "This is Jesus, 3306
	21:27	So they a Jesus, "We don't know." 646
	21:29	" 'I will not,' he a, 646
	21:30	He a, 'I will, sir,' but he did not go. 646
	21:31	"The first," they a. 3306
	24:4	Jesus a: "Watch out 646
	26:25	Jesus a, "Yes, it is you." 3306
	26:34	"I tell you the truth," Jesus a, 5774
	26:66	"He is worthy of death," they a. 646
	27:21	"Barabbas," they a. 3306
	27:22	They all a, "Crucify him!" 3306
	27:25	All the people a, 646
	27:65	"Take a guard," Pilate a. 5774
Mk	2:19	Jesus a, "How can the guests of 3306
	2:25	He a, "Have you never read what David did 3306
	5:31	his disciples a, "and yet you can ask, 3306
	6:24	"The head of John the Baptist," she a. 646
	6:37	he a, "You give them something to eat." 646
	8:4	His disciples a, "But where 646
	8:20	They a, "Seven." 3306
	8:29	Peter a, "You are the Christ." 646
	9:17	A man in the crowd a, "Teacher, 646
	9:21	"From childhood," he a. 3306

Mk	10:11	*He* **a,** "Anyone who divorces his wife	3306
	10:18	"Why do you call me good?" Jesus **a.**	3306
	10:39	"We can," they **a.**	3306
	11: 6	They **a** as Jesus had told them to,	3306
	11:22	"Have faith in God," Jesus **a.**	646
	11:33	So they **a** Jesus, "We don't know."	646
	12:29	"The most important one," Jesus **a,** "is this:	646
	12:34	When Jesus saw that *he* had **a** wisely,	646
	14:30	"I tell you the truth," Jesus **a,** "today—	3306
Lk	1:19	The angel **a,** "I am Gabriel.	646
	1:35	The angel **a,** "The Holy Spirit will come	646
	1:38	"I am the Lord's servant," Mary **a.**	3306
	3:11	John **a,** "The man with two	646
	3:16	John **a** them all, "I baptize you with water.	646
	4: 4	Jesus **a,** "It is written:	646
	4: 8	Jesus **a,** "It is written:	646
	4:12	Jesus **a,** "It says:	646
	5: 5	Simon **a,** "Master, we've worked hard all night	646
	5:31	Jesus **a** them, "It is not	646
	5:34	Jesus **a** them, "Can you make the guests of	3306
	6: 3	Jesus **a** them, "Have you never read what David did	646
	7:40	Jesus **a** him, "Simon, I have something	646
	9:13	They **a,** "We have only five loaves of bread	3306
	9:20	Peter **a,** "The Christ of God."	646
	10:27	He **a:** " 'Love the Lord your God with all	646
	10:28	"*You have* answered correctly," Jesus replied.	3306
	10:41	"Martha, Martha," the Lord **a,**	646
	11:45	One of the experts in the law **a** him,	646
	12:42	The Lord **a,** "Who then is the faithful	3306
	13: 2	Jesus **a,** "Do you think	646
	13:15	The Lord **a** him, "You hypocrites!	646
	15:29	But he **a** his father, 'Look!	646
	16:27	"*He* **a,** 'Then I beg you, father,	3306
	18:19	"Why do you call me good?" Jesus **a.**	3306
	19:19	"His master **a,** 'You take charge	3306
	20: 7	So they **a,** "We don't know	646
	22:34	Jesus **a,** "I tell you, Peter,	3306
	22:35	"Nothing," they **a.**	3306
	22:51	But Jesus **a,** "No more of this!"	646
	22:67	Jesus **a,** "If I tell you,	3306
	23:43	Jesus **a** him, "I tell you the truth,	3306
Jn	1:21	*He* **a,** "No."	646
	1:48	Jesus **a,** "I saw you while you were still	646
	2:19	Jesus **a** them, "Destroy this temple,	646
	3: 5	Jesus **a,** "I tell you the truth,	646
	4:10	Jesus **a** her, "If you knew the gift of God	646
	4:13	Jesus **a,** "Everyone who drinks this water will be thirsty again,	646
	6: 7	Philip **a** him, "Eight months' wages would	646
	6:26	Jesus **a,** "I tell you the truth,	646
	6:29	Jesus **a,** "The work of God is this:	646
	6:43	among yourselves," Jesus **a.**	646
	6:68	Simon Peter **a** him, "Lord,	646
	7:16	Jesus **a,** "My teaching is not my own.	646
	7:20	"You are demon-possessed," the crowd **a.**	646
	8:14	Jesus **a,** "Even if I testify	646
	8:33	*They* **a** him, "We are Abraham's descendants	646
	8:39	"Abraham is our father," *they* **a.**	646
	8:48	The Jews **a** him,	646
	8:58	"I tell you the truth," Jesus **a,**	3306
	9:20	"We know he is our son," the parents **a,**	646
	9:27	*He* **a,** "I have told you already and you did	646
	9:30	The man **a,** "Now that is remarkable!	646
	10:25	Jesus **a,** "I did tell you,	646
	10:34	Jesus **a** them, "Is it not written	646
	11: 9	Jesus **a,** "Are there not twelve hours	646
	11:24	Martha **a,** "I know he will rise again in	3306
	13: 8	Jesus **a,** "Unless I wash you,	646
	13:10	Jesus **a,** "A person who has had	3306
	13:26	Jesus **a,** "It is the one	646
	13:38	Then Jesus **a,** "Will you really lay	646
	14: 6	Jesus **a,** "I am the way and the truth and	3306
	14: 9	Jesus **a,** "Don't you know me,	3306
	16:31	"You believe at last!" Jesus **a.**	646
	18: 8	"I told you that I am he," Jesus **a.**	646
	18:37	Jesus **a,** "You are right in saying I am	646
	19: 6	But Pilate **a,** "You take him	3306
	19:11	Jesus **a,** "You would have no power	646
	19:15	the chief priests **a.**	646
	19:22	Pilate **a,** "What I have written,	646
	21: 5	"No," they **a.**	646
	21:16	*He* **a,** "Yes, Lord, you know	3306
	21:22	Jesus **a,** "If I want him to remain alive	3306
Ac	8:20	Peter **a:** "May your money perish with you,	3306
	8:24	Then Simon **a,** "Pray to the Lord for me so	646
	9:10	"Yes, Lord," he **a.**	3306
	9:13	Ananias **a,** "I have heard many reports	646
	10: 4	The angel **a,** "Your prayers and gifts to	3306
	10:30	Cornelius **a:** "Four days ago I was in my	5774
	13:46	Then Paul and Barnabas **a** them boldly:	3306
	19: 2	They **a,** "No, we have not even heard	NIG
	19:15	[One day] the evil spirit **a** them,	646
	21:13	Then Paul **a,** "Why are you weeping	646
	21:39	Paul **a,** "I am a Jew, from Tarsus in Cilicia,	3306
	22:27	"Yes, I am," he **a.**	5774
	25: 4	Festus **a,** "Paul is being held at Caesarea,	646
	25:10	Paul **a:** "I am now standing before Caesar's	3306
Rev	7:14	*I* **a,** "Sir, you know."	3306

ANSWERING (3) [ANSWER]

Job	32: 1	So these three men stopped **a** Job,	6699
	34:36	that Job might be tested to the utmost for **a**	9588
Jer	44:20	both men and women, who *were* **a** him,	6699

ANSWERS (14) [ANSWER]

1Sa	20:10	if your father **a** you harshly?"	6699
	28:15	*He* no longer **a** me,	6699
1Ki	18:24	The god who **a** by fire—he is God."	6699
Job	21:34	Nothing is left of your **a** but falsehood!"	9588
	33:13	Why do you complain to him that *he* **a** none	6699
Ps	3: 4	and *he* **a** me from his holy hill.	6699
	20: 6	*he* **a** him from his holy heaven with	6699
	120: 1	the Lord in my distress, and *he* **a** me.	6699
Pr	15:28	The heart of the righteous weighs its **a,**	6699
	18:13	*He who* **a** before listening—	1821+8740
	18:23	but a rich man **a** harshly.	6699
	22:21	you can give sound **a** to him who sent you?	609
Lk	2:47	at his understanding and his **a.**	647
	11: 7	"Then the one inside **a,** 'Don't bother me.	646

ANT (1) [ANTS]

Pr	6: 6	Go to the **a,** you sluggard;	5805

ANTELOPE (2)

Dt	14: 5	the ibex, the **a** and the mountain sheep.	9293
Isa	51:20	like *a caught in* a net.	9293

ANTHOTHIJAH (1)

1Ch	8:24	Hananiah, Elam, **A,**	6746

ANTICHRIST (4) [ANTICHRISTS]

1Jn	2:18	and as you have heard that the **a** is coming,	532
	2:22	Such a man is the **a**—	532
	4: 3	This is the spirit *of the* **a,**	532
2Jn	1: 7	Any such person is the deceiver and the **a.**	532

ANTICHRISTS (1) [ANTICHRIST]

1Jn	2:18	even now many **a** have come.	532

ANTICIPATING (1)

Ac	12:11	from everything the Jewish people were **a.**"	4660

ANTIOCH (21)

Ac	6: 5	and Nicolas *from* A, a convert to Judaism.	523
	11:19	as far as Phoenicia, Cyprus and A, telling	522
	11:20	went to A and began to speak to Greeks	522
	11:22	and they sent Barnabas to A.	522
	11:26	he brought him to A.	522
	11:26	disciples were called Christians first at A.	522
	11:27	down from Jerusalem to A.	522
	13: 1	In the church at A there were prophets	522
	13:14	From Perga they went on to Pisidian A.	522
	14:19	Then some Jews came from A and Iconium	522
	14:21	they returned to Lystra, Iconium and A,	522
	14:26	From Attalia they sailed back to A,	522
	15: 1	down from Judea to A and were teaching	NIG
	15:22	of their own men and send them to A	522
	15:23	To the Gentile believers in A,	522
	15:30	and went down to A,	522
	15:35	But Paul and Barnabas remained in A,	522
	18:22	the church and then went down to A.	522
	18:23	After spending some time in A,	NIG
Gal	2:11	When Peter came to A,	522
2Ti	3:11	what kinds of things happened to me in A,	522

ANTIPAS (1)

Rev	2:13	even in the days *of* A, my faithful witness,	525

ANTIPATRIS (1)

Ac	23:31	the night and brought him as far as A.	526

ANTIQUITY (KJV) See OLD

ANTOTHIJAH (KJV) See ANTHOTHIJAH

ANTOTHITE (KJV) See ANATHOTHITE

ANTS (1) [ANT]

Pr	30:25	**A** are creatures of little strength,	5805

ANUB (1)

1Ch	4: 8	who was the father of **A** and Hazzobebah	6707

ANVIL (1)

Isa	41: 7	the hammer spurs on him who strikes the **a.**	7193

ANXIETIES (1) [ANXIOUS]

Lk	21:34	drunkenness and the **a** of life,	3533

ANXIETY (6) [ANXIOUS]

Ps	94:19	When **a** was great within me,	8595
Ecc	11:10	banish **a** from your heart and cast off	4088
Eze	4:16	in **a** and drink rationed water in despair,	1796
	12:19	in **a** and drink their water in despair,	1796
Php	2:28	be glad and I may have **a** less **a.**	267
1Pe	5: 7	Cast all your **a** on him because he cares	3533

ANXIOUS (5) [ANXIETIES, ANXIETY,

ANXIOUSLY]

Dt	28:65	There the Lord will give you an **a** mind,	8076
Ps	139:23	test me and know my **a** thoughts.	8595
Pr	12:25	An **a** heart weighs a man down,	1796
Ecc	2:22	**a** striving with which he labors under	4213+8301
Php	4: 6	*Do not be* **a** about anything,	3534

ANXIOUSLY (1) [ANXIOUS]

Lk	2:48	Your father and I have been **a** searching	3849

ANY (582) [ANYBODY, ANYMORE, ANYONE, ANYONE'S, ANYTHING, ANYWHERE]

Ge	2:16	"You are free to eat from **a** tree in	3972
	3: 1	Now the serpent was more crafty than **a** *of*	3972
	3: 1	not eat from **a** tree in the garden'?"	3972
	6: 2	and they married **a** of them they chose.	3972
	13: 8	not have a quarreling between you and me,	NIH
	17:14	A uncircumcised male,	NIH
	27:36	"Haven't you reserved a blessing for me?"	NIH
	30: 1	that she was not bearing Jacob **a** children,	NIH
	30:33	A goat in my possession that is	3972
	30:33	or a lamb that is not dark-colored,	928
	31:14	"Do we still have a share in the inheritance	NIH
	31:50	if you take **a** wives besides my daughters,	NIH
	36:31	in Edom before a Israelite king reigned:	NIH
	37: 3	Now Israel loved Joseph more than **a**	3972
	37: 4	that their father loved him more than **a**	3972
	37:22	"Don't shed **a** blood.	NIH
	38:21	"There hasn't been a shrine prostitute here,"	NIH
	38:22	"There hasn't been a shrine prostitute here.'	NIH
	44: 9	If **a** of your servants is found to have it,	889
	47: 6	of **a** among them *with* special ability,	408
	48: 6	A children born to you after them will	NIH
Ex	3: 5	"*Do not* come **a** closer," God said.	AIT
	3:22	to ask her neighbor and **a** *woman living*	AIT
	4:18	in Egypt to see if **a** *of them* are still alive."	AIT
	5:10	'I will not give you **a** more straw.	NIH
	5:18	You will not be given **a** straw,	NIH
	9:28	you don't have to stay **a** longer."	3578
	11: 7	not a dog will bark at **a** man	4946
	12: 9	If a household is too small for	2021
	12:10	Do not leave **a** *of* it till morning;	4946
	12:44	A slave you have bought may eat of it	3972
	12:46	Do not break **a** of the bones.	NIH
	13: 7	to be seen among you, nor shall **a** *yeast*	AIT
	15:26	on you **a** *of* the diseases I brought on	3972
	16:19	"No one is to keep **a** *of* it until morning."	4946
	16:25	not find *a of* it on the ground today.	AIT
	16:26	the Sabbath, there will not be **a.**"	928
	20:10	On it you shall not do **a** work, neither you,	3972
	20:23	Do not make **a** gods to be alongside me;	NIH
	21:11	**without a payment** of money.	401+2855
	22: 9	or **a** *other* lost property	3972
	22:10	a sheep or **a** *other* animal to his neighbor	3972
	22:20	"Whoever sacrifices to a god other than	2021
	29:34	And if **a** *of* the meat of the ordination ram	4946
	29:34	of the ordination ram or **a** bread is left over	4946
	30: 9	Do not offer on this altar **a** other incense	NIH
	30: 9	or a burnt offering or grain offering,	NIH
	30:32	on men's bodies and do not make **a** oil with	NIH
	30:37	Do not make **a** incense with this formula	2021
	30:38	Whoever makes **a** like it	NIH
	31:14	whoever does **a** work on that day must	NIH
	31:15	Whoever does **a** work on	NIH
	32:24	I told them, 'Whoever has **a** gold jewelry,	NIH
	33: 4	to mourn and no one put on **a** ornaments.	2257[S]
	34:10	before done in a nation in all the world.	3972
	34:14	Do not worship **a** other god,	AIT
	34:25	and do not let **a** of the sacrifice from	NIH
	35: 2	Whoever does a work on it must be put	NIH
	35: 3	Do not light a fire in **a** *of* your dwellings	3972
	35:24	for **a** part of the work brought it.	3972
Lev	1: 2	**a** of you brings an offering to the Lord,	132
	2:11	for you are not to burn **a** yeast or honey in	3972
	3:17	You must not eat **a** fat or **a** blood.' "	3972
	3:17	You must not eat **a** fat or **a** blood.' "	3972
	4: 2	in **a** of the Lord's commands—	3972
	4:13	and does what is forbidden in **a** of	285+3972
	4:22	and does what is forbidden in **a** of	285+3972
	4:27	and does what is forbidden in **a** of	285
	5: 4	in a matter one might carelessly swear about	3972
	5: 4	of it, in a case when he learns of it he will	285
	5: 5	" 'When anyone is guilty in **a**	285
	5:13	for **a** of these sins he has committed,	285
	5:15	in regard to **a** of the Lord's holy things,	NIH
	5:17	and does what is forbidden in **a** of	285+3972
	6: 3	or if he commits **a** such sin	3972
	6: 7	be forgiven for **a** of these things he did	285
	6:18	A male descendant of Aaron may eat it.	3972
	6:27	Whatever touches **a** of	NIH
	6:27	if **a** of the blood is spattered on a garment,	4946
	6:29	A male in a priest's family may eat it;	3972
	6:30	But **a** sin offering whose blood is brought	3972
	7: 6	A male in a priest's family may eat it,	3972
	7:17	A meat of the sacrifice left over till	4946
	7:18	If **a** meat of the fellowship offering is eaten	4946
	7:18	the person who eats **a** *of* it will	4946
	7:20	But if anyone who is unclean eats **a** meat of	NIH
	7:21	or an unclean animal or **a** unclean,	3972
	7:21	and then eats **a** *of* the meat of	4946
	7:23	'Do not eat **a** of the fat of cattle,	3972
	7:24	be used for **a** other purpose,	3972
	7:26	not eat the blood of **a** bird or animal.	3972

Lev	11: 3	You may eat a animal that has	3972
	11: 9	you may eat a that have fins and scales.	3972
	11:14	the red kite, a kind of black kite,	NIH
	11:15	a kind of raven,	3972
	11:16	the screech owl, the gull, a kind of hawk,	NIH
	11:19	a kind of heron, the hoopoe and the bat.	NIH
	11:22	Of these you may eat a kind of locust,	NIH
	11:26	[the carcass of] a of them will be unclean.	3972
	11:29	the weasel, the rat, a kind of great lizard,	NIH
	11:34	A food that could be eaten but has water	3972
	11:34	and a liquid that could be drunk	3972
	11:37	If a carcass falls on a seeds that are to	3972
	11:42	not to eat a creature that moves about on	3972
	11:43	Do not defile yourselves by a of these	3972
	11:44	make yourselves unclean by a creature	3972
	13:47	"If a clothing is contaminated	2021
	13:47	a woolen or linen clothing,	NIH
	13:48	a woven or knitted material of linen	NIH
	13:48	a leather or anything made of leather—	NIH
	13:49	or a leather article, is greenish or reddish,	3972
	13:52	or a leather article that has	3972
	13:58	or a leather article that has been washed	3972
	13:59	or a leather article,	3972
	14:54	for a infectious skin disease,	3972
	15: 2	'When a man has a bodily discharge,	408+408
	15: 4	" 'A bed the man with a discharge lies	3972
	15:10	and whoever touches a of the things	3972
	15:12	a wooden article is to be rinsed with water.	3972
	15:17	A clothing or leather that has semen	3972
	15:24	a bed he lies on will be unclean.	3972
	15:26	A bed she lies on	3972
	16:29	and not do a work—	3972
	17: 3	A Israelite who sacrifices an ox,	408
	17: 7	They must no longer offer a	NIH
	17: 8	'A Israelite or any alien living	408
	17: 8	or a alien living among them who offers	4946
	17:10	" 'A Israelite or any alien living	408
	17:10	" 'Any Israelite or a alien living	4946
	17:10	among them who eats a blood—	3972
	17:13	" 'A Israelite or any alien living	408
	17:13	" 'Any Israelite or a alien living	4946
	17:13	among you who hunts a animal or bird	NIH
	17:14	"You must not eat the blood of a creature,	3972
	18: 6	" 'No one is to approach a close relative	3972
	18:21	not give a of your children to be sacrificed	4946
	18:24	not defile yourselves in a of these ways,	3972
	18:26	the aliens living among you must not do a	3972
	18:29	" 'Everyone who does a	3972
	18:30	Keep my requirements and do not follow a	4946
	19: 7	a of it is eaten on the third day,	AIT
	19:23	the land and plant a kind of fruit tree,	3972
	19:26	" 'Do not eat a meat with the blood still	NIH
	20: 2	'A Israelite or any alien living	408
	20: 2	or a alien living in Israel who gives any	4946
	20: 2	or any alien living in Israel who gives	4946
	20:25	by a animal or bird or anything that moves	2021
	21: 1	for a of his people who die,	NIH
	21:18	No man who has a defect may come near:	NIH
	21:20	or who has a eye defect,	NIH
	21:21	the priest who has a defect is to come near	NIH
	22: 3	'For the generations to come, if a	408+3972
	22: 5	or if he touches a crawling thing	3972
	22: 5	or a person who makes him unclean,	AIT
	22: 6	The one who touches a such thing will	2257S
	22: 6	He must not eat a of the sacred offerings	4946
	22:12	not eat a of the sacred contributions,	928
	22:13	however, may eat a of it.	928
	22:18	'If a of you—either and Israelite	408
	22:22	Do not place a of these on the altar as	4946
	23: 3	You are not to do a work;	3972
	23:14	You must not eat a bread,	NIH
	23:30	among his people anyone who does a work	3972
	25:14	of your countrymen or buy a from him,	NIH
	25:33	that is, a house sold in a town they hold—	NIH
	25:36	Do not take interest of a kind from him,	2256+5968+9552
	25:49	An uncle or a cousin or a blood relative	4946
	25:54	if he is not redeemed in a of these ways,	NIH
	27:31	If a man redeems a of his tithe,	4946
	27:33	from the bad or make a substitution.	5647S
Nu	5: 2	or a discharge of a kind,	3972
	5: 6	in a way and so is unfaithful to the LORD,	3972
	5:31	be innocent of a wrongdoing,	NIH
	7: 9	But Moses did not give a to the Kohathites,	NIH
	9:10	'When a of you or your descendants	408+408
	9:12	not leave a of it till morning or break any	4946
	9:12	not leave any of it till morning or break a	4946
	11:31	as far as a day's walk in a direction.	2256+3907+3907
	15:22	" 'Now if you unintentionally fail to keep a	3972
	15:23	a of the LORD's commands to you	3972
	16:15	nor have I wronged a of them."	285
	18:20	nor will you have a share among them;	NIH
	20:17	We will not go through a field or vineyard,	NIH
	20:17	or drink water from a well.	NIH
	20:19	if we or our livestock drink a of your water,	NIH
	21:22	not turn aside into a field or vineyard,	NIH
	21:22	or drink water from a well.	NIH
	30: 9	"A vow or obligation taken by a widow	3972
	30:13	or nullify a vow she makes	3972
	30:13	or a sworn pledge to deny herself.	3972
	32:19	not receive a inheritance with them on	AIT
	35:15	a other people living among them,	2021
	36: 8	in a Israelite tribe must marry someone	NIH
Dt	1:17	Do not be afraid of a man,	NIH
	1:17	Bring me a case too hard for you,	2021
	2: 5	for I will not give you a of their land,	4946

Dt	2: 9	for I will not give you a part of their land.	4946
	2:19	of a land belonging to the Ammonites.	4946
	2:37	you did not encroach on a of the land of	3972
	4:15	of a kind the day the LORD spoke to you	3972
	4:16	an image of a shape,	3972
	4:17	like a animal on earth or any bird that flies	3972
	4:17	like any animal on earth or a bird that flies	3972
	4:18	like a creature that moves along the ground	3972
	4:18	the ground or a fish in the waters below.	3972
	4:25	then become corrupt and make a kind	3972
	4:33	Has a other people heard the voice	NIH
	4:34	Has a god ever tried to take	NIH
	5:14	On it you shall not do a work, neither you,	3972
	5:14	your donkey or a a of your animals,	3972
	5:25	voice of the LORD our God a longer.	3578+6388
	7:14	be blessed more than a other people;	3972
	7:14	nor a of your livestock without young.	NIH
	10:16	and do not be stiff-necked a longer.	6388
	12:15	in a of your towns and eat as much of	3972
	14: 3	Do not eat a detestable thing.	3972
	14: 6	You may eat a animal that has	3972
	14: 9	you may eat a that has fins and scales.	3972
	14:11	You may eat a clean bird.	3972
	14:13	the red kite, the black kite, a kind of falcon,	NIH
	14:14	a kind of raven,	3972
	14:15	the screech owl, the gull, a kind of hawk,	NIH
	14:18	a kind of heron, the hoopoe and the bat.	NIH
	14:20	But a winged creature	3972
	14:21	You may give it to an alien living in a	NIH
	15: 3	you must cancel a debt your brother owes	AIT
	15: 7	among your brothers in a of the towns of	285
	15:21	is lame or blind, or has a serious flaw,	3972
	16: 4	Do not let a of the meat you sacrifice on	4946
	16: 5	in a town the LORD your God gives you	285
	16:21	not set up a wooden Asherah pole beside	3972
	17: 1	an ox or a sheep that has a defect or flaw	3972
	19:15	to convict a man accused of a crime	3972
	20: 8	"Is a man afraid or fainthearted?	408+2021+4769
	23: 2	No one born of a forbidden marriage nor a	4200
	23: 3	or a of his descendants may enter	4200
	23:18	of the LORD your God to pay a vow,	3972
	23:24	but do not put a in your basket.	NIH
	24: 5	not be sent to war or have a other duty laid	3972
	24:10	you make a loan of a kind to your neighbor,	4399
	26:13	nor have I forgotten a of them.	NIH
	26:14	I have not eaten a of the sacred portion	4946
	26:14	nor have I removed a of it	4946
	26:14	nor have I offered a of it to the dead.	4946
	27: 5	Do not use a iron tool upon them.	NIH
	27:21	"Cursed is the man who has sexual relations with a animal."	3972
	28:14	from a of the commands I give you today,	3972
	28:51	nor a calves of your herds or lambs	NIH
	28:55	to one of them a of the flesh of his children	4946
Jos	6:18	there was no longer a manna for	NIH
	6:18	about your own destruction by taking a	4946
	8:20	to escape in a direction,	2178+2178+2256
	11:13	Yet Israel did not burn a of the cities built	3972
	11:22	Gath and Ashdod did a survive.	AIT
	20: 9	A of the Israelites or any alien living	3972
	20: 9	Any of the Israelites or a alien living	3972
Jdg	2:21	I will no longer drive out before them a of	408
	3: 1	not experienced a of the wars in Canaan	3972
	11: 2	"You are not going to get a inheritance	AIT
	13:14	nor drink a wine or other fermented drink	NIH
	13:16	I will not eat a of your food.	928
	16: 7	I'll become as weak as a other man."	285
	16:11	I'll become as weak as a other man."	285
	16:13	I'll become as weak as a other man."	285
	16:17	I would become as weak as a other man."	3972
	21: 7	an oath by the LORD not to give them a	4946
Ru	1:11	Am I going to have a more sons,	6388
1Sa	4:20	she did not respond or pay a attention.	AIT
	5: 5	nor a others who enter Dagon's temple	3972
	9: 2	a head taller than a of the others.	3972
	10:23	the people he was a head taller than a of	3972
	12: 3	If I have done a of these,	NIH
	14:24	"Cursed be a man who eats food	2021
	14:28	'Cursed be a man who eats food today!'	2021
	21: 4	"I don't have a ordinary bread on hand;	NIH
	21: 8	my sword or a other weapon,	NIH
	22:15	Let not the king accuse your servant or a	3972
	30:12	not eaten a food or drunk any water	AIT
	30:12	not eaten any food or drunk a water	AIT
2Sa	6:20	of his servants as a vulgar fellow would!"	285
	7: 7	to a of their rulers whom I commanded	285
	12:17	he would not eat a food with them.	NIH
	14: 2	and don't use a cosmetic lotions.	NIH
	17:12	nor a of his men will be left alive.	3972
	18:22	You don't have a news that will bring you	NIH
	19:28	to make a more appeals to the king?"	6388
	19:42	Have we eaten a of the king's provisions?	4946
	23:23	He was held in greater honor than a of	NIH
1Ki	4:31	He was wiser than a other man,	3972
	6: 7	chisel or a other iron tool was heard at	3972
	8:16	not chosen a city in a tribe of Israel to have	3972
	8:37	an enemy besieges them in a of their cities,	NIH
	8:38	and when a prayer or plea is made by a	3972
	9:22	But Solomon did not make slaves of a of	NIH
	10:20	for a other kingdom.	3972
	15: 5	the LORD and had not failed to keep a of	3972
	17:10	of the LORD than a of those things.	3972
	17:12	she replied, "I don't have a bread—	NIH
	18: 5	not have to kill a of our animals."	4946
	19:17	to death a who escape the sword of Hazael,	2021
	19:17	and Elisha will put to death a who escape	2021
2Ki	5:12	better than a of the waters of Israel?	3972

2Ki	5:17	sacrifices to a other god but the LORD.	AIT
	6:33	for the LORD a longer?"	6388
	7: 2	"but you will not eat a of it!"	4946
	7:19	but you will not eat a of it!	4946
	10:24	of you lets a of the men I am placing	408
	12: 8	not collect a more money from the people	NIH
	12:13	trumpets or a other articles of gold or silver	3972
	13:11	the LORD and did not turn away from a	3972
	14:24	the LORD and did not turn away from a	3972
	17:35	"Do not worship a other gods or bow down	AIT
	18:33	the god of a nation ever delivered his land	2021
	23:22	had a such Passover been observed.	2021
1Ch	1:43	in Edom before a Israelite king reigned:	NIH
	11:25	He was held in greater honor than a of	NIH
	17: 6	to a of their leaders whom I commanded	285
	23:26	or a of the articles used in its service."	3972
	28:21	in a craft will help you in all the work.	3972
	29: 8	A who had precious stones gave them to	2257S
2Ch	2:14	and can execute a design given to him.	3972
	6: 5	not chosen a city in a tribe of Israel to have	3972
	6:28	or when enemies besiege them in a	NIH
	6:29	and when a prayer or plea is made by a	3972
	8:15	to the priests or to the Levites in a matter,	3972
	9:19	for a other kingdom.	3972
	11:21	of Absalom more than a of his other wives	3972
	19:11	the chief priest will be over you in a matter	3972
	19:11	over you in a matter concerning the king,	3972
	23: 8	for Jehoiada the priest had not released a of	NIH
	23:19	in a way unclean might enter.	3972
	25: 7	not with a of the people of Ephraim.	3972
	29: 7	or present a burnt offerings at the sanctuary	NIH
	31:19	around their towns or in a other towns,	3972
	32:15	of a nation or kingdom has been able	3972
Ezr	1: 4	the people of a place where survivors may	3972
	2:63	The governor ordered them not to eat a of	4946
	6:12	overthrow a king or people who lifts	10353
	7:13	that a of the Israelites in my kingdom,	10353
	7:24	tribute or duty on a of the priests, Levites,	10353
	7:25	who are to teach a who do not know them.	AIT
	9:12	a treaty of friendship with them at a time,	6409
Ne	2:16	or nobles or officials or a others who would	AIT
	2:20	you have no share in Jerusalem or a claim	NIH
	5:16	we did not acquire a land.	AIT
	7:65	not to eat a of the most sacred food	4946
	10:31	from them on the Sabbath or on a holy day.	NIH
Est	2:17	to Esther more than to a of	3972
	2:17	and approval more than a of	3972
	4:11	of the royal provinces know that for a man	3972
	8:11	to destroy, kill and annihilate a armed force	3972
	8:11	of a nationality or province	NIH
Job	2: 3	against him to ruin him without a reason."	2855
	3: 6	the year nor be entered in a of the months.	5031
	6:13	Do I have a power to help myself,	401S
	6:30	Is there a wickedness on my lips?	NIH
	10:18	I wish I had died before a eye saw me.	NIH
	17:15	Who can see a hope for me?	NIH
	32:21	nor will I flatter a man;	AIT
	34:27	from following him and had no regard for a	3972
	37:20	Would a man ask to be swallowed up?	NIH
	39: 8	and searches for a green thing.	3972
	41: 9	A hope of subduing him is false;	NIH
Ps	4: 6	"Who can show us a good?"	NIH
	14: 2	to see if there are a who understand,	AIT
	14: 2	a who seek God.	AIT
	53: 2	to see if there are a who understand,	AIT
	53: 2	a who seek God.	AIT
	139:24	See if there is a offensive way in me,	NIH
Pr	3:31	a violent man or choose a of his ways,	3972
	6:35	He will not accept a compensation;	3972
	8:26	before he made the earth or its fields or a	8031
	14:34	but sin is a disgrace to a people.	NIH
	26:10	a fool or a passer-by.	NIH
Ecc	5:19	God gives a man wealth and possessions,	3972
SS	4:10	the fragrance of your perfume than a spice!	3972
Isa	7:17	on the house of your father a time unlike a	NIH
	33:20	nor a of its ropes broken.	3972
	35: 9	nor will a ferocious beast get up on it;	AIT
	36:18	the god of a nation ever delivered his land	2021
	41:26	no one heard a words from you.	AIT
	43:24	You have not bought a fragrant calamus	AIT
	44: 8	Is there a God besides me?	NIH
	52:14	beyond that of a man and his form marred	AIT
	53: 9	nor was a deceit in his mouth.	NIH
	56: 2	and keeps his hand from doing a evil."	3972
	56: 3	And let not a eunuch complain,	2021
	64: 4	no eye has seen a God besides you,	NIH
Jer	2:24	A males that pursue her need	3972
	3: 2	Is there a place where you have	AIT
	3:19	the most beautiful inheritance of a nation.'	AIT
	5: 6	to tear to pieces a who venture out,	3972
	7:16	for this people nor offer a plea or petition	NIH
	10: 5	nor can they do a good."	AIT
	11:14	for this people nor offer a plea or petition	NIH
	12:17	But if a nation does not listen,	2085S
	14:22	Do a of the worthless idols of	928
	17:22	a load out of your houses or do a work on	3972
	17:24	the Sabbath day holy by not doing a work	3972
	17:27	the Sabbath day holy by not carrying a load	NIH
	18: 7	If at a time I announce that a nation	8092
	23: 4	nor will a be missing," declares the LORD.	AIT
	25: 4	you have not listened or paid a attention.	265+4200+5742+9048
	27: 8	a nation or kingdom will	2021
	27:11	if a nation will bow its neck under the yoke	2021
	27:13	the LORD has threatened a nation	2021
	29:26	you should put a madman who acts like	3972

Jer	34:14	you must free a fellow Hebrew who has sold himself	2257S
	35: 7	you must never have a of these things,	NIH
	37: 2	nor the people of the land paid a attention	AIT
	37:17	"Is there a word from the LORD?"	NIH
	38: 9	to death when there is no longer a bread in	2021
	51:26	nor a stone for a foundation,	NIH
La	1:12	Is a suffering like my suffering	NIH
	3:39	Why should a living man complain	1505S
	4:12	nor did a of the world's people,	3972
Eze	1:17	in a one of the four directions	NIH
	10:11	in a one of the four directions	NIH
	12:28	of my words will be delayed a longer;	6388
	14: 4	When an Israelite sets up idols in his heart	408
	14: 7	" 'When a Israelite or any alien living	408
	14: 7	or a alien living in Israel separates himself	2021
	15: 2	of a branch on a of the trees in the forest?	3972
	16: 5	or had compassion enough to do a	285
	18:10	or does a of these other things	285
	18:23	Do I take a pleasure in the death of	2911+2911
	20:28	and they saw a high hill or any leafy tree,	3972
	20:28	and they saw any high hill or a leafy tree,	3972
	24:16	Yet do not lament or weep or shed a tears.	3870S
	37:23	and vile images or with a of their offenses,	3972
	39:28	not leaving a behind.	4946+6388
	44:13	as priests or come near a of my holy things	3972
	44:17	they must not wear a woolen garment	NIH
	44:24	" 'In a dispute, the priests are to serve	NIH
	46:18	not take a of the inheritance of the people,	4946
	48:14	They must not sell or exchange a of it.	4946
Da	1: 4	young men without a physical defect,	3972
	1:15	and better nourished than a of	3972
	2:10	has ever asked such a thing of a magician	10353
	2:43	a more than iron mixes with clay.	10168+10195+10341
	3:28	or worship a god except their own God.	10353
	3:29	of a nation or language who say anything	10353
	6: 5	"We will never find a basis for charges	10353
	6: 7	to a god or man during the next thirty days,	10353
	6:12	to a god or man except to you,	10353
	6:18	and without a entertainment being brought	NIH
	6:22	Nor have I ever done a wrong before you,	NIH
	11:37	nor will he regard a god,	3972
Hos	3: 3	be a prostitute or be intimate with a man,	NIH
	12: 8	not find in me a iniquity or sin."	NIH
Jnh	3: 7	Do not let a man or beast, herd or flock,	2021
	4: 4	"Have you a right to be angry?"	3512
Zep	3:15	never again will you fear a harm.	NIH
Hag	2:19	Is there yet a seed left in the barn?	NIH
Zec	14:17	If a of the peoples of the earth do not go	907+4946
Mt	5:18	will by a means disappear from the Law	NIG
	10: 5	not go among the Gentiles or enter a town	NIG
	10: 9	Do not take along a gold or silver or copper	NIG
	12:11	"If a of you has a sheep and it falls into	5515
	16: 7	"It is because we didn't bring a bread."	NIG
	18:14	not willing that a of these little ones should	1651
	19: 3	to divorce his wife for a and every reason?"	4246
	22:46	to ask him a more questions.	4033
	25: 3	but did not take a oil with them.	NIG
	26:60	But they did not find a,	NIG
	26:65	Why do we need a more witnesses?	2285
Mk	4:13	How then will you understand a parable?	4246
	5: 3	and no one could bind him a more,	4033
	5:35	"Why bother the teacher a more?"	2285
	6: 5	He could not do a miracles there,	NIG
	6:11	And if a place will not welcome you	323+4005
	11:13	he went to find out if it had a fruit.	5516
	12:20	and died without leaving a children.	NIG
	12:22	In fact, none of the seven left a children.	NIG
	12:34	no one dared ask him a more questions.	NIG
	14: 7	and you can help them a time you want.	4020
	14:55	but they did not find a.	NIG
	14:63	"Why do we need a more witnesses?"	2285
Lk	3:13	"Don't collect a more than you are required	4123+4498
	4:26	Yet Elijah was not sent to a of them,	4029
	7:44	You did not give me a water for my feet,	NIG
	8:49	"Don't bother the teacher a more."	4029
	10:35	a extra expense you may have.'	323+4005+5516
	11:17	"A kingdom divided against itself will	4246
	13: 6	to look for fruit on it, but did not find a.	NIG
	13: 7	on this fig tree and haven't found a.	NIG
	13:33	In a case, I must keep going today	4440
	14:33	a of you who does not give	4246
	16: 2	because you cannot be manager a longer.'	2285
	18:34	The disciples did not understand a of this.	4029
	19:48	Yet they could not find a way to do it,	3836+5515
	20:40	no one dared to ask him a more	4033
	22:71	"Why do we need a more testimony?"	2285
Jn	7: 6	for you a time is right.	4121
	7: 7	"Has a of the rulers or of	5516
	8: 7	"If a one of you is without sin,	NIG
	8:46	Can a of you prove me guilty of sin?"	5515
	10:33	"We are not stoning you for a of these,	NIG
	17:14	world a more than I am of the world.	2777+4024
	21: 5	"Friends, haven't you a fish?"	5516
Ac	4:17	to stop this thing from spreading a further	2093+4498
	4:32	that a of his possessions was his own,	5516
	8:16	the Holy Spirit had not yet come upon a	4029
	9: 2	he found a there who belonged to the Way,	5516
	10:28	that I should not call a man impure	3594
	10:29	without raising a objection.	395
	22: 3	as zealous for God as a of you are today.	4246
	24:18	nor was I involved in a disturbance.	NIG
	25:10	I have not done a wrong to the Jews,	4029
	25:16	over a man before he has faced his accusers	5516

Ac	25:18	not charge him with a of the crimes	4029
	25:24	shouting that he ought not to live a longer.	3600
	26: 8	Why should a of you consider it incredible	NIG
	27:42	to prevent a of them from swimming away	5516
	28:18	because I was not guilty of a crime deserving death.	3594
	28:19	not that I had a charge to bring	5516
	28:21	"We have not received a letters from Judea	4046
Ro	3: 9	Are we a better?	NIG
	6: 2	how can we live in it a longer?	2285
	8:33	Who will bring a charge	1592
	8:38	the present nor the future, nor a powers,	NIG
	12: 2	conform a longer to the pattern of	AIT
	14:13	up your mind not to put a stumbling block	NIG
	15: 9	give her a help she may need from you,	3972
1Co	1: 7	not lack a spiritual gift as you eagerly wait	3594
	1:14	I am thankful that I did not baptize a	4029
	2:15	is not subject to a man's judgment:	4029
	3:11	For no one can lay a foundation other than	NIG
	3:12	If a man builds on this foundation using	5516
	3:18	If a one of you thinks he is wise by	5516
	4: 3	if I am judged by you or by a human court;	NIG
	6: 1	If a of you has a dispute with another,	5516
	7:12	If a brother has a wife who is not a believer	5516
	9:15	But I have not used a of these rights.	4029
2Co	1: 4	that we can comfort those in a trouble with	4246
	7: 9	not harmed in a way	3594
	8:20	We want to avoid a criticism of	5516
	9: 4	For if a Macedonians come with me	NIG
	11: 9	from being a burden to you in a way,	4246
	12:17	through a of the men I sent you?	5516
	13: 2	not spare those who sinned earlier or a of	4246
Gal	1:12	I did not receive it from a man,	NIG
	1:16	I did not consult a man,	NIG
	5: 6	nor uncircumcision has a value.	5516
Eph	4:29	Do not let a unwholesome talk come out	4246
	5: 3	or of a kind of impurity, or of greed,	4246
	5: 5	has a inheritance in the kingdom of Christ	NIG
	5:27	without stain or wrinkle or a other blemish,	5516
Php	1:28	in a way by those who oppose you.	3594
	2: 1	If you have a encouragement	5516
	2: 1	if a comfort from his love,	5516
	2: 1	if a fellowship with the Spirit,	5516
	2: 1	if a tenderness and compassion,	5516
	4:12	of being content in a and every situation,	4246
Col	2:23	but they lack a value	5516
2Th	2: 3	Don't let anyone deceive you in a way,	2848+3594+5573
	3: 8	that we would not be a burden to a of you.	5516
1Ti	1: 3	not to teach false doctrines a longer	NIG
	5:16	If a woman who is a believer has widows	5516
2Ti	2:21	the Master and prepared to do a good work.	4246
Phm	1:14	that a favor you do will be spontaneous and	3836
	1:18	If he has done you a wrong	5516
Heb	4:12	Sharper than a double-edged sword,	4246
	7:20	Others became priests without a oath,	NIG
	10:18	there is no longer a sacrifice for sin.	NIG
Jas	1: 5	If a of you lacks wisdom,	5516
	5:13	Is a one of you in trouble?	5516
	5:14	Is a one of you sick?	5516
1Pe	3: 1	if a of them do not believe the word,	5516
	4:15	not be as a murderer or thief or a other kind	NIG
2Jn	1: 7	A such person is the deceiver and	4047
Rev	2:24	not impose a other burden on you):	NIG
	7: 1	to prevent a wind from blowing on the land	4246
	7: 1	on the land or on the sea or on a tree.	4246
	7:16	nor a scorching heat.	4246
	9: 4	not to harm the grass of the earth or a plant	4246
	18: 4	that you will not receive a of her plagues;	NIG
	18:11	because no one buys their cargoes a more—	4033
	18:22	No workman of a trade will ever be found	4246
	21: 1	and there was no longer a sea.	NIG
	22: 3	No longer will there be a curse.	4246

ANYBODY (7) [ANY]

Lk	19: 8	and if I have cheated a out of anything,	5516
Ac	19:38	a grievance against a,	5516
1Co	11:21	ahead without waiting for a else.	NIG
	14:37	a thinks he is a prophet or spiritually gifted,	5516
Gal	1: 9	If a is preaching to you	5516
1Th	4:12	not be dependent on a.	3594
1Jn	2: 1	But if a does sin, we have one who speaks	5516

ANYMORE (17) [ANY]

Dt	3:26	Do not speak to me about this matter	3578+6388
	18:16	nor see this great fire a,	3578+6388
Jos	7:12	be with you a unless you destroy whatever	3578
2Sa	2:28	nor did they fight a.	3578+6388
	7:10	Wicked people will not oppress them a,	3578
	10:19	to help the Ammonites a.	6388
1Ch	17: 9	Wicked people will not oppress them a	3578
	19:19	not willing to help the Ammonites a.	6388
Isa	1: 5	Why should you be beaten a?	6388
	2: 4	nor will they train for war a.	6388
Jer	22:30	on the throne of David or rule a in Judah."	6388
Eze	14:11	nor will they defile themselves a	6388
	23:27	with longing or remember Egypt a.	6388
Am	7:13	Don't prophesy a at Bethel,	3578+6388
Mic	4: 3	nor will they train for war a.	6388
Jn	14:19	Before long, the world will not see me a,	4033
Rev	20: 3	to keep him from deceiving the nations a	2285

ANYONE (403) [ANY]

Ge	4:15	if a kills Cain, he will suffer vengeance	3972
	13:16	so that if a could count the dust,	408

Ge	19:12	"Do you have a else here—	4769
	19:12	or a else in the city who belongs to you?	3972
	26:11	"A who molests this man or his wife shall	2021
	31:32	But if you find a who has your gods,	AIT
	41:38	"Can we find a like this man,	NIH
	43:34	as much as a else's.	3972
Ex	10:23	No one could see a else or leave his place	278S
	20: 7	not hold a guiltless who misuses his name.	AIT
	21:12	"A who strikes a man and kills him shall	AIT
	21:15	"A who attacks his father or his mother	AIT
	21:16	"A who kidnaps another and either sells	AIT
	21:17	"A who curses his father or mother must	AIT
	22:19	"A who has sexual relations with an animal	AIT
	24:14	a involved in a dispute can go to them."	4769
	30:33	a other than a priest	2424
	31:14	A who desecrates it must be put to death;	AIT
	33: 7	A inquiring of the LORD would go to	3972
	33:20	How will a know that you are pleased	3972
Lev	4: 2	'When a sins unintentionally	5883
	5: 5	" 'When a is guilty in any of these ways,	AIT
	6: 2	"If a sins and is unfaithful to the LORD	5883
	7: 8	a burnt offering for a may keep its hide	408
	7:19	a ceremonially clean may eat it.	3972
	7:20	But if a who is unclean eats any meat of	5883
	7:21	If a touches something unclean—	5883
	7:25	A who eats the fat of an animal from which	3972
	7:27	If a eats blood,	3972+5883
	7:29	'A who brings a fellowship offering to	2021
	11:28	A who picks up their carcasses must wash his clothes,	2021
	11:36	but a who touches one	AIT
	11:39	a who touches the carcass will be unclean	2021
	11:40	A who eats some of the carcass	2021
	11:40	A who picks up the carcass	2021
	13: 2	"When a has a swelling or a rash or	132
	13: 9	"When a has an infectious skin disease,	132
	14:32	for a who has an infectious skin disease	2257
	14:46	"A who goes into the house	2021
	14:47	A who sleeps or eats in	2021
	15: 5	A who touches his bed must wash his clothes	408
	15:11	" 'A the man with a discharge touches	3972
	15:19	and a who touches her will be unclean	3972
	15:23	when a touches it, he will be unclean	2257
	15:32	for a made unclean by an emission	AIT
	17:14	a who eats it must be cut off."	3972
	17:15	" 'A, whether native-born or alien,	3972+5883
	20: 9	'If a curses his father or mother,	408+408
	22: 4	by a corpse or by a who has an emission	408
	22:12	a other than a priest,	2424
	22:14	" 'If a eats a sacred offering by mistake,	408
	22:21	When a brings from the herd or flock	408
	23:29	A who does not deny himself on	2021+3972+5883
	23:30	a who does any work on	2021+3972+5883
	24:15	Say to the Israelites: 'If a curses his God,	408+408
	24:16	a who blasphemes the name of	AIT
	24:17	" 'If a takes the life of a human being,	408
	24:18	A who takes the life of someone's animal	AIT
	24:19	If a injures his neighbor,	408
	27: 2	'If a makes a special vow	408
	27: 8	If a making the vow is too poor to pay	2085
Nu	1:51	A else who goes near it shall be put	2424
	3:10	a else who approaches the sanctuary must	2424
	3:38	A else who approached the sanctuary was	2424
	5: 2	to send away from the camp a who has	3972
	12: 3	more humble than a else on the face of	3972
	15:14	or a else living among you presents	889
	15:30	" 'But a who sins defiantly,	5883
	17:13	A who even comes near the tabernacle of	3972
	18: 7	A else who comes near the sanctuary must	2424
	19:11	"Whoever touches the dead body of a	132+3972
	19:13	of a and fails to purify himself defiles	132
	19:14	A who enters the tent and anyone who is	3972
	19:14	the tent and a who is in it will be unclean	3972
	19:16	"A out in the open who touches someone who has been killed	3972
	19:16	or a who touches a human bone or a grave,	NIH
	19:18	He must also sprinkle a who has touched	2021
	19:21	and a who touches the water	2021
	19:21	and a who touches it becomes unclean	5883
	21: 8	a who is bitten can look at it and live."	3972
	21: 9	when a was bitten by a snake and looked at	408
	31:19	"All of you who have killed a	5883
	31:19	touched a who was killed must stay outside	2021
	35:15	a who has killed another accidentally can flee there.	3972
	35:17	if a has a stone in his hand that could kill,	NIH
	35:18	Or if a has a wooden object in his hand	NIH
	35:20	a with malice aforethought shoves	AIT
	35:30	" 'A who kills a person is to be put to death	3972
	35:32	not accept a ransom for a who has fled	AIT
	36: 6	They may marry a they please as long	2021
Dt	4:42	a who had killed a person	AIT
	5:11	not hold a guiltless who misuses his name.	889
	18:12	A who does these things is detestable to	3972
	18:19	If a does not listen to my words that	408+2021
	19: 3	so that a who kills a man may flee there.	3972
	20: 5	"Has a built a new home and	408+2021+4769
	20: 6	Has a planted a vineyard	408+2021+4769
	20: 7	Has a become pledged to a woman and	408+2021+4769
	21:23	a who is hung on a tree is under God's curse	AIT
	22: 5	LORD your God detests a who does this.	3972
	25:16	LORD your God detests a who does these	3972
	25:16	a who deals dishonestly.	3972
Jos	2:19	If a goes outside your house into the street,	3972
	2:19	As for a who is in the house with you,	3972
	11:14	not sparing a that breathed.	3972

Jos	20: 3	so that a who kills a person accidentally	8357S
Jdg	4:20	by and asks you, 'Is a here?'	408
	7: 3	'A who trembles with fear may turn back	4769
	16: 7	"If a ties me with seven fresh thongs	AIT
	16:11	"If a ties me securely with new ropes	AIT
	18: 7	and had no relationship with a else.	132
	18:28	and had no relationship with a else.	132
	21: 5	a solemn oath that a who failed to assemble	AIT
	21:18	be a who gives a wife to a Benjamite.'	AIT
Ru	2: 2	and pick up the leftover grain behind a	889
	3:14	but got up before a could be recognized;	408
1Sa	2:13	with the people that whenever a offered	408+3972
	11: 7	to the oxen of a who does not follow Saul	2257
	26:12	nor did a wake up.	AIT
2Sa	5: 8	"A who conquers the Jebusites will have	3972
	6:21	who chose me rather than your father or a	3972
	9: 1	"Is there a still left of the house of Saul	889
	14:10	"If a says anything to you, bring him to me,	2021
	15: 2	Whenever a came with a complaint	408+2021+3972
	15: 5	whenever a approached him to bow down	408
	19:22	Should a be put to death in Israel today?	408
	21: 4	nor do we have the right to put a in Israel	408
1Ki	3:12	that there will never have been a like you,	NIH
	13:33	A who wanted to become	2021
	15:17	to prevent a from leaving or entering	AIT
	15:29	He did not leave Jeroboam a that breathed,	3972
	18:40	Don't let a get away!"	408
	22:31	"Do not fight with a, small or great,	963+4200
2Ki	4:29	If you meet a, do not greet him,	408
	4:29	do not greet him, and if a greets you,	408
	7:10	not a sound of a—	132
	9:15	don't let a slip out of the city to go and tell	7127S
	10: 5	We will not appoint a as king;	408
	10:19	A who fails to come will no longer live."	3972
	11: 8	A who approaches your ranks must be put	2021
	11:15	and put to the sword a who follows her."	2021
	23:18	"Don't let a disturb his bones."	408
2Ch	6: 5	nor have I chosen a to be the leader	408
	16: 1	to prevent a from leaving or entering	AIT
	18:30	"Do not fight with a, small or great,	NIH
	23: 7	A who enters the temple must be put	2021
	23:14	and put to the sword a who follows her."	2021
	36:23	A of his people among you—	4769
Ezr	1: 3	A of his people among you—	4769
	6:11	I decree that if a changes this edict,	10050+10353
	10: 8	A who failed to appear	3972
Ne	2:12	I had not told a what my God had put	132
Job	13:19	Can a bring charges against me?	4769
	21:22	"Can a teach knowledge to God,	AIT
	31:19	I have seen a perishing for lack of clothing,	AIT
	40:24	Can a capture him by the eyes,	AIT
Pr	20:24	How then can a understand his own way?	132
	27:11	a who treats me with contempt.	AIT
	28: 9	If a turns a deaf ear to the law,	AIT
Ecc	1:16	in wisdom more than a who has ruled	3972
	2: 7	I also owned more herds and flocks than a	3972
	2: 9	I became greater by far than a in Jerusalem	3972
	6:11	and how does that profit a?	132
	9: 4	A who is among the living has hope—	4769
Isa	47:14	Here are no coals to warm a;	NIH
	54:15	a does attack you, it will not be my doing;	AIT
Jer	6: 7	a give them a drink	AIT
	23:24	Can a hide in secret places so	408
	23:34	If a prophet or a priest or a else claims,	6639S
	26:19	"Did Hezekiah king of Judah or a else	3972
	27: 5	and I give it to a I please.	889
	36:19	Don't let a know where you are."	408
	38:24	"Do not let a know about this conversation,	408
	41: 4	before a knew about it,	408
Eze	9: 6	but do not touch a who has the mark.	408+3972
	16:15	You lavished your favors on a who passed	3972
	16:25	to a who passed by.	3972
	18: 7	He does not oppress a,	408
	18:16	not oppress a or require a pledge for a loan.	408
	18:32	I take no pleasure in the death of a,	2021+4637S
	33: 4	then if a hears the trumpet but does	AIT
	45:20	the month for a who sins unintentionally or	408
Da	4:17	gives them to a he wishes and sets	10168+10426
	4:25	and gives them to a he wishes.	10168+10426
	4:32	and gives them to a he wishes."	10168+10426
	5:21	and sets over them a he wishes.	10168+10426
	6: 7	that a who prays to any god or man during	10353
	6:12	during the next thirty days a who prays	10050+10353
Am	6:10	of the house and asks a still hiding there,	889
	6:10	"Is a with you?"	NIH
Na	3: 7	Where can I find a to comfort you?"	AIT
Hag	2:16	a came to a heap of twenty measures,	4392
	2:16	a went to a wine vat to draw fifty measures,	AIT
Zec	13: 3	And if a still prophesies,	408
Mt	5:19	A who breaks one of the least	1569
	5:21	and a who murders will be subject	323
	5:22	that a who is angry with his brother will	4246
	5:22	a who says to his brother, 'Raca,'	323+4005
	5:22	But a who says, 'You fool!'	323+4005
	5:28	But I tell you that a who looks at	4246
	5:31	'A who divorces his wife must give her	323+4005
	5:32	But I tell you that a who divorces his wife,	4246
	5:32	and a marries	1569+4005
	8: 4	"See that you don't tell a.	3594
	8:10	I have not found a in Israel	4029
	10:14	If a will not welcome you or listen	4005
	10:37	"A who loves his father	3836
	10:37	a who loves his son	3836
	10:38	and a who does not take his cross	4005
	10:41	A who receives a prophet because he is	3836

Mt	10:41	and a who receives a righteous man	3836
	10:42	if a gives even a cup of cold water to one	4005
	11:11	not risen a greater than John the Baptist;	NIG
	12:29	how can a enter a strong man's house	5516
	12:32	A who speaks a word against the Son	1569
	12:32	but a who speaks against	323
	13:19	When a hears the message about	4246
	15: 4	'A who curses his father or mother must	3836
	16:20	Then he warned his disciples not to tell a	3594
	16:24	"If a would come after me,	5516
	17: 9	"Don't tell a what you have seen,	3594
	18: 6	But if a causes one of these little ones	4005
	19: 9	I tell you that a who divorces his wife,	323
	21: 3	If a says anything to you,	5516
	22: 9	and invite to the banquet a you find.'	1569+4012
	23: 9	And do not call a on earth 'father,'	NIG
	23:16	You say, 'If a swears by the temple,	4005
	23:16	but if a swears by the gold of the temple,	4005
	23:18	You also say, 'If a swears by the altar,	4005
	23:18	but if a swears by the gift on it,	4005
	24:23	At that time if a says to you, 'Look,	5516
	24:26	"So if a tells you, 'There he is,	NIG
Mk	1:44	"See that you don't tell this to a.	3594
	4:23	If a has ears to hear, let him hear."	5516
	5:37	He did not let a follow him except Peter,	4029
	5:43	He gave strict orders not to let a know	3594
	7:10	'A who curses his father or mother must	3836
	7:24	He entered a house and did not want a	4246
	7:36	Jesus commanded them not to tell a.	3594
	8: 4	in this remote place can a get enough bread	5516
	8:30	Jesus warned them not to tell a about him.	3594
	8:34	"If a would come after me,	5516
	8:38	If a is ashamed of me and my words	4005
	9: 3	whiter than a in the world could bleach	NIG
	9: 8	they no longer saw a	4029
	9: 9	Jesus gave them orders not to tell a what they had seen	3594
	9:30	not want a to know where they were,	5516
	9:35	"If a wants to be first, he must be the very last, and the servant of all."	5516
	9:41	a who gives you a cup of water in my name	323
	9:42	"And if a causes one of these little ones	4005
	10:11	"A who divorces his wife	323
	10:15	a who will not receive the kingdom of God	323
	11: 3	If a asks you, 'Why are you doing this?'	5516
	11:16	not allow a to carry merchandise through	5516
	11:23	if a says to this mountain, 'Go,	4005
	11:25	if you hold anything against a, forgive him,	5516
	13:21	At that time if a says to you, 'Look,	5516
	16: 8	They said nothing to a,	4029
Lk	4: 6	and I can give it to a I want to.	1569+4005
	5:14	Then Jesus ordered him, "Don't tell a,	3594
	6:30	and if a takes what belongs to you,	3836
	8:51	he did not let a go in with him except Peter,	5516
	8:56	but he ordered them not to tell a what had happened.	3594
	9:21	not to tell this to a.	3594
	9:23	"If a would come after me,	5516
	9:26	If a is ashamed of me and my words,	4005
	10: 4	and do not greet a on the road.	3594
	12:10	but a who blasphemes against	3836
	12:21	be with a who stores up things for himself	3836
	14:26	"If a comes to me and does	5516
	14:27	And a who does not carry his cross	4015
	16:18	"A who divorces his wife	4246
	16:26	nor can a cross over from there to us.'	NIG
	18:17	a who will not receive the kingdom of God	323
	19:31	If a asks you, 'Why are you untying it?'	5516
Jn	6:51	If a eats of this bread, he will live forever.	5516
	7:17	If a chooses to do God's will,	5516
	7:37	"If a is thirsty, let him come to me	5516
	7:51	"Does our law condemn a	476+3836S
	8:33	and have never been slaves of a.	4029
	8:51	I tell you the truth, if a keeps my word,	5516
	8:52	yet you say that if a keeps your word,	5516
	9:22	a who acknowledged that Jesus was	1569+5516
	11:57	that if a found out where Jesus was,	5516
	13:20	whoever accepts a I send accepts me;	5516
	14: 9	A who has seen me has seen the Father.	3836
	14:12	a who has faith in me will do what I	3836
	14:23	Jesus replied, "If a loves me,	5516
	15: 6	If a does not remain in me,	5516
	16: 2	a who kills you will think he is offering	4246
	16:30	not even need to have a ask you questions.	5516
	18:31	"But we have no right to execute a,"	4029
	19:12	A who claims to be a king opposes Caesar."	4246
	20:23	If you forgive a his sins, they are forgiven;	5516
Ac	2:45	they gave to a as he had need.	4246
	3:23	A who does not listen to him	1569+4246+6034
	4:17	to speak no longer to a in this name."	3594
	4:35	and it was distributed to a as he had need.	1667
	9: 7	they heard the sound but did not see a.	3594
	10:47	"Can a keep these people from being	5516
	23:22	"Don't tell a that you have reported this	3594
	24:12	My accusers did not find me arguing with a	5516
Ro	5: 7	Very rarely will a die for a righteous man,	5516
	6: 7	a who has died has been freed from sin.	AIT
	8: 9	And if a does not have the Spirit of Christ,	5516
	10:11	"A who trusts in him will never be put	4246
	12:17	Do not repay a evil for evil.	3594
	14:14	But if a regards something as unclean,	3836
	14:18	because a who serves Christ	3836
1Co	1:16	I don't remember if I baptized a else.)	5516
	3:17	If a destroys God's temple,	5516
	4: 7	For who makes you different from a else?	NIG
	5:11	not associate with a who calls himself	1569+5516
	7:36	If a thinks he is acting improperly toward	5516

1Co	7:39	she is free to marry a she wishes,	4005
	8:10	For if a with a weak conscience sees you	5516
	9:15	I would rather die than have a deprive me	4029
	10:28	But if a says to you,	5516
	10:32	Do not cause a to stumble, whether Jews,	NIG
	11:16	If a wants to be contentious about this,	5516
	11:29	For a who eats and drinks	3836
	11:34	If a is hungry, he should eat at home,	5516
	14: 2	For a who speaks in a tongue does not speak to men but to God.	3836
	14: 7	how will a know what tune is being played	NIG
	14: 9	how will a know what you are saying?	NIG
	14:13	For this reason a who speaks in	3836
	14:27	If a speaks in a tongue, two—	5516
	16:22	If a does not love the Lord—	5516
2Co	2: 5	If a has caused grief,	5516
	2:10	If you forgive a, I also forgive him.	4005
	3:16	But whenever a turns to the Lord,	AIT
	5:17	if a is in Christ, he is a new creation;	5516
	10: 7	If a is confident that he belongs to Christ,	5516
	11: 9	I was not a burden to a,	4029
	11:20	up with a who enslaves you or exploits you	5516
	11:21	What a else dares to boast about—	5516
Gal	6: 3	If a thinks he is something	5516
	6: 6	A who receives instruction in	3836
Php	3: 4	If a else thinks he has reasons	5516
Col	2:16	not let a judge you by what you eat	5516
	2:18	Do not let a who delights in false humility	3594
	3:25	A who does wrong will be repaid	3836
1Th	2: 6	not from you or a else.	257
	2: 9	a burden to a while we preached the gospel	5516
2Th	2: 3	Don't let a deceive you in any way,	5516
	3:14	If a does not obey our instruction	5516
1Ti	3: 1	If a sets his heart on being an overseer,	5516
	3: 5	(If a does not know how	5516
	4:12	Don't let a look down on you	3594
	5: 8	If a does not provide for his relatives,	5516
	6: 3	If a teaches false doctrines and does	5516
2Ti	2: 5	Similarly, if a competes as an athlete,	5516
Tit	2:15	Do not let a despise you.	3594
Heb	4:10	for a who enters God's rest also rests	3836
	5:13	A who lives on milk, being still an infant,	4246
	10:28	A who rejected the law of Moses died	5516
	11: 6	because a who comes to him must believe	3836
Jas	1:13	nor does he tempt a;	1254+4029
	1:23	A who listens to the word but does	5516
	1:26	If a considers himself religious and	5516
	2:13	without mercy will be shown to a who has	3836
	3: 2	If a is never at fault in what he says,	5516
	4: 4	A who chooses to be a friend of	1569
	4:11	A who speaks against his brother	3836
	4:17	A, then, who knows the good he ought	NIG
	5:13	Is a happy? Let him sing songs of praise.	5516
1Pe	4:11	If a speaks, he should do it as one speaking	5516
	4:11	If a serves, he should do it with	5516
2Pe	1: 9	But if a does not have them,	4005
	3: 9	not wanting a to perish,	5516
1Jn	2: 5	But if a obeys his word,	4005
	2: 9	A who claims to be in the light	3836
	2:15	If a loves the world,	5516
	2:27	and you do not need a to teach you.	5516
	3: 7	Dear children, do not let a lead you astray.	3594
	3:10	A who does not do what is right is not	4246
	3:10	nor is a who does not love his brother.	NIG
	3:14	A who does not love remains in death.	3836
	3:15	A who hates his brother is a murderer,	4246
	3:17	If a has material possessions	4005
	4:15	If a acknowledges that Jesus is the Son	4005
	4:20	If a says, "I love God,"	5516
	4:20	For a who does not love his brother,	3836
	5:10	A who believes in the Son	3836
	5:10	A who does not believe God has made him out to be a liar,	3836
	5:16	If a sees his brother commit a sin that does	5516
	5:16	that a born of God will not continue to sin;	4246
2Jn	1: 9	A who runs ahead and does not continue in	4246
	1:10	If a comes to you and does	5516
	1:11	A who welcomes him shares	3836
3Jn	1:11	A who does what is good is from God.	3836
	1:11	A who does what is evil has not seen God.	3836
Rev	3:20	If a hears my voice and opens the door,	5516
	11: 5	If a tries to harm them, fire comes	5516
	11: 5	how a who wants to harm them must die.	5516
	13:10	If a is to go into captivity,	5516
	13:10	If a is to be killed with the sword,	5516
	13:18	If a has insight, let him calculate the number	3836S
	14: 9	"If a worships the beast and his image	5516
	14:11	for a who receives the mark of his name."	5516
	21:27	nor will a who does what is shameful	4246
	22:18	If a adds anything to them,	5516
	22:19	And if a takes words away from this book	5516

ANYONE'S (6) [ANY]

1Sa	12: 4	not taken anything from a hand."	408
Job	30:13	without a helping them.	AIT
Ac	20:33	I have not coveted a silver or gold	4029
2Co	6: 3	We put no stumbling block in a path,	3594
2Th	3: 8	nor did we eat a food without paying for it.	5515
Rev	20:15	If a name was not found written in	5516

ANYTHING (203) [ANY]

Ge	18:14	Is a too hard for the LORD?	1821
	19: 8	But don't do a to these men,	1821
	19:22	because I cannot do a until you reach it."	1821
	22:12	"Do not do a to him.	4399

Ge 30:31 "Don't give me **a**," Jacob replied. 4399
31:24 "Be careful not *to* say *a* to Jacob, AIT
31:29 'Be careful not to say a to Jacob, NIH
31:32 see for yourself whether there is a NIH
39:6 he did not concern himself with a except 4399
39:8 not concern himself with a in the house; 4537
39:23 The warden paid no attention to a 3972+4399
44:7 be it from your servants to do a like that! 1821
Ex 12:15 whoever eats **a with yeast in it** 2809
12:19 whoever eats **a with yeast in it** 4721
20:4 an idol in the form *of a* in heaven above or 3972
20:17 or a that belongs to your neighbor." 3972
21:2 he shall go free, **without paying a.** 2855
23:18 to me along with **a containing yeast.** 2809
34:25 to me along with **a containing yeast,** 2809
36:6 or woman is to make a else as an offering 4856
Lev 5:2 touches a ceremonially unclean— 1821+3972
5:3 a that would make him unclean— 3972
5:4 person thoughtlessly takes an oath to do a, NIH
7:16 but a left over may be eaten on 2021
7:19 that touches a ceremonially unclean must 3972
11:12 A living in the water that does not have fins 3972
11:35 A that one of their carcasses falls 3972
12:4 not touch a sacred or go to the sanctuary 3972
13:48 any leather or a made of leather— 3972
15:4 and a he sits on will be unclean. 2021+3972+3998
15:6 on a that the man with a discharge sat 3998
15:20 " 'A she lies on during her period will 3972
15:20 and a she sits on will be unclean. 3972
15:22 Whoever touches a she sits 3972+3998
15:23 Whether it is the bed or a she was sitting 3998
15:26 a she sits on will be unclean, 2021+3972+3998
17:15 who eats **a found dead** or torn 5577
19:6 a left over until the third day must 2021
19:16 Do not **do a that endangers** your
   neighbor's life. 1947+6584+6641
20:25 by any animal or bird or a that moves along 3972
22:8 He must not eat **a found dead** or torn 5577
22:20 Do not bring a with a defect, 3972
22:22 **a with warts** or festering or running sores. 3301
Nu 6:4 not eat a that comes from the grapevine, 3972
11:6 we never see a but this manna!" 3972
16:26 Do not touch a belonging to them, 3972
19:22 A that an unclean person touches becomes
   unclean, 3972
22:16 Do not let a **keep** you from coming to me, AIT
22:18 not do a **great** or small to go beyond AIT
22:38 "But can I say just a? 4399
24:13 a of my own accord, **good** AIT
31:23 and a else that can withstand fire must 1821+3972
Dt 2:7 and you have not lacked a. 1821
4:23 of a the LORD your God has forbidden. 3972
4:32 Has a so great as this ever happened, 1821
4:32 or has a like it ever been heard of? NIH
5:8 an idol in the form of a in heaven above or 3972
5:21 or a that belongs to your neighbor." 3972
14:10 But a that does not have fins 3972
14:21 Do not eat a you find already dead. 3972
14:26 or other fermented drink, or a you wish. 3972
18:20 in my name a I have not commanded him 1821
20:16 do not leave alive a that breathes. 3972
22:3 or his cloak or a he loses. 3972
23:14 that he will not see among you a indecent 1821
23:19 or food or a else that may earn interest. 1821+3972
Jos 11:11 not sparing a that breathed, 3972
Jdg 13:4 and that you do not eat a unclean. 3972
13:7 and do not eat a unclean, 3972
13:14 not eat a that comes from the grapevine, 3972
13:14 or other fermented drink nor eat a unclean. 3972
19:19 We don't need a." 1821+3972
Ru 1:17 if a but death separates you and me." 3954
1Sa 3:17 if you hide from me a he told you."
   1821+1821+2021+3972+4946
12:4 not taken a from anyone's hand." 4399
12:5 that you have not found a in my hand." 4399
20:2 Look, my father doesn't do a, 1821
21:2 'No one is to know a about your mission 4399
   plunder or a else they had taken. 3972
2Sa 3:35 so severely, if I taste bread or a else 3972+4399
13:2 it seemed impossible for him to do a to her. 4399
14:10 The king replied, "If anyone says a to you, NIH
14:19 or to the left from a my lord the king says. 3972
14:32 and if I am guilty of a, NIH
15:35 Tell them a you hear in the king's palace.
   1821+2021+3972
15:36 Send them to me with a you hear." 1821+3972
17:19 No one knew a about it. 1821
19:38 a you desire from me I will do for you." 3972
19:42 *Have we taken a for ourselves?"* 5951+5951
1Ki 14:13 the God of Israel, has found a good. 1821
22:8 because he never prophesies *a* good AIT
22:18 that he never prophesies *a* good about me, AIT
2Ki 10:5 and we will do a you say. 3972
2Ch 18:7 because he never prophesies *a* good AIT
18:17 that he never prophesies *a* good about me, AIT
Ezr 7:20 And a else needed for the temple 10692
Ne 5:12 we will not demand a more from them. NIH
Est 2:13 A she wanted was given her to take 889+3972
6:10 Do not neglect a you have recommended."
   1821+3972+4946
Job 21:34 never having enjoyed a good. 2021ˢ
33:32 If you have a to say, answer me; 4863
Ps 39:2 not even saying *a* good, AIT
Pr 14:15 A simple man believes a, 1821+3972
Ecc 1:10 Is there a of which one can say, "Look! 1821
5:2 do not be hasty in your heart to utter a 1821
6:5 Though it never saw the sun or knew a, 4202ˢ

Ecc 7:14 a man cannot discover a about his future. 4399
9:6 a part in a that happens under the sun. 3972
12:12 my son, of a in addition to them. 3463
Jer 2:10 see if there has ever been a like this: NIH
18:13 Who has ever heard a like this? NIH
18:18 and pay no attention to a he says." 3972
32:27 Is a too hard for me? 1821+3972
38:14 "Do not hide a from me." 1821
Eze 4:14 until now I have never eaten a found dead 5577
15:3 from it to make a **useful?** 4856
15:3 is it then useful for a? 4856
15:5 it was not useful for a when it was whole, 4856
44:18 not wear a that makes them perspire. NIH
44:31 The priests must not eat a, bird or animal, 3972
Da 3:29 or language who say a against the God 10712
Joel 1:2 Has a like this ever happened in your days NIH
Am 8:7 "I will never forget a they have done. 3972
Jnh 3:7 taste a; do not let them eat or drink. 4399
Mt 5:13 no longer good for a, 4029
5:37 a beyond this comes from the evil one. 3836
12:34 how can you who are evil say a good? NIG
13:34 he did **not** say a to them without using 4029
18:19 if two of you on earth agree about a you
   ask for, 1569+4005+4246+4547
21:3 If anyone says a to you, 5516
24:17 the roof of his house go down to take a out 5516
27:19 **"Don't** have a to do with 3594
Mk 2:12 saying, "We have never seen a like this!" NIG
4:34 not say a to them without using a parable. NIG
6:22 "Ask me for a you want, 1569+4005
7:12 then you no longer let him do a 4029
8:23 Jesus asked, "Do you see a?" 5516
9:22 you can do a, take pity on us and help us." 5516
9:39 in the next moment say a bad about me, NIG
11:25 if you hold a against anyone, forgive him, 5516
Lk 5:5 and **haven't** caught a. 4029
6:35 **without** expecting to get a 3594
11:7 I can't get up and give you a.' NIG
15:16 but no one gave him a. NIG
17:31 no one in the field should go back for a. 5516
19:8 and if I have cheated anybody out of a, 5516
22:35 bag or sandals, did you lack a?" 5516
24:41 "Do you have a here to eat?" 5516
Jn 1:46 Can a good come from there?" 5516
7:13 But no one would say a publicly about him NIG
14:14 You may ask me for a in my name, 1569+5516
16:23 In that day you will no longer ask me a 4029
16:23 now you have not asked for a in my name. 4029
Ac 9:9 and did not eat or drink a. NIG
10:14 "I have never eaten a impure or unclean." 4246
10:15 "Do not call a impure
11:9 'Do not call a impure that 4005
15:28 **not** to burden you with a 3594
17:25 as if he needed a, 5516
19:36 you ought to be quiet and **not** do a rash. 3594
19:39 If there is a further you want to bring up, 5516
20:20 to preach a that would be helpful to you NIG
23:14 "We have taken a solemn oath **not** to eat a 3594
24:19 before you and bring charges if they have a 5516
25:5 if he has done a wrong." 5516
25:11 I am guilty of doing a deserving death, 5516
26:31 "This man is **not** doing a 4029
27:33 you **haven't** eaten a. 3594
28:21 from there has reported or said a bad 5516
Ro 8:39 nor a else in all creation, 5516
9:11 the twins were born or had done a good 5516
14:20 for a man to eat a that causes someone else NIG
14:21 not to eat meat or drink wine or to do a else NIG
15:18 of a except what Christ has accomplished 5516
1Co 3:7 nor he who waters is a, 5516
6:12 but I will not be mastered by a. 5516
9:12 up with a rather than hinder the gospel 4246
10:19 then that a sacrifice offered to an idol is a, 5516
10:19 or that an idol is a? 5516
10:25 Eat a sold in the meat market 4246
2Co 1:13 For we do not write you a you cannot read 257
2:10 if there was a to forgive, 5516
3:5 in ourselves to claim a for ourselves, 5516
9:4 not to say a about you— NIG
13:7 to God that you will **not** do a wrong. 3590+3594
13:8 For we cannot do a against the truth, 5516
Gal 6:15 nor uncircumcision means a; 5516
Php 4:6 **not** be anxious about a, 3594
4:8 if a is excellent or praiseworthy— 5516
1Th 1:8 Therefore we do not need to say a about it, 5516
2Ti 1:9 not because of a we have done but because NIG
2:23 **Don't** have a to do with 4148
Tit 1:16 disobedient and unfit for doing a good. 4246
Phm 1:14 **not** want to do a without your consent, 4029
1:18 or owes you a, charge it to me. NIG
Jas 1:4 be mature and complete, **not** lacking a. 3594
1:7 That man should not think he will receive a 5516
5:12 not by heaven or by earth or by a else. 5516
1Jn 2:15 not love the world or a in the world. 3593+3836
3:22 and receive from him a we ask, 1569+4005
5:14 we ask according to his will, he hears us. 5516
Rev 22:18 If anyone adds a to them, God will add NIG

ANYWHERE (15) [ANY]

Ge 19:17 and don't stop a in the plain! 3972
Ex 10:19 Not a locust was left a in Egypt. 3972
13:7 among you, nor shall any yeast be seen a 3972
34:4 No one is to come with you or be seen a on 3972
Nu 18:31 You and your households may eat the rest
   of it a, 928+3972+5226

Dt 12:13 sacrifice your burnt offerings a you please.
   928+3972+5226
18:6 If a Levite moves from one of your towns a 3972
1Sa 27:1 Saul will give up searching for me a 1473+3972
2Sa 21:4 and have no place a in Israel, 928+1473+3972
1Ki 2:36 but do not go a else. 625+2025+2025+2256
2:42 'On the day you leave to go a else,
   625+625+2025+2025+2256
2Ki 5:25 "Your servant didn't go a,"
   625+625+2025+2025+2256
Jer 40:5 or go a else you please." 3972
44:26 'that no one from Judah living a 3972
Ac 24:12 up a crowd in the synagogues or a else in 2848

APACE (KJV) See HASTE

APART (62) [PART]

Ge 21:28 Abraham set a seven ewe lambs from 963+4200
21:29 these seven ewe lambs you have set a 963+4200
30:40 set a the young of the flock **by themselves,** 7233
Ex 19:23 set it a **as holy.' "** 7727
32:29 "You **have been** set a to the LORD today,
   3338+4848
Lev 20:24 who **has** set you a from the nations. 976
20:25 those which *I have* set a as unclean 976
20:26 and *I have* set you a from the nations to 976
Nu 3:13 *I* set a for myself every firstborn in Israel, 7727
8:14 In this way *you are to* set the Levites a 976
8:17 *I* set them a for myself. 7727
16:31 the ground under them **split a** 1324
23:9 I see a people who live a and do 970+4200
31:28 set a as tribute for the LORD one out 8123
31:42 which Moses set a from that of 2936
Dt 7:26 like it, will be **set a for destruction.** 3051
7:26 for it is **set a for destruction.** 3051
10:8 that time the LORD set a the tribe of Levi 976
15:19 **Set a for the LORD** your God every
   firstborn male 7727
Jos 20:7 So *they* set a Kedesh in Galilee in 7727
Jdg 13:5 to be a **Nazirite**, *set a to* God from birth, AIT
14:6 upon him in power so that *he* **tore** the lion a 9117
16:17 "because I have been a **Nazirite** *set a* AIT
20:17 Israel, a from Benjamin, 963+4200
1Ki 13:3 the altar *will* **be split a** and the ashes 7973
13:5 the altar **was split a** 7973
19:11 and powerful wind **tore** the mountains a 7293
2Ki 2:12 his own clothes and **tore** them a.
   4200+7973+7974+9109
1Ch 23:13 Aaron **was** set a, 976
25:1 set a some of the sons of Asaph, 976
Ezr 8:24 Then *I* set a twelve of the leading priests, 976
Ps 4:3 the LORD **has** set a the godly for himself; 7111
16:2 a from you I have no good thing." 6584
88:5 I am **set a** with the dead, 2930
Pr 18:18 **keeps** strong opponents a. 7233
Isa 7:6 *let us* **tear** it a and divide it 7763
23:18 Yet her profit and her earnings will be **set a** 7731
43:11 and a **from me** there is no savior. 1187+4946
44:6 a **from me** there is no God. 1187+4946
45:5 a **from me** there is no God. 2314
45:21 And there is no God a **from** me, 1187+4946
Jer 1:5 before you were born *I* set you a; 7727
12:3 **Set** them a for the day of slaughter! 7727
Hos 13:8 a wild animal *will* **tear** them a. 1324
Mic 1:4 and the valleys **split a,** 1324
Mt 10:29 the ground a **from** the will of your Father. 459
Mk 5:4 but he **tore** the chains a and broke the irons 1400
Jn 10:36 what about the one whom the Father **set a** 39
15:5 a **from** me you can do nothing. 6006
Ac 13:2 **"Set a** for me Barnabas and Saul for 928
Ro 1:1 to be an apostle and **set a** for the gospel 928
2:12 All who sin a **from the law** will 492
2:12 the law will also perish **a from the law,** 492
3:21 now a righteousness from God, **a from** law, 6006
3:28 a man is justified by faith **a from** observing 6006
4:6 to whom God credits righteousness **a from** 6006
7:8 For **a from** law, sin is dead. 6006
7:9 Once I was alive **a from** law; 6006
2Co 12:3 whether in the body or **a from** the body I do 6006
Gal 1:15 who **set** me a from birth and called me 928
Heb 7:26 blameless, pure, **set** a from sinners, 6004
1Pe 3:15 But in your hearts **set** a Christ as Lord. 39

APARTMENT (1)

Jer 36:22 and the king was sitting in the winter a, 1074

APELLES (1)

Ro 16:10 Greet A, tested and approved in Christ. 593

APES (2)

1Ki 10:22 silver and ivory, and a and baboons. 7761
2Ch 9:21 silver and ivory, and a and baboons. 7761

APHARSACHITES, APHARSITES (KJV)
See PERSIAN

APHARSATHCHITES (KJV) See
OFFICIALS

APHEK (9)

Jos 12:18 the king of A one the king of Lasharon one 707

Jos 13: 4 from Arah of the Sidonians as far as **A**, 707
  19:30 Ummah, **A** and Rehob. 707
Jdg 1:31 or Sidon or Ahlab or Aczib or Helbah or **A** 707
1Sa 4: 1 and the Philistines at **A**. 707
  29: 1 at **A**, and Israel camped by the spring 707
1Ki 20:26 and went up to **A** to fight against Israel. 707
  20:30 The rest of them escaped to the city of **A**, 707
2Ki 13:17 the Arameans at **A**." 707

APHEKAH (1)
Jos 15:53 Janim, Beth Tappuah, **A**, 708

APHIAH (1)
1Sa 9: 1 the son of **A** *of* Benjamin. 688

APHIK (KJV) See APHEK

APHRAH (KJV) See BETH OPHRAH

APHSES (KJV) See HAPPIZZEZ

APOLLONIA (1)
Ac 17: 1 through Amphipolis and **A**, 662

APOLLOS (11)
Ac 18:24 Meanwhile a Jew named **A**, 663
  18:27 When **A** wanted to go to Achaia, 899S
  19: 1 While **A** was at Corinth, 663
1Co 1:12 another, "I follow **A**"; 663
  3: 4 "I follow Paul," and another, "I follow **A**," 663
  3: 5 What, after all, is **A**? 663
  3: 6 I planted the seed, **A** watered it, 663
  3:22 or **A** or Cephas or the world or life or death 663
  4: 6 I have applied these things to myself and **A** 663
  16:12 Now about our brother **A**: 663
Tit 3:13 the lawyer and **A** on their way and see 663

APOLLYON (1)
Rev 9:11 in Hebrew is Abaddon, and in Greek, **A**. 661

APOSTLE (21) [APOSTLES, APOSTLES', APOSTLESHIP, APOSTOLIC, SUPER-APOSTLES]
Ro 1: 1 an **a** and set apart for the gospel of God— 693
  11:13 Inasmuch as I am the an to the Gentiles, 693
1Co 1: 1 called to be an **a** of Christ Jesus by the will 693
  9: 1 Am I not an **a**? 693
  9: 2 Even though I may not be an **a** to others, 693
  15: 9 and do not even deserve to be called an **a**, 693
2Co 1: 1 Paul, an **a** of Christ Jesus by the will of God, 693
  12:12 The things that mark an **a**— 693
Gal 1: 1 Paul, an **a**—sent not from men 693
  2: 8 **ministry of** Peter as an **a** 692
  2: 8 was also at work in my ministry as an **a** to NIG
Eph 1: 1 Paul, an **a** of Christ Jesus by the will of God, 693
Col 1: 1 Paul, an **a** of Christ Jesus by the will of God, 693
1Ti 1: 1 Paul, an **a** of Christ Jesus by the command 693
  2: 7 a herald and an **a**— 693
2Ti 1: 1 Paul, an **a** of Christ Jesus by the will of God, 693
  1:11 a herald and an **a** and a teacher. 693
Tit 1: 1 Paul, a servant of God and an **a** of Jesus 693
Heb 3: 1 the **a** and high priest whom we confess. 693
1Pe 1: 1 Peter, an **a** of Jesus Christ, To God's elect, 693
2Pe 1: 1 Simon Peter, a servant and **a** of Jesus Christ, 693

APOSTLES (57) [APOSTLE]
Mt 10: 2 These are the names of the twelve **a**: 693
Mk 3:14 He appointed twelve—designating them **a** 693
  6:30 The **a** gathered around Jesus and reported 693
Lk 6:13 whom he also designated **a**: 693
  9:10 When the **a** returned, 693
  11:49 'I will send them prophets and **a**, 693
  17: 5 The **a** said to the Lord, 693
  22:14 Jesus and his **a** reclined at the table. 693
  24:10 the others with them who told this to the **a**. 693
Ac 1: 2 the Holy Spirit *to* the **a** he had chosen. 693
  1:26 so he was added to the eleven **a**. 693
  2:37 the heart and said to Peter and the other **a**, 693
  2:43 and miraculous signs were done by the **a**. 693
  4: 2 because the **a** were teaching the people 899S
  4:33 the **a** continued to testify to the resurrection 693
  4:36 the **a** called Barnabas (which means Son 693
  5:12 The **a** performed many miraculous signs 693
  5:18 the **a** and put them in the public jail. 693
  5:21 and sent to the jail for the **a**. 899S
  5:26 with his officers and brought the **a**. 899S
  5:27 Having brought the **a**, 899S
  5:29 Peter and the other **a** replied: 693
  5:40 They called the **a** in and had them flogged. 693
  5:41 The **a** left the Sanhedrin, 3525+3836S
  6: 6 They presented these men to the **a**, 693
  8: 1 the **a** were scattered throughout Judea 693
  8:14 When the **a** in Jerusalem heard 693
  9:27 and brought him to the **a**. 693
  11: 1 The **a** and the brothers 693
  14: 4 with the Jews, others with the **a**. 693
  14:14 the **a** Barnabas and Paul heard of this, 693
  15: 2 to see the **a** and elders about this question. 693
  15: 4 by the church and the **a** and elders, 693
  15: 6 The **a** and elders met to consider this 693

Ac 15:22 Then the **a** and elders, 693
  15:23 The **a** and elders, your brothers, 693
  16: 4 the **a** and elders in Jerusalem for the people 693
Ro 16: 7 They are outstanding among the **a**, 693
1Co 4: 9 that God has put us **a** on display at the end 693
  9: 5 as do the other **a** and the Lord's brothers 693
  12:28 the church God has appointed first of all **a**, 693
  12:29 Are all **a**? 693
  15: 7 he appeared to James, then *to* all the **a**, 693
  15: 9 the **a** and do not deserve to be called 693
2Co 11:13 For such men are **false a**, 6013
  11:13 masquerading as **a** of Christ. 693
Gal 1:17 up to Jerusalem to see those who were **a** 693
  1:19 I saw none *of* the other **a**— 693
Eph 2:20 on the foundation *of* the **a** and prophets, 693
  3: 5 by the Spirit to God's holy **a** and prophets. 693
  4:11 It was he who gave some to be **a**, 693
1Th 2: 6 As **a** of Christ we could have been a burden 693
2Pe 3: 2 by our Lord and Savior *through* your **a**. 693
Jude 1:17 the **a** of our Lord Jesus Christ foretold. 693
Rev 2: 2 tested those who claim to be **a** but are not, 693
  18:20 Rejoice, saints and **a** and prophets! 693
  21:14 on them were the names *of* the twelve **a** of 693

APOSTLES' (5) [APOSTLE]
Ac 2:42 They devoted themselves to the **a'** teaching 693
  4:35 and put it at the **a'** feet, 693
  4:37 the money and put it at the **a'** feet. 693
  5: 2 but brought the rest and put it at the **a'** feet. 693
  8:18 at the laying on of the **a'** hands, 693

APOSTLESHIP (2) [APOSTLE]
Ro 1: 5 we received grace and **a** to call people from 692
1Co 9: 2 For you are the seal of my **a** in the Lord. 692

APOSTOLIC (1) [APOSTLE]
Ac 1:25 to take over this **a** ministry, 692

APOTHECARIES (KJV) See BLENDED, PERFUME-MAKERS

APOTHECARY (KJV) See PERFUMER

APPAIM (2)
1Ch 2:30 The sons of Nadab: Seled and **A**. 691
  2:31 The son of **A**: 691

APPALLED (22)
Lev 26:32 your enemies who live there *will be* **a**. 9037
1Ki 9: 8 all who pass by *will be* **a** and will scoff 9037
2Ch 7:21 all who pass by *will be* **a** and say, 9037
Ezr 9: 3 from my head and beard and sat down **a**. 9037
  9: 4 And I sat there **a** until the evening sacrifice. 9037
Job 17: 8 Upright men *are* **a** at this; 9037
  18:20 Men of the west *are* **a** at his fate; 9037
Ps 40:15 *be* **a** at their own shame. 9037
Isa 52:14 as there were many *who were* **a** at him— 9037
  59:16 he was **a** that there was no one to intervene; 9037
  63: 5 *I was* **a** that no one gave support; 9037
Jer 2:12 *Be* **a** at this, O heavens, 9037
  4: 9 and the prophets *will be* **a**." 9449
  18:16 *will be* **a** and will shake their heads. 9037
  19: 8 all who pass by *will be* **a** and will scoff 9037
  49:17 all who pass by *will be* **a** and will scoff 9037
Eze 4:17 *They will be* **a** at the sight of each other 9037
  26:16 trembling every moment, **a** at you. 9037
  27:35 All who live in the coastlands *are* **a** at you; 9037
  28:19 All the nations who knew you *are* **a** at you; 9037
  32:10 **cause** many peoples **to be a** 9037
Da 8:27 *I was* **a** by the vision; 9037

APPAREL (KJV) See CLOTHES, GARMENTS, ROBES

APPARENTLY (KJV) See CLEARLY

APPEAL (16) [APPEALED, APPEALING, APPEALS]
Dt 15: 9 He may then **a** to the Lord against you, 7924
Job 5: 8 "But if it were I, I *would* **a** to God; 2011
Ps 77:10 Then I thought, "To this I *will* **a**: 2704
Ac 25:11 I **a** to Caesar!" 2126
  25:21 When Paul **made** his **a** to be held over for 2126
  25:25 but *because* he **made** his **a** to 2126
  28:19 I was compelled *to* **a** to Caesar— 2126
1Co 1:10 I **a** to you, brothers, 4151
2Co 5:20 though God *were* **making** his **a** through us. 4155
  8:17 For Titus not only welcomed our **a**, 4155
  10: 1 I **a** to you—I, Paul, 4151
  13:11 Aim for perfection, **listen to** my **a**, 4151
1Th 2: 3 the **a** we make does not spring from error 4155
Phm 1: 9 yet I **a** to you on the basis of love. 4151
  1:10 I **a** to you for my son Onesimus, 4151
1Pe 5: 1 To the elders among you, I **a** 4151

APPEALED (7) [APPEAL]
Ex 5:15 Israelite foremen went and **a** to Pharaoh: 7590
Jos 10: 3 of Jerusalem **a** to Hoham king of Hebron, 8938
Est 2: 4 This advice **a** to the king, 928+3512+6524

Lk 23:20 Pilate **a** to them again. 4715
Ac 25:12 "You have **a** to Caesar. 2126
  26:32 if *he had* not **a** to Caesar." 2126
Ro 11: 2 how *he* **a** to God against Israel: 1961

APPEALING (1) [APPEAL]
2Pe 2:18 by **a** to the lustful desires NIG

APPEALS (1) [APPEAL]
2Sa 19:28 So what right do I have to **make** any more **a** 2410

APPEAR (50) [APPEARANCE, APPEARANCES, APPEARED, APPEARING, APPEARS, REAPPEARS]
Ge 1: 9 and let dry ground **a**." 8011
  27:12 I *would* **a** to be tricking 928+2118+3869+6524
Ex 4: 1 'The Lord *did* not **a** to you'?" 8011
  10:28 Make sure *you* do not **a** before me again! 8011
  10:29 "I will never **a** before you again." 8011
  22: 8 of the house *must* **a** before the judges 7928
  23:15 "No one is to **a** before me empty-handed. 8011
  23:17 "Three times a year all the men *are to* **a** 8011
  34:20 "No one is to **a** before me empty-handed. 8011
  34:23 Three times a year all your men *are to* **a** 8011
  34:24 when you go up three times each year to **a** 8011
Lev 9: 4 For today the Lord *will* **a** to you.'" 8011
  9: 6 that the glory of the Lord *may* **a** to you." 8011
  13: 4 the spot on his skin is white but does not **a** 5260
  13: 7 he *must* **a** before the priest again. 8011
  13:32 and it does not **a** to be more than skin deep, 5260
  14:37 that **a** to be deeper than the surface of 5260
  16: 2 I **a** in the cloud over the atonement cover. 8011
Nu 16:16 "You and all your followers *are to* **a** before 2118
Dt 16:16 Three times a year all your men *must* **a** 8011
  16:16 No man *should* **a** before the Lord empty-handed: 8011
  31:11 to **a** before the Lord your God at 8011
1Sa 3:21 The Lord continued to **a** at Shiloh, 8011
2Sa 9: 2 They called him to **a** before David, NIH
Ezr 2:21 Anyone who failed to **a** 995
Job 19:18 *when I* **a**, they ridicule me. 7756
Ps 102:16 For the Lord will rebuild Zion and **a** 8011
SS 2:12 Flowers **a** on the earth; 8011
Isa 1:12 When you come to **a** before me, 7156+8011
  58: 8 and your healing will quickly **a**; 7541
Eze 16:52 *they* **a** more *righteous* than you. 7405
  16:52 **made** your sisters **a** **righteous**. 7405
Da 7:23 a fourth kingdom *that will* **a** on earth. 10201
  11: 2 Three more kings *will* **a** in Persia, 6641
  11: 3 Then a mighty king *will* **a**, 6641
Hos 6: 3 As surely as the sun rises, he *will* **a**; 3922+4604
Zec 9:14 Then the Lord *will* **a** over them; 8011
Mt 23:28 the outside you *a* to people as righteous but 5743
  24:11 and many false prophets *will* **a** 1586
  24:24 For false Christs and false prophets *will* **a** 1586
  24:30 that time the sign of the Son of Man *will* **a** 5743
Mk 13:22 For false Christs and false prophets *will* **a** 1586
Lk 19:11 that the kingdom of God was going to **a** 428
Ac 5:27 *they* **made** them **a** before the Sanhedrin to 2705
  11:13 how he had seen an angel **a** in his house 2705
  19:30 Paul wanted to **a** before the crowd, NIG
2Co 5:10 For we must all **a** before the judgment seat 5746
Col 3: 4 then you also *will* **a** with him in glory. 5746
Heb 9:24 now *to* **a** for us in God's presence. 1872
  9:28 and *he will* **a** a second time, 3972

APPEARANCE (30) [APPEAR]
Lev 13:55 and if the mildew has not changed its **a**, 6524
1Sa 16: 7 "Do not consider his **a** or his height, 5260
  16: 7 Man looks at the **outward a**, 6524
  16:12 with a fine and handsome features. 6524
2Sa 14:25 a man so highly praised for his **handsome a** 3637
Ecc 8: 1 a man's face and changes its hard **a**. 7156
SS 5:15 His **a** is like Lebanon, choice as its cedars. 5260
Isa 52:14 his **a** was so disfigured beyond that 5260
  53: 2 nothing in his **a** that we should desire him. 5260
La 4: 7 their **a** like sapphires. 1619
Eze 1: 5 *In a* their form was that of a man, 5260
  1:13 The **a** of the living creatures was 5260
  1:16 This was the **a** and structure of the wheels: 5260
  1:28 Like the **a** of a rainbow in the clouds on 5260
  1:28 This was the **a** of the likeness of the glory 5260
  8: 2 up his **a** was as bright as glowing metal. 5260
  10:10 for their **a**, the four of them looked alike; 5260
  10:22 the same **a** as those I had seen by 1952
  40: 3 and I saw a man whose **a** was like bronze; 5260
Da 1:13 Then compare our **a** with that of 5260
  2:31 enormous, dazzling statue, awesome in **a**. 10657
Joel 2: 4 They have the **a** of horses; 5260
Mt 2: 4 You know how to interpret the **a** of the sky, 4725
  28: 3 His **a** was like lightning. 1624
Lk 9:29 he was praying, the **a** of his face changed, 1626
  12:56 to interpret the **a** of the earth and the sky. 4725
Gal 2: 6 God *does* not **judge by external a**— 476+3284+4725
Php 2: 8 And being found **in a** as a man, 5386
Col 2:23 Such regulations indeed have an **a** 3364
Rev 4: 3 the one who sat there had the **a** of jasper 3970

APPEARANCES (1) [APPEAR]
Jn 7:24 Stop judging by mere **a**, 4071

APPEARED (97) [APPEAR]

Ge	2: 5	the field had yet a on the earth and no plant	2118
	12: 7	The LORD a to Abram and said,	8011
	12: 7	the LORD, who had a to him.	8011
	15:17	with a blazing torch a and passed between	2180
	17: 1	the LORD a to him and said,	8011
	18: 1	The LORD a to Abraham near	8011
	26: 2	The LORD a to Isaac and said,	8011
	26:24	That night the LORD a to him and said,	8011
	35: 1	who a to you when you were fleeing	8011
	35: 9	God a to him again and blessed him.	8011
	46:29	As soon as Joseph a before him,	8011
	48: 3	"God Almighty a to me at Luz in the land	8011
Ex	3: 2	the angel of the LORD a to him in flames	8011
	3:16	God of Abraham, Isaac and Jacob—a to me	8011
	4: 5	the God of Jacob—has a to you."	8011
	6: 3	I a to Abraham, to Isaac and to Jacob	8011
	16:14	thin flakes like frost on the ground a on	2180
Lev	9:23	the glory of the LORD a to all the people.	8011
Nu	14:10	Then the glory of the LORD a at the Tent	8011
	16:19	the glory of the LORD a to the entire assembly.	8011
	16:42	and the glory of the LORD a.	8011
	20: 6	and the glory of the LORD a to them.	8011
Dt	31:15	LORD a at the Tent in a pillar of cloud,	8011
	32:17	not known, gods that recently a,	995
Jdg	6:12	When the angel of the LORD a to Gideon,	8011
	13: 3	The angel of the LORD a to her and said,	8011
	13:10	The man who a to me the other day!"	8011
	14:11	When he, as he was given thirty companions.	8011
1Ki	3: 5	At Gibeon the LORD a to Solomon during	8011
	9: 2	the LORD a to him a second time,	8011
	9: 2	as he had a to him at Gibeon.	8011
	11: 9	the God of Israel, who had a to him twice.	8011
2Ki	2:11	suddenly a chariot of fire and horses of fire	
		a and separated the two of them.	2180
2Ch	1: 7	That night God a to Solomon and said	8011
	3: 1	where the LORD had a to his father David.	8011
	7:12	the LORD a to him at night and said:	8011
Jer	31: 3	The LORD a to us in the past, saying:	8011
Eze	1:16	Each a to be made like a wheel intersecting	5260
	1:27	from what a to be his waist up he looked	5260
	8: 2	From what a to be his waist down he was	5260
	37: 8	and flesh a on them and skin covered them,	6590
Da	5: 5	the fingers of a human hand a and wrote on	10485
	8: 1	after the one that had already a to me.	8011
	11: 4	After he has a, his empire will be broken up	6641
Mt	1:20	of the Lord a to him in a dream and said,	5743
	2: 7	from them the exact time the star had a.	5743
	2:13	of the Lord a to Joseph in a dream.	5743
	2:19	of the Lord a in a dream to Joseph in Egypt	5743
	13:26	then the weeds also a.	5743
	17: 3	then there a before them Moses and Elijah,	3972
	27:53	into the holy city and a to many people.	1872
Mk	9: 4	And there a before them Elijah and Moses,	3972
	9: 7	Then a cloud a and enveloped them,	1181
	14:43	Judas, one of the Twelve, a.	4134
	16: 9	he a first to Mary Magdalene,	5743
	16:12	Afterward Jesus a in a different form	5746
	16:14	Later Jesus a to the Eleven	5746
Lk	1:11	Then an angel of the Lord a to him,	3972
	1:80	in the desert until he a publicly to Israel.	345
	2: 9	An angel of the Lord a to them,	2392
	2:13	a great company of the heavenly host a	1181
	7:16	"A great prophet has a among us,"	1586
	9: 8	others that Elijah had a,	5743
	9:31	in glorious splendor,	3972
	9:34	a cloud a and enveloped them,	1181
	22:43	An angel from heaven a to him	3972
	24:34	The Lord has risen and has a to Simon."	3972
Jn	8: 2	At dawn he a again in the temple courts,	4134
	21: 1	Jesus a again to his disciples,	1571+5746
	21:14	now the third time Jesus a to his disciples	5746
Ac	1: 3	He a to them over a period of forty days	3964
	5:36	Some time ago Theudas a,	482
	5:37	the Galilean a in the days of the census	482
	7: 2	The God of glory a to our father Abraham	3972
	7:30	an angel a to Moses in the flames of	3972
	7:35	through the angel who a to him in the bush.	3972
	8:40	however, a at Azotus and traveled about,	2351
	9:17	Jesus, who a to you on the road	3972
	12: 7	an angel of the Lord a and a light shone in	2392
	25: 2	a before him and presented the charges	1872
	25: 7	When Paul a, the Jews who had come down	4134
	26:16	I have a to you to appoint you as a servant	3972
	27:20	When neither sun nor stars a for many days	2210
1Co	15: 5	and that he a to Peter,	3972
	15: 6	he a to more than five hundred of	3972
	15: 7	Then he a to James, then to all the apostles,	3972
	15: 8	and last of all he a to me also,	3972
1Ti	3:16	He a in a body, was vindicated by the Spirit,	5746
Tit	2:11	the grace of God that brings salvation has a	2210
	3: 4	the kindness and love of God our Savior a,	2210
Heb	9:26	But now he has a once for all at the end of	5746
1Jn	1: 2	The life a; we have seen it	5746
	1: 2	which was with the Father and has a to us.	5746
	3: 5	But you know that he a so	5746
	3: 8	The reason the Son of God a was to destroy	5746
Rev	12: 1	A great and wondrous sign a in heaven:	3972
	12: 3	Then another sign a in heaven:	3972

APPEARING (9) [APPEAR]

Ex	16:10	and there was the glory of the LORD a in	8011
Ps	21: 9	the time of your a you will make them like	7156
Zec	5: 5	"Look up and see what this is that is a."	3655
Jn	8:13	a as your own witness;	3455

1Ti	6:14	until the a of our Lord Jesus Christ,	2211
2Ti	1:10	but it has now been revealed through the a	2211
	4: 1	and in view of his a and his kingdom,	2211
	4: 8	but also to all who have longed for his a.	2211
Tit	2:13	the glorious a of our great God and Savior,	2211

APPEARS (24) [APPEAR]

Ge	9:14	the earth and the rainbow a in the clouds,	8011
	9:16	Whenever the rainbow a in the clouds,	2118
Lev	13: 3	the sore has turned white and the sore a to	5260
	13:14	But whenever raw flesh a on him,	8011
	13:19	a white swelling or reddish-white spot a,	2118
	13:20	and if it a to be more than skin deep and	5260
	13:24	or white spot a in the raw flesh of the burn,	2118
	13:25	and it a to be more than skin deep,	5260
	13:30	and if it a to be more than skin deep and	5260
	13:34	and if it has not spread in the skin and a to	5260
Dt	13: 1	a among you and announces to you	7756
Ps	84: 7	till each a before God in Zion.	8011
Pr	27:25	the hay is removed and new growth a and	8011
SS	6:10	Who is this that a like the dawn,	9207
Isa	16:12	When Moab a at her high place,	8011
	60: 2	the LORD rises upon you and his glory a	8011
Na	3:17	but when the sun a they fly away,	2436
Mal	3: 2	Who can stand when he a?	8011
Col	3: 4	When Christ, who is your life, a,	5746
Heb	7:15	if another priest like Melchizedek a,	482
Jas	4:14	You are a mist that a for a little while and	5743
1Pe	5: 4	And when the Chief Shepherd a,	5746
1Jn	2:28	so that when he a we may be confident	5746
	3: 2	But we know that when he a,	5746

APPEASE (2)

Pr	16:14	but a wise man will a it.	4105
Ac	16:39	They came to a them and escorted them	4151

APPERTAIN (KJV) See DUE

APPETITE (6) [APPETITES]

Nu	11: 6	But now we have lost our a;	5883
Pr	16:26	The laborer's a works for him;	5883
Ecc	6: 7	yet his a is never satisfied.	5883
	6: 9	the eye sees than the roving of the a.	5883
Isa	5:14	the grave enlarges its a and opens its mouth	5883
Jer	50:19	his a will be satisfied on the hills	5883

APPETITES (2) [APPETITE]

Isa	56:11	They are dogs with mighty a;	5883
Ro	16:18	but their own a.	3120

APPHIA (1)

Phm	1: 2	to A our sister,	722

APPII (KJV) See APPIUS

APPIUS (1)

Ac	28:15	and they traveled as far as the Forum of A	716

APPLE (7) [APPLES]

Dt	32:10	he guarded him as the a of his eye,	413
Ps	17: 8	Keep me as the a of your eye;	413+1426
Pr	7: 2	guard my teachings as the a of your eye.	413
SS	2: 3	Like an a tree among the trees of	9515
	8: 5	Under the a tree I roused you;	9515
Joel	1:12	the pomegranate, the palm and the a tree—	9515
Zec	2: 8	for whoever touches you touches the a	949

APPLES (3) [APPLE]

Pr	25:11	A word aptly spoken is like a of gold	9515
SS	2: 5	refresh me with a, for I am faint with love.	9515
	7: 8	the fragrance of your breath like a,	9515

APPLIED (7) [APPLY]

2Ki	20: 7	They did so and a it to the boil,	8492
Pr	24:32	I a my heart to what I observed	8883
Ecc	1:17	Then I a myself to the understanding	5989
	8: 9	as I a my mind to everything done under	5989
	8:16	When I a my mind to know wisdom and	5989
Da	4:19	if only the dream a to your enemies	10378
1Co	4: 6	I have a these things to myself	3571

APPLIES (6) [APPLY]

Ex	12:49	The same law a to the native-born and to	2118
	21:31	also a if the bull gores a son or daughter.	6913
Lev	7: 7	"The same law a to both the sin offering	4200
Nu	8:24	"This a to the Levites:	4200
	15:29	One and the same law a	2118
	19:14	the law that a when a person dies in a tent:	NIH

APPLY (6) [APPLIED, APPLIES, APPLYING]

Nu	5:30	the LORD and is to a this entire law	6913
	15:16	The same laws and regulations will a both	2118
Job	5:27	So hear it and a it to yourself."	3359
Pr	22:17	a your heart to what I teach,	8883
	23:12	A your heart to instruction and your ears	995
Isa	38:21	"Prepare a poultice of figs and a it to	5302

APPLYING (2) [APPLY]

Pr	2: 2	and a your heart to understanding,	5742
Heb	9:10	external regulations a until the time of	2130

APPOINT (31) [APPOINTED, APPOINTING, APPOINTMENT, APPOINTS]

Ge	41:34	Let Pharaoh a commissioners over	7212
Ex	18:21	and a them as officials over thousands,	8492
Nu	1:50	a the Levites to be in charge of	7212
	3:10	A Aaron and his sons to serve as priests;	7212
	27:16	a a man over this community	7212
	34:18	And a one leader from each tribe	4374
Dt	1:13	A judges and officials for each	5989
	17:15	be sure to a over you the king	8492+8492
	20: 9	they shall a commanders over it.	7212
Jos	20: 7	A three men from each tribe.	2035
1Sa	2:36	"A me to some priestly office	6202
	8: 5	now a a king to lead us,	8492
2Ki	10: 5	We will not a anyone as king;	4887
1Ch	15:16	the leaders of the Levites to a their brothers	6641
Ezr	7:25	a magistrates and judges	10431
Ne	7: 3	Also a residents of Jerusalem as guards,	6641
Est	2: 3	the king a commissioners in every province	7212
Ps	61: 7	a your love and faithfulness to protect him.	4948
	89:27	I will also a him my firstborn,	5989
	109: 6	A an evil man to oppose him;	7212
Jer	15:	today I a you over nations and kingdoms	7212
	23:32	yet I did not send or a them.	7422
	49:19	Who is the chosen one I will a for this?	7212
	50:44	Who is the chosen one I will a for this?	7212
	51:27	A a commander against her;	7212
Da	6: 1	It pleased Darius to a 120 satraps to rule	10624
Hos	1:11	and they will a one leader and will come	8492
Ac	26:16	I have appeared to you to a you as a servant	4741
1Co	6: 4	a as judges even men of little account in	2767
1Th	5: 9	For God did not a us to suffer wrath but	5502
Tit	1: 5	and a elders in every town,	2770

APPOINTED (150) [APPOINT]

Ge	18:14	at the a time next year and Sarah will have	4595
Ex	5:14	The Israelite foremen a by Pharaoh's slave	8492
	13:10	a at the time year after year.	4595
	23:15	Do this at the a time in the month of Abib,	4595
	31: 6	I have a Oholiab son of Ahisamach,	5989
	34:18	Do this at the a time in the month of Abib,	4595
Lev	16:21	in the care of a man a for the task.	6967
	23: 2	'These are my a feasts,	4595
	23: 2	the a feasts of the LORD,	4595
	23: 4	"'These are the LORD's a feasts,	4595
	23: 4	to proclaim at their a times:	4595
	23:37	("'These are the LORD's a feasts,	4595
	23:44	to the Israelites the a feasts of the LORD.	4595
Nu	1:16	These were the men a from the community,	7924
	3:32	He was a over those who were responsible	7213
	3:36	The Merarites were a to take care of	7213
	9: 2	the Passover at the a time.	4595
	9: 3	Celebrate it at the a time,	4595
	9: 7	with the other Israelites at the a time?"	4595
	9:13	the LORD's offering at the a time.	4595
	10:10	your a feasts and New Moon festivals—	4595
	16: 2	well-known community leaders who had	
		been a members	7951
	28: 2	that you present to me at the a time the food	4595
	29:39	for the LORD at your a feasts:	4595
Dt	1:15	and a them to have authority over you—	5989
Jos	4: 4	the twelve men he had a from the Israelites,	3922
1Sa	8: 1	he a his sons as judges for Israel.	8492
	12: 6	"It is the LORD who a Moses and Aaron	6913
	13:14	a man after his own heart and a him leader	7422
	25:30	concerning him and has a him leader	7422
2Sa	6:21	from his house when he a me ruler over	7422
	7:11	the time I a leaders over my people Israel.	7422
	15: 4	"If only I were a judge in the land!	8492
	17:25	Absalom had a Amasa over the army	8492
	18: 1	and a over them commanders of thousands	8492
1Ki	1:35	I have a him ruler over Israel and Judah."	7422
	12:31	on high places and a priests from all sorts	6913
	13:33	but once more a priests for the high places	6913
2Ki	12:11	to the men a to supervise the work on	7212
	17:32	but they also a all sorts of their own people	6913
	22: 5	to the men a to supervise the work on	7212
	23: 5	the pagan priests a by the kings of Judah	5989
	25:22	of Babylon a Gedaliah son of Ahikam,	7212
	25:23	a Gedaliah as governor,	7212
1Ch	15:17	So the Levites a Heman son of Joel;	6641
	16: 4	He a some of the Levites to minister before	5989
	17:10	the time I a leaders over my people Israel.	7422
	22: 2	and from among them a stonecutters	6641
	23:31	and at New Moon festivals and at a feasts.	4595
	24: 3	for their a order of ministering.	7213
	24:19	This was their a order of ministering	7213
	26:10	his father had a him the first),	8492
2Ch	2: 4	and at the a feasts of the LORD our God.	4595
	8:14	he a the divisions of the priests	6641
	8:14	He also a the gatekeepers by divisions for	NIH
	11:15	And he a his own priests for the high places	6641
	11:22	Rehoboam a Abijah son of Maacah to be	6641
	19: 5	He a judges in the land,	6641
	19: 8	Jehoshaphat a some of the Levites,	6641
	20:21	Jehoshaphat a men to sing to the LORD	6641
	25:16	"Have we a you an adviser to the king?	5989
	31: 3	New Moons and a feasts as written in	4595
	32: 6	He a military officers over the people	5989
	34:10	to the men a to supervise the work on	7212

2Ch	35: 2	*He* a the priests to their duties	6641
	36:23	the earth and he *has* a me to build a temple	7212
Ezr	1: 2	the earth and he *has* a me to build a temple	7212
	3: 5	and the sacrifices for all the a sacred **feasts**	4595
	5:14	whom *he had* a governor,	10682
Ne	5:14	when I *was* a to be their governor in	7422
	6: 7	even a prophets to make this proclamation	6641
	7: 1	and the singers and the Levites **were** a.	7212
	9:17	and in their rebellion a a leader in order	5989
	10:33	New Moon festivals and a **feasts**;	4595
	12:44	At that time men **were** a to be in charge of	7212
Est	8: 2	And Esther a him over Haman's estate.	8492
	8:12	The day a for the Jews to do this in all	285
	9:27	in the way prescribed and at the **time** a.	2375
Job	7: 3	the heritage a *for* them by God."	609
	30:23	to the place a for all the living.	4595
	34:13	Who a him over the earth?	7212
Ps	75: 2	You say, "I choose the **a time**;	4595
	102:13	the **a time** has come.	4595
Pr	8:23	I was a from eternity,	5820
Isa	1:14	and your a **feasts** my soul hates.	4595
Jer	1: 5	I a you as a prophet to the nations."	5989
	6:17	I a watchmen over you and said,	7756
	8: 7	the stork in the sky knows her a **seasons**,	4595
	14:14	not sent them or a them or spoken to them.	7422
	29:26	'The LORD *has* a you priest in place	5989
	33:20	and night no longer come at their a **time**,	6961
	40: 5	of Babylon *has* a over the towns of Judah,	7212
	40: 7	a Gedaliah son of Ahikam **as governor**	7212
	40:11	a Gedaliah son of Ahikam, the son of	
		Shaphan, **as governor**	7212
	41: 2	king of Babylon *had* a **as governor** over	7212
	41:10	of the imperial guard *had* a Gedaliah son	7212
	41:18	king of Babylon *had* a **as governor** over	7212
La	1: 4	for no one comes to her a **feasts**.	4595
	2: 6	LORD *has* made Zion forget her a **feasts**	4595
	2: 7	of the LORD as on the day of an a **feast**.	4595
Eze	21:11	" 'The sword *is* a to be polished,	5989
	36:38	at Jerusalem during her a **feasts**.	4595
	44:24	and my decrees for all my a **feasts**,	4595
	45:17	at all the a **feasts** of the house of Israel.	4595
	46: 9	the LORD at the a **feasts**, whoever enters	4595
	46:11	" 'At the festivals and the a **feasts**,	4595
Da	1:11	to the guard whom the chief official *had* a	4948
	2:24	the king *had* a to execute the wise men	10431
	2:49	at Daniel's request the king a Shadrach,	10431
	5:11	a him chief of the magicians, enchanters,	10624
	8:19	the vision concerns the a **time** *of* the end.	4595
	11:27	because an end will still come at the a **time**.	4595
	11:29	the a **time** he will invade the South again,	4595
	11:35	for it will still come at the a **time**.	4595
Hos	2:11	her Sabbath days—all her a **feasts**.	4595
	6:11	"Also for you, Judah, a harvest *is* a.	8883
	9: 5	on the day of your a **feasts**,	4595
	12: 9	as in the days of your a **feasts**.	4595
Mic	6: 9	"Heed the rod and the One who a it.	3585
Hab	1:12	*you have* a them to execute judgment;	8492
	2: 3	For the revelation awaits an a **time**;	4595
Zep	2: 2	the a **time** arrives and that day sweeps on	2976
	3:18	"The sorrows for the a **feasts** I will remove	4595
Mt	8:29	to torture us before the a time?"	NIG
	26:18	My a time is near.	NIG
Mk	3:14	*He* a twelve—designating them apostles—	4472
	3:16	These are the twelve he a:	4472
Lk	10: 1	After this the Lord a seventy-two others	344
	12:14	who a me a judge or an arbiter	2770
	19:12	to a distant country *to have* himself a king	3284
Jn	15:16	and a you to go and bear fruit—	5502
Ac	3:20	*who has been* a for you—even Jesus.	4741
	10:42	the one whom God a as judge of the living	3988
	12:21	*On* a day Herod,	5414
	13:48	and all who were a for eternal life believed.	5435
	14:23	Paul and Barnabas a elders for them	5936
	15: 2	So Paul and Barnabas *were* a,	5435
	17:31	the world with justice by the man *he has* a.	3988
Ro	9: 9	"At the time I will return,	4047
1Co	4: 5	Therefore judge nothing before the a time;	NIG
	12:28	in the church God *has* a first of all apostles,	5502
Eph	1:22	and a him *to be* head over everything for	1443
1Ti	2: 7	And for this purpose I *was* a a herald and	5502
2Ti	1:11	And of this gospel I *was* a a herald and	5502
Tit	1: 3	at his a **season** he brought his word to light	2789
Heb	1: 2	whom *he* a heir of all things,	5502
	3: 2	He was faithful *to* the one who a him,	4472
	5: 1	among men and *is* a to represent them	2770
	7:28	which came after the law, a the Son,	NIG
	8: 3	Every high priest *is* a to offer both gifts	2770

APPOINTING (2) [APPOINT]

Ezr	3: 8	a Levites twenty years of age and older	6641
1Ti	1:12	considered me faithful, a me to his service.	5502

APPOINTMENT (1) [APPOINT]

2Ch	31:13	by a of King Hezekiah and Azariah	5152

APPOINTS (2) [APPOINT]

Jer	31:35	he who a the sun to shine by day,	5989
Heb	7:28	law a as high priests men who are weak;	2770

APPORTIONED (2) [PORTION]

Dt	4:19	the LORD your God *has* a to all	2745
Eph	4: 7	of us grace has been given as Christ a it.	3586

APPRAISED (1)

Job	28:27	then he looked at wisdom and a it;	6218

APPREHEND (KJV) See ARREST, TAKE, TOOK

APPREHENSIVE (1)

Lk	21:26	a of what is coming on the world,	4660

APPROACH (21) [APPROACHED, APPROACHES, APPROACHING]

Ex	19:22	Even the priests, who a the LORD,	5602
	24: 2	but Moses alone *is* to a the LORD;	5602
	28:43	or a the altar to minister in the Holy Place,	5602
	30:20	when they a the altar to minister	5602
Lev	10: 3	" 'Among *those who* a me I will show	
		myself holy;	7940
	18: 6	" 'No one *is* to a any close relative	7928
	18:19	not a woman to have sexual relations	7928
	21:23	not go near the curtain or a the altar,	5602
1Sa	15: 5	As you a the town,	995
Job	31:37	like a prince I would a him.)—	7928
	36:33	even the cattle make known *its* a.	6590
	40:19	yet his Maker *can* a him with his sword.	5602
	41:13	Who *would* a him with a bridle?	995
Ecc	12: 1	the days of trouble come and the years a	5595
Isa	5:19	*Let it* a, let the plan of the Holy One	7928
	41: 5	*They* a and come forward;	7928
La	2: 3	He has withdrawn his right hand at the a *of*	7156
Eze	42:13	where the priests who a the LORD will eat	7940
Hos	7: 6	*they* a him with intrigue.	7928
Eph	3:12	through faith in him *we may* a God	2400+4643
Heb	4:16	then a the throne of grace with confidence,	4665

APPROACHED (45) [APPROACH]

Ge	18:23	Then Abraham a him and said:	5602
	33: 3	the ground seven times as he a his brother.	5602
	33: 6	Then the maidservants and their children a	5602
Ex	14:10	As Pharaoh a, the Israelites looked up,	7928
	20:21	while Moses a the thick darkness	5602
	32:19	When Moses a the camp and saw the calf	7928
	40:32	the Tent of Meeting or a the altar,	7928
Lev	16: 1	two sons of Aaron who died when they a	7928
Nu	3:38	Anyone else who a the sanctuary was to	7929
	27: 1	Milcah and Tirzah. *They* a	7928
Dt	22:14	"I married this woman, but when *I* a her,	7928
Jos	8:11	up and the city and arrived in front of it.	5602
	14: 6	Now the men of Judah a Joshua at Gilgal,	5602
	21: 1	the family heads of the Levites a Eleazar	5602
Jdg	3:20	Ehud then a him while he was sitting alone	
			448+995
	9:52	*as* he a the entrance to the tower to set it	5602
	14: 5	As *they* a the vineyards of Timnah,	995+6330
	15:14	As he a Lehi, the Philistines came	995+6330
Ru	3: 7	Ruth a quietly, uncovered his feet	995
1Sa	9:18	Saul a Samuel in the gateway and asked,	5602
	17:40	with his sling in his hand, a the Philistine.	5602
	30:21	As David and his men a, he greeted them.	5602
2Sa	15: 5	whenever anyone a him to bow down	7928
	16: 5	As King David a Bahurim,	995+6330
2Ki	16:12	he a it and presented offerings on it.	7928
1Ch	21:21	David a, and when Araunah looked	995+6330
Est	5: 2	Esther a and touched the tip of the scepter.	7928
Jer	42: 1	the people from the least to the greatest a	5602
Da	3:26	then a the opening of the blazing furnace	10638
	7:13	*He* a the Ancient of Days and was led	10413
	7:16	I a one of those standing there	10638
Mt	14:15	As evening a, the disciples came to him	1181
	17:14	a man a Jesus and knelt before him.	4665
	21: 1	As *they* a Jerusalem and came	1581
	21:34	When the harvest time a,	1581
	27:57	As evening a, there came a rich man	1181
Mk	11: 1	As *they* a Jerusalem and came	1581
	15:42	So as evening a,	1181
Lk	7:12	As *he* a the town gate,	1581
	9:51	the time a for him to be taken up to heaven,	5230
	18:35	As Jesus a Jericho, a blind man was sitting	1581
	19:29	As *he* a Bethphage and Bethany at	1581
	19:41	As *he* a Jerusalem and saw the city,	1581
	22:47	*He* a Jesus to kiss him,	1581
	24:28	As *they* a the village	1581

APPROACHES (5) [APPROACH]

Lev	20:16	" 'If a woman a an animal	7928
Nu	3:10	anyone else who a the sanctuary must	7929
Dt	23:11	But as evening a he is to wash himself,	7155
2Ki	11: 8	Anyone *who* a your ranks must be put	448+995
Est	4:11	woman who a the king in the inner court	448+995

APPROACHING (10) [APPROACH]

Ge	24:63	and as he looked up, he saw camels a.	995
Lev	18:14	by a his wife to have sexual relations;	7928
2Ki	9:17	on the tower in Jezreel saw Jehu's troops a	995
Lk	22: 1	called the Passover, *was* a,	1581
Jn	1:47	When Jesus saw Nathanael a,	2262+4639
	6:19	they saw Jesus a the boat,	1181+1584
Ac	10: 9	as they were on their journey and a	1581
	27:27	the sailors sensed they *were* a land.	4642
Heb	10:25	and all the more as you see the Day a.	1581
1Jn	5:14	This is the confidence we have **in** a God;	4639

APPRAISED (1)

APPROPRIATE (2)

Ge	49:28	giving each the blessing a *to* him.	3869
1Ti	2:10	a for women who profess to worship God.	4560

APPROVAL (8) [APPROVE]

Jdg	18: 6	Your journey has the LORD's a."	5790
Est	2:17	and she won his favor and a more than any	2876
Hos	8: 4	they choose princes without *my* a."	3359
Jn	6:27	the Father has placed his seal of a.	NIG
Ac	8: 1	And Saul was there, **giving** a to his death.	5306
	22:20	I stood there **giving** my a and guarding	5306
1Co	11:19	to show which of you have God's a.	1511
Gal	1:10	**trying to win the** a of	4275

APPROVE (7) [APPROVAL, APPROVED, APPROVES]

1Sa	29: 6	but the rulers don't a of you.	928+3202+6524
Ps	49:13	and of their followers, *who* a their sayings.	8354
Lk	11:48	that *you* a of what your forefathers did;	5306
Ro	1:32	but also a of those who practice them.	5306
	2:18	if you know his will and a *of*	1507
	12: 2	be able *to* **test and** a what God's will is—	1507
1Co	16: 3	of introduction to the men *you* a	1507

APPROVED (5) [APPROVE]

Ro	14:18	in this way is pleasing to God and a	1511
	16:10	Greet Apelles, **tested and** a in Christ.	1511
2Co	10:18	the one who commends himself who is a,	1511
1Th	2: 4	we speak as men a by God to be entrusted	1507
2Ti	2:15	to present yourself to God as one a,	1511

APPROVES (1) [APPROVE]

Ro	14:22	not condemn himself by what *he* a.	1507

APRONS (1)

Ac	19:12	and a that had touched him were taken to	4980

APT (1) [APTITUDE, APTLY]

Pr	15:23	A man finds joy in **giving an** a reply	5101+7023

APTITUDE (1) [APT]

Da	1: 4	**showing** a for every kind of learning,	8505

APTLY (1) [APT]

Pr	25:11	A word a spoken is like apples of gold	698+6584

AQUEDUCT (3)

2Ki	18:17	and stopped at the a *of* the Upper Pool,	9498
Isa	7: 3	at the end of the a *of* the Upper Pool,	9498
	36: 2	When the commander stopped at the a *of*	9498

AQUILA (7)

Ac	18: 2	There he met a Jew named A,	217
	18:18	accompanied by Priscilla and A.	217
	18:19	where Paul left **Priscilla and** A.	1697S
	18:26	When Priscilla and A heard him,	217
Ro	16: 3	Greet Priscilla and A,	217
1Co	16:19	A and Priscilla greet you warmly in	217
2Ti	4:19	and A and the household of Onesiphorus.	217

AR (6)

Nu	21:15	the ravines that lead to the site of A and lie	6840
	21:28	It consumed A of Moab,	6840
Dt	2: 9	I have given A to the descendants of Lot as	6840
	2:18	to pass by the region of Moab at A.	6840
	2:29	and the Moabites, who live in A,	6840
Isa	15: 1	A *in* Moab is ruined, destroyed in a night!	6840

ARA (1)

1Ch	7:38	Jephunneh, Pispah and A.	736

ARAB (4) [ARABIA, ARABIAN, ARABS]

Jos	15:52	A, Dumah, Eshan,	742
Ne	2:19	and Geshem the A heard about it,	6861
	6: 1	Geshem the A and the rest of our enemies	6861
Isa	13:20	no A will pitch his tent there,	6862

ARABAH (28) [BETH ARABAH]

Dt	1: 1	east of the Jordan—that is, in the A—	6858
	1: 7	go to all the neighboring peoples in the A,	6858
	2: 8	We turned from the A road,	6858
	3:17	Its western border was the Jordan in the A,	6858
	3:17	from Kinnereth to the Sea of the A	6858
	4:49	and included all the A east of the Jordan,	6858
	4:49	as far as the Sea of the A,	6858
	11:30	of those Canaanites living in the A in	6858
Jos	3:16	the A (the Salt Sea) was completely cut off.	6858
	8:14	at a certain place overlooking the A.	6858
	11: 2	in the A south of Kinnereth,	6858
	11:16	of Goshen, the western foothills, the A and	6858
	12: 1	including all the eastern side of the A:	6858
	12: 3	the eastern A from the Sea of Kinnereth to	6858
	12: 3	the Sea of Kinnereth to the Sea of the A	6858
	12: 8	the western foothills, the A,	6858
	18:18	of Beth Arabah and on down into the A.	6858
1Sa	23:24	in the A south of Jeshimon.	6858
2Sa	2:29	and his men marched through the A.	6858

2Sa 4: 7 they traveled all night by way of the A. 6858
2Ki 14:25 from Lebo Hamath to the Sea of the A, 6858
    25: 4 They fled toward the A, 6858
Isa 33: 9 Sharon is like the A, 6858
Jer 39: 4 and headed toward the A. 6858
    52: 7 They fled toward the A, 6858
Eze 47: 8 and goes down into the A, 6858
Am 6:14 from Lebo Hamath to the valley of the A." 6858
Zec 14:10 south of Jerusalem, will become like the A. 6858

ARABIA (8) [ARAB]

2Ch 9:14 Also all the kings of A and the governors of 6851
Isa 21:13 An oracle concerning A: 6851
    21:13 who camp in the thickets of A, 6851
Jer 25:24 all the kings of A and all the kings of 6851
Eze 27:21 " 'A and all the princes 6851
    30: 5 Cush and Put, Lydia and all A, 6851
Gal 1:17 into A and later returned to Damascus. 728
    4:25 for Mount Sinai in A and corresponds to 728

ARABIAN (1) [ARAB]

1Ki 10:15 and from all the A kings and the governors 6851

ARABS (6) [ARAB]

2Ch 17:11 and the A brought him flocks; 6861
    21:16 the Philistines and of the A who lived near 6861
    22: 1 who came with the A into the camp, 6861
    26: 7 the Philistines and against the A who lived 6861
Ne 4: 7 But when Sanballat, Tobiah, the A, 6861
Ac 2:11 to Judaism); Cretans and A— 732

ARAD (5)

Nu 21: 1 When the Canaanite king of A, 6866
    33:40 The Canaanite king of A, 6866
Jos 12:14 the king of Hormah one the king of A one 6866
Jdg 1:16 of the Desert of Judah in the Negev near A. 6866
1Ch 8:15 Zebadiah, A, Eder, 6865

ARAH (5)

Jos 13: 4 from A of the Sidonians as far as Aphek, 6869
1Ch 7:39 The sons of Ulla: A, Hanniel and Rizia. 783
Ezr 2: 5 of A 775 783
Ne 6:18 he was son-in-law to Shecaniah son of A, 783
    7:10 of A 652 783

ARAM (69) [ARAM MAACAH, ARAM NAHARAIM, ARAM ZOBAH, ARAMAIC, ARAMEAN, ARAMEANS, PADDAN ARAM]

Ge 10:22 Elam, Asshur, Arphaxad, Lud and A. 806
    10:23 The sons of A: Uz, Hul, Gether and 806
    22:21 Buz his brother, Kemuel (the father of A), 806
Nu 23: 7 "Balak brought me from A, 806
Jdg 3:10 of A into the hands of Othniel, 806
    10: 6 and the gods of A, the gods of Sidon, 806
2Sa 15: 8 at Geshur in A, I made this vow: 806
1Ki 11:25 So Rezon ruled in A and was hostile 806
    15:18 the son of Hezion, the king of A, 806
    19:15 you get there, anoint Hazael king over A. 806
    20: 1 of A mustered his entire army. 806
    20:20 of A escaped on horseback with some 806
    20:22 the king of A will attack you again." 806
    20:23 the officials of the king of A advised him, 806
    22: 1 For three years there was no war between A 806
    22: 3 to retake it from the king of A?" 806
    22:31 the king of A had ordered his thirty-two chariot commanders, 806
2Ki 5: 1 of the army of the king of A. 806
    5: 1 the LORD had given victory to A. 806
    5: 2 from A had gone out and had taken captive 806
    5: 5 "By all means, go," the king of A replied. 806
    6: 8 Now the king of A was at war with Israel. 806
    6:11 This enraged the king of A. 806
    6:23 from A stopped raiding Israel's territory. 806
    6:24 of A mobilized his entire army 806
    8: 7 and Ben-Hadad king of A was ill. 806
    8: 9 of A has sent me to ask, 806
    8:13 that you will become king of A," 806
    8:28 against Hazael king of A at Ramoth Gilead. 806
    8:29 in his battle with Hazael king of A. 806
    9:14 against Hazael king of A. 806
    9:15 in the battle with Hazael king of A.) 806
    12:17 About this time Hazael king of A went up 806
    12:18 and he sent them to Hazael king of A, 806
    13: 3 under the power of Hazael king of A 806
    13: 4 the king of A was oppressing Israel. 806
    13: 5 and they escaped from the power of A. 806
    13: 7 of A had destroyed the rest and made them 806
    13:17 the arrow of victory over A!" 806
    13:19 then you would have defeated A 806
    13:22 of A oppressed Israel throughout the reign 806
    13:24 Hazael king of A died, 806
    15:37 the LORD began to send Rezin king of A 806
    16: 5 of A and Pekah son of Remaliah king 806
    16: 6 Rezin king of A recovered Elath for Aram 806
    16: 6 Rezin king of Aram recovered Elath for A 806
    16: 7 of the hand of the king of A and of the king 806
1Ch 1:17 Elam, Asshur, Arphaxad, Lud and A. 806
    1:17 The sons of A: 806
    2:23 (But Geshur and A captured Havvoth Jair, 806
    7:34 Ahi, Rohgah, Hubbah and A. 806
2Ch 16: 2 and sent it to Ben-Hadad king of A, 806
    16: 7 "Because you relied on the king of A and 806

2Ch 16: 7 the king of A has escaped from your hand. 806
    18:30 of A had ordered his chariot commanders, 806
    22: 5 against Hazael king of A at Ramoth Gilead. 806
    22: 6 in his battle with Hazael king of A. 806
    24:23 the army of A marched against Joash; 806
    28: 5 over to the king of A. 806
    28:23 gods of the kings of A have helped them, 806
Isa 7: 1 of A and Pekah son of Remaliah king 806
    7: 2 "A has allied itself with Ephraim"; 806
    7: 4 of Rezin and A and of the son of Remaliah. 806
    7: 5 A, Ephraim and Remaliah's son have plotted your ruin, 806
    7: 8 for the head of A is Damascus, 806
    17: 3 of A will be like the glory of the Israelites," 806
Eze 27:16 " 'A did business with you because 806
Hos 12:12 Jacob fled to the country of A; 806
Am 1: 5 The people of A will go into exile to Kir," 806

ARAM MAACAH (1) [ABEL BETH MAACAH, ARAM, MAACAH]

1Ch 19: 6 Aram Naharaim, A and Zobah. 807

ARAM NAHARAIM (5) [ARAM]

Ge 24:10 for A and made his way to 808
Dt 23: 4 from Pethor in A to pronounce 808
Jdg 3: 8 Cushan-Rishathaim king of A, to whom 808
1Ch 19: 6 chariots and charioteers from A, 808
Ps 60: T he fought A and Aram Zobah, 808

ARAM ZOBAH (1) [ARAM, ZOBAH]

Ps 60: T he fought Aram Naharaim and A, 809

ARAMAIC (13) [ARAM]

2Ki 18:26 "Please speak to your servants in A, 811
Ezr 4: 7 The letter was written in A script and in 811
    4: 7 in Aramaic script and in the A language. 811
Isa 36:11 "Please speak to your servants in A, 811
Da 2: 4 the astrologers answered the king in A, 811
Jn 5: 2 which in A is called Bethesda 1580
    19:13 Stone Pavement (which in A is Gabbatha). 1580
    19:17 the Skull (which in A is called Golgotha). 1580
    19:20 and the sign was written in A, 1580
    20:16 She turned toward him and cried out in A, 1580
Ac 21:40 he said to them in A: 1365+1579
    22: 2 they heard him speak to them in A, 1365+1579
    26:14 and I heard a voice saying to me in A, 1365+1579

ARAMEAN (17) [ARAM]

Ge 25:20 of Bethuel the A from Paddan Aram 812
    25:20 and sister of Laban the A. 812
    28: 5 to Laban son of Bethuel the A, 812
    31:20 Jacob deceived Laban the A by 812
    31:24 to Laban the A in a dream at night and said 812
Dt 26: 5 "My father was a wandering A, 812
2Sa 8: 6 He put garrisons in the A kingdom 806
    10: 6 they hired twenty thousand A foot soldiers 806
1Ki 20:29 on the A foot soldiers in one day. 806
2Ki 5:20 on Naaman, this A, by not accepting 812
    7:10 into the A camp and not a man was there— 806
    7:14 and the king sent them after the A army. 806
    24: 2 The LORD sent Babylonian, A, 806
1Ch 7:14 through his A concubine. 812
    18: 6 He put garrisons in the A kingdom 806
2Ch 24:24 the A army had come with only a few men, 806
Jer 35:11 to escape the Babylonian and A armies.' 806

ARAMEANS (48) [ARAM]

2Sa 8: 5 When the A of Damascus came 806
    8: 6 and the A became subject to him 806
    10: 8 the A of Zobah and Rehob and the men 806
    10: 9 in Israel and deployed them against the A. 806
    10:11 Joab said, "If the A are too strong for me, 806
    10:13 with him advanced to fight the A, 806
    10:14 the Ammonites saw that the A were fleeing, 806
    10:15 A saw that they had been routed by Israel, 806
    10:16 Hadadezer had A brought from beyond 806
    10:17 The A formed their battle lines 806
    10:19 So the A were afraid to help 806
1Ki 10:29 to all the kings of the Hittites and of the A. 806
    20:20 At that, the A fled, 806
    20:21 and inflicted heavy losses on the A. 806
    20:26 The next spring Ben-Hadad mustered the A 806
    20:27 while the A covered the countryside. 806
    20:28 the A think the LORD is a god of the hills 806
    22:11 the A until they are destroyed.' " 806
    22:35 up in his chariot facing the A. 806
2Ki 6: 9 because the A are going down there." 806
    7: 4 over to the camp of the A and surrender. 806
    7: 5 up and went to the camp of the A, 806
    7: 6 for the Lord had caused the A to hear 806
    7:12 "I will tell you what the A have done to us. 806
    7:15 and equipment the A had thrown away 806
    7:16 and plundered the camp of the A. 806
    8:28 The A wounded Joram; 812
    8:29 from the wounds the A had inflicted on him 812
    9:15 from the wounds the A had inflicted on him 812
    13:17 You will completely destroy the A 806
1Ch 18: 5 When the A of Damascus came 806
    18: 6 and the A became subject to him 806
    19:10 in Israel and deployed them against the A. 806
    19:12 Joab said, "If the A are too strong for me, 806
    19:14 with him advanced to fight the A, 806
    19:15 the Ammonites saw that the A were fleeing, 806

1Ch 19:16 A saw that they had been routed by Israel, 806
    19:16 and had A brought from beyond the River, 806
    19:17 David formed his lines to meet the A 806
    19:19 So the A were not willing to help 806
2Ch 1:17 to all the kings of the Hittites and of the A. 806
    18:10 the A until they are destroyed.' " 806
    18:34 up in his chariot facing the A until evening. 806
    22: 5 The A wounded Joram; 812
    24:25 When the A withdrew, 4392S
    28: 5 The A defeated him, and took many NIH
Isa 9:12 A from the east and Philistines from 806
Am 9: 7 the Philistines from Caphtor and the A 806

ARAMITESS (KJV) See ARAMEAN

ARAN (2)

Ge 36:28 The sons of Dishan: Uz and A. 814
1Ch 1:42 The sons of Dishan: Uz and A. 814

ARARAT (4)

Ge 8: 4 the ark came to rest on the mountains of A. 827
2Ki 19:37 and they escaped to the land of A. 827
Isa 37:38 and they escaped to the land of A. 827
Jer 51:27 A, Minni and Ashkenaz. 827

ARAUNAH (17)

2Sa 24:16 then at the threshing floor of A the Jebusite. 779
    24:18 to the LORD on the threshing floor of A 779
    24:20 When A looked and saw the king 779
    24:21 A said, "Why has my lord the king come 779
    24:22 A said to David, "Let my lord the king take 779
    24:23 O king, A gives all this to the king." 779
    24:23 A also said to him, "May the LORD 779
    24:24 But the king replied to A, "No, 779
1Ch 21:15 then standing at the threshing floor of A 821
    21:18 to the LORD on the threshing floor of A 821
    21:20 While A was threshing wheat, 821
    21:21 and when A looked and saw him, 821
    21:23 A said to David, "Take it! 821
    21:24 But King David replied to A, "No, 821
    21:25 So David paid A six hundred shekels 821
    21:28 on the threshing floor of A the Jebusite, 821
2Ch 3: 1 on the threshing floor of A the Jebusite, 821

ARBA (3) [KIRIATH ARBA]

Jos 14:15 to be called Kiriath Arba after A, NIH
    15:13 (A was the forefather of Anak.) NIH
    21:11 (A was the forefather of Anak.) NIH

ARBAH (KJV) See KIRIATH ARBA

ARBATHITE (2)

2Sa 23:31 Abi-Albon the A, Azmaveth 6863
1Ch 11:32 from the ravines of Gaash, Abiel the A, 6863

ARBEL See BETH ARBEL

ARBITE (1)

2Sa 23:35 Hezro the Carmelite, Paarai the A, 750

ARBITER (1) [ARBITRATE]

Lk 12:14 who appointed me a judge or an a 3537

ARBITRATE (1) [ARBITER]

Job 9:33 only there were someone to a between us, 3519

ARCHANGEL (2) [ANGEL]

1Th 4:16 the voice of the a and with the trumpet call 791
Jude 1: 9 But even the a Michael, 791

ARCHELAUS (1)

Mt 2:22 when he heard that A was reigning in Judea 793

ARCHER (4) [ARCHERS]

Ge 21:20 He lived in the desert and became an a 8009+8050
Pr 26:10 Like an a who wounds 8043
Jer 51: 3 Let not the a string his bow, 2005
Am 2:15 The a will not stand his ground, 8008+9530

ARCHERS (9) [ARCHER]

Ge 49:23 With bitterness a attacked him; 1251+2932
1Sa 31: 3 and when the a overtook him, 408+928+2021+4619+8008
2Sa 11:24 Then the a shot arrows at your servants 4619
1Ch 10: 3 and when the a overtook him, 928+2021+4619+8008
2Ch 35:23 A shot King Josiah, and he told his officers, 3452
Job 16:13 his a surround me. 8043
Isa 66:19 Libyans and Lydians (famous as a), 5432+8008
Jer 4:29 of horsemen and a every town takes 8008+8227
    50:29 "Summon a against Babylon, 8043

ARCHES (KJV) See PORTICO

ARCHEVITES (KJV) See ERECH

ARCHI, ARCHITE (KJV) See ARKITES

ARCHIPPUS (2)
Col 4:17 Tell A: "See to it that you complete   800
Phm 1: 2 to A our fellow soldier and to the church   800

ARCHITECT (1)
Heb 11:10 whose a and builder is God.   5493

ARCHIVES (3)
Ezr 4:15 made in the a of your predecessors. 10177+10515
      5:17 a search be made in the royal a of Babylon
                                          10103+10148
      6: 1 in the a stored in the treasury at Babylon.
                                          10103+10515

ARCTURUS (KJV) See BEAR

ARD (3) [ARDITE]
Ge 46:21 Ehi, Rosh, Muppim, Huppim and A.   764
Nu 26:40 of Bela through A and Naaman were: 764
     26:40 through A, the Ardite clan;   764

ARDENT (1)
2Co 7: 7 your deep sorrow, your a concern for me,   2419

ARDITE (1) [ARD]
Nu 26:40 through Ard, the A clan;   766

ARDON (1)
1Ch 2:18 These were her sons: Jesher, Shobab and A.   765

ARE (3890) [BE] See Index of Articles Etc.

AREA (55) [AREAS]
Ge 25:18 His descendants settled in the a   NIH
     34: 2 the ruler of that a, saw her,   824
Ex 10:14 in every a of the country in great numbers.   1473
Lev 10:17 the sin offering in the sanctuary a?   5226
     10:18 the goat in the sanctuary a,   NIH
     13:33 must be shaved except for the diseased a,   5999
     16: 3 how Aaron is to enter the sanctuary a: 7731
Nu 8: 2 to light the a in front of the lampstand.' "   NIH
     35: 5 They will have this a as pastureland for   AIT
Jos 13: 5 the a of the Gebalites;   824
     19:46 with the a facing Joppa.   1473
Jdg 19: 1 Now a Levite who lived in a remote a in   3752
     19:18 to a remote a in the hill country of Ephraim   3752
1Sa 9: 4 and through the a around Shalisha,   824
     14:14 in an a of about half an acre.   8441
     23:23 Then I will go with you; if he is in the a,   824
     27: 9 Whenever David attacked an a,   824
2Sa 5: 9 He built up the a around it,   6017
1Ch 5: 8 the a from Aroer to Nebo and Baal Meon,   NIH
Ne 12:29 and from the a of Geba and Azmaveth,   8441
Eze 40: 5 I saw a wall completely surrounding the
                  temple a.   2575+4946
     41: 9 The open a between the side rooms of   4965
     41:11 the open a, one on the north and another on   4965
     41:11 the open a was five cubits wide all around.   4965
     41:20 From the floor to the a above the entrance,   NIH
     42:15 inside the temple a, he led me out by   1074
     42:15 the east gate and measured the a all around: 2257S
     42:20 So he measured the a on all four sides.   2257S
     43:12 All the surrounding a on top of   1473
     43:21 the designated part of the temple a outside   1074
     45: 1 the entire a will be holy.   1473
     45: 1 An a 25,000 cubits long and 10,000   NIH
     45: 6 to give the city as its property an a 5,000   NIH
     45: 7 of the a formed by the sacred district and   NIH
     48:15 "The remaining a, 5,000   AIT
     48:18 What remains of the a,   NIH
     48:21 of the a formed by the sacred portion and   NIH
     48:22 of the city will lie in the center of the a   NIH
     48:22 The a belonging to the prince will lie   NIH
Mt   4:13 the lake in the a of Zebulun and Naphtali—   3990
     21:12 Jesus entered the temple a   2639
     21:15 and the children shouting in the temple a,   2639
Mk   5:10 and again not to send them out of the a.   6001
     11:15 Jesus entered the temple a   2639
Lk   4:37 throughout the surrounding a.   5536
     19:45 Then he entered the temple a   2639
Jn   2:15 and drove all from the temple a,   2639
     8:20 in the temple a near the place where   2639
     10:23 and Jesus was in the temple a walking   2639
     11:56 in the temple a they asked one another,   2639
Ac 16: 3 because of the Jews who lived in that a,   5536
     20: 2 He traveled through that a,   3538
     21:28 the temple a and defiled this holy place."   2639
     21:29 Paul had brought him into the temple a.)   2639
2Co 10:15 our a of activity among you   2834

AREAS (6) [AREA]
Jos 13: 1 and there are still very large a of land to   824

AREA (cont.)
Jos 14: 1 Now these are the a the Israelites received   889S
Jdg 19:29 and sent them into all the a of Israel.   1473
1Ki 20:34 "You may set up your own market a   2575
2Ch 27: 4 and forts and towers in the wooded a.   3091
Eze 48:21 Both these a running the length of   NIH

ARELI (2) [ARELITE]
Ge 46:16 Haggi, Shuni, Ezbon, Eri, Arodi and A.   739
Nu 26:17 through A, the Arelite clan.   739

ARELITE (1) [ARELI]
Nu 26:17 through Areli, the A clan.   740

AREN'T (17) [BE, NOT]
Jdg 8: 2 the gleanings of Ephraim's grapes better
                  than the full grape harvest of Abiezer?   4202
      9:38 A these the men you ridiculed?   4202
     18: 9 A you going to do something?   3120
1Sa 26:14 "A you going to answer me, Abner?"   4202
     26:15 David said, "You're a man, a you?   4202
2Sa 15:27 said to Zadok the priest, "A you a seer?   2022
2Ki 12: 7 "Why a you repairing the damage done to   401
2Ch 28:10 But a you also guilty of sins against   4202
Mt 13:55 and a his brothers James, Joseph,   NIG
     13:56 A all his sisters with us?   1639+4049
     22:16 You a swayed by men,   4024
Mk   6: 3 A his sisters here with us?"   1639+4024
     12:14 You a swayed by men,   4024
     15: 4 "A you going to answer?   4024
Lk 23:39 "A you the Christ?   1639+4049
Jn   8:48 "A we right in saying that you are a
                  Samaritan and demon-possessed?"   4024
Ac 21:38 "A you the Egyptian who started a revolt
                                          1639+4024

ARENA (1)
1Co 4: 9 like men condemned to die in the a.   NIG

AREOPAGITE (KJV) See AREOPAGUS

AREOPAGUS (3)
Ac 17:19 and brought him to a meeting of the A,   740
     17:22 Paul then stood up in the meeting of the A   740
     17:34 a member of the A,   741

ARETAS (1)
2Co 11:32 the governor under King A had the city of   745

ARGOB (5)
Dt   3: 4 the whole region of A,   758
      3:13 of A in Bashan used to be known as a land   758
      3:14 of A as far as the border of the Geshurites   758
1Ki 4:13 as well as the district of A in Bashan   758
2Ki 15:25 along with A and Arieh,   759

ARGUE (10) [ARGUED, ARGUING,
     ARGUMENT, ARGUMENTS]
Jdg 18:25 Danites answered; "Don't a with us,   7754+9048
Job 9:14 How can I find words to a with him?   NIH
     13: 3 to speak to the Almighty and to a my case   3519
     13: 8 Will you a the case for God?   8189
     13: 8 Would he a with useless words,   3519
Pr 25: 9 If you a your case with a neighbor,   8189
Isa 43:26 let us a the matter together;   9149
Jn   6:52 Then the Jews began to a sharply   3481
Ac   6: 9 These men began to a with Stephen,   5184
Ro   3: 7 Someone might a, "If my falsehood
                  enhances God's truthfulness   NIG

ARGUED (3) [ARGUE]
1Ki 3:22 And so they a before the king.   1819
Mk   9:34 on the way they had a about who was   1363
Ac 23: 9 Pharisees stood up and a vigorously.   1372

ARGUING (8) [ARGUE]
2Sa 19: 9 the people were all a with each other,   1906
Job 16: 3 What ails you that you keep on a?   6699
Mk   9:14 around them and the teachers of the law a   5184
      9:16 "What are you a with them about?"   5184
      9:33 "What were you a about on the road?"   1368
Ac 19: 8 a persuasively about the kingdom of God.   1363
     24:12 My accusers did not find me a with anyone   1363
Php 2:14 Do everything without complaining or a,   1369

ARGUMENT (5) [ARGUE]
Job 13: 6 Hear now my a;   9350
Lk   9:46 An a started among the disciples as   1369
Jn   3:25 An a developed between some   2428
Ro   3: 5 (I am using a human a.)   3306
Heb 6:16 and puts an end to all a.   517

ARGUMENTS (10) [ARGUE]
Job 6:25 But what do your a prove?   3519
     23: 4 before him and fill my mouth with a.   9350
     32:12 none of you has answered his a.   609
     32:14 and I will not answer him with your a.   609
Isa 41:21 "Set forth your a," says Jacob's King.   6802S
     59: 4 They rely on empty a and speak lies;   NIH

2Co 10: 5 We demolish a and every pretension   3361
Col 2: 4 that no one may deceive you by
                  fine-sounding a.   4391
2Ti 2:23 to do with foolish and stupid a,   2428
Tit 3: 9 and genealogies and a and quarrels about   2251

ARID (2)
Mt 12:43 through a places seeking rest and does   536
Lk 11:24 through a places seeking rest and does   536

ARIDAI (1)
Est 9: 9 Parmashta, Arisai, A and Vaizatha,   767

ARIDATHA (1)
Est 9: 8 Poratha, Adalia, A,   792

ARIEH (1)
2Ki 15:25 along with Argob and A,   794

ARIEL (5)
Ezr 8:16 So I summoned Eliezer, A, Shemaiah,   791
Isa 29: 1 Woe to you, A, Ariel,   790
     29: 1 Woe to you, Ariel, A,   790
     29: 2 Yet I will besiege A;   790
     29: 7 against A, that attack her and her fortress   790

ARIGHT (1) [RIGHT]
Ps 90:12 Teach us to number our days a,   4026

ARIMATHEA (4)
Mt 27:57 there came a rich man from A,   751
Mk 15:43 Joseph of A, a prominent member of   751
Lk 23:51 the Judean town of A and he was waiting   751
Jn 19:38 of A asked Pilate for the body of Jesus.   751

ARIOCH (6)
Ge 14: 1 A king of Ellasar,   796
     14: 9 Amraphel king of Shinar and A king   796
Da   2:14 When A, the commander of   10070
      2:15 A then explained the matter to Daniel.   10070
      2:24 Then Daniel went to A,   10070
      2:25 A took Daniel to the king at once and said, 10070

ARISAI (1)
Est 9: 9 Parmashta, A, Aridai and Vaizatha,   798

ARISE (33) [RISE]
Nu 23:18 Then he uttered his oracle: "A, Balak,   7756
Jdg 5:12 A, O Barak!   7756
2Ch 6:41 "Now a, O LORD God,   7756
Est 4:14 relief and deliverance for the Jews will a   6641
Ps   3: 7 A, O LORD! Deliver me, O my God!   7756
      7: 6 A, O LORD, in your anger;   7756
      9:19 A, O LORD, let not man triumph;   7756
     10:12 A, LORD! Lift up your hand, O God.   7756
     12: 5 I will now a," says the LORD.   7756
     35: 2 a and come to my aid.   7756
     59: 4 A to help me; look on my plight!   6424
     68: 1 May God a, may his enemies be scattered;   7756
     73:20 a dream when one awakes, so when you a,   6424
    102:13 You will a and have compassion on Zion,   7756
    132: 8 a, O LORD, and come   7756
Pr 31:28 Her children a and call her blessed;   7756
SS   2:10 My lover spoke and said to me, "A,   7756
      2:13 A, come, my darling;   7756
Isa 33:10 "Now will I a," says the LORD.   7756
     60: 1 "A, shine, for your light has come,   7756
Jer 6: 4 A, let us attack at noon!   7756
      6: 5 So a, let us attack at night   7756
     30:21 their ruler will a from among them.   3655
     49:28 "A, and attack Kedar and destroy   7756
     49:31 "A and attack a nation at ease,   7756
La   2:19 A, cry out in the night,   7756
Da   7:24 After them another king will a,   10624
      8:23 a master of intrigue, will a.   6641
     11: 7 "One from her family line will a   6641
     12: 1 Michael, the great prince who protects your
                  people, will a.   6641
Hab 2: 7 Will not your debtors suddenly a?   7756
Ac 20:30 Even from your own number men will a   482
Ro 15:12 one who will a to rule over the nations;   482

ARISEN (1) [RISE]
Dt 13:13 that wicked men have a among you   3655

ARISES (1) [RISE]
Ecc 10: 5 the sort of error that a from a ruler: 3655

ARISTARCHUS (5)
Ac 19:29 The people seized Gaius and A,   752
     20: 4 A and Secundus from Thessalonica,   752
     27: 2 A, a Macedonian from Thessalonica,   752
Col 4:10 fellow prisoner A sends you his greetings,   752
Phm 1:24 And so do Mark, A, Demas and Luke,   752

ARISTOBULUS (1)
Ro 16:10 to the household of A.   755

ARK (219)

Ge	6:14	So make yourself an a of cypress wood;	9310
	6:15	The a is to be 450 feet long,	9310
	6:16	for it and finish the a to within 18 inches of	9310
	6:16	a door in the side of the a and make lower,	9310
	6:18	and you will enter the a—	9310
	6:19	into the a two of all living creatures,	9310
	7: 1	LORD then said to Noah, "Go into the a,	9310
	7: 7	and his sons' wives entered the a to escape	9310
	7: 9	came to Noah and entered the a,	9310
	7:13	the wives of his three sons, entered the a.	9310
	7:15	in them came to Noah and entered the a.	9310
	7:17	the waters increased they lifted the a high	9310
	7:18	the a floated on the surface of the water.	9310
	7:23	and those with him in the a.	9310
	8: 1	the livestock that were with him in the a,	9310
	8: 4	of the seventh month a came to rest on	9310
	8: 6	the window he had made in the a	9310
	8: 9	so it returned to Noah in the a.	9310
	8: 9	and brought it back to himself in the a.	9310
	8:10	and again sent out the dove from the a.	9310
	8:13	Noah then removed the covering from the a	9310
	8:16	"Come out of the a, you and your wife	9310
	8:19	came out of the a, one kind after another.	9310
	9:10	all those that came out of the a with you—	9310
	9:18	of Noah who came out of the a were Shem,	9310
Ex	25:15	poles are to remain in the rings of this a;	778
	25:16	Then put in the a the Testimony,	778
	25:21	the cover on top of the a and put in the ark	778
	25:21	the cover on top of the ark and put in the a	778
	25:22	the two cherubim that are over the a of	778
	26:33	the clasps and place the a of the Testimony	778
	26:34	Put the atonement cover on the a of	778
	30: 6	in front of the curtain that is before the a of	778
	30:26	the a of the Testimony,	778
	31: 7	the a of the Testimony with	778
	35:12	the a with its poles and	778
	37: 1	Bezalel made the a of acacia wood—	778
	37: 5	the poles into the rings on the sides of the a	778
	39:35	the a of the Testimony with its poles and	778
	40: 3	the a of the Testimony in it and shield	778
	40: 3	of the Testimony in it and shield the a with	778
	40: 5	the gold altar of incense in front of the a of	778
	40:20	the Testimony and placed in the a,	778
	40:20	the a and put the atonement cover over it.	778
	40:21	Then he brought the a into the tabernacle	778
	40:21	the shielding curtain and shielded the a of	778
Lev	16: 2	in front of the atonement cover on the a,	778
Nu	3:31	They were responsible for the care of the a,	778
	4: 5	down the shielding curtain and cover the a	778
	7:89	above the atonement cover on the a of	778
	10:33	The a of the covenant of the LORD went	778
	10:35	Whenever the a set out, Moses said,	778
	14:44	nor the a of the LORD's covenant moved	778
Dt	10: 3	So I made the a out of acacia wood	778
	10: 5	and put the tablets in the a I had made,	778
	10: 8	of Levi to carry the a of the covenant of	778
	31: 9	the a of the covenant of the LORD:	778
	31:25	the a of the covenant of the LORD:	778
	31:26	and place it beside the a of the covenant of	778
Jos	3: 3	"When you see the a of the covenant of	778
	3: 4	a thousand yards between you and the a;	2257S
	3: 6	"Take up the a of the covenant and pass on	778
	3: 8	the priests who carry the a of the covenant:	778
	3:11	the a of the covenant of the Lord of all	778
	3:13	And as soon as the priests who carry the a	778
	3:14	the a of the covenant went ahead of them.	778
	3:15	as the priests who carried the a reached	778
	3:17	The priests who carried the a of	778
	4: 5	over before the a of the LORD your God	778
	4: 7	before the a of the covenant of the LORD.	778
	4: 9	the spot where the priests who carried the a	778
	4:10	the a remained standing in the middle of	778
	4:11	the a of the LORD and the priests came to	778
	4:16	the priests carrying the a of the Testimony	778
	4:18	the river carrying the a of the covenant of	778
	6: 4	of rams' horns in front of the a.	778
	6: 6	up the a of the covenant of the LORD	778
	6: 7	with the armed guard going ahead of the a	778
	6: 8	of the LORD's covenant	778
	6: 9	and the rear guard followed the a.	778
	6:11	So he had the a of the LORD carried	778
	6:12	the priests took up the a of the LORD.	778
	6:13	before the a of the LORD and blowing	778
	6:13	of them and the rear guard followed the a	778
	7: 6	to the ground before the a of the LORD,	778
	8:33	on both sides of the a of the covenant of	778
Jdg	20:27	the a of the covenant of God was there,	778
1Sa	3: 3	where the a of God was.	778
	4: 3	the a of the LORD's covenant	778
	4: 4	and they brought back the a of	778
	4: 4	were there with the a of the covenant	778
	4: 5	the a of the LORD's covenant came into	778
	4: 6	that the a of the LORD had come into	778
	4:11	The a of God was captured,	778
	4:13	because his heart feared for the a of God.	778
	4:17	and the a of God has been captured."	778
	4:18	When he mentioned the a of God,	778
	4:19	that the a of God had been captured and	778
	4:21	because of the capture of the a of God and	778
	4:22	for the a of God has been captured."	778
	5: 1	the Philistines had captured the a of God,	778
	5: 2	the a into Dagon's temple and set it	778
	5: 3	on the ground before the a of the LORD!	778
	5: 4	on the ground before the a of the LORD!	778
	5: 7	"The a of the god of Israel must	778

1Sa	5: 8	"What shall we do with the a of the god	778
	5: 8	the a of the god of Israel moved to Gath."	778
	5: 8	So they moved the a of the God of Israel.	778
	5:10	So they sent the a of God to Ekron.	778
	5:10	As the a of God was entering Ekron,	778
	5:10	the a of the god of Israel around to us	778
	5:11	"Send the a of the god of Israel away;	778
	6: 1	When the a of the LORD had been	778
	6: 2	"What shall we do with the a of the LORD?	778
	6: 3	"If you return the a of the god of Israel,	778
	6: 8	the a of the LORD and put it on the cart,	778
	6:11	the a of the LORD on the cart and along	778
	6:13	and when they looked up and saw the a,	778
	6:15	The Levites took down the a of	778
	6:18	on which they set the a of the LORD,	778
	6:19	to death because they had looked into the a	778
	6:20	To whom will the a go up from here?"	NIH
	6:21	"The Philistines have returned the a of	778
	7: 1	of Kiriath Jearim came and took up the a	778
	7: 1	to guard the a of the LORD.	778
	7: 2	that the a remained at Kiriath Jearim,	778
	14:18	Saul said to Ahijah, "Bring the a of God."	778
2Sa	6: 2	of Judah to bring up from there the a	778
	6: 2	between the cherubim that are on the a.	2257S
	6: 3	the a of God on a new cart and brought it	778
	6: 4	with the a of God on it,	778
	6: 6	Uzzah reached out and took hold of the a	778
	6: 7	and he died there beside the a of God.	778
	6: 9	can the a of the LORD ever come to me?"	778
	6:10	to take the a of the LORD to be with him	778
	6:11	The a of the LORD remained in the house	778
	6:12	because of the a of God."	778
	6:12	So David went down and brought up the a	778
	6:13	the a of the LORD had taken six steps,	778
	6:15	the entire house of Israel brought up the a	778
	6:16	the a of the LORD was entering the City	778
	6:17	the a of the LORD and set it in its place	778
	7: 2	while the a of God remains in a tent."	778
	11:11	a and Israel and Judah are staying in tents,	778
	15:24	with him were carrying the a of	778
	15:24	They set down the a of God,	778
	15:25	"Take the a of God back into the city.	778
	15:29	and Abiathar took the a of God back	778
1Ki	2:26	the a of the Sovereign LORD	778
	3:15	stood before the a of the Lord's covenant	778
	6:19	the a of the covenant of the LORD.	778
	8: 1	to bring up the a of the LORD's covenant	778
	8: 3	the priests took up the a,	778
	8: 4	and they brought up the a of the LORD	778
	8: 5	about him were before the a,	778
	8: 6	the a of the LORD's covenant to its place	778
	8: 7	over the place of the a and overshadowed	778
	8: 7	of the ark and overshadowed the a	778
	8: 9	in the a except the two stone tablets	778
	8:21	I have provided a place there for the a,	778
1Ch	6:31	of the LORD after the a came to rest there.	778
	13: 3	Let us bring the a of our God back to us,	778
	13: 5	to bring the a of God from Kiriath Jearim.	778
	13: 6	the a of God the LORD, who is enthroned	778
	13: 6	the a that is called by the Name.	NIH
	13: 7	the a of God from Abinadab's house on	778
	13: 9	Uzzah reached out his hand to steady the a,	778
	13:10	down because he had put his hand on the a.	778
	13:12	can I ever bring the a of God to me?"	778
	13:13	the a to be with him in the City of David.	778
	13:14	The a of God remained with the family	778
	15: 1	a place for the a of God and pitched a tent	778
	15: 2	"No one but the Levites may carry the a	778
	15: 2	the LORD chose them to carry the a of	778
	15: 3	to bring up the a of the LORD to the place	778
	15:12	to consecrate yourselves and bring up the a	778
	15:14	in order to bring up the a of the LORD,	778
	15:15	And the Levites carried the a of God with	778
	15:23	to be doorkeepers for the a.	778
	15:24	to blow trumpets before the a of God.	778
	15:24	also to be doorkeepers for the a.	778
	15:25	the a of the covenant of the LORD from	778
	15:26	the Levites who were carrying the a of	778
	15:27	the Levites who were carrying the a,	778
	15:28	up the a of the covenant of the LORD	778
	15:29	As the a of the covenant of the LORD	778
	16: 1	They brought the a of God and set it inside	778
	16: 4	of the Levites to minister before the a of	778
	16: 6	to blow the trumpets regularly before the a	778
	16:37	before the a of the covenant of the LORD	778
	17: 1	the a of the covenant of the LORD is	778
	22:19	so that you may bring the a of the covenant	778
	28: 2	to build a house as a place of rest for the a	778
	28:18	that spread their wings and shelter the a of	778
2Ch	1: 4	Now David had brought up the a of God	778
	5: 2	to bring up the a of the LORD's covenant	778
	5: 4	the Levites took up the a,	778
	5: 5	up the a and the Tent of Meeting and all	778
	5: 6	about him were before the a,	778
	5: 7	the a of the LORD's covenant to its place	778
	5: 8	over the place of the a and covered the ark	778
	5: 8	over the place of the ark and covered the a	778
	5: 9	from the a, could be seen from in front of	778
	5:10	There was nothing in the a except	778
	6:11	There I have placed the a,	778
	6:41	you and the a of your might.	778
	8:11	of the LORD has entered are holy."	778
	35: 3	the sacred a in the temple that Solomon son	778
Ps	78:61	He sent [the a of] his might into captivity,	NIH
	132: 8	you and the a of your might.	778
Jer	3:16	'The a of the covenant of the LORD.'	778
Mt	24:38	up to the day Noah entered the a;	3066

Lk	17:27	up to the day Noah entered the a.	3066
Heb	9: 4	and the gold-covered a of the covenant.	3066
	9: 4	This a contained the gold jar of manna,	4005S
	9: 5	Above the a were the cherubim of	899S
	11: 7	in holy fear built an a to save his family.	3066
1Pe	3:20	of Noah while the a was being built.	3066
Rev	11:19	and within his temple was seen the a	3066

ARKITE (5) [ARKITES]

2Sa	15:32	Hushai the A was there to meet him,	805
	16:16	Then Hushai the A, David's friend,	805
	17: 5	"Summon also Hushai the A,	805
	17:14	"The advice of Hushai the A is better than	805
1Ch	27:33	Hushai the A was the king's friend.	805

ARKITES (3) [ARKITE]

Ge	10:17	Hivites, A, Sinites,	6909
Jos	16: 2	over to the territory of the A in Ataroth,	805
1Ch	1:15	Hivites, A, Sinites,	6909

ARM (77) [ARMED, ARMIES, ARMLETS, ARMOR, ARMOR-BEARER, ARMOR-BEARERS, ARMORY, ARMRESTS, ARMS, ARMY]

Ex	6: 6	with an outstretched a and with mighty acts	2432
	15:16	By the power of your a they will be as still	2432
Nu	11:23	"Is the LORD's a too short?	3338
	20:11	Then Moses raised his a and struck	3338
	31: 3	"A some of your men to go to war against	2741
	32:17	But we are ready to a ourselves and go	2741
	32:20	if you will a yourselves before	2741
Dt	4:34	by a mighty hand and an outstretched a.	2432
	5:15	with a mighty hand and an outstretched a.	2432
	7:19	the mighty hand and outstretched a,	2432
	9:29	great power and your outstretched a."	2432
	11: 2	his mighty hand, his outstretched a;	2432
	26: 8	with a mighty hand and an outstretched a,	2432
	33:20	tearing at a or head.	2432
2Sa	1:10	that was on his head and the band on his a	2432
1Ki	8:42	mighty hand and your outstretched a—	2432
2Ki	5:18	to bow down and he is leaning on my a	3338
	7: 2	on whose a the king was leaning said to	3338
	7:17	on whose a he leaned in charge of the gate,	3338
	17:36	with mighty power and outstretched a,	2432
2Ch	6:32	and your outstretched a—	2432
	32: 8	With him is only the a of flesh,	2432
Job	26: 2	How you have saved the a that is feeble!	2432
	31:22	then let my a fall from the shoulder,	4190
	35: 9	for relief from the a of the powerful.	2432
	38:15	and their upraised a is broken.	2432
	40: 9	Do you have an a like God's,	2432
Ps	10:15	Break the a of the wicked and evil man;	2432
	44: 3	nor did their a bring them victory;	2432
	44: 3	it was your right hand, your a,	2432
	77:15	With your mighty a you redeemed your people,	2432
	79:11	of your a preserve those condemned to die.	2432
	89:10	with your strong a you scattered your enemies.	2432
	89:13	Your a is endued with power;	2432
	89:21	surely my a will strengthen him.	2432
	98: 1	and his holy a have worked salvation	2432
	136:12	with a mighty hand and outstretched a;	2432
SS	2: 6	His left a is under my head,	NIH
	2: 6	and his right a embraces me.	NIH
	8: 3	His left a is under my head	NIH
	8: 3	and his right a embraces me.	NIH
	8: 6	like a seal on your a;	2432
Isa	17: 5	and harvests the grain with his a—	2432
	30:30	and will make them see his a coming down	2432
	30:32	in battle with the blows of his a.	NIH
	40:10	and his a rules for him.	2432
	44:12	he forges it with the might of his a.	2432
	48:14	his a will be against the Babylonians.	2432
	50: 2	Was my a too short to ransom you?	3338
	51: 5	and my a will bring justice to the nations.	2432
	51: 5	to me and wait in hope for my a.	2432
	51: 9	O a of the LORD;	2432
	52:10	The LORD will lay bare his holy a in	2432
	53: 1	the a of the LORD been revealed?	2432
	59: 1	a of the LORD is not too short to save,	3338
	59:16	so his own a worked salvation for him,	2432
	60: 4	and your daughters are carried on the a,	7396
	62: 8	by his right hand and by his mighty a:	2432
	63: 5	so my own a worked salvation for me,	2432
	63: 5	who sent his glorious a of power to be	2432
	66:12	you will nurse and be carried on her a	7396
Jer	21: 5	with an outstretched hand and a mighty a	2432
	27: 5	and outstretched a I made the earth	2432
	32:17	by your great power and outstretched a.	2432
	32:21	by a mighty hand and an outstretched a and	274
	48:25	her a is broken," declares the LORD.	2432
Eze	4: 7	of Jerusalem and with bared a prophesy	2432
	17: 9	not take a strong a or many people to pull it	2432
	20:33	with a mighty hand and an outstretched a	2432
	20:34	with a mighty hand and an outstretched a	2432
	30:21	I have broken the a of Pharaoh king	2432
	30:22	the good a as well as the broken one,	NIH
Zec	11:17	the sword strike his a and his right eye!	2432
	11:17	May his a be completely withered,	2432
Lk	1:51	He has performed mighty deeds with his a;	1098
Jn	12:38	the a of the Lord been revealed?"	1098
1Pe	4: 1	a yourselves also with the same attitude,	3959

ARMAGEDDON (1)

Rev 16:16   to the place that in Hebrew is called A.   762

ARMED (48) [ARM]

Ex	13:18	up out of Egypt **a** for battle.	2821
Nu	31: 5	So twelve thousand men **a** for battle,	2741
	32:21	and if all of you will go **a** over the Jordan	2741
	32:27	But your servants, every man **a** for battle,	2741
	32:29	every man **a** for battle,	2741
	32:30	But if they do not cross over with you **a**,	2741
	32:32	over before the LORD into Canaan **a**,	2741
Dt	3:18	all your able-bodied men, **a** for battle,	2741
Jos	1:14	but all your fighting men, **fully a**,	2821
	4:12	**a**, in front of the Israelites,	2821
	4:13	About forty thousand **a** for battle crossed	2741
	6: 3	around the city once with all the **a** men.	4878
	6: 7	with the **a** guard going ahead of the ark of	2741
	6: 9	The **a** guard marched ahead of	2741
	6:13	The **a** men went ahead of them and	2741
Jdg	18:11	the Danites, **a** for battle, set out	2520+3998
	18:16	The six hundred Danites, **a** for battle,	2520+3998
	18:17	the six hundred **a** men stood at the entrance	2520+3998
	20: 2	four hundred thousand soldiers **a**	8990
	20:25	all of them **a** with swords.	8990
	20:35	Benjamites, all **a** with swords.	8990
1Sa	2: 4	but those who stumbled are **a** with strength.	273
2Sa	21:16	and who was **a** with a new [sword],	2520
	22:40	You **a** me with strength for battle;	273
2Ki	3:25	but men **a** with slings surrounded it	7847
1Ch	12: 2	they were **a** with bows and were able	5976
	12:23	of the men **a** for battle who came to David	2741
	12:24	6,800 **a** for battle;	2741
	12:37	**a** with every type of weapon—120,000.	AIT
	20: 1	Joab led out the **a** forces.	2657+7372
2Ch	14: 8	**a** with small shields and with bows.	5951
	17:17	with 200,000 men **a** with bows and shields;	5976
	17:18	Jehozabad, with 180,000 men **a** for battle.	2741
Est	8:11	to destroy, kill and annihilate any **a** force	2657
Ps	18:39	You **a** me with strength for battle;	273
	65: 6	having **a** yourself with strength,	273
	78: 9	men of Ephraim, though **a** with bows,	5976+8227
	93: 1	the LORD is robed in majesty and is **a**	273
Pr	6:11	like a bandit and scarcity like an **a** man.	4482
	24:34	like a bandit and scarcity like an **a** man.	4482
Isa	15: 4	Therefore the **a** men of Moab cry out,	2741
Jer	6:23	They are **a** with bow and spear;	2616
	50:42	They are **a** with bows and spears;	2616
Eze	38: 4	your horses, your horsemen fully **a**,	4229
Da	11:31	"His **a** forces will rise up to desecrate	2432
Mt	26:47	With him was a large crowd **a** with swords	NIG
Mk	14:43	With him was a crowd **a** with swords	NIG
Lk	11:21	"When a strong man, **fully a**,	2774

ARMENIA (KJV) See ARARAT

ARMIES (16) [ARM]

Ex	14:20	coming between the **a** of Egypt and Israel.	4722
Jdg	8:10	of the **a** of the eastern peoples;	4722
1Sa	17:26	that he should defy the **a** of the living God?"	5120
	17:36	he has defied the **a** of the living God.	5120
	17:45	the God of the **a** of Israel,	5120
1Ki	2: 5	to the two commanders of Israel's **a**,	7372
Ps	44: 9	you no longer go out with our **a**.	7372
	60:10	and no longer go out with our **a**?	7372
	68:12	"Kings and **a** flee in haste;	7372
	108:11	and no longer go out with our **a**?	7372
Isa	34: 2	his wrath is upon all their **a**.	7372
Jer	35:11	to escape the Babylonian and Aramean **a**.'	2657
Lk	21:20	being surrounded by **a**, you will know	5136
Heb	11:34	in battle and routed foreign **a**.	4213
Rev	19:14	The **a** of heaven were following him,	5128
	19:19	and their **a** gathered together to make war	5128

ARMLETS (1) [ARM]

Nu 31:50   **a**, bracelets, signet rings,   731

ARMONI (1)

2Sa 21: 8   But the king took A and Mephibosheth,   813

ARMOR (19) [ARM]

1Sa	14: 1	to the young man bearing his **a**,	3998
	17: 5	on his head and wore a **coat of scale a**	7989+9234
	17:38	a **coat of a** on him and a bronze helmet	9234
	31: 9	and stripped off his **a**,	3998
	31:10	They put his **a** in the temple of	3998
1Ki	20:11	'One who **puts on** his **a** should not boast	2520
	22:34	of Israel between the sections of his **a**.	9234
1Ch	10: 9	and took his head and his **a**,	3998
	10:10	They put his **a** in the temple of their gods	3998
2Ch	18:33	of Israel between the sections of his **a**.	9234
	26:14	spears, helmets, **coats of a**,	9234
Ne	4:16	with spears, shields, bows and **a**.	9234
Isa	45: 1	and to strip kings of their **a**, to open doors	5516
Jer	46: 4	Polish your spears, put on your **a**!	6246
	51: 3	nor let him put on his **a**.	6246
Lk	11:22	the **a** in which the man trusted and divides	4110
Ro	13:12	the deeds of darkness and put on the **a**	3960
Eph	6:11	Put on the **full a** of God so	4110
	6:13	Therefore put on the **full a** of God,	4110

ARMOR-BEARER (18) [ARM]

Jdg	9:54	Hurriedly he called to his **a**,	3998+5951
1Sa	14: 6	Jonathan said to his young **a**, "Come,	3998+5951
	14: 7	"Do all that you have in mind," his **a** said.	3998+5951
	14:12	outpost shouted to Jonathan and his **a**,	3998+5951
	14:12	Jonathan said to his **a**, "Climb up after me;	3998+5951
	14:13	with his **a** right behind him.	3998+5951
	14:13	his **a** followed and killed them.	3998+5951
	14:14	and his **a** killed some twenty men in	3998+5951
	14:17	it was Jonathan and his **a** who were	3998+5951
	31: 4	Saul said to his **a**,	3998+5951
	31: 4	But his **a** was terrified and would not do it;	3998+5951
	31: 5	When the **a** saw that Saul was dead,	3998+5951
	31: 6	and his **a** and all his men died together	3998+5951
2Sa	23:37	**a** of Joab son of Zeruiah,	3998+5951
1Ch	10: 4	Saul said to his **a**,	3998+5951
	10: 4	But his **a** was terrified and would not do it;	3998+5951
	10: 5	When the **a** saw that Saul was dead,	3998+5951
	11:39	the **a** of Joab son of Zeruiah,	3998+5951

ARMOR-BEARERS (2) [ARM]

1Sa	16:21	and David became one of his **a**.	3998+5951
2Sa	18:15	ten of Joab's **a** surrounded Absalom,	3998+5951

ARMORY (3) [ARM]

2Ki	20:13	his **a** and everything found	1074+3998
Ne	3:19	a point facing the ascent to the **a** as far as	5977
Isa	39: 2	the spices, the fine oil, his entire **a**	1074+3998

ARMRESTS (2) [ARM]

1Ki	10:19	On both sides of the seat were **a**,	3338
2Ch	9:18	On both sides of the seat were **a**,	3338

ARMS (49) [ARM]

Ge	16: 5	I put my servant in your **a**,	2668
	24:30	and the bracelets on his sister's **a**,	3338
	24:47	in her nose and the bracelets on her **a**,	3338
	33: 4	he **threw** his **a** around his neck	5877+6584
	45:14	Then he **threw** his **a** around	5877+6584+7418
	46:29	he **threw** his **a** around his father and wept	5877+6584+7418
	48:14	and crossing his **a**, he put his left hand	3338
	49:24	his **strong a** stayed limber,	2432+3338
Nu	11:12	Why do you tell me to carry them in my **a**,	2668
Dt	33:27	and underneath are the everlasting **a**.	2432
Jdg	6:35	**calling** them to **a**, and also into Asher,	339+2410
	10:17	When the Ammonites **were called to a**	7590
	15:14	on his **a** became like charred flax,	2432
	16:12	the ropes off his **a** as if they were threads.	2432
2Sa	12: 3	drank from his cup and even slept in his **a**.	2668
	12: 8	and your master's wives into your **a**.	2668
	22:33	It is God who **a** me with strength	273
	22:35	my **a** can bend a bow of bronze.	2432
1Ki	17:19	He took him from her **a**,	2668
2Ki	3:21	who could **bear a** was called up	2514+2520
	4:16	**hold** a son in your **a**."	2485
Ps	18:32	It is God who **a** me with strength	273
	18:34	my **a** can bend a bow of bronze.	2432
	129: 7	nor the one who gathers fill his **a**.	2950
Pr	31:17	her **a** are strong for her tasks.	2432
	31:20	She opens her **a** to the poor	4090
SS	5:14	His **a** are rods of gold set with chrysolite.	3338
Isa	40:11	in his **a** and carries them close to his heart;	2432
	49:22	they will bring your sons in their **a**	2950
Jer	38:12	worn-out clothes under your **a** to pad	723+3338
La	4:10	as their lives ebb away in their mothers' **a**.	2668
Eze	13:20	like birds and I will tear them from your **a**;	2432
	16:11	on your **a** and a necklace around your neck,	3338
	23:42	the rabble, and they put bracelets on the **a**	3338
	30:22	I will break both his **a**,	2432
	30:24	I will strengthen the **a** of the king	2432
	30:24	but I will break the **a** of Pharaoh,	2432
	30:25	I will strengthen the **a** of the king	2432
	30:25	but the **a** of Pharaoh will fall limp.	2432
	38: 8	many days you will **be called to a**.	7212
Da	2:32	its chest and **a** of silver,	10185
	10: 6	his **a** and legs like the gleam	2432
Hos	11: 3	taking them by the **a**;	2432
Mk	9:36	**Taking** him in his **a**,	1878
	10:16	took the children in his **a**,	1878
Lk	2:28	Simeon took him in his **a** and praised God,	44
	15:20	**threw** his **a** around him and kissed him.	2093+2158+3836+5549
Ac	20:10	the young man and **put** his **a** around him.	5227
Heb	12:12	strengthen your feeble **a** and weak knees.	5931

ARMY (250) [ARM]

Ex	14: 4	for myself through Pharaoh and all his **a**,	2657
	14: 6	and took his **a** with him.	6639
	14:17	through Pharaoh and all his **a**,	2657
	14:19	in front of Israel's **a**,	4722
	14:24	the pillar of fire and cloud at the Egyptian **a**	4722
	14:28	the entire **a** of Pharaoh that had followed	2657
	15: 4	Pharaoh's chariots and his **a** he has hurled	2657
	17:13	So Joshua overcame the Amalekite **a** with	6639
Nu	1: 3	or more who are able to serve in the **a**.	7372
	1:20	to serve in the **a** were listed by name,	7372
	1:22	in the **a** were counted and listed by name,	7372
	1:24	to serve in the **a** were listed by name,	7372
	1:26	to serve in the **a** were listed by name,	7372
	1:28	to serve in the **a** were listed by name,	7372
	1:30	to serve in the **a** were listed by name,	7372
	1:32	to serve in the **a** were listed by name,	7372
	1:34	to serve in the **a** were listed by name,	7372
	1:36	to serve in the **a** were listed by name,	7372
	1:38	to serve in the **a** were listed by name,	7372
	1:40	to serve in the **a** were listed by name,	7372
	1:42	to serve in the **a** were listed by name,	7372
	1:45	in Israel's **a** were counted according	7372
	20:20	against them with a large and powerful **a**.	6639
	21:23	He mustered his entire **a** and marched out	6639
	21:33	and his whole **a** marched out to meet them	6639
	21:34	with his whole **a** and his land.	6639
	21:35	together with his sons and his whole **a**,	6639
	26: 2	or more who are able to serve in the **a**	7372
	31:14	Moses was angry with the officers of the **a**	2657
	31:48	officers who were over the units of the **a**—	7372
Dt	2:32	and all his **a** came out to meet us in battle	6639
	2:33	together with his sons and his whole **a**.	6639
	3: 1	with his whole **a** marched out to meet us	6639
	3: 2	over to you with his whole **a** and his land.	6639
	3: 3	of Bashan and all his **a**.	6639
	11: 4	what he did to the Egyptian **a**,	2657
	20: 1	and chariots and an **a** greater than yours,	6639
	20: 2	and address the **a**.	6639
	20: 5	The officers shall say to the **a**:	6639
	20: 9	the officers have finished speaking to the **a**,	6639
Jos	5:14	of the **a** of the LORD I have now come."	7372
	5:15	The commander of the LORD's **a** replied,	7372
	8: 1	Take the whole **a** with you,	4878+6639
	8: 3	the whole **a** moved out to attack Ai.	4878+6639
	10: 7	up from Gilgal with his entire **a**,	6639
	10:21	The whole **a** then returned safely to Joshua	6639
	10:24	the **a** commanders who had come with him,	408+4878
	10:33	but Joshua defeated him and his **a**—	6639
	11: 4	a huge **a**, as numerous as the sand on	6639
	11: 7	So Joshua and his whole **a** came	4878+6639
Jdg	4: 2	The commander of his **a** was Sisera,	7372
	4: 7	the commander of Jabin's **a**,	7372
	4:15	and all his chariots and **a** by the sword,	4722
	4:16	But Barak pursued the chariots and **a** as far	4722
	7:22	The **a** fled to Beth Shittah toward Zererah	4722
	8:11	and fell upon the unsuspecting **a**.	4722
	8:12	routing their entire **a**.	4722
	9:29	'Call out your whole **a**!' "	7372
	20:10	to get provisions for the **a**.	6639
	20:10	when the **a** arrives at Gibeah in Benjamin,	4392S
1Sa	4:17	and the **a** has suffered heavy losses.	6639
	12: 9	the commander of the **a** of Hazor,	7372
	13: 6	and that their **a** was hard pressed,	6639
	14:15	Then panic struck the whole **a**—	6639
	14:16	in Benjamin saw the **a** melting away	2162
	14:25	The entire **a** entered the woods,	824
	14:28	"Your father bound the **a** under	6639
	14:38	all you who are leaders of the **a**,	6639
	14:50	the commander of Saul's **a** was Abner son	7372
	15: 9	the spared Agag and the best of the sheep	6639
	17:20	the **a** was going out to its battle positions,	2657
	17:46	of the Philistine **a** to the birds of the air and	4722
	17:55	he said to Abner, commander of the **a**,	7372
	18: 5	that Saul gave him a high rank in the **a**.	408+4878
	26: 5	the commander of the **a**, had lain down.	7372
	26: 5	with the **a** encamped around him.	6639
	26: 7	David and Abishai went to the **a** by night,	6639
	26:14	He called out to the **a** and to Abner son	6639
	28: 1	and your men will accompany me in the **a**."	4722
	28: 5	Saul saw the Philistine **a**, he was afraid;	4722
	28:19	over the **a** of Israel to the Philistines.	4722
	29: 6	to have you serve with me in the **a**.	4722
	31: 7	the Jordan saw that the Israelite **a** had fled	408
2Sa	2: 8	**a** of the LORD and the house of Israel,	6639
	2: 8	the commander of Saul's **a**,	7372
	5:24	in front of you to strike the Philistine **a**."	4722
	8: 9	that David had defeated the entire **a**	2657
	8:16	Joab son of Zeruiah was over the **a**;	7372
	10: 7	David sent Joab out with the entire **a**	7372
	10:16	of Hadadezer's **a** leading them.	7372
	10:18	down Shobach the commander of their **a**,	7372
	11: 1	the king's men and the whole Israelite **a**.	NIH
	11:17	some of the men in David's **a** fell;	6639
	12:29	So David mustered the entire **a** and went	6639
	12:31	and his entire **a** returned to Jerusalem.	6639
	17:25	Absalom had appointed Amasa over the **a**	7372
	18: 6	The **a** marched into the field to fight Israel,	6639
	18: 7	There the **a** of Israel was defeated	6639
	19: 2	the whole **a** the victory that day was turned	6639
	19:13	now on you are not the commander of my **a**	7372
	20:23	Joab was over Israel's entire **a**;	6639
	24: 2	the king said to Joab and the **a** commanders	2657
	24: 4	overruled Joab and the **a** commanders;	2657
1Ki	1:19	and Joab the commander of the **a**,	7372
	1:25	the commanders of the **a** and Abiathar	7372
	2:32	Abner son of Ner, commander of Israel's **a**,	7372
	2:32	commander of Judah's **a**—	7372
	2:35	of Jehoiada over the **a** in Joab's position	7372
	11:15	Joab the commander of the **a**,	7372
	11:21	and that Joab the commander of the **a** was	7372
	16:15	The **a** was encamped near Gibbethon,	6639
	16:16	the commander of the **a**,	7372
	20: 1	of Aram mustered his entire **a**.	2657
	20:13	'Do you see this vast **a**?	2162
	20:19	of the city with the **a** behind them	2657
	20:25	also raise an **a** like the one you lost—	2657
	20:28	I will deliver this vast **a** into your hands,	2162
	22:36	a cry spread through the **a**:	4722

2Ki	3: 9	the a had no more water for themselves or	4722
	4:13	to the king or the commander of the a?' "	7372
	5: 1	Now Naaman was commander of the a of	7372
	6:15	an a with horses and chariots	2657
	6:24	of Aram mobilized his entire a	4722
	7: 6	of chariots and horses and a great a,	2657
	7:14	and the king sent them after the Aramean a.	2657
	8:21	his a, however, fled back home.	6639
	9: 5	he found the a officers sitting together.	2657
	13: 7	of the a of Jehoahaz except fifty horsemen,	6639
	18:17	and his field commander with a large a,	2657
	25: 1	against Jerusalem with his whole a.	2657
	25: 4	whole a fled at night through the gate	408+4878
	25: 5	but the Babylonian a pursued the king	2657
	25:10	The whole Babylonian a,	2657
	25:23	When all the a officers and their men heard	2657
	25:26	together with the a officers,	2657
1Ch	10: 7	in the valley saw that the a had fled and	NIH
	12:14	These Gadites were a commanders;	7372
	12:21	and they were commanders in his a.	7372
	12:22	until he had a great a,	4722
	12:22	like the a of God.	4722
	14:15	in front of you to strike the Philistine a."	4722
	14:16	and they struck down the Philistine a,	4722
	18: 9	the entire a of Hadadezer king of Zobah,	2657
	18:15	Joab son of Zeruiah was over the a	7372
	19: 8	David sent Joab out with the entire a	7372
	19:16	of Hadadezer's a leading them.	7372
	19:18	the commander of their a.	7372
	20: 3	and his entire a returned to Jerusalem.	6639
	25: 1	together with the commanders of the a,	7372
	26:26	and by the other a commanders.	7372
	27: 1	that concerned the a divisions that were	4713
	27: 3	of Perez and chief of all the a officers for	7372
	27: 5	The third a commander,	7372
	27:34	Joab was the commander of the royal a.	7372
2Ch	13: 8	You are indeed a vast a and have with you	2162
	14: 8	an a of three hundred thousand men	2657
	14: 9	with a vast a and three hundred chariots,	2657
	14:11	we have come against this vast a.	2162
	14:13	Asa and his a pursued them as far as Gerar	6639
	16: 7	on the LORD your God, the a of the king	2657
	16: 8	and Libyans a mighty a with great numbers	2657
	20: 2	"A vast a is coming against you	2162
	20:12	For we have no power to face this vast a	2162
	20:15	or discouraged because of this vast a.	2162
	20:21	as they went out at the head of the a,	2741
	20:24	the desert and looked toward the vast a,	2162
	24:23	the a of Aram marched against Joash;	2657
	24:24	Aramean a had come with only a few men,	2657
	24:24	into their hands a much larger a.	2657
	25:11	then marshaled his strength and led his a to	6639
	25:12	The a of Judah also captured ten thousand	1201
	26:11	Uzziah had a well-trained a,	2657
	26:13	Under their command was an a of 307,500	2657+7372
	26:14	bows and slingstones for the entire a.	7372
	28: 9	to meet the a when it returned to Samaria.	7372
	32: 7	the king of Assyria and the vast a with him,	2162
	33:11	against them the a commanders of the king	7372
Ne	2: 9	also sent a officers and cavalry with me.	2657
	4: 2	in the presence of his associates and the a	2657
Ps	27: 3	an a besiege me, my heart will not fear;	4722
	33:16	No king is saved by the size of his a;	2657
	136:15	swept Pharaoh and his a into the Red Sea;	2657
Pr	30:31	and a king with his a around him.	554
Isa	13: 4	The LORD Almighty is mustering an a	7372
	36: 2	a large a from Lachish to King Hezekiah	2657
	43:17	the a and reinforcements together,	2657
Jer	4:16	besieging a is coming from a distant land,	AIT
	6:22	an a is coming from the land of the north;	6639
	32: 2	The a of the king of Babylon was	2657
	34: 1	and all his a and all the kingdoms	2657
	34: 7	the a of the king of Babylon was fighting	2657
	34:21	to the a of the king of Babylon,	2657
	37: 5	Pharaoh's a had marched out of Egypt,	2657
	37: 7	to inquire of me, 'Pharaoh's a,	2657
	37:10	to defeat the entire Babylonian a	2657
	37:11	After the Babylonian a had withdrawn	2657
	37:11	from Jerusalem because of Pharaoh's a,	2657
	38: 3	over to the a of the king of Babylon,	2657
	39: 1	with his whole a and laid siege to it.	2657
	39: 5	But the Babylonian a pursued them	2657
	40: 7	the a officers and their men who were still	2657
	40:13	the a officers still in the open country came	2657
	41:11	of Kareah and all the a officers who were	2657
	41:13	of Kareah and the a officers who were	2657
	41:16	of Kareah and all the a officers who were	2657
	42: 1	Then all the a officers,	2657
	42: 8	of Kareah and all the a officers who were	2657
	43: 4	the a officers and all the people disobeyed	2657
	43: 5	of Kareah and all the a officers led away all	2657
	46: 2	the a of Pharaoh Neco king of Egypt,	2657
	50:41	An a is coming from the north;	6639
	51: 3	completely destroy her a.	7372
	52: 4	against Jerusalem with his whole a.	2657
	52: 7	and the whole a fled.	408+4878
	52: 8	the Babylonian a pursued King Zedekiah	2657
	52:14	The whole Babylonian a under	2657
La	1:15	an a against me to crush my young men.	4595
Eze	1:24	like the tumult of an a,	4722
	17:15	to Egypt to get horses and a large a.	6639
	17:17	with his mighty a and great horde will be	2657
	26: 7	with horsemen and a great a.	2256+6639+7736
	27:10	Lydia and Put served as soldiers in your a.	2657
	29:18	of Babylon drove his a in a hard campaign	2657
	29:18	Yet he and his a got no reward from	2657

Eze	29:19	and plunder the land as pay for his a.	2657
	29:20	for his efforts because he and his a did it	AIT
	30:11	He and his a—the most ruthless	6639
	32:22	"Assyria is there with her whole a;	7736
	32:23	of the pit and her a lies around her grave.	7736
	32:31	"Pharaoh—he and all his a—	2657
	37:10	on their feet—a vast a.	2657
	38: 4	and bring you out with your whole a—	2657
	38:15	a great horde, a mighty a.	2657
Da	3:20	of the strongest soldiers in his a to tie	10264
	11:10	for war and assemble a great a,	2162+2657
	11:11	who will raise a large a,	2162
	11:12	When the a is carried off,	2162
	11:13	the king of the North will muster another a,	2162
	11:13	with a huge a fully equipped.	2657
	11:22	an overwhelming a will be swept away	2432
	11:25	"With a large a he will stir up his strength	2657
	11:25	with a large and very powerful a,	2657
	11:26	his a will be swept away,	2657
Joel	2: 2	the mountains a large and mighty a comes,	6639
	2: 5	like a mighty a drawn up for battle.	6639
	2:11	The LORD thunders at the head of his a;	2657
	2:20	"I will drive the **northern** a far from you,	AIT
	2:25	my great a that I sent among you.	2657
Mt	22: 7	He sent his a and destroyed those murderers	*5128*
Rev	19:19	against the rider on the horse and his a.	*5128*

ARNAN (1)

1Ch	3:21	of A, of Obadiah and of Shecaniah.	820

ARNON (24) [ARNON'S]

Nu	21:13	from there and camped alongside the A,	818
	21:13	The A is the border of Moab,	818
	21:14	"…Waheb in Suphah and the ravines, the A	818
	21:24	over his land from the A to the Jabbok,	818
	21:26	from him all his land as far as the A.	818
	22:36	at the Moabite town on the A border,	818
Dt	2:24	"Set out now and cross the A Gorge.	818
	2:36	From Aroer on the rim of the A Gorge,	818
	3: 8	from the A Gorge as far as Mount Hermon.	818
	3:12	the territory north of Aroer by the A Gorge,	818
	3:16	the A Gorge (the middle of the gorge being	818
	4:48	on the rim of the A Gorge to Mount Siyon	818
Jos	12: 1	from the A Gorge to Mount Hermon,	818
	12: 2	from Aroer on the rim of the A Gorge—	818
	13: 9	from Aroer on the rim of the A Gorge,	818
	13:16	from Aroer on the rim of the A Gorge,	818
Jdg	11:13	they took away my land from the A to	818
	11:18	and camped on the other side of the A.	818
	11:18	for the A was its border.	818
	11:22	capturing all of it from the A to the Jabbok	818
	11:26	and all the towns along the A.	818
2Ki	10:33	from Aroer by the A Gorge through Gilead	818
Isa	16: 2	the women of Moab at the fords of the A.	818
Jer	48:20	Announce by the A that Moab is destroyed.	818

ARNON'S (1) [ARNON]

Nu	21:28	the citizens of A heights.	818

ARODI (2) [ARODITE]

Ge	46:16	Haggi, Shuni, Ezbon, Eri, A and Areli.	771
Nu	26:17	through A, the Arodite clan;	771

ARODITE (1) [ARODI]

Nu	26:17	the A clan; through Areli, the Arelite clan.	772

AROER (16) [AROERITE]

Nu	32:34	The Gadites built up Dibon, Ataroth, A,	6876
Dt	2:36	From A on the rim of the Arnon Gorge,	6876
	3:12	and the Gadites the territory north of A by	6876
	4:48	This land extended from A on the rim of	6876
Jos	12: 2	from A on the rim of the Arnon Gorge—	6876
	13: 9	from A on the rim of the Arnon Gorge,	6876
	13:16	from A on the rim of the Arnon Gorge,	6876
	13:25	and half the Ammonite country as far as A,	6876
Jdg	11:26	A, the surrounding settlements and all	6876
	11:33	He devastated twenty towns from A to	6876
1Sa	30:28	to those in A, Siphmoth, Eshtemoa	6876
2Sa	24: 5	crossing the Jordan, they camped near A,	6876
2Ki	10:33	from A by the Arnon Gorge through Gilead	6876
1Ch	5: 8	in the area from A to Nebo and Baal Meon.	6876
Isa	17: 2	The cities of A will be deserted and left	6876
Jer	48:19	you who live in A.	6876

AROERITE (1) [AROER]

1Ch	11:44	Shama and Jeiel the sons of Hotham the A,	6901

AROMA (41) [AROMATIC]

Ge	8:21	the pleasing a and said in his heart:	8194
Ex	29:18	the LORD, a pleasing a, an offering made	8194
	29:25	with the burnt offering for a pleasing a to	8194
	29:41	a pleasing a, an offering made to	8194
Lev	1: 9	an a pleasing to the LORD.	8194
	1:13	an a pleasing to the LORD.	8194
	1:17	an a pleasing to the LORD.	8194
	2: 2	an a pleasing to the LORD.	8194
	2: 9	an a pleasing to the LORD.	8194
	2:12	to be offered on the altar as a pleasing a.	8194
	3: 5	an a pleasing to the LORD.	8194
	3:16	an offering made by fire, a pleasing a.	8194
	4:31	on the altar as an a pleasing to the LORD.	8194
	6:15	on the altar as an a pleasing to the LORD.	8194

Lev	6:21	in pieces as an a pleasing to the LORD.	8194
	8:21	the altar as a burnt offering, a pleasing a,	8194
	8:28	as an ordination offering, a pleasing a,	8194
	17: 6	the fat as an a pleasing to the LORD.	8194
	23:13	to the LORD by fire, a pleasing a—	8194
	23:18	an a pleasing to the LORD.	8194
	26:31	and I will take no delight in the pleasing a	8194
Nu	15: 3	as an a pleasing to the LORD—	8194
	15: 7	Offer it as an a pleasing to the LORD.	8194
	15:10	an a pleasing to the LORD.	8194
	15:13	an offering made by fire as an a pleasing to	8194
	15:14	an offering made by fire as an a pleasing to	8194
	15:24	for a burnt offering as an a pleasing to	8194
	18:17	an a pleasing to the LORD.	8194
	28: 2	as an a pleasing to me.'	8194
	28: 6	at Mount Sinai as a pleasing a.	8194
	28: 8	as an a pleasing to the LORD.	8194
	28:13	This is for a burnt offering, a pleasing a,	8194
	28:24	for seven days as an a pleasing to	8194
	28:27	a year old as an a pleasing to the LORD.	8194
	29: 2	As an a pleasing to the LORD,	8194
	29: 6	by fire—a pleasing a.	8194
	29: 8	Present as an a pleasing to the LORD	8194
	29:13	an offering made by fire as an a pleasing to	8194
	29:36	an offering made by fire as an a pleasing to	8194
Jer	48:11	and her a is unchanged.	8194
2Co	2:15	For we are to God the a of Christ	*2380*

AROMATIC (1) [AROMA]

Ge	2:12	a resin and onyx are also there.)	978

AROSE (11) [RISE]

Ge	13: 7	And quarreling a between Abram's	2118
Jdg	5: 7	Deborah, a, arose a mother in Israel.	7756
	5: 7	Deborah, arose, a a mother in Israel.	7756
1Sa	1:19	**Early** the next morning they a	8899
Est	8: 4	to Esther and she a and stood before him.	7756
SS	5: 5	I a to open for my lover,	7756
Jnh	1: 4	a violent storm a that the ship threatened	2118
Lk	22:24	Also a dispute a among them as to which	*1181*
Ac	6: 1	**Opposition** a, however,	*482*
	19:23	About that time there a a great disturbance	*1181+1254*
Gal	2: 4	[This matter a] because some false brothers	NIG

AROUND (404) [ROUNDABOUT]

Ge	19:31	and there is no man a here to lie with us,	928
	33: 4	he threw his arms a his neck and kissed him.	5877+6584
	35: 5	of God fell upon the towns all a them so	6017
	37: 7	while your sheaves **gathered** a mine	6015
	37:15	a man found him **wandering** a in the fields	9494
	41:42	in robes of fine linen and put a gold chain a	6584
	45:14	Then he **threw** his arms a	5877+6584+7418
	46:29	he **threw** his arms a his father and wept for	5877+6584+7418
	49: 1	"Gather a so I can tell you what will happen	665
Ex	13:18	So God **led** the people by the desert road	6015
	14: 3	**wandering** a the land in confusion,	1003
	16: 3	There we sat a pots of meat and ate all	6584
	16:13	in the morning there was a layer of dew a	6017
	18:13	and they stood a him from morning	6584
	18:14	while all these people stand a you	6584
	19:12	for the people a the mountain and tell them,	6017
	19:23	'Put limits a the mountain and set it apart	1487
	21:19	if the other gets up and **walks** a outside	2143
	25:11	and make a gold molding a it.	6017
	25:24	with pure gold and make a gold molding a	6017
	25:25	Also make a it a rim a handbreadth wide	6017
	27:17	All the posts a the courtyard are	6017
	28:32	There shall be a woven edge like a collar a	6017
	28:33	and scarlet yarn a the hem of the robe,	6017
	28:34	the pomegranates are to alternate a the hem	4059
	29:13	Then take all the fat a the inner parts,	4059
	29:22	the fat tail, the fat a the inner parts,	4059
	30: 3	and make a gold molding a it.	6017
	32: 1	they gathered a Aaron and said, "Come,	6584
	37: 2	and made a gold molding a it.	6017
	37:11	with pure gold and made a gold molding a	6017
	37:12	also made a it a rim a handbreadth wide	6017
	37:26	and made a gold molding a it.	6017
	38:16	All the curtains a the courtyard were	6017
	39:23	and a band a this opening,	6584
	39:24	and scarlet yarn and finely twisted linen a	6584
	39:25	of pure gold and attached them a the hem	6017
	39:26	and pomegranates alternated a the hem of	6017
	40: 8	Set up the courtyard a it and put the curtain	6017
	40:33	up the courtyard a the tabernacle and altar	6017
Lev	8: 7	**tied** the sash a him,	2520
	8:13	**tied** sashes a them and put headbands	2520
	8:16	Moses also took all the fat a the inner parts,	6584
	8:25	the fat tail, all the fat a the inner parts,	6584
	16: 4	tie the linen sash a	2520
	25:31	without walls a them are to be considered	6017
	25:44	to come from the nations a you;	6017
Nu	1:50	they are to take care of it and encamp a it.	6017
	1:53	are to set up their tents a the tabernacle of	6017
	2: 2	"The Israelites are to camp a the Tent	6017
	11: 8	The people **went** a gathering it,	8763
	11:24	of their elders and had them stand a	6017
	11:31	It brought them down all a the camp to	6017
	11:32	they spread them out all a the camp.	6017
	16:34	At their cries, all the Israelites a them fled,	6017
	21: 4	route to the Red Sea, to **go** a Edom.	6015
	22: 4	"This horde is going to lick up everything a	6017

Nu	32:33	with its cities and the territory **a** them.	6017
	35: 2	And give them pasturelands **a** the towns.	6017
	35: 4	"The pasturelands **a** the towns	6017
Dt	1:40	turn **a** and set out toward the desert along	7155
	2: 1	For a long time we **made** our **way a**	6015
	2: 3	"You have **made** your **way a**	6015
	2:37	the Jabbok nor that **a** the towns in the hills.	NIH
	6:14	the gods of the peoples **a** you;	6017
	7:22	or the wild animals will multiply **a** you.	6584
	12:10	rest from all your enemies **a** you	4946+6017
	13: 7	gods of the peoples **a** you,	6017
	17:14	a king over us like all the nations **a** us,"	6017
	22: 8	make a parapet **a** your roof so that you may	4200
	25:19	from all the enemies **a** you in	4946+6017
Jos	6: 3	**March a** the city once with all	5938+6015
	6: 4	**march a** the city seven times,	6015
	6: 7	"Advance! **March a** the city,	6015
	6:11	So he had the ark of the LORD **carried a**	6015
	6:14	second day they **marched a** the city once	6015
	6:15	they got up at daybreak and **marched a**	6015
	6:16	The seventh time **a**, when the priests	NIH
	8:21	they **turned a** and attacked the men of Ai.	8740
	10:38	with him turned **a** and attacked Debir.	8740
	15: 3	past Hezron up to Addar and **curved a**	6015
	15:12	These are the boundaries **a** the people	6017
	19: 8	and all the villages **a** these towns as far	6017
	19:14	There the boundary **went a** on the north	6015
	21:12	and **villages a** the city they had given	AIT
	23: 1	from all their enemies **a** them,	4946+6017
Jdg	2:12	various gods of the peoples **a** them.	6017
	2:14	he sold them to their enemies **all a**,	4946+6017
	6:31	Joash replied to the hostile crowd **a** him,	6584
	7:18	from all the camp blow yours and shout,	6017
	7:21	each man held his position **a** the camp,	6017
	11: 3	where a group of adventurers gathered **a**	448
	18:26	**turned a** and went back home.	7155
	20:29	Then Israel set an ambush **a** Gibeah.	6017
1Sa	5:10	**brought** the ark of the god of Israel **a**	6015
	9: 4	of Ephraim and through the area **a**	AIT
	17:39	over the tunic and tried **walking a**,	2143
	22: 2	or in debt or discontented gathered **a** him,	448
	22: 6	with all his officials standing **a** him.	6584
	25:12	David's men **turned a** and went back.	2200
	25:16	Night and day they were a wall **a** us all	6584
	26: 5	with the army encamped **a** him.	6017
	26: 7	Abner and the soldiers were lying **a** him.	6017
	26:16	**Look a** you. Where are the king's spear	8011
	31: 3	The fighting grew fierce **a** Saul,	448
2Sa	1: 7	When he turned **a** and saw me,	339
	5: 9	He built up the **area a** it,	6017
	5:23	but **circle a** behind them and attack them	6015
	7: 1	from all his enemies **a** him,	4946+6017
	11: 2	up from his bed and **walked a** on the roof	2143
	22: 6	The cords of the grave **coiled a** me;	6015
	22:12	He made darkness his canopy **a** him—	6017
	24: 6	and on to Dan Jaan and **a** toward Sidon.	6017
1Ki	2: 5	with that blood stained the belt **a** his waist	928
	3: 1	and the wall **a** Jerusalem.	6017
	6: 5	and inner sanctuary he built a structure **a**	6017
	6: 6	He made offset ledges **a** the outside of	6017
	6:29	On the walls all **a** the temple,	4990
	7:15	and twelve cubits **a**,	6015
	7:20	pomegranates in rows **all a**.	6017
	7:23	It took a line of thirty cubits to **measure a**	
		it.	6015+6017
	7:31	**A** its opening there was engraving,	6584
	7:36	with wreaths **all a**.	6017
	8:14	the king **turned a** and blessed them.	6015
	11:24	He gathered men **a** him and became	6584
	16:18	the royal palace and set the palace on fire **a**	6584
	18:26	And they danced **a** the altar they had made.	6584
	18:32	a trench **a** it large enough to hold two seahs	6017
	18:35	down **a** the altar and even filled the trench.	6017
	19: 6	He **looked a**, and there by his head was	5564
	19:19	Elijah went up to him and threw his cloak **a**	448
	20:31	with sackcloth **a** our waists and ropes	928
	20:31	around our waists and ropes **a** our heads.	928
	20:32	Wearing sackcloth **a** their waists and ropes	928
	20:32	around their waists and ropes **a** their heads,	928
	21:27	He lay in sackcloth and **went a** meekly.	2143
	22:19	with all the host of heaven standing **a** him	6584
	22:34	"**Wheel a** and get me out of the fighting.	
			2200+3338
2Ki	1: 8	of hair and with a leather belt **a** his waist."	928
	2:24	He turned **a**, looked at them and called	339
	4: 3	Go **a** and ask all your neighbors	2021+2575+4946
	6:17	of horses and chariots of fire **all a** Elisha.	6017
	10:23	"**Look a** and see that no servants of	2924
	11: 8	Station yourselves **a** the king,	6017
	11:11	stationed themselves **a** the king—	6017
	17:15	They imitated the nations **a** them although	6017
	23: 5	of Judah and on those **a** Jerusalem—	4990
	23:16	Then Josiah **looked a**,	7155
	25: 1	the city and built siege works **all a** it.	6017
	25:10	broke down the walls **a** Jerusalem.	6017
	25:17	and pomegranates of bronze all **a**.	6017
1Ch	4:33	the villages **a** these towns as far as Baalath.	AIT
	6:56	and **villages a** the city were given	AIT
	9:27	They would spend the night **stationed a**	6017
	10: 3	The fighting grew fierce **a** Saul,	6584
	11: 8	He built up the city **a** it,	6017
	14:14	but **circle a** and attack them in front	6015
2Ch	4: 2	It took a line of thirty cubits to **measure a**	
		it.	6015+6017
	6: 3	the king **turned a** and blessed them.	6015
	13: 7	Some worthless scoundrels gathered **a** him	6584
	13:13	Now Jeroboam had **sent** troops **a** to the rear,	6015

2Ch	14: 7	he said to Judah, "and **put** walls **a** them,	6015
	14:14	They destroyed all the villages **a** Gerar,	6017
	17: 9	they **went a** to all the towns of Judah	6015
	18:33	"**Wheel a** and get me out of the fighting.	
			2200+3338
	23: 7	The Levites are to station themselves **a**	6017
	23:10	with his weapon in his hand, **a** the king—	6017
	31:19	who lived on the **farm** lands **a** their towns	AIT
	34: 6	as far as Naphtali, and in the ruins **a** them,	6017
Ezr	3: 3	Despite their fear of the peoples **a** them,	824S
	4: 4	the peoples **a** them set out to discourage	824S
	9: 2	the holy race with the peoples **a** them.	824S
	9: 4	at the words of the God of Israel gathered **a**	448
	10: 1	and children—gathered **a** him.	448
	10: 2	from the peoples **a** us.	824S
	10:11	Separate yourselves from the peoples **a** you	824S
Ne	8:13	gathered **a** Ezra the scribe to give attention	448
	10:30	to the peoples **a** us or take their daughters	824S
	12:28	from the region **a** Jerusalem—	6017
	12:29	for themselves **a** Jerusalem.	6017
	12:44	the **fields a** the towns they were to bring	AIT
Job	1:10	not put a hedge **a** him and his household	
			1237+4946+6017
	8:17	it entwines its roots **a** a pile of rocks	6584
	12:18	by kings and ties a loincloth **a** their waist.	928
	19: 6	and drawn his net **a** me.	6584
	19:12	a siege ramp against me and encamp **a**	6017
	21: 8	They see their children established **a** them,	6640
	22:10	That is why snares are **all a** you,	6017
	29: 5	with me and my children were **a** me,	6017
	37:12	At his direction they swirl **a** over the face	4991
Ps	3: 3	But you are a shield **a** me, O LORD;	1237
	7: 7	Let the assembled peoples **gather a** you.	6015
	18: 5	The cords of the grave **coiled a** me;	6015
	18:11	his canopy **a** him—	6017
	34: 7	The LORD encamps **a** those who fear him,	6017
	44:13	the scorn and derision of those **a** us.	6017
	48:12	Walk about Zion, go **a** her,	5938
	50: 3	and **a** him a tempest rages,	6017
	78:28	inside their camp, **all a** their tents.	6017
	79: 3	like water **all a** Jerusalem,	6017
	79: 4	of scorn and derision to those **a** us.	6017
	109:19	like a belt **tied** forever **a** him.	2520
	118:12	They **swarmed a** me like bees,	6015
	128: 3	your sons will be like olive shoots **a**	6017
	139:11	and the light become night **a** me,"	1237
Pr	3: 3	bind them **a** your neck,	6584
	6:21	fasten them **a** your neck.	6584
	30:31	a he-goat, and a king with his army **a** him,	6640
Isa	11: 5	be his belt and faithfulness the **sash a**	AIT
	19:14	as a drunkard **staggers a** in his vomit.	9494
	20: 2	he did so, **going a** stripped and barefoot.	2143
	22:21	with your robe and **fasten** your sash **a** him	AIT
	28:20	the blanket too narrow to **wrap a** you.	4043
	29: 3	I will encamp against you **all a**;	1885+2021+3869
	32:11	**put** sackcloth **a** your waists.	2520
	49:18	Lift up your eyes and look **a**;	6017
	56:10	they **lie** and dream, they love to sleep.	8886
Jer	5: 1	**look a** and consider,	8011
	6: 3	they will pitch their tents **a** her,	6017
	13: 1	and buy a linen belt and put it **a** your waist,	6584
	13: 2	and put it **a** my waist.	6584
	13: 4	the belt you bought and are **wearing a**	6584
	13:11	For as a belt is bound **a** a man's waist,	448
	17:26	the towns of Judah and the villages **a**	4946+6017
	19:15	the villages **a** it every disaster I pronounced	3972
	21:14	that will consume everything **a** you.'"	6017
	26: 9	the people crowded **a** Jeremiah in the house	448
	31:26	At this I awoke and **looked a**.	AIT
	32:44	in the villages **a** Jerusalem,	6017
	33:13	in the villages **a** Jerusalem and in the towns	6017
	34:16	you have **turned a** and profaned my name;	8740
	40:15	and cause all the Jews who are gathered **a**	448
	43:12	**wraps** his garment **a** them,	6486
	43:12	so will he **wrap** Egypt **a himself** and depart	6486
	46:14	for the sword devours those **a** you.'	6017
	48:17	Mourn for her, all who live **a** her,	6017
	48:39	an object of horror to all those **a** her."	6017
	49: 5	I will bring terror on you from all those **a**	6017
	50:14	"Take up your positions **a** Babylon,	6017
	50:29	Encamp **all a** her; let no one escape.	6017
	50:32	that will consume all who are **a** her."	6017
	52: 4	the city and built siege works **all a** it.	6017
	52:14	down all the walls **a** Jerusalem.	6017
	52:22	and pomegranates of bronze all **a**.	6017
La	1:12	**Look a** and see. Is any suffering like my	5564
	2: 3	a flaming fire that consumes **everything a**	AIT
	2: 8	down the **wall a** the Daughter of Zion.	AIT
Eze	1:18	and all four rims were full of eyes **all a**.	6017
	1:28	so was the radiance **a** him.	6017
	2: 6	though briers and thorns are **all a** you	907
	4: 2	against it and put battering rams **a** it.	6017
	5: 2	and strike it with the sword **all a** the city.	6017
	5: 5	with countries **all a** her.	6017
	5: 6	the nations and countries **a** her.	6017
	5: 7	the nations **a** you and have	6017
	5: 7	to the standards of the nations **a** you.	6017
	5:14	a ruin and a reproach among the nations **a**	6017
	5:15	the nations **a** you when I inflict punishment	6017
	6: 5	and I will scatter your bones **a** your altars.	6017
	6:13	among their idols **a** their altars,	6017
	11:12	to the standards of the nations **a** you.	6017
	12:14	I will scatter to the winds all those **a** him—	6017
	16:11	on your arms and a necklace **a** your neck,	6584
	16:37	I will gather them against you from **all a**	6017
	16:57	all those **a** you who despise you.	6017
	23:15	with belts **a** their waists	928

Eze	23:42	"The noise of a carefree crowd was **a** her;	928
	27:11	They hung their shields **a** your walls;	6017
	31: 4	their streams flowed **all a** its base	6017
	32:23	in the depths of the pit and her army lies **a**	6017
	32:24	with all her hordes **a** her grave.	6017
	32:25	with all her hordes **a** her grave.	6017
	32:26	with all their hordes **a** their graves.	6017
	36: 4	ridiculed by the rest of the nations **a**	4946+6017
	36: 7	the nations **a** you will also suffer scorn	4946+6017
	36:36	the nations **a** you that remain will know	6017
	37:21	from **all a** and bring them back	6017
	38: 4	I will **turn** you **a**,	8740
	39: 2	I will **turn** you **a** and drag you along.	8740
	39:17	from **all a** to the sacrifice I am preparing	6017
	40:14	the faces of the projecting walls **all a**	6017+6017
	40:16	by narrow parapet openings **all a**,	6017+6017
	40:16	the openings **all a** faced inward.	6017+6017
	40:17	had been constructed **all a** the court;	6017+6017
	40:29	its portico had narrow openings **all a**,	6017+6017
	40:29	and its portico had openings **all a**.	6017+6017
	40:30	(The porticoes of the gateways **a**	6017+6017
	40:33	and its portico had openings **all a**.	6017+6017
	40:36	and it had openings **all a**.	6017+6017
	40:43	were attached to the wall **all a**.	6017+6017
	41: 5	and each side room **a**	6017+6017
	41: 6	There were ledges **all a** the wall of	6017+6017
	41: 7	The side rooms **all a**	6015
	41: 8	the temple had a raised base **all a** it,	6017+6017
	41:10	was twenty cubits wide **all a**	6017+6017
	41:11	open area was five cubits wide **all a**.	6017+6017
	41:12	building was five cubits thick **all a**,	6017+6017
	41:16	and the narrow windows and galleries **a**	6017
	41:17	on the walls at regular intervals **all a**	6017+6017
	41:19	They were carved **all a**.	6017
	42:15	east gate and measured the area **all a**:	6017+6017
	42:20	It had a wall **a** it,	6017
	43:13	with a rim of one span **a** the edge.	6017
	43:17	a cubit and a gutter of a cubit **all a**.	6017
	43:20	of the upper ledge and **a** the rim,	6017
	44:18	on their heads and linen undergarments **a**	6584
	45: 2	with 50 cubits **a** it for open land.	6017
	46:21	and **led** me **a** to its four corners,	6296
	46:23	**A** the inside of each of the four courts was	6017
	46:23	with places for fire built **all a** under	6017
	47: 2	the north gate and **led** me **a** the outside to	6015
	48:35	"The distance **all a** will be 18,000 cubits.	6017
Da	3:25	see four men **walking a** in the fire,	10207
	3:27	governors and royal advisers **crowded a**	10359
	5: 7	in purple and have a gold chain placed **a**	10542
	5:16	and have a gold chain placed **a** your neck,	10542
	5:29	a gold chain was placed **a** his neck,	10542
	9:16	an object of scorn to all those **a** us.	6017
	10: 5	with a belt of the finest gold **a** his waist.	NIH
Jnh	2: 5	seaweed was **wrapped a** my head.	2502
Na	3: 8	situated on the Nile, with water **a** her?	6017
Hab	2:16	from the LORD's right hand is **coming a**	6015
Zec	2: 5	And I myself will be a wall of fire **a** it,'	6017
Mt	3: 4	and he had a leather belt **a** his waist.	4309
	8:18	When Jesus saw the crowd **a** him,	4309
	13: 2	Such large crowds gathered **a** him	4639
	18: 6	to have a large millstone hung **a** his neck	4309
	20: 6	and found still others standing **a**.	NIG
	21:33	He **put** a wall **a** it,	4363
	27:27	the whole company of soldiers **a** him.	2093
Mk	1: 6	with a leather belt **a** his waist,	4309
	3: 5	He **looked a** at them in anger and,	4315
	3: 8	the regions across the Jordan and **a** Tyre	4309
	3:32	A crowd was sitting **a** him,	4309
	3:34	Then he looked at those seated in a circle **a**	4309
	4: 1	The crowd that gathered **a** him was so large	4639
	4:10	the Twelve and the others **a** him asked him	4309
	5:21	a large crowd gathered **a** him while he was	2093
	5:24	A large crowd followed and **pressed a** him.	5315
	5:30	He **turned a** in the crowd and asked,	2188
	5:32	But Jesus kept **looking a**	4315
	5:42	Immediately the girl stood up and walked **a**	NIG
	6: 6	Then he **went a** teaching from village	4310
	6:30	The apostles gathered **a** Jesus and reported	4639
	7: 1	from Jerusalem gathered **a** Jesus and	4639
	8:24	they look like trees **walking a**."	4344
	8:27	and his disciples went on to the villages **a**	NIG
	9: 8	Suddenly, when they **looked a**,	4315
	9:14	a large crowd **a** them and the teachers of	4309
	9:20	He fell to the ground and **rolled a**,	3244
	9:42	into the sea with a large millstone **tied a**	4329
	10:23	Jesus **looked a** and said to his disciples,	4315
	11:11	He **looked a** at everything,	4315
	12: 1	He **put** a wall **a** it,	4363
	12:38	to **walk a** in flowing robes and be greeted	4344
	14:69	she said again to those standing **a**,	4225
Lk	2: 9	and the glory of the Lord **shone a** them,	4334
	3: 3	He went into all the **country a** the Jordan,	4369
	5: 1	the people **crowding a** him and listening to	2130
	6:10	He **looked a** at them all,	4315
	10: 7	Do not **move a** from house to house.	3553
	13: 8	and I'll dig **a** it and fertilize it.	4309
	15: 1	"sinners" were all **gathering a**	1581
	15:20	**threw his arms a** him and kissed him.	
			2093+2158+3836+5549
	17: 2	the sea with a millstone **tied a** his neck than	4329
	20:46	like to **walk a** in flowing robes and love to	4344
Jn	1:38	**Turning a**, Jesus saw them following	5138
	7: 1	After this, Jesus **went a** in Galilee,	4344
	8: 2	where all the people gathered **a** him,	4639
	10:24	The Jews **gathered a** him, saying,	3240
	11:44	and a cloth **a** his face.	4317
	13: 4	**wrapped** a towel **a** his **waist**.	1346

Jn	13: 5	with the towel that was **wrapped** a him.	1346
18:18	and officials stood a fire they had made	NIG
20: 7	the burial cloth that had been a Jesus' head.	2093
20:14	she **turned** a and saw Jesus standing there,	1650+3836+3958+5138
21: 7	**wrapped** his outer garment a him	1346
Ac	5:16	Crowds gathered also from the towns a	4339
9: 3	suddenly a light from heaven **flashed** a	4313
9:39	All the widows **stood** a him,	4225
10:38	and how he **went** a doing good	1451
12: 8	"**Wrap** your cloak a you and follow me,"	4314
14:20	But *after* the disciples *had* **gathered** a him,	3240
16:18	so troubled that he **turned** a and said to	2188
17:23	For *as I* **walked** a and looked carefully	1451
19:13	Some Jews who **went** a	4320
20:10	on the young man and **put** *his* **arms** a him.	5227
22: 6	a bright light from heaven **flashed** a me.	4313
25: 7	down from Jerusalem **stood** a him,	4325
26:13	**blazing** a me and my companions.	4334
Ro	15:19	from Jerusalem all the way a to Illyricum,	3241
2Co	4:10	We always **carry** a in our body the death	4367
Eph	6:14	with the belt of truth **buckled** a your **waist**,	4322
2Ti	4: 3	*they will* **gather** a them a great number	2197
Heb	11:30	people *had* **marched** a them for seven days.	3240
1Pe	5: 8	Your enemy the devil **prowls** a like	4344
1Jn	2:11	the darkness and **walks** a in the darkness;	4344
Rev	1:12	*I* **turned** a to see the voice	2188
1:13	down to his feet and with a golden sash a	4639
4: 6	In the center, *around* the throne,	3241
4: 8	and was covered with eyes **all** a,	3239
7:11	the angels were standing a the throne and	3241
7:11	*around* the throne and the elders and	NIG
15: 6	shining linen and wore golden sashes a	4309

AROUSE (5) [ROUSE]
SS	2: 7	*Do* not a or awaken love until it so desires.	6424
3: 5	*Do* not a or awaken love until it so desires.	6424
8: 4	*Do* not a or awaken love until it so desires.	6424
Ro | 11:14 | a my own people **to envy** | 4143
1Co | 10:22 | a the Lord's **jealousy**? | 4143

AROUSED (15) [ROUSE]
Ex	22:24	My anger *will be* a,	3013
Nu	11: 1	and when he heard them his anger *was* a.	3013
32:10	The Lord's anger *was* a that day	3013
Dt	9: 8	At Horeb *you* a the Lord's **wrath** so	7911
2Ch	21:16	The Lord *against* Jehoram the hostility	6424
36:16	of the Lord *was* a against his people	6590
Job	17: 8	the innocent *are* a against the ungodly.	6424
32: 5	his anger *was* a.	3013
Ps	78:58	*they* a his **jealousy** with their idols.	7861
Jer	32:31	this city *has* so a my anger and wrath	2118+6584
51:39	But while they *are* a,	2801
Eze | 38:18 | my hot anger *will be* a, | 6590
Hos | 11: 8 | all my compassion *is* a. | 4023
Ac | 21:30 | The whole city *was* a, | 3075
Ro | 7: 5 | the sinful passions a by the law were | NIG

AROUSES (1) [ROUSE]
Pr | 6:34 | for jealousy a a husband's fury, | NIH

ARPAD (6)
2Ki	18:34	Where are the gods of Hamath and A?	822
19:13	is the king of Hamath, the king of A,	822
Isa	10: 9	Is not Hamath like A,	822
36:19	Where are the gods of Hamath and A?	822
37:13	is the king of Hamath, the king of A,	822
Jer | 49:23 | "Hamath and A are dismayed, | 822

ARPHAD (KJV) See ARPAD

ARPHAXAD (10)
Ge	10:22	Elam, Asshur, A, Lud and Aram.	823
10:24	A was the father of Shelah,	823
11:10	he became the father of A.	823
11:11	And after he became the father of A,	823
11:12	When A had lived 35 years,	823
11:13	A lived 403 years and had other sons	823
1Ch	1:17	Elam, Asshur, A, Lud and Aram.	823
1:18	A was the father of Shelah,	823
1:24	Shem, A, Shelah,	823
Lk | 3:36 | the son *of* A, the son of Shem, | 790

ARRANGE (4) [ARRANGED, ARRANGEMENT, ARRANGEMENTS]
Lev	1: 7	to put fire on the altar and a wood on	6885
1: 8	Aaron's sons the priests *shall* a the pieces,	6885
1:12	and the priest *shall* a them,	6885
6:12	to add firewood and a the burnt offering on	6885

ARRANGED (12) [ARRANGE]
Ge	15:10	and the halves opposite each other;	5989
22: 9	an altar there and a the wood on it.	6885
Jdg | 20:38 | men of Israel *had* a with the ambush | 2118+4595
2Sa | 23: 5 | a and secured in every part? | 6885
1Ki | 18:33 | He a the wood, cut the bull into pieces | 6885
2Ki | 9:30 | a her hair and looked out of a window. | 3512
2Ch | 35:10 | The service was a and the priests stood | 3922
Mt | 26:48 | Now the betrayer *had* a a signal with them: | 1443
Mk | 14:44 | Now the betrayer *had* a a signal with them | 1443
Ac | 28:23 | They a to meet Paul on a certain day, | 5435

1Co | 12:18 | But in fact God *has* a the parts in the body, | 5502
Heb | 9: 6 | *When* everything *had been* a like this, | 2941

ARRANGEMENT (2) [ARRANGE]
Eze | 43:11 | its a, its exits and entrances— | 9414
Ac | 20:13 | He had **made** this a | 1411

ARRANGEMENTS (1) [ARRANGE]
2Co | 9: 5 | and **finish** the a for the generous gift | 4616

ARRAY (2) [ARRAYED]
Ge | 2: 1 | in all their **vast** a. | 7372
Dt | 4:19 | all the heavenly a— | 7372

ARRAYED (2) [ARRAY]
Ps | 110: 3 | A in holy majesty, | 928
Isa | 61:10 | with garments of salvation and a me *in* | 3598

ARREST (16) [ARRESTED, ARRESTING]
Jer	36:26	and Shelemiah son of Abdeel to a Baruch	4374
Mt	10:19	But when they a you,	4140
21:46	They looked for a way *to* a him,	3195
26: 4	and they plotted to a Jesus in some sly way	3195
26:48	"The one I kiss is the man; a him."	3195
26:55	and *you* did not a me.	3195
Mk	12:12	*to* a him because they knew he had spoken	3195
14: 1	for some sly way *to* a Jesus and kill him.	3195
14:44	a him and lead him away under guard."	3195
14:49	and *you* did not a me.	3195
Lk	20:19	looked for a way *to* a him immediately,	2093+2095+3836+5931
Jn	7:32	the Pharisees sent temple guards to a him.	4389
11:57	he should report it so that *they might* a him.	4389
18:36	my servants would fight to prevent *my* a by	4140
Ac | 9:14 | from the chief priests *to* a all who call | 1313
2Co | 11:32 | the Damascenes guarded *in order to* a me. | 4389

ARRESTED (14) [ARREST]
Jer	37:13	the son of Hananiah, a him and said,	9530
37:14	instead, he a Jeremiah and brought him to	9530
Mt	14: 3	Now Herod *had* a John and bound him	3195
26:50	seized Jesus and a him.	3195
26:57	Those who *had* a Jesus took him	3195
Mk	6:17	to have John a,	3195
13:11	Whenever you *are* a and brought to trial,	4140
14:46	The men seized Jesus and a him.	3195
Jn	18:12	and the Jewish officials a Jesus.	5197
Ac	1:16	as guide *for* those who a Jesus—	5197
5:18	*They* a the apostles and	2093+2095+3836+5931
12: 1	King Herod a some who	2095+3836+5931
21:33	up and a him and ordered him to be bound	2138
28:17	I was a in Jerusalem and handed over to	1300

ARRESTING (2) [ARREST]
Ac	12: 4	*After* a him, he put him in prison,	4389
22: 4	a both men and women and throwing them	1297

ARRIVAL (3) [ARRIVE]
Ge | 43:25 | They prepared their gifts for Joseph's a | 995
Ezr | 3: 8 | of the second year after their a at the house | 995
Jn | 11:17 | On his a, Jesus found | 2262

ARRIVE (4) [ARRIVAL, ARRIVED, ARRIVES, ARRIVING]
Ex | 1:19 | and give birth before the midwives a." | 448+995
Ne | 2: 7 | until *I* a in Judah? | 995
Job | 6:20 | *they* a there, only to be disappointed. | 995+6330
1Co | 16: 3 | when *I* a, I will give letters of introduction | 4134

ARRIVED (89) [ARRIVE]
Ge	12: 5	for land of Canaan, and *they* a there.	995
19: 1	The two angels a at Sodom in the evening,	995
33:18	he a safely *at* the city of Shechem	995
37:14	When Joseph a at Shechem,	995
42: 6	So when Joseph's brothers a,	995
46:28	When *they* a in the region of Goshen,	995
Nu	10:21	to be set up before they a.	995
20: 1	the whole Israelite community a *at*	995
Dt	9: 7	the day you left Egypt until you a here,	995+6330
11: 5	in the desert until you a at this place,	995
Jos	8:11	and approached the city and a in front of it.	995
Jdg	3:27	When he a there,	995
7:13	Gideon a just as a man was telling	995
Ru	1:19	When they a *in* Bethlehem,	995
2: 4	then Boaz a from Bethlehem and greeted	995
1Sa	4:13	When he a, there was Eli sitting	995
10:10	When *they* a at Gibeah,	995
13:10	Samuel a, and Saul went out to greet him.	995
16: 4	When he a at Bethlehem,	995
16: 6	When they a, Samuel saw Eliab	995
25: 9	When David's men a,	995
25:12	When *they* a, they reported every word.	995
26: 4	and learned that Saul *had* definitely a.	995
30:26	When David a in Ziklag,	995
2Sa	1: 2	the third day a man a from Saul's camp,	995
2:32	and his men marched all night and a	NIH
3:23	When Joab and all the soldiers with him a,	995
4: 5	and *they* a there in the heat of the day	995
11:22	when he a he told David everything Joab	995
15:32	When David a at the summit,	995

2Sa	15:37	So David's friend Hushai a at Jerusalem	995
16:14	with him a at their destination exhausted.	995
18:31	Then the Cushite a and said,	995
19:30	that my lord the king *has* a home safely."	995
1Ki	1:22	Nathan the prophet a.	995
1:42	Jonathan son of Abiathar the priest a.	995
8: 3	When all the elders of Israel *had* a,	995
12:21	When Rehoboam a in Jerusalem,	995
22:15	he a, the king asked him, "Micaiah,	448+995
2Ki	6:32	but before he a, Elisha said to the elders,	448+995
9: 5	When *he* a, he found the army officers	995
10: 7	When the letter a, these men took	448+995
10: 8	When the messenger a, he told Jehu,	995
2Ch	5: 4	When all the elders of Israel *had* a,	995
11: 1	When Rehoboam a *in* Jerusalem,	995
18:14	he a, the king asked him, "Micaiah,	448+995
22: 7	When Ahaziah a, he went out with Joram	995
Ezr	2:68	When they a at the house of the Lord	995
7: 8	Ezra a *in* Jerusalem in the fifth month of	995
7: 9	and *he* a in Jerusalem on the first day of	995
	So we a in Jerusalem,	995
Est	6:14	the king's eunuchs a and hurried Haman	5595
Isa	30: 4	in Zoan and their envoys *have* a in Hanes,	5595
Eze	7:12	The time has come, the day *has* a.	5595
23:40	when *they* a you bathed yourself for them,	995
33:22	Now the evening before the man a,	995
47: 7	When I a there, I saw a great number	8740
Zec	6:10	who *have* a from Babylon.	995
Mt	8:28	When he a at the other side in the region of	2262
17:24	and his disciples a in Capernaum,	2262
25:10	to buy the oil, the bridegroom a.	2262
26:47	Judas, one of the Twelve, a.	2262
Mk	3:31	Then Jesus' mother and brothers a.	2262
11:27	*They* a again in Jerusalem,	1650+2262
14:17	Jesus a with the Twelve.	2262
Lk	8:51	*When* he a at the house of Jairus,	2262
Jn	4:45	When *he* a in Galilee,	2262
4:47	that Jesus *had* a in Galilee from Judea,	2457
12: 1	Jesus a at Bethany, where Lazarus lived,	2262
20: 6	a and went into the tomb.	2262
Ac	1:13	When *they* a, they went upstairs to	1656
5:21	*When* the high priest and his associates a,	4134
8:15	*When* *they* a, they prayed for them	2849
9:39	he a he was taken upstairs to the room.	4134
10:24	The following day *he* a in Caesarea.	1656
11:23	*When* he a and saw the evidence of	4134
13: 5	*When they* a at Salamis,	1181
18:19	*They* a at Ephesus, where Paul left	2918
19: 1	through the interior and a at Ephesus.	2982
20: 2	and finally a in Greece,	2262
20:15	from there and a off Kios.	2918
20:15	and on the following day a at Miletus.	2262
20:18	*When they* a, he said to them:	4134
21:17	*When* we a at Jerusalem,	1181
23:33	*When* the cavalry a *in* Caesarea,	1656
25:13	and Bernice a at Caesarea	2918
28:13	From there *we* set sail and a at Rhegium.	2918
1Co | 16:17 | Fortunatus and Achaicus a, | 3836+4242
Gal | 2:12 | But when *they* a, he began to draw back | 2262

ARRIVES (8) [ARRIVE]
Jdg | 20:10 | when the army a at Gibeah in Benjamin, | 995
1Sa | 16:11 | we will not sit down until he a." | 995+7024
1Ki | 14: 5 | When she a, she will pretend to | 995
Hos | 13:13 | when the time a, he does not come | NIH
Zep | 2: 2 | the appointed time a and that day sweeps | 3528
Mt | 12:44 | *When it* a, it finds the house unoccupied, | 2262
Lk | 11:25 | *When it* a, it finds the house swept clean | 2262
Heb | 13:23 | he a soon, I will come with him to see you. | 2262

ARRIVING (10) [ARRIVE]
Ru	1:22	a *in* Bethlehem as the barley harvest	995
1Ki	10: 2	A at Jerusalem with a very great caravan—	995
2Ch	9: 1	A with a very great caravan—	NIH
28:12	confronted those *who were* a from the war.	995
Ac	5:22	But *on* a at the jail,	4134
14:27	*On* a there, they gathered	4134
17:10	*On* a there, they went to	4134
18:27	*On* a, he was a great help to those who	4134
25: 1	Three days after a *in* the province,	2094
27: 7	and had difficulty a off Cnidus.	1181

ARROGANCE (17) [ARROGANT]
Dt	1:43	and *in your* a you marched up into	2326
1Sa	2: 3	so proudly or let your mouth speak such a,	6981
15:23	and a like the evil of idolatry.	7210
Job	35:12	when men cry out because of the a *of*	1454
Ps	10: 2	In his a the wicked man hunts down	1452
17:10	and their mouths speak with a.	1455
73: 8	in their a they threaten oppression.	5294
Pr	8:13	I hate pride and a,	1454
Isa	2:17	The a *of* man will be brought low	1471
9: 9	who say with pride and a *of* heart,	1542
13:11	I will put an end to the a *of* the haughty	1454
Jer	48:29	and a and the haughtiness of her heart.	1452
Eze	7:10	the rod has budded, a has blossomed!	2295
Hos	5: 5	Israel's a testifies against them;	1454
7:10	Israel's a testifies against him,	1454
Mk | 7:22 | deceit, lewdness, envy, slander, a and folly. | 5661
2Co | 12:20 | factions, slander, gossip, a and disorder. | 5883

ARROGANT (37) [ARROGANCE, ARROGANTLY]
2Ki | 14:10 | and now you are a. | 4213+5951

2Ch	25:19	and now you *are* a and proud.	4213+5951
Ne	9:16	our forefathers, *became* a and stiff-necked,	2326
	9:29	but they *became* a and disobeyed	2326
Ps	5: 5	The a cannot stand in your presence;	2147
	73: 3	the a when I saw the prosperity of	2147
	75: 4	To the a I say, 'Boast no more,'	2147
	86:14	The a are attacking me, O God;	2294
	94: 4	They pour out a words;	6981
	119:21	You rebuke the a, who are cursed	2294
	119:51	The a mock me without restraint,	2294
	119:69	Though the a have smeared me with lies,	2294
	119:78	the a be put to shame for wronging me	2294
	119:85	a dig pitfalls for me, contrary to your law.	2294
	119:122	let not the a oppress me.	2294
	123: 4	much contempt from the a.	1456
Pr	7: 7	A lips are unsuited to a fool—	3856
	21:24	The proud and a *man*—"Mocker"	3400
Isa	2:11	The eyes of the a man will be humbled and	1471
	5:15	the eyes of the a humbled.	1469
	33:19	You will see those a people no more,	3594
Jer	13:15	Hear and pay attention, *do not be* a,	1467
	43: 2	and all the a men said to Jeremiah,	2294
	50:31	"See, I am against you, O a one,"	2295
	50:32	The a *one* will stumble and fall	2295
Eze	16:49	She and her daughters were a,	1454
Da	5:20	his heart *became* a and hardened with pride,	10659
Hab	2: 5	he is a and never at rest.	3400
Zep	3: 4	Her prophets *are* a;	7069
Mal	3:15	But now we call the blessed.	2294
	4: 1	the a and every evildoer will be stubble,	2294
Ro	1:30	God-haters, insolent, a and boastful;	5662
	11:20	*Do not be* a, but be afraid.	5734+5858
1Co	4:18	Some of you *have become* a,	5881
	4:19	not only how these a *people* are talking,	5881
1Ti	6:17	not *to be* a nor to put their hope in wealth,	5735
2Pe	2:10	Bold and a, these men are not afraid	881

ARROGANTLY (4) [ARROGANT]

Ex	18:11	to *those* who had **treated** Israel a."	2326
Ne	9:10	knew how a the Egyptians **treated** them.	2326
Job	36: 9	that they have sinned a.	1504
Ps	31:18	for with pride and contempt they speak a	6981

ARROW (18) [ARROWS]

1Sa	20:36	As the boy ran, he shot an a beyond him.	2943
	20:37	to the place where Jonathan's a had fallen,	2943
	20:37	"Isn't the a beyond you?"	2943
	20:38	The boy picked up the a and returned	2943
2Ki	9:24	The a pierced his heart and he slumped	2943
	13:17	"The LORD's a of victory,	2932
	13:17	the a of victory over Aram!"	2932
	19:32	not enter this city or shoot an a here.	2932
Job	20:24	a bronze-tipped a pierces him.	8008
	34: 6	his a inflicts an incurable wound.'	2932
Ps	91: 5	nor the a that flies by day,	2932
Pr	7:23	till an a pierces his liver,	2932
	25:18	Like a club or a sword or a sharp a is	2932
Isa	7:24	Men will go there with bow and a,	2932
	37:33	not enter this city or shoot an a here.	2932
	49: 2	into a polished a and concealed me	2932
Jer	9: 8	Their tongue is a deadly a;	2932
Zec	9:14	his a will flash like lightning.	2932

ARROWS (46) [ARROW]

Ex	19:13	shall surely be stoned or **shot with a;**	3721+3721
Nu	24: 8	with their a they pierce them.	2932
Dt	32:23	upon them and spend my a against them.	2932
	32:42	I will make my a drunk with blood,	2932
1Sa	20:20	I will shoot three a to the side of it,	2932
	20:21	I will send a boy and say, 'Go, find the a.'	2932
	20:21	'Look, the a are on this side of you;	2932
	20:22	the a are beyond you,' then you must go,	2932
	20:36	"Run and find the a I shoot."	2932
2Sa	11:20	Didn't you know *they would* **shoot** a from	3721
	11:24	Then the archers **shot** a at your servants	3721
	22:15	He shot a and scattered [the enemies],	2932
2Ki	13:15	Elisha said, "Get a bow and *some* a,"	2932
	13:18	Then he said, "Take the a,"	2932
1Ch	12: 2	to shoot a or to sling stones right-handed	2932
2Ch	26:15	and on the corner defenses to shoot a	2932
Job	6: 4	The a of the Almighty are in me,	2932
	41:28	A do not make him flee;	1201+8008
Ps	7:13	he makes ready his flaming a.	2932
	11: 2	they set their a against the strings to shoot	2932
	18:14	He shot his a and scattered [the enemies],	2932
	38: 2	For your a have pierced me,	2932
	45: 5	Let your sharp a pierce the hearts of	2932
	57: 4	men whose teeth are spears and a,	2932
	58: 7	let their a be blunted.	2932
	64: 3	and aim their words like deadly a.	2932
	64: 7	But God will shoot them with a;	2932
	76: 3	There he broke the flashing a,	8008
	77:17	your a flashed back and forth.	2932
	120: 4	He will punish you with a warrior's sharp a,	2932
	127: 4	Like a in the hands of	2932
	144: 6	shoot your a and rout them.	2932
Pr	26:18	a madman shooting firebrands or deadly a	2932
Isa	5:28	Their a are sharp, all their bows are strung;	2932
Jer	50:14	Spare no a, for she has sinned against	2932
	51:11	"Sharpen the a, take up the shields!	2932
La	3:12	and made me the target for his a.	2932
	3:13	He pierced my heart with a *from* his quiver.	1201S
Eze	5:16	at you with my deadly and destructive a	2932
	21:21	He will cast lots with a,	2932

Eze	39: 3	from your left hand and make your a drop	2932
	39: 9	the small and large shields, the bows and a,	2932
Hab	3: 9	you called for many a.	4751
	3:11	in the heavens at the glint of your flying a,	2932
Eph	6:16	the flaming a of the evil one.	1018

ARSENAL (1)

Jer	50:25	The LORD has opened his a	238

ART (1) [ARTISANS, ARTISTIC, ARTS]

2Ch	2: 7	experienced in the **a of engraving**,	7334+7338

ARTAXERXES (15)

Ezr	4: 7	And in the days of A king of Persia,	831
	4: 7	rest of his associates wrote a letter to A.	831
	4: 8	against Jerusalem to A the king as follows:	10078
	4:11	To King A, From your servants,	10078
	4:23	as the copy of the letter of King A was read	10078
	6:14	Darius and A, kings of Persia.	10078
	7: 1	during the reign of A king of Persia,	831
	7: 7	to Jerusalem in the seventh year of King A.	831
	7:11	of the letter King A had given to Ezra	831
	7:12	A, king of kings, To Ezra the priest,	10078
	7:21	King A, order all the treasurers	10078
Ne	2: 1	from Babylon during the reign of King A:	831
	2: 1	of Nisan in the twentieth year of King A,	831
	5:14	from the twentieth year of King A,	831
	13: 6	of A king of Babylon I had returned to	831

ARTEMAS (1)

Tit	3:12	As soon as I send A or Tychicus to you,	782

ARTEMIS (5)

Ac	19:24	who made silver shrines *of* A,	783
	19:27	that the temple *of* the great goddess A will	783
	19:28	"Great is A of the Ephesians!"	783
	19:34	"Great is A of the Ephesians!"	783
	19:35	the temple *of* the great A and of her image,	783

ARTICLE (14) [ARTICLES]

Lev	11:32	that a, whatever its use, will be unclean,	3998
	13:49	or any leather a, is greenish or reddish,	3998
	13:50	and isolate the **affected** a for seven days.	5596
	13:51	destructive mildew; the a is unclean.	5596S
	13:52	or any leather a that has the contamination	3998
	13:52	the a must be burned up.	NIH
	13:53	or the leather a,	3998
	13:54	he shall order that the **contaminated** a	5596
	13:55	After the **affected** a has been washed,	5596
	13:56	after the a has been washed,	2257S
	13:57	or in the leather a, it is spreading,	3998
	13:58	or any leather a that has been washed	3998
	13:59	woven or knitted material, or any leather a,	3998
	15:12	any wooden a is to be rinsed with water.	3998

ARTICLES (79) [ARTICLE]

Ge	24:53	and silver jewelry and a **of clothing**	955
Ex	3:22	for a *of* silver and gold and for clothing,	3998
	11: 2	to ask their neighbors for a *of* silver	3998
	12:35	the Egyptians for a *of* silver and gold and	3998
	27:19	All the other a *used* in the service of	3998
	30:27	the table and all its a,	3998
	31: 8	the table and its a,	3998
	35:13	with its poles and all its a and the bread of	3998
	37:16	And they made from pure gold the a for	3998
	39:36	with all its a and the bread of the Presence;	3998
Nu	3:31	the a *of* the sanctuary used in ministering,	3998
	4:12	the a used for ministering in the sanctuary,	3998
	4:15	the holy furnishings and all the holy a,	3998
	4:16	including its holy furnishings and a."	3998
	31: 6	who took with him a *from* the sanctuary	3998
	31:50	an offering to the LORD the gold a each	3998
	31:51	all the crafted a.	3998
Jos	6:19	All the silver and gold and the a *of* bronze	3998
	6:24	and gold and the a *of* bronze and iron into	3998
2Sa	8:10	with him a *of* silver and gold and bronze.	3998
	8:11	King David dedicated **these** a to	4392S
	17:28	brought bedding and bowls and a	3998
1Ki	10:21	the **household** a in the Palace of the Forest	3998
	10:25	a *of* silver and gold, robes,	3998
	15:15	of the LORD the silver and gold and the a	3998
2Ki	12:13	trumpets or any other a *of* gold or silver	3998
	14:14	and silver and all the a found in the temple	3998
	23: 4	the a made for Baal and Asherah and all	3998
	24:13	the gold a that Solomon king	3998
	25:14	the bronze a used in the temple service.	3998
1Ch	9:28	Some of them were in charge of the a *used*	3998
	9:29	of the furnishings and all the other a *of*	3998
	18: 8	the pillars and various bronze a.	3998
	18:10	Hadoram brought all kinds of a *of* gold	3998
	18:11	King David dedicated **these** a to	4392S
	22:19	of the LORD and the sacred a *belonging*	3998
	23:26	to carry the tabernacle or any of the a *used*	3998
	28:13	as for all the a *to be used in* its service.	3998
	28:14	the gold a *to be used in* various kinds	3998
	28:14	and the weight of silver for all the silver a	3998
2Ch	4:16	shovels, meat forks and all related a.	3998
	9:20	the **household** a in the Palace of the Forest	3998
	9:24	a *of* silver and gold, and robes,	3998
	15:18	of God the silver and gold and the a that he	3998
	20:25	of equipment and clothing and also a	3998
	21: 3	of silver and gold and a **of value**,	4458

2Ch	24:14	and with it were made a for	3998
	24:14	a *for* the service and for	3998
	25:24	and silver and all the a found in the temple	3998
	29:18	the consecrated bread, with all its a.	3998
	29:19	We have prepared and consecrated all the a	3998
	36: 7	to Babylon a *from* the temple of the LORD	3998
	36:10	together with a *of* value from the temple of	3998
	36:18	to Babylon all the a *from* the temple	3998
Ezr	1: 6	All their neighbors assisted them with a	3998
	1: 7	King Cyrus brought out the a *belonging to*	3998
	1:10	30 matching silver bowls 410 other a	3998
	1:11	there were 5,400 a of gold and of silver.	3998
	5:14	the temple of Babylon the gold and silver a	10398
	5:15	'Take these a and go and deposit them in	10398
	6: 5	the gold and silver a *of* the house of God,	10398
	7:19	to the God of Jerusalem *all* the a entrusted	10398
	8:25	of silver and gold and the a that the king,	3998
	8:26	silver a weighing 100 talents,	3998
	8:27	darics, and two fine a of polished bronze,	3998
	8:28	"You as well as these a are consecrated to	3998
	8:30	and sacred a that had been weighed out to	3998
	8:33	and gold and the sacred a into the hands	3998
Ne	10:39	the a *for* the sanctuary are kept and where	3998
	13: 5	and incense and temple a,	3998
Jer	27:16	now the a *from* the LORD's house will	3998
	28: 3	the a *of* the LORD's house	3998
	28: 6	by bringing the a *of* the LORD's house	3998
	52:18	the bronze a used in the temple service.	3998
Eze	27:13	they exchanged slaves and a *of* bronze	3998
Da	1: 2	with some of the a *from* the temple of God.	3998
	11: 8	their metal images and their valuable a	3998
2Ti	2:20	In a large house there are a not only of gold	5007
Rev	18:12	and a of every kind made of ivory,	NIG

ARTIFICER, ARTIFICERS (KJV) See CRAFTSMEN

ARTIFICIAL (1)

Ne	3:16	as the a pool and the House of the Heroes.	6913

ARTILLERY (KJV) See WEAPONS

ARTISANS (4) [ART]

2Ki	24:14	and all the craftsmen and a—	4994
	24:16	and a thousand craftsmen and a.	4994
Jer	24: 1	and the a *of* Judah were carried into exile	4994
	29: 2	the craftsmen and the a had gone into exile	4994

ARTISTIC (3) [ART]

Ex	31: 4	to make a **designs** for work in gold,	4742
	35:32	to make a **designs** for work in gold,	4742
	35:33	to engage in all kinds of a **craftsmanship.**	4742

ARTS (7) [ART]

Ex	7:11	also did the same things by their **secret a:**	4268
	7:22	the same things by their **secret a;**	4319
	8: 7	the same things by their **secret a;**	4319
	8:18	to produce gnats by their **secret a,**	4319
Rev	9:21	their **magic a**, their sexual immorality	5760
	21: 8	**those who practice magic a,**	5761
	22:15	those who **practice magic a,**	5761

ARUBBOTH (1)

1Ki	4:10	in A (Socoh and all the land	749

ARUMAH (1)

Jdg	9:41	Abimelech stayed in A,	777

ARVAD (2) [ARVADITES]

Eze	27: 8	Men of Sidon and A were your oarsmen;	770
	27:11	Men of A and Helech manned your walls	770

ARVADITES (2) [ARVAD]

Ge	10:18	A, Zemarites and Hamathites.	773
1Ch	1:16	A, Zemarites and Hamathites.	773

ARZA (1)

1Ki	16: 9	getting drunk in the home of A,	825

AS (4006) See Index of Articles Etc.

ASA (52) [ASA'S]

1Ki	15: 8	And A his son succeeded him as king.	654
	15: 9	A became king of Judah,	654
	15:11	A did what was right in the eyes of	654
	15:13	A cut the pole down and burned it in	654
	15:16	There was war between A and Baasha king	654
	15:17	or entering the territory of A king of Judah.	654
	15:18	A then took all the silver and gold	654
	15:20	Ben-Hadad agreed with King A and sent	654
	15:22	Then King A issued an order to all Judah—	654
	15:22	With them King A built up Geba	654
	15:24	Then A rested with his fathers	654
	15:25	in the second year of A king of Judah,	654
	15:28	of A king of Judah and succeeded him	654
	15:32	There was war between A and Baasha king	654
	15:33	In the third year of A king of Judah,	654
	16: 8	In the twenty-sixth year of A king of Judah,	654

1Ki 16:10 the twenty-seventh year of A king of Judah. 654
16:15 the twenty-seventh year of A king of Judah. 654
16:23 In the thirty-first year of A king of Judah, 654
16:29 In the thirty-eighth year of A king of Judah 654
22:41 Jehoshaphat son of A became king of Judah 654
22:43 in the ways of his father A and did not stray 654
22:46 even after the reign of his father A. 654
1Ch 3:10 A his son, Jehoshaphat his son, 654
9:16 and Berekiah son of A, the son of Elkanah. 654
2Ch 14: 1 A his son succeeded him as king, 654
14: 2 A did what was good and right in the eyes 654
14: 8 A had an army of three hundred thousand 654
14:10 A went out to meet him, 654
14:11 A called to the LORD his God and said, 654
14:12 down the Cushites before A and Judah. 654
14:13 and A and his army pursued them as far 654
15: 2 He went out to meet A and said to him, 654
15: 2 A and all Judah and Benjamin. 654
15: 8 When A heard these words and 654
15:16 King A also deposed his grandmother
Maacah from her position 654
15:16 A cut the pole down, 654
16: 1 or entering the territory of A king of Judah. 654
16: 2 A then took the silver and gold out of 654
16: 4 Ben-Hadad agreed with King A and sent 654
16: 6 Then King A brought all the men of Judah, 654
16: 7 the seer came to A king of Judah and said 654
16:10 A was angry with the seer because of this; 654
16:10 the same time A brutally oppressed some of 654
16:12 of his reign A was afflicted with a disease 654
16:13 in the forty-first year of his reign A died 654
17: 2 of Ephraim that his father A had captured. 654
20:32 in the ways of his father A and did not stray 654
21:12 of your father Jehoshaphat or of A king 654
Jer 41: 9 the one King A had made as part 654
Mt 1: 7 Abijah the father of A, 809
1: 8 A the father of Jehoshaphat, 809

ASA'S (7) [ASA]

1Ki 15:14 A heart was fully committed to the LORD 654
15:23 As for all the other events of A reign, 654
2Ch 15:10 of the fifteenth year of A reign. 654
15:17 A heart was fully committed 654
15:19 until the thirty-fifth year of A reign. 654
16: 1 the thirty-sixth year of A reign Baasha king 654
16:11 The events of A reign, 654

ASAHEL (18) [ASAHEL'S]

2Sa 2:18 Joab, Abishai and A. 6915
2:18 A was as fleet-footed as a wild gazelle. 6915
2:20 behind him and asked, "Is that you, A?" 6915
2:21 But A would not stop chasing him. 6915
2:22 Again Abner warned A, "Stop chasing me! 6915
2:23 But A refused to give up the pursuit; NIH
2:23 to the place where A had fallen and died. 6915
2:30 Besides A, nineteen of David's 6915
2:32 They took A and buried him 6915
3:27 there, to avenge the blood of his brother A, 6915
3:30 because he had killed their brother A in 6915
23:24 A the brother of Joab, 6915
1Ch 2:16 Zeruiah's three sons were Abishai, Joab
and A. 6915
11:26 A the brother of Joab, 6915
27: 7 was A the brother of Joab; 6915
2Ch 17: 8 Shemaiah, Nethaniah, Zebadiah, A, 6915
31:13 Jehiel, Azaziah, Nahath, A, Jerimoth, 6915
Ezr 10:15 Only Jonathan son of A and Jahzeiah son 6915

ASAHEL'S (1) [ASAHEL]

2Sa 2:23 the butt of his spear into A stomach, 2084ˢ

ASAHIAH (KJV) See ASAIAH

ASAIAH (8)

2Ki 22:12 the secretary and A the king's attendant: 6919
22:14 Shaphan and A went to speak to 6919
1Ch 4:36 Jaakobah, Jeshohaiah, A, Adiel, Jesimiel, 6919
6:30 Haggiah his son and A his son. 6919
9: 5 A the firstborn and his sons. 6919
15: 6 A the leader and 220 relatives. 6919
15:11 and Uriel, A, Joel, Shemaiah, 6919
2Ch 34:20 the secretary and A the king's attendant: 6919

ASAPH (45) [ASAPH'S]

2Ki 18:18 and Joah son of A the recorder went out 666
18:37 Shebna the secretary and Joah son of A 666
1Ch 6:39 and Heman's associate A, who served 666
6:39 A son of Berekiah, the son of Shimea, 666
9:15 the son of Zicri, the son of A; 666
15:17 from his brothers, A son of Berekiah; 666
15:19 A and Ethan were to sound 666
16: 5 A was the chief, 666
16: 5 A was to sound the cymbals, 666
16: 7 to A and his associates this psalm of thanks 666
16:37 David left A and his associates before 666
25: 1 set apart some of the sons of A, 666
25: 2 From the sons of A: 666
25: 2 of A were under the supervision of Asaph, 666
25: 2 of Asaph were under the supervision of A, 666
25: 6 A, Jeduthun and Heman were under 666
25: 9 The first lot, which was for A, 666
26: 1 one of the sons of A. 666
2Ch 5:12 All the Levites who were musicians—A, 666

2Ch 20:14 a Levite and descendant of A, 666
29:13 from the descendants of A, 666
29:30 with the words of David and of A the seer. 666
35:15 The musicians, the descendants of A, 666
35:15 were in the places prescribed by David, A, 666
Ezr 2:41 The singers: the descendants of A 128 666
3:10 the Levites (the sons of A) with cymbals, 666
Ne 2: 8 And may I have a letter to A, 666
7:44 The singers: the descendants of A 148 666
11:17 the son of Zabdi, the son of A, 666
12:35 the son of Zaccur, the son of A, 666
12:46 For long ago, in the days of David and A, 666
Ps 50: T A psalm of A. 666
73: T A psalm of A. 666
74: T A maskil of A. 666
75: T A psalm of A. 666
76: T A psalm of A. 666
77: T For Jeduthun. Of A. 666
78: T A maskil of A. 666
79: T A psalm of A. 666
80: T "The Lilies of the Covenant." Of A. 666
81: T According to gittith. Of A. 666
82: T A psalm of A. 666
83: T A song. A psalm of A. 666
Isa 36: 3 Joah son of A the recorder went out to him. 666
36:22 and Joah son of A the recorder went 666

ASAPH'S (1) [ASAPH]

Ne 11:22 Uzzi was one of A descendants, 666

ASAREL (1)

1Ch 4:16 Ziph, Ziphah, Tiria and A. 832

ASARELAH (1)

1Ch 25: 2 Zaccur, Joseph, Nethaniah and A. 833

ASCEND (7) [ASCENDED, ASCENDING, ASCENT, ASCENTS]

Dt 30:12 "Who will a into heaven to get it 6590
Ps 24: 3 Who may a the hill of the LORD? 6590
Isa 14:13 "I will a to heaven; 6590
14:14 I will a above the tops of the clouds; 6590
Jn 6:62 the Son of Man a to where he was before! 326
Ac 2:34 For David did not a to heaven, 326
Ro 10: 6 'Who will a into heaven?' " 326

ASCENDED (8) [ASCEND]

Jdg 13:20 the angel of the LORD a in the flame. 6590
2Ki 19:23 "With my many chariots I have a 6590
Ps 47: 5 God has a amid shouts of joy, 6590
68:18 When you a on high, 6590
Isa 37:24 'With my many chariots I have a 6590
Eph 4: 8 This is why it says: "When he a on high, 326
4: 9 (What does "he a" mean except that he 326
4:10 the very one who a higher than all 326

ASCENDING (3) [ASCEND]

Ge 28:12 the angels of God were a and descending 6590
Eze 41: 7 the temple was built in a stages, 2025+2025+4200+4200+5087+5087
Jn 1:51 and the angels of God a and descending on 326

ASCENT (2) [ASCEND]

Ne 3:19 a point facing the a to the armory as far as 6590
12:37 up the steps of the City of David on the a to 5090

ASCENTS (15) [ASCEND]

Ps 120: T A song of a. 5092
121: T A song of a. 5092
122: T A song of a. Of David. 5092
123: T A song of a. 5092
124: T A song of a. Of David. 5092
125: T A song of a. 5092
126: T A song of a. 5092
127: T A song of a. Of Solomon. 5092
128: T A song of a. 5092
129: T A song of a. 5092
130: T A song of a. 5092
131: T A song of a. Of David. 5092
132: T A song of a. 5092
133: T A song of a. Of David. 5092
134: T A song of a. 5092

ASCRIBE (10)

1Ch 16:28 A to the LORD, O families of nations, 2035
16:28 a to the LORD glory and strength, 2035
16:29 a to the LORD the glory due his name. 2035
Job 36: 3 I will a justice to my Maker. 5989
Ps 29: 1 A to the LORD, O mighty ones, 2035
29: 1 a to the LORD glory and strength. 2035
29: 2 a to the LORD the glory due his name; 2035
96: 7 A to the LORD, O families of nations, 2035
96: 7 a to the LORD glory and strength. 2035
96: 8 a to the LORD the glory due his name; 2035

ASENATH (3)

Ge 41:45 and gave him A daughter of Potiphera, 664
41:50 to Joseph by A daughter of Potiphera, 664
46:20 to Joseph by A daughter of Potiphera, 664

ASER (KJV) See ASHER

ASH (4) [ASHES]

Lev 4:12 and burn it in a wood fire on the a heap. 2016
1Sa 2: 8 and lifts the needy from the a heap; 883
Ps 113: 7 and lifts the needy from the a heap; 883
La 4: 5 in purple now lie on a heaps. 883

ASHAMED (53) [SHAME]

2Sa 19: 3 the city that day as men steal in who are a 4007
2Ki 2:17 they persisted until he was too a to refuse. 1017
8:11 with a fixed gaze until Hazael felt a. 1017
2Ch 30:15 The priests and the Levites were a 4007
Ezr 8:22 I was a to ask the king for soldiers 1017
9: 6 I am too a and disgraced to lift up my face 1017
Ps 6:10 All my enemies will be a and dismayed; 1017
83:17 May they ever be a and dismayed; 1017
Isa 1:29 "You will be a because of the sacred oaks 1017
23: 4 Be a, O Sidon, and you, 1017
24:23 The moon will be abashed, the sun a; 1017
29:22 "No longer will Jacob be a; 1017
33: 9 Lebanon is a and withers; 2917
41:11 "All who rage against you will surely be a 1017
Jer 6:15 Are they a of their loathsome conduct? 1017
8:12 Are they a of their loathsome conduct? 1017
22:22 Then you will be a and disgraced because 1017
31:19 I was a and humiliated because I bore 1017
48:13 Then Moab will be a of Chemosh, 1017
48:13 of Israel was a when they trusted in Bethel. 1017
50:12 your mother will be greatly a; 1017
Eze 16:52 So then, be a and bear your disgrace, 1017
16:54 that you may bear your disgrace and be a 4007
16:61 and be a when you receive your sisters, 4007
16:63 and be a and never again open your mouth 1017
36:32 Be a and disgraced for your conduct, 1017
43:10 that they may be a of their sins. 4007
43:11 and if they are a of all they have done, 4007
Hos 10: 6 Israel will be a of its wooden idols. 1017
Mic 3: 7 be a and the diviners disgraced. 1017
7:16 Nations will see and be a, 1017
Zec 13: 4 "On that day every prophet will be a 1017
Mk 8:38 If anyone is a of me and my words 2049
8:38 of Man will be a of him when he comes 2049
Lk 9:26 If anyone is a of me and my words, 2049
9:26 of Man will be a of him when he comes 2049
16: 3 and I'm a to beg— 159
Ro 1:16 I am not a of the gospel, 2049
6:21 from the things you are now a of? 2049
2Co 9: 4 would be a of having been so confident. 2875
10: 8 I will not be a of it. 159
Php 1:20 and hope that I will in no way be a, 159
2Th 3:14 in order that he may feel a. 1956
2Ti 1: 8 So do not be a to testify about our Lord, 2049
1: 8 or a of me his prisoner. NIG
1:12 Yet I am not a, because I know whom I
have believed, 2049
1:16 and was not a of my chains. 2049
2:15 a workman who does not need to be a 454
Tit 2: 8 be a because they have nothing bad to say 1956
Heb 2:11 So Jesus is not a to call them brothers. 2049
11:16 God is not a to be called their God, 2049
1Pe 3:16 in Christ may be a of their slander. 2875
4:16 if you suffer as a Christian, do not be a, 159

ASHAN (4) [BOR ASHAN]

Jos 15:42 Libnah, Ether, A, 6941
19: 7 Rimmon, Ether and A— 6941
1Ch 4:32 Ain, Rimmon, Token and A— 6941
6:59 A, Juttah and Beth Shemesh, together 6941

ASHBEA See BETH ASHBEA

ASHBEL (3) [ASHBELITE]

Ge 46:21 Bela, Beker, A, Gera, Naaman, Ehi, Rosh, 839
Nu 26:38 through A, the Ashbelite clan; 839
1Ch 8: 1 A the second son, Aharah the third, 839

ASHBELITE (1) [ASHBEL]

Nu 26:38 through Ashbel, the A clan; 840

ASHCHENAZ (KJV) See ASHKENAZ

ASHDOD (21)

Jos 11:22 only in Gaza, Gath and A did any survive. 846
13: 3 A, Ashkelon, Gath and Ekron. 847
15:46 all that were in the vicinity of A, 846
15:47 A, its surrounding settlements and villages; 846
1Sa 5: 1 they took it from Ebenezer to A. 846
5: 3 the people of A rose early the next day, 847
5: 5 at A step on the threshold. 846
5: 6 upon the people of A and its vicinity; 847
5: 7 the men of A saw what was happening, 846
6:17 one each for A, Gaza, Ashkelon, 846
2Ch 26: 6 down the walls of Gath, Jabneh and A. 846
26: 6 He then rebuilt towns near A and elsewhere 846
Ne 4: 7 the Ammonites and the men of A heard that 847
13:23 of Judah who had married women from A, 847
13:24 of their children spoke the language of A 848
Isa 20: 1 came to A and attacked and captured it— 846
Jer 25:20 Gaza, Ekron, and the people left at A); 846
Am 1: 8 of A and the one who holds the scepter 846

Am 3: 9 to the fortresses of A and to the fortresses 846
Zep 2: 4 At midday A will be emptied 846
Zec 9: 6 Foreigners will occupy A, 846

ASHDODITES, ASHDOTHITES (KJV)
See MEN OF ASHDOD

ASHDOTHPISGAH (KJV) See PISGAH

ASHER (45) [ASHER'S]
Ge 30:13 So she named him A. 888
35:26 of Leah's maidservant Zilpah: Gad and A. 888
46:17 The sons of A: Imnah, Ishvah, Ishvi, and 888
Ex 1: 4 Dan and Naphtali; Gad and A. 888
Nu 1:13 from A, Pagiel son of Ocran; 888
1:40 From the descendants of A: 888
1:41 number from the tribe of A was 41,500. 888
2:27 The tribe of A will camp next to them. 888
2:27 The leader of the people of A is Pagiel son 888
7:72 the leader of the people of A, 888
10:26 over the division of the tribe of A, 888+1201
13:13 from the tribe of A, Sethur son of Michael; 888
26:44 The descendants of A by their clans were: 888
26:46 (A had a daughter named Serah.) 888
26:47 These were the clans of A; 888+1201
34:27 the leader from the tribe of A; 888+1201
Dt 27:13 Reuben, Gad, A, Zebulun. 888
33:24 About A he said: "Most blessed of sons 888
33:24 "Most blessed of sons is A; 888
Jos 17: 7 The territory of Manasseh extended from A 888
17:10 and bordered A on the north and Issachar 888
17:11 Within Issachar and A, 888
19:24 The fifth lot came out for the tribe of A, 888+1201
19:31 the inheritance of the tribe of A, 888+1201
19:34 A on the west and the Jordan on the east. 888
21: 6 A, Naphtali and the half-tribe of Manasseh 888
21:30 from the tribe of A, Mishal, Abdon, 888
Jdg 1:31 Nor did A drive out those living in Acco 888
1:32 and because of this the people of A lived 896
5:17 A remained on the coast and stayed 888
6:35 and also into A, Zebulun and Naphtali, 888
7:23 A and all Manasseh were called out, 888
1Ki 4:16 Baana son of Hushai—in A and in Aloth; 888
1Ch 2: 2 Joseph, Benjamin, Naphtali, Gad and A. 888
6:62 from the tribes of Issachar, A, Naphtali, 888
6:74 from the tribe of A they received Mashal, 888
7:30 sons of A: Imnah, Ishvah, Ishvi and Beriah. 888
7:40 All these were descendants of A— 888
12:36 men of A, experienced soldiers prepared 888
2Ch 30:11 Nevertheless, some men of A, 888
Eze 48: 2 "A will have one portion; 888
48: 3 it will border the territory of A from east 888
48:34 the gate of A and the gate of Naphtali. 888
Lk 2:36 the daughter of Phanuel, of the tribe of A. 818
Rev 7: 6 from the tribe of A 12,000, 818

ASHER'S (1) [ASHER]
Ge 49:20 "A food will be rich; 888+4946

ASHERAH (39) [ASHERAHS]
Ex 34:13 and cut down their A poles. 895
Dt 7: 5 cut down their A poles and burn their idols 895
12: 3 and burn their A poles in the fire; 895
16:21 Do not set up any wooden A pole beside 895
Jdg 6:25 to Baal and cut down the A pole beside it. 895
6:26 the wood of the A pole that you cut down, 895
6:28 with the A pole beside it cut down and 895
6:30 down Baal's altar and cut down the A pole 895
1Ki 14:15 the LORD to anger by making A poles. 895
14:23 and A poles on every high hill and 895
15:13 because she had made a repulsive A pole. 895
16:33 Ahab also made an A pole and did more 895
18:19 of Baal and the four hundred prophets of A, 895
2Ki 13: 6 the A pole remained standing in Samaria. 895
17:10 They set up sacred stones and A poles 895
17:16 in the shape of calves, and an A pole. 895
18: 4 and cut down the A poles. 895
21: 3 to Baal and made an A pole, 895
21: 7 the carved A pole he had made and put it 895
23: 4 the articles made for Baal and A and all 895
23: 6 the A pole from the temple of the LORD 895
23: 7 and where women did weaving for A. 895
23:14 the sacred stones and cut down the A poles 895
23:15 and burned the A pole also. 895
2Ch 14: 3 and cut down the A poles. 895
15:16 because she had made a repulsive A pole. 895
17: 6 the high places and the A poles 895
19: 3 for you have rid the land of the A poles 895
24:18 and worshiped A poles and idols. 895
31: 1 and cut down the A poles. 895
33: 3 to the Baals and made A poles. 895
33:19 and set up A poles and idols 895
34: 3 A poles, carved idols and cast images. 895
34: 4 and smashed the A poles, 895
34: 7 he tore down the altars and the A poles 895
Isa 17: 8 have no regard for the A poles 895
27: 9 to pieces, no A poles or incense altars will 895
Jer 17: 2 and A poles beside the spreading trees and 895
Mic 5:14 from among you your A poles 895

ASHERAHS (1) [ASHERAH]
Jdg 3: 7 and served the Baals and the A. 895

ASHERITES (KJV) See ASHER

ASHES (35) [ASH]
Ge 18:27 though I am nothing but dust and a, 709
Ex 27: 3 its pots to remove the a, and its shovels, 2014
Lev 1:16 east side of the altar, where the a are. 2016
4:12 where the a are thrown, 2016
6:10 and shall remove the a of the burnt offering 2016
6:11 and carry the a outside the camp to a place 2016
Nu 4:13 to remove the a from the bronze altar 2014
19: 9 "A man who is clean shall gather up the a 709
19:10 The man who gathers up the a of 709
19:17 put some a from the burned purification 6760
2Sa 13:19 Tamar put a on her head and tore 709
1Ki 13: 3 The altar will be split apart and the a 2016
13: 5 the altar was split apart and its a poured out 2016
2Ki 23: 4 the Kidron Valley and took the a to Bethel. 6760
Est 4: 1 he tore his clothes, put on sackcloth and a, 709
4: 3 Many lay in sackcloth and a. 709
Job 2: 8 with it as he sat among the a. 709
13:12 Your maxims are proverbs of a; 709
30:19 and I am reduced to dust and a. 709
42: 6 and repent in dust and a." 709
Ps 102: 9 For I eat a as my food and mingle my drink 709
147:16 like wool and scatters the frost like a. 709
Isa 44:20 on a, a deluded heart misleads him; 709
58: 5 a reed and for lying on sackcloth and a? 709
61: 3 on them a crown of beauty instead of a, 709
Jer 6:26 put on sackcloth and roll in a; 709
31:40 where dead bodies and a are thrown, 2016
Eze 27:30 on their heads and roll in a. 709
28:18 and I reduced you to a on the ground in 709
Da 9: 3 in fasting, and in sackcloth and a. 709
Mal 4: 3 be a under the soles of your feet on the day 709
Mt 11:21 repented long ago, in sackcloth and a. 5075
Lk 10:13 long ago, sitting in sackcloth and a. 5075
Heb 9:13 The blood of goats and bulls and the a of 5075
2Pe 2: 6 Sodom and Gomorrah by burning them to a 5491

ASHHUR (2)
1Ch 2:24 of Hezron bore him A the father of Tekoa. 858
4: 5 A the father of Tekoa had two wives, 858

ASHIMA (1)
2Ki 17:30 and the men from Hamath made A; 860

ASHKELON (13)
Jos 13: 3 Ashdod, A, Gath and Ekron— 885
Jdg 1:18 A and Ekron—each city with its territory. 884
14:19 He went down to A, 884
1Sa 6:17 one each for Ashdod, Gaza, A, 884
2Sa 1:20 proclaim it not in the streets of A, 884
Jer 25:20 all the kings of the Philistines (those of A, 884
47: 5 A will be silenced. 884
47: 7 when he has ordered it to attack A and 884
Am 1: 8 and the one who holds the scepter in A. 884
Zep 2: 4 Gaza will be abandoned and A left in ruins. 884
2: 7 down in the houses of A. 884
Zec 9: 5 A will see it and fear; 884
9: 5 Gaza will lose her king and A will 884

ASHKENAZ (3)
Ge 10: 3 A, Riphath and Togarmah. 867
1Ch 1: 6 A, Riphath and Togarmah. 867
Jer 51:27 Ararat, Minni and A. 867

ASHNAH (2)
Jos 15:33 In the western foothills: Eshtaol, Zorah, A, 877
15:43 Iphtah, A, Nezib, 877

ASHORE (2) [SHORE]
Lk 8:27 When Jesus stepped a, he was met 1178+2093
Jn 21:11 aboard and dragged the net a. 1178+1650+3836

ASHPENAZ (1)
Da 1: 3 Then the king ordered A, 881

ASHRIEL (KJV) See ASRIEL

ASHTAROTH (6)
Dt 1: 4 king of Bashan, who reigned in A. 6958
Jos 9:10 and Og king of Bashan, who reigned in A. 6958
12: 4 who reigned in A and Edrei. 6958
13:12 in A and Edrei and had survived as one of 6958
13:31 and A and Edrei (the royal cities of Og 6958
1Ch 6:71 also A, together with their pasturelands; 6958

ASHTERATHITE (1)
1Ch 11:44 the A, Shama and Jeiel the sons of Hotham 6960

ASHTEROTH KARNAIM (1)
Ge 14: 5 and defeated the Rephaites in A, 6959

ASHTORETH (3) [ASHTORETHS]
1Ki 11: 5 He followed A the goddess of 6956
11:33 and worshiped A the goddess of 6956
2Ki 23:13 of Israel had built for A the vile goddess of 6956

ASHTORETHS (6) [ASHTORETH]
Jdg 2:13 and served Baal and the A. 6956
10: 6 They served the Baals and the A, 6956
1Sa 7: 3 the A and commit yourselves to the LORD 6956
7: 4 the Israelites put away their Baals and A, 6956
12:10 the LORD and served the Baals and the A. 6956
31:10 of the A and fastened his body to the wall 6956

ASHURBANIPAL (1)
Ezr 4:10 and honorable A deported and settled in 10055

ASHUR (KJV) See ASHHUR

ASHURITES (KJV) See ASHURI

ASHURI (1)
2Sa 2: 9 A and Jezreel, and also over Ephraim, 856

ASHVATH (1)
1Ch 7:33 The sons of Japhlet: Pasach, Bimhal and A. 6937

ASIA (19)
Ac 2: 9 Judea and Cappadocia, Pontus and A, 823
6: 9 as well as the provinces of Cilicia and A. 823
16: 6 the word in the province of A. 823
19:10 in the province of A heard the word of 823
19:22 while he stayed in the province of A 823
19:26 in practically the whole province of A. 823
19:27 throughout the province of A and 823
20: 4 from the province of A, 824
20:16 in the province of A, 823
20:18 the first day I came into the province of A. 823
21:27 the province of A saw Paul at the temple. 823
24:19 from the province of A, 823
27: 2 along the coast of the province of A, 823
Ro 16: 5 to Christ in the province of A. 823
1Co 16:19 in the province of A send you greetings. 823
2Co 1: 8 in the province of A, 823
2Ti 1:15 in the province of A has deserted me, 823
1Pe 1: 1 Galatia, Cappadocia, A and Bithynia, 823
Rev 1: 4 the seven churches in the province of A: 823

ASIDE (72) [SIDE]
Ge 19: 2 "please turn a to your servant's house. 6073
Nu 18:11 whatever is set a from the gifts of all 9556
18:19 Whatever is set a from the holy offerings 9556
21:22 not turn a into any field or vineyard, 5742
23: 3 beside your offering while I go a. 2143
Dt 2:27 we will not turn a or to the right or 6073
4:41 Moses set a three cities east of the Jordan, 976
5:32 do not turn a to the right or to the left. 6073
9:16 You had turned a quickly from the way that 6073
14:22 Be sure to set a a tenth of all 6923+6923
17:11 Do not turn a from what they tell you, 6073
19: 2 then set a for yourselves three cities 976
19: 7 This is why I command you to set a 976
19: 9 then you are to set a three more cities. NIH
21:13 and put a the clothes she was wearing 6073
26:12 When you have finished setting a a tenth 5130+6923
26:13 I have not turned a from your commands 6296
28:14 Do not turn a from any of the commands 6073
Jos 16: 9 the towns and their villages that were set a 4426
23: 6 without turning a to the right or to the left. 6073
Jdg 14: 8 he turned a to look at the lion's carcass. 6073
1Sa 8: 3 They turned a after dishonest gain 5742
9:23 the one I told you to lay a." 6640
9:24 it was set a for you for this occasion, 9068
2Sa 2:21 "Turn a to the right or to the left; 5742
3:27 Joab took him a into the gateway, 5742
6:10 he took it a to the house of Obed-Edom 5742
18:30 The king said, "Stand a and wait here." 6015
18:30 So he stepped a and stood there. 6015
23: 6 evil men are all to be cast a like thorns, 5610
2Ki 22: 2 not turning a to the right or to the left. 6073
24:12 So Jehoiachin put a his prison clothes and 9101
1Ch 13:13 he took it a to the house of Obed-Edom 5742
2Ch 34: 2 not turning a to the right or to the left. 6073
35:12 They set a the burnt offerings to give them 6073
Ne 12:47 also set a the portion for the other Levites, 7727
12:47 and the Levites set a the portion for 7727
Job 6:18 Caravans turn a from their routes; 4369
23:11 I have kept to his way without turning a. 5742
29: 8 the young men saw me and stepped a and 2461
36:18 do not let a large bribe turn you a. 5742
Ps 14: 3 All have turned a, 6073
40: 4 to those who turn a to false gods. 8454
85: 3 You set a all your wrath and turned 665
102:10 for you have taken me up and thrown me a. 8959
Pr 5: 7 do not turn a from what I say. 6073
Jer 5:23 they have turned a and gone away. 6073
52:33 So Jehoiachin put a his prison clothes and 9101
Eze 26:16 from their thrones and lay a their robes 6073
31:11 according to its wickedness, I cast it a, 1763
48:20 As a special gift you will set a 8123
Mt 16:22 Peter took him a and began to rebuke him. 4689
20:17 he took the twelve disciples a and said to them, 2625+2848
Mk 7: 9 of setting a the commands of God in order 119
7:33 After he took him a, away from the crowd, 2625+2848
8:32 Peter took him a and began to rebuke him. 4689

Mk 10:32 Again he **took** the Twelve a 4161
10:50 **Throwing** his cloak a, 610
Lk 18:31 Jesus **took** the Twelve a and told them, 4161
Jn 2: 9 Then he called the bridegroom a NIG
11:28 she went back and called her sister Mary a. 3277
Ac 7:27 the other **pushed** Moses a and said, 723
23:19 drew him a and asked, 2625+2848
Ro 13:12 So let us **put** the deeds of darkness 700
1Co 16: 2 of you should **set** a sum of money 5502
Gal 2:21 I do not **set** a the grace of God, 119
3:15 Just as no one can **set** a or add to 119
3:17 does not **set** a 218
2Ti 4: 4 from the truth and **turn** a to myths. 1762
Heb 7:18 The former regulation is **set** a 120
10: 9 He **sets** a the first to establish the second. 359
2Pe 1:14 because I know that I will soon **put** it a, 629+1639

ASIEL (1)
1Ch 4:35 the son of Seraiah, the son of A, 6918

ASK (184) [ASKED, ASKING, ASKS]
Ge 23: 9 A him to sell it to me for the full price as NIH
24:57 "Let's call the girl and a her *about* it." 8626
32:29 But he replied, "Why *do you* a my name?" 8626
34:11 and I will give you whatever *you* a. 606
34:12 and I'll pay whatever *you* a me. 606
50:17 I a you to forgive your brothers the sins 626
Ex 3:13 and *they* a me, 'What is his name?' 606
3:22 *to* a her neighbor and any woman living 8626
11: 2 and women alike *are to* a their neighbors 8626
12:26 And when your children a you, 606
Lev 25:20 *You may* a, "What will we eat in 8626
Dt 4:32 A now about the former days, 8626
4:32 a from one end of the heavens to the other. NIH
10:12 the LORD your God of you but to fear 8626
29:24 All the nations *will* a: 606
30:12 so that *you have to* a, 606
30:13 so that *you have to* a, 606
31:17 and on that day *they will* a, 606
32: 7 A your father and he will tell you, 8626
Jos 4: 6 In the future, when your children a you, 8626
4:21 when your descendants a their fathers, 8626
15:18 she urged him to a her father for a field. 907+8626
Jdg 1:14 she urged him to a her father *for* a field. 8626
9: 2 "A all the citizens of Shechem, 1819
13: 6 I didn't a him where he came from, 8626
13:18 He replied, "Why *do you* a my name? 8626
18:24 How *can you* a, 'What's the matter 606
Ru 3:11 I will do for you all *you* a. 606
1Sa 25: 8 A your own servants and they will tell you. 8626
2Sa 11:20 anger may flare up, and *he may* a you, 606
14:18 the answer to what I *am going to* a you." 8626
14:32 so I can send you to the king to a, 606
16:10 who *can* a, 'Why *do you* do this?' " 606
19:11 "A the elders of Judah, 1819
1Ki 2:17 he continued, "Please a King Solomon— 8626
3: 5 "A for whatever you want me to give you." 8626
14: 5 "Jeroboam's wife is coming to a you 1821+2011
2Ki 1: 3 of the king of Samaria and a, 1819
4: 3 and a all your neighbors for empty jars. 8626
4: 3 Don't a for just a few. NIH
4:26 Run to meet her and a her, 606
4:28 "*Did I* a you for a son, my lord?" 8626
8: 8 a him, 'Will I recover from this illness?' " 606
8: 9 of Aram has sent me to a, 606
9:17 "Send him to meet them and a, 606
14:10 Why a for trouble and cause 1741
2Ch 1: 7 "A for whatever you want me to give you." 8626
25:19 Why a for trouble and cause 1741
32:31 by the rulers of Babylon to a him *about* 2011
Ezr 7:21 may a of you— 10689
8:21 and a him for a safe journey for us 1335
8:22 I was ashamed to a the king *for* soldiers 8626
Est 5:14 and a the king in the morning 606
Job 8: 8 "A the former generations 8626
12: 7 "But a the animals, 8626
35: 3 Yet *you* a him, 'What profit is it to me, 606
37:20 Would any man a to be swallowed up? 606
Ps 2: 8 A of me, and I will make 8626
27: 4 One thing I a of the LORD, 8626
Pr 30: 7 "Two things I a of you, O LORD; 8626
Ecc 7:10 For it is not wise *to* a such questions. 8626
Isa 7:11 "A the LORD your God for a sign, 8626
7:12 But Ahaz said, "I *will* not a; 8626
21:12 If *you would* a, then ask; 1239
21:12 If you would ask, then a; 1239
41:28 no one to give answer when I a them. 8626
58: 2 They a me *for just* decisions 8626
65: 1 "I revealed myself to *those who did* not a 8626
Jer 2: 6 They did *not* a, 'Where is the LORD, 606
2: 8 priests *did not* a, 'Where is the LORD?' 606
5:19 And when *the people* a, 606
6:16 a for the ancient paths, 8626
6:16 a where the good way is, and walk in it, NIH
13:22 And if *you* a yourself, 606
15: 2 And if *they* a you, 'Where shall we go?' 606
15: 5 Who will stop to a how you are? 8626
16:10 and *they* a you, 'Why has the LORD decreed 606
22: 8 by this city and *will* a one another, 606
23:33 a you, 'What is the oracle of the LORD?' 8626
30: 6 A and see: Can a man bear children? 8626
38:14 "I *am going to* a you something," 8626
48:19 A the man fleeing and the woman escaping, 8626
48:19 a them, 'What has happened?' 606
50: 5 *They will* a the way to Zion 8626

Eze 12: 9 *did* not that rebellious house of Israel a you, 606
13:12 the wall collapses, *will* people not a you, 606
18:19 "Yet *you* a, 'Why does the son not share 606
21: 7 when *they* a you, 'Why are you groaning?' 606
37:18 "When your countrymen a you, 606
Hag 2: 2 of the people. A them, 606
2:11 'A the priests what the law says: 8626
Zec 7: 5 "A all the people of the land and 606
10: 1 A the LORD for rain in the springtime; 8626
Mal 1: 2 "But *you* a, 'How have you loved us?' 606
1: 6 "But *you* a, 'How have we shown contempt 606
1: 7 "But *you* a, 'How have we defiled you?' 606
2:14 *You* a, "Why?" 606
2:17 "How have we wearied him?" *you* a. 606
3: 7 "But *you* a, 'How are we to return?' 606
3: 8 "But *you* a, 'How do we rob you?' 606
3:13 *you* a, 'What have we said against you?' 606
Mt 6: 8 before *you* a him. 160
7: 7 "A and it will be given to you; 160
7:11 *to* those who a him! 160
9:38 A the Lord of the harvest, therefore, 1289
11: 3 to a him, "Are you the one who was 3306
18:19 on earth agree about anything *you* a for, 160
19:17 "Why *do you* a me about what is good?" 2263
21:22 you will receive whatever *you* a for 160
21:24 "I *will* also a you one question. 2263
21:25 "If we say, 'From heaven,' he *will* a, 3306
22:46 a him any more **questions**. 2089
27:20 and the elders persuaded the crowd to a for 160
Mk 5:31 his disciples answered, "and yet *you can* a, 3306
6:22 "A me for anything you want, 160
6:23 "Whatever *you* a I will give you, 160
6:24 "What *shall I* a for?" 160
8:12 "Why *does* this generation a for 2426
9:32 and were afraid *to* a him *about* it. 2089
10:35 "we want you to do for us whatever *we* a." 160
11:24 whatever *you* a for in prayer, 160
11:29 Jesus replied, "I *will* a you one question. 2089
11:31 "If we say, 'From heaven,' he *will* a, 3306
12:34 a him any more **questions**. 2089
Lk 6: 9 Then Jesus said to them, "I a you, 2089
7:19 he sent them to the Lord to a, 3306
7:20 "John the Baptist sent us to you to a, 3306
9:45 and they were afraid *to* a him about it. 2263
10: 2 A the Lord of the harvest, therefore, 1289
11: 9 A and it will be given to you; 160
11:13 the Holy Spirit to those who a him!" 160
14:32 the other is still a long way off and will a 2263
20: 3 He replied, "I *will* also a you a question. 2263
20: 5 he *will* a, 'Why didn't you believe him?' 3306
20:40 no one dared *to* a him any more questions. 2089
Jn 1:19 and Levites to a him who he was. 2263
4: 9 How can *you* a me for a drink?" 160
7:25 of the people of Jerusalem *began* to a, 3306
8:22 This made the Jews a, "Will he kill himself? 3306
9:21 we don't know. A him. 2263
9:23 "He is of age; a him." 2089
11:22 now God will give you whatever *you* a." 160
13:24 "A him which one he means." 4785
14:13 And I will do whatever *you* a in my name, 160
14:14 *You may* a me for anything in my name, 160
14:16 And I *will* a the Father, 2263
15: 7 words remain in you, a whatever you wish, 160
15:16 the Father will give you whatever *you* a 160
16:19 that they wanted *to* a him about this, 2263
16:23 day *you will* no longer a me anything. 2263
16:23 my Father will give you whatever *you* a 160
16:24 A and you will receive, 160
16:26 In that day *you will* a in my name. 160
16:26 I am not saying that I *will* a the Father 2263
16:30 even need to have anyone a you **questions**. 2263
18:21 a those who heard me. 2263
21:12 None of the disciples dared a him, 2004
Ac 9:11 of Judas on Straight Street and a for a man 2426
10:29 May I a why you sent for me?" 4785
23:20 "The Jews have agreed to a you 2263
Ro 10:18 But I a: Did they not hear? 3306
10:19 Again I a: Did Israel not understand? 3306
10:20 *to* those who did *not* a for me." 2089
11: 1 I a then: Did God reject his people? 3306
11:11 Again I a: Did they stumble 3306
16: 2 I a you to receive her in the Lord in NIG
1Co 14:35 *they should* a their own husbands at home; 2089
15:35 someone *may* a, "How are the dead raised? 3306
Eph 3:13 I a you, therefore, not to be discouraged 160
3:20 to do immeasurably more than all *we* a 160
Php 4: 3 Yes, and I a you, loyal yokefellow, 2263
1Th 4: 1 Now *we* a you and urge you in 2263
5:12 Now *we* a you, brothers, 2263
2Th 2: 1 and our being gathered to him, *we* a you, 2263
1Ti 5: 5 and day to pray and *to* a God for help. 4666
Phm 1:21 that you will do even more than I a. 3306
Jas 1: 5 lacks wisdom, *he should* a God, 160
4: 2 because you *do not* a God. 160
4: 3 When *you* a, you *do not* receive, 160
4: 3 because *you* a with wrong motives, 160
1Jn 3:22 and receive from him anything *we* a, 160
5:14 that if *we* a anything according to his will, 160
5:15 that he hears us—whatever *we* a— 160
2Jn 1: 5 I a that we love one another. 2263

ASKED (552) [ASK]
Ge 18: 9 "Where is your wife Sarah?" *they* a him. 606
20:10 And Abimelech a Abraham, 606
21:29 and Abimelech a Abraham, 606
24: 5 The servant a him, "What if the woman 606

Ge 24:23 Then he a, "Whose daughter are you? 606
24:39 "Then I a my master, 606
24:47 "I a her, 'Whose daughter are you?' 8626
24:58 So they called Rebekah and a her, 606
24:65 and a the servant, "Who is that man 606
26: 7 the men of that place a him about his wife, 8626
26:27 Isaac a them, "Why have you come to me 606
27:20 Isaac a his son, "How did you find 606
27:24 "Are you really my son Esau?" *he* a. 606
27:32 His father Isaac a him, "Who are you?" 606
27:36 now he's taken my blessing!" Then *he* a, 606
29: 4 Jacob a the shepherds, "My brothers, 606
29: 5 Then Jacob a them, "Is he well?" 606
30:31 "What shall I give you?" *he* a. 606
31:36 "What is my crime?" he a Laban. 6699
32:27 The man a him, "What is your name?" 606
33: 5 "Who are these with you?" *he* a. 606
33: 8 Esau a, "What do you mean 606
33:15 "But why do that?" Jacob a. 606
37:15 around in the fields and a him, 8626
38: 6 to sleep with you?" *she* a. 606
38:17 until you send it?" *she* a. 606
38:21 *He* a the men who lived there, 8626
40: 7 So *he* a Pharaoh's officials who were 8626
41:38 So Pharaoh a them, "Can we find anyone 606
42: 7 "Where do you come from?" he a. 606
43: 6 Israel a, "Why did you bring this trouble 606
43: 7 'Is your father still living?' *he* a us. 606
43:27 He a them how they were, 4200+8626+8934
44:19 My lord a his servants, 8626
47: 3 Pharaoh a the brothers, 606
47: 8 Pharaoh a him, "How old are you?" 606
48: 8 When Israel saw the sons of Joseph, *he* a, 606
Ex 1:18 the midwives and a them, 606
2: 7 Then his sister a Pharaoh's daughter, 606
2:13 *He* a the one in the wrong, 606
2:18 he a them, "Why have you returned 606
2:20 he a his daughters. 606
5:14 were beaten and *were* a, "Why didn't you 606
8:13 And the LORD did what Moses a. 1821
8:31 and the LORD did what Moses a: 1821
12:35 The Israelites did as Moses instructed and a 8626
12:36 **gave** them what they a for; 8626
33:17 "I will do the very thing *you have* a, 1819
Lev 10:16 Aaron's remaining sons, and a, 606
Nu 11:11 he a the LORD, "Why have you brought this 606
12: 2 LORD spoken only through Moses?" *they* a. 606
14:20 "I have forgiven them, as you a. 1821
22: 9 God came to Balaam and a, 606
22:32 The angel of the LORD a him, 606
23:17 Balak a him, "What did the LORD say?" 606
31:15 allowed all the women to live?" he a them. 606
Dt 18:16 For this is what *you* a of the LORD 8626
Jos 5:13 Joshua went up to him and a, 606
5:14 to the ground in reverence, and a him, 606
9: 8 But Joshua a, "Who are you and 606
15:18 When she got off her donkey, Caleb a her, 606
19:50 They gave him the town *he* a for— 8626
Jdg 1: 1 the Israelites a the LORD, 8626
1:14 When she got off her donkey, Caleb a her, 606
5:25 *He* a for water, and she gave him milk; 8626
6:15 "But Lord," Gideon a, 606
6:29 *They* a each other, "Who did this?" 606
8: 1 Now the Ephraimites a Gideon, 606
8:18 Then *he* a Zebah and Zalmunna, 606
8:26 The weight of the gold rings he a for came 8626
12: 5 the men of Gilead a him, 606
13:12 So Manoah a him, 606
15: 6 When the Philistines a, "Who did this?" 606
15:10 The men of Judah a, 606
17: 9 Micah a him, "Where are you from?" 606
18: 3 so they turned in there and a him, 606
18: 3 their brothers a them, 606
19:17 the old man a, "Where are you going? 606
20:28 They a, "Shall we go up again to battle 606
21: 5 Then the Israelites a, 606
21: 8 Then *they* a, "Which one of the tribes 606
Ru 2: 5 Boaz a the foreman of his harvesters, 606
2:19 Her mother-in-law a her, 606
3: 9 "Who are you?" he a. 606
Ruth a her mother-in-law, Naomi a, 8626
1Sa 1:17 of Israel grant you what *you have* a 8626
1:20 saying, "Because I *a the* LORD for him." 8626
1:27 LORD has granted me what I a of him. 8626
3:17 "What was it he said to you?" Eli a. 606
4: 3 the elders of Israel a, 606
4: 6 Hearing the uproar, the Philistines a, 606
4:14 Eli heard the outcry and a, 606
4:16 Eli a, "What happened, my son?" 606
5: 8 the rulers of the Philistines and a them, 606
6: 4 The Philistines a, "What guilt offering 606
6:20 and the men of Beth Shemesh a, 606
9:11 and *they* a them, "Is the seer here?" 606
9:18 approached Samuel in the gateway and a, 606
10:11 they a each other, "What is this 606
10:14 Now Saul's uncle a him and his servant, 606
10:14 and he a, "What is wrong with the people? 606
11:12 "Who was it that a, 'Shall Saul reign 606
12:13 king you have chosen, the one *you a for*; 8626
12:17 in the eyes of the LORD when you a for 8626
13:11 "What have you done?" a Samuel. 606
14:37 So Saul a God, "Shall I go down 8626
16: 4 *They* a, "Do you come in peace?" 606
16:11 So he a Jesse, "Are these all the sons 606
17:26 David a the men standing near him, 606
17:28 he burned with anger at him and a, 606

1Sa	17:58	"Whose son are you, young man?" Saul a	606
	19:22	And he a, "Where are Samuel and David?"	8626
	20: 1	at Ramah and went to Jonathan and a,	606
	20: 6	**earnestly a** my **permission**	8626+8626
	20:10	David a, "Who will tell me	606
	20:28	**earnestly a** me **for permission**	8626+8626
	20:32	Jonathan a his father.	6699
	21: 1	and a, "Why are you alone?	606
	21: 8	David a Ahimelech, "Don't you have	606
	23:12	Again David a, "Will the citizens	606
	24:16	When David finished saying this, Saul a,	606
	26: 6	David then a Ahimelech the Hittite	6699
	27:10	When Achish a, "Where did you go	606
	28:11	Then the woman a, "Whom shall I bring up	606
	28:14	"What does he look like?" he a.	606
	29: 3	The commanders of the Philistines a,	606
	29: 8	"But what have I done?" a David.	606
	30:13	David a him, "To whom do you belong,	606
	30:15	David a him, "Can you lead me down	606
2Sa	1: 3	"Where have you come from?" David a him.	606
	1: 4	"What happened?" David a.	606
	1: 8	*"He a me, 'Who are you?'*	606
	1:14	David a him, "Why were you not afraid	606
	2: 1	of the towns of Judah?" he a.	606
	2: 1	David a, "Where shall I go?"	606
	2:20	Abner looked behind him and a,	606
	9: 1	David a, "Is there anyone still left of	606
	9: 3	The king a, "Is there no one still left of	606
	9: 4	"Where is he?" the king a.	606
	11: 7	David a him how Joab was,	8626
	11:10	"Uriah did not go home," he a.	606
	12:19	"Is the child dead?" he a.	606
	12:21	His servants a him,	606
	13: 4	He a Amnon, "Why do you, the king's son,	606
	13:26	The king a him, "Why are you acting this	606
	14: 5	The king a her, "What is troubling you?"	606
	14:19	The king a, "Isn't the hand of Joab	606
	16: 2	The king a Ziba, "Why have you brought	606
	16: 3	The king then a, "Where is your master's	606
	16:17	Absalom a Hushai, "Is this the love	606
	17:20	at the house, they a, "Where are Ahimaaz	606
	18:29	king a, "Is the young man Absalom safe?"	606
	18:32	The king a the Cushite, "Is the young man	606
	19:25	the king a him, "Why didn't you go with me	606
	20:17	He went toward her, and she a,	606
	21: 3	David a the Gibeonites, "What shall I do	606
	21: 4	want me to do for you?" David a.	606
1Ki	1:11	Nathan a Bathsheba, Solomon's mother,	606
	1:16	"What is it you want?" the king a.	606
	1:41	the sound of the trumpet, Joab a, "What's	606
	2:13	Solomon's mother. Bathsheba a him,	606
	3:10	The Lord was pleased that Solomon had a	8626
	3:11	"Since you have a for this and not	8626
	3:11	nor have a for the death of your enemies	8626
	3:12	I will do what you have a.	1821
	3:13	I will give you what you have not a for—	8626
	9:13	you have given me, my brother?" he a.	606
	10:13	the queen of Sheba all she desired and a	8626
	11:22	to your own country?" Pharaoh a.	606
	12: 6	to answer these people?" he a.	606
	12: 9	He a them, "What is your advice?	606
	13:12	Their father a them,	1819
	13:14	under an oak tree and a,	606
	17:10	He called to him and a,	606
	18: 9	"What have I done wrong," a Obadiah,	606
	20:14	"But who will do this?" a Ahab.	606
	20:14	"And who will start the battle?" he a.	606
	21: 5	His wife Jezebel came in and a him,	1819
	22: 4	So he a Jehoshaphat,	606
	22: 6	and a them, "Shall I go to war	606
	22: 7	But Jehoshaphat a, "Is there not a prophet	606
	22:15	When he arrived, the king a him, "Micaiah,	606
	22:22	"'By what means?' the LORD a.	606
	22:24	to speak to you?" he a.	606
2Ki	1: 5	messengers returned to the king, he a them,	606
	1: 7	The king a them, "What kind of man	1819
	2: 3	at Bethel came out to Elisha and a,	606
	2: 5	at Jericho went up to Elisha and a him,	606
	2:10	"You have a a difficult thing," Elijah said,	8626
	2:14	the God of Elijah?" he a.	606
	3: 8	"By what route shall we attack?" he a.	606
	3:11	But Jehoshaphat a, "Is there no prophet of	606
	4:14	"What can be done for her?" Elisha a.	606
	4:23	"Why go to him today?" he a.	606
	4:43	before a hundred men?" his servant a.	606
	5:21	"Is everything all right?" he a.	606
	5:25	"Where have you been, Gehazi?" Elisha a.	606
	6: 6	The man of God a, "Where did it fall?"	606
	6:15	what shall we do?" the servant a.	606
	6:18	as Elisha had a,	1821
	6:21	he a Elisha, "Shall I kill them, my father?	606
	6:28	Then he a her, "What's the matter?"	606
	8: 6	The king a the woman about it,	8626
	8:12	"Why is my lord weeping?" a Hazael.	606
	8:14	When Ben-Hadad a, "What did Elisha say	606
	9: 5	"For which of us?" a Jehu.	606
	9:11	one of them a him, "Is everything all right?	606
	9:22	When Joram saw Jehu he a,	606
	9:31	As Jehu entered the gate, she a,	606
	10:13	of Ahaziah king of Judah and a,	606
	12: 7	the priest and the other priests and a them,	606
	20: 8	Hezekiah had a Isaiah,	606
	20:14	the prophet went to King Hezekiah and a,	606
	20:15	The prophet a, "What did they see	606
	23:17	The king a, "What is that tombstone I see?"	606
1Ch	13:12	David was afraid of God that day and a,	606
2Ch	1:11	and you have not a for wealth,	8626

2Ch	1:11	and since you have not a for a long life but	8626
	9:12	of Sheba all she desired and a for;	8626
	10: 6	to answer these people?" he a.	606
	10: 9	He a them, "What is your advice?	606
	18: 3	Ahab king of Israel a Jehoshaphat king	606
	18: 5	and a them, "Shall we go to war	606
	18: 6	But Jehoshaphat a, "Is there not a prophet	606
	18:14	When he arrived, the king a him, "Micaiah,	606
	18:20	"'By what means?' the LORD a.	606
	18:23	he went from me to speak to you?" he a.	606
	25: 9	Amaziah a the man of God,	606
	31: 9	Hezekiah a the priests and Levites about	2011
Ezr	5: 3	and their associates went to them and a,	10042
	5: 4	They also a, "What are the names of	10042
	5: 9	We questioned the elders and a them,	10042
	5:10	We also a them their names,	10689
	7: 6	The king had granted him everything he a,	1336
Ne	2: 2	so the king a me, "Why does your face look	606
	2: 6	a me, "How long will your journey take,	606
	2:19	"What is this you are doing?" they a.	606
	13: 6	Some time later I a his permission	8626
	13:11	So I rebuked the officials and a them,	606
Est	1:15	what must be done to Queen Vashti?" he a.	NIH
	2:15	she a for nothing other than what Hegai,	1335
	3: 3	at the king's gate a Mordecai,	606
	5: 3	the king a, "What is it, Queen Esther?	606
	5: 6	the king again a Esther, "Now what	606
	6: 3	Mordecai received for this?" the king a.	606
	6: 6	When Haman entered, the king a him,	606
	7: 2	the king again a, "Queen Esther,	606
	7: 5	King Xerxes a Queen Esther, "Who is he?	606
Job	42: 3	[You a,] 'Who is this that obscures	NIH
Ps	21: 4	He a you for life, and you gave it to him—	8626
	105:40	They a, and he brought them quail	8626
	106:15	So he gave them what they a for,	8629
	137: 3	for there our captors a us for songs,	8626
Ecc	4: 8	"For whom am I toiling," he a,	NIH
Isa	1:12	who has a this of you,	1335
	38:22	Hezekiah had a, "What will be the sign	606
	39: 3	the prophet went to King Hezekiah and a,	606
	39: 4	The prophet a, "What did they see	606
Jer	24: 3	Then the LORD a me, "What do you see,	606
	36:17	Then they a Baruch, "Tell us,	8626
	37:17	where he a him privately,	8626
Eze	24:19	Then the people a me, "Won't you tell us	606
	37: 3	He a me, "Son of man, can these bones live?	606
	47: 6	He a me, "Son of man, do you see this?"	606
Da	1: 8	a the chief official for permission	1335
	2:10	has ever a such a thing of any magician	10689
	2:15	He a the king's officer,	10558
	2:16	Daniel went in to the king and a for time,	10114
	2:23	you have made known to me what we a,	10114
	2:26	king a Daniel (also called Belteshazzar),	10558
	2:27	to the king the mystery he has a about,	10689
	3:24	to his feet in amazement and a his advisers,	10558
	7:16	and a him the true meaning of all this.	10114
	12: 8	So I a, "My lord, what will the outcome	606
Am	7: 8	LORD a me, "What do you see, Amos?"	606
	8: 2	"What do you see, Amos?" he a.	606
Jnh	1: 8	So they a him, "Tell us,	606
	1:10	This terrified them and they a,	606
	1:11	So they a him, "What should we do to you	606
Zec	1: 9	I a, "What are these, my lord?"	606
	1:19	I a the angel who was speaking to me,	606
	1:21	I a, "What are these coming to do?"	606
	2: 2	I a, "Where are you going?"	606
	4: 2	He a me, "What do you see?"	606
	4: 4	I a the angel who talked with me,	6699
	4:11	Then I a the angel, "What are these two	6699
	4:12	Again I a him, "What are these two	6699
	5: 2	He a me, "What do you see?"	606
	5: 6	I a, "What is it?"	606
	5:10	I a the angel who was speaking to me.	606
Mt	2: 2	and a, "Where is the one who has been	
		born king of the Jews?	3306
	2: 4	he a where the Christ was to be born.	4785
	8:27	The men were amazed and a,	3306
	9:11	they a his disciples,	3306
	9:14	Then John's disciples came and a him,	3306
	9:28	the blind men came to him, and he a them,	3306
	12:10	to accuse Jesus, they a him, "Is it lawful	2089
	13:10	The disciples came to him and a,	3306
	13:28	"The servants a him, 'Do you want	3306
	13:51	"Have you understood all these things?"	
		Jesus a.	3306
	13:54	and these miraculous powers?" they a.	3306
	14: 7	with an oath to give her whatever she a.	160
	15: 1	to Jesus from Jerusalem and a,	3306
	15:12	Then the disciples came to him and a,	3306
	15:16	"Are you still so dull?" Jesus them.	3306
	15:34	"How many loaves do you have?" Jesus a.	3306
	16: 8	Aware of their discussion, Jesus a,	3306
	16:13	he a his disciples, "Who do people say	2263
	16:15	"But what about you?" he a.	3306
	17:10	disciples a him, "Why then do the teachers	2089
	17:19	disciples came to Jesus in private and a,	3306
	17:24	the two-drachma tax came to Peter and a,	3306
	17:25	"What do you think, Simon?" he a.	NIG
	18: 1	that time the disciples came to Jesus and a,	3306
	18:21	Then Peter came to Jesus and a, "Lord,	3306
	19: 3	They a, "Is it lawful for a man	3306
	19: 7	then," they a, "did Moses command that	3306
	19:16	Now a man came up to Jesus and a,	3306
	19:18	they were greatly astonished and a,	3306
	20: 6	He a them, "Why have you been standing	3306
	20:20	kneeling down, a a favor of him.	160

Mt	20:21	"What is it you want?" he a.	3306
	20:32	What do you want me to do for you?" he a.	3306
	21:10	the whole city was stirred and a,	3306
	21:16	what these children are saying?" they a him.	3306
	21:20	"How did the fig tree wither so quickly?"	
		they a.	3306
	21:23	"By what authority are you doing these	
		things?" they a.	3306
	22:12	he a, 'how did you get in here	3306
	22:20	and he a them, "Whose portrait is this?	3306
	22:41	While the Pharisees were gathered together,	
		Jesus a them,	2089
	24: 2	"Do you see all these things?" he a.	3306
	26: 8	"Why this waste?" they a.	3306
	26:15	and a, "What are you willing to give me	3306
	26:17	the disciples came to Jesus and a,	3306
	26:40	watch with me for one hour?" he a Peter.	3306
	27:11	and the governor a him,	2089
	27:13	Then Pilate a him, "Don't you hear	3306
	27:17	the crowd had gathered, Pilate a them,	3306
	27:21	to release to you?" a the governor.	646
	27:22	with Jesus who is called Christ?" Pilate a.	3306
	27:23	What crime has he committed?" a Pilate.	5774
	27:58	Going to Pilate, he a for Jesus' body,	160
Mk	1:27	so amazed that they a each other,	5184
	2:16	they a his disciples: "Why does he eat	3306
	2:18	Some people came and a Jesus,	3306
	3: 4	Then Jesus a them, "Which is lawful on	3306
	3:33	my mother and my brothers?" he a.	646
	4:10	and the others around him a him about	2263
	4:41	They were terrified and a each other,	3306
	5: 9	Then Jesus a him, "What is your name?"	2089
	5:30	He turned around in the crowd and a,	3306
	6: 2	"Where did this man get these things?" they	
		a.	3306
	6:38	"How many loaves do you have?" he a.	3306
	7: 5	Pharisees and teachers of the law a Jesus,	2089
	7:17	his disciples a him about this parable.	2089
	7:18	"Are you so dull?" he a.	3306
	8: 5	"How many loaves do you have?" Jesus a.	2263
	8:11	they a him for a sign from heaven.	2426
	8:17	Aware of their discussion, Jesus a them:	3306
	8:23	Jesus a, "Do you see anything?"	2089
	8:27	On the way he a them, "Who do people say	2089
	8:29	"But what about you?" he a.	2089
	9:11	And they a him, "Why do the teachers	2089
	9:16	arguing with them about?" he a.	2089
	9:18	your disciples to drive out the spirit,	3306
	9:21	Jesus a the boy's father, "How long	2089
	9:28	his disciples a him privately, "Why	2089
	9:33	When he was in the house, he a them,	2089
	10:10	the disciples a Jesus about this.	2089
	10:17	he a, "what must I do to inherit eternal life?	2089
	10:36	"What do you want me to do for you?" he a.	3306
	10:51	do you want me to do for you?" Jesus a	646
	11: 5	some people standing there a,	3306
	11:28	"By what authority are you doing these	
		things?" they a.	3306
	12:15	you trying to trap me?" he a.	3306
	12:16	They brought the coin, and he a them,	3306
	12:28	he a him, "Of all the commandments,	2089
	12:35	in the temple courts, he a, "How is it that	3306
	13: 3	James, John and Andrew a him privately,	2089
	14:12	Jesus' disciples a him,	3306
	14:60	up before them and a Jesus,	2089
	14:61	Again the high priest a him,	2089
	14:63	do we need any more witnesses?" he a.	3306
	15: 2	"Are you the king of the Jews?" a Pilate.	2089
	15: 4	So again Pilate a him, "Aren't you	2089
	15: 8	The crowd came up and a Pilate to do	160
	15: 9	to you the king of the Jews?" a Pilate,	646
	15:12	crime has he committed?" Pilate a them.	646
	15:14	What crime has he committed?" a Pilate.	3306
	15:43	to Pilate and a for Jesus' body.	160
	15:44	he a him if Jesus had already died.	2089
	16: 3	and they a each other, "Who will roll	3306
Lk	1:18	Zechariah a the angel, "How can I be sure	3306
	1:34	"How will this be," Mary a the angel,	3306
	1:63	He a for a writing tablet,	160
	2:49	"Why were you searching for me?" he a.	2089
	3:10	"What should we do then?" the crowd a.	2089
	3:12	"Teacher," they a, "what should we do?"	3306
	3:14	Then some soldiers a him,	2089
	4:22	"Isn't this Joseph's son?" they a.	3306
	4:38	and they a Jesus to help her.	2263
	5: 3	and a him to put out a little from shore.	2263
	5:22	Jesus knew what they were thinking and a,	646
	6: 2	Some of the Pharisees a,	3306
	8: 9	His disciples a him what this parable meant.	2089
	8:25	"Where is your faith?" he a his disciples.	3306
	8:25	In fear and amazement they a one another,	3306
	8:30	Jesus a him, "What is your name?"	2089
	8:37	of the Gerasenes a Jesus to leave them,	2263
	8:45	"Who touched me?" Jesus a.	3306
	9:18	he a them, "Who do the crowds say I am?"	2089
	9:20	"But what about you?" he a.	3306
	9:54	they a, "Lord, do you want us to call fire	3306
	10:25	he a, "what must I do to inherit eternal life?	3306
	10:29	so he a Jesus, "And who is my neighbor?"	3306
	10:40	She came to him and a, "Lord,	3306
	12:41	Peter a, "Lord, are you telling this parable	3306
	12:48	entrusted with much, much more will be a.	160
	13:18	Jesus a, "What is the kingdom of God like?	3306
	13:20	Again he a, "What shall I compare	3306
	13:23	Someone a him, "Lord, are only a few	3306
	14: 3	Jesus a the Pharisees and experts in the law,	646
	14: 5	Then he a them, "If one of you has a son	3306

Lk	15:26	the servants and a him what was going on.	4785
	16: 2	So he called him in and a him,	3306
	16: 5	He a the first, 'How much do you owe	3306
	16: 7	"Then he a the second, 'And how much	3306
	17:17	Jesus a, "Were not all ten cleansed?	646
	17:20	having been a by the Pharisees when	2089
	17:37	"Where, Lord?" they a.	646
	18:18	A certain ruler a him, "Good teacher,	2089
	18:26	Those who heard this a, "Who then can	3306
	18:36	he a what was happening.	4785
	18:40	When he came near, Jesus a him,	2089
	19:33	untying the colt, its owners a them,	3306
	20:17	Jesus looked directly at them and a,	3306
	21: 7	they a, "when will these things happen?	2089
	22: 9	want us to prepare for it?" they a.	3306
	22:31	Simon, Satan has a to sift you as wheat.	1977
	22:35	Then Jesus a them, "When I sent you	3306
	22:46	"Why are you sleeping?" he a them.	3306
	22:48	but Jesus a him, "Judas, are you betraying	3306
	22:68	and if I a you, you would not answer.	2263
	22:70	They all a, "Are you then the Son of God?"	3306
	23: 3	So Pilate a Jesus, "Are you the king	2263
	23: 6	Pilate a if the man was a Galilean.	2089
	23:25	the one they a for,	160
	23:52	Going to Pilate, he a for Jesus' body.	160
	24:17	He a them, "What are you discussing	3306
	24:18	One of them, named Cleopas, a him,	646
	24:19	"What things?" he a. "About Jesus	3306
	24:32	They a each other, "Were not our hearts	3306
	24:41	because of joy and amazement, he a them,	3306
Jn	1:21	They a him, "Then who are you?	2263
	1:38	Jesus saw them following and a,	3306
	1:46	good come from there?" Nathanael a.	3306
	1:48	"How do you know me?" Nathanael a.	3306
	3: 4	when he is old?" Nicodemus a.	3306
	3: 9	"How can this be?" Nicodemus a.	646
	4:10	you would have a him	160
	4:27	But no one a, "What do you want?"	3306
	5: 6	he a him, "Do you want to get well?"	3306
	5:12	So they a him, "Who is this fellow	2263
	6: 6	He a this only to test him,	3306
	6:25	on the other side of the lake, they a him,	3306
	6:28	Then they a him, "What must we do	3306
	6:30	So they a him, "What miraculous sign	3306
	6:67	Jesus a the Twelve.	3306
	7:15	The Jews were amazed and a,	3306
	7:41	Still others a, "How can the Christ come	3306
	7:45	the chief priests and Pharisees, who a them,	3306
	7:50	and who was one of their own number, a,	3306
	8:10	Jesus straightened up and a her, "Woman,	3306
	8:19	Then they a him, "Where is your father?"	3306
	8:25	"Who are you?" they a.	3306
	9: 2	His disciples a him, "Rabbi, who sinned,	2263
	9: 8	those who had formerly seen him begging a,	3306
	9:12	"Where is this man?" they a him.	3306
	9:15	also a him how he had received his sight	2263
	9:16	But others a, "How can a sinner do such	3306
	9:19	"Is this your son?" they a.	2263
	9:26	Then they a him, "What did he do to you?	3306
	9:36	"Who is he, sir?" the man a.	646
	9:40	with him heard him say this and a,	3306
	11:34	"Where have you laid him?" he a.	3306
	11:47	"What are we accomplishing?" they a.	3306
	11:56	in the temple area they a one another,	3306
	13:12	what I have done for you?" he a them.	3306
	13:25	Leaning back against Jesus, he a him,	3306
	13:36	Simon Peter a him, "Lord, where are you	3306
	13:37	Peter a, "Lord, why can't I follow you now?	3306
	16:24	Until now you have not a for anything	160
	18: 4	went out and a them, "Who is it you want?"	3306
	18: 7	Again he a them, "Who is it you want?"	2089
	18:17	the girl at the door a Peter.	3306
	18:25	he was a, "You are not one of his disciples,	3306
	18:29	So Pilate came out to them and a,	5774
	18:33	summoned Jesus and a him,	3306
	18:34	"Is that your own idea," Jesus a,	646
	18:38	"What is truth?" Pilate a.	3306
	19: 9	he a Jesus, but Jesus gave him no answer.	3306
	19:15	"Shall I crucify your king?" Pilate a.	3306
	19:31	they a Pilate the legs broken and	2263
	19:38	of Arimathea a Pilate for the body of Jesus.	2263
	20:13	They a her, "Woman, why are you crying?"	3306
	21:17	Peter was hurt because Jesus a him	3306
	21:21	When Peter saw him, he a, "Lord,	3306
Ac	1: 6	So when they met together, they a him,	2263
	2: 7	Utterly amazed, they a:	3306
	2:12	Amazed and perplexed, they a one another,	3306
	3: 3	he a them for money.	2263
	3:14	and Righteous One and a that a murderer	160
	4: 9	to a cripple and are a how he was healed,	NIG
	4:16	we going to do with these men?" they a.	3306
	5: 8	Peter a her, "Tell me, is this the price	646
	7: 1	high priest a him, "Are these charges true?"	3306
	7:46	who enjoyed God's favor and a	160
	8:30	"Do you understand what you are reading?" Philip a.	3306
	8:34	The eunuch a Philip, "Tell me, please,	646
	9: 2	and a him for letters to the synagogues	160
	9: 5	"Who are you, Lord?" Saul a.	3306
	9:21	and a, "Isn't he the man who raised havoc	3306
	10: 4	"What is it, Lord?" he a.	3306
	10:48	Then they a Peter to stay with them for	2263
	12:20	they a for peace,	160
	13:21	Then the people a for a king,	160
	13:28	they a Pilate to have him executed.	160
	16:30	He then brought them out and a, "Sirs,	5774
	17:18	Some of them a, "What is this babbler	3306

Ac	18:20	When they a him to spend more time	2263
	19: 2	a them, "Did you receive the Holy Spirit	3306
	19: 3	So Paul a, "Then what baptism did you receive?"	3306
	21:33	he a who he was and what he had done.	4785
	21:37	he a the commander, "May I say	3306
	22: 8	" 'Who are you, Lord?' I a.	646
	22:10	" 'What shall I do, Lord?' I a.	3306
	22:26	"What are you going to do?" he a.	3306
	22:27	The commander went to Paul and a,	3306
	23:18	for me and a me to bring this young man	2263
	23:19	drew him aside and a, "What is it	4785
	23:34	the letter and a what province he was from.	2089
	23:15	the Jews brought charges against him and a	160
	25:20	so I a if he would be willing to go	3306
	26:15	"Then I a, 'Who are you, Lord?'	3306
	28:20	For this reason I have a to see you and talk	4151
Gal	2:10	All they a was that we should continue	3667
1Jn	5:15	we know that we have what we a of him.	160+161
Rev	7:13	Then one of the elders a me,	646
	10: 9	So I went to the angel and a him to give me	3306
	13: 4	and they also worshiped the beast and a,	3306

ASKELON (KJV) See ASHKELON

ASKING (26) [ASK]

Ex	10:11	since that's what you have been a for."	1335
1Sa	8:10	the LORD to the people who were a him	8626
	10: 2	He is a, "What shall I do about my son?' '	606
	12:19	to all our other sins the evil of a for a king.	8626
	25:39	a her to become his wife.	1819
2Sa	15: 6	the Israelites who came to the king a	NIH
1Ki	1: 6	with him by a, "Why do you behave as	606
Ps	4: 6	Many are a, "Who can show us any good?"	606
Da	6:11	and a God for help.	10274
Zec	7: 3	by a the priests of the house of	606
Mt	8: 5	a centurion came to him, a for help.	4151
	16: 1	by a him to show them a sign from heaven.	2089
	20:22	"You don't know what you are a,"	160
Mk	10: 2	Some Pharisees came and tested him by a,	2089
	10:38	"You don't know what you are a,"	160
Lk	1:66	a, "What then is this child going to be?"	3306
	2:46	listening to them and a them questions.	2089
	7: 3	a him to come and heal his servant,	2263
	11:16	Others tested him by a for a sign	2426
Jn	7:11	the Jews were watching for him and a,	3306
	11:28	she said, "and is a for you."	5888
	16:18	They kept a, "What does he mean by	3306
	16:19	"Are you a one another what I meant	2426
Ac	10:18	a if Simon who was known as Peter	4785
Eph	1:17	I keep a that the God of our Lord Jesus	NIG
Col	1: 9	and a God to fill you with the knowledge	160

ASKS (33) [ASK]

Ge	32:17	"When my brother Esau meets you and a,	8626
	46:33	When Pharaoh calls you in and a,	606
Ex	13:14	"In days to come, when your son a you,	8626
Dt	6:20	In the future, when your son a you,	8626
Jdg	4:20	"If someone comes by and a you, 'Also,	8626
2Sa	11: 7	If he a you this, then say to him, 'Also,	NIH
	14:15	perhaps he will do what his servant a.	1821
1Ki	8:43	and do whatever the foreigner a of you,	7924
2Ch	6:33	and do whatever the foreigner a of you,	7924
Est	5: 5	"so that we may do what Esther a."	1821
Jer	39:12	but do for him whatever he a."	1819
Da	2:10	"There is not a man on earth who can do what the king a!	10418
	2:11	What the king a is too difficult.	10689
Am	6:10	of the house and a anyone still hiding there,	606
Zec	13: 6	If someone a him, 'What are these wounds	606
Mt	5:42	Give to the one who a you,	160
	7: 8	For everyone who a receives;	160
	7: 9	"Which of you, if his son a for bread,	160
	7:10	Or if he a for a fish, will give him a snake?	160
	12:39	"A wicked and adulterous generation a for	2118
Mk	11: 3	If anyone a you, 'Why are you doing this?'	3306
	14:14	of the house he enters, 'The Teacher a:	3306
Lk	6:30	Give to everyone who a you,	160
	6:30	For everyone who a receives;	160
	11:11	if your son a for a fish,	160
	11:12	Or if he a for an egg,	160
	11:29	It a for a miraculous sign,	2426
	19:31	If anyone a you, 'Why are you untying it?'	2263
	22:11	to the owner of the house, 'The Teacher a:	3306
Jn	4:10	of God and who it is that a you for a drink,	3306
	16: 5	yet none of you a me, 'Where are you	2263
Jas	1: 6	But when he a, he must believe	160
1Pe	3:15	to everyone who a you to give the reason	160

ASLEEP (27) [SLEEP]

Ge	41: 5	He fell a again and had a second dream:	3822
Jdg	4:21	to him while he lay fast a,	8101
1Sa	26: 7	lying inside the camp with his spear stuck	3825
1Ki	3:20	from my side while I your servant was a.	3825
	19: 5	he lay down under the tree and fell a.	3822
Job	3:13	I would be a and at rest	3822
Mt	9:24	The girl is not dead but a."	2761
	25: 5	and they all became drowsy and fell a.	2761
	28:13	and stole him away while we were a.'	3121
Mk	5:39	The child is not dead but a."	2761
	14:37	he said to Peter, "are you a?	2761
Lk	8:23	As they sailed, he fell a.	934
	8:52	"She is not dead but a."	2761
	22:45	he found them a, exhausted from sorrow.	3121

Jn	11:11	"Our friend Lazarus has fallen a;	3121
Ac	7:60	When he had said this, he fell a;	3121
	13:36	in his own generation, he fell a;	3121
	13:36	When he was a	608+2965+3836+5678
1Co	11:30	and a number of you have fallen a.	3121
	15: 6	though some have fallen a.	3121
	15:18	also who have fallen a in Christ are lost.	3121
	15:20	the firstfruits of those who have fallen a.	3121
1Th	4:13	to be ignorant about those who fall a,	3121
	4:14	with Jesus those who have fallen a.	3121
	4:15	not precede those who have fallen a.	3121
	5: 6	then, let us not be like others, who are a,	2761
	5:10	whether we are awake or a,	2761

ASNAH (1)

Ezr	2:50	A, Meunim, Nephussim,	663

ASNAPPER (KJV) See ASHURBANIPAL

ASP, ASPS (KJV) See COBRA, SERPENTS, VIPERS

ASPATHA (1)

Est	9: 7	They also killed Parshandatha, Dalphon, A,	672

ASRIEL (3) [ASRIELITE]

Nu	26:31	through A, the Asrielite clan;	835
Jos	17: 2	the clans of Abiezer, Helek, A, Shechem,	835
1Ch	7:14	A was his descendant	835

ASRIELITE (1) [ASRIEL]

Nu	26:31	through Asriel, the A clan;	834

ASS, ASS'S, ASSES (KJV) See DONKEY

ASSAIL (2) [ASSAILANT, ASSAILS]

Ps	17: 9	from the wicked who a me,	8720
	55: 4	the terrors of death a me.	5877+6584

ASSAILANT (1) [ASSAIL]

Dt	25:11	to rescue her husband from his a,	5782

ASSAILS (1) [ASSAIL]

Job	16: 9	God a me and tears me in his anger	8475

ASSAR See TEL ASSAR

ASSASSINATE (2) [ASSASSINATED, ASSASSINATION, ASSASSINS]

Est	2:21	and conspired to a King Xerxes.	928+3338+8938
	6: 2	had conspired to a King Xerxes.	928+3338+8938

ASSASSINATED (9) [ASSASSINATE]

2Ki	12:20	against him and a him at Beth Millo,	5782
	15:10	a him and succeeded him as king.	4637
	15:14	a him and succeeded him as king.	4637
	15:25	he a Pekahiah, along with Argob and Arieh,	5782
	15:30	He attacked and a him,	4637
	21:23	against him and a the king in his palace.	4637
	25:25	came with with ten men and a Gedaliah	2256+4637+5782
2Ch	33:24	against him and a him in his palace.	4637
Jer	41:16	of Nethaniah after he had a Gedaliah son	5782

ASSASSINATION (1) [ASSASSINATE]

Jer	41: 4	The day after Gedaliah's a,	4637

ASSASSINS (1) [ASSASSINATE]

2Ki	14: 6	he did not put the sons of the a to death,	5782

ASSAULT (2) [ASSAULTS]

Dt	21: 5	and to decide all cases of dispute and a.	5596
Ps	62: 3	How long will you a a man?	2109

ASSAULTED (KJV) See RUSHED TO

ASSAULTS (3) [ASSAULT]

Dt	17: 8	bloodshed, lawsuits or a—	4200+5596+5596
	19:11	lies in wait for him, a and kills him,	6584+7756
Job	28: 9	Man's hand a the flinty rock	928+8938

ASSAY (KJV) See VENTURES

ASSEMBLE (33) [ASSEMBLED, ASSEMBLIES, ASSEMBLING, ASSEMBLY]

Ge	49: 2	"A and listen, sons of Jacob;	7695
Ex	4:29	"Go, a the elders of Israel and say to them,	665
Nu	8: 9	to the front of the Tent of Meeting and a	7735
	10: 3	the whole community is to a before you at	3585
	10: 4	are to a before you.	3585
Dt	4:10	"A the people before me to hear my words	7735
	31:12	A the people—men, women and children	7735
	31:28	A before me all the elders of your tribes	7735

Jdg 21: 5 from all the tribes of Israel *has failed* to a
928+2021+6590+7736
   21: 5 a solemn oath that anyone who failed *to* a 6590
   21: 8 of the tribes of Israel failed *to* a before 6590
1Sa 7: 5 "A all Israel at Mizpah and I will intercede 7695
2Sa 3:21 and a all Israel for my lord the king, 7695
1Ch 22: 2 So David gave orders to a the aliens living 4043
   28: 1 **summoned** all the officials of Israel **to** a 7735
Ezr 10: 7 and Jerusalem for all the exiles to a 7695
Ne 7: 5 So my God put it into my heart *to* a 7695
Est 8:11 the right to a and protect themselves; 7735
Ps 47: 9 The nobles of the nations a as the people of 665
  102:22 the kingdoms a to worship the LORD. 3481+7695
Isa 45: 9 of Mount Zion and over *those who* a there 5246
  11:12 he will a the scattered people of Judah 7695
  43: 9 nations gather together and the peoples a. 665
  45:20 a, *you* fugitives from the nations. 3481+5602
  60: 4 All a and come to you; 7695
Jer 49:14 "A yourselves to attack it! 7695
Eze 39:17 'A and come together from all around to 7695
Da 11:10 His sons will prepare for war and a 665
Joel 3:11 from every side, and a there. 7695
Am 3: 9 "A yourselves on the mountains 665
Mic 4: 6 I will gather the lame, *I will* a the exiles 7695
Zep 3: 8 I have decided to a the nations, 665
Ac 22:30 the chief priests and all the Sanhedrin to a. *5302*

ASSEMBLED (48) [ASSEMBLE]

Ex 35: 1 Moses a the whole Israelite community 7735
Dt 33: 5 when the leaders of the people a, 665
  33:21 When the heads of the people a, 910
Jos 24: 1 Joshua a all the tribes of Israel at Shechem. 665
Jdg 9:47 Abimelech heard that they *had* a there, 7695
  10:17 the Israelites a and camped at Mizpah. 665
  16:23 of the Philistines a to offer a great sacrifice 665
  20: 1 of Gilead came out as one man and a 7735
1Sa 7: 6 When *they had* a at Mizpah, 7695
  7: 7 Philistines heard that Israel *had* a at Mizpah 7695
  13: 5 The Philistines a to fight Israel, 665
  14:20 Then Saul and all his men a and went to 2410
  17: 1 for war and a *at* Socoh in Judah. 665
  17: 2 the Israelites a and camped in the Valley 665
  25: 1 and all Israel a and mourned for him; 7695
  28: 4 The Philistines a and came and set up camp 7695
2Sa 2:30 from pursuing Abner and a all his men. 665
1Ki 18:20 throughout all Israel and a the prophets 7695
  20:15 Then *he* a the rest of the Israelites, 7,000 7212
1Ch 13: 5 So David a all the Israelites, 7735
  15: 3 David a all Israel in Jerusalem to bring up 7735
2Ch 12: 5 the leaders of Judah who *had* a in Jerusalem 665
  15: 9 Then *he* a all Judah and Benjamin and 7695
  15:10 They a *at* Jerusalem in the third month of 7695
  20:26 On the fourth day *they* a in the Valley 7735
  29: 4 a them in the square on the east side 665
  29:15 When *they had* a their brothers 665
  30: 3 and the people *had* not a in Jerusalem 665
  30:13 of people a *in* Jerusalem to celebrate 665
  30:25 Levites and all who *had* a from Israel, 995+7736
  32: 4 A large force of men a, 7695
  32: 6 over the people and a them before him in 7695
Ezr 3: 1 the people a as one man in Jerusalem. 665
  8:15 *I* a them at the canal that flows 7695
Ne 5:16 All my men **were** a there for the work; 7695
  8: 1 all the people a as one man in the square 665
Est 2:19 When the virgins **were** a a second time, 7695
  9: 2 The Jews a in their cities in all 7735
  9:16 also a to protect themselves and get relief 7735
  9:18 *had* a on the thirteenth and fourteenth, 7735
Ps 7: 7 Let the peoples gather around you. 6337
Da 3: 3 and all the other provincial officials a for 10359
Mt 26: 3 the people a in the palace of the high priest, *5251*
  26:57 the teachers of the law and the elders *had* a. *5251*
Lk 1:10 all the a **worshipers** were praying outside.
3295+3836+4436
  24:33 the Eleven and those with them, a **together** *125*
Ac 28:17 When they *had* a, Paul said to them: *5302*
1Co 5: 4 *When* you are a in the name *5251*

ASSEMBLIES (5) [ASSEMBLE]

Lev 23: 2 which you are to proclaim as sacred a. 5246
  23: 4 the sacred a you are to proclaim 5246
  23:37 as sacred a for bringing offerings made to 5246
Isa 1:13 I cannot bear your evil a. 6809
Am 5:21 I cannot stand your a. 6809

ASSEMBLING (1) [ASSEMBLE]

1Sa 13:11 and that the Philistines *were* a at Micmash, 665

ASSEMBLY (160) [ASSEMBLE]

Ge 49: 6 let me not join their a, 7736
Ex 12:16 On the first day hold a sacred a, 5246
  16: 3 into this desert to starve this entire a. 7736
Lev 4:14 the a must bring a young bull as 7736
  8: 3 and gather the entire a at the entrance to 6337
  8: 4 the a gathered at the entrance to the Tent 6337
  8: 5 Moses said to the a, 6337
  9: 5 and the entire a came near and stood before 6337
  19: 2 to the entire a *of* Israel and say to them: 6337
  23: 3 a day of sacred a. 5246
  23: 7 a sacred a and do no regular work. 5246
  23: 8 And on the seventh day hold a sacred a 5246
  23:21 a sacred a and do no regular work. 5246
  23:24 a day of rest, a sacred a commemorated 5246
  23:27 Hold a sacred a and deny yourselves, 5246

Lev 23:35 The first day is a sacred a; 5246
  23:36 a sacred a and present an offering made to 5246
  23:36 It is the **closing** a; do no regular work. 6809
  24:14 and the entire a is to stone him. 6337
  24:16 The entire a must stone him. 6337
Nu 10: 7 To gather the a, blow the trumpets, 6337
  13:26 to the whole a and showed them the fruit of 6337
  14: 2 and the whole a said to them, 6337
  14: 5 of the whole Israelite a gathered there. 6337
  14: 7 and said to the entire Israelite a, 6337
  14:10 But the whole a talked about stoning them. 6337
  15:33 to Moses and Aaron and the whole a, 6337
  15:35 The whole a must stone him outside 6337
  15:36 So the a took him outside the camp 6337
  16: 3 you set yourselves above the LORD's a?" 7736
  16:19 of the LORD appeared to the entire a. 6337
  16:21 from this a so I can put an end to them 6337
  16:22 with the entire a when only one man sins?" 6337
  16:24 "Say to the a, 'Move away from the tents 6337
  16:26 He warned the a, 'Move back from 6337
  16:42 when the a gathered in opposition to Moses 6337
  16:45 "Get away from this a so I can put an end 6337
  16:46 hurry to the a to make atonement for them. 6337
  16:47 and ran into the midst of the a. 6337
  20: 6 the a to the entrance to the Tent of Meeting 7736
  20: 8 your brother Aaron gather the a together. 6337
  20:10 and Aaron gathered the a in front 7736
  25: 6 the eyes of Moses and the whole a *of* Israel 6337
  25: 7 the priest, saw this, he left the a, 6337
  27: 2 the leaders and the whole a, and said, 6337
  27:19 before Eleazar the priest and the entire a 6337
  27:22 before Eleazar the priest and the whole a. 6337
  28:18 a sacred a and do no regular work. 5246
  28:25 On the seventh day hold a sacred a 5246
  28:26 hold a sacred a and do no regular work. 5246
  29: 1 of the seventh month hold a sacred a. 5246
  29: 7 of this seventh month hold a sacred a. 5246
  29:12 hold a sacred a and do no regular work. 5246
  29:35 " 'On the eighth day hold an a 6809
  31:12 the priest and the Israelite a at their camp 6337
  35:12 not die before he stands trial before the a. 6337
  35:24 the a must judge between him and 6337
  35:25 The a must protect the one accused 6337
Dt 5:22 in a loud voice to your whole a there on 7736
  9:10 on the day of the a. 7736
  10: 4 out of the fire, on the day of the a. 7736
  16: 8 and on the seventh day hold an a to 6809
  18:16 at Horeb on the day of the a when you said, 7736
  23: 1 or cutting may enter the a *of* the LORD. 7736
  23: 2 nor any of his descendants may enter the a 7736
  23: 3 or any of his descendants may enter the a 7736
  23: 8 of children born to them may enter the a *of* 7736
  31:30 in the hearing of the whole a *of* Israel: 7736
  33: 4 the possession of the a *of* Jacob. 7737
Jos 8:35 that Joshua did not read to the whole a 7736
  9:15 and the leaders of the a ratified it by oath. 6337
  9:18 because the leaders of the a had sworn 6337
  9:18 The whole a grumbled against the leaders, 6337
  18: 1 The whole a of the Israelites gathered 6337
  20: 6 that city until he has stood trial before the a 6337
  20: 9 of blood prior to standing trial before the a. 6337
  22:12 the whole a *of* Israel gathered at Shiloh 6337
  22:16 "The whole a *of* the LORD says: 6337
Jdg 20: 2 the tribes of Israel took their places in the a 7736
  21: 8 to the camp for the a. 7736
  21:10 So the a sent twelve thousand fighting men 6337
  21:13 Then the whole a sent an offer of peace to 6337
  21:16 And the elders of the a said, 6337
1Ki 8: 5 and the entire a *of* Israel that had gathered 6337
  8:14 the whole a *of* Israel was standing there, 7736
  8:22 of the LORD in front of the whole a 7736
  8:55 He stood and blessed the whole a *of* Israel 7736
  8:65 a vast a, people from Lebo Hamath to 6951
  12: 3 the whole a *of* Israel went to Rehoboam 6951
  12:20 and called him to the a and made him king 5712
2Ki 10:20 Jehu said, "Call an a in honor of Baal." 6809
1Ch 13: 2 He then said to the whole a *of* Israel, 7736
  13: 4 The whole a agreed to do this, 6951
  28: 8 of the a *of* the LORD, and in the hearing 6951
  29: 1 Then King David said to the whole a: 6951
  29:10 the LORD in the presence of the whole a, 6951
  29:20 Then David said to the whole a, 6951
2Ch 1: 3 and the whole a went to the high place 6951
  1: 5 Solomon and the a inquired of him there. 6951
  5: 6 and the entire a *of* Israel that had gathered 6337
  6: 3 the whole a *of* Israel was standing there, 6951
  6:12 the LORD in front of the whole a *of* Israel 6951
  6:13 and then knelt down before the whole a 6951
  7: 8 a vast a, people from Lebo Hamath to 6951
  7: 9 On the eighth day they held an a, 6809
  20: 5 the a *of* Judah and Jerusalem at the temple 6951
  20:14 as he stood in the a. 6951
  23: 3 the whole a made a covenant with the king 6951
  24: 6 of the LORD and by the a of Israel for 6951
  28:14 in the presence of the officials and all the a. 6951
  29:23 before the king and the a, 6951
  29:28 The whole a bowed in worship, 6951
  29:31 a brought sacrifices and thank offerings, 6951
  29:32 the a brought was seventy bulls, 6951
  30: 2 The king and his officials and the whole a 6951
  30: 4 both to the king and to the whole a. 6951
  30:23 The whole a then agreed to celebrate 6951
  30:24 and goats for the a, 6951
  30:25 The entire a *of* Judah rejoiced, 6951
Ezr 10: 8 and would himself be expelled from the a 6951
  10:12 The whole a responded with a loud voice: 6951
  10:14 Let our officials act for the whole a. 7736

Ne 5:13 At this the whole a said, "Amen," 7736
  8: 2 the priest brought the Law before the a, 7736
  8:18 with the regulation, there was an a. 6809
  13: 1 be admitted into the a *of* God, 7736
Job 30:28 I stand up in the a and cry for help. 7736
Ps 1: 5 nor sinners in the a *of* the righteous. 6337
  22:25 the theme of my praise in the great a; 7736
  26: 5 I abhor the a *of* evildoers and refuse to sit 7736
  26:12 in the **great** a I will praise the LORD. 5220
  35:18 I will give you thanks in the great a; 7736
  40: 9 I proclaim righteousness in the great a; 7736
  40:10 and your truth from the great a. 7736
  68:26 praise the LORD in the a *of* Israel. 5227
  82: 1 God presides in the great a; 6337
  89: 5 in the a *of* the holy ones. 6951
  107:32 Let them exalt him in the a *of* the people 7736
  111: 1 in the council of the upright and in the a. 6337
  149: 1 his praise in the a *of* the saints. 7736
Pr 5:14 utter ruin in the midst of the **whole a.**
2256+6337+7736
  24: 7 in the a **at the gate** he has nothing to say. 9133
  26:26 his wickedness will be exposed in the a. 7736
Isa 14:13 I will sit enthroned on the mount of a, 4595
Jer 26:17 and said to the entire a *of* people, 7736
  44:15 all the women who were present—a large a 7736
La 1:10 those you had forbidden to enter your a. 7736
Joel 1:14 Declare a holy fast; call a **sacred a.** 6809
  2:15 declare a holy fast, call a **sacred a.** 6809
  2:16 Gather the people, consecrate the a; 7736
Mic 2: 5 Therefore you will have no one in the a *of* 7736
Lk 23: 1 the whole a rose and led him off to Pilate. 4436
Ac 5:21 the full a of the **elders** of Israel— *1172*
  7:38 He was in the a in the desert, *1711*
  15:12 The whole a became silent as they listened *4436*
  19:32 The a was in confusion; *1711*
  19:39 it must be settled in a legal a. *1711*
  19:41 After he had said this, he dismissed the a. *1711*
  23: 7 and the a was divided. *4436*
Heb 12:22 upon thousands of angels *in* **joyful a,** *4108*

ASSENT (KJV) See MAN

ASSERTED (1) [ASSERTING]

Lk 22:59 About an hour later another a, *1462*

ASSERTING (1) [ASSERTED]

Ac 24: 9 a that these things were true. *5763*

ASSESSMENTS (1)

2Ki 23:35 the people of the land according to their a. 6886

ASSHUR (7) [ASSHURITES]

Ge 2:14 it runs along the east side of A. 855
  10:22 Elam, A, Arphaxad, Lud and Aram. 855
  25:18 as you go toward A. 855
Nu 24:22 be destroyed when A takes you captive." 855
  24:24 they will subdue A and Eber, 855
1Ch 1:17 Elam, A, Arphaxad, Lud and Aram. 855
Eze 27:23 A and Kilmad traded with you. 855

ASSHURITES (1) [ASSHUR]

Ge 25: 3 the descendants of Dedan were the A, 857

ASSIGN (12) [ASSIGNED, ASSIGNMENT, ASSIGNMENTS, ASSIGNS, REASSIGN]

Nu 4:19 and a to each man his work and what he is 8492
  4:27 *You shall* a to them as their responsibility 7212
  4:32 A to each man the specific things he is 7212
  8:26 is how *you are to* a the responsibilities of 6913
  34:13 "A this land by lot **as an inheritance.** 5706
  34:17 a the land for you **as an inheritance:** 5706
  34:18 from each tribe to **help** a the land. 5706
  34:29 to a the **inheritance** *to* the Israelites in 5706
1Sa 8:12 Some he *will* a to be commanders 8492
Job 22:24 and a your nuggets to the dust, 8883
Mt 24:51 He will cut him to pieces and a him a place *5502*
Lk 12:46 He will cut him to pieces and a him a place *5502*

ASSIGNED (47) [ASSIGN]

Ge 40: 4 The captain of the guard a them *to* Joseph, 7212
Nu 2: 9 All the *men* a to the camp of Judah, 7212
  2:16 All the *men* a to the camp of Reuben, 7212
  2:24 All the *men* a to the camp of Ephraim, 7212
  2:31 All the *men* a to the camp of Dan 7212
  4:49 each was a his work and told what to carry. 7212
Jos 13: 8 the servant of the LORD, *had* a it to them. 5989
  14: 2 Their inheritances *were* a by lot to NIH
  19:51 and the heads of the tribal clans of Israel a 5706
  21:10 (these towns were a to the descendants 4200
  24: 4 *I* a the hill country of Seir to Esau, 5989
1Sa 15:20 "I went on the mission the LORD a me. 8938
  27: 5 *be* a to me in one of the country towns, 5989
  29: 4 that he may return to the place *you* a him. 7212
1Ki 7:14 to King Solomon and did all the **work** a AIT
  14:27 and a these to an official to her case and said to him, 7212
2Ki 8: 6 He a an official to her case and said to him, 5989
1Ch 6:48 Their fellow Levites **were** a to all 5989
  6:54 as their territory (they were a to 4200
  9:22 gatekeepers *had been* a to their **positions** 3569
  9:29 Others were a to take care of the
furnishings 4948

1Ch	26:29	Kenaniah and his sons were a duties away	4200
2Ch	2:18	He a 70,000 of them to be carriers	6913
	12:10	and a these to the commanders of the guard	7212
	23: 6	to guard what the LORD has a to them.	5466
	25: 5	the people of Judah together and a them	6641
	30:22	For the seven days they ate their a portion	4595
	31: 2	Hezekiah a the priests and Levites	6641
	33: 8	the feet of the Israelites leave the land I a	6641
Ne	12:31	I also a two large choirs to give thanks.	6641
	13:10	that the portions a to the Levites had	AIT
	13:30	and a them duties, each to his own task.	6641
Est	2: 9	He a to her seven maids selected from	5989
	4: 5	one of the king's eunuchs a to attend her,	6641
Job	7: 3	and nights of misery have been a to me.	4948
Ps	16: 5	you have a me my portion and my cup;	4987
	104: 8	to the place you a for them.	3569
Isa	53: 9	He a a a grave with the wicked.	5989
Eze	4: 5	I have a you the same number of days as	5989
	4: 6	I have a you 40 days, a day for each year.	5989
Da	1: 5	The king a them a daily amount of food	4948
	1:10	who has a your food and drink.	4948
Mk	13:34	each with his a task,	NIG
Ac	22:10	be told all that you have been a to do.'	5435
1Co	3: 5	as the Lord has a to each his task.	1443
	7:17	the place in life that the Lord a to him and	3532
2Co	10:13	to the field God has a to us,	3532

ASSIGNMENT (1) [ASSIGN]

1Ch	23:11	as one family with one a.	7213

ASSIGNMENTS (1) [ASSIGN]

2Ch	23:18	to whom David had made a in the temple,	2745

ASSIGNS (1) [ASSIGN]

Mic	2: 4	He a our fields to traitors.' "	2745

ASSIR (4)

Ex	6:24	The sons of Korah were A,	661
1Ch	6:22	Korah his son, A his son,	661
	6:23	Ebiasaph his son, A his son,	661
	6:37	the son of A, the son of Ebiasaph,	661

ASSIST (9) [ASSISTANCE, ASSISTANT, ASSISTANTS, ASSISTED]

Nu	1: 5	the names of the men who are to a you:	907+6641
	3: 6	to Aaron the priest to a him.	9250
	8:26	They may a their brothers	9250
	18: 2	and a you when you and your sons minister	9250
2Ch	8:14	the Levites to lead the praise and to a	9250
	13:10	and the Levites a them.	4856
Ezr	8:20	and the officials had established to a	6275
Job	29:12	and the fatherless who had none to a him.	6468
Ro	15:24	a me on my journey	4636

ASSISTANCE (1) [ASSIST]

Ezr	8:36	then gave a to the people and to the house	5951

ASSISTANT (2) [ASSIST]

Dt	1:38	your a, Joshua son of Nun, will enter it.	4200+6641+7156
Ne	13:13	the son of Mattaniah, their a,	3338+6584

ASSISTANT (Anglicized) See also AIDE

ASSISTANTS (1) [ASSIST]

Ne	5:15	Their a also lorded it over the people.	5853

ASSISTED (3) [ASSIST]

2Ch	31:15	and Shecaniah a him faithfully in the towns	3338+6584
Ezr	1: 6	All their neighbors a them with articles	928+2616+3338
	6:22	he a them in the work on the house	2616+3338

ASSOCIATE (10) [ASSOCIATED, ASSOCIATES]

Jos	23: 7	Do not a with these nations that remain	928+995
	23:12	if you intermarry with them and a with	928+995
1Ch	6:39	and Heman's a Asaph, who served	278
Pr	22:24	do not a with one easily angered,	995
Jn	4: 9	(For Jews do not a with Samaritans.)	5178
Ac	10:28	that it is against our law for a Jew to a with	3140
Ro	12:16	but be willing to a with people	5270
1Co	5: 9	I have written you in my letter not to a with	5264
	5:11	not a with anyone who calls himself	5264
2Th	3:14	Do not a with him,	5264

ASSOCIATED (4) [ASSOCIATE]

Ne	13: 4	He was closely a with Tobiah,	7940
Eze	37:16	to Judah and the Israelites a with him.'	2492
	37:16	to Joseph and all the house of Israel a with	2492
	37:19	and of the Israelite tribes a with him,	2492

ASSOCIATES (28) [ASSOCIATE]

1Ch	6:44	from their a, the Merarites, at his left hand:	278
	16: 7	to Asaph and his a this psalm of thanks to	278
	16:37	and his a before the ark of the covenant of	278
	16:38	and his sixty-eight a to minister with them.	278

Ezr	3: 2	of Shealtiel and his a began to build	278
	4: 7	Tabeel and the rest of his a wrote a letter	4056
	4: 9	together with the rest of their a—	10360
	4:17	of their a living in Samaria and elsewhere	10360
	4:23	and Shimshai the secretary and their a,	10360
	5: 3	and Shethar-Bozenai and their a went	10360
	5: 6	and Shethar-Bozenai and their a,	10360
	6:13	and their a carried it out with diligence.	10360
Ne	2: 4	and in the presence of his a and the army	278
	10:10	and their a: Shebaniah,	278
	11:12	and his a, who carried on work for	278
	11:13	and his a, who were heads of families—	278
	11:14	and his a, who were able men—	278
	11:17	Bakbukiah, second among his a;	278
	11:19	Akkub, Talmon and their a,	278
	12: 7	the priests and their a in the days of Jeshua.	278
	12: 8	who, together with his a,	278
	12: 9	Bakbukiah and Unni, their a,	278
	12:24	Jeshua son of Kadmiel, and their a,	278
	12:36	and his a— Shemaiah, Azarel,	278
Job	34: 8	he a with wicked men.	2143
Zec	3: 8	O high priest Joshua and your a seated	8276
Ac	5:17	Then the high priest and all his a,	3836+5250
	5:21	When the high priest and his a arrived,	3836+5250

ASSOS (2)

Ac	20:13	on ahead to the ship and sailed for A,	840
	20:14	When he met us at A,	840

ASSUME (2) [ASSUMED]

Ne	10:32	a the responsibility for carrying out	6584+6641
	10:35	"We also a responsibility for bringing to	NIH

ASSUMED (2) [ASSUME]

1Sa	14:47	After Saul had a rule over Israel,	4334
Ac	21:29	with Paul and a that Paul had brought him	3787

ASSUR (KJV) See ASSYRIA

ASSURANCE (5) [ASSURE]

1Sa	17:18	and bring back some a from them.	6859
Est	9:30	words of goodwill and a—	622
Job	24:22	they have no a of life.	586
1Ti	3:13	and great a in their faith in Christ Jesus.	4244
Heb	10:22	near to God with a sincere heart in full a	4443

ASSURE (2) [ASSURANCE, ASSURED, ASSUREDLY, ASSURES, REASSURE, REASSURED]

Lk	4:25	I a you that there were many widows	237+2093+3306
Gal	1:20	I a you before God that what I am writing	2627

ASSURED (7) [ASSURE]

Dt	9: 3	But be a today that the LORD your God is	3359
Jos	2:14	"Our lives for your lives!" the men a her.	606
1Sa	10:16	"He a us that the donkeys had been found."	5583+5583
Job	36: 4	Be a that my words are not false;	597
Jer	26:15	Be a, however, that if you put me to death,	3359+3359
Ac	2:36	"Therefore let all Israel be a of this:	857+1182
Col	4:12	in all the will of God, mature and fully a.	4442

ASSUREDLY (1) [ASSURE]

Jer	32:41	in doing them good and will a plant them	622+928

ASSURES (1) [ASSURE]

Jer	5:24	who a us of the regular weeks of harvest.'	9068

ASSWAGE (KJV) See BRING RELIEF

ASSYRIA (122) [ASSYRIA'S, ASSYRIAN, ASSYRIANS]

Ge	10:11	From that land he went to A,	855
2Ki	15:19	Then Pul king of A invaded the land,	855
	15:20	of silver to be given to the king of A.	855
	15:20	So the king of A withdrew and stayed in	855
	15:29	Tiglath-Pileser king of A came	855
	15:29	and deported the people to A.	855
	16: 7	to say to Tiglath-Pileser king of A,	855
	16: 8	and sent it as a gift to the king of A.	855
	16: 9	of A complied by attacking Damascus	855
	16:10	to meet Tiglath-Pileser king of A.	855
	16:18	in deference to the king of A.	855
	17: 3	Shalmaneser king of A came up	855
	17: 4	of A discovered that Hoshea was a traitor,	855
	17: 4	he no longer paid tribute to the king of A,	855
	17: 5	The king of A invaded the entire land,	855
	17: 6	of A captured Samaria and deported	855
	17: 6	and deported the Israelites to A.	855
	17:23	from their homeland into exile in A,	855
	17:24	of A brought people from Babylon,	855
	17:26	It was reported to the king of A:	855
	17:27	Then the king of A gave this order:	855
	18: 7	against the king of A and did not serve him.	855
	18: 9	Shalmaneser king of A marched	855
	18:11	The king of A deported Israel to Assyria	855
	18:11	The king of Assyria deported Israel to A	855

2Ki	18:13	of A attacked all the fortified cities	855
	18:14	of Judah sent this message to the king of A	855
	18:14	The king of A exacted from Hezekiah king	855
	18:16	and gave it to the king of A.	855
	18:17	of A sent his supreme commander,	855
	18:19	the great king, the king of A, says:	855
	18:23	bargain with my master, the king of A:	855
	18:28	the word of the great king, the king of A!	855
	18:30	be given into the hand of the king of A.'	855
	18:31	This is what the king of A says:	855
	18:33	from the hand of the king of A?	855
	19: 4	whom his master, the king of A,	855
	19: 6	of the king of A have blasphemed me.	855
	19: 8	that the king of A had left Lachish,	855
	19:10	not be handed over to the king of A.'	855
	19:11	of A have done to all the countries,	855
	19:20	concerning Sennacherib king of A,	855
	19:32	the LORD says concerning the king of A:	855
	19:36	So Sennacherib king of A broke camp	855
	20: 6	from the hand of the king of A.	855
	23:29	the Euphrates River to help the king of A.	855
1Ch	5: 6	whom Tiglath-Pileser king of A took	855
	5:26	up the spirit of Pul king of A (that is,	855
	5:26	Tiglath-Pileser king of A),	855
2Ch	28:16	that time King Ahaz sent to the king of A	855
	28:20	Tiglath-Pileser king of A came to him,	855
	28:21	and presented them to the king of A,	855
	30: 6	from the hand of the kings of A.	855
	32: 1	of A came and invaded Judah.	855
	32: 4	of A come and find plenty of water?"	855
	32: 7	because of the king of A and the vast army	855
	32: 9	of A and all his forces were laying siege	855
	32:10	"This is what Sennacherib king of A says:	855
	32:11	from the hand of the king of A,'	855
	32:22	from the hand of Sennacherib king of A	855
	33:11	the army commanders of the king of A,	855
Ezr	4: 2	since the time of Esarhaddon king of A,	855
	6:22	by changing the attitude of the king of A,	855
Ne	9:32	from the days of the kings of A until today.	855
Ps	83: 8	Even A has joined them to lend strength to	855
Isa	7:17	he will bring the king of A."	855
	7:18	of Egypt and for bees from the land of A.	855
	7:20	hired from beyond the River—the king of A	855
	8: 4	be carried off by the king of A."	855
	8: 7	the king of A with all his pomp.	855
	10:12	of A for the willful pride of his heart and	855
	11:11	that is left of his people from A,	855
	11:16	his people that is left from A,	855
	19:23	be a highway from Egypt to A.	855
	19:23	to Egypt and the Egyptians to A.	855
	19:24	along with Egypt and A,	855
	19:25	be Egypt my people, A my handiwork,	855
	20: 1	sent by Sargon king of A	855
	20: 4	of A will lead away stripped and barefoot	855
	20: 6	and deliverance from the king of A!	855
	27:13	in A and those who were exiled	824+855
	30:31	The voice of the LORD will shatter A;	855
	31: 8	"A will fall by a sword that is not of man;	855
	36: 1	of A attacked all the fortified cities	855
	36: 2	the king of A sent his field commander	855
	36: 4	the great king, the king of A, says:	855
	36: 8	bargain with my master, the king of A:	855
	36:13	the great king, the king of A!	855
	36:15	be given into the hand of the king of A.'	855
	36:16	This is what the king of A says:	855
	36:18	from the hand of the king of A?	855
	37: 4	whom his master, the king of A,	855
	37: 6	of the king of A have blasphemed me.	855
	37: 8	that the king of A had left Lachish,	855
	37:10	not be handed over to the king of A.'	855
	37:11	of A have done to all the countries,	855
	37:21	to me concerning Sennacherib king of A,	855
	37:33	the LORD says concerning the king of A:	855
	37:37	So Sennacherib king of A broke camp	855
	38: 6	from the hand of the king of A.	855
	52: 4	lately, A has oppressed them.	855
Jer	2:18	why go to A to drink water from the River?	855
	2:36	by Egypt as you were by A.	855
	50:17	The first to devour him was the king of A;	855
	50:18	and his land as I punished the king of A.	855
La	5: 6	to Egypt and A to get enough bread.	855
Eze	31: 3	Consider A, once a cedar in Lebanon,	855
	32:22	"A is there with her whole army;	855
Hos	5:13	then Ephraim turned to A,	855
	7:11	now calling to Egypt, now turning to A.	855
	8: 9	to A like a wild donkey wandering alone.	855
	9: 3	to Egypt and eat unclean food in A.	855
	10: 6	be carried to A as tribute for the great king.	855
	11: 5	not A rule over them because they refuse	855
	11:11	like doves from A.	824+855
	12: 1	with A and sends olive oil to Egypt.	855
	14: 3	A cannot save us;	855
Mic	5: 6	They will rule the land of A with	855
	7:12	In that day people will come to you from A	855
Na	3:18	O king of A, your shepherds slumber;	855
Zep	2:13	against the north and destroy A,	855
Zec	10:10	from Egypt and gather them from A.	855

ASSYRIA'S (1) [ASSYRIA]

Zec	10:11	A pride will be brought down	855

ASSYRIAN (9) [ASSYRIA]

2Ki	19:17	the A kings have laid waste these nations	855
	19:35	in the A camp.	855
2Ch	32:21	and officers in the camp of the A king.	855

Isa	10: 5	"Woe to the A, the rod of my anger,	855
	14:25	I will crush the A in my land;	855
	37:18	A kings have laid waste all these peoples	855
	37:36	thousand men in the A camp.	855
Mic	5: 5	When the A invades our land and marches	855
	5: 6	from the A when he invades our land	855

ASSYRIANS (11) [ASSYRIA]

2Ki	18:10	At the end of three years the A took it.	NIH
Isa	10:24	do not be afraid of the A,	855
	19:23	The A will go to Egypt and the Egyptians	855
	19:23	The Egyptians and A will worship together.	855
	23:13	A have made it a place for desert creatures;	855
Eze	16:28	You engaged in prostitution with the A too,	855+1201
	23: 5	and she lusted after her lovers, the A—	855
	23: 7	A and defiled herself with all the idols	855+1201
	23: 9	the A, for whom she lusted.	855+1201
	23:12	She too lusted after the A—	855+1201
	23:23	and all the A with them,	855+1201

ASTAROTH (KJV) See ASHTAROTH

ASTIR (2) [STIR]

Ps	83: 2	See how your enemies are a,	2159
Isa	14: 9	The grave below is all a to meet you	8074

ASTONISHED (23) [ASTONISHMENT]

Job	21: 5	Look at me and be a;	9037
Mt	8:10	he was a and said to those following him,	2513
	12:23	All the people were a and said,	2014
	19:25	they were greatly a and asked,	1742
	22:33	they were a at his teaching.	1742
Mk	5:42	At this they were completely a.	1749+2014
	10:32	and the disciples were a,	2501
Lk	2:48	When his parents saw him, they were a.	1742
	5: 9	all his companions were a at the catch	2502+4321
	8:56	Her parents were a,	2014
	20:26	And a by his answer, they became silent.	2513
Jn	7:21	"I did one miracle, and you are all a.	2513
Ac	3:11	all the people were a and came running	1702
	4:13	they were a and they took note	2513
	8:13	a by the great signs and miracles he saw.	2014
	9:21	All those who heard him were a and asked,	2014
	10:45	with Peter were a that the gift of	2014
	12:16	the door and saw him, they were a.	2014
Gal	1: 6	I am a that you are so quickly deserting	2513
Rev	13: 3	The whole world was a and followed	2513
	17: 6	When I saw her, I was greatly a.	2512+2513
	17: 7	the angel said to me: "Why are you a?	2513
	17: 8	from the creation of the world will be a.	2513

ASTONISHING (1) [ASTONISHMENT]

Da	12: 6	be before these a things are fulfilled?"	7099

ASTONISHMENT (2) [ASTONISHED, ASTONISHING]

Ge	43:33	looked at each other in a.	9449
Lk	1:63	and to everyone's a he wrote,	2513

ASTOUND (1) [ASTOUNDED, ASTOUNDING]

Isa	29:14	Therefore once more I will a these people	7098

ASTOUNDED (1) [ASTOUND]

Ps	48: 5	they saw [her] and were a;	9449

ASTOUNDING (2) [ASTOUND]

La	1: 9	Her fall was a;	7099
Da	8:24	He will cause a devastation	7098

ASTRAY (50) [STRAY]

Nu	5:12	a man's wife goes a and is unfaithful to him	8474
	5:19	with you and you have not gone a	8474
	5:20	But if you have gone a while married	8474
	5:29	is the law of jealousy when a woman goes a	8474
Dt	13:13	led the people of their town a,	5615
	17:17	or his heart will be led a.	6073
	27:18	"Cursed is the man who leads the blind a on	8706
1Ki	11: 3	and his wives led him a.	4213+5742
2Ki	21: 9	Manasseh led them a,	9494
2Ch	21:11	and had led Judah a.	5615
	33: 9	led Judah and the people of Jerusalem a,	9494
Job	19: 4	If it is true that I have gone a,	8706
Ps	58: 3	Even from birth the wicked go a;	2319
	95:10	"They are a people whose hearts go a,	9494
	119:67	Before I was afflicted I went a,	8704
Pr	5:23	led a by his own great folly.	8706
	7:21	With persuasive words she led him a;	5742
	10:17	whoever ignores correction leads others a.	9494
	12:26	but the way of the wicked leads them a.	9494
	14:22	Do not those who plot evil go a?	9494
	20: 1	whoever is led a by them is not wise.	8706
Isa	3:12	O my people, your guides lead you a;	9494
	9:16	and those who are guided are led a.	1182
	19:13	of her peoples lead Egypt a.	9494
	30:28	of the peoples a bit that leads them a.	9494
	53: 6	We all, like sheep, have gone a,	9494
Jer	4: 1	of my sight and no longer go a,	5653
	23:13	led my people Israel a.	9494

Jer	23:32	"They tell them and lead my people a	9494
	50: 6	their shepherds have led them a	9494
Eze	13:10	"'Because they lead my people a, saying,	3246
	44:10	when Israel went a and who wandered	9494
	44:15	of my sanctuary when the Israelites went a	9494
	48:11	and did not go a as the Levites did when	9494
	48:11	the Levites did when the Israelites went a.	9494
Hos	4:12	A spirit of prostitution leads them a;	9494
Am	2: 4	they have been led a by false gods,	9494
Mic	3: 5	"As for the prophets who lead my people a,	9494
Jn	16: 1	so that you will not go a.	4997
Ac	19:26	and led a large numbers of people here	3496
1Co	12: 2	or other you were influenced and led a	552
2Co	11: 3	your minds may somehow be led a	5780
Gal	2:13	even Barnabas was led a.	5270
Heb	3:10	'Their hearts are always going a,	4414
	5: 2	those who are ignorant and are going a,	4414
1Pe	2:25	For you were like sheep going a,	4414
1Jn	2:26	about those who are trying to lead you a.	4414
	3: 7	do not let anyone lead you a.	4414
Rev	12: 9	Satan, who leads the whole world a.	4414
	18:23	your magic spell all the nations were led a.	4414

ASTROLOGER (1) [ASTROLOGERS]

Da	2:10	a thing of any magician or enchanter or a.	10373

ASTROLOGERS (9) [ASTROLOGER]

Isa	47:13	Let your a come forward,	2042+9028
Da	2: 2	and a to tell him what he had dreamed.	4169
	2: 4	Then the a answered the king in Aramaic,	4169
	2: 5	The king replied to the a,	10373
	2:10	The a answered the king,	10373
	3: 8	At this time some a came forward	10373
	4: 7	a and diviners came, I told them the dream,	10373
	5: 7	a and diviners to be brought and said	10373
	5:11	enchanters, a and diviners."	10373

ASUPPIM (KJV) See SHUPPIM, STOREHOUSE

ASUNDER (2)

Ps	136:13	the Red Sea a His love endures forever.	1617
Isa	24:19	The earth is broken up, the earth is split a,	7297+7297

ASWAN (3)

Isa	49:12	some from the region of A."	6059
Eze	29:10	and a desolate waste from Migdol to A,	6059
	30: 6	to A they will fall by the sword within her,	6059

ASYNCRITUS (1)

Ro	16:14	Greet A, Phlegon, Hermes, Patrobas,	850

AT (2217) See Index of Articles Etc.

ATAD (2)

Ge	50:10	they reached the threshing floor of A,	354
	50:11	the mourning at the threshing floor of A,	354

ATARAH (1)

1Ch	2:26	whose name was A;	6499

ATAROTH (4) [ATAROTH ADDAR]

Nu	32: 3	"A, Dibon, Jazer, Nimrah,	6500
	32:34	The Gadites built up Dibon, A, Aroer,	6500
Jos	16: 2	over to the territory of the Arkites in A,	6500
	16: 7	it went down from Janoah to A and Naarah,	6500

ATAROTH ADDAR (2) [ADDAR, ATAROTH]

Jos	16: 5	of their inheritance went from A in	6501
	18:13	and went down to A on the hill south	6501

ATAROTHADAR (KJV) See ATAROTH ADDAR

ATE (107) [EAT]

Ge	3: 6	she took some and a it.	430
	3: 6	who was with her, and he a it.	430
	3:12	from the tree, and I a it."	430
	3:13	"The serpent deceived me, and I a."	430
	3:17	"Because you listened to your wife and a	430
	18: 8	While they a, he stood near them under	430
	19: 3	baking bread without yeast, and they a.	430
	24:54	Then he and the men who were with him a	430
	25:34	He a and drank, and then got up and left.	430
	26:30	and they a and drank.	430
	27:25	Jacob brought it to him and he a;	430
	27:33	I a it just before you came	430
	31:46	and they a there by the heap.	430
	39: 6	with anything except the food he a.	430
	41: 4	the cows that were ugly and gaunt a up	430
	41:20	ugly cows a up the seven fat cows	430
	41:21	But even after they a them,	448+995+7931
	43:32	and the Egyptians who a with him	430
Ex	16: 3	There we sat around pots of meat and a all	430
	16:35	The Israelites a manna forty years,	430
	16:35	they a manna until they reached the border	430

Ex	24:11	they saw God, and they a and drank.	430
Nu	11: 5	We remember the fish we a in Egypt	430
	25: 2	The people a and bowed down	430
Dt	9: 9	I a no bread and drank no water.	430
	9:18	I a no bread and drank no water,	430
	29: 6	You a no bread and drank no wine	430
	32:38	the gods who a the fat of their sacrifices	430
Jos	5:11	they a some of the produce of the land:	430
	5:12	the day after they a this food from the land;	430
	5:12	that year they a of the produce of Canaan.	430
Jdg	14: 9	which he scooped out with his hands and a	430
	14: 9	he gave them some, and they too a it.	430
	19: 8	So the two of them a together.	430
Ru	2:14	She a all she wanted	430
1Sa	1:18	Then she went her way and a something,	430
	14:32	on the ground and a them,	430
	28:25	before Saul and his men, and they a.	430
	30:12	He a and was revived.	430
2Sa	9:11	So Mephibosheth a at David's table	430
	9:13	because he always a at the king's table,	430
	11:13	he a and drank with him,	430
	12:20	his request they served him food, and he a.	430
1Ki	4:20	they a, they drank and they were happy.	430
	13:19	So the man of God returned with him and a	430
	13:22	and a bread and drank water in the place	430
	19: 6	He a and drank and then lay down again.	430
	19: 8	So he got up and a and drank.	430
	19:21	and gave it to the people, and they a.	430
2Ki	4:44	and they a and had some left over,	430
	6:29	So we cooked my son and a him.	430
	7: 8	They a and drank, and carried away silver,	430
	9:34	Jehu went in and a and drank.	430
	23: 9	they a unleavened bread	430
	25:29	of his life a regularly at the king's table.	430
1Ch	29:22	They a and drank with great joy in	430
2Ch	30:18	yet they a the Passover,	430
	30:22	the seven days they a their assigned portion	430
Ezr	6:21	who had returned from the exile a it,	430
	10: 6	he a no food and drank no water,	430
Ne	5:14	nor my brothers a the food allotted to	430
	5:17	and fifty Jews and officials a at my table,	NIH
	9:25	They a to the full and were well-nourished;	430
Job	42:11	before came and a with him in his house.	430
Ps	78:25	Men a the bread of angels;	430
	78:29	They a till they had more than enough,	430
	105:35	they a up every green thing in their land,	430
	105:35	a up the produce of their soil.	430
	106:28	to the Baal of Peor and a sacrifices offered	430
Isa	44:19	I roasted meat and I a.	430
Jer	15:16	When your words came, I a them;	430
	52:33	of his life a regularly at the king's table.	430
La	4: 5	Those who once a delicacies are destitute in	430
Eze	3: 3	So I a it, and it tasted as sweet as honey	430
Da	1:15	of the young men who a the royal food.	430
	4:33	from people and a grass like cattle.	10030
	5:21	he lived with the wild donkeys and a grass	10301
	10: 3	I a no choice food;	430
Mt	9:10	and "sinners" came and a with him	5263
	12: 4	and he and his companions a	2266
	13: 4	and the birds came and a it up.	2983
	14:20	They all a and were satisfied.	2266
	14:21	The number of those who was	2266
	15:37	They all a and were satisfied.	2266
	15:38	of those who a was four thousand,	2266
Mk	1: 6	and he a locusts and wild honey.	2266
	2:26	of God and a the consecrated bread,	2266
	4: 4	and the birds came and a it up.	2983
	6:42	They all a and were satisfied,	2266
	8: 8	The people a and were satisfied.	2266
Lk	4: 2	He a nothing during those days,	2266
	6: 4	he a what is lawful only for priests to eat.	2266
	8: 5	and the birds of the air a it up.	2983
	9:17	They all a and were satisfied,	2266
	13:26	you will say, 'We a and drank with you,	2266
	24:43	and he took it and a it in their presence.	2266
Jn	6:26	because you a the loaves and had your fill.	2266
	6:31	Our forefathers a the manna in the desert;	2266
	6:49	Your forefathers a the manna in the desert,	2266
	6:58	Your forefathers a manna and died,	2266
Ac	2:46	and a together with glad and sincere hearts,	5575
	10:41	by us who a and drank with him	5303
	11: 3	the house of uncircumcised men and a with	5303
	20:11	and broke bread and a.	1174
	27:36	and a some food themselves.	4689
1Co	10: 3	They all a the same spiritual food	2266
Rev	10:10	from the angel's hand and a it.	2983

ATER (5)

Ezr	2:16	of A (through Hezekiah) 98	359
	2:42	the descendants of Shallum, A, Talmon,	359
Ne	7:21	of A (through Hezekiah) 98	359
	7:45	the descendants of Shallum, A, Talmon,	359
	10:17	A, Hezekiah, Azzur,	359

ATHACH (1)

1Sa	30:30	to those in Hormah, Bor Ashan, A	6973

ATHAIAH (1)

Ne	11: 4	A son of Uzziah, the son of Zechariah,	6970

ATHALIAH (17)

2Ki	8:26	His mother's name was A,	6976
	11: 1	When A the mother of Ahaziah saw	6975
	11: 2	in a bedroom to hide him from A;	6976

2Ki	11: 3	of the LORD for six years while A ruled	6975
	11:13	When A heard the noise made by	6975
	11:14	A tore her robes and called out, "Treason!	6975
	11:20	because A had been slain with the sword at	6976
1Ch	8:26	Shamsherai, Shehariah, A,	6975
2Ch	22: 2	His mother's name was A,	6976
	22:10	When A the mother of Ahaziah saw	6976
	22:11	the child from A so she could not kill him.	6976
	22:12	of God for six years while A ruled the land.	6975
	23:12	When A heard the noise of	6976
	23:13	A tore her robes and shouted, "Treason!	6976
	23:21	because A had been slain with the sword.	6976
	24: 7	of that wicked woman A had broken into	6976
Ezr	8: 7	Jeshaiah son of A, and with him 70 men;	6975

ATHARIM (1)

Nu	21: 1	that Israel was coming along the road to A,	926

ATHENIANS (1) [ATHENS]

Ac	17:21	(All the A and the foreigners who lived there	122

ATHENS (5) [ATHENIANS]

Ac	17:15	to A and then left with instructions for Silas	121
	17:16	While Paul was waiting for them in A,	121
	17:22	and said: "Men of A!	122
	18: 1	After this, Paul left A and went to Corinth.	121
1Th	3: 1	to be left by ourselves in A.	121

ATHLAI (1)

Ezr	10:28	Jehohanan, Hananiah, Zabbai and A.	6974

ATHLETE (1)

2Ti	2: 5	Similarly, if anyone competes as an a,	123

ATONE (3) [ATONEMENT]

Ex	30:15	to the LORD to a for your lives.	4105
2Ch	29:24	the altar for a sin offering to a for all Israel,	4105
Da	9:24	to put an end to sin, to a for wickedness,	4105

ATONED (6) [ATONEMENT]

Dt	21: 8	And the bloodshed will be a for.	4105
1Sa	3:14	of Eli's house will never be a for	4105
Pr	16: 6	Through love and faithfulness sin is a for;	4105
Isa	6: 7	your guilt is taken away and your sin a for."	4105
	22:14	this sin will not be a for,"	4105
	27: 9	By this, then, will Jacob's guilt be a for,	4105

ATONEMENT (105) [ATONE, ATONED, ATONING]

Ex	25:17	"Make an a cover of pure gold—	4114
	26:34	the a cover on the ark of the Testimony in	4114
	29:33	to eat these offerings by which a was made	4105
	29:36	a bull each day as a sin offering to make a.	4113
	29:36	Purify the altar by making a for it,	4105
	29:37	For seven days make a for the altar	4105
	30: 6	the a cover that is over the Testimony—	4114
	30:10	a year Aaron shall make a on its horns.	4105
	30:10	This annual a must be made with the blood	4105
	30:16	the a money from the Israelites and use it	4113
	30:16	making a for your lives."	4105
	31: 7	the ark of the Testimony with the a cover	4114
	32:30	perhaps I can make a for your sin."	4105
	35:12	the a cover and the curtain that shields it;	4114
	37: 6	He made the a cover of pure gold—	4114
	39:35	with its poles and the a cover;	4114
	40:20	the poles to the ark and put the a cover	4114
Lev	1: 4	accepted on his behalf to make a for him.	4105
	4:20	In this way the priest will make a for them,	4105
	4:26	the priest will make a for the man's sin,	4105
	4:31	In this way the priest will make a for him	4105
	4:35	In this way the priest will make a for him	4105
	5: 6	the priest shall make a for him for his sin.	4105
	5:10	in the prescribed way and make a for him	4105
	5:13	In this way the priest will make a for him	4105
	5:16	who will make a for him with the ram as	4105
	5:18	In this way the priest will make a for him	4105
	6: 7	In this way the priest will make a for him	4105
	6:30	to make a in the Holy Place is	4105
	7: 7	They belong to the priest who makes a	4105
	8:15	So he consecrated it to make a for it.	4105
	8:34	by the LORD to make a for you.	4105
	9: 7	and make a for yourself and the people;	4105
	9: 7	the offering that is for the people and make a for them,	4105
	10:17	by making a for them before the LORD	4105
	12: 7	before the LORD to make a for her,	4105
	12: 8	In this way the priest will make a for her,	4105
	14:18	the one to be cleansed and make a for him	4105
	14:19	to sacrifice the sin offering and make a for	4105
	14:20	and make a for him, and he will be clean.	4105
	14:21	as a guilt offering to be waved to make a	4105
	14:29	to make a for him before the LORD.	4105
	14:31	the priest will make a before the LORD	4105
	14:53	In this way he will make a for the house,	4105
	15:15	In this way he will make a before	4105
	15:30	In this way the priest will make a for her before	4105
	16: 2	behind the curtain in front of the a cover	4114
	16: 2	I appear in the cloud over the a cover.	4114
	16: 6	the bull for his own sin offering to make a	4105
	16:10	for making a by sending it into the desert as	4105
	16:11	the bull for his own sin offering to make a	4105

Lev	16:13	the incense will conceal the a cover above	4114
	16:14	on the front of the a cover;	4114
	16:14	before the a cover.	4114
	16:15	He shall sprinkle it on the a cover and	4114
	16:16	In this way he will make a for	4105
	16:17	from the time Aaron goes in to make a in	4105
	16:17	having made a for himself,	4105
	16:18	that is before the LORD and make a for it.	4105
	16:20	"When Aaron has finished making a for	4105
	16:24	to make a for himself and for the people.	4105
	16:27	to make a, must be taken outside the camp;	4105
	16:30	because on this day a will be made for you,	4105
	16:32	as high priest is to make a.	4105
	16:33	and make a for the Most Holy Place,	4105
	16:34	A is to be made once a year for all the sins	4105
	17:11	to you to make a for yourselves on the altar;	4105
	17:11	it is the blood that makes a for one's life.	4105
	19:22	of the guilt offering the priest is to make a	4105
	23:27	of this seventh month is the Day of A.	4113
	23:28	because it is the Day of A,	4113
	23:28	when a is made for you before	4105
	25: 9	on the Day of A sound the trumpet	4113
Nu	5: 8	the ram with which a is made for him.	4105+4113
	6:11	and the other as a burnt offering to make a	4105
	7:89	the a cover on the ark of the Testimony.	4114
	8:12	to make a for the Levites.	4105
	8:19	of the Israelites and to make a for them so	4105
	8:21	before the LORD and made a for them	4105
	15:25	The priest is to make a for	4105
	15:28	The priest is to make a before the LORD	4105
	15:28	and when a has been made for him,	4105
	16:46	hurry to the assembly to make a for them.	4105
	16:47	but Aaron offered the incense and made a	4105
	25:13	of his God and made a for the Israelites."	4105
	28:22	as a sin offering to make a for you.	4105
	28:30	Include one male goat to make a for you.	4105
	29: 5	as a sin offering to make a for you.	4105
	29:11	in addition to the sin offering for a and	4113
	31:50	to make a for ourselves before the LORD."	4105
	35:33	and a cannot be made for the land	4105
Dt	21: 8	Accept this a for your people Israel,	4105
	32:43	on his enemies and make a for his land	4105
1Ch	6:49	making a for Israel,	4105
	28:11	its inner rooms and the place of a.	4114
Ne	10:33	for sin offerings to make a for Israel;	4105
Eze	16:63	I make a for you for all you have done,	4105
	43:20	and so purify the altar and make a for it.	4105
	43:26	For seven days they are to make a for	4105
	45:15	and fellowship offerings to make a for	4105
	45:17	and fellowship offerings to make a for	4105
	45:20	so you are to make a for the temple.	4105
Ro	3:25	God presented him as a sacrifice of a,	2663
Heb	2:17	and that he might make a for the sins of	2661
	9: 5	overshadowing the a cover.	2663

ATONING (3) [ATONEMENT]

Ex	30:10	of the a sin offering for the generations	4113
1Jn	2: 2	He is the sacrifice for our sins,	2662
	4:10	and sent his Son as an a sacrifice	2662

ATROTH BETH JOAB (1)

1Ch	2:54	A, half the Manahathites,	6502

ATROTH SHOPHAN (1)

Nu	32:35	A, Jazer, Jogbehah,	6503

ATTACH (7) [ATTACHED, ATTACHING]

Ex	28:14	like a rope, and a the chains to the settings.	5989
	28:26	and a them to the other two corners of	8492
	28:27	Make two more gold rings and a them to	5989
	28:37	Fasten a blue cord to it to a it to the turban;	2118
	29: 6	on his head and a the sacred diadem to	5989
	39:31	Then they fastened a blue cord to it to a it	5989
Eze	37: 6	I will a tendons to you	5989

ATTACHED (15) [ATTACH]

Ge	29:34	at last my husband will become a to me,	4277
	32:32	the Israelites do not eat the tendon a to	6584
Ex	28: 7	It is to have two shoulder pieces a to two	2489
	39: 4	which were a to two of its corners,	2489
	39:19	They made two gold rings and a them to	8492
	39:20	and a them to the bottom of	5989
	39:25	of pure gold and a them around the hem	5989
	40:20	the poles to the ark and put	8492
1Ki	6:10	and they were a to the temple by beams	297
	7:28	They had side panels a to uprights.	1068
	7:32	the axles of the wheels were a to the stand.	928
	7:35	The supports and panels were a to the top	6584
2Ch	3:16	a hundred pomegranates and a them to	5989
	9:18	and a footstool of gold was a to it.	297
Eze	40:43	were a to the wall all around.	3922

ATTACHING (2) [ATTACH]

Ex	28:25	a them to the shoulder pieces of the ephod	5989
	39:18	a them to the shoulder pieces of the ephod	5989

ATTACK (101) [ATTACKED, ATTACKER, ATTACKERS, ATTACKING, ATTACKS]

Ge	14:15	the night Abram divided his men to a them	6584
	32:11	for I am afraid he will come and a me,	5782
	34:30	and if they join forces against me and a me,	5782
	43:18	to a us and overpower us and seize us	1670

Ge	49:19	but he will a them at their heels.	1574
Nu	13:31	"We can't a those people;	448+6590
	20:18	if you try, we will march out and a you	7925
Dt	20:10	When you march up to a a city,	4309
Jos	8: 1	and go up and a Ai.	6590
	8: 3	and the whole army moved out to a Ai.	6590
	9:18	But the Israelites did not a them,	5782
	10: 4	"Come up and help me a Gibeon," he said,	5782
	10:19	Pursue your enemies, a them from the rear	2386
Jdg	7:10	If you are afraid to a,	3718
	7:11	you will be encouraged to a the camp."	928+3718
	9:43	he rose to a them.	5782
	9:45	All that day Abimelech pressed his a	4309
	10:18	the a against the Ammonites will be	4309
	18: 9	They answered, "Come on, let's a them!	6584+6590
	18:25	or some hot-tempered men will a you,	7003
	20:34	of Israel's finest men made a frontal a	995
1Sa	7: 7	of the Philistines came up to a them.	448
	14:14	In that first a Jonathan	4804
	15: 3	Now go, a the Amalekites	5782
	17:48	As the Philistine moved closer to a him,	7925
	23: 2	saying, "Shall I go and a these Philistines?"	5782
	23: 2	"Go, a the Philistines and save Keilah."	5782
	24: 7	and did not allow them to a Saul.	448+7756
2Sa	5: 6	and his men marched to Jerusalem to a	448
	5:19	"Shall I go and a the Philistines?	448
	5:23	behind them and a them in front of	995+4200
	11:25	Press the a against the city and destroy it.'	4878
	17: 2	I would a him while he is weary	995+6584
	17: 9	If he should a your troops first,	928+5877
	17:12	we will a him wherever he may be found,	448+995
1Ki	20:12	and he ordered his men: "Prepare to a."	NIH
	20:12	So they prepared to a the city.	6584
	20:22	the king of Aram will a you again."	6584+6590
	22:12	"A Ramoth Gilead and be victorious,"	6590
	22:15	"A and be victorious," he answered,	6590
	22:32	So they turned to a him,	4309
2Ki	3: 8	"By what route shall we a?"	6590
	7: 6	the Hittite and Egyptian kings to a us!"	995+6584
	12:17	Then he turned to Jerusalem.	6584+6590
	17: 3	of Assyria came up to a Hoshea,	6584
	18:25	to a and destroy this place without word	6584
1Ch	11: 6	"Whoever leads the a on	5782
	14:10	"Shall I go and a the Philistines?"	6584
	14:14	circle around them and a them in front	995+4200
2Ch	18: 2	and urged him to a Ramoth Gilead.	448+6590
	18:11	"A Ramoth Gilead and be victorious,"	6590
	18:14	"A and be victorious," he answered,	6590
	18:31	So they turned to a him,	4309
Ne	4:12	"Wherever you turn, they will a us."	6584
Est	8:11	that might a them and their women	7444
	9: 2	to a those seeking their destruction.	928+3338+8938
Job	15:21	when all seems well, marauders a him.	995
	15:24	like a king poised to a,	3960
	19: 3	shamelessly you a me.	2686
	30:21	with the might of your hand you a me.	8475
Ps	27: 2	when my enemies and my foes a me,	4200
	56: 1	all day long they press their a.	4309
	59: 4	yet they are ready to a me.	8132
	109: 3	they a me without cause.	4309
	109:28	when they a they will be put to shame,	7756
Isa	21: 2	the looter takes loot. Elam, a!	6590
	29: 7	that a her and her fortress and besiege her,	7371
	36:10	have I come to a and destroy this land	6584
	54:15	anyone does a you, it will not be my doing;	1592+1592
Jer	5: 6	a lion from the forest will a them,	5782
	6: 4	Arise, let us a at noon!	6590
	6: 5	let us a at night	6590
	6:23	like men in battle formation to a you,	6584
	12: 9	that other birds of prey surround and a?	6584
	18:18	let's a him with our tongues	5782
	37: 8	the Babylonians will return and a this city;	4309
	37:19	of Babylon will not a you or this land'?	995+6584
	43:11	He will come and a Egypt,	5782
	46:13	of Babylon to a Egypt:	5782
	47: 7	when he has ordered it to a Ashkelon and	448
	49: 4	'Who will a me?'	448+995
	49:14	"Assemble yourselves to a it!	6584+6590
	49:28	a Kedar and destroy the people of the East.	448+6590
	49:31	"Arise and a a nation at ease,	448+6590
	50: 3	A nation from the north will a her	6584+6590
	50:21	"A the land of Merathaim	6584+6590
	50:42	like men in battle formation to a you,	6584
	51:48	out of the north destroyers will a her,"	995+4200
Eze	38:11	I will a a peaceful	995
Da	8: 7	I saw him a the ram furiously,	5595
	11: 7	He will a the forces of the king of	448+990
	11:39	He will a the mightiest fortresses with	4200+6913
Hos	13: 8	I will a them and rip them open.	7008
Joel	3: 9	Let all the fighting men draw near and a.	6590
Zec	12: 9	destroy all the nations that a Jerusalem.	995+6584
	14:13	and they will a each other.	3338+6584+6590
Ac	16:22	The crowd joined in the a against Paul	5308
	18:10	and no one is going to a and harm you,	2202
	18:12	the Jews made a united a on Paul	2987
2Ti	4:18	The Lord will rescue me from every evil a	NIG
Rev	11: 7	comes up from the Abyss will a them,	4472+4483

ATTACKED (61) [ATTACK]

Ge	4: 8	Cain a his brother Abel and killed him.	448+7756
	34:25	and the unsuspecting city,	995+6584
	49:19	"Gad will be a by a band of raiders,	1574

Ge	49:23	*With* **bitterness** archers a him;	5352
Ex	17: 8	The Amalekites came and a the Israelites	4309
Nu	14:45	and a them and beat them down all the way	5782
	21: 1	*he* a the Israelites and captured some	4309
Jos	8:21	they turned around and a the men of Ai.	5782
	10: 5	up positions against Gibeon and a it.	4309
	10:29	on from Makkedah to Libnah and a it.	4309
	10:31	he took up positions against it and a it.	4309
	10:34	they took up positions against it and a it.	4309
	10:36	up from Eglon to Hebron and a it.	4309
	10:38	with him turned around and a Debir.	4309
	11: 7	at the Waters of Merom and a them,	928+5877
	19:47	so they went up and a Leshem, took it,	4309
Jdg	1: 4	When Judah a, the LORD gave	6590
	1: 8	men of Judah a Jerusalem also and took it,	4309
	1:17	with the Simeonites their brothers and a	5782
	1:22	Now the house of Joseph a Bethel,	6590
	3:13	Eglon came and a Israel,	5782
	11:12	against us that *you* have a our country?"	4309
	15: 8	*He* a them **viciously** and slaughtered many	3751+5782+6584+8797
	18:27	*They* a them with the sword and burned	5782
1Sa	13:3	Jonathan a the Philistine outpost at Geba,	5782
	13: 4	"Saul *has* a the Philistine outpost,	5782
	15: 7	Then Saul a the Amalekites all the way	5782
	27: 9	Whenever David a an area,	5782
	30: 1	*They* had a Ziklag and burned it,	5782
2Sa	12:29	and a and captured it.	4309
1Ki	2:32	of my father David he a two men	7003
	9:16	of Egypt *had* a and captured Gezer.	6590
	14:25	Shishak king of Egypt a Jerusalem.	6584+6590
	20: 1	he went up and besieged Samaria and a it.	4309
2Ki	3:25	with slings surrounded it and a it as well.	5782
	12:17	up and a Gath and captured it.	4309
	14:11	so Jehoash king of Israel a.	6590
	15:10	*He* a him in front of the people,	5782
	15:14	*He* a Shallum son of Jabesh in Samaria,	5782
	15:16	a Tiphsah and everyone in the city	5782
	15:30	*He* a and assassinated him,	5782
	18:13	king of Assyria a all the fortified cities of Judah	6584+6590
1Ch	4:41	*They* a the Hamites in their dwellings and	5782
	20: 1	Joab a Rabbah and left it in ruins.	5782
2Ch	12: 2	Shishak king of Egypt a Jerusalem in	6584+6590
	12: 9	When Shishak king of Egypt a Jerusalem,	6584+6590
	13:14	that they were being a at both front	4878
	14:15	*They* also a the camps of the herdsmen	5782
	21:17	*They* a Judah, invaded it and carried off	928+6584
	25:21	So Jehoash king of Israel a.	6590
	28:17	The Edomites had again come and a Judah	5782
	36: 6	Nebuchadnezzar king of Babylon a him	6584+6590
Est	8: 7	"Because Haman a the Jews,	928+3338+8938
Job	1:15	and the Sabeans a and carried them off.	5877
Ps	53: 5	God scattered the bones of *those who* a you;	2837
	124: 2	not been on our side when men a us,	6584+7756
Isa	20: 1	came to Ashdod and a and captured it—	4309
	36: 1	king of Assyria a all the fortified cities of Judah	6584+6590
Jer	47: 1	the Philistines before Pharaoh a Gaza:	5782
	49:28	which Nebuchadnezzar king of Babylon a:	5782
Zec	14:16	nations that *have* a Jerusalem will go	995+6584

ATTACKER (1) [ATTACK]

Na	2: 1	An a advances against you, [Nineveh].	7046

ATTACKERS (1) [ATTACK]

Ps	35:15	a gathered against me when I was unaware.	5784

ATTACKING (13) [ATTACK]

1Ki	22:20	into a Ramoth Gilead and going	6590
2Ki	16: 7	who *are* a me."	6584+7756
	16: 9	of Assyria complied by a Damascus	448+6590
2Ch	18:19	of Israel into a Ramoth Gilead and going	6590
	20:12	to face this vast army that *is* a us.	995+6584
	35:21	It is not you I am a at this time,	6584
Ps	54: 3	Strangers *are* a me;	6584+7756
	56: 2	many *are* a me in their pride.	4309
	86:14	The arrogant are a me, O God;	6584+7756
Jer	21: 2	Nebuchadnezzar king of Babylon *is* a us.	4309
	32:24	over to the Babylonians who *are* a it.	4309
	32:29	The Babylonians who *are* a this city	4309
	37:10	the entire Babylonian army that *is* a you	4309

ATTACKS (14) [ATTACK]

Ge	32: 8	"If Esau comes and a one group,	5782
Ex	21:15	"*Anyone who* a his father or his mother	5782
Dt	22:26	case is like that of someone *who* a	6584+7756
Jos	15:16	in marriage to the man who a	5782
Jdg	1:12	in marriage to the man who a	5782
2Sa	22:44	"You have delivered me from the a	8190
Job	30:12	On my right the tribe a;	7756
Ps	18:43	You have delivered me from the a *of*	8190
	55:20	My companion a his friends;	928+3338+8938
Pr	21:22	A wise man a the city of the mighty	6590
Isa	54:15	whoever a you will surrender to you.	1592
Eze	38:18	When Gog a the land of Israel,	995+6584
Lk	11:22	someone stronger a and overpowers him,	2088
Jn	10:12	Then the wolf a the flock and scatters it.	773

ATTAI (4)

1Ch	2:35	and she bore him A.	6968
	2:36	A was the father of Nathan,	6968

1Ch	12:11	A the sixth, Eliel the seventh,	6968
2Ch	11:20	who bore him Abijah, A,	6968

ATTAIN (4) [ATTAINED, ATTAINING, ATTAINS]

Ps	139: 6	too lofty for *me* to a.	3523
Pr	2:19	None who go to her return or a the paths	5952
Gal	3: 3	*are you* now *trying to* a your **goal**	2200
Php	3:11	to a to the resurrection from the dead.	2918

ATTAINED (4) [ATTAIN]

Pr	16:31	*it* is a by a righteous life.	5162
Ro	9:31	law of righteousness, *has* not a it.	5777
Php	3:16	up to what *we have already* a.	5777
Heb	7:11	If perfection could have been a through	*NIG*

ATTAINING (2) [ATTAIN]

Pr	1: 2	for a wisdom and discipline;	3359
Eph	4:13	a to the whole measure of the fullness	*1650*

ATTAINS (1) [ATTAIN]

Pr	11:19	The truly righteous man a life.	4200

ATTALIA (2)

Ac	14:25	they went down to A.	877
	14:26	From A they sailed back to Antioch,	*NIG*

ATTEMPT (1)

Ac	27:30	*In* an a to escape from the ship,	*2426*

ATTEND (3) [ATTENDANCE, ATTENDANT, ATTENDANTS, ATTENDED, ATTENDING, ATTENDS]

Ge	39:11	One day he went into the house to a to	6913
1Ki	1: 2	a young virgin *to* a the king and take care	4200+6641+7156
Est	4: 5	one of the king's eunuchs assigned to a her,	4200+7156

ATTENDANCE (1) [ATTEND]

SS	8:13	in the gardens with friends *in* a,	7992

ATTENDANT (6) [ATTEND]

Ge	39: 4	in his eyes and *became* his a.	9250
1Ki	19:21	to follow Elijah and *became* his a.	9250
2Ki	22:12	the secretary and Asaiah the king's a:	6269
2Ch	34:20	the secretary and Asaiah the king's a:	6269
Lk	4:20	gave it back *to* the a and sat down.	5677
Ac	13: 7	who was an a of the proconsul,	5250

ATTENDANTS (26) [ATTEND]

Ge	45: 1	no longer control himself before all his a,	5893
Ex	2: 5	her a were walking along the river bank.	5855
Jdg	3:19	And all his a left him.	6584+6641
1Sa	8:14	and olive groves and give them to his a	6269
	8:15	and give it to his officials and a.	6269
	16:15	Saul's a said to him, "See,	6269
	16:17	So Saul said to his a,	6269
	18:22	Then Saul ordered his a:	6269
	18:22	and his a all like you;	6269
	18:26	When the a told David these things,	6269
	19: 1	Saul told his son Jonathan and all the a	6269
	28: 7	Saul then said to his a,	6269
2Ki	5:15	and all his a went back to the man of God.	4722
	24:12	Jehoiachin king of Judah, his mother, his a,	6269
Ezr	8:17	that they might bring a to us for the house	9250
Est	1:12	when the a delivered the king's command,	6247
	2: 2	Then the king's **personal** a proposed,	5853+9250
	6: 3	for him," his a answered.	5853+9250
	6: 5	His a answered, "Haman is standing in	5853
Jer	25:19	his a, his officials and all his people,	6269
	36:24	all his a who heard all these words showed no fear,	6269
	36:31	I will punish him and his children and his a	6269
	37: 2	Neither he nor his a nor the people of	6269
Mt	14: 2	he said to his a, "This is John the Baptist;	4090
	22:13	"Then the king told the a,	1356
Ac	10: 7	and a devout soldier who *was one of* his a.	4674

ATTENDED (6) [ATTEND]

Ge	40: 4	and *he* a them.	9250
Jdg	14:20	a him at his **wedding**.	9250
1Sa	25:42	a by her five maids,	2143+4200+8079
Da	7:10	Thousands upon thousands a him;	10727
Mt	4:11	devil left him, and angels came and a him.	*1354*
Mk	1:13	and angels a him.	*1354*

ATTENDING (6) [ATTEND]

1Sa	4:20	As she was dying, the *women* a her said,	5893
1Ki	1:15	where Abishag the Shunammite *was* a him.	9250
	10: 5	the a servants in their robes, his cupbearers,	5096
2Ch	9: 4	the a servants in their robes,	5096
	22: 8	relatives, *who had been* a Ahaziah,	9250
Est	7: 1	and Harbona, one of the eunuchs a the king	4200+7156

ATTENDS (1) [ATTEND]

Jn	3:29	The friend who a the bridegroom waits	*NIG*

ATTENTION (78) [ATTENTIVE, ATTENTIVELY]

Ge	39:23	The warden **paid** no a to anything	8011
Ex	4: 8	"If they do not believe you or **pay** a to	9048
	5: 9	so that they keep working and **pay** no a	9120
	15:26	if *you* **pay** a to his commands	263
	16:20	some of them **paid** no a to Moses;	9048
	23:21	**Pay** a to him and listen to what he says.	9068
Nu	5:15	a reminder offering to **draw** a to guilt.	2349
Dt	1:45	but he **paid** no a to your weeping	9048
	7:12	If *you* **pay** a to these laws and are careful	9048
	17: 4	**been brought** to your a,	2256+5583+9048
	28:13	If *you* **pay** a to the commands of	9048
Jdg	11:28	**paid** no a to the message	9048
Ru	4: 4	**bring** the matter to your a	265+1655
1Sa	4:20	But she did not respond or pay *any* a.	4213
	25:25	May my lord pay no a to	4213
1Ki	8:28	Yet **give** a to your servant's prayer	7155
	18:29	no one answered, no one **paid** a.	7993
2Ch	6:19	Yet **give** a to your servant's prayer	7155
	33:10	but *they* **paid** no a.	7992
Ne	8:13	gathered around Ezra the scribe to **give** a to	8505
	9:30	Yet *they* **paid** no a,	263
	9:34	*they* did not **pay** a to your commands or	7992
Est	9:25	But when the plot came to the king's a	4200+7156
Job	7:17	that you give him so much a,	4213
	32:12	gave you *my* **full** a.	1067
	33: 1	**pay** a to everything I say.	263
	33:31	"**Pay** a, Job, and listen to me;	7992
	35:13	the Almighty **pays** no a to it.	8800
Pr	4: 1	**pay** a and gain understanding.	7992
	4:20	My son, **pay** a to what I say;	7992
	5: 1	My son, **pay** a to my wisdom,	7992
	7:24	my sons, listen to me; **pay** a to what I say.	7992
	17: 4	a liar **pays** a to a malicious tongue.	263
	22:17	**Pay** a and listen to the sayings of the wise;	265+5742
	27:23	give **careful** a to your herds;	4213
Ecc	7:21	*Do* not pay a to every word people say,	4213
Isa	28:23	**pay** a and hear what I say.	7992
	34: 1	Come near, you nations, and listen; **pay** a,	7992
	42:20	but *have* **paid** no a;	9068
	42:23	Which of you will listen to this or **pay close** a	2256+7992+9048
	48:18	If only *you had* **paid** a to my commands,	7992
Jer	7:24	But they did not listen or **pay** a;	265+5742
	7:26	But they did not listen to me or **pay** a.	265+5742
	11: 8	But they did not listen or **pay** a;	265+5742
	13:15	Hear and **pay** a, do not be arrogant,	263
	17:23	Yet they did not listen or **pay** a;	265+5742
	18:18	and **pay** no a to anything he says."	7992
	25: 4	you have not listened or **paid** *any* a.	265+4200+5742+9048
	34:14	did not listen to me or **pay** a to me.	265+5742
	35:15	*you have* not **paid** a or listened to me.	265+5742
	37: 2	nor the people of the land **paid** *any* a to	9048
	44: 5	But they did not listen or **pay** a;	265+5742
Eze	40: 4	and pay a to everything I am going	4213
	44: 5	and give a to everything I tell you	4213
	44: 5	**Give** a to the entrance of the temple and all	4213
Da	3:12	who pay no a to you, O king.	10302
	6:13	pays no a to you, O king.	10302
	9:13	from our sins and **giving** a to your truth.	8505
	11:18	Then he will turn his a to the coastlands	7156
Hos	5: 1	**Pay** a, *you* Israelites!	7992
Zec	1: 4	But they would not listen or **pay** a to me,	7992
	7:11	"But they refused to **pay** a;	7992
Mal	2:13	and wail because *he* no longer **pays** a	7155
Mt	7: 3	and **pay** no a to the plank in your own eye?	2917
	22: 5	"But they **paid** no a and went off—	*288*
	22:16	**pay** no a to **who they are**.	476+1063+4725
	24: 1	up to him to **call** his a to its buildings.	*2109*
Mk	12:14	**pay** no a to **who they are**;	476+1063+4725
Lk	6:41	and **pay** no a to the plank in your own eye?	2917
Ac	3: 5	So the man **gave** them his a,	2091
	6: 4	and *will* **give** our a to prayer and	4674
	8: 6	*they* all **paid close** a to what he said.	4668
	8:10	gave him *their* a and exclaimed,	4668
Tit	1:14	and *will* **pay** no a to Jewish myths or to	4668
Heb	2: 1	**pay** more careful a, therefore, to	4668
Jas	2: 3	*If you* **show** special a to	2098
2Pe	1:19	and you will do well to **pay** a to it,	4668
3Jn	1:10	*I will* **call** a to what he is doing,	*5703*

ATTENTIVE (7) [ATTENTION]

2Ch	6:40	may your eyes be open and your ears a to a	7995
	7:15	Now my eyes will be open and my ears a	7995
Ne	1: 6	let your ear be a and your eyes open to hear	7994
	1:11	be a to the prayer of this your servant and	7994
Ps	34:15	the righteous and his ears are a to their cry;	448
	130: 2	Let your ears be a to my cry for mercy.	7995
1Pe	3:12	on the righteous and his ears are a	*NIG*

ATTENTIVELY (2) [ATTENTION]

Ne	8: 3	And all the people **listened** a to the Book of the Law.	265+448
Jer	8: 6	I have listened a, but they do not say	7992

ATTESTED (1)

1Sa	3:20	to Beersheba recognized that Samuel was a	586

ATTIRE (KJV) See DRESSED, WEDDING ORNAMENTS

ATTITUDE (8) [ATTITUDES]
Ge	31: 2	And Jacob noticed that Laban's **a**	7156
	31: 5	"I see that your father's **a** toward me is	7156
1Ki	11:11	"Since this is your **a** and you have	6640
Ezr	6:22	by changing the **a** of the king of Assyria,	4213
Da	3:19	and his **a** toward them changed.	10049+10614
Eph	4:23	to be made new *in* the **a** of your minds;	4460
Php	2: 5	Your **a** *should be* the same as that	5858
1Pe	4: 1	arm yourselves also with the same **a**,	1936

ATTITUDES (1) [ATTITUDE]
Heb	4:12	it judges the thoughts and **a** of the heart.	1936

ATTRACT (1) [ATTRACTED, ATTRACTIVE]
Isa	53: 2	He had no beauty or majesty *to* **a** us	8011

ATTRACTED (2) [ATTRACT]
Dt	21:11	the captives a beautiful woman and *are* **a**	3137
Est	2:17	the king *was* **a** *to* Esther more than to any	170

ATTRACTIVE (3) [ATTRACT]
Jdg	15: 2	Isn't her younger sister more **a**?	3202
Zec	9:17	How **a** and beautiful they will be!	3206
Tit	2:10	**make** the teaching about God our Savior **a**.	3175

AUDIENCE (5)
1Ki	10:24	The whole world sought **a** with Solomon	7156
2Ch	9:23	of the earth sought **a** with Solomon to hear	7156
Pr	29:26	Many **seek an a** with a ruler,	1335+7156
Ac	12:20	they now joined together and **sought an a**	4205
	25:23	the **a room** with the high ranking officers	211

AUGMENT (KJV) See MORE

AUGUSTUS (1)
Lk	2: 1	In those days Caesar **A** issued a decree that	880

AUL (KJV) See AWL

AUNT (2)
Lev	18:14	to have sexual relations; she is your **a**.	1860
	20:20	" 'If a man sleeps with his **a**,	1860

AUSTERE (KJV) See HARD

AUTHOR (3)
Ac	3:15	You killed the **a** of life,	795
Heb	2:10	should make the **a** of their salvation perfect	795
	12: 2	the **a** and perfecter of our faith,	795

AUTHORITIES (13) [AUTHORITY]
Lk	12:11	before synagogues, rulers and **a**, do	2026
Jn	7:26	the **a** really concluded that he is the Christ?	807
Ac	16:19	into the marketplace to face the **a**.	807
Ro	13: 1	must submit himself *to* the governing **a**,	2026
	13: 1	The **a** that exist have been established	NIG
	13: 5	it is necessary to submit to the **a**,	NIG
	13: 6	for the **a** are God's servants,	NIG
Eph	3:10	*to* the rulers and **a** in the heavenly realms,	2026
	6:12	but against the rulers, against the **a**,	2026
Col	1:16	whether thrones or powers or rulers or **a**;	2026
	2:15	And having disarmed the powers and **a**,	2026
Tit	3: 1	the people to be subject *to* rulers and **a**,	2026
1Pe	3:22	**a** and powers in submission to him.	2026

AUTHORITY (88) [AUTHORITIES, AUTHORIZATION, AUTHORIZED]
Ge	41:35	up the grain under the **a** *of* Pharaoh,	3338
Nu	27:20	Give him some of your **a** so	2086
Dt	1:15	and appointed them to have **a** over you—	8031
Ezr	7:24	You are also to know that you have no **a**	10718
Ne	3: 7	the **a** of the governor of Trans-Euphrates.	4058
Est	9:29	with full **a** to confirm this second letter	9549
Isa	22:21	around him and hand your **a** over to him.	4939
Jer	5:31	the priests rule by their own **a**,	3338
Da	4:31	Your **royal a** has been taken from you.	10424
	7: 6	and it was given **a** **to rule**.	10717
	7:12	of their **a**, but were allowed to live for	10717
	7:14	He was given **a**, glory	10717
Mt	7:29	because he taught as one who had **a**,	2026
	8: 9	For I myself am a man under **a**,	2026
	9: 6	Son of Man has **a** on earth to forgive sins	2026
	9: 8	who had given such **a** to men.	2026
	10: 1	and gave them **a** to drive out evil spirits	2026
	20:25	their high officials **exercise a** over them.	2980
	21:23	"By what **a** are you doing these things?"	2026
	21:23	"And who gave you this **a**?"	2026
	21:24	by what **a** I am doing these things.	2026
	21:27	by what **a** I am doing these things.	2026
	28:18	"All **a** in heaven and on earth	2026
Mk	1:22	because he taught them as one who had **a**,	2026
	1:27	A new teaching—and with **a**!	2026
	2:10	Son of Man has **a** on earth to forgive sins	2026
	3:15	and to have **a** to drive out demons.	2026
	6: 7	by two and gave them **a** over evil spirits.	2026
	10:42	their high officials **exercise a** over them.	2980
	11:28	"By what **a** are you doing these things?"	2026
	11:28	"And who gave you **a** to do this?"	2026

Mk	11:29	by what **a** I am doing these things,	2026
	11:33	by what **a** I am doing these things."	2026
Lk	4: 6	"I will give you all their **a** and splendor,	2026
	4:32	because his message **had a**.	1639+1877+2026
	4:36	With **a** and power he gives orders	2026
	5:24	Son of Man has **a** on earth to forgive sins	2026
	7: 8	For I myself am a man under **a**,	2026
	9: 1	and **a** to drive out all demons and	2026
	10:19	I have given you **a** to trample on snakes	2026
	20: 2	by what **a** you are doing these things,"	2026
	20: 2	"Who gave you this **a**?"	2026
	20: 8	by what **a** I am doing these things."	2026
	20:20	over *to* the power and **a** of the governor.	2026
	22:25	and those who **exercise a** over	2027
Jn	2:18	to prove your **a** to do all this?"	NIG
	5:27	And he has given him **a** to judge	2026
	10:18	I have **a** to lay it down and authority	2026
	10:18	to lay it down and **a** to take it up again.	2026
	17: 2	For you granted him **a** over all people	2026
Ac	1: 7	or dates the Father has set by his own **a**.	2026
	9:14	And he has come here **with a** from	2026+2400
	26:10	**On** the **a** of the chief priests I put many of the saints in prison,	2026+3284
	26:12	to Damascus with the **a** and commission of	2026
Ro	7: 1	that the law *has* **a** over a man only as long	3259
	13: 1	for there is no **a** except	2026
	13: 2	he who rebels against the **a** is rebelling	2026
	13: 3	to be free from fear of the one in **a**?	2026
1Co	11:10	the woman ought to have a sign of **a**	2026
	15:24	after he has destroyed all dominion, **a**	2026
2Co	10: 8	even if I boast somewhat freely about the **a**	2026
	13:10	not have to be harsh in my use of **a**—	2026
	13:10	the **a** the Lord gave me for building you up,	4005S
Eph	1:21	far above all rule and **a**,	2026
Col	2:10	who is the head over every power and **a**,	2026
1Th	4: 2	you know what instructions we gave you **by the a of** the Lord	1328
1Ti	2: 2	for kings and all those in **a**,	5667
	2:12	a woman to teach or *to* **have a** over a man;	883
Tit	2:15	Encourage and rebuke with all **a**.	2198
Heb	13:17	Obey your leaders and submit to their **a**.	NIG
1Pe	2:13	for the Lord's sake to every **a** instituted	3232
	2:13	whether to the king, as the **supreme a**,	5660
2Pe	2:10	of the sinful nature and despise **a**.	3262
Jude	1: 6	not keep their **positions of a**	794
	1: 8	reject **a** and slander celestial beings.	3262
	1:25	majesty, power and **a**,	2026
Rev	2:26	I will give **a** over the nations—	2026
	2:27	just as I have received **a** from my Father,	NIG
	12:10	and the **a** of his Christ.	2026
	13: 2	and his throne and great **a**.	2026
	13: 4	the dragon because he had given **a** to	2026
	13: 5	and to exercise his **a** for forty-two months.	2026
	13: 7	And he was given **a** over every tribe,	2026
	13:12	He exercised all the **a** of the first beast	2026
	17:12	for one hour will receive **a** as kings along	2026
	17:13	and will give their power and **a** to	2026
	18: 1	He had great **a**,	2026
	20: 4	seated those who had been given **a** to judge.	NIG

AUTHORIZATION (1) [AUTHORITY]
Ac	15:24	that some went out from us without our **a**	1403

AUTHORIZED (3) [AUTHORITY]
Ezr	3: 7	as **a** by Cyrus king of Persia.	8397
	5: 3	"Who **a** you to rebuild this temple	10302+10682
	5: 9	"Who **a** you to rebuild this temple	10302+10682

AUTUMN (7)
Dt	11:14	both **a** and spring rains,	3453
Ps	84: 6	the **a** rains also cover it with pools.	4620
Jer	5:24	who gives **a** and spring rains in season,	3453
Joel	2:23	for he has given you the **a** rains	4620
	2:23	both **a** and spring rains, as before.	4620
Jas	5: 7	how patient he is for the **a** and spring **rains**.	4611
Jude	1:12	**a** trees, without fruit and uprooted—	5781

AVA (KJV) See AVVA

AVAIL (2) [AVAILABLE]
Isa	16:12	*it is to* no **a**.	3523
Da	11:27	but *to* no **a**,	7503

AVAILABLE (1) [AVAIL]
1Ki	7:36	in every **a** space, with wreaths all around.	5113

AVEN (1) [BETH AVEN]
Am	1: 5	in the Valley of **A** and the one who holds	225

AVENGE (17) [VENGEANCE]
Lev	26:25	I will bring the sword upon you *to* **a**	5933+5934
Dt	32:35	It is mine *to* **a**; I will repay.	5934
	32:43	for *he will* **a** the blood of his servants;	5933
1Sa	24:12	the LORD **a** the **wrongs** you have **done**	5933
2Sa	3:27	there, to **a** the blood of his brother Asahel.	928
2Ki	9: 7	and *I will* **a** the blood of my servants	5933
Est	8:13	that day to **a** **themselves** on their enemies.	5933
Ps	79:10	make known among the nations that *you* **a**	5935
Isa	1:24	from my foes and **a** myself on my enemies.	5933
Jer	5: 9	"Should *I* not **a** myself on such a nation	5933
	5:29	"Should *I* not **a** myself on such a nation	5933
	9: 9	"Should *I* not **a** myself on such a nation	5933

Jer	15:15	**A** me on my persecutors.	5933
	51:36	I will defend your cause and **a** you;	5933+5935
Ro	12:19	"It is mine *to* **a**;	1689
Heb	10:30	we know him who said, "It is mine to **a**;	1689
Rev	6:10	of the earth and **a** our blood?"	1688

AVENGED (11) [VENGEANCE]
Ge	4:24	If Cain is **a** seven times,	5933
Jos	10:13	till the nation **a** *itself on* its enemies,	5933
Jdg	9:24	*might be* **a** on their brother Abimelech and	8492
	11:36	the LORD **has a** you of your enemies,	5935+6913
1Sa	14:24	before *I have* **a** **myself** on my enemies!"	5933
	25:31	or *of having* **a** himself.	3828
2Sa	4: 8	This day the LORD **has a** my lord the king	5935+5989
Ps	58:10	The righteous will be glad when they are **a**,	5934
Eze	5:13	and *I will* **be a**.	5714
Ac	7:24	so *he* went to his defense and **a** him	1689+4472
Rev	19: 2	He **has a** on her the blood of his servants."	1688

AVENGER (14) [VENGEANCE]
Nu	35:12	They will be places of refuge from the **a**,	1457
	35:19	The **a** of blood shall put the murderer to death;	1457
	35:21	The **a** of blood shall put the murderer	1457
	35:24	between him and the **a** of blood according	1457
	35:25	from the **a** of blood and send him back to	1457
	35:27	the **a** of blood finds him outside the city,	1457
	35:27	the **a** of blood may kill the accused	1457
Dt	19: 6	the **a** of blood might pursue him in a rage,	1457
	19:12	and hand him over to the **a** of blood to die.	1457
Jos	20: 3	and find protection from the **a** of blood.	1457
	20: 5	If the **a** of blood pursues him,	1457
	20: 9	the **a** of blood prior to standing trial before	1457
2Sa	14:11	to prevent the **a** of blood from adding to	1457
Ps	8: 2	to silence the foe and the **a**.	5933

AVENGES (5) [VENGEANCE]
2Sa	22:48	He is the God who **a** me,	5935+5989
Ps	9:12	For *he who* **a** blood remembers;	2011
	18:47	He is the God who **a** me,	5935+5989
	94: 1	O LORD, the God who **a**,	5935
	94: 1	the God who avenges, O God who **a**,	5935

AVENGING (3) [VENGEANCE]
1Sa	25:26	and from **a** yourself with your own hands,	3828
	25:33	from bloodshed this day and from **a** myself	3828
Na	1: 2	The LORD is a jealous and **a** God;	5933

AVERSE (KJV) See RETURNING

AVERT (1)
Jer	11:15	*Can* consecrated meat **a** [your punishment]?	4946+6296+6584

AVIM (KJV) See AVVIM

AVIMS, AVITES (KJV) See AVVITES

AVITH (2)
Ge	36:35	His city was named **A**.	6400
1Ch	1:46	His city was named **A**.	6400

AVOID (18) [AVOIDS]
Ne	5: 9	to **a** the reproach of our Gentile enemies?	4946
Ps	38:11	My friends and companions **a** me because	6641
Pr	4:15	**A** it, do not travel on it;	7277
	19: 7	how much more *do* his friends **a** him!	8178
	20: 3	It is *to* a man's honor *to* **a** strife,	3782+4926
	20:19	so **a** a man who talks too much.	4200+4202+6843
Ecc	7:18	The man who fears God *will* **a** all [extremes].	3655
Eze	46:20	to **a** bringing them into the outer court	1194
Zep	1: 9	that day I will punish all who **a** **stepping** on	1925
Jn	18:28	to **a** ceremonial uncleanness the Jews did	3590
Ac	15:29	You will do well *to* **a** these things.	1413
	20:16	to **a** spending time in the province of Asia,	3590
2Co	8:20	*We want to* **a** any criticism of	5097
Gal	6:12	to **a** being persecuted for the cross	3590
1Th	4: 3	that you should **a** sexual immorality;	600
	5:22	**A** every kind of evil.	600
2Ti	2:16	**A** godless chatter,	4325
Tit	3: 9	But **a** foolish controversies and genealogies	4325

AVOIDS (2) [AVOID]
Pr	16: 6	through the fear of the LORD **a** man evil.	6073
	16:17	The highway of the upright **a** evil;	6073

AVVA (1)
2Ki	17:24	from Babylon, Cuthah, **A**, Hamath	6379

AVVIM (1)
Jos	18:23	**A**, Parah, Ophrah,	6399

AVVITES (3)
Dt	2:23	the **A** who lived in villages as far as Gaza,	6398
Jos	13: 3	Gath and Ekron—that of the **A**);	6398
2Ki	17:31	the **A** made Nibhaz and Tartak,	6398

AWAIT (5) [WAIT]

Isa	24:17	Terror and pit and snare a you,	6584
Jer	48:43	Terror and pit and snare a you,	6584
Hos	9: 8	yet snares a him on all his paths,	NIH
Gal	5: 5	by faith eagerly a through the Spirit the righteousness for	587
Php	3:20	And we eagerly a Savior from there,	587

AWAITS (8) [WAIT]

Job	17: 1	my days are cut short, the grave a me.	4200
Ps	65: 1	Praise a you, O God, in Zion;	1875
Pr	15:10	Stern discipline a him who leaves the path;	4200
	28:22	and is unaware that poverty a him.	995
Ecc	3:19	the same fate a them both:	4200
	9: 1	no man knows whether love or hate a him.	4200+7156
Ob	1: 5	Oh, what a disaster a you—	1950
Hab	2: 3	For the revelation a an appointed time;	6388

AWAKE (28) [WAKE]

Job	14:12	the heavens are no more, men will not a	7810
Ps	7: 6	A, my God; decree justice.	6424
	17:15	when I a, I will be satisfied	7810
	35:23	A, and rise to my defense!	6424
	44:23	A, O Lord!	6424
	57: 8	A, my soul!	6424
	57: 8	A, harp and lyre!	6424
	102: 7	I lie a; I have become like a	9193
	108: 2	A, harp and lyre! I will awaken the dawn.	6424
	139:18	When I a, I am still with you.	7810
Pr	6:22	when you a, they will speak to you.	7810
	20:13	stay a and you will have food to spare.	6524+7219
SS	4:16	A, north wind, and come, south wind!	6424
	5: 2	I slept but my heart was a.	6424
Isa	51: 9	A, awake! Clothe yourself with strength,	6424
	51: 9	a! Clothe yourself with strength,	6424
	51: 9	a, as in days gone by,	6424
	51:17	A, awake! Rise up, O Jerusalem,	6424
	51:17	a! Rise up, O Jerusalem,	6424
	52: 1	A, awake, O Zion, clothe yourself	6424
	52: 1	a, O Zion, clothe yourself with strength.	6424
Jer	51:39	then sleep forever and not a,"	7810
	51:57	they will sleep forever and not a,"	7810
Da	12: 2	in the dust of the earth will a:	7810
Zec	13: 7	"A, O sword, against my shepherd,	6424
Lk	9:32	but when they became fully a,	1340
1Th	5:10	whether we are a or asleep,	1213
Rev	16:15	Blessed is he who stays a	1213

AWAKEN (6) [WAKE]

Ps	57: 8	I will a the dawn.	6424
	80: 2	A your might; come and save us.	6424
	108: 2	Awake, harp and lyre! I will a the dawn.	6424
SS	2: 7	Do not arouse or a love until it so desires.	6424
	3: 5	Do not arouse or a love until it so desires.	6424
	8: 4	Do not arouse or a love until it so desires.	6424

AWAKENED (2) [WAKE]

1Ki	18:27	Maybe he is sleeping and must be a."	3699
2Ki	4:31	"The boy has not a."	7810

AWAKENS (2) [WAKE]

Isa	29: 8	but he a, and his hunger remains;	7810
	29: 8	but he a faint, with his thirst unquenched.	7810

AWAKES (1) [WAKE]

Ps	73:20	As a dream when one a, so when you arise,	7810

AWARD (1)

2Ti	4: 8	will a to me on that day—	625

AWARE (21)

Ge	19:33	He was not a of it when she lay down or	3359
	19:35	Again he was not a of it when she lay	3359
	28:16	and I was not a of it."	3359
Ex	34:29	he was not a that his face was radiant	3359
Lev	4:14	they become a of the sin they committed,	3359
	4:23	When he is made a of the sin he committed,	3359
	4:28	When he is made a of the sin he committed,	3359
Nu	15:24	without the community being a	4946+6524
1Sa	22: 8	No one was a that Jonathan had left.	3359
1Ki	8:38	each one a of the afflictions	3359
2Ch	6:29	each one a of his afflictions and pains,	3359
Ne	4:15	When our enemies heard that we were a	3359
Mt	12:15	A of this, Jesus withdrew from that place.	1182
	16: 8	A of their discussion, Jesus asked,	1182
	24:50	and at an hour he is not a of.	1182
	26:10	A of this, Jesus said to them,	1182
Mk	8:17	A of their discussion, Jesus asked them:	1182
Lk	12:46	and at an hour he is not a of.	1182
Jn	6:61	that his disciples were grumbling	3857
Ac	10:28	"You are well a that it is against our law	2179
Gal	4:21	are you not a of what the law says?	201

AWAY (798)

Ge	5:24	he was no more, because God took him a.	4374
	6:21	be eaten and store it a as food for you and	665
	14:11	then they went a.	2143
	15:11	but Abram drove them a.	5959
	16: 8	"I'm running a from my mistress Sarai,"	1368
	18:22	men turned a and went toward Sodom,	4946+9004

Ge	18:23	"Will you sweep a the righteous with	6200
	18:24	Will you really sweep it a and not spare	6200
	19:15	or you will be swept a when	6200
	19:17	to the mountains or you will be swept a!"	6200
	21:16	about a bowshot a, for she thought,	8178
	25: 6	the sons of his concubines and sent them a	8938
	26:16	Abimelech said to Isaac, "Move a from us;	4946+6640
	26:17	So Isaac moved a from there and encamped	4946
	26:27	you were hostile to me and sent me a?"	907+4946
	26:29	but always treated you well and sent you a	8938
	27:39	"Your dwelling will be a from	4946
	27:39	a from the dew of heaven above.	4946
	29: 3	the shepherds would roll the stone a from the well's mouth	4946+6584
	29: 8	the stone has been rolled a from the mouth of the well.	4946+6584
	29:10	and rolled the stone a from the mouth of the well	4946+6584
	30:15	that you took a my husband?	4374
	30:23	"God has taken a my disgrace."	665
	31: 9	So God has taken a your father's livestock	5911
	31:16	that God took a from our father belongs	5911
	31:20	by not telling him he was running a.	1368
	31:27	so I could send you a with joy and singing	8938
	31:31	I thought you would take your daughters a from me by force.	4946+6640
	31:42	surely have sent me a empty-handed.	8938
	31:49	and me when we are a from each other.	6259
	40:19	And the birds will eat a your flesh."	430
	42:24	He turned a from them and began to weep,	6015
	44:28	One of them went a from me, and I said,	3655
	45:24	Then he sent his brothers a,	8938
	47:13	Canaan wasted a because of the famine.	3532
Ex	2:17	along and drove them a,	1763
	5: 4	why are you taking the people a	7277
	8: 8	to take the frogs a from me and my people,	6073
	10:17	take this deadly plague a"	6073
	14:25	"Let's get a from the Israelites!	5674
	15:15	the people of Canaan will melt a;	4570
	16:21	and when the sun grew hot, it melted a.	5022
	18: 2	After Moses had sent a his wife Zipporah,	8933
	21:14	take him a from my altar and put him	4946+6640
	22:10	or is taken a while no one is looking,	8647
	23:25	I will take a sickness from among you,	6073
	32: 8	to turn a from what I commanded them	6073
	33: 7	the camp some distance a,	4946+8178
Lev	10: 4	a from the front of the sanctuary."	907+4946
	10:17	to you to take a the guilt of the community	5951
	16:21	He shall send the goat a into the desert in	8938
	26:16	and drain a your life.	1853
	26:39	Those of you who are left will waste a in	5245
	26:39	of their fathers' sins they will waste a.	5245
Nu	5: 2	to send a from the camp anyone who has	8938
	5: 3	Send a male and female alike;	8938
	5:21	to waste a and your abdomen to swell.	5877
	5:22	and your thigh wastes a."	5877
	5:27	and her thigh waste a,	5877
	9:10	of a dead body or are a on a journey,	8158
	12:12	with its flesh half eaten a."	430
	14:43	you have turned a from the LORD,	8740
	16:24	'Move a from the tents of Korah,	6590
	16:26	or you will be swept a because	6200
	16:27	So they moved a from the tents of Korah,	6590
	16:37	and scatter the coals some distance a, for	2134
	16:45	"Get a from this assembly so I can put	8250
	20:21	Israel turned a from them.	4946+6584
	21: 7	that the LORD will take the snakes a	6073
	22:11	be able to fight them and drive them a.' "	1763
	22:33	and turned a from me these three times.	5742
	22:33	If she had not turned a,	5742
	25: 4	that the LORD's fierce anger may turn a	8740
	25:11	has turned my anger a from the Israelites;	8740
	31:16	turning the Israelites a	5086
	32:15	If you turn a from following him,	8740
	36: 3	to us will be taken a.	1757
Dt	7: 4	for they will turn your sons a	6073
	9:12	They have turned a quickly	6073
	11:16	to turn a and worship other gods and bow	6073
	12:21	to put his Name is too far a from you,	8178
	12:32	do not add to it or take a from it.	1757
	13:10	to turn you a from the LORD your God,	5615
	14:24	to put his Name is so far a),	8178
	15:13	do not send him a empty-handed.	4946+6640
	23: 9	keep a from everything impure.	4946
	23:14	and turn a from you.	339+4946
	28:26	there will be no one to frighten them a.	3006
	28:49	a nation against you from far a,	8158
	29:18	among you today whose heart turns a from	7155
	30:17	But if your heart turns a and you are	7155
	30:17	and if you are drawn a to bow down	5615
Jos	2:21	So she sent them a and they departed.	8938
	3:16	It piled up in a heap a great distance a,	8178
	5: 9	"Today I have rolled a the reproach	1670
	6:18	But keep a from the devoted things,	9068
	8: 6	until we have lured them a from the city,	5998
	8: 6	'They are running a from us	5674
	8:16	and they pursued Joshua and were lured a	5998
	22: 6	Then Joshua blessed them and sent them a,	8938
	22:16	How could you turn a from the LORD	8740
	22:18	are you now turning a from the LORD?	8740
	22:23	If we have built our own altar to turn a	8740
	22:29	and turn a from him today by building	8740
	24:14	"But if you turn a and ally yourselves	8740+8740
	24:14	Throw a the gods your forefathers worshiped beyond the River and in Egypt,	6073
	24:23	"throw a the foreign gods that are	6073

(right column)

Jos	24:28	Then Joshua sent the people a,	8938
Jdg	3:26	While they waited, Ehud got a.	4880
	5:21	The river Kishon swept them a,	1759
	6:18	Please do not go a until I come back	4631
	11: 2	they drove Jephthah a.	1763
	11:13	they took a my land from the Arnon to	4374
	12: 9	gave his daughters a in marriage	8938
	15:17	he threw the jawbone,	8959
	18:21	they turned a and left.	7155
	18:24	and my priest, and went a.	2143
	20:31	to meet them and were drawn a from	5998
	20:32	"Let's retreat and draw them a from the city	5998
Ru	1:21	I went a full, but the LORD has brought me	2143
	2: 8	in another field and don't go a from here.	6296
1Sa	2: 5	but she who has had many sons pines a.	581
	5:11	"Send the ark of the god of Israel a;	8938
	6: 3	do not send it a empty,	8938
	6: 7	but take their calves a and pen them up.	8740
	7: 4	Israelites put a their Baals and Ashtoreths,	6073
	12:20	yet do not turn a from the LORD,	6073
	12:21	Do not turn a after useless idols.	6073
	12:25	both you and your king will be swept a."	6200
	14:16	in Benjamin saw the army melting a	2143+2256+4570
	15: 6	Then he said to the Kenites, "Go a,	6073
	15: 6	the Kenites moved a from the Amalekites.	6073
	15:11	because he has turned a from me	339+4946
	17:30	then turned a to someone else and	725+4946
	18:13	So he sent David a from him	6073
	19:17	and send my enemy a so that he escaped?"	8938
	19:17	"He said to me, 'Let me get a,	8938
	20:13	not let you know and send you a safely.	2143
	20:22	because the LORD has sent you a.	8938
	20:29	let me get a to see my brothers.'	4880
	21: 6	by hot bread on the day it was taken a.	4374
	23:26	hurrying to get a from Saul.	2143
	24:19	does he let him get a unharmed?	928+2006+8938
	25:10	Many servants are breaking a	7287
	25:29	the lives of your enemies he will hurl a as	7843
	26:13	and stood on top of the hill some distance a;	4946+8158
	28:15	and God has turned a from me.	6073
	28:16	now that the LORD has turned a from you	6073
	30:17	and none of them got a,	4880
2Sa	3:15	and had her taken a	4374
	3:21	David sent Abner a, and he went in peace.	8938
	3:22	because David had sent him a,	8938
	3:23	king had sent him a and that he had gone	8938
	4: 6	Recab and his brother Baanah slipped a.	4880
	7:15	my love will never be taken a from him,	6073
	7:15	as I took it a from Saul,	6073
	10: 4	and sent them a.	8938
	12:13	"The LORD has taken a your sin.	6296
	13:16	"Sending me a would be	8938
	13:19	She put her hand on her head and went a,	2143
	14:14	But God does not take a life;	5951
	15:17	and they halted at a place some distance a.	5305
	19:41	steal the king a and bring him	1704
	22:23	I have not turned a from his decrees.	6073
	24:10	I beg you, take a the guilt of your servant.	6296
1Ki	2:40	So Shimei went a and brought	2143
	5: 9	and you can take them a.	5951
	8:46	to his own land, far a or near;	8158
	8:66	On the following day he sent the people a.	8938
	9: 6	if you or your sons turn a from me	8740+8740
	11: 9	because his heart had turned a from	5742
	11:11	most certainly tear the kingdom a	7973+7973
	12: 5	"Go a for three days and then come back	2143
	12: 5	So the people went a.	2143
	14: 8	I tore the kingdom a from the house	7973
	15:22	and they carried a from Ramah the stones	5951
	17:15	She went a and did as Elijah had told her.	2143
	18:40	Don't let anyone get a!"	4880
	20: 6	and carry it a.' "	4374
	20:36	And after the man went a,	725+4946
2Ki	3: 3	he did not turn a from them.	6073
	4:27	Gehazi came over to push her a,	2074
	4:35	Elisha turned a and walked back and forth	8740
	5:11	But Naaman went a angry and said,	2143
	5:24	the servants and put them a in the house.	7212
	5:24	He sent the men a and they left.	8938
	6:23	he sent them a,	8938
	7: 8	ate and drank, and carried a silver,	4946+9004
	7:15	and equipment the Arameans had thrown a	8959
	8: 1	"Go a with your family and stay for a	2143
	8: 2	She and her family went a and stayed in	2143
	9: 2	get him a from his companions	7756
	10:21	not one stayed a.	995+4202
	10:29	not turn a from the sins of Jeroboam son	6073
	10:31	not turn a from the sins of Jeroboam,	6073
	11: 2	took Joash son of Ahaziah and stole him a	1704
	13: 2	and he did not turn a from them.	6073
	13: 6	But they did not turn a from the sins of	6073
	13:11	the LORD and did not turn a from any of	6073
	14:24	the LORD and did not turn a from any of	6073
	15: 9	not turn a from the sins of Jeroboam son	6073
	15:18	not turn a from the sins of Jeroboam son	6073
	15:24	not turn a from the sins of Jeroboam son	6073
	15:28	not turn a from the sins of Jeroboam son	6073
	16:17	King Ahaz took a the side panels	7915
	16:18	He took a the Sabbath canopy	6015
	17:21	he tore Israel a from the house of David,	7973
	17:21	Jeroboam enticed Israel a from following	4946
	17:22	of Jeroboam and did not turn a from them	6073
	20:18	that will be born to you, will be taken a,	4374
	23: 5	He did a with the pagan priests	8697

2Ki 23:26	not **turn a** from the heat of his fierce anger,	8740
24:13	and **took a** all the gold articles	7915
25:14	*They* also **took a** the pots, shovels,	4374
25:15	of the imperial guard **took a** the censers	4374
25:21	**a** from her land.	4946+6584
1Ch 12:19	after consultation, their rulers **sent** him **a.**	8938
12:40	their neighbors from **as far a** as Issachar,	6330
17:13	I will never **take** my love **a** from him,	6073
17:13	as *I* took it **a** from your predecessor.	6073
19: 4	and **sent** them **a.**	8938
21: 8	I beg you, **take a** the guilt of your servant.	6296
21:12	of **being swept a** before your enemies,	6200
26:29	and his sons were assigned duties **a** from	2667
2Ch 6:36	who takes them captive to a land **far a**	8158
7:19	"But if you **turn a** and forsake the decrees	8740
10: 5	So the people **went a.**	2143
16: 6	and *they* **carried a** from Ramah the stones	5951
18:31	God **drew** them **a** from him,	6077
20:10	so *they* **turned a** from them and did	6073
20:25	more than *they* could **take a.**	5362+5911
21:20	*He* **passed a,** to no one's regret,	2143
22:11	took Joash son of Ahaziah and **stole** him **a**	1704
25:27	that Amaziah **turned a** from following	6073
28:17	and attacked Judah and **carried a** prisoners,	8647
28:24	from the temple of God and **took** them **a.**	7915
29: 6	*They* **turned** their faces **a** from	6015
29:10	that his fierce anger *will* **turn a** from us.	8740
30: 8	that his fierce anger *will* **turn a** from you.	8740
30:14	the altars in Jerusalem and **cleared a**	6073
35:22	however, *would* not **turn a** from him,	6015+7156
35:23	and he told his officers, "**Take** me **a;**	6296
Ezr 1: 7	which Nebuchadnezzar *had* **carried a**	3655
3:13	And the sound was heard **far a.**	4200+4946+6330+8158
6: 6	stay **a** from there.	10663
10: 3	before our God to **send a** all these women	3655
10:14	of our God in this matter *is* **turned a**	8740
10:19	in pledge to **put a** their wives,	3655
Ne 6:11	But I said, "*Should a* man like me **run a?**	1368
8:12	Then all the people **went a** to eat and drink,	2143
12:43	in Jerusalem could be heard **far a.**	4946+8158
13:28	And *I* **drove** him **a** from me.	1368
Est 4:17	So Mordecai **went a** and carried out all	6296
6:14	and hurried Haman **a** to	995
Job 1:21	and the LORD *has* **taken a;**	4374
5:13	and the schemes of the wily **are swept a.**	4554
6:27	for the fatherless and **barter a** your friend.	4126
7:19	Will you never look **a from** me,	4946
8:19	Surely its life **withers a,**	5376
9:12	If he **snatches a,** who can stop him?	3166
9:25	*they* **fly a** without a glimpse of joy.	1368
10:20	Turn **a from** me so I can have	4946
11:14	if *you* **put a** the sin that is in your hand	8178
12:17	*He* **leads** counselors **a** stripped	2143
12:19	*He* **leads** priests **a** stripped	2143
12:20	the lips of trusted advisers and **takes a**	4374
13:28	"So man **wastes a** like something rotten,	1162
14: 2	He springs up like a flower and **withers a;**	4908
14: 6	So look **a from** him and let him alone,	4946+6584
14:19	as water **wears a** stones	8835
14:19	and torrents **wash a** the soil,	8851
14:20	and **send** him **a.**	8938
15:12	Why *has* your heart **carried** you **a,**	4374
15:30	of God's mouth *will* **carry** *him* **a.**	6073
16: 6	and if I refrain, it does not go **a.**	4946
18:13	It eats **a** parts of his skin;	430
19:14	My kinsmen *have* **gone a;**	2532
20: 8	Like a dream he **flies a,**	6414
21:18	like chaff **swept a** by a gale?	1704
22: 9	And *you* **sent** widows **a** empty-handed	8938
22:16	their foundations **washed a** by a flood.	3668
24: 3	*They* **drive a** the orphan's donkey and take	5627
24:19	heat and drought **snatch a** the melted snow,	1608
24:19	grave snatches **a** those who have sinned.	NIH
24:22	But God **drags a** the mighty by his power;	5432
27: 8	when God **takes a** his life?	8923
27:20	a tempest **snatches** him **a** in the night.	1704
30:15	my dignity *is* **driven a** as by the wind,	8103
30:16	my life **ebbs a;** days of suffering grip me.	9161
32:22	my Maker *would* soon **take** me **a.**	5951
33:21	His flesh **wastes a** to nothing,	3983
34:20	the people are shaken and *they* **pass a;**	6296
36:20	to **drag** people **a** *from* their homes.	6590
39:22	he does not shy **a** from the sword.	8740
Ps 1: 4	They are like chaff that the wind **blows a.**	5622
6: 8	**A** from me, all you who do evil,	6073
18:22	I *have* not **turned a** from his decrees.	6073
22:14	it *has* **melted a** within me.	5022
25:18	and my distress and **take a** all my sins.	5951
26: 9	*Do* not **take a** my soul along with sinners,	665
27: 9	*do* not **turn** your servant **a** in anger;	5742
28: 3	*Do* not **drag** me **a** with the wicked,	5432
32: 3	my bones **wasted a**	1162
34: T	*who* **drove** him **a,** and he left.	1763
35: 5	the angel of the LORD **driving** them **a;**	1890
36:11	nor the hand of the wicked **drive** me **a.**	5653
37: 2	like green plants *they* will soon **die a.**	5570
37:36	but *he* soon **passed a** and was no more;	6296
38:11	my neighbors stay **far a.**	4946+8158
39:13	Look **a from** me,	4946
51: 2	**Wash a** all my iniquity and cleanse me	3891
53: 3	Everyone *has* **turned a,**	6047
55: 6	I would **fly a** and be at rest—	6414
55: 7	I would **flee far a** and stay in the desert;	8178
57: 1	Let them vanish like water *that* **flows a;**	2143
58: 8	Like a slug **melting a** as it moves along,	9468
58: 9	the wicked *will be* **swept a.**	8548

Ps 65: 8	Those living **far a** fear your wonders;	7921
68: 2	As smoke **is blown a** by the wind,	5622
68: 2	*may you* **blow** them **a;**	5622
71: 9	*Do* not **cast** me **a** when I am old;	8959
73:19	completely **swept a** by terrors!	6200
80:18	Then *we will* not **turn a** from you;	6047
85: 4	and **put a** your displeasure toward us.	7296
90: 5	*You* **sweep** men **a** in the sleep of death;	2441
90: 9	All our days **pass a** under your wrath;	7155
90:10	for they quickly pass, and *we* **fly a.**	6414
102:11	I **wither a** like grass.	3312
102:24	So I said: "*Do* not **take** me **a,** O my God,	6590
104:22	The sun rises, and *they* **steal a;**	665
104:29	*when you* **take a** their breath,	665
106:43	on rebellion and *they* **wasted a** in their sin.	4812
107: 5	and their lives **ebbed a.**	6494
107:14	the deepest gloom and **broke a** their chains.	5998
107:26	in their peril their courage **melted a.**	4570
109:23	*I* **fade a** like an evening shadow;	2143
110:10	he will gnash his teeth and **waste a.**	5022
119:37	**Turn** my eyes **a** from worthless things;	6296
119:39	**Take a** the disgrace I dread,	6296
119:115	**A** from me, *you* evildoers,	6073
124: 5	the raging waters *would have* **swept** us **a.**	6296
139:19	**A** from me, *you* bloodthirsty men!	6073
148: 6	he gave a decree *that will* never **pass a.**	6296
Pr 1:19	it **takes a** the lives of those who get it.	4374
4:24	**Put a** perversity from your mouth;	6073
6:33	and his shame *will* never **be wiped a;**	4681
13:11	Dishonest money **dwindles a,**	5070
13:23	but injustice **sweeps** it **a.**	6200
14: 7	Stay **a from** a foolish man,	4946+5584
15: 1	A gentle answer **turns a** wrath,	8740
20:30	Blows and wounds **cleanse a** evil,	5347
21: 7	violence of the wicked *will* **drag** them **a,**	1760
24:11	Rescue those **being led a** to death;	4374
24:18	and disapprove and **turn** his wrath **a**	8740
25:20	Like *one* who **takes a** a garment on	6334
27:10	a neighbor nearby than a brother **far a.**	8158
29: 8	but wise men **turn a** anger.	8740
Ecc 3: 6	a time to keep and a time to **throw a,**	8959
SS 1: 4	**Take** me **a** with you—let us hurry!	5432
5: 7	they **took a** my cloak,	4946+6584
8: 7	rivers cannot **wash** it **a.**	8851
8:14	**Come a,** my lover, and be like a gazelle or	1368
Isa 1:25	*I will* **thoroughly purge a** your dross	1342+2021+3869+7671
2:20	In that day men *will* **throw a** to the rodents	8959
3:18	the Lord *will* **snatch a** their finery:	6073
4: 1	**Take a** our disgrace!"	665
4: 4	The Lord *will* **wash a** the filth of	8175
5: 5	*I will* **take a** its hedge,	6073
5:24	and their flowers **blow a** like dust;	6590
5:25	Yet for all this, his anger *is* not **turned a,**	8740
6: 7	your guilt *is* **taken a**	6073
6:12	until the LORD *has* **sent** everyone **far a**	8178
7:17	a time unlike any since Ephraim **broke a**	6073
9:12	Yet for all this, his anger *is* not **turned a,**	8740
9:17	Yet for all this, his anger *is* not **turned a,**	8740
9:21	Yet for all this, his anger *is* not **turned a,**	8740
10: 4	Yet for all this, his anger *is* not **turned a,**	8740
10:18	as *when* a sick man **wastes a.**	5022
12: 1	your anger *has* **turned a**	8740
14:31	**Melt a,** all you Philistines!	4570
15: 7	and stored up *they* **carry a** over the Ravine	5951
16:10	and gladness *are* **taken a** from the orchards;	665
17: 4	the fat of his body *will* **waste a.**	8135
17:13	when he rebukes them they flee **far a,**	4946+5305
19: 7	*will* **blow a** and be no more.	5622
19: 8	on the water *will* **pine a.**	581
20: 4	the king of Assyria *will* **lead a** stripped	5627
22: 3	while the enemy was still **far a.**	4946+8158
22: 4	Therefore I said, "**Turn a** from me;	9120
22: 8	the defenses of Judah *are* **stripped a.**	1655
22:17	take firm hold of you and **hurl** you **a,**	3214+3232
24:16	But I said, "**I waste a,** I waste away!	8140
24:16	But I said, "I waste away, **I waste a!**	8140
25: 8	The Sovereign LORD *will* **wipe a**	4681
28:17	hail *will* **sweep a** your refuge, the lie,	3589
28:19	As often as it comes *it will* **carry** you **a;**	4374
30:17	at the threat of five *you will* all **flee a,**	5674
30:22	*you will* **throw** them like	2430
30:22	like a menstrual cloth and say to them, "**A**	3655
33: 9	The land mourns and **wastes a,**	581
33:13	You who are **far a,** hear what I have done;	8158
34:12	all her princes will **vanish a.**	700
35:10	and sorrow and sighing *will* **flee a.**	5674
39: 7	*will be* **taken a,**	4374
40:24	and a whirlwind **sweeps** them **a** like chaff.	5951
41:16	and a gale *will* **blow** them **a.**	7046
42:22	all of them trapped in pits or **hidden a**	2461
44:22	*I have* **swept a** your offenses like a cloud,	4681
46:13	it is not **far a;**	8178
47:11	and you will not know how *to* **conjure** it **a.**	8838
49:19	those who devoured you *will be* **far a.**	8178
50: 1	of divorce with which I **sent** her **a?**	8938
50: 1	because of your transgressions your mother was **sent a.**	8938
51:11	and sorrow and sighing *will* **flee a.**	5674
52: 5	my people *have* **been taken a** for nothing,	4374
52: 5	oppression and judgment *he* **was taken a.**	4374
57: 1	devout men *are* **taken a,**	665
57: 1	that the righteous *are* **taken a** to be spared	665
57: 9	You sent your ambassadors **far a;**	4946+8158
57:13	a mere breath *will* **blow** them **a.**	4374
58: 7	*to* **turn a** from your own flesh and blood?	6623

Isa 58: 9	"If *you* **do a** with the yoke of oppression,	4946+6073+9348
59:11	for deliverance, but *it is* **far a.**	8178
64: 6	and like the wind our sins **sweep** us **a.**	5951
64: 7	and **made** us **waste a** because of our sins.	4570
65: 5	say, '**Keep a;** don't come near	448+3870+7928
Jer 1:13	**tilting a** from the north," I answered.	4946+7156
3: 8	and **sent** her **a** because of all her adulteries.	8938
3:19	and not **turn a** from following me.	8740
4: 1	of the LORD *has* not **turned a** from us.	8740
4:25	every bird in the sky *had* **flown a.**	5610
5:23	they have turned aside and **gone a.**	2143
5:25	Your wrongdoings *have* **kept** these **a;**	5742
6: 8	or I *will* **turn a** from you	3697
6:29	The bellows blow fiercely *to* **burn a**	9462
7:29	Cut off your hair and **throw** it **a;**	8959
7:33	there will be no *one* to **frighten** them **a.**	3006
8: 4	When *a* man **turns a,** does he not return?	8740
8: 5	Why then *have* these people **turned a?**	8740
8: 5	Why does Jerusalem always **turn a?**	5412
8:13	" '*I will* **take a** their harvest,	665
8:19	to the cry of my people from a land **far a:**	5305
9: 2	that I might leave my people and go **a from** them;	907+4946
13:19	be carried into exile, **carried** completely **a.**	1655
15: 1	**Send** them **a** from my presence!	8938
15: 3	to kill and the dogs to **drag a** and the birds	6079
15:15	You are long-suffering—*do* not **take** me **a;**	4374
17: 3	and all your treasures *I will* **give a**	5989
17: 5	and whose heart **turns a** from the LORD.	6073
17:13	*Those who* **turn a** from you will be written	6073
17:16	I have not **run a** from being your shepherd;	4946
18:20	in their behalf to **turn** your wrath **a**	8740
20: 4	*who will* **carry** them **a** to Babylon	1655
20: 5	*They will* **take** it **a** as plunder	4374
22:19	**dragged a** and thrown outside the gates	6079
22:22	**drive** all your shepherds **a,**	8286
23: 2	and **driven** them **a** and have	5615
23:23	"and not a God **far a?**	4946+8158
24: 1	from Judah, whom *I* **sent a** from this place	8938
27:20	not **take a** when he carried Jehoiachin son	4374
29:20	all you exiles whom *I have* **sent a**	8938
32:40	so that they *will* never **turn a** from me.	6073
41:16	with him **led a** all the survivors	4374
43: 5	the army officers **led a** all the remnant	4374
43: 6	They also **led a** all the men,	NIH
44:12	*I will* **take a** the remnant	4374
46:16	**a from** the sword of the oppressor.'	4946+7156
49: 5	"Every one of *you will* **be driven a,**	5615
49:20	The young of the flock *will be* **dragged a;**	6079
49:30	"Flee quickly **a!**	5653
50: 3	both men and animals will **flee a.**	2143
50:17	a scattered flock that lions *have* **chased a.**	5615
50:45	The young of the flock *will be* **dragged a;**	6079
52:18	*They* also **took a** the pots, shovels,	4374
52:19	of the imperial guard **took a** the basins,	4374
52:27	**a** from her land.	4946+6584
La 1: 8	she herself groans and **turns a.**	294
2: 8	together *they* **wasted a.**	581
2:12	as their lives **ebb a** in their mothers' arms.	9161
3: 2	*He has* **driven** me **a** and made me walk	5627
4: 9	*they* **waste a** for lack of food from the field.	2307
4:15	"**Go a!** You are unclean!"	6073
4:15	men cry to them. "**A!**	6073
4:15	men cry to them. "Away! **A!**	6073
Eze 3:14	The Spirit then lifted me up and **took** me **a,**	4374
4:17	at the sight of each other and *will* **waste a**	5245
5: 3	a few strands of hair and **tuck** them **a** in	7443
6: 9	which have **turned a** from me,	4946+6584
6:12	He *that* is **far a** will die of the plague,	8158
7:22	I will turn my face **a** from them,	4946
10: 5	of the cherubim could be heard as **far a** as	6330
11:15	'They are **far a** from the LORD;	8178
11:16	Although *I* **sent** them **far a** among	8178
16:42	and my jealous anger *will* **turn a**	6073
16:50	*I* **did a** with them as you have seen.	6073
17: 4	and **carried** it **a** to a land of merchants,	995
17:10	**wither a** in the plot where it grew?' "	3312
17:13	also **carried a** the leading men of the land,	4374
18:21	"But if a wicked man **turns a** from all	8740
18:27	But if a wicked man **turns a** from	8740
18:28	and **turns a** from them, he will surely live;	8740
18:30	**Turn a** from all your offenses;	8740
22: 5	near and those *who* are **far a** will mock you,	8158
23:10	**took a** her sons and daughters	4374
23:17	**turned a** from them **in disgust.**	3697
23:18	**turned a** from her **in disgust,**	3697
23:18	just as I *had* **turned a** from her sister.	5936
23:22	**turned a** from **in disgust,**	5936
23:25	They *will* **take a** your sons and daughters,	4374
23:28	**turned a** from **in disgust.**	5936
23:29	and **take a** everything you have worked for.	4374
23:40	for men who came from **far a,**	5305
24: 6	whose deposit will not go **a!**	4946
24:11	be melted and its deposit **burned a.**	9462
24:16	*to* **take a** from you the delight of your eyes.	4374
24:16	but *will* **waste a** because of your sins	5245
24:25	on the day I **take a** their stronghold,	4374
26: 4	I will **scrape a** her rubble and make her	6081
30: 4	her wealth *will be* **carried a**	4374
31:15	and all the trees of the field **withered a.**	6634
33: 6	that man *will* **be taken a** because of his sin,	4374
33:10	and we *are* **wasting a** because of them.	5245
33:14	but *he* then **turns a** from his sin	8740
33:19	a wicked man **turns a** from his wickedness	8740
34:21	you have **driven** them **a,**	448+2021+2025+2575
38:13	to **take a** livestock and goods and	4374

Eze	43: 9	Now *let them* **put a** from me 8178
Da	1:16	So the guard **took a** their choice food and 5951
	2:35	The wind **swept** them **a** without leaving 10492
	4:25	*be* **driven a** from people and will live with 10304
	4:32	*be* **driven a** from people and will live with 10304
	4:33	*He was* **driven a** from people and ate grass 10304
	5:21	*He was* **driven a** from people and given 10304
	7:14	that *will* not **pass a**, 10528
	7:26	and his power *will be* **taken a** 10528
	8:11	*it* **took a** the daily sacrifice from him, 8123
	9: 5	we *have* **turned a** from your commands 6073
	9:11	and **turned a**, refusing 6073
	9:16	**turn a** your anger and your wrath 8740
	11:22	an overwhelming army *will be* **swept a** 8851
	11:26	his army *will be* **swept a**, 8851
Hos	2: 9	"Therefore I *will* **take a** my grain 4374
	4: 3	and all who live in it **waste a**; 581
	4:11	which **take a** the understanding 4374
	4:19	A whirlwind *will* **sweep** them **a**, 928+4053+7674
	5:14	I will tear them to pieces and **go a**; 2143
	7:14	and new wine but **turn a** from me. 6073
	8:10	to **waste a** under the oppression of 5071
	9:11	Ephraim's glory *will* **fly a** like a bird— 6414
	9:12	Woe to them when I **turn a** from them! 6073
	10: 7	and its king *will* **float a** like a twig on 1950
	13:11	and in my wrath I **took** him **a**. 4374
	14: 4	for my anger *has* **turned a** from them. 8740
Joel	1: 7	and **thrown** it **a**, 8959
	1:12	Surely the joy of mankind *is* **withered a**. 3312
	3: 8	a nation **far a**." 8158
Am	2:15	the fleet-footed soldier *will* not **get a**, 4880
	4: 2	surely come when you *will be* **taken a** 5951
	4: 7	when the harvest was still three months **a**. NIH
	5:23	**A** with the noise of your songs! 6073
	6: 5	You **strum a** on your harps like David 7260
	7:11	**a** from their native land.'" 4946+6584
	7:17	**a** from their native land.'" 4946+6584
	8: 4	you who trample the needy and **do a** with 8697
	9: 1	Not one *will* **get a**, none will escape. 5674+5674
Jnh	1: 3	But Jonah **ran a** from the LORD 1368
	1:10	(They knew he *was* **running a** from 1368
	2: 7	"When my life *was* **ebbing a**, 6494
	4: 3	Now, O LORD, **take a** my life, 4946
Mic	2: 9	You **take a** my blessing 4374
	2:10	Get up, **go a**! 2143
	4: 7	those **driven a** a strong nation. 2133
Na	1: 5	before him and the hills **melt a**. 4570
	1:12	they will be cut off and **pass a**. 6296
	1:13	from your neck and **tear** your shackles **a**." 5998
	2: 7	that [the city] be exiled and **carried a**. 6590
	2: 8	and its water is **draining a**. 5674
	3:16	the land and then **fly a**. 6414
	3:17	but when the sun appears *they* **fly a**, 5610
Zep	1: 2	"I will **sweep a** everything from the face of the earth," 665+6066
	1: 3	"I will **sweep a** both men and animals; 6066
	1: 3	I will **sweep a** the birds of the air and 6066
	3:15	The LORD *has* **taken a** your punishment, 6073
Hag	2: 9	What you brought home, I **blew a**. 5870
Zec	3: 4	"See, I have **taken a** your sin, 6296
	6:15	*Those who are* **far a** will come and help 8158
	9: 4	But the Lord *will* **take a** her **possessions** 3769
	9:10	I will **take a** the chariots from Ephraim 4162
	10:11	down and Egypt's scepter *will* **pass a**. 6073
Mal	3: 7	of your forefathers *you have* **turned a** 6073
Mt	4:10	Jesus said to him, "**A** from me, Satan! 5632
	5:29	gouge it out and throw it **a**. 608
	5:30	cut it off and throw it **a**. 608
	5:42	and *do* not **turn a** from the one who wants 695
	6:26	they do not sow or reap or **store a** in barns, 5251
	7:23	**A** from me, you evildoers!' 713
	9:16	the patch *will* **pull a** from the garment, 149
	9:24	he said, "**Go a**. The girl is 432
	11: 6	the man who *does* not **fall a** on account 4997
	13:19	and **snatches a** what was sown in his heart. 773
	13:21	he quickly **falls a**. 4997
	13:25	among the wheat, and **went a**. 599
	13:46	he **went a** and sold everything he had 599
	13:48	but threw the bad **a**. 2032
	14:15	**Send** the crowds **a**, 668
	14:16	Jesus replied, "They do not need *to* **go a**. 599
	15:23	"**Send** her **a**, for she keeps crying out 668
	15:32	I do not want *to* **send** them **a** hungry, 668
	15:39	After Jesus *had* **sent** the crowd **a**, 668
	16: 4	Jesus then left them and **went a**. 599
	18: 8	cut it off and throw it **a**. 608
	18: 9	gouge it out and throw it **a**. 608
	18:12	and one of them **wanders a**, 4414
	19: 7	a certificate of divorce and **send** her **a**?" 668
	19:22	he **went a** sad, because he had great wealth. 599
	21: 3	and he will send them **right a**." 2317
	21:33	**went a** on a journey. 623
	21:43	of God *will be* **taken a** from you and given 149
	22:22	So *they* left him and **went a**. 599
	24: 1	and *was* **walking a** when his disciples came 4513
	24:10	that time many *will* **turn a** from the faith 4997
	24:34	this generation *will* certainly not **pass a** 4216
	24:35	Heaven and earth *will* **pass a**, 4216
	24:35	but my words *will* never **pass a**. 4216
	24:39	until the flood came and **took** them all **a**. 149
	24:48	'My master is **staying a** a long time,' 5988
	25:46	they will **go a** to eternal punishment, 599
	26: 2	the Passover is two days **a**— 3552
	26:31	"This very night you *will* all **fall a** 4997
	26:33	"Even if all **fall a** on account of you, 4997
	26:42	He **went a** a second time and prayed, 599
	26:42	for this cup *to be* **taken a** unless I drink it, 4216

Mt	26:44	So he left them and **went a** once more 599
	26:73	for your accent **gives** you **a**." 1316+4472
	27: 2	**led** him **a** and handed him over to Pilate. 552
	27: 5	Then he **went a** and hanged himself. 599
	27:31	Then *they* **led** him **a** to crucify him. 552
	27:60	of the entrance to the tomb and **went a**. 599
	28: 8	the women **hurried a** from the tomb, 599+5444
	28:13	and stole him **a** while we were asleep.' NIG
Mk	1:43	Jesus **sent** him **a** at once with 1675
	2:21	the new piece will **pull a** from the old, 149
	4:15	and **takes a** the word that was sown 149
	4:17	*they* quickly **fall a**. 4997
	5:20	So the man **went a** and began to tell in 599
	6:32	So *they* **went a** by themselves in a boat to 599
	6:36	**Send** the people so they can go to 668
	7:33	**took** him aside, **a** from 655
	8: 9	And having **sent** them **a**, 668
	10: 4	a certificate of divorce and **send** her **a**." 668
	10:22	He **went a** sad, because he had great wealth. 599
	12: 1	and **went a** on a journey. 623
	12: 3	beat him and **sent** him **a** empty-handed. 690
	12:12	so *they* left him and **went a**. 599
	13:30	this generation *will* certainly not **pass a** 4216
	13:31	Heaven and earth *will* **pass a**, 4216
	13:31	but my words *will* never **pass a**. 4216
	13:34	It's like a man **going a**: 624
	14: 1	of Unleavened Bread were only two days **a**, 3552
	14:27	"*You will* all **fall a**," Jesus told them, 4997
	14:29	Peter declared, "Even if all **fall a**, 4997
	14:39	Once more he **went a** and prayed 599
	14:44	arrest him and **lead** him **a** under guard." 552
	15: 1	**led** him **a** and handed him over to Pilate. 708
	15:16	The soldiers **led** Jesus **a** into the palace 552
	16: 3	"Who *will* **roll** the stone **a** from 653
	16: 4	which was very large, *had been* **rolled a**. 653
Lk	1:25	and **taken a** my disgrace among 904
	1:53	but *has* **sent** the rich **a** empty. 1990
	5: 8	"**Go a** from me, Lord; I am a sinful man!" 2002
	7:23	the man who *does* not **fall a** on account 4997
	8:12	then the devil comes and **takes a** the word 149
	8:13	but in the time of testing *they* **fall a**. 923
	8:38	but Jesus **sent** him **a**, saying, 668
	8:39	So the man **went a** and told all over town 599
	9:12	"**Send** the crowd **a** so they can go to 668
	10:30	beat him and **went a**, leaving him half dead. 599
	10:42	and it *will* not *be* **taken a** from her." 904
	11:22	he **takes a** the armor in which 149
	11:52	*you have* **taken a** the key to knowledge. 149
	13:27	**A** from me, all you evildoers!' 923
	14: 4	he healed him and **sent** him **a**. 668
	16: 3	My master *is* **taking a** my job. 904
	16:23	he looked up and saw Abraham **far a**, 608+3427
	19:20	I have kept it **laid a** in a piece of cloth. 641
	19:24	'**Take** his mina **a** from him and give it to 149
	19:26	even what he has *will be* **taken a**. 149
	20: 9	to some farmers and **went a** for a long time. 623
	20:10	and **sent** him **a** empty-handed. 1990
	20:11	and **sent a** empty-handed. 1990
	21: 9	but the end will not come **right a**." 2311
	21:32	this generation *will* certainly not **pass a** 4216
	21:33	Heaven and earth *will* **pass a**, 4216
	21:33	but my words *will* never **pass a**. 4216
	22:54	*they* **led** him **a** and took him into the house 72
	23:18	"**A** with this man! 149
	23:26	As *they* **led** him **a**, 552
	23:48	*they* beat their breasts and **went a**. 5715
	24: 2	They found the stone **rolled a** from 653
	24:12	and he **went a**, 599
Jn	1:29	who **takes a** the sin of the world! 149
	5:13	for Jesus *had* **slipped a** into the crowd 1728
	5:15	The man **went a** and told the Jews 599
	6:22	but that they *had* **gone a** alone. 599
	6:37	whoever comes to me I will never **drive a**. 2032
	7: 1	purposely **staying a** from Judea 1877+4024+4344
	8: 9	those who heard began to **go a** one at 2002
	8:21	"I am **going a**, and you will look for me, 5632
	8:59	**slipping a** from the temple grounds. 2002
	10: 5	*they* will **run a** from him because they do 5771
	10:12	he abandons the sheep and **runs a**. 5771
	10:13	The man **runs a** because he is a hired hand NIG
	11:39	"**Take a** the stone," he said. 149
	11:41	So *they* **took a** the stone. 149
	11:48	and then the Romans will come and **take a** 149
	14:28	'I am **going a** and I am coming back 5632
	15: 6	like a branch that is thrown **a** and withers; 2032
	16: 7	It is for your good that I am **going a**. 599
	16: 7	Unless *I* **go a**, the Counselor will 599
	16:22	and no one will **take a** your joy. 149
	18:11	"Put your sword **a**! 1650+2557+3836ˢ
	19:15	But they shouted, "**Take** him **a**! 149
	19:15	**Take** him **a**! 149
	19:38	he came and **took** the body **a**. 149
	20:13	"*They have* **taken** my Lord **a**," she said, 149
	20:15	she said, "Sir, if you *have* **carried** him **a**, 1002
Ac	7:42	But God **turned a** and gave them over to 5138
	8:39	**suddenly took** Philip **a**, 773
	17:10	**sent** Paul and Silas **a** 1734
	20:30	in order to **draw a** disciples after them. 685
	21: 1	*After we had* **torn** ourselves **a** from them, 685
	21:21	among the Gentiles to **turn a** from Moses, 686
	21:36	that followed kept shouting, "**A** with him!" 149
	22:16	Get up, be baptized and **wash** your sins **a**, 666
	22:21	I will send you **far a** to the Gentiles.'" 3426
	23:10	the troops to go down and **take** him **a** from 1666
	27:32	that held the lifeboat and let it **fall a**. 1738
	27:42	to prevent any of them *from* **swimming a** 1713
Ro	3:12	All *have* **turned a**, 1712

Ro	6: 6	that the body of sin *might be* **done a** with, 2934
	11:26	**turn** godlessness **a** from 695
	11:27	with them when I **take a** their sins." 904
	16:17	*Keep* **a** from them. 1712
1Co	7:31	this world in its present form *is* **passing a**. 4135
	13: 8	where there is knowledge, *it will* **pass a**. 2934
2Co	3:11	And if what *was* **fading a** came with glory, 2934
	3:13	at it *while the radiance was* **fading a**. 2934
	3:14	because only in Christ *is it* **taken a**. 2934
	3:16	the veil *is* **taken a**. 4311
	4:16	Though outwardly we *are* **wasting a**, 1425
	5: 6	at home in the body we *are* **a** from the Lord. 1685
	5: 8	*to be* **a** from the body and at home with 1685
	5: 9	at home in the body or **a** from it. 1685
	10: 1	to face with you, but "bold" when **a**! 582
	12: 8	with the Lord to **take** it **a** from me. 923
Gal	3:17	by God and thus do **a** with the promise. 2934
	5: 4	*you have* **fallen a** from grace. 1738
Eph	2:13	in Christ Jesus you who once were **far a** have been brought near 3426
	2:17	and preached peace to you who were **far a** 3426
Col	2:14	he **took** it **a**, nailing it to the cross. 149
1Th	2:17	when we were **torn a** from you for 682
2Th	3: 6	to **keep a** from every brother who is idle 5097
1Ti	1: 6	Some *have* **wandered a** from these 1762
	5:15	in fact already **turned a** to follow Satan. 1762
	6:20	**Turn a** from godless chatter and 1762
2Ti	2:19	who *have* **wandered a** from the truth. 846
	2:19	the Lord *must* **turn a** from wickedness." 923
	4: 4	**turn** their ears **a** from the truth 695
Heb	2: 1	so that we do not **drift a**. 4184
	3:12	unbelieving heart that **turns a** from 923
	6: 6	*if they* **fall a**, to be brought back 4178
	8: 9	and I **turned a** from them, 288
	9:26	to do **a** with sin by the sacrifice of himself. 120
	9:28	so Christ was sacrificed once to **take a** 429
	10: 4	the blood of bulls and goats *to* **take a** sins. 904
	10:11	which can never **take a** sins. 4311
	10:35	So do not **throw a** your confidence; 610
	11: 5	because God *had* **taken** him **a**. 3572
	12:25	*if we* **turn a** from him who warns us 695
	13: 9	*Do not be* **carried a** by all kinds 4195
Jas	1:10	because *he will* **pass a** like a wild flower. 4216
	1:11	the rich man *will* **fade a** even 3447
	1:14	he is **dragged a** and enticed. 1999
	1:24	and, after looking at himself, **goes a** 599
1Pe	5: 4	the crown of glory that will never **fade a**. 277
2Pe	3:17	not *be* **carried a** by the error of lawless men 5270
1Jn	2:17	The world and its desires **pass a**, 4135
	3: 5	so that he *might* **take a** our sins. 149
Rev	7:17	**wipe a** every tear **from** their eyes." 1981
	12:15	**sweep** her **a** **with** the torrent. 4472+4533
	16:20	Every island **fled a** and 5771
	17: 3	Then the angel **carried** me **a** in the Spirit 708
	21: 1	first heaven and the first earth *had* **passed a**, 599
	21: 4	for the old order of things *has* **passed a**." 599
	21:10	And he **carried** me **a** in the Spirit to 708
	22:19	if anyone **takes** words **a** **from** this book 904
	22:19	God *will* **take a** from him his share in 904

AWE (16) [AWESOME, OVERAWED]

1Sa	12:18	all the people **stood in a** *of* the LORD 3707+4394
1Ki	3:28	**held** the king **in a**, 3707
Job	25: 2	"Dominion and **a** belong to God; 7065
Ps	119:120	*I* **stand in a** of your laws. 3707
Ecc	5: 7	Therefore **stand in a** *of* God. 3707
Isa	29:23	and *will* **stand in a** of the God of Israel. 6907
Jer	2:19	the LORD your God and have no **a** 7067
	33: 9	and *they will be* **in a** and will tremble at 7064
Hab	3: 2	*I* **stand in a** of your deeds, O LORD. 3707
Mal	2: 5	and he revered me and **stood in a** 3169
Mt	9: 8	*they were* **filled with a**; 5828
Lk	1:65	The neighbors were all **filled with a**, 5832
	5:26	They were **filled** *with* **a** and said, 5832
	7:16	They were all **filled with a** 3284+5832
Ac	2:43	Everyone was **filled with a**, 5832
Heb	12:28	with reverence and **a**, 1290

AWESOME (34) [AWE]

Ge	28:17	"How **a** is this place! 3707
Ex	15:11	majestic in holiness, **a** in glory, 3707
	34:10	among will see how **a** is the work that I, 3707
Dt	4:34	or by great and **a deeds**, 4616
	7:21	who is among you, is a great and **a** God. 3707
	10:17	the great God, mighty and **a**, 3707
	10:21	**a wonders** you saw with your own eyes. 3707
	28:58	do not revere this glorious and **a** name— 3707
	34:12	the mighty power or performed the **a deeds** 4616
Jdg	13: 6	He looked like an angel of God, very **a**. 3707
2Sa	7:23	and **a wonders** by driving out nations 3707
1Ch	17:21	and **a wonders** by driving out nations from 3707
Ne	1: 5	God of heaven, the great and **a** God, 3707
	4:14	Remember the Lord, who is great and **a**, 3707
	9:32	O our God, the great, mighty and **a** God, 3707
Job	10:16	like a lion and again **display** *your* **power** 7098
	37:22	God comes in **a** majesty. 3707
Ps	45: 4	let your right hand display **a deeds**. 3707
	47: 2	How **a** is the LORD Most High, 3707
	65: 5	with **a deeds** of righteousness, 3707
	66: 3	Say to God, "How **a** are your deeds! 3707
	66: 5	how **a** his works in man's behalf! 3707
	68:35	*You are* **a**, O God, in your sanctuary; 3707
	89: 7	he is more **a** than all who surround him. 3707
	99: 3	Let them praise your great and **a** name— 3707
	106:22	miracles in the land of Ham and **a deeds** by 3707

Ps 111: 9 holy and **a** *is* his name. 3707
145: 6 They will tell of the power of your **a works**, 3707
Isa 64: 3 you did *a* *things* that we did not expect, 3707
Eze 1:18 Their rims were high and **a**, 3711
1:22 sparkling like ice, and **a**. 3707
Da 2:31 enormous, dazzling statue, **a** in appearance. 10167
9: 4 "O Lord, the great and **a** God, 3707
Zep 2:11 be **a** to them when he destroys all the gods 3707

AWFUL (5)
Jdg 20: 3 "Tell us how this **a thing** happened." 8288
20:12 about this **a crime** that was committed 8288
Ne 9:18 or when they committed **a blasphemies**. 1524
9:26 they committed **a blasphemies**. 1524
Jer 30: 7 How **a** that day will be! 1524+2098

AWHILE (3) [WHILE]
Ge 47: 4 "We have come to **live here a**, 1591
1Sa 9:27 "but you stay here **a**, 2021+3427+3869
1Co 16: 6 Perhaps *I* will **stay** with you **a**, 4169

AWL (2)
Ex 21: 6 the doorpost and pierce his ear with an **a**. 5345
Dt 15:17 an **a** and push it through his ear lobe into 5345

AWNINGS (1)
Eze 27: 7 your **a** were of blue and purple from 4833

AWOKE (7) [WAKE]
Ge 9:24 When Noah **a** from his wine 3699
28:16 When Jacob **a** from his sleep, he thought, 3699
Jdg 16:14 *He* **a** from his sleep and pulled up the pin 3699
16:20 *He* **a** from his sleep and thought, 3699
1Ki 3:15 Then Solomon **a**—and he realized it had been a dream. 3699
Ps 78:65 Then the Lord **a** as from sleep, 3699
Jer 31:26 At this *I* **a** and looked around. 7810

AX (8) [AXES, AXHEAD]
Dt 19: 5 and as he swings his **a** to fell a tree, 1749
20:19 do not destroy its trees by putting an **a** 1749
Jdg 9:48 He took an **a** and cut off some branches, 7935
Ecc 10:10 If the **a** is dull and its edge unsharpened, 1366
Isa 10:15 the **a** raise itself above him who swings it, 1749
10:34 down the forest thickets with an **a**; 1366
Mt 3:10 The **a** is already at the root of the trees, 544
Lk 3: 9 The **a** is already at the root of the trees, 544

AXES (7) [AX]
1Sa 13:20 mattocks, **a** and sickles sharpened. 7935
13:21 of a shekel for sharpening forks and **a** and 7935
2Sa 12:31 with saws and with iron picks and **a**, 4477
1Ch 20: 3 with saws and with iron picks and **a**, 4490
Ps 74: 5 like men wielding **a** to cut through a thicket 7935
74: 6 the carved paneling with their **a** 4172
Jer 46:22 they will come against her with **a**, 7935

AXHEAD (1) [AX]
2Ki 6: 5 the iron **a** fell into the water. 1366

AXLES (3)
1Ki 7:30 with bronze **a**, and each had a basin resting 6248
7:32 **a** of the wheels were attached to the stand. 3338
7:33 the **a**, rims, spokes and hubs were all 3338

AXLETREES (KJV) See AXEL

AYYAH (1)
1Ch 7:28 and its villages all the way to **A** 6509

AZAL (KJV) See AZEL

AZALIAH (2)
2Ki 22: 3 Shaphan son of **A**, the son of Meshullam, 729
2Ch 34: 8 he sent Shaphan son of **A** and Maaseiah 729

AZANIAH (1)
Ne 10: 9 The Levites: Jeshua son of **A**, 271

AZARAEL, AZAREEL (KJV) See AZAREL

AZAREL (6)
1Ch 12: 6 **A**, Joezer and Jashobeam the Korahites; 6475
25:18 the eleventh to **A**, his sons and relatives, 12 6475
27:22 **A** son of Jeroham. 6475
Ezr 10:41 **A**, Shelemiah, Shemariah, 6475
Ne 11:13 Amashsai son of **A**, the son of Ahzai, 6475
12:36 Shemaiah, **A**, Milalai, Gilalai, Maai, 6475

AZARIAH (46) [AZARIAH'S, UZZIAH]
1Ki 4: 2 **A** son of Zadok— 6482
4: 5 **A** son of Nathan— 6482
2Ki 14:21 Then all the people of Judah took **A**, 6481
15: 1 **A** son of Amaziah king of Judah began 6481
15: 7 **A** rested with his fathers and was buried 6481
15: 8 In the thirty-eighth year of **A** king of Judah, 6481

2Ki 15:17 In the thirty-ninth year of **A** king of Judah, 6481
15:23 In the fiftieth year of **A** king of Judah, 6481
15:27 In the fifty-second year of **A** king of Judah, 6481
1Ch 2: 8 The son of Ethan: **A**. 6481
2:38 Jehu the father of **A**, 6481
2:39 **A** the father of Helez, 6481
3:12 **A** his son, Jotham his son, 6481
6: 9 Ahimaaz the father of **A**, 6481
6: 9 **A** the father of Johanan, 6481
6:10 of **A** (it was he who served as priest in 6481
6:11 **A** the father of Amariah, 6481
6:13 Hilkiah the father of **A**, 6481
6:14 **A** the father of Seraiah, 6481
6:36 the son of **A**, the son of Zephaniah, 6481
9:11 **A** son of Hilkiah, the son of Meshullam, 6481
2Ch 15: 1 The Spirit of God came upon **A** son 6482
15: 8 the prophecy of **A** son of Oded the prophet, 6482
21: 2 the sons of Jehoshaphat, were **A**, Jehiel, 6481
23: 1 **A** son of Jeroham, 6481
23: 1 Ishmael son of Jehohanan, **A** son of Obed, 6481
26:17 **A** the priest with eighty other courageous priests 6482
26:20 When **A** the chief priest and all 6482
28:12 son of Jehohanan, Berekiah son 6482
29:12 Mahath son of Amasai and Joel son of **A**; 6482
29:12 Kish son of Abdi and **A** son of Jehallelel; 6482
31:10 and **A** the chief priest, 6482
31:13 and **A** the official in charge of the temple 6482
Ezr 7: 1 Ezra son of Seraiah, the son of **A**, 6481
7: 3 the son of **A**, the son of Meraioth, 6481
Ne 3:23 and next to them, **A** son of Maaseiah 6481
7: 7 **A**, Raamiah, Nahamani, Mordecai, Bilshan, 6481
8: 7 Shabbethai, Hodiah, Maaseiah, Kelita, **A**, 6481
10: 2 Seraiah, **A**, Jeremiah, 6481
12:33 along with **A**, Ezra, Meshullam, 6481
Jer 43: 2 **A** son of Hoshaiah and Johanan son 6481
Da 1: 6 Daniel, Hananiah, Mishael and **A**. 6481
1: 7 to Mishael, Meshach; and to **A**, 6481
1:11 Hananiah, Mishael and **A**, 6481
1:19 Hananiah, Mishael and **A**; 6481
2:17 to his friends Hananiah, Mishael and **A**. 10538

AZARIAH'S (2) [AZARIAH]
2Ki 15: 6 As for the other events of **A** reign, 6482
Ne 3:24 from **A** house to the angle and the corner, 6481

AZARIAHU (1)
2Ch 21: 2 Zechariah, **A**, Michael and Shephatiah. 6482

AZAZ (1)
1Ch 5: 8 and Bela son of **A**, 6452

AZAZIAH (3)
1Ch 15:21 Jeiel and **A** were to play the harps, 6453
27:20 Hoshea son of **A**; 6453
2Ch 31:13 Jehiel, **A**, Nahath, Asahel, Jerimoth, 6453

AZBUK (1)
Ne 3:16 Beyond him, Nehemiah son of **A**, 6443

AZEKAH (7)
Jos 10:10 down all the way to **A** and Makkedah. 6467
10:11 on the road down from Beth Horon to **A**, 6467
15:35 Jarmuth, Adullam, Socoh, **A**, 6467
1Sa 17: 1 between Socoh and **A**, 6467
2Ch 11: 9 Adoraim, Lachish, **A**, 6467
Ne 11:30 and in **A** and its settlements. 6467
Jer 34: 7 that were still holding out—Lachish and **A**. 6467

AZEL (7)
1Ch 8:37 Eleasah his son and **A** his son. 727
8:38 **A** had six sons, and these were their names: 727
8:38 All these were the sons of **A**. 727
9:43 Eleasah his son and **A** his son. 727
9:44 **A** had six sons, and these were their names: 727
9:44 These were the sons of **A**. 727
Zec 14: 5 for it will extend to **A**. 728

AZEM (KJV) See EZEM

AZGAD (4)
Ezr 2:12 of **A** 1,222 6444
8:12 of the descendants of **A**, Johanan son 6444
Ne 7:17 of **A** 2,322 6444
10:15 Bunni, **A**, Bebai, 6444

AZIEL (1)
1Ch 15:20 **A**, Shemiramoth, Jehiel, Unni, Eliab, 6456

AZIZA (1)
Ezr 10:27 Mattaniah, Jeremoth, Zabad and **A**. 6461

AZMAVETH (8) [BETH AZMAVETH]
2Sa 23:31 Abi-Albon the Arbathite, **A** the Barhumite, 6462
1Ch 8:36 of Alemeth, **A** and Zimri, and Zimri was 6462
9:42 of Alemeth, **A** and Zimri, and Zimri was 6462
11:33 **A** the Baharumite, Eliahba the Shaalbonite, 6462
12: 3 Jeziel and Pelet the sons of **A**; 6462
27:25 **A** son of Adiel was in charge of 6462

Ezr 2:24 of **A** 42 6463
Ne 12:29 and from the area of Geba and **A**, 6463

AZMON (2)
Nu 34: 4 to Hazar Addar and over to **A**, 6801
Jos 15: 4 then passed along to **A** and joined the Wadi 6801

AZNOTH TABOR (1) [TABOR]
Jos 19:34 through **A** and came out at Hukkok. 268

AZOR (2)
Mt 1:13 Eliakim the father of **A**, *110*
1:14 **A** the father of Zadok, *110*

AZOTUS (1)
Ac 8:40 however, appeared at **A** and traveled about, *111*

AZRIEL (3)
1Ch 5:24 Epher, Ishi, Eliel, **A**, Jeremiah, 6480
27:19 Jerimoth son of **A**; 6480
Jer 36:26 Seraiah son of **A** and Shelemiah son 6480

AZRIKAM (6)
1Ch 3:23 Elioenai, Hizkiah and **A**— three in all. 6483
8:38 **A**, Bokeru, Ishmael, Sheariah, 6483
9:14 Shemaiah son of Hasshub, the son of **A**, 6483
9:44 **A**, Bokeru, Ishmael, Sheariah, 6483
2Ch 28: 7 **A** the officer in charge of the palace, 6483
Ne 11:15 Shemaiah son of Hasshub, the son of **A**, 6483

AZUBAH (4)
1Ki 22:42 His mother's name was **A** daughter 6448
1Ch 2:18 of Hezron had children by his wife **A** (and 6448
2:19 When **A** died, Caleb married Ephrath, 6448
2Ch 20:31 His mother's name was **A** daughter 6448

AZUR (KJV) See AZZUR

AZZAH (KJV) See GAZA

AZZAN (1)
Nu 34:26 of **A**, the leader from the tribe of Issachar; 6464

AZZUR (3)
Ne 10:17 Ater, Hezekiah, **A**, 6473
Jer 28: 1 the prophet Hananiah son of **A**, 6473
Eze 11: 1 and I saw among them Jaazaniah son of **A** 6473

B

BAAL (63) [BAAL GAD, BAAL HAMON, BAAL HAZOR, BAAL HERMON, BAAL MEON, BAAL PEOR, BAAL PERAZIM, BAAL SHALISHAH, BAAL TAMAR, BAAL ZEPHON, BAAL'S, BAAL-BERITH, BAAL-HANAN, BAAL-ZEBUB, BAALS, BAMOTH BAAL]
Nu 25: 3 Israel joined in worshiping the **B** *of* Peor. 1251
25: 5 in worshiping the **B** *of* Peor." 1251
Dt 4: 3 among you everyone who followed the **B** 1251
Jdg 2:13 because they forsook him and served **B** and 1251
6:25 down your father's altar to **B** and cut down 1251
6:31 If **B** really is a god, 2085[S]
6:32 saying, "Let **B** contend with him," 1251
1Ki 16:31 and began to serve **B** and worship him. 1251
16:32 for **B** *in* the temple of Baal that he built 1251
16:32 in the temple of **B** that he built in Samaria. 1251
18:19 the four hundred and fifty prophets of **B** 1251
18:21 but if **B** is God, follow him." 1251
18:22 but **B** has four hundred and fifty prophets. 1251
18:25 Elijah said to the prophets of **B**, 1251
18:26 on the name of **B** from morning till noon. 1251
18:26 "O **B**, answer us!" 1251
18:40 "Seize the prophets of **B**. 1251
19:18 all whose knees have not bowed down to **B** 1251
22:53 He served and worshiped **B** and provoked 1251
2Ki 3: 2 He got rid of the sacred stone of **B** 1251
10:18 "Ahab served **B** a little; 1251
10:19 Now summon all the prophets of **B**, 1251
10:19 I am going to hold a great sacrifice for **B**. 1251
10:19 in order to destroy the ministers of **B**. 1251
10:20 Jehu said, "Call an assembly in honor of **B**." 1251
10:21 and all the ministers of **B** came; 1251
10:21 **B** until it was full from one end to 1251
10:22 "Bring robes for all the ministers of **B**." 1251
10:23 of Recab went into the temple of **B**. 1251
10:23 Jehu said to the ministers of **B**, 1251
10:23 only ministers of **B**." 1251

2Ki	10:25	the inner shrine of the temple of **B**.	1251
	10:26	the sacred stone out of the temple of **B**	1251
	10:27	of **B** and tore down the temple of Baal,	1251
	10:27	of Baal and tore down the temple of **B**,	1251
	10:28	So Jehu destroyed **B** worship in Israel.	1251
	11:18	to the temple of **B** and tore it down.	1251
	11:18	and killed Mattan the priest of **B** in front of	1251
	17:16	and they worshiped **B**.	1251
	21: 3	he also erected altars to **B** and made	1251
	23: 4	the articles made for **B** and Asherah and all	1251
	23: 5	those who burned incense to **B**,	1251
1Ch	5: 5	Micah his son, Reaiah his son, **B** his son,	1252
	8:30	followed by Zur, Kish, **B**, Ner, Nadab,	1252
	9:36	followed by Zur, Kish, **B**, Ner, Nadab,	1252
2Ch	23:17	All the people went to the temple of **B**	1251
	23:17	and killed Mattan the priest of **B** in front of	1251
Ps	106:28	to the **B** of Peor and ate sacrifices offered	1251
Jer	2: 8	The prophets prophesied by **B**,	1251
	7: 9	to **B** and follow other gods you have	1251
	11:13	to burn incense to that shameful god **B** are	1251
	11:17	to anger by burning incense to **B**.	1251
	12:16	they once taught my people to swear by **B**—	1251
	19: 5	the high places of **B** to burn their sons in	1251
	19: 5	in the fire as offerings to **B**—	1251
	23:13	by **B** and led my people Israel astray.	1251
	23:27	as their fathers forgot my name through **B** worship.	1251
	32:29	by burning incense on the roofs to **B** and	1251
	32:35	They built high places for **B** in the Valley	1251
Hos	2: 8	which they used for **B**.	1251
	13: 1	But he became guilty of **B** worship and died.	1251
Zep	1: 4	from this place every remnant of **B**,	1251
Ro	11: 4	not bowed the knee *to* **B**."	955

BAAL GAD (3) [BAAL, GAD]

Jos	11:17	to **B** in the Valley	1254
	12: 7	from **B** in the Valley of Lebanon	1254
	13: 5	the east, from **B** below Mount Hermon	1254

BAAL HAMON (1) [BAAL]

SS	8:11	Solomon had a vineyard in **B**;	1255

BAAL HAZOR (1) [BAAL, HAZOR]

2Sa	13:23	at **B** near the border of Ephraim,	1258

BAAL HERMON (2) [BAAL, HERMON, SENIR]

Jdg	3: 3	from Mount **B** to Lebo Hamath.	1259
1Ch	5:23	in the land from Bashan to **B**,	1259

BAAL MEON (3) [BETH BAAL MEON, BETH MEON]

Nu	32:38	and **B** (these names were changed)	1260
1Ch	5: 8	the area from Aroer to Nebo and **B**.	1260
Eze	25: 9	Beth Jeshimoth, **B** and Kiriathaim—	1260

BAAL PEOR (2) [BAAL, PEOR]

Dt	4: 3	the LORD did at **B**.	1261
Hos	9:10	But when they came to **B**,	1261

BAAL PERAZIM (4) [BAAL, PERAZIM]

2Sa	5:20	So David went to **B**,	1262
	5:20	So that place was called **B**.	1262
1Ch	14:11	David and his men went up to **B**,	1262
	14:11	So that place was called **B**.	1262

BAAL SHALISHAH (1) [BAAL]

2Ki	4:42	A man came from **B**,	1264

BAAL TAMAR (1) [BAAL, TAMAR]

Jdg	20:33	and took up positions at **B**,	1265

BAAL ZEPHON (3) [BAAL, ZEPHON]

Ex	14: 2	directly opposite **B**.	1263
	14: 9	near Pi Hahiroth, opposite **B**.	1263
Nu	33: 7	to the east of **B**,	1263

BAAL'S (4) [BAAL]

Jdg	6:28	there was **B** altar, demolished,	1251
	6:30	because he has broken down **B** altar and cut	1251
	6:31	"Are you going to plead **B** cause?"	1251S
	6:32	because he broke down **B** altar.	2257S

BAAL-BERITH (2) [BAAL]

Jdg	8:33	They set up **B** as their god	1253
	9: 4	of silver from the temple of **B**,	1253

BAAL-HANAN (5) [BAAL]

Ge	36:38	**B** son of Acbor succeeded him as king.	1257
	36:39	When **B** son of Acbor died,	1257
1Ch	1:49	**B** son of Acbor succeeded him as king.	1257
	1:50	**B** died, Hadad succeeded him as king.	1257
	27:28	**B** the Gederite was in charge of the olive	1257

BAAL-ZEBUB (4) [BAAL, BEELZEBUB]

2Ki	1: 2	"Go and consult **B**, the god of Ekron,	1256

2Ki	1: 3	that you are going off to consult **B**,	1256
	1: 6	that you are sending men to consult **B**,	1256
	1:16	that you have sent messengers to consult **B**,	1256

BAALAH (6) [KIRIATH JEARIM]

Jos	15: 9	of Mount Ephron and went down toward **B**	1267
	15:10	it curved westward from **B** to Mount Seir,	1267
	15:11	along to Mount **B** and reached Jabneel.	1267
	15:29	**B**, Iim, Ezem,	1267
2Sa	6: 2	He and all his men set out from **B** *of* Judah	1267
1Ch	13: 6	to **B** of Judah (Kiriath Jearim) to bring up	1267

BAALATH (4) [BAALATH BEER]

Jos	19:44	Eltekeh, Gibbethon, **B**,	1272
1Ki	9:18	**B**, and Tadmor in the desert,	1272
1Ch	4:33	the villages around these towns as far as **B**.	1272
2Ch	8: 6	as well as **B** and all his store cities, and all	1272

BAALATH BEER (1) [BAALATH]

Jos	19: 8	as far as **B** (Ramah in the Negev).	1273

BAALI (KJV) See MY MASTER

BAALIM (KJV) See BAALS

BAALIS (1)

Jer	40:14	"Don't you know that **B** king of	1271

BAALS (18) [BAAL]

Jdg	2:11	in the eyes of the LORD and served the **B**.	1251
	3: 7	the LORD their God and served the **B** and	1251
	8:33	prostituted themselves to the **B**.	1251
	10: 6	They served the **B** and the Ashtoreths,	1251
	10:10	forsaking our God and serving the **B**."	1251
1Sa	7: 4	Israelites put away their **B** and Ashtoreths,	1251
	12:10	and served the **B** and the Ashtoreths.	1251
1Ki	18:18	and have followed the **B**.	1251
2Ch	17: 3	He did not consult the **B**	1251
	24: 7	even its sacred objects for the **B**.	1251
	28: 2	also made cast idols for worshiping the **B**.	1251
	33: 3	to the **B** and made Asherah poles.	1251
	34: 4	the altars of the **B** were torn down;	1251
Jer	2:23	I have not run after the **B**'?	1251
	9:14	they have followed the **B**,	1251
Hos	2:13	for the days she burned incense to the **B**;	1251
	2:17	the names of the **B** from her lips;	1251
	11: 2	to the **B** and they burned incense to images.	1251

BAANA (3)

1Ki	4:12	**B** son of Ahilud—	1275
	4:16	**B** son of Hushai—in Asher and in Aloth;	1275
Ne	3: 4	to him Zadok son of **B** also made repairs.	1275

BAANAH (9)

2Sa	4: 2	One was named **B** and the other Recab;	1276
	4: 5	Now Recab and **B**,	1276
	4: 6	Recab and his brother **B** slipped away.	1276
	4: 9	David answered Recab and his brother **B**,	1276
	23:29	Heled son of **B** the Netophathite,	1276
1Ch	11:30	Heled son of **B** the Netophathite,	1276
Ezr	2: 2	Bilshan, Mispar, Bigvai, Rehum and **B**):	1276
Ne	7: 7	Mispereth, Bigvai, Nehum and **B**):	1276
	10:27	Malluch, Harim and **B**.	1276

BAARA (1)

1Ch	8: 8	after he had divorced his wives Hushim and **B**.	1281

BAASEIAH (1)

1Ch	6:40	the son of **B**, the son of Malkijah,	1283

BAASHA (25) [BAASHA'S]

1Ki	15:16	There was war between Asa and **B** king	1284
	15:17	**B** king of Israel went up against Judah	1284
	15:19	Now break your treaty with **B** king of Israel	1284
	15:21	When **B** heard this,	1284
	15:22	and timber **B** had been using there.	1284
	15:27	son of Ahijah of the house	1284
	15:28	**B** killed Nadab in the third year	1284
	15:32	There was war between Asa and **B** king	1284
	15:33	son of Ahijah became king of all Israel	1284
	16: 1	to Jehu son of Hanani against **B**:	1284
	16: 3	So I am about to consume **B** and his house,	1284
	16: 4	Dogs will eat those belonging to **B** who die	1284
	16: 6	**B** rested with his fathers and was buried	1284
	16: 7	of Hanani to **B** and his house, because	1284
	16: 8	Elah son of **B** became king of Israel,	1284
	16:12	So Zimri destroyed the whole family of **B**,	1284
	16:12	the word of the LORD spoken against **B**	1284
	16:13	the sins of **B** and his son Elah had committed	1284
	21:22	of Jeroboam son of Nebat and that of **B** son	1284
2Ki	9: 9	and like the house of **B** son of Ahijah.	1284
2Ch	16: 1	the thirty-sixth year of Asa's reign **B** king	1284
	16: 3	Now break your treaty with **B** king of Israel	1284
	16: 5	When **B** heard this,	1284
	16: 6	the stones and timber **B** had been using.	1284
Jer	41: 9	of his defense against **B** king of Israel.	1284

BAASHA'S (2) [BAASHA]

1Ki	16: 5	As for the other events of **B** reign,	1284
	16:11	he killed off **B** whole family.	1284

BABBLER (1) [BABBLING]

Ac	17:18	"What is this **b** trying to say?"	5066

BABBLING (1) [BABBLER]

Mt	6: 7	you pray, *do not keep on* **b** like pagans,	1006

BABBLINGS (KJV) See CHATTER

BABE, BABES (KJV) See CHILDREN

BABEL (1) [BABYLON]

Ge	11: 9	That is why it was called **B**—	951

BABIES (5) [BABY]

Ge	25:22	The **b** jostled each other within her,	1201
Ex	2: 6	"This is one of the Hebrew **b**," she said.	3529
Lk	18:15	People were also bringing **b** to Jesus	1100
Ac	7:19	to throw out their **newborn b** so	1100
1Pe	2: 2	Like newborn **b**, crave pure spiritual milk,	1100

BABOONS (2)

1Ki	10:22	silver and ivory, and apes and **b**.	9415
2Ch	9:21	silver and ivory, and apes and **b**.	9415

BABY (16) [BABIES, BABY'S]

Ex	2: 6	She opened it and saw the **b**.	3529
	2: 7	the Hebrew women to nurse the **b** for you?"	3529
	2: 9	"Take this **b** and nurse him for me,	3529
	2: 9	So the woman took the **b** and nursed him.	3529
1Ki	3:17	*I* had a **b** while she was there with me.	3528
	3:18	this woman also had a **b**.	3528
	3:26	"Please, my lord, give her the living **b**!	3528
	3:27	"Give the living **b** to the first woman.	3528
Isa	49:15	the **b** at her breast and have no compassion	6403
Lk	1:41	the **b** leaped in her womb,	1100
	1:44	the **b** in my womb leaped for joy.	1100
	1:57	for Elizabeth *to have her* **b**,	5503
	2: 6	the time came for the **b** to be born,	5503
	2:12	You will find a **b** wrapped in cloths	1100
	2:16	and the **b**, who was lying in the manger.	1100
Jn	16:21	when her **b** is born she forgets the anguish	4086

BABY'S (1) [BABY]

Ex	2: 8	And the girl went and got the **b** mother.	3529

BABYLON (281) [BABEL, BABYLON'S, BABYLONIA, BABYLONIAN, BABYLONIANS, BABYLONIANS']

Ge	10:10	The first centers of his kingdom were **B**,	951
2Ki	17:24	of Assyria brought people from **B**,	951
	17:30	The men from **B** made Succoth Benoth,	951
	20:12	of Baladan king of **B** sent Hezekiah letters	951
	20:14	"They came from **B**."	951
	20:17	will be carried off to **B**.	951
	20:18	in the palace of the king of **B**."	951
	24: 1	Nebuchadnezzar king of **B** invaded	951
	24: 7	the king of **B** had taken all his territory,	951
	24:10	of **B** advanced on Jerusalem and laid siege	951
	24:12	of the reign of the king of **B**,	951
	24:15	Nebuchadnezzar took Jehoiachin captive to **B**.	951
	24:15	from Jerusalem to **B** the king's mother,	951
	24:16	The king of **B** also deported to Babylon	951
	24:16	The king of Babylon also deported to **B**	951
	24:20	Zedekiah rebelled against the king of **B**.	951
	25: 1	Nebuchadnezzar king of **B** marched	951
	25: 6	He was taken to the king of **B** at Riblah,	951
	25: 7	with bronze shackles and took him to **B**.	951
	25: 8	of Nebuchadnezzar king of **B**,	951
	25: 8	an official of the king of **B**,	951
	25:11	over to the king of **B**.	951
	25:13	and they carried the bronze to **B**.	951
	25:20	and brought them to the king of **B**	951
	25:22	of **B** appointed Gedaliah son of Ahikam,	951
	25:23	that the king of **B** had appointed Gedaliah	951
	25:24	down in the land and serve the king of **B**,	951
	25:27	the year Evil-Merodach became king of **B**,	951
	25:28	of the other kings who were with him in **B**.	951
1Ch	9: 1	of Judah were taken captive to **B** because	951
2Ch	32:31	of **B** to ask him about the miraculous sign	951
	33:11	with bronze shackles and took him to **B**.	951
	36: 6	Nebuchadnezzar king of **B** attacked him	951
	36: 6	with bronze shackles to take him to **B**.	951
	36: 7	to **B** articles from the temple of the LORD	951
	36:10	for him and brought him to **B**.	951
	36:18	to **B** all the articles from the temple of God,	951
	36:20	He carried into exile to **B** the remnant,	951
Ezr	1:11	the exiles came up from **B** to Jerusalem.	951
	2: 1	of **B** had taken captive	951
	2: 1	to **B** (they returned to Jerusalem and Judah,	951
	4: 9	Persia, Erech and **B**, the Elamites of Susa,	10094
	5:12	king of **B**, who destroyed this temple	10093
	5:12	and deported the people to **B**.	10093
	5:13	in the first year of Cyrus king of **B**,	10093
	5:14	the temple of **B** the gold and silver articles	10093

Ezr	5:14	and brought to the temple in B. 10093
	5:17	a search be made in the royal archives of B 10093
	6: 1	in the archives stored in the treasury at B. 10093
	6: 5	the temple in Jerusalem and brought to B, 10093
	7: 6	this Ezra came up from B. 951
	7: 9	from B on the first day of the first month, 951
	7:16	from the province of B, 10093
	8: 1	with them who came up with me from B 951
Ne	7: 6	of B had taken captive (they returned 951
	13: 6	of Artaxerxes king of B I had returned to 951
Est	2: 6	by Nebuchadnezzar king of B, 951
Ps	87: 4	"I will record Rahab and B 951
	137: 1	By the rivers of B we sat and wept 951
	137: 8	O Daughter of B, doomed to destruction, 951
Isa	13: 1	concerning B that Isaiah son of Amoz saw: 951
	13:19	the jewel of kingdoms, 951
	14: 4	up this taunt against the king of B: 951
	14:22	from B her name and survivors, 951
	21: 9	'B has fallen, has fallen!' 951
	39: 1	of Baladan king of B sent Hezekiah letters 951
	39: 3	"They came to me from B." 951
	39: 6	will be carried off to B. 951
	39: 7	in the palace of the king of B." 951
	43:14	"For your sake I will send to B and bring 951
	47: 1	sit in the dust, Virgin Daughter of B; 951
	48:14	The LORD's chosen ally will carry out his purpose against B; 951
	48:20	Leave B, flee from the Babylonians! 951
Jer	20: 4	I will hand all Judah over to the king of B, 951
	20: 4	who will carry them away to B or put them 951
	20: 5	as plunder and carry it off to B. 951
	20: 6	in your house will go into exile to B. 951
	21: 2	of B is attacking us. 951
	21: 4	which you are using to fight the king of B 951
	21: 7	to Nebuchadnezzar king of B and 951
	21:10	be given into the hands of the king of B, 951
	22:25	to Nebuchadnezzar king of B and to 951
	24: 1	to B by Nebuchadnezzar king of Babylon, 951
	24: 1	to Babylon by Nebuchadnezzar king of B, 951
	25: 1	the first year of Nebuchadnezzar king of B. 951
	25: 9	and my servant Nebuchadnezzar king of B," 951
	25:11	the king of B seventy years. 951
	25:12	I will punish the king of B and his nation, 951
	27: 6	to my servant Nebuchadnezzar king of B; 951
	27: 8	not serve Nebuchadnezzar king of B 951
	27: 9	'You will not serve the king of B.' 951
	27:11	the yoke of the king of B and serve him, 951
	27:12	under the yoke of the king of B; 951
	27:14	that will not serve the king of B? 951
	27:14	'You will not serve the king of B,' 951
	27:16	be brought back from B.' 951
	27:17	Serve the king of B, and you will live. 951
	27:18	and in Jerusalem not be taken to B. 951
	27:20	which Nebuchadnezzar king of B did 951
	27:20	of Judah into exile from Jerusalem to B, 951
	27:22	be taken to B and there they will remain 951
	28: 2	'I will break the yoke of the king of B. 951
	28: 3	that Nebuchadnezzar king of B removed 951
	28: 3	from here and took to B. 951
	28: 4	from Judah who went to B,' 951
	28: 4	'for I will break the yoke of the king of B.' 951
	28: 6	and all the exiles back to this place from B. 951
	28:11	the yoke of Nebuchadnezzar king of B off 951
	28:14	to make them serve Nebuchadnezzar king of B, 951
	29: 1	into exile from Jerusalem to B. 951
	29: 3	to King Nebuchadnezzar in B. 951
	29: 4	into exile from Jerusalem to B: 951
	29:10	"When seventy years are completed for B, 951
	29:15	LORD has raised up prophets for us in B," 951
	29:20	from Jerusalem to B. 951
	29:21	over to Nebuchadnezzar king of B, 951
	29:22	in B will use this curse: 951
	29:22	whom the king of B burned in the fire.' 951
	29:28	He has sent this message to us in B: 951
	32: 2	of B was then besieging Jerusalem, 951
	32: 3	to hand this city over to the king of B, 951
	32: 4	be handed over to the king of B, 951
	32: 5	He will take Zedekiah to B, 951
	32:28	and to Nebuchadnezzar king of B, 951
	32:36	be handed over to the king of B': 951
	34: 1	of B and all his army and all the kingdoms 951
	34: 2	to hand this city over to the king of B, 951
	34: 3	the king of B with your own eyes, 951
	34: 3	And you will go to B. 951
	34: 7	of B was fighting against Jerusalem and 951
	34:21	to the army of the king of B, 951
	35:11	of B invaded this land, 951
	36:29	that the king of B would certainly come 951
	37: 1	of Judah by Nebuchadnezzar king of B; 951
	37:17	"you will be handed over to the king of B." 951
	37:19	of B will not attack you or this land'? 951
	38: 3	over to the army of the king of B, 951
	38:17	the officers of the king of B, your life will 951
	38:18	the king of B, this city will be handed over 951
	38:22	to the officials of the king of B; 951
	38:23	but will be captured by the king of B; 951
	39: 1	Nebuchadnezzar king of B marched 951
	39: 3	Then all the officials of the king of B came 951
	39: 3	and all the other officials of the king of B. 951
	39: 5	and took him to Nebuchadnezzar king of B 951
	39: 6	at Riblah the king of B slaughtered the sons 951
	39: 7	with bronze shackles to take him to B. 951
	39: 9	of the imperial guard carried into exile to B 951
	39:11	of B had given these orders about Jeremiah 951
	39:13	and all the other officers of the king of B 951
	40: 1	who were being carried into exile to B. 951

Jer	40: 4	Come with me to B, if you like, 951
	40: 5	the king of B has appointed over the towns 951
	40: 7	the king of B had appointed Gedaliah son 951
	40: 7	not been carried into exile to B, 951
	40: 9	down in the land and serve the king of B, 951
	40:11	the king of B had left a remnant in Judah 951
	41: 2	the one whom the king of B had appointed 951
	41:18	the king of B had appointed as governor 951
	42:11	Do not be afraid of the king of B, 951
	43: 3	they may kill us or carry us into exile to B." 951
	43:10	for my servant Nebuchadnezzar king of B, 951
	44:30	over to Nebuchadnezzar king of B, 951
	46: 2	of B in the fourth year of Jehoiakim son 951
	46:13	the coming of Nebuchadnezzar king of B 951
	46:26	to Nebuchadnezzar king of B 951
	49:28	which Nebuchadnezzar king of B attacked: 951
	49:30	"Nebuchadnezzar king of B has plotted 951
	50: 1	through Jeremiah the prophet concerning B 951
	50: 2	but say, 'B will be captured; 951
	50: 8	"Flee out of B! 951
	50: 9	against B an alliance of great nations from 951
	50:13	All who pass B will be horrified and scoff 951
	50:14	"Take up your positions around B, 951
	50:16	Cut off from B the sower, 951
	50:17	the last to crush his bones was Nebuchadnezzar king of B." 951
	50:18	"I will punish the king of B and his land 951
	50:23	How desolate is B among the nations! 951
	50:24	I set a trap for you, O B, 951
	50:28	fugitives and refugees from B declaring 824+951
	50:29	"Summon archers against B, 951
	50:34	but unrest to those who live in B. 951
	50:35	"against those who live in B and 951
	50:42	to attack you, O Daughter of B. 951
	50:43	king of B has heard reports about them, 951
	50:44	I will chase B from its land in an instant. 4392S
	50:45	against B, what he has purposed against 951
	51: 1	up the spirit of a destroyer against B and 951
	51: 2	I will send foreigners to B to winnow her 951
	51: 4	They will fall down slain in B, 824+4169
	51: 6	"Flee from B! 951
	51: 7	B was a gold cup in the LORD's hand; 951
	51: 8	B will suddenly fall and be broken. 951
	51: 9	" 'We would have healed B, 951
	51:11	because his purpose is to destroy B. 951
	51:12	Lift up a banner against the walls of B! 951
	51:12	his decree against the people of B. 951
	51:24	"Before your eyes I will repay B 951
	51:29	the LORD's purposes against B stand— 951
	51:29	the land of B so that no one will live there. 951
	51:31	of B that his entire city is captured, 951
	51:33	"The Daughter of B is like a threshing floor 951
	51:34	of B has devoured us, 951
	51:35	the violence done to our flesh be upon B," 951
	51:37	B will be a heap of ruins, 951
	51:41	What a horror B will be among the nations! 951
	51:42	The sea will rise over B; 951
	51:44	I will punish Bel in B 951
	51:44	And the wall of B will fall. 951
	51:47	when I will punish the idols of B; 951
	51:48	that is in them will shout for joy over B, 951
	51:49	"B must fall because of Israel's slain, 951
	51:49	in all the earth have fallen because of B. 951
	51:53	Even if B reaches the sky 951
	51:54	"The sound of a cry comes from B, 951
	51:55	The LORD will destroy B; 951
	51:56	A destroyer will come against B; 951
	51:59	when he went to B with Zedekiah king 951
	51:60	the disasters that would come upon B— 951
	51:60	all that had been recorded concerning B. 951
	51:61	He said to Seraiah, "When you get to B, 951
	51:64	'So will B sink to rise no more because of 951
	52: 3	Zedekiah rebelled against the king of B. 951
	52: 4	Nebuchadnezzar king of B marched 951
	52: 9	He was taken to the king of B at Riblah 951
	52:10	at Riblah the king of B slaughtered the sons 951
	52:11	with bronze shackles and took him to B, 951
	52:12	of Nebuchadnezzar king of B, 951
	52:12	who served the king of B, 951
	52:15	over to the king of B. 951
	52:17	and they carried all the bronze to B. 951
	52:26	and brought them to the king of B 951
	52:31	the year Evil-Merodach became king of B, 951
	52:32	of the other kings who were with him in B. 951
	52:34	Day by day the king of B gave Jehoiachin 951
Eze	17:12	'The king of B went to Jerusalem 951
	17:12	bringing them back with him to B. 951
	17:16	he shall die in B, 951
	17:20	I will bring him to B and execute judgment 951
	19: 9	a cage and brought him to the king of B. 951
	21:19	for the sword of the king of B to take, 951
	21:21	king of B will stop at the fork in the road, 951
	24: 2	because the king of B has laid siege 951
	26: 7	against Tyre Nebuchadnezzar king of B, 951
	29:18	Nebuchadnezzar king of B drove his army 951
	29:19	to Nebuchadnezzar king of B. 951
	30:10	by the hand of Nebuchadnezzar king of B. 951
	30:24	the arms of the king of B and put my sword 951
	30:25	I will strengthen the arms of the king of B, 951
	30:25	of B and he brandishes it against Egypt. 951
	32:11	" 'The sword of the king of B will come 951
Da	1: 1	of B came to Jerusalem and besieged it. 951
	2:12	the execution of all the wise men of B. 10093
	2:14	to put to death the wise men of B, 10093
	2:18	with the rest of the wise men of B, 10093
	2:24	to execute the wise men of B, 10093
	2:24	"Do not execute the wise men of B. 10093

Da	2:48	the entire province of B and placed him 10093
	2:49	over the province of B, 10093
	3: 1	on the plain of Dura in the province of B. 10093
	3:12	over the affairs of the province of B— 10093
	3:30	and Abednego in the province of B. 10093
	4: 6	So I commanded that all the wise men of B 10093
	4:29	on the roof of the royal palace of B, 10093
	4:30	"Is not this the great B I have built as 10093
	5: 7	and said to these wise men of B. 10093
	7: 1	In the first year of Belshazzar king of B, 10093
Mic	4:10	You will go to B; 951
Zec	2: 7	Escape, you who live in the Daughter of B!" 951
	6:10	who have arrived from B. 951
Mt	1:11	at the time of the exile to B. 956
	1:12	After the exile to B: 956
	1:17	fourteen from David to the exile to B. 956
Ac	7:43	into exile' beyond B. 956
1Pe	5:13	She who is in B, chosen together with you, 956
Rev	14: 8	Fallen is B the Great, 956
	16:19	God remembered B the Great and gave her 956
	17: 5	B THE GREAT THE MOTHER OF PROSTITUTES AND OF THE ABOMINATIONS OF THE EARTH. 956
	18: 2	Fallen is B the Great! 956
	18:10	Woe, O great city, O B, city of power! 956
	18:21	"With such violence the great city of B will 956

BABYLON'S (3) [BABYLON]

Jer	50:46	of B capture the earth will tremble; 951
	51:30	B warriors have stopped fighting; 951
	51:58	"B thick wall will be leveled 951

BABYLONIA (10) [BABYLON]

Jos	7:21	in the plunder a beautiful robe from B, 9114
Isa	11:11	from Cush, from Elam, from B, 9114
Jer	50:10	So B will be plundered; 4169
	51:24	in B for all the wrong they have done 4169
	51:35	"May our blood be on those who live in B," 4169
Eze	11:24	to the exiles in B in the vision given by 4169
	12:13	I will bring him to B, 951
	16:29	to include B, a land of merchants, but even 4169
Da	1: 2	to the temple of his god in B and put in 824+9114
Zec	5:11	"To the country of B to build a house for it. 9114

BABYLONIAN (13) [BABYLON]

2Ki	24: 2	The LORD sent B, Aramean, 4169
	25: 5	but the B army pursued the king 4169
	25:10	The whole B army, 4169
	25:24	"Do not be afraid of the B officials," 4169
Jer	35:11	we must go to Jerusalem to escape the B 4169
	37:10	if you were to defeat the entire B army 4169
	37:11	the B army had withdrawn from Jerusalem 4169
	39: 5	But the B army pursued them 4169
	41: 3	as well as the B soldiers who were there. 4169
	52: 8	but the B army pursued King Zedekiah 4169
	52:14	The whole B army under the commander of 4169
Eze	23:15	of them looked like B chariot officers, 951+1201
Da	9: 1	who was made ruler over the B kingdom— 4169

BABYLONIANS (53) [BABYLON]

2Ki	25: 4	though the B were surrounding the city. 4169
	25:13	The B broke up the bronze pillars, 4169
	25:25	also the men of Judah and the B who were 4169
	25:26	fled to Egypt for fear of the B. 4169
2Ch	36:17	up against them the king of the B, 4169
Isa	23:13	Look at the land of the B, 4169
	43:14	and bring down as fugitives all the B, 4169
	47: 1	without a throne, Daughter of the B. 4169
	47: 5	go into darkness, Daughter of the B; 4169
	48:14	his arm will be against the B. 4169
	48:20	Leave Babylon, flee from the B! 4169
Jer	21: 4	of Babylon and the B who are outside 4169
	21: 9	to the B who are besieging you will live; 4169
	22:25	of Babylon and to the B, 4169
	24: 5	from this place to the land of the B. 4169
	25:12	the land of the B, for their guilt," 4169
	32: 4	of the B but will certainly be handed over 4169
	32: 5	If you fight against the B, 4169
	32:24	over to the B who are attacking it. 4169
	32:25	the city will be handed over to the B, 4169
	32:28	over to the B and to Nebuchadnezzar king 4169
	32:29	The B who are attacking this city will come 4169
	32:43	for it has been handed over to the B.' 4169
	37: 5	in the fight with the B: 4169
	37: 5	the B who were besieging Jerusalem heard 4169
	37: 8	Then the B will return and attack this city; 4169
	37: 9	thinking, 'The B will surely leave us.' 4169
	37:13	"You are deserting to the B!" 4169
	37:14	"I am not deserting to the B." 4169
	38: 2	but whoever goes over to the B will live. 4169
	38:18	over to the B and they will burn it down; 4169
	38:19	of the Jews who have gone over to the B, 4169
	38:19	for the B may hand me over to them NIH
	38:23	and children will be brought out to the B. 4169
	38: 3	The B set fire to the royal palace and 4169
	40: 9	"Do not be afraid to serve the B," he said. 4169
	40:10	to represent you before the B who come 4169
	41:18	to escape the B. 4169
	43: 3	against us to hand us over to the B, 4169
	50: 1	concerning Babylon and the land of the B: 4169
	50: 8	leave the land of the B, 4169
	50:25	to do in the land of the B, 4169
	50:35	"A sword against the B!" 4169
	50:45	against the land of the B: 4169
	51:54	of great destruction from the land of the B. 4169

Jer	52: 7	though the **B** were surrounding the city.	4169
	52:17	The **B** broke up the bronze pillars,	4169
Eze	1: 3	by the Kebar River in the land of the **B.**	4169
	23:17	the **B** came to her, to the bed of love,	951+1201
	23:23	the **B** and all the Chaldeans,	951+1201
Da	1: 4	the language and literature of the **B.**	4169
	5:30	That very night Belshazzar, king of the **B,**	10373
Hab	1: 6	I am raising up the **B,**	4169

BABYLONIANS' (1) [BABYLON]

Isa	13:19	the glory of the **B'** pride,	4169

BABYLONISH (KJV) See BABYLONIA

BACA (1)

Ps	84: 6	As they pass through the Valley of **B,**	1133

BACHRITES (KJV) See BEKER

BACK (619) [BACKBONE, BACKGROUND, BACKS, BACKSLIDING, BACKSLIDINGS, BACKWARD]

Ge	3:24	and a flaming sword **flashing b and forth**	2200
	8: 7	and it kept flying **b** and forth until	8740
	8: 9	the dove and **brought** it **b** to himself in	995
	14: 7	Then *they* **turned b** and went to En Mishpat	8740
	14:16	the goods and **brought b** his relative Lot	8740
	15:16	fourth generation your descendants *will* come **b** here,	8740
	16: 9	"**Go b** to your mistress and submit to her."	8740
	19:10	and **pulled** Lot **b** into the house and shut	995
	19:17	Don't look **b**, and don't stop anywhere in	339
	19:26	But Lot's wife looked **b**,	339+4946
	22: 5	We will worship and then *we will* **come b**	8740
	24: 5	"What if the woman is unwilling to come **b**	339
	24: 5	*Shall I then* **take** your son **b** to	8740+8740
	24: 6	that *you do not* **take** my son **b** there,"	8740
	24: 8	If the woman is unwilling to come **b**	339
	24: 8	Only *do not* **take** my son **b** there."	8740
	24:20	ran to the well to draw more water **b**	6388
	24:39	if the woman will not come **b** *with me?'*	339
	24:61	and mounted their camels and went **b** *with*	339
	27: 5	to hunt game and **bring** it **b**,	995
	27:45	I'll send word for you *to* **come b** from there.	4374
	28:15	and *I will* **bring** you **b** to this land.	8740
	29: 7	the sheep and **take** them **b** *to* pasture."	2143
	30:25	so *I can* **go b** to my own homeland.	2143
	31: 3	"**Go b** to the land of your fathers and	8740
	31:13	at once and **go b** to your native land.' "	8740
	32: 9	'**Go b** to your country and your relatives,	8740
	33:16	**started** on his way **b**	8740
	37:14	and **bring** word **b** *to* me."	8740
	37:22	to rescue him from them and **take** him **b**	8740
	37:30	*He* **went b** to his brothers and said,	8740
	37:32	**took** the ornamented robe **b**	995+2256+8938
	38:20	the Adullamite in order to **get** his pledge **b**	4374
	38:22	So *he* **went b** to Judah and said,	8740
	38:29	But when *he* **drew b** his hand,	8740
	42:19	while the rest of you go and **take** grain **b**	995
	42:24	but then **turned b** and spoke to them again.	8740
	42:25	put each man's silver **b**	8740
	42:34	Then *I will* **give** your brother **b** to you,	5989
	42:37	of my sons to death if *I do not* **bring** him **b**	995
	42:37	and *I will* **bring** him **b**."	8740
	43: 2	"**Go b** and buy us a little more food."	8740
	43: 9	not **bring** him **b** and set him here	995
	43:12	the silver that *was* **put b** into the mouths	8740
	43:13	Take your brother also and **go b** to the man	8740
	43:14	and Benjamin **come b** with you.	8938
	43:18	that *was* **put b** into our sacks the first time.	8740
	43:21	So *we have* **brought** it **b** with us.	8740
	44: 8	*We even* **brought b** to you from the land	8740
	44:17	**go b** to your father in peace."	6590
	44:24	When *we* **went b** to your servant my father,	6590
	44:25	'**Go b** and buy a little more food.'	8740
	44:30	when I **go b** to your servant my father and	995
	44:32	I said, '*If I do not* **bring** him **b** to you,	995
	44:34	How *can I* **go b** to my father if the boy is	6590
	45: 9	Now hurry **b** to my father and say to him,	6590
	45:18	bring your father and your families **b** to me.	995
	45:27	the carts Joseph had sent to **carry** him **b**,	5951
	46: 4	and *I will* **surely bring** you **b** again.	6590+6590
	48:21	but God will be with you and **take** you **b** to	8740
	50:15	grudge against us and **pays** us **b** *for* all	8740+8740
Ex	4: 4	of the snake and *it* **turned b** into a staff	AIT
	4: 7	"Now **put** it **b** into your cloak," he said.	8740
	4: 7	So Moses **put** his hand **b** into his cloak,	8740
	4:18	Then Moses **went b**	8740
	4:18	"Let me **go b** to my own people in Egypt	8740
	4:19	"**Go b** to Egypt,	8740
	4:20	on a donkey and **started b** to Egypt.	8740
	5: 4	**Get b** to your work!"	2143
	9: 2	and continue *to* **hold** them **b**,	2616
	9:24	hail fell and lightning **flashed b and forth.**	928+4374+9348
	10: 8	Then Moses and Aaron were **brought b**	8740
	14: 2	"Tell the Israelites *to* **turn b** and encamp	8740
	14:21	that night the LORD **drove** the sea **b** with	2143
	14:26	the sea so that the waters *may* **flow b** over	8740
	14:27	and at daybreak the sea **went b** to its place.	8740
	14:28	The water **flowed b** and covered	8740
	15:19	**brought** the waters of the sea **b**	8740
	19: 7	So Moses **went b** and summoned the elders	995

Ex	19: 8	Moses **brought** their answer **b**	8740
	22: 1	*he must* **pay b** five head of cattle for the ox	8966
	22: 4	*he must* **pay b** double.	8966
	22: 7	if he is caught, *must* **pay b** double.	8966
	22: 9	judges declare guilty *must* **pay b** double	8966
	22:29	not **hold b** offerings from your granaries	336
	23: 4	**be sure to take** it **b**	8740+8740
	24:14	"Wait here for us until *we* **come b** to you.	8740
	32:15	on both sides, front and **b.**	2296S
	32:27	**Go b** and forth through the camp	8740
	32:31	So Moses **went b** to the LORD and said,	8740
	33:23	and you will see my **b**;	294
	34:31	leaders of the community **came b** to him,	8740
	34:35	Then Moses *would* **put** the veil **b**	8740
Lev	19:13	**hold b** the wages of a hired man **overnight.**	1332+4328+6330
	25:27	*he can* then **go b** to his own property.	8740
	25:28	and *he can* then **go b** to his property.	8740
	25:41	and *he will* **go b** to his own clan and to	8740
	27:27	*he may* **buy** it **b** at its set value,	7009
Nu	10:30	*I am going* **b** to my own land	2143
	12:14	after that *she can* be **brought b.**"	665
	12:15	not move on till she *was* **brought b.**	665
	13:20	Do your best *to* **bring b** some of the fruit of	4374
	13:26	*They* **came b** to Moses and Aaron and the whole Israelite community	995+2143+2256
	14: 3	Wouldn't it be better for us *to* **go b**	8740
	14: 4	"We should choose a leader and **go b**	8740
	14:25	**turn b** tomorrow and set out toward	7155
	16:26	"**Move b** from the tents	6073
	17:10	"**Put b** Aaron's staff in front of	8740
	22: 8	"and *I will* **bring** you **b** the answer	8740
	22:13	"**Go b** to your own country,	2143
	22:23	Balaam beat her to get her **b** on the road.	5742
	22:34	Now if you are displeased, *I will* **go b.**"	8740
	23: 5	"**Go b** to Balak and give him this message."	8740
	23: 6	So *he* **went b** to him and found him	8740
	23:16	"**Go b** to Balak and give him this message."	8740
	24:14	Now *I am going* **b** to my people, but come,	2143
	33: 7	They left Etham, **turned b** to Pi Hahiroth,	8740
	35:25	and **send** him **b** to the city of refuge	8740
	35:32	a city of refuge and so *allow* him to **go b**	8740
Dt	1:22	ahead to spy out the land for us and **bring b**	8740
	1:45	*You* **came b** and wept before the LORD,	8740
	2: 1	Then *we* **turned b** and set out toward	7155
	3:20	each of *you may* **go b**	8740
	10: 5	Then *I* **came b** down the mountain and put	7155
	17:16	"*You are* not to **go b** that way again."	8740
	19:12	**bring** him **b** from the city,	4374
	22: 1	**be sure to take** it **b**	8740+8740
	22: 2	Then **give** it **b** to him.	8740
	24:19	*do not* **go b** to get it.	8740
	28:68	The LORD *will* **send** you **b** in ships	8740
	30: 4	and **bring** you **b**,	4374
Jos	1:15	*you may* **go b** and occupy your own land,	8740
	2:23	Then the two men **started b.**	8740
	8:15	**let themselves be driven b**	8740
	8:20	men of Ai looked **b** and saw the smoke	339+7155
	8:20	toward the desert *had* **turned b**	2200
	8:26	not draw **b** the hand that held out his javelin	8740
	11:10	At that time Joshua **turned b**	8740
	14: 7	And *I* **brought** him **b** a report according	8740
	19:29	The boundary then **turned b** *toward* Ramah	8740
	20: 6	Then he *may* **go b** to his own home in	8740
Jdg	1: 7	God has **paid** me **b** *for* what I did to them."	8966
	3:19	At the idols near Gilgal *he himself* **turned b**	8740
	3:22	which came out his **b.**	7307
	6:18	Please do not go away until I **come b**	8740
	7: 3	'Anyone who trembles with fear *may* **turn b**	8740
	8:29	Jerub-Baal son of Joash **went b** home	2143
	11: 9	"Suppose you **take** me **b** to fight	8740
	11:13	Now **give** it **b** peaceably."	8740
	11:14	Jephthah **sent b** messengers to	3578+6388
	14: 8	when *he* **went b** to marry her,	8740
	16:18	"**Come b** once more;	6590
	16:31	*They* **brought** him **b** and buried him	6590
	17: 3	*I will* **give** it **b** to you."	8740
	18:26	turned around and **went b** home.	8740
	19: 2	and went **b** to her father's house	NIH
	19:26	At daybreak the woman **went b** *to*	995
	20:48	of Israel **went b** to Benjamin and put all	8740
Ru	1: 7	that *would* **take** them **b** to the land of Judah.	8740
	1: 8	"**Go b**, each of you, to your mother's home.	8740
	1:10	"*We will* **go b** with you to your people."	8740
	1:15	"your sister-in-law *is going* **b** to her people	8740
	1:15	**Go b** with her."	8740
	1:16	"Don't urge me to leave you or to **turn b**	8740
	1:21	but the LORD *has* **brought** me **b** empty.	8740
	2: 4	*they* **called b.**	606
	2: 6	the Moabitess who **came b** from Moab	8740
	2:18	She carried it **b** *to* town,	8740
	3:15	Then *he* **went b** to town.	995
	3:17	of barley, saying, 'Don't **go b**	8740
	4: 3	"Naomi, who *has* **come b** from Moab,	8740
1Sa	1:19	the LORD and then **went b** to their home	8740
	3: 5	Eli said, "I did not call; **go b** and lie down."	8740
	3: 5	**go b** and lie down."	8740
	4: 4	they **brought b** the ark of the covenant	4946+9004
	5: 3	They took Dagon and **put** him **b**	8740
	5:11	*let* it **go b** to its own place,	8740
	6: 2	how *we should* **send** it **b** to its place."	8938
	6: 7	the gold objects *you are* **sending b** to him as	8740
	7:17	But he always **went b** to Ramah,	9588
	8:22	"Everyone **go b** to his town."	2143
	9: 5	*let's* **go b**, or my father will stop thinking	8740
	13: 2	of the men *he* **sent b** to their homes.	8938
	15:20	and **brought b** Agag their king.	995

1Sa	15:25	forgive my sin and **come b** with me,	8740
	15:26	"*I will* not **go b** with you.	8740
	15:30	**come b** with me,	8740
	15:31	So Samuel **went b** with Saul,	8740
	17: 6	a bronze javelin was **slung** on his **b.**	1068+4190
	17:15	but David **went b** and forth from Saul	8740
	17:18	and **bring b** some assurance from them.	4374
	19:15	Then Saul **sent** the men **b** to see David	8938
	20:40	"Go, **carry** them **b** *to* town.	995
	20:42	and Jonathan **went b** to the town.	995
	23:23	and **come b** to me with definite information.	8740
	24: 3	David and his men were **far b** in the cave.	928+3752
	25:12	David's men turned around and **went b.**	8740
	25:21	*He has* **paid** me **b** evil for good.	8740
	26:21	**Come b**, David my son.	8740
	29: 4	"**Send** the man **b**,	8740
	29: 7	**Turn b** and go in peace;	8740
	29:11	up early in the morning to **go b** to the land	8740
	30:19	David **brought** everything **b.**	8740
2Sa	1:22	the bow of Jonathan did not **turn b,**	294
	2:23	and the spear came out through his **b.**	339
	3:16	Then Abner said to him, "**Go b** home!"	8740
	3:16	So *he* **went b.**	8740
	3:26	*they* **brought** him **b** from the well of Sirah.	8740
	10: 5	and then **come b.**"	8740
	11: 4	Then *she* **went b** home.	8740
	11:12	and tomorrow *I will* **send** you **b.**"	8740
	11:23	but *we* **drove** them **b** to the entrance to	2118+6584
	12:23	Can I **bring** him **b** again?	8740
	13: 4	king *has* not **brought b** his banished son?	8938
	14:21	Go, **bring b** the young man Absalom."	8740
	14:23	and **brought** Absalom **b** to Jerusalem.	995
	15: 8	'If the LORD **takes** me **b** *to* Jerusalem,	8740+8740
	15:19	**Go b** and stay with King Absalom.	8740
	15:20	**Go b**, and take your countrymen.	8740
	15:25	"**Take** the ark of God **b**	8740
	15:25	*he will* **bring** me **b** and let me see it	8740
	15:27	**Go b** *to* the city in peace,	8740
	15:29	took the ark of God **b**	8740
	16: 3	the house of Israel *will* **give** me **b** my grandfather's kingdom.' "	8740
	17: 3	**bring** all the people **b**	8740
	19:10	about **bringing** the king **b?**"	8740
	19:11	be the last to **bring** the king **b** to his palace,	8740
	19:12	So why should you be the last to **bring b**	8740
	19:43	the first to speak of **bringing b** our king?"	8740
	20:22	And Joab **went b** to the king in Jerusalem.	8740
	22:38	*I did not* **turn b** till they were destroyed.	8740
	23:16	near the gate of Bethlehem and carried it **b**	995
	24: 8	*they* **came b** to Jerusalem at the end	995
1Ki	2:26	"**Go b** to your fields in Anathoth.	2143
	2:40	and **brought** the slaves **b** from Gath.	995
	5: 2	Solomon **sent b** this message to Hiram:	8938
	7: 8	set **farther b**, was similar in design.	337+2021+2958
	8:33	*they* **turn b** to you and confess your name,	8740
	8:34	of your people Israel and **bring** them **b** to	8740
	8:48	and if *they* **turn b** to you with all their heart	8740
	9:28	to Ophir and **brought b** 420 talents of gold,	4946+9004
	10:19	and its **b** had a rounded top.	339+4946
	11:22	to **go b** to your own country?"	2143
	12: 5	"Go away for three days and then **come b**	8740
	12:12	"**Come b** to me in three days."	8740
	13: 4	so that he could not pull it **b.**	8740
	13:16	"I cannot **turn b** and go with you,	8740
	13:18	'**Bring** him **b** with you to your house so	8740
	13:20	to the old prophet who *had* **brought** him **b.**	8740
	13:22	*You* **came b** and ate bread and drank water	8740
	13:23	the prophet who *had* **brought** him **b**	8740
	13:26	When the prophet who *had* **brought** him **b**	8740
	13:29	and **brought** it **b** to his own city to mourn	8740
	14: 9	to anger and thrust me behind your **b.**	1567
	14:12	"As for you, **go b** home.	2143
	14:37	that you are turning their hearts **b** again."	345
	18:43	Seven times Elijah said, "**Go b.**"	8740
	19: 7	of the LORD **came** a second time	8740
	19:15	"**Go b** the way you came,	8740
	19:20	"**Go b**," Elijah replied.	8740
	19:21	So Elisha left him and **went b.**	8740
	20: 9	and took the answer **b** *to* Ben-Hadad.	8740
	22:26	**send** him **b** to Amon the ruler of the city	8740
2Ki	1: 5	he asked them, "Why *have you* **come b?**"	8740
	1: 6	'**Go b** to the king who sent you	8740
	2:13	that had fallen from Elijah and **went b**	8740
	4:31	Gehazi **went b** to meet Elisha and told him,	8740
	4:35	Elisha turned away and walked **b and forth**	285+285+2178+2178+2256
	5: 7	Can I kill and **bring b** to life?	2649
	5:15	Then Naaman and all his attendants **went b**	8740
	6:13	*The* **report came b:** "He is in Dothan."	5583
	6:22	that they may eat and drink and then **go b**	2143
	8: 3	the seven years she **came b** from the land of	8740
	8: 5	the woman whose son Elisha *had* **brought** **b to life** came	2649
	8: 6	"**Give** everything that belonged to her.	8740
	8:21	his army, however, **fled b** home.	5674
	9:18	but he isn't **coming b.**"	8740
	9:20	but he isn't **coming b** either.	8740
	9:36	*They* **went b** and told Jehu, who said,	8740
	14:20	*He was* **brought b** by horse and was buried	5951
	16:12	the king **came b** from Damascus and saw	995
	17:27	from Samaria go **b** to live there and teach	2025+9004S
	20: 5	"**Go b** and tell Hezekiah, the leader	8740
	20: 9	or *shall it* **go b** ten steps?"	8740

2Ki	20:10	"Rather, *have* it **go b** ten steps."	345+8740
	20:11	**made** the shadow **go b**	8740
	22:20	So *they* **took** her answer **b** *to* the king.	8740
	23:20	Then *he* **went b** *to* Jerusalem.	8740
1Ch	11:18	near the gate of Bethlehem and carried it **b**	995
	11:19	they risked their lives *to* **bring** it **b,**	995
	13: 3	**bring** the ark of our God **b**	6015
	19: 5	and then **come b."**	8740
	19:15	So Joab **went b** *to* Jerusalem.	995
	21: 2	Then **report** it to me so that I may know	995
	21: 4	and went throughout Israel and then **came b**	995
	21:27	and *he* **put** his sword **b** into its sheath.	8740
2Ch	6:24	when *they* **turn b** and confess your name,	8740
	6:25	of your people Israel and **bring them b** to	8740
	6:38	and if *they* **turn b** to you with all their heart	8740
	8:18	and brought **b** four hundred and fifty talents	4946+9004
	10: 5	"**Come b** to me in three days."	8740
	10:12	"**Come b** to me in three days."	8740
	11: 4	of the LORD and **turned b** from marching	8740
	15:11	from the plunder *they had* **brought b.**	995
	18:25	**send** him **b** to Amon the ruler of the city	8740
	19: 4	and **turned** them **b** to the LORD,	8740
	24:11	the chest and carry it **b** to its place.	8740
	24:19	to the people to **bring** them **b** to him,	8740
	25:13	Amaziah *had* **sent b** and had not allowed	8740
	25:14	*he* **brought b** the gods of the people of Seir.	995
	25:28	He *was* **brought b** by horse and was buried	5951
	28: 8	which *they* **carried b** to Samaria.	995
	28:11	**Send b** your fellow countrymen you have	8740
	28:15	So *they* **took** them **b**	995
	30: 9	by their captors and *will* **come b**	8740
	33:13	so *he* **brought** him **b** *to* Jerusalem and	8740
	34: 7	Then *he* **went b** *to* Jerusalem.	8740
	34:28	So *they* **took** her answer **b** *to* the king.	8740
Ne	1: 3	"Those who survived the exile and are **b** in	9004
	2: 6	and when *will you* **get b?"**	8740
	2:15	*I* **turned b** and reentered through	8740
	4: 2	**bring** the stones **b** to life	2649
	4: 4	**Turn** their insults **b** on their own heads.	8740
	5: 8	we *have* **bought b** our Jewish brothers who were sold	7864
	5: 8	only for *them to* **be sold b** to us!"	4835
	5:11	**Give b** to them immediately their fields,	8740
	5:12	"*We will* **give b,**" they said.	8740
	6: 7	Now this report *will* **get b** to the king;	9048
	8:15	into the hill country and **bring b** branches	995
	8:16	the people went out and **brought b** branches	995
	9:26	in order to **turn** them **b** to you;	8740
	13: 7	and **came b** to Jerusalem.	995
	13: 9	and then *I* **put b** *into* them the equipment	8740
	13:10	the service *had* **gone b** to their own fields.	1368
Est	2:11	Every day he **walked b** and forth near	2143
	4: 9	Hathach **went b** and reported	995
	4:13	he **sent b** this answer:	8740
	9:25	*should* **come b** onto his own head,	8740
Job	1: 7	through the earth and **going b and forth**	2143
	2: 2	through the earth and **going b and forth**	2143
	12:15	If *he* **holds b** the waters, there is drought;	6806
	20:10	his own hands *must* **give b** his wealth.	8740
	20:18	What he toiled for *he must* **give b** uneaten;	8740
	20:25	He pulls it out of his **b,**	1576
	33:30	to **turn b** his soul from the pit,	8740
	37: 4	his voice resounds, *he* **holds** nothing **b.**	6810
	41:15	His **b** has rows of shields tightly sealed	1568
Ps	6:10	*they* *will* **turn b** in sudden disgrace.	8740
	9: 3	My enemies turn **b;**	294
	18:37	*I* did not let *till they* were destroyed.	294
	28: 4	for what their hands have done and **bring b**	8740
	31:23	but the proud *he* **pays b** in full.	8966
	35: 4	may those who plot my ruin be turned **b**	294
	38: 7	My **b** is filled with searing pain;	4072
	40:14	may all who desire my ruin be turned **b**	294
	44: 5	Through you *we* **push b** our enemies;	5590
	44:18	Our hearts had not turned **b;**	294
	51:13	and sinners *will* **turn b** to you.	8740
	56: 9	my enemies will turn **b** when I call for help.	294
	70: 2	may all who desire my ruin be turned **b**	294
	70: 3	**turn b** because of their shame.	8740
	74:11	Why *do you* **hold b** your hand,	8740
	77:17	your arrows **flashed b and forth.**	2143
	78: 9	**turned b** on the day of battle;	2200
	78:66	He beat **b** his enemies;	294
	79:12	**Pay b** into the laps	8966
	89:43	*You have* **turned b** the edge of his sword	8740
	90: 3	*You* **turn** men **b** to dust, saying,	8740
	94: 2	**pay b** to the proud what they deserve.	8740
	114: 3	sea looked and fled, the Jordan turned **b;**	294
	114: 5	that you fled, O Jordan, that you turned **b,**	294
	118:13	I *was* **pushed b** and about to fall,	1890+1890
	126: 1	the LORD **brought b** the captives *to* Zion,	8740
	129: 3	Plowmen have plowed my **b**	1461
	129: 5	May all who hate Zion be turned **b**	294
Pr	3:28	not say to your neighbor, "**Come b** later;	8740
	10:13	rod is for the **b** of him who lacks judgment.	1568
	14: 3	A fool's talk brings a rod to his **b,**	1452
	17:13	If a *man* **pays b** evil for good,	8740
	19:24	*he* will not even **bring** it **b** to his mouth!	8740
	20:22	"*I'll* **pay** you **b** for this wrong!"	8966
	24:11	**hold b** those staggering toward slaughter.	3104
	24:29	*I'll* **pay** that man **b** *for* what he did."	8740
	26:15	he is too lazy to **bring** it **b** to his mouth.	8740
	26:27	*it will* **roll b** on him.	8740
Ecc	1: 5	and **hurries b** to where it rises.	8634
SS	6:13	**Come b,** come back, O Shulammite;	8740
	6:13	Come back, **come b,** O Shulammite;	8740
	6:13	**come b,** come back, that we may gaze	8740

SS	6:13	**come b,** that we may gaze on you!	8740
Isa	3:11	They *will* **be paid b**	6913
	14:27	and who *can* **turn** it **b?**	8740
	21: 9	And he **gives b** *the* answer:	6699
	21:12	and come **b** yet **again."**	8740
	28: 6	of strength to *those who* **turn b** the battle at	8740
	31: 2	*he* does not **take b** his words.	6073
	38: 8	I will make the shadow cast by the sun **go b**	345
	38: 8	So the sunlight **went b**	8740
	38:17	you have put all my sins behind your **b.**	1568
	42:14	I have been quiet and **held myself b.**	706
	42:17	will be turned **b** in utter shame.	294
	42:22	with no one to say, "**Send them b.**"	8740
	43: 6	and to the south, '*Do* not **hold** them **b.**'	3973
	48: 9	the sake of my praise *I* **hold** it **b** from you,	2641
	49: 5	the womb to be his servant to **bring** Jacob **b**	8740
	49: 6	and **bring b** those of Israel I have kept.	8740
	49:17	Your sons hasten **b,**	8740
	50: 5	*I have* not **drawn b.**	294+6047
	50: 6	I offered my **b** to those who beat me,	1568
	51:23	And you made your **b** like the ground,	1568
	54: 2	*do* not **hold b;**	3104
	54: 6	The LORD *will* **call** you **b** as	7924
	54: 7	with deep compassion *I will* **bring** you **b.**	7695
	58: 1	"Shout it aloud, *do* not **hold b.**	3104
	59: 14	So justice **is driven b,**	294+6047
	64:12	O LORD, *will you* **hold yourself b?**	706
	65: 6	not keep silent but *will* **pay b in full;**	8966
	65: 6	*I will* **pay** it **b** into their laps—	8966
Jer	4:28	I have decided and *will* not **turn b.**"	8740
	12:15	**bring** each of them **b,**	8740
	18:17	I will show them my **b** and not my face in	6902
	22:27	*You* will never **come b** to the land you long	8740
	23: 3	and *will* **bring** them **b** to their pasture,	8740
	23:20	The anger of the LORD *will* not **turn b**	8740
	24: 6	and *I will* **bring** them **b** to this land.	8740
	27:16	from the LORD's house *will* **be brought b**	8740
	27:22	'Then *I will* **bring** them **b**	6590
	28: 3	Within two years *I will* **bring b**	8740
	28: 4	also **bring b** to this place Jehoiachin son	8740
	28: 6	**bringing** the articles of the LORD's house and all the exiles **b**	8740
	29:10	to **bring** you **b** to this place.	8740
	29:14	"and *will* **bring** you **b** *from* captivity,	8740
	29:14	"and *will* **bring** you **b** to the place	8740
	30: 3	**bring** my people Israel and Judah **b**	8740
	30:24	not **turn b** until he fully accomplishes	8740
	31: 9	they will pray *as* I **bring** them **b.**	3297
	31:23	"When I **bring** them **b** *from* captivity,	8740
	32:37	*I will* **bring** them **b** to this place	8740
	33: 7	**bring** Judah and Israel **b**	8740
	34:11	and took **b** the slaves they had freed	8740
	34:16	each of *you has* **taken b** the male	8740
	34:22	and *I will* **bring** them **b** to this city.	8740
	37: 7	*will* **go b** to its own land, to Egypt.	8740
	37:20	*Do* not **send** me **b** *to* the house of Jonathan	8740
	38:26	me **b** *to* Jonathan's house	8740
	39:14	to **take** him **b** to his home.	3655
	40: 5	"**Go b** to Gedaliah son of Ahikam,	8740
	40:12	they all **came b** to the land of Judah,	8740
	42: 4	the LORD says and *will* **keep** nothing **b**	4979
	43: 5	remnant of Judah who *had* **come b** to live	8740
	46: 5	They flee in terror without **looking b,**	7155
	46:16	*let us* **go b** to our own people	8740
	48:39	How Moab turns her **b** in shame!	6902
	50: 2	**keep** nothing **b,** but say,	3948
	50:19	But *I will* **bring** Israel **b**	8740
La	1:13	a net for my feet and turned me **b.**	294
	3:64	**Pay** them **b** what they deserve, O LORD.	8740
Eze	1:13	Fire **moved b and forth** among	2143
	1:14	The creatures sped **b** and forth like flashes	2143
	9:11	the writing kit at his side **brought b** word,	8740
	11:17	from the nations and **bring** you **b** from	665
	11:17	and *I will* **give** you **b** the land	5989
	17:12	**bringing** them *b* with him to Babylon.	AIT
	23:35	and thrust me behind your **b,**	1567
	24:14	*I will* not **hold b;**	7277
	29:14	*I will* **bring** them **b** *from* captivity	8740
	31:15	*I* **held b** its streams,	4979
	33:15	if he **gives b** what he took in pledge for	8740
	34: 4	not **brought b** the strays or searched for	8740
	34:16	I will search for the lost and **bring b**	8740
	36:24	from all the countries and **bring** you **b**	995
	37: 2	He led me **b** and forth among them,	6017+6017
	37:12	*I will* **bring** you **b** to the land of Israel.	995
	37:21	and **bring** them **b** into their own land.	995
	39:25	*I will* now **bring** Jacob **b** *from* captivity	8740
	39:27	When *I have* **brought** them **b** from	8740
	40:49	and twelve cubits from **front to b.**	8145
	44: 1	the man **brought** me **b** to the outer gate of	8740
	47: 1	The man **brought** me **b** to the entrance of	8740
	47: 6	then led me **b** *to* the bank of the river.	8740
Da	4:35	No one *can* **hold b** his hand or say to him:	10411
	7: 6	And on its **b** it had four wings like those of	10128
	11:18	and *will* **turn** his insolence **b** upon him.	8740
	11:19	*he* will **turn b** toward the fortresses	8740
	11:30	Then *he* will **turn b** and vent his fury	8740
Hos	2: 7	'I will **go b** to my husband as at first,	8740
	2: 9	*I will* **take b** my wool and my linen,	5911
	2:15	There *I will* **give** her **b** her vineyards,	5989
	5:15	Then I will **go b** to my place	8740
Joel	3: 4	If *you are* **paying** me **b,**	1694
Am	1: 3	*I will* not **turn b** [my wrath].	8740
	1: 6	*I will* not **turn b** [my wrath].	8740
	1: 9	*I will* not **turn b** [my wrath].	8740
	1:11	*I will* not **turn b** [my wrath].	8740
	1:13	*I will* not **turn b** [my wrath].	8740

Am	2: 1	*I will* not **turn b** [my wrath].	8740
	2: 4	*I will* not **turn b** [my wrath].	8740
	2: 6	*I will* not **turn b** [my wrath].	8740
	7:12	**Go b** to the land of Judah.	1368
	9:14	*I will* **bring b** my exiled people Israel;	8740
Jnh	1:13	the men did their best to row **b** to land.	8740
Na	2: 4	**rushing b and forth** through the squares.	9212
	2: 8	they cry, but no *one* **turns b.**	7155
Zep	1: 6	those *who* **turn b** from following	6047
	3:15	*he* **has turned b** your enemy.	7155
Zec	8: 8	and *he* **pushed** her **b** into the basket	8959
	8: 8	*I will* **bring** them **b** to live in Jerusalem;	995
	10:10	*I will* **bring** them **b** from Egypt	8740
Mt	2:12	in a dream not *to* **go b** to Herod.	366
	11: 4	"**Go b** and report to John what you hear	NIG
	18:26	he begged, 'and *I will* **pay b** everything.'	625
	18:28	'**Pay b** what you owe me!'	625
	18:29	*I will* **pay** you **b.'**	625
	18:34	until *he* should **pay b** all he owed.	625
	21:18	*as he was* on *his* **way b** to the city,	2056
	24:18	Let no one in the field go **b** to get his cloak.	3958
	25:27	when I returned I would *have* **received** it **b**	3152
	26:43	*When he* **came b,**	2262
	26:52	"**Put** your sword **b** in its place,"	695
	28: 2	**rolled b** the stone and sat on it.	653
	28:17	and brought **b** his head on a platter.	NIG
Mk	6:28	got **b** into the boat and crossed to	4099
	8:13	*I will* **send** it **b** here shortly.' "	690
	11: 3	Let no one in the field go **b** to get his cloak.	1650+3836+3958
	13:16		
	13:35	when the owner of the house *will* **come b**—	2262
	14:40	*When he* **came b,**	2262
Lk	1:16	of the people of Israel *will he* **bring b** to	2188
	2:45	*they* **went b** to Jerusalem to look for him.	5715
	4:20	**gave** it **b** to the attendant and sat down.	625
	6:30	*do* not **demand** it **b.**	555
	6:35	**expecting to get** anything **b.**	594
	7:15	and Jesus gave him **b** to his mother.	NIG
	7:22	"**Go b** and report to John	NIG
	7:42	of them had the money *to* **pay** him **b,**	625
	9: 8	the prophets of long ago *had* **come b to life.**	482
	9:19	of long ago *has* **come b to life.**"	482
	9:42	the boy and gave him **b** to his father.	625
	9:61	but first let me go **b** and say good-by	NIG
	9:62	and looks **b** is fit for service in the kingdom	1650+3836+3958
	14:12	they *may* **invite** you **b** and so you will	511
	14:21	"The servant **came b** and reported this	4134
	15:18	and **go b** to my father and say to him:	4513
	15:27	the fattened calf because *he has* him **b** safe	655
	17: 4	and seven times **comes b** to you and says,	2188
	17:15	**came b,** praising God in a loud voice.	5715
	17:31	in the field should go **b** for anything.	1650+3836+3958
	19: 8	*I will* **pay b** four times the amount."	625
	19:13	he said, 'until *I* **come b.'**	2262
	19:23	so that *when* I **came b,**	2262
	22:32	And when you *have* **turned b,**	2188
	22:45	When he rose from prayer and **went b** to	2262
	23:11	*they* **sent** him **b** to Pilate.	402
	23:15	Neither has Herod, for *he* **sent** him **b** to us;	402
	24: 9	*When they* **came b** from the tomb,	5715
Jn	1:22	an answer to **take b** to those who sent us.	1443
	4: 3	he left Judea and **went b** once more	599
	4:16	"**Go,** call your husband and **come b.**"	1924
	4:28	the woman **went b** to the town and said to	599
	6:66	From this time many of his disciples **turned b**	599+1650+3836+3958
	7:45	the temple guards **went b** to the chief priests	2262
	10:40	Then Jesus **went b** across the Jordan to	4099
	11: 7	"Let us go **b** to Judea."	4099
	11: 8	and yet *you are* **going b** there?"	5632
	11:28	she **went b** and called her sister Mary aside.	599
	13:25	**Leaning b** against Jesus, he asked him,	404
	14: 3	I will come **b** and take you to be with me	4099
	14:28	'I am going away and *I am* **coming b**	2262
	16:28	now I am leaving the world and going **b** to	NIG
	18: 6	drew **b** and fell to the ground.	1650+3836+3958
	18:16	who was known to the high priest, came **b,**	NIG
	18:33	Pilate then **went b** inside the palace,	4099
	18:40	They shouted **b,** "No, not him!	4099
	19: 9	and he **went b** inside the palace.	4099
	20:10	Then the disciples **went b** to their homes,	599
	21:20	the one who *had* **leaned b** against Jesus at	404
Ac	1:11	*will* **come b** in the same way you have seen	2262
	4:23	Peter and John **went b** to their own people	2262
	5: 2	With his wife's full knowledge *he* **kept b** part of the money	3802
	5:22	So they **went b** and reported,	418
	7:16	Their bodies *were* **brought b** to Shechem	3572
	7:34	Now come, *I will* **send** you **b** to Egypt.'	690
	7:39	and in their hearts **turned b** to Egypt.	5138
	10: 5	Now send men to Joppa *to* **bring b**	3569
	10:16	and immediately the sheet *was* **taken b**	377
	12:14	so overjoyed she ran **b** without opening it	NIG
	14:20	he got up and went **b** into the city.	NIG
	14:26	From Attalia they sailed **b** to Antioch,	NIG
	15:36	"Let us **go b** and visit the brothers in all	2188
	18:21	"*I will* **come b** if it is God's will."	366
	20: 3	he decided *to* **go b** through Macedonia.	5715
Ro	9:20	who are you, O man, to **talk b** to God?	503
1Co	15:34	**Come b** to *your* **senses**	1729
2Co	1:16	on my way to Macedonia and to come **b**	4099
Gal	2:12	*he* began to **draw b** and separate himself	5713
		that you are turning **b** to those weak	4099
Eph	4:14	tossed **b** and forth by the waves,	3115
Php	2:25	But I think it is necessary to send **b**	NIG

1Th	5:15	that nobody **pays b** wrong for wrong,	625
2Th	1: 6	*He will* **pay b** trouble	500
	2: 6	now you know what *is* **holding** him **b**,	2988
	2: 7	the one who now **holds** it **b** will continue	2988
Tit	2: 9	to try to please them, not to **talk b** to them,	515
Phm	1:12	**sending** him—who is my very heart—**b**	402
	1:15	a little while was that *you might* **have** him **b**	600
	1:19	I *will* **pay** it **b**—	702
Heb	6: 6	*to be* **brought b** to repentance,	362
	10:38	he **shrinks b**, I will not be pleased with him."	5713
	10:39	not *of* those who **shrink b** and are destroyed,	5714
	11:19	he **did receive** Isaac **b** from death.	3152
	11:35	Women received **b** their dead,	NIG
	13:20	the blood of the eternal covenant **brought b**	343
Jas	5:19	the truth and someone **should bring** him **b**,	2188
2Pe	2:13	They will be paid **b** with harm for	NIG
	2:22	that is washed goes **b** to her wallowing in	NIG
Rev	4: 6	in front and in **b**.	3957
	7: 1	**holding b** the four winds of the earth	3195
	12: 7	and the dragon and his angels fought **b**.	NIG
	18: 6	**Give b** to her as she has given;	625
	18: 6	**pay** her **b double** for what she has done.	1486+1488

BACKBITING, BACKBITINGS (KJV)
See SLY, SLANDER

BACKBONE (1) [BACK, BONE]
Lev	3: 9	the entire fat tail cut off close to the **b**,	6782

BACKGROUND (2) [BACK]
Est	2:10	not revealed her nationality and **family b**,	4580
	2:20	But Esther had kept secret her **family b**	4580

BACKS (24) [BACK]
Ex	23:27	I will make all your enemies turn their **b**	6902
Jos	7:12	they turn their **b** and run	6902
	23:13	whips on your **b** and thorns in your eyes,	7396
2Sa	22:41	You made my enemies turn their **b** in flight,	6902
2Ch	29: 6	and turned their **b** on him.	6902
Ne	9:26	they put your law behind their **b**.	1567
	9:29	Stubbornly they turned their **b** on you,	4190
Ps	18:40	You made my enemies turn their **b** in flight,	6902
	21:12	for you will make them turn their **b**	8900
	66:11	into prison and laid burdens on our **b**.	5516
	69:23	and their **b** be bent forever.	5516
Pr	19:29	and beatings for the **b** *of* fools.	1568
	26: 3	and a rod for the **b** *of* fools!	1568
Isa	1: 4	the Holy One of Israel and turned their **b**	294
	30: 6	the envoys carry their riches on donkeys' **b**,	4190
	59:13	turning our **b** on our God,	339
Jer	2:27	They have turned their **b** to me and	6902
	32:33	They turned their **b** to me and	6902
Eze	8:16	*With* their **b** toward the temple of	294
	10:12	Their entire bodies, including their **b**,	1461
	29: 7	you broke and their **b** were wrenched.	5516
Zec	7:11	stubbornly they turned their **b** and stopped	4190
Ro	11:10	and their **b** be bent forever."	3822
2Pe	2:21	to have known it and then *to* **turn their b**	5715

BACKSLIDERS, BACKSLIDING (KJV)
See also FAITHLESS, STUBBORN, UNFAITHFUL, WAYWARDNESS

BACKSLIDING (5) [BACK]
Jer	2:19	your **b** will rebuke you.	5412
	3:22	I will cure you of **b**."	5412
	14: 7	our **b** is great; we have sinned against you.	5412
	15: 6	"You keep on **b**.	294
Eze	37:23	for I will save them from all their sinful **b**,	5412

BACKSLIDINGS (1) [BACK]
Jer	5: 6	for their rebellion is great and their **b** many.	5412

BACKWARD (5) [BACK]
Ge	9:23	in **b** and covered their father's nakedness.	345
	49:17	the horse's heels so that its rider tumbles **b**.	294
1Sa	4:18	Eli fell **b** off his chair by the side of	345
Isa	28:13	so that they will go and fall **b**,	294
Jer	7:24	They went **b** and not forward.	294+4200

BACUTH See ALLON BACUTH

BAD (65) [BADLY]
Ge	18:21	down and see if what they have done is as **b**	3986
	31:24	anything to Jacob, either good or **b**."	8273
	31:29	to say anything to Jacob, either good or **b**.'	8273
	37: 2	and he brought their father a **b** report	8273
Ex	7:21	and the river **smelled** so **b**	944
Lev	27:10	or substitute a good one for a **b** *one*,	8273
	27:10	or a **b** *one* for a good one;	8273
	27:12	who will judge its quality as good or **b**.	8273
	27:14	judge its quality as good or **b**.	8273
	27:33	He must not pick out the good from the **b**	8273
Nu	13:19	Is it good or **b**?	8273
	13:32	among the Israelites a **b** report *about*	1804
	14:36	against them by spreading a **b** report	1804
Nu	14:37	the **b** report about the land were struck	8273
	24:13	good or **b**, to go beyond the command of	8288
Dt	1:39	not yet know good from **b**—	8273
	22:14	and slanders her and gives her a **b** name,	8273
	22:19	an Israelite virgin a **b** name.	8273
2Sa	13:22	word to Amnon, either good or **b**;	8273
1Ki	14: 6	I have been sent to you with **b news**.	7997
	22: 8	about me, but always **b**.	8273
	22:18	about me, but only **b**?"	8273
2Ki	2:19	water is **b** and the land is unproductive."	8273
2Ch	18: 7	about me, but always **b**.	8288
	18:17	about me, but only **b**?"	8273
Ne	6:13	and then they would give me a **b** name	8273
Ps	112: 7	He will have no fear of **b news**;	8273
Pr	25:10	and you will never lose your **b reputation.**	1804
	25:19	Like a **b** tooth or a lame foot is reliance on	8317
Ecc	7:14	but when times are **b**, consider:	8288
	8: 3	Do not stand up for a **b** cause,	8273
	9: 2	the good and the **b**,	8273
	10: 1	give perfume a **b** smell,	944+5580
Isa	5: 2	but it yielded only **b** fruit.	946
	5: 4	why did it yield only **b**?	946
	41:23	Do something, whether good or **b**,	8317
Jer	24: 2	so **b** they could not be eaten.	8278
	24: 3	poor ones are so **b** they cannot be eaten."	8278
	24: 8	which are so **b** they cannot be eaten,'	8278
	29:17	like poor figs that are so **b** they cannot	8278
	49:23	for they have heard **b** news.	8273
Zep	1:12	will do nothing, either good or **b**.'	8317
Mt	6:23	But if your eyes are **b**,	4505
	7:17	but a **b** tree bears bad fruit.	4911
	7:17	but a bad tree bears **b** fruit.	4505
	7:18	A good tree cannot bear **b** fruit,	4505
	7:18	and a **b** tree cannot bear good fruit.	4911
	12:33	or make a tree **b** and its fruit will be bad,	4911
	12:33	or make a tree bad and its fruit will be **b**,	4911
	13:48	but threw the **b** away.	4911
	22:10	both good and **b**,	4505
Mk	9:39	the next moment **say** anything **b** about me,	2800
Lk	6:43	"No good tree bears **b** fruit.	4911
	6:43	nor does a **b** tree bear good fruit.	4911
	11:34	But when they are **b**,	4505
	16:25	while Lazarus received **b** *things*,	2805
Jn	11:39	"by this time *there is* a **b** odor,	3853
Ac	17: 5	up some **b** characters from the marketplace,	4505
	28:21	from there has reported or said anything **b**	4505
Ro	9:11	or had done anything good or **b**—	5765
1Co	15:33	"**B** company corrupts good character."	2805
2Co	5:10	whether good or **b**.	5765
	6: 8	**b report** and good report;	1556
2Ti	3:13	and impostors will go **from b to worse,**	2093+3836+5937
Tit	2: 8	be ashamed because they have nothing **b**	5765

BADGERS' (KJV) See SEA COWS

BADLY (4) [BAD]
Ge	50:17	wrongs they committed in treating you *so* **b**.	8288
1Sa	24:17	but I have treated you **b**.	8288
2Ch	35:23	I am **b** wounded."	4394
Mk	12:27	You are **b** mistaken!"	4498

BAFFLED (2)
Da	5: 9	His nobles *were* **b**.	10698
Ac	9:22	and more powerful and **b** the Jews living	5177

BAG (13) [BAGS, BAGGAGE]
Dt	25:13	not have two differing weights in your **b**—	3967
1Sa	17:40	put them in the pouch of his shepherd's **b**	3998
	17:49	Reaching into his **b** and taking out a stone,	3998
Job	14:17	My offenses will be sealed up in a **b**;	7655
Pr	16:11	all the weights in the **b** are of his making.	3967
Mic	6:11	with a **b** *of* false weights?	3967
Mt	10:10	take no **b** for the journey, or extra tunic,	4385
Mk	6: 8	no bread, no **b**, no money in your belts.	4385
Lk	9: 3	no staff, no **b**, no bread, no money,	4385
	10: 4	Do not take a purse or **b** or sandals;	4385
	22:35	**b** or sandals, did you lack anything?"	4385
	22:36	take it, and also a **b**;	4385
Jn	12: 6	keeper of the **money b**,	1186+2400

BAGGAGE (1) [BAG]
1Sa	10:22	"Yes, he has hidden himself among the **b**."	3998

BAGS (5) [BAG]
Ge	42:25	Joseph gave orders to fill their **b** with grain,	3998
	43:11	in your **b** and take them down to the man as	3998
2Ki	5:23	tied up the two talents of silver in two **b**,	3038
	12:10	the temple of the LORD and **put** it **into b.**	7443
Isa	46: 6	from their **b** and weigh out silver on	3967

BAHARUMITE (1)
1Ch	11:33	Azmaveth the **B**, Eliahba the Shaalbonite,	1049

BAHURIM (5)
2Sa	3:16	weeping behind her all the way to **B**.	1038
	16: 5	As King David approached **B**,	1038
	17:18	and went to the house of a man in **B**.	1038
	19:16	Shimei son of Gera, the Benjamite from **B**,	1038
1Ki	2: 8	the Benjamite from **B**,	1038

BAJITH (KJV) See TEMPLE

BAKBAKKAR (1)
1Ch	9:15	**B**, Heresh, Galal and Mattaniah son	1320

BAKBUK (2)
Ezr	2:51	**B**, Hakupha, Harhur,	1317
Ne	7:53	**B**, Hakupha, Harhur,	1317

BAKBUKIAH (3)
Ne	11:17	**B**, second among his associates;	1319
	12: 9	**B** and Unni, their associates,	1319
	12:25	Mattaniah, **B**, Obadiah, Meshullam,	1319

BAKE (9) [BAKED, BAKER, BAKERS, BAKES, BAKING]
Ge	11: 3	let's make bricks and **b** them **thoroughly**."	4200+8596+8599
	18: 6	and knead it and **b** some bread.	6913
Ex	16:23	So **b** what you want to bake	684
	16:23	*to* **b** and boil what you want to boil.	684
Lev	24: 5	"Take fine flour and **b** twelve loaves	684
	26:26	ten women *will be able to* **b** your bread	684
Eze	4:12	**b** it in the sight of the people,	6383
	4:15	"I will let you **b** your bread	6913
	46:20	the guilt offering and the sin offering and **b**	684

BAKED (14) [BAKE]
Ge	40:17	In the top basket were all kinds of **b** goods	685+4407+5126
Ex	12:39	they **b** cakes of unleavened bread.	684
Lev	2: 4	"'If you bring a grain offering **b** *in*	4418
	6:17	*It must not be* **b** with yeast;	684
	7: 9	Every grain offering **b** in an oven or cooked	684
	23:17	of an ephah of fine flour, **b** with yeast, as	684
1Sa	28:24	kneaded it and **b** bread without yeast.	684
2Sa	13: 8	made the bread in his sight and **b** it.	1418
1Ki	19: 6	a cake of bread **b** *from* hot coals,	8363
2Ki	4:42	of barley bread **b** *from* the first ripe grain,	4312
Isa	44:19	I even **b** bread over its coals,	684
Da	2:33	its feet partly of iron and partly of **b** clay,	10279
	2:41	of **b** clay and partly of iron, so this will be	10279
	2:43	you saw the iron mixed with **b** clay,	10279+10298

BAKEMEATS (KJV) See BAKED GOODS

BAKER (8) [BAKE]
Ge	40: 1	the cupbearer and the **b** of the king	685
	40: 2	the chief cupbearer and the chief **b**,	685
	40: 5	cupbearer and the **b** of the king of Egypt,	685
	40:16	When the chief **b** saw that Joseph had given	685
	40:20	the chief **b** in the presence of his officials:	685
	40:22	but he hanged the chief **b**,	685
	41:10	and the chief **b** in the house of the captain	685
Hos	7: 4	an oven whose fire the **b** need not stir from	685

BAKERS (2) [BAKE]
1Sa	8:13	to be perfumers and cooks and **b**.	685
Jer	37:21	from the street of the **b** each day until all	685

BAKES (1) [BAKE]
Isa	44:15	he kindles a fire and **b** bread.	684

BAKING (3) [BAKE]
Ge	19: 3	**b** bread without yeast, and they ate.	684
1Ch	9:31	was entrusted with the responsibility for **b**	5126
	23:29	the **b** and the mixing,	4679

BALAAM (59) [BALAAM'S]
Nu	22: 5	sent messengers to summon **B** son of Beor,	1189
	22: 7	When they came to **B**,	1189
	22: 8	"Spend the night here," **B** said to them,	1189
	22: 9	God came to **B** and asked, "Who are these	1189
	22:10	**B** said to God, "Balak son of Zippor,	1189
	22:12	But God said to **B**, "Do not go with them.	1189
	22:13	The next morning **B** got up and said	1189
	22:14	"**B** refused to come with us."	1189
	22:16	They came to **B** and said: "This is what	1189
	22:18	But **B** answered them, "Even if Balak gave	1189
	22:20	That night God came to **B** and said,	1189
	22:21	**B** got up in the morning,	1189
	22:22	**B** was riding on his donkey,	2085S
	22:23	**B** beat her to get her back on the road.	1189
	22:27	she lay down under **B**,	1189
	22:28	and she said to **B**, "What have I done to you	1189
	22:29	**B** answered the donkey, "You made a fool	1189
	22:30	The donkey said to **B**, "Am I not your own	1189
	22:34	**B** said to the angel of the LORD,	1189
	22:35	The angel of the LORD said to **B**,	1189
	22:35	So **B** went with the princes of Balak.	1189
	22:36	When Balak heard that **B** was coming,	1189
	22:37	Balak said to **B**, "Did I not send you	1189
	22:38	"Well, I have come to you now," **B** replied.	1189
	22:39	Then **B** went with Balak to Kiriath Huzoth.	1189
	22:40	to **B** and the princes who were with him.	1189
	22:41	The next morning Balak took **B** up	1189
	23: 1	**B** said, "Build me seven altars here,	1189
	23: 2	Balak did as **B** said,	1189
	23: 3	Then **B** said to Balak, "Stay here	1189

Nu 23: 4 God met with him, and **B** said, 1189
23: 7 Then **B** uttered his oracle: NIH
23:11 Balak said to **B**, "What have you done 1189
23:15 **B** said to Balak, "Stay here NIH
23:16 The LORD met with **B** and put a message 1189
23:25 Then Balak said to **B**, "Neither curse them 1189
23:26 **B** answered, "Did I not tell you 1189
23:27 Then Balak said to **B**, "Come, 1189
23:28 And Balak took **B** to the top of Peor, 1189
23:29 **B** said, "Build me seven altars here, 1189
23:30 Balak did as **B** had said, 1189
24: 1 when **B** saw that it pleased the LORD 1189
24: 2 When **B** looked out and saw Israel 1189
24: 3 "The oracle of **B** son of Beor, 1189
24:10 Then Balak's anger burned against **B**. 1189
24:12 **B** answered Balak, "Did I not tell 1189
24:15 "The oracle of **B** son of Beor, 1189
24:20 Then **B** saw Amalek and uttered his oracle: NIH
24:25 Then **B** got up and returned home 1189
31: 8 also killed **B** son of Beor with the sword. 1189
Dt 23: 4 and they hired **B** son of Beor from Pethor 1189
23: 5 the LORD your God would not listen to **B** 1189
Jos 13:22 the Israelites had put to death **B** son 1189
24: 9 for **B** son of Beor to put a curse on you. 1189
24:10 But I would not listen to **B**, 1189
Ne 13: 2 with food and water but had hired **B** to call 1189
Mic 6: 5 of Moab counseled and what **B** son 1189
2Pe 2:15 to follow the way of **B** son of Beor, 962
Rev 2:14 hold to the teaching of **B**, 962

BALAAM'S (5) [BALAAM]

Nu 22:25 crushing **B** foot against it. 1189
22:31 Then the LORD opened **B** eyes, 1189
23: 5 The LORD put a message in **B** mouth 1189
31:16 the ones who followed **B** advice and were 1189
Jude 1:11 they have rushed for profit into **B** error; 962

BALAC (KJV) See BALAK

BALADAN (2)

2Ki 20:12 that time Merodach-Baladan son of **B** king 1156
Isa 39: 1 that time Merodach-Baladan son of **B** king 1156

BALAH (1)

Jos 19: 3 Hazar Shual, **B**, Ezem, 1163

BALAK (36) [BALAK'S]

Nu 22: 2 Now **B** son of Zippor saw all that Israel 1192
22: 4 So **B** son of Zippor, who was king of Moab 1192
22: 5 **B** said: "A people has come out of Egypt; NIH
22: 7 they told him what **B** had said. 1192
22:10 Balaam said to God, "**B** son of Zippor, 1192
22:14 the Moabite princes returned to **B** and said, 1192
22:15 Then **B** sent other princes, 1192
22:16 "This is what **B** son of Zippor says: 1192
22:18 if **B** gave me his palace filled with silver 1192
22:35 So Balaam went with the princes of **B**. 1192
22:36 When **B** heard that Balaam was coming, 1192
22:37 **B** said to Balaam, "Did I not send you 1192
22:39 Balaam went with **B** to Kiriath Huzoth. 1192
22:40 **B** sacrificed cattle and sheep, 1192
22:41 The next morning **B** took Balaam up 1192
23: 2 **B** did as Balaam said, 1192
23: 3 Then Balaam said to **B**, "Stay here 1192
23: 5 "Go back to **B** and give him this message." 1192
23: 7 "**B** brought me from Aram, 1192
23:11 **B** said to Balaam, "What have you done 1192
23:13 Then **B** said to him, "Come with me 1192
23:15 Balaam said to **B**, "Stay here 1192
23:16 "Go back to **B** and give him this message." 1192
23:17 **B** asked him, "What did the LORD say?" 1192
23:18 Then he uttered his oracle: "Arise, **B**, 1192
23:25 Then **B** said to Balaam, "Neither curse 1192
23:27 Then **B** said to Balaam, "Come, 1192
23:28 And **B** took Balaam to the top of Peor, 1192
23:30 **B** did as Balaam had said, 1192
24:12 Balaam answered **B**, "Did I not tell 1192
24:13 if **B** gave me his palace filled with silver 1192
24:25 and **B** went his own way. 1192
Jos 24: 9 When **B** son of Zippor, the king of Moab, 1192
Jdg 11:25 Are you better than **B** son of Zippor, 1192
Mic 6: 5 remember what **B** king of Moab counseled 1192
Rev 2:14 who taught **B** to entice the Israelites to sin 963

BALAK'S (2) [BALAK]

Nu 22:13 up and said to **B** princes, 1192
24:10 Then **B** anger burned against Balaam. 1192

BALANCE (3) [BALANCES]

Lev 25:27 since he sold it and refund the **b** to the man 6369
Ps 62: 9 if weighed on a **b**, they are nothing; 4404
Isa 40:12 on the scales and the hills in a **b**? 4404

BALANCES (1) [BALANCE]

Pr 16:11 Honest scales and **b** are from the LORD; 7144

BALD (5) [BALDHEAD, BALDNESS]

Lev 13:40 "When a man has lost his hair and is **b**, 7944
13:41 the front of his scalp and has a **b** forehead, 1477
13:42 if he has a reddish-white sore on his **b** head 7949
Isa 3:17 the LORD will make their scalps **b**." 6867

BALDHEAD (2) [BALD]

2Ki 2:23 "Go on up, you **b**!" 7944
2:23 "Go on up, you **b**!" 7944

BALDNESS (1) [BALD]

Isa 3:24 instead of well-dressed hair, **b**; 7947

BALL (1)

Isa 22:18 like a **b** and throw you into a large country. 1885

BALM (7)

Ge 37:25 **b** and myrrh, and they were on their way 7661
43:11 a little **b** and a little honey, 7661
2Ch 28:15 food and drink, and healing **b**. 6057
Jer 8:22 Is there no **b** in Gilead? 7661
46:11 "Go up to Gilead and get **b**, 7661
51: 8 Get **b** for her pain; 7661
Eze 27:17 honey, oil and **b** for your wares. 7661

BALSAM (4)

2Sa 5:23 and attack them in front of the **b** trees. 1132
5:24 of marching in the tops of the **b** trees, 1132
1Ch 14:14 and attack them in front of the **b** trees. 1132
14:15 of marching in the tops of the **b** trees, 1132

BAMAH (1)

Eze 20:29 (It is called **B** to this day.) 1196

BAMOTH (2) [BAMOTH BAAL]

Nu 21:19 from Nahaliel to **B**, 1199
21:20 from **B** to the valley in Moab where the top 1199

BAMOTH BAAL (2) [BAAL, BAMOTH]

Nu 22:41 Balak took Balaam up to **B**, 1200
Jos 13:17 including Dibon, **B**, Beth Baal Meon, 1200

BAN (1)

1Ch 2: 7 on Israel by violating the **b** 5085

BAND (16) [BANDED, BANDS]

Ge 49:19 "Gad will be attacked by a **b** of raiders, 1522
Ex 39:23 and a **b** around this opening, 8557
2Sa 1:10 that was on his head and the **b** on his arm 731
23:13 while a **b** of Philistines was encamped in 2653
1Ki 7:35 the stand there was a **circular b** half 6017+6318
11:24 of a **b** of rebels when David destroyed 1522
2Ki 13:21 suddenly they saw a **b** of raiders; 1522
19:31 and out of Mount Zion a **b** of survivors. 7129
1Ch 11:15 while a **b** of Philistines was encamped in 4722
Ps 22:16 a **b** of evil men has encircled me, 6337
78:49 a **b** of destroying angels. 5449
86:14 a **b** of ruthless men seeks my life— 6337
94:21 They **b** together against the righteous 1518
Isa 31: 4 a **whole b** of shepherds is called together 4850
37:32 and out of Mount Zion a **b** of survivors. 7129
Ac 5:37 the days of the census and led a **b** of people NIG

BANDAGED (2)

Isa 1: 6 not cleansed or **b** or soothed with oil. 2502
Lk 10:34 He went to him and **b** his wounds, 2866

BANDED (4) [BAND]

Nu 14:35 which has **b** together against me. 3585
16:11 and all your followers have **b** together. 3585
27: 3 who **b** together against the LORD, 3585
2Sa 23:11 When the Philistines **b** together at a place 665+2021+2653+4200

BANDIT (3) [BANDITS]

Pr 6:11 like a **b** and scarcity like an armed man. 2143
23:28 Like a **b** she lies in wait, 3167
24:34 like a **b** and scarcity like an armed man. 2143

BANDITS (3) [BANDIT]

Ezr 8:31 and he protected us from enemies and **b** 741
Hos 7: 1 **b** rob in the streets; 1522
2Co 11:26 in danger from **b**, in danger 3334

BANDS (17) [BAND]

Ex 27:10 and with silver hooks and **b** on the posts. 3122
27:11 and with silver hooks and **b** on the posts. 3122
27:17 around the courtyard are to have silver **b** 3138
36:38 the tops of the posts and their **b** with gold 3122
38:10 and with silver hooks and **b** on the posts. 3122
38:11 with silver hooks and **b** on the posts. 3122
38:12 with silver hooks and **b** on the posts. 3122
38:17 The hooks and on the posts were silver, 3122
38:17 all the posts of the courtyard had silver **b**. 3138
38:19 Their hooks and **b** were silver, 3122
38:28 and to make their **b**. 3138
2Sa 4: 2 Now Saul's son had two men who were leaders of raiding **b**, 1522
2Ki 5: 2 Now **b** from Aram had gone out 1522
6:23 So the **b** from Aram stopped raiding 1522
1Ch 12:18 and made them leaders of his raiding **b**. 1522

Mic 1:16 make yourselves as **b** as the vulture, 7947+8143

BANGLES (1)

Isa 3:18 **b** and headbands and crescent necklaces, 6577

BANI (14)

1Ch 6:46 the son of **B**, the son of Shemer, 1220
9: 4 the son of Imri, the son of **B**, 1220
Ezr 2:10 of **B** 642 1220
8:10 of the descendants of **B**, Shelomith son NIH
10:29 From the descendants of **B**: 1220
10:34 From the descendants of **B**: 1220
Ne 3:17 by the Levites under Rehum son of **B**. 1220
8: 7 Jeshua, **B**, Sherebiah, Jamin, Akkub, 1220
9: 4 Jeshua, **B**, Kadmiel, Shebaniah, Bunni, 1220
9: 4 Bunni, Sherebiah, **B** and Kenani— 1220
9: 5 And the Levites—Jeshua, Kadmiel, **B**, 1220
10:13 Hodiah, **B** and Beninu. 1220
10:14 Parosh, Pahath-Moab, Elam, Zattu, **B**, 1220
11:22 in Jerusalem was Uzzi son of **B**, 1220

BANISH (11) [BANISHED, BANISHMENT]

2Ki 13:23 or **b** them from his presence. 8959
Ps 5:10 **B** them for their many sins, 5615
125: 1 to crooked ways the LORD will **b** with 2143
Ecc 11:10 **b** anxiety from your heart and cast off 6073
Jer 8: 3 Wherever I **b** them, 5615
24: 9 wherever I **b** them, 5615
25:10 I will **b** from them the sounds of joy 6
27:10 I will **b** you and you will perish. 5615
27:15 I will **b** you and you will perish, 5615
32:37 where I **b** them in my furious anger 5615
Zec 13: 2 I will **b** the names of the idols from 4162

BANISHED (16) [BANISH]

Ge 3:23 So the LORD God **b** him from the Garden 8938
Dt 30: 4 if you have been **b** to the most distant land 5615
2Sa 14:13 for the king has not brought back his **b** son? 5615
14:14 so that a **b** person may not remain estranged 5615
1Ch 12: 1 while he was **b** from the presence 6806
Job 18:18 into darkness and is **b** from the world. 5610
20: 8 **b** like a vision of the night. 5610
30: 5 They were **b** from their fellow men, 1763
Isa 24:11 all gaiety is **b** from the earth. 1655
Jer 16:15 of all the countries where he had **b** them.' 5615
23: 8 of all the countries where he had **b** them.' 5615
23:12 be **b** to darkness and there they will fall. 5615
29:14 and places where I have **b** you," 5615
Jnh 2: 4 I said, 'I have been **b** from your sight; 1763
Zec 5: 3 every thief will be **b**, 5927
5: 3 everyone who swears falsely will be **b**. 5927

BANISHMENT (1) [BANISH]

Ezr 7:26 **b**, confiscation of property, 10744

BANK (13) [BANKERS, BANKS, EMBANKMENT]

Ge 41:17 "In my dream I was standing on the **b** of 8557
Ex 2: 3 in it and put it among the reeds along the **b** 8557
2: 5 along the river **b**. 3338
7:15 Wait on the **b** of the Nile to meet him, 8557
Jos 13:23 of the Reubenites was the **b** of the Jordan. 1473
2Ki 2:13 and went back and stood on the **b** of 8557
Eze 47: 6 Then he led me back to the **b** of the river. 8557
Da 10: 4 I was standing on the **b** of the great river, 3338
12: 5 one on this **b** of the river and one on 8557
12: 5 of the river and one on the opposite **b**. 8557
Mt 8:32 the whole herd rushed down the **steep b** into 3204
Mk 5:13 the **steep b** into the lake and were drowned. 3204
Lk 8:33 the **steep b** into the lake and was drowned. 3204

BANKERS (1) [BANK]

Mt 25:27 on deposit with the **b**, 5545

BANKS (3) [BANK]

1Ch 12:15 when it was overflowing all its **b**, 1536
Isa 8: 7 run over all its **b** 1536
Eze 47:12 Fruit trees of all kinds will grow on both **b** 8557

BANNER (15) [BANNERS]

Ex 17:15 an altar and called it The LORD is my **B**. 5812
Ps 60: 4 you have raised a **b** to be unfurled against 5812
SS 2: 4 and his **b** over me is love. 1840
Isa 5:26 He lifts up a **b** for the distant nations, 5812
11:10 that day the Root of Jesse will stand as a **b** 5812
11:12 He will raise a **b** for the nations and gather 5812
13: 2 Raise a **b** on a bare hilltop, shout to them; 5812
18: 3 when a **b** is raised on the mountains, 5812
30:17 like a **b** on a hill." 5812
49:22 I will lift up my **b** to the peoples; 5812
62:10 Raise a **b** for the nations. 5812
Jer 50: 2 lift up a **b** and proclaim it; 5812
51:12 Lift up a **b** against the walls of Babylon! 5812
51:27 "Lift up a **b** in the land! 5812
Eze 27: 7 and served as your **b**; 5812

BANNERS (3) [BANNER]

Nu 2: 2 each man under his standard with the **b** 253
Ps 20: 5 and will **lift up** our **b** in the name 1839

SS   6: 4   majestic as **troops** with **b**.   1839

BANQUET (31) [BANQUETS]

1Sa	25:36	he was in the house holding a **b** like that of	5492
Est	1: 3	of his reign he gave a **b** for all his nobles	5492
	1: 5	the king gave a **b**, lasting seven days,	5492
	1: 9	Queen Vashti also gave a **b** for the women	5492
	2:18	And the king gave a great **b**,	5492
	2:18	the king gave a great banquet, Esther's **b**,	5492
	5: 4	come today to a **b** I have prepared for him."	5492
	5: 5	to the **b** Esther had prepared.	5492
	5: 8	to the **b** I will prepare for them.	5492
	5:12	to accompany the king to the **b** she gave.	5492
	6:14	to the **b** Esther had prepared.	5492
	7: 8	from the palace garden to the **b** hall,	3516+5492
SS	2: 4	He has taken me to the **b** hall,	1074+3516
Isa	25: 6	a **b** of aged wine—	5492
Da	5: 1	a great **b** for a thousand of his nobles	10389
	5:10	came into the **b** hall.	10447
Mt	22: 2	king who prepared a wedding **b** for his son.	1141
	22: 3	to those who had been invited to the **b**	1141
	22: 4	Come to the **wedding b**.'	1141
	22: 8	'The **wedding b** is ready,	1141
	22: 9	and invite to the **b** anyone you find.'	1141
	25:10	in with him to the **wedding b**.	1141
Mk	6:21	On his birthday Herod gave a **b**	1270
Lk	5:29	Levi held a great **b** for Jesus at his house,	1531
	12:36	for their master to return from a **wedding b**,	1270
	14:13	But when you give a **b**, invite the poor,	1531
	14:16	"A certain man was preparing a great **b**	1270
	14:17	At the time of the **b** he sent his servant	1270
	14:24	a taste of my **b**.'"	1270
Jn	2: 8	and take it to the **master of the b**."	804
	2: 9	and the **master of the b** tasted the water	804

BANQUETS (4) [BANQUET]

Isa	5:12	They have harps and lyres at their **b**,	5492
Mt	23: 6	of honor at **b** and the most important seats	1270
Mk	12:39	and the places of honor at **b**.	1270
Lk	20:46	and the places of honor at **b**.	1270

BAPTISM (20) [BAPTIZE]

Mt	21:25	John's **b**—where did it come from?	967
Mk	1: 4	in the desert region and preaching a **b**	967
	10:38	be baptized with the **b** I am baptized with?"	967
	10:39	be baptized with the **b** I am baptized with,	967
	11:30	John's **b**—was it from heaven, or from men?	967
Lk	3: 3	a **b** of repentance for the forgiveness	967
	12:50	But I have a **b** to undergo,	966+967
	20: 4	John's **b**—was it from heaven,	967
Ac	1:22	beginning from John's **b** to the time	967
	10:37	in Galilee after the **b** that John preached—	967
	13:24	John preached repentance and **b** to all	967
	18:25	though he knew only the **b** of John.	967
	19: 3	"Then what **b** did you receive?"	966
	19: 3	"John's **b**," they replied.	967
	19: 4	"John's **b** was a baptism of repentance.	966
	19: 4	"John's baptism was a **b** of repentance.	967
Ro	6: 4	with him through **b** into death in order that,	967
Eph	4: 5	one Lord, one faith, one **b**;	967
Col	2:12	in **b** and raised with him through your faith	967
1Pe	3:21	and this water symbolizes **b** that	967

BAPTISMS (1) [BAPTIZE]

Heb	6: 2	instruction about **b**, the laying on	968

BAPTIST (14) [BAPTIZE]

Mt	3: 1	In those days John the **B** came,	969
	11:11	not risen anyone greater than John the **B**;	969
	11:12	From the days of John the **B** until now,	969
	14: 2	"This is John the **B**;	969
	14: 8	on a platter the head of John the **B**."	969
	17:13	They replied, "Some say John the **B**;	969
	17:13	to them about John the **B**.	969
Mk	6:14	"John the **B** has been raised from the dead,	966
	6:24	"The head of John the **B**," she answered.	969
	6:25	now the head of John the **B** on a platter."	969
	8:28	They replied, "Some say John the **B**;	969
Lk	7:20	they said, "John the **B** sent us to you to ask,	969
	7:33	For John the **B** came neither eating bread	969
	9:19	They replied, "Some say John the **B**;	969

BAPTIZE (12) [BAPTISM, BAPTISMS, BAPTIST, BAPTIZED, BAPTIZING]

Mt	3:11	"I **b** you with water for repentance.	966
	3:11	He will **b** you with the Holy Spirit and	966
Mk	1: 8	I **b** you with water,	966
	1: 8	but he will **b** you with the Holy Spirit."	966
Lk	3:16	"I **b** you with water.	966
	3:16	He will **b** you with the Holy Spirit and	966
Jn	1:25	then do you **b** if you are not the Christ,	966
	1:26	"I **b** with water," John replied,	966
	1:33	except that the one who sent me to **b**	966
	1:33	down and remain is he who will **b** with	966
1Co	1:14	not **b** any of you except Crispus and Gaius,	966
	1:17	For Christ did not send me to **b**,	966

BAPTIZED (50) [BAPTIZE]

Mt	3: 6	they were **b** by him in the Jordan River.	966
	3:13	Galilee to the Jordan to be **b** by John.	966+3836
	3:14	saying, "I need to be **b** by you,	966
	3:16	As soon as Jesus was **b**,	966

Mk	1: 5	they were **b** by him in the Jordan River.	966
	1: 9	from Nazareth in Galilee and was **b** by John	966
	10:38	"Can you drink the cup I drink or be **b** with	966
	10:38	be baptized with the baptism I am **b** with?"	966
	10:39	be **b** with the baptism I am baptized with,	966
	10:39	be baptized with the baptism I am **b** with,	966
	16:16	Whoever believes and is **b** will be saved,	966
Lk	3: 7	John said to the crowds coming out to be **b**	966
	3:12	Tax collectors also came to be **b**.	966
	3:21	When all the people were being **b**,	966
	3:21	Jesus was **b** too.	966
	7:29	because they had been **b** by John.	966+967
	7:30	because they had not been **b** by John.)	966+967
Jn	3:22	where he spent some time with them, and **b**.	966
	3:23	and people were constantly coming to be **b**.	966
	4: 2	although in fact it was not Jesus who **b**,	966
Ac	1: 5	For John **b** with water,	966
	1: 5	but in a few days you will be **b** with	966
	2:38	Peter replied, "Repent and be **b**,	966
	2:41	Those who accepted his message were **b**,	966
	8:12	they were **b**, both men and women.	966
	8:13	Simon himself believed and was **b**.	966
	8:16	they had simply been **b** into the name	966+5639
	8:36	Why shouldn't I be **b**?"	966
	8:38	down into the water and Philip **b** him.	966
	9:18	He got up and was **b**,	966
	10:47	from being **b** with water?	966
	10:48	that they be **b** in the name of Jesus Christ.	966
	11:16	'John **b** with water,	966
	11:16	but you will be **b** with the Holy Spirit.'	966
	16:15	and the members of her household were **b**,	966
	16:33	immediately he and all his family were **b**.	966
	18: 8	many of the Corinthians who heard him believed and were **b**.	966
	19: 5	they were **b** into the name of the Lord Jesus.	966
	22:16	Get up, be **b** and wash your sins away,	966
Ro	6: 3	Or don't you know that all of us who were **b**	966
	6: 3	into Christ Jesus were **b** into his death?	966
1Co	1:13	Were you **b** into the name of Paul?	966
	1:15	so no one can say that you were **b**	966
	1:16	(Yes, I also **b** the household of Stephanas,	966
	1:16	I don't remember if I **b** anyone else.)	966
	10: 2	They were all **b** into Moses in the cloud and	966
	12:13	we were all **b** by one Spirit into one body—	966
	15:29	what will those do who are **b** for the dead?	966
	15:29	why are people **b** for them?	966
Gal	3:27	for all of you who were **b** into Christ	966

BAPTIZING (9) [BAPTIZE]

Mt	3: 7	and Sadducees coming to where he was **b**,	967
	28:19	**b** them in the name of the Father and of	966
Mk	1: 4	**b** in the desert region and preaching	966
Jn	1:28	where John was **b**.	966
	1:31	but the reason I came **b** with water was	966
	3:23	Now John also was **b** at Aenon near Salim,	966
	3:26	he is **b**, and everyone is going to him."	966
	4: 1	and **b** more disciples than John,	966
	10:40	where John had been **b** in the early days.	966

BAR (3) [BARRED, BARS]

Jdg	16: 3	and tore them loose, **b** and all.	1378
Ne	7: 3	have them shut the doors and **b** them,	296
Isa	9: 4	the **b** across their shoulders,	4751

BAR-JESUS (1)

Ac	13: 6	and false prophet named **B**,	979

BARABBAS (12)

Mt	27:16	a notorious prisoner, called **B**.	972
	27:17	**B**, or Jesus who is called Christ?"	972
	27:20	the elders persuaded the crowd to ask for **B**	972
	27:21	"**B**," they answered.	972
	27:26	Then he released **B** to them.	972
Mk	15: 7	A man called **B** was in prison with	972
	15:11	the crowd to have Pilate release **B** instead.	972
	15:15	Pilate released **B** to them.	972
Lk	23:18	Release **B** to us!"	972
	23:19	(**B** had been thrown into prison for	4015S
Jn	18:40	Give us **B**!"	972
	18:40	Now **B** had taken part in a rebellion.	972

BARACHEL (KJV) See BARAKEL

BARACHIAS (KJV) See BARACHIAH

BARAH   See BETH BARAH

BARAK (13) [BARAK'S]

Jdg	4: 6	for **B** son of Abinoam from Kedesh	1399
	4: 8	**B** said to her, "If you go with me, I will go;	1399
	4: 9	So Deborah went with **B** to Kedesh,	1399
	4:12	that **B** son of Abinoam had gone up	1399
	4:14	Then Deborah said to **B**, "Go!	1399
	4:14	So **B** went down Mount Tabor,	1399
	4:16	But **B** pursued the chariots and army as far	1399
	4:22	**B** came by in pursuit of Sisera,	1399
	5: 1	and **B** son of Abinoam sang this song:	1399
	5:12	Arise, O **B**!	1399
	5:15	yes, Issachar was with **B**,	1399
1Sa	12:11	Then the LORD sent Jerub-Baal, **B**,	1399
Heb	11:32	I do not have time to tell about Gideon, **B**,	973

BARAK'S (1) [BARAK]

Jdg	4:15	At **B** advance, the LORD routed Sisera	1399

BARAKEL (2)

Job	32: 2	But Elihu son of **B** the Buzite,	1387
	32: 6	So Elihu son of **B** the Buzite said:	1387

BARBARIAN (1)

Col	3:11	circumcised or uncircumcised, **b**, Scythian,	975

BARBARIANS (KJV) See FOREIGNER, ISLANDER, NON-GREEKS

BARBAROUS (KJV) See ISLANDERS

BARBER'S (1)

Eze	5: 1	and use it as a **b** razor to shave your head	1647

BARBS (1)

Nu	33:55	those you allow to remain will become **b**	8493

BARE (28) [BARED, BAREFOOT, BARELY, BARREN]

Jdg	14: 6	that he tore the lion apart with his **b** hands	401+928+4399
2Sa	22:16	and the foundations of the earth laid **b** at	1655
2Ki	9:13	and spread them under him on the steps.	1752
Job	28: 9	and lays **b** the roots of the mountains.	2200
Ps	18:15	and the foundations of the earth laid **b**	1655
	29: 9	the oaks and **strips** the forests **b**.	3106
Isa	13: 2	a banner on a **b** hilltop, shout to them;	9142
	23:13	**stripped** its fortresses **b**	6910
	27:10	they **strip** its branches **b**.	3983
	47: 2	Lift up your skirts, **b** your legs,	1655
	52:10	The LORD will lay **b** his holy arm in	3106
Jer	2:25	until your feet are **b** and your throat is dry.	3504
	3: 6	But I will **strip** Esau **b**.	3106
Eze	13:14	so that its foundation will be laid **b**.	1655
	16: 7	you who were naked and **b**.	6880
	16:22	when you were naked and **b**,	6880
	16:39	and leave you naked and **b**.	6880
	23:29	They will leave you naked and **b**,	6880
	24: 7	She poured it on the **b** rock;	7460
	24: 8	I put her blood on the **b** rock,	7460
	26: 4	and make her a **b** rock.	7460
	26:14	I will make you a **b** rock,	7460
	26:14	every head was **rubbed b**	7942
Hos	2: 3	and **make** her as **b** as on	3657
Mic	1: 6	into the valley and **lay b** her foundations.	1655
1Co	14:25	and the secrets of his heart will be laid **b**.	5745
Heb	4:13	and **laid b** before the eyes of him	5548
2Pe	3:10	earth and everything in it will be laid **b**.	2351

BARED (2) [BARE]

Isa	20: 4	with buttocks **b**—to Egypt's shame.	3106
Eze	4: 7	of Jerusalem and with **b** arm prophesy	3106

BAREFOOT (5) [BARE, FOOT]

2Sa	15:30	his head was covered and he was **b**.	3504
Isa	20: 2	And he did so, going around stripped and **b**.	3504
	20: 3	and **b** for three years,	3504
	20: 4	of Assyria will lead away stripped and **b**	3504
Mic	1: 8	I will go about **b** and naked.	8768

BARELY (2) [BARE]

1Sa	3: 2	so weak that he could **b** see,	4202
Isa	26:16	they could **b** whisper a prayer.	4318+7440

BARGAIN (2)

2Ki	18:23	" 'Come now, **make a b** with my master,	6842
Isa	36: 8	" 'Come now, **make a b** with my master,	6842

BARHUMITE (1)

2Sa	23:31	Abi-Albon the Arbathite, Azmaveth the **B**,	1372

BARIAH (1)

1Ch	3:22	Hattush, Igal, **B**, Neariah and Shaphat—	1377

BARK (4)

Ge	30:37	on them by **peeling** the **b** and exposing	AIT
Ex	11: 7	among the Israelites not a dog will **b**;	3076+4383
Isa	56:10	they are all mute dogs, they cannot **b**;	5560
Joel	1: 7	It has **stripped off** their **b**	3106+3106

BARKOS (2)

Ezr	2:53	**B**, Sisera, Temah,	1401
Ne	7:55	**B**, Sisera, Temah,	1401

BARLEY (36)

Ex	9:31	(The flax and **b** were destroyed,	8555
	9:31	**b** had headed and the flax was in bloom.	8555
Lev	27:16	fifty shekels of silver to a homer of **b** seed.	8555
Nu	5:15	a tenth of an ephah of **b** flour on her behalf.	8555
Dt	8: 8	a land with wheat and **b**, vines	8555
Jdg	7:13	"A round loaf of **b** bread came tumbling	8555
Ru	1:22	as the **b** harvest was beginning.	8555

Ru	2:17	Then she threshed the **b** she had gathered,	8555
	2:23	the servant girls of Boaz to glean until the **b**	8555
	3: 2	be winnowing **b** on the threshing floor.	8555
	3:15	into it six measures of **b** and put it on her.	8555
	3:17	"He gave me these six measures of **b**,	8555
2Sa	14:30	and he has **b** there.	8555
	17:28	They also brought wheat and **b**,	8555
	21: 9	just as the **b** harvest was beginning.	8555
1Ki	4:28	the proper place their quotas of **b** and straw	8555
2Ki	4:42	of **b** bread baked from the first ripe grain,	8555
	7: 1	for a shekel and two seahs of **b** for a shekel	8555
	7:16	and two seahs of **b** sold for a shekel	8555
	7:18	for a shekel and two seahs of **b** for a shekel	8555
1Ch	11:13	At a place where there was a field full of **b**,	8555
2Ch	2:10	twenty thousand cors of **b**,	8555
	2:15	the wheat and **b** and the olive oil	8555
	27: 5	of wheat and ten thousand cors of **b**.	8555
Job	31:40	instead of wheat and weeds instead of **b**."	8555
Isa	28:25	**b** in its plot, and spelt in its field?	8555
Jer	41: 8	We have wheat and **b**, oil and honey,	8555
Eze	4: 9	"Take wheat and **b**, beans and lentils,	8555
	4:12	Eat the food as you would a **b** cake;	8555
	13:19	for a few handfuls of **b** and scraps of bread.	8555
	45:13	a sixth of an ephah from each homer of **b**.	8555
Hos	3: 2	and about a homer and a lethek of **b**.	8555
Joel	1:11	grieve for the wheat and the **b**,	8555
Jn	6: 9	"Here is a boy with five **small b** loaves	3209
	6:13	with the pieces of the five **b** loaves left over	3209
Rev	6: 6	and three quarts *of* **b** for a day's wages,	3208

BARN (5) [BARNS]

Hag	2:19	Is there yet any seed left in the **b**?	4476
Mt	3:12	gathering his wheat into the **b** and burning	630
	13:30	the wheat and bring it into my **b**.' "	630
Lk	3:17	and to gather the wheat into his **b**,	630
	12:24	they have no storeroom or **b**;	630

BARNABAS (34)

Ac	4:36	called **B** (which means Son of Encouragement),	982
	9:27	But **B** took him and brought him to	982
	11:22	and they sent **B** to Antioch.	982
	11:25	Then **B** went to Tarsus to look for Saul,	NIG
	11:26	So for a whole year **B and Saul** met with	899S
	11:30	sending their gift to the elders by **B**	982
	12:25	**B** and Saul had finished their mission,	982
	13: 1	**B**, Simeon called Niger, Lucius of Cyrene,	982
	13: 2	"Set apart for me **B** and Saul for the work	982
	13: 7	for **B** and Saul because he wanted to hear	982
	13:42	As **Paul and B** were leaving	899S
	13:43	to Judaism followed Paul and **B**,	982
	13:46	Then Paul and **B** answered them boldly:	982
	13:50	up persecution against Paul and **B**,	982
	14: 1	At Iconium **Paul and B** went as usual into	899S
	14: 3	and **B** spent considerable time there,	NIG
	14:12	**B** they called Zeus,	982
	14:14	when the apostles **B** and Paul heard of this,	982
	14:20	The next day he and **B** left for Derbe.	982
	14:23	Paul and **B** appointed elders for them	NIG
	15: 2	This brought Paul and **B** into sharp dispute	982
	15: 2	So Paul and **B** were appointed,	982
	15:12	as they listened to **B** and Paul telling about	982
	15:22	and send them to Antioch with Paul and **B**.	982
	15:25	to you with our dear friends **B** and Paul—	982
	15:35	But Paul and **B** remained in Antioch,	982
	15:36	Some time later Paul said to **B**,	982
	15:37	**B** wanted to take John, also called Mark,	982
	15:39	**B** took Mark and sailed for Cyprus,	982
1Co	9: 6	Or is it only I and **B** who must work for	982
Gal	2: 1	again to Jerusalem, this time with **B**.	982
	2: 9	gave me and **B** the right hand of fellowship	982
	2:13	by their hypocrisy even **B** was led astray.	982
Col	4:10	as does Mark, the cousin of **B**.	982

BARNEA   See KADESH BARNEA

BARNS (5) [BARN]

Dt	28: 8	The Lᴏʀᴅ will send a blessing on your **b**	662
Ps	144:13	Our **b** will be filled with every kind	4646
Pr	3:10	then your **b** will be filled to overflowing,	662
Mt	6:26	they do not sow or reap or store away in **b**,	630
Lk	12:18	down my **b** and build bigger ones,	630

BARRACKS (6)

Ac	21:34	he ordered that Paul be taken into the **b**.	4213
	21:37	about to take Paul into the **b**,	4213
	22:24	to be taken into the **b**.	4213
	23:10	by force and bring him into the **b**.	4213
	23:16	he went into the **b** and told Paul.	4213
	23:32	while they returned to the **b**.	4213

BARRED (4) [BAR]

Pr	18:19	disputes are like the **b gates** *of* a citadel.	1378
Isa	24:10	the entrance to every house is **b**.	6037
La	3: 9	*He has* **b** my way with blocks of stone;	1553
Jnh	2: 6	the earth beneath **b** me **in** forever.	1237+1378

BARREL, BARRELS (KJV) See JAR, JARS

BARREN (29) [BARE]

Ge	11:30	Now Sarai was **b**; she had no children.	6829
	25:21	because she was **b**.	6829
	29:31	he opened her womb, but Rachel was **b**.	6829
Ex	23:26	and none will miscarry or be **b** in your land.	6829
Nu	23: 3	Then he went off to a **b height.**	9155
Dt	32:10	in a **b** and howling waste.	9332
1Sa	2: 5	*She who was* **b** has borne seven children,	6829
Job	3: 7	May that night be **b**;	6829
	15:34	For the company of the godless will be **b**,	1678
	24:21	They prey on the **b** and childless woman,	6829
Ps	113: 9	the **b woman** in her home as a happy mother	6829
Pr	30:16	the **b** womb, land, which is never satisfied	6808
Isa	41:18	I will make rivers flow on **b heights**,	9155
	49: 9	the roads and find pasture on every **b hill**.	9155
	49:21	I was bereaved and **b**;	1678
	54: 1	O **b** woman, you who never bore a child;	6829
Jer	2: 6	and led us through the **b wilderness**,	4497
	3: 2	"Look up to the **b heights** and see.	9155
	3:21	A cry is heard on the **b heights**,	9155
	4:11	"A scorching wind from the **b heights** in	9155
	7:29	take up a lament on the **b heights**,	9155
	12:12	Over all the **b heights** in	9155
	14: 6	on the **b heights** and pant like jackals;	9155
Joel	2:20	pushing it into a parched and **b** land,	9039
Lk	1: 7	because Elizabeth was **b**;	5096
	1:36	and she who was said to be **b** is	5096
	23:29	'Blessed are the **b women**,	5096
Gal	4:27	For it is written: "Be glad, O **b woman**,	5096
Heb	11:11	and Sarah herself was **b**—	5096

BARRIER (2)

| Jer | 5:22 | an everlasting **b** it cannot cross. | 2976 |
| Eph | 2:14 | the two one and has destroyed the **b**, | 5850 |

BARS (23) [BAR]

Lev	26:13	the **b** *of* your yoke and enabled you to walk	4574
Dt	3: 5	with high walls and with gates and **b**,	1378
1Sa	23: 7	by entering a town with gates and **b**."	1378
1Ki	4:13	with bronze **gate b**);	1378
2Ch	8: 5	with walls and with gates and **b**,	1378
	14: 7	with towers, gates and **b**.	1378
Ne	3: 3	and put its doors and bolts and **b** in place.	1378
	3: 6	and put its doors and bolts and **b** in place.	1378
	3:13	and put its doors and bolts and **b** in place.	1378
	3:14	and put its doors and bolts and **b** in place.	1378
	3:15	over and putting its doors and bolts and **b**	1378
Job	38:10	for it and set its doors and **b** in place,	1378
Ps	68:30	Humbled, may it bring **b** of silver.	8349
	107:16	down gates of bronze and cuts through **b**	1378
	147:13	the **b** *of* your gates and blesses your people	1378
Isa	45: 2	down gates of bronze and cut through **b**	1378
Jer	49:31	"a nation that has neither gates nor **b**;	1378
	51:30	the **b** *of* her **gates** are broken.	1378
La	2: 9	their **b** he has broken and destroyed.	1378
Eze	34:27	the **b** *of* their yoke and rescue them from	4574
	38:11	without walls and without gates and **b**,	1378
Hos	11: 6	will destroy the **b** of their **gates** and put	964
Na	3:13	fire has consumed their **b**.	1378

BARSABBAS (2)

| Ac | 1:23 | Joseph called **B** (also known as Justus) | 984 |
| | 15:22 | They chose Judas (called **B**) and Silas, | 984 |

BARTER (3)

Job	6:27	for the fatherless and **b** *away* your friend.	4126
	41: 6	*Will* traders **b** for him?	4126
La	1:11	*they* **b** their treasures for food	5989

BARTHOLOMEW (4)

Mt	10: 3	Philip and **B**; Thomas	978
Mk	3:18	Philip, **B**, Matthew, Thomas,	978
Lk	6:14	his brother Andrew, James, John, Philip, **B**,	978
Ac	1:13	Philip and Thomas, **B** and Matthew;	978

BARTIMAEUS (1) [TIMAEUS]

| Mk | 10:46 | **B** (that is, the Son of Timaeus), | 985 |

BARUCH (28)

Ne	3:20	Next to him, **B** son of Zabbai	1358
	10: 6	Daniel, Ginnethon, **B**,	1358
	11: 5	and Maaseiah son of **B**,	1358
Jer	32:12	and I gave this deed to **B** son of Neriah,	1358
	32:13	In their presence I gave **B** these instructions:	1358
	32:16	to **B** son of Neriah, I prayed to the Lᴏʀᴅ:	1358
	36: 4	So Jeremiah called **B** son of Neriah,	1358
	36: 4	**B** wrote them on the scroll.	1358
	36: 5	Then Jeremiah told **B**, "I am restricted;	1358
	36: 8	**B** son of Neriah did everything Jeremiah	1358
	36:10	**B** read to all the people at	1358
	36:13	Micaiah told them everything he had heard **B** read	1358
	36:14	the son of Cushi, to say to **B**,	1358
	36:14	So **B** son of Neriah went to them with	1358
	36:15	So **B** read it to them.	1358
	36:16	at each other in fear and said to **B**,	1358
	36:17	Then they asked **B**, "Tell us,	1358
	36:18	**B** replied, "he dictated all these words	1358
	36:19	Then the officials said to **B**,	1358
	36:26	and Shelemiah son of Abdeel to arrest **B**	1358
	36:27	that **B** had written at Jeremiah's dictation,	1358
	36:32	and gave it to the scribe **B** son of Neriah,	1358

Jer	36:32	**B** wrote on it all the words of the scroll	NIH
	43: 3	But **B** son of Neriah is inciting you	1358
	43: 6	Jeremiah the prophet and **B** son of Neriah.	1358
	45: 1	the prophet told **B** son of Neriah in	1358
	45: 1	after **B** had written on a scroll	2257S
	45: 2	the God of Israel, says to you, **B**:	1358

BARZILLAI (13)

2Sa	17:27	and **B** the Gileadite from Rogelim	1367
	19:31	**B** the Gileadite also came down	1367
	19:32	**B** was a very old man, eighty years of age.	1367
	19:33	The king said to **B**, "Cross over with me	1367
	19:34	But **B** answered the king, "How many more	1367
	19:39	The king kissed **B**	1367
	19:39	and **B** returned to his home.	NIH
	21: 8	whom she had borne to Adriel son of **B**	1367
1Ki	2: 7	to the sons of **B** of Gilead and let them be	1367
Ezr	2:61	and **B** (a man who had married a daughter	1367
	2:61	(a man who had married a daughter of **B**	1367
Ne	7:63	the descendants of Hobaiah, Hakkoz and **B**	1367
	7:63	(a man who had married a daughter of **B**	1367

BASE (21) [BASED, BASES, BASIC, BASING, BASIS]

Ex	25:31	and hammer it out, **b** and shaft;	3751
	29:12	pour out the rest of it at the **b** *of* the altar.	3572
	37:17	and hammered it out, **b** and shaft;	3751
	38:27	one talent for each **b**.	149
Lev	4: 7	of the bull's blood he shall pour out at the **b**	3572
	4:18	of the blood he shall pour out at the **b** *of*	3572
	4:25	and pour out the rest of the blood at the **b**	3572
	4:30	and pour out the rest of the blood at the **b**	3572
	4:34	and pour out the rest of the blood at the **b**	3572
	5: 9	of the blood must be drained out at the **b** *of*	3572
	8:15	He poured out the rest of the blood at the **b**	3572
	9: 9	the rest of the blood he poured out at the **b**	3572
Nu	8: 4	from its **b** to its blossoms.	3751
2Ki	16:17	that supported it and set it on a stone **b**.	5346
Job	30: 8	A **b** and nameless brood,	5572
SS	3:10	Its posts he made of silver, its **b** *of* gold.	8339
Isa	3: 5	the **b** against the honorable.	7829
Eze	31: 4	around its **b** and sent their channels to all	4760
	41: 8	that the temple had a **raised** *b* all around it,	AIT
	41:11	and the **b** *adjoining*	5226
	41:22	its corners, its **b** and its sides were of wood.	149

BASED (6) [BASE]

Lev	25:50	**b** on the rate paid to a hired man	3427+3869
Nu	26:53	to be allotted to them as an inheritance **b** on	928
Ro	2: 2	against those who do such things is **b** on	2848
	10: 2	but their zeal is not **b** on knowledge.	2848
Gal	3:12	The law is not **b** on faith;	1666
Col	2:22	because they are **b** on human commands	2848

BASEMATH (7)

Ge	26:34	and also **B** daughter of Elon the Hittite.	1412
	36: 3	also **B** daughter of Ishmael and sister	1412
	36: 4	Adah bore Eliphaz to Esau, **B** bore Reuel,	1412
	36:10	and Reuel, the son of Esau's wife **B**.	1412
	36:13	These were grandsons of Esau's wife **B**.	1412
	36:13	they were grandsons of Esau's wife **B**.	1412
1Ki	4:15	in Naphtali (he had married **B** daughter	1412

BASER (KJV) See BAD CHARACTERS

BASEST (KJV) See LOWLIEST

BASES (41) [BASE]

Ex	26:19	and make forty silver **b** to go under them—	149
	26:19	two **b** for each frame,	149
	26:21	and forty silver **b**—two under each frame.	149
	26:25	be eight frames and sixteen silver **b**—	149
	26:32	with gold and standing on four silver **b**.	149
	26:37	And cast five bronze **b** for them.	149
	27:10	with twenty posts and twenty bronze **b**	149
	27:11	with twenty posts and twenty bronze **b** and	149
	27:12	with ten posts and ten **b**.	149
	27:14	with three posts and three **b**,	149
	27:15	with three posts and three **b**,	149
	27:16	with four posts and four **b**.	149
	27:17	and hooks, and bronze **b**.	149
	27:18	and with bronze **b**.	149
	35:11	clasps, frames, crossbars, posts and **b**;	149
	35:17	of the courtyard with its posts and **b**, and	149
	36:24	and made forty silver **b** to go under them—	149
	36:24	two **b** for each frame,	149
	36:26	and forty silver **b**—two under each frame.	149
	36:30	there were eight frames and sixteen silver **b**	149
	36:36	for them and cast their four silver **b**.	149
	36:38	with gold and made their five **b** *of* bronze.	149
	38:10	with twenty posts and twenty bronze **b**,	149
	38:11	and had twenty posts and twenty bronze **b**,	149
	38:12	with ten posts and ten **b**,	149
	38:14	with three posts and three **b**,	149
	38:15	with three posts and three **b**.	149
	38:17	The **b** for the posts were bronze.	149
	38:19	with four posts and four bronze **b**.	149
	38:27	to cast the **b** *for* the sanctuary and for	149
	38:27	100 **b** from the 100 talents,	149
	38:30	They used it to make the **b** *for* the entrance	149
	38:31	the **b** *for* the surrounding courtyard	149
	39:33	its clasps, frames, crossbars, posts and **b**;	149

Ex	39:40	of the courtyard with its posts and **b**, and	149
	40:18	he put the **b** in place, erected the frames,	149
Nu	3:36	its crossbars, posts, **b**, all its equipment,	149
	3:37	of the surrounding courtyard with their **b**,	149
	4:31	its crossbars, posts and **b**,	149
	4:32	of the surrounding courtyard with their **b**,	149
SS	5:15	His legs are pillars of marble set on **b**	149

BASEWORK (1)

1Ki	7:31	its **b** it measured a cubit and a half.	4029+5126

BASHAN (60)

Nu	21:33	and went up along the road toward **B**,	1421
	21:33	of **B** and his whole army marched out	1421
	32:33	and the kingdom of Og king of **B**—	1421
Dt	1: 4	and at Edrei had defeated Og king of **B**,	1421
	3: 1	and went up along the road toward **B**,	1421
	3: 1	of **B** with his whole army marched out	1421
	3: 3	also gave into our hands Og king of **B**	1421
	3: 4	of Argob, Og's kingdom in **B**.	1421
	3:10	and all **B** as far as Salecah and Edrei,	1421
	3:10	towns of Og's kingdom in **B**.	1421
	3:11	(Only Og king of **B** was left of the remnant	1421
	3:13	The rest of Gilead and also all of **B**,	1421
	3:13	of Argob in **B** used to be known as a land	1421
	3:14	so that to this day **B** is called Havvoth Jair.)	1421
	4:43	and Golan in **B**, for the Manassites.	1421
	4:47	of his land and the land of Og king of **B**,	1421
	29: 7	of Heshbon and Og king of **B** came out	1421
	32:14	of **B** and the finest kernels of wheat.	1421
	33:22	"Dan is a lion's cub, springing out of **B**."	1421
Jos	9:10	Sihon king of Heshbon, king of **B**,	1421
	12: 4	And the territory of Og king of **B**,	1421
	12: 5	of **B** to the border of the people of Geshur	1421
	13:11	all of Mount Hermon and all **B** as far	1421
	13:12	the whole kingdom of Og in **B**,	1421
	13:30	from Mahanaim and including all of **B**,	1421
	13:30	the entire realm of Og king of **B**—	1421
	13:30	all the settlements of Jair in **B**, sixty towns,	1421
	13:31	and Edrei (the royal cities of Og in **B**).	1421
	17: 1	who had received Gilead and **B** because	1421
	17: 5	of land besides Gilead and **B** east of	1421
	20: 8	and Golan in **B** in the tribe of Manasseh.	1421
	21: 6	and the half-tribe of Manasseh in **B**.	1421
	21:27	of Manasseh, Golan in **B** (a city of refuge	1421
	22: 7	of Manasseh Moses had given land in **B**,	1421
1Ki	4:13	in **B** and its sixty large walled cities	1421
	4:19	and the country of Og king of **B**,	1421
2Ki	10:33	by the Arnon Gorge through Gilead to **B**.	1421
1Ch	5:11	The Gadites lived next to them in **B**,	824+1421
	5:12	then Janai and Shaphat, in **B**.	1421
	5:16	in **B** and its outlying villages,	1421
	5:23	in the land from **B** to Baal Hermon,	1421
	6:62	of the tribe of Manasseh that is in **B**.	1421
	6:71	of Manasseh they received Golan in **B** and	1421
Ne	9:22	and the country of Og king of **B**.	1421
Ps	22:12	strong bulls of **B** encircle me.	1421
	68:15	mountains of **B** are majestic mountains;	1421
	68:15	rugged are the mountains of **B**.	1421
	68:22	The Lord says, "I will bring them from **B**;	1421
	135:11	Og king of **B** and all the kings of Canaan—	1421
	136:20	and Og king of **B**—	1421
Isa	2:13	tall and lofty, and all the oaks of **B**,	1421
	33: 9	and **B** and Carmel drop their leaves.	1421
Jer	22:20	let your voice be heard in **B**,	1421
	50:19	and he will graze on Carmel and **B**;	1421
Eze	27: 6	Of oaks from **B** they made your oars;	1421
	39:18	all of them fattened animals from **B**.	1421
Am	4: 1	you cows of **B** on Mount Samaria,	1421
Mic	7:14	in **B** and Gilead as in days long ago.	1421
Na	1: 4	**B** and Carmel wither and the blossoms	1421
Zec	11: 2	the stately trees are ruined! Wail, oaks of **B**;	1421

BASHAN-HAVOTH-JAIR (KJV) See
HAVVOTH JAIR

BASHEMATH (KJV) See BASEMATH

BASIC (3) [BASE]

Gal	4: 3	we were in slavery under the **b** principles	5122
Col	2: 8	the **b** principles of this world rather than	5122
	2:20	to the **b** principles of this world, why, as	5122

BASIN (14) [BASINS, WASHBASIN]

Ex	12:22	the **b** and put some of the blood on the top	6195
	30:18	"Make a bronze **b**,	3963
	30:28	and the **b** with its stand.	3963
	31: 9	the **b** with its stand—	3963
	35:16	the bronze **b** with its stand;	3963
	38: 8	the bronze **b** and its bronze stand from	3963
	39:39	the **b** with its stand;	3963
	40: 7	place the **b** between the Tent of Meeting	3963
	40:11	the **b** and its stand and consecrate them.	3963
	40:30	the **b** between the Tent of Meeting and	3963
Lev	8:11	and all its utensils and the **b** with its stand,	3963
1Ki	7:30	and each had a **b** resting on four supports,	3963
	7:38	one **b** to go on each of the ten stands.	3963
Jn	13: 5	a **b** and began to wash his disciples' feet,	3781

BASING (3) [BASE]

2Ki	18:19	**On** what *are you* **b** this confidence of yours	1053
2Ch	32:10	**On** what *are you* **b** your **confidence**,	1053

Isa	36: 4	**On** what *are you* **b** this confidence of yours	1053

BASINS (9) [BASIN]

1Ki	7:38	He then made ten bronze **b**,	3963
	7:40	the **b** and shovels and sprinkling bowls.	3963
	7:43	the ten stands with their ten **b**;	3963
	7:50	the pure gold **b**,	6195
2Ki	12:13	not spent for making silver **b**,	6195
	16:17	the side panels and removed the **b** from	3963
2Ch	4: 6	He then made ten **b** for washing	3963
	4:14	the stands with their **b**;	3963
Jer	52:19	of the imperial guard took away the **b**,	6195

BASIS (15) [BASE]

Lev	25:15	to buy from your countryman **on the b of**	928
	25:15	to you **on the b of** the number of years left	928
1Ki	20:34	"**On the b of** a treaty I will set you free."	928
Eze	16:61	but not **on the b of** my covenant with you.	4946
Da	6: 5	"We will never find any **b** for charges	10544
Lk	23: 4	"I find no **b** for a charge against this man."	165
	23:14	in your presence and have found no **b**	165
Jn	8: 6	in order to have a **b** for accusing him.	NIG
	18:38	"I find no **b** for a charge against him.	162
	19: 4	to let you know that I find no **b** for a		
		charge against him."	162
	19: 6	I find no **b** for a charge against him."	162
Phm	1: 9	yet I appeal to you **on the b** of love.	1328
Heb	7:11	the Levitical priesthood (for **on the b of** it	2093
	7:16	a priest not **on the b of** a regulation as	2848
	7:16	to his ancestry but **on the b of** the power of	2848

BASKET (34) [BASKETFULS, BASKETS]

Ge	40:17	In the top **b** were all kinds of baked goods	6130
	40:17	but the birds were eating them out of the **b**	6130
Ex	2: 3	a papyrus **b** for him and coated it with tar	9310
	2: 5	She saw the **b** among the reeds	9310
	29: 3	Put them in a **b** and present them in it—	6130
	29:23	From the **b** of bread made without yeast,	6130
	29:32	of the ram and the bread that is in the **b**.	6130
Lev	8: 2	and the **b** *containing* bread made	6130
	8:26	from the **b** of bread made without yeast,	6130
	8:31	and eat it there with the bread from the **b**	6130
Nu	6:15	and a **b** of bread made without yeast—	6130
	6:17	to present the **b** of unleavened bread and is	6130
	6:19	and a cake and a wafer from the **b**,	6130
Dt	23:24	but do not put any in your **b**.	3998
	26: 2	and put them in a **b**.	3244
	26: 4	The priest shall take the **b** from your hands	3244
	26:10	Place the **b** before the LORD your God	2257S
	28: 5	Your **b** and your kneading trough will	3244
	28:17	Your **b** and your kneading trough will	3244
Jdg	6:19	Putting the meat in a **b** and its broth in	6130
Ps	81: 6	their hands were set free from the **b**.	1857
Isa	40:12	Who has held the dust of the earth in a **b**,	8955
Jer	24: 2	One **b** had very good figs,	1857
	24: 2	the other **b** had very poor figs,	1857
Am	8: 1	a **b** of ripe fruit.	3990
	8: 2	"A **b** *of* ripe fruit," I answered.	3990
Zec	5: 6	He replied, "It is a **measuring b**."	406
	5: 7	and there in the **b** sat a woman!	406
	5: 8	into the **b** and pushed the lead cover down	406
	5: 9	and they lifted up the **b** between heaven	406
	5:10	"Where are they taking the **b**?"	406
	5:11	the **b** will be set there in its place."	NIH
Ac	9:25	and lowered him in a **b** through an opening	5083
2Co	11:33	But I was lowered in a **b** from a window in	4914

BASKETFULS (9) [BASKET]

Mt	14:20	and the disciples picked up twelve **b**	3186+4441
	15:37	the disciples picked up seven **b**	4441+5083
	16: 9	and how many **b** you gathered?	3186
	16:10	and how many **b** you gathered?	5083
Mk	6:43	up twelve **b** of broken pieces of bread	3186+4445
	8: 8	Afterward the disciples picked up seven **b**	5083
	8:19	how many **b** of pieces did you pick up?"		
			3186+4441
	8:20	how many **b** of pieces did you pick up?"		
			4445+5083
Lk	9:17	and the disciples picked up twelve **b**	3186

BASKETS (6) [BASKET]

Ge	40:16	On my head were three **b** *of* bread.	6130
	40:18	"The three **b** are three days.	6130
2Ki	10: 7	They put their heads in **b** and sent them	1857
Jer	24: 1	the LORD showed me two **b**	1857
Mt	13:48	down and collected the good fish in **b**,	35
Jn	6:13	So they gathered them and filled twelve **b**	3186

BASMATH (KJV) See BASEMATH

BASON, BASONS (KJV) See BASIN,
BASINS, DISH, BOWLS

BASTARD, BASTARDS (KJV) See
BORN OF A FORBIDDEN MARRIAGE,
FOREIGNERS

BAT (2) [BATS]

Lev	11:19	any kind of heron, the hoopoe and the **b**.	6491
Dt	14:18	any kind of heron, the hoopoe and the **b**.	6491

BATCH (4)

Ro	11:16	then the whole **b** is holy;	5878
1Co	5: 6	through the whole **b** of dough?	5878
	5: 7	that you may be a new **b** without yeast—	5878
Gal	5: 9	through the whole **b** of dough."	5878

BATH (7) [BATHE]

Isa	5:10	A ten-acre vineyard will produce only a **b**	1427
Eze	45:10	an accurate ephah and an accurate **b**.	1427
	45:11	ephah and the **b** are to be the same size,	1427
	45:11	the **b** containing a tenth of a homer and	1427
	45:14	measured by the **b**,	1427
	45:14	a tenth of a **b** from each cor (which consists	1427
Jn	13:10	"A person who *has* **had a b** needs only	3374

BATH RABBIM (1)

SS	7: 4	of Heshbon by the gate of **B**.	1442

BATHE (26) [BATH, BATHED, BATHING, BATHS]

Ex	2: 5	down to the Nile to **b**,	8175
Lev	14: 8	shave off all his hair and **b** with water;	8175
	14: 9	and **b** with water,	8175
	15: 5	on must wash his clothes and **b** with water,	8175
	15: 7	a discharge must wash his clothes and **b**	8175
	15: 8	that person must wash his clothes and **b**	8175
	15:10	up those things must wash his clothes and **b**	8175
	15:11	with water must wash his clothes and **b**	8175
	15:13	he must wash his clothes and **b** himself	8175
	15:16	*he must* **b** his whole body with water,	8175
	15:18	*both must* **b** with water,	8175
	15:21	and **b** with water,	8175
	15:22	on must wash his clothes and **b** with water,	8175
	15:27	he must wash his clothes and **b** with water,	8175
	16: 4	so *he must* **b** himself with water	8175
	16:24	*He shall* **b** himself with water in	8175
	16:26	and **b** himself with water;	8175
	16:28	and **b** with water, and he will	8175
	17:15	and **b** with water, and he will	8175
	17:16	he does not wash his clothes and **b** himself,	8175
Nu	19: 7	and **b** himself with water.	8175
	19: 8	also wash his clothes and **b** with water,	8175
	19:19	and **b** with water,	8175
Dt	33:24	and *let him* **b** his feet in oil.	3188
Ps	58:10	*they* **b** their feet in the blood of the wicked.	8175

BATHED (5) [BATHE]

Lev	22: 6	the sacred offerings unless *he has* **b** himself	8175
1Ki	22:38	a pool in Samaria (where the prostitutes **b**),	8175
Isa	34: 6	The sword of the LORD *is* **b** in blood,	4848
Eze	16: 9	" '*I* **b** you with water and washed	8175
	23:40	and when they arrived *you* **b** *yourself*	8175

BATHING (2) [BATHE]

2Sa	11: 2	From the roof he saw a woman **b**.	8175
Job	36:30	**b** the depths of the sea.	4059

BATHS (10) [BATHE]

1Ki	5:11	to twenty thousand **b** *of* pressed olive oil.	1427
	7:26	It held two thousand **b**.	1427
	7:38	each holding forty **b**	1427
2Ch	2:10	twenty thousand **b** of wine	1427
	2:10	and twenty thousand **b** of olive oil."	1427
	4: 5	It held three thousand **b**.	1427
Ezr	7:22	a hundred **b** of wine,	10126
	7:22	a hundred **b** of olive oil,	10126
Eze	45:14	from each cor (which consists of ten **b**	1427
	45:14	for ten **b** are equivalent to a homer).	1427

BATHSHEBA (13)

2Sa	11: 3	The man said, "Isn't this **B**,	1444
	12:24	Then David comforted his wife **B**,	1444
1Ki	1:11	Then Nathan asked **B**, Solomon's mother,	1444
	1:15	So **B** went to see the aged king in his room,	1444
	1:16	**B** bowed low and knelt before the king.	1444
	1:28	Then King David said, "Call in **B**."	1444
	1:31	Then **B** bowed low with her face to	1444
	2:13	Adonijah, the son of Haggith, went to **B**,	1444
	2:13	**B** asked him, "Do you come peaceably?"	NIH
	2:18	"Very well," **B** replied,	1444
	2:19	When **B** went to King Solomon to speak	1444
1Ch	3: 5	These four were by **B** daughter of Ammiel.	1444
Ps	51: T	after David had committed adultery with **B**.	1444

BATS (1) [BAT]

Isa	2:20	throw away to the rodents and **b** their idols	6491

BATTERED (1) [BATTERING]

Isa	24:12	city is left in ruins, its gate *is* **b** to pieces.		
			4198+8625

BATTERING (7) [BATTERED]

2Sa	20:15	While *they were* **b** the wall to bring it down,	8845
Isa	22: 5	a day of **b** down walls and of crying out to	7982
Eze	4: 2	to it, set up camps against it and put **b** rams	4119
	21:22	where he is to set up **b** rams,	4119
	21:22	to set **b** rams against the gates,	4119
	26: 9	the blows of his **b** rams against your walls	7692
Ac	27:18	**took** such a violent **b from the storm**	5928

BATTLE (210) [BATTLEMENTS, BATTLES]

Ge	14: 8	marched out and drew up their **b** lines	4878
Ex	13:18	went up out of Egypt **armed for b.**	2821
Nu	10: 9	When you go into **b** in your own land	4878
	21:33	to meet them in **b** at Edrei.	4878
	31: 4	Send into **b** a thousand men from each of	7372
	31: 5	So twelve thousand men armed for **b,**	7372
	31: 6	Moses sent them into **b,**	7372
	31:14	who returned from the **b.**	4878+7372
	31:21	into **b,** "This is the requirement of the law	4878
	31:27	between the soldiers who took part in the **b**	7372
	31:28	From the soldiers who fought in the **b,**	7372
	31:36	of those who fought in the **b** was:	7372
	32:20	before the LORD for **b**	4878
	32:27	But your servants, every man armed for **b,**	7372
	32:29	every man armed for **b,**	4878
Dt	2:24	take possession of it and engage him in **b.**	4878
	2:32	and all his army came out to meet us in **b**	4878
	3: 1	to meet us in **b** at Edrei.	4878
	3:18	But all your able-bodied men, **armed for b,**	2741
	20: 2	When you arc about to go into **b,**	4878
	20: 3	"Hear, O Israel, today you are going into **b**	4878
	20: 5	in **b** and someone else may dedicate it.	4878
	20: 6	in **b** and someone else enjoy it.	4878
	20: 7	in **b** and someone else marry her."	4878
	20:12	to make peace and they engage you in **b,**	4878
Jos	4:13	About forty thousand armed for **b** crossed	7372
	8:14	in the morning to meet Israel in **b** at	4878
	11:19	who took them all in **b.**	4878
	13:22	In addition to *those* **slain in b,**	2728
	14:11	I'm just as vigorous to go out to **b** now	4878
Jdg	3: 2	not had previous **b** experience):	4392S
	8:13	of Joash then returned from the **b** by	4878
	18:11	the clan of the Danites, armed for **b,** set out	4878
	18:16	The six hundred Danites, armed for **b,**	4878
	20:20	the Benjamites and took up **b** positions	4878
	20:23	up again to **b** against the Benjamites,	4878
	20:28	up again to **b** with Benjamin our brother,	4878
	20:39	then the men of Israel would turn in the **b.**	4878
	20:39	"We are defeating them as in the first **b."**	4878
	20:42	but they could not escape the **b.**	4878
1Sa	4: 2	and as the **b** spread,	4878
	4:12	a Benjamite ran from the **b line** and went	5120
	4:16	"I have just come from the **b line;**	5120
	7:10	near to engage Israel in **b.**	4878
	13:22	on the day of the **b** not a soldier with Saul	4878
	14:20	and went to the **b.**	4878
	14:22	they joined the **b** in hot pursuit.	4878
	14:23	and the **b** moved on beyond Beth Aven.	4878
	17: 2	the Valley of Elah and drew up their **b** line	4878
	17: 8	"Why do you come out and line up for **b?**	4878
	17:20	the army was going out to its **b positions.**	5120
	17:22	ran to the **b lines** and greeted his brothers.	5120
	17:28	you came down only to watch the **b."**	4878
	17:47	for the **b** is the LORD's,	4878
	17:48	David ran quickly toward the **b line**	5120
	18:30	commanders continued to go out to **b,**	NIH
	23: 8	And Saul called up all his forces for **b,**	4878
	26:10	or he will go into **b** and perish.	4878
	29: 4	He must not go with us into **b,**	4878
	29: 9	'He must not go up with us into **b.'**	4878
	30:24	as that of him who went down to the **b.**	4878
2Sa	1: 4	He said, "The men fled from the **b.**	4878
	1:25	"How the mighty have fallen in **b!**	4878
	2:17	The **b** that day was very fierce,	4878
	3:30	in the **b** at Gibeon.)	4878
	8:10	and congratulate him on his victory *in* **b**	4309
	10: 8	and drew up in **b formation** at the entrance	4878
	10: 9	that there were **b lines** in front of him and	4878
	10:17	The Arameans **formed** *their* **b** lines	6885
	11:18	Joab sent David a full account of the **b.**	4878
	11:19	the king this account of the **b,**	4878
	17:11	with you yourself leading them into **b.**	7930
	18: 6	the **b** took place in the forest of Ephraim.	4878
	18: 8	The **b** spread out over	4878
	19: 3	in who are ashamed when they flee from **b.**	4878
	19:10	anointed to rule over us, has died in **b.**	4878
	21:15	a **b** between the Philistines and Israel.	4878
	21:17	"Never again will you go out with us to **b,**	4878
	21:18	there was another **b** with the Philistines,	4878
	21:19	In another **b** with the Philistines at Gob,	4878
	21:20	In still another **b,** which took place at Gath,	4878
	22:35	He trains my hands for **b;**	4878
	22:40	You armed me with strength for **b;**	4878
	23: 9	[at Pas Dammim]	4878
1Ki	2: 5	in peacetime as if in **b,**	4878
	20:14	"And who will start the **b?"**	4878
	20:29	and on the seventh day the **b** was joined.	4878
	20:39	"Your servant went into the thick of the **b,**	4878
	22:30	"I will enter the **b** in disguise,	4878
	22:30	of Israel disguised himself and went into **b.**	4878
	22:35	All day long the **b** raged,	4878
2Ki	3:26	the king of Moab saw that the **b** had gone	4878
	8:29	on him at Ramoth in his **b** with Hazael king	4309
	9:15	on him in the **b** with Hazael king of Aram.)	4309
	13:25	of Hazael the times he had taken in **b**	4878
	14: 7	in the Valley of Salt and captured Sela in **b,**	4878
	23:29	King Josiah marched out to **meet** him in **b,**	7925
1Ch	5:18	and who were trained for **b.**	4878
	5:20	because they cried out to him during the **b,**	4878
	5:22	because the **b** was God's.	4878
	7: 4	had 36,000 **men ready for b,**	1522+4878+7372
	7:40	The number of men **ready for b,**	928+2021+4878+7372
	11:13	when the Philistines gathered there for **b.**	4878
	12: 1	among the warriors who helped him in **b;**	4878

1Ch	12: 8	They were brave warriors, **ready for b**	408+2021+4200+4878+7372
	12:23	of the men armed for **b** who came to David	7372
	12:24	6,800 armed for **b;**	7372
	12:25	of Simeon, warriors ready for **b—7,100;**	7372
	12:33	experienced soldiers prepared for **b**	4878
	12:35	men of Dan, ready for **b—28,600;**	4878
	12:36	experienced soldiers prepared for **b—**	4878
	14:15	move out to **b,**	4878
	18:10	and congratulate him on his victory *in* **b**	4309
	19: 7	from their towns and moved out for **b.**	4878
	19: 9	and drew up in **b formation** at the entrance	4878
	19:10	that there were **b lines** in front of him and	4878
	19:17	and **formed** *his* **b** lines opposite them.	6885
	19:17	to meet the Arameans *in* **b,**	4878
	20: 5	In another **b** with the Philistines,	4878
	20: 6	In still another **b,** which took place at Gath,	4878
	26:27	of the plunder taken in **b** they dedicated for	4878
2Ch	13: 3	Abijah went into **b** with a force	4878
	13: 3	and Jeroboam drew up a **b** line against him	4878
	13:12	with their trumpets will sound the **b cry**	9558
	13:15	and the men of Judah **raised the b cry.**	8131
	13:15	**sound of** their **b** cry,	8131
	14:10	and they took up **b** positions in the Valley	4878
	17:18	Jehozabad, with 180,000 men armed for **b.**	7372
	18:29	"I will enter the **b** in disguise,	4878
	18:29	of Israel disguised himself and went into **b.**	4878
	18:34	All day long the **b** raged,	4878
	20:15	For the **b** is not yours, but God's.	4878
	20:17	You *will* not *have* to **fight** this **b.**	4309
	22: 6	on him at Ramoth in his **b** with Hazael king	4309
	25: 8	Even if you go and fight courageously in **b,**	4878
	35:20	and Josiah marched out to **meet** him in **b.**	7925
	35:22	but disguised himself to **engage** him **in b.**	4309
Job	5:20	and in **b** from the stroke of the sword.	4878
	38:23	for days of war and **b?**	4878
	39:25	He catches the scent of **b** from afar,	4878
	39:25	the shout of commanders and the **b cry.**	9558
Ps	18:34	He trains my hands for **b;**	4878
	18:39	You armed me with strength for **b;**	4878
	24: 8	the LORD mighty in **b.**	4878
	55:18	from the **b** waged against me,	7930
	78: 9	turned back on the day of **b;**	7930
	89:43	and have not supported him in **b.**	7930
	110: 3	be willing on your day of **b.**	2657
	140: 7	who shields my head in the day of **b,**	5977
	144: 1	trains my hands for war, my fingers for **b.**	4878
Pr	21:31	The horse is made ready for the day of **b,**	4878
Ecc	9:11	or the **b** to the strong, nor does food come	4878
SS	3: 8	all experienced in **b,**	4878
Isa	3:25	your warriors in **b.**	4878
	8: 9	**Prepare for b,** and be shattered!	273
	8: 9	**Prepare for b,** and be shattered!	273
	9: 5	in **b** and every garment rolled in blood will	8323
	21:15	from the bent bow and from the heat of **b.**	4878
	22: 2	nor did they die in **b.**	4878
	27: 4	I would march against them in **b;**	4878
	28: 6	of strength to those who turn back the **b** at	4878
	30:32	as he fights them in **b** with the blows	4878
	31: 4	to do **b** on Mount Zion and on its heights.	7371
	31: 9	**b standard** their commanders will panic,"	5812
	42:13	with a shout *he will* **raise the b cry**	7658
Jer	4:19	I have heard the **b cry.**	4878
	4:21	the **b standard** and hear the sound of	5812
	6: 4	"Prepare for **b** against her!	4878
	6:23	like men in **b** formation to attack you,	4878
	8: 6	like a horse charging into **b.**	4878
	18:21	their young men slain by the sword in **b.**	4878
	20:16	a **b cry** at noon.	9558
	46: 3	both large and small, and march out for **b!**	4878
	48:14	'We are warriors, men valiant in **b'?**	4878
	49: 2	"when I will sound the **b cry**	4878
	49:14	Rise up for **b!"**	4878
	50:22	The noise of **b** is in the land,	4878
	50:42	like men in **b** formation to attack you,	4878
	51:20	"You are my war club, my weapon for **b—**	4878
	51:27	Prepare the nations for **b** against her;	NIH
	51:28	Prepare the nations for **b** against her—	NIH
Eze	7:14	no one will go into **b,**	4878
	13: 5	so that it will stand firm in the **b** on the day	4878
	21:22	to sound the **b cry,**	9558
Da	11:10	**carry the b** as far as his fortress	1741+2256+8740
	11:20	yet not in anger or in **b.**	4878
	11:26	and many *will* **fall in b.**	2728+5877
	11:40	the king of the South *will* **engage** him in **b,**	5590
Hos	1: 7	not by bow, sword or **b,**	4878
	2:18	Bow and sword and **b** I will abolish from	4878
	5: 8	**Raise the b cry** in Beth Aven;	8131
	10:14	the **roar of b** will rise against your people,	8623
	10:14	war cries on the day of **b,**	4878
Joel	2: 5	like a mighty army drawn up for **b.**	4878
Am	1:14	on the day of **b,**	4878
Ob	1: 1	"Rise, and let us go against her for **b"—**	4878
Mic	2: 8	like men returning from **b.**	4878
Zep	1:16	and **b cry** against the fortified cities and	9558
Zec	9:10	and the **b** bow will be broken.	4878
	10: 3	and make them like a proud horse in **b.**	4878
	10: 4	from him the tent peg, from him the **b** bow,	4878
	10: 5	the muddy streets in **b.**	4878
	14: 3	as he fights in the day of **b.**	7930
1Co	14: 8	who will get ready for **b?**	4483
Heb	11:34	and who became powerful in **b**	4483
Jas	4: 1	Don't they come from your desires that **b**	5129
Rev	9: 7	like horses prepared for **b.**	4483
	9: 9	of many horses and chariots rushing into **b.**	4483
	16:14	for the **b** on the great day of God Almighty.	4483
	20: 8	to gather them for **b.**	4483

BATTLEFIELD (2) [FIELD]

Jdg	20:21	cut down twenty-two thousand Israelites on the **b** that day.	824
1Sa	4: 2	about four thousand of them on the **b.**	5120+8441

BATTLEMENT (KJV) See PARAPET

BATTLEMENTS (1) [BATTLE]

Isa	54:12	I will make your **b** of rubies,	9087

BATTLES (4) [BATTLE]

1Sa	8:20	and to go out before us and fight our **b."**	4878
	18:17	only serve me bravely and fight the **b** *of*	4878
	25:28	because he fights the LORD's **b.**	4878
2Ch	32: 8	to help us and to fight our **b."**	4878

BAVAI (KJV) See BINNUI

BAY (4)

Jos	15: 2	Their southern boundary started from the **b**	4383
	15: 5	the **b** *of* the sea at the mouth of the Jordan,	4383
	18:19	and came out at the northern **b** *of*	4383
Ac	27:39	but they saw a **b** with a sandy beach,	3146

BAZLUTH (2)

Ezr	2:52	**B,** Mehida, Harsha,	1296
Ne	7:54	**B,** Mehida, Harsha,	1296

BDELLIUM (KJV) See RESIN

BE (5161) [AM, ARE, AREN'T, BEEN, BEING, WAS, WASN'T, WERE, WEREN'T] See Index of Articles Etc.

BE ESHTARAH (1)

Jos	21:27	and **B,** together with their pasturelands—	1285

BEACH (3)

Ac	21: 5	and there on the **b** we knelt to pray.	129
	27:39	but they saw a bay with a **sandy b,**	129
	27:40	the foresail to the wind and made for the **b.**	129

BEACON (KJV) See FLAGSTAFF

BEAK (1)

Ge	8:11	in its **b** was a freshly plucked olive leaf!	7023

BEALIAH (1)

1Ch	12: 5	**B,** Shemariah and Shephatiah	1270

BEALOTH (1)

Jos	15:24	Ziph, Telem, **B,**	1268

BEAM (1) [BEAMS]

Ezr	6:11	a **b** is to be pulled from his house and he is	10058

BEAMS (18) [BEAM]

1Ki	6: 9	roofing it with **b** and cedar planks.	1464
	6:10	and they were attached to the temple by **b**	6770
	6:36	and one course of **trimmed** cedar **b.**	4164
	7: 2	columns supporting **trimmed** cedar **b.**	4164
	7: 3	above the **b** that rested on the columns—	7521
	7: 3	forty-five **b,** fifteen to a row.	NIH
	7:11	cut to size, and **cedar** *b.*	AIT
	7:12	and one course of **trimmed** cedar **b.**	4164
2Ch	3: 7	He overlaid the **ceiling b,** doorframes,	7771
	34:11	and timber for joists and **b** *for* the buildings	7936
Ne	2: 8	to **make b** *for* the gates of the citadel by	7936
	3: 3	They **laid** its **b** and put its doors and bolts	7936
	3: 6	They **laid** its **b** and put its doors and bolts	7936
Ps	104: 3	and **lays** *the* **b** *of* his upper chambers	7936
SS	1:17	The **b** *of* our house are cedars;	7771
Jer	22:14	up your fine **cedar** *b* and throw them into	AIT
Hab	2:11	and the **b** of the woodwork will echo it.	4096
Zep	2:14	the **b** of cedar will be exposed.	781

BEANS (2)

2Sa	17:28	flour and roasted grain, **b** and lentils,	7038
Eze	4: 9	"Take wheat and barley, **b** and lentils,	7038

BEAR (125) [AFTERBIRTH, BEARABLE, BEARER, BEARING, BEARS, BIRTH, BIRTHDAY, BIRTHRIGHT, BORE, BORN, BORNE, CHILDBEARING, CHILDBIRTH, FIRSTBORN, HIGHBORN, LOWBORN, NATIVE-BORN, NEWBORN, REBIRTH, STILLBORN, UNBORN]

Ge	1:11	and trees on the land *that* **b** fruit with seed	6913
	4:13	"My punishment is more than I can **b.**	5951
	17:17	*Will* Sarah **b** a child at the age of ninety?"	3528
	17:19	but your wife Sarah *will* **b** you a son,	3528
	17:21	Isaac, whom Sarah *will* **b** to you	3528

Ge	30: 3	with her so that *she can* **b children** for me	3528
	43: 9	*I will* **b the blame** before you all my life.	2627
	44:32	*I will* **b the blame** before you, my father,	2627
Ex	16:29	**B in mind** that the LORD has given you	8011
	28:12	Aaron *is to* **b** the names on his shoulders	5951
	28:29	he *will* **b** the names of the sons of Israel	5951
	28:30	Thus Aaron *will* always **b** the means	5951
	28:38	and he *will* **b** the guilt involved in	5951
Lev	19:18	not seek revenge or **b a grudge against** one	5757
Nu	5:31	but the woman *will* **b** the consequences	5951
	9:13	That man *will* **b** the consequences	5951
	18: 1	your sons and your father's family *are to* **b**	5951
	18: 1	*to* **b** the responsibility for offenses against	5951
	18:22	or they *will* **b** the consequences	5951
	18:23	the Tent of Meeting and **b** the responsibility	5951
Dt	1:12	But how *can I* **b** your problems	5951
	21:15	both **b** him sons that the firstborn is the son	3528
Jdg	5:14	from Zebulun *those who* **b** a commander's	5432
	10:16	**b** Israel's misery **no longer.**	7918
1Sa	17:34	a lion or a **b** came and carried off a sheep	1800
	17:36	both the lion and the **b;**	1800
	17:37	and the paw of the **b** will deliver me from	1800
2Sa	17: 8	and as fierce as a wild **b** robbed of her cubs.	1800
2Ki	3:21	old, *who could* **b arms** was called up	2514+2520
	19:30	and **b** fruit above.	6913
Est	8: 6	*can I* **b** to see disaster fall on my people?	3523
	8: 6	How *can I* **b** to see the destruction	3523
Job	9: 9	He is the Maker of the **B** and Orion,	6933
	20:13	though *he cannot* **b** to let it go and keeps it	2798
	21: 3	**B** with me while I speak,	5951
	36: 2	"**B** with me a little longer	4192
	38:32	in their seasons or lead out the **B**	6568
	39: 2	Do you count the months till *they* **b?**	4848
Ps	38: 4	like a burden too heavy to **b.**	NIH
	89:50	I **b** in my heart the taunts of all the nations,	5951
	92:14	*They will* still **b fruit** in old age,	5649
Pr	17:12	Better to meet a **b** robbed of her cubs than	1800
	18:14	but a crushed spirit *who can* **b?**	5951
	28:15	or a charging **b** is a wicked man ruling over	1800
	30:21	under four it cannot **b up:**	5951
Isa	1:13	*I cannot* **b** your evil assemblies.	3523+4202
	11: 1	from his roots a Branch *will* **b fruit.**	7238
	11: 7	The cow will feed with the **b,**	1800
	24: 6	its people *must* **b** their **guilt.**	870
	37:31	and **b** fruit above.	6913
	53:11	and he *will* **b** their iniquities.	6022
	65:23	not toil in vain or **b children** doomed	3528
Jer	12: 2	they grow and **b** fruit.	6913
	12:13	So **b** *the shame* of your harvest because of	954
	14: 9	we **b** your name; do not forsake us!	6584+7924
	15:16	for I **b** your name,	6584+7924
	17: 8	of drought and never fails *to* **b** fruit."	6913
	30: 6	Ask and see: *Can* a man **b children?**	3528
La	3:10	Like a **b** lying in wait, like a lion in hiding,	1800
	3:27	for a man *to* **b** the yoke while he is young.	5951
	5: 7	and we **b** their punishment.	6022
Eze	4: 4	*You are to* **b** their sin for the number	5951
	4: 5	So for 390 days *you will* **b** the sin of	5951
	4: 6	and **b** the sin of the house of Judah.	5951
	14:10	*They will* **b** their guilt—	5951
	16:52	**B** your disgrace, for you have furnished	5951
	16:52	So then, be ashamed and **b** your disgrace,	5951
	16:54	so that *you may* **b** your disgrace and	5951
	16:58	You *will* **b** the consequences	5951
	17: 8	**b** fruit and become a splendid vine.'	6213
	17:23	and **b** fruit and become a splendid cedar.	6913
	23:35	behind your back, you *must* **b**	5951
	23:49	for your lewdness and the consequences	5951
	32:24	*They* **b** their shame with those who go	5951
	32:25	*they* **b** their shame with those who go down	5951
	32:30	and **b** their shame with those who go down	5951
	34:29	in the land or **b** the scorn of the nations.	5951
	44:10	after their idols *must* **b** the consequences	5951
	44:12	with uplifted hand that *they must* **b**	5951
	44:13	*they must* **b** the shame	5951
	47:12	Every month *they will* **b,**	1144
Da	7: 5	which looked like a **b.**	10155
	9:19	your city and your people **b** your Name."	6584+7924
Hos	9:16	Even if *they* **b children,**	3528
	10: 2	and now *they* must **b** *their* **guilt.**	870
	13: 8	Like a **b** robbed of her cubs,	1800
	13:16	people of Samaria *must* **b** their **guilt,**	870
Am	5:19	a man fled from a lion only to meet a **b,**	1800
	7:10	The land cannot **b** all his words.	3920
	9:12	and all the nations that **b** my name,"	6584+7924
Mic	6:16	*you will* **b** the scorn of the nations."	5951
	7: 9	*I will* **b** the LORD's wrath,	5951
Na	1:14	to **b** your name.	NIH
Mt	7:18	A good tree cannot **b** bad fruit,	4472
	7:18	and a bad tree cannot **b** good fruit.	4472
	7:19	Every tree that *does not* **b** good fruit is cut	4472
	21:19	"*May* you never **b** fruit again!"	1181
Mk	4: 7	so that *they* did not **b** grain.	1443
Lk	1:13	Your wife Elizabeth *will* **b** you a son,	1164
	1:42	blessed is the **child** you *will* **b!**	2843+3120+3836
	6:43	nor *does* a bad tree **b** good fruit.	4472
Jn	15: 2	*that does* **b** fruit he prunes so that it will be	5770
	15: 4	No branch can **b** fruit by itself;	5770
	15: 4	Neither can you **b** fruit unless you remain	NIG
	15: 5	he *will* **b** much fruit;	5770
	15: 8	that you **b** much fruit,	5770
	15:16	and appointed you to go and **b** fruit—	5770
	16:12	more than you can now **b.**	1002
Ac	15:10	nor our fathers have been able *to* **b?**	1002
	15:17	and all the Gentiles who **b** my name,	2126
Ro	7: 4	in order that *we might* **b fruit** to God.	2844

Ro	13: 4	for *he does* not **b** the sword for nothing.	5841
	13: 4	to **b** with the failings of the weak and not	1002
1Co	10:13	be tempted beyond what you can **b.**	NIG
	15:49	so *shall* we **b** the likeness of the man	5841
Gal	6:17	for I **b** on my body the marks of Jesus.	1002
Col	3:13	**B** with each other and forgive	462
Heb	9:28	he will appear a second time, not to **b** sin,	NIG
	12:20	*they* could not **b** what was commanded:	5770
	13:22	to **b** with my word of exhortation,	462
Jas	3:12	My brothers, can a fig tree **b** olives,	4472
	3:12	or a grapevine **b** figs?	NIG
1Pe	4:16	but praise God that you **b** that name.	NIG
2Pe	3:15	**B in mind** that our Lord's patience means salvation,	2451
Rev	13: 2	but had feet like those of a **b** and a mouth	759

BEARABLE (5) [BEAR]

Mt	10:15	it will be **more b** for Sodom and Gomorrah	445
	11:22	be **more b** for Tyre and Sidon on the day	445
	11:24	that it will be **more b** for Sodom on the day	445
Lk	10:12	it will be **more b** on that day for Sodom	445
	10:14	But it will be **more b** for Tyre and Sidon at	445

BEARD (12) [BEARDS]

Lev	14: 9	he must shave his head, his **b,**	2417
	19:27	of your head or clip off the edges of your **b.**	2417
1Sa	21:13	the gate and letting saliva run down his **b.**	2417
2Sa	10: 4	shaved off half of each man's **b,**	2417
	20: 9	by the **b** with his right hand to kiss him.	2417
Ezr	9: 3	from my head and **b** and sat down appalled.	2417
Ps	133: 2	running down on the **b,**	2417
	133: 2	running down on Aaron's **b,**	2417
Isa	15: 2	Every head is shaved and every **b** cut off.	2417
	50: 6	my cheeks to *those who* **pulled out** my **b;**	5307
Jer	48:37	Every head is shaved and every **b** cut off;	2417
Eze	5: 1	to shave your head and your **b.**	2417

BEARDS (5) [BEARD]

Lev	21: 5	the edges of their **b** or cut their bodies.	2417
2Sa	10: 5	"Stay at Jericho till your **b** have grown,	2417
1Ch	19: 5	"Stay at Jericho till your **b** have grown,	2417
Isa	7:20	and to take off your **b** also.	2417
Jer	41: 5	eighty men who had shaved off their **b,**	2417

BEARER (2) [BEAR]

1Sa	17: 7	His shield **b** went ahead of him.	5951
	17:41	with his shield **b** in front of him,	5951

BEARING (18) [BEAR]

Ge	1:12	plants **b** seed according to their kinds	2445
	1:12	and trees **b** fruit with seed in it according	6913
	30: 1	that *she was* not **b** Jacob any **children,**	3528
Nu	13:23	they cut off a branch **b** a single cluster	2256
Jdg	8:18	"each one with the **b** of a prince."	9307
1Sa	14: 1	of Saul said to the young man **b** his armor,	5951
2Ch	12:11	the guards went with him, **b** the shields,	5951
Pr	30:29	four that move *with* **stately b:**	3512
Isa	1:14	I am weary of **b** them.	5951
	60: 6	**b** gold and incense and proclaiming	5951
Jer	4: 31	a groan as of *one* **b** her **first child—**	1144
Joel	2:22	The trees *are* **b** their fruit;	5951
Ro	2:15	their consciences also **b witness,**	5210
Eph	4: 2	be patient, **b** with one another in love.	462
Col	1: 6	All over the world this gospel is **b fruit**	2844
	1:10	**b fruit** in every good work,	2844
Heb	13:13	the disgrace he bore.	5770
Rev	22: 2	**b** twelve crops of fruit,	4472

BEARS (27) [BEAR]

Ge	49:21	a doe set free that **b** beautiful fawns.	5989
Ex	21: 4	a wife and *she* **b** him sons or daughters,	3528
Dt	25: 6	The first son *she* **b** shall carry on the name	3528
	28:57	from her womb and the children *she* **b.**	3528
1Ki	8:43	this house I have built **b** your Name.	6584+7924
2Ki	2:24	Then two **b** came out of the woods	1800
2Ch	6:33	this house I have built **b** your Name.	6584+7924
	20: 9	that *by* your Name and will cry out to you	928
Job	39: 1	Do you watch when the doe **b** her fawn?	2655
Ps	68:19	God our Savior, *who* daily **b** our **burdens.**	6673
Isa	59:11	We all growl like **b;**	1800
Jer	7:10	which **b** my Name, and say,	6584+7924
	7:11	Has this house, which **b** my Name,	6584+7924
	7:14	now do to the house that **b** my Name,	6584+7924
	7:30	that **b** my Name and have defiled it.	6584+7924
	25:29	on the city that **b** my Name,	6584+7924
	32:34	house that **b** my Name and defiled it.	6584+7924
	34:15	in the house that **b** my Name.	6584+7924
Da	9:18	the desolation of the city that **b** your Name.	6584+7924
Mt	7:17	Likewise every good tree **b** good fruit,	4472
	7:17	but a bad tree **b** good fruit.	4472
Lk	6:43	"No good tree **b** bad fruit,	1639+4472
	13: 9	If *it* **b** fruit next year, fine!	4472
Jn	15: 2	cuts off every branch in me *that* **b** no fruit,	5770
Gal	4:24	from Mount Sinai and **b children** who are	1164
	4:27	O barren woman, who **b** no **children;**	5503
1Pe	2:19	For it is commendable if a *man* **b up under**	5722

BEAST (58) [BEASTS]

2Ki	14: 9	Then a wild **b** in Lebanon came along	2651
2Ch	25:18	Then a wild **b** in Lebanon came along	2651
Ps	36: 6	O LORD, you preserve both man and **b.**	989

Ps	68:30	Rebuke the **b** *among* the reeds,	2651
	73:22	I was a **brute b** before you.	989
Isa	35: 9	nor will *any* ferocious **b** get up on it;	2651
Jer	7:20	be poured out on this place, on man and **b,**	989
Da	7: 5	"And there before me was a second **b,**	10263
	7: 6	and there before me was another **b,**	NIH
	7: 6	This **b** had four heads,	10263
	7: 7	and there before me was a fourth **b—**	10263
	7:11	until the **b** was slain and its body destroyed	10263
	7:19	the fourth **b,** which was different from all	10263
	7:19	the **b** that crushed and devoured its victims	NIH
	7:23	'The fourth **b** is a fourth kingdom	10263
Jnh	3: 7	Do not let any man or **b,** herd or flock,	989
	3: 8	let man and **b** be covered with sackcloth.	989
Zec	8:10	that time there were no wages for man or **b.**	989
2Pe	2:16	for his wrongdoing by a **donkey—a b**	5689
Rev	11: 7	the **b** that comes up from the Abyss	2563
	13: 1	And I saw a **b** coming out of the sea.	2563
	13: 2	The **b** I saw resembled a leopard,	2563
	13: 2	The dragon gave the **b** his power	899S
	13: 3	*of* the **b** seemed to have had a fatal wound,	899S
	13: 3	and followed the **b.**	2563
	13: 4	because he had given authority *to* the **b,**	2563
	13: 4	and they also worshiped the **b** and asked,	2563
	13: 4	"Who is like the **b?**	2563
	13: 5	The **b** was given a mouth	899S
	13: 8	of the earth will worship the **b—**	899S
	13:11	I saw another **b,** coming out of the earth.	2563
	13:12	He exercised all the authority *of* the first **b**	2563
	13:12	and its inhabitants worship the first **b,**	2563
	13:14	to do on behalf of the first **b,**	2563
	13:14	the **b** who was wounded by the sword and	2563
	13:15	to give breath to the image *of* the first **b,**	2563
	13:17	which is the name *of* the **b** or the number	2563
	13:18	let him calculate the number *of* the **b,**	2563
	14: 9	the **b** and his image and receives his mark	2563
	14:11	for those who worship the **b** and his image,	2563
	15: 2	those who had been victorious over the **b**	2563
	16: 2	the mark *of* the **b** and worshiped his image.	2563
	16:10	on the throne *of* the **b,**	2563
	16:13	the mouth *of* the **b** and out of the mouth *of*	2563
	17: 3	There I saw a woman sitting on a scarlet **b**	2563
	17: 7	of the woman and *of* the **b** she rides,	2563
	17: 8	The **b,** which you saw, once was,	2563
	17: 8	be astonished when they see the **b,**	2563
	17:11	The **b** who once was, and now is not,	2563
	17:12	authority as kings along with the **b.**	2563
	17:13	and authority *to* the **b.**	2563
	17:16	The **b** and the ten horns you saw will hate	2563
	17:17	by agreeing to give the **b** their power	2563
	19:19	Then I saw the **b** and the kings of the earth	2563
	19:20	But the **b** was captured,	2563
	19:20	the mark *of* the **b** and worshiped his image.	2563
	20: 4	They had not worshiped the **b** or his image	2563
	20:10	where the **b** and the false prophet had been thrown.	2563

BEASTS (58) [BEAST]

Ge	1:30	the **b** *of* the earth and all the birds of the air	2651
	2:19	the **b** *of* the field and all the birds of the air.	2651
	2:20	the birds of the air and all the **b** *of* the field.	2651
	9: 2	upon all the **b** *of* the earth and all the birds	2651
	31:39	**animals torn by wild b;**	3274
Ex	22:31	**animal torn by** wild **b;**	3274
Lev	26: 6	I will remove savage **b** from the land,	2651
Dt	28:26	be food for all the birds of the air and the **b**	989
	32:24	against them the fangs of **wild b,**	989
1Sa	17:44	the birds of the air and the **b** *of* the field!"	989
	17:46	to the birds of the air and the **b** of the earth,	2651
Job	5:22	and need not fear the **b** *of* the earth.	2651
	28: 8	**Proud b** do not set foot on it,	1201+8832
	35:11	the **b** of the earth and makes us wiser than	989
Ps	8: 7	all flocks and herds, and the **b** of the field,	989
	49:12	he is like the **b** that perish.	989
	49:20	without understanding is like the **b**	989
	57: 4	I lie among **ravenous b—**	4266
	74:19	over the life of your dove to **wild b;**	2651
	79: 2	the flesh of your saints to the **b** of the earth.	2651
	104:11	They give water to all the **b** of the field;	2651
	104:20	and all the **b** of the forest prowl.	2651
Pr	30:30	among **b,** who retreats before nothing;	989
Isa	46: 1	their idols are borne by **b** of burden.	989+2256+2651
	56: 9	Come, all you **b** of the field,	2651
	56: 9	come and devour, all you **b** of the forest!	2651
Jer	7:33	the birds of the air and the **b** of the earth,	989
	12: 9	Go and gather all the wild **b;**	2651
	15: 3	of the air and the **b** of the earth to devour	989
	16: 4	the birds of the air and the **b** of the earth."	989
	19: 7	to the birds of the air and the **b** of the earth.	989
	34:20	the birds of the air and the **b** of the earth.	989
Eze	5:17	I will send famine and wild **b** against you,	2651
	14:15	"Or if I send wild **b** through that country	2651
	14:15	through it because of the **b,**	2651
	14:21	sword and famine and wild **b** and plague—	2651
	29: 5	to the **b** of the earth and the birds of the air.	2651
	31: 6	all the **b** of the field gave birth	2651
	31:13	the **b** of the field were among its branches.	2651
	32: 4	the **b** of the earth gorge themselves on you.	2651
	34:25	of wild **b** so that they may live in the desert	2651
	38:20	the **b** of the field, the	2651
Da	2:38	the **b** of the field and the birds of the air.	10263
	4:12	Under it the **b** *of* the field found shelter,	10263
	4:21	giving shelter to the **b** of the field,	10263
	7: 3	Four great **b,** each different from the others,	10263
	7: 7	It was different from all the former **b,**	10263

Da	7:12	(The other *b* had been stripped	10263
	7:17	'The four great *b* are four kingdoms	10263
Hos	2:18	a covenant for them with the *b* of the field	2651
	4: 3	the *b* of the field and the birds of the air	2651
Mic	5: 8	like a lion among the *b* of the forest,	989
Zep	2:15	a lair for **wild b!**	2651
Ac	11: 6	**wild b,** reptiles, and birds of the air.	2563
1Co	15:32	If *I* **fought wild b** in Ephesus	2562
2Pe	2:12	They are like brute *b,* creatures of instinct,	2442
	2:12	and like *b* they too will perish.	NIG
Rev	6: 8	and by the **wild b** of the earth.	2563

BEAT (42) [BEATEN, BEATING, BEATINGS, BEATS]

Ex	9:25	it *b* **down** everything growing in the fields	5782
Nu	14:45	down and attacked them and *b* them **down**	4198
	22:23	Balaam *b* her to get her back on the road.	5782
	22:25	So *he b* her again.	5782
	22:27	and he was angry and *b* her with his staff.	5782
	22:28	*to make you b* me these three times?"	5782
Dt	1:44	and *b* you **down** from Seir all the way	5782
	24:20	When *you b* the olives from your trees,	2468
2Sa	22:43	*I b* them as **fine** as the dust of the earth;	8835
Ne	13:25	*I b* some of the men	5782
Ps	18:42	*I b* them as **fine** as dust borne on the wind;	8835
	78:66	He *b* back his enemies;	5782
Pr	23:35	They *b* me, but I don't feel it!	2150
SS	5: 7	They *b* me, they bruised me;	5782
Isa	2: 4	They will *b* their swords into plowshares	4198
	10:24	the Assyrians, *who b* you with a rod and lift	5782
	32:12	**B** your breasts for the pleasant fields,	6199
	49:10	the desert heat or the sun *b* **upon** them.	5782
	50: 6	I offered my back to *those who b* me,	5782
Jer	31:19	after I came to understand, *I b* my breast.	6215
Eze	21:12	Therefore *b* your breast.	6215
Joel	3:10	**B** your plowshares into swords	4198
Mic	4: 3	They will *b* their swords into plowshares	4198
Na	2: 7	Its slave girls moan like doves and *b*	9528
Mt	7:25	the winds blew and *b* **against** that house;	4700
	7:27	the winds blew and *b* **against** that house,	4684
	21:35	*they b* one, killed another,	1296
	24:49	and he then begins *to b* his fellow servants	5597
Mk	12: 3	*b* him and sent him away empty-handed.	1296
	12: 5	some of them *they b,* others they killed.	1296
	14:65	And the guards took him and *b* him.	4825
Lk	10:30	*b* him and went away,	2202+4435
	12:45	*to b* the menservants and maidservants and	5597
	18:13	but *b* his breast and said, 'God,	5597
	20:10	But the tenants *b* him	1296
	20:11	that one also they *b* and treated shamefully	1296
	23:48	they *b* their breasts and went away.	5597
Ac	16:37	"They *b* us publicly without a trial,	1296
	18:17	the synagogue ruler and *b* him in front of	5597
	22:19	*to* imprison and *b* those who believe	1296
1Co	9:27	*I b* my body and make it my slave so that	5724
Rev	7:16	The sun *will* not *b* upon them,	4406

BEATEN (18) [BEAT]

Ex	5:14	by Pharaoh's slave drivers **were** *b*	5782
	5:16	Your servants *are* **being b,**	5782
Nu	22:32	"Why *have you b* your donkey these three times?	5782
Dt	25: 2	If the guilty man deserves *to be b,*	5782
Jdg	20:36	Then the Benjamites saw that *they* **were b.**	5597
1Ki	6:32	the cherubim and palm trees with *b* gold.	8096
Isa	1: 5	Why *should you* **be b** anymore?	5782
	17: 6	as when an olive tree is *b,*	5939
	24:13	as when an olive tree is *b,*	5939
	28:18	you will be *b* **down** by it.	5330
	28:27	caraway **is b out** with a rod,	2468
Jer	20: 2	he **had** Jeremiah the prophet *b*	5782
	37:15	and **had** him *b* and imprisoned in the house	5782
Lk	12:47	*will be b* **with** many **blows.**	1296
	12:48	*will be b* **with** few **blows.**	1296
Ac	16:22	to be stripped and *b,*	4810
2Co	6: 9	*b,* and yet not killed;	4084
	11:25	Three times *I* was *b* **with rods,**	4810

BEATING (7) [BEAT]

Ex	2:11	He saw an Egyptian *b* a Hebrew,	5782
Pr	18: 6	and his mouth invites a *b.*	4547
Lk	22:63	The men who were guarding Jesus began mocking and *b* him.	1296
Ac	19:16	*He* **gave** them such a *b*	2710
	21:32	they stopped *b* Paul.	5597
1Co	9:26	I do not fight like a man *b* the air.	1296
1Pe	2:20	how is it to your credit if you **receive a b**	3139

BEATINGS (3) [BEAT]

Pr	19:29	and *b* for the backs of fools.	4547
	20:30	and *b* purge the inmost being.	4804
2Co	6: 5	in *b,* imprisonments and riots;	4435

BEATS (1) [BEAT]

Ex	21:20	a man *b* his male or female slave with a rod	5782

BEAUTIFUL (71) [BEAUTY]

Ge	6: 2	that the daughters of men were *b,*	3202
	12:11	"I know what a *b* woman you are.	3637+5260
	12:14	that she was a very *b* woman.	3637
	24:16	The girl was very *b,* a virgin;	3202+5260
	26: 7	because she is *b."*	3202+5260
	29:17	but Rachel was lovely in form, and *b.*	3637+5260
Ge	49:21	a doe set free that bears *b* fawns.	9183
Nu	24: 5	"How *b* **are** your tents,	3201
Dt	21:11	captives a *b* woman and are attracted	3637+9307
Jos	7:21	in the plunder a *b* robe from Babylonia,	3202
1Sa	25: 3	She was an intelligent and *b* woman,	3637+9307
2Sa	11: 2	The woman was very *b,*	3202+5260
	13: 1	The *b* sister of Absalom son of David.	3637
	14:27	and she became a *b* woman.	3637+5260
1Ki	1: 3	for a *b* girl and found Abishag,	3637
	1: 4	The girl was very *b;*	3637
Est	2: 2	"Let a search be made for *b* young virgins	3202+5260
	2: 3	bring all these *b* girls into the harem	3202+5260
Job	38:31	"Can you bind the *b* Pleiades?	5051
	42:15	in all the land were there found women as *b*	3637
Ps	48: 2	It is *b* in its loftiness,	3637
Pr	11:22	a *b* woman who shows no discretion.	3637
	24: 4	with rare and *b* treasures.	5833
Ecc	3:11	He has made everything *b* in its time.	3637
SS	1: 8	If you do not know, *most b* of women,	3637
	1:10	Your cheeks *are b* with earrings,	5533
	1:15	How *b* you are, my darling!	3637
	1:15	Oh, how *b!*	3637
	2:10	my darling, my *b* one, and come with me.	3637
	2:13	my *b* one, come with me."	3637
	4: 1	How *b* you are, my darling!	3637
	4: 1	Oh, how *b!*	3637
	4: 7	All *b* you are, my darling;	3637
	5: 9	*most b* of women?	3637
	6: 1	has your lover gone, *most b* of women?	3637
	6: 4	You are *b,* my darling, as Tirzah,	3637
	7: 1	*b* your sandaled feet, O prince's daughter!	3636
	7: 6	How *b you are* and how pleasing, O love,	3636
Isa	4: 2	that day the Branch of the LORD will be *b*	7382
	28: 5	a *b* wreath for the remnant of his people.	7382
	52: 7	How *b* on the mountains *are* the feet	5533
Jer	3:19	the *most b* inheritance of any nation.'	7382+7382
	6: 2	so *b* and delicate.	5534
	11:16	a thriving olive tree with fruit *b* in form.	3637
	46:20	"Egypt is a *b* heifer,	3645
Eze	7:20	They were proud of their *b* jewelry	6344+7382
	16: 7	and became the *most b* of jewels.	6344+6344
	16:12	on your ears and a *b* crown on your head.	9514
	16:13	*You became* very *b* and rose to be a queen.	3636
	20: 6	the *most b* of all lands.	7382
	20:15	*most b* of all lands—	7382
	23:42	and her sister and *b* crowns on their heads.	9514
	27:24	they traded with you *b* **garments,**	4815
	31: 3	*with b* branches overshadowing the forest;	3637
	31: 9	I made it *b* with abundant branches.	3637
	33:32	a *b* voice and plays an instrument well,	3637
Da	4:12	Its leaves were *b,* its fruit abundant,	10736
	4:21	with *b* leaves and abundant fruit,	10736
	8: 9	and to the east and toward the **B** Land.	7382
	11:16	He will establish himself in the **B** Land.	7382
	11:41	He will also invade the **B** Land.	7382
	11:45	between the seas at the *b* holy mountain.	7382
Zec	9:17	How attractive and *b* they will be!	3642
Mt	23:27	which look *b* on the outside but on the	6053
	26:10	She has done a *b* thing to me.	2819
Mk	14: 6	She has done a *b* thing to me.	2819
Lk	21: 5	how the temple was adorned *with b* stones	2819
Ac	3: 2	to the temple gate called **B,**	6053
	3:10	to sit begging at the temple gate called **B,**	6053
Ro	10:15	"How *b* are the feet of those who bring	6053
1Pe	3: 5	in God *used to* **make** themselves *b.*	3175

BEAUTIFULLY (1) [BEAUTY]

Rev	21: 2	as a bride *b* **dressed** for her husband.	3175

BEAUTY (33) [BEAUTIFUL, BEAUTIFULLY]

Est	1:11	to display her *b* to the people and nobles,	3642
	2: 3	and let *b* **treatments** be given to them.	9475
	2: 9	with her *b* **treatments** and special food.	9475
	2:12	of *b* **treatments** prescribed for the women,	5299
Ps	27: 4	**upon** the *b* of the LORD and to seek him	5840
	37:20	The LORD's enemies will be like the *b* of	3701
	45:11	The king is enthralled by your *b;*	3642
	50: 2	From Zion, perfect in *b,* God shines forth.	3642
Pr	6:25	Do not lust in your heart after her *b*	3642
	31:30	Charm is deceptive, and *b* is fleeting;	3642
Isa	3:24	instead of *b,* branding.	3642
	28: 1	to the fading flower, his glorious *b,*	7382
	28: 4	That fading flower, his glorious *b,*	7382
	33:17	in his *b* and view a land that stretches afar.	3642
	53: 2	He had no *b* or majesty to attract us to him,	9307
	61: 3	to bestow on them a **crown of** *b* instead	6996
La	2:15	the city that was called the perfection of *b,*	3642
Eze	16:14	among the nations on account of your *b,*	3642
	16:14	splendor I had given you made your *b* perfect,	NIH
	16:15	in your *b* and used your fame to become	3642
	16:15	who passed by and your *b* became his.	NIH
	16:25	and degraded your *b,*	3642
	27: 3	"'You say, O Tyre, "I am perfect in *b."*	3642
	27: 4	your builders brought your *b* to perfection.	3642
	27:11	they brought your *b* to perfection.	3642
	28: 7	they will draw their swords against your *b*	3642
	28:12	full of wisdom and perfect in *b.*	3642
	28:17	on account of your *b,*	3642
	31: 7	It was majestic in *b,*	1542
	31: 8	in the garden of God could match its *b.*	3642
Jas	1:11	its blossom falls and its *b* is destroyed.	2346
1Pe	3: 3	Your *b* should not come	NIG
	3: 4	the unfading *b* of a gentle and quiet spirit,	NIG

BEBAI (6)

Ezr	2:11	of **B** 623	950
	8:11	of the descendants of **B,** Zechariah son	950
	8:11	Zechariah son of **B,** and with him 28 men;	950
	10:28	From the descendants of **B:**	950
Ne	7:16	of **B** 628	950
	10:15	Bunni, Azgad, **B,**	950

BECAME (329) [BECOME]

Ge	2: 7	and the man *b* a living being.	2118
	4: 1	and *she b* **pregnant** and gave birth to Cain.	AIT
	4:17	*she b* **pregnant** and gave birth to Enoch.	AIT
	5: 6	he *b* the **father** of Enosh.	AIT
	5: 7	And after he *b* the **father** of Enosh,	AIT
	5: 9	he *b* the **father** of Kenan.	AIT
	5:10	And after he *b* the **father** of Kenan,	AIT
	5:12	he *b* the **father** of Mahalalel.	AIT
	5:13	And after he *b* the **father** of Mahalalel,	AIT
	5:15	he *b* the **father** of Jared.	AIT
	5:16	And after he *b* the **father** of Jared,	AIT
	5:18	he *b* the **father** of Enoch.	AIT
	5:19	And after he *b* the **father** of Enoch,	AIT
	5:21	he *b* the **father** of Methuselah.	AIT
	5:22	And after he *b* the **father** of Methuselah,	AIT
	5:25	he *b* the **father** of Lamech.	AIT
	5:26	And after he *b* the **father** of Lamech,	AIT
	5:32	he *b* the **father** of Shem, Ham and Japheth.	AIT
	8: 5	the tops of the mountains *b* **visible.**	AIT
	9:21	he *b* **drunk** and lay uncovered inside his tent.	AIT
	11:10	he *b* the **father** of Arphaxad.	AIT
	11:11	And after he *b* the **father** of Arphaxad,	AIT
	11:12	he *b* the **father** of Shelah.	AIT
	11:13	And after he *b* the **father** of Shelah,	AIT
	11:14	he *b* the **father** of Eber.	AIT
	11:15	And after he *b* the **father** of Eber,	AIT
	11:16	he *b* the **father** of Peleg.	AIT
	11:17	And after he *b* the **father** of Peleg,	AIT
	11:18	he *b* the **father** of Reu.	AIT
	11:19	And after he *b* the **father** of Reu,	AIT
	11:20	And after he *b* the **father** of Serug,	AIT
	11:21	And after he *b* the **father** of Serug,	AIT
	11:22	he *b* the **father** of Nahor.	AIT
	11:23	And after he *b* the **father** of Nahor,	AIT
	11:24	he *b* the **father** of Terah.	AIT
	11:25	And after he *b* the **father** of Terah,	AIT
	11:26	he *b* the **father** of Abram,	AIT
	11:27	Terah *b* the **father** of Abram,	AIT
	11:27	And Haran *b* the **father** of Lot.	AIT
	19:26	and *she b* a pillar of salt.	2118
	19:36	So both of Lot's daughters *b* **pregnant**	AIT
	20:12	and *she b* my wife.	2118
	21: 2	Sarah *b* **pregnant** and bore a son	AIT
	21:20	He lived in the desert and *b* an archer.	2118
	22:23	Bethuel *b* the **father** of Rebekah.	AIT
	24:67	So *she b* his wife, and he loved her;	2118
	25:19	Abraham *b* the **father** of Isaac,	AIT
	25:21	and his wife Rebekah *b* **pregnant.**	AIT
	25:27	and Esau *b* a skillful hunter,	2118
	26:13	The man *b* **rich,** and his wealth	AIT
	26:13	to grow until *he b* very **wealthy.**	AIT
	29:32	Leah *b* **pregnant** and gave birth to a son.	AIT
	30: 1	she *b* **jealous** of her sister.	AIT
	30: 2	Jacob *b* **angry** with her and said,	AIT
	30: 5	and she *b* **pregnant** and bore him a son.	AIT
	30:17	she *b* **pregnant** and bore Jacob a fifth son.	AIT
	30:23	She *b* **pregnant** and gave birth to a son	AIT
	36:32	Bela son of Beor *b* **king** of Edom.	AIT
	38: 3	*she b* **pregnant** and gave birth to a son,	AIT
	38:18	and *she b* **pregnant** by him.	AIT
	39: 4	in his eyes and *b* his **attendant.**	AIT
	47:20	The land *b* Pharaoh's,	2118
Ex	1: 7	*b* exceedingly **numerous,**	AIT
	1:20	*b* even more **numerous.**	AIT
	2: 2	and she *b* **pregnant** and gave birth to a son.	AIT
	2:10	to Pharaoh's daughter and *he b* her son.	2118
	4: 3	Moses threw it on the ground and *it b*	2118
	7:10	and *it b* a snake.	2118
	7:12	Each one threw down his staff and it *b*	2118
	7:13	Yet Pharaoh's heart *b* **hard** and he would	AIT
	7:22	and Pharaoh's heart *b* **hard;**	AIT
	8:17	throughout the land of Egypt *b* gnats.	2118
	15:25	and the water *b* **sweet.**	AIT
Lev	18:24	to drive out before you *b* **defiled.**	3237
	18:27	and the land *b* **defiled.**	AIT
Nu	6:12	because *he b* **defiled** during his separation.	AIT
	11:10	The LORD *b* exceedingly **angry,**	AIT
	16: 1	and On son of Peleth—*b* **insolent**	AIT
	16:15	Then Moses *b* very **angry** and said to	AIT
Dt	1:37	the LORD *b* **angry** with me also and said,	AIT
	26: 5	with a few people and lived there and *b*	2118
	32:15	filled with food, *he b* **heavy** and sleek.	AIT
Jos	7: 5	of the people melted and *b* **like water.**	2118
	24:32	*This b* the inheritance of Joseph's	2118
Jdg	1:28	When Israel *b* **strong,**	AIT
	1:33	and Beth Anath *b* **forced laborers** for them.	2118
	3:10	so that *he b* Israel's **judge** and went to war.	AIT
	8:27	and *it b* a snare to Gideon and his family.	2118
	9: 4	*who b* his **followers.**	AIT
	10: 7	he *b* **angry** with them.	AIT
	15:14	The ropes on his arms *b* **like charred flax,**	2118
	17:12	and the young man *b* his **priest** and lived	2118
Ru	4:13	So Boaz took Ruth and *she b* his wife.	2118
1Sa	10:12	So *it b* a saying: "Is Saul also among	2118
	13: 1	Saul was [thirty] years old when he *b* **king,**	AIT

1Sa	16:21	and David b one of his armor-bearers.	2118
	18: 1	b one in spirit with	8003
	18:29	Saul b still more afraid of him,	AIT
	18:30	and his name b well known.	AIT
	22: 2	and he b their leader.	2118
	25:37	his heart failed him and he b like a stone.	2118
	25:42	with David's messengers and b his wife.	2118
	30:13	when I b ill three days ago.	AIT
2Sa	2:10	of Saul was forty years old when he b king	AIT
	4: 1	he lost courage, and all Israel b alarmed.	AIT
	4: 4	he fell and b crippled.	7174
	5: 4	David was thirty years old when he b king,	AIT
	5:10	And he b more and more powerful,	1524+2143+2143+2256
	8: 2	So the Moabites b subject to David	2118
	8: 6	and the Arameans b subject to him	2118
	8:13	And David b famous after he returned	6913+9005
	8:14	and all the Edomites b subject to David.	2118
	10:19	with the Israelites and b subject to them.	AIT
	11:27	and she b his wife and bore him a son.	2118
	12:15	borne to David, and he b ill.	AIT
	13: 2	Amnon b frustrated to the point of illness	AIT
	14:26	to time when it b too heavy for him—	NIH
	14:27	and she b a beautiful woman.	2118
	21:15	and he b exhausted.	AIT
	23:18	and so he b as famous as the Three.	4200
	23:19	He b their commander,	2118
1Ki	11: 9	The LORD b angry with Solomon	AIT
	11:24	around him and b the leader of a band	2118
	12:30	And this thing b a sin;	2118
	13: 6	and the king's hand was restored and b	2118
	14: 1	that time Abijah son of Jeroboam b ill,	AIT
	14:21	He was forty-one years old when he b king,	AIT
	15: 1	Abijah b king of Judah,	AIT
	15: 9	Asa b king of Judah,	AIT
	15:23	In his old age, however, his feet b diseased.	AIT
	15:25	Nadab son of Jeroboam b king of Israel in	AIT
	15:33	Baasha son of Ahijah b king of all Israel	AIT
	16: 8	Elah son of Baasha b king of Israel,	AIT
	16:22	So Tibni died and Omri b king.	AIT
	16:23	Omri b king of Israel,	AIT
	16:29	Ahab son of Omri b king of Israel,	AIT
	17:17	the woman who owned the house b ill.	AIT
	19:21	to follow Elijah and b his attendant.	AIT
	22:41	Jehoshaphat son of Asa b king of Judah in	AIT
	22:42	years old when he b king,	AIT
	22:51	Ahaziah son of Ahab b king of Israel in Samaria	AIT
2Ki	3: 1	Joram of Ahab b king of Israel in Samaria	AIT
	4:17	But the woman b pregnant,	AIT
	5:14	and his flesh was restored and b clean like	AIT
	8:17	years old when he b king,	AIT
	8:26	years old when he b king,	AIT
	12: 1	In the seventh year of Jehu, Joash b king,	AIT
	13: 1	Jehoahaz son of Jehu b king of Israel	AIT
	13:10	Jehoash son of Jehoahaz b king of Israel	AIT
	14: 2	years old when he b king,	AIT
	14:23	of Jehoash king of Israel b king in Samaria,	AIT
	15: 2	He was sixteen years old when he b king,	AIT
	15: 8	Zechariah son of Jeroboam b king of Israel	AIT
	15:13	of Jabesh b king in the thirty-ninth year	AIT
	15:17	Menahem son of Gadi b king of Israel,	AIT
	15:23	Pekahiah son of Menahem b king of Israel,	AIT
	15:27	of Remaliah b king of Israel in Samaria,	AIT
	15:33	years old when he b king,	AIT
	16: 2	Ahaz was twenty years old when he b king,	AIT
	17: 1	Hoshea son of Elah b king of Israel	AIT
	17:15	and themselves b worthless.	AIT
	18: 2	years old when he b king,	AIT
	20: 1	In those days Hezekiah b ill and was at	AIT
	21: 1	years old when he b king,	AIT
	21:19	years old when he b king,	AIT
	22: 1	Josiah was eight years old when he b king,	AIT
	23:31	years old when he b king,	AIT
	23:36	years old when he b king,	AIT
	24: 1	and Jehoiakim b his vassal for three years.	2118
	24: 8	years old when he b king,	AIT
	24:18	years old when he b king,	AIT
	25:27	the year Evil-Merodach b king of Babylon,	AIT
1Ch	2: 9	and she b pregnant and gave birth to a son.	AIT
	11: 9	David b more and more powerful,	1524+2143+2143+2256
	11:20	and so he b as famous as the Three.	NIH
	11:21	above the Three and b their commander,	2118
	14: 3	and b the father of more sons	AIT
	18: 2	they b subject to him and brought tribute.	2118
	18: 6	and the Arameans b subject to him	2118
	18:13	and all the Edomites b subject to David.	2118
	19:19	they made peace with David and b subject	AIT
2Ch	12:13	He was forty-one years old when he b king,	AIT
	13: 1	Abijah b king of Judah,	AIT
	17:12	Jehoshaphat b more and more powerful;	2118
	20:31	He was thirty-five years old when he b king	AIT
	21: 5	years old when he b king,	AIT
	21:20	years old when he b king,	AIT
	22: 2	years old when he b king,	AIT
	22: 4	after his father's death they b his advisers,	2118
	24: 1	Joash was seven years old when he b king,	AIT
	25: 1	years old when he b king,	AIT
	26: 3	years old when he b king,	AIT
	26:15	he was greatly helped until he b powerful.	AIT
	26:16	But after Uzziah b powerful,	2621
	26:19	in his hand ready to burn incense, b angry.	AIT
	27: 1	years old when he b king,	AIT
	27: 8	years old when he b king,	AIT
	28: 1	Ahaz was twenty years old when he b king,	AIT
	28:22	King Ahaz b even more unfaithful	AIT

2Ch	29: 1	years old when he b king,	AIT
	32:24	In those days Hezekiah b ill and was at	AIT
	33: 1	years old when he b king,	AIT
	33:21	years old when he b king,	AIT
	34: 1	Josiah was eight years old when he b king,	AIT
	35:25	These b a tradition in Israel and are written	5989
	36: 2	years old when he b king,	AIT
	36: 5	years old when he b king,	AIT
	36: 9	years old when he b king,	AIT
	36:11	years old when he b king,	AIT
	36:13	He b stiff-necked and hardened his heart	AIT
	36:14	b more and more unfaithful,	AIT
	36:20	and they b servants to him and his sons	2118
Ne	4: 1	he b angry and was greatly incensed.	AIT
	9:16	b arrogant and stiff-necked,	AIT
	9:17	They b stiff-necked and	AIT
	9:29	but they b arrogant	AIT
	9:29	b stiff-necked and refused to listen.	AIT
Est	1:12	the king b furious and burned with anger.	AIT
	2:21	b angry and conspired	AIT
	8:17	of other nationalities b Jews because fear of	3366
	9: 4	he b more and more powerful.	1524+2143+2256
Job	26:13	By his breath the skies b fair;	NIH
	32: 2	b very angry with Job	AIT
Ps	83:10	who perished at Endor and b like refuse on	2118
	106:36	which b a snare to them.	2118
	107:17	Some b fools through their rebellious ways	NIH
	114: 2	Judah b God's sanctuary,	2118
Ecc	2: 9	I b greater by far than anyone	AIT
Isa	23: 3	and she b the marketplace of the nations.	2118
	38: 1	In those days Hezekiah b ill and was at	2118
	63: 8	and so he b their Savior.	2118
	63:10	So he turned and b their enemy	2200
Jer	2: 5	and b worthless themselves.	AIT
	44:22	your land b an object of cursing and	2118
	52: 1	years old when he b king,	AIT
	52:31	the year Evil-Merodach b king of Babylon,	4895
La	3:14	I b the laughingstock of all my people;	2118
	4:10	who b their food	2118
Eze	16: 7	up and developed and b the most beautiful	995
	16: 8	and you b mine.	2118
	16:13	You b very beautiful and rose to be	AIT
	16:15	by and your beauty b his.	2118
	16:47	in all your ways you soon b more depraved than they.	AIT
	17: 6	and it sprouted and b a low,	2118
	17: 6	So it b a vine and produced branches	2118
	19: 3	and he b a strong lion.	2118
	23: 3	They b prostitutes in Egypt,	AIT
	23:10	She b a byword among women,	2118
	23:19	Yet she b more and more promiscuous	AIT
	25:12	on the house of Judah and b very guilty	AIT
	28:17	Your heart b proud on account	AIT
	34: 5	and when they were scattered they b food	2118
	35:15	of the house of Israel b desolate,	AIT
	36: 3	so that you b the possession of the rest of	2118
Da	2:35	to pieces at the same time and b like chaff	10201
	2:35	that struck the statue b a huge mountain	10201
	4:36	b even greater than before.	10323+10339+10650
	5: 9	So King Belshazzar b even more terrified	6584
	5:20	when his heart b arrogant and hardened	AIT
	8: 4	He did as he pleased and b great.	AIT
	8: 8	The goat b very great,	AIT
Hos	9:10	to that shameful idol and b as vile as	2118
	13: 1	But he b guilty of Baal worship and died.	AIT
	13: 6	when they were satisfied, they b proud;	AIT
Jnh	4: 1	Jonah was greatly displeased and b angry.	AIT
Mt	17: 2	and his clothes b as white as the light.	1181
	25: 5	and they all b drowsy and fell asleep.	3818
	28: 4	of him that they shook and b like dead men.	1181
Mk	9: 3	His clothes b dazzling white,	1181
	10:41	they b indignant with James and John.	806
Lk	1:24	After this his wife Elizabeth b pregnant	AIT
	1:80	And the child grew and b strong in spirit;	AIT
	2:40	And the child grew and b strong;	3194
	6:16	and Judas Iscariot, who b a traitor.	1181
	9:29	and his clothes b as bright as a flash	NIG
	9:32	but when they b fully awake,	AIT
	13:19	It grew and b a tree,	1181+1650
	14:21	the house b angry and ordered his servant,	AIT
	15:28	"The older brother b angry and refused	AIT
	18:23	When he heard this, he b very sad,	1181
	20:26	astonished by his answer, they b silent.	AIT
	23:12	That day Herod and Pilate b friends—	1181
Jn	1:14	The Word b flesh and made his dwelling	1181
	4:41	of his words many more b believers.	4409
Ac	3: 7	the man's feet and ankles b strong.	AIT
	6: 7	and a large number of priests b obedient to	AIT
	7: 8	And Abraham b the father of Isaac	1164
	7: 8	Later Isaac b the father of Jacob,	NIG
	7: 8	Jacob b the father of the twelve patriarchs.	NIG
	7:18	who knew nothing about Joseph, b ruler of Egypt.	482
	9:37	About that time she b sick and died,	AIT
	9:42	This b known all over Joppa,	1181
	10:10	He b hungry and wanted something to eat,	1181
	15:12	The whole assembly b silent	AIT
	16:18	Finally Paul b so troubled that he turned	AIT
	17:34	A few men b followers of Paul	3140
	18: 6	when the Jews opposed Paul and b abusive,	AIT
	19: 9	But some of them b obstinate;	AIT
	19:17	When this b known to the Jews	1181
	22: 2	they b very quiet.	4218
	23:10	The dispute b so violent that	1181
Ro	1:21	but their thinking b futile	AIT
	1:22	they claimed to be wise, they b fools	AIT
	4:18	and so b the father of many nations,	1181

1Co	4:15	for in Christ Jesus I b your father through	1164
	9:20	To the Jews I b like a Jew,	1181
	9:20	To those under the law I b like one under	NIG
	9:21	not having the law I b like one not having	NIG
	9:22	To the weak I b weak, to win the weak.	1181
	13:11	I b a man, I put childish ways behind me.	1181
	15:45	"The first man Adam b a living being";	1181+1650
2Co	7: 9	For you b sorrowful as God intended and	AIT
	8: 9	yet for your sakes he b poor,	AIT
Gal	4:12	brothers, become like me, for I b like you.	NIG
Eph	3: 7	I b a servant of this gospel by the gift	1181
Php	2: 8	he humbled himself and b obedient	1181
1Th	1: 6	You b imitators of us and of the Lord;	1181
	1: 7	And so you b a model to all the believers	1181
	2:14	b imitators of God's churches in Judea,	1181
1Ti	2:14	it was the woman who was deceived and b a sinner.	1181
Phm	1:10	who b my son while I was in chains.	1164
Heb	1: 4	So he b as much superior to the angels as	1181
	5: 9	he b the source of eternal salvation	1181
	7:20	Others b priests without any oath,	1181+1639
	7:21	but he b a priest with an oath	NIG
	11: 7	and b heir of the righteousness that comes	1181
	11:34	and who b powerful in battle	1181
Rev	16: 4	springs of water, and they b blood.	1181
	18:19	where all who had ships on the sea b rich	AIT

BECAUSE (1672)

Ge	2: 3	b on it he rested from all the work	3954
	3:10	and I was afraid b I was naked; so I hid."	3954
	3:14	"B you have done this,	3954
	3:17	"B you listened to your wife and ate from	3954
	3:17	"Cursed is the ground b of you;	6288
	3:20	b she would become the mother of all	3954
	5:24	he was no more, b God took him away.	3954
	6:13	the earth is filled with violence b of them.	4946+7156
	7: 1	b I have found you righteous	3954
	8: 9	the dove could find no place to set its feet b	3954
	8:21	"Never again will I curse the ground b of	6288
	10:25	b in his time the earth was divided;	3954
	11: 9	b there the LORD confused the language	3954
	12:10	down to Egypt to live there for a while b	3954
	12:13	and my life will be spared b of you."	1673
	12:17	his household b of Abram's wife Sarai	1821+6584
	18:28	Will you destroy the whole city b of	928
	19:13	we are going to destroy this place.	3954
	19:14	b the LORD is about to destroy the city!"	3954
	19:22	b I cannot do anything until you reach it."	3954
	20: 3	as dead b of the woman you have taken;	6584
	20:11	and they will kill me b of my wife.'	1821+6584
	20:18	in Abimelech's household b of	1821+6584
	21:11	The matter distressed Abraham greatly b of	6584
	21:12	b it is through Isaac that your offspring will	3954
	21:13	b he is your offspring."	3954
	21:31	b the two men swore an oath there.	3954
	22:12	b you have not withheld from me your son,	2256
	22:16	that b you have done this and have	889+3610
	22:18	b you have obeyed me."	889+6813
	25:21	b she was barren.	3954
	26: 5	b Abraham obeyed me	889+6813
	26: 7	"She is my sister," b he was afraid to say,	3954
	26: 7	b she is beautiful."	3954
	26: 9	"B I thought I might lose my life	3954
	26:12	b the LORD blessed him.	2256
	26:20	b they disputed with him.	3954
	27:41	Esau held a grudge against Jacob b of	6584
	27:46	with living b of these Hittite women.	4946+7156
	28:11	he stopped for the night b the sun had set.	3954
	29: 2	with three flocks of sheep lying near it b	3954
	29:15	"Just b you are a relative of mine,	3954
	29:20	like only a few days to him b of his love	928
	29:32	"It is b the LORD has seen my misery.	3954
	29:33	"B the LORD heard that I am not loved,	3954
	29:34	b I have borne him three sons."	3954
	30: 6	B of this she named him Dan.	6584
	30:20	b I have borne him six sons."	3954
	30:27	that the LORD has blessed me b of you."	928+1673
	31:30	Now you have gone off b you longed	3954
	31:31	Jacob answered Laban, "I was afraid, b	3954
	31:49	It was also called Mizpah, b he said,	889
	32:28	b you have struggled with God and	3954
	32:30	saying, "It is b I saw God face to face,	3954
	32:31	and he was limping b of his hip.	6584
	32:32	b the socket of Jacob's hip was touched	3954
	33:11	And b Jacob insisted, Esau accepted it.	2256
	34: 7	b Shechem had done a disgraceful thing	3954
	34:13	B their sister Dinah had been defiled,	889
	34:19	b he was delighted with Jacob's daughter.	3954
	35: 7	b it was there that God revealed himself	3954
	36: 7	not support them both b of their livestock.	4946+7156
	37: 3	b he had been born to him in his old age;	3954
	37: 8	And they hated him all the more b of	6584
	39: 5	the household of the Egyptian b of Joseph.	1673
	39: 9	b you are his wife.	889+928
	39:23	b the LORD was with Joseph	889+928
	41:31	b the famine that follows it will be	4946+7156
	41:49	so much that he stopped keeping records b	3954
	41:51	firstborn Manasseh and said, "It is b	3954
	41:52	"It is b God has made me fruitful in	3954
	41:57	b the famine was severe in all the world.	3954
	42: 4	b he was afraid that harm might come	3954
	42:21	"Surely we are being punished b of	6584
	43: 5	we will not go down, b the man said to us,	3954

Ref	Text	Number
Ge 43:18	"We were brought here **b** of the silver	1821+6584
43:25	**b** they had heard that they were to eat there.	3954
43:32	**b** Egyptians could not eat with Hebrews,	3954
45: 3	**b** they were terrified at his presence.	3954
45: 5	**b** it was to save lives that God sent me	3954
45:11	**b** five years of famine are still to come.	3954
45:20	**b** the best of all Egypt will be yours.' "	3954
47: 4	**b** the famine is severe in Canaan	3954
47:13	the whole region **b** the famine was severe;	3954
47:13	Canaan wasted away **b** of the famine.	4946+7156
47:20	**b** the famine was too severe for them.	3954
47:22	**b** they received a regular allotment	3954
48:10	Israel's eyes were failing **b** of old age,	4946
49:24	**b** of the hand of the Mighty One of Jacob,	4946
49:24	**b** of the Shepherd, the Rock of Israel,	4946+9004
49:25	**b** of your father's God,	4946
49:25	who helps you, **b** of the Almighty,	907
Ex 1:21	And **b** the midwives feared God,	3954
2:23	for help **b** of their slavery went up to God.	4946
3: 6	**b** he was afraid to look at God.	3954
3: 7	I have heard them crying out **b** of	4946+7156
6: 1	**B** of my mighty hand he will let them go;	928
6: 1	**b** of my mighty hand he will drive them out of his country."	928
6: 9	not listen to him **b** of their discouragement	4946
7:24	**b** they could not drink the water of	3954
9:11	before Moses **b** of the boils that were	4946+7156
9:19	**b** the hail will fall on every man and animal	2256
9:32	were not destroyed, **b** they ripen later.)	3954
10: 9	**b** we are to celebrate a festival to	3954
12:17	**b** it was on this very day	3954
12:39	without yeast **b** they had been driven out	3954
12:42	**B** the LORD kept vigil that night	NIH
13: 3	**b** the LORD brought you out of it with	3954
13: 8	'I do this **b** of what the LORD did for me	6288
13:19	Moses took the bones of Joseph with him **b**	3954
14:11	"Was it **b** there were no graves in Egypt	4946
15:23	not drink its water **b** it was bitter.	3954
16: 7	**b** he has heard your grumbling against him.	928
16: 8	**b** he has heard your grumbling against him.	928
16:25	"**b** today is a Sabbath to the LORD.	3954
17: 7	and Meribah **b** the Israelites quarreled and	6584
17: 7	the Israelites quarreled and **b** they tested	6584
17:14	**b** I will completely blot out the memory	3954
18:15	"**B** the people come to me	3954
18:22	**b** they will share it with you.	2256
19:11	**b** on that day the LORD will come down	3954
19:18	**b** the LORD descended on it in fire.	4946+7156
19:23	**b** you yourself warned us,	3954
21: 8	**b** he has broken faith with her.	928
22:27	**b** his cloak is the only covering he has	3954
23: 9	**b** you were aliens in Egypt.	3954
23:29	**b** the land would become desolate and	7153
23:33	**b** the worship of their gods will certainly be	3954
29:33	**b** they are sacred.	3954
29:34	It must not be eaten, **b** it is sacred.	3954
31:14	" 'Observe the Sabbath, **b** it is holy to you.	3954
32: 7	"Go down, **b** your people,	3954
32:35	the people with a plague **b of** what they did	6584
33: 3	**b** you are a stiff-necked people	3954
33:17	**b** I am pleased with you and I know you	3954
34:29	he was not aware that his face was radiant **b**	928
36: 7	**b** what they already had was more than enough	2256
40:35	the Tent of Meeting **b** the cloud had settled	3954
Lev 5: 1	" 'If a person sins **b** he does not speak up	561
5:11	**b** it is a sin offering.	3954
10: 7	**b** the LORD's anointing oil is on you."	3954
10:13	**b** it is your share and your sons' share of	3954
11:13	to detest and not eat **b** they are detestable:	NIH
11:44	consecrate yourselves and be holy, **b**	3954
11:45	therefore be holy, **b** I am holy.	3954
13:11	**b** he is already unclean.	3954
13:44	The priest shall pronounce him unclean **b of**	928
13:52	**b** the mildew is destructive;	3954
14:48	**b** the mildew is gone.	3954
15:15	the LORD for the man **b of** his discharge.	4946
16: 2	on the ark, or else he will die, **b** I appear in	3954
16:16	the Most Holy Place **b of** the uncleanness	4946
16:30	**b** on this day atonement will be made	3954
17:14	**b** the life of every creature is its blood.	3954
17:14	**b** the life of every creature is its blood;	3954
18:13	**b** she is your mother's close relative.	3954
18:24	**b** this is how the nations that I am going	3954
19: 2	'Be holy **b** I, the LORD your God,	3954
19: 8	Whoever eats it will be held responsible **b**	3954
19:20	**b** she had not been freed.	3954
20: 7	**b** I am the LORD your God.	3954
20:23	**B** they did all these things,	3954
20:26	You are to be holy to me **b** I, the LORD,	3954
21: 6	**B** they present the offerings made to	3954
21: 7	**b** priests are holy to their God.	3954
21: 8	**b** he offers up the food of your God.	3954
21: 8	**b** I the LORD am holy—	3954
21:12	**b** he has been dedicated by the anointing oil	3954
21:23	yet **b of** his defect,	3954
22:20	**b** it will not be accepted on your behalf.	3954
22:25	**b** they are deformed and have defects.' "	3954
23:28	**b** it is the Day of Atonement.	3954
24: 9	**b** it is a most holy part of their regular share	3954
25:16	**b** what he is really selling you is	3954
25:23	**b** the land is mine and you are but aliens	3954
25:33	in the Jubilee, **b** the houses in the towns of	3954
25:42	**B** the Israelites are my servants,	3954
26:16	**b** your enemies will eat it.	2256
26:20	your soil will not yield its crops,	2256
26:39	in the lands of their enemies **b** of their sins;	928
Lev 26:39	**b** of their fathers' sins they will waste away.	928
26:43	pay for their sins **b** they rejected my laws	928+2256+3610+3610
Nu 5: 2	or who is ceremonially unclean **b of**	4200
5:15	**b** it is a grain offering for jealousy,	3954
5:30	over a man **b** he suspects his wife.	2256
6: 7	**b** the symbol of his separation to God is	3954
6:11	to make atonement for him **b** he sinned	889+4946
6:12	**b** he became defiled during his separation.	3954
7: 9	**b** they were to carry on their shoulders	3954
9: 6	that day **b** they were ceremonially unclean	NIH
9: 7	"We have become unclean **b of**	4200
9:10	or your descendants are unclean **b of**	4200
9:13	from his people **b** he did not present	3954
11: 3	**b** fire from the LORD had burned	3954
11:20	**b** you have rejected the LORD,	3610+3954
11:34	**b** there they buried	3954
12: 1	Aaron began to talk against Moses **b of**	128+6584
13:24	the Valley of Eshcol **b of** the cluster	128+6584
14: 9	**b** we will swallow them up.	3954
14:24	But **b** my servant Caleb has	6813
14:42	Do not go up, **b** the LORD is not with you.	3954
14:43	**B** you have turned away from the LORD,	3954+4027+6584
15:26	**b** all the people were involved in	3954
15:31	**B** he has despised the LORD's word	3954
15:34	**b** it was not clear what should be done	3954
16:26	you will be swept away **b of** all their sins."	928
16:49	in addition to those who had died **b of** Korah.	1821+6584
19:13	**B** the water of cleansing has	3954
19:20	**b** he has defiled the sanctuary of	3954
20:12	"**B** you did not trust in me enough	3610
20:24	**b** both of you rebelled	889+6584
21:24	**b** their border was fortified.	3954
22: 3	and Moab was terrified **b** there were	4946+7156
22: 3	Moab was filled with dread **b of**	4946+7156
22: 6	**b** they are too powerful for me.	3954
22:12	**b** they are blessed."	3954
22:17	**b** I will reward you handsomely	3954
22:32	to oppose you **b** your path is a reckless one	3954
25:13	**b** he was zealous for the honor of his God	889+9393
25:18	**b** they treated you as enemies	3954
26:62	not counted along with the other Israelites	3954
27: 4	from his clan **b** he had no son?	3954
30: 5	the LORD will release her **b**	3954
32:11	'B they have not followed me wholeheartedly,	3954
32:19	**b** our inheritance has come to us on	3954
34:14	the families of the tribe of Reuben,	3954
Dt 1:36	**b** he followed the LORD wholeheartedly	889+3610
1:37	**B of** you the LORD became angry	928+1673
1:38	**b** he will lead Israel to inherit it.	3954
1:42	**b** I will not be with you.	3954
2:25	will tremble and be in anguish **b of**	4946+7156
3:26	But **b of** you the LORD was angry	5100
4:21	The LORD was angry with me **b of** you	1821+6584
4:37	**B** he loved your forefathers	3954+9393
5: 5	**b** you were afraid of the fire and did not go	3954
7: 7	on you and choose you **b**	4946
7: 8	But it was **b** the LORD loved you and kept	4946
9: 4	of this land **b of** my righteousness."	928
9: 5	It is not **b of** your righteousness	928
9: 6	that it is not **b of** your righteousness that	928
9:12	**b** your people whom you brought out	3954
9:18	**b of** all the sin you had committed,	6584
9:25	and forty nights **b**	3954
9:28	'B the LORD was not able to take them	4946
9:28	and **b** he hated them,	4946
12: 7	**b** the LORD your God has blessed you.	889
12:23	**b** the blood is the life,	3954
12:25	**b** you will be doing what is right in the eyes	3954
12:28	**b** you will be doing what is good and right	3954
12:31	**b** in worshiping their gods,	3954
13: 5	**b** he preached rebellion against	3954
13:10	**b** he tried to turn you away from	3954
13:18	**b** you obey the LORD your God,	3954
14:24	and cannot carry your tithe (**b** the place	3954
15: 2	**b** the LORD's time	3954
15:10	then **b of** this	1673
15:16	**b** he loves you and your family	3954
15:18	to set your servant free, **b** his service	3954
16: 1	**b** in the month of Abib he brought you out	3954
16: 3	**b** you left Egypt in haste—	3954
18:12	and **b of** these detestable practices	1673
19: 9	**b** you carefully follow all these laws I command you today—	3954
20: 1	**b** the LORD your God,	3954
20:19	**b** you can eat their fruit.	3954
21:23	**b** anyone who is hung on a tree is	3954
22:19	**b** this man has given an Israelite virgin	3954
22:24	the girl **b** she was in a town and did	1821+6584
22:24	man **b** he violated another man's wife.	1821+6584
23: 5	**b** the LORD your God loves you.	3954
23: 7	**b** you lived as an alien in his country.	3954
23:10	If one of your men is unclean **b of**	4946
23:14	**b** the LORD your God detests them both.	3954
23:23	**b** you made your vow freely to	NIH
24: 1	to him **b** he finds something indecent	3954
24: 6	**b** that would be taking a man's livelihood	3954
24:15	**b** he is poor and is counting on it.	3954
28:20	to sudden ruin **b of** the evil you have done	4946+7156
28:38	**b** locusts will devour it.	3954
28:39	**b** worms will eat them.	3954
28:40	**b** the olives will drop off.	3954
Dt 28:41	**b** they will go into captivity.	3954
28:45	**b** you did not obey the LORD your God	3954
28:47	**B** you did not serve the LORD your God	889+9393
28:53	**B of** the suffering that your enemy	928
28:55	It will be all he has left **b of**	928
28:62	**b** you did not obey the LORD your God.	3954
28:67	**b of** the terror that will fill your hearts and	4946
29:25	"It is **b** this people abandoned the covenant	6584
31: 6	Do not be afraid or terrified **b of** them,	4946+7156
31:17	'Have not these disasters come upon us **b**	3954+6584
31:18	that day **b of** all their wickedness in turning	6584
31:21	**b** it will not be forgotten	3954
31:29	upon you **b** you will do evil in the sight of	3954
32:19	The LORD saw this and rejected them **b**	4946
32:51	This is **b** both of you broke faith with me in	6584
32:51	and **b** you did not uphold my holiness	6584
34: 9	of wisdom **b** Moses had laid his hands	3954
Jos 1: 6	**b** you will lead these people to inherit	3954
2: 1	and entered your house, **b** they have come	3954
2: 9	country is melting in fear **b of** you.	4946+7156
2:11	everyone's courage failed **b of** you,	4946+7156
2:12	**b** I have shown kindness to you.	3954
2:24	all the people are melting in fear **b of** us.	4946+7156
5: 7	They were still uncircumcised **b** they had	3954
6: 1	Now Jericho was tightly shut up **b of**	4946+7156
6:17	**b** she hid the spies we sent.	3954
6:25	**b** she hid the men Joshua had sent as spies	3954
7:12	and run **b** they have been made liable	3954
9: 9	from a very distant country **b of** the fame	4200
9:18	**b** the leaders of the assembly had sworn	3954
9:24	So we feared for our lives **b of** you,	4946+7156
10: 2	**b** Gibeon was an important city,	3954
10: 4	"**b** it has made peace with Joshua and	3954
10: 6	**b** all the Amorite kings from	3954
10:42	**b** the LORD, the God of Israel,	3954
11: 6	**b** by this time tomorrow I will hand all	3954
14: 9	**b** you have followed	3954
14:14	**b** he followed the LORD,	889+3610
17: 1	who had received Gilead and Bashan **b**	3954
17: 6	**b** the daughters of the tribe	3954
18: 7	**b** the priestly service of	3954
19: 9	from the share of Judah, **b**	3954
20: 5	**b** he killed his neighbor unintentionally and	3954
21:10	**b** the first lot fell to them):	3954
22:31	**b** you have not acted unfaithfully toward	889
23:10	**b** the LORD your God fights for you,	3954
24:18	**b** he is our God."	3954
Jdg 1:19	**b** they had iron chariots.	3954
1:32	and **b of** this the people of Asher lived	3954
2:13	**b** they forsook him and served Baal and	2256
2:20	**B** this nation has violated the covenant	889+3610
3:12	**b** they did this evil	3954+6584
4: 3	**B** he had nine hundred iron chariots.	3954
4: 9	But **b of** the way you are going about this,	6584
4:17	**b** there were friendly relations	3954
5:23	**b** they did not come to help the LORD,	3954
6: 2	**B** the power of Midian was so oppressive,	4946+7156
6: 7	the Israelites cried to the LORD **b of**	128+6584
6:27	But **b** he was afraid of his family and	889+3869
6:30	**b** he has broken down Baal's altar and cut	3954
6:32	**b** he broke down Baal's altar.	3954
7: 9	**b** I am going to give it into your hands.	3954
8:20	**b** he was only a boy and was afraid.	3954
8:22	**b** you have saved us out of the hand	3954
9:18	king over the citizens of Shechem **b**	3954
9:21	**b** he was afraid of	4946+7156
10: 6	And **b** the Israelites forsook the LORD	2256
11: 2	"**b** you are the son of another woman."	3954
11:35	**b** I have made a vow to the LORD	2256
11:37	**b** I will never marry."	6584
11:38	the hills and wept **b** she would never marry.	6584
12: 4	The Gileadites struck them down **b**	3954
12: 6	**b** he could not pronounce	2256
13: 5	**b** you will conceive and give birth to a son.	3954
13: 5	**b** the boy is to be a Nazirite.	3954
13: 7	**b** the boy will be a Nazirite of God	3954
14:17	**b** she continued to press him.	3954
15: 6	**b** his wife was given to his friend."	3954
15:18	**B** he was very thirsty,	2256
16:17	"**b** I have been a Nazirite set apart to God	3954
18: 1	**b** they had not yet come into an inheritance	3954
18:28	to rescue them **b** they lived a long way	3954
20: 6	**b** they committed this lewd	3954
20:36	**b** they relied on the ambush they had set	3954
20:41	**b** they realized that disaster had come	3954
21:15	**b** the LORD had made a gap in the tribes	3954
21:22	**b** we did not get wives for them during	3954
Ru 1:13	**b** the LORD's hand has gone out	3954
1:19	the whole town was stirred **b of** them,	6584
1:20	"Call me Mara, **b** the Almighty has made my life very bitter.	3954
2:22	**b** in someone else's field you might	2256+4202
4: 6	"Then I cannot redeem it **b**	7153
1Sa 1: 5	But to Hannah he gave a double portion **b**	3954
1: 6	And **b** the LORD had closed her womb,	3954
1:20	saying, "**B** I asked the LORD for him."	3954
3:13	that I would judge his family forever **b of**	928
4:13	his heart feared for the ark of God.	3954
4:21	**b of** the capture of the ark of God and	448
5: 7	**b** his hand is heavy upon us and	3954
6: 4	the same plague has struck both you	3954
6:19	to death **b** they had looked into the ark of	3954
6:19	The people mourned **b of** the heavy blow	3954
7: 7	they were afraid **b of** the Philistines.	4946+7156

1Sa	9: 9	b the prophet of today used to be called	3954
	9:13	b he must bless the sacrifice;	3954
	9:24	b it was set aside for you for this occasion,	3954
	12: 7	b I am going to confront you with evidence	2256
	12:21	nor can they rescue you, b they are useless.	3954
	12:22	b the LORD was pleased	3954
	13:14	and appointed him leader of his people, b	3954
	13:19	b the Philistines had said,	3954
	14:10	b that will be our sign that	2256
	14:24	b Saul had bound the people under an oath,	2256
	14:26	b they feared the oath.	3954
	15:11	b he has turned away from me and has	3954
	15:23	B you have rejected the word of	3610
	17:36	like one of them, b he has defied the armies	3954
	17:39	b he was not used to them.	3954
	17:39	he said to Saul, "b I am not used to them."	3954
	18: 3	with David b he loved him as himself.	928
	18:12	b the LORD was with David	3954
	18:14	b the LORD was with him.	2256
	18:16	b he led them in their campaigns.	3954
	20: 6	b an annual sacrifice is being made there	3954
	20:17	b he loved him as he loved himself.	3954
	20:18	b your seat will be empty.	3954
	20:21	bring them here,' then come, b,	3954
	20:22	b the LORD has sent you away.	3954
	20:29	b our family is observing a sacrifice in	3954
	20:34	the month he did not eat, b he was grieved	3954
	21: 8	the king's business was urgent."	3954
	22:17	b they too have sided with David.	3954
	22:17	b he is the LORD's anointed.'	3954
	25:17	b disaster is hanging over our master	3954
	25:28	b he fights the LORD's battles.	3954
	26:12	b the LORD had put them into	3954
	26:16	b you did not guard your master,	889
	26:21	B you considered my life precious today,	889+9393
	28:18	B you did not obey the LORD	889+3869
	28:20	filled with fear b of Samuel's words.	4946
	30: 6	David was greatly distressed b	3954
	30: 6	each one was bitter in spirit b of his sons	6584
	30:16	drinking and reveling b of the great amount	928
	30:22	"B they did not go out with us,	889+3610
2Sa	1:10	I knew that after he had fallen he could	3954
	1:12	b they had fallen by the sword.	3954
	2: 6	and I too will show you the same favor b	889
	3: 8	Abner was very angry b of	6584
	3:11	b he was afraid of him.	4946
	3:22	b David had sent him away,	3954
	3:30	and his brother Abishai murdered Abner b	6584
	4: 3	b the people of Beeroth fled to Gittaim	2256
	5:10	b the LORD God Almighty was with him.	2256
	5:24	b that will mean the LORD has gone out	3954
	6: 6	b the oxen stumbled.	3954
	6: 7	against Uzzah b of his irreverent act;	6584
	6: 8	Then David was angry b	6584
	6:12	b of the ark of God."	6288
	9:13	b he always ate at the king's table,	3954
	12: 6	b he did such a thing and had no pity."	889+6813
	12:10	b you despised me and took the wife	3954+6813
	12:14	But b by doing this you have made	3954
	12:25	and b the LORD loved him,	6288
	13:22	he hated Amnon b	1821+6584
	14:15	the king b the people have made me afraid.	3954
	14:22	in your eyes, my lord the king, b	889
	16: 3	"He is staying in Jerusalem, b he thinks,	3954
	16: 8	You have come to ruin b you are a man	3954
	16:10	If he is cursing b the LORD said to him,	3954
	18:20	b the king's son is dead."	3954+4027+6584
	19: 2	b on that day the troops heard it said,	3954
	19: 9	he has fled the country b of Absalom;	4946+6584
	19:42	"We did this b the king is closely related	3954
	21: 1	it is b he put the Gibeonites to death."	889+6584
	21: 7	b of the oath before the LORD	6584
	22: 8	they trembled b he was angry.	3954
	22:20	he rescued me b he delighted in me.	3954
	24:16	the LORD was grieved b of the calamity	448
1Ki	2:26	b you carried the ark of	3954
	2:32	b without the knowledge	889
	3: 2	b a temple had not yet been built for	3954
	3: 6	b he was faithful to you and righteous	889+3869
	3:19	"During the night this woman's son died b	889
	3:28	b they saw that he had wisdom from God	3954
	5: 1	b he had always been on friendly terms	3954
	5: 3	"You know that b of the wars waged	4946+7156
	7:47	b there were so many;	4946
	8:11	not perform their service b of the cloud,	4946+7156
	8:18	'B it was in your heart to build a temple	889+3610
	8:33	an enemy b they have sinned against you,	889
	8:35	there is no rain b your people have sinned	3954
	8:35	from their sin b you have afflicted them,	3954
	8:41	but has come from a distant land b of	5100
	8:64	b the bronze altar before the LORD	3954
	9: 9	'B they have forsaken the LORD	889+6584
	9:11	b Hiram had supplied him with all	NIH
	10: 9	B of the LORD's eternal love for Israel,	928
	10:21	b silver was considered of little value	NIH
	11: 2	b they will surely turn your hearts	434
	11: 9	The LORD became angry with Solomon b	3954
	11:33	I will do this b they have forsaken me	889+3610
	11:39	I will humble David's descendants b of	5100
	14: 4	his sight was gone b of his age.	4946
	14:10	b of this, I am going to bring disaster	4027+4200
	14:13	b he is the only one in the house	3610
	14:15	b they provoked the LORD to anger	889+3610
	14:16	up b of the sins Jeroboam has committed	1673
	15:13	b she had made a repulsive Asherah pole.	889

1Ki	15:30	b of the sins Jeroboam had committed	6584
	15:30	and b he provoked the LORD,	928
	16: 7	b of all the evil he had done in the eyes of	6584
	16: 7	and also b he destroyed it.	889+6584
	16:13	b of all the sins Baasha	448
	16:19	b of the sins he had committed,	6584
	17: 7	the brook dried up b there had been no rain	3954
	20:22	b next spring the king	3954
	20:28	B the Arameans think the LORD is a god	889+3610
	20:36	"B you have not obeyed the LORD,	889+3610
	21: 4	and angry b Naboth the Jezreelite had said,	6584
	21: 6	"B I said to Naboth the Jezreelite,	3954
	21:20	"b you have sold yourself to do evil in	3610
	21:22	b you have provoked me to anger	448
	21:29	B he has humbled himself,	3610+3954
	22: 8	but I hate him b	3954
	22:52	b he walked in the ways of his father	2256
2Ki	1: 3	'Is it b there is no God in Israel	4946
	1: 6	Is it b there is no God in Israel	4946
	1:16	Is it b there is no God in Israel for you	4946
	1:16	B you have done this,	889+3610
	1:17	B Ahaziah had no son,	3954
	3:13	the king of Israel answered, "b it was	3954
	5: 1	of his master and highly regarded, b	3954
	6: 9	the Arameans are going down there."	3954
	8: 1	b the LORD has decreed a famine in	3954
	8:12	"B I know the harm you will do to	3954
	8:29	b he had been wounded.	3954
	9:16	b Joram was resting there and Ahaziah king	3954
	10:19	b I am going to hold a great sacrifice	3954
	10:30	"B you have done well	889+3610
	11:20	b Athaliah had been slain with the sword at	2256
	12:15	b they acted with complete honesty.	3954
	13:23	for them b of his covenant with Abraham,	5100
	15: 7	All this took place b	3954
	17:26	b the people do	889+3869
	18:12	This happened b they had not obeyed	889+6584
	18:36	b the king had commanded,	3954
	19:28	B you rage against me	3610
	20: 1	b you are going to die;	3954
	20:12	b he had heard of Hezekiah's illness.	3954
	21:15	b they have done evil in my eyes	889+3610
	22: 7	b they are acting faithfully."	3954
	22:13	LORD's anger that burns against us b	889+6584
	22:17	B they have forsaken me	889+9393
	22:19	B your heart was responsive	3610
	22:19	and b you tore your robes and wept	NIH
	23:26	which burned against Judah b of all	6584
	24: 3	to remove them from his presence b of	928
	24: 7	from his own country again, b the king	3954
	24:20	It was b of the LORD's anger	6584
1Ch	1:19	b in his time the earth was divided;	3954
	4:14	It was called this b	3954
	4:41	b there was pasture for their flocks.	3954
	5: 9	b their livestock had increased in Gilead.	3954
	5:20	b they cried out to him during the battle.	3954
	5:20	b they trusted in him.	3954
	5:22	b the battle was God's.	3954
	6:54	b the first lot was for them):	3954
	7:23	b there had been misfortune in his family.	3954
	9: 1	to Babylon b of their unfaithfulness.	928
	9:27	b they had to guard it;	3954
	9:33	from other duties b they were responsible	3954
	10:13	Saul died b he was unfaithful to	928
	11: 9	b the LORD Almighty was with him.	2256
	11:19	B they risked their lives to bring it back,	3954
	12:19	and his men did not help the Philistines b,	3954
	13: 4	b it seemed right to all the people.	3954
	13: 9	b the oxen stumbled.	3954
	13:10	down b he had put his hand on the ark.	889+6584
	13:11	Then David was angry b	3954
	14:15	b that will mean God has gone out	3954
	15: 2	b the LORD chose them to carry the ark of	3954
	15:13	It was b you, the Levites,	3954+4200+4537
	15:22	that was his responsibility b he was skillful	3954
	15:26	B God had helped	928
	19: 2	b his father showed kindness to me."	3954
	21: 6	b the king's command was repulsive	3954
	21:15	and was grieved b of the calamity and said	3954
	21:30	b he was afraid of the sword of the angel of	3954
	22: 8	b you have shed much blood on the earth	3954
	26: 6	who were leaders in their father's family b	3954
	27:23	b the LORD had promised to make Israel	3954
	28: 3	b you are a warrior and have shed blood.'	3954
	29: 1	b this palatial structure is not for man but	3954
2Ch	1: 4	b he had pitched a tent for it in Jerusalem	3954
	2: 5	b our God is greater than all other gods.	3954
	2: 9	b the temple I build must be large	3954
	2:11	"B the LORD loves his people,	928
	5:14	not perform their service b of the cloud,	4946+7156
	6: 8	'B it was in your heart to build a temple	889+3610
	6:24	an enemy b they have sinned against you	3954
	6:26	up and there is no rain b	3954
	6:26	from their sin b you have afflicted them,	3954
	6:32	from a distant land b of your great name	5100
	7: 2	the temple of the LORD b the glory of	3954
	7: 7	the bronze altar he had made could	3954
	7:22	'B they have forsaken the LORD,	889+6584
	8:11	b the places the ark of	3954
	8:14	b this was what David the man	3954
	9: 8	B of the love of your God for Israel	928
	9:20	b silver was considered of little value	NIH
	11:14	to Judah and Jerusalem b Jeroboam	3954
	12: 2	B they had been unfaithful to the LORD,	3954
	12:12	B Rehoboam humbled himself,	928

2Ch	12:14	He did evil b he had not set his heart	3954
	13:18	of Judah were victorious b they relied on	3954
	14: 7	b we have sought the LORD our God;	3954
	15: 6	b God was troubling them with every kind	3954
	15:15	All Judah rejoiced about the oath b	3954
	15:16	b she had made a repulsive Asherah pole.	889
	16: 7	"B you relied on the king of Aram and not	
		on the LORD your God,	4027+6584
	16:10	Asa was angry with the seer b of this;	6584
	17: 3	The LORD was with Jehoshaphat b	3954
	18: 7	but I hate him b	3954
	19: 2	B of this, the wrath of the LORD is	928
	19: 6	b you are not judging for man but for	3954
	20:15	'Do not be afraid or discouraged b of	4946+7156
	20:37	"B you have made an alliance	3869
	21: 3	but he had given the kingdom to Jehoram b	3954
	21: 7	b of the covenant the LORD had made	5100
	21:10	b Jehoram had forsaken the LORD,	3954
	21:19	his bowels came out b of the disease,	6640
	22: 6	down to Jezreel to see Joram son of Ahab b	3954
	22:11	B Jehosheba, the daughter of King Jehoram	2256
	23: 6	they may enter b they are consecrated,	3954
	23:21	b Athaliah had been slain with the sword.	2256
	24:16	b of the good he had done in Israel for God	3954
	24:18	B of their guilt,	928
	24:20	B you have forsaken the LORD,	3954
	24:24	b Judah had forsaken the LORD,	3954
	25:16	b you have done this and have not listened	3954
	25:20	b they sought the gods of Edom.	3954
	26: 8	b he had become very powerful.	3954
	26:10	b he had much livestock in the foothills and	3954
	26:20	b the LORD had afflicted him.	3954
	27: 6	Jotham grew powerful b	3954
	28: 6	b Judah had forsaken the LORD,	928
	28: 9	He said to them, "B the LORD,	3954
	28:19	The LORD had humbled Judah b of	6288
	29:24	b the king had ordered the burnt offering	3954
	29:36	b it was done so quickly.	3954
	30: 3	to celebrate it at the regular time b	3954
	31:10	b the LORD has blessed his people,	3954
	32: 7	discouraged b of the king of Assyria	4946+7156
	34:21	b our fathers have not kept the word	889+6584
	34:25	B they have forsaken me	889+9393
	34:27	B your heart was responsive	3610
	34:27	and b you humbled yourself before me	NIH
	35:14	the priests, the descendants of Aaron,	3954
	35:15	b their fellow Levites made	3954
	36:15	b he had pity on his people and	3954
Ezr	3:11	b the foundation of the house of	6584
	3:13	b the people made so much noise.	3954
	4: 2	"Let us help you build b, like you,	3954
	5:12	b our fathers angered the God of heaven,	
			10168+10427
	6:13	Then, b of the decree King Darius had sent,	
			10168+10378+10619
	6:22	b the LORD had filled them with joy	3954
	7:28	B the hand of the LORD my God was	3869
	8:18	B the gracious hand of our God was on us,	3869
	8:22	b we had told the king,	3954
	9: 4	the God of Israel gathered around me b of	6584
	9: 6	to lift up my face to you, my God, b	3954
	9: 7	B of our sins,	928
	9:15	though b of it not one of us can stand	6584
	10: 6	he continued to mourn over	3954
	10: 9	greatly distressed by the occasion and b of	4946
	10:13	b we have sinned greatly in this thing.	3954
Ne	2: 8	And b the gracious hand of my God was	3869
	2:16	b as yet I had said nothing to the Jews or	2256
	5: 5	b our fields and our vineyards belong	2256
	5: 8	b they could find nothing to say.	2256
	5:18	b the demands were heavy on these people.	3954
	6:10	b men are coming to kill you—	3954
	6:12	that he had prophesied against me b Tobiah	2256
	6:14	O my God, b of what they have done;	3869
	6:16	and lost their self-confidence, b	2256
	7: 2	b he was a man of integrity	3954
	8: 5	the people could see him b he was standing	3954
	8:12	b they now understood the words	3954
	9: 8	You have kept your promise b	3954
	9:19	"B of your great compassion you did	928
	9:37	B of our sins, its abundant harvest goes	928
	12:43	rejoicing b God had given them great joy.	3954
	13: 2	b they had not met the Israelites with food	3954
	13:13	b these men were considered trustworthy.	3954
	13:26	Was it not b of marriages like these	6584
	13:29	b they defiled the priestly office and	6584
Est	2: 7	up b she had neither father nor mother.	3954
	2:10	b Mordecai had forbidden her to do so.	3954
	4: 2	b no one clothed in sackcloth was allowed	3954
	4:13	that b you are in the king's house you alone	NIH
	7: 4	b no such distress would justify disturbing	3954
	8: 7	"B Haman attacked the Jews,	889+6584
	8:17	of other nationalities became Jews b fear of	3954
	9: 2	the people of all	3954
	9: 3	b fear of Mordecai had seized them.	3954
	9:26	B of everything written in this letter	4027+6584
	9:26	this letter and b of what they had seen	3970+6584
	10: 3	b he worked for the good of his people	NIH
Job	2:13	b they saw how great his suffering was.	3954
	6:20	b they had been confident;	3954
	11:18	You will be secure, b there is hope;	3954
	15:25	b he shakes his fist at God	3954
	20: 2	to answer b I am greatly disturbed.	6288
	29:12	I rescued the poor who cried for help,	3954
	31:34	b I so feared the crowd and so dreaded	3954
	32: 1	b he was righteous in his own eyes.	3954
	32: 3	b they had found no way to refute Job,	889+6584

Job 32: 4	to Job **b** they were older than he.	3954
34:25	**B** he takes note of their deeds,	4027+4200
34:27	**b** they turned from following him	4027+6584
35:12	He does not answer when men cry out **b of**	4946+7156
37:19	we cannot draw up our case **b of**	4946+7156
42: 7	**b** you have not spoken of me what is right,	3954
Ps 3: 5	I wake again, **b** the LORD sustains me.	3954
5: 8	in your righteousness **b of** my enemies—	5100
6: 4	save me **b of** your unfailing love.	5100
6: 7	they fail **b of** all my foes.	928
7:17	I will give thanks to the LORD **b of**	3869
8: 2	and infants you have ordained praise **b of**	5100
12: 5	"**B of** the oppression of the weak and	4946
16: 8	**B** he is at my right hand,	3954
16:10	**b** you will not abandon me to the grave,	3954
18: 7	they trembled **b** he was angry.	3954
18:19	he rescued me **b** he delighted in me.	3954
25:21	**b** my hope is in you.	3954
27:11	in a straight path **b of** my oppressors.	5100
31:10	my strength fails **b of** my affliction,	928
31:11	**B** of all my enemies,	4946
37: 1	Do not fret **b of** evil men or be envious	928
37:40	**b** they take refuge in him.	3954
38: 3	**B of** your wrath there is no health	4946+7156
38: 3	my bones have no soundness **b of** my sin.	4946+7156
38: 5	My wounds fester and are loathsome **b of**	4946+7156
38:11	My friends and companions avoid me **b of**	4946+5584
44:16	**b of** the enemy, who is bent on revenge.	4946+7156
44:26	redeem us **b of** your unfailing love.	5100
48:11	of Judah are glad **b of** your judgments.	5100
63: 3	**B** your love is better than life,	3954
63: 7	**B** you are my help,	3954
68:29	**B of** your temple	4946
69: 6	in you not be disgraced **b of** me, O Lord,	928
69: 6	not be put to shame **b of** me,	928
69:18	redeem me **b of** my foes.	5100
70: 3	turn back **b of** their shame.	6584+6813
74:20	**b** haunts of violence fill the dark places of	3954
91:14	"**B** he loves me," says the LORD,	3954
97: 8	of Judah are glad **b of** your judgments,	5100
102: 5	**B of** my loud groaning I am reduced	4946
102:10	**b of** your great wrath,	4946+7156
105:38	**b** dread of Israel had fallen on them.	3954
106:32	and trouble came to Moses **b of** them;	6288
107:17	and suffered affliction **b of** their iniquities,	4946
107:34	**b of** the wickedness of those	4946
115: 1	**b of** your love and faithfulness.	6584
116: 2	**B** he turned his ear to me,	3954
119:47	I delight in your commands **b** I love them.	889
119:53	Indignation grips me **b of** the wicked,	4946
119:127	**B** I love your commands more than gold,	4027+6584
119:128	**b** I consider all your precepts right,	4027+6584
139:14	I praise you **b** I am fearfully	3954+4268
142: 7	the righteous will gather about me **b of**	3954
Pr 3:12	**b** the LORD disciplines those he loves,	3954
21:25	**b** his hands refuse to work.	3954
22:22	not exploit the poor **b** they are poor and do	3954
24: 1	Do not fret **b of** evil men or be envious of	928
Ecc 2:17	**b** the work that is done under	3954
2:18	**b** I must leave them to the one who comes	8611
3:22	**b** that is his lot.	3954
4: 9	**b** they have a good return for their work;	889
5:20	**b** God keeps him occupied with gladness	3954
7: 3	**b** a sad face is good for the heart.	3954
8: 2	I say, **b** you took an oath before God.	1826+6584
8:13	Yet **b** the wicked do not fear God,	889
8:15	**b** nothing is better for a man under	889
10:20	**b** a bird of the air may carry your words,	3954
12: 3	when the grinders cease **b** they are few,	3954
SS 1: 6	Do not stare at me **b** I am dark,	8611
1: 6	**b** I am darkened by the sun.	8611
Isa 1:29	"You will be ashamed **b of** the sacred oaks	4946
1:29	you will be disgraced **b of** the gardens	4946
7: 4	Do not lose heart **b of**	4946
7: 4	**b of** the fierce anger of Rezin and Aram	928
7:22	**b of** the abundance of the milk they give,	4946
8: 6	"**B** this people has rejected	3610+3954
10:13	and by my wisdom, **b** I have understanding.	3954
10:27	the yoke will be broken **b** you have grown	4946+7156
13: 7	**B of** this, all hands will go limp,	4027+6584
17: 9	which they left **b of** the Israelites,	4946+7156
19:17	**b of** what the LORD Almighty is planning	4946+7156
19:20	When they cry out to the LORD **b of**	4946+7156
26: 3	whose mind is steadfast, **b** he trusts in you.	3954
30: 5	to shame **b of** a people useless to them,	6584
30:12	"**B** you have rejected this message,	3610
31: 9	Their stronghold will fall **b of** terror;	4946
36:21	**b** the king had commanded,	3954
37:21	**B** you have prayed to me	889
37:29	**B** you rage against me and	3610
37:29	and **b** your insolence has reached my ears,	NIH
38: 1	**b** you are going to die;	3954
38:15	I will walk humbly all my years **b of**	6584
39: 1	**b** he had heard of his illness and recovery.	2256
40: 7	**b** the breath of the LORD blows on them.	3954
40:26	**B of** his great power and mighty strength,	4946
43: 4	and **b** I love you,	NIH
43:20	**b** I provide water in the desert and streams	3954
49: 7	**b of** the LORD, who is faithful,	5100
Isa 50: 1	**B of** your sins you were sold;	928
50: 1	**b of** your transgressions your mother was sent away.	928
50: 7	**B** the Sovereign LORD helps me,	4027+6584
51:13	in constant terror every day **b of** the wrath of the oppressor,	4946+7156
52:15	and kings will shut their mouths **b of** him.	6584
53:12	**b** he poured out his life unto death,	889+9393
54: 1	**b** more are the children of	3954
55: 5	**b of** the LORD your God,	5100
57:11	not **b** I have long been silent that you do	NIH
61: 1	**b** the LORD has anointed me	3610
64: 7	and made us waste away **b of** our sins.	928+3338
65: 7	"**B** they burned sacrifices on the mountains	889
66: 5	and exclude you **b of** my name, have said,	5100
66:18	I, **b of** their actions and their imaginations,	NIH
Jer 1:16	**b of** their wickedness	3954
2:35	But I will pass judgment on you **b** you say,	6584
3: 8	sent her away **b of** all her adulteries.	128+6584
3: 9	**B** Israel's immorality mattered so little	2256
3:21	**b** they have perverted their ways	3954
4: 4	like fire **b of** the evil you have done—	4946+7156
4:17	**b** she has rebelled against me,' "	3954
4:28	**b** I have spoken and will not relent,	3954+6584
5:14	"**B** the people have spoken these words,	3610
6:19	on this people, the fruit of their schemes, **b**	3954
6:30	**b** the LORD has rejected them."	3954
7:12	see what I did to it **b of** the wickedness	4946+7156
8:14	**b** we have sinned against him.	3954
9: 7	test them, for what else can I do **b of**	4946+7156
9:13	"It is **b** they have forsaken my law,	6584
9:19	We must leave our land **b** our houses are	3954
10: 5	they must be carried **b** they cannot walk.	3954
10:19	Woe to me **b of** my injury!	6584
11:14	**b** I will not listen when they call to me in	3954
11:17	**b** the house of Israel and the house	1673
11:18	**B** the LORD revealed their plot to me,	2256
11:23	**b** I will bring disaster on the men	3954
12: 4	**B** those who live in it are wicked,	4946
12:11	be laid waste **b** there is no one who cares.	3954
12:13	So bear the shame of your harvest **b of**	4946
13:17	I will weep in secret **b of** your pride;	4946+7156
13:17	the LORD's flock will be taken captive.	3954
13:22	it is **b of** your many sins	928
13:25	"**b** you have forgotten me and trusted	889
14: 4	The ground is cracked **b** there is no rain in	3954
14: 5	in the field deserts her newborn fawn **b**	3954
14:16	Jerusalem **b of** the famine and sword.	4946+7156
15: 4	of the earth **b of** what Manasseh son	1673
15:13	**b of** all your sins throughout your country.	928
15:17	I sat alone **b** your hand was on me	4946+7156
16: 5	**b** I have withdrawn my blessing,	3954
16:11	'It is **b** your fathers forsook me,'	889+6584
16:18	**b** they have defiled my land with	6584
17: 3	of sin throughout your country.	928
17:13	be written in the dust **b** they have forsaken	3954
19: 8	by will be appalled and will scoff **b of**	6584
19:15	**b** they were stiff-necked and would	3954
21: 2	the LORD for us **b** Nebuchadnezzar king	3954
21:12	like fire **b of** the evil you have done—	4946+7156
22: 9	'**B** they have forsaken the covenant of	889+6584
22:10	for him who is exiled, **b**	3954
22:22	and disgraced **b of** all your wickedness.	4946
23: 2	"**B** you have scattered my flock	NIH
23: 9	**B of** the LORD and his holy words.	4946+7156
23:10	**b of** the curse the land lies parched	3954+4946+7156
23:15	and drink poisoned water, **b** from	3954
23:36	'the oracle of the LORD' again, **b**	3954
25: 8	"**B** you have not listened to my words,	889+3610
25:16	and go mad **b of** the sword I will send	4946+7156
25:27	rise no more **b of** the sword I will send	4946+7156
25:37	be laid waste **b of** the fierce anger of	4946+7156
25:38	their land will become desolate **b of**	4946+7156
25:38	the sword of the oppressor and **b of**	4946+7156
26: 3	the disaster I was planning **b of**	4946+7156
26:11	be sentenced to death **b** he has prophesied	3954
28:16	**b** you have preached rebellion against	3954
29: 7	Pray to the LORD for it, **b** if it prospers,	3954
29:22	**B of** them, all the exiles	3954
29:31	**B** Shemaiah has prophesied to you,	889+3610
29:32	**b** he has preached rebellion against me.' "	3954
30:14	**b** your guilt is so great and your sins	6584
30:15	**B of** your great guilt	6584
30:17	'**b** you are called an outcast,	3954
31: 9	**b** I am Israel's father,	3954
31:15	**b** her children are no more."	3954
31:18	**b** you are the LORD my God.	3954
31:19	I was ashamed and humiliated **b** I bore	3954
31:32	**b** they broke my covenant,	889
31:34	**b** they will all know me,	3954
31:37	of Israel **b of** all they have done,"	6584
32: 7	**b** as nearest relative it is your right and duty	3954
32:24	**B of** the sword, famine and plague,	4946+7156
32:44	**b** I will restore their fortunes,	3954
33: 5	I will hide my face from this city **b of**	6584
35: 6	**b** our forefather Jonadab son	3954
35:14	**b** they obey their forefather's command.	3954
36:31	**b** they have not listened.' "	2256
37:11	from Jerusalem **b of** Pharaoh's army,	4946+7156
39:18	**b** you trust in me, declares the LORD.' "	3954
40: 3	All this happened **b** you people sinned	NIH
41:18	They were afraid of them **b** Ishmael son	3954
43: 4	**b of** the evil they have done.	4946
44:23	**B** you have burned incense	4946+7156
48: 8	**b** the LORD has spoken.	889
48:42	Moab will be destroyed as a nation **b**	3954
Jer 49:17	by will be appalled and will scoff **b of**	6584
49:20	he will completely destroy their pasture **b of**	6584
50:11	"**B** you rejoice and are glad,	3954
50:11	**b** you frolic like a heifer threshing grain	3954
50:13	**B of** the LORD's anger she will not	4946
50:13	be horrified and scoff **b of** all her wounds.	6584
50:16	**B of** the sword of the oppressor	4946+7156
50:24	and captured **b** you opposed the LORD.	3954
50:45	he will completely destroy their pasture **b of**	6584
51: 6	Do not be destroyed **b of** her sins.	928
51:11	**b** his purpose is to destroy Babylon.	3954
51:49	"Babylon must fall **b of** Israel's slain,	NIH
51:49	as the slain in all the earth have fallen **b of**	4200
51:51	**b** foreigners have entered the holy places of	3954
51:64	rise no more **b of** the disaster I will bring	4946+7156
52: 3	It was **b of** the LORD's anger	6584
La 1: 5	The LORD has brought her grief **b of**	6584
1:16	My children are destitute **b**	3954
1:22	as you have dealt with me **b of** all my sins.	6584
2:11	on the ground **b** my people are destroyed,	6584
2:11	**b** children and infants faint in the streets of	928
3:22	**B of** the LORD's great love we are	NIH
3:48	from my eyes **b** my people are destroyed.	6584
3:51	What I see brings grief to my soul **b of** all	4946
4: 4	**B of** thirst the infant's tongue sticks to	928
4:13	But it happened **b of** the sins	4946
5: 9	our lives **b of** the sword in the desert.	4946+7156
5:17	**B of** this our hearts are faint,	6584
5:17	**b of** these things our eyes grow dim	6584
Eze 1:20	**b** the spirit of the living creatures was in	3954
1:21	**b** the spirit of the living creatures was in	3954
3: 7	to you **b** they are not willing to listen to me,	3954
3:21	he will surely live **b** he took warning,	3954
4:17	of each other and will waste away **b of**	928
5: 9	**B of** all your detestable idols,	3610
5:11	**b** you have defiled my sanctuary	561+3610+4202
6:11	**b of** all the wicked and detestable practices	448
7:13	**B of** their sins, not one of them	928
7:16	each **b of** his sins.	928
7:23	**b** the land is full of bloodshed and	3954
10:17	the cherubim rose, they rose with them, **b**	3954
12:19	in it **b of** the violence of all who live there.	4946
13: 8	**B of** your false words and lying visions,	3610
13:10	" '**B** they lead my people astray, saying,	3610
13:10	"Peace," when there is no peace, and **b**,	928+3610
13:22	**B** you disheartened the righteous	3610
13:22	and **b** you encouraged the wicked not	NIH
14:15	so that no one can pass through it **b of**	4946+7156
15: 8	I will make the land desolate **b**	3610
16:14	the nations on account of your beauty, **b**	3954
16:28	**b** you were insatiable;	4946
16:31	**b** you scorned payment.	4200
16:36	**B** you poured out your wealth	3610
16:36	and **b of** all your detestable idols,	6584
16:36	and **b** you gave them your children's blood,	3869
16:43	" '**B** you did not remember the days	889+3610
16:52	**B** your sins were more vile than theirs,	928
16:59	**b** you despised my oath by breaking	889
16:63	and never again open your mouth **b of**	4946+7156
17:18	**B** he had given his hand in pledge and	2256
17:20	upon him there **b** he was unfaithful to me.	889
18:13	**B** he has done all these detestable things,	NIH
18:18	**b** he practiced extortion,	3954
18:22	**B of** the righteous things he has done,	928
18:24	**B of** the unfaithfulness he is guilty of and	928
18:24	the unfaithfulness he is guilty of and	928
18:26	**b of** the sin he has committed he will die.	928
18:28	**B** he considers all	2256
19:10	and full of branches **b of** abundant water.	4946
20:16	**b** they rejected my laws and did	3610
20:24	**b** they had not obeyed my laws	3610
21: 4	**B** I am going to cut off the righteous	889+3610
21: 7	'**B of** the news that is coming.	448
21:24	'**B** you people have brought	3610
21:24	**b** you have done this,	3610
22: 4	you have become guilty **b of**	928
22:19	'**B** you have all become dross,	3610
23:30	**b** you lusted after the nations	928
23:45	**b** they are adulterous and blood is	3954
24: 2	**b** the king of Babylon has laid siege	NIH
24:13	**B** I tried to cleanse you but you would not	3610
24:23	or weep but will waste away **b of** your sins	928
25: 3	**B** you said "Aha!"	3610
25: 6	**B** you have clapped your hands	3610
25: 8	'**B** Moab and Seir said, "Look,	3610
25:12	'**B** Edom took revenge on the house	3610
25:15	'**B** the Philistines acted in revenge	3610
26: 2	**b** Tyre has said of Jerusalem, 'Aha!	889+3610
27:12	with you **b of** your great wealth of goods;	4946
27:16	" 'Aram did business with you **b of**	4946
27:18	**b of** your many products and great wealth	928
27:31	They will shave their heads **b of** you	448
28: 5	**b of** your wealth your heart has grown proud	928
28: 6	" '**B** you think you are wise,	3610
28:17	and you corrupted your wisdom **b of**	6584
29: 9	" '**B** you said, "The Nile is mine;	3610
29:20	for his efforts **b** he and his army did it	889
31: 5	spreading **b of** abundant waters.	4946
31:10	**B** it towered on high,	889+3610
31:10	and **b** it was proud of its height,	NIH
31:15	**B of** it I clothed Lebanon with gloom,	6584
32:10	with horror **b of** you	6584
32:25	**B** their terror had spread in the land of	3954
32:26	by the sword **b** they spread their terror in	3954
33: 6	that man will be taken away **b of** his sin,	928
33:10	and we are wasting away **b of** them.	928

Eze 33:12	to live **b** of his former righteousness.'	928
33:29	the land a desolate waste **b** of all	6584
34: 5	So they were scattered **b**	4946
34: 8	**b** my flock lacks a shepherd and	4946
34: 8	and **b** my shepherds did not search	NIH
34:21	**B** you shove with flank and shoulder,	3610
35: 5	" '**B** you harbored an ancient hostility	3610
35:10	" '**B** you have said, "These two nations	3610
35:15	**B** you rejoiced when the inheritance of	3869
36: 3	**B** they ravaged and hounded you	928+3610+3610
36: 6	in my jealous wrath **b** you have suffered	3610
36:13	**B** people say to you,	3954
36:18	on them **b** they had shed blood in the land	6584
36:18	and **b** they had defiled it with their idols.	NIH
36:30	disgrace among the nations **b**	AIT
39:10	**b** they will use the weapons for fuel.	3954
39:11	**b** Gog and all his hordes will	2256
39:23	**b** they were unfaithful to me.	889+6584
44: 2	It is to remain shut **b** the LORD,	3954
44:12	But **b** they served them in the presence	889+3610
47: 5	**b** the water had risen and was deep enough	3954
47: 9	**b** this water flows there and makes	3954
47:12	**b** the water from the sanctuary flows	3954
47:14	**B** I swore with uplifted hand to give it	889
48:14	**b** it is holy to the LORD.	3954
Da 1:10	king would then have my head **b** of you."	2549
2: 8	are trying to gain time,	10168+10353+10619
2:30	this mystery has been revealed to me, not **b**	10089
4:18	**b** the spirit of the holy gods is in you."	10168
4:37	everything he does is right	10168
5:19	**B** of the high position he gave him,	10427
6: 4	**b** he was trustworthy and neither corrupt	10168+10353+10619
6:22	**b** I was found innocent in his sight.	10168+10353+10619
6:23	**b** he had trusted in his God.	10168
7:11	to watch **b** of the boastful words	10427
8:12	**B** of rebellion, the host [of the saints] and	928
8:19	**b** the vision concerns the appointed time of	3954
9: 7	where you have scattered us **b** of	928
9: 7	with shame **b** we have sinned against you.	889
9:11	**b** we have sinned against you.	3954
9:18	We do not make requests of you **b**	6584
9:18	but **b** of your great mercy.	6584
9:19	For your sake, O my God, do not delay, **b**	3954
10:13	**B** I was detained there with the king	2256
10:16	"I am overcome with anguish **b** of	928
11: 4	**b** his empire will be uprooted and given	3954
11:25	to stand **b** of the plots devised against him.	3954
11:27	**b** an end will still come at	3954
12: 9	**b** the words are closed up and sealed until	3954
Hos 1: 2	**b** the land is guilty of the vilest adultery	3954
1: 4	**b** I will soon punish the house of Jehu for	3954
2: 4	**b** they are the children of adultery.	3954
4: 1	**b** the LORD has a charge to bring	3954
4: 3	**B** of this the land mourns,	6584
4: 6	"**B** you have rejected knowledge,	3954
4: 6	**b** you have ignored the law of your God,	2256
4:10	but not increase, **b** they have deserted	3954
4:14	**b** the men themselves consort with harlots	3954
7:13	Woe to them, **b** they have strayed from me!	3954
7:13	**b** they have rebelled against me!	3954
7:16	Their leaders will fall by the sword **b** of	4946
8: 1	An eagle is over the house of the LORD **b**	3610
9: 7	**B** your sins are so many and your hostility	6584
9:15	"**B** of all their wickedness in Gilgal,	NIH
9:15	**B** of their sinful deeds,	6584
9:17	My God will reject them **b** they have	3954
10: 3	"We have no king **b** we did not revere	3954
10: 5	**b** it is taken from them into exile.	3954
10:13	**B** you have depended on your own strength	3954
10:15	O Bethel, **b** your wickedness is great.	4946+7156
11: 5	not Assyria rule over them **b** they refuse	3954
13: 9	**b** you are against me, against your helper.	3954
13:16	**b** they have rebelled against their God.	3954
Joel 1: 5	wail **b** of the new wine,	6584
1:11	**b** the harvest of the field is destroyed.	3954
1:18	herds mill about **b** they have no pasture;	3954
3:19	**b** of violence done to the people of Judah,	4946
Am 1: 3	**B** she threshed Gilead	6584
1: 6	**B** she took captive whole communities	6584
1: 9	**B** she sold whole communities of captives	6584
1:11	**B** he pursued his brother with a sword,	6584
1:11	**b** his anger raged continually	2256
1:13	**B** he ripped open the pregnant women	6584
2: 1	**B** he burned, as if to lime,	6584
2: 4	**B** they have rejected the law of the LORD	6584
2: 4	**b** they have been led astray by false gods,	6584
4:12	Israel, and **b** I will do this to you,	3954+6813
7:13	**b** this is the king's sanctuary and the temple	3954
8:13	and strong young men will faint **b** of thirst.	928
Ob 1:10	**B** of the violence	4946
Jnh 1: 2	**b** its wickedness has come up before me."	3954
1: 9	**b** he had already told them so.)	3954
Mic 1: 5	All this is **b** of Jacob's transgression,	928
1: 5	**b** of the sins of the house of Israel.	928
1: 8	**B** of this I will weep and wail;	6584
1:12	**b** disaster has come from the LORD,	3954
2: 1	At morning's light they carry it out **b** it is	3954
2:10	this is not your resting place, **b** it is defiled,	6288
3: 4	from them **b** of the evil they have done.	889+3869
3: 7	They will all cover their faces **b**	3954
3:12	Therefore **b** of you,	1673
6:13	to ruin you **b** of your sins.	6584
6:14	**b** what you save I will give to the sword.	2256
7: 9	**B** I have sinned against him,	3954
7:13	The earth will become desolate **b** of	6584
Na 3: 4	all **b** of the wanton lust of a harlot,	4946
Hab 2: 5	**B** he is as greedy as the grave and	889
2: 8	**B** you have plundered many nations,	3954
Zep 3:11	**b** I will remove from this city	3954
Hag 1: 9	"**B** of my house, which remains a ruin,	3610
1:10	Therefore, **b** of you the heavens have withheld their dew	6584
1:12	**b** the LORD their God had sent him,	889+3869
Zec 2: 4	without walls **b** of the great number of men	4946
2:13	**b** he has roused himself	3954
8: 4	each with cane in hand **b** of his age.	4946
8:10	about his business safely **b** of his enemy,	4946
8:23	**b** we have heard that God is with you.' "	3954
9:11	**b** of the blood of my covenant with you,	928
10: 5	**B** the LORD is with them,	3954
10: 6	I will restore them **b** I have compassion	3954
12: 5	**b** the LORD Almighty is their God.'	928
13: 3	**b** you have told lies in the LORD's name.'	3954
Mal 1:11	**b** my name will be great among	3954
2: 2	**b** you have not set your heart to honor me.	3954
2: 3	"**B** of you I will rebuke your descendants;	4200
2: 7	**b** he is the messenger of	3954
2: 9	**b** you have not followed my ways	889+3869+7023
2:13	and wail **b** he no longer pays attention	4946
2:14	the LORD is acting as the witness	3954+6584
2:14	**b** you have broken faith with her,	889
2:15	**B** he was seeking godly offspring.	NIH
3: 9	**b** you are robbing me.	2256
Mt 1:19	**B** Joseph her husband was	AIT
1:20	**b** what is conceived in her is from	1142
1:21	**b** he will save his people from their sins."	1142
2:18	**b** they are no more."	4022
5:10	Blessed are those who are persecuted **b**	1915
5:11	of evil against you **b** of me.	1915
5:12	**b** great is your reward in heaven,	4022
6: 7	for they think they will be heard **b** of	1877
7:25	**b** it had its foundation on the rock.	1142
7:29	**b** he taught as one who had authority,	1142
9:36	**b** they were harassed and helpless,	4022
10:22	All men will hate you **b** of me,	1328
10:41	a prophet **b** he is a prophet will receive	NIG
10:41	and anyone who receives a righteous man **b**	NIG
10:42	of cold water to one of these little ones **b**	NIG
11:20	**b** they did not repent.	4022
11:25	**b** you have hidden these things from	4022
13: 5	**b** the soil was shallow.	1328
13: 6	and they withered **b** they had no root.	1328
13:16	But blessed are your eyes **b** they see,	4022
13:16	and your ears **b** they hear.	4022
13:21	When trouble or persecution comes **b** of	1328
13:29	'**b** while you are pulling the weeds,	3607
13:58	And he did not do many miracles there **b** of their lack of faith.	1328
14: 3	and bound him and put him in prison **b** of	1328
14: 5	**b** they considered him a prophet.	4022
14: 9	but **b** of his oaths and his dinner guests,	1328
14:24	by the waves **b** the wind was against it.	1142
16: 7	"It is **b** we didn't bring any bread."	4022
17:20	He replied, "**B** you have so little faith.	1328
18: 7	the world **b** of the things that cause people	608
18:32	that debt of yours **b** you begged me to.	2075
19: 8	to divorce your wives **b**	4639
19:12	For some are eunuchs **b** they were born	NIG
19:12	and others have renounced marriage **b** of	1328
19:22	he went away sad, **b** he had great wealth.	1142
20: 7	" '**B** no one has hired us,' they answered.	4022
20:15	Or are you envious **b** I am generous?'	4022
21:46	of the crowd **b** the people held that he was	2075
22:16	**b** you pay no attention to who they are.	1142
22:29	**b** you do not know the Scriptures	AIT
24: 9	you will be hated by all nations **b** of me.	1328
24:12	**B** of the increase of wickedness,	1328
24:42	**b** you do not know	4022
24:44	**b** the Son of Man will come at an hour	4022
25:13	**b** you do not know the day or the hour.	4022
26:43	**b** their eyes were heavy.	1142
27:19	a great deal today in a dream **b** of him."	1328
Mk 1:22	**b** he taught them as one who had authority,	1142
1:34	the demons speak **b** they knew who he was.	4022
2: 4	Since they could not get him to Jesus **b** of	1328
3: 9	**B** of the crowd he told his disciples to have	1328
3:30	He said this **b** they were saying,	4022
4: 5	**b** the soil was shallow.	1328
4: 6	and they withered **b** they had no root.	1328
4:17	When trouble or persecution comes **b** of	1328
4:29	**b** the harvest has come."	4022
5:28	**b** she thought, "If I just touch his clothes,	1142
6:17	He did this **b** of Herodias,	1328
6:20	**b** Herod feared John and protected him,	1142
6:26	but **b** of his oaths and his dinner guests,	1328
6:31	**b** so many people were coming and going	1142
6:34	**b** they were like sheep without a shepherd.	4022
6:48	**b** the wind was against them.	1142
6:50	**b** they all saw him and were terrified.	1142
8: 3	some of them have come	2779
8:16	"It is **b** we have no bread."	4022
9:31	**b** he was teaching his disciples.	1142
9:38	But they kept quiet **b** no	1142
9:38	**b** he was not one of us."	4022
9:41	a cup of water in my name **b** you belong	4022
10: 5	"It was **b** your hearts were hard	4639
10:22	He went away sad, **b** he had great wealth.	1142
11:13	**b** it was not the season for figs.	1142
11:18	**b** the whole crowd was amazed	1142
12:12	Then they looked for a way to arrest him **b**	1142
12:14	**b** you pay no attention to who they are;	1142
Mk 12:24	**b** you do not know the Scriptures or	1328+4047
13:13	All men will hate you **b** of me,	1328
13:19	**b** those will be days of distress unequaled	1142
13:35	"Therefore keep watch **b** you do not know	1142
14:40	**b** their eyes were heavy.	1142
16: 8	**b** they were afraid.	1142
Lk 1: 7	**b** Elizabeth was barren;	2776
1:14	and many will rejoice **b** of his birth,	2093
1:20	**b** you did not believe my words,	505+4005
1:68	**b** he has come and has redeemed	4022
1:78	**b** of the tender mercy of our God,	1328
2: 4	**b** he belonged to the house and line	1484
2: 7	**b** there was no room for them in the inn.	1484
3:19	when John rebuked Herod the tetrarch **b** of	4309
4:18	**b** he has anointed me to preach good news to the poor.	1641+4005
4:32	**b** his message had authority.	4022
4:41	**b** they knew he was the Christ.	4022
4:43	**b** that is why I was sent."	4022
5: 5	But **b** you say so, I will let down the nets."	2093
5:19	not find a way to do this **b** of the crowd,	1328
6:19	**b** power was coming from him	4022
6:22	**b** of the Son of Man.	1915
6:23	**b** great is your reward in heaven.	1142
6:35	**b** he is kind to the ungrateful and wicked.	4022
6:48	**b** it was well built.	1328+3836
7: 5	**b** he loves our nation	1142
7:29	*b they had been* **baptized**	AIT
7:30	*b they had not been* **baptized**	AIT
8: 6	the plants withered **b** they had no moisture.	1328
8:19	but they were not able to get near him **b** of	1328
8:30	**b** many demons had gone into him.	4022
8:37	**b** they were overcome with fear.	4022
8:42	**b** his only daughter,	4022
9: 7	**b** some were saying	1328
9:12	**b** we are in a remote place here."	4022
9:49	**b** he is not one of us."	4022
9:53	**b** he was heading for Jerusalem.	4022
10:21	**b** you have hidden these things from	4022
11: 6	**b** a friend of mine on a journey has come	2076
11: 8	give him the bread **b** he is his friend,	1328+3836
11: 8	yet **b** of the man's boldness he will get up	1328
11:18	say this **b** you claim that I drive out demons	4022
11:42	**b** you give God a tenth of your mint,	4022
11:43	**b** you love the most important seats in	4022
11:44	**b** you are like unmarked graves,	4022
11:46	**b** you load people down	4022
11:47	**b** you build tombs for the prophets,	4022
11:49	**B** of this, God in his wisdom said,	1328
11:52	**b** you have taken away the key	4022
12:40	**b** the Son of Man will come at an hour	4022
13: 2	other Galileans **b** they suffered this way?	4022
13:14	Indignant **b** Jesus had healed on the Sabbath,	4022
13:24	**b** many, I tell you, will try to enter	4022
15:27	the fattened calf **b** he has him back safe	4022
15:32	**b** this brother of yours was dead	4022
16: 2	**b** you cannot be manager any longer.'	1142
16: 8	commended the dishonest manager **b**	4022
16:24	**b** I am in agony in this fire.'	4022
17: 9	the servant **b** he did what he was told to do?	4022
17:21	the kingdom of God is within you."	1142
18: 5	yet **b** this widow keeps bothering me,	1328
18:23	**b** he was a man of great wealth.	1142
19: 3	**b** of the crowd	608
19: 9	**b** this man, too, is a son of Abraham.	2776
19:11	**b** he was near Jerusalem and	1328+3836
19:17	'**B** you have been trustworthy in	4022
19:21	I was afraid of you, **b** you are a hard man.	4022
19:44	**b** you did not recognize the time	505+4005
19:48	**b** all the people hung on his words.	1142
20: 6	**b** they are persuaded that John was	1142
20:19	**b** they knew he had spoken this parable	1142
21:17	All men will hate you **b** of me.	1328
21:28	**b** your redemption is drawing near."	1484
23: 8	**b** for a long time he had been wanting	1142
24:11	**b** their words seemed to them	2779
24:41	And while they still did not believe it **b** of	608
Jn 1:15	after me has surpassed me **b** he was	4022
1:30	after me has surpassed me **b** he was	4022
1:50	"You believe **b** I told you I saw you under	4022
3:18	not believe stands condemned already **b**	4022
3:19	but men loved darkness instead of light **b**	1142
3:23	**b** there was plenty of water,	4022
4:39	in him **b** of the woman's testimony,	1328
4:41	**b** of his words many more became believers	1328
4:42	"We no longer believe just **b** of	1328
5:16	**b** Jesus was doing these things on	1328+4047
5:19	**b** whatever the Father does the Son	1142
5:27	And he has given him authority to judge **b**	4022
5:39	You diligently study the Scriptures **b**	4022
6: 2	and a great crowd of people followed him **b**	4022
6:26	not **b** you saw miraculous signs but	4022
6:26	not because you saw miraculous signs but **b**	4022
6:41	the Jews began to grumble about him **b**	4022
6:57	as the living Father sent me and I live **b** of	1328
6:57	the one who feeds on me will live **b** of me.	1328
7: 1	from Judea **b** the Jews there were waiting	4022
7: 7	but it hates me **b** I testify	4022
7: 8	**b** for me the right time has not yet come."	4022
7:22	**b** Moses gave you circumcision	1328+4047
7:29	but I know him **b** I am from him	4022
7:30	**b** his time had not yet come.	4022
7:43	Thus the people were divided **b** of Jesus.	1328
8:16	my decisions are right, **b** I am not alone.	4022
8:20	**b** his time had not yet come.	4022
8:37	**b** you have no room for my word.	4022

Jn	8:43	**B** you are unable to hear what I say.	4022
	8:45	**b** I tell the truth, you do not believe me!	4022
	9:22	His parents said this **b** they were afraid of	4022
	10: 4	and his sheep follow him **b**	4022
	10: 5	they will run away from him **b** they do	4022
	10:13	The man runs away **b** he is a hired hand	4022
	10:26	you do not believe **b** you are not my sheep.	4022
	10:33	"but for blasphemy, **b** you, a mere man,	4022
	10:36	then do you accuse me of blasphemy **b**	4022
	12: 6	not say this **b** he cared about the poor but	4022
	12: 6	because he cared about the poor but **b**	4022
	12: 9	not only **b** of him but also to see Lazarus.	1328
	12:18	Many people, **b** they had heard	4022
	12:39	For this reason they could not believe, **b,**	4022
	12:41	Isaiah said this **b** he saw Jesus' glory	4022
	12:42	But **b** of the Pharisees they would	1328
	14:12	**b** I am going to the Father.	4022
	14:17	**b** it neither sees him nor knows him.	4022
	14:19	**B** I live, you also will live.	4022
	15: 3	You are already clean **b** of the word	1328
	15:15	**b** a servant does not know his master's	4022
	15:21	They will treat you this way **b** of my name,	1328
	16: 3	They will do such things **b** they have	4022
	16: 4	not tell you this at first **b** I was with you.	4022
	16: 6	**B** I have said these things,	4022
	16: 9	**b** men do not believe in me;	4022
	16:10	**b** I am going to the Father,	4022
	16:11	**b** the prince of this world	4022
	16:17	and '**B** I am going to the Father'?"	4022
	16:21	A woman giving birth to a child has pain **b**	1328
	16:21	the anguish **b** of her joy that a child is born	1328
	16:27	the Father himself loves you **b**	4022
	17:24	the glory you have given me **b**	4022
	18: 2	**b** Jesus had often met there	4022
	18:15	**B** this disciple was known to	1254
	19: 7	**b** he claimed to be the Son of God."	4022
	19:31	**B** the Jews did not want the bodies left on	2671
	19:38	but secretly **b** he feared the Jews.	1328
	19:42	**B** it was the Jewish day of Preparation and	1328
	20:29	Then Jesus told him, "**B** you have seen me,	4022
	21: 6	the net in **b** of the large number of fish.	608
	21:17	Peter was hurt **b** Jesus asked him	4022
	21:23	**B** of this, the rumor spread among	4036
Ac	2: 6	**b** each one heard them speaking	4022
	2:24	**b** it was impossible for death	2776
	2:25	**B** he is at my right hand,	4022
	2:27	**b** you will not abandon me to the grave,	4022
	4: 2	They were greatly disturbed **b**	1328
	4: 3	and **b** it was evening,	1142
	4:21	**b** all the people were praising God	1328
	5:26	**b** they feared that the people would stone	1142
	5:41	rejoicing **b** they had been counted worthy	4022
	6: 1	against the Hebraic Jews **b** their widows	4022
	7: 9	"**B** the patriarchs *were* **jealous of**	AIT
	8:11	They followed him **b** he had amazed them	1328+3836
	8:16	**b** the Holy Spirit had not yet come	1142
	8:20	with you, **b** you thought you could buy	4022
	8:21	**b** your heart is not right before God.	1142
	10:38	**b** God was with him.	4022
	12:20	**b** they depended on the king's country	1328
	12:23	**b** Herod did not give praise to God,	505+4005
	13: 7	for Barnabas and Saul **b** he wanted to hear	NIG
	14:12	and Paul they called Hermes **b** he was	2076
	14:13	to the city gates **b** he and the crowd wanted	NIG
	15:38	*b* he had **deserted** them in Pamphylia	AIT
	16: 3	so he circumcised him **b** of the Jews	1328
	16:27	and was about to kill himself *b* he **thought**	AIT
	16:34	*b* he had **come to believe**	AIT
	17:18	They said this **b** Paul was preaching	4022
	17:25	*b* he himself **gives** all men life and breath	AIT
	18: 2	**b** Claudius had ordered all the Jews	1328+3836
	18: 3	**b** he was a tentmaker as they were,	1328+3836
	18:10	**b** I have many people in this city."	1484
	18:18	he had his hair cut off at Cenchrea **b** of	1142
	19:40	in danger of being charged with rioting **b**	4309
	20: 3	**B** the Jews **made** a plot against him just	AIT
	20: 7	*b* he **intended** to leave the next day,	AIT
	20:13	He had made this arrangement *b* he was **going** there	AIT
	21:34	not get at the truth **b** of the uproar,	1328
	22:11	**b** the brilliance of the light had blinded me.	608
	22:18	**b** they will not accept your testimony	1484
	23: 6	on trial **b** of my hope in the resurrection of	4309
	23:18	to you *b* he **has** something to tell you."	AIT
	23:21	**b** more than forty of them are waiting	1142
	24:27	*b* Felix **wanted** to grant a favor to the Jews,	AIT
	25:25	*b* he **made** his **appeal** to the Emperor	AIT
	26: 3	and especially **b** you **are** well acquainted	1639
	26: 6	And now it is **b** of my hope	2093
	26: 7	it is **b** of this hope that	4309
	26:26	**b** it was not done in a corner.	1142
	27: 4	Cyprus **b** the winds were against us.	1328+3836
	27: 9	sailing had already become dangerous **b**	1328+3836
	27:22	**b** not one of you will be lost;	1142
	28: 2	a fire and welcomed us all **b** it was raining	1328
	28:18	**b** I was not guilty	1328+3836
	28:20	It is **b** of the hope of Israel that I am bound	1915
Ro	1: 8	**b** your faith is being reported all over	4022
	1:16	**b** it is the power of God for the salvation	1142
	1:19	**b** God has made it plain to them.	1142
	1:26	**B** of this, God gave them over	1328
	2: 1	**b** you who pass judgment do	1142
	2: 5	But **b** of your stubbornness	2848
	2:18	superior *b you are* **instructed** by the law;	AIT
	2:20	*b you* **have** in the law the embodiment	AIT

Ro	2:24	among the Gentiles **b** of you."	1328
	3:25	**b** in his forbearance he had left	1328
	4:15	**b** law brings wrath.	1142
	5: 3	also rejoice in our sufferings, *b we* **know**	AIT
	5: 5	**b** God has poured out his love	4022
	5:12	in this way death came to all men, **b**	2093+4005
	6: 7	**b** anyone who has died has been freed	1142
	6:14	**b** you are not under law, but under grace.	1142
	6:15	Shall we sin **b** we are not under law but	4022
	6:19	I put this in human terms **b** you are weak	1328
	8: 2	**b** through Christ Jesus the law of the Spirit	1142
	8:10	Christ is in you, your body is dead **b** of sin,	1328
	8:10	yet your spirit is alive **b** of righteousness.	1328
	8:14	**b** those who are led by the Spirit	1142
	8:27	**b** the Spirit intercedes for the saints	4022
	9: 7	Nor **b** they are his descendants are they all Abraham's children.	4022
	9:32	**B** they pursued it not by faith but as	4022
	11:11	*b* of their **transgression,**	AIT
	11:20	But they were broken off *b* of **unbelief,**	AIT
	13: 5	not only **b** of possible punishment but also	1328
	13: 5	of possible punishment but also **b** of	1328
	13:11	**b** our salvation is nearer now than	1142
	14:15	If your brother is distressed **b** of	1328
	14:18	**b** anyone who serves Christ	1142
	14:23	**b** his eating is not from faith;	4022
	15:15	**b** of the grace God gave me	1328
1Co	1: 4	**b** of his grace given you in Christ Jesus.	2093
	1: 6	**b** our testimony about Christ was confirmed in you.	2777
	1:30	It is **b** of him that you are in Christ Jesus,	1666
	2:14	**b** they are spiritually discerned.	4022
	3:13	**b** the Day will bring it to light.	1142
	7: 5	that Satan will not tempt you **b** of your lack	1328
	7:26	**B** of the present crisis,	1328
	9:10	**b** when the plowman plows and	4022
	10:17	**B** there is one loaf, we, who are many,	4022
	10:30	why am I denounced **b** of	5642
	11:10	For this reason, and **b** of the angels,	1328
	12:15	If the foot should say, "**B** I am not a hand,	4022
	12:16	if the ear should say, "**B** I am not an eye,	4022
	15: 9	**b** I persecuted the church of God.	1484
	15:58	*b you* **know** that your labor in the Lord is	AIT
	16: 9	**b** a great door for effective work	1142
	16:17	**b** they have supplied what was lacking	4022
2Co	1: 7	*b we* **know** that just as you share	AIT
	1:15	**B** I was **confident** of this,	AIT
	1:24	**b** it is by faith you stand firm.	1142
	2:13	*b* I **did** not **find** my brother Titus	AIT
	3: 7	not look steadily at the face of Moses **b** of	1328
	3:14	**b** only in Christ is it taken away.	4022
	4:14	*b we* **know** that the one who raised	AIT
	5: 3	*b when we are* **clothed,**	AIT
	5: 4	**b** we do not wish to be unclothed	2093+4005
	5:14	*b we are* **convinced** that one died for all,	AIT
	7: 9	not **b** you were made sorry,	4022
	7: 9	but **b** your sorrow led you to repentance.	4022
	7:13	**b** his spirit has been refreshed by all of you.	4022
	8:22	*b* of his **great confidence**	AIT
	9:13	**B** of the service by which you have proved	1328
	9:14	their hearts will go out to you, **b** of	1328
	11:11	**B** I do not love you?	4022
	12: 6	**b** I would be speaking the truth.	1142
	12: 7	*b* of these **surpassingly great**	AIT
	12:14	**b** what I want is not your possessions	1142
Gal	1:24	And they praised God **b** of me.	1877
	2: 4	[This matter arose] **b** some false brothers	1328
	2:11	**b** he was clearly in the wrong.	4022
	2:12	*b* he *was* **afraid of** those who belonged to	AIT
	2:16	**b** by observing the law no one will	4022
	3: 5	among you **b** you observe the law,	1666
	3: 5	or **b** you believe what you heard?	1666
	3:11	**b,** "The righteous will live by faith."	4022
	3:19	It was added **b** of transgressions until	5920
	4: 6	**B** you are sons, God sent the Spirit	4022
	4:13	it was **b** of an illness that I first preached	1328
	4:20	**b** I am perplexed about you!	4022
	4:25	**b** she is in slavery with her children.	1142
	4:27	**b** more are the children of the desolate	4022
Eph	2: 4	But **b** of his great love for us, God,	1328
	3:13	be discouraged **b** of my sufferings for you,	1877
	4:18	the life of God **b** of the ignorance that is	1328
	5: 3	**b** these are improper for God's holy people.	2777
	5: 6	for **b** of such things God's wrath comes	1328
	5: 1	every opportunity, **b** the days are evil.	4022
	6: 8	*b you* **know** that the Lord will reward	AIT
Php	1: 5	**b** of your partnership in the gospel from	2093
	1:14	**B** of my **chains,**	AIT
	1:18	And **b** of this I rejoice.	1877
	2:22	**b** as a son with his father he has served	NIG
	2:26	and is distressed **b** you heard he was ill.	1484
	2:30	**b** he almost died for the work of Christ,	4022
	4:11	I am not saying this **b** I am in need,	4022
Col	1: 4	*b we have* **heard** of your faith in Christ Jesus	AIT
	1:21	in your minds **b** of your evil behavior.	1877
	2:22	**b** they are based on human commands	NIG
	3: 6	**B** of these, the wrath of God is coming.	1328
	4: 1	*b you* **know** that you also have a Master	AIT
1Th	1: 5	**b** our gospel came to you not simply	4022
	2: 8	**b** you had become so dear to us.	1484
	2:13	And we also thank God continually **b,**	4022
	3: 7	about you **b** of your faith.	1328
	3: 9	in the presence of our God **b** of you?	1328
	5:13	the highest regard in love **b** of their work.	1328
2Th	1: 3	**b** your faith is growing more and more,	4022
	1:10	**b** you believed our testimony to you.	4022

2Th	2:10	They perish **b** they refused to love the truth	505+4005
	2:13	**b** from the beginning God chose you to	4022
	3: 9	not **b** we do not have the right to such help,	4022
1Ti	1:13	I was shown mercy **b** I acted in ignorance	4022
	4: 5	**b** it is consecrated by the word of God	1142
	4:12	Don't let anyone look down on you **b**	NIG
	4:16	Persevere in them, **b** if you do,	1142
	5:12	**b** they have broken their first.pledge.	4022
	5:23	and use a little wine **b** of your stomach	1328
	6: 2	not to show less respect for them **b**	4022
	6: 2	**b** those who benefit from their service	4022
2Ti	1: 9	not **b** of anything we have done but	2848
	1: 9	because of anything we have done but **b** of	2848
	1:12	**b** I know whom I have believed,	1142
	1:16	**b** he often refreshed me and was	4022
	2:16	**b** those who indulge in it will become more	1142
	2:23	*b you* **know** they produce quarrels.	AIT
	3: 9	But they will not get very far **b,**	1142
	3:14	*b you* **know** those from whom you learned	AIT
	4:10	*b* he **loved** this world,	AIT
	4:11	**b** he is helpful to me in my ministry.	1142
	4:15	**b** he strongly opposed our message.	1142
Tit	1:11	*b* they *are* **ruining** whole households	AIT
	2: 8	be ashamed *b* they **have** nothing bad to say	AIT
	3: 5	not **b** of righteous things we had done,	1666
	3: 5	but **b** of his mercy.	2848
	3: 9	**b** these are unprofitable and useless.	1142
	3:12	**b** I have decided to winter there.	1142
Phm	1: 5	*b* I **hear** about your faith in the Lord Jesus	AIT
	1: 7	**b** you, brother, have refreshed the hearts of	1328
	1:22	a guest room for me, **b** I hope to be restored	1142
Heb	2: 9	with glory and honor **b** he suffered death,	1328
	2:18	**B** he himself suffered when he was tempted	1142
	3:19	**b** of their unbelief.	1328
	4: 2	of no value to them, **b** those who heard did	NIG
	4: 6	**b** of their disobedience.	1328
	5: 7	he was heard **b** of his reverent submission.	608
	5:11	but it is hard to explain **b** you are slow	2075
	6: 6	*b* to their loss *they are* **crucifying** the Son of God **all over again**	AIT
	6:17	**B** God wanted to make	1877+4005
	7:10	**b** when Melchizedek met Abraham,	1142
	7:18	The former regulation is set aside **b**	1328+3836
	7:22	**B** of this oath,	2848
	7:24	but **b** Jesus lives forever,	1328+3836
	7:25	*b* he always **lives** to intercede for them.	AIT
	8: 9	**b** they did not remain faithful	4022
	8:11	'Know the Lord,' **b** they will all know me,	4022
	9:17	**b** a will is in force only	1142
	10: 4	**b** it is impossible for the blood of bulls	1142
	10:14	**b** by one sacrifice he has made perfect forever those who are being made holy.	1142
	10:34	*b you* **knew** that you yourselves had better	AIT
	11: 5	**b** God had taken him away.	1484
	11: 6	**b** anyone who comes to him must believe	1142
	11:11	was enabled to become a father **b**	2075
	11:23	**b** they saw he was no ordinary child,	1484
	11:26	**b** he was looking ahead to his reward.	1142
	11:27	persevered **b** he saw him who is invisible.	1142
	11:31	*b* she **welcomed** the spies,	AIT
	12: 6	**b** the Lord disciplines those he loves,	1142
	12:20	**b** they could not bear what was commanded	1142
	13: 5	**b** God has said, "Never will I leave you;	1142
Jas	1: 3	*b you* **know** that the testing	AIT
	1: 6	**b** he who doubts is like a wave of the sea,	1142
	1:10	**b** he will pass away like a wild flower.	4022
	1:12	**b** when he has stood the test,	4022
	2:13	**b** judgment without mercy will be shown	1142
	3: 1	*b you* **know** that we who teach will	AIT
	4: 2	You do not have, **b** you do not ask God.	1328
	4: 3	**b** you ask with wrong motives,	1484
	5: 1	and wail **b** of the misery that is coming	2093
	5: 8	**b** the Lord's coming is near.	4022
1Pe	2: 8	They stumble **b** they **disobey** the message—	AIT
	2:19	up under the pain of unjust suffering **b**	1328
	2:21	**b** Christ suffered for you,	4022
	3: 9	**b** to this you were called so	4022
	4: 1	**b** he who has suffered in his body is done	4022
	4: 8	**b** love covers over a multitude of sins.	4022
	4:14	If you are insulted **b** of the name of Christ,	1877
	5: 2	not **b** you **must,** but because you are willing,	AIT
	5: 2	because you must, but **b** you are **willing,**	AIT
	5: 5	**b,** "God opposes the proud but gives grace	4022
	5: 7	Cast all your anxiety on him **b** he cares	4022
	5: 9	*b you* **know** that your brothers throughout	AIT
2Pe	1:14	*b* I **know** that I will soon put it aside,	AIT
1Jn	2: 8	in him and you, **b** the darkness is passing	4022
	2:11	**b** the darkness has blinded him.	4022
	2:12	**b** your sins have been forgiven on account	4022
	2:13	**b** you have known him who is from	4022
	2:13	**b** you have overcome the evil one.	4022
	2:13	**b** you have known the Father.	4022
	2:14	**b** you have known him who is from	4022
	2:14	young men, **b** you are strong,	4022
	2:21	I do not write to you **b** you do not know	4022
	2:21	but **b** you do know it and	4022
	2:21	because you know it and **b** no lie comes	4022
	3: 8	**b** the devil has been sinning from	4022
	3: 9	**b** God's seed remains in him;	4022
	3: 9	**b** he has been born of God.	4022
	3:12	**B** his own actions were evil	4022
	3:14	**b** we love our brothers.	4022
	3:22	**b** we obey his commands	4022
	4: 1	**b** many false prophets have gone out into	4022
	4: 4	**b** the one who is in you is greater than	4022

1Jn 4: 8 does not know God, **b** God is love. 4022
4:13 **b** he has given us of his Spirit. 4022
4:17 **b** in this world we are like him. 4022
4:18 **b** fear has to do with punishment. 4022
4:19 We love **b** he first loved us. 4022
5: 6 **b** the Spirit is the truth. 4022
5: 9 but God's testimony is greater **b** it is 4022
5:10 **b** he has not believed 4022
2Jn 1: 2 **b** of the truth, which lives in us and will be 1328
Rev 1: 3 **b** the time is near. 1142
1: 7 the peoples of the earth will mourn **b** of 2093
1: 9 was on the island of Patmos **b** of the word 1328
3:16 So, **b** you are lukewarm— 4022
5: 4 I wept and wept **b** no one was found 4022
5: 9 to take the scroll and to open its seals, **b** 4022
6: 9 the souls of those who had been slain **b** of 1328
8:13 **b** of the trumpet blasts about to be sounded NIG
11: 2 **b** it has been given to the Gentiles, 4022
11:10 by sending each other gifts, **b** 4022
11:17 **b** you have taken your great power 4022
12:12 **b** the devil has gone down to you! 4022
12:12 *b* he **knows** that his time is short." AIT
13: 4 the dragon **b** he had given authority to 4022
13:14 **B** of the signs he was given power to do 1328
14: 7 **b** the hour of his judgment has come. 4022
14:15 **b** the time to reap has come, 4022
14:18 **b** its grapes are ripe." 4022
15: 1 last, **b** with them God's wrath is completed. 4022
16: 5 the Holy One, **b** you have so judged; 4022
16:11 of heaven **b** of their pains and their sores, 1666
16:21 **b** the plague was so terrible. 4022
17: 8 **b** he once was, now is not, 4022
17:14 the Lamb will overcome them **b** he is Lord 4022
18:11 of the earth will weep and mourn over her **b** 4022
20: 4 of those who had been beheaded **b** of 1328
20: 4 of their testimony for Jesus and **b** of 1328
21:22 **b** the Lord God Almighty and 1142
22:10 **b** the time is near. 1142

BECHER (KJV) See BEKER

BECHORATH (KJV) See BECORATH

BECKON (2)
Isa 13: 2 *b* to them to enter the gates of the nobles. 3338+5677
49:22 "See, I will **b** to the Gentiles, 3338+5951

BECOME (398) [BECAME, BECOMES, BECOMING]
Ge 2:24 and *they will b* one flesh. 2118
3:20 she would **b** the mother of all the living. 2118
3:22 "The man *has* now **b** like one of us, 2118
6: 5 man's wickedness on the earth had **b**, NIH
6:12 **corrupt** the earth had **b**, AIT
9:15 Never again will the waters **b** a flood 2118
13: 2 Abram *had b* very **wealthy** in livestock and AIT
18:18 Abraham *will* **surely b** a great 2118+2118
24:35 and *he has b* **wealthy.** AIT
24:51 and let her **b** the wife of your master's son, 2118
26:16 *you have b* too **powerful** for us." AIT
28: 3 and increase your numbers until *you b* 2118
29:34 at last my husband *will b* **attached** to me, AIT
32: 7 but now *I have b* two groups. 2118
34:15 that *you b* like us 2118
34:16 We'll settle among you and **b** one people 2118
34:23 and all their other animals **b** ours? NIH
38:23 or we will **b** a laughingstock. 2118
44: 9 and the rest of us *will b* my lord's slaves." 2118
44:10 to have it will **b** my slave; 2118
44:17 to have the cup will **b** my slave. 2118
45:11 to you will **b destitute.'** AIT
47:19 and that the land *may* not **b desolate."** AIT
47:26 of the priests that *did* not **b** Pharaoh's. 2118
48:19 He too will **b** a people, 2118
48:19 and he too will **b great.** AIT
48:19 his descendants *will b* a group of nations." 2118
49:13 "Zebulun will live by the seashore and **b** 4200
Ex 1: 9 Israelites have **b** much too numerous for us. NIH
1:10 or they will **b even more numerous** and, AIT
2:14 "What I did *must have* **b known.**" 3359
2:22 saying, "I have **b** an alien in a foreign land." 2118
4: 9 from the river *will* **b** blood on the ground." 2118
7: 9 and *it will* **b** a snake." 2118
8:16 the land of Egypt the dust *will* **b** gnats." 2118
9: 9 *It will* **b** fine dust over the whole land 2118
9:24 the land of Egypt since *it had* **b** a nation, 2118
15: 2 *he has* **b** my salvation. 2118
18: 3 "I have **b** an alien in a foreign land"; 2118
22:24 your wives *will* **b** widows 2118
23:29 because the land *would* **b** desolate and 2118
32: 7 up out of Egypt, have **b corrupt.** AIT
32:25 and so **b** a laughingstock to their enemies. 4200
Lev 4:14 they **b aware** of the sin they committed, 3359
5: 2 he has **b unclean** and is guilty. AIT
6:18 Whatever touches them *will b* **holy.'** " AIT
6:27 of the flesh *will b* **holy,** AIT
10: 6 "Do not let your hair **b unkempt,** AIT
13: 2 a rash or a bright spot on his skin that *may b* 2118
21:10 *must* not let his hair **b unkempt** AIT
22: 8 and so **b unclean** through it. AIT
22: 9 not **b guilty** and die 2628+5951+6584
25:45 and *they will b* your property. 2118
27:10 both it and the substitute **b** holy. 2118

Lev 27:15 and the house *will again* **b** his. 2118
27:19 and the field *will again* **b** his. 7756
27:21 it *will b* holy, like a field devoted to 2118
27:21 *it will* **b** the property of the priests. 2118
27:33 both the animal and its substitute **b** holy 2118
Nu 5:19 not gone astray and **b** impure while married NIH
5:27 and she *will* **b** accursed among her people. 2118
9: 7 "We have **b** unclean because of NIH
16:38 before the LORD and *have b* **holy.** AIT
16:40 or he would **b** like Korah and his followers. 2118
33:55 those you allow to remain *will* **b** barbs 2118
Dt 4:16 not **b corrupt** and make for yourselves AIT
4:25 then **b corrupt** and make any kind of idol, AIT
8:14 then your heart *will* **b proud** AIT
9:12 of Egypt have **b corrupt.** AIT
15:17 and *he will* **b** your servant for life. 2118
20: 7 *Has* anyone **b pledged** to a woman and AIT
20: 8 not **b disheartened** too." AIT
23:17 or woman *is to* **b** a shrine prostitute. 2118
27: 9 now **b** the people of the LORD your God. 2118
28:25 and *you will* **b** a thing of horror to all 2118
28:37 You *will* **b** a thing of horror and an object 2118
31:17 On that day I will **b angry** with them AIT
31:29 *you are* **sure to b utterly corrupt** 8845+8845
Jos 14: 4 for the sons of Joseph *had b* two tribes— 2118
23:13 *they will* **b** snares and traps for you, 2118
Jdg 16: 7 *I'll* **b** as weak as any other man." 2118
16:11 *I'll* **b** as weak as any other man." 2118
16:13 *I'll* **b** as weak as any other man." 2118
16:17 and *I would* **b** as weak as any other man." 2118
17:13 since this Levite *has* **b** my priest." 2118
Ru 1:11 *who could* **b** your husbands? 2118
4: 7 and transfer of property to **b final,** AIT
4:14 *May* he **b famous** throughout Israel! AIT
1Sa 8:17 and you yourselves *will* **b** his slaves. 2118
8:17 Israel *has b* a **stench** to the Philistines." AIT
15:17 not **b** the head of the tribes of Israel? NIH
17: 9 *we will* **b** your subjects; 2118
17: 9 *you will* **b** our subjects and serve us." 2118
18:18 that *I should* **b** the king's son-in-law?" 2118
18:21 a second opportunity *to b* my **son-in-law.**" AIT
18:22 now *b* his **son-in-law.'** " AIT
18:23 *b* the king's **son-in-law?** AIT
18:26 *b* the king's **son-in-law.** AIT
18:27 *b* the king's **son-in-law.** AIT
25:39 asking her to *b* his **wife.** 851+4200+4374
25:40 to you to take you to **b** his wife." NIH
27:12 "He *has b* so **odious** to his people, AIT
28:16 from you and **b** your enemy? 2118
2Sa 5: 2 and you *will* **b** their ruler.' " 2118
6:22 even more **undignified** 7837
7:24 and you, O LORD, *have* **b** their God. 2118
10: 6 that *they had b* a **stench** in David's nostrils, AIT
16: 2 to refresh those who **b** exhausted in NIH
17:29 "The people *have b* hungry and tired NIH
19:22 This day *you have b* my adversaries! NIH
1Ki 1:11 the son of Haggith, *has* **king** AIT
1:13 Why then *has* Adonijah *b* **king?'** AIT
1:18 But now Adonijah *has b* **king,** and you, AIT
8:46 and *you b* **angry** with them and give them AIT
9: 7 Israel *will* then **b** a byword and an object 2118
13:33 to *b* a priest he consecrated for 2118
2Ki 8:13 that you will **b** king of Aram," NIH
9:29 Ahaziah *had b* **king** of Judah.) AIT
20:18 and *they will* **b** eunuchs in the palace of 2118
22:19 that they would **b** accursed and laid waste, 2118
25: 3 the famine in the city had *b so* **severe** AIT
1Ch 4:27 so their entire clan *did* not *b* as **numerous** AIT
11: 2 and you *will* **b** their ruler.' " 2118
11: 6 the Jebusites *will* **b** commander-in-chief." AIT
17:22 and you, O LORD, *have* **b** their God. 2118
19: 6 that *they had b* a **stench** in David's nostrils, AIT
2Ch 6:36 and *you b* **angry** with them and give them AIT
12: 1 and he had **b strong,** 2621
12: 8 *They* will, however, **b** subject to him, 2118
13: 9 may **b** a priest of what are not gods. 2118
26: 8 because he had **b** very **powerful.** AIT
Ne 6: 6 *about* to **b** their king 2093
9:21 not wear out nor *did* their feet **b** swollen. AIT
Est 1:17 For the queen's conduct *will* **b known** to all 3655
Job 3: 9 *May* its morning stars **b dark;** AIT
7:20 *Have I b* a burden to you? 2118
11:12 But a witless man *can* no more **b wise** than 4220
11:17 and darkness *will* **b** like morning. 2118
11:20 their hope will **b** a dying gasp." NIH
12: 4 "I have **b** a laughingstock to my friends, 2118
16: 8 and it has **b** a witness; 2118
20:14 it will **b** the venom of serpents within him. NIH
24:22 though *they* **b established,** AIT
30: 9 I have **b** a byword among them. 2118
30:29 I have **b** a brother of jackals, 2118
37:10 and the broad waters **b** frozen. NIH
38:30 when the waters **b hard** as stone, 2461
Ps 2: 7 today I *have b* your **Father.** AIT
14: 3 *they have* together **b corrupt;** AIT
31:12 I have **b** like broken pottery. 2118
38:14 I have **b** like a man who does not hear, 2118
53: 3 *they have* together **b corrupt;** AIT
63:10 over to the sword and **b** food for jackals, 2118
69:22 May the table set before them **b** a snare; 2118
69:22 may it **b** retribution and a trap. NIH
71: 7 I have **b** like a portent to many, 2118
89:41 he *has* **b** the scorn of his neighbors. 2118
94: 8 you fools, when will you **b wise?** AIT
94:22 But the LORD *has* **b** my fortress, 2118
102: 7 I have **b** like a bird alone on a roof. 2118
118:14 *he has* **b** my salvation. 2118

Ps 118:21 *you have b* my salvation. 2118
118:22 the builders rejected *has b* the capstone; 2118
139:11 and the light **b** night around me," NIH
140: 8 or *they will* **b proud.** AIT
Pr 21:17 He who loves pleasure will **b** poor; NIH
21:18 The wicked **b** a ransom for the righteous, NIH
23:21 for drunkards and gluttons *b* **poor,** AIT
29:12 all his officials **b** wicked. NIH
30: 9 Or I *may* **b** poor and steal, 3769
SS 8:10 Thus I *have* **b** in his eyes 2118
Isa 1: 9 *we would have* **b** like Sodom, 2118
1:14 *They have* **b** a burden to me; 2118
1:21 See how the faithful city *has* **b** a harlot! 2118
1:22 Your silver *has* **b** dross, 2118
1:31 The mighty man *will* **b** tinder 2118
5: 9 "Surely the great houses *will* **b** desolate, 2118
7:25 *they will* **b** places where cattle are turned 2118
8:21 *they will* **b enraged** and, looking upward, AIT
10:17 The Light of Israel *will* **b** a fire, 2118
12: 2 he has **b** my salvation. 2118
14:10 they will say to you, "You also *have b* **weak,** AIT
14:10 *you have b* like us." 5439
17: 1 be a city but *will* **b** a heap of ruins. 2118
19: 7 along the Nile *will* **b parched,** AIT
19:13 The officials of Zoan have **b** fools, 3282
21: 4 the twilight I longed for *has* **b** a horror 8492
28:13 the word of the LORD to them *will* **b:** 2118
28:22 or your chains *will* **b heavier;** AIT
29: 5 your many enemies *will* **b** like fine dust, 2118
30:13 this sin *will* **b** for you like a high wall, 2118
32:14 citadel and watchtower *will* **b** 2118
34: 9 her land *will* **b** blazing pitch! 2118
34:13 She *will* **b** a haunt for jackals, 2118
35: 7 The burning sand *will* **b** a pool, 2118
39: 7 and *they will* **b** eunuchs in the palace of 2118
40: 4 the rough ground *shall* **b** level, 2118
42:22 *They have* **b** plunder, with no one 2118
42:24 Who handed Jacob over to **b** loot, NIH
51: 4 my justice *will* **b** a light to the nations. 8088
58:10 and your night *will* **b** like the noonday. NIH
60:22 The least of you *will* **b** a thousand, 2118
64: 6 All of us *have* **b** like one who is unclean, 2118
64:10 Your sacred cities *have* **b** a desert; 2118
65:10 Sharon *will* **b** a pasture for flocks, 2118
Jer 2:14 Why then *has* he **b** plunder? 2118
5:27 *they have* **b rich** and powerful AIT
7:11 **b** a den of robbers to you? 2118
7:33 the carcasses of this people *will* **b** food for 2118
7:34 for the land *will* **b** desolate. 2118
12: 8 My inheritance *has* **b** to me like a lion in 2118
12: 9 Has not my inheritance **b** to me like NIH
16: 4 and their dead bodies *will* **b** food for 2118
22: 5 by myself that this palace *will* **b** a ruin.' " 2118
23:12 "Therefore their path *will* **b** slippery; 2118
25:11 whole country *will* **b** a desolate wasteland, 2118
25:38 and their land *will* **b** desolate because of 2118
26:18 Jerusalem *will* **b** a heap of rubble, 2118
27:17 Why *should* this city *b* a ruin? 2118
34:16 to **b** your slaves again. 2118
34:20 Their dead bodies *will* **b** food for the birds 2118
44:12 *They will* **b** an object of cursing 2118
47: 2 *they will* **b** an overflowing torrent. 2118
48: 6 **b** like a bush in the desert. 2118
48: 9 her towns *will* **b** desolate, 2118
48:39 Moab *has* **b** an object of ridicule, 2118
49: 2 *it will* **b** a mound of ruins. 2118
49:13 "that Bozrah *will* **b** a ruin and an object 2118
49:17 "Edom *will* **b** an object of horror; 2118
49:24 Damascus *has b* **feeble,** AIT
49:32 Their camels *will* **b** plunder, 2118
49:33 "Hazor *will* **b** a haunt of jackals, 2118
50:36 *They will* **b** fools. 3282
50:37 *They will* **b** women. 2118
51:30 *they have* **b** like women. 2118
52: 6 the famine in the city had *b so* **severe** AIT
La 1: 1 among the provinces *has* now **b** a slave. 2118
1: 2 *they have* **b** her enemies. 2118
1: 5 Her foes *have* **b** her masters; 2118
1: 8 and so *has* **b** unclean. 2118
1:17 for Jacob that his neighbors **b** his foes; NIH
1:17 Jerusalem *has* **b** an unclean thing 2118
1:21 the day you have announced so *they may* **b** 2118
4: 1 the fine gold *b* **dull!** AIT
4: 3 but my people have **b** heartless NIH
4: 8 it has **b** as dry as a stick. 2118
4: 8 *We have* **b** orphans and fatherless, AIT
Eze 7:17 and every knee *will b* as **weak** as water. AIT
16:15 and used your fame *to b* a **prostitute.** AIT
17: 8 bear fruit and **b** a splendid vine.' 2118
17:23 and bear fruit and **b** a splendid cedar. 2118
20:26 I let them **b defiled** through their gifts— 3237
21: 7 every spirit *will* **b faint** AIT
21: 7 and every knee *b* as **weak** as water.' AIT
22: 4 *you have b* **guilty** because of AIT
22: 4 the blood you have shed and *have* **b defiled** AIT
22:18 the house of Israel *has* **b** dross to me; 2118
22:19 'Because you *have* all **b** dross, AIT
25: 8 of Judah has **b** like all the other nations, NIH
26: 5 Out in the sea *she* will **b** a place 2118
26:14 and *you will* **b** a place to spread fishnets. 2118
29: 9 Egypt *will* **b** a desolate wasteland. 2118
30:11 in a splint so as to **b strong enough** to hold AIT
33:28 the mountains of Israel *will b* **desolate** so AIT
34: 8 so has been plundered and *has b* food for all 2118
36: 2 The ancient heights *have* **b** our possession." 2118

Eze	36:11	and they will be fruitful and *b* **numerous.**	AIT
	36:35	"This land that was laid waste *has* **b** like	2118
	37:17	into one stick so that *they* will **b** one	2118
	37:19	and *they* will **b** one in my hand.'	2118
	47:11	the swamps and marshes *will* not **b** fresh;	AIT
	47:14	this land *will* **b** your inheritance.	5877
Da	4:22	*You* have **b** **great** and strong;	AIT
	8:23	when rebels *have* **b** **completely** wicked,	AIT
	8:24	*He will* **b** **very strong,**	AIT
	11: 5	"The king of the South will **b** **strong,**	AIT
	11: 5	one of his commanders will **b** even	
		stronger than he	AIT
	11: 6	After some years, *they* will **b** **allies.**	AIT
Hos	4:15	O Israel, *let* not Judah **b** **guilty.**	AIT
	7: 5	of our king the princes **b** **inflamed**	AIT
	8:11	*these* have **b** altars for sinning,	2118
	12: 8	*I have* **b** wealthy.	5162
Am	7:17	"'Your wife *will* **b** *a* **prostitute** in	AIT
Jnh	1:12	he replied, "and it *will* **b** **calm.**	AIT
Mic	3:12	Jerusalem *will* **b** a heap of rubble,	2118
	7:13	The earth *will* **b** desolate because	2118
	7:16	on their mouths and their ears *will* **b** **deaf.**	AIT
Na	3:11	You too *will* **b** **drunk;**	AIT
Hab	2: 7	Then *you* will **b** their victim.	2118+4200
Zep	2: 9	"surely Moab *will* **b** like Sodom,	2118
	2:15	What a ruin *she* has **b,** a lair for wild beasts!	2118
Hag	2:12	oil or other food, *does it* **b** **consecrated?'** "	AIT
	2:13	*does it* **b** **defiled?"**	AIT
Zec	2:11	in that day and *will* **b** my people.	2118
	4: 7	Before Zerubbabel *you* will **b** level ground.	4200
	8:19	seventh and tenth months *will* **b** joyful	2118
	9: 7	to our God and **b** leaders in Judah,	2118
	10: 7	The Ephraimites *will* **b** like mighty men,	2118
	14:10	south of Jerusalem, *will* **b** like the Arabah.	6015
Mt	4: 3	tell these stones *to* **b** bread."	1181
	5:32	causes her *to* **b** an **adulteress,**	3658
	13:15	For this people's heart *has* **b** **calloused;**	AIT
	18: 3	unless you change and **b** like little children,	1181
	19: 5	and the two will **b** one flesh'?	1639+1650
	20:26	*to* **b** great among you must be your servant,	1181
	21:42	builders rejected *has* **b** the capstone;	1181+1650
	27:57	who *had* himself **b** **a disciple** of Jesus.	3411
Mk	6:14	for Jesus' name *had* **b** well known.	1181
	10: 8	and the two will **b** one flesh.'	1639+1650
	10:43	*to* **b** great among you must be your servant,	1181
	12:10	builders rejected *has* **b** the capstone;	1181+1650
Lk	3: 5	The crooked roads *shall* **b** straight,	1639
	4: 3	tell this stone *to* **b** bread."	1181
	20:17	builders rejected *has* **b** the capstone'?	1181+1650
Jn	1:12	he gave the right *to* **b** children of God—	1181
	3:30	He must **b** **greater;** I must become less.	889
	3:30	He must become greater; I must **b** less.	AIT
	4:14	the water I give him *will* **b** in him a spring	1181
	7: 4	No one who wants *to* **b** a public figure acts	1181
	9:27	Do you want *to* **b** his disciples, too?"	1181
	9:39	and those who see *will* **b** blind."	1181
	12:36	so that *you* may **b** sons of light."	1181
Ac	1:22	For one of these *must* **b** a witness with us	1181
	4:11	which *has* **b** the capstone.'	1181
	12:18	among the soldiers as to what *had* **b** of	1181
	13:33	today I *have* **b** your **Father.'**	1164
	26:29	to me today *may* **b** what I am,	1181
	27: 9	and sailing *had* already **b** dangerous	1639
	28:27	For this people's heart *has* **b** **calloused;**	AIT
Ro	1:29	*They* have **b** **filled** with every kind	AIT
	2:25	you *have* **b** as though you had	1181
	3:12	*they* have together **b** **worthless;**	946
	3:20	through the law we **b** conscious of sin.	NIG
	6:18	and have **b** slaves to righteousness.	1530
	6:22	from sin and have **b** slaves to God,	1530
	7:13	*Did* that which is good, then, **b** death to me?	1181
	7:13	sin *might* **b** utterly sinful.	1181
	9:29	we would have **b** like Sodom,	1181
	11: 9	"May their table **b** a snare and a trap,	1181+1650
	11:31	so they too have now **b** **disobedient** in order	AIT
	15: 8	For I tell you that Christ *has* **b** a servant of	1181
	15:16	the Gentiles *might* **b** an offering acceptable	1181
1Co	1:30	who *has* **b** for us wisdom from God—	1181
	3:18	he should **b** a "fool" so he may	1181
	3:18	a "fool" so that *he* may **b** wise.	1181
	4: 8	Already *you* have **b** rich!	AIT
	4: 8	*You* have **b** **kings**—and that without us!	AIT
	4: 8	that *you* really had **b** **kings** so that we might	AIT
	4:13	Up to this moment *we* have **b** the scum of	1181
	4:18	Some of you have **b** **arrogant,**	AIT
	6:16	it is said, "The two *will* **b** one flesh."	1639+1650
	7:18	*He should* not **b** **uncircumcised.**	2177
	7:23	*do* not **b** slaves of men.	1181
	8: 9	that the exercise of your freedom *does* not **b**	1181
	9:22	*I have* **b** all things to all men so that	1181
2Co	5:21	in him we *might* **b** the righteousness of God.	1181
	8: 9	that you through his poverty *might* **b** rich.	4456
Gal	4:12	I plead with you, brothers, **b** like me,	1181
	4:16	now *I* **b** your enemy by telling you the truth?	1181
	5:26	*Let us* not **b** conceited,	1181
	6: 9	*Let us* not **b** **weary** in doing good,	1591
Eph	2:21	and rises *to* **b** a holy temple in the Lord.	NIG
	2:22	in him you too are being built together *to* **b**	NIG
	4:13	of the Son of God and **b** mature,	1650
	5:31	and the two *will* **b** one flesh."	1639+1650
Php	1:13	it *has* **b** clear throughout	1181
	2:15	so that *you* may **b** blameless and pure,	1181
Col	1:23	and of which I, Paul, *have* **b** a servant.	1181
	1:25	*I have* **b** its servant by the commission God	1181
	3:21	or *they* will **b** **discouraged.**	126
1Th	1: 8	your faith in God *has* **b** **known** everywhere.	AIT
	2: 8	because you had **b** so dear to us.	1181

2Th	2: 2	not *to* **b** easily **unsettled** or alarmed	AIT
1Ti	3: 6	or *he* may **b** **conceited** and fall under	5605
	5:13	And not only do they **b** idlers,	NIG
2Ti	2:16	because those who indulge in it will **b** more	NIG
	3:14	and *have* **b** **convinced** of,	AIT
Tit	3: 7	we might **b** heirs having the hope	1181
Phm	1:11	now he has **b** useful both to you and to me.	NIG
Heb	1: 5	today I *have* **b** your **Father"?**	1164
	2:17	in order that *he might* **b** a merciful	1181
	5: 5	today I *have* **b** your **Father."**	1164
	6:12	We do not want *you to* **b** lazy,	1181
	6:20	*He has* **b** a high priest forever,	1181
	7: 5	of Levi who **b** priests to collect a tenth from	3284
	7:16	one who *has* **b** a priest not on the basis of	1181
	7:22	Jesus *has* **b** the guarantee of	1181
	11:11	was enabled to **b** a father	2856+3284+5065
Jas	1:19	slow to speak and slow to **b** angry,	AIT
	2: 4	and **b** judges with evil thoughts?	1181
	2:11	*you have* **b** a lawbreaker.	1181
1Pe	2: 7	builders rejected *has* **b** the capstone,"	1181+1650
	4:18	what *will* **b** of the ungodly and the sinner?"	5743
Rev	3:18	so *you can* **b** rich;	AIT
	8:11	from the waters that *had* **b** bitter.	AIT
	11:15	of the world *has* **b** the kingdom of our Lord	1181
	18: 2	*She has* **b** a home for demons and a haunt	1181

BECOMES (35) [BECOME]

Lev	6: 4	when he thus sins and **b** **guilty,**	AIT
	11:35	of their carcasses falls on **b** **unclean;**	AIT
	12: 2	'A woman who **b** **pregnant** and gives birth	AIT
	22:13	priest's daughter **b** a widow or is divorced,	2118
	25:25	of your countrymen **b** **poor** and sells some	AIT
	25:35	of your countrymen **b** **poor** and is unable	AIT
	25:39	of your countrymen **b** **poor** among you	AIT
	25:47	or a temporary resident among you **b** **rich**	AIT
	25:47	and one of your countrymen **b** **poor**	AIT
Nu	19:22	such an animal given to the LORD **b** holy.	2118
	19:22	that an unclean person touches **b** **unclean,**	AIT
	19:22	and anyone who touches it **b** **unclean**	AIT
Dt	24: 1	If a man marries a woman who **b**	
		displeasing to him	2118
	24: 2	if after she leaves his house *she* **b** the wife	2118
Job	14:11	the sea or a riverbed **b** **parched** and dry,	2118
	18: 6	The light in his tent **b** **dark;**	AIT
	30:18	In his great power [God] **b** like clothing	2924
	38:38	when the dust **b** **hard** and the clods	AIT
Ps	104:20	You bring darkness, *it* **b** night,	2118
Pr	30:22	a servant who **b** **king,**	AIT
Isa	18: 5	when the blossom is gone and the flower **b**	2118
	32:15	and the desert **b** a fertile field,	2118
	59:15	and whoever shuns evil **b** *a* **prey.**	8964
Jer	23:36	because every man's own word **b** his oracle	2118
Eze	15: 5	and they leave it childless and it **b** desolate	2118
	24:11	the coals till *it* **b** **hot** and its copper glows	AIT
	47: 8	the water there **b** **fresh.**	AIT
Hag	2:13	"Yes," the priests replied, "*it* **b** **defiled."**	AIT
Mt	13:32	the largest of garden plants and **b** a tree,	1181
		and when *he* **b** one,	1181
Mk	4:32	and **b** the largest of all garden plants,	1181
	9:18	gnashes his teeth and **b** **rigid.**	3830
Gal	2:17	*it* **b** **evident** that we ourselves are sinners,	AIT
Eph	5:13	everything exposed by the light **b** **visible,**	AIT
Jas	4: 4	be a friend of the world **b** an enemy of God.	2770

BECOMING (8) [BECOME]

Lev	21: 9	by **b** a **prostitute,** she disgraces her father;	AIT
1Sa	3: 2	whose eyes *were* **b** so weak	2725
1Ki	16: 7	and **b** like the house of Jeroboam—	2118
Joel	2:22	for the open pastures *are* **b** green.	AIT
2Co	5: 7	To keep me from **b** **conceited** because	AIT
Gal	3:13	the law by **b** a curse for us, for it is written:	1181
Php	3:10	**b** like him in his death,	5214
Heb	7:11	upon himself the glory *of* **b** a high priest.	1181

BECORATH (1)

1Sa	9: 1	the son of Zeror, the son of **B,**	1138

BED (76) [BEDDING, BEDRIDDEN, BEDROOM, BEDROOMS, BEDS, SICKBED]

Ge	19: 4	Before *they had* **gone to b,**	8886
	39: 7	**"Come to b with me!"**	6640+8886
	39:10	he refused to **go to b** with her	725+8886
	39:12	**"Come to b with me!"**	6640+8886
	48: 2	and sat up on the **b.**	4753
	49: 4	for you went up onto your father's **b,**	5435
	49:33	he drew his feet up into the **b,**	4753
Ex	8: 3	and your bedroom and onto your **b,**	4753
	21:18	and he does not die but is confined to **b,**	5435
Lev	15: 4	" 'Any **b** the man with a discharge lies	5435
	15: 5	Anyone who touches his **b** must wash his	
		clothes	5435
	15:21	Whoever touches her **b** must wash his	
		clothes	5435
	15:23	the **b** or anything she was sitting on,	5435
	15:24	any **b** he lies on will be unclean.	5435
	15:26	Any **b** she lies on while her discharge	5435
	15:26	as is her **b** during her monthly period,	5435
Dt	3:11	His **b** was *made of* iron	6911
	22:30	*he must* not **dishonor** his father's **b.**	1655+4053
	27:20	for *he* **dishonors** his father's **b."**	1655+4053
1Sa	19:13	Michal took an idol and laid it on the **b,**	4753
	19:15	up to me in his **b** so that I may kill him."	4753

1Sa	19:16	the men entered, there was the idol in the **b,**	4753
2Sa	4: 7	while he was lying on the **b** in his bedroom.	4753
	4:11	in his own house and on his own **b**—	5435
	11: 2	from his **b** and walked around on the roof	5435
	13: 5	"Go to **b** and pretend to be ill,"	5435
	13:11	"Come *to* **b** with me, my sister."	6640+8886
1Ki	1:47	And the king bowed in worship on his **b**	5435
	17:19	and laid him on his **b.**	4753
	21: 4	He lay on his **b** sulking and refused to eat.	4753
2Ki	1: 4	'You will not leave the **b** you are lying on.	4753
	1: 6	not leave the **b** you are lying on.	4753
	1:16	you will never leave the **b** you are lying on.	4753
	4:10	a small room on the roof and put in it a **b**	4753
	4:21	and laid him on the **b** *of* the man of God,	4753
	4:34	Then he got on the **b** and lay upon the boy,	NIH
	4:35	and forth in the room and then got on the **b**	NIH
1Ch	—	he defiled his father's **marriage b,**	3661
2Ch	24:25	and they killed him in his **b.**	4753
Job	7:13	When I think my **b** will comfort me	6911
	17:13	if I spread out my **b** in darkness,	3661
	33:19	Or a man may be chastened on a **b** of pain	5435
Ps	6: 6	all night long I flood my **b** with weeping	4753
	36: 4	Even on his **b** he plots evil;	5435
	41: 3	on his sickbed and restore him from his **b**	5435
	63: 6	On my **b** I remember you;	3661
	132: 3	"I will not enter my house or go to my **b**—	3661+6911
	139: 8	if *I* **make** *my* **b** in the depths, you are there.	3667
Pr	7:16	I have covered my **b** with colored linens	6911
	7:17	I have perfumed my **b** with myrrh,	5435
	22:27	your very **b** will be snatched from	
	26:14	so a sluggard turns on his **b.**	4753
	31:22	She makes **coverings** for her **b;**	5267
SS	1:16	And our **b** is verdant.	6911
	3: 1	All night long on my **b** I looked for	5435
Isa	28:20	The **b** is too short to stretch out on,	5201
	57: 7	You have made your **b** on a high	5435
	57: 8	Forsaking me, you uncovered your **b,**	5435
Eze	22:10	**dishonor** their fathers' **b;**	1655+6872
	23:17	Babylonians came to her, to the **b** *of* love,	5435
	32:25	A **b** is made for her among the slain,	5435
Da	2:28	as you lay on your **b** are these:	10444
	4: 5	As I was lying in my **b,**	10444
	4:10	the visions I saw while lying in my **b:**	10444
	4:13	"In the visions I saw while lying in my **b,**	10444
	7: 1	through his mind as he was lying on his **b.**	10444
Mt	8:14	he saw Peter's mother-in-law lying in **b**	NIG
Mk	1:30	Simon's mother-in-law *was* in **b** with	2879
	4:21	in a lamp to put it under a bowl or a **b?**	3109
	7:30	and found her child lying on the **b,**	3109
Lk	8:16	and hides it in a jar or puts it under a **b.**	3109
	11: 7	and my children are with me in **b.**	3130
	17:34	on that night two people will be in one **b;**	3109
Ac	28: 8	His father was **sick in b,**	2879
Heb	13: 4	and the **marriage b** kept pure,	3130
Rev	2:22	So I will cast her on a **b of suffering,**	3109

BEDAD (2)

Ge	36:35	When Husham died, Hadad son of **B,**	971
1Ch	1:46	When Husham died, Hadad son of **B,**	971

BEDAN (1)

1Ch	7:17	The son of Ulam: **B.**	979

BEDCHAMBER (KJV) See BEDROOM

BEDDING (1) [BED]

2Sa	17:28	brought **b** and bowls and articles of pottery.	5435

BEDEIAH (1)

Ezr	10:35	Benaiah, **B,** Keluhi,	973

BEDRIDDEN (1) [BED]

Ac	9:33	a paralytic *who had been* **b** for eight years.	
			2093+2879+3187

BEDROOM (8) [BED, ROOM]

Ex	8: 3	up into your palace and your **b**	2540+5435
2Sa	4: 7	while he was lying on the bed in his **b.**	2540+5435
	13:10	"Bring the food here into my **b** so I may eat	2540
	13:10	to her brother Amnon in his **b.**	2540
2Ki	6:12	the very words you speak in your **b."**	2540+5435
	11: 2	in a **b** to hide him from Athaliah;	2540+4753
2Ch	22:11	and put him and his nurse in a **b.**	2540+4753
Ecc	10:20	or curse the rich in your **b,**	2540+5435

BEDROOMS (1) [BED, ROOM]

Ps	105:30	which went up into the **b** *of* their rulers.	2540

BEDS (12) [BED]

Job	30: 6	to live in the dry **stream b,**	5707
	33:15	on men as they slumber in their **b,**	5435
Ps	4: 4	when you are on your **b,**	5435
	149: 5	in this honor and sing for joy on their **b.**	5435
SS	5:13	like **b** of spice yielding perfume,	6870
	6: 2	to the **b** *of* spices.	6870
Isa	57: 8	a pact with those whose **b** you love,	5435
Hos	7:14	from their hearts but wail upon their **b.**	5435
Am	3:12	on the edge of their **b** and in Damascus	4753
	6: 4	You lie on **b** *inlaid with* ivory and lounge	4753
Mic	2: 1	to those who plot evil on their **b!**	5435

Ac   5:15   into the streets and laid them on **b** and mats   *3108*

BEELIADA (1)

1Ch 14: 7   Elishama, **B** and Eliphelet.   1269

BEELZEBUB (7) [BAAL-ZEBUB]

Mt   10:25   If the head of the house *has been* called **B**,   *1015*
     12:24   "It is only by **B**, the prince of demons,   *1015*
     12:27   And if I drive out demons by **B**,   *1015*
Mk   3:22   "He is possessed by **B**!   *1015*
Lk   11:15   But some of them said, "By **B**,   *1015*
     11:18   that I drive out demons by **B**.   *1015*
     11:19   Now if I drive out demons by **B**,   *1015*

BEEN (890) [BE] See Index of Articles Etc.

BEER (13) [BAALATH BEER, BEER LAHAI ROI, BEER ELIM]

Nu   21:16   From there they continued on to **B**,   932
Jdg   9:21   Then Jotham fled, escaping to **B**,   932
1Sa   1:15   I have not been drinking wine or **b**;   8911
Pr   20: 1   Wine is a mocker and **b** a brawler;   8911
     31: 4   not for rulers to crave **b**,   8911
     31: 6   Give **b** to those who are perishing,   8911
Isa   24: 9   the **b** is bitter to its drinkers.   8911
     28: 7   also stagger from wine and reel from **b**:   8911
     28: 7   from **b** and are befuddled with wine;   8911
     28: 7   they reel from **b**,   8911
     29: 9   but not from wine, stagger, but not from **b**.   8911
     56:12   Let us drink our fill of **b**!   8911
Mic   2:11   for you plenty of wine and **b**,'   8911

BEER ELIM (1) [BEER, ELIM]

Isa   15: 8   their lamentation as far as **B**.   935

BEER LAHAI ROI (3) [BEER]

Ge   16:14   the well was called **B**;   936
     24:62   Now Isaac had come from **B**,   936
     25:11   who then lived near **B**.   936

BEERA (1)

1Ch   7:37   Hod, Shamma, Shilshah, Ithran and **B**.   938

BEERAH (2)

1Ch   5: 6   and **B** his son,   939
     5: 6   **B** was a leader of the Reubenites.   2085ˢ

BEERI (2)

Ge   26:34   he married Judith daughter of **B** the Hittite,   941
Hos   1: 1   of the LORD that came to Hosea son of **B**   941

BEEROTH (6) [BEEROTHITE]

Jos   9:17   Gibeon, Kephirah, **B** and Kiriath Jearim.   940
     18:25   Gibeon, Ramah, **B**,   940
2Sa   4: 2   **B** is considered part of Benjamin,   940
     4: 3   because the **people of B** fled to Gittaim   943
Ezr   2:25   of Kiriath Jearim, Kephirah and **B** 743   940
Ne   7:29   of Kiriath Jearim, Kephirah and **B** 743   940

BEEROTHITE (4) [BEEROTH]

2Sa   4: 2   they were sons of Rimmon the **B** from   943
     4: 5   the sons of Rimmon the **B**,   943
     4: 9   the sons of Rimmon the **B**,   943
     23:37   the **B**, the armor-bearer of Joab son   943

BEERSHEBA (34)

Ge   21:14   and wandered in the desert of **B**.   937
     21:31   So that place was called **B**,   937
     21:32   After the treaty had been made at **B**,   937
     21:33   Abraham planted a tamarisk tree in **B**,   937
     22:19   and they set off together for **B**.   937
     22:19   And Abraham stayed in **B**.   937
     26:23   From there he went up to **B**.   937
     26:33   the name of the town has been **B**.   937
     28:10   Jacob left **B** and set out for Haran.   937
     46: 1   and when he reached **B**,   937
     46: 5   Then Jacob left **B**,   937
Jos   15:28   Hazar Shual, **B**, Biziothiah,   937
     19: 2   It included: **B** (or Sheba), Moladah,   937
Jdg   20: 1   to **B** and from the land of Gilead came out   937
1Sa   3:20   to **B** recognized that Samuel was attested as   937
     8: 2   and they served at **B**.   937
2Sa   3:10   over Israel and Judah from Dan to **B**."   937
     17:11   Let all Israel, from Dan to **B**—   937
     24: 2   from Dan to **B** and enroll the fighting men,   937
     24: 7   they went on to **B** in the Negev of Judah.   937
     24:15   of the people from Dan to **B** died.   937
1Ki   4:25   from Dan to **B**, lived in safety,   937
     19: 3   When he came to **B** in Judah,   937
2Ki   12: 1   mother's name was Zibiah; she was from **B**.   937
     23: 8   from Geba to **B**.   937
1Ch   4:28   They lived in **B**, Moladah, Hazar Shual,   937
     21: 2   "Go and count the Israelites from **B** to Dan.   937
2Ch   19: 4   from **B** to the hill country of Ephraim   937
     24: 1   she was from **B**.   937
     30: 5   throughout Israel, from **B** to Dan,   937
Ne   11:27   in Hazar Shual, in **B** and its settlements,   937
     11:30   So they were living all the way from **B** to   937
Am   5: 5   do not go to Gilgal, do not journey to **B**.   937

Am   8:14   or, 'As surely as the god of **B** lives'—   937

BEES (4)

Dt   1:44   like a **swarm of b** and beat you down   1805
Jdg   14: 8   In it was a swarm of **b** and some honey,   1805
Ps   118:12   They swarmed around me like **b**,   1805
Isa   7:18   of Egypt and for **b** from the land of Assyria.   1805

BEESH-TERAH (KJV) See BE ESHTARAH

BEETLE (KJV) See CRICKET

BEEVES (KJV) See CATTLE

BEFALL (2) [BEFALLS]

Job   5:19   in seven no harm *will* **b** you.   5595
Ps   91:10   then no harm *will* **b** you,   448+628

BEFALLS (1) [BEFALL]

Pr   12:21   No harm **b** the righteous,   628+4200

BEFORE (1295) [BEFOREHAND]

Ge   10: 9   He was a mighty hunter **b** the LORD;   4200+7156
     10: 9   a mighty hunter **b** the LORD."   4200+7156
     13: 9   Is not the whole land **b** you?   4200+7156
     13:10   This was **b** the LORD destroyed Sodom   4200+7156
     17: 1   walk **b** me and be blameless.   4200+7156
     18: 8   and set these **b** them.   4200+7156
     18:22   Abraham remained standing **b** the LORD.   4200+7156
     19: 4   **B** they had gone to bed,   3270
     19:27   place where he had stood **b** the LORD.   907+7156
     20:15   Abimelech said, "My land is **b** you;   4200
     20:16   This is to cover the offense against you **b**   4200
     21:23   Now swear to me here **b** God that you will   928
     23: 7   and bowed down **b** the people of the land,   4200
     23:12   Abraham bowed down **b** the people   4200+7156
     24: 7   he will send his angel **b** you so   4200+7156
     24:15   **B** he had finished praying,   3270
     24:33   Then food was set **b** him, but he said,   4200+7156
     24:40   'The LORD, **b** whom I have walked,   4200+7156
     24:45   "**B** I finished praying in my heart,   3270
     24:52   down to the ground **b** the LORD.   4200
     27: 4   I may give you my blessing **b** I die."   928+3270
     27: 7   in the presence of the LORD **b** I die.'   4200+7156
     27:10   so that he may give you his blessing **b**   4200+7156
     27:33   I ate it **just b** you came   928+3270
     29:26   to give the younger daughter in marriage **b**   4200+7156
     30:30   The little you had **b** I came   4200+7156
     31: 5   toward me is not what it was **b**,   8997+9453
     33:14   slowly at the pace of the droves **b** me   4200+7156
     36:31   in Edom **b** any Israelite king reigned: 4200+7156
     37:10   and bow down to the ground **b** you?"   4200
     37:18   and **b** he reached them,   928+3270
     41:14   he came **b** Pharaoh.   448
     41:21   they looked just as ugly as **b**.   928+2021+9378
     41:43   and men shouted **b** him, "Make way!"   4200+7156
     41:50   **B** the years of famine came,   928+3270
     42:24   from them and bound **b** their eyes.   4200
     43: 9   to you and set him here **b** you,   4200+7156
     43: 9   I will bear the blame **b** you all my life.   4200
     43:14   may God Almighty grant you mercy **b**   4200+7156
     43:26   and they bowed down **b** him to the ground.   4200
     43:33   The men had been seated **b** him,   4200+7156
     44:14   they threw themselves to the ground **b** him.   4200
     44:32   I will bear the blame **b** you, my father,   4200
     45: 1   Joseph could no longer control himself **b**   4200
     45:28   I will go and see him **b** I die."   928+3270
     46:29   As soon as Joseph appeared **b** him,   448
     47: 2   of his brothers and presented them **b**   4200+7156
     47: 6   and the land of Egypt is **b** you;   4200+7156
     47: 7   in and presented him **b** Pharaoh.   4200+7156
     47:15   Why should we die **b** your eyes?   5584
     47:19   Why should we perish **b** your eyes—   4200
     48: 5   to you in Egypt **b** I came to you here will   6330
     48:15   the God **b** whom my fathers Abraham   4200+7156
     50:16   "Your father left these instructions **b**   4200+7156
     50:18   and threw themselves down **b** him.   4200+7156
Ex   1:19   and give birth **b** the midwives arrive."   928+3270
     4:21   see that you perform **b** Pharaoh all   4200+7156
     4:30   also performed the signs **b** the people,   4200+6524
     5: 8   make the same number of bricks as **b**;   8997+9453
     5:14   of bricks yesterday or today, as **b**?"   8997+9453
     7: 9   'Take your staff and throw it down **b**   4200+7156
     9:10   from a furnace and stood **b** Pharaoh.   4200+7156
     9:11   magicians could not stand **b** Moses   4200+7156
     10: 3   to humble yourself **b** me?   4946+7156
     10:14   Never **b** had there been such a plague   4200+7156
     10:29   "I will never appear **b** you again."   7156
     11: 8   bowing down **b** me and saying, 'Go,   4200
     11:10   Aaron performed all these wonders **b**   4200+7156
     12:34   So the people took their dough **b**   3270
     16: 9   'Come **b** the LORD,   4200+7156
     16:33   Then place it **b** the LORD to be kept for   4200+7156
     17: 6   I will stand there **b** you by the rock   4200+7156
     19: 7   You must be **b** the people's representative   4578
     19: 7   people and set **b** them all the words   4200+7156
     20: 3   "You shall have no other gods **b** me.   6584+7156
     21: 1   are the laws you are to set **b** them: 4200+7156

Ex   21: 6   then his master must take him **b** the judges.   448
     22: 8   of the house must appear **b** the judges   448
     22: 9   parties are to bring their cases **b** the judges.   6330
     22:11   an **oath** *b* the LORD that the neighbor did   AIT
     23:15   "No one is to appear **b** me empty-handed.   7156
     23:17   to appear **b** the Sovereign LORD.   448+7156
     23:24   not bow down **b** their gods or worship them   4200
     23:30   Little by little I will drive them out **b** you,   7156
     23:31   the land and you will drive them out **b** you.   7156
     25:30   the Presence on this table to be **b** me   4200+7156
     27:21   to keep the lamps burning **b** the LORD   4200+7156
     28:12   names on his shoulders as a memorial **b** the LORD.   4200+7156
     28:29   as a continuing memorial **b** the LORD.   4200+7156
     28:30   Israelites over his heart **b** the LORD.   4200+7156
     28:35   heard when he enters the Holy Place **b**   4200+7156
     29:23   which is **b** the LORD, take a loaf,   4200+7156
     29:24   his sons and wave them **b** the LORD   4200+7156
     29:26   wave it **b** the LORD as a wave offering,   4200+7156
     29:42   the entrance to the Tent of Meeting **b**   4200+7156
     30: 6   Put the altar in front of the curtain that is **b**   6584
     30: 6   **b** the atonement cover that is over   4200+7156
     30: 8   so incense will burn regularly **b** the LORD   4200+7156
     30:16   memorial for the Israelites **b** the LORD,   4200+7156
     32: 1   "Come, make us gods who will go **b** us.   4200+7156
     32:23   'Make us gods who will go **b** us.   4200+7156
     32:34   and my angel will go **b** you.   4200+7156
     33: 2   I will send an angel **b** you and drive   4200+7156
     34:10   **B** all your people I will do wonders never   5584
     34:10   all your people I will do wonders never **b**   NIH
     34:11   I will drive out **b** you the Amorites,   4946+7156
     34:20   "No one is to appear **b** me empty-handed.   7156
     34:23   a year all your men are to appear **b**   907+7156
     34:24   I will drive out nations **b** you   4946+7156
     34:24   up three times each year to appear **b**   907+7156
     40:23   and set out the bread on it **b** the LORD,   4200+7156
     40:25   and set up the lamps **b** the LORD,   4200+7156
Lev   1: 5   slaughter the young bull **b** the LORD,   4200+7156
     1:11   to slaughter it at the north side of the altar **b** the LORD,   4200+7156
     3: 1   he is to present it **b** the LORD an animal   4200+7156
     3: 7   he is to present it **b** the LORD.   4200+7156
     3:12   he is to present it **b** the LORD.   4200+7156
     4: 4   the entrance to the Tent of Meeting **b**   4200+7156
     4: 4   on its head and slaughter it **b** the LORD.   4200+7156
     4: 6   and sprinkle some of it seven times **b**   4200+7156
     4: 7   is **b** the LORD in the Tent of Meeting.   4200+7156
     4:14   a sin offering and present it **b** the Tent   4200+7156
     4:15   to lay their hands on the bull's head **b**   4200+7156
     4:15   bull shall be slaughtered **b** the LORD.   4200+7156
     4:17   and sprinkle it **b** the LORD seven times   4200+7156
     4:18   horns of the altar that is **b** the LORD in   4200+7156
     4:24   the burnt offering is slaughtered **b**   4200+7156
     6: 7   priest will make atonement for him **b**   4200+7156
     6:14   Aaron's sons are to bring it **b** the LORD,   4200+7156
     6:25   be slaughtered **b** the LORD in the place   4200+7156
     7:30   breast **b** the LORD as a wave offering.   4200+7156
     8:26   which was **b** the LORD,   4200+7156
     8:27   his sons and waved them **b** the LORD   4200+7156
     8:29   waved it **b** the LORD as a wave offering,   4200+7156
     9: 2   and present them **b** the LORD.   4200+7156
     9: 4   for a fellowship offering to sacrifice **b**   4200+7156
     9: 5   entire assembly came near and stood **b**   4200+7156
     9:21   breasts and the right thigh **b** the LORD   4200+7156
     10: 1   and they offered unauthorized fire **b**   4200+7156
     10: 2   and they died **b** the LORD.   4200+7156
     10:15   waved **b** the LORD as a wave offering.   4200+7156
     10:17   by making atonement for them **b**   4200+7156
     10:19   and their burnt offering **b** the LORD,   4200+7156
     12: 7   He shall offer them **b** the LORD   4200+7156
     13: 7   he must appear **b** the priest again.   448
     14:11   cleansed and his offerings **b** the LORD   4200+7156
     14:12   he shall wave them **b** the LORD as   4200+7156
     14:16   with his finger sprinkle some of it **b**   4200+7156
     14:18   make atonement for him **b** the LORD.   4200+7156
     14:23   the entrance to the Tent of Meeting, **b**   4200+7156
     14:24   and wave them **b** the LORD as a   4200+7156
     14:27   from his palm seven times **b** the LORD.   4200+7156
     14:29   make atonement for him **b** the LORD.   4200+7156
     14:31   the priest will make atonement **b**   4200+7156
     14:36   order the house to be emptied **b** he goes   928+3270
     15:14   come **b** the LORD to the entrance to   4200+7156
     15:15   In this way he will make atonement **b**   4200+7156
     15:30   for her **b** the LORD for the uncleanness   4200+7156
     16: 4   so he must bathe himself with water **b**   2256
     16: 7   take the two goats and present them **b**   4200+7156
     16:10   presented alive **b** the LORD to be used   4200+7156
     16:12   the altar **b** the LORD and   4200+4946+7156
     16:12   put the incense on the fire **b** the LORD,   4200+7156
     16:14   of it with his finger seven times **b**   4200+7156
     16:18   is **b** the LORD and make atonement   4200+7156
     16:23   and take off the linen garments he put on **b**   928
     16:30   Then, **b** the LORD, you will be clean   4200+7156
     18:24   nations that I am going to drive out **b**   4946+7156
     18:27   people who lived in the land **b** you,   4200+7156
     18:28   it vomited out the nations that were **b**   4200+7156
     18:30   the detestable customs that were practiced **b**   4200+7156
     19:22   priest is to make atonement for him **b**   4200+7156
     20:17   be cut off **b** the eyes of their people.   4200
     20:23   nations I am going to drive out **b** you.   4946+7156
     23:11   to wave the sheaf **b** the LORD so it will   4200+7156
     23:20   to wave the two lambs the **b** the LORD as   4200+7156

Lev	23:28	when atonement is made for you **b**	7156
	23:40	and rejoice **b** the LORD your God	4200+7156
	24: 3	Aaron is to tend the lamps **b** the LORD	4200+7156
	24: 4	the pure gold lampstand **b** the LORD	4200+7156
	24: 6	on the table of pure gold **b** the LORD.	4200+7156
	24: 8	to be set out **b** the LORD regularly,	4200+7156
	25:30	not redeemed **b** a full year has passed,	6330
	26: 1	a carved stone in your land to bow down **b**	6584
	26: 7	and they will fall by the sword **b** you.	4200+7156
	26: 8	enemies will fall by the sword **b** you.	4200+7156
	26:37	not be able to stand **b** your enemies.	4200+7156
Nu	3: 4	fell dead **b** the LORD when they made	4200+7156
	3: 4	offering with unauthorized fire **b** him	4200+7156
	5:16	and have her stand **b** the LORD.	4200+7156
	5:18	After the priest has had the woman stand **b** the LORD	4200+7156
	5:25	wave it **b** the LORD and bring it to	4200+7156
	5:30	The priest is to have her stand **b** the LORD	4200+7156
	6:16	to present them **b** the LORD and make	4200+7156
	6:20	The priest shall then wave them **b**	4200+7156
	7: 3	their gifts **b** the LORD six covered carts	4200+7156
	7: 3	These they presented **b** the tabernacle.	4200+7156
	7:10	for its dedication and presented them **b**	4200+7156
	8:10	are to bring the Levites **b** the LORD,	4200+7156
	8:11	Levites **b** the LORD as a wave offering	4200+7156
	8:21	as a wave offering **b** the LORD	4200+7156
	10: 3	the whole community is to assemble **b** you	448
	10: 4	are to assemble **b** you.	448
	10:10	and they will be a memorial for you **b**	4200+7156
	10:21	The tabernacle was to be set up **b**	6330
	10:33	The ark of the covenant of the LORD went **b** them	4200+7156
	10:35	may your foes flee **b** you."	4946+7156
	11:20	among you, have wailed **b** him,	4200+7156
	11:33	the meat was still between their teeth and **b**	3270
	13:22	(Hebron had been built seven years **b** Zoan	4200+7156
	13:30	Then Caleb silenced the people **b** Moses	448
	14:14	that you go **b** them in a pillar of cloud	4200+7156
	14:37	down and died of a plague **b** the LORD.	4200+7156
	15:15	the alien shall be the same **b** the LORD:	4200+7156
	15:28	to make atonement **b** the LORD for	4200+7156
	16: 7	and incense in them **b** the LORD.	4200+7156
	16: 9	to stand **b** the community and minister	4200+7156
	16:16	"You and all your followers are to appear **b** the LORD	4200+7156
	16:17	and present it **b** the LORD.	4200+7156
	16:38	for they were presented **b** the LORD	4200+7156
	16:40	Aaron should come to burn incense **b**	4200+7156
	17: 7	Moses placed the staffs **b** the LORD	4200+7156
	18: 2	when you and your sons minister **b** the Tent	4200+7156
	18:19	It is an everlasting covenant of salt **b**	4200+7156
	20: 3	our brothers fell dead **b** the LORD!	4200+7156
	20: 8	Speak to that rock **b** their eyes	4200
	22:32	your path is a reckless one **b** me.	4200+5584
	25: 2	The people ate and bowed down **b**	4200
	25: 4	and expose them in broad daylight **b**	4200
	25: 6	to his family a Midianite woman **right b**	4200
	26:61	they made an offering **b** the LORD	4200+7156
	27: 2	Tent of Meeting and stood **b** Moses,	4200+7156
	27: 5	Moses brought their case **b** the LORD	4200+7156
	27:14	to honor me as holy **b** their eyes."	4200
	27:17	to go out and come in **b** them,	4200+7156
	27:19	Have him stand **b** Eleazar the priest	4200+7156
	27:21	He is to stand **b** Eleazar the priest,	4200+7156
	27:21	by inquiring of the Urim **b** the LORD.	4200+7156
	27:22	had him stand **b** Eleazar the priest	4200+7156
	31:50	to make atonement for ourselves **b**	4200+7156
	31:54	memorial for the Israelites **b** the LORD.	4200+7156
	32: 4	land the LORD subdued **b** the people	4200+7156
	32:20	if you will arm yourselves **b** the LORD	4200+7156
	32:21	you will go armed over the Jordan **b**	4200+7156
	32:21	until he has driven his enemies out **b** him—	4946+7156
	32:22	when the land is subdued **b** the LORD,	4200+7156
	32:22	this land will be your possession **b**	4200+7156
	32:27	will cross over to fight **b** the LORD,	4200+7156
	32:29	over the Jordan with you **b** the LORD,	4200+7156
	32:29	then when the land is subdued **b** you,	4200+7156
	32:32	over **b** the LORD into Canaan armed,	4200+7156
	33:52	drive out all the inhabitants of the land **b** you.	4946+7156
	35:12	a person accused of murder may not die **b**	6330
	35:12	before he stands trial **b** the assembly.	4200+7156
	35:32	and live on his own land **b** the death of	6330
	36: 1	and spoke **b** Moses and the leaders,	4200+7156
Dt	1:30	The LORD your God, who is going **b** you,	4200+7156
	1:30	did for you in Egypt, **b** your very eyes,	4200
	1:45	You came back and wept **b** the LORD,	4200+7156
	2:12	They destroyed the Horites from **b** them	7156
	2:21	The LORD destroyed them from **b**	7156
	2:22	when he destroyed the Horites from **b** them.	7156
	4: 8	as this body of laws I am setting **b**	4200+7156
	4:10	day you stood **b** the LORD your God	4200+7156
	4:10	the people **b** me to hear my words so	4200
	4:32	long **b** your time, from	4200+7156
	4:34	for you in Egypt **b** your very eyes?	4200
	4:38	to drive out **b** you nations greater	4946+7156
	4:44	This is the law Moses set **b** the Israelites.	4200+7156
	5: 7	"You shall have no other gods **b** me.	6584+7156
	6:19	thrusting out all your enemies **b** you,	4946+7156
	6:22	**B** our eyes the LORD sent miraculous signs	4200
	6:25	if we are careful to obey all this law **b**	4200+7156

Dt	7: 1	and drives out **b** you many nations—	4946+7156
	7:22	The LORD your God will drive out those nations **b** you,	4946+7156
	8:20	Like the nations the LORD destroyed **b**	4946+7156
	9: 3	he will subdue them **b** you.	4200+7156
	9: 4	the LORD your God has driven them out **b** you,	4200+4946+7156
	9: 4	the LORD is going to drive them out **b**	4946+7156
	9: 5	the LORD your God will drive them out **b** you,	4946+7156
	9:17	breaking them to pieces **b** your eyes.	4200
	9:18	Then once again I fell prostrate **b**	4200+7156
	9:25	I lay prostrate **b**	4200+7156
	10: 4	on these tablets what he had written **b**,	8037
	10: 8	to stand **b** the LORD to minister and	4200+7156
	11:23	the LORD will drive out all these nations **b** you,	4200+4946+7156
	11:26	I am setting **b** you today a blessing	4200+7156
	11:32	the decrees and laws I am setting **b**	4200+7156
	12:12	there rejoice **b** the LORD your God,	4200+7156
	12:18	to rejoice **b** the LORD your God	4200+7156
	12:29	The LORD your God will cut off **b** you	4946+7156
	12:30	after they have been destroyed **b** you,	4946+7156
	16:11	And rejoice **b** the LORD your God at	4200+7156
	16:16	a year all your men must appear **b**	907+7156
	16:16	No man should appear **b**	907+7156
	17: 8	If cases come **b** your courts	928
	18:12	the LORD your God will drive out those nations **b** you.	4946+7156
	18:13	be blameless **b** the LORD your God.	6640
	19:17	the presence of the LORD **b** the priests	4200+7156
	20: 3	not be terrified or give way to panic **b** them.	4946+7156
	22:17	Then her parents shall display the cloth **b** the elders	4200+7156
	24:15	Pay him his wages each day **b** sunset,	4202
	26: 5	shall declare **b** the LORD your God:	4200+7156
	26:10	Place the basket **b** the LORD your God	4200+7156
	26:10	your God and bow down **b** him.	4200+7156
	28: 7	up against you will be defeated **b** you,	4200+7156
	28:25	The LORD will cause you to be defeated **b** your enemies.	4200+7156
	28:31	Your ox will be slaughtered **b** your eyes,	4200
	30: 1	curses I have set **b** you come upon you	4200+7156
	30:15	I set **b** you today life and prosperity,	4200+7156
	30:19	witnesses against you that I have set **b**	4200+7156
	31: 3	He will destroy these nations **b** you,	4200+4946+7156
	31: 8	The LORD himself goes **b** you and	4200+7156
	31:11	to appear **b** the LORD your God at	907+7156
	31:11	you shall read this law **b** them	5584
	31:21	even **b** I bring them into the land	928+3270
	31:28	Assemble **b** me all the elders of your tribes	448
	33: 1	of God pronounced on the Israelites **b**	4200+7156
	33:10	He offers incense **b** you	678+928
	33:27	He will drive out your enemy **b** you,	4946+7156
	33:29	Your enemies will cower **b** you,	4200
Jos	2: 8	**B** the spies lay down for the night,	3270
	3: 1	where they camped **b** crossing over.	7156
	3: 4	you have never been this way **b**.	4946+8997+9453
	3:10	that he will certainly drive out **b** you	4946+7156
	4: 5	"Go over **b** the ark of the LORD your God	4200+7156
	4: 7	the flow of the Jordan was cut off **b** the ark	4200+7156
	4:13	**b** the plains of Jericho	4200+7156
	4:18	their place and ran at flood stage as **b**.	8997+9453
	4:23	the LORD your God dried up the Jordan **b** you	4946+7156
	4:23	the Red Sea when he dried it up **b** us	4946+7156
	5: 1	the LORD had dried up the Jordan **b**	4946+7156
	6: 8	the seven trumpets **b**	4200+7156
	6:13	marching **b** the ark of the LORD	4200+7156
	6:26	"Cursed **b** the LORD is the man	4200+7156
	7: 6	fell facedown to the ground **b** the ark	4200+7156
	7:23	all the Israelites and spread them out **b**	4200+7156
	8: 5	as they did **b**, we will flee from them.	928+2021+8037
	8: 6	from us as they did **b**.'	928+2021+8037
	8:10	leaders of Israel marched **b** them to Ai	4200+7156
	8:15	be driven back **b** them,	4200+7156
	9:24	to wipe out all its inhabitants from **b** you.	7156
	10:10	The LORD threw them into confusion **b** Israel,	4200+7156
	10:11	As they fled **b** Israel on the road down	4946+7156
	10:14	There has never been a day like it **b** or	4200+7156
	13: 6	will drive them out **b** the Israelites.	4946+7156
	18: 3	"How long will you wait **b** you begin	NIH
	20: 4	city gate and state his case **b** the elders	265+928
	20: 6	in that city until he has stood trial **b**	4200+7156
	20: 9	of blood prior to standing trial **b**	4200+7156
	22:29	of the LORD our God that stands **b**	4200+7156
	23: 5	He will push them out **b** you,	4200+4946+7156
	23: 9	"The LORD has driven out **b** you great	4946+7156
	23:13	LORD your God will no longer drive out these nations **b** you.	4200+4946+7156
	24: 1	and they presented themselves **b** God.	4200+7156
	24: 8	I destroyed them out **b** you,	7156
	24:12	which drove them out **b** you—	4946+7156
	24:17	and performed those great signs **b** our eyes.	4200
	24:18	LORD drove out **b** us all the nations,	4946+7156
Jdg	2: 3	that I will not drive them out **b** you;	4946+7156
	2:21	I will no longer drive out **b** them any	4946+7156
	4:23	the Canaanite king, **b** the Israelites.	4200+7156
	5: 5	The mountains quaked **b** the LORD,	4946+7156
	5: 5	**b** the LORD, the God of Israel.	4946+7156
	6: 9	from **b** you and gave you their land.	7156

Jdg	6:18	bring my offering and set it **b** you."	4200+7156
	8:28	Midian was subdued **b** the Israelites	4200+7156
	11:11	he repeated all his words **b** the LORD	4200+7156
	11:23	the Amorites out **b** his people Israel,	4200+7156
	14:18	**B** sunset on the seventh day the men of	928+3270
	16:20	"I'll go out as **b** and shake myself free."	928+3869+7193+7193
	20: 1	as one man and assembled **b** the LORD	448
	20:23	up and wept **b** the LORD until evening,	4200+7156
	20:26	and there they sat weeping **b** the LORD.	4200+7156
	20:28	the son of Aaron, ministering **b** it.)	4200+7156
	20:30	as they had **done b**.	928+3869+7193+7193
	20:31	to inflict casualties on the Israelites **as b,**	928+3869+7193+7193
	20:32	"We are defeating them as **b,"**	928+2021+8037
	20:35	The LORD defeated Benjamin **b** Israel,	4200+7156
	20:36	men of Israel had given way **b** Benjamin,	4200
	20:42	fled **b** the Israelites in the direction	4200+7156
	21: 2	where they sat **b** God until evening,	4200+7156
	21: 5	has failed to assemble **b** the LORD?"	448
	21: 5	that anyone who failed to assemble **b**	448
	21: 8	of the tribes of Israel failed to assemble **b**	448
Ru	2:11	live with a people you did not know **b**.	8997+9453
	3:14	got up **b** anyone could be recognized;	928+3270
1Sa	1:19	and worshiped **b** the LORD and	907+7156
	1:22	I will take him and present him **b**	907+7156
	2:11	the boy ministered **b** the LORD under Eli	907
	2:15	But even the fat was burned,	928+3270
	2:18	Samuel was ministering **b** the LORD—	907+7156
	2:30	your father's house would minister **b**	4200+7156
	2:35	minister **b** my anointed one always.	4200+7156
	2:36	down **b** him for a piece of silver and a crust	4200
	3: 1	The boy Samuel ministered **b** the LORD	907
	4: 3	the LORD bring defeat upon us today **b**	4200+7156
	4: 7	Nothing like this has happened **b**.	919+8997
	4:17	"Israel fled **b** the Philistines,	4200+7156
	5: 3	fallen on his face on the ground **b** the ark of the LORD!	4200
	5: 4	fallen on his face on the ground **b** the ark of the LORD!	4200+7156
	7: 6	they drew water and poured it out **b**	4200+7156
	7:10	such a panic that they were routed **b**	4200+7156
	8:20	to go out **b** us and fight our battles."	4200+7156
	8:21	he repeated it **b** the LORD.	265+928
	9:13	you will find him **b** he goes up to	928+3270
	9:15	Now the day **b** Saul came,	4200+7156
	10: 5	flutes and harps being played **b** them,	4200+7156
	10:19	So now present yourselves **b** the LORD	4200+7156
	10:25	a scroll and deposited it **b** the LORD.	4200+7156
	11:15	they sacrificed fellowship offerings **b**	4200+7156
	12: 7	to confront you with evidence **b** the LORD	4200+7156
	12:16	the LORD is about to do **b** your eyes!	4200
	14:13	The Philistines fell **b** Jonathan,	4200+7156
	14:24	"Cursed be any man who eats food **b**	6330
	14:24	**b** I have avenged myself on my enemies!"	NIH
	15:30	But please honor me **b** the elders	5584
	15:30	before the elders of my people and **b** Israel;	5584
	15:33	And Samuel put Agag to death **b**	4200+7156
	16: 6	the LORD's anointed stands here **b**	5584
	16:10	Jesse had seven of his sons pass **b** Samuel,	4200+7156
	17:30	and the men answered him as **b**.	8037
	17:57	Abner took him and brought him **b** Saul,	4200+7156
	18:26	**b** the allotted time **elapsed,**	4202+4848
	19: 7	and David was with Saul as **b**.	919+8997
	19: 8	with such force that they fled **b** him.	4946+7156
	20: 8	into a **covenant** with you **b** the LORD.	AIT
	20:41	and **bowed** down **b** Jonathan three times,	AIT
	21: 6	had been removed from **b** the LORD!	4200+7156
	21: 7	detained **b** the LORD;	4200+7156
	23:18	of them made a covenant **b** the LORD.	4200+7156
	25:23	bowed down **b** David with her face to the ground.	678+4200
	26:19	may they be cursed **b** the LORD!	4200+7156
	28:25	set it **b** Saul and his men, and they ate.	4200+7156
	30:15	to me **b** God that you will not kill me	928
	31: 1	the Israelites fled **b** them,	4946+7156
2Sa	2:26	How long **b** you order your men	4202
	3:28	"I and my kingdom are forever innocent **b** the LORD	4946+6640
	3:34	You fell as one falls **b** wicked men."	4200+7156
	3:35	if I taste bread or anything else **b**	4200+7156
	5: 3	with them at Hebron **b** the LORD,	4200+7156
	5:20	against my enemies **b** me."	4200+7156
	6: 5	with all their might **b** the LORD,	4200+7156
	6:14	danced **b** the LORD with all his might,	4200+7156
	6:16	and dancing **b** the LORD,	4200+7156
	6:17	and fellowship offerings **b** the LORD.	4200+7156
	6:21	David said to Michal, "It was **b** the LORD,	4200+7156
	6:21	I will celebrate **b** the LORD.	4200+7156
	7: 9	I have cut off all your enemies from **b** you.	7156
	7:15	whom I removed from **b** you.	4200+7156
	7:16	kingdom will endure forever **b** me;	4200+7156
	7:18	David went in and sat **b** the LORD,	4200+7156
	7:23	and their gods from **b** your people,	7156
	7:26	house of your servant David will be established **b** you.	4200+7156
	9: 2	They called him to appear **b** David,	448
	10:13	and they fled **b** him.	4946+7156
	10:14	they fled **b** Abishai and went inside	4946+7156
	10:18	But they fled **b** Israel,	4946+7156
	12:11	**B** your very eyes I will take your wives	4200
	12:12	but I will do this thing in broad daylight **b**	5584
	14:33	with his face to the ground **b** the king.	4200+7156

2Sa 15: 2 with a complaint to be placed **b** the king for 448
15: 5 to bow down **b** him, 4200
15:18 from Gath marched **b** the king. 6584+7156
18:21 The Cushite bowed down **b** Joab 4200
18:28 down **b** the king with his face to the ground 4200
19: 8 they all came **b** him. 4200+7156
19:18 he fell prostrate **b** the king 4200+7156
21: 6 to us to be killed and exposed **b** the LORD 4200
21: 7 of the **oath** *b* the LORD between David AIT
21: 9 exposed them on a hill **b** the LORD. 4200+7156
22:23 All his laws are **b** me; 4200+5584
22:24 I have been blameless **b** him 4200
23:16 instead, he poured it out **b** the LORD. 4200
24:11 **B** David got up the next morning, 2256
24:20 and bowed down **b** the king with his face to 4200

1Ki 1:16 Bathsheba bowed low and knelt **b** the king. 4200
1:23 So he went **b** the king and bowed 4200+7156
1:28 the king's presence and stood **b** him. 4200+7156
1:31 kneeling **b** the king, said, 4200
1:32 When they came **b** the king, 4200+7156
2: 4 and if they walk faithfully **b** me 4200+7156
2:26 the Sovereign LORD **b** my father David 4200+7156
2:45 David's throne will remain secure **b** 4200+7156
3:15 stood **b** the ark of the Lord's covenant 4200+7156
3:16 to the king and stood **b** him. 4200+7156
3:22 And so they argued **b** the king. 4200+7156
8: 5 gathered about him were **b** the ark, 4200+7156
8:22 Then Solomon stood **b** the altar of 4200+7156
8:25 'You shall never fail to have a man to sit **b** 4200+4946+7156
      me on the throne
8:25 to walk **b** me as you have done.' 4200+7156
8:31 and he comes and swears the oath **b** 4200+7156
8:54 he rose from **b** the altar of the LORD, 4200+7156
8:59 which I have prayed **b** the LORD, 4200+7156
8:62 all Israel with him offered sacrifices **b** 4200+7156
8:64 bronze altar **b** the LORD was too small 4200+7156
8:65 They celebrated it **b** the LORD our God 4200+7156
9: 3 prayer and plea you have made **b** me; 4200+7156
9: 4 if you walk **b** me in integrity of heart 4200+7156
9:25 burning incense **b** the LORD along . 4200+7156
10: 8 who continually stand **b** you 4200+7156
11:36 a lamp **b** me in Jerusalem, 4200+7156
13: 6 and became as it was **b**. 928+2021+8037
14: 9 You have done more evil than all who lived
      b you. 4200+7156
14:24 the nations the LORD had driven out **b** 4946+7156
15: 3 the sins his father had done **b** him; 4200+7156
16:25 and sinned more than all those **b** him, 4200+7156
16:30 eyes of the LORD than any of those **b** 4200+7156
16:33 to anger than did all the kings of Israel **b** 4200+7156
      him.
18:21 Elijah went **b** the people and said, 448
18:44 'Hitch up your chariot and go down **b** 4202
19:11 and shattered the rocks **b** the LORD, 4200+7156
21:13 and brought charges against Naboth **b** 5584
21:26 like the Amorites the LORD drove out **b** 4946+7156
      Israel.)
21:29 how Ahab has humbled himself **b** me? 4200+4946+7156
22:10 all the prophets prophesying **b** them. 4200+7156
22:21 stood **b** the LORD and said, 4200+7156

2Ki 1:13 up and fell on his knees **b** Elijah. 4200+5584
2: 9 what can I do for you **b** I am taken 928+3270
2:15 to meet him and bowed to the ground **b** 4200
4:12 So he called her, and she stood **b** him. 4200+7156
4:43 "How can I set this **b** a hundred men?" 4200+7156
4:44 Then he set it **b** them, 4200+7156
5:15 He stood **b** him and said, 4200+7156
5:25 he went in and stood **b** his master Elisha. 448
6:22 and water **b** them so that they may eat 4200+7156
6:32 **b** he arrived, Elisha said to the elders, 928+3270
8: 9 He went in and stood **b** him, and said, 4200+7156
10: 9 He stood **b** all the people and said, 448
13: 5 in their own homes as they had **b**. 8997+9453
16: 3 the nations the LORD had driven out **b** 4946+7156
16:11 and finished it **b** King Ahaz returned. 6330
16:14 that stood **b** the LORD he brought from 4200+7156
17: 8 the nations the LORD had driven out **b** 4946+7156
17:11 the LORD had driven out **b** 4946+7156
18: 5 either **b** him or after him. 4200+7156
18:22 "You must worship **b** this altar 4200+7156
19:14 and spread it out **b** the LORD. 4200+7156
19:26 scorched **b** it grows up. 4200+7156
19:32 *He will* not **come b** it with shield or build 7709
20: 3 how I have walked **b** you faithfully 4200+7156
20: 4 **B** Isaiah had left the middle court, 4202
21: 2 the nations the LORD had driven out **b** 4946+7156
21: 9 LORD had destroyed **b** the Israelites. 4946+7156
22:19 and you humbled yourself **b** the LORD 4946+7156
23:25 Neither **b** nor after Josiah was there a king
      like him 4200+7156
25: 7 They killed the sons of Zedekiah **b** his eyes. 4200

1Ch 1:43 in Edom **b** any Israelite king reigned: 4200+7156
5:25 whom God had destroyed **b** them. 4946+7156
6:32 They ministered with music **b** 4200+7156
10: 1 the Israelites fled **b** them, 4946+7156
11: 3 he made a compact with them at Hebron **b** 4200+7156
      the LORD,
11:18 instead, he poured it out **b** the LORD. 4200
13: 8 with all their might **b** God, 4200+7156
13:10 So he died **b** God. 4200+7156
15: 2 the LORD and to **minister** *b* him forever." AIT
15:24 priests were to blow trumpets **b** the ark 4200+7156
16: 1 and fellowship offerings **b** God. 4200
16: 4 of the Levites to minister **b** the ark 4200+7156
16: 6 blow the trumpets regularly **b** the ark 4200+7156
16:27 Splendor and majesty are **b** him; 4200+7156

1Ch 16:29 Bring an offering and come **b** him; 4200+7156
16:30 Tremble **b** him, all the earth! 4200+4946+7156
16:33 will sing for joy **b** the LORD, 4200+4946+7156
16:37 his fellow priests **b** the ark of the covenant 4200+7156
16:39 his fellow priests **b** the tabernacle of 4200+7156
17: 8 I have cut off all your enemies from **b** you. 7156
17:16 David went in and sat **b** the LORD, 4200+7156
17:21 by driving out nations from **b** your people, 7156
17:24 of your servant David will be established **b** 4200+7156
      you.
19:14 and they fled **b** him. 4946+7156
19:15 they too fled **b** his brother Abishai 4946+7156
19:18 But they fled **b** Israel, 4946+7156
21:12 of being swept away by your enemies, 4946+7156
21:21 down **b** David with his face to the ground. 4200
21:30 David could not go **b** it to inquire of God, 4200+7156
22: 5 So David made extensive preparations **b** his
      death. 4200+7156
23:13 to offer sacrifices **b** the LORD, 4200+7156
23:13 to **minister** *b* him AIT
23:31 were to serve **b** the LORD regularly 4200+7156
24: 2 Nadab and Abihu died **b** their father did, 4200+7156
29:20 they bowed low and fell prostrate **b** 4200
29:22 anointing him **b** the LORD to be ruler 4200
29:25 as no king over Israel ever had **b**. 4200

2Ch 1: 6 the bronze altar **b** the LORD in the Tent 4200+7156
1:12 riches and honor, such as no king who was
      b you ever had 4200+7156
1:13 from **b** the Tent of Meeting. 4200+7156
2: 4 for burning fragrant incense **b** him, 4200+7156
2: 6 as a place to burn sacrifices **b** him? 4200+7156
5: 6 gathered about him were **b** the ark, 4200+7156
6:12 Then Solomon stood **b** the altar of 4200+7156
6:13 and then knelt down **b** the whole assembly 5584
6:16 'You shall never fail to have a man to sit **b** 4200+4946+7156
      me on the throne
6:16 in all they do to walk **b** me according 4200+7156
6:22 and he comes and swears the oath **b** 4200+7156
6:24 praying and making supplication **b** you 4200+7156
7: 4 people offered sacrifices **b** the LORD. 4200+7156
7:17 if you walk **b** me as David your father did, 4200+7156
9: 7 who continually stand **b** you 4200+7156
13:15 God routed Jeroboam and all Israel **b** 4946+7156
13:16 The Israelites fled **b** Judah, 4946+7156
14:12 The LORD struck down the Cushites **b** 4200+7156
14:13 they were crushed **b** the LORD 4200+7156
18: 9 all the prophets prophesying **b** them. 4200+7156
18:20 stood **b** the LORD and said, 4200+7156
19:10 In every case that comes **b** you 6584
19:11 Levites will serve as officials **b** you. 4200+7156
20: 7 not drive out the inhabitants of this land **b**
      your people 4200+4946+7156
20: 9 we will stand in your presence **b** 4200+7156
20:13 stood there **b** the LORD. 4200+7156
20:18 and Jerusalem fell down in worship **b** 4946+7156
20:20 He stood **b** the people and said, 4946+6584
25: 8 God will overthrow you **b** the enemy, 4200+7156
26:19 in their presence **b** the incense altar in 4946+6584
27: 6 because he walked steadfastly **b** 4200+7156
28: 3 the nations the LORD had driven out **b** 4946+7156
28:13 "or we must worship **b** the LORD. AIT
29:11 the LORD has chosen you to stand **b** him
29:11 to minister **b** him and to burn incense." 4200
29:23 sin offering were brought **b** the king 4200+7156
31:20 and faithful **b** the LORD his God. 4200+7156
32: 6 over the people and assembled them **b** him 448
32:12 'You must worship **b** one altar 4200+7156
33: 2 the nations the LORD had driven out **b** 4946+7156
33: 9 LORD had destroyed **b** the Israelites. 4946+7156
33:12 and humbled himself greatly **b** the God 4200+4946+7156
33:19 and set up Asherah poles and idols **b** 4200+7156
33:23 he did not humble himself **b** the LORD; 4200+4946+7156
34:27 you humbled yourself **b** God 4200+4946+7156
34:27 because you humbled yourself **b** me 4200+7156
36:12 not humble himself **b** Jeremiah the prophet, 4200+4946+7156

Ezr 7:28 to me **b** the king and his advisers 4200+7156
8:21 that we might humble ourselves **b** our God
8:29 the house of the LORD in Jerusalem **b** 4200+7156
9:15 Here we are **b** you in our guilt, 4200+7156
10: 1 down **b** the house of God, 4200+7156
10: 1 Now let us make a covenant **b** our God 4200
10: 6 Then Ezra withdrew from **b** the house 4200+7156
10: 9 all the people were sitting in the **square** *b* AIT

Ne 1: 4 and prayed **b** the God of heaven. 4200+7156
1: 6 hear the prayer your servant is praying **b**
      you day and night 4200+7156
2: 1 I had not been sad in his presence **b**; NIH
4:11 "**B** they know it or see us, 4202
8: 1 in the square **b** the Water Gate. 4200+7156
8: 2 Ezra the priest brought the Law **b** the 4200+7156
      assembly,
8: 3 the square **b** the Water Gate 4200+7156
9:11 You divided the sea **b** them, 4200+7156
9:24 You subdued **b** them the Canaanites, 4200+7156
13: 4 **B** this, Eliashib the priest had been put 4200+7156
13:19 the gates of Jerusalem **b** the Sabbath, 4200+7156

Est 1:11 to bring **b** him Queen Vashti, 4200+7156
1:17 to be brought **b** you, 4200+7156
2:12 **B** a girl's turn came to go in 928

Est 6: 9 through the city streets, proclaiming **b** him, 4200+7156
6:11 through the city streets, proclaiming **b** him, 4200+7156
6:13 **b** whom your downfall has started, 4200+7156
7: 6 Haman was terrified **b** the king and queen. 4200+4946+7156
8: 4 and she arose and stood **b** him. 4200+7156

Job 1: 6 the angels came to present themselves **b** 6584
2: 1 the angels came to present themselves **b** 6584
2: 1 also came with them to present himself **b** 6584
4:16 A form stood **b** my eyes, 4200+5584
5: 8 I would lay my cause **b** him. 448
7: 4 I lie down I think, '**How long** *b* I get up?' AIT
9: 2 But how can a mortal be righteous **b** God? 6640
10:18 I wish I had died **b** any eye saw me. 4200
10:21 **b** I go to the place of no return, 928+3270
13:16 no godless man would dare come **b** him! 4200+7156
14: 3 Will you bring him **b** you for judgment? 6640
15: 7 Were you brought forth **b** the hills? 4200+7156
15:32 **B** his time he will be paid in full, 928+4202
16:22 a few years will pass **b** I go on the journey 2256
21: 8 their offspring **b** them, 4200
21:18 How often are they like straw **b** the wind, 4200+7156
21:33 and a countless throng goes **b** him. 4200+7156
22:16 They were carried off **b** their time, 4202
23: 4 I would state my case **b** him 4200+7156
23: 7 an upright man could present his case **b** 6640
23:15 That is why I am terrified **b** him; 4946+7156
25: 4 How then can a man be righteous **b** God? 6640
26: 6 Death is naked **b** God; 5584
30:22 You snatch me up and drive me **b** the wind; 448
32: 4 Now Elihu had waited **b** speaking to Job NIH
33: 6 I am just like you **b** God; 4200
34:23 that they should come **b** him for judgment. 448
34:28 They caused the cry of the poor to come **b** 6584
35:14 your case is **b** him and you must wait 4200+7156
41:22 dismay goes **b** him. 4200+7156
41:25 they retreat **b** his thrashing. 4946
42:10 and gave him twice as much as he had **b**. NIH
42:11 everyone who had known him **b** came 4200+7156

Ps 5: 3 in the morning I lay my requests **b** you 4200
5: 8 make straight your way **b** me. 4200+7156
9: 3 they stumble and perish **b** you. 4946+7156
16: 8 I have set the LORD always **b** me. 4200+5584
18: 6 my cry came **b** him, into his ears. 4200+7156
18:22 All his laws are **b** me; 4200+5584
18:23 I have been blameless **b** him 6640
18:44 foreigners cringe **b** me. 4200
22:25 **b** those who fear you will I fulfill my vows. 5584
22:27 the families of the nations will bow down **b**
      him, 4200+7156
22:29 all who go down to the dust will kneel **b**
      him— 4200+7156
23: 5 You prepare a table **b** me in the presence of
      my enemies. 4200+7156
26: 3 for your love is ever **b** me, 4200+5584+6524
34: T pretended to be insane **b** Abimelech, 4200+7156
35: 5 May they be like chaff **b** the wind, 4200+7156
36: 1 There is no fear of God **b** his eyes. 4200+5584
37: 7 Be still **b** the LORD and wait patiently 4200
38: 9 All my longings lie open **b** you, O Lord; 5584
39: 5 the span of my years is as nothing **b** you. 5584
39:13 that I may rejoice again **b** I depart 928+3270
44:10 You made us retreat **b** the enemy, 4974
44:15 My disgrace is **b** me all day long, 5584
50: 3 a fire devours **b** him, 4200+7156
50: 8 which are ever **b** me. 4200+5584
51: 3 and my sin is always **b** me. 5584
56:13 I may walk **b** God in the light of life. 4200+7156
58: 9 **B** your pots can feel [the heat of] 928+3270
59:10 God *will* **go b** me and will let me gloat 7709
66: 3 that your enemies cringe **b** you. 4200
68: 1 may his foes flee **b** him. 4946+7156
68: 2 as wax melts **b** the fire, 4946+7156
68: 2 may the wicked perish **b** God. 4946+7156
68: 3 But may the righteous be glad and rejoice **b**
      God; 4200+7156
68: 4 and rejoice **b** him. 4200+7156
68: 7 you went out **b** your people, O God, 4200+7156
68: 8 the heavens poured down rain, O God, 4946+7156
68: 8 **b** God, the God of Israel. 4946+7156
68:28 O God, as you have done **b**. NIH
69:19 all my enemies are **b** you. 5584
69:22 the table set **b** them become a snare; 4200+7156
72: 9 The desert tribes will bow **b** him 4200+7156
73:22 I was a brute beast **b** you. 6640
76: 7 Who can stand **b** you when you are angry? 4200+7156
78:30 **b** they turned from the food they craved, 4202
78:55 He drove out nations **b** them 4946+7156
79:10 **B** our eyes, make known among the nations 4200
79:11 May the groans of the prisoners come **b**
      you; 4200+7156
80: 2 **b** Ephraim, Benjamin 4200+7156
81:15 Those who hate the LORD would cringe **b** 4200
83:13 O my God, like chaff **b** the wind. 4200+7156
84: 7 till each appears **b** God in Zion. 448
85:13 Righteousness goes **b** him 4200+7156
86: 9 and worship **b** you, O Lord; 4200+7156
88: 1 day and night I cry out **b** you. 5584
88: 2 May my prayer come **b** you; 4200+7156
88:13 in the morning my prayer **comes b** you. 7709
89:14 love and faithfulness go **b** you. 7156
89:23 I will crush his foes **b** him and strike 4946+7156

Ps	89:36	and his throne endure **b** me like the sun;	5584
	90: 2	**B** the mountains were born	928+3270
	90: 8	You have set our iniquities **b** you,	4200+5584
	95: 2	Let us come **b** him with thanksgiving	7156
	95: 6	let us kneel **b** the LORD our Maker;	4200+7156
	96: 6	Splendor and majesty are **b** him;	4200+7156
	96: 9	tremble **b** him, all the earth.	4946+7156
	96:13	they will sing **b** the LORD,	4200+7156
	97: 3	Fire goes **b** him and consumes his foes	4200+7156
	97: 5	The mountains melt like wax **b** the LORD,	4200+4946+7156
	97: 5	**b** the Lord of all the earth.	4200+4946+7156
	98: 6	shout for joy **b** the LORD, the King.	4200+7156
	98: 9	let them sing **b** the LORD,	4200+7156
	100: 2	come **b** him with joyful songs.	4200+7156
	101: 3	I will set **b** my eyes no vile thing.	4200+5584
	102: T	and pours out his lament **b** the LORD	4200+7156
	102:28	their descendants will be established **b**	4200+7156
	105:17	and he sent a man **b** them—	4200+7156
	106:23	stood in the breach **b** him	4200+7156
	109:14	of his fathers be remembered **b** the LORD;	448
	109:15	May their sins always remain **b** the LORD,	5584
	116: 9	that I may walk **b** the LORD in the land of the living.	4200+7156
	119:46	of your statutes **b** kings and will not be put	5584
	119:67	**B** I was afflicted I went astray,	3270
	119:147	I rise **b** dawn and cry for help;	928
	119:169	May my cry come **b** you, O LORD;	4200+7156
	119:170	May my supplication come **b** you;	4200+7156
	129: 6	which withers **b** it can grow;	7712
	138: 1	**b** the "gods" I will sing your praise.	5584
	139: 4	**B** a word is	401+3954
	139: 5	You hem me in—behind and **b**;	7710
	139:16	in your book **b** one of them came to be.	4202
	140:13	and the upright will live **b** you.	907+7156
	141: 2	May my prayer be set **b** you like incense;	4200+7156
	142: 2	I pour out my complaint **b** him;	4200+7156
	142: 2	**b** him I tell my trouble.	4200+7156
	143: 2	for no one living is righteous **b** you.	4200+7156
Pr	2:17	and ignored the **covenant** she made **b** God.	AIT
	4:25	fix your gaze directly **b** you.	5584
	8:22	**b** his deeds of old;	7710
	8:23	from the beginning, **b** the world **began**.	7710
	8:25	**b** the mountains were settled in place,	928+3270
	8:25	**b** the hills, I was given birth,	4200+7156
	8:26	**b** he made the earth or its fields	4202+6330
	15:11	and Destruction lie open **b** the LORD—	5584
	15:33	and humility comes **b** honor.	4200+7156
	16:18	Pride goes **b** destruction,	4200+7156
	16:18	a haughty spirit **b** a fall.	4200+7156
	17:14	drop the matter **b** a dispute breaks out.	4200+7156
	18:12	**B** his downfall a man's heart is proud,	4200+7156
	18:12	but humility comes **b** honor.	4200+7156
	18:13	He who answers **b** listening—	928+3270
	22:29	He will serve **b** kings;	4200+7156
	22:29	he will not serve **b** obscure men.	4200+7156
	23: 1	note well what is **b** you,	4200+7156
	25: 7	to humiliate you **b** a nobleman.	4200+7156
	27: 4	but who can stand **b** jealousy?	4200+7156
	30: 7	do not refuse me **b** I die:	928+3270
	30:30	who retreats **b** nothing;	4946+7156
Ecc	1:10	it was here **b** our **time**.	4200+4946+7156
	1:16	over Jerusalem **b** me;	4200+7156
	2: 7	flocks than anyone in Jerusalem **b** me.	4200+7156
	2: 9	by far than anyone in Jerusalem **b** me.	4200+7156
	3:15	and what will be has been **b**;	3893
	4:16	to all the people who were **b** them,	4200+7156
	5: 2	do not be hasty in your heart to utter anything **b** God.	4200+7156
	6: 8	by knowing how to conduct himself **b**	5584
	7:17	why die **b** your time?	928+4202
	8: 2	I say, because you took an **oath** *b* God.	AIT
	8:12	who are reverent **b** God.	4200+4946+7156
	10:11	If a snake bites **b** it is charmed,	928+4202
	12: 1	**b** the days of trouble come and	889+4202+6330
	12: 2	**b** the sun and the light and the moon and the stars grow dark,	889+4202+6330
	12: 6	**b** the silver cord is severed,	889+4202+6330
	12: 6	**b** the pitcher is shattered at the spring,	NIH
SS	6:12	**B** I realized it,	4202
Isa	1: 7	by foreigners **right b** you,	4200+5584
	1:12	When you come to **appear b** me,	7156+8011
	1:23	the widow's case does not come **b** them.	448
	7:16	But **b** the boy knows enough to reject	928+3270
	8: 4	**B** the boy knows how to say 'My father'	928+3270
	9: 3	they rejoice **b** you as people rejoice at	4200+7156
	10:34	Lebanon will fall **b** the Mighty One.	928
	13:16	Their infants will be dashed to pieces **b**	4200
	17:13	driven **b** the wind like chaff	4200+7156
	17:13	like tumbleweed **b** a gale.	4200+7156
	17:14	**B** the morning, they are gone!	928+3270
	18: 5	For, **b** the harvest, when the blossom is gone	4200+7156
	19: 1	The idols of Egypt tremble **b** him,	4946+7156
	23:18	Her profits will go to those who live **b**	4200+7156
	24:23	and **b** its elders, gloriously.	5584
	28: 4	will be like a fig ripe **b** harvest—	928+3270
	31: 8	They will flee **b** the sword	4946+7156
	36: 7	"You must worship **b** this altar'"?	7709
	37:14	the LORD and spread it out **b** the LORD.	4200+7156
	37:27	scorched **b** it grows up.	4200+7156
	37:33	*He will* not **come b** it with shield or build	7709
	38: 3	how I have walked **b** you faithfully	4200+7156
	40:17	**B** him all the nations are as nothing;	5584
	41: 1	"Be silent **b** me, you islands!	448
	41: 2	over to him and subdues kings **b** him.	4200+7156

Isa	41: 3	by a path his feet have not traveled **b**.	NIH
	42: 9	**b** they spring into being	928+3270
	42:16	I will turn the darkness into light **b** them	4200+7156
	43:10	**B** me no god was formed,	4200+7156
	44: 7	and lay out **b** me what has happened	4200
	45: 1	to subdue nations **b** him	4200+7156
	45: 1	to open doors **b** him so that gates	4200+7156
	45: 2	I will go **b** you and will level	4200+7156
	45:14	down **b** you and plead with you, saying,	448
	45:23	**B** me every knee will bow;	4200
	48: 5	**b** they happened I announced them to you	928+3270
	48: 7	you have not heard of them today.	4200+7156
	48:19	be cut off nor destroyed from **b** me."	4200+7156
	49: 1	**B** I was born the LORD called me;	4946
	49:16	your walls are ever **b** me.	5584
	49:23	They will bow down **b** you with their faces	4200
	52:12	for the LORD will go **b** you,	4200+7156
	53: 2	He grew up **b** him like a tender shoot,	4200+7156
	53: 7	and as a sheep **b** her shearers is silent,	4200+7156
	55:12	and hills will burst into song **b** you,	4200+7156
	57:16	the spirit of man would grow faint **b** me—	4200+4946+7156
	58: 8	then your righteousness will go **b** you,	4200+7156
	60:14	of your oppressors will come bowing **b**	448
	61:11	and praise spring up **b** all nations.	5584
	63:12	who divided the waters **b** them,	4946+7156
	64: 1	the mountains would tremble **b** you!	4946+7156
	64: 2	and cause the nations to quake **b** you!	4946+7156
	64: 3	and the mountains trembled **b** you.	4946+7156
	65: 6	"See, it stands written **b** me:	4200+7156
	65:24	**B** they call I will answer;	3270
	66: 7	"**B** she goes into labor, she gives birth;	928+3270
	66: 7	**b** the pains come upon her,	928+3270
	66:22	the new earth that I make will endure **b**	4200+7156
	66:23	all mankind will come and bow down **b**	4200+7156
Jer	1: 5	"**B** I formed you in the womb I knew you,	928+3270
	1: 5	**b** you were born I set you apart;	928+3270
	1:17	or I will terrify you **b** them.	4200+7156
	2:22	the stain of your guilt is still **b** me,"	4200+7156
	4:26	all its towns lay in ruins **b** the LORD,	4946+7156
	4:26	before the LORD, **b** his fierce anger.	4200+7156
	6: 7	sickness and wounds are ever **b** me.	6584+7156
	6:21	"I will put obstacles **b** this people.	448
	7:10	come and stand **b** me in this house,	4200+7156
	9:13	which I set **b** them;	4200+7156
	12: 1	O LORD, when I bring a case **b** you.	448
	12:11	parched and desolate **b** me;	6584
	13:16	Give glory to the LORD your God **b**	928+3270
	13:16	**b** your feet stumble on the darkening hills.	928+3270
	15: 1	if Moses and Samuel were to stand **b** me,	4200+7156
	15: 9	to the sword **b** their enemies,"	4200+7156
	16: 9	**B** your eyes and in your days I will bring	4200
	17:16	What passes my lips is **open b** you.	5790+7156
	18:17	I will scatter them **b** their enemies;	4200+7156
	18:20	I stood **b** you and spoke in their behalf	4200+7156
	18:23	Let them be overthrown **b** you;	4200+7156
	19: 7	I will make them fall by the sword **b**	4200+7156
	21: 8	I am setting **b** you the way of life and	4200+7156
	26: 4	which I have set **b** you,	4200+7156
	28: 5	the prophet Hananiah **b** the priests	4200+6524
	28:11	and he said **b** all the people,	4200+6524
	29:21	he will put them to death **b** your very eyes.	4200
	30:20	their community will be established **b** me;	4200+7156
	31:36	Israel ever cease to be a nation **b** me."	4200+7156
	33: 7	will rebuild them as they were **b**.	928+2021+8037
	33: 9	and honor **b** all nations on earth that hear	4200
	33:11	the fortunes of the land as they were **b**,'	928+2021+8037
	33:18	to have a man to stand **b** me continually	4200+4946+7156
	33:21	the Levites who are priests **ministering** *b*	AIT
	33:22	the Levites *who* **minister** *b* me as countless	AIT
	34:15	made a covenant **b** me in the house	4200+7156
	34:18	terms of the covenant they made **b** me,	4200+7156
	35: 5	of wine and some cups **b** the men of	4200+7156
	36: 7	Perhaps they will bring their petition **b**	4200+7156
	36: 9	of fasting **b** the LORD was proclaimed	4200+7156
	37:20	Let me bring my petition **b** you:	4200+7156
	38:10	the prophet out of the cistern **b** he dies."	928+3270
	39: 6	slaughtered the sons of Zedekiah **b** his eyes	4200
	39:16	they will be fulfilled **b** your eyes.	4200+7156
	40: 4	Look, the whole country lies **b** you;	4200+7156
	40: 5	However, **b** Jeremiah turned to go,	4202+6388
	40:10	at Mizpah to represent you **b**	4200+7156
	41: 4	**b** anyone knew about it,	4202
	44:10	decrees I set **b** you and your fathers.	4200+7156
	47: 1	Philistines **b** Pharaoh attacked Gaza:	928+3270
	49:37	I will shatter Elam **b** their foes,	4200+7156
	49:37	**b** those who seek their lives;	4200+7156
	50:24	and you were caught **b** you knew it;	4202
	51: 5	though their land is full of guilt **b**	4946
	51:24	"**B** your eyes I will repay Babylon	4200
	52:10	the sons of Zedekiah **b** his eyes;	4200
La	1: 5	captive to the foe.	4200+7156
	1: 6	in weakness they have fled **b** the pursuer.	4200+7156
	1:22	"Let all their wickedness come **b** you;	4200+7156
	3:35	deny a man his rights **b** the Most High,	5584+7156
Eze	2:10	which he unrolled **b** me.	4200+7156
	3: 1	eat what *is* **b** you, eat this scroll;	5162

Eze	3:20	and I put a stumbling block **b** him,	4200+7156
	5: 9	I will do to you what *I have* never **done** *b*	AIT
	8: 1	the elders of Judah were sitting **b** me,	4200+7156
	8: 4	And there **b** me was the glory of the God	NIH
	14: 3	and put wicked stumbling blocks **b**	5790
	14: 4	a wicked stumbling block **b** his face and	5790
	14: 7	a wicked stumbling block **b** his face and	5790
	16:18	offered my oil and incense **b** them.	4200+7156
	16:19	offered as fragrant incense **b** them.	4200+7156
	16:50	and did detestable things **b** me.	4200+7156
	16:55	will return to *what* they were **b**;	7712
	16:55	to *what* you were **b**.	7712
	16:57	**b** your wickedness was uncovered.	928+3270
	21: 6	Groan **b** them with broken heart	4200+6524
	22:30	and stand **b** me in the gap on behalf of	4200+7156
	23:41	with a table spread **b** it on which	4200+7156
	28:17	I made a spectacle of you **b** kings.	4200+7156
	30:24	and he will groan **b** him like	4200+7156
	32:10	when I brandish my sword **b** them.	6584+7156
	33:22	Now the evening **b** the man arrived,	4200+7156
	33:22	and he opened my mouth **b** the man came	6330
	33:31	and sit **b** you to listen to your words,	4200+7156
	36:11	and will make you prosper more than **b**.	8035
	36:23	when I show myself holy through you **b**	4200
	37:20	Hold **b** their eyes the sticks	4200
	38:16	when I show myself holy through you **b**	4200
	40:46	near to the LORD to **minister** *b* him."	AIT
	41:22	"This is the table that is **b** the LORD."	4200+7156
	42:14	They are to put on other clothes **b** they go	2256
	43:19	Write these down **b** them so that	4200+6524
	43:19	who come near to **minister** *b* me,	AIT
	43:24	You are to offer them **b** the LORD,	4200+7156
	44:11	sacrifices for the people and stand **b**	4200+7156
	44:15	are to come near to **minister** *b* me;	AIT
	44:15	are to stand **b** me to offer sacrifices	AIT
	44:16	to **minister** *b* me and perform my service.	AIT
	45: 4	and who draw near to **minister** *b*	AIT
	46: 9	people of the land come **b** the LORD	4200+7156
Da	2: 2	they came in and stood **b** the king,	4200+7156
	2:31	there **b** you stood a large statue,	10378+10619
	2:46	Then King Nebuchadnezzar fell prostrate **b**	NIH
	3: 3	and they stood **b** it.	10378+10619
	3:13	So these men were brought **b** the king,	10621
	3:16	we do not need to **defend** ourselves *b* you	AIT
	4: 6	the wise men of Babylon be brought **b** me	10621
	4:10	and there **b** me stood a tree in the middle of	NIH
	4:13	I looked, and there **b** me was a messenger,	NIH
	4:36	and became even greater than **b**.	NIH
	5:13	So Daniel was brought **b** the king,	10621
	5:15	and enchanters were brought **b** me	10621
	6:10	just as he had done **b**.	10180+10427+10622
	6:22	Nor have I ever done any wrong **b** you,	10621
	6:24	and **b** they reached the floor of the den,	10379
	7: 2	"In my vision at night I looked, and there **b**	NIH
	7: 5	"And there **b** me was a second beast,	NIH
	7: 6	I looked, and there **b** me was another beast,	NIH
	7: 7	and there **b** me was a fourth beast—	NIH
	7: 8	there **b** me was another horn, a little one,	NIH
	7: 8	three of the first horns were uprooted **b** it.	10427+10621
	7:10	coming out from **b** him.	10621
	7:10	ten thousand times ten thousand stood **b**	10621
	7:13	and there **b** me was one like a son of man,	NIH
	7:20	**b** which three of them fell—	10427+10621
	8: 3	and there **b** me was a ram with two horns,	NIH
	8:15	there **b** me stood one who looked like	4200+5584
	10: 5	and there **b** me was a man dressed in linen,	NIH
	10:12	and to humble yourself **b** your God,	4200+7156
	10:16	I said to the one standing **b** me,	4200+5584
	11:22	be swept away **b** him;	4200+4946+7156
	11:29	be different from what it was **b**.	8037
	12: 5	looked, and there **b** me stood two others,	NIH
	12: 6	be **b** these astonishing things are fulfilled?"	NIH
Hos	2:10	now I will expose her lewdness **b** the eyes	4200
	7: 2	they are always **b** me.	5584+7156
Joel	1: 9	*those who* **minister** *b* the LORD.	AIT
	1:13	wail, *you who* **minister** *b* the altar.	AIT
	1:13	*you who* **minister** *b* my God;	AIT
	1:16	not the food been cut off **b** our very eyes—	5584
	2: 3	**B** them fire devours,	4200+7156
	2: 3	**B** them the land is like the garden of Eden,	4200+7156
	2:10	**B** them the earth shakes, the sky trembles,	4200+7156
	2:17	Let the priests, *who* **minister** *b* the LORD,	AIT
	2:23	both autumn and spring rains, as **b**.	8037
	2:31	the moon to blood **b** the coming	4200+7156
Am	1: 1	what he saw concerning Israel two years **b** the earthquake,	4200+7156
	2: 9	"I destroyed the Amorite **b** them,	4946+7156
Jnh	1: 2	its wickedness has come up **b** me."	4200+7156
	1:13	for the sea grew even wilder than **b**.	NIH
Mic	1: 4	like wax **b** the fire,	4946+7156
	2:13	One who breaks open the way will go up **b** them,	4200+7156
	2:13	Their king will pass through **b** them,	4200+7156
	6: 1	**plead** *your* **case** *b* the mountains;	AIT
	6: 6	With what *shall I* **come b** the LORD	7709
	6: 6	before the LORD and bow down **b**	4200
	6: 6	Shall I **come b** him with burnt offerings,	7709
Na	1: 5	The mountains quake **b** him and	4946
	1: 5	the rocks are shattered **b** him.	4946
Hab	2: 3	Destruction and violence are **b** me;	4200+5584
	2:20	let all the earth be silent **b** him."	4946+7156
	3: 5	Plague went **b** him;	4200+7156
Zep	1: 7	Be silent **b** the Sovereign LORD,	4946+7156
	2: 2	**b** the appointed time arrives and	928+3270

Zep	2: 2	**b** the fierce anger of the LORD comes	928+3270+4202
	2: 2	**b** the day of the LORD's wrath comes	928+3270+4202
	3:20	I restore your fortunes **b** your very eyes,"	4200
Hag	2:15	how things were **b** one stone was laid	3270+4946
Zec	1: 8	there **b** me was a man riding a red horse!	NIH
	1:18	and there **b** me were four horns!	NIH
	2: 1	and there **b** me was a man with	NIH
	2:13	Be still **b** the LORD, all mankind,	4946+7156
	3: 1	the high priest standing **b** the angel of	4200+7156
	3: 3	filthy clothes as he stood **b** the angel.	4200+7156
	3: 4	to those who were standing **b** him,	4200+7156
	3: 8	and your associates seated **b** you,	4200+7156
	4: 7	**B** Zerubbabel you will become level ground.	4200+7156
	5: 1	and there **b** me was a flying scroll!	NIH
	5: 9	and there **b** me were two women,	NIH
	6: 1	and there **b** me were four chariots coming out from between two mountains—	NIH
	8:10	**B** that time there were no wages	4200+7156
	10: 8	they will be as numerous as **b**.	8049S
	12: 8	like the Angel of the LORD going **b** them.	4200+7156
Mal	2: 9	be despised and humiliated **b** all the people,	4200
	3: 1	who will prepare the way **b** me.	4200+7156
	3:14	like mourners **b** the LORD Almighty?"	4946+7156
	4: 5	I will send you the prophet Elijah **b**	4200+7156
Mt	1:18	but **b** they came together,	2445+4570
	5:12	the prophets who were **b** you.	4574
	5:16	In the same way, let your light shine **b** men,	1869
	6: 1	to do your 'acts of righteousness' **b** men,	1869
	6: 8	for your Father knows what you need **b**	4574
	8: 2	with leprosy came and **knelt b** him and said,	4665
	8:29	"Have you come here to torture us **b**	4574
	9:18	a ruler came and **knelt b** him and said,	4686
	10:18	On my account you will be brought **b**	2093
	10:23	cities of Israel **b** the Son of Man comes.	323+2401
	10:32	"Whoever acknowledges me **b** men,	1869
	10:32	I will also acknowledge him **b** my Father	1869
	10:33	But whoever disowns me **b** men,	1869
	10:33	I will disown him **b** my Father in heaven.	1869
	11:10	who will prepare your way **b** you.'	1869
	15: 2	They don't wash their hands **b** they eat!"	4020
	15:25	The woman came and **knelt b** him.	4686
	16:28	not taste death **b** they see the Son	323+2401
	17: 2	There he was transfigured **b** them.	1869
	17: 3	Just then there appeared **b** them Moses	AIT
	17:14	a man approached Jesus and **knelt b** him.	1206
	18:26	"The servant fell **on** *his* **knees b** him.	4686
	24:38	For in the days **b** the flood,	4574
	25:32	All the nations will be gathered **b** him,	1869
	26:34	"this very night, **b** the rooster crows,	4570
	26:70	But he denied it **b** them all.	1869
	26:75	"**B** the rooster crows,	4570
	27:11	Meanwhile Jesus stood **b** the governor,	1869
Mk	3:11	*they* **fell down b** him and cried out,	4700
	6:41	He gave them to his disciples to **set b**	4192
	8: 6	and gave them to his disciples to **set b**	4192
	9: 1	not taste death **b** they see the kingdom	323+2401
	9: 2	There he was transfigured **b** them.	1869
	9: 4	there appeared *b* them Elijah and Moses,	AIT
	9:17	and **fell on** his **knees b** him.	1206
	13: 9	of me you will stand **b** governors and kings	2093
	14:30	**b** the rooster crows twice you yourself will disown me three times.	4570
	14:60	high priest stood up **b** them and asked Jesus,	1650+3545
	14:72	"**B** the rooster crows twice you will disown me three times."	4570
	15:42	the **day b** the Sabbath).	4640
Lk	1: 8	on duty and he was serving as priest **b** God,	1882
	1:17	And he will go on **b** the Lord,	1967
	1:75	and righteousness **b** him all our days.	1967
	1:76	on **b** the Lord to prepare the way for him,	1967
	2:21	the name the angel had given him **b**	4574
	2:26	by the Holy Spirit that he would not die **b** he had seen the Lord's Christ.	323+2445+4570
	4:35	the demon threw the man down **b** them all	1650+3545+3836
	5:18	to take him into the house to lay him **b**	1967
	7:27	who will prepare your way **b** you.'	1967
	9:16	Then he gave them to the disciples *to* **set b**	4192
	9:27	not taste death **b** they see the kingdom	323+2401
	10: 8	eat what **is** set **b** you.	4192
	11: 6	and I have nothing *to* **set b** him.'	4192
	11:38	that Jesus did not first wash **b** the meal,	4574
	12: 8	whoever acknowledges me **b** men,	1869
	12: 8	also acknowledge him **b** the angels of God.	1869
	12: 9	But he who disowns me **b** men will	1967
	12: 9	before men will be disowned **b** the angels	1967
	12:11	"When you are brought **b** synagogues,	2093
	18:14	went home **justified b** God.	1467
	21:12	"But **b** all this, they will lay hands on you	4574
	21:12	you will be brought **b** kings and governors,	2093
	21:36	and that you may be able to stand **b** the Son	1869
	22:15	to eat this Passover with you **b** I suffer.	4574
	22:34	"I tell you, Peter, the rooster crows today,	2401
	22:61	"**B** the rooster crows today,	4570
	22:66	met together, and Jesus was led **b** them.	1650
	23:12	**b** this *they* had **been**	1639+4732
	24:19	in word and deed **b** God and all the people.	1883
Jn	1:15	because he was **b** me."	4755
	1:30	because he was **b** me.'	4755
	1:48	while you were still under the fig tree **b**	4574
	3:24	(This was **b** John was put in prison.)	4037
	4:49	"Sir, come down **b** my child dies."	4570

Jn	5:45	do not think I will accuse you **b** the Father.	4639
	6:62	the Son of Man ascend to where he was **b**!	4728
	8: 3	They made her stand **b** the group	1877+3545
	8:58	Jesus answered, "**b** Abraham was born, I am!"	4570
	10: 8	All who ever came **b** me were thieves	4574
	11:55	ceremonial cleansing **b** the Passover.	4574
	12: 1	Six days **b** the Passover,	4574
	12:35	**b** darkness overtakes you.	2671+3590
	13: 1	It was just **b** the Passover Feast.	4574
	13:19	"I am telling you now **b** it happens,	4574
	13:38	I tell you the truth, **b** the rooster crows,	2401+4005
	14:19	**B** long, the world will	2285+3625
	14:29	I have told you now **b** it happens,	4574
	17: 5	the glory I had with you **b** the world began.	4574
	17:24	because you loved me **b** the creation of	4574
Ac	1: 9	he was taken up **b** their very eyes,	899+1063
	2:20	the moon to blood **b** the coming of the great	4570
	2:25	" 'I saw the Lord always **b** me.	1967
	3:13	and you disowned him **b** Pilate,	2848+4725
	4: 7	They had Peter and John brought **b** them	1877+3545+3836
	4:10	that this man stands **b** you healed.	1967
	5: 4	Didn't it belong to you **b** it was sold?	NIG
	5:27	they made them appear **b** the Sanhedrin	1877
	6:12	They seized Stephen and brought him **b**	1650
	7: 2	**b** he lived in Haran.	2445+4570
	7:40	'Make us gods who *will* go **b** us.	4638
	7:45	the land from the nations God drove out **b** them.	608+4725
	8:21	because your heart is not right **b** God.	1882
	8:32	and as a lamb **b** the shearer is silent,	1883
	9:15	to carry my name **b** the Gentiles	1967
	9:15	and their kings and the people of Israel.	NIG
	10: 4	up as a memorial offering **b** God.	1869
	10:30	Suddenly a man in shining clothes stood **b**	1967
	12: 6	The night **b** Herod was to bring him to trial,	4021
	13:24	**B** the coming of Jesus,	4574+4725
	16:20	They **brought** them **b** the magistrates	4642
	16:29	in and **fell** trembling **b** Paul and Silas.	4574
	16:34	into his house and **set a meal b** them;	4192+5544
	17: 6	and some other brothers **b** the city officials,	2093
	18:18	**B** he sailed, he had his hair cut off	NIG
	19:30	Paul wanted to appear **b** the crowd,	NIG
	19:33	in order to make a defense *b* **the people.**	AIT
	22:30	he brought Paul and had him stand **b** them.	1650
	23:15	the commander to bring him **b** you on	1650
	23:15	We are ready to kill him **b** he gets here."	4575
	23:20	to bring Paul **b** the Sanhedrin tomorrow on	1650
	24: 1	against Paul *b* the **governor.**	AIT
	24: 2	Tertullus presented his case **b** Felix:	NIG
	24:16	to keep my conscience clear **b** God	4639
	24:19	to be here **b** you and bring charges	2093
	24:20	in me when I stood **b** the Sanhedrin—	2093
	24:21	the dead that I am on trial **b** you today.' "	2093
	25: 2	and Jewish leaders appeared *b* **him**	AIT
	25: 6	and ordered that Paul be brought **b** him.	NIG
	25: 9	up to Jerusalem and stand trial **b** me there	2093
	25:10	"I am now standing **b** Caesar's court,	2093
	25:16	not the Roman custom to hand over any man **b** he has faced his accusers	2445+4570
	25:26	Therefore *I* have **brought** him **b** all of you,	4575
	25:26	and especially **b** you, King Agrippa,	2093
	26: 2	to stand **b** you today as I make my defense	2093
	27:14	**B** very long, a wind of hurricane force,	3552+4024+4498
	27:21	Paul stood up **b** them and said:	1877+3545
	27:24	You must **stand trial b** Caesar;	4225
	27:33	**Just b** dawn Paul urged them all to eat.	948+4005
Ro	3:18	"There is no fear of God **b** their eyes."	595
	4: 2	but not **b** God.	4639
	4:10	Was it after he was circumcised, or **b**?	NIG
	4:10	It was not after, but **b**!	NIG
	4:12	the faith our father Abraham had **b** he was **circumcised.**	213+1877
	5:13	for **b** the law was given,	948
	9:11	Yet, **b** the twins were born	3609
	14:10	we will all **stand b** God's judgment seat.	4225
	14:11	says the Lord, 'every knee will bow **b** me;	AIT
	16: 7	and they were in Christ **b** I was.	4574
1Co	1:29	so that no one may boast **b** him.	1967
	2: 7	and that God destined for our glory **b**	4574
	4: 5	judge nothing **b** the appointed time;	4574
	6: 1	dare he take it **b** the ungodly	2093
	6: 1	the ungodly for judgment instead of **b**	2093
	10:27	eat whatever *is* **put b** you	4192
	11:28	A man ought to examine himself **b** he eats	NIG
2Co	2:17	in Christ we speak **b** God with sincerity,	2978
	3: 4	as this is ours through Christ **b** God.	4639
	5:10	For we must all appear **b** the judgment seat	1869
	7: 3	*I have* **said b** that you have such a place	4625
	7:12	that **b** God you could see for yourselves	1967
	12:21	I come again my God will humble me **b**	4639
Gal	1:17	to see those who were apostles **b** I was,	4574
	1:20	I assure you **b** God	1967
	2: 2	I went in response to a revelation and **set b**	423
	2:12	**B** certain men came from James,	4574
	3: 1	**B** your very eyes Jesus Christ was clearly portrayed as crucified.	2848
	3:11	Clearly no one is justified **b** God by	4123
	3:23	**B** this faith came, we were held prisoners	4574
	5:21	I warn you, as *I did* **b**,	4625S
Eph	1: 4	For he chose us in him **b** the creation of	4574
	3:14	For this reason I kneel **b** the Father,	4639
Php	3:18	as I have often told you **b** and	NIG
Col	1:17	He is **b** all things,	4574
1Th	1: 3	We continually remember **b** our God	1869

1Th	5:27	*I* **charge** you **b** the Lord	1941
1Ti	6:13	who while testifying **b** Pontius Pilate made	2093
2Ti	1: 9	This grace was given us in Christ Jesus **b**	4574
	2:14	Warn them **b** God against quarreling	1967
	4:21	Do your best to get here **b** winter.	4574
Tit	1: 2	promised **b** the beginning of time,	4574
Heb	4: 7	as *was* said **b**: "Today, if you hear	4625
	4:13	and laid bare **the eyes** of him	AIT
	6:20	who **went b** us, has entered on our behalf.	4596
	11: 5	For **b** he was taken,	4574
	12: 2	who for the joy **set b** him endured the cross,	4618
Jas	4:10	Humble yourselves **b** the Lord,	1967
1Pe	1:20	*He was* **chosen b** the creation of the world,	4589
	2:20	this is commendable **b** God.	4123
1Jn	2:28	and unashamed **b** him at his coming.	608
	3:21	we have confidence **b** God	4639
Jude	1:24	and to present you **b** his glorious presence	2979
	1:25	through Jesus Christ our Lord, **b** all ages,	4574
Rev	1: 4	and from the seven spirits **b** his throne,	1967
	3: 5	but will acknowledge his name **b** my Father	1967
	3: 8	I have placed **b** you an open door	1967
	4: 1	and **there b** me was a door standing open	2627
	4: 2	and **there b** me was a throne in heaven	2627
	4: 5	**B** the throne, seven lamps were blazing.	1967
	4: 6	Also **b** the throne there was what looked	1967
	4:10	down **b** him who sits on the throne,	1967
	4:10	They lay their crowns **b** the throne and say:	1967
	5: 8	and the twenty-four elders fell down **b**	1967
	6: 2	I looked, and **there b** me was a white horse!	2627
	6: 5	I looked, and **there b** me was a black horse!	2627
	6: 8	I looked, and **there b** me was a pale horse!	2627
	7: 9	After this I looked and **there b** me was	2627
	7: 9	standing **b** the throne and in front of	1967
	7:11	They fell down on their faces **b** the throne	1967
	7:15	"they are **b** the throne of God	1967
	8: 2	I saw the seven angels who stand **b** God,	1967
	8: 3	on the golden altar **b** the throne.	1967
	8: 4	went up **b** God from the angel's hand.	1967
	9:13	the horns of the golden altar that is **b** God.	1967
	11: 4	the two lampstands that stand **b** the Lord of	1967
	11:16	who were seated on their thrones **b** God,	1967
	12:10	who accuses them **b** our God day and night,	1967
	14: 1	I looked, and **there b** me was the Lamb,	2627
	14: 3	And they sang a new song **b** the throne and	1967
	14: 3	the throne and the four living creatures	1967
	14:14	I looked, and **there b** me was a white cloud,	2627
	15: 4	All nations will come and worship **b** you,	1967
	19:11	I saw heaven standing open and **there b**	2627
	20:12	great and small, standing **b** the throne,	1967

BEFOREHAND (7) [BEFORE]

Isa	41:26	or **b**, so we could say, 'He was right'?	4200+4946+7156
Mk	13:11	*do* not **worry b** about what to say.	4628
	14: 8	on my body **b** to prepare for my burial.	4624
Lk	21:14	*to* **worry b** how you will defend yourselves.	4627
Ac	4:28	and will *had* **decided b** should happen.	4633
Ro	1: 2	the gospel *he* **promised b** through his prophets	4600
	3:25	the sins **committed b** unpunished—	4588

BEFUDDLED (1)

Isa	28: 7	and prophets stagger from beer and *are* **b**	1182

BEG (19) [BEGGAR, BEGGARS, BEGGED, BEGGING]

Jdg	13: 8	"O Lord, **I b** you, let the man of God	5528
1Sa	15:25	Now **I b** you, forgive my sin	5528
2Sa	24:10	Now, O LORD, **I b** you, take away the guilt	5528
2Ki	1: 9	of the Philistines went to the king to **b**	7590
	8: 5	to life came *to* **b** the king for her house	7590
1Ch	21: 8	**I b** you, take away the guilt of your servant.	5528
Est	8: 3	into the king's presence to **b** for mercy	2858
	7: 7	behind to **b** Queen Esther for his life.	1335
Job	19:16	though *I* **b** him with my own mouth.	2858
La	4: 4	the children **b** *for* bread,	8626
Am	7: 5	I cried out, "Sovereign LORD, **I b** you,	5528
Lk	8:28	*I b* you, don't torture me!"	1289
	9:38	"Teacher, *I* **b** you to look at my son,	1289
	16: 3	and I'm ashamed *to* **b**—	2050
	16:27	"He answered, 'Then *I* **b** you, father,	2263
Jn	9: 8	the same man who *used to* sit and **b**?"	4644
Ac	3: 2	where he was put every day to **b**	160+1797+3836
	9: 8	*I* **b** you to listen to me patiently.	1289
2Co	10: 2	*I* **b** you that when I come I may not have	1289

BEGAN (175) [BEGIN]

Ge	4:26	At that time *men* **b** to call on the name of the LORD.	2725
	6: 1	When men **b** to increase in number on	2725
	16: 4	she **b** to **despise** her mistress.	AIT
	21:16	And as she sat there nearby, *she* **b** to sob.	906+5951+7754
	29:11	Jacob kissed Rachel and **b** to **weep** aloud.	AIT
	35:16	Rachel **b** to **give birth**	AIT
	41:54	and the seven years of famine **b**,	2725
	41:55	**b** to **feel** the famine,	AIT
	42:24	He turned away from them and **b** to **weep**,	AIT
Ex	16:20	but it was full of maggots and **b** to **smell**.	AIT
Nu	25: 1	the men **b** to indulge in sexual immorality	2725
	3: 7	*they* **b** to **mourn**, and no one put	AIT
	11: 4	**b** to **crave other food**,	AIT
	12: 1	and Aaron **b** to **talk** against Moses	AIT
Dt	1: 5	Moses **b** to expound this law, saying:	3283

Jos	16: 1	The allotment for Joseph *b* at the Jordan	3655
	18:12	On the north side their boundary *b* at	2118
	18:15	The southern side *b* at the outskirts	3655
Jdg	13:25	and the Spirit of the LORD *b* to stir him	2725
	16:19	and so *b* to subdue him.	2725
	16:22	But the hair on his head *b* to grow *again*	2725
	20:31	*They b* to inflict casualties on the Israelites	2725
	20:40	the column of smoke *b* to rise from the city,	2725
Ru	2: 3	and *b to* **glean** in the fields behind	AIT
1Sa	13: 8	and Saul's men *b to* **scatter.**	AIT
	20:19	where you hid **when** this trouble *b,*	928+3427
	23:25	Saul and his men *b* the search.	2143
1Ki	6: 1	he *b to* **build** the temple of the LORD.	AIT
	15:29	As soon as he *b to* **reign,**	AIT
	16:11	As soon as he *b to* **reign** and was seated on	AIT
	16:31	and *b* to serve Baal and worship him.	2143
	18:27	At noon Elijah *b to* **taunt** them.	AIT
2Ki	4:40	but as they *b to* **eat** it, they cried out,	AIT
	6: 4	They went to the Jordan and *b to* **cut down**	AIT
	8:11	Then the man of God *b to* **weep.**	AIT
	8:16	of Jehoshaphat *b his* **reign** as king of Judah.	AIT
	8:25	of Jehoram king of Judah *b to* **reign.**	AIT
	10:32	the LORD *b* to reduce the size of Israel.	2725
	11:21	when he *b to* **reign.**	AIT
	14: 1	of Joash king of Judah *b to* **reign.**	AIT
	15: 1	of Amaziah king of Judah *b to* **reign.**	AIT
	15:32	of Uzziah king of Judah *b to* **reign.**	AIT
	15:37	the LORD *b* to send Rezin king of Aram	2725
	16: 1	of Jotham king of Judah *b to* **reign.**	AIT
	18: 1	of Ahaz king of Judah *b to* **reign.**	AIT
1Ch	27:24	Joab son of Zeruiah *b* to count the men	2725
2Ch	3: 1	Then Solomon *b* to build the temple of	2725
	3: 2	*He b* building on the second day of	2725
	20:22	As *they* **b** to sing and praise,	2725
	22: 1	of Jehoram king of Judah *b to* **reign.**	AIT
	29:17	*They b* the consecration on the first day of	2725
	29:27	the offering *b,* singing to the LORD	2725
	29:27	singing to the LORD *b* also,	2725
	31: 7	*They b* doing this in the third month	2725
	31:10	the people *b* to bring their contributions to	2725
	34: 3	he *b* to seek the God of his father David.	2725
	34: 3	In his twelfth year he *b* to purge Judah	2725
Ezr	3: 2	of Shealtiel and his associates to build	7756
	3: 6	the first day of the seventh month *they* **b**	2725
	3: 8	from the captivity to Jerusalem) *b* the work,	2725
Ne	2:18	So they *b* this good work.	2616+3338
Job	2:12	*they* **b** weep aloud,	AIT
Pr	8:23	from the beginning, **before** the world *b.*	7710
Ecc	2:20	So my heart *b* to despair	6015
SS	5: 4	my heart *b* to **pound** for him.	AIT
Jer	36: 2	the other nations from the time *I* **b** **speaking**	AIT
Eze	9: 6	So *they* **b** with the elders who were in front	2725
	9: 7	So they went out and *b* **killing** throughout	AIT
	23: 8	not give up the prostitution she *b* in Egypt,	NIH
	23:27	to the lewdness and prostitution you *b*	NIH
Da	9:23	As soon as you *b* to pray,	9378
	10:16	and I opened my mouth and *b to* **speak.**	AIT
Hos	1: 2	*When* the LORD *b* to speak through Hosea,	2725
Hag	1:14	They came and *b to* work on the house of	6913
Mt	4:17	From that time on Jesus *b* to preach,	806
	5: 2	and *he b to* **teach** them, saying:	AIT
	8:15	and she got up and *b to* **wait on** him.	AIT
	11: 7	Jesus *b* to speak to the crowd about John:	806
	11:20	Then Jesus *b* to denounce the cities	806
	12: 1	and *b* to pick some heads of grain,	806
	13:54	*he b* **teaching** the people in their synagogue,	AIT
	16:21	on Jesus *b* to explain to his disciples	806
	16:22	Peter took him aside and *b* to rebuke him.	806
	18:24	As he *b* the settlement,	AIT
	18:28	He grabbed him and *b to* **choke** him.	AIT
	20:11	*they* **b** to **grumble** against the landowner.	AIT
	26:22	*They* were very sad and *b* to say to him one	806
	26:37	and he *b* to be sorrowful and troubled.	806
	26:74	Then he *b* to call down curses on himself	806
Mk	1:21	into the synagogue and *b to* **teach.**	AIT
	1:31	The fever left her and *she b to* **wait on**	AIT
	1:45	Instead *he* went out and *b* to talk freely,	806
	2:13	and *he b to* **teach** them.	AIT
	2:23	*they* **b** to pick some heads of grain.	806
	3: 6	Then the Pharisees went out and *b to* **plot**	AIT
	4: 1	Again Jesus *b* to teach by the lake.	806
	5:17	Then the *people* **b** to plead with Jesus	806
	5:20	So the man went away and *b* to tell in	806
	6: 2	*he b* to teach in the synagogue,	806
	6:34	So *he b* teaching them many things.	AIT
	7:35	and *he b to* **speak** plainly.	AIT
	8:11	The Pharisees came and *b*	806
	8:31	*He* then *b* to teach them that the Son	806
	8:32	Peter took him aside and *b* to rebuke him.	806
	10:47	he *b* to shout, "Jesus, Son of David,	806
	11:15	and *b* driving out those who were buying	806
	11:18	and *b* **looking** for a way to kill him,	AIT
	12: 1	*He* then *b* to speak to them in parables:	806
	14:33	*he b* to be deeply distressed and troubled.	806
	14:65	Then some *b* to spit at him;	806
	14:71	He *b* to call down curses on himself,	806
	15:18	and *they* **b** to call out to him, "Hail,	806
Lk	1:64	and *he b to* **speak,** praising God.	AIT
	2:44	Then *they* **b** **looking** for him	AIT
	3:23	Jesus himself was about thirty years old	
		when he **b** his ministry.	806
	4:21	and *b* by saying to them,	806
	4:31	and on the Sabbath *b* to teach the people.	1639
	4:39	*She* got up at once and *b to* **wait on** them.	AIT
	5: 6	of fish that their nets *b to* **break.**	AIT
	5: 7	both boats so full that *they b to* **sink.**	AIT
	5:21	and the teachers of the law *b* thinking	806

Lk	6: 1	his disciples *b to* **pick** some heads of grain,	AIT
	6:11	But they were furious and *b to* **discuss**	AIT
	7:15	The dead man sat up and *b to* talk,	806
	7:24	Jesus *b* to speak to the crowd about John:	806
	7:38	*she* **b** to wet his feet with her tears.	806
	7:49	The other guests *b* to say	806
	11:53	the Pharisees and the teachers of the law *b*	806
	12: 1	Jesus *b* to speak first to his disciples,	806
	14:18	"But *they* all alike *b* to make excuses.	806
	14:30	'This fellow *b* to build and was not able	806
	15:14	and he *b* to be in need.	806
	15:24	So *they* **b** to celebrate.	806
	19: 7	All the people saw this and *b to* **mutter,**	AIT
	19:37	the whole crowd of disciples *b* joyfully	806
	19:45	and *b* driving out those who were selling.	806
	22:23	*They* **b** to question among themselves	806
	22:63	The men who were guarding Jesus *b*	
		mocking and beating him.	AIT
	23: 2	And *they* **b** to accuse him, saying,	806
	24:30	broke it and *b to* **give** it to them.	AIT
Jn	6:14	*they b to* **say,** "Surely this is the Prophet	AIT
	6:41	At this the Jews *b to* **grumble** about him	AIT
	6:52	Then the Jews *b to* **argue** sharply	AIT
	7:25	of the people of Jerusalem *b to* **ask,**	AIT
	8: 9	those who heard it *b to* **go away** one at	AIT
	13: 5	a basin and *b to* **wash** his disciples' feet,	AIT
	17: 5	the glory I had with you before the world *b.*	1639
	18:27	and at that moment a rooster *b to* **crow.**	AIT
Ac	1: 1	about all that Jesus *b* to do and to teach	806
	2: 4	with the Holy Spirit and *b* to speak	806
	3: 8	He jumped to his feet and *b* to **walk.**	AIT
	4: 7	before them and *b to* **question** them:	AIT
	5:21	and *b* to **teach** the people.	AIT
	6: 9	These men *b* to argue with Stephen,	NIG
	7:58	of the city and *b to* **stone** him.	AIT
	8: 3	But Saul *b* to **destroy** the church.	3381
	8:35	Then Philip *b* with that very passage	806
	9:20	At once he *b* to **preach** in the synagogues	AIT
	10:34	Then Peter *b* to speak:	487+3306+3836+5125
	11: 4	Peter *b* and explained everything	806
	11:15	"As I *b* to speak, the Holy Spirit came on	806
	11:20	went to Antioch and *b* to **speak** to Greeks	AIT
	14:10	At that, the *man* jumped up and *b to* **walk.**	AIT
	16:13	*We* sat down and *b to* **speak** to	AIT
	17:18	and Stoic philosophers *b to* **dispute with**	AIT
	18:26	He *b* to speak boldly in the synagogue.	806
	19:28	they were furious and *b to* **shouting:**	AIT
	26: 1	with his hand and *b* his **defense:**	AIT
	27:13	**gentle** south wind *b to* **blow,**	AIT
	27:18	the storm that the next day *they* **b** to throw	4472
	27:35	Then he broke it and *b* to eat.	806
	28:25	among themselves and *b to* **leave**	AIT
1Co	2: 7	for our glory before time *b.*	NIG
Gal	2:12	*b to* **draw back** and **separate**	AIT
Php	1: 6	that he who *b* a good work in you	1887

BEGAT, BEGET, BEGETTEST, BEGETTETH (KJV) See FATHER

BEGGAR (3) [BEG]

Lk	16:20	At his gate was laid a *b* named Lazarus,	4777
	16:22	when the *b* died and the angels carried him	4777
Ac	3:11	While the *b* held on to Peter and John,	899S

BEGGARS (1) [BEG]

Ps	109:10	May his children be wandering *b;*	8626

BEGGED (23) [BEG]

2Ki	1:13	"Man of God," he *b,*	2858
Est	8: 3	*She b* him to put an end to the evil plan	2858
Hos	12: 4	he wept and *b* for his **favor.**	2858
Mt	8:31	The demons *b* Jesus, "If you drive us out,	
			3306+4151
	14:36	and *b* him to let the sick just touch the edge	4151
	18:26	'Be patient with me,' he *b,*	3306
	18:29	to his knees and *b* him,	4151
	18:32	that debt of yours because *you* **b** me to.	4151
Mk	1:40	A man with leprosy came to him and *b* him	4151
	5:10	And *he b* Jesus again and again not	4151
	5:12	The demons *b* Jesus, "Send us among	4151
	5:18	the man who had been demon-possessed *b*	4151
	6:56	*They* **b** him to let them touch even the edge	4151
	7:26	*She b* Jesus to drive the demon out	2263
	7:32	*they* **b** him to place his hand on the man.	4151
	8:22	a blind man *b* Jesus to touch him.	4151
Lk	5:12	with his face to the ground and *b* him,	1289
	8:31	And *they b* him *repeatedly* not	4151
	8:32	The demons *b* Jesus to let them go	4151
	8:38	the demons had gone out *b* to go with him,	1289
	9:40	*I b* your disciples to drive it out,	1289
Jn	4:47	to him and *b* him to come and heal his son,	2263
Heb	12:19	heard it *b* that no further word be spoken	4148

BEGGING (8) [BEG]

Job	41: 3	Will he keep *b* you **for mercy?**	9384
Ps	37:25	or their children *b* bread.	1335
Mk	10:46	was sitting by the roadside *b.*	4644
Lk	18:35	a blind man was sitting by the roadside *b.*	2050
Jn	9: 8	How was this man who formerly sat him *b* asked,	4645
Ac	3:10	to sit *b* at the temple gate called Beautiful,	
			1797+3836+4639
	16: 9	of a man of Macedonia standing and *b* him,	4151
	19:31	sent him a message *b* him not to venture	4151

BEGIN (21) [BEGAN, BEGINNING, BEGINNINGS, BEGINS, BEGUN]

Dt	2:24	*B* to take possession of it and engage him	2725
	2:25	This very day *I will* **b** to put the terror	2725
	2:31	Now *b* to conquer and possess his land."	2725
	16: 9	Count off seven weeks from the time you *b*	2725
	28:30	but *you* will not *even b* to **enjoy** its fruit.	AIT
Jos	3: 7	"Today *I will* **b** to exalt you in the eyes	2725
	18: 3	before you *b* to take possession of the land	995
Jdg	13: 5	and he *will b* the deliverance of Israel	2725
1Sa	9:13	The people *will* not *b* eating	AIT
1Ch	22:16	*b* the work, and the LORD be with you."	7756
	22:19	*B* to build the sanctuary of the LORD God,	7756
Ps	81: 2	*B* the music, strike the tambourine,	5951
La	2:19	as the watches of the night *b;*	8031
Eze	9: 6	*B* at my sanctuary."	2725
	39:14	the seven months *they will b* their **search.**	AIT
Hos	8:10	*They will* **b** to waste away under	2725
Lk	3: 8	And *do* not *b* to say to yourselves,	806
	21:28	When these things *b* to take place,	806
	23:54	and the Sabbath *was* **about to** *b.*	2216
Jn	7:14	up to the temple courts and *b to* **teach.**	AIT
1Pe	4:17	for judgment *to b* with the family of God;	806

BEGINNING (90) [BEGIN]

Ge	1: 1	In the *b* God created the heavens and	8040
	44:12	*b* with the oldest and ending with	2725
Lev	23:39	" 'So *b* with the fifteenth day of	928
Dt	11:12	on it from the *b of* the year to its end.	8040
	31:24	a book the words of this law from *b* to end,	6330
	31:30	of this song *from b* to end in the hearing of	6330
Jdg	7:19	of the camp at the *b of* the middle watch,	8031
Ru	1:22	in Bethlehem as the barley harvest was *b.*	9378
1Sa	3:12	from *b* to end.	2725
2Sa	21: 9	oppress them anymore, as they did at the *b*	8037
	21: 9	just as the barley harvest was *b.*	9378
	21:10	the *b of* the harvest till the rain poured	9378
1Ch	17: 9	as they did at the *b*	8037
	29:29	events of King David's reign, from *b* to end,	8037
2Ch	9:29	events of Solomon's reign, from *b* to end,	8037
	12:15	events of Rehoboam's reign, from *b* to end,	8037
	16:11	The events of Asa's reign, from *b* to end,	8037
	20:34	of Jehoshaphat's reign, from *b* to end,	8037
	25:26	events of Amaziah's reign, from *b* to end,	8037
	26:22	events of Uzziah's reign, from *b* to end,	8037
	28:26	his reign and all his ways, from *b* to end,	8037
	35:27	all the events, from *b* to end,	8037
Ezr	4: 6	At the *b of* the reign of Xerxes,	9378
Ps	102:25	the *b* you laid the foundations of the earth,	7156
	111:10	The fear of the LORD is the *b of* wisdom;	8040
Pr	1: 7	fear of the LORD is the *b of* knowledge,	8040
	8:23	from the *b,* before the world began.	8031
	9:10	fear of the LORD is the *b of* wisdom,	9378
	20:21	An inheritance quickly gained at the *b* will	8037
Ecc	3:11	what God has done from *b* to end.	8031
	7: 8	The end of a matter is better than its *b,*	8040
	10:13	At the *b* his words are folly;	9378
Isa	1:26	your counselors as at the *b.*	9378
	40:21	Has it not been told you from the *b?*	8031
	41: 4	calling forth the generations from the *b?*	8031
	41:26	Who told of this from the *b,*	8031
	46:10	I make known the end from the *b,*	8040
Jer	17:12	A glorious throne, exalted from the *b,*	8037
	25:29	I am *b* to bring disaster on the city	2725
Eze	25: 9	*b* at its frontier towns—	NIH
	40: 1	at the *b of* the year,	8031
	42:12	the *b of* the passageway that was parallel to	8031
	48:30	*B* on the north side, which is 4,500	NIH
Da	12: 1	as has not happened from the *b of* nations	2118
Mic	1:13	You were the *b of* sin to the Daughter	8040
Mt	14:30	he was afraid and, *b* to sink, cried out,	806
	19: 4	"that at the *b* the Creator 'made them male	794
	19: 8	But it was not this way from the *b.*	794
	20: 8	*b* with the last ones hired and going on to	806
	24: 8	All these are the *b* of birth pains.	794
	24:21	from the *b* of the world until now—	794
Mk	1: 1	The *b* of the gospel about Jesus Christ,	794
	10: 6	at the *b of* creation God 'made them male	794
	13: 8	These are the *b* of birth pains.	794
	13:19	be days of distress unequaled from the *b,*	794
Lk	1: 3	I myself have carefully investigated	
		everything **from the** *b,*	540
	11:50	that has been shed since the *b* of the world,	2856
	24:27	And *b* with Moses and all the Prophets,	806
	24:47	in his name to all nations, *b* at Jerusalem.	806
Jn	1: 1	In the *b* was the Word,	794
	1: 2	He was with God in the *b.*	794
	6:64	from the *b* which of them did not believe	794
	8:44	He was a murderer from the *b,*	794
	15:27	for you have been with me from the *b.*	794
Ac	1:22	from John's baptism to the time	806
	10:37	*b* in Galilee after the baptism	806
	11:15	on them as he had come on us at the *b.*	794
	26: 4	from the *b of* my life in my own country,	794
2Co	3: 1	*Are we b* to commend ourselves again?	806
Gal	3: 3	*After b* with the Spirit,	1887
Col	1:18	he is the *b* and the firstborn from among	794
2Th	2:13	from the *b* God chose you to be saved	794
2Ti	1: 9	in Christ Jesus before the *b* of time,	173+5989
Tit	1: 2	promised before the *b* of time,	173+5989
Heb	1:10	He also says, "In the *b,* O Lord,	794
	7: 3	without *b* of days or end of life,	
2Pe	2:20	at the end than they were at the *b.*	4755
	3: 4	everything goes on as it has since the *b*	794

1Jn	1: 1	That which was from the **b**,	794
	2: 7	which you have had since the **b**.	794
	2:13	you have known him who is from the **b**.	794
	2:14	you have known him who is from the **b**.	794
	2:24	from the **b** remains in you.	794
	3: 8	the devil has been sinning from the **b**.	794
	3:11	This is the message you heard from the **b**:	794
2Jn	1: 5	but one we have had from the **b**.	794
	1: 6	As you have heard from the **b**,	794
Rev	21: 6	the **B** and the End.	794
	22:13	the First and the Last, the **B** and the End.	794

BEGINNINGS (1) [BEGIN]

Job	8: 7	Your **b** will seem humble,	8040

BEGINS (7) [BEGIN]

Lev	23: 5	The LORD's Passover **b** at twilight on	NIH
	23: 6	the LORD's Feast of Unleavened Bread **b**;	NIH
	23:34	the LORD's Feast of Tabernacles **b**,	NIH
Eze	45:25	which **b** in the seventh month on	NIH
Mt	24:49	and *he* then **b** to beat his fellow servants and	806
Lk	12:45	and *he* then **b** to beat the menservants	806
1Pe	4:17	and if it **b** with us,	4754

BEGOTTEN (1)

Isa	45:10	'What *have* you **b**?'	3528

BEGRUDGE (1)

Dt	28:56	*will* **b** the husband she loves	6524+8317

BEGUILE, BEGUILED, BEGUILING
(KJV) See DECEIVE, DISQUALIFY

BEGUN (9) [BEGIN]

Ge	11: 6	the same language they *have* **b** to do this,	2725
Dt	2:31	*I have* **b** to deliver Sihon and his country	2725
	3:24	you *have* **b** to show to your servant	2725
	20: 6	a vineyard and not *b* to **enjoy** it?	AIT
Jdg	20:39	The Benjamites *had* **b** to inflict casualties	2725
Ezr	7: 9	He *had* **b** his journey from Babylon on	3569
Est	9:23	to continue the celebration *they had* **b**,	2725
Mic	6:13	Therefore, *I have* **b** to destroy you,	2725
Rev	11:17	and *have* **b** to **reign**.	AIT

BEHALF (46)

Ge	23: 8	with Ephron son of Zohar on my **b**	4200
	25:21	Isaac prayed to the LORD on **b** of	4200+5790
Lev	1: 4	be accepted **on** his **b** to make atonement	4200
	14:31	the LORD **on b** of the one to be cleansed."	6584
	19: 5	a way that it will be **accepted** *on* your **b**.	AIT
	22:19	in order that it may be **accepted** *on* your *b*.	AIT
	22:20	because it will not be accepted on your **b**.	4200
	22:25	They will not be accepted on your **b**,	4200
	22:29	a way that it will be **accepted** *on* your *b*.	AIT
	23:11	so it will be **accepted** *on* your *b*;	AIT
	24: 8	**on b** of the Israelites, as a lasting covenant.	907+4946
Nu	3:38	of the sanctuary **on b of** the Israelites.	4200+5466
	5:15	a tenth of an ephah of barley flour on her **b**.	6584
	8:19	**work** at the Tent of Meeting *on b*	AIT
1Sa	7: 9	He cried out to the LORD **on** Israel's **b**,	1237
	14: 6	Perhaps the LORD will act in our **b**.	4200
2Sa	3:12	Then Abner sent messengers on his **b** to say	9393
	14: 8	and I will issue an order **in** your **b**."	6584
	21:14	God answered prayer **in b** of the land.	4200
	24:25	LORD answered prayer **in b** of the land,	4200
2Ki	4:13	Can we speak **on** your **b** to the king or	4200
Est	8: 8	in the king's name **in b** of the Jews	6584
Job	6:22	Have I ever said, 'Give something on my **b**,	4200
	8: 6	even now he will rouse himself **on** your **b**	6584
	13: 7	Will you speak wickedly on God's **b**?	4200
	16:21	**on b** of a man he pleads with God as	4200
	36: 2	that there is more to be said in God's **b**.	4200
Ps	45: 4	In your majesty ride forth victoriously **in b of** truth,	1821+6584
	66: 5	how awesome his works **in** man's **b**!	6584
Isa	8:19	Why consult the dead **on b** of the living?	1237
	58:10	if you spend yourselves **in b** of the hungry	4200
	64: 4	who acts **on b of** those who wait for him.	4200
	65: 8	so will I do **in b** of my servants;	5100
Jer	7: 9	I stood before you and spoke in their **b**	3208+6584
Eze	22:30	and stand before me in the gap **on b of**	1237
Jn	8:14	"Even if I testify **on** my own **b**,	4309
	16:26	that I will ask the Father on your **b**.	4309
Ro	15: 8	a servant of the Jews **on b of** God's truth,	5642
2Co	1:11	Then many will give thanks on our **b** for	5642
	5:20	We implore you **on** Christ's **b**:	5642
Php	1:29	to you **on b of** Christ not only to believe	5642
Col	1: 7	a faithful minister of Christ **on** our **b**,	5642
Heb	6:20	who went before us, has entered **on** our **b**.	5642
Rev	13:12	the authority of the first beast **on** his **b**,	1967
	13:14	the signs he was given power to do **on b of**	1967
	19:20	the miraculous signs **on** his **b**.	1967

BEHAVE (2) [BEHAVED, BEHAVES, BEHAVIOR]

1Ki	1: 6	"Why *do you* **b** as you do?"	6913
Ro	13:13	*Let us* **b** decently, as in the daytime,	4344

BEHAVED (5) [BEHAVE]

2Sa	15: 6	Absalom **b** in this way toward all	6913
1Ki	21:26	*He* **b** in the **vilest manner**	4394+9493
Ps	74: 5	*They* **b** like men wielding axes to cut	3359
Jer	2:23	See **how** you **b** in the valley;	2006
	16:12	you *have* **b** more wickedly than your fathers.	6913

BEHAVES (1) [BEHAVE]

Pr	21:24	he **b** with overweening pride.	6913

BEHAVIOR (5) [BEHAVE]

Est	3: 4	about it to see whether Mordecai's **b** would	1821
Pr	8:13	evil **b** and perverse speech.	2006
Col	1:21	in your minds because of your evil **b**.	2240
1Pe	3: 1	over without words by the **b** of their wives,	419
	3:16	against your good **b** in Christ may	419

BEHEADED (5)

Mt	14:10	and *had* John **b** in the prison.	642
Mk	6:16	he said, "John, the man I **b**,	642
	6:27	The man went, **b** John in the prison,	642
Lk	9: 9	But Herod said, "I **b** John.	642
Rev	20: 4	the souls of those who *had been* **b** because	4284

BEHELD (1) [BEHOLD]

Ps	63: 2	in the sanctuary and **b** your power	8011

BEHEMOTH (1)

Job	40:15	"Look at the **b**, which I made along with you	990

BEHIND (101)

Ge	18:10	which was **b** him.	339
	19: 6	to meet them and shut the door **b** him	339
	32:18	and he is coming **b** us.' "	339
	32:20	'Your servant Jacob is coming **b** us.' "	339
Ex	10:24	**leave** your flocks and herds **b**."	3657
	10:26	not a hoof *is to be* **left b**.	8636
	14:19	withdrew and went **b** them.	339+4946
	14:19	moved from in front and stood **b** them,	339+4946
	26:33	the ark of the Testimony **b** the curtain.	1074+4946
Lev	16: 2	the Most Holy Place **b** the curtain	1074+4946
	16:12	and take them **b** the curtain.	1074+4946
	16:15	and take its blood **b** the curtain	1074+4946
Nu	3:23	to camp on the west, **b** the tabernacle.	339
Dt	25:18	and cut off all who were lagging **b**;	339
Jos	8: 2	Set an ambush **b** the city."	339+4946
	8: 4	You are to set an ambush **b** the city.	339+4946
	8:14	an ambush had been set against him **b**	339+4946
Jdg	3:23	of the upper room **b** him and locked them.	1237
	5:28	**b** the lattice she cried out,	1237
Ru	2: 2	to the fields and pick up the leftover grain **b**	339
	2: 3	to glean in the fields **b** the harvesters.	339
	2: 7	among the sheaves **b** the harvesters.'	339
1Sa	11: 5	**b** his oxen, and he asked,	339
	14:13	with his armor-bearer **right b** him.	339
	14:13	his armor-bearer followed and killed **b** him.	339
	21: 9	it is wrapped in a cloth **b** the ephod.	339
	24: 8	When Saul looked **b** him,	339
	30: 9	where some **stayed b**,	6641
	30:21	and who were **left b** at the Besor Ravine.	8740
2Sa	2:20	Abner looked **b** him and asked,	339
	2:25	Then the men of Benjamin rallied **b** Abner.	339
	3:16	weeping **b** her all the way to Bahurim.	339
	3:31	King David himself walked **b** the bier.	339
	5:23	around **b** them and attack them in front of	339
	10: 9	in front of him and **b** him;	294+4946
	18:22	please let me run **b** the Cushite."	339
1Ki	14: 9	to anger and thrust me **b** your back.	339
	20:19	of the city with the army **b** them	339
2Ki	4: 4	Then go inside and shut the door **b** you	1237
	4: 5	She left him and afterward shut the door **b**	1237
	6:32	the sound of his master's footsteps **b** him?"	339
	9:18	"Fall in **b** me."	339
	9:19	Fall in **b** me."	339
	9:25	and I were riding together in chariots **b**	339
	11: 6	and a third at the gate **b** the guard,	339
	25:12	But the commander **left b** some of	8636
	25:22	be over the people he had **left b** in Judah.	8636
1Ch	19:10	in front of him and **b** him;	294
	28: 9	and understands every **motive** *b*	AIT
2Ch	13:13	front of Judah the ambush was **b** them.	339+4946
Ne	4:13	people **b** the lowest points of the wall	339+4946
	4:16	The officers posted themselves **b** all	339
	9:26	they put your law **b** their backs.	339
Est	7: 7	**stayed b** to beg Queen Esther for his life.	6641
Job	21:21	about the family he **leaves b**	339
	38: 8	up the sea **b** doors when it burst forth from	928
	39:10	Will he till the valleys **b** you?	339
	41:32	**B** him he leaves a glistening wake;	339
Ps	50:17	and cast my words **b** you.	339
	139: 5	You hem me in—**b** and before;	294
SS	2: 9	There he stands **b** our wall,	339
	4: 1	Your eyes *b* your veil are doves.	1237+4946
	4: 3	Your temples **b** your veil are like	1237+4946
	6: 7	Your temples *b* your veil are like	1237+4946
Isa	26:20	enter your rooms and shut the doors **b** you;	1237
	30:21	your ears will hear a voice **b** you,	339+4946
	38:17	you have put all my sins **b** your back.	339
	45:14	they will trudge **b** you,	339
	57: 8	**B** your doors and your doorposts you have put your pagan symbols.	339

Jer	9:22	like cut grain **b** the reaper,	339+4946
	39:10	the guard **left b** in the land of Judah some	8636
	40: 6	the people who were **left b** in the land.	8636
	52:16	But Nebuzaradan **left b** the rest of	8636
Eze	3:12	and I heard **b** me a loud rumbling sound—	339
	23:35	and thrust me **b** your back,	339
	24:21	and daughters *you* **left b** will fall by	6440
	39:28	not leaving any **b**.	9004
	42:14	to go into the outer court until they leave **b**	9004
Joel	2: 3	**b** them a flame blazes.	339
	2: 3	**b** them, a desert waste—	339
	2:14	He may turn and have pity and leave **b**	339
Zec	1: 8	**B** him were red, brown and white horses.	339
	7:14	so desolate **b** them that no one could come	339
Mt	9:20	up **b** him and touched the edge of his cloak.	3957
	16:23	Jesus turned and said to Peter, "Get **b** me,	3958
Mk	4:36	**Leaving** the crowd **b**,	918
	5:27	she came up **b** him in the crowd	3957
	8:33	"Get **b** me, Satan!"	3958
	14:52	he fled naked, **leaving** his garment **b**.	2901
Lk	2:43	the boy Jesus **stayed b** in Jerusalem.	5702
	7:38	and as she stood **b** him at his feet weeping,	3958
	8:44	up **b** him and touched the edge of his cloak,	3957
	23:26	the cross on him and made him carry it **b**	3957
Jn	20: 6	Then Simon Peter, *who was* **b** him,	199
1Co	13:11	I became a man, *I* **put** childish ways **b** me.	2934
Php	3:13	Forgetting what is **b** and straining	3958
1Ti	5:24	the sins of others **trail b** them.	2051
Heb	6:19	It enters the inner sanctuary **b** the curtain,	NIG
	9: 3	**B** the second curtain was a room called	3552
Rev	1:10	I heard **b** me a loud voice like a trumpet,	3958
	6: 8	and Hades *was* **following** close **b** him.	199

BEHOLD (6) [BEHELD]

Nu	24:17	*I* **b** him, but not near.	8800
Isa	65:17	"**B**, I will create new heavens and	2180
Rev	1:18	and **b** I am alive for ever and ever!	2627
	16:15	"**B**, I come like a thief!	2627
	22: 7	"**B**, I am coming soon!	2627
	22:12	"**B**, I am coming soon!	2627

BEHOVED (KJV) See HAD TO, HAVE TO

BEING (165) [BE, BEINGS]

Ge	2: 7	and the man became a living **b**.	5883
	38:25	*As* she **was** *b* **brought** out,	AIT
	40: 5	who *were* *b* held in prison—	AIT
	40:15	*to deserve* *b* **put** in a dungeon."	AIT
	42:21	"Surely we are *b* **punished** because	NIH
	50:20	for good to accomplish what is now *b* done,	NIH
Ex	5:16	Your servants *are* *b* **beaten**,	5782
	6: 6	I will free you from *b* slaves to them,	NIH
	23: 1	a wicked man by *b* a malicious witness.	2118
Lev	24:17	" If anyone takes the life of a **human b**,	132
Nu	6:11	because he sinned by *b* in the presence of	NIH
	15:24	**without** the community *b* **aware**	4946+6524
	19:19	The person *b* cleansed must wash his clothes	NIH
	24:11	the LORD has kept you from *b* rewarded."	NIH
	35:27	the accused without *b* guilty of murder.	NIH
Dt	3:16	the Arnon Gorge (the middle of the gorge **b**	NIH
	22:21	in Israel by *b* **promiscuous** while still	AIT
1Sa	2:13	and the meat *was* *b* **boiled**,	AIT
	10: 5	flutes and harps **b** played before them,	NIH
	20: 6	because an annual sacrifice is *b* **made** there	NIH
2Sa	13:13	not keep me from *b* married to you."	NIH
	17:17	they could not risk *b* **seen** entering the city.	8011
	19:11	to his palace, since what is *b* said	NIH
	20:10	Without *b* stabbed again, Amasa died.	NIH
1Ki	6: 7	at the temple site while it *was b* built.	AIT
1Ch	9:18	*b* stationed at the King's Gate on the east,	NIH
	21:12	of *b* **swept away** before your enemies,	6200
	24: 6	one family *b* **taken** from Eleazar and	296
	28: 7	as is *b* done at this time.'	NIH
2Ch	21:19	that they were *b* **attacked** at both front	NIH
	15: 6	One nation *was b* **crushed** by another	AIT
Ezr	3:12	**the foundation** *of* this temple *b* **laid**,	AIT
	5: 8	The work *is b* **carried** on with diligence	10522
Ne	4: 7	ahead and that the gaps *were* *b* **closed**,	6258
	8: 8	people could understand what was *b* read.	NIH
	13:27	and *are b* **unfaithful** to our God	AIT
Est	4:11	in the inner court without *b* **summoned**	7924
Job	4: 7	Who, *b* innocent, has ever perished?	NIH
	10:19	If only *I had* never **come into** *b*,	2118+2118
	33:20	so that his *very b* finds food repulsive	2652
Ps	11: 3	When the foundations *are b* **destroyed**,	2238
	35:10	My whole *b* will exclaim,	6795
	103: 1	all my **inmost b**, praise his holy name.	7931
	119:126	your law *is b* **broken**.	AIT
	139:13	For you created my **inmost b**;	4000
Pr	3:26	and will keep your foot from *b* snared.	NIH
	6:27	into his lap without his clothes *b* **burned**?	8596
	6:28	on hot coals without his feet *b* **scorched**?	3917
	20:27	it searches out his **inmost b**.	1061+2540
	20:30	and beatings purge the **inmost b**.	1061+2540
	23:16	my **inmost b** will rejoice	4000
	24:11	Rescue *those b* **led** away to death;	4374
Ecc	2:15	What then do I gain *by b* **wise**?"	AIT
Isa	1: 7	your fields *are b* **stripped**	AIT
	16:11	my **inmost b** for Kir Hareseth.	7931
	42: 9	before *they* **spring into b** I announce them	7541
	50: 4	wakens my ear to listen like one *b* **taught**.	NIH
	66: 2	and so they **came into b**?	2118
Jer	6:22	a great nation *is b* **stirred up** from the ends	AIT
	17:16	I have not run away from *b* your **shepherd**;	AIT

Jer	40: 1	and Judah who *were* **b carried into exile**	1655
	50:41	and many kings *are* **b stirred up** from	6424
Eze	3: 5	not **b sent** to a people of obscure speech	8938
	10:13	I heard the wheels **b called**	7924
	14:13	by **b unfaithful** and I stretch out my hand	AIT
	20: 9	from **b profaned** in the eyes of	2725
	20:14	from **b profaned** in the eyes of the nations	2725
	20:22	from **b profaned** in the eyes of the nations	2725
	43:13	that cubit **b** a cubit and a handbreadth:	NIH
Da	4:27	and your wickedness by **b kind** *to*	AIT
	6:18	and without any entertainment **b brought**	AIT
Mt	20:13	'Friend, *I am* not **b unfair** to you.	AIT
	23:33	How will you escape **b condemned** to hell?	NIG
Mk	1:10	he saw heaven **b torn open** and	AIT
	1:13	**b tempted** by Satan.	AIT
Lk	3:21	When all the people *were* **b baptized,**	AIT
	7:12	a dead person *was* **b carried out**—	AIT
	8:23	so that the boat *was* **b swamped,**	AIT
	14: 1	he was **b carefully watched.**	AIT
	16:16	**the good news** of the kingdom of God *is b* **preached,**	AIT
	17:27	marrying and **b given in marriage** up to	AIT
	19: 3	but **b** a short man he could not,	1639
	21:13	This will result in your **b witnesses** to them.	NIG
	21:20	"When you see Jerusalem **b surrounded**	AIT
	22:44	And **b** in anguish,	1181
Jn	13: 2	The evening meal *was* **b served,**	1181
Ac	2:47	the Lord added to their number daily those who *were* **b saved.**	AIT
	3: 2	a man crippled from birth *was* **b carried** to	AIT
	4: 9	**b called** to account	AIT
	6: 1	because their widows *were* **b overlooked** in	AIT
	7:24	of them **b mistreated** by an Egyptian,	AIT
	10:10	and *while* the meal *was* **b prepared,**	AIT
	10:11	like a large sheet **b let down** to earth	AIT
	10:47	from **b baptized** with water?	AIT
	11: 5	like a large sheet **b let down** from heaven	AIT
	17:28	in him we live and move and **have our b.'**	1639
	17:29	**the divine b** is like gold or silver or stone—	2521
	19:40	in danger of **b charged with** rioting because	1592
	22:30	to find out exactly why Paul *was* **b accused**	AIT
	25: 4	"Paul is **b held** at Caesarea,	AIT
	27:20	we finally gave up all hope of **b saved.**	AIT
	27:27	fourteenth night we were *still* **b driven**	AIT
Ro	1: 8	your faith is **b reported** all over the world.	AIT
	1:18	of God is **b revealed** from heaven	AIT
	1:20	**b understood** from what has been made,	AIT
	2: 9	for every **human b** who does evil;	476
	3: 1	What advantage, then, is there in **b** a Jew,	NIG
	3: 8	**b slanderously reported**	NIG
	4:21	**b fully persuaded** that God had power	AIT
	7:22	For in my inner **b** I delight in God's law;	476
1Co	1:18	but to us who *are b* **saved** it is the power	AIT
	11:32	we are **b disciplined** so that we will not	AIT
	14: 7	will anyone know what tune *is b* **played**	AIT
	15:45	"The first man Adam became a living **b**";	6034
2Co	2:15	of Christ among those who *are b* **saved**	AIT
	3:18	*are b* **transformed into** his likeness.	AIT
	4:11	we who are alive *are* always **b given over**	AIT
	4:16	yet inwardly we *are b* **renewed** day by day.	AIT
	11: 9	I have kept myself from **b** a burden to you	NIG
Gal	3:22	**b given** through faith in Jesus Christ,	NIG
	5:11	why *am I* still **b persecuted?**	NIG
	6:12	to avoid **b persecuted** for the cross	AIT
Eph	2:22	And in him you too *are b* **built together**	AIT
	3:16	through his Spirit in your inner **b,**	476
	3:17	**b rooted and established**	AIT
	4:22	which *is b* **corrupted**	AIT
Php	1: 6	**b confident** of this,	AIT
	1:26	that through my **b** with you again your joy	4242
	1:28	without **b frightened** in any way	AIT
	2: 1	from **b united** with Christ,	NIG
	2: 2	make my joy complete by **b like-minded,** 899+3836+5858	
	2: 2	**b** one in spirit and purpose.	NIG
	2: 6	**b** in very nature God,	5639
	2: 7	**b made** in human likeness.	AIT
	2: 8	And **b found** in appearance as a man,	AIT
	2: 8	**b poured out** like a drink offering	AIT
	2:17	**b poured out** like a drink offering	AIT
	4:12	I have learned the secret of **b content** in any	NIG
Col	1:11	**b strengthened** with all power according	AIT
	3:10	which *is b* **renewed** in knowledge in	AIT
	4: 2	**b watchful** and thankful.	AIT
2Th	1: 7	and our **b gathered** to him,	AIT
1Ti	3: 1	sets his heart on **b**	3977
	5:13	**get into the habit of b**	3443
2Ti	2: 9	to the point of **b chained** like a criminal.	AIT
	3:13	deceiving and **b deceived.**	AIT
	4: 6	**b poured out** like a drink offering,	AIT
Tit	1: 6	and are not open to the charge of **b wild**	NIG
	3: 3	**b hated and hating** one another.	NIG
Heb	1: 3	and the exact representation of his **b,**	5712
	2:18	he is able to help those who *are b* **tempted.**	AIT
	5:13	Anyone who lives on milk, **b** still an infant,	1639
	6: 8	and is in danger of **b cursed.**	2932
	9: 9	that the gifts and sacrifices **b offered** were	AIT
	10: 2	would they not have stopped **b offered?**	AIT
	10:14	by one sacrifice he has made perfect forever those who *are b* **made holy.**	AIT
	11: 1	Now faith is **b sure** of what we hope for	AIT
Jas	1:27	and to keep oneself from **b polluted** by	834
	3: 7	reptiles and creatures of the sea *are b* **tamed**	AIT
1Pe	2: 5	*are b* **built** into a spiritual house to be	AIT
	3:20	of Noah *while* the ark *was b* **built.**	1181
	5: 3	but **b** examples to the flock.	1181
2Pe	1: 8	they will keep you from **b ineffective**	NIG
	3: 7	**b kept** for the day of judgment	AIT

Rev	3: 1	you have a reputation of **b alive,**	AIT
	4:11	they were created and have *their* **b.**"	1639

BEINGS (5) [BEING]

Ps	8: 5	a little lower than the **heavenly b**	466
	89: 6	like the LORD among the **heavenly b?**	446+1201
2Pe	2:10	not afraid to slander **celestial b;**	1518
	2:11	against **such b** in the presence of the Lord.	899
Jude	1: 8	reject authority and slander **celestial b.**	1518

BEKA (2) [BEKAS]

Ge	24:22	a gold nose ring weighing a **b**	1325
Ex	38:26	one **b** per person,	1325

BEKAS (3) [BEKA]

1Ki	10:16	six hundred **b** of gold went into each shield.	NIH
2Ch	9:15	six hundred **b** of hammered gold went	NIH
	9:16	with three hundred **b** of gold in each shield.	NIH

BEKER (5) [BEKERITE]

Ge	46:21	Bela, **B,** Ashbel, Gera, Naaman, Ehi, Rosh,	1146
Nu	26:35	through **B,** the Bekerite clan;	1146
1Ch	7: 6	Bela, **B** and Jediael.	1146
	7: 8	The sons of **B:**	1146
	7: 8	All these were the sons of **B.**	1146

BEKERITE (1) [BEKER]

Nu	26:35	through Beker, the **B** clan;	1151

BEL (3)

Isa	46: 1	**B** bows down, Nebo stoops low;	1155
Jer	50: 2	**B** will be put to shame,	1155
	51:44	I will punish **B** in Babylon	1155

BELA (14) [BELAITE, ZOAR]

Ge	14: 2	and the king of **B** (that is, Zoar).	1186
	14: 8	the king of Zeboiim and the king of **B**	1186
	36:32	**B** son of Beor became king of Edom.	1185
	36:33	When **B** died, Jobab son of Zerah	1185
	46:21	The sons of Benjamin: **B,** Beker, Ashbel,	1185
Nu	26:38	through **B,** the Belaite clan;	1185
	26:40	**B** through Ard and Naaman were:	1185
1Ch	1:43	**B** son of Beor,	1185
	1:44	When **B** died, Jobab son of Zerah	1185
	5: 8	and **B** son of Azaz,	1185
	7: 6	Three sons of Benjamin: **B,**	1185
	7: 7	The sons of **B:**	1185
	8: 1	Benjamin was the father of **B** his firstborn,	1185
	8: 3	The sons of **B** were: Addar, Gera, Abihud,	1185

BELAH (KJV) See BELA

BELAITE (1) [BELA]

Nu	26:38	through Bela, the **B** clan;	1188

BELCH (KJV) See SPEW

BELIAL (1)

2Co	6:15	harmony is there between Christ and **B?**	1016

BELIEF (1) [BELIEVE]

2Th	2:13	of the Spirit and through **b** in the truth.	4411

BELIEFS (1) [BELIEVE]

Job	11: 4	'My **b** are flawless and I am pure	4375

BELIEVE (160) [BELIEF, BELIEFS, BELIEVED, BELIEVER, BELIEVERS, BELIEVES, BELIEVING]

Ge	45:26	Jacob was stunned; he did not **b** them.	586
Ex	4: 1	if *they do* not **b** me or listen to me and say,	586
	4: 5	"is so that *they may* **b** that the LORD,	586
	4: 8	"If *they do* not **b** you or pay attention to	586
	4: 8	*they may* **b** the second.	586
	4: 9	But if *they do* not **b** these two signs or listen	586
Nu	14:11	How long *will they* refuse to **b** in me,	586
1Ki	10: 7	But *I did* not **b** these things until I came	586
2Ch	9: 6	But *I did* not **b** what they said until I came	586
	32:15	*Do* not **b** him, for no god of any nation	586
Job	9:16	I *do* not **b** he would give me a hearing.	586
Ps	78:22	not **b** in God or trust in his deliverance.	586
	78:32	in spite of his wonders, *they did* not **b.**	586
	106:24	*they did* not **b** his promise.	586
	119:66	for *I* **b** in your commands.	586
Pr	26:25	his speech is charming, *do* not **b** him,	586
Isa	43:10	and **b** me and understand that I am he.	586
Jer	29:31	and *has led* you to **b** a lie,	1053
	40:14	Gedaliah son of Ahikam *did* not **b** them.	586
La	4:12	The kings of the earth *did* not **b,**	586
Hab	1: 5	in your days *that you would* not **b.**	586
Mt	9:28	"Do you **b** that I am able to do this?"	4409
	18: 6	of these little ones who **b** in me, to sin,	4409
	21:22	If you **b,** you will receive whatever you ask	4409
	21:25	he will ask, 'Then why didn't *you* **b** him?'	4409
	21:32	and *you did* not **b** him,	4409
	21:32	you did not repent and **b** him.	4409
	24:23	'There he is!' *do* not **b** it.	4409

Mt	24:26	'Here he is, in the inner rooms,' *do* not **b** it.	4409
	27:42	and *we will* **b** in him.	4409
Mk	1:15	Repent and **b the good news!**	1877+4409
	5:36	"Don't be afraid; just **b.**"	4409
	9:24	"*I do* **b;** help me overcome my unbelief!"	4409
	9:42	of these little ones who **b** in me to sin,	4409
	11:24	**b** that you have received it,	4409
	11:31	he will ask, 'Then why didn't *you* **b** him?'	4409
	13:21	'Look, there he is!' *do* not **b** it.	4409
	15:32	that we may see and **b.**"	4409
	16:11	*they did* not **b** it.	601
	16:13	but *they did* not **b** them either.	4409
	16:14	to **b** those who had seen him	4409
	16:16	whoever *does* not **b** will be condemned.	601
	16:17	these signs will accompany those who **b:**	4409
Lk	1:20	because *you did* not **b** my words,	4409
	8:12	so that they may not **b** and be saved.	4409
	8:13	They **b** for a while,	4409
	8:50	just **b,** and she will be healed."	4409
	20: 5	he will ask, 'Why didn't *you* **b** him?'	4409
	22:67	"If I tell you, *you will* not **b** me,	4409
	24:11	But *they did* not **b** the women,	601
	24:25	to **b** all that the prophets have spoken!	4409
	24:41	*while* they still *did* not **b** it because of joy	601
Jn	1: 7	so that through him all men *might* **b.**	4409
	1:50	"You **b** because I told you I saw you under	4409
	3:12	to you of earthly things and *you do* not **b;**	4409
	3:12	*will you* **b** if I speak of heavenly things?	4409
	3:18	not **b** stands condemned already	4409
	4:21	Jesus declared, "**B** me, woman,	4409
	4:42	"*We* no longer **b** just because	4409
	4:48	Jesus told him, "*you will* never **b.**"	4409
	5:38	for you *do* not **b** the one he sent.	4409
	5:44	How can you **b** if you accept praise	4409
	5:46	If you believed Moses, *you would* **b** me,	4409
	5:47	But since *you do* not **b** what he wrote,	4409
	5:47	how *are you going to* **b** what I say?"	4409
	6:29	to **b** in the one he has sent."	4409
	6:30	that we may see it and **b** you?	4409
	6:36	you have seen me and still *you do* not **b.**	4409
	6:64	Yet there are some of you who *do* not **b.**"	4409
	6:64	from the beginning which of them *did* not **b**	4409
	6:69	We **b** and know that you are the Holy One	4409
	7: 5	For even his own brothers *did* not **b** in him.	4409
	8:24	if *you do* not **b** that I am [the one I claim to	4409
	8:45	because I tell the truth, *you do* not **b** me!	4409
	8:46	I am telling the truth, why don't you **b** me?	4409
	9:18	not **b** that he had been blind	4409
	9:35	he said, "Do you **b** in the Son of Man?"	4409
	9:36	"Tell me so that *I may* **b** in him."	4409
	9:38	Then the man said, "Lord, *I* **b,**"	4409
	10:25	"I did tell you, but *you do* not **b.**	4409
	10:26	*you do* not **b** because you are not my sheep.	4409
	10:37	not **b** me unless I do what my Father does.	4409
	10:38	But if I do it, even though *you do* not **b** me,	4409
	10:38	even though you do not believe me, **b**	4409
	11:15	so that *you may* **b.**	4409
	11:26	*Do you* **b** this?"	4409
	11:27	"I **b** that you are the Christ, the Son of God,	4409
	11:42	that *they may* **b** that you sent me."	4409
	11:48	everyone *will* **b** in him,	4409
	12:37	*they* still *would* not **b** in him.	4409
	12:39	For this reason they could not **b,** because,	4409
	12:44	he *does* not **b** in me only,	4409
	13:19	it does happen *you will* **b** that I am He.	4409
	14:10	Don't *you* **b** that I am in the Father,	4409
	14:11	**B** me when I say that I am in the Father and	4409
	14:11	or at least **b** on the evidence of	4409
	14:29	so that when it does happen *you will* **b.**	4409
	16: 9	in regard to sin, because *men do* not **b** in me;	4409
	16:30	This makes *us* **b** that you came from God."	4409
	16:31	"*You* **b** at last!" Jesus answered.	4409
	17:20	I pray also for those who *will* **b** in me	4409
	17:21	that the world *may* **b** that you have sent me.	4409
	19:35	and he testifies so that you also *may* **b.**	4409
	20:25	*I will* not **b** it."	4409
	20:27	Stop doubting and **b.**"	4412
	20:31	that *you may* **b** that Jesus is the Christ,	4409
Ac	13:41	in your days that *you would* never **b,**	4409
	14: 2	But the Jews who **refused to b** stirred up	578
	15: 7	the message of the gospel and **b.**	4409
	15:11	*We* **b** it is through the grace	4409
	16:31	They replied, "**B** in the Lord Jesus,	4409
	16:34	with joy *because* he had **come to b** in God	4409
	19: 4	the people to **b** in the one coming after him,	4409
	19: 9	*they* **refused to b** and publicly maligned	578
	22:19	to another to imprison and beat those who **b**	4409
	24:14	*I* **b** everything that agrees with the Law	4409
	26:27	King Agrippa, *do you* **b** the prophets?"	4409
	28:24	but others *would* not **b.**	601
Ro	3:22	through faith in Jesus Christ to all who **b.**	4409
	4:11	he is the father of all who **b** but have	4409
	4:24	for us who **b** in him who raised Jesus	4409
	6: 8	we **b** that we will also live with him.	4409
	10: 9	and **b** in your heart that God raised him	4409
	10:10	with your heart that *you* **b** and are justified,	4409
	10:14	And how *can* they **b** in the one	4409
	14:22	So whatever you **b** about these things	2400+4411
	16:26	so that all nations might **b** and obey him—	4411
1Co	1:21	of what was preached to save those who **b.**	4409
	3: 5	through whom *you came* to **b**—	4409
	11:18	and to some extent *I* **b** it.	4409
2Co	4:13	With that same spirit of faith we also **b** and	4409
Gal	3: 6	or because you **b** what you heard?	4409
	3: 7	those who **b** are children of Abraham.	1666+4411
	3:22	might be given *to* those who **b.**	4409

Eph	1:19	his incomparably great power for us who **b**.	4409
Php	1:29	on behalf of Christ not only *to* **b** on him,	4409
1Th	2:13	which is at work in you who **b**.	4409
	4:14	*We* **b** that Jesus died and rose again and	4409
	4:14	that Jesus died and rose again and so we **b**	NIG
2Th	2:11	a powerful delusion so that they *will* **b**	4409
1Ti	1:16	an example for those who would **b** on him	4409
	4:3	*by* those who **b** and who know the truth.	4412
	4:10	and especially *of* those who **b**.	4412
Tit	1:6	a man whose children **b** and are not open to	4412
	1:15	*to* those who are corrupted and do **not b**,	603
Heb	10:39	but *of* those who **b** and are saved.	4411
	11:6	because anyone who comes to him must **b**	4409
Jas	1:6	But when he asks, *he must* **b** and not doubt,	4411
	2:19	You **b** that there is one God.	4409
	2:19	Even the demons **b** that—and shudder.	4409
1Pe	1:8	even though you do not see him now, you **b**	4409
	1:21	Through him you **b** in God,	4412
	2:7	Now to you who **b**, this stone is precious.	4409
	2:7	But *to* those who do **not b**,	601
	3:1	if any of them **do not b** the word,	578
1Jn	3:23	to **b** in the name of his Son, Jesus Christ,	4409
	4:1	Dear friends, *do* not **b** every spirit,	4409
	5:10	not **b** God has made him out to be a liar,	4409
	5:13	to you who **b** in the name of the Son of God	4409
Jude	1:5	but later destroyed those who *did* not **b**.	4409

BELIEVED (66) [BELIEVE]

Ge	15:6	Abram **b** the LORD, and he credited to him	
		as righteousness.	586
Ex	4:31	and they **b**. And when they heard	586
Job	29:24	When I smiled at them, *they* scarcely **b** it;	586
Ps	106:12	*they* **b** his promises and sang his praise.	586
	116:10	*I* **b**; therefore I said,	586
Isa	53:1	Who *has* **b** our message and to whom has	586
Jnh	3:5	The Ninevites **b** God.	586
Mt	8:13	It will be done just as *you* **b** it would."	4409
Lk	1:45	Blessed is she who *has* **b** that what	4409
Jn	1:12	to those who **b** in his name,	4409
	2:22	Then *they* **b** the Scripture and the words	4409
	2:23	the miraculous signs he was doing and **b**	4409
	3:18	because he has not **b** in the name	4409
	4:39	of the Samaritans from that town **b** in him	4409
	4:53	So he and all his household **b**.	4409
	5:46	If *you* **b** Moses, you would believe me,	4409
	7:39	whom those who **b** in him were later	4409
	7:48	of the rulers or of the Pharisees **b** in him?	4409
	8:31	To the Jews who *had* **b** him, Jesus said,	4409
	10:42	And in that place many **b** in Jesus.	4409
	11:40	Jesus said, "Did I not tell you that if *you* **b**,	4409
	12:38	who *has* **b** our message and to whom has	4409
	12:42	even among the leaders **b** in him.	4409
	16:27	because you have loved me and *have* **b**	4409
	17:8	and *they* **b** that you sent me.	4409
	20:8	He saw and **b**.	4409
	20:29	"Because you have seen me, *you* have **b**;	4409
	20:29	who have not seen and yet *have* **b**."	4409
Ac	4:4	But many who heard the message **b**,	4409
	5:14	and women **b** in the Lord and were added	4409
	8:12	But when *they* **b** Philip as he preached	4409
	8:13	Simon himself **b** and was baptized.	4409
	9:42	and many people **b** in the Lord.	4409
	11:17	*who* **b** in the Lord Jesus Christ,	4409
	11:21	and a great number of people **b** and turned	4409
	13:12	the proconsul saw what had happened, he **b**,	4409
	13:48	all who were appointed for eternal life **b**.	4409
	14:1	that a great number of Jews and Gentiles **b**.	4409
	17:12	Many of the Jews **b**,	4409
	17:34	A few men became followers of Paul and **b**.	4409
	18:8	and his entire household **b** in the Lord;	4409
	18:8	of the Corinthians who heard him **b** and	4409
	18:27	a great help to those who by grace *had* **b**.	4409
	19:2	the Holy Spirit *when you* **b**?"	4409
	19:18	Many of those who **b** now came	4409
	21:20	how many thousands of Jews *have* **b**,	4409
Ro	4:3	"Abraham **b** God, and it was credited	4409
	4:17	in the sight of God, in whom *he* **b**—	4409
	4:18	in hope **b** and so became the father	4409
	10:14	on the one *they have* not **b** in?	4409
	10:16	"Lord, who *has* **b** our message?"	4409
	13:11	now than when *we* first **b**.	4409
1Co	15:2	Otherwise, *you* have **b** in vain.	4409
	15:11	and this is what *you* **b**.	4409
2Co	4:13	It is written: *"I* **b**; therefore I have spoken."	4409
Gal	3:6	Consider Abraham: *"He* **b** God,	4409
Eph	1:13	Having **b**, you were marked in him with	4409
1Th	2:10	and blameless we were among you who **b**.	4409
2Th	1:10	be marveled at among all those who *have* **b**.	4409
	1:10	because you **b** our testimony to you.	4409
	2:12	that all will be condemned who *have* not **b**	4409
1Ti	3:16	*was* **b** on in the world,	4409
2Ti	1:12	because I know whom *I have* **b**,	4409
Heb	4:3	Now we who *have* **b** enter that rest,	4409
Jas	2:23	"Abraham **b** God, and it was credited	4409
1Jn	5:10	not **b** the testimony God has given	4409

BELIEVER (7) [BELIEVE]

1Ki	18:3	(Obadiah was a devout **b** *in* the LORD.	3707
Ac	16:1	whose mother was a Jewess and a **b**,	4412
	16:15	"If you consider me a **b** in the Lord,"	1639+4412
1Co	7:12	If any brother has a wife who is **not a b**	603
	7:13	a husband who is **not a b** and he is willing	603
2Co	6:15	a **b** have in common with an unbeliever?	4412
1Ti	5:16	If any woman who is a **b** has widows	4412

BELIEVERS (21) [BELIEVE]

Jn	4:41	because of his words many more **became b**.	4409
Ac	1:15	up among the **b** (a group numbering about	81
	2:44	All the **b** were together and had everything	4409
	4:32	All the **b** were one in heart and mind.	4409
	5:12	And all the **b** used to meet together	NIG
	9:41	the **b** and the widows and presented her	41
	10:45	The circumcised **b** who had come	4412
	11:2	the circumcised **b** criticized him	NIG
	15:2	along with some other **b**,	899+1666S
	15:5	of the **b** who belonged to the party of	4409
	15:23	your brothers, *To* the Gentile **b** in Antioch,	81
	21:25	As for the Gentile **b**,	4409
1Co	6:5	to judge a dispute between **b**?	81
	14:22	are a sign, not *for* **b** but for unbelievers;	4409
	14:22	prophecy, however, is *for* **b**,	4409
Gal	6:10	to those who belong to the family of **b**.	3836+4411
1Th	1:7	And so you became a model *to* all the **b**	4409
1Ti	4:12	but set an example *for* the **b** in speech,	4412
Jas	2:1	as **b** in our glorious Lord Jesus Christ,	2400+3836+4411
1Pe	2:17	Love the **brotherhood of b**, fear God,	82

BELIEVES (24) [BELIEVE]

Pr	14:15	A simple man **b** anything,	586
Mk	9:23	"Everything is possible *for* him who **b**."	4409
	11:23	and does not doubt in his heart but **b**	4409
	16:16	Whoever **b** and is baptized will be saved,	4409
Jn	3:15	that everyone who **b**	4409
	3:16	that whoever **b** in him shall not perish	4409
	3:18	Whoever **b** in him is not condemned	4409
	3:36	Whoever **b** in the Son has eternal life,	4409
	5:24	and **b** him who sent me has eternal life	4409
	6:35	and he who **b** in me will never be thirsty.	4409
	6:40	the Son and **b** in him shall have eternal life,	4409
	6:47	he who **b** has everlasting life.	4409
	7:38	Whoever **b** in me, as the Scripture has said,	4409
	11:25	He who **b** in me will live,	4409
	11:26	whoever lives and **b** in me will never die.	4409
	12:44	Then Jesus cried out, *"When* a man **b** in me,	4409
	12:46	so that no one who **b** in me should stay	4409
Ac	10:43	about him that everyone who **b**	4409
	13:39	Through him everyone who **b** is justified	4409
Ro	1:16	for the salvation *of* everyone who **b**:	4409
	10:4	be righteousness for everyone who **b**.	4409
1Jn	5:1	Everyone who **b** that Jesus is the Christ	4409
	5:5	Only he who **b** that Jesus is the Son of God.	4409
	5:10	Anyone who **b** in the Son	4409

BELIEVING (7) [BELIEVE]

Jn	20:31	that *by* **b** you may have life in his name.	4409
Ac	9:26	not **b** that he really was a disciple.	4409
1Co	7:14	sanctified through her **b** husband.	NIG
	7:15	A **b** **man** or woman is not bound	81
	9:5	Don't we have the right to take a **b** wife	80+1222
Gal	3:2	or by **b** what you heard?	4411
1Ti	6:2	Those who have **b** masters are not	4412

BELLOW (1) [BELLOWS]

Job	6:5	or an ox **b** when it has fodder?	1716

BELLOWS (1) [BELLOW]

Jer	6:29	The **b** blow fiercely to burn away the lead	5135

BELLS (6)

Ex	28:33	with gold **b** between them.	7194
	28:34	The gold **b** and the pomegranates are	7194
	28:35	of the **b** will be heard when he enters	2257S
	39:25	And they made **b** of pure gold.	7194
	39:26	The **b** and pomegranates alternated around	7194
Zec	14:20	be inscribed on the **b** *of* the horses,	5197

BELLY (9)

Ge	3:14	on your **b** and you will eat dust all the days	1623
Lev	11:42	whether it moves on its **b** or walks	1623
Jdg	3:21	and plunged it into the king's **b**.	1061
2Sa	20:10	and Joab plunged it into his **b**,	2824
Job	15:2	with empty notions or fill his **b** with	1061
	20:23	When he has filled his **b**,	1061
	40:16	what power in the muscles of his **b**!	1061
Da	2:32	its **b** and thighs of bronze,	10435
Mt	12:40	and three nights in the **b** of a huge fish,	3120

BELONG (81) [BELONGED, BELONGING, BELONGINGS, BELONGS]

Ge	32:17	*'To* whom do you **b**,	4200
	32:18	'They **b** to your servant Jacob.	4200
	40:8	"Do not interpretations **b** to God?	4200
	45:11	and your household and all who **b** to	4200
Ex	13:12	the firstborn males of your livestock **b** to	4200
	21:4	and her children *shall* **b** to her master,	2118+4200
	29:27	of the ordination ram that **b** to Aaron	4200
	29:29	"Aaron's sacred garments *will* **b** to	2118+4200
Lev	5:13	of the offering *will* **b** to the priest,	2118+4200
	7:7	*They* **b** to the priest who makes atonement	
			2118+4200
	25:30	in the walled city *shall* **b** permanently to	7756
	25:55	for the Israelites **b** to me as servants.	4200
Nu	5:9	the Israelites bring to a priest *will* **b** to	2118+4200
	5:10	what he gives to the priest *will* **b**	2118+4200
	6:20	they are holy and **b** to the priest,	4200
Dt	10:14	**To** the LORD your God **b**	4200
	20:15	at a distance from you and do not **b** to	4946
	29:29	The secret things **b** to the LORD our God,	4200
	29:29	but the things revealed **b** to us and	4200
	33:8	and Urim **b** to the man you favored.	4200
Jos	2:13	and all who **b** to them,	4200
	6:25	and bring her out and all who **b** to her,	4200
1Sa	25:22	of all who **b** to him!"	4200
	30:13	"To whom do you **b**,	4200
1Ki	8:41	not **b** to your people Israel but has come	4946
2Ch	6:32	not **b** to your people Israel but has come	4946
Ne	5:5	because our fields and our vineyards **b** to	4200
Job	12:13	"To God **b** wisdom and power;	6640
	12:16	**To** him **b** strength and victory;	6640
	25:2	"Dominion and awe **b** to God;	6640
Ps	47:9	for the kings of the earth **b** to God;	4200
	95:4	and the mountain peaks **b** to him.	4200
	104:18	The high mountains **b** to the wild goats;	4200
	115:16	The highest heavens **b** to the LORD,	4200
Pr	16:1	To man **b** the plans of the heart,	4200
SS	7:10	I **b** to my lover, and his desire is for me.	4200
Isa	44:5	One will say, 'I **b** to the LORD';	4200
Jer	5:10	for these people do not **b** to the LORD.	4200
Eze	13:9	not **b** to the council of my people or	928+2118
	13:9	both alike **b** to me.	4200
	44:29	in Israel devoted to the LORD *will* **b** to	2118+4200
	44:30	and of all your special gifts *will* **b** to	2118+4200
	45:5	cubits wide *will* **b** to the Levites,	2118
	45:6	it *will* **b** to the whole house of Israel.	2118+4200
	46:16	it *will* also **b** to his descendants;	2118+4200
	48:21	and the city property *will* **b** to the prince,	4200
	48:21	of the tribal portions *will* **b** to the prince,	4200
Zep	2:7	It *will* **b** to the remnant of the house	2118+4200
Zec	9:7	Those who are left *will* **b** to our God	4200
Mt	20:23	**b** to *those for whom*	AIT
Mk	9:41	a cup of water in my name because *you* **b**	1639
	10:40	These places **b** to those	NIG
	13:14	where *it does* not **b**—	1256
Jn	8:44	You **b** to your father, the devil,	1639+1666
	8:47	not hear is that *you do* not **b** to God."	1639+1666
	14:24	they *b* to the **Father** who sent me.	AIT
	15:19	As it is, *you do* not **b** to the world,	1639+1666
Ac	5:4	Didn't *it* **b** to you before it was sold?	3531
Ro	1:6	to *b* to **Jesus Christ**.	AIT
	7:4	that you *might* **b** to another,	1181
	8:9	he **does** not **b** to Christ.	1639
	14:8	whether we live or die, *we* **b** to the **Lord**.	
			1639+3261
	16:10	Greet those who **b** to the household	1666
1Co	6:14	not **b** to her alone but also to her husband,	2027
	7:4	not **b** to him alone but also to his wife.	2027
	7:39	but he must **b** to the Lord.	1877
	9:19	free and **b** to no man,	1666+1801+4246
	12:15	I do not **b** to the body,"	1666
	12:16	I do not **b** to the body,"	1666
	15:23	then, when he comes, those who *b* **to him**.	AIT
2Co	10:7	that we *b* to **Christ** just as much as he.	AIT
Gal	3:29	If you *b* to **Christ**,	AIT
	5:24	Those who *b* to **Christ Jesus** have crucified	AIT
	6:10	to those who **b** to the **family** of believers.	3858
Php	4:22	especially those who **b** to	1666
1Th	5:5	We do not **b** to the night or to	1639
	5:8	But *since* we **b** to the day,	1639
Jas	2:7	the noble name of him to whom you **b**?	2126
1Jn	2:19	but *they did* not really **b** to us.	1639+1666
	3:19	then is how we know that *we* **b** to the truth,	1639
Rev	19:1	and glory and power *b* **to** our **God**,	AIT

BELONGED (51) [BELONG]

Ge	30:40	and dark-colored **animals** that **b** to Laban.	AIT
	31:1	from what **b** to our father."	4200
Nu	3:21	**To** Gershon **b** the clans of the Libnites	4200
	3:27	**To** Kohath **b** the clans of the Amramites,	4200
	3:33	**To** Merari **b** the clans of the Mahlites and	4200
	27:1	**b** to the clans of Manasseh son of Joseph.	4200
Dt	11:6	tents and every living thing that **b** to	928+8079
	30:5	He will bring you to the land that **b**	3769
Jos	6:23	and mother and brothers and all who **b** to	4200
	6:25	with her family and all who **b** to her,	4200
	14:14	So Hebron *has* **b** to Caleb son	2118+4200
	17:8	Gilead **b** to the rest of the descendants	2118+4200
	17:8	**b** to the Ephraimites.)	4200
	17:10	On the south the land **b** to Ephraim,	4200
Jdg	6:11	under the oak in Ophrah that **b** to Joash	4200
Ru	4:3	of land that **b** to our brother Elimelech.	4200
1Sa	27:6	and it *has* **b** to the kings	2118+4200
2Sa	8:7	the gold shields that **b** to the officers	448+2118
	8:8	**towns** *that* **b** to Hadadezer,	AIT
	9:7	the **land** *that* **b** to your grandfather Saul,	AIT
	9:9	that **b** to Saul and his family.	2118+4200
	12:4	the **ewe lamb** *that* **b** to the poor man	AIT
	16:4	"All that **b** to Mephibosheth is now yours."	4200
1Ki	6:22	also overlaid with gold the altar that **b** to	4200
2Ki	8:6	"Give back everything that **b** to her,	4200
	9:21	**plot of ground** *that* had **b**	AIT
	9:25	the **field** *that* **b** to Naboth the Jezreelite.	AIT
	11:10	that had **b** to King David and that were in	4200
	12:16	*it* **b** to the priests.	2118+4200
	14:28	which had **b** to Yaudi,	4200
1Ch	5:2	the rights of the firstborn **b** to Joseph)—	4200
	8:8	**towns** *that* **b** to Hadadezer,	AIT
2Ch	23:9	and small shields that had **b** to King David	4200
	26:23	near them in a field for burial that **b** to,	AIT
Eze	23:41	the incense and **oil** *that* **b** to me.	AIT
	46:19	which **b** to the priests,	448

Lk	1: 5	who **b** to the priestly division of Abijah;	1666
	2: 4	because he **b** to the house and line	1639+1666
	5:30	the teachers of the law who **b** to their sect	899
Jn	15:19	If *you* **b** to the world,	1639+1666
Ac	9: 2	that if he found any there who **b** to the Way,	1639
	12: 1	that King Herod arrested some who **b** to	608
	15: 5	of the believers who **b** to the party of	608
	27: 1	*b to* the Imperial **Regiment.**	AIT
	28: 7	was an estate nearby that **b**	5639
Gal	2:12	of those who **b** to the circumcision group.	1666
Col	2:20	why, as though *you still* **b** to it,	2409
Heb	7:13	*He* of whom these things are said **b** to	3576
1Jn	2:19	For if *they had* **b** to us,	1639+1666
	2:19	that none of them **b** to us.	1639+1666
	3:12	who **b** to the evil one	1666

BELONGING (37) [BELONG]

Ge	14:23	that I will accept nothing **b** to you,	4200
	50: 8	*b to* his father's **household.**	AIT
Ex	9: 4	no animal **b** to the Israelites will die.' "	4200
	9: 6	but not one animal **b** to the Israelites died.	4946
Lev	7:20	of the fellowship offering **b** to the LORD,	4200
	7:21	of the fellowship offering **b** to the LORD,	4200
	25:34	But the **pastureland** *b to* their towns must	AIT
Nu	1:50	over all its furnishings and everything **b** to	4200
	16:26	Do not touch anything **b** to them,	4200
	17: 5	The **staff** *b to* the man I choose	AIT
	31:42	The **half** *b to* the Israelites,	AIT
Dt	2:19	not give you possession of any **land** *b to*	AIT
Jos	17: 9	There were towns **b** to Ephraim lying	4200
Ru	2: 3	she found herself working in a field **b** to	4200
1Sa	6:18	of Philistine towns **b** to the five rulers—	4200
	9: 3	donkeys **b** to Saul's father Kish were lost,	4200
	25:34	not one male **b** to Nabal	4200
	30:14	and the territory **b** to Judah and the Negev	4200
1Ki	14:11	Dogs will eat those **b** to Jeroboam who die	4200
	14:13	He is the only one **b** to Jeroboam who will	4200
	16: 4	Dogs will eat those **b** to Baasha who die in	4200
	21: 1	a vineyard **b** to Naboth the Jezreelite.	2118+4200
	21:24	"Dogs will eat those **b** to Ahab who die in	4200
1Ch	7: 5	The relatives who were fighting men **b** to	4200
	9:18	These were the gatekeepers **b** to the camp	4200
	22:19	of the LORD and the sacred **articles** *b*	AIT
	23: 7	**B** to the Gershonites: Ladan and Shimei.	4200
	26:21	and who were heads of families **b** to Ladan	4200
	28: 1	and livestock **b** to the king and his sons,	4200
2Ch	34:33	from all the territory **b** to the Israelites,	4200
Ezr	1: 7	King Cyrus brought out the **articles** *b to*	AIT
Eze	37:16	'B to Judah and the Israelites associated	4200
	37:16	**b** to Joseph and all the house	4200
	48:22	The area **b** to the prince will lie between	4200
Lk	5: 3	the one **b** to Simon,	1639+4981
1Pe	2: 9	a holy nation, a people **b** to God,	1650+4348
Rev	13: 8	book of life *b to* **the Lamb** that was slain	AIT

BELONGINGS (8) [BELONG]

Ge	45:20	Never mind about your **b,**	3998
Jdg	14:19	of their **b** and gave their clothes	2723
Jer	10:17	Gather up your **b** to leave the land,	4045
	46:19	Pack your **b** *for* exile.	3998
Eze	12: 3	pack your **b** *for* exile and in the daytime,	3998
	12: 4	bring out your **b** packed for exile.	3998
	12: 5	dig through the wall and take your **b** out	NIH
	12: 7	I took my **b** out at dusk,	NIH

BELONGS (58) [BELONG]

Ge	14:24	and the **share** *that b to* the men who went	AIT
	19:12	or anyone else in the city who **b** to you?	4200
	23: 9	which **b** to him and is at the end	4200
	31:16	that God took away from our father **b** to us	4200
	31:37	what have you found that **b** to	4946
	47:18	and our livestock **b** to you,	448
	47:26	that a fifth of the produce **b** to Pharaoh.	4200
	49:10	until he comes **to** whom it **b** and	4200
Ex	13: 2	of every womb among the Israelites **b** to	4200
	20:17	or anything that **b** to your neighbor."	4200
	34:19	first offspring of every womb **b** to me,	4200
	40: 4	Bring in the table and set out **what b** *on* it.	6886
Lev	2: 3	the grain offering **b** to Aaron and his sons;	4200
	2:10	the grain offering **b** to Aaron and his sons;	4200
	7: 9	on a griddle **b** to the priest who offers it,	2118+4200
	7:10	**b** equally to all the sons of Aaron.	2118
	7:14	*it* **b** to the priest who sprinkles the blood	2118+4200
	7:31	but the breast **b** to Aaron and his sons.	2118+4200
	14:13	the guilt offering **b** to the priest;	4200
	24: 9	*It* **b** to Aaron and his sons,	2118+4200
	27:26	**firstborn** already **b** to the LORD	1144+4200
	27:30	**b** to the LORD; it is holy to the LORD.	4200
Nu	5: 8	the restitution **b** to the LORD and must	4200
	16: 5	the LORD will show who **b** to him	4200
	16:30	with everything that **b** to them,	4200
	18: 9	that part **b** to you and your sons.	4200
Dt	1:17	for judgment **b** to God.	4200
	5:21	or anything that **b** to your neighbor."	4200
	21:17	The right of the firstborn **b** to him.	4200
Jos	7:15	along with all that **b** to him.	4200
1Sa	15: 3	and totally destroy everything that **b** to	4200
1Ki	22: 3	"Don't you know that Ramoth Gilead **b** to	4200
1Ch	29:16	and all of it **b** to you.	4200
Job	41:11	Everything under heaven **b** to me.	4200
Ps	22:28	for dominion **b** to the LORD and he rules	4200
	89:18	Indeed, our shield **b** to the LORD,	4200
	111:10	*To* him *b* eternal **praise.**	AIT

Jer	46:10	But that day **b** to the Lord,	4200
Eze	18: 4	For every living soul **b** to me,	4200
	21:27	to whom it rightfully **b;**	4200
	46:17	His inheritance **b** to his sons only;	NIH
	48:22	the center of the area that **b** to the prince.	4200
Mt	19:14	the kingdom of heaven **b** to such as these."	1639
	25:25	See, here is what **b** **to** you.'	2400+5050
Mk	10:14	for the kingdom of God **b** to such as these.	1639
Lk	6:30	and if anyone takes what **b** to you,	5050
	18:16	for the kingdom of God **b** to such as these.	1639
Jn	3:29	The bride **b** to the bridegroom.	2400
	3:31	who is from the earth **b** to the earth,	1639+1666
	8:35	but a son **b** to it forever.	3531
	8:47	He who **b** to God hears what God says	1639+1666
	16:15	All that **b** to the Father is mine.	2400
Ac	1:25	which Judas left to go where he **b**."	2625
Ro	12: 5	and each member **b** to all the others.	NIG
2Co	10: 7	If anyone is confident that he **b** to Christ,	1639+5986
Col	3: 5	whatever **b** to your earthly nature:	NIG
Rev	7:10	"Salvation *b to* our **God,**	AIT
	17:11	*He* **b** to the seven and is going	1639+1666

BELOVED (4) [LOVE]

Dt	33:12	the **b** *of* the LORD rest secure in him,	3351
SS	5: 9	How is your **b** better than others,	1856
	5: 9	How is your **b** better than others,	1856
Jer	11:15	"What is my **b** doing in my temple	3351

BELOW (42)

Ge	35: 8	was buried under the oak **b** Bethel.	4946+9393
	49:25	blessings of the deep that lies **b,**	9393
Ex	20: 4	the earth beneath or in the waters **b.**	4946+9393
	30: 4	Make two gold rings for the altar **b**	4946+9393
	37:27	made two gold rings **b** the molding—	4946+9393
Dt	3:17	**b** the slopes of Pisgah.	9393
	4:18	the ground or any fish in the waters **b.**	4946+9393
	4:39	in heaven above and on the earth **b.**	4946+9393
	4:49	**b** the slopes of Pisgah.	9393
	5: 8	the earth beneath or in the waters **b.**	4946+9393
	32:22	one that burns to the realm of death **b.**	9397
	33:13	above and with the deep waters that lie **b;**	9393
Jos	2:11	in heaven above and on the earth **b.**	4946+9393
	11: 3	and to the Hivites **b** Hermon in the region	9393
	11:17	in the Valley of Lebanon **b** Mount Hermon.	9393
	12: 3	and then southward **b** the slopes of Pisgah.	9393
	13: 5	the east, from Baal Gad **b** Mount Hermon	9393
Jdg	7: 8	the camp of Midian lay **b** him in the valley.	4946+9393
1Sa	7:11	along the way to a point **b** Beth Car.	4946+9393
1Ki	4:12	Beth Shan next to Zarethan **b** Jezreel,	4946+9393
	7:24	**B** the rim, gourds encircled it—	4946+9393
	7:29	and **b** the lions and bulls were wreaths	4946+9393
	8:23	like you in heaven above or on earth **b**	4946+9393
2Ki	19:30	of the house of Judah will take root **b**	4200+4752
2Ch	4: 3	**B** the rim, figures of bulls encircled it—	9393
Job	18:16	up **b** and his branches wither above.	4946+9393
	28: 5	is transformed **b** as by fire;	9393
Isa	14: 9	The grave **b** is all astir to meet you	4946+9393
	14:21	and the kings on the earth **b.**	141+2021+6584
	37:31	of the house of Judah will take root **b**	4200+4752
Jer	31:37	the earth **b** be searched out	4200+4752
Eze	26:20	I will make you dwell in the earth **b,**	9397
	31:14	for the earth **b,** among mortal men,	9397
	31:16	were consoled in the earth **b.**	9397
	31:18	down with the trees of Eden to the earth **b;**	9397
	32:18	of Egypt and consign to the earth **b** both her	9397
	32:24	down uncircumcised to the earth **b.**	9397
Am	2: 9	I destroyed his fruit above and his roots **b.**	4946+9393
Jnh	1: 5	But Jonah had gone **b** deck,	2021+3752+6208
Mk	14:66	While Peter was **b** in the courtyard,	3004
Jn	8:23	But he continued, "You are from **b;**	3004
Ac	2:19	the heaven above and signs on the earth **b,**	3004

BELSHAZZAR (6) [BELSHAZZAR'S]

Da	5: 1	King **B** gave a great banquet for a thousand	10109
	5: 2	While **B** was drinking his wine,	10109
	5: 9	So King **B** became even more terrified	10109
	5:22	"But you his son, O **B,**	10109
	5:30	That very night **B,** king of the Babylonians,	10105
	7: 1	In the first year of **B** king of Babylon,	10105

BELSHAZZAR'S (2) [BELSHAZZAR]

Da	5:29	Then at **B** command,	10109
	8: 1	In the third year of King **B** reign, I, Daniel,	1157

BELT (25) [BELTS]

Ex	12:11	**cloak tucked into** your **b,**	2520+5516
1Sa	18: 4	and even his sword, his bow and his **b.**	2512
2Sa	18:11	of silver and a **warrior's b."**	2514
	20: 8	over it at his waist was a **b** with a dagger	2512
1Ki	2: 5	that blood stained the **b** around his waist	2514
	18:46	**tucking** his **cloak** into *his* **b,**	5516+9113
2Ki	1: 8	with a garment of hair and with a leather **b**	2520+5516
	4:29	**"Tuck** your **cloak into** your **b,**	2520+5516
	9: 1	**"Tuck** *your* **cloak into** your **b,**	2520+5516
Ps	109:19	like a **b** tied forever around him.	4652
Isa	5:27	not a **b** is loosened at the waist,	258
	11: 5	Righteousness will be his **b** and	258+5516
Jer	13: 1	a linen **b** and put it around your waist,	258
	13: 2	So I bought a **b,** as the LORD directed,	258
	13: 4	"Take the **b** you bought and are wearing	258
	13: 6	"Go now to Perath and get the **b** I told you	258

Jer	13: 7	to Perath and dug up the **b** and took it from	258
	13:10	will be like this **b**—completely useless!	258
	13:11	For as a **b** is bound around a man's waist,	258
Da	10: 5	with a **b** of the finest gold around his waist.	2520
Mt	3: 4	and he had a leather **b** around his waist.	2438
Mk	1: 6	with a leather **b** around his waist;	2438
Ac	21:11	Coming over to us, he took Paul's **b,**	2438
	21:11	the owner of this **b** and will hand him over	2438
Eph	6:14	the **b** of truth buckled around your waist,	4019

BELTESHAZZAR (10)

Da	1: 7	to Daniel, the name **B;**	1171
	2:26	The king asked Daniel (also called **B**),	10108
	4: 8	(He is called **B,** after the name of my god,	10108
	4: 9	I said, "**B,** chief of the magicians,	10108
	4:18	Now, **B,** tell me what it means,	10108
	4:19	(also called **B**) was greatly perplexed for	10108
	4:19	So the king said, "**B,**	10108
	4:19	**B** answered, "My lord,	10108
	5:12	This man Daniel, whom the king called **B,**	10108
	10: 1	to Daniel (who was called **B**).	1171

BELTS (3) [BELT]

Eze	23:15	with **b** around their waists	258+2513
Mt	10: 9	or silver or copper in your **b;**	2438
Mk	6: 8	no bread, no bag, no money in your **b.**	2438

BEMOAN, BEMOANED, BEMOANING
(KJV) See MOURN, SHOW SYMPATHY

BEN HINNOM (10)

Jos	15: 8	Valley of **B** along the southern slope of	1208
	18:16	of the hill facing the Valley of **B,**	1208
2Ki	23:10	which was in the Valley of **B,**	1208
2Ch	28: 3	of **B** and sacrificed his sons in	1208
	33: 6	in the fire in the Valley of **B,**	1208
Jer	7:31	the Valley of **B** to burn their sons	1208
	7:32	or the Valley of **B,**	1208
	19: 2	and go out to the Valley of **B,**	1208
	19: 6	or the Valley of **B,**	1208
	32:35	for Baal in the Valley of **B**	1208

BEN-ABINADAB (1) [ABINADAB]

1Ki	4:11	**B**—in Naphoth Dor (he was married to	1203

BEN-AMMI (1)

Ge	19:38	and she named him **B;**	1214

BEN-DEKER (1)

1Ki	4: 9	**B**—in Makaz, Shaalbim,	1206

BEN-GEBER (1) [GEBER]

1Ki	4:13	**B**—in Ramoth Gilead	1205

BEN-HADAD (28) [BEN-HADAD'S, HADAD]

1Ki	15:18	and sent them to **B** son of Tabrimmon,	1207
	15:20	**B** agreed with King Asa and sent	1207
	20: 1	**B** king of Aram mustered his entire army.	1207
	20: 2	saying, "This is what **B** says:	1207
	20: 5	"This is what **B** says:	1207
	20: 9	They left and took the answer back to **B.**	2084S
	20:10	Then **B** sent another message to Ahab:	1207
	20:12	**B** heard this message while he and	NIH
	20:16	at noon while **B** and the 32 kings allied	1207
	20:17	Now **B** had dispatched scouts,	1207
	20:20	But **B** king of Aram escaped on horseback	1207
	20:26	The next spring **B** mustered the Arameans	1207
	20:30	And **B** fled to the city and hid in	1207
	20:32	"Your servant **B** says:	1207
	20:33	"Yes, your brother **B!**"	1207
	20:33	When **B** came out,	1207
	20:34	from your father," **B** offered.	NIH
2Ki	6:24	**B** king of Aram mobilized his entire army	1207
	8: 7	and **B** king of Aram was ill.	1207
	8: 9	"Your son **B** king of Aram has sent me	1207
	8:14	**B** asked, "What did Elisha say to you?"	NIH
	13: 3	of Hazael king of Aram and **B** his son.	1207
	13:24	and **B** his son succeeded him as king.	1207
	13:25	of Jehoahaz recaptured from **B** son	1207
2Ch	16: 2	and of his own palace and sent it to **B** king	1207
	16: 4	**B** agreed with King Asa and sent	1207
Jer	49:27	it will consume the fortresses of **B.**"	1207
Am	1: 4	that will consume the fortresses of **B.**	1207

BEN-HADAD'S (1) [BEN-HADAD]

1Ki	20: 9	So he replied to **B** messengers,	1207

BEN-HAIL (1)

2Ch	17: 7	of his reign he sent his officials **B,**	1211

BEN-HANAN (1) [HANAN]

1Ch	4:20	Amnon, Rinnah, **B** and Tilon.	1212

BEN-HESED (1)

1Ki	4:10	**B**—in Arubboth (Socoh	1213

BEN-HUR (1) [HUR]

1Ki	4: 8	These are their names: **B**—	1210

BEN-ONI (1)
Ge 35:18   she named her son **B**.   1204

BEN-ZOHETH (1)
1Ch 4:20   The descendants of Ishi: Zoheth and **B**.   1209

BENAIAH (45)
2Sa	8:18	**B** son of Jehoiada was over the Kerethites	1226
	20:23	**B** son of Jehoiada was over the Kerethites	1225
	23:20	**B** son of Jehoiada was a valiant fighter	1226
	23:21	**B** went against him with a club.	NIH
	23:22	the exploits of **B** son of Jehoiada;	1226
	23:30	**B** the Pirathonite, Hiddai from the ravines	1226
1Ki	1: 8	But Zadok the priest, **B** son of Jehoiada,	1226
	1:10	not invite Nathan the prophet or **B** or	1226
	1:26	and **B** son of Jehoiada,	1226
	1:32	Nathan the prophet and **B** son of Jehoiada."	1226
	1:36	**B** son of Jehoiada answered the king,	1226
	1:38	Nathan the prophet, **B** son of Jehoiada,	1226
	1:44	Nathan the prophet, **B** son of Jehoiada,	1226
	2:25	So King Solomon gave orders to **B** son	1226
	2:29	Then Solomon ordered **B** son of Jehoiada,	1226
	2:30	So **B** entered the tent of the LORD	1226
	2:30	**B** reported to the king,	1226
	2:31	the king commanded **B**, "Do as he says.	2257S
	2:34	So **B** son of Jehoiada went up and struck	1226
	2:35	The king put **B** son of Jehoiada over	1226
	2:46	king gave the order to **B** son of Jehoiada.	1226
	4: 4	**B** son of Jehoiada—	1226
1Ch	4:36	Jeshohaiah, Asaiah, Adiel, Jesimiel, **B**,	1225
	11:22	**B** son of Jehoiada was a valiant fighter	1225
	11:23	**B** went against him with a club.	NIH
	11:24	the exploits of **B** son of Jehoiada;	1226
	11:31	of Ribai from Gibeah in Benjamin, **B**	1225
	15:18	Eliab, **B**, Maaseiah, Mattithiah, Eliphelehu,	1226
	15:20	and **B** were to play the lyres according	1225
	15:24	**B** and Eliezer the priests were	1226
	16: 5	Mattithiah, Eliab, **B**, Obed-Edom and Jeiel.	1226
	16: 6	**B** and Jahaziel the priests were to blow	1226
	18:17	**B** son of Jehoiada was over the Kerethites	1226
	27: 5	was **B** son of Jehoiada the priest.	1226
	27: 6	This was the **B** who was a mighty man	1226
	27:14	was **B** the Pirathonite, an Ephraimite.	1225
	27:34	by Jehoiada son of **B** and by Abiathar.	1226
2Ch	20:14	the son of **B**, the son of Jeiel,	1225
	31:13	and **B** were supervisors under Conaniah	1226
Ezr	10:25	Mijamin, Eleazar, Malkijah and **B**.	1225
	10:30	Adna, Kelal, **B**, Maaseiah, Mattaniah,	1225
	10:35	**B**, Bedeiah, Keluhi,	1225
	10:43	Zabad, Zebina, Jaddai, Joel and **B**.	1225
Eze	11: 1	of Azzur and Pelatiah son of **B**,	1226
	11:13	Pelatiah son of **B** died.	1225

BENCHES (2)
Mt	21:12	the tables of the money changers and the **b**	2756
Mk	11:15	the tables of the money changers and the **b**	2756

BEND (9) [BENDING, BENT]
Ge	49:15	he will **b** his shoulder to the burden	5742
2Sa	22:35	my arms *can* **b** a bow of bronze.	5737
Ps	7:12	he will **b** and string his bow.	2005
	11: 2	For look, the wicked **b** their bows;	2005
	18:34	my arms *can* **b** a bow of bronze.	5737
	37:14	The wicked draw the sword and **b** the bow	2005
Isa	65:12	and you will all **b** down for the slaughter;	4156
Zec	9:13	I will **b** Judah as I bend my bow and fill it	2005
	9:13	I will bend Judah as I **b** my bow and fill it	NIH

BENDING (1) [BEND]
Lk 24:12   **B** over, he saw the strips of linen lying   4160

BENE BERAK (1)
Jos 19:45   Jehud, **B**, Gath Rimmon,   1222

BENE JAAKAN (2) [JAAKANITES]
Nu	33:31	and camped at **B**.	1223
	33:32	They left **B** and camped	1223

BENEATH (22) [UNDERNEATH]
Ex	20: 4	on the earth **b** or in the waters below.	4946+9393
Lev	26:19	like iron and the **ground** *b* you like bronze.	AIT
Dt	5: 8	on the earth **b** or in the waters below.	4946+9393
	28:23	the ground **b** you iron.	9393
2Sa	22:37	You broaden the path **b** me,	9393
	22:39	they fell **b** my feet.	9393
1Ki	8: 6	and put it **b** the wings of the cherubim.	9393
2Ch	5: 7	and put it **b** the wings of the cherubim.	9393
Job	26: 5	those **b** the waters and all that live in them.	4946+9393
	37: 3	He unleashes his lightning **b**	9393
Ps	18:36	You broaden the path **b** me,	9393
	18:38	they fell **b** my feet.	9393
	45: 5	let the nations fall **b** your feet.	9393
Isa	14:11	maggots are spread out **b** you	9393
	44:23	shout aloud, O earth **b**;	9397
	51: 6	look at the earth **b**;	4946+9393
Eze	10: 2	"Go in among the wheels **b** the cherubim.	9393
	10:20	These were the living creatures I had seen **b**	9393
	24: 5	Pile wood **b** it for the bones;	9393
Joel	1:17	The seeds are shriveled **b** the clods.	9393
Jnh	2: 6	the earth **b** barred me in forever.	NIH

BENEFACTORS (1)
Lk 22:25   over them call themselves **B**.   2309

BENEFICIAL (2) [BENEFIT]
1Co	6:12	but not everything *is* **b**.	5237
	10:23	but not everything **is b**.	5237

BENEFIT (16) [BENEFICIAL, BENEFITED, BENEFITS]
Job	22: 2	"Can a man **be of b** to God?	6122
	22: 2	*Can* even a wise man **b** him?	6122
Ecc	5:11	And what **b** are they to the owner except	4179
Isa	38:11	it was for my **b** that I suffered such anguish.	8934
	57:12	and *they will* not **b** you.	3603
Jer	23:32	"they do not **b** these people **in the least**,"	3603+3603
Jn	11:42	but I said this **for the b** of	1328
	12:30	Jesus said, "This voice came **for** your **b**,	1328
Ro	6:21	What **b** did you reap at that time from	2843
	6:22	the **b** you reap leads to holiness,	2843
1Co	4: 6	to myself and Apollos **for** your **b**,	1328
2Co	1:15	I planned to visit you first so that *you might* **b** twice.	2400+5921
	4:15	All this is **for** your **b**,	1328
Eph	4:29	that *it may* **b** those who listen.	1443+5921
1Ti	6: 2	because those who **b**	514
Phm	1:20	*I may have* some **b** from you in the Lord;	3949

BENEFITED (1) [BENEFIT]
1Sa 19: 4   and what he has done has **b** you greatly.   3202

BENEFITS (5) [BENEFIT]
Dt	18: 8	He is to share equally in their **b**,	2750
Ps	103: 2	O my soul, and forget not all his **b**—	1691
Pr	11:17	A kind man **b** himself,	1694
Ecc	7:11	is a good thing and **b** those who see the sun.	3463
Jn	4:38	and you *have* **reaped the b** of their labor."	1656

BENINU (1)
Ne 10:13   Hodiah, Bani and **B**.   1231

BENJAMIN (136) [BENJAMIN'S, BENJAMITE, BENJAMITES]
Ge	35:18	But his father named him **B**.	1228
	35:24	The sons of Rachel: Joseph and **B**.	1228
	42: 4	But Jacob did not send **B**, Joseph's brother,	1228
	42:36	and now you want to take **B**.	1228
	43:14	and **B** come back with you.	1228
	43:15	the amount of silver, and **B** also.	1228
	43:16	When Joseph saw **B** with them,	1228
	43:29	As he looked about and saw his brother **B**,	1228
	45:12	and so can my brother **B**,	1228
	45:14	around his brother **B** and wept,	1228
	45:14	and **B** embraced him, weeping.	1228
	45:22	to **B** he gave three hundred shekels of silver	1228
	46:19	sons of Jacob's wife Rachel: Joseph and **B**.	1228
	46:21	The sons of **B**:	1228
	49:27	"**B** is a ravenous wolf;	1228
Ex	1: 3	Issachar, Zebulun and **B**;	1228
Nu	1:11	from **B**, Abidan son of Gideoni;	1228
	1:36	From the descendants of **B**:	1228
	1:37	number from the tribe of **B** was 35,400.	1228
	2:22	The tribe of **B** will be next.	1228
	2:22	The leader of the people of **B** is Abidan son	1228
	7:60	the leader of the people of **B**,	1228
	10:24	over the division of the tribe of **B**.	1201+1228
	13: 9	from the tribe of **B**, Palti son of Raphu;	1228
	26:38	The descendants of **B** by their clans were:	1228
	26:41	These were the clans of **B**;	1201+1228
	34:21	Elidad son of Kislon, from the tribe of **B**;	1228
Dt	27:12	Levi, Judah, Issachar, Joseph and **B**.	1228
	33:12	About **B** he said:	1228
Jos	18:11	The lot came up for the tribe of **B**,	1201+1228
	18:20	the inheritance of the clans of **B**	1201+1228
	18:21	The tribe of **B**, clan by clan,	1201+1228
	18:28	the inheritance of **B** for its clans.	1201+1228
	21: 4	from the tribes of Judah, Simeon and **B**.	1228
	21:17	from the tribe of **B** they gave them Gibeon,	1228
Jdg	1:21	**B** was with the people who followed you.	1228
	10: 9	**B** and the house of Ephraim;	1228
	19:14	and the sun set as they neared Gibeah in **B**.	1228
	20: 4	"I and my concubine came to Gibeah in **B**	1228
	20:10	when the army arrives at Gibeah in **B**,	1228
	20:12	throughout the tribe of **B**,	1228
	20:17	Israel, apart from **B**, mustered four hundred thousand swordsmen,	1228
	20:24	drew near to **B** the second day.	1201+1228
	20:28	up again to battle with **B** our brother,	1201+1228
	20:35	The LORD defeated **B** before Israel,	1228
	20:36	the men of Israel had given way before **B**,	1228
	20:41	and the men of **B** were terrified,	1228
	20:48	to **B** and put all the towns to the sword	1201+1228
	21:15	The people grieved for **B**,	1228
	21:16	"With the women of **B** destroyed,	1228
	21:21	the girls of Shiloh and go to the land of **B**.	1228
1Sa	9: 1	the son of Aphiah of **B**.	408+1201+3549
	9: 4	Then he passed through the territory of **B**,	3549
	9:16	a man from the land of **B**.	1228
	9:21	the least of all the clans of the tribe of **B**?	1228
	10: 2	at Zelzah on the border of **B**.	1228
	10:20	the tribe of **B** was chosen.	1228
	10:21	Then he brought forward the tribe of **B**,	1228
	13: 2	with Jonathan at Gibeah in **B**.	1228
	13:15	and went up to Gibeah in **B**,	1228
	13:16	with them were staying in Gibeah in **B**,	1228
	14:16	at Gibeah in **B** saw the army melting away	1228
	22: 7	Saul said to them, "Listen, **men of B**!	1229
2Sa	2: 9	and also over Ephraim, **B** and all Israel.	1228
	2:15	twelve men for **B** and Ish-Bosheth son	1228
	2:25	Then the men of **B** rallied behind Abner.	1228
	3:19	that Israel and the whole house of **B** wanted	1228
	4: 2	the Beerothite from the tribe of **B**—	1228
	4: 2	Beeroth is considered part of **B**,	1228
	21:14	Saul's father Kish, at Zela in **B**,	824+1228
	23:29	Ithai son of Ribai from Gibeah in **B**,	1201+1228
1Ki	4:18	Shimei son of Ela—in **B**;	1228
	12:21	whole house of Judah and the tribe of **B**—	1228
	12:23	to the whole house of Judah and **B**,	1228
	15:22	With them King Asa built up Geba in **B**	1228
1Ch	2: 2	Dan, Joseph, **B**, Naphtali, Gad and Asher.	1228
	6:60	the tribe of **B** they were given Gibeon,	1228
	6:65	Simeon and **B** they allotted	1201+1228
	7: 6	Three sons of **B**: Bela, Beker and Jediael.	1228
	7:10	The sons of Bilhan: Jeush, **B**, Ehud,	1228
	8: 1	**B** was the father of Bela his firstborn,	1228
	8:40	All these were the descendants of **B**.	1228
	9: 3	Those from Judah, from **B**,	1201+1228
	9: 9	the **people from B**,	278+2157
	11:31	Ithai son of Ribai from Gibeah in **B**,	1201+1228
	12: 2	of Saul from the **tribe of B**):	1228
	12:29	men of **B**, Saul's kinsmen—	1228
	21: 6	not include Levi and **B** in the numbering,	1228
	27:21	Iddo son of Zechariah; over **B**:	1228
2Ch	11: 1	he mustered the house of Judah and **B**—	1228
	11: 3	and to all the Israelites in Judah and **B**,	1228
	11:10	These were fortified cities in Judah and **B**.	1228
	11:12	So Judah and **B** were his.	1228
	11:23	throughout the districts of Judah and **B**,	1228
	14: 8	two hundred and eighty thousand from **B**,	1228
	15: 2	"Listen to me, Asa and all Judah and **B**.	1228
	15: 8	and **B** and from the towns he had captured	1228
	15: 9	Then he assembled all Judah and **B** and	1228
	17:17	From **B**: Eliada, a valiant soldier,	1228
	25: 5	of hundreds for all Judah and **B**.	1228
	31: 1	and the altars throughout Judah and **B** and	1228
	34: 9	and from all the people of Judah and **B** and	1228
	34:32	in Jerusalem and **B** pledge themselves to it;	1228
Ezr	1: 5	Then the family heads of Judah and **B**,	1228
	4: 1	heard that the exiles were building	1228
	10: 9	of Judah and **B** had gathered in Jerusalem.	1228
	10:32	**B**, Malluch and Shemariah.	1228
Ne	3:23	**B** and Hasshub made repairs in front	1228
	11: 4	from both Judah and **B** lived in Jerusalem):	1228
	11: 7	From the descendants of **B**:	1228
	11:36	of the Levites of Judah settled in **B**.	1228
	12:34	Judah, **B**, Shemaiah, Jeremiah,	1228
Est	2: 5	citadel of Susa a Jew of the **tribe of B**,	408+3549
Ps	68:27	There is the little **tribe of B**, leading them,	1228
	80: 2	before Ephraim, **B** and Manasseh.	1228
Jer	1: 1	the priests at Anathoth in the territory of **B**.	1228
	6: 1	"Flee for safety, people of **B**!	1228
	17:26	the territory of **B** and the western foothills,	1228
	20: 2	in the stocks at the Upper Gate of **B** at	1228
	32: 8	at Anathoth in the territory of **B**.	1228
	32:44	sealed and witnessed in the territory of **B**,	1228
	33:13	in the territory of **B**,	1228
	37:12	to go to the territory of **B** to get his share of	1228
	37:13	But when he reached the **B** Gate,	1228
	38: 7	While the king was sitting in the **B** Gate,	1228
Eze	48:22	the border of Judah and the border of **B**.	1228
	48:23	**B** will have one portion;	1228
	48:24	it will border the territory of **B** from east	1228
	48:32	the gate of **B** and the gate of Dan.	1228
Hos	5: 8	lead on, O **B**.	1228
Ob	19	and **B** will possess Gilead.	1228
Zec	14:10	the **B** Gate to the site of the First Gate,	1228
Ac	13:21	of the tribe *of* **B**, who ruled forty years.	1021
Ro	11: 1	from the tribe *of* **B**.	1021
Php	3: 5	of the people of Israel, of the tribe *of* **B**,	1021
Rev	7: 8	from the tribe *of* **B** 12,000.	1021

BENJAMIN'S (2) [BENJAMIN]
Ge	43:34	**B** portion was five times as much	1228
	44:12	And the cup was found in **B** sack.	1228

BENJAMITE (14) [BENJAMIN]
Jdg	3:15	a left-handed man, the son of Gera the **B**.	1229
	20:46	day twenty-five thousand **B** swordsmen fell,	1228
	21: 1	in marriage to a **B**."	1228
	21:17	The **B** survivors must have heirs,"	1228
	21:18	be anyone who gives a wife to a **B**.'	1228
1Sa	4:12	That same day a **B** ran from the battle line	408+1228
	9: 1	There was a **B**, a man of standing,	1228+4946
	9:21	Saul answered, "But am I not a **B**,	1229
2Sa	16: 5	How much more, then, this **B**!	1229
	16:11	Shimei son of Gera, the **B** from Bahurim,	1229
	20: 1	Sheba son of Bicri, a **B**,	408+3549
1Ki	2: 8	Shimei son of Gera, the **B** from Bahurim,	1229
1Ch	27:12	was Abiezer the Anathothite, a **B**.	1229
Ps	7: T	to the LORD concerning Cush, a **B**.	1229

BENJAMITES (33) [BENJAMIN]
Jdg	1:21	The **B**, however, failed to dislodge	1201+1228
	1:21	the Jebusites live there with the **B**.	1201+1228
	19:16	in Gibeah (the men of the place were **B**),	1229

Jdg	20: 3	(The **B** heard that the Israelites had gone up	1201+1228
	20:13	**B** would not listen to their fellow Israelites.	1201+1228
	20:15	**B** mobilized twenty-six thousand swordsmen	1201+1228
	20:18	shall go first to fight against the **B**?"	1201+1228
	20:20	to fight the **B** and took up battle positions	1228
	20:21	The **B** came out of Gibeah and cut	1201+1228
	20:23	up again to battle against the **B**,	1201+1228
	20:25	**B** came out from Gibeah to oppose them,	1228
	20:30	went up against the **B** on the third day	1201+1228
	20:31	The **B** came out to meet them	1201+1228
	20:32	While the **B** were saying,	1201+1228
	20:34	The fighting was so heavy that the **B** did	2156S
	20:35	**B**, all armed with swords.	1228
	20:36	Then the **B** saw that they were beaten.	1201+1228
	20:39	The **B** had begun to inflict casualties on	1228
	20:40	the **B** turned and saw the smoke of	1228
	20:43	They surrounded the **B**,	1228
	20:44	Eighteen thousand **B** fell,	1228
	20:45	after the **B** as far as Gidom and struck	2257S
	21: 6	Israelites grieved for their brothers, the **B**.	1228
	21:13	peace to the **B** at the rock of Rimmon.	1201+1228
	21:14	the **B** returned at that time and were given	1228
	21:20	So they instructed the **B**, saying,	1201+1228
	21:23	So that is what the **B** did.	1201+1228
2Sa	2:31	three hundred and sixty **B** who were with Abner.	408+1228+4946
	3:19	Abner also spoke to the **B** in person.	1228
	19:17	With him were a thousand **B**,	1228+4946
1Ch	9: 7	Of the **B**: Sallu son of Meshullam,	1201+1228
	12:16	Other **B** and some men from Judah	1201+1228
Ne	11:31	The descendants of the **B** from Geba lived	1228

BENO (2)

1Ch	24:26	The son of Jaaziah: **B**.	1217
	24:27	**B**, Shoham, Zaccur and Ibri.	1217

BENOTH   See SUCCOTH BENOTH

BENT (21) [BEND]

Ex	10:10	Clearly you are **b** on evil.	5584+7156
1Sa	24: 9	'David *is* **b** on harming you'?	1335
1Ki	18:42	**b** down to the ground and put his face	1566
Ps	44:16	because of the enemy, *who is* **b** on revenge.	5933
	69:23	and their backs *be* **b** forever.	5048
	106:43	but they were **b** on rebellion	928+6783
Pr	16:30	he who purses his lips *is* **b** on evil.	3983
	17:11	An evil man *is* **b** only on rebellion;	1335
Isa	21:15	from the **b** bow and from the heat of battle,	2005
	51:13	who *is* **b** on destruction?	3922
Eze	22: 9	In you are slanderous men **b** on	5100
Da	11:27	The two kings, with their hearts **b** on evil,	4200
Hos	11: 4	from their neck and **b** down to feed them.	5742
Hab	1: 9	they all come **b** on violence.	4200
Lk	4:39	So he **b** over her and rebuked the fever,	2392
	13:11	She was **b** over and could not straighten up	5174
Jn	8: 6	But Jesus **b** down and started to write on	3252
	20: 5	He **b** over and looked in at the strips	4160
	20:11	she **b** over to look into the tomb	4160
Ro	11:10	and their backs *be* **b** forever."	5159
Rev	6: 2	he rode out as a conqueror **b** on conquest.	2671

BEON (1)

Nu	32: 3	Heshbon, Elealeh, Sebam, Nebo and **B**—	1274

BEOR (11)

Ge	36:32	Bela son of **B** became king of Edom.	1242
Nu	22: 5	to summon Balaam son of **B**,	1242
	24: 3	"The oracle of Balaam son of **B**,	1242
	24:15	"The oracle of Balaam son of **B**,	1242
	31: 8	also killed Balaam son of **B** with the sword.	1242
Dt	23: 4	of **B** from Pethor in Aram Naharaim	1242
Jos	13:22	to the sword Balaam son of **B**,	1242
	24: 9	for Balaam son of **B** to put a curse on you.	1242
1Ch	1:43	Bela son of **B**,	1242
Mic	6: 5	and what Balaam son of **B** answered.	1242
2Pe	2:15	to follow the way of Balaam son *of* **B**,	1027

BERA (1)

Ge	14: 2	went to war against **B** king of Sodom,	1396

BERACAH (3)

1Ch	12: 3	**B**, Jehu the Anathothite,	1389
2Ch	20:26	in the Valley of **B**,	1390
	20:26	This is why it is called the Valley of **B**	1390

BERACHIAH, BERECHIAH (KJV) See BEREKIAH

BERAIAH (1)

1Ch	8:21	**B** and Shimrath were the sons of Shimei.	1349

BERAK   See BENE BERAK

BEREA (4) [BEREANS]

Ac	17:10	the brothers sent Paul and Silas away to **B**.	1023
	17:13	the word of God at **B**,	1023

Ac	17:14	but Silas and Timothy stayed at **B**.	1695S
	20: 4	by Sopater son of Pyrrhus **from B**,	1024

BEREANS (1) [BEREA]

Ac	17:11	Now the **B** were of more noble character	4047S

BEREAVE (1) [BEREAVED, BEREAVEMENT, BEREAVES]

Hos	9:12	*I will* **b** them of every one.	8897

BEREAVED (3) [BEREAVE]

Ge	43:14	As for me, if *I am* **b**, I am bereaved."	8897
	43:14	As for me, if I am bereaved, *I am* **b**."	8897
Isa	49:21	I was **b** and barren;	8892

BEREAVEMENT (2) [BEREAVE]

Isa	49:20	during your **b** will yet say in your hearing,	8898
Jer	15: 7	*I will* **bring** **b** and destruction	8897

BEREAVES (1) [BEREAVE]

La	1:20	Outside, the sword **b**;	8897

BERED (2)

Ge	16:14	it is still there, between Kadesh and **B**.	1354
1Ch	7:20	Shuthelah, **B** his son, Tahath his son,	1355

BEREKIAH (12)

1Ch	3:20	Ohel, **B**, Hasadiah and Jushab-Hesed.	1392
	6:39	Asaph son of **B**, the son of Shimea,	1393
	9:16	and **B** son of Asa, the son of Elkanah,	1392
	15:17	from his brothers, Asaph son of **B**;	1393
	15:23	**B** and Elkanah were to be doorkeepers for	1392
2Ch	28:12	**B** son of Meshillemoth,	1393
Ne	3: 4	Next to him Meshullam son of **B**,	1392
	3:30	Meshullam son of **B** made repairs opposite his living quarters.	1392
	6:18	the daughter of Meshullam son of **B**.	1392
Zec	1: 1	to the prophet Zechariah son of **B**, the son	1392
	1: 7	to the prophet Zechariah son of **B**,	1393
Mt	23:35	to the blood of Zechariah son *of* **B**,	974

BERI (1) [BERITES]

1Ch	7:36	Suah, Harnepher, Shual, **B**, Imrah,	1373

BERIAH (11) [BERIITE]

Ge	46:17	Imnah, Ishvah, Ishvi and **B**.	1380
	46:17	The sons of **B**: Heber and Malkiel.	1380
Nu	26:44	through **B**, the Beriite clan;	1380
	26:45	and through the descendants of **B**:	1380
1Ch	7:23	He named him **B**,	1380
	7:30	sons of Asher: Imnah, Ishvah, Ishvi and **B**.	1380
	7:31	The sons of **B**:	1380
	8:13	and **B** and Shema,	1380
	8:16	Ishpah and Joha were the sons of **B**.	1380
	23:10	sons of Shimei: Jahath, Ziza, Jeush and **B**.	1380
	23:11	but Jeush and **B** did not have many sons;	1380

BERIITE (1) [BERIAH]

Nu	26:44	through Beriah, the **B** clan;	1381

BERITES (1) [BERI]

2Sa	20:14	and through the entire region of the **B**,	1379

BERITH (KJV) See EL-BERITH

BERNICE (3)

Ac	25:13	and **B** arrived at Caesarea	1022
	25:23	and **B** came with great pomp and entered	1022
	26:30	the governor and **B** and those sitting	1022

BERODACHBALADAN (KJV) See MERODACH-BALADAN

BEROTHAH (1)

Eze	47:16	**B** and Sibraim (which lies on the border	1363

BEROTHAI (1) [BEROTHITE]

2Sa	8: 8	From Tebah and **B**,	1408

BEROTHITE (1) [BEROTHAI]

1Ch	11:39	the **B**, the armor-bearer of Joab son	1409

BERRIES (KJV) See OLIVES

BERYL (4)

Ex	28:17	a topaz and a **b**;	1403
	39:10	a topaz and a **b**;	1403
Eze	28:13	onyx and jasper, sapphire, turquoise and **b**.	1404
Rev	21:20	the seventh chrysolite, the eighth **b**,	1039

BESAI (2)

Ezr	2:49	Uzza, Paseah, **B**,	1234
Ne	7:52	**B**, Meunim, Nephussim,	1234

BESEECH, BESEECHING, BESOUGHT
(KJV) See APPEAL, ASKING, BEG, BEGGED, PLEAD, PLEASE, URGE

BESET (2)

Ps	41: 8	"A vile disease *has* **b** him;	3668
	55: 5	Fear and trembling *have* **b** me;	928+995

BESIDE (88) [BESIDES, SIDE]

Ge	16: 7	it was the spring that is **b** the road to Shur.	928
	23: 3	Abraham rose from **b** his dead wife	6584+7156
	24:13	See, I am standing **b** this spring,	6584
	24:43	See, I am standing **b** this spring;	6584
	38:21	"Where is the shrine prostitute who was **b**	6584
	39:15	he left his cloak **b** me and ran out of	725
	39:16	She kept his cloak **b** her	725
	39:18	he left his cloak **b** me and ran out of	725
	41: 3	the Nile and stood **b** those on the riverbank.	725
	48: 7	So I buried her there **b** the road to Ephrath"	928
Lev	6:10	on the altar and place them **b** the altar.	725
	10:12	and eat it prepared without yeast **b** the altar,	725
Nu	23: 3	"Stay here **b** your offering while I go aside.	6584
	23: 6	and found him standing **b** his offering,	6584
	23:15	"Stay here **b** your offering while I meet	6584
	23:17	and found him standing **b** his offering,	6584
	24: 6	like gardens **b** a river,	6584
	24: 6	like cedars **b** the waters.	6584
Dt	12:27	of your sacrifices must be poured **b** the altar	6584
	16:21	Do not set up any wooden Asherah pole **b**	725
	22: 6	If you come across a bird's nest **b** the road,	928
	31:26	"Take this Book of the Law and place it **b** the ark of the covenant	4946+7396
Jdg	6:25	to Baal and cut down the Asherah pole **b** it.	6584
	6:28	with the Asherah pole **b** it cut down and	6584
	6:30	and cut down the Asherah pole **b** it."	6584
	9: 6	and Beth Millo gathered **b** the great tree at	6640
1Sa	1:26	the woman who stood here **b** you praying	6640
	5: 2	into Dagon's temple and set it **b** Dagon.	725
	6: 8	put **b** it in a chest	4946+7396
	6:14	and there it stopped **b** a large rock.	9004
	26: 3	Saul made his camp **b** the road on the hill	5921
2Sa	6: 7	down and he died there **b** the ark of God.	6640
	12:17	of his household stood **b** him to get him up	6584
	18: 4	So the king stood **b** the gate while all	448+3338
	20:11	One of Joab's men stood **b** Amasa and said,	6584
1Ki	1: 2	She can lie **b** him so that our lord	928+2668
	2:29	the tent of the Lᴏʀᴅ and was **b** the altar.	725
	10:19	with a lion standing **b** each of them.	725
	13:24	both the donkey and the lion standing **b** it.	725
	13:25	with the lion standing **b** the body,	725
	13:28	with the donkey and the lion standing **b** it.	725
	13:31	lay my bones **b** his bones.	725
2Ki	11:14	The officers and the trumpeters were **b**	448
	12: 9	He placed it **b** the altar,	725
2Ch	9:18	with a lion standing **b** each of them.	6584
	23:13	The officers and the trumpeters were **b**	6584
Ne	2: 6	Then the king, with the queen sitting **b** him,	725
	3:17	**B** him, Hashabiah, ruler of half the district	3338+6584
	3:23	made repairs **b** his house.	725
	8: 4	**B** him on his right stood Mattithiah,	725
Job	18: 6	the lamp **b** him goes out.	6584
Ps	23: 2	he leads me **b** quiet waters,	6584
	110: 7	He will drink from a brook **b** the way;	928
Pr	8:34	the doors leading into the city, at	3338+4200
SS	1: 7	Why should I be like a veiled woman **b**	6584
Isa	49: 9	"They will feed **b** the roads and find pasture	6584
	49:10	on them will guide them and lead them **b**	6584
Jer	17: 2	and Asherah poles **b** the spreading trees and	6584
	31: 9	I will lead them **b** streams of water on	448
	36:21	the king and all the officials standing **b** him.	4946+6584
Eze	1:15	I saw a wheel on the ground **b** each creature	725
	1:19	the wheels **b** them moved;	725
	3:13	and the sound of the wheels **b** them,	4200+6645
	9: 2	They came in and stood **b** the bronze altar.	725
	10: 6	the man went in and stood **b** a wheel.	725
	10: 9	and I saw **b** the cherubim four wheels,	725
	10: 9	one **b** each of the cherubim.	725
	10:16	the wheels **b** them moved;	725
	11:22	the cherubim, with the wheels **b** them,	4200+6645
	32:13	from **b** abundant waters no longer to	6584
	39:15	he will set up a marker **b** it until	725
	43: 6	While the man was standing **b** me,	725
	43: 8	to my threshold and their doorposts **b**	725
Da	8: 2	in the vision I was **b** the Ulai Canal.	6584
	8: 3	standing **b** the canal,	4200+7156
	8: 6	the two-horned ram I had seen standing **b** the canal	4200+7156
Am	2: 8	down **b** every altar on garments taken	725
Zec	4:12	"What are these two olive branches **b**	928+3338
Mt	4:18	As Jesus was walking **b** the Sea of Galilee,	4123
Mk	1:16	As Jesus **walked b** the Sea of Galilee,	4135
	2:13	Once again Jesus went out **b** the lake.	4123
Lk	9:47	took a little child and had him stand **b** him.	4123
	24: 4	that gleamed like lightning **stood b** them.	2392
Ac	1:10	in white **stood b** them	4225
	5:10	carried her out and buried her **b**	4639
	22:13	He **stood b** me and said, 'Brother Saul,	2392
	27:23	and whom I serve **stood b** me	4225
Rev	15: 2	standing **b** the sea,	2093

BESIDES (42) [BESIDE]

Ge	20:12	**B**, she really is my sister,	1685+2256
	26: 1	**b** the earlier famine of Abraham's time—	963+4200+4946
	31:50	or if you take any wives **b** my daughters.	6584
	38:22	**B**, the men who lived there said,	1685+2256
	46:15	**b** his daughter Dinah.	2256
	50: 8	**b** all the members of Joseph's household	2256
Ex	12:37	**b** women and children.	963+4200+4946
Nu	28:15	**B** the regular burnt offering	6584
Dt	4: 35	**b** him there is no other.	963+4200+4946
	32:39	There is no god **b** me.	6643
Jos	17: 5	of land **b** Gilead and Bashan east of	963+4200
1Sa	2: 2	there is no one **b** you;	1194
2Sa	2:30	**B** Asahel, nineteen of David's	2256
	17: 8	**B**, your father is an experienced fighter;	2256
	19:43	and **b**, we have a greater claim	1685
	22:32	For who is God **b** the LORD?	1187+4946
1Ki	10:13	**b** what he had given her out	963+4200+4946
	11: 1	Solomon, however, loved many foreign	
		women **b** Pharaoh's daughter—	2256
2Ki	21:16	**b** the sin that he had caused Judah to	
		commit,	963+4200+4946
1Ch	3: 9	**b** his sons by his concubines,	963+4200+4946
	29: 3	**B**, in my devotion to the temple	6388
2Ch	17:19	**b** those he stationed in the fortified cities	
			963+4200+4946
Ezr	2:65	**b** their 7,337 menservants	963+4200+4946
	10:13	**B**, this matter cannot be taken care of	2256
Ne	7:67	**b** their 7,337 menservants	963+4200+4946
Ps	18:31	For who is God **b** the LORD?	1187+4946
	73:25	And earth has nothing I desire **b** you.	6640
	120: 3	What will he do to you, and what **more b**,	3578
Isa	26:13	other lords **b** you have ruled over us,	2314
	44: 8	Is there any God **b** me?	1187+4946
	45: 6	men may know there is none **b** me.	1187
	47: 8	'I am, and there is none **b** me.	6388
	47:10	'I am, and there is none **b** me.'	6388
	56: 8	to them **b** those already gathered."	4200
	64: 4	no eye has seen any God **b** you,	2314
Zep	2:15	"I am, and there is none **b** me."	6388
Mt	14:21	**b** women and children.	6006
	15:38	**b** women and children.	6006
Lk	16:26	And **b** all this,	1877
Ac	2:14	And **b**, he has brought Greeks into	2285
2Co	11:28	**B** everything else, I face daily the pressure	
		of my concern for all	3836+4211+6006
1Ti	5:13	**B**, they get into the habit of being idle	275

BESIEGE (10) [SIEGE]

Dt	20:19	that you **should b** them?	928+995+2021+5189
	28:52	*They will* **b** all the cities throughout	7674
1Sa	23: 8	down to Keilah to **b** David and his men.	7443
2Sa	12:28	and **b** the city and capture it.	2837+6584
2Ch	6:28	when enemies **b** them in any of their cities,	7443
Ps	27: 3	an army to me, my heart will not fear;	2837+6584
Isa	29: 2	Yet *I will* **b** Ariel;	7439
	29: 7	that attack her and her fortress and **b** her,	7439
Eze	4: 3	It will be under siege, and *you shall* **b** it.	7439
Lk	11:53	and *to* **b** him **with questions,**	694+4309+4498

BESIEGED (11) [SIEGE]

Jdg	9:50	Abimelech went to Thebez and **b** it	928+2837
1Sa	11: 1	up and **b** Jabesh Gilead.	2837+6584
2Sa	11: 1	the Ammonites and **b** Rabbah.	7443
	20:15	All the troops with Joab came and **b** Sheba	7443
1Ki	20: 1	he went up and **b** Samaria and attacked it.	7443
2Ki	16: 5	up to fight against Jerusalem and **b** Ahaz,	7443
1Ch	20: 1	and went to Rabbah and **b** it,	7443
Ps	31:21	to me when I was in a **b** city.	5189
La	3: 5	*He has* **b** me and surrounded me	1215+6584
Da	1: 1	of Babylon came to Jerusalem and **b** it.	7443
Zec	12: 2	Judah will be **b** as well as Jerusalem.	5189

BESIEGES (1) [SIEGE]

1Ki	8:37	an enemy **b** them in any of their cities,	7443

BESIEGING (7) [SIEGE]

1Ki	15:27	while Nadab and all Israel *were* **b** it.	7443
2Ki	24:11	up to the city while his officers *were* **b** it.	7443
Jer	4:16	'A **b** army is coming from a distant land,	7443
	21: 4	who are outside the wall **b** you.	7443
	21: 9	to the Babylonians who *are* **b** you will live;	7443
	32: 2	the king of Babylon *was* then **b** Jerusalem,	7443
	37: 5	Babylonians who *were* **b** Jerusalem heard	7443

BESODEIAH (1)

Ne	3: 6	of Paseah and Meshullam son of **B**.	1233

BESOM (KJV) See BROOM

BESOR (2)

1Sa	30: 9	with him came to the **B** Ravine,	1410
	30:21	and who were left behind at the **B** Ravine.	1410

BEST (69) [GOOD]

Ge	16: 6	"Do with her whatever you think **b**."	3202
	27:15	the **b** clothes of Esau her older son,	2776
	43:11	of the **b** products *of* the land in your bags	2380
	45:18	I will give you the **b** of the land of Egypt	3206
	45:20	because the **b** *of* all Egypt will be yours.' "	3206

Ge	45:23	ten donkeys loaded with the **b** things	3206
	47: 6	and your brothers in the **b** *part of* the land.	4774
	47:11	and gave them property in the **b** *part of*	4774
Ex	14: 7	He took six hundred of the **b** chariots,	1047
	15: 4	The **b** of Pharaoh's officers are drowned in	4436
	22: 5	from the **b** of his own field or vineyard.	4774
	23:19	"Bring the **b** of the firstfruits of your soil to	8040
	34:26	"Bring the **b** of the firstfruits of your soil to	8040
Nu	13:20	**Do** your **b** to bring back some of the fruit of	2616
	18:29	the LORD's portion the **b** and holiest part	2693
	18:30	'When you present the **b** part,	2693
	18:32	By presenting the **b** part of it you will not	2693
Dt	33:14	the **b** the sun brings forth and the finest	4458
	33:16	with the **b** gifts *of* the earth and its fullness	4458
	33:21	He chose the **b** land for himself;	8040
Jos	8: 3	his **b fighting men** and sent them out	1475+2657
	10: 7	including all the **b fighting men**.	1475+2657
Jdg	10:15	Do with us whatever you think **b**,	3202
Ru	3: 3	and put on your **b clothes**.	8529
1Sa	1:23	"Do what seems **b** to you,"	3202
	8:14	the **b** of your fields and vineyards	3202
	8:16	and maidservants and the **b** of your cattle	3202
	14:36	"Do whatever seems **b** to you,"	3202
	14:40	"Do what seems **b** to you," the men replied.	3202
	15: 9	the **b** of the sheep and cattle, the fat calves	4774
	15:15	the **b** of the sheep and cattle to sacrifice to	4774
	15:21	the **b** *of* what was devoted to God,	8040
	27: 1	The **b** thing I can do is to escape to the land	3202
2Sa	10: 9	of the **b** troops *in* Israel and deployed them	1047
	18: 4	"I will do whatever seems **b** to you."	3512
	23:20	He struck down two of Moab's **b** men.	738
1Ki	20: 3	and the **b** of your wives	3202
2Ki	10: 3	choose the **b** and most worthy	3202
	10: 5	you do whatever you think **b**."	3202
1Ch	11:22	He struck down two of Moab's **b** men.	738
	19:10	so he selected some of the **b** troops in Israel	1047
Ezr	7:18	then do whatever *seems* **b** with the rest of	10320
Est	2: 9	and her maids into the **b** *place in*	3202
	2: 9	in the king's **b** interest	8750
	8: 8	the Jews as seems **b** to you, and seal it with	3202
Pr	5: 9	lest you give your **b strength** to others	2086
SS	7: 9	and your mouth like the **b** wine.	3202
Isa	1:19	you will eat the **b** *from* the land;	3206
	25: 6	the **b** of meats and the finest of wines.	9043
	48:17	who teaches you *what is* **b** for you,	3603
Jer	18: 4	shaping it as seemed **b** to him.	3837
Eze	24: 4	Fill it with the **b** of these bones;	4436
	31:16	the choicest and **b** of Lebanon,	3202
	44:30	The **b** of all the firstfruits and	8040
	48:14	This is the **b** of the land and must not pass	8040
Da	11:15	even their **b** troops will not have	4436
Jnh	1:13	the men *did their* **b** to **row** back to land.	AIT
Mic	7: 4	The **b** *of* them is like a brier,	3202
Zec	11:12	I told them, "If you think it **b**,	3202
Lk	15:22	Bring the **b** robe and put it on him.	4755
Jn	2:10	but you have saved the **b** till now."	2819
2Co	5: 9	And here is my advice about what is **b**	5237
Php	1:10	you may be able to discern **what is b**	1422+3836
1Th	5:13	*we* **thought it b** to be left by ourselves	2305
2Ti	2:15	**Do** your **b** to present yourself to God	5079
	4: 9	**Do** your **b** to come to me quickly,	5079
	4:21	**Do** your **b** to get here before winter.	5079
Tit	3:12	**do** your **b** to come to me at Nicopolis,	5079
Heb	12:10	for a little while as they thought **b**;	NIG

BESTOW (6) [BESTOWED, BESTOWER, BESTOWING, BESTOWS]

Ps	3: 3	you **b** glory on me and lift up my head.	NIH
	31:19	which *you* **b** in the sight of men	7188
Isa	45: 4	**b** on you **a title of honor,**	4033
	61: 3	to **b** on them a crown of beauty instead	5989
	62: 2	that the mouth of the LORD *will* **b**.	5918
Jer	23: 2	on them, I *will* **b** punishment on you *for*	7212

BESTOWED (4) [BESTOW]

1Ch	29:25	and **b** on him royal splendor such	5989
Ps	21: 5	*you have* **b** on him splendor and majesty.	8751
	89:19	"I *have* **b** strength on a warrior;	8751
Jer	23: 2	and *have* not **b** care on them,"	7212

BESTOWER (1) [BESTOW]

Isa	23: 8	against Tyre, the **b** of **crowns**,	6497

BESTOWING (1) [BESTOW]

Pr	8:21	**b** wealth on those who love me	5706

BESTOWS (3) [BESTOW]

Job	5:10	He **b** rain on the earth;	5989
Ps	84:11	the LORD **b** favor and honor;	5989
	133: 3	For there the LORD **b** his blessing,	7422

BETEN (1)

Jos	19:25	Their territory included: Helkath, Hali, **B**,	1062

BETH (1)

1Sa	31:12	through the night to **B** Shan.	NIH

BETH ANATH (3) [ANATH]

Jos	19:38	Horem, **B** and Beth Shemesh.	1117
Jdg	1:33	in Beth Shemesh or **B**;	1117
	1:33	and **B** became forced laborers.	1117

BETH ANOTH (1)

Jos	15:59	**B** and Eltekon—	1116

BETH ARABAH (4) [ARABAH]

Jos	15: 6	of **B** to the Stone of Bohan son	1098
	15:61	In the desert: **B**, Middin, Secacah,	1098
	18:18	of **B** and on down into the Arabah.	1098
	18:22	**B**, Zemaraim, Bethel,	1098

BETH ARBEL (1)

Hos	10:14	as Shalman devastated **B** on the day	1079

BETH ASHBEA (1)

1Ch	4:21	the clans of the linen workers at **B**,	1080

BETH AVEN (7) [AVEN]

Jos	7: 2	which is near **B** to the east of Bethel,	1077
	18:12	coming out at the desert of **B**.	1077
1Sa	13: 5	camped at Micmash, east of **B**.	1077
	14:23	and the battle moved on beyond **B**.	1077
Hos	4:15	do not go up to **B**.	1077
	5: 8	Raise the battle cry in **B**;	1077
	10: 5	for the calf-idol of **B**.	1077

BETH AZMAVETH (1) [AZMAVETH]

Ne	7:28	of **B** 42	1115

BETH BAAL MEON (1) [BAAL MEON]

Jos	13:17	Bamoth Baal, **B**,	1081

BETH BARAH (2)

Jdg	7:24	ahead of them as far as **B**."	1083
	7:24	the waters of the Jordan as far as **B**.	1083

BETH BIRI (1)

1Ch	4:31	Hazar Susim, **B** and Shaaraim.	1082

BETH CAR (1)

1Sa	7:11	along the way to a point below **B**.	1105

BETH DAGON (2) [DAGON]

Jos	15:41	**B**, Naamah and Makkedah—	1087
	19:27	It then turned east toward **B**,	1087

BETH DIBLATHAIM (1) [ALMON DIBLATHAIM]

Jer	48:22	to Dibon, Nebo and **B**,	1086

BETH EDEN (1) [EDEN]

Am	1: 5	the one who holds the scepter in **B**.	1114

BETH EKED (2)

2Ki	10:12	At **B** of the Shepherds,	1118
	10:14	by the well of **B**—	1118

BETH EMEK (1)

Jos	19:27	and went north to **B** and Neiel,	1097

BETH EZEL (1) [EZEL]

Mic	1:11	**B** is in mourning;	1089

BETH GADER (1)

1Ch	2:51	and Hareph the father of **B**.	1084

BETH GAMUL (1) [GAMUL]

Jer	48:23	to Kiriathaim, **B** and Beth Meon,	1085

BETH GILGAL (1) [GILGAL]

Ne	12:29	from **B**, and from the area of Geba	1090

BETH HAGGAN (1)

2Ki	9:27	he fled up the road to **B**.	1091

BETH HAKKEREM (2)

Ne	3:14	ruler of the district of **B**.	1094
Jer	6: 1	Raise the signal over **B**!	1094

BETH HARAM (1)

Jos	13:27	**B**, Beth Nimrah,	1099

BETH HARAN (1) [HARAN]

Nu	32:36	and **B** as fortified cities,	1100

BETH HOGLAH (3) [HOGLAH]

Jos	15: 6	went up to **B** and continued north	1102
	18:19	to the northern slope of **B**	1102
	18:21	Jericho, **B**, Emek Keziz,	1102

BETH HORON (14) [HORONITE]

Jos	10:10	the road going up to **B** and cut them	1103
	10:11	on the road down from **B** to Azekah,	1103

Jos	16: 3	as far as the region of Lower **B** and	1103
	16: 5	in the east to Upper **B**	1103
	18:13	on the hill south of Lower **B**.	1103
	18:14	From the hill facing **B** on the south	1103
	21:22	Kibzaim and **B**, together	1103
1Sa	13:18	another toward **B**,	1103
1Ki	9:17	He built up Lower **B**	1103
1Ch	6:68	Jokmeam, **B**,	1103
	7:24	who built Lower and Upper **B**	1103
2Ch	8: 5	He rebuilt Upper **B**	1103
	8: 5	and Lower **B** as fortified cities,	1103
	25:13	from Samaria to **B**.	1103

BETH JESHIMOTH (4)

Nu	33:49	along the Jordan from **B**	1093
Jos	12: 3	to **B**, and then southward below	1093
	13:20	the slopes of Pisgah, and **B**	1093
Eze	25: 9	**B**, Baal Meon and Kiriathaim—	1093

BETH LEBAOTH (1) [LEBAOTH]

Jos	19: 6	**B** and Sharuhen—	1106

BETH MARCABOTH (2)

Jos	19: 5	Ziklag, **B**, Hazar Susah,	1096
1Ch	4:31	**B**, Hazar Susim, Beth Biri	1112

BETH MEON (1) [BAAL MEON]

Jer	48:23	to Kiriathaim, Beth Gamul and **B**,	1110

BETH MILLO (4)

Jdg	9: 6	and **B** gathered beside the great tree	1109
	9:20	citizens of Shechem and **B**,	1109
	9:20	citizens of Shechem and **B**,	1109
2Ki	12:20	and assassinated him at **B**,	1109

BETH NIMRAH (2) [NIMRAH]

Nu	32:36	**B** and Beth Haran	1113
Jos	13:27	Beth Haram, **B**,	1113

BETH OPHRAH (1) [OPHRAH]

Mic	1:10	In **B** roll in the dust.	1108

BETH PAZZEZ (1)

Jos	19:21	En Gannim, En Haddah and **B**.	1122

BETH PELET (2) [PELET]

Jos	15:27	Hazar Gaddah, Heshmon, **B**,	1120
Ne	11:26	in Jeshua, in Moladah, in **B**,	1120

BETH PEOR (4) [PEOR]

Dt	3:29	So we stayed in the valley near **B**.	1121
	4:46	in the valley near **B** east of the Jordan,	1121
	34: 6	in the valley opposite **B**,	1121
Jos	13:20	**B**, the slopes of Pisgah,	1121

BETH RAPHA (1) [RAPHA]

1Ch	4:12	Eshton was the father of **B**,	1125

BETH REHOB (2) [REHOB]

Jdg	18:28	The city was in a valley near **B**.	1124
2Sa	10: 6	from **B** and Zobah,	1124

BETH SHAN (9)

Jos	17:11	Manasseh also had **B**,	1126
	17:16	in **B** and its settlements and those in	1126
Jdg	1:27	the people of **B** or Taanach or Dor	1126
1Sa	31:10	fastened his body to the wall of **B**.	1126
	31:10	the wall of **B** and went to Jabesh,	1126
2Sa	21:12	from the public square at **B**,	1126
1Ki	4:12	of **B** next to Zarethan below Jezreel,	1126
	4:12	to Zarethan below Jezreel, from **B**	1126
1Ch	7:29	the borders of Manasseh were **B**,	1126

BETH SHEMESH (22)

Jos	15:10	continued down to **B** and crossed	1127
	19:22	Shahazumah and **B**,	1127
	19:38	Horem, Beth Anath and **B**.	1127
	21:16	Juttah and **B**,	1127
Jdg	1:33	in **B** or Beth Anath;	1127
	1:33	of the land, and those living in **B**	1127
1Sa	6: 9	up to its own territory, toward **B**,	1127
	6:12	cows went straight up toward **B**,	1127
	6:12	as far as the border of **B**.	1127
	6:13	of **B** were harvesting their wheat	1127
	6:14	to the field of Joshua of **B**,	1127
	6:15	of **B** offered burnt offerings	1127
	6:18	in the field of Joshua **of B**.	1128
	6:19	down some of the men of **B**,	1127
	6:20	and the men of **B** asked,	1127
1Ki	4:19	Shaalbim, **B** and Elon Bethhanan;	1127
2Ki	14:11	of Judah faced each other at **B**.	1127
	14:13	the son of Ahaziah, at **B**.	1127
1Ch	6:59	Juttah and **B**,	1127
2Ch	25:21	of Judah faced each other at **B**	1127
	25:23	the son of Ahaziah, at **B**.	1127
	28:18	They captured and occupied **B**,	1127

BETH SHITTAH (1)

Jdg	7:22	The army fled to **B** toward Zererah	1101

BETH TAPPUAH (1) [TAPPUAH]

Jos	15:53	Janim, **B**, Aphekah,	1130

BETH TOGARMAH (2) [TOGARMAH]

Eze	27:14	of **B** exchanged work horses,	1129
	38: 6	and **B** from the far north	1129

BETH ZUR (4) [ZUR]

Jos	15:58	Halhul, **B**, Gedor,	1123
1Ch	2:45	and Maon was the father of **B**.	1123
2Ch	11: 7	Soco, Adullam,	1123
Ne	3:16	ruler of a half-district of **B**,	1123

BETH-HACCEREM (KJV) See BETH HAKKEREM

BETH-HOGLA (KJV) See BETH HOGLAH

BETH-LEHEM-JUDAH (KJV) See BETHLEHEM, JUDAH

BETH-MEON (KJV) See BETH BAAL MEON, BAAL MEON

BETH-PALET (KJV) See BETH PELET

BETH-SHEAN (KJV) See BETH SHAN

BETH-SHEMITE (KJV) See BETH SHEMESH

BETHABARA (KJV) See BETHANY

BETHANY (12)

Mt	21:17	he left them and went out of the city to **B**,	1029
	26: 6	in **B** in the home of a man known as Simon	1029
Mk	11: 1	to Bethphage and **B** at the Mount of Olives,	1029
	11:11	he went out to **B** with the Twelve.	1029
	11:12	The next day as they were leaving **B**,	1029
	14: 3	While he was in **B**, reclining at the table	1029
Lk	19:29	As he approached Bethphage and **B** at	1029
	24:50	he had led them out to the vicinity of **B**,	1029
Jn	1:28	This all happened at **B** on the other side of	1029
	11: 1	He was from **B**, the village of Mary	1029
	11:18	**B** was less than two miles from Jerusalem,	1029
	12: 1	Jesus arrived at **B**, where Lazarus lived,	1029

BETHARAM (KJV) See BETH HARAM

BETHBIREI (KJV) See BETH BIRI

BETHEL (71) [EL BETHEL, LUZ]

Ge	12: 8	the hills east of **B** and pitched his tent,	1078
	12: 8	with **B** on the west and Ai on the east.	1078
	13: 3	from place to place until he came to **B**,	1078
	13: 3	to the place between **B** and Ai	1078
	28:19	He called that place **B**,	1078
	31:13	I am the God of **B**,	1078
	35: 1	"Go up to **B** and settle there.	1078
	35: 3	Then come, let us go up to **B**,	1078
	35: 6	Luz (that is, **B**) in the land of Canaan.	1078
	35: 8	and was buried under the oak below **B**.	1078
	35:15	where God had talked with him at **B**.	1078
	35:16	Then they moved on from **B**.	1078
Jos	7: 2	which is near Beth Aven to the east of **B**,	1078
	8: 9	between **B** and Ai, to the west of Ai—	1078
	8:12	and set them in ambush between **B** and Ai,	1078
	8:17	a man remained in Ai or **B** who did not go	1078
	12: 9	the king of Ai (near **B**) one	1078
	12:16	king of Makkedah one the king of **B** one	1078
	16: 1	the desert into the hill country of **B**.	1078
	16: 2	It went on from **B** (that is, Luz),	1078
	18:13	slope of Luz (that is, **B**) and went down	1078
	18:22	Beth Arabah, Zemaraim, **B**,	1078
Jdg	1:22	Now the house of Joseph attacked **B**,	1078
	1:23	to spy out **B** (formerly called Luz),	1078
	4: 5	between Ramah and **B** in the hill country	1078
	20:18	The Israelites went up to **B** and inquired	1078
	20:26	the Israelites, all the people, went up to **B**,	1078
	20:31	the one leading to **B** and the other	1078
	21: 2	The people went to **B**,	1078
	21:19	to the north of **B**,	1078
	21:19	of the road that goes from **B** to Shechem,	1078
1Sa	7:16	on a circuit from **B** to Gilgal to Mizpah,	1078
	10: 3	up to God at **B** will meet you there.	1078
	13: 2	at Micmash and in the hill country of **B**,	1078
	30:27	He sent it to those who were in **B**,	1078
1Ki	12:29	One he set up in **B**, and the other in Dan.	1078
	12:32	This he did in **B**,	1078
	12:32	And at **B** he also installed priests at	1078
	12:33	on the altar he had built at **B**.	1078
	13: 1	a man of God came from Judah to **B**,	1078

1Ki	13: 4	of God cried out against the altar at **B**,	1078
	13:10	not return by the way he had come to **B**.	1078
	13:11	there was a certain old prophet living in **B**,	1078
	13:32	the altar in **B** and against all the shrines on	1078
	16:34	In Ahab's time, Hiel of **B** rebuilt Jericho.	1088
2Ki	2: 2	the LORD has sent me to **B**."	1078
	2: 2	So they went down to **B**.	1078
	2: 3	The company of the prophets at **B** came out	1078
	2:23	From there Elisha went up to **B**.	1078
	10:29	the worship of the golden calves at **B**	1078
	17:28	in **B** and taught them how to worship	1078
	23: 4	the Kidron Valley and took the ashes to **B**.	1078
	23:15	Even the altar at **B**,	1078
	23:17	the altar of **B** the very things you have done	1078
	23:19	Just as he had done at **B**,	1078
1Ch	7:28	Their lands and settlements included **B**	1078
2Ch	13:19	and took from him the towns of **B**,	1078
Ezr	2:28	of **B** and Ai 223	1078
Ne	7:32	of **B** and Ai 123	1078
	11:31	Aija, **B** and its settlements,	1078
Jer	48:13	when they trusted in **B**.	1078
Hos	10:15	Thus will it happen to you, O **B**,	1078
	12: 4	at **B** and talked with him there—	1078
Am	3:14	I will destroy the altars of **B**;	1078
	4: 4	"Go to **B** and sin;	1078
	5: 5	do not seek **B**;	1078
	5: 5	and **B** will be reduced to nothing."	1078
	5: 6	and **B** will have no one to quench it.	1078
	7:10	of **B** sent a message to Jeroboam king	1078
	7:13	Don't prophesy anymore at **B**,	1078
Zec	7: 2	of **B** had sent Sharezer and Regem-Melech,	1078

BETHELITE (KJV) See BETHEL

BETHESDA (1)

Jn	5: 2	which in Aramaic is called **B**	1031

BETHHANAN See ELON BETHHANAN

BETHLEHEM (51) [BETHLEHEMITE, EPHRATH]

Ge	35:19	on the way to Ephrath (that is, **B**).	1107
	48: 7	beside the road to Ephrath" (that is, **B**).	1107
Jos	19:15	Nahalal, Shimron, Idalah and **B**.	1107
Jdg	12: 8	After him, Ibzan of **B** led Israel.	1107
	12:10	Then Ibzan died, and was buried in **B**.	1107
	17: 7	A young Levite from **B** in Judah,	1107
	17: 9	"I'm a Levite from **B** in Judah," he said,	1107
	19: 1	of Ephraim took a concubine from **B**	1107
	19: 2	and went back to her father's house in **B**,	1107
	19:18	"We are on our way to **B** in Judah to	1107
	19:18	to **B** in Judah and now I am going to	1107
Ru	1: 1	and a man from **B** in Judah,	1107
	1: 2	They were Ephrathites from **B**, Judah.	1107
	1:19	two women went on until they came to **B**.	1107
	1:19	When they arrived in **B**,	1107
	1:22	in **B** as the barley harvest was beginning.	1107
	2: 4	Just then Boaz arrived from **B** and greeted	1107
	4:11	in Ephrathah and be famous in **B**.	1107
1Sa	16: 1	I am sending you to Jesse of **B**.	1107
	16: 4	When he arrived at **B**,	1107
	16:18	a son of Jesse of **B** who knows how to play	1095
	17:12	who was from **B** in Judah.	1107
	17:15	from Saul to tend his father's sheep at **B**.	1107
	17:58	"I am the son of your servant Jesse **of B**."	1095
	20: 6	to hurry to **B**,	1107
	20:28	for permission to go to **B**.	1107
2Sa	2:32	and buried him in his father's tomb at **B**.	1107
	23:14	and the Philistine garrison was at **B**.	1107
	23:15	of water from the well near the gate of **B**!"	1107
	23:16	drew water from the well near the gate of **B**	1107
	23:24	Elhanan son of Dodo from **B**,	1107
1Ch	2:51	Salma the father of **B**,	1107
	2:54	**B**, the Netophathites, Atroth Beth Joab,	1107
	4: 4	the firstborn of Ephrathah and father of **B**.	1107
	11:16	and the Philistine garrison was at **B**,	1107
	11:17	of water from the well near the gate of **B**!"	1107
	11:18	drew water from the well near the gate of **B**	1107
	11:26	Elhanan son of Dodo from **B**,	1107
2Ch	11: 6	**B**, Etam, Tekoa,	1107
Ezr	2:21	the men of **B** 123	1107
Ne	7:26	the men of **B** and Netophah 188	1107
Jer	41:17	at Geruth Kimham near **B** on their way	1107
Mic	5: 2	"But you, **B** Ephrathah,	1107
Mt	2: 1	After Jesus was born in **B** in Judea,	1033
	2: 5	"In **B** in Judea," they replied,	1033
	2: 6	**B**, in the land of Judah,	1033
	2: 8	He sent them to **B** and said,	1033
	2:16	and he gave orders to kill all the boys in **B**	1033
Lk	2: 4	to **B** the town of David,	1033
	2:15	and see this thing that has happened,	1033
Jn	7:42	from David's family and from **B**,	1033

BETHLEHEMITE (1) [BETHLEHEM]

2Sa	21:19	of Jaare-Oregim the **B** killed Goliath	1095

BETHPHAGE (3)

Mt	21: 1	and came to **B** on the Mount of Olives,	1036
Mk	11: 1	to **B** and Bethany at the Mount of Olives,	1036
Lk	19:29	As he approached **B** and Bethany at	1036

BETHPHELET (KJV) See BETH PELET

BETHSAIDA (7)

Mt	11:21	Woe to you, **B**!	1034
Mk	6:45	into the boat and go on ahead of him to **B**,	1034
	8:22	They came to **B**,	1034
Lk	9:10	by themselves to a town called **B**,	1034
	10:13	Woe to you, **B**!	1034
Jn	1:44	was from the town of **B**.	1034
	12:21	who was from **B** in Galilee, with a request.	1034

BETHUEL (10)

Ge	22:22	Kesed, Hazo, Pildash, Jidlaph and **B**.”	1432
	22:23	**B** became the father of Rebekah.	1432
	24:15	She was the daughter of **B** son of Milcah,	1432
	24:24	“I am the daughter of **B**,	1432
	24:47	‘The daughter of **B** son of Nahor,	1432
	24:50	Laban and **B** answered,	1432
	25:20	when he married Rebekah daughter of **B**	1432
	28: 2	to the house of your mother’s father **B**.	1432
	28: 5	to Laban son of **B** the Aramean.	1432
1Ch	4:30	**B**, Hormah, Ziklag,	1433

BETHUL (1)

Jos	19: 4	Eltolad, **B**, Hormah,	1434

BETIMES (KJV) See AGAIN, EARLY, CAREFUL, FORAGING, LOOK

BETONIM (1)

Jos	13:26	and **B**, and from Mahanaim to the territory	1064

BETRAY (24) [BETRAYED, BETRAYER, BETRAYING, BETRAYS]

1Ch	12:17	if you have come to **b** me to my enemies	8228
Ps	89:33	nor *will I* ever **b** my faithfulness.	9213
Pr	16:10	and his mouth *should* not **b** justice.	5085
	25: 9	*do* not **b** another man’s confidence,	1655
Isa	16: 3	Hide the fugitives, *do* not **b** the refugees.	1655
	24:16	The treacherous **b**!	953
	24:16	With treachery the treacherous **b**!”	953
Mt	10:21	“Brother *will* **b** brother to death,	4140
	24:10	the faith and *will* **b** and hate each other,	4140
	26:21	one of you *will* **b** me.”	4140
	26:23	into the bowl with me *will* **b** me.	4140
	26:25	Then Judas, the one who *would* **b** him,	4140
Mk	13:12	“Brother *will* **b** brother to death,	4140
	14:10	went to the chief priests to **b** Jesus to them.	4140
	14:18	one of you *will* **b** me.”	4140
Lk	22: 4	with them how *he might* **b** Jesus.	4140
	22:21	*of* him who *is going to* **b** me is with mine	4140
Jn	6:64	and who *would* **b** him.	1639+3836+4140
	6:71	one of the Twelve, was later *to* **b** him.)	4140
	12: 4	Judas Iscariot, who was later *to* **b** him,	4140
	13: 2	son of Simon, to **b** Jesus.	4140
	13:11	For he knew who *was going to* **b** him,	4140
	13:21	one of you *is going to* **b** me.”	4140
	21:20	“Lord, who *is going to* **b** you?”)	4140

BETRAYED (22) [BETRAY]

2Sa	19:26	But Ziba my servant **b** me.	8228
Ps	73:15	*I would have* **b** your children.	953
Isa	33: 1	O traitor, you *who have* not *been* **b**!	953
	33: 1	when you stop betraying, you *will be* **b**.	953
Jer	12: 6	even they *have* **b** you;	953
La	1: 2	All her friends *have* **b** her;	953
	1:19	“I called to my allies but they **b** me.	8228
Mt	10: 4	the Zealot and Judas Iscariot, who **b** him.	4140
	17:22	of Man is going to *be* **b** into the hands	4140
	20:18	*be* **b** to the chief priests and the teachers of	4140
	26:45	Son of Man *is* **b** into the hands of sinners.	4140
	27: 3	When Judas, who *had* **b** him,	4140
	27: 4	he said, *“for I have* **b** innocent blood.”	4140
Mk	3:19	and Judas Iscariot, who **b** him.	4140
	9:31	of Man *is going to be* **b** into the hands	4140
	10:33	*be* **b** to the chief priests and teachers of	4140
	14:41	Son of Man *is* **b** into the hands of sinners.	4140
Lk	9:44	of Man is going to *be* **b** into the hands	4140
	21:16	*You will be* **b** even by parents, brothers,	4140
Jn	18: 2	Now Judas, who **b** him, knew the place,	4140
Ac	7:52	now you *have* **b** and murdered him—	1181+4595
1Co	11:23	The Lord Jesus, on the night *he was* **b**,	4140

BETRAYER (4) [BETRAY]

Mt	26:46	Rise, let us go! Here comes my **b**!”	4140
	26:48	Now the **b** had arranged a signal with them:	4140
Mk	14:42	Rise! Let us go! Here comes my **b**!”	4140
	14:44	Now the **b** had arranged a signal with them:	4140

BETRAYING (2) [BETRAY]

Isa	33: 1	when you stop **b**, you will be betrayed.	953
Lk	22:48	*are you* **b** the Son of Man with a kiss?”	4140

BETRAYS (7) [BETRAY]

Pr	11:13	A gossip **b** a confidence,	1655
	20:19	A gossip **b** a confidence;	1655
Isa	21: 2	The traitor **b**, the looter takes loot.	953
Hab	2: 5	wine **b** him; he is arrogant and never at rest.	953
Mt	26:24	woe to that man who **b** the Son of Man!	4140
Mk	14:21	woe to that man who **b** the Son of Man!	4140
Lk	22:22	but woe to that man who **b** him.”	4140

BETROTH (3) [BETROTHED]

Hos	2:19	*I will* **b** you to me forever;	829
	2:19	*I will* **b** you in righteousness and justice,	829
	2:20	*I will* **b** you in faithfulness,	829

BETROTHED (2) [BETROTH]

Dt	22:27	and though the **b** girl screamed,	829
2Sa	3:14	whom *I* **b** to myself for the price of	829

BETTER (133) [GOOD]

Ge	29:19	“It’s **b** that I give her to you than	3202
Ex	14:12	It would have been **b** for us to serve	3202
Nu	11:18	We were **b** off in Egypt!”	3202
	14: 3	Wouldn’t it be **b** for us to go back	3202
Dt	17:20	and not **consider** himself **b** than his brothers	4222+8123
Jdg	8: 2	the gleanings of Ephraim’s grapes **b** than	3202
	9: 2	‘Which is **b** for you:	3202
	11:25	Are you **b** than Balak son of Zippor,	3201+3201
	18:19	Isn’t it **b** that you serve a tribe and clan	3202
Ru	4:15	and who is **b** to you than seven sons,	3202
1Sa	14:30	**How much** it would have been if	677+3954
	15:22	To obey is **b** than sacrifice,	3202
	15:22	and to heed is **b** than the fat of rams.	4946
	15:28	to one **b** than you.	3202
	16:16	and you *will* feel **b**.”	3201
	16:23	he *would* feel **b**,	3201
	29: 4	**b** could he regain his master’s favor **than**	4202
2Sa	14:32	It would be **b** for me if I were still there!” ’	3202
	17:14	“The advice of Hushai the Arkite is **b** than	3202
	18: 3	be **b** now for you to give us support from	3202
1Ki	2:32	were **b** *men* and more upright than he.	3202
	19: 4	I am no **b** than my ancestors.”	3202
	21: 2	In exchange I will give you a **b** vineyard or,	3202+4946
2Ki	5:12	than any of the waters of Israel?	3202
2Ch	21:13	men *who* were **b** than you.	3202
Est	1:19	to someone else who is **b** than she.	3202
Ps	37:16	**B** the little that the righteous have than	3202
	63: 3	Because your love is **b** than life,	3202
	84:10	**B** is one day in your courts than	3202
	118: 8	It is **b** to take refuge in the LORD than	3202
	118: 9	It is **b** to take refuge in the LORD than	3202
Pr	3:14	and yields **b** returns **than** gold.	4946
	8:19	My fruit is **b** than fine gold;	3202
	12: 9	**B** to be a nobody and yet have a servant	3202
	15:16	**B** a little with the fear of the LORD than	3202
	15:17	**B** a meal of vegetables where there is love	3202
	16: 8	**B** a little with righteousness	3202
	16:16	How much **b** to get wisdom than gold,	3202
	16:19	**B** to be lowly in spirit and among	3202
	16:32	**B** a patient man than a warrior,	3202
	17: 1	**B** a dry crust with peace and quiet than	3202
	17:12	**B** to meet a bear robbed of her cubs **than**	440
	19: 1	**B** a poor man whose walk is blameless than	3202
	19:22	**b** to be poor than a liar.	3202
	21: 9	**B** to live on a corner of the roof than share	3202
	21:19	**B** to live in a desert than with	3202
	22: 1	to be esteemed is **b** than silver or gold.	3202
	25: 7	it is **b** for him to say to you,	3202
	25:24	**B** to live on a corner of the roof than share	3202
	27: 5	**B** is open rebuke than hidden love.	3202
	27:10	**b** a neighbor nearby than	3202
	28: 6	**B** a poor man whose walk is blameless than	3202
Ecc	2:13	I saw that wisdom is **b** than folly,	3862
	2:13	just as light is **b** than darkness.	3862
	2:24	A man can do nothing **b** than to eat	3202
	3:12	I know that there is nothing **b** for men than	3202
	3:22	that there is nothing **b** for a man than	3202
	4: 3	But **b** than both is he who has not yet been,	3202
	4: 6	**B** one handful with tranquillity	3202
	4: 9	Two are **b** than one,	3202
	4:13	**B** a poor but wise youth than an old	3202
	5: 5	It is **b** not to vow than to make a vow and	3202
	6: 3	I say that a stillborn child is **b** off than he.	3202
	6: 9	**B** what the eye sees than the roving of	3202
	7: 1	A good name is **b** than fine perfume,	3202
	7: 1	and the day of death **b than** the day of birth.	4946
	7: 2	It is **b** to go to a house of mourning than	3202
	7: 3	Sorrow is **b** than laughter,	3202
	7: 5	It is **b** to heed a wise man’s rebuke than	3202
	7: 8	The end of a matter is **b** than its beginning,	3202
	7: 8	and patience is **b** than pride.	3202
	7:10	“Why were the old days **b** than these?”	3202
	8:12	that it will go **b** with God-fearing men,	3202
	8:15	because nothing is **b** for a man under	3202
	9: 4	even a live dog is **b** off than a dead lion!	3202
	9:16	So I said, “Wisdom is **b** than strength.”	3202
	9:18	Wisdom is **b than** weapons of war,	3202
SS	5: 9	How is your beloved **b than** others,	4946
	5: 9	How is your beloved **b than** others,	4946
Isa	56: 5	and a name **b** than sons and daughters;	3202
	56:12	tomorrow will be like today, or even far **b**.”	1524
La	4: 9	by the sword are **b** off than those who die	3202
Eze	15: 2	of a vine **b** than that of a branch on any of	4946
Da	1:15	and **b** nourished **than** any of	4946
	1:20	he found them ten times **b than** all	6584
Hos	2: 7	for then I was **b** off than now.’	3202
Am	6: 2	Are *they* **b** off than your two kingdoms?	3202
Jnh	4: 3	for it is **b** for me to die than to live.”	3202
	4: 8	“It would be **b** for me to die than to live.”	3202
Na	3: 8	Are you **b** than Thebes,	3512
Mt	5:29	*It is* **b** for you to lose one part	5237
	5:30	*It is* **b** for you to lose one part	5237
	18: 6	*be* **b** for him to have a large millstone hung	5237

Mt	18: 8	It is **b** for you to enter life maimed	2819
	18: 9	It is **b** for you to enter life	2819
	19:10	*it is* **b** not to marry.”	5237
	26:24	be **b** for him if he had not been born.”	2819
Mk	5:26	yet instead of **getting b** she grew worse.	6067
	9:42	be **b** for him to be thrown into the sea with	2819
	9:43	It is **b** for you to enter life maimed than	2819
	9:45	It is **b** for you to enter life crippled than	2819
	9:47	It is **b** to enter the kingdom of God	2819
	14:21	be **b** for him if he had not been born.”	2819
Lk	5:39	for he says, ‘The old is **b**.’ ”	5982
	10:42	Mary has chosen what is **b**,	19
	14:10	‘Friend, move up to a **b** place.’	NIG
	17: 2	*be* **b** for him to be thrown into the sea with	3387
Jn	2:10	as to the time when his son got **b**,	3153
	11:12	“Lord, if he sleeps, *he will* get **b**.”	5392
	11:50	that *it is* **b** for you that one man die for	5237
Ro	3: 9	*Are we* any **b**? Not at all!	4604
	14:21	It is **b** not to eat meat or drink wine or	2819
1Co	7: 9	it is **b** to marry than to burn with passion.	3202
	7:38	but he who does not marry her does even **b**.	3202
	8: 8	and no **b** if we do.	4355
Eph	1:17	so that you may **know** him **b**.	2106
Php	1:23	be with Christ, which is **b** by far;	3202+3437
	2: 3	in humility consider others **b** than yourselves.	5660
1Ti	6: 2	Instead, they are to serve them even **b**,	NIG
Phm	1:16	but **b** than a slave, as a dear brother.	5642
Heb	6: 9	we are confident of **b** *things* in your case—	3202
	7:19	and a **b** hope is introduced,	3202
	7:22	the guarantee *of* a **b** covenant.	3202
	8: 6	and it is founded on **b** promises.	3202
	9:23	*with* **b** sacrifices than these.	3202
	10:34	you knew that you yourselves had **b** and lasting possessions.	3202
	11: 4	a **b** sacrifice than Cain did.	4498
	11:16	they were longing for a **b** country—	3202
	11:35	so that they might gain a **b** resurrection.	3202
	11:40	God had planned something **b** for us so	3202
	12:24	that speaks a **b** word than the blood	3202
1Pe	3:17	It is **b**, if it is God’s will, to suffer for doing good	3202
2Pe	2:21	It would have been **b** for them not to have known the way of righteousness,	3202

BETWEEN (223)

Ge	1: 6	expanse **b** the waters to separate water	928+9348
	3:15	I will put enmity **b** you and the woman,	1068
	3:15	and **b** your offspring and hers;	1068
	9:12	of the covenant I am making **b** me and you	1068
	9:13	the sign of the covenant **b** me and the earth.	1068
	9:15	I will remember my covenant **b** me and you	1068
	9:16	and remember the everlasting covenant **b**	1068
	9:17	of the covenant I have established **b** me	1068
	10:12	which is **b** Nineveh and Calah;	1068
	13: 3	to the place **b** Bethel and Ai	1068
	13: 7	And quarreling arose **b** Abram’s herdsmen	1068
	13: 8	not have any quarreling **b** you and me,	1068
	13: 8	or **b** your herdsmen and mine,	1068
	15:17	with a blazing torch appeared and passed **b**	1068
	16: 5	May the LORD judge **b** you and me!”	1068
	16:14	it is still there, **b** Kadesh and Bered.	1068
	17: 2	I will confirm my covenant **b** me and you	1068
	17: 7	as an everlasting covenant **b** me and you	1068
	17:11	and it will be the sign of the covenant **b** me	1068
	20: 1	the region of the Negev and lived **b** Kadesh	1068
	23:15	but what is that **b** me and you?	1068
	26:28	‘There ought to be a sworn agreement **b** us	1068
	26:28	sworn agreement **b** us and you,	1068
	30:36	Then he put a three-day journey **b** himself	1068
	31:37	and let them judge **b** the two of us.	1068
	31:44	and let it serve as a witness **b** us.”	1068
	31:48	a witness **b** you and me today.”	1068
	31:49	“May the LORD keep watch **b** you and me	1068
	31:50	remember that God is a witness **b** you	1068
	31:51	and here is this pillar I have set up **b** you	1068
	31:53	the God of their father, judge **b** us.”	1068
	32:16	and keep some space **b** the herds.	1068
	49:10	nor the ruler’s staff from **b** his feet,	1068
	49:14	a rawboned donkey lying down **b**	1068
Ex	8:23	a distinction **b** my people and your people.	1068
	9: 4	But the LORD will make a distinction **b**	1068
	11: 7	the LORD makes a distinction **b** Egypt	1068
	14: 2	**b** Migdol and the sea.	1068
	14:20	coming **b** the armies of Egypt and Israel.	1068
	16: 1	which is **b** Elim and Sinai.	1068
	18:16	and I decide **b** the parties and inform them	1068
	22:11	the issue **b** them will be settled by	1068
	25:22	above the cover **b** the two cherubim	1068+4946
	28:33	with gold bells **b** them.	928+9348
	30:18	Place it **b** the Tent of Meeting and the altar,	1068
	31:13	be a sign **b** me and you for the generations	1068
	31:17	be a sign **b** me and the Israelites forever,	1068
	39:25	around the hem **b** the pomegranates.	928+9348
	40: 7	place the basin **b** the Tent of Meeting and	1068
	40:30	He placed the basin **b** the Tent of Meeting	1068
Lev	10:10	You must distinguish **b** the holy and	1068
	10:10	**b** the unclean and the clean,	1068
	11:47	You must distinguish **b** the unclean and	1068
	11:47	**b** living creatures that may be eaten	1068
	20:25	“ ‘You must therefore make a distinction **b**	1068
	20:25	between clean and unclean animals and **b**	1068
		and a fight broke out in the camp **b** him and	NIH
Lev	26:46	on Mount Sinai **b** himself and the Israelites	1068
	27: 3	set the value of a male **b** the ages of twenty	2256+4946+6330

Lev 27: 5 b the ages of five and twenty, 2256+4946+6330
  27: 6 If it is a person b one month and five years, 2256+4946+6330
Nu 7:89 he heard the voice speaking to him from b 1068
  11:33 But while the meat was still b their teeth, 1068
  13:23 Two of them carried it on a pole b them, 928
  16:48 He stood b the living and the dead, 1068
  21:13 b Moab and the Amorites. 1068
  22:24 of the LORD stood in a **narrow path** b AIT
  30:16 **relationships** b a man and his wife, 1068
  30:16 and b a father and his your daughter 1068
  31:27 the spoils b the soldiers who took part in 1068
  35:24 the assembly must judge b him and 1068
Dt 1: 1 opposite Suph, b Paran and Tophel, Laban, 1068
  1:16 Hear the disputes b your brothers 1068
  1:16 whether the case is b brother Israelites or 1068
  1:16 between brother Israelites or b one of them 1068
  5: 5 (At that time I stood b the LORD and you 1068
  33:12 the LORD loves rests b his shoulders." 1068
Jos 3: 4 a distance of about a thousand yards b you 1068
  8: 9 in wait b Bethel and Ai, to the west of Ai— 1068
  8:11 with the valley b them and the city. 1068
  8:12 and set them in ambush b Bethel and Ai, 1068
  18:11 Their allotted territory lay b the tribes 1068
  22:25 the Jordan a boundary b us and you— 1068
  22:27 a witness b us and you and the generations 1068
  22:28 but as a witness b us and you.' 1068
  22:34 A Witness B Us that the LORD is God. 1068
  23: 4 b the Jordan and the Great Sea in the west. 4946
  24: 7 he put darkness b you and the Egyptians; 1068
Jdg 4: 5 She held court under the Palm of Deborah b 1068
  4:17 because there were friendly relations b 1068
  9:23 an evil spirit b Abimelech and the citizens 1068
  11:27 decide the dispute this day b the Israelites 1068
  13:25 b Zorah and Eshtaol. 1068
  16:31 They brought him back and buried him b 1068
1Sa 4: 4 who is **enthroned** b the cherubim. AIT
  7:12 Then Samuel took a stone and set it up b 1068
  7:14 there was peace b Israel and the Amorites. 1068
  14:42 "Cast the lot b me and Jonathan my son." 1068
  17: 1 b Socoh and Azekah. 1068
  17: 3 with the valley b them. 1068
  20: 3 there is only a step b me and death." 1068
  20:23 LORD is witness b you and me forever." 1068
  20:42 'The LORD is witness b you and me, 1068
  20:42 and b your descendants 1068
  24:12 May the LORD judge b you and me. 1068
  24:15 May he be our judge and decide b 1068
  26:13 there was a wide space b them. 1068
2Sa 3: 1 The war b the house of Saul and the house 1068
  3: 6 While the war b the house of Saul and the house 1068
  6: 2 who is **enthroned** b the cherubim AIT
  18:24 While David was sitting b the inner 1068
  19:35 Can I tell the difference b what is good 1068
  21: 7 because of the oath before the LORD b 1068
  21:15 a battle b the Philistines and Israel. 4200
1Ki 3: 9 to govern your people and to distinguish b 1068
  5:12 There were peaceful relations b Hiram 1068
  7:29 On the panels b the uprights were lions, 1068
  7:46 in clay molds in the plain of the Jordan b 1068
  8:32 **Judge** b your servants, AIT
  14:30 There was continual warfare b Rehoboam 1068
  15: 6 There was war b Rehoboam and Jeroboam 1068
  15: 7 There was war b Abijah and Jeroboam. 1068
  15:16 There was war b Asa and Baasha king 1068
  15:19 "Let there be a treaty b me and you," 1068
  15:19 "as there was b my father and your father. 1068
  15:32 There was war b Asa and Baasha king 1068
  18:21 "How long will you waver b two opinions? 6584
  18:42 bent down to the ground and put his face b 1068
  22: 1 For three years there was no war b Aram 1068
  22:34 and hit the king of Israel b the sections 1068
2Ki 9:24 Then Jehu drew his bow and shot Joram b 1068
  11:15 "Bring her out b the ranks and put to 4200
  11:17 then made a covenant b the LORD and 1068
  11:17 He also made a covenant b the king and 1068
  16:14 from b the new altar and the temple of 1068
  19:15 God of Israel, **enthroned** b the cherubim, AIT
  25: 4 at night through the gate b the two walls 1068
1Ch 13: 6 who is **enthroned** b the cherubim— AIT
  21:16 and saw the angel of the LORD standing b 1068
  21:16 in clay molds in the plain of the Jordan b 1068
2Ch 4:17 There was continual **warfare** b Rehoboam AIT
  6:23 **Judge** b your servants, AIT
  12: 8 **learn the difference** b serving me and 3359
  12:15 There was continual **warfare** b Rehoboam AIT
  13: 2 There was war b Abijah and Jeroboam. 1068
  16: 3 "Let there be a treaty b me and you," 1068
  16: 3 "as there was b my father and your father. 1068
  18:33 and hit the king of Israel b the sections 1068
  23:14 "Bring her out b the ranks and put to AIT
  35:21 "What **quarrel** is there b you and me, 4200
Ne 3:32 and b the room above the corner and 1068
Job 4:20 B dawn and dusk they are broken to pieces; 4946
  9:33 only there were someone to arbitrate b us, 1068
  26:10 the face of the waters for a **boundary** b AIT
    light and darkness.
  41:16 so close to the next that no air can pass b. 1068
Ps 80: 1 you who **sit enthroned** b the cherubim, AIT
  99: 1 he **sits enthroned** b the cherubim, AIT
  104:10 it flows b the mountains. 1068
SS 1:13 a sachet of myrrh resting b my breasts. 1068
Isa 2: 4 He will judge b the nations 1068
  5: 3 judge b me and my vineyard. 1068
  22:11 a reservoir b the two walls for the water of 1068
  37:16 God of Israel, **enthroned** b the cherubim, AIT
Jer 34:18 the calf they cut in two and then walked b 1068
  34:19 and all the people of the land who walked b 1068

Jer 39: 4 through the gate b the two walls, 1068
  52: 7 at night through the gate b the two walls 1068
Eze 4: 3 place it as an iron wall b you and the city 1068
  8: 3 The Spirit lifted me up b earth and heaven 1068
  8:16 b the portico and the altar, 1068
  18: 8 from doing wrong and judges fairly b man 1068
  20:12 Also I gave them my Sabbaths as a sign b 1068
  20:20 that they may be a sign b us. 1068
  22:26 not distinguish b the holy and the common; 1068
  22:26 that there is no **difference** b the unclean and 1068
  34:17 I will judge b one sheep and another, 1068
  34:17 and b rams and goats. 4200
  34:20 See, I myself will judge b the fat sheep and 1068
  34:22 I will judge b one sheep and another. 1068
  40: 7 and the projecting walls b 1068
  41: 9 The open area b the side rooms of 1075
  43: 8 with only a wall b me and, 1068
  44:23 to teach my people **the difference** b the
    holy and the common 1068
  44:23 to distinguish b the unclean and the clean. 1068
  47:16 on the border b Damascus and Hamath), 1068
  47:18 the east side the boundary will run b 1068+4946
  47:18 Jordan b Gilead and the land of Israel, 1068+4946
  48:22 the prince will lie b the border of Judah and 1068
Da 7: 5 and it had three ribs in its mouth b its teeth. 10099
  8: 5 suddenly a goat with a prominent horn b 1068
  8:21 the large horn b his eyes is the first king. 1068
  11:45 He will pitch his royal tents b the seas at 1068
Hos 2: 2 from her face and the unfaithfulness from b 1068
Joel 2:17 weep b the temple porch and the altar. 1068
Mic 4: 3 He will judge b many peoples 1068
Zec 5: 9 and they lifted up the basket b heaven 1068
  6: 1 from b two mountains— 1068
  6:13 And there will be harmony b the two.' 1068
  9: 7 the forbidden food from b their teeth. 1068
  11:14 the brotherhood b Judah and Israel. 1068
Mal 2:14 the LORD is acting as the witness b you 1068
  3:18 and you will again see the **distinction** b 1068
  3:18 b those who serve God 1068
Mt 18:15 just b the two of you. 3568
  19:10 "If this is the situation b a husband 3552
  23:35 whom you murdered b the temple and 3568
Lk 11:51 who was killed b the altar and 3568
  12:14 who appointed me a judge or an arbiter b 2093
  15:12 So he **divided** his property b them. 1349
  16:26 b us and you a great chasm has been fixed, 3568
  17:11 Jesus traveled along the border b Samaria 3545
Jn 3:25 An argument developed b some 3552
Ac 12: 6 Peter was sleeping b two soldiers, 3568
  15: 9 He made no distinction b us and them, 3568
  23: 7 b **the Pharisees** and the Sadducees, AIT
Ro 10:12 there is no difference b Jew and Gentile— 5445
  14:22 about these things keep b yourself and God. NIG
1Co 6: 5 to judge a dispute b believers? 324+3545
  12:10 to another **distinguishing** b spirits, 1360
2Co 6:15 What harmony is there b Christ and Belial? NIG
  6:16 What agreement is there b the temple 3552
Php 1:23 I am torn b the two: 1666
1Ti 2: 5 For there is one God and one **mediator** b 3542
  6: 5 **constant friction** b men of corrupt mind, 1384

BEULAH (1)
Isa 62: 4 called Hephzibah, and your land B; 1241

BEWAIL, BEWAILED (KJV) See
GRIEVED, MOURN, MOURNED, WEEP

BEWARE (7)
2Ki 6: 9 "B of passing that place, 9068
Job 36:21 B of turning to evil, 440+9068
Isa 22:17 "B, the LORD is about to take firm hold 2180
Jer 7:32 So b, the days are coming, 2180
  9: 4 "B of your friends; 9068
  19: 6 So b, the days are coming, 2180
Lk 20:46 "B of the teachers of the law. 4668

BEWILDERED (3) [BEWILDERMENT]
Est 3:15 but the city of Susa was b. 1003
Isa 21: 3 I am b by what I see. 987
Mk 16: 8 and b, the women went out and fled from 1749

BEWILDERMENT (1) [BEWILDERED]
Ac 2: 6 a crowd came together in b, 5177

BEWITCHED (1) [WITCHCRAFT]
Gal 3: 1 Who has b you? 1001

BEWRAY (KJV) See BETRAY

BEYOND (65)
Ge 35:21 and pitched his tent b Migdal Eder. 2134+4946
  41:49 because it was b measure. 401
Lev 15:25 a discharge that continues b her period, 6584
Nu 22:18 not do anything great or small to **go b** 6296
  24:13 to **go b** the command of the LORD— 6296
Dt 3:25 and see the good land b the Jordan— 928+6298
  30:11 not too difficult for you or b your **reach**. 8158
  30:13 Nor is it b the sea, so that you have to ask, 4946+6298
Jos 24: 2 lived b the River and worshiped other gods. 928+6298

Jos 24: 3 from the **land** b the River and led him 6298
  24:14 the gods your forefathers worshiped b 928+6298
  24:15 the gods your forefathers served b 928+6298
Jdg 1:36 from Scorpion Pass to Sela and b. 2025+5087
  5:17 Gilead stayed b the Jordan. 928+6298
  13:18 It is b **understanding**." 7100
1Sa 14:23 and the battle **moved on** b Beth Aven. 6296
  20:22 the arrows are b you,' then you must go, 2134+2256+4946
  20:36 As the boy ran, he shot an arrow b him. 6296
  20:37 "Isn't the arrow b you?" 2134+2256+4946
2Sa 10:16 Hadadezer had Arameans brought from b 6298
  16: 1 When David had gone a short distance b 4946
1Ki 14:15 to their forefathers and scatter them b 4946+6298
1Ch 19:16 and had Arameans brought from b 6298
  22:16 and iron—craftsmen b number. 401
Ne 3:16 B him, Nehemiah son of Azbuk, 339
  3:23 B them, Benjamin 339
Job 28:18 the price of wisdom is b rubies. 4946
  36:26 How great is God—b our understanding! 4202
  37: 5 he does great things b our understanding. 4202
  37:23 The Almighty is b our reach and exalted 4202
Ps 104:25 teeming with creatures b number— 401
Ecc 7:23 but this was b me. 8158
SS 6: 8 and virgins b number; 401
Isa 7:20 the Lord will use a razor hired from b 6298
  52:14 his appearance was so disfigured b that 4946
  52:14 and his form marred b human likeness— 4946
  64: 9 Do not be angry b **measure**, O LORD; 4394+6330
  64: 9 and punish us b **measure**? 4394+6330
Jer 17: 9 above all things and b **cure**. 631
  30:12 your injury b **healing**. 2703
La 5:22 and are angry with us b **measure**. 4394+6330
Eze 41:16 everything b and including 5584
Da 8:27 it was b understanding. 401
Joel 2:11 his forces are b **number**, 4394+8041
Am 5:27 I will send you into exile b Damascus," 2134+4200+4946
Mic 2:10 it is ruined, b **all remedy**. 5344
Zep 3:10 From b the rivers of Cush my worshipers, 6298
Mal 1: 5 even b the borders of Israel!' 4946+6584
Mt 5:37 anything b this comes from the evil one. 4356
Lk 22:41 He withdrew about a stone's throw b them, 608
Ac 7:43 Therefore I will send you into exile b 2084
  15:28 and to us not to burden you with anything b 4440
  26:22 I am saying nothing b what the prophets 1760
Ro 11:11 Did they stumble so as to fall b recovery? NIG
  11:33 and his paths b **tracing out**! 453
1Co 1:16 b that, I don't remember 3370
  4: 6 "Do not go b what is written." 5642
  10:13 not let you be tempted b what you can bear. 5642
2Co 1: 8 far b our ability to endure, 5642
  8: 3 and even b their ability. 4123
  10:13 however, will not boast b proper **limits**, 296+1650+3836
  10:15 Neither do we go b our **limits** by boasting
    of work done by others. 296+1650+3836
  10:16 the gospel in the regions b you. 5654
Gal 1:14 I was advancing in Judaism b many Jews 5642
1Ti 3: 16 B **all question,** the mystery 3935

BEZAI (3)
Ezr 2:17 of B 323 1291
Ne 7:23 of B 324 1291
  10:18 Hodiah, Hashum, B, 1291

BEZALEL (9)
Ex 31: 2 I have chosen B son of Uri, the son of Hur, 1295
  35:30 "See, the LORD has chosen B son of Uri, 1295
  36: 1 So B, Oholiab and every skilled person 1295
  36: 2 Then Moses summoned B and Oholiab 1295
  37: 1 B made the ark of acacia wood— 1295
  38:22 (B son of Uri, the son of Hur, 1295
1Ch 2:20 and Uri the father of B. 1295
2Ch 1: 5 But the bronze altar that B son of Uri, 1295
Ezr 10:30 Kelal, Benaiah, Maaseiah, Mattaniah, B, 1295

BEZEK (2) [ADONI-BEZEK]
Jdg 1: 4 down ten thousand men at B. 1028
1Sa 11: 8 When Saul mustered them at B, 1028

BEZER (5)
Dt 4:43 B in the desert plateau, for the Reubenites, 1311
Jos 20: 8 of the Jordan of Jericho they designated B 1311
  21:36 from the tribe of Reuben, B, Jahaz, 1311
1Ch 6:78 the Jordan east of Jericho they received B 1311
  7:37 B, Hod, Shamma, Shilshah, Ithran 1310

BICRI (8)
2Sa 20: 1 a troublemaker named Sheba son of B, 1152
  20: 2 to follow Sheba son of B. 1152
  20: 6 Sheba son of B will do us more harm than Absalom did. 1152
  20: 7 from Jerusalem to pursue Sheba son of B. 1152
  20:10 and his brother Abishai pursued Sheba son of B. 1152
  20:13 on with Joab to pursue Sheba son of B. 1152
  20:21 A man named Sheba son of B, 1152
  20:22 and they cut off the head of Sheba son of B 1152

BID, BIDDEN, BIDDETH (KJV) See
SAID, SAY, SAYS

BIDDING (2)
Ps	103:20	you mighty ones who do his **b**,	1821
	148: 8	stormy winds that do his **b**,	1821

BIDKAR (1)
2Ki	9:25	Jehu said to **B**, his chariot officer,	982

BIER (2)
2Sa	3:31	King David himself walked behind the **b**.	4753
2Ch	16:14	They laid him on a **b** covered with spices	5435

BIG (14) [BIGGER]
Ex	29:20	and on the **b** toes of their right feet.	991
Lev	8:23	and on the **b** of his right foot.	991
	8:24	of their right hands and on the **b** toes	991
	14:14	and on the **b** toe of his right foot.	991
	14:17	and on the **b** toe of his right foot.	991
	14:25	and on the **b** toe of his right foot.	991
	14:28	and on the **b** toe of his right foot.	991
Jdg	1: 6	and cut off his thumbs and **b** toes.	8079
	1: 7	and **b** toes cut off have picked up scraps	8079
	9:38	"Where is your **b** talk now, you who said,	7023
2Sa	18:17	into a **b** pit in the forest and piled up	1524
Mt	27:60	He rolled a **b** stone in front of the entrance	3489
Mk	4:32	with such **b** branches that the birds of	3489
Ac	22:28	"I had to pay a **b** price for my citizenship."	4498

BIGGER (2) [BIG]
Lk	7:43	the one who had the **b** debt canceled."	4498
	12:18	I will tear down my barns and build **b** ones,	3505

BIGTHA (1)
Est	1:10	Mehuman, Biztha, Harbona, **B**, Abagtha,	960

BIGTHANA (2)
Est	2:21	at the king's gate, **B** and Teresh, two of	961
	6: 2	that Mordecai had exposed **B** and Teresh,	962

BIGVAI (6)
Ezr	2: 2	Bilshan, Mispar, **B**, Rehum and Baanah):	958
	2:14	of **B** 2,056	958
	8:14	of the descendants of **B**,	958
Ne	7: 7	Mispereth, **B**, Nehum and Baanah):	958
	7:19	of **B** 2,067	958
	10:16	Adonijah, **B**, Adin,	958

BILDAD (5)
Job	2:11	**B** the Shuhite and Zophar the Naamathite,	1161
	8: 1	Then **B** the Shuhite replied:	1161
	18: 1	Then **B** the Shuhite replied:	1161
	25: 1	Then **B** the Shuhite replied:	1161
	42: 9	**B** the Shuhite and Zophar	1161

BILEAM (1)
1Ch	6:70	the Israelites gave Aner and **B**,	1190

BILGAH (2) [BILGAH'S]
1Ch	24:14	the fifteenth to **B**, the sixteenth to Immer,	1159
Ne	12: 5	Mijamin, Moadiah, **B**,	1159

BILGAH'S (1) [BILGAH]
Ne	12:18	of **B**, Shammua; of Shemaiah's,	1159

BILGAI (1)
Ne	10: 8	**B** and Shemaiah. These were the priests.	1160

BILHAH (10)
Ge	29:29	Laban gave his servant girl **B** to his	1167
	30: 3	Then she said, "Here is **B**, my maidservant.	1167
	30: 4	So she gave him her servant **B** as a wife.	1167
	30: 7	Rachel's servant **B** conceived again	1167
	35:22	in and slept with his father's concubine **B**,	1167
	35:25	The sons of Rachel's maidservant **B**:	1167
	37: 2	the sons of **B** and the sons of Zilpah,	1167
	46:25	These were the sons born to Jacob by **B**,	1167
1Ch	4:29	**B**, Ezem, Tolad,	1168
	7:13	the descendants of **B**.	1167

BILHAN (4)
Ge	36:27	The sons of Ezer: **B**, Zaavan and Akan.	1169
1Ch	1:42	The sons of Ezer: **B**, Zaavan and Akan.	1169
	7:10	The son of Jediael: **B**.	1169
	7:10	The sons of **B**: Jeush, Benjamin, Ehud,	1169

BILL (2)
Lk	16: 6	"The manager told him, 'Take your **b**,	1207
	16: 7	'Take your **b** and make it eight hundred.'	1207

BILLOWED (1) [BILLOWS]
Ex	19:18	The smoke **b** up from it like smoke from	6590

BILLOWS (2) [BILLOWED]
Joel	2:30	blood and fire and **b** of smoke.	9406
Ac	2:19	blood and fire and **b** of smoke.	874

BILSHAN (2)
Ezr	2: 2	Nehemiah, Seraiah, Reelaiah, Mordecai, **B**,	1193
Ne	7: 7	**B**, Mispereth, Bigvai, Nehum and Baanah):	1193

BIMHAL (1)
1Ch	7:33	Pasach, **B** and Ashvath.	1197

BIND (19) [BINDING, BINDINGS, BINDS, BOUND]
Dt	6: 8	and **b** them on your foreheads	2118+3213+4200
	11:18	and **b** them on your foreheads	2118+3213+4200
Ne	10:29	**b** themselves with a curse and an oath	928+995
Job	38:31	"Can you **b** the beautiful Pleiades?	8003
Ps	119:61	Though the wicked **b** me with ropes,	6386
	149: 8	to **b** their kings with fetters,	673
Pr	3: 3	**b** them around your neck,	8003
	6:21	**B** them upon your heart forever;	8003
	7: 3	**B** them on your fingers;	8003
Isa	8:16	**B** up the testimony and seal up the law	7674
	56: 6	And foreigners who **b** themselves to	4277
	61: 1	He has sent me to **b** up the brokenhearted,	2502
Jer	50: 5	They will come and **b** themselves to	4277
Eze	34:16	I will **b** up the injured and strengthen	2502
Hos	6: 1	he has injured us but he will **b** up	2502
Mt	16:19	whatever you **b** on earth will be bound	1313
	18:18	whatever you **b** on earth will be bound	1313
Mk	5: 3	and no one could **b** him any more,	1313
Ac	21:11	of Jerusalem will **b** the owner of this belt	1313

BIND, BINDS, BOUND (Anglicized) See also OBLIGATE, OBLIGATED, OBLIGATES

BINDING (7) [BIND]
Ge	37: 7	We were **b** sheaves of grain out in the field	520
Nu	30: 9	by a widow or divorced woman will be **b**	7756
	30:14	or the pledges **b** on her.	6584
Jos	2:17	the oath you made us swear will not be **b**	5929
Jdg	16:21	**B** him with bronze shackles,	673
Ne	9:38	we are making a **b** agreement,	591
Heb	2: 2	For if the message spoken by angels was **b**,	1010

BINDINGS (1) [BIND]
Jdg	15:14	and the **b** dropped from his hands.	657

BINDS (5) [BIND]
Job	5:18	For he wounds, but he also **b** up;	2502
	30:18	he **b** me like the neck of my garment.	273
Ps	147: 3	the brokenhearted and **b** up their wounds.	2502
Isa	30:26	the LORD **b** up the bruises of his people	2502
Col	3:14	love, which **b** them all **together** in perfect unity.	1639+5278

BINEA (2)
1Ch	8:37	Moza was the father of **B**;	1232
	9:43	Moza was the father of **B**;	1232

BINNUI (8)
Ezr	8:33	of Jeshua and Noadiah son of **B**.	1218
	10:30	Mattaniah, Bezalel, **B** and Manasseh.	1218
	10:38	From the descendants of **B**: Shimei,	1218
Ne	3:18	by their countrymen under **B** son	1218
	3:24	**B** son of Henadad repaired another section,	1218
	7:15	of **B** 648	1218
	10: 9	**B** of the sons of Henadad, Kadmiel,	1218
	12: 8	The Levites were Jeshua, **B**, Kadmiel,	1218

BIRD (38) [BIRD'S, BIRDS]
Ge	1:21	and every winged **b** according to its kind.	6416
	6:20	Two of every kind of **b**,	6416
	7: 3	and also seven of every kind of **b**,	6416
	7:14	according to its kind and every **b** according	6416
Lev	7:26	not eat the blood of any **b** or animal.	6416
	14: 6	He is then to take the live **b** and dip it,	7606
	14: 6	of the **b** that was killed over the fresh water.	7606
	14: 7	he is to release the live **b** in the open fields.	7606
	14:51	the hyssop, the scarlet yarn and the live **b**,	7606
	14:51	the blood of the dead **b** and the fresh water,	7606
	14:52	the fresh water, the live **b**, the cedar wood,	7606
	14:53	the live **b** in the open fields outside	7606
	17:13	among you who hunts any animal or **b**	6416
	20:25	Do not defile yourselves by any animal or **b**	6416
Dt	4:17	any animal on earth or any **b** that flies	4053+7606
	14:11	You may eat any clean **b**.	7606
Job	28: 7	No **b** of prey knows that hidden path,	6416
	41: 5	like a **b** or put him on a leash for your girls?	7606
Ps	11: 1	"Flee like a **b** to your mountain.	7606
	50:11	I know every **b** in the mountains,	6416
	102: 7	I have become like a **b** alone on a roof.	7606
	124: 7	like a **b** out of the fowler's snare;	7606
Pr	6: 5	like a **b** from the snare of the fowler.	7606
	7:23	like a **b** darting into a snare,	7606
	27: 8	Like a **b** that strays from its nest is	6416
Ecc	10:20	a **b** of the air may carry your words,	6416
	10:20	a **b** on the wing may report what you say.	1251+4053
Isa	46:11	From the east I summon a **b** of prey;	6514
Jer	4:25	every **b** in the sky had flown away.	6416
	12: 9	like a speckled **b** of prey that other birds	6514
La	3:52	without cause hunted me like a **b**.	7606
Eze	39:17	to every kind of **b** and all the wild animals;	7606

BIRD'S (2) [BIRD]
Lev	14:52	He shall purify the house with the **b** blood,	7606
Dt	22: 6	If you come across a **b** nest beside the road,	7606

BIRDS (97) [BIRD]
Ge	1:20	and let **b** fly above the earth across	6416
	1:22	and let **b** increase on the earth."	6416
	1:26	over the fish of the sea and the **b** of the air,	6416
	1:28	over the fish of the sea and the **b** of the air	6416
	1:30	the beasts of the earth and all the **b** of the air	6416
	2:19	the beasts of the field and all the **b** of the air	6416
	2:20	the **b** of the air and all the beasts of	6416
	6: 7	and **b** of the air—	6416
	7: 8	of **b** and of all creatures that move along	6416
	7:21	**b**, livestock, wild animals,	6416
	7:23	the ground and the **b** of the air were wiped	6416
	8:17	the **b**, the animals, and all the creatures	6416
	8:19	that move along the ground and all the **b**—	6416
	8:20	of all the clean animals and clean **b**,	6416
	9: 2	the beasts of the earth and all the **b** of the air	6416
	9:10	the **b**, the livestock and all	6416
	15:10	the **b**, however, he did not cut in half.	7606
	15:11	**b** of prey came down on the carcasses,	6514
	40:17	but the **b** were eating them out of the basket	6416
	40:19	And the **b** will eat away your flesh."	6416
Lev	1:14	to the LORD is a burnt offering of **b**,	6416
	11:13	" 'These are the **b** you are to detest and	6416
	11:46	concerning animals, **b**, every living thing	6416
	14: 4	that two live clean **b** and some cedar wood,	7606
	14: 5	Then the priest shall order that one of the **b**	7606
	14:49	To purify the house he is to take two **b**	7606
	14:50	He shall kill one of the **b** over fresh water	7606
	20:25	and between unclean and clean **b**.	6416
Dt	28:26	Your carcasses will be food for all the **b** of	6416
1Sa	17:44	the **b** of the air and the beasts of the field!"	6416
	17:46	the carcasses of the Philistine army to the **b**	6416
2Sa	21:10	not let the **b** of the air touch them by day or	6416
1Ki	4:33	He also taught about animals and **b**,	6416
	14:11	the **b** of the air will feed on those who die	6416
	16: 4	the **b** of the air will feed on those who die	6416
	21:24	the **b** of the air will feed on those who die	6416
Job	12: 7	and they will teach you, or the **b** of the air,	6416
	28:21	concealed even from the **b** of the air.	6416
	35:11	the earth and makes us wiser than the **b** of	6416
Ps	8: 8	the **b** of the air,	7606
	78:27	flying **b** like sand on the seashore.	6416
	79: 2	of your servants as food to the **b** of the air,	6416
	104:12	The **b** of the air nest by the waters;	7606
	104:17	There the **b** make their nests;	7606
	148:10	small creatures and flying **b**,	7606
Pr	1:17	to spread a net in full view of all the **b**!	1251+4053
Ecc	9:12	or **b** are taken in a snare,	7606
	12: 4	when men rise up at the sound of **b**,	7606
Isa	16: 2	Like fluttering **b** pushed from the nest,	6416
	18: 6	be left to the mountain **b** of prey and to	6514
	18: 6	the **b** will feed on them all summer,	6514
	31: 5	Like **b** hovering overhead,	7606
Jer	5:26	in wait like **men who snare b** and	3687
	5:27	Like cages full of **b**,	6416
	7:33	of this people will become food for the **b** of	6416
	9:10	The **b** of the air have fled and	6416
	12: 4	the animals and **b** have perished.	6416
	12: 9	that other **b** of prey surround and attack?	6514
	15: 3	to kill and the dogs to drag away and the **b**	6416
	16: 4	the **b** of the air and the beasts of the earth."	6416
	19: 7	as food to the **b** of the air and the beasts of	6416
	34:20	the **b** of the air and the beasts of the earth.	6416
Eze	13:20	like **b** and I will tear them from your arms;	7256
	13:20	the people that you ensnare like **b**.	7256
	17:23	**B** of every kind will nest in it;	4053+7606
	29: 5	the beasts of the earth and the **b** of the air.	6416
	31: 6	All the **b** of the air nested in its boughs,	6416
	31:13	the **b** of the air settled on the fallen tree,	6416
	32: 4	I will let all the **b** of the air settle on you	6416
	38:20	The fish of the sea, the **b** of the air,	6416
	39: 4	as food to all kinds of **carrion b** and to	6514+7606
Da	2:38	the beasts of the field and the **b** of the air	10533
	4:12	and the **b** of the air lived in its branches;	10616
	4:14	Let the animals flee from under it and the **b**	10616
	4:21	in its branches for the **b** of the air—	10616
Hos	2:18	the **b** of the air and the creatures that move	6416
	4: 3	the **b** of the field and the fish of the	6416
	7:12	I will pull them down like **b** of the air.	6416
	11:11	They will come trembling like **b**	7606
Zep	1: 3	the **b** of the air and the fish of the sea.	6416
Mt	6:26	Look at the **b** of the air;	4374
	8:20	"Foxes have holes and **b** of the air	4374
	13: 4	and the **b** came and ate it up.	4374
	13:32	so that the **b** of the air come and perch	4374
Mk	4: 4	and the **b** came and ate it up.	4374
	4:32	that the **b** of the air can perch in its shade."	4374
Lk	8: 5	and the **b** ate it up.	4374
	9:58	"Foxes have holes and **b** of the air	4374
	12:24	how much more valuable you are than **b**!	4374
	13:19	the **b** of the air perched in its branches."	4374
Ac	10:12	as well as reptiles of the earth and **b** of	4374
	11: 6	wild beasts, reptiles, and **b** of the air.	4374
Ro	1:23	to look like mortal man and **b** and animals	4374

Eze 44:31   priests must not eat anything, **b** or animal,   6416
Da   4:33   an eagle and his nails like the claws of a **b**.   10616
   7: 6   four wings like those of a **b**.   10533
Hos 9:11   Ephraim's glory will fly away like a **b**—   6416
Am   3: 5   Does a **b** fall into a trap on the ground   7606
Rev 18: 2   a haunt for every unclean and detestable **b**.   3997

1Co	15:39	**b** another and fish another.	4764
Jas	3: 7	All kinds of animals, **b**,	4374
Rev	19:17	who cried in a loud voice *to* all the **b** flying	3997
	19:21	all the **b** gorged themselves on their flesh.	3997

BIRI See BETH BIRI

BIRSHA (1)

| Ge | 14: 2 | **B** king of Gomorrah, | 1407 |

BIRTH (143) [BEAR]

Ge	3:16	with pain you will give **b** to children.	3528
	4: 1	she became pregnant and gave **b** to Cain.	3528
	4: 2	Later she gave **b** to his brother Abel.	3528
	4:17	she became pregnant and gave **b** to Enoch.	3528
	4:20	Adah gave **b** to Jabal;	3528
	4:25	*she* gave **b** to a son and named him Seth,	4580
	11:28	in the land of his **b**.	4580
	25:13	listed in the **order of** their **b**:	9352
	25:24	When the time came for her to give **b**,	3528
	25:26	when Rebekah gave **b** to them.	3528
	29:32	Leah became pregnant and gave **b** to	3528
	29:33	and when *she* gave **b** to a son she said,	3528
	29:34	and when *she* gave **b** to a son she said,	3528
	29:35	and when *she* gave **b** to a son she said,	3528
	30:21	Some time later *she* gave **b** to a daughter	3528
	30:23	She became pregnant and gave **b** to a son	3528
	30:25	After Rachel gave **b** to Joseph,	3528
	31: 8	all the flocks gave **b** to speckled young;	3528
	35:16	to give **b** and had great difficulty.	3528
	38: 3	she became pregnant and gave **b** to a son,	3528
	38: 4	and gave **b** *to* a son and named him Onan.	3528
	38: 5	*She* gave **b** to still another son	3528
	38: 5	It was at Kezib that she gave **b** to him.	3528
	38:27	When the time came for her *to* give **b**,	3528
	38:28	As she *was* **giving b**,	3528
	50:23	of Manasseh *were* **placed at b**	3528
Ex	1:19	and give **b** before the midwives arrive."	3528
	2: 2	she became pregnant and gave **b** to a son.	3528
	2:22	Zipporah gave **b** *to* a son,	3528
	21:22	and she **gives b** prematurely	3529+3655
	28:10	in the *order of* their **b**—	9352
Lev	12: 2	and **gives b** to a son will	3528
	12: 5	If *she* **gives b** to a daughter,	3528
	12: 7	the regulations for the *woman who* **gives b**	3528
Nu	11:12	*Did* I **give** them **b?**	2655
Dt	32:18	you forgot the God *who* **gave** you **b**.	2655
Jdg	13: 5	you will conceive and give **b** to a son.	3528
	13: 5	set apart to God from **b**,	1061
	13: 7	'You will conceive and give **b** to a son.	3528
	13: 7	of God from **b** until the day of his death.'"	1061
	13:24	The woman gave **b** to a boy	3528
	16:17	a Nazirite set apart to God since **b**.	562+1061
Ru	1:12	if I had a husband tonight and then **gave b**	3528
	4:13	and *she* **gave b** to a son.	3528
	4:15	has **given** him **b**."	3528
1Sa	1:20	of time Hannah conceived and **gave b** to	3528
	2:21	she conceived and **gave b** to three sons	3528
	4:19	she went into labor and **gave b**,	3528
	4:20	*you have* **given b** to a son."	3528
2Sa	12:24	*She* **gave b** to a son,	3528
1Ki	11: 3	He had seven hundred wives **of royal b**	8576
2Ki	4:17	about that same time *she* **gave b** to a son,	3528
	19: 3	to the **point of b** and there is no strength	5402
1Ch	2:49	*She* also **gave b** to Shaaph the father	3528
	4: 9	saying, "I **gave b** to him in pain."	3528
	4:17	One of Mered's wives **gave b** to Miriam,	2225
	4:18	(His Judean wife **gave b** to Jered the father	3528
	7:14	*She* **gave b** to Makir the father of Gilead.	3528
	7:16	Makir's wife Maacah **gave b** to a son	3528
	7:18	His sister Hammoleketh **gave b** to Ishhod,	3528
	7:23	she became pregnant and **gave b** to a son.	3528
Job	3: 1	and cursed the day of his **b**.	NIH
	3: 3	"May the day of *my* **b** perish,	3205
	3:11	"Why did I not perish at **b**,	8167
	15:35	They conceive trouble and give **b** to evil;	3528
	31:18	and from my **b** I guided the widow—	562+1061
	38:29	Who **gives b** *to* the frost from the heavens	3528
	39: 1	when the mountain goats **give b?**	3528
	39: 2	Do you know the time they **give b?**	3528
Ps	7:14	with evil and conceives trouble **gives b**	3528
	22:10	From **b** I was cast upon you;	8167
	51: 5	Surely *I was* sinful **at b**,	2655
	58: 3	Even from **b** the wicked go astray;	8167
	71: 6	From **b** I have relied on you;	1061
Pr	8:24	When there were no oceans, *I was* given **b**,	2655
	8:25	before the hills, *I was* given **b**,	2655
	23:25	may *she who* **gave** you **b** rejoice!	3528
Ecc	7: 1	the day of death better than the day of **b**.	3528
	10:17	of noble **b** and whose princes eat at	1201
SS	8: 5	there *she* who was in labor **gave** you **b**.	3528
Isa	7:14	be with child and *will* **give b** to a son,	3528
	8: 3	and she conceived and **gave b** to a son.	3528
	23: 4	"I have neither been in labor nor **given b**;	3528
	26:17	to **give b** writhes and cries out in her pain,	3528
	26:18	we writhed in pain, but *we* **gave b** to wind.	3528
	26:18	we have not **given b** to people of the world.	5877
	26:19	the earth *will* **give b** to her dead.	5877
	33:11	You conceive chaff, *you* **give b** to straw;	3528
	37: 3	to the **point of b** and there is no strength	5402
	45:10	'What *have you* **brought to b?'**	2655
	46: 3	and have carried since your **b**.	8167
	48: 8	you were called a rebel from **b**.	1061
	49: 1	from my **b** he has made mention	562+5055
	51: 2	your father, and to Sarah, *who* **gave** you **b**.	2655
Isa	59: 4	they conceive trouble and give **b** to evil.	3528
	66: 7	"Before she goes into labor, *she* **gives b;**	3528
	66: 8	in labor than *she* **gives b** to her children.	3528
	66: 9	Do I **bring to** the moment of **b**	8689
Jer	2:14	Is Israel a servant, a **slave by b?**	1074+3535
	2:27	and to stone, 'You **gave** me **b.'**	3528
	15:10	Alas, my mother, that *you* **gave** me **b**,	3528
	22:26	and the mother who **gave** you **b**	3528
	50:12	*she who* **gave** you **b** will be disgraced.	3528
Eze	16: 3	*were* in the land of the Canaanites;	4580
	23: 4	They were mine and **gave b** to sons	3528
	31: 6	of the field **gave b** under its branches;	3528
Hos	1: 6	Gomer conceived again and **gave b** to	3528
	5: 7	*they* **give b** to illegitimate children.	3528
	9:11	no **b**, no pregnancy, no conception.	4256
Mic	5: 3	the time when she who is in labor **gives b**	3528
Mt	1:18	how the **b** of Jesus Christ came about:	1161
	1:21	*She will* **give b** to a son,	5503
	1:23	be with child and *will* **give b** to a son,	5503
	1:25	with her until *she* **gave b** to a son.	5503
	24: 8	All these are the beginning of **b pains**.	6047
Mk	13: 8	These are the beginning *of* **b pains**.	6047
Lk	1:14	and many will rejoice because *of* his **b**,	1161
	1:15	filled with the Holy Spirit even from **b**	3120+3613
	1:31	You will be with child and **give b** to a son,	5503
	1:57		1164
	2: 7	and *she* **gave b** to her firstborn,	5503
	11:27	"Blessed is the mother who **gave** you **b**	1002
	19:12	*of* **noble b** went to a distant country	2302
Jn	3: 6	Flesh **gives b** to flesh,	1164
	3: 6	but the Spirit **gives b** to spirit.	1164
	9: 1	he saw a man blind from **b**.	1162
	9:34	"You *were* steeped in sin at **b;**	1164
	16:21	A woman **giving b** to a child has pain	5503
Ac	3: 2	a man crippled from **b** was being carried to the temple gate	3120+3613
	7: 8	and circumcised him eight days after his **b**.	NIG
	14: 8	from **b** and had never walked.	3120+3613
1Co	1:26	not many were of **noble b**.	2302
Gal	1:15	who set me apart from **b** and called me	3120+3613
	2:15	**by b** and not 'Gentile sinners'	5882
Eph	2:11	that formerly you are Gentiles by **b**	4922
Jas	1:15	desire has conceived, *it* **gives b** to sin;	5503
	1:15	when it is full-grown, **gives b** to death.	652
	1:18	*He* chose *to* **give** us **b** through the word	652
1Pe	1: 3	In his great mercy he *has* **given** us **new b**	335
Rev	12: 2	in pain *as she was about to* **give b**.	5503+6048
	12: 4	of the woman who was about to **give b**,	5503
	12: 5	*She* **gave b** to a son, a male child,	5503
	12:13	he pursued the woman who *had* **given b** to	5503

BIRTHDAY (3) [BEAR]

Ge	40:20	Now the third day was Pharaoh's **b**,	3427+3528
Mt	14: 6	On Herod's **b** the daughter	1160
Mk	6:21	*On* his **b** Herod gave a banquet	1160

BIRTHRIGHT (6) [BEAR]

Ge	25:31	Jacob replied, "First sell me your **b**."	1148
	25:32	"What good is the **b** to me?"	1148
	25:33	selling his **b** to Jacob.	1148
	25:34	So Esau despised his **b**.	1148
	27:36	He took my **b**,	1148
1Ch	5: 1	in accordance with his **b**,	1148

BIRZAITH (1)

| 1Ch | 7:31 | who was the father of **B**. | 1365 |

BISHLAM (1)

| Ezr | 4: 7 | in the days of Artaxerxes king of Persia, **B**, | 1420 |

BISHOPRICK (KJV) See LEADERSHIP

BIT (5) [BITES, BIT]

Nu	21: 6	*they* **b** the people and many Israelites died.	5966
2Ki	19:28	I will put my hook in your nose and my **b**	5496
Ps	32: 9	be controlled by **b** and bridle or they will	5496
Isa	30:28	of the peoples a **b** that leads them astray.	8270
	37:29	I will put my hook in your nose and my **b**	5496

BITE (4) [BIT, BITES, BITING, BITTEN]

Jer	8:17	and *they will* **b** you," declares the LORD.	5966
Am	5:19	on the wall only to have a snake **b** him.	5966
	9: 3	the serpent *to* **b** them.	5966
Jn	6: 7	for each one to have a **b!**"	NIG

BITES (3) [BITE]

Ge	49:17	that **b** the horse's heels so	5966
Pr	23:32	the end *it* **b** like a snake and poisons like	5966
Ecc	10:11	If a snake **b** before it is charmed,	5966

BITHIAH (1)

| 1Ch | 4:18 | the children of Pharaoh's daughter **B**, | 1437 |

BITHRON (1)

| 2Sa | 2:29 | continued through the whole **B** and came | 1443 |

BITHYNIA (2)

| Ac | 16: 7 | they tried to enter **B**, | 1049 |
| 1Pe | 1: 1 | Galatia, Cappadocia, Asia and **B**, | 1049 |

BITING (1) [BITE]

| Gal | 5:15 | *on* **b** and devouring each other, | 1231 |

BITS (2) [BIT]

| Am | 6:11 | into pieces and the small house into **b**. | 1323 |
| Jas | 3: 3 | When we put **b** into the mouths of horses | 5903 |

BITTEN (3) [BITE]

Nu	21: 8	anyone who is **b** can look at it and live."	5966
	21: 9	when anyone *was* **b** by a snake and looked	5966
Ecc	10: 8	whoever breaks through a wall *may be* **b** by	5966

BITTER (44) [BITTERLY, BITTERNESS, EMBITTER, EMBITTERED]

Ge	27:34	with a loud and **b** cry and said to his father,	5253
Ex	1:14	*They* **made** their lives **b** with hard labor	5352
	12: 8	along with **b herbs**,	5353
	15:23	not drink its water because it was **b**.	5253
Nu	5:18	while he himself holds the **b** water	5253
	5:19	may this **b** water that brings a curse	5253
	5:23	and then wash them off into the **b** water.	5253
	5:24	He shall have the woman drink the **b** water	5253
	5:24	and cause **b suffering**.	5253
	5:27	it will go into her and cause **b suffering;**	5253
	9:11	with unleavened bread and **b herbs**.	5353
Dt	29:18	among you that produces such **b** poison.	4360
Ru	1:13	It is more **b** for me than for you,	5253
	1:20	the Almighty **made** my life very **b**.	5352
1Sa	14:52	of Saul there was **b** war with the Philistines,	2617
	30: 6	each one *was* **b** in spirit because of his sons	5352
1Ki	2: 8	down **b** curses on me the day I went	5344
2Ki	4:27	She *is* in **b distress**,	5352
Job	3:20	and life to the **b** of soul,	5253
	13:26	For you write down **b things** against me	5353
	23: 2	"Even today my complaint is **b;**	5308
Ps	71:20	many and **b**, you will restore my life again;	8273
	107:12	So he subjected them to **b labor;**	6662
Pr	5: 4	but in the end she is **b** as gall,	5253
	27: 7	to the hungry even *what is* **b** tastes sweet.	5253
Ecc	7:26	I find more **b** than death the woman who is	5253
Isa	5:20	who put **b** for sweet and sweet for bitter.	5253
	5:20	who put bitter for sweet and sweet for **b**.	5253
	24: 9	the beer *is* **b** to its drinkers.	5352
Jer	2:19	then and realize how evil and **b** it is for you	5253
	4:18	How **b** it is!	5253
	6:26	mourn with **b** wailing as for an only son,	9476
	9:15	"See, I will make this people eat **b** food	4360
	23:15	"I will make them eat **b** food	4360
La	1: 4	her maidens grieve, and she is in **b anguish**.	5253
	3:15	He has filled me with **b herbs** and sated	5353
Eze	21: 6	before them with broken heart and **b grief**.	5320
	27:31	with anguish of soul and with **b mourning**.	5253
Am	8:10	an only son and the end of it like a **b day**.	5253
Zep	1:14	The cry on the day of the LORD will be **b**,	5253
Heb	12:15	and that no **b** root grows up to cause trouble	4394
Jas	3:14	if you harbor **b** envy and selfish ambition	4395
Rev	8:11	A third of the waters turned **b**,	952
	8:11	from the waters that *had become* **b**.	4393

BITTERLY (21) [BITTER]

Ge	50:10	they lamented loudly and **b**;	3878+4394
Nu	14:39	to all the Israelites, they mourned **b**.	4394
Jdg	5:23	'Curse its people **b**,	826+826
	21: 2	raising their voices and weeping **b**.	1524
2Sa	13:36	too, and all his servants wept very **b**.	1524
2Ki	14:26	how **b** everyone in Israel, whether slave	5253
	20: 3	And Hezekiah wept **b**.	1524
Ezr	10: 1	They too **wept b**.	1134+1135+2221
Est	3: 3	wailing loudly and **b**.	5289
Isa	22: 4	*let me* weep **b**.	5352
	33: 7	the envoys of peace weep **b**.	5253
	38: 3	And Hezekiah wept **b**.	1524
Jer	13:17	my eyes *will* weep **b**,	1963+1963
	22:10	rather, **weep b** for him who is exiled,	1134+1134
	48:32	**weeping b** as they go;	1140+1140
La	1: 2	**B** *she* weeps at night,	1134+1134
Eze	27:30	They will raise their voice and cry **b**	5352
Hos	12:14	But Ephraim has **b** provoked him to anger;	9476
Zec	12:10	and grieve **b** for him as one grieves for	5352
Mt	26:75	And he went outside and wept **b**.	4396
Lk	22:62	And he went outside and wept **b**.	4396

BITTERN (KJV) See OWL

BITTERNESS (19) [BITTER]

Ge	49:23	*With* **b** archers **attacked** him;	5352
Dt	32:32	and their clusters with **b**.	5353
1Sa	1:10	In **b** of soul Hannah wept much and prayed	5253
	15:32	thinking, "Surely the **b** *of* death is past."	5253
2Sa	2:26	Don't you realize that this will end in **b?**	5253
Job	7:11	I will complain in the **b** of my soul.	5253
	10: 1	to my complaint and speak out in the **b**	5253
	21:25	Another man dies in **b** of soul,	5253
	27: 2	*who has* **made** me taste **b** of soul,	5352
Pr	14:10	Each heart knows its own **b**,	4933
	17:25	to his father and **b** to the one who bore him.	4933
La	3: 5	and surrounded me with **b** and hardship.	8032
	3:19	the **b** and the gall.	8032
Eze	3:14	I went *in* **b** and in the anger of my spirit,	5253
Am	5: 7	into **b** and cast righteousness to the ground	4360
	6:12	and the fruit of righteousness into **b**—	4360
Ac	8:23	For I see that you are full of **b**	4394+5958

Ro	3:14	"Their mouths are full of cursing and **b**."	4394
Eph	4:31	Get rid of all **b**, rage and anger,	4394

BITUMEN (Anglicized) See TAR

BIZIOTHIAH (1)
Jos	15:28	Hazar Shual, Beersheba, **B**,	1026

BIZJOTHJAH (KJV) See BIZIOTHIAH

BIZTHA (1)
Est	1:10	Mehuman, **B**, Harbona, Bigtha, Abagtha,	1030

BLACK (16) [BLACKENED, BLACKER, BLACKEST, BLACKNESS]
Ex	10:15	They covered all the ground until it *was* **b**.	3124
Lev	11:13	the eagle, the vulture, the **b vulture,**	6465
	11:14	the red kite, any kind of **b kite,**	370
	13:31	and there is no **b** hair in it,	8839
	13:37	and **b** hair has grown in it,	8839
Dt	4:11	with **b** clouds and deep darkness.	3125
	14:12	the eagle, the vulture, the **b vulture,**	6465
	14:13	the red kite, the **b kite,** any kind of falcon,	370
1Ki	18:45	Meanwhile, the sky **grew b** with clouds,	7722
Job	30:30	My skin **grows b** and peels;	8837
SS	5:11	his hair is wavy and **b** as a raven.	8839
Zec	6:2	first chariot had red horses, the second **b**,	8839
	6:6	The one with the **b** horses is going toward	8839
Mt	5:36	you cannot make even one hair white or **b**.	3506
Rev	6:5	and there before me was a **b** horse!	3506
	6:12	The sun turned **b** like sackcloth made	3506

BLACKENED (1) [BLACK]
Job	30:28	I go about **b**, but not by the sun;	7722

BLACKER (1) [BLACK]
La	4:8	But now they *are* **b** than soot;	3124

BLACKEST (3) [BLACK]
Job	28:3	for ore in the **b** darkness.	7516
2Pe	2:17	**B** darkness is reserved for them.	2432
Jude	1:13	whom **b** darkness has been reserved forever.	2432

BLACKNESS (4) [BLACK]
Job	3:5	may **b** overwhelm its light.	4025
Joel	2:2	a day of clouds and **b**.	6906
Am	5:8	who turns **b** into dawn and darkens day	7516
Zep	1:15	a day of clouds and **b**,	6906

BLACKSMITH (3)
1Sa	13:19	Not a **b** could be found in the whole land	3093
Isa	44:12	The **b** takes a tool and works with it	1366+3093
	54:16	it is I who created the **b** who fans the coals	3093

BLADE (2)
Jdg	3:22	Even the handle sank in after the **b**,	4258
Eze	21:16	then to the left, wherever your **b** is turned.	7156

BLAINS (KJV) See FESTERING

BLAME (8) [BLAMELESS, BLAMELESSLY]
Ge	43:9	*I will* **bear the b** before you all my life.	2627
	44:10	the rest of you will be **free from b**."	5929
	44:32	*I will* **bear the b** before you, my father,	2627
1Sa	25:24	"My lord, let the **b** be on me alone.	6411
2Sa	14:9	the **b** rest on me and on my father's family,	6411
Ro	9:19	"Then why *does* God still **b** us?	3522
1Ti	5:7	**no** one may be **open to b**.	455
	6:14	to keep this command without spot or **b**	455

BLAMELESS (55) [BLAME]
Ge	6:9	**b** among the people of his time,	9459
	17:1	walk before me and be **b**.	9459
Dt	18:13	be **b** before the LORD your God.	9459
2Sa	22:24	I have been **b** before him	9459
	22:26	to the **b** you show yourself blameless,	1475+9459
	22:26	to the blameless *you* **show yourself b**,	9462
Job	1:1	This man was **b** and upright;	9447
	1:8	he is **b** and upright,	9447
	2:3	he is **b** and upright,	9447
	4:6	and your **b** ways your hope?	9448
	8:20	not reject a **b** *man* or strengthen the hands	9447
	9:20	if I were **b**, it would pronounce me guilty.	9447
	9:21	I am **b**, I have no concern for myself;	9447
	9:22	'He destroys both the **b** and the wicked.'	9447
	12:4	though righteous and **b**!	9459
	22:3	What would he gain if your ways *were* **b**?	9462
	31:6	and he will know that I am **b**—	9450
Ps	15:2	He whose walk is **b**	9459
	18:23	I have been **b** before him	9459
	18:25	to the **b** you show yourself blameless,	1505+9459
	18:25	to the blameless *you* **show yourself b**,	9462
	19:13	Then *will* I be **b**,	9462
	26:1	O LORD, for I have led a **b** life	9448
	26:11	But I lead a **b** life;	9448
	37:18	The days of the **b** are known to the LORD,	9459
	37:37	Consider the **b**, observe the upright;	9447
	84:11	from those whose walk is **b**.	9459

Ps	101:2	I will be careful to lead a **b** life—	9459
	101:2	I will walk in my house with **b** heart.	9448
	101:6	he whose walk is **b** will minister to me.	9459
	119:1	Blessed are *they* whose ways are **b**,	9459
	119:80	May my heart be **b** toward your decrees,	9459
Pr	2:7	he is a shield to those whose walk is **b**,	9448
	2:21	and the **b** will remain in it;	9459
	11:5	of the **b** makes a straight way for them,	9459
	11:20	but he delights in *those whose* ways are **b**.	9459
	19:1	Better a poor man whose walk is **b** than	9448
	20:7	The righteous man leads a **b** life;	9459
	28:6	Better a poor man whose walk is **b** than	9448
	28:10	but the **b** will receive a good inheritance.	9459
	28:18	He whose walk is **b** is kept safe,	9459
Eze	28:15	You were **b** in your ways from	9459
1Co	1:8	on the day of our Lord Jesus Christ.	441
Eph	1:4	the creation of the world to be holy and **b**	320
	5:27	or any other blemish, but holy and **b**.	320
Php	1:10	be pure and **b** until the day of Christ,	718
	2:15	so that you may become **b** and pure,	289
1Th	2:10	and **b** we were among you who believed.	290
	3:13	that you will be **b** and holy in the presence	289
	5:23	soul and body be kept **b** at the coming	290
Tit	1:6	An elder must be **b**,	441
	1:7	he must be **b**—not overbearing,	441
Heb	7:26	one who is holy, **b**, pure,	179
2Pe	3:14	**b** and at peace with him.	318
Rev	14:5	in their mouths; they are **b**.	320

BLAMELESSLY (1) [BLAME]
Lk	1:6	observing all the Lord's commandments and regulations **b**.	289

BLANKET (1) [BLANKETS]
Isa	28:20	the **b** too narrow to wrap around you.	5012

BLANKETS (2) [BLANKET]
Jdg	5:10	sitting on your **saddle b**,	4496
Eze	27:20	" 'Dedan traded in saddle **b** with you.	955+2927

BLASPHEME (5) [BLASPHEMED, BLASPHEMER, BLASPHEMES, BLASPHEMIES, BLASPHEMING, BLASPHEMOUS, BLASPHEMY]
Ex	22:28	not **b** God or curse the ruler of your people.	7837
Ac	26:11	and I tried to force them to **b**.	1059
1Ti	1:20	over to Satan to be taught not *to* **b**.	1059
2Pe	2:12	But these men **b** in matters they do	1059
Rev	13:6	He opened his mouth to **b** God,	1060

BLASPHEMED (9) [BLASPHEME]
Lev	24:11	The son of the Israelite woman **b** the Name	5919
2Ki	19:6	of the king of Assyria *have* **b** me.	1552
	19:22	Who is it you have insulted and **b**?	1552
Isa	37:6	of the king of Assyria *have* **b** me.	1552
	37:23	Who is it you have insulted and **b**?	1552
	52:5	"And all day long my name is constantly **b**.	5540
Eze	20:27	also your fathers **b** me by forsaking me:	1552
Ac	19:37	nor **b** our goddess.	1059
Ro	2:24	"God's name *is* **b** among the Gentiles	1059

BLASPHEMER (3) [BLASPHEME]
Lev	24:14	"Take the **b** outside the camp.	7837
	24:23	the **b** outside the camp and stoned him.	7837
1Ti	1:13	though I was once a **b** and a persecutor and	1061

BLASPHEMES (5) [BLASPHEME]
Lev	24:16	*anyone who* **b** the name of the LORD must	5919
	24:16	when he **b** the Name,	5919
Nu	15:30	whether native-born or alien, **b** the LORD,	1552
Mk	3:29	But whoever **b** against the Holy Spirit	1059
Lk	12:10	but anyone who **b** against the Holy Spirit	1059

BLASPHEMIES (4) [BLASPHEME]
Ne	9:18	or when they committed awful **b**.	5542
	9:26	they committed awful **b**.	5542
Mk	3:28	and **b** of men will be forgiven them,	1059+1060
Rev	13:5	a mouth to utter proud words and **b** and	1060

BLASPHEMING (2) [BLASPHEME]
Mt	9:3	"This fellow *is* **b**!"	1059
Mk	2:7	"Why does this fellow talk like that? *He's* **b**!	1059

BLASPHEMOUS (2) [BLASPHEME]
Rev	13:1	and on each head a **b** name.	1060
	17:3	with **b** names and had seven heads	1060

BLASPHEMY (9) [BLASPHEME]
Mt	12:31	every sin and **b** will be forgiven men,	1060
	12:31	the Spirit will not be forgiven.	1060
	26:65	"He has **spoken b**!	1059
	26:65	Look, now you have heard the **b**.	1060
Mk	14:64	"You have heard the **b**.	1060
Lk	5:21	"Who is this fellow who speaks **b**?	1060
Jn	10:33	replied the Jews, "but for **b**, because you,	1059
	10:36	then do you accuse me of **b** because I said,	1059
Ac	6:11	"We have heard Stephen speak words *of* **b**	1061

BLAST (19) [BLASTS]
Ex	15:8	the **b** of your nostrils the waters piled up.	8120
	19:13	ram's horn **sounds a long b** may they go	5432
	19:16	and a very loud trumpet **b**.	7754
Nu	10:5	When a **trumpet b** is sounded,	9558
	10:6	At the sounding of a second **b**,	9558
	10:6	The **b** will be the signal for setting out.	9558
	10:7	**sound** a **b** on the trumpets.	8131
Jos	6:5	When you hear them sound a long **b**	7754+8795
	6:16	**sounded** the trumpet **b**,	9546
2Sa	22:16	at the **b** of breath from his nostrils.	5972
Job	4:9	at the **b** of his anger they perish.	8120
	39:25	**At the b** *of* the trumpet he snorts, 'Aha!	928+1896
Ps	18:15	at the **b** of breath from your nostrils.	5972
	98:6	and the **b** of the ram's horn—	7754
	147:17	Who can withstand his **icy b**?	7938
Isa	27:8	with his fierce **b** he drives her out,	8120
Eze	22:20	into a furnace to melt it with a fiery **b**,	5870
Am	2:2	amid war cries and the **b** of the trumpet.	7754
Heb	12:19	*to* a trumpet **b** or to such	2491

BLASTS (2) [BLAST]
Lev	23:24	a sacred assembly commemorated with **trumpet b**.	9558
Rev	8:13	of the trumpet **b** about to be sounded by	5889

BLASTUS (1)
Ac	12:20	Having secured the support *of* **B**,	1058

BLAZE (2) [BLAZED, BLAZES, BLAZING]
Nu	21:28	a **b** from the city of Sihon.	4259
Jer	48:45	a **b** from the midst of Sihon;	4259

BLAZED (7) [BLAZE]
Dt	4:11	the foot of the mountain while it **b** with fire	1277
Jdg	13:20	As the flame **b up** from the altar	6590
2Sa	22:9	burning coals **b** out of it.	1277
	22:13	of his presence bolts of lightning **b forth.**	1277
Ps	18:8	burning coals **b** out of it.	1277
	106:18	Fire **b** among their followers;	1277
Jnh	4:8	sun **b** on Jonah's head so that he grew faint.	5782

BLAZES (2) [BLAZE]
Hos	7:6	in the morning it **b** like a flaming fire.	1277
Joel	2:3	behind them a flame **b**.	4265

BLAZING (22) [BLAZE]
Ge	15:17	with a **b** torch appeared and passed between	836
SS	8:6	It burns like fire, like a mighty flame.	8404
Isa	10:16	a fire will be kindled like a **b** flame.	3679
	34:9	her land will become **b** pitch!	1277
	62:1	her salvation like a **b** torch.	1277
Eze	20:47	The **b** flame will not be quenched,	4259
Da	3:6	be thrown into a **b** furnace."	10328+10471
	3:11	be thrown into a **b** furnace.	10328+10471
	3:15	be thrown immediately into a **b** furnace	10328+10471
	3:17	If we are thrown into the **b** furnace,	10328+10471
	3:20	and throw them into the **b** furnace.	10328+10471
	3:21	were bound and thrown into the **b** furnace.	10328+10471
	3:23	firmly tied, fell into the **b** furnace.	10328+10471
	3:26	the opening of the **b** furnace and shouted,	10328+10471
	7:11	and thrown into the **b** fire.	10329
Ac	26:13	**b around** me and my companions.	4334
2Th	1:7	in **b** fire with his powerful angels.	5825
Rev	1:14	and his eyes were like **b** fire	5825
	2:18	the Son of God, whose eyes are like **b** fire	5825
	4:5	Before the throne, seven lamps were **b**.	2794
	8:10	and a great star, **b** like a torch.	2794
	19:12	His eyes are like **b** fire,	5825

BLEACH (1)
Mk	9:3	in the world could **b** them.	3326

BLEAT (1) [BLEATING]
Isa	34:14	and wild goats *will* **b** to each other;	7924

BLEATING (1) [BLEAT]
1Sa	15:14	"What then is this **b** *of* sheep in my ears?	7754

BLEEDING (8) [BLOOD]
Lev	12:4	to be purified from her **b**.	1947
	12:5	to be purified from her **b**.	1947
Mt	9:20	then a woman *who had been* **subject** to **b**	137
Mk	5:25	woman was there who had been **subject** to **b** for twelve years.	135+1877+4868
	5:29	Immediately her **b** stopped.	135+3836+4380
Lk	8:43	woman was there who had been **subject** to **b** for twelve years,	135+1877+4868
	8:44	immediately her **b** stopped.	135+3836+4868
Ac	19:16	that they ran out of the house naked and **b**.	5547

BLEMISH (6) [BLEMISHED, BLEMISHES]
Lev	22:21	be without defect or **b** to be acceptable.	4583
Nu	19:2	to bring you a red heifer without defect or **b**	4583
2Sa	14:25	the sole of his foot there was no **b** in him.	4583
Eph	5:27	stain or wrinkle or any other **b**,	3836+5525[S]

Col 1:22 **without b** and free from accusation— 320
1Pe 1:19 a lamb **without b** or defect. 320

BLEMISHED (1) [BLEMISH]

Mal 1:14 but then sacrifices a **b** *animal* to the Lord. 8845

BLEMISHES (2) [BLEMISH]

2Pe 2:13 They are blots and **b**, 3700
Jude 1:12 These men are **b** at your love feasts, 5069

BLEND (2) [BLENDED]

Ex 30:25 a fragrant **b**, the work of a perfumer. 8381
   30:35 and make a **fragrant b** of incense, 8381

BLENDED (2) [BLEND]

2Ch 16:14 with spices and various **b** perfumes, 8379
SS 7: 2 a rounded goblet that never lacks **b** wine. 4641

BLESS (95) [BLESSED, BLESSEDNESS, BLESSES, BLESSING, BLESSINGS]

Ge 12: 2 into a great nation and *I* will **b** you; 1385
   12: 3 *I* will **b** those who bless you, 1385
   12: 3 I will bless *those who* **b** you, 1385
   17:16 I will **b** her and will surely give you a son 1385
   17:16 I will **b** her so that she will be the mother 1385
   17:20 *I* will surely **b** him; 1385
   22:17 *I* will **surely** b you 1385+1385
   26: 3 and I will be with you and *will* **b** you. 1385
   26:24 *I* will **b** you and will increase the number 1385
   27:29 be cursed and *those who* **b** you be blessed." 1385
   27:34 "**B** me—me too, my father!" 1385
   27:38 **B** me too, my father!" 1385
   28: 3 *May* God Almighty **b** you 1385
   32:26 "I will not let you go unless *you* **b** me." 1385
   48: 9 "Bring them to me so *I may* **b** them." 1385
   48:16 *may* he **b** these boys. 1385
Ex 12:32 And also **b** me." 1385
   20:24 I will come to you and **b** you. 1385
Nu 6:23 'This is how *you are to* **b** the Israelites. 1385
   6:24 " '"The LORD **b** you and keep you; 1385
   6:27 and I *will* **b** them. 1385
   22: 6 For I know that those *you* **b** are blessed, 1385
   23:11 *you have* **done nothing but b** them!" 1385+1385
   23:20 I have received a command *to* **b**; 1385
   23:25 at all nor **b** them **at all!**" 1385+1385
   24: 1 that it pleased the LORD to **b** Israel, 1385
   24: 9 *"May those who* **b** you be blessed 1385
Dt 1:11 increase you a thousand times and **b** you 1385
   7:13 and **b** you and increase your numbers. 1385
   7:13 *He* will **b** the fruit of your womb, 1385
   14:29 and so that the LORD your God *may* **b** you 1385
   15: 4 he *will* **richly** b you, 1385+1385
   15: 6 For the LORD your God *will* **b** you 1385
   15:10 of this the LORD your God *will* **b** you 1385
   15:18 And the LORD your God *will* **b** you 1385
   16:15 For the LORD your God *will* **b** you 1385
   23:20 so that the LORD your God *may* **b** you 1385
   24:19 that the LORD your God *may* **b** you in all 1385
   26:15 and **b** your people Israel and 1385
   27:12 on Mount Gerizim to **b** the people: 1385
   28: 8 The LORD your God *will* **b** you in 1385
   28:12 on your land in season and to **b** all the work 1385
   30:16 and the LORD your God *will* **b** you in 1385
   33:11 **B** all his skills, O LORD, 1385
   33:13 *"May the* LORD **b** his land with 1385
Jos 8:33 when he gave instructions to **b** the people 1385
Jdg 17: 2 Then his mother said, "The LORD **b** you, 1385
Ru 2: 4 "The LORD **b** you!" 1385
   2:20 "The LORD **b** him!" 1385
   3:10 "The LORD **b** you, my daughter," 1385
1Sa 2:20 Eli *would* **b** Elkanah and his wife, saying, 1385
   9:13 because he *must* **b** the sacrifice; 1385
   15:13 Saul said, "The LORD **b** you! 1385
   23:21 "The LORD **b** you for your concern 1385
2Sa 2: 5 "The LORD **b** you 1385
   6:20 David returned home to **b** his household, 1385
   7:29 be pleased *to* **b** the house of your servant, 1385
   21: 3 so that *you* will **b** the LORD's inheritance?" 1385
1Ch 4:10 *you would* **b** me and enlarge my territory! 1385+1385
   16:43 and David returned home to **b** his family. 1385
   17:27 Now you have been pleased to **b** the house 1385
2Ch 30:27 The priests and the Levites stood *to* **b** 1385
Job 31:20 and his heart *did* not **b** me for warming him 1385
Ps 5:12 For surely, O LORD, you **b** the righteous; 1385
   28: 9 Save your people and **b** your inheritance; 1385
   41: 2 he *will* **b** him in the land and 887
   62: 4 With their mouths *they* **b**, 1385
   65:10 you soften it with showers and **b** its crops. 1385
   67: 1 and **b** us and make his face shine upon us, 1385
   67: 6 and God, our God, *will* **b** us. 1385
   67: 7 God *will* **b** us, 1385
   72:15 for him and **b** him all day long. 1385
   109:28 They may curse, but you *will* **b**; 1385
   115:12 The LORD remembers us and *will* **b** us: 1385
   115:12 *He* will **b** the house of Israel, 1385
   115:12 *he* will **b** the house of Aaron, 1385
   115:13 *he* will **b** those who fear the LORD— 1385
   118:26 From the house of the LORD *we* **b** you. 1385
   128: 5 the LORD **b** you from Zion all the days 1385
   129: 8 *we* **b** you in the name of the LORD." 1385
   132:15 *I* will **b** her *with* **abundant** provisions; 1385+1385
   134: 3 **b** you from Zion. 1385

Pr 30:11 and *do* not **b** their mothers; 1385
Isa 19:25 The LORD Almighty *will* **b** them, saying, 1385
Jer 31:23 'The LORD **b** you, O righteous dwelling, 1385
Eze 34:26 *I* will **b** them and the places 1388+5989
Hag 2:19 " 'From this day on *I* will **b** you.' " 1385
Zec 4: 7 the capstone to shouts of 'God **b** it! 2834
   4: 7 God **b** it!' " 2834
Lk 6:28 **b** those who curse you, 2328
Ac 3:26 to you *to* **b** you by turning each of you 2328
Ro 12:14 **B** those who persecute you; 2328
   12:14 **b** and do not curse. 2328
1Co 4:12 When we are cursed, *we* **b**; 2328
Heb 6:14 *"I* will surely **b** you 2328+2328

BLESSED (234) [BLESS]

Ge 1:22 God **b** them and said, 1385
   1:28 God **b** them and said to them, 1385
   2: 3 God **b** the seventh day and made it holy, 1385
   5: 2 and female and **b** them. 1385
   9: 1 Then God **b** Noah and his sons, 1385
   9:26 He also said, "**B** be the LORD, 1385
   12: 3 and all peoples on earth *will* be **b** 1385
   14:19 and he **b** Abram, 1385
   14:19 saying, "**B** be Abram by God Most High, 1385
   14:20 And **b** *be* God Most High, 1385
   18:18 all nations on earth *will* be **b** through him. 1385
   22:18 on earth *will* be **b**, 1385
   24: 1 and the LORD *had* **b** him in every way. 1385
   24:31 "Come, *you who are* **b** by the LORD," 1385
   24:35 The LORD *has* **b** my master abundantly, 1385
   24:60 And *they* **b** Rebekah and said to her, 1385
   25:11 God **b** his son Isaac, 1385
   26: 4 on earth *will* be **b**, 1385
   26:12 because the LORD **b** him. 1385
   26:29 And now you are **b** by the LORD." 1385
   27:23 so he **b** him. 1385
   27:27 he **b** him and said, "Ah, 1385
   27:27 the smell of a field that the LORD *has* **b**. 1385
   27:29 be cursed and those who bless you be **b**." 1385
   27:33 I ate it just before you came and *I* **b** him— 1385
   27:33 and indeed he will **b**!" 1385
   28: 1 for Jacob and **b** him and commanded him: 1385
   28: 6 Now Esau learned that Isaac *had* **b** Jacob 1385
   28: 6 that when he **b** him he commanded him, 1385
   28:14 All peoples on earth *will* be **b** through you 1385
   30:27 that the LORD *has* **b** me because of you." 1385
   30:30 LORD *has* **b** you wherever I have been. 1385
   31:55 and his daughters and **b** them. 1385
   32:29 Then he **b** him there. 1385
   35: 9 God appeared to him again and **b** him. 1385
   39: 5 the LORD **b** the household of the Egyptian 1385
   47: 7 After Jacob **b** Pharaoh, 1385
   47:10 Then Jacob **b** Pharaoh and went out 1385
   48: 3 and there *he* **b** me 1385
   48:15 Then *he* **b** Joseph and said, 1385
   48:20 *He* **b** them that day and said, 1385
   49:28 to them when *he* **b** them, 1385
Ex 20:11 Therefore the LORD **b** the Sabbath day 1385
   32:29 and he *has* **b** you this day." 1388+5989
   39:43 So Moses **b** them. 1385
Lev 9:22 toward the people and **b** them. 1385
   9:23 When they came out, *they* **b** the people; 1385
Nu 22: 6 For I know that those *you* bless *are* **b**, 1385
   22:12 because they *are* **b**." 1385
   23:20 *he has* **b**, and I cannot change it. 1385
   24: 9 "May those who bless you *be* **b** 1385
   24:10 but *you have* **b** them these three times. 1385+1385
Dt 2: 7 The LORD your God *has* **b** you in all 1385
   7:14 You will be **b** more than any other people; 1385
   12: 7 because the LORD your God *has* **b** you. 1385
   14:24 and you *have been* **b** by 1385
   15:14 to him as the LORD your God *has* **b** you. 1385
   16:17 the way the LORD your God *has* **b** you. 1388+5989
   28: 3 You *will* be **b** in the city and blessed in 1385
   28: 3 be blessed in the city and **b** in the country. 1385
   28: 4 The fruit of your womb *will* be **b**, 1385
   28: 5 and your kneading trough *will* be **b**. 1385
   28: 6 You *will* be **b** when you come in 1385
   28: 6 when you come in and **b** when you go out. 1385
   33:20 "**B** is he who enlarges Gad's domain! 1385
   33:24 *"Most* **b** of sons is Asher," 1385
   33:29 **B** are you, O Israel! 897
Jos 14:13 Then Joshua **b** Caleb son of Jephunneh 1385
   17:14 and the LORD *has* **b** us abundantly." 1385
   22: 6 Then Joshua **b** them and sent them away, 1385
   22: 7 When Joshua sent them home, *he* **b** them, 1385
   24:10 **b** you **again and again**, 1385+1385
Jdg 5:24 "Most **b** of women be Jael, 1385
   5:24 most **b** of tent-dwelling women. 1385
   13:24 He grew and the LORD **b** him, 1385
Ru 2:19 **B** be the man who took notice of you!" 1385
1Sa 25:33 *May* you be **b** *for* your good judgment and 1385
   26:25 then Saul said to David, *"May* you be **b**, 1385
2Sa 6:11 the LORD **b** him and his entire household. 1385
   6:12 "The LORD *has* **b** the household 1385
   6:18 *he* **b** the people in the name of the LORD 1385
   7:29 of your servant *will* be **b** forever." 1385
   12:24 and *he* **b** the king. 1385
1Ki 2:45 But King Solomon *will* be **b**, 1385
   8:14 the king turned around and **b** them. 1385
   8:55 and **b** the whole assembly of Israel in 1385
   8:66 *They* **b** the king and then went home, 1385
1Ch 13:14 and the LORD **b** his household 1385
   16: 2 *he* **b** the people in the name of the LORD. 1385
   17:27 for you, O LORD, *have* **b** it, 1385
   17:27 have **blessed** it, and *it* will *be* **b** forever." 1385

1Ch 26: 5 (For God *had* **b** Obed-Edom.) 1385
2Ch 6: 3 the king turned around and **b** them. 1385
   31: 8 the LORD and **b** his people Israel. 1385
   31:10 because the LORD *has* **b** his people. 1385
Ne 9: 5 "**B** be your glorious name, 1385
Job 1:10 *You have* **b** the work of his hands, 1385
   5:17 "**B** is the man whom God corrects; 897
   29: 4 God's intimate friendship **b** my house, 6584
   29:13 The man who was dying **b** me; 995+1388
   42:12 The LORD **b** the latter part 1385
Ps 1: 1 **B** is the man who does not walk in 897
   2:12 **B** are all who take refuge in him. 897
   32: 1 **B** is he whose transgressions are forgiven, 897
   32: 2 **B** is the man whose sin the LORD does 897
   33:12 **B** is the nation whose God is the LORD, 897
   34: 8 **b** is the man who takes refuge in him. 897
   37:26 their children will be **b**. 1388
   40: 4 **B** is the man who makes 897
   41: 1 **B** is he who has regard for the weak; 897
   45: 2 since God *has* **b** you forever. 1385
   49:18 Though while he lived *he* **counted** himself **b**— 1385
   65: 4 **B** are those you choose and bring near 897
   72:17 All nations *will* be **b** through him, 1385
   72:17 and *they* will **call** him **b**. 887
   84: 4 **B** are those who dwell in your house; 897
   84: 5 **B** are those whose strength is in you, 897
   84:12 **b** is the man who trusts in you. 897
   89:15 **B** are those who have learned 897
   94:12 **B** is the man you discipline, O LORD, 897
   106: 3 **B** are they who maintain justice, 897
   107:38 *he* **b** them, and their numbers greatly increased, 1385
   112: 1 **B** is the man who fears the LORD, 897
   112: 2 the generation of the upright *will* be **b**. 1385
   115:15 *May* you be **b** by the LORD, 1385
   118:26 **B** *is* he who comes in the name of 1385
   119: 1 **B** are they whose ways are blameless, 897
   119: 2 **B** are they who keep his statutes 897
   127: 5 **B** is the man whose quiver is full of them. 897
   128: 1 **B** are all who fear the LORD, 897
   128: 4 Thus is the man **b** who fears the LORD. 1385
   144:15 **B** are the people of whom this is true; 897
   144:15 **b** are the people whose God is the LORD. 897
   146: 5 **B** is he whose help is the God of Jacob, 897
Pr 3:13 **B** is the man who finds wisdom, 897
   3:18 those who lay hold of her *will* be **b**. 887
   5:18 May your fountain be **b**, 1385
   8:32 **b** are those who keep my ways. 897
   8:34 **B** is the man who listens to me, 897
   14:21 but **b** is he who is kind to the needy. 897
   16:20 and **b** is he who trusts in the LORD. 897
   20: 7 **b** are his children after him. 897
   20:21 at the beginning *will* not *be* **b** at the end. 1385
   22: 9 A generous man *will* himself *be* **b**, 1385
   28:14 **B** is the man who always fears the LORD, 897
   28:20 A faithful man will be richly **b**, 1388
   29:18 but **b** is he who keeps the law. 890
   31:28 Her children arise and **call** her **b**; 887
Ecc 10:17 **B** are you, O land whose king is 897
SS 6: 9 The maidens saw her and **called** her **b**; 887
Isa 19:25 saying, "**B** be Egypt my people, 1385
   30:18 **B** are all who wait for him! 897
   32:20 how **b** you will be, 897
   51: 2 and *I* **b** him and made him many. 1385
   56: 2 **B** is the man who does this, 897
   61: 9 that they are a people the LORD *has* **b**." 1385
   65:23 for they will be a people **b** by the LORD, 1385
Jer 4: 2 then the nations *will* be **b** by him and 1385
   17: 7 **b** *is* the man who trusts in the LORD, 1385
   20:14 May the day my mother bore me not be **b**! 1385
Da 12:12 **B** is the one who waits for and reaches 897
Mal 3:12 "Then all the nations *will* **call** you **b**, 887
   3:15 But now we **call** the arrogant **b**. 887
Mt 5: 3 "**B** are the poor in spirit, 3421
   5: 4 **B** are those who mourn, 3421
   5: 5 **B** are the meek, 3421
   5: 6 **B** are those who hunger and thirst 3421
   5: 7 **B** are the merciful, 3421
   5: 8 **B** are the pure in heart, 3421
   5: 9 **B** are the peacemakers, 3421
   5:10 **B** are those who are persecuted because 3421
   5:11 "**B** are you when people insult you, 3421
   11: 6 **B** is the man who does not fall away 3421
   13:16 But **b** are your eyes because they see, 3421
   16:17 Jesus replied, "**B** are you, 3421
   21: 9 "**B** is he who comes in the name of the Lord 2328
   23:39 '**B** is he who comes in the name of the Lord 2328
   25:34 'Come, *you who are* **b** by my Father; 2328
Mk 10:16 put his hands on them and **b** them. 2986
   11: 9 "**B** is he who comes in the name of the Lord 2328
   11:10 "**B** is the coming kingdom 2328
   14:61 the Son of the **B** One?" 2329
Lk 1:42 "**B** *are* you among women, 2328
   1:42 and **b** *is* the child you will bear! 2328
   1:45 **B** is she who has believed that what 3421
   1:48 now on all generations *will* **call** me **b**, 3420
   2:34 Then Simeon **b** them and said to Mary, 2328
   6:20 "**B** are you who are poor, 3421
   6:21 **B** are you who hunger now, 3421
   6:21 **B** are you who weep now, 3421
   6:22 **B** are you when men hate you, 3421
   7:23 **B** is the man who does not fall away 3421
   10:23 "**B** are the eyes that see what you see. 3421
   11:27 "**B** is the mother who gave you birth 3421
   11:28 "**B** rather are those who hear the word 3421
   13:35 '**B** is he who comes in the name of 2328

Lk	14:14	and you will be b. 3421
	14:15	"B is the man who will eat at the feast in 3421
	19:38	"B is the king who comes in the name of 2328
	23:29	'B are the barren women, 3421
	24:50	he lifted up his hands and b them. 2328
Jn	12:13	"B is he who comes in the name of the Lord 2328
	12:13	"B is the King of Israel!" NIG
	13:17	you will be b if you do them. 3421
	20:29	b are those who have not seen and yet have believed. 3421
Ac	3:25	all peoples on earth will be b.' 1922
	20:35	'It is more b to give than to receive.'" 3421
Ro	4:7	"B are they whose transgressions are forgiven, 3421
	4:8	B is the man whose sin the Lord will never count against him." 3421
	14:22	B is the man who does not condemn himself 3421
Gal	3:8	"All nations will be b through you." 1922
	3:9	So those who have faith are b along 2328
Eph	1:3	who has b us in the heavenly realms 2328
1Ti	1:11	to the glorious gospel of the b God, 3421
	6:15	God, the b and only Ruler, 3421
Tit	2:13	while we wait for the b hope— 3421
Heb	7:1	from the defeat of the kings and b him, 2328
	7:6	a tenth from Abraham and b him who had 2328
	7:7	And without doubt the lesser person is b 2328
	11:20	By faith Isaac b Jacob and Esau in regard 2328
	11:21	b each of Joseph's sons, 2328
Jas	1:12	B is the man who perseveres under trial, 3421
	1:25	he will be b in what he does. 3421
	5:11	we consider b those who have persevered. 3420
1Pe	3:14	suffer for what is right, you are b. 3421
	4:14	insulted because of the name of Christ, you are b, 3421
Rev	1:3	B is the one who reads the words 3421
	1:3	and b are those who hear it and take NIG
	14:13	B are the dead who die in the Lord 3421
	16:15	B is he who stays awake and keeps 3421
	19:9	'B are those who are invited to the wedding 3421
	20:6	B and holy are those who have part in the first resurrection. 3421
	22:7	B is he who keeps the words of the prophecy 3421
	22:14	"B are those who wash their robes, 3421

BLESSEDNESS (2) [BLESS]

Ro	4:6	the same thing when he speaks of the b of 3422
	4:9	Is this b only for the circumcised, 3422

BLESSES (8) [BLESS]

Ge	49:25	who b you with blessings of the heavens 1385
Ps	10:3	he b the greedy and reviles the LORD. 1385
	29:11	the LORD b his people with peace. 1385
	37:22	those the LORD b will inherit the land, 1385
	147:13	of your gates and b your people within you. 1385
Pr	3:33	but he b the home of the righteous. 1385
	27:14	If a man loudly b his neighbor early in 1385
Ro	10:12	of all and richly b all who call on him, NIG

BLESSING (65) [BLESS]

Ge	12:2	and you will be a b. 1388
	17:18	"If only Ishmael might live under your b!" 4200+7156
	27:4	so that I may give you my b before I die." 1385
	27:7	so that I may give you my b in the presence 1385
	27:10	that he may give you his b before he dies." 1385
	27:12	down a curse on myself rather than a b." 1388
	27:19	so that you may give me your b." 1385
	27:25	so that I may give you my b." 1385
	27:30	After Isaac finished b him 1385
	27:31	so that you may give me your b." 1385
	27:35	and took your b." 1388
	27:36	and now he's taken my b!" 1388
	27:36	"Haven't you reserved any b for me?" 1388
	27:38	"Do you have only one b, my father? 1388
	27:41	because of the b his father had given him. 1388
	28:4	and your descendants the b given 1388
	39:5	The b of the LORD was on everything 1388
	48:20	"In your name will Israel pronounce this b: 1385
	49:28	giving each the b appropriate to him. 1385+1388
Ex	23:25	and his b will be on your food and water. 1385
Lev	25:21	I will send you such a b in the sixth year 1388
Dt	11:26	I am setting before you today a b and 1388
	11:27	the b if you obey the commands of 1388
	12:15	to the b the LORD your God gives you. 1388
	23:5	to Balaam but turned the curse into a b 1388
	28:8	The LORD will send a b on your barns 1388
	29:19	he invokes a b on himself 1385
	33:1	This is the b that Moses the man 1388
	33:23	the favor of the LORD and is full of his b; 1388
2Sa	7:29	with your b the house of your servant will 1388
	13:25	he still refused to go, but gave him his b. 1385
	19:39	and gave him his b, 1385
Ne	9:5	may it be exalted above all b and praise. 1388
	13:2	however, turned the curse into a b.) 1388
Ps	3:8	May your b be on your people. 1388
	24:5	He will receive b from the LORD 1388
	109:17	he found no pleasure in b— 1388
	129:8	"The b of the LORD be upon you; 1388
	133:3	For there the LORD bestows his b, 1388
Pr	10:7	The memory of the righteous will be a b, 1388
	10:22	The b of the LORD brings wealth, 1388
	11:11	the b of the upright a city is exalted, 1388
	11:26	but b crowns him who is willing to sell. 1388
	24:25	and rich b will come upon them. 1388
Isa	19:24	a b on the earth. 1388

Isa	44:3	and my b on your descendants. 1388
	65:16	Whoever invokes a b in the land will do so 1388
Jer	16:5	because I have withdrawn my b, 8934
Eze	34:26	there will be showers of b. 1388
	44:30	of your ground meal so that a b may rest 1388
Joel	2:14	and have pity and leave behind a b— 1388
Mic	2:9	You take away my b from their children 2077
Zec	8:13	so will I save you, and you will be a b. 1388
Mal	3:10	and pour out so much b that you will 1388
Lk	24:51	While he was b them, 2328
Jn	1:16	of his grace we have all received one b 5921
Ac	15:33	by the brothers with the b of peace to return 1645
Ro	15:29	I will come in the full measure of the b 2330
Gal	3:14	that the b given to Abraham might come to 2330
Eph	1:3	the heavenly realms with every spiritual b 2330
Heb	6:7	for whom it is farmed receives the b 2330
	12:17	when he wanted to inherit this b, 2330
	12:17	though he sought the b with tears. 899S
1Pe	3:9	but with b, because to this you were called 2328
	3:9	so that you may inherit a b. 2330

BLESSINGS (24) [BLESS]

Ge	49:25	who blesses you with b of the heavens 1388
	49:25	b of the deep that lies below, 1388
	49:25	b of the breast and womb. 1388
	49:26	Your father's b are greater than 1388
	49:26	the b of the ancient mountains, 1388
Dt	10:8	to minister and to pronounce b in his name, 1385
	11:29	to proclaim on Mount Gerizim the b, 1388
	16:10	b the LORD your God has given 1385
	21:5	to minister and to pronounce b in the name 1385
	28:2	All these b will come upon you 1388
	30:1	When all these b and curses I have set 1388
	30:19	that I have set before you life and death, b 1388
Jos	8:34	the b and the curses— 1388
1Ch	23:13	to minister before him and to pronounce b 1385
Ps	21:3	with rich b and placed a crown of pure gold 1388
	21:6	Surely you have granted him eternal b 1388
	128:2	b and prosperity will be yours. 897
Pr	10:6	B crown the head of the righteous, 1388
Hos	3:5	to the LORD and to his b in the last days. 3206
Mal	2:2	and I will curse your b. 1388
Ac	13:34	holy and sure b promised 4008
Ro	15:27	Gentiles have shared in the Jews' spiritual b, NIG
	15:27	to share with them their material b. NIG
1Co	9:23	that I may share in its b. NIG

BLEW (13) [BLOW]

Ex	15:10	But you b with your breath, 5973
Jos	6:9	ahead of the priests who b the trumpets, 9546
Jdg	3:27	he b a trumpet in the hill country 9546
	6:34	and he b a trumpet, 9546
	7:19	They b their trumpets and broke the jars 9546
	7:20	The three companies b the trumpets 9546
2Sa	2:28	So Joab b the trumpet, 9546
2Ki	9:13	Then they b the trumpet and shouted, 9546
2Ch	7:6	the priests b their trumpets, 2955
	13:14	The priests b their trumpets 2955
Hag	1:9	What you brought home, I b away. 5870
Mt	7:25	the winds b and beat against that house; 4463
	7:27	and the winds b and beat against that house, 4463

BLIGHT (5) [BLIGHTED]

Dt	28:22	with b and mildew, 8730
1Ki	8:37	or b or mildew, locusts or grasshoppers, 8730
2Ch	6:28	or b or mildew, locusts or grasshoppers, 8730
Am	4:9	I struck them with b and mildew. 8730
Hag	2:17	I struck all the work of your hands with b, 8730

BLIGHTED (2) [BLIGHT]

Ps	102:4	My heart is b and withered like grass; 5782
Hos	9:16	Ephraim is b, their root is withered, 5782

BLIND (82) [BLINDED, BLINDFOLDS, BLINDNESS, BLINDS]

Ex	4:11	Who gives him sight or makes him b? 6426
Lev	19:14	or put a stumbling block in front of the b, 6426
	21:18	no man who is b or lame, 6426
	22:22	Do not offer to the LORD the b, 6428
Dt	15:21	If an animal has a defect, is lame or b, 6426
	27:18	"Cursed is the man who leads the b astray 6426
	28:29	about like a b man in the dark. 6426
1Sa	5:6	be spared only to b your eyes with tears and 3983
2Sa	5:6	even the b and the lame can ward you off." 6426
	5:8	and b' who are David's enemies." 6426
	5:8	'b and lame' will not enter the palace." 6426
Job	29:15	I was eyes to the b and feet to the lame. 6426
Ps	146:8	the LORD gives sight to the b, 6426
Isa	29:9	b yourselves and be sightless; 9129
	29:18	and darkness the eyes of the b will see. 6426
	35:5	the eyes of the b be opened and the ears of 6426
	42:7	to open eyes that are b, 6426
	42:16	the b by ways they have not known, 6426
	42:18	"Hear, you deaf; look, you b, and see! 6426
	42:19	Who is b but my servant, 6426
	42:19	Who is b like the one committed to me, 6426
	42:19	b like the servant of the LORD? 6426
	43:8	Lead out those who have eyes but are b, 6426
	44:9	Those who would speak up for them are b; 1153+8011
	56:10	Israel's watchmen are b, 6426
	59:10	Like the b we grope along the wall, 6426
Jer	31:8	Among them will be the b and the lame, 6426

La	4:14	through the streets like men who are b. 6426
Zep	1:17	on the people and they will walk like b men, 6426
Zec	12:4	but I will b all the horses of the nations. 928+2021+5782+6427
Mal	1:8	When you bring b animals for sacrifice, 6426
Mt	9:27	two b men followed him, calling out, 5603
	9:28	the b men came to him, and he asked them, 5603
	11:5	The b receive sight, 5603
	12:22	a demon-possessed man who was b 5603
	15:14	Leave them; they are b guides. 5603
	15:14	If a b man leads a blind man, 5603
	15:14	If a blind man leads a b man, 5603
	15:30	bringing the lame, the b, the crippled, 5603
	15:31	the lame walking and the b seeing. 5603
	20:30	Two b men were sitting by the roadside. 5603
	21:14	The b and the lame came to him at 5603
	23:16	"Woe to you, b guides! 5603
	23:17	You b fools! 5603
	23:19	You b men! 5603
	23:24	You b guides! 5603
	23:26	B Pharisee! First clean the inside of the cup 5603
Mk	8:22	a b man and begged Jesus to touch him. 5603
	8:23	the b man by the hand and led him outside 5603
	10:46	were leaving the city, a b man, 5603
	10:49	So they called to the b man, "Cheer up! 5603
	10:51	The b man said, "Rabbi, I want to see." 5603
Lk	4:18	and recovery of sight for the b, 5603
	6:39	"Can a b man lead a blind man? 5603
	6:39	"Can a blind man lead a b man? 5603
	7:21	and gave sight to many who were b. 5603
	7:22	The b receive sight, the lame walk, 5603
	14:13	the crippled, the lame, the b, 5603
	14:21	the crippled, the b and the lame.' 5603
	18:35	a b man was sitting by the roadside begging. 5603
Jn	5:3	the b, the lame, the paralyzed. 5603
	9:1	he saw a man b from birth. 5603
	9:2	that he was born b?" 5603
	9:13	to the Pharisees the man who had been b. 5603
	9:17	Finally they turned again to the b man, 5603
	9:18	not believe that he had been b 5603
	9:19	"Is this the one you say was born b? 5603
	9:20	"and we know he was born b. 5603
	9:24	the man who had been b. 5603
	9:25	I was b but now I see!" 5603
	9:32	of opening the eyes of a man born b. 5603
	9:39	so that the b will see 1063+3590
	9:39	and those who see will become b." 5603
	9:40	Are we b too?" 5603
	9:41	Jesus said, "If you were b, 5603
	10:21	Can a demon open the eyes of the b?" 5603
	11:37	the b man have kept this man from dying?" 5603
Ac	9:9	For three days he was b, 1063+3590
	13:11	You are going to be b, 5603
Ro	2:19	that you are a guide for the b, 5603
2Pe	1:9	he is nearsighted and b. 5603
Rev	3:17	pitiful, poor, b and naked. 5603

BLINDED (5) [BLIND]

Zec	11:17	his right eye totally b!" 3908+3908
Jn	12:40	"He has b their eyes 5604
Ac	22:11	because the brilliance of the light had b me. 1838+4024
2Co	4:4	The god of this age has b the minds of unbelievers, 5604
1Jn	2:11	because the darkness has b him. 5604

BLINDFOLDED (2)

Mk	14:65	they b him, struck him with their fists, 3836+4328+4725
Lk	22:64	They b him and demanded, "Prophesy! 4328

BLINDFOLDS (1) [BLIND]

Job	9:24	he b its judges. 4059+7156

BLINDNESS (4) [BLIND]

Ge	19:11	with b so that they could not find the door. 6177
Dt	28:28	b and confusion of mind. 6427
2Ki	6:18	"Strike these people with b." 6177
	6:18	he struck them with b, as Elisha had asked. 6177

BLINDS (2) [BLIND]

Ex	23:8	for a bribe b those who see and twists 6422
Dt	16:19	for a bribe b the eyes of the wise and twists 6422

BLOCK (13) [BLOCKED, BLOCKING, BLOCKS]

Lev	19:14	or put a stumbling b in front of the blind, 4842
Isa	44:19	Shall I bow down to a b of wood?" 1005
Eze	3:20	and I put a stumbling b before him, 4842
	14:4	in his heart and puts a wicked stumbling b 4842
	14:7	in his heart and puts a wicked stumbling b 4842
	39:11	It will b the way of travelers, 2888
Hos	2:6	Therefore I will b her path 8455
Mt	16:23	You are a stumbling b to me; 4998
Ro	11:9	a stumbling b and a retribution for them. 4998
	14:13	up your mind not to put any stumbling b 4682
1Co	1:23	a stumbling b to Jews and foolishness 4998
	8:9	not become a stumbling b to the weak. 4682
2Co	6:3	We put no stumbling b in anyone's path, 4683

BLOCKED (5) [BLOCK]

Lev	15:3	from his body or is b, 3159

2Ch 32: 4 and *they* **b** all the springs and the stream 6258
   32:30 It was Hezekiah *who* **b** the upper outlet of 6258
Job 19: 8 He has **b** my way so I cannot pass; 1553
Pr 15:19 The way of the sluggard is **b** *with* thorns, 5379

BLOCKING (1) [BLOCK]
2Ch 32: 3 and military staff about **b** off the water 6258

BLOCKS (5) [BLOCK]
1Ki 5:17 from the quarry large **b** of quality stone 74
   6: 7 only **b** dressed at the quarry were used, 74
   7: 9 were made of **b** of high-grade **stone** cut AIT
La 3: 9 He has barred my way with **b** of stone; 1607
Eze 14: 3 in their hearts and put wicked **stumbling b** 4842

BLOOD (405) [AKELDAMA, BLEEDING, BLOOD-STAINED, BLOODSHED, BLOODSHOT, BLOODSTAINS, BLOODTHIRSTY, LIFEBLOOD]
Ge 4:10 Your brother's **b** cries out to me from 1947
   4:11 to receive your brother's **b** from your hand. 1947
   9: 6 "Whoever sheds the **b** of man, 1947
   9: 6 by man shall his **b** be shed; 1947
   29:14 "You are my own flesh and **b**." 6795
   37:22 "Don't shed any **b**. 1947
   37:26 if we kill our brother and cover up his **b**? 1947
   37:27 all, he is our brother, our own **flesh and b**. 1414
   37:31 a goat and dipped the robe in the **b**. 1947
   42:22 Now we must give an accounting for his **b**." 1947
   49:11 his robes in the **b** of grapes. 1947
Ex 4: 9 the river will become **b** on the ground." 1947
   4:25 "Surely you are a bridegroom of **b** to me," 1947
   4:26 (At that time she said "bridegroom of **b**," 1947
   7:17 and it will be changed into **b**. 1947
   7:19 and they will turn to **b**. 1947
   7:19 **B** will be everywhere in Egypt, 1947
   7:20 and all the water was changed into **b**. 1947
   7:21 **B** was everywhere in Egypt. 1947
   12: 7 to take some of the **b** and put it on the sides 1947
   12:13 The **b** will be a sign for you on the houses 1947
   12:13 and when I see the **b**, I will pass over you. 1947
   12:22 the **b** in the basin and put some of the blood 1947
   12:22 blood in the basin and put some of the **b** 1947
   12:23 the **b** on the top and sides of the doorframe 1947
   23:18 not offer the **b** of a sacrifice to me along 1947
   24: 6 Moses took half of the **b** and put it 1947
   24: 8 Moses then took the **b**, 1947
   24: 8 "This is the **b** of the covenant that 1947
   29:12 of the bull's **b** and put it on the horns of 1947
   29:16 Slaughter it and take the **b** and sprinkle it 1947
   29:20 take some of its **b** and put it on the lobes of 1947
   29:20 sprinkle **b** against the altar on all sides. 1947
   29:21 And take some of the **b** on the altar 1947
   30:10 with the **b** of the atoning sin offering for 1947
   34:25 not offer the **b** of a sacrifice to me along 1947
Lev 1: 5 the priests shall bring the **b** and sprinkle it 1947
   1:11 the priests shall sprinkle its **b** against 1947
   1:15 its **b** shall be drained out on the side of 1947
   3: 2 the priests shall sprinkle the **b** against 1947
   3: 8 Then Aaron's sons shall sprinkle its **b** 1947
   3:13 Then Aaron's sons shall sprinkle its **b** 1947
   3:17 You must not eat any fat or any **b**.' " 1947
   4: 5 of the bull's **b** and carry it into the Tent 1947
   4: 6 the **b** and sprinkle some of it seven times 1947
   4: 7 The priest shall then put some of the **b** on 1947
   4: 7 the bull's **b** he shall pour out at the base of 1947
   4:16 to take some of the bull's **b** into the Tent 1947
   4:17 He shall dip his finger into the **b** 1947
   4:18 the **b** on the horns of the altar that is before 1947
   4:18 of the **b** he shall pour out at the base of 1947
   4:25 Then the priest shall take some of the **b** of 1947
   4:25 and pour out the rest of the **b** at the base of 1947
   4:30 the **b** with his finger and put it on the horns 1947
   4:30 and pour out the rest of the **b** at the base of 1947
   4:34 Then the priest shall take some of the **b** of 1947
   4:34 and pour out the rest of the **b** at the base of 1947
   5: 9 to sprinkle some of the **b** of the sin offering 1947
   5: 9 of the **b** must be drained out at the base of 1947
   6:27 if any of the **b** is spattered on a garment, 1947
   6:30 But any sin offering whose **b** is brought 1947
   7: 2 and its **b** is to be sprinkled against the altar 1947
   7:14 It belongs to the priest who sprinkles the **b** 1947
   7:26 not eat the **b** of any bird or animal. 1947
   7:27 If anyone eats **b**, 1947
   7:33 of Aaron who offers the **b** and the fat of 1947
   8:15 the bull and took *some* of the **b**, 1947
   8:15 He poured out the rest of the **b** at the base 1947
   8:19 the ram and sprinkled the **b** against the altar 1947
   8:23 and took some of its **b** and put it on the lobe 1947
   8:24 of the **b** on the lobes of their right ears, 1947
   8:24 he sprinkled **b** against the altar on all sides. 1947
   8:30 of the anointing oil and some of the **b** from 1947
   9: 9 His sons brought the **b** to him, 1947
   9: 9 the **b** and put it on the horns of the altar; 1947
   9: 9 the rest of the **b** he poured out at the base of 1947
   9:12 His sons handed him the **b**, 1947
   9:18 His sons handed him the **b**, 1947
   10:18 its **b** was not taken into the Holy Place, 1947
   12: 7 be ceremonially clean from her flow of **b**. 1947
   14:14 the **b** of the bird that was killed over 1947
   14:14 to take some of the **b** of the guilt offering 1947
   14:17 on top of the **b** of the guilt offering. 1947
   14:25 and take some of its **b** and put it on the lobe 1947
   14:28 to put on the same places he put the **b** of 1947

Lev 14:51 the **b** of the dead bird and the fresh water, 1947
   14:52 He shall purify the house with the bird's **b**, 1947
   15:19 a woman has her regular flow of **b**, 1947
   15:25 " 'When a woman has a discharge of **b** 1947
   16:14 the bull's **b** and with his finger sprinkle it 1947
   16:15 the sin offering for the people and take its **b** 1947
   16:15 and do with it as he did with the bull's **b**: 1947
   16:18 He shall take some of the bull's **b** and some 1947
   16:18 of the bull's blood and some of the goat's **b** 1947
   16:19 of the **b** on it with his finger seven times 1947
   16:27 whose **b** was brought into 1947
   17: 4 he has shed **b** and must be cut off 1947
   17: 6 the **b** against the altar of the LORD at 1947
   17:10 among you who eats any **b**— 1947
   17:10 that person who eats **b** and will cut him off 1947
   17:11 For the life of a creature is in the **b**, 1947
   17:11 the **b** that makes atonement for one's life. 1947
   17:12 "None of you may eat **b**, 1947
   17:12 nor may an alien living among you eat **b**." 1947
   17:13 be eaten must drain out the **b** and cover it 1947
   17:14 because the life of every creature is its **b**. 1947
   17:14 "You must not eat the **b** of any creature, 1947
   17:14 because the life of every creature is its **b**." 1947
   19:26 " 'Do not eat any meat with the **b** still in it. 1947
   20: 9 and his **b** will be on his own head. 1947
   20:11 their **b** will be on their own heads. 1947
   20:12 their **b** will be on their own heads. 1947
   20:13 their **b** will be on their own heads. 1947
   20:16 their **b** will be on their own heads. 1947
   20:27 their **b** will be on their own heads.' " 1947
   25:49 An uncle or a cousin or any **b** relative 1414+8638
Nu 18:17 Sprinkle their **b** on the altar 1947
   19: 4 to take some of its **b** on his finger 1947
   19: 5 its hide, flesh, **b** and offal. 1947
   23:24 till he devours his prey and drinks the **b** 1947
   35:19 The avenger of **b** shall put the murderer 1947
   35:21 the avenger of **b** shall put the murderer 1947
   35:24 of **b** according to these regulations. 1947
   35:25 of **b** and send him back to the city of refuge 1947
   35:27 the avenger of **b** finds him outside the city, 1947
   35:27 the avenger of **b** may kill the accused 1947
   35:33 for the land on which **b** has been shed, 1947
   35:33 except by the **b** of the one who shed it. 1947
Dt 12:16 But you must not eat the **b**; 1947
   12:23 But be sure you do not eat the **b**, 1947
   12:23 because the **b** is the life, 1947
   12:24 You must not eat **the b**; 5647S
   12:27 both the meat and the **b**. 1947
   12:27 The **b** of your sacrifices must be poured 1947
   15:23 But you must not eat the **b**; 1947
   19: 6 avenger of **b** might pursue him in a rage, 1947
   19:10 Do this so that innocent **b** will not be shed 1947
   19:12 hand him over to the avenger of **b** to die. 1947
   19:13 **guilt of shedding** innocent **b**, 1947
   21: 7 "Our hands did not shed this **b**, 1947
   21: 8 not hold your people **guilty of** the **b** of 1947
   21: 9 **guilt of shedding** innocent **b**, 1947
   32:14 You drank the foaming **b** of the grape. 1947
   32:42 I will make my arrows drunk with **b**, 1947
   32:42 the **b** of the slain and the captives, 1947
   32:43 for he will avenge the **b** of his servants; 1947
Jos 2:19 his **b** will be on his own head; 1947
   2:19 his **b** will be on our head if a hand is laid 1947
   20: 3 and find protection from the avenger of **b**. 1947
   20: 5 If the avenger of **b** pursues him, 1947
   20: 9 and not be killed by the avenger of **b** prior 1947
Jdg 9: 2 Remember, I am your flesh and **b**." 6795
   9:24 the **shedding of** their **b**, 1947
1Sa 14:32 together with the **b**. 1947
   14:33 the LORD by eating meat that has **b** in it." 1947
   14:34 the LORD by eating meat with **b** still 1947
   26:20 Now do not let my **b** fall to the ground far 1947
2Sa 1:16 "Your **b** be on your own head. 1947
   1:22 From the **b** of the slain, 1947
   3:27 to avenge the **b** of his brother Asahel, 1947
   3:28 the LORD concerning the **b** of Abner son 1947
   3:29 May his **b** fall upon the head of Joab and NIH
   4:11 now demand his **b** from your hand and rid 1947
   5: 1 "We are your own flesh and **b**. 6795
   14:11 to prevent the avenger of **b** from adding to 1947
   16: 7 get out, you man of **b**, you scoundrel! 1947
   16: 8 the **b** you **shed** *in* the household of Saul, 1947
   16: 8 to ruin because you are a man of **b**!" 1947
   19:12 You are my brothers, my own flesh and **b**. 6795
   19:13 'Are you not my own flesh and **b**? 6795
   20:12 Amasa lay wallowing in his **b** in the middle 1947
   23:17 "Is it not the **b** of men who went at the risk 1947
1Ki 2: 5 shedding their **b** in peacetime *as if* 1947
   2: 5 with that **b** stained the belt around his waist 1947
   2: 9 Bring his gray head down to the grave 1947
   in **b**." 1947
   2:31 **guilt of** the innocent **b** 1947
   2:32 for the **b** he shed, 1947
   2:33 May the **guilt of** their **b** rest on the head 1947
   2:37 your **b** will be on your own head." 1947
   8:19 but your son, who *is* your own
   flesh and b— 2743+3655+4946
   18:28 as was their custom, until their **b** flowed. 1947
   21:19 the place where dogs licked up Naboth's **b**, 1947
   21:19 dogs will lick up your **b**—yes, yours!' " 1947
   22:35 The **b** *from* his wound ran onto the floor of 1947
   22:38 and the dogs licked up his **b**, 1947
2Ki 3:22 the water looked red—like **b**. 1947
   3:23 "That's **b**!" they said. "Those kings 1947
   9: 7 and I will avenge the **b** of my servants 1947
   9: 7 of my servants the prophets and the **b** of all 1947
   9:26 the **b** of Naboth and the blood of his sons, 1947

2Ki 9:26 the blood of Naboth and the **b** of his sons, 1947
   9:33 of her **b** spattered the wall and the horses 1947
   16:13 the **b** of his fellowship offerings on 1947
   16:15 on the altar all the **b** of the burnt offerings 1947
   20:18 **your own flesh and b**, 1947
   21:16 so much innocent **b** that he filled Jerusalem 1947
   24: 4 including the shedding of innocent **b**, 1947
   24: 4 with innocent **b**, and the LORD was 1947
   25:25 the son of Elishama, who was of royal **b**, 2446
1Ch 11: 1 "We are your own flesh and **b**. 6795
   11:19 the **b** of these men who went at the risk 1947
   22: 8 'You have shed much **b** 1947
   22: 8 because you have shed much **b** on the earth 1947
   28: 3 because you are a warrior and have shed **b**.' 1947
2Ch 6: 9 but your son, who *is* your own
   flesh and b— 2743+3655+4946
   29:22 and the priests took the **b** and sprinkled it 1947
   29:22 the rams and sprinkled their **b** on the altar; 1947
   29:22 the lambs and sprinkled their **b** on the altar. 1947
   29:24 the goats and presented their **b** on the altar 1947
   30:16 The priests sprinkled the **b** handed to them 1947
   35:11 the priests sprinkled the **b** handed to them, NIH
Ne 5: 5 of the same **flesh and b** as our countrymen 1414
Job 16:18 "O earth, do not cover my **b**; 1947
   39:30 His young ones feast on **b**, 1947
Ps 9:12 For he who avenges **b** remembers; 1947
   16: 4 not pour out their libations of **b** or take 1947
   50:13 the flesh of bulls or drink the **b** of goats? 1947
   58:10 they bathe their feet in the **b** of the wicked. 1947
   68:23 that you may plunge your feet in the **b** 1947
   72:14 for precious is their **b** in his sight. 1947
   78:44 He turned their rivers to **b**; 1947
   79: 3 They have poured out **b** like water all 1947
   79:10 the nations that you avenge the outpoured **b** 1947
   105:29 He turned their waters into **b**, 1947
   106:38 They shed innocent **b**, 1947
   106:38 the **b** of their sons and daughters, 1947
   106:38 and the land was desecrated by their **b**. 1947
Pr 1:11 let's lie in wait for someone's **b**, 1947
   1:16 they are swift to shed **b**. 1947
   1:18 These men lie in wait for their own **b**; 1947
   6:17 a lying tongue, hands that shed innocent **b**, 1947
   12: 6 The words of the wicked lie in wait for **b**, 1947
   30:33 and as twisting the nose produces **b**, 1947
Isa 1:11 in the **b** of bulls and lambs and goats. 1947
   1:15 Your hands are full of **b**; 1947
   9: 5 In battle and every garment rolled in **b** will 1947
   15: 9 Dimon's waters are full of **b**, 1947
   26:21 The earth will disclose the **b** *shed upon* her; 1947
   34: 3 the mountains will be soaked with their **b**. 1947
   34: 6 The sword of the LORD is bathed in **b**, 1947
   34: 6 the **b** of lambs and goats, 1947
   34: 7 Their land will be drenched with **b**, 1947
   39: 7 **your own flesh and b** 3655+3870+4946
   49:26 they will be drunk on their own **b**, 1947
   58: 7 to turn away from your own **flesh and b**? 1414
   59: 3 For your hands are stained with **b**, 1947
   59: 7 they are swift to shed innocent **b**. 1947
   63: 3 their **b** spattered my garments, 5906
   63: 6 and poured their **b** on the ground." 5906
   66: 3 like one who presents pig's **b**, 1947
Jer 7: 6 or the widow and do not shed innocent **b** 1947
   19: 4 and they have filled this place with the **b** of 1947
   22: 3 and do not shed innocent **b** in this place. 1947
   22:17 on shedding innocent **b** and on oppression 1947
   26:15 the **guilt of** innocent **b** on yourselves and 1947
   41: 1 who was of royal **b** and had been one of 2446
   46:10 till it has quenched its thirst with **b**. 1947
   51:35 "May our **b** be on those who live 1947
La 4:13 who shed within her the **b** of the righteous. 1947
   4:14 They are so defiled with **b** that no one dares 1947
Eze 3:18 and I will hold you accountable for his **b**. 1947
   3:20 and I will hold you accountable for his **b**. 1947
   11:15 your brothers who are your **b** relatives 408+1460
   16: 6 by and saw you kicking about in your **b**, 1947
   16: 6 and as you lay there in your **b** I said to you, 1947
   16: 9 the **b** from you and put ointments on you. 1947
   16:22 kicking about in your **b**. 1947
   16:36 because you gave them your children's **b**, 1947
   16:38 and who shed **b**; 1947
   16:38 upon you the **vengeance of** my wrath 1947
   18:10 who sheds **b** or does any 1947
   18:13 he will surely be put to death and his **b** will 1947
   21:32 your **b** will be shed in your land, 1947
   22: 3 on herself doom by shedding **b** in her midst 1947
   22: 4 because of the **b** you have shed 1947
   22: 6 in you uses his power to shed **b**. 1947
   22: 9 In you are slanderous men bent on
   shedding **b**; 1947
   22:12 In you men accept bribes to shed **b**; 1947
   22:13 and at the **b** you have shed in your midst. 1947
   22:27 they shed **b** and kill people 1947
   23:37 for they have committed adultery and **b** is 1947
   23:45 and shed **b**, because they are adulterous 1947
   23:45 they are adulterous and **b** is on their hands. 1947
   24: 7 "For the **b** she shed is in her midst: 1947
   24: 8 up wrath and take revenge I put her **b** 1947
   28:23 upon her and make **b** flow in her streets. 1947
   32: 6 the land with your flowing **b** all the way to 1947
   33: 4 his **b** will be on his own head. 1947
   33: 5 his **b** will be on his own head. 1947
   33: 6 the watchman accountable for his **b**.' 1947
   33: 8 and I will hold you accountable for his **b**. 1947
   33:25 with the **b** still in it and look to your idols 1947
   33:25 in it and look to your idols and shed **b**, 1947
   36:18 because they had shed **b** in the land and 1947
   39:17 There you will eat flesh and drink **b**. 1947

Eze 39:18 the flesh of mighty men and drink the **b** *of* 1947
39:19 till you are glutted and drink **b** 1947
43:18 and sprinkling **b** upon the altar 1947
43:20 You are to take some of its **b** and put it on 1947
44: 7 fat and **b**, and you broke my covenant; 1947
44:15 before me to offer sacrifices of fat and **b**, 1947
45:19 to take some of the **b** of the sin offering 1947
Hos 6: 8 stained with footprints of **b**. 1947
Joel 2:30 **b** and fire and billows of smoke. 1947
2:31 be turned to darkness and the moon to **b** 1947
3:19 in whose land they shed innocent **b**. 1947
Mic 7: 2 All men lie in wait to shed **b**; 1947
Na 3: 1 Woe to the city of **b**, full of lies, 1947
Hab 2: 8 For you have shed man's **b**; 1947
2:17 For you have shed man's **b**. 1947
Zep 1:17 Their **b** will be poured out like dust 1947
Zec 9: 7 I will take the **b** from their mouths, 1947
9:11 because of the **b** *of* my covenant with you, 1947
Mt 23:30 in shedding the **b** of the prophets.' 135
23:35 the righteous **b** that has been shed on earth, 135
23:35 from the **b** of righteous Abel to the blood 135
23:35 of righteous Abel to the **b** of Zechariah son 135
26:28 This is my **b** of the covenant, 135
27: 4 he said, "for I have betrayed innocent **b**." 135
27: 6 since it is **b** money." 135+5507
27: 8 the Field *of* B to this day. 135
27:24 "I am innocent of this man's **b**," he said. 135
27:25 "Let his **b** be on us and on our children!" 135
Mk 14:24 "This is my **b** of the covenant, 135
Lk 11:50 the **b** of all the prophets that has been shed 135
11:51 the **b** of Abel to the blood of Zechariah, 135
11:51 the blood of Abel to the **b** of Zechariah, 135
13: 1 the Galileans whose **b** Pilate had mixed 135
22:20 "This cup is the new covenant in my **b**, 135
22:44 and his sweat was like drops of **b** falling to 135
Jn 6:53 the flesh of the Son of Man and drink his **b**, 135
6:54 and drinks my **b** has eternal life, 135
6:55 my flesh is real food and my **b** is real drink. 135
6:56 and drinks my **b** remains in me, 135
19:34 bringing a sudden flow of **b** and water. 135
Ac 1:19 Akeldama, that is, Field *of* **B**.) 135
2:19 **b** and fire and billows of smoke. 135
2:20 be turned to darkness and the moon to **b** 135
5:28 to make us guilty of this man's **b**." 135
15:20 the meat of strangled animals and from **b**. 135
15:29 *from* **b**, from the meat of strangled animals 135
18: 6 "Your **b** be on your own heads! 135
20:26 to you today that I am innocent of the **b** 135
20:28 which he bought with his own **b**. 135
21:25 from **b**, from the meat of strangled animals 135
22:20 the **b** of your martyr Stephen was shed, 135
Ro 3:15 "Their feet are swift *to* shed **b**; 135
3:25 through faith in his **b**. 135
5: 9 Since we have now been justified by his **b**, 135
1Co 10:16 a participation *in* the **b** of Christ? 135
11:25 "This cup is the new covenant in my **b**; 135
11:27 be guilty of sinning against the body and **b** 135
15:50 that flesh and **b** cannot inherit the kingdom 135
Eph 1: 7 In him we have redemption through his **b**, 135
2:13 near through the **b** of Christ. 135
6:12 For our struggle is not against flesh and **b**, 135
Col 1:20 by making peace through his **b**, 135
Heb 2:14 Since the children have flesh and **b**, 135
9: 7 and never without **b**, 135
9:12 He did not enter by means of the **b** of goats 135
9:12 for all by his own **b**, 135
9:13 The **b** of goats and bulls and the ashes of 135
9:14 How much more, then, will the **b** of Christ, 135
9:18 not put into effect without **b**. 135
9:19 he took the **b** of calves, together with water, 135
9:20 He said, "This is the **b** of the covenant, 135
9:21 he sprinkled *with* the **b** both the tabernacle 135
9:22 that nearly everything was cleansed with **b**, 136
9:22 the **shedding of b** there is no forgiveness. 135
9:25 the Most Holy Place every year with **b** 135
10: 4 the **b** of bulls and goats to take away sins. 135
10:19 the Most Holy Place by the **b** of Jesus, 135
10:29 who has treated as an unholy thing the **b** of 135
11:28 the Passover and the sprinkling *of* **b**, 135
12: 4 yet resisted to the point of **shedding** your **b**. 135
12:24 *and to* the sprinkled **b** that speaks NIG
12:24 that speaks a better word than the **b** NIG
13:11 The high priest carries the **b** of animals into 135
13:12 to make the people holy through his own **b**. 135
13:20 the **b** of the eternal covenant brought back 135
1Pe 1: 2 to Jesus Christ and sprinkling *by* his **b**: 135
1:19 but *with* the precious **b** of Christ, 135
1Jn 1: 7 and the **b** of Jesus, his Son, 135
5: 6 This is the one who came by water and **b**— 135
5: 6 but by water and **b**. 135
5: 8 the water and the **b**; 135
Rev 1: 5 and has freed us from our sins by his **b**, 135
5: 9 with your **b** you purchased men for God 135
6:10 of the earth and avenge our **b**?" 135
6:12 the whole moon turned **b** red, 135+6055
7:14 and made them white in the **b** of the Lamb. 135
8: 7 and there came hail and fire mixed with **b**, 135
8: 8 A third of the sea turned into **b**, 135
11: 6 the waters into **b** and to strike the earth 135
12:11 They overcame him by the **b** of the Lamb 135
14:20 and **b** flowed out of the press, 135
16: 3 and it turned into **b** like that of a dead man, 135
16: 4 and they became **b**. 135
16: 6 for they have shed the **b** of your saints 135
16: 6 and you have given them **b** to drink 135
17: 6 I saw that the woman was drunk with the **b** 135
17: 6 the **b** of those who bore testimony to Jesus. 135

Rev 18:24 In her was found the **b** of prophets and of 135
19: 2 on her for the **b** of his servants." 135
19:13 He is dressed in a robe dipped *in* **b**, 135

BLOOD-STAINED (1) [BLOOD]

2Sa 21: 1 "It is on account of Saul and his **b** house; 1947

BLOODGUILT (2) [GUILT]

Ps 51:14 Save me from **b**, O God, 1947
Joel 3:21 Their **b**, which I have not pardoned, 1947

BLOODSHED (30) [BLOOD]

Ex 22: 2 the defender is not **guilty of b**; 1947
22: 3 he is **guilty of b**. 1947
Lev 17: 4 that man shall be considered **guilty of b**; 1947
Nu 35:33 **B** pollutes the land, 1947
Dt 17: 8 whether **b**, lawsuits or assaults 1947+1947+4200
19:10 and so that you will not be **guilty of b**. 1947
21: 8 And the **b** will be atoned for. 1947
22: 8 so that you may not bring the **guilt of b** 1947
1Sa 25:26 and from avenging himself 928+995+1947
25:31 burden of needless **b** or of having avenged 1947+9161
25:33 keeping me from **b** this day and from
avenging myself 928+995+1947
2Ch 19:10 or other concerns of the law, 1947+1947+4200
Isa 5: 7 And he looked for justice, but saw **b**; 5384
Jer 48:10 on him who keeps his sword from **b**! 1947
Eze 5:17 Plague and **b** will sweep through you, 1947
7:23 the land is full of **b** and the city is full 1947+5477
9: 9 the land is full of **b** and the city is full 1947
14:19 and pour out my wrath upon it through **b**, 1947
22: 2 Will you judge this city of **b**? 1947
24: 6 "Woe to the city of **b**, 1947
24: 9 "Woe to the city of **b**! 1947
35: 6 over to **b** and it will pursue you. 1947
35: 6 Since you did not hate **b**, 1947
35: 6 **b** will pursue you. 1947
38:22 upon him with plague and **b**; 1947
Hos 4: 2 and **b** follows bloodshed. 1947
4: 2 and bloodshed follows **b**. 1947
12:14 the **guilt of** his **b** and will repay him 1947
Mic 3:10 who build Zion with **b**, 1947
Hab 2:12 "Woe to him who builds a city with **b** 1947

BLOODSHOT (1) [BLOOD]

Pr 23:29 Who has **b** eyes? 2680

BLOODSTAINS (1) [BLOOD]

Isa 4: 4 he will cleanse the **b** from Jerusalem by 1947

BLOODTHIRSTY (6) [BLOOD]

Ps 5: 6 **b** and deceitful men the LORD abhors. 1947
26: 9 my life with **b** men, 1947
55:23 **b** and deceitful men will 1947
59: 2 from evildoers and save me from **b** men. 1947
139:19 Away from me, you **b** men! 1947
Pr 29:10 **B** men hate a man of integrity and seek 1947

BLOOM (5)

Ex 9:31 the barley had headed and the flax was in **b**. 1499
SS 2:15 our vineyards that are **in b**. 6163
6:11 or the pomegranates were **in b**. 5914
7:12 and if the pomegranates *are* **in b**— 5914
Isa 35: 2 *it will* **burst into b**; 7255+7255

BLOSSOM (8) [BLOSSOMED, BLOSSOMING, BLOSSOMS]

1Ki 7:26 like the rim of a cup, like a lily **b**. 7258
2Ch 4: 5 like the rim of a cup, like a lily **b**. 7258
Isa 18: 5 when the **b** is gone and the flower becomes 7258
27: 6 Israel will bud and **b** and fill all the world 7255
35: 1 the wilderness will rejoice and **b**. 7255
Hos 14: 5 he will **b** like a lily. 7255
14: 7 He will **b** like a vine, 7255
Jas 1:11 its **b** falls and its beauty is destroyed. 470

BLOSSOMED (3) [BLOSSOM]

Ge 40:10 As soon as it budded, it **b**, 5890+6590
Nu 17: 8 **b** and produced almonds. 7437+7488
Eze 7:10 the rod has budded, arrogance *has* **b**! 7255

BLOSSOMING (1) [BLOSSOM]

SS 2:13 the **b** vines spread their fragrance. 6163

BLOSSOMS (12) [BLOSSOM]

Ex 25:31 buds and **b** shall be of one piece with it. 7258
25:33 like almond flowers with buds and **b** are to 7258
25:34 like almond flowers with buds and **b**. 7258
37:17 buds and **b** were of one piece with it. 7258
37:19 like almond flowers with buds and **b** were 7258
37:20 like almond flowers with buds and **b**. 7258
Nu 8: 4 from its base to its **b**. 7258
Job 15:33 like an olive tree shedding its **b**. 5900
Ecc 12: 5 when the almond tree **b** and 5914
SS 1:14 My lover is to me a cluster of *henna* **b** from 4110
7:12 if their **b** have opened, 6163
Na 1: 4 Bashan and Carmel wither and the **b** 7258

BLOT (14) [BLOTS, BLOTTED]

Ex 17:14 because *I will* **completely b out** 4681+4681
32:32 **b** me out of the book you have written." 4681
32:33 against me I will **b** out of my book. 4681
Dt 9:14 and **b** out their name from under heaven. 4681
25:19 *you shall* **b** out the memory of Amalek 4681
29:20 and the LORD will **b** out his name from 4681
32:26 and **b** out their memory from mankind, 8697
2Ki 14:27 not said he *would* **b** out the name of Israel 4681
Ne 4: 5 not cover up their guilt or **b** out their sins 4681
13:14 not **b** out what I have so faithfully done for 4681
Ps 51: 1 to your great compassion **b** out my
transgressions. 4681
51: 9 from my sins and **b** out all my iniquity. 4681
Jer 18:23 not forgive their crimes or **b** out their sins 4681
Rev 3: 5 never **b** out his name **from** the book of life, 1981

BLOTS (2) [BLOT]

Isa 43:25 am he *who* **b** out your transgressions, 4681
2Pe 2:13 They are **b** and blemishes, 5070

BLOTTED (5) [BLOT]

Dt 25: 6 that his name *will* not **be b** out from Israel. 4681
Ps 9: 5 *you have* **b** out their name for ever 4681
69:28 *May they* **be b** out of the book of life and 4681
109:13 their names **b** out from the next generation. 4681
109:14 *may* the sin of his mother never **be b out**. 4681

BLOW (31) [BLEW, BLOWING, BLOWN, BLOWS, WINDBLOWN]

Ex 10:13 **made** an east wind **b** 5627
21:19 the one who **struck** the **b** will not 5782
Nu 10: 7 To gather the assembly, **b** the **trumpets**, 9546
10: 8 the priests, *are to* **b** the trumpets. 9546
Jdg 7:18 I and all who are with me **b** our trumpets, 9546
7:18 then from all around the camp **b** yours 9546
7:20 the trumpets *they were to* **b**, 9546
16:28 with **one b** get revenge on the Philistines AIT
1Sa 6:19 of the heavy **b** the LORD had dealt them, 4804
1Ki 1:34 **B** the trumpet and shout, 9546
1Ch 15:24 and Eliezer the priests *were to* **b** trumpets 2955
16: 6 to **b** the trumpets regularly before the ark of NIH
2Ch 21:14 with a heavy **b**. 4487
Ps 39:10 I am overcome by the **b** *of* your hand. 9327
68: 2 *may you* **b** them **away**; 5622
SS 4:16 **B** *on* my garden, 7031
Isa 5:24 and their flowers **b away** like dust; 6590
19: 7 *will* **b away** and be no more. 5622
41:16 and a gale *will* **b** them **away**. 7046
57:13 a mere breath *will* **b** them **away**. 4374
Jer 6:29 The bellows **b fiercely** to burn away 5723
14:17 a grievous wound, a crushing **b**. 4804
51:27 **B** the trumpet among the nations! 9546
Eze 7: 9 that it is I the LORD *who* **strikes the b**. 5782
7:14 Though *they* **b** the trumpet, 9546
22:21 and *I will* **b** on you with my fiery wrath, 5870
24:16 with **one b** I am about to take away 4487
33: 6 not **b** the trumpet to warn the people and 9546
Joel 2: 1 **B** the trumpet in Zion; 9546
2:15 **B** the trumpet in Zion, declare a holy fast, 9546
Ac 27:13 **gentle** south wind *began to* **b**, 5710

BLOWING (9) [BLOW]

Jos 6: 4 with the priests **b** the trumpets. 9546
6: 8 the LORD went forward, **b** their trumpets, 9546
6:13 the ark of the LORD and **b** the trumpets. 9546
2Ki 11:14 of the land *were* rejoicing and **b** trumpets. 9546
2Ch 23:13 of the land *were* rejoicing and **b** trumpets, 9546
Hos 13:15 **b** in from the desert; 6590
Jn 6:18 A strong wind *was* **b** and 4463
Ac 2: 2 the **b** of a violent wind came from heaven 5770
Rev 7: 1 **prevent** any wind **from b** 3590+4463

BLOWN (6) [BLOW]

1Sa 13: 3 Then Saul *had* the trumpet **b** throughout 9546
Ps 68: 2 As smoke **is b away** by the wind, 5622
Isa 29: 5 the ruthless hordes like **b** chaff. 6296
Eph 4:14 and **b** here and there by every wind 4367
Jas 1: 6 **b** and tossed **by the wind**. 448
Jude 1:12 **b along** by the wind; 4195

BLOWS (18) [BLOW]

Job 20:23 against him and rain down his **b** upon him. 4303
Ps 1: 4 They are like chaff *that* the wind **b away**. 5622
103:16 the wind **b** over it and it is gone, 6296
Pr 6:33 **B** and disgrace are his lot, 5596
20:30 **B** and wounds cleanse away evil, 2467
Ecc 1: 6 wind **b** to the south and turns to the north; 2143
Isa 1: 6 down peoples with unceasing **b**, 4804
27: 8 as on a day the east wind **b**. NIH
30:32 as he fights them in battle with the **b** 9485
40: 7 the breath of the LORD **b** on them. 5959
40:24 than *he* **b** on them and they wither, 5973
Jer 1:11 in the desert to warn my people, but not NIH
Eze 26: 9 He will direct the **b** *of* his battering rams 4693
33: 3 against the land and the trumpet to warn 9546
Lk 12:47 *be* **beaten with** many **b**. 1296
12:48 *be* **beaten with** few **b**. 1296
12:55 And when the south wind **b**, you say, 4463
Jn 3: 8 The wind **b** wherever it pleases. 4463

BLUE (50)

Ex	25: 4	**b**, purple and scarlet yarn and fine linen;	9418
	26: 1	of finely twisted linen and **b**,	9418
	26: 4	Make loops of **b material** along the edge	9418
	26:31	"Make a curtain of **b**,	9418
	26:36	the entrance to the tent make a curtain of **b**,	9418
	27:16	provide a curtain twenty cubits long, of **b**,	9418
	28: 5	Have them use gold, and **b**,	9418
	28: 6	"Make the ephod of gold, and of **b**,	9418
	28: 8	and with **b**, purple and scarlet yarn,	9418
	28:15	of gold, and of **b**, purple and scarlet yarn,	9418
	28:28	to the rings of the ephod with **b** cord,	9418
	28:31	the robe of the ephod entirely of **b cloth**,	9418
	28:33	Make pomegranates of **b**,	9418
	28:37	a **b** cord to it to attach it to the turban;	9418
	35: 6	**b**, purple and scarlet yarn and fine linen;	9418
	35:23	Everyone who had **b**,	9418
	35:25	**b**, purple or scarlet yarn or fine linen.	9418
	35:35	designers, embroiderers in **b**,	9418
	36: 8	of finely twisted linen and **b**,	9418
	36:11	Then they made loops of **b material** along	9418
	36:35	They made the curtain of **b**,	9418
	36:37	to the tent they made a curtain of **b**, purple	9418
	38:18	for the entrance to the courtyard was of **b**,	9418
	38:23	and an embroiderer in **b**,	9418
	39: 1	From the **b**, purple	9418
	39: 2	They made the ephod of gold, and of **b**,	9418
	39: 3	and cut strands to be worked into the **b**,	9418
	39: 5	and with **b**, purple and scarlet yarn,	9418
	39: 8	of gold, and of **b**, purple and scarlet yarn,	9418
	39:21	with **b** cord, connecting it to the waistband	9418
	39:22	the robe of the ephod entirely of **b cloth**—	9418
	39:24	They made pomegranates of **b**,	9418
	39:29	The sash of finely twisted linen and **b**,	9418
	39:31	Then they fastened a **b** cord to it to attach it	9418
Nu	4: 6	a cloth of solid **b** over that and put the poles	9418
	4: 7	of the Presence they are to spread a **b** cloth	9418
	4: 9	to take a **b** cloth and cover the lampstand	9418
	4:11	the gold altar they are to spread a **b** cloth	9418
	4:12	wrap them in a **b** cloth,	9418
	15:38	with a **b** cord on each tassel.	9418
2Ch	2: 7	and in purple, crimson and **b yarn**,	9418
	2:14	and with purple and **b** and crimson **yarn**	9418
	3:14	**b**, purple and crimson **yarn**	9418
Est	1: 6	garden had hangings of white and **b** linen,	9418
	8:15	royal garments of **b** and white,	9418
Jer	10: 9	then dressed in **b** and purple—	9418
Eze	23: 6	in **b**, governors and commanders, all	9418
	27: 7	of **b** and purple from the coasts of Elishah.	9418
	27:24	with you beautiful garments, **b** fabric,	9418
Rev	9:17	Their breastplates were fiery red, **dark b**,	5610

BLUNTED (1)

Ps	58: 7	let their arrows **be b**.	4908

BLURTS (1)

Pr	12:23	but the heart of fools **b** out folly.	7924

BLUSH (3)

Jer	3: 3	you refuse *to* **b with shame**.	4007
	6:15	they do not even know how *to* **b**.	4007
	8:12	they do not even know how *to* **b**.	4007

BLUSTERING (1)

Job	8: 2	Your words are a **b** wind.	3888

BOANERGES (1)

Mk	3:17	the name **B**, which means Sons	1065

BOARD (5) [ABOARD, BOARDED, BOARDS]

Eze	27: 9	Veteran craftsmen of Gebal were **on b**	928
	27:27	and everyone else **on b** will sink into	928+9348
Ac	21: 2	**went on b** and set sail.	2094
	27: 6	for Italy and **put us on b**.	899+1650+1837
	27:37	Altogether there were 276 of us **on b**.	1877+3836+4450

BOARDED (1) [BOARD]

Ac	27: 2	We **b** a ship from Adramyttium about to sail	2094

BOARDS (4) [BOARD]

Ex	27: 8	Make the altar hollow, out of **b**.	4283
	38: 7	They made it hollow, out of **b**.	4283
1Ki	6:15	He lined its interior walls with cedar **b**,	7521
	6:16	with cedar **b** from floor to ceiling to form	7521

BOARS (1)

Ps	80:13	**B** from the forest ravage it and	2614

BOAST (56) [BOASTED, BOASTERS, BOASTFUL, BOASTFULLY, BOASTING, BOASTS]

Jdg	7: 2	In order that Israel *may* not **b** against me	6995
1Ki	20:11	'One who puts on his armor *should* not **b**	2146
Ps	34: 2	My soul will **b** in the LORD;	2146
	44: 8	In God we make our **b** all day long,	2146
	49: 6	in their wealth and **b** of their great riches?	2146
	52: 1	Why do you **b** of evil, you mighty man?	2146

Ps	52: 1	Why do you **b** all day long,	NIH
	75: 4	'**B** no more,' and to the wicked,	2147
	97: 7	those who **b** in idols—	2146
Pr	27: 1	*Do* not **b** about tomorrow,	2146
Isa	10:15	or the saw **b** against him who uses it?	1540
	28:15	You **b**, "We have entered into a covenant	606
	61: 6	and in their riches *you will* **b**.	607
Jer	9:23	"*Let* not the wise man **b** of his wisdom or	2146
	9:23	or the strong man **b** of his strength or	2146
	9:23	of his strength or the rich man **b**	2146
	9:24	but let him who boasts **b** about this:	2146
	49: 4	Why *do you* **b** of your valleys,	2146
	49: 4	so **b** of your valleys so fruitful?	NIH
	51:41	the **b** of the whole earth seized!	9335
Am	4: 5	**b** *about* them, you Israelites,	9048
Ob	1:12	nor **b so much** in the day of their trouble.	1540+3870+7023
Ro	2: 6	have **something to b about**—	3017
	11:18	*do* not **b over** those branches.	2878
1Co	1:29	so that no one *may* **b** before him.	3016
	1:31	"*Let* him who boasts **b** in the Lord."	3016
	4: 7	why *do you* **b** as though you did not?	3016
	9:15	I would rather die than have anyone deprive me of this **b**.	3017
	9:16	Yet when I preach the gospel, I cannot **b**,	3017
	13: 4	It does not envy, *it does* not **b**,	4371
2Co	1:12	Now this is our **b**:	3018
	1:14	to understand fully that you can **b** in	NIG
	1:14	just as *we will* **b** of you in the day of	1639+3017
	10: 8	if *I* **b** somewhat freely about the authority	3016
	10:13	however, *will* not **b** beyond proper limits,	3016
	10:16	not *want to* **b about** work already done	3016
	10:17	But, "*Let* him who boasts **b** in the Lord."	3016
	11:12	with us in the things *they* **b about**.	3016
	11:18	I too *will* **b**.	3016
	11:21	What anyone else dares to **b about**—	NIG
	11:21	I also dare to **b about**.	NIG
	11:30	If I must **b**, I will boast of the things	3016
	11:30	*I will* **b** of the things that show my weakness	3016
	12: 5	*I will* **b** about a man like that,	3016
	12: 5	but *I will* not **b** about myself,	3016
	12: 6	Even if I should choose to **b**,	3016
	12: 9	Therefore *I will* **b** all the more gladly	3016
Gal	6:13	to be circumcised that *they may* **b**	3016
	6:14	May I never **b** except in the cross	3016
Eph	2: 9	not by works, so that no one *can* **b**.	3016
Php	2:16	that I may **b** on the day of Christ that I did	3017
2Th	1: 4	among God's churches we **b** about your	1595
Heb	3: 6	to our courage and the hope of which we **b**.	3017
Jas	3:14	*do* not **b** about it or deny the truth.	2878
	4:16	As it is, you **b** and brag.	3016
Jude	1:16	they **b** about themselves and flatter others	3281+5665

BOASTED (7) [BOAST]

Ex	15: 9	"The enemy **b**, 'I will pursue.	606
Est	5:11	Haman **b** to them *about* his vast wealth,	6218
Isa	20: 5	in Cush and **b** in Egypt will be afraid	9514
Jer	13:20	the sheep of which you **b**?	9514
Eze	35:13	You **b** against me and spoke against me	928+1540+7023
Ac	8: 9	He **b** that he was someone great,	3306
2Co	7:14	I had **b** to him about you,	3016

BOASTERS (1) [BOAST]

Jer	48:45	the skulls of the **noisy b**.	1201+8623

BOASTFUL (5) [BOAST]

Ps	12: 3	and every **b** tongue	1524+1819
Da	7:11	of the **b** words the horn was speaking.	10647
Ro	1:30	God-haters, insolent, arrogant and **b**;	225
2Ti	3: 2	lovers of money, **b**, proud, abusive,	225
2Pe	2:18	For they mouth empty, **b** words and,	5665

BOASTFULLY (2) [BOAST]

Da	7: 8	the eyes of a man and a mouth that spoke **b**.	10647
	7:20	and that had eyes and a mouth that spoke **b**.	10647

BOASTING (17) [BOAST]

Ps	94: 4	all the evildoers *are* **full of b**.	607
Ro	3:27	Where, then, is **b**?	3018
1Co	3:21	So then, no more **b** about men!	3016
	5: 6	Your **b** is not good.	3017
2Co	7:14	so our **b about** you to Titus has proved to	3018
	9: 2	and *I have been* **b about** it to	3016
	9: 3	that our **b about** you in this matter should	3017
	10:13	but will confine our **b** to	NIG
	10:14	We are not going too far in our **b**,	NIG
	10:15	Neither do we go beyond our limits *by* **b** of	3016
	11:10	in the regions of Achaia will stop this **b**	3018
	11:16	so that *I may* do a little **b**.	3016
	11:18	many *are* **b** in the way the world does,	3016
	12: 1	I must go on **b**.	3016
Jas	4:16	All such **b** is evil.	3018
1Jn	2:16	the lust of his eyes and the **b** of what he has	224

BOASTS (12) [BOAST]

1Sa	2: 1	My mouth **b** over my enemies,	8143
Ps	10: 3	He **b** of the cravings of his heart;	2146
Pr	20:14	then off he goes and **b** *about* his purchase.	2146
	25:14	without rain is a man *who* **b** of gifts he does	2146
Isa	16: 6	but her **b** are empty.	966

Jer	9:24	but *let* him *who* **b** boast about this:	2146
	48:30	"and her **b** accomplish nothing.	966
Hos	12: 8	Ephraim **b**, "I am very rich;	606
1Co	1:31	"Let him who **b** boast in the Lord."	3016
2Co	10:17	But, "*Let* him who **b** boast in the Lord."	3016
Jas	3: 5	but *it* **makes** great **b**.	902
Rev	18: 7	In her heart *she* **b**, 'I sit as queen;	3306

BOAT (43) [BOATS, LIFEBOAT]

Mt	4:21	They were in a **b** with their father Zebedee,	4450
	4:22	the **b** and their father and followed him.	4450
	8:23	into the **b** and his disciples followed him.	4450
	8:24	so that the waves swept over the **b**.	4450
	9: 1	Jesus stepped into a **b**,	4450
	13: 2	around him that he got into a **b** and sat in it,	4450
	14:13	by **b** privately to a solitary place.	4450
	14:22	the disciples get into the **b** and go on ahead	4450
	14:24	the **b** was already a considerable distance	4450
	14:29	Then Peter got down out of the **b**,	4450
	14:32	And when they climbed into the **b**,	4450
	14:33	those who were in the **b** worshiped him,	4450
	15:39	the **b** and went to the vicinity of Magadan.	4450
Mk	1:19	of Zebedee and his brother John in a **b**,	4450
	1:20	the **b** with the hired men and followed him.	4450
	3: 9	to have a **small b** ready for him,	4449
	4: 1	around him was so large that he got into a **b**	4450
	4:36	just as he was, in the **b**.	4450
	4:37	and the waves broke over the **b**,	4450
	5: 2	When Jesus got out of the **b**,	4450
	5:18	As Jesus was getting into the **b**,	4450
	5:21	When Jesus had again crossed over by **b** to	4450
	6:32	So they went away by themselves in a **b** to	4450
	6:45	the **b** and go on ahead of him to Bethsaida,	4450
	6:47	the **b** was in the middle of the lake,	4450
	6:51	Then he climbed into the **b** with them,	4450
	6:54	As soon as they got out of the **b**,	4450
	8:10	he got into the **b** with his disciples and went	4450
	8:13	into the **b** and crossed to the other side.	4450
	8:14	for one loaf they had with them in the **b**.	4450
Lk	5: 3	down and taught the people from the **b**.	4450
	5: 7	in the other **b** to come and help them,	4450
	8:22	So they got into a **b** and set out.	4450
	8:23	so that the **b** was being swamped,	NIG
	8:37	So he got into the **b** and left.	4450
Jn	6:17	where they got into a **b** and set off across	4450
	6:19	they saw Jesus approaching the **b**,	4450
	6:21	they were willing to take him into the **b**,	4450
	6:21	and immediately the **b** reached the shore	4450
	6:22	that only one **b** had been there,	4449
	21: 3	So they went out and got into the **b**,	4450
	21: 6	"Throw your net on the right side *of* the **b**	4450
	21: 8	The other disciples followed *in* the **b**,	4449

BOATS (9) [BOAT]

Job	9:26	They skim past like **b** of papyrus,	641
Isa	18: 2	which sends envoys by sea in papyrus **b**	3998
Mk	4:36	There were also other **b** with him.	4450
Lk	5: 2	he saw at the water's edge two **b**,	4450
	5: 3	He got into one of the **b**,	4450
	5: 7	and filled both **b** so full that they began	4450
	5:11	So they pulled their **b** up on shore,	4450
Jn	6:23	Then some **b** from Tiberias landed near	4449
	6:24	into the **b** and went to Capernaum in search	4449

BOAZ (29)

Ru	2: 1	a man of standing, whose name was **B**.	1244
	2: 3	in a field belonging to **B**,	1244
	2: 4	then **B** arrived from Bethlehem and greeted	1244
	2: 5	**B** asked the foreman of his harvesters,	1244
	2: 8	**B** said to Ruth, "My daughter, listen to me.	1244
	2:11	**B** replied, "I've been told all	1244
	2:14	At mealtime **B** said to her,	1244
	2:15	**B** gave orders to his men,	1244
	2:19	of the man I worked with today is **B**,"	1244
	2:23	to the servant girls of **B** to glean until	1244
	3: 2	Is not **B**, with whose	1244
	3: 7	When **B** had finished eating and drinking	1244
	3:16	she told her everything **B** had done for her	408+2021S
	4: 1	Meanwhile **B** went up to the town gate	1244
	4: 1	**B** said, "Come over here, my friend,	1244
	4: 2	**B** took ten of the elders of the town	NIH
	4: 5	Then **B** said, "On the day you buy the land	1244
	4: 8	So the kinsman-redeemer said to **B**,	1244
	4: 9	Then **B** announced to the elders and all	1244
	4:13	So **B** took Ruth and she became his wife.	1244
	4:21	Salmon the father of **B**,	1244
	4:21	**B** the father of Obed,	1244
1Ki	7:21	and the one to the north **B**.	1245
1Ch	2:11	Salmon the father of **B**,	1244
	2:12	**B** the father of Obed and Obed the father	1244
2Ch	3:17	and the one to the north **B**.	1245
Mt	1: 5	Salmon the father of **B**,	1067
	1: 5	**B** the father of Obed,	1067
Lk	3:32	the son *of* **B**, the son of Salmon,	1078

BOCHERU (KJV) See BOKERU

BOCHIM (KJV) See BOKIM

BODIES (70) [BODY]

Ge	34:27	of Jacob came upon the **dead b** and looted	2728
	47:18	except for our lord except our **b** and our land.	1581

Ex	30:32	on men's **b** and do not make any oil with	1414
Lev	19:28	" 'Do not cut your **b** for the dead	1414
	21: 5	the edges of their beards or cut their **b**.	1414
	26:30	and pile your **dead b** on the lifeless forms	7007
Nu	8: 7	then have them shave their whole **b**	1414
	14:29	In this desert your **b** will fall—	7007
	14:32	But you—your **b** will fall in this desert.	7007
	14:33	until the last of your **b** lies in the desert.	7007
1Sa	31:12	They took down the **b** *of* Saul and his sons	1581
2Sa	4:12	and hung the **b** by the pool in Hebron.	NIH
	21:10	down from the heavens on the **b**,	2157S
2Ki	10:25	The guards and officers threw the **b** out and	NIH
	19:35	there were all the dead **b**!	7007
1Ch	10:12	all their valiant men went and took the **b**	1590
2Ch	20:24	they saw only **dead b** lying on the ground;	7007
Ne	9:37	over our **b** and our cattle as they please.	1581
Ps	44:25	our **b** cling to the ground.	1061
	73: 4	their **b** are healthy and strong.	214
	79: 2	the **dead b** *of* your servants as food to	5577
Isa	5:25	and the **dead b** are like refuse in the streets.	5577
	26:19	But your dead will live; their **b** will rise.	5577
	34: 3	their **dead b** will send up a stench;	7007
	37:36	there were all the dead **b**!	7007
	66:24	upon the **dead b** *of* those who rebelled	7007
Jer	9:22	" 'The **dead b** *of* men will lie like refuse on	5577
	16: 4	and their **dead b** will become food for	5577
	31:40	where **dead b** and ashes are thrown,	7007
	33: 5	'They will be filled with the **dead b** *of*	7007
	34:20	Their **dead b** will become food for the birds	5577
	41: 9	Now the cistern where he threw all the **b** *of*	7007
La	4: 7	their **b** more ruddy than rubies,	6795
Eze	6: 5	I will lay the **dead b** *of* the Israelites in front	7007
	10:12	Their entire **b**, including their backs,	1414
	11: 7	The **b** you have thrown there are the meat	2728
Da	3:27	the fire had not harmed their **b**, nor was	10151
Am	4:10	And if a relative who is to burn the **b** comes	6795
	8: 3	Many, many **b**—flung everywhere!	7007
Na	2:10	Hearts melt, knees give way, **b** tremble,	5516
	3: 3	piles of dead, **b** without number,	1581
Hab	2:15	so that he can gaze on their **naked b**.	5067
Mt	24:29	and the heavenly **b** will be shaken.'	NIG
	27:52	The tombs broke open and the **b**	5393
Mk	13:25	and the heavenly **b** will be shaken.'	1539
Lk	21:26	the **heavenly b** will be shaken.	1539+3836+4041
Jn	19:31	the **b** left on the crosses during the Sabbath,	5393
	19:31	the legs broken and the **b** taken down.	NIH
Ac	7:16	Their **b** were brought back to Shechem	NIG
	7:42	over to the worship *of* the heavenly **b**.	5131
Ro	1:24	the degrading of their **b** with one another.	5393
	7: 5	by the law were at work in our **b**,	3517
	8:11	the dead will also give life *to* your mortal **b**	5393
	8:23	the redemption *of* our **b**.	5393
	12: 1	to offer your **b** as living sacrifices,	5393
1Co	6:15	that your **b** are members of Christ himself?	5393
	10: 5	their **b** were scattered over the desert.	NIG
	15:40	There are also heavenly **b**	5393
	15:40	and there are earthly **b**;	5393
	15:40	the splendor of the heavenly **b** is one kind,	NIG
	15:40	and the splendor of the earthly **b** is another.	NIG
Eph	5:28	to love their wives as their own **b**.	5393
Php	3:21	will transform our lowly **b** so that they will	5393
Heb	11: 8	whose **b** fell in the desert?	3265
	10:22	and having our **b** washed with pure water.	5393
	13:11	but the **b** are burned outside the camp.	5393
Jude	1: 8	these dreamers pollute their own **b**,	4922
Rev	11: 8	Their **b** will lie in the street of	4773
	11: 9	language and nation will gaze on their **b**	4773
	18:13	and **b** and souls of men.	5393

BODILY (4) [BODY]

Lev	15: 2	'When any man has a **b** discharge,	1414+4946
	22: 4	an infectious skin disease or a **b discharge**,	2307
Lk	3:22	on him *in* **b** form like a dove.	5394
Col	2: 9	the fullness of the Deity lives **in b form**,	5395

BODY (253) [BODIES, BODILY, EMBODIMENT]

Ge	15: 4	but a son coming from your own **b** will	5055
	25:25	and his **whole b** was like a hairy garment;	AIT
	35:11	and kings will come from your **b**.	2743
Ex	22:27	the only covering he has for his **b**.	6425
	28:42	as a covering for the **b**,	1414+6872
Lev	6:10	with linen undergarments next to his **b**,	1414
	13:13	and if the disease has covered his whole **b**,	1414
	15: 3	Whether it continues flowing from his **b**	1414
	15:16	he must bathe his whole **b** with water,	1414
	16: 4	with linen undergarments next to his **b**;	1414
	21:11	not enter a place where there is a dead **b**.	5883
Nu	5: 2	because of a **dead b**.	5883
	5:22	that brings a curse enter your **b** so	5055
	6: 6	to the LORD he must not go near a dead **b**.	5883
	6:11	by being in the presence of the **dead b**.	5883
	9: 6	on account of a dead **b**.	132
	9: 7	because of a dead **b**.	132
	9:10	of a **dead b** or are away on a journey,	5883
	19:11	the dead **b** of anyone will be unclean	5883
	19:13	Whoever touches the dead **b** *of* anyone	5883
	25: 8	the Israelite and into the woman's **b**.	7687
Dt	4: 8	and laws as this **b** *of* laws I am setting	3972
	21: 2	and measure the distance from the **b** to	2728
	21: 3	of the town nearest the **b** shall take a heifer	2728
	21: 6	the **b** shall wash their hands over	2728
	21:22	to death and **his b** is hung on a tree,	2257S
	21:23	not leave his **b** on the tree overnight.	5577
Jos	8:29	Joshua ordered them to take his **b** from	5577

1Sa	5: 4	only **his b** remained.	1837S
	31:10	and fastened his **b** to the wall of Beth Shan.	1581
2Sa	7:12	who will come from your own **b**,	5055
1Ki	13:22	Therefore your **b** will not be buried in	5577
	13:24	and his **b** was thrown down on the road,	5577
	13:25	by saw the **b** thrown down there,	5577
	13:25	with the lion standing beside the **b**,	5577
	13:28	and found the **b** thrown down on the road,	5577
	13:28	The lion had neither eaten the **b** nor mauled	5577
	13:29	prophet picked up the **b** *of* the man of God,	5577
	13:30	Then he laid the **b** in his own tomb,	5577
2Ki	4:34	the boy's **b** grew warm.	1414
	6:30	underneath, he had sackcloth on his **b**.	1414
	9:37	Jezebel's **b** will be like refuse on	5577
	13:21	they threw the **man's b** into Elisha's tomb.	408
	13:21	When the **b** touched Elisha's bones,	NIH
	23:30	Josiah's servants brought *his* **b** in a chariot	5577
Ezr	8:20	a **b** *that* David and the officials	8611S
Job	4:15	and the hair on my **b** stood on end.	1414
	7: 5	My **b** is clothed with worms and scabs,	1414
	7:15	rather than this **b** *of* mine.	6795
	14:22	of his own **b** and mourns only for himself."	1414
	21: 6	trembling seizes my **b**.	1414
	21:24	his **b** well nourished,	6489
	30:30	my **b** burns with fever.	6795
Ps	16: 9	my **b** also will rest secure,	1414
	31: 9	my soul and my **b** with grief.	1061
	38: 3	of your wrath there is no health in my **b**;	1414
	38: 7	there is no health in my **b**.	1414
	63: 1	my soul thirsts for you, my **b** longs for you,	1414
	109:18	it entered into his **b** like water,	7931
	109:24	my **b** is thin and gaunt.	1414
	139:16	your eyes saw my **unformed b**.	1677
Pr	3: 8	to your **b** and nourishment to your bones.	9219
	4:22	and health to a man's whole **b**.	1414
	5:11	when your flesh and **b** are spent.	8638
	14:30	A heart at peace gives life to the **b**,	1414
Ecc	11: 5	how the **b** is formed in a mother's womb,	6795
	11:10	and cast off the troubles of your **b**,	1414
	12:12	and much study wearies the **b**.	1414
SS	5:14	His **b** is like polished ivory decorated	5055
Isa	17: 4	the fat of his **b** will waste away.	1414
	20: 2	the sackcloth from your **b** and the sandals	5516
	21: 3	At this my **b** is racked with pain,	5516
Jer	13:22	and your **b** mistreated.	6811
	26:23	down with a sword and his **b** thrown into	5577
	36:30	his **b** will be thrown out and exposed to	5577
Eze	1:11	and two wings covering its **b**.	1581
	1:23	and each had two wings covering its **b**.	1581
	16:25	**offering** your **b** with increasing promiscuity	906+7316+8079
Da	4:33	His **b** was drenched with the dew of heaven	10151
	5:21	his **b** was drenched with the dew of heaven,	10151
	7:11	until the beast was slain and its **b** destroyed	10151
	10: 6	His **b** was like chrysolite,	1581
Mic	6: 7	the fruit of my **b** for the sin of my soul?	1061
Hag	2:13	with a **dead b** touches one of these things,	5883
Zec	13: 6	'What are these wounds on your **b**?'	3338
Mt	5:29	for you to lose one **part of** your **b** than	3517
	5:29	for your whole **b** to be thrown into hell.	5393
	5:30	for you to lose one **part of** your **b** than	3517
	5:30	of your body than for your whole **b** to go	5393
	6:22	"The eye is the lamp *of* the **b**.	5393
	6:22	your whole **b** will be full of light.	5393
	6:23	your whole **b** will be full of darkness.	5393
	6:25	or about your **b**, what you will wear.	5393
	6:25	and the **b** more important than clothes?	5393
	10:28	Do not be afraid of those who kill the **b**	5393
	10:28	of the One who can destroy both soul and **b**	5393
	14:12	John's disciples came and took his **b**	4773
	15:17	into the stomach and then out of the **b**?	NIG
	26:12	When she poured this perfume on my **b**,	5393
	26:26	"Take and eat; this is my **b**."	5393
	26:41	The spirit is willing, but the **b** is weak."	4922
	27:58	Going to Pilate, he asked for Jesus' **b**,	5393
	27:59	Joseph took the **b**,	5393
	27:64	his disciples may come and steal the **b**	899S
Mk	5:29	and she felt *in* her **b** that she was freed	5393
	6:29	John's disciples came and took his **b**	4773
	7:19	and then out of his **b**."	NIG
	14: 8	She poured perfume on my **b** beforehand	5393
	14:22	"Take it; this is my **b**."	5393
	14:38	The spirit is willing, but the **b** is weak."	4922
	15:43	to Pilate and asked for Jesus' **b**.	4773
	15:45	he gave the **b** to Joseph.	5393
	15:46	took down the **b**, wrapped it in the linen,	899S
	16: 1	so that they might go to anoint **Jesus' b**.	899S
Lk	11:34	Your eye is the lamp *of* the **b**.	5393
	11:34	your whole **b** also is full of light.	5393
	11:34	they are bad, your **b** also is full of darkness.	5393
	11:36	Therefore, if your whole **b** is full of light,	5393
	12: 4	do not be afraid of those who kill the **b** and	5393
	12: 5	Fear him who, after the killing of the **b**,	NIG
	12:22	or about your **b**, what you will wear.	5393
	12:23	and the **b** more than clothes.	5393
	17:37	He replied, "Where there is a **dead b**,	5393
	22:19	saying, "This is my **b** given for you;	5393
	23:52	Going to Pilate, he asked for Jesus' **b**.	5393
	23:55	and saw the tomb and how his **b** was laid	5393
	24: 3	they did not find the **b** of the Lord Jesus.	5393
	24:23	but didn't find his **b**.	5393
Jn	2:21	But the temple he had spoken of was his **b**.	5393
	13:10	his whole **b** is clean.	NIG
	19:38	Joseph of Arimathea asked Pilate for the **b**	5393
	19:38	he came and took the **b** away.	5393
	19:40	Taking Jesus' **b**, the two	5393
	20:12	seated where Jesus' **b** had been,	5393

Ac	1:18	there he fell headlong, his **b** burst open	NIG
	2:26	my **b** also will live in hope,	4922
	2:31	nor did his **b** see decay.	4922
	5: 6	wrapped up his **b**,	NIG
	9:37	and her **b** was washed and placed in	NIG
	13:36	with his fathers and *his* **b** decayed.	1426+3972
Ro	4:19	the fact that his **b** was as good as dead—	5393
	6: 6	that the **b** of sin might be done away with,	5393
	6:12	not let sin reign in your mortal **b** so	5393
	6:13	Do not offer the **parts of** your **b** to sin,	3517
	6:13	the **parts of** your **b** to him as instruments	3517
	6:19	the **parts of** your **b** in slavery to impurity	3517
	7: 4	also died to the law through the **b** of Christ,	5393
	7:23	at work in the **members of** my **b**,	3517
	7:24	Who will rescue me from this **b** of death?	5393
	8:10	your **b** is dead because of sin,	5393
	8:13	to death the misdeeds of the **b**,	5393
	12: 4	of us has one **b** with many members,	5393
	12: 5	so in Christ we who are many form one **b**,	5393
1Co	6:13	The **b** is not meant for sexual immorality,	5393
	6:13	but for the Lord, and the Lord *for* the **b**.	5393
	6:16	with a prostitute is one with her in **b**?	5393
	6:18	a man commits are outside his **b**,	5393
	6:18	who sins sexually sin against his own **b**.	5393
	6:19	know that your **b** is a temple of the Holy Spirit, who is in you,	5393
	6:20	Therefore honor God with your **b**.	5393
	7: 4	The wife's **b** does not belong to her alone	5393
	7: 4	the husband's **b** does not belong	5393
	7:34	be devoted to the Lord *in* both **b** and spirit.	5393
	9:27	I beat my **b** and make it my slave so that	5393
	10:16	that we break a participation *in* the **b**	5393
	10:17	are one **b**, for we all partake of the one loaf.	5393
	11:24	he broke it and said, "This is my **b**,	5393
	11:27	be guilty of sinning against the **b** and blood	5393
	11:29	the **b** of the Lord eats and drinks judgment	5393
	12:12	The **b** is a unit, though it is made up of many parts;	5393
	12:12	all its parts are many, they form one **b**.	5393
	12:13	by one Spirit into one **b**—	5393
	12:14	Now the **b** is not made up of one part but	5393
	12:15	I do not belong to the **b**,"	5393
	12:15	not for that reason cease to be part of the **b**.	5393
	12:16	I do not belong to the **b**,"	5393
	12:16	not for that reason cease to be part of the **b**.	5393
	12:17	If the whole **b** were an eye,	5393
	12:17	If the whole **b** were an ear,	NIG
	12:18	in fact God has arranged the parts in the **b**,	5393
	12:19	where would the **b** be?	5393
	12:20	As it is, there are many parts, but one **b**.	5393
	12:22	those parts *of* the **b** that seem to	5393
	12:24	of the **b** and has given greater honor to	5393
	12:25	so that there should be no division in the **b**,	5393
	12:27	Now you are the **b** of Christ,	5393
	13: 3	the poor and surrender my **b** to the flames,	5393
	15:35	With what kind of **b** will they come?"	5393
	15:37	you do not plant the **b** that will be,	5393
	15:38	But God gives it a **b** as he has determined,	5393
	15:38	and to each kind of seed he gives its own **b**.	5393
	15:42	The **b** that is sown is perishable,	NIG
	15:44	it is sown a natural **b**,	5393
	15:44	it is raised a spiritual **b**.	5393
	15:44	If there is a natural **b**,	5393
	15:44	there is also a spiritual **b**.	NIG
2Co	4:10	We always carry around in our **b** the death	5393
	4:10	life of Jesus may also be revealed in our **b**.	5393
	4:11	his life may be revealed in our mortal **b**.	4922
	5: 6	as we are at home in the **b** we are away	5393
	5: 8	and would prefer to be away from the **b** and	5393
	5: 9	whether we are at home in the **b** or away	NIG
	5:10	for the things done while in the **b**,	5393
	7: 1	from everything that contaminates **b**	4922
	7: 5	this **b** of ours had no rest,	4922
	12: 2	in the **b** or out of the body I do not know—	5393
	12: 2	in the body or out of the **b** I do not know—	5393
	12: 3	whether in the **b** or apart from the body I do	5393
	12: 3	whether in the body or apart from the **b** I do	5393
Gal	2:20	The life I live in the **b**,	4922
	6:17	for I bear on my **b** the marks of Jesus.	5393
Eph	1:23	which is his **b**, the fullness of him	5393
	2:11	(that done in the **b** by the hands of men)—	4922
	2:16	and in this one **b** to reconcile both of them	5393
	3: 6	**members together of one b**,	5362
	4: 4	There is one **b** and one Spirit—	5393
	4:12	so that the **b** of Christ may be built up	5393
	4:16	From him the whole **b**,	5393
	4:25	for we are all members *of* **one b**.	253
	5:23	his **b**, of which he is the Savior.	5393
	5:29	After all, no one ever hated his own **b**,	4922
	5:30	for we are members *of* his **b**.	5393
Php	1:20	as always Christ will be exalted in my **b**,	5393
	1:22	If I am to go on living in the **b**,	4922
	1:24	for you that I remain in the **b**.	4922
	3:21	so that they will be like his glorious **b**.	5393
Col	1:18	And he is the head *of* the **b**, the church;	5393
	1:22	by Christ's physical **b** through death	5393
	1:24	for the sake of his **b**, which is the church.	5393
	2: 5	For though I am absent from you in **b**,	4922
	2:19	from whom the whole **b**,	5393
	2:23	and their harsh treatment *of* the **b**,	5393
	3:15	members of one **b** you were called to peace.	5393
1Th	4: 4	of you should learn to control his own **b** in	5007
	5:23	soul and **b** be kept blameless at the coming	5393
1Ti	3:16	He appeared in a **b**,	4922
	4:14	the **b of elders** laid their hands on you.	4564
Heb	7:10	Levi was still in the **b** of his ancestor.	4019
	10: 5	but a **b** you prepared for me;	5393

Heb	10:10	the sacrifice *of* the **b** of Jesus Christ once	5393
	10:20	for us through the curtain, that is, his **b**,	4922
Jas	2:26	As the **b** without the spirit is dead,	5393
	3: 2	able to keep his whole **b** in check.	5393
	3: 5	the tongue is a small **part of the b**,	3517
	3: 6	a world of evil among the **parts of the b**.	3517
1Pe	2:24	in his **b** on the tree, so that we might die	5393
	3:18	He was put to death *in* the **b** but made alive	4922
	3:21	the **b** but the pledge of a good conscience	4922
	4: 1	Therefore, since Christ suffered *in* his **b**,	4922
	4: 1	who has suffered *in* his **b** is done with sin.	4922
	4: 6	according to men *in regard to* the **b**,	4922
2Pe	1:13	as long as I live in the tent of this **b**,	NIG
Jude	1: 9	with the devil about the **b** of Moses,	5393

BODYGUARD (4) [GUARD]

1Sa	22:14	captain of your **b** and highly respected	5463
	28: 2	I will make you my **b** for life."	4200+8031+9068
2Sa	23:23	And David put him in charge of his **b**.	5463
1Ch	11:25	And David put him in charge of his **b**.	5463

BOHAN (2)

Jos	15: 6	of Beth Arabah to the Stone of **B** son	992
	18:17	ran down to the Stone of **B** son of Reuben.	992

BOIL (10) [BOILED, BOILING, BOILS]

Ex	16:23	to bake and **b** what you want to boil.	1418
	16:23	to bake and boil *what you want to* **b**,	1418
Lev	13:18	"When someone has a **b** on his skin	8825
	13:19	and in the place where the **b** was,	8825
	13:20	that has broken out where the **b** was.	8825
	13:23	it is only a scar from the **b**,	8825
2Ki	20: 7	They did so and applied it to the **b**,	8825
Isa	38:21	a poultice of figs and apply it to the **b**,	8825
	64: 2	fire sets twigs ablaze and **causes** water to **b**,	1240
Eze	24: 5	**bring** it **to a b** and cook the bones	8409+8410

BOILED (4) [BOIL]

Nu	6:19	in his hands a **b** shoulder of the ram,	1419
1Sa	2:13	a sacrifice and while the meat *was being* **b**,	1418
	2:15	he won't accept **b** meat from you,	1418
2Ch	35:13	and **b** the holy offerings in pots,	1418

BOILING (3) [BOIL]

Job	41:20	from his nostrils as from a **b** pot over a fire	5870
	41:31	He makes the depths churn like a **b** caldron	NIH
Jer	1:13	"I see a **b** pot, tilting away from the north,"	5870

BOILS (5) [BOIL]

Ex	9: 9	and festering **b** will break out on men	8825
	9:10	festering **b** broke out on men and animals.	8825
	9:11	before Moses because of the **b** that were	8825
Dt	28:27	The LORD will afflict you with the **b**	8825
	28:35	with painful **b** that cannot be cured,	8825

BOKERU (2)

1Ch	8:38	Azrikam, **B**, Ishmael, Sheariah,	1150
	9:44	Azrikam, **B**, Ishmael, Sheariah,	1150

BOKIM (2)

Jdg	2: 1	of the LORD went up from Gilgal to **B**	1141
	2: 5	and they called that place **B**.	1141

BOLD (10) [BOLDLY, BOLDNESS, EMBOLDENED]

Ge	18:27	"Now *that I have been so* **b** *as* to speak to	3283
	18:31	"Now *that I have been so* **b** *as* to speak to	3283
Ps	138: 3	you **made** me **b** and stouthearted.	8104
Pr	21:29	A wicked man **puts up a b** front,	928+6451+7156
	28: 1	but the righteous *are* as **b** as a lion.	1053
2Co	3:12	since we have such a hope, *we are* very **b**.	4244+5968
	10: 1	to face with you, but **"b"** when away!	2509
	10: 2	that when I come I *may* not have *to be* as **b**	2509
Phm	1: 8	although in Christ I could **be b** and order	2400+4244+4498
		you to do what you ought	
2Pe	2:10	**B** and arrogant, these men are not afraid	5532

BOLDLY (12) [BOLD]

Ex	14: 8	who were marching out **b**.	928+3338+8123
Nu	33: 3	They marched out **b** in full view of all the	928+3338+8123
		Egyptians,	
Mk	15:43	went **b** to Pilate and asked for Jesus' body.	5528
Ac	4:31	and spoke the word of God **b**.	3552+4244
	9:28	**speaking b** in the name of the Lord.	4245
	13:46	Then Paul and Barnabas answered them **b**:	4245
	14: 3	**speaking b** for the Lord,	4245
	18:26	He began *to* speak **b** in the synagogue.	4245
	19: 8	and **spoke b** there for three months,	4245
	28:31	**B** and without hindrance he preached	4244
Ro	10:20	And Isaiah **b** says, "I was found	703
	15:15	I have written you **quite b** on some points,	5529

BOLDNESS (2) [BOLD]

Lk	11: 8	of the man's **b** he will get up and give him	357
Ac	4:29	to speak your word with great **b**.	4244

BOLSTER (KJV) See HEAD

BOLT (1) [BOLTED, BOLTS]

2Sa	13:17	"Get this woman out of here and **b** the door	5835

BOLTED (1) [BOLT]

2Sa	13:18	So his servant put her out and **b** the door	5835

BOLTS (12) [BOLT]

Dt	33:25	**b** of your **gates** will be iron and bronze,	4981
2Sa	22:13	of his presence **b** of lightning blazed forth.	1624
	22:15	**b** of lightning and routed them.	1398
Ne	3: 3	They laid its beams and put its doors and **b**	4980
	3: 6	They laid its beams and put its doors and **b**	4980
	3:13	and put its doors and **b** and bars in place.	4980
	3:14	and put its doors and **b** and bars in place.	4980
	3:15	roofing it over and putting its doors and **b**	4980
Job	38:35	Do you send the **lightning b** on their way?	1398
Ps	18:12	with hailstones and **b** of lightning.	1624
	18:14	great **b** of lightning and routed them.	1398
	78:48	their livestock to **b** of lightning.	8404

BOND (3) [BONDAGE, BONDS]

Eze	20:37	I will bring you into the **b** of the covenant.	5037
Ac	17: 9	Then they made Jason and the others **post b**	2653
Eph	4: 3	to keep the unity of the Spirit through the **b**	5278

BONDAGE (9) [BOND]

Ge	47:19	we with our land will be in **b** to Pharaoh.	6269
	47:25	we will be in **b** to Pharaoh."	6269
Ex	6: 9	of their discouragement and cruel **b**.	6275
Ezr	9: 8	to our eyes and a little relief in our **b**.	6285
	9: 9	our God has not deserted us in our **b**.	6285
Isa	14: 3	suffering and turmoil and cruel **b**,	6268+6275
Jer	34: 9	**hold** a fellow Jew in **b**.	6268
	34:10	and no longer **hold** them in **b**.	6268
Ro	8:21	be liberated from its **b** to decay and brought	1525

BONDMAID, BONDMAIDS (KJV) See SLAVE GIRL, SLAVES

BONDMAN, BONDMEN (KJV) See SLAVE, SERVANT

BONDS (4) [BOND]

Jer	2:20	and tore off your **b**;	4593
	5: 5	the yoke and torn off the **b**.	4593
	30: 8	and will tear off their **b**;	4593
Hos	10:10	be gathered against them *to* **put** them in **b**	673

BONDSERVANT (KJV) See SLAVE

BONDWOMAN, BONDWOMEN (KJV) See SLAVE

BONE (7) [BACKBONE, BONES]

Ge	2:23	now **b** of my bones and flesh of my flesh;	6795
Nu	19:16	anyone who touches a human **b** or a grave	6795
	19:18	anyone who touches a human **b** or a grave	6795
Pr	25:15	and a gentle tongue can break a **b**.	1752
Eze	37: 7	and the bones came together, **b** to bone.	6795
	37: 7	and the bones came together, bone to **b**.	6795
	39:15	the land and one of them sees a human **b**,	6795

BONES (90) [BONE]

Ge	2:23	now bone of my **b** and flesh of my flesh;	6795
	50:25	and then you must carry my **b** up	6795
Ex	12:46	Do not break any of the **b**.	6795
	13:19	Moses took the **b** of Joseph with him	6795
	13:19	and then you must carry my **b** up with you	6795
Nu	9:12	of it till morning or break any of its **b**.	6795
	24: 8	and break their **b** in pieces;	6795
Jos	24:32	And Joseph's **b**, which	6795
1Sa	31:13	Then they took their **b** and buried them	6795
2Sa	21:12	and took the **b** of Saul and his son Jonathan	6795
	21:13	the **b** of Saul and his son Jonathan	6795
	21:13	and the **b** of those who had been killed	6795
	21:14	the **b** of Saul and his son Jonathan in	6795
1Ki	13: 2	and human **b** will be burned on you.' "	6795
	13:31	lay my **b** beside his bones.	6795
	13:31	lay my bones beside his **b**.	6795
2Ki	13:21	When the body touched Elisha's **b**,	6795
	23:14	and covered the sites with human **b**.	6795
	23:16	he removed them from and burned on	6795
	23:18	"Don't let anyone disturb his **b**."	6795
	23:18	So they spared his **b** and those of	6795
	23:20	on the altars and burned human **b** on them.	6795
1Ch	10:12	Then they buried their **b** under	6795
2Ch	34: 5	the **b** of the priests on their altars	6795
Job	2: 5	and strike his flesh and **b**,	6795
	4:14	and made all my **b** shake.	6795
	10:11	and knit me together with **b** and sinews?	6795
	19:20	I am nothing but skin and **b**;	6795
	20:11	that fills his **b** will lie with him in the dust.	6795
	21:24	his **b** rich with marrow.	6795
	30:17	Night pierces my **b**;	6795
	33:19	a bed of pain with constant distress in his **b**,	6795
	33:21	and his **b**, once hidden, now stick out.	6795

Job	40:18	His **b** are tubes of bronze,	6795
Ps	6: 2	O LORD, heal me, for my **b** are in agony.	6795
	22:14	and all my **b** are out of joint.	6795
	22:17	I can count all my **b**;	6795
	31:10	and my **b** grow weak.	6795
	32: 3	my **b** wasted away	6795
	34:20	he protects all his **b**,	6795
	38: 3	my **b** have no soundness because of my sin.	6795
	42:10	My **b** suffer mortal agony	6795
	51: 8	let the **b** you have crushed rejoice.	6795
	53: 5	the **b** of those who attacked you;	6795
	102: 3	my **b** burn like glowing embers.	6795
	102: 5	I am reduced to skin and **b**.	6795
	109:18	into his **b** like oil.	6795
	141: 7	so our **b** have been scattered at the mouth	6795
Pr	3: 8	to your body and nourishment to your **b**.	6795
	12: 4	but a disgraceful wife is like decay in his **b**.	6795
	14:30	but envy rots the **b**.	6795
	15:30	and good news gives health to the **b**.	6795
	16:24	sweet to the soul and healing to the **b**.	6795
	17:22	but a crushed spirit dries up the **b**.	1752
Isa	38:13	but like a lion he broke all my **b**;	6795
Jer	8: 1	the **b** of the kings and officials of Judah,	6795
	8: 1	the **b** of the priests and prophets,	6795
	8: 1	and the **b** of the people of Jerusalem will	6795
	20: 9	a fire shut up in my **b**.	6795
	23: 9	heart is broken within me; all my **b** tremble.	6795
	50:17	*to* **crush** his **b** was Nebuchadnezzar king	6793
La	1:13	sent it down into my **b**.	6795
	3: 4	and has broken my **b**.	6795
	4: 8	Their skin has shriveled on their **b**;	6795
Eze	6: 5	and I will scatter your **b** around your altars.	6795
	24: 4	Fill it with the best of these **b**;	6795
	24: 5	Pile wood beneath it for the **b**;	6795
	24: 5	bring it to a boil and cook the **b** in it.	6795
	24:10	and let the **b** be charred.	6795
	32:27	for their sins rested on their **b**.	6795
	37: 1	the middle of a valley; it was full of **b**.	6795
	37: 2	a great many **b** on the floor of the valley,	NIH
	37: 2	**b** that were very dry.	NIH
	37: 3	"Son of man, can these **b** live?"	6795
	37: 4	"Prophesy to these **b** and say to them,	6795
	37: 4	'Dry **b**, hear the word of the LORD!	6795
	37: 5	the Sovereign LORD says to these **b**:	6795
	37: 7	a rattling sound, and the **b** came together,	6795
	37:11	these **b** are the whole house of Israel.	6795
	37:11	'Our **b** are dried up and our hope is gone;	6795
Da	6:24	and crushed all their **b**.	10150
Am	2: 1	as if to lime, the **b** *of* Edom's king,	6795
	3:12	the lion's mouth only two **leg b** or a piece	4157
Mic	3: 2	from my people and the flesh from their **b**;	6795
	3: 3	strip off their skin and break their **b**	6795
Hab	3:16	decay crept into my **b**,	6795
Mt	23:27	but on the inside are full *of* dead men's **b**	4014
Lk	24:39	a ghost does not have flesh and **b**,	4014
Jn	19:36	"Not one of his **b** will be broken,"	4014
Heb	11:22	and gave instructions about his **b**.	4014

BONNETS (KJV) See HEADBANDS, HEADDRESSES, TURBANS

BOOK (130) [BOOKS]

Ex	24: 7	Then he took the **B** of the Covenant	6219
	32:32	then blot me out of the **b** you have written."	6219
	32:33	against me I will blot out of my **b**.	6219
Nu	21:14	the **B** of the Wars of the LORD says:	6219
Dt	28:58	which are written in this **b**,	6219
	28:61	and disaster not recorded in this **B** *of*	6219
	29:20	All the curses written in this **b** will fall	6219
	29:21	the curses of the covenant written in this **B**	6219
	29:27	on it all the curses written in this **b**.	6219
	30:10	and decrees that are written in this **B** *of*	6219
	31:24	in a **b** the words of this law from beginning	6219
	31:26	"Take this **B** of the Law and place it beside	6219
Jos	1: 8	Do not let this **B** of the Law depart	6219
	8:31	according to what is written in the **B** *of*	6219
	8:34	just as it is written in the **B** of the Law.	6219
	10:13	as it is written in the **B** of Jashar?	6219
	23: 6	to obey all that is written in the **B** *of*	6219
	24:26	And Joshua recorded these things in the **B**	6219
2Sa	1:18	of the bow (it is written in the **B** of Jashar):	6219
1Ki	11:41	are they not written in the **b** *of* the annals	6219
	14:19	in the **b** of the annals of the kings of Israel.	6219
	14:29	in the **b** of the annals of the kings of Judah?	6219
	15: 7	in the **b** of the annals of the kings of Judah?	6219
	15:23	in the **b** of the annals of the kings of Judah?	6219
	15:31	in the **b** of the annals of the kings of Israel?	6219
	16: 5	in the **b** of the annals of the kings of Israel?	6219
	16:14	in the **b** of the annals of the kings of Israel?	6219
	16:20	in the **b** of the annals of the kings of Israel?	6219
	16:27	in the **b** of the annals of the kings of Israel?	6219
	22:39	in the **b** of the annals of the kings of Israel?	6219
	22:45	in the **b** of the annals of the kings of Judah?	6219
2Ki	1:18	in the **b** of the annals of the kings of Israel?	6219
	8:23	in the **b** of the annals of the kings of Judah?	6219
	10:34	in the **b** of the annals of the kings of Israel?	6219
	12:19	in the **b** of the annals of the kings of Judah?	6219
	13:12	in the **b** of the annals of the kings of Israel?	6219
	14: 6	in accordance with what is written in the **B**	6219
	14:15	in the **b** of the annals of the kings of Israel?	6219
	14:18	in the **b** of the annals of the kings of Judah?	6219
	14:28	in the **b** of the annals of the kings of Israel?	6219
	15: 6	in the **b** of the annals of the kings of Judah?	6219
	15:11	in the **b** of the annals of the kings of Israel.	6219

2Ki	15:15	in the **b** of the annals of the kings of Israel.	6219
	15:21	in the **b** of the annals of the kings of Israel?	6219
	15:26	in the **b** of the annals of the kings of Israel?	6219
	15:31	in the **b** of the annals of the kings of Israel?	6219
	15:36	in the **b** of the annals of the kings of Judah?	6219
	16:19	in the **b** of the annals of the kings of Judah?	6219
	20:20	in the **b** of the annals of the kings of Judah?	6219
	21:17	in the **b** of the annals of the kings of Judah?	6219
	21:25	in the **b** of the annals of the kings of Judah?	6219
	22: 8	"I have found the **B** of the Law in	6219
	22:10	"Hilkiah the priest has given me a **b**."	6219
	22:11	When the king heard the words of the **B** of	6219
	22:13	for all Judah about what is written in this **b**	6219
	22:13	not obeyed the words of this **b**;	6219
	22:16	according to everything written in the **b**	6219
	23: 2	in their hearing all the words of the **B** of	6219
	23: 3	the words of the covenant written in this **b**.	6219
	23:21	as it is written in this **B** of the Covenant."	6219
	23:24	the requirements of the law written in the **b**	6219
	23:28	the **b** of the annals of the kings of Judah?	6219
	24: 5	the **b** of the annals of the kings of Judah?	6219
1Ch	9: 1	in the genealogies recorded in the **b** of	6219
	27:24	and the number was not recorded in the **b** of	6219
2Ch	16:11	are written in the **b** of the kings of Judah	6219
	17: 9	with them the **B** of the Law of the LORD;	6219
	20:34	which are recorded in the **b** of the kings of	6219
	24:27	in the annotations on the **b** of the kings.	6219
	25: 4	in the **B** of Moses,	6219
	25:26	not written in the **b** of the kings of Judah	6219
	27: 7	are written in the **b** of the kings of Israel	6219
	28:26	are written in the **b** of the kings of Judah	6219
	32:32	the prophet Isaiah son of Amoz in the **b** of	6219
	34:14	Hilkiah the priest found the **B** of the Law	6219
	34:15	"I have found the **B** of the Law in	6219
	34:16	the **b** to the king and reported to him:	6219
	34:18	"Hilkiah the priest has given me a **b**."	6219
	34:21	and Judah about what is written in this **b**	6219
	34:21	with all that is written in this **b**."	6219
	34:24	the **b** that has been read in the presence of	6219
	34:30	in their hearing all the words of the **B** of	6219
	34:31	the words of the covenant written in this **b**.	6219
	35:12	as is written in the **B** of Moses.	6219
	35:27	are written in the **b** of the kings of Israel	6219
	36: 8	are written in the **b** of the kings of Israel	6219
Ezr	6:18	to what is written in the **B** of Moses.	10515
Ne	8: 1	They told Ezra the scribe to bring out the **B**	6219
	8: 3	the people listened attentively to the **B** of	6219
	8: 5	Ezra opened the **b**.	6219
	8: 8	They read from the **B** of the Law of God,	6219
	8:18	Ezra read from the **B** of the Law of God.	6219
	9: 3	the **B** of the Law of the LORD their God	6219
	12:23	of Eliashib were recorded in the **b** of	6219
	13: 1	On that day the **B** of Moses was read aloud	6219
Est	2:23	All this was recorded in the **b** of the annals	6219
	6: 1	so he ordered the **b** of the chronicles,	6219
	10: 2	in the **b** of the annals of the kings of Media	6219
Ps	69:28	May they be blotted out of the **b** of life and	6219
	139:16	in your **b** before one of them came to be.	6219
Jer	25:13	all that are written in this **b** and prophesied	6219
	30: 2	in a **b** all the words I have spoken to you.	6219
Da	10:21	written in the **B** of Truth.	4181
	12: 1	everyone whose name is found written in the **b**—	6219
Na	1: 1	**b** of the vision of Nahum the Elkoshite.	6219
Mk	12:26	have you not read in the **b** of Moses,	1047
Lk	3: 4	As is written in the **b** of the words of Isaiah	1047
	20:42	David himself declares in the **B** of Psalms:	1047
Jn	20:30	which are not recorded in this **b**.	1046
Ac	1: 1	In my former **b**, Theophilus,	3364
	1:20	said Peter, "it is written in the **b** of Psalms,	1047
	7:42	This agrees with what is written in the **b** of	1047
	8:28	in his chariot reading the **b** of Isaiah	NIG
Gal	3:10	to do everything written in the **B** of	1046
Php	4: 3	whose names are in the **b** of life.	1047
Rev	3: 5	I will never blot out his name from the **b**	1047
	13: 8	not been written in the **b** of life belonging	1046
	17: 8	not been written in the **b** of life from	1046
	20:12	Another **b** was opened,	1046
	20:12	which is the **b** of life.	NIG
	20:15	not found written in the **b** of life,	1047
	21:27	in the Lamb's **b** of life.	1046
	22: 7	the words of the prophecy *in* this **b**."	1046
	22: 9	and of all who keep the words *of* this **b**.	1046
	22:10	up the words of the prophecy *of* this **b**,	1046
	22:18	the words of the prophecy *of* this **b**:	1046
	22:18	to him the plagues described in this **b**.	1046
	22:19	if anyone takes words away from this **b**	1046
	22:19	which are described in this **b**.	1046

BOOKS (5) [BOOK]

Ecc	12:12	Of making many **b** there is no end,	6219
Da	7:10	court was seated, and the **b** were opened.	10515
Jn	21:25	not have room for the **b** that would	1046
Rev	20:12	before the throne, and **b** were opened.	1046
	20:12	to what they had done as recorded in the **b**.	1046

BOOSTING (1)

Am	8: 5	the measure, **b** the price and cheating	1540

BOOT (1)

Isa	9: 5	Every warrior's **b** used in battle	6007

BOOTH (3) [BOOTHS]

Mt	9: 9	at the **tax collector's b**.	5468

Mk	2:14	at the **tax collector's b**.	5468
Lk	5:27	by the name of Levi sitting at his **tax b**.	5468

BOOTHS (7) [BOOTH]

Lev	23:42	Live in **b** for seven days:	6109
	23:42	All native-born Israelites are to live in **b**	6109
	23:43	in **b** when I brought them out of Egypt.	6109
Ne	8:14	in **b** during the feast of the seventh month	6109
	8:15	palms and shade trees, to make **b**"—	6109
	8:16	and built themselves **b** on their own roofs,	6109
	8:17	from exile built **b** and lived in them.	6109

BOOTY (2)

2Ch	14:14	since there was much **b** there.	1023
Jer	49:32	and their large herds will be **b**.	8965

BOOZ (KJV) See BOAZ

BOR ASHAN (1) [ASHAN]

1Sa	30:30	to those in Hormah, **B**, Athach	1016

BORDER (59) [BORDERED, BORDERING, BORDERS]

Ge	25:18	near the **b** of Egypt,	7156
	49:13	his **b** will extend toward Sidon.	3752
Ex	16:35	they ate manna until they reached the **b**	7895
Nu	20:23	At Mount Hor, near the **b** of Edom,	1473
	21:13	The Arnon is the **b** of Moab,	1473
	21:15	that lead to the site of Ar and lie along the **b**	1473
	21:24	because their **b** was fortified.	1473
	22:36	at the Moabite town on the Arnon **b**,	1473
	33:37	on the **b** of Edom.	7895
	33:44	on the **b** of Moab.	1473
	34: 3	of the Desert of Zin along the **b** of Edom.	3338
Dt	3:14	the whole region of Argob as far as the **b** of	1473
	3:16	(the middle of the gorge being the **b**)	1473
	3:16	which is the **b** of the Ammonites.	1473
	3:17	Its western **b** was the Jordan in the Arabah,	1473
Jos	4:19	and camped at Gilgal on the eastern **b**	7895
	12: 2	which is the **b** of the Ammonites.	1473
	12: 5	the **b** of the people of Geshur and Maacah,	1473
	12: 5	and half of Gilead to the **b** of Sihon king	1473
	13:10	out to the **b** of the Ammonites.	1473
	16: 8	the **b** went west to the Kanah Ravine	1473
	22:11	as the **b** at Geliloth near the Jordan	4578
Jdg	7:22	as the **b** of Abel Meholah near Tabbath.	8557
	11:18	for the Arnon was its **b**.	1473
1Sa	6:12	the Philistines followed them as far as the **b**	1473
	10: 2	at Zelzah on the **b** of Benjamin.	1473
2Sa	13:23	at Baal Hazor near the **b** of Ephraim,	NIH
1Ki	4:21	as far as the **b** of Egypt.	1473
2Ki	3:21	up and stationed on the **b**.	1473
2Ch	9:26	as far as the **b** of Egypt.	1473
	26: 8	his fame spread as far as the **b** of Egypt,	995
Ps	78:54	Thus he brought them to the **b**	1473
Isa	15: 8	Their outcry echoes along the **b** of Moab;	1473
	19:19	and a monument to the LORD at its **b**.	1473
Eze	29:10	from the **b** of Cush.	1473
	45: 7	the western to the eastern **b** parallel to one	1473
	47:16	Berothah and Sibraim (which lies on the **b**	1473
	47:16	which is on the **b** of Hauran.	1473
	47:17	along the northern **b** of Damascus.	1473
	47:17	with the **b** of Hamath to the north.	1473
	48: 1	and the northern **b** of Damascus next	1473
	48: 1	of its **b** *from* the east side to the west side.	6991
	48: 2	it will **b** the territory of Dan from east	6584
	48: 3	it will **b** the territory of Asher from east	6584
	48: 4	it will **b** the territory of Naphtali from east	6584
	48: 5	it will **b** the territory of Manasseh from east	6584
	48: 6	it will **b** the territory of Ephraim from east	6584
	48: 7	it will **b** the territory of Reuben from east	6584
	48:21	cubits of the sacred portion to the eastern **b**,	1473
	48:21	cubits to the western **b**.	1473
	48:22	the **b** of Judah and the border of Benjamin.	1473
	48:22	the border of Judah and the **b** of Benjamin.	1473
	48:24	it will **b** the territory of Benjamin from east	6584
	48:25	it will **b** the territory of Simeon from east	6584
	48:26	it will **b** the territory of Issachar from east	6584
	48:27	it will **b** the territory of Zebulun from east	6584
Ob	1: 7	All your allies will force you to the **b**;	1473
Lk	17:11	Jesus traveled along the **b** between Samaria	NIG
Ac	16: 7	When they came to the **b** of Mysia,	NIG

BORDERED (1) [BORDER]

Jos	17:10	of Manasseh reached the sea and **b** Asher	7003

BORDERING (4) [BORDER]

Eze	45: 7	" 'The prince will have the land **b** each side	2256+2296+2296+4946+4946ˢ
	48: 8	"**B** the territory of Judah from east	6584
	48:12	**b** the territory of the Levites.	448
	48:18	**b** *on* the sacred portion and running	4200+6645

BORDERLAND (1) [LAND]

1Sa	13:18	and the third toward the **b** overlooking	1473

BORDERS (14) [BORDER]

Ge	10:19	and the **b** of Canaan reached from Sidon	1473
	23:17	and all the trees within the **b** of the field—	1473
Ex	13: 7	be seen anywhere within your **b**.	1473
	23:31	"I will establish your **b** from the Red Sea to	1473

1Ch	7:29	Along the **b** of Manasseh were Beth Shan,	3338
Ps	147:14	He grants peace to your **b** and satisfies you	1473
Isa	26:15	you have extended all the **b** of the land.	7898
	60:18	nor ruin or destruction within your **b**,	1473
Eze	11:10	and I will execute judgment on you at the **b**	1473
	11:11	I will execute judgment on you at the **b**	1473
Am	1:13	of Gilead in order to extend his **b**,	1473
Mic	5: 6	and marches into our **b**.	1473
Zec	9: 2	*which* **b** on it, and upon Tyre and Sidon,	1487
Mal	1: 5	even beyond the **b** of Israel!'	1473

BORE (62) [BEAR]

Ge	16:15	So Hagar **b** Abram a son,	3528
	16:16	when Hagar **b** him Ishmael.	3528
	21: 2	and **b** a son to Abraham in his old age,	3528
	21: 3	the name Isaac to the son Sarah **b** him,	3528
	22:23	Milcah **b** these eight sons.	3528
	24:24	the son that Milcah **b** to Nahor."	3528
	24:47	whom Milcah **b** to him.'	3528
	25: 2	*She* **b** him Zimran, Jokshan, Medan,	3528
	25:12	Hagar the Egyptian, **b** to Abraham.	3528
	30: 5	and she became pregnant and **b** him a son.	3528
	30: 7	and **b** Jacob a second son.	3528
	30:10	Leah's servant Zilpah **b** Jacob a son.	3528
	30:12	Leah's servant Zilpah **b** Jacob a second son.	3528
	30:17	and she became pregnant and **b** him	3528
	30:19	Leah conceived again and **b** Jacob	3528
	30:39	And they **b** *young* that were streaked	3528
	31: 8	then all the flocks **b** streaked young.	3528
	31:39	I **b** the loss myself.	2627
	36: 4	Adah **b** Eliphaz to Esau,	3528
	36: 4	to Esau, Basemath **b** Reuel,	3528
	36: 5	and Oholibamah **b** Jeush,	3528
	36:12	Timna, *who* **b** him Amalek.	3528
	36:14	Zibeon, whom *she* **b** to Esau:	3528
	44:27	'You know that my wife **b** me two sons.	3528
	46:15	the sons Leah **b** to Jacob in Paddan Aram,	3528
Ex	6:20	who **b** him Aaron and Moses.	3528
	6:23	and *she* **b** him Nadab and Abihu,	3528
	6:25	and *she* **b** him Phinehas.	3528
Nu	26:59	To Amram *she* **b** Aaron,	3528
Jdg	8:31	who lived in Shechem, also **b** him a son,	3528
	11: 1	Gilead's wife also **b** him sons,	3528
Ru	4:12	whom Tamar **b** to Judah."	3528
1Sa	20:30	and to the shame of the **mother** *who* **b** you?	AIT
2Sa	11:27	and she became his wife and **b** him a son.	3528
1Ki	11:20	of Tahpenes **b** him a son named Genubath,	3528
	14:28	the guards **b** the shields,	5951
1Ch	2: 4	**b** him Perez and Zerah.	3528
	2:19	Caleb married Ephrath, *who* **b** him Hur.	3528
	2:21	and *she* **b** him Segub.	3528
	2:24	the wife of Hezron **b** him Ashhur the father	3528
	2:29	*who* **b** him Ahban and Molid.	3528
	2:35	and *she* **b** him Attai.	3528
	4: 6	Naarah **b** him Ahuzzam, Hepher,	3528
2Ch	11:19	*She* **b** him sons:	3528
	11:20	*who* **b** him Abijah, Attai,	3528
Pr	17:25	and bitterness to the *one who* **b** him.	3528
SS	6: 9	the favorite of the *one who* **b** her.	3528
Isa	49:21	'Who **b** me these?	3528
	51:18	the sons *she* **b** there was none to guide her;	5951
	53:12	For he **b** the sin of many,	5951
	54: 1	O barren woman, *you* who never **b a child**;	3528
Jer	20:14	the day my mother **b** me not be blessed!	3528
	31:19	I was ashamed and humiliated because *I* **b**	5951
Eze	16:20	and daughters whom *you* **b** to me	3528
	23:37	whom *they* **b** to me, as food for them.	3528
Hos	1: 3	and she conceived and **b** him a son.	3528
Lk	23: 9	so that *we* **b fruit** for death.	1164
Ro	7: 5	**b** with great patience the objects	2844
	9:22	bearing the disgrace he **b**.	5770
Heb	13:13	He himself **b** our sins in his body on	NIG
1Pe	2:24		429
Rev	17: 6	the blood *of* those who **b testimony**	3459

BORED (1) [BEAR]

2Ki	12: 9	Jehoiada the priest took a chest and **b** a hole	5918

BORN (144) [BEAR]

Ge	4:18	To Enoch *was* **b** Irad,	3528
	5: 4	After Seth *was* **b**,	3528
	5:30	After Noah *was* **b**,	3528
	6: 1	and daughters were **b** to them,	3528
	10:21	*Sons* were also **b** to Shem:	3528
	10:25	Two sons were **b** to Eber:	3528
	14:14	the 318 trained men **b** *in* his household	3535
	17:12	including *those* **b** *in* your household	3535
	17:13	Whether **b** *in* your household or bought	3528
	17:17	a son be **b** to a man a hundred years old?	3528
	17:23	and all *those* **b** *in* his household or bought	3535
	17:27	including *those* **b** *in* his household	3535
	21: 5	when his son Isaac *was* **b** to him.	3528
	35:26	who *were* **b** to him in Paddan Aram.	3528
	36: 5	who *were* **b** to him in Canaan.	3528
	37: 3	he had been **b** to him in his old age;	1201
	41:50	two sons *were* **b** to Joseph	3528
	44:20	a young *son* **b** to him *in* his old age.	AIT
	46:18	These were the children **b** to Jacob	3528
	46:20	Manasseh and Ephraim *were* **b** to Joseph	3528
	46:22	These were the sons of Rachel who *were* **b**	3528
	46:25	These were the sons **b** to Jacob by Bilhah,	3528
	46:27	the two sons who *had been* **b** to Joseph	3528
	48: 5	your two sons **b** to you in Egypt	3528
	48: 6	Any children **b** *to* you after them will	3528
Ex	1:22	"Every boy that is **b** you must throw into	3533

Ex	12:48	then he may take part like one **b** in	275
	23:12	**slave b in** your **household,**	563+1201
Lev	18:9	**b in the same home**	1074+4580
	18:11	**b** to your **father;** she is your sister.	4580
	22:11	or if a slave is **b** in his household,	3535
	22:27	a lamb or a goat is **b,**	3528
	25:45	among you and members of their clans **b**	3528
Nu	26:59	who was **b** to the Levites in Egypt.	3528
Dt	23:2	one **b of a forbidden marriage**	4927
	23:8	The third generation of children **b**	3528
Jos	5:5	but all the people **b** in the desert during	3533
Jdg	13:8	how to bring up the boy who is to be **b."**	3528
	18:29	who was **b** to Israel—	3528
2Sa	3:2	Sons were **b** to David in Hebron.	3528
	3:5	These were **b** to David in Hebron.	3528
	5:13	and more sons and daughters were **b** to him.	3528
	5:14	the names of the **children b** to him there:	3533
	12:14	the son to you will die."	3533
	14:27	and a daughter were **b** to Absalom.	3528
1Ki	1:6	He was also very handsome and was **b** next	3528
	3:18	The third day after my **child was b,**	3528
	13:2	'A son named Josiah will **be b** to the house	3528
2Ki	20:18	that will be **b** to you, will be taken away,	3528
1Ch	1:19	Two sons were **b** to Eber:	3528
	1:32	The sons **b** to Keturah.	3528
	2:3	These three were **b** to him by	3528
	2:9	The sons **b** to Hezron were:	3528
	3:1	These were the sons of David **b** to him	3528
	3:4	These six were **b** to David in Hebron,	3528
	3:5	and these were the children **b** to him there:	3528
	8:8	Sons were **b** to Shaharaim in Moab	3528
	8:8	the names of the **children b** to him there:	3528
Job	3:3	and the night it was said, 'A boy **is b!'**	2225
	5:7	Yet man is **b** to trouble as surely	3528
	5:7	for we were **b** only yesterday	NIH
	11:12	a wild donkey's colt *can* be **b** a man.	3528
	14:1	"Man **b** of woman is of few days and full	3528
	15:7	"Are you the first man ever **b?**	3528
	15:14	that he could be pure, or one **b** of woman,	3528
	25:4	How can one **b** of woman be pure?	3528
	38:21	Surely you know, for *you* were already **b!**	3528
Ps	78:6	even the children yet to be **b,**	3528
	87:4	and will say, 'This one was **b** in Zion.' "	3528
	87:5	"This one and that one were **b** in her,	3528
	87:6	"This one was **b** in Zion."	3528
	90:2	the mountains were **b** or you brought forth	3528
	127:4	of a warrior are **sons** *b* in one's youth.	AIT
Pr	17:17	and a brother is **b** for adversity.	3528
Ecc	2:7	and had other slaves *who* were **b**	1201
	3:2	a time to be **b** and a time to die,	3528
	4:14	or *he may* have **been b** in poverty	3528
Isa	9:6	For to us a child is **b,** to us a son is given,	3528
	39:7	your own flesh and blood *who will* be **b**	3528
	49:1	Before I was **b** the LORD called me;	1061
	49:20	The **children** *b* during your bereavement	AIT
	66:8	*Can* a country be **b** in a day or a nation	2655
Jer	1:5	before *you* were **b** I set you apart;	3655+4946+8167
	16:3	about the sons and daughters **b** in this land	3533
	20:14	Cursed be the day *I* was **b!**	3528
	20:15	saying, "A child is **b** to you—a son!"	3528
	22:26	where neither *of* you was **b,**	3528
Eze	16:4	the day you were **b** your cord was not cut,	3528
	16:5	on the day you were **b** you were despised.	3528
Hos	2:3	as bare as on the day she was **b;**	3528
Zec	13:3	his father and mother, to whom he was **b,**	3528
Mt	1:16	the husband of Mary, of whom was **b** Jesus,	1164
	2:1	*After* Jesus was **b** in Bethlehem in Judea,	1164
	2:2	is the one who has **been b** king of the Jews?	5503
	2:4	where the Christ was to be **b.**	1164
	11:11	Among *those* **b** of women there has	1168
	19:12	For some are eunuchs because *they* were **b**	1164
	26:24	be better for him if he *had* not **been b."**	1164
Mk	7:26	**b** in Syrian Phoenicia.	1169
	14:21	be better for him if he *had* not **been b."**	1164
Lk	1:35	the holy one *to* be **b** will be called the Son	1164
	2:6	the time came for the **baby** to be **b,**	5503
	2:11	town of David a Savior *has* been **b** to you;	5503
	7:28	I tell you, among *those* **b**	1168
Jn	1:13	children **b** not of natural descent,	1164
	1:13	but **b** of God.	NIG
	3:3	the kingdom of God unless he *is* **b** again."	1164
	3:4	"How can a man be **b** when he is old?"	1164
	3:4	into his mother's womb to be **b!"**	1164
	3:5	the kingdom of God unless he *is* **b** of water	1164
	3:7	'You must *be* **b** again.'	1164
	3:8	So it is with everyone **b** of the Spirit."	1164
	8:58	Jesus answered, "before Abraham **was b,**	1181
	9:2	that *he was* **b** blind?"	1164
	9:19	"Is this the one you say *was* **b** blind.	1164
	9:20	"and we know he *was* **b** blind.	1164
	9:32	of opening the eyes *of a man* **b** blind.	1164
	16:21	when her baby is **b** she forgets the anguish	1164
	16:21	of her joy that a child *is* **b** into the world.	1164
	18:37	In fact, for this reason *I* was **b,**	1164
Ac	7:20	"At that time Moses was **b,**	1164
	22:3	**b** in Tarsus of Cilicia,	1164
	22:28	"But I *was* **b** a citizen," Paul replied.	1164
Ro	9:11	the twins were **b** or had done anything good	1164
1Co	11:12	so also man is **b** of woman.	NIG
	15:8	as to one **abnormally b.**	1765
Gal	4:4	God sent his Son, **b** of a woman,	1181
	4:4	born of woman, **b** under law,	1181
	4:23	the slave woman was **b** in the ordinary way;	1164
	4:23	by the free woman was **b** as the result of	NIG
	4:29	the son **b** in the ordinary way persecuted	1164
	4:29	in the ordinary way persecuted the son **b** by	NIG

Heb	11:23	for three months *after* he was **b,**	1164
1Pe	1:23	*For* you have been **b** again,	335
2Pe	2:12	**b** only to be caught and destroyed,	1164
1Jn	2:29	everyone who does what is right *has been* **b**	1164
	3:9	No one who is **b** of God will continue	1164
	3:9	because *he has been* **b** of God.	1164
	4:7	Everyone who loves *has been* **b** of God	1164
	5:1	that Jesus is the Christ *is* **b** of God,	1164
	5:4	everyone **b** of God overcomes the world.	1164
	5:18	that anyone **b** of God does not continue	1164
	5:18	the one who *was* **b** of God keeps him safe,	1164
Rev	12:4	the moment *it was* **b.**	5503

BORNE (21) [BEAR]

Ge	16:1	Sarai, Abram's wife, *had* **b** him no **children.**	3528
	16:15	the name Ishmael to the son she had **b.**	3528
	21:7	Yet *I have* **b** him a son in his old age."	3528
	21:9	the son whom Hagar the Egyptian *had* **b**	3528
	22:20	she *has* **b** sons to your brother Nahor:	3528
	24:36	My master's wife Sarah *has* **b** him a son	3528
	29:34	because *I have* **b** him three sons."	3528
	30:20	because *I have* **b** him six sons."	3528
	31:43	or about the children they *have* **b?**	3528
	34:1	Dinah, the daughter Leah *had* **b** to Jacob,	3528
1Sa	2:5	She who was barren *has* **b** seven **children,**	3528
2Sa	12:15	the child that Uriah's wife *had* **b** to David,	3528
	21:8	whom *she had* **b** to Saul,	3528
	21:8	whom *she had* **b** to Adriel son of Barzillai	3528
1Ki	3:21	I saw that it wasn't the son *I had* **b."**	3528
Ps	18:42	I beat them as fine as dust **b** on the wind;	6584+7156
Isa	46:1	their idols are **b** by beasts of burden.	4200
	49:15	on the child she has **b?**	1061
Hag	2:19	and the olive tree *have* not **b fruit.**	5951
Mt	20:12	to us who *have* **b** the burden of the work	1002
1Co	15:49	just as *we have* **b** the likeness of the earthly man,	5841

BORROW (5) [BORROWED, BORROWER, BORROWS]

Dt	15:6	to many nations but *will* **b** from none.	6292
	28:12	You will lend to many nations but *will* **b**	4278
Ne	5:4	*to* **b** money to pay the king's tax	4278
Ps	37:21	The wicked **b** and do not repay,	4278
Mt	5:42	not turn away from the one who wants *to* **b**	1247

BORROWED (2) [BORROW]

| 2Ki | 6:5 | "Oh, my lord," he cried out, "it was **b!"** | 8626 |
| Jer | 15:10 | I have neither lent nor **b,** | 928+5957 |

BORROWER (3) [BORROW]

Ex	22:15	the **b** will not have to pay.	NIH
Pr	22:7	and the **b** is servant to the lender.	4278
Isa	24:2	for seller as for buyer, for **b** as for lender,	4278

BORROWS (1) [BORROW]

| Ex | 22:14 | "If a man **b** an animal from his neighbor | 8626 |

BOSCATH (KJV) See BOZKATH

BOSOM (3) [BOSOMS]

Pr	5:20	Why embrace the **b** *of* another man's wife?	2668
Eze	23:8	caressed her virgin **b**	1843
	23:21	when in Egypt your **b** was caressed	1843

BOSOMS (1) [BOSOM]

| Eze | 23:3 | and their virgin **b** caressed. | 1843 |

BOSOR (KJV) See BEOR

BOTH (289)

Ge	2:25	The man and his wife were **b** naked,	9109
	3:7	Then the eyes of **b** *of* them were opened,	9109
	6:13	I am surely going to destroy **b** them and	907
	11:29	Abram and Nahor **b** married.	2157S
	11:29	the father of **b** Milcah **and** Iscah.	2256
	17:26	Abraham and his son Ishmael were *b* **circumcised** on that same day.	AIT
	19:4	**b** young **and** old—surrounded the house.	2256
	19:36	So **b** of Lot's daughters became pregnant	9109
	23:17	**b** the field **and** the cave in it,	2256
	27:45	Why should I lose **b** of you in one day?"	9109
	36:7	not support them **b** because	AIT
	39:5	**b** in the house **and** in the field.	2256
	40:8	"We **b** had dreams," they answered,	AIT
	42:37	"You may put **b** of my sons to death if I do	9109
	47:13	**b** Egypt and Canaan wasted away because	2256
	48:13	And Joseph took **b** of them,	9109
Ex	4:15	I will help **b** of you speak	2084+2256+3870
	9:25	**b** men **and** animals;	2256
	12:12	**b** men **and** animals—	2256
	12:22	on the top and on **b** sides *of* the doorframe,	9109
	12:38	**b** flocks **and** herds.	2256
	13:15	**b** man **and** animal.	2256
	21:35	to sell the live one and divide **b** the money	2256
	23:4	**b** *parties* in their cases before	9109
	25:11	Overlay it with pure gold, **b** inside **and** out,	2256
	26:13	cubit longer on **b** sides;	2256+2296+2296+4946S
	26:24	**b** shall be like that.	9109

Ex	29:13	and **b** kidneys with the fat on them,	9109
	29:22	**b** kidneys with the fat on them,	9109
	31:10	**b** the sacred garments for Aaron the priest	2256
	32:15	They were inscribed on **b** sides,	9109
	35:19	**b** the sacred garments for Aaron the priest **and** the garments	2256
	35:34	And he has given **b** him **and** Oholiab son	2256
	36:29	**b** were made alike.	9109
	37:2	**b** inside **and** out,	2256
	39:41	**b** the sacred garments for Aaron the priest **and** the garments	2256
Lev	3:4	**b** kidneys with the fat on them near	9109
	3:10	**b** kidneys with the fat on them near	9109
	3:15	**b** kidneys with the fat on them near	9109
	4:9	**b** kidneys with the fat on them near	9109
	7:4	**b** kidneys with the fat on them near	9109
	7:7	**b** the sin offering **and** the guilt offering:	3869
	8:16	and **b** kidneys and their fat,	9109
	8:25	**b** kidneys and their fat and the right thigh.	9109
	9:2	**b** without defect, and present them before	AIT
	9:3	*b* a year old and without defect—	AIT
	14:11	**b** the one to be cleansed **and**	2256
	15:18	*b* must bathe with water,	AIT
	16:21	to lay **b** hands on the head of the live goat	9109
	18:17	with **b** a woman and her daughter.	2256
	20:5	and will cut off from their people **b** him **and**	2256
	20:10	**b** the adulterer **and** the adulteress must	2256
	20:11	**B** the man and the woman must be put	9109
	20:12	**b** of them must be put to death.	9109
	20:13	**b** of them have done what is detestable.	9109
	20:14	a man marries **b** a woman **and** her mother,	2256
	20:14	**B** he **and** they must be burned in the fire,	2256
	20:16	kill **b** the woman **and** the animal.	2256
	20:18	**B** of them must be cut off	9109
	20:19	*b* of you would be held responsible.	AIT
	27:10	**b** it and the substitute become holy.	2256
	27:33	**b** the animal and its substitute become holy	2256
Nu	6:19	**b** made without yeast.	NIH
	7:13	**b** according to the sanctuary shekel,	NIH
	7:19	**b** according to the sanctuary shekel,	NIH
	7:25	**b** according to the sanctuary shekel,	NIH
	7:31	**b** according to the sanctuary shekel,	NIH
	7:37	**b** according to the sanctuary shekel,	NIH
	7:43	**b** according to the sanctuary shekel,	NIH
	7:49	**b** according to the sanctuary shekel,	NIH
	7:55	**b** according to the sanctuary shekel,	NIH
	7:61	**b** according to the sanctuary shekel,	NIH
	7:67	**b** according to the sanctuary shekel,	NIH
	7:73	**b** according to the sanctuary shekel,	NIH
	7:79	**b** according to the sanctuary shekel,	NIH
	10:3	When **b** are sounded,	2177S
	12:5	When **b** *of* them stepped forward,	9109
	15:16	and regulations will apply **b** to you and to	2256
	18:3	or **b** they and you will die.	1685
	18:15	**b** man **and** animal,	2256
	18:19	the LORD for **b** you **and** your offspring."	2256
	19:10	**b** for the Israelites and	2256
	20:24	because **b** of you **rebelled**	AIT
	22:24	walls on **b** sides.	2256+2296+2296+4946+4946S
	25:8	He drove the spear through **b** of them—	9109
	27:14	**b** of you **disobeyed** my command	AIT
Dt	1:17	**b** small *and* great **alike.**	3869
	11:3	**b** to Pharaoh king of Egypt **and**	2256
	11:14	**b** autumn **and** spring rains,	2256
	12:15	**B** the ceremonially unclean **and**	2256
	12:22	**B** the ceremonially unclean **and**	3481
	12:27	**b** the meat **and** the blood.	2256
	13:15	**b** its people **and** its livestock.	2256
	15:22	**B** the ceremonially unclean **and**	3481
	21:15	**b** bear him two sons but	170+2021+2021+2256+8533S
	22:22	**b** the man who slept with her **and**	9109
	22:24	you shall take **b** *of* them to the gate of	9109
	23:18	the LORD your God detests them **b.**	9109
	28:66	filled with dread **b** night **and** day,	2256
	32:51	*b* of you **broke faith**	AIT
Jos	8:22	with Israelites on **b** sides.	2256+2296+2296+4946+4946S
	8:33	were standing on **b** sides of the ark	2256+2296+2296+4946+4946S
	17:16	**b** those in Beth Shan and its settlements	NIH
Jdg	9:9	by which **b** gods **and** men are honored,	2256
	9:13	which cheers **b** gods **and** men,	2256
	19:19	We have **b** straw and fodder	1685
Ru	1:5	**b** Mahlon and Kilion also died,	9109
1Sa	2:34	they will **b** die on the same day.	9109
	5:9	**b** young **and** old,	4946
	6:4	the same plague has struck **b** you **and**	2256
	12:14	and if **b** you and the king who reigns	1685
	12:25	**b** you and your king will be swept away."	1685
	14:11	So **b** *of* them showed themselves to	9109
	17:36	Your servant has killed **b** the lion **and**	1685
	25:43	and they **b** were his wives.	9109
	28:19	The LORD will hand over **b** Israel **and** you	1685
	30:2	**b** young **and** old.	4946
2Sa	4:4	of Saul had a son who was lame in **b** feet.	AIT
	6:19	**b** men **and** women.	4946
	9:3	he is crippled in **b** feet."	AIT
	9:13	and he was crippled in **b** feet.	9109
	14:16	of the man who is trying to cut off **b** me	3480
	16:23	how **b** David and Absalom regarded all	1685
1Ki	2:32	with the sword. **B** of them—	NIH
	3:13	**b** riches **and** honor,	1685
	6:29	in **b** the inner **and** outer rooms,	2256
	6:30	of **b** the inner **and** outer rooms,	2256
	7:20	On the capitals of **b** pillars,	9109
	10:19	On **b** sides of the seat were armrests,	2256+2296+2296+4946+4946S

1Ki 13:24 with **b** the donkey and the lion standing 2256
21:10 that he has cursed **b** God **and** the king. 2256
21:13 "Naboth has cursed **b** God **and** the king." 2256
2Ki 14:28 for Israel **b** Damascus **and** Hamath, 2256
21: 5 In **b** courts of the temple of the LORD, 9109
1Ch 24: 5 the descendants of **b** Eleazar **and** Ithamar. 2256
2Ch 9:18 On **b** sides of the seat were armrests,
2256+2296+2296+4946+4946S
13:14 that they were being attacked at **b** front **and** 2256
30: 4 **b** to the king **and** 2256
33: 5 In **b** courts of the temple of the LORD, 9109
36:18 **b** large **and** small, 2256
Ezr 3: 3 **b** the morning **and** evening sacrifices. 2256
Ne 11: 4 while other people from **b** Judah **and** 2256
Job 9:22 'He destroys **b** the blameless **and** 2256
9:33 to lay his hand upon us **b**, 9109
12:16 **b** deceived **and** deceiver are his. 2256
21:26 and worms cover them **b**. AIT
31:15 the same one form us **b** within our mothers? AIT
Ps 36: 6 O LORD, you preserve **b** man **and** beast. 2256
36: 7 **B** high **and** low among men find refuge in 2256
49: 2 **b** low **and** high, rich **and** poor alike; 1685
74:17 you made **b** summer **and** winter. 2256
76: 6 **b** horse **and** chariot lie still. 2256
104:25 living things **b** large **and** small. 6640
113: 2 **b** now **and** forevermore. 2256
115:14 **b** you **and** your children. 2256
115:18 **b** now **and** forevermore. 2256
121: 8 over your coming **and** going **b** now **and** 2256
125: 2 the LORD surrounds his people **b** now **and** 2256
131: 3 put your hope in the LORD **b** now **and** 2256
Pr 17:15 the LORD detests them **b**. 9109
20:10 the LORD detests them **b**. 9109
20:12 the LORD has made them **b**. 9109
22:16 **b** come to poverty. 421
27: 3 but provocation by a fool is heavier than **b**. 9109
29:13 The LORD gives sight to the eyes of **b**. 9109
Ecc 2:14 that the same fate overtakes them **b**. 3972
2:16 in days to come **b** will be forgotten. 3972
3:17 to judgment the righteous **and** the wicked, 2256
3:19 the same fate awaits them **b**: AIT
4: 3 better than **b** is he who has not yet been, 9109
5: 8 and over them **b** are others higher still. AIT
7:15 of mine I have seen **b** of these: 3972
11: 6 or whether **b** will do equally well. 9109
SS 7:13 new **and** old, 1685
Isa 1:28 But rebels **and** sinners will be **b** broken, 3481
1:31 **b** will burn together, 9109
3: 1 from Jerusalem **and** Judah **b** supply **and** 2256
8:14 but for **b** houses of Israel he will be a stone 9109
9:14 from Israel **b** head **and** tail, 2256
9:14 **b** palm branch **and** reed in a single day; 2256
31: 3 **b** will perish together. 3972
47: 9 **B** of these will overtake you in a moment, 9109
65: 7 **b** your sins **and** the sins of your fathers," 3481
Jer 3:25 **b** we **and** our fathers; 2256
6:11 **b** husband **and** wife will be caught in it, 1685
11:10 **B** the house of Israel **and** 2256
14:18 **B** prophet **and** priest have gone to 1685
16: 6 "B high **and** low will die in this land. 2256
21: 6 **b** men **and** animals, 2256
22:26 and there you **b** will **die.** AIT
23:11 "B prophet **and** priest are godless; 1685
27:15 **b** you **and** the prophets who prophesy 2256
32:14 Take these documents, **b** the sealed **and** 2256
32:20 **b** in Israel **and** among all mankind, 2256
34: 9 **b** male **and** female; 2256
36:29 and destroy this land and cut off **b** men **and** 2256
44:20 **b** men **and** women, 2256
46: 3 **b** large **and** small, and march out for battle! 2256
46:12 **b** will fall down together." 9109
50: 3 **b** men **and** animals will flee away. 4946
La 2: 6 in his fierce anger he has spurned **b** king
and priest. 2256
3:38 that **b** calamities **and** good things come? 2256
Eze 2:10 On **b** sides of it were written words of
lament 294+2256+7156
7:13 as long as **b** of **them** live, AIT
15: 4 on the fire as fuel and the fire burns **b** ends 9109
16:61 **b** those who are older than you **and** 448
18: 4 **b** alike belong to me. 2179
20:47 **b** green **and** dry. 2256
21: 3 from you the righteous **and** the wicked. 2256
21:19 **b** starting from the same country. 9109
23:13 **b** of them went the same way. 9109
30:22 I will break **b** his **arms,** AIT
32:18 to the earth below **b** her **and** the daughters 2256
41:23 **B** the outer sanctuary **and** 2256
42: 3 **B** in the section twenty cubits from the
inner court **and** 2256
43:23 and a ram from the flock, **b** without defect. NIH
43:25 and a ram from the flock, **b** without defect. AIT
45:11 to be the standard measure for **b**. 2257S
47:12 Fruit trees of all kinds will grow on **b** banks
2256+2296+2296+4946+4946
48:21 "What remains on **b** sides of the area
formed by 2256+2296+2296+4946+4946S
48:21 **B** these areas running the length of NIH
Da 9: 7 of Jerusalem and all Israel, **b** near **and** far, 2256
11:22 **b** it and a prince of the covenant will 2256
Hos 4: 9 I will punish **b** of **them** for their ways AIT
Joel 2:23 **b** autumn **and** spring rains, as before. 2256
2:29 Even on my servants, **b** men **and** women, 2256
Mic 7: 3 **B** hands are skilled in doing evil; AIT
Zep 1: 3 "I will sweep away **b** men **and** animals; 2256
Zec 5: 4 **b** its timbers **and** its stones.' " 2256
13: 2 "I will remove **b** the prophets and the spirit 1685

Mt 6:24 You cannot serve **b** God and Money. NIG
9:17 and **b** are preserved." 317
10:28 be afraid of the One who can destroy **b** soul 2779
12:22 so that he could **b** talk and see. NIG
13:30 Let **b** grow together until the harvest. 317
15:14 **b** will fall into a pit." 317
22:10 **b** good and bad, 5445
25: 9 'there may not be enough for **b** us and you. NIG
Mk 2:22 **and b** the wine and the wineskins will 2779
Lk 1: 6 **B** of them were upright in the sight of God, 317
1: 7 and they were **b** well along in years. 317
5: 7 and filled **b** boats so full that they began 317
6:39 Will they not **b** fall into a pit? 317
7:42 so he canceled the debts of **b**. 317
14: 9 the host who invited **b** of you will come
899+2779+5148
16:13 You cannot serve **b** God and Money." NIG
22:66 **b** the chief priests and teachers of the law, 5445
23:32 Two other men, **b** criminals, NIG
Jn 2:15 **b** sheep and cattle; 5445
11:48 and take away **b** our place and our nation." 2779
15:24 yet they have hated **b** me and my Father. 2779
20: 4 **B** were running, but the other disciple
outran Peter 1545+3836S
Ac 2:11 (**b** Jews and converts to Judaism); 5445
2:18 Even on my servants, **b** men and women, NIG
2:36 whom you crucified, **b** Lord and Christ." 2779
8:10 **b** high and low, 608
8:12 they were baptized, **b** men and women. 5445
8:38 Then **b** Philip and the eunuch went down 317
20:21 to **b** Jews and Greeks that they must turn 5445
22: 4 arresting **b** men and women 5445
24:15 be a resurrection of **b** the righteous and 5445
27:12 facing **b** southwest and northwest. NIG
Ro 1:14 I am obligated **b** to Greeks and non-Greeks, 5445
1:14 **b** to the wise and the foolish. 5445
14: 9 that he might be the Lord of **b** the dead and 2779
1Co 1:24 **b** Jews and Greeks, 5445
6:13 but God will destroy them **b**. 2779+4047
7:34 be devoted to the Lord in **b** body and spirit. 2779
10:21 you cannot have a part in **b** the Lord's table NIG
10:28 **b** for the sake of the man who told you and NIG
2Co 1:21 Now it is God who makes **b** us NIG
Eph 2:16 and in this one body to reconcile **b** of them 317
2:18 through him we **b** have access to the Father 317
6: 9 that he who is **b** their Master and yours is 2779
1Ti 4: 8 holding promise for **b** the present life and NIG
4:16 you will save **b** yourself and your hearers. 2779
Tit 1:15 In fact, **b** their minds and consciences 2779
Phm 1:11 he has become useful **b** to you and to me. NIG
1:16 **b** as a man and as a brother in the Lord. 2779
Heb 2:11 **B** the one who makes men holy 5445
8: 3 Every high priest is appointed to offer **b** 5445
9:21 he sprinkled with the blood **b** the tabernacle 2779
Jas 3:11 Can **b** fresh water and salt water flow from NIG
2Pe 3: 1 I have written **b** of them as reminders 1877+4005
3:18 To him be glory **b** now and forever! 2779
2Jn 1: 9 the teaching has **b** the Father and the Son. 2779
Rev 5: 1 on the throne a scroll with writing on **b**
sides 2277+2779+3957
11:18 **b** small and great— NIG
19: 5 you who fear him, **b** small and great!" NIG

BOTHER (4) [BOTHERING]

2Sa 14:10 and he will not **b** you again." 5595
Mk 5:35 "Why **b** the teacher any more?" 5035
Lk 8:49 "Don't **b** the teacher any more." 5035
11: 7 the one inside answers, 'Don't **b** me. 3160+4218

BOTHERING (3) [BOTHER]

Mt 26:10 "Why are you **b** this woman? 3160+4218
Mk 14: 6 "Why are you **b** her? 3160+4218
Lk 18: 5 yet because this widow keeps **b** me, 3160+4218

BOTTLED-UP (1)

Job 32:19 inside I am like **b** wine, 4202+7337

BOTTLES (1)

Isa 3:20 the perfume **b** and charms, 1074

BOTTOM (9)

Ex 26:24 be double from the **b** all the way to the top, 4752
28:27 the **b** of the shoulder pieces 4200+4752+4946
36:29 from the **b** all the way to the top and fitted 4752
39:20 the **b** of the shoulder pieces 4200+4752+4946
Dt 28:13 never at the **b**. 4752
Am 9: 3 Though they hide from me at the **b** of 7977
Mt 27:51 of the temple was torn in two from top to **b**. 3004
Mk 15:38 of the temple was torn in two from top to **b**. 3004
Jn 19:23 woven in one piece from top to **b**. 1328+3910

BOTTOMLESS (KJV) See ABYSS

BOUGHS (10)

Ps 80:11 It sent out its **b** to the Sea, 7908
118:27 With **b** in hand, join the festal procession 6291
Isa 10:33 will lop off the **b** with great power. 6998
17: 6 four or five on the fruitful **b**," 6187
Eze 17: 6 and put out leafy **b**. 6997
31: 5 its **b** increased and its branches grew long, 6250
31: 6 All the birds of the air nested in its **b**, 6190
31: 7 with its spreading **b**, 1936

Eze 31: 8 nor could the pine trees equal its **b**, 6190
31:12 Its **b** fell on the mountains and in all 1936

BOUGHT (47) [BUY]

Ge 17:12 including those born in your household or **b** 5239
17:13 in your household or **b** with your money, 5239
17:23 and all those born in his household or **b** 5239
17:27 those born in his household or **b** 4084+5239
25:10 the field Abraham had **b** from the Hittites. 7864
33:19 he **b** from the sons of Hamor, 7864
39: 1 the captain of the guard, **b** him from 7864
47:20 Joseph **b** all the land in Egypt for Pharaoh. 7864
47:23 that I have **b** you and your land today 7864
49:30 which Abraham **b** as a burial place 7864
49:32 and the cave in it were **b** from the Hittites." 5238
50:13 which Abraham had **b** as a burial place. 7864
Ex 21: 2 Any slave you have **b** may eat of it 4084+5239
15:16 O LORD, until the people you **b** pass by. 7864
Lev 27:22 to the LORD a field he has **b**, 5239
27:24 to the person from whom he **b** it, 7864
Jos 24:32 at Shechem in the tract of land that Jacob **b** 7864
Ru 4: 9 that I have **b** from Naomi all the property 7864
2Sa 12: 3 poor man had nothing except one little ewe
lamb he had **b**. 7864
24:24 So David **b** the threshing floor and the oxen 7864
1Ki 16:24 He **b** the hill of Samaria from Shemer 7864
Ne 5: 8 we have **b** back our Jewish brothers who
were sold 7864
Job 28:15 It cannot be **b** with the finest gold, 5989
28:16 It cannot be **b** with the gold of Ophir, 6137
28:19 it cannot be **b** with pure gold. 6137
Ecc 2: 7 I **b** male and female slaves 7864
Isa 43:24 You have not **b** any fragrant calamus for me,
928+2021+4084+7864
Jer 13: 2 So I **b** a belt, as the LORD directed, 7864
13: 4 "Take the belt you **b** and are wearing 7864
32: 9 so I **b** the field at Anathoth 7864
32:15 and vineyards will again be **b** in this land.' 7864
32:43 Once more fields will be **b** in this land 7864
32:44 Fields will be **b** for silver, 7864
Eze 27:19 and Greeks from Uzal **b** your merchandise; NIH
Hos 3: 2 So I **b** her for fifteen shekels of silver and 4126
Mt 13:44 in his joy went and sold all he had and **b** 60
13:46 and sold everything he had and **b** it. 60
Mk 15:46 So Joseph **b** some linen cloth, 60
16: 1 and Salome **b** spices so that they might go 60
Lk 14:18 The first said, 'I have just **b** a field, 3227
14:19 'I have just **b** five yoke of oxen, 60
Ac 1:18 got for his wickedness; Judas **b** a field; 3227
7:16 that Abraham had **b** from the sons of Hamor 6050
20:28 which he **b** with his own blood. 4347
1Co 6:20 you were **b** at a price. 60
7:23 You were **b** at a price; do not become slaves 60
2Pe 2: 1 denying the sovereign Lord who **b** them— 60

BOULDER (1)

Rev 18:21 a **b** the size of a large millstone and threw it 3345

BOUND (58) [BIND]

Ge 22: 9 He **b** his son Isaac and laid him on the altar, 6818
42:24 He had Simeon taken from them and **b** 673
44:30 whose life is closely **b** up with the boy's 8003
Jdg 15:13 So they **b** him with two new ropes 673
1Sa 14:24 **b** the people under an oath, 457
14:27 **b** the people with the oath, 8678
14:28 **b** the army under a strict oath, 8678+8678
25:29 be **b** securely in the bundle of the living by 7674
2Sa 3:34 Your hands were not **b**, 673
2Ki 25: 7 **b** him with bronze shackles and took him 673
2Ch 33:11 **b** him with bronze shackles and took him 673
36: 6 and **b** him with bronze shackles to take him 673
Job 16: 8 You have **b** me— 7855
36: 8 But if men are **b** in chains, 673
Pr 22:15 Folly is **b** up in the heart of a child, 8003
Isa 16:14 servant **b** by contract would count 8502
21:16 servant **b** by contract would count 8502
24:22 be herded together like prisoners **b** in AIT
56: 3 Let no foreigner who has **b** himself to 4277
Jer 13:11 For as a belt is **b** around a man's waist, 1815
13:11 so I **b** the whole house of Israel and 1815
39: 7 and **b** him with bronze shackles to take him 673
40: 1 He had found Jeremiah **b** in chains 673
52:11 **b** him with bronze shackles and took him 673
La 1:14 "My sins have been **b** into a yoke; 8567
Eze 3:25 you will be **b** so that you cannot go out 673
30:21 not been **b** up for healing or put in a splint 2502
34: 4 or healed the sick or **b** up the injured. 2502
Da 3:21 were **b** and thrown into the blazing furnace. 10366
4:15 **b** with iron and bronze, 10054
4:23 **b** with iron and bronze, 10054
Jnh 1: 3 where he found a ship **b** for that port. 995
Mt 14: 3 and **b** him and put him in prison because 1313
16:19 whatever you bind on earth will be **b** 1313
18:18 whatever you bind on earth will be **b** 1313
23:16 he is **b** by his oath.' 4053
23:18 he is **b** by his oath.' 4053
27: 2 They **b** him, led him away and handed him 1313
Mk 6:17 and he had him **b** and put in prison. 1313
15: 1 They **b** Jesus, led him away 1313
Lk 13:16 whom Satan has kept **b** 1301
13:16 on the Sabbath day from what **b** her?" 1301
17: 1 cause people to sin are to come, 450+2262+3590
Jn 18:12 arrested Jesus. They **b** him 1313
18:24 Then Annas sent him, still **b**, 1313
Ac 12: 6 **b** with two chains, and sentries stood guard 1313

Ac	21:13	I am ready not only *to be* **b**,	1313
	21:33	and arrested him and ordered him *to be* **b**	1313
	23:12	**b** themselves **with an oath**	354
	28:20	because of the hope of Israel that *I am* **b**	4329
Ro	7: 2	a married woman *is* **b** to her husband	1313
	7: 6	But now, by dying to what once **b** *us*,	2988
	11:32	For God *has* **b** all men **over** to disobedience	5168
1Co	7:15	or woman *is* not **b** in such circumstances;	1530
	7:39	A woman *is* **b** to her husband as long	1313
Jude	1: 6	**b** with everlasting chains for judgment on	NIG
Rev	9:14	"Release the four angels who *are* **b** at	1313
	20: 2	or Satan, and **b** him for a thousand years.	1313

BOUNDARIES (11) [BOUNDARY]

Nu	34: 2	to you as an inheritance will have these **b**:	1473
	34:12	with its **b** on every side.' "	1473
Dt	32: 8	he set up **b** *for* the peoples according to	1473
Jos	15:12	These are the **b** around the people of Judah	1473
	18:20	the **b** that marked out the inheritance of	1473
2Ki	14:25	He was the one who restored the **b** *of* Israel	1473
Ps	74:17	It was you who set all the **b** of the earth;	1473
Pr	15:25	but he keeps the widow's **b** intact.	1473
Isa	10:13	*of* nations,	1473
Eze	47:13	"These are the **b** by which you are to divide	1473
Mic	7:11	the day for extending your **b**.	2976

BOUNDARY (59) [BOUNDARIES, BOUNDLESS, BOUNDS]

Nu	34: 3	your southern **b** will start from the end of	1473
	34: 6	" 'Your western **b** will be the coast of	1473
	34: 6	This will be your **b** *on* the west.	1473
	34: 7	" 'For your northern **b**,	1473
	34: 8	Then the **b** will go to Zedad,	1473
	34: 9	This will be your **b** *on* the north.	1473
	34:10	" 'For your eastern **b**, run a line	1473
	34:11	The **b** will go down from Shepham	1473
	34:11	Then the **b** will go down along the Jordan	1473
Dt	19:14	Do not move your neighbor's **b** stone set up	1473
	27:17	man who moves his neighbor's **b** stone."	1473
Jos	13:23	The **b** *of* the Reubenites was the bank of	1473
	15: 2	Their southern **b** started from the bay at	1473
	15: 4	This is their southern **b**.	1473
	15: 5	The eastern **b** is the Salt Sea as far as	1473
	15: 5	The northern **b** started from the bay of	1473
	15: 7	The **b** then went up to Debir from	1473
	15: 9	the hilltop the **b** headed toward the spring	1473
	15:11	The **b** ended at the sea.	1473
	15:12	The western **b** is the coastline of	1473
	15:21	the tribe of Judah in the Negev toward the **b**	1473
	16: 5	The **b** *of* their inheritance went	1473
	17: 7	The **b** ran southward from there to include	1473
	17: 8	but Tappuah itself, on the **b** *of* Manasseh,	1473
	17: 9	**b** continued south to the Kanah Ravine.	1473
	17: 9	the **b** *of* Manasseh was the northern side of	1473
	18:12	the north side their **b** began at the Jordan,	1473
	18:14	the **b** turned south along the western side	1473
	18:15	the **b** came out at the spring of the waters	1473
	18:16	The **b** went down to the foot of	1473
	18:19	This was the southern **b**.	1473
	18:20	Jordan formed the **b** on the eastern side.	1487
	19:10	The **b** *of* their inheritance went as far	1473
	19:14	There the **b** went around on the north	1473
	19:22	The **b** touched Tabor,	1473
	19:26	the **b** touched Carmel and Shihor Libnath.	NIH
	19:29	The **b** then turned back toward Ramah	1473
	19:33	Their **b** went from Heleph and the large tree	1473
	19:34	The **b** ran west through Aznoth Tabor	1473
	22:25	the Jordan a **b** between us and you—	1473
Jdg	1:36	The **b** of the Amorites was	1473
Job	24: 2	Men move **b** stones;	1474
	26:10	the horizon on the face of the waters for a **b**	9417
Ps	16: 6	The **b** lines have fallen for me	2475
	104: 9	You set a **b** they cannot cross;	1473
Pr	8:29	the sea its **b** so the waters would	2976
	22:28	Do not move an ancient **b** stone set up	1473
	23:10	Do not move an ancient **b** stone or encroach	1473
Jer	5:22	I made the sand a **b** for the sea,	1473
Eze	47:15	"This is to be the **b** *of* the land:	1473
	47:17	The **b** will extend from the sea	1473
	47:17	This will be the north **b**.	6991
	47:18	the east side the **b** will run between Hauran	1473
	47:18	This will be the east **b**.	6991
	47:19	This will be the south **b**.	6991
	47:20	be the **b** to a point opposite Lebo Hamath.	1473
	47:20	This will be the west **b**.	6991
	48:28	"The southern **b** *of* Gad will run south	1473
Hos	5:10	like those who move **b** stones.	1473

BOUNDING (1)

SS	2: 8	leaping across the mountains, **b** over the hills.	7890

BOUNDLESS (2) [BOUNDARY]

Ps	119:96	but your commands are **b**.	4394+8146
Na	3: 9	Cush and Egypt were her **b** strength;	401+7897

BOUNDS (2) [BOUNDARY]

Hos	4: 2	*they* break all **b**,	7287
2Co	7: 4	in all our troubles my joy **knows no b**.	5668

BOUNTY (7)

Ge	49:26	than the **b** of the age-old hills.	9294
Dt	28:12	the heavens, the storehouse of his **b**,	3202

1Ki	10:13	what he had given her out of his royal **b**.	3338
Ps	65:11	You crown the year with your **b**,	3208
	68:10	Your people settled in it, and from your **b**,	3208
Jer	31:12	they will rejoice in the **b** of the LORD—	3206
	31:14	and my people will be filled with my **b**,"	3206

BOW (105) [BOWED, BOWING, BOWMEN, BOWS, BOWSHOT]

Ge	27: 3	your quiver and **b**—	8008
	27:29	May nations serve you and peoples **b down**	2556
	27:29	*may* the sons of your mother **b down** to you.	2556
	37:10	your brothers actually come and **b down**	2556
	48:22	the Amorites with my sword and my **b**."	8008
	49: 8	your father's sons *will* **b down** to you.	2556
	49:24	But his **b** remained steady,	8008
Ex	20: 5	not **b down** to them or worship them;	2556
	23:24	*Do* not **b down** before their gods	2556
Lev	26: 1	a carved stone in your land to **b down**	2556
Dt	5: 9	not **b down** to them or worship them;	2556
	8:19	and worship and **b down** to them,	2556
	11:16	worship other gods and **b down** to them,	2556
	26:10	before the LORD your God and **b down**	2556
	30:17	*to* **b down** to other gods and worship them,	2556
	33: 3	At your feet they all **b down**,	9413
Jos	23: 7	You must not serve them or **b down**	2556
	23:16	and serve other gods and **b down** to them,	2556
	24:12	not do it with your own sword and **b**.	8008
1Sa	2:36	and **b down** before him for a piece of silver	2556
	18: 4	and even his sword, his **b** and his belt.	8008
2Sa	1:18	this lament of the **b** (it is written in the Book of Jashar):	8008
	1:22	the **b** of Jonathan did not turn back,	8008
	15: 5	to **b down** before him,	2556
	16: 4	"*I* humbly **b**," Ziba said.	2556
	22:35	my arms can bend a **b** *of* bronze.	8008
	22:40	you **made** my adversaries **b** at my feet.	4156
1Ki	22:34	But someone drew his **b** at random and hit	8008
2Ki	5:18	of Rimmon to **b down** and he is leaning	2556
	5:18	on my arm and *I* **b** there also—	2556
	5:18	when I **b down** in the temple of Rimmon,	2556
	6:22	with your own sword or **b**?	8008
	9:24	Then Jehu drew his **b** and shot Joram	8008
	13:15	Elisha said, "Get a **b** and some arrows,"	8008
	13:16	"Take the **b** in your hands,"	8008
	17:35	"Do not worship any other gods or **b down**	2556
	17:36	To him *you shall* **b down** and	2556
1Ch	5:18	who could use a **b**,	8008
	8:40	brave warriors who could handle the **b**.	8008
2Ch	18:33	But someone drew his **b** at random and hit	8008
Job	29:20	my **b** ever new in my hand.'	8008
	30:11	God has unstrung my **b** and afflicted me,	3857
Ps	5: 7	in reverence *will I* **b down**	2556
	7:12	he will bend and string his **b**.	8008
	18:34	my arms can bend a **b** *of* bronze.	8008
	18:39	you **made** my adversaries **b** at my feet.	4156
	21:12	when you aim at them with **drawn b**.	4798
	22:27	the families of the nations *will* **b down**	2556
	37:14	The wicked draw the sword and bend the **b**	8008
	44: 6	I do not trust in my **b**,	8008
	46: 9	he breaks the **b** and shatters the spear,	8008
	58: 7	*when* they **draw the b**,	2005
	60: 4	a banner to be unfurled against the **b**.	8000
	72: 9	The desert tribes *will* **b** before him	4156
	72:11	All kings *will* **b down** to him	2556
	78:57	as unreliable as a faulty **b**.	8008
	81: 9	*you shall* not **b down** to an alien god.	2556
	95: 6	Come, *let us* **b down** in worship,	4156
	138: 2	*I will* **b down** toward your holy temple	2556
Pr	14:19	Evil men *will* **b down** in the presence of	8820
Isa	2: 8	they **b down** to the work of their hands,	2556
	7:24	Men will go there with **b** and arrow,	8008
	21:15	from the bent **b** and from the heat of battle.	8008
	22: 3	without using the **b**.	8008
	41: 2	to windblown chaff with his **b**.	8008
	44:19	*Shall I* **b down** to a block of wood?"	6032
	45:14	*They* will **b down** before you and plead	2556
	45:23	Before me every knee *will* **b**;	4156
	46: 2	They stoop and **b down** together;	4156
	46: 6	and *they* **b down** and worship it.	6032
	49: 7	princes will see and **b down**,	2556
	49:23	*They* will **b down** before you	2556
	60:14	all who despise you *will* **b down**	2556
	66:23	all mankind will come and **b down**	2556
Jer	6:23	They are armed with **b** and spear;	8008
	9: 3	"They make ready their tongue like a **b**,	8008
	27: 8	of Babylon or **b** its neck under his yoke,	5989
	27:11	if any nation *will* **b** its neck under the yoke	995
	27:12	"**B** your neck under the yoke of the king	995
	46: 9	men of Lydia who draw the **b**.	8008
	49:35	"See, I will break the **b** *of* Elam,	8008
	50:14	all you who draw the **b**.	8008
	50:29	all those who draw the **b**.	8008
	51: 3	Let not the archer string his **b**,	8008
La	2: 4	Like an enemy he has strung his **b**;	8008
	3:12	He drew his **b** and made me the target	8008
Eze	39: 3	Then I will strike your **b**	8008
Hos	1: 5	that day I will break Israel's **b** in the Valley	8008
	1: 7	not by **b**, sword or battle,	8008
	2:18	**B** and sword and battle I will abolish from	8008
	7:16	they are like a faulty **b**.	8008
Mic	5:13	*you will* no longer **b down** to the work	2556
	6: 6	before the LORD and **b down** before	4104
Hab	3: 9	You uncovered your **b**,	8008
Zep	1: 5	**b down** on the roofs **to worship**	2556
	1: 5	those *who* **b down** and swear by the LORD	2556
Zec	9:10	and the battle **b** will be broken.	8008

Zec	9:13	I will bend Judah as I bend my **b** and fill it	8008
	10: 4	from him the battle **b**,	8008
Mt	4: 9	"if you will **b down** and worship me."	4406
Ac	27:29	to lower some anchors from the **b**.	4749
	27:41	The **b** stuck fast and would not move,	4749
Ro	14:11	'every knee *will* **b** before me;	2828
Php	2:10	at the name of Jesus every knee **should b**,	2828
Rev	6: 2	Its rider held a **b**,	5534

BOWED (68) [BOW]

Ge	18: 2	to meet them and **b** low to the ground.	2556
	19: 1	and **b** down *with* his face to the ground.	2556
	23: 7	he **b** down before the people of the land,	2556
	23:12	Again Abraham **b** down before the people	2556
	24:26	the man **b** down and worshiped the LORD,	7702
	24:48	and *I* **b** down and worshiped the LORD.	7702
	24:52	he **b** down to the ground before the LORD.	2556
	33: 3	and **b** down to the ground seven times	2556
	33: 6	and their children approached and **b down**.	2556
	33: 7	Leah and her children came and **b down**.	2556
	33: 7	and *they* too **b down**.	2556
	37: 7	around mine and **b down** to it."	2556
	42: 6	they **b down** to him with their faces to	2556
	43:26	and *they* **b down** before him to the ground.	2556
	43:28	And *they* **b** low to pay him honor.	7702
	48:12	and **b down** *with* his face to the ground.	2556
Ex	4:31	they **b down** and worshiped.	7702
	12:27	Then the people **b down** and worshiped.	7702
	18: 7	to meet his father-in-law and **b down**	2556
	32: 8	They have **b down** to it and sacrificed to it	2556
	34: 8	Moses **b** to the ground at once	7702
Nu	22:31	So he **b** low and fell facedown.	2556
	25: 2	and **b down** before these gods.	2556
Dt	29:26	and worshiped other gods and **b down**	2556
Ru	2:10	she **b** down with her face to the ground.	2556
1Sa	20:41	up from the south side [of the stone] and **b**	2556
	24: 8	David **b** down and prostrated himself	7702
	25:23	she quickly got off her donkey and **b down**	2556
	25:41	She **b** down *with* her face to the ground	2556
	28:14	and *he* **b** down and prostrated himself	7702
2Sa	9: 6	he **b** down to pay him honor.	5877+6584+7156
	9: 8	Mephibosheth **b** down and said,	2556
	14:33	and he came in and **b down** *with* his face to	2556
	18:21	Cushite **b** down before Joab and ran off.	2556
	18:28	He **b** down before the king with his face to	2556
	24:20	and **b** down before the king with his face to	2556
1Ki	1:16	Bathsheba **b** low and knelt before the king.	7702
	1:23	the king and **b** with his face to the ground.	2556
	1:31	Then Bathsheba **b** low with her face to	7702
	1:47	And the king **b** in worship on his bed	2556
	1:53	And Adonijah came and **b down**	2556
	2:19	**b** down to her and sat down on his throne.	2556
	18: 7	**b** down to the ground,	5877+6584+7156
	19:18	all whose knees *have* not **b** down to Baal	4156
2Ki	2:15	And they went to meet him and **b** to	2556
	4:37	fell at his feet and **b** to the ground.	2556
	17:16	They **b** down to all the starry hosts,	2556
	21: 3	He **b** down to all the starry hosts	2556
	21:21	and **b** down to them.	2556
1Ch	21:21	threshing floor and **b** down before David	2556
	29:20	they **b** low and fell prostrate before	7702
2Ch	20:18	Jehoshaphat **b** with his face to the ground,	7702
	25:14	**b** down to them and burned sacrifices	2556
	29:28	The whole assembly **b** in worship,	2556
	29:30	and **b** *their* heads and worshiped.	7702
	33: 3	He **b** down to all the starry hosts	2556
Ne	8: 6	Then *they* **b down** and worshiped	7702
Ps	35:14	*I* **b** *my* head in grief as though weeping	8820
	38: 6	*I am* **b** down and brought very low;	6390
	57: 6	I *was* **b** down in distress.	4104
	145:14	and lifts up all who **are b down**.	4104
	146: 8	the LORD lifts up *those who* **are b** down,	4104
La	2:10	of Jerusalem *have* **b** their heads to	3718
Da	10:15	I **b** with my face toward the ground	5989
Mt	2:11	and they **b** down and worshiped him.	4406
Lk	24: 5	the *women* **b** down with their faces to	3111
Jn	19:30	he **b** his head and gave up his spirit.	3111
Ro	11: 4	for myself seven thousand who *have* not **b**	2828

BOWELS (4)

2Ch	21:15	be very ill with a lingering disease of the **b**,	5055
	21:15	the disease causes your **b** to come out.' "	5055
	21:18	with an incurable disease of the **b**.	5055
	21:19	his **b** came out because of the disease,	5055

BOWING (7) [BOW]

Ge	37: 9	and moon and eleven stars *were* **b** down	2556
Ex	11: 8	**b** down before me and saying, 'Go,	2556
Dt	4:19	into **b** down to them and worshiping things	2556
	17: 3	**b** down to them or to the sun or the moon or	2556
Isa	58: 5	Is it only for **b** one's head like a reed and	4104
	60:14	of your oppressors will come **b** before you;	8820
Eze	8:16	they *were* **b** down to the sun in the east.	2556

BOWL (31) [BOWL-SHAPED, BOWLFUL, BOWLS]

Nu	7:13	one silver **sprinkling b** weighing seventy shekels,	4670
	7:19	one silver **sprinkling b** weighing seventy shekels,	4670
	7:25	one silver **sprinkling b** weighing seventy shekels,	4670
	7:31	one silver **sprinkling b** weighing seventy shekels,	4670

Nu	7:37	one silver **sprinkling b** weighing seventy shekels,	4670
	7:43	one silver **sprinkling b** weighing seventy shekels,	4670
	7:49	one silver **sprinkling b** weighing seventy shekels,	4670
	7:55	one silver **sprinkling b** weighing seventy shekels,	4670
	7:61	one silver **sprinkling b** weighing seventy shekels,	4670
	7:67	one silver **sprinkling b** weighing seventy shekels,	4670
	7:73	one silver **sprinkling b** weighing seventy shekels,	4670
	7:79	one silver **sprinkling b** weighing seventy shekels,	4670
	7:85	and each **sprinkling b** seventy shekels.	4670
Jdg	5:25	in a **b** fit for nobles	6210
2Ki	2:20	"Bring me a new **b**," he said.	7504
Ecc	12: 6	or the golden **b** is broken;	1657
Zec	4: 2	a solid gold lampstand with a **b** at the top	1657
	4: 3	the right of the **b** and the other on its left."	1657
	9:15	will be full like a **b used for sprinkling**	4670
Mt	5:15	a lamp and put it under a **b.**	3654
	26:23	into the **b** with me will betray me.	5581
Mk	4:21	"Do you bring in a lamp to put it under a **b**	3654
	14:20	"one who dips bread into the **b** with me.	5581
Lk	11:33	where it will be hidden, or under a **b.**	3654
Rev	16: 2	The first angel went and poured out his **b**	5786
	16: 3	The second angel poured out his **b** on	5786
	16: 4	The third angel poured out his **b** on	5786
	16: 8	The fourth angel poured out his **b** on	5786
	16:10	The fifth angel poured out his **b** on	5786
	16:12	The sixth angel poured out his **b** on	5786
	16:17	The seventh angel poured out his **b** into	5786

BOWL-SHAPED (7) [BOWL]

1Ki	7:20	above the **b part** next to the network,	1061
	7:41	the two **b** capitals on top of the pillars;	1657
	7:41	of network decorating the two **b** capitals	1657
	7:42	the **b** capitals on top of the pillars;	1657
2Ch	4:12	the two **b** capitals on top of the pillars;	1657
	4:12	of network decorating the two **b** capitals	1657
	4:13	the **b** capitals on top of the pillars);	1657

BOWLFUL (3) [BOWL]

Jdg	6:38	wrung out the dew—a **b** of water.	4850+6210
Ps	80: 5	you have made them drink tears by the **b.**	8955
Am	6: 6	by the **b** and use the finest lotions.	4670

BOWLS (35) [BOWL]

Ex	24: 6	of the blood and put it in **b,**	110
	25:29	as its pitchers and **b** for the pouring out	4984
	27: 3	**sprinkling b,** meat forks and firepans.	4670
	37:16	its plates and dishes and **b** and its pitchers	4984
	38: 3	its pots, shovels, **sprinkling b,**	4670
Nu	4: 7	and **b,** and the jars for drink offerings;	4984
	4:14	meat forks, shovels and **sprinkling b.**	4670
	7:84	twelve silver **sprinkling b**	4670
2Sa	17:28	brought bedding and **b** and articles	6195
1Ki	7:40	the basins and shovels and **sprinkling b.**	4670
	7:45	shovels and **sprinkling b.**	4670
	7:50	**sprinkling b,** dishes and censers;	4670
2Ki	12:13	wick trimmers, **sprinkling b,**	4670
	25:15	the censers and **sprinkling b—**	4670
1Ch	28:17	**sprinkling b** and pitchers;	4670
2Ch	4: 8	He also made a hundred gold **sprinkling b.**	4670
	4:11	the pots and shovels and **sprinkling b.**	4670
	4:22	**sprinkling b,** dishes and censers;	4670
Ezr	1:10	gold **b** 30 matching silver bowls 410	4094
	1:10	gold bowls 30 matching silver **b** 410	4094
	8:27	20 **b** of gold valued at 1,000	4094
Ne	7:70	50 **b** and 530 garments for priests.	4670
Pr	23:30	who go to sample **b of mixed wine.**	4932
Isa	22:24	from the **b** to all the jars.	110
	65:11	a table for Fortune and fill **b of mixed wine**	4932
Jer	35: 5	Then I set **b** full of wine and some cups	1483
	52:18	shovels, wick trimmers, **sprinkling b,**	4670
	52:19	censers, **sprinkling b,** pots, lampstands,	4670
	52:19	**b used for drink offerings.**	4984
Zec	14:20	be like the **sacred b** in front of the altar.	4670
Rev	5: 8	a harp and they were holding golden **b** full	5786
	15: 7	the seven angels seven golden **b** filled with	5786
	16: 1	the seven **b** of God's wrath on the earth."	5786
	17: 1	the seven angels who had the seven **b** came	5786
	21: 9	the seven angels who had the seven **b** full	5786

BOWMEN (1) [BOW]

Isa	21:17	The survivors of the **b,**	5031+8008

BOWS (19) [BOW]

1Sa	2: 4	"The **b** of the warriors are broken,	8008
1Ch	12: 2	with **b** and were able to shoot arrows or	8008
2Ch	14: 8	armed with small shields and **with b.**	2005+8008
	17:17	men armed with **b** and shields;	8008
	26:14	**b** and slingstones for the entire army.	8008
Ne	4:13	with their swords, spears and **b.**	8008
	4:16	with spears, shields, **b** and armor.	8008
Ps	11: 2	For look, the wicked bend their **b;**	8008
	37:15	and their **b** will be broken.	8008
	66: 4	All the earth **b down** to you;	2556
	78: 9	The men of Ephraim, though armed with **b,**	8008
Isa	5:28	all their **b** are strung;	8008
	13:18	Their **b** will strike down the young men;	8008

Isa	44:15	he makes an idol and **b down** to it.	6032
	44:17	he **b down** to it and worships.	6032
	46: 1	Bel **b down,** Nebo stoops low;	4156
Jer	50:42	They are armed with **b** and spears;	8008
	51:56	and their **b** will be broken.	8008
Eze	39: 9	the **b** and arrows, the war clubs and spears.	8008

BOWSHOT (1) [BOW]

Ge	21:16	about a **b** away, for she thought,	3217+8008

BOX (KJV) See CHEST, HORN, FLASK

BOY (79) [BOY'S, BOYHOOD, BOYS]

Ge	21:12	"Do not be so distressed about the **b**	5853
	21:14	and then sent her off with the **b.**	3529
	21:15	she put the **b** under one of the bushes.	3529
	21:16	for she thought, "I cannot watch the **b** die."	3529
	21:17	God heard the **b** crying,	5853
	21:17	God has heard the **b** crying as he lies there.	5853
	21:18	Lift the **b** up and take him by the hand,	5853
	21:19	the skin with water and gave the **b** a drink.	5853
	21:20	God was with the **b** as he grew up.	5853
	22: 5	the donkey while I and the **b** go over there.	5853
	22:12	"Do not lay a hand on the **b,**" he said.	5853
	37:30	"The **b** isn't there!	3529
	42:22	"Didn't I tell you not to sin against the **b?**	3529
	43: 8	the **b** along with me and we will go at once,	5853
	44:22	'The **b** cannot leave his father;	5853
	44:30	if the **b** is not with us when I go back	5853
	44:31	sees that the **b** isn't there,	5853
	44:33	as my lord's slave in place of the **b,**	5853
	44:33	and let the **b** return with his brothers.	5853
	44:34	How can I go back to my father if the **b** is	5853
Ex	1:16	if it is a **b,** kill him;	1201
	1:22	"Every **b** that is born you must throw into	1201
Lev	12: 3	the eighth day the **b** is to be circumcised.	2257S
	12: 7	the woman who gives birth to a **b** or a girl.	2351
Jdg	8:20	because he was only a **b** and was afraid.	5853
	13: 5	because the **b** is to be a Nazirite.	5853
	13: 7	the **b** will be a Nazirite of God from birth	5853
	13: 8	to teach us how to bring up the **b** who is to	5853
	13:24	to a **b** and named him Samson.	1201
1Sa	1:22	"After the **b** is weaned,	5853
	1:24	she took the **b** with her, young as he was,	5853
	1:25	they brought the **b** to Eli,	5853
	2:11	but the **b** ministered before the LORD	5853
	2:18	a **b** wearing a linen ephod.	5853
	2:21	the **b** Samuel grew up in the presence of	5853
	2:26	the **b** Samuel continued to grow in stature	5853
	3: 1	The **b** Samuel ministered before	5853
	3: 8	that the LORD was calling the **b.**	5853
	4:21	She named the **b** Ichabod, saying,	5853
	17:33	you are only a **b,** and he has been a fighting	5853
	17:42	over and saw that he was only a **b,**	5853
	20:21	Then I will send a **b** and say, 'Go,	5853
	20:22	But if I say to the **b,** 'Look,	6624
	20:35	He had a small **b** with him,	5853
	20:36	and he said to the **b,**	5853
	20:36	As the **b** ran, he shot an arrow beyond him.	5853
	20:37	When the **b** came to the place	5853
	20:38	The **b** picked up the arrow and returned	5853
	20:39	(The **b** knew nothing of all this;	5853
	20:40	Then Jonathan gave his weapons to the **b**	5853
	20:41	After the **b** had gone,	5853
	30:19	young or old, **b** or girl,	1201
1Ki	11:17	But Hadad, still only a **b,**	5853+7783
	14: 3	He will tell you what will happen to the **b.**"	5853
	14:12	you set foot in your city, the **b** will die.	3529
	14:17	over the threshold of the house, the **b** died.	5853
	17:21	the **b** three times and cried to the LORD,	3529
2Ki	4:20	the **b** sat on her lap until noon,	NIH
	4:31	"The **b** has not awakened."	5853
	4:32	there was the **b** lying dead on his couch.	5853
	4:34	Then he got on the bed and lay upon the **b,**	3529
	4:35	The **b** sneezed seven times and opened his	5853
	5:14	and became clean like that of a young **b.**	5853
Job	3: 3	and the night it was said, 'A **b** is born!'	1505
Pr	4: 3	When I was a **b** in my father's house,	1201
Isa	7:16	But before the **b** knows enough to reject	5853
	8: 4	Before the **b** knows how to say 'My father'	5853
Mt	17:18	Bring the **b** here to me."	899S
	17:18	and it came out of the **b,**	4090
Mk	9:19	Bring the **b** to me."	899S
	9:20	it immediately threw the **b** into	899S
	9:26	The **b** looked so much like a corpse	NIG
	10:20	"all these I have kept since I was a **b.**"	3744
Lk	2:43	the **b** Jesus stayed behind in Jerusalem	4090
	9:42	Even while the **b** was coming,	899S
	9:42	and he gave him back to his father.	4090
	18:21	"All these I have kept since I was a **b,**"	3744
Jn	4:51	with the news that his **b** was living.	4090
	6: 9	"Here is a **b** with five small barley loaves	4081

BOY'S (10) [BOY]

Ge	44:30	is closely bound up with the **b** life,	2257S
	44:32	Your servant guaranteed the **b** safety	5853
Jdg	13:12	to be the rule for the **b** life and work?"	5853
1Ki	17:21	let this **b** life return to him!"	3529
	17:22	and the **b** life returned to him, and he lived.	3529
2Ki	4:29	Lay my staff on the **b** face."	5853
	4:31	on ahead and laid the staff on the **b** face.	5853
	4:34	the **b** body grew warm.	3529
Mk	9:21	Jesus asked the **b** father, "How long	899S
	9:24	Immediately the **b** father exclaimed,	4086

BOYHOOD (1) [BOY]

Ge	46:34	have tended livestock from our **b** on,	5830

BOYS (14) [BOY]

Ge	25:24	there were **twin** b in her womb.	AIT
	25:27	The **b** grew up,	5853
	38:27	there were **twin** b in her womb.	AIT
	48:16	may he bless these **b.**	5853
Ex	1:17	they let the **b** live.	3529
	1:18	Why have you let the **b** live?"	3529
Nu	31:17	Now kill all the **b.**	2351+3251
2Ki	4: 1	to take my two **b** as his slaves."	3529
Job	19:18	Even the **little b** scorn me;	6396
Isa	3: 4	I will make **b** their officials;	5853
La	5:13	**b** stagger under loads of wood.	5853
Joel	3: 3	for my people and traded **b** for prostitutes;	3529
Zec	8: 5	be filled with **b** and girls playing there."	3529
Mt	2:16	and he gave orders to kill all the **b**	4090

BOZEZ (1)

1Sa	14: 4	one was called **B,** and the other Seneh.	1010

BOZKATH (2)

Jos	15:39	Lachish, **B,** Eglon,	1304
2Ki	22: 1	she was from **B.**	1304

BOZRAH (8)

Ge	36:33	Jobab son of Zerah from **B** succeeded him	1313
1Ch	1:44	Jobab son of Zerah from **B** succeeded him	1313
Isa	34: 6	For the LORD has a sacrifice in **B** and	1313
	63: 1	Who is this coming from Edom, from **B,**	1313
Jer	48:24	to Kerioth and **B—**	1313
	49:13	"that **B** will become a ruin and an object	1313
	49:22	spreading its wings over **B.**	1313
Am	1:12	that will consume the fortresses of **B.**"	1313

BRACE (3) [BRACING]

Job	38: 3	**B** yourself like a man;	273+2743
	40: 7	"**B** yourself like a man;	273+2743
Na	2: 1	**b** yourselves, marshal all your strength!	2616+5516

BRACELETS (7)

Ge	24:22	and two gold **b** weighing ten shekels.	3338+6584+7543
	24:30	and the **b** on his sister's arms,	7543
	24:47	the ring in her nose and the **b** on her arms,	7543
Nu	31:50	armlets, **b,** signet rings,	7543
Isa	3:19	the earrings and **b** and veils,	9217
Eze	16:11	I put **b** on your arms and a necklace	7543
	23:42	from the rabble, and they put **b** on the arms	7543

BRACING (1) [BRACE]

Jdg	16:29	**B** himself against them,	6164

BRAG (4)

Am	4: 5	and **b** about your freewill offerings—	7924
Ro	2:17	on the law and **b about** your relationship	3016
	2:23	You who **b** about the law,	3016
Jas	4:16	As it is, you boast and **b.**	224+1877+3836

BRAIDED (5) [BRAIDS]

Ex	28:14	and two **b** chains of pure gold,	4456
	28:22	the breastpiece make **b** chains of pure gold,	1491
	39:15	For the breastpiece they made **b** chains	1491
1Ti	2: 9	not with **b** hair or gold or pearls	4427
1Pe	3: 3	as **b** hair and the wearing of gold jewelry	1862

BRAIDS (3) [BRAIDED]

Jdg	16:13	"If you weave the seven **b** of my head into	4710
	16:13	Delilah took the seven **b** of his head,	4710
	16:19	a man to shave off the seven **b** of his hair,	4710

BRAMBLE (KJV) See THORNBUSH

BRAMBLES (1)

Isa	34:13	nettles and **b** her strongholds.	2560

BRANCH (26) [BRANCHES]

Ge	49:11	his colt to the **choicest b;**	8605
Ex	25:33	with buds and blossoms are to be on one **b,**	7866
	25:33	three on the next **b,**	7866
	37:19	with buds and blossoms were on one **b,**	7866
	37:19	three on the next **b** and the next **b—**	7866
Nu	4: 2	a census of the Kohathite **b** of the Levites	4946+9348
	13:23	they cut off a **b** bearing a single cluster	2367
Isa	4: 2	the **B** of the LORD will be beautiful	7542
	9:14	both **palm b** and reed in a single day;	4093
	11: 1	from his roots a **B** will bear fruit.	5916
	14:19	of your tomb like a rejected **b;**	5916
	19:15	head or tail, **palm b** or reed.	4093
Jer	1:11	"I see the **b** of an almond tree," I replied.	5234
	23: 5	I will raise up for David a righteous **B,**	7542
	33:15	that time I will make a righteous **B** sprout	7542
Eze	8:17	Look at them putting the **b** to their nose!	2367
	15: 2	that of a **b** on any of the trees in the forest?	2367
	19:14	No strong **b** is left on it fit for	4751

Zec	3: 8	I am going to bring my servant, the **B**.	7542
	6:12	'Here is the man whose name is the **B**,	7542
	6:12	and *he will* **b out** from his place and build	7541
Mal	4: 1	"Not a root or a **b** will be left to them.	6733
Jn	15: 2	He cuts off every **b** in me that bears no fruit,	*3097*
	15: 2	while every **b** that does bear fruit he prunes	*NIG*
	15: 4	No **b** can bear fruit by itself;	*3097*
	15: 6	like a **b** that is thrown away and withers;	*3097*

BRANCHES (80) [BRANCH]

Ge	30:37	however, took fresh-cut **b** *from* poplar,	5234
	30:37	the white inner wood of the **b**.	5234
	30:38	the peeled **b** in all the watering troughs,	5234
	30:39	they mated in front of the **b**.	5234
	30:41	the **b** in the troughs in front of the animals	5234
	30:41	the animals so they would mate near the **b**,	5234
	40:10	and on the vine were three **b**.	8585
	40:12	"The three **b** are three days.	8585
	49:22	whose **b** climb over a wall.	1426
Ex	25:32	Six **b** are to extend from the sides of	7866
	25:33	for all six **b** extending from the lampstand.	7866
	25:35	be under the first pair of **b** extending from	7866
	25:35	six **b** in all.	7866
	25:36	The buds and **b** shall all be of one piece	7866
	37:18	Six **b** extended from the sides of	7866
	37:19	for all six **b** extending from the lampstand.	7866
	37:21	under the first pair of **b** extending from	7866
	37:21	under the third pair—six **b** in all.	7866
	37:22	The buds and the **b** were all of one piece	7866
Lev	23:40	and palm fronds, leafy **b** and poplars,	6733
Dt	24:20	not **go over the b a second time**.	339+6994
Jdg	9:48	He took an ax and cut off *some* **b**,	6770+8457
	9:49	all the men cut **b** and followed Abimelech.	8456
2Sa	18: 9	mule went under the **thick b** *of* a large oak,	8449
Ne	8:15	the hill country and bring back **b** *from* olive	6591
	8:16	So the people went out and brought back **b**	*NIH*
Job	15:32	and his **b** will not flourish.	4093
	18:16	up below and his **b** wither above.	7908
	29:19	and the dew will lie all night on my **b**.	7908
Ps	80:10	the mighty cedars with its **b**.	6733
	104:12	they sing among the **b**.	6751
Isa	17: 6	or three olives on the topmost **b**,	580
	18: 5	cut down and take away the **spreading b**.	5746
	27:10	they strip its **b** bare.	6187
Jer	5:10	Strip off her **b**,	5746
	6: 9	pass your hand over the **b** again,	6151
	11:16	and its **b** will be broken.	1936
	48:32	Your **b** spread as far as the sea;	5746
Eze	17: 6	Its **b** turned toward him,	1936
	17: 6	and produced **b** and put out leafy boughs.	964
	17: 7	where it was planted and stretched out its **b**	1936
	17: 8	so that it would produce **b**,	6733
	17:23	it will produce **b** and bear fruit and become	6733
	17:23	they will find shelter in the shade of its **b**.	1936
	19:10	and **full of b** because of abundant water.	6734
	19:11	Its **b** were strong, fit for a ruler's scepter.	4751
	19:11	for its height and for its many **b**.	1936
	19:12	its strong **b** withered	4751
	19:14	of its **main b** and consumed its fruit.	964+4751
	21:19	a signpost where the road **b off** *to* the city.	8031
	31: 3	with beautiful **b** overshadowing the forest;	6733
	31: 5	its boughs increased and its **b** grew long,	6997
	31: 6	of the field gave birth under its **b**;	6997
	31: 8	nor could the plane trees compare with its **b**	6997
	31: 9	I made it beautiful with abundant **b**,	1936
	31:12	its **b** lay broken in all the ravines of	6997
	31:13	the beasts of the field were among its **b**.	6997
	36: 8	will produce **b** and fruit	6733
Da	4:12	and the birds of the air lived in its **b**;	10561
	4:14	'Cut down the tree and trim off its **b**;	10561
	4:14	from under it and the birds from its **b**.	10561
	4:21	and having nesting places in its **b** for	10561
Joel	1: 7	leaving their **b** white.	8585
Zec	4:12	"What are these two olive **b** beside	8672
Mt	13:32	the birds of the air come and perch in its **b**."	*3080*
	21: 8	while others cut **b** from the trees	*3080*
Mk	4:32	with such big **b** that the birds of	*3080*
	11: 8	others spread **b** they had cut in the fields.	*5115*
Lk	13:19	and the birds of the air perched in its **b**."	*3080*
Jn	12:13	They took palm **b** and went out	*961*
	15: 5	"I am the vine; you are the **b**.	*3097*
	15: 6	such **b** are picked up,	*NIG*
Ro	11:16	if the root is holy, so are the **b**.	*3080*
	11:17	If some of the **b** have been broken off,	*3080*
	11:18	do not boast over those **b**.	*3080*
	11:19	"**B** were broken off so that I could	*3080*
	11:21	For if God did not spare the natural **b**,	*3080*
	11:24	the natural **b**, be grafted	*NIG*
Heb	9:19	scarlet wool and **b of hyssop**,	5727
Rev	7: 9	and were holding **palm b** in their hands.	*5836*

BRAND (KJV) See BURNING STICK

BRANDING (1)

| Isa | 3:24 | instead of beauty, **b**. | 3953 |

BRANDISH (3) [BRANDISHED, BRANDISHES, BRANDISHING]

Ps	35: 3	**B** spear and javelin	8197
Isa	10:15	or a club **b** him who is not wood!	8123
Eze	32:10	of you when I **b** my sword before them.	6758

BRANDISHED (1) [BRANDISH]

| Na | 2: 3 | the spears of pine *are* **b**. | 8302 |

BRANDISHES (1) [BRANDISH]

| Eze | 30:25 | the hand of the king of Babylon and *he* **b** it | 5742 |

BRANDISHING (1) [BRANDISH]

| Eze | 38: 4 | all of them **b** their swords. | 9530 |

BRASEN, BRASS (KJV) See BRONZE

BRAVE (15) [BRAVELY, BRAVEST]

1Sa	14:52	whenever Saul saw a mighty or **b** man,	1201+2657
	16:18	He is a **b man** and a warrior.	1475+2657
2Sa	2: 7	Now then, be strong and **b**,	1201+2657
	13:28	Be strong and **b**."	1201+2657
	17:10	a fighter and that those with him are **b**.	1201+2657
1Ch	5:24	They were **b** warriors, famous men,	2657
	7:40	**b** warriors and outstanding leaders.	1475+2657
	8:40	were **b** warriors who could handle	1475+2657
	12: 8	They were **b** warriors,	1475+2657
	12:21	for all of them were **b** warriors	1475+2657
	12:28	a **b** young warrior, with 22 officers	1475+2657
	28: 1	the mighty men and all the **b** warriors.	1475+2657
2Ch	14: 8	All these were **b fighting** men.	1475+2657
Isa	33: 7	Look, their **b** men cry aloud in the streets;	737

BRAVELY (3) [BRAVE]

1Sa	18:17	serve me **b** and fight the battles	1201+2657+4200
2Sa	10:12	and *let us* **fight b** for our people and	2616
1Ch	19:13	and *let us* **fight b** for our people and	2616

BRAVERY (KJV) See FINERY

BRAVEST (2) [BRAVE]

| 2Sa | 17:10 | Then even the **b soldier**, | 1201+2657 |
| Am | 2:16 | **b** warriors will flee naked on that day," | 579+4213 |

BRAWLER (1) [BRAWLERS, BRAWLING]

| Pr | 20: 1 | Wine is a mocker and beer a **b**; | 2159 |

BRAWLERS (1) [BRAWLER]

| Isa | 5:14 | and masses with all their **b** and revelers. | 8623 |

BRAWLING (1) [BRAWLER]

| Eph | 4:31 | rage and anger, **b** and slander, | *3199* |

BRAY (1) [BRAYED]

| Job | 6: 5 | *Does* a wild donkey **b** when it has grass, | 5640 |

BRAYED (1) [BRAY]

| Job | 30: 7 | *They* **b** among the bushes and huddled in | 5640 |

BRAZEN (3)

Pr	7:13	and kissed him and *with* a **b** face she said:	6451
Jer	3: 3	Yet you have the **b look** *of* a prostitute;	5195
Eze	16:30	acting like a **b** prostitute!	8951

BRAZIER (Anglicized) See FIRE POT

BREACH (2) [BREAK]

| Job | 30:14 | They advance as through a gaping **b**; | 7288 |
| Ps | 106:23 | stood in the **b** before him to keep his wrath | 7288 |

BREACHES (1) [BREAK]

| Isa | 22: 9 | of David had many **b in** its defenses; | 1323 |

BREACHING (2) [BREAK]

| Ps | 144:14 | There will be no **b of** walls, | 7288 |
| Pr | 17:14 | Starting a quarrel is like a **b** dam; | 7080 |

BREAD (271)

Ge	14:18	of Salem brought out **b** and wine.	4312
	18: 6	of fine flour and knead it and bake *some* **b**."	6314
	19: 3	baking **b without yeast**, and they ate.	5174
	25:34	Then Jacob gave Esau *some* **b**	4312
	27:17	the tasty food and the **b** she had made.	4312
	40:16	On my head were three baskets of **b**.	3035
	45:23	and **b** and other provisions for his journey.	4312
Ex	12: 8	and **b made without yeast**.	5174
	12:15	to eat **b made without yeast**.	5174
	12:17	**Feast of Unleavened B**,	5174
	12:18	to eat **b made without yeast**,	5174
	12:20	you must eat **unleavened b**."	5174
	12:39	they baked cakes of **unleavened b**.	5174
	13: 6	For seven days eat **b made without yeast**	5174
	13: 7	Eat **unleavened b** during those seven days;	5174
	16: 4	"I will rain down **b** from heaven for you.	4312
	16: 8	to eat in the evening and all the **b** you want	4312
	16:12	in the morning you will be filled with **b**.	4312
	16:15	"It is the **b** the LORD has given you to eat.	4312
	16:29	that is why on the sixth day he gives you **b**	4312
	16:31	The people of Israel called the **b** manna.	2257S
	16:32	to come, so they can see the **b** I gave you	4312
Ex	18:12	of Israel to eat **b** with Moses' father-in-law	4312
	23:15	"Celebrate the Feast of **Unleavened B**;	5174
	23:15	for seven days eat **b made without yeast**,	5174
	25:30	Put the **b** *of* the Presence on this table to be	4312
	29: 2	make **b**, and cakes mixed with oil,	4312
	29:23	From the basket of **b made without yeast**,	5174
	29:32	to eat the meat of the ram and the **b** that is	4312
	29:34	of the ordination ram or any **b** is left over	4312
	34:18	"Celebrate the Feast of **Unleavened B**.	5174
	34:18	For seven days eat **b made without yeast**,	5174
	34:28	without eating **b** or drinking water.	4312
	35:13	with its poles and all its articles and the **b**	4312
	39:36	the table with all its articles and the **b** *of*	4312
	40:23	and set out the **b** on it before the LORD,	4312
Lev	7:12	offer cakes of **b made without yeast**	5174
	7:13	to present an offering with cakes of **b** made	4312
	8: 2	the basket containing **b made without yeast**,	5174
	8:26	from the basket of **b made without yeast**, and	5174
	8:26	he took a cake of **b**, and one made with oil,	5174
	8:31	of Meeting and eat it there with the **b** from	4312
	8:32	Then burn up the rest of the meat and the **b**.	4312
	23: 6	of **Unleavened B** begins;	5174
	23: 6	seven days you must eat **b made without yeast**.	5174
	23:14	You must not eat any **b**,	4312
	23:18	Present with this **b** seven male lambs,	4312
	23:20	together with the **b** of the firstfruits.	4312
	24: 5	and bake twelve **loaves of b**,	2705
	24: 7	as a memorial portion to represent the **b** and	4312
	24: 8	This **b** is to be set out before	5647S
	26:26	When I cut off your supply of **b**,	4312
	26:26	ten women will be able to bake your **b**	4312
	26:26	and they will dole out the **b** by weight.	4312
Nu	4: 7	the **b** that is continually there is to remain	4312
	6:15	and a basket of **b made without yeast**—	5174
	6:17	He is to present the basket of **unleavened b**	5174
	9:11	with **unleavened b** and bitter herbs.	5174
	21: 5	There is no **b**!	4312
	28:17	for seven days eat **b made without yeast**.	5174
Dt	8: 3	on **b** alone but on every word that comes	4312
	8: 9	a land where **b** will not be scarce	4312
	9: 9	I ate no **b** and drank no water.	4312
	9:18	I ate no **b** and drank no water,	4312
	16: 3	Do not eat it with **b made with yeast**,	2809
	16: 3	but for seven days eat **unleavened b**,	5174
	16: 3	the **b** *of* affliction, because you left Egypt	4312
	16: 8	For six days eat **unleavened b** and on	5174
	16:16	at the Feast of **Unleavened B**,	5174
	23: 4	to meet you with **b** and water on your way	4312
	29: 6	You ate no **b** and drank no wine	4312
Jos	5:11	**unleavened b** and roasted grain.	5174
	9: 5	All the **b** *of* their food supply was dry	4312
	9:12	This **b** *of* ours was warm	4312
Jdg	6:19	an ephah of flour he made **b without yeast**.	5174
	6:20	"Take the meat and the **unleavened b**,	5174
	6:21	the meat and the **unleavened b**.	5174
	6:21	consuming the meat and the **b**.	5174
	7:13	"A round loaf of barley **b** came tumbling	4312
	8: 5	"Give my troops *some* **b**;	3971+4312
	8: 6	Why should we give **b** to your troops?"	4312
	8:15	Why should we give **b**	4312
	19:19	and fodder for our donkeys and **b** and wine	4312
Ru	2:14	Have some **b** and dip it in the wine vinegar	4312
1Sa	2:36	a piece of silver and a crust of **b** and plead,	4312
	10: 3	another three loaves of **b**,	4312
	10: 4	and offer you two loaves of **b**,	4312
	16:20	So Jesse took a donkey loaded with **b**,	4312
	17:17	of roasted grain and these ten **loaves of b**	4312
	21: 3	Give me five **loaves of b**,	4312
	21: 4	"I don't have any ordinary **b** on hand;	4312
	21: 4	there is *some* consecrated **b**—	4312
	21: 6	So the priest gave him the consecrated **b**,	NIH
	21: 6	since there was no **b** there except the bread	4312
	21: 6	since there was no bread there except the **b**	4312
	21: 6	before the LORD and replaced by hot **b** on	4312
	22:13	giving him **b** and a sword and inquiring	4312
	25:11	Why should I take my **b** and water,	4312
	25:18	She took two hundred **loaves of b**,	4312
	28:24	kneaded it and baked **b without yeast**.	5174
2Sa	3:35	with me, be it ever so severely, if I taste **b**	4312
	6:19	Then he gave a loaf of **b**,	4312
	13: 6	and **make** some **special b** in my sight,	4221+4223
	13: 8	**made** *the* **b** in his sight and baked it.	4221
	13: 9	she took the pan and served him the **b**,	NIH
	13:10	And Tamar took the **b** she had prepared	4223
	16: 1	and loaded with two hundred **loaves of b**,	4312
	16: 2	the **b** and fruit are for the men to eat,	4312
1Ki	7:48	the golden table on which was the **b** *of*	4312
	13: 8	nor would I eat **b** or drink water here.	4312
	13: 9	'You must not eat **b** or drink water or return	4312
	13:16	nor can I eat **b** or drink water with you	4312
	13:17	not eat **b** or drink water there or return by	4312
	13:18	with you to your house so that he may eat **b**	4312
	13:22	You came back and ate **b** and drank water	4312
	14: 3	Take ten **loaves of b** with you,	4312
	17: 6	The ravens brought him **b** and meat in	4312
	17: 6	the morning and **b** and meat in the evening,	4312
	17:11	"And bring me, please, a piece of **b**."	4312
	17:12	she replied, "I don't have any **b**—	5056
	17:13	But first make a small **cake of b** for me	6314
	19: 6	and there by his head was a **cake of b** baked	6314
	22:27	but **b** and water until I return safely."	4312
2Ki	4:42	of God twenty **loaves of b** of barley baked	4312
	18:32	a land of **b** and vineyards,	4312
	23: 9	they ate **unleavened b** with their fellow	5174
1Ch	9:31	the responsibility for baking the **offering b**.	2503

1Ch	9:32	for every Sabbath the **b** set out on the table.	4312
	16: 3	Then he gave a loaf of **b**,	4312
	23:29	They were in charge of the **b** set out on	4312
	28:16	of gold for each table for **consecrated b**;	5121
2Ch	2: 4	for setting out the **consecrated b** regularly,	5121
	4:19	on which was the **b** of the Presence,	4312
	8:13	the Feast of **Unleavened B**,	5174
	13:11	the **b** on the ceremonially clean table	4312
	18:26	but **b** and water until I return safely.' "	4312
	29:18	**setting out the consecrated b**,	5121
	30:13	to celebrate the Feast of **Unleavened B** in	5174
	30:21	the Feast of **Unleavened B** for seven days	5174
	35:17	the Feast of **Unleavened B** for seven days.	5174
Ezr	6:22	with joy the Feast of **Unleavened B**,	5174
Ne	9:15	In their hunger you gave them **b**	4312
	10:33	for the **b** set out on the table;	4312
Job	23:12	of his mouth more than my **daily b**.	2976
	31:17	if I have kept my **b** to myself, not sharing it	7326
Ps	14: 4	those who devour my people as men eat **b**	4312
	37:25	or their children begging for **b**.	4312
	41: 9	whom I trusted, he who shared my **b**,	4312
	53: 4	those who devour my people as men eat **b**	4312
	78:25	Men ate the **b** of angels;	4312
	80: 5	You have fed them with the **b** of tears;	4312
	104:15	and **b** that sustains his heart.	4312
	105:40	and satisfied them with the **b** of heaven.	4312
Pr	4:17	They eat the **b** of wickedness and drink	4312
	6:26	for the prostitute reduces you to a loaf of **b**,	4312
	28:21	yet a man will do wrong for a piece of **b**.	4312
	30: 8	but give me only my **daily b**.	2976+4312
	31:27	of her household and does not eat the **b**	4312
Ecc	11: 1	Cast your **b** upon the waters,	4312
Isa	28:28	Grain must be ground to make **b**;	4312
	30:20	the Lord gives you the **b** of adversity and	4312
	33:16	His **b** will be supplied,	4312
	36:17	a land of **b** and vineyards.	4312
	44:15	he kindles a fire and bakes **b**.	4312
	44:19	I even baked **b** over its coals,	4312
	51:14	nor will they lack **b**.	4312
	55: 2	Why spend money on *what* is not **b**,	4312
	55:10	so that it yields seed for the sower and **b** for	4312
Jer	7:18	and make **cakes of b** for the Queen	3924
	37:21	given **b** from the street of the bakers	3971+4312
	37:21	of the bakers each day until all the **b** in the city."	4312
	38: 9	when there is no longer any **b** in the city."	4312
	42:14	or hear the trumpet or be hungry for **b**,'	4312
La	1:11	All her people groan as they search for **b**;	4312
	2:12	"Where is **b** and wine?"	1841
	4: 4	the children beg for **b**,	4312
	5: 6	to Egypt and Assyria to get enough **b**.	4312
	5: 9	We get our **b** at the risk of our lives because	4312
Eze	4: 9	in a storage jar and use them to make **b**	4312
	4:15	"I will let you bake your **b** over cow manure	4312
	13:19	a few handfuls of barley and scraps of **b**.	4312
	45:21	which you shall eat **b made without yeast**.	5174
Hos	9: 4	Such sacrifices will be to them like the **b**	4312
Am	4: 5	Burn **leavened b** as a thank offering	2809
	4: 6	in every city and lack of **b** in every town,	4312
	7:12	Earn your **b** there and do your prophesying	4312
Ob	1: 7	those who eat your **b** will set a trap for you,	4312
Hag	2:12	and that fold touches some **b** or stew,	4312
Mt	4: 3	tell these stones to become **b**."	788
	4: 4	'Man does not live on **b** alone,	788
	6:11	Give us today our daily **b**.	788
	7: 9	"Which of you, if his son asks for **b**,	788
	12: 4	and his companions ate the consecrated **b**—	788
	14:17	"We have here only five **loaves of b**	788
	15:26	not right to take the children's **b** and toss it	788
	15:33	"Where could we get enough **b**	788
	16: 5	the disciples forgot to take **b**.	788
	16: 7	"It is because we didn't bring any **b**."	788
	16: 8	among yourselves about having no **b**?	788
	16:11	that I was not talking to you about **b**?	788
	16:12	to guard against the yeast used *in* **b**,	788
	26:17	**Feast of Unleavened B**,	109
	26:26	While they were eating, Jesus took **b**,	788
Mk	2:26	the house of God and ate the consecrated **b**,	788
	6: 8	no **b**, no bag, no money in your belts.	788
	6:37	that much on **b** and give it to them to eat?"	788
	6:43	up twelve basketfuls of broken pieces of **b**	NIG
	7:27	not right to take the children's **b** and toss it	788
	8: 4	this remote place can anyone get enough **b**	788
	8:14	The disciples had forgotten to bring **b**,	788
	8:16	"It is because we have no **b**."	788
	8:17	"Why are you talking about having no **b**?	788
	14: 1	**Feast of Unleavened B**	109
	14:12	**Feast of Unleavened B**,	109
	14:20	"one who dips **b** into the bowl with me.	NIG
	14:22	While they were eating, Jesus took **b**,	788
Lk	4: 3	tell this stone to become **b**."	788
	4: 4	'Man does not live on **b** alone.' "	788
	6: 4	and taking the consecrated **b**,	788
	7:33	For John the Baptist came neither eating **b**	788
	9: 3	no staff, no bag, no **b**, no money,	788
	9:13	"We have only five **loaves of b**	788
	11: 3	Give us each day our daily **b**.	788
	11: 5	'Friend, lend me three **loaves of b**,	788
	11: 8	and give him the **b** because he is his friend,	NIG
	22: 1	Now the Feast *of* **Unleavened B**,	109
	22: 7	Then came the day *of* **Unleavened B**	109
	22:19	And he took **b**, gave thanks and broke it,	788
	24:30	he took **b**, gave thanks,	788
	24:35	by them when he broke the **b**.	788
Jn	6: 5	shall we buy **b** for these people to eat?"	788
	6: 7	not buy enough **b** for each one to have	788
	6:23	the place where the people had eaten the **b**	788
	6:31	'He gave them **b** from heaven to eat.' "	788

Jn	6:32	it is not Moses who has given you the **b**	788
	6:32	but it is my Father who gives you the true **b**	788
	6:33	For the **b** of God is he who comes down	788
	6:34	they said, "from now on give us this **b**."	788
	6:35	Then Jesus declared, "I am the **b** of life.	788
	6:41	"I am the **b** that came down from heaven."	788
	6:48	I am the **b** of life.	788
	6:50	here is the **b** that comes down from heaven,	788
	6:51	the living **b** that came down from heaven.	788
	6:51	If anyone eats of this **b**, he will live forever.	788
	6:51	This **b** is my flesh, which I give	788
	6:58	This is the **b** that came down from heaven.	788
	6:58	he who feeds on this **b** will live forever."	788
	13:18	'He who shares my **b** has lifted up his heel	788
	13:26	the one to whom I will give this **piece of b**	6040
	13:26	Then, dipping the **piece of b**,	6040
	13:27	As soon as Judas took the **b**,	6040
	13:30	As soon as Judas had taken the **b**,	6040
	21: 9	with fish on it, and some **b**.	788
	21:13	Jesus came, took the **b** and gave it to them,	788
Ac	2:42	to the breaking of **b** and to prayer.	788
	2:46	They broke **b** in their homes	788
	12: 3	**Feast of Unleavened B**.	109
	20: 6	**Feast of Unleavened B**,	109+2465
	20: 7	of the week we came together to break **b**.	788
	20:11	he went upstairs again and broke **b** and ate.	788
	27:35	he took some **b** and gave thanks to God	788
1Co	5: 8	but with **b without yeast**,	109
	5: 8	the **b** of sincerity and truth.	NIG
	10:16	not the **b** that we break a participation in	788
	11:23	on the night he was betrayed, took **b**,	788
	11:26	whenever you eat this **b** and drink this cup,	788
	11:27	whoever eats the **b** or drinks the cup of	788
	11:28	to examine himself before he eats of the **b**	788
2Co	9:10	to the sower and **b** for food will also supply	788
2Th	3:12	to settle down and earn the **b** they eat.	788
Heb	9: 2	the table and the **consecrated b**;	788+4606

BREADTH (5)

Ge	13:17	walk through the length and **b** of the land,	8145
1Ki	4:29	and a **b** of understanding as measureless as	8145
Isa	8: 8	Its outspread wings will cover the **b**	8145
	40:12	the **b** of his **hand** marked off the heavens?	2455
Rev	20: 9	the **b** of the earth and surrounded the camp	4424

BREAK (96) [BREACH, BREACHES, BREACHING, BREAKERS, BREAKING, BREAKS, BROKE, BROKEN, BROKENNESS, LAWBREAKER, LAWBREAKERS]

Ge	19: 9	and moved forward to **b** down the door.	8689
Ex	9: 9	and festering boils will **b** out on men	7255
	12:46	*Do* not **b** any of the bones.	8689
	13:13	but if you do not redeem it, **b** its **neck**.	6904
	19:22	or the LORD *will* **b** out against them."	7287
	19:24	or *he will* **b** out against them."	7287
	23:24	**b** their sacred stones **to pieces**.	8689+8689
	34:13	**B** down their altars,	5997
	34:20	but if you do not redeem it, **b** its **neck**.	6904
Lev	11:33	and *you* must **b** the pot.	8689
	26:19	*I will* **b** down your stubborn pride	8689
Nu	9:12	not leave any of it till morning or **b** any	8689
	24: 8	**b** their bones **in pieces**;	1751
	30: 2	he must not **b** his word	2725
Dt	1: 7	**B camp** and advance into the hill country of	7155
	7: 5	**B** down their altars,	5997
	12: 3	**B** down their altars,	5997
	21: 4	in the valley *they are* to **b** the heifer's **neck**.	6904
	31:16	and **b** the covenant I made with them.	7296
Jos	22:16	'How could you **b faith** with the God	5085+5086
Jdg	2: 1	'I will never **b** my covenant with you,	7296
	2: 2	but *you* shall **b** down their altars.'	5997
	5:12	Wake up, wake up, **b** out *in* song!	1819
	11:35	a vow to the LORD that I cannot **b**."	8740
2Sa	5:20	He said, "As waters **b** out,	7288
1Ki	15:19	Now **b** your treaty with Baasha king	7296
2Ki	3:26	to **b through** to the king of Edom,	1324
1Ch	14:11	He said, "As waters **b** out,	7288
2Ch	16: 3	Now **b** your treaty with Baasha king	7296
Ezr	9:14	Shall we again **b** your commands	7296
Ne	4: 3	*he would* **b** down their wall of stones!"	7287
Job	24:16	In the dark, *men* **b** into houses,	3168
	30:13	*They* **b** up my road;	5995
Ps	2: 3	"Let us **b** their chains," they say,	5998
	3: 7	**b** the teeth of the wicked.	8689
	10:15	**B** the arm of the wicked and evil man;	8689
	27: 3	though war **b** out against me,	7756
	46: 5	God will help her at **b** of **day**.	1332+7155
	58: 6	**B** the teeth in their mouths, O God;	2238
Pr	25:15	and a gentle tongue *can* **b** a bone.	8689
Isa	5: 5	I *will* **b** down its wall,	7287
	11:15	*He will* **b** it **up** into seven streams so	5782
	14: 7	*they* **b** *into* singing.	7200
	30:14	It will **b in pieces** like pottery,	8691
	42: 3	A bruised reed *he will* not **b**,	8689
	45: 2	I *will* **b** down gates of bronze and cut	8689
	58: 6	to set the oppressed free and **b** every yoke?	5998
	58: 8	Then your light *will* **b forth** like the dawn,	1324
Jer	4: 3	"**B up** your unplowed ground and do	5774
	4: 4	or my wrath *will* **b** out and burn like fire	3655
	14:21	with us and *do* not **b** it.	7296
	15:12	"*Can a man* **b** iron—	8318
	19:10	"Then **b** the jar while those who go	8689
	21:12	or my wrath *will* **b** out and burn like fire	3655

Jer	28: 2	'I will **b** the yoke of the king of Babylon.	8689
	28: 4	'for *I will* **b** the yoke of the king	8689
	28:11	'In the same way *will I* **b** the yoke	8689
	30: 8	'I will **b** the yoke off their necks.	8689
	33:20	'If *you can* **b** my covenant with the day	7296
	49:35	"See, I will **b** the bow of Elam,	8689
	50:26	**B** open her granaries;	7337
Eze	17:22	*I will* **b off** a tender sprig	7786
	26:12	*they will* **b down** your walls	2238
	27:26	But the east wind *will* **b** you **to pieces** in	8689
	30:18	Dark will be the day at Tahpanhes when I **b**	8689
	30:24	*I will* **b** both his arms,	8689
	30:24	but *I will* **b** the arms of Pharaoh,	8689
	34:27	when I **b** the bars of their yoke	8689
Da	2:40	so it will crush and **b** all the others.	10671
Hos	1: 5	In that day *I will* **b** Israel's bow in	8689
	4: 2	*they* **b all bounds**,	7287
	7: 1	They practice deceit, thieves **b** into houses,	995
	10:11	and Jacob *must* **b up the ground**.	8440
	10:12	and **b up** your unplowed ground;	5774
Am	1: 5	*I will* **b down** the gate of Damascus;	8689
Jnh	1: 4	that the ship threatened to **b up**.	8689
Mic	2:13	*they will* **b** through the gate and go out.	7287
	3: 3	**b** their bones **in pieces**;	7200
	4:13	and *you will* **b to pieces** many nations."	1990
Na	1:13	Now *I will* **b** their yoke from your neck	8689
Mal	2:15	*do* not **b faith** with the wife of your youth.	953
	2:16	and *do* not **b faith**.	953
Mt	5:33	'Do not **b** your **oath**,	2155
	6:19	and where thieves **b in** and steal.	1482
	6:20	and where thieves *do* not **b in** and steal.	1482
	12:20	A bruised reed *he will* not **b**,	2862
	15: 2	"Why *do* your disciples **b** the tradition of	4124
	15: 3	"And why *do* you **b** the command of God	4124
Lk	5: 6	of fish that their nets *began to* **b**.	1396
Jn	19:33	*they did* not **b** his legs.	2862
Ac	20: 7	of the week we came together *to* **b** bread.	3089
Ro	2:25	but if *you* **b** the law,	1639+4127
1Co	10:16	not the bread that *we* **b** a participation in	3089
Gal	4:27	**b forth** and cry aloud,	4838
Rev	5: 2	"Who is worthy *to* **b** the seals and open	3395

BREAKERS (3) [BREAK]

Ps	42: 7	all your waves and **b** have swept over me.	1644
	93: 4	mightier than the **b** *of* the sea—	5403
Jnh	2: 3	all your waves and **b** swept over me.	5403

BREAKFAST (1)

Jn	21:12	Jesus said to them, "Come and *have* **b**."	753

BREAKING (23) [BREAK]

Ex	22: 2	"If a thief is caught **b in** and is struck so	4747
	32:19	**b** them **to pieces** at the foot of	8689
Lev	13:42	it is an infectious disease **b out** on his head	7255
	26:25	upon you to avenge the **b** of the covenant.	NIH
	26:44	**b** my covenant with them.	7296
Dt	9:17	**b** them **to pieces** before your eyes.	8689
	31:20	rejecting me and **b** my covenant.	7296
Jos	9:20	on us for the oath we swore to them."	NIH
1Sa	25:10	Many servants *are* **b away**	7287
Isa	28:24	*Does he keep on* **b up** and harrowing	7337
	58:13	"If you keep your feet from **b** the Sabbath	NIH
Jer	2:34	though you did not catch them **b in**.	4747
Eze	16:59	because you have despised my oath by **b**	7296
	17:18	He despised the oath by **b** the covenant.	7296
Joel	2: 8	through defenses without **b ranks**.	1298
Zec	11:14	**b** the brotherhood between Judah	7296
Mal	2:10	of our fathers *by* **b faith** with one another?	953
Jn	5:18	not only *was* he **b** the Sabbath,	3395
Ac	2:42	to the **b** of bread and to prayer.	3082
	21:13	"Why are you weeping and **b** my heart?	5316
Ro	2:23	do you dishonor God by **b** the law?	4126
	5:14	even over those who did not sin by **b** a **command**,	4126
Jas	2:10	at just one point is guilty of **b** all of it.	NIG

BREAKS (23) [BREAK]

Ex	1:10	if war **b** out, will join our enemies,	7925
	22: 6	a fire **b** out and spreads into thornbushes so	3655
Lev	13:12	the disease **b** out all over his skin	7255+7255
Jdg	6:31	when *someone* **b** down his altar."	5997
Ps	29: 5	The voice of the LORD **b** the cedars;	8689
	29: 5	the LORD **b in pieces** the cedars	8689
	46: 9	*he* **b** the bow and shatters the spear,	8689
	76:12	*He* **b** the spirit of rulers;	1306
	107:16	for *he* **b down** gates of bronze and cuts	8689
	141: 7	"As one plows and **b up** the earth,	1324
Pr	17:14	so drop the matter before a dispute **b** out.	1679
Ecc	10: 8	whoever **b** through a wall may be bitten by	7287
SS	2:17	Until the day **b** and the shadows flee, turn,	7031
	4: 6	Until the day **b** and the shadows flee,	7031
Isa	66: 3	like *one who* **b** a dog's **neck**;	6904
Jer	23:29	**b** a rock **in pieces**?	7207
Eze	13: 5	to the **b** in the wall to repair it for the house	7288
Da	2:40	for iron **b** and smashes everything—	10182
	2:40	and as iron **b** things **to pieces**,	10671
Am	4: 3	through **b in the wall**,	7288
Mic	2:13	One *who* **b open** the way will go up	7287
Mt	5:19	Anyone *who* **b** one of the least	3395
1Jn	3: 4	Everyone who sins **b** the **law**;	490+4472

BREAST (22) [BREASTPIECE, BREASTPLATE, BREASTPLATES, BREASTS]

Ge	49:25	blessings of the **b** and womb.	8716
Ex	29:26	the **b** of the ram for Aaron's ordination,	2601
	29:27	the **b** that was waved and the thigh	2601
Lev	7:30	he is to bring the fat, together with the **b**,	2601
	7:30	the **b** before the LORD as a wave offering.	2601
	7:31	but the **b** belongs to Aaron and his sons.	2601
	7:34	I have taken the **b** that is waved and	2601
	8:29	He also took the **b**—	2601
	10:14	that was waved and the thigh	2601
	10:15	the **b** that was waved must be brought with	2601
Nu	6:20	and belong to the priest, together with the **b**	2601
	18:18	just as the **b** of the wave offering and	2601
1Ki	3:20	by her **b** and put her dead son by my breast.	2668
	3:20	by her breast and put her dead son by my **b**.	2668
Job	24: 9	The fatherless child is snatched from the **b**;	8718
Ps	22: 9	in you even at my mother's **b**.	8716
Isa	28: 9	to those just taken from the **b**?	8716
	49:15	the **baby** at her **b** and have no compassion	6403
Jer	31:19	after I came to understand, I beat my **b**.	3751
Eze	21:12	Therefore beat your **b**.	3751
Joel	2:16	gather the children, those nursing at the **b**.	8716
Lk	18:13	but beat his **b** and said, 'God,	5111

BREASTPIECE (23) [BREAST]

Ex	25: 7	to be mounted on the ephod and **b**.	3136
	28: 4	a **b**, an ephod, a robe, a woven tunic,	3136
	28:15	"Fashion a **b** for making decisions—	3136
	28:22	the **b** make braided chains of pure gold,	3136
	28:23	and fasten them to two corners of the **b**.	3136
	28:24	to the rings at the corners of the **b**,	3136
	28:26	the **b** on the inside edge next to the ephod.	3136
	28:28	the **b** are to be tied to the rings of the ephod	3136
	28:28	the **b** will not swing out from the ephod.	3136
	28:29	of Israel over his heart on the **b** of decision	3136
	28:30	put the Urim and the Thummim in the **b**,	3136
	29: 5	the ephod itself and the **b**.	3136
	35: 9	to be mounted on the ephod and **b**.	3136
	35:27	to be mounted on the ephod and **b**.	3136
	39: 8	They fashioned the **b**—	3136
	39:15	For the **b** they made braided chains	3136
	39:16	the rings to two of the corners of the **b**.	3136
	39:17	to the rings at the corners of the **b**,	3136
	39:19	the **b** on the inside edge next to the ephod.	3136
	39:21	the rings of the **b** to the rings of the ephod	3136
	39:21	so that the **b** would not swing out from	3136
Lev	8: 8	He placed the **b** on him and put the Urim	3136
	8: 8	and put the Urim and Thummim in the **b**.	3136

BREASTPLATE (3) [BREAST]

Isa	59:17	He put on righteousness as his **b**,	9234
Eph	6:14	with the **b** of righteousness in place,	2606
1Th	5: 8	putting on faith and love as a **b**,	2606

BREASTPLATES (3) [BREAST]

Rev	9: 9	They had **b** like breastplates of iron,	2606
	9: 9	They had breastplates like **b** of iron,	2606
	9:17	Their **b** were fiery red, dark blue,	2400+2606

BREASTS (25) [BREAST]

Lev	9:20	these they laid on the **b**,	2601
	9:21	the **b** and the right thigh before the LORD	2601
Job	3:12	to receive me and **b** that I might be nursed?	8716
Pr	5:19	may her **b** satisfy you always,	1843
SS	1:13	a sachet of myrrh resting between my **b**.	8716
	4: 5	Your two **b** are like two fawns,	8716
	7: 3	Your **b** are like two fawns,	8716
	7: 7	and your **b** like clusters of fruit.	8716
	7: 8	May your **b** be like the clusters of the vine,	8716
	8: 1	who was nursed at my mother's **b**!	8716
	8: 8	and her **b** are not yet grown.	8716
	8:10	I am a wall, and my **b** are like towers.	8716
Isa	32:12	Beat your **b** for the pleasant fields,	8718
	60:16	of nations and be nursed at royal **b**.	8718
	66:11	and be satisfied at her comforting **b**;	8718
La	4: 3	jackals offer their **b** to nurse their young,	8716
Eze	16: 7	Your **b** were formed and your hair grew,	8716
	23: 3	In that land their **b** were fondled	8716
	23:21	and your young **b** fondled	8716
	23:34	you will dash it to pieces and tear your **b**.	8716
Hos	2: 2	and the unfaithfulness from between her **b**.	8716
	9:14	Give them wombs that miscarry and **b**	8716
Na	2: 7	like doves and beat upon their **b**.	4222
Lk	23:29	the wombs that never bore and the **b**	3466
	23:48	they beat their **b** and went away.	5111

BREATH (60) [BREATHE, BREATHED, BREATHES, BREATHING, GOD-BREATHED]

Ge	1:30	everything that has the **b** of life in it—	5883
	2: 7	and breathed into his nostrils the **b** of life,	5972
	6:17	every creature that has the **b** of life in it.	8120
	7:15	Pairs of all creatures that have the **b** of life	8120
	7:22	that had the **b** of life in its nostrils died.	5972+8120
Ex	15:10	But you blew with your **b**,	8120
2Sa	22:16	at the blast of **b** from his nostrils.	8120
Job	4: 9	At the **b** of God they are destroyed;	5972
	7: 7	Remember, O God, that my life is but a **b**;	8120
	9:18	He would not let me regain my **b**	8120
	12:10	of every creature and the **b** of all mankind.	8120
	15:30	the **b** of God's mouth will carry him away.	8120
	19:17	My **b** is offensive to my wife;	8120
	26:13	By his **b** the skies became fair;	8120
	27: 3	the **b** of God in my nostrils,	8120
	32: 8	the **b** of the Almighty,	5972
	33: 4	the **b** of the Almighty gives me life.	5972
	34:14	and he withdrew his spirit and **b**,	5972
	37:10	The **b** of God produces ice,	5972
	41:21	His **b** sets coals ablaze,	5883
Ps	18:15	at the blast of **b** from your nostrils.	8120
	33:6	their starry host by the **b** of his mouth.	8120
	39: 5	Each man's life is but a **b**.	2039
	39:11	each man is but a **b**.	2039
	62: 9	Lowborn men are but a **b**, the highborn are	2039
	62: 9	together they are only a **b**;	2039
	104:29	when you take away their **b**,	8120
	135:17	nor is there **b** in their mouths.	8120
	144: 4	Man is like a **b**;	2039
	150: 6	Let everything that has **b** praise	5972
Ecc	3:19	All have the same **b**;	8120
SS	7: 8	the fragrance of your **b** like apples,	678
Isa	2:22	who has but a **b** in his nostrils.	5972
	11: 4	the **b** of his lips he will slay the wicked.	8120
	25: 4	the **b** of the ruthless is like a storm driving	8120
	30:28	His **b** is like a rushing torrent.	8120
	30:33	the **b** of the LORD,	5972
	33:11	your **b** is a fire that consumes you.	8120
	40: 7	the **b** of the LORD blows on them.	8120
	42: 5	who gives **b** to its people,	5972
	57:13	a **mere b** will blow them away.	2039
	57:16	the **b** of man that I have created.	5972
	59:19	that the **b** of the LORD drives along.	8120
Jer	4:31	cry of the Daughter of Zion **gasping for b**,	3640
	10:14	they have no **b** in them.	8120
	38:16	who has given us **b**,	5883
	51:17	they have no **b** in them.	8120
La	4:20	the LORD's anointed, our very **life b**,	678+8120
Eze	37: 5	I will make **b** enter you,	8120
	37: 6	I will put **b** in you,	8120
	37: 8	but there was no **b** in them.	8120
	37: 9	Then he said to me, "Prophesy to the **b**;	8120
	37: 9	Come from the four winds, O **b**,	8120
	37:10	and **b** entered them;	8120
Hab	2:19	there is no **b** in it.	8120
Ac	17:25	because he himself gives all men life and **b**	4466
2Co	1:17	so that in the same **b** I say,	NIG
2Th	2: 8	the Lord Jesus will overthrow *with the* **b**	4460
Rev	11:11	after the three and a half days a **b** of life	4460
	13:15	He was given power to give **b** to the image	4460

BREATHE (4) [BREATH]

Jer	15: 9	of seven will grow faint and **b** her last.	5870+5883
Eze	21:31	and **b** out my fiery anger against you;'	7032
	37: 9	and **b** into these slain, that they may live."	7032
Da	10:17	My strength is gone and I **can hardly b**."	4202+5972+8636

BREATHED (13) [BREATH]

Ge	2: 7	the ground and **b** into his nostrils the breath	5870
	25: 8	Then Abraham **b** his last and died at	1588
	25:17	He **b** his last and died,	1588
	35:18	As she **b** her last—	3655+5883
	35:29	Then he **b** his last and died	1588
	49:33	**b** his last and was gathered to his people.	1588
Jos	10:40	He totally destroyed all who **b**,	5972
	11:11	not sparing anything that **b**,	5972
	11:14	not sparing anyone that **b**.	5972
1Ki	15:29	He did not leave Jeroboam anyone that **b**,	5972
Mk	15:37	With a loud cry, Jesus **b** his last.	1743
Lk	23:46	When he had said this, *he* **b** his last.	1743
Jn	20:22	And with that *he* **b** on them and said,	1874

BREATHES (2) [BREATH]

Dt	20:16	do not leave alive anything that **b**.	5972
Job	14:10	he **b** his last and is no more.	1588

BREATHING (3) [BREATH]

1Ki	17:17	and finally stopped **b**.	5972
Ps	27:12	up against me, **b** out violence.	3641
Ac	9: 1	Saul *was* still **b** out murderous threats	1863

BRED (1) [BREED]

Est	8:10	who rode fast horses **especially b** for the king.	1201+2021+8247

BREEChES (KJV) See UNDERGARMENT

BREED (1) [BRED, BREEDING, BREEDS]

Job	21:10	Their bulls never fail *to* **b**;	6296

BREEDING (1) [BREED]

Ge	31:10	"In **b** season I once had a dream	2021+3501+7366

BREEDS (1) [BREED]

Pr	13:10	Pride only **b** quarrels,	5989

BREEZE (1) [BREEZES]

Ps	78:39	a passing **b** that does not return.	8120

BREEZES (1) [BREEZE]

Ps	147:18	he stirs up his **b**, and the waters flow.	8120

BRETHREN (KJV) See BROTHERS

BRIBE (16) [BRIBERY, BRIBES, BRIBING]

Ex	23: 8	"Do not accept a **b**,	8816
	23: 8	for a **b** blinds those who see and twists	8816
Dt	16:19	Do not accept a **b**,	8816
	16:19	a **b** blinds the eyes of the wise and twists	8816
	27:25	"Cursed is the man who accepts a **b** to kill	8816
1Sa	12: 3	From whose hand have I accepted a **b**	4111
Job	36:18	do not let a large **b** turn you aside.	4111
Ps	15: 5	without usury and does not accept a **b**	8816
Pr	6:35	he will refuse the **b**, however great it is.	8816
	17: 8	A **b** is a charm to the one who gives it;	8816
	17:23	a **b** in secret to pervert the course of justice.	8816
	21:14	a **b** concealed in the cloak pacifies	8816
Ecc	7: 7	and a **b** corrupts the heart.	5510
Isa	5:23	who acquit the guilty for a **b**,	8816
Mic	3:11	Her leaders judge for a **b**,	8816
Ac	24:26	that Paul would offer him a **b**,	5975

BRIBERY (1) [BRIBE]

2Ch	19: 7	there is no injustice or partiality or **b**."	5228+8816

BRIBES (11) [BRIBE]

Dt	10:17	who shows no partiality and accepts no **b**.	8816
1Sa	8: 3	and accepted **b** and perverted justice.	8816
Job	15:34	the tents of **those who love b**.	8816
Ps	26:10	whose right hands are full of **b**.	8816
Pr	15:27	but he who hates **b** will live.	5510
	29: 4	but one who is greedy for **b** tears it down.	9556
Isa	1:23	they all love **b** and chase after gifts.	8816
	33:15	and keeps his hand from accepting **b**,	8816
Eze	22:12	In you men accept **b** to shed blood;	8816
Am	5:12	the righteous and take **b** and you deprive	4111
Mic	7: 3	ruler demands gifts, the judge accepts **b**,	8936

BRIBING (1) [BRIBE]

Eze	16:33	**b** them to come to you from everywhere	8815

BRICK (4) [BRICKMAKING, BRICKS, BRICKWORK]

Ge	11: 3	They used **b** instead of stone,	4246
Ex	1:14	in **b** and mortar and with all kinds of work	4246
Isa	65: 3	and burning incense on **altars of b**;	4246
Jer	43: 9	and bury them in clay in the **b** pavement at	4861

BRICKKILN (KJV) See BRICK PAVEMENT, BRICKWORK, BRICKMAKING

BRICKMAKING (1) [BRICK]

2Sa	12:31	and he made them work at **b**.	4861

BRICKS (8) [BRICK]

Ge	11: 3	*let's* **make b** and bake them thoroughly."	4236+4246
Ex	5: 7	the people with straw for **making b**;	4236+4246
	5: 8	to make the same number of **b** as before;	4246
	5:14	of **b** yesterday or today,	4236
	5:16	yet we are told, 'Make **b**!'	4246
	5:18	yet you must produce your full quota of **b**."	4246
	5:19	to reduce the number of **b** *required of* you	4246
Isa	9:10	"The **b** have fallen down,	4246

BRICKWORK (1) [BRICK]

Na	3:14	tread the mortar, repair the **b**!	4861

BRIDAL (1) [BRIDE]

Ge	29:27	Finish this daughter's **b week**;	8651

BRIDE (25) [BRIDAL]

Ge	34:12	the **price for the b** and the gift I am to bring	4558
1Sa	18:25	king wants no other **price for** *the* **b** than	4558
Ps	45: 9	at your right hand is the **royal b** in gold	8712
SS	4: 8	Come with me from Lebanon, my **b**;	3987
	4: 9	You have stolen my heart, my sister, my **b**;	3987
	4:10	delightful is your love, my sister, my **b**!	3987
	4:11	as the honeycomb, my **b**;	3987
	4:12	a garden locked up, my sister, my **b**;	3987
	5: 1	into my garden, my sister, my **b**;	3987
Isa	49:18	you will put them on, like a **b**.	3987
	61:10	and as a **b** adorns herself with her jewels.	3987
	62: 5	as a bridegroom rejoices over his **b**,	3987
Jer	2: 2	a **b** you loved me and followed me through	3994
	2:32	a **b** her wedding ornaments?	3987
	7:34	of **b** and bridegroom in the towns of Judah	3987
	16: 9	of joy and gladness and to the voices of **b**	3987
	25:10	the voices of **b** and bridegroom,	3987
	33:11	the voices of **b** and bridegroom,	3987
Joel	2:16	and the **b** her chamber.	3987
Jn	3:29	The **b** belongs to the bridegroom.	3811
Rev	18:23	The voice of bridegroom and **b** will never	3811
	19: 7	and his **b** has made herself ready.	1222
	21: 2	as a **b** beautifully dressed for her husband.	3811
	21: 9	"Come, I will show you the **b**,	3811
	22:17	The Spirit and the **b** say, "Come!"	3811

BRIDE-PRICE (2)

Ex	22:16	he **must pay** the **b**, and she shall be his	
		wife.	4555+4555
	22:17	he must still pay the **b** for virgins.	4558

BRIDECHAMBER (KJV) See
BRIDEGROOM

BRIDEGROOM (24) [BRIDEGROOM'S, BRIDEGROOMS]

Ex	4:25	"Surely you are a **b** of blood to me,"	3163
	4:26	(At that time she said "**b** of blood,"	3163
Ps	19: 5	like a **b** coming forth from his pavilion.	3163
Isa	61:10	as a **b** adorns his head like a priest,	3163
	62: 5	as a **b** rejoices over his bride,	3163
Jer	7:34	and **b** in the towns of Judah and the streets	3163
	16: 9	to the voices of bride and **b** in this place.	3163
	25:10	the voices of bride and **b**,	3163
	33:11	the voices of bride and **b**,	3163
Joel	2:16	Let the **b** leave his room and	3163
Mt	9:15	of the **b** mourn while he is with them?	3813
	9:15	when the **b** will be taken from them;	3812
	25: 1	and went out to meet the **b**.	3812
	25: 5	The **b** was a long time in coming,	3812
	25: 6	At midnight the cry rang out: 'Here's the **b**!	3812
	25:10	on their way to buy the **b** arrived.	3812
Mk	2:19	of the **b** fast while he is with them?	3813
	2:20	the time will come when the **b** will be taken	3812
Lk	5:34	"Can you make the guests of the **b** fast	3813
	5:35	the time will come when the **b** will be taken	3812
Jn	2: 9	Then he called the **b** aside	3812
	3:29	The bride belongs to the **b**.	3812
	3:29	The friend who attends the **b** waits	3812
Rev	18:23	The voice of **b** and bride will never	3812

BRIDEGROOM'S (1) [BRIDEGROOM]

Jn	3:29	and is full of joy when he hears the **b** voice.	3812

BRIDEGROOMS (1) [BRIDEGROOM]

Jdg	14:10	as was customary for **b**.	1033

BRIDLE (2) [BRIDLES]

Job	41:13	Who would approach him with a **b**?	4101+8270
Ps	32: 9	by bit and **b** or they will not come to you.	6344+8270

BRIDLES (1) [BRIDLE]

Rev	14:20	rising as high as the horses' **b** for a distance	5903

BRIEF (3) [BRIEFLY]

Ezr	9: 8	"But now, for a **b** moment is,	5071
Job	20: 5	that the mirth of the wicked is **b**,	4946+7940
Isa	54: 7	"For a **b** moment I abandoned you,	7785

BRIEFLY (3) [BRIEF]

Ac	24: 4	that you be kind enough to hear us **b**.	5339
Eph	3: 3	as I have already written **b**.	1877+3900
1Pe	5:12	I have written to you **b**,	1328+3900

BRIER (1) [BRIERS]

Mic	7: 4	The best of them is like a **b**,	2537

BRIERS (16) [BRIER]

Jdg	8: 7	with desert thorns and **b**."	1402
	8:16	by punishing them with desert thorns and **b**.	1402
Job	31:40	then let **b** come up instead of wheat	2560
Isa	5: 6	and **b** and thorns will grow there.	9031
	7:23	there will be only **b** and thorns.	9031
	7:24	the land will be covered with **b** and thorns.	9031
	7:25	you will no longer go there for fear of the **b**	9031
	9:18	it consumes **b** and thorns,	9031
	10:17	and consume his thorns and his **b**.	9031
	27: 4	If only there were **b** and thorns confronting	9031
	32:13	a land overgrown with thorns and **b**—	9031
	55:13	and instead of **b** the myrtle will grow.	6252
Eze	2: 6	though **b** and thorns are all around you	6235
	28:24	people of Israel have malicious neighbors who are painful **b**	6141
Hos	9: 6	of silver will be taken over by **b**,	7853
Lk	6:44	or grapes from **b**.	1003

BRIGANDINE (KJV) See ARMOR

BRIGHT (12) [BRIGHTENED, BRIGHTENS, BRIGHTER, BRIGHTLY, BRIGHTNESS]

Lev	13: 2	a swelling or a rash or a **b** spot on his skin	994
	14:56	and for a swelling, a rash or a **b** spot,	994
Job	25: 5	the moon is not **b** and the stars are not pure	183
	37:21	**b** as it is in the skies after	986
SS	6:10	fair as the moon, **b** as the sun,	1338
Eze	1:13	it was **b**, and lightning flashed out of it.	5586
	8: 2	and from there up his appearance was as **b**	2303
Mt	17: 5	a **b** cloud enveloped them,	5893
Lk	9:29	and his clothes became as **b** as a flash	3328
Ac	22: 6	a **b** light from heaven flashed around me.	2653
Rev	19: 8	Fine linen, **b** and clean,	3287
	22:16	and the **b** Morning Star."	3287

BRIGHTENED (2) [BRIGHT]

1Sa	14:27	and his eyes **b**.	239
	14:29	See how my eyes **b** when I tasted a little	239

BRIGHTENS (2) [BRIGHT]

Pr	16:15	When a king's face **b**, it means life;	240
Ecc	8: 1	Wisdom **b** a man's face	239

BRIGHTER (5) [BRIGHT]

Job	11:17	Life will be **b** than noonday,	7756
Pr	4:18	**shining ever b** till the full light of day.	239+2143+2256
Isa	30:26	and the sunlight will be seven times **b**,	AIT
La	4: 7	Their princes were **b** than snow	2348
Ac	26:13	I saw a light from heaven, **b** than the sun,	3288+5642

BRIGHTLY (1) [BRIGHT]

Pr	13: 9	The light of the righteous **shines b**,	8523

BRIGHTNESS (8) [BRIGHT]

2Sa	22:13	Out of the **b** of his presence bolts	5586
	23: 4	the **b** after rain that brings the grass from	5586
Ps	18:12	of the **b** of his presence clouds advanced,	5586
Isa	59: 9	for **b**, but we walk in deep shadows.	5588
	60: 3	and kings to the **b** of your dawn.	5586
	60:19	nor will the **b** of the moon shine on you,	5586
Da	12: 3	Those who are wise will shine like the **b** of the heavens,	2303
Am	5:20	pitch-dark, without a **ray of b**?	5586

BRILLIANCE (3) [BRILLIANT]

Ac	22:11	because the **b** of the light had blinded me.	1518
Rev	1:16	like the sun shining in all its **b**.	1539
	21:11	its **b** was like that of a very precious jewel,	5891

BRILLIANT (3) [BRILLIANCE]

Ecc	9:11	or wealth to the **b** or favor to the learned;	1067
Eze	1: 4	and surrounded by **b** light.	5586
	1:27	and **b** light surrounded him.	5586

BRIM (2)

Pr	3:10	and your vats will **b** over with new wine.	7287
Jn	2: 7	so they filled them to the **b**.	539

BRIMSTONE (KJV) See SULPHUR

BRING (728) [BRINGING, BRINGS, BROUGHT]

Ge	6:17	I am going to **b** floodwaters on the earth	995
	6:19	to **b** into the ark two of all living creatures,	995
	8:17	**B out** every kind of living creature that is	3655
	9:14	Whenever I **b clouds** over the earth	6725+6727
	15: 9	So the LORD said to him, "**B** me a heifer,	4374
	18:19	so that the LORD will **b** about	995
	19: 5	**B** them **out** to us so that we can have sex	3655
	19: 8	Let me **b** them **out** to you,	3655
	27: 4	the kind of tasty food I like and **b** it to me	995
	27: 5	to hunt game and **b** it **back**,	995
	27: 7	"**B** me some game	995
	27: 9	the flock and **b** me two choice young goats,	4374
	27:12	be tricking him and would **b down** a curse	995
	27:25	"My son, **b** me some of your game to eat,	5602
	28:15	and I will **b** you **back** to this land.	8740
	31:39	not **b** you animals torn by wild beasts;	995
	34:12	the price for the bride and the gift I am to **b**	AIT
	37:14	and **b** word **back** to me."	8740
	38:24	"**B** her **out** and have her burned to death!"	3655
	42:20	you must **b** your youngest brother to me,	995
	42:34	But **b** your youngest brother to me	995
	42:37	of my sons to death if I do not **b** him **back**	995
	42:37	and I will **b** him **back**."	8740
	42:38	**b** my gray head **down** to the grave	3718
	43: 6	"Why did you **b** this **trouble** on me	8317
	43: 7	'**B** your brother **down** here'?"	3718
	43: 9	not **b** him **back** to you and set him here	995
	44:21	'**B** him **down** to me so I can look	3718
	44:29	**b** my gray head **down** to the grave	3718
	44:31	**b** the gray head of our father **down**	3718
	44:32	I said, 'If I do not **b** him **back** to you,	995
	45:13	and my father **down** here quickly."	3718
	45:18	**b** your father and your families back to me.	4374
	46: 4	and I will surely **b** you **back** again.	6590+6590
	47:16	"Then **b** your livestock," said Joseph.	2035
	48: 9	"**B** them to me so I may bless them."	4374
Ex	3: 8	the hand of the Egyptians and to **b** them **up**	6590
	3:10	**b** my people the Israelites **out**	3655
	3:11	and **b** the Israelites **out** of Egypt?"	3655
	3:17	to **b** you **up** out of your misery in Egypt	6590
	6: 6	and I will **b** you **out** from under the yoke	3655
	6: 8	And I will **b** you to the land I swore	995
	6:13	to **b** the Israelites **out** of Egypt.	3655
	6:26	"**B** the Israelites **out** of Egypt	3655
	7: 4	of judgment I will **b** out my divisions,	3655
	7: 5	against Egypt and **b** the Israelites **out** of it."	3655
	9: 3	of the LORD will **b** a terrible plague	2118
	9:19	**b** your livestock and everything you have in the field **to a place of shelter**,	6395
	9:20	of the LORD **hurried to b** their slaves	5674
	10: 4	I will **b** locusts into your country	995
Ex	11: 1	"I will **b** one more plague on Pharaoh and	995
	12:12	and I will **b** judgment on all the gods	6913
	12:42	that night to **b** them **out** of Egypt,	3655
	14:13	the LORD will **b** you today.	6913
	15:17	You will **b** them **in** and plant them on	995
	15:26	not **b** on you any of the diseases I brought	8492
	16: 5	to prepare what they **b in**,	995
	17: 3	"Why did you **b** us **up** out of Egypt	6590
	18:19	before God and **b** their disputes to him.	995
	18:22	but have them **b** every difficult case to you;	995
	19:24	"Go down and **b** Aaron **up** with you.	AIT
	22: 9	both parties are to **b** their cases before	995
	22:13	he shall **b** in the remains as evidence	995
	23:19	"**B** the best of the firstfruits of your soil to	995
	23:20	to guard you along the way and to **b** you to	995
	23:23	My angel will go ahead of you and **b** you to	995
	25: 2	"Tell the Israelites to **b** me an offering.	4374
	27:20	"Command the Israelites to **b** you clear oil	4374
	29: 4	Then **b** Aaron and his sons to the entrance	7928
	29: 8	**B** his sons and dress them in tunics.	7928
	29:10	"**B** the bull to the front of the Tent	7928
	32: 2	and **b** them to me."	995
	32:12	relent and do not **b** disaster on your people	5714
	32:14	Then the LORD relented and did not **b**	6913
	34:26	"**B** the best of the firstfruits of your soil to	995
	35: 5	to **b** to the LORD an offering of gold,	995
	36: 3	to **b** freewill offerings morning	995
	40: 4	**B** in the table and set out what belongs	995
	40: 4	**b** in the lampstand and set up its lamps.	995
	40:12	"**B** Aaron and his sons to the entrance to	7928
	40:14	**B** his sons and dress them in tunics.	7928
Lev	1: 2	to the LORD, **b** as your offering an animal	7928
	1: 5	the priests shall **b** the blood and sprinkle it	7928
	1:13	and the priest is to **b** all of it and burn it	7928
	1:15	The priest shall **b** it to the altar,	7928
	2: 4	" 'If you **b** a grain offering baked in	7928
	2: 8	**B** the grain offering made of these things to	995
	2:11	" 'Every grain offering you **b** to	7928
	2:12	You may **b** them to the LORD as	7928
	2:14	" 'If you **b** a grain offering of firstfruits to	7928
	3: 3	to **b** a sacrifice made to the LORD by fire:	7928
	3: 9	to **b** a sacrifice made to the LORD by fire:	7928
	4: 3	he must **b** to the LORD a young bull	7928
	4:14	the assembly must **b** a young bull as	7928
	4:23	he must **b** as his offering a male goat	995
	4:28	he must **b** as his offering for	995
	4:32	he is to **b** a female without defect.	995
	5: 6	he must **b** to the LORD a female lamb	995
	5: 7	he is to **b** two doves or two young pigeons	995
	5: 8	He is to **b** them to the priest,	995
	5:11	he is to **b** as an offering for his sin a tenth	995
	5:12	He is to **b** it to the priest,	995
	5:15	he is to **b** to the LORD as a penalty a ram	995
	5:18	to **b** to the priest as a guilt offering a ram	995
	6: 6	And as a penalty he must **b** to the priest,	995
	6:14	Aaron's sons are to **b** it before the LORD,	7928
	6:20	the offering Aaron and his sons are to **b** to	7928
	6:21	**b** it well-mixed and present	995
	7:14	He is to **b** one of each kind as an offering,	7928
	7:29	to **b** part of it as his sacrifice to	995
	7:30	to **b** the offering made to the LORD	995
	7:30	he is to **b** the fat, together with the breast,	995
	7:38	the Israelites to **b** their offerings to	7928
	8: 2	"**B** Aaron and his sons,	4374
	12: 6	to **b** to the priest at the entrance to the Tent	995
	12: 8	to **b** two doves or two young pigeons,	4374
	14:10	the eighth day he must **b** two male lambs	4374
	14:23	"On the eighth day he must **b** them	995
	15: 3	This is how his discharge will **b** about	928+2118
	15:29	and **b** them to the priest at the entrance to	995
	16: 9	Aaron shall **b** the goat whose lot falls to	7928
	16:11	"Aaron shall **b** the bull	7928
	16:20	he shall **b forward** the live goat.	7928
	17: 5	so the Israelites will **b** to the LORD	995
	17: 5	They must **b** them to the priest, that is,	995
	17: 9	and does not **b** it to the entrance to the Tent	995
	19:21	must **b** a ram to the entrance to the Tent	995
	22:16	to eat the sacred offerings and so **b upon**	5951
	22:20	Do not **b** anything with a defect,	7928
	23:10	to give you and reap its harvest, **b**	995
	23:14	until the very day you **b** this offering	995
	23:17	**b** two loaves made of two-tenths of	995
	24: 2	"Command the Israelites to **b** you clear oil	4374
	26:16	I will **b** upon you sudden terror,	7212
	26:25	And I will **b** the sword upon you	995
Nu	3: 6	"**B** the tribe of Levi and present them	7928
	5: 9	All the sacred contributions the Israelites **b**	7928
	5:16	" 'The priest shall **b** her and have her stand	7928
	5:25	before the LORD and **b** it to the altar.	7928
	6:10	on the eighth day he must **b** two doves	995
	6:12	for the period of his separation and must **b**	995
	7:11	"Each day one leader is to **b** his offering	7928
	8: 9	**B** the Levites to the front of the Tent	7928
	8:10	You are to **b** the Levites before the LORD,	7928
	11:16	"**B** me seventy of Israel's elders	665
	13:20	Do your best to **b back** some of the fruit of	4374
	14:16	'The LORD was not able to **b** these people	995
	14:24	I will **b** him into the land he went to,	995
	14:31	I will **b** them **in** to enjoy	995
	15: 9	**b** with the bull a grain offering	7928
	15:10	**b** half a hin of wine as a drink offering.	7928
	15:27	he must **b** a year-old female goat for	7928
	18: 2	**B** your fellow Levites	7928
	18: 9	the gifts they **b** me as most holy offerings,	8740
	18:13	that they **b** to the LORD will be yours.	995
	19: 2	Tell the Israelites to **b** you a red heifer	4374
	20: 4	Why did you **b** the LORD's community	995

Nu	20: 5	Why *did you* **b** us **up** out of Egypt	6590
	20: 8	*You* will **b** water **out** of the rock for	3655
	20:10	*must we* **b** you water **out** of this rock?"	3655
	20:12	*you* will not **b** this community into	995
	22: 8	"and *I* will **b** you **back** the answer	8740
	27:17	one who will lead them out and **b** them **in**,	995
Dt	1:17	**B** me any case too hard for you,	7928
	1:22	ahead to spy out the land for us and **b** back	8740
	4:38	to **b** you **into** their land to give it to you	995
	6:23	But he brought us out from there to **b** us **in**	995
	7:26	*Do* not **b** a detestable thing into your house	995
	12: 6	there **b** your burnt offerings and sacrifices,	995
	12:11	to **b** everything I command you:	995
	14:28	**b** all the tithes of that year's produce	3655
	16:17	Each of you must **b** a gift in proportion to	NIH
	19:12	**b** him **back** from the city,	4374
	21:12	**B** her into your home	995
	21:19	of him and **b** him to the elders at the gate	3655
	22: 8	so that your **b** may not **b** the guilt of bloodshed	8492
	22:15	the girl's father and mother *shall* **b** proof	
		that she was a virgin 2256+3655+4374	
	23:18	*not* **b** the earnings of a female prostitute or	995
	24: 4	*Do* not **b** sin *upon* the land	2627
	24: 5	stay at home and **b** happiness *to* the wife	8523
	24:11	the loan or the pledge **out** to you.	3655
	26:10	now *I* **b** the firstfruits of the soil that you,	995
	28:49	The LORD *will* **b** a nation against you	5951
	28:60	*He will* **b** upon you all the diseases	8740
	28:61	The LORD *will* also **b** on you every kind	6623
	29:19	This *will* **b** disaster *on* the watered land	6200
	30: 4	and **b** you **back.**	4374
	30: 5	He *will* **b** you to the land that belonged	995
	31:21	even before *I* **b** them into	995
	31:23	"Be strong and courageous, for you *will* **b**	995
	32:39	I put to death and *I* **b** to **life,**	2649
	33: 7	**b** him to his people.	995
Jos	2: 3	"**B** out the men who came to you	3655
	6:18	**b** about *your own* destruction	3049
	6:18	to destruction and **b** trouble *on* it.	6579
	6:22	and **b** her **out** and all who belong to her,	3655
	7: 7	why *did you ever* **b** this people **across** 6296+6296	
	7:25	LORD *will* **b** trouble *on* you today."	6579
	10:22	**b** those five kings **out**	3655
	18: 6	**b** them here to me and I will cast lots	995
	23:15	so the LORD *will* **b** on you all	995
	24:20	he will turn and **b** disaster on you and make	8317
Jdg	6:13	'*Did* not the LORD **b** us **up** out of Egypt?'	6590
	6:18	and my offering and set it before you."	3655
	6:30	"**B** out your son.	3655
	13: 8	to teach us how to **b** up the boy who is to	6913
	16:25	"**B** out Samson to entertain us."	7924
	19:22	"**B** out the man who came to your house"	3655
	19:24	*I will* **b** them **out** to you now,	3655
Ru	3:15	"**B** me the shawl you are wearing	2035
	4: 4	**b** the matter **to your attention** 265+1655	
1Sa	4: 3	the LORD **b** defeat upon us today before	5597
	4: 3	*Let us* **b** the ark of the LORD's covenant	4374
	9:23	"**B** the piece of meat I gave you,	5989
	11: 2	of you and so **b** disgrace on all Israel."	8492
	11:12	**B** these men to us and we will put them	5989
	13: 9	"**B** me the burnt offering and	5602
	14:18	Saul said to Ahijah, "**B** the ark of God."	5602
	14:34	'Each of you **b** me your cattle and sheep,	5602
	15:32	"**B** me Agag king of the Amalekites."	5602
	16:17	"Find someone who plays well and **b** him	995
	17:18	and **b** back some assurance from them.	4374
	19:15	"**B** him **up** to me in his bed so	6590
	20:21	**b** them here,' then come, because,	4374
	20:31	Now send and **b** him to me,	4374
	21:14	Why **b** him to me?	995
	21:15	that *you have* to **b** this fellow here to carry	995
	23: 9	to Abiathar the priest, "**B** the ephod."	5602
	28: 8	he said, "and **b** up for me the one I name."	6590
	28: 9	a trap for my life to **b** about my **death?"**	4637
	28:11	"Whom *shall I* **b** up for you?"	6590
	28:11	"**B** up Samuel," he said.	6590
2Sa	3:12	I will help you **b** all Israel **over** to you."	6015
	3:13	unless you **b** Michal daughter of Saul	995
	6: 2	of Judah to **b** up from there the ark of God,	6590
	9:10	to farm the land for him and **b** in the crops,	995
	12:11	to **b** calamity upon you.	7756
	12:23	Can *I* **b** him **back** again?	8740
	13:10	"**B** the food here **into**	995
	14:10	**b** him to me,	995
	14:17	word of my lord the king **b** me rest, 2118+4200	
	14:21	Go, **b** back the young man Absalom."	8740
	15:14	to overtake us and **b** ruin upon us and put	5616
	15:25	*he will* **b** me **back** and let me see it	8740
	17: 3	**b** all the people **back**	8740
	17:13	then all Israel *will* **b** ropes to that city,	5951
	17:14	of Ahithophel in order to **b** disaster	995
	18:22	*that will* **b** a **reward."**	5162
	19:11	be the last to **b** the king **back** to his palace,	8740
	19:12	So why should you be the last to **b** back	8740
	19:15	the king and **b** him across the Jordan.	6296
	19:41	**b** him and his household **across**	6296
	20:15	they were battering the wall to **b** it **down,**	5877
	22:28	on the haughty to **b** them **low.**	9164
	23: 5	*Will he* not **b** to **fruition** my salvation?	7541
1Ki	2: 9	**B** his gray head **down**	3718
	2:24	Then the king said, "**B** me a sword."	4374
	8: 1	to **b** up the ark of the LORD's covenant	6590
	8:34	of your people Israel and **b** them **back** to	8740
	13:18	'**B** him **back** with you to your house so	8740
	14:10	to **b** disaster on the house of Jeroboam.	995
	17:10	"*Would you* **b** me a little water in a jar	4374

1Ki	17:11	"And **b** me, please, a piece of bread."	4374
	17:13	for me from what you have and **b** it to me,	3655
	18:19	And **b** the four hundred and fifty prophets	7695
	21:21	'*I am going to* **b** disaster on you.	995
	21:29	*I will* not **b** this disaster in his day,	995
	21:29	but *I will* **b** it on his house in the days	995
	22: 9	"**B** Micaiah son of Imlah **at once."**	4554
2Ki	2:20	"**B** me a new bowl," he said,	4374
	3:15	But now **b** me a harpist."	995
	4: 6	she said to her son, "**B** me another one."	5602
	5: 7	Can I kill and **b** back to **life?**	2649
	10:22	"**B** robes for all the ministers of Baal."	3655
	11:15	"**B** her **out** between the ranks and put to	3655
	21:12	to **b** such disaster on Jerusalem and Judah	995
	22:16	to **b** disaster on this place and its people,	995
	22:20	the disaster *I am going to* **b** on this place.' "	995
1Ch	11:19	Because they risked their lives to **b** it **back,**	995
	13: 3	**b** the ark of our God **back**	6015
	13: 5	to **b** the ark of God from Kiriath Jearim.	995
	13: 6	of Judah (Kiriath Jearim) to **b** up from there	6590
	13:12	"How can *I* ever **b** the ark of God to me?"	995
	15: 3	in Jerusalem to **b** up the ark of the LORD	6590
	15:12	to consecrate yourselves and **b** up the ark of	6590
	15:13	*did* not **b** it up the first time	NIH
	15:14	in order to **b** up the ark of the LORD,	6590
	15:25	of units of a thousand went to **b** up the ark	6590
	16:29	**B** an offering and come before him;	5951
	21: 3	Why *should he* **b** guilt on Israel?" 2118+4200	
	22:19	so that you *may* **b** the ark of the covenant of	995
2Ch	5: 2	to **b** up the ark of the LORD's covenant	6590
	6:25	of your people Israel and **b** them **back** to	8740
	18: 8	"**B** Micaiah son of Imlah **at once.**	4554
	23:14	"**B** her **out** *between* the ranks and put to	3655
	24: 6	to **b** in from Judah and Jerusalem	995
	24: 9	in Judah and Jerusalem that they *should* **b**	995
	24:19	to the people to **b** them **back** to him,	8740
	28:13	"*You must* not **b** those prisoners here,"	995
	29:31	Come and **b** sacrifices and thank offerings	995
	31:10	the people began to **b** their contributions *to*	995
	34:24	*I am going to* **b** disaster on this place and its people—	995
	34:28	the disaster *I am going to* **b** on this place	995
Ezr	3: 7	so that they *would* **b** cedar logs by sea	995
	7:27	into the king's heart to **b** honor to the house	6995
	8:17	so that they *might* **b** attendants to us for	995
Ne	1: 9	I will gather them from there and **b** them to	995
	4: 2	**b** the stones **back to life**	2649
	8: 1	They told Ezra the scribe to **b** out the Book	995
	8:15	into the hill country and **b** back branches	995
	10:31	the neighboring peoples **b** merchandise	995
	10:34	when each of our families is to **b** to	995
	10:36	we *will* **b** the firstborn of our sons and	995
	10:37	we *will* **b** to the storerooms of the house	995
	10:37	we *will* **b** a tithe of our crops to the Levites,	NIH
	10:38	**b** a tenth of the tithes **up**	6590
	10:39	*are* to **b** their contributions of grain,	995
	11: 1	the rest of the people cast lots to **b** one out	995
	12:44	the fields around the towns they were to **b**	4043
Est	1:11	to **b** before him Queen Vashti,	995
	2: 3	to **b** all these beautiful girls into the harem	7695
	5: 5	"**B** Haman **at once,"** the king said,	4554
	5: 5	"**B** him **in,"** the king ordered.	995
	6: 8	*have them* **b** a royal robe the king has worn	995
Job	8:10	*Will they* not **b** forth words	3655
	10:17	*You* **b** new witnesses against me	2542
	10:18	"Why then *did you* **b** me **out** of the womb?	3655
	12:12	Does not long life **b** understanding?	995
	13:19	*Can* anyone **b** charges against me?	8189
	14: 3	*Will you* **b** him before you for judgment?	995
	14: 4	Who *can* **b** what is pure from the impure?	995
	16: 5	comfort from my lips *would* **b** you **relief.**	3104
	19:29	for wrath will **b** punishment by the sword,	NIH
	30:23	I know *you* will **b** me **down** *to* death,	8740
	38:32	*Can you* **b** forth the constellations	3655
	39: 3	They crouch down and **b** forth their young;	7114
	39:12	Can you trust him *to* **b** in your grain	8740
	40:11	look at every proud man and **b** him **low,**	9164
	40:20	The hills **b** him their produce,	5951
Ps	7: 9	**b** to an **end** the violence of the wicked	1698
	17:13	O LORD, confront them, **b** them **down;**	4156
	18:27	but **b** low those whose eyes are haughty.	8214
	28: 4	for what their hands have done and **b** back	8740
	37:14	the bow to **b** down the poor and needy,	5877
	43: 3	*let them* **b** me to your holy mountain,	995
	44: 3	nor *did their* arm **b** them **victory;**	3828
	44: 6	my sword *does* not **b** me **victory;**	3828
	51:16	or *I would* **b** it;	5989
	52: 5	**b** you **down** to everlasting **ruin:**	5997
	55: 3	*for they* **b** down suffering upon me	4572
	55:23	*will* **b** down the wicked into the pit	3718
	56: 7	in your anger, O God, **b** down the nations.	3718
	59:11	and **b** them **down.**	3718
	60: 9	Who *will* **b** me to the fortified city?	3297
	64: 8	against them and **b** them to **ruin;**	4173
	65: 4	Blessed are those you choose and **b** near	7928
	68:22	Lord says, "*I will* **b** them from Bashan;	8740
	68:22	*I will* **b** them from the depths of the sea,	8740
	68:29	at Jerusalem kings *will* **b** you gifts.	3297
	68:30	Humbled, may it **b** bars of silver.	NIH
	71:20	of the earth you will again **b** me **up.**	6590
	72: 3	mountains *will* **b** prosperity to the people,	5951
	72:10	and of distant shores *will* **b** tribute to him.	8740
	74:12	*you* **b** salvation upon the earth.	7188
	76:11	the neighboring lands **b** gifts to the One to	2986
	86: 4	**B** joy *to* your servant, for to you, O Lord,	8523
	86: 9	*they will* **b** glory to your name.	3877
	96: 8	**b** an offering and come into his courts.	5951
	104:20	*You* **b** darkness, it becomes night,	8883

Ps	108:10	Who *will* **b** me *to* the fortified city?	3297
	143: 2	*Do* not **b** your servant into judgment, 907+995	
	143: 8	*Let* the morning **b** me word	9048
	143:11	in your righteousness, **b** me **out** of trouble.	3655
Pr	3: 2	and **b** you prosperity.	3578
	3: 8	*This will* **b** health to your body	2118
	10: 4	but diligent hands **b** wealth.	6947
	10:16	The wages of the righteous **b** them life,	4200
	13: 5	but the wicked **b** shame and disgrace.	944
	18: 6	A fool's lips **b** him strife,	995
	19:24	*he will* not even **b** it **back** to his mouth!	995
	22: 4	of the LORD **b** wealth and honor and life.	6813
	24:22	who knows what calamities they can **b?**	NIH
	25: 8	*do* not **b** hastily to court,	3655
	26:15	he is too lazy to **b** it **back** to his mouth.	8740
	27: 1	you do not know what a day may **b** forth.	3528
	27: 9	Perfume and incense **b** joy *to* the heart,	8523
	27:11	Be wise, my son, and **b** joy *to* my heart;	8523
	29:17	*he will* **b** delight to your soul.	5989
	29:21	*he will* **b** grief in the end.	2118
	31:31	and *let* her works **b** her **praise** at	2146
Ecc	3:17	"God *will* **b** to judgment both	9149
	3:22	For who *can* **b** him to see what will happen	995
	10:10	but skill *will* **b** success.	4178
	11: 9	that for all these things God *will* **b** you	995
	12:14	For God *will* **b** every deed into judgment,	995
SS	1: 4	*Let* the king **b** me **into** his chambers.	995
	8: 2	and **b** you to my mother's house—	995
	8:11	*to* **b** for its fruit a thousand shekels	995
Isa	1:25	the Lord *will* **b** sores on the heads of	8558
	7:17	The LORD *will* **b** on you and	995
	7:17	he will **b** the king of Assyria."	NIH
	8: 7	*to* **b** against them the mighty floodwaters	6590
	14: 2	Nations will take them and **b** them	995
	15: 9	but *I will* **b** still more upon Dimon—	8883
	17:11	*you* **b** them **to bud,**	7255
	19: 3	**b** their plans **to nothing;**	1182
	19:17	Judah *will* **b** terror *to* the Egyptians; 2118+4200	
	21: 2	*I will* **b** to an **end** all	8697
	21:14	**b** water for the thirsty;	910
	21:14	**b** food for the fugitives.	7709
	23: 9	to **b** low the pride of all glory and	2725
	25:11	God *will* **b** down their pride despite	9164
	25:12	He *will* **b** down your high fortified walls	8820
	25:12	*he will* **b** them **down** to the ground,	5595
	28:19	of this message *will* **b** sheer terror.	2118
	30: 3	Egypt's shade will **b** you disgrace.	NIH
	30: 5	who **b** neither help nor advantage,	NIH
	31: 2	Yet he too is wise and *can* **b** disaster;	995
	40: 9	You *who* **b** good **tidings** *to* Zion,	1413
	40: 9	You *who* **b** good **tidings** *to* Jerusalem,	1413
	41:22	"**B** in [your idols] to tell us what is going	5602
	42: 1	on him and *he will* **b** justice to the nations.	3655
	42: 3	In faithfulness *he will* **b** forth justice;	3655
	43: 5	*I will* **b** your children from the east	995
	43: 6	**B** my sons from afar and my daughters	995
	43: 9	*Let them* **b** in their witnesses	5989
	43:14	and **b** down as fugitives all the Babylonians	3718
	45: 7	I **b** prosperity and create disaster;	6913
	46:11	What I have said, that *will I* **b** about;	995
	48:15	*I will* **b** him,	995
	49: 5	the womb to be his servant to **b** Jacob **back**	8740
	49: 6	and **b** back those of Israel I have kept.	8740
	49:22	that *you may* **b** my salvation to the ends of	2118
	49:22	*they will* **b** your sons in their arms	995
	50: 8	Who then *will* **b** charges against me?	8189
	51: 5	and my arm *will* **b** justice to the nations.	9149
	52: 7	the feet of *those who* **b** good **news,**	1413
	52: 7	*who* **b** good **tidings,** who proclaim	
		salvation,	1413
	54: 7	with deep compassion *I will* **b** you **back.**	7695
	56: 7	these *I will* **b** to my holy mountain	995
	60:11	men *may* **b** you the wealth of the nations—	995
	60:17	Instead of bronze *I will* **b** you gold,	995
	60:17	Instead of wood *I will* **b** you bronze,	995
	65: 9	*I will* **b** forth descendants from Jacob,	3655
	66: 4	and *will* **b** upon them what they dread.	995
	66: 9	**b** to the moment of **birth**	8689
	66: 9	up the womb when I **b** to **delivery?"**	3528
	66:15	*he will* **b** down his anger with fury,	8740
	66:20	And *they will* **b** all your brothers,	995
	66:20	"They will **b** them,	NIH
	66:20	as the Israelites **b** their grain offerings,	995
Jer	2: 9	"Therefore *I* **b** charges against you again,"	8189
	2: 9	"And *I will* **b** charges	8189
	2:29	"Why *do you* **b** charges against me?	8189
	3:14	and **b** you *to* Zion.	995
	7:34	*I will* **b** an end to the sounds of joy	8697
	10:18	*I will* **b** distress on them so that they may	7674
	11:11	'I will **b** on them	995
	11:23	because *I will* **b** disaster on the men	995
	12: 1	O LORD, when *I* **b** a case before you.	8189
	12: 9	**b** them to devour.	910
	12:15	**b** each of them **back**	8740
	14:22	the worthless idols of the nations **b** rain?	1772
	15: 7	*I will* **b** bereavement and destruction	8897
	15: 8	At midday *I will* **b** a destroyer against	995
	15: 8	suddenly *I will* **b** down on them anguish	5877
	16: 9	in your days *I will* **b** an end *to* the sounds	8697
	17:18	**B** on them the day of disaster;	995
	17:21	on the Sabbath day or **b** it through the gates	995
	17:22	*Do* not **b** a load **out** of your houses	3655
	17:24	and **b** no load through the gates of this city	995
	18:22	when *you* suddenly **b** invaders	995
	19: 3	*to* **b** a disaster on this place that will make	995
	19:15	I am going to **b** on this city and the villages	8740
	23: 3	and *will* **b** them **back** to their pasture,	8740

Jer	23:12	I will **b** disaster on them in	995
	23:40	I will **b** upon you everlasting disgrace—	5989
	24: 6	and I will **b** them **back** to this land.	8740
	25: 9	"and I will **b** them against this land	995
	25:13	I will **b** upon that land all	995
	25:29	I am beginning to **b** disaster on the city	8317
	25:31	for the LORD will **b** charges against	NIH
	25:31	he will **b** judgment on all mankind and put	9149
	26: 3	not **b** on them the disaster I was planning	6913
	26:13	Then the LORD will **relent and not b**	5714
	26:15	you will **b** the guilt of innocent blood	5989
	26:19	**relent,** so that he **did not b**	5714
	26:19	to **b** a terrible disaster on ourselves!"	6913
	27:22	"Then I will **b** them and restore them	6590
	28: 3	Within two years I will **b back**	8740
	28: 4	also **b back** to this place Jehoiachin son	8740
	29:10	to **b** you **back** to this place.	8740
	29:14	"and I will **b** you **back from** captivity.	8740
	29:14	I will **b** you **back** to the place	8740
	30: 3	**b** my people Israel and Judah **back**	8740
	30:19	I will **b** them **honor,**	3877
	30:21	I will **b** him **near** and he will come close	7928
	31: 8	I will **b** them from the land of the north	995
	31: 9	they will pray as I **b** them **back.**	3297
	31:23	"When I **b** them **back from** captivity,	8740
	31:28	and to overthrow, destroy and **b disaster,**	8317
	32:18	but **b** the **punishment** for the fathers' sins	8966
	32:37	I will **b** them **back** to this place	8740
	33: 6	I will **b** health and healing to it;	6590
	33: 7	**b** Judah and Israel **back**	8740
	33: 9	Then this city will **b** me renown, joy,	2118+4200
	33:11	the voices of those who **b** thank offerings to	995
	34:22	and I will **b** them **back** to this city.	8740
	35:17	to **b** on Judah and on everyone living	995
	36: 7	Perhaps they will **b** their petition before	5877
	36:14	"**B** the scroll from which you have read to	4374
	36:31	I will **b** on them and those living	995
	37:20	Let me **b** my petition before you:	5877
	42:17	or escape the disaster I will **b** on them.'	995
	44: 7	Why **b** such great disaster on yourselves	6913
	44:11	I am determined to **b** disaster on you and	NIH
	45: 5	For I will **b** disaster on all people,	995
	46:25	"I am about to **b punishment** on Amon god	7212
	48:44	for I will **b** upon Moab the year	995
	49: 5	I will **b** terror on you from all those	995
	49: 8	for I will **b** disaster on Esau at	995
	49:16	from there I will **b** you **down,"**	3718
	49:32	in distant places and will **b** disaster	995
	49:36	I will **b** against Elam the four winds from	995
	49:37	I will **b** disaster upon them,	995
	50: 9	For I will stir up and **b** against Babylon	6590
	50:19	But I will **b** Israel **back** to his own pasture	8740
	50:34	so that he may **b rest** to their land,	8089
	51:40	"I will **b** them **down** like lambs to	3718
	51:64	because of the disaster I will **b** upon her.	995
La	1:21	May you **b** the day you have announced	995
	3:33	For he does not willingly **b affliction**	6700
Eze	5:16	I will **b** more and more famine upon you	3578
	5:17	and I will **b** the sword against you.	995
	6: 3	I am about to **b** a sword against you,	995
	6:10	I did not threaten in vain to **b** this calamity	6913
	7:24	I will **b** the most wicked of the nations	995
	9: 1	"**B** the guards of the city **here,**	7928
	9:10	but I will **b down** on their own heads	5989
	11: 8	the sword is what I will **b** against you,	995
	11:17	from the nations and **b** you **back** from	665
	11:21	I will **b down** on their own heads	5989
	12: 4	**b out** your belongings packed for exile.	3655
	12:13	I will **b** him to Babylonia,	995
	14:17	if I **b** a sword against that country and say,	995
	16:38	I will **b** upon you the blood vengeance	5989
	16:40	They will **b** a mob against you,	995
	16:43	I will surely **b down**	5989
	17:19	I will **b down** on his head my oath	5989
	17:20	I will **b** him to Babylon	995
	17:24	the LORD **b down** the tall tree and make	9164
	20: 6	to them that I would **b** them **out** of Egypt	3655
	20:15	not **b** them into the land I had given them—	995
	20:34	I will **b** you from the nations	3655
	20:35	I will **b** you into the desert of the nations	995
	20:37	and I will **b** you into the bond of	995
	20:38	Although I will **b** them **out** of the land	3655
	20:41	as fragrant incense when I **b** you **out** from	3655
	20:42	when I **b** you into the land of Israel,	995
	23:22	in disgust, and I will **b** them against you	995
	23:32	it will **b** scorn and derision,	2118+4200
	23:46	**B** a mob against them and give them over	6590
	24: 5	**b** it **to a boil** and cook the bones	8409+8410
	26: 3	and I will **b** many nations against you,	6590
	26: 7	to **b** against Tyre Nebuchadnezzar king	995
	26:19	like cities no longer inhabited, and when I **b**	6590
	26:20	then I will **b** you **down** with those who go	3718
	26:21	I will **b** you **to a horrible end**	5989
	28: 7	I am going to **b** foreigners against you,	995
	28: 8	They will **b** you **down** to the pit,	3718
	29: 8	I will **b** a sword against you	995
	29:14	I will **b** them **back from** captivity	8740
	32: 8	I will **b** darkness over your land,	5989
	32: 9	the hearts of many peoples when I **b about**	995
	33: 2	'When I **b** the sword against a land,	995
	34:13	I will **b** them **out** from the nations	3655
	34:13	and I will **b** them into their own land.	995
	34:16	I will search for the lost and **b back**	8740
	36:24	from all the countries and **b** you **back**	995
	36:29	and make it plentiful and will not **b** famine	5989
	37:12	to open your graves and **b** you **up**	6590
	37:12	I will **b** you **back** to the land of Israel.	995

Eze	37:13	when I open your graves and **b** you **up**	6590
	37:21	and **b** them **back** into their own land.	995
	38: 4	and **b** you **out** with your whole army—	3655
	38:16	O Gog, I will **b** you against my land,	995
	38:17	for years that I would **b** you against them.	995
	39: 2	I will **b** you from the far north	6590
	39:25	I will now **b** Jacob **back** from captivity	8740
Da	1: 3	to **b in** some of the Israelites from	995
	1:18	of the time set by the king to **b** them **in,**	995
	2:44	**b** them **to an end,**	10508
	5: 2	to **b in** the gold and silver goblets	10085
	9:14	not hesitate to **b** the disaster upon us, for	995
	9:24	to **b in** everlasting righteousness,	995
Hos	4: 1	because the LORD has a charge to **b**	NIH
	4: 4	"But let no man **b** a charge,	8189
	4: 4	for your people are like those who **b**	
		charges against a priest.	8189
	4:19	and their sacrifices will **b** them **shame.**	1017
	9:13	But Ephraim will **b out** their children to	3655
	12: 2	The LORD has a charge to **b**	NIH
	12:13	The LORD used a prophet to **b** Israel **up**	6590
Joel	2:16	**b together** the elders, gather the children,	7695
	3: 2	I will gather all nations and **b** them **down** to	3718
	3:11	**B down** your warriors, O LORD!	5737
Am	4: 1	"**B** us some drinks!"	995
	4: 4	**B** your sacrifices every morning,	995
	5:22	Even though you **b** me burnt offerings	6590
	5:22	Though you **b** choice fellowship offerings,	NIH
	5:25	"Did you **b** me sacrifices	5602
	6: 3	You put off the evil day and **b near** a reign	5602
	9: 1	**B** them **down** on the heads of all the people;	1298
	9: 2	from there I will **b** them **down.**	3718
	9: 7	"Did I not **b** Israel **up** from Egypt,	6590
	9:14	I will **b back** my exiled people Israel;	8740
Ob	1: 3	'Who can **b** me **down** to the ground?'	3718
	1: 4	from there I will **b** you **down,"**	3718
Jnh	3:10	he had compassion and did not **b** upon them	6913
Mic	1:15	I will **b** a conqueror against you who live	995
	2:12	I will **surely b together** the remnant	7695+7695
	2:12	I will **b** them together like sheep in a pen,	8492
	7: 9	He will **b** me **out** into the light;	3655
Na	1: 9	against the LORD he will **b** to an end;	6913
Zep	1:17	I will **b distress** on the people	7674
	3:10	my scattered people, will **b** me offerings.	3297
	3:20	at that time I will **b** you **home.**	995
Hag	1: 8	the mountains and **b down** timber and build	995
Zec	3: 8	I am going to **b** my servant, the Branch.	995
	4: 7	Then he will **b out** the capstone to shouts	3655
	8: 8	I will **b** them **back** to live in Jerusalem;	995
	8:14	as I had determined to **b disaster** upon you	8317
	10:10	I will **b** them **back** from Egypt	8740
	10:10	I will **b** them to Gilead and Lebanon,	995
	13: 9	This third I will **b** into the fire;	995
	14:18	The LORD will **b** on them	2118
Mal	1: 8	When you **b** blind animals for sacrifice,	5602
	1:13	"When you **b** injured,	995
	3: 3	LORD will have men who will **b** offerings	5602
	3:10	**B** the whole tithe into the storehouse,	995
Mt	10:34	not suppose that I have come to **b** peace to	965
	10:34	I did not come to **b** peace, but a sword.	965
	13:30	the wheat and **b** it into my barn.' "	NIG
	14:18	"**B** them here to me," he said.	5770
	16: 7	"It is because we didn't **b** any bread."	3284
	17:17	**B** the boy here to me."	5770
	21: 2	Untie them and **b** them to me.	72
	21:41	those wretches to a wretched **end,"**	660
Mk	4:21	"*Do* you **b** in a lamp to put it under a bowl	2262
	6:27	with orders to **b** John's head.	5770
	8:14	The disciples had forgotten to **b** bread,	3284
	9:19	**B** the boy to me."	5770
	11: 2	Untie it and **b** it here.	5770
	12:15	"**B** me a denarius and let me look at it."	5770
Lk	1:16	of the people of Israel will he **b back** to	2188
	2:10	I **b** you **good news** of great joy that will be	2294
	9:31	which he was about to **b** to **fulfillment**	4444
	9:41	**B** your son here."	4642
	12:49	"I have come to **b** fire on the earth,	965
	12:51	Do you think I came to **b** peace on earth?	1443
	14:21	the streets and alleys of the town and **b in**	1652
	15:22	**B** the best robe and put it on him.	1766
	15:23	**B** the fattened calf and kill it.	5770
	18: 7	And will not God **b about** justice	4472
	19:27	**b** them here and kill them in front of me.' "	72
	19:30	Untie it and **b** it here.	72
	19:42	on this day what would **b** you **peace**—	NIG
Jn	7:45	"Why didn't *you* **b** him in?"	72
	10:16	I must **b** them also.	72
	11:52	to **b together** and make them one.	5251
	14:13	so that the Son may **b glory** to the Father.	1519
	16:14	He will **b glory** to me by taking	1519
	21:10	"**B** some of the fish you have just caught."	5770
Ac	7:42	" 'Did you **b** me sacrifices	4712
	10: 5	Now send men to Joppa to **b** back	3569
	11:14	He will **b** you a **message** through	3281+4839
	12: 4	to **b** him **out** for public trial after	343
	12: 6	The night before Herod was to **b** him	4575
	13:47	the Gentiles, that you may **b** salvation	1639+1650
	17: 5	of Paul and Silas in order to **b** them **out** to	4575
	19:39	If there is anything further *you* **want to b**	
		up,	2118
	22: 5	to **b** these people as prisoners to Jerusalem	72
	23:10	by force and **b** him into the barracks.	72
	23:15	the commander to **b** him before you on	2864
	23:18	for me and asked me to **b** this young man	72
	23:20	to **b** Paul before the Sanhedrin tomorrow on	2864
	24:17	I came to Jerusalem to **b** my people gifts	4472
	24:19	to be here before you and **b charges**	2989

Ac	27:10	to be disastrous and **b** great loss to ship	NIG
	28:19	not that I had any **charge to b against**	2989
Ro	5:21	through righteousness to **b** eternal life	1650
	7:10	commandment that was intended to **b** life	
		actually brought death.	1650
	8:33	Who will **b** any **charge**	1592
	10: 6	(that is, to **b** Christ **down**)	2864
	10: 7	(that is, to **b** Christ **up** from the dead).	343
	10:15	the feet of those who **b** good news!"	2294
	11:12	much greater riches will their fullness **b**!	NIG
	13: 2	and those who do so will **b** judgment	3284
	13: 4	**agent** of wrath to **b** punishment	1690
	15: 7	in order to **b** praise to God.	NIG
1Co	3:13	because the Day will **b** it to **light.**	1317
	4: 5	He will **b** to light what is hidden	5894
	8: 8	But food *does* not **b** us near to God;	4225
	14: 6	unless I **b** you some revelation	3281
2Co	8: 6	to **b** also **to completion** this act of grace	2200
Eph	1:10	**b** all things in heaven and on earth **together**	
		under one head,	368
	6: 4	**b** them **up** in the training and instruction of	1763
Php	3:21	**b** everything **under** his control,	5718
1Th	4:14	and so we believe that God will **b**	72
1Ti	5:12	Thus *they* **b** judgment on themselves,	2400
	6:15	which God will **b** about in his own time—	1259
2Ti	4:11	Get Mark and **b** him with you,	72
	4:13	the cloak that I left with Carpus at Troas,	5770
	4:18	and will **b** me **safely**	5392
Heb	9:28	but to **b** salvation to those who are waiting	1650
	12:17	He could **b** about no change of mind,	2351
Jas	1:20	for man's anger *does* not **b** about	2237
	5:19	the truth and someone *should* **b** him **back,**	2188
1Pe	3:18	to **b** you to God.	4642
2Pe	2: 2	**b** the way of truth **into disrepute.**	1059
	2:11	*do* not **b** slanderous accusations	5770
	3:12	That day will **b** about the destruction of	1328
2Jn	1:10	to you and *does* not **b** this teaching,	5770
Jude	1: 9	**b** a slanderous accusation **against**	2214
	1:21	the mercy of our Lord Jesus Christ to **b** you	NIG
Rev	1:19	O Lord, and **b glory** to your name?	1519
	17:16	They will **b** her to ruin	4472
	21:24	the kings of the earth will **b** their splendor	5770

BRING UP, BRINGING UP (Anglicized)
See REAR, REARING

BRINGING (67) [BRING]

Ge	19: 9	*They kept* **b** pressure on Lot	4394+7210
Ex	6:27	about **b** the Israelites **out** of Egypt.	3655
	14:11	What have you done to us by **b** us **out**	3655
	36: 5	"The people *are* **b** more than enough	995
	36: 6	so the people were restrained from **b** more,	995
Lev	4: 3	**b** guilt on the people,	4200
	17: 4	instead of **b** it to the entrance to the Tent	995
	18: 3	where I *am* **b** you.	995
	20:22	that the land where I *am* **b** you to live may	995
	23:37	as sacred assemblies for **b** offerings made	7928
Nu	14: 3	Why *is* the LORD **b** us to this land only	995
Dt	8: 7	For the LORD your God *is* **b** you into	995
1Sa	2:14	"Why have you disturbed me by me **up?**"	6590
2Sa	4:10	and thought he was **b** good news,	1413
	18:26	The king said, "He *must* be **b** good news,	1413
	19:10	about **b** the king **back?**"	8740
	19:43	not the first to speak of **b back** our king?"	8740
1Ki	1:42	like you *must* be **b** good news."	1413
	8:32	condemning the guilty and **b down**	5989
2Ki	4:42	**b** the man of God twenty loaves	995
1Ch	12:40	and Naphtali *came* **b** food on donkeys,	995
2Ch	6:23	repaying the guilty by **b down**	5989
	34:14	While they *were* **b out** the money	3655
Ne	10:35	for **b** to the house of the LORD each year	995
	13:15	on the Sabbath and **b in** grain and loading it	995
	13:15	And *they were* **b** all this **into** Jerusalem on	995
	13:16	from Tyre who lived in Jerusalem *were* **b in**	995
Est	2:20	as she had done when he was **b** her **up.**	594
Ps	104:14	**b forth** food from the earth:	3655
Pr	31:14	**b** her food from afar.	995
SS	8:10	in his eyes like *one* **b** contentment	3655
Isa	1:13	Stop **b** meaningless offerings!	995
	46:13	**b** my righteousness **near,**	7928
	60: 9	**b** your sons from afar,	995
Jer	4: 6	For I *am* **b** disaster from the north,	995
	5:15	"I *am* **b** a distant nation against you—	995
	6:19	I am **b** disaster on this people,	995
	17:26	**b** burnt offerings and sacrifices,	995
	28: 6	**b** the articles of the LORD's house and all	
		the exiles **back**	8740
	41: 5	**b** grain offerings and incense with them to	995
	43:11	**b** death to those destined for death,	NIH
Eze	17:12	**b** them **back** with him to Babylon.	995
	20: 9	to the Israelites by **b** them **out** of Egypt.	3655
	22:31	with my fiery anger, **b down**	5989
	27:10	and helmets on your walls, **b** you splendor.	5989
	46:20	to avoid **b** them into the outer court	3655
Da	9:12	against us and against our rulers by **b**	995
Mt	15:30	Great crowds came to him, **b** the lame,	1571+2400+3552
	26:62	**testimony** that these men *are* **b against**	2909
	27:13	**testimony** that these men *are* **b against**	2909
Mk	2: 3	Some men came, **b** to him a paralytic,	5770
	10:13	*People were* **b** little children to Jesus	4712
	14:60	What *is* this **testimony** *that* these men *are*	
		b against you?"	2909
Lk	18:15	*People were* also **b** babies to Jesus	4712
Jn	18:29	"What charges *are* you **b**	5770

Jn	19: 4	*I am* **b** him out to you to let you know	72
	19:34	**b** a sudden flow of blood and water.	2002
Ac	5:16	**b** their sick and those tormented	5770
	7:11	**b** great suffering, and our fathers could	NIG
	14:15	We are **b** you **good news,**	2294
	17:20	**b** some strange ideas **to**	1662
	24: 8	charges we *are* **b against**	2989
	25: 7	**b** many serious charges **against**	2965
Ro	3: 5	That God is unjust in **b** his wrath on us?	2214
1Ti	5:10	such as **b up children,** showing hospitality,	5452
Heb	2:10	In **b** many sons to glory,	72
2Pe	2: 1	**b** swift destruction **on** themselves.	2042

BRINGS (85) [BRING]

Ex	13: 5	When the LORD **b** you into the land of	995
	13:11	"After the LORD **b** you into the land of	995
Lev	1: 2	any of you **b** an offering to the LORD,	7928
	2: 1	" 'When someone **b** a grain offering to	7928
	4:32	" 'If *he* **b** a lamb as his sin offering,	995
	7:29	'Anyone *who* **b** a fellowship offering to	7928
	22:21	When anyone **b** from the herd or flock	7928
Nu	5:18	the bitter water that **b a curse.**	826
	5:19	may this bitter water that **b a curse**	826
	5:22	that **b a curse** enter your body so	826
	5:24	the bitter water that **b a curse,**	826
	5:27	to drink the water that **b a curse,** it will go	826
	15: 4	then the *one who* **b** his offering shall present	7928
	15:13	in this way when *he* **b** an offering made	7928
	16:30	the LORD **b about** something totally new,	1343
Dt	6:10	When the LORD your God **b** you into	995
	7: 1	When the LORD your God **b** you into	995
	33:14	with the best the sun **b forth** and the finest	9311
1Sa	2: 6	"The LORD **b death** and makes alive;	4637
	2: 6	he **b down** *to* the grave and raises up.	3718
2Sa	23: 4	like the brightness after rain that **b** the grass	NIH
Job	9:23	When a scourge **b** sudden **death,**	4637
	12:22	of darkness and **b** deep shadows into	3655
	22: 4	that he rebukes you and **b** charges	995
	28:11	of the rivers and **b** hidden things *to* light.	3655
	34:11	he **b upon** him what his conduct deserves.	5162
	37:13	*He* **b** the clouds to punish men,	5162
Ps	75: 7	*He* **b** one **down,** he exalts another.	9164
	76:10	your wrath against men **b** you **praise,**	3344
	94:20	*one that* **b on** misery by its decrees?	3670
	135: 7	he sends lightning with the rain and **b out**	3655
Pr	10: 1	A wise son **b joy** *to* his father,	8523
	10:16	income of the wicked **b** them punishment.	4200
	10:22	The blessing of the LORD **b wealth,**	6947
	10:31	mouth of the righteous **b forth** wisdom,	5649
	11:17	but a cruel man **b trouble** *on* himself.	6579
	11:29	*He who* **b trouble** on his family	6579
	12:18	but the tongue of the wise **b** healing.	NIH
	13:17	but a trustworthy envoy **b** healing.	NIH
	14: 3	A fool's talk **b** a rod to his back,	928
	14:23	All hard work **b** a profit,	2118
	15: 4	The tongue that **b** healing is a tree of life,	NIH
	15: 6	the income of the wicked **b** them **trouble.**	6579
	15:20	A wise son **b joy** *to* his father,	8523
	15:27	A greedy man **b trouble** *to* his family,	6579
	15:30	A cheerful look **b joy** *to* the heart,	8523
	16:22	but folly **b** punishment to fools.	NIH
	17:21	To have a fool for a son **b** grief;	4200
	17:25	A foolish son **b** grief to his father	NIH
	19: 4	Wealth **b** many friends,	3578
	19:15	Laziness **b on** deep sleep,	5877
	19:26	a son who **b shame** and disgrace.	1017
	21:12	**b** the wicked **to ruin.**	2021+4200+6156+8273
	21:15	it **b** joy to the righteous but terror	NIH
	25:23	As a north wind **b** rain,	2655
	25:23	so a sly tongue **b** angry looks.	NIH
	29: 3	man who loves wisdom **b joy** *to* his father,	8523
	29:23	A man's pride **b** him **low,**	9164
	31:12	*She* **b** him good, not harm,	1694
Isa	40:23	He **b** princes to naught and reduces	5989
	40:26	He *who* **b out** the starry host one by one,	3655
Jer	10:13	He sends lightning with the rain and **b out**	3655
	13:16	before he **b** the **darkness,**	3124
	51:16	He sends lightning with the rain and **b out**	3655
La	3:32	Though he **b grief,**	3324
	3:51	What I see **b grief** to my soul because of all	6618
Eze	22: 3	*that* **b on** herself doom by shedding blood	995
	46: 4	The burnt offering the prince **b** to	7928
Am	5: 9	on the stronghold and **b** the fortified city	995
Na	1:15	the feet of *one who* **b good news,**	1413
Mal	2:12	he **b** offerings to the LORD Almighty.	5602
Mt	12:35	The good man **b** good things out of	1675
	12:35	and the evil man **b** evil things out of	1675
	13:52	like the owner of a house who **b out**	1675
Lk	6:45	The good man **b** good things out of	4734
	6:45	and the evil man **b** evil things out of	4734
Jn	2:10	"Everyone **b out** the choice wine first and	5502
Ro	3: 5	**b out** God's righteousness **more clearly,**	5319
	4:15	because law **b** wrath.	2981
	5:18	*that* **b** life for all men.	2437
2Co	3: 9	the ministry that **b** righteousness!	NIG
	7:10	Godly sorrow **b** repentance that leads	3337
	7:10	but worldly sorrow **b** death.	2981
Tit	2:11	that **b** salvation has appeared to all men.	NIG
Heb	1: 6	God **b** his firstborn **into** the world,	1650+1652

BRINK (1)

Pr	5:14	I have come to the **b** of utter ruin in	5071

BRITTLE (1)

Da	2:42	be partly strong and partly **b.**	10752

BROAD (11) [BROADEN]

Nu	25: 4	kill them and expose them in **b daylight**	9087
2Sa	12:11	he will lie with your wives in **b daylight.**	2021+2021+2296+4200+6524+9087
	12:12	but I will do this thing in **b daylight**	2021+5584+9087
Ne	3: 8	as far as the **B** Wall.	8146
	12:38	past the Tower of the Ovens to the **B** Wall,	8146
Job	37:10	and the **b** waters become frozen.	8145
Isa	30:23	your cattle will graze in **b** meadows.	8143
	33:21	be like a place of **b** rivers and streams.	3338+8146
Am	8: 9	at noon and darken the earth in **b daylight.**	240+3427
Mt	7:13	and **b** is the road that leads to destruction,	2353
2Pe	2:13	of pleasure is to carouse in **b daylight.**	2465

BROADEN (2) [BROAD]

2Sa	22:37	*You* **b** the path beneath me,	8143
Ps	18:36	*You* **b** the path beneath me,	8143

BROIDED   (KJV) See BRAIDED HAIR

BROILED (1)

Lk	24:42	They gave him a piece *of* **b** fish,	3966

BROKE (81) [BREAK]

Ex	9:10	festering boils **b out** on men and animals.	7255
	34: 1	that were on the first tablets, which *you* **b.**	8689
Lev	24:10	and a fight **b out** in the camp between him	5897
	26:13	*I* **b** the bars of your yoke and enabled you	8689
Dt	10: 2	that were on the first tablets, which *you* **b.**	8689
	32:51	*of you* **b** faith with me in the presence of	5085
Jos	3:14	when the people **b camp** to cross the	185+4946+5825
		Jordan,	
Jdg	6:32	because *he* **b down** Baal's altar.	5997
	7:19	They blew their trumpets and **b** the jars	5879
1Sa	11:11	during the last watch of the night *they* **b**	995
	19: 8	Once more war **b** out,	2118
	23:28	Then Saul **b off** his pursuit of David	4946+8740
2Sa	23:16	So the three mighty men **b** through	1324
2Ki	8:21	but he rose up and **b** through by night;	5782
	14:13	Then Jehoash went to Jerusalem and **b**	7287
		down the wall	
	18: 4	*He* **b into pieces** the bronze snake	4198
	19:36	So Sennacherib king of Assyria **b camp**	5825
	23: 8	*He* **b down** the shrines at the gates—	5997
	25:10	**b down** the walls around Jerusalem	5997
	25:13	The Babylonians **b up** the bronze pillars,	8689
1Ch	11:18	So the Three **b** through the Philistine lines,	1324
	15:13	that the LORD our God **b out in anger**	7287
	20: 4	war **b out** with the Philistines, at Gezer.	6641
2Ch	15:16	**b** it **up** and burned it in the Kidron Valley.	1990
	21: 9	but he rose up and **b through** by night.	5782
	25:23	and **b down** the wall of Jerusalem from	7287
	26: 6	against the Philistines and **b down** the walls	7287
	26:19	leprosy **b out** on his forehead.	2436
	34: 4	These he **b to pieces** and scattered over	1990
	36:19	They set fire to God's temple and **b down**	5997
Job	29:17	and the strength of the fatherless.	1917
	29:17	*I* **b** the fangs of the wicked and snatched	8689
Ps	74:13	*you* **b** the heads of the monster in	8689
	76: 3	There he **b** the flashing arrows,	8689
	78:21	his fire **b out** against Jacob,	5956
	102:23	In the course of my life he **b** my strength;	6700
	106:29	and a plague **b out** among them.	7287
	107:14	the deepest gloom and **b away** their chains.	5998
Isa	7:17	a time unlike any since Ephraim **b away**	6073
	37:37	So Sennacherib king of Assyria **b camp**	5825
	38:13	but like a lion he **b** all my bones;	8689
Jer	2:20	"Long ago *you* **b** off your yoke	8689
	28:10	the neck of the prophet Jeremiah and **b** it,	8689
	31:32	because they **b** my covenant,	7296
	39: 8	and the houses of the people and **b down**	5997
	52:14	of the imperial guard **b down** all the walls	5997
	52:17	The Babylonians **b up** the bronze pillars,	8689
Eze	17: 4	he **b off** its topmost shoot	7786
	17:16	and whose treaty *he* **b.**	7296
	17:19	that he despised and my covenant that *he* **b.**	7296
	19: 7	*He* **b down** their strongholds	1548
	29: 7	*you* **b** and their backs were wrenched.	8689
	44: 7	fat and blood, and *you* **b** my covenant.	7296
Da	2:45	**b** the iron, the bronze, the clay, the silver	10182
		and the gold **to pieces.**	
Zec	11:10	Then I took my staff called Favor and **b** it,	1548
	11:14	Then *I* **b** my second staff called Union,	1548
Mt	14:19	he gave thanks and **b** the loaves.	3089
	15:36	he **b** them and gave them to the disciples,	3089
	26:26	Jesus took bread, gave thanks and **b** it,	3089
	27:52	The tombs **b open** and the bodies	487
Mk	4:37	and the waves **b** over the boat,	2095
	5: 4	the chains apart and **b** the irons on his feet.	5341
	6:41	he gave thanks and **b** the loaves.	2880
	8: 6	he **b** them and gave them to his disciples	3089
	8:19	*I* **b** the five loaves for the five thousand,	3089
	8:20	*I* **b** the seven loaves for the four thousand,	NIG
	14: 3	She **b** the jar and poured the perfume	5341
	14:22	Jesus took bread, gave thanks and **b** it,	3089
	14:72	And he **b down** and wept.	2095
Lk	9:16	he gave thanks and **b** them.	2880
	22:19	And *he* took bread, gave thanks and **b** it,	3089
	24:30	**b** it and began to give it to them,	3089
	24:35	by them when he **b** the bread.	3082
Jn	19:32	The soldiers therefore came and **b** the legs	2862
Ac	2:46	They **b** bread in their homes	3089

Ac	8: 1	a great persecution **b out** against the church	1181
	20:11	*he* went upstairs again and **b** bread and ate.	3089
	23: 7	a dispute **b out** between the Pharisees and	1181
	27:35	Then he **b** it and began to eat.	3089
1Co	11:24	*he* **b** it and said, "This is my body,	3089
Rev	16: 2	and ugly and painful sores **b out** on	1181

BROKEN (130) [BREAK]

Ge	17:14	he *has* **b** my covenant."	7296
	38:29	"So this is how *you have* **b out!**"	7287+7288
Ex	21: 8	because he *has* **b** faith with her.	953
Lev	6:21	and present the grain offering **b** *in* pieces	9519
	6:28	the meat is cooked in *must be* **b;**	8689
	11:35	an oven or cooking pot *must be* **b up.**	5997
	13:20	an infectious skin disease *that has* **b out**	7255
	13:25	it is an infectious disease *that has* **b out** in	7255
	13:39	a harmless rash *that has* **b out** on the skin;	7255
	15:12	that the man touches *must be* **b,**	8689
Nu	15:31	the LORD's word and *has* **b** his commands,	7296
Dt	21: 6	the heifer whose **neck** *was* **b** in the valley,	6904
Jdg	6:30	because *he has* **b down** Baal's altar and cut	5997
1Sa	2: 4	"The bows of the warriors are **b,**	3146
	4:18	His neck *was* **b** and he died,	8689
	5: 4	and hands *had been* **b off** and were lying on	4162
	14:33	"*You have* **b faith,**" he said.	953
2Sa	5:20	the LORD *has* **b out** *against* my enemies	7287
	6: 8	because the LORD's wrath *had* **b out**	7287
1Ki	19:10	**b down** your altars,	2238
	19:14	**b down** your altars,	2238
2Ki	25: 4	Then the city wall *was* **b through,**	1324
1Ch	13:11	because the LORD's wrath *had* **b out**	7287
	14:11	God *has* **b out** *against* my enemies	7287
2Ch	24: 7	of that wicked woman Athaliah *had* **b into**	7287
	32: 5	the **b** *sections* of the wall	7287
Ne	1: 3	The wall of Jerusalem is **b down,**	7287
	2:13	which *had been* **b down,** and its gates,	7287
Job	2: 8	a piece of **b** pottery and scraped himself	3084
	4:10	yet the teeth of the great lions are **b.**	5996
	4:20	and dusk they *are* **b to pieces;**	4198
	7: 5	my skin is **b** and festering.	8090
	17: 1	My spirit is **b,** my days are cut short,	2472
	24:20	but *are* **b** like a tree.	8689
	30:24	a hand on a **b man** when he cries for help	6505
	31:22	*let it be* **b off** at the joint.	8689
	31:39	without payment or **b** the spirit	5870
	38:15	and their upraised arm is **b.**	8689
Ps	31:12	I have become like **b** pottery.	6
	34:20	not one of them *will be* **b.**	8689
	37:15	and their bows *will be* **b.**	8689
	37:17	for the power of the wicked *will be* **b,**	8689
	51:17	The sacrifices of God are a **b** spirit;	8689
	51:17	a **b** and contrite heart, O God,	8689
	69:20	Scorn *has* **b** my heart	8689
	80:12	Why *have you* **b down** its walls so	7287
	89:40	*You have* **b through** all his walls	7287
	119:126	your law *is being* **b.**	7296
	124: 7	the snare *has been* **b,** and we have escaped.	8689
Pr	25:28	Like a city whose walls *are* **b down** is	7287
Ecc	4:12	A cord of three strands is not quickly **b.**	5998
	12: 6	or the golden bowl *is* **b;**	8368
	12: 6	or the wheel **b** at the well,	8368
Isa	1:28	But rebels and sinners will both be **b,**	8691
	5:27	not a sandal thong *is* **b.**	5998
	8:15	they will fall and be **b,**	8689
	10:27	the yoke *will be* **b** because you have grown	2472
	14: 5	The LORD *has* **b** the rod of the wicked,	8689
	14:29	that the rod that struck you *is* **b;**	8689
	24: 5	the statutes and **b** the everlasting covenant.	7296
	24:19	The earth *is* **b up,** the earth is split asunder,	8318+8318
	27:11	*they are* **b off** and women come	8689
	33: 8	The treaty *is* **b,** its witnesses are despised,	7296
	33:20	nor any of its ropes *is* **b.**	5998
	58:12	you will be called Repairer of **B** Walls,	7288
	59: 5	and *when* one *is* **b,** an adder is hatched.	2318
Jer	2:13	**b** cisterns that cannot hold water.	8689
	5: 5	with one accord they too *had* **b off** the yoke	8689
	11:10	of Israel and the house of Judah *have* **b**	7296
	11:16	and its branches *will be* **b.**	8318
	22:28	Is this man Jehoiachin a despised, **b** pot,	7046
	23: 9	My heart is **b** within me;	8689
	28:13	Shortly after the prophet Hananiah *had* **b**	8689
	28:13	*You have* **b** a wooden yoke,	8689
	33:21	*can be* **b** and David will no longer have	7296
	39: 2	the city wall *was* **b through.**	1324
	48: 4	Moab *will be* **b;**	8689
	48:17	say, 'How **b** *is* the mighty scepter,	8689
	48:17	how **b** the glorious staff!'	NIH
	48:25	her arm *is* **b,**" declares the LORD.	8689
	48:38	for *I have* **b** Moab like a jar	8689
	50:23	How **b** and shattered is the hammer of	1548
	51: 8	Babylon will suddenly fall and be **b.**	8689
	51:30	the bars of her gates are **b.**	8689
	51:56	and their bows *will be* **b.**	3169
	52: 7	Then the city wall *was* **b through,**	1324
La	2: 9	their bars *he has* **b** and destroyed.	8689
	3: 4	and my flesh grow old and *has* **b** my bones.	8689
	3:16	*He has* **b** my teeth with gravel,	1756
Eze	6: 6	your incense altars **b down,**	1548
	21: 6	before them with **b** heart and bitter grief.	8695
	26: 2	The gate to the nations is **b,**	8689
	26:10	a city whose walls *have been* **b through.**	1324
	30:21	*I have* **b** the arm of Pharaoh king of Egypt.	8689
	30:22	the good arm as well as the **b one,**	8689
	31:12	its branches *lay* **b** in all the ravines of	8689
	32:28	*will be* **b** and will lie among	8689

Da	2:35	the gold *were* **b** to pieces at the same time	10182
	8: 8	of his power his large horn was **b** off,	8689
	8:22	*that* was **b** off represent four kingdoms	8689
	11: 4	his empire *will* be **b** up and parceled out	8689
	12: 7	of the holy people *has been* finally **b**,	5879
Hos	6: 7	Like Adam, they *have* **b** the covenant—	6296
	8: 1	the people *have* **b** my covenant and rebelled	6296
	8: 6	It will be **b** in pieces, that calf of Samaria	8646
Joel	1:17	the granaries *have* been **b** down,	2238
Am	9:11	I will repair its **b places**, restore its ruins,	7288
Mic	1: 7	All her idols *will* be **b** to pieces;	4198
Zec	9:10	and the battle bow *will* be **b**.	4162
Mal	2:11	Judah *has* **b** faith.	953
	2:14	because you *have* **b** faith with her,	953
Mt	14:20	up twelve basketfuls *of* **b pieces**	3083
	15:37	up seven basketfuls *of* **b pieces**	3083
	21:44	on this stone *will* be **b** to pieces,	5314
	24:43	and would not have let his house be **b** into.	1482
Mk	6:43	up twelve basketfuls *of* **b pieces** of bread	3083
	8: 8	up seven basketfuls *of* **b pieces**	3083
Lk	8:29	*he had* **b** his chains and had been driven by	1396
	9:17	up twelve basketfuls *of* **b pieces**	3083
	12:39	he would not have let his house be **b** into.	1482
	20:18	on that stone *will* be **b** to pieces,	5314
Jn	7:23	so that the law of Moses *may* not be **b**,	3395
	10:35	and the Scripture cannot be **b**—	3395
	19:31	they asked Pilate to *have* the legs be **b** and	2862
	19:36	"Not one of his bones *will* be **b**,"	5341
Ac	27:41	the stern *was* **b** to pieces by the pounding of	3395
Ro	11:17	If some of the branches *have been* **b** off,	1709
	11:19	"Branches *were* **b** off so that I could	1709
	11:20	But *they were* **b** off because of unbelief,	1709
1Ti	5:12	because *they have* **b** their first pledge.	119

BROKENHEARTED (4) [HEART]

Ps	34:18	the **b** and saves those who are crushed	4213+8689
	109:16	the poor and the needy and the **b**	3874+4222
	147: 3	He heals the **b** and binds up their wounds.	
			4213+8689
Isa	61: 1	He has sent me to bind up the **b**,	4213+8689

BROKENNESS (1) [BREAK]

Isa	65:14	from anguish of heart and wail in **b**	8691

BRONZE (159) [BRONZE-TIPPED]

Ge	4:22	who forged all kinds of tools out of **b**	5733
Ex	25: 3	gold, silver and **b**;	5733
	26:11	Then make fifty **b** clasps and put them in	5733
	26:37	And cast five **b** bases for them.	5733
	27: 2	and overlay the altar with **b**.	5733
	27: 3	Make all its utensils of **b**—	5733
	27: 4	Make a grating for it, a **b** network,	5733
	27: 4	a **b** ring at each of the four corners of	5733
	27: 6	for the altar and overlay them with **b**.	5733
	27:10	with twenty posts and twenty **b** bases and	5733
	27:11	with twenty posts and twenty **b** bases and	5733
	27:17	and hooks, and **b** bases.	5733
	27:18	and with **b** bases.	5733
	27:19	those for the courtyard, are to be of **b**.	5733
	30:18	"Make a **b** basin, with its bronze stand,	5733
	30:18	with its **b** stand, for washing,	5733
	31: 4	for work in gold, silver and **b**,	5733
	35: 5	an offering of gold, silver and **b**;	5733
	35:16	of burnt offering with its **b** grating, its poles	5733
	35:16	the **b** basin with its stand;	NIH
	35:24	or **b** brought it as an offering to the LORD,	5733
	35:32	for work in gold, silver and **b**,	5733
	36:18	They made fifty **b** clasps to fasten	5733
	36:38	with gold and made their five bases of **b**.	5733
	38: 2	and they overlaid the altar with **b**.	5733
	38: 3	They made all its utensils of **b**—	5733
	38: 4	a **b** network, to be under its ledge,	5733
	38: 5	They cast **b** rings to hold the poles for	NIH
	38: 5	for the four corners of the **b** grating.	5733
	38: 6	of acacia wood and overlaid them with **b**.	5733
	38: 8	They made the **b** basin and its bronze stand	5733
	38: 8	They made the bronze basin and its **b** stand	5733
	38:10	with twenty posts and twenty **b** bases,	5733
	38:11	and had twenty posts and twenty **b** bases,	5733
	38:17	The bases for the posts were **b**.	5733
	38:19	with four posts and four **b** bases.	5733
	38:20	and of the surrounding courtyard were **b**.	5733
	38:29	The **b** *from* the wave offering was 70 talents	5733
	38:30	the **b** altar with its bronze grating	5733
	38:30	with its **b** grating and all its utensils,	5733
	39:39	the **b** altar with its bronze grating, its poles	5733
	39:39	the bronze altar with its **b** grating, its poles	5733
Lev	6:28	but if it is cooked in a **b** pot,	5733
	26:19	like iron and the ground beneath you like **b**.	5733
Nu	4:13	the **b** altar and spread a purple cloth over it.	NIH
	16:39	the priest collected the **b** censers brought	5733
	21: 9	So Moses made a **b** snake and put it up on	5733
	21: 9	by a snake and looked at the **b** snake,	5733
	31:22	Gold, silver, **b**, iron, tin, lead	5733
Dt	28:23	The sky over your head will be **b**,	5733
	33:25	The bolts of your gates will be iron and **b**,	5733
Jos	6:19	All the silver and gold and the articles of **b**	5733
	6:24	the articles of **b** and iron into the treasury of	5733
	22: 8	with silver, gold, **b** and iron,	5733
Jdg	16:21	Binding him with **b** *shackles*,	5733
1Sa	17: 5	He had a **b** helmet on his head and wore	5733
	17: 5	of **b** weighing five thousand shekels;	5733
	17: 6	on his legs he wore **b** greaves,	5733
	17: 6	and a **b** javelin was slung on his back.	5733
	17:38	a coat of armor on him and a **b** helmet	5733

2Sa	8: 8	King David took a great quantity of **b**.	5733
	8:10	with him articles of silver and gold and **b**.	5733
	21:16	**b** spearhead weighed three hundred shekels	5733
	22:35	my arms can bend a bow of **b**.	5703
1Ki	4:13	with **b** gate bars);	5733
	7:14	a man of Tyre and a craftsman in **b**.	5733
	7:14	and experienced in all kinds of **b** work.	5733
	7:15	He cast two **b** pillars,	5733
	7:16	He also made two capitals of cast **b** to set	5733
	7:27	He also made ten movable stands of **b**;	5733
	7:30	Each stand had four **b** wheels	5733
	7:30	with **b** axles, and each had a basin resting	5733
	7:38	He then made ten **b** basins,	5733
	7:45	of the LORD were of burnished **b**.	5733
	7:47	the weight of the **b** was not determined.	5733
	8:64	the **b** altar before the LORD was too small	5733
	14:27	So King Rehoboam made **b** shields	5733
2Ki	16:14	The **b** altar that stood before	5733
	16:15	I will use the **b** altar for seeking guidance."	5733
	16:17	from the **b** bulls that supported it and set it	5733
	18: 4	into pieces the **b** snake Moses had made,	5733
	25: 7	with **b** shackles and took him to Babylon.	5733
	25:13	The Babylonians broke up the **b** pillars,	5733
	25:13	the movable stands and the **b** Sea that were	5733
	25:13	of the LORD and they carried the **b**	5733
	25:14	the **b** articles used in the temple service.	5733
	25:16	The **b** *from* the two pillars,	5733
	25:17	The **b** capital on top of one pillar was four	5733
	25:17	and pomegranates of **b** all around.	5733
1Ch	15:19	and Ethan were to sound the **b** cymbals;	5733
	18: 8	David took a great quantity of **b**,	5733
	18: 8	which Solomon used to make the **b** Sea,	5733
	18: 8	the pillars and various **b** articles.	5733
	18:10	of articles of gold and silver and **b**.	5733
	22: 3	and more **b** than could be weighed.	5733
	22:14	of **b** and iron too great to be weighed,	5733
	22:16	**b** and iron—craftsmen beyond number.	5733
	29: 2	silver for the silver, **b** for the bronze,	5733
	29: 2	silver for the silver, bronze for the **b**,	5733
	29: 7	of **b** and a hundred thousand talents of iron.	5733
2Ch	1: 5	But the **b** altar that Bezalel son of Uri,	5733
	1: 6	to the **b** altar before the LORD in the Tent	5733
	2: 7	**b** and iron, and in purple,	5733
	2:14	**b** and iron, stone and wood,	5733
	4: 1	He made a **b** altar twenty cubits long,	5733
	4: 9	and overlaid the doors with **b**.	5733
	4:16	of the LORD were of polished **b**.	5733
	4:18	that the weight of the **b** was not determined.	5733
	6:13	Now he had made a **b** platform,	5733
	7: 7	the **b** altar he had made could not hold	5733
	12:10	So King Rehoboam made **b** shields	5733
	24:12	workers in iron and **b** to repair the temple.	5733
	33:11	with **b** shackles and took him to Babylon.	5733
	36: 6	and bound him with **b** shackles to take him	5733
Ezr	8:27	darics, and two fine articles of polished **b**,	5733
Job	6:12	Is my flesh **b**?	5702
	37:18	hard as a mirror of **cast b**?	4607
	40:18	His bones are tubes of **b**,	5703
	41:27	like straw and **b** like rotten wood.	5703
Ps	18:34	my arms can bend a bow of **b**,	5703
	107:16	for he breaks down gates of **b** and cuts	5733
Isa	45: 2	down gates of **b** and cut through bars	5703
	48: 4	your forehead was **b**.	5703
	60:17	Instead of **b** I will bring you gold,	5733
	60:17	Instead of wood I will bring you **b**,	5733
Jer	1:18	a **b** wall to stand against the whole land—	5733
	6:28	They are **b** and iron; they all act corruptly.	5733
	15:12	from the north—or **b**?	5733
	15:20	a fortified wall of **b**;	5733
	39: 7	and bound him with **b** shackles to take him	5733
	52:11	with **b** shackles and took him to Babylon.	5733
	52:17	The Babylonians broke up the **b** pillars,	5733
	52:17	the movable stands and the **b** Sea that were	5733
	52:17	of the LORD and they carried all the **b**	5733
	52:18	the **b** articles used in the temple service.	5733
	52:20	The **b** *from* the two pillars,	5733
	52:20	the Sea and the twelve **b** bulls under it,	5733
	52:22	The **b** capital on top of	5733
	52:22	and pomegranates of **b** all around.	5733
Eze	1: 7	of a calf and gleamed like burnished **b**.	5733
	9: 2	They came in and stood beside the **b** altar.	5733
	27:13	they exchanged slaves and articles of **b**	5733
	40: 3	a man whose appearance was like **b**;	5733
Da	2:32	its belly and thighs of **b**,	10473
	2:35	Then the iron, the clay, the **b**,	10473
	2:39	Next, a third kingdom, one of **b**,	10473
	2:45	a rock that broke the iron, the **b**, the clay,	10473
	4:15	bound with iron and **b**,	10473
	4:23	but leave the stump, bound with iron and **b**,	10473
	5: 4	of **b**, iron, wood and stone.	10473
	5:23	of **b**, iron, wood and stone,	10473
	7:19	with its iron teeth and **b** claws—	10473
	10: 6	and legs like the gleam of burnished **b**,	5733
Mic	4:13	I will give you hoofs of **b**	5733
Zec	6: 1	between two mountains—mountains of **b**!	5733
Rev	1:15	His feet were like **b** glowing in a furnace,	5909
	2:18	and whose feet are like **burnished b**.	5909
	9:20	silver, **b**, stone and wood—	5905
	18:12	costly wood, **b**, iron and marble;	5910

BRONZE-TIPPED (1) [BRONZE]

Job	20:24	a **b** arrow pierces him.	5703

BROOCHES (1)

Ex	35:22	**b**, earrings, rings and ornaments.	2626

BROOD (9)

Nu	32:14	"And here you are, a **b** of sinners,	9551
Job	30: 8	A base and nameless **b**,	1201
Isa	1: 4	a people loaded with guilt, a **b** of evildoers,	2446
	57: 4	Are you not a **b** of rebels,	3529
Mt	3: 7	"*You* **b** of vipers! Who warned you to flee	1165
	12:34	*You* **b** of vipers, how can you who are evil	1165
	23:33	*You* **b** of vipers! How will you escape	1165
Lk	3: 7	"*You* **b** of vipers! Who warned you to flee	1165
2Pe	2:14	experts in greed—an accursed **b**!	5451

BROOK (7)

2Sa	17:20	"They crossed over the **b**."	4782+4784
1Ki	17: 4	You will drink from the **b**,	5707
	17: 6	and he drank from the **b**.	5707
	17: 7	Some time later the **b** dried up	5707
Ps	110: 7	He will drink from a **b** beside the way;	5707
Pr	18: 4	but the fountain of wisdom is a bubbling **b**.	5707
Jer	15:18	Will you be to me like a deceptive **b**,	NIH

BROOKS (KJV) See BROOK, RAVINES, RIVERS, WADI

BROOM (4)

1Ki	19: 4	He came to a **b** tree,	8413
Job	30: 4	and their food was the root of the **b** tree.	8413
Ps	120: 4	with burning coals of the **b** tree.	8413
Isa	14:23	I will sweep her with the **b** of destruction,"	4748

BROTH (3)

Jdg	6:19	Putting the meat in a basket and its **b** in	5348
	6:20	place them on this rock, and pour out the **b**.	5348
Isa	65: 4	and whose pots hold **b** of unclean meat;	5348

BROTHER (327) [BROTHER-IN-LAW, BROTHER'S, BROTHERHOOD, BROTHERLY, BROTHERS]

Ge	4: 2	Later she gave birth to his **b** Abel.	278
	4: 8	Now Cain said to his **b** Abel,	278
	4: 8	Cain attacked his **b** Abel and killed him.	278
	4: 9	"Where is your **b** Abel?"	278
	10:21	whose older **b** was Japheth;	278
	10:25	his **b** was named Joktan.	278
	14:13	a **b** of Eshcol and Aner,	278
	20: 5	and didn't he also say, 'He is my **b**'?	278
	20:13	say of me, "He is my **b**." '"	278
	24:16	"I am giving your **b** a thousand shekels	278
	22:20	she has borne sons to your **b** Nahor:	278
	22:21	Buz his **b**, Kemuel (the father of Aram),	278
	22:23	to Abraham's **b** Nahor.	278
	24:15	who was the wife of Abraham's **b** Nahor.	278
	24:29	Now Rebekah had a **b** named Laban,	278
	24:48	to get the granddaughter of my master's **b**	278
	24:53	he also gave costly gifts to her **b** and	278
	24:55	But her **b** and her mother replied,	278
	25:26	After this, his **b** came out,	278
	27: 6	I overheard your father say to your **b** Esau,	278
	27:11	"But my **b** Esau is a hairy man,	278
	27:23	like those of his **b** Esau;	278
	27:30	his **b** Esau came in from hunting.	278
	27:35	"Your **b** came deceitfully	278
	27:40	by the sword and you will serve your **b**.	278
	27:41	then I will kill my **b** Jacob.	278
	27:42	"Your **b** Esau is consoling himself with	278
	27:43	Flee at once to my **b** Laban in Haran.	278
	27:45	When your **b** is no longer angry with you	278
	28: 2	the daughters of Laban, your mother's **b**.	278
	28: 5	the Aramean, the **b** of Rebekah,	278
	29:10	his mother's **b**, and Laban's sheep,	278
	32: 3	of him to his **b** Esau in the land of Seir,	278
	32: 6	they said, "We went to your **b** Esau,	278
	32:11	I pray, from the hand of my **b** Esau,	278
	32:13	with him he selected a gift for his **b** Esau:	278
	32:17	"When my **b** Esau meets you and asks,	278
	33: 3	as he approached his **b**.	278
	33: 9	Esau said, "I already have plenty, my **b**.	278
	35: 1	when you were fleeing from your **b** Esau."	278
	35: 7	to him when he was fleeing from his **b**.	278
	36: 6	to a land some distance from his **b** Jacob.	278
	37:26	if we kill our **b** and cover up his blood?	278
	37:27	all, he is our **b**, our own flesh and blood."	278
	38: 8	to produce offspring for your **b**."	278
	38: 9	to keep from producing offspring for his **b**.	278
	38:29	his **b** came out, and she said,	278
	38:30	Then his **b**, who had the scarlet thread	278
	42: 4	Jacob did not send Benjamin, Joseph's **b**,	278
	42:15	unless your youngest **b** comes here.	278
	42:16	Send one of your number to get your **b**;	278
	42:20	But you must bring your youngest **b** to me,	278
	42:21	punished because of our **b**.	278
	42:34	But bring your youngest **b** to me	278
	42:34	Then I will give your **b** back to you,	278
	42:38	his **b** is dead and he is the only one left.	278
	43: 3	not see my face again unless your **b** is	278
	43: 4	If you will send our **b** along with us,	278
	43: 5	not see my face again unless your **b** is	278
	43: 6	by telling the man you had another **b**?"	278
	43: 7	'Do you have another **b**?'	278
	43: 7	'Bring your **b** down here'?	278
	43:13	Take your **b** also and go back to the man	278
	43:14	the man so that he will let your other **b**	278
	43:29	he looked about and saw his **b** Benjamin,	278

Ge 43:29 he asked, "Is this your youngest **b,** 278
43:30 Deeply moved at the sight of his **b,** 278
44:19 'Do you have a father or a **b?**' 278
44:20 His **b** is dead, 278
44:23 your youngest **b** comes down with you, 278
44:26 if our youngest **b** is with us we will go. 278
44:26 the man's face unless our youngest **b** is 278
45: 4 he said, "I am your **b** Joseph, 278
45:12 and so can my **b** Benjamin. 278
45:14 around his **b** Benjamin and wept, 278
48:19 his younger **b** will be greater than he, 278
Ex 4:14 "What about your **b,** Aaron the Levite? 278
7: 1 and your **b** Aaron will be your prophet. 278
7: 2 and your **b** Aaron is to tell Pharaoh to let 278
28: 1 "Have Aaron your **b** brought to you from 278
28: 2 Make sacred garments for your **b** Aaron, 278
28: 4 for your **b** Aaron and his sons, 278
28:41 on your **b** Aaron and his sons, 278
32:27 each killing his **b** and friend 278
Lev 16: 2 "Tell your **b** Aaron not to come whenever 278
18:14 " 'Do not dishonor your father's **b** 278
18:16 that would dishonor your **b.** 278
19:17 " 'Do not hate your **b** in your heart. 278
20:21 he has dishonored his **b.** 278
21: 2 his son or daughter, his **b,** 278
Nu 6: 7 his own father or mother or **b** or sister dies, 278
20: 8 and you and your **b** Aaron gather 278
20:14 "This is what your **b** Israel says: 278
27:13 as your **b** Aaron was, 278
36: 2 to give the inheritance of our **b** Zelophehad 278
Dt 1:16 whether the case is between **b** **Israelites** or 278
3:18 must cross over ahead of your **b** Israelites. 278
13: 6 If your **very own b,** 278+562+1201+3870
15: 2 from his fellow Israelite or **b,** 278
15: 3 you must cancel any debt your **b** owes you. 278
15: 7 or tightfisted toward your poor **b.** 278
15: 9 toward your needy **b** and give him nothing. 278
17:15 one who is not a **b** Israelite. 278
19:18 giving false testimony against his **b,** 278
19:19 then do to him as he intended to do to his **b.** 278
22: 1 If the **b** does not live near you or if you do 278
23: 7 Do not abhor an Edomite, for he is your **b.** 278
23:19 Do not charge your **b** interest, 278
23:20 but not a **b** **Israelite.** 278
24: 7 of his **b** Israelites and treats him as a slave 278
24:14 a **b** **Israelite** or an alien living in one 278
25: 3 your **b** will be degraded in your eyes. 278
25: 5 Her **husband's b** shall take her and marry her 3303
25: 6 of the dead **b** so that his name will not 278
25: 7 "My **husband's b** refuses to carry 3303
28:54 on his own **b** or the wife he loves 278
32:50 just as your **b** Aaron died on Mount Hor 278
Jos 15:17 Othniel son of Kenaz, Caleb's **b,** took it; 278
Jdg 1:13 Othniel son of Kenaz, Caleb's younger **b,** 278
3: 9 Othniel son of Kenaz, Caleb's younger **b,** 278
9: 3 for they said, "He is our **b.**" 278
9:18 of Shechem because he is your **b)**— 278
9:21 because he was afraid of his **b** Abimelech. 278
9:24 might be avenged on their **b** Abimelech and 278
20:28 up again to battle with Benjamin our **b,** 278
Ru 1:19 of land that belonged to our **b** Elimelech. 278
1Sa 14: 3 He was a son of Ichabod's **b** Ahitub son 278
17:28 When Eliab, David's oldest **b,** 278
20:29 in the town and my **b** has ordered me to 278
26: 6 Joab's **b,** "Who will go down into the camp 278
2Sa 1:26 I grieve for you, Jonathan my **b;** 278
2:22 How could I look your **b** Joab in the face?" 278
3:27 there, to avenge the blood of his **b** Asahel, 278
3:30 (Joab and his **b** Abishai murdered Abner 278
3:30 because he had killed their **b** Asahel in 278
4: 6 Recab and his **b** Baanah slipped away. 278
4: 9 David answered Recab and his **b** Baanah, 278
10:10 of Abishai his **b** and deployed them against 278
13: 3 Jonadab son of Shimea, David's **b.** 278
13: 4 my **b** Absalom's sister." 278
13: 7 of your **b** Amnon and prepare some food 278
13: 8 Tamar went to the house of her **b** Amnon, 278
13:10 to her **b** Amnon in his bedroom. 278
13:12 "Don't, my **b!**" she said to him. 278
13:20 Her **b** Absalom said to her, 278
13:20 "Has that Amnon, your **b,** been with you? 278
13:20 Be quiet now, my sister; he is your **b.** 278
13:20 And Tamar lived in her **b** Absalom's house, 278
13:26 please let my **b** Amnon come with us." 278
13:32 But Jonadab son of Shimea, David's **b,** 278
14: 7 'Hand over the one who struck his **b** down, 278
14: 7 for the life of his **b** whom he killed; 278
18: 2 of Joab, a third under Joab's **b** Abishai son 278
20: 9 Joab said to Amasa, "How are you, my **b?**" 278
20:10 and his **b** Abishai pursued Sheba son 278
21:21 Jonathan son of Shimeah, David's **b,** 278
23:18 the **b** of Joab son of Zeruiah was chief of 278
23:24 Asahel the **b** of Joab, 278
1Ki 1:10 or the special guard or his **b** Solomon. 278
2: 7 by me when I fled from your **b** Absalom. 278
2:15 and the kingdom has gone to my **b;** 278
2:21 be given in marriage to your **b** Adonijah." 278
2:22 after all, he is my older **b**— 278
9:13 towns are these you have given me, my **b?**" 278
13:30 over him and said, "Oh, my **b!**" 278
20:32 "Is he still alive? He is my **b.**" 278
20:33 "Yes, your **b** Ben-Hadad!" 278
1Ch 1:19 his **b** was named Joktan. 278
2:32 The sons of Jada, Shammai's **b:** 278
2:42 The sons of Caleb the **b** of Jerahmeel: 278
4:11 Shuhah's **b,** was the father of Mehir, 278

1Ch 7:16 His **b** was named Sheresh, 278
7:35 The sons of his **b** Helem, 278
8:39 The sons of his **b** Eshek: 278
11:20 the **b** of Joab was chief of the Three. 278
11:26 Asahel the **b** of Joab, 278
11:38 Joel the **b** of Nathan, Mibhar son of Hagri, 278
11:45 Jediael son of Shimri, his **b** Joha the Tizite, 278
19:11 under the command of Abishai his **b,** 278
19:15 they too fled before his **b** Abishai and went 278
20: 5 Elhanan son of Jair killed Lahmi the **b** 278
20: 7 Jonathan son of Shimea, David's **b,** 278
24:25 the **b** of Micah: 278
24:31 the oldest **b** were treated the same as those 278
26:22 Zetham and his **b** Joel. 278
27: 7 was Asahel the **b** of Joab; 278
27:18 Elihu, a **b** of David; 278
2Ch 31:12 and his **b** Shimei was next in rank. 278
31:13 under Conaniah and Shimei his **b,** 278
36: 4 a **b** of Jehoahaz, 278
36: 4 But Neco took Eliakim's **b** Jehoahaz 278
Ezr 7:18 You and your **b** **Jews** may 10017
Ne 7: 2 I put in charge of Jerusalem my **b** Hanani, 278
Job 30:29 I have become a **b** of jackals, 278
Ps 35:14 as though for my friend or **b.** 278
50:20 You speak continually against your **b** 278
Pr 17:17 and a **b** is born for adversity. 278
18: 9 in his work is **b** to one who destroys. 278
18:19 An offended **b** is more unyielding than 278
18:24 a friend who sticks closer than a **b.** 278
27:10 better a neighbor nearby than a **b** far away. 278
Ecc 4: 8 he had neither son nor **b.** 278
SS 8: 1 If only you were to me like a **b,** 278
Isa 9:19 no one will spare his **b.** 278
19: 2 **b** will fight against brother, 408
19: 2 brother will fight against **b,** 278
41: 6 each helps the other and says to his **b,** 278
Jer 9: 4 For every **b** is a deceiver, 278
22:18 for him: 'Alas, my **b!** 278
31:34 or a man his **b,** saying, 'Know the LORD,' 278
Eze 18:18 robbed his **b** and did what was wrong 278
38:21 Every man's sword will be against his **b.** 278
44:25 son or daughter, **b** or unmarried sister, 278
Am 1:11 Because he pursued his **b** with a sword, 278
Ob 1:10 of the violence against your **b** Jacob, 278
1:12 You should not look down on your **b** in 278
Mic 7: 2 each hunts his **b** with a net. 278
Hag 2:22 each by the sword of his **b.** 278
Mal 1: 2 "Was not Esau Jacob's **b?**" 278
Mt 4:18 Simon called Peter and his **b** Andrew. 81
4:21 James son of Zebedee and his **b** John. 81
5:22 that anyone who is angry with his **b** 81
5:22 Again, anyone who says to his **b,** 'Raca,' 81
5:23 that your **b** has something against you, 81
5:24 First go and be reconciled to your **b;** 81
7: 4 How can you say to your **b,** 81
10: 2 (who is called Peter) and his **b** Andrew; 81
10: 2 James son of Zebedee, and his **b** John; 81
10:21 "**B** will betray brother to death, 81
10:21 "Brother will betray **b** to death, 81
12:50 in heaven is my **b** and sister and mother." 81
14: 3 Herodias, his **b** Philip's wife, 81
17: 1 James and John the **b** of James, 81
18:15 "If your **b** sins against you, 81
18:15 you have won your **b** over. 81
18:21 how many times shall I forgive my **b** 81
18:35 unless you forgive your **b** from your heart." 81
22:24 **b** must marry the widow 81
22:25 he left his wife to his **b.** 81
22:26 to the second and third **b,** NIG
Mk 1:16 he saw Simon and his **b** Andrew casting 81
1:19 of Zebedee and his **b** John in a boat, 81
3:17 of Zebedee and his **b** John (to them he gave 81
3:35 Whoever does God's will is my **b** and sister 81
5:37 James and John the **b** of James. 81
6: 3 Isn't this Mary's son and the **b** of James, 81
6:17 his **b** Philip's wife, whom he had married. 81
12:19 "Moses wrote for us that if a man's **b** dies 81
12:19 the widow and have children for his **b.** 81
13:12 "**B** will betray brother to death, 81
13:12 "Brother will betray **b** to death, 81
Lk 3: 1 of Galilee, his **b** Philip tetrarch of Iturea 81
6:14 his **b** Andrew, James, John, Philip, 81
6:42 How can you say to your **b,** 'Brother, 81
6:42 How can you say to your brother, '**B,** 81
12:13 tell my **b** to divide the inheritance 81
15:27 'Your **b** has come,' he replied, 81
15:28 "The older **b** became angry and refused NIG
15:32 this **b** of yours was dead and is alive again; 81
17: 3 "If your **b** sins, rebuke him, 81
20:28 "Moses wrote for us that if a man's **b** dies 81
20:28 the widow and raise children for his **b.** 81
Jn 1:40 Andrew, Simon Peter's **b,** 81
1:41 to find his **b** Simon and tell him, 81
6: 8 Andrew, Simon Peter's **b,** spoke up, 81
11: 2 This Mary, whose **b** Lazarus now lay sick, 81
11:19 to comfort them in the loss of their **b.** 81
11:21 my **b** would not have died. 81
11:23 Jesus said to her, "Your **b** will rise again." 81
11:32 my **b** would not have died. 81
Ac 9:17 Placing his hands on Saul, he said, "**B** Saul, 81
12: 2 He had James, the **b** of John, 81
21:20 Then they said to Paul: "You see, **b,** 81
22:13 He stood beside me and said, '**B** Saul, 81
Ro 14:10 You, then, why do you judge your **b?** 81
14:10 Or why do you look down on your **b?** 81
14:15 If your **b** is distressed because 81
14:15 Do not by your eating destroy **your b** 1697S

Ro 14:21 or to do anything else that will cause your **b** 81
16:23 and my **b** Quartus send you their greetings. 81
1Co 1: 1 and our **b** Sosthenes, 81
5:11 a **b** but is sexually immoral or greedy, 81
6: 6 one **b** goes to law against another— 81
7:12 If any **b** has a wife who is not a believer 81
8:11 So this weak **b,** for whom Christ died, 81
8:13 if what I eat causes my **b** to fall into sin, 81
16:12 Now about our **b** Apollos: 81
2Co 1: 1 and Timothy our **b,** To the church of God 81
2:13 because I did not find my **b** Titus there. 81
8:18 along with him the **b** who is praised by all 81
8:22 with them our **b** who has often proved to us 81
12:18 I urged Titus to go to you and I sent our **b** 81
Gal 1:19 only James, the Lord's **b.** 81
Eph 6:21 the dear **b** and faithful servant in the Lord, 81
Php 2:25 my **b,** fellow worker and fellow soldier, 81
Col 1: 1 and Timothy our **b,** 81
4: 7 He is a dear **b,** a faithful minister 81
4: 9 our faithful and dear **b,** who is one of you. 81
1Th 3: 2 who is our **b** and God's fellow worker 81
4: 6 in this matter no one should wrong his **b** 81
2Th 3: 6 from every **b** who is idle and does not live 81
3:15 as an enemy, but warn him as a **b.** 81
Phm 1: 1 and Timothy our **b,** 81
1: 7 **b,** have refreshed the hearts of the saints. 81
1:16 but better than a slave, as a dear **b.** 81
1:16 both as a man and as a **b** in the Lord. NIG
1:20 **b,** that I may have some benefit from you 81
Heb 8:11 or a man his **b,** saying, 'Know the Lord,' 81
13:23 that our **b** Timothy has been released. 81
Jas 1: 9 The **b** in humble circumstances ought 81
2:15 Suppose a **b** or sister is without clothes 81
4:11 against his **b** or judges him speaks against 81
1Pe 5:12 whom I regard as a faithful **b,** 81
2Pe 3:15 just as our dear **b** Paul also wrote you with 81
1Jn 2: 9 to be in the light but hates his **b** is still in 81
2:10 Whoever loves his **b** lives in the light, 81
2:11 But whoever hates his **b** is in the darkness 81
3:10 nor is anyone who does not love his **b.** 81
3:12 to the evil one and murdered his **b.** 81
3:15 Anyone who hates his **b** is a murderer, 81
3:17 and sees his **b** in need but has no pity 81
4:20 anyone says, "I love God," yet hates his **b,** 81
4:20 For anyone who does not love his **b,** 81
4:21 Whoever loves God must also love his **b.** 81
5:16 If anyone sees his **b** commit a sin that does 81
Jude 1: 1 a servant of Jesus Christ and a **b** of James, 81
Rev 1: 9 your **b** and companion in the suffering 81

BROTHER'S (28) [BROTHER]

Ge 4: 9 "Am I my **b** keeper?" 278
4:10 Your **b** blood cries out to me from 278
4:11 to receive your **b** blood from your hand. 278
4:21 His **b** name was Jubal; 278
27:44 for a while until your **b** fury subsides. 278
38: 8 with your **b** wife and fulfill your duty to her 278
38: 9 so whenever he lay with his **b** wife, 278
Lev 18:16 not have sexual relations with your **b** wife; 278
20:21 " 'If a man marries his **b** wife, 278
Dt 22: 1 If you see your **b** ox or sheep straying, 278
22: 3 Do the same if you find **your b** donkey 2257S
22: 4 If you see your **b** donkey or his ox fallen on 278
25: 7 if a man does not want to marry his **b** wife, 3304
25: 7 to carry on his **b** name in Israel. 278
25: 9 his **widow** shall go up to him in 3304
25: 9 not build up his **b** family line." 278
Job 1:13 and drinking wine at the oldest **b** house, 278
1:18 and drinking wine at the oldest **b** house, 278
Pr 27:10 to your **b** house when disaster strikes you— 278
Hos 12: 3 In the womb he grasped his **b** heel; 278
Mt 7: 3 at the speck of sawdust in your **b** eye 81
7: 5 to remove the speck from your **b** eye. 81
Mk 3:19 the tetrarch because of Herodias, his **b** wife, 81
Lk 6:41 at the speck of sawdust in your **b** eye 81
6:42 to remove the speck from your **b** eye. 81
Ro 14:13 or obstacle in your **b** way. 81
1Jn 3:12 and his **b** were righteous. 81

BROTHER-IN-LAW (4) [BROTHER]

Ge 38: 8 **fulfill** *your* **duty to her as a b** 3302
Dt 25: 5 **fulfill the duty of a b** to her. 3302
25: 7 not **fulfill the duty of a b** to me." 3302
Jdg 4:11 the descendants of Hobab, Moses' **b,** 3162

BROTHERHOOD (3) [BROTHER]

Am 1: 9 disregarding a treaty of **b,** 278
Zec 11:14 breaking the **b** between Judah and Israel. 288
1Pe 2:17 Love the **b** of **believers,** fear God, 82

BROTHERLY (4) [BROTHER]

Ro 12:10 Be devoted to one another *in* **b** love. 5789
1Th 4: 9 Now about **b** **love** we do not need to write 5789
2Pe 1: 5 **b** kindness; and to brotherly kindness, love. 5789
1: 7 and to **b** **kindness,** love. 5789

BROTHERS (429) [BROTHER]

Ge 9:22 and told his two **b** outside. 278
9:25 The lowest of slaves will he be to his **b.**" 278
13: 8 your herdsmen and mine, for we are **b.** 278
16:12 he will live in hostility toward all his **b.**" 278
25:18 they lived in hostility toward all their **b.** 278
27:29 Be lord over your **b,** and may the sons 278

Ge	29: 4	Jacob asked the shepherds, "My **b**,	278
	34:11	Shechem said to Dinah's father and **b**,	278
	34:25	Simeon and Levi, Dinah's **b**,	278
	37: 2	was tending the flocks with his **b**,	278
	37: 4	When his **b** saw that their father loved him	278
	37: 5	and when he told it to his **b**,	278
	37: 8	His **b** said to him,	278
	37: 9	and he told it to his **b**.	278
	37:10	When he told his father as well as his **b**,	278
	37:10	and your **b** actually come and bow down to	278
	37:11	His **b** were jealous of him,	278
	37:12	Now his **b** had gone	278
	37:13	your **b** are grazing the flocks near Shechem.	278
	37:14	and see if all is well with your **b** and with	278
	37:16	He replied, "I'm looking for my **b**.	278
	37:17	So Joseph went after his **b** and found them	278
	37:23	So when Joseph came to his **b**,	278
	37:26	Judah said to his **b**,	278
	37:27	His **b** agreed.	278
	37:28	his **b** pulled Joseph up out of the cistern	NIH
	37:30	He went back to his **b** and said,	278
	38: 1	Judah left his **b** and went down to stay with	278
	38:11	he thought, "He may die too, just like his **b**.	278
	42: 3	of Joseph's **b** went down to buy grain	278
	42: 6	So when Joseph's **b** arrived,	278
	42: 7	As soon as Joseph saw his **b**,	278
	42: 8	Although Joseph recognized his **b**,	278
	42:13	they replied, "Your servants were twelve **b**,	278
	42:19	let one of your **b** stay here in prison,	278
	42:28	he said to his **b**,	278
	42:32	We were twelve **b**, sons of one father.	278
	42:33	Leave one of your **b** here with me,	278
	43:32	the **b** by themselves,	2157S
	44:14	in the house when Judah and his **b** came in,	278
	44:33	and let the boy return with his **b**.	278
	45: 1	when he made himself known to his **b**.	278
	45: 3	Joseph said to his **b**, "I am Joseph!	278
	45: 3	But his **b** were not able to answer him,	278
	45: 4	Joseph said to his **b**, "Come close to me."	278
	45:15	And he kissed all his **b** and wept over them.	278
	45:15	Afterward his **b** talked with him.	278
	45:16	that Joseph's **b** had come,	278
	45:17	Pharaoh said to Joseph, "Tell your **b**,	278
	45:24	Then he sent his **b** away,	278
	46:31	to his **b** and to his father's household,	278
	46:31	'My **b** and my father's household,	278
	47: 1	"My father and **b**, with their flocks	278
	47: 2	of his **b** and presented them before Pharaoh.	278
	47: 3	Pharaoh asked the **b**, "What is your	278
	47: 5	"Your father and your **b** have come to you,	278
	47: 6	settle your father and your **b** in the best part	278
	47:11	and his **b** in Egypt and gave them property	278
	47:12	Joseph also provided his father and his **b**	278
	48: 6	be reckoned under the names of their **b**.	278
	48:22	And to you, as one who is over your **b**,	278
	49: 5	"Simeon and Levi are **b**—	278
	49: 8	"Judah, your **b** will praise you;	278
	49:26	on the brow of the prince among his **b**.	278
	50: 8	of Joseph's household and his **b**	278
	50:14	with his **b** and all the others who had gone	278
	50:15	Joseph's **b** saw that their father was dead,	278
	50:17	I ask you to forgive your **b** the sins and	278
	50:18	His **b** then came and threw themselves	278
	50:24	Joseph said to his **b**, "I am about to die.	278
Ex	1: 6	and all his **b** and all that generation died,	278
	32:29	for you were against your own sons and **b**,	278
Lev	21:10	the one among his **b** who has had	278
Nu	8:26	They may assist their **b** in performing	278
	20: 3	"If only we had died when our **b** fell dead	278
	27: 9	give his inheritance to his **b**.	278
	27:10	If he has no **b**, give his inheritance	278
	27:10	give his inheritance to his father's **b**.	278
	27:11	If his father had no **b**,	278
Dt	1:16	Hear the disputes between your **b**	278
	1:28	Our **b** have made us lose heart.	278
	2: 4	about to pass through the territory of your **b**	278
	2: 8	So we went on past our **b** the descendants	278
	3:20	The LORD gives rest to your **b** as he has	278
	10: 9	or inheritance among their **b**;	278
	15: 7	If there is a poor man among your **b** in any	278
	15:11	be openhanded toward your **b** and toward	278
	17:15	He must be from among your own **b**.	278
	17:20	and not consider himself better than his **b**	278
	18: 2	shall have no inheritance among their **b**;	278
	18:15	a prophet like me from among your own **b**.	278
	18:18	a prophet like you from among their **b**;	278
	20: 8	Let him go home so that his **b** will	278
	25: 5	If **b** are living together and one of them dies	278
	33: 9	He did not recognize his **b**	278
	33:16	on the brow of the prince among his **b**.	278
	33:24	let him be favored by his **b**,	278
Jos	1:14	must cross over ahead of your **b**.	278
	1:14	You are to help **your b**	4392S
	2:13	my father and mother, my **b** and sisters,	278
	2:18	your **b** and all your family into your house.	278
	6:23	and mother and **b** and all who belonged	278
	14: 8	but my **b** who went up with me made	278
	17: 4	to give us an inheritance among our **b**."	278
	17: 4	along with the **b** of their father,	278
	22: 3	not deserted your **b** but have carried out	278
	22: 4	the LORD your God has given your **b** rest	278
	22: 7	on the west side of the Jordan with their **b**.)	278
	22: 8	and divide with your **b** the plunder	278
Jdg	1: 3	of Judah said to the Simeonites their **b**	278
	1:17	of Judah went with the Simeonites their **b**	278
	8:19	Gideon replied, "Those were my **b**,	278
	9: 1	to his mother's **b** in Shechem and said	278

Jdg	9: 3	the **b** repeated all this to the citizens	278+562
	9: 5	and on one stone murdered his seventy **b**,	278
	9:24	who had helped him murder his **b**.	278
	9:26	of Ebed moved with his **b** into Shechem,	278
	9:31	of Ebed and his **b** have come to Shechem	278
	9:41	and Zebul drove Gaal and his **b** out	278
	9:56	to his father by murdering his seventy **b**.	278
	11: 3	So Jephthah fled from his **b** and settled in	278
	16:31	Then his **b** and his father's whole family	
		went down to get him.	278
	18: 8	their **b** asked them, "How did you find	278
	18:14	the land of Laish said to their **b**,	278
	20:23	to battle against the Benjamites, our **b**?"	278
	21: 6	Now the Israelites grieved for their **b**,	278
	21:22	When their fathers or **b** complain to us,	278
1Sa	16:13	and anointed him in the presence of his **b**,	278
	17:17	of bread for your **b** and hurry to their camp.	278
	17:18	See how your **b** are and bring back	278
	17:22	ran to the battle lines and greeted his **b**.	278
	20:29	let me get away to see my **b**.'	278
	22: 1	of Adullam. When his **b**	278
	30:23	David replied, "No, my **b**,	278
2Sa	2:26	to stop pursuing their **b**?"	278
	2:27	the pursuit of their **b** until morning."	278
	19:12	You are my **b**, my own flesh and blood.	278
	19:41	"Why did our **b**, the men of Judah,	278
1Ki	1: 9	He invited all his **b**, the king's sons,	278
	12:24	Do not go up to fight against your **b**,	278
1Ch	4: 9	Jabez was more honorable than his **b**.	278
	4:27	but his **b** did not have many children;	278
	5: 2	and though Judah was the strongest of his **b**	278
	9:17	Akkub, Talmon, Ahiman and their **b**,	278
	9:25	Their **b** in their villages had to come	278
	9:32	Some of their Kohathite **b** were in charge	278
	13: 2	of our **b** throughout the territories of Israel,	278
	15:16	the leaders of the Levites to appoint their **b**	278
	15:17	from his **b**, Asaph son of Berekiah;	278
	15:17	and from their **b** the Merarites,	278
	15:18	and with them their **b** next in rank:	278
	23:32	under their **b** the descendants of Aaron,	278
	24:31	just as their **b** the descendants of Aaron did,	278
	28: 2	"Listen to me, my **b** and my people.	278
2Ch	11: 4	Do not go up to fight against your **b**.	278
	11:22	to be the chief prince among his **b**,	278
	19:10	his wrath will come on you and your **b**.	278
	21: 2	Jehoram's **b**, the sons of Jehoshaphat,	278
	21: 4	he put all his **b** to the sword along	278
	21:13	You have also murdered your own **b**,	278
	29:15	When they had assembled their **b**	278
	30: 7	Do not be like your fathers and **b**,	278
	30: 9	then your **b** and your children will	278
	35: 9	his **b**, and Hashabiah, Jeiel and Jozabad,	278
Ezr	3: 8	and the rest of their **b** (the priests and	278
	3: 9	Jeshua and his sons and Kadmiel	278
	3: 9	the sons of Henadad and their sons and **b**—	278
	6:20	for their **b** the priests and for themselves.	278
	8:18	and Sherebiah's sons and **b**, 18 men;	278
	8:19	and his **b** and nephews, 20 men.	278
	8:24	Hashabiah and ten of their **b**,	278
	10:18	of Jeshua son of Jozadak, and his **b**:	278
Ne	1: 2	Hanani, one of my **b**, came from Judah	278
	4:14	and fight for your **b**,	278
	4:23	nor my **b** nor my men nor the guards	278
	5: 1	a great outcry against their Jewish **b**.	278
	5: 8	we have bought back our Jewish **b** who	
		were sold	278
	5: 8	Now you are selling your **b**,	278
	5:10	I and my **b** and my men are also lending	278
	5:14	neither I nor my **b** ate the food allotted to	278
	10:29	all these now join their **b** the nobles,	278
	13:13	for distributing the supplies to their **b**.	278
Job	6:15	But my **b** are as undependable	278
	19:13	"He has alienated my **b** from me;	278
	19:17	I am loathsome to my own **b**.	1061+1201
	22: 6	You demanded security from your **b**	278
	42:11	All his **b** and sisters	278
	42:15	an inheritance along with their **b**.	278
Ps	22:22	I will declare your name to my **b**;	278
	69: 8	I am a stranger to my **b**,	278
	122: 8	For the sake of my **b** and friends, I will say,	278
	133: 1	and pleasant it is when **b** live together	278
Pr	6:19	a man who stirs up dissension among **b**.	278
	17: 2	will share the inheritance as one of the **b**.	278
Isa	3: 6	A man will seize one of his **b**	278
	66: 5	"Your **b** who hate you,	278
	66:20	And they will bring all your **b**,	278
Jer	7:15	just as I did all your **b**,	278
	9: 4	do not trust your **b**,	278
	12: 6	Your **b**, your own family—	278
	35: 3	and his **b** and all his sons—	278
Eze	11:15	"Son of man, your **b**—	278
	11:15	your **b** who are your blood relatives and	278
Hos	2: 1	"Say of your **b**, 'My people,'	278
	13:15	even though he thrives among his **b**.	278
Mic	5: 3	the rest of his **b** return to join the Israelites.	278
Mt	1: 2	Jacob the father of Judah and his **b**,	81
	1:11	the father of Jeconiah and his **b** at the time	81
	4:18	he saw two **b**, James son of Zebedee	81
	4:21	Going on from there, he saw two other **b**,	81
	5:47	And if you greet only your **b**,	81
	12:46	his mother and **b** stood outside,	81
	12:47	"Your mother and **b** are standing outside,	81
	12:48	"Who is my mother, and who are my **b**?"	81
	12:49	he said, "Here are my mother and my **b**.	81
	13:55	and aren't his **b** James, Joseph,	81
	19:29	And everyone who has left houses or **b**	81
	20:24	they were indignant with the two **b**.	81

Mt	22:25	Now there were seven **b** among us.	81
	23: 8	you have only one Master and you are all **b**.	81
	25:40	for one of the least of these **b** of mine,	81
	28:10	Go and tell my **b** to go to Galilee.	81
Mk	3:31	Then Jesus' mother and **b** arrived.	81
	3:32	"Your mother and **b** are outside looking	81
	3:33	"Who are my mother and my **b**?" he asked.	81
	3:34	"Here are my mother and my **b**!	81
	10:29	"no one who has left home or **b** or sisters	81
	10:30	**b**, sisters, mothers, children and fields—	81
	12:20	Now there were seven **b**.	81
Lk	8:19	Now Jesus' mother and **b** came to see him,	81
	8:20	"Your mother and **b** are standing outside,	81
	8:21	and **b** are those who hear God's word	81
	14:12	your **b** or relatives, or your rich neighbors;	81
	14:26	his wife and children, his **b** and sisters—	81
	16:28	for I have five **b**.	81
	18:29	or **b** or parents or children for the sake of	81
	20:29	Now there were seven **b**.	81
	21:16	You will be betrayed even by parents, **b**,	81
	22:32	you have turned back, strengthen your **b**."	81
Jn	2:12	down to Capernaum with his mother and **b**	81
	7: 3	Jesus' **b** said to him, "You ought to leave	81
	7: 5	For even his own **b** did not believe in him.	81
	7:10	However, after his **b** had left for the Feast,	81
	20:17	Go instead to my **b** and tell them,	81
	21:23	the **b** that this disciple would never die.	81
Ac	1:14	Mary the mother of Jesus, and with his **b**.	81
	1:16	"**B**, the Scripture had to be fulfilled which	81+467
	2:29	"**B**, I can tell you confidently that	81
	2:37	"**B**, what shall we do?"	81+467
	3:17	**b**, I know that you acted in ignorance,	81
	6: 3	**B**, choose seven men from	81
	7: 2	"**B** and fathers, listen to me!	81+467
	7:13	Joseph told his **b** who he was,	81
	7:26	by saying, 'Men, you are **b**;	81
	9:30	When the **b** learned of this,	81
	10:23	and some of the **b** from Joppa went along.	81
	11: 1	and the **b** throughout Judea heard that	81
	11:12	These six **b** also went with me,	81
	11:29	to provide help for the **b** living in Judea.	81
	12:17	"Tell James and the **b** about this," he said,	81
	13:15	to them, saying, "**B**, if you have a message	81+467
	13:26	"**B**, children of Abraham,	81+467
	13:38	"Therefore, my **b**, I want you to know that	81+467
	14: 2	and poisoned their minds against the **b**.	81
	15: 1	to Antioch and were teaching the **b**:	81
	15: 3	This news made all the **b** very glad.	81
	15: 7	"**B**, you know that some time ago God	
		made a choice among you	81+467
	15:13	When they finished, James spoke up: "**B**,	81+467
	15:22	two men who were leaders among the **b**.	81
	15:23	The apostles and elders, your **b**,	81
	15:32	to encourage and strengthen the **b**.	81
	15:33	by the **b** with the blessing of peace to return	81
	15:36	the **b** in all the towns where we preached	81
	15:40	commended by the **b** to the grace of	81
	16: 2	The **b** at Lystra and Iconium spoke well	81
	16:40	they met with the **b** and encouraged them.	81
	17: 6	they dragged Jason and some other **b** before	81
	17:10	the **b** sent Paul and Silas away to Berea.	81
	17:14	The **b** immediately sent Paul to the coast,	81
	18:18	Then he left the **b** and sailed for Syria,	81
	18:27	the **b** encouraged him and wrote to	81
	21: 7	the **b** and stayed with them for a day.	81
	21:17	the **b** received us warmly.	81
	22: 1	"**B** and fathers, listen now to my defense."	81+467
	22: 5	I even obtained letters from them to their **b**	81
	23: 1	and said, "My **b**, I have fulfilled my duty	81+467
	23: 5	"**B**, I did not realize that he was	81
	23: 6	called out in the Sanhedrin, "My **b**,	81+467
	28:14	There we found some **b** who invited us	81
	28:15	The **b** there had heard that we were coming,	81
	28:17	"My **b**, although I have done nothing	81+467
	28:21	and none of the **b** who have come	81
Ro	1:13	I do not want you to be unaware, **b**,	81
	7: 1	Do you not know, **b**—	81
	7: 4	So, my **b**, you also died to the law through	81
	8:12	Therefore, **b**, we have an obligation—	81
	8:29	be the firstborn among many **b**.	81
	9: 3	from Christ for the sake of my **b**,	81
	10: 1	**B**, my heart's desire and prayer to God for	81
	11:25	**b**, so that you may not be conceited:	81
	12: 1	Therefore, I urge you, **b**,	81
	15:14	I myself am convinced, my **b**,	81
	15:30	**b**, by our Lord Jesus Christ and by the love	81
	16:14	Patrobas, Hermas and the **b** with them.	81
	16:17	I urge you, **b**, to watch out	81
1Co	1:10	I appeal to you, **b**, in the name of our Lord	81
	1:11	My **b**, some from Chloe's	81
	1:26	**B**, think of what you were	81
	2: 1	When I came to you, **b**,	81
	3: 1	**B**, I could not address you as spiritual but	81
	4: 6	**b**, I have applied these things to myself	81
	6: 8	and you do this to your **b**.	81
	7:24	**B**, each man, as responsible to God,	81
	7:29	What I mean, **b**, is that the time is short.	81
	8:12	When you sin against your **b** in this way	81
	9: 5	as do the other apostles and the Lord's **b**	81
	10: 1	of the fact, **b**, that our forefathers were all	81
	11:33	my **b**, when you come together to eat,	81
	12: 1	Now about spiritual gifts, **b**,	81
	14: 6	**b**, if I come to you and speak in tongues,	81
	14:20	**B**, stop thinking like children.	81
	14:26	What then shall we say, **b**?	81
	14:39	Therefore, my **b**, be eager to prophesy,	81
	15: 1	Now, **b**, I want to remind you of	81

1Co 15: 6	*to* more than five hundred of the **b** at	81
15:31	I die every day—I mean that, **b**—	81
15:50	I declare to you, **b**, that flesh and blood	
	cannot inherit	81
15:58	Therefore, my dear **b**, stand firm.	81
16:11	I am expecting him along with the **b**.	81
16:12	to go to you with the **b**.	81
16:15	of the saints. I urge you, **b**,	81
16:20	All the **b** here send you greetings.	81
2Co 1: 8	We do not want you to be uninformed, **b**,	81
8: 1	And now, **b**, we want you to know about	81
8:23	as for our **b**, they are representatives	81
9: 3	the **b** in order that our boasting about you	81
9: 5	the **b** to visit you in advance and finish	81
11: 9	for the **b** who came from Macedonia	81
11:26	and in danger from **false b**.	6012
13:11	Finally, **b**, good-by.	81
Gal 1: 2	the **b** with me, To the churches in Galatia:	81
1:11	I want you to know, **b**, that the gospel	81
2: 4	some **false b** had infiltrated our ranks	6012
3:15	**B**, let me take an example	81
4:12	I plead with you, **b**, become like me,	81
4:28	you, **b**, like Isaac, are children of promise.	81
4:31	**b**, we are not children of the slave woman,	81
5:11	**B**, if I am still preaching circumcision,	81
5:13	You, my **b**, were called to be free.	81
6: 1	**B**, if someone is caught in a sin,	81
6:18	The grace of our Lord Jesus Christ be with	
	your spirit, **b**.	81
Eph 6:23	Peace *to* the **b**, and love with faith	81
Php 1:12	Now I want you to know, **b**,	81
1:14	*of* the **b** in the Lord have been encouraged	81
3: 1	Finally, my **b**, rejoice in the Lord!	81
3:13	**B**, I do not consider myself yet	81
3:17	in following my example, **b**, and take note	81
4: 1	my **b**, you whom I love and long for,	81
4: 8	Finally, **b**, whatever is true,	81
4:21	The **b** who are with me send greetings.	81
Col 1: 2	the holy and faithful **b** in Christ at Colosse:	81
4:15	Give my greetings to the **b** at Laodicea,	81
1Th 1: 4	For we know, **b** loved by God,	81
2: 1	**b**, that our visit to you was not a failure.	81
2: 9	you remember, **b**, our toil and hardship;	81
2:14	**b**, became imitators of God's churches	81
2:17	But, **b**, when we were torn away from you	81
3: 7	Therefore, **b**, in all our distress	81
4: 1	**b**, we instructed you how to live in order	81
4:10	the **b** throughout Macedonia.	81
4:10	we urge you, **b**, to do so more and more.	81
4:13	**B**, we do not want you to be ignorant	81
5: 1	**b**, about times and dates we do not need	81
5: 4	But you, **b**, are not in darkness so	81
5:12	Now we ask you, **b**, to respect those	81
5:14	And we urge you, **b**, warn those	81
5:25	**B**, pray for us.	81
5:26	Greet all the **b** with a holy kiss.	81
5:27	the Lord to have this letter read *to* all the **b**.	81
2Th 1: 3	We ought always to thank God for you, **b**,	81
2: 1	to him, we ask you, **b**,	81
2:13	**b** loved by the Lord,	81
2:15	So then, **b**, stand firm and hold to	81
3: 1	**b**, pray for us that the message of	81
3: 6	the Lord Jesus Christ, we command you, **b**,	81
3:13	for you, **b**, never tire of doing what is right.	81
1Ti 4: 6	If you point these things out *to* the **b**,	81
5: 1	Treat younger men as **b**,	81
6: 2	for them because they are **b**.	81
2Ti 4:21	Linus, Claudia and all the **b**.	81
Heb 2:11	So Jesus is not ashamed to call them **b**.	81
2:12	"I will declare your name *to* my **b**;	81
2:17	For this reason he had to be made like his **b**	81
3: 1	holy **b**, who share in the heavenly calling.	81
3:12	See to it, **b**, that none of you has a sinful,	81
7: 5	that is, their **b**—	81
7: 5	their **b** are descended from Abraham.	NIG
10:19	Therefore, **b**, since we have confidence	81
13: 1	Keep on **loving each other as b**.	5789
13:22	**B**, I urge you to bear with my word	81
Jas 1: 2	Consider it pure joy, my **b**,	81
1:16	Don't be deceived, my dear **b**.	81
1:19	My dear **b**, take note of this:	81
2: 1	My **b**, as believers in our	81
2: 5	my dear **b**: Has God not chosen	81
2:14	What good is it, my **b**, if a man claims	81
3: 1	to be teachers, my **b**, because you know	81
3:10	My **b**, this should not be.	81
3:12	My **b**, can a fig tree bear olives,	81
4:11	**B**, do not slander one another.	81
5: 7	Be patient, then, **b**, until the Lord's coming.	81
5: 9	Don't grumble against each other, **b**,	81
5:10	**B**, as an example of patience in the face	81
5:12	Above all, my **b**, do not swear—	81
5:19	My **b**, if one of you should wander from	81
1Pe 1:22	so that you have sincere **love for** your **b**,	5789
3: 8	be sympathetic, **love as b**,	5790
5: 9	because you know that your **b** throughout	82
2Pe 1:10	Therefore, my **b**, be all the more eager	81
1Jn 3:13	Do not be surprised, my **b**,	81
3:14	because we love our **b**.	81
3:16	we ought to lay down our lives for our **b**.	81
3Jn 1: 3	It gave me great joy to have some **b** come	81
1: 5	in what you are doing for the **b**,	81
1:10	he refuses to welcome the **b**.	81
Rev 6:11	of their fellow servants and **b** who were to	81
12:10	For the accuser *of* our **b**,	81
19:10	and with your **b** who hold to the testimony	81
22: 9	with you and with your **b** the prophets and	81

BROUGHT (763) [BRING]

Ge 2:19	*He* **b** them to the man	995
2:22	and *he* **b** her to the man.	995
4: 1	the help of the Lord *I* have **b** forth	7865
4: 3	the course of time Cain **b** some of the fruits	995
4: 4	But Abel **b** fat portions from some of	995
8: 9	the dove and **b** it **back** to himself in the ark.	995
14:16	the goods and **b back** his relative Lot	8740
14:18	of Salem **b** out bread and wine.	3655
15: 7	who **b** you out of Ur of the Chaldeans	3655
15:10	Abram **b** all these to him,	4374
18: 4	*Let* a little water **be b**,	4374
18: 8	*He* then **b** some curds and milk and the calf	4374
19:17	As soon as they *had* **b** them out,	3655
19:29	and *he* **b** Lot out of the catastrophe	8938
20: 9	that *you* have **b** such great guilt upon me	995
20:14	Then Abimelech **b** sheep and cattle	4374
21: 6	Sarah said, "God *has* **b** me laughter,	6913
21:27	So Abraham **b** sheep and cattle	4374
24: 7	who **b** me out of my father's household	4374
24:32	Straw and fodder *were* **b** for the camels,	5989
24:53	the servant **b** out gold and silver jewelry	3655
24:67	Isaac **b** her into the tent	995
26:10	and *you would have* **b** guilt upon us."	995
27:14	and got them and **b** them to his mother,	995
27:25	Jacob **b** it to him and he ate;	5602
27:25	and *he* **b** some wine and he drank.	995
27:31	He too prepared some tasty food and **b** it	995
27:33	then, that hunted game and **b** it to me?	995
29:13	and kissed him and **b** him to his home,	995
29:22	So Laban **b together** all the people of	665
30:14	which *he* **b** to his mother Leah.	995
33:11	Please accept the present that *was* **b** to you,	995
34:30	"You have **b trouble** *on* me by making me	6579
37: 2	*he* **b** their father a bad report about them.	995
38:25	*As* she *was being* **b** out,	3655
39:14	"this Hebrew *has been* **b** to us	995
39:17	"That Hebrew slave *you* **b** us came to me	995
41:14	and he *was* **quickly b** from the dungeon.	8132
43: 2	when they had eaten all the grain *they had* **b**	995
43:18	"We *were* **b** here because of the silver	995
43:21	So *we have* **b** it **back** with us.	8740
43:22	also **b** additional silver with us to buy food.	3718
43:23	Then *he* **b** Simeon **out** to them.	3655
43:26	him the gifts they had **b** into the house,	928+3338
44: 8	even **b back** to you from the land of Canaan	8740
46:32	and *they have* **b along** their flocks and herds	995
47: 7	**b** his father Jacob **in**	995
47:14	and he **b** it to Pharaoh's palace.	995
47:17	So *they* **b** their livestock to Joseph,	995
47:17	And *he* **b** them through that year with food	5633
48:10	So Joseph **b** his sons **close** to him,	5602
48:13	and **b** them **close** to him.	5602
Ex 3:12	When you *have* **b** the people **out** of Egypt,	3655
4:29	Moses and Aaron **b together** all the elders	665
5:22	why *have you* **b trouble** upon this people?	8317
5:23	*he has* **b trouble** upon this people,	8317
6: 7	who **b** you **out** from under the yoke of	3655
8:12	to the Lord about the frogs *he had* **b**	8492
9:19	every man and animal that *has* not **been b**	665
10: 8	Moses and Aaron *were* **b back** to Pharaoh.	8740
10:13	By morning the wind *had* **b** the locusts;	5951
12:17	on this very day that *I* **b** your divisions **out**	3655
12:39	With the dough *they* had **b** from Egypt,	3655
12:51	the Lord **b** the Israelites **out** of Egypt	3655
13: 3	Lord **b** you **out** of it with a mighty hand.	3655
13: 9	For the Lord **b** you **out** of Egypt	3655
13:14	'With a mighty hand the Lord **b** us **out**	3655
13:16	on your forehead that the Lord **b** us **out**	3655
14:11	in Egypt *that you* **b** us to the desert to die?	4374
14:20	Throughout the night the cloud **b** darkness	2118
15:19	**b** the waters of the sea **back**	8740
15:26	not bring on you any of the diseases *I* **b** on	8492
16: 3	but *you have* **b** us **out** into this desert	3655
16: 6	that it was the Lord *who* **b** you **out**	3655
16:32	in the desert when I **b** you **out** of Egypt.' "	3655
18: 1	how the Lord *had* **b** Israel **out** of Egypt.	3655
18:12	**b** a burnt offering and other sacrifices	4374
18:16	a dispute, *it is* **b** to me,	995
18:26	The difficult cases *they* **b** to Moses,	995
19: 4	on eagles' wings and **b** you to myself.	995
19: 8	Moses **b** their answer **back** to the Lord.	8740
20: 2	who **b** you **out** of Egypt,	3655
28: 1	"Have Aaron your brother **b** to you from	7928
29:46	who **b** them **out** of Egypt so	3655
32: 1	As for this fellow Moses who **b** us **up** out	6590
32: 3	and **b** them to Aaron.	995
32: 4	O Israel, who **b** you **up** out of Egypt."	6590
32: 7	whom *you* **b up** out of Egypt,	6590
32: 8	O Israel, who **b** you **up** out of Egypt.'	6590
32:11	whom *you* **b** us **out** of Egypt	3655
32:12	'It was with evil intent *that he* **b** them **out,**	3655
32:23	As for this fellow Moses who **b** us **up** out	6590
33: 1	you and the people *you* **b up** out of Egypt,	6590
35:21	and whose heart moved him came and **b**	995
35:22	came and **b** gold jewelry of all kinds:	995
35:23	or hides of sea cows **b** them.	995
35:24	or bronze **b** it as an offering to the Lord,	995
35:24	for any part of the work **b** it.	995
35:25	with her hands and **b** what she had spun—	995
35:27	The leaders **b** onyx stones and other gems	995
35:28	They also **b** spices and olive oil for the light	NIH
35:29	and women who were **b** to carry out	995
36: 3	the offerings the Israelites *had* **b** to carry out	995
39:33	Then *they* **b** the tabernacle to Moses:	995
40:21	Then *he* **b** the ark into the tabernacle	995

Lev 6:30	But any sin offering whose blood is **b** into	995
8: 6	**b** Aaron and his sons **forward**	7928
8:13	**b** Aaron's sons **forward,**	7928
8:24	**b** Aaron's sons **forward**	7928
9: 9	His sons **b** the blood to him,	7928
9:15	then **b** the offering that was for the people.	7928
9:16	**b** the burnt offering and offered it in	7928
9:17	*He* also **b** the grain offering,	7928
10:15	the breast that was waved *must* **be b** with	995
11:45	I am the Lord who **b** you **up** out of Egypt	6590
13: 2	*he must* be **b** to Aaron the priest or to one	995
13: 9	*he must* **be b** to the priest.	995
14: 2	when *he* is **b** to the priest:	995
14: 4	and hyssop *be* **b** for the one to be cleansed.	4374
16:27	whose blood was **b** into	995
19:36	who **b** you **out** of Egypt.	3655
22:33	who **b** you **out** of Egypt to be your God.	3655
23:15	the day you **b** the sheaf of	995
23:43	in booths when I **b** them **out** of Egypt.	3655
24:11	so *they* **b** him to Moses.	995
25:38	who **b** you **out** of Egypt to give you	3655
25:42	whom *I* **b** out of Egypt,	3655
25:55	whom *I* **b** out of Egypt.	3655
26:13	who **b** you **out** of Egypt so	3655
26:45	with their ancestors whom *I* **b** out	3655
Nu 6:13	*be* **b** to the entrance to the Tent of Meeting.	995
7: 3	*They* **b** as their gifts before	995
7:10	the leaders **b** their offerings	7928
7:12	The *one who* **b** his offering on	7928
7:18	the leader of Issachar, **b** his **offering.**	7928
7:19	offering *he* was one silver plate weighing	7928
7:24	of the people of Zebulun, **b** his offering.	NIH
7:30	of the people of Reuben, **b** his offering.	NIH
7:36	of the people of Simeon, **b** his offering.	NIH
7:42	of the people of Gad, **b** his offering.	NIH
7:48	of the people of Ephraim, **b** his offering.	NIH
7:54	of the people of Manasseh, **b** his offering.	NIH
7:60	of the people of Benjamin, **b** his offering.	NIH
7:66	of the people of Dan, **b** his offering.	NIH
7:72	of the people of Asher, **b** his offering.	NIH
7:78	of the people of Naphtali, **b** his offering.	NIH
11:11	"Why *have* you **b** *this* **trouble**	8317
11:24	He **b together** seventy of their elders	665
11:31	*It* **b** them **down** all around the camp to	5759
12:14	after that *she can* **be b back**."	665
12:15	people did not move on till she was **b back.**	665
14:13	By your power *you* **b** these people **up** from	6590
15:25	for it was not intentional and they *have* **b** to	995
15:33	Those who found him gathering wood **b**	
	him to Moses	7928
15:41	who **b** you **out** of Egypt to be your God.	3655
16: 9	of the Israelite community and **b** you **near**	7928
16:10	**b** you and all your fellow Levites **near**	7928
16:13	Isn't it enough that *you have* **b** us **up** out of	6590
16:14	*you* haven't **b** us into a land flowing	995
16:39	the priest collected the bronze censers **b**	7928
17: 9	Then Moses **b** out all the staffs from	3655
20:16	and sent an angel and **b** us **out** of Egypt.	3655
21: 5	"Why *have you* **b** us **up** out of Egypt to die	6590
23: 7	"Balak **b** me from Aram,	5663
23:11	*I* **b** you to curse my enemies,	4374
23:22	God **b** them **out** of Egypt;	3655
24: 8	"God **b** them **out** of Egypt;	3655
25: 6	Then an Israelite man **b** to his family	7928
27: 5	So Moses **b** their case before the Lord	7928
31:12	and **b** the captives, spoils and plunder	995
31:50	So *we have* **b** as an offering to the Lord	7928
31:54	and commanders of hundreds and **b** it into	995
32:17	ahead of the Israelites until *we have* **b** them	995
33: 4	the Lord *had* **b** judgment on their gods.	6913
Dt 1:25	*they* **b** it **down** to us and reported,	3718
1:27	so *he* **b** us **out** of Egypt to deliver us into	3655
4:20	and **b** you **out** of the iron-smelting furnace,	3655
4:37	*he* **b** you **out** of Egypt by his Presence	3655
5: 6	who **b** you **out** of Egypt,	3655
5:15	and that the Lord your God **b** you **out**	3655
6:12	who **b** you **out** of Egypt,	3655
6:21	in Egypt, but the Lord **b** us **out** of Egypt	3655
6:23	But *he* **b** us **out** from there to bring us in	3655
7: 8	to your forefathers that he **b** you **out** with	3655
7:19	the Lord your God **b** you **out.**	3655
8:14	who **b** you **out** of Egypt,	3655
8:15	He **b** you water **out** of hard rock.	3655
9: 4	"The Lord *has* **b** me here	995
9:12	because your people whom *you* **b** out	3655
9:28	by your great power and **b** of Egypt	3655
9:28	the country from which *you* **b** us will say,	3655
9:28	*he* **b** them **out** to put them to death in	3655
9:29	that *you* **b** out by your great power	3655
11: 4	and how the Lord **b** lasting **ruin** *on* them.	6
11:29	When the Lord your God *has* **b** you into	995
13: 5	who **b** you **out** of Egypt and redeemed you	3655
13:10	who **b** you **out** of Egypt,	3655
16: 1	in the month of Abib he **b** you **out** of Egypt	3655
17: 4	**been b** to your **attention,**	2256+5583+9048
20: 1	who **b** you **up** out of Egypt,	6590
22:21	*be* **b** to the door of her father's house	3655
26: 8	So the Lord **b** us **out** of Egypt with	3655
26: 9	He **b** us to this place and gave us this land,	995
29:25	with them when he **b** them **out** of Egypt.	3655
29:27	*he* **b** on it all the curses written in this book.	995
31:20	When I *have* **b** them into the land flowing	995
Jos 2:18	unless *you have* **b** your father and mother,	665
6:23	the spying went in and **b** out Rahab,	3655
6:23	*They* **b out** her entire family and put them	3655
7:23	**b** them to Joshua and all the Israelites	995
7:25	"Why *have you* **b** *this* **trouble** on us?	6579

Jos	8:23	the king of Ai alive and **b** him to Joshua.	7928
	10:23	**b** the five kings **out**	3655
	10:24	When they had **b** these kings to Joshua,	3655
	14: 7	And I **b** him **back** a report according	8740
	18: 1	was **b** under their **control,**	3899
	24: 5	and I **b** you **out.**	3655
	24: 6	When I **b** your fathers **out** of Egypt,	3655
	24: 7	he **b** the sea over them and covered them.	995
	24: 8	" 'I **b** you to the land of	995
	24:17	**b** us and our fathers **up**	6590
	24:32	which the Israelites had **b** **up** from Egypt,	6590
Jdg	1: 7	They **b** him to Jerusalem, and he died there.	995
	2: 1	"I **b** you **up** out of Egypt and led you into	6590
	2:12	who had **b** them **out** of Egypt.	3655
	5:25	for nobles she **b** him curdled milk.	7928
	6: 8	I **b** you **up** out of Egypt,	6590
	6:19	he **b** them **out** and offered them to him	3655
	7:25	the Midianites and **b** the heads of Oreb	995
	12: 9	**b** in thirty young women **as wives**	995
	16: 8	of the Philistines **b** her seven fresh thongs	6590
	16:31	They **b** him **back** and buried him	6590
	18: 3	in there and asked him, "Who **b** you here?	995
Ru	1:21	but the LORD has **b** me **back** empty.	8740
	1:21	the Almighty has **b** misfortune upon me."	8317
	2:18	also **b** out and gave her what she had left	3655
1Sa	1:24	**b** him to the house of the LORD at Shiloh.	995
	1:25	they **b** the boy to Eli,	995
	2:14	for himself whatever the fork **b** **up.**	6590
	4: 4	and they **b** back the ark of the covenant of	5951
	4:17	The man who **b** the **news** replied,	1413
	5: 6	he **b** devastation upon them	9037
	5:10	**b** the ark of the god of Israel **around**	6015
	6: 9	the LORD has **b** this great disaster on us.	6913
	8: 8	from the day I **b** them **up** out of Egypt	6590
	9:22	Then Samuel **b** Saul and his servant into	995
	10:18	'I **b** Israel **up** out of Egypt,	6590
	10:20	**b** all the tribes of Israel **near,**	7928
	10:21	Then he **b** forward the tribe of Benjamin,	7928
	10:23	They ran and **b** him **out,**	4374
	10:27	They despised him and **b** him no gifts.	995
	12: 6	and Aaron and your forefathers **up** **out**	6590
	12: 8	**b** your forefathers **out**	3655
	14:34	So everyone **b** his ox that night	5602
	14:45	he who has **b** about this great deliverance	6913
	15:15	"The soldiers **b** them from the Amalekites;	995
	15:20	the Amalekites and **b** **back** Agag their king.	995
	16:12	So he sent and had him **b** **in.**	995
	17:30	then turned away to someone else and **b** **up**	606
	17:54	the Philistine's head and **b** it to Jerusalem,	995
	17:57	Abner took him and **b** him before Saul,	995
	18:27	He **b** their foreskins and presented	995
	19: 7	He **b** him to Saul,	995
	20: 8	for you have **b** him into a covenant	995
	21: 8	I haven't **b** my sword	4374
	23: 6	of Ahimelech had **b** the ephod **down**	3718
	25:27	which your servant has **b** to my master,	995
	25:31	when the LORD has **b** my master **success,**	3512
	25:35	from her hand what she had **b** him and said,	995
	25:39	Nabal's wrongdoing **down**	8740
	27:11	not leave a man or woman alive to be **b**	995
	30: 7	Abiathar **b** it to him,	5602
	30:11	an Egyptian in a field and **b** him to David.	4374
	30:19	David **b** everything **back.**	8740
2Sa	1: 5	to the young man who **b** him the **report,**	5583
	1:10	the band on his arm and have **b** them here	995
	1:13	to the young man who **b** him the **report,**	5583
	2: 8	of Saul and **b** him over to Mahanaim.	6296
	3:22	from a raid and **b** with them a great deal	995
	3:26	and they **b** him **back** from the well of Sirah.	8740
	4: 8	They **b** the head of Ish-Bosheth to David	995
	6: 1	David again **b** together out	665
	6: 3	the ark of God on a new cart and **b** it from	5951
	6:12	and **b** up the ark of God from the house	6590
	6:15	while he and the entire house of Israel **b** **up**	6590
	6:17	They **b** the ark of the LORD and set it	995
	7: 6	in a house from the day I **b** the Israelites **up**	6590
	7:18	that you have **b** me this far?	995
	8: 2	to David and **b** tribute.	5951
	8: 6	to him and **b** tribute.	5951
	8: 7	to the officers of Hadadezer and **b** them	995
	8:10	Joram **b** with him articles of silver and gold	928+2118+3338
	9: 5	So King David had him **b** from Lo Debar,	2256+4374+8938
	10:16	Hadadezer had Arameans **b** from beyond	3655
	11:27	David had her **b** to his house,	665
	12:31	and **b** out the people who were there,	3655
	13:10	the bread she had prepared and **b** it	995
	14: 2	had a wise woman **b**	4374
	14:13	the king has not **b** back his banished son?	8740
	14:23	and **b** Absalom **back** to Jerusalem.	995
	16: 2	"Why have you **b** these?"	4200
	17:28	**b** bedding and bowls and articles of pottery.	NIH
	17:28	They also **b** wheat and barley,	5602
	21:13	David **b** the bones of Saul	6590
	22:20	He **b** me **out** into a spacious place;	3655
	23:10	The LORD **b** about a great victory.	6913
	23:12	and the LORD **b** about a great victory.	6913
1Ki	1: 3	a Shunammite, and her to the king.	995
	1:53	and they **b** him **down** from the altar.	3718
	2:19	He had a throne **b** for the king's mother,	8492
	2:40	So Shimei went away and **b** the slaves **back**	935
	3: 1	He **b** her to the City of David	995
	3:24	So they **b** a sword for the king.	995
	4:21	These countries **b** tribute	5602
	4:28	They also **b** to the proper place their quotas	995
	7:13	King Solomon sent to Tyre and **b** Huram,	4374

1Ki	7:51	of the LORD was finished, he **b** **in**	995
	8: 4	and they **b** **up** the ark of the LORD and	6590
	8: 6	then **b** the ark of the LORD's covenant	995
	8:16	**b** my people Israel **out**	3655
	8:21	with our fathers when he **b** them **out**	3655
	8:51	whom you **b** **out** of Egypt,	3655
	8:53	**b** our fathers **out** of Egypt."	3655
	9: 9	who **b** their fathers **out** of Egypt,	3655
	9: 9	the LORD **b** all this disaster on them.' "	935
	9:28	They sailed to Ophir and **b** back 420 talents	4374
	10:10	so many spices **b** **in** as those the queen	995
	10:11	(Hiram's ships **b** gold from Ophir;	5951
	10:11	and from there they **b** great cargoes	995
	10:25	everyone who came **b** a gift—	995
	11:20	whom Tahpenes **b** **up** in the royal palace.	1694
	12:28	O Israel, who **b** you **up** out of Egypt."	6590
	13:20	to the old prophet who had **b** him **back.**	8740
	13:23	the prophet who had **b** him **back** saddled his donkey	8740
	13:26	When the prophet who had **b** him **back**	8740
	13:29	and **b** it **back** to his own city to mourn	8740
	15:15	He **b** into the temple of the LORD	935
	17: 6	The ravens **b** him bread and meat in	995
	17:20	have you **b** tragedy also	8317
	18:40	and Elijah had them **b** **down** to	3718
	21:13	and sat opposite him and **b** charges against	6386
	22: 6	the king of Israel **b** together the prophets—	7695
	22:37	So the king died and was **b** to Samaria,	995
2Ki	2:20	So they **b** it to him.	4374
	4: 5	They **b** the jars to her and she kept pouring,	5602
	5:20	by not accepting from him what he **b.**	995
	8: 5	the woman whose son Elisha had **b** **back** to life came	2649
	10: 8	"They have **b** the heads of the princes."	995
	10:18	**b** all the people **together**	7695
	10:22	So he **b** out robes for them.	3655
	10:26	**b** the sacred stone **out**	3655
	11: 4	the Carites and the guards and had them **b**	995
	11:12	Jehoiada **b** out the king's son and put	3655
	11:19	and together they **b** the king **down** from	3718
	12: 4	that is **b** as sacred offerings to the temple of	995
	12: 4	and the money is voluntarily **b** to the temple.	995
	12: 9	into the chest all the money that was **b** to	995
	12:10	the money that had been **b** into the temple	5162
	12:13	The money **b** into the temple was not spent	995
	12:16	and sin offerings was not **b** into the temple	995
	14:20	He was **b** back by horse and was buried	5951
	16:14	before the LORD he **b** from the front of	7928
	17: 7	who had **b** them **up** out of Egypt from under	6590
	17:24	of Assyria **b** people from Babylon,	995
	17:33	of the nations from which they had been **b.**	1655
	17:36	who **b** you **up** out of Egypt	6590
	19:25	now I have **b** it to pass,	995
	20:20	the tunnel by which he **b** water into the city,	995
	22: 4	the money that has been **b** into the temple	995
	23: 8	Josiah **b** all the priests from the towns	995
	23:30	Josiah's servants **b** his body in a chariot	995
	25:20	the commander took them all and **b** them to	2143
1Ch	2: 7	who **b** trouble on Israel by violating	6579
	9:28	they counted them when they were **b** **in** and	995
	10:12	the bodies of Saul and his sons and **b** them	995
	11:14	The LORD **b** about a great **victory.**	3828+9591
	15:28	So all Israel **b** **up** the ark of the covenant of	6590
	16: 1	They **b** the ark of God and set it inside	995
	17: 5	in a house from the day I **b** Israel **up** out	6590
	17:16	that you have **b** me this far?	995
	18: 2	they became subject to him and **b** tribute.	5951
	18: 6	to him and **b** tribute.	5951
	18: 7	by the officers of Hadadezer and **b** them	995
	18:10	Hadoram **b** all kinds of articles of gold	NIH
	19:16	had Arameans **b** from beyond the River,	3655
	20: 3	and **b** out the people who were there,	3655
	22: 4	and Tyrians had **b** large numbers of them	995
2Ch	1: 4	Now David had **b** **up** the ark of God	6590
	5: 1	temple of the LORD was finished, he **b** **in**	995
	5: 5	and they **b** **up** the ark and the Tent	6590
	5: 7	then **b** the ark of the LORD's covenant	995
	6: 5	the day I **b** my people **out** of Egypt,	3655
	7:22	who **b** them **out** of Egypt,	3655
	7:22	that is why he **b** all this disaster on them.' "	995
	8:11	Pharaoh's daughter **up**	6590
	8:18	and **b** back four hundred and fifty talents	4374
	9: 10	of Hiram and the men of Solomon **b** gold	995
	9:10	also **b** algumwood and precious stones.	995
	9:12	he gave her more than she had **b** to him.	995
	9:14	the revenues **b** in by merchants and traders.	995
	9:14	the governors of the land **b** gold and silver	995
	9:24	everyone who came **b** a gift—	995
	15:11	and goats from the plunder they had **b** **back.**	995
	15:18	He **b** into the temple of God the silver	995
	16: 6	Then King Asa **b** all the men of Judah,	4374
	17: 5	and all Judah **b** gifts to Jehoshaphat,	5989
	17:11	Some Philistines **b** Jehoshaphat gifts	995
	17:11	and the Arabs **b** him flocks:	995
	18: 5	the king of Israel **b** together the prophets—	7695
	22: 7	God **b** about Ahaziah's downfall.	2118+4946
	22: 9	He was **b** to Jehu and put to death.	995
	23:11	Jehoiada and his sons **b** out the king's son	3655
	23:20	the people of the land and **b** the king **down**	3718
	24:10	the people **b** their contributions gladly,	995
	24:11	Whenever the chest was **b** in by the Levites	995
	24:14	they **b** the rest of the money to the king	995
	25:14	he **b** back the gods of the people of Seir.	995
	25:23	Then Jehoash **b** to Jerusalem	995
	25:28	He was **b** back by horse and was buried	5951
	26: 8	The Ammonites **b** tribute to Uzziah	5989
	27: 5	The Ammonites **b** him the same amount	8740

2Ch	28: 5	as prisoners and **b** them to Damascus.	995
	29: 4	He **b** in the priests and the Levites,	995
	29:16	They **b** out to the courtyard of	3655
	29:21	They **b** seven bulls, seven rams,	995
	29:23	The goats for the sin offering were **b** before	5602
	29:31	assembly **b** sacrifices and thank offerings,	995
	29:31	all whose hearts were willing **b** burnt offerings.	NIH
	29:32	The assembly **b** was seventy bulls,	995
	29:36	the people rejoiced at what God had **b** **about**	3922
	30:15	and **b** burnt offerings to the temple of	995
	31: 5	They **b** a great amount,	995
	31: 6	also **b** a tithe of their herds and flocks and	995
	31:12	Then they faithfully **b** in the contributions,	995
	32:23	Many **b** offerings to Jerusalem for	995
	33:11	So the LORD **b** against them	995
	33:13	so he **b** him **back** to Jerusalem and	8740
	34: 9	gave him the money that had **been b** into	995
	35:24	in the other chariot he had **b** and him	2143
	36:10	for him and **b** him to Babylon,	995
	36:17	He **b** up against them the king of	6590
Ezr	1: 7	King Cyrus **b** out the articles belonging to	3655
	1: 8	of Persia had them **b** by Mithredath	3655
	1:11	Sheshbazzar **b** all these along when	5605+5607
	3: 5	**b** as freewill offerings to the LORD	5605+5607
	4: 2	king of Assyria, who **b** us here."	6590
	5:14	the temple in Jerusalem and **b** to the temple	10308
	6: 5	the temple in Jerusalem and **b** to Babylon,	10308
	8:18	they **b** us Sherebiah, a capable man,	995
	8:20	They also **b** 220 of the temple servants—	NIH
Ne	2: 1	when wine was **b** for him,	NIH
	8: 2	the seventh month Ezra the priest **b** the Law	995
	8:16	So the people went out and **b** back branches	995
	9: 7	who chose Abram and **b** him out of Ur of	3318
	9:15	and in their thirst you **b** them water from	3318
	9:18	who **b** you **up** out of Egypt,'	6590
	9:23	and you **b** them into the land	935
	12:27	where they lived and were **b** to Jerusalem	995
	12:28	The singers also were **b** together from	665
	13:12	All Judah **b** the tithes of grain,	935
	13:18	that our God **b** all this calamity upon us and	935
	13:19	the gates so that no load could be **b** in on	935
Est	1:17	Queen Vashti to be **b** before him,	935
	2: 7	Hadassah, whom he had **b** up	587
	2: 8	many girls were **b** to the citadel of Susa	7695
	6: 1	to be **b** in and read to him.	935
Job	4:12	"A word was secretly **b** to me,	1704
	14:21	if they are **b** low, he does not see it.	7592
	15: 7	Were you **b** forth before the hills?	2655
	22:29	men are **b** low and you say, 'Lift them up!'	9164
	24:24	they are **b** low and gathered up	4812
	42:11	the trouble the LORD had **b** upon him,	995
Ps	18:19	He **b** me out into a spacious place;	3655
	20: 8	They are **b** to their knees and fall,	4156
	22: 9	Yet you **b** me out of the womb;	1631
	30: 3	O LORD, you **b** me **up** from the grave;	6590
	37:33	be condemned when **b** to trial.	9149
	38: 6	I am bowed down and very low;	8820
	44:25	We are **b** down to the dust;	AIT
	45:14	her virgin companions follow her and are **b**	995
	46: 8	the desolations he has **b** on the earth.	8492
	66:11	You **b** us into prison and laid burdens	995
	66:12	but you **b** us to a place of abundance.	3655
	71: 6	you **b** me **forth** from my mother's womb.	1602
	74: 3	destruction the enemy has **b**	8317
	78:16	he **b** streams out of a rocky crag	3655
	78:52	But he **b** his people out like a flock;	5825
	78:54	Thus he **b** them to the border	995
	78:71	from tending the sheep he **b** him to be	995
	80: 8	You **b** a vine out of Egypt;	5825
	81:10	who **b** you **up** out of Egypt.	6590
	90: 2	the mountains were born or you **b** forth	2655
	94:19	your consolation **b** joy to my soul.	9130
	105:37	He **b** out Israel, laden with silver and gold,	3655
	105:40	and he **b** them quail and satisfied them with	995
	105:43	He **b** out his people with rejoicing,	3655
	107:14	He **b** them out of darkness and	3655
	107:28	and he **b** them out of their distress.	3655
	107:36	**b** the hungry to live,	3782
	126: 1	the LORD **b** back the captives to Zion,	8740
	136:11	and **b** Israel out from	3655
	136:14	and **b** Israel through the midst of it,	6296
Pr	7:26	Many are the victims she has **b** **down;**	5877
	8:22	LORD **b** me forth as the first of his works,	7865
	11: 5	but the wicked are **b** down	5877
	14:32	calamity comes, the wicked are **b** down,	1890
	21:27	how much more so when **b** with evil intent!	995
	24:16	but the wicked are **b** down by calamity.	4173
SS	3: 4	and would not let him go till I had **b** him	995
Isa	1: 2	"I reared children and **b** them, **up,**	8123
	2: 9	So man will be **b** low	8820
	2:11	be humbled and the pride of men **b** low;	8820
	2:17	The arrogance of man will be **b** low and	8820
	3: 9	They have **b** disaster upon themselves.	1694
	5:15	man will be **b** low and mankind humbled,	8820
	10:33	the tall ones will be **b** low.	9164
	14:11	All your pomp has been **b** down to	3718
	14:15	But you are **b** down to the grave,	3718
	18: 7	At that time gifts will be **b** to	3297
	18: 7	the gifts will be **b** to Mount Zion,	NIH
	23: 4	I have neither reared sons nor **b** up	8123
	26:14	You punished them and **b** them to ruin;	9012
	26:18	We have not **b** salvation to the earth;	6913
	29: 4	**b** low, you will speak from the ground;	9164
	29:10	The LORD has **b** over you a deep sleep:	5818
	37:26	now I have **b** it to pass,	995

Isa	43:23	not **b** me sheep for burnt offerings,	995
	44:11	*they will be* **b** *down to terror* and infamy.	7064
	45:10	to his mother, 'What *have you* **b** *to birth?*'	2655
	49:21	Who **b** these **up?**	1540
	53: 5	**punishment** *that* **b** us peace was upon him,	AIT
	60: 5	the wealth on the seas *will be* **b** to you,	2200
	63:11	where is he *who* **b** them through the sea,	6590
	66: 8	in a day or a nation be **b** forth in a moment?	3528
Jer	2: 6	who **b** us **up** out of Egypt and led us	6590
	2: 7	*I* **b** you into a fertile land to eat its fruit	995
	2:17	not **b** this on yourselves by forsaking	6913
	4:18	"Your own conduct and actions *have* **b** this	6913
	6:15	*they will be* **b** *down* when I punish them,"	4173
	7:22	**b** your forefathers **out**	3655
	8:12	*they will be* **b** *down*	4173
	10: 9	Hammered silver is **b** from Tarshish	995
	11: 4	when I **b** them **out** of Egypt,	3655
	11: 7	the time I **b** your forefathers **up** from Egypt	6590
	16:14	So I **b** on them all the curses of	995
	16:14	who **b** the Israelites **up** out of Egypt,'	6590
	16:15	who **b** the Israelites **up** out of the land of	6590
	20: 5	So the word of the LORD *has* **b** me insult	2118
	20:15	**b** my father **the news,**	1413
	23: 7	who **b** the Israelites **up** out of Egypt,'	6590
	23: 8	**b** the descendants of Israel **up**	6590
	25: 7	and you have **b** harm to yourselves."	NIH
	26:23	*They* **b** Uriah **out** of Egypt and took him	3655
	27:16	from the LORD's house *will be* **b** *back*	8740
	32:21	**b** your people Israel **out**	3655
	32:23	**b** all this disaster **upon**	7925
	32:42	As *I have* **b** all this great calamity	995
	34:13	with your forefathers when *I* **b** them **out**	3655
	35: 4	*I* **b** them into the house of the LORD,	995
	36:21	and Jehudi **b** it from the room of Elishama	4374
	37:14	instead, they arrested Jeremiah and **b** him to	995
	37:17	for him and *had* him to the palace,	4374
	38:14	for Jeremiah the prophet and *had* him **b** to	4374
	38:22	of Judah *will be* **b** *out* to the officials of	3655
	38:23	and children *will be* **b** *out* to	3655
	40: 3	And now the LORD *has* **b** it **about;**	995
	41:16	and court officials he *had* **b** from Gibeon.	8740
	44: 2	the great disaster *I* **b** on Jerusalem and	995
	50:25	**b** **out** the weapons of his wrath,	3655
	52:26	the commander took them all and **b** them to	2143
La	1: 5	The LORD *has* **b** her grief because	3324
	1:12	that the LORD **b** on me in the day	3324
	2: 2	**b** her kingdom and its princes **down**	5595
Eze	8: 7	Then *he* **b** me to the entrance to the court.	995
	8:14	Then *he* **b** me to the entrance to	995
	8:16	then **b** me into the inner court of the house	995
	9:11	with the writing kit at his side **b** *back* word,	8740
	11: 1	the Spirit lifted me up and **b** me to the gate	995
	11:24	up and **b** me to the exiles in Babylonia in	995
	12: 7	the day I **b** **out** my things packed for exile.	3655
	13:22	when I *had* **b** them no **grief,**	3872
	14:22	sons and daughters who *will be* **b** *out* of it.	3655
	14:22	be consoled regarding the disaster *I have* **b**	995
	14:22	every disaster *I have* **b** upon it.	995
	17:14	so that the kingdom would be *b low,*	AIT
	19: 3	She **b** **up** one of her cubs,	6590
	19: 9	a cage and **b** them to the king of Babylon.	995
	20:10	of Egypt and **b** them into the desert.	995
	20:14	in whose sight *I had* **b** them **out.**	3655
	20:22	in whose sight *I had* **b** them **out.**	3655
	20:28	When *I* **b** them into the land I had sworn	995
	21:24	how people have **b** to **mind** your guilt	2349
	21:26	be exalted and the exalted *will be* **b** *low.*	9164
	22: 4	**b** your days **to a close,**	7928
	22:30	*have* **b** this upon you,	6913
	23:42	Sabeans *were* **b** from the desert along	995
	27: 4	**b** your beauty **to perfection.**	4005
	27:11	**b** your beauty **to perfection.**	4005
	30:11	*will be* **b** *in* to destroy the land.	995
	31:15	the day it *was* **b** *down* to the grave	3718
	31:16	at the sound of its fall when I **b** it **down** to	3718
	31:18	*will be* **b** *down* with the trees of Eden to	3718
	34: 4	You have not **b** *back* the strays or searched	8740
	37: 1	and *he* **b** me **out** by the Spirit of the LORD	3655
	38: 8	They *had* **been** **b** **out** from the nations,	3655
	39:27	When I *have* **b** them *back* from the nations	8740
	40: 4	for that is why *you have been* **b** here.	995
	40:17	Then *he* **b** me into the outer court.	995
	40:28	Then *he* **b** me into the inner court through	995
	40:32	*he* **b** me to the inner court on the east side,	995
	40:35	*he* **b** me to the north gate and measured it.	995
	40:48	*He* **b** me to the portico of the temple	995
	41: 1	Then the man **b** me to the outer sanctuary	995
	42: 1	into the outer court and **b** me to	995
	43: 1	Then the man **b** me to the gate facing east,	2143
	43: 5	Then the Spirit lifted me up and **b** me into	995
	44: 1	Then the man **b** me *back* to the outer gate	8740
	44: 4	the man **b** me by way of the north gate to	995
	44: 7	you **b** foreigners uncircumcised in heart	995
	46:19	Then the man **b** me through the entrance at	995
	46:21	*He* then **b** me to the outer court and led me	8740
	47: 1	The man **b** me *back* to the entrance of	8740
	47: 2	*He* then **b** me **out** through the north gate	3655
Da	3:13	So these men were **b** before the king,	10085
	4: 6	the wise men of Babylon be **b** before me	10549
	5: 3	So *they* **b** in the gold goblets	10085
	5: 7	astrologers and diviners to be **b** and said	10549
	5:13	So Daniel *was* **b** before the king,	10549
	5:13	the exiles my father the king **b** from Judah?	10085
	5:15	The wise men and enchanters *were* **b**	10549
	5:23	You had the goblets from his temple **b**	10085
	5:26	days of your reign and **b** it to an end.	10719
	6:16	and *they* **b** Daniel and threw him into	10085

Da	6:17	A stone *was* **b** and placed over the mouth of	10085
	6:18	without any entertainment *being* **b** to him.	10549
	6:24	the men who had falsely accused Daniel *were* **b** *in*	10085
	8:11	and the place of his sanctuary *was* **b** low.	8959
	9:15	who **b** your people **out** of Egypt with	3655
Hos	10: 1	he **b** forth fruit for himself.	8751
	12: 1	[*who* **b** you] out of Egypt;	NIH
	13: 4	[*who* **b** you] out of Egypt.	NIH
Am	2:10	"I **b** you **up** out of Egypt,	6590
	3: 1	the whole family I **b up** out of Egypt:	6590
Jnh	2: 6	But *you* **b** my life **up** from the pit,	6590
Mic	4: 6	the exiles and those *I have* **b** to grief.	8317
	4: 6	*I* **b** you **up** out of Egypt and redeemed you	6590
Hag	1: 9	What *you* **b** home, I blew away.	995
Zec	1: 9	Assyria's pride *will be* **b** *down*	3718
Mal	1:11	and pure offerings *will be* **b** to my name,	5602
Mt	4:24	and people **b** to him all who were ill	4712
	8:16	many who were demon-possessed *were* **b** to	4712
	9: 2	*Some men* **b** to him a paralytic,	4712
	9:32	and could not talk *was* **b** to Jesus,	4712
	10:18	be before governors and kings	72
	12:22	Then *they* **b** him a demon-possessed man	4712
	14:11	His head *was* **b** in on a platter and given to	5770
	14:35	*People* **b** all their sick to him	4712
	17:16	*I* **b** him to your disciples,	4712
	18:24	man who owed him ten thousand talents *was* **b** to him.	4712
	19:13	Then little children *were* **b** to Jesus for him	4712
	19:13	the disciples rebuked those who **b** them.	NIG
	21: 7	*They* **b** the donkey and the colt,	72
	22:19	They **b** him a denarius,	4712
	25:20	the five talents **b** the other five.	4712
Mk	1:32	That evening after sunset the *people* **b**	5770
	4:22	to be **b** out into the open.	2262
	6:28	and **b** back his head on a platter.	5770
	7:32	There *some people* **b** to him	5770
	8:22	and *some people* **b** a blind man	5770
	9:17	"Teacher, *I* **b** you my son,	5770
	9:20	So *they* **b** him.	5770
	11: 7	When *they* **b** the colt to Jesus	5770
	12:16	They **b** the coin, and he asked them,	5770
	13:11	Whenever you are arrested and **b** to **trial,**	72
	15:22	*They* **b** Jesus to the place called Golgotha	5770
Lk	1:52	*He has* **b** *down* rulers from their thrones	2524
	2:27	When the parents **b** *in* the child Jesus to do	1652
	4:16	where he had been **b** **up,**	5555
	4:40	When the sun was setting, the people **b**	5555
	7:37	*she* **b** an alabaster jar of perfume,	3152
	8:17	not be known or **b** out into the open.	2262
	12:11	"When you are **b** before synagogues,	1662
	18:40	Jesus stopped and ordered the man *to be* **b**	72
	19:35	*They* **b** it to Jesus,	72
	21:12	*you will be* **b** before kings and governors,	552
	23:14	"You **b** me this man as one who was inciting the people to rebellion.	4712
Jn	1:42	And *he* **b** him to Jesus.	72
	4:33	"Could someone *have* **b** him food?"	5770
	8: 3	The teachers of the law and the Pharisees **b**	72
	9:13	*They* **b** to the Pharisees	72
	10: 4	When *he has* **b** *out* all his own,	1675
	17: 4	*I have* **b** you **glory** on earth by completing	1519
	17:23	May they be **b** to complete unity to let	NIG
	18:13	and **b** him first to Annas,	72
	18:16	to the girl on duty there and **b** Peter **in.**	1652
	19:13	*he* **b** Jesus out and sat down on	1652
	19:39	Nicodemus **b** a mixture of myrrh and aloes,	5770
Ac	4: 7	*They had* Peter and John **b** before them	2705
	4:34	**b** the money from the sales	5770
	4:37	a field he owned and **b** the money and put it	5770
	5: 2	but **b** the rest and put it at the apostles' feet.	5770
	5:15	people **b** the sick into the streets	1766
	5:19	the doors of the jail and **b** them **out.**	1974
	5:26	the captain went with his officers and **b**	72
	5:27	*Having* **b** the apostles,	72
	6:12	They seized Stephen and **b** him before	72
	7:16	Their bodies *were* **b** *back* to Shechem	3572
	7:21	Pharaoh's daughter took him and **b** him **up**	427
	7:41	*They* **b** sacrifices to it and held	343
	7:45	when Joshua **b** it with them when they took	1652
	9:27	But Barnabas took him and **b** him to	72
	11:24	great number of people *were* **b** to the Lord.	4707
	11:26	he **b** him to Antioch.	72
	12:17	and described how the Lord *had* **b** him out	1974
	13: 1	Manaen (who had been **b** **up with** Herod	5343
	13:23	"From this man's descendants God *has* **b**	72
	14:13	**b** bulls and wreaths to the city gates	5770
	15: 2	This **b** Paul and Barnabas into sharp dispute	1181
	16:20	They **b** them **before** the magistrates	4642
	16:30	He then **b** them out and asked, "Sirs,	4575
	16:34	The jailer **b** them into his house and set	343
	17:15	The men who escorted Paul **b** him	72
	17:19	Then *they* took him and **b** him to a meeting	72
	18:12	a united attack on Paul and **b** him	72
	19:19	**b** their scrolls **together**	5237
	19:24	**b** *in* no little business for the craftsmen.	4218
	19:37	*You have* **b** these men here,	72
	21:16	from Caesarea accompanied us and **b** us to	72
	21:28	*he has* **b** Greeks **into** the temple area	1652
	21:29	that Paul had **b** him **into** the temple area.)	1652
	22: 3	but **b** up in this city.	427
	22:30	he **b** Paul and had him stand before them.	2864
	23:28	so *I* **b** him to their Sanhedrin.	2864
	23:31	with them during the night and **b** him as far	72
	24: 1	and they **b** their **charges** against Paul before	1872
	24: 2	under you, and your foresight *has* **b** **about**	1181
	25: 6	and ordered that Paul *be* **b** before him.	72

Ac	25:11	the **charges** **b** **against** me by these Jews are	2989
	25:15	elders of the Jews **b** **charges** against me	1872
	25:17	and ordered the man *to be* **b** in.	72
	25:23	At the command of Festus, Paul *was* **b** in.	72
	25:26	Therefore *I have* **b** him **before** all of you,	4575
Ro	5:16	followed one sin and **b** condemnation.	1650
	5:16	but the gift followed many trespasses and **b** justification.	1650
	6:13	**b** from death **to life;**	2409
	7:10	to bring life actually **b** death.	1650
	8:21	to decay and **b** into the glorious freedom of	NIG
2Co	3: 7	Now if the ministry that **b** death,	NIG
Eph	2:13	in Christ Jesus you who once were far away *have been* **b** near	1181
Col	1:13	and **b** us into the kingdom of the Son	3496
1Th	1: 5	to us from you and *has* **b** good news about	2294
1Ti	4: 6	**b** **up** in the truths of the faith and of	1957
	5:19	an accusation against an elder unless it is **b**	NIG
	6: 7	For *we* **b** nothing **into** the world,	1662
2Ti	1:10	**b** life and immortality **to light**	5894
Tit	1: 3	**b** his word **to light**	5746
Heb	6: 6	to be **b** **back** to repentance,	362
	13:20	the blood of the eternal covenant **b** *back*	343
Jas	5:11	have seen what the Lord finally **b** about.	NIG
2Pe	2: 5	*when he* **b** the flood **on** its ungodly people,	2042
Rev	18:17	In one hour such great wealth *has been* **b** to ruin!'	2246
	18:19	In one hour *she has been* **b** to ruin!	2246
	21:26	and honor of the nations *will be* **b** into it.	5770

BROUGHT (Anglicized) See also TOOK

BROUGHT UP (Anglicized) See REARED

BROW (5)

Ge	3:19	the sweat of your **b** you will eat your food	678
	49:26	on the **b** *of* the prince among his brothers.	7721
Dt	33:16	on the **b** *of* the prince among his brothers.	7721
Job	16:15	over my skin and buried my **b** in the dust.	7967
Lk	4:29	and took him to the **b** of the hill on which	4059

BROWN (1)

Zec	1: 8	Behind him were red, **b** and white horses.	8601

BROWSE (2) [BROWSES]

SS	4: 5	like twin fawns of a gazelle that **b** among	8286
	6: 2	to **b** in the gardens and to gather lilies.	8286

BROWSES (2) [BROWSE]

SS	2:16	he **b** among the lilies.	8286
	6: 3	he **b** among the lilies.	8286

BRUISE (2) [BRUISED, BRUISES]

Ex	21:25	wound for wound, **b** for bruise.	2467
	21:25	wound for wound, bruise for **b.**	2467

BRUISED (5) [BRUISE]

Lev	22:24	the LORD an animal whose testicles *are* **b,**	5080
Ps	105:18	*They* **b** his feet with shackles,	6700
SS	5: 7	They beat me, *they* **b** me;	7205
Isa	42: 3	A **b** reed he will not break,	8368
Mt	12:20	A **b** reed he will not break,	5341

BRUISES (2) [BRUISE]

Pr	23:29	Who has needless **b?**	7206
Isa	30:26	the LORD binds up the **b** *of* his people	8691

BRUISES (Anglicized) See also WELTS

BRUIT (KJV) See REPORT, NEWS

BRUSH (1) [BRUSHWOOD, UNDERBRUSH]

Job	30: 4	In the **b** they gathered salt herbs,	8489

BRUSHING (1)

Eze	3:13	the living creatures **b** against each other and	5976

BRUSHWOOD (1) [BRUSH, WOOD]

Ac	28: 3	Paul gathered a pile of **b** and,	5866

BRUTAL (2) [BRUTE]

Eze	21:31	I will hand you over to **b** men,	1279
2Ti	3: 3	slanderous, without self-control, **b,**	466

BRUTALLY (3) [BRUTE]

2Ch	16:10	At the same time Asa **b** **oppressed** some of	8368
Eze	34: 4	You have ruled them harshly and **b.**	928+7266
1Co	4:11	we are **b** treated, we are homeless.	3139

BRUTE (2) [BRUTAL, BRUTALLY, BRUTES]

Ps	73:22	I was a **b** beast before you.	989
2Pe	2:12	They are like **b** beasts, creatures of instinct,	263

BRUTES (1) [BRUTE]
Tit 1:12 "Cretans are always liars, evil **b**, 2563

BUBASTIS (1)
Eze 30:17 of Heliopolis and **B** will fall by the sword, 7083

BUBBLING (2)
Pr 18: 4 but the fountain of wisdom is a **b** brook. 5580
Isa 35: 7 the thirsty ground **b** springs. 4432+4784

BUCKET (1) [BUCKETS]
Isa 40:15 Surely the nations are like a drop in a **b**; 1932

BUCKETS (2) [BUCKET]
Ex 7:19 even in the **wooden** *b* and stone jars." AIT
Nu 24: 7 Water will flow from their **b**; 1932

BUCKLED (1) [BUCKLER]
Eph 6:14 with the belt of truth **b around** your **waist,** 4322

BUCKLER (1) [BUCKLED]
Ps 35: 2 Take up shield and **b**; 7558

BUCKLERS (KJV) See SHIELDS

BUD (11) [BUDDED, BUDS]
Ex 25:35 One **b** shall be under the first pair 4117
25:35 a second **b** under the second pair, 4117
25:35 and a third **b** under the third pair— 4117
37:21 One **b** was under the first pair 4117
37:21 a second **b** under the second pair, 4117
37:21 and a third **b** under the third pair— 4117
Job 14: 9 of water *it will* **b** and put forth shoots like 7255
Isa 17:11 *you* bring them to **b**, 7255
27: 6 Israel *will* **b** and blossom and fill all 7437
55:10 without watering the earth and **making** it **b** 3528
Hab 3:17 not **b** and there are no grapes on the vines, 7255

BUDDED (6) [BUD]
Ge 40:10 As soon as it **b**, it blossomed, 7255
Nu 17: 8 had not only sprouted but *had* **b**, 3655+7258
SS 6:11 if the vines *had* **b** or the pomegranates were 7255
7:12 to the vineyards to see if the vines *have* **b**, 7255
Eze 7:10 Doom has burst forth, the rod *has* **b**, 7437
Heb 9: 4 Aaron's staff that *had* **b**, 1056

BUDS (8) [BUD]
Ex 25:31 its flowerlike cups, **b** and blossoms shall be 4117
25:33 with **b** and blossoms are to be 4117
25:34 like almond flowers with **b** and blossoms. 4117
25:36 The **b** and branches shall all be of one piece 4117
37:17 **b** and blossoms were of one piece with it. 4117
37:19 with **b** and blossoms were on one branch, 4117
37:20 like almond flowers with **b** and blossoms. 4117
37:22 The **b** and the branches were all 4117

BUFFET (KJV) See BEAT, STRUCK, TORMENT

BUFFETED (1)
Mt 14:24 **b** by the waves because the wind was 989

BUILD (152) [BUILDER, BUILDERS, BUILDING, BUILDINGS, BUILDS, BUILT, REBUILD, REBUILDING, REBUILT, WELL-BUILT]
Ge 6:15 This is how *you are to* **b** it: 6913
11: 4 "Come, *let us* **b** ourselves a city, 1215
16: 2 perhaps *I can* **b** a **family** through her." 1215
30: 3 and that through her I too *can* **b a family."** 1215
35: 1 and **b** an altar there to God, 6913
35: 3 where *I will* **b** an altar to God, 6913
Ex 20:25 *do not* **b** it *with* dressed stones, 1215
27: 1 "**B** an altar of acacia wood, 6913
Nu 23: 1 Balaam said, "**B** me seven altars here, 1215
23:29 Balaam said, "**B** me seven altars here, 1215
32:16 *to* **b** pens here for our livestock and cities 1215
32:24 **B** cities for your women and children, 1215
Dt 6:10 flourishing cities *you did* not **b**, 1215
8:12 when you **b** fine houses and settle down, 1215
16:21 the altar *you* to the LORD your God, 6913
19: 3 **B** roads to them and divide into three parts 3922
20:20 *to* **b** siege works until the city at war 1215
22: 8 When *you* **b** a new house, 1215
25: 9 not **b up** his brother's family line." 1215
27: 5 **B** there an altar to the LORD your God, 1215
27: 6 **B** the altar of the LORD your God 6913
28:30 *You will* **b** a house, 1215
Jos 22:16 from the LORD and **b** yourselves an altar 1215
22:26 'Let us get ready and **b** an altar— 1215
24:13 not toil and cities *you did not* **b**; 1215
Jdg 6:26 Then **b** a proper kind of altar to 1215
2Sa 7: 5 the one to **b** me a house to dwell in? 1215
7:13 the one *who will* **b** a house for my Name, 1215
7:27 saying, '*I will* **b** a house for you.' 1215
24:18 "Go up and **b** an altar to the LORD on 7756
24:21 "so I *can* **b** an altar to the LORD, 1215

1Ki 2:36 "**B** yourself a house in Jerusalem 1215
5: 3 he could not **b** a temple for the Name of 1215
5: 5 to **b** a temple for the Name of 1215
5: 5 the throne in your place *will* **b** the temple 1215
6: 1 *he began to* **b** the temple of the LORD. 1215
8:17 to **b** a temple for the Name of the LORD, 1215
8:18 'Because it was in your heart to **b** a temple 1215
8:19 you *are* not *the one to* **b** the temple, 1215
8:19 he *is the one who will* **b** the temple 1215
9:15 to **b** the LORD's temple, 1215
9:19 whatever he desired to **b** in Jerusalem, 1215
11:38 *I will* **b** you a dynasty as enduring as 1215
2Ki 6: 2 and *let us* **b** a place there for us to live." 6913
19:32 He will not come before it with shield or **b** 9161
1Ch 14: 1 stonemasons and carpenters to **b** a palace 1215
17: 4 not the one *to* **b** me a house to dwell in. 1215
17:10 " 'I declare to you that the LORD *will* **b** 1215
17:12 He *is* the one who will **b** a house for me, 1215
17:25 to your servant that you will **b** a house 1215
21:18 to go up and **b** an altar to the LORD on 7756
21:22 of your threshing floor so I *can* **b** an altar 1215
22: 6 for his son Solomon and charged him to **b** 1215
22: 7 "My son, I had it in my heart to **b** a house 1215
22: 8 *You are* not *to* **b** a house for my Name, 1215
22:10 *the one who will* **b** a house for my Name. 1215
22:11 and may you have success and **b** the house 1215
22:19 *to* **b** the sanctuary of the LORD God, 1215
28: 2 to **b** a house as a place of rest for the ark of 1215
28: 2 and I made plans to **b** it. 1215
28: 3 'You are not *to* **b** a house for my Name, 1215
28: 6 the one *who will* **b** my house 1215
28:10 the LORD has chosen you to **b** a temple as 1215
29:19 to do everything to **b** the palatial structure 1215
2Ch 2: 1 to **b** a temple for the Name of the LORD 1215
2: 3 when you sent him cedar to **b** a palace 1215
2: 4 *about to* **b** a temple for the Name of 1215
2: 5 "The temple *I am going to* **b** will be great, 1215
2: 6 But who is able to **b** a temple for him, 1215
2: 6 Who then am I *to* **b** a temple for him, 1215
2: 9 temple I **b** must be large and magnificent. 1215
2:12 who *will* **b** a temple for the LORD and 1215
3: 1 to **b** the temple of the LORD in Jerusalem 1215
6: 7 to **b** a temple for the Name of the LORD. 1215
6: 8 'Because it was in your heart to **b** a temple 1215
6: 9 you are not *the one to* **b** the temple, 1215
6: 9 he is *the one who will* **b** the temple 1215
8: 6 whatever he desired to **b** in Jerusalem, 1215
14: 7 "*Let us* **b up** these towns," 1215
36:23 to **b** a temple for him at Jerusalem in Judah. 1215
Ezr 1: 2 to **b** a temple for him at Jerusalem in Judah. 1215
1: 3 up to Jerusalem in Judah and **b** the temple 1215
1: 5 to go up and **b** the house of the LORD 1215
3: 2 of Shealtiel and his associates began to **b** 1215
4: 2 "*Let us* help you **b** because, like you, 1215
4: 3 We alone *will* **b** it for the LORD, 1215
6:14 So the elders of the Jews *continued to* **b** 10111
Job 19:12 *they* **b** a siege ramp against me and encamp 6148
20:19 he has seized houses *he did* not **b**. 1215
30:12 *they* **b** their siege ramps against me. 6148
39:27 **b** his nest **on high**? 8123
Ps 28: 5 down and never **b** them **up** *again*. 1215
51:18 **b up** the walls of Jerusalem. 1215
Pr 24:27 after that, **b** your house. 1215
Ecc 3: 3 a time to tear down and a time to **b**, 1215
SS 8: 9 *we will* **b** towers of silver on her. 1215
Isa 37:33 with shield or **b** a siege ramp against it. 9161
54:11 I will **b** you with stones of turquoise, 8069
57:14 "**B up,** build up, prepare the road! 6148
57:14 "Build up, **b up,** prepare the road! 6148
62:10 **B up,** build up the highway! 6148
62:10 Build up, **b up** the highway! 6148
65:21 *They will* **b** houses and dwell in them; 1215
65:22 No longer *will they* **b** houses 1215
66: 1 Where is the house *you will* **b** for me? 1215
Jer 1:10 to **b** and to plant." 1215
6: 6 "Cut down the trees and **b** siege ramps 9161
22:14 I will **b** myself a great palace 1215
24: 6 *I will* **b** them **up** and not tear them down; 1215
29: 5 "**B** houses and settle down; 1215
29:28 Therefore **b** houses and settle down; 1215
31: 4 I will **b** you **up** again and you will 1215
31:28 I will watch over them to **b** and to plant," 1215
35: 7 Also *you must* never **b** houses, 1215
42:10 *I will* **b** you **up** and not tear you down; 1215
49:16 **b** your nest as **high** 1467
Eze 4: 2 **b** a ramp up to it, 9161
11: 3 'Will it not soon be time *to* **b** houses? 1215
21:22 to **b** a ramp and to erect siege works, 9161
22:30 a man among them *who would* **b up** the wall 1553
26: 8 he will set up siege works against you, **b** 9161
28:26 and *will* **b** houses and plant vineyards; 1215
Da 11:15 the North will come and **b up** siege ramps 9161
Am 9:11 restore its ruins, and **b** it as it used to be, 1215
Mic 3:10 who **b** Zion with bloodshed, 1215
Hab 1:10 *they* **b** earthen ramps and capture them. 7392
Zep 1:13 *They will* **b** houses but not live in them; 1215
Hag 1: 8 the mountains and bring down timber and **b** 1215
Zec 5:11 the country of Babylonia to **b** a house for it. 1215
6:12 and he will branch out from his place and **b** 1215
6:13 It is he *who will* **b** the temple of 1215
6:13 and help *to* **b** the temple of the LORD, 1215
Mal 1: 4 "They *may* **b**, but I will demolish. 1215
Mt 16:18 and on this rock I will **b** my church, 3868
23:29 *You* **b** tombs for the prophets and decorate 3868
27:40 to destroy the temple and **b** it in three days, 3868
Mk 14:58 and in three days *will* **b** another, 3868
15:29 to destroy the temple and **b** it in three days, 3868

Lk 11:47 because *you* **b** tombs for the prophets, 3868
11:48 and *you* **b** their tombs. 3868
12:18 down my barns and **b** bigger ones, 3868
14:28 "Suppose one of you wants *to* **b** a tower. 3868
14:30 'This fellow began *to* **b** and was not able 3868
19:43 when your enemies *will* **b** an embankment 4212
Jn 2:20 *to* **b** this temple, 3868
Ac 7:49 What kind of house *will you* **b** for me? 3868
20:32 which can **b** you **up** and give you 3868
Ro 15: 2 to **b** him **up**. 3869
1Co 14:12 try to excel in gifts that **b up** the church. 3869
1Th 5:11 encourage one another and **b** each other **up,** 3868
Heb 8: 5 when he was about to **b** the tabernacle: 2200
Jude 1:20 **b** yourselves **up** in your most holy faith 2224

BUILDER (4) [BUILD]
1Co 3:10 I laid a foundation as an expert **b**, 802
Heb 3: 3 as the **b** of a house has greater honor than 2941
3: 4 but God is the **b** of everything. 2941
11:10 whose architect and **b** is God. 1321

BUILDERS (14) [BUILD]
2Ki 12:11 the carpenters and **b**, 1215
22: 6 the **b** and the masons. 1215
2Ch 34:11 also gave money to the carpenters and **b** 1215
Ezr 3:10 the **b** laid the foundation of the temple of 1215
Ne 4: 5 in the face of the **b**. 1215
4:18 and each of the **b** wore his sword at his side 1215
Ps 118:22 the **b** rejected has become the capstone; 1215
127: 1 its **b** labor in vain. 1215
Eze 27: 4 your **b** brought your beauty to perfection. 1215
Mt 21:42 the **b** rejected has become the capstone; 3868
Mk 12:10 the **b** rejected has become the capstone; 3868
Lk 20:17 the **b** rejected has become the capstone'? 3868
Ac 4:11 He is " 'the stone you **b** rejected, 3871
1Pe 2: 7 the **b** rejected has become the capstone," 3868

BUILDING (50) [BUILD]
Ge 4:17 Cain was then **b** a city, 1215
11: 5 the city and the tower that the men *were* **b**. 1215
11: 8 and they stopped **b** the city. 1215
Jos 22:19 or against us by **b** an altar for yourselves, 1215
22:29 and turn away from him today by **b** an altar 1215
1Ki 3: 1 of David until he finished **b** his palace and 1215
5:18 and prepared the timber and stone for the **b** 1215
6: 5 a structure around the **b**, 1074
6: 7 In **b** the temple, 1215
6:12 "As for this temple you *are* **b**, 1215
6:38 *He had spent* seven years in it. 1215
9: 1 When Solomon had finished **b** the temple 1215
15:21 he stopped **b** Ramah and withdrew 1215
2Ki 25: 9 Every important he burned down. 1074
1Ch 22: 2 to prepare dressed stone for **b** the house 1215
29:16 that we have provided for **b** you a temple 1215
2Ch 3: 2 He began to **b** on the second day of 1215
3: 3 The foundation Solomon laid for **b** 1215
3: 4 the width of the **b** and twenty cubits high. 1074
16: 5 he stopped **b** Ramah 1215
32: 5 the broken sections of the wall and **b** towers 6590
Ezr 4: 8 and older to supervise the **b** of the house of 4856
4: 1 the exiles *were* **b** a temple for the LORD, 1215
4: 3 "You have no part with us in **b** a temple 1215
4: 4 of Judah and make them afraid to *go on* **b**. 1215
5: 4 the names of the men constructing this **b**?" 10112
5: 8 The people *are* **b** it with large stones 10111
6:14 They finished **b** the temple according to 10111
Ne 3: 1 **b** as far as the Tower of the Hundred, NIH
4: 3 who was at his side, said, "What they *are* **b** 1215
4:17 who *were* **b** the wall. 1215
6: 6 and therefore you *are* **b** the wall. 1215
Jer 52:13 Every important he burned down. 1074
Eze 41:12 The **b** facing the temple courtyard on 1230
41:12 The wall of the **b** was five cubits thick all 1230
41:13 and the temple courtyard and the **b** 1224
41:15 Then he measured the length of the **b** facing 1230
42: 1 The **b** whose door faced north was NIH
42: 5 on the lower and middle floors of the **b**. 1230
Mic 7:11 The day for **b** your walls will come, 1215
Lk 6:48 He is like a man **b** a house, 3868
17:28 buying and selling, planting and **b**. 3868
Ro 15:20 not **b** on someone else's foundation. 3868
1Co 3: 9 you are God's field, God's **b**. 3869
3:10 and someone else *is* **b** on it. 2224
2Co 5: 1 we have a **b** from God, 3869
10: 8 the authority the Lord gave us for **b** you **up** 3869
13:10 authority the Lord gave me for **b** you **up,** 3869
Eph 2:21 the whole **b** is joined together and rises 3869
4:29 for **b** others **up** according to their needs, 3869

BUILDINGS (12) [BUILD]
1Ki 9:10 during which Solomon built these two **b**— 1074
1Ch 15: 1 After David had constructed **b** for himself 1074
28:11 its **b**, its storerooms, its upper parts, 1074
29: 4 for the overlaying of the walls of the **b**, 1074
2Ch 32:28 also made **b** to store the harvest of grain, 5016
34:11 for joists and beams for the **b** that the kings 1074
Isa 22:10 the **b** in Jerusalem and tore down houses 1074
Jer 22:23 who are nestled in cedar **b**, NIH
Eze 40: 2 on whose south side were *some* **b** 4445
Mt 24: 1 up to him to call his attention to its **b**. 3869
Mk 13: 1 What magnificent **b**!" 3869
13: 2 "Do you see all these great **b**?" 3869

BUILDS (13) [BUILD]

Job	27:18	The house he **b** is like a moth's cocoon,	1215
Ps	127: 1	Unless the LORD **b** the house,	1215
	147: 2	The LORD **b** up Jerusalem;	1215
Pr	14: 1	The wise woman **b** her house,	1215
	17:19	he who **b** a high gate invites destruction.	1467
Jer	22:13	to him who **b** his palace by unrighteousness,	1215
Am	9: 6	he who **b** his lofty palace in the heavens	1215
Hab	2: 9	"Woe to him who **b** his realm by unjust gain	1298
	2:12	"Woe to him who **b** a city with bloodshed	1215
1Co	3:10	But each one should be careful how he **b**.	2224
	3:12	If any man **b** on this foundation using gold,	2224
	8: 1	Knowledge puffs up, but love **b up**.	3868
Eph	4:16	grows and **b** itself **up** in love,	3869

BUILT (200) [BUILD]

Ge	8:20	Then Noah **b** an altar to the LORD and,	1215
	10:11	where he **b** Nineveh, Rehoboth Ir,	1215
	12: 7	So he **b** an altar there to the LORD,	1215
	12: 8	There he **b** an altar to the LORD and called	1215
	13: 4	and where he had first **b** an altar.	6913
	13:18	where he **b** an altar to the LORD.	1215
	22: 9	Abraham **b** an altar there and arranged	1215
	26:25	Isaac **b** an altar there and called on	1215
	33:17	where he **b** a place for himself	1215
	35: 7	There he **b** an altar,	1215
Ex	1:11	and they **b** Pithom and Rameses	1215
	17:15	Moses **b** an altar and called it	1215
	24: 4	up early the next morning and **b** an altar at	1215
	32: 5	he **b** an altar in front of the calf	1215
	38: 1	They **b** the altar of burnt offering	6913
Nu	13:22	(Hebron had been **b** seven years before Zoan	1215
	23:14	and there he **b** seven altars and offered	1215
	32:34	The Gadites **b** up Dibon, Ataroth, Aroer,	1215
	32:36	and **b** pens for their flocks.	NIH
Dt	20: 5	"Has anyone **b** a new house and	1215
Jos	8:30	Then Joshua **b** on Mount Ebal an altar to	1215
	8:31	He **b** it according to what is written in	6641
	11:13	Yet Israel did not burn any of the cities **b**	6641
	19:50	And he **b** up the town and settled there.	1215
	22:10	of Manasseh **b** an imposing altar there by	1215
	22:11	the Israelites heard that they had **b** the altar	1215
	22:23	If we have our own altar to turn away	1215
	22:28	of the LORD's altar, which our fathers **b**,	6913
Jdg	1:26	where he **b** a city and called it Luz,	1215
	6:24	So Gideon **b** an altar to the LORD there	1215
	6:28	on the newly **b** altar!	1215
	21: 4	Early the next day the people **b** an altar	1215
Ru	4:11	who together **b up** the house of Israel.	1215
1Sa	7:17	And he **b** an altar there to the LORD.	1215
	14:35	Then Saul **b** an altar to the LORD;	1215
2Sa	5: 9	He **b** up the area around it,	1215
	5:11	and they **b** a palace for David.	1215
	7: 7	"Why have you not **b** me a house	1215
	20:15	They **b** a siege ramp up to the city,	9161
	24:25	David **b** an altar there to the LORD	1215
1Ki	3: 2	not yet been **b** for the Name of the LORD.	1215
	6: 2	The temple that King Solomon **b** for	1215
	6: 5	and inner sanctuary he **b** a structure around	1215
	6: 7	at the temple site while it was being **b**.	1215
	6: 9	So he **b** the temple and completed it,	1215
	6:10	he **b** the side rooms all along the temple.	1215
	6:14	So Solomon **b** the temple and completed it.	1215
	6:36	And he **b** the inner courtyard	1215
	7: 2	He **b** the Palace of the Forest of Lebanon	1215
	7: 7	He **b** the throne hall, the Hall of Justice,	6913
	8:13	I have indeed **b** a magnificent temple	1215+1215
	8:16	to have a temple **b** for my Name to be there,	1215
	8:20	and I have **b** the temple for the Name of	1215
	8:27	How much less this temple I have **b**!	1215
	8:43	that this house I have **b** bears your Name.	1215
	8:44	and the temple I have **b** for your Name,	1215
	8:48	and the temple I have **b** for your Name;	1215
	9: 3	this temple, which you have **b**,	1215
	9:10	during which Solomon **b** these two buildings—	1215
	9:17	He **b** up Lower Beth Horon,	NIH
	9:24	of David to the palace Solomon had **b**	1215
	9:25	fellowship offerings on the altar he had **b**	1215
	9:26	King Solomon also **b** ships at Ezion Geber,	6913
	10: 4	of Solomon and the palace he had **b**,	1215
	11: 7	Solomon **b** a high place for Chemosh	1215
	11:27	Solomon had **b** the supporting terraces	1215
	11:38	the one I **b** for David and will give Israel	1215
	12:25	From there he went out and **b up** Peniel.	1215
	12:31	Jeroboam **b** shrines on high places	6913
	12:33	he offered sacrifices on the altar he had **b**	6913
	15:22	With them King Asa **b** up Geba	1215
	15:23	all he did and the cities he **b**,	1215
	16:24	from Shemer for two talents of silver and **b**	1215
	16:32	in the temple of Baal that he **b** in Samaria.	1215
	18:32	With the stones he **b** an altar in the name of	1215
	22:39	the palace he **b** and inlaid with ivory,	1215
	22:48	Now Jehoshaphat **b** a fleet of trading ships	6913
2Ki	16:11	So Uriah the priest **b** an altar in accordance	1215
	16:18	that had been **b** at the temple and removed	1215
	17: 9	fortified city they **b** themselves high places	1215
	21: 4	He **b** altars in the temple of the LORD,	1215
	21: 5	he **b** altars to all the starry hosts.	1215
	23:12	the altars Manasseh had **b** in the two courts	6913
	23:13	the ones Solomon king of Israel had **b**	6913
	23:19	the high places that the kings of Israel had **b**	6913
	25: 1	the city and **b** siege works all around it.	1215
1Ch	6:10	in the temple Solomon **b** in Jerusalem),	1215
1Ch	6:32	until Solomon **b** the temple of the LORD	1215
	7:24	who **b** Lower and Upper Beth Horon as well	1215
	8:12	Eber, Misham, Shemed (who **b** Ono	1215
	11: 8	He **b** up the city around it,	1215
	17: 6	"Why have you not **b** me a house	1215
	21:26	David **b** an altar to the LORD there	1215
	22: 5	the house to be **b** for the LORD should be	1215
	22:19	into the temple that will be **b** for the Name	1215
2Ch	3: 8	He **b** the Most Holy Place,	6913
	6: 2	I have **b** a magnificent temple for you,	1215
	6: 5	to have a temple for my Name to be there,	1215
	6:10	and I have **b** the temple for the Name of	1215
	6:18	How much less this temple I have **b**!	1215
	6:33	that this house I have **b** bears your Name.	1215
	6:34	and the temple I have **b** for your Name,	1215
	6:38	toward the temple I have **b** for your Name;	1215
	8: 1	during which Solomon **b** the temple of	1215
	8: 4	He also **b** up Tadmor in the desert and all	1215
	8: 4	in the desert and all the store cities he had **b**	1215
	8:11	the City of David to the palace he had **b**	1215
	8:12	the altar of the LORD that he had **b** in front	1215
	9: 3	as well as the palace he had **b**,	1215
	11: 5	in Jerusalem and **b** up towns for defense	1215
	14: 6	He **b** up the fortified cities of Judah,	1215
	14: 7	So they **b** and prospered.	1215
	16: 9	With them he **b** up Geba and Mizpah.	1215
	17:12	he **b** forts and store cities in Judah	1215
	20: 8	and have **b** in it a sanctuary for your Name,	1215
	20:36	After these were **b** at Ezion Geber,	1215
	21:11	also **b** high places on the hills of Judah	6913
	26: 9	Uzziah **b** towers in Jerusalem at	1215
	26:10	He also **b** towers in the desert	1215
	27: 4	He **b** towns in the Judean hills and forts	1215
	28:25	in Judah he **b** high places to burn sacrifices	6913
	32: 5	He **b** another wall outside that one	NIH
	32:29	He **b** villages and acquired great numbers	6913
	33: 4	He **b** altars in the temple of the LORD,	1215
	33: 5	In both courtyards he **b** altars to all the starry hosts.	1215
	33:15	as all the altars he had **b** on the temple hill	1215
	33:19	and the sites where he **b** high places and set	1215
	35: 3	that Solomon son of David king of Israel **b**.	1215
Ezr	3: 3	they **b** the altar on its foundation	3922
	4:13	the king should know that if this city is **b**	10111
	4:16	if this city is **b** and its walls are restored,	10111
	5:11	the temple that was **b** many years ago,	10111
	5:11	that a great king of Israel **b** and finished.	10111
Ne	3: 2	The men of Jericho **b** the adjoining section,	1215
	3: 2	and Zaccur son of Imri **b** next to them.	1215
	8: 4	a high wooden platform **b** for the occasion.	6913
	8:16	and **b** themselves booths	6913
	8:17	from exile **b** booths and lived in them.	6913
	12:29	for the singers had **b** villages for themselves	1215
Est	5:14	"Have a gallows **b**, seventy-five feet high,	6913
	7: 9	and he had **b** the gallows **b**.	6913
Job	3:14	who **b** for themselves places now lying	1215
Ps	78:69	He **b** his sanctuary like the heights,	1215
	122: 3	Jerusalem is **b** like a city	1215
Pr	9: 1	Wisdom has **b** her house;	1215
	24: 3	By wisdom a house is **b**,	1215
Ecc	2: 4	I **b** houses for myself	1215
	9:14	surrounded it and **b** huge siegeworks	1215
SS	4: 4	like the tower of David, **b** with elegance;	1215
Isa	5: 2	He **b** a watchtower in it and cut out	1215
	22:11	You **b** a reservoir between the two walls for	6913
	44:26	of the towns of Judah, 'They shall be **b**,'	1215
Jer	7:31	They have **b** the high places of Topheth in	1215
	18: 9	that a nation or kingdom is to be **b up**	1215
	18:15	in bypaths and on roads not **b up**.	6148
	19: 5	They have **b** the high places of Baal	1215
	32:24	"See how the siege ramps are **b** up to take	995
	32:31	From the day it was **b** until now,	1215
	32:35	They **b** high places for Baal in the Valley	1215
	35: 9	or **b** houses to live in or had vineyards.	1215
	45: 4	I will overthrow what I have **b**	1215
	52: 4	the city and **b** siege works all around it.	1215
Eze	13:10	and because, when a flimsy wall is **b**,	1215
	16:24	you **b** a mound for yourself and made	1215
	16:25	of every street you **b** your lofty shrines	1215
	16:31	When you **b** your mounds at the head	1215
	17:17	when ramps are **b** and siege works erected	9161
	41: 7	The structure surrounding the temple was **b**	NIH
	43:18	upon the altar when it is **b**:	6913
	46:23	with places for fire **b** all around under	6913
Da	4:30	"Is not this the great Babylon I have **b** as	10111
Hos	8:11	Ephraim **b** many altars for sin offerings,	8049
	8:14	Israel has forgotten his Maker and **b** palaces;	1215
	10: 1	As his fruit increased, he **b** more altars;	8049
Am	5:11	though you have **b** stone mansions,	1215
	7: 7	by a wall that had been **b** true to plumb,	NIH
Hag	1: 2	yet come for the LORD's house to be **b**.'"	1215
Zec	8: 9	be strong so that the temple may be **b**.	1215
	9: 3	Tyre has **b** herself a stronghold;	1215
Mt	7:24	a wise man who **b** his house on the rock.	3868
	7:26	like a foolish man who **b** his house on sand.	3868
	21:33	dug a winepress in it and **b** a watchtower.	3868
Mk	12: 1	a pit for the winepress and **b** a watchtower.	3868
Lk	4:29	of the hill on which the town was **b**,	3868
	6:48	because it was well **b**.	3868
	6:49	into practice is like a man who **b** a house on	3868
	7: 5	and has **b** our synagogue."	3868
Ac	7:47	it was Solomon who **b** the house for him.	3868
	17:24	and does not live in temples **b** by hands.	5935
	28: 2	They **b** a fire and welcomed us all	721
1Co	3:14	If what he has **b** survives,	2224
2Co	5: 1	an eternal house in heaven, **not b by human hands**.	942
Eph	2:20	**b on** the foundation of the apostles	2224
	2:22	And in him you too are being **b together**	5325
	4:12	so that the body of Christ may be **b up**	3869
Col	2: 7	rooted and **b up** in him,	2224
Heb	3: 4	For every house is **b** by someone,	2941
	11: 7	in holy fear **b** an ark to save his family.	2941
1Pe	2: 5	are being **b** into a spiritual house to be	3868
	3:20	the days of Noah while the ark was being **b**.	2941

BUKKI (5)

Nu	34:22	**B** son of Jogli, the leader from the tribe	1321
1Ch	6: 5	Abishua the father of **B**,	1321
	6: 5	**B** the father of Uzzi,	1321
	6:51	**B** his son, Uzzi his son, Zerahiah his son,	1321
Ezr	7: 4	the son of Uzzi, the son of **B**,	1321

BUKKIAH (2)

1Ch	25: 4	As for Heman, from his sons: **B**,	1322
	25:13	the sixth to **B**, his sons and relatives,	1322

BUL (1)

1Ki	6:38	In the eleventh year in the month of **B**,	1004

BULGES (1) [BULGING]

Job	15:27	with fat and his waist **b with flesh**,	6913+7089

BULGING (1) [BULGES]

Isa	30:13	cracked and **b**, that collapses suddenly,	1240

BULL (98) [BULL'S, BULLS]

Ex	21:28	"If a **b** gores a man or a woman to death,	8802
	21:28	the **b** must be stoned to death,	8802
	21:28	of the **b** will not be held responsible.	8802
	21:29	the **b** has had the habit of goring and	8802
	21:29	the **b** must be stoned and the owner	8802
	21:31	This law also applies if the **b** gores a son	NIH
	21:32	If the **b** gores a male or female slave,	8802
	21:32	and the **b** must be stoned.	8802
	21:35	"If a man's **b** injures the bull of another	8802
	21:35	If a man's bull injures the **b** of another	8802
	21:36	if it was known that the **b** had the habit	8802
	29: 1	young **b** and two rams without defect.	1330+7228
	29: 3	along with the **b** and the two rams.	7228
	29:10	the **b** to the front of the Tent of Meeting,	7228
	29:36	Sacrifice a **b** each day as a sin offering	7228
Lev	1: 5	to slaughter the young **b** before the LORD,	1330
	4: 3	to the LORD a young **b** without defect	1330+7228
	4: 4	the **b** at the entrance to the Tent of Meeting	7228
	4: 8	He shall remove all the fat from the **b** of	7228
	4:11	But the hide of the **b** and all its flesh,	7228
	4:12	all the rest of the **b**—	7228
	4:14	young **b** as a sin offering and present	1330+7228
	4:15	and the **b** shall be slaughtered before	7228
	4:20	with this **b** just as he did with the bull for	7228
	4:20	with this bull just as he did with the **b** for	7228
	4:21	Then he shall take the **b** outside the camp	7228
	4:21	and burn it as he burned the first **b**.	7228
	8: 2	the anointing oil, the **b** for the sin offering,	7228
	8:14	He then presented the **b** for the sin offering,	7228
	8:15	Moses slaughtered the **b** and took some of	NIH
	8:17	But the **b** with its hide and its flesh	7228
	9: 2	"Take a **b** calf for your sin offering	1201+1330
	16: 3	young **b** for a sin offering and a ram	1330+7228
	16: 6	to offer the **b** for his own sin offering	7228
	16:11	the **b** for his own sin offering	7228
	16:11	to slaughter the **b** for his own sin offering.	7228
	16:27	The **b** and the goat for the sin offerings,	7228
	23:18	one young **b** and two rams.	1330+7228
Nu	7:15	one young **b**, one ram and one male	1330+7228
	7:21	one young **b**, one ram and one male	1330+7228
	7:27	one young **b**, one ram and one male	1330+7228
	7:33	one young **b**, one ram and one male	1330+7228
	7:39	one young **b**, one ram and one male	1330+7228
	7:45	one young **b**, one ram and one male	1330+7228
	7:51	one young **b**, one ram and one male	1330+7228
	7:57	one young **b**, one ram and one male	1330+7228
	7:63	one young **b**, one ram and one male	1330+7228
	7:69	one young **b**, one ram and one male	1330+7228
	7:75	one young **b**, one ram and one male	1330+7228
	7:81	one young **b**, one ram and one male	1330+7228
	8: 8	a young **b** with its grain offering	1330+7228
	8: 8	a second young **b** for a sin offering.	7228
	15: 8	a young **b** as a burnt offering or sacrifice,	1330
	15: 9	with the **b** a grain offering of three-tenths of	1330
	15:11	Each **b** or ram, each lamb or young goat,	8802
	15:24	whole community is to offer a young **b**	1330+7228
	23: 2	then offered a **b** and a ram on each altar.	7228
	23: 4	on each altar I have offered a **b** and a ram."	7228
	23:14	and offered a **b** and a ram on each altar.	7228
	23:30	and offered a **b** and a ram on each altar.	7228
	28:12	With each **b** there is to be a grain offering	7228
	28:14	With each **b** there is to be a drink offering	7228
	28:20	With each **b** prepare a grain offering	7228
	28:28	With each **b** there is to be a grain offering	7228
	29: 2	a burnt offering of one young **b**,	1330+7228
	29: 3	With the **b** prepare a grain offering	7228
	29: 8	a burnt offering of one young **b**,	1330+7228
	29: 9	With the **b** prepare a grain offering	7228
	29:36	a burnt offering of one **b**,	7228
	29:37	With the **b**, the ram and the lambs,	7228
Dt	18: 3	the people who sacrifice a **b** or a sheep:	8802
	33:17	In majesty he is like a firstborn **b**;	8802
Jdg	6:25	"Take the second **b** from your father's herd,	7228

Jdg 6:26 offer the second *b* as a burnt offering." 7228
    6:28 down and the second *b* sacrificed on 7228
1Sa 1:24 along with a three-year-old *b*, 7228
    1:25 When they had slaughtered the **b**, 7228
2Sa 6:13 he sacrificed a *b* and a fattened calf. 8802
1Ki 18:23 I will prepare the other *b* and put it on 7228
    18:26 they took the *b* given them and prepared it. 7228
    18:33 the *b* into pieces and laid it on the wood. 7228
2Ch 13: 9 a young *b* and seven rams may become 1330
Ps 50: 9 I have no need of a *b* from your stall or 7228
    69:31 more than a *b* with its horns and hoofs. 7228
    106:20 for an image of a *b*, 8802
Isa 34: 7 the *b* calves and the great bulls. 7228
    66: 3 a *b* is like one who kills a man, 7228
Eze 43:19 are to give a young *b* as a sin offering 1330+7228
    43:21 to take the *b* for the sin offering and burn it 7228
    43:22 to be purified as it was purified with the **b**. 7228
    43:23 a young *b* and a ram from the flock, 1330+7228
    43:25 also to provide a young *b* and a ram 1330+7228
    45:18 take a young *b* without defect and purify
        the sanctuary. 1330+7228
    45:22 the prince is to provide a *b* as a sin offering 7228
    45:24 as a grain offering an ephah for each *b* and 7228
    46: 6 New Moon he is to offer a young *b*, 1330+7228
    46: 7 as a grain offering one ephah with the *b*, 7228
    46:11 grain offering is to be an ephah with a *b*, 7228

BULL'S (9) [BULL]
Ex 29:12 of the *b* blood and put it on the horns of 7228
    29:14 the *b* flesh and its hide and its offal outside 7228
Lev 4: 5 of the *b* blood and carry it into the Tent 7228
    4: 7 the *b* blood he shall pour out at the base of 7228
    4:15 to lay their hands on the *b* head before 7228
    4:16 to take some of the *b* blood into the Tent 7228
    16:14 the *b* blood and with his finger sprinkle it 7228
    16:14 and do with it as he did with the *b* blood: 7228
    16:18 He shall take some of the *b* blood and some 7228

BULLOCK (KJV) See BULL

BULLS (64) [BULL]
Ge 32:15 forty cows and ten **b**, 7228
Ex 24: 5 and sacrificed **young b** 7228
Nu 7:87 the burnt offering came to twelve **young b**, 7228
    8:12 on the heads of the **b**, 7228
    23: 1 and prepare seven **b** and seven rams 7228
    23:29 and prepare seven **b** and seven rams 7228
    28:11 a burnt offering of two young **b**, 1330+7228
    28:19 a burnt offering of two young **b**, 1330+7228
    28:27 Present a burnt offering of two young **b**, 1330+7228
    29:13 a burnt offering of thirteen young **b**, 1330+7228
    29:14 of the thirteen **b** prepare a grain offering 7228
    29:17 second day prepare twelve young **b**, 1330+7228
    29:18 With the **b**, rams and lambs, 7228
    29:20 " 'On the third day prepare eleven **b**, 7228
    29:21 With the **b**, rams and lambs, 7228
    29:23 " 'On the fourth day prepare ten **b**, 7228
    29:24 With the **b**, rams and lambs, 7228
    29:26 " 'On the fifth day prepare nine **b**, 7228
    29:27 With the **b**, rams and lambs, 7228
    29:29 " 'On the sixth day prepare eight **b**, 7228
    29:30 With the **b**, rams and lambs, 7228
    29:32 " 'On the seventh day prepare seven **b**, 7228
    29:33 With the **b**, rams and lambs, 7228
1Ki 7:25 The Sea stood on twelve **b**, 1330
    7:29 the uprights were lions, **b** and cherubim— 1330
    7:29 and **b** were wreaths of hammered work. 1330
    7:44 the Sea and the twelve **b** under it; 1330
    18:23 Get two **b** for us. 1330
    18:25 "Choose one of the **b** and prepare it first, 7228
2Ki 16:17 the Sea from the bronze **b** that supported it 1330
1Ch 15:26 seven **b** and seven rams were sacrificed. 7228
    29:21 a thousand **b**, a thousand rams and 7228
2Ch 4: 3 Below the rim, figures of **b** encircled it— 1330
    4: 3 The **b** were cast in two rows in one piece 1330
    4: 4 The Sea stood on twelve **b**, 1330
    4:15 the Sea and the twelve **b** under it; 1330
    29:21 They brought seven **b**, seven rams, 7228
    29:22 So they slaughtered the **b**, 1330
    29:32 the assembly brought was seventy **b**, 1330
    29:33 to six hundred **b** and three thousand sheep 1330
    30:24 a thousand **b** and seven thousand sheep 7228
    30:24 with a thousand **b** and ten thousand sheep 7228
Ezr 6: 9 Whatever is needed—young **b**, rams, 10756
    6:17 of God they offered a hundred **b**, 10756
    7:17 With this money be sure to buy **b**, 10756
    8:35 twelve **b** for all Israel, ninety-six rams, 7228
Job 21:10 Their **b** never fail to breed; 8802
    42: 8 So now take seven **b** and seven rams and go 7228
Ps 22:12 Many **b** surround me; 7228
    22:12 strong **b** of Bashan encircle me. NIH
    50:13 the flesh of **b** or drink the blood of goats? 52
    51:19 then **b** will be offered on your altar. 7228
    66:15 I will offer **b** and goats. 1330
    68:30 herd of **b** among the calves of the nations. 52
Isa 1:11 in the blood of **b** and lambs and goats. 7228
    34: 7 the bull calves and the great **b**. NIH
Jer 50:27 Kill all her **young b**; 7228
    52:20 the Sea and the twelve bronze **b** under it, 1330
Eze 39:18 as if they were rams and lambs, goats and **b** 7228
    45:23 of the Feast he is to provide seven **b** 7228
Hos 12:11 Do they sacrifice **b** in Gilgal? 8802
Ac 14:13 brought **b** and wreaths to the city gates 5436
Heb 9:13 The blood of goats and **b** and the ashes of 5436

Heb 10: 4 the blood of *b* and goats to take away sins. 5436

BULRUSH, BULRUSHES (KJV) See PAPYRUS

BULWARKS (KJV) See SEIGEWORKS, CORNER DEFENSES

BUNAH (1)
1Ch 2:25 Ram his firstborn, **B**, Oren, 1007

BUNCH (1)
Ex 12:22 Take a *b* of hyssop, 99

BUNDLE (1) [BUNDLES]
1Sa 25:29 be bound securely in the *b* of the living by 7655

BUNDLES (2) [BUNDLE]
Ru 2:16 from the *b* and leave them for her to pick 7395
Mt 13:30 First collect the weeds and tie them in *b* to 1299

BUNNI (3)
Ne 9: 4 Jeshua, Bani, Kadmiel, Shebaniah, **B**, 1221
    10:15 **B**, Azgad, Bebai, 1221
    11:15 the son of Hashabiah, the son of **B**; 1221

BURDEN (37) [BURDENED, BURDENS, BURDENSOME]
Ge 49:15 to the *b* and submit to forced labor. 6022
Nu 11:11 that you put the *b* of all these people 5362
    11:14 the *b* is too heavy for me. NIH
    11:17 of the people so that you will 5362
Dt 1: 9 **too heavy a b** for me **to carry** 3523+4202+5951
1Sa 25:31 not have on his conscience the **staggering**
        b of needless bloodshed 2256+4842+7050
2Sa 13:25 we would only be a *b* to you." 3877
    15:33 "If you go with me, you will be a *b* to me. 5362
    19:35 Why should your servant be an added *b* 5362
Ne 5:15 **placed a heavy** *b* on the people 3877
Job 7:20 Have I become a *b* to you? 5362
Ps 38: 4 like a *b* too heavy to bear. 5362
    81: 6 "I removed the *b* from their shoulders; 6023
Pr 3: 5 Stone is heavy and sand a *b*, 5748
Ecc 1:13 What a heavy *b* God has laid on men! 6701+6721
    3:10 I have seen the *b* God has laid on men. 6701+6721
Isa 1:14 They have become a *b* to me; 3268
    10:27 In that day their *b* will be lifted 6024
    14:25 and his *b* removed from their shoulders." 6024
    46: 1 idols are borne by **beasts of b**. 989+2256+2651
    46: 1 a *b* for the weary. 5362
    46: 2 unable to rescue the **b**, 5362
Zep 3:18 they are a *b* and a reproach to you. 5368
Mal 1:13 And you say, 'What a *b*!' 9430
Mt 11:30 For my yoke is easy and my *b* is light." 5845
    20:12 to us who have borne the *b* of the work and 983
Ac 15:28 to us not to *b* you with anything beyond 983+2202
2Co 11: 9 I was not a *b* to anyone, 2915
    11: 9 I have kept myself from being a *b* to you 4
    12:13 except that I was never a *b* to you? 2915
    12:14 and I will not be a *b* to you, 2915
    12:16 I have not been a *b* to you. 2851
1Th 2: 6 of Christ we could have been a *b* to you, 983
    2: 9 not to be a *b* to anyone while we preached 2096
2Th 3: 8 so that we would not be a *b* to any of you. 2096
Heb 13:17 so that their work will be a joy, not a *b*, for 5100
Rev 2:24 not impose any other *b* on you): 983

BURDENED (7) [BURDEN]
Isa 43:23 I have not *b* you with grain offerings 6268
    43:24 But you have *b* me with your sins 6268
Mic 6: 3 How have I *b* you? 4206
Mt 11:28 "Come to me, all you who are weary and *b*, 5844
2Co 5: 4 we groan and are *b*, 976
Gal 5: 1 not let yourselves be *b* again by a yoke 1923
1Ti 5:16 and not let the church be *b* with them, 976

BURDENS (8) [BURDEN]
Nu 4:24 as they work and carry **b**: 5362
Dt 1:12 and your *b* and your disputes all by myself? 5362
Ps 66:11 You brought us into prison and laid *b* 4601
    68:19 to God our Savior, who daily bears our **b**. 6673
    73: 5 They are free from the *b* common to man; 6662
Isa 9: 4 you have shattered the yoke that *b* them, 6024
Lk 11:46 down with *b* they can hardly carry, 5845
Gal 6: 2 Carry each other's **b**, 983

BURDENSOME (2) [BURDEN]
Isa 46: 1 The images that are carried about are **b**, 6673
1Jn 5: 3 And his commands are not **b**, 987

BURIAL (18) [BURY]
Ge 23: 4 for a *b* site here so I can bury my dead." 7700
    23: 9 to sell it to me for the full price as a *b* site 7700
    23:20 to Abraham by the Hittites as a *b* site. 7700
    49:30 as a *b* place from Ephron the Hittite, 7700
    50:13 which Abraham had bought as a *b* place 7700
2Ch 26:23 near them in a field for *b* that belonged to 7690
Ecc 6: 3 and does not receive **proper b**, 7690

Isa 14:20 you will not join them in **b**, 7690
Jer 22:19 He will have the *b* of a donkey— 7690+7699
    26:23 into the *b* **place** of the common people.) 7700
Eze 39:11 that day I will give Gog a *b* place in Israel, 7700
Mt 26:12 she did it to **prepare** me **for b**. 1946
    27: 7 to buy the potter's field as a *b* **place** 5438
Mk 14: 8 to prepare for my **b**. 1947
Jn 12: 7 for the day of my **b**. 1947
    19:40 in accordance with Jewish customs. 1946
    20: 7 as well as the *b* **cloth** that had been 5051
Rev 11: 9 gaze on their bodies and refuse them **b**.
        1650+3645+5502

BURIED (112) [BURY]
Ge 15:15 will go to your fathers in peace and be *b* at 7699
    23:19 Afterward Abraham *b* his wife Sarah in 7699
    25: 9 His sons Isaac and Ishmael *b* him in 7699
    25:10 There Abraham was *b* with his wife Sarah. 7699
    35: 4 Jacob *b* them under the oak at Shechem. 3243
    35: 8 died and was *b* under the oak below Bethel. 7699
    35:19 and was *b* on the way to Ephrath (that is, 7699
    35:29 And his sons Esau and Jacob *b* him. 7699
    47:30 of Egypt and bury me where they are **b**." 7690
    48: 7 So I *b* her there beside the road 7699
    49:31 There Abraham and his wife Sarah were **b**, 7699
    49:31 there Isaac and his wife Rebekah were **b**, 7699
    49:31 and there I *b* Leah. 7699
    50:13 of Canaan and *b* him in the cave in the field 7699
Nu 11:34 because there they *b* 7699
    20: 1 There Miriam died and was **b**. 7699
Dt 10: 6 There Aaron died and was **b**, 7699
    34: 6 He *b* him in Moab, 7699
Jos 24:30 they *b* him in the land of his inheritance, 7699
    24:32 were *b* at Shechem in the tract of land 7699
    24:33 And Eleazar son of Aaron died and was *b* 7699
Jdg 2: 9 they *b* him in the land of his inheritance, 7699
    8:32 of Joash died at a good old age and was *b* in 7699
    10: 2 then he died, and was *b* in Shamir. 7699
    10: 5 When Jair died, he was *b* in Kamon. 7699
    12: 7 and was *b* in a town in Gilead. 7699
    12:10 Then Ibzan died, and was *b* in Bethlehem. 7699
    12:12 and was *b* in Aijalon in the land of Zebulun. 7699
    12:15 and was *b* at Pirathon in Ephraim, 7699
    16:31 and *b* him between Zorah and Eshtaol in 7699
Ru 1:17 and there I will be **b**. 7699
1Sa 25: 1 and they *b* him at his home in Ramah. 7699
    28: 3 and *b* him in his own town of Ramah. 7699
    31:13 and *b* them under a tamarisk tree at Jabesh, 7699
2Sa 2: 4 the men of Jabesh Gilead who had *b* Saul, 7699
    2:32 and *b* him in his father's tomb 7699
    3:32 They *b* Abner in Hebron. 7699
    4:12 of Ish-Bosheth and *b* it in Abner's tomb 7699
    17:23 So he died and was *b* in his father's tomb. 7699
    21:14 They *b* the bones of Saul 7699
1Ki 2:10 with his fathers and was *b* in the City 7699
    2:34 and he was *b* on his own land in the desert. 7699
    11:43 Then he rested with his fathers and was *b* in 7699
    13:22 not be *b* in the tomb of your fathers.' " 995
    13:31 in the grave where the man of God is *b*; 7700
    14:13 to Jeroboam who will be **b**, 448+995+7700
    14:18 They *b* him, and all Israel mourned for him, 7699
    14:31 and was *b* with them in the City of David. 7699
    15: 8 with his fathers and was *b* in the City 7699
    15:24 Then Asa rested with his fathers and was *b* 7699
    16: 6 Baasha rested with his fathers and was *b* 7699
    16:28 Omri rested with his fathers and was *b* 7699
    22:37 and they *b* him there. 7699
    22:50 with his fathers and was *b* with them in 7699
2Ki 8:24 and was *b* with them in the City of David. 7699
    9:28 and *b* him with his fathers in his tomb in 7699
    10:35 with his fathers and was *b* in Samaria. 7699
    12:21 and was *b* with his fathers in the City 7699
    13: 9 Jehoahaz rested with his fathers and was *b* 7699
    13:13 Jehoash rested with his fathers and was *b* 7699
    13:20 Elisha died and was **b**. 7699
    14:16 with his fathers and was *b* in Samaria with 7699
    14:20 He was brought back by horse and was *b* 7699
    15: 7 and was *b* near them in the City of David. 7699
    15:38 and was *b* with them in the City of David. 7699
    16:20 and was *b* with them in the City of David. 7699
    21:18 Manasseh rested with his fathers and was *b* 7699
    21:26 He was *b* in his grave in the garden 7699
    22:20 and you will be *b* in peace. 448+665+7700
    23:30 to Jerusalem and *b* him in his own tomb. 7699
1Ch 10:12 Then they *b* their bones under the great tree 7699
2Ch 9:31 Then he rested with his fathers and was *b* in 7699
    12:16 Rehoboam rested with his fathers and was *b* 7699
    14: 1 with his fathers and was *b* in the City 7699
    16:14 They *b* him in the tomb that he had cut out 7699
    21: 1 and was *b* with his fathers in the City of David. 7699
    21:20 and was *b* in the City of David, 7699
    22: 9 They *b* him, for they said, 7699
    24:16 He was *b* with the kings in the City 7699
    24:25 So he died and was *b* in the City of David, 7699
    25:28 He was brought back by horse and was *b* 7699
    26:23 Uzziah rested with his fathers and was *b* 7699
    27: 9 Jotham rested with his fathers and was *b* in 7699
    28:27 Ahaz rested with his fathers and was *b* in 7699
    32:33 with his fathers and was *b* on the hill where 7699
    33:20 Manasseh rested with his fathers and was *b* 7699
    34:28 and you will be *b* in peace. 448+665+7700
    35:24 He was *b* in the tombs of his fathers, 7699
Ne 2: 3 the city where my fathers are *b* lies in ruins, 7700
    2: 5 the city in Judah where my fathers are *b* so 7700
Job 16:15 over my skin and *b* my brow in the dust. 6619
Ps 106:17 it *b* the company of Abiram. 4059

Ecc	8:10	Then too, I saw the wicked **b**—	7699
Jer	8: 2	They will not be gathered up or **b**,	7699
	16: 4	They will not be mourned or **b** but will be	7699
	16: 6	*They* will not **be b** or mourned,	7699
	20: 6	There you will die and **be b,**	7699
	25:33	not be mourned or gathered up or **b,**	7699
	43:10	over these stones *I have* **b** here;	3243
Eze	39:11	Gog and all his hordes *will be* **b** there.	7699
	39:15	beside it until the gravediggers *have* **b** it in	7699
Mt	14:12	and took his body and **b** it.	2507
Lk	16:22	The rich man also died and *was* **b.**	2507
Ac	2:29	that the patriarch David died and *was* **b,**	2507
	5: 6	and carried him out and **b** him.	2507
	5: 9	of the men who **b** your husband are at	2507
	5:10	and **b** her beside her husband.	2507
	8: 2	Godly men **b** Stephen and mourned deeply	5172
	13:36	*he was* **b** with his fathers	4707
Ro	6: 4	therefore **b** with him through baptism	5313
1Co	15: 4	that *he was* **b,** that he was raised	2507
Col	2:12	*having been* **b** with him in baptism	5313

BURIES (2) [BURY]

Pr	19:24	The sluggard **b** his hand in the dish;	3243
	26:15	The sluggard **b** his hand in the dish;	3243

BURN (136) [BURNED, BURNED-OUT, BURNING, BURNS, BURNT]

Ex	3: 2	though the bush was on fire it *did* not **b** up.	430
	3: 3	why the bush *does* not **b** up."	1277
	12:10	if some is left till morning, *you must* **b** it. 836+928+2021+8596	
	21:25	**b** for burn, wound for wound, bruise	3918
	21:25	burn for **b,** wound for wound, bruise	3918
	29:13	and **b** them on the altar.	7787
	29:14	But **b** the bull's flesh and its hide 836+928+2021+8596	
	29:18	Then **b** the entire ram on the altar.	7787
	29:25	from their hands and **b** them on the altar	7787
	29:34	over till morning, **b** it **up.** 836+928+2021+8596	
	30: 7	"Aaron *must* **b** fragrant incense on	7787
	30: 8	*He must* **b** incense again when he lights	7787
	30: 8	at twilight so incense will **b** regularly	NIH
	32:10	Now leave me alone so that my anger *may* **b**	3013
	32:11	"why *should* your anger **b**	3013
Lev	1: 9	and the priest is to **b** all of it on the altar.	7787
	1:13	and the priest is to bring all of it and **b** it on	7787
	1:15	wring off the head and **b** it on the altar;	7787
	1:17	then the priest *shall* **b** it on the wood that is	7787
	2: 2	**b** this as a memorial portion on the altar,	7787
	2: 9	from the grain offering and **b** it on the altar	7787
	2:11	for *you are* not to **b** any yeast or honey in	7787
	2:16	The priest *shall* **b** the memorial portion of	7787
	3: 5	Then Aaron's sons *are to* **b** it on the altar	7787
	3:11	The priest *shall* **b** them on the altar	7787
	3:16	The priest *shall* **b** them on the altar	7787
	4:10	Then the priest *shall* **b** them on the altar	7787
	4:12	and **b** it in a wood fire on the ash heap.	8596
	4:19	He shall remove all the fat from it and **b** it	7787
	4:21	the camp and **b** it as he burned the first bull.	8596
	4:26	*He shall* **b** all the fat on the altar	7787
	4:31	and the priest *shall* **b** it on the altar as	7787
	4:35	and the priest *shall* **b** it on the altar on top	7787
	5:12	as a memorial portion and **b** it on the altar	7787
	6:12	the burnt offering on the fire and **b** the fat	7787
	6:15	and **b** the memorial portion on the altar as	7787
	7: 5	The priest *shall* **b** them on the altar as	7787
	7:31	The priest *shall* **b** the fat on the altar,	7787
	8:32	**b** up the rest of the meat and the bread. 836+928+2021+8596	
	13:24	"When someone has a **b** on his skin 836+4805	
	13:24	in the raw flesh of the **b,**	4805
	13:25	that has broken out in the **b.**	4805
	13:28	it is a swelling from the **b,**	4805
	13:28	it is only a scar from the **b.**	4805
	13:52	*He must* **b** up the clothing,	8596
	13:55	**B** it with fire,	8596
	16:25	also **b** the fat of the sin offering on the altar.	7787
	17: 6	at the entrance to the Tent of Meeting and **b**	7787
Nu	5:26	as a memorial offering and **b** it on the altar;	7787
	16:40	of Aaron should come to **b** incense before	7787
	18:17	the altar and **b** their fat as an offering made	7787
Dt	6:15	is a jealous God and his anger *will* **b**	3013
	7: 4	and the LORD's anger *will* **b** against you	3013
	7: 5	down their Asherah poles and **b** their idols	8596
	7:25	The images of their gods *you are to* **b** in	8596
	11:17	the LORD's anger *will* **b** against you,	3013
	12: 3	and **b** their Asherah poles in the fire;	8596
	12:31	**b** their sons and daughters in the fire as sacrifices	8596
	13:16	and completely **b** the town 836+928+2021+8596	
	29:20	his wrath and zeal *will* **b** against that man.	6939
Jos	11: 6	and **b** their chariots. 836+928+2021+8596	
	11:13	Yet Israel *did* not **b** any of the cities built	8596
	23:16	the LORD's anger *will* **b** against you,	3013
Jdg	12: 1	to **b** down your house over your head." 836+928+2021+8596	
	14:15	**b** you and your father's household **to death.** 836+928+2021+8596	
1Sa	2:28	to go up to my altar, to **b** incense,	7787
1Ki	1: 4	*I will* **b** up the house of Jeroboam	1277
	22:43	to offer sacrifices and **b** incense there.	7787
2Ki	12: 3	to offer sacrifices and **b** incense there.	7787
	14: 4	to offer sacrifices and **b** incense there.	7787
	15: 4	to offer sacrifices and **b** incense there.	7787
	15:35	to offer sacrifices and **b** incense there.	7787

2Ki	22:17	my anger *will* **b** against this place and will	3675
	23: 5	*to* **b** incense on the high places of the towns	7787
1Ch	14:12	and David gave orders *to* **b** them in the fire.	8596
2Ch	2: 6	as a place to **b** sacrifices before him?	7787
	4:20	to **b** in front of the inner sanctuary	1277
	26:16	the temple of the LORD to **b** incense on	7787
	26:18	Uzziah, to **b** incense to the LORD.	7787
	26:18	who have been consecrated to **b** incense.	7787
	26:19	a censer in his hand *ready* to **b** incense,	7787
	28:25	in Judah he built high places to **b** sacrifices	7787
	29: 7	not **b** incense or present any burnt offerings	7787
	29:11	to minister before him and *to* **b** incense."	7787
	32:12	before one altar and **b** sacrifices on it'?	7787
Ne	10:34	a contribution of wood to **b** on the altar of	1277
Ps	79: 5	How long *will* your jealousy **b** like fire?	1277
	89:46	How long *will* your wrath **b** like fire?	1277
	102: 3	my bones like glowing embers.	3081
Isa	1:31	both *will* **b** together,	1277
	10:17	in a single day *it will* **b**	1277
	47:14	The fire *will* **b** them **up.**	8596
	57: 5	You **b** with lust among the oaks and	2801
Jer	4: 4	or my wrath will break out and **b** like fire	1277
	4: 4	**b** with no one to quench it.	NIH
	6:29	The bellows blow fiercely *to* **b** away	9462
	7: 9	**b** incense to Baal	7787
	7:20	and *it will* **b** and not be quenched.	1277
	7:31	in the Valley of Ben Hinnom to **b** their sons	8596
	11:12	to the gods to whom they **b** incense,	7787
	11:13	and the altars you have set up to **b** incense	7787
	15:14	for my anger will kindle a fire *that will* **b**	3678
	17: 4	and *it will* **b** forever."	3678
	18:15	*they* **b** incense to worthless idols,	7787
	19: 5	the high places of Baal to **b** their sons in	8596
	21:12	or my wrath will break out and **b** like fire	1277
	21:12	**b** with no one to quench it.	NIH
	32:29	*they will* **b** it **down,**	8596
	33:18	to **b** grain offerings and	7787
	34: 2	and *he will* **b** it **down.** 836+928+2021+8596	
	34:22	take it and **b** it **down.** 836+928+2021+8596	
	36:25	and Gemariah urged the king not *to* **b**	8596
	37: 8	they will capture it and **b** it **down.'** 836+928+2021+8596	
	37:10	they would come out and **b** this city **down."** 836+928+2021+8596	
	38:18	the Babylonians and *they will* **b** it **down;** 836+928+2021+8596	
	43:12	*he will* **b** their temples	8596
	43:13	and *will* **b** down the temples of the gods 836+928+2021+8596	
	44:17	We *will* **b** incense to the Queen of Heaven	7787
	44:25	to **b** incense and pour out drink offerings to	7787
	48:35	the high places and **b** incense to their gods,"	7787
Eze	5: 2	**b** a third of the hair with fire inside the city.	1277
	5: 4	and throw them into the fire and **b** them **up.** 836+928+2021+8596	
	16:41	*They will* **b** down your houses 836+928+2021+8596	
	23:47	and daughters and **b** down their houses. 836+928+2021+8596	
	39: 9	use the weapons for fuel and **b** them **up**—	5956
	43:21	to take the bull for the sin offering and **b** it	8596
Hos	4:13	on the mountaintops and **b** offerings on	7787
Am	4: 5	**B** leavened bread as a thank offering	7787
	6:10	*to* **b** the bodies comes to carry them out of	6251
Na	2:13	"I will **b** up your chariots in smoke,	1277
Mal	4: 1	the day is coming; *it will* **b** like a furnace.	1277
Lk	1: 9	into the temple of the Lord and **b** incense.	2594
	3:17	but *he will* **b** up the chaff	2876
1Co	7: 9	it is better to marry than *to* **b** with passion.	4792
2Co	11:29	and *I do* not **inwardly** **b**?	4792
Rev	17:16	they will eat her flesh and **b** her with fire.	2876

BURNED (150) [BURN]

Ge	38:24	"Bring her out and *have her* **b** to death!"	8596
	39:19	he **b** with anger.	3013
Ex	4:14	Then the LORD's anger **b** against Moses	3013
	32:19	his anger **b** and he threw the tablets out	3013
	32:20	And he took the calf they had made and **b** it	8596
	40:27	and **b** fragrant incense on it,	7787
Lev	4:21	the bull outside the camp and burn it as *he* **b**	8596
	4:26	He shall burn all the fat on the altar as he **b**	NIH
	6:22	and *is to* **be b** completely.	7787
	6:23	of a priest shall **be b** completely;	NIH
	6:30	*it must* **be b.** 836+928+2021+8596	
	7:17	over till the third day *must* **be b up.** 836+928+2021+8596	
	7:19	must not be eaten; *it must* **be b up.** 836+928+2021+8596	
	8:16	and **b** it on the altar.	7787
	8:17	and its flesh and its offal *he* **b up** outside 836+928+2021+8596	
	8:20	He cut the ram into pieces and **b** the head,	7787
	8:21	with water and **b** the whole ram on the altar	7787
	8:28	from their hands and **b** them on the altar	7787
	9:10	On the altar *he* **b** the fat,	7787
	9:11	and the hide *he* **b** up outside the camp. 836+928+2021+8596	
	9:13	and *he* **b** them on the altar.	7787
	9:14	and **b** them on top of the burnt offering on	7787
	9:17	took a handful of it and **b** it on the altar	7787
	9:20	and then Aaron **b** the fat on the altar.	7787
	10:16	and found that *it had* **been b** up,	8596
	10:16	the article *must* **be b.** 836+928+2021+8596	
	13:52	and whatever has the mildew *must be* **b**	8596
	13:57	their hides, flesh and offal *are to be* **b up.** 836+928+2021+8596	

Lev	19: 6	over until the third day *must* **be b** up.	
		836+928+2021+8596	
	20:14	Both he and they *must* **be b** in the fire,	8596
	21: 9	*she must* **be b** in the fire.	8596
Nu	11: 1	Then fire from the LORD **b** among them	1277
	11: 3	fire from the LORD *had* **b** among them.	1277
	11:33	of the LORD **b** against the people,	3013
	12: 9	The anger of the LORD **b** against them,	3013
	16:39	by those who *had* **been b** up,	8596
	19: 5	While he watches, the heifer *is to be* **b**—	8596
	19:17	from the **b** purification offering into a jar	8599
	24:10	Then Balak's anger **b** against Balaam.	3013
	25: 3	And the LORD's anger **b** against them.	3013
	31:10	*They* **b** all the towns where 836+928+2021+8596	
	32:13	The LORD's anger **b** against Israel	3013
Dt	9:21	the calf you had made, and **b** it in the fire.	8596
	29:27	the LORD's anger **b** against this land,	3013
Jos	6:24	*they* **b** the whole city and everything in it,	
		836+928+2021+8596	
	7: 1	So the LORD's anger **b** against Israel.	3013
	7:25	after they had stoned the rest, *they* **b** them.	
		836+928+2021+8596	
	8:28	So Joshua **b** Ai and made it	8596
	11: 9	and **b** their chariots. 836+928+2021+8596	
	11:11	and *he* **b** up Hazor itself. 836+928+2021+8596	
	11:13	except Hazor, which Joshua **b.**	8596
Jdg	3: 8	The anger of the LORD **b** against Israel so	3013
	15: 5	**b** up the shocks and standing grain,	1277
	15: 6	**b** her and her father **to death.**	
		836+928+2021+8596	
	18:27	with the sword and **b** down their city.	
		836+928+2021+8596	
1Sa	2:15	But even before the fat was **b,**	7787
	2:16	said to him, "Let the fat be **b** up first, 7787+7787	
	11: 6	and he **b** with anger.	3013+4394
	17:28	he **b** *with* anger at him and asked,	3013
	30: 1	attacked Ziklag and **b** it, 836+928+2021+8596	
	30:14	And *we* **b** Ziklag."	8596
	31:12	where *they* **b** them.	8596
2Sa	6: 7	The LORD's anger **b** against Uzzah	3013
	12: 5	David **b** *with* anger against the man 3013+4394	
	23: 7	*they* **are b** up where they lie."	
		836+928+2021+8596+4806	
	24: 1	the anger of the LORD **b** against Israel,	3013
1Ki	3: 3	that he offered sacrifices and **b** incense on	7787
	11: 8	who **b** incense and offered sacrifices	7787
	13: 2	and human bones *will be* **b** on you.' "	8596
	15:13	down and **b** it in the Kidron Valley.	8596
	18:38	Then the fire of the LORD fell and **b** up	430
	19:21	**b** the plowing equipment **to cook**	1418
2Ki	10:26	of the temple of Baal and **b** it.	8596
	13: 3	So the LORD's anger **b** against Israel,	3013
	16: 4	He offered sacrifices and **b** incense at	7787
	17:11	At every high place *they* **b** incense,	7787
	17:31	**b** their children in the fire **as sacrifices**	8596
	22:17	and **b** incense to other gods	7787
	23: 4	*He* **b** them outside Jerusalem in the fields of	8596
	23: 5	those *who* **b** incense to Baal,	7787
	23: 6	and **b** it there.	8596
	23: 8	where the priests *had* **b** incense.	7787
	23:11	then **b** the chariots dedicated to the sun.	
		836+928+2021+8596	
	23:15	*He* **b** the high place and ground it	8596
	23:15	and **b** the Asherah pole also.	8596
	23:16	he had the bones removed from them and **b**	8596
	23:20	on the altars and **b** human bones on them.	8596
	23:26	which **b** against Judah because of all	3013
	25: 9	Every important building he **b** down.	
		836+928+2021+8596	
1Ch	13:10	The LORD's anger **b** against Uzzah,	3013
2Ch	15:16	broke it up and **b** it in the Kidron Valley.	8596
	25:14	down to them and **b** sacrifices to them.	7787
	25:15	of the LORD **b** against Amaziah,	3013
	28: 3	He **b** sacrifices in the Valley	7787
	28: 4	He offered sacrifices and **b** incense at	7787
	34: 5	*He* **b** the bones of the priests on their altars,	8596
	34:25	and **b** incense to other gods	7787
	36:19	*they* **b** all the palaces 836+928+2021+8596	
Ne	1: 3	and its gates *have* **been b** with fire."	3675
	2:17	and its gates *have* **been b** with fire.	3675
	4: 2	**b** as they are?"	8596
Est	1:12	the king became furious and **b** *with* anger.	1277
Job	1:16	the sky and **b** up the sheep and the servants,	1277
Ps	39: 3	and as I meditated, the fire **b;**	1277
	74: 7	*They* **b** your sanctuary to the ground;	
		836+928+2021+8938	
	74: 8	*They* **b** every place where God	8596
	80:16	Your vine is cut down, *it is* **b** with fire;	8596
Pr	6:27	into his lap without his clothes *being* **b?**	8596
Isa	1: 7	your cities **b** with fire;	8596
	24: 6	Therefore earth's inhabitants *are* **b** up,	3081
	33:12	The peoples will be **b** *as if to* lime;	5386
	43: 2	*you will* not **be b;**	3917
	64:11	has been **b** with fire,	8599
	65: 7	"Because *they* **b** sacrifices on	7787
Jer	2:15	his towns **are b** and deserted.	3675
	19: 4	*they* have **b** sacrifices in it to gods	7787
	19:13	where *they* **b** incense on the roofs to all	7787
	29:22	whom the king of Babylon **b** in the fire.'	7828
	36:23	until the entire scroll *was* **b** in the fire.	9462
	36:27	the king **b** the scroll containing the words	8596
	36:28	which Jehoiakim king of Judah **b** up.	8596
	36:29	You **b** that scroll and said,	8596
	36:32	scroll that Jehoiakim king of Judah *had* **b**	8596
	38:17	be spared and this city *will* not **be b** down;	
		836+928+2021+8596	
	38:23	and this city *will be* **b** down." 836+2021+8596	

Jer	44:19	"When we **b** incense to the Queen	7787
	44:21	and think about the incense **b** in the towns	7787
	44:23	Because *you* have **b** incense	7787
	52:13	Every important building he **b** down.	
			836+928+2021+8596
La	2: 3	*He has* **b** in Jacob like a flaming fire	1277
Eze	15: 5	into something useful *when* the fire *has* **b** it	430
	24:11	be melted and its deposit **b** away.	9462
Da	11:33	the sword or be **b** or captured or plundered.	4259
Hos	2:13	I will punish her for the days *she* **b** incense	7787
	11: 2	to the Baals and *they* **b** incense to images.	7787
Joel	1:19	the open pastures and flames *have* **b** up all	4265
Am	2: 1	Because he **b**, as if to lime,	8596
Mic	1: 7	all her temple gifts *will* **be b** with fire;	8596
Mt	13:30	the weeds and tie them in bundles to *be* **b**;	2876
	13:40	the weeds are pulled and **b** in the fire,	2876
	22: 7	and **b** their city.	1856
Jn	5:35	John was a lamp that **b** and gave light,	2794
	15: 6	thrown into the fire and **b**.	2794
Ac	19:19	and **b** them publicly.	2876
1Co	3:15	If it is **b** up, he will suffer loss;	2876
Heb	6: 8	In the end it will be **b**.	3011
	13:11	but the bodies *are* **b** outside the camp.	2876
Rev	8: 7	A third of the earth *was* **b** up,	2876
	8: 7	a third of the trees *were* **b** up,	2876
	8: 7	and all the green grass *was* **b** up.	2876

BURNED-OUT (1) [BURN]

Jer	51:25	and make you a **b** mountain.	8599

BURNING (77) [BURN]

Ge	19:24	the LORD rained down **b** sulfur on Sodom	836
Ex	15: 7	You unleashed your **b** anger;	3019
	27:20	the light so that the lamps *may be* kept **b**.	6590
	27:21	and his sons are to keep the lamps **b** before	NIH
	30: 1	an altar of acacia wood for **b** incense.	5230
Lev	1: 8	on the **b** wood that is on the altar.	836+2021+6584
	1:12	on the **b** wood that is on the altar.	836+2021+6584
	3: 5	the burnt offering that is on the **b** wood,	
			836+2021+6584
	6: 9	and the fire *must* be kept **b** on the altar.	3678
	6:12	The fire on the altar *must* be kept **b**;	3678
	6:13	The fire *must* be kept **b** on	3678
	16:12	a censer full of **b** coals from the altar before	836
	24: 2	so that the lamps *may be* **kept b** continually.	6590
Nu	19: 6	and throw them onto the **b** heifer.	8599
Dt	29:23	The whole land will be a **b** waste *of* salt	8599
	29:24	Why this fierce, **b** anger?"	3034
	33:16	the favor of him who dwelt in the **b** bush.	NIH
Jdg	14:19	**B** with anger, he went up	3013
2Sa	14: 7	the only **b** coal I have left,	1625
	22: 9	**b** coals blazed out of it.	1624
1Ki	9:25	**b** incense before the LORD along	7787
2Ki	18: 4	the Israelites had been **b** incense to it.	7787
2Ch	2: 4	to dedicate it to him for **b** fragrant incense	7787
Job	18: 5	the flame of his fire stops **b**.	5585
	18:15	**b** sulfur is scattered over his dwelling.	1730
	20:23	God will vent his **b** anger against him	3019
Ps	11: 6	On the wicked he will rain fiery coals and **b** sulfur;	1730
	18: 8	**b** coals blazed out of it.	1624
	18:28	You, O LORD, **keep** my lamp **b**;	239
	118:12	but they died out as quickly as **b** thorns;	836
	120: 4	with **b** coals *of* the broom tree.	1624
	140:10	Let **b** coals fall upon them;	1624
Pr	25:22	you will heap **b** coals on his head,	1624
Isa	9: 5	in blood will be destined for **b**,	8599
	13:13	in the day of his **b** anger.	3019
	30:27	with **b** anger and dense clouds of smoke;	1277
	30:33	like a stream of **b** sulfur, sets it ablaze.	1730
	33:14	Who of us can dwell with everlasting **b**?"	4611
	34: 9	her dust into **b** sulfur;	1730
	35: 7	The **b** sand will become a pool,	9220
	42:25	So he poured out on them his **b** anger,	2779
	44:15	It is man's fuel for **b**;	1277
	65: 3	offering sacrifices in gardens and **b** incense	7787
	65: 5	a fire *that* keeps **b** all day.	3678
Jer	1:16	*in* **b** incense to other gods and	7787
	11:17	and provoked me to anger by **b** incense	7787
	32:29	to anger by **b** incense on the roofs to Baal	7787
	36:22	with a fire **b** in the firepot in front of him.	1277
	44: 3	by **b** incense and by worshiping other gods	7787
	44: 5	from their wickedness or stop **b** incense	7787
	44: 8	**b** incense to other gods in Egypt,	7787
	44:15	that their wives *were* **b** incense	7787
	44:18	since we stopped **b** incense to the Queen	7787
Eze	1:13	the living creatures was like **b** coals of fire	1277
	10: 2	Fill your hands with **b** coals from among	836
	36: 5	In my **b** zeal I have spoken against the rest	836
	38:22	of rain, hailstones and **b** sulfur on him and	836
Hos	7: 4	**b** like an oven whose fire the baker need	1277
	13: 5	in the land of **b** heat.	9429
Am	4:11	You were like a **b** stick snatched from	202
Zec	3: 2	Is not this man a **b** stick snatched from	202
	8: 2	I am **b** *with* jealousy for her."	2779
Mt	3:12	and **b** up the chaff with unquenchable fire."	2876
Lk	1:10	when the time *for* the **b** of incense came,	2592
	12:35	for service and *keep* your lamps **b**,	2794
	24:32	not our hearts **b** within us while he talked	2794
Jn	21: 9	they saw a **fire** of **b** coals there with fish	471
Ac	7:30	*of* a **b** bush in the desert near Mount Sinai.	4786
Ro	12:20	you will heap **b** coals on his head,"	4786
Heb	12:18	that can be touched and that *is* **b** with fire;	2794
2Pe	2: 6	Sodom and Gomorrah *by* **b** them **to ashes**,	5491
Rev	14:10	be tormented with **b** sulfur in the presence	4786

Rev	18: 9	the smoke *of* her **b**,	4796
	18:18	When they see the smoke *of* her **b**,	4796
	19:20	into the fiery lake *of* **b** sulfur.	2794
	20:10	was thrown into the lake *of* **b** sulfur.	4786
	21: 8	be in the fiery lake *of* **b** sulfur.	2794

BURNISHED (4)

1Ki	7:45	the temple of the LORD were of **b** bronze.	5307
Eze	1: 7	of a calf and gleamed like **b** bronze.	7838
Da	10: 6	and legs like the gleam of **b** bronze,	7838
Rev	2:18	and whose feet are like **b** bronze.	5909

BURNS (20) [BURN]

Ex	22: 6	that *it* **b** shocks of grain or standing grain	430
Lev	16:28	The *man who* **b** them must wash his clothes	8596
Nu	19: 8	The *man who* **b** it must also wash his clothes	8596
Dt	32:22	*one that* **b** to the realm of death below.	3678
1Ki	14:10	up the house of Jeroboam as *one* **b** dung,	1277
2Ki	22:13	that **b** against us because our fathers have	3675
Job	19:11	His anger **b** against me;	3013
	30:30	my body **b** with fever.	3081
	31:12	It is a fire *that* **b** to Destruction;	430
Ps	46: 9	he **b** the shields with fire.	8596
SS	8: 6	It **b** like blazing fire, like a mighty flame.	8404
Isa	5:25	the LORD's anger **b** against his people;	3013
	9:18	Surely wickedness **b** like a fire;	1277
	44:16	Half of the wood he **b** in the fire;	8596
	66: 3	and *whoever* **b** **memorial** incense,	2349
Jer	48:45	*it* **b** the foreheads of Moab,	430
Eze	15: 4	on the fire as fuel and the fire **b** both ends	430
Hos	8: 5	My anger **b** against them!	3013
Hab	1:16	to his net and **b** incense to his dragnet.	7787
Zec	10: 3	"My anger **b** against the shepherds,	3013

BURNT (275) [BURN]

Ge	8:20	he sacrificed **b** offerings on it.	6592
	22: 2	Sacrifice him there as a **b** offering on one	6592
	22: 3	he had cut enough wood for the **b** offering,	6592
	22: 6	Abraham took the wood for the **b** offering	6592
	22: 7	"but where is the lamb for the **b** offering?"	6592
	22: 8	the lamb for the **b** offering,	6592
	22:13	and sacrificed it as a **b** offering instead	6592
Ex	10:25	to have sacrifices and **b** offerings to present	6592
	18:12	brought a **b** offering and other sacrifices	6592
	20:24	for me and sacrifice on it your **b** offerings	6592
	24: 5	and they offered **b** offerings	6592
	29:18	It is a **b** offering to the LORD,	6592
	29:25	with the **b** offering for a pleasing aroma to	6592
	29:42	the generations to come this **b** offering is	6592
	30: 9	or any **b** offering or grain offering,	6592
	30:28	the altar of **b** offering and all its utensils,	6592
	31: 9	of **b** offering and all its utensils, the basin	6592
	32: 6	and sacrificed **b** offerings	6592
	35:16	of **b** offering with its bronze grating,	6592
	38: 1	the altar of **b** offering *of* acacia wood,	6592
	40: 6	"Place the altar of **b** offering in front of	6592
	40:10	the altar of **b** offering and all its utensils,	6592
	40:29	the altar of **b** offering near the entrance to	6592
	40:29	on it **b** offerings and grain offerings,	6592
Lev	1: 3	the offering is a **b** offering from the herd,	6592
	1: 4	on the head of the **b** offering,	6592
	1: 6	to skin the **b** offering and cut it into pieces.	6592
	1: 9	It is a **b** offering, an offering made by fire,	6592
	1:10	the offering is a **b** offering from the flock,	6592
	1:13	It is a **b** offering, an offering made by fire,	6592
	1:14	the offering to the LORD is a **b** offering	6592
	1:17	It is a **b** offering, an offering made by fire,	6592
	3: 5	the **b** offering that is on the burning wood,	6592
	4: 7	of the altar of **b** offering at the entrance to	6592
	4:10	on the altar of **b** offering.	6592
	4:18	of the altar of **b** offering at the entrance to	6592
	4:24	where the **b** offering is slaughtered before	6592
	4:25	the altar of **b** offering and pour out the rest	6592
	4:29	at the place of the **b** offering.	6592
	4:30	the altar of **b** offering and pour out the rest	6592
	4:33	where the **b** offering is slaughtered.	6592
	4:34	the altar of **b** offering and pour out the rest	6592
	5: 7	and the other for a **b** offering.	6592
	5:10	then offer the other as a **b** offering in	6592
	6: 9	the regulations for the **b** offering:	6592
	6: 9	The **b** offering is to remain on	6592
	6:10	of the **b** offering that the fire has consumed	6592
	6:12	to add firewood and arrange the **b** offering	6592
	6:25	in the place the **b** offering is slaughtered	6592
	7: 2	where the **b** offering is slaughtered,	6592
	7: 8	a **b** offering *for* anyone may keep its hide	6592
	7:37	then, are the regulations for the **b** offering,	6592
	8:18	then presented the ram for the **b** offering,	6592
	8:21	the whole ram on the altar as a **b** offering,	6592
	8:28	of the **b** offering as an ordination offering,	6592
	9: 2	and a ram for your **b** offering,	6592
	9: 3	for a **b** offering,	6592
	9: 7	and your **b** offering and make atonement	6592
	9:12	Then he slaughtered the **b** offering.	6592
	9:13	They handed him the **b** offering piece	6592
	9:14	and burned them on top of the **b** offering	6592
	9:16	He brought the **b** offering and offered it in	6592
	9:17	in addition to the morning's **b** offering.	6592
	9:22	the **b** offering and the fellowship offering,	6592
	9:24	the LORD and consumed the **b** offering	6592
	10:19	and their **b** offering before the LORD,	6592
	12: 6	of Meeting a year-old lamb for a **b** offering	6592
	12: 8	one for a **b** offering and the other for	6592
	14:13	and the **b** offering are slaughtered.	6592

Lev	14:19	the priest shall slaughter the **b** offering	6592
	14:22	and the other for a **b** offering.	6592
	14:31	a sin offering and the other as a **b** offering	6592
	15:15	and the other for a **b** offering.	6592
	15:30	and the other for a **b** offering.	6592
	16: 3	a sin offering and a ram for a **b** offering.	6592
	16: 5	a sin offering and a ram for a **b** offering.	6592
	16:24	and sacrifice the **b** offering *for* himself and	6592
	16:24	for himself and the **b** offering *for*	6592
	17: 8	among them who offers a **b** offering	6592
	22:18	a gift for a **b** offering to the LORD,	6592
	23:12	as a **b offering** to the LORD a lamb	6592
	23:18	They will be a **b** offering to the LORD,	6592
	23:37	the **b** offerings and grain offerings,	6592
Nu	6:11	as a **b** offering to make atonement for him	6592
	6:14	without defect for a **b** offering,	6592
	6:16	the sin offering and the **b** offering.	6592
	7:15	one male lamb a year old, for a **b** offering;	6592
	7:21	one male lamb a year old, for a **b** offering;	6592
	7:27	one male lamb a year old, for a **b** offering;	6592
	7:33	one male lamb a year old, for a **b** offering;	6592
	7:39	one male lamb a year old, for a **b** offering;	6592
	7:45	one male lamb a year old, for a **b** offering;	6592
	7:51	one male lamb a year old, for a **b** offering;	6592
	7:57	one male lamb a year old, for a **b** offering;	6592
	7:63	one male lamb a year old, for a **b** offering;	6592
	7:69	one male lamb a year old, for a **b** offering;	6592
	7:75	one male lamb a year old, for a **b** offering;	6592
	7:81	one male lamb a year old, for a **b** offering;	6592
	7:87	the **b** offering came to twelve young bulls,	6592
	8:12	the LORD and the other for a **b** offering,	6592
	10:10	to sound the trumpets over your **b** offerings	6592
	15: 3	whether **b** offerings or sacrifices,	6592
	15: 5	With each lamb for the **b** offering or	6592
	15: 8	a young bull as a **b** offering or sacrifice,	6592
	15:24	for a **b** offering as an aroma pleasing to	6592
	28: 3	as a regular **b** offering each day.	6592
	28: 6	This is the regular **b** offering instituted	6592
	28:10	This is the **b** offering *for* every Sabbath,	6592
	28:10	in addition to the regular **b** offering	6592
	28:11	present to the LORD a **b** offering	6592
	28:13	This is for a **b** offering, a pleasing aroma,	6592
	28:14	This is the monthly **b** offering to be made	6592
	28:15	Besides the regular **b** offering	6592
	28:19	a **b** offering of two young bulls,	6592
	28:23	to the regular morning **b** offering.	6592
	28:24	in addition to the regular **b** offering.	6592
	28:27	Present a **b** offering of two young bulls,	6592
	28:31	in addition to the regular **b** offering	6592
	29: 2	prepare a **b** offering of one young bull,	6592
	29: 6	to the monthly and daily **b** offerings	6592
	29: 8	the LORD a **b** offering of one young bull,	6592
	29:11	for atonement and the regular **b** offering	6592
	29:13	a **b** offering of thirteen young bulls,	6592
	29:16	in addition to the regular **b** offering	6592
	29:19	in addition to the regular **b** offering	6592
	29:22	in addition to the regular **b** offering	6592
	29:25	in addition to the regular **b** offering	6592
	29:28	in addition to the regular **b** offering	6592
	29:31	in addition to the regular **b** offering	6592
	29:34	in addition to the regular **b** offering	6592
	29:36	a **b** offering of one bull,	6592
	29:38	in addition to the regular **b** offering	6592
	29:39	your **b** offerings, grain offerings,	6592
Dt	12: 6	there bring your **b** offerings and sacrifices,	6592
	12:11	your **b** offerings and sacrifices,	6592
	12:13	not to sacrifice your **b** offerings anywhere you please.	6592
	12:27	Present your **b** offerings on the altar of	6592
	13:16	and all its plunder as a **whole b** offering to	4003
	27: 6	with fieldstones and offer **b** offerings on it	6592
	33:10	and **whole b** offerings on your altar.	4003
Jos	8:31	to the LORD **b** offerings	6592
	22:23	and to offer **b** offerings and grain offerings,	6592
	22:26	but not for **b** offerings or sacrifices.'	6592
	22:27	at his sanctuary with our **b** offerings,	6592
	22:28	not for **b** offerings and sacrifices,	6592
	22:29	by building an altar for **b** offerings,	6592
Jdg	6:26	offer the second bull as a **b** offering."	6592
	11:31	and I will sacrifice it as a **b** offering."	6592
	13:16	But if you prepare a **b** offering,	6592
	13:23	he would not have accepted a **b** offering	6592
	20:26	until evening and presented **b** offerings	6592
	21: 4	an altar and presented **b** offerings	6592
1Sa	6:14	and sacrificed the cows as a **b** offering to	6592
	6:15	of Beth Shemesh offered **b** offerings	6592
	7: 9	and offered it up as a whole **b** offering to	6592
	7:10	Samuel was sacrificing the **b** offering,	6592
	10: 8	down to you to sacrifice **b** offerings	6592
	13: 9	"Bring me the **b** offering and	6592
	13: 9	And Saul offered up the **b** offering.	6592
	13:12	So I felt compelled to offer the **b** offering."	6592
	15:22	"Does the LORD delight in **b** offerings	6592
2Sa	6:17	and David sacrificed **b** offerings	6592
	6:18	the **b** offerings and fellowship offerings,	6592
	24:22	Here are oxen for the **b** offering,	6592
	24:24	to the LORD my God **b** offerings	6592
	24:25	the LORD there and sacrificed **b** offerings	6592
1Ki	3: 4	a thousand **b** offerings on that altar.	6592
	3:15	and sacrificed **b** offerings	6592
	8:64	and there he offered **b** offerings,	6592
	8:64	to hold the **b** offerings,	6592
	9:25	a year Solomon sacrificed **b** offerings	6592
	10: 5	and the **b** offerings he made at the temple	6592
2Ki	5:17	your servant will never again make **b** offerings and sacrifices to any other god	6592
	10:24	in to make sacrifices and **b** offerings.	6592

2Ki	10:25	the **b** offering, he ordered the guards	6592
	16:13	up his **b offering** and grain offering,	6592
	16:15	offer the morning **b offering** and	6592
	16:15	the king's **b offering**	6592
	16:15	the **b offering** *of* all the people of the land,	6592
	16:15	on the altar all the blood of the **b offerings**	6592
1Ch	6:49	on the altar of **b offering** and on the altar	6592
	16: 1	and they presented **b offerings**	6592
	16: 2	the **b offerings** and fellowship offerings,	6592
	16:40	to present **b offerings** to the Lord on	6592
	16:40	on the altar of **b offering** regularly,	6592
	21:23	I will give the oxen for the **b offerings,**	6592
	21:24	a **b offering** that costs me nothing."	6592
	21:26	the Lord there and sacrificed **b offerings**	6592
	21:26	from heaven on the altar of **b offering.**	6592
	21:29	and the altar of **b offering** were at that time	6592
	22: 1	and also the altar of **b offering** for Israel."	6592
	23:31	and whenever **b offerings** were presented	6592
	29:21	to the Lord and presented **b offerings**	6592
2Ch	1: 6	and offered a thousand **b offerings** on it.	6592
	2: 4	and for making **b offerings** every morning	6592
	4: 6	to be used for the **b offerings** were rinsed,	6592
	7: 1	from heaven and consumed the **b offering**	6592
	7: 7	and there he offered **b offerings** and the fat	6592
	7: 7	not hold the **b offerings,**	6592
	8:12	Solomon sacrificed **b offerings** to	6592
	9: 4	in their robes and the **b offerings** he made	6592
	13:11	and evening they present **b offerings**	6592
	23:18	the **b offerings** *of* the Lord as written in	6592
	24:14	for the service and for the **b offerings,**	6592
	24:14	**b offerings** were presented continually in	6592
	29: 7	not burn incense or present any **b offerings**	6592
	29:18	the altar of **b offering** with all its utensils,	6592
	29:24	the king had ordered the **b offering** and	6592
	29:27	the order to sacrifice the **b offering** on	6592
	29:28	of the **b offering** was completed.	6592
	29:31	all whose hearts were willing brought **b offerings.**	6592
	29:32	The number of **b offerings**	6592
	29:32	all of them for **b offerings** to the Lord.	6592
	29:34	were too few to skin all the **b offerings;**	6592
	29:35	There were **b offerings** in abundance,	6592
	29:35	that accompanied the **b offerings.**	6592
	30:15	and brought **b offerings** to the temple of	6592
	31: 2	to offer **b offerings**	6592
	31: 3	the morning and evening **b offerings** and	6592
	31: 3	and for the **b offerings** on the Sabbaths,	6592
	35:12	They set aside the **b offerings** to give them	6592
	35:14	were sacrificing the **b offerings** and	6592
	35:16	the Passover and the offering of **b offerings**	6592
Ezr	3: 2	of the God of Israel to sacrifice **b offerings**	6592
	3: 3	on its foundation and sacrificed **b offerings**	6592
	3: 4	of **b offerings** prescribed for each day.	6592
	3: 5	they presented the regular **b offerings,**	6592
	3: 6	to offer **b offerings** to the Lord,	6592
	6: 9	male lambs for **b offerings** to the God	10545
	8:35	from captivity sacrificed **b offerings** to	6592
	8:35	All this was a **b offering** to the Lord.	6592
Ne	10:33	the regular grain offerings and **b offerings;**	6592
Job	1: 5	a **b offering** for each of them,	6592
	42: 8	and sacrifice a **b offering** for yourselves.	6592
Ps	20: 3	and accept your **b offerings.**	6592
	40: 6	**b offerings** and sin offerings you did	6592
	50: 8	for your sacrifices or your **b offerings,**	6592
	51:16	you do not take pleasure in **b offerings.**	6592
	51:19	whole **b offerings** to delight you;	6592
	66:13	I will come to your temple with **b offerings**	6592
Isa	1:11	"I have more than enough of **b offerings,**	6592
	40:16	nor its animals enough for **b offerings.**	6592
	43:23	not brought me sheep for **b offerings,**	6592
	56: 7	Their **b offerings** and sacrifices will	6592
Jer	6:20	Your **b offerings** are not acceptable;	6592
	7:21	Go ahead, add your **b offerings**	6592
	7:22	about **b offerings** and sacrifices,	6592
	14:12	though they offer **b offerings**	6592
	17:26	bringing **b offerings** and sacrifices,	6592
	33:18	before me continually to offer **b offerings,**	6592
Eze	40:38	where the **b offerings** were washed.	6592
	40:39	on which the **b offerings,**	6592
	40:42	of dressed stone for the **b offerings,**	6592
	40:42	the utensils for slaughtering the **b offerings**	6592
	43:18	the regulations for sacrificing **b offerings**	6592
	43:24	on them and sacrifice them as a **b offering**	6592
	43:27	the priests are to present your **b offerings**	6592
	44:11	the **b offerings** and sacrifices for the people	6592
	45:15	**b offerings** and fellowship offerings	6592
	45:17	to provide the **b offerings,** grain offerings	6592
	45:17	**b offerings** and fellowship offerings	6592
	45:23	without defect as a **b offering** to	6592
	45:25	**b offerings,** grain offerings and oil.	6592
	46: 2	The priests are to sacrifice his **b offering**	6592
	46: 4	The **b offering** the prince brings to	6592
	46:12	a **b offering** or fellowship offerings—	6592
	46:12	He shall offer his **b offering**	6592
	46:13	without defect for a **b offering** to	6592
	46:15	by morning for a regular **b offering.**	6592
Hos	6: 6	of God rather than **b offerings.**	6592
Am	5:22	Even though you bring me **b offerings**	6592
Mic	6: 6	Shall I come before him with **b offerings,**	6592
Mk	12:33	love your neighbor as yourself is more important than all **b offerings**	3906
Heb	10: 6	with **b offerings** and sin offerings you were	3906
	10: 8	**b offerings** and sin offerings you did not	3906

BURNT-OUT (Anglicized) See
BURNED-OUT

BURST (21) [BURSTS]

Ge	7:11	the springs of the great deep **b forth,**	1324
	27:34	he **b** out with a loud and bitter cry and said	7590
Job	26: 8	yet the clouds *do* not **b** under their weight.	1324
	32:19	like new wineskins **ready to b.**	1324
	38: 8	the sea behind doors when it **b** forth from	1631
Ps	60: 1	O God, and **b forth** upon us;	7287
	98: 4	**b** into jubilant song with music;	7200
Isa	35: 2	it will **b** into bloom;	7255+7255
	44:23	**B** into song, you mountains,	7200
	49:13	**b** into song, O mountains!	7200
	52: 9	**B** into songs of joy together,	7200
	54: 1	**b** into song, shout for joy,	7200
	55:12	the mountains and hills *will* **b** *into* song	7200
Jer	23:19	storm of the Lord *will* **b** out in wrath,	3655
	30:23	storm of the Lord *will* **b** out in wrath,	3655
Eze	7:10	Doom *has* **b** forth, the rod has budded,	3655
	13:11	and violent winds *will* **b forth.**	1324
Mt	9:17	If they do, the skins *will* **b,**	4838
Mk	2:22	If he does, the wine *will* **b** the skins,	4838
Lk	5:37	If he does, the new wine *will* **b** the skins,	4838
Ac	1:18	there he fell headlong, his body **b** open	3279

BURSTS (1) [BURST]

Job	16:14	**Again and again** he **b** upon me	7287+7288+7288

BURY (38) [BURIAL, BURIED, BURIES, BURYING]

Ge	23: 4	for a burial site here so *I can* **b** my dead."	7699
	23: 6	**B** your dead in the choicest of our tombs.	7699
	23: 8	"If you are willing to *let* me **b** my dead,	7699
	23:11	**B** your dead."	7699
	23:13	from me so *I can* **b** my dead there."	7699
	23:15	**B** your dead."	7699
	47:29	*Do* not **b** me in Egypt,	7699
	47:30	of Egypt and **b** me where they are buried."	7699
	49:29	**B** me with my fathers in the cave in	7699
	50: 5	**b** me in the tomb I dug for myself in	7699
	50: 5	Now let me go up and **b** my father."	7699
	50: 6	Pharaoh said, "Go up and **b** your father,	7699
	50: 7	So Joseph went up to **b** his father.	7699
	50:14	with him to **b** his father.	7699
Dt	21:23	**Be sure to b** him that same day,	7699+7699
1Ki	2:31	Strike him down and **b** him,	7699
	11:15	who had gone up to **b** the dead,	7699
	13:29	to his own city to mourn for him and **b** him.	7699
	13:31	**b** me in the grave where the man	7699
	14:13	All Israel will mourn for him and **b** him.	7699
2Ki	9:10	and no *one will* **b** her.' "	7699
	9:34	"and **b** her, for she was a king's daughter."	7699
	9:35	But when they went out to **b** her,	7699
Job	27:15	The plague *will* **b** those who survive him,	7699
	40:13	**B** them all in the dust together;	3243
Ps	79: 3	and there is no *one to* **b** the dead.	7699
Jer	7:32	for *they will* **b** the dead in Topheth	7699
	14:16	be no *one to* **b** them or their wives,	7699
	19:11	*They will* **b** the dead in Topheth	7699
	43: 9	take some large stones with you and **b** them	3243
La	3:29	*Let him* **b** his face in the dust—	5989
Eze	39:13	All the people of the land *will* **b** them,	7699
	39:14	*others will* **b** those that remain on	7699
Hos	9: 6	and Memphis *will* **b** them.	7699
Mt	8:21	"Lord, first let me go and **b** my father."	2507
	8:22	and let the dead **b** their own dead."	2507
Lk	9:59	"Lord, first let me go and **b** my father."	2507
	9:60	"Let the dead **b** their own dead,	2507

BURYING (7) [BURY]

Ge	23: 6	his tomb for **b** your dead."	7699
	50:14	After **b** his father, Joseph returned to Egypt,	7699
Nu	33: 4	who *were* **b** all their firstborn, whom	7699
2Sa	3:35	to Saul your master *by* **b** him.	7699
1Ki	13:31	After **b** him, he said to his sons,	7699
2Ki	13:21	Once *while* some Israelites *were* **b** a man,	7699
Eze	39:12	of Israel *will* be **b** them in order to cleanse	7699

BUSH (11) [BUSHES]

Ex	3: 2	to him in flames of fire from within a **b.**	6174
	3: 2	though the **b** was on fire it did not burn up.	6174
	3: 3	why the **b** does not burn up."	6174
	3: 4	God called to him from within the **b,**	6174
Dt	33:16	of him who dwelt in the burning **b.**	6174
Jer	17: 6	He will be like a **b** in the wastelands;	6899
	48: 6	become like a **b** in the desert.	6899
Mk	12:26	the book of Moses, in the account *of* the **b,**	1003
Lk	20:37	But in the account *of* the **b,**	1003
Ac	7:30	a burning **b** in the desert near Mount Sinai.	1003
	7:35	the angel who appeared to him in the **b.**	1003

BUSHELS (1)

Lk	16: 7	'A thousand **b** of wheat,' he replied.	1669+3174

BUSHES (2) [BUSH]

Ge	21:15	she put the boy under one of the **b.**	8489
Job	30: 7	They brayed among the **b** and huddled in	8489

BUSHY (KJV) See WAVY

BUSINESS (17)

1Sa	21: 8	because the king's **b** was urgent."	1821
Est	3: 9	for the men who carry out this **b.**"	4856
Ecc	4: 8	This too is meaningless—a miserable **b!**	6721
Eze	27:12	" 'Tarshish **did b with** you because	6086
	27:16	" 'Aram **did b with** you because	6086
	27:18	**did b with** you in wine from Helbon	6086
	27:21	*they* **did b** with you in lambs,	6086
Da	8:27	Then I got up and went about the king's **b.**	4856
Zec	8:10	No one *could* go about his **b** safely	995+2256+3655
Mt	22: 5	one to his field, another to his **b.**	1865
Jn	15:15	a servant does not know his master's **b.**	4472+5515
Ac	19:24	brought in no little **b** for the craftsmen,	2238
	19:25	a good income from this **b.**	2238
1Co	5:12	**What b** is it of mine to judge	1609+5515
1Th	4:11	to **mind** your own **b** and to work	4556
Jas	1:11	even while he **goes about his b.**	4512
	4:13	**carry on b** and make money."	1864

BUSTLES (1)

Ps	39: 6	He **b about,** but only in vain;	2159

BUSY (6)

1Ki	18:27	Perhaps he is deep in thought, or **b,**	8485
	20:40	While your servant was **b** here and there,	6913
Isa	32: 6	fool speaks folly, his mind *is* **b** with evil:	6913
Hag	1: 9	while each of you *is* **b** with his own house.	8132
2Th	3:11	*They are* not **b;** they are busybodies.	2237
Tit	2: 5	to be **b at home,** to be kind,	3877

BUSYBODY (KJV) See MEDDLER

BUSYBODIES (2)

2Th	3:11	They are not busy; *they are* **b.**	4318
1Ti	5:13	but also gossips and **b,**	4319

BUT (3983) See Index of Articles Etc.

BUTCHERED (4)

1Sa	14:32	they **b** them on the ground and ate them,	8821
	28:24	which *she* **b** at once.	2284
Jer	12: 3	Drag them off like sheep to be **b!**	3186
Mt	22: 4	My oxen and fattened cattle *have been* **b,**	2604

BUTLER (KJV) See CUPBEARER

BUTT (1) [BUTTING]

2Sa	2:23	the **b** *of* his spear into Asahel's stomach,	339

BUTTER (2)

Ps	55:21	His speech is smooth as **b,**	4717
Pr	30:33	For as churning the milk produces **b,**	2772

BUTTING (1) [BUTT]

Eze	34:21	**b** all the weak sheep with your horns	5590

BUTTOCKS (3)

2Sa	10: 4	in the middle at the **b,**	9268
1Ch	19: 4	in the middle at the **b,**	5156
Isa	20: 4	with **b** bared—to Egypt's shame.	9268

BUY (54) [BOUGHT, BUYER, BUYERS, BUYING, BUYS]

Ge	41:57	the countries came to Egypt to **b grain**	8690
	42: 2	Go down there and **b** some for us,	8690
	42: 3	of Joseph's brothers went down to **b grain**	8690
	42: 5	among those who went to **b grain,**	8690
	42: 7	they replied, "to **b** food."	8690
	42:10	"Your servants have come to **b** food.	8690
	43: 2	"Go back and **b** us a little more food."	8690
	43: 4	we will go down and **b** food for you.	8690
	43:20	down here the first time to **b** food.	8690
	43:22	with us to **b** food.	8690
	44:25	'Go back and **b** a little more food.'	8690
	47:19	**B** us and our land in exchange for food,	7864
	47:22	he did not **b** the land of the priests,	7864
Ex	21: 2	"If *you* **b** a Hebrew servant,	7864
Lev	25:14	of your countrymen or **b** any from him,	7864
	25:15	to **b** from your countryman on the basis of	7864
	25:44	from them *you may* **b** slaves.	7864
	25:45	*You may* also **b** some of	7864
	27:27	he may **b** it **back** at its set value,	7009
Dt	14:26	*Use* the silver to **b** whatever you like:	5989
	28:68	but no *one will* **b** you.	7864
Ru	4: 4	to your attention and suggest that *you* **b** it	7864
	4: 5	"On the day you **b** the land from Naomi	7864
	4: 8	to Boaz, "**B** it yourself."	7864
2Sa	24:21	"To **b** your threshing floor,"	7864
Ezr	7:17	With this money be sure *to* **b** bulls,	10632
Ne	10:31	*we will* not **b** from them on the Sabbath or	4374
Pr	23:23	**B** the truth and do not sell it;	7864
Isa	55: 1	you who have no money, come, and eat!	8690
	55: 1	**b** wine and milk without money and	8690
Jer	13: 1	"Go and **b** a linen belt and put it	7864
	19: 1	"Go and **b** a clay jar from a potter.	7864
	32: 7	'**B** my field at Anathoth,	7864
	32: 7	and duty to **b** it.'	7864
	32: 8	'**B** my field at Anathoth in the territory	7864
	32: 8	**b** it for yourself.'	7864
	32:25	'**B** the field with silver and have	7864
La	5: 4	We must **b** the water we drink;	928+4084

Mt	14:15	the villages and **b** themselves some food."	60
	25: 9	go to those who sell oil and **b** some	60
	25:10	while they were on their way *to* **b** the oil,	60
	27: 7	to use the money to **b** the potter's field as	60
	27:10	and *they* used them to **b** the potter's field,	1443
Mk	6:36	and villages and **b** themselves something	60
Lk	9:13	unless we go and **b** food for all this crowd."	60
	22:36	sell your cloak and **b** one.	60
Jn	4: 8	into the town to **b** food.)	60
	6: 5	*shall we* **b** bread for these people to eat?"	60
	6: 7	not **b** enough bread for each one to have	NIG
	13:29	*to* **b** what was needed for the Feast,	60
Ac	8:20	because you thought *you could* **b** the gift	3227
1Co	7:30	those who **b** something,	60
Rev	3:18	I counsel you *to* **b** from me gold refined in	60
	13:17	so that no one could **b** or sell unless he had	60

BUYER (6) [BUY]

Lev	25:28	in the possession of the **b** until the Year	7864
	25:30	to the **b** and his descendants.	7864
	25:50	He and his **b** are to count the time from	7864
Pr	20:14	it's no good!" says the **b**;	7864
Isa	24: 2	for mistress as for maid, for seller as for **b**,	7864
Eze	7:12	Let not the **b** rejoice nor the seller grieve,	7864

BUYERS (1) [BUY]

Zec	11: 5	Their **b** slaughter them and go unpunished.	7864

BUYING (5) [BUY]

Ge	47:14	in payment for the grain they *were* **b**,	8690
Am	8: 6	**b** the poor with silver and the needy for	7864
Mt	21:12	and drove out all who *were* **b**	4797
Mk	11:15	and began driving out those who *were* **b**	4797
Lk	17:28	**b** and selling, planting and building.	60

BUYS (3) [BUY]

Lev	22:11	But if a priest **b** a slave *with* money,	7864+7871
Pr	31:16	She considers a field and **b** it;	4374
Rev	18:11	because no one **b** their cargoes any more—	60

BUZ (3) [BUZITE]

Ge	22:21	**B** his brother, Kemuel (the father of Aram),	998
1Ch	5:14	the son of Jahdo, the son of **B**.	998
Jer	25:23	Tema, **B** and all who are in distant places;	998

BUZI (1)

Eze	1: 3	Ezekiel the priest, the son of **B**,	1001

BUZITE (2) [BUZ]

Job	32: 2	But Elihu son of Barakel the **B**,	1000
	32: 6	So Elihu son of Barakel the **B** said:	1000

BY (2431) See Index of Articles Etc.

BYPATHS (1) [PATH]

Jer	18:15	They made them walk in **b** and on roads	5986

BYWORD (9) [WORD]

1Ki	9: 7	then become a **b** and an object of ridicule	5442
2Ch	7:20	I will make it a **b** and an object of ridicule	5442
Job	17: 6	"God has made me a **b** to everyone,	5439
	30: 9	I have become a **b** among them.	4863
Ps	44:14	You have made us a **b** among the nations;	5442
Jer	24: 9	a reproach and a **b**,	5442
Eze	14: 8	and make him an example and a **b**.	5442
	23:10	She became a **b** among women,	9005
Joel	2:17	a **b** among the nations.	5442

C

CAB (1)

2Ki	6:25	quarter of a **c** *of* seed pods for five shekels.	7685

CABBON (1)

Jos	15:40	**C**, Lahmas, Kitlish,	3887

CABINS (KJV) See VAULTED CELL

CABUL (2)

Jos	19:27	passing **C** on the left.	3886
1Ki	9:13	And he called them the Land of **C**,	3886

CAESAR (20) [CAESAR'S]

Mt	22:17	Is it right to pay taxes *to* **C** or not?"	2790
	22:21	"Give to **C** what is Caesar's,	2790
Mk	12:14	Is it right to pay taxes *to* **C** or not?	2790
	12:17	"Give *to* **C** what is Caesar's and	2790
Lk	2: 1	In those days **C** Augustus issued a decree	2790
	3: 1	fifteenth year of the reign *of* Tiberius **C**—	2790

Lk	20:22	Is it right for us to pay taxes *to* **C** or not?"	2790
	20:25	"Then give *to* **C** what is Caesar's,	2790
	23: 2	of taxes to **C** and claims to be Christ,	2790
Jn	19:12	you are no friend *of* **C**.	2790
	19:12	to be a king opposes **C**."	2790
	19:15	"We have no king but **C**,"	2790
Ac	25: 8	Jews or against the temple or against **C**."	2790
	25:11	I appeal to **C**!"	2790
	25:12	"You have appealed *to* **C**.	2790
	25:12	To **C** you will go!"	2790
	25:21	until I could send him to **C**."	2790
	26:32	if he had not appealed to **C**."	2790
	27:24	You must stand trial before **C**;	2790
	28:19	I was compelled to appeal to **C**—	2790

CAESAR'S (9) [CAESAR]

Mt	22:21	"**C**," they replied.	2790
	22:21	"Give to Caesar what is **C**,	2790
Mk	12:16	"**C**," they replied.	2790
	12:17	"Give to Caesar what *is* **C** and	2790
Lk	20:25	"**C**," they replied.	2790
	20:25	"Then give to Caesar what *is* **C**,	2790
Ac	17: 7	They are all defying **C** decrees,	2790
	25:10	"I am now standing before **C** court,	2790
Php	4:22	especially those who belong to **C** household	2790

CAESAREA (19)

Mt	16:13	to the region *of* **C** Philippi,	2791
Mk	8:27	on to the villages around **C** Philippi.	2791
Ac	8:40	in all the towns until he reached **C**.	2791
	9:30	they took him down to **C** and sent him off	2791
	10: 1	At **C** there was a man named Cornelius,	2791
	10:24	The following day he arrived in **C**.	2791
	11:11	to me from **C** stopped at the house	2791
	12:19	from Judea to **C** and stayed there a while.	2791
	18:22	When he landed at **C**,	2791
	21: 8	we reached **C** and stayed at the house	2791
	21:16	from **C** accompanied us and brought us to	2791
	23:23	and two hundred spearmen to go to **C**	2791
	23:33	When the cavalry arrived in **C**,	2791
	24: 1	the high priest Ananias went down to **C**	NIG
	25: 1	Festus went up from **C** to Jerusalem,	2791
	25: 4	Festus answered, "Paul is being held at **C**,	2791
	25: 6	he went down to **C**,	2791
	25:13	at **C** to pay their respects to Festus.	2791
	25:24	about him in Jerusalem and here in **C**,	NIG

CAGE (1) [CAGES]

Eze	19: 9	With hooks they pulled him into a **c**	6050

CAGES (1) [CAGE]

Jer	5:27	Like **c** full of birds,	3990

CAIAPHAS (9)

Mt	26: 3	high priest, whose name was **C**,	2780
	26:57	to **C**, the high priest, where the teachers of	2780
Lk	3: 2	during the high priesthood of Annas and **C**,	2780
Jn	11:49	Then one of them, named **C**,	2780
	18:13	who was the father-in-law of **C**,	2780
	18:14	**C** was the one who had advised the Jews	2780
	18:24	still bound, to **C** the high priest.	2780
	18:28	the Jews led Jesus from **C** to the palace of	2780
Ac	4: 6	and so were **C**, John, Alexander	2780

CAIN (20)

Ge	4: 1	she became pregnant and gave birth to **C**.	7803
	4: 2	Abel kept flocks, and **C** worked the soil.	7803
	4: 3	In the course of time **C** brought some of	7803
	4: 5	but on **C** and his offering he did not look	7803
	4: 5	So **C** was very angry,	7803
	4: 6	LORD said to **C**, "Why are you angry?	7803
	4: 8	Now **C** said to his brother Abel.	7803
	4: 8	**C** attacked his brother Abel and killed him.	7803
	4: 9	Then the LORD said to **C**,	7803
	4:13	**C** said to the LORD,	7803
	4:15	if anyone kills **C**,	7803
	4:15	Then the LORD put a mark on **C** so	7803
	4:16	So **C** went out from the LORD's presence	7803
	4:17	**C** lay with his wife,	7803
	4:17	**C** was then building a city,	NIH
	4:24	If **C** is avenged seven times,	7803
	4:25	since **C** killed him."	7803
Heb	11: 4	a better sacrifice than **C** did.	2782
1Jn	3:12	Do not be like **C**.	2782
Jude	1:11	They have taken the way *of* **C**;	2782

CAINAN (1)

Lk	3:36	the son *of* **C**,	2783

CAKE (13) [CAKES]

Ex	29:23	and a **c** *made* with oil, and a wafer.	2705+4312
Lev	8:26	he took a **c** of bread,	2705
Nu	6:19	and a **c** and a wafer from the basket,	2705
	15:20	a **c** from the first of your ground meal	2705
1Sa	30:12	a **c** **of** pressed figs and two cakes of raisins.	1811
2Sa	6:19	a **c** of dates and a **c** of raisins	882
	6:19	of dates and a **c** **of** raisins to each person in	862
1Ki	17:13	But first make a small **c** of bread for me	6314
	19: 6	by his head was a **c** of bread baked	6314
1Ch	16: 3	a **c** of dates and a cake of raisins	882
	16: 3	and a **c** **of** raisins to each Israelite man	862
Eze	4:12	Eat the food as you would a barley **c**;	6314

Hos	7: 8	Ephraim is a **flat c** not turned over.	6314

CAKES (19) [CAKE]

Ex	12:39	they baked **c** *of* unleavened bread.	6314
	29: 2	make bread, and **c** mixed with oil,	2705
Lev	2: 4	**c** *made* without yeast and mixed with oil,	2705
	7:12	with this thank offering he is to offer **c**	2705
	7:12	and **c** *of* fine flour well-kneaded and mixed	2705
	7:13	to present an offering with **c** *of* bread made	2705
Nu	6:15	**c** *made* *of* fine flour mixed with oil,	2705
	11: 8	They cooked it in a pot or made it into **c**.	6314
1Sa	25:18	a hundred **c** of raisins,	7540
	25:18	and two hundred **c** *of* pressed figs,	1811
	30:12	a cake of pressed figs and two **c** *of* raisins,	7540
2Sa	16: 1	a hundred **c** of raisins,	7540
	16: 1	a hundred **c** *of* figs and a skin of wine.	7811
1Ki	14: 3	*some* **c** and a jar of honey, and go to him.	5926
1Ch	12:40	**fig c**, raisin cakes, wine, oil,	1811
	12:40	**raisin c**, wine, oil, cattle and sheep,	7540
Jer	7:18	and make **c** *of* bread for the Queen	3924
	44:19	that we were making **c** like her image	3924
Hos	3: 1	to other gods and love the **sacred** raisin **c**."	862

CALAH (2)

Ge	10:11	where he built Nineveh, Rehoboth Ir, **C**	3996
	10:12	which is between Nineveh and **C**;	3996

CALAMITIES (8) [CALAMITY]

Dt	29:22	the **c** that have fallen on the land and	4804
	32:23	"I will heap **c** upon them	8288
1Sa	10:19	who saves you out of all your **c**	8288
2Sa	19: 7	This will be worse for you than all the **c**	8288
Job	5:19	From six **c** he will rescue you;	7650
Pr	24:22	and who knows what **c** they can bring?	7085
Isa	51:19	These double **c** have come upon you—	NIH
La	3:38	the mouth of the Most High that both **c**	8288

CALAMITY (29) [CALAMITIES]

2Sa	12:11	to bring **c** upon you.	8288
	24:16	the LORD was grieved because of the **c**	8288
1Ch	21:15	and was grieved because of the **c** and said	8288
2Ch	20: 9	'If **c** comes upon us,	8288
Ne	13:18	that our God brought all this **c** upon us and	8288
Job	18:12	**C** is hungry for him;	224
	21:17	How often does **c** come upon them,	369
	21:30	the evil man is spared from the day of **c**,	369
Ps	107:39	and they were humbled by oppression, **c**	8288
Pr	1:26	I will mock when **c** overtakes you—	7065
	1:27	when **c** overtakes you like a storm,	7065
	14:32	When **c** comes, the wicked are brought	8288
	21:23	and his tongue keeps himself from **c**.	7650
	24:16	but the wicked are brought down by **c**.	8288
Isa	47:11	A **c** will fall upon you	2096
Jer	14:16	I will pour out on them the **c** they *deserve*.	8288
	32:42	As I have brought all this great **c**	8288
	48:16	her **c** will come quickly.	8288
Eze	6:10	not threaten in vain to bring this **c** on them.	8288
	7:26	**C** upon calamity will come,	2096
	7:26	Calamity upon **c** will come,	2096
	35: 5	over to the sword at the time of their **c**,	369
Joel	2:13	and he relents from sending **c**.	8288
Ob	1:13	nor look down on them in their **c** in the day	8288
Jnh	1: 7	to find out who is responsible for this **c**."	8288
	4: 2	a God who relents from sending **c**.	8288
Mic	2: 3	for it will be a time of **c**,	8288
Hab	3:16	Yet I will wait patiently for the day of **c**	7650
Zec	1:15	but they added to the **c**.'	8288

CALAMUS (4)

SS	4:14	**c** and cinnamon, with every kind	7866
Isa	43:24	You have not bought *any* **fragrant c**	7866
Jer	6:20	from Sheba or sweet **c** from a distant land?	7866
Eze	27:19	cassia and **c** for your wares.	7866

CALCOL (2)

1Ki	4:31	wiser than Heman, **C** and Darda,	4004
1Ch	2: 6	Zimri, Ethan, Heman, **C** and Darda—	4004

CALCULATE (1) [CALCULATED]

Rev	13:18	*let him* **c** the number of the beast,	6028

CALCULATED (1) [CALCULATE]

Ac	19:19	When *they* **c** the value of the scrolls,	5248

CALDRON (2) [CALDRONS]

1Sa	2:14	into the pan or kettle or **c** or pot,	7831
Job	41:31	He makes the depths churn like a boiling **c**	6105

CALDRONS (1) [CALDRON]

2Ch	35:13	**c** and pans and served them quickly to all	1857

CALEB (33) [CALEB EPHRATHAH, CALEB'S, CALEBITE]

Nu	13: 6	**C** son of Jephunneh	3979
	13:30	Then **C** silenced the people before Moses	3979
	14: 6	of Nun and **C** son of Jephunneh,	3979
	14:24	because my servant **C** has a different spirit	3979
	14:30	except **C** son of Jephunneh and Joshua son	3979
	14:38	of Nun and **C** son of Jephunneh survived.	3979

Nu	26:65	and not one of them was left except C son 3979
	32:12	not one except C son of Jephunneh 3979
	34:19	These are their names: C son of Jephunneh 3979
Dt	1:36	except C son of Jephunneh 3979
Jos	14: 6	and C son of Jephunneh the Kenizzite said 3979
	14:13	Then Joshua blessed C son of Jephunneh 3979
	14:14	to C son of Jephunneh the Kenizzite ever 3979
	15:13	to C son of Jephunneh a portion in Judah— 3979
	15:14	From Hebron C drove out 3979
	15:16	And C said, "I will give my daughter Acsah in marriage 3979
	15:17	so C gave his daughter Acsah to him NIH
	15:18	When she got off her donkey, C asked her, 3979
	15:19	So C gave her the upper and lower springs. NIH
	21:12	to C son of Jephunneh as his possession. 3979
Jdg	1:12	And C said, "I will give my daughter Acsah in marriage 3979
	1:13	so C gave his daughter Acsah to him NIH
	1:14	When she got off her donkey, C asked her, 3979
	1:15	C gave her the upper and lower springs. 3979
	1:20	Hebron was given to C, 3979
1Sa	30:14	to Judah and the Negev of C. 3979
1Ch	2: 9	Jerahmeel, Ram and C. 3992
	2:18	C son of Hezron had children 3979
	2:19	When Azubah died, C married Ephrath, 3979
	2:42	The sons of C the brother of Jerahmeel— 3979
	2:50	These were the descendants of C. 3979
	4:15	The sons of C son of Jephunneh: 3979
	6:56	the city were given to C son of Jephunneh. 3979

CALEB EPHRATHAH (1) [CALEB, EPHRATHAH]

1Ch 2:24 After Hezron died in C, 3980

CALEB'S (6) [CALEB]

Jos	15:17	Othniel son of Kenaz, C brother, took it; 3979
Jdg	1:13	Othniel son of Kenaz, C younger brother, 3979
	3: 9	Othniel son of Kenaz, C younger brother, 3979
1Ch	2:46	C concubine Ephah was the mother 3979
	2:48	C concubine Maacah was the mother 3979
	2:49	C daughter was Acsah. 3979

CALEBITE (1) [CALEB]

1Sa 25: 3 a C, was surly and mean in his dealings. 3982

CALF (33) [CALF-IDOL, CALF-IDOLS, CALVE, CALVED, CALVES]

Ge	18: 7	tender c and gave it to a servant, 1201+1330
	18: 8	milk and the c that had been prepared, 1201+1330
Ex	32: 4	into an idol cast in the shape of a c, 6319
	32: 5	an altar in front of the c and announced, 2257S
	32: 8	an idol cast in the shape of a c. 6319
	32:19	the camp and saw the c and the dancing, 6319
	32:20	the c they had made and burned it in 6319
	32:24	and out came this c!" 6319
	32:35	with the c Aaron had made. 6319
Lev	9: 2	"Take a bull c for your sin offering and 6319
	9: 3	a sin offering, a c and a lamb— 6319
	9: 8	and slaughtered the c as a sin offering 6319
	22:27	a c, lamb or a goat is born, it is to remain 8802
Dt	9:16	an idol cast in the shape of a c. 6319
	9:21	the c you had made, 6319
1Sa	28:24	The woman had a fattened c at the house, 6319
2Sa	6:13	he sacrificed a bull and a fattened c. 5309
2Ch	11:15	and for the goat and c idols he had made. 6319
Ne	9:18	for themselves an image of a c and said, 6319
Ps	29: 6	He makes Lebanon skip like a c, 6319
	106:19	a c and worshiped an idol cast from metal. 6319
Pr	15:17	where there is love than a fattened c. 8802
Isa	11: 6	the c and the lion and the yearling together; 6319
Jer	31:18	'You disciplined me like an unruly c, 6319
	34:18	like the c they cut in two and then walked 6319
	34:19	between the pieces of the c, 6319
Eze	1: 7	of a c and gleamed like burnished bronze. 6319
Hos	8: 5	They are from Israel! This c— NIH
	8: 6	that c of Samaria. 6319
Lk	15:23	Bring the fattened c and kill it. 3675
	15:27	the fattened c because he has him back safe 3675
	15:30	you kill the fattened c for him!' 3675
Ac	7:41	made an idol in the form of a c. 3674

CALF-IDOL (2) [CALF, IDOL]

Hos	8: 5	Throw out your c, O Samaria! 6319
	10: 5	in Samaria fear for the c of Beth Aven. 6319

CALF-IDOLS (1) [CALF, IDOL]

Hos 13: 2 "They offer human sacrifice and kiss the c." 6319

CALL (192) [CALLED, CALLING, CALLS, SO-CALLED]

Ge	4:26	At that time men began to c on the name of 7924
	17:15	you are no longer to c her Sarai; 7924+9005
	17:19	and you will c him Isaac. 7924+9005
	24:57	"Let's c the girl and ask her about it." 7924
	30:13	The women will c me happy." 887
Dt	3: 9	the Amorites c it Senir; 7924
	4:26	c heaven and earth as witnesses 6386
	18:19	I myself will c him to account. 2011+4946+6640
	30:19	c heaven and earth as witnesses 6386
	31:14	C Joshua and present yourselves at 7924
	31:28	c heaven and earth to testify 6386

Jos	22:23	may the LORD himself c us to account. 1335
Jdg	8: 1	Why didn't you c us when you went 7924
	9:29	'C out your whole army!'" 3655
Ru	1:20	"Don't c me Naomi," she told them. 7924
	1:20	"C me Mara, because the Almighty has made my life very bitter. 7924
	1:21	Why c me Naomi? 7924
1Sa	3: 5	But Eli said, "I did not c; 7924
	3: 6	"My son," Eli said, "I did not c; 7924
	12:17	I will c upon the LORD to send thunder 7924
	20:16	c David's enemies to account." 1335+3338+4946
	23:28	That is why they c this place Sela Hammahlekoth. 7924
2Sa	15: 2	Absalom would c out to him, 7924
	22: 4	I c to the LORD, 7924
1Ki	1:28	Then King David said, "C in Bathsheba." 7924
	1:32	King David said, "C in Zadok the priest, 7924
	18:24	Then you c on the name of your god, 7924
	18:24	and I will c on the name of the LORD. 7924
	18:25	C on the name of your god, 7924
2Ki	4:12	to his servant Gehazi, "C 7924
	4:15	Elisha said, "C her." 7924
	4:36	and said, "C the Shunammite." 7924
	5:11	and c on the name of the LORD his God, 7924
	10:20	"C an assembly in honor of 4200+7727
1Ch	16: 8	c on his name; 7924
2Ch	24:22	the LORD see this and c you to account." 2011
Ne	13: 2	but had hired Balaam to c a curse down 7837
Job	5: 1	"C if you will, but who will answer you? 7924
	14:15	You will c and I will answer you; 7924
	19: 7	though I c for help, there is no justice. 8775
	27:10	Will he c upon God at all times? 7924
Ps	4: 1	Answer me when I c to you, 7924
	4: 3	the LORD will hear when I c to him. 7924
	10:13	"He won't c me to account"? 2011
	10:15	c him to account for his wickedness 2011
	14: 4	as men eat bread and who do not c on 7924
	17: 6	I c on you, O God, for you will answer me; 7924
	18: 3	I c to the LORD, 7924
	20: 9	Answer us when we c! 7924
	27: 7	Hear my voice when I c, O LORD; 7924
	28: 1	To you I c, O LORD my Rock; 7924
	28: 2	c to you for help, 8775
	50:15	and c upon me in the day of trouble; 7924
	53: 4	as men eat bread and who do not c on God? 7924
	55:16	But I c to God, and the LORD saves me. 7924
	56: 9	when I c for help. 7924
	61: 2	From the ends of the earth I c to you, 7924
	61: 2	I c as my heart grows faint; NIH
	65: 8	c forth songs of joy. 8264
	72:17	and they will c him blessed. 887
	79: 6	the kingdoms that do not c on your name; 7924
	80:18	revive us, and we will c on your name. 7924
	86: 3	O Lord, for I c to you all day long. 7924
	86: 5	abounding in love to all who c to you. 7924
	86: 7	In the day of my trouble I will c to you, 7924
	88: 9	I c to you, O LORD, every day; 7924
	89:26	He will c out to me, 'You are my Father, 7924
	91:15	He will c upon me, and I will answer him; 7924
	102: 2	when I c, answer me quickly. 7924
	105: 1	Give thanks to the LORD, c on his name; 7924
	116: 2	I will c on him as long as I live. 7924
	116:13	up the cup of salvation and c on the name 7924
	116:17	a thank offering to you and c on the name 7924
	119:145	I c with all my heart; 7924
	119:146	I c out to you; 7924
	120: 1	I c on the LORD in my distress, 7924
	141: 1	O LORD, I c to you; 7924
	141: 1	Hear my voice when I c to you. 7924
	145:18	The LORD is near to all who c on him, 7924
	145:18	to all who c on him in truth. 7924
	147: 9	and for the young ravens when they c. 7924
Pr	1:28	they will c to me but I will not answer; 7924
	2: 3	and if you c out for insight and cry aloud 7924
	7: 4	and understanding your kinsman; 7924
	8: 1	Does not wisdom c out? 7924
	8: 4	I c out; I raise my voice to all mankind. 7924
	31:28	Her children arise and c her blessed; 887
Ecc	3:15	c the past to account. 1335
Isa	5:20	Woe to those who c evil good and good evil, 606
	7:14	and will c him Immanuel. 7924+9005
	8: 2	c in Uriah the priest and Zechariah son of Jeberekiah as reliable witnesses 6332+6386
	8:12	"Do not c conspiracy everything 606
	8:12	that these people c conspiracy; 606
	12: 4	"Give thanks to the LORD, c on his name; 7924
	30: 7	Therefore I c her Rahab the Do-Nothing. 7924
	44: 5	another will c himself by the name 7924
	48: 2	you who c yourselves citizens of 7924
	54: 6	The LORD will c you back as if you were 7924
	55: 6	c on him while he is near. 7924
	58: 5	Is that what you c a fast, 7924
	58: 9	you will c, and the LORD will answer; 7924
	58:13	if you c the Sabbath a delight and 7924
	60:14	down at your feet and will c you the City 7924
	60:18	but you will c your walls Salvation 7924
	62: 4	No longer will they c you Deserted, 606
	62: 6	You who c on the LORD, 2349
	65: 1	To a nation that did not c on my name, 7924
	65:24	Before they c I will answer; 7924
Jer	3:17	At that time they will c Jerusalem 7924
	3:19	I thought you would c me 'Father' and 7924
	7:27	when you c to them, they will not answer. 7924
	7:32	when people will no longer c it Topheth 606
	9:17	C for the wailing women to come; 7924
	10:25	on the peoples who do not c on your name. 7924
	11:14	because I will not listen when they c to me 7924

Jer	19: 6	people will no longer c this place Topheth 7924
	29:12	Then you will c upon me and come 7924
	33: 3	'C to me and I will answer you 7924
La	3: 8	Even when I c out or cry for help, 2410
	3:21	this I c to mind and therefore I have hope: 448+4213+8740
Eze	9: 1	Then I heard him c out in a loud voice, 7924
	36:29	I will c for the grain and make it plentiful 7924
	39:17	C out to every kind of bird and all 606
Da	5:12	C for Daniel, and he will tell you what 10637
Hos	1: 4	LORD said to Hosea, "C him Jezreel, 7924+9005
	1: 6	to Hosea, "C her Lo-Ruhamah, 7924+9005
	1: 9	the LORD said, "C him Lo-Ammi, 7924+9005
	2:16	"you will c me 'my husband'; 7924
	2:16	you will no longer c me 'my master.' 7924
	11: 7	Even if they c to the Most High, 7924
Joel	1:14	Declare a holy fast; c a sacred assembly. 7924
	1:19	To you, O LORD, I c, 7924
	2:15	declare a holy fast, c a sacred assembly. 7924
Jnh	1: 6	Get up and c on your god!' 7924
	3: 8	Let everyone c urgently on God. 7924
Hab	1: 2	How long, O LORD, must I c for help, 8775
Zep	3: 9	of them may c on the name of the LORD 7924
Zec	13: 9	They will c on my name 7924
Mal	3:12	"Then all the nations will c you blessed, 887
	3:15	c the arrogant blessed. 887
Mt	1:23	and they will c him Immanuel 2813+3836+3950
	9:13	For I have not come to c the righteous, 2813
	20: 8	'C the workers and pay them their wages, 2813
	23: 7	and to have men c them 'Rabbi.' 2813
	23: 9	And do not c anyone on earth 'father,' 2813
	24: 1	to him to c his attention to its buildings. 2109
	24:31	with a loud trumpet c, 4894
	26:53	Do you think I cannot c on my Father, 4151
	26:74	Then he began to c down curses on himself 2874
Mk	2:17	I have not come to c the righteous, 2813
	3:31	they sent someone in to c him. 2813
	10:18	"Why do you c me good?" 3306
	10:49	Jesus stopped and said, "C him." 5888
	14:71	He began to c down curses on himself, 354
	15:12	with the one you c the king of the Jews?" 3306
	15:18	And they began to c out to him, "Hail, 832
Lk	1:48	now on all generations will c me blessed, 3420
	5:32	I have not come to c the righteous, 2813
	6:46	"Why do you c me, 'Lord, Lord,' 2813
	9:54	do you want us to c fire down 3306
	18:19	"Why do you c me good?" 3306
	22:25	over them c themselves Benefactors. 2813
Jn	4:16	"Go, c your husband and come back." 5888
	9:11	"The man they c Jesus made some mud 3306
	13:13	"You c me 'Teacher' and 'Lord,' 5888
	15:15	I no longer c you servants, 3306
Ac	2:39	for all whom the Lord our God will c." 4673
	9:14	from the chief priests to arrest all who c on 2126
	9:21	in Jerusalem among those who c on 2126
	10:15	"Do not c anything impure 3123
	10:28	that I should not c any man impure 3306
	11: 9	'Do not c anything impure 3123
	24:14	which they c a sect. 3306
Ro	1: 1	and apostleship to c people from among all NIG
	2:17	Now you, if you c yourself a Jew; 2226
	9:25	"I will c them 'my people' who are 2813
	9:25	and I will c her 'my loved one' who is NIG
	10:12	of all and richly blesses all who c on him, 2126
	10:14	can they c on the one they have 2126
	11:29	for God's gifts and his c are irrevocable. 3104
1Co	1: 2	with all those everywhere who c on 2126
	14: 8	if the trumpet does not sound a clear c, 5889
2Co	1:23	I c God as my witness that it was in order 2126
Eph	2:11	by those who c themselves 3306
1Th	4: 7	For God did not c us to be impure, 2813
	4:16	of the archangel and with the trumpet c 4894
2Ti	2:22	along with those who c on the Lord out of 2126
Heb	2:11	Jesus is not ashamed to c them brothers. 2813
Jas	5:14	He should c the elders of the church to pray 4673
1Pe	2:11	Since you c on a Father who judges each 2126
3Jn	1:10	I will c attention to what he is doing, 5703
Rev	8:13	an eagle that was flying in midair c out in 3306

CALL (Anglicized) See also GET

CALLED (502) [CALL]

Ge	1: 5	God c the light "day," 7924
	1: 5	and the darkness he c "night." 7924
	1: 8	God c the expanse "sky." 7924
	1:10	God c the dry ground "land," 7924
	1:10	and the gathered waters he c "seas." 7924
	2:19	whatever the man c each living creature, 7924
	2:23	she shall be c 'woman.' 7924
	3: 9	But the LORD God c to the man, 7924
	5: 2	they were created, he c them "man." 7924+9005
	11: 9	That is why it was c Babel— 7924+9005
	12: 8	an altar to the LORD and c on the name 7924
	13: 4	There Abram c on the name of the LORD. 7924
	14:14	he c out the 318 trained men born 8197
	16:14	That is why the well was c Beer Lahai Roi; 7924
	17: 5	No longer will you be c Abram; 7924+9005
	19: 5	They c to Lot, 7924
	19:22	(That is why the town was c Zoar.) 7924+9005
	20: 9	Then Abimelech c Abraham in and said, 7924
	21:17	the angel of God c to Hagar from heaven 7924
	21:31	So that place was c Beersheba, 7924
	21:33	and there he c upon the name 7924
	22:11	But the angel of the LORD c out to him 7924
	22:14	So Abraham c that place 7924+9005

Ge	22:15	of the LORD c to Abraham from heaven	7924
	24:58	So they c Rebekah and asked her,	7924
	25:30	(That is why he was also c Edom.)	7924+9005
	26:25	Isaac built an altar there and c on the name	7924
	26:33	He c it Shibah,	7924
	27: 1	he c for Esau his older son and said to him,	7924
	28: 1	So Isaac c Jacob and blessed him	7924
	28:19	He c that place Bethel,	7924+9005
	28:19	though the city used to be c Luz.	9005
	31:47	Laban c it Jegar Sahadutha,	7924
	31:47	and Jacob c it Galeed.	7924
	31:48	That is why it was c Galeed.	7924+9005
	31:49	It was also c Mizpah, because he said,	NIH
	32:30	So Jacob c the place Peniel, saying,	7924+9005
	33:17	That is why the place is c Succoth.	7924+9005
	33:20	up an altar and c it El Elohe Israel.	7924
	35: 7	and he c the place El Bethel,	7924
	35:10	but you will no longer be c Jacob;	7924+9005
	35:15	Jacob c the place where God had talked	7924+9005
	39:14	she c her household servants.	7924
	47:29	he c for his son Joseph and said to him,	7924
	48:16	May they be c by my name and the names	7924
	49: 1	Then Jacob c for his sons and said:	7924
	50:11	near the Jordan is c Abel Mizraim.	7924+9005
Ex	3: 4	God c to him from within the bush,	7924
	15:23	(That is why the place is c Marah.)	7924+9005
	16:31	people of Israel c the bread manna.	7924
	17: 7	he c the place Massah and Meribah	7924+9005
	17:15	altar and c it The LORD is my Banner.	7924+9005
	19: 3	and the LORD c to him from the mountain	7924
	19:20	of Mount Sinai and c Moses to the top of	7924
	24:16	on the seventh day the LORD c to Moses	7924
	34:31	But Moses c to them;	7924
Lev	1: 1	The LORD c to Moses and spoke to him	7924
Nu	1:18	c the whole community together	7735
	11: 3	So that place was c Taberah,	7924+9005
	13:24	That place was c the Valley of Eshcol	7924
	32:41	and c them Havvoth Jair.	7924
	32:42	and c it Nobah after himself.	7924
Dt	2:11	but the Moabites c them Emites.	7924
	2:20	but the Ammonites c them Zamzummites.	7924
	3: 9	(Hermon is c Sirion by the Sidonians;	7924
	3:14	that to this day Bashan is c Havvoth Jair.)	NIH
	28:10	on earth will see that you are c by the name	7924
Jos	3:16	a town c Adam in the vicinity of Zarethan,	NIH
	4: 4	So Joshua c together	7924
	5: 9	So the place has been c Gilgal to this day.	7924+9005
	6: 6	So Joshua son of Nun c the priests and	7924
	7:26	Therefore that place has been c the Valley of Achor	7924+9005
	8:16	All the men of Ai were c to pursue them,	2410
	14:15	(Hebron used to be c Kiriath Arba	9005
	15:15	in Debir (formerly c Kiriath Sepher).	9005
Jdg	1:10	in Hebron (formerly c Kiriath Arba)	9005
	1:11	in Debir (formerly c Kiriath Sepher).	9005
	1:17	Therefore it was c Hormah.	7924+9005
	1:23	to spy out Bethel (formerly c Luz),	9005
	1:26	where he built a city and c it Luz,	7924+9005
	2: 5	and they c that place Bokim.	7924+9005
	6:24	an altar to the LORD there and c it	7924
	6:32	So that day they c Gideon "Jerub-Baal,"	7924
	7:15	to the camp of Israel and c out,	606
	7:23	Asher and all Manasseh were c out,	7590
	7:24	So all the men of Ephraim were c out	7590
	9:54	Hurriedly he c to his armor-bearer,	7924
	10: 4	which to this day are c Havvoth Jair.	7924
	10:17	the Ammonites were c to arms and camped	7590
	12: 1	The men of Ephraim c out their forces,	7590
	12: 2	and although I c,	2410
	12: 4	Jephthah then c together the men of Gilead	7695
	15:17	and the place was c Ramath Lehi.	7924
	15:19	So the spring was c En Hakkore,	7924+9005
	16: 9	With men hidden in the room, she c to him,	606
	16:12	with men hidden in the room, she c to him,	606
	16:14	Again she c to him, "Samson,	606
	16:19	she c a man to shave off the seven braids	7924
	16:20	Then she c, "Samson,	606
	16:25	So they c Samson out of the prison,	7924
	18:12	of Kiriath Jearim is c Mahaneh Dan	7924
	18:22	near Micah were c together and overtook	2410
	18:23	c out your men to fight?"	2410
	18:29	though the city used to be c Laish.	9005
Ru	2: 4	"The LORD bless you!" they c back.	606
1Sa	1: 2	one was c Hannah and the other Peninnah.	9005
	3: 4	Then the LORD c Samuel.	7924
	3: 5	"Here I am; you c me."	7924
	3: 6	Again the LORD c, "Samuel!"	7924
	3: 6	"Here I am; you c me."	7924
	3: 8	The LORD c Samuel a third time,	7924
	3: 8	"Here I am; you c me."	7924
	3:16	but Eli c him and said,	7924
	5: 8	So they c together all the rulers	665+2256+8938
	5:11	So they c together all the rulers	665+2256+8938
	6: 2	the Philistines c for the priests and	7924
	9: 9	the prophet of today used to be c a seer.)	7924
	9:26	about daybreak and Samuel c to Saul on	7924
	12:18	Then Samuel c upon the LORD,	7924
	14: 4	one was c Bozez, and the other Seneh.	9005
	16: 8	Then Jesse c Abinadab and had him pass	7924
	19: 7	So Jonathan c David and told him	7924
	20:37	Jonathan c out after him,	606
	23: 8	And Saul c up all his forces for battle,	9048
	24: 8	Then David went out of the cave and c out	7924
	26:14	He c out to the army and to Abner son	7924
	28:15	So I have c on you to tell me what to do."	7924
	29: 6	So Achish c David and said to him,	7924
2Sa	1: 7	he c out to me, and I said, 'What can I do?'	7924
	1:15	Then David c one of his men and said,	7924
	2:16	in Gibeon was c Helkath Hazzurim.	7924
	2:26	Abner c out to Joab,	7924
	5: 9	up residence in the fortress and c it the City	7924
	5:20	So that place was c Baal Perazim.	7924+9005
	6: 2	which is c by the Name,	7924
	6: 8	and to this day that place is c Perez Uzzah.	7924
	9: 2	They c him to appear before David,	7924
	13:17	He c his personal servant and said,	7924
	18:18	it is c Absalom's Monument to this day.	7924
	18:25	The watchman c out to the king	7924
	18:26	and he c down to the gatekeeper, "Look,	7924
	18:28	Ahimaaz c out to the king, "All is well!"	7924
	20:16	a wise woman c from the city,	7924
	22: 7	In my distress I c to the LORD;	7924
	22: 7	I c out to my God.	7924
1Ki	2: 8	who c down bitter curses on me	7837+7839
	9:13	And he c them the Land of Cabul,	7924
	12:20	they sent and c him to the assembly	7924
	17:10	He c to her and asked,	7924
	18: 1	As he was going to get it, he c,	7924
	18:26	Then they c on the name of Baal	7924
	20:39	the prophet c out to him,	7590
	22: 9	So the king of Israel c one of his officials	7590
2Ki	2:24	looked at them and c down a curse on them	7837
	3:10	c us three kings together	7924
	3:13	c us three kings together	7924
	3:21	who could bear arms was c up and stationed	7590
	4:12	So he c her, and she stood before him.	7924
	4:15	So he c her, and she stood in the doorway.	7924
	4:22	She c her husband and said,	7924
	7:10	and c out to the city gatekeepers	7924
	9:17	he c out, "I see some troops coming."	606
	9:32	He looked up at the window and c out,	606
	11:14	Then Athaliah tore her robes and c out,	7924
	18: 4	(It was c Nehushtan.)	7924
	18:18	They c for the king;	7924
	18:28	the commander stood and c out in Hebrew:	928+1524+7754+7924
	20:11	Then the prophet Isaiah c on the LORD,	7924
	23: 1	the king c together all the elders of Judah	665+2256+8938
1Ch	4:14	It was c this because its people	NIH
	9:23	the house c the Tent.	NIH
	11: 7	and so it was c the City of David.	7924
	13: 6	the ark that is c by the Name.	7924
	13:11	and to this day that place is c Perez Uzzah.	7924
	14:11	So that place was c Baal Perazim.	7924+9005
	15: 4	He c together the descendants of Aaron	665
	21:26	He c on the LORD,	7924
	22: 6	Then he c for his son Solomon	7924
2Ch	7:14	who are c by my name,	7924
	14:11	Asa c to the LORD his God and said,	7924
	18: 8	So the king of Israel c one of his officials	7924
	20:26	is why it is c the Valley of Beracah	7924+9005
	24: 5	He c together the priests and Levites	7695
	25: 5	c the people of Judah together	7695
	32:18	Then they c out in Hebrew to the people	928+1524+7754+7924
	34:29	the king c together all the elders of Judah	665+2256+8938
Ezr	2:61	of Barzillai the Gileadite and was c by	7924
Ne	5: 7	So I c together a large meeting to deal	5989
	7:63	of Barzillai the Gileadite and was c by	7924
	9: 4	who c with loud voices to	2410
	13:11	Then I c them together and stationed them	7695
	13:25	I rebuked them and c curses down on them.	7837
Est	4:11	But thirty days have passed since I was c	7924
	9:26	(Therefore these days were c Purim,	7924
Job	12: 4	though I c upon God and he answered—	7924
	31:14	What will I answer when c to account?	7212
Ps	18: 6	In my distress I c to the LORD;	7924
	30: 2	c to you for help	8775
	30: 8	To you, O LORD, I c;	7924
	31:22	c to you for help.	8775
	34: 6	This poor man c, and	7924
	81: 7	In your distress you c and I rescued you,	7924
	99: 6	among those who c on his name;	7924
	99: 6	they c on the LORD	7924
	105:16	He c down famine on the land	7924
	116: 4	Then I c on the name of the LORD:	7924
	138: 3	When I c, you answered me;	7924
Pr	1:24	But since you rejected me when I c	7924
	16:21	The wise in heart are c discerning,	7924
SS	5: 6	I c him but he did not answer.	7924
	6: 9	The maidens saw her and c her blessed;	887
Isa	1:26	Afterward you will be c the City	7924
	4: 1	only let us be c by your name.	7924
	4: 3	who remain in Jerusalem, will be c holy,	606
	9: 6	And he will be c Wonderful Counselor	7924+9005
	19:18	of them will be c the City of Destruction.	606
	22:12	c you on that day to weep and to wail,	7924
	31: 4	of shepherds is c together against him, he is	7924
	32: 5	No longer will the fool be c noble nor	7924
	34:12	Her nobles will have nothing there to be c	7924
	35: 8	it will be c the Way of Holiness.	7924
	36:13	the commander stood and c out in Hebrew,	928+1524+7754+7924
	41: 9	from its farthest corners I c you.	7924
	42: 6	the LORD, have c you in righteousness;	7924
	43: 7	everyone who is c by my name,	7924
	43:22	"Yet you have not c upon me, O Jacob,	7924
	47: 1	No more will you be c tender or delicate.	7924
	47: 5	no more will you be c queen of kingdoms.	7924
	48: 1	you who are c by the name of Israel	7924
	48: 8	you were c a rebel from birth.	7924
Isa	48:12	O Jacob, Israel, whom I have c:	7924
	48:15	I, even I, have spoken; yes, I have c him.	7924
	49: 1	Before I was born the LORD c me;	7924
	50: 2	I c, why was there no one to answer?	7924
	51: 2	When I c him he was but one,	7924
	54: 5	he is c the God of all the earth.	7924
	56: 7	for my house will be c a house of prayer	7924
	58:12	you will be c Repairer of Broken Walls,	7924
	61: 3	They will be c oaks of righteousness,	7924
	61: 6	And you will be c priests of the LORD,	7924
	62: 2	you will be c by a new name that	7924
	62: 4	But you will be c Hephzibah,	7924
	62:12	They will be c the Holy People,	7924
	62:12	and you will be c Sought After,	7924
	63:19	they have not been c by your name.	7924
	65:12	for I c but you did not answer,	7924
	66: 4	For when I c, no one answered,	7924
Jer	3: 4	Have you not just c to me:	7924
	6:30	They are c rejected silver,	7924
	7:13	I c you, but you did not answer.	7924
	11:16	The LORD c you a thriving olive tree	7924+9005
	23: 6	This is the name by which he will be c:	7924
	30:17	'because you are c an outcast,	7924
	33:16	This is the name by which it will be c:	7924
	35:17	I c to them, but they did not answer.' "	7924
	36: 4	So Jeremiah c Baruch son of Neriah,	7924
	42: 8	So he c together Johanan son of Kareah	7924
La	1:19	"I c to my allies but they betrayed me.	7924
	2:15	the city that was c the perfection of beauty,	606
	3:55	I c on your name, O LORD,	7924
	3:57	You came near when I c you,	7924
Eze	9: 3	Then the LORD c to the man clothed	7924
	10:13	the wheels being c "the whirling wheels."	7924
	20:29	(It is c Bamah to this day.)	7924+9005
	38: 8	After many days you will be c to arms.	7212
	39:11	So it will be c the Valley of Hamon Gog.	7924
	39:16	(Also a town c Hamonah will be there.)	9005
Da	2:26	king asked Daniel (also c Belteshazzar),	10721
	4: 8	(He is c Belteshazzar),	10721
	4:14	He c in a loud voice:	10637
	4:19	(also c Belteshazzar) was greatly perplexed	10721
	5: 7	The king c out for the enchanters,	10637
	5:12	whom the king c Belteshazzar,	10682+10721
	6:20	he c to Daniel in an anguished voice,	10237
	10: 1	to Daniel (who was c Belteshazzar).	7924+9005
Hos	1:10	they will be c 'sons of the living God.'	606
	2:23	to the one I c 'Not my loved one.'	NIH
	2:23	I will say to those c 'Not my people,'	NIH
	11: 1	I loved him, and out of Egypt I c my son.	7924
	11: 2	But the more I c Israel,	7924
Jnh	2: 2	He said: "In my distress I c to the LORD,	7924
	2: 2	From the depths of the grave I c for help,	8775
Hab	3: 9	you c for many arrows.	606
Hag	1:11	I c for a drought on the fields and	7924
Zec	6: 8	Then he c to me, "Look,	2410
	7:13	" 'When I c, they did not listen;	7924
	7:13	so when they c, I would not listen,'	7924
	8: 3	Jerusalem will be c the City of Truth,	7924
	8: 3	of the LORD Almighty will be c	NIH
	11: 7	Then I took two staffs c one Favor and	7924
	11:10	Then I took my staff c Favor and broke it,	NIH
	11:14	Then I broke my second staff c Union,	NIH
Mal	1: 4	They will be c the Wicked Land,	7924
	2: 5	this c for reverence and he revered me	NIH
Mt	1:16	of whom was born Jesus, who is c Christ.	3306
	2: 4	When he had c together all	5251
	2: 7	Then Herod c the Magi secretly	2813
	2:15	"Out of Egypt I c my son."	2813
	2:23	he went and lived in a town c Nazareth.	3306
	2:23	"He will be c a Nazarene."	3306
	4:18	Simon c Peter and his brother Andrew.	3306
	4:21	preparing their nets. Jesus c them,	2813
	5: 9	for they will be c sons of God.	2813
	5:19	the same will be c least in the kingdom	2813
	5:19	be c great in the kingdom of heaven.	2813
	10: 1	c his twelve disciples to him	4673
	10: 2	first, Simon (who is c Peter)	3306
	10:25	head of the house has been c Beelzebub,	2126
	15:10	Jesus c the crowd to him and said,	4673
	15:32	Jesus c his disciples to him and said,	4673
	18: 2	He c a little child and had him stand	4673
	18:32	"Then the master c the servant in.	4673
	20:25	Jesus c them together and said,	4673
	20:32	Jesus stopped and c them.	5888
	21:13	" 'My house will be c a house of prayer,'	2813
	23: 8	"But you are not to be c 'Rabbi,	2813
	23:10	Nor are you to be c 'teacher,'	2813
	25:14	who c his servants	2813
	26:14	the one c Judas Iscariot—	3306
	26:36	with his disciples to a place c Gethsemane,	3306
	27: 8	That is why it has been c the Field	2813
	27:16	a notorious prisoner, c Barabbas.	3306
	27:17	Barabbas, or Jesus who is c Christ?"	3306
	27:22	then, with Jesus who is c Christ?"	3306
	27:33	to a place c Golgotha (which means	3306
Mk	1:20	Without delay he c them,	2813
	3:13	Jesus went up on a mountainside and c to	4673
	3:23	So Jesus c them and spoke to them	4673
	7:14	Again Jesus c the crowd to him and said,	4673
	8: 1	Jesus c his disciples to him and said,	4673
	8:34	Then he c the crowd to him along	4673
	9:35	Sitting down, Jesus c the Twelve and	5888
	10:42	Jesus c them together and said,	4673
	10:49	So they c to the blind man, "Cheer up!	5888
	11:17	" 'My house will be c a house of prayer	2813
	14:32	went to a place c Gethsemane,	3836+3950+4005
	15: 7	A man c Barabbas was in prison with	3306

Mk	15:16	and **c together** the whole company	5157
	15:22	to the place **c** Golgotha (which means	NIG
Lk	1:32	He will be great and *will be* **c** the Son of	2813
	1:35	the holy one to be born *will be* **c** the Son	2813
	1:60	He is to be **c** John."	2813
	1:76	*will be* **c** a prophet of the Most High;	2813
	2:25	was a man in Jerusalem **c** Simeon,	3950+4005
	6:13	he **c** his disciples **to** him and chose twelve	4715
	6:15	Simon who *was* **c** the Zealot,	2813
	7:11	Jesus went to a town **c** Nain,	2813
	8: 2	Mary (**c** Magdalene) from whom seven demons had come out;	2813
	8: 8	When he said this, *he* **c** out,	5888
	9: 1	**c** the Twelve **together**,	5157
	9:10	by themselves to a town **c** Bethsaida,	2813
	9:38	A man in the crowd **c** out, "Teacher,	1066
	10:39	She had a sister **c** Mary,	2813
	11:27	a woman in the crowd **c** out,	2048+5889
	13:12	he **c** her **forward** and said to her, "Woman,	4715
	15:19	I am no longer worthy *to be* **c** your son;	2813
	15:21	I am no longer worthy *to be* **c** your son.'	2813
	15:26	So he **c** one of the servants	4673
	16: 2	So he **c** him **in** and asked him,	5888
	16: 5	he **c** in each one of his master's debtors.	4673
	16:24	So he **c** to him, 'Father Abraham,	5888
	17:13	**c** out in a loud voice,	149+5889
	18:16	But Jesus **c** the children *to him* and said,	4673
	18:38	He **c** out, "Jesus, Son of David,	1066
	19:13	So he **c** ten of his servants	2813
	19:29	and Bethany at the hill **c** the Mount	2813
	21:37	the night on the hill **c** the Mount of Olives,	2813
	22: 1	Feast of Unleavened Bread, **c** the Passover,	3306
	22: 3	Then Satan entered Judas, **c** Iscariot,	2813
	22:47	and the man who *was* **c** Judas,	3306
	23:13	Pilate **c together** the chief priests,	5157
	23:33	When they came to the place **c** the Skull,	2813
	23:46	Jesus **c** out with a loud voice, "Father,	5888
	24:13	of them were going to a village **c** Emmaus,	3950
Jn	1:42	You *will be* **c** Cephas" (which,	2813
	1:48	under the fig tree before Philip **c** you."	5888
	2: 9	Then he **c** the bridegroom aside	5888
	4: 5	So he came to a town in Samaria **c** Sychar,	3306
	4:25	that Messiah" (**c** Christ) "is coming.	3306
	5: 2	which in Aramaic *is* **c** Bethesda	2141
	10:35	If *he* **c** them 'gods,'	3306
	11:16	Then Thomas (**c** Didymus) said to the rest	3306
	11:28	she went back and **c** her sister Mary aside.	5888
	11:43	Jesus **c** in a loud voice, "Lazarus,	3198
	11:47	the Pharisees **c** a **meeting** of the Sanhedrin.	5251
	11:54	to a village **c** Ephraim,	3306
	12:17	with him when *he* **c** Lazarus from the tomb	5888
	15:15	Instead, I have **c** you friends,	3306
	19:17	in Aramaic *is* **c** Golgotha).	3306
	20:24	Now Thomas (**c** Didymus),	3306
	21: 2	Thomas (**c** Didymus),	3306
	21: 5	He **c** out to them, "Friends,	3306
Ac	1:12	to Jerusalem from the hill **c** the Mount	2813
	1:19	so they **c** that field	2813
	1:23	Joseph **c** Barsabbas (also known as Justus)	2813
	3: 2	to the temple gate **c** Beautiful,	3306
	3:10	at the temple gate **c** Beautiful,	NIG
	3:11	in the place **c** Solomon's Colonnade.	2813
	4: 9	If we *are being* **c** to account today for	373
	4:18	Then *they* **c** them in again	2813
	4:36	the apostles **c** Barnabas (which means Son	2126
	5:21	*they* **c together** the Sanhedrin—	5157
	5:40	*They* **c** the apostles **in**	4673
	6: 9	of the Freedmen (as *it was* **c**)—	3306
	9:10	The Lord **c** to him in a vision, "Ananias!"	3306
	9:41	Then he **c** the believers and the widows	5888
	10: 5	a man named Simon who *is* **c** Peter.	2126
	10: 7	Cornelius **c** two of his servants and	5888
	10:18	*They* **c** out, asking	5888
	10:24	and *had* **c together** his relatives	5157
	10:32	Send to Joppa for Simon who *is* **c** Peter.	2126
	11:13	'Send to Joppa for Simon who *is* **c** Peter.	2126
	11:26	The disciples *were* **c** Christians first	5976
	12:12	of Mary the mother of John, also **c** Mark,	2126
	12:25	taking with them John, also **c** Mark.	2126
	13: 1	Barnabas, Simeon **c** Niger,	2813
	13: 2	for the work to which *I have* **c** them."	4673
	13: 9	Then Saul, who was also **c** Paul,	NIG
	14:10	and **c** out, "Stand up	3306+3489+5889
	14:12	Barnabas *they* **c** Zeus,	2813
	14:12	and Paul they **c** Hermes because he was	NIG
	15:22	They chose Judas (**c** Barsabbas) and Silas,	2813
	15:37	Barnabas wanted to take John, also **c** Mark,	2813
	16:10	concluding that God *had* **c** us to preach	4673
	16:29	The jailer **c** for lights,	160
	17: 7	that there is another king, one **c** Jesus."	NIG
	19:25	He **c** them **together**, along with	5255
	23: 6	**c** out in the Sanhedrin, "My brothers,	3189
	23:17	Then Paul **c** one of the centurions and said,	4673
	23:23	Then he **c** two of his centurions	4673
	24: 2	*When* Paul *was* **c** in,	2813
	27: 8	and came to a place **c** Fair Havens,	2813
	27:14	of hurricane force, **c** the "northeaster,"	2813
	27:16	to the lee of a small island **c** Cauda,	2813
	28: 1	we found out that the island *was* **c** Malta.	2813
	28:17	Three days later he **c together** the leaders	5157
Ro	1: 1	**c** to be an apostle and set apart for	3105
	1: 6	also are among those who are **c** to belong	3105
	1: 7	in Rome who are loved by God and **c** to	3105
	7: 3	*she is* **c** an adulteress.	5976
	8:28	who have been **c** according to his purpose.	3105
	8:30	And those he predestined, *he* also **c**;	2813
	8:30	those *he* **c**, he also justified;	2813

Ro	9:24	even us, whom *he* also **c**,	2813
	9:26	they will be **c** 'sons of the living God.' "	2813
1Co	1: 1	**c** to be an apostle of Christ Jesus by	3105
	1: 2	to those sanctified in Christ Jesus and **c**	3105
	1: 9	who has **c** you into fellowship	2813
	1:24	but to those whom God has **c**,	3105
	1:26	think of what you were when you were **c**.	3104
	7:15	God has **c** us to live in peace.	2813
	7:17	to him and to which God has **c** him.	2813
	7:18	a man already circumcised when *he was* **c**?	2813
	7:18	Was a man uncircumcised when *he was* **c**?	2813
	7:20	which he was in when God **c** him.	2813
	7:21	Were you a slave when *you were* **c**?	2813
	7:22	For he who was a slave when *he was* **c** by	2813
	7:22	a free man *when he was* **c** is Christ's slave.	2813
	7:24	should remain in the situation God **c** him to.	2813
	15: 9	and do not even deserve *to be* **c** an apostle,	2813
Gal	1: 6	so quickly deserting the one who **c** you by	2813
	1:15	who set me apart from birth and **c** me	2813
	5:13	You, my brothers, *were* **c** to be free.	2813
Eph	1:18	the hope to which he has **c** you,	3104
	2:11	by birth and **c** "uncircumcised"	3306
	4: 4	just as *you were* **c** to one hope	2813
	4: 4	to one hope when you were **c**	3104
Php	3:14	for which God has **c** me heavenward	3104
Col	3:15	members of one body you were **c** to peace.	2813
	4:11	Jesus, who *is* **c** Justus,	3306
2Th	2:14	that is **c** God or is worshiped,	3306
	2:14	*He* **c** you to this through our gospel,	2813
1Ti	6:12	of the eternal life to which *you were* **c**	2813
	6:20	of what is **falsely c** knowledge,	6024
2Ti	1: 9	who has saved us and **c** us to a holy life—	2813
Heb	3:13	as long as *it is* **c** Today,	2813
	5: 4	*he* must be **c** by God, just as Aaron was.	2813
	9: 2	this *was* **c** the Holy Place.	3306
	9: 3	Behind the second curtain was a room the Most Holy Place,	3306
	9:15	that those who are **c** may receive	2813
	11: 8	By faith Abraham, *when* **c** to go	2813
	11:16	God is not ashamed *to be* **c** their God,	2126
Jas	2:23	and *he was* **c** God's friend.	2813
1Pe	1:15	But just as he who **c** you is holy,	2813
	2: 9	of him who **c** you out of darkness	2813
	2:21	To this *you were* **c**,	2813
	3: 6	and **c** him her master.	2813
	3: 9	to this *you were* **c** so that you may inherit	2813
	5:10	who **c** you to his eternal glory in Christ,	2813
2Pe	1: 3	through our knowledge of him who **c** us	2813
1Jn	3: 1	that *we should be* **c** children of God!	2813
Jude	1: 1	To those who *have been* **c**,	3105
Rev	6:10	*They* **c** out in a loud voice, "How long,	3189
	6:16	*They* **c** to the mountains and the rocks,	3306
	7: 2	*He* **c** out in a loud voice to the four angels	3189
	11: 8	which *is* figuratively **c** Sodom and Egypt,	2813
	12: 9	that ancient serpent **c** the devil, or Satan,	2813
	14:15	of the temple and **c** in a loud voice	3189
	14:18	came from the altar and **c** in a loud voice	5888
	16:16	the place that in Hebrew is **c** Armageddon.	2813
	17:14	and with him will be his **c**,	3105
	19:11	whose rider *is* **c** Faithful and True.	2813

CALLING (43) [CALL]

Ex	33: 7	**c** it the "tent of meeting."	7924
Nu	10: 2	**c** the community **together**	5246
Jdg	6:35	**c** them **to arms**, and also into Asher,	339+2410
	12: 1	to fight the Ammonites without **c** us to go	7924
1Sa	3: 8	Eli realized that the LORD *was* **c** the boy.	7924
	3:10	**c** as at the other times, "Samuel!	7924
1Ki	16:24	**c** it Samaria, after Shemer,	7924+9005
2Ki	9:23	**c** out to Ahaziah, "Treachery, Ahaziah!"	606
	14: 7	**c** it Joktheel, the name it has to this day.	7924
2Ch	30: 5	**c** the people to come to Jerusalem	NIH
Est	5:10	**C together** his friends and Zeresh, his wife,	995+2256+8938
Ps	69: 3	I am worn out **c** for help;	7924
Pr	9:15	**c** out to those who pass by,	7924
Isa	6: 3	And *they were* **c** to one another:	7924
	40: 3	A voice of one **c**: "In the desert prepare	7924
	41: 2	**c** him in righteousness to his service?	7924
	41: 4	**c** forth the generations from	7924
Jer	25:29	for I *am* **c down** a sword upon all who live	7924
Da	8:16	And I heard a man's voice from the Ulai **c**,	7924
Hos	7:11	now **c** to Egypt, now turning to Assyria.	7924
Am	7: 4	The Sovereign LORD *was* **c** for judgment	7924
Mic	6: 9	The LORD *is* **c** to the city—	7754+7924
Mt	3: 3	"A voice *of one* **c** in the desert,	1066
	9:27	**c** out, "Have mercy on us, Son of David!"	3189
	11:16	in the marketplaces and **c** out to others:	4715
	27:47	they said, "He's **c** Elijah."	5888
Mk	1: 3	"a voice *of one* **c** in the desert,	1066
	6: 7	**C** the Twelve **to** him,	4673
	10:49	On your feet! He's **c** you."	5888
	12:43	**C** his disciples **to** him, Jesus said,	4673
	15:35	they said, "Listen, he's **c** Elijah.	5888
Lk	3: 4	"A voice *of one* **c** in the desert,	1066
	7:18	**C** two of them,	4673
	7:32	in the marketplace and **c** out to each other:	4715
Jn	1:23	"I am the voice *of one* **c** in the desert,	1066
	5:18	but *he was* even **c** God his own Father,	3306
Ac	22:16	and wash your sins away, **c** on his name.'	2126
Eph	4: 1	live a life worthy of the **c** you have **received.**	2813+3104
2Th	1:11	our God may count you worthy of his **c**,	3104
Heb	3: 1	holy brothers, who share in the heavenly **c**,	3104
	4: 7	God again set a certain day, **c** it Today,	NIG
	8:13	By **c** this covenant "new,"	3306

2Pe	1:10	be all the more eager to make your **c**	3104

CALLOUS (3) [CALLOUSED]

Ps	17:10	They close up their **c** hearts,	2693
	73: 7	From their **c** hearts comes iniquity;	2693
	119:70	Their hearts are **c** and unfeeling,	2021+2693+3869

CALLOUSED (3) [CALLOUS]

Isa	6:10	**Make** the heart of this people **c**;	9042
Mt	13:15	For this people's heart *has become* **c**;	4266
Ac	28:27	For this people's heart *has become* **c**;	4266

CALLS (40) [CALL]

Ge	46:33	When Pharaoh **c** you **in** and asks,	7924
1Sa	3: 9	"Go and lie down, and if *he* **c** you, say,	7924
	26:14	"Who are you *who* **c** to the king?"	7924
Ps	42: 7	Deep **c** to deep in the roar	7924
	147: 4	the number of the stars and **c** them each	7924
Pr	1:20	Wisdom **c aloud** in the street,	8264
	9: 3	and *she* **c** from the highest point of the city.	7924
Isa	21:11	*Someone* **c** to me from Seir, "Watchman,	7924
	40:26	and **c** them each by name.	7924
	41:25	one from the rising sun *who* **c** on my name.	7924
	59: 4	No *one* **c** for justice;	7924
	64: 7	No *one* **c** on your name or strives	7924
Hos	7: 7	and none of them **c** on me.	7924
Joel	2:32	everyone who **c** on the name of the LORD	7924
	2:32	among the survivors whom the LORD **c**.	7924
Am	5: 8	who **c** for the waters of the sea	7924
	9: 6	who **c** for the waters of the sea	7924
Zep	2:14	Their **c** will echo through the windows,	7754
Mt	22:43	speaking by the Spirit, **c** him 'Lord'?	2813
	22:45	If then David **c** him 'Lord,'	2813
Mk	12:37	David himself **c** him 'Lord.'	3306
Lk	15: 6	**c** his friends and neighbors **together**	5157
	15: 9	**c** her friends and neighbors **together**	5157
	20:37	for *he* **c** the Lord 'the God of Abraham,	3306
	20:44	David **c** him 'Lord.'	2813
Jn	10: 3	*He* **c** his own sheep by name	5888
Ac	2:21	And everyone who **c** on the name of	2126
Ro	4:17	to the dead and **c** things that are not as	2813
	9:12	not by works but by him who **c**—	2813
	10:13	"Everyone who **c** on the name of the Lord	2126
1Co	5:11	not associate with anyone who **c** *himself*	3951
Gal	4: 6	the Spirit who **c** out, "Abba, Father."	3189
	5: 8	not come from the one who **c** you.	2813
1Th	2:12	who **c** you into his kingdom and glory.	2813
	5:24	one who **c** you is faithful and he will do it.	2813
Rev	2:20	who **c** herself a prophetess.	3306
	13:10	This **c** for patient endurance.	1639
	13:18	This **c** for wisdom.	1639
	14:12	This **c** for patient endurance on the part of	1639
	17: 9	"This **c** for a mind with wisdom.	6045

CALM (9) [CALMED, CALMNESS, CALMS]

Ps	107:30	They were glad when *it grew* **c**,	9284
Isa	7: 4	'Be careful, *keep* **c** and don't be afraid.	9200
Eze	16:42	*I will be* **c** and no longer angry.	9200
Jnh	1:11	to you *to make* the sea **c down** for us?"	9284
	1:12	he replied, "and it *will become* **c**.	9284
	1:15	and the raging sea *grew* **c**.	6641
Mt	8:26	and it was completely **c**.	1132
Mk	4:39	wind died down and it was completely **c**.	1132
Lk	8:24	the storm subsided, and all was **c**.	1132

CALMED (1) [CALM]

Ne	8:11	The Levites **c** all the people, saying,	3120

CALMNESS (1) [CALM]

Ecc	10: 4	**c** can lay great errors to rest.	5341

CALMS (1) [CALM]

Pr	15:18	but a patient man **c** a quarrel.	9200

CALNEH (2)

Ge	10:10	Erech, Akkad and **C**, in Shinar.	4011
Am	6: 2	Go to **C** and look at it;	4011

CALNO (1)

Isa	10: 9	'Has not **C** fared like Carchemish?	4012

CALVARY (KJV) See SKULL

CALVE (1) [CALF]

Job	21:10	their cows **c** and do not miscarry.	7117

CALVED (1) [CALF]

1Sa	6: 7	*that have* **c** and have never been yoked.	6402

CALVES (25) [CALF]

Dt	7:13	the **c** of your herds and the lambs	8715
	28: 4	the **c** of your herds and the lambs	8715
	28:18	and all the **c** of your herds and the lambs	8715
	28:51	nor any **c** of your herds or lambs	8715
1Sa	6: 7	but take their **c** away and pen them up.	1201
	6:10	to the cart and penned up their **c**.	1201
	14:32	taking sheep, cattle and **c**,	1201+1330
	15: 9	the **fat c** and lambs—	AIT
1Ki	1: 9	and **fattened c** at the Stone of Zoheleth	5309

1Ki	1:19	fattened c, and sheep,	5309
	1:25	fattened c, and sheep.	5309
	12:28	the king made two golden c.	6319
	12:32	sacrificing to the c he had made.	6319
2Ki	10:29	the worship of the golden c at Bethel	6319
	17:16	two idols cast in the shape of c,	6319
2Ch	13: 8	a vast army and have with you the golden c	6319
Ps	68:30	herd of bulls among the c of the nations.	6319
Isa	34: 7	the bull c and the great bulls.	7228
Jer	46:21	in her ranks are like fattened c,	6319
Am	6: 4	You dine on choice lambs and fattened c.	6319
Mic	6: 6	with c a year old?	6319
Mal	4: 2	and leap like c released *from* the stall.	6319
Heb	9:12	by means of the blood of goats and c;	*3675*
	9:19	he took the blood *of* c,	*3675*

CAME (1193) [COME]

Ge	2: 6	but streams c up from the earth	6590
	7: 6	when the floodwaters c on the earth.	2118
	7: 9	c to Noah and entered the ark,	995
	7:10	And after the seven days the floodwaters	2118
	7:15	in them c to Noah and entered the ark.	995
	8: 4	of the seventh month the ark c to rest on	5663
	8:18	So Noah c out, together with his sons	3655
	8:19	c out of the ark, one kind after another.	3655
	9:10	all *those that* c out of the ark with you—	3655
	9:18	of Noah who c out of the ark were Shem,	3655
	9:19	from them c the people who were scattered	NIH
	10:14	Casluhites (from whom the Philistines c)	3655
	11: 5	the LORD c down to see the city and	3718
	11:31	when *they* c to Haran, they settled there.	995
	12:14	When Abram c to Egypt,	995
	13: 3	from place to place until he c to Bethel,	NIH
	14:13	*One* who had escaped c and reported this	995
	14:17	of Sodom c out to meet him in the Valley	3655
	15: 1	the word of the LORD c to Abram in	2118
	15: 4	Then the word of the LORD c to him:	NIH
	15:11	birds of prey c down on the carcasses,	3718
	15:12	a thick and dreadful darkness c over him.	5877
	19: 5	"Where are the men who c to you tonight?	995
	19: 9	they said, "This fellow c here as an alien,	995
	20: 3	But God c to Abimelech in	995
	24: 5	to the country *you* c from?"	3655
	24:15	Rebekah c out with her jar	3655
	24:16	filled her jar and c up again.	6590
	24:42	"When *I* c to the spring today, I said,	995
	24:45	Rebekah c out, with her jar	3655
	25:24	When the time c for her to give birth,	4848
	25:26	After this, his brother c out,	3655
	25:29	Esau c in from the open country, famished.	995
	26:32	That day Isaac's servants c and told him	995
	27:30	his brother Esau c in from hunting.	995
	27:33	before *you* c and I blessed him—	995
	27:35	"Your brother c deceitfully	995
	29: 1	Then Jacob continued on his journey and c	2143
	29: 9	Rachel c with her father's sheep,	995
	29:23	But when evening c,	2118
	29:25	When morning c, there was Leah!	2118
	30:16	Jacob c in from the fields that evening,	995
	30:30	before I c he has increased greatly,	NIH
	30:38	be directly in front of the flocks when they c	995
	30:38	the flocks were in heat and c to drink,	995
	30:43	and c to *own* large flocks,	AIT
	31:24	Then God c to Laban the Aramean in	995
	31:33	After *he* c out of Leah's tent,	3655
	33: 7	Leah and her children c and bowed down.	5602
	33: 7	Last of all c Joseph and Rachel,	5602
	33:18	After Jacob c from Paddan Aram,	995
	34: 5	so he kept quiet about it until they c **home.**	995
	34:27	of Jacob c upon the dead bodies and looted	995
	35: 6	Jacob and all the people with him c to Luz	995
	35:27	Jacob c **home** to his father Isaac in Mamre,	995
	37:23	So when Joseph c to his brothers,	995
	37:28	So when the Midianite merchants c **by,**	6296
	37:35	and daughters c to comfort him,	7756
	38:27	When the time c for her to give birth,	2118
	38:28	"This one c **out** first."	3655
	38:29	his brother c out, and she said,	3655
	38:30	c out and he was given the name Zerah.	3655
	39:14	*He* c in here to sleep with me,	995
	39:16	beside her until his master c home.	995
	39:17	"That Hebrew slave you brought us c to me	995
	40: 6	When Joseph c to them the next morning,	995
	41: 2	out of the river there c up seven cows,	6590
	41: 3	c up out of the Nile and stood beside those	6590
	41:14	he c before Pharaoh.	995
	41:18	out of the river there c up seven cows,	6590
	41:19	After them, seven other cows c **up—**	6590
	41:20	ugly cows ate up the seven fat cows that c	NIH
	41:27	that c up afterward are seven years, and	6590
	41:50	Before the years of famine c,	995
	41:53	of abundance in Egypt c **to an end,**	3983
	41:57	the countries c to Egypt to buy grain	995
	42:29	When they c to their father Jacob in	995
	43:20	*we* c **down** here the first time to buy food.	3718+3718
	43:26	When Joseph c home,	995
	43:31	After he had washed his face, *he* c out and,	3655
	44:14	the house when Judah and his brothers c in,	995
	45:25	up out of Egypt and c to their father Jacob	995
	47:15	all Egypt c to Joseph and said,	995
	47:18	*they* c to him the following year and said,	995
	48: 5	to you in Egypt before I c to you here will	995
	50:17	When their **message** c to him, Joseph wept.	1819
	50:18	His brothers then c and threw themselves	2143
Ex	1: 8	c **to power** in Egypt.	7756
	1:12	so the Egyptians *c to* **dread** the Israelites	AIT
	2:16	and *they* c to draw water and fill	995
	2:17	Some shepherds c **along**	995
	2:17	but Moses got up and c to their **rescue**	3828
	3: 1	to the far side of the desert and c to Horeb,	995
	8: 6	and the frogs c **up** and covered the land.	6590
	8:17	gnats c **upon** men and animals.	2118
	13: 3	the day *you* c **out** of Egypt,	3655
	13: 8	the LORD did for me when I c **out**	3655
	15:23	When *they* c to Marah,	995
	15:27	Then *they* c to Elim,	995
	16: 1	from Elim and c to the Desert of Sin,	995
	16:13	That evening quail c and covered the camp,	6590
	16:35	until they c to a land that was settled;	995
	17: 8	The Amalekites c and attacked	995
	18: 5	c to him in the desert,	995
	18:12	and Aaron c **with** all the elders of Israel	995
	19: 1	*they* c to the Desert of Sinai.	995
	23:15	for in that month *you* c out of Egypt.	3655
	32:24	and out c this calf!"	3655
	34: 5	Then the LORD c **down** in the cloud	3718
	34:18	for in that month *you* c **out** of Egypt.	3655
	34:29	When Moses c **down** from Mount Sinai	3718
	34:31	the leaders of the community c **back** to him,	8740
	34:32	Afterward all the Israelites c **near** him,	5602
	34:34	he removed the veil until he c **out.**	3655
	34:34	And when *he* c **out** and told	3655
	35:21	and whose heart moved him c and brought	995
	35:22	c and brought gold jewelry of all kinds:	995
Lev	9: 5	the entire assembly c **near** and stood before	7928
	9: 8	So Aaron c to the altar and slaughtered	7928
	9:23	When *they* c **out,** they blessed the people;	3655
	9:24	Fire c **out** from the presence of the LORD	3655
	10: 2	So fire c **out** from the presence of	3655
	10: 5	So *they* c and carried them,	7928
	18:30	before you c and do not defile yourselves	NIH
Nu	1: 1	of the second year after the Israelites c **out**	3655
	4:35	from thirty to fifty years of age who c	995
	4:39	from thirty to fifty years of age who c	995
	4:43	from thirty to fifty years of age who c	995
	4:47	from thirty to fifty years of age who c to do	995
	7:87	the burnt offering c to twelve young bulls,	NIH
	7:88	for the sacrifice of the fellowship offering c	NIH
	8:22	the Levites c to do their work at the Tent	995
	9: 1	the second year after they c **out** of Egypt.	3655
	9: 6	*they* c to Moses and Aaron that same day	995
	10:12	from place to place until the cloud c **to rest**	8905
	10:36	Whenever it c **to rest,** he said, "Return,	5663
	11:25	the LORD c **down** in the cloud and spoke	3718
	12: 4	So the three of them c **out.**	3655
	12: 5	the LORD c **down** in a pillar of cloud;	3718
	13:22	up through the Negev and c to Hebron,	995
	13:26	*They* c **back** to Moses and Aaron	995+2143+2256
	14:45	that hill country c **down** and attacked them	3718
	16: 3	*They* c **as a group** to oppose Moses	7735
	16:35	And fire c **out** from the LORD	3655
	20:20	Then Edom c **out** against them with a large	3655
	20:22	from Kadesh and c *to* Mount Hor.	995
	20:28	and Eleazar c **down** from the mountain,	3718
	21: 7	The people c to Moses and said,	995
	22: 7	When *they* c to Balaam,	995
	22: 9	God c to Balaam and asked,	995
	22:16	*They* c to Balaam and said:	995
	22:20	That night God c to Balaam and said,	995
	24: 2	the Spirit of God c **upon** him	2118
	25:18	when the plague c as a result of Peor."	NIH
	26: 4	These were the Israelites who c **out**	3655
	30:12	or pledges that c **from** her lips will stand.	4604
	32: 2	So they c to Moses and Eleazar the priest	995
	32:11	the men twenty years old or more who c **up**	6590
	32:16	Then *they* c **up** to him and said,	5602
	33: 1	of the Israelites when *they* c **out** of Egypt	3655
	33:38	of the fortieth year after the Israelites c **out**	3655
	36: 1	c and spoke before Moses and the leaders,	7928
Dt	1:22	Then all of you c to me and said,	7928
	1:24	c to the Valley of Eshcol and explored it.	995
	1:44	in those hills c **out** against you;	3655
	1:45	*You* c **back** and wept before the LORD,	8740
	2:32	and all his army c **out** to meet us in battle	3655
	4:11	*You* c **near** and stood at the foot of	7928
	4:45	when they c **out** of Egypt	3655
	4:46	by Moses and the Israelites as they c **out**	3655
	5:23	of your tribes and your elders c to me.	7928
	10: 5	Then I c **back** down the mountain and put	AIT
	23: 4	and water on your way when you c **out**	3655
	24: 9	to Miriam along the way after you c **out**	3655
	25:17	along the way when you c **out** of Egypt.	3655
	29: 7	of Heshbon and Og king of Bashan c **out**	3655
	31:14	and Joshua c and presented themselves at	2143
	32:44	Moses with Joshua son of Nun	995
	33: 2	"The LORD c **from** Sinai and dawned	995
	33: 2	*He* c with myriads of holy ones from	910
Jos	2: 3	"Bring out the men who c to you	995
	2: 4	She said, "Yes, the men c to me,	995
	2:10	of the Red Sea for you when you c **out**	3655
	2:23	forded the river and c to Joshua son of Nun	995
	4:11	priests c **to the other side**	6296
	4:18	the priests c **up** out of the river carrying	6590
	5: 5	All those who c **out** of Egypt—	3655
	5: 5	that c **out** had been circumcised,	3655
	6: 1	No one went out and no one c **in.**	995
	7:17	The clans of Judah c **forward,**	7928
	8:22	The men of the ambush also c **out** of the city	3655
Jos	9: 2	*they* c **together** to make war against Joshua	3481+7695
	9:17	the Israelites set out and on the third day c	995
	10:24	So they c **forward** and placed their feet	7928
	11: 4	They c **out** with all their troops and	3655
	11: 7	So Joshua and his whole army c	995
	15: 7	to the waters of En Shemesh and c **out**	2118
	15: 9	c **out** at the towns of Mount Ephron	3655
	15:18	One day when she c to Othniel,	995
	16: 7	touched Jericho and c **out** at the Jordan.	3655
	18:11	The lot c **up** for the tribe of Benjamin,	6590
	18:14	the western side and c **out** at Kiriath Baal	2118
	18:15	and the boundary c **out** at the spring of	3655
	18:19	c **out** at the northern bay of	2118
	19: 1	The second lot c **out** for the tribe	3655
	19:10	The third lot c **up** for Zebulun,	6590
	19:13	*it* c **out** at Rimmon and faced	3655
	19:17	fourth lot c **out** for Issachar, clan by clan.	3655
	19:24	The fifth lot c **out** for the tribe of Asher,	3655
	19:29	turned toward Hosah and c **out** at the sea in	2118
	19:32	sixth lot c **out** for Naphtali, clan by clan:	3655
	19:34	through Aznoth Tabor and c **out**	3655
	19:40	The seventh lot c **out** for the tribe of Dan,	3655
	21: 4	The first lot c **out** for the Kohathites,	3655
	22:10	When *they* c to Geliloth near the Jordan in	995
	24: 6	*you* c to the sea, and the Egyptians pursued	995
	24:11	you crossed the Jordan and c to Jericho.	995
Jdg	1:14	One day when she c *to* Othniel,	995
	3:10	The Spirit of the LORD c **upon** him,	2118
	3:13	Eglon c and attacked Israel,	2143
	3:22	blade, *which* c out his back.	3655
	3:24	the servants c and found the doors of	995
	3:31	After Ehud c Shamgar son of Anath,	2118
	4: 5	and the Israelites c to her	6590
	4:22	Barak c **by in pursuit** *of* Sisera,	8103
	5: 8	war c to the city gates,	NIH
	5:13	the men who were left c **down** to the nobles;	3718
	5:13	of the LORD c to me with the mighty.	3718
	5:14	Some c from Ephraim,	NIH
	5:14	From Makir captains c **down,**	3718
	5:19	"Kings c, they fought;	995
	6: 5	They c **up** with their livestock	6590
	6:11	the LORD c and sat down under the oak	995
	6:34	the Spirit of the LORD c **upon** Gideon,	4252
	7:13	"A round loaf of barley bread c **tumbling**	2200
	8: 4	c to the Jordan and crossed it.	995
	8:15	Gideon c and said to the men of Succoth,	995
	8:26	for c seventeen hundred shekels,	2118
	9:35	as Abimelech and his soldiers c **out**	7756
	9:57	The curse of Jotham son of Jerub-Baal c	995
	11:13	"When Israel c **up** out of Egypt,	6590
	11:16	But when they c **up** out of Egypt,	6590
	11:29	the Spirit of the LORD c **upon** Jephthah.	2118
	13: 6	"A man of God c to me.	995
	13: 6	I didn't ask him where he c from,	NIH
	13: 9	and the angel of God c again to the woman	995
	13:11	When *he* c to the man, he said,	995
	14: 5	suddenly a young lion c roaring **toward**	7925
	14: 6	Spirit of the LORD c **upon** him **in power**	7502
	14:19	Spirit of the LORD c **upon** him **in power.**	7502
	15:14	the Philistines c **toward** him shouting.	7925
	15:14	Spirit of the LORD c **upon** him **in power.**	7502
	15:19	and water c **out** of it.	3655
	16:30	and **down** c the temple on the rulers and all	5877
	17: 8	On his way *he* c to Micah's house in	995
	18: 2	of Ephraim and c to the house of Micah,	NIH
	18: 7	So the five men left and c to Laish,	995
	18:13	on to the hill country of Ephraim and c	995
	19:16	c **in** from his work in the fields.	995
	19:22	"Bring out the man who c to your house	995
	19:30	the day the Israelites c **up** out of Egypt.	6590
	20: 1	of Gilead c **out** as one man and assembled	3655
	20: 4	and my concubine c to Gibeah in Benjamin	995
	20: 5	the night the men of Gibeah c after me	7756
	20:14	From their towns they c **together** at Gibeah	665
	20:21	The Benjamites c **out** of Gibeah and cut	3655
	20:25	when the Benjamites c **out** from Gibeah	3655
	20:31	The Benjamites c **out** to meet them	3655
	20:42	of Israel who c **out** of the towns cut them	NIH
	20:48	All the towns they c **across** they set on fire.	5162
Ru	1:19	So the two women went on until they c	995
	2: 6	the Moabitess who c **back** from Moab	8740
	2:11	and your homeland and c to live with	2143
	3:14	"Don't let it be known that a woman c *to*	995
	3:16	When Ruth c to her mother-in-law,	995
	4: 1	the kinsman-redeemer he had mentioned c **along,**	6296
1Sa	1: 4	the day c for Elkanah to sacrifice,	2118
	2:14	how they treated all the Israelites who c	995
	2:27	Now a man of God c to Eli and said to him,	995
	3:10	The LORD c and stood there,	995
	4: 1	And Samuel's word c to all Israel.	2118
	4: 5	of the LORD's covenant c into the camp,	995
	6:14	The cart c to the field of Joshua	995
	7: 1	So the men of Kiriath Jearim c and took up	995
	7: 7	of the Philistines c **up** to attack them.	6590
	8: 4	of Israel gathered together and c to Samuel	995
	9:15	Now the day before Saul c,	995
	9:25	After they c **down** from the high place to	3718
	10:10	Spirit of God c **upon** him **in power,**	7502
	11: 4	When the messengers c to Gibeah of Saul	995
	11: 6	Spirit of God c **upon** him **in power,**	7502
	15: 2	when they waylaid them as they c **up**	6590
	15: 6	the Israelites c **up** out of Egypt."	6590
	15:10	Then the word of the LORD c to Samuel:	2118
	15:32	Agag c to him confidently, thinking,	2143
	16:13	Spirit of the LORD c **upon** David **in power.**	7502

Ref	Text	No.
1Sa 16:21	David c to Saul and entered his service.	995
16:23	Whenever the spirit from God c upon Saul,	2118
17: 4	c out of the Philistine camp.	3655
17:16	the Philistine c forward every morning	5602
17:28	you c down only to watch the battle."	3718
17:34	a lion or a bear c and carried off a sheep	995
18: 6	the women c out from all the towns	3655
18:10	an evil spirit from God c forcefully	7502
18:19	So when the time c for Merab,	2118
19: 9	an evil spirit from the LORD c upon Saul	2118
19:19	Word c to Saul: "David is in Naioth	5583
19:20	the Spirit of God upon Saul's men	2118
19:23	But the Spirit of God c even upon him,	2118
19:23	and he walked along prophesying until he c	995
20:24	and when the New Moon festival c,	2118
20:37	When the boy c to the place	995
22:11	and they all c to the king.	995
23:27	a messenger c to Saul,	995
24: 3	He c to the sheep pens along the way;	995
25:20	As she c riding her donkey into	8206
26:15	Someone c to destroy your lord the king.	995
28: 4	The Philistines assembled and c and set	995
28:21	When the woman c to Saul and saw	995
29: 6	From the day you c to me until now,	995
29: 8	against your servant from the day I c	2118
30: 3	When David and his men c to Ziklag,	995
30: 9	David and the six hundred men with him c	995
30:21	Then David c to the two hundred men	995
30:21	They c out to meet David and the people	3655
30:23	and handed over to us the forces that c	995
31: 7	And the Philistines c and occupied them.	995
31: 8	when the Philistines c to strip the dead,	995
2Sa 1: 2	When he c to David,	995
2: 4	Then the men of Judah c to Hebron	995
2:23	and the spear c out through his back.	3655
2:23	And every man stopped when he c to	995
2:24	they c to the hill of Ammah,	995
2:28	and all the men c to a halt;	6641
2:29	continued through the whole Bithron and c	995
3:20	c to David at Hebron,	995
3:24	Look, Abner c to you.	995
3:25	he c to deceive you	995
3:35	Then they all c and urged David	995
4: 4	when the news about Saul and Jonathan c	995
5: 1	All the tribes of Israel c to David at Hebron	995
5:22	the Philistines c up and spread out in	6590
6: 6	they c to the threshing floor of Nacon,	995
6:20	Michal daughter of Saul c out to meet him	3655
7: 4	the word of the LORD c to Nathan,	2118
8: 5	of Damascus c to help Hadadezer king	995
9: 6	the son of Saul, c to David,	995
10: 2	When David's men c to the land of	995
10: 8	The Ammonites c out and drew up	3655
10:14	the Ammonites and c to Jerusalem.	995
11: 4	She c to him, and he slept with her.	995
11: 7	When Uriah c to him,	995
11: 7	When the men of the city c out and fought	3655
11:23	"The men overpowered us and c out	3655
12: 1	When he c to him, he said,	995
12: 4	"Now a traveler c to the rich man,"	995
13: 6	When the king c to see him,	995
13:30	the report c to David:	995
13:36	the king's sons c in, wailing loudly.	995
14:33	and he c in and bowed down with his face	995
15: 2	Whenever anyone c with a complaint to	2118
15: 6	in this way toward all the Israelites who c	995
15:13	A messenger c and told David,	995
15:20	You c only yesterday.	995
16: 5	from the same clan as Saul's family c out	995
16: 5	and he cursed as he c out.	3655+3655
16:15	and all the men of Israel c to Jerusalem,	995
17: 6	When Hushai c to him, Absalom said,	995
17:20	When Absalom's men c to the woman at	995
17:27	When David c to Mahanaim,	995
18:25	And the man c closer and closer.	2143
19: 8	they all c before him.	995
19:25	When he c from Jerusalem to meet the king,	995
19:31	the Gileadite also c down from Rogelim	3718
20: 8	Amasa c to meet them.	995
20:12	that all the troops c to a halt	6641
20:12	that everyone who c up to Amasa stopped,	995
20:15	the troops with Joab c and besieged Sheba	995
21:17	of Zeruiah c to David's rescue;	6468
22: 7	my cry c to his ears.	NIH
22: 9	consuming fire c from his mouth,	NIH
22:10	He parted the heavens and c down;	3718
23:13	of the thirty chief men c down to David at	995
24: 8	they c back to Jerusalem at the end	995
1Ki 1:28	So she c into the king's presence and stood	995
1:32	When they c before the king,	995
1:53	And Adonijah c and bowed down	995
2: 8	When he c down to meet me at the Jordan,	3718
3:16	Now two prostitutes c to the king and stood	995
4:27	for King Solomon and all who c to	7929
4:34	Men of all nations c to listen	995
6:11	The word of the LORD c to Solomon:	2118
7:14	He c to King Solomon and did all	995
8: 2	of Israel c together to King Solomon at	7735
8: 9	the Israelites after they c out of Egypt.	3655
10: 1	she c to test him with hard questions.	995
10: 2	c to Solomon and talked with him	995
10: 7	But I did not believe these things until I c	995
10:25	everyone who c brought a gift—	NIH
12:22	of God c to Shemaiah the man of God:	2118
13: 1	By the word of the LORD a man of God c	995
13: 9	or return by the way you c.' "	2143
13:11	whose sons c and told him all that the man	995
1Ki 13:14	the man of God who c from Judah?"	995
13:17	or return by the way you c.' "	2143
13:20	the word of the LORD c to	2118
13:22	You c back and ate bread and drank water	8740
16: 1	Then the word of the LORD c to Jehu son	2118
16: 7	the LORD c through the prophet Jehu son	2118
16:10	Zimri c in, struck him down and killed him	995
17: 2	Then the word of the LORD c to Elijah:	2118
17: 8	Then the word of the LORD c to him:	2118
17:10	When he c to the town gate,	995
18: 1	the word of the LORD c to Elijah:	2118
18:30	They c to him,	5602
18:45	a heavy rain c on and Ahab rode off	2118
18:46	The power of the LORD c upon Elijah	2118
19: 3	When he c to Beersheba in Judah,	995
19: 4	He c to a broom tree,	995
19: 7	of the LORD c back a second time	8740
19: 9	And the word of the LORD c to him:	606
19:12	After the earthquake c a fire,	NIH
19:12	And after the fire c a gentle whisper.	NIH
19:15	"Go back the way you c,	NIH
20: 5	The messengers c again and said,	8740
20:13	Meanwhile a prophet c to Ahab king	5602
20:22	the prophet c to the king of Israel and said,	5602
20:28	of God c up and told the king of Israel,	5602
20:33	When Ben-Hadad c out,	3655
20:39	someone c to me with a captive and said,	995
21: 5	His wife Jezebel c in and asked him,	995
21:13	Then two scoundrels c	995
21:17	Then the word of the LORD c to Elijah	2118
21:28	Then the word of the LORD c to Elijah	2118
22:21	Finally, a spirit c forward,	3655
2Ki 1: 6	"A man c to meet us," they replied.	6590
1: 7	of man was it who c to meet you	6590
2: 3	of the prophets at Bethel c out to Elisha	3655
2:23	some youths c out of the town and jeered	3655
2:24	Then two bears c out of the woods	3655
3:15	the hand of the LORD c upon Elisha	2118
3:24	when the Moabites c to the camp of Israel,	995
4: 8	So whenever he c by,	6296
4:11	One day when Elisha c,	995
4:25	and c to the man of God at Mount Carmel.	995
4:27	Gehazi c over to push her away,	5602
4:36	When she c, he said, "Take your son."	995
4:37	She c in, fell at his feet and bowed to	995
4:42	A man c from Baal Shalishah,	995
5:24	When Gehazi c to the hill,	995
6:13	The report c back: "He is in Dothan."	5583
6:18	As the enemy c down toward him,	3718
6:33	the messenger c down to him.	3718
7:17	of God had foretold when the king c down	3718
8: 3	the seven years she c back from the land of	8740
8: 5	to life c to beg the king for her house	NIH
9:19	When he c to them he said,	995
10:15	he c upon Jehonadab son of Recab,	5162
10:17	When Jehu c to Samaria,	995
10:21	and all the ministers of Baal c;	995
11: 9	and c to Jehoiada the priest.	995
12:10	the royal secretary and the high priest c,	6590
13:21	the man c to life and stood up on his feet.	2649
14: 9	Then a wild beast in Lebanon c	6296
15:29	Tiglath-Pileser king of Assyria c	995
16:12	the king c back from Damascus and saw	995
17: 3	Shalmaneser king of Assyria c up	6590
17:28	from Samaria c to live in Bethel	995
18:17	They c up to Jerusalem and stopped at	995
19: 5	King Hezekiah's officials c to Isaiah,	995
19:28	I will make you return by the way you c.'	995
19:33	By the way that he c he will return;	995
20: 4	the word of the LORD c to him:	2118
20:14	"They c from Babylon."	995
21:15	the day their forefathers c out of Egypt	3655
23:17	of God who c from Judah and pronounced	995
24:11	and Nebuchadnezzar himself c up to	995
25: 8	of the king of Babylon, c to Jerusalem.	995
25:23	they c to Gedaliah at Mizpah—	995
25:25	c with ten men and assassinated Gedaliah	995
1Ch 1:12	Casluhites (from whom the Philistines c)	3655
2:55	the Kenites who c from Hammath,	995
4:41	The men whose names were listed c in	995
5: 2	the strongest of his brothers and a ruler c	NIH
6:31	of the LORD after the ark c to rest there.	4955
7:22	and his relatives c to comfort him.	995
10: 7	And the Philistines c and occupied them.	995
10: 8	when the Philistines c to strip the dead,	995
11: 1	All Israel c together to David at Hebron	7695
11:15	the thirty chiefs c down to David to the rock	3718
12: 1	These were the men who c to David	995
12:16	and some men from Judah also c to David	995
12:18	Then the Spirit c upon Amasai,	4252
12:22	Day after day men c to help David,	995
12:23	of the men armed for battle who c to David	995
12:38	They c to Hebron fully determined	995
12:40	and Naphtali c bringing food on donkeys,	995
13: 9	they c to the threshing floor of Kidon,	995
17: 3	That night the word of God c to Nathan,	2118
18: 5	of Damascus c to help Hadadezer king	995
19: 2	When David's men c to Hanun in the land	995
19: 5	someone c and told David about the men,	2143
19: 9	who c and camped near Medeba,	995
19: 9	The Ammonites c out and drew up	3655
21: 4	and went throughout Israel and then c back	995
22: 8	But this word of God c to me:	2118
27:24	Wrath c on Israel on account	2118
2Ch 5: 3	of Israel c together to the king at the time	7735
5:10	the Israelites after they c out of Egypt.	3655
7: 1	fire c down from heaven and consumed	3718
2Ch 9: 1	she c to Jerusalem to test him	995
9: 1	she c to Solomon and talked with him	995
9: 6	until I c and saw with my own eyes.	995
9:24	everyone who c brought a gift—	NIH
11: 2	But this word of the LORD c to Shemaiah	2118
11:14	and c to Judah and Jerusalem	2143
12: 2	and Cushites that c with him from Egypt,	995
12: 4	the fortified cities of Judah and c as far	995
12: 5	Then the prophet Shemaiah c to Rehoboam	995
12: 7	this word of the LORD c to Shemaiah:	2118
14: 9	and c as far as Mareshah.	995
15: 1	The Spirit of God c upon Azariah son	2118
16: 7	At that time Hanani the seer c to Asa king	995
18:20	Finally, a spirit c forward,	3655
20: 1	with some of the Meunites c to make war	995
20: 2	Some men c and told Jehoshaphat,	995
20: 4	The people of Judah c together to seek help	7695
20: 4	indeed, they c from every town in Judah	995
20:10	not allow Israel to invade when they c	995
20:14	of the LORD c upon Jahaziel son	2118
20:24	When the men of Judah c to the place	995
20:29	The fear of God c upon all the kingdoms of	2118
21:19	his bowels c out because of the disease,	3655
22: 1	who c with the Arabs into the camp,	995
23: 2	When they c to Jerusalem,	995
24:17	the officials of Judah c and paid homage to	995
24:18	God's anger c upon Judah and Jerusalem.	2118
24:20	of God c upon Zechariah son of Jehoiada	4252
25: 7	But a man of God c to him and said,	995
25:18	Then a wild beast in Lebanon c along	6296
28:20	Tiglath-Pileser king of Assyria c to him,	995
30:18	Although most of the many people who c	NIH
31: 8	When Hezekiah and his officials c and saw	995
32: 1	of Assyria c and invaded Judah.	995
36:20	until the kingdom of Persia c to power.	4887
Ezr 1:11	the exiles c up from Babylon to Jerusalem.	6590
2: 1	the province who c up from the captivity of	6590
2:59	The following c up from the towns	6590
3: 1	When the seventh month c and	5595
4: 2	they c to Zerubbabel and to the heads of	5602
4:12	that the Jews who c up to us	10513
4:24	of God in Jerusalem c to a standstill	10098
5:16	So this Sheshbazzar c and laid	10085
7: 6	this Ezra c up from Babylon.	6590
7: 7	also c up to Jerusalem in the seventh year	6590
8: 1	with them who c up with me from Babylon	6590
9: 1	the leaders c to me and said,	5602
Ne 1: 2	c from Judah with some other men,	995
4:12	near them c and told us ten times over,	995
4:21	the first light of dawn till the stars c out.	3655
5:17	as well as those who c to us from	995
6: 1	When word c to Sanballat, Tobiah,	9048
7: 6	the province who c up from the captivity of	6590
7:61	The following c up from the towns	6590
7:73	When the seventh month c and	5595
9:13	"You c down on Mount Sinai;	3718
13: 7	and c back to Jerusalem.	995
13:21	From that time on they no longer c on	995
Est 2:12	a girl's turn to c to go in to King Xerxes,	5595
2:15	When the turn c for Esther	5595
4: 3	to which the edict and order of the king c,	5595
4: 4	When Esther's maids and eunuchs c	995
8: 1	And Mordecai c into the presence of	995
9:15	in Susa c together on the fourteenth day of	7735
9:25	But when the plot c to the king's attention,	995
Job 1: 6	One day the angels c to present themselves	995
1: 6	and Satan also c with them.	995
1:14	a messenger c to Job and said,	995
1:16	another messenger c and said,	995
1:17	another messenger c and said,	995
1:18	yet another messenger c and said,	995
1:21	"Naked I c from my mother's womb,	3655
2: 1	the angels c to present themselves before	995
2: 1	also c with them to present himself	995
3:11	and die as I c from the womb?	3655
30:26	Yet when I hoped for good, evil c;	995
30:26	when I looked for light, then c darkness.	995
31:29	or gloated over the trouble that c to him—	5162
42:11	and everyone who had known him before c	995
Ps 18: 6	my cry c before him, into his ears.	995
18: 8	consuming fire c from his mouth,	NIH
18: 9	He parted the heavens and c down;	3718
33: 9	For he spoke, and it c to be;	2118
51: T	When the prophet Nathan c to him	995
105:19	till what he foretold c to pass,	995
105:31	He spoke, and there c swarms of flies,	995
105:34	He spoke, and the locusts c,	995
106:32	and trouble c to Moses because of them;	8317
106:33	and rash words c from Moses' lips.	1051
114: 1	When Israel c out of Egypt,	3655
116: 3	the anguish of the grave c upon me;	5162
132: 6	we c upon it in the fields of Jaar:	5162
139:16	in your book before one of them c to be.	NIH
Pr 7:10	out c a woman to meet	7925
7:15	So I c out to meet you;	3655
Ecc 2:14	but I c to realize that	AIT
4:16	But those who c later were not pleased	NIH
9:14	And a powerful king c against it,	995
12: 7	the dust returns to the ground it c from,	2118
Isa 11:16	as there was for Israel when they c up	6590
14:28	This oracle c in the year King Ahaz died:	2118
20: 1	c to Ashdod and attacked and captured it—	995
23: 3	the great waters c the grain of the Shihor,	NIH
26:16	LORD, they c to you in their distress;	7212
37: 5	King Hezekiah's officials c to Isaiah,	995
37:29	I will make you return by the way you c.	995
37:34	By the way that he c he will return;	995

Isa 38: 4 Then the word of the LORD c to Isaiah: 2118
39: 3 *"They* c to me from Babylon." 995
48: 3 then suddenly I acted, and *they* c **to pass.** 995
50: 2 When I c, why was there no one? 995
64: 3 *you* c **down,** and the mountains trembled 3718
66: 2 and so they c **into being?"** 2118
Jer 1: 2 the LORD c to him in the thirteenth year 2118
1: 4 The word of the LORD c to me, saying, 2118
1:11 The word of the LORD c to me: 2118
1:13 The word of the LORD c to me again: 2118
2: 1 The word of the LORD c to me: 2118
2: 7 But *you* c and defiled my land 995
7: 1 This is the word that c to Jeremiah from 2118
11: 1 This is the word that c to Jeremiah from 2118
13: 3 word of the LORD c to me a second time: 2118
13: 8 Then the word of the LORD c to me: 2118
15:16 *When* your words c, I ate them; 5162
16: 1 Then the word of the LORD c to me: 2118
18: 1 This is the word that c to Jeremiah from 2118
18: 5 Then the word of the LORD c to me: 2118
21: 1 The word c to Jeremiah from the LORD 2118
24: 4 Then the word of the LORD c to me: 2118
25: 1 The word c to Jeremiah concerning all 2118
26: 1 this word c from the LORD: 2118
27: 1 this word c to Jeremiah from the LORD: 2118
28:12 the word of the LORD c to Jeremiah: 2118
29:30 the word of the LORD c to Jeremiah: 2118
30: 1 This is the word that c to Jeremiah from 2118
31:19 after I c to **understand,** I beat my breast. AIT
32: 1 This is the word that c to Jeremiah from 2118
32: 6 "The word of the LORD c to me: 2118
32: 8 my cousin Hanamel c to me in 995
32:23 They c in and took possession of it, 995
32:26 the word of the LORD c to Jeremiah: 2118
33: 1 of the LORD c to him a second time: 2118
33:19 the word of the LORD c to Jeremiah: 2118
33:23 The word of the LORD c to Jeremiah: 2118
34: 1 this word c to Jeremiah from the LORD: 2118
34: 8 The word c to Jeremiah from the LORD 2118
34:12 the word of the LORD c to Jeremiah 2118
35: 1 that c to Jeremiah from the LORD during 2118
35:12 word of the LORD c to Jeremiah, saying: 2118
36: 1 this word c to Jeremiah from the LORD: 2118
36:27 the word of the LORD c to Jeremiah: 2118
37: 6 Then the word of the LORD c to Jeremiah 2118
39: 3 of the king of Babylon c and took seats in 995
39:15 the word of the LORD c to him: 2118
40: 1 The word c to Jeremiah from the LORD 2118
40: 8 *they* c to Gedaliah at Mizpah— 995
40:12 they all c **back** to the land of Judah, 8740
40:13 the army officers still in the open country c 995
41: 1 c with ten men to Gedaliah son of Ahikam 995
41: 5 torn their clothes and cut themselves c 995
42: 7 Ten days later the word of the LORD c 2118
43: 8 In Tahpanhes the word of the LORD c 2118
44: 1 This word c to Jeremiah concerning all 2118
44:28 the whole remnant of Judah who c to live 995
46: 1 the word of the LORD that c to Jeremiah 2118
47: 1 the word of the LORD that c to Jeremiah 2118
49: 9 If grape pickers c to you, 995
49: 9 If thieves c during the night, NIH
49:34 the word of the LORD that c to Jeremiah 2118
52:12 the king of Babylon, c to Jerusalem. 995
La 3:57 You c **near** when I called you, and you said, 7928
Eze 1: 3 the word of the LORD c to Ezekiel 2118+2118
1:25 Then *there* c a voice from above 2118
2: 2 the Spirit c into me and raised me 995
3:15 I c to the exiles who lived at Tel Abib 995
3:16 of seven days the word of the LORD c 2118
3:24 Spirit c into me and raised me to my feet. 995
6: 1 The word of the LORD c to me: 2118
7: 1 The word of the LORD c to me: 2118
8: 1 of the Sovereign LORD c upon me there. 5877
9: 2 *They* c in and stood beside the bronze altar. 995
11: 5 Then the Spirit of the LORD c upon me, 5877
11:14 The word of the LORD c to me: 2118
12: 1 The word of the LORD c to me: 2118
12: 8 In the morning the word of the LORD c 2118
12:17 The word of the LORD c to me: 2118
12:21 The word of the LORD c to me: 2118
12:26 The word of the LORD c to me: 2118
13: 1 The word of the LORD c to me: 2118
14: 1 Some of the elders of Israel c to me and sat 995
14: 2 Then the word of the LORD c to me: 2118
14:12 The word of the LORD c to me: 2118
15: 1 The word of the LORD c to me: 2118
16: 1 The word of the LORD c to me: 2118
17: 1 The word of the LORD c to me: 2118
17: 3 and full plumage of varied colors c 995
17:11 Then the word of the LORD c to me: 2118
18: 1 The word of the LORD c to me: 2118
19: 8 Then the nations c against him, 5989
20: 1 some of the elders of Israel c to inquire of 995
20: 2 Then the word of the LORD c to me: 2118
20:45 The word of the LORD c to me: 2118
21: 1 The word of the LORD c to me: 2118
21: 8 The word of the LORD c to me: 2118
21:18 The word of the LORD c to me: 2118
22: 1 The word of the LORD c to me: 2118
22:17 Then the word of the LORD c to me: 2118
22:23 Again the word of the LORD c to me: 2118
23: 1 The word of the LORD c to me: 2118
23:17 Then the Babylonians c to her, 995
23:40 "They even sent messengers for men *who* c 995
24: 1 the word of the LORD c to me: 2118
24:15 The word of the LORD c to me: 2118
24:20 "The word of the LORD c to me: 2118

Eze 25: 1 The word of the LORD c to me: 2118
26: 1 the word of the LORD c to me: 2118
27: 1 The word of the LORD c to me: 2118
27: 9 the sea and their sailors c alongside to trade 2118
28: 1 The word of the LORD c to me: 2118
28:11 The word of the LORD c to me: 2118
28:20 The word of the LORD c to me: 2118
29: 1 the word of the LORD c to me: 2118
29:17 the word of the LORD c to me: 2118
30: 1 the word of the LORD c to me: 2118
30:20 the word of the LORD c to me: 2118
31: 1 the word of the LORD c to me: 2118
31:12 of the earth c **out** from under its shade 3718
32: 1 the word of the LORD c to me: 2118
32:17 the word of the LORD c to me: 2118
33: 1 The word of the LORD c to me: 2118
33:21 a man who had escaped from Jerusalem c 995
33:22 and he opened my mouth before the man c 995
33:23 Then the word of the LORD c to me: 2118
34: 1 The word of the LORD c to me: 2118
35: 1 The word of the LORD c to me: 2118
36:16 Again the word of the LORD c to me: 2118
37: 7 a rattling sound, and the bones c **together,** 7928
37:10 *they* c **to life** and stood up on their feet— 2649
37:15 The word of the LORD c to me: 2118
38: 1 The word of the LORD c to me: 2118
43: 3 the vision I had seen when he c to destroy 995
Da 1: 1 of Babylon c *to* Jerusalem and besieged it. 995
2: 2 When *they* c **in** and stood before the king, 995
3: 8 At this time some astrologers c **forward** 10638
3:26 Meshach and Abednego c **out** of the fire, 10485
4: 7 enchanters, astrologers and diviners c, 10549
4: 8 Daniel c **into** my presence and I told him 10549
4:31 on his lips *when* a voice c from heaven, 10484
5: 8 Then all the king's wise men c **in,** 10549
5:10 c into the banquet hall. 10549
6:20 When he c **near** the den, 10638
7: 3 c **up** out of the sea. 10513
7: 8 a little one, *which* c **up** among them; 10513
7:20 that c **up,** before which three of them fell— 10513
7:22 of Days c and pronounced judgment 10085
7:22 time c when they possessed the kingdom. 10413
8: 5 a prominent horn between his eyes c then 995
8: 6 *He* c toward the two-horned ram I had seen 995
8: 8 Out of one of them c another horn, 3655
8:17 *he* c near the place where I was standing, 995
9:21 c to me in swift flight about the time of 5595
10: 1 The understanding of the message c to him NIH
10:13 one of the chief princes, c to help me, 995
Hos 1: 1 of the LORD that c to Hosea son of Beeri 2118
2:15 as in the day she c **up** out of Egypt. 6590
9:10 But when they c *to* Baal Peor, 995
Joel 1: 1 of the LORD that c to Joel son of Pethuel. 2118
Ob 1: 5 thieves c to you, if robbers in the night— 995
1: 5 If grape pickers c to you, 995
Jnh 1: 1 of the LORD that c to Jonah son of Amittai 2118
3: 1 Then the word of the LORD c to Jonah 2118
Mic 1: 1 the LORD that c to Micah of Moresheth 2118
7:15 "As in the days when you c **out** of Egypt, 3655
Hab 3: 3 God c from Teman, 995
3:13 *You* c **out** to deliver your people, 3655
Zep 1: 1 that c to Zephaniah son of Cushi, the son 2118
Hag 1: 1 the LORD c through the prophet Haggai 2118
1: 3 the LORD c through the prophet Haggai: 2118
1:14 *They* c and began to work on the house of 995
2: 1 the LORD c through the prophet Haggai: 2118
2: 5 with you when you c **out** of Egypt. 3655
2:10 of the LORD c to the prophet Haggai 2118
2:16 anyone c to a heap of twenty measures, 995
2:20 the LORD c to Haggai a second time on 2118
Zec 1: 1 the LORD c to the prophet Zechariah son 2118
1: 7 the LORD c to the prophet Zechariah son 2118
2: 3 and another angel c to meet him 3655
4: 8 Then the word of the LORD c to me: 2118
5: 5 to me c **forward** and said to me, 3655
6: 9 The word of the LORD c to me: 2118
7: 1 the word of the LORD c to Zechariah on 2118
7: 4 the word of the LORD Almighty c to me: 2118
7: 8 word of the LORD c again to Zechariah: 2118
8: 1 the word of the LORD Almighty c to me. 2118
8:18 the word of the LORD Almighty c to me. 2118
Mt 1:18 how the birth of Jesus Christ c **about:** 1639
1:18 but before they c **together,** 5302
2: 1 Magi from the east c to Jerusalem 4134
3: 1 In those days John the Baptist c, 4134
3:13 Then Jesus c from Galilee to the Jordan to 4134
4: 3 The tempter c to him and said, 4665
4:11 and angels c and attended him. 4665
5: 1 His disciples c to him, 4665
7:25 The rain c **down,** the streams rose, 2849
7:27 The rain c **down,** the streams rose, 2849
8: 1 *When* he c **down** from the mountainside, 2849
8: 2 A man with leprosy c and knelt before him 4665
8: 5 a centurion c to him, asking for help. 4665
8:14 *When* Jesus c into Peter's house, 2262
8:16 *When* evening c, many who were demon-possessed were brought to him, 1181
8:19 a teacher of the law c to him and said, 4665
8:24 a furious storm c **up** on the lake, 1181
8:32 So they c **out** and went into the pigs, 2002
9: 1 crossed over and c to his own town. 2262
9:10 many tax collectors and "sinners" c and ate 2262
9:14 Then John's disciples c and asked him, 4665
9:18 a ruler c and knelt before him and said, 2262
9:20 for twelve years c **up** behind him 4665
9:28 the blind men c to him, and he asked them, 4665
11:18 For John c neither eating nor drinking, 2262

Mt 11:19 The Son of Man c eating and drinking, 2262
12:42 for *she* c from the ends of the earth to listen 2262
13: 4 and the birds c and ate it up. 2262
13: 6 But *when* the sun c **up,** 422
13:10 The disciples c to him and asked, 4665
13:25 his enemy c and sowed weeds among 2262
13:27 "The owner's servants c to him and said, 4665
13:36 His disciples c to him and said, 4665
14:12 John's disciples c and took his body 4665
14:15 the disciples c to him and said, 4665
14:23 *When* evening c, he was there alone, 1181
14:29 walked on the water and c toward Jesus. 2262
15: 1 of the law c to Jesus from Jerusalem 4665
15:12 Then the disciples c to him and asked, 4665
15:22 A Canaanite woman from that vicinity c 2002
15:23 So his disciples c to him and urged him, 4665
15:25 The woman c and knelt before him. 2262
15:30 Great crowds c to him, bringing the lame, 4665
16: 1 and Sadducees c to Jesus and tested him 4665
16:13 *When* Jesus c to the region 2262
17: 7 But Jesus c and touched them. 4665
17:14 *When they* c to the crowd, 2262
17:18 and it c **out** of the boy, 2002
17:19 disciples c to Jesus in private and asked, 4665
17:22 *When* they c **together** in Galilee, 5370
17:24 the two-drachma tax c to Peter and asked, 4665
17:25 *When* Peter c into the house, 2262
18: 1 At that time the disciples c to Jesus 4665
18:21 Then Peter c to Jesus and asked, "Lord, 4665
19: 3 Some Pharisees c to him to test him. 4665
19:16 Now a man c **up** to Jesus and asked, 4665
20: 8 *"When* evening c, the owner of 1181
20: 9 the eleventh hour c and each received 2262
20:10 So *when* those c who were hired first, 2262
20:20 of Zebedee's sons c to Jesus with her sons 4665
21: 1 As they approached Jerusalem and c 2262
21:14 and the lame c to him at the temple, 4665
21:23 and the elders of the people c to him. 4665
21:32 For John c to you to show you the way 2262
22:11 "But *when* the king c **in** to see the guests, 1656
22:23 c to him with a question. 4665
24: 1 when his disciples c **up** to him 4665
24: 3 the disciples c to him privately. 4665
24:39 about what would happen until the flood c 2262
25:11 "Later the others also c. 2262
25:22 "The man with the two talents also c. 2262
25:24 the man who had received the one talent c. 4665
25:36 I was in prison and *you* c to visit me.' 2262
26: 7 a woman c to him with an alabaster jar 4665
26:17 the disciples c to Jesus and asked, 4665
26:20 *When* evening c, Jesus was reclining at 1181
26:43 *When* he c **back,** 2262
26:50 Jesus replied, "Friend, *do* what *you* c **for."** 4205
26:60 *though* many false witnesses c **forward.** 4665
26:60 Finally two c **forward** 4665
26:69 and a servant girl c to him. 4665
27: 1 of the people c to the decision to put Jesus 1181
27:33 *They* c to a place called Golgotha 2262
27:45 the ninth hour darkness c over all the land. 1181
27:53 *They* c **out of** the tombs, 2002
27:57 *there* c a rich man from Arimathea, 2262
28: 2 angel of the Lord c **down** from heaven and, 2849
28: 9 They c to him, 4665
28:13 'His disciples c during the night 2262
28:18 Then Jesus c to them and said, 4665
Mk 1: 4 And so John c, baptizing in the desert 1181
1: 9 that time Jesus c from Nazareth in Galilee 2262
1:11 And a voice c from heaven: 1181
1:21 and when the Sabbath c, NIG
1:26 the man violently and c **out** of him with 2002
1:40 with leprosy c to him and begged him 2262
1:45 the *people* still c to him from everywhere. 2262
2: 3 Some *men* c, bringing to him a paralytic, 2262
2:13 A large crowd c to him, 2262
2:18 Some *people* c and asked Jesus, 2262
3: 8 many people c to him from Judea, 2262
3:13 and *they* c to him. 599
3:22 of the law who c **down** from Jerusalem said, 2849
4: 4 and the birds c and ate it up. 2262
4: 6 But when the sun c **up,** 422
4: 8 It c **up,** grew and produced a crop, 326
4:35 That day *when* evening c, 1181
4:37 A furious squall c **up,** 1181
5: 2 an evil spirit c from the tombs to meet him. NIG
5:13 the evil spirits c **out** and went into the pigs. 2002
5:15 When *they* c to Jesus, 2262
5:22 the synagogue rulers, named Jairus, c there. 2262
5:27 *she* c up behind him in the crowd 2262
5:33 c and fell at his feet and, 2262
5:35 *some men* c from the house of Jairus, 2262
5:38 When *they* c to the home of 2262
6: 2 *When* the Sabbath c, 1181
6:21 Finally the opportune time c. 1181
6:22 the daughter of Herodias c **in** and danced, 1656
6:29 John's disciples c and took his body 2262
6:35 so his disciples c to him. 4665
6:47 *When* evening c, the boat was in the middle 1181
7:25 by an evil spirit c and fell at his feet. 2262
8:11 The Pharisees c and began 2002
8:22 *They* c to Bethsaida, 2262
9: 7 and a voice c from the cloud: 1181
9:14 *When* they c to the other disciples, 2262
9:26 convulsed him violently and c **out.** 2002
9:33 *They* c to Capernaum. 2262
10: 1 Again crowds of people c to him, 5233
10: 2 Some Pharisees c and tested him by asking, 4665
10:35 the sons of Zebedee, c to him. 4702

Mk	10:46	Then *they* c to Jericho.	2262
	10:50	he jumped to his feet and c to Jesus.	2262
	11: 1	As they approached Jerusalem and c	NIG
	11:19	When evening c, they went out of the city.	1181
	11:27	the teachers of the law and the elders c	2262
	12:14	They c to him and said, "Teacher,	2262
	12:18	c to him with a question.	2262
	12:28	of the law c and heard them debating.	4665
	12:42	But a poor widow c and put	2262
	14: 3	a woman c with an alabaster jar	2262
	14:17	*When* evening c, Jesus arrived with	1181
	14:40	*When* he c **back**, he again found them	2262
	14:53	elders and teachers of the law c **together.**	5302
	14:66	of the servant girls of the high priest c by.	2262
	15: 8	The crowd c **up** and asked Pilate to do	326
	15:33	At the sixth hour darkness c over	1181
Lk	1:10	when the time for the burning of incense c,	NIG
	1:22	*When* he c **out**, he could not speak to them.	2002
	1:59	On the eighth day *they* c to circumcise	2262
	2: 6	the time for the baby to be born,	4398
	3: 2	the word of God c to John son of Zechariah	1181
	3:12	Tax collectors also c to be baptized.	2262
	3:22	And a voice c from heaven:	1181
	4:22	at the gracious words that c **from** his lips.	1744
	4:35	the man down before them all and c **out**	2002
	4:41	Moreover, demons c **out** of many people,	2002
	4:42	for him and when *they* c to where he was,	2262
	5: 7	and *they* c and filled both boats so full	2262
	5:12	a man c along who was covered	NIG
	5:15	so that crowds of people c to hear him and	5302
	5:18	Some men c carrying a paralytic on a mat	NIG
	6:13	When morning c, he called his disciples	1181
	6:48	*When* a flood c, the torrent struck	1181
	7: 4	*When* they c to Jesus,	4134
	7:20	When the men c to Jesus, they said,	4134
	7:33	For John the Baptist c neither eating bread	2262
	7:34	The Son of Man c eating and drinking,	2262
	7:44	I c **into** your house.	1656
	8: 6	Some fell on rock, and *when* it c **up,**	5886
	8: 8	*It* c **up** and yielded a crop,	5886
	8:19	Jesus' mother and brothers c to see him,	4134
	8:23	A squall c **down** on the lake,	2849
	8:33	*When* the demons c **out** of the man,	2002
	8:35	When *they* c to Jesus,	2262
	8:41	c and fell at Jesus' feet,	2262
	8:44	She c **up** behind him and touched the edge	4665
	8:47	c trembling and fell at his feet.	2262
	8:49	someone c from the house of Jairus,	2262
	9:12	Late in the afternoon the Twelve c to him	4665
	9:35	A voice c from the cloud, saying,	1181
	9:37	*when* they c **down** from the mountain,	2982
	10:32	*when* he c to the place and saw him,	1181
	10:33	as he traveled, c where the man was;	2262
	10:38	he c to a village where	1656
	10:40	She c to him and asked, "Lord,	2392
	11:31	for *she* c from the ends of the earth to listen	2262
	12:51	Do you think *I* c to bring peace on earth?	4134
	13:31	At that time some Pharisees c to Jesus	4665
	14:21	"The servant c **back** and reported this	4134
	15:17	*"When* he c to his senses, he said,	2262
	15:25	When he c near the house,	2262
	16:21	Even the dogs c and licked his sores.	2262
	16:22	**"The time c when** the beggar died	1181+1254
	17:15	c **back,** praising God in a loud voice.	5715
	17:27	Then the flood c and destroyed them all.	2262
	18:40	*When* he c **near,** Jesus asked him,	1581
	19: 6	So he c **down** at once	2849
	19:10	For the Son of Man c to seek and	2262
	19:16	"The first one c and said, 'Sir,	4134
	19:18	"The second c and said, 'Sir,	2262
	19:20	"Then another servant c and said, 'Sir,	2262
	19:23	so that *when* I c **back,**	2262
	19:37	*When* he c **near** the place where	1581
	20: 1	together with the elders, c **up** to him.	2392
	20:27	c to Jesus with a question.	4665
	21:38	c **early in the morning**	3983
	22: 7	Then c the day of Unleavened Bread	2262
	22:14	When the hour c,	1181
	22:47	While he was still speaking a crowd c up,	NIG
	23:33	*When they* c to the place called the Skull,	2262
	23:36	The soldiers also c **up** and mocked him.	4665
	23:44	and darkness c over the whole land until	1181
	23:51	He c from the Judean town of Arimathea	NIG
	24: 9	*When they* c **back** from the tomb,	5715
	24:15	Jesus himself c **up** and walked along	1581
	24:23	and told us that they had seen	2262
Jn	1: 6	*There* c a man who was sent from God;	1181
	1: 7	He c as a witness to testify concerning	2262
	1: 8	he c only as a witness to the light.	NIG
	1:11	*He* c to that which was his own,	2262
	1:14	who c from the Father,	NIG
	1:17	grace and truth c through Jesus Christ.	1181
	1:31	but the reason I c baptizing with water was	2262
	3: 2	He c to Jesus at night and said, "Rabbi,	2262
	3:13	into heaven except the one who c	2849
	3:26	*They* c to John and said to him, "Rabbi,	2262
	4: 5	So *he* c to a town in Samaria called Sychar,	2262
	4: 7	When a Samaritan woman c to draw water,	2262
	4:30	*They* c **out** of the town and made their way	2002
	4:40	So when the Samaritans c to him,	2262
	6:16	When evening c, his disciples went down	2262
	6:41	"I am the bread that c **down** from heaven."	2849
	6:42	can he now say, *'I* c **down** from heaven'?	2849
	6:51	the living bread that c **down** from heaven.	2849
	6:58	This is the bread that c **down** from heaven.	2849
	8:14	where I c **from** and where I am going.	2262
	8:42	for I c **from** God and now am here.	2002

Jn	9: 7	man went and washed, and c home seeing.	2262
	10: 8	All who ever c before me were thieves	2262
	10:22	c the Feast of Dedication at Jerusalem.	1181
	10:35	to whom the word of God c—	1181
	10:41	and many people c to him.	2262
	11:38	once more deeply moved, c to the tomb.	2262
	11:44	The dead man c **out,**	2002
	12: 9	that Jesus was there and c,	2262
	12:21	They c to Philip,	4665
	12:27	it was for this very reason *I* c to this hour.	2262
	12:28	Then a voice c from heaven,	2262
	13: 6	*He* c to Simon Peter, who said to him,	2262
	16:27	and have believed that I c from God.	2002
	16:28	*I* c from the Father and entered the world;	2002
	16:30	This makes us believe that *you* c	2002
	17: 8	They knew with certainty that *I* c	2002
	18: 3	So Judas c to the grove,	2262
	18:16	who was known to the high priest, c back,	2002
	18:29	So Pilate c **out** to them and asked,	2002
	18:37	and for this *I* c into the world,	2002
	19: 1	Once more Pilate c **out** and said to	2002
	19: 5	When Jesus c **out** wearing the crown	2002
	19:32	The soldiers therefore c and broke the legs	2262
	19:33	But *when they* c to Jesus and found	2262
	19:38	he c and took the body away.	2262
	20: 2	So *she* c running to Simon Peter and	2262
	20:19	Jesus c and stood among them and said,	2262
	20:24	was not with the disciples when Jesus c.	2262
	20:26	Jesus c and stood among them and said,	2262
	21:13	Jesus c, took the bread and gave it to them,	2262
Ac	2: 1	When the day of Pentecost c,	5230
	2: 2	of a violent wind c from heaven and filled	1181
	2: 3	of fire that separated and c **to rest** on each	2767
	2: 6	a crowd c **together** in bewilderment,	5302
	3:11	the people were astonished and c **running**	5340
	4: 1	and the Sadducees c **up** to Peter and John	2392
	5: 6	Then the young men c **forward,**	482
	5: 7	About three hours later his wife c **in,**	1656
	5:10	Then the young men c **in** and,	1656
	5:25	Then someone c and said, "Look!	4134
	5:36	and *it* all c to nothing.	1181
	7:26	The next day Moses c **upon**	3972
	8: 7	With shrieks, evil spirits c **out** of many,	2002
	8:36	*they* c to some water and the eunuch said,	2262
	8:39	When *they* c **up** out of the water,	326
	9:26	*When* he c to Jerusalem,	4134
	10: 3	who c to him and said, "Cornelius!"	1656
	10:29	*I* c without raising any objection.	2262
	10:44	Holy Spirit c **on** all who heard the message.	2158
	11: 5	and *it* c **down** to where I was.	2262
	11:15	the Holy Spirit c **on** them as he had come	2158
	11:27	During this time some prophets c **down**	2982
	12:10	and c to the iron gate leading to the city.	2262
	12:11	Then Peter c to himself and said,	1181
	12:13	and a servant girl named Rhoda c to answer	4665
	13: 6	the whole island until they c to Paphos.	NIG
	13:11	Immediately mist and darkness c over him,	4406
	14:19	Then some Jews c from Antioch	2088
	14:24	*they* c into Pamphylia,	2262
	15: 1	Some men c **down** from Judea to Antioch	2982
	15: 4	*When they* c to Jerusalem,	4134
	16: 1	He c to Derbe and then to Lystra,	2918
	16: 7	*When they* c to the border of Mysia,	2262
	16:26	and everybody's chains c **loose.**	479
	16:39	*They* c to appease them and escorted them	2262
	16:40	*After* Paul and Silas c **out** of the prison,	2002
	17: 1	*they* c to Thessalonica,	2262
	18: 5	and Timothy c from Macedonia,	2982
	18:24	a native of Alexandria, c to Ephesus.	2918
	19: 6	the Holy Spirit c **on** them,	2262
	19:18	Many of those who believed now c	2262
	19:19	the total to fifty thousand drachmas.	NIG
	20: 7	On the first day of the week we c **together**	5251
	20:18	the first day *I* c into the province of Asia.	2094
	21:10	prophet named Agabus c **down** from Judea.	2982
	21:30	the people c **running** from all directions.	1181
	21:33	The commander c **up** and arrested him	1581
	22: 6	"About noon *as* I c near Damascus,	4513
	22:12	"A man named Ananias c to see me.	2262
	23:27	but I c with my troops and rescued him,	2392
	24:17	*I* c to Jerusalem to bring my people gifts	4134
	24:24	Several days later Felix c	4134
	25:17	*When* they c **here with me,**	5302
	25:23	and Bernice c with great pomp and entered	2262
	27: 8	along the coast with difficulty and c to	2262
	27:39	When daylight c, they did not recognize	1181
	28: 9	of the sick on the island c and were cured.	4665
	28:13	The next day the south wind c **up,**	2104
	28:14	And so *we* c to Rome.	2262
	28:23	and c in even larger numbers to the place	2262
	28:30	and welcomed all who c to see him.	1660
Ro	3:24	by his grace through the redemption that c	NIG
	5:12	and in this way death c to all men,	1451
	5:15	the gift that c by the grace of the one man,	NIG
	7: 9	but *when* the commandment c,	2262
1Co	2: 1	When I c to you, brothers,	2262
	2: 3	I c to you in weakness and fear,	1181
	3: 5	through whom *you* c **to believe—**	AIT
	8: 6	from whom all things c and	NIG
	8: 6	through whom all things c and	NIG
	11:12	For as woman c from man,	NIG
	15:21	For since death c through a man,	NIG
2Co	2: 3	so that *when I* c I should not be distressed	2262
	3: 7	c with glory, so that the Israelites could	1181
	3:11	And if what was fading c with glory,	NIG
	7: 5	For *when* we c into Macedonia,	2262
	11: 9	for the brothers *who* c from Macedonia	2262

Gal	2:11	When Peter c to Antioch,	2262
	2:12	Before certain men c from James,	2262
	3:23	Before this faith c, we were held prisoner	2262
Eph	2:17	He c and preached peace	2262
1Th	1: 5	our gospel c to you not simply with words,	1181
1Ti	1:15	Christ Jesus c into the world	2262
2Ti	4:16	no one c to my **support,**	4134
Heb	7:28	but the oath, which c after the law,	NIG
	9:11	*When* Christ c as high priest of	4134
	10: 5	*when* Christ c **into** the world, he said:	1656
	11:12	c **descendants** as numerous as the stars in	1164
2Pe	1:17	the voice c to him from the Majestic Glory,	5770
	1:18	that c from heaven when we were with him	5770
	1:20	that no prophecy of Scripture c **about** by	1181
1Jn	5: 6	This is the one who c by water and blood—	2262
Rev	1:16	**out** of his mouth c a sharp double-edged sword.	1744
	2: 8	who died and c **to life** again.	2409
	4: 5	**From** the throne c flashes of lightning,	1744
	5: 7	*He* c and took the scroll from the right hand	2262
	6: 1	Then another horse c **out,** a fiery red one.	2002
	8: 3	c and stood at the altar.	2262
	8: 5	and *there* c peals of thunder, rumblings,	1181
	8: 7	and *there* c hail and fire mixed with blood,	1181
	9: 3	**out** of the smoke locusts c	2002
	9:17	**out** of their mouths c fire, smoke and sulfur.	1744
	9:18	and sulfur that c **out** of their mouths.	1744
	11:19	And *there* c flashes of lightning,	1181
	14:15	Then another angel c **out** of the temple	2002
	14:18	Another angel c **out** of the temple	2002
	14:18	c from the altar and called in a loud voice	NIG
	15: 6	**Out** of the temple c the seven angels	2002
	16:13	they c **out** of the mouth of the dragon,	NIG
	16:17	**out** of the temple c a loud voice	2002
	16:18	Then *there* c flashes of lightning,	1181
	17: 1	the seven bowls c and said to me,	2262
	19: 5	Then a voice c from the throne, saying:	2002
	19:21	with the sword that c **out** of the mouth of	2002
	20: 4	*They* c **to life** and reigned with Christ	2409
	20: 9	But fire c **down** from heaven	2849
	21: 9	of the seven last plagues c and said to me,	2262

CAMEL (7) [CAMEL'S, CAMEL-LOADS, CAMELS, CAMELS', SHE-CAMEL]

Ge	24:64	She got down from her c	1695
Lev	11: 4	The c, though it chews the cud,	1695
Dt	14: 7	not eat the c, the rabbit or the coney.	1695
Mt	19:24	it is easier for a c to go through the eye of	2823
	23:24	You strain out a gnat but swallow a c.	2823
Mk	10:25	It is easier for a c to go through the eye of	2823
Lk	18:25	It is easier for a c to go through the eye of	2823

CAMEL'S (3) [CAMEL]

Ge	31:34	inside her c saddle and was sitting on them.	1695
Mt	3: 4	John's clothes were made of c hair,	2823
Mk	1: 6	John wore clothing made *of* c hair,	2823

CAMEL-LOADS (1) [LOAD]

2Ki	8: 9	taking with him as a gift forty c of all	1695+5362

CAMELS (48) [CAMEL]

Ge	12:16	menservants and maidservants, and c.	1695
	24:10	servant took ten of his master's c and left,	1695
	24:11	to kneel down near the well outside	1695
	24:14	'Drink, and I'll water your c too'—	1695
	24:19	she said, "I'll draw water for your c too,	1695
	24:22	When the c had finished drinking,	1695
	24:30	to the man and found him standing by the c	1695
	24:31	the house and a place for the c."	1695
	24:32	and the c were unloaded.	1695
	24:32	Straw and fodder were brought for the c,	1695
	24:35	and c and donkeys.	1695
	24:44	"Drink, and I'll draw water for your c too,"	1695
	24:46	'Drink, and I'll water your c too.'	1695
	24:46	So I drank, and she watered my c also.	1695
	24:61	and mounted their c and went back with	1695
	24:63	and as he looked up, he saw c approaching.	1695
	30:43	and c and donkeys.	1695
	31:17	Jacob put his children and his wives on c,	1695
	32: 7	and the flocks and herds and c as well.	1695
	32:15	thirty female c with their young,	1695
	37:25	Their c were loaded with spices,	1695
Ex	9: 3	on your horses and donkeys and c and	1695
Jdg	6: 5	to count the men and their c;	1695
	7:12	Their c could no more be counted than	1695
1Sa	15: 3	cattle and sheep, c and donkeys.' "	1695
	27: 9	but took sheep and cattle, donkeys and c,	1695
	30:17	who rode off on c and fled.	1695
1Ki	10: 2	with c carrying spices,	1695
1Ch	5:21	of the Hagrites—fifty thousand c,	1695
	12:40	Naphtali came bringing food on donkeys, c,	1695
	27:30	Obil the Ishmaelite was in charge of the c.	1695
2Ch	9: 1	with c carrying spices,	1695
	14:15	of sheep and goats and c.	1695
Ezr	2:67	435 c and 6,720 donkeys.	1695
Ne	7:69	435 c and 6,720 donkeys.	1695
Job	1: 3	three thousand c, five hundred yoke	1695
	1:17	down on your c and carried them off.	1695
	42:12	six thousand c, a thousand yoke of oxen	1695
Isa	21: 7	riders on donkeys or riders on c,	1695
	30: 6	their treasures on the humps of c,	1695
	60: 6	Herds of c will cover your land,	1695
	60: 6	**young** c *of* Midian and Ephah.	1145

Isa	66:20	and on mules and **c**," says the LORD.	4140
Jer	49:29	be carried off with all their goods and **c**.	1695
	49:32	Their **c** will become plunder,	1695
Eze	25: 5	I will turn Rabbah into a pasture for **c**	1695
Zec	14:15	the **c** and donkeys,	1695

CAMELS' (2) [CAMEL]

Jdg	8:21	and took the ornaments off their **c**' necks.	1695
	8:26	or the chains that were on their **c**' necks.	1695

CAMON (KJV) See KAMON

CAMP (180) [CAMPED, CAMPFIRES, CAMPING, CAMPS, ENCAMP, ENCAMPED, ENCAMPS]

Ge	32: 2	he said, "This is the **c** of God!"	4722
	32:21	but he himself spent the night in the **c**.	4722
Ex	16:13	That evening quail came and covered the **c**,	4722
	16:13	a layer of dew around the **c**.	4722
	19:16	Everyone in the **c** trembled.	4722
	19:17	the people out of the **c** to meet with God,	4722
	29:14	and its hide and its offal outside the **c**.	4722
	32:17	"There is the sound of war in the **c**."	4722
	32:19	When Moses approached the **c** and saw	4722
	32:26	he stood at the entrance to the **c** and said,	4722
	32:27	through the **c** from one end to the other,	4722
	33: 7	the **c** some distance away,	4722
	33: 7	to the tent of meeting outside the **c**.	4722
	33:11	Then Moses would return to the **c**,	4722
	36: 6	and they sent this word throughout the **c**:	4722
Lev	4:12	the **c** to a place ceremonially clean,	4722
	4:21	the **c** and burn it as he burned the first bull.	4722
	6:11	and carry the ashes outside the **c** to a place	4722
	8:17	and its offal he burned up outside the **c**,	4722
	9:11	and the hide he burned up outside the **c**.	4722
	10: 4	carry your cousins outside the **c**,	4722
	10: 5	still in their tunics, outside the **c**,	4722
	13:46	he must live outside the **c**.	4722
	14: 3	to go outside the **c** and examine him.	4722
	14: 8	After this he may come into the **c**,	4722
	16:26	afterward he may come into the **c**.	4722
	16:27	must be taken outside the **c**;	4722
	16:28	afterward he may come into the **c**.	4722
	17: 3	a lamb or a goat in the **c** or outside of it	4722
	24:10	and a fight broke out in the **c** between him	4722
	24:14	"Take the blasphemer outside the **c**.	4722
	24:23	and they took the blasphemer outside the **c**	4722
Nu	1:52	in his own **c** under his own standard.	4722
	2: 2	"The Israelites *are to* **c** around the Tent	2837
	2: 3	the divisions of the **c** of Judah are	4722
	2: 5	The tribe of Issachar *will* **c** next to them.	2837
	2: 9	All the men assigned to the **c** of Judah,	4722
	2:10	On the south will be the divisions of the **c**	4722
	2:12	The tribe of Simeon *will* **c** next to them.	2837
	2:16	All the men assigned to the **c** of Reuben,	4722
	2:17	Then the tent of Meeting and the **c** of	4722
	2:18	of the **c** of Ephraim under their standard.	4722
	2:24	All the men assigned to the **c** of Ephraim,	4722
	2:25	On the north will be the divisions of the **c**	4722
	2:27	The tribe of Asher *will* **c** next to them.	2837
	2:31	to the **c** of Dan number 157,600.	4722
	3:23	Gershonite clans *were to* **c** on the west,	2837
	3:29	*to* **c** on the south side of the tabernacle.	2837
	3:35	*to* **c** on the north side of the tabernacle.	2837
	3:38	Moses and Aaron and his sons *were to* **c** to	2837
	4: 5	When the **c** is to move,	4722
	4:15	and when the **c** is ready to move,	4722
	5: 2	to send away from the **c** anyone who has	4722
	5: 3	the **c** so they will not defile their camp,	4722
	5: 3	the camp so they will not defile the **c**,	4722
	5: 4	they sent them outside the **c**.	4722
	9:18	*they* **remained in** the **c**.	2837
	9:22	the Israelites *would* **remain in c** and	2837
	10:14	The divisions of the **c** of Judah went first,	4722
	10:18	divisions of the **c** of Reuben went next,	4722
	10:22	divisions of the **c** of Ephraim went next,	4722
	10:25	the divisions of the **c** of Dan set out,	4722
	10:31	You know where we *should* **c** in the desert,	2837
	10:34	by day when they set out from the **c**.	4722
	11: 1	of the outskirts of the **c**.	4722
	11: 9	When the dew settled on the **c** at night,	4722
	11:26	had remained in the **c**.	4722
	11:26	and they prophesied in the **c**.	4722
	11:27	and Medad are prophesying in the **c**."	4722
	11:30	and the elders of Israel returned to the **c**.	4722
	11:31	the **c** to about three feet above the ground,	4722
	11:32	Then they spread them out all around the **c**.	4722
	12:14	Confine her outside the **c** for seven days;	4722
	12:15	So Miriam was confined outside the **c**	4722
	14:44	the LORD's covenant moved from the **c**.	4722
	15:35	assembly must stone him outside the **c**."	4722
	15:36	So the assembly took him outside the **c**	4722
	19: 3	to be taken outside the **c** and slaughtered	4722
	19: 7	He may then come into the **c**,	4722
	19: 9	in a ceremonially clean place outside the **c**.	4722
	31:12	and the Israelite assembly at their **c** on	4722
	31:13	to meet them outside the **c**.	4722
	31:19	must stay outside the **c** for seven days.	4722
	31:24	Then you may come into the **c**."	4722
Dt	1: 7	**Break c** and advance into the hill country of	7155
	1:33	to search out places for you to **c** and	2837
	2:14	of fighting men had perished from the **c**,	4722
	2:15	until he had completely eliminated them	
		from the **c**.	4722

Dt	23:10	he is to go outside the **c** and stay there.	4722
	23:11	and at sunset he may return to the **c**.	4722
	23:12	the **c** where you can go to relieve yourself.	4722
	23:14	about in your **c** to protect you and	4722
	23:14	Your **c** must be holy,	4722
Jos	1:11	"Go through the **c** and tell the people,	4722
	3: 2	the officers went throughout the **c**,	4722
	3:14	when the people **broke c** to cross the	
		Jordan,	185+4946+5825
	4: 8	they carried them over with them to their **c**,	4869
	5: 8	they remained where they were in **c**	4722
	6:11	Then the people returned to **c** and spent	4722
	6:14	around the city once and returned to the **c**.	4722
	6:18	the **c** of Israel liable to destruction	4722
	6:23	and put them in a place outside the **c**	4722
	8:11	*They* **set up c** north of Ai,	2837
	8:13	all those in the **c** to the north of the city and	4722
	9: 6	the **c** at Gilgal and said to him and the men	4722
	10: 6	then sent word to Joshua in the **c** at Gilgal:	4722
	10:15	with all Israel to the **c** at Gilgal.	4722
	10:21	then returned safely to Joshua in the **c**	4722
	10:43	with all Israel to the **c** at Gilgal.	4722
	11: 5	and **made c** together at the Waters	2837
	18: 9	and returned to Joshua in the **c** at Shiloh.	4722
Jdg	7: 1	The **c** of Midian was north of them in	4722
	7: 8	**c** of Midian lay below him in the valley.	4722
	7: 9	"Get up, go down against the **c**,	4722
	7:10	go down to the **c** with your servant Purah	4722
	7:11	you will be encouraged to attack the **c**."	4722
	7:11	down to the outposts of the **c**.	4722
	7:13	into the Midianite **c**.	4722
	7:14	and the whole **c** into his hands."	4722
	7:15	to the **c** of Israel and called out,	4722
	7:15	The LORD has given the Midianite **c**	4722
	7:17	When I get to the edge of the **c**,	4722
	7:18	from all around the **c** blow yours and shout,	4722
	7:19	the **c** at the beginning of the middle watch,	4722
	7:21	each man held his position around the **c**,	4722
	7:22	throughout the **c** to turn on each other	4722
	18:12	On their way *they* **set up c**	2837
	20:19	the Israelites got up and **pitched c**	2837
	21: 8	from Jabesh Gilead had come to the **c** for	4722
	21:12	and they took them to the **c** *at* Shiloh	4722
1Sa	4: 3	When the soldiers returned to **c**,	4722
	4: 5	of the LORD's covenant came into the **c**,	4722
	4: 6	in the Hebrew **c**?"	4722
	4: 6	the ark of the LORD had come into the **c**,	4722
	4: 7	"A god has come into the **c**," they said.	4722
	11:11	of the night they broke into the **c** of	4722
	13:17	from the Philistine **c** in three detachments.	4722
	14:15	those in the **c** and field,	4722
	14:19	the Philistine **c** increased more and more.	4722
	14:21	and had gone up with them to their **c** went	4722
	17: 1	*They* **pitched c** at Ephes Dammim,	2837
	17: 4	came out of the Philistine **c**.	4722
	17:17	for your brothers and hurry to their **c**.	4722
	17:20	He reached the **c** as the army was going out	5046
	17:53	they plundered their **c**.	4722
	26: 3	Saul **made** *his* **c** beside the road on the hill	2837
	26: 5	Saul was lying inside the **c**,	5046
	26: 6	"Who will go down into the **c** with me	4722
	26: 7	the **c** with his spear stuck in the ground	5046
	28: 4	and came and **set up c** at Shunem,	2837
	28: 4	the Israelites and **set up c** at Gilboa.	2837
2Sa	1: 2	the third day a man arrived from Saul's **c**,	4722
	1: 3	"I have escaped from the Israelite **c**."	4722
1Ki	16:16	the **c** heard that Zimri had plotted against	2837
	16:16	king over Israel that very day there in the **c**.	4722
2Ki	3:24	when the Moabites came to the **c** of Israel,	4722
	6: 8	"I will **set up** my **c** in such and such	9381
	7: 4	So let's go over to the **c** of the Arameans	4722
	7: 5	At dusk they got up and went to the **c** of	4722
	7: 5	When they reached the edge of the **c**,	4722
	7: 7	the **c** as it was and ran for their lives.	4722
	7: 8	of the **c** and entered one of the tents.	4722
	7:10	the Aramean **c** and not a man was there—	4722
	7:12	so they have left the **c** to hide in	4722
	7:16	the people went out and plundered the **c** of	4722
	19:35	men in the Assyrian **c**.	4722
	19:36	So Sennacherib king of Assyria **broke c**	5825
1Ch	9:18	the gatekeepers belonging to the **c** of	4722
2Ch	22: 1	who came with the Arabs into the **c**,	4722
	32:21	and officers in the **c** of the Assyrian king.	4722
Ps	78:28	He made them come down inside their **c**,	4722
	106:16	In the **c** they grew envious of Moses and	4722
Isa	10:29	and say, "We will **c** overnight at Geba."	4869
	21:13	*who* **c** in the thickets of Arabia,	4328
	37:36	in the Assyrian **c**.	4722
	37:37	So Sennacherib king of Assyria **broke c**	5825
Mic	4:10	for now you must leave the city *to* **c** in	8905
Heb	13:11	but the bodies are burned outside the **c**.	*4213*
	13:13	Let us, then, go to him outside the **c**,	*4213*
Rev	20: 9	and surrounded the **c** of God's people,	*4213*

CAMPAIGN (3) [CAMPAIGNS]

Jos	10:42	and their lands Joshua conquered in one **c**,	7193
Eze	29:18	of Babylon drove his army in a hard **c**	6275
	29:18	from the **c** he led against Tyre.	6275

CAMPAIGNS (4) [CAMPAIGN]

1Sa	18:13	**led** the troops **in** their **c**.	
		995+2256+3655+4200+7156
	18:16	**led** them **in** their **c**. 995+2256+3655+4200+7156
2Sa	5: 2	**led** Israel **on** their **military c**. 995+2256+3655
1Ch	11: 2	**led** Israel **on** their **military c**. 995+2256+3655

CAMP (Anglicized) See also ENCAMP

CAMPED (79) [CAMP]

Ge	31:25	and Laban and his relatives **c** there too.	9546
	33:18	of Shechem in Canaan and **c** within sight	2837
Ex	13:20	After leaving Succoth *they* **c** at Etham on	2837
	14: 9	the Israelites and overtook them *as they* **c**	2837
	15:27	and *they* **c** there near the water.	2837
	17: 1	*They* **c** at Rephidim,	2837
	18: 5	where he *was* **c** near the mountain of God.	2837
	19: 2	and Israel **c** there in the desert in front of	2837
Nu	21:10	The Israelites moved on and **c** at Oboth.	2837
	21:11	Then they set out from Oboth and **c**	2837
	21:12	From there they moved on and **c** in	2837
	21:13	They set out from there and **c** alongside	2837
	22: 1	and **c** along the Jordan across from Jericho.	2837
	33: 5	The Israelites left Rameses and **c**	2837
	33: 6	They left Succoth and **c** at Etham,	2837
	33: 7	and **c** near Migdol.	2837
	33: 8	*they* **c** at Marah.	2837
	33: 9	and *they* **c** there.	2837
	33:10	They left Elim and **c** by the Red Sea.	2837
	33:11	They left the Red Sea and **c** in the Desert	2837
	33:12	the Desert of Sin and **c** at Dophkah.	2837
	33:13	They left Dophkah and **c** at Alush.	2837
	33:14	They left Alush and **c** at Rephidim,	2837
	33:15	They left Rephidim and **c** in the Desert	2837
	33:16	of Sinai and **c** at Kibroth Hattaavah.	2837
	33:17	They left Kibroth Hattaavah and **c**	2837
	33:18	They left Hazeroth and **c** at Rithmah.	2837
	33:19	They left Rithmah and **c** at Rimmon Perez.	2837
	33:20	They left Rimmon Perez and **c** at Libnah.	2837
	33:21	They left Libnah and **c** at Rissah.	2837
	33:22	They left Rissah and **c** at Kehelathah.	2837
	33:23	They left Kehelathah and **c**	2837
	33:24	They left Mount Shepher and **c** at Haradah.	2837
	33:25	They left Haradah and **c** at Makheloth.	2837
	33:26	They left Makheloth and **c** at Tahath.	2837
	33:27	They left Tahath and **c** at Terah.	2837
	33:28	They left Terah and **c** at Mithcah.	2837
	33:29	They left Mithcah and **c** at Hashmonah.	2837
	33:30	They left Hashmonah and **c** at Moseroth.	2837
	33:31	They left Moseroth and **c** at Bene Jaakan.	2837
	33:32	They left Bene Jaakan and **c**	2837
	33:33	They left Hor Haggidgad and **c**	2837
	33:34	They left Jotbathah and **c** at Abronah.	2837
	33:35	They left Abronah and **c** at Ezion Geber.	2837
	33:36	They left Ezion Geber and **c** at Kadesh,	2837
	33:37	They left Kadesh and **c** at Mount Hor,	2837
	33:41	They left Mount Hor and **c** at Zalmonah.	2837
	33:42	They left Zalmonah and **c** at Punon.	2837
	33:43	They left Punon and **c** at Oboth.	2837
	33:44	They left Oboth and **c** at Iye Abarim,	2837
	33:45	They left Iyim and **c** at Dibon Gad.	2837
	33:46	and **c** at Almon Diblathaim.	2837
	33:47	They left Almon Diblathaim and **c** in	2837
	33:48	and **c** on the plains of Moab by the Jordan	2837
	33:49	the plains of Moab *they* **c** along the Jordan	2837
Jos	3: 1	where *they* **c** before crossing over.	4328
	4:19	the people went up from the Jordan and **c**	2837
	5:10	*while* **c** at Gilgal on the plains of Jericho,	2837
Jdg	6: 4	*They* **c** on the land and ruined the crops all	2837
	6:33	the Jordan and **c** in the Valley of Jezreel.	2837
	7: 1	and all his men **c** at the spring of Harod.	2837
	10:17	the Ammonites were called to arms and **c**	2837
	10:17	the Israelites assembled and **c** at Mizpah.	2837
	11:18	and **c** on the other side of the Arnon.	2837
	15: 9	The Philistines went up and **c** in Judah,	2837
1Sa	4: 1	The Israelites **c** at Ebenezer,	2837
	13: 5	They went up and **c** at Micmash,	2837
	13:16	while the Philistines **c** at Micmash.	2837
	17: 2	the Israelites assembled and **c** in the Valley	2837
	26: 5	and went to the place where Saul *had* **c**.	2837
	29: 1	and Israel by the spring in Jezreel.	2837
2Sa	11:11	and my lord's men *are* **c** in the open fields.	2837
	17:26	The Israelites and Absalom **c** *in* the land	2837
	24: 5	crossing the Jordan, *they* **c** near Aroer,	2837
1Ki	20:27	The Israelites **c** opposite them	2837
	20:29	For seven days they **c** opposite each other,	2837
1Ch	19: 7	who came and **c** near Medeba,	2837
Ezr	8:15	and we **c** there three days.	2837
Jer	52: 4	*They* **c** outside the city	2837

CAMPFIRES (2) [CAMP, FIRE]

Jdg	5:16	the **c** to hear the whistling for the flocks?	5478
Ps	68:13	Even while you sleep among the **c**,	9190

CAMPHIRE (KJV) See HENNA

CAMPING (1) [CAMP]

Nu	10: 5	the tribes **c** on the east are to set out.	2837

CAMPS (13) [CAMP]

Ge	25:16	according to their settlements and **c**.	3227
Nu	2:17	in the middle of the **c**,	4722
	2:32	All those in the **c**, by their divisions,	4722
	10: 2	and for having the **c** set out.	4722
	10: 6	the **c** on the south are to set out.	4722
	31:10	as well as all their **c**.	3227
Dt	23:10	in your **c** who chop your wood	4722
2Ch	14:15	They also attacked the **c** of the herdsmen	185
Ps	68:12	in the **c** men divide the plunder.	1074+5661
Eze	4: 2	set up **c** against it and put battering rams	4722

Eze 25: 4 They will set up their **c** and pitch their tents 3227
Am 4:10 with the stench of your **c**, 4722
Zec 14:15 and all the animals in those **c**. 4722

CAN (718) [CAN'T, CANNOT]

Ge 4:13 "My punishment is more than I **c** bear. AIT
8:17 so *they* **c** multiply on the earth and AIT
15: 2 what **c** you give me AIT
15: 5 if indeed you **c** count them." 3523
15: 8 how **c** I know that I will gain possession AIT
16: 2 perhaps I **c** build a family through her." AIT
18: 5 so you **c** be refreshed and then go AIT
18:30 What if only thirty **c** be found there?" AIT
18:31 so what if only twenty **c** be found there?" AIT
18:32 What if only ten **c** be found there?" AIT
19: 2 *You* **c** wash your feet and spend the night AIT
19: 5 to us so that *we* **c** have sex with them." AIT
19: 8 and *you* **c** do what you like with them. AIT
19:34 with him so *we* **c** preserve our family line AIT
20:13 'This is how *you* **c** show your love to me: AIT
23: 4 for a burial site here so I **c** bury my dead." AIT
23:13 from me so I **c** bury my dead there." AIT
24: 7 so that *you* **c** get a wife for my son AIT
24:40 so that *you* **c** get a wife for my son AIT
24:50 *we* **c** say nothing to you one way or 3523
27: 9 I **c** prepare some tasty food for your father, AIT
27:21 "Come near so I **c** touch you, my son, AIT
27:37 So what *c* I possibly do for you, AIT
30: 3 with her so that *she* **c** bear children for me AIT
30: 3 that through her I too *c* build a family." AIT
30:15 "*he* **c** sleep with you tonight in return AIT
30:25 so I **c** go back to my own homeland. AIT
31:43 Yet what **c** I do today AIT
34:10 *You* **c** settle among us; AIT
34:21 We **c** marry their daughters AIT
34:21 and they **c** marry ours. AIT
37:16 **C** you tell me where they are AIT
37:30 Where **c** I turn now?" AIT
41:15 "I had a dream, and no *one* **c** interpret it. AIT
41:15 when you hear a dream *you* **c** interpret it." AIT
41:38 "**C** we find anyone like this man, AIT
42:34 and *you* **c** trade in the land.' " AIT
43: 9 I **c** hold me personally responsible AIT
44: 1 with as much food as *they* **c** carry, 3523
44:15 **c** find things out by divination?" AIT
44:16 "What *c* we say to my lord?" AIT
44:16 "What *c* we say? AIT
44:16 *c* we prove *our* innocence? AIT
44:21 down to me so I **c** see him for myself.' AIT
44:34 How **c** I go back to my father if the boy is AIT
45:12 "*You* **c** see for yourselves, AIT
45:12 and so **c** my brother Benjamin, NIH
45:18 the land of Egypt and *you* **c** enjoy the fat AIT
47:23 here is seed for you so *you* **c** plant AIT
49: 1 around so I **c** tell you what will happen AIT
Ex 4:14 I know he **c** speak well. AIT
4:17 so *you* **c** perform miraculous signs with it." AIT
5:11 get your own straw wherever *you* **c** find it, AIT
10:21 darkness *that* **c** be felt." AIT
14:16 the water so that the Israelites **c** go through AIT
16:32 to come, so *they* **c** see the bread I gave you AIT
18:22 the simple cases *they* **c** decide themselves. AIT
24:14 anyone involved in a dispute **c** go to them." AIT
28: 7 so *it* **c** be fastened. AIT
29:29 so that they **c** be anointed and ordained AIT
32:30 perhaps I **c** make atonement for your sin." AIT
Lev 13:12 so far as the priest **c** see, NIH
14:22 which he **c** afford, AIT
14:30 which the person **c** afford, AIT
25:27 he **c** then go back to his own property. AIT
25:28 and *he* **c** then go back to his property. AIT
25:31 They **c** be redeemed, AIT
25:35 so he **c** continue to live among you. AIT
25:46 *You* **c** will them to your children AIT
25:46 and **c** make them slaves for life, AIT
27: 8 to what the man making the vow **c** afford. AIT
27:20 *it* **c** never be redeemed. AIT
Nu 5: 8 to whom restitution **c** be made *for* AIT
6:21 in addition to whatever else he **c** afford. AIT
10:31 and *you* **c** be our eyes. AIT
11:13 Where **c** I get meat for all these people? AIT
12:14 after that *she* **c** be brought back." AIT
13:30 for *we* **c** certainly do it." 3523+3523
16:21 from this assembly so I **c** put an end AIT
16:45 from this assembly so I **c** put an end AIT
20: 8 so they and their livestock **c** drink." AIT
21: 8 anyone who is bitten **c** look *at* it and live." AIT
22:38 "But I **c** say just anything? 3523+3523
23: 8 *c* I curse those whom God has not cursed? AIT
23: 8 How **c** I denounce those whom AIT
23:10 Who **c** count the dust of Jacob or number AIT
23:13 to another place where *you* **c** see them; AIT
24:23 "Ah, who **c** live when God does this? AIT
31:23 and anything else that **c** withstand fire must AIT
35:15 anyone who has killed another accidentally **c** flee there. AIT
Dt 1:12 But how **c** I bear your problems AIT
1:28 Where **c** we go? AIT
3:24 in heaven or on earth who **c** do the deeds AIT
5:24 a man **c** live even if God speaks with him. AIT
7:17 How **c** *we* drive them out?" 3523
8: 9 the rocks are iron and *you* **c** dig copper out AIT
9: 2 "Who **c** stand up against the Anakites?" AIT
18:21 "How **c** *we* know when a message has AIT
20:19 because *you* **c** eat their fruit. AIT
22:20 of the girl's virginity **c** be found, AIT

Dt 22:29 He **c** never divorce her as long as he lives. 3523
23:12 a place outside the camp where *you* **c** go AIT
31:12 so *they* **c** listen and learn to fear AIT
31:28 that I **c** speak these words in their hearing AIT
32:39 and no *one* **c** deliver out of my hand. AIT
33:14 and the finest the moon **c** yield; NIH
Jos 7: 8 O Lord, what **c** I say, AIT
9: 7 How then **c** *we* make a treaty with you?" AIT
15:18 Caleb asked her, "What **c** I do for you?" NIH
16:10 *you* **c** drive them out." AIT
Jdg 1:14 Caleb asked her, "What **c** I do for you?" NIH
6:15 Gideon asked, "how **c** I save Israel? AIT
6:31 *he* **c** defend himself when someone breaks AIT
7:14 "This **c** be nothing other than the sword NIH
11: 6 so *we* **c** fight the Ammonites." AIT
14:12 **c** give me *the* answer AIT
16: 5 "*See if* you **c** lure him *into* showing you AIT
16: 5 how *we* **c** overpower him so we may tie him up AIT
16: 6 and how *you* **c** be tied up and subdued." AIT
16:10 Come now, tell me how *you* **c** be tied." AIT
16:13 Tell me how *you* **c** be tied." AIT
16:15 Then she said to him, "How *c* you say, AIT
16:26 where I **c** feel the pillars that support AIT
18:24 How **c** you ask, AIT
19: 5 then *you* **c** go." AIT
19: 9 **Early** tomorrow **morning** *you* **c** get up AIT
19:22 to your house so *we* **c** have sex with him." AIT
19:24 and *you* **c** use them and do AIT
20:10 it **c** give them what they deserve AIT
21: 7 *c* we provide wives for those who are left, AIT
Ru 1:19 "**C** this be Naomi?" NIH
1Sa 2:36 *c* have food *to eat*.' " ' AIT
6:20 "Who **c** stand in the presence of 3523
9: 7 "If we go, what *c* we give the man? AIT
10:27 "How *c* this fellow save us?" AIT
11: 3 so *we* **c** send messengers throughout Israel; AIT
11:10 and *you* **c** do to us whatever seems good AIT
12:21 *c* do you no good, AIT
12:21 nor *c* they rescue you, AIT
14: 6 Nothing **c** hinder the LORD from saving, NIH
16: 2 But Samuel said, "How *c* I go? AIT
16:16 to search for someone *who* **c** play the harp. 3359
18: 8 What more **c** he get but the kingdom?" NIH
20: 7 *you* **c** be sure that he is determined AIT
21: 3 or whatever *you* **c** find." AIT
25: 8 and your son David whatever *you* **c** find AIT
25:17 Now think it over and see what *you* **c** do, AIT
25:17 a wicked man that no *one* **c** talk to him." AIT
26: 9 Who **c** lay a hand on AIT
27: 1 The best thing I **c** do is to escape to NIH
28: 2 for yourself what your servant **c** do." AIT
30:15 "*C* you lead me down AIT
2Sa 1: 7 and I said, '**What** **c** I do?' 2180
5: 6 the blind and the lame **c** ward you off." AIT
6: 9 **c** the ark of the LORD *ever* come AIT
7:10 so that *they* **c** have a home *of* their own AIT
7:20 "What more **c** David say to you?" AIT
9: 1 of Saul to whom I **c** show kindness AIT
9: 3 of Saul to whom I **c** show God's kindness?" AIT
12:18 How **c** *we* tell him the child is dead? AIT
12:23 **C** I bring him back again? 3523
14:19 no one **c** turn to the right or to the left NIH
14:32 'Come here so I **c** send you to the king AIT
15:34 **c** help me by frustrating AIT
16:10 who **c** ask, 'Why do you do this?' " AIT
17: 5 so *we* **c** hear what he has to say." AIT
17:13 until not even a piece of it **c** be found." AIT
19:26 so I **c** go with the king.' AIT
19:35 **C** I tell the difference AIT
19:35 **C** your servant **taste** what he eats AIT
19:35 **C** I still **hear** the voices of men AIT
20:16 Tell Joab to come here so I **c** speak AIT
22:30 With your help I **c** advance *against* AIT
22:30 with my God I **c** scale a wall. AIT
22:35 my arms **c** bend a bow of bronze. AIT
24:21 "so I **c** build an altar to the LORD, AIT
1Ki 1: 2 *She* **c** lie beside him so that our lord AIT
1:12 how *you* **c** save your own life and the life AIT
2:37 *you* **c** be sure you will die; AIT
2:42 *you* **c** be sure you will die'? AIT
5: 9 and you **c** take them **away**. AIT
13:16 nor **c** I eat bread or drink water with you AIT
18: 5 Maybe *we* **c** find some grass to keep AIT
20:25 so *we* **c** fight Israel on the plains. AIT
22: 7 of the LORD here whom *we* **c** inquire of?" AIT
22: 8 through whom *we* **c** inquire of the LORD, AIT
22:14 I **c** tell him only what AIT
2Ki 2: 9 what **c** I do for you before I am taken AIT
2:19 this town is well situated, as you **c** see, AIT
4: 2 Elisha replied to her, "How **c** I help you? AIT
4:10 he **c** stay there whenever he comes to us." AIT
4:13 Now what **c** be done for you? AIT
4:13 **C** we **speak** on your behalf to the king or AIT
4:14 "What **c** be done for her?" AIT
4:22 *c* go to the man of God quickly AIT
4:43 "How **c** I set this before a hundred men?" AIT
5: 1 **C** I kill and bring back to life? AIT
5:17 as much earth as a pair of mules **c** carry, NIH
6: 2 where each of *us* **c** get a pole; AIT
6:13 "so I **c** send men and capture him." AIT
6:20 open the eyes of these men so *they* **c** see." AIT
6:27 *c* I get help for you? AIT
8: 1 and stay for a while wherever *you* **c**, 1591S
9:22 "How **c** there be peace," Jehu replied, NIH
10: 4 not resist him, how **c** we?" 6641S

2Ki 18:23 if *you* **c** put riders on them! 3523
18:24 How **c** *you* repulse one officer of the least AIT
18:35 How then **c** the LORD **deliver** Jerusalem AIT
1Ch 13:12 **c** I ever **bring** the ark of God to me?" AIT
17: 9 so that *they* **c** have a home *of* their own AIT
17:18 "What more **c** David say to you NIH
21:22 of your threshing floor so I **c** build AIT
2Ch 2:14 and **c** execute any design given to him. AIT
2:16 **c** then **take** them **up** AIT
18: 6 of the LORD here whom *we* **c** inquire of?" AIT
18: 7 through whom *we* **c** inquire of the LORD, AIT
18:13 I **c** tell him only what my God says." AIT
20: 6 and no one **c** withstand you. AIT
25: 9 "The LORD **c** give you much more than that." AIT
29: 8 as you **c** see with your own eyes. AIT
32:14 then **c** your god deliver you from my hand? 3523
Ezr 9:10 now, O our God, what **c** we say after this? AIT
9:15 though because of it not one of us **c** stand AIT
Ne 2: 2 This **c** be nothing but sadness of heart." NIH
2: 5 so that I **c** rebuild it." AIT
4: 2 **C** they **bring** the stones **back to life** AIT
4: 9 so *they* **c** serve us as guards by night AIT
Est 8: 6 **c** I bear to see disaster fall on my people? AIT
8: 6 How **c** I bear to see the destruction NIH
8: 8 and sealed with his ring **c** be revoked." AIT
Job 4: 2 But who **c** keep from speaking? 3523
4:17 '**C** a mortal *be* more righteous AIT
4:17 **C** a man *be* more **pure**? AIT
6:30 **C** my mouth not **discern** AIT
8:11 **C** papyrus **grow tall** AIT
8:11 **C** reeds **thrive** without water? AIT
9: 2 *c* a mortal *be* righteous AIT
9:12 If he snatches away, who **c** stop him? AIT
9:12 Who **c** say to him, 'What are you doing?' AIT
9:14 "How then **c** I dispute with him? AIT
9:14 How **c** I find words to argue with him? AIT
10: 7 that no *one* **c** rescue me from your hand? AIT
10:20 **c** have a moment's **joy** AIT
11: 7 "**C** you fathom the mysteries of God? AIT
11: 7 **C** you probe the limits of the Almighty? AIT
11: 8 what *c* you **do**? AIT
11: 8 what *c* you **know**? AIT
11:10 who **c** oppose him? AIT
11:12 **c** no more become wise AIT
11:12 a wild donkey's colt **c** be born a man. AIT
13:19 **c** anyone bring charges AIT
14: 4 Who **c** bring what is pure from the impure? AIT
17:15 Who **c** see any hope for me? AIT
18: 2 Be sensible, and then *we* **c** talk. AIT
21:22 "**C** anyone teach knowledge to God, AIT
21:34 *c* you **console** me *with* your nonsense? AIT
22: 2 "**C** a man *be* of benefit AIT
22: 2 **C** even a wise man **benefit** AIT
22:17 What *c* the Almighty do to us?' AIT
23:13 he stands alone, and who **c** oppose him? AIT
24:25 who **c** prove me false AIT
25: 3 **C** his forces be numbered? AIT
25: 4 *c* a man *be* righteous AIT
25: 4 one born of woman *be* **pure**? AIT
26:14 Who then **c** understand the thunder AIT
28:12 "But where **c** wisdom **be found**? AIT
28:15 *c* its price be weighed AIT
28:17 Neither gold nor crystal **c** compare *with* it, AIT
28:17 nor **c** it be had for jewels of gold. NIH
33: 5 Answer me then, if *you* **c**; 3523
34:17 **C** he who hates justice govern? AIT
34:22 no deep shadow, where evildoers **c** hide. AIT
34:26 where *everyone* **c** see them, AIT
34:29 if he remains silent, who **c** condemn him? AIT
34:29 If he hides his face, who **c** see him? AIT
36:29 *Who c* understand how he spreads out AIT
37:18 *c* you join him in **spreading out** AIT
37:21 Now no *one* **c** look at the sun, AIT
38:20 **C** you take them to their places? AIT
38:31 "**C** you bind the beautiful Pleiades? AIT
38:31 **C** you loose the cords of Orion? AIT
38:32 **C** you bring forth the constellations AIT
38:33 **C** you set up [God's] dominion over AIT
38:34 "**C** you raise your voice to the clouds AIT
38:37 Who **c** tip over the water jars of AIT
39:10 **C** you hold him to the furrow with AIT
39:12 **C** you trust him to bring in your grain AIT
40: 4 how **c** I reply to you? AIT
40: 9 and *your* voice **thunder** like his? AIT
40:14 to you that your own right hand **c** save you. AIT
40:19 his Maker **c** approach him with his sword. AIT
40:24 **C** anyone capture him by the eyes, AIT
41: 1 "**C** you pull in the leviathan with AIT
41: 2 **C** you put a cord through his nose AIT
41: 5 **C** you make a pet AIT
41: 7 **C** you fill his hide with harpoons AIT
41:13 Who **c** strip off his outer coat? AIT
41:16 to the next that no air **c** pass between. AIT
42: 2 "I know that *you* **c** do all things; 3523
42: 2 no plan of yours **c** be thwarted. AIT
Ps 2:12 for his wrath **c** flare up in a moment. AIT
4: 6 "Who **c** show us any good?" AIT
5: 9 Not a *word* from their mouth **c** be trusted; AIT
11: 1 How then **c** *you* say to me: AIT
11: 3 what **c** the righteous do?" AIT
18:29 With your help I **c** advance *against* AIT
18:29 with my God I **c** scale a wall. AIT
18:34 my arms **c** bend a bow of bronze. AIT
19:12 Who **c** discern his errors? AIT
22:17 I **c** count all my bones; AIT
38:14 whose mouth **c** offer no reply. NIH

Ref		Text	Strong
Ps	40:5	for us no *one* c **recount** to you;	AIT
	42:2	When c *I* **go** and meet with God?	AIT
	49:7	No man c **redeem** the life of another or give	AIT
	49:10	For *all* c **see** that wise men die;	AIT
	56:4	What mortal man **do** to me?	AIT
	56:11	What c man **do** to me?	AIT
	58:9	Before your pots c **feel** [the heat of] the thorns—	AIT
	59:7	and they say, "Who c **hear** us?"	AIT
	71:3	to which I c always **go**;	AIT
	73:11	They say, "How c God **know?**	AIT
	75:6	the west or from the desert c **exalt** a man.	AIT
	76:5	not one of the warriors c **lift** his hands.	AIT
	76:7	Who c **stand** before you	AIT
	78:19	"C God spread a table in the desert?	3523
	78:20	But c he also give us food?	3523
	78:20	C he **supply** meat for his people?"	AIT
	86:8	no deeds c **compare** with yours.	NIH
	89:6	For who in the skies above c **compare** with	AIT
	89:48	What man c **live** and not see death,	AIT
	94:20	C a corrupt throne **be allied** with	AIT
	104:5	it c never **be moved.**	AIT
	106:2	Who c **proclaim** the mighty acts of	AIT
	115:7	c they **utter** a sound	AIT
	116:12	How c I **repay** the LORD	AIT
	118:6	What c man **do** to me?	AIT
	119:9	c a young man **keep** his way **pure?**	AIT
	119:165	and nothing c **make** them stumble.	NIH
	129:6	which withers before *it* c **grow;**	AIT
	137:4	How c we **sing** the songs of the LORD	AIT
	139:7	Where c I **go** from your Spirit?	AIT
	139:7	Where c I **flee** from your presence?	AIT
	145:3	his greatness no one c **fathom.**	NIH
	147:17	Who c **withstand** his icy blast?	AIT
Pr	3:15	nothing you desire c **compare** with her.	AIT
	6:27	C a man **scoop** fire into his lap	AIT
	6:28	C a **man** walk on hot coals	AIT
	8:11	and nothing you desire c **compare** with her.	AIT
	14:10	and no one else c **share** its joy.	AIT
	18:14	but a crushed spirit who c **bear?**	AIT
	20:6	but a faithful man who c **find?**	AIT
	20:9	Who c **say,** "I have kept my heart pure;	AIT
	20:24	then c anyone **understand** his own way?	AIT
	21:30	no plan that c **succeed** against the LORD.	NIH
	22:21	so that *you* c **give** sound answers	AIT
	23:35	will I wake up so I c **find** another drink?"	AIT
	24:22	who knows what calamities they c **bring?**	NIH
	25:15	Through patience a ruler c **be persuaded,**	AIT
	25:15	and a gentle tongue c **break** a bone.	AIT
	27:4	but who c **stand** before jealousy?	AIT
	27:6	Wounds from a friend c **be trusted,**	AIT
	27:11	then *I* c **answer** anyone who treats me	AIT
	29:6	but a righteous one c **sing** and be glad.	AIT
	30:28	a lizard c be **caught** with the hand,	AIT
	31:10	A wife of noble character who c **find?**	AIT
	31:25	she c **laugh** at the days to come.	AIT
Ecc	1:8	more than one c say.	3523
	1:10	Is there anything of which *one* c **say,**	AIT
	2:12	c the king's successor **do**	AIT
	2:24	A man c **do** nothing better than to eat	NIH
	2:25	who c **eat** or find enjoyment?	AIT
	3:14	nothing c be **added** to it and nothing taken	AIT
	3:22	For who c **bring** him	AIT
	4:10	his friend c **help** him **up.**	AIT
	4:11	But how c one *keep* **warm** alone?	AIT
	4:12	two c **defend** *themselves.*	AIT
	5:15	from his labor that *he* c **carry** in his hand.	AIT
	6:10	no man c **contend**	3523
	6:12	Who c **tell** him what will happen under	AIT
	7:13	Who c **straighten** what he has made crooked?	3523
	7:24	who c **discover** it?	AIT
	8:4	a king's word is supreme, who c **say** to him,	AIT
	8:7	who c **tell** him what is to come?	AIT
	8:17	No one c comprehend what goes on under	3523
	10:4	c **lay** great errors to rest.	AIT
	10:14	who c **tell** him what will happen	AIT
Isa	11:15	into seven streams so that *men* c **cross over**	AIT
	14:27	and who c **thwart** him?	AIT
	14:27	and who c **turn** it **back?**	AIT
	19:11	How c *you* **say** to Pharaoh,	AIT
	19:15	There is nothing Egypt c **do—**	AIT
	20:6	How then c we **escape?'"**	AIT
	22:22	what he opens no one c **shut,**	AIT
	22:22	and what he shuts no one c **open.**	AIT
	29:11	give the scroll to *someone who* c **read,**	3359+6219
	29:16	C the **pot** say of the potter,	AIT
	31:2	Yet he too is wise and c **bring** disaster;	AIT
	33:14	of us c **dwell** *with* the consuming fire?	AIT
	33:14	of us c **dwell** *with* everlasting burning?"	AIT
	36:8	if *you* c **put** riders on them!	3523
	36:9	then c *you* **repulse** one officer of the least	AIT
	36:20	c the LORD **deliver**	AIT
	38:15	But what I c **say?**	AIT
	40:28	and his understanding no one c **fathom.**	NIH
	43:13	No *one* c **deliver** out of my hand.	AIT
	43:13	When I act, who c **reverse** it?"	AIT
	44:10	*which* c **profit** him nothing?	AIT
	47:15	That is all *they* c **do** for you—	AIT
	47:15	there is not *one that* c **save** you.	AIT
	48:11	c I *let* myself **be defamed?**	AIT
	49:15	"C a mother **forget** the baby at her breast	AIT
	49:24	C plunder **be taken** from warriors?	AIT
	51:19	who c **comfort** you?—	AIT
	51:19	who c **console** you?	AIT
	53:8	And who c **speak** *of* his descendants?	AIT
	64:5	How then c we **be saved?**	AIT
Isa	66:8	C *a* country **be born** in a day	AIT
Jer	2:23	"How c *you* **say,** 'I am not defiled;	AIT
	2:24	in her heat who c **restrain** her?	AIT
	2:28	if *they* c **save** you when you are in trouble!	AIT
	2:33	of women c **learn** *from* your ways.	AIT
	3:5	but you do all the evil *you* **c.**"	3523
	5:1	If *you* c **find** but one person	AIT
	6:8	so no *one* c **live** in *it.*	AIT
	6:10	To whom c *I* **speak** and give warning?	AIT
	8:8	" 'How c *you* **say,** "We are wise,	AIT
	9:7	and test them, for what else c *I* **do** because	AIT
	9:11	of Judah so no *one* c **live** there.	AIT
	9:12	by the LORD and c **explain** it?	AIT
	9:12	like a desert that no *one* c **cross?**	AIT
	10:5	*they* c **do** no harm	AIT
	10:5	c *they* **do** *any* good."	AIT
	11:15	C consecrated meat **avert**	AIT
	12:5	how c *you* **compete** with horses?	AIT
	13:23	C the Ethiopian **change**	AIT
	13:23	Neither c you do good who are accustomed	3523
	15:6	*I* c **no longer** show compassion.	4206
	15:12	"C a man **break** iron—	AIT
	17:9	Who c **understand** it?	AIT
	18:6	c *I* **not** do with you as this potter does?	3523
	21:13	you who say, "Who c **come** against us?	AIT
	21:13	Who c **enter** our refuge?"	AIT
	23:24	C anyone **hide** in secret places so	AIT
	25:5	and you c **stay** in the land the LORD gave	AIT
	30:6	C a man **bear children?**	AIT
	31:37	"Only if the heavens above c **be measured**	AIT
	33:20	'If you c **break** my covenant with the day	AIT
	33:21	c **be broken** and David will no longer have	AIT
	34:22	of Judah so no *one* c **live** there.	AIT
	38:5	"The king c **do** nothing to oppose you."	3523
	47:7	But how c it **rest** when	AIT
	48:14	"How c *you* **say,** 'We are warriors,	AIT
	49:11	Your widows too c **trust** in me."	AIT
	49:19	Who is like me and who c **challenge** me?	AIT
	49:19	And what shepherd c **stand** against me?"	AIT
	50:44	Who is like me and who c **challenge** me?	AIT
	50:44	And what shepherd c **stand** against me?"	AIT
	51:8	perhaps *she* c **be healed.**	AIT
La	2:13	What c *I* **say** for you?	AIT
	2:13	What c *I* **compare** you,	AIT
	2:13	To what c *I* **liken** you,	AIT
	2:13	Who c **heal** you?	AIT
	3:37	Who c **speak** and have it happen if	AIT
	3:44	a cloud so that no prayer c **get through.**	AIT
	4:15	*"They* c **stay** here no longer."	AIT
	5:4	our wood c **be had** only at a price.	AIT
Eze	14:15	so that no *one* c **pass through** it because of	AIT
	15:5	how much less c it **be made**	AIT
	31:2	" 'Who c **be compared** with *you*	AIT
	31:18	the trees of Eden c **be compared** with *you*	AIT
	33:10	How then c we **live?'** '	AIT
	34:10	the shepherds c **no longer** **feed** themselves.	AIT
	37:3	"Son of man, c these bones **live?"**	AIT
Da	2:9	I will know that you c **interpret** it *for* me."	AIT
	2:10	on earth who c **do** what the king asks!	AIT
	2:11	No one c **reveal** it to the king except	AIT
	2:25	among the exiles from Judah who c **tell**	AIT
	2:27	magician or diviner c **explain** to the king	10321
	3:29	for no other god c **save** in this way."	10321
	4:18	the wise men in my kingdom c **interpret** it	10321
	4:18	But you c, because the spirit of	10346
	4:35	No one c **hold back** his hand or say to him:	AIT
	5:16	If *you* c **read** this writing	10321
	6:15	or edict that the king issues c **be changed."**	10321
	10:17	How c I, your servant, talk with you,	3523
	10:17	My strength is gone and I c **hardly breathe."**	4202+5972+8636
Hos	4:16	then c the LORD **pasture** them like lambs	AIT
	6:4	"What c *I* **do** with you, Ephraim?	AIT
	6:4	What c *I* **do** with you, Judah?	AIT
	11:8	c *I* **give** you **up,**	AIT
	11:8	c *I* **hand** you **over,**	AIT
	11:8	How c *I* **treat** you like Admah?	AIT
	11:8	How c *I* **make** you like Zeboiim?"	AIT
Joel	2:11	Who c **endure** it?	AIT
Am	2:8	who c but **prophesy?**	AIT
	7:2	How c Jacob **survive?**	AIT
	7:5	How c Jacob **survive?**	AIT
Ob	1:3	'Who c **bring** me **down** to the ground?'	AIT
Jnh	1:6	"How c *you* **sleep?**	AIT
Mic	5:8	and no one c **rescue.**	AIT
Na	1:6	Who c **withstand** his indignation?	AIT
	1:6	Who c **endure** his fierce anger?	AIT
	3:7	Where c *I* **find** anyone to comfort you?"	AIT
	3:19	Nothing c **heal** your wound,	NIH
Hab	2:15	so that *he* c **gaze** on their naked bodies.	AIT
	2:19	C it **give guidance?**	AIT
Mal	3:2	But who c **endure** the day of his coming?	AIT
	3:2	Who c **stand** when he appears?	AIT
Mt	3:9	And do not think you c **say** to yourselves,	NIG
	3:9	of these stones God c **raise up** children	1538
	5:13	c it be **made salty**	AIT
	6:24	"No one c **serve** two masters.	1538
	6:27	by worrying c **add** a single hour to his life?	1538
	7:4	How c you **say** to your brother,	4802
	8:2	if you are willing, *you* c **make** me clean."	1538
	9:15	"How c the **guests** of	1538
	10:28	the One who c **destroy** both soul and body	1538
	11:16	"To what c *I* **compare** this generation?	NIG
	12:26	c his kingdom **stand?**	AIT
	12:29	anyone enter a strong man's house	1538
	12:29	Then *he* c **rob** his house.	AIT
	12:34	c *you* who are evil say anything good?"	1538
Mt	14:15	c **go** to the villages and **buy**	AIT
	16:26	Or what c a man **give** in exchange	AIT
	17:20	you c **say** to this mountain,	NIG
	19:11	"Not everyone c **accept** this word,	NIG
	19:12	one who c **accept** this should accept it."	1538
	19:25	"Who then c **be saved?"**	1538
	20:22	"C *you* **drink** the cup I am going to drink?"	1538
	20:22	*"We* c," they answered.	1538
	21:21	not only c *you* **do** what was done to	AIT
	21:21	but also *you* c **say** to this mountain, 'Go,	AIT
	22:45	how c he be his son?"	4802
Mk	1:38	so *I* c **preach** there also.	AIT
	1:40	"If you are willing, *you* c **make** me clean."	1538
	2:7	Who c **forgive** sins but God alone?"	1538
	2:19	"How c the guests of the bridegroom fast	1538
	3:23	"How c Satan drive out Satan?	1538
	3:27	no one c **enter** a strong man's house	1538
	3:27	Then he c rob his house.	NIG
	4:32	the birds of the air c **perch** in its shade."	1538
	5:31	his disciples answered, "and yet you c **ask,**	NIG
	6:36	c go to the surrounding countryside and villages and buy themselves something *to* **eat."**	AIT
	7:15	a man c **make** him 'unclean' by going	1538
	7:18	from the outside c **make** him 'unclean'?	1538
	8:4	this remote place c anyone get enough bread	1538
	8:37	Or what c a man **give** in exchange	NIG
	9:22	But if *you* c **do** anything,	1538
	9:23	" 'If *you* **c'?**	1538
	9:29	"This kind c **come** out only by prayer."	1538
	9:39	"No one who does a miracle in my name c	1538
	9:50	c *you* **make** it salty	AIT
	10:26	"Who then c **be saved?"**	1538
	10:38	"C *you* **drink** the cup I drink or be baptized	1538
	10:39	*"We* c," they answered.	1538
	12:37	How then c he be his son?	4470
	14:7	and *you* c **help** them any time you want.	1538
Lk	1:18	"How c I **be** sure of this?	AIT
	3:8	of these stones God c **raise up** children	1538
	4:6	and *I* c **give** it to anyone I want to.	AIT
	5:12	if you are willing, *you* c **make** me clean."	1538
	5:21	Who c **forgive** sins but God alone?"	1538
	5:34	"C *you* **make** the guests of	1538
	6:39	"C a blind man lead a blind man?	1538
	6:42	How c you say to your brother, 'Brother,	1538
	7:31	c *I* **compare** the people of this generation?	AIT
	8:16	so that those who come in c **see** the light.	AIT
	9:12	so *they* c **go** to the surrounding villages	AIT
	11:18	c his kingdom **stand?**	AIT
	11:46	down with burdens *they* c **hardly carry,**	AIT
	12:4	the body and after that c do no more.	2400S
	12:25	by worrying c **add** a single hour to his life?	1538
	12:36	and knocks *they* c immediately **open**	AIT
	13:33	surely no prophet c **die** outside Jerusalem!	1896
	14:34	c it be **made salty**	AIT
	16:10	"Whoever c **be trusted** with very little can	4412
	16:10	with very little c also **be trusted** with much,	4412
	16:13	"No servant c **serve** two masters.	1538
	16:26	nor c anyone cross over from there to us.'	NIG
	17:6	*you* c **say** to this mulberry tree,	AIT
	18:26	"Who then c **be saved?"**	1538
	20:36	and *they* c **no longer die;**	1538
	20:44	How then c he be his son?"	AIT
	21:30	c **see** for yourselves and **know**	AIT
	23:15	as *you* c **see,**	2627
Jn	1:46	C anything good come from there?"	1538
	2:18	c *you* **show** us *to prove*	AIT
	3:3	no one c **see** the kingdom of God	1538
	3:4	"How c a man be born when he is old?"	1538
	3:5	no *one* c **enter** the kingdom of God	1538
	3:9	"How c **this be?"** Nicodemus asked.	1538
	3:27	"A man c **receive** only what is given him	1538
	3:28	You yourselves c **testify** that I said,	AIT
	4:9	How c *you* **ask** me for a drink?"	NIG
	4:11	Where c *you* **get** this living water?	AIT
	4:19	*"I* c **see** that you are a prophet.	2555
	5:19	the Son c **do** nothing by himself;	1538
	5:19	he c do only what he sees his Father doing,	NIG
	5:30	By myself I c do nothing;	1538
	5:44	How c you believe if you accept praise	1538
	6:42	How c he now say,	4802
	6:44	"No one c **come** to me unless	1538
	6:52	"How c this man give us his flesh to eat?"	1538
	6:60	Who c **accept** it?	1538
	6:65	"This is why I told you that no one c **come**	1538
	7:23	a child c **be circumcised** on the Sabbath so	AIT
	7:41	"How c the Christ **come** from Galilee?	AIT
	8:33	How c *you* **say** that we shall be set free?"	AIT
	8:46	C any of you **prove** me guilty	AIT
	9:4	Night is coming, when no one c **work.**	1538
	9:16	c a sinner do such miraculous signs?"	1538
	9:19	How is it that now he c **see?"**	AIT
	9:21	But how *he* c **see** now,	AIT
	9:21	you claim *you* c **see,** your guilt remains.	AIT
	10:21	C a demon open the eyes of the blind?"	1538
	10:28	no one c **snatch** them out of my hand.	AIT
	10:29	no one c **snatch** them out	AIT
	12:34	so how c *you* **say,**	AIT
	12:40	so *they* c neither **see** with their eyes,	AIT
	14:5	so how c we **know** the way?"	AIT
	14:9	How c *you* **say,** 'Show us the Father'?	AIT
	15:4	No branch c **bear fruit** by itself;	1538
	15:4	Neither c you **bear fruit** unless you remain	NIG
	15:5	apart from me *you* c **do** nothing.	1538
	16:10	where *you* c **see** me no longer;	AIT
	16:12	more than *you* c **now bear.**	1538
	16:30	Now *we* c **see** that you know all things and	3857

Ac	2:29	I c tell you confidently that	2003
	3:16	as **you** c all see.	595+5148
	8:31	"How c I," he said,	1538
	8:33	Who c **speak of** his descendants?	AIT
	10:47	"C anyone keep these people	1538
	16:36	Now **you** c leave.	AIT
	19:38	*They* c **press charges.**	AIT
	20:32	which c build you up and give you	1538
	21:24	c **have** their heads **shaved.**	AIT
	22: 5	high priest and all the Council c **testify.**	AIT
	24:11	You c easily verify	1538
	26: 5	for a long time and c testify,	NIG
	26:26	and I c speak freely to him.	NIG
	26:28	that in such a short time *you* c **persuade** me	AIT
	27:10	I c see that our voyage is going to	AIT
Ro	6: 2	how c we **live** in it any longer?	AIT
	8: 7	not submit to God's law, nor c it do so.	1538
	8:31	If God is for us, who c be against us?	NIG
	10: 2	For I c **testify** about them	AIT
	10:14	c they **call on** the one they have	AIT
	10:14	And how c they **believe in** the one	AIT
	10:14	how c they **hear** without someone preaching	AIT
	10:15	how c they **preach** unless they are sent?"	AIT
1Co	1:15	so no one c **say** that you were baptized	AIT
	3:11	For no one c lay any foundation other than	1538
	7:21	if *you* c gain your freedom, do so.	1538
	7:32	how he c **please** the Lord.	AIT
	7:33	how he c **please** his wife—	AIT
	7:34	how *she* c **please** her husband.	AIT
	10:13	be tempted beyond what *you* c bear.	1538
	10:13	also provide a way out so that you c stand	1538
	12: 3	"Jesus be cursed," and no one c say,	1538
	13: 2	of prophecy and c fathom all mysteries	NIG
	13: 2	and if I have a faith that c move mountains,	NIG
	14:16	how c one who finds himself	NIG
	14:31	For *you* c all prophesy in turn so	1538
	15:12	**how** c some of you say	4802
	16: 9	so that you c help me on my journey,	NIG
2Co	1: 4	that we c comfort those in any trouble with	1538
	1:14	that you c boast of us just as we will boast	NIG
	5:12	so that *you* c answer those who take pride	2400
	6:14	Or what fellowship c light have	NIG
	7:16	I am glad I c have complete confidence	NIG
	8:24	so that the churches c **see it.**	4725S
	9:11	that you c be generous on every occasion,	NIG
	10:16	that we c preach the gospel in the regions	NIG
Gal	3:15	Just as no one c **set aside** or add to	AIT
	4:15	I c testify that, if you could have done so,	NIG
	6: 4	Then *he* c take **pride** in himself,	AIT
Eph	1:21	**title** *that* c be **given,**	AIT
	2: 9	not by works, so that no one c **boast.**	AIT
	5: 5	For of this *you* c **be sure:**	AIT
	6:11	so that you c take your stand against	1538
	6:16	with which *you* c extinguish all	1538
Php	1: 8	God c **testify** how I long for all of you with	NIG
	1:17	that they c stir up trouble for me while I am	NIG
	4:13	I c **do** everything	2710
1Th	3: 9	How c *we* thank God enough for you	1538
1Ti	3: 5	how *he* c **take care of** God's church?)	AIT
	5:16	church c **help** those widows who are really	AIT
	6: 7	and *we* c take nothing out of it.	1538
	6:16	whom no one has seen or c see.	1538
Tit	1: 9	so that *he* c encourage others	1543+1639
	2: 4	Then *they* c **train** the younger women	AIT
	2:10	but to show that they c be fully trusted,	NIG
	3:13	Do **everything you** c to help Zenas	5081
Heb	10: 1	For this reason it c never,	1538
	10:11	which c never take away sins.	1538
	12:18	not come to a mountain that c be touched	NIG
	12:27	the removing of what c be **shaken**—	AIT
	13: 6	What c man **do** to me?"	AIT
Jas	1:21	which c save you.	1538
	2:14	C such faith save him?	1538
	3: 3	*we* c turn the whole animal.	NIG
	3: 8	but no man c tame the tongue.	1538
	3:11	C both fresh water and salt water **flow**	AIT
	3:12	My brothers, c a fig tree bear olives,	1538
	3:12	Neither c a salt spring produce fresh water.	NIG
1Pe	1: 4	into an inheritance that c **never perish,**	
		spoil or fade—	915
	4: 7	and self-controlled so that you c pray.	NIG
1Jn	3:17	**how** c the love of God be in him?	4802
	4: 2	how *you* c **recognize** the Spirit of God:	AIT
Rev	3: 7	What he opens no one c shut,	NIG
	3: 7	and what he shuts no one c open.	NIG
	3: 8	before you an open door that no one c shut.	1538
	3:18	so *you* c *become* **rich;**	AIT
	3:18	so *you* c **cover** your shameful nakedness;	AIT
	3:18	and salve to put on your eyes, so *you* c **see.**	AIT
	6:17	and who c stand?"	1538
	13: 4	Who c make war against him?"	1538

CAN'T (16) [CAN, CANNOT, NOT]

Ge	19:19	But I c flee to the mountains;	3523+4202
	29: 8	"We c," they replied, "until all	3523+4202
	34:14	They said to them, "We c do such a thing;	
			3523+4202
	34:14	we c give our sister to a man who is	NIH
Nu	13:31	"We c attack those people;	3523+4202
Jdg	9:54	so that they c say, 'A woman killed him.'"	7153
	14:13	If *you* c tell me the answer,	3523+4202
	21:18	We c give them our daughters as wives,	
			3523+4202
1Sa	17:29	"C I even speak?"	4202
	29: 8	Why c I go and fight against the enemies	3523+4202
Isa	29:11	he will answer, "I c; it is sealed."	3523+4202

Mt	27:42	they said, "but he c save himself!	1538+4024
Mk	15:31	they said, "but *he* c save himself!	1538+4024
Lk	11: 7	I c get up and give you anything.'	1538+4024
	14:20	'I just got married, so I c come.'	1538+4024
Jn	13:37	"Lord, why c I follow you now?"	1538+4024

CANA (4)

Jn	2: 1	On the third day a wedding took place at C	2830
	2:11	Jesus performed at C in Galilee.	2830
	4:46	Once more he visited C in Galilee,	2830
	21: 2	Nathanael from C in Galilee,	2830

CANAAN (84) [CANAANITE, CANAANITES]

Ge	9:18	(Ham was the father of C.)	4046
	9:22	Ham, the father of C,	4046
	9:25	he said, "Cursed be C!	4046
	9:26	May C be the slave of Shem.	4046
	9:27	and may C be his slave."	4046
	10: 6	Cush, Mizraim, Put and C.	4046
	10:15	C was the father of Sidon his firstborn,	4046
	10:19	and the borders of C reached from Sidon	4050
	11:31	from Ur of the Chaldeans to go to C.	824+4046
	12: 5	and they set out for the land of C,	4046
	13:12	Abram lived in the land of C,	4046
	16: 3	Abram had been living in C ten years,	824+4046
	17: 8	The whole land of C,	4046
	23: 2	Hebron) in the land of C,	4046
	23:19	at Hebron) in the land of C.	4046
	31:18	to go to his father Isaac in the land of C.	4046
	33:18	of Shechem in C and camped	824+4046
	35: 6	Bethel) in the land of C.	4046
	36: 2	Esau took his wives from the women of C:	4046
	36: 5	who were born to him in C.	4046
	36: 6	and all the goods he had acquired in C,	824+4046
	37: 1	where his father had stayed, the land of C.	4046
	42: 5	for the famine was in the land of C also.	4046
	42: 7	"From the land of C," they replied,	4046
	42:13	who lives in the land of C.	4046
	42:29	to their father Jacob in the land of C,	4046
	42:32	youngest is now with our father in C.'	824+4046
	44: 8	of C the silver we found inside the mouths	4046
	45:17	and return to the land of C,	4046
	45:25	to their father Jacob in the land of C.	4046
	46: 6	the possessions they had acquired in C,	824+4046
	46:12	and Onan had died in the land of C).	4046
	46:31	who were living in the land of C	4046
	47: 1	have come from the land of C and are now	4046
	47: 4	because the famine is severe in C	4046
	47:13	C wasted away because of the famine.	824+4046
	47:14	to be found in Egypt and C in payment	824+4046
	47:15	of the people of Egypt and C was gone,	824+4046
	48: 3	to me at Luz in the land of C,	4046
	48: 7	to my sorrow Rachel died in the land of C	4046
	49:30	Machpelah, near Mamre in C,	824+4046
	50: 5	the tomb I dug for myself in the land of C."	4046
	50:13	of C and buried him in the cave in the field	4046
Ex	6: 4	with them to give them the land of C,	4046
	15:15	the people of C will melt away;	4046
	16:35	until they reached the border of C.	824+4046
Lev	14:34	"When you enter the land of C,	4046
	18: 3	not do as they do in the land of C,	4046
	25:38	of Egypt to give you the land of C and to	4046
Nu	13: 2	"Send some men to explore the land of C,	4046
	13:17	When Moses sent them to explore C,	824+4046
	26:19	but they died in C.	824+4046
	32:30	possession with you in C."	4046
	32:32	over before the LORD into C armed,	824+4046
	33:40	who lived in the Negev of C,	824+4046
	33:51	'When you cross the Jordan into C,	824+4046
	34: 2	'When you enter C, the land that will	824+4046
	34:29	to the Israelites in the land of C.	4046
	35:10	'When you cross the Jordan into C,	824+4046
	35:14	on this side of the Jordan and three in C	824+4046
Dt	32:49	across from Jericho, and view C,	4046
Jos	5:12	that year they ate of the produce of C.	824+4046
	14: 1	as an inheritance in the land of C,	4046
	21: 2	at Shiloh in C and said to them,	824+4046
	22: 9	the Israelites at Shiloh in C to return	824+4046
	22:10	to Geliloth near the Jordan in the land of C,	4046
	22:11	the altar on the border of C at Geliloth	824+4046
	22:32	and the leaders returned to C	824+4046
	24: 3	the River and led him throughout C	824+4046
Jdg	3: 1	not experienced any of the wars in C	4046
	4: 2	a king of C, who reigned in Hazor.	4046
	5:19	of C fought at Taanach by the waters	4046
	21:12	took them to the camp at Shiloh in C.	824+4046
1Ch	1: 8	sons of Ham: Cush, Mizraim, Put and C.	4046
	1:13	C was the father of Sidon his firstborn,	4046
	16:18	of C as the portion you will inherit."	4046
Ps	105:11	of C as the portion you will inherit."	4046
	106:38	whom they sacrificed to the idols of C,	4046
	135:11	Og king of Bashan and all the kings of C—	4046
Isa	19:18	the language of C and swear allegiance to	4046
Ob	1:20	of Israelite exiles who are **in** C will possess	4050
Zep	2: 5	word of the LORD is against you, O C,	4046
Ac	7:11	"Then a famine struck all Egypt and C,	5913
	13:19	in C and gave their land to his people	1178+5913

CANAANITE (19) [CANAAN]

Ge	10:18	Later the C clans scattered	4050
	28: 1	"Do not marry a C woman.	4046
	28: 6	"Do not marry a C woman,"	4046
	28: 8	the C women were to his father Isaac;	4046
	38: 2	the daughter of a C man named Shua.	4050
	46:10	Zohar and Shaul the son of a C *woman.*	4050

Ex	6:15	Zohar and Shaul the son of a C *woman.*	4050
Nu	21: 1	When the C king of Arad,	4050
	33:40	The C king of Arad,	4050
Jos	5: 1	and all the C kings along the coast heard	4050
	13: 3	all of it counted as C (the territory of	4050
Jdg	1:32	of Asher lived among the C inhabitants of	4050
	1:33	among the C inhabitants of the land,	4050
	4:23	the C king, before the Israelites.	4046
	4:24	the C king, until they destroyed him.	4046
1Ki	9:16	He killed its C inhabitants and then gave it	4050
1Ch	2: 3	to him by a C *woman,*	4050
Zec	14:21	And on that day there will no longer be a C	4050
Mt	15:22	A C woman from that vicinity came	5914

CANAANITES (57) [CANAAN]

Ge	12: 6	At that time the C were in the land.	4050
	13: 7	The C and Perizzites were also living in	4050
	15:21	Amorites, C, Girgashites and Jebusites."	4050
	24: 3	for my son from the daughters of the C,	4050
	24:37	for my son from the daughters of the C,	4050
	34:30	on me by making me a stench to the C	4050
	50:11	the C who lived there saw the mourning at	4050
Ex	3: 8	the home of the C, Hittites, Amorites,	4050
	3:17	in Egypt into the land of the C,	4050
	13: 5	of the C, Hittites, Amorites, Hivites	4050
	13:11	into the land of the C and gives it to you,	4050
	23:23	Perizzites, C, Hivites and Jebusites,	4050
	23:28	C and Hittites out of your way.	4050
	33: 2	an angel before you and drive out the C,	4050
	34:11	I will drive out before you the Amorites, C,	4050
Nu	13:29	C live near the sea and along the Jordan."	4050
	14:25	Amalekites and C are living in the valleys,	4050
	14:43	the Amalekites and C will face you there.	4050
	14:45	and C who lived in that hill country came	4050
	21: 3	to Israel's plea and gave the C over	4050
Dt	1: 7	to the land of the C and to Lebanon,	4050
	7: 1	the Hittites, Girgashites, Amorites, C,	4050
	11:30	the territory of those C living in the Arabah	4050
	20:17	the Hittites, Amorites, C, Perizzites,	4050
Jos	3:10	drive out before you the C,	4050
	7: 9	The C and the other people of	4050
	9: 1	C, Perizzites, Hivites and Jebusites)—	4050
	11: 3	to the C in the east and west;	4050
	12: 8	the lands of the Hittites, Amorites, C,	4050
	13: 4	all the land of the C,	4050
	16:10	not dislodge the C living in Gezer;	4050
	16:10	the C live among the people of Ephraim	4050
	17:12	C were determined to live in that region.	4050
	17:13	they subjected the C to forced labor but did	4050
	17:16	and all the C who live in	4050
	17:18	though the C have iron chariots and	4050
	24:11	as did also the Amorites, Perizzites, C,	4050
Jdg	1: 1	to go up and fight for us against the C?"	4050
	1: 3	to fight against the C.	4050
	1: 4	the LORD gave the C and Perizzites	4050
	1: 5	putting to rout the C and Perizzites.	4050
	1: 9	against the C living in the hill country,	4050
	1:10	They advanced against the C living	4050
	1:17	and attacked the C living in Zephath,	4050
	1:27	the C were determined to live in that land.	4050
	1:28	they pressed the C into forced labor	4050
	1:29	Nor did Ephraim drive out the C living	4050
	1:29	the C continued to live there among them.	4050
	1:30	Neither did Zebulun drive out the C living	4050
	3: 3	all the C, the Sidonians,	4050
	3: 5	The Israelites lived among the C, Hittites,	4050
2Sa	24: 7	and all the towns of the Hivites and C.	4050
Ezr	9: 1	like those of the C, Hittites, Perizzites,	4050
Ne	9: 8	to his descendants the land of the C,	4050
	9:24	You subdued before them the C,	4050
	9:24	you handed **the** C over to them,	4392S
Eze	16: 3	and birth were in the land of the C;	4050

CANAL (6) [CANALS]

Ezr	8:15	I assembled them at the c that flows	5643
	8:21	There, by the Ahava C, I proclaimed a fast,	5643
	8:31	from the Ahava C to go to Jerusalem.	5643
Da	8: 2	in the vision I was beside the Ulai C.	67
	8: 3	standing beside the c,	67
	8: 6	the c and charged at him in great rage.	67

CANALS (3) [CANAL]

Ex	7:19	over the streams and c,	3284
	8: 5	with your staff over the streams and c	3284
Isa	19: 6	The c will stink;	5643

CANCEL (4) [CANCELED, CANCELING]

Dt	15: 1	of every seven years *you* must c debts.	6913+9024
	15: 2	Every creditor *shall* c	9023
	15: 3	*you* must c *any* **debt** your brother owes you.	9023
Ne	10:31	the land and will c all debts.	NIH

CANCELED (5) [CANCEL]

Mt	18:27	c the debt and let him go.	918
	18:32	'I c all that debt of yours	918
Lk	7:42	so *he* c the debts of both.	5919
	7:43	the one who *had* the bigger debt c."	5919
Col	2:14	*having* c the written code,	1981

CANCELING (3) [CANCEL]

Dt	15: 2	the LORD's **time for** c debts has been	
		proclaimed.	9024
	15: 9	"The seventh year, the year for c debts,	9024

Dt 31:10 in the year for **c** debts, 9024

CANDACE (1)
Ac 8:27 in charge of all the treasury *of* C, 2833

CANDLE (KJV) See LAMP

CANDLESTICK, CANDLESTICK (KJV)
See LAMPSTAND, LAMPSTANDS

CANE (2)
Ex 30:23 250 shekels of fragrant **c**, 7866
Zec 8: 4 each with **c** in hand because of his age. 5475

CANKER (KJV) See GANGRENE

CANKERWORM (KJV) See LOCUST, GRASSHOPPER

CANNEH (1)
Eze 27:23 C and Eden and merchants of Sheba, 4034

CANNOT (249) [CAN]
Ge 19:22 I **c** do anything until you reach it." 3523+4202
21:16 for she thought, "I **c** watch the boy die." 440
31:35 that I **c** stand up in your presence; 3523+4202
32:12 which **c** be counted.' " 4202
41:16 "I **c** do it," Joseph replied to Pharaoh, 1187
44:22 'The boy **c** leave his father; 3523+4202
44:26 But we said, 'We **c** go down. 3523+4202
44:26 We **c** see the man's face 3523+4202
47:18 "We **c** hide from our lord the fact that 4202
Ex 10: 5 They will cover the face of the ground so that it **c** be seen. 3523+4202
18:18 *you* **c** handle it alone. 4202
19:23 "The people **c** come up Mount Sinai, 3523+4202
33:20 But," he said, "*you* **c** see my face, 3523+4202
Lev 5: 7 " 'If he **c** afford a lamb, 4202
5:11 he **c** afford two doves 4202
12: 8 If she **c** afford a lamb, 4202
14:21 "If, however, he is poor and **c** afford these, 401
14:32 an infectious skin disease and who **c** afford 4202
27:33 and its substitute become holy and **c** 4202
Nu 11:14 I **c** carry all these people by myself; 3523+4202
23:20 he has blessed, and I **c** change it. 4202
31:23 And whatever **c** withstand fire must be put 4202
35:33 and atonement **c** be made for the land 4202
Dt 4:28 which **c** see or hear or eat or smell. 4202
14:24 and **c** carry your tithe 3523+4202
28:27 from which *you* **c** be cured. 3523+4202
28:35 legs with painful boils that **c** be cured, 3523+4202
Jos 7:12 Israelites **c** stand against their enemies; 3523+4202
7:13 *You* **c** stand against your enemies 3523+4202
9:19 and we **c** touch them now. 4202
Jdg 11:35 a vow to the LORD that I **c** break." 4202
Ru 4: 6 "Then I **c** redeem it 3523+4202
4: 6 I **c** do it." 3523+4202
1Sa 17:39 "I **c** go in these," he said to Saul, 3523+4202
2Sa 5: 6 They thought, "David **c** get in here." 4202
14:14 which **c** be recovered, so we must die. 4202
1Ki 8:27 even the highest heaven, **c** contain you. 4202
13:16 "I **c** turn back and go with you, 3523+4202
20: 9 but this demand I **c** meet.' " 3523+4202
2Ki 18:29 He **c** deliver you from my hand. 3523+4202
1Ch 16:30 it **c** be moved. 1153
2Ch 2: 6 even the highest heavens, **c** contain him? 4202
6:18 even the highest heavens, **c** contain you. 4202
Ezr 10:13 so we **c** stand outside. 401+3946
10:13 this matter **c** be taken care of in a day 4202
Ne 4:10 there is so much rubble that we **c** rebuild the wall." 3523+4202
6: 3 on a great project and **c** go down. 3523+4202
Est 1:19 which **c** be repealed, 4202
6:13 *you* **c** stand against him— 3523+4202
Job 5: 9 He performs wonders that **c** be fathomed, 401
5: 9 miracles that **c** be counted. 401
9:10 He performs wonders that **c** be fathomed, 401
9:10 miracles that **c** be counted. 401
9:11 When he passes me, I **c** see him; 4202
9:11 when he goes by, I **c** perceive him. 4202
9:35 but as it now stands with me, I **c**. 4202
10:15 Even if I am innocent, I **c** lift my head, 4202
12:14 What he tears down **c** be rebuilt; 4202
12:14 the man he imprisons **c** be released. 4202
14: 5 and have set limits he **c** exceed. 4202
19: 8 He has blocked my way so I **c** pass; 4202
20:13 though he **c** bear to let it go and keeps it 4202
20:20 he **c** save himself by his treasure. 4202
22:11 why it is so dark you **c** see, 4202
28:13 it **c** be found in the land of the living. 4202
28:15 It **c** be bought with the finest gold, 4202
28:16 It **c** be bought with the gold of Ophir, 4202
28:19 The topaz of Cush **c** compare with it; 4202
28:19 it **c** be bought with pure gold. 4202
33: 7 Teach me what I **c** see; 1187
37:19 we **c** draw up our case because 4202
39:13 but they **c** compare with the pinions 561
39:24 he **c** stand still when the trumpet sounds. 4202
41:17 they cling together and **c** be parted. 4202
Ps 5: 4 with you the wicked **c** dwell. 4202
5: 5 The arrogant **c** stand in your presence; 4202

Ps 21:11 and devise wicked schemes, they **c** succeed; 1153
22:29 those who **c** keep themselves alive. 4202
33:17 despite all its great strength it **c** save. 4202
38:13 I am like a deaf man, who **c** hear, 4202
38:13 like a mute, who **c** open his mouth; 4202
40:12 sins have overtaken me, and I **c** see. 3523+4202
69:23 May their eyes be darkened so they **c** see, 4946
88: 8 I am confined and **c** escape; 4202
93: 1 it **c** be moved. 1153
96:10 it **c** be moved; 1153
104: 9 You set a boundary they **c** cross; 1153
115: 5 They have mouths, but **c** speak, eyes, 4202
115: 5 but cannot speak, eyes, but they **c** see; 4202
115: 6 but **c** hear, noses, but they cannot smell; 4202
115: 6 but cannot hear, noses, but they **c** smell; 4202
115: 7 but **c** feel, feet, but they cannot walk; 4202
115: 7 but cannot feel, feet, but they **c** walk; 4202
125: 1 which **c** be shaken but endures forever. 4202
129: 7 with it the reaper **c** fill his hands, 4202
135:16 They have mouths, but **c** speak, eyes, 4202
135:16 but cannot speak, eyes, but they **c** see; 4202
135:17 but **c** hear, nor is there breath 4202
146: 3 in mortal men, who **c** save. 401
Pr 4:16 For they **c** sleep till they do evil; 4202
12: 3 man **c** be established through wickedness, 4202
12: 3 but the righteous **c** be uprooted. 1153
29:19 A servant **c** be corrected by mere words; 4202
30:21 under four *it* **c** bear up: 3523+4202
31: 8 up for those who **c** speak *for themselves*, 522
Ecc 1:15 What is twisted **c** be straightened; 3523+4202
1:15 what is lacking **c** be counted. 3523+4202
3:11 yet they **c** fathom what God has done 4202
6: 3 if he **c** enjoy his prosperity and does 4202
7:14 a man **c** discover anything about his future. 4202
8:17 man **c** discover its meaning. 4202
8:17 *he* **c** really comprehend it. 3523+4202
11: 5 so you **c** understand the work of God, 4202
SS 8: 7 Many waters **c** quench love; 3523+4202
8: 7 rivers **c** wash it away. 4202
Isa 1:13 I **c** bear your evil assemblies. 3523+4202
28:15 it **c** touch us, 4202
29:12 you give the scroll to someone *who* **c** read, 3359+4202+6219
36:14 He **c** deliver you! 3523+4202
38:18 For the grave **c** praise you, 4202
38:18 death **c** sing your praise; NIH
38:18 to the pit **c** hope for your faithfulness. 4202
44:18 their eyes are plastered over *so* they **c** see, 4946
44:18 their minds closed *so* they **c** understand. 4946
44:20 he **c** save himself, or say, 4202
45:20 who pray to gods that **c** save. 4202
46: 7 From that spot it **c** move. 4202
46: 7 it **c** save him from his troubles. 4202
47:11 that *you* **c** ward off with a ransom; 3523+4202
47:11 a catastrophe you **c** foresee will suddenly come 4202
47:14 They **c** even save themselves from 4202
48: 7 So you **c** say, 'Yes, I knew of them.' 7153
56:10 they are all mute dogs, *they* **c** bark; 3523+4202
57:20 the wicked are like the tossing sea, *which* **c** rest, 3523+4202
58: 4 You **c** fast as you do today 4202
59: 6 they **c** cover themselves 4202
59:14 in the streets, honesty **c** enter. 4202
Jer 2:13 broken cisterns that **c** hold water. 4202
4:19 My heart pounds within me, I **c** keep silent. 4202
5:22 an everlasting barrier it **c** cross. 4202
5:22 The waves may roll, but *they* **c** prevail; 4202
5:22 they may roar, but they **c** cross it. 4202
6:10 Their ears are closed *so they* **c** hear. 3523+4202
6:11 and I **c** hold it in. 4206
8:17 vipers that **c** be charmed, 401
10: 5 their idols **c** speak; 4202
10: 5 they must be carried because they **c** walk. 4202
10:10 the nations **c** endure his wrath. 4202
11:11 on them a disaster *they* **c** escape. 3523+4202
14:19 Why have you afflicted us so that we **c** 401
19:11 as this potter's jar is smashed and **c** 3523+4202
20: 9 I am weary of holding it in; indeed, I **c.** 3523+4202
23:24 in secret places so I **c** see him?" 4202
24: 3 the poor ones are so bad they **c** be eaten." 4202
24: 8 which are so bad they **c** be eaten,' 4202
29:17 like poor figs that are so bad they **c** 4202
36: 5 I **c** go to the LORD's temple. 3523+4202
46: 6 "The swift **c** flee nor the strong escape. 440
46:15 **c** stand, for the LORD will push them down. 4202
46:23 they **c** be counted. 401
49:10 so that *he* **c** conceal himself. 3523+4202
51: 9 but she **c** be healed; 4202
La 1:14 over to those I **c** withstand. 3523+4202
3: 7 He has walled me in so I **c** escape; 4202
Eze 3: 6 whose words you **c** understand. 4202
3:25 so that you **c** go out among the people. 4202
4: 8 with ropes so that you **c** turn from one side 4202
12: 6 Cover your face so that you **c** see the land, 4202
12:12 He will cover his face so that he **c** see 4202
Da 5:23 which **c** see or hear or understand. 10379
6: 8 the decree and put it in writing so that it **c** 10379
6: 8 and Persians, which **c** be repealed." 10379
6:12 and Persians, which **c** be repealed." 10379
Hos 1:10 **c** be measured or counted. 4202
2: 6 I will wall her in so that she **c** find her way. 4202
14: 3 Assyria **c** save us; 4202
Am 5:21 I **c** stand your assemblies. 4202
7:10 The land **c** bear all his words. 3523+4202
Jnh 4:11 twenty thousand people who **c** tell their right hand from their left, 4202

Mic 2: 3 from which you **c** save yourselves. 4202
Hab 1:13 *you* **c** tolerate wrong. 3523+4202
2:18 he makes idols that **c** speak. 522
Mt 5:14 A city on a hill **c** be hidden. 1538+4024
5:36 *you* **c** make even one hair white or black. 1538+4024
6:24 *You* **c** serve both God and Money. 1538+4024
7:18 A good tree **c** bear bad fruit, 1538+4024
7:18 and a bad tree **c** bear good fruit. NIG
10:28 of those who kill the body but **c** kill 1538+3590
16: 3 you **c** interpret the signs of the times. 1538+4024
26:53 Do you think I **c** call on my Father, 1538+4024
Mk 2:19 *They* **c**, so long as they have him 1538+4024
3:24 that kingdom **c** stand. 1538+4024
3:25 that house **c** stand. 1538+4024
3:26 he **c** stand; his end has come. 1538+4024
Lk 12:26 Since *you* **c** do this very little thing, 1538+4028
14:14 Although *they* **c** repay you, 2400+4024
14:26 he **c** be my disciple. 1538+4024
14:27 not carry his cross and follow me **c** 1538+4024
14:33 up everything he has **c** be my disciple. 1538+4024
16: 2 because *you* **c** be manager any longer.' 1538+4024
16:13 *You* **c** serve both God and Money." 1538+4024
16:26 who want to go from here to you **c**, 1538+3590
Jn 3: 4 "Surely *he* **c** enter a second time 1538+3590
3: 8 but *you* **c** tell where it comes from or 4024
7: 7 The world **c** hate you, 1538+4024
7:34 and where I am, you **c** come." 1538+4024
7:35 to go that we **c** find him? 4024
7:36 and 'Where I am, you **c** come'?" 1538+4024
8:21 Where I go, you **c** come." 1538+4024
8:22 'Where I go, you **c** come'?" 1538+4024
10:35 and the Scripture **c** be broken— 1538+4024
13:33 Where I am going, you **c** come. 1538+4024
13:36 "Where I am going, you **c** follow now, 1538+4024
14:17 The world **c** accept him, 1538+4024
Ac 4:16 and *we* **c** deny it. 1538+4024
4:20 For *we* **c** help speaking 1538+4024
15: 1 to the custom taught by Moses, *you* **c** 1538+4024
24:13 And *they* **c** prove to you 1538+4028
27:31 you **c** be saved." 1538+4024
Ro 6: 9 he **c** die *again*; 4033
7:18 but I **c** carry it out. 4024
8: 8 by the sinful nature **c** please God. 1538+4024
8:26 for us with groans *that* **words c** express. 227
11:10 May their eyes be darkened so they **c** see, 3590
1Co 2:14 and *he* **c** understand them, 1538+4024
7: 9 But if they **c** control themselves, 4024
9:16 when I preach the gospel, I **c** boast, 1639+4024
10:21 *You* **c** drink the cup of the Lord and the cup of demons 1538+4024
10:21 *you* **c** have a part in both the Lord's table of demons. 1538+4024
12:21 The eye **c** say to the hand, 1538+4024
12:21 And the head **c** say to the feet, NIG
15:50 flesh and blood **c** inherit the kingdom 1538+4024
2Co 1:13 not write you anything you **c** read NIG
4: 4 so that they **c** see the light of the gospel of 3590
13: 8 For *we* **c** do anything against the truth, 1538+4024
Gal 6: 7 Do not be deceived: God **c** be mocked. 4024
1Ti 6: 7 even those that are not **c** be hidden. 1538+4024
2Ti 2:13 for *he* **c** disown himself. 1538+4024
Tit 2: 8 soundness of speech *that* **c** be condemned, 183
Heb 9: 5 But we discuss these things in detail 1639+4024
12:27 so that what **c** be shaken may remain. 3590
12:28 a kingdom that **c** be shaken, 810
Jas 1:13 For God **c** be tempted by evil, 585
4: 2 but *you* **c** have what you want. 1538+4024
1Jn 3: 9 *he* **c** go on sinning, 1538+4024
4:20 **c** love God, whom he has not seen. 1538+4024
5:18 and the evil one **c** harm him. 4024
Rev 2: 2 I know that *you* **c** tolerate wicked men, 1538+4024
9:20 idols that **c** see or hear or walk. 1538+4046

CANOPY (6)
2Sa 22:12 He made darkness his **c** around him— 6109
2Ki 16:18 the Sabbath **c** that had been built at 4590
Ps 18:11 his **c** around him— 6109
Isa 4: 5 over all the glory will be a **c**. 2903
40:22 He stretches out the heavens like a **c**, 1988
Jer 43:10 he will spread his *royal* **c** above them. 9188

CAPABLE (6)
Ex 18:21 But select **c** men from all the people— 2657
18:25 He chose **c** men from all Israel 2657
1Ch 26: 6 because they were very **c** men. 1475+2657
26: 8 and their relatives were **c** men with 2657
26:31 and **c** men among 1475+2657
Ezr 8:18 they brought us Sherebiah, a **c** man, 8507

CAPERNAUM (16)
Mt 4:13 Leaving Nazareth, he went and lived in C, 3019
8: 5 When Jesus had entered C, 3019
11:23 you, C, will you be lifted up to the skies? 3019
17:24 After Jesus and his disciples arrived in C, 3019
Mk 1:21 They went to C, 3019
2: 1 when Jesus again entered C, 3019
9:33 They came to C. 3019
Lk 4:23 that you did in C.' " 3019
4:31 Then he went down to C, 3019
7: 1 in the hearing of the people, he entered C. 3019
10:15 you, C, will you be lifted up to the skies? 3019
Jn 2:12 down to C with his mother and brothers 3019
4:46 And there was a certain royal official whose son lay sick at C. 3019

Jn 6:17 into a boat and set off across the lake for C. 3019
  6:24 the boats and went to C in search of Jesus. 3019
  6:59 while teaching in the synagogue in C. 3019

CAPES (1)
Isa 3:22 the fine robes and the c and cloaks, 5074

CAPHTOR (3) [CAPHTORITES]
Dt 2:23 from C destroyed them and settled 4116
Jer 47:4 the remnant from the coasts of C. 4116
Am 9:7 the Philistines from C and the Arameans 4116

CAPHTORITES (3) [CAPHTOR]
Ge 10:14 (from whom the Philistines came) and C. 4118
Dt 2:23 the C coming out from Caphtor 4118
1Ch 1:12 (from whom the Philistines came) and C. 4118

CAPITAL (7) [CAPITALS]
Dt 21:22 If a man guilty of a c offense is put to death 4638+5477
1Ki 7:16 each c was five cubits high. 4196
  7:17 seven for each c. 4196
  7:18 He did the same for each c. 4196
2Ki 25:17 The bronze c on top of one pillar was four 4196
2Ch 3:15 each with a c on top measuring five cubits. 7633
Jer 52:22 The bronze c on top of 4196

CAPITALS (12) [CAPITAL]
1Ki 7:16 He also made two c of cast bronze to set on 4196
  7:17 of interwoven chains festooned the c on top 4196
  7:18 to decorate the c on top of the pillars 4196
  7:19 The c on top of the pillars in 4196
  7:20 On the c of both pillars, 4196
  7:22 The c on top were in the shape of lilies. NIH
  7:41 the two bowl-shaped c on top of the pillars; 4196
  7:41 the two bowl-shaped c on top of the pillars; 4196
  7:42 the bowl-shaped c on top of the pillars); 4196
2Ch 4:12 the two bowl-shaped c on top of the pillars; 4196
  4:12 the two bowl-shaped c on top of the pillars; 4196
  4:13 the bowl-shaped c on top of the pillars); 4196

CAPPADOCIA (2)
Ac 2:9 residents of Mesopotamia, Judea and C, 2838
1Pe 1:1 scattered throughout Pontus, Galatia, C, 2838

CAPSTONE (7) [STONE]
Ps 118:22 The stone the builders rejected has become the c; 7157+8031
Zec 4:7 Then he will bring out the c to shouts 74+8036
Mt 21:42 " 'The stone the builders rejected has become the c; 1224+3051
Mk 12:10 " 'The stone the builders rejected has become the c; 1224+3051
Lk 20:17 " 'The stone the builders rejected has become the c'? 1224+3051
Ac 4:11 " 'the stone you builders rejected, which has become the c.' 1224+3051
1Pe 2:7 " 'The stone the builders rejected has become the c," 1224+3051

CAPTAIN (22) [CAPTAINS]
Ge 37:36 the c of the guard. 8569
  39:1 the c of the guard, 8569
  40:3 in custody in the house of the c of 8569
  40:4 The c of the guard assigned them 8569
  41:10 and the chief baker in the house of the c of 8569
  41:12 a servant of the c of the guard. 8569
1Sa 22:14 c of your bodyguard and highly respected 6233
2Ki 1:9 a c with his company of fifty men. 2822+8569
  1:9 The c went up to Elijah, NIH
  1:10 Elijah answered the c, 2822+8569
  1:10 and consumed the c and his men. 2257S
  1:11 this the king sent to Elijah another c 2822+8569
  1:11 The c said to him, "Man of God, NIH
  1:13 king sent a third c with his fifty men. 2822+8569
  1:13 third c went up and fell on his knees 2822+8569
Isa 3:3 the c of fifty and man of rank, 8569
Jer 37:13 the c of the guard, 1251
Jnh 1:6 The c went to him and said, 2021+2480+8042
Ac 4:1 The priests and the c of the temple guard 5130
  5:24 the c of the temple guard and 5130
  5:26 the c went with his officers and brought 5130
Rev 18:17 "Every sea c, and all who travel by ship, 3237

CAPTAINS (4) [CAPTAIN]
Jdg 5:14 From Makir c came down, 2980
1Ki 9:22 his government officials, his officers, his c, 8957
2Ki 1:14 and consumed the first two c 2822+8569
2Ch 8:9 commanders of his c, 8957

CAPTIVATE (1) [CAPTURE]
Pr 6:25 after her beauty or let her c you 4374

CAPTIVATED (2) [CAPTURE]
Pr 5:19 may you ever be c by her love. 8706
  5:20 Why be c, my son, by an adulteress? 8706

CAPTIVE (43) [CAPTURE]
Ge 14:14 that his relative had been taken c, 8647
Nu 24:22 be destroyed when Asshur takes you c." 8647
Dt 1:39 little ones that you said would be taken c, 1020
Jdg 5:12 Take c your captives, O son of Abinoam.' 8647
1Sa 30:2 and had taken c the women 8647
  30:3 and sons and daughters taken c. 8647
1Ki 8:46 who takes them c to his own land, 8647+8647
  8:47 the land where they are held c, and repent 8647
  8:48 of their enemies who took them c, and pray 8647
  20:39 and someone came to me with a c and said, 408
2Ki 5:2 from Aram had gone out and had taken c 8647
  17:27 "Have one of the priests you took c 1655
  24:15 Nebuchadnezzar took Jehoiachin c 1655
1Ch 3:17 The descendants of Jehoiachin the c: 660
  5:21 also took one hundred thousand people c, NIH
  9:1 of Judah were taken c to Babylon because 1655
2Ch 6:36 who takes them c to a land far away or near; 8647+8647
  6:37 the land where they are held c, and repent 8647
  28:8 The Israelites took c 8647
Ezr 2:1 king of Babylon had taken c 1655
Ne 7:6 king of Babylon had taken c 1655
Est 2:6 among those taken c with Jehoiachin king 1655
Ps 69:33 and does not despise his c people. 659
  106:46 to be pitied by all who held them c. 8647
SS 7:5 the king is held c by its tresses. 673
Isa 52:2 O c Daughter of Zion. 8665
Jer 13:17 the LORD's flock will be taken c. 8647
  22:12 in the place where they have led him c; 1655
  41:10 Ishmael son of Nethaniah took them c 8647
  41:14 All the people Ishmael had taken c 8647
  43:12 and take their gods c. 8647
  48:7 you too will be taken c, 4334
La 1:5 c before the foe. NIH
Eze 6:9 the nations where they have been carried c, 8647
  21:23 of their guilt and take them c. 9530
  21:24 you have done this, you will be taken c. 928+2021+4090+9530
Am 1:6 Because she took c whole communities 1655
Na 3:10 Yet she was taken c and went into exile. 1583
Hab 2:5 to himself all the nations and takes c all 7695
Ac 8:23 you are full of bitterness and c to sin." 5278
2Co 10:5 and we take c every thought 170
Col 2:8 See to it that no one takes you c through hollow and deceptive 1639+5194
2Ti 2:26 who has taken them c to do his will. 2436

CAPTIVES (25) [CAPTURE]
Ge 31:26 and you've carried off my daughters like c 8647
Nu 21:29 and his daughters as c to Sihon king of 8669
  31:12 and brought the c, 8660
  31:19 third and seventh days you must purify yourselves and your c. 8660
Dt 21:10 into your hands and you take c, 8647+8660
  21:11 the c a beautiful woman and are attracted 8664
  32:42 the blood of the slain and the c, 8664
Jdg 5:12 Take captive your c, O son of Abinoam.' 8660
Job 3:18 C also enjoy their ease; 659
Ps 68:18 you led c in your train; 8660
  126:1 the LORD brought back the c to Zion, 8860
Isa 10:4 but to cringe among the c or fall among 660
  14:2 They will make c of their captors and rule 8647
  14:17 and would not let his c go home?" 659
  20:4 the Egyptian c and Cushite exiles, young 8660
  42:7 to free c from prison and to release from 660
  49:9 to say to the c, 673
  49:24 or c rescued from the fierce? 8660
  49:25 "Yes, c will be taken from warriors, 8660
  61:1 to proclaim freedom for the c and release 8647
Jer 40:1 in chains among all the c from Jerusalem 1661
  41:10 Ishmael made c of all the rest of 8647
Eze 12:11 They will go into exile as c. 8660
Am 1:6 she sold whole communities of c to Edom, 1661
Eph 4:8 he led c in his train; 168+169

CAPTIVITY (32) [CAPTURE]
Dt 28:41 because they will go into c. 8660
Jdg 18:30 for the tribe of Dan until the time of the c 1655
2Ki 25:21 So Judah went into c, away from her land. 1655
2Ch 6:37 and plead with you in the land of their c 8660
  6:38 of their c where they were taken, and pray 8660
  29:9 and daughters and our wives are in c. 8660
Ezr 2:1 of the province who came up from the c of 8660
  3:8 from the c to Jerusalem) began the work, 8660
  8:35 from c sacrificed burnt offerings to the God 8660
  9:7 to the sword and c, 8660
Ne 4:4 Give them over as plunder in a land of c. 8664
  7:6 of the province who came up from the c of 8660
Ps 78:61 He sent [the ark of] his might into c, 8660
  144:14 no going into c, 3448
Isa 46:2 they themselves go off into c. 8660
Jer 15:2 those for c, to captivity.' 8660
  15:2 those for captivity, to c.' 8660
  29:14 "and will bring you back from c. 8654
  30:3 and Judah back from c and restore them to 8654
  31:23 "When I bring them back from c, 8654
  33:7 I will bring Judah and Israel back from c 8654
  43:11 c to those destined for captivity, 8660
  43:11 captivity to those destined for c, 8660
  48:46 into exile and your daughters into c. 8660
  52:27 So Judah went into c, away from her land. 1655
La 2:14 not expose your sin to ward off your c. 8654
Eze 29:14 from c and return them to Upper Egypt, 8654
  30:17 and the cities themselves will go into c. 8660
  30:18 and her villages will go into c. 8660
  39:25 from c and will have compassion on all 8654

Rev 13:10 If anyone is to go into c, 168
  13:10 into c he will go. 168

CAPTORS (4) [CAPTURE]
2Ch 30:9 by their c and will come back to this land, 8647
Ps 137:3 for there our c asked us for songs, 8647
Isa 14:2 They will make captives of their c and rule 8647
Jer 50:33 All their c hold them fast, 8647

CAPTURE (19) [CAPTIVATE, CAPTIVATED, CAPTIVE, CAPTIVES, CAPTIVITY, CAPTORS, CAPTURED, CAPTURES, CAPTURING, RECAPTURE, RECAPTURED]
Dt 20:19 fighting against it to c it, 9530
1Sa 4:21 of the c of the ark of God and the deaths 4374
  19:14 When Saul sent the men to c David, 4374
  19:20 so he sent men to c him. 4374
  23:26 in on David and his men to c them, 9530
2Sa 12:28 of the troops and besiege the city and c it. 4334
2Ki 6:13 "so I can send men and c him." 4374
2Ch 32:18 and make them afraid in order to c the city. 4334
Job 40:24 Can anyone c him by the eyes, 4374
Jer 18:22 to c me and have hidden snares for my feet. 4334
  32:3 and he will c it. 4334
  32:28 of Babylon, who will c it. 4334
  37:8 they will c it and burn it down.' 4334
  38:3 of the king of Babylon, who will c it.' " 4334
  50:46 of Babylon's c the earth will tremble; 9530
Da 11:15 up siege ramps and will c a fortified city. 4334
Hab 1:10 they build earthen ramps and c them. 4334
Mt 26:55 with swords and clubs to c me? 5197
Mk 14:48 with swords and clubs to c me? 5197

CAPTURED (75) [CAPTURE]
Nu 21:1 he attacked the Israelites and c some 8647+8660
  21:25 Israel c all the cities of the Amorites 4374
  21:32 the Israelites c its surrounding settlements 4334
  31:9 The Israelites c the Midianite women 8647
  31:26 the people and animals that were c. 8660
  32:39 c it and drove out the Amorites 4334
  32:41 of Manasseh, c their settlements 4334
  32:42 And Nobah c Kenath 4334
Dt 2:35 from the towns we had c we carried off 4334
  21:13 the clothes she was wearing when c. 8660
Jos 8:19 the city and c it and quickly set it on fire. 4334
  10:35 They c it that same day and put it to 4334
  11:10 and c Hazor and put its king to the sword. 4334
  11:17 He c all their kings and struck them down, 4334
Jdg 7:25 They also c two of the Midianite leaders, 4334
  8:12 fled, but he pursued them and c them, 4334
  9:45 city until he had c it and killed its people. 4334
  9:50 to Thebez and besieged it and c it. 4334
  12:5 The Gileadites c the fords of 4334
1Sa 4:11 The ark of God was c, and Eli's two sons, 4374
  4:17 are dead, and the ark of God has been c." 4374
  4:19 the ark of God had been c and that her father-in-law 4374
  4:22 for the ark of God has been c." 4374
  5:1 After the Philistines had c the ark of God, 4374
  7:14 to Gath that the Philistines had c 4374
  30:5 David's two wives had been c— 8647
2Sa 8:4 David c a thousand of his chariots, 4334
  12:26 of the Ammonites and c the royal citadel. 4334
   and attacked and c it. 4334
1Ki 9:16 of Egypt had attacked and c Gezer. 4334
2Ki 6:22 "Would you kill men you have c 8647
  12:17 up and attacked Gath and c it. 4334
  14:7 in the Valley of Salt and c Sela in battle, 9530
  14:13 Jehoash king of Israel c Amaziah king 9530
  17:6 the king of Assyria c Samaria and deported 4334
  18:10 So Samaria was c in Hezekiah's sixth year, 4334
  18:13 the fortified cities of Judah and c them. 9530
  25:6 and he was c. 9530
1Ch 2:23 (But Geshur and Aram c Havvoth Jair, 4374
  11:5 Nevertheless, David c the fortress of Zion, 4334
  18:4 David c a thousand of his chariots, 4334
2Ch 8:3 then went to Hamath Zobah and c it. 2616
  12:4 he c the fortified cities of Judah and came 4334
  15:8 and Benjamin and from the towns he had c 4334
  17:2 of Ephraim that his father Asa had c. 4334
  22:9 and his men c him while he was hiding 8647
  25:12 of Judah also c ten thousand men alive, 4334
  25:23 Jehoash king of Israel c Amaziah king 9530
  28:18 They c and occupied Beth Shemesh, 4334
Ne 9:25 They c fortified cities and fertile land; 4334
Isa 8:15 they will be snared and c." 4334
  13:15 Whoever is c will be thrust through; 5162
  20:1 came to Ashdod and attacked and c it— 4334
  22:3 they have been c without using the bow. 673
  28:13 be injured and snared and c, 4334
  36:1 the fortified cities of Judah and c them. 9530
Jer 10:18 on them so that they may be c." 5162
  34:3 but will surely be c and handed over 9530+9530
  38:23 from their hands but will be c by the king 9530
  38:28 of the guard until the day Jerusalem was c. 4334
  39:5 They c him and took him 4374
  48:1 Kiriathaim will be disgraced and c; 4334
  48:41 Kerioth will be c and 4334
  50:2 but say, 'Babylon will be c; 4334
  50:9 and from the north she will be c. 4334
  50:24 you were found and c because you opposed 9530

Jer	51:31	the king of Babylon that his entire city **is c,** 4334
	51:41	"How Sheshach *will* **be c,** 4334
	51:56	her warriors *will* **be c,** 4334
	52: 9	and he *was* **c.** 9530
Da	11:33	the sword or be burned or **c** or plundered. 8660
Am	4:10	along with your **c** horses. 8660
Zec	14: 2	the city *will* **be c,** the houses ransacked, 4334
Rev	19:20	But the beast *was* **c,** 4389

CAPTURES (2) [CAPTURE]
Jos	15:16	the man who attacks and **c** Kiriath Sepher." 4334
Jdg	1:12	the man who attacks and **c** Kiriath Sepher." 4334

CAPTURING (2) [CAPTURE]
Jdg	11:22	**c** all of it from the Arnon to the Jabbok and 3769
2Ki	16: 9	by attacking Damascus and **c** it. 9530

CAR See BETH CAR

CARAVAN (3) [CARAVANS]
Ge	37:25	a **c** of Ishmaelites coming from Gilead. 785
1Ki	10: 2	Arriving at Jerusalem with a very great **c—** 2657
2Ch	9: 1	Arriving with a very great **c—** 2657

CARAVANS (3) [CARAVAN]
Job	6:18	**C** turn aside from their routes; 785
	6:19	The **c** of Tema look for water, 785
Isa	21:13	You **c** of Dedanites, 785

CARAWAY (3)
Isa	28:25	does he not sow **c** and scatter cummin? 7902
	28:27	**C** is not threshed with a sledge, 7902
	28:27	**c** is beaten out with a rod, 7902

CARBUNCLE, CARBUNCLES (KJV)
See BERYL, JEWELS

CARCAS (1)
Est	1:10	Harbona, Bigtha, Abagtha, Zethar and **C—** 4139

CARCASE, CARCASES (KJV) See
CARCASSES, BODIES, CORPSES

CARCASS (9) [CARCASSES]
Lev	11:26	whoever touches [the **c** of] any of them will NIH
	11:37	a **c** falls on any seeds that are to be planted, 5577
	11:38	on the seed and a **c** falls on it, 5577
	11:39	anyone who touches the **c** will be unclean 5577
	11:40	of the **c** must wash his clothes, 5577
	11:40	up the **c** must wash his clothes, 5577
Jdg	14: 8	he turned aside to look at the lion's **c.** 5147
	14: 9	the honey from the lion's **c.** 1581
Mt	24:28	Wherever there is a **c,** 4773

CARCASSES (15) [CARCASS]
Ge	15:11	Then birds of prey came down on the **c,** 7007
Lev	5: 2	whether the **c** of unclean wild animals or 5577
	11: 8	not eat their meat or touch their **c;** 5577
	11:11	and you must detest their **c.** 5577
	11:24	whoever touches their **c** will be unclean 5577
	11:25	up one of their **c** must wash his clothes, 5577
	11:27	whoever touches their **c** will be unclean 5577
	11:28	up their **c** must wash his clothes, 5577
	11:35	of their **c** falls on becomes unclean; 5577
	11:36	of these **c** is unclean. 5577
Dt	14: 8	not to eat their meat or touch their **c.** 5577
	28:26	Your **c** will be food for all the birds of 5577
1Sa	17:46	the **c** of the Philistine army to the birds of 7007
Jer	7:33	Then the **c** *of* this people will become food 5577
	19: 7	and I will give their **c** as food to the birds 5577

CARCHEMISH (3)
2Ch	35:20	Neco king of Egypt went up to fight at **C** 4138
Isa	10: 9	'Has not Calno fared like **C?** 4138
Jer	46: 2	of Egypt, which was defeated at **C** on 4138

CARE (91) [CARED, CAREFREE, CAREFUL, CAREFULLY, CARELESS, CARELESSLY, CARES, CARING]
Ge	2:15	the Garden of Eden to work it and **take c of** 9068
	30:29	how your livestock has fared **under** my **c.** 907
	30:35	and he placed them in the **c** *of* his sons. 3338
	32:16	He put them in the **c** of his servants, 3338
	33:13	and that I must **c for** the ewes and cows 6584
	39: 4	he entrusted to his **c** everything he owned. 3338
	39: 6	So he left in Joseph's **c** everything he had; 3338
	39: 8	everything he owns he has entrusted to my **c** 3338
	39:23	to anything under Joseph's **c,** 3338
	42:37	Entrust him to my **c,** 3338
Ex	12: 6	**Take c of** them until the fourteenth day 2118+4200+5466
Lev	6: 2	to him or left in his **c** or stolen, 3338
	16:21	into the desert in the **c** *of* a man appointed 3338
Nu	1:50	*to* **take c of** it and encamp around it. 9250
	1:53	be responsible for the **c** of the tabernacle of 5466
	3: 8	*They are to* **take c of** all the furnishings of 9068
	3:25	the Gershonites were **responsible for** the **c** 5466

Nu	3:28	The Kohathites were responsible for the **c** 9068
	3:31	They were **responsible for** the **c** *of* the ark, 5466
	3:32	over *those who* were responsible for the **c** 9068
	3:36	The Merarites were appointed to **take c of** 5466
	3:38	for the **c** of the sanctuary on behalf of 9068
	4: 4	the **c** of the most holy things. NIH
	18: 4	to join you and be responsible for the **c** of 5466
	18: 5	to be responsible for the **c** *of* the sanctuary 5466
	31:30	for the **c** of the LORD's tabernacle." 5466
	31:47	for the **c** of the LORD's tabernacle. 5466
Dt	7:11	Therefore, **take c** to follow the commands, 9068
2Sa	15:16	but he left ten concubines to **take c of** 9068
	16:21	to **take c of** the palace. 9068
	18: 3	*they* won't **c about** us. 448+4213+8492
	18: 3	if half of us die, *they* won't **c;** 448+4213+8492
	19:24	*He had* not **taken c** of his feet 6913
	20: 3	the ten concubines he had left to **take c of** 9068
1Ki	1: 2	to attend the king and **take c of** him. 2118+6125
	1: 4	*she* **took c of** the king and waited on him, 2118+6125
2Ki	9:34	**"Take c of** that cursed woman," he said, 7212
1Ch	9:29	to **take c of** the furnishings and all 6584
	9:30	the priests **took c of** mixing the spices. 5351+8379
	26:28	the other dedicated things were in the **c** 3338
	27:32	of Hacmoni **took c of** the king's sons. 6640
2Ch	25:24	the temple of God that had been **in the c of** 6640
	32:22	*He* **took c of** them on every side. 5633
Ezr	10:13	this matter cannot be taken **c** of in a day NIH
Est	2: 3	Let them be placed under the **c** of Hegai, 3338
	2: 8	to the citadel of Susa and put under the **c** 3338
	2:14	to another part of the harem to the **c** 3338
Job	3: 4	*may* God above not **c** about it; 2011
	21:21	For what does he **c** about 2914
Ps	8: 4	the son of man that *you* **c** for him? 7212
	65: 9	*You* **c for** the land and water it; 7212
	88: 5	who are cut off from your **c.** 3338
	95: 7	the flock **under** his **c.** 3338
	144: 3	O LORD, what is man that *you* **c for** him, 3359
Pr	29: 7	The righteous **c about** justice for the poor, 3359
SS	1: 6	and made me **take c of** the vineyards; 5757
Isa	13:17	who do not **c for** silver and have no delight 3108
	34:15	and **c for** *her* young under the shadow 1842
Jer	6:20	What do I **c** about 2296+3276+4200+4200+4537
	15:15	remember me and **c for** me. 7212
	23: 2	and *have* not **bestowed c** on them, 7212
	30:14	*they* **c** nothing **for** you. 2011
Eze	34: 2	the shepherds of Israel who *only* **take c of** 8286
	34: 2	*Should* not shepherds **take c of** the flock? 8286
	34: 3	but *you* do not **take c of** the flock. 8286
Hos	14: 8	I will answer him and **c for** him. 8800
Am	7:14	and I also took **c of** sycamore-fig trees. 1179
Mic	2: 8	from those who pass by **without a c,** 1055
Zep	2: 7	The LORD their God *will* **c for** them; 7212
Zec	10: 3	the LORD Almighty *will* **c for** his flock, 7212
	11:16	a shepherd over the land *who will* not **c for** 7212
Mt	27:55	from Galilee to **c for** his needs. 1354
Mk	4:38	"Teacher, don't *you* **c** if we drown?" 3508
	5:26	She had suffered a great deal under the **c** NIG
Lk	10:34	took him to an inn and **took c of** him. 2150
	10:40	don't you **c** that my sister has left me to do 3508
	13: 7	**took c of the vineyard,** 307
	15: 7	though I don't fear God or **c about** men, 1956
Jn	21:16	Jesus said, **"Take c of** my sheep." 4477
Ac	9:34	**take c of** *your* mat." 4932+5143
	13:40	**Take c** that what 1063
	24:23	**take c of his needs.** 5676
1Co	4: 3	I **c** very little if I am judged by you 1639+1650+1788
Php	2:25	whom you sent to **take c of** my needs. 3313
1Ti	3: 5	how **can he take c of** God's church?) 2150
	6:20	what has been **entrusted to** *your* **c.** 4146
Heb	2: 6	the son of man that *you* **c for** him? 2170
1Pe	1:10	**searched intently and with the greatest c,** 1699+2001+2779
	5: 2	that is under your **c,** serving as overseers— NIG
Rev	12: 6	where she *might* be **taken c of** for 1,260 5555
	12:14	where she *would* be **taken c of** for a time, 5555

CAREAH (KJV) See KAREAH

CARED (11) [CARE]
Dt	32:10	He shielded him and **c for** him; 1067
Ru	4:16	laid him in her lap and **c for** him. 587
La	2:20	the children they have **c for?** 3259
	2:22	those *I* **c for** and reared, 3254
Eze	34: 8	not search for my flock but **c for** 8286
Hos	12:13	by a prophet *he* **c for** *him.* 9068
	13: 5	I **c for** you in the desert, 3359
Mk	15:41	and **c for** his needs. 1354
Lk	18: 2	nor **c about** men. 1956
Jn	12: 6	not say this because he **c about** the poor but 3508
Ac	7:20	For three months he *was* **c for** 427

CAREFREE (3) [CARE]
Ps	73:12	always **c,** they increase in wealth. 8929
Eze	23:42	"The noise of a **c** crowd was around her; 8929
Zep	2:15	This is the **c** city that lived in safety. 6611

CAREFUL (78) [CARE]
Ge	31:24	**"Be c** not to say anything to Jacob, 9068
	31:29	'**Be c** not to say anything to Jacob, 9068
Ex	19:12	'Be **c** *that* you do not go up the mountain 9068
	23:13	"Be **c to do** everything I have said to you. 9068
	34:12	Be **c** not to make a treaty 9068

Ex	34:15	"Be **c** not to make a treaty NIH
Lev	18: 4	You must obey my laws and be **c** 9068
	25:18	" 'Follow my decrees and be **c** 9068
	26: 3	" 'If you follow my decrees and are **c** 9068
Dt	2: 4	They will be afraid of you, but be very **c.** 9068
	4: 9	Only be **c,** and watch yourselves closely so 9068
	4:23	Be **c** not to forget the covenant of 9068
	5:32	So be **c** to do what 9068
	6: 3	and be **c** to obey so that it may go well 9068
	6:12	be **c** that you do not forget the LORD, 9068
	6:25	And if *we are* **c** to obey all this law before 9068
	7:12	If you pay attention to these laws and *are* **c** 9068
	8: 1	**Be c** to follow every command I am giving you today, 9068
	8:11	Be **c** that you do not forget 9068
	11:16	Be **c,** or you will be enticed to turn away 9068
	12: 1	be **c** to follow in the land that the LORD, 9068
	12:13	Be **c** not to sacrifice 9068
	12:19	Be **c** not to neglect the Levites as long 9068
	12:28	Be **c** to obey all these regulations I am giving you, 9068
	12:30	be **c** not to be ensnared by inquiring 9068
	15: 5	the LORD your God and *are* **c** 9068
	15: 9	Be **c** not to harbor this wicked thought: 9068
	17:10	Be **c** to do everything they direct you 9068
	24: 8	leprous diseases be very **c** to do exactly as the priests, 9068+9068
Jos	1: 7	Be **c** to obey all the law 9068
	1: 8	*you may* be **c** to do everything written in it. 9068
	22: 5	But be very **c** to keep the commandment 9068
	23: 6	be **c** to obey all that is written in the Book 9068
	23:11	So *be* very **c** to love the LORD your God. 9068
1Ki	2: 4	if only your sons *are* **c** in all they do 9068
2Ki	10:31	Yet Jehu *was* not **c** to keep the law of 9068
	17:37	*You must* always *be* **c** to keep the decrees 9068
	21: 8	*be* **c** to do everything I commanded them 9068
1Ch	22:13	Then you will have success if *you are* **c** 9068
	28: 8	*Be* **c** to follow all the commands of 9068
2Ch	6:16	if only your sons *are* **c** in all they do 9068
	33: 8	*be* **c** to do everything I commanded them 9068
Ezr	4:22	Be **c** not to neglect this matter. 10224
Job	36:18	Be **c** that no one entices you by riches; 2778
Ps	101: 2	*I will be* **c** to lead a blameless life— 8505
Pr	13:24	he who loves him *is* **c** to discipline him. 8838
	27:23	give **c attention** to your herds; 4213
Isa	7: 4	Say to him, '*Be* **c,** 9068
Jer	17:21	*Be* **c** not to carry a load on the Sabbath day 9068
	17:24	But if *you are* **c to obey** me, 9048+9048
	22: 4	if *you are* **c to carry out** these commands, 6913+6913
Eze	11:20	Then they will follow my decrees and *be* **c** 9068
	18:19	and *has been* **c** to keep all my decrees, 9068
	20:19	follow my decrees and *be* **c** 9068
	20:21	*they were* not **c** to keep my laws— 9068
	36:27	to follow my decrees and *be* **c** 9068
	37:24	They will follow my laws and *be* **c** 9068
Mic	7: 5	with *her* who lies in your embrace *be* **c** 9068
Hag	1: 5	**"Give c thought** to your ways. 4222+8492
	1: 7	**"Give c thought** to your ways. 4222+8492
	2:15	" 'Now **give c thought** to this 4222+8492
	2:18	**give c thought** to the day when 4222+8492
	2:18	**Give c thought:** 4222+8492
Mt	2: 8	"Go and make a **c** search for the child. 209
	6: 1	"Be **c** not to do your 'acts of righteousness' 4668
	16: 6	"Be **c,**" Jesus said to them. 3972
Mk	8:15	"Be **c,**" Jesus warned them. 3972
Lk	17:20	not come with your **c observation,** 4191
	21:34	"Be **c,** or your hearts will be weighed down 4668
Ro	12:17	Be **c,** to do what is right in the eyes 4629
1Co	3:10	But each one *should be* **c** how he builds. 1063
	8: 9	Be **c,** however, that the exercise 1063
	10:12	*be* **c** that you don't fall! 1063
Eph	5:15	Be very **c,** then, how you live— 209
2Ti	4: 2	with great patience and **c instruction.** 1439
Tit	3: 8	in God *may be* **c** to devote themselves 5863
Heb	2: 1	We must pay **more** attention, therefore, 4359
	4: 1	*let us be* **c** that none of you be found 5828

CAREFULLY (41) [CARE]
Ge	27: 8	my son, **listen c** and do what I tell you: 928+7754+9048
Ex	15:26	"If *you* **listen c** to the voice of 9048+9048
	23:22	If *you* **listen c** to what he says and do 9048+9048
Dt	4: 6	Observe them **c,** for this will show your wisdom 9068
	4:15	**watch** yourselves very **c,** 9068
	11:22	If *you* **c observe** all these commands I am giving you 9068+9068
	16:12	and follow **c** these decrees. 9068
	17:19	and follow **c** all the words of this law 9068
	19: 9	*you* **c** follow all these laws I command you today— 9068
	24: 8	You must follow **c** what I have commanded 9068
	26:16	**c** observe them with all your heart and 9068
	28: 1	**c** follow all his commands I give you today, 9068
	28:13	that I give you this day and follow them, 9068
	28:15	and do not **c** follow all his commands 9068
	28:58	not **c** follow all the words of this law, 9068
	29: 9	**C** follow the terms of this covenant, 9068
	31:12	and follow **c** all the words of this law. 9068
Jos	8: 4	with these orders: "**Listen c.** 8011
Jdg	6:29	When *they* **c investigated,** 1335+2011+2256
2Ch	19: 6	He told them, "**Consider c** what you do, 8011
	19: 7	Judge **c,** for with the LORD our God there is no injustice 9068

Ezr	8:29	Guard them c until you weigh them out in	9068
Ne	10:29	of God and to obey c all the commands,	9068
Job	13:17	**Listen c** to my words;	9048+9048
	21: 2	"**Listen c** to my words;	9048+9048
Eze	3:10	listen c and take to heart all	265+928+9048
	44: 5	"Son of man, **look c,**	928+6524+8011
Da	10:11	**consider c** the words I am about to speak	1067
Mk	4:24	"**Consider c** what you hear," he continued.	1063
Lk	1: 3	I myself have c investigated everything	209
	4:10	concerning you *to guard* you c;	1428+3836
	8:18	Therefore **consider c** how you listen.	1063
	9:44	"**Listen c** to what I am about to tell you:	1650+3836+4044+5148+5148+5502
	14: 1	he was *being* c **watched.**	4190
	15: 8	the house and search c until she finds it?	2151
Ac	2:14	**listen c** to what I say.	1969
	5:35	"Men of Israel, **consider c** what you intend	4668
	16:23	the jailer was commanded to guard them c.	857
	17:23	and **looked c at** your objects of worship, I	355
1Co	14:29	and the others *should* **weigh c** what is said.	1359

CARELESS (1) [CARE]
Mt	12:36	for every c word they have spoken.	734

CARELESSLY (1) [CARE]
Lev	5: 4	in any matter one *might* c swear about—	1051

CARES (12) [CARE]
Dt	11:12	It is a land the LORD your God c for;	2011
Job	39:16	she c not that her labor was in vain,	7065
Ps	55:22	Cast your c on the LORD	3365
	142: 4	I have no refuge; no *one* c for my life.	2011
Pr	12:10	A righteous man c **for** the needs	2011
Ecc	5: 3	As a dream comes when there are many c,	6721
Jer	12:11	be laid waste because there is no one *who* c.	4213+6584+8492
	30:17	Zion for whom no *one* c.'	2011
Na	1: 7	*He* c **for** those who trust in him,	3359
Jn	10:13	a hired hand and c nothing for the sheep.	3508
Eph	5:29	but *he* feeds and c **for** it,	2499
1Pe	5: 7	Cast all your anxiety on him because he c	3508

CARESSED (3) [CARESSING]
Eze	23: 3	and their virgin bosoms c.	6914
	23: 8	c her virgin bosom	6914
	23:21	when in Egypt your bosom *was* c	6914

CARESSING (1) [CARESSED]
Ge	26: 8	and saw Isaac c his wife Rebekah.	7464

CARGO (5) [CARGOES]
Eze	27:25	You are filled with **heavy** c in the heart of	AIT
Jnh	1: 5	And they threw the c into the sea to lighten	641+889+928+2021+3998
Ac	21: 3	where our ship was to unload its c.	1203
	27:10	and bring great loss to ship and c,	5845
	27:18	**throw the c overboard.**	1678

CARGOES (4) [CARGO]
1Ki	10:11	and from there they brought **great** *c*	AIT
Rev	18:11	because no one buys their c any more—	1203
	18:12	c of gold, silver, precious stones	1203
	18:13	c of cinnamon and spice, of incense, myrrh	NIG

CARING (2) [CARE]
1Th	2: 7	like a mother c **for** her little children.	2499
1Ti	5: 4	**put** *their* **religion into practice by** c **for**	2355

CARITES (2)
2Ki	11: 4	the C and the guards and had them brought	4133
	11:19	the C, the guards and all the people of	4133

CARMEL (27) [CARMELITE]
Jos	12:22	the king of Jokneam in C one	4151
	15:55	Maon, C, Ziph, Juttah,	4150
	19:26	On the west the boundary touched C	4151
1Sa	15:12	but he was told, "Saul has gone to C.	4150
	25: 2	who had property there at C,	4150
	25: 2	which he was shearing in C.	4150
	25: 5	to Nabal at C and greet him in my name.	4150
	25: 7	and the whole time they were at C nothing	4150
	25:40	His servants went to C and said to Abigail,	4150
	27: 3	Ahinoam of Jezreel and Abigail **of** C,	4153
	30: 5	the widow of Nabal **of** C.	4153
2Sa	2: 2	the widow of Nabal **of** C.	4153
	3: 3	of Abigail the widow of Nabal **of** C;	4153
1Ki	18:19	over Israel to meet me on Mount C.	4151
	18:20	and assembled the prophets on Mount C.	4151
	18:42	but Elijah climbed to the top of C,	4151
2Ki	2:25	on to Mount C and from there returned	4151
	4:25	came to the man of God at Mount C.	4151
1Ch	3: 1	second, Daniel the son of Abigail **of** C;	4153
SS	7: 5	Your head crowns you like Mount C.	4151
Isa	33: 9	and Bashan and C drop their leaves.	4151
	35: 2	the splendor of C and Sharon;	4151
Jer	46:18	like C by the sea.	4151
	50:19	to his own pasture and he will graze on C	4151
Am	1: 2	and the top of C withers."	4151
	9: 3	on the top of C,	4151
Na	1: 4	Bashan and C wither and the blossoms	4151

CARMELITE (2) [CARMEL]
2Sa	23:35	Hezro the C, Paarai the Arbite,	4153
1Ch	11:37	Hezro the C, Naarai son of Ezbai,	4153

CARMI (8) [CARMITE]
Ge	46: 9	Hanoch, Pallu, Hezron and C.	4145
Ex	6:14	and Pallu, Hezron and C.	4145
Nu	26: 6	through C, the Carmite clan.	4145
Jos	7: 1	Achan son of C, the son of Zimri,	4145
	7:18	and Achan son of C, the son of Zimri,	4145
1Ch	2: 7	The son of C:	4145
	4: 1	Perez, Hezron, C, Hur and Shobal.	4145
	5: 3	Hanoch, Pallu, Hezron and C.	4145

CARMITE (1) [CARMI]
Nu	26: 6	through Carmi, the C clan.	4146

CARNAL (KJV) See UNSPIRITUAL, SINFUL NATURE, SINFUL, MATERIAL, WORLDLY, MERE MEN

CARNALLY (KJV) See SINFUL MAN, INTERCOURSE

CARNELIAN (2)
Rev	4: 3	the appearance of jasper and c.	4917
	21:20	the sixth c, the seventh chrysolite,	4917

CAROUSE (1) [CAROUSING]
2Pe	2:13	of pleasure is to c in broad daylight.	5588

CAROUSING (1) [CAROUSE]
1Pe	4: 3	orgies, c and detestable idolatry.	4542

CARPENTER (2) [CARPENTER'S, CARPENTERS]
Isa	44:13	The c measures with a line and makes	3093+6770
Mk	6: 3	Isn't this the c?	5454

CARPENTER'S (1) [CARPENTER]
Mt	13:55	"Isn't this the c son?	5454

CARPENTERS (8) [CARPENTER]
2Sa	5:11	with cedar logs and c and stonemasons	3093+6770
2Ki	12:11	the c and builders,	3093+6770
	22: 6	the c, the builders and	3093
1Ch	14: 1	stonemasons and c to build a palace	3093+6770
	22:15	stonecutters, masons and c,	6770
2Ch	24:12	and c to restore the LORD's temple,	3093
	34:11	They also gave money to the c and builders	3093
Ezr	3: 7	they gave money to the masons and c,	3093

CARPUS (1)
2Ti	4:13	bring the cloak that I left with C at Troas,	2842

CARRIAGE (2) [CARRIAGES]
SS	3: 7	It is Solomon's c,	4753
	3: 9	King Solomon made for himself the c;	712

CARRIAGES (1) [CARRIAGE]
Rev	18:13	horses and c; and bodies and souls of men.	4832

CARRIED (156) [CARRY]
Ge	14:12	*They* also c off Abram's nephew Lot	4374
	22: 6	and *he* himself c the fire and the knife.	928+3338+4374
	31:26	and *you've* c off my daughters	5627
	34:29	*They* c off all their wealth	8647
	40:15	For *I* **was forcibly** c off from the land	1704+1704
	50:13	They c him to the land of Canaan	5951
Ex	10:19	up the locusts and c them into the Red Sea	9546
	12:34	and c it on their shoulders	NIH
	19: 4	and how *I* c you on eagles' wings	5951
	27: 7	be on two sides of the altar when it *is* c.	5951
	34: 4	and *he* c the two stone tablets in his hands.	4374
Lev	10: 5	So they came and c them,	5951
Nu	10:17	and the Gershonites and Merarites, *who* c it,	5951
	13:23	Two of them c it on a pole between them,	5951
Dt	1:31	how the LORD your God c you,	5951
	2:35	from the towns we had captured *we* c off	1024
	3: 7	and the plunder from their cities *we* c off	1024
	31: 9	who c the ark of the covenant and	5951
	31:25	the Levites who c the ark of the covenant of	5951
	33:21	he c out the LORD's righteous will,	6913
Jos	3:15	the priests *who* c the ark reached the Jordan	5951
	3:17	The priests *who* c the ark of the covenant of	5951
	4: 8	*they* c them over with them to their camp,	6296
	4: 9	at the spot where the priests *who* c the ark of	5951
	4:10	the priests *who* c the ark remained standing	5951
	6:11	So he had the ark of the LORD c **around**	6015
	8:33	facing *those who* c it—	5951
	11:14	The Israelites c **off** for themselves all	1024
	22: 3	not deserted your brothers but *have* c **out**	9068
Jdg	3:18	he sent on their way the men *who had* c it.	5951
	5:19	but *they* c off no silver, no plunder.	4374
	16: 3	He lifted them on his shoulders and c them	6590
Jdg	21:23	each man caught one and c her **off** to	5951
Ru	2:18	*She* c it back to town,	5951
1Sa	5: 2	Then they c the ark *into* Dagon's temple	4374
	15:11	and *has* not c **out** my instructions."	7756
	15:13	*I have* c **out** the LORD's instructions."	7756
	17:34	and c off a sheep	5951
	23: 5	the Philistines and c **off** their livestock.	5627
	30: 2	but c them **off** as they went on their way.	5627
2Sa	5:21	and David and his men c them **off.**	5951
	23:16	near the gate of Bethlehem and c it back	5951
1Ki	2:26	because *you* c the ark of the Sovereign	5951
	8: 4	The priests and Levites c them **up,**	6590
	14:26	*He* c **off** the treasures of the temple of	4374
	15:22	and *they* c **away** from Ramah the stones	5951
	16:20	and the rebellion *he* c **out,**	8003
	17:19	c him to the upper room	5951
	17:23	up the child and c him **down** from the room	3718
2Ki	4:20	the servant had lifted him up and c him	995
	5:23	and *they* c them ahead of Gehazi.	5951
	7: 8	They ate and drank, and c **away** silver,	5951
	18:12	to the commands nor c them **out.**	6913
	20:17	*will* **be** c **off** to Babylon.	5951
	23:34	he took Jehoahaz and c him **off** *to* Egypt,	995
	24:14	*He* c **into exile** all Jerusalem:	1655+1655
	25:11	the commander of the guard c **into exile**	1655
	25:13	at the temple of the LORD and *they* c	5951
1Ch	11:18	near the gate of Bethlehem and c it back	5951
	15:15	the Levites c the ark of God with the poles	5951
	18: 7	the gold shields c by the officers	2118+6584
	23:32	the Levites c **out** their responsibilities	9068
2Ch	5: 5	The priests, who were Levites, c them **up;**	6590
	8:16	All Solomon's work was c out,	3922
	12: 9	*he* c **off** the treasures of the temple of	4374
	14:13	of Judah c off a large amount of plunder.	5951
	14:15	of the herdsmen and c **off** droves of sheep	8647
	16: 6	and *they* c **away** from Ramah the stones	5951
	21:17	invaded it and c **off** all the goods found in	8647
	24:12	to the *men who* c **out** the work required for	6913
	25:13	and c **off** great quantities of plunder.	1024
	28: 8	which *they* c **back** to Samaria.	995
	28:17	and attacked Judah and c **away** prisoners,	8647
	29:16	The Levites took it and c it **out** to	3655
	35: 3	It is not to be c **about** on your shoulders.	5362
	35:16	the LORD **was** c **out** for the celebration of	3922
	36: 4	and c him **off** to Egypt.	995
	36:18	*He* c to Babylon all the articles from	995
	36:20	*He* c **into exile** to Babylon the remnant,	1655
Ezr	1: 7	which Nebuchadnezzar *had* c **away**	3655
	5: 8	The work *is* being c on with diligence	10522
	6:12	*Let it* **be** c **out** with diligence.	10522
	6:13	and their associates c it **out** with diligence.	10522
Ne	3:17	c out **repairs** for his district.	2616
	4:17	Those *who* c materials did their work	5951+6673
	11:12	*who* c **on** work for the temple—	6913
Est	2: 6	who *had* **been** c **into exile** from Jerusalem	1655
	4:17	So Mordecai went away and c **out** all	6913
	9: 1	by the king was to be c **out.**	6913
Job	1:15	and the Sabeans attacked and c them **off.**	4374
	1:17	down on your camels and c them **off.**	4374
	10:19	or *had* **been** c straight from the womb to	3297
	15:12	Why *has* your heart c you **away,**	4374
	21:32	He is c to the grave,	3297
	22:16	They **were** c **off** before their time,	7855
Ecc	8:11	is not quickly c **out,**	6913
Isa	8: 4	and the plunder of Samaria *will* **be** c **off**	5951
	39: 6	*will* **be** c **off** to Babylon.	5951
	41: 4	Who has done this and c it **through,**	6913
	46: 1	**images that are** c **about**	5953
	46: 3	and *have* c since your birth.	5951
	53: 4	up our infirmities and c our sorrows,	6022
	60: 4	and your daughters **are** c on the arm.	587
	63: 9	he lifted them up and c them all the days	5951
	66:12	you will nurse and **be** c on her arm	5951
Jer	10: 5	*they* **must be** c because they cannot walk.	5951+5951
	13:19	All Judah *will* **be** c **into exile,**	1655
	13:19	be carried into exile, c completely **away.**	1655
	24: 1	and the artisans of Judah *were* c **into exile**	1655
	27:20	c Jehoiachin son of Jehoiakim king of Judah **into exile**	1655
	29: 1	people Nebuchadnezzar *had* c **into exile**	1655
	29: 4	to all those *I* c **into exile** from Jerusalem	1655
	29: 7	the city to which *I have* c you **into exile.**	1655
	29:14	the place from which *I* c you **into exile.**"	1655
	35:16	of Jonadab son of Recab *have* c **out**	7756
	39: 9	the imperial guard c **into exile** *to* Babylon	1655
	40: 1	and Judah who *were* **being** c **into exile**	1655
	40: 7	the land and who *had* not **been** c **into exile**	1655
	49:29	*be* c **off** with all their goods and camels.	5951
	52:15	of the guard c **into exile** some of	1655
	52:17	at the temple of the LORD and *they* c all	5951
	52:28	the people Nebuchadnezzar c **into exile:**	1655
Eze	6: 9	where *they have* **been** c captive,	8647
	16:16	c on your **prostitution.**	2388
	17: 4	he broke off its topmost shoot and c it **away**	995
	17:12	and c **off** her king and her nobles,	4374
	17:13	*He* also c **away** the leading men of the land,	4374
	23:14	c her prostitution **still further.**	3578
	23:18	c on her prostitution **openly**	1655
	30: 4	*be* c **away** and her foundations torn down.	4374
	44:11	and *they* **faithfully** c **out** the duties	9068
Da	1: 2	These *he* c **off** *to* the temple of his god	995
	11:12	When the army *is* c **off,**	5951
Hos	10: 6	It *will* **be** c to Assyria as tribute for	3297
Joel	3: 5	and my gold and c **off** my finest treasures	995
Ob	1:11	while strangers c **off** his wealth	8647
Na	2: 7	that [the city] be exiled and c **away.**	6590

Mal 2: 3 and you *will be* c off with it. 5951
Mt 8:17 up our infirmities and c our diseases." 1002
  14:11 *who* c it to her mother. 5770
Mk 2: 3 paralytic, c by four of them. 149
  6:55 throughout that whole region and c the sick 4367
Lk 7:12 a dead person *was being* c out— 1714
  16:22 when the beggar died and the angels c him 708
Jn 20:15 she said, "Sir, if you *have* c him **away,** 1002
Ac 3: 2 Now a man crippled from birth *was being* c 1002
  5: 6 and c him **out** and buried him. 1766
  5:10 c her **out** and buried her 1766
  13:29 When *they had* c **out** all that was written 5464
  21:35 of the mob was so great he had to be c by 1002
    When I was informed of a plot to be c out NIG
Heb 13: 9 be c **away** by all kinds of strange teachings. 4195
2Pe 1:21 but men spoke from God *as they were* c 5770
  3:17 so that you may not *be* c **away** by the error 5270
Rev 17: 3 angel c me **away** in the Spirit into a desert. 708
  21:10 And *he* c me **away** in the Spirit to 708

CARRIERS (7) [CARRY]

Jos 9:21 but let them be woodcutters and water c for 8612
  9:23 as woodcutters and water c for the house 8612
  9:27 the Gibeonites woodcutters and water c for 8612
1Ki 5:15 Solomon had seventy thousand c 5951+6025
2Ch 2: 2 as c and eighty thousand as stonecutters in 6025
  2:18 of them to be c and 80,000 6025
Eze 27:25 of Tarshish *serve as* c *for* your wares. 8801

CARRIES (9) [CARRY]

Nu 11:12 as a nurse c an infant, 5951
Dt 1:31 as a father c his son, 5951
  32:11 to catch them and c them on its pinions 5951
Job 23:14 *He* c out his decree against me, 8966
  27:21 The east wind c him **off,** and he is gone; 5951
Isa 40:11 in his arms and c them close to his heart; 5951
  44:26 *who* c **out** the words of his servants 7756
Hag 2:12 If a person c consecrated meat in the fold 5951
Heb 13:11 The high priest c the blood of animals into 1662

CARRION (1)

Eze 39: 4 as food to all kinds of c **birds** and to 6514+7606

CARRY (132) [CARRIED, CARRIERS, CARRIES, CARRYING]

Ge 44: 1 with as much food as they can c, 5951
  45:27 the carts Joseph had sent to c him **back,** 5951
  47:30 c me out of Egypt and bury me 5951
  50:25 and then *you must* c my bones **up** 6590
Ex 13:19 then *you must* c my bones **up** with you 6590
  25:14 the rings on the sides of the chest to c it. 5951
  25:28 overlay them with gold and c the table 5951
  30: 4 to hold the poles used to c it. 5951
  36: 1 how to c **out** all the work of constructing 6213
  36: 3 the Israelites had brought to c **out** the work 6213
  37: 5 into the rings on the sides of the ark to c it. 5951
  37:27 to hold the poles used to c it. 5951
Lev 4: 5 of the bull's blood and c it into the Tent 995
  6:11 and c the ashes outside the camp to a place 3655
  10: 4 c your cousins outside the camp, 5951
  16:22 The goat will c on itself all their sins to 5951
  26:14 to me and c **out** all these commands, 6213
  26:15 and fail *to* c **out** all my commands and 6213
Nu 1:50 *to* c the tabernacle and all its furnishings, 5951
  4:15 The Kohathites are to c those things 5362
  4:19 **what** he is to c. 5362
  4:24 as they work and c burdens: NIH
  4:25 *They are to* c the curtains of the tabernacle, 5951
  4:27 as their responsibility all they are to c. 5362
  4:31 to c the frames of the tabernacle, 5362
  4:32 to each man the specific things he is to c. 5362
  4:49 and told **what** to c. 5362
  7: 9 because *they were to* c on their shoulders 5951
  11:12 Why do you tell me *to* c them in my arms, 5951
  11:14 I cannot c all these people by myself, 5375
  11:17 *They will* help you c the burden of 5375
  11:17 so that *you will* not have to c it alone. 5375
  31: 3 to c **out** the LORD's vengeance on them. 5989
Dt 1: 9 **too heavy a burden** for me *to* c 3523+4202+5951
  10: 8 to c the ark of the covenant of the LORD, 5951
  14:24 and cannot c your tithe (because the place 5951
  25: 6 The first son she bears *shall* c **on** the name 6584+7756
    of the dead brother
  25: 7 "My husband's brother refuses *to* c **on** 7756
  29:11 and c your water. 8612
Jos 3: 8 the priests *who* c the ark of the covenant: 5951
  3:13 as the priests *who* c the ark of the LORD— 5951
  4: 3 where the priests stood and *to* c them **over** 6296
  6: 4 *Have* seven priests c trumpets 5951
  6: 6 and *have* seven priests c trumpets in front 5951
  8: 2 except that *you may* c **off** their plunder 1024
  8:27 But Israel *did* c **off** for themselves 1024
1Sa 3:12 At that time *I will* c out 7756
  20:40 "Go, c them **back** *to* town." 995
  21:15 to bring this fellow here to c **on** like this 8713
  28:18 the LORD or c **out** his fierce wrath 6213
2Sa 18:18 "I have no son *to* c **on the memory** 2349
  24:12 of them *for me to* c **out** against you.'" 6213
1Ki 1:30 surely c **out** today what I swore to you by 6213
  3: 7 and do not know how *to* c **out** my **duties.** 995+2256+3655
  6:12 c **out** my regulations 6213
  18:12 of the LORD *may* c you when I leave you. 5375
  20: 6 and c it **away.'"** 4374

2Ki 4:19 "C him to his mother." 5951
  5:17 as much earth as a pair of mules can c, 5362
1Ch 15: 2 "No one but the Levites *may* c the ark 5951
  15: 2 because the LORD chose them to c the ark 5951
  21:10 of them *for me to* c **out** against you.'" 6913
  23:26 the Levites no *longer* need to c 5951
2Ch 20:25 and his men went to c **off** their plunder, 1024
  24:11 the chest and c it back to its place. 5951
Est 3: 9 for the *men who* c **out** this business." 6213
  9:13 to c **out** this day's edict tomorrow also, 6213
Job 12: 6 *those* who c their god in their hands. 995
  15:30 of God's mouth *will* c him **away.** 6073
  20:28 A flood *will* c **off** his house, 1655
  24:10 *they* c the sheaves, but still go hungry. 5951
Ps 28: 9 be their shepherd and c them forever. 5375
  37: 7 when they c **out** their wicked schemes. 6213
  149: 9 to c **out** the sentence written against them. 6213
Ecc 5:15 from his labor that *he can* c in his hand. 2143
  10:20 because a bird of the air *may* c your words, 2143
Isa 5:29 as they seize their prey and c it **off** 7117
  10:23 *will* c **out** the destruction decreed upon 6213
  13: 3 to c **out** my wrath— NIH
  15: 7 and stored up *they* c **away** over the Ravine 5951
  28:19 As often as it comes *it will* c you **away;** 4374
  30: 1 "to those *who* c **out** plans that are not mine, 6213
  30: 6 envoys of their riches on donkeys' backs, 5951
  33:23 and even the lame *will* c **off** plunder. 1024
  45:20 Ignorant are those *who* c **about** idols 5951
  46: 4 I have made you and I *will* c you; 5951
  46: 7 They lift it to their shoulders and c it; 6022
  48:14 LORD's chosen *will* c **out** his purpose 6213
  49:22 and c your daughters on their shoulders. 5951
  52:11 you *who* c the vessels of the LORD. 5375
  57:13 c all of them **off,** 5375
Jer 17:21 *to* c a load on the Sabbath day or bring it 5951
  20: 4 *who will* c them **away** to Babylon, 1655
  20: 5 as plunder and c it **off** to Babylon. 995
  22: 4 *you are* **careful to** c **out** these commands, 6213+6213
  43: 3 so they may kill us or c us **into exile** 1655
  44:25 you said, 'We *will* **certainly** c **out** 6213+6213
  46: 9 men of Cush and Put *who* c shields, 8610
  51:12 The LORD *will* c **out** his purpose, 2372
Eze 12: 6 as they are watching and c them **out** 3655
  25:17 *I will* c **out** great vengeance on them 6213
  29:19 and *he will* c **off** its wealth. 5375
  38:13 to c **off** silver and gold, 5375
Da 11: 8 and gold and c them **off** to Egypt. 5951
  11:10 and c **the battle** as far as his 1741+2256+8740
Hos 5:14 *I will* c them **off,** 5375
  11: 9 *I will* not c **out** my fierce anger, 6213
Am 6:10 to burn the bodies comes *to* c them out of 5375
Mic 2: 1 At morning's light *they* c it **out** 6213
Mt 3:11 whose sandals I am not fit *to* c. 1002
  12:29 and c **off** his possessions 773
  27:32 and they forced him *to* c the cross. 149
Mk 3:27 and c **off** his possessions 1395
  11:16 not allow anyone *to* c merchandise 1422
  15:21 and they forced *him to* c it. 149
Lk 11:46 down with burdens *they can* **hardly** c, 1546
  14:27 And anyone *who does* not c his cross 1002
  23:26 and put the cross on him and made him c it 5770
Jn 5:10 the law forbids you *to* c your mat." 149
  8:44 and you want *to* c **out** your father's desire. 4472
Ac 9:15 to c my name before the Gentiles 1002
Ro 7:18 but *I* cannot c it **out.** 2981
  9:28 the Lord *will* c **out** his sentence on earth 4472
2Co 4:10 We always c **around** in our body the death 4367
  8:19 by the churches to accompany us as we c NIG
Gal 6: 2 C each other's burdens, 1002
  6: 5 for each one *should* c his own load. 1002
Php 1: 6 c **it on** to completion 2200
Heb 9: 6 into the outer room *to* c **on** their ministry. 2200
Jas 4:13 c **on business** and make money." 1864

CARRYING (50) [CARRY]

Ex 25:27 to the rim to hold the poles *used in* c 5951
  37:14 the rim to hold the poles used in c the table. 5951
  37:15 for c the table were made of acacia wood 5951
  38: 7 be on the sides of the altar for c it. 5951
Nu 4:10 of sea cows and put it on a c **frame.** 4573
  4:12 of sea cows and put them on a c **frame.** 4573
  4:15 the Kohathites are to come to *do the* c. 5951
  4:27 whether c or doing other work, 5362
  4:47 to do the work of serving and c the Tent 5362
  10:21 the Kohathites set out, c the holy things. 5951
Dt 27:26 the words of this law by c them **out."** 6913
Jos 3: 3 and the priests, who are Levites, c it, 5951
  3:14 the priests c the ark of the covenant went 5951
  4:16 the priests c the ark of the Testimony 5951
  4:18 up out of the river c the ark of the covenant 5951
  6: 8 the seven priests c the seven trumpets 5951
  6:13 The seven priests c the seven trumpets 5951
1Sa 10: 3 One *will be* c three young goats, 5375
2Sa 15:24 When *those who were* c the ark of 5375
  15:24 with him *were* c the ark of the covenant 5375
1Ki 8: 3 and overshadowed the ark and its c **poles.** 964
  8: 7 with camels c spices, large quantities 5951
  10: 2 with camels c spices, large quantities 5951
  10:22 Once every three years it returned, c gold, 5951
1Ch 12:24 c shield and spear— 5375
  12:34 men c shields and spears; 928
  15:26 the Levites *who were* c the ark of 5951
  15:27 as were all the Levites *who were* c the ark, 5951

1Ch 28: 7 if he is unswerving in c **out** my commands 6913
2Ch 5: 8 the ark and covered the ark and its c **poles.** 964
  7:11 and *had* **succeeded in** c **out** all he had 7503
  9: 1 with camels c spices, large quantities 5951
  9:21 Once every three years it returned, c gold, 5951
Ne 6: 3 "I am c on a great project 6913
  10:32 **assume the responsibility for** c **out** 6584+6641
Ps 126: 6 He who goes out weeping, c seed to sow, 5951
  126: 6 c sheaves with him. 5951
Jer 17:27 the Sabbath day holy by not c any load 5951
Eze 12: 7 c them on my shoulders 5951
  44: 8 Instead of c **out** *your* duty in regard 9068
Mal 3:14 by c **out** his requirements and going about 9068
Mk 14:13 and a man c a jar of water will meet you. 1002
Lk 5:18 Some men came c a paralytic on a mat 5770
  7:14 and those c it stood still. 1002
  22:10 a man c a jar of water will meet you. 1002
Jn 18: 3 They were c torches, lanterns and weapons. NIG
  19:17 C his own cross, 1002
Ac 23:31 So the soldiers, c **out** their orders, 2848
  27:43 and kept them from c **out** their plan. NIG
1Co 16:10 for *he is* c **on** the work of the Lord. 2237
1Jn 5: 2 by loving God and c **out** his commands. 4472

CARSHENA (1)

Est 1:14 C, Shethar, Admatha, Tarshish, Meres, 4161

CART (14) [CARTS, CARTWHEEL]

Nu 7: 3 from each leader and a c from every two. 6322
1Sa 6: 7 "Now then, get a new c ready, 6322
  6: 7 Hitch the cows to the c, 6322
  6: 8 the ark of the LORD and put it on the c, 6322
  6:10 and hitched them to the c and penned 6322
  6:11 They placed the ark of the LORD on the c 6322
  6:14 The c came to the field of Joshua 6322
  6:14 The people chopped up the wood of the c 6322
2Sa 6: 3 on a new c and brought it from the house 6322
  6: 3 were guiding the new c 6322
1Ch 13: 7 of God from Abinadab's house on a new c, 6322
Isa 5:18 and wickedness as with c ropes, 6322
  28:28 the wheels of his **threshing** c over it, 6322
Am 2:13 I will crush you as a c crushes when loaded 6322

CARTS (9) [CART]

Ge 45:19 Take *some* c from Egypt for your children 6322
  45:21 Joseph gave them c, 6322
  45:27 the c Joseph had sent to carry him back, 6322
  46: 5 and their children and their wives in the c 6322
Nu 7: 3 before the LORD six covered c 6322
  7: 6 the c and oxen and gave them to 6322
  7: 7 He gave two c and four oxen to 6322
  7: 8 and he gave four c and eight oxen to 6322
Ps 65:11 and your c overflow with abundance. 5047

CARTWHEEL (1) [CART]

Isa 28:27 nor is a c rolled over cummin; 236+6322

CARVED (26) [CARVES, CARVINGS]

Lev 26: 1 not place a c stone in your land to bow 5381
Nu 33:52 Destroy all their c **images** 5381
Jdg 17: 3 to the LORD for my son to make a c **image** 7181
  18:14 a c **image** and a cast idol? 7181
  18:17 the land went inside and took the c **image,** 7181
  18:18 into Micah's house and took the c **image,** 7181
  18:20 the c **image** and went along with the people. 7181
1Ki 6:18 c *with* gourds and open flowers. 5237
  6:29 and outer rooms, *he* c cherubim, 5237+7844
  6:32 two olive wood doors *he* c cherubim, 5237+7844
  6:35 *He* c cherubim, palm trees and open flowers 7844
2Ki 21: 7 the c Asherah pole he had made and put it 7181
2Ch 3: 7 and *he* c cherubim on the walls. 7338
  33: 7 He took the c image he had made and put it 7181
  34: 3 Asherah poles, c idols and cast images. 7178
Ps 74: 6 They smashed all the c **paneling** 7334
  144:12 and our daughters will be like pillars c 2624
Eze 41:18 were c cherubim and palm trees. 6913
  41:19 *They were* c all around the whole temple. 6913
  41:20 cherubim and palm trees *were* c on the wall 6913
  41:25 of the outer sanctuary *were* c cherubim 6913
  41:25 and palm trees like *those* c on the walls, 6913
  41:26 with palm trees c on each side. NIH
Mic 5:13 I will destroy your c **images** 7178
Na 1:14 I will destroy the c **images** and cast idols 7181
Hab 2:18 since a man *has* c it? 7180

CARVES (1) [CARVED]

Dt 27:15 "Cursed is the man who c an image or casts 6913

CARVINGS (1) [CARVED]

1Ki 6:35 with gold hammered evenly over the c. 2977

CASE (58) [CASES]

Ex 18:22 have them bring every difficult c to you; 1821
Lev 5: 1 of it, in any c when he learns of it he will 465S
  5:13 **as in the** c of the grain offering.'" 3869
Nu 27: 5 Moses brought their c before the LORD 5477
Dt 1:16 whether the c is between brother Israelites NIH
  1:17 Bring me any c too hard for you, 1821
  6:24 **as is the** c today. 3869
  22:26 This c is like that of someone who attacks 1821
  25: 1 to court and the judges will decide the c, 4392S
Jos 20: 4 and state his c before the elders of that city. 1821

2Sa	15: 4	or c could come to me and I would see	5477
	20:21	That is not the c.	1821
1Ki	15: 5	except in the c of Uriah the Hittite.	1821
2Ki	8: 6	Then he assigned an official to her c	NIH
2Ch	19:10	In every c that comes before you	8190
Job	13: 3	the Almighty and to argue my c with God.	3519
	13: 8	Will you argue the c for God?	8189
	13:18	Now that I have prepared my c,	5477
	23: 4	I would state my c before him	5477
	23: 7	There an upright man could present his c	3519
	29:16	I took up the c of the stranger.	8190
	35:14	that your c is before him and you must wait	1907
	37:19	we cannot draw up our c because	6885
Pr	18:17	The first to present his c seems right,	8190
	22:23	for the LORD will take up their c	8190
	23:11	he will take up their c against you.	8190
	25: 9	If you argue your c with a neighbor,	8190
Isa	1:17	plead the c of the widow.	8189
	1:23	the widow's c does not come before them.	8190
	41:21	"Present your c," says the LORD.	8190
	43:26	state the c for your innocence.	AIT
	59: 4	no one pleads his c with integrity.	9149
Jer	5:28	not plead the c of the fatherless to win it,	1907
	12: 1	O LORD, when I bring a c before you.	8189
La	3:58	O Lord, you took up my c;	8190
Mic	6: 1	plead your c before the mountains;	8189
	6: 2	For the LORD has a c against his people;	8190
	7: 9	until he pleads my c	8190
Lk	13:33	In any c, I must keep going today	4440
Ac		Therefore, in the present c I advise you:	NIG
	19:40	In that c we would not be able to account	4005+4309
	23:15	of wanting more accurate information about his c.	NIG
	23:30	to present to you their c against him.	NIG
	23:35	"I will hear your c	1358
	24: 2	Tertullus presented his c before Felix:	2989
	24:22	he said, "I will decide your c."	2848+3836
	25:14	Festus discussed Paul's c with the king.	2848+3836
	25:17	I did not delay the c,	NIG
1Co	5:10	In that c you would have to leave	726+2075
	14: 7	Even in the c of lifeless things	3940
2Co	10:14	as would be the c if we had not come	NIG
Gal	3:15	so it is in this c.	NIG
	5:11	the offense of c	726
2Ti	3: 9	as in the c of those men,	NIG
Heb	6: 9	we are confident of better things in your c—	NIG
	7: 8	In the one c, the tenth is collected	3525+6045
	7: 8	but in the other c, by him	1254+1695
	9:16	In the c of a will,	3963

CASEMENT (KJV) See LATTICE

CASES (9) [CASE]

Ex	18:22	The simple c they can decide themselves.	1821
	18:26	The difficult c they brought to Moses,	1821
	22: 9	In all c of illegal possession of an ox,	1821
	22: 9	both parties are to bring their c before	1821
Dt	17: 8	If c come before your courts	1821+8191
	21: 5	and to decide all c of dispute and assault.	8190
	24: 8	In c of leprous diseases be very careful	NIH
Ezr	10:16	down to investigate the c,	1821
1Co	6: 2	are you not competent to judge trivial c?	3215

CASIPHIA (2)

Ezr	8:17	I sent them Iddo, the leader in C.	4085
	8:17	the temple servants in C,	4085

CASLUHITES (2)

Ge	10:14	C (from whom the Philistines came)	4078
1Ch	1:12	C (from whom the Philistines came)	4078

CASSIA (3)

Ex	30:24	500 shekels of c—	7703
Ps	45: 8	with myrrh and aloes and c;	7904
Eze	27:19	c and calamus for your wares.	7703

CAST (90) [CASTING, CASTS, OUTCAST]

Ex	25:12	C four gold rings for it and fasten them	3668
	26:37	And c five bronze bases for them.	3668
	32: 4	and made it into an idol in the shape of	5011
	32: 8	and have made themselves an idol c in	5011
	34:17	"Do not make c idols.	5011
	36:36	for them and c their four silver bases.	3668
	37: 3	He c four gold rings for it	3668
	37:13	They c four gold rings for the table	3668
	38: 5	They c bronze rings to hold the poles for	3668
	38:27	The 100 talents of silver were used to c	3668
Lev	16: 8	He is to c lots for the two goats—	5989
	19: 4	not turn to idols or make gods of c metal	5011
Nu	33:52	and their c idols,	5011
Dt	9:12	and have made a c idol for themselves."	5011
	9:16	you had made for yourselves an idol c in	5011
Jos	18: 6	and I will c lots for you in the presence	3721
	18: 8	and I will c lots for you here at Shiloh in	8959
	18:10	Joshua then c lots for them in Shiloh in	8959
Jdg	17: 3	to make a carved image and a c idol.	5011
	18:14	a carved image and a c idol?	5011
	18:17	the other household gods and the c idol	5011
	18:18	the other household gods and the c idol,	5011
1Sa	14:42	"C the lot between me	5877
2Sa	23: 6	evil men are all to be c aside like thorns,	5610

1Ki	7:15	He c two bronze pillars,	7445
	7:16	also made two capitals of c bronze to set on	4607
	7:23	He made the Sea of c metal,	4607
	7:24	The gourds were c in two rows in one piece	3668
	7:30	c with wreaths on each side.	3668
	7:33	rims, spokes and hubs were all of c metal.	4607
	7:37	c in the same molds	4607
	7:46	The king had them c in clay molds in	3668
2Ki	17:16	and made for themselves two idols c in	5011
1Ch	24:31	They also c lots,	5877
	25: 8	c lots for their duties.	5877
	26:13	Lots were c for each gate,	5877
	26:14	Then lots were c for his son Zechariah,	5877
2Ch	4: 2	He made the Sea of c metal,	4607
	4: 3	The bulls were c in two rows in one piece	3668
	4:17	The king had them c in clay molds in	3668
	28: 2	of the kings of Israel and also made c idols	5011
	34: 3	Asherah poles, carved idols and c images.	5011
Ne	9:18	even when they c for themselves an image	6913
	10:34	have c lots to determine when each	5877
	11: 1	the rest of the people c lots to bring one out	5877
Est	3: 7	the month of Nisan, they c the pur (that is,	5877
	9:24	against the Jews to destroy them and had c	5877
Job	6:27	You would even c lots for the fatherless	5877
	37:18	hard as a mirror of c bronze?	4607
Ps	22:10	From birth I was c upon you;	8959
	22:18	among them and c lots for my clothing.	5877
	50:17	You hate my instruction and c my words	8959
	51:11	Do not c me from your presence	8959
	55:22	C your cares on the LORD	8959
	71: 9	Do not c me away when I am old;	8959
	73:18	you c them down to ruin.	5877
	89:44	an end to his splendor and c his throne to	4489
	106:19	and worshiped an idol c from metal.	5011
Pr	16:33	The lot is c into the lap,	3214
	23: 5	C but a glance at riches, and they are gone,	6414
	29:18	the people c off restraint;	7277
Ecc	11: 1	C your bread upon the waters,	8938
	11:10	banish anxiety from your heart and c off	6296
Isa	14:12	You have been c down to the earth,	1548
	14:19	But you are c out of your tomb like	8959
	19: 8	all who c hooks into the Nile;	8959
	38: 8	the shadow c by the sun go back	NIH
	57:20	whose waves c up mire and mud.	1764
Jer	22:28	c into a land they do not know?	8959
	23:39	and c you out of my presence along with	5759
La	3:31	For men are not c off by the Lord forever.	2396
Eze	21:21	He will c lots with arrows,	7837
	31:11	according to its wickedness, I c it aside,	1763
	32: 3	a great throng of people I will c my net	7298
Joel	3: 3	They c lots for my people and traded boys	3341
Am	4: 3	and you will be c out toward Harmon,"	8959
	5: 7	into bitterness and c righteousness to	5663
Ob		and foreigners entered his gates and c lots	3341
Jnh	1: 7	let us c lots to find out who is responsible	5877
	1: 7	They c lots and the lot fell on Jonah.	5877
Mic	5:12	and you will no longer c spells.	6726
Na	1:14	the carved images and c idols that are in	5011
	3:10	Lots were c for her nobles,	3341
Mal	3:11	in your fields will not c their fruit,"	8897
Mk	15: 7	they c lots to see what each would get.	965
Jn	19:24	among them and c lots for my clothing."	965
Ac	1:26	they c lots, and the lot fell to Matthias;	1443
	26:10	I c my vote against them.	2965
1Pe	5: 7	C all your anxiety on on him because he cares for you.	2166
Rev	2:22	So I will c her on a bed of suffering,	965

CASTAWAY (KJV) See DISQUALIFIED

CASTING (7) [CAST]

Pr	18:18	C the lot settles disputes	NIH
Eze	24: 6	Empty it piece by piece without c lots	5877
	26: 3	like the sea c up its waves.	6590
Mt	4:18	They were c a net into the lake,	965
	27:35	they divided up his clothes by c lots.	965
Mk	1:16	and his brother Andrew c a net into	311
Lk	23:34	And they divided up his clothes by c lots.	965

CASTLE, CASTLES (KJV) See FORT, FORTRESS

CASTOR (1)

Ac	28:11	twin gods C and Pollux.	1483

CASTS (7) [CAST]

Dt	18:11	or c spells, or who is a medium	2489+2490
	27:15	the man who carves an image or c	NIH
Ps	15: 3	and c no slur on his fellowman,	5951
	147: 6	the humble but c the wicked to the ground.	9164
Isa	26: 5	he levels it to the ground and c it down to	5595
	40:19	As for an idol, a craftsman c it,	5818
	44:10	Who shapes a god and c an idol,	5818

CASUALTIES (7)

Jdg	20:31	They began to inflict c on the Israelites as	2728
	20:39	The Benjamites had begun to inflict c on	2728
2Sa	18: 7	and the c that day were great—	4487
1Ki	20:21	inflicted a hundred thousand c	5782
2Ch	13:17	so that there were five hundred thousand c	2728
	28: 5	who inflicted heavy c on him.	4804
Na	3: 3	Many c, piles of dead,	2728

CATASTROPHE (2)

Ge	19:29	of the c that overthrew the cities	2202
Isa	47:11	a c you cannot foresee will suddenly come	8739

CATCH (19) [CATCHES, CAUGHT]

Ge	44: 4	and when you c up with them, say to them,	5952
Dt	32:11	to c and carries them on its pinions.	4374
Jos	2: 5	You may c up with them."	5952
Job	23: 9	I c no glimpse of him.	8011
Ps	10: 9	he lies in wait to c the helpless;	2642
SS	2:15	C for us the foxes,	296
Jer	2:34	though you did not c them breaking in.	5162
	5:26	and like those who set traps to c men.	4334
	16:16	"and they will c them.	1899
Hos	2: 7	after her lovers but not c them;	5952
	7:12	I will c them.	3579
Am	3: 5	when there is nothing to c?	4334+4334
Mt	17:27	Take the first fish you c;	NIG
Mk	12:13	and Herodians to Jesus to c him	65
Lk	5: 4	and let down the nets for a c."	62
	5: 9	at the c of fish they had taken,	62
	5:10	from now on you will c men."	1639+2436
	11:54	to c him in something he might say.	2561
	20:20	to c Jesus in something he said so	2138

CATCHES (5) [CATCH]

Job	5:13	He c the wise in their craftiness,	4334
	39:25	He c the scent of battle from afar,	8193
Ps	10: 9	he c the helpless and drags them off	2642
Hab	1:15	he c them in his net,	1760
1Co	3:19	"He c the wise in their craftiness";	1533

CATERPILLER, CATERPILLERS (KJV)
See GRASSHOPPER, GRASSHOPPERS

CATTLE (85)

Ge	12:16	and Abram acquired sheep and c,	1330
	20:14	Then Abimelech brought sheep and c	1330
	21:27	and c and gave them to Abimelech,	1330
	24:35	He has given him sheep and c,	1330
	32: 5	I have c and donkeys, sheep and goats,	8802
	47:17	sheep and goats, their c and donkeys.	1330+5238
Ex	9: 3	and donkeys and camels and on your c	1330
	11: 5	and all the firstborn of the c as well.	989
	20:24	your sheep and goats and your c.	1330
	22: 1	he must pay back five head of c for the ox	1330
	22:30	Do the same with your c and your sheep.	8802
Lev	7:23	'Do not eat any of the fat of c,	8802
	22:19	a male without defect from the c,	1330
	26:22	destroy your c and make you so few	989
Nu	22:40	Balak sacrificed c and sheep,	1330
	31:28	whether persons, c, donkeys,	1330
	31:30	c, donkeys, sheep, goats or other animals.	1330
	31:33	72,000 c,	1330
	31:38	36,000 c, of which the tribute for	1330
	31:44	36,000 c,	1330
	35: 3	to live in and pasturelands for their c,	989
Dt	11:15	I will provide grass in the fields for your c,	1330
	14:26	Use the silver to buy whatever you like: c,	1330
Jos	6:21	men and women, young and old, c,	8802
	7:24	his sons and daughters, his c,	8802
Jdg	6: 4	neither sheep nor c nor donkeys.	8802
1Sa	8:16	the best of your c and donkeys he will take	1330
	14:32	taking sheep, c and calves,	8802
	14:34	'Each of you bring me your c and sheep,	8802
	15: 3	c and sheep, camels and donkeys.' "	8802
	15: 9	the sheep and c, the fat calves and lambs—	1330
	15:14	What is this lowing of c that I hear?"	1330
	15:15	and c to sacrifice to the LORD your God,	1330
	15:21	The soldiers took sheep and c from	1330
	22:19	its children and infants, and its c,	8802
	27: 9	but took sheep and c, donkeys and camels,	8802
2Sa	12: 2	a very large number of sheep and c,	1330
	12: 4	of his own sheep or c to prepare a meal for	1330
1Ki	1: 9	c and fattened calves at the Stone	1330
	1:19	He has sacrificed great numbers of c,	8802
	1:25	down and sacrificed great numbers of c,	8802
	4:23	ten head of stall-fed c,	1330
	4:23	of pasture-fed c and a hundred sheep	1330
	8: 5	so many sheep and c that they could not	1330
	8:63	twenty-two thousand c and a hundred	1330
2Ki	3:17	your c and your other animals will drink.	5238
1Ch	12:40	oil, c and sheep, for there was joy in Israel.	1330
2Ch	5: 6	so many sheep and c that they could not	1330
	7: 5	of twenty-two thousand head of c and	1330
	15:11	of c and seven thousand sheep and goats	1330
	18: 2	and c for him and the people with him	1330
	32:28	made stalls for various kinds of c,	989+989+2256
	35: 7	and also three thousand c—	1330
	35: 8	and three hundred c.	1330
	35: 9	and five hundred head of c for the Levites.	1330
	35:12	They did the same with the c.	1330
Ne	9:37	over our bodies and our c as they please.	989
	10:36	the firstborn of our sons and of our c,	989
Job	18: 3	as c and considered stupid in your sight?	989
	36:33	even the c make known its approach.	5238
Ps	50:10	and the c on a thousand hills.	989
	78:48	He gave over their c to the hail,	1248
	104:14	He makes grass grow for the c,	989
	147: 9	He provides food for the c and for	989
	148:10	wild animals and all c,	989
Isa	7:25	where c are turned loose and	8802
	22:13	slaughtering of c and killing of sheep,	1330

Isa	30:23	In that day your c will graze	5238
	32:20	and letting your c and donkeys range free.	8802
	63:14	like c that go down to the plain,	989
Jer	9:10	and the lowing of c is not heard.	5238
Eze	32:13	I will destroy all her c from	989
	32:13	of man or muddied by the hoofs of c.	989
Da	4:25	you will eat grass like c and be drenched	10756
	4:32	you will eat grass like c.	10756
	4:33	from people and ate grass like c.	10756
	5:21	with the wild donkeys and ate grass like c;	10756
Joel	1:18	How the c moan!	989
Jnh	4:11	and many as well.	989
Hab	3:17	in the pen and no c in the stalls,	1330
Hag	1:11	on men and c,	989
Mt	22: 4	and fattened c have been butchered,	4990
Jn	2:14	the temple courts he found men selling c,	1091
	2:15	both sheep and c;	1091
Rev	18:13	and wheat; c and sheep;	3229

CAUDA (1)
Ac	27:16	to the lee of a small island called C,	3007

CAUGHT (57) [CATCH]
Ge	22:13	and there in a thicket he saw a ram c	296
	27:27	When Isaac c the smell of his clothes,	8193+8194
	31:23	he pursued Jacob for seven days and c up	1815
	39:12	She c him by his cloak and said,	9530
	44: 6	When he c up with them,	5952
Ex	10:19	which c up the locusts and carried them into	5951
	21:16	or still has him when he is c must be put	5162
	22: 2	"If a thief is c breaking in and is struck so	5162
	22: 7	the thief, if he is c, must pay back double.	5162
Nu	5:13	she has not been c in the act),	9530
	11:22	if all the fish in the sea were c for them?"	665
Dt	24: 7	If a man is c kidnapping one	5162
Jos	7:15	He who is c with the devoted things shall	4334
	8:22	so that there were c in the middle,	2118
Jdg	1: 6	but they chased him and c him,	296
	8:14	He c a young man of Succoth	4334
	15: 4	So he went out and c three hundred foxes	4334
	21:23	each man c one and carried her off to	1608
1Sa	9:17	When Samuel c sight of Saul,	8011
	15:27	Saul c hold of the hem of his robe,	2616
2Sa	18: 9	Absalom's head got c in the tree.	2616
Job	4:12	my ears c a whisper of it.	4374
Ps	9:15	their feet are c in the net they have hidden.	4334
	10: 2	who are c in the schemes he devises.	9530
	59:12	let them be c in their pride.	4334
Pr	6:31	Yet if he is c, he must pay sevenfold,	5162
	30:28	a lizard can be c with the hand,	9530
Ecc	9:12	As fish are c in a cruel net,	296
Isa	13:15	all who are c will fall by the sword.	6200
	22: 3	All you who were c were taken prisoner together,	5162
	24:18	whoever climbs out of the pit will be c in	4334
	51:20	like antelope c in a net.	AIT
Jer	2:26	"As a thief is disgraced when he is c,	5162
	6:11	both husband and wife will be c in it,	4334
	41:12	They c up with him near the great pool	5162
	48:27	Was she c among thieves,	5162
	48:44	whoever climbs out of the pit will be c in	4334
	50:24	and you were c before you knew it;	4334
La	4:20	our very life breath, was c in their traps.	4334
Eze	12:13	and he will be c in my snare;	9530
	17:20	and he will be c in my snare.	9530
Am	3: 4	in his den when he has c nothing?	4334
Mt	13:47	down into the lake and c all kinds of fish.	5251
	14:31	Immediately Jesus reached out his hand and c him.	2138
Lk	5: 5	and haven't c anything.	3284
	5: 6	they c such a large number of fish	5168
Jn	8: 3	and the Pharisees brought in a woman c	2898
	8: 4	this woman was c in the act of adultery.	900+2093+2898
	21: 3	but that night they c nothing.	4389
	21:10	"Bring some of the fish you have just c."	4389
Ac	27:15	The ship was c by the storm and could	5275
2Co	12: 2	a man in Christ who fourteen years ago was c up to the third heaven.	773
	12: 4	was c up to paradise.	773
	12:16	I c you by trickery!	3284
Gal	6: 1	Brothers, if someone is c in a sin,	4624
1Th	4:17	be c up together with them in the clouds	773
2Pe	2:12	born only to be c and destroyed,	274

CAUL, CAULS (KJV) See COVERING

CAULK (1)
Eze	27: 9	on board as shipwrights to c your seams.	2616

CAUSE (87) [CAUSED, CAUSES, CAUSING]
Ex	20:24	c my name to be honored,	2349
	23:33	or they will c you to sin against me,	2627
	33:19	c all my goodness to pass	6296
Nu	5:21	"may the LORD c your people to curse	5989
	5:24	and c bitter suffering,	4200
	5:27	it will go into her and c bitter suffering;	4200
	16: 5	The man he chooses he will c to come near	7928
	32:15	c of their destruction."	8845
Dt	3:28	across and will c them to inherit the land	5706
	10:18	He defends the c of the fatherless and	5477
	28:25	The LORD will c you to be defeated	5989
Dt	33: 7	With his own hands he defends his c.	8189
Jos	22:25	your descendants might c ours to stop fearing the LORD.	8697
Jdg	6:31	"Are you going to plead Baal's c?	8189
1Sa	24:15	May he consider my c and uphold it;	8190
	25:39	who has upheld my c against Nabal	8190
1Ki	8:45	and uphold their c.	5477
	8:49	and uphold their c.	5477
	8:50	c their conquerors to show them mercy;	5989
	8:59	that he may uphold the c of his servant and	5477
	8:59	of his servant and the c of his people Israel	5477
2Ki	2:21	Never again will it c death or make	2118+4946
	14:10	c your own downfall	AIT
2Ch	6:35	and uphold their c.	5477
	6:39	and uphold their c.	5477
	20:27	given them c to rejoice	8523
	25:19	c your own downfall	AIT
Job	5: 8	I would lay my c before him.	1826
Ps	9: 4	or without c have robbed my foe—	8200
	9: 4	For you have upheld my right and my c;	1907
	35: 7	Since they hid their net for me without c	2855
	35: 7	for me without cause and without c dug	2855
	35:19	over me who are my enemies without c;	9214
	37: 6	the justice of your c like the noonday sun.	5477
	43: 1	and plead my c against an ungodly nation;	8190
	69: 4	many are my enemies without c,	9214
	74:22	Rise up, O God, and defend your c;	8190
	82: 3	Defend the c of the weak and fatherless;	9149
	109: 3	they attack me without c.	2855
	119:78	to shame for wronging me without c;	9214
	119:86	help me, for men persecute me without c.	9214
	119:154	Defend my c and redeem me;	8190
	119:161	Rulers persecute me without c,	2855
	140:12	the poor and upholds the c of the needy.	5477
	146: 7	the c of the oppressed and gives food to	5477
Pr	24:28	not testify against your neighbor without c,	2855
Ecc	8: 3	Do not stand up for a bad c,	1821
Isa	1:17	Defend the c of the fatherless,	9149
	1:23	They do not defend the c of the fatherless;	9149
	16: 5	in judging seeks justice and speeds the c	NIH
	30:30	The LORD will c men to hear his majestic voice	9048
	34: 8	a year of retribution, to uphold Zion's c.	8189
	40:27	my c is disregarded by my God"?	5477
	47:12	perhaps you will c terror.	6907
	53:10	to crush him and c him to suffer,	2703
	58:14	and I will c you to ride on the heights of	8206
	64: 2	c the nations to quake	AIT
Jer	11:20	for to you I have committed my c.	8190
	20:12	for to you I have committed my c.	8190
	22:16	He defended the c of the poor and needy,	1907
	30:13	There is no one to plead your c,	1907
	40:15	c all the Jews who are gathered around you to be scattered	AIT
	50:34	He will vigorously defend their c so	8190
	51:36	"See, I will defend your c and avenge you;	8190
La	3:52	Those who were my enemies without c hunted me	2855
	3:59	Uphold my c!	5477
Eze	14:23	that I have done nothing in it without c,	2855
	32:10	c many peoples to be appalled	9037
	32:12	c your hordes to fall	5877
	33:12	of the wicked man will not c him to fall	AIT
	36:12	c people, my people Israel, to walk	2143
	36:15	c your nation to fall,	4173
Da	8:24	c astounding devastation	8845
	8:25	He will c deceit to prosper,	928+3338
Mt	18: 7	things that c people to sin!	4998
Lk	2:34	"This child is destined to c the falling	1650
	17: 1	that c people to sin are bound to come,	4998
	17: 2	c one of these little ones to sin.	4997
Ro	14:21	c your brother to fall.	4684
	16:17	for those who c divisions and put obstacles	4472
1Co	8:13	so that I will not c him to fall.	4997
	10:32	not c anyone to stumble,	718
2Co	4:15	and more people may c thanksgiving	NIG
Gal	6:17	Finally, let no one c me trouble,	4218
Php	4: 3	at my side in the c of the gospel,	1877
Heb	12:15	that no bitter root grows up to c trouble	1943
Rev	13:15	and c all who refused to worship the image	4472

CAUSED (48) [CAUSE]
Ge	2:21	c the man to fall into a deep sleep;	5877
	5:29	painful toil of our hands c by the ground	4946
Jdg	9:24	c the men throughout the country to turn	8492
1Ki	11:25	adding to the trouble c by Hadad.	6913
	14:16	and has c Israel to commit."	2627
	15:26	in his sin, which he had c Israel to commit;	2627
	15:30	and had c Israel to commit,	2627
	15:34	in his sin, which he had c Israel to commit.	2627
	16: 2	c my people Israel to sin	2627
	16:13	and had c Israel to commit,	2627
	16:19	and had c Israel to commit,	2627
	16:26	in his sin, which he had c Israel to commit,	2627
	21:22	to anger and have c Israel to sin.'	2627
	22:52	who c Israel to sin.	2627
2Ki	3: 3	which he had c Israel to commit;	2627
	7: 6	c the Arameans to hear	9048
	10:29	which he had c Israel to commit—	2627
	10:31	which he had c Israel to commit.	2627
	13: 2	which he had c Israel to commit.	2627
	13: 6	which he had c Israel to commit.	2627
	13:11	which he had c Israel to commit.	2627
	14:24	which he had c Israel to commit.	2627
	15: 9	which he had c Israel to commit.	2627
	15:18	which he had c Israel to commit.	2627
2Ki	15:24	which he had c Israel to commit.	2627
	15:28	which he had c Israel to commit.	2627
	17:21	the LORD and c them to commit	2627
	21:16	the sin that he had c Judah to commit,	2627
	23:15	who had c Israel to sin—	2627
2Ch	21:11	c the people of Jerusalem to prostitute themselves	2388
Ezr	6:12	c his Name to dwell	10709
Job	34:28	c the cry of the poor to come	995
Ps	106:46	He c them to be pitied	5989
	111: 4	He has c his wonders to be remembered;	6913
	140: 9	trouble their lips have c.	AIT
Isa	21: 2	to an end all the groaning she c.	NIH
Jer	50: 6	and c them to roam on the mountains.	8740
Eze	32:30	the slain in disgrace despite the terror c by	4946
Da	1: 9	Now God had c the official to show favor	5989
Am	3: 6	has not the LORD c it?	6913
Mal	2: 8	by your teaching have c many to stumble;	4173
	2: 9	"So I have c you to be despised	5989
Ac	10:40	from the dead on the third day and c him to	1443
	17: 6	"These men who have c trouble all over	415
2Co	2: 5	If anyone has c grief,	3382
	7: 8	Even if I c you sorrow by my letter,	3382
Jas	4: 5	the spirit he c to live in us envies intensely?	NIG
2Pe	1: 4	and escape the corruption in the world c by	1877

CAUSED (Anglicized) See also RAISED

CAUSES (31) [CAUSE]
Nu	5:21	and denounce you when he c your thigh	5989
2Ch	21:15	the disease c your bowels to come out.'"	4946
Ps	7:16	The trouble he c recoils on himself;	AIT
Pr	10:10	He who winks maliciously c grief,	5989
Isa	8:14	a stone that c men to stumble and a rock	5598
	61:11	up and a garden c seeds to grow,	7541
	64: 2	fire sets twigs ablaze and c water to boil,	1240
Da	8:13	the rebellion that c desolation,	9037
	9:27	up an abomination that c desolation,	9037
	11:31	up the abomination that c desolation.	9037
	12:11	the abomination that c desolation is set	9037
Mt	5:29	If your right eye c you to sin,	4997
	5:30	And if your right hand c you to sin,	4997
	5:32	c her to become an adulteress,	4472
	5:45	He c his sun to rise	422
	13:41	of his kingdom everything that c sin	4998
	18: 6	c one of these little ones who believe in me to sin,	4997
	18: 8	If your hand or your foot c you to sin,	4997
	18: 9	And if your eye c you to sin,	4997
	24:15	that c desolation,' spoken of through	AIT
Mk	9:42	c one of these little ones who believe in me to sin,	4997
	9:43	If your hand c you to sin, cut it off.	4997
	9:45	And if your foot c you to sin, cut it off.	4997
	9:47	And if your eye c you to sin, pluck it out.	4997
	13:14	that c desolation' standing where it does	AIT
Ro	9:33	I lay in Zion a stone that c men to stumble	4682
	14:20	a man to eat anything that c someone else	1328
1Co	8:13	c my brother to fall into sin,	4997
Col	2:19	grows as God c it to grow.	NIG
Jas	4: 1	What c fights and quarrels among you?	4470
1Pe	2: 8	"A stone that c men to stumble and a rock	4682

CAUSEWAY (KJV) See ROAD

CAUSING (4) [CAUSE]
Dt	8: 3	c you to hunger and then feeding you	8279
1Ki	17:20	c her son to die?"	4637
Ps	105:29	c their fish to die.	4637
Rev	13:13	even c fire to come down from heaven	4472

CAUTIONED (1) [CAUTIOUS]
Ac	23:22	the young man and c him,	4133

CAUTIOUS (1) [CAUTIONED]
Pr	12:26	A righteous man is c in friendship,	9365

CAVALRY (7)
Ne	2: 9	The king had also sent army officers and c	7305
Da	11: 40	with chariots and c and a great fleet	7305
Joel	2: 4	they gallop along like c.	7305
Na	3: 3	Charging c, flashing swords	7305
Hab	1: 8	Their c gallops headlong;	7305
Ac	23:32	The next day they let the c go on with him,	2689
	23:33	When the c arrived in Caesarea,	4015s

CAVE (35) [CAVERNS, CAVES]
Ge	19:30	He and his two daughters lived in a c.	5117
	23: 9	so he will sell me the c of Machpelah,	5117
	23:11	and I give you the c that is in it.	5117
	23:17	both the field and the c in it,	5117
	23:19	in the c in the field of Machpelah	5117
	23:20	and the c in it were deeded to Abraham by	5117
	25: 9	in the c of Machpelah near Mamre,	5117
	49:29	in the c in the field of Ephron the Hittite,	5117
	49:30	the c in the field of Machpelah.	5117
	49:32	The field and the c in it were bought from	5117
	50:13	land of Canaan and buried him in the c	5117
Jos	10:16	the five kings had fled and hidden in the c	5117
	10:17	in the c at Makkedah.	5117
	10:18	"Roll large rocks up to the mouth of the c,	5117
	10:22	the c and bring those five kings out to me."	5117

Jos	10:23	So they brought the five kings out of the **c**—	5117
	10:27	from the trees and threw them into the **c**	5117
	10:27	the mouth of the **c** they placed large rocks,	5117
Jdg	15: 8	Then he went down and stayed in a **c** *in*	6186
	15:11	down to the **c** in the rock of Etam and said	6186
1Sa	22: 1	David left Gath and escaped to the **c**	5117
	24: 3	a **c** was there,	5117
	24: 3	David and his men were far back in the **c**.	5117
	24: 7	And Saul left the **c** and went his way.	5117
	24: 8	of the **c** and called out to Saul,	5117
	24:10	into my hands in the **c**.	5117
2Sa	17: 9	he is hidden in a **c** or some other place.	7074
	23:13	down to David at the **c** of Adullam,	5117
1Ki	19: 9	There he went into a **c** and spent the night.	5117
	19:13	and stood at the mouth of the **c**.	5117
1Ch	11:15	to David to the rock at the **c** of Adullam,	5117
Ps	57: T	When he had fled from Saul into the **c**.	5117
	142: T	When he was in the **c**.	5117
Jer	48:28	that makes its nest at the mouth of a **c**.	7074
Jn	11:38	a **c** with a stone laid across the entrance.	*5068*

CAVERNS (1) [CAVE]

Isa	2:21	They will flee to **c** *in* the rocks and to	5942

CAVES (10) [CAVE]

Jdg	6: 2	in mountain clefts, **c** and strongholds.	5117
1Sa	13: 6	they hid in **c** and thickets, among the rocks,	5117
1Ki	18: 4	and hidden them in two **c**,	5117
	18:13	of the LORD's prophets in two **c**,	5117
Isa	2:19	Men will flee to **c** in the rocks and to holes	5117
Jer	49: 8	Turn and flee, hide in deep **c**,	NIH
	49:30	Stay in deep **c**, you who live in Hazor,"	NIH
Eze	33:27	and those in strongholds and **c** will die of	5117
Heb	11:38	and in **c** and holes in the ground.	*5068*
Rev	6:15	and every slave and every free man hid in **c**	*5068*

CEASE (17) [CEASED, CEASING]

Ge	8:22	day and night *will* never **c**."	8697
Jos	9:23	You *will* never **c** to serve as woodcutters	4162
2Ki	18: 6	to the LORD and *did* not **c** to follow him;	6073
Ne	9:19	the pillar of cloud *did* not **c** to guide them	6073
Est	9:28	And these days of Purim *should* never **c** to	6296
Job	3:17	There the wicked **c** *from* turmoil,	2532
	6:17	but that **c to flow** in the dry season,	7551
Ps	46: 9	He **makes** wars **c** to the ends of the earth;	8697
Ecc	12: 3	when the grinders **c** because they are few,	1060
Isa	16: 4	and destruction *will* **c**;	3983
Jer	18:14	from distant sources *ever* **c** to flow?	5980
	31:36	"will the descendants of Israel ever **c** to be	8697
	47: 6	Return to your scabbard; **c** and be still.'	8089
Eze	5:13	"Then my anger *will* **c** and my wrath	3983
1Co	12:15	*it would* not for that reason **c to be** part of	
		the body.	*1639+4024*
	12:16	*it would* not for that reason **c to be** part of	
		the body.	*1639+4024*
	13: 8	where there are prophecies, *they will* **c**;	*2934*

CEASED (3) [CEASE]

Jdg	5: 7	Village life in Israel **c**, ceased until I,	2532
	5: 7	Village life in Israel ceased, **c** until I,	2532
Ps	36: 3	*he has* **c** to be wise and to do good.	2532

CEASING (2) [CEASE]

Ps	35:15	They slandered me without **c**.	1957
Jer	14:17	with tears night and day without **c**;	1949

CEDAR (57) [CEDARS]

Lev	14: 4	that two live clean birds and some **c** wood,	780
	14: 6	together with the **c** wood,	780
	14:49	to take two birds and some **c** wood,	780
	14:51	Then he is to take the **c** wood, the hyssop,	780
	14:52	the **c** wood, the hyssop and the scarlet yarn.	780
Nu	19: 6	The priest is to take some **c** wood,	780
2Sa	5:11	along with **c** logs and carpenters	780
	7: 2	"Here I am, living in a palace of **c**,	780
	7: 2	not built me a house of **c**?" '	780
1Ki	4:33	from the **c** of Lebanon to the hyssop	780
	5: 8	and will do all you want in providing the **c**	780
	5:10	with all the **c** and pine logs he wanted,	780
	6: 9	roofing it with beams and **c** planks.	780
	6:10	to the temple by beams of **c**.	780
	6:15	He lined its interior walls with **c** boards,	780
	6:16	with **c** boards from floor to ceiling to form	780
	6:18	The inside of the temple was **c**,	780
	6:18	Everything was **c**; no stone was to be seen.	780
	6:20	and he also overlaid the altar of **c**.	780
	6:36	and one course of trimmed **c** beams.	780
	7: 2	**c** columns supporting trimmed cedar beams.	780
	7: 2	cedar columns supporting trimmed **c** beams.	780
	7: 3	with **c** above the beams that rested on	780
	7: 7	he covered it with **c** from floor to ceiling.	780
	7:11	cut to size, and **c** beams.	780
	7:12	and one course of trimmed **c** beams,	780
	9:11	with all the **c** and pine and gold he wanted.	780
	10:27	and **c** as plentiful as sycamore-fig trees in	780
2Ki	14: 9	"A thistle in Lebanon sent a message to a **c**	780
1Ch	17: 1	along with **c** logs,	780
	17: 1	"Here I am, living in a palace of **c**,	780
	17: 6	not built me a house of **c**?" '	780
	22: 4	He also provided more **c** logs than could	780
2Ch	1:15	and **c** as plentiful as sycamore-fig trees in	780
	2: 3	"Send me **c** logs as you did	NIH
	2: 3	for my father David when you sent him **c**	780
	2: 8	"Send me also **c**, pine and algum logs	780
	9:27	and **c** as plentiful as sycamore-fig trees in	780
Ezr	3: 7	so that they would bring **c** logs by sea	780
Job	40:17	His tail sways like a **c**;	780
Ps	92:12	they will grow like a **c** of Lebanon;	780
SS	8: 9	we will enclose her with panels of **c**.	780
Isa	41:19	I will put in the desert the **c** and the acacia,	780
Jer	22: 7	up your fine **c** beams and throw them into	780
	22:14	panels it with **c** and decorates it in red.	780
	22:15	a king to have more and more **c**?	780
	22:23	who are nestled in **c** buildings.	780
Eze	17: 3	Taking hold of the top of a **c**,	780
	17:22	from the very top of a **c** and plant it;	780
	17:23	and bear fruit and become a splendid **c**.	780
	27: 5	they took a **c** from Lebanon to make a mast	780
	31: 3	Consider Assyria, once a **c** in Lebanon,	780
Hos	14: 5	Like a **c** of Lebanon he will send	4248
	14: 6	his fragrance like a **c** of Lebanon.	4248
Zep	2:14	the **beams of c** will be exposed.	781
Zec	11: 2	Wail, O pine tree, for the **c** has fallen;	780

CEDARS (19) [CEDAR]

Nu	24: 6	like **c** beside the waters.	780
Jdg	9:15	of the thornbush and consume the **c**	780
1Ki	5: 6	"So give orders that **c** of Lebanon be cut	780
2Ki	19:23	I have cut down its tallest **c**,	780
Ps	29: 5	The voice of the LORD breaks the **c**;	780
	29: 5	the LORD breaks in pieces the **c**	780
	80:10	the mighty **c** with its branches.	780
	104:16	the **c** of Lebanon that he planted.	780
	148: 9	fruit trees and all **c**,	780
SS	1:17	The beams of our house are **c**;	780
	5:15	choice as its **c**.	780
Isa	2:13	for all the **c** *of* Lebanon,	780
	9:10	but we will replace them with **c**."	780
	14: 8	the **c** of Lebanon exult over you and say,	780
	37:24	I have cut down its tallest **c**,	780
	44:14	He cut down **c**,	780
Eze	31: 8	**c** in the garden of God could not rival it,	780
Am	2: 9	he was tall as the **c** and strong as the oaks.	780
Zec	11: 1	O Lebanon, so that fire may devour your **c**!	780

CEDRON (KJV) See KIDRON

CEILING (4)

1Ki	6:15	from the floor of the temple to the **c**,	6212
	6:16	with cedar boards from floor to **c** to form	7815
	7: 7	he covered it with cedar from floor to **c**.	6212
2Ch	3: 7	He overlaid the **c beams**, doorframes,	7771

CELEBRATE (53) [CELEBRATED, CELEBRATING, CELEBRATION, CELEBRATIONS]

Ex	10: 9	because we are to **c** a festival to	NIH
	12:14	for the generations to come you shall **c** it	2510
	12:17	"**C** the Feast of Unleavened Bread,	9068
	12:17	**C** this day as a lasting ordinance for	9068
	12:47	The whole community of Israel *must* **c** it.	6913
	12:48	"An alien living among you who wants to **c**	6913
	23:14	a year *you are to* **c a festival** to me.	2510
	23:15	"**C** the Feast of Unleavened Bread,	9068
	23:16	"**C** the Feast of Harvest with the firstfruits	NIH
	23:16	"**C** the Feast of Ingathering at the end of	NIH
	34:18	"**C** the Feast of Unleavened Bread.	9068
	34:22	"**C** the Feast of Weeks with the firstfruits	6913
Lev	23:39	**c** the festival to the LORD for seven days;	2510
	23:41	**C** this as a festival to the LORD	2510
	23:41	**c** it in the seventh month.	2510
Nu	9: 2	"*Have* the Israelites **c** the Passover at	6913
	9: 3	**C** it at the appointed time,	6913
	9: 4	Moses told the Israelites to **c** the Passover,	6913
	9: 6	But some of them could not **c** the Passover	6913
	9:10	*they may still* **c** the LORD's Passover.	6913
	9:11	*They are to* **c** it on the fourteenth day of	6913
	9:12	*When they* **c** the Passover,	6913
	9:13	and not on a journey fails to **c** the Passover,	6913
	9:14	*to* **c** the LORD's Passover must do so	6913
	29:12	**C** a festival to the LORD for seven days.	2510
Dt	16: 1	the month of Abib and **c** the Passover of	6913
	16:10	Then **c** the Feast of Weeks to	6913
	16:13	**C** the Feast of Tabernacles for seven days	6913
	16:15	For seven days **c the Feast** to	2510
Jdg	16:23	to Dagon their god and to **c**,	8525
2Sa	6:21	*I will* **c** before the LORD.	8471
2Ki	23:21	"**C** the Passover to the LORD your God,	6913
2Ch	30: 1	in Jerusalem and **c** the Passover to	6913
	30: 2	in Jerusalem decided to **c** the Passover in	6913
	30: 3	not been able to **c** it at the regular time	6913
	30: 5	to come to Jerusalem and **c** the Passover to	6913
	30:13	of people assembled in Jerusalem to **c**	6913
	30:23	The whole assembly then agreed to **c**	6913
Ne	8:12	to send portions of food and to **c**	6913
	12:27	and were brought to Jerusalem to **c** joyfully	6913
Est	9:21	to have them **c** annually the fourteenth	6913
Ps	145: 7	*They will* **c** your abundant goodness	2352+5580
Isa	30:29	as on the night you **c** a **holy** festival;	7727
Na	1:15	**C** your festivals, O Judah,	2510
Zec	14:16	and to **c** the Feast of Tabernacles.	2510
	14:18	the nations that do not go up to **c** the Feast	2510
	14:19	the nations that do not go up to **c** the Feast	2510
Mt	26:18	*to* **c** the Passover with my disciples	4472
Lk	15:23	*Let's* have a feast and **c**.	2370
	15:24	So they began *to* **c**.	2370
	15:29	even a young goat so *I could* **c**	2370
	15:32	But we had *to* **c** and be glad,	2370
Rev	11:10	the earth will gloat over them and *will* **c**	2370

CELEBRATED (18) [CELEBRATE]

Jos	5:10	the Israelites **c** the Passover.	6913
1Ki	8:65	They **c** it before the LORD our God	NIH
2Ki	23:23	this Passover **was c** to the LORD	6913
2Ch	7: 9	for *they had* **c** the dedication of the altar	6913
	30: 5	not *been* **c** in large numbers according	6913
	30:21	in Jerusalem **c** the Feast	6913
	30:23	so for another seven days *they* **c** joyfully.	6913
	35: 1	Josiah **c** the Passover to the LORD	6913
	35:17	The Israelites who were present **c**	6913
	35:18	of the kings of Israel *had ever* **c** such	6913
	35:19	This Passover **was c** in the eighteenth year	6913
Ezr	3: 4	*they* **c** the Feast of Tabernacles with	6913
	6:16	**c** the dedication of the house of God	10522
	6:19	the exiles **c** the Passover.	6913
	6:22	For seven days *they* **c** with joy the Feast	6913
Ne	8:17	the Israelites **had** not **c** it like this.	6913
	8:18	*They* **c** the feast for seven days,	6913
Est	9:28	of Purim should never cease to be **c** by	NIH

CELEBRATING (5) [CELEBRATE]

Ex	31:16	**c** it for the generations to come as	6913
2Sa	6: 5	David and the whole house of Israel *were* **c**	8471
1Ch	13: 8	the Israelites *were* **c** with all their might	8471
	15:29	when she saw King David dancing and **c**,	8471
Est	8:17	with feasting and **c**.	3202+3427

CELEBRATION (7) [CELEBRATE]

1Sa	11:15	Saul and all the Israelites **held a** great **c**.	8523
2Ch	35:16	of the LORD was carried out for the **c** of	6913
Est	8:15	And the city of Susa **held a** joyous **c**.	7412
	9:22	into joy and their mourning into a day of **c**.	3202
	9:23	to continue the **c** they had begun,	889S
Ac	7:41	They brought sacrifices to it and **held a c**	2370
Col	2:16	a **New Moon c** or a Sabbath day.	3741

CELEBRATIONS (1) [CELEBRATE]

Hos	2:11	I will stop all her **c**:	5375

CELESTIAL (2)

2Pe	2:10	not afraid to slander **c** beings;	1518
Jude	1: 8	reject authority and slander **c** beings.	1518

CELL (3)

Jer	37:16	Jeremiah was put into a **vaulted c** in	2844
Ac	12: 7	and a light shone in the **c**.	3862
	16:24	in the inner **c** and fastened their feet in	5871

CELLARS (KJV) See VATS, SUPPLIES

CENCHREA (2)

Ac	18:18	he had his hair cut off at **C** because of	3020
Ro	16: 1	a servant of the church in **C**.	3020

CENSER (8) [CENSERS]

Lev	16:12	He is to take a **c** full of burning coals from	4746
Nu	16:17	Each man is to take his **c** and put incense	4746
	16:18	So each man took his **c**,	4746
	16:46	"Take your **c** and put incense in it,	4746
2Ch	26:19	a **c** in his hand ready to burn incense,	5233
Eze	8:11	Each had a **c** in his hand,	5233
Rev	8: 3	Another angel, who had a golden **c**,	3338
	8: 5	Then the angel took the **c**,	3338

CENSERS (13) [CENSER]

Lev	10: 1	and Abihu took their **c**, put fire in them	4746
Nu	16: 6	your followers are to do this: Take **c**	4746
	16:17	250 **c** in all—	4746
	16:17	You and Aaron are to present your **c** also."	4746
	16:37	to take the **c** out of the smoldering remains	4746
	16:37	for the **c** are holy—	NIH
	16:38	the **c** *of* the men who sinned at the cost	4746
	16:38	Hammer **the c** into sheets to overlay	4392S
	16:39	the priest collected the bronze **c** brought	4746
1Ki	7:50	sprinkling bowls, dishes and **c**;	4746
2Ki	25:15	of the imperial guard took away the **c**	4746
2Ch	4:22	sprinkling bowls, dishes and **c**;	4746
Jer	52:19	**c**, sprinkling bowls, pots, lampstands,	4746

CENSUS (17)

Ex	30:12	"When *you* take a **c** of the Israelites	906+5951+8031
	38:25	**were counted in the c**	7212
Nu	1: 2	"Take a **c** *of* the whole Israelite	5951+8031
	1:49	**include** them **in the c**	906+5951+8031
	4: 2	"Take a **c** *of* the Kohathite branch of the Levites	906+5951+8031
	4:22	"Take a **c** also *of* the Gershonites	5951+8031
	14:29	in the **c** and who has grumbled against me.	5031
	26: 2	"Take a **c** *of* the whole Israelite	906+5951+8031
	26: 4	a **c** of the men twenty years and over,	NIH
2Sa	24: 1	"Go and **take a c** *of* Israel and Judah."	4948
2Ki	12: 4	the money collected in the **c**,	408+6296
1Ch	21: 1	against Israel and incited David to **take a c**	4948
2Ch	2:17	Solomon **took a c** *of* all the aliens	6218

2Ch	2:17	c his father David had taken;	6218+6222
Lk	2: 1	c should be taken of	616
	2: 2	(This was the first c that took place	615
Ac	5:37	of the c and led a band of people in revolt.	615

CENTER (20) [CENTERS, CENTRAL, CENTRALLY]

Ex	26:28	The c crossbar is to extend from end to end	9399
	28:32	with an opening for the head in its c.	9348
	36:33	the c crossbar so that it extended from end	9399
	39:23	with an opening in the c of the robe like	9348
Nu	35: 5	with the town in the c.	9348
Jdg	9:37	"Look, people are coming down from the c	3179
1Ki	7:25	and their hindquarters were toward the c.	1074
2Ch	4: 4	and their hindquarters were toward the c.	1074
	6:13	and had placed it in the c of	9348
Eze	1: 4	The c of the fire looked like	9348
	5: 5	which I have set in the c of the nations,	3179
	38:12	living at the c of the land."	3179
	48: 8	the sanctuary will be in the c of it.	9348
	48:10	In the c of it will be the sanctuary of	9348
	48:15	The city will be in the c of it	9348
	48:21	with the temple sanctuary will be in the c	9348
	48:22	the c of the area that belongs to the prince.	9348
Rev	4: 6	In the c, around the throne,	3545
	5: 6	standing in the c of the throne,	3545
	7:17	at the c of the throne will be their shepherd;	3545

CENTERS (1) [CENTER]

Ge	10:10	The first c of his kingdom were Babylon,	AIT

CENTRAL (1) [CENTER]

Jdg	16:29	the two c pillars on which the temple stood.	9348

CENTRALLY (1) [CENTER]

Dt	19: 2	for yourselves three cities c located in	928+9348

CENTURION (21) [CENTURION'S, CENTURIONS]

Mt	8: 5	a c came to him, asking for help.	1672
	8: 8	The c replied, "Lord, I do not deserve	1672
	8:13	Then Jesus said to the c, "Go!	1672
	27:54	When the c and those with him	1672
Mk	15:39	And when the c, who stood there	3035
	15:44	Summoning the c, he asked him	3035
	15:45	When he learned from the c that it was so,	3035
Lk	7: 3	The c heard of Jesus and sent some elders	NIG
	7: 6	the house when the c sent friends to say	1672
	23:47	The c, seeing what had happened,	1672
Ac	10: 1	Cornelius, a c in what was known as	1672
	10:22	"We have come from Cornelius the c.	1672
	22:25	Paul said to the c standing there,	1672
	22:26	When the c heard this,	1672
	23:18	The c said, "Paul, the prisoner,	NIG
	24:23	He ordered the c to keep Paul under guard	1672
	27: 1	over to a c named Julius,	1672
	27: 6	the c found an Alexandrian ship sailing	1672
	27:11	But the c, instead of listening	1672
	27:31	Then Paul said to the c and the soldiers,	1672
	27:43	But the c wanted to spare Paul's life	1672

CENTURION'S (1) [CENTURION]

Lk	7: 2	There a c servant, whom his master valued	1672

CENTURIONS (2) [CENTURION]

Ac	23:17	Then Paul called one of the c and said,	1672
	23:23	he called two of his c and ordered them,	1672

CEPHAS (4) [PETER]

Jn	1:42	You will be called C" (which, when translated, is Peter).	3064
1Co	1:12	another, "I follow C";	3064
	3:22	whether Paul or Apollos or C or the world	3064
	9: 5	and the Lord's brothers and C?	3064

CEREMONIAL (9) [CEREMONY]

Lev	14: 2	of his c cleansing, when he is brought to	3200
	15:13	for his c cleansing;	3200
Mk	7: 3	unless they give their hands a c washing,	4778
Jn	2: 6	the kind used by the Jews for c washing,	2752
	3:25	a certain Jew over the matter of c washing.	2752
	11:55	for their c cleansing before the Passover.	49
	18:28	and to avoid c uncleanness the Jews did	3620
Heb	9:10	of food and drink and various c washings,	968
	13: 9	strengthened by grace, not by c foods,	NIG

CEREMONIALLY (40) [CEREMONY]

Lev	4:12	the camp to a place c clean,	3196
	5: 2	if a person touches anything c unclean—	3238
	6:11	the camp to a place that is c clean.	3196
	7:19	that touches anything c unclean must not	3238
	7:19	anyone c clean may eat it.	3196
	10:14	Eat them in a c clean place;	3196
	11: 4	it is c unclean for you.	3238
	12: 2	to a son will be c unclean for seven days,	3237
	12: 7	then she will be c clean from her flow	3197
	13: 2	pronounce him c unclean.	3237
	14: 8	then he will be c clean.	3197
	15:28	and after that she will be c clean.	3197
	15:33	with a woman who is c unclean.	3238

Lev	17:15	and he will be c unclean till evening;	3237
	21: 1	make himself c unclean	3237
	22: 3	if any of your descendants is c unclean	3240
	27:11	If what he vowed is a c unclean animal—	3238
Nu	5: 2	who is c unclean because of a dead body.	3238
	6: 7	make himself c unclean	3237
	8: 6	the other Israelites and make them c clean.	3197
	9: 6	on that day because they were c unclean	3238
	9:13	But if a man who is c clean and not on	3196
	18:11	in your household who is c clean may eat it.	3196
	18:13	in your household who is c clean may eat it.	3196
	19: 7	but he will be c unclean till evening.	3237
	19: 9	and put them in a c clean place outside	3196
	19:19	Then a man who is c clean is	3196
Dt	12:15	the c unclean and the clean may eat it.	3238
	12:22	Both the c unclean and the clean may eat.	3238
	14: 7	they are c unclean for you.	3238
	15:22	the c unclean and the clean may eat it,	3238
1Sa	20:26	to David to make him c unclean—	1194+3196
2Ch	13:11	on the c clean table and light the lamps on	3196
	30:17	for all those who were not c clean	3196
Ezr	6:20	and were all c clean.	3196
Ne	12:30	purified themselves c,	3197
Isa	66:20	of the LORD in c clean vessels.	3196
Eze	22:10	when they are c unclean.	3238
Ac	24:18	I was c clean when they found me in	49
Heb	9:13	on those who are c unclean sanctify them	3124

CEREMONIES (1) [CEREMONY]

Heb	9:21	the tabernacle and everything used in its c.	3311

CEREMONY (4) [CEREMONIAL, CEREMONIALLY, CEREMONIES]

Ge	50:11	a solemn c of mourning."	65
Ex	12:25	as he promised, observe this c.	6275
	12:26	'What does this c mean to you?'	6275
	13: 5	you are to observe this c in this month:	6275

CERTAIN (37) [CERTAINTY, CERTAINLY]

Ge	15:13	"Know for c that your descendants	3359+3359
	28:11	When he reached a c place,	2021
Nu	16: 1	the son of Levi, and c Reubenites—	NIH
Jos	8:14	at a c place overlooking the Arabah.	4595
Jdg	13: 2	A c man of Zorah, named Manoah,	285
1Sa	1: 1	There was a c man from Ramathaim,	285
	21: 2	"The king charged me with a c matter	AIT
	21: 2	I have told them to meet me at a c place	532+7141
	25: 2	A c man in Maon,	NIH
2Sa	12: 1	he said, "There were two men in a c town,	285
1Ki	13:11	there was a c old prophet living in Bethel,	285
2Ki	19: 7	in him that when he hears a c report,	NIH
2Ch	17: 8	With them were c Levites—	2021
Ne	7:73	along with c of the people and the rest of	4946
Est	3: 8	a c people dispersed and scattered among	285
Isa	37: 7	in him so that when he hears a c report,	NIH
Da	2: 8	"I am c that you are trying to gain time,	10313+10327+10427
Hos	5: 9	the tribes of Israel I proclaim what is c.	586
Mt	26:18	"Go into the city to a c man and tell him,	1265
Mk	15:21	A c man from Cyrene, Simon,	5516
Lk	7:41	"Two men owed money to a c moneylender.	5516
	11: 1	One day Jesus was praying in a c place.	5516
	12:16	"The ground of a c rich man produced	5516
	14:16	"A c man was preparing a great banquet.	5516
	18: 2	"In a c town there was a judge	5516
	18:18	A c ruler asked him, "Good teacher,	5516
Jn	3:25	of John's disciples and a c Jew over	5516
	4:46	a c royal official whose son lay sick	5516
Ac	7:16	the sons of Hamor at Shechem for a c sum	NIG
	28:23	They arranged to meet Paul on a c day,	NIG
Gal	2:12	Before c men came from James,	5516
1Ti	1: 3	so that you may command c men not	NIG
	4: 3	and order them to abstain from c foods,	NIG
Heb	4: 7	Therefore God again set a c day,	5516
	11: 1	of what we hope for and c of what we do	1793
2Pe	1:19	the word of the prophets made more c,	1010
Jude	1: 4	c men whose condemnation was written	5516

CERTAINLY (49) [CERTAIN]

Ex	22: 3	"A thief must c make restitution,	8966+8966
	22:23	I will c hear their cry.	9048+9048
	22:33	because the worship of their gods will c be	3954
Nu	13:30	for we can c do it."	3523+3523
	22:33	I would c have killed you by now,	3954
	27: 7	You must c give them property as	5989+5989
Dt	4:26	not live there long but will c be destroyed.	9012+9012
	13: 9	must c put him to death.	2222+2222
	13:15	you must c put to the sword all who live in that town.	5782+5782
	23:21	the LORD your God will c demand it	2011+2011
	30:18	that you will c be destroyed.	6+6
	31:18	And I will c hide my face on that day	6259+6259
Jos	3:10	that he will c drive out before you	3769+3769
Jdg	11:10	we will c do as you say."	561+4202
	21: 5	be put to death.	4637+4637
1Sa	25:28	the LORD will c make a lasting dynasty	6913+6913
	30: 8	"You will c overtake them and	5952+5952
1Ki	11:11	most c tear the kingdom away	7973+7973
	13:32	towns of Samaria will c come true."	2118+2118
2Ki	1: 4	You will c die!' "	4637+4637
	1: 6	You will c die!' " "	4637+4637
	1:16	You will c die!' ';	4637+4637
	8:10	'You will c recover';	2649+2649

2Ki	8:14	He told me that you would c recover.	2649+2649
Jer	32: 4	the Babylonians but will c be handed over	928+3338+5989+5989
	36:29	that the king of Babylon would c come	995+995
	38: 3	'This city will c be handed over to the army	928+3338+5989+5989
	42: 4	"I will c pray to the LORD your God	2180
	44:17	We will c do everything we said we would:	6913+6913
	44:25	'We will c carry out the vows we made	6913+6913
Da	3:24	They replied, "C, O king."	10002+10327
Am	7:17	And Israel will c go into exile,	1655+1655
Hab	2: 3	it will c come and will not delay.	995+995
Mal	3:15	C the evildoers prosper,	1685
Mt	5:20	you will c not enter the kingdom	3590+4024
	10:42	he will c not lose his reward."	3590+4024
	24:34	this generation will c not pass away	3590+4024
Mk	9:41	because you belong to Christ will c not lose his reward.	3590+4024
	13:30	this generation will c not pass away	3590+4024
Lk	21:32	this generation will c not pass away	3590+4024
	22:59	"C this fellow was with him,	237+2093
Ac	21:22	They will c hear that you have come,	4122
Ro	3: 6	C not! If that were so,	1181+3590
	6: 5	we will c also be united with him	247
	7: 7	Is the law sin? C not!	1181+3590
1Co	11:22	Shall I praise you for this? C not!	NIG
Gal	3:21	then righteousness would c have come by	3953
1Th	2:18	c I, Paul, did, again and again—	3525
	4:15	will c not precede those who have fallen asleep.	3590+4024

CERTAINTY (2) [CERTAIN]

Lk	1: 4	the c of the things you have been taught.	854
Jn	17: 8	They knew with c that I came from you,	242

CERTIFICATE (7) [CERTIFIED]

Dt	24: 1	and he writes her a c of divorce,	6219
	24: 3	and writes her a c of divorce,	6219
Isa	50: 1	"Where is your mother's c of divorce	6219
Jer	3: 8	I gave faithless Israel her c of divorce	6219
Mt	5:31	must give her a c of divorce.'	687
	19: 7	that a man give his wife a c of divorce	1046
Mk	10: 4	to write a c of divorce and send her away."	1046

CERTIFIED (1) [CERTIFICATE]

Jn	3:33	The man who has accepted it has c that God is truthful.	3456+3836+5381

CHAFF (18)

Job	13:25	Will you chase after dry c?	7990
	21:18	like c swept away by a gale?	5161
	41:28	slingstones are like c to him.	7990
Ps	1: 4	They are like c that the wind blows away.	5161
	35: 5	May they be like c before the wind,	5161
	83:13	O my God, like c before the wind.	7990
Isa	17:13	driven before the wind like c on the hills,	5161
	29: 5	the ruthless hordes like blown c.	5161
	33:11	You conceive c, you give birth to straw;	3143
	40:24	and a whirlwind sweeps them away like c.	7990
	41: 2	to windblown c with his bow.	7990
	41:15	and reduce the hills to c.	5161
Jer	13:24	"I will scatter you like c driven by	7990
Da	2:35	like c on a threshing floor in the summer.	10534
Hos	13: 3	like c swirling from a threshing floor,	5161
Zep	2: 2	and that day sweeps on like c,	5161
Mt	3:12	into the barn and burning up the c	949
Lk	3:17	up the c with unquenchable fire."	949

CHAIN (9) [CHAINED, CHAINS]

Ge	41:42	in robes of fine linen and put a gold c	8054
2Ch	3: 5	with palm tree and c designs.	9249
Pr	1: 9	be a garland to grace your head and a c	6736
Da	5: 7	and have a gold c placed around his neck,	10212
	5:16	and have a gold c placed around your neck,	10212
	5:29	a gold c was placed around his neck,	10212
Mk	5: 3	not even with a c.	268
Ac	28:20	of Israel that I am bound with this c."	268
Rev	20: 1	and holding in his hand a great c.	268

CHAINED (5) [CHAIN]

Mk	5: 4	For he had often been c hand and foot,	268+1313
Lk	8:29	and though he was c hand and foot	268+1297
2Ti	2: 9	even to the point of being c like a criminal.	1301
	2: 9	But God's word is not c.	1313
Heb	11:36	while still others were c and put in prison.	1301

CHAINS (50) [CHAIN]

Ex	28:14	and two braided c of pure gold,	9249
	28:14	and attach the c to the settings.	6310+9249
	28:22	"For the breastpiece make braided c	9249
	28:24	the two gold c to the rings at the corners of	6310
	28:25	the other ends of the c to the two settings,	6310
	39:15	For the breastpiece they made braided c	9249
	39:17	They fastened the two gold c to the rings at	6310
	39:18	the other ends of the c to the two settings,	6310
Jdg	8:26	or the c that were on their camels' necks.	6736
1Ki	6:21	and extended gold c across the front of	8411
	7:17	of interwoven c festooned the capitals	5126+9249
2Ki	23:33	Pharaoh Neco put him in c at Riblah in	673
2Ch	3:16	He made interwoven c and put them on top	9249

2Ch	3:16	and attached them to the **c**.	9249
Job	36: 8	But if men are bound in **c**,	2414
Ps	2: 3	"Let us break their **c**," they say,	4593
	107:10	prisoners suffering in **iron c**,	1366
	107:14	the deepest gloom and broke away their **c**.	4593
	116:16	you have freed me from my **c**.	4591
Ecc	7:26	a trap and whose hands are **c**.	657
Isa	3:20	the headdresses and **ankle c** and sashes,	7578
	28:22	or your **c** will become heavier;	4591
	40:19	with gold and fashions silver **c** for it.	8416
	45:14	coming over to you in **c**.	2414
	52: 2	Free yourself from the **c** *on* your neck,	4591
	58: 6	the **c** *of* injustice and untie the cords of	3078
Jer	40: 1	in **c** among all the captives from Jerusalem	272
	40: 4	But today I am freeing you from the **c**	272
La	3: 7	he has weighed me down with **c**.	5733
Eze	7:23	"Prepare **c**, because the land is full	8408
Na	3:10	all her great men **were put in c**.	928+2414+8415
Mk	5: 4	the **c** apart and broke the irons on his feet.	268
Lk	8:29	he had broken his **c** and had been driven by	1301
Ac	12: 6	bound *with* two **c**,	268
	12: 7	he said, and the **c** fell off Peter's wrists.	268
	16:26	and everybody's **c** came loose.	1301
	21:33	and ordered him to be bound *with* two **c**.	268
	22:29	**put** Paul, a Roman citizen, **in c**.	1313
	26:29	except for these **c**."	1301
Eph	6:20	for which I am an ambassador in **c**.	268
Php	1: 7	for whether I am in **c** or defending	1301
	1:13	to everyone else that I am in **c** for Christ.	1301
	1:14	*Because of* my **c**,	1301
	1:17	up trouble for me while I am *in* **c**.	1301
Col	4: 3	for which *I am* **in c**.	1313
	4:18	Remember my **c**.	1301
2Ti	1:16	and was not ashamed of my **c**.	268
Phm	1:10	who became my son while I was in **c**.	1301
	1:13	in helping me while I am in **c** for	1301
Jude	1: 6	bound *with* everlasting **c** for judgment	1301

CHAIR (4)

1Sa	1: 9	the priest was sitting on a **c** by the doorpost	4058
	4:13	there was Eli sitting on his **c** *by* the side of	4058
	4:18	Eli fell backward off his **c** by the side of	4058
2Ki	4:10	a **c** and a lamp for him.	4058

CHALCEDONY (1)

Rev	21:19	the second sapphire, the third **c**,	5907

CHALCOL (KJV) See CALCOL

CHALDAEANS (KJV) See BABYLON, BABYLONIA

CHALDEA (2) [CHALDEAN, CHALDEANS]

Eze	23:15	Babylonian chariot officers, natives of C.	4169
	23:16	and sent messengers to them in C.	4169

CHALDEAN (1) [CHALDEA]

Ezr	5:12	over to Nebuchadnezzar the C,	10373

CHALDEANS (9) [CHALDEA]

Ge	11:28	Haran died in Ur of the C,	4169
	11:31	and together they set out from Ur of the C	4169
	15: 7	who brought you out of Ur of the C	4169
Ne	9: 7	of Ur of the C and named him Abraham.	4169
Job	1:17	"The C formed three raiding parties	4169
Eze	12:13	the land of the C, but he will not see it,	4169
	23:14	figures of C portrayed in red,	4169
	23:23	the Babylonians and all the C,	4169
Ac	7: 4	"So he left the land of the C and settled	5900

CHALDEES (KJV) See CHALDEAN

CHALK (1)

Isa	27: 9	the altar stones to be like **c** stones crushed	1732

CHALLENGE (5) [CHALLENGED]

2Ki	14: 8	*with the* **c**: "Come, meet me face to face."	606
2Ch	25:17	he sent this **c** to Jehoash son of Jehoahaz,	606
Jer	49:19	Who is like me and who *can* **c** me?	3585
	50:44	Who is like me and who *can* **c** me?	3585
Mal	3:15	and even *those who* **c** God escape.' "	1043

CHALLENGED (2) [CHALLENGE]

Jn	8:13	The Pharisees **c** him, "Here you are,	3306
	18:26	the man whose ear Peter had cut off, **c** him,	3306

CHAMBER (3) [CHAMBERS]

Job	37: 9	The tempest comes out from its **c**,	2540
Ps	45:13	All glorious is the princess within [her **c**];	NIH
Joel	2:16	and the bride her **c**.	2903

CHAMBERLAIN (KJV) See EUNUCH, OFFICERS

CHAMBERS (5) [CHAMBER]

Ezr	8:29	until you weigh them out in the **c** *of*	4384
Ps	104: 3	the beams of his **upper c** on their waters.	6608

Ps	104:13	He waters the mountains from his **upper c**;	6608
Pr	7:27	leading down to the **c** of death.	2540
SS	1: 4	Let the king bring me into his **c**.	2540

CHAMELEON (1)

Lev	11:30	the wall lizard, the skink and the **c**.	9491

CHAMOIS (KJV) See MOUNTAIN SHEEP

CHAMPAIGN (KJV) See ARABAH

CHAMPION (3) [CHAMPIONS]

1Sa	17: 4	A **c** named Goliath, who was from Gath,	408+1227+2021
	17:23	Goliath, the Philistine **c** from Gath,	408+1227+2021
Ps	19: 5	like a **c** rejoicing to run his course.	1475

CHAMPIONS (1) [CHAMPION]

Isa	5:22	at drinking wine and **c** at mixing drinks,	408+2657

CHANAAN (KJV) See CANAAN

CHANCE (5)

Jos	8:20	but they **had** no **c** to escape in any direction,	928+2118+3338
1Sa	6: 9	and that it happened to us by **c**."	5247
	19: 2	"My father Saul *is* **looking for a c**	1335
Ecc	9:11	but time and **c** happen to them all.	7004
Mk	6:31	and going that they did not even **have a c**	2320

CHANCELLOR (KJV) See COMMANDING OFFICER

CHANGE (33) [CHANGED, CHANGERS, CHANGES, CHANGING]

Ge	35: 2	and purify yourselves and **c** your clothes.	2736
Ex	13:17	they might **c** *their* **minds** and return	5714
Lev	13:16	Should the raw flesh **c** and turn white,	8740
Nu	23:19	nor a son of man, that *he should* **c** *his* **mind**.	5714
	23:20	he has blessed, and *I* cannot **c** it.	8740
1Sa	15:29	of Israel does not lie or **c** *his* **mind**;	5714
	15:29	he is not a man, that *he should* **c** *his* **mind**."	5714
2Sa	14:20	Your servant Joab did this to **c**	6015
1Ki	8:47	and if *they have* a **c** of heart in the land	8740
	11:33	after this, Jeroboam *did* not **c** his evil ways,	8740
2Ch	6:37	and if *they have* a **c** of heart in the land	8740
Ezr	6:12	or people who lifts a hand to **c** this decree	10731
Job	9:27	*I will* **c** my expression, and smile,'	6440
	14:20	you **c** his countenance and send him away.	9101
Ps	55:19	men who never **c** their ways	2722
	102:26	Like clothing you will **c** them	2736
	110: 4	LORD has sworn and *will* not **c** *his* mind:	5714
Jer	7: 5	If *you* **really c** your ways	3512+3512
	13:16	but he will turn it to thick darkness and **c** it	8883
	13:23	Can the Ethiopian **c** his skin or	2200
Da	2: 9	hoping the situation *will* **c**.	10731
	7:25	and try to **c** the set times and the laws.	10731
Mal	3: 6	"I the LORD *do* not **c**.	9101
Mt	18: 3	*you* **c** and become like little children,	5138
Ac	6:14	of Nazareth will destroy this place and **c**	248
Gal	4:20	be with you now and **c** my tone,	248
Heb	7:12	For *when there is* a **c** of the priesthood,	3572
	7:12	there must also be a **c** of the law.	3557
	7:21	Lord has sworn and *will* not **c** *his* mind:	3564
	12:17	He could bring about no **c** of mind,	3567
Jas	1:17	who *does* not **c** like shifting shadows.	1913+4164
	4: 9	**C** your laughter to mourning and your joy	3573
Jude	1: 4	who **c** the grace of our God into a license	3572

CHANGED (32) [CHANGE]

Ge	31:41	and *you* **c** my wages ten times.	2736
	41:14	When he had shaved and **c** his clothes,	2736
Ex	7:15	and take in your hand the staff that **was c**	2200
	7:17	and *it will* be **c** into blood.	2200
	7:20	and all the water **was c** into blood.	2200
	10:19	And the LORD **c** the wind *to*	2200
	14: 5	and his officials **c** their minds about them	2200
Lev	13:55	and *if* the mildew *has* not **c** its appearance,	2200
Nu	32:38	and Baal Meon (these names **were c**)	6015
Jdg	7:19	just after *they had* **c** the guard.	7756+7756
1Sa	10: 6	and *you will* be **c** into a different person.	2200
	10: 9	God **c** Saul's heart,	337+2200
2Sa	12:20	put on lotions and **c** his clothes,	2736
1Ki	2:15	But *things* **c**, and the kingdom has gone	6015
2Ki	23:34	of his father Josiah and **c** Eliakim's name	6015
	24: 1	But then *he* **c** his **mind** and rebelled	8740
	24:17	in his place and **c** his name *to* Zedekiah.	6015
2Ch	36: 4	and Jerusalem and **c** Eliakim's name	6015
Jer	2:11	Has a nation *ever* **c** its gods?	3558
	15: 7	for *they have* not **c** their ways.	8740
	34:11	But afterward *they* **c** *their* **minds**	8740
Da	3:19	and his attitude toward them **c**.	10731
	4:16	Let his mind *be* **c** from that of a man	10731
	6:15	or edict that the king issues *can be* **c**."	10731
	6:17	so that Daniel's situation *might* not be **c**.	10731
Hos	11: 8	My heart *is* **c** within me;	2200
Mt	21:29	but later *he* **c** *his* **mind** and went.	3564
Lk	9:29	the appearance of his face **c**,	1181+2283
Ac	28: 6	they **c** *their* **minds** and said he was a god.	3554

1Co	15:51	We will not all sleep, but *we will* all be **c**—	248
	15:52	raise imperishable, and we *will* be **c**.	248
Heb	1:12	like a garment *they will* be **c**.	248

CHANGERS (3) [CHANGE]

Mt	21:12	He overturned the tables *of* the **money c** and	3142
Mk	11:15	He overturned the tables *of* the **money c** and	3142
Jn	2:15	*of* the **money c** and overturned their tables.	3142

CHANGES (3) [CHANGE]

Ezr	6:11	I decree that if anyone **c** this edict,	10731
Ecc	8: 1	a man's face and **c** its hard appearance.	9101
Da	2:21	He **c** times and seasons;	10731

CHANGING (3) [CHANGE]

Ge	31: 7	*by* **c** my wages ten times.	2736
Ezr	6:22	the LORD had filled them with joy *by* **c**	6015
Jer	2:36	about so much, **c** your ways?	9101

CHANNEL (1) [CHANNELED, CHANNELS]

Job	38:25	Who cuts a **c** for the torrents of rain,	9498

CHANNELED (1) [CHANNEL]

2Ch	32:30	the upper outlet of the Gihon spring and **c**	3837

CHANNELS (4) [CHANNEL]

Job	6:17	and in the heat vanish from their **c**.	5226
Isa	8: 7	It will overflow all its **c**,	692
Eze	31: 4	and sent their **c** to all the trees of the field.	9498
Zec	4: 2	with seven **c** to the lights.	4609

CHANT (3)

Eze	32:16	"This is the lament *they will* **c** *for* her.	7801
	32:16	The daughters of the nations *will* **c** it;	7801
	32:16	for Egypt and all her hordes *they will* **c** it,	7801

CHAOS (1)

Isa	34:11	the measuring line of **c** and the plumb line	9332

CHAPEL (KJV) See SANCTUARY

CHAPITER, CHAPITERS (KJV) See CAPITALS, TOPS

CHARACTER (7) [CHARACTERS]

Ru	3:11	that you are a woman of **noble c**.	2657
Pr	12: 4	A wife of **noble c** is her husband's crown,	2657
	31:10	A wife of **noble c** who can find?	2657
Ac	17:11	the Bereans were **of more noble c** than	2302
Ro	5: 4	perseverance, **c**; and character, hope.	1509
	5: 4	perseverance, character; and **c**, hope.	1509
1Co	15:33	"Bad company corrupts good **c**."	2456

CHARACTERS (1) [CHARACTER]

Ac	17: 5	up some bad **c** from the marketplace,	467

CHARASHIM (KJV) See GE HARASHIM

CHARCHEMISH (KJV) See CARCHEMISH

CHARCOAL (1)

Pr	26:21	As **c** to embers and as wood to fire,	7073

CHARGE (162) [CHARGED, CHARGES, CHARGING]

Ge	24: 2	the *one* in **c** of all that he had,	5440
	39: 4	Potiphar **put** him **in c** of his household,	7212
	39: 5	the time *he* put him **in c** of his household	7212
	39: 6	with Joseph in **c**,	NIH
	39: 8	"With me in **c**," he told her,	NIH
	39:22	warden put Joseph **in c** of all those held	928+3338
	41:33	and wise man and put him **in c** of the land	6584
	41:40	You shall be **in c** of my palace,	6584
	41:41	"I hereby put you **in c** of the whole land	6584
	41:43	Thus he put him **in c** of the whole land	6584
	47: 6	put them **in c** of my own livestock."	8569
Ex	5: 6	to the slave drivers and foremen **in c** of	928
	22:25	**c** him no interest.	8492
	23: 7	Have nothing to do with a false **c** and do	1821
Lev	5: 1	not speak up when he hears a **public c**	460
Nu	1:50	the Levites to be **in c** of the tabernacle of	6584
	4:16	is to have **c** *of* the oil for the light,	7213
	4:16	He is to be **in c** *of* the entire tabernacle	7213
	7: 2	who were the tribal leaders **in c**	6584+6641
	18: 8	"I myself have put you **in c** *of*	5466
Dt	22:20	the **c** is true and no proof of	1821
	23:19	**c** your brother **interest**,	5967+5968
	23:20	**c** a foreigner **interest**,	5967
2Sa	20:24	Adoniram was **in c** of forced labor;	6584
	20:24	and David put him **in c** of his bodyguard.	448
1Ki	2: 1	*he gave* a **c** *to* Solomon his son.	7422
	4: 5	**in c** of the district officers;	6584
	4: 6	**in c** of the palace;	6584
	4: 6	**in c** of forced labor.	6584
	5:14	Adoniram was **in c** of the forced labor.	6584
	9:23	They were also the chief officials **in c** of	6584

1Ki	11:28	*he* **put** him **in c** of the whole labor force of	7212
	12:18	who was **in c** of forced labor,	6584
	16: 9	the man **in c** of the palace at Tirzah.	6584
	18: 3	who was **in c** of his palace.	6584
2Ki	7:17	**put** the officer on whose arm he leaned **in c**	7212
	11:15	*who were* **in c** of the troops:	7212
	15: 5	Jotham the king's son **had c** of the palace	6584
	25:19	he took the officer **in c** of the fighting men	7224
	25:19	in **c** of conscripting the people of the land	NIH
1Ch	6:31	the men David **put in c** *of* the music	
			3338+6584+6641
	9:11	the **official in c** of the house of God;	5592
	9:20	of Eleazar was **in c** of the gatekeepers,	5592
	9:23	They and their descendants were **in c** of	6584
	9:27	and they **had c** of the key	6584
	9:28	Some of them were **in c** of the articles used	6584
	9:32	of their Kohathite brothers were **in c** of	6584
	11:25	And David put him **in c** of his bodyguard.	6584
	15:22	the head Levite *was* **in c** of the singing;	6254
	15:27	who was **in c** of the singing of the choirs.	8569
	23:28	to be **in c** of the courtyards, the side rooms,	6584
	23:29	They were **in c** of the bread set out on	4200
	26:20	Their fellow Levites were **in c** of	6584
	26:22	They were **in c** of the treasuries of	6584
	26:24	was the officer **in c** of the treasuries.	6584
	26:26	Shelomith and his relatives were **in c** of all	6584
	26:32	and King David **put** them **in c** of	7212
	27: 2	**In c** of the first division,	6584
	27: 4	**In c** of the division for	6584
	27: 6	His son Ammizabad was **in c**	NIH
	27:25	of Adiel was **in c** of the royal storehouses.	6584
	27:25	of Uzziah was **in c** of the storehouses in	6584
	27:26	Ezri son of Kelub was **in c** of	6584
	27:27	the Ramathite was **in c** of the vineyards.	6584
	27:27	was **in c** of the produce of	6584
	27:28	Baal-Hanan the Gederite was **in c** of	6584
	27:28	Joash was **in c** of the supplies of olive oil.	6584
	27:29	the Sharonite was **in c** of the herds grazing	6584
	27:29	Shaphat son of Adlai was **in c** of the herds	6584
	27:30	Obil the Ishmaelite was **in c** of the camels.	6584
	27:30	the Meronothite was **in c** of the donkeys.	6584
	27:31	Jaziz the Hagrite was **in c** of the flocks.	6584
	27:31	All these were the **officials in c**	8569
	28: 1	of hundreds, and the **officials in c** *of* all	8569
	28: 8	now I **c** you in the sight of all Israel and of	NIH
	29: 6	and the **officials in c** *of*	8569
2Ch	10:18	who was **in c** of forced labor,	6584
	23:14	*who were* **in c** of the troops,	7212
	24:13	The **men in c** of the work were diligent,	6913
	26:21	Jotham his son **had c** of the palace	6584
	28: 7	Azrikam the **officer in c** of the palace,	5592
	31:12	a Levite, was **in c** of these things,	5592
	31:13	the **official in c** *of* the temple of God.	5592
	31:14	was **in c** of the freewill offerings given	6584
	34:13	**had c** of the laborers and supervised all	6584
Ne	7: 2	*I* **put in c** of Jerusalem my brother Hanani,	7422
	11:16	who **had c** of the outside work of the house	6584
	11:21	and Ziha and Gishpa were **in c** of them.	6584
	12: 8	was **in c** of the songs of thanksgiving.	6584
	12:44	that time men were appointed to be **in c** of	6584
	13: 4	Eliashib the priest had been put **in c** of	928
	13:13	**put** Shelemiah the priest, Zadok the scribe,	
		and a Levite named Pedaiah **in c** of the	
		storerooms	238+732+6584
Est	2: 3	*who is* **in c** of the women;	9068
	2: 8	*who* **had c** of the harem.	9068
	2:14	the king's eunuch *who was* **in c** of	9068
	2:15	king's eunuch *who was* **in c** of the harem,	9068
Job	34:13	Who **put** him **in c** of the whole world?	8492
Ps	69:27	**C** them with crime upon crime;	5989
SS	2: 7	*I* **c** you by the gazelles and by the does of	8678
	3: 5	*I* **c** you by the gazelles and by the does of	8678
	5: 8	O daughters of Jerusalem, *I* **c** you—	8678
	5: 9	that *you* **c** us so?	8678
	8: 4	Daughters of Jerusalem, *I* **c** you:	8678
Isa	3: 6	**take c** of this heap of ruins!'	3338+9393
	22:15	to Shebna, who is **in c** of the palace:	6584
	33:18	Where is the **officer in c** of the towers?"	6221
Jer	15:13	without **c**, because of all your sins	4697
	29:26	in place of Jehoiada to be **in c** *of* the house	7224
	40: 7	the land and *had* **put** him **in c** of the men,	7212
	46: 9	**C**, O horses!	6590
	52:25	he took the officer **in c** of the fighting men,	7224
	52:25	in **c** of conscripting the people of the land	NIH
Eze	40:45	the priests *who* **have c** of the temple,	5466+9068
	40:46	the priests *who* **have c** of the altar.	5466+9068
	44: 8	you put *others* **in c** of my sanctuary.	9068
	44:11	**having c** of the gates of the temple	7213
	44:14	Yet I will put them **in c** of the duties of	9068
Da	2:48	placed him **in c** of all its wise men.	10505+10647
Hos	4: 1	because the LORD has a **c** to bring	8190
	4: 4	"But *let* no man **bring a c**,	8189
	12: 2	The LORD has a **c** to bring against Judah;	8190
Joel	2: 7	They **c** like warriors;	8132
Mic	6: 2	*he is* **lodging** a **c** against Israel.	3519
Zec	3: 6	of the LORD **gave** *this* **c** to Joshua:	6386
	3: 7	and **have c** of my courts,	9068
Mt	24:45	the master *has* **put in c** of the servants	2770
	24:47	*he will* **put** him **in c** of all his possessions.	2770
	25:21	*I* **will put** you **in c** of many things.	2770
	25:23	*I* **will put** you **in c** of many things.	2770
	26:63	"*I* **c** you **under oath** by the living God:	2019
	27:14	Jesus made no reply, not even to a single **c**	4839
	27:37	the written **c** against him:	162
Mk	3:21	they went *to* **take c** of him, for they said,	3195
	13:34	and puts his servants **in c**,	2026
	15:26	The written notice of the **c**	162

Lk	12:42	whom the master **puts in c** of his servants	2770
	12:44	*he will* **put** him **in c** of all his possessions.	2770
	19:17	take **c** of ten cities.'	2026
	19:19	'You take **c** of five cities.'	1181+2062
	23: 4	"I find no **basis for a c** against this man."	165
Jn	13:29	Since Judas **had c** of the money,	2400
	18:38	I find no **basis for a c** against him.	162
	19: 4	to let you know that I find no **basis for a c**	162
	19: 6	I find no **basis for a c** against him."	162
	19:16	So the soldiers **took c** of Jesus.	4161
Ac	8:27	an important official **in c** of all the treasury	
			1639+2093
	23:29	but there was no **c** against him	1598
	25:18	*they* **did** not **c** him with any of	162+5770
	28:19	not that I had any **c** to bring against	2989
Ro	3: 9	We have **already made the c** that Jews	4577
	8:33	Who **will bring** any **c**	1592
1Co	9:18	the gospel I may offer it **free of c**,	78
2Co	11: 7	the gospel of God to you **free of c**?	1562
Gal	3:24	So the law was **put in c** to **lead** us to Christ	4080
1Th	5:27	*I* **c** you **before the Lord**	1941
1Ti	5:21	*I* **c** you, in the sight of God,	1371
	6:13	the good confession, *I* **c** you	4133
2Ti	4: 1	*I* **give** you this **c**:	1371
Tit	1: 6	and are not open to the **c** of being wild	2990
Phm	1:18	owes you anything, **c** it to me.	1823
Rev	14:18	Still another angel, who had **c** of the fire,	2026
	16: 5	I heard the angel in **c** of the waters say:	NIG

CHARGED (10) [CHARGE]

Dt	1:16	And *I* **c** your judges at that time:	7422
Jos	6:20	so every man **c** straight in,	6590
Jdg	20:33	and the Israelite ambush **c** out of its place	1631
1Sa	21: 2	"The king **c** me **with** a certain matter	7422
1Ch	22: 6	and **c** him to build a house for the LORD,	7422
Eze	18:20	of the wicked will be **c** against him.	6584
Da	8: 4	I watched the ram *as he* **c** toward the west	5590
	8: 6	beside the canal and **c** at him in great rage.	8132
Ac	18:13	they **c**, "is persuading the people	3306
	19:40	in danger of **being c with** rioting because	1592

CHARGER (KJV) See PLATE, PLATTER

CHARGES (34) [CHARGE]

1Ki	21:13	and sat opposite him and **brought c against**	6386
Ne	5: 6	When I heard their outcry and these **c**,	1821
Job	4:18	if *he* **c** his angels with error,	8492
	10: 2	but tell me what *you* **have against** me.	8189
	13:19	*Can* anyone **bring c** against me?	8189
	22: 4	that he rebukes you and **brings c**	5477
	23: 6	No, he *would* not **press c** against me.	8492
	24:12	But God **c** no one *with* wrongdoing.	8492
	39:21	and **c** into the fray.	3655
Isa	50: 8	Who then *will* **bring c** against me?	8189
Jer	2: 9	"Therefore *I* **bring c** against you again,"	8189
	2: 9	"And *I will* **bring c** against your	8189
	2:29	"Why *do you* **bring c** against me?	8189
	25:31	the LORD will bring **c** against the nations;	8190
Da	6: 4	and the satraps tried to find **grounds for c**	10544
	6: 5	"We will never find any **basis for c**	10544
Hos	4: 4	for your people are like *those who* **bring c**	8189
Lk	23:14	and have found no basis for *your* **c**	2989
Jn	18:29	"What **c** are you bringing	2990
Ac	7: 1	high priest asked him, "Are these **c** true?"	NIG
	19:38	*They can* **press c**.	1592
	24: 1	and they **brought** their **c** against Paul before	1872
	24: 8	**c** we *are* **bringing against**	2989
	24:13	**c** they are now **making against**	2989
	24:19	to be here before you and **bring c**	2989
	25: 2	**appeared** before him **and presented the c**	1872
	25: 7	with me and **press c** against the man there,	2989
	25: 9	and stand trial before me there on these **c**?"	NIG
	25:11	the **c brought against** me by these Jews are	2989
	25:15	the Jews **brought c** against him and asked	1872
	25:16	to defend himself against their **c**.	1598
	25:20	and stand trial there on these **c**.	NIG
	25:27	without specifying the **c** against him."	162

CHARGING (6) [CHARGE]

Ne	5:11	and also *the* **usury** you *are* **c** them—	5957
Job	1:22	Job did not sin *by* **c** God *with* wrongdoing.	5989
	15:26	defiantly **c** against him with a thick,	8132
Pr	28:15	or a **c** bear is a wicked man ruling over	9212
Jer	8: 6	Each pursues his own course like a horse **c**	8851
Na	3: 3	**C** cavalry, flashing swords	6590

CHARIOT (65) [CHARIOTEERS, CHARIOTS]

Ge	41:43	in a **c** as his second-in-command,	5324
	46:29	Joseph had his **c** made ready and went	5324
Ex	14: 6	So he had his **c** made ready	8207
Jdg	4:15	Sisera abandoned his **c** and fled on foot.	5324
	5:28	'Why is his **c** so long in coming?	8207
2Sa	8: 4	but a hundred of the **c horses.**	8207
	15: 1	a **c** and horses and with fifty men to run	5324
1Ki	4:26	Solomon had four thousand stalls for **c**	5323
		horses,	
	4:28	of barley and straw for the **c horses** and	8224
	7:33	The wheels were made like a **c** wheels;	5324
	10:26	the **c** cities and also with him in Jerusalem.	8207
	10:29	a **c** from Egypt for six hundred shekels	5324
	12:18	to get into his **c** and escape to Jerusalem.	5324

1Ki	18:44	'Hitch up your **c** and go down before	NIH
	20:25	horse for horse and **c** for chariot—	8207
	20:25	horse for horse and chariot for **c**—	8207
	20:33	Ahab had him come up into his **c**.	5324
	22:31	the king of Aram had ordered his thirty-two	
		c commanders,	8207
	22:32	When the **c** commanders saw Jehoshaphat,	8207
	22:33	the **c** commanders saw that he was not	8207
	22:34	The king told his **c** driver,	8208
	22:35	and the king was propped up in his **c** facing	5324
	22:35	from his wound ran onto the floor of the **c**,	8207
	22:38	They washed the **c** at a pool in Samaria	8207
2Ki	2:11	a **c** of fire and horses of fire appeared	8207
	5:21	he got down from the **c** to meet him.	5324
	5:26	the man got down from his **c** to meet you?	5324
	8:21	and his **c** commanders, but he rose up	8207
	9:16	Then he **got into** his **c** and rode to Jezreel.	8206
	9:21	"Hitch up my **c**," Joram ordered.	8207
	9:21	each in his own **c**, to meet Jehu.	8207
	9:24	and he slumped down in his **c**.	8207
	9:25	Jehu said to Bidkar, his **c officer**,	8957
	9:27	in his **c** on the way up to Gur near Ibleam,	5324
	9:28	His servants **took** him **by c** to Jerusalem.	8206
	10:15	he did, and Jehu helped him up into the **c**.	5324
	10:16	Then he had him ride along in his **c**.	8207
	23:30	Josiah's servants brought his body **in a c**	8206
1Ch	18: 4	but a hundred of the **c horses.**	8207
	28:18	He also gave him the plan for the **c**, that is,	5324
2Ch	1:14	the **c** cities and also with him in Jerusalem.	8207
	1:17	a **c** from Egypt for six hundred shekels	5324
	9:25	the **c** cities and also with him in Jerusalem.	8207
	10:18	to get into his **c** and escape to Jerusalem.	5324
	18:30	of Aram had ordered his **c** commanders,	8207
	18:31	When the **c** commanders saw Jehoshaphat,	8207
	18:32	when the **c** commanders saw that he was	8207
	18:33	The king told the **c** driver,	8208
	18:34	of Israel propped himself up in his **c** facing	5324
	21: 9	and his **c** commanders,	8207
	35:24	So they took him out of his **c**,	5324
	35:24	in the other **c** he had and brought him	8207
Ps	76: 6	O God of Jacob, both horse and **c** lie still.	8207
	104: 3	the clouds his **c** and rides on the wings of	8213
Isa	5:28	their **c** wheels like a whirlwind.	1649
	21: 9	here comes a man in a **c** with a team	8207
Jer	51:21	with you I shatter **c** and driver,	8207
Eze	23:23	of them looked like Babylonian **c officers**,	8957
	23:23	**c** officers and men of high rank,	8957
Mic	1:13	harness the team to the **c**.	5324
Zec	6: 2	The first **c** had red horses,	5324
Ac	8:28	in his **c** reading the book of Isaiah	761
	8:29	"Go to that **c** and stay near it."	761
	8:30	to the **c** and heard the man reading Isaiah	NIG
	8:38	And he gave orders to stop the **c**.	761

CHARIOTEERS (11) [CHARIOT]

1Sa	13: 5	six thousand **c**, and soldiers as numerous as	7305
2Sa	8: 4	of his chariots, seven thousand **c**	7305
	10:18	and David killed seven hundred of their **c**	8207
1Ki	9:22	and the commanders of his chariots and **c**.	7305
1Ch	18: 4	of his chariots, seven thousand **c**	7305
	19: 6	of silver to hire chariots and **c**	7305
	19: 7	They hired thirty-two thousand **chariots and c**,	8207
	19:18	and David killed seven thousand of their **c**	8207
2Ch	8: 9	and commanders of his chariots and **c**.	7305
Isa	22: 6	with her **c** and horses;	132+8207
Jer	46: 9	Drive furiously, O **c**!	8207

CHARIOTS (102) [CHARIOT]

Ge	50: 9	**C** and horsemen also went up with him.	8207
Ex	14: 7	He took six hundred of the best **c**,	8207
	14: 7	along with all the other **c** *of* Egypt.	8207
	14: 9	all Pharaoh's horses and **c**,	8207
	14:17	through his **c** and his horsemen.	8207
	14:18	his **c** and his horsemen."	8207
	14:23	and **c** and horsemen followed them into	8207
	14:25	He made the wheels of their **c** come off so	5324
	14:26	the Egyptians and their **c** and horsemen."	8207
	14:28	The water flowed back and covered the **c**	8207
	15: 4	Pharaoh's **c** and his army he has hurled	5324
	15:19	**c** and horsemen went into the sea,	8207
Dt	11: 4	to its horses and **c**,	8207
	20: 1	against your enemies and see horses and **c**	8207
Jos	11: 4	and a large number of horses and **c**—	8207
	11: 6	to hamstring their horses and burn their **c**."	5324
	11: 9	and burned their **c**.	5324
	17:16	in the plain have iron **c**,	8207
	17:18	though the Canaanites have iron **c** and	8207
	24: 6	with **c** and horsemen as far as the Red Sea.	8207
Jdg	1:19	because they had iron **c**.	8207
	4: 3	Because he had nine hundred iron **c**	8207
	4: 7	Jabin's army, with his **c** and his troops	8207
	4:13	Sisera gathered together his nine hundred	
		iron **c**	8207
	4:15	the LORD routed Sisera and all his **c**	8207
	4:16	But Barak pursued the **c** and army as far	8207
	5:28	Why is the clatter of his **c** delayed?'	5324
1Sa	8:11	and make them serve with his **c** and horses,	5324
	8:11	and they will run in front of his **c**.	5324
	8:12	of war and equipment for his **c**.	8207
	13: 5	with three thousand **c**,	8207
2Sa	1: 6	with the **c** and riders almost upon him,	8207
	1: 6	David captured a thousand of his **c**,	8207
1Ki	1: 5	So he got **c** and horses ready,	8207
	9:19	and the towns for his **c** and for his horses—	8207

1Ki	9:22	the commanders of his c and charioteers.	8207
	10:26	Solomon accumulated c and horses;	8207
	10:26	he had fourteen hundred c	8207
	16: 9	who had command of half his c,	8207
	20: 1	by thirty-two kings with their horses and c,	8207
	20:21	the horses and c and inflicted heavy losses	8207
2Ki	2:12	The c and horsemen of Israel!"	8207
	5: 9	So Naaman went with his horses and c	8207
	6:14	and c and a strong force there.	8207
	6:15	an army with horses and c had surrounded	8207
	6:17	of horses and c of fire all around Elisha.	8207
	7: 6	the sound of c and horses and a great army,	8207
	7:14	So they selected two c with their horses,	8207
	8:21	So Jehoram went to Zair with all his c.	8207
	9:25	how you and I were riding together in c	8206
	10: 2	with you and you have c and horses,	8207
	13: 7	ten c and ten thousand foot soldiers,	8207
	13:14	"The c and horsemen of Israel!"	8207
	18:24	though you are depending on Egypt for c	8207
	19:23	"With my many c I have ascended	8207
	23:11	then burned the c dedicated to the sun.	5324
1Ch	18: 4	David captured a thousand of his c,	8207
	19: 6	a thousand talents of silver to hire c	8207
	19: 7	They hired thirty-two thousand c and charioteers,	8207
2Ch	1:14	Solomon accumulated c and horses.	8207
	1:14	he had fourteen hundred c	8207
	8: 6	all the cities for his c and for his horses—	8207
	8: 9	and commanders of his c and charioteers.	8207
	9:25	for horses and c,	5324
	12: 3	With twelve hundred c	8207
	14: 9	with a vast army and three hundred c,	5324
	16: 8	with great numbers of c and horsemen?	8207
	21: 9	with his officers and all his c.	8207
Ps	20: 7	Some trust in c and some in horses,	8207
	68:17	The c of God are tens of thousands	8207
SS	1: 9	to a mare harnessed to one of the c	8207
	6:12	my desire set me among the royal c	5324
Isa	2: 7	there is no end to their c.	5324
	21: 7	When he sees c with teams of horses,	8207
	22: 7	Your choicest valleys are full of c,	8207
	22:18	and there your splendid c will remain—	5324
	31: 1	who trust in the multitude of their c and in	8207
	36: 9	though you are depending on Egypt for c	8207
	37:24	'With my many c I have ascended	8207
	43:17	who drew out the c and horses, the army	8207
	66:15	and his c are like a whirlwind;	5324
	66:20	on horses, in c and wagons,	8207
Jer	4:13	his c come like a whirlwind,	5324
	17:25	and their officials will come riding in c and	8207
	22: 4	riding in c and on horses,	8207
	47: 3	of enemy c and the rumble of their wheels.	8207
	50:37	A sword against her horses and c and all	8207
Eze	23:24	c and wagons and with a throng of people;	8207
	26: 7	king of kings, with horses and c,	8207
	26:10	wagons and c when he enters your gates	8207
Da	11:40	the North will storm out against him with c	8207
Joel	2: 5	that of c they leap over the mountaintops,	5324
Mic	5:10	from among you and demolish your c.	5324
Na	2: 3	The metal on the c flashes on	8207
	2: 4	The c storm through the streets,	8207
	2:13	"I will burn up your c in smoke,	8207
	3: 2	galloping horses and jolting c!	5324
Hab	3: 8	with your horses and your victorious c?	5324
Hag	2:22	I will overthrow c and their drivers;	5324
Zec	6: 1	before me were four c coming out from	5324
	9:10	I will take away the c from Ephraim and	8207
Rev	9: 9	of many horses and c rushing into battle.	761

CHARITY (KJV) See LOVE

CHARM (2) [CHARMED, CHARMER, CHARMING, CHARMS]

Pr	17: 8	A bribe is a c to the one who gives it;	74+2834
	31:30	C is deceptive, and beauty is fleeting;	2834

CHARMED (2) [CHARM]

Ecc	10:11	If a snake bites before it is c,	4318
Jer	8:17	vipers that cannot be c,	4318

CHARMER (2) [CHARM]

Ps	58: 5	that will not heed the tune of the c,	4317
Ecc	10:11	there is no profit for the c.	1251+4383

CHARMING (2) [CHARM]

Pr	26:25	Though his speech is c,	2858
SS	1:16	Oh, how c!	5833

CHARMS (3) [CHARM]

Isa	3:20	the perfume bottles and c,	4318
Eze	13:18	Woe to the women who sew magic c	4086
	13:20	I am against your magic c	4086

CHARRAN (KJV) See HARAN

CHARRED (3) [CHARS]

Jdg	15:14	The ropes on his arms became like c flax,	836+928+1277+2021
Eze	15: 5	when the fire has burned it and it is c?	3081
	24:10	and let the bones be c.	3081

CHARS (1) [CHARRED]

Eze	15: 4	the fire burns both ends and c the middle,	3081

CHASE (8) [CHASED, CHASES, CHASING]

Lev	26: 8	Five of you will c a hundred,	8103
	26: 8	and a hundred of you will c ten thousand,	8103
Dt	32:30	How could one man c a thousand,	8103
Job	13:25	Will you c after dry chaff?	8103
Isa	1:23	they all love bribes and c after gifts.	8103
Jer	49:19	I will c Edom from its land in an instant.	8132
	50:44	I will c Babylon from its land in	8132
Hos	2: 7	She will c after her lovers but	8103

CHASED (10) [CHASE]

Dt	1:44	they c you like a swarm of bees	8103
Jos	7: 5	They c the Israelites from the city gate	8103
	8:24	and in the desert where they had c them,	8103
Jdg	1: 6	but they c him and caught him,	8103
	9:40	Abimelech c him, and many fell wounded	8103
	20:43	c them and easily overran them in	8103
2Sa	2:19	He c Abner, turning neither to the right nor	8103
2Ki	9:27	Jehu c him, shouting, "Kill him too!"	8103
Jer	50:17	a scattered flock that lions have c away.	5615
La	4:19	they c us over the mountains and lay	1944

CHASES (2) [CHASE]

Pr	12:11	but he who c fantasies lacks judgment.	8103
	28:19	but the one who c fantasies will have his fill	8103

CHASING (12) [CHASE]

1Sa	17:53	Israelites returned from c the Philistines	339+1944
2Sa	2:21	But Asahel would not stop c him.	339
	2:22	Again Abner warned Asahel, "Stop c me!	339
Ecc	1:14	meaningless, a c after the wind.	8296
	1:17	too, is a c after the wind.	8301
	2:11	meaningless, a c after the wind;	8296
	2:17	All of it is meaningless, a c after the wind.	8296
	2:26	meaningless, a c after the wind.	8296
	4: 4	meaningless, a c after the wind.	8296
	4: 6	with toil and c after the wind.	8296
	4:16	meaningless, a c after the wind.	8301
	6: 9	meaningless, a c after the wind.	8296

CHASM (1)

Lk	16:26	between us and you a great c has been fixed,	5926

CHASTE (KJV) See PURE

CHASTENED (2)

Job	33:19	Or a man may be c on a bed of pain	3519
Ps	118:18	The LORD has c me severely,	3579+3579

CHASTISE (KJV) See PUNISH, SCOURGE, CATCH, TRAINED

CHATTER (2) [CHATTERING]

1Ti	6:20	from godless c and the opposing ideas	3032
2Ti	2:16	Avoid godless c,	3032

CHATTERING (2) [CHATTER]

Pr	10: 8	but a c fool comes to ruin.	8557
	10:10	and a c fool comes to ruin.	8557

CHEAPER (1)

Jn	2:10	the choice wine first and then the c wine	1781

CHEAT (2) [CHEATED, CHEATING, CHEATS]

Mal	1:14	the c who has an acceptable male	5792
1Co	6: 8	Instead, you yourselves c and do wrong,	691

CHEATED (5) [CHEAT]

Ge	31: 7	yet your father has c me	9438
1Sa	12: 3	Whom have I c?	6943
	12: 4	"You have not c or oppressed us,"	6943
Lk	19: 8	and if I have c anybody out of anything,	5193
1Co	6: 7	Why not rather be c?	691

CHEATING (1) [CHEAT]

Am	8: 5	the measure, boosting the price and c	6430

CHEATS (1) [CHEAT]

Lev	6: 2	or if he c him,	6943

CHEBAR (KJV) See KEBAR

CHECK (2) [CHECKED]

Ge	30:33	whenever you c on the wages	995+4200+7156
Jas	3: 2	keep his whole body in c.	5902

CHECKED (3) [CHECK]

2Ki	6:10	king of Israel on the place indicated	448+8938
Ezr	8:15	I c among the people and the priests,	1067
Ps	106:30	and the plague was c.	6806

CHECKER WORK (KJV) See INTERWOVEN CHAINS

CHEDORLAOMER (KJV) See KEDORLAOMER

CHEEK (5) [CHEEKS]

Job	16:10	they strike my c in scorn and unite together	4305
La	3:30	Let him offer his c	4305
Mic	5: 1	They will strike Israel's ruler on the c with	4305
Mt	5:39	If someone strikes you on the right c,	4965
Lk	6:29	If someone strikes you on one c,	4965

CHEEKS (4) [CHEEK]

SS	1:10	Your c are beautiful with earrings,	4305
	5:13	His c are like beds of spice	4305
Isa	50: 6	my c to those who pulled out my beard;	4305
La	1: 2	tears are upon her c.	4305

CHEER (2) [CHEERED, CHEERFUL, CHEERFULLY, CHEERING, CHEERS]

1Ki	21: 7	Get up and eat! C up.	3512+4213
Mk	10:49	So they called to the blind man, "C up!	2510

CHEERED (1) [CHEER]

Php	2:19	that I also may be c when I receive news	2379

CHEERFUL (5) [CHEER]

Pr	15:13	A happy heart makes the face c,	3512
	15:15	but the c heart has a continual feast.	3202
	15:30	A c look brings joy to the heart,	4401
	17:22	A c heart is good medicine,	8524
2Co	9: 7	for God loves a c giver.	2659

CHEERFULLY (1) [CHEER]

Ro	12: 8	if it is showing mercy, let him do it c.	1877+2660

CHEERING (3) [CHEER]

1Ki	1:45	From there they have gone up c,	8524
2Ch	23:12	the noise of the people running and c	2146
Ecc	2: 3	I tried c myself with wine,	5432

CHEERS (2) [CHEER]

Jdg	9:13	my wine, which c both gods and men,	8523
Pr	12:25	but a kind word c him up.	8523

CHEESE (2) [CHEESES]

2Sa	17:29	and c from cows' milk for David	9147
Job	10:10	like milk and curdle me like c,	1482

CHEESES (1) [CHEESE]

1Sa	17:18	Take along these ten c to the commander	2692+3043

CHELAL (KJV) See KELAL

CHELLUH (KJV) See KELUHI

CHELUB (KJV) See KELUB

CHELUBAI (KJV) See CALEB

CHEMARIMS (KJV) See PAGAN

CHEMOSH (8)

Nu	21:29	You are destroyed, O people of C!	4019
Jdg	11:24	not take what your god C gives you?	4019
1Ki	11: 7	a high place for C the detestable god	4019
	11:33	C the god of the Moabites,	4019
2Ki	23:13	for C the vile god of Moab,	4019
Jer	48: 7	and C will go into exile,	4019
	48:13	Then Moab will be ashamed of C,	4019
	48:46	The people of C are destroyed;	4019

CHENAANAH (KJV) See KENAANAH

CHENANI (KJV) See KENANI

CHENANIAH (KJV) See KENANIAH

CHEPHAR-HAAMMONAI (KJV) See KEPHAR AMMONI

CHEPHIRAH (KJV) See KEPHIRAH

CHERAN (KJV) See KERAN

CHERETHIMS, CHERETHITES (KJV) See KERETHITES

CHERISH (2) [CHERISHED, CHERISHES]

Ps	17:14	You still the hunger of those you c;	7621
	83: 3	they plot against *those* you c.	7621

CHERISHED (2) [CHERISH]

Ps	66:18	If *I had* c sin in my heart,	8011
Hos	9:16	I will slay their c offspring."	4718

CHERISHES (1) [CHERISH]

Pr	19: 8	he who c understanding prospers.	9068

CHERITH (KJV) See KERITH

CHERUB (16) [CHERUBIM]

Ex	25:19	Make one c on one end and	4131
	25:19	on one end and the second c on the other;	4131
	37: 8	He made one c on one end and	4131
	37: 8	on one end and the second c on the other;	4131
1Ki	6:24	of the first c was five cubits long, and	4131
	6:25	The second c also measured ten cubits,	4131
	6:26	The height of each c was ten cubits.	4131
	6:27	The wing of one c touched one wall,	4131
2Ch	3:11	One wing of the first c was five cubits long	NIH
	3:11	touched the wing of the other c.	4131
	3:12	of the second c was five cubits long	4131
	3:12	touched the wing of the first c.	4131
Eze	10:14	One face was that of a c,	4131
	28:14	You were anointed as a guardian c,	4131
	28:16	O guardian c, from among the fiery stones.	4131
	41:18	Each c had two faces:	4131

CHERUBIM (73) [CHERUB]

Ge	3:24	the east side of the Garden of Eden c and	4131
Ex	25:18	And make two c out of hammered gold at	4131
	25:19	make the c of one piece with the cover,	4131
	25:20	The c are to have their wings spread upward	4131
	25:20	The c are to face each other,	4131
	25:22	above the cover between the two c that are	4131
	26: 1	with c worked into them by	4131
	26:31	with c worked into it by	4131
	36: 8	with c worked into them by	4131
	36:35	with c worked into it by	4131
	37: 7	Then he made two c out of hammered gold	4131
	37: 9	The c had their wings spread upward,	4131
	37: 9	The c faced each other,	4131
Nu	7:89	the two c above the atonement cover on	4131
1Sa	4: 4	who is enthroned between the c.	4131
2Sa	6: 2	who is enthroned between the c that are on	4131
	22:11	He mounted the c and flew;	4131
1Ki	6:23	In the inner sanctuary he made a pair of c	4131
	6:25	The two c were identical in size and shape.	4131
	6:27	He placed the c inside the innermost room	4131
	6:28	He overlaid the c with gold.	4131
	6:29	he carved c, palm trees and open flowers.	4131
	6:32	on the two olive wood doors he carved c,	4131
	6:32	the c and palm trees with beaten gold.	4131
	6:35	He carved c, palm trees and open flowers	4131
	7:29	bulls and c—and on the uprights as well.	4131
	7:36	He engraved c, lions and palm trees on	4131
	8: 6	and put it beneath the wings of the c.	4131
	8: 7	The c spread their wings over the place of	4131
2Ki	19:15	God of Israel, enthroned between the c,	4131
1Ch	13: 6	who is enthroned between the c—	4131
	28:18	the c of gold that spread their wings	4131
2Ch	3: 7	and he carved c on the walls.	4131
	3:10	a pair of sculptured c and overlaid them	4131
	3:11	of the c was twenty cubits.	4131
	3:13	wings of these c extended twenty cubits.	4131
	3:14	with c worked into it.	4131
	5: 7	and put it beneath the wings of the c.	4131
	5: 8	The c spread their wings over the place of	4131
Ps	18:10	He mounted the c and flew;	4131
	80: 1	you who sit enthroned between the c,	4131
	99: 1	he sits enthroned between the c,	4131
Isa	37:16	God of Israel, enthroned between the c,	4131
Eze		of Israel went up from above the c,	4131
	10: 1	that was over the heads of the c.	4131
	10: 2	"Go in among the wheels beneath the c.	4131
	10: 2	from among the c and scatter them over	4131
	10: 3	Now the c were standing on the south side	4131
	10: 4	above the c and moved to the threshold of	4131
	10: 5	The sound of the wings of the c could	4131
	10: 6	from among the c,"	4131
	10: 7	Then one of the c reached out his hand to	4131
	10: 8	of the c could be seen what looked like	4131
	10: 9	I saw beside the c four wheels,	4131
	10: 9	one beside each of the c;	4131
	10:11	of the four directions the c faced;	2157^S
	10:11	the wheels did not turn about as the c went.	4392^S
	10:11	The c went in whatever direction	NIH
	10:14	Each of the c had four faces:	NIH
	10:15	Then the c rose upward.	4131
	10:16	When the c moved, the wheels	4131
	10:16	when the c spread their wings to rise from	4131
	10:17	When the c stood still, they also stood still;	4392^S
	10:17	and when the c rose, they rose with them,	4392^S
	10:18	of the temple and stopped above the c.	4131
	10:19	the c spread their wings and rose from	4131
	10:20	and I realized that they were c.	4131
	11:22	Then the c, with the wheels beside them,	4131
	41:18	were carved c and palm trees.	4131
	41:18	Palm trees alternated with c.	4131
	41:20	c and palm trees were carved on the wall of	4131

Eze	41:25	of the outer sanctuary were carved c	4131
Heb	9: 5	Above the ark were the c of the Glory,	5938

CHESALON (KJV) See KESALON

CHESED (KJV) See KESED

CHESIL (KJV) See KESIL

CHESNUT (KJV) See PLANE

CHEST (17) [CHESTS]

Ex	25:10	"Have them make a c *of* acacia wood—	778
	25:14	the poles into the rings on the sides of the c	778
Dt	10: 1	Also make a wooden c.	778
	10: 2	Then you are to put them in the c."	778
1Sa	6: 8	and in a c beside it put	761
	6:11	along with it the c containing the gold rats	761
	6:15	with the c containing the gold objects.	761
2Ki	12: 9	Jehoiada the priest took a c and bored	778
	12: 9	in **the** c all the money that was brought	9004^S
	12:10	a large amount of money in the c,	778
2Ch	24: 8	a c was made and placed outside,	778
	24:10	dropping them into the c until it was full.	778
	24:11	the c was brought in by the Levites to	778
	24:11	and carry it back to its place.	778
Job	41:24	His c is hard as rock,	4213
Da	2:32	its c and arms of silver,	10249
Rev	1:13	and with a golden sash around his c.	3466

CHESTS (1) [CHEST]

Rev	15: 6	and wore golden sashes around their c.	5111

CHESULLOTH (KJV) See KESULLOTH

CHEW (6) [CHEWED, CHEWS]

Lev	11: 4	" 'There are some *that* only c the cud	6590
	11: 7	*does* not c the cud; it is unclean for you.	1760
	11:26	*that does* not c the cud is unclean for you;	6590
Dt	14: 7	of *those that* c the cud or that have	6590
	14: 7	Although they c the cud,	6590
	14: 8	it does not c the cud.	NIH

CHEWED (1) [CHEW]

Jnh	4: 7	*which* c the vine so that it withered.	5782

CHEWS (5) [CHEW]

Lev	11: 3	a split hoof completely divided and *that* c	6590
	11: 4	The camel, though it c the cud,	6590
	11: 5	The coney, though it c the cud,	6590
	11: 6	The rabbit, though it c the cud,	6590
Dt	14: 6	a split hoof divided in two and that c	6590

CHEZIB (KJV) See KEZIB

CHICKENS (KJV) See CHICKS

CHICKS (2)

Mt	23:37	as a hen gathers her c under her wings,	3800
Lk	13:34	as a hen gathers her c under her wings,	3799

CHIDE (KJV) See QUARREL; CRITICIZED, ACCUSE

CHIDON (KJV) See KIDON

CHIEF (145) [CHIEFS]

Ge	24: 2	He said to the c servant *in* his household,	2418
	40: 2	the c cupbearer and the chief baker,	8569
	40: 2	the chief cupbearer and the c baker,	8569
	40: 9	So the c cupbearer told Joseph his dream.	8569
	40:16	the c baker saw that Joseph had given	8569
	40:20	He lifted up the heads of the c cupbearer	8569
	40:20	and the c baker in the presence of his officials:	8569
	40:21	He restored the c cupbearer to his position,	8569
	40:22	but he hanged the c baker,	8569
	40:23	The c cupbearer, however,	8569
	41: 9	Then the c cupbearer said to Pharaoh,	8569
	41:10	and the c baker in the house of the captain	8569
Nu	3:32	The c **leader** *of* the Levites	5954+5954
	25:15	a tribal c of a Midianite family.	8031
Dt	29:10	your leaders and c **men,**	8657
Jos	22:14	With him they sent ten of the c **men,**	5954
2Sa	23: 8	a Tahkemonite, was c of the Three;	8031
	23:13	of the thirty c **men** came down to David at	8031
	23:18	the brother of Joab son of Zeruiah was c *of*	8031
1Ki	4: 2	And these were his c **officials:**	8569
	4: 4	of Jehoiada—**commander in** c;	2021+6584+7372
	4: 5	They were also the c officials in charge	8569
2Ki	10:11	as well as all his c **men,**	1524
	15:25	One of his c **officers,**	8957
	18:17	his c officer and his field commander with	8042
	25:18	as prisoners Seraiah the c priest,	8031
	25:19	the secretary who was c **officer** in charge	2021+7372+8569
1Ch	5: 7	Jeiel the c, Zechariah,	8031

1Ch	5:12	Joel was the c, Shapham the second,	8031
	9:17	and their brothers, Shallum their c	8031
	11:11	a Hacmonite, was c of the officers;	8031
	11:20	the brother of Joab was c of the Three.	8031
	11:42	who was c of the Reubenites,	8031
	12: 3	Ahiezer their c and Joash the sons	8031
	12: 9	Ezer was the c,	8031
	12:18	Spirit came upon Amasai, c of the Thirty,	8031
	16: 5	Asaph was the c,	8031
	18:17	and David's sons were c **officials** at	8037
	26:12	through their c men,	8031
	26:31	Jeriah was their c according to	8031
	27: 3	He was a descendant of Perez and c of all	8031
	27: 5	He was c and there were 24,000	8031
2Ch	8:10	also King Solomon's c officials—	8569
	11:22	to be the c prince among his brothers,	8031
	19:11	the c priest will be over you in any matter	8031
	24: 6	the king summoned Jehoiada the c priest	8031
	24:11	and the officer of the c priest would come	8031
	26:20	the c priest and all the other priests looked	8031
	31:10	and Azariah the c priest,	8031
Ezr	7: 5	the son of Aaron the c priest—	8031
Ne	11:11	Seraiah son of Hilkiah... was c **officer,**	7224
	11:14	Their c **officer** was Zabdiel son	7224
	11:22	The c **officer** *of* the Levites	7224
Job	29: 9	The c **men** refrained from speaking	8569
	29:25	I chose the way for them and sat as their c;	8031
Isa	2: 2	be established as c *among* the mountains;	8031
	33:18	"Where is that c **officer?**	6221
Jer	20: 1	the c officer in the temple of the LORD,	5592
	39: 3	Nebo-Sarsekim a c officer,	8042
	39:13	Nebushazban a c officer,	8042
	52:24	as prisoners Seraiah the c priest,	8031
	52:25	the secretary who was c **officer** in charge	2021+7372+8569
Eze	38: 2	the c prince of Meshech and Tubal;	8031
	38: 3	O Gog, c prince of Meshech and Tubal.	8031
	39: 1	O Gog, c prince of Meshech and Tubal.	8031
Da	1: 3	c *of* his court officials,	8041
	1: 7	The c official gave them new names:	8569
	1: 8	and he asked the c official for permission	8569
	1:11	the c official had appointed over Daniel,	8569
	1:18	the c official presented them	8569
	4: 9	I said, "Belteshazzar, c *of* the magicians,	10647
	5:11	appointed him c of the magicians,	10647
	10:13	Then Michael, one of the c princes,	8037
Mic	4: 1	be established as c *among* the mountains;	8031
Mt	2: 4	the people's c **priests** and teachers of	797
	16:21	c priests and teachers of the law,	797
	20:18	*to* the c priests and the teachers of the law.	797
	21:15	the c priests and the teachers of the law saw	797
	21:23	the c priests and the elders of	797
	21:45	When the c priests and the Pharisees	797
	26: 3	Then the c priests and the elders of	797
	26:14	went to the c priests	797
	26:47	the c priests and the elders of the people.	797
	26:59	The c priests and the whole Sanhedrin	797
	27: 1	all the c priests and the elders of	797
	27: 3	the thirty silver coins *to* the c priests and	797
	27: 6	The c priests picked up the coins and said,	797
	27:12	When he was accused by the c priests and	797
	27:20	But the c priests and the elders persuaded	797
	27:41	In the same way the c priests,	797
	27:62	c priests and the Pharisees went to Pilate.	797
	28:11	the c priests everything that had happened.	797
	28:12	When the c priests had met with the elders	NIG
Mk	8:31	c priests and teachers of the law,	797
	10:33	be betrayed *to* the c priests and teachers of	797
	11:18	The c priests and the teachers of	797
	11:27	the temple courts, the c priests, the teachers	797
	14: 1	and the c priests and the teachers of	797
	14:10	to the c priests to betray Jesus to them.	797
	14:43	sent from the c priests, the teachers	797
	14:53	and all the c priests, elders and teachers	797
	14:55	The c priests and the whole Sanhedrin	797
	15: 1	Very early in the morning, the c priests,	797
	15: 3	The c priests accused him of many things.	797
	15:10	the c priests had handed Jesus over to him.	797
	15:11	But the c priests stirred up the crowd	797
	15:31	the same way the c priests and the teachers	797
Lk	9:22	c priests and teachers of the law,	797
	19: 2	a c **tax collector** and was wealthy.	803
	19:47	But the c priests, the teachers of the law	797
	20: 1	the c priests and the teachers of the law,	797
	20:19	the law and the c priests looked for a way	797
	22: 2	and the c priests and the teachers of	797
	22: 4	And Judas went *to* the c priests and	797
	22:52	Then Jesus said to the c priests,	797
	22:66	both the c priests and teachers of the law,	797
	23: 4	Then Pilate announced *to* the c priests and	797
	23:10	The c priests and the teachers of	797
	23:13	Pilate called together the c priests,	797
	24:20	The c priests and our rulers handed him	797
Jn	7:32	Then the c priests and the Pharisees	797
	7:45	the temple guards went back to the c priests	797
	11:47	Then the c priests and the Pharisees called	797
	11:57	the c priests and Pharisees had given orders	797
	12:10	c priests made plans to kill Lazarus as well,	797
	18: 3	and some officials from the c priests	797
	18:35	and your c priests who handed you over	797
	19: 6	as the c priests and their officials saw him,	797
	19:15	the c priests answered.	797
	19:21	The c priests of the Jews protested	797
Ac	4:23	the c priests and elders had said to them.	797
	5:24	and the c priests were puzzled,	797
	9:14	from the c priests to arrest all who call	797
	9:21	to take them as prisoners to the c priests?"	797

Ac	14:12	because he was the c speaker.	2451
	19:14	Seven sons of Sceva, a Jewish c priest,	797
	22:30	he released him and ordered the c priests	797
	23:14	They went to the c priests and elders	797
	25: 2	the c priests and Jewish leaders appeared	797
	25:15	the c priests and elders of the Jews	797
	26:10	On the authority of the c priests I put many	797
	26:12	and commission of the c priests.	797
	28: 7	the c official of the island.	4755
Eph	2:20	himself as the c cornerstone.	214+1639
1Pe	5: 4	And when the C Shepherd appears,	799

CHIEFS (25) [CHIEF]

Ge	36:15	These were the c among Esau's descendants:	477
	36:15	C Teman, Omar, Zepho, Kenaz,	477
	36:16	These were the c descended from Eliphaz	477
	36:17	C Nahath, Zerah, Shammah and Mizzah.	477
	36:17	These were the c descended from Reuel	477
	36:18	C Jeush, Jalam and Korah.	477
	36:18	These were the c descended	477
	36:19	Edom), and these were their c.	477
	36:21	These sons of Seir in Edom were Horite c.	477
	36:29	These were the Horite c:	477
	36:30	These were the Horite c,	477
	36:40	These were the c descended from Esau,	477
	36:43	These were the c of Edom.	477
Ex	15:15	The c of Edom will be terrified,	477
Jos	13:21	and the Midianite c, Evi, Rekem, Zur, Hur	5954
1Ki	8: 1	the tribes and the c of the Israelite families.	5954
1Ch	1:51	The c of Edom were:	477
	1:54	These were the c of Edom.	477
	7: 3	All five of them were c.	8031
	8:28	c as listed in their genealogy,	8031
	9:34	c as listed in their genealogy,	8031
	11:10	These were the c of David's mighty men—	8031
	11:15	the thirty c came down to David to the rock	8031
	12:32	200 c, with all their relatives	8031
2Ch	5: 2	the tribes and the c of the Israelite families.	5954

CHILD (121) [CHILD'S, CHILDHOOD, CHILDISH, CHILDLESS, CHILDREN, CHILDREN'S, GRANDCHILDREN]

Ge	4:25	"God has granted me another c in place	2446
	16:11	"You are now with c and you will have	2226
	17:17	Will Sarah bear a c at the age of ninety?"	3528
	18:13	'Will I really have a c,	3528
	21: 8	The c grew and was weaned,	3529
Ex	2: 2	When she saw that he was a fine c,	AIT
	2: 3	the c in it and put it among the reeds along	3529
	2:10	When the c grew older,	3529
Jdg	11:34	She was an only c.	3495
Ru	4:16	Then Naomi took the c,	3529
1Sa	1:27	I prayed for this c.	5853
2Sa	12:15	the c that Uriah's wife had borne to David,	3529
	12:16	David pleaded with God for the c.	5853
	12:18	On the seventh day the c died.	3529
	12:18	to tell him that the c was dead,	3529
	12:18	"While the c was still living,	3529
	12:18	How can we tell him the c is dead?	3529
	12:19	and he realized that the c was dead.	3529
	12:19	"Is the c dead?"	3529
	12:21	While the c was alive, you fasted and wept,	3529
	12:21	but now that the c is dead,	3529
	12:22	He answered, "While the c was still alive,	3529
	12:22	be gracious to me and let the c live.'	3529
1Ki	3: 7	But I am only a little c and do not know	5853
	3:18	The third day after my c was born,	3528
	3:25	the living c in two and give half to one	3529
	17:23	the c and carried him down from the room	3529
2Ki	4:18	The c grew, and one day he went out	3529
	4:26	Is your c all right?"	3529
2Ch	22:11	she hid the c from Athaliah so she could	2084S
Job	3:16	in the ground like a stillborn c,	5878
	24: 9	fatherless c is snatched from the breast;	3846
Ps	58: 8	like a stillborn c,	851+5878
	131: 2	like a weaned c with its mother,	AIT
	131: 2	like a weaned c is my soul within me.	AIT
Pr	4: 3	still tender, and an only c of my mother,	3495
	20:11	Even a c is known by his actions,	5853
	22: 6	Train a c in the way he should go,	5853
	22:15	Folly is bound up in the heart of a c,	5853
	23:13	Do not withhold discipline from a c;	5853
	29:15	but a c left to himself disgraces his mother.	5853
Ecc	4:15	that a stillborn c is better off than he.	5878
Isa	7:14	The virgin will be with c and will give birth to a son,	2226
	9: 6	For to us a c is born, to us a son is given,	3529
	10:19	be so few that a c could write them down.	5853
	11: 6	and a little c will lead them.	5853
	11: 8	young c put his hand into the viper's nest.	1694
	26:17	As a woman with c and about	2225
	26:18	We were with c, we writhed in pain,	2225
	49:15	on the c she has borne?	1201
	54: 1	O barren woman, you who never bore a c;	3528
	66:13	As a mother comforts her c,	408
Jer	1: 6	I am only a c."	5853
	1: 7	'Do not say, 'I am only a c.'	5853
	4:31	a groan as of one bearing her first c—	1144
	20:15	saying, "A c is born to you—a son!"	1201
	31:20	the c in whom I delight?	3529
Hos	11: 1	"When Israel was a c, I loved him,	5853
	11:13	but he is a c without wisdom;	1201
Zec	12:10	for him as one mourns for an only c,	3495
Mt	1:18	she was found to be with c through the Holy Spirit.	1143+1877+2400

Mt	1:23	"The virgin will be with c and will give birth to a son,	1143+1877+2400
	2: 8	"Go and make a careful search for the c.	4086
	2: 9	over the place where the c was.	4086
	2:11	they saw the c with his mother Mary,	4086
	2:13	the c and his mother and escape to Egypt.	4086
	2:13	for Herod is going to search for the c	4086
	2:14	took the c and his mother during the night	4086
	2:20	take the c and his mother and go to the land	4086
	2:21	the c and his mother and went to the land	4086
	10:21	and a father his c;	5451
	18: 2	He called a little c and had him stand	4086
	18: 4	like this c is the greatest in the kingdom	4086
	18: 5	"And whoever welcomes a little c	4086
Mk	5:39	The c is not dead but asleep."	4086
	5:40	and went in where the c was.	4086
	7:30	She went home and found her c lying on	4086
	9:36	He took a little c and had him stand	4086
	10:15	of God like a little c will never enter it."	4086
	12:21	but he also died, leaving no c.	5065
	13:12	and a father his c.	5451
Lk	1:31	You will be with c and give birth to a son,	1143+1877+5197
	1:36	to have a c in her old age,	5626
	1:42	blessed is the c you will bear!	2843+3120+3836
	1:59	to circumcise the c,	4086
	1:62	like to name the c.	899S
	1:66	asking, "What then is this c going to be?"	4086
	1:76	my c, will be called a prophet of	4086
	1:80	the c grew and became strong in spirit;	4086
	2: 5	be married to him and was expecting a c.	1607
	2:17	what had been told them about this c,	4086
	2:27	the c Jesus to do for him what the custom	4086
	2:34	"This c is destined to cause the falling	NIG
	2:38	about the c to all who were looking forward	899S
	2:40	And the c grew and became strong;	4086
	8:54	he took her by the hand and said, "My c,	4090
	9:38	for he is my only c.	3666
	9:47	a little c and had him stand beside him.	4086
	9:48	"Whoever welcomes this little c	4086
	18:17	of God like a little c will never enter it."	4086
Jn	4:49	"Sir, come down before my c dies."	4086
	7:22	you circumcise a c on the Sabbath.	476
	7:23	if a c can be circumcised on the Sabbath so	476
	16:21	A woman giving birth to a c has pain	5503
	16:21	of her joy that a c is born into the world.	476
Ac	7: 5	though at that time Abraham had no c.	5451
	7:20	and he was no ordinary c.	NIG
	13:10	a c of the devil and an enemy of everything	5626
	26: 4	the way I have lived ever since I was a c,	3744
1Co	13:11	When I was a c, I talked like a child,	3758
	13:11	When I was a child, I talked like a c,	3758
	13:11	I thought like a c, I reasoned like a child.	3758
	13:11	I thought like a child, I reasoned like a c.	3758
Gal	4: 1	that as long as the heir is a c,	3758
Heb	11:23	because they saw he was no ordinary c,	4086
1Jn	3:10	not do what is right is not a c of God;	NIG
	5: 1	the father loves his c as well.	1164
Rev	12: 4	so that he might devour her c	5451
	12: 5	She gave birth to a son, a male c,	NIG
	12: 5	And her c was snatched up to God and	5451
	12:13	who had given birth to the male c.	NIG

CHILD'S (6) [CHILD]

2Ki	4:30	But the c mother said,	5853
Job	33:25	then his flesh is renewed like a c;	5854
Mt	2:20	to take the c life are dead."	4086
Mk	5:40	he took the c father and mother and	4086
Lk	2:33	The c father and mother marveled	899S
	8:51	and the c father and mother.	4090

CHILDBEARING (3) [BEAR]

Ge	3:16	"I will greatly increase your pains in c;	2228
	18:11	Sarah was past the age of c.	784+851+2021+3869
1Ti	2:15	But women will be saved through c—	5450

CHILDBIRTH (6) [BEAR]

Ge	35:17	And as she was having great difficulty in c,	3528
Ex	1:19	help the Hebrew women in c	3528
Isa	42:14	like a woman in c, I cry out, I gasp and pant.	3528
Hos	13:13	Pains as of a woman in c come to him,	3528
Ro	8:22	groaning as in the pains of c	5349
Gal	4:19	for whom I am again in the pains of c	6048

CHILDHOOD (4) [CHILD]

Ge	8:21	every inclination of his heart is evil from c	5830
Isa	47:12	which you have labored at since c.	5830
	47:15	with and trafficked with since c.	5830
Mk	9:21	"From c," he answered.	4085

CHILDISH (1) [CHILD]

1Co	13:11	I became a man, I put c ways behind me.	3758+3836

CHILDLESS (16) [CHILD]

Ge	15: 2	what can you give me since I remain c and	6884
Lev	20:20	they will die c.	6884
	20:21	They will be c.	6884
Dt	7:14	none of your men or women will be c,	6829
	25: 5	In the street they would will make them c;	3846
Jdg	13: 2	wife who was sterile and remained c.	3528+4202
	13: 3	"You are sterile and c,	3528+4202
1Sa	15:33	"As your sword has made women c,	8897

1Sa	15:33	so will your mother be c among women."	8897
Job	24:21	They prey on the barren and c woman,	3528+4202
Jer	18:21	Let their wives be made c and widows;	8891
	22:30	"Record this man as if c,	6884
Eze	5:17	through that country and they leave it c	8897
	14:15	or make your nation c,	8897
	36:14	or make your nation c,	8897
Lk	20:29	The first one married a woman and died c.	866

CHILDREN (435) [CHILD]

Ge	3:16	with pain you will give birth to c.	1201
	6: 4	to the daughters of men and had c by them.	3528
	11:30	Now Sarai was barren; she had no c.	2263
	15: 3	Abram said, "You have given me no c,	2446
	16: 1	Sarai, Abram's wife, had borne him no c.	3528
	16: 2	"The LORD has kept me from having c.	3528
	18:19	that he will direct his c and his household	3528
	20:17	so they could have c again,	3528
	21: 7	to Abraham that Sarah would nurse c?	1201
	21:23	with me or my c or my descendants.	5769
	29:35	Then she stopped having c.	3528
	30: 1	that she was not bearing Jacob any c,	3528
	30: 1	she said to Jacob, "Give me c, or I'll die!"	1201
	30: 2	who has kept you from having c?"	1061+7262
	30: 3	Sleep with her so that she can bear c for me	3528
	30: 9	Leah saw that she had stopped having c,	3528
	30:26	Give me my wives and c,	3529
	31:16	from our father belongs to us and our c.	1201
	31:17	Jacob put his c and his wives on camels,	1201
	31:43	the c are my children,	1201
	31:43	the children are my c,	1201
	31:43	or about the c they have borne?	1201
	32:11	and also the mothers with their c.	1201
	33: 1	so he divided the c among Leah,	3529
	33: 2	the maidservants and their c in front,	3529
	33: 2	Leah and her c next,	3529
	33: 5	Esau looked up and saw the women and c.	3529
	33: 5	c God has graciously given your servant."	3529
	33: 6	and their c approached and bowed down.	3529
	33: 7	Leah and her c came and bowed down.	3529
	33:13	that the c are tender and that I must care for	3529
	33:14	of the droves before me and that of the c,	3529
	34:29	and all their women and c,	3251
	36:25	The c of Anah:	1201
	42:36	deprived me of my c.	8897
	43: 8	we and you and our c may live and not die.	3251
	45:10	you, your c and grandchildren,	1201
	45:19	Take some carts from Egypt for your c	3251
	46: 5	and their c and their wives in the carts	3251
	46:18	These were the c born to Jacob by Zilpah,	1201
	47:12	according to the number of their c.	3251
	47:24	and your households and your c."	3251
	48: 6	Any c born to you after them will be yours;	4580
	48:11	God has allowed me to see your c too."	2446
	50: 8	Only their c and their flocks	3251
	50:21	I will provide for you and your c."	3251
	50:23	saw the third generation of Ephraim's c.	1201
	50:23	Also the c of Makir son of Manasseh	1201
Ex	10: 2	that you may tell your c and grandchildren	1201
	10:10	I let you go, along with your women and c!	3251
	10:24	Even your women and c may go with you;	3251
	12:26	And when your c ask you,	1201
	12:37	besides women and c.	3251
	17: 3	to make us and our c and livestock die	1201
	20: 5	punishing the c for the sin of the fathers to	1201
	21: 4	and her c shall belong to her master,	3529
	21: 5	'I love my master and my wife and c	1201
	22:24	and your c fatherless.	1201
	34: 7	he punishes the c and their children for	1201
	34: 7	he punishes the children and their c for	1201
Lev	10:14	they have been given to you and your c	1201
	10:15	be the regular share for you and your c,	1201
	18:21	not give any of your c to be sacrificed	2446
	20: 2	of his c to Molech must be put to death.	2446
	20: 3	for by giving his c to Molech,	2446
	20: 4	when that man gives one of his c to Molech	2446
	22:13	yet has no c,	2446
	25:41	Then he and his c are to be released,	1201
	25:46	to your c as inherited property	1201
	25:54	he and his c are to be released in the Year	1201
	26:22	rob you of your c,	8897
Nu	5:28	and will be able to have c.	2445+2446
	14: 3	Our wives and c will be taken as plunder.	3251
	14:18	he punishes the c for the sin of the fathers	1201
	14:31	As for your c that you said would be taken	3251
	14:33	Your c will be shepherds here	1201
	16:27	c and little ones at the entrances	1201
	31: 9	the Midianite women and c and took all	3251
	32:16	and cities for our women and c.	3251
	32:17	Meanwhile our women and c will live	3251
	32:24	Build cities for your women and c,	3251
	32:26	Our c and wives,	3251
Dt	1:39	your c who do not yet know good	1201
	2:34	men, women and c.	3251
	3: 6	men, women and c.	3251
	3:19	However, your wives, your c	3251
	4: 9	Teach them to your c and to their children	1201
	4: 9	Teach them to your children and to their c	1201
	4:10	in the land and may teach them to their c."	1201
	4:25	After you have had c and grandchildren	1201
	4:40	so that it may go well with you and your c	1201
	5: 9	punishing the c for the sin of the fathers to	1201
	5:29	with them and their c forever!	1201
	6: 2	your c and their children	1201
	6: 2	and their c after them may fear	1201
	6: 7	Impress them on your c.	1201

Dt	11: 2	that your c were not the ones who saw	1201
	11: 5	not your c who saw what he did for you in	NIH
	11:19	Teach them to your c,	1201
	11:21	the days of your c may be many in the land	1201
	12:25	so that it may go well with you and your c	1201
	12:28	with you and your c after you,	1201
	14: 1	You are the c of the LORD your God.	1201
	20:14	As for the women, the c,	3251
	23: 8	of c born to them may enter the assembly	1201
	24:16	Fathers shall not be put to death for their c,	1201
	24:16	nor c put to death for their fathers;	1201
	28:54	or the wife he loves or his surviving c,	1201
	28:55	to one of them any of the flesh of his c	1201
	28:57	from her womb and the c she bears.	1201
	29:11	together with your c and your wives,	3251
	29:22	Your c who follow you in later generations	1201
	29:29	to us and to our c forever,	1201
	30: 2	and your c return to the LORD your God	1201
	30:19	so that you and your c may live	2446
	31:12	Assemble the people—men, women and c,	3251
	31:13	Their c, who do not know this law,	1201
	32: 5	to their shame they are no longer his c,	1201
	32:20	a perverse generation, c who are unfaithful.	1201
	32:46	so that you may command your c	1201
	33: 9	or acknowledge his own c.	1201
Jos	1:14	your c and your livestock may stay in	3251
	4: 6	In the future, when your c ask you,	1201
	8:35	including the women and c,	3251
	14: 9	and that of your c forever.	1201
Jdg	18:21	Putting their **little** c,	3251
	21:10	including the women and c.	3251
1Sa	1: 2	Peninnah had c, but Hannah had none.	3529
	2: 5	She who was barren *has* **borne** seven c,	3528
	2:20	the LORD give you c by this woman	2446
	15: 3	put to death men and women, c and infants,	6407
	22:19	with its men and women, its c and infants,	6407
	30:22	each man may take his wife and c and go."	1201
2Sa	3: 2	the names of the c **born** to him there:	3533
	6:23	And Michal daughter of Saul had no c to	3529
	12: 3	and it grew up with him and his c.	1201
1Ki	11:20	with Pharaoh's own c.	1201
	20: 3	the best of your wives and c are mine.' "	1201
	20: 5	your wives and your c.	1201
	20: 7	When he sent for my wives and my c,	1201
2Ki	8:12	dash their **little** c to the ground,	6407
	10: 1	**guardians** of Ahab's c.	587
	14: 6	be put to death for their c, nor children put	1201
	14: 6	nor c put to death for their fathers;	1201
	17:31	the Sepharvites burned their c in the fire	1201
	17:41	To this day their c and grandchildren	1201
	19: 3	and disgrace, as when c come to the point	1201
1Ch	2:18	of Hezron **had** c by his wife Azubah (and	3528
	2:30	Seled died without c.	1201
	2:32	Jether died without c.	1201
	3: 5	and these were *the* c **born** to him there:	AIT
	4:18	the c of Pharaoh's daughter Bithiah,	1201
	4:27	but his brothers did not have many c;	1201
	6: 3	The c of Amram:	1201
	7: 4	for they had many wives and c,	1201
	14: 4	the names of the c **born** to him there:	3528
2Ch	20:13	with their wives and c and little ones,	1201
	25: 4	be put to death for their c, nor children put	1201
	25: 4	nor c put to death for their fathers;	1201
	30: 9	and your c will be shown compassion	1201
Ezr	8:21	for a safe journey for us and our c,	3251
	9:12	to your c as an everlasting inheritance.'	1201
	10: 1	men, women and c—gathered around him.	3529
	10: 3	to send away all these women and their c,	3528
	10:44	and some of them had c by these wives.	1201
Ne	12:43	The women and c also rejoiced.	3529
	13:24	of their c spoke the language of Ashdod or	1201
Est	3:13	young and old, women and **little** c—	3251
	8:11	and their women and c;	3251
Job	1: 5	"Perhaps my c have sinned and cursed God	1201
	5: 4	His c are far from safety.	1201
	5:25	You will know that your c will be many,	2446
	8: 4	When your c sinned against him,	1201
	17: 5	the eyes of his c will fail.	1201
	20:10	His c must make amends to the poor;	1201
	21: 8	They see their c established around them,	2446
	21:11	They send forth their c as a flock;	6396
	24: 5	the wasteland provides food for their c.	5853
	27:14	many his c, their fate is the sword;	1201
	29: 5	when me and my c were around me,	5853
	42:16	he saw his c and their children to	1201
	42:16	and their c to the fourth generation.	1201
Ps	8: 2	of c and infants you have ordained praise	6407
	17:14	and they store up wealth for their c.	6407
	34:11	Come, my c, listen to me;	1201
	37:25	or their c begging bread.	2446
	37:26	their c will be blessed.	2446
	69:36	the c *of* his servants will inherit it,	2446
	72: 4	the people and save the c of the needy;	1201
	73:15	I would have betrayed your c.	1201+1887
	78: 4	We will not hide them from their c;	1201
	78: 5	to teach their c,	1201
	78: 6	even the c yet to be born,	1201
	78: 6	and they in turn would tell their c.	1201
	90:16	your splendor to their c.	1201
	102:28	The c of your servants will live	1201
	103:13	As a father has compassion on his c,	1201
	103:17	his righteousness with their children's c—	1201
	109: 9	May his c be fatherless and his wife	1201
	109:10	May his c be wandering beggars;	1201
	109:12	to him or take pity on his **fatherless** c.	3846
	112: 2	His c will be mighty in the land;	2446
	113: 9	in her home as a happy mother of c.	1201

Ps	115:14	both you and your c.	1201
	127: 3	c a reward from him.	1061+2021+7262
	128: 6	and may you live to see your children's c.	1201
	148:12	young men and maidens, old men and c.	5853
Pr	13:22	an inheritance for his children's c,	1201
	14:26	and for his c it will be a refuge.	1201
	17: 6	Children's c are a crown to the aged,	1201
	17: 6	and parents are the pride of their c.	1201
	20: 7	blessed are his c after him.	1201
	31:28	Her c arise and call her blessed;	1201
Ecc	6: 3	A man *may* **have** a hundred c	3528
Isa	1: 2	"I reared c and brought them up,	1201
	1: 4	a brood of evildoers, c given to corruption!	1201
	3: 4	**mere** c will govern them.	9500
	8:18	and the c the LORD has given me.	3529
	13:18	nor will they look with compassion on c.	1201
	28: 9	To c weaned from their milk,	AIT
	29:23	When they see among them their c,	3529
	30: 1	"Woe to the obstinate c,"	1201
	30: 9	These are rebellious people, deceitful c,	1201
	30: 9	c unwilling to listen to	1201
	37: 3	and disgrace, as when c come to the point	1201
	38:19	fathers tell their c about your faithfulness.	1201
	43: 5	I will bring your c from the east	2446
	45:11	do you question me about my c,	1201
	47: 8	be a widow or suffer the **loss of** c.'	8890
	47: 9	**loss of** c and widowhood.	8890
	48:19	your c like its numberless grains;	5055+7368
	49:20	The c *born during* your bereavement will	1201
	49:25	and your c I will save.	1201
	54: 1	the c of the desolate woman than	1201
	57: 5	you sacrifice your c in the ravines and	3529
	59:21	or from the mouths of your c,	2446
	65:23	They will not toil in vain or **bear** c doomed	3528
	66: 8	in labor than she gives birth to her c.	1201
Jer	2: 9	against your children's c.	1201
	4:22	They are senseless c;	1201
	5: 7	Your c have forsaken me and sworn	1201
	6:11	"Pour it out on the c in the street and on	6408
	7:18	The c gather wood,	1201
	9:21	the c from the streets and the young men	6408
	17: 2	Even their c remember their altars	1201
	18:21	So give their c over to famine;	1201
	22:28	Why will he and his c be hurled out,	2446
	30: 6	Ask and see: *Can* a man **bear** c?	3528
	30:20	Their c will be as in days of old,	1201
	31:15	Rachel weeping for her c and refusing to	1201
	31:15	because her c are no more."	1201
	31:17	"Your c will return to their own land.	1201
	32:18	for the fathers' sins into the laps of their c	1201
	32:39	for their own good and the good of their c	1201
	36:31	and his c and his attendants	2446
	38:23	"All your wives and c will be brought out	1201
	40: 7	and c who were the poorest in the land	3251
	41:16	c and court officials he had brought	3251
	43: 6	led away all the men, women and c and	3251
	44: 7	the men and women, the c and infants,	6407
	47: 3	Fathers will not turn to help their c;	1201
	49:10	His c, relatives and neighbors will perish,	2446
La	1: 5	Her c have gone into exile,	6408
	1:16	My c are destitute because	1201
	2:11	c and infants faint in the streets of the city.	6407
	2:19	to him for the lives of your c,	6408
	2:20	the c they have cared for?	6407
	3:33	or grief to the c of men.	1201
	4: 4	c beg for bread, but no one gives it to them.	6408
	4:10	With their own hands compassionate	
		women have cooked their own c,	3529
Eze	5:10	in your midst fathers will eat their c,	1201
	5:10	and c will eat their fathers.	1201
	9: 6	young men and maidens, women and c,	3251
	16:21	You slaughtered my c and sacrificed them	1201
	16:45	who despised her husband and her c;	1201
	16:45	who despised their husbands and their c.	1201
	20:18	I said to their c in the desert,	1201
	20:21	" 'But the c rebelled against me:	1201
	23:37	they even sacrificed their c,	1201
	23:39	On the very day they sacrificed their c	1201
	36:12	**deprive** them **of** their c.	8897
	36:13	**deprive** your nation **of** *its* c,"	8897
	37:25	They and their c	1201
	37:25	their children's c will live there forever,	1201
	47:22	among you and who have c.	1201
Da	6:24	along with their wives and c.	10120
Hos	1: 2	an adulterous wife and c of unfaithfulness,	3529
	2: 4	I will not show my love to her c,	1201
	2: 4	because they are the c of adultery.	1201
	4: 6	I also will ignore your c.	1201
	5: 7	They give birth to illegitimate c.	1201
	9:12	Even if they rear c,	1201
	9:13	But Ephraim will bring out their c to	1201
	9:16	Even if they **bear** c,	3528
	10:14	to the ground with their c.	1201
	11:10	his c will come trembling from the west.	1201
Joel	1: 3	Tell it to your c,	1201
	1: 3	and let your c tell it to their children,	1201
	1: 3	and let your children tell it to their c,	1201
	1: 3	and their c to the next generation.	1201
	2:16	bring together the elders, gather the c,	6408
Mic	1:16	in mourning for the c *in whom* you delight;	1201
	2: 9	from their c forever.	6408
Zec	10: 7	Their c will see it and be joyful;	1201
	10: 9	They and their c will survive,	1201
Mal	4: 6	of the fathers to their c, and the hearts of	1201
	4: 6	and the hearts of the c to their fathers;	1201
Mt	2:18	Rachel weeping for her c and refusing to	5451
	3: 9	that out of these stones God can raise up c	5451

Mt	7:11	know how to give good gifts *to* your c,	5451
	10:21	c will rebel against their parents	5451
	11:16	They are like c sitting in the marketplaces	4086
	11:25	and revealed them *to* **little** c.	3758
	14:21	besides women and c.	4086
	15:38	besides women and c.	4086
	18: 3	you change and become like **little** c,	4086
	18:25	and his wife and his c and all that he had	5451
	19:13	Then **little** c were brought to Jesus	4086
	19:14	Jesus said, "Let the **little** c come to me,	4086
	19:29	or sisters or father or mother or c or fields	5451
	21:15	and the c shouting in the temple area,	4090
	21:16	"Do you hear what these c are saying?"	NIG
	21:16	" 'From the lips *of* c and infants	3758
	22:24	that if a man dies without having c,	5451
	22:24	the widow and **have** c for him.	482+5065
	22:25	and since he had no c,	5065
	23:37	to gather your c together,	5451
	27:25	"Let his blood be on us and on our c!"	5451
Mk	7:27	"First let the c eat all they want,"	5451
	9:37	"Whoever welcomes one *of* these **little** c	4086
	10:13	People were bringing **little** c to Jesus	4086
	10:14	"Let the **little** c come to me,	4086
	10:16	And he took the c in his arms,	899S
	10:24	But Jesus said again, "C,	5451
	10:29	or mother or father or c or fields for me and	5451
	10:30	brothers, sisters, mothers, c and fields—	5451
	12:19	and leaves a wife but no c,	5451
	12:19	must marry the widow and **have** c	1985+5065
	12:20	and died without leaving any c.	5065
	12:22	In fact, none of the seven left any c.	5065
	13:12	C will rebel against their parents	5451
Lk	1: 7	But they had no c,	5451
	1:17	of the fathers to their c and the disobedient	5451
	3: 8	that out of these stones God can raise up c	5451
	7:32	They are like c sitting in the marketplace	4086
	7:35	But wisdom is proved right by all her c."	5451
	10:21	and revealed them *to* **little** c.	3758
	11: 7	and my c are with me in bed.	4086
	11:13	know how to give good gifts *to* your c,	5451
	13:34	to gather your c together,	5451
	14:26	his wife and c, his brothers and sisters—	5451
	18:16	But Jesus called the c to him and said,	899S
	18:16	"Let the **little** c come to me,	4086
	18:29	or parents or c for the sake of the kingdom	5451
	19:44	you and the c within your walls.	5451
	20:28	and leaves a wife but no c,	866
	20:28	must marry the widow and **have** c	1985+5065
	20:31	the same way the seven died, leaving no c.	5451
	20:36	They are God's c,	5626
	20:36	since they are c of the resurrection.	5626
	23:28	weep for yourselves and for your c.	5451
Jn	1:12	he gave the right to become c of God—	5451
	1:13	c born not of natural descent,	4005S
	8:39	"If you were Abraham's c," said Jesus,	5451
	8:41	"We *are* not **illegitimate** c,"	1164+1666+4518
	11:52	for that nation but also for the scattered c	5451
	13:33	"My c, I will be with you only	5448
Ac	2:39	and your c and for all who are far off—	5451
	13:26	"Brothers, c of Abraham,	1169+5626
	13:33	their c, by raising up Jesus.	5451
	21: 5	and their wives and c accompanied us out	5451
	21:21	not to circumcise their c or live according	5451
Ro	8:16	with our spirit that we are God's c.	5451
	8:17	Now if we are c, then we are heirs—	5451
	8:21	into the glorious freedom *of* the c of God.	5451
	9: 7	Nor because they are his descendants are	
		they all Abraham's c.	5451
	9: 8	not the natural c who are God's children,	5451
	9: 8	not the natural children who are God's c,	5451
	9: 8	the c of the promise who are regarded	5451
	9:10	Rebekah's c had one and the same father,	NIG
1Co	4:14	but to warn you, as my dear c,	5451
	7:14	Otherwise your c would be unclean,	5451
	14:20	Brothers, stop thinking *like* c.	4086
2Co	6:13	As a fair exchange—I speak as *to* my c—	5451
	12:14	c should not have to save up	5451
	12:14	but parents *for* their c.	5451
Gal	3: 7	that those who believe are c of Abraham.	5626
	4: 3	So also, when we were c,	3758
	4:19	My **dear** c, for whom I am again in	5451
	4:24	from Mount Sinai and **bears** c who are to	1164
	4:25	because she is in slavery with her c.	5451
	4:27	O barren woman, who **bears** no c;	5503
	4:27	the c of the desolate woman than	5451
	4:28	you, brothers, like Isaac, are c of promise.	5451
	4:31	brothers, we are not c of the slave woman,	5451
Eph	5: 1	Be imitators of God, therefore, as dearly	
		loved c	5451
	5: 8	Live as c of light	5451
	6: 1	C, obey your parents in the Lord,	5451
	6: 4	Fathers, do not exasperate your c;	5451
Php	2:15	c of God without fault in a crooked	5451
Col	3:20	C, obey your parents in everything,	5451
	3:21	Fathers, do not embitter your c,	5451
1Th	2: 7	like a mother caring for her little c.	5451
	2:11	of you as a father deals with his own c,	5451
1Ti	3: 4	that his c obey him with proper respect.	5451
	3:12	of but one wife and must manage his c	5451
	5: 4	But if a widow has c or grandchildren,	5451
	5:10	such as **bringing up** c, showing hospitality,	5452
	5:14	to marry, *to* **have** c, to manage their homes	5449
Tit	1: 6	a man whose c believe and are not open to	5451
	2: 4	to love their husbands and c,	5817
Heb	2:13	"Here am I, and the c God has given me."	4086
	2:14	Since the c have flesh and blood,	4086
	12: 8	you are **illegitimate** c and not true sons.	3785

1Pe	1:14	As obedient c, do not conform to the evil	5451
1Jn	2: 1	My dear c, I write this to you so	5448
	2:12	I write to you, dear c,	5448
	2:13	I write to you, dear c,	4086
	2:18	Dear c, this is the last hour;	4086
	2:28	And now, dear c, continue in him,	5448
	3: 1	that we should be called c of God!	5451
	3: 2	Dear friends, now we are c of God,	5451
	3: 7	Dear c, do not let anyone lead you astray.	5448
	3:10	This is how we know who the c of God are	5451
	3:10	of God are and who the c of the devil are:	5451
	3:18	Dear c, let us not love with words	5448
	4: 4	You, dear c, are from God	5448
	5: 2	how we know that we love the c of God:	5451
	5:19	We know that we are c of God,	NIG
	5:21	Dear c, keep yourselves from idols.	5448
2Jn	1: 1	The elder, To the chosen lady and her c,	5451
	1: 4	to find some of your c walking in the truth,	5451
	1:13	c of your chosen sister send their greetings.	5451
3Jn	1: 4	to hear that my c are walking in the truth.	5451
Rev	2:23	I will strike her c dead.	5451

CHILDREN'S (13) [CHILD]

Ps	103:17	his righteousness with their c children—	1201
	128: 6	may you live to see your c children.	1201+4200
Pr	13:22	an inheritance for his c children,	1201
	17: 6	C children are a crown to the aged,	1201
Isa	54:13	and great will be your c peace.	1201
Jer	2: 9	I will bring charges against your c children.	1201
	31:29	and the c teeth are set on edge.'	1201
Eze	16:36	and because you gave them your c blood,	1201
	18: 2	and the c teeth are set on edge"?	1201
	37:25	and their c children will live there forever,	1201
Mt	15:26	not right to take the c bread and toss it	5451
Mk	7:27	not right to take the c bread and toss it	5451
	7:28	the dogs under the table eat the c crumbs."	4086

CHILEAB (KJV) See KILEAB

CHILION (KJV) See KILION

CHILMAD (KJV) See KILMAD

CHIMHAM (KJV) See KIMHAM

CHIMNEY (KJV) See WINDOW

CHIN (2)

Lev	13:29	a sore on the head or on the c,	2417
	13:30	an infectious disease of the head or c.	2417

CHINNERETH, CHINNEROTH (KJV)
See KINNERETH

CHIOS (KJV) See KIOS

CHIRP (1)

Isa	10:14	or opened its mouth to c.' "	7627

CHISEL (4) [CHISELED, CHISELING, CHISELS]

Ex	34: 1	"C out two stone tablets like the first ones,	7180
Dt	10: 1	"C out two stone tablets like the first ones	7180
1Ki	6: 7	or any other iron tool was heard at	1749
Jer	10: 3	and a craftsman shapes it with his c.	5108

CHISELED (2) [CHISEL]

Ex	34: 4	So Moses c out two stone tablets like	7180
Dt	10: 3	of acacia wood and c out two stone tablets	7180

CHISELING (1) [CHISEL]

Isa	22:16	on the height and c your resting place in	2980

CHISELS (1) [CHISEL]

Isa	44:13	with c and marks it with compasses.	5244

CHISLEU (KJV) See KISLEV

CHISLON (KJV) See KISLON

CHISLOTH-TABOR (KJV) See KISLOTH
TABOR

CHITTIM (KJV) See KITTIM

CHIUN (KJV) See PEDESTAL

CHLOE'S (1)

1Co	1:11	some from C household have informed me	5951

CHOICE (34) [CHOOSE]

Ge	18: 7	Then he ran to the herd and selected a c,	3202
	27: 9	the flock and bring me two c young goats,	3202

Lev	23:40	On the first day you are to take c fruit from	2077
Dt	12:11	and all the c possessions you have vowed to	4436
	32:14	with c rams of Bashan and	1201
1Sa	2:29	on the c parts of every offering made	8040
1Ki	4:23	gazelles, roebucks and c fowl.	80
1Ch	7:40	heads of families, c men,	1405
	21:11	"This is what the LORD says: 'Take your c:	7691
Ne	5:18	Each day one ox, six c sheep	1405
	8:10	"Go and enjoy c food and sweet drinks,	5460
Job	36:16	of your table laden with c food.	2016
Pr	8:10	knowledge rather than c gold,	1047
	8:19	what I yield surpasses c silver.	1047
	10:20	The tongue of the righteous is c silver,	1047
	18: 8	The words of a gossip are like c morsels;	4269
	21:20	In the house of the wise are stores of c food	2773
	26:22	The words of a gossip are like c morsels;	4269
SS	4:13	an orchard of pomegranates with c fruits,	4458
	4:16	into his garden and taste its c fruits.	4458
	5:15	c as its cedars.	1047
Isa	1:22	your c wine is diluted with water.	6011
Jer	2:21	like a c vine of sound and reliable stock.	8603
Eze	20:40	and your c gifts,	8040
	24: 4	all the c pieces—the leg and the shoulder.	3202
	34: 3	with the wool and slaughter the c animals,	1374
Da	1:15	So the guard took away their c food and	7329
	10: 3	I ate no c food;	2776
Am	5:22	Though you bring c fellowship offerings,	5309
	6: 4	You dine on c lambs and fattened calves.	4119+4946+7366
Zec	11:16	but will eat the meat of the c sheep,	1374
Jn	2:10	the c wine first and then the cheaper wine	2819
Ac	15: 7	you know that some time ago God made a c	1721
Ro	8:20	not by its own c, but by the will of the one	1776

CHOICEST (12) [CHOOSE]

Ge	23: 6	Bury your dead in the c of our tombs.	4436
	49:11	his colt to the c branch;	8605
Dt	33:15	with the c gifts of the ancient mountains	8031
2Ki	19:23	the c of its pines.	4435
Job	22:25	the c silver for you.	9361
	33:20	and his soul loathes the c meal.	9294
Isa	5: 2	of stones and planted it with the c vines.	8603
	16: 8	down the c vines,	8602
	22: 7	Your c valleys are full of chariots,	4436
	37:24	the c of its pines.	4436
Eze	31:16	the c and best of Lebanon,	4436
Hab	1:16	in luxury and enjoys the c food.	1374

CHOIR (1) [CHOIRS]

Ne	12:38	The second c proceeded in	9343

CHOIRS (4) [CHOIR]

1Ch	15:27	who was in charge of the singing of the c.	8876
Ne	12:31	I also assigned two large c to give thanks.	9343
	12:40	The two c that gave thanks	9343
	12:42	The c sang under the direction of Jezrahiah.	8876

CHOKE (3) [CHOKED]

Mt	13:22	and the deceitfulness of wealth c it,	5231
	18:28	He grabbed him and began to c him.	4464
Mk	4:19	the desires for other things come in and c	5231

CHOKED (4) [CHOKE]

Mt	13: 7	which grew up and c the plants.	4464
Mk	4: 7	which grew up and c the plants,	5231
Lk	8: 7	which grew up with it and c the plants.	678
	8:14	on their way they are c by life's worries,	5231

CHOLER (KJV) See FURIOUSLY, RAGE

CHOOSE (66) [CHOICE, CHOICEST, CHOOSES, CHOOSING, CHOSE, CHOSEN]

Ex	12: 5	The animals you c must be year-old males	4200
	17: 9	"C some of our men and go out to fight	1047
	34:16	c some of their daughters as wives	4374
Nu	14: 4	"We should c a leader and go back	5989
	17: 5	to the man I c will sprout,	1047
Dt	1:13	C some wise, understanding	2035
	7: 7	not set his affection on you and c you	1047
	12: 5	the place the LORD your God will c	1047
	12:11	the LORD your God will c as a dwelling	1047
	12:14	the LORD will c in one of your tribes,	1047
	12:18	at the place the LORD your God will c—	1047
	12:26	and go to the place the LORD will c.	1047
	14:23	the LORD your God at the place he will c	1047
	14:24	the LORD will c to put his Name is	1047
	14:25	to the place the LORD your God will c.	1047
	15:20	at the place he will c.	1047
	16: 2	the place the LORD will c as a dwelling	1047
	16: 6	except in the place he will c as a dwelling	1047
	16: 7	at the place the LORD your God will c,	1047
	16:11	at the place he will c as a dwelling	1047
	16:15	at the place the LORD will c.	1047
	16:16	at the place he will c:	1047
	17: 8	to the place the LORD your God will c.	1047
	17:10	at the place the LORD will c.	1047
	18: 6	to the place the LORD will c,	1047
	26: 2	the LORD your God will c as a dwelling	1047
	30:19	Now c life, so that you and your children	1047
	31:11	at the place he will c,	1047
Jos	3:12	then, c twelve men from the tribes of Israel,	4374

Jos	4: 2	"C twelve men from among the people,	4374
	9:27	at the place the LORD would c.	1047
	24:15	if serving the LORD seems undesirable to you, then c for yourselves this day whom	1047
1Sa	17: 8	C a man and have him come down to me.	1405
2Sa	17: 1	"I would c twelve thousand men	1047
	24:12	C one of them for me to carry out	1047
1Ki	18:23	Let them c one for themselves,	1047
	18:25	"C one of the bulls and prepare it first,	1047
2Ki	10: 3	c the best and most worthy	8011
	18:32	C life and not death!	2649
1Ch	21:10	C one of them for me to carry out	1047
Ps	65: 4	Blessed are those you c and bring near	1047
	75: 2	You say, "I c the appointed time;	4374
	78:67	he did not c the tribe of Ephraim;	1047
Pr	1:29	Since they hated knowledge and did not c	1047
	3:31	Do not envy a violent man or c any	1047
	8:10	c my instruction instead of silver,	1047
	16:16	to c understanding rather than silver!	1047+7864
Isa	7:15	to reject the wrong and c the right,	1047
	7:16	to reject the wrong and c the right,	1047
	14: 1	once again he will c Israel	1047
	56: 4	who c what pleases me and hold fast	1047
	66: 4	so I also will c harsh treatment for them	1047
Jer	3:14	I will c you—one from a town	4374
	33:26	and will not c one of his sons to rule over	4374
Eze	33: 2	the people of the land c one of their men	4374
Hos	5: 1	they c princes without my approval.	8606
Zec	1:17	and the LORD will again comfort Zion and c Jerusalem.' "	1047
	2:12	the holy land and will again c Jerusalem.	1047
Jn	15:16	You did not c me, but I chose you	1721
Ac	1:24	to c one of the men who have been with us	NIG
	6: 3	c seven men from among you	2170
	15:22	to c some of their own men and send them	1721
	15:25	to c some men and send them to you	1721
2Co	12: 6	Even if I should c to boast,	2527
Php	1:22	Yet what shall I c?	145
1Pe	4: 3	in the past doing what pagans c to do—	1088

CHOOSES (13) [CHOOSE]

Lev	16: 2	not to come whenever he c into	NIH
Nu	16: 5	The man he c will cause to come	1047
	16: 7	the LORD c will be the one who is holy.	1047
Dt	17:15	If the place where the LORD your God c	1047
	17:15	over you the king the LORD your God c.	1047
	23:16	and in whatever town he c.	1047
2Sa	15:15	to do whatever our lord the king c."	1047
Ps	68:16	at the mountain where God c to reign,	2773
Isa	41:24	he who c you is detestable.	1047
Mt	11:27	and those to whom the Son c to reveal him.	1089
Lk	10:22	the Son and those to whom the Son c	1089
Jn	7:17	If anyone c to do God's will,	2527
Jas	4: 4	Anyone who c to be a friend of the world	1089

CHOOSING (2) [CHOOSE]

1Ki	12:33	a month of his own c,	968
Ro	9:22	What if God, c to show his wrath	2527

CHOP (3) [CHOPPED]

Dt	29:11	in your camps who c your wood	2634
Jer	46:23	They will c down her forest,"	4162
Mic	3: 3	who c them up like meat for the pan,	7298

CHOPPED (1) [CHOP]

1Sa	6:14	The people c up the wood of the cart	1324

CHORASHAN (KJV) See BOR ASHAN

CHORAZIN (KJV) See KORAZIN

CHOSE (45) [CHOOSE]

Ge	6: 2	and they married any of them they c.	1047
	13:11	So Lot c for himself the whole plain of	1047
	47: 2	He c five of his brothers and presented them	4374
Ex	18:25	He c capable men from all Israel	1047
Dt	4:37	and c their descendants after them,	1047
	10:15	and he c you, their descendants,	1047
	33:21	He c the best land for himself;	8011
Jos	8: 3	He c thirty thousand of his best fighting	1047
Jdg	5: 8	When they c new gods,	1047
1Sa	8: 3	I c your father out of all the tribes of Israel	1047
	13: 2	Saul c three thousand men from Israel;	1047
	17:40	c five smooth stones from the stream,	1047
2Sa	6:21	who c me rather than your father or anyone	1047
1Ki	11:34	the sake of David my servant, whom I c	1047
	11:36	the city where I c to put my Name.	1047
2Ki	23:27	and I will reject Jerusalem, the city I c,	1047
1Ch	15: 2	because the LORD c them to carry the ark	1047
	28: 4	c me from my whole family to be king	1047
	28: 4	He c Judah as leader,	1047
	28: 4	from the house of Judah he c my family,	NIH
2Ch	24: 3	Jehoiada c two wives for him,	5951
Ne	9: 7	who c Abram and brought him out of Ur of	1047
Job	29:25	I c the way for them and sat as their chief;	1047
Ps	33:12	the people he c for his inheritance.	1047
	47: 4	He c our inheritance for us,	1047
	78:68	but he c the tribe of Judah,	1047
	78:70	He c David his servant and took him from	1047
Isa	65: 12	in my sight and c what displeases me.	1047
	66: 4	in my sight and c what displeases me."	1047
Jer	33:24	the two kingdoms he c'?	1047

Eze 20: 5 On the day I c Israel, 1047
Lk 6:13 he called his disciples to him and c twelve 1721
Jn 5:35 and you c for a time to enjoy his light. 2527
  15:16 but I c you and appointed you to go 1721
Ac 6: 5 They c Stephen, a man full of faith and of 1721
  13:17 God of the people of Israel c our fathers; 1721
  15:22 They c Judas (called Barsabbas) and Silas, NIG
  15:40 but Paul c Silas and left, 2141
1Co 1:27 But God c the foolish things of the world 1721
  1:27 God c the weak things of the world 1721
  1:28 He c the lowly things of this world and 1721
Eph 1: 4 For he c us in him before the creation of 1721
2Th 2:13 from the beginning God c you to be saved 145
Heb 11:25 He c to be mistreated along with the people 145
Jas 1:18 He c to give us birth through the word 1089

CHOSEN (125) [CHOOSE]

Ge 18:19 For I have c him, 3359
  24:14 the one you have c for your servant Isaac. 3519
  24:44 the LORD has c for my master's son.' 3519
Ex 31: 2 I have c Bezalel son of Uri, 928+7924+9005
  35:30 "See, the LORD has c Bezalel 928+7924+9005
Lev 16:10 But the goat c by lot as the scapegoat shall 6590
Dt 7: 6 The LORD your God has c you out of all 1047
  14: 2 the LORD has c you to be his treasured 1047
  18: 5 for the LORD your God has c them 1047
  21: 5 for the LORD your God has c them 1047
Jos 24:22 against yourselves that you have c to serve 1047
Jdg 10:14 Go and cry out to the gods you have c. 1047
  20:15 to seven hundred c men from those living 1047
  20:16 seven hundred c men who were left-handed, 1047
1Sa 8:18 for relief from the king you have c, 1047
  10:20 the tribe of Benjamin was c. 4334
  10:21 clan by clan, and Matri's clan was c. 4334
  10:21 Finally Saul son of Kish was c. 4334
  10:24 "Do you see the man the LORD has c? 1047
  12:13 Now here is the king you have c, 1047
  16: 1 I have c one of his sons to be king. 8011
  16: 8 "The LORD has not c this one either." 1047
  16: 9 "Nor has the LORD c this one." 1047
  16:10 "The LORD has not c these." 1047
  24: 2 So Saul took three thousand c men 1047
  26: 2 with his three thousand c men of Israel, 1047
2Sa 6: 1 brought together out of Israel c men, 1047
  16:18 the one c by the LORD, by these people, 1047
  21: 6 at Gibeah of Saul—the LORD's c one." 1040
1Ki 3: 8 among the people you have c, 1047
  8:16 not c a city in any tribe of Israel to have 1047
  8:16 I have c David to rule my people Israel.' 1047
  8:44 the LORD toward the city you have c and 1047
  8:48 toward the city you have c and 1047
  11:13 Jerusalem, which I have c." 1047
  11:32 which I have c out of all the tribes 1047
  14:21 the LORD had c out of all the tribes 1047
2Ki 21: 7 which I have c out of all the tribes 1047
1Ch 9:22 those c to be gatekeepers at 1405
  16:13 O sons of Jacob, his c ones. 1040
  16:41 the rest of those c and designated by name 1405
  28: 5 he has c my son Solomon to sit on 1047
  28: 6 for I have c him to be my son, 1047
  28:10 for the LORD has c you to build a temple 1047
  29: 1 the one whom God has c, 1047
2Ch 6: 5 not c a city in any tribe of Israel to have 1047
  6: 5 nor have I c anyone to be the leader 1047
  6: 6 But now I have c Jerusalem for my Name 1047
  6: 6 I have c David to rule my people Israel.' 1047
  6:34 to you toward this city you have c and 1047
  6:38 toward the city you have c and toward 1047
  7:12 and have c this place for myself as a temple 1047
  7:16 I have c and consecrated this temple so 1047
  12:13 the LORD had c out of all the tribes 1047
  29:11 the LORD has c you to stand before him 1047
  33: 7 which I have c out of all the tribes 1047
Ne 1: 9 and bring them to the place I have c as 1047
Ps 25:12 He will instruct him in the way c for him. 1047
  89: 3 "I have made a covenant with my c one, 1040
  105: 6 O sons of Jacob, his c ones. 1040
  105:26 and Aaron, whom he had c. 1047
  105:43 his c ones with shouts of joy; 1040
  106: 5 I may enjoy the prosperity of your c ones, 1040
  106:23 had not Moses, his c one, 1040
  119:30 I have c the way of truth; 1047
  119:173 for I have c your precepts. 1047
  132:13 For the LORD has c Zion, 1047
  135: 4 For the LORD has c Jacob to be his own, 1047
Isa 1:29 because of the gardens you have c. 1047
  41: 8 my servant, Jacob, whom I have c, 1047
  41: 9 I have c you and have not rejected you. 1040
  42: 1 my c one in whom I delight; 1040
  43:10 "and my servant whom I have c, 1047
  43:20 to give drink to my people, my c, 1040
  44: 1 my servant, Israel, whom I have c. 1047
  44: 2 my servant, Jeshurun, whom I have c. 1047
  45: 4 sake of Jacob my servant, of Israel my c, 1040
  48:14 LORD's c ally will carry out his purpose 170
  49: 7 the Holy One of Israel, who has c you." 1047
  58: 5 Is this the kind of fast I have c, 1047
  58: 6 "Is not this the kind of fasting I have c: 1047
  65: 9 my c people will inherit them, 1040
  65:15 You will leave your name to my c ones as 1040
  65:22 my c ones will long enjoy the works 1040
  66: 3 they have chosen their own ways, 1047
Jer 49:19 Who is the c one I will appoint for this? 1047
  50:44 Who is the c one I will appoint for this? 1047
Am 3: 2 "You only have I c of all the families of 3359
Hag 2:23 for I have c you,' 1047

Zec 3: 2 The LORD, who has c Jerusalem, 1047
Mt 12:18 "Here is my servant whom I have c, 147
  22:14 "For many are invited, but few are c." 1723
  27:15 at the Feast to release a prisoner c by 2527
Mk 13:20 for the sake of the elect, whom he has c, 1721
Lk 1: 9 he was c by lot, 3275
  9:35 saying, "This is my Son, whom I have c; 1721
  10:42 Mary has c what is better, 1721
  18: 7 not God bring about justice for his c ones, 1723
  23:35 if he is the Christ of God, the C One." 1723
Jn 6:70 Jesus replied, "Have I not c you, the Twelve? 1721
  13:18 I know those I have c. 1721
  15:19 but I have c you out of the world. 1721
Ac 1: 2 the Holy Spirit to the apostles he had c. 1721
  1:24 Show us which of these two you have c 1721
  9:15 This man is my c instrument 1724
  10:41 but by witnesses whom God had already c 4742
  22:14 of our fathers has c you to know his will 4741
Ro 8:33 against those whom God has c? 1723
  11: 5 at the present time there is a remnant c 1724
  16:13 Greet Rufus, c in the Lord, and his mother, 1723
2Co 8:19 he was c by the churches to accompany us 5936
Eph 1:11 In him we were also c, 3103
Col 1:27 To them God has c to make known among 2527
  3:12 Therefore, as God's c people, 1723
1Th 1: 4 brothers loved by God, that he has c you, 1724
Jas 2: 5 not God c those who are poor in the eyes of 1721
1Pe 1: 2 have been c according to the foreknowledge NIG
  1:20 He was c before the creation of the world, 4589
  2: 4 rejected by men but c by God and precious 1723
  2: 6 a c and precious cornerstone, 1723
  2: 9 But you are a c people, a royal priesthood, 1723
  5:13 She who is in Babylon, c together with you, 5293
2Jn 1: 1 The elder, To the c lady and her children, 1723
  1:13 of your c sister send their greetings. 1723
Rev 17:14 c and faithful followers." 1723

CHOZEBA (KJV) See COZEBA

CHRIST (530) [CHRIST'S, CHRISTIAN, CHRISTIANS, CHRISTS, MESSIAH]

Mt 1: 1 the genealogy of Jesus C the son of David, 5986
  1:16 of whom was born Jesus, who is called C. 5986
  1:17 and fourteen from the exile to the C. 5986
  1:18 how the birth of Jesus C came about: 5986
  2: 4 he asked them where the C was to be born. 5986
  11: 2 in prison what C was doing, 5986
  16:16 Simon Peter answered, "You are the C, 5986
  16:20 not to tell anyone that he was the C. 5986
  22:42 "What do you think about the C? 5986
  23:10 for you have one Teacher, the C. 5986
  24: 5 'I am the C,' and will deceive many. 5986
  24:23 'Look, here is the C!' 5986
  26:63 Tell us if you are the C, the Son of God." 5986
  26:68 and said, "Prophesy to us, C. 5986
  27:17 Barabbas, or Jesus who is called C?" 5986
  27:22 then, with Jesus who is called C?" 5986
Mk 1: 1 beginning of the gospel about Jesus C, 5986
  8:29 Peter answered, "You are the C." 5986
  9:41 because you belong to C will certainly 5986
  12:35 that the teachers of the law say that the C is 5986
  13:21 'Look, here is the C!' 5986
  14:61 "Are you the C, the Son of the Blessed One 5986
  15:32 Let this C, this King of Israel, 5986
Lk 2:11 he is C the Lord. 5986
  2:26 not die before he had seen the Lord's C. 5986
  3:15 if John might possibly be the C. 5986
  4:41 because they knew he was the C. 5986
  9:20 Peter answered, "The C of God." 5986
  20:41 "How is it that they say the C is the Son 5986
  22:67 "If you are the C," they said, "tell us." 5986
  23: 2 of taxes to Caesar and claims to be C, 5986
  23:35 let him save himself if he is the C of God, 5986
  23:39 "Aren't you the C? 5986
  24:26 Did not the C have to suffer these things 5986
  24:46 The C will suffer and rise from the dead on 5986
Jn 1:17 grace and truth came through Jesus C. 5986
  1:20 but confessed freely, "I am not the C." 5986
  1:25 then do you baptize if you are not the C, 5986
  1:41 the Messiah" (that is, the C). 5986
  3:28 'I am not the C but am sent ahead of him.' 5986
  4:25 that Messiah" (called C) "is coming. 5986
  4:29 Could this be the C?" 5986
  7:26 that he is the C? 5986
  7:27 when the C comes, 5986
  7:31 They said, "When the C comes, 5986
  7:41 Others said, "He is the C." 5986
  7:41 "How can the C come from Galilee? 5986
  7:42 not the Scripture say that the C will come 5986
  9:22 the C would be put out of the synagogue. 5986
  10:24 If you saw the C, tell us plainly." 5986
  11:27 she told him, "I believe that you are the C, 5986
  12:34 the Law that the C will remain forever, 5986
  17: 3 and Jesus C, whom you have sent. 5986
  20:31 that you may believe that Jesus is the C, 5986
Ac 2:31 he spoke of the resurrection of the C, 5986
  2:36 whom you crucified, both Lord and C." 5986
  3: 6 In the name of Jesus C of Nazareth, walk." 5986
  3:18 saying that his C would suffer. 5986
  3:20 the C, who has been appointed for you— 5986
  4:10 It is by the name of Jesus C of Nazareth, 5986
  5:42 the good news that Jesus is the C. 5986

Ac 8: 5 in Samaria and proclaimed the C there. 5986
  8:12 of God and the name of Jesus C, 5986
  9:22 in Damascus by proving that Jesus is the C. 5986
  9:34 Peter said to him, "Jesus C heals you. 5986
  10:36 the good news of peace through Jesus C, 5986
  10:48 be baptized in the name of Jesus C. 5986
  11:17 who believed in the Lord Jesus C, 5986
  15:26 for the name of our Lord Jesus C. 5986
  16:18 "In the name of Jesus C I command you 5986
  17: 3 the C had to suffer and rise from the dead. 5986
  17: 3 I am proclaiming to you is the C," 5986
  18: 5 testifying to the Jews that Jesus was the C. 5986
  18:28 from the Scriptures that Jesus was the C. 5986
  24:24 to him as he spoke about faith in C Jesus. 5986
  26:23 that the C would suffer and, 5986
  28:31 of God and taught about the Lord Jesus C. 5986
Ro 1: 1 Paul, a servant of C Jesus, 5986
  1: 4 Jesus C our Lord. 5986
  1: 6 to belong to Jesus C. 5986
  1: 7 and from the Lord Jesus C. 5986
  1: 8 I thank my God through Jesus C for all 5986
  2:16 when God will judge men's secrets through Jesus C, 5986
  3:22 through faith in Jesus C to all who believe. 5986
  3:24 the redemption that came by C Jesus. 5986
  5: 1 with God through our Lord Jesus C, 5986
  5: 6 C died for the ungodly. 5986
  5: 8 While we were still sinners, C died for us. 5986
  5:11 in God through our Lord Jesus C, 5986
  5:15 Jesus C, overflow to the many! 5986
  5:17 in life through the one man, Jesus C. 5986
  5:21 through Jesus C our Lord. 5986
  6: 3 into C Jesus were baptized into his death? 5986
  6: 4 just as C was raised from the dead through 5986
  6: 8 Now if we died with C, 5986
  6: 9 For we know that since C was raised from 5986
  6:11 to sin but alive to God in C Jesus. 5986
  6:23 of God is eternal life in C Jesus our Lord. 5986
  7: 4 also died to the law through the body of C, 5986
  7:25 through Jesus C our Lord! 5986
  8: 1 for those who are in C Jesus, 5986
  8: 2 through C Jesus the law of the Spirit 5986
  8: 9 if anyone does not have the Spirit of C, 5986
  8: 9 he does not belong to C. 899S
  8:10 But if C is in you, 5986
  8:11 he who raised C from the dead will 5986
  8:17 heirs of God and co-heirs with C, 5986
  8:34 C Jesus, who died— 5986
  8:35 Who shall separate us from the love of C? 5986
  8:39 the love of God that is in C Jesus our Lord. 5986
  9: 1 I speak the truth in C—I am not lying, 5986
  9: 3 cut off from C for the sake of my brothers, 5986
  9: 5 the human ancestry of C, 5986
  10: 4 C is the end of the law so that there may 5986
  10: 6 (that is, to bring C down) 5986
  10: 7 (that is, to bring C up from the dead). 5986
  10:17 message is heard through the word of C. 5986
  12: 5 so in C we who are many form one body, 5986
  13:14 clothe yourselves with the Lord Jesus C, 5986
  14: 9 C died and returned to life so that he might 5986
  14:15 your brother for whom C died. 5986
  14:18 because anyone who serves C 5986
  15: 3 For even C did not please himself but, 5986
  15: 5 among yourselves as you follow C Jesus, 5986
  15: 6 the God and Father of our Lord Jesus C. 5986
  15: 7 then, just as C accepted you, 5986
  15: 8 For I tell you that C has become a servant 5986
  15:16 to be a minister of C Jesus to the Gentiles 5986
  15:17 I glory in C Jesus in my service to God. 5986
  15:18 not venture to speak of anything except what C has accomplished 5986
  15:19 I have fully proclaimed the gospel of C. 5986
  15:20 the gospel where C was not known, 5986
  15:29 in the full measure of the blessing of C. 5986
  15:30 by our Lord Jesus C and by the love of 5986
  16: 3 my fellow workers in C Jesus, 5986
  16: 5 the first convert to C in the province 5986
  16: 7 and they were in C before I was. 5986
  16: 9 Greet Urbanus, our fellow worker in C, 5986
  16:10 Greet Apelles, tested and approved in C, 5986
  16:16 All the churches of C send greetings. 5986
  16:18 such people are not serving our Lord C, 5986
  16:25 and the proclamation of Jesus C, 5986
  16:27 be glory forever through Jesus C! 5986
1Co 1: 1 an apostle of C Jesus by the will of God, 5986
  1: 2 to those sanctified in C Jesus and called to 5986
  1: 2 on the name of our Lord Jesus C— 5986
  1: 3 from God our Father and the Lord Jesus C. 5986
  1: 4 because of his grace given you in C Jesus. 5986
  1: 6 about C was confirmed in you. 5986
  1: 7 as you eagerly wait for our Lord Jesus C to 5986
  1: 8 on the day of our Lord Jesus C. 5986
  1: 9 with his Son Jesus C our Lord, 5986
  1:10 brothers, in the name of our Lord Jesus C, 5986
  1:12 still another, "I follow C." 5986
  1:13 Is C divided? Was Paul crucified for you? 5986
  1:17 For C did not send me to baptize, 5986
  1:17 lest the cross of C be emptied of its power. 5986
  1:23 but we preach C crucified: 5986
  1:24 C the power of God and the wisdom 5986
  1:30 It is because of him that you are in C Jesus, 5986
  2: 2 with you except Jesus C and him crucified. 5986
  2:16 But we have the mind of C. 5986
  3: 1 as worldly—mere infants in C. 5986
  3:11 one already laid, which is Jesus C. 5986
  3:23 and you are of C, and Christ is of God. 5986
  3:23 and you are of Christ, and C is of God. 5986

1Co	4: 1	men ought to regard us as servants *of* C	5986
	4:10	We are fools for C,	5986
	4:10	but you are so wise in C!	5986
	4:15	in C, you do not have many fathers, for	5986
	4:15	for in C Jesus I became your father through	5986
	4:17	of my way of life in C Jesus,	5986
	5: 7	C, our Passover lamb, has been sacrificed.	5986
	6:11	in the name *of* the Lord Jesus C and by	5986
	6:15	that your bodies are members *of* C himself?	5986
	6:15	then take the members *of* C and unite them	5986
	8: 6	and there is but one Lord, Jesus C,	5986
	8:11	So this weak brother, for whom C died,	5986
	8:12	wound their weak conscience, you sin against C.	5986
	9:12	rather than the gospel *of* C.	5986
	10: 4	and that rock was C.	5986
	10:16	a participation in the blood *of* C?	5986
	10:16	a participation in the body *of* C?	5986
	11: 1	as I follow the example *of* C.	5986
	11: 3	to realize that the head of every man is C,	5986
	11: 3	and the head *of* C is God.	5986
	12:12	So it is with C.	5986
	12:27	Now you are the body *of* C,	5986
	15: 3	that C died for our sins according to	5986
	15:12	if it is preached that C has been raised from	5986
	15:13	then not even C has been raised.	5986
	15:14	And if C has not been raised,	5986
	15:15	about God that he raised C from the dead.	5986
	15:16	then C has not been raised either.	5986
	15:17	if C has not been raised, your faith is futile;	5986
	15:18	also who have fallen asleep in C are lost.	5986
	15:19	If only for this life we have hope in C,	5986
	15:20	C has indeed been raised from the dead,	5986
	15:22	so in C all will be made alive.	5986
	15:23	But each in his own turn: C, the firstfruits;	5986
	15:27	who put everything under C.	899S
	15:31	as I glory over you in C Jesus our Lord.	5986
	15:57	the victory through our Lord Jesus C.	5986
	16:24	My love to all of you in C Jesus. Amen.	5986
2Co	1: 1	an apostle *of* C Jesus by the will of God,	5986
	1: 2	from God our Father and the Lord Jesus C.	5986
	1: 3	to the God and Father *of* our Lord Jesus C.	5986
	1: 5	For just as the sufferings *of* C flow over	5986
	1: 5	so also through C our comfort overflows.	5986
	1:19	For the Son of God, Jesus C,	5986
	1:20	they are "Yes" in C.	899S
	1:21	both us and you stand firm in C.	5986
	2:10	I have forgiven in the sight *of* C	5986
	2:12	and found that the Lord had opened	5986
	2:14	in C and through us spreads everywhere	5986
	2:15	*of* C among those who are being saved	5986
	2:17	in C we speak before God with sincerity,	5986
	3: 3	You show that you are a letter *from* C,	5986
	3: 4	Such confidence as this is ours through C	5986
	3:14	because only in C is it taken away.	5986
	4: 4	the light of the gospel of the glory *of* C,	5986
	4: 5	but Jesus C as Lord,	5986
	4: 6	of the glory of God in the face *of* C.	5986
	5:10	before the judgment seat *of* C,	5986
	5:16	Though we once regarded C in this way,	5986
	5:17	if anyone is in C, he is a new creation;	5986
	5:18	who reconciled us to himself through C	5986
	5:19	the world to himself in C,	5986
	6:15	What harmony is there between C	5986
	8: 9	you know the grace of our Lord Jesus C,	5986
	8:23	of the churches and an honor *to* C.	5986
	9:13	confession of the gospel *of* C,	5986
	10: 1	By the meekness and gentleness *of* C,	5986
	10: 5	to make it obedient *to* C.	5986
	10: 7	is confident that he **belongs to** C,	1639+5986
	10: 7	that we *belong to* C just as much as he.	5986
	10:14	as far as you with the gospel *of* C.	5986
	11: 2	I promised you to one husband, *to* C,	5986
	11: 3	from your sincere and pure devotion to C.	5986
	11:10	As surely as the truth *of* C is in me,	5986
	11:13	masquerading as apostles *of* C.	5986
	11:23	Are they servants *of* C?	5986
	12: 2	in C who fourteen years ago was caught up	5986
	12:19	in the sight of God as those in C;	5986
	13: 3	that C is speaking through me.	5986
	13: 5	Do you not realize that C Jesus is in you—	5986
	13:14	May the grace *of* the Lord Jesus C,	5986
Gal	1: 1	but by Jesus C and God the Father,	5986
	1: 3	from God our Father and the Lord Jesus C,	5986
	1: 6	the one who called you by the grace *of* C	5986
	1: 7	and are trying to pervert the gospel *of* C.	5986
	1:10	I would not be a servant *of* C.	5986
	1:12	I received it by revelation *from* Jesus C.	5986
	1:22	to the churches of Judea that are in C.	5986
	2: 4	to spy on the freedom we have in C Jesus	5986
	2:16	but by faith in Jesus C.	5986
	2:16	in C Jesus that we may be justified by faith	5986
	2:16	by faith *in* C and not by observing the law,	5986
	2:17	"If, while we seek to be justified in C,	5986
	2:17	does that mean that C promotes sin?	5986
	2:20	I have been crucified with C	5986
	2:20	but C lives in me.	5986
	2:21	gained through the law, C died for nothing!	5986
	3: 1	Before your very eyes Jesus C was clearly portrayed as crucified.	5986
	3:13	C redeemed us from the curse of the law	5986
	3:14	to the Gentiles through C Jesus,	5986
	3:16	meaning one person, who is C.	5986
	3:22	being given through faith in Jesus C,	5986
	3:24	to lead us to C that we might be justified	5986
	3:26	of God through faith in C Jesus,	5986
	3:27	into C have clothed yourselves with Christ.	5986

Gal	3:27	into Christ have clothed yourselves with C.	5986
	3:28	for you are all one in C Jesus.	5986
	3:29	If you *belong to* C, then you are Abraham's	5986
	4:14	as if I were C Jesus himself.	5986
	4:19	in the pains of childbirth until C is formed	5986
	5: 1	It is for freedom that C has set us free.	5986
	5: 2	C will be of no value to you at all.	5986
	5: 4	by law have been alienated from C;	5986
	5: 6	For in C Jesus neither circumcision	5986
	5:24	*to* C Jesus have crucified the sinful nature	5986
	6: 2	in this way you will fulfill the law *of* C.	5986
	6:12	for the cross *of* C.	5986
	6:14	in the cross of our Lord Jesus C,	5986
	6:18	*of* our Lord Jesus C be with your spirit,	5986
Eph	1: 1	an apostle *of* C Jesus by the will of God,	5986
	1: 1	the faithful in C Jesus:	5986
	1: 2	from God our Father and the Lord Jesus C.	5986
	1: 3	to the God and Father *of* our Lord Jesus C,	5986
	1: 3	with every spiritual blessing in C.	5986
	1: 5	as his sons through Jesus C, in accordance	5986
	1: 9	which he purposed in C,	899S
	1:10	on earth together under one head, even C.	5986
	1:12	who were the first to hope in C,	5986
	1:13	also were included in C when you heard	4005S
	1:17	that the God of our Lord Jesus C,	5986
	1:20	which he exerted in C when he raised him	5986
	2: 5	with C even when we were dead	5986
	2: 6	And God raised us up with C and seated us	NIG
	2: 6	with him in the heavenly realms in C Jesus,	5986
	2: 7	expressed in his kindness to us in C Jesus.	5986
	2:10	created in C Jesus to do good works,	5986
	2:12	that at that time you were separate from C,	5986
	2:13	in C Jesus you who once were far away have been brought near	5986
	2:13	near through the blood *of* C.	5986
	2:20	C Jesus himself as the chief cornerstone.	5986
	3: 1	*of* C Jesus for the sake of you Gentiles—	5986
	3: 4	into the mystery *of* C,	5986
	3: 6	sharers together in the promise in C Jesus.	5986
	3: 8	the Gentiles the unsearchable riches *of* C,	5986
	3:11	accomplished in C Jesus our Lord.	5986
	3:17	C may dwell in your hearts through faith.	5986
	3:18	and high and deep is the love *of* C,	5986
	3:21	and in C Jesus throughout all generations,	5986
	4: 7	grace has been given as C apportioned it.	5986
	4:12	so that the body *of* C may be built up	5986
	4:13	to the whole measure of the fullness *of* C.	5986
	4:15	up into him who is the Head, that is, C.	5986
	4:20	did not come to know C that way.	5986
	4:32	just as in C God forgave you.	5986
	5: 2	as C loved us and gave himself up for us as	5986
	5: 5	has any inheritance in the kingdom *of* C	5986
	5:14	and C will shine on you."	5986
	5:20	in the name of our Lord Jesus C.	5986
	5:21	to one another out of reverence *for* C.	5986
	5:23	the husband is the head of the wife as C is	5986
	5:24	Now as the church submits *to* C,	5986
	5:25	just as C loved the church and gave himself	5986
	5:29	just as C does the church—	5986
	5:32	but I am talking about C and the church.	5986
	6: 5	just as you would obey C.	5986
	6: 6	but like slaves *of* C, doing the will of God	5986
	6:23	from God the Father and the Lord Jesus C.	5986
	6:24	Grace to all who love our Lord Jesus C	5986
Php	1: 1	Paul and Timothy, servants *of* C Jesus,	5986
	1: 1	To all the saints in C Jesus at Philippi,	5986
	1: 2	from God our Father and the Lord Jesus C.	5986
	1: 6	to completion until the day *of* C Jesus.	5986
	1: 8	for all of you with the affection *of* C Jesus.	5986
	1:10	be pure and blameless until the day *of* C,	5986
	1:11	that comes through Jesus C—	5986
	1:13	to everyone else that I am in chains for C.	5986
	1:15	that some preach C out of envy and rivalry,	5986
	1:17	former preach C out of selfish ambition,	5986
	1:18	from false motives or true, C is preached.	5986
	1:19	and the help given by the Spirit *of* Jesus C,	5986
	1:20	as always C will be exalted in my body,	5986
	1:21	For to me, to live is C and to die is gain.	5986
	1:23	I desire to depart and be with C,	5986
	1:26	in C Jesus will overflow on account of me.	5986
	1:27	in a manner worthy of the gospel *of* C.	5986
	1:29	on behalf of C not only to believe on him,	5986
	2: 1	from being united with C,	5986
	2: 5	be the same as that of C Jesus:	5986
	2:11	every tongue confess that Jesus C is Lord,	5986
	2:16	*of* C that I did not run or labor for nothing.	5986
	2:21	not those of Jesus C.	5986
	2:30	because he almost died for the work *of* C,	5986
	3: 3	who glory in C Jesus,	5986
	3: 7	now consider loss for the sake of C.	5986
	3: 8	of knowing C Jesus my Lord,	5986
	3: 8	that I may gain C	5986
	3: 9	but that which is through faith *in* C—	5986
	3:10	I want to know C and the power	899S
	3:12	of that for which C Jesus took hold of me.	5986
	3:14	God has called me heavenward in C Jesus.	5986
	3:18	many live as enemies of the cross *of* C.	5986
	3:20	the Lord Jesus C,	5986
	4: 7	and your minds in C Jesus.	5986
	4:19	according to his glorious riches in C Jesus.	5986
	4:21	Greet all the saints in C Jesus.	5986
	4:23	*of* the Lord Jesus C be with your spirit.	5986
Col	1: 1	an apostle *of* C Jesus by the will of God,	5986
	1: 2	To the holy and faithful brothers in C	5986
	1: 3	the Father of our Lord Jesus C,	5986
	1: 4	in C Jesus and of the love you have for all	5986
	1: 7	a faithful minister *of* C on our behalf,	5986

Col	1:27	which is C in you, the hope of glory.	5986
	1:28	that we may present everyone perfect in C.	5986
	2: 2	the mystery of God, namely, C,	5986
	2: 5	and how firm your faith in C is.	5986
	2: 6	then, just as you received C Jesus as Lord,	5986
	2: 8	of this world rather than on C.	5986
	2: 9	For in C all the fullness of the Deity lives	899S
	2:10	and you have been given fullness in C,	899S
	2:11	but with the circumcision done *by* C,	5986
	2:13	God made you alive with C.	899S
	2:17	the reality, however, is found in C.	5986
	2:20	with C to the basic principles of this world,	5986
	3: 1	Since, then, you have been raised with C,	5986
	3: 1	where C is seated at the right hand of God.	5986
	3: 3	and your life is now hidden with C in God.	5986
	3: 4	When C, who is your life, appears,	5986
	3:11	slave or free, but C is all, and is in all.	5986
	3:15	Let the peace *of* C rule in your hearts,	5986
	3:16	Let the word *of* C dwell in you richly	5986
	3:24	It is the Lord C you are serving.	5986
	4: 3	so that we may proclaim the mystery *of* C,	5986
	4:12	who is one of you and a servant *of* C Jesus,	5986
1Th	1: 1	in God the Father and the Lord Jesus C:	5986
	1: 3	by hope *in* our Lord Jesus C.	5986
	2: 6	*of* C we could have been a burden to you,	5986
	2:14	which are in C Jesus:	5986
	3: 2	in spreading the gospel *of* C,	5986
	4:16	and the dead in C will rise first.	5986
	5: 9	through our Lord Jesus C.	5986
	5:18	for this is God's will for you in C Jesus.	5986
	5:23	at the coming of our Lord Jesus C.	5986
	5:28	grace of our Lord Jesus C be with you.	5986
2Th	1: 1	in God our Father and the Lord Jesus C:	5986
	1: 2	from God the Father and the Lord Jesus C.	5986
	1:12	the grace of our God and the Lord Jesus C.	5986
	2: 1	the coming of our Lord Jesus C	5986
	2:14	in the glory of our Lord Jesus C.	5986
	2:16	May our Lord Jesus C himself	5986
	3: 6	In the name of the Lord Jesus C,	5986
	3:12	and urge in the Lord Jesus C to settle down	5986
	3:18	grace *of* our Lord Jesus C be with you all.	5986
1Ti	1: 1	an apostle *of* C Jesus by the command	5986
	1: 1	and *of* C Jesus our hope,	5986
	1: 2	from God the Father and C Jesus our Lord.	5986
	1:12	I thank C Jesus our Lord,	5986
	1:14	with the faith and love that are in C Jesus.	5986
	1:15	C Jesus came into the world to save sinners	5986
	1:16	C Jesus might display his unlimited patience as an example	5986
	2: 5	between God and men, the man C Jesus,	5986
	3:13	in their faith in C Jesus.	5986
	4: 6	you will be a good minister *of* C Jesus,	5986
	5:11	when their sensual desires overcome their dedication to C,	5986
	5:21	of God and C Jesus and the elect angels,	5986
	6: 3	*of* our Lord Jesus C and to godly teaching,	5986
	6:13	and *of* C Jesus, who while testifying	5986
	6:14	until the appearing of our Lord Jesus C,	5986
2Ti	1: 1	an apostle *of* C Jesus by the will of God,	5986
	1: 1	to the promise of life that is in C Jesus,	5986
	1: 2	from God the Father and C Jesus our Lord.	5986
	1: 9	This grace was given us in C Jesus before	5986
	1:10	the appearing *of* our Savior, C Jesus,	5986
	1:13	with faith and love in C Jesus.	5986
	2: 1	be strong in the grace that is in C Jesus.	5986
	2: 3	with us like a good soldier *of* C Jesus.	5986
	2: 8	Remember Jesus C, raised from the dead,	5986
	2:10	the salvation that is in C Jesus,	5986
	3:12	a godly life in C Jesus will be persecuted,	5986
	3:15	for salvation through faith in C Jesus.	5986
	4: 1	In the presence of God and *of* C Jesus,	5986
Tit	1: 1	a servant of God and an apostle *of* Jesus C	5986
	1: 4	the Father and C Jesus our Savior.	5986
	2:13	*of* our great God and Savior, Jesus C,	5986
	3: 6	through Jesus C our Savior,	5986
Phm	1: 1	Paul, a prisoner *of* C Jesus,	5986
	1: 3	from God our Father and the Lord Jesus C.	5986
	1: 6	of every good thing we have in C.	5986
	1: 8	in C I could be bold and order you	5986
	1: 9	and now also a prisoner *of* C Jesus—	5986
	1:20	refresh my heart in C.	5986
	1:23	Epaphras, my fellow prisoner in C Jesus,	5986
	1:25	*of* the Lord Jesus C be with your spirit.	5986
Heb	3: 6	But C is faithful as a son over God's house.	5986
	3:14	to share in C if we hold firmly till the end	5986
	5: 5	So C also did not take upon himself	5986
	6: 1	the elementary teachings *about* C and go	5986
	9:11	When C came as high priest of	5986
	9:14	much more, then, will the blood *of* C,	5986
	9:15	For this reason C is the mediator of	NIG
	9:24	For C did not enter a man-made sanctuary	5986
	9:26	C would have had to suffer many times	899S
	9:28	so C was sacrificed once to take away	5986
	10: 5	when C came into the world, he said:	NIG
	10:10	the sacrifice of the body of Jesus C once	5986
	11:26	He regarded disgrace *for the sake of* C as	5986
	13: 8	Jesus C is the same yesterday and today	5986
	13:21	through Jesus C, to whom be glory for ever	5986
Jas	1: 1	a servant of God and of the Lord Jesus C,	5986
	2: 1	as believers *in* our glorious Lord Jesus C,	5986
1Pe	1: 1	Peter, an apostle *of* Jesus C,	5986
	1: 2	for obedience *to* Jesus C and sprinkling	5986
	1: 3	to the God and Father of our Lord Jesus C!	5986
	1: 3	the resurrection of Jesus C from the dead,	5986
	1: 7	glory and honor when Jesus C is revealed.	5986
	1:11	and circumstances to which the Spirit *of* C	5986
	1:11	when he predicted the sufferings *of* C and	5986

1Pe	1:13	to be given you when Jesus C is revealed.	5986
	1:19	but with the precious blood of C,	5986
	2: 5	acceptable to God through Jesus C.	5986
	2:21	because C suffered for you,	5986
	3:15	But in your hearts set apart C as Lord.	5986
	3:16	in C may be ashamed of their slander.	5986
	3:18	For C died for sins once for all,	5986
	3:21	It saves you by the resurrection of Jesus C,	5986
	4: 1	Therefore, since C suffered in his body,	5986
	4:11	be praised through Jesus C.	5986
	4:13	that you participate in the sufferings of C,	5986
	4:14	you are insulted because of the name of C,	5986
	5:10	who called you to his eternal glory in C,	5986
	5:14	Peace to all of you who are in C.	5986
2Pe	1: 1	a servant and apostle of Jesus C,	5986
	1: 1	and Savior Jesus C have received a faith	5986
	1: 8	in your knowledge of our Lord Jesus C.	5986
	1:11	of our Lord and Savior Jesus C.	5986
	1:14	as our Lord Jesus C has made clear to me.	5986
	1:16	and coming of our Lord Jesus C.	5986
	2:20	and Savior Jesus C and are again entangled	5986
	3:18	of our Lord and Savior Jesus C.	5986
1Jn	1: 3	with the Father and with his Son, Jesus C.	5986
	2: 1	Jesus C, the Righteous One.	5986
	2:22	It is the man who denies that Jesus is the C.	5986
	3:16	**Jesus** C laid down his life for us.	1697S
	3:23	to believe in the name of his Son, Jesus C,	5986
	4: 2	that acknowledges that Jesus C has come in	5986
	5: 1	that Jesus is the C is born of God,	5986
	5: 6	by water and blood—Jesus C.	5986
	5:20	even in his Son Jesus C.	5986
2Jn	1: 3	from God the Father and from Jesus C,	5986
	1: 7	not acknowledge Jesus C as coming in	5986
	1: 9	in the teaching of C does not have God;	5986
Jude	1: 1	servant of Jesus C and a brother of James,	5986
	1: 1	by God the Father and kept by Jesus C:	5986
	1: 4	and deny Jesus C our only Sovereign	5986
	1:17	the apostles of our Lord Jesus C foretold.	5986
	1:21	the mercy of our Lord Jesus C to bring you	5986
	1:25	through Jesus C our Lord, before all ages,	5986
Rev	1: 1	The revelation of Jesus C,	5986
	1: 2	word of God and the testimony of Jesus C.	5986
	1: 5	and from Jesus C,	5986
	11:15	the kingdom of our Lord and of his C,	5986
	12:10	and the authority of his C.	5986
	20: 4	to life and reigned with C a thousand years.	5986
	20: 6	be priests of God and of C and will reign	5986

CHRIST'S (11) [CHRIST]

1Co	7:22	a free man when he was called is C slave.	5986
	9:21	from God's law but am under C law),	5986
2Co	5:14	For C love compels us,	5986
	5:20	We are therefore C ambassadors,	5642+5986
	5:20	We implore you on C behalf:	5986
	12: 9	so that C power may rest on me.	5986
	12:10	That is why, for C sake,	5986
Col	1:22	by C physical body through death	899S
	1:24	in regard to C afflictions.	5986
2Th	3: 5	into God's love and C perseverance.	5986
1Pe	5: 1	of C sufferings and one who also will share	5986

CHRISTIAN (2) [CHRIST]

Ac	26:28	you can persuade me to be a C?"	5985
1Pe	4:16	However, if you suffer as a C,	5985

CHRISTIANS (1) [CHRIST]

Ac	11:26	The disciples were called C first at Antioch.	5985

CHRISTS (2) [CHRIST]

Mt	24:24	For **false** C and false prophets will appear	6023
Mk	13:22	For **false** C and false prophets will appear	6023

CHRONIC (1)

Lev	13:11	it is a c skin disease and the priest shall	3823

CHRONICLES (1)

Est	6: 1	so he ordered the book of the c,	2355

CHRYSOLITE (8)

Ex	28:20	in the fourth row a c,	9577
	39:13	in the fourth row a c,	9577
SS	5:14	His arms are rods of gold set with c.	9577
Eze	1:16	They sparkled like c,	9577
	10: 9	the wheels sparkled like c,	74+9577
	28:13	ruby, topaz and emerald, c,	9577
Da	10: 6	His body was like c, his face like lightning,	9577
Rev	21:20	the sixth carnelian, the seventh c,	5994

CHRYSOPRASE (1)

Rev	21:20	the tenth c, the eleventh jacinth,	5995

CHUB (KJV) See LIBYA

CHUN (KJV) See CUN

CHURCH (79) [CHURCHES]

Mt	16:18	and on this rock I will build my c,	1711
	18:17	refuses to listen to them, tell it to the c;	1711
	18:17	and if he refuses to listen even to the c,	1711
Ac	5:11	fear seized the whole c and all who heard	1711

Ac	8: 1	a great persecution broke out against the c	1711
	8: 3	But Saul began to destroy the c.	1711
	9:31	Then the c throughout Judea,	1711
	11:22	News of this reached the ears of the c	1711
	11:26	the c and taught great numbers of people.	1711
	12: 1	that King Herod arrested some who	
		belonged to the c, intending	1711
	12: 5	the c was earnestly praying to God for him.	1711
	13: 1	In the c at Antioch there were prophets	1711
	14:23	elders for them in each c and,	1711
	14:27	gathered the c together and reported all	1711
	15: 3	The c sent them on their way,	1711
	15: 4	by the c and the apostles and elders,	1711
	15:22	the apostles and elders, with the whole c,	1711
	15:30	the c together and delivered the letter.	4436
	18:22	he went up and greeted the c and then went	1711
	20:17	Paul sent to Ephesus for the elders of the c.	1711
	20:28	Be shepherds of the c of God,	1711
Ro	16: 1	a servant of the c in Cenchrea.	1711
	16: 5	Greet also the c that meets at their house.	1711
	16:23	and the whole c here enjoy,	1711
1Co	1: 2	the c of God in Corinth, to those sanctified	1711
	4:17	with what I teach everywhere in every c.	1711
	5:12	of mine to judge those outside the c?	NIG
	6: 4	even men of little account in the c!	1711
	10:32	whether Jews, Greeks or the c of God—	1711
	11:18	I hear that when you come together as a c,	1711
	11:22	Or do you despise the c of God	1711
	12:28	And in the c God has appointed first	1711
	14: 4	but he who prophesies edifies the c.	1711
	14: 5	so that the c may be edified.	1711
	14:12	try to excel in gifts that build up the c.	1711
	14:19	But in the c I would rather speak five	
		intelligible words	1711
	14:23	So if the whole c comes together	1711
	14:26	be done for the strengthening of the c.	NIG
	14:28	in the c and speak to himself and God.	1711
	14:35	for a woman to speak in the c.	1711
	15: 9	because I persecuted the c of God.	1711
	16:19	and so does the c that meets at their house.	1711
2Co	1: 1	To the c of God in Corinth,	1711
Gal	1:13	how intensely I persecuted the c of God	1711
Eph	1:22	to be head over everything for the c,	1711
	3:10	His intent was that now, through the c,	1711
	3:21	to him be glory in the c and in Christ Jesus	1711
	5:23	of the wife as Christ is the head of the c,	1711
	5:24	Now as the c submits to Christ,	1711
	5:25	just as Christ loved the c and gave himself	1711
	5:27	and to present her to himself as a radiant c,	1711
	5:29	just as Christ does the c—	1711
	5:32	but I am talking about Christ and the c.	1711
Php	3: 6	as for zeal, persecuting the c;	1711
	4:15	not one c shared with me in the matter	1711
Col	1:18	And he is the head of the body, the c;	1711
	1:24	for the sake of his body, which is the c.	1711
	4:15	and to Nympha and the c in her house.	1711
	4:16	also read in the c of the Laodiceans and	1711
1Th	1: 1	To the c of the Thessalonians in God	1711
2Th	1: 1	To the c of the Thessalonians	1711
1Ti	3: 5	how can he take care of God's c?)	1711
	3:15	which is the c of the living God,	1711
	5:16	and not let the c be burdened with them,	1711
	5:16	the c can help those widows who are really	NIG
	5:17	of the c well are worthy of double honor,	NIG
Phm	1: 2	and to the c that meets in your home:	1711
Heb	12:23	to the c of the firstborn,	1711
Jas	5:14	He should call the elders of the c to pray	1711
3Jn	1: 6	They have told the c about your love.	1711
	1: 9	I wrote to the c, but Diotrephes,	1711
	1:10	to do so and puts them out of the c.	1711
Rev	2: 1	"To the angel of the c in Ephesus write:	1711
	2: 8	"To the angel of the c in Smyrna write:	1711
	2:12	"To the angel of the c in Pergamum write:	1711
	2:18	"To the angel of the c in Thyatira write:	1711
	3: 1	"To the angel of the c in Sardis write:	1711
	3: 7	"To the angel of the c in Philadelphia write:	1711
	3:14	"To the angel of the c in Laodicea write:	1711

CHURCHES (35) [CHURCH]

Ac	15:41	and Cilicia, strengthening the c.	1711
	16: 5	So the c were strengthened in the faith	1711
Ro	16: 4	the c of the Gentiles are grateful to them.	1711
	16:16	All the c of Christ send greetings.	1711
1Co	7:17	This is the rule I lay down in all the c.	1711
	11:16	nor do the c of God.	1711
	14:34	women should remain silent in the c.	1711
	16: 1	Do what I told the Galatian c to do.	1711
	16:19	The c in the province of Asia	1711
2Co	8: 1	that God has given the Macedonian c.	1711
	8:18	by all the c for his service to the gospel.	1711
	8:19	he was chosen by the c to accompany us	1711
	8:23	they are representatives of the c and	1711
	8:24	so that the c can see it.	1711
	11: 8	I robbed other c by receiving support	1711
	11:28	the pressure of my concern for all the c.	1711
	12:13	How were you inferior to the other c,	1711
Gal	1: 2	To the c in Galatia.	1711
	1:22	to the c of Judea that are in Christ.	1711
1Th	2:14	became imitators of God's c in Judea,	1711
	2:14	the same things those c suffered from	NIG
2Th	1: 4	among God's c we boast	1711
Rev	1: 4	To the seven c in the province of Asia:	1711
	1:11	and send it to the seven c:	1711
	1:20	seven stars are the angels of the seven c,	1711
	1:20	and the seven lampstands are the seven c.	1711
	2: 7	let him hear what the Spirit says to the c.	1711

Rev	2:11	let him hear what the Spirit says to the c.	1711
	2:17	let him hear what the Spirit says to the c.	1711
	2:23	Then all the c will know	1711
	2:29	let him hear what the Spirit says to the c.	1711
	3: 6	let him hear what the Spirit says to the c.	1711
	3:13	let him hear what the Spirit says to the c.	1711
	3:22	let him hear what the Spirit says to the c."	1711
	22:16	to give you this testimony for the c.	1711

CHURN (1) [CHURNED, CHURNING, CHURNS]

Job	41:31	He **makes** the depths c like a boiling	
		caldron	8409

CHURNED (1) [CHURN]

Job	26:12	By his power he c up the sea;	8088

CHURNING (5) [CHURN]

Job	30:27	The c inside me never stops;	8409
Pr	30:33	For as c the milk produces butter,	4790
Eze	32: 2	the seas thrashing about in your streams, c	1931
Da	7: 2	the four winds of heaven c up the great sea.	10137
Hab	3:15	c the great waters.	2816

CHURNS (1) [CHURN]

Isa	51:15	who c up the sea so that its waves roar—	8088

CHUSHAN-RISHATHAIM (KJV) See CUSHAN-RISHATHAIM

CHUZA (Anglicized, KJV) See CUZA

CIELED (KJV) See COVERED, PANELED, PANELS

CILICIA (8)

Ac	6: 9	as well as the **provinces of** C and Asia.	3070
	15:23	Syria and C: Greetings.	3070
	15:41	He went through Syria and C,	3070
	21:39	"I am a Jew, from Tarsus in C,	3070
	22: 3	born in Tarsus of C,	3070
	23:34	Learning that he was from C,	3070
	27: 5	across the open sea off the coast of C	3070
Gal	1:21	Later I went to Syria and C.	3070

CINNAMON (4)

Ex	30:23	250 shekels) of fragrant c,	7872
Pr	7:17	with myrrh, aloes and c.	7872
SS	4:14	and c, with every kind of incense tree,	7872
Rev	18:13	cargoes of c and spice, of incense, myrrh	3077

CINNEROTH (KJV) See KINNEROTH

CIRCLE (4) [CIRCLED, CIRCLING, CIRCUIT, CIRCULAR, CIRCUMFERENCE, ENCIRCLE, ENCIRCLED, ENCIRCLING]

2Sa	5:23	but c **around** behind them and attack them	6015
1Ch	14:14	but c **around** them and attack them in front	6015
Isa	40:22	He sits enthroned above the c of the earth,	2553
Mk	3:34	at those seated **in a** c around him and said,	3241

CIRCLED (1) [CIRCLE]

Jos	6:15	that on that day they c the city seven times.	6015

CIRCLING (1) [CIRCLE]

Jos	6:11	around the city, c it once.	5938

CIRCUIT (2) [CIRCLE]

1Sa	7:16	on a c from Bethel to Gilgal to Mizpah,	6015
Ps	19: 6	of the heavens and makes its c to the other;	9543

CIRCULAR (4) [CIRCLE]

1Ki	7:23	He made the Sea of cast metal, c in shape,	6017+6318
	7:31	that had a c frame one cubit deep.	4196
	7:35	top of the stand there was a c band	6017+6318
2Ch	4: 2	He made the Sea of cast metal, c in shape,	6017+6318

CIRCULATED (1)

Mt	28:15	And this story **has been widely** c among	1424

CIRCUMCISE (9) [CIRCUMCISED, CIRCUMCISING, CIRCUMCISION]

Dt	10:16	C your hearts, therefore,	4576+6889
	30: 6	The LORD your God will c your hearts	4576
Jos	5: 2	and c the Israelites again."	4909
Jer	4: 4	C yourselves to the LORD,	4576
	4: 4	c your hearts, you men of Judah	6073+6889
Lk	1:59	On the eighth day they came to c the child,	4362
	2:21	when it was time to c him,	4362
Jn	7:22	you c a child on the Sabbath.	4362
Ac	21:21	telling them not to c their children or live	4362

CIRCUMCISED (51) [CIRCUMCISE]

Ge	17:10	Every male among you *shall* be **c.**	4576
	17:12	among you who is eight days old *must* be **c,**	4576
	17:13	*they* must be **c.**	4576+4576
	17:14	who *has* not **been c** *in* the flesh,	4576+6889
	17:23	every male in his household, and **c** them, as	
		God told him.	1414+4576+6889
	17:24	Abraham was ninety-nine years old when	
		he was **c,**	1414+4576+6889
	17:26	Abraham and his son Ishmael were *both* **c**	4576
	17:27	was **c** with him.	4576
	21: 4	Abraham **c** him, as God commanded him.	4576
	34:14	to a man who is **not c.**	2257+4200+6889
	34:17	But if you will not agree to be **c,**	4576
	34:22	on the condition that our males be **c,**	4576
	34:24	and every male in the city was **c.**	4576
Ex	12:44	of it after *you* have **c** him,	4576
	12:48	the males in his household **c;**	4576
Lev	12: 3	On the eighth day the boy *is to* be **c.**	
			1414+4576+6889
Jos	5: 3	and **c** the Israelites at Gibeath Haaraloth.	4576
	5: 5	All the people that came out *had* been **c,**	4576
	5: 7	and these were the ones Joshua **c.**	4576
	5: 7	because they *had* not been **c** on the way.	4576
	5: 8	And after the whole nation had been **c,**	4576
Jer	9:25	"when I will punish all *who are* **c** only in	4576
Jn	7:23	Now if a child *can be* **c** on the Sabbath	3284+4364
Ac	7: 8	the father of Isaac and **c** him eight days	4362
	10:45	The **c** believers who had come	1666+4364
	11: 2	the **c** believers criticized him	1666+4364
	15: 1	"Unless *you are* **c,** according to the custom	4362
	15: 5	"The Gentiles must *be* **c** and required	4362
	16: 3	so he **c** him because of the Jews	3284+4362
Ro	2:25	as though you had not been **c.**	213
	2:26	If those who are **not c** keep	213
	2:26	not be regarded as though they were **c?**	4364
	2:27	The one who is **not c** physically and	213
	3:30	who will justify the **c** by faith and	4364
	4: 9	Is this blessedness only for the **c,**	4364
	4:10	Was it **after he was c,** or before?	1639+1877+4364
	4:11	of all who believe but have **not** been **c,**	213
	4:12	father of the **c** who not only are circumcised	4364
	4:12	of the circumcised who not only are **c**	1666+4364
	4:12	father Abraham had **before** he was **c.**	213+1877
1Co	7:18	*Was* a man *already* **c** when he was called?	4362
	7:18	*He* should not be **c.**	4362
Gal	2: 3	who was with me, was compelled *to be* **c,**	4362
	5: 2	tell you that if *you let yourselves* be **c,**	4362
	5: 3	to every man *who lets himself* be **c**	4362
	6:12	trying to compel you *to be* **c.**	4362
	6:13	Not even those who *are* **c** obey the law,	4362
	6:13	be **c** that they may boast about your flesh.	4362
Php	3: 5	**c** on the eighth day, of the people of Israel,	4364
Col	2:11	In him *you* were also **c,**	4362
	3:11	**c** or uncircumcised, barbarian, Scythian,	4364

CIRCUMCISING (1) [CIRCUMCISE]

| Ge | 34:15 | you become like us by **c** all your males. | 4576 |

CIRCUMCISION (21) [CIRCUMCISE]

Ge	17:11	You *are* to **undergo c,**	906+1414+4576+6889
Ex	4:26	"bridegroom of blood," referring to **c.)**	4581
Jn	7:22	because Moses gave you **c**	4364
Ac	7: 8	Then he gave Abraham the covenant *of* **c.**	4364
Ro	2:25	**C** has value if you observe the law,	4364
	2:27	though you have the written code and **c,**	4364
	2:28	nor is **c** merely outward and physical.	4364
	2:29	and **c** is circumcision of the heart,	4364
	2:29	and circumcision is **c** of the heart,	NIG
	3: 1	or what value is there in **c?**	4364
	4:11	And he received the sign *of* **c,**	4364
1Co	7:19	**C** is nothing and uncircumcision is nothing.	4364
Gal	2:12	of those who belonged to the **c** group.	4364
	5: 6	For in Christ Jesus neither **c**	4364
	5:11	Brothers, if I am still preaching **c,**	4364
	6:15	Neither **c** nor uncircumcision means	
		anything;	4364
Eph	2:11	"the **c"** (that done in the body by the hands	4364
Php	3: 3	For it is we who are the **c,**	4364
Col	2:11	*with* a **c** done by the hands of men but with	4364
	2:11	by the hands of men but with the **c** done	4364
Tit	1:10	especially those of the **c** group.	4364

CIRCUMFERENCE (1) [CIRCLE]

| Jer | 52:21 | and twelve cubits *in* **c;** | 2562+6015 |

CIRCUMSPECT (KJV) See CAREFUL

CIRCUMSTANCES (8)

1Ch	29:30	and the **c** that surrounded him and Israel	6961
Ro	4:10	**Under what c** was it credited?	4802
1Co	7:15	or woman is not bound in such **c;**	AIT
Php	4:11	I have learned to be content whatever the **c.**	NIG
Col	4: 8	that you may know about our **c** and	3836
1Th	5:18	give thanks in **all** *c,*	AIT
Jas	1: 9	The brother **in humble** *c* ought to take pride	5424
1Pe	1:11	to find out the time and **c** to **which** the Spirit	AIT

CIS (KJV) See KISH

CISTERN (20) [CISTERNS]

Ge	37:22	Throw him into *this* **c** here in the desert,	1014
	37:24	they took him and threw him into the **c.**	1014
	37:24	the **c** was empty; there was no water in it.	1014
	37:28	his brothers pulled Joseph up out of the **c**	1014
	37:29	to the **c** and saw that Joseph was not there,	1014
Lev	11:36	or a **c** *for* collecting water remains clean,	1014
1Sa	19:22	for Ramah and went to the great **c** at Secu.	1014
2Ki	18:31	and drink water from his own **c,**	1014
Pr	5:15	Drink water from your own **c,**	1014
Isa	30:14	from a hearth or scooping water out of a **c."**	1465
	36:16	and drink water from his own **c,**	1014
Jer	38: 6	and put him into the **c** of Malkijah,	1014
	38: 6	lowered Jeremiah by ropes into the **c;**	1014
	38: 7	heard that they had put Jeremiah into the **c.**	1014
	38: 9	They have thrown him into a **c,**	1014
	38:10	and lift Jeremiah the prophet out of the **c**	1014
	38:11	down with ropes to Jeremiah in the **c.**	1014
	38:13	with the ropes and lifted him out of the **c.**	1014
	41: 7	and threw them into a **c.**	1014
	41: 9	Now the **c** where he threw all the bodies of	1014

CISTERNS (6) [CISTERN]

Ge	37:20	and throw him into one of these **c** and say	1014
1Sa	13: 6	among the rocks, and in pits and **c.**	1014
2Ch	26:10	in the desert and dug many **c,**	1014
Jer	2:13	and have dug their own **c,**	1014
	2:13	broken **c** that cannot hold water.	1014
	14: 3	they go to the **c** but find no water.	1463

CITADEL (20) [CITADELS]

2Sa	12:26	of the Ammonites and captured the royal **c.**	6551
1Ki	16:18	the **c** of the royal palace and set the palace	810
2Ki	15:25	in the **c** of the royal palace at Samaria.	810
Ezr	6: 2	the **c** of Ecbatana in the province of Media,	10101
Ne	1: 1	while I was in the **c** of Susa,	1072
	2: 8	of the **c** by the temple and for the city wall	1072
	7: 2	with Hananiah the commander of the **c,**	1072
Est	1: 2	from his royal throne in the **c** of Susa,	1072
	1: 5	who were in the **c** of Susa.	1072
	2: 3	into the harem at the **c** of Susa.	1072
	2: 5	Now there was in the **c** of Susa a Jew of	1072
	2: 8	many girls were brought to the **c** of Susa	1072
	3:15	and the edict was issued in the **c** of Susa.	1072
	8:14	the edict was also issued in the **c** of Susa.	1072
	9: 6	In the **c** of Susa,	1072
	9:11	of those slain in the **c** of Susa was reported	1072
	9:12	and the ten sons of Haman in the **c** of Susa.	1072
Pr	18:19	disputes are like the barred gates of a **c.**	810
Isa	32:14	**c** and watchtower will become	6755
Da	8: 2	In my vision I saw myself in the **c** of Susa	1072

CITADELS (4) [CITADEL]

Ps	48: 3	God is in her **c;**	810
	48:13	view her **c,** that you may tell of them to	810
	122: 7	and security within your **c."**	810
Isa	34:13	Thorns will overrun her **c,**	810

CITIES (150) [CITY]

Ge	13:12	while Lot lived among the **c** *of* the plain	6551
	19:25	Thus he overthrew those **c** and	6551
	19:25	including all those living in the **c**—	6551
	19:29	So when God destroyed the **c** *of* the plain,	6551
	19:29	that overthrew the **c** where Lot had lived.	6551
	22:17	of the **c** of their enemies,	9133
	41:35	to be kept in the **c** for food.	6551
	41:48	in Egypt and stored it in the **c.**	6551
Ex	1:11	and Rameses as store **c** for Pharaoh.	6551
Lev	26:31	When you withdraw into your **c,**	6551
	26:31	I will turn your **c** into ruins.	6551
	26:33	and your **c** will lie in ruins.	6551
Nu	13:28	and the **c** are fortified and very large.	6551
	21: 2	we will totally destroy their **c."**	6551
	21:25	the **c** of the Amorites conquered them,	6551
	32:16	to build pens here for our livestock and **c**	6551
	32:17	and children will live in fortified **c,**	6551
	32:24	Build **c** for your women and children,	6551
	32:26	and herds will remain here in the **c**	6551
	32:33	the whole land with its **c** and the territory	6551
	32:36	Beth Nimrah and Beth Haran as fortified **c,**	6551
	32:38	They gave names to the **c** they rebuilt.	6551
	35: 6	of the towns you give the Levites will be **c**	6551
	35:11	select some towns to be your **c** of refuge,	6551
	35:13	These six towns you give will be your **c**	6551
	35:14	of the Jordan and three in Canaan as **c**	6551
Dt	1:28	the **c** are large, with walls up to the sky.	6551
	3: 4	At that time we took all his **c.**	6551
	3: 4	not one of the sixty **c** that we did not take	6551
	3: 5	All these **c** were fortified with high walls	6551
	3: 7	and the plunder from their **c** we carried off	6551
	4:41	Moses set aside three **c** east of the Jordan,	6551
	4:42	into one of these **c** and save his life.	6551
	4:43	The **c** were these:	NIH
	6:10	flourishing **c** you did not build,	6551
	9: 1	with large **c** that have walls up to the sky.	6551
	19: 2	for yourselves three **c** centrally located in	6551
	19: 5	That man may flee to one of these **c**	6551
	19: 7	to set aside for yourselves three **c.**	6551
	19: 9	then you are to set aside three more **c.**	6551
	19:11	and then flees to one of these **c,**	6551
	20:15	the **c** that are at a distance from you and do	6551
	20:16	in the **c** of the nations	6551
	28:52	to all the **c** throughout your land until	9133
	28:52	They will besiege all the **c** throughout	9133
	28:55	on you during the siege of all your **c.**	9133
	28:57	inflict on you in your **c.**	9133

Jos	9:17	and on the third day came to their **c:**	6551
	10: 2	like one of the royal **c;**	6551
	10:19	the rear and don't let them reach their **c,**	6551
	10:20	few who were left reached their fortified **c.**	6551
	11:12	Joshua took all these royal **c**	6551
	11:13	Yet Israel did not burn any of the **c** built	6551
	11:14	the plunder and livestock of these **c,**	6551
	13:31	and Ashtaroth and Edrei (the royal **c** *of* Og	6551
	14:12	and their **c** were large and fortified,	6551
	18:21	clan by clan, had the following **c:**	6551
	19:35	The fortified **c** were Ziddim, Zer,	6551
	20: 2	the Israelites to designate the **c** *of* refuge,	6551
	20: 4	"When he flees to one of these **c,**	6551
	20: 9	to these designated **c** and not be killed by	6551
	24:13	on which you did not toil and **c** you did	6551
2Sa	10:12	for our people and the **c** of our God.	6551
	20: 6	he will find fortified **c** and escape from us."	6551
1Ki	4:13	in Bashan and its sixty large walled **c**	6551
	8:37	enemy besieges them in any of their **c,**	824+9133
	9:19	as well as all his store **c** and the towns	6551
	10:26	which he kept in the chariot **c** and also	6551
	15:23	all he did and the **c** he built,	6551
	20:34	the **c** my father took from your father,"	6551
	22:39	and the **c** he fortified,	6551
2Ki	18:13	the fortified **c** of Judah and captured them.	6551
	19:25	that you have turned fortified **c** into piles	6551
1Ch	19:13	for our people and the **c** of our God.	6551
2Ch	1:14	which he kept in the chariot **c** and also	6551
	6:28	besiege them in any of their **c,**	824+9133
	8: 4	in the desert and all the store **c** he had built	6551
	8: 5	and Lower Beth Horon as fortified **c,**	6551
	8: 6	as well as Baalath and all his store **c,**	6551
	8: 6	the **c** *for* his chariots and for his horses—	6551
	9:25	which he kept in the chariot **c** and also	6551
	11:10	These were fortified **c** in Judah	6551
	11:12	He put shields and spears in all the **c,**	
			2256+6551+6551
	11:23	and to all the fortified **c.**	6551
	12: 4	the fortified **c** of Judah and came as far	6551
	14: 6	He built up the fortified **c** of Judah,	6551
	16: 4	Abel Maim and all the store **c** of Naphtali.	6551
	17: 2	the fortified **c** of Judah and put garrisons	6551
	17:12	he built forts and store **c** in Judah	6551
	17:19	besides those he stationed in the fortified **c**	6551
	19: 5	in each of the fortified **c** of Judah.	6551
	19:10	fellow countrymen who live in the **c**—	6551
	21: 3	as well as fortified **c** in Judah,	6551
	32: 1	He laid siege to the fortified **c,**	6551
	33:14	in all the fortified **c** in Judah.	6551
Ne	9:25	They captured fortified **c** and fertile land;	6551
Est	9: 2	The Jews assembled in their **c** in all	6551
Ps	9: 6	you have uprooted their **c;**	6551
	69:35	for God will save Zion and rebuild the **c**	6551
Isa	1: 7	your **c** burned with fire;	6551
	6:11	the **c** lie ruined and without inhabitant,	6551
	14:17	who overthrew its **c** and would	6551
	14:21	the land and cover the earth with their **c.**	6551
	17: 2	The **c** of Aroer will be deserted and left	6551
	17: 9	In that day their strong **c,**	6551
	19:18	In that day five **c** in Egypt will speak	6551
	25: 3	**c** of ruthless nations will revere you.	7953
	36: 1	the fortified **c** of Judah and captured them.	6551
	37:26	that you have turned fortified **c** into piles	6551
	54: 3	and settle in their desolate **c.**	6551
	61: 4	the ruined **c** that have been devastated	6551
	64:10	Your sacred **c** have become a desert;	6551
Jer	4: 5	Let us flee to the fortified **c!'**	6551
	4:16	raising a war cry against the **c** of Judah.	6551
	5:17	the sword they will destroy the fortified **c**	6551
	8:14	to the fortified **c** and perish there!	6551
	13:19	The **c** *in* the Negev will be shut up,	6551
	14: 2	"Judah mourns, her **c** languish;	9133
	34: 7	against Jerusalem and the other **c** *of* Judah.	6551
	34: 7	These were the only fortified **c** left	6551
	46: 8	I will destroy **c** and their people.'	6551
	48:18	up against you and ruin your **fortified c.**	4448
Eze	26:19	like **c** no longer inhabited,	6551
	29:12	and her **c** will lie desolate forty years	6551
	29:12	and her cities will lie desolate forty years	
		among ruined **c.**	6551
	30: 7	and their **c** will lie among ruined cities.	6551
	30: 7	and their cities will lie among ruined **c.**	6551
	30:17	and the **c** themselves will go into captivity.	NIH
	36:35	the **c** that were lying in ruins,	6551
	36:38	the ruined **c** be filled with flocks of people.	6551
Hos	8:14	But I will send fire upon their **c**	6551
	11: 6	Swords will flash in their **c,**	6551
Am	9:14	they will rebuild the ruined **c** and live	6551
Mic	5:11	I will destroy the **c** of your land and tear	6551
	5:14	and demolish your **c.**	6551
	7:12	to you from Assyria and the **c** *of* Egypt,	6551
Hab	1:10	They laugh at all **fortified c;**	4448
	2: 8	you have destroyed lands and **c**	7953
	2: 8	you have destroyed lands and **c**	7953
Zep	1:16	and battle cry against the fortified **c** and	6551
	3: 6	Their **c** are destroyed;	6551
Zec	8:20	the inhabitants of many **c** will yet come,	6551
Mt	10:23	you will not finish going through the **c**	4484
	11:20	Then Jesus began to denounce the **c** in	
		which most of his miracles	4484
Lk	19:17	take charge of ten **c.**	4484
	19:19	'You take charge of five **c.'**	4484
Ac	14: 6	the Lycaonian **c** of Lystra and Derbe and to	4484
	26:11	I even went to foreign **c** to persecute them.	4484
2Pe	2: 6	if he condemned the **c** of Sodom and	
		Gomorrah	4484
Rev	16:19	and the **c** of the nations collapsed.	4484

CITIZEN (8) [CITIZENS, CITIZENSHIP]
Lk	15:15	and hired himself out to a **c** of that country,	4489
Ac	21:39	a **c** of no ordinary city.	4489
	22:25	for you to flog a **Roman c** who hasn't	476+4871
	22:26	"This man is a **Roman c**."	4871
	22:27	"Tell me, are you a **Roman c**?"	4871
	22:28	"But I was born a **c**," Paul replied.	NIG
	22:29	put Paul, a **Roman c**, in chains.	4871
	23:27	for I had learned that he is a **Roman c**.	4871

CITIZENS (24) [CITIZEN]
Nu	21:28	the **c** of Arnon's heights.	1251
Jos	8:33	All Israel, aliens and **c** alike,	275
	24:11	The **c** of Jericho fought against you,	1251
Jdg	9: 2	the **c** of Shechem, 'Which is better for you:	1251
	9: 3	When the brothers repeated all this to the **c**	1251
	9: 6	the **c** of Shechem and Beth Millo gathered	1251
	9: 7	"Listen to me, **c** of Shechem.	1251
	9:18	king over the **c** of Shechem	1251
	9:20	**c** of Shechem and Beth Millo,	1251
	9:20	**c** of Shechem and Beth Millo,	1251
	9:23	between Abimelech and the **c** of Shechem,	1251
	9:24	on their brother Abimelech and on the **c**	1251
	9:25	to him these **c** of Shechem set men on	1251
	9:26	and its **c** put their confidence in him.	1251
	9:39	the **c** of Shechem and fought Abimelech.	1251
	9:46	the **c** in the tower of Shechem went into	1251
1Sa	23:11	Will the **c** of Keilah surrender me to him?	1251
	23:12	the **c** of Keilah surrender me and my men	1251
2Sa	21:12	of Saul and his son Jonathan from the **c**	1251
Isa	48: 2	you who call yourselves **c** of the holy city	4946S
Eze	26:17	you and your **c**;	3782
Ac	16:37	even though we are **Roman c**,	476+4871
	16:38	that Paul and Silas were **Roman c**,	4871
Eph	2:19	but **fellow c** with God's people	5232

CITIZENSHIP (3) [CITIZEN]
Ac	22:28	"I had to pay a big price for my **c**."	4486
Eph	2:12	excluded **from** **c** in Israel and foreigners to	4486
Php	3:20	But our **c** is in heaven.	4487

CITRON (1)
Rev	18:12	every sort of **c** wood,	2591

CITY (718) [CITIES, CITY'S]
Ge	4:17	Cain was then building a **c**,	6551
	10:12	that is the great **c**.	6551
	11: 4	"Come, let us build ourselves a **c**,	6551
	11: 5	But the LORD came down to see the **c**	6551
	11: 8	and they stopped building the **c**.	6551
	18:24	if there are fifty righteous people in the **c**?	6551
	18:26	"If I find fifty righteous people in the **c**	6551
	18:28	Will you destroy the whole **c** because	6551
	19: 1	and Lot was sitting in the gateway of **the c**.	6042S
	19: 4	from every part of the **c** of Sodom—	6551
	19:12	or anyone else in the **c** who belongs	6551
	19:14	the LORD is about to destroy the **c**!"	6551
	19:15	be swept away when the **c** is punished."	6551
	19:16	and led them safely out of the **c**,	6551
	23:10	to the gate of his **c**.	6551
	23:18	to the gate of the **c**.	6551
	28:19	though the **c** used to be called Luz.	6551
	33:18	at the **c** of Shechem in Canaan and camped	6551
	33:18	and camped within sight of the **c**.	6551
	34:20	to the gate of their **c** to speak	6551
	34:24	the men who went out of the **c** gate agreed	6551
	34:24	and every male in the **c** was circumcised.	6551
	34:25	and attacked the unsuspecting **c**,	6551
	34:27	the **c** where their sister had been defiled.	6551
	34:28	of theirs in the **c** and out in the fields.	6551
	36:32	His **c** was named Dinhabah.	6551
	36:35	His **c** was named Avith.	6551
	36:39	His **c** was named Pau,	6551
	41:48	In each **c** he put the food grown in	6551
	44: 4	from the **c** when Joseph said to his steward,	6551
	44:13	and returned to the **c**.	6551
Ex	9:29	"When I have gone out of the **c**,	6551
	9:33	Moses left Pharaoh and went out of the **c**	6551
Lev	25:29	" 'If a man sells a house in a walled **c**,	6551
	25:30	in the walled **c** shall belong permanently to	6551
Nu	21:26	the **c** of Sihon king of the Amorites,	6551
	21:27	let Sihon's **c** be restored.	6551
	21:28	a blaze from the **c** of Sihon.	7953
	24:19	of Jacob and destroy the survivors of the **c**."	6551
	35:25	and send him back to the **c** of refuge	6551
	35:26	of the **c** of refuge to which he has fled	6551
	35:27	avenger of blood finds him outside the **c**,	6551
	35:28	The accused must stay in his **c** of refuge	6551
	35:32	a **c** of refuge and so allow him to go back	6551
Dt	3: 6	of Heshbon, destroying every **c**—	6551
	17: 5	to your **c** gate and stone that person	9133
	19:12	bring him back from **the c**,	9004S
	20:10	When you march up to attack a **c**,	6551
	20:12	lay siege to **that c**.	2023S
	20:14	the livestock and everything else in the **c**,	6551
	20:19	When you lay siege to a **c** for a long time,	6551
	20:20	to build siege works until the **c** at war	6551
	28: 3	You will be blessed in the **c** and blessed in	6551
	28:16	You will be cursed in the **c** and cursed in	6551
	34: 3	the **C** of Palms, as far as Zoar.	6551
Jos	2: 5	when it was time to close the **c** gate,	9133
	2:15	house she lived in was part of the **c** wall.	7815
	6: 3	around the **c** once with all the armed men.	6551
	6: 4	march around the **c** seven times,	6551
Jos	6: 5	of the **c** will collapse and the people will go	6551
	6: 7	March around the **c**,	6551
	6:11	the ark of the LORD carried around the **c**,	6551
	6:14	the **c** once and returned to the camp.	6551
	6:15	and marched around the **c** seven times in	6551
	6:15	on that day they circled the **c** seven times.	6551
	6:16	For the LORD has given you the **c**!	6551
	6:17	The **c** and all that is in it are to be devoted	6551
	6:20	and they took the **c**.	6551
	6:21	the **c** to the LORD and destroyed with	6551
	6:24	the whole **c** and everything in it,	6551
	6:26	the man who undertakes to rebuild this **c**,	6551
	7: 5	from the **c** gate as far as the stone quarries	9133
	8: 1	his people, his **c** and his land.	6551
	8: 2	Set an ambush behind the **c**."	6551
	8: 4	You are to set an ambush behind the **c**.	6551
	8: 5	with me will advance on the **c**,	6551
	8: 6	until we have lured them away from the **c**,	6551
	8: 7	to rise up from ambush and take the **c**.	6551
	8: 8	When you have taken the **c**, set it on fire.	6551
	8:11	with him marched up and approached the **c**	6551
	8:11	with the valley between them and the **c**.	6504S
	8:12	to the west of the **c**.	6551
	8:13	all those in the camp to the north of the **c**	6551
	8:14	and all the men of the **c** hurried out early in	6551
	8:14	against him behind the **c**.	6551
	8:16	and were lured away from the **c**.	6551
	8:17	They left the **c** open and went in pursuit	6551
	8:18	for into your hand I will deliver **the c**."	5626S
	8:19	the **c** and captured it and quickly set it	6551
	8:20	and saw the smoke of the **c** rising against	6551
	8:21	the **c** and that smoke was going up from the	6551
	8:21	and that smoke was going up from the **c**,	6551
	8:22	of the ambush also came out of the **c**	6551
	8:27	the livestock and plunder of this **c**,	6551
	8:29	down at the entrance of the **c** gate.	6551
	10: 2	because Gibeon was an important **c**,	6551
	10:28	He put the **c** and its king to the sword	2023S
	10:30	The LORD also gave **that** **c** and its king	2023S
	10:30	**The c** and everyone in it Joshua put to	2023S
	10:32	**The c** and everyone in it he put to	2023S
	10:37	They took **the c** and put it to the sword,	2023S
	10:39	They took **the c**, its king and its villages,	2023S
	11:19	not one **c** made a treaty of peace with	6551
	15: 8	the southern slope of the Jebusite **c** (that is,	NIH
	15:62	the **C** of Salt and En Gedi—	6551
	18:16	the southern slope of the **Jebusite** **c** and so	AIT
	18:28	Haeleph, the **Jebusite** **c** (that is, Jerusalem),	AIT
	19:29	toward Ramah and went to the fortified **c**	6551
	20: 4	the entrance of the **c** gate and state his case	6551
	20: 4	before the elders of that **c**.	6551
	20: 4	into their **c** and give him a place to live	6551
	20: 6	to stay in that **c** until he has stood trial	6551
	21:12	around the **c** they had given to Caleb son	6551
	21:13	(a **c** of refuge for one accused of murder)	6551
	21:21	(a **c** of refuge for one accused of murder)	6551
	21:27	(a **c** of refuge for one accused of murder)	6551
	21:32	(a **c** of refuge for one accused of murder)	6551
	21:38	(a **c** of refuge for one accused of murder),	6551
Jdg	1: 8	They put the **c** to the sword and set it	6551
	1:16	from the **C** of Palms with the men of Judah	6551
	1:17	and they totally destroyed the **c**.	6551
	1:18	each **c** with its territory.	NIH
	1:24	a man coming out of the **c** and they said	6551
	1:24	how to get into the **c** and we will see	6551
	1:25	and they put the **c** to the sword but spared	6551
	1:26	where he built a **c** and called it Luz.	6551
	3:13	they took possession of the **C** of Palms.	6551
	5: 8	war came to the **c** gates,	9133
	5:11	of the LORD went down to the **c** gates.	9133
	9:30	of the **c** heard what Gaal son of Ebed said,	6551
	9:31	and are stirring up the **c** against you.	6551
	9:33	advance against the **c**.	6551
	9:35	the entrance to the **c** gate just as Abimelech	6551
	9:43	he saw the people coming out of the **c**,	6551
	9:44	to a position at the entrance to the **c** gate.	6551
	9:45	against the **c** until he had captured it	6551
	9:45	he destroyed the **c** and scattered salt over it.	6551
	9:51	Inside the **c**, however, was a strong tower,	6551
	9:51	all the people of the **c**—fled.	6551
	16: 2	in wait for him all night at the **c** gate.	6551
	16: 3	up and took hold of the doors of the **c** gate,	6551
	18:27	with the sword and burned down their **c**.	6551
	18:28	The **c** was in a valley near Beth Rehob.	2085S
	18:28	The Danites rebuilt the **c** and settled there.	6551
	18:29	though the **c** used to be called Laish.	6551
	19:11	at this **c** of the Jebusites and spend	6551
	19:12	We won't go into an alien **c**,	6551
	19:15	They went and sat in the **c** square,	6551
	19:17	and saw the traveler in the **c** square,	6551
	19:22	of the wicked men of the **c** surrounded	6551
	20:11	and united as one man against the **c**.	6551
	20:31	and were drawn away from the **c**.	6551
	20:32	and draw them away from the **c** to	6551
	20:37	and put the whole **c** to the sword.	6551
	20:38	up a great cloud of smoke from the **c**,	6551
	20:40	column of smoke began to rise from the **c**,	6551
	20:40	and saw the smoke of the whole **c** going up	6551
1Sa	5: 9	the LORD's hand was against that **c**,	6551
	5: 9	He afflicted the people of the **c**,	6551
	5:11	For death had filled the **c** with panic;	6551
	5:12	and the outcry of the **c** went up to heaven.	6551
	15: 5	to the **c** of Amalek and set an ambush in	6551
2Sa	5: 7	fortress of Zion, the **C** of David.	6551
	5: 9	in the fortress and called it the **C** of David.	6551
	6:10	of the LORD to be with him in the **C**	6551
2Sa	6:12	the house of Obed-Edom to the **C** of David	6551
	6:16	the LORD was entering the **C** of David,	6551
	10: 3	the **c** and spy it out and overthrow it?"	6551
	10: 8	at the entrance to their **c** gate,	9133
	10:14	before Abishai and went inside the **c**.	6551
	11:16	So while Joab had the **c** under siege,	6551
	11:17	of the **c** came out and fought against Joab,	6551
	11:20	'Why did you get so close to the **c** to fight?	6551
	11:23	to the entrance to the **c** gate.	9133
	11:25	the attack against the **c** and destroy it.'	6551
	12:28	the troops and besiege the **c** and capture it.	6551
	12:28	Otherwise I will take the **c**,	6551
	12:30	a great quantity of plunder from the **c** gate.	6551
	15: 2	the side of the road leading to the **c** gate.	9133
	15:14	and bring ruin upon us and put the **c** to	6551
	15:24	the people had finished leaving the **c**.	6551
	15:25	"Take the ark of God back into the **c**.	6551
	15:27	Go back to the **c** in peace.	6551
	15:34	if you return to the **c** and say to Absalom,	6551
	15:37	as Absalom was entering the **c**.	6551
	17:13	If he withdraws into a **c**,	6551
	17:13	then all Israel will bring ropes to that **c**,	6551
	17:17	not risk being seen entering the **c**.	6551
	18: 3	now for you to give us support from the **c**."	6551
	19: 3	The men stole into the **c** that day	6551
	20:15	They built a siege ramp up to the **c**,	6551
	20:16	a wise woman called from the **c**,	6551
	20:19	to destroy a **c** that is a mother in Israel.	6551
	20:21	and I'll withdraw from the **c**."	6551
	20:22	and his men dispersed from the **c**,	6551
1Ki	1:41	the meaning of all the noise in the **c**?"	7953
	1:45	and the **c** resounds with it.	7953
	2:10	with his fathers and was buried in the **C**	6551
	3: 1	He brought her to the **C** of David	6551
	8: 1	from Zion, the **C** of David.	6551
	8:16	not chosen a **c** in any tribe of Israel to have	6551
	8:44	the LORD toward the **c** you have chosen	6551
	8:48	toward the **c** you have chosen and	6551
	9:24	up from the **C** of David to	6551
	11:27	and had filled in the gap in the wall of the **c**	6551
	11:32	for the sake of my servant David and the **c**	6551
	11:36	the **c** where I chose to put my Name.	6551
	11:43	and was buried in the **c** of David his father.	6551
	13:25	and they went and reported it in the **c**	6551
	13:29	and brought it back to his own **c** to mourn	6551
	14:11	to Jeroboam die in the **c**,	6551
	14:12	When you set foot in your **c**,	6551
	14:21	the **c** the LORD had chosen out of all	6551
	14:31	and was buried with his fathers in the **C**	6551
	15: 8	with his fathers and was buried in the **C**	6551
	15:24	with them in the **c** of his father David.	6551
	16: 4	to Baasha who die in the **c**,	6551
	16:18	When Zimri saw that the **c** was taken,	6551
	16:24	for two talents of silver and built a **c** on	6551
	20: 2	He sent messengers into the **c** to Ahab king	6551
	20:12	So they prepared to attack the **c**.	6551
	20:19	of the **c** with the army behind them	6551
	20:30	The rest of them escaped to the **c** of Aphek,	6551
	20:30	And Ben-Hadad fled to the **c** and hid in	6551
	21: 8	and nobles who lived in Naboth's **c**	6551
	21:11	and nobles who lived in Naboth's **c** did	6551
	21:13	So they took him outside the **c**	6551
	21:24	to Ahab who die in the **c**,	6551
	22:26	to Amon the ruler of the **c** and to Joash	6551
	22:50	with them in the **c** of David his father.	6551
2Ki	2:19	The men of the **c** said to Elisha, "Look,	6551
	3:19	You will overthrow every fortified **c**	6551
	3:27	offered him as a sacrifice on the **c** wall.	2570
	6:14	They went by night and surrounded the **c**.	6551
	6:15	and chariots had surrounded the **c**.	6551
	6:19	"This is not the road and this is not the **c**.	6551
	6:20	After they entered **the c**, Elisha said,	9076S
	6:25	There was a great famine in the **c**	9076S
	7: 3	with leprosy at the entrance of the **c** gate.	9133
	7: 4	If we say, 'We'll go into the **c**'—	6551
	7:10	the **c** gatekeepers and told them, "We went	6551
	7:12	and get into the **c**.' "	6551
	7:13	of the horses that are left in **the c**.	2023S
	8:24	and was buried with them in the **C**	6551
	9:15	of the **c** to go and tell the news in Jezreel."	6551
	9:28	with his fathers in his tomb in the **C**	6551
	10: 2	a fortified **c** and weapons,	6551
	10: 5	So the palace administrator, the **c** governor,	6551
	10: 6	were with the leading men of the **c**,	6551
	10: 8	the entrance of the **c** gate until morning."	9133
	11:20	And the **c** was quiet,	6551
	12:21	and was buried with his fathers in the **C**	6551
	14:20	in the **C** of David.	6551
	15: 7	and was buried near them in the **C**	6551
	15:16	attacked Tiphsah and everyone in **the c**	2023S
	15:38	and was buried with them in the **C**	6551
	15:38	the **c** of his father.	NIH
	16:20	and was buried with them in the **C**	6551
	17: 9	fortified **c** they built themselves high places	6551
	18: 8	From watchtower to fortified **c**,	6551
	18:30	this **c** will not be given into the hand of	6551
	19:13	the king of the **c** of Sepharvaim,	6551
	19:32	not enter this **c** or shoot an arrow here.	6551
	19:33	he will not enter this **c**,	6551
	19:34	I will defend this **c** and save it,	6551
	20: 6	And I will deliver you and this **c** from	6551
	20: 6	I will defend this **c** for my sake and for	6551
	20:20	by which he brought water into the **c**,	6551
	23: 8	to the Gate of Joshua, the **c** governor,	6551
	23: 8	which is on the left of the **c** gate.	6551
	23:17	The men of the **c** said,	6551
	23:27	and I will reject Jerusalem, the **c** I chose,	6551

2Ki	24:11	to the c while his officers were besieging it.	6551
	25: 1	He encamped outside **the c**	2023S
	25: 2	The c was kept under siege until	6551
	25: 3	the famine in the c had become so severe	6551
	25: 4	Then the c wall was broken through,	6551
	25: 4	the Babylonians were surrounding the c.	6551
	25:11	the people who remained in the c,	6551
	25:19	Of those still in the c,	6551
	25:19	of his men who were found in the c.	6551
1Ch	1:43	whose c was named Dinhabah.	6551
	1:46	His c was named Avith.	6551
	1:50	His c was named Pau,	6551
	6:56	around the c were given to Caleb son	6551
	6:57	of Aaron were given Hebron (a c	6551
	6:67	of Ephraim they were given Shechem (a c	6551
	11: 5	fortress of Zion, the C of David.	6551
	11: 7	and so it was called the C of David.	6551
	11: 8	He built up the c around it,	6551
	11: 8	while Joab restored the rest of the c.	6551
	13:13	the ark to be with him in the C of David.	6551
	15: 1	for himself in the C of David,	6551
	15:29	the LORD was entering the C of David,	6551
	19: 9	at the entrance to their c,	6551
	19:15	and went inside the c.	6551
	20: 2	a great quantity of plunder from the c	6551
2Ch	5: 2	from Zion, the C of David.	6551
	6: 5	not chosen a c in any tribe of Israel to have	6551
	6:34	to you toward this c you have chosen and	6551
	6:38	toward the c you have chosen and toward	6551
	8:11	the C of David to the palace he had built	6551
	9:31	and was buried in the c of David his father.	6551
	12:13	the c the LORD had chosen out of all	6551
	12:16	with his fathers and was buried in the C	6551
	14: 1	with his fathers and was buried in the C	6551
	15: 6	by another and *one* c by another,	6551
	16:14	that he had cut out for himself in the C	6551
	18:25	to Amon the ruler of the c and to Joash	6551
	21: 1	was buried with them in the C	6551
	21:20	and was buried in the C of David,	6551
	23:21	And the c was quiet,	6551
	24:16	He was buried with the kings in the C	6551
	24:25	he died and was buried in the C of David,	6551
	25:28	and was buried with his fathers in the C	6551
	27: 9	with his fathers and was buried in the C	6551
	28:15	the C of Palms, and returned to Samaria.	6551
	28:27	with his fathers and was buried in the c	6551
	29:20	the c officials together and went up to	6551
	32: 3	the water from the springs outside the c,	6551
	32: 5	the supporting terraces of the C of David.	6551
	32: 6	before him in the square at the c gate.	6551
	32:18	in order to capture the c.	6551
	32:30	down to the west side of the C of David.	6551
	33:14	Afterward he rebuilt the outer wall of the C	6551
	33:15	and he threw them out of the c.	6551
	34: 8	of Azaliah and Maaseiah the ruler of the c,	6551
Ezr	4:10	in the c of Samaria and elsewhere	10640
	4:12	that rebellious and wicked c.	10640
	4:13	the king should know that if this c is built	10640
	4:15	In these records you will find that this c is	10640
	4:15	that this city is a rebellious c,	10640
	4:15	That is why this c was destroyed.	10640
	4:16	if this c is built and its walls are restored,	10640
	4:19	that this c has a long history of revolt	10640
	4:21	this c will not be rebuilt until I so order.	10640
Ne	2: 3	when the c where my fathers are buried lies	6551
	2: 5	the c in Judah where my fathers are buried	6551
	2: 8	the citadel by the temple and for the c wall	6551
	3:15	the steps going down from the C of David.	6551
	7: 4	Now the c was large and spacious,	6551
	11: 1	the holy c, while the remaining nine were	6551
	11: 9	over the Second District of the c.	6551
	11:18	The Levites in the holy c totaled 284.	6551
	12:37	the steps of the C of David on the ascent to	6551
	13:18	upon us and upon this c?	6551
Est	3:15	but the c of Susa was bewildered.	6551
	4: 1	and went out into the c,	6551
	4: 6	to Mordecai in the open square of the c	6551
	6: 9	on the horse through the c streets,	6551
	6:11	led him on horseback through the c streets,	6551
	8:11	the Jews in every c the right to assemble	6551
	8:15	the c of Susa held a joyous celebration.	6551
	8:17	In every province and in every c,	6551
	9:28	every province and in **every c.**	2256+6551+6551
Job	24:12	The groans of the dying rise from the c,	6551
	29: 7	the c and took my seat in the public square,	7984
Ps	31:21	to me when I was in a besieged c.	6551
	46: 4	a river whose streams make glad the c	6551
	48: 1	in the c of our God, his holy mountain.	6551
	48: 2	the c of the Great King.	7953
	48: 8	the c of the LORD Almighty, in the city	6551
	48: 8	in the c of our God:	6551
	55: 9	for I see violence and strife in the c.	6551
	55:11	Destructive forces are at work in **the c;**	2023S
	59: 6	snarling like dogs, and prowl about the c.	6551
	59:14	snarling like dogs, and prowl about the c.	6551
	60: 9	Who will bring me to the fortified c?	6551
	87: 3	Glorious things are said of you, O c of God:	6551
	101: 8	I will cut off every evildoer from the c of	6551
	107: 4	to a c where they could settle.	6551
	107: 7	He led them by a straight way to a c	6551
	107:36	they founded a c where they could settle.	6551
	108:10	Who will bring me to the fortified c?	6551
	122: 3	like a c that is closely compacted together.	6551
	127: 1	Unless the LORD watches over the c,	6551
Pr	1:21	of the c she makes her speech:	6551
	8: 3	into the c, at the entrances, she cries aloud:	7984
	9: 3	she calls from the highest point of the c.	7984

Pr	9:14	on a seat at the highest point of the c,	7984
	10:15	The wealth of the rich is their fortified c,	7953
	11:10	When the righteous prosper, the c rejoices;	7953
	11:11	the blessing of the upright a c is exalted,	7984
	16:32	a man who controls his temper than one who takes a c.	6551
	18:11	The wealth of the rich is their fortified c;	7953
	18:19	a fortified c, and disputes are like	7953
	21:22	A wise man attacks the c of the mighty	6551
	25:28	Like a c whose walls are broken down is	6551
	29: 8	Mockers stir up a c,	7953
	31:23	Her husband is respected at the c gate,	9133
	31:31	her works bring her praise at the c gate.	9133
Ecc	7:19	Wisdom makes one wise man more powerful than ten rulers in a c.	6551
	8:10	the holy place and receive praise in the c	6551
	9:14	a small c with only a few people in it.	6551
	9:15	there lived in **that** c a man poor but wise,	2023S
	9:15	and he saved the c by his wisdom.	6551
SS	3: 2	I will get up now and go about the c,	6551
	3: 3	as they made their rounds in the c.	6551
	5: 7	as they made their rounds in the c.	6551
Isa	1: 8	like a c under siege.	6551
	1:21	See how the faithful c has become a harlot!	7953
	1:26	Afterward you will be called the C	7953
	1:26	the City of Righteousness, the Faithful C."	7953
	14:31	Howl, O c!	6551
	17: 1	be a c but will become a heap of ruins.	6551
	17: 3	The fortified c will disappear	NIH
	19: 2	c against city, kingdom against kingdom.	6551
	19: 2	city against c, kingdom against kingdom.	6551
	19:18	One of them will be called the C	7953
	22: 2	O c of tumult and revelry!	6551
	22: 7	and horsemen are posted at the c gates;	9133
	22: 9	that the C of David had many breaches	6551
	23: 7	Is this your c of revelry, the old, old city,	NIH
	23: 7	Is this your city of revelry, the old, old c,	2023S
	23:16	walk through the c, O prostitute forgotten;	6551
	24:10	The ruined c lies desolate,	7953
	24:12	The c is left in ruins,	6551
	25: 2	You have made the c a heap of rubble,	6551
	25: 2	the foreigners' stronghold a c no more;	6551
	26: 1	We have a strong c;	6551
	26: 5	he lays the lofty c low;	7953
	27:10	The fortified c stands desolate,	6551
	28: 1	to that c, the pride of those laid low	NIH
	29: 1	Ariel, Ariel, the c where David settled!	7953
	32:13	for all houses of merriment and for this c	7953
	32:14	the noisy c deserted;	6551
	32:19	the forest and the c is leveled completely,	6551
	33:20	Look upon Zion, the c of our festivals;	7953
	36:15	this c will not be given into the hand of	6551
	37:13	the king of the c of Sepharvaim,	6551
	37:33	not enter this c or shoot an arrow here.	6551
	37:34	he will not enter this c,"	6551
	37:35	"I will defend this c and save it,	6551
	38: 6	And I will deliver you and this c from	6551
	38: 6	I will defend this c.	6551
	45:13	He will rebuild my c	6551
	48: 2	the holy c and rely on the God of Israel—	6551
	52: 1	O Jerusalem, the holy c.	6551
	54:11	"O afflicted c, lashed by storms and	NIH
	60:14	down at your feet and will call you the C	6551
	62:12	the C No Longer Deserted.	6551
	66: 6	Hear that uproar from the c,	6551
Jer	1:18	Today I have made you a fortified c,	6551
	5: 1	I will forgive **this c.**	2023S
	6: 6	This c must be punished;	6551
	8:16	the c and all who live there."	6551
	14:18	if I go into the c,	6551
	15: 7	with a winnowing fork at the c gates of	9133
	17:24	through the gates of this c on the Sabbath,	6551
	17:25	the gates of this c with their officials.	6551
	17:25	and this c will be inhabited forever.	6551
	19: 8	I will devastate this c and make it an object	6551
	19:11	I will smash this nation and this c just	6551
	19:12	I will make this c like Topheth.	6551
	19:15	to bring on this c and the villages	6551
	20: 5	to their enemies all the wealth of this c—	6551
	21:, 4	And I will gather them inside this c.	6551
	21: 6	I will strike down those who live in this c—	6551
	21: 7	the people in this c who survive the plague,	6551
	21: 9	Whoever stays in this c will die by	6551
	21:10	I have determined to do this c harm and	6551
	22: 8	from many nations will pass by this c	6551
	22: 8	a thing to this great c?'	6551
	23:39	with the c I gave to you and your fathers.	6551
	25:29	I am beginning to bring disaster on the c	6551
	26: 6	like Shiloh and this c an object of cursing	6551
	26: 9	and this c will be desolate and deserted?"	6551
	26:11	because he has prophesied against this c.	6551
	26:12	to prophesy against this house and this c all	6551
	26:15	and on this c and on those who live in it,	6551
	26:20	against this c and this land as Jeremiah did.	6551
	27:17	Why should this c become a ruin?	6551
	27:19	the other furnishings that are left in this c,	6551
	29: 7	the c to which I have carried you into exile.	6551
	29:16	in this c, your countrymen who did not go	6551
	30:18	the c will be rebuilt on her ruins,	6551
	31:38	"when this c will be rebuilt for me from	6551
	31:40	The c will never again be uprooted	NIH
	32: 3	to hand this c over to the king of Babylon,	6551
	32:24	the siege ramps are built up to take the c.	6551
	32:24	the c will be handed over to	6551
	32:25	And though the c will be handed over to	6551
	32:28	to hand this c over to the Babylonians and	6551
	32:29	The Babylonians who are attacking this c	6551

Jer	32:31	this c has so aroused my anger and wrath	6551
	32:36	"You are saying about this c,	6551
	33: 4	the houses in this c and the royal palaces	6551
	33: 5	from this c because of all its wickedness.	6551
	33: 9	Then this c will bring me renown, joy,	NIH
	34: 2	to hand this c over to the king of Babylon,	6551
	34:22	and I will bring them back to this c,	6551
	37: 8	Babylonians will return and attack this c;	6551
	37:10	and burn this c down."	6551
	37:12	Jeremiah started to leave the c to go to	3731S
	37:21	until all the bread in the c was gone.	6551
	38: 2	'Whoever stays in this c will die by	6551
	38: 3	'This c will certainly be handed over to	6551
	38: 4	the soldiers who are left in this c,	6551
	38: 9	when there is no longer any bread in the c."	6551
	38:17	your life will be spared and this c will not	6551
	38:18	this c will be handed over to	6551
	38:23	and this c will be burned down."	6551
	39: 2	the c wall was broken through.	6551
	39: 4	at night by way of the king's garden,	6551
	39: 9	the people who remained in the c,	6551
	39:16	about to fulfill my words against this c	6551
	41: 7	When they went into the c,	6551
	49:25	the c of renown not been abandoned,	6551
	51:31	of Babylon that his entire c is captured,	6551
	52: 4	They camped outside the c	2023S
	52: 5	The c was kept under siege until	6551
	52: 6	the famine in the c had become so severe	6551
	52: 7	Then the c wall was broken through,	6551
	52: 7	They left the c at night through the gate	6551
	52: 7	the Babylonians were surrounding the c.	6551
	52:15	and those who remained in the c,	6551
	52:25	Of those still in the c,	6551
	52:25	of his men who were found in the c.	6551
La	1: 1	deserted lies the c, once so full of people!	6551
	1:19	My priests and my elders perished in the c	6551
	2:11	and infants faint in the streets of the c,	7953
	2:12	like wounded men in the streets of the c,	7953
	2:15	"Is this the c that was called the perfection	6551
	3:51	because of all the women of my c.	6551
		The elders are gone from the c gate;	9133
Eze	4: 1	in front of you and draw the c of Jerusalem	6551
	4: 3	between you and the c and turn your face	6551
	5: 2	a third of the hair with fire inside the c.	6551
	5: 2	with the sword all around the c.	2023S
	7:15	by the sword, and those in the c will	6551
	7:23	of bloodshed and the c is full of violence.	6551
	9: 1	"Bring the guards of the c here,	6551
	9: 4	"Go throughout the c of Jerusalem and put	6551
	9: 5	"Follow him through the c and kill,	6551
	9: 7	and began killing throughout the c.	6551
	9: 9	of bloodshed and the c is full of injustice.	6551
	10: 2	the cherubim and scatter them over the c."	6551
	11: 2	and giving wicked advice in this c.	6551
	11: 3	**This** c is a cooking pot,	2085S
	11: 6	in this c and filled its streets with the dead.	6551
	11: 7	the meat and **this** c is the pot,	2085S
	11: 9	I will drive you out of **the** c and hand you	2023S
	11:11	**This** c will not be a pot for you,	2085S
	11:23	and stopped above the mountain east	6551
	17: 4	where he planted it in a c of traders.	6551
	21:19	where the road branches off to the c.	6551
	22: 2	Will you judge this c of bloodshed?	6551
	22: 3	O c that brings on herself doom	6551
	22: 5	O infamous c, full of turmoil.	NIH
	22:20	and my wrath and put you inside the c	NIH
	24: 6	" 'Woe to the c of bloodshed,	6551
	24: 9	" 'Woe to the c of bloodshed!	6551
	26:10	a c whose walls have been broken through.	6551
	26:17	'How you are destroyed, O c of renown,	6551
	26:19	When I make you a desolate c,	6551
	33:21	"The c has fallen!"	6551
	40: 1	the fourteenth year after the fall of the c—	6551
	40: 2	that looked like a c.	6551
	43: 3	when he came to destroy the c and like	6551
	45: 6	to give the c as its property an area 5,000	6551
	45: 7	the sacred district and the property of the c.	6551
	48:15	will be for the common use of the c,	6551
	48:15	The c will be in the center of it	6551
	48:17	The pastureland for the c will be 250 cubits	6551
	48:18	for the workers of the c.	6551
	48:19	from the c who farm it will come from all	6551
	48:20	along with the property of the c.	6551
	48:21	and the c property will belong to the prince.	6551
	48:22	the property of the c will lie in the center of	6551
	48:30	"These will be the exits of the c:	6551
	48:31	of the c will be named after the tribes	6551
	48:35	the name of the c from that time on will be:	6551
Da	9:16	Jerusalem, your c, your holy hill.	6551
	9:18	of the c that bears your Name.	6551
	9:19	your c and your people bear your Name."	6551
	9:24	and your holy c to finish transgression,	6551
	9:26	the ruler who will come will destroy the c	6551
	11:15	and will capture a fortified c.	6551
Hos	6: 8	Gilead is a c of wicked men,	7953
Joel	2: 9	They rush upon the c;	6551
Am	3: 6	When a trumpet sounds in a c,	6551
	3: 6	When disaster comes to a c,	6551
	4: 6	in every c and lack of bread in every town,	6551
	5: 3	"The c that marches out a thousand strong	6551
	5: 9	the stronghold and brings the **fortified** c	4448
	6: 8	I will deliver up the c and everything in it."	6551
	7:17	a prostitute in the c,	6551
Jnh	1: 2	"Go to the great c of Nineveh and preach	6551
	3: 2	to the great c of Nineveh and proclaim to it	6551
	3: 3	Now Nineveh was a very important c—	6551
	3: 4	On the first day, Jonah started into the c.	6551

Jnh 4: 5 and sat down at a place east of the **c**. 6551
   4: 5 to see what would happen to the **c**. 6551
   4:11 not be concerned about that great **c**?" 6551
Mic 4:10 for now you must leave the **c** to camp in 7953
   5: 1 Marshal your troops, O **c** *of troops*, 1426
   6: 9 The LORD is calling to the **c**— 6551
Na 2: 5 They dash to the **c wall**; 2570
   2: 7 that [the **c**] be exiled and carried away. NIH
   3: 1 Woe to the **c** of blood, full of lies, 6551
Hab 2:12 a **c** with bloodshed and establishes a town 6551
Zep 2:15 This is the carefree **c** that lived in safety. 6551
   3: 1 Woe to the **c** of oppressors, 6551
   3: 7 I said to the **c**, 'Surely you will fear me NIH
   3:11 from **this c** those who rejoice in their pride. 3871S
Zec 2: 4 'Jerusalem will be a **c without walls** 7252
   8: 3 Jerusalem will be called the **C** *of* Truth, 6551
   8: 5 The **c** streets will be filled with boys 6551
   8:21 the inhabitants of one **c** will go to another NIH
   14: 2 the **c** will be captured, 6551
   14: 2 Half of the **c** will go into exile, 6551
   14: 2 of the people will not be taken from the **c**. 6551
Mt 4: 5 Then the devil took him to the holy **c** 4484
   5:14 A **c** on a hill cannot be hidden. 4484
   5:35 for it is the **c** of the Great King. 4484
   12:25 and every **c** or household divided 4484
   21:10 the whole **c** was stirred and asked, 4484
   21:17 And he left them and went out of the **c** 4484
   21:18 as he was on his way back to the **c**, 4484
   22: 7 and burned their **c**. 4484
   26:18 into the **c** to a certain man and tell him, 4484
   27:53 the holy **c** and appeared to many people. 4484
   28:11 of the guards went into the **c** and reported 4484
Mk 10:46 were leaving the **c**, a blind man, NIG
   11:19 they went out *of* the **c**. 4484
   14:13 telling them, "Go into the **c**, 4484
   14:16 went into the **c** and found things just 4484
Lk 19:41 As he approached Jerusalem and saw the **c**, 4484
   21:21 let those in the **c** get out, 899S
   21:21 and let those in the country not enter **the c**. 899S
   22:10 He replied, "As you enter the **c**, 4484
   23:19 into prison for an insurrection in the **c**, 4484
   24:49 in the **c** until you have been clothed 4484
Jn 19:20 where Jesus was crucified was near the **c**, 4484
Ac 1:12 a Sabbath day's walk from the **c**. NIG
   4:27 and the people of Israel in this **c** to conspire 4484
   7:58 dragged him out *of* the **c** and began 4484
   8: 5 down to a **c** in Samaria and proclaimed 4484
   8: 8 So there was great joy in that **c**. 4484
   8: 9 the **c** and amazed all the people of Samaria. 4484
   9: 6 "Now get up and go into the **c**, 4484
   9:24 on the **c gates** in order to kill him. 4783
   10: 9 on their journey and approaching the **c**, 4484
   11: 5 "I was in the **c** of Joppa praying, 4484
   12:10 and came to the iron gate leading to the **c**. 4484
   13:44 the whole **c** gathered to hear the word of 4484
   13:50 and the leading men *of* the **c**. 4484
   14: 4 The people *of* the **c** were divided; 4484
   14:13 whose temple was just outside the **c**, 4484
   14:13 and wreaths to the **c** gates because he and NIG
   14:19 and dragged him outside the **c**, 4484
   14:20 he got up and went back into the **c**. 4484
   14:21 that **c** and won a large number of disciples. 4484
   15:21 For Moses has been preached in every **c** 4484
   16:12 the leading **c** of that district of Macedonia. 4484
   16:13 On the Sabbath we went outside the **c gate** 4783
   16:14 in purple cloth *from* the **c** of Thyatira, 4484
   16:20 and are throwing our **c** into an uproar 4484
   16:39 requesting them to leave the **c**. 4484
   17: 5 formed a mob and started a riot *in* the **c**. 4484
   17: 6 before the **c officials**, shouting: 4485
   17: 8 the crowd and the **c officials** were thrown 4485
   17:16 to see that the **c** was full of idols. 4484
   18:10 because I have many people in this **c**." 4484
   19:29 Soon the whole **c** was in an uproar. 4484
   19:35 The **c** clerk quieted the crowd and said: NIG
   19:35 the world know that the **c** of Ephesus is 4484
   20:23 that in every **c** the Holy Spirit warns me 4484
   21: 5 and children accompanied us out of the **c**, 4484
   21:29 in the **c** with Paul and assumed 4484
   21:30 The whole **c** was aroused, 4484
   21:31 that the whole **c of Jerusalem** was in 2647
   21:39 a citizen of no ordinary **c**. 4484
   22: 3 but brought up in this **c**. 4484
   24:12 the synagogues or anywhere else in the **c**. 4484
   25:23 and the leading men *of* the **c**. 4484
2Co 11:26 in danger in the **c**, in danger in the country, 4484
   11:32 the governor under King Aretas had the **c** 4484
Gal 4:25 *to* the present **c of Jerusalem**, 2647
Heb 11:10 For he was looking forward to the **c** 4484
   11:16 for he has prepared a **c** for them. 4484
   12:22 the **c** of the living God, 4484
   13:12 so Jesus also suffered outside the **c gate** 4783
   13:14 For here we do not have an enduring **c**, 4484
   13:14 but we are looking for the **c** that is to come. NIH
Jas 4:13 or tomorrow we will go to this or that **c**, 4484
Rev 2:13 who was put to death in your **c**— NIG
   3:12 the name of my God and the name *of* the **c** 4484
   11: 2 They will trample on the holy **c** 4484
   11: 8 in the street of the great **c**, 4484
   11:13 and a tenth of the **c** collapsed. 4484
   14:20 in the winepress outside the **c**, 4484
   16:19 The great **c** split into three parts, 4484
   17:18 the great **c** that rules over the kings of 4484
   18:10 Woe! Woe, O great **c**, O Babylon, city of power! 4484
   18:10 Woe, O great city, O Babylon, **c** of power! 4484
   18:16 Woe, O great **c**, dressed in fine linen, 4484
   18:18 'Was there ever a **c** like this great city?' NIG

Rev 18:18 'Was there ever a city like this great **c**?' 4484
   18:19 O great **c**, where all who had ships on 4484
   18:21 the great **c** of Babylon will be thrown 4484
   20: 9 camp of God's people, the **c** he loves. 4484
   21: 2 I saw the Holy **C**, the new Jerusalem, 4484
   21:10 and showed me the Holy **C**, Jerusalem, 4484
   21:14 The wall of the **c** had twelve foundations, 4484
   21:15 a measuring rod of gold to measure the **c**, 4484
   21:16 The **c** was laid out like a square, 4484
   21:16 the **c** with the rod and found it to be 12,000 4484
   21:18 and the **c** of pure gold, as pure as glass. 4484
   21:19 the **c** walls were decorated with every kind 4484
   21:21 The great street *of* the **c** was of pure gold, 4484
   21:22 I did not see a temple in the **c**, 899S
   21:23 The **c** does not need the sun or the moon 4484
   22: 2 the middle of the great street *of* **the c**. 899S
   22: 3 of God and of the Lamb will be in the **c**, 899S
   22:14 and may go through the gates into the **c**. 4484
   22:19 in the tree of life and in the holy **c**, 4484

CITY'S (1) [CITY]
Ro 16:23 who is the **c** director of public works, 4484

CIVILIAN (1)
2Ti 2: 4 a soldier gets involved in **c affairs**— 1050+4548

CLAD (2)
Na 2: 3 the warriors *are* **c in scarlet**. 9443
Zep 1: 8 and the king's sons and all those **c** 4252

CLAIM (23) [CLAIMED, CLAIMING, CLAIMS, RECLAIM, RECLAIMED]
2Sa 19:43 **have a** greater **c on** David than you have. 928
Ne 2:20 you have no share in Jerusalem or any **c** 7407
Job 3: 5 and deep shadow **c** it once more; 1457
   41:11 Who **has a c against** me that I must pay? 7709
Ps 73: 9 Their mouths **lay c** to heaven, 9286
Pr 25: 6 and *do not* **c** a place among great men; 6641
Jer 23:38 Although *you* **c**, 'This is the oracle of 606
   23:38 though I told you that *you must not* **c**, 606
Lk 11:18 because *you* **c** that I drive out demons 3306
Jn 4:20 but you Jews **c** that the place 3306
   8:24 if you do not believe that I am [the one I **c** NIG
   8:28 then you will know that I am [the one I **c** to NIG
   8:54 My Father, whom you **c** as your God, 3306
   9:41 that *you* can see, your guilt remains. 3306
   10:33 because you, a mere man, **c** to be God. 4472+4932
Ro 8: 2 as saying and as some **c** that we say— 5774
2Co 3: 5 in ourselves *to* **c** anything for ourselves, 3357
Tit 1:16 *They* **c** to know God, 3933
1Jn 1: 6 If *we* **c** to have fellowship with him 3306
   1: 8 If *we* **c** to be without sin, 3306
   1:10 If *we* **c** we have not sinned, 3306
Rev 2: 2 that you have tested those who **c** to 3306
   3: 9 who **c** to be Jews though they are not, 3306

CLAIMED (9) [CLAIM]
2Sa 18: 8 forest **c** more lives that day than the sword. 430
1Ki 18:10 a nation or kingdom **c** you were not there, 606
Mk 6:15 And still others **c**, "He is a prophet, 3306
Jn 9: 9 Some **c** that he was. 3306
   19: 7 because *he* **c to be** the Son of God." 1571+4472
   19:21 but that this man **c** to be king of the Jews." 3306
Ac 4:32 No one **c** that any of his possessions 3306
   25:19 about a dead man named Jesus who Paul **c** was alive. 5763
Ro 1:22 *Although they* **c** to be wise, 5763

CLAIMING (5) [CLAIM]
Mt 24: 5 For many will come in my name, **c**, 3306
Mk 13: 6 Many will come in my name, **c**, 'I am he,' 3306
Lk 21: 8 For many will come in my name, **c**, 3306
Jn 8:25 "Just what *I have been* **c** all along," 3281
Ac 5:36 **c** to be somebody, 3306

CLAIMS (9) [CLAIM]
2Sa 15: 3 "Look, your **c** are valid and proper, 1821
Pr 20: 6 Many a man **c** to have unfailing love, 7924
Ecc 8:17 Even if a wise man **c** he knows, 606
Jer 23:34 If a prophet or a priest or anyone else **c**, 606
Lk 23: 2 of taxes to Caesar and **c** to be Christ, 3306
Jn 19:12 Anyone who **c to be** a king 1571+4472
Jas 2:14 if a man **c** to have faith but has no deeds? 3306
1Jn 2: 9 Whoever **c** to live in him must walk 3306
   2: 9 Anyone who **c** to be in the light 3306

CLAMOR (2)
Ps 74:23 Do not ignore the **c** of your adversaries, 7754
Isa 31: 4 by their shouts or disturbed by their **c**— 2162

CLAN (170) [CLANS]
Ge 24:38 go to my father's family and to my own **c**, 5476
   24:40 a wife for my son from my own **c** and 5476
   24:41 Then, when you go to my **c**, 5476
Ex 6:25 the heads of the Levite families, **c** by clan. NIH
   6:25 the heads of the Levite families, clan by **c**. 5476
Lev 25:10 and each to his own **c**. 5476
   25:41 and he will go back to his own **c** and to 5476
   25:47 among you or to a member of the alien's **c**, 5476
   25:49 in his **c** may redeem him. 5476
Nu 2:34 each with his **c** and family. 5476

Nu 26: 5 through Hanoch, the Hanochite **c**; 5476
   26: 5 through Pallu, the Palluite **c**; 5476
   26: 6 through Hezron, the Hezronite **c**; 5476
   26: 6 through Carmi, the Carmite **c**. 5476
   26:12 through Nemuel, the Nemuelite **c**; 5476
   26:12 through Jamin, the Jaminite **c**; 5476
   26:12 through Jakin, the Jakinite **c**; 5476
   26:13 through Zerah, the Zerahite **c**; 5476
   26:13 through Shaul, the Shaulite **c**. 5476
   26:15 through Zephon, the Zephonite **c**; 5476
   26:15 through Haggi, the Haggite **c**; 5476
   26:15 through Shuni, the Shunite **c**; 5476
   26:16 through Ozni, the Oznite **c**; 5476
   26:16 through Eri, the Erite **c**; 5476
   26:17 through Arodi, the Arodite **c**; 5476
   26:17 through Areli, the Arelite **c**. 5476
   26:20 through Shelah, the Shelanite **c**; 5476
   26:20 through Perez, the Perezite **c**; 5476
   26:20 through Zerah, the Zerahite **c**. 5476
   26:21 through Hezron, the Hezronite **c**; 5476
   26:21 through Hamul, the Hamulite **c**. 5476
   26:23 through Tola, the Tolaite **c**; 5476
   26:23 through Puah, the Puite **c**; 5476
   26:24 through Jashub, the Jashubite **c**; 5476
   26:24 through Shimron, the Shimronite **c**. 5476
   26:26 through Sered, the Seredite **c**; 5476
   26:26 through Elon, the Elonite **c**; 5476
   26:26 through Jahleel, the Jahleelite **c**. 5476
   26:29 through Makir, the Makirite **c** (Makir was 5476
   26:29 through Gilead, the Gileadite **c**. 5476
   26:30 through Iezer, the Iezerite **c**; 5476
   26:30 through Helek, the Helekite **c**. 5476
   26:31 through Asriel, the Asrielite **c**; 5476
   26:31 through Shechem, the Shechemite **c**; 5476
   26:32 through Shemida, the Shemidaite **c**; 5476
   26:32 through Hepher, the Hepherite **c**. 5476
   26:35 through Shuthelah, the Shuthelahite **c**; 5476
   26:35 through Beker, the Bekerite **c**; 5476
   26:35 through Tahan, the Tahanite **c**. 5476
   26:36 through Eran, the Eranite **c**. 5476
   26:38 through Bela, the Belaite **c**; 5476
   26:38 through Ashbel, the Ashbelite **c**; 5476
   26:38 through Ahiram, the Ahiramite **c**; 5476
   26:39 through Shupham, the Shuphamite **c**; 5476
   26:39 through Hupham, the Huphamite **c**. 5476
   26:40 through Ard, the Ardite **c**; 5476
   26:40 through Naaman, the Naamite **c**. 5476
   26:42 through Shuham, the Shuhamite **c**. 5476
   26:44 through Imnah, the Imnite **c**; 5476
   26:44 through Ishvi, the Ishvite **c**; 5476
   26:44 through Beriah, the Beriite **c**; 5476
   26:45 through Heber, the Heberite **c**; 5476
   26:45 through Malkiel, the Malkielite **c**. 5476
   26:48 through Jahzeel, the Jahzeelite **c**; 5476
   26:48 through Guni, the Gunite **c**; 5476
   26:49 through Jezer, the Jezerite **c**; 5476
   26:49 through Shillem, the Shillemite **c**. 5476
   26:57 through Gershon, the Gershonite **c**; 5476
   26:57 through Kohath, the Kohathite **c**; 5476
   26:57 through Merari, the Merarite **c**. 5476
   26:58 These also were Levite clans: the Libnite **c**, 5476
   26:58 the Libnite clan, the Hebronite **c**, 5476
   26:58 the Hebronite clan, the Mahlite **c**, 5476
   26:58 the Mushite **c**, the Korahite clan. 5476
   26:58 the Mushite clan, the Korahite **clan**. 5476
   27: 4 from his **c** because he had no son? 5476
   27:11 to the nearest relative in his **c**, 5476
   36: 1 The family heads of the **c** *of* Gilead son 5476
   36: 6 as long as they marry within the tribal **c** 5476
   36: 8 in her father's tribal **c**, 5476
   36:12 in their father's **c** and tribe. 5476
Dt 29:18 or woman, **c** or tribe 5476
Jos 7:14 that the LORD takes shall come forward **c** NIH
   7:14 that the LORD takes shall come forward clan by **c**; 5476
   7:14 the **c** that the LORD takes shall come forward family by family; 5476
   7:17 the **c** *of the* Zerahites come forward 5476
   13:15 to the tribe of Reuben, **c** by clan: NIH
   13:15 to the tribe of Reuben, clan by **c**: 5476
   13:23 the inheritance of the Reubenites, **c** NIH
   13:23 of the Reubenites, clan by **c**. 5476
   13:24 to the tribe of Gad, **c** by clan: NIH
   13:24 to the tribe of Gad, clan by **c**: 5476
   13:28 the inheritance of the Gadites, **c** by clan. NIH
   13:28 the inheritance of the Gadites, clan by **c**. 5476
   13:29 of the descendants of Manasseh, **c** by clan: NIH
   13:29 of the descendants of Manasseh, clan by **c**: 5476
   13:31 for half of the sons of Makir, **c** by clan. NIH
   13:31 for half of the sons of Makir, clan by **c**. 5476
   15: 1 for the tribe of Judah, **c** by clan, extended NIH
   15: 1 for the tribe of Judah, clan by **c**, extended 5476
   15:20 the inheritance of the tribe of Judah, **c** NIH
   15:20 of the tribe of Judah, clan by **c**; 5476
   16: 5 the territory of Ephraim, **c** by clan: NIH
   16: 5 the territory of Ephraim, clan by **c**: 5476
   16: 8 of the tribe of the Ephraimites, **c** by clan. NIH
   16: 8 of the tribe of the Ephraimites, clan by **c**. 5476
   18:11 up for the tribe of Benjamin, **c** by clan. NIH
   18:11 up for the tribe of Benjamin, clan by **c**. 5476
   18:21 The tribe of Benjamin, **c** by clan, NIH
   18:21 The tribe of Benjamin, clan by **c**, 5476
   19: 1 for the tribe of Simeon, **c** by clan. NIH
   19: 1 for the tribe of Simeon, clan by **c**. 5476
   19: 8 of the tribe of the Simeonites, **c** by clan. NIH
   19: 8 of the tribe of the Simeonites, clan by **c**. 5476
   19:10 The third lot came up for Zebulun, **c** NIH

Jos	19:10	up for Zebulun, clan by **c**:	5476
	19:16	the inheritance of Zebulun, **c** by clan.	NIH
	19:16	the inheritance of Zebulun, clan by **c**.	5476
	19:17	fourth lot came out for Issachar, **c** by clan.	NIH
	19:17	fourth lot came out for Issachar, clan by **c**.	5476
	19:23	the inheritance of the tribe of Issachar, **c**	NIH
	19:23	of the tribe of Issachar, clan by **c**.	5476
	19:24	for the tribe of Asher, **c** by clan.	NIH
	19:24	for the tribe of Asher, clan by **c**.	5476
	19:31	the inheritance of the tribe of Asher, **c**	NIH
	19:31	of the tribe of Asher, clan by **c**.	5476
	19:32	sixth lot came out for Naphtali, **c** by clan:	NIH
	19:32	sixth lot came out for Naphtali, clan by **c**:	5476
	19:39	the inheritance of the tribe of Naphtali, **c**	NIH
	19:39	of the tribe of Naphtali, clan by **c**.	5476
	19:40	for the tribe of Dan, **c** by clan.	NIH
	19:40	for the tribe of Dan, clan by **c**.	5476
	19:48	the inheritance of the tribe of Dan, **c**	NIH
	19:48	of the tribe of Dan, clan by **c**.	5476
	21: 4	The first lot came out for the Kohathites, **c**	NIH
	21: 4	for the Kohathites, clan by **c**.	5476
	21: 7	The descendants of Merari, **c** by clan,	NIH
	21: 7	The descendants of Merari, clan by **c**,	5476
Jdg	4:17	of Hazor and the **c** of Heber the Kenite.	1074
	6:15	My **c** is the weakest in Manasseh,	548
	9: 1	to them and to all his mother's **c**,	3+1074+5476
	12: 9	in marriage to those **outside** his **c**,	AIT
	12: 9	as wives from **outside** his **c**.	AIT
	13: 2	named Manoah, from the **c** of the Danites,	5476
	17: 7	who had been living within the **c** of Judah,	5476
	18:11	six hundred men from the **c** of the Danites,	5476
	18:19	Isn't it better that you serve a tribe and **c**	5476
Ru	2: 1	from the **c** of Elimelech,	5476
	2: 3	who was from the **c** of Elimelech.	5476
1Sa	9:21	and is not my **c** the least of all the clans of	5476
	10:21	**c** by clan, and Matri's clan was chosen.	NIH
	10:21	clan by **c**, and Matri's clan was chosen.	5476
	10:21	clan by clan, and Matri's **c** was chosen.	5476
	18:18	and what is my family or my father's **c**	5476
	20: 6	for his whole **c**.'	5476
2Sa	14: 7	Now the whole **c** has risen up	5476
	16: 5	from the *same* **c** as Saul's family came out	5476
1Ch	4:27	so their entire **c** did not become	5476
	6:54	of Aaron who were from the Kohathite **c**,	5476
	6:62	descendants of Gershon, **c** by clan,	4200+5476
	6:62	descendants of Gershon, **clan by c**,	4200+5476
	6:63	The descendants of Merari, **c** by clan,	4200+5476
	6:63	The descendants of Merari, **clan by c**,	4200+5476
	6:71	From the **c** of the half-tribe	5476
Jer	3:14	one from a town and two from a **c**—	5476
Zec	12:12	The land will mourn, **each c** by itself,	5476+5476
	12:12	**c** of the house of David and their wives,	5476
	12:12	the **c** of the house of Nathan and their wives,	5476
	12:13	the **c** of the house of Levi and their wives,	5476
	12:13	the **c** of Shimei and their wives,	5476

CLANGING (1)

1Co	13: 1	I am only a resounding gong or a **c** cymbal.	226

CLANS (137) [CLAN]

Ge	10: 5	by their **c** within their nations,	5476
	10:18	Later the Canaanite **c** scattered	5476
	10:20	the sons of Ham by their **c** and languages,	5476
	10:31	the sons of Shem by their **c** and languages,	5476
	10:32	These are the **c** of Noah's sons,	5476
	36:40	by name, according to their **c** and regions:	5476
Ex	6:14	These were the **c** of Reuben.	5476
	6:15	These were the **c** of Simeon.	5476
	6:17	The sons of Gershon, by **c**,	5476
	6:19	the **c** of Levi according to their records.	5476
	6:24	These were the Korahite **c**.	5476
Lev	25:45	among you and members of their **c** born	5476
Nu	1: 2	of the whole Israelite community by their **c**	5476
	1:16	They were the heads of the **c** of Israel.	548
	1:18	by their **c** and families,	5476
	1:20	by one, according to the records of their **c**	5476
	1:22	by one, according to the records of their **c**	5476
	1:24	by name, according to the records of their **c**	5476
	1:26	by name, according to the records of their **c**	5476
	1:28	by name, according to the records of their **c**	5476
	1:30	by name, according to the records of their **c**	5476
	1:32	by name, according to the records of their **c**	5476
	1:34	by name, according to the records of their **c**	5476
	1:36	by name, according to the records of their **c**	5476
	1:38	by name, according to the records of their **c**	5476
	1:40	by name, according to the records of their **c**	5476
	1:42	by name, according to the records of their **c**	5476
	3:15	"Count the Levites by their families and **c**.	5476
	3:18	These were the names of the Gershonite **c**:	5476
	3:19	The Kohathite **c**: Amram,	5476
	3:20	The Merarite **c**: Mahli and Mushi.	5476
	3:20	These were the Levite **c**,	5476
	3:21	To Gershon belonged the **c** of the Libnites	5476
	3:21	these were the Gershonite **c**.	5476
	3:23	Gershonite **c** were to camp on the west,	5476
	3:27	To Kohath belonged the **c** of	5476
	3:27	these were the Kohathite **c**.	5476
	3:29	The Kohathite **c** were to camp on	5476
	3:30	of the Kohathite **c** was Elizaphan son	5476
	3:33	To Merari belonged the **c** of the Mahlites	5476
	3:33	these were the Merarite **c**.	5476
	3:35	of the Merarite **c** was Zuriel son of Abihail;	5476
	3:39	by Moses and Aaron according to their **c**,	5476
	4: 2	of the Levites by their families and **c**.	5476
	4:18	the Kohathite tribal **c** are not cut off from	5476

Nu	4:22	of the Gershonites by their families and **c**.	5476
	4:24	"This is the service of the Gershonite **c**	5476
	4:28	of the Gershonite **c** at the Tent of Meeting.	5476
	4:29	the Merarites by their **c** and families.	5476
	4:33	the service of the Merarite **c** as they work	5476
	4:34	the Kohathites by their **c** and families.	5476
	4:36	counted by **c**, were 2,750.	5476
	4:37	of all those in the Kohathite **c** who served	5476
	4:38	The Gershonites were counted by their **c**	5476
	4:40	counted by their **c** and families,	5476
	4:41	in the Gershonite **c** who served at the Tent	5476
	4:42	The Merarites were counted by their **c**	5476
	4:44	counted by their **c**, were 3,200.	5476
	4:45	the total of those in the Merarite **c**.	5476
	4:46	of Israel counted all the Levites by their **c**	5476
	10: 4	the heads of the **c** of Israel—	548
	26: 7	These were the **c** of Reuben;	5476
	26:12	descendants of Simeon by their **c** were:	5476
	26:14	These were the **c** of Simeon;	5476
	26:15	The descendants of Gad by their **c** were:	5476
	26:18	These were the **c** of Gad;	5476
	26:20	the descendants of Judah by their **c** were:	5476
	26:22	These were the **c** of Judah;	5476
	26:23	descendants of Issachar by their **c** were:	5476
	26:25	These were the **c** of Issachar;	5476
	26:26	descendants of Zebulun by their **c** were:	5476
	26:27	These were the **c** of Zebulun;	5476
	26:28	of Joseph by their **c** through Manasseh	5476
	26:34	These were the **c** of Manasseh;	5476
	26:35	the descendants of Ephraim by their **c**:	5476
	26:37	These were the **c** of Ephraim;	5476
	26:37	the descendants of Joseph by their **c**.	5476
	26:38	descendants of Benjamin by their **c** were:	5476
	26:41	These were the **c** of Benjamin;	5476
	26:42	the descendants of Dan by their **c**:	5476
	26:42	These were the **c** of Dan:	5476
	26:43	All of them were Shuhamite **c**;	5476
	26:44	The descendants of Asher by their **c** were:	5476
	26:47	These were the **c** of Asher;	5476
	26:48	descendants of Naphtali by their **c** were:	5476
	26:50	These were the **c** of Naphtali;	5476
	26:57	the Levites who were counted by their **c**:	5476
	26:58	These also were Levite **c**:	5476
	27: 1	of Manasseh son of Joseph.	5476
	31: 5	were supplied from the **c** of Israel.	548
	33:54	according to your **c**.	5476
	36: 1	from the **c** of the descendants of Joseph,	5476
	36:12	the **c** of the descendants of Manasseh son	5476
Jos	7:17	of Judah came forward,	5476
	14: 1	the heads of the tribal **c** of Israel allotted	3
	15:12	around the people of Judah by their **c**.	5476
	17: 2	of Abiezer, Helek, Asriel, Shechem,	1201
	17: 2	of Manasseh son of Joseph by their **c**.	5476
	18:20	that marked out the inheritance of the **c**	5476
	18:28	the inheritance of Benjamin for its **c**.	5476
	19:51	the heads of the tribal **c** of Israel assigned	3
	21: 5	from the **c** of the tribes of Ephraim,	5476
	21: 6	from the **c** of the tribes of Issachar,	5476
	21:10	of Aaron who were from the Kohathite **c** of	5476
	21:20	The rest of the Kohathite **c** of	5476
	21:26	to the rest of the Kohathite **c**.	5476
	21:27	The Levite **c** of the Gershonites	5476
	21:33	the towns of the Gershonite **c** were thirteen,	5476
	21:34	The Merarite **c** (the rest of	5476
	21:40	All the towns allotted to the Merarite **c**,	5476
	22:14	of a family division among the Israelite **c**.	548
	22:21	of Manasseh replied to the heads of the **c**	548
	22:30	the heads of the **c** of the Israelites—	548
Jdg	18: 2	These men represented all their **c**.	5476
	21:24	and went home to their tribes and **c**,	5476
1Sa	9:21	and is not my **c** the least of all the **c** *of*	5476
	10:19	before the LORD by your tribes and **c**."	548
	23:23	I will track him down among all the **c**	548
1Ch	2:53	and the **c** of Kiriath Jearim.	5476
	2:55	and the **c** of scribes who lived at Jabez:	5476
	4: 2	These were the **c** of the Zorathites.	5476
	4: 8	and of the **c** of Aharhel son of Harum.	5476
	4:21	Laadah the father of Mareshah and the **c** *of*	5476
	4:38	above by name were leaders of their **c**.	5476
	5: 7	Their relatives by **c**, listed according	5476
	6:19	the **c** of the Levites listed according	5476
	6:60	among the Kohathite **c**,	5476
	6:61	from the **c** of half the tribe of Manasseh.	5476
	6:66	Some of the Kohathite **c** were given	5476
	6:70	to the rest of the Kohathite **c**.	5476
	7: 5	to all the **c** of Issachar,	5476
	12:30	brave warriors, famous in their own **c**—	3+1074
Job	31:34	the contempt of the **c** that I kept silent	5476
Jer	2: 4	all you of the house of Israel.	5476
	31: 1	"I will be the God of all the **c** of Israel,	5476
Mic	5: 2	you are small among the **c** of Judah,	548
Zec	12:14	and all the rest of the **c** and their wives.	5476

CLAP (6) [CLAPPED, CLAPS]

Job	21: 5	**c** your hand over your mouth.	8492
Ps	47: 1	**C** your hands, all you nations;	9546
	98: 8	*Let* the rivers **c** their hands,	4673
Pr	30:32	**c** your hand over your mouth!	NIH
Isa	55:12	all the trees of the field *will* **c** their hands.	4673
La	2:15	All who pass your way **c** their hands	6215

CLAPPED (2) [CLAP]

2Ki	11:12	and the people **c** their hands and shouted,	5782
Eze	25: 6	Because you *have* **c** your hands	4673

CLAPS (3) [CLAP]

Job	27:23	**c** its hands **in derision**	8562
	34:37	**scornfully** *he* **c** *his* **hands**	6215
Na	3:19	the news about you **c** his hands at your fall,	9546

CLASH (1)

Ps	150: 5	praise him with the **c** *of* cymbals,	9049

CLASP (1) [CLASPED, CLASPS]

Isa	2: 6	the Philistines and **c hands** with pagans.	8562

CLASPED (1) [CLASP]

Mt	28: 9	**c** his feet and worshiped him.	*3195*

CLASPS (7) [CLASP]

Ex	26: 6	Then make fifty gold **c** and use them	7971
	26:11	Then make fifty bronze **c** and put them in	7971
	26:33	the curtain from the **c** and place the ark of	7971
	35:11	**c**, frames, crossbars, posts and bases;	7971
	36:13	Then they made fifty gold **c** and used them	7971
	36:18	They made fifty bronze **c** to fasten	7971
	39:33	the tent and all its furnishings, its **c**,	7971

CLASSIFY (1)

2Co	10:12	We do not dare *to* **c** or compare ourselves	*1605*

CLATTER (2)

Jdg	5:28	Why is the **c** of his chariots delayed?'	7193
Na	3: 2	The crack of whips, the **c** *of* wheels,	7754+8323

CLAUDA (KJV) See CAUDA

CLAUDIA (1)

2Ti	4:21	Linus, **C** and all the brothers.	*3086*

CLAUDIUS (3)

Ac	11:28	(This happened during the reign of **C**.)	*3087*
	18: 2	**C** had ordered all the Jews to leave Rome.	*3087*
	23:26	**C** Lysias, To His Excellency,	*3087*

CLAVE (KJV) See CUT, SPLIT, DIVIDED, DRAWN, CLUNG

CLAWS (2)

Da	4:33	of an eagle and his nails like the **c** of a bird.	NIH
	7:19	with its iron teeth and bronze **c**—	10303

CLAY (40)

Lev	6:28	The **c** pot the meat is cooked in must	3084
	11:33	If one of them falls into a **c** pot,	3084
	14: 5	be killed over fresh water in a **c** pot,	3084
	14:42	to replace these and take new **c** and plaster	6760
	14:50	of the birds over fresh water in a **c** pot.	3084
	15:12	" '' A **c** pot that the man touches must	3084
Nu	5:17	in a **c** jar and put some dust from	3084
1Ki	7:46	The king had them cast in **c** molds in	141
2Ch	4:17	The king had them cast in **c** molds in	141
Job	4:19	much more those who live in houses of **c**,	2817
	10: 9	Remember that you molded me like **c**.	2817
	13:12	your defenses are defenses of **c**,	2817
	27:16	like dust and clothes like piles of **c**,	2817
	33: 6	I too have been taken from **c**.	2817
	38:14	The earth takes shape like **c** *under* a seal;	2817
Ps	12: 6	like silver refined in a furnace of **c**,	824
Isa	29:16	if the potter were thought to be like the **c!**	2817
	41:25	as if he were a potter treading the **c**.	3226
	45: 9	Does the **c** say to the potter,	2817
	64: 8	We are the **c**, you are the potter;	2817
Jer	18: 4	from the **c** was marred in his hands;	2817
	18: 6	"Like **c** in the hand of the potter,	2817
	19: 1	"Go and buy a **c** jar from a potter.	3084
	32:14	and put them in a **c** jar so they will last	3084
	43: 9	and bury them in **c** in the brick pavement at	4879
La	4: 2	are now considered as pots of **c**,	3084
Eze	4: 1	"Now, son of man, take a **c tablet**,	4246
Da	2:33	its feet partly of iron and partly of **baked c**,	10279
	2:34	on its feet of iron and **c** and smashed them.	10279
	2:35	Then the iron, the **c**, the bronze,	10279
	2:41	of **baked c** and partly of iron, so this will be	10279
	2:41	even as you saw iron mixed with **c**.	10279+10298
	2:42	As the toes were partly iron and partly **c**,	10279
	2:43	saw the iron mixed with **baked c**,	10279+10298
	2:43	any more than iron mixes with **c**.	10279
	2:45	the **c**, the silver and the gold to pieces.	10279
Na	3:14	Work the **c**, tread the mortar,	3226
Ro	9:21	of the same **lump of c** some pottery	5878
2Co	4: 7	But we have this treasure in jars of **c**	*4017*
2Ti	2:20	but also of wood and **c**;	*4017*

CLEAN (120) [CLEANNESS, CLEANSE, CLEANSED, CLEANSES, CLEANSING]

Ge	7: 2	with you seven of every kind of **c** animal,	3196
	7: 8	Pairs of **c** and unclean animals,	3196
	8:20	of all the **c** animals and clean birds,	3196
	8:20	of all the clean animals and **c** birds,	3196
	20: 5	with a clear conscience and **c** hands."	5931
Lev	4:12	the camp to a place **ceremonially c**,	3196

Lev	6:11	the camp to a place that is **ceremonially c.**	3196
	7:19	anyone **ceremonially c** may eat it.	3196
	10:10	between the unclean and the **c,**	3196
	10:14	Eat them in a **ceremonially c** place;	3196
	11:32	and then *it will be* **c.**	3197
	11:36	or a cistern for collecting water remains **c,**	3196
	11:37	that are to be planted, they remain **c.**	3196
	11:47	between the unclean and the **c,**	3196
	12: 7	*be* **ceremonially c** from her flow of blood.	3197
	12: 8	and *she will be* **c.** "	3197
	13: 6	the priest *shall* **pronounce** him **c;**	3197
	13: 6	and he will be **c.**	3197
	13: 7	to the priest to be **pronounced c,**	3200
	13:13	**pronounce** that person **c.**	3197
	13:13	Since it has all turned white, he is **c.**	3196
	13:17	**pronounce** the infected person **c;**	3197
	13:17	then he will be **c.**	3196
	13:23	and the priest *shall* **pronounce** him **c.**	3197
	13:28	and the priest *shall* **pronounce** him **c;**	3197
	13:34	the priest *shall* **pronounce** him **c.**	3197
	13:34	and *he will be* **c.**	3197
	13:35	in the skin after he is **pronounced c,**	3200
	13:37	He is **c,** and the priest shall pronounce him clean.	3196
	13:37	and the priest *shall* **pronounce** him **c.**	3197
	13:39	that person is **c.**	3196
	13:40	a man has lost his hair and is bald, he is **c.**	3196
	13:41	and has a bald forehead, he is **c.**	3196
	13:58	must be washed again, and *it will be* **c.**"	3197
	13:59	for **pronouncing** them **c** or unclean.	3196
	14: 4	that two live **c** birds and some cedar wood,	3196
	14: 7	and **pronounce** him **c.**	3197
	14: 8	then *he will be* **ceremonially c.**	3197
	14: 9	and *he will be* **c.**	3197
	14:11	The priest who **pronounces** him **c** shall	3197
	14:20	and *he will be* **c.**	3197
	14:48	**pronounce** the house **c,**	3197
	14:53	and *it will be* **c.**"	3197
	14:57	to determine when something is **c**	3196
	15: 8	the discharge spits on someone who is **c,**	3196
	15:13	and *he will be* **c.**	3197
	15:28	and after that *she will be* **ceremonially c.**	3197
	16:30	you will be **c** from all your sins.	3197
	17:15	then *he will be* **c.**	3197
	20:25	therefore make a distinction between **c**	3196
	20:25	and between unclean and **c** birds.	3196
	22: 7	When the sun goes down, *he will be* **c,**	3197
Nu	8: 6	**make** them **ceremonially c.**	3196
	9:13	if a man who is **ceremonially c** and not on	3196
	18:11	in your household who is **ceremonially c** may eat it.	3196
	18:13	in your household who is **ceremonially c** may eat it.	3196
	19: 9	"A man who is **c** shall gather up the ashes	3196
	19: 9	a **ceremonially c** place outside the camp.	3196
	19:12	then *he will be* **c.**	3197
	19:12	he will not be **c.**	3197
	19:18	Then a man who is **ceremonially c** is	3196
	19:19	The *man* who is **c** is to sprinkle	3196
	19:19	and that evening *he will be* **c.**	3197
	31:23	and then *it will be* **c.**	3197
	31:24	and *you will be* **c.**	3197
Dt	12:15	ceremonially unclean and the **c** may eat it.	3196
	12:22	ceremonially unclean and the **c** may eat.	3196
	14:11	You may eat any **c** bird.	3196
	14:20	any winged creature that is **c** you may eat.	3196
	15:22	ceremonially unclean and the **c** may eat it,	3196
2Ki	5:14	and his flesh was restored and *became* **c**	3197
2Ch	13:11	the bread on the **ceremonially c** table	3196
	30:17	for all *those who* were not **ceremonially c**	3196
	30:19	even if he is not **c** according to the rules of	3200
Ezr	6:20	and were all **ceremonially c.**	3196
Job	11: 4	and those with **c** hands will grow stronger.	3198
	33: 9	I am **c** and free from guilt.	2899
	37:21	the skies after the wind has swept them **c.**	3197
Ps	24: 4	*He who* has **c** hands and a pure heart,	5929
	51: 7	Cleanse me with hyssop, and *I will be* **c;**	3197
Pr	20: 9	*I am* **c** and without sin"?	3197
Ecc	9: 2	the **c** and the unclean,	3196
Isa	1:16	wash and **make yourselves c.**	2342
	66:20	of the LORD in **ceremonially c** vessels.	2342
Eze	16: 4	with water to **make** you **c,**	5470
	22:26	between the unclean and the **c;**	3196
	24:13	you will not be **c** again until my wrath	3197
	36:25	I will sprinkle **c** water on you,	3196
	36:25	and *you will be* **c;**	3197
	44:23	between the unclean and the **c.**	3196
Am	7: 2	When *they had* **stripped** the land **c,**	430
Zec	3: 5	Then I said, "Put a **c** turban on his head."	3196
	3: 5	a **c** turban on his head and clothed him;	3196
Mt	8: 2	if you are willing, you can **make** me **c.**"	2751
	8: 3	"I am willing," he said. "*Be* **c!**"	2751
	12:44	**swept c** and put in order.	4924
	23:25	*You* **c** the outside of the cup and dish,	2751
	23:26	First **c** the inside of the cup and dish,	2751
	23:26	and then the outside also will be **c.**	2754
	27:59	wrapped it in a **c** linen cloth,	2754
Mk	1:40	"If you are willing, you can **make** me **c.**"	2751
	1:41	"I am willing," he said. "*Be* **c!**"	2751
	7:19	Jesus declared all foods "**c.**")	2751
Lk	5:12	if you are willing, you can **make** me **c.**"	2751
	5:13	"I am willing," he said. "*Be* **c!**"	2751
	11:25	it finds the house **swept c** and put in order.	4924
	11:39	you Pharisees **c** the outside of the cup	2751
	11:41	and everything will be **c** for you.	2751
Jn	13:10	his whole body is **c.**	2754
	13:10	you are **c,** though not every one of you."	2754

Jn	13:11	that was why he said not every one was **c.**	2754
	15: 3	You are already **c** because of the word	2754
Ac	10:15	that God *has* **made c.**"	2751
	11: 9	that God *has* **made c.**'	2751
Ro	14:20	All food is **c,** but it is wrong for a man to	2754
Heb	9:13	so that they are outwardly **c.**	2755
Rev	15: 6	They were dressed in **c,**	2754
	19: 8	Fine linen, bright and **c,**	2754
	19:14	and dressed in fine linen, white and **c.**	2754

CLEANNESS (5) [CLEAN]

2Sa	22:21	to the **c** *of* my hands he has rewarded me.	1341
	22:25	according to my **c** in his sight.	1341
Job	22:30	be delivered through the **c** *of* your hands."	1341
Ps	18:20	to the **c** *of* my hands he has rewarded me.	1341
	18:24	according to the **c** *of* my hands in his sight.	1341

CLEANSE (20) [CLEAN]

Lev	16:19	on it with his finger seven times *to* **c** it and	3197
	16:30	be made for you, to **c** you.	3197
Ps	51: 2	Wash away all my iniquity and **c** me	3197
	51: 7	**C** me with hyssop, and I will be clean;	2627
Pr	20:30	Blows and wounds **c away** evil,	5347
Isa	4: 4	*he will* **c** the bloodstains from Jerusalem	1866
Jer	4:11	but not to winnow or **c;**	1405
	33: 8	*I will* **c** them from all	3197
Eze	24:13	Because *I tried to* **c** you but you would	3197
	36:25	*I will* **c** you from all your impurities and	3197
	36:33	On the day *I* **c** you from all your sins,	3197
	37:23	and *I will* **c** them.	3197
	39:12	of Israel will be burying them in order to **c**	3197
	39:14	" 'Men will be regularly employed to **c**	3197
	39:16	And so *they will* **c** the land.	3197
	43:26	to make atonement for the altar and **c** it;	3197
Zec	13: 1	to **c** them from sin and impurity.	NIH
Mt	10: 8	raise the dead, **c** those who have leprosy,	2751
Heb	9:14	**c** our consciences from acts that lead	2751
	10:22	*having* our hearts **sprinkled to c** us from	4822

CLEANSED (30) [CLEAN]

Lev	14: 4	and hyssop be brought for the *one to* **be c.**	3197
	14: 7	the *one to* **be c** of the infectious disease	3197
	14: 8	"The *person to* **be c** must wash his clothes,	3197
	14:11	*to* **be c** and his offerings before the LORD	3197
	14:14	the lobe of the right ear of the *one to* **be c,**	3197
	14:17	the lobe of the right ear of the *one to* **be c,**	3197
	14:18	*to* **be c** and make atonement for him before	3197
	14:19	for the *one to* **be c** from his uncleanness.	3197
	14:25	the lobe of the right ear of the *one to* **be c,**	3197
	14:28	the lobe of the right ear of the *one to* **be c,**	3197
	14:29	on the head of the *one to* **be c,**	3197
	14:31	the LORD on behalf of the *one to* **be c.**"	3197
	15:13	" 'When a man *is* **c** from his discharge,	3197
	15:28	" 'When *she is* **c** from her discharge,	3197
	22: 4	not eat the sacred offerings until *he is* **c.**	3197
Nu	19:19	The person being **c** must wash his clothes	NIH
Jos	22:17	Up to this very day *we* have not **c** ourselves	3197
2Ki	5:10	be restored and *you will be* **c.**"	3197
	5:12	Couldn't I wash in them and *be* **c?**"	3197
	5:13	then, when he tells you, 'Wash and *be* **c**'!"	3197
Pr	30:12	in their own eyes and yet *are* not **c**	8175
Isa	1: 6	not **c** or bandaged or soothed with oil.	2318
Eze	24:13	to cleanse you but *you* would not *be* **c**	3197
	44:26	After he is **c,** he must wait seven days.	3200
Lk	4:27	yet not one of them *was* **c**—	2751
	17:14	And as they went, *they were* **c.**	2751
	17:17	Jesus asked, *"Were* not all ten **c?**	2751
Heb	9:22	the law requires that nearly everything *be* **c**	2751
	10: 2	For the worshipers *would have been* **c** once	2751
2Pe	1: 9	that he has been **c** from his past sins.	2752

CLEANSES (1) [CLEAN]

2Ti	2:21	If a man **c** himself from the latter,	1705

CLEANSING (16) [CLEAN]

Lev	14: 2	of his **ceremonial c,** when he is brought to	3200
	14:23	the eighth day he must bring them for his **c**	3200
	14:32	the regular offerings for his **c.**	3200
	15:13	seven days for his **ceremonial c;**	3200
Nu	6: 9	he must shave his head on the day of his **c**—	3200
	8: 7	Sprinkle the water of **c** on them;	2633
	19: 9	for use in the water of **c;**	5614
	19:13	water of **c** has not been sprinkled on him,	5614
	19:20	water of **c** has not been sprinkled on him,	5614
	19:21	the water of **c** must also wash his clothes,	5614
	19:21	and anyone who touches the water of **c** will	5614
	31:23	it must also be purified with the water of **c.**	5614
Mk	1:44	that Moses commanded for your **c,**	2752
Lk	5:14	that Moses commanded for your **c,**	2752
Jn	11:55	for their **ceremonial c** before the Passover.	49
Eph	5:26	**c** her by the washing with water through	2751

CLEAR (41) [CLEARED, CLEARLY]

Ge	20: 5	with a **c** conscience and clean hands."	9448
	20: 6	I know you did this with a **c** conscience,	9448
Ex	24:10	made of sapphire, **c** as the sky itself.	3198
	27:20	"Command the Israelites to bring you **c** oil	2341
Lev	24: 2	"Command the Israelites to bring you **c** oil	2341
	24:12	of the LORD *should be* **made c** to them.	7300
Nu	15:34	*it was* not **c** what should be done to him.	7300
Jos	17:15	and **c** *land* for yourselves in the land	1345
	17:18	**C** it, and its farthest limits will be yours;	1345

2Sa	19: 6	*You* have **made** *it* **c** today that	5583
1Ki	2:31	so **c** me and my father's house *of* the guilt	6073
Ne	8: 8	**making** it **c** and giving the meaning so that	7300
Isa	32: 4	the stammering tongue will be fluent and **c.**	7456
Eze	34:18	Is it not enough for you to drink **c** water?	5488
Mt	3:12	and he will **c** his threshing floor,	1351
Lk	3:17	in his hand *to* **c** his threshing floor and	1350
Jn	8:43	Why *is* my language **not c** to you?	1182+4024
Ac	18: 6	I am **c** of my responsibility.	2754
	24:16	So I strive always to keep my conscience **c**	718
1Co	4: 4	My **conscience** is **c,**	4029+5323
	14: 8	if the trumpet does **not** sound a **c** call,	83
	15:27	it is **c** that this does	1316
2Co	7:11	what **eagerness** to **c** yourselves,	665
	11: 6	*We have* **made** this perfectly **c** to you	5746
Php	1:13	it has become **c** throughout	5745
	3:15	that too God *will* **make c** to you.	636
1Th	3:11	and Father himself and our Lord Jesus **c**	2985
1Ti	3: 9	of the faith with a **c** conscience.	2754
2Ti	1: 3	as my forefathers did, with a **c** conscience,	2754
	3: 9	their folly will be **c** to everyone.	1684
Heb	6:17	**make** the unchanging nature of his purpose very **c** to the heirs	2109
	7:14	For *it is* **c** that our Lord descended	4593
	7:15	And what we have said is even more **c**	2867
	9: 9	*to* **c** the conscience of the worshiper.	5457
	13:18	a **c** conscience and desire to live honorably	2819
1Pe	3:16	keeping a **c** conscience,	2754
	4: 7	Therefore *be* **c minded** and self-controlled	5404
2Pe	1:14	as our Lord Jesus Christ *has* **made c** to me.	1317
Rev	4: 6	like a sea of glass, **c** as crystal.	NIG
	21:11	like a jasper, **c as crystal.**	3222
	22: 1	river of the water of life, as **c** as crystal,	3287

CLEARED (7) [CLEAR]

Nu	5:28	she *will be* **c** of guilt and will be able	5927
1Sa	14:41	and the men *were* **c.**	3655
2Ch	30:14	in Jerusalem and **c away** the incense altars	6073
Job	33:32	speak up, for I want you *to be* **c.**	7405
	35: 2	You say, 'I will be **c** by God.'	7406
Ps	80: 9	*You* **c** *the* ground for it,	7155
Isa	5: 2	up and **c** it *of* stones and planted it with	6232

CLEARLY (20) [CLEAR]

Ge	26:28	*We* **saw c** that the LORD was with you;	8011+8011
Ex	10:10	**C** you are bent on evil.	3954+8011
Nu	12: 8	face to face, **c** and not in riddles;	5260
	24: 3	the oracle of one whose eye *sees* **c,**	9280
	24:15	the oracle of one whose eye *sees* **c,**	9280
Dt	27: 8	And you shall write very **c** all the words	930
Jos	9:24	"Your servants were **c** told how	5583+5583
1Sa	2:27	not **c** reveal myself to your father's house	1655+1655
Jer	23:20	In days to come *you will* **understand** it **c.**	1067+1069
Mt	7: 5	then *you will* **see c** to remove the speck	1332
Mk	8:25	and he saw everything **c.**	5495
Lk	6:42	then *you will* **see c** to remove the speck	1332
Jn	16:29	"Now you are speaking **c** and	1877+4244
Ro	1:20	have **been c seen,**	2775
	3: 5	**brings out** God's righteousness **more c,**	5319
Gal	2:11	because he was **c in the wrong.**	2861
	3: 1	Before your very eyes Jesus Christ was **c** portrayed as crucified.	NIG
	3:11	**C** no one is justified before God by	1316
Col	4: 4	Pray that *I may* **proclaim** it **c,** as I should.	5746
1Ti	4: 1	The Spirit **c** says that	4843

CLEAVE, CLEAVED, CLEAVETH (KJV)
ALLY, CLING, CLUNG, DIVIDED, HELD
FAST, HOLD FAST, REMAIN TRUE,
STICK, STUCK, UNITED

CLEFT (1) [CLEFTS]

Ex	33:22	in a **c** *in* the rock and cover you	5942

CLEFTS (4) [CLEFT]

Jdg	6: 2	for themselves in **mountain c,**	2215
SS	2:14	My dove in the **c** of the rock,	2511
Jer	49:16	you who live in the **c** of the rocks,	2511
Ob	1: 3	the **c** of the rocks and make your home on	2511

CLEMENCY (KJV) See KIND

CLEMENT (1)

Php	4: 3	with **C** and the rest of my fellow workers,	3098

CLEOPAS (1)

Lk	24:18	One of them, named **C,** asked him,	3093

CLEOPHAS (KJV) See CLOPAS

CLERESTORY (1)

1Ki	6: 4	He made narrow **c** windows in the temple.	9209

CLERK (1)

Ac	19:35	The city **c** quieted the crowd and said:	1208

CLEVER (2) [CLEVERLY, CLEVERNESS]
Isa 3: 3 skilled craftsman and c enchanter. 1067
　　5:21 in their own eyes and c in their own sight. 1067

CLEVERLY (2) [CLEVER]
Hos 13: 2 from their silver, c fashioned images, 9312
2Pe 1:16 We did not follow c invented stories 5054

CLEVERNESS (1) [CLEVER]
Isa 25:11 down their pride despite the c 747

CLIFF (5) [CLIFFS]
1Sa 14: 4 to reach the Philistine outpost was a c; 6152+9094
　　14: 5 One c stood to the north toward Micmash, 9094
2Ch 25:12 took them to the top of a c and threw them 6152
Job 39:28 He dwells on a c and stays there at night; 6152
Lk 4:29 throw him down the c. 2889

CLIFFS (3) [CLIFF]
Ps 141: 6 be thrown down from the c, 6152
Jer 51:25 roll you off the c, 6152
Eze 38:20 the c will crumble and every wall will fall 4533

CLIFT (KJV) See CLEFT

CLIMAX (3)
Eze 21:25 of punishment has reached its c, 7891
　　21:29 of punishment has reached its c. 7891
　　35: 5 the time their punishment reached its c, 7891

CLIMB (7) [CLIMBED, CLIMBING, CLIMBS]
Ge 49:22 whose branches c over a wall. 7575
1Sa 14:10 if they say, 'Come up to us,' we will c up, 6590
　　14:12 "C up after me; 6590
SS 7: 8 I said, "I will c the palm tree; 6590
Jer 4:29 some c up among the rocks. 6590
Joel 2: 9 They c into the houses; 6590
Am 9: 2 Though they c up to the heavens, 6590

CLIMBED (17) [CLIMB]
Dt 32:50 the mountain that you have c you will die 6590
　　34: 1 Then Moses c Mount Nebo from the plains 6590
Jos 15: 8 From there it c to the top of the hill west of 6590
Jdg 9: 7 he c up on the top of Mount Gerizim 2143
　　9:51 They locked themselves in and c up on 6590
1Sa 14:13 Jonathan c up, using his hands and feet, 6590
2Sa 17:18 and they c down into it. 3718
　　17:21 the two c out of the well and went 6590
1Ki 18:42 but Elijah c to the top of Carmel, 6590
Ne 4: 3 if even a fox c up on it, 6590
Isa 57: 8 you c into it and opened it wide; 6590
Jer 9:21 Death has c in through our windows 6590
Eze 40: 6 He c its steps and measured the threshold of 6590
Mt 14:32 they c into the boat, the wind died down, 326
Mk 6:51 Then he c into the boat with them, 326
Lk 19: 4 ahead and c a sycamore-fig tree to see him, 326
Jn 21:11 Simon Peter c aboard and dragged 326

CLIMBING (1) [CLIMB]
2Ch 20:16 They will be c up by the Pass of Ziz, 6590

CLIMBS (3) [CLIMB]
Isa 24:18 whoever c out of the pit will be caught in 6590
Jer 48:44 whoever c out of the pit will be caught in 6590
Jn 10: 1 but c in by some other way, 326

CLING (10) [CLINGING, CLINGS, CLUNG]
Dt 28:60 and they will c to you. 1815
2Ki 5:27 Naaman's leprosy will c to you and 1815
Job 41:17 they c together and cannot be parted. 4334
Ps 31: 6 I hate those who c to worthless idols; 9068
　　44:25 our bodies c to the ground. 1815
　　101: 3 they will not c to me. 1815
　　137: 6 May my tongue c to the roof of my mouth 1815
Jer 8: 5 They c to deceit; they refuse to return. 2616
Jnh 2: 8 "Those who c to worthless idols forfeit 9068
Ro 12: 9 Hate what is evil; c to what is good. 3140

CLINGING (1) [CLING]
1Ki 1:51 of King Solomon and is c to the horns of 296

CLINGS (2) [CLING]
Job 8:15 he c to it, but it does not hold. 2616
Ps 63: 8 My soul c to you; 1815

CLIP (1)
Lev 19:27 at the sides of your head or c off the edges 8845

CLOAK (51) [CLOAKS]
Ge 39:12 She caught him by his c and said, 955
　　39:12 But he left his c in her hand and ran out of 955
　　39:13 When she saw that he had left his c 955
　　39:15 he left his c beside me and ran out of 955
　　39:16 She kept his c beside her 955
　　39:18 he left his c beside me and ran out of 955
Ex 4: 6 LORD said, "Put your hand inside your c." 2668
　　4: 6 So Moses put his hand into his c, 2668

Ex 4: 7 "Now put it back into your c," he said. 2668
　　4: 7 So Moses put his hand back into his c, 2668
　　12:11 c tucked into your belt, 2520+5516
　　22:26 If you take your neighbor's c as a pledge. 8515
　　22:27 because his c is the only covering he has 8529
Dt 22: 3 if you find your brother's donkey or his c 8529
　　22:12 on the four corners of the c you wear. 4064
　　24:13 Return his c to him by sunset so 8515
　　24:17 or take the c of the widow as a pledge. 955
1Ki 11:29 wearing a new c. 8515
　　11:30 of the new c he was wearing and tore it 8515
　　18:46 tucking his c into his belt, 5516+9113
　　19:13 he pulled his c over his face and went out 168
　　19:19 up to him and threw his c around him. 168
2Ki 2: 8 Elijah took his c, 168
　　2:13 up the c that had fallen from Elijah 168
　　2:14 Then he took the c that had fallen from him 168
　　4:29 "Tuck your c into your belt, 2520+5516
　　4:39 of its gourds and filled the fold of his c. 955
　　9: 1 "Tuck your c into your belt, 2520+5516
Ezr 9: 3 When I heard this, I tore my tunic and c, 5077
　　9: 5 with my tunic and c torn, 5077
Ps 109:19 May it be like a c wrapped about him, 955
　　109:29 and wrapped in shame as in a c. 5077
Pr 21:14 in the c pacifies great wrath. 2668
　　30: 4 Who has wrapped up the waters in his c? 8529
SS 5: 7 they took away my c, 8100
Isa 3: 6 and say, "You have a c, you be our leader; 8529
　　59:17 and wrapped himself in zeal as in a c. 5077
Mt 5:40 let him have your c as well. 2668
　　9:20 behind him and touched the edge of his c. 2668
　　9:21 She said to herself, "If I only touch his c, 2668
　　14:36 to let the sick just touch the edge of his c, 2668
　　24:18 Let no one in the field go back to get his c. 2668
Mk 5:27 behind him in the crowd and touched his c, 2668
　　6:56 to let them touch even the edge of his c, 2668
　　10:50 Throwing his c aside, 2668
　　13:16 Let no one in the field go back to get his c. 2668
Lk 6:29 If someone takes your c, 2668
　　8:44 behind him and touched the edge of his c, 2668
　　22:36 sell your c and buy one. 2668
Ac 12: 8 "Wrap your c around you and follow me," 2668
2Ti 4:13 bring the c that I left with Carpus at Troas, 5742

CLOAKS (9) [CLOAK]
2Ki 9:13 and took their c and spread them under him 955
Isa 3:22 the fine robes and the capes and c, 4762
Mt 21: 7 placed their c on them, 2668
　　21: 8 A very large crowd spread their c on 2668
Mk 11: 7 the colt to Jesus and threw their c over it, 2668
　　11: 8 Many people spread their c on the road, 2668
Lk 19:35 threw their c on the colt and put Jesus on it. 2668
　　19:36 people spread their c on the road. 2668
Ac 22:23 and throwing off their c and flinging dust 2668

CLODS (2)
Job 38:38 and the c of earth stick together? 8073
Joel 1:17 The seeds are shriveled beneath the c. 4493

CLOPAS (1)
Jn 19:25 Mary the wife of C, and Mary Magdalene. 3116

CLOSE (65) [CLOSED, CLOSELY, CLOSER, CLOSES, CLOSEST, CLOSING, ENCLOSE, ENCLOSED]
Ge 27:22 Jacob went c to his father Isaac, 5602
　　45: 4 Joseph said to his brothers, "Come c to me." 5602
　　46: 4 And Joseph's own hand will c your eyes." 8883
　　48:10 So Joseph brought his sons c to him, 5602
　　48:13 and brought them c to him. 5602
Ex 25:27 to be c to the rim to hold the poles 4200+6645
　　28:27 c to the seam just above the waistband 4200+6645
　　37:14 The rings were put c to the rim to hold 4200+6645
　　39:20 c to the seam just above the waistband 4200+6645
Lev 3: 9 entire fat tail cut off c to the backbone, 4200+6645
　　14:38 of the house and c it up for seven days. 6037
　　18: 6 'No one is to approach any c relative 1414+8638
　　18:12 she is your father's c relative. 8638
　　18:13 because she is your mother's c relative. 8638
　　18:17 they are her c relatives. 8638
　　20: 4 If the people of the community c their eyes 6623+6623
　　20:19 for that would dishonor a c relative; 8638
　　21: 2 except for a c relative, 7940+8638
Nu 5: 8 But if that person has no c relative 1457
　　22:25 she pressed c to the wall, 4315
Jos 2: 5 when it was time to c the city gate, 6037
Jdg 16: 9 of string snaps when it comes c to a flame. 8193
Ru 2:20 She added, "That man is our c relative; 7940
　　2:23 So Ruth stayed c to the servant girls 1815
2Sa 11:20 'Why did you get so c to the city to fight? 5602
　　11:21 Why did you get so c to the wall?' 5602
　　12:11 and give them to one who is c to you, 8276
1Ki 21: 1 c to the palace of Ahab king of Samaria. 725
　　21: 2 since it is c to my palace. 725+7940
2Ki 10:11 his c friends and his priests, 3359
　　11: 8 Stay c to the king wherever he goes." 907
2Ch 23: 7 Stay c to the king wherever he goes." 907
Ne 6:10 and let us c the temple doors, 6037
Job 13:27 you keep c watch on all my paths 9068
　　33:11 he keeps c watch on all my paths.' 9068
　　41:16 each is so c to the next 5602

Ps 17:10 They c up their callous hearts, 6037
　　34:18 The LORD is c to the brokenhearted 7940
　　41: 9 Even my c friend, whom I trusted, 408+8934
　　55:13 my companion, my c friend, 3359
　　69:15 up or the pit c its mouth over me. 358
　　88:15 and c to death; 1588
　　148:14 of Israel, the people c to his heart. 7940
Pr 16:28 and a gossip separates c friends. 476
　　17: 9 the matter separates c friends. 476
Isa 6:10 make their ears dull and c their eyes. 9129
　　40:11 the lambs in his arms and carries them c to 928
　　42:23 listen to this or pay c attention 2256+7992+9048
　　56: 1 and do what is right, for my salvation is c 7940
　　66: 9 "Do I c up the womb when I bring 6806
Jer 30:21 I will bring him near and he will come c 5602
　　30:21 to be c to me?' 5602
La 3:56 "Do not c your ears to my cry for relief." 6623
Eze 22: 4 brought your days to a c, 7928
Da 12: 4 c up and seal the words of the scroll until 6258
Joel 2: 1 It is c at hand— 7940
Zec 13: 7 against the man who is c to me!" 6660
Mt 6: 6 c the door and pray to your Father, 3091
Lk 20:20 Keeping a c watch on him, they sent spies, 4190
　　21:34 day will c on you unexpectedly like a trap. 2392
Jn 4:47 who was c to death. 3516
Ac 8: 6 they all paid c attention to what he said. 4668
　　9:24 Day and night they kept c watch on 4190
　　10:24 called together his relatives and c friends. 338
Rev 6: 8 and Hades was following c behind him. 3552

CLOSE-KNIT (1) [KNIT]
Job 40:17 the sinews of his thighs are c. 8571

CLOSED (18) [CLOSE]
Ge 2:21 he took one of the man's ribs and c up 6037
　　8: 2 the floodgates of the heavens had been c, 6126
　　20:18 for the LORD had c up every womb 6806+6806
Lev 14:46 the house while it is c up will be unclean 6037
Nu 16:33 the earth c over them, 4059
Jdg 3:22 and the fat c in over it. 6037
1Sa 1: 5 and the LORD had c her womb. 6037
　　1: 6 And because the LORD had c her womb, 6037
Ne 4: 7 ahead and that the gaps were being c, 6258
Job 17: 4 You have c their minds to understanding; 7621
Ecc 12: 4 the doors to the street are c and the sound 6037
Isa 32: 3 eyes of those who see will no longer be c, 9129
　　44:18 their minds c so they cannot understand. NIH
Jer 6:10 Their ears are c so they cannot hear. 6888
La 3:54 the waters c over my head, 7429
Da 12: 9 the words are c up and sealed until the time 6258
Mt 13:15 and they have c their eyes. 2826
Ac 28:27 and they have c their eyes. 2826

CLOSELY (18) [CLOSE]
Ge 24:21 the man watched her c to learn whether or 8617
　　43: 7 man questioned us c about ourselves 8626+8626
　　44:30 whose life is c bound up with 8003
Dt 4: 9 and watch yourselves c so that you do 4394
2Sa 19:42 "We did this because the king is c related 7940
1Ki 10: 1 I looked at him c in the morning light, 1067
Ne 13: 4 He was c associated with Tobiah, 7940
Job 23:11 My feet have c followed his steps; 296
Ps 122: 3 like a city that is c compacted together. 2489
Pr 4:20 listen c to my words. 265+5742
Jer 2:10 send to Kedar and observe c; 4394
Eze 44: 5 listen c and give attention 265+928+9048
Mk 3: 2 so they watched him c to see 4190
　　14:67 she looked c at him. 1838
Lk 6: 7 so they watched him c to see 4190
　　22:56 She looked c at him and said, 867
Ac 7:31 As he went over to look more c, 2917
1Ti 4:16 Watch your life and doctrine c. 2091

CLOSER (6) [CLOSE]
Ex 3: 5 "Do not come any c," God said. 7928
1Sa 17:41 kept coming c to David. 7929
　　17:48 As the Philistine moved c to attack him, 7940
2Sa 18:25 the man came c and closer. 2143+2256+7929
　　18:25 the man came closer and c. 2143+2256+7929
Pr 18:24 but there is a friend who sticks c than 1816

CLOSES (2) [CLOSE]
Pr 28:27 but he who c his eyes 6623
Lk 13:25 Once the owner of the house gets up and c 643

CLOSEST (4) [CLOSE]
Dt 13: 6 or your c friend secretly entices you, 889+3869+3870+5883+8276
Est 1:14 and were c to the king— 7940
Ps 88: 8 You have taken from me my c friends 3359
　　88:18 the darkness is my c friend. 3359

CLOSET (KJV) See CHAMBER, ROOM

CLOSING (4) [CLOSE]
Lev 23:36 It is the c assembly; do no regular work. 6809
1Sa 23:26 As Saul and his forces were c in on David 6496
Ps 77: 4 kept my eyes from c; 296+9073
Eze 21:14 c in on them from every side. 253

CLOTH (27) [CLOTHS]

Ex	28:31	the robe of the ephod entirely in **blue c,**	9418
	39:22	the robe of the ephod entirely of **blue c—**	9418
Lev	11:32	whether it is made of wood, **c,**	955
Nu	4: 6	a **c** of solid blue over that and put the poles	955
	4: 7	of the Presence they are to spread a blue **c**	955
	4: 8	Over these they are to spread a scarlet **c,**	955
	4: 9	to take a blue **c** and cover the lampstand	955
	4:11	to spread a blue **c** and cover that with hides	955
	4:12	wrap them in a blue **c,**	955
	4:13	from the bronze altar and spread a purple **c**	955
Dt	22:17	Then her parents shall display the **c** before	8529
1Sa	21: 9	it is wrapped in a **c** behind the ephod.	8529
2Ki	8:15	But the next day he took a **thick c,**	4802
Isa	19:10	The **workers in c** will be dejected,	9271
	30:22	like a **menstrual c** and say to them,	1865
Eze	16:13	and costly fabric and **embroidered c.**	8391
Mt	9:16	a patch of unshrunk **c** on an old garment,	4820
	27:59	wrapped it in a clean **linen c,**	4984
Mk	2:21	a patch of unshrunk **c** on an old garment,	4820
	15:46	So Joseph bought some **linen c.**	4984
Lk	19:20	I have kept it laid away in a **piece of c.**	5051
	23:53	in **linen c** and placed it in a tomb cut in	4984
Jn	11:44	and a **c** around his face.	5051
	20: 7	as well as the **burial c** that had been	5051
	20: 7	The **c** was folded up by itself,	NIG
Ac	16:14	a **dealer in purple c** from the city	4527
Rev	18:12	fine linen, purple, silk and scarlet **c;**	NIG

CLOTHE (21) [CLOTHED, CLOTHES, CLOTHING]

Job	10:11	**c** me with skin and flesh	4252
	39:19	the horse his strength or **c** his neck with	4252
	40:10	and **c** yourself in honor and majesty.	4252
Ps	45: 3	**c** yourself with splendor and majesty.	NIH
	73: 6	they **c** themselves with violence.	6493+8884
	132:16	I will **c** her priests with salvation,	4252
	132:18	I will **c** his enemies with shame,	4252
Isa	22:21	I will **c** him with your robe	4252
	50: 3	I **c** the sky with darkness	4252
	51: 9	**C** yourself with strength,	4252
	52: 1	awake, O Zion, **c** yourself with strength.	4252
	58: 7	when you see the naked, to **c** him,	4059
Eze	34: 3	**c** yourselves with the wool and slaughter	4252
Mt	6:30	will he not much more **c** you,	NIG
	25:38	or needing clothes and **c** you?	4314
	25:43	I needed clothes and you did not **c** me,	4314
Lk	12:28	how much more will he **c** you,	NIG
Ro	13:14	**c** yourselves with the Lord Jesus Christ,	1907
1Co	15:53	For the perishable must **c** itself with	1907
Col	3:12	**c** yourselves with compassion, kindness,	1907
1Pe	5: 5	**c** yourselves with humility	1599

CLOTHED (47) [CLOTHE]

Ge	3:21	of skin for Adam and his wife and **c** them.	4252
Lev	8: 7	**c** him with the robe and put the ephod	4252
2Sa	1:24	who **c** you in scarlet and finery,	4252
1Ch	15:27	Now David was **c** in a robe of fine linen,	4124
	21:16	Then David and the elders, **c** in sackcloth,	4059
2Ch	6:41	O LORD God, be **c** with salvation,	4252
	28:15	the plunder they **c** all who were naked.	4252
Est	4: 2	because no one **c** in sackcloth was allowed	4230
Job	7: 5	My body is **c** with worms and scabs,	4252
	8:22	Your enemies will be **c** in shame,	4252
Ps	30:11	you removed my sackcloth and **c** me	273
	35:26	may all who exalt themselves over me be **c**	4252
	65: 13	the hills are **c** with gladness.	2520
	104: 1	you are **c** with splendor and majesty.	4252
	109:29	be **c** with disgrace and wrapped in shame	4252
	132: 9	May your priests be **c** with righteousness;	4252
Pr	31:21	for all of them are **c** in scarlet.	4229
	31:22	she is **c** in fine linen and purple.	4230
	31:25	She is **c** with strength and dignity;	4230
Ecc	9: 8	Always be **c** in white,	955
Isa	61:10	For he has **c** me with garments of salvation,	4252
Eze	7:18	They will put on sackcloth and be **c**	4059
	7:27	the prince will be **c** with despair.	4252
	9: 2	With them was a man **c** in linen who had	4229
	9: 3	the man **c** in linen who had the writing kit	4229
	10: 2	The LORD said to the man **c** in linen,	4229
	16:10	I **c** you with an embroidered dress	4252
	23: 6	**c** in blue, governors and commanders, all	4229
	26:16	**C** with terror, they will sit on the ground,	4252
	31:15	**c** Lebanon with gloom,	7722
Da	5: 7	and tells me what it means will be **c**	10383
	5:16	you will be **c** in purple and have	10383
	5:29	Daniel was **c** in purple,	10383
	12: 6	One of them said to the man **c** in linen,	4229
	12: 7	The man **c** in linen,	4229
Zec	3: 5	a clean turban on his head and **c** him,	955+4252
	6:13	and he will be **c** with majesty and will sit	5951
Mt	25:36	I needed clothes and you **c** me,	4314
Lk	24:49	the city until you have been **c** with power	1907
Jn	19: 2	They **c** him in a purple robe	4314
1Co	15:54	When the perishable has been **c** with	1907
2Co	5: 2	to be **c** with our heavenly dwelling,	2086
	5: 3	because when we are **c,**	1907
	5: 4	but to be **c** with our heavenly dwelling,	2086
Gal	3:27	into Christ have **c** yourselves with Christ.	1907
	11: 3	they will prophesy for 1,260 days, **c** in	4314
	1	a woman **c** with the sun,	4314

...ES (169) [CLOTHE]

		...e best **c** of Esau her older son,	955

Ge	27:27	When Isaac caught the smell of his **c,**	955
	28:20	and will give me food to eat and **c** to wear	955
	35: 2	and purify yourselves and change your **c.**	8529
	37:29	saw that Joseph was not there, he tore his **c.**	955
	37:34	Then Jacob tore his **c,** put on sackcloth	8529
	38:14	she took off her widow's **c,**	955
	38:19	and put on her widow's **c** again.	955
	41:14	When he had shaved and changed his **c,**	8529
	44:13	At this, they tore their **c.**	8529
	45:22	of silver and five sets of **c.**	8529
Ex	19:10	Have them wash their **c**	8529
	19:14	and they washed their **c.**	8529
	28:41	After you put these **c** on	4252
Lev	6:10	The priest shall then put on his linen **c,**	4496
	6:11	he is to take off these **c** and put on others,	955
	10: 6	and do not tear your **c,**	955
	11:25	up one of their carcasses must wash his **c,**	955
	11:28	up their carcasses must wash his **c,**	955
	11:40	of the carcass must wash his **c,**	955
	11:40	up the carcass must wash his **c,**	955
	13: 6	The man must wash his **c,**	955
	13:34	He must wash his **c,** and he will be clean.	955
	13:45	an infectious disease must wear torn **c,**	955
	14: 8	to be cleansed must wash his **c,**	955
	14: 9	He must wash his **c** and bathe himself	955
	14:47	or eats in the house must wash his **c.**	955
	15: 5	who touches his bed must wash his **c**	955
	15: 5	on must wash his **c** and bathe with water,	955
	15: 7	a discharge must wash his **c** and bathe	955
	15: 8	that person must wash his **c** and bathe	955
	15:10	up those things must wash his **c** and bathe	955
	15:11	with water must wash his **c** and bathe	955
	15:13	he must wash his **c** and bathe himself	955
	15:21	Whoever touches her bed must wash his **c**	955
	15:22	on must wash his **c** and bathe with water,	955
	15:27	he must wash his **c** and bathe with water,	955
	16:26	the goat as a scapegoat must wash his **c**	955
	16:28	The man who burns them must wash his **c**	955
	17:15	by wild animals must wash his **c** and bathe	955
	17:16	if he does not wash his **c** and bathe himself,	NIH
	21:10	let his hair become unkempt or tear his **c.**	955
Nu	8: 7	shave their whole bodies and wash their **c,**	955
	8:21	purified themselves and washed their **c.**	955
	14: 6	the land, tore their **c**	955
	19: 7	the priest must wash his **c**	955
	19: 8	The man who burns it must also wash his **c**	955
	19:10	of the heifer must also wash his **c,**	955
	19:19	The person being cleansed must wash his **c**	955
	19:21	of cleansing must also wash his **c,**	955
	31:24	the seventh day wash your **c** and you will	955
Dt	8: 4	Your **c** did not wear out and your feet did	8529
	21:13	the **c** she was wearing when captured.	8529
	22:11	Do not wear **c** of wool and linen	4252
	29: 5	your **c** did not wear out,	8515
Jos	7: 6	Then Joshua tore his **c** and fell facedown to	8529
	9: 5	on their feet and their **c** were old **c.**	8515
	9:13	And our **c** and sandals are worn out by	8515
Jdg	11:35	When he saw her, he tore his **c** and cried,	955
	14:12	and thirty sets of **c.**	955
	14:13	and thirty sets of **c."**	955
	14:19	of their belongings and gave their **c**	2722
	17:10	your **c** and your food."	955+6886
Ru	3: 3	and put on your **best c.**	8529
1Sa	4:12	his **c** torn and dust on his head.	4496
	27: 9	donkeys and camels, and **c.**	955
	28: 8	Saul disguised himself, putting on other **c,**	955
2Sa	1: 2	with his **c** torn and with dust on his head.	955
	1:11	the men with him took hold of their **c**	955
	3:31	"Tear your **c** and put on sackcloth and walk	955
	12:20	put on lotions and changed his **c,**	8529
	13:31	tore his **c** and lay down on the ground;	955
	13:31	all his servants stood by with their **c** torn.	955
	14: 2	Dress in mourning **c,**	955
	19:24	or washed his **c** from the day the king left	955
1Ki	21:27	he tore his **c,** put on sackcloth and fasted.	955
2Ki	2:12	of his own **c** and tore them apart.	955
	5:26	or to accept **c,** olive groves, vineyards,	955
	7: 8	and gold and **c,** and went off and hid them.	955
	18:37	with their **c** torn,	955
	19: 1	he tore his **c** and put on sackcloth and went	955
	25:29	So Jehoiachin put aside his prison **c** and for	955
2Ch	28:15	They provided them with **c** and sandals,	4252
Ne	4:23	nor the guards with me took off our **c;**	955
	9:21	they lacked nothing, their **c** did	8515
Est	4: 1	he tore his **c,** put on sackcloth and ashes,	955
	4: 4	She sent **c** for him to put on instead	955
Job	9:31	so that even my **c** would detest me.	8515
	24: 7	Lacking **c,** they spend the night naked;	4230
	24:10	Lacking **c,** they go about naked;	4230
	27:16	up silver like dust and **c** like piles of clay,	4860
	37:17	in your **c** men find the land lies hushed under	955
Pr	6:27	into his lap without his **c** being burned?	4252
	23:21	and drowsiness **c** them in rags.	4252
Isa	4: 1	we will provide our own **c;**	8529
	23:18	for abundant food and fine **c.**	4833
	32:11	**Strip off** your **c,**	2256+6910+7320
	36:22	with their **c** torn,	955
	37: 1	he tore his **c** and put on sackcloth and went	955
Jer	2:34	On your **c** men find the lifeblood of	4053
	36:24	nor did they tear their **c.**	955
	38:11	and worn-out **c** from there and let them	4874
	38:12	and worn-out **c** under your arms to pad	4874
	41: 5	torn their **c** and cut themselves came	955
	52:33	So Jehoiachin put aside his prison **c** and for	955
Eze	16:13	your **c** were of fine linen and costly fabric	4860
	16:18	And you took your embroidered **c** to put	955
	16:39	of your **c** and take your fine jewelry	955

Eze	23:26	of your **c** and take your fine jewelry	955
	42:14	They are to put on other **c** before they go	955
	44:17	they are to wear linen **c;**	955
	44:19	to take off the **c** they have been ministering	955
	44:19	and put on other **c,**	955
Da	3:21	trousers, turbans and other **c,**	10382
Zep	1: 8	and all those clad in foreign **c.**	4860
Hag	1: 6	You put on **c,** but are not warm.	4252
Zec	3: 3	in filthy **c** as he stood before the angel.	955
	3: 4	"Take off his filthy **c."**	955
Mt	3: 4	John's **c** were made of camel's hair,	1903
	6:25	and the body more important than **c?**	1903
	6:28	"And why do you worry about **c?**	1903
	6:30	If that is how God **c** the grass of the field,	314
	11: 8	A man dressed in **fine c?**	3434
	11: 8	those who wear **fine c** are	3434
	17: 2	and his **c** became as white as the light.	2668
	22:11	not wearing wedding **c?**	1903
	22:12	in here without wedding **c?"**	1903
	25:36	I **needed c** and you clothed me,	1218
	25:38	or **needing c** and clothe you?	1218
	25:43	I **needed c** and you did not clothe me,	1218
	25:44	a stranger or **needing c** or sick or in prison,	1218
	26:65	Then the high priest tore his **c** and said,	2668
	27:31	they took off the robe and put his own **c**	2668
	27:35	they divided up his **c** by casting lots.	2668
	28: 3	and his **c** were white as snow.	1903
Mk	5:28	"If I just touch his **c,** I will be healed."	2668
	5:30	"Who touched my **c?"**	2668
	9: 3	His **c** became dazzling white,	2668
	14:63	The high priest tore his **c.**	5945
	15:20	the purple robe and put his own **c** on him.	2668
	15:24	Dividing up his **c,** they cast lots	2668
Lk	7:25	A man dressed in fine **c?**	2668
	7:25	those who wear expensive **c** and indulge	2669
	8:27	For a long time this man had not worn **c**	2668
	9:29	and his **c** became as bright as a flash	2669
	10:30	**stripped** him of his **c,**	1694
	12:23	and the body more than **c.**	1903
	12:28	If that is how God **c** the grass of the field,	313
	23:34	And they divided up his **c** by casting lots.	2668
	24: 4	in **c** that gleamed like lightning stood	2264
Jn	11:44	"Take off the grave **c** and let him go."	NIG
	13:12	he put on his **c** and returned to his place.	2668
	19:23	they took his **c,** dividing them into four	2668
Ac	7:58	the witnesses laid their **c** at the feet of	2668
	10:30	a man in shining **c** stood before me	2264
	12: 8	**"Put on** your **c** and sandals."	2439
	14:14	they tore their **c** and rushed out into	2668
	18: 6	he shook out his **c** in protest and said	2668
	22:20	the **c** of those who were killing him.'	2668
1Ti	2: 9	or gold or pearls or expensive **c,**	2669
Jas	2: 2	a gold ring and fine **c,**	2264
	2: 2	and a poor man in shabby **c** also comes in.	2264
	2: 3	to the man wearing fine **c** and say,	2264
	2:15	Suppose a brother or sister is **without c**	1218
	5: 2	and moths have eaten your **c.**	2668
1Pe	3: 3	and the wearing of gold jewelry and fine **c.**	2668
Rev	3: 4	in Sardis who have not soiled their **c.**	2668
	3:18	and white to wear,	2668
	16:15	and keeps his **c** with him,	2668

CLOTHING (52) [CLOTHE]

Ge	24:53	and silver jewelry and **articles of c**	955
	45:22	To each of them he gave new **c,**	8529
Ex	3:22	for articles of silver and gold and for **c,**	8529
	12:34	in kneading troughs wrapped in **c.**	8529
	12:35	for articles of silver and gold and for **c,**	8529
	21:10	**c** and marital rights.	4064
Lev	13:47	"If any **c** is contaminated with mildew—	955
	13:47	any woolen or linen **c,**	955
	13:49	and if the contamination in the **c,**	955
	13:51	and if the mildew has spread in the **c,**	955
	13:52	He must burn up the **c,**	955
	13:53	the mildew has not spread in the **c,**	955
	13:56	to tear the contaminated part out of the **c,**	955
	13:57	But if it reappears in the **c,**	955
	13:58	The **c,** or the woven or knitted material,	955
	13:59	by mildew in woolen or linen **c,**	955
	14:55	for mildew in **c** or in a house,	955
	15:17	Any **c** or leather that has semen on it must	955
	19:19	not wear **c** woven of two kinds of material.	955
Dt	10:18	and loves the alien, giving him food and **c.**	8529
	22: 5	A woman must not wear men's **c,**	3998
	22: 5	nor a man wear women's **c,**	955
Jos	22: 8	bronze and iron, and a great quantity of **c—**	8515
Jdg	3:16	to his right thigh under his **c.**	4496
2Ki	5: 5	of gold and ten sets of **c.**	955
	5:22	a talent of silver and two sets of **c.'"**	955
	5:23	with two sets of **c.**	955
	7:15	the whole road strewn with the **c**	955
2Ch	20:25	a great amount of equipment and **c** and	955
Job	22: 6	you stripped men of their **c,**	955
	29:14	**put on** righteousness as **my c;**	4252
	30:18	In his great power [God] becomes like a	4230
	31:19	I have seen anyone perishing for lack of **c,**	4230
Ps	22:18	among them and cast lots for my **c.**	4230
	102:26	Like a you will change them and they will	4230
Pr	27:26	the lambs will provide you with **c,**	4230
Isa	3: 7	I have no food or **c** in my house;	8529
	3:24	instead of **fine c,** sackcloth;	7345
	59: 6	Their cobwebs are useless for **c;**	955
	63: 3	and I stained all my **c.**	4860
Eze	18: 7	to the hungry and provides **c** for the naked.	955
	18:16	to the hungry and provides **c** for the naked.	955
Da	7: 9	His **c** was as white as snow;	10382

Zec 14:14 great quantities of gold and silver and c.   955
Mt 7:15 They come to you in sheep's c,   1903
Mk 1: 6 John **wore** c made of camel's hair,   1639+1907
Jn 13: 4 took off his **outer** c,   2668
   19:24 among them and cast lots for my c."   2668
Ac 9:39 the robes and other c that Dorcas had made   2668
   20:33 not coveted anyone's silver or gold or c.   2669
1Ti 6: 8 But if we have food and c,   5004
Jude 1:23 even the c stained by corrupted flesh.   5945

CLOTHS (3) [CLOTH]

Eze 16: 4 with salt or **wrapped in** c.   3156+3156
Lk 2: 7 *She* **wrapped** him **in** c and placed him in   5058
   2:12 a baby **wrapped in** c and lying in a
     manger."   5058

CLOUD (97) [CLOUDBURST, CLOUDLESS, CLOUDS, THUNDERCLOUD]

Ex 13:21 a pillar of c to guide them on their way and   6727
   13:22 Neither the pillar of c by day nor the pillar   6727
   14:19 The pillar of c also moved from in front   6727
   14:20 the c brought darkness to the one side   6727
   14:24 the pillar of fire and c at the Egyptian army   6727
   16:10 the glory of the LORD appearing in the c.   6727
   19: 9 "I am going to come to you in a dense c,   6727
   19:16 with a thick c over the mountain,   6727
   24:15 went up on the mountain, the c covered it,   6727
   24:16 For six days the c covered the mountain,   6727
   24:16 to Moses from within the c.   6727
   24:18 Then Moses entered the c as he went on up   6727
   33: 9 the pillar of c would come down and stay   6727
   33:10 the people saw the pillar of c standing at   6727
   34: 5 down in the c and stood there with him   6727
   40:34 Then the c covered the Tent of Meeting,   6727
   40:35 of Meeting because the c had settled   6727
   40:36 the c lifted from above the tabernacle,   6727
   40:37 if the c did not lift, they did not set out—   6727
   40:38 So the c of the LORD was over   6727
   40:38 and fire was in **the** c by night,   2257S
Lev 16: 2 I appear in the c over the atonement cover.   6727
Nu 9:15 was set up, the c covered it.   6727
   9:15 the c above the tabernacle looked like fire.   NIH
   9:16 c covered it, and at night it looked like fire.   6265
   9:17 Whenever the c lifted from above the Tent,   6727
   9:17 wherever the c settled,   6727
   9:18 As long as the c stayed over the tabernacle,   6727
   9:19 When the c remained over the tabernacle   6727
   9:20 the c was over the tabernacle only   6727
   9:21 Sometimes the c stayed only from evening   6727
   9:21 whenever the c lifted, they set out.   6727
   9:22 Whether the c stayed over the tabernacle   6727
   10:11 the c lifted from above the tabernacle of   6727
   10:12 from place to place until the c came to rest   6727
   10:34 The c of the LORD was over them by day   6727
   11:25 the LORD came down in the c and spoke   6727
   12: 5 the LORD came down in a pillar of c;   6727
   12:10 When the c lifted from above the Tent,   6727
   14:14 that your c stays over them,   6727
   14:14 and that you go before them in a pillar of c   6727
   16:42 suddenly the c covered it and the glory of   6727
Dt 1:33 in fire by night and in a c by day,   6727
   5:22 the c and the deep darkness;   6727
   31:15 at the Tent in a pillar of c,   6727
   31:15 the c stood over the entrance to the Tent.   6727
Jdg 20:38 that they should send up a great c of smoke   5368
1Ki 8:10 the c filled the temple of the LORD.   6727
   8:11 not perform their service because of the c,   6727
   8:12 that he would dwell in a **dark** c."   6906
   18:44 "A c as small as a man's hand is rising   6265
2Ch 5:13 temple of the LORD was filled with a c,   6727
   5:14 not perform their service because of the c,   6727
   6: 1 that he would dwell in a **dark** c;   6906
Ne 9:12 By day you led them with a pillar of c,   6727
   9:19 the pillar of c did not cease to guide them   6727
Job 3: 5 may a c settle over it;   6729
   7: 9 As a c vanishes and is gone,   6727
   30:15 my safety vanishes like a c.   6265
Ps 78:14 He guided them with the c by day and   6727
   99: 7 He spoke to them from the pillar of c;   6727
   105:39 He spread out a c as a covering,   6727
Pr 16:15 his favor is like a rain c in spring.   6265
Isa 4: 5 and over those who assemble there a c   6727
   14:31 A c **of smoke** comes from the north,   6940
   18: 4 like a c of dew in the heat of harvest."   6265
   19: 1 on a swift c and is coming to Egypt.   6265
   25: 5 as heat is reduced by the shadow of a c,   6265
   44:22 I have swept away your offenses like a c,   6265
La 2: 1 covered the Daughter of Zion **with the** c   6380
   3:44 with a c so that no prayer can get through.   6727
Eze 1: 4 an immense c with flashing lightning   6727
   8:11 and a fragrant c of incense was rising.   6727
   10: 3 and a c filled the inner court.   6727
   10: 4 The c filled the temple,   6727
   32: 7 I will cover the sun with a c,   6727
   38: 9 you will be like a c covering the land.   6727
   38:16 against my people Israel like a c that covers   6727
Mt 17: 5 a bright c enveloped them,   3749
   17: 5 and a voice from the c said,   3749
Mk 9: 7 Then a c appeared and enveloped them,   3749
   9: 7 and a voice came from the c: 3749
Lk 9:34 a c appeared and enveloped them,   3749
   9:34 and they were afraid as they entered the c.   3749
   9:35 A voice came from the c, saying,   3749
   12:54 "When you see a c rising in the west,   3749
   21:27 the Son of Man coming in a c with power   3749

Ac 1: 9 and a c hid them from their sight.   3749
1Co 10: 1 that our forefathers were all under the c and   3749
   10: 2 They were all baptized into Moses in the c   3749
Heb 12: 1 since we are surrounded by such a great c   3751
Rev 10: 1 He was robed in a c,   3749
   11:12 And they went up to heaven in a c,   3749
   14:14 and there before me was a white c,   3749
   14:14 on the c was one "like a son of man" with   3749
   14:15 to him who was sitting on the c,   3749
   14:16 on the c swung his sickle over the earth,   3749

CLOUDBURST (1) [CLOUD]

Isa 30:30 with c, thunderstorm and hail.   5881

CLOUDLESS (1) [CLOUD]

2Sa 23: 4 of morning at sunrise on a c morning,   4202+6265

CLOUDS (67) [CLOUD]

Ge 9:13 I have set my rainbow in the c,   6727
   9:14 Whenever I **bring** c over the earth and   6725+6727
   9:14 the earth and the rainbow appears in the c,   6727
   9:16 Whenever the rainbow appears in the c,   6727
Dt 4:11 with black c and deep darkness.   6727
   33:26 on the heavens to help you and on the c   8836
Jdg 5: 4 the c poured down water.   6265
2Sa 22:10 **dark** c were under his feet.   6906
   22:12 the dark rain c **of the sky.**   6265+8836
1Ki 18:45 Meanwhile, the sky grew black with c,   6265
Job 20: 6 to the heavens and his head touches the c,   6265
   22:14 **Thick** c veil him,   6265
   26: 8 He wraps up the waters in his c,   6265
   26: 8 yet the c do not burst under their weight.   6727
   26: 9 spreading his c over it.   6727
   35: 5 gaze at the c so high above you.   8836
   36:28 the c pour down their moisture   8836
   36:29 how he spreads out the c,   6265
   37:11 He loads the c with moisture;   6265
   37:13 He brings **the** c to punish men,   2084S
   37:15 Do you know how God controls the c   6727
   37:16 Do you know how the c hang poised,   6265
   38: 9 the c its garment and wrapped it   6727
   38:34 to the c and cover yourself with a flood   6265
   38:37 Who has the wisdom to count the c?   8836
Ps 18: 9 **dark** c were under his feet.   6906
   18:11 the dark rain c **of the sky.**   6265+8836
   18:12 the brightness of his presence c advanced,   6265
   68: 4 extol him who rides on the c—   6265
   77:17 The c poured down water,   6265
   97: 2 C and thick darkness surround him;   6727
   104: 3 He his chariot and rides on the wings of c   6265
   135: 7 He makes c rise from the ends of the earth;   5955
   147: 8 He covers the sky with c;   6265
   148: 8 and hail, snow and c, stormy winds   7798
Pr 3:20 and the c let drop the dew.   8836
   8:28 when he established the c above   8836
   25:14 Like c and wind without rain is   5955
Ecc 11: 3 If c are full of water,   6265
   11: 4 whoever looks at the c will not reap.   6265
   12: 2 and the c return after the rain;   6265
Isa 5: 6 I will command the c not to rain on it."   6265
   5:30 even the light will be darkened by the c.   6882
   14:14 I will ascend above the tops of the c;   6265
   30:27 with burning anger and dense c **of smoke;**   5366
   45: 8 let the c shower it down.   8836
   60: 8 "Who are these that fly along like c,   6265
Jer 4:13 He advances like the c,   6727
   10:13 he makes c rise from the ends of the earth.   5955
   51: 9 it rises as high as the c.'   8836
   51:16 he makes c rise from the ends of the earth.   5955
Eze 1:28 Like the appearance of a rainbow in the c   6727
   30: 3 a day of c, a time of doom for the nations.   6727
   30:18 She will be covered with c,   6727
   34:12 where they were scattered on a day of c   6727
Da 7:13 coming with the c of heaven.   10560
Joel 2: 2 a day of c and blackness.   6727
Na 1: 3 and c are the dust of his feet.   6727
Zep 1:15 a day of c and blackness,   6727
Zec 10: 1 it is the LORD who makes the **storm** c.   2613
Mt 24:30 the Son of Man coming on the c of the sky,   3749
   26:64 and coming on the c of the Mighty One   3749
Mk 13:26 of Man coming in c with great power   3749
   14:62 of the Mighty One and coming on the c   3749
1Th 4:17 be caught up together with them in the c   3749
Jude 1:12 They are c without rain,   3749
Rev 1: 7 Look, he is coming with the c,   3749

CLOVEN (KJV) See DIVIDED, SEPARATED

CLUB (8) [CLUBS]

2Sa 23:21 Benaiah went against him with a c.   8657
1Ch 11:23 Benaiah went against him with a c.   8657
Job 41:29 A c seems to him but a piece of straw;   9371
Pr 25:18 Like a c or a sword or a sharp arrow is   5138
Isa 10: 5 in whose hand is the c of my wrath!   4751
   10:15 or a c brandish him who is not wood!   4751
   10:24 who beat you with a rod and lift up a c   4751
Jer 51:20 "You are my **war** c,   5151

CLUBS (6) [CLUB]

Eze 39: 9 bows and arrows, the **war** c and spears   3338+5234
Mt 26:47 a large crowd armed with swords and c,   3833
   26:55 that you have come out with swords and c   3833
Mk 14:43 a crowd armed with swords and c,   3833

Mk 14:48 "that you have come out with swords and c   3833
Lk 22:52 that you have come with swords and c?   3833

CLUNG (3) [CLING]

Ru 1:14 but Ruth c to her.   1815
2Ki 3: 3 *he* c to the sins of Jeroboam son of Nebat,   1815
La 1: 9 Her filthiness c to her skirts;   928

CLUSTER (5) [CLUSTERS]

Nu 13:23 they cut off a branch bearing a single c   864
   13:24 the c of grapes the Israelites cut off there.   864
SS 1:14 a c of henna blossoms from the vineyards   864
Isa 65: 8 when juice is still found in a c **of grapes**   864
Mic 7: 1 there is no c **of grapes** to eat,   864

CLUSTERS (5) [CLUSTER]

Ge 40:10 it blossomed, and its c ripened into grapes.   864
Dt 32:32 and their c **with** bitterness.   864
SS 7: 7 and your breasts like c **of fruit.**   864
   7: 8 May your breasts be like the c **of** the vine,   864
Rev 14:18 the c **of grapes** from the earth's vine,   1084

CLUTCHES (5)

Job 5:15 he saves them from the c of the powerful.   3338
   6:23 ransom me from the c of the ruthless'?   3338
   16:11 over to evil men and thrown me into the c   3338
Hab 2: 9 to escape the c **of** ruin!   4090
Ac 12:11 from Herod's c and from everything   5931

CNIDUS (1)

Ac 27: 7 and had difficulty arriving off C.   3118

CO-HEIRS (1) [INHERIT]

Ro 8:17 heirs of God and c **with** Christ,   5169

COAL (2) [COALS]

2Sa 14: 7 the only **burning** c I have left,   1625
Isa 6: 6 of the seraphs flew to me with a **live** c   8365

COALS (21) [COAL]

Lev 16:12 He is to take a censer full of burning c from   1624
Nu 16:37 and scatter the c some distance away, for   836
2Sa 22: 9 **burning** c blazed out of it.   1624
1Ki 19: 6 a cake of bread **baked over hot** c,   8363
Job 41:21 His breath sets c ablaze,   1624
Ps 11: 6 On the wicked he will rain fiery c   7073
   18: 8 **burning** c blazed out of it.   1624
   120: 4 with **burning** c **of** the broom tree.   1624
   140:10 Let **burning** c fall upon them;   1624
Pr 6:28 on **hot** c without his feet being scorched?   1624
   25:22 you will heap **burning** c on his head,   1624
Isa 30:14 a fragment will be found for taking c from   836
   44:12 a tool and works with it in the c;   7073
   44:19 I even baked bread over its c,   1624
   47:14 Here are no c to warm anyone;   1625
   54:16 the blacksmith who fans the c into flame   7073
Eze 1:13 of the living creatures was like burning c   1624
   10: 2 Fill your hands with burning c from among   1624
   24:11 the empty pot on the c till it becomes hot   1624
Jn 21: 9 they saw a **fire of burning** c there with fish   471
Ro 12:20 you will heap burning c on his head."   472

COARSE (1)

Eph 5: 4 foolish talk or c joking,   2365

COAST (15) [COASTLANDS, COASTLINE, COASTS]

Nu 34: 6 " 'Your western boundary will be the c of   1473
Dt 1: 7 in the Negev and along the c,   2572+3542
Jos 5: 1 the Canaanite kings along the c heard how   3542
   9: 1 the western foothills, and along the entire c   2572
Jdg 5:17 Asher remained on the c and stayed   2572+3542
2Ch 8:17 to Ezion Geber and Elath on the c   3542+8557
Isa 20: 6 the people who live on this c will say,   362
Jer 47: 7 to attack Ashkelon and the c?"   2572+3542
Eze 25:16 destroy those remaining along the c.   2572+3542
   26:16 then all the princes of the c will step down   3542
Lk 6:17 and from the c of Tyre and Sidon,   4163
Ac 17:14 to the c, but Silas and Timothy stayed   2498
   27: 2 to sail for ports along the c of the province   NIG
   27: 5 across the open sea off the c of Cilicia   NIG
   27: 8 along the c with difficulty and came to   NIG

COASTLANDS (9) [COAST]

Jer 25:22 the kings of the c across the sea;   362
   31:10 proclaim it in distant c: 362
Eze 26:15 not the c tremble at the sound of your fall,   362
   26:18 Now the c tremble on the day of your fall;   362
   27:15 and many c were your customers;   362
   27:35 All who live in the c are appalled at you;   362
   39: 6 and on those who live in safety in the c,   362
Da 11:18 Then he will turn his attention to the c   362
   11:30 Ships of the **western** c will oppose him,   4183

COASTLINE (2) [COAST]

Jos 15:12 The western boundary is the c of   !
   15:47 as far as the Wadi of Egypt and the c of

COASTS (5) [COAST]
Jer	2:10	Cross over to the **c** of Kittim and look,	362
	47: 4	the remnant from the **c** of Caphtor.	362
Eze	27: 3	merchant of peoples on many **c,**	362
	27: 6	from the **c** of Cyprus they made your deck,	362
	27: 7	of blue and purple from the **c** of Elishah.	362

COAT (6) [COATED, COATING, COATS]
Ge	6:14	make rooms in it and **c** it with pitch inside	4106
Dt	27: 2	set up some large stones and **c** them	8486
	27: 4	and **c** them with plaster.	8486
1Sa	17: 5	his head and wore a **c of scale armor**	7989+9234
	17:38	a **c of armor** on him and a bronze helmet	9234
Job	41:13	Who can strip off his outer **c**?	4230

COAT OF MANY COLOURS (KJV) See RICHLY ORNAMENTED ROBE

COATED (1) [COAT]
Ex	2: 3	a papyrus basket for him and **c** it with tar	2814

COATING (1) [COAT]
Pr	26:23	Like a **c** of glaze	7596

COATS (1) [COAT]
2Ch	26:14	spears, helmets, **c** of armor,	9234

COAX (1)
Jdg	14:15	"**C** your husband *into* explaining	7331

COBRA (3) [COBRAS]
Ps	58: 4	like that of a **c** that has stopped its ears,	7352
	91:13	You will tread upon the lion and the **c**;	7352
Isa	11: 8	The infant will play near the hole of the **c**,	7352

COBRAS (1) [COBRA]
Dt	32:33	the deadly poison of **c**.	7352

COBWEBS (1) [WEB]
Isa	59: 6	Their **c** are useless for clothing;	7770

COCK (Anglicized, KJV) See ROOSTER

COCKATRICE (KJV) See VIPER

COCKCROWING (KJV) See ROOSTER, CROWING

COCKLE (KJV) See WEED

COCOON (1)
Job	27:18	The house he builds is like a **moth's c,**	6931

CODE (4)
Ro	2:27	you have the written **c** and circumcision,	NIG
	2:29	by the Spirit, not by the written **c**.	NIG
	7: 6	and not in the old way of the **written c**.	1207
Col	2:14	the **written c,** with its regulations, that was	5934

COFFER (KJV) See CHEST

COFFIN (2)
Ge	50:26	he was placed in a **c** in Egypt.	778
Lk	7:14	Then he went up and touched the **c,**	5049

COGNITIONS (KJV) See THOUGHTS

COHORTS (1)
Job	9:13	even the **c** of Rahab cowered at his feet.	6468

COILED (2) [COILING]
2Sa	22: 6	The cords of the grave **c around** me;	6015
Ps	18: 5	The cords of the grave **c around** me;	6015

COILING (1) [COILED]
Isa	27: 1	Leviathan the **c** serpent;	6825

COIN (4) [COINS]
Mt	17:27	and you will find a **four-drachma c**.	5088
	22:19	Show me the **c** used for paying the tax."	3790
Mk	12:16	They brought the **c,** and he asked them:	NIG
Lk	15: 9	I have found my lost **c**.'	1534

...INS (9) [COIN]
		counted out for him thirty **silver c.**	736
		..hirty **silver c** to the chief priests and	736
		..hief priests picked up the **c** and said,	736
		..took the thirty **silver c,**	736
		..n two very **small copper c,**	3321
		..day he took out two **silver c**	1324
		..has ten **silver c** and loses one.	1534

Lk	21: 2	in two very **small copper c.**	3321
Jn	2:15	he scattered the **c** of the money changers	3047

COL-HOZEH (2)
Ne	3:15	by Shallun son of **C,**	3997
	11: 5	the son of **C,** the son of Hazaiah,	3997

COLD (15)
Ge	8:22	seedtime and harvest, **c** and heat,	7923
	31:40	in the daytime and the **c** at night,	7943
Job	24: 7	to cover themselves in the **c**.	7938
	37: 9	the **c** from the driving winds.	7938
Pr	25:20	a garment on a **c** day,	7938
	25:25	Like **c** water to a weary soul is good news	7922
Na	3:17	that settle in the walls on a **c** day—	7938
Zec	14: 6	no **c** or frost.	7938
Mt	10:42	And if anyone gives even a cup *of* **c** water	6037
	24:12	the love of most *will* **grow c,**	6038
Jn	18:18	It was **c**, and the servants	6036
Ac	28: 2	because it was raining and **c**.	6036
2Co	11:27	I have been **c** and naked.	6036
Rev	3:15	that you are neither **c** nor hot.	6037
	3:16	neither hot nor **c**—	6037

COLLAPSE (5) [COLLAPSED, COLLAPSES]
Jos	6: 5	the city *will* **c** and the people will go up,	5877
Ps	10:10	His victims are crushed, *they* **c**;	8820
Eze	26:18	in the sea are terrified at your **c**.'	3655
Mt	15:32	or *they* may **c** on the way."	1725
Mk	8: 3	*they* will **c** on the way,	1725

COLLAPSED (8) [COLLAPSE]
Jos	6:20	the people gave a loud shout, the wall **c**;	5877
Jdg	7:13	that the tent overturned and **c**."	5877
1Ki	20:30	where the wall **c** on twenty-seven thousand	5877
Job	1:19	*It* **c** on them and they are dead,	5877
Hab	3: 6	and the age-old hills **c**.	8820
Lk	6:49	*it* **c** and its destruction was complete."	5229
Rev	11:13	and a tenth of the city **c**.	4406
	16:19	and the cities of the nations **c**.	4406

COLLAPSES (3) [COLLAPSE]
Isa	30:13	cracked and bulging, that **c** suddenly,	995+8691
Eze	13:12	When the wall **c,** will people not ask you,	5877
Na	2: 6	and the palace **c**.	4570

COLLAR (3)
Ex	28:32	a woven edge like a **c** around this	7023+9389
	39:23	of the robe like the opening of a **c,**	9389
Ps	133: 2	down upon the **c** of his robes.	7023

COLLECT (13) [COLLECTED, COLLECTING, COLLECTION, COLLECTIONS, COLLECTOR, COLLECTOR'S, COLLECTORS, COLLECTS]
Ge	41:35	*They should* **c** all the food	7695
Nu	3:47	**c** five shekels for each one,	4374
2Ki	12: 4	"**C** all the money that is brought	NIH
	12: 8	not **c** any more money from the people and	4374
2Ch	20:25	that it took three days *to* **c** it.	1024
	24: 5	of Judah and **c** the money due annually	7695
Ne	10:37	the Levites who **c** *the* **tithes** in all the towns	6923
Mt	13:30	First **c** the weeds and tie them in bundles to	5198
	17:25	the kings of the earth **c** duty and taxes—	3284
	21:34	to the tenants *to* **c** his fruit.	3284
Mk	12: 2	the tenants to **c** from them some of the fruit	3284
Lk	3:13	"Don't **c** any more than you are required	4556
Heb	7: 5	*to* **c a tenth from** the people—	620+2400

COLLECTED (15) [COLLECT]
Ge	41:48	Joseph **c** all the food produced	7695
	47:14	Joseph **c** all the money that was to be found	4377
Nu	3:49	So Moses **c** the redemption money	4374
	3:50	of the Israelites *he* **c** silver weighing 1,365	4374
	16:39	the priest **c** the bronze censers brought	4374
2Ki	12: 4	the **money** *c* in the census,	AIT
	22: 4	the doorkeepers *have* **c** from the people.	665
2Ch	24:11	and **c** a great amount of money.	665
	34: 9	the Levites who were the doorkeepers *had* **c**	665
Ecc	12:11	their **c sayings** like firmly embedded nails—	670+1251
Zec	14:14	of all the surrounding nations *will* **be c**—	665
Mt	13:48	Then *they* sat down and **c** the good fish	5198
Lk	19:23	*I* could *have* **c** it with interest?'	4556
Heb	7: 6	yet *he* **c a tenth** from Abraham	1282
	7: 8	the tenth is **c** by men who die;	3284

COLLECTING (1) [COLLECT]
Lev	11:36	or a cistern for **c** water remains clean,	5224

COLLECTION (2) [COLLECT]
Isa	57:13	let your **c** [of idols] save you!	7689
1Co	16: 1	Now about the **c** for God's people:	3356

COLLECTIONS (1) [COLLECT]
1Co	16: 2	when I come no **c** will have to be made.	3356

COLLECTOR (8) [COLLECT]
Da	11:20	a **tax c** to maintain the royal splendor.	5601
Mt	10: 3	Thomas and Matthew the **tax c**;	5467
	18:17	treat him as you would a pagan or a **tax c**.	5467
Lk	5:27	and saw a **tax c** by the name of Levi sitting	5467
	18:10	one a Pharisee and the other a **tax c**.	5467
	18:11	or even like this **tax c**.	5467
	18:13	"But the **tax c** stood at a distance.	5467
	19: 2	he was a **chief tax c** and was wealthy.	803

COLLECTOR'S (2) [COLLECT]
Mt	9: 9	at the **tax c booth**.	5468
Mk	2:14	of Alphaeus sitting at the **tax c booth**.	5468

COLLECTORS (16) [COLLECT]
Mt	5:46	Are not even the **tax c** doing that?	5467
	9:10	many **tax c** and "sinners" came and ate	5467
	9:11	"Why does your teacher eat with **tax c**	5467
	11:19	a friend *of* **tax c** and "sinners." '	5467
	17:24	**c** of the two-drachma **tax**	3284
	21:31	the **tax c** and the prostitutes are entering	5467
	21:32	but the **tax c** and the prostitutes did.	5467
Mk	2:15	many **tax c** and "sinners" were eating	5467
	2:16	and **tax c,** they asked his disciples:	5467
	2:16	"Why does he eat with **tax c**	5467
Lk	3:12	**Tax c** also came to be baptized.	5467
	5:29	*of* **tax c** and others were eating with them.	5467
	5:30	"Why do you eat and drink with **tax c**	5467
	7:29	(All the people, even the **tax c,**	5467
	7:34	a friend *of* **tax c** and "sinners." '	5467
	15: 1	the **tax c** and "sinners" were all gathering	5467

COLLECTS (1) [COLLECT]
Heb	7: 9	who **c** the tenth,	3284

COLLEGE (KJV) See SECOND DISTRICT

COLONNADE (4) [COLUMN]
1Ki	7: 6	a **c** fifty cubits long and thirty wide.	395+6647
Jn	10:23	in the temple area walking in Solomon's **C**.	5119
Ac	3:11	to them in the place called Solomon's **C**.	5119
	5:12	to meet together in Solomon's **C**.	5119

COLONNADES (1) [COLUMN]
Jn	5: 2	and which is surrounded by five **covered c**.	5119

COLONY (1)
Ac	16:12	a **Roman c** and the leading city of	3149

COLORED (1) [COLORFUL, COLORS, DARK-COLORED, MULTICOLORED]
Pr	7:16	I have covered my bed with **c** linens	2635

COLORFUL (2) [COLORED]
Jdg	5:30	**c garments** as plunder for Sisera,	7389
	5:30	**c garments** embroidered,	7389

COLORS (2) [COLORED]
1Ch	29: 2	turquoise, stones of **various c,**	8391
Eze	17: 3	and full plumage *of* **varied c** came	8391

COLOSSE (1)
Col	1: 2	and faithful brothers in Christ at **C:**	3145

COLT (15)
Ge	49:11	his **c** to the choicest branch;	912+1201
Job	11:12	a wild donkey's **c** can be born a man.	6555
Zec	9: 9	gentle and riding on a donkey, on a **c,**	6555
Mt	21: 2	with her **c** by her.	4798
	21: 5	gentle and riding on a donkey, on a **c,**	4798
	21: 7	They brought the donkey and the **c,**	4798
Mk	11: 2	you will find a **c** tied there,	4798
	11: 4	They went and found a **c** outside in	4798
	11: 5	"What are you doing, untying that **c**?"	4798
	11: 7	the **c** to Jesus and threw their cloaks	4798
Lk	19:30	you will find a **c** tied there,	4798
	19:33	As they were untying the **c,**	4798
	19:33	"Why are you untying the **c**?"	4798
	19:35	threw their cloaks on the **c** and put Jesus	4798
Jn	12:15	seated on a donkey's **c**."	4798

COLUMN (3) [COLONNADE, COLONNADES, COLUMNS]
Jdg	20:40	the **c** of smoke began to rise from the city,	6647
SS	3: 6	up from the desert like a **c** of smoke,	9406
Isa	9:18	so that it rolls upward in a **c** of smoke.	1455

COLUMNS (5) [COLUMN]
1Ki	7: 2	of cedar **c** supporting trimmed cedar beams	6647
	7: 3	above the beams that rested on the **c**—	6647
Jer	36:23	Whenever Jehudi had read three or four **c**	1946
Joel	2:20	with its **front c** going into the eastern sea	7156
Zep	2:14	and the screech owl will roost on her **c**.	4117

COMB (2) [COMBED]
Ps	19:10	than honey from the **c**.	7430

Pr 24:13 **honey from the** c **is sweet to your taste.** 5885

COMBED (1) [COMB]
Isa 19: 9 Those who work with c flax will despair, 8591

COMBINE (1) [COMBINED]
Heb 4: 2 those who heard *did* not c it with faith. 5166

COMBINED (1) [COMBINE]
1Co 12:24 But God *has* c the members of the body 5166

COME (1463) [CAME, COMES, COMING]
Ge 6:20 that moves along the ground *will* c to you 995
8:16 "C out of the ark, 3655
9:12 a covenant for all generations **to c:** 6409
11: 3 They said to each other, "C, 2035
11: 4 "C, let us build ourselves a city, 2035
11: 7 C, let us go down 2035
15:14 and afterward *they will* c out 3655
15:16 fourth generation your descendants *will* c back here, 8740
16: 8 servant of Sarai, where *have you* c from, 995
17: 6 and kings *will* c from you. 3655
17: 7 after you for the **generations to c,** 1887
17: 9 after you for the **generations to c.** 1887
17:12 For the **generations to c** every male 1887
17:16 kings of peoples *will* c from her." 2118
18: 5 now that *you have* c to your servant." 6296
19: 8 for *they have* c under the protection 995
22: 5 We will worship and then *we will* c back 8740
23:10 hearing of all the Hittites *who had* c to 995
23:18 the Hittites *who had* c to the gate of the city. 995
24: 5 "What if the woman is unwilling to c back 2143
24: 8 the woman is unwilling to c back with you, 2143
24:31 "C, you who are blessed by the LORD," 995
24:39 if the woman *will* not c back with me?' 2143
24:42 to the journey on which I have c. 2143
24:62 Now Isaac *had* c from Beer Lahai Roi, 995
25:25 The first to c out was red, 3655
26:26 Abimelech *had* c to him from Gerar, 2143
26:27 Isaac asked them, "Why *have you* c to me, 995
27:21 "C near so I can touch you, my son. 5602
27:26 Then his father Isaac said, "C here, 5602
27:45 I'll send word for you *to* c back from there. 4374
31: 4 to c out to the fields where his flocks were. NIH
31:44 C now, let's make a covenant, you and I, 2143
32:11 for I am afraid he *will* c and attack me, 995
33:14 until *I* c to my lord in Seir." 995
34: 7 Now Jacob's sons *had* c in from the fields 995
35: 3 Then c, let us go up to Bethel, 7756
35:11 a community of nations *will* c from you, 2118
35:11 and kings *will* c from your body. 3655
37:10 and your brothers **actually** c and bow 995+995
37:13 C, I am going to send you to them." 2143
37:20 "C now, let's kill him and throw him 2143
37:27 "C, let's sell him to the Ishmaelites and 2143
38:16 "C now, let me sleep with you." 2035
39: 7 "C to bed with me!" 6640+8886
39:12 "C to bed with me!" 6640+8886
41:36 the seven years of famine that *will* c 2118
42: 4 he was afraid that harm *might* c to him. 7925
42: 7 "Where *do you* c from?" 995
42: 9 *You have* c to see 995
42:10 "Your servants *have* c to buy food. 995
42:12 *"You have* c to see 995
42:21 that's why this distress *has* c upon us." 995
43:14 and Benjamin c back with you. 8938
44:34 not let me see the misery that *would* c upon 5162
45: 4 "C close to me." 5602
45: 9 C down to me; don't delay. 3718
45:11 five years of famine are **still** *to* c. AIT
45:16 that Joseph's brothers *had* c, 995
45:19 and get your father and c. 995
46:31 have c to me. 995
47: 1 have c from the land of Canaan and are 995
47: 4 "We have c to live here awhile, 995
47: 5 "Your father and your brothers *have* c 995
48: 2 "Your son Joseph *has* c to you," 995
49: 1 to you in days to c. 344
50:24 **surely** c to your aid 7212+7212
50:25 **surely** c to your aid, 7212+7212
Ex 1:10 C, we must deal shrewdly with them 2035
3: 5 "Do not c any closer," God said. 7928
3: 8 So *I have* c down to rescue them from 3718
3: 8 *They will* c up into your palace 995
8: 3 and **make** frogs c up on the land of Egypt.' 6590
8: 7 also **made** frogs c up on the land of Egypt. 6590
11: 8 All these officials of yours *will* c to me, 3718
12:14 the **generations to c** you shall celebrate it 1887
12:17 for the **generations to c.** 1887
12:42 the LORD for the **generations to c.** 1887
13:14 "*In days to* c, when your son asks you, 4737
13:19 **surely** c to your aid, 7212+7212
14:25 **made** the wheels of their chariots c off 6073
16: 1 of the second month after they *had* c out 3655
16: 9 'C before the LORD, 7928
16:32 and keep it for the **generations to c,** 1887
16:33 to be kept for the **generations to c.** 1887
17: 6 and water *will* c out of it for the people 3655
18:15 the people c to me to seek God's will. 995
18:18 You and these people who c NIH
19: 9 "*I am going to* c to you in a dense cloud, 995
19:11 the LORD *will* c down on Mount Sinai in 3718
19:23 "The people cannot c up Mount Sinai, 6590

Ex 19:24 not force their way through to c up to 6590
20:20 God *has* c to test you, 995
20:24 *I will* c to you and bless you. 995
23: 4 "If *you* c across your enemy's ox 7003
24: 1 he said to Moses, "C up to the LORD, 6590
24: 2 the others *must* not c near. 5602
24: 2 And the people *may* not c up with him." 6590
24:12 "C up to me on the mountain and stay here, 6590
24:14 "Wait here for us until *we* c back to you. 8740
27:21 the Israelites for the **generations to c.** 1887
29:42 the **generations to c** this burnt offering is 1887
30: 8 before the LORD for the **generations to c.** 1887
30:10 for the **generations to c.** 1887
30:12 Then no plague *will* c on them 2118
30:21 for the **generations to c."** 1887
30:31 for the **generations to c.** 1887
31:13 and you for the **generations to c,** 1887
31:16 the **generations to c** as a lasting covenant. 1887
32: 1 they gathered around Aaron and said, "C, 7756
32:26 "Whoever is for the LORD, c to me." NIH
33: 9 the pillar of cloud *would* c down and stay at 3718
34: 2 and then c up on Mount Sinai. 6590
34: 3 *to* c with you or be seen anywhere on 6590
34:30 and they were afraid *to* c near him. 5602
35:10 among you *are to* c and make everything 995
36: 2 and who was willing to c and do the work. 7928
40:15 that will continue for all **generations to c."** 1887
Lev 3:17 the **generations to c,** wherever you live: 1887
6:18 the LORD by fire for the **generations to c.** 1887
7:36 for the **generations to c.** 1887
9: 7 "C to the altar and sacrifice 7928
10: 4 and said to them, "C here; 7928
10: 9 for the **generations to c.** 1887
14: 8 After this he *may* c into the camp. 995
15:14 and c before the LORD to the entrance to 995
16: 2 not to c whenever he chooses into 995
16:18 "Then *he shall* c out to the altar that is 3655
16:24 Then *he shall* c out and sacrifice 3655
16:26 afterward *he may* c into the camp. 995
16:28 afterward *he may* c into the camp. 995
17: 7 for them and for the **generations to c.'** 1887
21:17 'For the **generations to c** none 1887
21:17 a defect *may* c near to offer the food 7928
21:18 No man who has any defect *may* c near: 7928
21:21 the priest who has any defect *is to* c near 5602
21:21 not c near to offer the food of his God. 5602
22: 3 "Say to them: 'For the **generations to c,** 1887
23:14 for the **generations to c,** 1887
23:21 for the **generations to c,** 1887
23:31 for the **generations to c,** 1887
23:41 for the **generations to c;** 1887
24: 3 for the **generations to c.** 1887
25:25 his nearest relative *is to* c 995
25:44 and female slaves *are to* c from the nations 2118
Nu 4: 3 of age *who* c to serve in the work in the Tent 995
4:15 the Kohathites *are to* c to do the carrying. 995
4:19 when they c near the most holy things, 5602
4:23 from thirty to fifty years of age *who* c 995
4:30 from thirty to fifty years of age *who* c 995
5:14 if feelings of jealousy c over her husband 6296
5:30 or when feelings of jealousy c over a man 6296
8:15 they *are to* c to do their work at the Tent 995
8:24 Men twenty-five years old or more *shall* c 995
10: 8 for you and the **generations to c.** 1887
10:29 C with us and we will treat you well, 2143
10:32 If *you* c with us, 2143
11:16 **Have** them c to the Tent of Meeting, 4374
11:17 *I will* c down and speak with you there, 3718
11:17 or not what I say *will* c **true** *for* you." 7936
12: 4 "C out to the Tent of Meeting, 3655
13:33 (the descendants of Anak c from NIH
15:14 For the **generations to c.** 1887
15:15 for the **generations to c.** 1887
15:21 Throughout the **generations to c** you are 1887
15:23 through the **generations to c—** 1887
15:38 'Throughout the **generations to c** you are 1887
16: 5 have that person c near 7928
16: 5 The man he chooses he will **cause** to c near 7928
16:12 But they said, "We will not c! 6590
16:14 No, we will not c!" 6590
16:27 and Abiram *had* c out and were standing 3655
16:40 of Aaron *should* c to burn incense before 7928
16:46 Wrath *has* c out from the LORD; 3655
18: 4 and no *one* else *may* c near where you are. 7928
18:23 for the **generations to c.** 1887
19: 7 *He may* then c into the camp, 995
20:14 about all the hardships that *have* c upon us. 5162
21:27 "C to Heshbon and let it be rebuilt; 995
22: 5 Balak said: "A people *has* c out of Egypt; 3655
22:11 Now c and put a curse on these people, 2143
22:11 that *has* c out of Egypt covers the face of 3655
22:11 Now c and put a curse on them for me. 2143
22:14 "Balaam refused *to* c with us." 2143
22:17 C and put a curse on these people for me." 2143
22:20 "Since these men *have* c to summon you, 995
22:32 *I have* c here to oppose you 3655
22:37 Why didn't *you* c to me? 2143
22:38 "Well, *I have* c to you now," 995
23: 3 the LORD *will* c to meet with me. 7936
23: 7 'C,' he said, 'curse Jacob for me; 2143
23: 7 "Come,' he said, 'curse Jacob for me; 2143
23:13 "C with me to another place 2143
23:27 Then Balak said to Balaam, "C, 2143
24:14 Now I am going back to my people, but c, 2143
24:14 to your people in days to c." 344
24:17 A star *will* c out of Jacob; 2005
24:19 A ruler *will* c out of Jacob and destroy NIH

Nu 24:20 but he *will* c to ruin at last." 6330
24:24 Ships *will* c from the shores of Kittim; NIH
24:24 but they too *will* c to ruin." 6330
27:17 to go out and c in before them, 995
27:21 and at his command *they will* c in." 995
31:24 Then *you may* c into the camp." 995
32:19 because our inheritance *has* c to us on 995
35:29 for you throughout the **generations to c,** 1887
Dt 1:22 to take and the towns *we will* c to." 995
2:19 When *you* c to the Ammonites, 7928
10: 1 like the first ones and c up to me on 6590
11:10 from which *you have* c, 3655
14:29 the widows who live in your towns *may* c 995
17: 8 If cases c before your courts NIH
18:22 the LORD does not take place or c **true,** 995
20: 2 the priest *shall* c **forward** and address 5602
22: 6 *you* **across** a bird's nest beside the road, 4200+7156+7925
23: 4 For *they did* not c to meet you with bread 7709
26: 3 that *I have* c to the land the LORD swore 995
28: 2 All these blessings *will* c upon you 995
28: 2 be blessed when you c in and blessed 995
28: 7 *They will* c at you from one direction 3655
28:15 all these curses *will* c upon you 995
28:15 when you c in and cursed when you go out. 995
28:20 and c to sudden **ruin** because of 6
28:24 *it will* c down from the skies 3718
28:25 *You will* c at them from one direction 3655
28:45 All these curses *will* c upon you. 995
29:22 in later generations and foreigners who c 995
30: 1 before you c upon you and you take them 995
31:17 and difficulties *will* c upon them, 5162
31:17 'Have not these disasters c upon us 5162
31:21 and difficulties c upon them, 5162
31:29 In days to c, disaster will fall upon you 344
Jos 2: 2 the Israelites *have* c here tonight to spy out 995
2: 3 *they have* c to spy out the whole land." 995
2: 4 but I did not know where they *had* c from. NIH
3: 9 "C here and listen to the words of 5602
4:16 the Testimony *to* c up out of the Jordan." 6590
4:17 "C up out of the Jordan. 6590
5:14 of the army of the LORD I *have* now c." 995
7:14 that the LORD takes *shall* c **forward** clan 7928
7:14 the LORD takes *shall* c **forward** family 7928
7:14 that the LORD takes *shall* c **forward** 7928
7:16 next morning Joshua **had** Israel c **forward** 7928
7:17 **had** the clan of the Zerahites c **forward** 7928
7:18 **had** his family c **forward** 7928
8: 5 and when the men c out against us, 3655
9: 6 *"We have* c from a distant country; 995
9: 8 "Who are you and where *do you* c from?" 995
9: 9 "Your servants *have* c from 995
10: 4 at home on the day we left to c to you. 2143
10: 4 "C up and help me attack Gibeon," he said, 6590
10: 6 C up to us quickly and save us! 6590
10:24 said to the army commanders who *had* c 2143
10:24 "C here and put your feet on the necks 7928
10:33 of Gezer *had* c up to help Lachish, 6590
22:19 c **over** to the LORD's land, 6296
22:20 *did* not wrath c upon the whole community 2118
23:15 of the LORD your God *has* c **true,** 995
Jdg 1: 3 "C up with us into the territory allotted 6590
1:34 not allowing them to c **down** into the plain. 3718
4:18 "C, my lord, come right in. 6073
4:18 "Come, my lord, c right in. 6073
4:22 "C," she said, "I will show you 2143
5:23 because *they did* not c to help the LORD, 995
6:18 Please do not go away until I c back 995
7:24 "C **down** against the Midianites and seize 3718
8:21 Zebah and Zalmunna said, "C, 7756
9:10 'C and be our king.' 2143
9:12 trees said to the vine, 'C and be our king.' 2143
9:14 'C and be our king.' 2143
9:15 c and take refuge in my shade; 995
9:15 if not, then *let* fire c out of the thornbush 3655
9:20 *let* fire c out from Abimelech 3655
9:20 and *let* fire c out from you, 3655
9:31 of Ebed and his brothers *have* c to Shechem 995
9:32 and your men *should* c and lie in wait in 7756
9:33 When Gaal and his men c out against you, 3655
11: 6 "C," they said, "be our commander, 2143
11: 7 Why *do you* c to me now, 995
11: 8 c with us to fight the Ammonites, 2143
11:34 *who should* c out to meet him 3655
12: 3 why *have you* c up today to fight me?" 6590
13: 8 *let* the man of God you sent to us c again 995
15:10 "Why *have you* c to fight us?" 6590
15:12 "We *have* c to take Samson prisoner," 6590
15:12 "We've c to tie you up and hand you over to 3718
16:10 C now, tell me how you can be tied." 5528+6964
16:18 "C back once more; 6590
18: 1 c **into** an inheritance among the tribes 928+5877
18: 9 They answered, "C, **on,** let's attack them! 7756
18:19 "C with us, and be our father and priest. 2143
19:13 "C, let's try to reach Gibeah or Ramah 2143
19:17 "Where *did you* c from?" 995
20:41 they realized that disaster *had* c upon them. 5595
21: 8 from Jabesh Gilead *had* c to the camp for 995
21:21 When the girls of Shiloh c out to join in 3655
Ru 1: 6 the LORD *had* c **to the aid** of his people 7212
1:11 Why *would you* c with me? 2143
2:12 under whose wings you *have* c 995
2:14 At mealtime Boaz said to her, "C 5602
4: 1 "C **over** here, my friend, and sit down." 6073
4: 3 "Naomi, who *has* c back from Moab, 8740
1Sa 2:13 the servant of the priest *would* c with 995

1Sa	2:15	the servant of the priest *would* c and say to	995
	2:36	in your family line *will* c and bow down	995
	4: 6	the ark of the LORD *had* c into the camp,	995
	4: 7	"A god *has* c into the camp," they said.	995
	4:16	"I *have just* c from the battle line;	995
	6:21	C down and take it up to your place."	3718
	9: 5	to the servant who was with him, "C,	2143
	9: 9	he would say, "C, let us go to the seer,"	2143
	9:10	"C, let's go."	2143
	9:12	Hurry now; *he has just* c to our town today,	995
	10: 6	c upon you **in power,**	7502
	10: 8	I *will* surely c **down** to you	3718
	10: 8	until I c to you and tell you what you are	995
	10:22	"*Has* the man c here yet?"	995
	11: 9	They told the messengers who *had* c,	995
	11:14	Then Samuel said to the people, "C,	2143
	13: 8	but Samuel *did not* c to Gilgal,	995
	13:11	and that you *did not* c at the set time,	995
	13:12	the Philistines *will* c **down** against me	3718
	14: 1	"C, let's go over to the Philistine outpost	2143
	14: 6	to his young armor-bearer, "C, let's go	2143
	14: 8	Jonathan said, "C, then;	2180
	14: 9	'Wait there until we c to you,'	5595
	14:10	But if they say, 'C up to us,'	6590
	14:12	"C up to us and we'll teach you a lesson."	6590
	14:38	Saul therefore said, "C here,	5602
	15:25	forgive my sin and c **back** with me,	8740
	15:30	c **back** with me, so that I may worship	8740
	16: 2	'*I have* c to sacrifice to the LORD.'	995
	16: 4	They asked, "*Do* you c in peace?"	995
	16: 5	I *have* c to sacrifice to the LORD.	995
	16: 5	Consecrate yourselves and c to the sacrifice	995
	16:23	Then **relief** *would* c to Saul;	8118
	17: 8	"Why *do you* c out and line up for battle?	3655
	17: 8	Choose a man and *have him* c **down** to me.	3718
	17:28	"Why *have you* c **down** here?	3718
	17:43	"Am I a dog, that you c at me with sticks?"	995
	17:44	"C here," he said, "and I'll give your flesh	2143
	17:45	"You c against me with sword and spear	995
	17:45	but I c against you in the name of	995
	20:11	"C," Jonathan said, "let's go out into	2143
	20:21	bring them here,' then c, because,	995
	20:27	"Why hasn't the son of Jesse c to the meal,	995
	20:29	That is why *he has not* c to	995
	21:15	*Must* this man c into my house?"	995
	22: 3	"*Would you let* my father and mother c	3655
	22: 9	"I saw the son of Jesse c to Ahimelech son	995
	23:10	that Saul plans to c to Keilah and destroy	995
	23:11	*Will* Saul c **down,**	3718
	23:15	that Saul *had* c out to take his life.	3655
	23:20	c **down** whenever it pleases you to do so,	3718
	23:23	and c **back** to me with definite information.	8740
	23:27	to Saul, saying, "C quickly!	2143
	24:13	'From evildoers c evil deeds,'	3655
	24:14	the king of Israel c out?	3655
	25: 8	since *we* c at a festive time.	995
	25:34	if *you had* not c quickly to meet me,	995
	26:10	either his time *will* c and he will die,	995
	26:20	The king of Israel *has* c out to look for	3655
	26:21	C **back,** David my son.	8740
	26:22	of your young men c **over** and get it.	6296
	29:10	with your master's servants who *have* c	995
	30:13	and where do you c from?"	NIH
	31: 4	or these uncircumcised fellows *will* c	995
2Sa	1: 3	"Where *have you* c from?"	995
	3:13	*Do not* c into my **presence**	906+7156+8011
	3:13	of Saul when you c to see me."	995
	3:23	that Abner son of Ner *had* c to the king and	995
	5: 3	of Israel *had* c to King David at Hebron,	995
	5:18	Now the Philistines *had* c and spread out in	995
	6: 9	can the ark of the LORD c to me?"	995
	7:12	who *will* c from your own body,	3655
	10: 5	and then c **back.**"	8740
	10:11	then *you are to* c to my rescue;	2118
	10:11	then *I will* c to rescue you.	2143
	11:10	"Haven't you *just* c from a distance?	995
	12: 4	to prepare a meal for the traveler who *had* c	995
	12: 4	and prepared it for the one who *had* c	995
	13: 5	*to* c and give me something to eat.	995
	13: 6	"I would like my sister Tamar *to* c	995
	13:11	"C to bed with me, my sister."	995
	13:23	he invited all the king's sons *to* c there.	NIH
	13:24	"Your servant has had shearers c.	2180
	13:26	please *let* my brother Amnon c with us."	2143
	14:15	"And now *I have* c to say this to my lord	995
	14:29	but Joab refused to c to him.	995
	14:29	he sent a second time, but he refused to c.	995
	14:32	'C here so I can send you to the king	995
	14:32	"Why *have I* c from Geshur?	995
	15: 4	or case *could* c to me and I would see	995
	15:12	David's counselor, to c from Giloh,	NIH
	15:14	with him in Jerusalem, "C!	7756
	15:19	"Why *should you* c along with us?	2143
	16: 8	You have c to ruin because you are a man	NIH
	18:22	again said to Joab, "C what may,	2118+4537
	18:23	He said, "C what may, I want to run."	2118+4537
	19: 7	for you than all the calamities that *have* c	995
	19:15	of Judah *had* c to Gilgal to go out and meet	995
	19:20	but today *I have* c here as the first of	995
	19:20	of the whole house of Joseph to c **down**	3718
	20: 4	"Summon the men of Judah to c to me	NIH
	20:16	Tell Joab *to* c here so I can speak to him."	7928
		and foreigners c **cringing** to me;	3950
		y c **trembling** from their strongholds.	3004
		the LORD *had* c to Gad the prophet,	2118
		ll there c upon you three years	995
		has my lord the king c	995

1Ki	1:14	I *will* c in and confirm what you have said	995
	1:35	and he *is to* c and sit on my throne	995
	1:42	Adonijah said, "C in.	995
	1:47	the royal officials *have* c	995
	2:13	"*Do you* c peacefully?"	995
	2:15	for it *has* c to him from the LORD.	2118
	2:30	"The king says, 'C out!'"	3655
	6: 1	after the Israelites *had* c out of Egypt,	3655
	8:26	let your word that you promised your	
		servant David my father c **true.**	586
	8:37	whatever disaster or disease *may* c,	2118
	8:41	not belong to your people Israel but *has* c	995
	9:24	After Pharaoh's daughter *had* c up from	6590
	12: 5	"Go away for three days and then c **back**	8740
	12:12	"C **back** to me in three days."	8740
	13: 7	"C home with me and have something	995
	13:10	not return by the way *he had* c to Bethel.	995
	13:15	"C home with me and eat."	2143
	13:21	of God who *had* c from Judah, "This is what	995
	13:32	of Samaria *will* **certainly** c **true.**"	2118+2118
	14: 6	he said, "C in, wife of Jeroboam.	995
	17:18	*Did you* c to remind me of my sin	995
	18:30	Elijah said to all the people, "C here to	
		me."	5602
	18:31	to whom the word of the LORD *had* c,	2118
	19:20	he said, "and then *I will* c with you."	2143
	20:18	He said, "If *they have* c out for peace,	3655
	20:18	if *they have* c out for war,	3655
	20:33	Ahab *had* him c up into his chariot.	6590
2Ki	1: 5	he asked them, "Why *have you* c **back?**"	8740
	1: 9	"Man of God, the king says, 'C **down!**'"	3718
	1:10	*may* fire c **down** from heaven	3718
	1:11	'C **down** at once!'"	3718
	1:12	"*may* fire c **down** from heaven	3718
	3:21	the Moabites had heard that the kings *had* c	6590
	5: 8	*Have* the man c to me and he will know	995
	5:11	that he *would* **surely** c out to me and	3655+3655
	5:22	the company of the prophets *have* just c	995
	6: 3	"*Won't* you please c with your servants?"	2143
	7:12	thinking, 'They *will* **surely** c out,	3655
	8: 7	"The man of God *has* c all the way	995
	9:11	Why *did* this madman c to you?"	995
	9:17	'Do you c in peace?'"	8934
	9:18	'Do you c in peace?'"	8934
	9:19	'Do you c in peace?'"	8934
	9:22	"Have you c in peace, Jehu?"	8934
	9:31	she asked, "Have you c in peace, Zimri,	8934
	10: 6	the heads of your master's sons and c to me	995
	10:13	and we have c **down** to greet the families of	3718
	10:16	"C with me and see my zeal for	2143
	10:19	Anyone who **fails** to c will no longer live."	7212
	14: 8	"C, meet me face to face."	2143
	16: 7	C up and save me out of the hand of	6590
	18:23	"'C **now,** make a bargain with my master,	
			5528+6964
	18:25	*have I* c to attack and destroy this place	6590
	18:31	Make peace with me and c out to me.	3655
	18:32	until I c and take you to a land	995
	19: 3	as when children c to the point of birth	995
	19: 7	where you stay and *when* you c and go and	995
	19:31	For out of Jerusalem *will* c a remnant,	3655
	19:32	*He will* not c **before** it with shield or build	7709
	20:14	and where *did they* c from?"	995
	20:17	surely c when everything in your palace,	995
	23:18	of the prophet who *had* c from Samaria.	995
1Ch	9:25	in their villages had to c from time to time	995
	10: 4	or these uncircumcised fellows *will* c	995
	11: 3	of Israel *had* c to King David at Hebron,	995
	12:17	"If *you have* c to me in peace, to help me,	995
	12:17	if you have c to betray me to my enemies	NIH
	12:31	by name to c and make David king—	995
	13: 2	to c **and join** us.	7695
	14: 9	the Philistines *had* c and raided the Valley	995
	16:29	Bring an offering and c before him;	995
	19: 3	Haven't his men c to you to explore	995
	19: 5	and then c **back.**"	8740
	19: 9	the kings who *had* c were by themselves in	995
	23:25	and *has* c to dwell in Jerusalem forever,	8905
2Ch	1: —	Wealth and honor c from you;	NIH
	6:17	you promised your servant David c **true.**	586
	6:28	whatever disaster or disease *may* c,	2118
	6:32	not belong to your people Israel but *has* c	995
	6:41	O LORD God, and c to your resting place,	NIH
	10: 5	"C **back** to me in three days."	8740
	10:12	"C **back** to me in three days."	8740
	14:11	and in your name *we have* c	995
	19:10	for large numbers *had* c **over** to him	5877
	19:10	otherwise his wrath *will* c on you	2118
	21:15	the disease causes your bowels *to* c **out.**'"	3655
	24:11	and the officer of the chief priest *would* c	995
	24:24	Aramean army *had* c with only a few men,	995
	25:10	So Amaziah dismissed the troops who *had* c	995
	25:17	"C, meet me face to face."	2143
	28:17	The Edomites *had* again c	995
	29:31	C and bring sacrifices and thank offerings	5602
	30: 1	inviting them to c to the temple of	995
	30: 5	the people to c to Jerusalem and celebrate	995
	30: 8	C to the sanctuary,	995
	30: 9	by their captors and *will* c **back**	8740
	30:25	including the aliens who *had* c from Israel	995
	32: 2	When Hezekiah saw that Sennacherib *had* c	995
	32: 4	of Assyria c and find plenty of water?"	995
	32:26	the LORD's wrath *did* not c upon them	995
Ezr	10:14	a foreign woman c at a set time,	995
Ne	2:10	that someone *had* c to promote the welfare	995
	2:17	C, let us rebuild the wall of Jerusalem,	2143
	4: 8	to c and fight against Jerusalem and stir	995

Ne	6: 2	"C, let us meet together in one of	2143
	6: 7	so c, let us confer together."	2143
	9:32	the hardship that *has* c upon us,	5162
Est	1:12	Queen Vashti refused to c.	995
	1:17	but *she would* not c."	995
	4:14	that *you have* c to royal position for such	5595
	5: 4	c today to a banquet I have prepared	995
	5: 8	*let* the king and Haman c tomorrow to	995
	6:13	*you will* **surely** c to ruin!"	5877+5877
	9:25	the Jews *should* c **back** onto his own head,	8740
Job	1: 7	"Where *have you* c from?"	995
	2: 2	"Where *have you* c from?"	995
	2:11	about all the troubles that *had* c upon him,	995
	3:21	to those who long for death that does not c,	NIH
	3:25	What I feared *has* c upon me;	910
	5:26	You will c to the grave in full vigor,	995
	7: 6	and *they* c to an end without hope.	3983
	7:10	*He will* never c into his house again;	8740
	9: 4	and c out **unscathed?**	AIT
	10:17	your forces c against me wave upon wave.	NIH
	10:19	If only I *had* never c **into being,**	2118+2118
	13:13	then *let* c to me what may.	6296
	13:16	no godless man *would dare* c before him!	995
	14:14	for my renewal *to* c.	995
	17:10	"But c on, all of you, try again!	995
	20:22	the full force of misery *will* c upon him.	995
	20:25	Terrors *will* c over him;	2143
	21:17	How often *does* calamity c upon them,	995
	21:21	when his allotted months c **to an end?**	2951
	22:21	in this way prosperity *will* c to you.	995
	23:10	I will c **forth** as gold.	3655
	28: 6	sapphires c from its rocks,	NIH
	28:20	"Where then *does* wisdom c from?	995
	30:14	amid the ruins *they* c **rolling in.**	1670
	31:40	then *let* briers c **up** instead of wheat	3655
	33: 3	My words c from an upright heart;	NIH
	34:23	they *should* c before him for judgment.	2143
	34:28	**caused** the cry of the poor **to** c	995
	38:11	'This far *you may* c and no farther;	995
Ps	5: 7	*will* c **into** your house;	995
	14: 7	that salvation for Israel *would* c out	NIH
	17: 2	*May* my vindication c from you;	3655
	18:45	they c **trembling** from their strongholds.	3004
	22:19	O my Strength, c **quickly** to help me.	2590
	24: 7	that the King of glory *may* c **in.**	995
	24: 9	that the King of glory *may* c **in.**	995
	31: 2	c quickly to my **rescue;**	5911
	32: 9	by bit and bridle or they *will* not c to you.	7928
	34:11	C, my children, listen to me;	2143
	35: 2	**arise and** c to my aid.	7756
	35:11	Ruthless witnesses c **forward;**	7756
	36:11	*May* the foot of the proud not c *against* me,	995
	38: 2	and your hand *has* c **down** upon me.	5737
	38:22	C **quickly** to help me, O Lord my Savior.	2590
	40: 7	Then I said, "Here I am, *I have* c—	995
	40:13	O LORD, c **quickly** to help me.	2590
	45:12	The Daughter of Tyre will c with a gift,	NIH
	46: 8	C and see the works of the LORD,	2143
	49: 5	Why should I fear when evil days c,	NIH
	53: 6	salvation for Israel *would* c out of Zion!	NIH
	65: 2	to you all men *will* c.	995
	66: 5	C and see what God has done,	2143
	66: 6	c, *let us* **rejoice** in him.	AIT
	66:13	I *will* c to your temple	995
	66:16	C and listen, all you who fear God;	2143
	68:17	Lord [has c] from Sinai into his sanctuary.	NIH
	68:24	Your procession *has* c **into view,** O God,	8011
	68:31	Envoys *will* c from Egypt;	910
	69: 1	for the waters *have* c up to my neck.	995
	69: 2	*I have* c into the deep waters;	995
	69:18	C **near** and rescue me;	7928
	70: 1	O LORD, c **quickly** to help me.	2590
	70: 5	c **quickly** to me, O God.	2590
	71:12	c **quickly,** O my God, to help me.	2590
	71:16	I *will* c and proclaim your mighty acts,	995
	71:18	your might to all *who are to* c,	995
	78:28	He **made** them c **down** inside their camp,	5877
	79: 8	*may* your mercy c quickly **to meet** us,	7709
	79:11	the groans of the prisoners c before you;	995
	80: 2	Awaken your might; c and save us.	2143
	83: 4	"C," they say, "let us destroy them as	2143
	86: 9	All the nations you have made *will* c	995
	88: 2	*May* my prayer c before you;	995
	91: 7	but it *will* not c **near** you.	5602
	91:10	no disaster *will* c **near** your tent.	7928
	95: 1	C, *let us* sing for joy to the LORD;	2143
	95: 2	*Let us* c before him with thanksgiving	7709
	95: 6	C, let us bow down in worship,	995
	96: 8	bring an offering and c into his courts.	995
	100: 2	c before him with joyful songs.	995
	101: 2	when *will you* c to me?	995
	102: 1	*let* my cry for help c to you.	995
	102:13	the appointed time *has* c.	995
	106: 4	c to my **aid** when you save them,	7212
	106:31	for endless **generations to** c.	1887+1887+2256
	109:19	*may* it c on him;	995
	112: 5	Good will c to him who is generous	NIH
	112:10	longings of the wicked *will* c **to nothing.**	6
	119:13	With my lips I recount all the **laws** *that* c	AIT
	119:41	*May* your unfailing love c *to* me,	995
	119:77	*Let* your compassion c *to* me	995
	119:143	Trouble and distress *have* c **upon** me,	5162
	119:169	*May* my cry c before you, O LORD;	7928
	119:170	*May* my supplication c before you;	995
	121: 1	where *does* my help c from?	995
	132: 8	O LORD, and c to your resting place,	NIH
	141: 1	O LORD, I call to you; c **quickly** to me.	2590

Ref	Text	Num
Ps 143: 1	and righteousness c to my **relief.**	6699
144: 5	Part your heavens, O LORD, and c **down;**	3718
146: 4	on that very day their plans c to **nothing.**	6
Pr 1:11	If they say, "C along with us;	2143
2: 6	and from his mouth c knowledge	NIH
3:28	Do not say to your neighbor, "C back later;	2143
5:14	I have c to the brink of utter ruin in	2118
6:11	and poverty will c on you like a bandit	995
7:18	C, let's drink deep of love till morning;	2143
9: 4	"Let all who are simple c in here!"	6073
9: 5	"C, eat my food and drink	2143
9:16	"Let all who are simple c in here!"	6073
10:28	but the hopes of the wicked c to **nothing.**	6
13: 3	but he who speaks rashly will c to ruin.	NIH
18:24	A man of many companions may c to ruin,	8318
22:16	both c to poverty.	NIH
24:25	and rich blessing will c upon them.	995
24:31	thorns had c up everywhere,	6590
24:34	and poverty will c on you like a bandit	995
25: 7	"C up here," than for him to humiliate you	6590
26: 2	an undeserved curse does not c to rest.	995
30: 4	Who has gone up to heaven and c **down?**	3718
31:25	she can laugh at the days **to c.**	340
Ecc 1: 4	Generations c and generations go,	2143
1: 7	To the place the streams c from,	2143
1:11	and even those who are yet to c will not	340
2: 1	I thought in my heart, "C now,	2143
2:16	in days to c both will be forgotten.	995
3:20	all c from dust, and to dust all return.	2118
4:14	The youth may have c from prison to	3655
8: 5	Whoever obeys his command will c to	3359
8: 7	who can tell him what is to c?	2118
8:10	those who used to c and go from	2143
9:11	or the battle to the strong, nor does food c	NIH
9:12	no man knows when his hour will c:	NIH
11: 2	for you do not know what disaster may c	2118
11: 8	Everything to c is meaningless.	995
12: 1	of trouble c and the years approach	995
SS 2:10	my beautiful one, and c with me.	2143
2:12	the season of singing has c,	5595
2:13	Arise, c, my darling;	2143
2:13	my beautiful one, c with me."	2143
3:11	C out, you daughters of Zion,	3655
4: 8	C with me from Lebanon, my bride,	NIH
4: 8	my bride, c with me from Lebanon.	995
4:16	Awake, north wind, and c, south wind!	995
4:16	Let my lover c into his garden	995
5: 1	I have c into my garden, my sister,	995
6:13	C back, come back, O Shulammite;	8740
6:13	Come back, c back, O Shulammite;	8740
6:13	c back, that we may gaze	8740
6:13	c back, that we may gaze on you!	8740
7:11	C, my lover, let us go to the countryside,	2143
8:14	C away, my lover, and be like a gazelle or	1368
Isa 1:12	When you c to appear before me,	995
1:18	"C now, let us reason together,"	2143
1:23	the widow's case does not c before them.	995
2: 3	Many peoples will c and say, "Come,	2143
2: 3	Many peoples will come and say, "C,	2143
2: 5	C, O house of Jacob,	2143
5:19	let the plan of the Holy One of Israel c,	995
5:26	Here they c, swiftly and speedily!	995
7:19	They will all c and settle in	995
11: 1	A shoot will c up from the stump of Jesse;	3655
13: 5	They c from faraway lands,	995
13: 6	it will c like destruction from	995
14: 4	How the oppressor has c to an end!	8697
16: 4	The oppressor will c to an end,	699
21:12	and c back yet again."	910
21:16	all the pomp of Kedar will c to an end.	3983
23: 1	the land of Cyprus word has c to then..	1655
26: 9	When your judgments c on the earth,	NIH
27: 5	Or else let them c to me for refuge;	2616
27: 6	In days to c Jacob will take root,	995
27:11	and women c and make fires with them.	995
27:13	and those who were exiled in Egypt will c	995
29: 4	Your voice will c ghostlike from	2118
29: 6	the LORD Almighty will c with thunder	7212
29:13	"These people c near to me	5602
30: 8	days to c it may be an everlasting witness.	340
31: 4	so the LORD Almighty will c down	3718
32:10	and the harvest of fruit will not c.	995
34: 1	C near, you nations, and listen;	NIH
35: 4	your God, he will come	NIH
35: 4	he will c with vengeance;	995
35: 4	with divine retribution he will c	995
36: 8	" "C now, make a bargain with my master,	5528+6964
36:10	have I c to attack and destroy this land	6590
36:16	Make peace with me and c out to me.	3655
36:17	until I c and take you to a land	995
37: 3	as when children c to the point of birth	995
37:28	"But I know where you stay and when you c	995
37:32	For out of Jerusalem will c a remnant,	3655
37:33	He will not c before it with shield or build	7709
38:14	I am troubled; O Lord, c to my **aid!"**	6842
39: 3	and where did they c from?	995
39: 6	surely c when everything in your palace,	995
41: 1	Let them c forward and speak;	5602
41: 5	They approach and c forward;	910
41:22	Or declare to us the things to c,	995
42:23	to this or pay close attention in time to c?	294
44: 7	and what is yet to c—	910
44: 7	yes, let him foretell what will c.	995
44:11	Let them all c together	7695
45:11	Concerning things to c,	910
45:14	they will c over to you and will be yours;	6296
Isa 45:20	"Gather together and c;	995
45:24	All who have raged against him will c	995
46:10	from ancient times, what is still to c.	4202+6913
47: 9	They will c upon you in full measure,	995
47:11	Disaster will c upon you,	995
47:11	a catastrophe you cannot foresee will c suddenly c upon you.	995
47:13	Let your astrologers c forward,	6641
48: 1	by the name of Israel and c from the line	3655
48:14	"C together, all of you, and listen:	7695
48:16	"C near me and listen to this:	7928
49: 9	'C out,' and to those in darkness,	3655
49:12	See, they will c from afar—	995
49:18	all your sons gather and c to you.	995
49:21	where have they c from?' "	NIH
51:19	These double calamities have c upon you—	7925
52:11	C out from it and be pure,	3655
54:14	it will not c near you.	7928
55: 1	"C, all you who are thirsty,	2098
55: 1	all you who are thirsty, c to the waters;	2143
55: 1	you who have no money, c, buy and eat!	2143
55: 1	C, buy wine and milk without money and	2143
55: 3	Give ear and c to me;	2143
55:10	the rain and the snow c down from heaven,	3718
56: 9	C, all you beasts of the field,	910
56: 9	c and devour, all you beasts of the forest!	NIH
56:12	"C," each one cries, "let me get wine!	910
57: 3	"But you—c here, you sons of a sorceress,	7928
58: 2	and seem eager for God to c near them.	7932
59:19	For he will c like a pent-up flood that	995
59:20	"The Redeemer will c to Zion,	995
60: 1	"Arise, shine, for your light has c,	995
60: 3	Nations will c to your light,	2143
60: 4	All assemble and c to you;	995
60: 4	your sons c from afar,	995
60: 5	to you the riches of the nations will c.	995
60: 6	And all from Sheba will c,	995
60:13	"The glory of Lebanon will c to you,	995
60:14	The sons of your oppressors will c bowing	2143
61:11	**makes** the sprout c up	3655
63: 4	and the year of my redemption has c.	995
64: 1	you would rend the heavens and c down,	3718
64: 2	c down to make your name known	NIH
64: 5	You c to the **help of**	7003
65: 5	don't c near me,	5602
65:17	nor will they c to mind.	6590
66: 7	before the pains c upon her,	995
66:18	to c and gather all nations and tongues,	995
66:18	and they will c and see my glory.	995
66:23	all mankind will c and bow down	995
Jer 1:15	"Their kings will c and set	995
1:15	they will c against all her surrounding walls	NIH
2:27	they say, 'C and save us!'	7756
2:28	Let them c if they can save you	7756
2:31	we will c to you no more'?	995
3:18	and together they will c from	995
3:22	"Yes, we will c to you,	910
4: 7	A lion has c out of his lair;	6590
4:13	his chariots c like a whirlwind,	NIH
5:12	No harm will c to us;	995
6: 3	with their flocks will c against her;	995
6:23	they c like men in battle formation	NIH
6:26	for suddenly the destroyer will c upon us.	995
7: 2	the LORD, all you people of Judah who c	995
7:10	then c and stand before me in this house,	995
8:15	We hoped for peace but no good has c,	NIH
8:16	They have c to devour the land	995
9:17	Call for the wailing women to c;	995
9:18	Let them c quickly and wail over us	4554
13:18	"C down from your thrones,	9164
14:19	We hoped for peace but no good has c,	NIH
16:19	to you the nations will c from the ends of	995
17:20	in Jerusalem who c through these gates.	995
17:25	on David's throne will c through the gates	995
17:25	and their officials will c riding in chariots	NIH
17:26	People will c from the towns of Judah	995
17:27	as you c through the gates of Jerusalem on	995
18:18	"C, let's make plans against Jeremiah;	2143
18:18	So c, let's attack him with our tongues	2143
20:18	Why did I ever c out of the womb	3655
21:13	you who say, "Who can c against us?	5737
22: 2	and your people who c through these gates.	995
22: 4	on David's throne will c through the gates	995
22:23	you will groan when pangs c upon you,	995
22:27	You will never c back to the land you long	8740
23:17	'No harm will c to you.'	995
23:20	In days to c you will understand it clearly.	344
25: 3	the LORD has c to me and I have spoken	2118
25:34	For your time to be slaughtered has c;	4848
26: 2	of the towns of Judah who c to worship in	995
27: 3	and Sidon through the envoys who have c	995
27:22	and there they will remain until the day I c	7212
29:10	for Babylon, I will c to you	7212
29:12	Then you will call upon me and c and pray	2143
30:19	From them will c songs of thanksgiving	3655
30:21	I will bring him near and he will c **close**	5602
30:24	In days to c you will understand this.	344
31: 2	I will c to give rest to Israel."	2143
31: 6	'C, let us go up to Zion,	7756
31: 9	They will c with weeping,	995
31:12	They will c and shout for joy on	995
32: 7	of Shallum your uncle is going to c to you	995
32:29	The Babylonians who are attacking this city will c	995
33:20	the night, so that day and night no longer c	2118
35: 2	to the Recabite family and invite them to c	995
35:11	of Babylon invaded this land, we said, 'C,	995
Jer 36: 6	of Judah who c in from their towns.	995
36: 9	the people in Jerusalem and those who had c	995
36:14	to the people and c."	2143
36:17	"Tell us, how did you c to write all this?	AIT
36:29	the king of Babylon would **certainly** c	995+995
37: 4	Now Jeremiah was free to c and go among	995
37:10	they would c out and burn this city down."	7756
38:25	and they c to you and say,	995
38:27	All the officials c to Jeremiah	995
40: 4	C with me to Babylon, if you like,	995
40: 4	but if you do not want to, then don't c.	995
40:10	before the Babylonians who c to us,	995
41: 6	he said, "C to Gedaliah son of Ahikam."	995
43: 5	remnant of Judah who had c **back** to live	8740
43:11	He will c and attack Egypt,	995
44: 8	where you have c to live?	995
44:23	this disaster has c upon you,	7925
46:18	"one who c who is like Tabor among	995
46:22	they will c against her with axes,	995
47: 4	the day has c to destroy all the Philistines	995
48: 2	'C, let us put an end to that nation.'	2143
48: 8	The destroyer will c against every town,	995
48:16	her calamity will c quickly.	4394+4554
48:18	"C down from your glory and sit on	3718
48:18	for he who destroys Moab will c up	6590
48:21	Judgment has c to the plateau—	995
48:47	the fortunes of Moab in days to c,"	344
49:39	the fortunes of Elam in days to c,"	344
50: 5	They will c and bind themselves to	995
50:26	C against her from afar.	995
50:27	For their day has c,	995
50:31	the LORD Almighty, "for your day has c,	995
50:42	they c like men in battle formation	NIH
51:10	" 'The LORD has vindicated us; c,	995
51:13	your end has c,	995
51:33	the time to harvest her will soon c."	995
51:45	"C out of her, my people!	3655
51:47	the time will surely c when I will punish	995
51:56	A destroyer will c against Babylon;	995
51:60	the disasters that would c upon Babylon—	995
La 1:14	They have c upon my neck and	6590
1:22	"Let all their wickedness c before you;	995
3:38	that both calamities and good things c?	3655
4:18	our days were numbered, for our end had c.	995
Eze 5: 2	When the days of your siege c to an end,	4848
7: 2	end has c upon the four corners of the land.	995
7: 6	The end has c!	995
7: 6	The end has c!	995
7: 6	It has roused itself against you. It has c!	995
7: 7	Doom has c upon you—	995
7: 7	The time has c, the day is near;	995
7:10	"The day is here! It has c!	995
7:12	The time has c, the day has arrived.	995
7:26	Calamity upon calamity will c,	995
13:11	Rain will c in torrents,	2118
14:22	They will c to you,	3655
15: 7	although they have c out of the fire,	3655
16:33	bribing them to c to you from everywhere	995
20: 3	Have you c to inquire of me?	995
21:13	" '**Testing** will surely c.	AIT
21:20	to c against Rabbah of the Ammonites	995
21:22	Into his right hand will c the lot	2118
21:25	wicked prince of Israel, whose day has c,	995
21:29	are to be slain, whose day has c,	995
22: 4	and the end of your years has c.	995
23:24	They will c against you with weapons,	995
24:14	The time has c for me to act.	995
24:26	on that day a fugitive will c to tell you	995
27:36	you have c to a horrible end and will	2118
28:18	made a fire c out, and it consumed you,	3655
28:19	you have c to a horrible end and will	2118
30: 4	A sword will c against Egypt,	995
30: 4	and anguish will c upon Cush.	2118
30: 9	for it is sure to c.	995
30:18	there her proud strength will c to an end.	8697
32:11	of the king of Babylon will c against you.	995
32:21	'They have c down and they lie with	3718
33:28	and her proud strength will c to an end,	8697
33:30	'C and hear the message that has come	995
33:30	the message that has c from the LORD.'	3655
33:31	My people c to you, as they usually do,	995
35: 7	and cut off from it all who c and go.	6296
36: 8	for they will soon c **home.**	995
37: 5	and you will c to life.	2649
37: 6	I will attach tendons to you and **make** flesh c upon you	6590
37: 6	and you will c to life.	2649
37: 9	C from the four winds, O breath,	995
38:10	that day thoughts will c into your mind	6590
38:13	"Have you c to plunder?	995
38:15	You will c from your place in	995
38:16	In days to c, O Gog,	344
39:17	'Assemble and c together from all around	995
43:19	who c near to minister before me,	7940
44:13	to c near to serve me as priests or come	5602
44:13	as priests or c near any of my holy things	5602
44:15	are to c near to minister before me;	7928
44:16	to c near my table to minister before me	7928
46: 8	and he is to c out the same way.	3655
46: 9	the people of the land c before the LORD	995
46: 9	from the city who farm it will c from all	NIH
Da 2:28	in days to c,	10022
2:29	O king, your mind turned to things to c,	10021+10180+10201
3: 2	and all the other provincial officials to c to	10085
3:26	servants of the Most High God, c out!	10485
3:26	of the Most High God, come out! C here!	10085

Da	7:24	The ten horns are ten kings *who will* **c**	10624
	9:13	all this disaster *has* **c** upon us,	995
	9:22	*I have* now **c** to give you insight	3655
	9:23	which *I have* **c** to tell you,	995
	9:26	the ruler who *will* **c** will destroy the city	995
	9:26	The end will **c** like a flood:	NIH
	10:12	and I *have* **c** in response to them.	995
	10:14	Now *I have* **c** to explain	995
	10:14	for the vision concerns a time *yet to* **c**."	6388
	10:20	"Do you know why *I have* **c** to you?	995
	10:20	the prince of Greece *will* **c**;	995
	11:15	the North *will* **c** and build up siege ramps	995
	11:17	to **c** with the might of his entire kingdom	995
	11:27	an end will still **c** at the appointed time.	NIH
	11:35	for it will still **c** at the appointed time.	NIH
	11:45	Yet *he will* **c** to his end,	995
Hos	1:11	and *will* **c** **up** out of the land,	6590
	3: 5	*They will* **c trembling** to the LORD and	7064
	4:14	without understanding *will* **c to ruin!**	4231
	6: 1	"**C**, let us return to the LORD.	2143
	6: 3	he will **c** to us like the winter rains,	995
	9: 4	not **c into** the temple of the LORD.	995
	11: 9	*I will* not **c** in wrath.	995
	11:10	his children *will* **c trembling** from	3006
	11:11	*They will* **c trembling** like birds	3006
	13: 7	So *I will* **c** upon them like a lion,	2118
	13:13	Pains as of a woman in childbirth **c** to him,	995
	13:13	he *does* not **c** to the opening of the womb.	6641
	13:15	An east wind from the LORD *will* **c**,	995
Joel	1:13	**C**, spend the night in sackcloth,	995
	1:15	it will **c** like destruction from	995
	2: 2	nor ever will be in ages *to* **c**.	1887+1887+2256
	3:11	**C** quickly, all you nations from every side,	995
	3:13	**C**, trample the grapes,	995
Am	4: 2	"The time *will* surely **c** when you will	995
	6: 1	to whom the people of Israel **c!**	995
Jnh	1: 2	its wickedness *has* **c up** before me."	6590
	1: 7	Then the sailors said to each other, "**C**,	2143
	1: 8	Where *do you* **c** from?	995
	1:12	that it is my fault that this great storm *has*	NIH
	1:12	her wound is incurable; *it has* **c** to Judah.	995
Mic	1:11	Those who live in Zaanan *will* not **c out**.	3655
	1:12	because disaster *has* **c** from the LORD,	3718
	1:15	the glory of Israel *will* **c** to Adullam.	995
	3: 6	Therefore night will **c** over you,	NIH
	3:11	No disaster *will* **c** upon us."	995
	4: 2	Many nations *will* **c** and say, "Come,	2143
	4: 2	Many nations will **c** and say, "**C**,	2143
	4: 8	kingship *will* **c** to the Daughter	995
	5: 2	of you *will* **c** for me one who will be ruler	3655
	6: 6	With what shall *I* **c before** the LORD	7709
	6: 6	Shall *I* **c before** him with burnt offerings,	7709
	7: 4	The day of your watchmen *has* **c**,	995
	7:11	The day for building your walls will **c**,	NIH
	7:12	that day *people will* **c** to you from Assyria	995
	7:17	*They will* **c trembling** out of their dens;	8074
Na	1: 9	trouble *will* not **c** a second time.	7756
	1:11	*has* one **c forth** who plots evil against	3655
Hab	1: 8	their horsemen **c** from afar.	995
	1: 9	they all **c** bent on violence.	995
	2: 3	it will **certainly c** and will not delay.	995+995
	2:19	to him who says to wood, '**C to life!**'	7810
	3:16	of calamity to **c** on the nation invading us.	6590
Zep	3: 7	nor all *my* **punishments c** upon her.	7212
Hag	1: 2	*yet* **c** for the LORD's house to be built.' "	995
	2: 7	and the desired of all nations *will* **c**,	995
Zec	1:21	but the craftsmen *have* **c** to terrify them	995
	2: 6	"**C!** Come! Flee from the	2098
	2: 6	**C!** Flee from the land of the	2098
	2: 7	"**C**, O Zion!	2098
	3: 8	men **symbolic of things to c:**	4603
	6:15	Those who are far away *will* **c** and help	995
	7:14	behind them that no *one could* **c** or go.	8740
	8:20	the inhabitants of many cities *will* yet **c**,	995
	8:22	and powerful nations *will* **c** to Jerusalem	995
	10: 4	From Judah *will* **c** the cornerstone,	3655
	14: 5	Then the LORD my God *will* **c**,	995
	14:21	and all who **c** to sacrifice will take some of	995
Mal	3: 1	the Lord you are seeking *will* **c**	995
	3: 1	*will* **c**," says the LORD Almighty.	995
	3: 5	"So *I will* **c near** to you for judgment.	7928
	4: 6	or else *I will* **c** and strike the land with	995
Mt	2: 2	in the east and *have* **c** to worship him."	2262
	2: 6	*out of* you *will* **c** a ruler	2002
	3:11	me *will* **c** one who is more powerful than I,	2262
	3:14	and *do you* **c** to me?"	2262
	4:19	"**C**, follow me," Jesus said,	1307
	5:17	not think that *I have* **c** to abolish the Law	2262
	5:17	not to abolish them but to fulfill them.	2262
	5:24	then **c** and offer your gift.	2262
	6:10	your kingdom **c**, your will be done on earth	2262
	7:15	They **c** to you in sheep's clothing,	2262
	8: 8	not deserve to have *you* **c** under my roof.	1656
	8: 9	and that one, '**C**,' and he comes.	2262
	8:11	I say to you that many *will* **c** from the east	2457
	8:29	"*Have you* **c** here to torture us before	2262
	9:13	For *I have* not **c** to call the righteous,	2262
	9:15	The time *will* **c** when the bridegroom will	2262
	9:18	But **c** and put your hand on her,	2262
	10:34	not suppose that *I have* **c** to bring peace to	2262
	10:34	*I did* not **c** to bring peace, but a sword.	2262
	10:35	*I have* **c** to turn " 'a man against his father,	2262
	11: 3	"Are you the one who *was* to **c**,	2262
	11:14	he is the Elijah who *was* **to c**.	2262+3516
		"**C** to me, all *you* who are weary	1307
		hen the kingdom of God *has* **c** upon you.	5777
		ther in this age or in the age *to* **c**.	3516

Mt	13:27	Where then did the weeds **c** from?'	2400
	13:32	birds of the air **c** and perch in its branches."	2262
	13:49	The angels *will* **c** and separate the wicked	2002
	14:28	tell me *to* **c** to you on the water."	2262
	14:29	"**C**," he said.	2262
	15:18	the things that **c out** of the mouth come	1744
	15:18	that come out of the mouth **c from**	2002
	15:19	**out of** the heart **c**	2002
	16:24	"*If anyone would* **c** after me,	2262
	16:27	of Man is going to **c** in his Father's glory	2262
	17:10	of the law say that Elijah must **c** first?"	2262
	17:12	But I tell you, Elijah *has* already **c**,	2262
	18: 7	Such things must **c**,	2262
	18: 7	but woe to the man through whom they **c!**	2262
	18:20	two or three **c together** in my name,	1639+5251
	19:14	Jesus said, "Let the little children **c** to me,	2262
	19:21	Then **c**, follow me."	1306
	20:28	as the Son of Man *did* not **c** to be served,	2262
	21:25	John's baptism—where did it **c**	NIG
	21:38	**C**, let's kill him and take his inheritance.'	1307
	22: 3	to the banquet to tell them to **c**,	NIG
	22: 3	but they refused *to* **c**.	2262
	22: 4	**C** to the wedding banquet.'	1307
	22: 8	but those *I* invited did not deserve to **c**.	NIG
	23:35	so upon you *will* **c** all the righteous blood	2262
	23:36	all this *will* **c** upon this generation.	2457
	24: 5	For many *will* **c** in my name, claiming,	2262
	24: 6	but the end is **still to c**.	4037
	24:14	and then the end *will* **c**.	2457
	24:32	as its twigs get tender and its leaves **c out**,	1770
	24:42	not know on what day your Lord *will* **c**.	2262
	24:44	because the Son of Man *will* **c** at an hour	2262
	24:50	The master of that servant *will* **c** on a day	2457
	25: 6	**C out** to meet him!'	2002
	25:21	**C** and share your master's happiness!'	1656
	25:23	**C** and share your master's happiness!'	1656
	25:34	the King will say to those on his right, '**C**,	1307
	26:55	that *you have* **c out** with swords and clubs	2002
	27:40	**C down** from the cross,	2849
	27:42	*Let him* **c down** now from the cross,	2849
	27:64	his disciples *may* **c** and steal the body	2262
	28: 6	**C** and see the place where he lay.	1307
Mk	1: 7	"After me *will* **c** one more powerful than I,	2262
	1:15	"The time *has* **c**," he said.	4444
	1:17	"**C**, follow me," Jesus said,	1307
	1:24	*Have you* **c** to destroy us?	2262
	1:25	"**C out** of him!"	2002
	1:38	That is why I *have* **c**."	2002
	2: 1	the people heard that *he had* **c** home.	1639
	2:17	*I have* not **c** to call the righteous,	2262
	2:20	the time *will* **c** when the bridegroom will	2262
	3:26	his end has **c**.	NIG
	4:19	the desires for other things **c in** and choke	1656
	4:29	because the harvest *has* **c**."	4225
	5: 8	Jesus had said to him, "**C out** of this man,	2002
	5:23	Please **c** and put your hands on her so	2262
	6:31	"**C** with me by yourselves to a quiet place	1307
	7: 1	the law who had **c** from Jerusalem gathered	2262
	7: 4	When *they* **c** from the marketplace they do	2262
	7:21	*out* of men's hearts, **c** evil thoughts,	1744
	7:23	All these evils **c** from inside and make	1744
	8: 3	some of them *have* **c** a long distance."	2457
	8:34	"*If anyone would* **c** after me,	199
	9: 1	before they see the kingdom of God **c**	2262
	9:11	of the law say that Elijah must **c** first?"	2262
	9:12	Elijah *does* **c** first, and restores all things.	2262
	9:13	But I tell you, Elijah *has* **c**,	2262
	9:25	**c out** of him and never enter him again."	2002
	9:29	"This kind can **c out** only by prayer."	2002
	10:14	"Let the little children **c** to me,	2262
	10:21	Then **c**, follow me."	1306
	10:30	persecutions) and in the age *to* **c**,	2262
	10:45	even the Son of Man *did* not **c** to be served,	2262
	12: 7	**C**, let's kill him, and the inheritance will	1307
	12: 9	*He will* **c** and kill those tenants and give	2262
	13: 6	Many *will* **c** in my name, claiming,	2262
	13: 7	but the end is **still to c**.	4037
	13:28	as its twigs get tender and its leaves **c out**,	1770
	13:33	You do not know when that time *will* **c**.	1639
	13:35	when the owner of the house *will* **c back—**	2262
	14:41	The hour *has* **c**.	2262
	14:48	"that *you have* **c out** with swords and clubs	2002
	15:30	**c down** from the cross and save yourself!"	2849
	15:32	**c down** now from the cross,	2849
	15:41	Many other women who *had* **c up** with him	5262
Lk	1:20	which *will* **c true** at their proper time."	4444
	1:35	"The Holy Spirit *will* **c upon** you,	2088
	1:43	the mother of my Lord *should* **c** to me?	2262
	1:68	he *has* **c** and has redeemed his people.	2170
	1:78	the rising sun *will* **c** to us from heaven	2170
	3:16	But one more powerful than I *will* **c**,	2262
	4:34	*Have you* **c** to destroy us?	2262
	4:35	"**C out** of him!"	2002
	4:36	to evil spirits and *they* **c out!"**	2002
	5: 7	in the other boat to **c** and help them,	2262
	5:17	who had **c** from every village of Galilee	2262
	5:32	*I have* not **c** to call the righteous,	2262
	5:35	the time *will* **c** when the bridegroom will	2262
	6:18	who *had* **c** to hear him and to be healed	2262
	7: 3	asking him to **c** and heal his servant.	2262
	7: 6	not deserve to have *you* **c** under my roof.	1656
	7: 7	even consider myself worthy *to* **c** to you.	2262
	7: 8	and that one, '**C**,' and he comes.	2262
	7:16	"God *has* **c to help** his people."	2170
	7:19	"Are you the one who *was* to **c**,	2262
	7:20	'Are you the one who *was* to **c**,	2262
	8: 2	from whom seven demons had **c out;**	2002

Lk	8:16	so that those who **c in** can see the light.	1660
	8:29	the evil spirit *to* **c out** of the man.	2002
	8:41	pleading with him *to* **c** to his house	1656
	9: 8	the prophets of long ago *had* **c back to life**.	482
	9:19	of long ago *has* **c back to life**."	482
	9:23	"*If anyone would* **c** after me,	2262
	11: 2	hallowed be your name, your kingdom **c**.	2262
	11: 6	a friend of mine on a journey *has* **c** to me,	4134
	11:20	then the kingdom of God *has* **c** to you.	5777
	11:33	so that those who **c in** may see the light.	1660
	12:37	at the table and *will* **c** and wait on them.	4216
	12:40	because the Son of Man *will* **c** at an hour	2262
	12:46	The master of that servant *will* **c** on a day	2457
	12:49	"*I have* **c** to bring fire on the earth,	2262
	13:14	So **c** and be healed on those days,	2262
	13:25	'I don't know you or where *you* **c** from.'	1639
	13:27	'I don't know you or where *you* **c** from.	1639
	13:29	*People will* **c** from east and west	2457
	14: 9	the host who invited both of you *will* **c**	2262
	14:17	'**C**, for everything is now ready.'	2262
	14:20	'I just got married, so I can't **c**.'	2262
	14:23	and country lanes and make them **c in**,	1656
	15:27	'Your brother *has* **c**,' he replied,	2457
	16:28	so that they *will* not also **c** to this place	2262
	17: 1	"Things that cause people to sin are **bound** **to c**,	450+2262+3590
	17: 1	woe to that person through whom *they* **c**.	2262
	17: 7	'**C along** now and sit down to eat'?	4216
	17:20	when the kingdom of God *would* **c**,	2262
	17:20	not **c** with your careful observation,	2262
	18:16	"Let the little children **c** to me,	2262
	18:22	Then **c**, follow me."	1306
	18:30	in the age *to* **c**, eternal life."	2262
	19: 5	"Zacchaeus, **c down** immediately.	2849
	19: 9	"Today salvation *has* **c** to this house,	1181
	19:13	he said, 'until *I* **c back**.'	2262
	19:43	The days *will* **c** upon you	2457
	20:16	*He will* **c** and kill those tenants and give	2262
	21: 6	the time *will* **c** when not one stone will	2262
	21: 8	For many *will* **c** in my name, claiming,	2262
	21: 9	but the end will not **c** right away."	NIG
	21:35	For *it will* **c upon** all those who live on	2082
	22:52	and the elders, who *had* **c** for him,	4134
	22:52	that *you have* **c** with swords and clubs?	2002
	23: 5	in Galilee and *has* **c** all the way here."	NIG
	23:29	For the time *will* **c** when you will say,	2262
	23:42	when *you* **c** into your kingdom."	2262
	23:55	The women who *had* **c with** Jesus	5302
Jn	1:32	the Spirit **c down** from heaven as a dove	2849
	1:33	on whom you see the Spirit **c down**	2849
	1:39	"**C**," he replied, "and you will see."	2262
	1:46	Can anything good **c** from there?"	1639
	1:46	"**C and see**," said Philip.	2262
	2: 4	"My time *has* not yet **c**."	2457
	2: 9	He did not realize where *it had* **c** from,	1639
	3: 2	we know *you* are a teacher who *has* **c**	2262
	3:19	Light *has* **c** into the world,	2262
	3:20	and *will* not **c** into the light for fear	2262
	4:16	"Go, call your husband and **c back**."	2262
	4:23	Yet a time *is* coming and *has* now **c** when	1639
	4:29	"**C**, see a man who told me everything I ever did.	1307
	4:47	and begged him *to* **c** and heal his son,	2849
	4:49	"Sir, **c down** before my child dies."	2849
	4:54	having **c** from Judea to Galilee.	2262
	5:25	now **c** when the dead will hear the voice of	1639
	5:29	and **c out**—those who have done good will rise to live,	1744
	5:40	yet you refuse *to* **c** to me to have life.	2262
	5:43	*I have* **c** in my Father's name,	2262
	6:14	"Surely this is the Prophet who *is to* **c** into	2262
	6:15	that they intended *to* **c** and make him king	2262
	6:37	All that the Father gives me *will* **c** to me,	2457
	6:38	For *I have* **c down** from heaven not	2849
	6:44	"No one can **c** to me unless	2262
	6:65	"This is why I told you that no one can **c**	2262
	7: 6	"The right time for me *has* not yet **c**;	4205
	7: 8	because for me the right time *has* not yet **c**."	4444
	7:22	(though actually *it did* not **c** from Moses,	1639
	7:30	because his time *had* not yet **c**.	2262
	7:34	and where I am, you cannot **c**."	2262
	7:36	and 'Where I am, you cannot **c'**?"	2262
	7:37	*let him* **c** to me and drink.	2262
	7:41	"How *can* the Christ **c** from Galilee?	2262
	7:42	not the Scripture say that the Christ *will* **c**	2262
	7:52	that a prophet *does* not **c** out of Galilee."	1586
	8:14	But you have no idea where *I* **c** from or	2262
	8:20	because his time *had* not yet **c**.	2262
	8:21	Where I go, you cannot **c**."	2262
	8:22	'Where I go, you cannot **c'**?"	2262
	8:42	*I have* not **c** on my own; but he sent me.	2262
	9:39	"For judgment *I have* **c** into this world,	2262
	10: 9	*He will* **c in** and go out, and find pasture.	1656
	10:10	*I have* **c** that they may have life,	2262
	11:19	and many Jews *had* **c** to Martha and Mary	2262
	11:27	who *was to* **c** into the world."	2262
	11:33	and the Jews who *had* **c along with** her	5302
	11:34	"**C and see**, Lord," they replied.	2262
	11:43	in a loud voice, "Lazarus, **c out!**"	1306
	11:45	many of the Jews who *had* **c** to visit Mary,	2262
	11:48	and then the Romans *will* **c** and take away	4205
	12:12	that *had* **c** for the Feast heard that Jesus was	2262
	12:23	"The hour *has* **c** for the Son of Man to	2262
	12:46	*I have* **c** into the world as a light,	2262
	12:47	For *I did* not **c** to judge the world,	2262
	13: 1	the time *had* **c** for him to leave this world	2262
	13: 3	that *he had* **c** from God and was returning	2002

Jn	13:33	Where I am going, you cannot **c**.	2262
	14: 3	*I will* **c** back and take you to be with me	2262
	14:18	*I will* **c** to you.	2262
	14:23	and *we will* **c** to him and make our home	2262
	14:31	"**C** now; let us leave.	1586
	15:22	If *I had* not **c** and spoken to them,	2262
	16: 7	the Counselor *will* not **c** to you;	2262
	16:13	and he will tell you what *is* yet to **c**.	2262
	16:21	to a child has pain because her time has **c**;	2262
	16:32	"But a time is coming, and has **c**,	2262
	17: 1	"Father, the time has **c**.	2262
	17:10	And **glory** has **c** to *me* through them.	1519
	18:20	where all the Jews **c together.**	5302
	19: 9	"Where *do you* **c** from?"	1639
	21:12	Jesus said to them, "**C** and have breakfast."	1307
Ac	1:11	*will* **c** back in the same way	2262
	3:19	times of refreshing *may* **c** from the Lord,	2262
	5:24	wondering what would **c** of this.	1181
	7: 7	'and afterward *they will* **c** out of	2002
	7:34	I have heard their groaning and *have* **c down** to set them free.	2849
	7:34	Now **c**, I will send you back to Egypt.'	1306
	8:16	Holy Spirit *had* not yet **c upon** any of them;	1639+2158
	8:31	he invited Philip to **c** up and sit with him.	326
	9:12	he has seen a man named Ananias **c**	1656
	9:14	And he has **c** here with authority from	NIG
	9:21	And *hasn't* he **c** here to take them	2262
	9:38	to him and urged him, "Please **c** at once!"	1451
	10: 4	the poor *have* **c** up as a memorial offering	326
	10:21	Why *have* you **c**?"	4205
	10:22	"We have **c** from Cornelius the centurion.	NIG
	10:22	A holy angel told him to *have* you **c**	3569
	10:33	and it was good of you to **c**.	4134
	10:45	The circumcised believers who *had* **c with**	5302
	11:15	on them as he had **c** on us at the beginning.	NIG
	14:11	"The gods *have* **c down** to us	2849
	16: 9	"**C over** to Macedonia and help us."	1329
	16:15	she said, "**c** and stay **at** my house."	1656
	16:18	of Jesus Christ I command you to **c** out	2002
	16:34	*because* he had **c** to believe in God—	4409
	16:37	Let them **c** themselves and escort us out."	2262
	17: 6	over the world *have* **c** now here,	4205
	18: 2	who *had* recently **c** from Italy	2262
	18:21	"*I will* **c** back if it is God's will."	366
	19:13	command you to **c** out."	3991
	20:29	savage wolves *will* **c in** among you	1656
	21:22	They will certainly hear that *you have* **c**,	2262
	24:25	self-control and the judgment to **c**,	3516
	25: 5	of your leaders **c with** me and press charges	5160
	25: 7	the Jews *who had* **c down**	2849
	28:21	and none of the brothers *who have* **c from**	4134
Ro	1:10	the way may be opened for me to **c** to you.	2262
	1:13	that I planned many times to **c** to you	2262
	5:14	who was a pattern *of* the one to **c**.	3516
	11:11	salvation has **c** to the Gentiles	NIG
	11:25	the full number of the Gentiles has **c in**.	1656
	11:26	"The deliverer *will* **c** from Zion;	2457
	13:11	The hour has **c** for you to wake up	NIG
	14:23	everything that does not **c** from faith is sin.	NIG
	15:29	I know that *when* I **c** to you,	2262
	15:29	*I will* **c** in the full measure of the blessing	2262
	15:32	that by God's will I may **c** to you with joy	2262
1Co	2: 1	not **c** with eloquence or superior wisdom	2262
	2:14	not accept the things that **c** *from* **the Spirit**	AIT
	4:19	But *I will* **c** to you very soon,	2262
	4:21	Shall *I* **c** to you with a whip,	2262
	7: 5	Then **c together** again so that Satan will	899+1639+2093+3836
	10:11	on whom the fulfillment of the ages *has* **c**.	2918
	11: 8	For man *did* not **c** from woman,	1639
	11:18	I hear that *when* you **c together** as a church,	5302
	11:20	*When* you **c together,**	5302
	11:31	*we* would not **c under** judgment.	3212
	11:33	my brothers, *when* you **c together** to eat,	5302
	11:34	when *I* **c** I will give further directions.	2262
	14: 6	if *I* **c** to you and speak in tongues,	2262
	14:23	not understand or some unbelievers **c in**,	1656
	14:26	When you **c together,**	5302
	15:24	Then the end will **c**,	NIG
	15:34	**C** back to *your* **senses**	1729
	15:35	With what kind of body *will* they **c**?"	2262
	15:36	What you sow *does* not **c** to **life**	2443
	15:46	The spiritual did not **c** first, but the natural,	NIG
	15:54	then the saying that is written *will* **c true**:	1181
	16: 2	*I* **c** no collections will have to be made.	2262
	16: 5	*I will* **c** to you—	2262
	16:22	**C**, O **Lord**!	3448
2Co	1:14	*you* will **c** to **understand** fully	2105
	1:16	on my way to Macedonia and to **c** back	2262
	1:22	guaranteeing what is to **c**.	NIG
	5: 2	guaranteeing what is to **c**.	NIG
	5:17	the old has gone, the new has **c**!	1181
	6:17	**c** out from them and be separate,	2002
	9: 4	For if any Macedonians **c** with me	2262
	10: 2	that *when* I **c** I may not have to be as bold	4205
	10:14	as would be the case if *we had* not **c** to you,	2391
	12:20	*when I* **c** I may not find you as I want	2262
	12:21	that *when* I **c** again my God will humble me	2262
	13:10	that *when I* **c** I may not have to be harsh	4205
Gal	3:14	that the blessing given to Abraham *might* **c**	1181
	3:19	to whom the promise referred *had* **c**,	2262
	3:21	then righteousness would certainly *have* **c**	1639
	3:25	Now that faith has **c**,	2262
	4: 4	But when the time *had* fully **c**,	2262
	5: 8	That kind of persuasion does not **c** from	NIG
Eph	1:21	in the present age but also in the one to **c**.	3516

Eph	4:20	however, *did* not **c** to **know** Christ that way.	AIT
	4:29	*Do* not *let* any unwholesome talk **c** out	1744
Php	1:27	whether I **c** and see you or only hear	2262
	2:24	in the Lord that I myself *will* **c** soon.	2262
Col	1: 6	that *has* **c** to you.	4205
	2:17	a shadow *of* the things that *were* to **c**;	3516
1Th	2:16	The wrath of God has **c** upon them at last.	5777
	2:18	For we wanted to **c** to you—	2262
	3: 6	But Timothy *has* just now **c** to us from you	2262
	3:11	and our Lord Jesus clear the way for us to **c**	NIG
	4:16	the Lord himself *will* **c down** from heaven,	2849
	5: 2	of the Lord *will* **c** like a thief in the night.	2262
	5: 3	destruction *will* **c on** them suddenly,	2392
2Th	2: 2	report or letter supposed to *have* **c** from us,	NIG
	2: 2	that the day of the Lord *has* already **c**.	1931
	2: 3	not **c**] until the rebellion occurs and	NIG
1Ti	2: 4	who wants all men to be saved and to **c** to	2262
	3:14	Although I hope to **c** to you soon,	2262
	4: 2	Such teachings **c** through hypocritical liars,	NIG
	4: 8	for both the present life and the life to **c**.	3516
	4:13	Until *I* **c**, devote yourself to	2262
2Ti	2:26	that *they will* **c** to *their* **senses** and escape	392
	3: 2	For the time *will* **c** when men will not put	1639
	4: 6	and the time has **c** for my departure.	2392
	4: 9	Do your best to **c** to me quickly,	2262
	4:13	*When* you **c**, bring the cloak that I left	2262
Tit	3:12	do your best to **c** to me at Nicopolis,	2262
Heb	3: 3	that he has subjected the world **to c**,	3516
	3:14	*We have* **c** to share in Christ	1181
	7:11	for another priest to **c**—	482
	7:25	to save completely those who **c** to God	4665
	10: 7	*I have* **c** to do your will, O God.' "	2457
	10: 9	"Here I am, *I have* **c** to do your will."	2457
	10:37	"He who is coming *will* **c** and will	2457
	12:18	not **c** to a mountain that can be touched	4665
	12:22	But *you have* **c** to Mount Zion,	4665
	12:22	You have **c** to thousands upon thousands	NIG
	12:23	You have **c** to God, the judge of all men,	NIG
	13:14	but we are looking for the city that *is* to **c**.	3516
	13:23	I will **c** with him to see you.	NIG
Jas	3:10	**Out** of the same mouth **c**	2002
	3:15	not **c down** from heaven but is earthly,	2982
	4: 1	Don't they **c** from your desires that battle	NIG
	4: 8	**C near** to God and he will come near	1581
	4: 8	near to God and *he will* **c near** to you.	1581
1Pe	1: 7	These have **c** so that your faith—	NIG
	1:10	who spoke of the grace that was to **c**	NIG
	2: 4	*As* you **c** to him, the living Stone,	4665
	2: 4	not **c** from outward appearance,	1639
2Pe	3: 3	that in the last days scoffers *will* **c**,	2262
	3: 9	but everyone to **c** to repentance.	6003
	3:10	But the day of the Lord *will* **c** like a thief.	2457
1Jn	2: 3	We know that *we have* **c** to **know** him	AIT
	2:18	even now many antichrists *have* **c**.	1181
	4: 2	that acknowledges that Jesus Christ *has* **c** in	2262
	5: 6	He did not **c** by water only,	NIG
	5:20	We know also that the Son of God *has* **c**	2457
3Jn	1: 3	to have some brothers **c** and tell	2262
	1:10	So if *I* **c**, I will call attention	2262
Rev	1: 4	and who was, and who *is* to **c**,	2262
	1: 8	"who is, and who was, and who *is* to **c**,	2262
	2: 5	*I will* **c** to you	2262
	2:16	*I will* soon **c** to you and will fight	2262
	2:25	Only hold on to what you have until *I* **c**.	2457
	3: 3	you do not wake up, *I will* **c** like a thief.	2457
	3: 3	not know at what time *I will* **c** to you.	2457
	3: 9	I will make them **c** and fall down	2457
	3:10	that is going to **c** upon the whole world	2262
	3:20	*I will* **c in** and eat with him,	1656
	4: 1	to me like a trumpet said, "**C up** here,	326
	4: 8	who was, and is, and *is to* **c**."	2262
	6: 1	in a voice like thunder, "**C**!"	2262
	6: 3	I heard the second living creature say, "**C**!"	2262
	6: 5	I heard the third living creature say, "**C**!"	2262
	6: 7	of the fourth living creature say, "**C**!"	2262
	6:17	For the great day of their wrath has **c**,	2262
	7:13	who are these, and where *did* they **c** from?"	2262
	7:14	"These are they who *have* **c** out of	2262
	9:12	two other woes are yet to **c**.	2262
	11:12	from heaven saying to them, "**C up** here."	326
	11:18	and your wrath has **c**.	2262
	11:18	The time has **c** for judging the dead,	NIG
	12:10	"Now *have* **c** the salvation and the power	1181
	13:13	to **c down** from heaven to earth in full view	2849
	14: 7	because the hour of his judgment has **c**.	2262
	14:15	because the time to reap has **c**,	2262
	15: 4	All nations *will* **c** and worship before you,	2457
	16:15	"Behold, *I* **c** like a thief!	2262
	17: 1	to me, "**C**, I will show you the punishment	1306
	17: 8	and will **c up** out of the Abyss and go	326
	17: 8	now is not, and yet *will* **c**.	4205
	17:10	one is, the other *has* not yet **c**;	2262
	17:10	*he does,* he must remain for a little while.	2262
	18: 4	"**C out** of her, my people,	2002
	18:10	In one hour your doom *has* **c**!'	2262
	19: 7	For the wedding of the Lamb *has* **c**,	2262
	19:17	"**C**, gather together for the great supper	1307
	20: 5	(The rest of the dead *did* not **c** to **life** until	2409
	21: 9	"**C**, I will show you the bride,	1306
	22:17	The Spirit and the bride say, "**C**!"	2262
	22:17	And let him who hears say, "**C**!"	2262
	22:17	Whoever is thirsty, *let him* **c**;	2262
	22:20	**C**, Lord Jesus.	2262

COMES (290) [COME]

Ge	24:43	if a maiden **c out** to draw water and I say	3655

Ge	29: 6	here **c** his daughter Rachel with the sheep."	995
	32: 8	"If Esau **c** and attacks one group,	995
	37:19	"Here **c** that dreamer!"	995
	37:20	Then we'll see what **c** of his dreams."	2118
	42:15	unless your youngest brother **c** here.	995
	42:38	If harm *to* him on the journey	7925
	44:23	your youngest brother **c down** with you,	3718
	44:29	from me too and harm **c** *to* him,	7936
	47:24	But when the **crop** **c** in,	9311
	49:10	until *he* **c** to whom it belongs and	995
Ex	21: 3	If *he* **c** alone, he is to go free alone;	995
	21: 3	but if he has a wife when he **c**,	NIH
	28:35	before the LORD and when he **c out**,	3655
	29:30	and **c** to the Tent of Meeting to minister in	995
	32:34	when the time **c** for me to punish,	NIH
Lev	14:48	"But if the priest **c** to examine it and	995+995
	16:17	in the Most Holy Place until he **c out**,	3655
	22: 3	and yet **c near** the sacred offerings that	7928
	25:22	until the harvest of the ninth year **c in**.	995
Nu	6: 4	not eat anything that **c** from the grapevine,	6913
	11:20	until *it* **c out** of your nostrils	3655
	17:13	who *even* **c near** the tabernacle	7929+7929
	18: 7	Anyone else who **c near** the sanctuary must	7929
	36: 4	the Year of Jubilee for the Israelites,	2118
Dt	2: 8	which **c** up from Elath and Ezion Geber,	NIH
	8: 3	but on every **word that c** from the mouth of	4604
	18: 6	and **c** in all earnestness to the place	995
	22: 2	with you and keep it until he **c looking for**	2011
	25:11	of one of them **c** to rescue her husband	7928
	31:11	when all Israel **c** to appear before	995
	32:32	Their vine **c** from the vine of Sodom and	NIH
Jdg	4:20	"If someone **c by** and asks you,	995
	11:31	whatever **c out** of the door of my house	3655
	11:39	From this **c** the Israelite custom	2118
	13:14	not eat anything that **c** from the grapevine,	3655
	13:17	when your word **c true**?"	995
	16: 9	of string snaps when it **c close** *to* a flame.	8193
1Sa	8:18	When that day **c**,	995
	9: 6	and everything he says **c true**.	995+995
	9:13	The people will not begin eating until he **c**,	995
	11: 3	if no one **c** to rescue us,	NIH
	14:24	be any man who eats food before evening **c**,	NIH
	16:16	when the evil spirit from God **c** upon you,	2118
	17:25	*He* **c out** to defy Israel.	6590
2Sa	13: 5	"When your father **c** to see you, say to him,	995
	15:28	until word **c** from you to inform me."	995
	18:27	"*He* **c** with good news."	995
1Ki	8:31	to take an oath and he **c** and swears the oath	995
	8:37	"When famine or plague **c** to the land,	2118
	8:42	when *he* **c** and prays toward this temple,	995
2Ki	4: 9	that this man *who* often **c** our way is	6296
	4:10	he can stay there whenever he **c** to us."	995
	6:32	Look, when the messenger **c**,	995
1Ch	16:33	for he **c** to judge the earth.	995
	29:14	Everything **c** from you,	NIH
	29:14	and we have given you only what **c**	NIH
	29:16	it **c** from your hand,	NIH
2Ch	6:22	to take an oath and he **c** and swears the oath	995
	6:28	"When famine or plague **c** to the land,	2118
	6:32	when *he* **c** and prays toward this temple,	995
	13: 9	Whoever **c** to consecrate himself with	995
	19:10	In every case that **c** before you	995
	20: 9	'If calamity **c** upon us,	995
Job	3:24	For sighing **c** to me instead of food;	995
	4: 5	trouble **c** to you, and you are discouraged;	995
	5:14	Darkness **c** upon them in the daytime;	7008
	5:21	and need not fear when destruction **c**,	995
	11:10	"If he **c along** and confines you in prison	2736
	27: 9	Does God listen to his cry when distress **c**	995
	28: 5	The earth, from which food **c**,	3655
	33:27	Then *he* **c** to men and says, 'I sinned,	8801
	37: 2	to the rumbling that **c** from his mouth.	3655
	37: 4	**c** the sound of *his* **roar**;	8613
	37: 9	The tempest **c** out from its chamber,	995
	37:22	Out of the north **c** in golden splendor;	910
	37:22	God **c** in awesome majesty.	NIH
	38:29	From whose womb **c** the ice?	3655
Ps	3: 8	From the LORD **c** deliverance.	NIH
	7:16	his violence **c down** on his own head.	3718
	22:25	From you you **c** the theme of my praise in	NIH
	30: 5	but rejoicing **c** in the morning.	NIH
	37:39	The salvation of the righteous **c** from	NIH
	41: 6	Whenever one **c** to see me,	995
	50: 3	Our God **c** and will not be silent;	995
	62: 1	my salvation **c** from him.	NIH
	62: 5	my hope **c** from him.	NIH
	68:20	the Sovereign LORD **c** escape from death.	NIH
	73: 7	From their callous hearts **c** iniquity;	3655
	88:13	in the morning my prayer **c before** you.	7709
	96:13	for he **c**, he comes to judge the earth.	995
	96:13	for he comes, he **c** to judge the earth.	995
	98: 9	for he **c** to judge the earth.	995
	118:26	Blessed be who **c** in the name of	995
	121: 2	My help **c** from the LORD.	NIH
Pr	10: 8	but a chattering fool **c** to ruin.	4231
	10:10	and a chattering fool **c** to ruin.	4231
	11: 2	*When* pride **c**, then comes disgrace,	995
	11: 2	When pride comes, then **c** disgrace,	995
	11: 2	but with humility **c** wisdom.	NIH
	11: 7	from his power **c** to nothing.	6
	11: 8	and it **c** on the wicked instead.	995
	11:24	another withholds unduly, but **c** to poverty.	NIH
	11:27	but evil **c** *to* him who searches for it.	995
	13:18	He who ignores discipline **c** to poverty	NIH
	14: 4	the strength of an ox **c** an abundant harvest.	NIH
	14: 6	but knowledge **c easily** to the discerning.	7837
	14:32	When calamity **c**, the wicked are brought	NIH

Pr	15:33	and humility c before honor.	NIH
	16: 1	from the LORD c the reply of the tongue.	NIH
	18: 3	When wickedness c, so does contempt,	995
	18: 3	and with shame c disgrace.	NIH
	18:12	but humility c before honor.	NIH
	18:17	till another c forward and questions him.	995
	21:16	from the path of understanding c to rest in	5663
	25: 4	and out c material for the silversmith;	3655
Ecc	1:18	For with much wisdom c much sorrow;	NIH
	2:18	because I must leave them to the one who c	2118
	5: 3	As a dream c when there are many cares,	995
	5:15	Naked a man c from his mother's womb,	3655
	5:15	and as he c, so he departs.	995
	5:16	This too is a grievous evil: As a man c,	995
	6: 4	It c without meaning,	995
SS	2: 8	Here he c, leaping across the mountains,	995
Isa	10: 3	when disaster c from afar?	995
	14: 8	no woodsman c to cut us down."	6590
	14:31	A cloud of smoke c from the north,	995
	21: 1	an invader c from the desert,	995
	21: 9	here c a man in a chariot with a team	995
	23: 5	When word c to Egypt,	NIH
	28:19	As often as it c it will carry you away;	6296
	28:29	All this also c from the LORD Almighty,	3655
	30:27	the food that c from the land will be rich	9311
	30:27	See, the Name of the LORD c from afar,	995
	34: 1	the world, and all that c out of it!	7368
	40:10	See, the Sovereign LORD c with power,	995
	41:25	up one from the north, and he c—	910
	42: 5	the earth and all that c out of it,	7368
	62:11	the Daughter of Zion, 'See, your Savior c!	995
Jer	4:12	a wind too strong for that c from me.	995
	10:15	when their judgment c, they will perish.	NIH
	17: 6	he will not see prosperity when it c.	995
	17: 8	It does not fear when heat c;	995
	27: 7	until the time for his land c;	995
	28: 9	by the LORD only if his prediction c true."	995
	51:18	when their judgment c, they will perish.	NIH
	51:46	one rumor c this year, another the next,	995
	51:54	"The sound of a cry c from Babylon,	NIH
La	1: 4	for no one c to her appointed feasts,	995
Eze	7:25	When terror c, they will seek peace,	995
	12:22	by and every vision c to nothing'?	6
	21:27	until he c to whom it rightfully belongs;	995
	33: 4	but does not take warning and the sword c	995
	33: 6	and the sword c and takes the life of one	995
	33:33	"When all this c true—	995
Da	9:25	the ruler, c, there will be seven 'sevens,'	NIH
Hos	10:12	for it is time to seek the LORD, until he c	995
	14: 8	your fruitfulness c from me."	5162
Joel	2: 2	the mountains a large and mighty army c,	NIH
Am	3: 6	When disaster c to a city,	2118
	6:10	the bodies to carry them out of the house	NIH
Jnh	2: 9	Salvation c from the LORD."	NIH
Mic	1: 3	he c down and treads the high places of	3718
	2:11	If a liar and deceiver c and says,	2143
Zep	2: 2	the fierce anger of the LORD c upon you,	995
	2: 2	the day of the LORD's wrath c upon you.	995
Zec	9: 9	See, your king c to you,	995
	14: 7	When evening c, there will be light.	2118
Mal	4: 5	and dreadful day of the LORD c.	995
Mt	4: 4	but on every word that c from the mouth	1744
	5:37	anything beyond this c from the evil one.	1639
	8: 9	and that one, 'Come,' and he c,	2262
	10:23	the cities of Israel before the Son of Man c.	2262
	12:43	"When an evil spirit c out of a man,	2002
	13:19	the evil one c and snatches away	2262
	13:21	When trouble or persecution c because of	1181
	15:11	but what c out of his mouth,	1744
	16: 2	He replied, "When evening c, you say,	1181
	17:11	Elijah c and will restore all things.	2262
	21: 5	'See, your king c to you,	2262
	21: 9	Blessed is he who c in the name of the Lord!	2262
	21:40	when the owner of the vineyard c,	2262
	23:39	Blessed is he who c in the name of the Lord.	2262
	24:27	as lightning that c from the east is visible	2002
	25:31	"When the Son of Man c in his glory,	2262
	26:46	Rise, let us go! Here c my betrayer!"	1581
	27:49	Let's see if Elijah c to save him."	2262
Mk	4:15	Satan c and takes away the word	2262
	4:17	When trouble or persecution c because of	1181
	7:15	c out of a man that makes him 'unclean.'	1744
	7:20	c out of a man is what makes him 'unclean.'	1744
	8:38	of him when he c in his Father's glory with	2262
	11: 9	Blessed is he who c in the name of the Lord!	2262
	13:36	If he c suddenly,	2262
	14:42	Rise! Let us go! Here c my betrayer!"	1581
	15:36	Let's see if Elijah c to take him down,"	2262
Lk	6:47	I will show you what he is like who c to me	2262
	7: 8	and that one, 'Come,' and he c.	2262
	8:12	then the devil c and takes away the word	2262
	9:26	of Man will be ashamed of him when he c	2262
	11:24	"When an evil spirit c out of a man,	2002
	12:33	no thief c near and no moth destroys.	1581
	12:36	so that when he c	2262
	12:37	master finds them watching when he c.	2262
	12:38	even if he c in the second or third watch of	2262
	13:35	Blessed is he who c in the name of the Lord.	2262
	14:10	so that when your host c,	2262
	14:26	"If anyone c to me and does	2262
	15:30	with prostitutes c home,	2262
	17: 4	and seven times c back to you and says,	2188
	17: 7	to the servant when he c in from the field,	1656
	18: 8	However, when the Son of Man c,	2262
	19:38	Blessed is the king who c in the name of	2262
	22:18	of the vine until the kingdom of God c."	2262
Jn	1:15	'He who c after me has surpassed me	2262

Jn	1:27	He is the one who c after me,	2262
	1:30	'A man who c after me has surpassed me	2262
	3: 8	but you cannot tell where it c from or	2262
	3:21	whoever lives by the truth c into the light,	2262
	3:31	"The one who c from above is above all;	2262
	3:31	The one who c from heaven is above all.	2262
	4:25	he c, he will explain everything to us."	2262
	5:43	but if someone else c in his own name,	2262
	5:44	the praise that c from the only God?	NIG
	6:33	For the bread of God is he who c down	2849
	6:35	He who c to me will never go hungry,	2262
	6:37	whoever c to me I will never drive away.	2262
	6:45	to the Father and learns from him c to me.	2262
	6:50	here is the bread that c down from heaven,	2849
	7:16	It c from him who sent me.	NIG
	7:17	he will find out whether my teaching c	1639
	7:27	when the Christ c,	2262
	7:31	They said, "When the Christ c,	2262
	9:29	we don't even know where he c from."	1639
	9:30	You don't know where he c from,	1639
	10:10	thief c only to steal and kill and destroy;	2262
	12:13	"Blessed is he who c in the name of	2262
	14: 6	No one c to the Father except through me.	2262
	15:26	"When the Counselor c,	2262
	16: 4	so that when the time c you will remember	2262
	16: 8	When he c, he will convict the world	2262
	16:13	But when he, the Spirit of truth, c,	2262
	17: 7	that everything you have given me c	1639
Ac	1: 8	when the Holy Spirit c on you;	2088
	3:16	It is Jesus' name and the faith that c	NIG
	3:21	He must remain in heaven until the time c	NIG
	24:22	"When Lysias the commander c," he said,	2849
Ro	1: 5	the Gentiles to the obedience c	NIG
	3:22	from God c through faith in Jesus Christ	NIG
	3:22	through the righteousness that c by faith.	NIG
	4:16	Therefore, the promise c by faith,	NIG
	10: 3	the righteousness that c from God	NIG
	10:17	faith c from hearing the message,	NIG
1Co	4: 5	wait till the Lord c.	2262
	11:12	But everything c from God.	NIG
	11:26	you proclaim the Lord's death until he c.	2262
	13:10	but when perfection c,	2262
	14:23	whole church c together	899+2093+3836+5302
	14:24	or someone who does not understand c in	1656
	14:30	And if a revelation c	636
	15:21	the resurrection of the dead c also through	NIG
	15:23	then, when he c, those who belong to him.	4242
	16:10	If Timothy c, see to it that he has nothing	2262
2Co	3: 5	but our competence c from God.	NIG
	3:18	which c from the Lord, who is the Spirit.	NIG
	11: 4	For if someone c to you and preaches	2262
Eph	5: 6	for because of such things God's wrath c	2262
	6:13	so that when the day of evil c,	NIG
	6:15	with the readiness that c from the gospel	NIG
Php	1:11	filled with the fruit of righteousness that c	NIG
	3: 9	a righteousness of my own that c from	NIG
	3: 9	the righteousness that c from God and is	NIG
Col	4:10	if he c to you, welcome him.)	2262
1Th	2:19	the presence of our Lord Jesus when he c?	4242
	3:13	and Father when our Lord Jesus c	4242
2Th	1:10	on the day he c to be glorified	2262
1Ti	1: 5	which c from a pure heart and	NIG
Heb	11: 6	because anyone who c to him must believe	4665
	11: 7	and became heir of the righteousness that c	NIG
Jas	2: 2	a man c into your meeting wearing	1656
	2: 2	and a poor man in shabby clothes also c in.	1656
	3:13	by deeds done in the humility that c	NIG
	3:17	But the wisdom that c from heaven is first	NIG
1Jn	2:16	c not from the Father but from the world.	1639
	2:21	and because no lie c from the truth.	1639
	4: 7	for love c from God.	1639
2Jn	1:10	If anyone c to you and does	2262
Rev	11: 5	fire c from their mouths	1744
	11: 7	that c up from the Abyss will attack them,	326
	19:15	Out of his mouth c a sharp sword	1744

COMFORT (47) [COMFORTED, COMFORTER, COMFORTERS, COMFORTING, COMFORTS]

Ge	5:29	"He will c us in the labor and painful toil	5714
	37:35	All his sons and daughters came to c him,	5714
Ru	2:13	"You have given me c	5714
1Ch	7:22	and his relatives came to c him.	5714
Job	2:11	to go and sympathize with him and c him.	5714
	7:13	When I think my bed will c me	5714
	16: 5	But my lips would bring you relief.	5764
	36:16	the c of your table laden with choice food.	5739
Ps	23: 4	your rod and your staff, they c me.	5714
	71:21	and c me once again.	5714
	119:50	My c in my suffering is this:	5717
	119:52	O LORD, and I find c in them.	5714
	119:76	May your unfailing love be my c,	5714
	119:82	I say, "When will you c me?"	5714
Isa	40: 1	C, comfort my people, says your God.	5714
	40: 1	Comfort, c my people, says your God.	5714
	51: 3	The LORD will surely c Zion	5714
	51:19	who can c you?—	5653
	57:18	I will guide him and restore c to him,	5719
	61: 2	to c all who mourn,	5714
	66:13	mother comforts her child, so will I c you;	5714
Jer	16: 7	to c those who mourn for the dead—	5714
	31:13	I will give them c and joy instead	5714
La	1: 2	Among all her lovers there is none to c her.	5714
	1: 9	there was none to c her.	5714
	1:16	No one is near to c me,	5714

La	1:17	but there is no one to c her.	5714
	1:21	but there is no one to c me.	5714
		To what can I liken you, that I may c you,	5714
Eze	16:54	of all you have done in giving them c.	5714
Na	3: 7	Where can I find anyone to c you?"	5714
Zec	1:17	and the LORD will again c Zion	5714
	10: 2	they give c in vain.	5714
Lk	6:24	for you have already received your c.	4155
Jn	11:19	to Martha and Mary to c them in the loss	4170
1Co	14: 3	encouragement and c.	4171
2Co	1: 3	Father of compassion and the God of all c,	4155
	1: 4	so that we can c those in any trouble with	4151
	1: 4	with the c we ourselves have received	4155
	1: 5	so also through Christ our c overflows.	4155
	1: 6	it is for your c and salvation;	4155
	1: 6	if we are comforted, it is for your c,	4155
	1: 7	so also you share in our c.	4155
	2: 7	instead, you ought to forgive and c him,	4151
	7: 7	but also by the c you had given him.	4155
Php	2: 1	if any c from his love,	4172
Col	4:11	and they have proved a c to me.	4219

COMFORTED (17) [COMFORT]

Ge	24:67	and Isaac was c after his mother's death.	5714
	37:35	but he refused to be c.	5714
2Sa	12:24	Then David c his wife Bathsheba,	5714
Job	42:11	They c and consoled him over all	5653
Ps	77: 2	and my soul refused to be c.	5714
	86:17	O LORD, have helped me and c me.	5714
Isa	12: 1	and you have c me.	5714
	52: 9	for the LORD has c his people,	5714
	54:11	lashed by storms and not c,	5714
	66:13	and you will be c over Jerusalem."	5714
Jer	31:15	for her children and refusing to be c,	5714
Mt	2:18	for her children and refusing to be c,	4151
	5: 4	for they will be c.	4151
Lk	16:25	but now he is c here and you are in agony.	4151
Ac	20:12	and were greatly c.	4151
2Co	1: 6	if we are c, it is for your comfort,	4151
	7: 6	c us by the coming of Titus,	4151

COMFORTER (3) [COMFORT]

Ecc	4: 1	and they have no c;	5714
	4: 1	and they have no c.	5714
Jer	8:18	O my C in sorrow,	4443

COMFORTER (KJV) See COUNSELOR

COMFORTERS (2) [COMFORT]

Job	16: 2	miserable c are you all!	5714
Ps	69:20	but there was none, but I found none.	5714

COMFORTING (4) [COMFORT]

Isa	66:11	and be satisfied at her c breasts;	9488
Zec	1:13	So the LORD spoke kind and c words to	5719
Jn	11:31	with Mary in the house, c her, noticed	4170
1Th	2:12	c and urging you to live lives worthy	4170

COMFORTS (6) [COMFORT]

Job	29:25	I was like one who c mourners.	5714
Isa	49:13	For the LORD c his people	5714
	51:12	"I, even I, am he who c you.	5714
	66:13	a mother c her child, so will I comfort you;	5714
2Co	1: 4	who c us in all our troubles,	4151
	7: 6	But God, who c the downcast,	4151

COMING (245) [COME]

Ge	7:17	For forty days the flood kept c on	2118
	15: 4	"This man will not be your heir, but a son c	3655
	15:19	With the c of dawn, the angels urged Lot,	6590
	24:13	the daughters of the townspeople are c out	3655
	24:65	that man in the field c to meet us?"	2143
	32: 6	and now he is c to meet you,	2143
	32:18	and he is c behind us.'"	NIH
	32:20	'Your servant Jacob is c behind us.'	NIH
	33: 1	c with his four hundred men;	995
	37:25	a caravan of Ishmaelites c from Gilead.	995
	41:29	Seven years of great abundance are c	995
	41:35	of these good years that are c and store up	995
Ex	14:20	c between the armies of Egypt and Israel.	995
	18: 6	am c to you with your wife	995
	32: 1	that Moses was so long in c down from	3718
Nu	12:12	a stillborn infant c from its mother's womb	3718
	21: 1	that Israel was c along the road to Atharim,	995
	22:16	Do not let anything keep you from c to me,	2143
	22:36	When Balak heard that Balaam was c,	995
	33:40	heard that the Israelites were c.	995
Dt	32: 6	the Caphtorites c out	3655
Jos	18:12	c out at the desert of Beth Aven.	2118
Jdg	1:24	a man c out of the city and they said	3655
	5:28	'Why is his chariot so long in c?	995
	9:36	people are c down from the tops of	3718
	9:37	"Look, people are c down from the center	3718
	9:37	the center of the land, and a company c	995
	9:43	When he saw the people c out of the city,	3655
Ru	1:22	the LORD make the woman who c	995
1Sa	2:31	The time is c when I will cut short	995
	9:11	they met some girls c out to draw water,	3655
	9:11	c toward them on his way up to	3655
	10: 5	of prophets c down from the high place	3718
	17:25	"Do you see how this man keeps c out?	6590
	17:41	kept c closer to David.	2143+2143

Column 1

1Sa	25:11	give it to men **c** from who knows where?"	NIH
	28:13	"I see a spirit **c up** out of the ground."	6590
	28:14	"An old man wearing a robe *is* **c up**,"	6590
2Sa	13:34	**c** down the side of the hill.	2143
	19:41	of Israel *were* **c** to the king and saying	995
	24:20	the king and his men **c** toward him,	6296
1Ki	14: 5	"Jeroboam's wife *is* **c** to ask you	995
2Ki	4: 1	now his creditor *is* **c** to take my two boys	995
	9:17	he called out, "I see some troops **c**."	NIH
	9:18	but *he* isn't **c back**."	8740
	9:20	but *he* isn't **c back** either.	8740
2Ch	7: 3	the fire **down** and the glory of the LORD	3718
	20: 2	"A vast army *is* **c** against you from Edom,	995
	20:11	See how they are repaying us by **c**	995
Ne	6:10	because *men are* **c** to kill you—	995
	6:10	by night *they are* **c** to kill you."	995
	6:17	and replies from Tobiah *kept* **c** to me.	995
Job	36:33	His thunder announces **the c storm;**	2257S
Ps	19: 5	a bridegroom **c forth** from his pavilion,	3655
	37:13	for he knows their day *is* **c**.	995
	121: 8	the LORD will watch over your **c**	995
Ecc	10:14	No one knows what *is* **c**—	2118
SS	3: 6	Who is this **c up** from the desert like	6590
	4: 2	**c up** from the washing.	6590
	6: 6	Your teeth are like a flock of sheep **c up**	6590
	8: 5	Who is this **c up** from the desert leaning	6590
Isa	13: 9	See, the day of the LORD *is* **c**—	995
	14: 9	to meet you *at* your **c;**	995
	19: 1	the LORD rides on a swift cloud and *is* **c**	995
	21:12	The watchman replies, "Morning *is* **c**,	910
	26:21	the LORD *is* **c** out of his dwelling	3655
	30:30	and will make them see his arm **c down**	5738
	45:14	**c over** to you in chains.	6296
	47:13	let them save you from what *is* **c**	995
	63: 1	Who is this **c** from Edom, from Bozrah,	995
	66:15	See, the LORD *is* **c** with fire,	995
Jer	4:16	'A besieging army *is* **c** from a distant land,	995
	6:22	an army *is* **c** from the land of the north;	995
	7:32	So beware, the days *are* **c**,	995
	9:25	"The days *are* **c**," declares the LORD,	995
	10:22	The report *is* **c**—	995
	13:20	up your eyes and see those *who are* **c** from	995
	16:14	"However, the days *are* **c**,"	995
	19: 6	So beware, the days *are* **c**,	995
	23: 5	"The days *are* **c**," declares the LORD,	995
	23: 7	"So then, the days *are* **c**,"	995
	30: 3	The days *are* **c**,' declares the LORD,	995
	31:27	"The days *are* **c**," declares the LORD,	995
	31:31	"The time *is* **c**," declares the LORD,	995
	31:38	"The days *are* **c**," declares the LORD,	995
	33:14	" 'The days *are* **c**,' declares the LORD,	995
	46:13	the **c** of Nebuchadnezzar king of Babylon	995
	46:20	a gadfly *is* **c** against her from the north.	995
	46:21	for the day of disaster *is* **c** upon them,	995
	48:12	But days *are* **c**," declares the LORD,	995
	49: 2	But days *are* **c**," declares the LORD, ·	995
	49:19	"Like a lion **c up** from Jordan's thickets to	6590
	50:41	An army *is* **c** from the north;	995
	50:44	Like a lion **c up** from Jordan's thickets to	6590
	51:52	"But days *are* **c**," declares the LORD,	995
Eze	1: 4	and I saw a windstorm **c** out of the north—	995
	7: 5	An unheard-of disaster *is* **c**.	995
	9: 2	And I saw six men **c** from the direction of	995
	21: 7	'Because of the news that *is* **c**.	995
	21: 7	*It is* **c**! It will surely take place,	995
	33: 3	and he sees the sword **c** against the land	995
	33: 6	the sword **c** and does not blow the trumpet	995
·	39: 8	*It is* **c**! It will surely take place,	995
	43: 2	and I saw the glory of the God of Israel **c**	995
	47: 1	and I saw water **c** out from under	3655
	47: 1	The water *was* **c down** from under	3718
Da	4:13	a holy one, **c down** from heaven.	10474
	4:23	a holy one, **c down** from heaven and saying,	10474
	7:10	**c** out from before him.	10485
	7:13	**c** with the clouds of heaven.	10085
	11:23	After **c to an agreement** with him,	2489
Hos	9: 7	The days of punishment *are* **c**,	995
Joel	2: 1	for the day of the LORD *is* **c**.	995
	2:31	the moon to blood before the **c** of the great	995
Am	7: 1	and just as the second crop *was* **c up**.	6590
	8:11	"The days *are* **c**," declares	995
	9:13	"The days *are* **c**," declares the LORD,	995
Mic	1: 3	The LORD *is* **c** from his dwelling place;	3655
Hab	2:16	from the LORD's right hand *is* **c around**	6015
Zep	1:14	near and **c quickly**.	4394+4554
Zec	1:21	I asked, "What are these **c** to do?"	995
	2:10	For *I am* **c**, and I will live among you,"	995
	6: 1	before me were four chariots **c out** from	3655
	14: 1	of the LORD *is* **c** when your plunder will	995
Mal	3: 2	But who can endure the day of his **c**?	995
	4: 1	the day *is* **c;** it will burn like a furnace.	995
	4: 1	that day that **c** will set them on fire,"	995
Mt	2:11	*On* **c** to the house,	2262
	3: 7	of the Pharisees and Sadducees **c**	2262
	3: 7	Who warned you to flee from the **c** wrath?	3516
	8:28	two demon-possessed men **c from**	2002
	13:54	**C** to his hometown,	2262
	16:28	the Son of Man **c** in his kingdom."	2262
	17: 9	*As they were* **c down** the mountain,	2849
	24: 3	and what will be the sign of your **c** and of	4242
	24:27	so will be the **c** of the Son of Man.	2262
	24:30	the Son of Man **c** on the clouds of the sky,	2262
	24:37	so it will be at the **c** of the Son of Man.	4242
	24:39	is how it will be at the **c** of the Son of Man.	4242
	24:43	at what time of night the thief *was* **c**,	2262
	25: 5	The bridegroom *was* **a long time in c**,	5988
	26:64	the right hand of the Mighty One and **c** on	2262

Column 2

Mk	1:10	*As* Jesus *was* **c up** out of the water,	326
	6:31	because so many people were **c** and going	2262
	9: 9	*As* they *were* **c down** the mountain,	2849
	11:10	the **c** kingdom of our father David!"	2262
	13:26	that time men will see the Son of Man **c**	2262
	14:62	the right hand of the Mighty One and **c** on	2262
Lk	3:38	**C up** to them at that very moment,	2392
	3: 7	*to* the crowds **c out** to be baptized by him,	1744
	3: 7	Who warned you to flee from the **c** wrath?	3516
	6:19	because power *was* **c** from him	2002
	8: 4	and people *were* **c** to Jesus from town	2164
	9:42	Even *while* the boy *was* **c**,	4465
	12:39	at what hour the thief *was* **c**,	2262
	12:45	'My master is taking a long time in **c**,'	2262
	13: 7	'For three years now *I've been* **c** to look	2262
	14:31	with ten thousand men to oppose the one **c**	2262
	17:22	"The time *is* **c** when you will long	2262
	18: 3	that town *who kept* **c** to him with the plea,	2262
	18: 5	that she won't eventually wear me out *with her* **c**! "	2262
	19: 9	since Jesus *was* **c** that way.	1451+3516
	19:44	not recognize the time *of* God's **c** to you."	2175
	21:26	apprehensive *of* what *is* **c** on the world,	2088
	21:27	At that time they will see the Son of Man **c**	2262
Jn	1: 9	that gives light to every man *was* **c** into	2262
	1:29	The next day John saw Jesus **c** toward him	2262
	3:23	and *people* were constantly **c** to	4134
	4:15	have *to keep* **c** here to draw water."	1451
	4:21	a time *is* **c** when you will worship	2262
	4:23	Yet a time *is* **c** and has now come when	2262
	4:25	"I know that Messiah (called Christ) "*is* **c**.	2262
	5:25	a time *is* **c** and has now come when	2262
	5:28	for a time *is* **c** when all who are	2262
	6: 5	up and saw a great crowd **c** toward him,	2262
	9: 4	Night *is* **c**, when no one can work.	2262
	10:12	So when he sees the wolf **c**,	2262
	11:20	When Martha heard that Jesus *was* **c**,	2262
	11:56	Isn't *he* **c** to the Feast at all?"	2262
	12:15	see, your king *is* **c**,	2262
	14:28	'I am going away and *I am* **c back** to you.'	2262
	14:30	for the prince of this world *is* **c**.	2262
	16: 2	a time *is* **c** when anyone who kills you	2262
	16:25	a time *is* **c** when I will no longer use	2262
	16:32	"But a time *is* **c**, and has come,	2262
	17:11	and *I am* **c** to you.	2262
	17:13	"*I am* **c** to you now,	2262
Ac	2:20	the moon to blood before the **c** of the great	2262
	7:52	They even killed those who predicted the **c**	1803
	9:17	to you on the road *as you were* **c** here—	2262
	13:24	Before the **c** of Jesus,	1658
	13:25	No, but *he is* **c** after me,	2262
	19: 4	the people to believe in the one **c** after him,	2262
	21:11	**C** over to us, he took Paul's belt,	2262
	28:15	brothers there had heard that we were **c**,	NIG
Ro	15:22	hindered from **c** to you.	2262+3836
1Co	2: 6	who *are* **c to nothing.**	2934
	4: 5	as if *I* were not **c** to you.	2262
2Co	7: 6	comforted us by the **c** of Titus,	4242
	7: 7	and not only by his **c** but also by	4242
	8:17	but *he is* **c** to you with much enthusiasm	2002
Eph	2: 7	in order that in the **c** ages he might show	2088
Php	2:17	the sacrifice and service **c** *from* your **faith**,	AIT
Col	3: 6	Because of these, the wrath of God *is* **c**	2262
	4: 9	He is **c** with Onesimus,	NIG
1Th	1:10	Jesus, who rescues us from the **c** wrath.	2262
	4:15	who are left till the **c** of the Lord,	4242
	5:23	soul and body be kept blameless at the **c**	4242
2Th	2: 1	Concerning the **c** of our Lord Jesus Christ	4242
	2: 8	and destroy by the splendor *of his* **c**.	4242
	2: 9	The **c** of the lawless one will be in	4242
1Ti	6:19	as a firm foundation for the **c** age,	3516
Heb	6: 5	of God and the powers *of the* **c** age,	3516
	8: 8	"The time *is* **c**, declares the LORD,	2262
	10: 1	a shadow *of* the good things **that are c**—	3516
	10:37	"He who is **c** will come and will not delay.	2262
Jas	1:17	**c down** from the Father of	2849
	5: 1	because of the misery that *is* **c** upon you.	2088
	5: 7	then, brothers, until the Lord's **c**.	4242
	5: 8	because the Lord's **c** is near.	4242
1Pe	1: 5	by God's power until the **c** of the salvation	NIG
2Pe	1:16	the power and **c** of our Lord Jesus Christ,	4242
	3: 4	"Where is this '**c**' he promised?	4242
	3:12	to the day of God and speed its **c**.	4242
1Jn	2:18	as you have heard that the antichrist *is* **c**,	2262
	2:28	and unashamed before him at his **c**.	4242
	4: 3	which you have heard *is* **c** and even	2262
2Jn	1: 7	who do not acknowledge Jesus Christ as **c**	2262
Jude	1:14	"See, the Lord is **c** with thousands	2262
Rev	1: 7	Look, he *is* **c** with the clouds,	2262
	3:11	*I am* **c** soon.	2262
	3:12	which *is* **c down** out of heaven	2849
	7: 2	I saw another angel **c up** from the east,	326
	9:13	a voice *from* the horns of the golden altar	NIG
	10: 1	Then I saw another mighty angel **c down**	2849
	11:14	the third woe *is* **c** soon.	2262
	13: 1	And I saw a beast **c** out of the sea.	326
	13:11	I saw another beast, **c** out of the earth.	326
	18: 1	After this I saw another angel **c down**	2849
	20: 1	And I saw an angel **c down** out of heaven,	2849
	21: 2	**c down** out of heaven from God,	2849
	21:10	**c down** out of heaven from God.	2849
	22: 7	"Behold, *I am* **c** soon!	2262
	22:12	"Behold, *I am* **c** soon!	2262
	22:20	"Yes, *I am* **c** soon."	2262

COMMAND (195) [COMMANDED,

Column 3

Ex	7: 2	You are to say everything *I* **c** you,	7422
	27:20	"**C** the Israelites to bring you clear oil	7422
	34:11	Obey what *I* **c** you today.	7422
	38:21	which were recorded at Moses' **c** by	7023
Lev	6: 9	"**Give** Aaron and his sons *this* **c:**	7422
	10: 1	before the LORD, contrary to *his* **c**.	7422
	24: 2	"**C** the Israelites to bring you clear oil	7422
Nu	3:39	at the LORD's **c** *by* Moses and Aaron	7023
	4:37	to the LORD's **c** through Moses.	7023
	4:41	according to the LORD's **c**.	7023
	4:45	to the LORD's **c** through Moses.	7023
	4:49	At the LORD's **c** through Moses,	7023
	5: 2	"**C** the Israelites to send away from	7422
	9:18	At the LORD's **c** the Israelites set out,	7023
	9:18	and at his **c** they encamped.	7023
	9:20	at the LORD's **c** they would encamp,	7023
	9:20	and then at his **c** they would set out.	7023
	9:23	At the LORD's **c** they encamped,	7023
	9:23	and at the LORD's **c** they set out.	7023
	9:23	in accordance with his **c** through Moses.	7023
	10:13	at the LORD's **c** through Moses.	7023
	10:14	Nahshon son of Amminadab was in **c**.	6584+7372
	10:18	Elizur son of Shedeur was in **c**.	6584+7372
	10:22	Elishama son of Ammihud was in **c**.	6584+7372
	10:25	Ahiezer son of Ammishaddai was in **c**.	6584+7372
	13: 3	So at the LORD's **c** Moses sent them out	7023
	14:41	"Why are you disobeying the LORD's **c**?	7023
	20:24	because both of you rebelled against my **c**	7023
	22:18	to go beyond the **c** *of* the LORD my God.	7023
	23:20	I have received a **c** to bless;	NIH
	24:13	to go beyond the **c** *of* the LORD—	7023
	27:14	of you disobeyed my **c** to honor me as holy	7023
	27:21	At his **c** he and the entire community of	7023
	27:21	and at his **c** they will come in."	7023
	28: 2	"**Give** *this* **c** to the Israelites and say	7422
	31:49	the soldiers under our **c**,	3338
	33: 2	the LORD's **c** Moses recorded the stages	7023
	33:38	At the LORD's **c** Aaron the priest went	7023
	34: 2	"**C** the Israelites and say to them:	7422
	35: 2	"**C** the Israelites to give the Levites towns	7422
	36: 5	at the LORD's **c** Moses gave this order to	7023
Dt	1:26	against the **c** *of* the LORD your God.	7023
	1:43	You rebelled against the LORD's **c** and	7023
	2:37	with the **c** *of* the LORD our God,	7422
	4: 2	to what *I* **c** you and do not subtract from it,	7422
	8: 1	to follow every **c** *I* am giving you today,	5184
	9:23	against the **c** *of* the LORD your God.	7023
	11:28	that *I* **c** you today by following other gods,	7422
	12:11	there you are to bring everything *I* **c** you:	7422
	12:14	and there observe everything *I* **c** you.	7422
	12:32	See that you do all *I* **c** you;	7422
	15:11	Therefore *I* **c** you to be openhanded	7422
	15:15	That is why *I* give you this **c** today.	1821
	17: 3	contrary to *my* **c** has worshiped other gods,	7422
	18:18	and he will tell them everything *I* **c** him.	7422
	19: 7	This is why *I* **c** you to set aside	7422
	19: 9	carefully follow all these laws *I* **c** you today	7422
	24:18	That is why *I* **c** you to do this.	7422
	24:22	That is why *I* **c** you to do this.	7422
	27: 4	as *I* **c** you today,	7422
	30: 2	according to everything *I* **c** you today,	7422
	30:16	I **c** you today to love the LORD your God,	7422
	31:23	The LORD **gave** *this* **c** to Joshua son	7422
	31:25	he **gave** *this* **c** to the Levites who carried	7422
	32:46	so that *you may* **c** your children	7422
Jos	1:13	"Remember the **c** that Moses the servant of	1821
	1:18	whatever *you may* **c** them,	7422
	4:16	"**C** the priests carrying the ark of	7422
	15:13	In accordance with the LORD's **c** to him,	7023
	17: 4	according to the LORD's **c**.	7023
	22: 9	with the **c** *of* the LORD through Moses.	7023
Jdg	9:29	If only this people were under my **c**!	3338
1Sa	13:13	the **c** the LORD your God gave you;	5184
	13:14	because you have not kept the LORD's **c**."	7422
	15:24	the LORD's **c** and your instructions.	7023
	16:16	*Let* our lord **c** his servants here to search	606
	18:13	and gave him **c** *over* a thousand men,	8569
2Sa	10:10	the men under the **c** of Abishai his brother	3338
	18: 2	a third under the **c** of Joab,	3338
	20: 7	the mighty warriors went out **under the c** of	339
1Ki	2:43	to the LORD and obey the **c** *I* gave you?"	5184
	5:17	At the king's **c** they removed from	7422
	9: 4	and do all *I* **c** and observe my decrees	7422
	11:10	Solomon did not keep the LORD's **c**	7422
	11:38	If you do whatever *I* **c** you and walk	7422
	13:21	of the LORD and have not kept the **c**	5184
	16: 9	who had *c* of half his chariots,	8569
	18:36	and have done all these things at your **c**.	1821
2Ki	24: 3	to Judah according to the LORD's **c**,	7023
1Ch	11: 6	and so he received the **c**.	8031
	12: 9	Obadiah the **second in c**, Eliab the third,	9108
	12:32	with all their relatives under their **c**;	7023
	19:11	the men under the **c** *of* Abishai his brother,	3338
	21: 6	because the king's **c** was repulsive to him;	1821
	21: 7	This **c** was also evil in the sight of God;	1821
	22:12	and understanding when *he* **puts** you in **c**	7422
	22:19	and all the people will obey your every **c**."	1821
2Ch	7:13	or **c** locusts to devour the land or send	7422
	7:17	and do all *I* **c**,	7422
	24: 8	*At* the king's **c**,	606

2Ch 26:13 Under their c was an army of 307,500　3338
30: 6 At the king's c, couriers went　5184
35:22 not listen to what Neco had said at God's c　7023
Ezr 6:14 according to the c of the God of Israel and　10302
Est 1: 8 By the king's c each guest was allowed　2017
1:12 when the attendants delivered the king's c,　1821
1:15 "She has not obeyed the c of King Xerxes　4411
3: 3 "Why do you disobey the king's c?"　5184
3:15 Spurred on by the king's c,　1821
8:14 raced out, spurred on by the king's c.　1821
Job 39:27 the eagle soar at your c and build his nest　7023
Ps 71: 3 give the c to save me,　7422
78:23 Yet he gave a c to the skies above　7422
91:11 For he will c his angels concerning you　7422
147:15 He sends his c to the earth;　614
Pr 8:29 so the waters would not overstep his c,　7023
13:13 but he who respects a c is rewarded.　5184
Ecc 8: 2 Obey the king's c, I say,　7023
8: 5 Whoever obeys his c will come to no harm,　5184
Isa 5: 6 I will c the clouds not to rain on it."　7422
Jer 1: 7 and say whatever I c you.　7422
1:17 Stand up and say to them whatever I c you.　7422
7:23 but I gave them this c:　7422
7:23 Walk in all the ways I c you,　7422
7:31 something I did not c,　7422
11: 4 'Obey me and do everything I c you,　7422
19: 5 something I did not c or mention,　7422
26: 2 Tell them everything I c you;　7422
35: 6 of Recab gave us this c:　7422
35:14 not to drink wine and this c has been kept.　1821
35:14 because they obey their forefather's c.　5184
35:16 the c their forefather gave them,　5184
35:18 the c of your forefather Jonadab　5184
43: 4 the LORD's c to stay in the land of Judah.　7754
La 1:18 yet I rebelled against his c.　7023
Eze 21:22 to give the c to slaughter,　7023+7337
38: 7 and take c of them.　2118+4200+5464
Da 3:22 The king's c was so urgent and the furnace　10418
3:28 They trusted in him and defied the king's c　10418
4:26 The c to leave the stump of the tree　10042
5:29 Then at Belshazzar's c,　10042
6:24 At the king's c,　10042
Joel 2:11 and mighty are those who obey his c.　1821
Am 6:11 For the LORD has given the c,　7422
9: 3 there I will c the serpent to bite them.　7422
9: 4 there I will c the sword to slay them.　7422
9: 9 "For I will give the c,　7422
Na 1:14 The LORD has given a c concerning you,　7422
Mt 4: 6 " 'He will c his angels concerning me,　1948
15: 3 the c of God for the sake of your tradition?　1953
19: 7 "did Moses c that a man give his wife　1948
Mk 9:25 he said, "I c you,　2199
10: 3 "What did Moses c you?" he replied.　1948
Lk 4:10 " 'He will c his angels concerning you　1948
Jn 10:18 This c I received from my Father."　1953
12:50 I know that his c leads to eternal life.　1953
13:34 "A new c I give you: Love one another.　1953
14:15 "If you love me, you will obey what I c.　1953
15:12 My c is this: Love each other as I have　1953
15:14 You are my friends if you do what I c.　1948
15:17 This is my c: Love each other.　1948
Ac 1: 4 he gave them this c:　4133
16:18 "In the name of Jesus Christ I c you　4133
19:13 c you to come out."　3991
25:23 At the c of Festus, Paul was brought in.　3027
Ro 5:14 over those who did not sin by breaking a c,　4126
16:26 through the prophetic writings by the c of　2198
1Co 7: 6 I say this as a concession, not as a c.　2198
7:10 To the married I give this c (not I,　4133
7:25 I have no c from the Lord,　2198
14:37 to you is the Lord's c.　1953
Gal 5:14 The entire law is summed up in a single c:　3364
1Th 4:16 with a loud c,　3026
2Th 3: 4 and will continue to do the things we c.　4133
3: 6 the Lord Jesus Christ, we c you, brothers,　4133
3:12 Such people we c and urge in　4133
1Ti 1: 1 of Christ Jesus by the c of God our Savior　2198
1: 3 in Ephesus so that you may c certain men　4133
1: 5 The goal of this c is love,　4132
4:11 C and teach these things.　4133
6:14 to keep this c without spot or blame until　1953
6:17 C those who are rich in this present world　4133
6:18 C them to do good,　NIG
Tit 1: 3 the preaching entrusted to me by the c　2198
Heb 11: 3 that the universe was formed at God's c,　4839
2Pe 2:21 on the sacred c that was passed on to them.　1953
3: 2 past by the holy prophets and the c given　1953
1Jn 2: 7 not writing you a new c but an old one,　1953
2: 7 This old c is the message you have heard.　1953
2: 8 Yet I am writing you a new c;　1953
3:23 And this is his c: to believe in the name　1953
4:21 And he has given us this c:　1953
2Jn 1: 5 a new c but one we have had from　1953
1: 6 his c is that you walk in love.　1953
Rev 3:10 you have kept my c to endure patiently,　3364

COMMANDED (271) [COMMAND]

Ge 2:16 And the LORD God c the man,　7422
3:11 from the tree that I c you not to eat from?"　7422
3:17 the tree about which I c you, 'You must　7422
6:22 Noah did everything just as God c him.　7422
7: 5 And Noah did all that the LORD c him.　7422
7: 9 as God had c Noah.　7422
7:16 as God had c Noah.　7422
Abraham circumcised him, as God c him.　7422
for Jacob and blessed him and c him:　7422

Ge 28: 6 and that when he blessed him he c him,　7422
45:21 Joseph gave them carts, as Pharaoh had c,　7023
50:12 So Jacob's sons did as he had c them:　7422
Ex 4:28 about all the miraculous signs he had c him　7422
6:13 and he c them to bring the Israelites out　7422
7: 6 and Aaron did just as the LORD c them.　7422
7:10 to Pharaoh and did just as the LORD c.　7422
7:20 and Aaron did just as the LORD had c.　7422
12:28 the LORD c Moses and Aaron.　7422
12:50 the LORD had c Moses and Aaron.　7422
16:16 This is what the LORD has c:　7422
16:23 "This is what the LORD c:　1819
16:24 So they saved it until morning, as Moses c,　7422
16:32 "This is what the LORD has c:　7422
16:34 As the LORD c Moses,　7422
17: 1 from place to place as the LORD c.　7023
19: 7 the words the LORD had c him to speak.　7422
23:15 without yeast, as I c you.　7422
29:35 and his sons everything I have c you,　7422
31: 6 to make everything I have c you:　7422
31:11 They are to make them just as I c you."　7422
32: 8 to turn away from what I c them　7422
32:28 The Levites did as Moses c,　1821
34: 4 as the LORD had c him;　7422
34:18 eat bread made without yeast, as I c you.　7422
34:34 and told the Israelites what he had been c,　7422
35: 1 "These are the things the LORD has c you　7422
35: 4 "This is what the LORD has c:　7422
35:10 and make everything the LORD has c:　7422
35:29 the LORD through Moses had c them　7422
36: 1 to do the work just as the LORD has c."　7422
36: 5 the work the LORD c to be done."　7422
38:22 made everything the LORD c Moses;　7422
39: 1 as the LORD c Moses.　7422
39: 5 as the LORD c Moses.　7422
39: 7 as the LORD c Moses.　7422
39:21 as the LORD c Moses.　7422
39:26 as the LORD c Moses.　7422
39:29 as the LORD c Moses.　7422
39:31 as the LORD c Moses.　7422
39:32 as the LORD c Moses.　7422
39:42 as the LORD had c Moses.　7422
39:43 as the LORD had c.　7422
40:16 as the LORD c him.　7422
40:19 as the LORD c him.　7422
40:21 as the LORD c him.　7422
40:23 as the LORD c him.　7422
40:25 as the LORD c him.　7422
40:27 as the LORD c him.　7422
40:29 as the LORD c him.　7422
40:32 as the LORD c him.　7422
Lev 7:36 the LORD c that the Israelites give this　7422
7:38 on Mount Sinai on the day he c　7422
8: 4 Moses did as the LORD c,　7422
8: 5 "This is what the LORD has c to be done."　7422
8: 9 on the front of it, as the LORD c Moses.　7422
8:13 as the LORD c Moses.　7422
8:17 as the LORD c Moses.　7422
8:21 as the LORD c Moses.　7422
8:29 as the LORD c Moses.　7422
8:31 the basket of ordination offerings, as I c,　7422
8:34 What has been done today was c by　7422
8:35 for that is what I have been c."　7422
8:36 and his sons did everything the LORD c　7422
9: 5 the things Moses c to the front of the Tent　7422
9: 6 "This is what the LORD has c you to do,　7422
9: 7 as the LORD has c."　7422
9:10 as the LORD c Moses;　7422
9:21 the LORD as a wave offering, as Moses c.　7422
10:13 for so I have been c.　7422
10:15 as the LORD has c."　7422
10:18 the goat in the sanctuary area, as I c."　7422
16:34 And it was done, as the LORD c Moses.　7422
17: 2 'This is what the LORD has c:　7422
24:23 The Israelites did as the LORD c Moses.　7422
Nu 1:19 as the LORD c Moses.　7422
1:54 as the LORD c Moses.　7422
2:33 as the LORD c Moses.　7422
2:34 the LORD c Moses;　7422
3:16 as he was c by the word of the LORD.　7422
3:42 as the LORD c him.　7422
3:51 as he was c by the word of the LORD.　7422
4:49 as the LORD c Moses.　7422
8: 3 just as the LORD c Moses.　7422
8:20 the Levites just as the LORD c Moses.　7422
8:22 the Levites just as the LORD c Moses.　7422
9: 5 as the LORD c Moses.　7422
15:36 as the LORD c Moses.　7422
17:11 Moses did just as the LORD c him.　7422
19: 2 of the law that the LORD has c:　7422
20: 9 just as he c him.　7422
20:27 Moses did as the LORD c:　7422
26: 4 as the LORD c Moses."　7422
27:11 as the LORD c Moses.' "　7422
27:22 Moses did as the LORD c him.　7422
29:40 the Israelites all that the LORD c him.　7422
31: 7 as the LORD c Moses,　7422
31:31 the priest did as the LORD c Moses.　7422
31:41 as the LORD c Moses.　7422
31:47 as the LORD c him,　7422
34:13 Moses c the Israelites:　7422
34:29 These are the men the LORD c to assign　7422
36: 2 the LORD c my lord to give the land as　7422
36:10 as the LORD c Moses.　7422
Dt 1: 3 that the LORD had c him concerning them.　7422
1:19 Then, as the LORD our God c us,　7422
1:41 as the LORD our God c us."　7422

Dt 3:18 I c you at that time:　7422
3:21 At that time I c Joshua:　7422
4: 5 and laws as the LORD my God c me,　7422
4:13 which he c you to follow and　7422
5:12 as the LORD your God has c you.　7422
5:15 the LORD your God has c you to observe　7422
5:16 as the LORD your God has c you,　7422
5:32 to do what the LORD your God has c you;　7422
5:33 that the LORD your God has c you,　7422
6:20 and laws the LORD our God has c you?"　7422
6:24 The LORD c us to obey all these decrees　7422
6:25 as he has c us,　7422
9:12 from what I c them and have made　7422
9:16 from the way that the LORD had c you.　7422
10: 5 as the LORD c me,　7422
12:21 as I have c you,　7422
13: 5 from the way the LORD your God c you　7422
18:20 in my name anything I have not c him　7422
20:17 as the LORD your God has c you.　7422
24: 8 You must follow carefully what I have c them.　7422
26:13 according to all you c.　5184+7422
26:14 I have done everything you c me.　7422
27: 1 Moses and the elders of Israel c the people:　7422
27:11 On the same day Moses c the people:　7422
29: 1 the covenant the LORD c Moses to make　7422
31: 5 must do to them all that I have c you.　5184+7422
31:10 Then Moses c them:　7422
31:29 and to turn from the way I have c you.　7422
34: 9 and did what the LORD had c Moses.　7422
Jos 1: 9 Have I not c you?　7422
1:16 "Whatever you have c us we will do,　7422
4: 8 So the Israelites did as Joshua c them.　7422
4:10 the LORD had c Joshua was done by　7422
4:17 So Joshua c the priests,　7422
6:10 But Joshua had c the people,　7422
6:16 Joshua c the people, "Shout!　606
7:11 which I c them to keep.　7422
8: 8 Do what the LORD has c.　1821
8:31 as Moses the servant of the LORD had c　7422
8:33 the servant of the LORD had formerly c　7422
8:35 that Moses had c that Joshua did not read to　7422
9:24 LORD your God had c his servant Moses　7422
10:40 just as the LORD, the God of Israel, had c.　7422
11:12 as Moses the servant of the LORD had c.　7422
11:15 As the LORD c his servant Moses,　7422
11:15 so Moses c Joshua, and Joshua did it;　7422
11:15 of all that the LORD c Moses.　7422
11:20 as the LORD had c Moses.　7422
14: 2 as the LORD had c through Moses.　7422
14: 5 just as the LORD had c Moses.　7422
17: 4 "The LORD c Moses to give us　7422
19:50 as the LORD had c.　7023
21: 2 "The LORD c through Moses　7422
21: 3 So, as the LORD had c,　7023
21: 8 as the LORD had c through Moses.　7422
22: 2 that Moses the servant of the LORD c,　7422
22: 2 and you have obeyed me in everything I c.　7422
23:16 which he c you,　7422
Jdg 13:14 She must do everything I have c her."　7422
2Sa 5:25 So David did as the LORD c him,　7422
7: 7 to any of their rulers whom I c　7422
18: 5 The king c Joab, Abishai and Ittai,　7422
18:12 In our hearing the king c you and Abishai　7422
21:14 and did everything the king c.　7422
24:19 as the LORD had c through Gad.　7422
1Ki 2:31 Then the king c Benaiah, "Do as he says.　606
11:11 which I c you,　7422
13: 9 For I was c by the word of the LORD:　7422
17: 9 I have c a widow in that place　7422
18:40 Elijah c them, "Seize the prophets of Baal.　606
2Ki 7:14 He c the drivers,　606
11: 5 He c them, saying, "This is what you are　7422
14: 6 of the Law of Moses where the LORD c:　7422
17:13 the entire Law that I c your fathers to obey　7422
17:35 a covenant with the Israelites, he c them:　7422
18:12 all that Moses the servant of the LORD c.　7422
18:36 because the king had c,　5184
21: 8 to do everything I c them and will keep　7422
1Ch 6:49 that Moses the servant of God had c.　7422
14:16 So David did as God c him,　7422
15:15 as Moses had c in accordance with the word　7422
16:15 the word he c, for a thousand generations,　7422
17: 6 to any of their leaders whom I c　7422
24:19 as the LORD, the God of Israel, had c him.　7422
2Ch 8:13 to the daily requirement for offerings c　5184
8:18 Hiram sent him ships c by his own officers,　3338
14: 4 He c Judah to seek the LORD,　606
25: 4 in the Book of Moses, where the LORD c:　7422
29:21 The king c the priests,　606
29:25 this was c by the LORD	5184
33: 8 to do everything I c them concerning all　7422
35: 6 doing what the LORD c through Moses."　1821
Ezr 4: 3 as King Cyrus, the king of Persia, c us."　7422
Ne 8: 1 which the LORD had c for Israel.　7422
8:14 which the LORD had c through Moses,	7422
13:22 Then I c the Levites to purify themselves　606
Est 1:10 he c the seven eunuchs who served him—　606
1:17 'King Xerxes c Queen Vashti to be brought　606
2: 8 for the king had c this concerning him.　7422
6:10 "Go at once," the king c Haman.　606
9: 1 the edict c by the king was to　1821
9:14 So the king c that this be done.　606
Ps 33: 9 he c, and it stood firm.　7422
78: 5 which he c our forefathers　7422
105: 8 the word he c, for a thousand generations,　7422
106:34 the peoples as the LORD had c them,　606

Ps	148: 5	for he c and they were created.	7422
Isa	13: 3	I have c my holy ones;	7422
	36:10	because the king had c,	5184
Jer	11: 4	the terms I c your forefathers	7422
	11: 8	of the covenant I had c them to follow but	7422
	17:22	as I c your forefathers.	7422
	26: 8	the people everything the LORD had c him	7422
	32:23	they did not do what you c them to do.	7422
	32:35	though I never c,	7422
	35: 8	Jonadab son of Recab c us.	7422
	35:10	have fully obeyed everything our forefather
		Jonadab c us.	7422
	36:26	Instead, the king c Jerahmeel,	7422
	38:10	Then the king c Ebed-Melech the Cushite,	7422
	47: 7	how can it rest when the LORD has c it,	7422
	50:21	"Do everything I have c you.	7422
Eze	9:11	saying, "I have done as you c."	7422
	10: 6	When the LORD c the man in linen,	7422
	12: 7	So I did as I was c.	7422
	24:18	The next morning I did as I had been c.	7422
	37: 7	So I prophesied as I was c.	7422
	37:10	So I prophesied as he c me,	7422
Da	3: 4	"This is what you are c to do, O peoples,	10042
	3:20	and c some of the strongest soldiers	10042
	4: 6	So I c that all the wise men of Babylon	10302+10682
Am	2:12	the Nazirites drink wine and c the prophets	7422
Jnh	2:10	And the LORD c the fish,	606
Zec	1: 6	which I c my servants the prophets,	7422
Mt	1:24	he did what the angel of the Lord had c him	4705
	8: 4	to the priest and offer the gift Moses c,	4705
	27:10	buy the potter's field, as the Lord c me."	5332
	28:20	to obey everything I have c you.	1948
Mk	1:44	and offer the sacrifices that Moses c	4705
	7:36	Jesus c them not to tell anyone.	1403
Lk	5:14	and offer the sacrifices that Moses c	4705
	8:29	For Jesus had c the evil spirit to come out of	4133
Jn	8: 5	the Law Moses c us to stone such women.	1948
	12:49	Father who sent me c me what to say	1443+1953
	14:31	that I do exactly what my Father has c me.	1948
	18:11	Jesus c Peter, "Put your sword away!	3306
Ac	4:18	Then they called them in again and c them	4133
	10:33	to everything the Lord has c you to tell us."	4705
	10:42	He c us to preach to the people and	4133
	13:47	For this is what the Lord has c us:	1948
	16:23	and the jailer was c to guard them carefully.	4133
1Co	9:14	the Lord has c that those who preach	1411
Heb	9:20	which God has c you to keep."	1948
	12:20	because they could not bear what was c:	1403
1Jn	3:23	and to love one another as he c us.	1443+1953
2Jn	1: 4	just as the Father c us.	1953+3284

COMMANDER (105) [COMMAND]

Ge	21:22	At that time Abimelech and Phicol the c	8569
	21:32	the c of his forces returned to the land of	8569
	26:26	and Phicol c of his forces.	8569
Jos	5:14	"but as c of the army of the LORD I have	8569
	5:15	The c of the LORD's army replied,	8569
Jdg	4: 2	The c of his army was Sisera.	8569
	4: 7	I will lure Sisera, the c of Jabin's army,	8569
	11: 6	"Come," they said, "be our c,	7903
	11:11	the people made him head and c over them.	7903
1Sa	9: 2	the c of the army of Hazor,	8569
	14:50	the c of Saul's army was Abner son of Ner,	8569
	17:18	Take along these ten cheeses to the c	8569
	17:55	he said to Abner, the c of the army, "Abner,	8569
	26: 5	the c of the army, had lain down.	8569
2Sa	2: 8	Abner son of Ner, the c of Saul's army,	8569
	10:16	the c of Hadadezer's army leading them.	8569
	10:18	He also struck down Shobach the c	8569
	19:13	from now on you are not the c of my army	8569
	23:19	He became their c,	8569
1Ki	1:19	the priest and Joab the c of the army,	8569
	2:32	Abner son of Ner, c of Israel's army,	8569
	2:32	of Jether, c of Judah's army—	8569
	4: 4	Benaiah son of Jehoiada—c in chief;	
			2021+6584+7372
	11:15	Joab the c of the army,	8569
	11:21	that Joab the c of the army was also dead.	8569
	16:16	they proclaimed Omri, the c of the army,	8569
2Ki	4:13	on your behalf to the king or the c of	8569
	5: 1	Now Naaman was c of the army of	8569
	9: 5	"I have a message for you, c," he said.	8569
	9: 5	"For you, c," he replied.	8569
	18:17	The king of Assyria sent his **supreme c**,	9580
	18:17	his chief officer and his **field c** with	8072
	18:19	The **field c** said to them, "Tell Hezekiah,	8072
	18:26	and Shebna and Joah said to the **field c**,	8072
	18:27	the c replied, "Was it only to your master	8072
	18:28	Then the c stood and called out in Hebrew,	8072
	18:37	and told him what the **field c** had said.	8072
	19: 4	the words of the **field c**,	8072
	19: 8	When the **field c** heard that the king	8072
	25: 8	Nebuzaradan c of the imperial guard,	8042
	25:10	under the c of the imperial guard.	8042
	25:11	Nebuzaradan the c of the guard carried	8042
	25:12	But the c left behind some of	8042
	25:15	The c of the imperial guard took away	8042
	25:18	The c of the guard took	8042
	25:20	the c took them all and brought them to	8042
1Ch	11:21	above the Three and became their c,	8569
	19:16	the c of Hadadezer's army leading them.	8569
	19:18	also killed Shophach the c of their army.	8569
	27: 5	The third army c, for the third month,	8569
	27: 8	was the c Shamhuth the Izrahite.	8569
	27:34	Joab was the c of the royal army.	

2Ch	17:14	Adnah the c, with 300,000 fighting men;	8569
	17:15	next, Jehohanan the c, with 280,000;	8569
Ne	7: 2	along with Hananiah the c of the citadel,	8569
Pr	6: 7	It has no c, no overseer or ruler,	7903
Isa	20: 1	In the year that the **supreme c**,	9580
	36: 2	Then the king of Assyria sent his **field c**	8072
	36: 2	When the c stopped at the aqueduct of	NIH
	36: 4	The **field c** said to them, "Tell Hezekiah,	8072
	36:11	Shebna and Joah said to the **field c**,	8072
	36:12	the c replied, "Was it only to your master	8072
	36:13	Then the c stood and called out in Hebrew,	8072
	36:22	and told him what the **field c** had said.	8072
	37: 4	the words of the **field c**,	8072
	37: 8	When the **field c** heard that the king	8072
	55: 4	a leader and c of the peoples.	7422
Jer	39: 9	Nebuzaradan c of the imperial guard carried
		into exile	8042
	39:10	the c of the guard left behind in the land	8042
	39:11	about Jeremiah through Nebuzaradan c of	8042
	39:13	So Nebuzaradan the c of the guard,	8042
	40: 1	from the LORD after Nebuzaradan c of	8042
	40: 2	When the c of the guard found Jeremiah,	8042
	40: 5	the c gave him provisions and a present	8042
	41:10	over whom Nebuzaradan c	8042
	43: 6	the king's daughters whom Nebuzaradan c	8042
	51:27	Appoint a c against her;	3261
	52:12	Nebuzaradan c of the imperial guard,	8042
	52:14	The whole Babylonian army under the c of	8042
	52:15	the c of the guard carried into exile some	8042
	52:19	The c of the imperial guard took away	8042
	52:24	The c of the guard took	8042
	52:26	the c took them all and brought them to	8042
	52:30	into exile by Nebuzaradan the c of	8042
Da	2:14	When Arioch, the c of the king's guard,	10647
	11:18	but a c will put an end to his insolence	7903
Jn	18:12	Then the detachment of soldiers with its c	5941
Ac	21:31	news reached the c of the Roman troops	5941
	21:32	When the rioters saw the c and his soldiers,	5941
	21:33	The c came up and arrested him	5941
	21:34	and since the c could not get at the truth	899S
	21:37	he asked the c,	5941
	22:24	the c ordered Paul to be taken into	5941
	22:26	he went to the c and reported it.	5941
	22:27	The c went to Paul and asked, "Tell me,	5941
	22:28	Then the c said,	5941
	22:29	The c himself was alarmed	5941
	22:30	since the c wanted to find out	NIG
	23:10	so violent that the c was afraid Paul would	5941
	23:15	the c to bring him before you on the pretext	5941
	23:17	"Take this young man to the c;	5941
	23:18	So he took him to the c.	5941
	23:19	The c took the young man by the hand,	5941
	23:22	The c dismissed the young man	5941
	24:22	"When Lysias the c comes," he said,	5941

COMMANDER'S (2) [COMMAND]

Jdg	5:14	from Zebulun those who bear a c staff.	6221
Ac	21:40	Having received **the** c permission,	899S

COMMANDER-IN-CHIEF (1) [COMMAND]

1Ch	11: 6	"Whoever leads the attack on the Jebusites
		will become c."	2256+8031+8569

COMMANDERS (88) [COMMAND]

Nu	31:14	the c of thousands and commanders	8569
	31:14	the commanders of thousands and c	8569
	31:48	the c of thousands and commanders	8569
	31:48	the commanders of thousands and c	8569
	31:52	from the c of thousands and commanders	8569
	31:52	of thousands and c of hundreds that Moses	8569
	31:54	from the c of thousands and commanders	8569
	31:54	from the commanders of thousands and c	NIH
Dt	1:15	as c of thousands, of hundreds,	8569
	20: 9	they shall appoint c over it.	7372+8569
Jos	10:24	to the army c who had come with him,	7903
1Sa	8:12	Some he will assign to be c of thousands	8569
	8:12	to be commanders of thousands and c	8569
	18:30	The Philistine c continued to go out	8569
	22: 7	of you c of thousands and commanders	8569
	22: 7	of you commanders of thousands and c	8569
	29: 3	The c of the Philistines asked,	8569
	29: 4	Philistine c were angry with him and said,	8569
	29: 9	nevertheless, the Philistine c have said,	8569
2Sa	18: 1	over them c of thousands and commanders	8569
	18: 1	over them commanders of thousands and c	8569
	18: 5	concerning Absalom to each of the c.	8569
	19: 6	the c and their men mean nothing to you.	8569
	24: 2	king said to Joab and the army c with him,	8569
	24: 4	however, overruled Joab and the army c;	8569
1Ki	1:25	the c of the army and Abiathar the priest.	8569
	2: 5	what he did to the two c of Israel's armies,	8569
	9:22	and the c of his chariots and charioteers.	8569
	14:27	to replace them and assigned these to the c	8569
	15:20	with King Asa and sent the c of his forces	8569
	20:14	of the provincial c will do it.'"	8569
	20:15	the young officers of the provincial c,	8569
	20:17	of the provincial c went out first.	8569
	20:19	of the provincial c marched out of the city	8569
	22:31	the king of Aram had ordered his thirty-two
		chariot c,	8569
	22:32	When the chariot c saw Jehoshaphat,	8569
	22:33	the chariot c saw that he was not the king	8569
2Ki	8:21	and his chariot c, but he rose up and broke	8569
	11: 4	In the seventh year Jehoiada sent for the c	8569
	11: 9	The c of units of a hundred did just	8569

2Ki	11:10	Then he gave the c the spears and shields	8569
	11:15	Jehoiada the priest ordered the c of units of	8569
	11:19	He took with him the c of hundreds,	8569
1Ch	12:14	These Gadites were army c;	8031
	12:21	and they were c in his army.	8569
	13: 1	the c of thousands and commanders	8569
	13: 1	the commanders of thousands and c	NIH
	15:25	So David and the elders of Israel and the c	8569
	21: 2	David said to Joab and the c of the troops,	8569
	25: 1	David, together with the c of the army,	8569
	26:26	of families who were the c of thousands	8569
	26:26	the commanders of thousands and c	NIH
	26:26	and by the other army c.	8569
	27: 1	heads of families, c of thousands	8569
	27: 1	commanders of thousands and c	NIH
	28: 1	over the tribes, the c of the divisions	8569
	28: 1	the service of the king, the c of thousands	8569
	28: 1	the commanders of thousands and c	8569
	29: 6	the c of thousands and commanders	8569
	29: 6	the commanders of thousands and c	NIH
2Ch	1: 2	to the c of thousands and commanders	8569
	1: 2	and c of hundreds, to the judges and to all	NIH
	8: 9	they were his fighting men, c	8569
	8: 9	and c of his chariots and charioteers.	8569
	11:11	He strengthened their defenses and put c	5592
	12:10	to replace them and assigned these to the c	8569
	16: 4	with King Asa and sent the c of his forces	8569
	17:14	From Judah, c of units of 1,000:	8569
	18:30	the king of Aram had ordered his chariot c,	8569
	18:31	When the chariot c saw Jehoshaphat,	8569
	18:32	for when the chariot c saw that he was not	8569
	21: 9	surrounded him and his chariot c,	8569
	23: 1	He made a covenant with the c of units of	8569
	23: 9	the c of units of a hundred the spears and	8569
	23:14	Jehoiada the priest sent out the c of units	8569
	23:20	He took with him the c of hundreds,	8569
	25: 5	to c of thousands and commanders	8569
	25: 5	to commanders of thousands and c	8569
	33:11	against them the army c of the king	8569
	33:14	He stationed military c in all	8569
Job	39:25	the shout of c and the battle cry.	8569
Isa	10: 8	'Are not my c all kings?' he says.	8569
	31: 9	of the battle standard their c will panic,"	8569
Eze	23: 6	and c, all of them handsome young men,	6036
	23:12	governors and c, warriors in full dress,	6036
	23:23	all of them governors and c,	6036
Da	11: 5	of his c will become even stronger than he	8569
Mk	6:21	for his high officials and **military** c and	5941

COMMANDING (7) [COMMAND]

Dt	30:11	Now what I am c you today is	7422
Ezr	4: 8	Rehum the c **officer** and Shimshai	10116+10302
	4: 9	Rehum the c **officer** and Shimshai	10116+10302
	4:17	To Rehum the c **officer**,	10116+10302
Ac	23: 3	yet **you** yourself violate the law by c that I	3027
2Co	8: 8	I **am** not c you,	2198+2848+3306
2Ti	2: 4	he wants to please his c **officer.**	5133

COMMANDMENT (15) [COMMAND]

Jos	22: 5	the c and the law that Moses the servant of	5184
Mt	22:36	which is the greatest c in the Law?"	1953
	22:38	This is the first and greatest c.	1953
Mk	12:31	There is no c greater than these."	1953
Lk	23:56	on the Sabbath in obedience to the c.	1953
Ro	7: 8	seizing the opportunity afforded by the c,	1953
	7: 9	the c came, sin sprang to life and I died.	1953
	7:10	I found that the very c that was intended	1953
	7:11	seizing the opportunity afforded by the c,	1953
	7:11	and through **the** c put me to death.	899S
	7:12	So then, the law is holy, and the c is holy,	1953
	7:13	the sin might become utterly sinful.	1953
	13: 9	and whatever other c there may be,	1953
Eph	6: 2	which is the first c with a promise—	1953
Heb	9:19	When Moses had proclaimed every c of	1953

COMMANDMENTS (20) [COMMAND]

Ex	20: 6	of those who love me and keep my c	5184
	34:28	of the covenant—the Ten C.	1821
Dt	4:13	the Ten C, which he commanded you	1821
	5:10	of those who love me and keep my c.	5184
	5:22	These are the c the LORD proclaimed in	1821
	6: 6	These c that I give you today are to be	1821
	9:10	the c the LORD proclaimed to you on	1821
	10: 4	the Ten C he had proclaimed to you on	1821
Ecc	12:13	Fear God and keep his c,	5184
Mt	5:19	the least of these c and teaches others to do	1953
	19:17	If you want to enter life, obey the c."	1953
	22:40	and the Prophets hang on these two c."	1953
Mk	10:19	You know the c:	1953
	12:28	he asked him, "Of all the c,	1953
Lk	1: 6	the Lord's c and regulations blamelessly.	1953
	18:20	You know the c:	1953
Ro	13: 9	The c, "Do not commit adultery,"	NIG
Eph	2:15	by abolishing in his flesh the law with its c	1953
Rev	12:17	those who obey God's c and hold to	1953
	14:12	on the part of the saints who obey God's c	1953

COMMANDS (183) [COMMAND]

Ge	26: 5	my c, my decrees and my laws."	5184
Ex	8:27	as he c us.	606
	15:26	to his c and keep all his decrees,	5184
	16:28	"How long will you refuse to keep my c	5184
	18:23	If you do this and God so c,	7422
	24:12	and c I have written for their instruction."	5184

Ex	25:22	I will meet with you and give you all my c	7422
	34:32	gave them all the c	7422
Lev	4: 2	in any of the LORD's c—	5184
	4:13	in any of the LORD's c,	5184
	4:22	and does what is forbidden in any of the c	5184
	4:27	in any of the LORD's c,	5184
	5:17	in any of the LORD's c,	5184
	22:31	"Keep my c and follow them.	5184
	26: 3	and are careful to obey my c,	5184
	26:14	not listen to me and carry out all these c	5184
	26:15	and fail to carry out all my c and	5184
	27:34	These are the c LORD gave Moses	5184
Nu	9: 8	"Wait until I find out what the LORD	7422
	15:22	of these c the LORD gave Moses—	5184
	15:23	any of the LORD's c to you through him,	7422
	15:31	and broken his c, that person must surely	5184
	15:39	at and so you will remember all the c of	5184
	15:40	Then you will remember to obey all my c	5184
	30: 1	"This is what the LORD c:	7422
	32:25	"We your servants will do as our lord c.	7422
	36: 6	the LORD c for Zelophehad's daughters:	7422
	36:13	the c and regulations the LORD gave	5184
Dt	4: 2	but keep the c of the LORD your God	5184
	4:40	Keep his decrees and c,	5184
	5:29	to fear me and keep all my c always,	5184
	5:31	with me so that I may give you all the c,	5184
	6: 1	These are the c, decrees and laws	5184
	6: 2	as you live by keeping all his decrees and c	5184
	6:17	to keep the c of the LORD your God and	5184
	7: 9	of those who love him and keep his c.	5184
	7:11	Therefore, take care to follow the c,	5184
	8: 2	whether or not you would keep his c.	5184
	8: 6	Observe the c of the LORD your God,	5184
	8:11	failing to observe his c,	5184
	10:13	and to observe the LORD's c and decrees	5184
	11: 1	his decrees, his laws and his c always.	5184
	11: 8	therefore all the c I am giving you today,	5184
	11:13	the c I am giving you today—	5184
	11:22	If you carefully observe all these c I am giving you	5184
	11:27	if you obey the c of the LORD your God	5184
	11:28	the c of the LORD your God and turn	5184
	13: 4	Keep his c and obey him;	5184
	13:18	keeping all his c that I am giving you today	5184
	15: 5	to follow all these c I am giving you today.	5184
	26:13	from your c nor have I forgotten any	5184
	26:16	The LORD your God c you this day	7422
	26:17	that you will keep his decrees, c and laws,	5184
	26:18	and that you are to keep all his c.	5184
	27: 1	"Keep all these c that I give you today.	5184
	27:10	the LORD your God and follow his c	5184
	28: 1	carefully follow all his c I give you today,	5184
	28: 9	if you keep the c of the LORD your God	5184
	28:13	to the c of the LORD your God	5184
	28:14	from any of the c I give you today,	1821
	28:15	and do not carefully follow all his c	5184
	28:45	and observe the c and decrees he gave you.	5184
	30: 8	and follow all his c I am giving you today.	5184
	30:10	and keep his c and decrees that are written	5184
	30:16	to walk in his ways, and to keep his c,	5184
Jos	22: 5	to walk in all his ways, to obey his c,	5184
Jdg	2:17	the way of obedience to the LORD's c.	5184
	3: 4	see whether they would obey the LORD's c,	5184
	4: 6	"The LORD, the God of Israel, c you:	7422
1Sa	12:14	not rebel against his c, and if both you and	7023
	12:15	and if you rebel against his c,	7023
2Sa	9:11	the king c his servant to do."	7422
1Ki	2: 3	and keep his decrees and c,	5184
	3:14	in my ways and obey my statutes and c	5184
	6:12	carry out my regulations and keep all my c	5184
	8:58	to walk in all his ways and to keep the c,	5184
	8:61	to live by his decrees and obey his c,	5184
	9: 6	the c and decrees I have given you	5184
	11:34	whom I chose and who observed my c	5184
	11:38	in my eyes by keeping my statutes and c,	5184
	14: 8	who kept my c and followed me	5184
	15: 5	not failed to keep any of the LORD's c all	7422
	18:18	You have abandoned the LORD's c	5184
	20:24	the kings from their c and replace them	5226
2Ki	17:13	Observe my c and decrees,	5184
	17:16	the c of the LORD their God and made	5184
	17:19	not keep the c of the LORD their God.	5184
	17:34	and c that the LORD gave the descendants	5184
	17:37	the laws and c he wrote for you.	5184
	18: 6	he kept the c the LORD had given Moses.	5184
	18:12	They neither listened to the c	NIH
	23: 3	to follow the c and keep his c,	5184
1Ch	28: 7	if he is unswerving in carrying out my c	5184
	28: 8	to follow all the c of the LORD your God,	5184
	29:19	the wholehearted devotion to keep your c,	5184
2Ch	7:19	the decrees and c I have given you	5184
	8:15	not deviate from the king's c to the priests	5184
	14: 4	and to obey his laws and c,	5184
	17: 4	and followed his c rather than the practices	5184
	19:10	c, decrees or ordinances—	5184
	24:20	'Why do you disobey the LORD's c?	5184
	31:21	and in obedience to the law and the c,	5184
	34:31	to follow the c and keep his c,	5184
Ezr	7:11	concerning the c and decrees of the LORD	5184
	9:10	For we have disregarded the c	5184
	9:14	Shall we again break your c and intermarry	5184
	10: 3	and of those who fear the c of our God.	5184
Ne	1: 5	with those who love him and obey his c,	5184
	1: 7	We have not obeyed the c,	5184
	1: 9	but if you return to me and obey my c,	5184
	9:13	and decrees and c that are good.	5184
	9:13	and gave them c,	5184

Ne	9:16	and did not obey your c.	5184
	9:29	and disobeyed your c.	5184
	9:34	to your c or the warnings you gave them.	5184
	10:29	of God and to obey carefully all the c,	5184
	10:32	the c to give a third of a shekel each year	5184
	12:45	to the c of David and his son Solomon.	5184
Job	23:12	I have not departed from the c of his lips;	5184
	36:10	to correction and c them to repent	606
	36:32	with lightning and c it to strike its mark.	7422
	37:12	the whole earth to do whatever he c them.	7422
Ps	19: 8	The c of the LORD are radiant,	5184
	78: 7	not forget his deeds but would keep his c.	5184
	89:31	and fail to keep my c,	5184
	112: 1	who finds great delight in his c.	5184
	119: 6	be put to shame when I consider all your c.	5184
	119:10	do not let me stray from your c.	5184
	119:19	do not hide your c from me.	5184
	119:21	who are cursed and who stray from your c.	5184
	119:32	I run in the path of your c,	5184
	119:35	Direct me in the path of your c,	5184
	119:47	for I delight in your c because I love them.	5184
	119:48	I lift up my hands to your c, which I love,	5184
	119:60	I will hasten and not delay to obey your c.	5184
	119:66	for I believe in your c.	5184
	119:73	give me understanding to learn your c.	5184
	119:86	All your c are trustworthy;	5184
	119:96	but your c are boundless.	5184
	119:98	Your c make me wiser than my enemies,	5184
	119:115	that I may keep the c of my God!	5184
	119:127	Because I love your c more than gold,	5184
	119:131	longing for your c.	5184
	119:143	but your c are my delight.	5184
	119:151	O LORD, and all your c are true.	5184
	119:166	O LORD, and I follow your c.	5184
	119:172	for all your c are righteous.	5184
	119:176	for I have not forgotten your c.	5184
Pr	2: 1	if you accept my words and store up my c	5184
	3: 1	but keep my c in your heart,	5184
	4: 4	keep my c and you will live.	5184
	6:20	keep your father's c and do	5184
	6:23	For these c are a lamp,	5184
	7: 1	keep my words and store up my c	5184
	7: 2	Keep my c and you will live;	5184
	10: 8	The wise in heart accept c,	5184
Isa	48:18	If only you had paid attention to my c,	5184
	58: 2	and has not forsaken the c of its God.	5477
Jer	7:22	not just give them c about burnt offerings	7422
	22: 4	For if you are careful to carry out these c,	1821
	22: 5	But if you do not obey these c,	1821
Da	9: 4	with all who love him and obey his c,	5184
	9: 5	we have turned away from your c and laws.	5184
Zep	2: 3	you who do what he c.	5477
Mt	5:19	and teaches these c will be called great in	NIG
Mk	7: 8	of the c of God and are holding on to	1953
	7: 9	"You have a fine way of setting aside the c	1953
Lk	8:25	He c even the winds and the water,	2199
Jn	14:21	Whoever has my c and obeys them,	1953
	15:10	If you obey my c, you will remain in my love,	1953
	15:10	as I have obeyed my Father's c and remain	1953
Ac	17:30	now he c all people everywhere to repent.	4133
1Co	7:19	Keeping God's c is what counts.	1953
Col	2:22	they are based on human c and teachings.	1945
Tit	1:14	or to the c of those who reject the truth.	1953
1Jn	2: 3	to know him if we obey his c.	1953
	2: 4	but does not do what he c is a liar,	1953
	3:22	we obey his c and do what pleases him.	1953
	3:24	Those who obey his c live in him,	1953
	5: 2	by loving God and carrying out his c.	1953
	5: 3	This is love for God: to obey his c.	1953
	5: 3	And his c are not burdensome,	1953
2Jn	1: 6	that we walk in obedience to his c.	1953

COMMEMORATE (4) [COMMEMORATED]

Ex	12:14	"This is a day you are to c;	2355
	13: 3	Then Moses said to the people, "C this day,	2349
Jdg	11:40	to c the daughter of Jephthah the Gileadite.	9480
2Ch	35:25	and women singers c Josiah in the laments.	606

COMMEMORATED (1) [COMMEMORATE]

Lev	23:24	a sacred assembly c with trumpet blasts.	2355

COMMEND (10) [COMMENDABLE, COMMENDED, COMMENDS]

Ps	145: 4	One generation will c your works	8655
Ecc	8:15	So I c the enjoyment of life,	8655
Ro	13: 3	do what is right and he will c you.	2047+2400
	16: 1	I c to you our sister Phoebe,	5319
2Co	3: 1	Are we beginning to c ourselves again?	5319
	4: 2	the truth plainly we c ourselves	5319
	5:12	not trying to c ourselves to you again,	5319
	6: 4	of God we c ourselves in every way:	5319
	10:12	with some who c themselves.	5319
1Pe	2:14	and to c those who do right.	2047

COMMENDABLE (2) [COMMEND]

1Pe	2:19	For it is c if a man bears up under the pain	5921
	2:20	this is c before God.	5921

COMMENDED (9) [COMMEND]

Ne	11: 2	The people c all the men who volunteered	1385
Job	29:11	and those who saw me c me,	6386
Lk	16: 8	"The master c the dishonest manager	2046

Ac	15:40	c by the brothers to the grace of the Lord.	4140
2Co	12:11	I ought to have been c by you,	5319
Heb	11: 2	This is what the ancients were c for.	3455
	11: 4	By faith he was c as a righteous man,	3455
	11: 5	he was c as one who pleased God.	3455
	11:39	These were all c for their faith,	3455

COMMENDS (3) [COMMEND]

Pr	15: 2	The tongue of the wise c knowledge,	3512
2Co	10:18	not the one who c himself who is approved,	5319
	10:18	but the one whom the Lord c.	5319

COMMISSION (5) [COMMISSIONED, COMMISSIONERS]

Nu	27:19	and the entire assembly and c him	7422
Dt	3:28	But c Joshua, and encourage	7422
	31:14	where I will c him.	7422
Ac	26:12	with the authority and c of the chief priests.	2207
Col	1:25	by the c God gave me to present to you	3873

COMMISSIONED (1) [COMMISSION]

Nu	27:23	Then he laid his hands on him and c him,	7422

COMMISSIONERS (2) [COMMISSION]

Ge	41:34	Let Pharaoh appoint c over the land to take	7224
Est	2: 3	Let the king appoint c in every province	7224

COMMIT (56) [COMMITS, COMMITTED, COMMITTING]

Ex	20:14	"You shall not c adultery.	5537
Dt	5:18	"You shall not c adultery.	5537
1Sa	7: 3	the Ashtoreths and c yourselves to the LORD	3922
1Ki	14:16	and has caused Israel to c."	2627
	15:26	his sin, which he had caused Israel to c.	2627
	15:30	and had caused Israel to c,	2627
	15:34	his sin, which he had caused Israel to c,	2627
	16:13	and had caused Israel to c,	2627
	16:19	and had caused Israel to c,	2627
	16:26	his sin, which he had caused Israel to c,	2627
	16:31	not only considered it trivial to c the sins of Jeroboam	928+2143
2Ki	3: 3	which he had caused Israel to c;	2627
	10:29	which he had caused Israel to c—	2627
	10:31	which he had caused Israel to c;	2627
	13: 2	which he had caused Israel to c;	2627
	13: 6	which he had caused Israel to c;	2627
	13:11	which he had caused Israel to c;	2627
	14:24	which he had caused Israel to c.	2627
	15: 9	which he had caused Israel to c.	2627
	15:18	which he had caused Israel to c.	2627
	15:24	which he had caused Israel to c.	2627
	15:28	which he had caused Israel to c.	2627
	17:21	the LORD and caused them to c	2627
	21:16	the sin that he had caused Judah to c,	2627
Ezr	9:14	the peoples who c such detestable practices?	AIT
Ne	6:13	to intimidate me so that I would c a sin	2627
Ps	31: 5	Into your hands I c my spirit;	7212
	37: 5	C your way to the LORD;	1670
Pr	16: 3	C to the LORD whatever you do,	1670
Jer	7: 9	c adultery and perjury,	5537
	23:14	They c adultery and live a lie.	5537
Eze	16:38	to the punishment of women who c adultery	5537
	16:51	Samaria did not c half the sins you did.	2627
	18: 7	He does not c robbery but gives his food to the hungry	1608+1611
	18:16	He does not c robbery but gives his food to the hungry	1608+1611
	22: 9	at the mountain shrines and c lewd acts.	6913
	22:29	practice extortion and c robbery;	1608+1610
	23:45	to the punishment of women who c adultery	5537
Hos	4:14	when they c adultery, because	5537
	4:15	"Though you c adultery, O Israel,	2388
Mt	5:27	'Do not c adultery.'	3658
	19:18	" 'Do not murder, do not c adultery,	3658
Mk	10:19	'Do not murder, do not c adultery,	3658
Lk	18:20	'Do not c adultery, do not murder,	3658
	23:46	"Father, into your hands I c my spirit."	4192
Ac	20:32	"Now I c you to God and to the word	4192
Ro	2:22	that people should not c adultery,	3658
	2:22	do you c adultery?	3658
	13: 9	The commandments, "Do not c adultery,"	3658
1Co	10: 8	not c sexual immorality,	4519
Jas	2:11	For he who said, "Do not c adultery,"	3658
	2:11	not c adultery but do commit murder,	3658
	2:11	not commit adultery but do c murder,	5839
1Pe	4:19	to God's will should c themselves	4192
1Jn	5:16	If anyone sees his brother c a sin that does not lead to death,	279+281
Rev	2:22	and I will make those who c adultery	3658

COMMITS (20) [COMMIT]

Lev	5:15	"When a person c a violation	5085+5086
	6: 3	if he c any such sin that people may do—	2627
	20:10	" 'If a man c adultery	5537
Ps	10:14	The victim c himself to you;	6440
	36: 4	he c himself to a sinful course and does	3656
Pr	6:32	But a man who c adultery lacks judgment;	5537
	29:22	and a hot-tempered one c many sins.	NIH
Ecc	8:12	Although a wicked man c a hundred crimes	6913
Eze	18:12	He c robbery.	1608+1611
	18:14	a son who sees all the sins his father c, and	6913
	18:24	man turns from his righteousness and c sin	6913

Eze 18:26   turns from his righteousness and c sin,   6913
    22:11   In you one man c a detestable offense   6913
Mt   5:32   the divorced woman c adultery,   3656
    19: 9   and marries another woman c adultery."   3656
Mk 10:11   and marries another woman c adultery   3656
    10:12   and marries another man, *she* c adultery."   3656
Lk   16:18   and marries another woman c adultery,   3658
    16:18   a divorced woman c adultery.   3658
1Co   6:18   All other sins a man c are outside his body,   4472

COMMITTED (89) [COMMIT]
Ge   31:36   "What sin have I c that you hunt me down?   AIT
    50:17   and the wrongs *they* c in *treating* you   1694
Ex   32:30   "You *have* c a great sin.   2627+2631
    32:31   a great sin these people *have* c!   2627+2631
Lev   4: 3   as a sin offering for the sin *he has* c.   2627
    4:14   When they become aware of the sin *they* c,   2627
    4:23   When he is made aware of the sin *he* c,   2627
    4:28   When he is made aware of the sin *he* c,   2627
    4:28   as his offering for the sin *he* c a female goat   2627
    4:35   for him for the sin *he has* c,   2627
    5: 6   as a penalty for the sin *he has* c,   2627
    5:10   for him for the sin *he has* c,   2627
    5:13   for him for any of these sins *he has* c,   2627
    5:18   **wrong** he has c **unintentionally,**   8704+8705
    19:22   before the LORD for the sin *he has* c,   2627
Nu   5: 7   and must confess the sin *he has* c.   6913
    12:11   against us the sin *we have* so foolishly c.   2627
Dt   9:18   because of all the sin *you had* c,   2627
    19:15   any crime or offense *he may have* c.   2627+2628
    22:26   she has c no sin deserving death.   NIH
Jdg   20: 6   because *they* c this lewd   6913
    20:12   "What about this awful crime that *was* c   2118
1Sa   14:38   let us find out what sin *has been* c today.   2118
1Ki   8:50   the offenses *they have* c against you,   7321
    8:61   be **fully** c to the LORD our God,   8969
    14:16   up because of the sins Jeroboam *has* c   2627
    14:22   By the sins *they* c they stirred   2627
    15: 3   *He* c all the sins his father had done   928+2143
    15:14   Asa's heart was **fully** c to   8969
    15:30   because of the sins Jeroboam *had* c   2627
    16:13   and his son Elah *had* c and had caused Israel   2627
    16:19   because of the sins *he had* c,   2627
    16:19   ways of Jeroboam and in the sin *he had* c   6913
2Ki   21:11   of Judah *has* c these detestable sins   6913
    21:17   and all he did, including the sin *he* c,   2627
1Ch   16: 7   That day David first c to Asaph   5989
2Ch   16: 9   Asa's heart was **fully** c [to   8969
    16: 9   to strengthen those whose hearts are **fully** c   8969
    34:16   that *has been* c to them.   5989
Ne   1: 6   *have* c against you.   2627
    9:18   or when *they* c awful blasphemies.   6913
    9:26   *they* c awful blasphemies.   6913
Job   13:23   How many wrongs and sins have I c?   4200
Ps   51: T   David *had* c adultery with Bathsheba.   448+995
Isa   42:19   Who is blind like the *one* c to me,   8966
Jer   2:13   "My people *have* c two sins: 6913
    3: 6   and *has* c adultery there.   2388
    3: 8   she also went out and c adultery.   2388
    3: 9   and c adultery with stone and wood.   5537
    5: 7   yet *they* c adultery and thronged to   5537
    11:20   for to you I *have* c my cause.   1655
    16:10   What sin have *we* c against   2627
    20:12   for to you I *have* c my cause.   1655
    29:23   *they have* c adultery   5537
    33: 8   from all the sin *they have* c against me   2627
    37:18   "What **crime** *have I* c against you   2627
    41:11   the crimes Ishmael son of Nethaniah *had* c,   6913
    44: 9   the wickedness c by your fathers and by   6913
    44: 9   the wickedness c by you and your wives in   NIH
Eze   18:21   the sins *he has* c and keeps all my decrees   6913
    18:22   of the offenses *he has* c will be remembered   6913
    18:24   of and because of the sins *he has* c,   2627
    18:26   because of the sin *he has* c he will die.   6913
    18:27   from the wickedness *he has* c   6913
    18:28   the offenses *he has* c and turns away   6913
    18:31   of all the offenses *you have* c,   7321
    23:37   for *they have* c adultery and blood is   5537
    23:37   They c adultery with their idols;   5537
    33:16   of the sins *he has* c will be remembered   2627
Mal   2:11   A detestable thing *has been* c in Israel and   6913
Mt   5:28   who looks at a woman lustfully *has* already c adultery with her in his heart.   3658
    11:27   "All things *have been* c to me   4140
    27:23   What **crime** *has* he c?"   4472
Mk   15: 7   with the insurrectionists who *had* c murder   4472
    15:14   What crime *has* he c?"   4472
Lk   10:22   "All things *have been* c to me   4140
    23:22   What crime *has* this man c?   4472
Ac   14:23   with prayer and fasting, c them to the Lord,   4192
    14:26   where they had been c to the grace of God   4140
Ro   1:27   Men c indecent acts with other men,   2981
    3:25   the sins c **beforehand** unpunished—   4588
1Co   9:17   I am simply discharging the trust c to *me*.   4409
2Co   5:19   he *has* c to us the message of reconciliation.   5502
Heb   9: 7   sins the people had c in ignorance.   52
    9:15   as a ransom to set them free from the sins c   NIG
1Pe   2:22   "He c no sin, and no deceit was found   4472
Rev   17: 2   the earth c adultery and the inhabitants of   4519
    18: 3   The kings of the earth c adultery with her,   4519
    18: 9   the kings of the earth who c adultery   4519

COMMITTING (2) [COMMIT]
Hos   6: 9   on the road to Shechem, c shameful crimes.   6913
Rev   2:14   and by c sexual immorality.   4519

COMMON (26)
Ge   11: 1   world had one language and a c speech.   285
Lev   10:10   between the holy and the c,   2687
2Sa   16:10   king said, "What do you and I have in c,   4200
    19:22   "What do you and I have in c,   4200
1Ki   10:27   silver as c in Jerusalem as stones,   3869
2Ki   23: 6   dust over the graves of the c **people.**   1201+6639
2Ch   1:15   gold as c in Jerusalem as stones,   3869
    9:27   silver as c in Jerusalem as stones,   3869
Ne   7: 5   the c people for registration by families.   6639
Ps   73: 5   They are free from the **burdens** c to man;   AIT
Pr   1:14   and we will share a c purse"—   285
    22: 2   Rich and poor have *this* in c: 7008
    29:13   poor man and the oppressor have *this* in c: 7008
Ecc   9: 2   All share a c destiny—   285
Jer   26:23   into the burial place of the c people.)   1201+6639
Eze   22:26   not distinguish between the holy and the c;   2687
    42:20   to separate the holy from the c.   2687
    44:23   between the holy and the c and show them   2687
    48:15   cubits long, will be for the c use of the city,   2687
Ac   2:44   and had everything in c.   3123
Ro   9:21   for noble purposes and some for c use?   871
1Co   10:13   No temptation has seized you except what is c to man.   474
    12: 7   of the Spirit is given for the c good.   NIG
2Co   6:14   and wickedness have in c?   3580
    6:15   a believer have in c with an unbeliever?   3535
Tit   1: 4   my true son in our c faith: 3123

COMMONWEALTH (KJV) See CITIZENSHIP

COMMOTION (8)
Job   39: 7   He laughs at the c *in* the town;   2162
Isa   22: 2   O town full of c,   9583
Jer   3:23   Surely the [idolatrous] c on the hills   2162
    10:22   a great c from the land of the north!   8323
Mk   5:38   Jesus saw a c,   2573
    5:39   "Why all this c and wailing?   2572
Ac   12:18   there was no small c among the soldiers as   5431
    19:40   not be able to account for this c,   5371

COMMUNION (KJV) See PARTICIPATION, FELLOWSHIP

COMMUNITIES (2) [COMMUNITY]
Am   1: 6   Because she took captive whole c   1661
    1: 9   she sold whole c **of captives** to Edom,   1661

COMMUNITY (86) [COMMUNITIES, COMMUNITY'S]
Ge   28: 3   until you become a c *of* peoples.   7736
    35:11   and a c *of* nations will come from you,   7736
    48: 4   I will make you a c *of* peoples,   7736
Ex   12: 3   the whole c *of* Israel that on the tenth day   6337
    12: 6   of the c *of* Israel must slaughter them   6337
    12:19   with yeast in it must be cut off from the c   6337
    12:47   The whole c *of* Israel must celebrate it.   6337
    16: 1   The whole Israelite c set out from Elim   6337
    16: 2   the whole c grumbled against Moses   6337
    16: 9   "Say to the entire Israelite c,   6337
    16:10   to the whole Israelite c,   6337
    16:22   the leaders of the c came and reported this   6337
    17: 1   The whole Israelite c set out from   6337
    34:31   the leaders of the c came back to him,   6337
    35: 1   Moses assembled the whole Israelite c   6337
    35: 4   Moses said to the whole Israelite c,   6337
    35:20   Then the whole Israelite c withdrew   6337
    38:25   from those of the c who were counted in   6337
Lev   4:13   the whole Israelite c sins unintentionally   6337
    4:13   even though the c is unaware of the matter,   7736
    4:15   The elders of the c are to lay their hands on   6337
    4:21   This is the sin offering for the c.   7736
    4:27   " 'If a member of the c sins unintentionally   824+2021+6639
    10: 6   the LORD will be angry with the whole c.   6337
    10:17   the c by making atonement for them before   6337
    16: 5   the Israelite c he is to take two male goats   6337
    16:17   his household and the whole c of Israel.   7736
    16:33   for the priests and all the people of the c.   7736
    20: 2   The people of the c are to stone him.   824
    20: 4   If the people of the c close their eyes when   824
Nu   1: 2   "Take a census of the whole Israelite c   6337
    1:16   These were the men appointed from the c,   6337
    1:18   and they called the whole c together on   6337
    1:53   so that wrath will not fall on the Israelite c.   6337
    3: 7   and for the whole c at the Tent of Meeting   6337
    4:34   the c counted the Kohathites by their clans   6337
    8: 9   and assemble the whole Israelite c.   6337
    8:20   Aaron and the whole Israelite c did with   6337
    10: 2   and use them for calling the c together and   6337
    10: 3   the whole c is to assemble before you at   6337
    13:26   and the whole Israelite c at Kadesh in   6337
    14: 1   of the c raised their voices and wept aloud.   6337
    14:27   "How long will this wicked c grumble   6337
    14:35   to this whole wicked c,   6337
    14:36   and made the whole c grumble against him   6337
    15:15   The c is to have the same rules for you and   7736
    15:24   without the c being aware of it,   6337
    15:24   then the whole c is to offer a young bull for   6337
    15:25   for the whole Israelite c,   6337
    15:26   The whole Israelite c and the aliens living   6337

Nu   16: 2   well-known c leaders who had been appointed members of the council.   6337
    16: 3   The whole c is holy, every one of them,   6337
    16: 9   the Israelite c and brought you near himself   6337
    16: 9   to stand before the c and minister to them?   6337
    16:33   they perished and were gone from the c.   7736
    16:41   the whole Israelite c grumbled   6337
    19: 9   They shall be kept by the Israelite c for use   6337
    19:20   he must be cut off from the c,   7736
    20: 1   the first month the whole Israelite c arrived   6337
    20: 2   Now there was no water for the c,   6337
    20: 4   Why did you bring the LORD's c   7736
    20: 8   the c so they and their livestock can drink."   6337
    20:11   and the c and their livestock drank.   6337
    20:12   not bring this c into the land I give them."   7736
    20:22   The whole Israelite c set out from Kadesh   6337
    20:27   up Mount Hor in the sight of the whole c.   6337
    20:29   the whole c learned that Aaron had died,   6337
    26: 2   "Take a census of the whole Israelite c   6337
    26: 9   the c officials who rebelled against Moses   6337
    27:14   the c rebelled at the waters in the Desert   6337
    27:16   appoint a man over this c   6337
    27:20   so the whole Israelite c will obey him.   6337
    27:21   and the entire c of the Israelites will go out,   6337
    31:13   the c went to meet them outside the camp.   6337
    31:26   the priest and the family heads of the c are   6337
    31:27   in the battle and the rest of the c.   6337
    32: 2   the priest and to the leaders of the c,   6337
Jos   9:21   and water carriers for the entire c."   6337
    9:27   and water carriers for the c and for the altar   6337
    22:17   a plague fell on the c of the LORD!   6337
    22:18   be angry with the whole c of Israel.   6337
    22:20   did not wrath come upon the whole c   6337
    22:30   Phinehas the priest and the leaders of the c   6337
2Ch   31:18   the sons and daughters of the whole c listed   7736
Jer   30:20   and their c will be established before me;   6337
Ac   25:24   The whole **Jewish** c has petitioned me   2681+4436

COMMUNITY'S (1) [COMMUNITY]
Nu   31:43   the c half—was 337,500 sheep,   6337

COMPACT (3) [COMPACTED]
2Sa   3:21   so that they may make a c with you,   1382
    5: 3   the king made a c with them at Hebron   1382
1Ch   11: 3   he made a c with them at Hebron before   1382

COMPACTED (1) [COMPACT]
Ps   122: 3   like a city that **is** closely c together.   2489

COMPANIES (8) [COMPANY]
Jdg   7:16   the three hundred men into three c,   8031
    7:20   The three c blew the trumpets and smashed   8031
    9:34   near Shechem in four c.   8031
    9:43   into three c and set an ambush in the fields.   8031
    9:44   the c with him rushed forward to a position   8031
    9:44   Then two c rushed upon those in the fields   8031
2Ki   11: 5   You who are in the three c that are going   NIH
    11: 7   and you who are in the other two c   3338

COMPANION (8) [COMPANIONS]
1Ki   20:35   of the sons of the prophets said to his c,   8276
Job   30:29   a c of owls.   8276
Ps   55:13   But it is you, a man like myself, my c,   476
    55:20   **My** c attacks his friends;   2257S
Pr   13:20   but a c of fools suffers harm.   8287
    28: 7   but a c of gluttons disgraces his father.   8287
    29: 3   but a c *of* prostitutes squanders his wealth.   8287
Rev   1: 9   and c in the suffering and kingdom   5171

COMPANIONS (27) [COMPANION]
Jdg   14:11   When he appeared, he was given thirty c.   5335
2Ki   9: 2   from his c and take him into an inner room.   278
Ps   38:11   and c avoid me because of my wounds;   8276
    45: 7   above your c by anointing you with the oil   2492
    45:14   her virgin c follow her and are brought   8292
    88:18   You have taken my c and loved ones   8276
Pr   18:24   A man of *many* c may come to ruin,   8276
Isa   1:23   Your rulers are rebels, c of thieves;   2492
Mt   12: 3   when he and his c were hungry?   3552+3836
    12: 4   he and his c ate the consecrated bread   3552+3836
    26:51   one *of* Jesus' c reached for his sword,   3552+3836
Mk   1:36   Simon and his c went to look for him,   3552+3836
    2:25   and his c were hungry and in need?   3552+3836
    2:26   he also gave some *to* his c."   1639+3836+5250
Lk   6: 3   all his c were astonished at the catch   3836+5250
    6: 3   when he and his c were hungry?   1639+3552+3836
    6: 4   And he also gave some *to* his c."   3552
    9:32   Peter and his c were very sleepy,   3836+5250
    24:24   some *of* our c went to the tomb   1609+3836+5250
Ac   13:13   and his c sailed to Perga in Pamphylia,   3836+4309
    16: 6   and his c traveled throughout the region   NIG
    19:29   Paul's **traveling** c from Macedonia,   5292
    20:34   and the needs of my c.   1639+3552+3836
    22: 9   My c saw the light,   1639+3836+5250
    22:11   My c led me by the hand into Damascus,   5289
    26:13   blazing around me and my c.   4513+5250
Heb   1: 9   above your c by anointing you with the oil   3581

COMPANY (36) [COMPANIES]
Ge   13: 9   *Let's* part c.   7233
    13:11   The two men **parted** c: 7233
    50: 9   It was a very large c.   4722

Jdg	9:37	the center of the land, and a c is coming	8031
2Ki	1:9	to Elijah a captain with his c of fifty men.	AIT
	2:3	The c of the prophets at Bethel came out	1201
	2:5	The c of the prophets at Jericho went up	1201
	2:7	of the c of the prophets went and stood at	1201
	2:15	The c of the prophets from Jericho.	1201
	4:1	a man from the c of the prophets cried out	1201
	4:38	c of the prophets was meeting with him,	1201
	5:22	the c of the prophets have just come to me	1201
	6:1	The c of the prophets said to Elisha,	1201
	9:1	from the c of the prophets and said to him,	1201
Ezr	2:2	in c with Zerubbabel,	6640
	2:64	The whole c numbered 42,360,	7736
Ne	7:7	in c with Zerubbabel,	6640
	7:66	The whole c numbered 42,360,	7736
	7:66	The whole c that had returned	7736
Job	15:34	For the c of the godless will be barren,	6337
	34:8	He keeps c with evildoers;	782+2495+4200
Ps	14:5	for God is present in the c of the righteous.	1887
	68:11	great was the c of those who proclaimed it:	7372
	106:17	it buried the c of Abiram.	6337
Pr	21:16	of understanding comes to rest in the c of	7736
	24:1	do not desire their c;	907+2118
Jer	15:17	I never sat in the c of revelers,	6051
Eze	27:34	your wares and all your c have gone down	7736
Ob	1:20	This c of Israelite exiles who are	2657
Mt	27:27	and gathered the whole c of soldiers	5061
Mk	15:16	the whole c of soldiers.	5061
Lk	2:13	a great c of the heavenly host appeared	4436
	2:44	Thinking he was in their c,	5322
Ac	15:39	They had a sharp disagreement that they parted c.	253+608+714
Ro	15:24	after I have enjoyed your c for a while.	1855
1Co	15:33	"Bad c corrupts good character."	3918

COMPARE (20) [COMPARED, COMPARING, COMPARISON]

Job	28:17	Neither gold nor crystal can c with it,	6885
	28:19	The topaz of Cush cannot c with it;	6885
	39:13	but they cannot c with the pinions	NIH
Ps	86:8	no deeds can c with yours.	3869
	89:6	in the skies above can c with the LORD?	6885
Pr	3:15	nothing you desire can c with her.	8750
	8:11	and nothing you desire can c with her.	8750
Isa	40:18	To whom, then, will you c God?	1948
	40:18	What image will you c him to?	6885
	40:25	"To whom will you c me	1948
	46:5	"To whom will you c me	1948
La	2:13	With what can I c you,	1948
Eze	31:8	the plane trees c with its branches—	2118+3869
Da	1:13	Then c our appearance with that of	8011
Mt	11:16	"To what can I c this generation?	3929
Lk	7:31	then, can I c the people of this generation?	3929
	13:18	What shall I c it to?	3929
	13:20	"What shall I c the kingdom of God to?	3929
2Co	10:12	We do not dare to classify or c ourselves	5173
	10:12	and c themselves with themselves,	5173

COMPARED (6) [COMPARE]

Jdg	8:2	"What have I accomplished c to you?	3869
	8:3	What was I able to do c to you?"	3869
Isa	46:5	that we may be c?	1948
Eze	31:2	" 'Who can be c with you in majesty?	1948
	31:18	be c with you in splendor and majesty?	1948
Php	3:8	a loss c to the surpassing greatness	1328

COMPARING (3) [COMPARE]

Ro	8:18	not worth c with the glory that will	4639
2Co	8:8	of your love by c it with the earnestness	NIG
Gal	6:4	without c himself to somebody else,	NIG

COMPARISON (1) [COMPARE]

2Co	3:10	now in c with the surpassing glory.	3538

COMPASS (KJV) See AROUND

COMPASSES (1)

Isa	44:13	with chisels and marks it with c.	4684

COMPASSION (77) [COMPASSIONATE, COMPASSIONS]

Ex	33:19	and I will have c on whom I will have	8163
	33:19	compassion on whom I will have c.	8163
Dt	13:17	he will show you mercy, have c on you,	8163
	28:54	among you will have no c	6524+8317
	30:3	and have c on you and gather you again	8163
	32:36	and have c on his servants	5714
Jdg	2:18	the LORD had c on them as they groaned	5714
1Ki	3:26	with c for her son and said to the king,	8171
2Ki	13:23	the LORD was gracious to them and had c	8163
2Ch	30:9	and your children will be shown c	8171
Ne	9:19	of your great c you did not abandon them	8171
	9:27	in your great c you gave them deliverers,	8171
	9:28	and in your c you delivered them time	8171
Ps	51:1	to your great c blot out my transgressions.	8171
	77:9	Has he in anger withheld his c?"	8171
	90:13	Have c on your servants.	5714
	102:13	You will arise and have c on Zion,	8163
	103:4	the pit and crowns you with love and c,	8171
	103:13	As a father has c on his children,	8163
	103:13	so the LORD has c on those who fear him;	8163
	116:5	our God is full of c.	8163
Ps	119:77	Let your c come to me that I may live,	8171
	119:156	Your c is great, O LORD;	8171
	135:14	and have c on his servants.	5714
	145:9	he has c on all he has made.	8171
Isa	13:18	nor will they look with c on children.	2571+6524
	14:1	The LORD will have c on Jacob;	8163
	27:11	so their Maker has no c on them,	8163
	30:18	he rises to show you c.	8163
	49:10	He who has c on them will guide them	8163
	49:13	and will have c on his afflicted ones.	8163
	49:15	and have no c on the child she has borne?	8163
	51:3	surely comfort Zion and will look with c	5714
	54:7	but with deep c I will bring you back.	8171
	54:8	with everlasting kindness I will have c	8163
	54:10	says the LORD, who has c on you.	8163
	60:10	in favor I will show you c.	8163
	63:7	according to his c and many kindnesses.	8171
	63:15	Your tenderness and c are withheld	8171
Jer	12:15	I will again have c and will bring each	8163
	13:14	or c to keep me from destroying them.' "	8163
	15:6	I can no longer show c.	5714
	21:7	he will show them no mercy or pity or c.'	8163
	30:18	the fortunes of Jacob's tents and have c	8163
	31:20	I have great c for him,"	8163+8163
	33:26	For I will restore their fortunes and have c	8163
	42:12	I will show you c so	8171
	42:12	that he will have c on you and restore you	8163
La	3:32	Though he brings grief, he will show c,	8163
Eze	5:11	without showing pity or c.	2798
	16:5	on you with pity or had c enough to do any	2798
	39:25	and will have c on all the people of Israel,	8163
Hos	2:19	in righteousness and justice, in love and c.	8171
	11:8	all my c is aroused.	5719
	13:14	"I will have no c,	5716
	14:3	for in you the fatherless find c."	8163
Am	1:11	with a sword, stifling all c,	8171
Jnh	3:9	and with c turn from his fierce anger so	5714
	3:10	he had c and did not bring upon them	5714
Mic	7:19	You will again have c on us;	8163
Zec	7:9	show mercy and c to one another.	8171
	10:6	I will restore them because I have c	8163
Mal	3:17	as in c a man spares his son	2798
Mt	9:36	When he saw the crowds, he had c on them,	5072
	14:14	he had c on them and healed their sick.	5072
	15:32	"I have c for these people;	5072
	20:34	Jesus had c on them and touched their eyes.	5072
Mk	1:41	Filled with c, Jesus reached out his hand	5072
	6:34	he had c on them,	5072
	8:2	"I have c for these people;	5072
Lk	15:20	and was filled with c for him;	5072
Ro	9:15	"I will have c on whom I have compassion."	3882
	9:15	I will have compassion on whom I have."	3882
2Co	1:3	the Father of c and the God of all comfort,	3880
Php	2:1	if any tenderness and c,	3880
Col	3:12	clothe yourselves with c, kindness,	3880
Jas	5:11	The Lord is full of c and mercy.	4499

COMPASSIONATE (14) [COMPASSION]

Ex	22:27	I will hear, for I am c.	2843
	34:6	the c and gracious God, slow to anger,	8157
2Ch	30:9	for the LORD your God is gracious and c.	8157
Ne	9:17	you are a forgiving God, gracious and c,	8157
Ps	86:15	But you, O LORD, are a c and gracious God,	8157
	103:8	The LORD is c and gracious,	8157
	111:4	the LORD is gracious and c.	8157
	112:4	for the gracious and c and righteous man.	8157
	145:8	The LORD is gracious and c,	8157
La	4:10	With their own hands c women have cooked their own children,	8172
Joel	2:13	for he is gracious and c,	8157
Jnh	4:2	I knew that you are a gracious and c God,	8157
Eph	4:32	Be kind and c to one another,	2359
1Pe	3:8	love as brothers, be c and humble.	2359

COMPASSIONS (1) [COMPASSION]

La	3:22	for his c never fail.	8171

COMPEL (1) [COMPELLED, COMPELS, COMPULSION]

Gal	6:12	to c you to be circumcised.	337

COMPELLED (6) [COMPEL]

1Sa	13:12	So I felt c to offer the burnt offering."	706
Ezr	4:23	the Jews in Jerusalem and c them by force	10264
Ac	20:22	"And now, c by the Spirit,	1313
	28:19	I was c to appeal to Caesar—	337
1Co	9:16	I cannot boast, for I am c to preach.	340+2130
Gal	2:3	who was with me, was c to be circumcised,	337

COMPELS (3) [COMPEL]

Ex	3:19	not let you go unless a mighty hand c him.	928
Job	32:18	and the spirit within me c me;	7439
2Co	5:14	For Christ's love c us,	5309

COMPENSATE (2) [COMPENSATION]

Ex	21:26	he must let the servant go free to c for	9393
	21:27	he must let the servant go free to c for	9393

COMPENSATION (1) [COMPENSATE]

Pr	6:35	He will not accept any c;	4111

COMPETE (1) [COMPETES]

Jer	12:5	how can you c with horses?	3013

COMPETENCE (1) [COMPETENT]

2Co	3:5	but our c comes from God.	2654

COMPETENT (4) [COMPETENCE]

Ro	15:14	in knowledge and c to instruct one another.	1538
1Co	6:2	are you not c to judge trivial cases?	396
2Co	3:5	that we are c in ourselves to claim anything	2653
	3:6	He has made us c as ministers of	2655

COMPETES (3) [COMPETE]

1Co	9:25	Everyone who c in the games goes	76
2Ti	2:5	Similarly, if anyone c as an athlete,	123
	2:5	the victor's crown unless he c according to	123

COMPLACENCY (2) [COMPLACENT]

Pr	1:32	and the c of fools will destroy them;	8932
Eze	30:9	in ships to frighten Cush out of her c.	1055

COMPLACENT (4) [COMPLACENCY]

Isa	32:9	You women who are so c,	8633
	32:11	Tremble, you c women;	8633
Am	6:1	Woe to you who are c in Zion,	8633
Zep	1:12	with lamps and punish those who are c,	7884

COMPLAIN (7) [COMPLAINED, COMPLAINING, COMPLAINT, COMPLAINTS]

Jdg	21:22	When their fathers or brothers c to us,	8189
Job	7:11	I will c in the bitterness of my soul.	8488
	33:13	Why do you c to him that he answers none	8189
Isa	29:24	those who c will accept instruction.	8087
	40:27	Why do you say, O Jacob, and c, O Israel,	1819
	56:3	And let not any eunuch c,	606
La	3:39	Why should any living man c	645

COMPLAINED (4) [COMPLAIN]

Ge	21:25	Then Abraham c to Abimelech about	3519
Nu	11:1	Now the people c about their hardships in	645
Lk	5:30	of the law who belonged to their sect c	1197
Ac	6:1	Grecian Jews among them c against	1181+1198

COMPLAINING (1) [COMPLAIN]

Php	2:14	Do everything without c or arguing,	1198

COMPLAINT (11) [COMPLAIN]

2Sa	15:2	with a c to be placed before the king	8190
	15:4	a c or case could come to me	8190
Job	7:13	and my couch will ease my c,	8490
	9:27	If I say, 'I will forget my c,	8490
	10:1	to my c and speak out in the bitterness	8490
	21:4	"Is my c directed to man?	8490
	23:2	"Even today my c is bitter;	8490
Ps	64:1	Hear me, O God, as I voice my c;	8490
	142:2	I pour out my c before him;	8490
Hab	2:1	and what answer I am to give to this c.	9350
Ac	18:14	"If you Jews were making a c about	1639S

COMPLAINTS (2) [COMPLAIN]

Nu	14:27	the c of these grumbling Israelites.	9442
Pr	23:29	Who has c? Who has needless bruises?	8490

COMPLETE (29) [COMPLETED, COMPLETELY, COMPLETING, COMPLETION]

Ex	5:13	"C the work required of you for each day,	3983
Dt	16:15	and your joy will be c.	421
1Ki	7:1	to c the construction of his palace.	3983
2Ki	12:15	because they acted with c honesty.	575
Est	2:12	she had to c twelve months	2118+4946+7891
Zec	4:9	his hands will also c it.	1298
Lk	6:49	it collapsed and its destruction was c."	3489
	14:28	to see if he has enough money to c it?	568
Jn	3:29	That joy is mine, and it is now c.	4444
	15:11	be in you and that your joy may be c.	4444
	16:24	and your joy will be c.	4444
	17:23	be brought to c unity to let the world know	5457
Ac	3:16	through him that has given this c healing	3907
	20:24	if only I may finish the race and c the task	NIG
Ro	15:14	in knowledge and competent	4246+4444
2Co	7:16	I am glad I can have c confidence in you.	1877+4246
	8:7	in c earnestness and in your love for us—	4246
	10:6	once your obedience is c.	4444
Php	2:2	then make my joy c by being like-minded,	4444
Col	2:2	the full riches of c understanding,	4443
	4:17	to it that you c the work you have received	4444
Jas	1:4	so that you may be mature and c,	3908
	2:22	and his faith was made c by what he did.	5457
1Jn	1:4	We write this to make our joy c.	1639+4444
	2:5	God's love is truly made c in him.	5457
	4:12	God lives in us and his love is made c in us.	5457
	4:17	love is made c among us so	5457
2Jn	1:12	so that our joy may be c.	4444
Rev	3:2	for I have not found your deeds c in the sight of my God.	4444

COMPLETED (26) [COMPLETE]

Ge	2: 1	and the earth were c in all their vast array.	3983
	29:21	My time is c, and I want to lie with her."	4848
Ex	39:32	the Tent of Meeting, was c.	3983
Lev	8:33	until the days of your ordination are c,	4848
Jos	3:17	by until the whole nation had c the crossing	9462
1Ki	6: 9	So he built the temple and c it,	3983
	6:14	So Solomon built the temple and c it.	3983
	7:22	And so the work on the pillars was c.	9462
2Ch	29:28	the sacrifice of the burnt offering was c.	3983
	36:21	until the seventy years were c in fulfillment	4848
Ezr	6:15	The temple was c on the third day of	10707
Ne	6: 9	and it will not be c."	6913
	6:15	the wall was c on the twenty-fifth of Elul,	8966
Isa	40: 2	to her that her hard service has been c,	4848
Jer	29:10	"When seventy years are c for Babylon,	4848
Da	11:36	be successful until the time of wrath is c,	3983
	12: 7	all these things will be c."	3983
Lk	1:23	When his time of service was c,	4398
	2:22	according to the Law of Moses had been c,	4398
	12:50	and how distressed I am until it is c!	5464
Jn	19:28	Later, knowing that all was now c,	5464
Ac	14:26	of God for the work they had now c.	4444
Ro	15:28	So after I have c this task	2200
Rev	6:11	to be killed as they had been was c.	4444
	15: 1	last, because with them God's wrath is c.	5464
	15: 8	seven plagues of the seven angels were c.	5464

COMPLETELY (91) [COMPLETE]

Ge	8:14	of the second month the earth was c dry.	3312
	20:16	you are c vindicated."	3972
Ex	11: 1	and when he does, he will drive you out c.	3986
	17:14	because I will c blot out the memory	4681+4681
	21:19	see that he is c healed.	8324+8324
Lev	1:17	not severing it c,	976
	5: 8	not severing it c,	976
	6:22	and is to be burned c.	4003
	6:23	of a priest shall be burned c;	4003
	11: 3	a split hoof c divided and that chews	9117+9118
	11: 7	the pig, though it has a split hoof c divided,	9117+9118
	11:26	a split hoof not c divided or that does	9117+9118
	26:44	or abhor them so as to destroy them c,	3983
Nu	21: 3	They c destroyed them and their towns;	3049
Dt	2:15	against them until he had c eliminated them	9462
	2:34	and c destroyed them.	3049
	3: 6	We c destroyed them, as we had done	3049
	12: 2	Destroy c all the places on	6+6
	13:15	Destroy it c, both its people	3049
	13:16	the middle of the public square and c burn	NIH
	14: 7	or that have a split hoof c divided you may	9117
	20:17	C destroy them—the Hittites,	3049+3049
Jos	2:10	whom you c destroyed.	3049
	3:16	of the Arabah (the Salt Sea) was c cut off.	3983
	10:20	Joshua and the Israelites destroyed them c—	3983
	11:14	to the sword until they c destroyed them,	9012
	17:13	but did not drive them out c.	3769+3769
Jdg	1:28	but never drove them out c.	3769+3769
1Sa	15: 9	These they were unwilling to destroy c,	3049
	15:18	'Go and c destroy those wicked people,	3049
	15:20	I c destroyed the Amalekites	3049
2Sa	22:39	I crushed them c,	430+2256+4730
1Ki	11: 6	did not follow the LORD c,	4848
2Ki	13:17	"You will c destroy the Arameans	3983+6330
	13:19	and c destroyed it.	3983+6330
	19:11	to all the countries, destroying them c.	3049
1Ch	4:41	and c destroyed them,	3049
Job	19:13	my acquaintances are c estranged from me.	421
	21:23	c secure and at ease,	3972
Ps	73:19	c swept away by terrors!	9462
	74: 8	"We will crush them c!"	3480
	78:59	he rejected Israel c.	4394
	88:17	they have c engulfed me.	3480
	139: 4	a word is on my tongue you know it c,	3972
Isa	10:18	and fertile fields it will c destroy,	1414+2256+4946+5883+6330
	24: 3	The earth will be c laid waste	1327+1327
	32:19	the forest and the city is leveled c,	928+2021+9164+9168
	37:11	to all the countries, destroying them c.	3049
Jer	3: 1	Would not the land be c defiled?	2866+2866
	4:10	how c you have deceived this people	5958+5958
	4:27	though I will not destroy it c.	3986+6913
	5:10	but do not destroy them c.	3986+6913
	5:18	"I will not destroy you c.	3986+6913
	10:25	they have devoured him c	3983
	12:17	I will c uproot and destroy it,"	6004+6004
	13: 7	now it was ruined and c useless.	2021+3972+4200
	13:10	like this belt—c useless!	2021+3972+4200
	13:19	be carried into exile, carried c away.	8934
	14:19	Have you rejected Judah c?	4415+4415
	25: 9	I will c destroy them and make them	3049
	30:11	'Though I c destroy all the nations	3986+6913
	30:11	I will not c destroy you.	3986+6913
	46:28	"Though I c destroy all the nations	3986+6913
	46:28	I will not c destroy you.	3986+6913
	49:20	he will c destroy their pasture because	9037
	50:13	not be inhabited but will be c desolate.	3972
	50:21	Pursue, kill and c destroy them.	3049
	50:26	C destroy her and leave her no remnant.	3049
	50:45	he will c destroy their pasture because	9037
	51: 3	c destroy her army.	3049
Eze	10:12	c full of eyes, as were their four wheels.	6017
	11:13	Will you c destroy the remnant of Israel?"	3986+6913

COMPLETING (2) [COMPLETE]

Jn	17: 4	on earth by c the work you gave me to do.	5457
Ac	13:25	As John was c his work, he said:	4444

COMPLETION (4) [COMPLETE]

2Ch	8:16	of the LORD was laid until its c.	3983
2Co	8: 6	to bring also to c this act of grace	2200
	8:11	to do it may be matched by your c of it,	2200
Php	1: 6	who began a good work in you will carry it on to c	2200

COMPLIED (1) [COMPLY]

2Ki	16: 9	of Assyria c by attacking Damascus	9048

COMPLIMENTS (1)

Pr	23: 8	and will have wasted your c.	1821+5833

COMPLY (1) [COMPLIED]

Est	3: 4	to him but he refused to c.	9048

COMPOSED (1) [COMPOSE]

2Ch	35:25	Jeremiah c laments for Josiah,	7801

COMPREHEND (3) [COMPREHENDED]

Job	28:13	Man does not c its worth;	3359
Ecc	8:17	No one can c what goes on under the sun.	5162
	8:17	he cannot really c it.	5162

COMPREHENDED (1) [COMPREHEND]

Job	38:18	Have you c the vast expanses of the earth?	1067

COMPULSION (2) [COMPEL]

1Co	7:37	who is under no c but has control	340
2Co	9: 7	not reluctantly or under c,	340

COMPUTE (1)

Lev	25:52	he is to c that and pay	3108

CONANIAH (3)

2Ch	31:12	C, a Levite, was in charge of these things,	4042
	31:13	and Benaiah were supervisors under C	4042
	35: 9	Also C along with Shemaiah and Nethanel,	4042

CONCEAL (8) [CONCEALED, CONCEALS]

Lev	16:13	of the incense will c the atonement cover	4059
Job	14:13	and c me till your anger has passed!	6259
	27:11	the ways of the Almighty I will not c.	3948
	40:22	The lotuses c him in their shadow;	6114
Ps	40:10	I do not c your love and your truth nor	3948
Pr	25: 2	It is the glory of God to c a matter;	6259
Isa	26:21	she will c her slain no longer.	4059
Jer	49:10	so that he cannot c himself.	2464

CONCEALED (13) [CONCEAL]

Jdg	9:34	and took up c positions near Shechem	741
Job	10:13	"But this is what you c in your heart,	7621
	24:15	and he keeps his face c.	6260
	28:21	c even from the birds of the air.	6259
	31:33	if I have c my sin as men do,	4059
Pr	21:14	a bribe c in the cloak pacifies great wrath.	928
	26:26	His malice may be c by deception,	4059
Isa	49: 2	he made me into a polished arrow and c me	6259
Jer	16:17	nor is their sin c from my eyes.	7621
Mt	10:26	There is nothing c that will not be disclosed,	2821
Mk	4:22	and whatever is c is meant to	649
Lk	8:17	and nothing c that will not be known	649
	12: 2	There is nothing c that will not be disclosed,	5158

CONCEALS (2) [CONCEAL]

Pr	10:18	He who c his hatred has lying lips,	4059
	28:13	He who c his sins does not prosper,	4059

CONCEDE (1) [CONCESSION]

Dt	32:31	as even our enemies c.	7130

CONCEIT (3) [CONCEITED, CONCEITS]

Isa	16: 6	her overweening pride and c,	1452
Jer	48:29	her overweening pride and c,	1470
Php	2: 3	of selfish ambition or vain c,	3029

CONCEITED (8) [CONCEIT]

1Sa	17:28	I know how c you are and	2295
Ro	11:25	brothers, so that you may not be c:	5861
	12:16	Do not be c.	4123+4932+5861
2Co	12: 7	To keep me from becoming c because	5643
Gal	5:26	Let us not become c,	3030
1Ti	3: 6	or he may become c and fall under	5605
	6: 4	he is c and understands nothing.	5605
2Ti	3: 4	c, lovers of pleasure rather than lovers	5605

CONCEITS (1) [CONCEIT]

Ps	73: 7	the evil c of their minds know no limits.	5381

CONCEIVE (8) [CONCEIVED, CONCEIVES, CONCEPTION]

Nu	11:12	Did I c all these people?	2225
Jdg	13: 3	but you are going to c and have a son.	2225
	13: 5	because you will c and give birth to a son.	2225
	13: 7	'You will c and give birth to a son.	2225
Ru	4:13	and the LORD enabled her to c,	2231
Job	15:35	They c trouble and give birth to evil;	2225
Isa	33:11	You c chaff, you give birth to straw;	2225
	59: 4	they c trouble and give birth to evil.	2225

CONCEIVED (23) [CONCEIVE]

Ge	16: 4	He slept with Hagar, and she c.	2225
	29:33	She c again, and when she gave birth to	2225
	29:34	Again she c, and when she gave birth to	2225
	29:35	She c again, and when she gave birth to	2225
	30: 7	Rachel's servant Bilhah c again	2225
	30:19	Leah c again and bore Jacob a sixth son.	2225
	38: 4	She c again and gave birth to a son	2225
1Sa	1:20	the course of time Hannah c and gave birth	2225
	2:21	she c and gave birth to three sons	2225
2Sa	11: 5	The woman c and sent word to David,	2225
Ps	51: 5	sinful from the time my mother c me.	3501
SS	3: 4	to the room of the one who c me.	2225
	8: 5	there your mother c you,	2473
Isa	8: 3	and she c and gave birth to a son.	2225
	46: 3	you whom I have upheld since you were c,	1061
	59:13	uttering lies our hearts have c.	5861
Hos	1: 3	and she c and bore him a son.	2225
	1: 6	Gomer c again and gave birth to	2225
	2: 5	and has c them in disgrace.	2225
Mt	1:20	what is c in her is from the Holy Spirit.	1164
Lk	2:21	before he had been c.	1877+3120+3836+5197
1Co	2: 9	no mind has c what God has prepared	326
Jas	1:15	after desire has c, it gives birth to sin;	5197

CONCEIVES (1) [CONCEIVE]

Ps	7:14	and c trouble gives birth to disillusionment.	2225

CONCEPTION (1) [CONCEIVE]

Hos	9:11	no birth, no pregnancy, no c.	2231

CONCERN (18) [CONCERNED, CONCERNING, CONCERNS]

Ge	39: 6	with Joseph in charge, he did not c himself	3359
	39: 8	not c himself with anything in the house;	3359
1Sa	23:21	"The LORD bless you for your c for me.	2798
2Ki	13:23	and had compassion and showed c for them	448+7155
Job	9:21	I am blameless, I have no c for myself;	3359
	19: 4	my error remains my c alone.	907
Ps	131: 1	I do not c myself with great matters	2143
Pr	29: 7	but the wicked have no such c.	1067+1981
Eze	36:21	I had c for my holy name,	2798
Ac	15:14	how God at first showed his c by taking	2170
	18:17	But Gallio showed no c whatever.	3508
1Co	7:32	I would like you to be free from c.	291
	12:25	its parts should have equal c for each other.	3534
2Co	7: 7	your deep sorrow, your ardent c for me,	2419
	7:11	what c, what readiness to see justice done.	2419
	8:16	the heart of Titus the same c I have for you.	5082
	11:28	the pressure of my c for all the churches.	3533
Php	4:10	at last you have renewed your c for me.	5858

CONCERNED (21) [CONCERN]

Ge	21:11	because it c his son.	128
Ex	2:25	on the Israelites and was c about them.	3359
	3: 7	and I am c about their suffering.	3359
	4:31	that the LORD was c about them	7212
1Sa	22: 8	None of you is c about me or tells me	2703
2Sa	13:33	the king should not be c about the report	448+4213+8492
1Ch	27: 1	in all that c the army divisions that were	1821
Ps	142: 4	no one is c for me.	5795
Eze	36: 9	I am c for you and will look on you	448
Da	10: 1	Its message was true and it c a great war.	NIH
Jnh	4:10	"You have been c about this vine,	2571
	4:11	Should I not be c about that great city?"	2571
Ro	11:28	As far as the gospel is c,	2848
	11:28	but as far as election is c,	2848
1Co	7:32	An unmarried man is c about	3534
	7:33	But a married man is c about the affairs	3534

CONCEAL

(Eze 17:10 ... portion at top of column 2)

Eze	17:10	not wither c when the east wind strikes it—	3312+3312
	40: 5	a wall c surrounding the temple area.	6017+6017
Da	7:26	his power will be taken away and c destroyed forever.	10005+10221+10722
	8:23	when rebels have become c wicked,	9462
Hos	10:15	the king of Israel will be c destroyed.	1950+1950
Na	1:15	they will be c destroyed.	3972
Zec	11:17	May his arm be c withered,	3312+3312
Mt	8:26	and it was c calm.	3489
	12:13	So he stretched it out and it was c restored,	635
Mk	3: 5	and his hand was c restored.	635
	4:39	the wind died down and it was c calm.	3489
	5:42	At this they were c astonished.	3489
	6:51	They were c amazed,	1666+3336+4356
Lk	6:10	He did so, and his hand was c restored.	635
	11:36	and no part of it dark, it will be c lighted,	3910
Ac	3:23	not listen to him will be c cut off from	2017
1Co	6: 7	lawsuits among you means you have been c defeated already.	3914
Eph	4: 2	Be c humble and gentle;	4246
Heb	7:25	save c those who come to God	1650+3836+4117

1Co	7:34	An unmarried woman or virgin *is* **c** about	3534
	7:34	a married woman *is* **c** about the affairs	3534
	9: 9	Is it about oxen that God *is* **c**?	3508
Php	4:10	Indeed, *you have been* **c**,	5858
2Ti	3: 8	who, as far as the faith is **c**, are rejected.	4309

CONCERNING (111) [CONCERN]

Ge	24: 9	and swore an oath to him **c** this matter.	6584
	47:26	So Joseph established it as a law **c** land	6584
Lev	11:46	"These are the **regulations** *c* animals,	AIT
	13:59	These are the **regulations** *c* contamination	AIT
Nu	9: 8	the LORD commands **c** you."	4200
	18:24	That is why I said **c** them:	4200
	30:16	the regulations the LORD gave Moses **c**	NIH
Dt	1: 3	the LORD had commanded him **c** them.	448
	19: 4	the **rule** *c* the man who kills another	AIT
	33:21	and his judgments **c** Israel."	6640
1Sa	1:27	my master every good thing he promised **c**	6584
2Sa	1:17	up this lament **c** Saul and his son Jonathan,	6584
	3:28	the LORD **c** the blood of Abner son	4946
	7:25	keep forever the promise you have made **c**	6584
	10: 2	to express his sympathy to Hanun **c**	448
	13:39	for he was consoled **c** Amnon's death.	6584
	18: 5	the king giving orders **c** Absalom	1821+6584
1Ki	21:23	"And also **c** Jezebel the LORD says:	4200
2Ki	19:20	I have heard your prayer **c** Sennacherib	448
	19:32	"Therefore this is what the LORD says **c**	448
	22:13	in accordance with all that is written there **c**	6584
	22:18	says **c** the words you heard:	NIH
1Ch	17:23	the promise you have made **c** your servant	6584
	19: 2	to express his sympathy to Hanun **c**	6584
2Ch	9:29	the visions of Iddo the seer **c** Jeroboam son	6584
	19:11	be over you in any **matter** *c* the LORD,	AIT
	19:11	will be over you in any **matter** *c* the king,	AIT
	23: 3	as the LORD promised **c** the descendants	6584
	33: 8	to do everything I commanded them **c** all	4200
	34:26	says **c** the words you heard:	NIH
Ezr	6: 3	king issued a **decree** *c* the temple of God	AIT
	7:11	in **matters** *c* the commands and decrees of	AIT
Est	3: 2	for the king had commanded this **c** him.	4200
	9:29	to confirm this second **letter** *c* Purim.	AIT
Ps	7: T	which he sang to the LORD **c** Cush,	1821+6584
	36: 1	**oracle** is within my heart **c**	AIT
	91:11	For he will command his angels **c** you	4200
Isa	1: 1	The vision **c** Judah and Jerusalem	6584
	2: 1	This is what Isaiah son of Amoz saw **c**	6584
	13: 1	An **oracle** *c* Babylon that Isaiah son	AIT
	15: 1	An **oracle** *c* Moab:	AIT
	16:13	the word the LORD has already spoken **c**	448
	17: 1	An **oracle** *c* Damascus:	AIT
	19: 1	An **oracle** *c* Egypt:	AIT
	21: 1	An **oracle** *c* the Desert by the Sea:	AIT
	21:11	An **oracle** *c* Dumah:	AIT
	21:13	An **oracle** *c* Arabia:	928
	22: 1	An **oracle** *c* the Valley of Vision:	AIT
	23: 1	**oracle** *c* Tyre: Wail, O ships of Tarshish!	AIT
	23:11	an order **c** Phoenicia that her fortresses	448
	30: 6	An **oracle** *c* the animals of the Negev:	AIT
	32: 6	and spreads error **c** the LORD;	448
	37:21	to me **c** Sennacherib king of Assyria,	448
	37:33	"Therefore this is what the LORD says **c**	448
	45:11	**C** things to come,	NIH
Jer	9:10	and take up a lament **c** the desert pastures.	6584
	14: 1	of the LORD to Jeremiah **c** the drought:	1821+6584
	23: 9	**C** the prophets: My heart is broken within	4200
	23:15	the LORD Almighty says **c** the prophets:	6584
	25: 1	The word came to Jeremiah **c** all the people	6584
	30: 4	These are the words the LORD spoke **c**	448
	34: 4	This is what the LORD says **c** you:	6584
	36: 2	on it all the words I have spoken to you **c**	6584
	44: 1	This word came to Jeremiah **c** all	448
	46: 1	to Jeremiah the prophet **c** the nations:	6584
	46: 2	**C** Egypt: This is the message against the	4200
	47: 1	to Jeremiah the prophet **c** the Philistines	448
	48: 1	**C** Moab: This is what the LORD Almighty,	4200
	49: 1	**C** the Ammonites: This is what the LORD says:	4200
	49: 7	**C** Edom: This is what the LORD Almighty says:	4200
	49:23	**C** Damascus: "Hamath and Arpad are	4200
	49:28	**C** Kedar and the kingdoms of Hazor,	4200
	49:34	that came to Jeremiah the prophet **c** Elam,	448
	50: 1	through Jeremiah the prophet **c** Babylon	448
	51:60	all that had been recorded **c** Babylon.	448
Eze	7:13	for the vision **c** the whole crowd will not	448
	19: 1	"Take up a lament **c** the princes of Israel	448
	21:29	Despite false visions **c** you	4200
	26:17	Then they will take up a lament **c** you	6584
	27: 2	"Son of man, take up a lament **c** Tyre.	6584
	27:32	they will take up a lament **c** you:	6584
	28:12	take up a lament **c** the king of Tyre and say	6584
	32: 2	a lament **c** Pharaoh king of Egypt and say	6584
	36: 6	Therefore prophesy **c** the land of Israel	4200
	44: 5	and give attention to everything I tell you **c**	4200
Da	2:18	from the God of heaven **c** this mystery,	10542
	8:13	the vision **c** the daily sacrifice,	NIH
Joel	3: 2	against them **c** my inheritance,	6584
Am	1: 1	what he saw **c** Israel two years before	6584
	5: 1	this lament I take up **c** you:	6584
Mic	1: 1	the vision he saw **c** Samaria and Jerusalem.	6584
Na	1: 1	An **oracle** *c* Nineveh.	AIT
	1:14	The LORD has given a command **c** you,	6584
Zec	12: 1	An Oracle This is the word of the LORD **c**	6584
Mal	3:16	in his presence **c** those who feared	4200
	4: 6	"He will command his angels **c** you	4309
	3:17	they spread the word **c** what *had been* **told**	AIT

Lk	4:10	"'He will command his angels **c** you	4309
	24:27	in all the Scriptures **c** himself.	4309
Jn	1: 7	He came as a witness to testify **c** that light,	4309
	1:15	John testifies **c** him.	4309
	5:37	Father who sent me has himself testified **c**	4309
Ac	1:16	the mouth of David **c** Judas, who served	4309
	13:22	He testified **c** him:	AIT
	24:21	'It is **c** the resurrection of the dead	4309
	28:21	not received any letters from Judea **c** you,	4309
Ro	9:27	Isaiah cries out **c** Israel:	5642
	10:21	But **c** Israel he says,	4639
2Th	2: 1	**C** the coming of our Lord Jesus Christ	5642
1Pe	1:10	**C** this salvation, the prophets,	4309
1Jn	1: 1	this we proclaim **c** the Word of life.	4309

CONCERNS (6) [CONCERN]

2Ch	19:10	whether bloodshed or other **c** of the law,	NIH
Eze	12:10	This **oracle** *c* the prince in Jerusalem and	AIT
Da	8:17	"understand that the vision **c** the time of	4200
	8:19	the vision **c** the appointed time of the end.	4200
	8:26	for it **c** the distant future."	4200
	10:14	for the vision **c** a time yet to come."	4200

CONCESSION (1) [CONCEDE]

1Co	7: 6	I say this as a **c**, not as a command.	5152

CONCISION (KJV) See MUTILATORS OF THE FLESH

CONCLUDE (1) [CONCLUDED, CONCLUDES, CONCLUDING, CONCLUSION]

Ro	3: 9	What shall we **c** then?	4036

CONCLUDED (2) [CONCLUDE]

Ecc	9: 1	on all this and **c** that the righteous and	1013
Jn	7:26	the authorities really **c** that he is the Christ?	1182

CONCLUDES (1) [CONCLUDE]

Ps	72:20	*This* **c** the prayers of David son of Jesse.	3983

CONCLUDING (1) [CONCLUDE]

Ac	16:10	**c** that God had called us to preach	5204

CONCLUSION (1) [CONCLUDE]

Ecc	12:13	here is the **c** *of* the matter: Fear God	6067

CONCORD (KJV) See HARMONY

CONCOURSE (KJV) See COMMOTION, NOISY

CONCUBINE (21) [CONCUBINES]

Ge	22:24	His **c**, whose name was Reumah,	7108
	35:22	in and slept with his father's **c** Bilhah,	7108
	36:12	also had a **c** named Timna,	7108
Jdg	8:31	His **c**, who lived in Shechem,	7108
	19: 1	in the hill country of Ephraim took a **c**	7108
	19: 9	when the man, with his **c** and his servant,	7108
	19:10	with his two saddled donkeys and his **c**.	7108
	19:24	here is my virgin daughter, and his **c**.	7108
	19:25	So the man took his **c** and sent her outside	7108
	19:27	there lay his **c**,	7108
	19:29	he took a knife and cut up his **c**,	7108
	20: 4	"I and my **c** came to Gibeah in Benjamin	7108
	20: 5	They raped my **c**, and she died.	7108
	20: 6	I took my **c**,	7108
2Sa	3: 7	a **c** named Rizpah daughter of Aiah.	7108
	3: 7	"Why did you sleep with my father's **c**?"	7108
	21:11	When David was told what Aiah's daughter Rizpah, Saul's **c**,	7108
1Ch	1:32	The sons born to Keturah, Abraham's **c**:	7108
	2:46	Caleb's **c** Ephah was the mother of Haran,	7108
	2:48	Caleb's **c** Maacah was the mother	7108
	7:14	through his Aramean **c**.	7108

CONCUBINES (17) [CONCUBINE]

Ge	25: 6	to the sons of his **c** and sent them away	7108
2Sa	5:13	David took more **c** and wives in Jerusalem,	7108
	15:16	but he left ten **c** to take care of the palace.	7108
	16:21	"Lie with your father's **c** whom he left	7108
	16:22	with his father's **c** in the sight of all Israel.	7108
	19: 5	and the lives of your wives and **c**.	7108
	20: 3	he took the ten **c** he had left to take care of	7108
1Ki	11: 3	of royal birth and three hundred **c**,	7108
1Ch	3: 9	besides his sons by his **c**.	7108
2Ch	11:21	of his other wives and **c**.	7108
	11:21	In all, he had eighteen wives and sixty **c**.	7108
Est	2:14	king's eunuch who was in charge of the **c**.	7108
SS	6: 8	Sixty queens there may be, and eighty **c**,	7108
	6: 9	the queens and **c** praised her.	7108
Da	5: 2	his wives and his **c** might drink from them.	10390
	5: 3	his wives and his **c** drank from them.	10390
	5:23	and your **c** drank wine from them.	10390

CONCUPISCENCE (KJV) See COVETOUS DESIRE, EVIL DESIRE, LUST

CONDEMN (26) [CONDEMNATION, CONDEMNED, CONDEMNING, CONDEMNS, SELF-CONDEMNED]

Job	9:20	if I were innocent, my mouth *would* **c** me;	8399
	10: 2	I will say to God: Do not **c** me,	8399
	34:17	*Will you* **c** the just and mighty One?	8399
	34:29	But if he remains silent, who can **c** him?	8399
	40: 8	*Would you* **c** me to justify yourself?	8399
Ps	94:21	the righteous and **c** the innocent to death.	8399
	109: 7	and *may* his prayers **c** him.	2118+2631+4200
	109:31	to save his life from *those who* **c** him.	9149
Isa	50: 9	Who is he *that will* **c** me?	8399
Mt	12:41	the judgment with this generation and **c** it;	2891
	12:42	the judgment with this generation and **c** it;	2891
	20:18	*They will* **c** him to death	2891
Mk	10:33	*They will* **c** him to death	2891
Lk	6:37	Do not **c**, and you will not be condemned.	2868
	11:31	with the men of this generation and **c** them;	2891
	11:32	the judgment with this generation and **c** it;	2891
Jn	3:17	not send his Son into the world to **c**	3212
	7:51	"Does our law **c** anyone without first	3212
	8:11	"Then neither do I **c** you," Jesus declared.	2891
	12:48	that very word which I spoke *will* **c** him at	3212
Ro	2:27	and yet obeys the law *will* **c** you,	3212
	14: 3	not eat everything *must* not **c** the man	3212
	14:22	Blessed is the man who *does* not **c** himself	3212
2Co	7: 3	I do not say this to **c** you,	2892
1Jn	3:20	whenever our hearts **c** us.	2861
	3:21	Dear friends, if our hearts *do* not **c** us,	2861

CONDEMNATION (8) [CONDEMN]

Jer	42:18	of **c** and reproach;	7839
	44:12	of **c** and reproach.	7839
Ro	3: 8	Their **c** is deserved.	3210
	5:16	judgment followed one sin and brought **c**,	2890
	5:18	the result of one trespass was **c** for all men,	2890
	8: 1	now no **c** for those who are in Christ Jesus,	2890
2Pe	2: 3	Their **c** has long been hanging over them,	3210
Jude	1: 4	For certain men whose **c** was written	3210

CONDEMNED (35) [CONDEMN]

Dt	13:17	None of *those* **c** *things* shall be found	3051
Job	32: 3	and yet *had* **c** him.	8399
Ps	34:21	the foes of the righteous *will be* **c**.	870
	34:22	no one *will be* **c** who takes refuge in him.	870
	37:33	or *let* them *be* **c** when brought to trial.	8399
	79:11	of your arm preserve *those* **c** to die.	1201
	102:20	the prisoners and release *those* **c** to death."	1201
Mt	12: 7	*you* would not *have* **c** the innocent.	2868
	12:37	and by your words you *will be* **c**."	2868
	23:33	How will you escape being **c** to hell?	3213
	27: 3	saw that Jesus *was* **c**,	2891
Mk	14:64	They all **c** him as worthy of death.	2891
	16:16	but whoever does not believe *will be* **c**.	2891
Lk	6:37	Do not condemn, and *you will* not *be* **c**.	2868
Jn	3:18	Whoever believes in him *is* not **c**,	3212
	3:18	not believe *stands* **c** already	3212
	5:24	and *will* not *be* **c**;	1650+2262+3213
	5:29	those who have done evil will rise to *be* **c**.	3213
	8:10	*Has* no one **c** you?"	2891
	16:11	the prince of this world *now stands* **c**.	3212
Ac	25:15	against him and asked that he *be* **c**.	2869
Ro	3: 7	why *am* I still **c** as a sinner?"	3212
	8: 3	And so *he* **c** sin in sinful man,	2891
	14:23	But the man who has doubts *is* **c** if he eats,	2891
1Co	4: 9	like *men* **c** to die in the arena.	2119
	11:32	so that *we will* not *be* **c** with the world.	2891
Gal	1: 8	let him be **eternally c!**	353
	1: 9	let him be **eternally c!**	353
2Th	2:12	so that all *will be* **c** who have not believed	3212
Tit	2: 8	and soundness of speech *that* **cannot** *be* **c**,	183
Heb	11: 7	By his faith *he* **c** the world and became heir	2891
Jas	5: 6	*You have* **c** and murdered innocent men,	2868
	5:12	your "No," no, or *you will be* **c**.	3213+4406+5679
2Pe	2: 6	if *he* **c** the cities of Sodom and Gomorrah	2891
Rev	19: 2	He has **c** the great prostitute who corrupted	3212

CONDEMNING (5) [CONDEMN]

Dt	25: 1	acquitting the innocent and **c** the guilty.	8399
1Ki	8:32	**c** the guilty and bringing down	8399
Pr	17:15	Acquitting the guilty and **c** the innocent—	8399
Ac	13:27	yet *in* **c** him they fulfilled the words of	3212
Ro	2: 1	*you are* **c** yourself,	2891

CONDEMNS (4) [CONDEMN]

Job	15: 6	Your own mouth **c** you, not mine;	8399
Pr	12: 2	but the LORD **c** a crafty man.	8399
Ro	8:34	Who is he that **c**?	2891
2Co	3: 9	If the ministry that **c** men is glorious,	2892

CONDESCEND (KJV) See WILLING TO ASSOCIATE

CONDITION (7) [CONDITIONS]

Ge	34:15	to you on one **c** only:	2296S
	34:22	to live with us as one people only on the **c**	2296S
1Sa	11: 2	with you only **on the c that** I gouge out	928+2296
Pr	27:23	Be sure you know the **c** of your flocks,	7156
Mt	12:45	**final** **c** of that man is worse than the first.	AIT
Lk	11:26	the **final c** of that man is worse than	AIT
Jn	5: 6	that he had been in this **c** for a long time,	NIG

CONDITIONS (1) [CONDITION]
Jer 32:11 the sealed copy containing the terms and c,   2976

CONDUCT (31) [CONDUCTED, CONDUCTS, SAFE-CONDUCT]
Est 1:17 For the queen's c will become known to all   1821
    1:18 about the queen's c will respond to all   1821
Job 21:31 Who denounces his c to his face?   2006
    34:11 he brings upon him what his c deserves.   784
Pr 10:23 A fool finds pleasure in evil c,   6913
    20:11 by whether his c is pure and right.   7189
    21: 8 but the c of the innocent is upright.   7189
Ecc 6: 8 how to c himself before others?   2143
Jer 4:18 "Your own c and actions have brought this   2006
    6:15 Are they ashamed of their loathsome c?   6913
    8:12 Are they ashamed of their loathsome c?   6913
    17:10 to reward a man according to his c,   2006
    32:19 you reward everyone according to his c and   2006
Eze 7: 3 I will judge you according to your c   2006
    7: 4 for your c and the detestable practices   2006
    7: 8 I will judge you according to your c   2006
    7: 9 I will repay you in accordance with your c   2006
    7:27 I will deal with them according to their c,   2006
    14:22 and when you see their c and their actions,   2006
    14:23 You will be consoled when you see their c   2006
    16:27 who were shocked by your lewd c.   2006
    20:43 There you will remember your c and all   2006
    24:14 You will be judged according to your c   2006
    36:17 they defiled it by their c and their actions.   2006
    36:17 Their c was like a woman's monthly   2006
    36:19 according to their c and their actions.   2006
    36:32 Be ashamed and disgraced for your c,   2006
Da 6: 4 for charges against Daniel in his c   NIH
Ac 13:18 he endured their c for about forty years in   NIG
Php 1:27 c yourselves in a manner worthy   4488
1Ti 3:15 to c themselves in God's household,   418

CONDUCTED (1) [CONDUCT]
2Co 1:12 that we have c ourselves in the world,   418

CONDUCTS (1) [CONDUCT]
Ps 112: 5 who c his affairs with justice.   3920

CONDUIT (KJV) See AQUEDUCT, TUNNEL

CONEY (2) [CONEYS]
Lev 11: 5 The c, though it chews the cud,   9176
Dt 14: 7 the rabbit or the c.   9176

CONEYS (2) [CONEY]
Ps 104:18 the crags are a refuge for the c.   9176
Pr 30:26 c are creatures of little power,   9176

CONFECTION (KJV) See PERFUMER

CONFECTIONARIES (KJV) See PERFUMERS

CONFECTIONS (1)
Eze 27:17 they exchanged wheat from Minnith and c,   7154

CONFEDERACY (KJV) See CONSPIRACY, ALLIES

CONFER (2) [CONFERRED, CONFERRING]
Ne 6: 7 so come, let us c together."   3619
Lk 22:29 And I c on you a kingdom,   1416

CONFERRED (6) [CONFER]
2Sa 3:17 Abner c with the elders of Israel and said,   1821
1Ki 1: 7 Adonijah c with Joab son of Zeruiah   1821+2118
1Ch 13: 1 David c with each of his officers,   3619
Lk 22:29 just as my Father c one on me,   1416
Ac 4:15 from the Sanhedrin and then c together.   5202
    25:12 After Festus had c with his council,   5196

CONFERRING (1) [CONFER]
2Ki 6: 8 After c with his officers, he said,   3619

CONFESS (21) [CONFESSED, CONFESSES, CONFESSING, CONFESSION]
Lev 5: 5 he must c in what way he has sinned   3344
    16:21 on the head of the live goat and c over it all   3344
    26:40 " 'But if they will c their sins and the sins   3344
Nu 5: 7 and must c the sin he has committed.   3344
1Ki 8:33 they turn back to you and c your name,   3344
    8:35 toward this place and c your name and turn   3344
2Ch 6:24 and when they turn back and c your name,   3344
    6:26 toward this place and c your name and turn   3344
Ne 1: 6 I c the sins we Israelites,   3344
Ps 32: 5 "I will c my transgressions to   3344
    38:18 I c my iniquity; I am troubled by my sin.   5583
Jn 1:20 He did not fail to c, but confessed freely,   3933

Jn 12:42 because of the Pharisees they would not c their faith   3933
Ro 10: 9 That if you c with your mouth,   3933
    10:10 with your mouth that you c and are saved.   3933
    14:11 every tongue will c to God.' "   2018
Php 2:11 every tongue c that Jesus Christ is Lord,   2018
Heb 3: 1 the apostle and high priest whom we c.   3934
    13:15 the fruit of lips that c his name.   3934
Jas 5:16 Therefore c your sins to each other   2018
1Jn 1: 9 If we c our sins, he is faithful and just   3933

CONFESSED (5) [CONFESS]
1Sa 7: 6 On that day they fasted and there they c,   606
Ne 9: 2 They stood in their places and c their sins   3344
Da 9: 4 I prayed to the LORD my God and c: 3344
Jn 1:20 He did not fail to confess, but c freely,   3933
Ac 19:18 now came and openly c their evil deeds.   334+2018

CONFESSES (2) [CONFESS]
Pr 28:13 whoever c and renounces them finds mercy.   3344
2Ti 2:19 and, "Everyone who c the name of   3951

CONFESSING (4) [CONFESS]
Ezr 10: 1 While Ezra was praying and c,   3344
Da 9:20 c my sin and the sin of my people Israel   3344
Mt 3: 6 C their sins, they were baptized by him in   2018
Mk 1: 5 C their sins, they were baptized by him in   2018

CONFESSION (5) [CONFESS]
Ezr 10:11 Now make c to the LORD,   9343
Ne 9: 3 and spent another quarter in c and   3344
2Co 9:13 for the obedience that accompanies your c   3934
1Ti 6:12 when you made your good c in the presence of many witnesses,   3933+3934
    6:13 before Pontius Pilate made the good c,   3934

CONFIDE (1) [CONFIDES, CONFIDING]
Jdg 16:15 'I love you,' when you won't c in me?   907+4213

CONFIDENCE (36) [CONFIDENT, CONFIDENTLY, SELF-CONFIDENCE, SELF-CONFIDENT]
Jdg 9:26 and its citizens put their c in him.   1053
2Ki 18:19 On what are you basing this c of yours?   1059
2Ch 32: 8 the people gained c from what Hezekiah   6164
    32:10 On what are you basing your c,   1053
Job 4: 6 Should not your piety be your c   4074
Ps 71: 5 O Sovereign LORD, my c since my youth.   4440
Pr 3:26 be your c and will keep your foot   4073
    3:32 but takes the upright into his c.   6051
    11:13 A gossip betrays a c,   6051
    20:19 A gossip betrays a c;   6051
    25: 9 do not betray another man's c,   6051
    31:11 Her husband has full c in her   1053+4213
Isa 32:17 be quietness and c forever.   1055
    36: 4 On what are you basing this c of yours?   1059
Jer 17: 7 whose c is in him.   4440
    49:31 which lives in c," declares the LORD,   1055
Eze 29:16 Egypt will no longer be a source of c for   4440
Mic 7: 5 put no c in a friend.   1053
2Co 2: 3 I had c in all of you,   4275
    3: 4 Such c as this is ours through Christ   4301
    7: 4 I have great c in you;   4244
    7:16 I am glad I can have complete c in you.   2509
    8:22 more so because of his great c in you.   4301
Eph 3:12 with freedom and c.   4301
Php 3: 3 and who put no c in the flesh—   4275
    3: 4 though I myself have reasons for such c.   4301
    3: 4 to put c in the flesh, I have more: 4275
2Th 3: 4 We have c in the Lord that you are doing   4275
Heb 3:14 if we hold firmly till the end the c we had   5712
    4:16 then approach the throne of grace with c,   4244
    10:19 we have c to enter the Most Holy Place   4244
    10:35 So do not throw away your c;   4244
    13: 6 So we say with c, "The Lord is my helper;   2509
1Jn 3:21 we have c before God   4244
    4:17 that we will have c on the day of judgment,   4244
    5:14 This is the c we have in approaching God: 4244

CONFIDENT (15) [CONFIDENCE]
Job 6:20 because they had been c;   1053
Ps 27: 3 even then will I be c.   1053
    27:13 I am still c of this: I will see the goodness   586
Lk 18: 9 To some who were c of their own   4275
2Co 1:15 Because I was c of this,   4301
    5: 6 Therefore we are always c and know that   2509
    5: 8 We are c, I say, and would prefer to be   2509
    9: 4 would be ashamed of having been so c.   1877+5712
    10: 7 If anyone is c that he belongs to Christ,   4275
Gal 5:10 I am c in the Lord that you will take no   4275
Php 1: 6 being c of this, that he who began a good   4275
    2:24 And I am c in the Lord   4275
Phm 1:21 C of your obedience, I write to you,   4275
Heb 6: 9 we are c of better things in your case—   4275
1Jn 2:28 so that when he appears we may be c   2400+4244

CONFIDENTLY (3) [CONFIDENCE]
1Sa 15:32 Agag came to him c, thinking,   5051
Ac 2:29 I can tell you c that the patriarch   3552+4244
1Ti 1: 7 about or what they so c affirm.   1331

CONFIDES (1) [CONFIDE]
Ps 25:14 The LORD c in those who fear him;   6051

CONFIDING (1) [CONFIDE]
1Sa 20: 2 great or small, without c in me.   265+906+1655

CONFINE (2) [CONFINED, CONFINEMENT, CONFINES]
Nu 12:14 C her outside the camp for seven days;   6037
2Co 10:13 but will c our boasting to the field God has   NIG

CONFINED (9) [CONFINE]
Ge 39:20 the place where the king's prisoners were c.   673
    40: 3 in the same prison where Joseph was c.   673
Ex 21:18 or with his fist and he does not die but is c   5877
Nu 12:15 So Miriam was c outside the camp   6037
Jdg 1:34 Amorites c the Danites to the hill country,   4315
Ps 88: 8 I am c and cannot escape;   3973
Jer 32: 2 the prophet was c in the courtyard of   3973
    33: 1 While Jeremiah was still c in the courtyard   6806
    39:15 While Jeremiah had been c in the courtyard   6806

CONFINEMENT (1) [CONFINE]
2Sa 20: 3 They were kept in c till the day   7674

CONFINES (1) [CONFINE]
Job 11:10 and c you in prison and convenes a court,   6037

CONFIRM (9) [CONFIRMED, CONFIRMING, CONFIRMS]
Ge 17: 2 I will c my covenant between me   5989
    26: 3 and will c the oath I swore   7756
Nu 30:13 Her husband may c   7756
Dt 29:13 to c you this day as his people,   7756
1Ki 1:14 I.will come in and c what you have said."   4848
Est 9:29 to c this second letter concerning Purim.   7756
Da 9:27 He will c a covenant with many   1504
Ac 15:27 and Silas to c by word   550
Ro 15: 8 to c the promises made to the patriarchs   1011

CONFIRMED (13) [CONFIRM]
Dt 4:31 which he c to them by oath.   8678
1Sa 11:15 the people went to Gilgal and c Saul as king   4887
1Ch 16:17 He c it to Jacob as a decree,   6641
2Ch 1: 9 let your promise to my father David be c,   586
Est 9:32 Esther's decree c these regulations   7756
Job 28:27 he c it and tested it.   3922
Ps 105:10 He c it to Jacob as a decree,   6641
    119:106 I have taken an oath and c it,   7756
Mk 16:20 the Lord worked with them and c his word   1011
Ac 14: 3 who c the message of his grace   3455
1Co 1: 6 our testimony about Christ was c in you.   1011
Heb 2: 3 was c to us by those who heard him.   1011
    6:17 he c it with an oath.   3541

CONFIRMING (2) [CONFIRM]
2Ki 23: 3 thus c the words of the covenant written   7756
Php 1: 7 in chains or defending and c the gospel,   1012

CONFIRMS (5) [CONFIRM]
Nu 30:14 then he c all her vows or   7756
    30:14 He c them by saying nothing to her   7756
Dt 8:18 and so c his covenant,   7756
Ro 9: 1 my conscience c it in the Holy Spirit—   5210
Heb 6:16 and the oath c what is said and   1012+1650

CONFISCATION (2)
Ezr 7:26 c of property, or imprisonment.   10562
Heb 10:34 in prison and joyfully accepted the c   771

CONFLICT (2) [CONFLICTS]
Hab 1: 3 there is strife, and c abounds.   4506
Gal 5:17 They are in c with each other,   512

CONFLICTS (1) [CONFLICT]
2Co 7: 5 c on the outside, fears within.   3480

CONFORM (2) [CONFORMED, CONFORMITY, CONFORMS]
Ro 12: 2 c any longer to the pattern of this world,   5372
1Pe 1:14 do not c to the evil desires you had   5372

CONFORMED (3) [CONFORM]
Eze 5: 7 not even c to the standards of the nations   3869+6913
    11:12 or kept my laws but have c to the standards of the nations   3869+6913
Ro 8:29 predestined to be c to the likeness of his Son   5215

CONFORMITY (1) [CONFORM]
Eph 1:11 of him who works out everything in c with   2848

CONFORMS (1) [CONFORM]
1Ti 1:11 c to the glorious gospel of the blessed God   2848

CONFOUND (1)
Ps 55: 9 O Lord, **c** their speech,   7103

CONFRONT (13) [CONFRONTED, CONFRONTING, CONFRONTS]
Ex   8:20 "Get up early in the morning and **c** Pharaoh 3656
      9:13 **c** Pharaoh and say to him,   3656
Jdg 14: 4 who was seeking an occasion to **c**   4946
1Sa 12: 7 because *I am going to* **c** you **with evidence** 9149
Job 9:32 that *we might* **c** each other in court.   995
   30:27 days of suffering **c** me.   7709
   33: 5 prepare yourself and **c** me.   3656
Ps 17:13 Rise up, O LORD, **c** them,   7709
Isa 50: 8 *Let him* **c** me!   5602
Eze 16: 2 **c** Jerusalem *with* her detestable practices 3359
   20: 4 Then **c** them *with* the detestable practices 3359
   22: 2 Then **c** her *with* all her detestable practices 3359
   23:36 Then **c** them *with* their detestable practices, 5583

CONFRONTED (6) [CONFRONT]
2Sa 22: 6 the snares of death **c** me,   7709
   22:19 *They* **c** me in the day of my disaster,   7709
2Ch 26:18 *They* **c** him and said,   6584+6641
   28:12 **c** those who were arriving from the war. 6584+7756
Ps 18: 5 the snares of death **c** me.   7709
   18:18 *They* **c** me in the day of my disaster,   7709

CONFRONTING (2) [CONFRONT]
Isa 27: 4 If only there were briers and thorns **c** me! NIH
   30:11 stop **c** us *with* the Holy One of Israel!" 4946+7156

CONFRONTS (1) [CONFRONT]
Job 31:14 what will I do when God **c** me?   7756

CONFUSE (2) [CONFUSED, CONFUSING, CONFUSION]
Ge 11: 7 down and **c** their language so they will 1176
Ps 55: 9 **C** the wicked, O Lord,   1182

CONFUSED (1) [CONFUSE]
Ge 11: 9 because there the LORD **c** the language of 1176

CONFUSING (1) [CONFUSE]
Pr 23:33 and your mind imagine **c things**.   9337

CONFUSION (19) [CONFUSE]
Ex 14: 3 **wandering around** the land **in c**,   1003
   14:24 at the Egyptian army and **threw** it **into c**. 2169
   23:27 **throw into c** every nation you encounter. 2169
Dt   7:23 **throwing** them **into** great **c** 2169+4539
   28:20 The LORD will send on you curses, **c** 4539
   28:28 blindness and **c** *of* mind.   9451
Jos 10:10 The LORD **threw** them **into c**   2169
1Sa 14:20 They found the Philistines in total **c**,   4539
2Sa 18:29 "I saw great **c** just as Joab was about 2162
Ps 35:26 over my distress be put to shame and **c** 2917
   40:14 to take my life be put to shame and **c**; 2917
   70: 2 be put to shame and **c**;   2917
   71:24 to harm me have been put to shame and **c**. 2917
Isa 41:29 their images are but wind and **c**.   9332
Jer 51:34 *he has* **thrown** us into **c**,   2169
Mic 7: 4 Now is the time of their **c**.   4428
Ac 19:32 The assembly was *in* **c**:   *5177*
Gal 1: 7 some people are **throwing** you **into c** *5429*
   5:10 The one who *is* **throwing** you **into** will pay the penalty, *5429*

CONGEALED (1)
Ex 15: 8 the deep waters **c** in the heart of the sea. 7884

CONGRATULATE (3)
2Sa 8:10 to King David to greet him and **c** him 1385
1Ki 1:47 to **c** our lord King David,   1385
1Ch 18:10 to King David to greet him and **c** him 1385

CONGREGATION (4) [CONGREGATIONS]
Ps 22:22 in the **c** I will praise you.   7736
   68:26 Praise God in the **great c**;   5220
Ac 13:43 When the **c** was dismissed   *5252*
Heb 2:12 *of* the **c** I will sing your praises."   *1711*

CONGREGATIONS (1) [CONGREGATION]
1Co 14:33 As in all the **c** of the saints,   *1711*

CONIES (Anglicized, KJV) See CONEYS

CONJURE (1)
Isa 47:11 and you will not know how *to* **c** it **away**. 8838

CONNECTED (4) [CONNECTING, CONNECTION]
Lev 3: 3 the fat that covers the inner parts or is **c** to 6584
   3: 9 the fat that covers the inner parts or is **c** to 6584
   3:14 the fat that covers the inner parts or is **c** to 6584
   4: 8 the fat that covers the inner parts or is **c** to 6584

CONNECTING (2) [CONNECTED]
Ex 28:28 **c** it to the waistband,   2118
   39:21 **c** it to the waistband so that   2118

CONNECTION (4) [CONNECTED]
Nu 18: 7 and your sons may serve as priests **in c with** 4200
1Ch 6:49 of incense **in c with** all that was done in 4200
Ac 11:19 those who had been scattered by the persecution **in c with** Stephen *2093*
Col 2:19 He has **lost c** with the Head,   *3195+4024*

CONONIAH (KJV) See CONIAH

CONQUER (3) [CONQUERED, CONQUEROR, CONQUERORS, CONQUERS, CONQUEST]
Dt   2:31 Now begin *to* **c** and possess his land." 3769
2Ch 32: 1 thinking to **c** them for himself.   1324
Rev 13: 7 against the saints and *to* **c** them.   *3771*

CONQUERED (11) [CONQUER]
Ge 14: 7 and *they* **c** the whole territory of   5782
Nu 24:18 Edom will be **c**;   3771
   24:18 Seir, his enemy, will be **c**,   3771
Jos 10:42 and their lands Joshua **c** in one campaign, 4334
   12: 6 and the Israelites **c** them.   5782
   12: 7 the land that Joshua and the Israelites **c** on 5782
   23: 4 the nations *I* **c**—   4162
1Ki 15:20 *He* **c** Ijon, Dan, Abel Beth Maacah 5782
2Ch 16: 4 *They* **c** Ijon, Dan, Abel Maim and all 5782
   27: 5 the king of the Ammonites and **c** them. 2616+6584
Heb 11:33 who through faith **c** kingdoms,   *2865*

CONQUEROR (2) [CONQUER]
Mic 1:15 a **c** against you who live in Mareshah. 3769
Rev 6: 2 and he rode out as a **c** bent on conquest. *3771*

CONQUERORS (3) [CONQUER]
1Ki 8:47 and plead with you in the land of their **c** 8647
   8:50 and cause their **c** to show them mercy; 8647
Ro   8:37 in all these things *we are* **more than** **c** *5664*

CONQUERS (1) [CONQUER]
2Sa 5: 8 "Anyone *who* **c** the Jebusites will have 5782

CONQUEST (2) [CONQUER]
Am   6:13 you who rejoice in the **c** of Lo Debar NIH
Rev 6: 2 and he rode out as a conqueror bent on **c**. *3771*

CONSCIENCE (29) [CONSCIENCE', CONSCIENCE-STRICKEN, CONSCIENCES, CONSCIENTIOUS]
Ge 20: 5 with a clear **c** and clean hands."   4222
   20: 6 "Yes, I know you did this with a clear **c**, 4222
1Sa 25:31 not have on his **c** the staggering burden 4213
Job 27: 6 my **c** will not reproach me as long as I live. 4222
Ac 23: 1 to God *in* all good **c** to this day."   *5287*
   24:16 to keep my **c** clear before God and man. *5287*
Ro   9: 1 my **c** confirms it in the Holy Spirit— *5287*
   13: 5 but also because of **c**.   *5287*
1Co 8: 7 My **c is clear**,   *4029+5323*
   8: 7 and since their **c** is weak, it is defiled. *5287*
   8:10 if anyone with a weak **c** sees you who have this knowledge eating *5287*
   8:12 in this way and wound their weak **c**,   *5287*
   10:25 without raising questions of **c**,   *5287*
   10:27 before you without raising questions of **c**. *5287*
   10:29 the other man's **c**, I mean, not yours. *5287*
   10:29 be judged by another's **c**?   *5287*
2Co 1:12 **c** testifies that we have conducted ourselves in the world, *5287*
   4: 2 to every man's **c** in the sight of God. *5287*
   5:11 and I hope it is also plain to your **c**. *5287*
1Ti 1: 5 from a pure heart and a good **c** and *5287*
   1:19 holding on to faith and a good **c**.   *5287*
   3: 9 of the deep truths of the faith with a clear **c**. *5287*
2Ti 1: 3 as my forefathers did, with a clear **c**, *5287*
Heb 9: 9 not able to clear the **c** of the worshiper. *5287*
   10:22 to cleanse us from a **guilty c** and   *4505+5287*
   13:18 a clear **c** and desire to live honorably *5287*
1Pe 3:16 keeping a clear **c**,   *5287*
   3:21 from the body but the pledge *of* a good **c** *5287*

CONSCIENCE' [CONSCIENCE]
1Co 10:28 of the man who told you and for **c** sake— *5287*

CONSCIENCE-STRICKEN (2) [CONSCIENCE]
1Sa 24: 5 David *was* **c** for having cut off a corner 4213+5782
2Sa 24:10 David *was* **c** after he had counted   4213+5782

CONSCIENCES (4) [CONSCIENCE]
Ro   2:15 their **c** also bearing witness,   *5287*
1Ti 4: 2 whose **c** have been seared as with   *5287*
Tit 1:15 both their minds and **c** are corrupted. *5287*
Heb 9:14 cleanse our **c** from acts that lead to death, *5287*

CONSCIENTIOUS (1) [CONSCIENCE]
2Ch 29:34 for the Levites had been more **c** 3838+4222

CONSCIOUS (2)
Ro   3:20 rather, through the law we become **c** of sin. *2106*
1Pe 2:19 the pain of unjust suffering because he is **c** *5287*

CONSCRIPTED (5) [CONSCRIPTING]
1Ki 5:13 King Solomon **c** laborers from all Israel— 6590
   9:15 the forced labor King Solomon **c** to build 6590
   9:21 these Solomon **c** for his slave labor force, 6590
2Ch 2: 2 He **c** seventy thousand men as carriers 6218
   8: 8 these Solomon **c** for his slave labor force, 6590

CONSCRIPTING (2) [CONSCRIPTED]
2Ki 25:19 in charge of **c** the people of the land 7371
Jer 52:25 in charge of **c** the people of the land 7371

CONSECRATE (43) [CONSECRATED, CONSECRATING, CONSECRATION, RECONSECRATED]
Ex 13: 2 "**C** to me every firstborn male.   7727
   19:10 the people and **c** them today and tomorrow. 7727
   19:22 the LORD, *must* **c themselves,** or   7727
   28:38 in the sacred gifts the Israelites **c**,   7727
   28:41 **C** them so they may serve me as priests. 7727
   29: 1 "This is what you are to do to **c** them, 7727
   29:27 "**C** those parts of the ordination ram 7727
   29:36 and anoint it to **c** it.   7727
   29:37 for the altar and it.   7727
   29:44 "So *I will* **c** the Tent of Meeting and 7727
   29:44 and the altar and *will* **c** Aaron and his sons 7727
   30:29 *You shall* **c** them so they will   7727
   30:30 "Anoint Aaron and his sons and **c** them 7727
   40: 9 **c** it and all its furnishings,   7727
   40:10 **c** the altar, and it will be most holy. 7727
   40:11 Anoint the basin and its stand and **c** them. 7727
   40:13 anoint him and **c** him so he may serve me 7727
Lev 8:11 and the basin with its stand, to **c** them. 7727
   8:12 and anointed him to **c** him.   7727
   11:44 **c yourselves** and be holy,   7727
   16:19 and *to* **c** it from the uncleanness of   7727
   20: 7 "'**C yourselves** and be holy,   7727
   22: 2 the sacred offerings the Israelites **c** to me, 7727
   22: 3 the sacred offerings that the Israelites **c** to 7727
   25:10 **C** the fiftieth year and proclaim liberty 7727
Nu   6:11 That same day *he is to* **c** his head.   7727
   11:18 "'**C yourselves** in preparation   7727
Jos 3: 5 Joshua told the people, "**C yourselves,** 7727
   7:13 "Go, **c** the people.   7727
   7:13 "**C yourselves** in preparation   7727
Jdg 17: 3 "*I solemnly* **c** my silver to the LORD 7727+7727
1Sa 16: 5 **C yourselves** and come to the sacrifice 7727
1Ch 15:12 *to* **c yourselves** and bring up the ark of 7727
   23:13 to **c** the most holy things,   7727
   29: 5 who is willing to **c himself** today to the LORD? 2257+3338+4848
2Ch 13: 9 Whoever comes to **c himself** with   3338+4848
   29: 5 **C yourselves** now and consecrate   7727
   29: 5 now and **c** the temple of the LORD,   7727
   30:17 not **c** [their lambs] to the LORD.   7727
   35: 6 **c yourselves** and prepare [the lambs] 7727
Isa 66:17 "Those *who* **c** and purify themselves to go 7727
Eze 44:19 so that *they do* not **c** the people by means 7727
Joel 2:16 Gather the people, **c** the assembly; 7727

CONSECRATED (57) [CONSECRATE]
Ex 19:14 *he* **c** them, and they washed their clothes. 7727
   29:21 and his sons and their garments *will be* **c**. 7727
   29:43 and the place *will be* **c** by my glory. 7727
Lev 8:10 and so **c** them.   7727
   8:15 So *he* **c** it to make atonement for it.   7727
   8:30 So *he* **c** Aaron and his garments   7727
Nu 6: 8 of his separation he is **c** to the LORD. 7705
   7: 1 and **c** it and all its furnishings.   7727
   7: 1 and **c** the altar and all its utensils.   7727
   15:40 to obey all my commands and will be **c** 7705
Dt 12:26 But take your **c things**   7731
1Sa 7: 1 on the hill and his son Eleazar his son to guard 7727
   16: 5 Then *he* **c** Jesse and his sons   7727
   21: 4 however, there is some **c** bread here— 7731
   21: 6 So the priest gave him the **c** bread, 7731
1Ki 8:64 On that same day the king **c** the middle part 7727
   9: 3 *I have* **c** this temple, which you have built, 7727
   9: 7 and will reject this temple *I have* **c** 7727
   13:33 a priest *he* **c** for the high places. 906+3338+4848
1Ch 15:14 and Levites **c themselves** in order to bring 7727
   28:16 of gold for each table for **c** bread; 5121
2Ch 2: 4 for setting out the **c** bread regularly, 5121
   5:11 priests who were there had **c themselves,** 7727
   7: 7 Solomon **c** the middle part of the courtyard 7727
   7:16 and **c** this temple so that my Name may 7727
   7:20 and will reject this temple *I have* **c** 7727
   23: 6 they may enter because they are **c**,   7731
   26:18 who *have* **been c** to burn incense.   7731
   29:15 and **c themselves**, they went in to purify 7727
   29:17 For eight more days *they* **c** the temple of 7727
   29:18 **setting out the c** bread,   5121
   29:19 We have prepared and **c** all the articles 7727
   29:33 The *animals* **c** as sacrifices amounted 7731
   29:34 and until other priests *had* **been c**, 7727
   30: 3 not enough priests *had* **c themselves** 7727

2Ch 30: 8	the sanctuary, which *he has* **c** forever.	7727
30:15	the Levites were ashamed and **c themselves**	7727
30:17	many in the crowd *had* not **c themselves,**	7727
30:24	A great number of priests **c themselves.**	7727
31:14	to the LORD and also the **c gifts.**	7731+7731
35: 3	and who had been **c** to the LORD:	7705
36:14	which *he had* **c** in Jerusalem.	7727
Ezr 8:28	"You as well as these articles are **c** to	7731
Ps 50: 5	"Gather to me my **c** ones,	2883
106:16	who was **c** *to* the LORD.	7705
Jer 11:15	Can **c** meat avert [your punishment]?	7731
Eze 48:11	This will be for the **c** priests, the Zadokites,	7727
Hos 9:10	*they* **c themselves** to that shameful idol	5692
Zep 1: 7	*he has* **c** those he has invited.	7727
Hag 2:12	If a person carries **c** meat in the fold	7731
2:12	oil or other food, *does it become* **c?**"	7727
Mt 12: 4	he and his companions ate the **c** bread—	4606
Mk 2:26	the house of God and ate the **c** bread,	4606
Lk 2:23	"Every firstborn male is *to be* **c** to	41+2813
6: 4	and taking the **c** bread,	4606
1Ti 4: 5	it is **c** by the word of God and prayer.	39
Heb 9: 2	the table and the **c bread;**	788+4606

CONSECRATING (3) [CONSECRATE]

2Ch 29:34	in **c themselves** than the priests had been.	7727
31:18	For they *were* faithful in **c themselves.**	7727+7731
Eze 46:20	into the outer court and **c** the people."	7727

CONSECRATION (3) [CONSECRATE]

Ex 28: 3	for his **c,** so he may serve me as priest.	7727
29:33	for their ordination and **c.**	7727
2Ch 29:17	the **c** on the first day of the first month,	7727

CONSENT (8) [CONSENTED]

Ge 34:15	*We will give our* **c** to you	252
34:22	But the men *will* **c** to live with us	252
34:23	So *let us give our* **c** to them,	252
Job 39: 9	"Will the wild ox **c** to serve you?	14
Hos 8: 4	They set up kings without my **c;**	4946
Ac 23:21	waiting for your **c** to their request."	2039
1Co 7: 5	not deprive each other except by **mutual c**	5247
Phm 1:14	not want to do anything without your **c,**	1191

CONSENTED (3) [CONSENT]

Mt 3:15	Then John **c.**	918
Lk 22: 6	*He* **c,** and watched for an opportunity	2018
23:51	who had not **c** to their decision and action.	5163

CONSEQUENCES (8) [CONSEQUENTLY]

Nu 5:31	but the woman will bear the **c** of her sin.'"	6411
9:13	That man will bear the **c** of his sin.	2628
18:22	or they will bear the **c** of their sin	2628
Eze 16:58	You will bear the **c** of your lewdness	2365
23:35	the **c** of your lewdness and prostitution."	2365
23:49	and bear the **c** of your sins *of* idolatry.	2628
44:10	after their idols must bear the **c** of their **sin.**	6411
44:12	that they must bear the **c** of their **sin,**	6411

CONSEQUENTLY (4) [CONSEQUENCES]

Ro 5:18	C, just as the result of one trespass	726+4036
10:17	C, faith comes from hearing the message,	726
13: 2	C, he who rebels against the authority	6063
Eph 2:19	C, you are no longer foreigners	726+4036

CONSIDER (92) [CONSIDERABLE, CONSIDERATE, CONSIDERED, CONSIDERS, RECONSIDER]

Ex 30:32	It is sacred, and you *are to* **c** it sacred.	2118+4200
30:37	**c** it holy to the LORD.	2118+4200
Lev 19:23	three years you *are to* **c** it forbidden;	2118+4200
21: 8	**C** them holy, because I	2118+4200
Nu 23: 9	and *do* not **c themselves** one of the nations.	3108
Dt 15:18	Do not **c** it a hardship to set your servant free,	928+6524
17:20	not **c** himself **better** than his brothers	4222+8123
32: 7	**c** the generations long past.	1067
Jdg 5:10	and you who walk along the road, **c**	8488
19:30	Think about it! **C** it!	6418
1Sa 12:24	**c** what great things he has done for you.	8011
16: 7	"Do not **c** his appearance or his height,	5564
24:15	May he **c** my cause and uphold it;	8011
1Ki 2: 9	But now, *do* not **c** him **innocent.**	5927
1Ch 28:10	C now, for the LORD has chosen you	8011
2Ch 19: 6	He told them, "C carefully what you do,	8011
Job 4: 7	"C now: Who, being innocent,	2349
13:24	and **c** me your enemy?	3108
23: 5	and **c** what he would say.	1067
37:14	stop and **c** God's wonders.	1067
Ps 5: 1	O LORD, **c** my sighing.	1067
8: 3	When *I* **c** your heavens,	8011
10:14	*you* **c** it to take it in hand.	5564
37:37	C the blameless, observe the upright;	9068
45:10	Listen, O daughter, **c** and give ear:	8011
48:13	**c well** her ramparts,	4213+8883
50:22	"C this, *you* who forget God,	1067
77:12	and **c** all your mighty deeds.	8488
107:43	and **c** the great love of the LORD.	1067
119: 6	to shame when I **c** all your commands.	5564
119:15	on your precepts and **c** your ways.	5564
119:128	**c** all your precepts **right,**	3837
137: 6	if *I do* not **c** Jerusalem my highest joy.	6590
143: 5	and **c** what your hands have done.	8488

Pr 6: 6	**c** its ways and be wise!	8011
20:25	and only later to **c** his vows.	1329
Ecc 2:12	Then I turned my thoughts to **c** wisdom,	8011
7:13	C what God has done:	8011
7:14	but when times are bad, **c:**	8011
Isa 41:20	*may* **c** and understand,	8492
41:22	so that we *may* **c** them	4213+8492
47: 7	But *you did* not **c** these things	4213+6584+8492
Jer 2:19	C then and realize how evil and bitter it is	3359
2:23	**c** what you have done.	3359
2:31	**c** the word of the LORD:	8011
5: 1	look around and **c,**	3359
9:17	This is what the LORD Almighty says: "C now!	1067
La 1: 9	*she did* not **c** her future.	2349
1:11	"Look, O LORD, and **c,**	5564
1:20	"Look, O LORD, and **c:**	5564
Eze 31: 3	C Assyria, once a cedar in Lebanon,	2180
43:10	*Let them* **c** the plan,	4499
47:22	You *are to* **c** them as native-born Israelites;	2118+4200
Da 8:25	and he will **c himself** superior.	928+4222
9:23	**c** the message and understand the vision;	1067
10:11	**c** carefully the words I am about	1067
Hag 2:15	**c** how things were before one stone was laid	NIH
Mk 4:24	"C carefully what you hear,"	1063
Lk 7: 7	That is why *I did* not even **c** myself **worthy**	546
8:18	Therefore **c carefully** how you listen.	1063
12:24	C the ravens: They do not sow or reap,	2917
12:27	"C how the lilies grow.	2917
14:31	not first sit down and **c** whether he is able	1086
Ac 4:29	**c** their threats and enable your servants	2078
5:35	of Israel, **c carefully** what you intend	4668
13:46	not **c** yourselves worthy of eternal life,	3212
15: 6	and elders met *to* **c** this question.	3972+4309
16:15	"If *you* **c** me a believer in the Lord,"	3212
20:24	However, I **c** my life worth nothing to me,	4472
26: 2	I **c** myself fortunate to stand	2451
26: 8	Why *should* any of you **c** it incredible	3212
Ro 8:18	I **c** that our present sufferings are	3357
11:18	If you do, **c** this:	NIG
11:22	C therefore the kindness and sternness	3972
14:16	Do not allow what you **c** good to be spoken	NIG
1Co 10:18	C the people of Israel:	1063
2Co 10: 7	*he should* **c** again that we belong	3357
Gal 3: 6	C Abraham: "He believed God,	NIG
Php 2: 3	in humility **c** others better than yourselves.	2451
2: 6	*did* not **c** equality with God something to	2451
3: 7	But whatever was to my profit I *now* **c** loss	2451
3: 8	I **c** everything a loss compared to	2451
3: 8	I **c** them rubbish,	2451
3:13	not **c** myself yet to have taken hold of it.	3357
1Ti 6: 1	of slavery *should* **c** their masters worthy	2451
Phm 1:17	So if *you* **c** me a partner,	2400
Heb 10:24	And *let us* **c** how we may spur one another on toward love	2917
12: 3	C him who endured such opposition	382
13: 7	C the outcome of their way of life	355
Jas 1: 2	C it pure joy, my brothers,	2451
3: 5	C what a great forest is set on fire by	2627
5:11	*we* **c blessed** those who have persevered.	3420

CONSIDERABLE (2) [CONSIDER]

Mt 14:24	boat was already a **c** distance from land,	4498
Ac 14: 3	So Paul and Barnabas spent **c** time there,	2653

CONSIDERATE (4) [CONSIDER]

Tit 3: 2	to be peaceable and **c,**	2117
Jas 3:17	then peace-loving, **c,** submissive,	2117
1Pe 2:18	not only *to* those who are good and **c,**	2117
3: 7	be **c** as you live with your wives,	1194+2848

CONSIDERED (31) [CONSIDER]

Ge 30:33	*will* be **c** stolen."	1704
Lev 17: 4	that man *shall* be **c** guilty of bloodshed;	3108
25:31	around them *are to* be **c** as open country.	3108
Dt 2:11	they too **were c** Rephaites,	3108
2:20	(That too *was* **c** a land of the Rephaites,	3108
1Sa 26:21	Because you **c** my life precious today,	928+6524
2Sa 4: 2	Beeroth is **c** part of Benjamin,	3108
1Ki 10:21	because silver **was c** of little value	3108
16:31	not only *a* bit **trivial** for him to commit the sins	7837
2Ch 9:20	because silver **was c** of little value	3108
Ne 13:13	because *these men* **were c** trustworthy.	3108
Job 1: 8	"Have you **c** my servant Job?	4213+8492
2: 3	"Have you **c** my servant Job?	4213+8492
18: 3	Why are we regarded as cattle and **c stupid**	3241
34: 6	Although I am right, *I am* **c** a liar;	3941
Ps 44:22	*we* are **c** as sheep to be slaughtered.	3108
119:59	I have **c** my ways	3108
Isa 53: 4	yet we **c** him stricken by God,	3108
65:20	to reach a hundred *will* be **c accursed.**	7837
La 4: 2	are now **c** as pots of clay,	3108
Hos 9: 7	the prophet is **c** a fool,	NIH
Mt 1:20	But *after* he had **c** this,	1926
14: 5	because *they* **c** him a prophet.	2400+6055
Lk 20:35	But those who *are* **c worthy of** taking part	2921
22:24	among them as to which of them was **c** to	1506
Ro 8:36	*we* are **c** as sheep to be slaughtered."	3357
2Co 11:12	an opportunity to *be* **c** equal with us in	2351
1Ti 1:12	that *he* **c** me faithful,	2451
Heb 11:11	because *he* **c** him faithful who had made	2451
Jas 2:21	*Was* not our ancestor Abraham **c righteous**	1467
2:25	the prostitute **c righteous** for what she did	1467

CONSIDERS (7) [CONSIDER]

Job 33:10	*he* **c** me his enemy.	3108
Ps 33:15	who **c** everything they do.	1067
Pr 31:16	*She* **c** a field and buys it;	2372
Eze 18:28	Because *he* **c** all the offenses	8011
Ro 14: 5	One man **c** one day more sacred than another;	3212
14: 5	another man **c** every day alike.	3212
Jas 1:26	If anyone **c himself** religious and yet	1506+1639

CONSIGN (2) [CONSIGNING]

Isa 43:28	and *I will* **c** Jacob to destruction	5989
Eze 32:18	of Egypt and **c** to the earth below both her	3718

CONSIGNING (2) [CONSIGN]

2Sa 12:31	**c** them **to labor** with saws and	8492
1Ch 20: 3	**c** them **to labor** with saws and	8492

CONSIST (3) [CONSISTED, CONSISTING, CONSISTS]

Lev 2: 4	it is to **c** of fine flour:	NIH
Eze 45:12	The shekel *is to* **c** of twenty gerahs.	2118
Lk 12:15	not **c** in the abundance of his possessions."	1639

CONSISTED (2) [CONSIST]

Jos 17: 5	Manasseh's share **c** of ten tracts	5877
1Ch 27: 1	Each division **c** of 24,000 men.	NIH

CONSISTING (1) [CONSIST]

Eze 46:14	**c** of a sixth of an ephah with a third of	NIH

CONSISTS (2) [CONSIST]

Eze 45:14	is a tenth of a bath from each cor (which **c**	NIH
Eph 5: 9	(for the fruit of the light **c** in all goodness,	NIG

CONSOLATION (4) [CONSOLE]

Job 6:10	Then I would still have this **c**—	5717
21: 2	let this be the **c** you give me.	9487
Ps 94:19	your **c** brought joy to my soul.	9488
Lk 2:25	He was waiting for the **c** of Israel,	4155

CONSOLATIONS (1) [CONSOLE]

Job 15:11	Are God's **c** not enough for you,	9487

CONSOLE (4) [CONSOLATION, CONSOLATIONS, CONSOLED, CONSOLING]

Job 21:34	how *can you* **c** me *with* your nonsense?	5714
Isa 22: 4	to **c** me over the destruction of my people."	5714
51:19	who *can* **c** you?	5714
Jer 16: 7	will anyone give them a drink to **c** them.	9488

CONSOLED (6) [CONSOLE]

2Sa 13:39	for *he* **was c** concerning Amnon's death.	5714
Job 42:11	They comforted and **c** him over all	5714
Eze 14:22	*you will* be **c** regarding	5714
14:23	You *will* be **c** when you see their conduct	5714
31:16	**were c** in the earth below.	5714
32:31	and *he will* be **c** for all his hordes	5714

CONSOLING (1) [CONSOLE]

Ge 27:42	"Your brother Esau *is* **c himself** with	5714

CONSORT (2)

Ps 26: 4	nor *do I* **c** with hypocrites;	995
Hos 4:14	because the men themselves **c** with harlots	7233

CONSPICUOUS (1)

Eze 19:11	**c** for its height and for its many branches.	8011

CONSPIRACY (9) [CONSPIRE]

2Sa 15:12	And so the **c** gained strength,	8004
2Ki 15:15	and the **c** he **led,**	8003+8004
Ps 64: 2	Hide me from the **c** *of* the wicked,	6051
Isa 8:12	"Do not call **c** everything	8004
8:12	that these people call **c;**	8004
Jer 11: 9	"There is a **c** among the people of Judah	8004
Eze 22:25	There is a **c** *of* her princes within her like	8004
Am 7:10	"Amos is **raising a c** against you in	8003
Ac 23:12	the Jews formed a **c** and bound themselves	5371

CONSPIRATORS (1) [CONSPIRE]

2Sa 15:31	among the **c** with Absalom."	8003

CONSPIRE (9) [CONSPIRACY, CONSPIRATORS, CONSPIRED]

Ps 2: 1	the nations **c** and the peoples plot in vain?	8093
31:13	they **c** against me and plot to take my life.	3570
56: 6	*They* **c,** they lurk, they watch my steps,	1592
59: 3	Fierce men **c** against me for no offense	1592
71:10	those who wait to kill me **c** together.	3619
83: 3	With cunning they **c** against your people;	6051
105:25	to **c** against his servants.	5792
Mic 7: 3	*they all* **c** together.	6309
Ac 4:27	and the people of Israel in this city to **c**	NIG

CONSPIRED (19) [CONSPIRE]

1Sa	22: 8	Is that why you *have* all *c* against me?	8003
	22:13	"Why *have you* c against me,	8003
1Ki	2:28	who *had* c with Adonijah though not	5742
2Ki	9:14	the son of Nimshi, c against Joram.	8003
	10: 9	It was I *who* c against my master	8003
	12:20	His officials *c against* him	8003+8004
	14:19	*They* c against him in Jerusalem,	8003+8004
	15:10	Shallum son of Jabesh c against Zechariah.	8003
	15:25	Pekah son of Remaliah, c against him.	8003
	15:30	c against Pekah son of Remaliah.	8003+8004
	21:23	Amon's officials c against him	8003
2Ch	24:25	His officials c against him for murdering	8003
	24:26	Those *who* c against him were Zabad,	8003
	25:27	*they,* c against him in Jerusalem and	8003+8004
	33:24	Amon's officials c against him	8003
Est	2:21	and c to assassinate King Xerxes.	1335
	6: 2	who *had* c to assassinate King Xerxes.	1335
Da	2: 9	*You have* c to tell me misleading	10231
Ac	9:23	the Jews c to kill him,	5205

CONSTANT (10) [CONSTANTLY]

Nu	17: 5	I will rid myself of this *c* **grumbling**	4296+9442
Dt	28:66	You will live in *c* suspense,	4946+5584
Job	33:19	a bed of pain with *c* distress in his bones,	419
Pr	19:13	quarrelsome wife is like a *c* **dripping.**	1942+3265
	27:15	quarrelsome wife is like a *c* **dripping**	1942+3265
Isa	51:13	that you live in *c* terror every day because	9458
Eze	30:16	Memphis will be in *c* distress.	3429
Ac	27:33	"you have been in *c* suspense	NIG
1Ti	6: 5	*c* **friction between** men of corrupt mind,	1384
Heb	5:14	who by *c* use have trained themselves	NIG

CONSTANTLY (9) [CONSTANT]

Ps	106: 3	who c do what is right.	928+3972+6961
	119:109	Though I c take my life in my hands,	9458
Isa	52: 5	all day long my name is c blasphemed.	9458
Jn	3:23	and *people were* c **coming** to be baptized.	AIT
Ac	1:14	They all **joined** together c in prayer,	4674
Ro	1: 9	is my witness how c I remember you	90
2Co	11:26	I have been c on the move.	4490
2Th	1:11	With this in mind, we c pray for you,	4121
2Ti	1: 3	and day I c remember you in my prayers.	89

CONSTELLATIONS (4)

2Ki	23: 5	to the c and to all the starry hosts.	4655
Job	9: 9	the Pleiades and the c *of* the south.	2540
	38:32	Can you bring forth the c in their seasons	4666
Isa	13:10	and their c will not show their light.	4068

CONSTRAIN (KJV) See COMPEL

CONSTRUCT (1) [CONSTRUCTED, CONSTRUCTING, CONSTRUCTION, CONSTRUCTIVE]

2Ch	20:36	with him to c a fleet of trading ships.	6913

CONSTRUCTED (3) [CONSTRUCT]

1Ki	9:24	he c the supporting terraces.	1215
1Ch	15: 1	After David *had* c buildings for himself in	6913
Eze	40:17	and a pavement *that had* **been** c all around	6913

CONSTRUCTING (3) [CONSTRUCT]

Ex	36: 1	of c the sanctuary are to do the work just as	6275
	36: 3	to carry out the work of c the sanctuary.	6275
Ezr	5: 4	the names of the men c this building?"	10111

CONSTRUCTION (4) [CONSTRUCT]

1Ki	7: 1	however, to complete the c *of* his palace.	1215
2Ki	16:10	with detailed plans for its c.	5126
Ezr	5:16	to the present it has been **under** c but is not	10111
	6: 8	of the Jews in the c of this house of God:	10111

CONSTRUCTIVE (1) [CONSTRUCT]

1Co	10:23	is permissible"—but not everything *is* c.	3868

CONSULT (19) [CONSULTATION, CONSULTED, CONSULTING, CONSULTS]

1Sa	28: 8	"C a spirit for me," he said,	7876
	28:16	Samuel said, "Why *do you* c me,	8626
2Ki	1: 2	Go and c Baal-Zebub, the god of Ekron	928+2011
	1: 3	that you are going off to c Baal-Zebub,	928+2011
	1: 6	you are sending men to c Baal-Zebub,	928+2011
	1:16	is no God in Israel for you to c	928+1821+2011
	1:16	to c Baal-Zebub, the god of Ekron?	928+2011
	8: 8	C the LORD through him;	2011
2Ch	17: 3	*He did* not c the Baals	2011
	25:15	"Why *do you* c this people's gods,	2011
Est	1:13	the king to c experts in matters of law	4200+7156
Pr	15:12	he will not c the wise.	448+2143
Isa	8:19	When men tell you to c mediums	2011
	8:19	Why c the dead on behalf of the living?	448
	19: 3	*they* will c the idols and the spirits of	2011
	40:14	Whom *did* the LORD c to enlighten him,	3619
Eze	21:21	he will c his idols,	8626
Hos	4:12	*They* c a wooden idol and are answered by	8626
Gal	1:16	*I did* not c any man,	4651

CONSULTATION (1) [CONSULT]

1Ch	12:19	after c, their rulers sent him away.	6783

CONSULTED (10) [CONSULT]

1Ki	12: 6	Then King Rehoboam c the elders	3619
	12: 8	and c the young men who had grown up	3619
2Ki	21: 6	and c mediums and spiritists.	6913
1Ch	10:13	of the LORD and even c a medium	8626
2Ch	10: 6	Then King Rehoboam c the elders	3619
	10: 8	and c the young men who had grown up	3619
	25:17	Amaziah king of Judah c *his* **advisers,**	3619
	32: 3	*he* c with his officials and military staff	3619
	33: 6	and c mediums and spiritists.	6913
Jer	8: 2	and which they have followed and c	2011

CONSULTING (2) [CONSULT]

2Ch	20:21	After c the people,	3619
Isa	30: 2	who go down to Egypt without c me;	7023+8626

CONSULTS (2) [CONSULT]

Dt	18:11	or who is a medium or spiritist or *who* c	2011
Eze	14:10	be as guilty as the *one who* c him.	2011

CONSUME (39) [CONSUMED, CONSUMES, CONSUMING]

Dt	5:25	This great fire *will* c us,	430
Jdg	9:15	of the thornbush and c the cedars	430
	9:20	from Abimelech and c you,	430
	9:20	and Beth Millo, and c Abimelech!"	430
1Ki	16: 3	So I *am* about to c Baasha and his house,	1277
	21:21	I will c your descendants and cut off	1277
2Ki	1:10	and c you and your fifty men!"	430
	1:12	and c you and your fifty men!"	430
Job	5: 5	The hungry c his harvest,	430
	15:34	and fire *will* c the tents	430
	20:26	A fire unfanned *will* c him	430
Ps	21: 9	and his fire *will* c them.	430
	39:11	*you* c their wealth like a moth—	4998
	59:13	c them in wrath,	3983
	59:13	c them till they are no more.	3983
Ecc	5:11	As goods increase, so do *those who* c them.	430
Isa	5:11	in a single day it will burn and c his thorns	430
	26:11	the fire reserved for your enemies c them.	430
Jer	17:27	of Jerusalem *that will* c her fortresses.' "	430
	21:14	*that will* c everything around you.' "	430
	49:27	*it will* c the fortresses of Ben-Hadad.'	430
	50:32	a fire in her towns *that will* c all who are	430
Eze	15: 7	the fire *will yet* c them.	430
	20:47	and *it will* c all your trees,	430
	21:28	polished to c and to flash like lightning!	430
	22:31	on them and c them with my fiery anger,	3983
Hos	8:14	*that will* c their fortresses."	430
Am	1: 4	*that will* c the fortresses of Ben-Hadad.	430
	1: 7	of Gaza *that will* c her fortresses.	430
	1:10	of Tyre *that will* c her fortresses."	430
	1:12	I will send fire upon Teman *that will* c	430
	1:14	*that will* c her fortresses amid war cries	430
	2: 2	I will send fire upon Moab *that will* c	430
	2: 5	*that will* c the fortresses of Jerusalem."	430
Ob	1:18	and they will set it on fire and c it.	430
Na	3:15	like grasshoppers, c you.	430
Zec	12: 6	*They will* c right and left all	430
Jn	2:17	"Zeal for your house *will* c me."	2983
Heb	10:27	of judgment and of raging fire *that* will c	2266

CONSUMED (33) [CONSUME]

Ge	31:40	The heat c me in the daytime and the cold	430
Ex	15: 7	*it* c them like stubble.	430
Lev	6:10	of the burnt offering that the fire *has* c on	430
	9:24	and c the burnt offering and the fat portions	430
	10: 2	the presence of the LORD and c them,	430
Nu	11: 1	among them and c some of the outskirts of	430
	11:33	and before *it could* be c,	4162
	16:35	And fire came out from the LORD and c	430
	21:28	*It* c Ar of Moab,	430
2Ki	1:10	from heaven and c the captain and his men.	430
	1:12	the fire of God fell from heaven and c him	430
	1:14	from heaven and c the first two captains	430
2Ch	7: 1	down from heaven and c the burnt offering	430
Ps	31:10	My life is c by anguish and my years	3983
	78:63	Fire c their young men,	430
	90: 7	*We are* c by your anger and terrified	3983
	106:18	a flame c the wicked.	4265
	119:20	My soul *is* c with longing for your laws	1756
Ecc	10:12	but a fool *is* c by his own lips.	1180
Isa	42:25	*it* c them, but they did not take it to heart.	1277
Jer	3:24	From our youth shameful gods *have* c	430
La	3:22	of the LORD's great love *we* are not c,	9462
	4:11	a fire in Zion that c her foundations.	430
Eze	19:12	and fire c them.	430
	19:14	of its main branches and c its fruit.	430
	23:25	and those of you who are left *will* be c	430
	28:18	and *it* c you,	430
Na	1:10	*they* will be c like dry stubble.	430
	3:13	fire *has* c their bars.	430
Zep	1:18	of his jealousy the whole world *will* be c,	430
	3: 8	The whole world *will* be c by the fire	430
Zec	9: 4	and she *will* be c by fire.	430
Rev	18: 8	*She* will be c by fire,	2876

CONSUMES (8) [CONSUME]

Ps	69: 9	for zeal for your house c me,	430

(right column)

Ps	83:14	As fire c the forest or a flame sets	1277
	97: 3	before him and c his foes on every side.	4265
Isa	9:18	*it* c briers and thorns,	430
	24: 6	Therefore a curse c the earth;	430
	33:11	your breath is a fire *that* c you.	430
Jer	5:14	a fire and these people the wood *it* c.	430
La	2: 3	a flaming fire *that* c everything around it.	430

CONSUMING (11) [CONSUME]

Ex	24:17	glory of the LORD looked like a c fire on	430
Dt	4:24	LORD your God is a c fire, a jealous God.	430
	32:24	c pestilence and deadly plague;	4310
Jdg	6:21	c the meat and the bread.	430
2Sa	22: 9	c fire came from his mouth,	430
Ps	18: 8	c fire came from his mouth,	430
Isa	30:27	and his tongue *is* a c fire,	430
	30:30	down with raging anger and c fire,	430
	33:14	"Who of us can dwell with the c fire?	430
Joel	2: 5	like a crackling fire c stubble,	430
Heb	12:29	for our "God is a c fire."	2914

CONSUMMATION (KJV) See END

CONSUMPTION (KJV) See DISEASE, DESTRUCTION

CONTACT (1)

Hag	2:13	"If a *person* defiled by c with a dead body	AIT

CONTAIN (5) [CONTAINED, CONTAINER, CONTAINING, CONTAINS]

1Ki	8:27	even the highest heaven, cannot c you.	3920
2Ch	2: 6	even the highest heavens, cannot c him?	3920
	6:18	even the highest heavens, cannot c you.	3920
Ecc	8: 8	No man has power over the wind to c it;	3973
2Pe	3:16	His letters c some things that are hard	NIG

CONTAINED (2) [CONTAIN]

Ac	10:12	It c all kinds of four-footed animals,	1877+5639
Heb	9: 4	This ark c the gold jar of manna,	1877+2400

CONTAINER (1) [CONTAIN]

Nu	19:15	and every open c without a lid fastened	3998

CONTAINING (9) [CONTAIN]

Ex	13: 3	Eat nothing c **yeast.**	2809
	23:18	to me along with **anything** c **yeast.**	2809
	34:25	to me along with **anything** c **yeast,**	2809
Lev	8: 2	and the **basket** c bread made without yeast,	AIT
1Sa	6: 8	the chest c the gold rats and the models of	NIH
	6:15	together with the chest c the gold objects,	928
Jer	32:11	the sealed copy c the terms and conditions,	NIH
	36:27	After the king burned the scroll c the words	NIH
Eze	45:11	the bath c a tenth of a homer and the ephah	5951

CONTAINS (2) [CONTAIN]

Job	28: 6	and its dust c nuggets of gold.	4200
Pr	15: 6	The house of the righteous c great treasure,	NIH

CONTAMINATED (4) [CONTAMINATES, CONTAMINATION]

Lev	13:47	"If any clothing is c *with* mildew—	5596
	13:54	he shall order that the c **article**	5596
	13:56	he is to tear **the** c part out of the clothing,	2257S
	14:40	he is to order that the c stones be torn out	5596

CONTAMINATES (1) [CONTAMINATED]

2Co	7: 1	from everything **that** c body and spirit,	3663

CONTAMINATION (3) [CONTAMINATED]

Lev	13:49	and if the c in the clothing,	5596
	13:52	or any leather article that has the c in it,	5596
	13:59	the regulations concerning c *by* mildew	5596

CONTEMN (KJV) See REVILE, DESPISES

CONTEMPLATING (1) [CONTEMPLATE]

Isa	33:15	and shuts his eyes against c evil—	8011

CONTEMPT (31) [CONTEMPTIBLE, CONTEMPTUOUS, CONTEMPTUOUSLY]

Lev	22: 9	and die for **treating** them **with** c.	2725
Nu	14:11	"How long *will* these people **treat** me **with** c?	5540
	14:23	No one *who has* **treated** me **with** c will ever see it.	5540
	16:30	these men *have* **treated** the LORD **with** c."	5540
Dt	17:12	The man who shows c for the judge or for	2295
1Sa	2:17	**treating** the LORD's offering **with** c.	5540
	25:39	against Nabal for **treating** me with c.	3075
2Sa	12:14	*you have* **made** the enemies of the LORD **show utter** c,	5540+5540
	19:43	So why *do you* **treat** us **with** c?	7837
Job	12: 5	at ease have c for misfortune as the fate	997
	12:21	He pours c on nobles and disarms	997
	31:34	the crowd and so dreaded the c *of* the clans	997

Column 1

Ps   31:11   I am the utter **c** of my neighbors;   3075
      31:18   for with pride and **c** they speak arrogantly   997
    107:40   he who pours **c** on nobles   997
    119:22   Remove from me scorn and **c,**   997
    123: 3   for we have endured much **c.**   997
    123: 4   much **c** from the arrogant.   997
Pr   14:31   He who oppresses the poor **shows c**   3070
    17: 5   the poor **shows c** for their Maker;   3070
    18: 3   When wickedness comes, so does **c,**   997
    27:11   I can answer *anyone who* **treats me with c.**   3070
Eze 22: 7   **treated** father and mother **with c;**   7837
Da 12: 2   others to shame and everlasting **c.**   1994
Hos 12:14   and will repay him for his **c.**   3075
Na   3: 6   *I will* **treat** you **with c** and make you   5571
Mal 1: 6   O priests, *who* **show c** *for* my name.   1022
    1: 6   'How *have we* **shown c** *for* your name?'   1022
Ro   2: 4   Or *do you* **show c** *for* the riches   2969
Gal 4:14   *you did* not **treat** me **with c** or scorn.   2024
1Th 5:20   *do not* **treat** prophecies **with c.**   2024

CONTEMPTIBLE (5) [CONTEMPT]

1Sa 3:13   his sons **made** themselves **c,**   7837
Eze 35:12   the **c things** you have said against   5542
Da 11:21   by a **c** *person* who has not been given   1022
Mal 1: 7   "By saying that the LORD's table *is* **c.**   1022
    1:12   'It is defiled,' and of its food, 'It *is* **c.'**   1022

CONTEMPTUOUS (2) [CONTEMPT]

Dt 17:13   and *will* not *be* **c** again.   2326
Pr 19:16   but *he who is* **c** of his ways will die.   1022

CONTEMPTUOUSLY (1) [CONTEMPT]

Mal 1:13   and *you* **sniff** at it **c,"**   5870

CONTEND (11) [CONTENDED, CONTENDING, CONTENDS, CONTENTION, CONTENTIOUS]

Ge   6: 3   "My Spirit *will* not **c** with man forever,   1906
Jdg 6:32   saying, "*Let Baal* **c** with him,"   8189
Ps 35: 1   **C,** O LORD, with those who contend   8189
    35: 1   O LORD, with *those who* **c** with me;   3742
    35:23   **C** for me, my God and Lord.   8190
   127: 5   to shame when *they* **c** with their enemies in   1819
Ecc 6:10   no man can **c** with one who is stronger   1906
Isa 27: 8   By warfare and exile *you* **c** with her—   8189
    49:25   I *will* **c** with those who contend with you,   8189
    49:25   I will contend with *those who* **c** with you,   3742
Jude 1: 3   I felt I had to write and urge you *to* **c** for   2043

CONTENDED (2) [CONTEND]

Dt 33: 8   *you* **c** with him at the waters of Meribah.   8189
Php 4: 3   help these women who *have* **c** at my **side** in the cause of the gospel,   5254

CONTENDING (1) [CONTEND]

Php 1:27   **c** as one man for the faith of the gospel   5254

CONTENDS (2) [CONTEND]

Job 40: 2   "*Will* the *one who* **c** with   8189
Jer 15:10   with whom the whole land strives and **c!**   4506

CONTENT (9) [CONTENTED, CONTENTMENT, CONTENTS]

Jos   7: 7   If only *we had been* **c** to stay on   3283
Pr 13:25   The righteous eat to their hearts' **c,**   8427
    19:23   Then one rests **c,** untouched by trouble.   8428
Ecc 4: 8   yet his eyes *were* not **c** *with* his wealth.   8425
Lk   3:14   *be* **c** *with* your pay."   758
Php 4:11   to be **c** whatever the circumstances.   895
    4:12   I have learned the secret of being **c** in any   NIG
1Ti 6: 8   *we will be* **c** with that.   758
Heb 13: 5   of money and *be* **c** with what you have,   758

CONTENTED (1) [CONTENT]

Da   4: 4   at home in my palace, **c** and prosperous.   10710

CONTENTION (1) [CONTEND]

Ps 80: 6   You have made us a **source of c**   4506

CONTENTIOUS (1) [CONTEND]

1Co 11:16   If anyone wants to be **c** about this,   5809

CONTENTMENT (3) [CONTENT]

Job 36:11   in prosperity and their years in **c.**   5833
SS   8:10   in his eyes like one bringing **c.**   8934
1Ti 6: 6   But godliness with **c** is great gain.   894

CONTENTS (1) [CONTENT]

Lev 1:16   to remove the crop with its **c** and throw it   5901

CONTEST (1)

Heb 10:32   when you stood your ground in a great **c** in   124

CONTINUAL (4) [CONTINUE]

1Ki 14:30   There was **c** warfare between Rehoboam and Jeroboam.   2021+3427+3972

Column 2

2Ch 12:15   There was **c** warfare between Rehoboam and Jeroboam.   2021+3427+3972
Pr 15:15   but the cheerful heart has a **c** feast.   9458
Eph 4:19   with a **c** lust for more.   NIG

CONTINUALLY (26) [CONTINUE]

Ex 28:38   be on Aaron's forehead **c** so that they will   9458
Lev 24: 2   so that the lamps may be kept burning **c.**   9458
    24: 3   the LORD from evening till morning, **c.**   9458
    24: 4   before the LORD must be tended **c.**   9458
Nu   4: 7   the bread that is **c** there is to remain on it.   9458
Dt 11:12   the eyes of the LORD your God are **c** on it   9458
1Ki 10: 8   who **c** stand before you   9458
2Ch 9: 7   who **c** stand before you   9458
    24:14   burnt offerings were presented **c** in   9458
Ps 26: 3   and I walk **c** in your truth.   2143
    50:20   You speak **c** against your brother   3782
    74:23   the uproar of your enemies, which rises **c.**   9458
Isa 27: 3   I water it **c.**   4200+8092
    28:24   does he plow **c?**   2021+3427+3972
    65: 3   a people who **c** provoke me   9458
Jer 33:18   ever fail to have a man to stand before me **c** to offer burnt offerings,   2021+3427+3972
Eze 8:17   with violence and **c** provoke me to anger?   8740
Da   6:16   "May your God, whom you serve **c,** rescue you!"   10002+10089+10753
    6:20   has your God, whom you serve **c,** been able to rescue you   10002+10089+10753
Am 1:11   because his anger raged **c**   4200+6329
Ob 1:16   so all the nations will drink **c;**   9458
Lk 24:53   stayed **c** at the temple, praising God.   1328+4246
1Th 1: 3   We **c** remember before our God   90
    2:13   And we also thank God **c** because,   90
    5:17   pray **c;**   90
Heb 13:15   **c** offer to God a sacrifice of praise—   1328+4246

CONTINUE (65) [CONTINUAL, CONTINUALLY, CONTINUED, CONTINUES, CONTINUING, CONTINUOUSLY]

Ex   9: 2   to let them go and **c** to hold them back,   6388
    33:13   so I may know you and **c** to **find** favor   AIT
    40:15   a priesthood that will **c** for all generations   6409
Lev 25:22   from the old crop and will **c** to **eat** *from* it   AIT
    25:35   so he can **c** to **live** among you.   AIT
    25:36   so that your countryman *may* **c** to **live**   AIT
    26: 5   Your threshing *will* **c until** grape harvest   5952
    26: 5   the grape harvest *will* **c until** planting,   5952
    26:23   not accept my correction but **c** to   2143
    26:27   of this you still do not listen to me but **c** to   2143
Nu 34: 4   **c** on to Zin and go south of Kadesh Barnea.   6296
    34: 9   **c** to Ziphron and end at Hazar Enan.   3655
    34:11   to Riblah on the east side of Ain and **c**   4682
Dt 22:19   *She shall* **c** to **be** his wife;   AIT
Jos 13:13   so they **c** to **live** among the Israelites   AIT
Jdg 19:27   the house and stepped out to **c** on his way,   2143
Ru   2:13   "*May I* **c** to **find** favor in your eyes,   AIT
2Sa 7:29   that *it may* **c** forever in your sight;   2118
1Ki 8:23   with your servants who **c** wholeheartedly   2143
2Ki 17:41   and grandchildren **c** to **do**   AIT
1Ch 17:27   that *it may* **c** forever in your sight;   2118
2Ch 6:14   with your servants who **c** wholeheartedly   2143
Est 9:23   to **c** the celebration they had begun,   6913
Ps 36:10   **C** your love to those who know you,   5432
    72:17   *may* it **c** as long as the sun.   5672
    89:36   that his line *will* **c** forever   2118
Isa 47: 7   You said, '*I will* **c** forever'—   2118
Jer   3: 5   *Will* your wrath **c** forever?'   9068
    18:12   *We will* **c** with our own plans;   2143
    23:26   How long *will* this **c** in the hearts   3780
Eze 20:31   **c** to **defile** yourselves   AIT
    21:13   which the sword despises, *does* not **c?**   2118
Da   4:27   It may be that then your prosperity will **c."**   10073
    9:26   War will **c** until the end,   NIH
    12:10   but the wicked *will* **c** to **be** wicked.   AIT
Hos 4:18   **c** their **prostitution.**   2388+2388
Mal 2: 4   so that my covenant with Levi *may* **c,"**   2118
Jn 17:26   **c** to **make** you **known**   AIT
Ac 13:43   with them and urged them *to* **c** in the grace   4693
Ro   1:32   *they* not only **c** to **do** these very things but   AIT
    11:22   provided that *you* **c** in his kindness.   AIT
2Co 1:10   On him we have set our hope that he will **c**   2285
    11: 9   and *will* **c** to **do** so.   AIT
Gal 2:10   that *we should* **c** to **remember** the poor,   2152
    3:10   not **c** to do everything written in the Book   1844
Php 1:18   Yes, and *I will* **c** to **rejoice,**   4169
    1:25   and *I will* **c** with all of you   4169
    2:12   **c** to **work out** your salvation with fear   AIT
Col 1:23   if *you* **c** in your faith,   2152
    2: 6   **c** to **live** in him,   AIT
2Th 2: 7   the one who now holds it back will **c** to do   NIG
    3: 4   and *will* **c** to **do** the things we command.   AIT
1Ti 2:15   if *they* **c** in faith,   3531
2Ti 3:14   **c** in what you have learned   3531
Heb 6:10   and **c** to **help** them.   AIT
1Pe 4:19   to their faithful Creator and **c** to do good.   NIG
1Jn 2:28   And now, dear children, **c** in him,   3531
    3: 9   No one who is born of God *will* **c** to **sin,**   AIT
    3: 9   that anyone born of God does not **c** to **sin;**   AIT
2Jn 1: 9   Anyone who runs ahead and *does* not **c** in   3531
3Jn 1: 3   to the truth and how you **c** to **walk** in   AIT
Rev 22:11   Let him who does wrong **c** to do wrong;   2285
    22:11   let him who is vile **c** to be vile;   2285
    22:11   let him who does right **c** to do right;   2285

Column 3

Rev 22:11   and let him who is holy **c** to be holy."   2285

CONTINUED (77) [CONTINUE]

Ge   8: 5   The waters **c** to recede until   2118+2143
    12: 9   Abram set out and **c** toward the Negev.   2143
    26:13   and his wealth **c** to grow   2143
    29: 1   Then Jacob **c** on his **journey** and   5951+8079
    30:36   Jacob **c** to **tend** the rest of Laban's flocks.   AIT
    42: 2   *He* **c,** "I have heard that there is grain   606
Ex 36: 3   the people **c** to bring freewill offerings   6388
Nu   9:16   That is how it **c** to be: 9458
    21:16   From there they **c** on to Beer,   NIH
Jos 9:21   They **c,** "Let them live,   606
    15: 3   **c** on to Zin and went over to the south   6296
    15: 6   to Beth Hoglah and **c** north of Beth Arabah   6296
    15: 7   It **c** along to the waters of En Shemesh   6296
    15:10   **c** down *to* Beth Shemesh and crossed   3718
    16: 6   and **c** to the sea.   3655
    17: 9   the boundary **c** south to the Kanah Ravine.   3718
    18:16   *It* **c** down the Hinnom Valley along   3718
    18:17   went to En Shemesh, **c** to Geliloth,   3655
    18:18   *It* **c** to the northern slope of Beth Arabah   6296
    19:13   Then *it* **c** eastward to Gath Hepher   6296
Jdg 1:29   Canaanites **c** to **live** there among them.   AIT
    14:17   because *she* **c** to **press** him.   AIT
    18:31   They **c** to **use** the idols Micah had made,   AIT
1Sa 2:26   And the boy Samuel **c** to **grow** in stature   2143
    3:21   The LORD **c** to appear at Shiloh,   3578
    7:15   Samuel **c** *as* **judge** *over* Israel all the days   AIT
    18:30   The Philistine commanders **c** to **go out**   AIT
    30:10   and four hundred men **c** the **pursuit.**   AIT
2Sa 2:27   The men *would have* **c** the pursuit   6590
    2:29   **c** through the whole Bithron and came   2143
    15:30   But David **c** **up** the Mount of Olives,   AIT
    16:13   So David and his men **c** along the road   2143
    20:18   She **c,** "Long ago they used to say,   606
1Ki 2:12   So he **c,** "Please ask King Solomon—   606
    3: 6   *You have* **c** this great kindness to him   9068
    5:11   Solomon **c** to **do** this for Hiram year   AIT
    18:29   **c** their **frantic prophesying**   AIT
    22:19   Micaiah **c,** "Therefore hear the word of   606
    22:43   and the people **c** to offer sacrifices   6388
2Ki 12: 3   the people **c** to offer sacrifices   6388
    13: 6   *they* **c** in them.   2143
    13:11   *he* **c** in them.   2143
    14: 4   the people **c** to offer sacrifices   6388
    15: 4   the people **c** to offer sacrifices   6388
    15:35   the people **c** to offer sacrifices   6388
2Ch 12:13   in Jerusalem and **c** *as* **king.**   AIT
    18:18   Micaiah **c,** "Therefore hear the word of   606
    27: 2   people, however, **c** their corrupt practices.   6388
    29:28   All this **c** until the sacrifice of the burnt   NIH
    33:17   however, **c** to sacrifice at the high places,   6388
Ezr 6:14   of the Jews **c** to **build** and prosper under   AIT
    10: 6   because *he* **c** to **mourn** over   AIT
Ne   4:21   So we **c** the work with half   6913
    5: 9   So I **c,** "What you are doing is not right.   606
    12:37   At the Fountain Gate *they* **c** directly **up**   6590
Est 2:20   she **c** to **follow** Mordecai's instructions   AIT
Job 27: 1   And Job **c** his discourse: 3578
    29: 1   Job **c** his discourse: 3578
    36: 1   Elihu **c:**   3578
Ps 78:17   But *they* **c** to sin against him,   3578+6388
Isa 64: 5   But when we **c** to sin against them,   6409
Jer 32:20   and wonders in Egypt and have **c** them   NIH
Da   7:11   "Then *I* **c** to watch because of   10201
    10:12   Then *he* **c,** "Do not be afraid, Daniel.   606
Mk 4:24   "Consider carefully what you hear," he **c.**   3306
Lk   4:24   "I tell you the truth," *he* **c,**   3306
    15:11   Jesus **c:** "There was a man who had two sons.   3306
Jn   8:23   But *he* **c,** "You are from below;   3306
    12:17   **c** to **spread** the word.   AIT
Ac 2:46   Every day *they* **c** to meet together in   4674
    4:33   the apostles **c** to **testify** to the resurrection   AIT
    12:24   the word of God **c** to **increase** and spread.   AIT
    14: 7   where *they* **c** to preach the good news.   1639
    15:38   in Pamphylia and *had* not **c** with them in   5302
    21: 5   our time was up, *we* left and **c** on *our* **way.**   4513
    21: 7   We **c** our voyage from Tyre and landed   1382
    27:20   for many days and the storm **c** raging,   2130+3900+4024

CONTINUES (10) [CONTINUE]

Lev 15: 3   Whether it **c** flowing *from* his body   AIT
    15:25   or has a discharge that *beyond* her period,   NIH
    15:26   while her discharge **c** will be unclean,   3427+3972
Ps 100: 5   his faithfulness **c** through all generations.   NIH
   119:90   Your faithfulness **c** through all generations;   NIH
2Co 10:15   Our hope is that, *as* your faith **c** to **grow,**   AIT
1Ti 5: 5   and night and day to pray and to ask God   4693
Jas 1:25   and **c** to do this, not forgetting   4169
1Jn 3: 6   No one who **c** to **sin** has either seen him   AIT
2Jn 1: 9   whoever **c** in the teaching has both   3531

CONTINUING (5) [CONTINUE]

Ex 28:29   the breastpiece of decision as a **c** memorial   9458
Nu 15:23   from the day the LORD gave them and **c**   2134
Ro 13: 8   except the **c** debt to love one another,   NIG
Heb 7:23   since death prevented them from **c**   4169
2Pe 2: 9   *while* **c** their **punishment.**   AIT

CONTINUOUSLY (1) [CONTINUE]

Lev 6:13   fire must be kept burning on the altar **c;**   9458

CONTRACT (2)
Isa 16:14 as a **servant bound by** c would count them, 8502
21:16 as a **servant bound by** c would count it, 8502

CONTRADICT (1)
Lk 21:15 be able to resist or c. 515

CONTRARIWISE (KJV) See INSTEAD, CONTRARY, BUT

CONTRARY (23)
Lev 10: 1 before the LORD, c to his command. 4202
Dt 17: 3 c to my command has worshiped other gods 4202
Jos 22:27 **On the c,** it is to be a witness between us 3954
2Ch 30:18 c to what was written. 928+3869+4202
Ps 119:85 arrogant dig pitfalls for me, c to your law. 3869+4202
Ac 18:13 the people to worship God in ways c to 4123
Ro 9: 7 **On the c,** "It is through Isaac 247
11:24 and c to nature were grafted into 4123
12:20 **On the c:** "If your enemy is hungry, 247
16:17 that are c to the teaching you have learned. 4123
1Co 9:12 **On the c,** we put up 247
12:22 **On the c,** those parts of the body that seem to be weaker 247+3437+4498
2Co 2:17 **On the c,** in Christ we speak before God 247
4: 2 **On the c,** by setting forth 247
10: 4 **On the c,** they have divine power 247
Gal 2: 7 **On the c,** they saw that I had been entrusted with the task 247+1883
3:12 The law is not based on faith; **on the c,** 247
5:17 sinful nature desires what is c to the Spirit, 2848
5:17 and the Spirit what is c to the sinful nature. 2848
1Th 2: 4 **On the c,** we speak as men approved 247
2Th 3: 8 **On the c,** we worked night and day, 247
1Ti 1:10 whatever else is c to the sound doctrine 512
2Ti 1:17 **On the c,** when he was in Rome, 247

CONTRIBUTE (1) [CONTRIBUTED, CONTRIBUTING, CONTRIBUTION, CONTRIBUTIONS]
2Ki 15:20 Every wealthy man had to c fifty shekels 6584

CONTRIBUTED (4) [CONTRIBUTE]
2Ch 31: 3 The king c from his own possessions for 4987
35: 8 also c voluntarily to the people and 8123
Ne 7:70 of the heads of the families c to the work. 5989
12:47 all Israel c the daily portions for the singers 5989

CONTRIBUTING (1) [CONTRIBUTE]
Ro 12: 8 if it is c to the needs of others, 3556

CONTRIBUTION (5) [CONTRIBUTE]
Ex 29:28 It is the c the Israelites are to make to 9556
Lev 7:14 a c to the LORD; 9556
7:32 to the priest as a c. 9556
Ne 10:34 at set times each year a c of wood to burn 7934
Ro 15:26 to make a c for the poor among the saints 3126

CONTRIBUTIONS (10) [CONTRIBUTE]
Lev 22:12 she may not eat any of the sacred c. 9556
Nu 5: 9 All the sacred c the Israelites bring to 9556
2Ch 24:10 and all the people brought their c gladly, NIH
31:10 "Since the people began to bring their c to 9556
31:12 Then they faithfully brought in the c, 9556
31:14 distributing the c made to the LORD and 9556
Ne 10:39 are to bring their c of grain, 9556
12:44 to be in charge of the storerooms for the c, 9556
13: 5 as well as the c for the priests. 9556
13:31 I also made provision for c of wood 7934

CONTRITE (4)
Ps 51:17 a broken and c heart, O God, 1920
Isa 57:15 also with him who is c and lowly in spirit, 1918
57:15 the lowly and to revive the heart of the c. 1917
66: 2 he who is humble and c in spirit, 5783

CONTROL (23) [CONTROLLED, CONTROLLING, CONTROLS, SELF-CONTROL, SELF-CONTROLLED]
Ge 45: 1 Then Joseph could no longer c himself 706
Ex 32:25 that Aaron had let them **get out of** c and 7277
Jos 18: 1 The country **was brought under** their c, 3899
2Sa 8: 1 and he took Metheg Ammah from the c of 3338
8: 3 to restore his c along the Euphrates River. 3338
1Ki 11:24 where they settled and **took** c. 4887
1Ch 18: 1 and its surrounding villages from the c of 3338
18: 3 when he went to establish his c along 3338
2Ch 17: 5 the kingdom under his c; 3338
25: 3 After the kingdom was firmly in his c, 6584
Pr 29:11 but a wise man keeps himself **under** c. 294+928
Ecc 2:19 Yet he will **have** c over all the work 8948
Jer 28:14 even give him c over the wild animals.'" NIH
Da 11:43 He will **gain** c of the treasures of gold 5440
Ro 6:20 you were free from the c of righteousness, NIG
1Co 7: 9 But if they cannot c **themselves,** 1603
7:37 who is under no compulsion but has c 2026
14:32 The spirits of prophets are **subject to the** c 5718

CONTROLLED (7) [CONTROL]
Jdg 10: 4 They c thirty towns in Gilead, 4200
1Ch 2:22 who c twenty-three towns in Gilead, 2118+4200
Ps 32: 9 but must be c by bit and bridle or they will 1178
Ro 7: 5 For when we were c by the sinful nature, NIG
8: 6 the mind c by the Spirit is life and peace; NIG
8: 8 Those c by the sinful nature cannot please God. 1639
8: 9 are c not by the sinful nature but by 1639

CONTROLLING (1) [CONTROL]
Ge 43:31 c himself, said, "Serve the food." 706

CONTROLS (2) [CONTROL]
Job 37:15 Do you know how God c the clouds 8492
Pr 16:32 a man who c his temper than one who takes 5440

CONTROVERSIES (4)
Ac 26: 3 with all the Jewish customs and c. 2427
1Ti 1: 4 These promote c rather than God's work— 1700
6: 4 in c and quarrels about words that result 2428
Tit 3: 9 But avoid foolish c and genealogies 2428

CONVENED (2) [CONVENES]
Ac 25: 6 and the next day he c **the court** and ordered 1037+2093+2767+3836
25:17 but c the court the next day and ordered 2767

CONVENES (1) [CONVENED]
Job 11:10 and confines you in prison and c **a court,** 7735

CONVENIENT (1)
Ac 24:25 When I **find** it c, I will send for you." 2789+3561

CONVERSATION (4)
1Sa 19: 7 and told him the whole c. 1821
Jer 38:24 "Do not let anyone know about this c, 1821
38:27 for no one had heard his c with the king. 1821
Col 4: 6 Let your c be always full of grace, 3364

CONVERT (4) [CONVERTED, CONVERTS]
Mt 23:15 over land and sea to win a single c, 4670
Ac 6: 5 and Nicolas from Antioch, a c to **Judaism.** 4670
Ro 16: 5 the **first** c to Christ in the province 569
1Ti 3: 6 He must not be a **recent** c, 3745

CONVERTED (1) [CONVERT]
Ac 15: 3 they told how the Gentiles **had been** c. 2189+3836

CONVERTS (3) [CONVERT]
Ac 2:11 (both Jews and c to **Judaism);** 4670
13:43 and devout c to **Judaism** followed Paul 4670
1Co 16:15 the household of Stephanas were the first c NIG

CONVEY (KJV) See FLOAT, SAFE-CONDUCT

CONVICT (5) [CONVICTED, CONVICTION, CONVICTIONS]
Dt 19:15 to c a man accused of any crime 7756
2Sa 14:13 does he not c himself, 872
Pr 24:25 it will go well with those who c the guilty, 3519
Jn 16: 8 c the world **of guilt** 1794
Jude 1:15 and to c all the ungodly of all 1794

CONVICTED (1) [CONVICT]
Jas 2: 9 and are c by the law as lawbreakers. 1794

CONVICTION (1) [CONVICT]
1Th 1: 5 with the Holy Spirit and with deep c. 4443

CONVICTIONS (1) [CONVICT]
Jos 14: 7 a report according to my c, 4222+6640

CONVINCE (1) [CONVINCED, CONVINCING]
Ac 28:23 the kingdom of God and **tried to** c them 4275

CONVINCED (16) [CONVINCE]
Ge 45:28 And Israel said, "I'm c. 8041
Lk 16:31 they will not be c even if someone rises 4275
Ac 19:26 and hear how this fellow Paul has c 4275
26: 9 "I too was c that I ought to do all 1506
26:26 I am c that none of this has escaped his 4275
26:26 Some were c by what he said, 4275
Ro 2:19 if you are c that you are a guide for 4275
8:38 For I am c that neither death nor life, 4275
14: 5 Each one should be **fully** c 4442

CONTROLLED (continued — right column top)
Ro 14:14 I am **fully** c that no food is unclean 2779+3857+4275
15:14 I myself am c, my brothers, 4275
1Co 15:24 c by all **that** he **is a sinner** 1794
2Co 5:14 because we are c that one died for all, 3212
Php 1:25 C of this, I know that I will remain, 4275
2Ti 1:12 and am c that he is able to guard 4275
3:14 you have learned and have become c of, 4413

CONVINCING (1) [CONVINCE]
Ac 1: 3 and gave many c **proofs** that he was alive. 5447

CONVOCATIONS (1)
Isa 1:13 New Moons, Sabbaths and c— 5246+7924

CONVULSED (2) [CONVULSION]
Ps 77:16 the very depths were c. 8074
Mk 9:26 c him violently and came out. 5057

CONVULSION (2) [CONVULSED, CONVULSIONS]
Mk 9:20 it immediately **threw** the boy **into a** c. 5360
Lk 9:42 the demon threw him to the ground **in a** c. 5360

CONVULSIONS (1) [CONVULSION]
Lk 9:39 it throws him **into** c so that he foams at 5057

COOING (1)
SS 2:12 the c of doves is heard in our land. 7754

COOK (14) [COOKED, COOKING, COOKS]
Ex 23:19 "Do not c a young goat in its mother's milk. 1418
29:31 the ram for the ordination and c the meat in 1418
34:26 not c a young goat in its mother's milk. 1418
Lev 8:31 "C the meat at the entrance to the Tent 1418
Dt 14:21 Do not c a young goat in its mother's milk. 1418
1Sa 9:23 Samuel said to the c, 3184
9:24 the c took up the leg with what was on it 3184
1Ki 19:21 **burned** the plowing equipment to c 1418
2Ki 4:38 "Put on the large pot and c some stew, 1418
Eze 24: 5 bring it to a boil and c the bones in it. 1418
24:10 C the meat **well,** mixing in the spices; 9462
46:20 "This is the place where the priests will c 1418
46:24 at the temple will c the sacrifices of 1418
Zec 14:21 to sacrifice will take some of the pots and c 1418

COOKED (8) [COOK]
Ex 12: 9 Do not eat the meat raw or c in water, 1418+1419
Lev 2: 7 If your grain offering is c in a pan, NIH
6:28 The clay pot the meat is c in must 1418
6:28 but if it is c in a bronze pot, 1418
7: 9 Every grain offering baked in an oven or c 6913
Nu 11: 8 They c it in a pot or made it into cakes. 1418
2Ki 6:29 So we c my son and ate him. 1418
La 4:10 With their own hands compassionate women have c their own children, 1418

COOKING (5) [COOK]
Ge 25:29 Once when Jacob was c some stew, 2326
Lev 11:35 an oven or c pot must be broken up. 3968
Eze 11: 3 This city is a c **pot,** and we are the meat.' 6105
24: 3 " 'Put on the c pot; 6105
Zec 14:20 and the c pots in the LORD's house will 6105

COOKS (1) [COOK]
1Sa 8:13 to be perfumers and c and bakers. 3185

COOL (3) [COOLNESS]
Ge 3: 8 as he was walking in the garden in the c of 8120
Jer 18:14 Do its c waters from distant sources 7922
Lk 16:24 of his finger in water and c my tongue, 2976

COOLNESS (1) [COOL]
Pr 25:13 Like the c of snow at harvest time is 7557

COOS (KJV) See COS

COPIED (3) [COPY]
Jos 8:32 Joshua c on stones the law of Moses, 4180+5467
Pr 25: 1 c by the men of Hezekiah king of Judah: 6980
Eze 16:47 and c their detestable practices, 6913

COPIES (2) [COPY]
Jer 32:14 both the sealed and **unsealed** c of the deed AIT
Heb 9:23 the c of the heavenly things to be purified 5682

COPPER (8)
Dt 8: 9 the rocks are iron and you can dig c out of 5733
Job 28: 2 and c is smelted from ore. 5703
Eze 22:18 all of them are the c, tin, 5733
22:20 As men gather silver, c, iron, 5733
24:11 the coals till it becomes hot and its c glows 5733
Mt 10: 9 along any gold or silver or c in your belts; 5910
Mk 12:42 and put in two very **small** c coins, 3321
Lk 21: 2 in two very **small** c coins. 3321

COPPERSMITH (KJV) See METALWORKER

COPULATION (KJV) See EMISSION

COPY (14) [COPIED, COPIES]

Dt	17:18	he is to write for himself on a scroll a c	5467
2Ki	11:12	he presented him with a c of the covenant	6343
2Ch	23:11	with a c of the covenant	6343
Ezr	4:11	(This is a c of the letter they sent him.)	10598
	4:23	As soon as the c of the letter	10598
	5: 6	This is a c of the letter that Tattenai,	10598
	7:11	a c of the letter King Artaxerxes had given	7306
Est	3:14	A c of the text of the edict was to be issued	7358
	4: 8	also gave him a c of the text of the edict	7358
	8:13	A c of the text of the edict was to be issued	7358
Jer	32:11	the sealed c containing the terms	AIT
	32:11	as well as the unsealed c—	AIT
Heb	8: 5	that is a c and shadow of what is in heaven.	5682
	9:24	a man-made sanctuary that was only a c of	531

COR (1) [CORS]

Eze	45:14	from each c (which consists of ten baths	4123

CORAL (2)

Job	28:18	C and jasper are not worthy of mention;	8029
Eze	27:16	c and rubies for your merchandise.	8029

CORBAN (1)

Mk	7:11	from me is C' (that is, a gift devoted to God),	3167

CORD (15) [CORDS]

Ge	38:18	"Your seal and its c,	7348
	38:25	"See if you recognize whose seal and c	7348
Ex	28:28	to the rings of the ephod with blue c,	7348
	28:37	a blue c to it to attach it to the turban;	7348
	39:21	with blue c, connecting it to the waistband	7348
	39:31	Then they fastened a blue c to it to attach it	7348
Nu	15:38	with a blue c on each tassel.	7348
Jos	2:18	have tied this scarlet c in the window	2562+9535
	2:21	And she tied the scarlet c in the window.	9535
2Sa	8: 2	and measured them off with a length of c.	2475
Job	41: 2	a c through his nose or pierce his jaw with	109
Ecc	4:12	A c of three strands is not quickly broken.	2562
	12: 6	before the silver c is severed,	2475
Eze	16: 4	the day you were born your c was not cut,	9219
	40: 3	a linen c and a measuring rod in his hand.	7348

CORDIAL (1) [CORDIALLY]

Ezr	5: 7	To King Darius: C greetings.	10002+10002+10353+10720

CORDIALLY (2) [CORDIAL]

Ps	28: 3	who speak c with their neighbors	8934
Jer	9: 8	With his mouth each speaks c	8934

CORDS (17) [CORD]

2Sa	22: 6	The c of the grave coiled around me;	2475
Est	1: 6	with c of white linen and purple material	2475
Job	4:21	Are not the c of their tent pulled up,	3857
	36: 8	held fast by c of affliction,	2475
	38:31	Can you loose the c of Orion?	5436
Ps	18: 4	The c of death entangled me;	2475
	18: 5	The c of the grave coiled around me;	2475
	116: 3	The c of death entangled me,	2475
	129: 4	he has cut me free from the c of	6310
	140: 5	the c of their net and have set traps for me	2475
Pr	5:22	the c of his sin hold him fast.	2475
Isa	5:18	Woe to those who draw sin along with c	2475
	54: 2	lengthen your c, strengthen your stakes.	4798
	58: 6	the chains of injustice and untie the c of	99
Eze	27:24	and multicolored rugs with c twisted	2475
Hos	11: 4	I led them with c of human kindness,	2475
Jn	2:15	So he made a whip out of c,	5389

CORIANDER (2)

Ex	16:31	like c seed and tasted like wafers made	1512
Nu	11: 7	The manna was like c seed and looked	1512

CORINTH (7) [CORINTHIANS]

Ac	18: 1	After this, Paul left Athens and went to C.	3172
	18:18	Paul stayed on in C for some time.	NIG
	19: 1	While Apollos was at C,	3172
1Co	1: 2	the church of God in C, to those sanctified	3172
2Co	1: 1	To the church of God in C,	3172
	1:23	to spare you that I did not return to C.	3172
2Ti	4:20	Erastus stayed in C,	3172

CORINTHIANS (2) [CORINTH]

Ac	18: 8	and many of the C who heard him believed	3171
2Co	6:11	We have spoken freely to you, C,	3171

CORMORANT (2)

Lev	11:17	the little owl, the c, the great owl,	8960
Dt	14:17	the desert owl, the osprey, the c,	8960

CORN [EARS OF] (Anglicized, KJV) See GRAIN [HEADS OF], KERNEL

CORNELIUS (10)

Ac	10: 1	At Caesarea there was a man named C,	3173
	10: 3	who came to him and said, "C!"	3173
	10: 4	C stared at him in fear.	1254+3836S
	10: 7	C called two of his servants and	NIG
	10:17	by C found out where Simon's house was	3173
	10:22	"We have come from C the centurion.	3173
	10:24	C was expecting them	3173
	10:25	C met him and fell at his feet in reverence.	3173
	10:30	C answered: "Four days ago I was in my	3173
	10:31	and said, 'C, God has heard your prayer	3173

CORNER (26) [CORNERS, CORNERSTONE, CORNERSTONES]

Ru	3: 9	"Spread the c of your garment over me,	4053
1Sa	24: 4	up unnoticed and cut off a c of Saul's robe.	4053
	24: 5	for having cut off a c of his robe.	4053
	24:11	the c of your robe but did not kill you.	4053
1Ki	7:34	one on each c, projecting from the stand.	7157
	7:39	at the southeast c of the temple.	4578
2Ki	14:13	from the Ephraim Gate to the C Gate—	7157
2Ch	4:10	at the southeast c.	4578
	25:23	from the Ephraim Gate to the C Gate—	7157
	26: 9	in Jerusalem at the C Gate,	7157
	26:15	for use on the towers and on the c defenses	7157
	28:24	up altars at every street c in Jerusalem.	7157
Ne	3:24	to the angle and the c,	7157
	3:31	and as far as the room above the c;	7157
	3:32	the room above the c and the Sheep Gate	7157
Pr	7: 8	He was going down the street near her c,	7157
	7:12	now in the squares, at every c she lurks.)	7157
	21: 9	to live on a c of the roof than share a house	7157
	25:24	to live on a c of the roof than share a house	7157
Jer	31:38	from the Tower of Hananel to the C Gate	7157
	31:40	the Kidron Valley on the east as far as the c	7157
Eze	16: 8	I spread the c of my garment over you	4053
	46:21	and I saw in each c another court.	928+928+5243+5243
Zep	1:16	the fortified cities and against the c towers.	7157
Zec	14:10	Tower of Hananel to the C Gate,	7157
Ac	26:26	because this was not done in a c.	1224

CORNERS (36) [CORNER]

Ex	25:26	for the table and fasten them to the four c,	6991
	26:23	make two frames for the c at the far end.	7910
	26:24	At these two c they must be double from	5243
	27: 2	Make a horn at each of the four c,	7157
	27: 4	a bronze ring at each of the four c	7896
	28: 7	to two of its c,	7896
	28:23	for it and fasten them to two c of	7896
	28:24	the two gold chains to the rings at the c of	7896
	28:26	to the other two c of the breastpiece on the	7896
	36:28	for the c of the tabernacle at the far end.	7910
	36:29	At these two c the frames were double	5243
	37:13	the table and fastened them to the four c,	6991
	38: 2	They made a horn at each of the four c,	7157
	38: 5	for the four c of the bronze grating.	7921
	39: 4	which were attached to two of its c,	7896
	39:16	the rings to two of the c of the breastpiece.	7896
	39:17	the two gold chains to the rings at the c of	7896
	39:19	to the other two c of the breastpiece on the	7896
Nu	15:38	to make tassels on the c of your garments,	4053
Dt	22:12	on the four c of the cloak you wear.	4053
Job	1:19	in from the desert and struck the four c of	7157
Isa	41: 9	from its farthest c I called you.	721
Eze	7: 2	end has come upon the four c of the land.	4053
	41:22	its c, its base and its sides were of wood.	5243
	43:20	the four c of the upper ledge and all around	7157
	45:19	on the four c of the upper ledge of the altar	7157
	46:21	and led me around to its four c,	5243
	46:22	In the four c of the outer court	5243
	46:22	the courts in the four c was the same size.	7910
Zec	9:15	be full like a bowl used for sprinkling the c	2312
Mt	6: 5	in the synagogues and on the street c to	1224
	22: 9	Go to the street c and invite to	1447
Ac	10:11	down to earth by its four c.	794
	11: 5	down from heaven by its four c,	794
Rev	7: 1	at the four c of the earth,	1224
	20: 8	the nations in the four c of the earth—	1224

CORNERSTONE (6) [CORNER, STONE]

Job	38: 6	or who laid its c—	74+7157
Isa	28:16	a precious c for a sure foundation;	7157
Jer	51:26	No rock will be taken from you for a c,	7157
Zec	10: 4	From Judah will come the c,	7157
Eph	2:20	with Christ Jesus himself as the chief c.	214+1639
1Pe	2: 6	a chosen and precious c,	214

CORNERSTONES (1) [CORNER, STONE]

Isa	19:13	the c of her peoples have led Egypt astray.	7157

CORNET, CORNETS (KJV) See RAM'S HORNS, HORN

CORNFIELD, CORNFIELDS (Anglicized) See GRAINFIELD, GRAINFIELDS

CORNFLOOR (KJV) See THRESHING FLOOR

CORPSE (3) [CORPSES]

Lev	22: 4	by a c or by anyone who has an emission	5883
Isa	14:19	Like a c trampled underfoot,	7007
Mk	9:26	The boy looked so much like a c	3738

CORPSES (1) [CORPSE]

Na	3: 3	people stumbling over the c—	1581

CORRECT (4) [CORRECTED, CORRECTING, CORRECTION, CORRECTIONS, CORRECTLY, CORRECTS]

Job	6:26	Do you mean to c what I say,	3519
	40: 2	with the Almighty c him?	3574
Jer	10:24	C me, LORD, but only with justice—	3579
2Ti	4: 2	c, rebuke and encourage—	1794

CORRECTED (1) [CORRECT]

Pr	29:19	A servant cannot be c by mere words;	3579

CORRECTING (1) [CORRECT]

2Ti	3:16	rebuking, c and training in righteousness,	2061

CORRECTION (16) [CORRECT]

Lev	26:23	not accept my c but continue to be hostile	3579
Job	36:10	to c and commands them to repent	4592
Pr	5:12	How my heart spurned c!	9350
	10:17	but whoever ignores c leads others astray.	9350
	12: 1	but he who hates c is stupid.	9350
	13:18	but whoever heeds c is honored.	9350
	15: 5	but whoever heeds c shows prudence.	9350
	15:10	he who hates c will die.	9350
	15:12	A mocker resents c;	3519
	15:32	but whoever heeds c gains understanding.	9350
	29:15	The rod of c imparts wisdom,	9350
Jer	2:30	they did not respond to c.	4592
	5: 3	you crushed them, but they refused c.	4592
	7:28	the LORD its God or responded to c.	4592
Zep	3: 2	She obeys no one, she accepts no c.	4592
	3: 7	'Surely you will fear me and accept c!'	4592

CORRECTIONS (1) [CORRECT]

Pr	6:23	and the c of discipline are the way to life,	9350

CORRECTLY (5) [CORRECT]

Jdg	12: 6	he could not pronounce the word c,	4026
Jer	1:12	The LORD said to me, "You have seen c,	3512
Lk	7:43	"You have judged c," Jesus said.	3987
	10:28	"You have answered c," Jesus replied.	3987
2Ti	2:15	who does not need to be ashamed and who c handles the word	3982

CORRECTS (2) [CORRECT]

Job	5:17	"Blessed is the man whom God c;	3519
Pr	9: 7	"Whoever c a mocker invites insult;	3579

CORRESPONDING (3) [CORRESPONDS]

1Ch	23: 6	David divided the Levites into groups c to	4200
2Ch	3: 8	length c to the width of the temple—	6584+7156
Eze	42:12	to the c wall extending eastward,	2054

CORRESPONDS (1) [CORRESPONDING]

Gal	4:25	and c to the present city of Jerusalem,	5368

CORRODED (1) [CORROSION]

Jas	5: 3	Your gold and silver are c.	2995

CORROSION (1) [CORRODED]

Jas	5: 3	Their c will testify against you	2675

CORRUPT (26) [CORRUPTED, CORRUPTION, CORRUPTLY, CORRUPTS]

Ge	6:11	the earth was c in God's sight and was full	8845
	6:12	God saw how the earth had become,	8845
Ex	32: 7	up out of Egypt, have become c.	8845
Dt	4:16	not become c and make for yourselves	8845
	4:25	then become c and make any kind of idol,	8845
	9:12	of Egypt have become c.	8845
	31:29	you are sure to become utterly c	8845+8845
Jdg	2:19	even more c than those of their fathers,	8845
2Ch	27: 2	however, continued their c practices.	8845
Job	15:16	who is vile and c,	480
Ps	14: 1	They are c, their deeds are vile;	8845
	14: 3	they have together become c;	480
	53: 1	They are c, and their ways are vile;	8845
	53: 3	they have together become c;	480
	94:20	Can a c throne be allied with you—	2095
Pr	4:24	keep c talk far from your lips.	4299
	6:12	who goes about with a c mouth,	6838
	19:28	A c witness mocks at justice,	1175
Jer	2:21	did you turn against me into a c, wild vine?	6074
Eze	20:44	to your evil ways and your c practices,	8845
Da	6: 4	because he was trustworthy and neither c	10705

Da 11:32 With flattery he will **c** those who have
      violated the covenant; 2866
Hos 5: 3 turned to prostitution; Israel *is* **c.** 3237
Ac 2:40 "Save yourselves from this **c** generation." 5021
1Ti 6: 5 constant friction between men *of* **c** mind, 1425
2Pe 2:10 of those who follow the **c** desire of 3622

CORRUPTED (8) [CORRUPT]

Ge 6:12 for all the people on earth had **c** their ways. 8845
Eze 28:17 and *you* **c** your wisdom because 8845
2Co 7: 2 *we have* **c** no one, 5780
Eph 4:22 which *is being* **c** by its deceitful desires; 5780
Tit 1:15 but *to* those who *are* **c** and do not believe, 3620
   1:15 both their minds and consciences *are* **c.** 3620
Jude 1:23 hating even the clothing stained by **c** flesh. 4922
Rev 19: 2 the great prostitute who **c** the earth 5780

CORRUPTION (9) [CORRUPT]

2Ki 23:13 of Jerusalem on the south of the Hill of C— 5422
Ezr 9:11 a land polluted by the **c** of its peoples. 5614
Job 17:14 if I say to **c,** 'You are my father,' 8846
Ps 55:23 down the wicked into the pit of **c;** 8846
Isa 1: 4 a brood of evildoers, children **given to c!** 8845
Da 6: 4 They could find no **c** in him, 10705
Hos 9: 9 They have sunk deep into **c,** 8845
2Pe 1: 4 in the world caused by evil desires. 5785
   2:20 the **c** of the world by knowing our Lord 3621

CORRUPTLY (3) [CORRUPT]

Dt 32: 5 *They have* **acted c** toward him; 8845
Jer 6:28 They are bronze and iron; they all **act c.** 8845
Zep 3: 7 But they were still eager *to* **act c** 8845

CORRUPTS (3) [CORRUPT]

Ecc 7: 7 and a bribe **c** the heart. 6
1Co 15:33 "Bad company **c** good character." 5780
Jas 3: 6 It **c** the whole person, 5071

CORS (8) [COR]

1Ki 4:22 Solomon's daily provisions were thirty **c** 4123
   4:22 of fine flour and sixty **c** *of* meal, 4123
   5:11 Solomon gave Hiram twenty thousand **c** 4123
2Ch 2:10 twenty thousand **c** of ground wheat, 4123
   2:10 twenty thousand **c** of barley, 4123
   27: 5 ten thousand **c** of wheat 4123
   27: 5 of wheat and ten thousand **c** of barley. NIH
Ezr 7:22 a hundred **c** of wheat, 10367

COS (1)

Ac 21: 1 we put out to sea and sailed straight to **C.** 3271

COSAM (1)

Lk 3:28 the son *of* **C,** the son of Elmadam, 3272

COSMETIC (1) [COSMETICS]

2Sa 14: 2 and don't use any **c** lotions. 9043

COSMETICS (1) [COSMETIC]

Est 2:12 of myrrh and six with perfumes and **c.** 9475

COST (14) [COSTLY, COSTS]

Nu 11: 5 the fish we ate in Egypt at no **c—** 2855
   16:38 the men who sinned **at the c of** their lives. 928
Jos 6:26 **"At the c of** his firstborn son will he lay 928
   6:26 **at the c of** his youngest will he set 928
2Sa 24:24 burnt offerings that **c me nothing."** 2855
1Ki 16:34 He laid its foundations **at the c of** 928
   16:34 and he set up its gates **at the c of** 928
1Ch 12:19 "It will **c us** our heads if he deserts 928
Pr 4: 7 it **c** all you have, get understanding. 928
   7:23 little knowing it will **c** him his life. 928
   23: 7 of man who is always thinking about the **c.** 5883
Isa 55: 1 and milk without money and without **c.** 4697
Lk 14:28 Will he not first sit down and estimate the **c** 1252
Rev 21: 6 to drink **without c** from the spring of 1562

COSTLY (8) [COST]

Ge 24:53 he also gave **c** gifts to her brother and 4458
Est 1: 6 marble, mother-of-pearl and other **c** stones. 6090
Ps 49: 8 a life *is* **c,** no payment is ever enough— 3700
Eze 16:10 and covered you with **c** garments. 5429
   16:13 and **c** fabric and embroidered cloth. 5429
Da 11:38 with precious stones and **c** gifts. 2776
1Co 3:12 silver, **c** stones, wood, hay or straw, 5508
Rev 18:12 **c** wood, bronze, iron and marble; 5508

COSTS (3) [COST]

1Ch 21:24 a burnt offering that **c me nothing."** 2855
Ezr 6: 4 The **c** are to be paid by the royal treasury. 10486
Pr 6:31 though *it* **c** him all the wealth of his house. 5989

COTES (KJV) See PEN

COUCH (7) [COUCHES]

Ge 49: 4 onto my **c** and defiled it. 3661
1Sa 28:23 He got up from the ground and sat on the **c.** 4753
2Ki 4:32 there was the boy lying dead on his **c.** 4753
Est 7: 8 on the **c** where Esther was reclining. 4753

Job 7:13 and my **c** will ease my complaint, 5435
Ps 6: 6 with weeping and drench my **c** with tears. 6911
Eze 23:41 You sat on an elegant **c,** 4753

COUCHES (3) [COUCH]

Est 1: 6 There were **c** of gold and silver on 4753
Am 3:12 of their beds and in Damascus on their **c."** 6911
   6: 4 with ivory and lounge on your **c.** 6911

COULD (285) [COULDN'T]

Ge 8: 9 But the dove **c find** no place to set its feet AIT
   13: 6 But the land **c** not **support** them AIT
   13:16 so that if anyone **c** count the dust, 3523
   13:16 then your offspring **c be counted.** AIT
   19:11 with blindness so that *they* **c** not **find** 4206
   20:17 so *they* **c have children** again, AIT
   27: 1 so weak that *he* **c** no longer **see,** AIT
   31:27 so *I* **c send** you **away** with joy and singing AIT
   31:35 but **c** not **find** the household gods. AIT
   32:25 the man saw that *he* **c** not **overpower** him, AIT
   36: 7 where they were staying **c** not support them 3523
   37: 4 they hated him and **c** not speak a kind word 3523
   39: 9 then **c** I **do** such a wicked thing and sin AIT
   41: 8 but no one **c interpret** them for him. AIT
   41:21 no one **c tell** that they had done so; AIT
   41:24 but none **c explain** it to me." AIT
   42:23 not realize that Joseph **c understand** them, AIT
   43:10 **c have gone and returned** AIT
   43:32 because Egyptians **c** not eat with Hebrews, 3523
   45: 1 Then Joseph **c** no longer control himself 3523
   48:10 and *he* **c** hardly see. 3523
Ex 2: 3 But when *she* **c** hide him no longer, 3523
   7:21 that the Egyptians **c** not drink its water. 3523
   7:24 *they* **c** not drink the water of the river. 3523
   8:18 by their secret arts, *they* **c** not. 3523
   9:11 The magicians **c** not stand before Moses 3523
   9:15 For by now I **c have stretched out** my hand AIT
   10:23 No one **c see** anyone else or leave his place AIT
   13:21 so that they **c travel** by day or night. AIT
   15:23 *they* **c** not drink its water 3523
   39: 4 so it **c be fastened.** AIT
   40:35 Moses **c** not enter the Tent of Meeting 3523
Lev 11:34 that **c be eaten** but has water on it AIT
   11:34 any liquid that **c be drunk** from it is
      unclean. AIT
Nu 9: 6 who **c** not celebrate the Passover on 3523
   11:33 and before *it* **c be consumed,** AIT
   22:18 I **c** not do anything great or small to go 3523
   24:13 I **c** not do anything of my own accord, 3523
   35:17 anyone has a stone in his hand that **c kill,** AIT
   35:18 a wooden object in his hand that **c kill,** AIT
   35:23 drops a stone on him that **c kill** him, AIT
Dt 4:42 anyone who had killed a person **c flee** AIT
   4:42 *He* **c flee** into one of these cities AIT
   32:30 How **c** one man **chase** a thousand, AIT
Jos 15:63 Judah **c** not dislodge the Jebusites, 3523
   20: 9 among them who killed someone
      accidentally **c flee** AIT
   22:16 'How **c you break faith** with the God AIT
   22:16 How **c** you turn away from the LORD NIH
Jdg 7:12 Their camels **c** no more be counted than NIH
   10:16 **c** bear Israel's misery **no longer.** AIT
   12: 6 he **c** not pronounce the word correctly, 3922
   14:14 For three days *they* **c** not give the answer. 3523
   20:16 each of whom **c sling** a stone at a hair and AIT
   20:42 but they **c not escape** the battle. AIT
Ru 1:11 who **c become** your husbands? AIT
   3:14 but got up before anyone **c be recognized;** AIT
1Sa 3: 2 so weak that *he* **c** barely see, 3523
   4:15 and whose eyes were set so that *he* **c** AIT
   6: 6 **c go on** *their* **way?** AIT
   13:19 a blacksmith **c be found** in the whole land AIT
   29: 4 *c* he **regain** his master's favor. AIT
2Sa 1:10 that after he had fallen he **c** not **survive.** AIT
   2:22 **c** I **look** your brother Joab **in the face?"** AIT
   11:11 How **c** I **go** to my house to eat and drink AIT
   13:13 **c** I **get rid of** my disgrace? AIT
   15: 4 or case **c** anyone **come** to me and I would see AIT
   17:17 *they* **c** not **risk** being seen entering the city. 3523
   22:39 and *they* **c** not **rise;** AIT
   24: 9 able-bodied men who **c handle** a sword, AIT
1Ki 1: 1 he **c** not **keep warm** even AIT
   5: 3 he **c** not build a temple for the Name of 3523
   8: 5 that *they* **c** not **be recorded** or counted. AIT
   8: 8 their ends **c be seen** from the Holy Place AIT
   8:11 And the priests **c** not perform their service 3523
   9:21 whom the Israelites **c** not exterminate— 3523
   13: 4 so that he **c** not pull it back. 3523
   14: 4 Now Ahijah **c** not see; 3523
   18:10 he made them swear they **c** not **find** you. AIT
2Ki 3:21 who **c bear arms** was called up AIT
   4:40 And *they* **c** not eat it. 3523
   7: 2 of the heavens, **c** this **happen?"** AIT
   7:19 of the heavens, **c** this **happen?"** AIT
   8:13 **c** your servant, a mere dog, **accomplish** AIT
   10: 4 "If two kings **c** not **resist** him, AIT
   16: 5 but *they* **c** not **overpower** him. 3523
   23:10 **c** use it to **sacrifice** AIT
   25:16 was more than **c be weighed.** NIH
1Ch 5: 1 **c** not **be listed in the genealogical record** AIT
   5:18 able-bodied men who **c handle** shield AIT
   5:18 who **c use** a bow, AIT
   8:40 of Ulam were brave warriors who **c handle** AIT
   21: 5 men who **c handle** a sword, AIT
   21:30 David **c** not go before it to inquire of God, 3523

1Ch 22: 3 and more bronze than **c** be weighed. NIH
   22: 4 He also provided more cedar logs than **c** NIH
2Ch 5: 6 that *they* **c** not **be recorded** or counted. AIT
   5: 9 **c be seen** from in front of AIT
   5:14 and the priests **c** not perform their service 3523
   7: 2 The priests **c** not enter the temple of 3523
   7: 7 the bronze altar he had made **c** not hold 3523
   14:13 a great number of Cushites fell that they **c** NIH
   20:25 more than *they* **c take away.** AIT
   22:11 from Athaliah so *she* **c** not **kill** him. AIT
   25:15 which **c** not **save** their own people AIT
   30:17 and **c** not **consecrate** [their lambs] to AIT
   31: 4 so they **c devote** *themselves* to the Law of AIT
Ezr 2:59 but *they* **c** not show 3523
   2:62 but they **c** not **find** *them* and AIT
   3:13 No one **c distinguish** the sound of the
      shouts AIT
   5: 5 a report **c go** to Darius and his written reply AIT
   5:10 so that *we* **c write down** the names AIT
Ne 5: 8 because *they* **c find** nothing to say. AIT
   7:61 but *they* **c** not show 3523
   7:64 but they **c** not **find** *them* and AIT
   8: 3 women and others *who* **c understand.** AIT
   8: 5 All the people **c** see him NIH
   8: 8 people **c understand** what was being read. AIT
   9:36 so they **c** eat its fruit and AIT
   12:43 **sound** of rejoicing in Jerusalem **c be heard** AIT
   13:19 the gates so that no load **c be brought in** on AIT
Est 6: 1 That night the king **c** not sleep; 5610
   9: 2 No one **c stand** against them. AIT
Job 2:12 *they* **c** hardly **recognize** him; AIT
   4:16 It stopped, but *I* **c** not **tell** what it was. AIT
   6: 2 "If only my anguish **c be weighed** AIT
   9: 3 *he* **c** not **answer** him one time out of AIT
   9:15 *I* **c** not **answer** him. AIT
   9:15 **c** only **plead** with my Judge **for mercy.** AIT
   13: 9 **C** you **deceive** him AIT
   15:14 "What is man, that *he* **c be pure,** AIT
   15:14 that *he* **c be righteous?** AIT
   16: 4 I also **c speak** like you, AIT
   16: 4 I **c make fine speeches** against you AIT
   23: 3 if only I **c go** to his dwelling! AIT
   23: 7 There an upright man **c present** his **case** AIT
   31:23 fear of his splendor I **c** not **do** such things. 3523
Ps 18:38 I crushed them so that *they* **c** not rise; 3523
   37:36 though I looked for him, *he* **c** not **be found.** AIT
   55:12 I **c endure** it; AIT
   55:12 I **c hide** from him. AIT
   78:25 **all** the food they **c eat.** 8427
   78:44 *they* **c** not **drink** *from* their streams. AIT
   78:64 and their widows **c** not **weep.** AIT
   107: 4 to a city where they **c** settle. NIH
   107: 7 a straight way to a city where they **c** settle. NIH
   107:36 and they founded a city where they **c** settle. NIH
   130: 3 O Lord, who **c stand?** AIT
Isa 5: 4 What more **c have been done** AIT
   7: 1 but *they* **c** not overpower it. 3523
   10:19 be so few that a child **c write** them **down.** AIT
   26:16 **c barely whisper** a prayer. AIT
   41:26 so *we* **c know,** or beforehand, AIT
   41:26 or beforehand, so *we* **c say,** 'He was right'? AIT
   48: 5 so that *you* **c say,** 'My idols did them; AIT
Jer 24: 2 so bad *they* **c** not **be eaten.** AIT
   44:22 the LORD **c** no longer endure your wicked
      actions 3523
   47: 4 and to cut off all survivors *who* **c help** Tyre AIT
   52:20 was more than **c** be weighed. NIH
La 4:12 and foes **c enter** the gates of Jerusalem. AIT
   4:17 for a nation *that* **c** not **save** us. AIT
   4:18 so *we* **c** not **walk** in our streets. AIT
Eze 10: 5 of the cherubim **c be heard** as far away as AIT
   10: 8 of the cherubim **c be seen** what looked like AIT
   14:14 were in it, they **c save** only themselves AIT
   14:16 *they* **c** not **save** their own sons AIT
   14:18 *they* **c** not **save** their own sons AIT
   14:20 *they* **c save** neither son nor daughter. AIT
   20:25 not good and laws *they* **c** not **live** by; AIT
   31: 8 cedars in the garden of God **c** not rival it, AIT
   31: 8 **c** the pine trees **equal** AIT
   31: 8 **c** the plane trees **compare with** AIT
   31: 8 in the garden of God **c match** its beauty. AIT
   47: 5 but now it was a river that I **c** not cross, 3523
   47: 5 a river that no one **c cross.** AIT
Da 1:17 And Daniel **c understand** visions AIT
   2: 1 mind was troubled and he **c not** sleep. 2118+6584
   4: 7 but *they* **c** not **interpret** it for me. AIT
   5: 8 but *they* **c** not read the writing or tell 10346
   5:15 but *they* **c** not explain it. 10346
   6: 4 *They* **c find** no corruption in him, AIT
   6:18 And he **c** not sleep. 10463
   8: 4 No animal **c stand** against him, AIT
   8: 4 and none **c rescue** from his power. AIT
   8: 7 and none **c rescue** the ram from his power. AIT
Hos 10: 3 even if we had a king, what **c** he **do** for us?" AIT
Jnh 1:13 But *they* **c** not, 3523
   2: 8 forfeit the grace that **c** be theirs. NIH
Zec 1:21 so that no one **c raise** his head, AIT
   7:14 so desolate behind them that no *one* **c come** AIT
   7:14 **c go about** *his* **business** AIT
Mt 8:28 They were so violent that no one **c** pass 2710
   9:32 and **c** not talk was brought to Jesus. 3273
   12:22 **c** both **talk and see.** AIT
   12:23 "**C** this be the Son of David?" NIG
   15:33 "Where **c** we get enough bread NIG
   17:16 but *they* **c** not heal him." 1538
   18:30 the man thrown into prison until he **c pay** AIT
   22:10 and gathered all the people they **c** find, NIG

Mt	22:46	No one c say a word in reply, 1538
	26:9	"This perfume c have been sold at 1538
	26:40	"C you men not keep watch with me 2710
	26:59	c put him to death. AIT
Mk	1:45	Jesus c no longer enter a town openly 1538
	2:4	*Since they* c not get him to Jesus because 1538
	4:33	as much as *they* c understand. 1538
	5:3	and no one c bind him any more, 1538
	6:5	He c not do any miracles there, 1538
	7:24	yet he c not keep his presence secret. 1538
	7:32	a man who was deaf and c **hardly talk,** 3652
	9:3	in the world c bleach them. 1538
	9:18	but *they* c not." 2710
	14:5	It c have been sold for more than 1538
	14:8	She did what *she* c. 2400
	14:37	C you not keep watch for one hour? 2710
	14:55	against Jesus so that they c put him NIG
Lk	1:22	When he came out, he c not speak to them. 1538
	5:19	When they c not find a way to do this NIG
	6:48	torrent struck that house but c not shake it, 2710
	8:43	but no one c heal her. 2710
	8:47	woman, seeing that *she* c not **go unnoticed,** AIT
	9:40	but *they* c not." 1538
	13:11	She was bent over and c not straighten up 1538
	15:29	even a young goat so *I* c **celebrate** AIT
	19:3	but being a short man *he* c not, 1538
	19:23	I c have collected it with interest?' 323
	19:48	Yet *they* c not **find** any way to do it, AIT
	24:45	*so they* c **understand** the Scriptures. AIT
Jn	3:2	For no one c perform the miraculous 1538
	4:29	C this be the Christ?" NIG
	4:33	"C someone have brought him food?" NIG
	9:11	So I went and washed, and then *I* c **see."** AIT
	9:33	he c do nothing." 1538
	11:37	"C not he who opened the eyes of 1538
	12:39	For this reason *they* c not believe, because, 1538
Ac	4:14	But *since they* c **see** AIT
	4:14	there was nothing they c say. NIG
	4:21	They c not decide how to punish them, NIG
	5:9	c you **agree** to test the Spirit of the Lord? AIT
	6:10	but *they* c not stand up against his wisdom 2710
	7:11	and our fathers c not **find** food. AIT
	8:20	with you, because you thought *you* c **buy** AIT
	9:8	when he opened his eyes he c **see** nothing. AIT
	9:18	and he c **see again.** AIT
	10:22	so that they c **hear** what you have to say." AIT
	11:17	who was I to think that I c oppose God?" 1543
	13:39	from everything *you* c not be justified 1538
	21:34	*since* the commander c not get at the truth 1538
	25:7	which *they* c not prove. 2710
	25:21	I ordered him held until *I* c **send** him AIT
	26:32	"This man c have been set free if he had 1538
	27:15	by the storm and c not head into the wind; 1538
	27:39	to run the ship aground if *they* c. 1538
	27:43	He ordered those who c swim 1538
Ro	3:6	how c God **judge** the world? AIT
	9:3	For *I* c **wish** that I myself were cursed AIT
	11:8	a spirit of stupor, eyes so that *they* c not **see** AIT
	11:8	not see and ears so that *they* c not **hear,** AIT
	11:19	so that *I* c be **grafted in."** AIT
1Co	3:1	I c not address you as spiritual but 1538
2Co	3:7	the Israelites c not look steadily at the face 1538
	3:12	that before God you c see for yourselves NIG
Gal	2:21	righteousness c be gained through the law, NIG
	3:21	if a law had been given that c impart life, 1538
	4:15	I can testify that, if you c **have done so,** 1543
	4:20	how I wish *I* c be with you now NIG
Php	2:30	to make up for the help you c not **give me.** 5729
1Th	2:6	of Christ *we* c have been a burden to you, 1538
	3:1	So *when we* c **stand** it no longer, AIT
	3:5	For this reason, *when I* c **stand** it no longer, AIT
Phm	1:8	in Christ *I* c be bold and order you NIG
	1:13	c take your place in **helping** AIT
Heb	5:7	to the one who c save him from death, 1538
	7:11	If perfection c have been attained through AIT
	10:2	If it c, would they have stopped 2075
	11:5	he c not be **found,** AIT
	11:19	Abraham reasoned that God c raise 1543
	12:17	*He* c **bring about** no change of mind, AIT
	12:20	*they* c not **bear** what was commanded; AIT
Rev	5:3	on earth or under the earth c open the scroll 1538
	7:9	a great multitude that no one c count, 1538
	13:15	so that it c **speak** and **cause** all who refused AIT
	13:17	so that no one c buy or sell unless he had 1538
	14:3	No one c learn the song except the 144,000 1538
	15:8	and no one c enter the temple until 1538
	16:20	and the mountains c not *be* **found.** AIT

COULDN'T (3) [COULD, NOT]

2Ki	5:12	C I wash in them and be cleansed?" 4202
Mt	17:19	"Why c we drive it out?" 1538+4024
Mk	9:28	"Why c we drive it out?" 1538+4024

COUNCIL (16) [COUNCILS]

Ge	49:6	Let me not enter their c, 6051
Nu	16:2	who had been appointed members of the c. 4595
Job	15:8	Do you listen in on God's c? 6051
Ps	89:7	In the c of the holy ones 6051
	107:32	of the people and praise him in the c of 4632
	111:1	in the c of the upright and in the assembly. 6051
Jer	23:18	of them has stood in the c of the LORD 6051
	23:22	But if they had stood in my c, 6051
Eze	13:9	They will not belong to the c of my people 1085
Mk	15:43	a prominent **member of the C,** 1085
Lk	22:66	At daybreak the c **of the elders** 4564

Lk	23:50	Joseph, a **member of the C,** a good and upright man, 1085
Jn	3:1	a member of the Jewish ruling c. NIG
Ac	17:33	At that, Paul left the C. 899S
	22:5	the high priest and all the C can testify. 4564
	25:12	After Festus had conferred with his c, 5206

COUNCILS (2) [COUNCIL]

Mt	10:17	they will hand you over to the **local** c 5284
Mk	13:9	the local c and flogged in the synagogues. 5284

COUNSEL (33) [COUNSELED, COUNSELOR, COUNSELORS, COUNSELS]

2Sa	15:31	turn Ahithophel's c into foolishness." 6783
1Ki	22:5	"First seek the c *of the* LORD." 1821
2Ch	18:4	"First seek the c *of the* LORD." 1821
	22:5	He also followed their c when he went 6783
	25:16	and have not listened to my c." 6783
Ezr	10:3	in accordance with the c *of* my lord and 6783
Job	12:13	c and understanding are his. 6783
	21:16	so I stand aloof from the c *of the* wicked. 6783
	22:18	so I stand aloof from the c *of the* wicked. 6783
	29:21	waiting in silence for my c. 6783
	38:2	"Who is this that darkens my c with words 6783
	42:3	that obscures my c without knowledge?' 6783
Ps	1:1	not walk in the c *of the* wicked or stand in 6783
	32:8	*I will* c you and watch over you. 3619
	73:24	You guide me with your c, 6783
	106:13	and did not wait for his c. 6783
	107:11	the words of God and despised the c of 6783
Pr	8:14	C and sound judgment are mine; 6783
	15:22	Plans fail for lack of c, 6051
	22:20	sayings of c and knowledge, 4600
	27:9	of one's friend springs from his earnest c. 6783
Isa	11:2	the Spirit of c and of power, 6783
	16:3	"Give us c, render a decision. 6783
	28:29	wonderful in c and magnificent in wisdom. 6783
	41:28	**one** among them **to give** c, 3446
	45:21	*let them* **take** c together. 3619
	47:13	c you have *received* has only worn you out! 6783
Jer	18:18	nor will c from the wise, 6783
	38:15	Even if *I did* **give** you c, 3619
	49:7	Has c perished from the prudent? 6783
Eze	7:26	as will the c of the elders. 6783
1Ti	5:14	So *I* c younger widows to marry, 1089
Rev	3:18	*I* c you to buy from me gold refined in 5205

COUNSELED (1) [COUNSEL]

Mic	6:5	remember what Balak king of ᴀ 3619

COUNSELOR (13) [COUNSEL]

2Sa	15:12	Ahithophel the Gilonite, David's c, 3446
1Ch	26:14	a wise c, and the lot for the North Gate fell 3446
	27:32	Jonathan, David's uncle, was a c, 3446
	27:33	Ahithophel was the king's c. 3446
Isa	3:3	the captain of fifty and man of rank, the c, 3446
	9:6	And he will be called Wonderful C, 3446
	40:13	or instructed him as his c? 408+6783
Mic	4:9	Has your c perished, 3446
Jn	14:16	he will give you another C to be with you 4156
	14:26	But the C, the Holy Spirit, 4156
	15:26	"When the C comes, whom I will send 4156
	16:7	the C will not come to you; 4156
Ro	11:34	Or who has been his c?" 5207

COUNSELORS (6) [COUNSEL]

Ezr	4:5	They hired c to work against them 3446
Job	3:14	with kings and c of the earth, 3446
	12:17	He leads c away stripped and makes fools 3446
Ps	119:24	they are my c, 408+6783
Isa	1:26	your c as at the beginning. 3446
	19:11	wise c *of* Pharaoh give senseless advice. 3446

COUNSELS (2) [COUNSEL]

Ps	16:7	I will praise the LORD, who c me; 3619
Na	1:11	against the LORD and c wickedness. 3619

COUNT (45) [COUNTED, COUNTING, COUNTLESS, COUNTS]

Ge	13:16	so that if anyone could c the dust, 4948
	15:5	"Look up at the heavens and c the stars— 6218
	15:5	if indeed you can c them." 6218
	16:10	that *they will be* too numerous to c." 6218
Ex	30:12	a census of the Israelites to c them, 7212
Lev	15:13	he is to c **off** seven days 6218
	15:28	she must c **off** seven days, 6218
	23:15	c **off** seven full weeks. 6218
	23:16	c **off** fifty days up to the day after 6218
	25:8	" 'C **off** seven sabbaths of years— 6218
	25:50	*to* c the time from the year he sold himself 3108
Nu	1:49	not c the tribe of Levi or include them in 7212
	3:15	"C the Levites by their families and clans. 7212
	3:15	C every male a month old or more." 7212
	3:40	"C all the firstborn Israelite males who are 7212
	4:3	C all the men from thirty to fifty years NIH
	4:23	C all the men from thirty to fifty years 7212
	4:29	"C the Merarites by their clans 7212
	4:30	C all the men from thirty to fifty years 7212
	6:12	The previous days **do not** c, 5877
	23:10	Who *can* c the dust of Jacob or number 4948

Nu	31:26	heads of the community *are to* c all the people 906+5951+8031
Dt	16:9	C **off** seven weeks from 6218
Jdg	6:5	It was impossible to c the men 5031
1Ki	3:8	too numerous to c or number. 6218
1Ch	21:2	and c the Israelites from Beersheba to Dan. 6218
	27:24	Joab son of Zeruiah began to c the men 4948
Job	14:16	Surely then you will c my steps but 6218
	19:15	and my maidservants c me a stranger; 3108
	31:4	not see my ways and c my every step? 6218
	38:37	Who has the wisdom *to* c the clouds? 6218
	39:2	*Do you* c the months till they bear? 6218
Ps	22:17	*I can* c all my bones; 6218
	32:2	the man whose sin the LORD *does not* c 3108
	48:12	go around her, c her towers, 6218
	139:18	*Were I to* c them, 6218
	139:22	I c *them* my enemies. 2118+4200
Isa	16:14	a servant bound by contract would c them, NIH
	21:16	as a servant bound by contract would c it, NIH
	46:5	or c me **equal?** 8750
Ro	4:8	the man whose sin the Lord *will never* c 3357
	6:11	c yourselves dead to sin but alive to God 3357
2Th	1:11	our God *may* c you **worthy** of his calling, 546
Rev	7:9	a great multitude that no one could c, 749
	11:1	and c the worshipers there. NIG

COUNTED (67) [COUNT]

Ge	13:16	then your offspring *could be* c. 4948
	32:12	which cannot *be* c.' " 6218
Ex	30:12	a ransom for his life at the time he *is* c. 7212
	30:13	to those *already* c is to give a half shekel, 7212
	38:25	the community who **were** c **in the** census 7212
	38:26	who had crossed over to those c, 7212
Nu	1:19	And so *he* c them in the Desert of Sinai: 7212
	1:22	in the army **were** c and listed by name, 7212
	1:44	the **men** c **by Moses and Aaron** 7212+2186
	1:45	to serve in Israel's army were c according 7212
	1:47	however, **were** not c along with the others. 7212
	2:32	according to their families. 7212
	2:33	**were** not c along with the other Israelites, 7212
	3:16	So Moses c them, 7212
	3:22	a month old or more who **were** c was 7,500. 7212
	3:34	a month old or more who **were** c was 6,200. 7212
	3:39	of Levites c at the LORD's command 7212
	3:42	Moses c all the firstborn of the Israelites, 7212
	4:34	Aaron and the leaders of the community c 7212
	4:36	c by clans, were 2,750. 7212
	4:37	Moses and Aaron c them according to 7212
	4:38	The Gershonites **were** c by their clans 7212
	4:40	c by their clans and families, were 2,630. 7212
	4:41	Moses and Aaron c them according to 7212
	4:42	The Merarites **were** c by their clans 7212
	4:44	c by their clans, were 3,200. 7212
	4:45	Moses and Aaron c them according to 7212
	4:46	and the leaders of Israel c all the Levites 7212
	4:49	Thus they **were** c, 7212
	7:2	in charge of those *who* **were** c 7212
	14:29	of you twenty years old or more *who was* c 7212
	26:57	the Levites *who* **were** c by their clans: 7212
	26:62	They **were** not c along with 7212
	26:63	These are the *ones* c by Moses and Eleazar 7212
	26:63	when *they* c the Israelites on the plains 7212
	26:64	of them was among *those* c *by* Moses 7212
	26:64	by Moses and Aaron the priest when *they* c 7212
	31:49	Your servants *have* c the soldiers 906+5951+8031
Jos	13:3	all of *it* c as Canaanite (the territory of 3108
Jdg	7:12	Their camels could no more be c than 5031
1Sa	13:15	and Saul c the men who were with him. 7212
2Sa	2:15	So they stood up and *were* c **off** 928+5031+6296
	24:10	David was conscience-stricken after he had c the fighting men, 6218
1Ki	8:5	that they could not be recorded or c. 4948
2Ki	12:10	c the money that had been brought into 4948
1Ch	9:28	they c them when they were brought in and 5031
	21:17	the fighting men to be c? 4948
	22:4	be c, for the Sidonians 5031
	23:3	The Levites thirty years old or more **were** c, 6218
	23:11	so they were c as one family NIH
	23:14	of Moses the man of God **were** c as part of 7924
	23:24	under their names and c individually, 5031
	23:27	the Levites were c 5031
2Ch	5:6	that they could not be recorded or c. 4948
Ezr		*who* c them **out** to Sheshbazzar the prince 6218
Job	5:9	miracles that cannot be c. 5031
	9:10	miracles that cannot be c. 5031
Ps	49:18	Though while he lived *he* c himself **blessed—** 1385
	88:4	*I am* among those who go down to 3108
Ecc	1:15	what is lacking cannot *be* c. 4948
Isa	22:10	*You* c the buildings in Jerusalem and tore 6218
Jer	46:23	they cannot be c. 5031
Hos	1:10	which cannot be measured or c. 6218
Mt	26:15	So they c **out** for him thirty silver coins. 2705
Ac	5:41	rejoicing because *they had been* c **worthy** 2921
2Th	1:5	and as a result you *will be* c **worthy** of 2921

COUNTENANCE (1)

Job	14:20	you change his c and send him away. 7156

COUNTERFEIT (2)

2Th	2:9	in all kinds of c miracles, 6022
1Jn	2:27	and as that anointing is real, not c— 6022

COUNTING (4) [COUNT]

Ge	46:26	**not** c his sons' wives— 963+4200+4946
Dt	24:15	because he is poor and *is* c on it. 448+906+5883+5951
Jdg	8:26	**not** c the ornaments, 963+4200+4946
2Co	5:19	not c men's sins against them. 3357

COUNTLESS (4) [COUNT]

Nu	10:36	O LORD, to the c thousands of Israel." 8047
Job	21:33	and a c throng goes before him. 401+5031
Jer	33:22	**make** the descendants of David my servant and the Levites who minister before me as c 889+4202+6218+8049
Heb	11:12	as numerous as the stars in the sky and as c 410

COUNTRIES (43) [COUNTRY]

Ge	41:57	And all the c came to Egypt to buy grain 824
Dt	29:16	in Egypt and how we passed through the c 1580
1Ki	4:21	These c brought tribute NIH
2Ki	18:35	of these c has been able to save his land 824
	19:11	the kings of Assyria have done to all the c, 824
2Ch	9:28	from Egypt and from all other c. 824
	20:29	the kingdoms of the c when they heard 824
Isa	10:14	so I gathered all the c; 824
	36:20	of these c has been able to save his land 824
	37:11	the kings of Assyria have done to all the c, 824
Jer	16:15	of the land of the north and out of all the c 824
	23:3	the remnant of my flock out of all the c 824
	23:8	of the land of the north and out of all the c 824
	27:6	Now I will hand all your c over 824
	28:8	against many c and great kingdoms. 824
	40:11	and all the other c heard that the king 824
	40:12	the c where they had been scattered. 5226
	51:28	and all the c they rule. 824
Eze	5:5	with all around her. 824
	5:6	and decrees more than the nations and c 824
	11:16	and scattered them among the c 824
	11:16	for them in the c where they have gone.' 824
	11:17	from the c where you have been scattered, 824
	12:15	the nations and scatter them through the c 824
	20:23	the nations and scatter them through the c 824
	20:34	from the nations and gather you from the c 824
	20:41	from the nations and gather you from the c 824
	22:4	the nations and a laughingstock to all the c. 824
	22:15	the nations and scatter you through the c; 824
	25:7	the nations and exterminate you from the c. 824
	29:12	the nations and scatter them through the c 824
	30:23	the nations and scatter them through the c. 824
	30:26	the nations and scatter them through the c, 824
	34:13	the nations and gather them from the c, 824
	35:10	"These two nations and c will be ours 824
	36:19	and they were scattered through the c; 824
	36:24	from all the c and bring you back 824
	39:27	and have gathered them from the c 824
Da	9:7	and all Israel, both near and far, in all the c 824
	11:40	He will invade *many* c and sweep 824
	11:41	**Many** c will fall, but Edom, AIT
	11:42	He will extend his power over *many* c; 824
Zec	8:7	"I will save my people from the c of 824

COUNTRY (245) [COUNTRIES, COUNTRYSIDE, COUNTRYMAN, COUNTRYMAN]

Ge	10:30	in the eastern **hill** c. 2215
	12:1	to Abram, "Leave your c, your people 824
	14:6	and the Horites in the **hill** c of Seir, 2215
	15:13	be strangers in a c not their own, 824
	21:23	Show to me and the c where you are living 824
	24:4	but will go to my c and my own relatives 824
	24:5	to the c you came from?" 824
	25:27	a man of the **open** c, 8441
	25:29	Esau came in from the **open** c, famished. 8441
	27:3	the **open** c to hunt some wild game for me. 8441
	27:5	When Esau left for the **open** c to hunt game 8441
	31:21	he headed for the **hill** c of Gilead. 2215
	31:23	and caught up with him in the **hill** c 2215
	31:25	Jacob had pitched his tent in the **hill** c 2215
	31:54	He offered a sacrifice there in the **hill** c 2215
	32:3	the c of Edom. 8441
	32:9	'Go back to your c and your relatives, 824
	36:8	Edom) settled in the **hill** c of Seir. 2215
	36:9	the father of the Edomites in the **hill** c 2215
	36:35	who defeated Midian in the c of Moab, 8441
	41:36	be held in reserve for the c, 824
	41:36	the c may not be ruined by the famine." 824
	41:56	the famine had spread over the whole c, 824
Ex	1:10	fight against us and leave the c." 824
	6:1	Because of my mighty hand he will drive them out of his c." 824
	6:11	of Egypt to let the Israelites go out of his c." 824
	7:2	to let the Israelites go out of his c. 824
	8:2	I will plague your whole c with frogs. 1473
	10:4	I will bring locusts into your c tomorrow. 1473
	10:14	in every area of the c in great numbers. 5213
	11:10	not let the Israelites go out of his c. 824
	12:33	the people to hurry and leave the c. 824
	13:17	on the road through the Philistine c, 824
	18:27	and Jethro returned to his own c. 824
Lev	25:24	the c *that* you hold as a possession. 824
	25:31	to be considered as open c. 824
	25:45	and members of their clans born in your c, 824
	26:6	and the sword will not pass through your c. 824
	26:34	that it lies desolate and you are in the c 824
Nu	13:17	through the Negev and on into the **hill** c. 2215
	13:29	Jebusites and Amorites live in the **hill** c; 2215
	14:40	up toward the high **hill** c. 2215
	14:44	up toward the high **hill** c, 2215
	14:45	that **hill** c came down and attacked them 2215
	20:17	Please let us pass through your c. 824
	21:22	"Let us pass through your c. 824
	22:6	to defeat them and drive them out of the c. 824
	22:13	"Go back to your own c, 824
Dt	1:7	Break camp and advance into the **hill** c 2215
	1:19	from Horeb and went toward the **hill** c of 2215
	1:20	"You have reached the **hill** c of 2215
	1:24	They left and went up into the **hill** c, 2215
	1:41	thinking it easy to go up into the **hill** c. 2215
	1:43	up into the **hill** c. 2215
	2:1	around the **hill** c of Seir. 2215
	2:3	around this **hill** c long enough; 2215
	2:5	I have given Esau the **hill** c of Seir 2215
	2:24	king of Heshbon, and his c. 824
	2:27	"Let us pass through your c. 824
	2:31	I have begun to deliver Sihon and his c 824
	3:12	including half the **hill** c of Gilead, 2215
	3:25	that fine **hill** c and Lebanon. 2215
	9:28	the c from which you brought us will say, 824
	11:3	of Egypt and to his whole c; 824
	22:25	the c a man happens to meet a girl pledged 8441
	22:27	for the man found the girl out in the c, 8441
	23:7	because you lived as an alien in his c. 824
	28:3	be blessed in the city and blessed in the c. 8441
	28:16	be cursed in the city and cursed in the c, 8441
	28:24	the rain of your c into dust and powder; 824
	28:40	You will have olive trees throughout your c 1473
Jos	1:4	all the Hittite c— 824
	2:9	in this c are melting in fear because of you. 824
	7:9	and the other people of the c will hear 824
	9:1	those in the **hill** c, 2215
	9:6	"We have come from a distant c; 824
	9:9	from a very distant c because of the fame 824
	9:11	and all those living in our c said to us, 824
	10:6	the **hill** c have joined forces against us." 2215
	10:40	including the **hill** c, the Negev, 2215
	11:3	Perizzites and Jebusites in the **hill** c; 2215
	11:16	So Joshua took this entire land: the **hill** c, 2215
	11:21	the Anakites from the **hill** c: 2215
	11:21	from all the **hill** c of Judah, 2215
	11:21	and from all the **hill** c of Israel. 2215
	12:8	the **hill** c, the western foothills, 2215
	13:21	who lived in that c. 824
	13:25	of Gilead and half the Ammonite c as far 824
	14:12	Now give me this **hill** c that 2215
	15:48	In the **hill** c: Shamir, Jattir, Socoh, 2215
	16:1	the desert into the **hill** c of Bethel. 2215
	17:15	"and if the **hill** c of Ephraim is too small 2215
	17:16	"The **hill** c is not enough for us, 2215
	17:18	but the forested **hill** c as well. 2215
	18:1	The c was brought under their control, 824
	18:12	and headed west into the **hill** c, 2215
	19:50	Timnath Serah in the **hill** c of Ephraim. 2215
	20:7	in Galilee in the **hill** c of Naphtali, 2215
	20:7	Shechem in the **hill** c of Ephraim 2215
	20:7	Hebron) in the **hill** c of Judah. 2215
	21:11	in the **hill** c of Judah. 2215
	21:21	In the **hill** c of Ephraim they were given 2215
	22:33	to devastate the c where the Reubenites and 824
	24:4	I assigned the **hill** c of Seir to Esau, 2215
	24:30	at Timnath Serah in the **hill** c 2215
	24:33	to his son Phinehas in the **hill** c 2215
Jdg	1:9	against the Canaanites living in the **hill** c, 2215
	1:19	They took possession of the **hill** c, 2215
	1:34	the Danites to the **hill** c, 2215
	2:9	at Timnath Heres in the **hill** c 2215
	3:27	a trumpet in the **hill** c of Ephraim, 2215
	4:5	between Ramah and Bethel in the **hill** c 2215
	6:3	and other eastern peoples invaded **the** c. 2257S
	7:24	throughout the **hill** c of Ephraim, 2215
	10:1	in the **hill** c of Ephraim. 2215
	11:12	against us that you have attacked our c?" 824
	11:17	'Give us permission to go through your c,' 824
	11:18	along the eastern side of the c of Moab, 824
	11:19	through your c to our own place.' 824
	11:21	of the Amorites who lived in that c, 824
	12:15	in the **hill** c of the Amalekites. 2215
	17:1	Now a man named Micah from the **hill** c 2215
	17:8	to Micah's house in the **hill** c 2215
	18:2	The men entered the **hill** c of Ephraim 2215
	18:13	on to the **hill** c of Ephraim and came 2215
	19:1	in the **hill** c of Ephraim took a concubine 2215
	19:16	That evening an old man from the **hill** c 2215
	19:18	to a remote area in the **hill** c of Ephraim 2215
Ru	1:1	went to live for a while in the c of Moab. 8441
1Sa	1:1	a Zuphite from the **hill** c of Ephraim, 2215
	6:5	and of the rats that are destroying the c, 824
	6:18	the fortified towns with their c villages. 7253
	9:4	the **hill** c of Ephraim and through 2215
	13:2	at Micmash and in the **hill** c of Bethel, 2215
	14:22	the Israelites who had hidden in the **hill** c 2215
	14:29	"My father has made trouble for the c. 824
	27:5	be assigned to me in one of the c towns, 8441
2Sa	10:8	by themselves in the **open** c. 8441
	19:9	now he has fled the c because of Absalom; 824
	20:21	from the **hill** c of Ephraim 2215
1Ki	4:8	in the **hill** c of Ephraim; 2215
	4:19	(the c of Sihon king of the Amorites and 824
	4:19	of Sihon king of the Amorites and the c NIH
	10:6	in my own c about your achievements 824
	10:13	and returned with her retinue to her own c. 824
	11:21	"Let me go, that I may return to my own c." 824
1Ki	11:22	that you want to go back to your own c?" 824
	11:29	The two of them were alone out in the c, 8441
	12:25	in the **hill** c of Ephraim and lived there. 2215
	14:11	the air will feed on those who die in the c." 8441
	16:4	the air will feed on those who die in the c." 8441
	21:24	the air will feed on those who die in the c." 8441
2Ki	5:22	to me from the **hill** c of Ephraim. 2215
	8:6	from her land from the day she left the c 824
	13:20	to enter the c every spring. 824
	17:26	not know what the god of that c requires. 824
	18:25	to march against this c and destroy it.' " 824
	19:7	he will return to his own c, 824
	24:7	not march out from his own c again, 824
1Ch	1:46	who defeated Midian in the c of Moab, 8441
	4:42	invaded the **hill** c of Seir. 2215
	6:67	In the **hill** c of Ephraim they were given 2215
	19:3	and spy out the c and overthrow it?" 824
	19:9	by themselves in the **open** c. 8441
2Ch	9:5	in my own c about your achievements 824
	9:12	and returned with her retinue to her own c. 824
	13:4	in the **hill** c of Ephraim, and said, 2215
	14:1	in his days the c was at peace for ten years. 824
	19:4	from Beersheba to the **hill** c of Ephraim 2215
Ne	8:15	into the **hill** c and bring back branches 2215
	9:22	over the c of Sihon king of Heshbon and 824
	9:22	of Sihon king of Heshbon and the c 824
Ps	78:54	to the **hill** c his right hand had taken. 2215
	105:31	and gnats throughout their c. 1473
	105:33	and shattered the trees of their c. 1473
Pr	28:2	When a c is rebellious, it has many rulers, 824
	29:4	By justice a king gives c stability, 824
Isa	1:7	Your c is desolate, your cities burned 824
	13:5	to destroy the whole c. 824
	22:18	like a ball and throw you into a large c. 824
	36:10	to march against this c and destroy it.' " 824
	37:7	he will return to his own c, 824
	63:13	Like a horse in **open** c, 4497
	66:8	Can a c be born in a day or a nation 824
Jer	12:5	If you stumble in safe c, 824
	12:15	to his own inheritance and his own c. 824
	14:18	If I go into the c, 8441
	15:13	because of all your sins throughout your c. 1473
	17:3	because of sin throughout your c. 1473
	17:26	from the **hill** c and the Negev, 2215
	22:26	into another c, where neither 824
	25:11	This whole c will become a desolate 824
	32:44	of Judah and in the towns of the **hill** c, 2215
	33:13	In the towns of the **hill** c, 2215
	40:4	Look, the whole c lies before you; 824
	40:7	in the **open** c heard that the king 8441
	40:13	in the **open** c came to Gedaliah at Mizpah 8441
Eze	7:14	those in the c will die by the sword, 8441
	14:13	if a c sins against me by being unfaithful 824
	14:15	through that c and they leave it childless 824
	14:17	if I bring a sword against that c and say, 824
	21:19	both starting from the same c. 824
	33:27	by the sword, those out in the c I will give 8441
Da	11:9	of the South but will retreat to his own c. 141
	11:19	the fortresses of his own c but will stumble 824
	11:28	of the North will return to his own c 824
	11:28	against it and then return to his own c. 824
Hos	12:12	Jacob fled to the c of Aram; 8441
Am	7:17	and you yourself will die in a pagan c. 141
Jnh	1:8	What is your c? 824
Zec	5:11	the c of Babylonia to build a house for it. 824
	6:6	toward the north c, 824
	6:8	the north c have given my Spirit rest in 824
Mt	2:12	they returned to their c by another route. 6001
	14:35	they sent word to all the **surrounding** c, 4369
Mk	5:21	was passing by on his way in from the c, 69
	6:12	of them while they were walking in the c. 69
Lk	1:39	and hurried to a town in the **hill** c 3978
	1:65	the **hill** c of Judea people were talking 3978
	3:3	He went into all the c around the Jordan, 4369
	7:17	throughout Judea and the **surrounding** c. 4369
	14:23	the roads and c lanes and make them come 5850
	15:4	the ninety-nine in the **open** c and go after 2245
	15:13	a distant c and there squandered his wealth 6001
	15:14	there was a severe famine in that whole c, 6001
	15:15	and hired himself out to a citizen *of* that c, 6001
	19:12	a distant c to have himself appointed king 6001
	21:21	and let those in the c not enter the city. 6001
	23:26	who was on his way in from the c, 69
Jn	4:44	that a prophet has no honor in his own c.) 4258
	11:55	many went up from the c to Jerusalem 6001
Ac	7:3	'Leave your c and your people,' God said, 1178
	7:6	'Your descendants will be strangers in a c 1178
	7:7	'and afterward they will come out of that c NIG
	9:32	As Peter **traveled** about the c, 1328+1451+4246
	10:39	of everything he did in the c of the Jews 6001
	12:20	because they depended on the king's c NIG
	13:17	with mighty power he led them out of that c, 899S
	14:6	and Derbe and to the **surrounding** c, 4369
	26:4	from the beginning of my life in my own c, 1620
2Co	11:26	in danger in the city, in danger in the c, 2244
Heb	11:9	like a stranger in a foreign c; NIG
	11:14	that they are looking for a c of their own. 4258
	11:15	of the c they had left, NIG
	11:16	Instead, they were longing for a better c— NIG

COUNTRYMAN (3) [COUNTRY, MAN]

Lev	25:15	You are to buy from your c on the basis of 6660
	25:25	to come and redeem what his c has sold. 278
	25:36	your c may continue to live among you. 278

COUNTRYMEN (27) [COUNTRY, MAN]

Lev	25:14	to one of your c or buy any from him,	6660
	25:25	of your c becomes poor and sells some	278
	25:35	of your c becomes poor and is unable	278
	25:39	of your c becomes poor among you	278
	25:47	of your c becomes poor and sells himself to	278
Nu	32: 6	"Shall your c go to war while you sit here?	278
2Sa	15:20	Go back, and take your c.	278
2Ch	19:10	before you from your fellow c who live	278
	28:11	Send back your fellow c you have taken	278
	28:15	So they took them back to their fellow c	278
	35: 5	of the families of your fellow c,	278
	35: 6	[the lambs] for your fellow c,	278
Ne	3:18	by their c under Binnui son of Henadad,	278
	5: 5	and blood as our c and though our sons are	278
	5: 7	"You are exacting usury from your own c!"	278
Jer	22:13	making his c work for nothing,	8276
	29:16	your c who did not go with you	278
	34:15	Each of you proclaimed freedom to his c.	8276
	34:17	not proclaimed freedom for your fellow c.	8276
Eze	3:11	to your c in exile and speak to them.	1201+6639
	33: 2	speak to your c and say to them:	1201+6639
	33:12	"Therefore, son of man, say to your c,	1201+6639
	33:17	"Yet your c say,	1201+6639
	33:30	your c are talking together about you	1201+6639
	37:18	"When your c ask you,	1201+6639
2Co	11:26	in danger from my own c,	1169
1Th	2:14	You suffered from your own c	5241

COUNTRYSIDE (15) [COUNTRY]

1Sa	30:16	and there they were, scattered over the c,	824
2Sa	15:23	The whole c wept aloud as all	824
	18: 8	The battle spread out over the whole c,	824
1Ki	20:27	while the Arameans covered the c.	824
2Ki	7:12	so they have left the camp to hide in the c,	8441
Job	5:10	he sends water upon the c.	2575
SS	7:11	Come, my lover, let us go to the c,	8441
Mk	1: 5	The whole Judean c and all the people	6001
	5:14	and reported this in the town and c,	69
	6:36	so they can go to the surrounding c	69
	6:56	into villages, towns or c—	69
Lk	4:14	about him spread through the whole c.	4369
	8:34	and reported this in the town and c,	69
	9:12	to the surrounding villages and c	69
Jn	3:22	disciples went out into the Judean c,	1178

COUNTS (6) [COUNT]

Job	19:11	he c me among his enemies.	3108
Jer	33:13	under the hand of the one who c them,'	4948
Jn	6:63	Spirit gives life; the flesh c for nothing.	6067
1Co	7:19	Keeping God's commands is what c.	NIG
Gal	5: 6	that c is faith expressing itself	NIG
	6:15	what c is a new creation.	NIG

COURAGE (21) [COURAGEOUS, COURAGEOUSLY]

Jos	2:11	our hearts melted and everyone's c failed	8120
	5: 1	and they no longer had the c to face	8120
2Sa	4: 1	he lost c, and all Israel became alarmed.	3338+8332
	7:27	So your servant has found c	4213
1Ch	17:25	So your servant has found c to pray to you.	5162
2Ch	15: 8	of Oded the prophet, he took c.	2616
	19:11	Act with c, and may the LORD be	2616
Ezr	7:28	I took c and gathered leading men	2616
	10: 4	We will support you, so take c and do it."	2616
Ps	107:26	in their peril their c melted away.	5883
Eze	22:14	Will your c endure or your hands be strong	4213
Da	11:25	up his strength and c against the king of	4222
Mt	14:27	Jesus immediately said to them: "Take c!	2510
Mk	6:50	to them and said, "Take c!	2510
Ac	4:13	When they saw the c of Peter and John	4244
	23:11	the Lord stood near Paul and said, "Take c!	2510
	27:22	But now I urge you to keep up your c,	2313
	27:25	So keep up your c, men,	2313
1Co	16:13	be men of c; be strong.	437
Php	1:20	but will have sufficient c so that now	4244
Heb	3: 6	on to our c and the hope of which we boast.	4244

COURAGEOUS (12) [COURAGE]

Dt	31: 6	Be strong and c.	599
	31: 7	"Be strong and c,	599
	31:23	"Be strong and c,	599
Jos	1: 6	"Be strong and c,	599
	1: 7	Be strong and very c.	599
	1: 9	Be strong and c.	599
	1:18	Only be strong and c!"	599
	10:25	Be strong and c.	599
1Ch	22:13	Be strong and c.	599
	28:20	"Be strong and c, and do the work.	599
2Ch	26:17	Azariah the priest with eighty other c	1201+2657
		priests of the LORD	
	32: 7	"Be strong and c.	599

COURAGEOUSLY (2) [COURAGE]

2Ch	25: 8	Even if you go and fight c in battle,	2616
Php	1:14	the word of God more c and fearlessly.	5528

COURIER (1) [COURIERS]

Jer	51:31	One c follows another	8132

COURIERS (6) [COURIER]

2Ch	30: 6	c went throughout Israel and Judah	8132
	30:10	The c went from town to town in Ephraim	8132
Est	3:13	by c to all the king's provinces with	8132
	3:15	the c went out,	8132
	8:10	and sent them by mounted c,	8132
	8:14	The c, riding the royal horses, raced out,	8132

COURSE (33) [COURSES]

Ge	4: 3	In the c of time Cain brought some of	7891
Dt	2:37	the land along the c of the Jabbok nor that	5707
1Sa	1:20	So in the c of time Hannah conceived	9543
	22:15	Of c not!	2721
2Sa	2: 1	In the c of time,	339+4027
	8: 1	In the c of time,	339+4027
	10: 1	In the c of time,	339+4027
	13: 1	In the c of time,	339+4027
	15: 1	In the c of time,	339+4027+4946
	21:18	In the c of time,	339+4027
1Ki	6:36	of three courses of dressed stone and one c	3215
	7:12	of three courses of dressed stone and one c	3215
1Ch	18: 1	In the c of time,	339+4027
	19: 1	In the c of time,	339+4027
	20: 4	In the c of time,	339+4027
2Ch	21:19	In the c of time,	3427+3427+4200+4946
Job	1: 5	When a period of feasting had run its c,	5938
Ps	19: 5	like a champion rejoicing to run his c.	784
	36: 4	he commits himself to a sinful c and does	2006
	102:23	In the c of my life he broke my strength;	2006
Pr	2: 8	for he guards the c of the just and protects	784
	15:21	a man of understanding keeps a straight c.	2143
	16: 9	In his heart a man plans his c,	2006
	17:23	a bribe in secret to pervert the c of justice.	784
Ecc	1: 6	ever returning on its c.	6017
Jer	8: 6	Each pursues his own c like	5297
	23:10	an evil c and use their power unjustly.	5297
Joel	2: 7	not swerving from their c.	784
Ac	27: 7	allow us to hold our c,	4661
Ro	10:18	Of c they did:	3529
2Co	12:18	in the same spirit and follow the same c?	2717
	13: 5	unless, of c, you fail the test?	NIG
Jas	3: 6	sets the whole c of his life on fire,	5580

COURSES (4) [COURSE]

Jdg	5:20	from their c they fought against Sisera.	5019
1Ki	6:36	And he built the inner courtyard of three c	3215
	7:12	of three c of dressed stone and one course	3215
Ezr	6: 4	with three c of large stones and one	10462

COURTEOUS (KJV) See HUMBLE

COURT (90) [COURTS, COURTYARD, COURTYARDS]

Ge	50: 4	Joseph said to Pharaoh's c,	1074
	50: 7	of his c and all the dignitaries of Egypt—	1074
Ex	21:22	and the c allows.	7130
Dt	25: 1	to take it to c and the judges will decide	5477
Jdg	4: 5	She held c under the Palm of Deborah	3782
1Ki	3:15	Then he gave a feast for all his c.	6269
2Ki	20: 4	Before Isaiah had left the middle c,	2958
	23:11	They were in the c near the room of	7247
1Ch	26:18	As for the c to the west,	7232
	26:18	at the road and two at the c itself.	7232
2Ch	4: 9	and the large c and the doors for the court,	6478
	4: 9	and the large court and the doors for the c,	6478
	6:13	in the center of the outer c.	6478
Ne	3:25	the upper palace near the c of the guard.	2958
Est	4:11	in the inner c without being summoned	2958
	5: 1	on her royal robes and stood in the inner c	2958
	5: 2	he saw Queen Esther standing in the c,	2958
	6: 4	The king said, "Who is in the c?"	2958
	6: 4	Now Haman had just entered the outer c of	2958
	6: 5	"Haman is standing in the c."	2958
Job	5: 4	crushed in c without a defender.	9133
	9:32	that we might confront each other in c.	5477
	11:10	in prison and convenes a c,	7735
	11:19	and many will c your favor.	2704+7156
	31:21	knowing that I had influence in c,	9133
Pr	22:22	and do not crush the needy in c,	9133
	25: 8	do not bring hastily to c,	8190
	29: 9	If a wise man goes to c with a fool,	9149
Isa	3:13	The LORD takes his place in c;	8189
	29:21	in c and with false testimony deprive	9133
Jer	19:14	and stood in the c of the LORD's temple	2958
	29: 2	the c officials and the leaders of Judah	6247
	34:19	and Jerusalem, the c officials, the priests	6247
	41:16	children and c officials he had brought	6247
Eze	8: 3	to the north gate of the inner c,	NIH
	8: 7	he brought me to the entrance to the c.	2958
	8:16	into the inner c of the house of the LORD,	2958
	10: 3	and a cloud filled the inner c.	2958
	10: 4	the c was full of the radiance of the glory	2958
	10: 5	be heard as far away as the outer c,	2958
	40:17	Then he brought me into the outer c.	2958
	40:17	that had been constructed all around the c;	2958
	40:19	to the outside of the inner c.	2958
	40:20	leading into the outer c.	2958
	40:23	a gate to the inner c facing the north gate,	2958
	40:27	The inner c also had a gate facing south,	2958
	40:28	into the inner c through the south gate,	2958
	40:30	the inner c were twenty-five cubits wide	NIH
	40:31	Its portico faced the outer c;	2958
	40:32	Then he brought me to the inner c on	2958

Eze	40:34	Its portico faced the outer c;	2958
	40:37	Its portico faced the outer c;	2958
	40:44	Outside the inner gate, within the inner c,	2958
	40:47	Then he measured the c:	2958
	41:15	and the portico facing the c,	2958
	42: 1	the man led me northward into the outer c	2958
	42: 3	from the inner c and in the section opposite	2958
	42: 3	the pavement of the outer c;	2958
	42: 7	to the rooms and the outer c;	2958
	42: 8	to the outer c was fifty cubits long,	2958
	42: 9	as one enters them from the outer c.	2958
	42:10	along the length of the wall of the outer c,	2958
	42:14	not to go into the outer c until they leave	2958
	43: 5	up and brought me into the inner c,	2958
	44:17	"When they enter the gates of the inner c,	2958
	44:17	while ministering at the gates of the inner c	2958
	44:19	When they go out into the outer c where	2958
	44:21	to drink wine when he enters the inner c	2958
	44:27	into the inner c of the sanctuary to minister	2958
	45:19	the altar and on the gateposts of the c ordered	2958
	46: 1	of the inner c facing east is to be shut on	2958
	46:20	the outer c and consecrating the people."	2958
	46:21	then brought me to the outer c and led me	2958
	46:21	and I saw in each corner another c.	2958
	46:22	of the outer c were enclosed courts,	2958
Da	1: 3	chief of his c officials,	6247
	2:49	Daniel himself remained at the royal c.	10776
	7:10	c was seated, and the books were opened.	10170
	7:26	"'But the c will sit,	10170
Am	5:10	in c and despise him who tells the truth.	9133
Mt	5:25	adversary who is taking you to c.	508
Ac	18:12	on Paul and brought him into c.	1037
	18:16	So he had them ejected from the c.	1037
	18:17	and beat him in front of the c.	1037
	25: 6	the next day he convened the c and ordered	1037+2093+2767+3836
	25:10	"I am now standing before Caesar's c,	1037
	25:17	but convened the c the next day	1037+2093
1Co	4: 3	if I am judged by you or by any human c,	2465
Jas	2: 6	not the ones who are dragging you into c?	3215
Rev	11: 2	But exclude the outer c;	885

COURTS (51) [COURT]

Dt	17: 8	before your c that are too difficult for you	9133
2Ki	21: 5	In both c of the temple of the LORD,	2958
	23:12	the altars Manasseh had built in the two c	2958
1Ch	28: 6	the one who will build my house and my c,	2958
	28:12	that the Spirit had put in his mind for the c	2958
2Ch	33: 5	In both c of the temple of the LORD,	2958
Ne	8:16	the c of the house of God and in the square	2958
	13: 7	in providing Tobiah a room in the c of	2958
Ps	65: 4	and bring near to live in your c!	2958
	84: 2	even faints, for the c of the LORD;	2958
	84:10	in your c than a thousand elsewhere;	2958
	92:13	they will flourish in the c of our God.	2958
	96: 8	bring an offering and come into his c.	2958
	100: 4	Enter his gates with thanksgiving and his c	2958
	116:19	in the c of the house of the LORD—	2958
	135: 2	in the c of the house of our God.	2958
Isa	1:12	this trampling of my c?	2958
	62: 9	the grapes will drink it in the c	2958
Eze	9: 7	the temple and fill the c with the slain.	2958
	42: 6	had no pillars, as the c had;	2958
	46:22	of the outer court were enclosed c,	2958
	46:22	the c in the four corners was the same size.	4392S
	46:23	Around the inside of each of the four c was	4392S
Am	5:12	and you deprive the poor of justice in the c.	9133
	5:15	maintain justice in the c.	9133
Zec	3: 7	and have charge of my c,	2958
	8:16	and sound judgment in your c;	9133
Mt	21:23	Jesus entered the temple c, and,	2639
	26:55	Every day I sat in the temple c teaching,	2639
Mk	11:16	to carry merchandise through the temple c.	2639
	11:27	while Jesus was walking in the temple c,	2639
	12:35	While Jesus was teaching in the temple c,	2639
	14:49	teaching in the temple c,	2639
Lk	2:27	he went into the temple c.	2639
	2:46	they found him in the temple c,	2639
	20: 1	in the temple c and preaching the gospel,	2639
	22:53	Every day I was with you in the temple c,	2639
Jn	2:14	the temple c he found men selling cattle,	2639
	7:14	the Feast did Jesus go up to the temple c	2639
	7:28	Then Jesus, still teaching in the temple c,	2639
	8: 2	he appeared again in the temple c,	2639
Ac	2:46	to meet together in the temple c.	2639
	3: 2	to beg from those going into the temple c.	2639
	3: 8	Then he went with them into the temple c,	2639
	5:20	"Go, stand in the temple c," he said,	2639
	5:21	At daybreak they entered the temple c,	2639
	5:25	in jail are standing in the temple c teaching	2639
	5:42	in the temple c and from house to house,	2639
	19:38	the c are open and there are proconsuls.	61+72
	24:18	in the temple c doing this.	2639
	26:21	in the temple c and tried to kill me.	2639

COURTYARD (73) [COURT]

Ex	27: 9	"Make a c for the tabernacle.	2958
	27:12	of the c shall be fifty cubits wide.	2958
	27:13	the c shall also be fifty cubits wide.	2958
	27:16	"For the entrance to the c	2958
	27:17	the c are to have silver bands and hooks,	2958
	27:18	The c shall be a hundred cubits long	2958
	27:19	the tent pegs for it and those for the c,	2958
	35:17	of the c with its posts and bases, and	2958
	35:17	and the curtain for the entrance to the c;	2958

Ex	35:18	for the tabernacle and for the c, 2958
	38: 9	Next they made the c. 2958
	38:15	on the other side of the entrance to the c, 2958
	38:16	around the c were of finely twisted linen. 2958
	38:17	so all the posts of the c had silver bands. 2958
	38:18	to the c was of blue, purple and scarlet yarn 2958
	38:18	like the curtains of the c, five cubits high, 2958
	38:20	and of the surrounding c were bronze. 2958
	38:31	the surrounding c and those for its entrance 2958
	38:31	and those for the surrounding c. 2958
	39:40	of the c with its posts and bases, and 2958
	39:40	and the curtain for the entrance to the c; 2958
	39:40	the ropes and tent pegs for **the c;** 2023S
	40: 8	Set up the c around it and put the curtain in 2958
	40: 8	and put the curtain at the entrance to the c. 2958
	40:33	up the c around the tabernacle and altar 2958
	40:33	up the curtain at the entrance to the c. 2958
Lev	6:16	to eat it in the c of the Tent of Meeting. 2958
	6:26	in the c of the Tent of Meeting. 2958
Nu	3:26	of the c, the curtain at the entrance to 2958
	3:26	the c surrounding the tabernacle and altar, 2958
	3:37	as well as the posts of the surrounding c, 2958
	4:26	the c surrounding the tabernacle and altar, 2958
	4:32	as well as the posts of the surrounding c. 2958
2Sa	17:18	He had a well in his c, 2958
1Ki	6:36	the inner c of three courses of dressed stone 2958
	7: 9	to the great c and from foundation to eaves, 2958
	7:12	The great c was surrounded by a wall 2958
	7:12	the inner c of the temple of the LORD 2958
	8:64	the c in front of the temple of the LORD, 2958
2Ch	4: 9	He made the c of the priests, 2958
	7: 7	the c in front of the temple of the LORD, 2958
	20: 5	of the LORD in the front of the new c 2958
	24:21	the king they stoned him to death in the c 2958
	29:16	They brought out to the c of 2958
Est	2:11	near the c of the harem to find out 2958
Jer	26: 2	in the c of the LORD's house and speak 2958
	32: 2	in the c of the guard in the royal palace 2958
	32: 8	my cousin Hanamel came to me in the c of 2958
	32:12	of all the Jews sitting in the c of the guard. 2958
	33: 1	While Jeremiah was still confined in the c 2958
	36:10	the upper c at the entrance of the New Gate 2958
	36:20	to the king in the c and reported everything 2958
	37:21	in the c of the guard and given bread from 2958
	37:21	Jeremiah remained in the c of the guard. 2958
	38: 6	which was in the c of the guard. 2958
	38:13	Jeremiah remained in the c of the guard. 2958
	38:28	And Jeremiah remained in the c of 2958
	39:14	sent and had Jeremiah taken out of the c of 2958
	39:15	While Jeremiah had been confined in the c 2958
Eze	40:14	up to the portico facing the c. 2958
	41:12	The building facing the temple c on 1619
	41:13	a hundred cubits long, and the temple c and 1619
	41:14	The width of the temple c on the east, 1619
	41:15	of the building facing the c at the rear of 1619
	42: 1	the temple c and opposite the outer wall on 1619
	42:10	the temple c and opposite the outer wall, 1619
	42:13	and south rooms facing the temple c are 1619
Mt	26:58	right up to the c of the high priest. 885
	26:69	Now Peter was sitting out in the c, 885
Mk	14:54	right into the c of the high priest. 885
	14:66	While Peter was below in the c, 885
Lk	22:55	a fire in the middle *of* the c and had sat 885
Jn	18:15	he went with Jesus into the high priest's c, 885

COURTYARDS (4) [COURT]

Ex	8:13	in the c and in the fields. 2958
1Ch	23:28	to be in charge of the c, the side rooms, 2958
2Ch	23: 5	to be in the c of the temple of the LORD. 2958
Ne	8:16	in their c, in the courts of the house of God 2958

COUSIN (6) [COUSINS]

Lev	25:49	An uncle or a c or any blood relative 1201+1856
Est	2: 7	Mordecai had a c named Hadassah, 1426+1856
Jer	32: 8	my c Hanamel came to me in the courtyard 1201+1856
	32: 9	field at Anathoth from my c Hanamel 1201+1856
	32:12	in the presence of my c Hanamel and of 1856
Col	4:10	as does Mark, the c of Barnabas. *463*

COUSINS (3) [COUSIN]

Lev	10: 4	carry your c outside the camp, 278
Nu	36:11	**c on their father's side.** 1201+1856
1Ch	23:22	Their c, the sons of Kish, married them. 278

COVENANT (297) [COVENANTED, COVENANTS]

Ge	6:18	But I will establish my c with you, 1382
	9: 9	"I now establish my c with you and 1382
	9:11	I establish my c with you: 1382
	9:12	of the c I am making between me and you 1382
	9:12	a c for all generations to come: NIH
	9:13	the sign of the c between me and the earth. 1382
	9:15	I will remember my c between me and you 1382
	9:16	I will see it and remember the everlasting c 1382
	17: 2	"This is the sign of the c I have established 1382
	15:18	the LORD made a c with Abram and said, 1382
	17: 2	I will confirm my c between me and you 1382
	17: 4	this is my c with you: 1382
	17: 7	I will establish my c as an everlasting 1382
	17: 7	as an everlasting c between me and you 1382
	17: 9	"As for you, you must keep my c, 1382
	17:10	This is my c with you 1382
	17:10	**the c you are to keep:** 889S
Ge	17:11	and it will be the sign of the c between me 1382
	17:13	My c in your flesh is to be an everlasting 1382
	17:13	in your flesh is to be an everlasting c. 1382
	17:14	he has broken my c." 1382
	17:19	I will establish my c with him as 1382
	17:19	as an everlasting c for his descendants 1382
	17:21	But my c I will establish with Isaac, 1382
	31:44	Come now, let's make a c, you and I, 1382
Ex	2:24	and he remembered his c with Abraham, 1382
	6: 4	I also established my c with them 1382
	6: 5	and I have remembered my c. 1382
	19: 5	Now if you obey me fully and keep my c, 1382
	23:32	not make a c with them or with their gods. 1382
	24: 7	the Book of the C and read it to the people. 1382
	24: 8	of the c that the LORD has made with you 1382
	31:16	for the generations to come as a lasting c. 1382
	34:10	LORD said: "I am making a c with you 1382
	34:27	with these words I have made a c with you 1382
	34:28	he wrote on the tablets the words of the c— 1382
Lev	2:13	not leave the salt of the c of your God out 1382
	24: 8	on behalf of the Israelites, as a lasting c. 1382
	26: 9	and I will keep my c with you. 1382
	26:15	and so violate my c, 1382
	26:25	upon you to avenge the breaking of the c. 1382
	26:42	I will remember my c *with* Jacob 1382
	26:42	and my c *with* Isaac and my covenant 1382
	26:42	and my covenant with Isaac and my c 1382
	26:44	breaking my c with them. 1382
	26:45	But for their sake I will remember the c 1382
Nu	10:33	of the c of the LORD went before them 1382
	14:44	nor the ark of the LORD's c moved from 1382
	18:19	an everlasting c *of* salt before the LORD 1382
	25:12	Therefore tell him I am making my c 1382
	25:13	He and his descendants will have a c *of* 1382
Dt	4:13	He declared to you his c, 1382
	4:23	the c of the LORD your God that he made 1382
	4:31	not abandon or destroy you or forget the c 1382
	5: 2	The LORD our God made a c with us 1382
	5: 3	that the LORD made this c, 1382
	7: 9	the faithful God, keeping his c *of* love to 1382
	7:12	then the LORD your God will keep his c 1382
	8:18	and so confirms his c, 1382
	9: 9	the c that the LORD had made with you, 1382
	9:11	the tablets of the c. 1382
	9:15	the two tablets of the c were in my hands. 1382
	10: 8	the tribe of Levi to carry the ark of the c 1382
	17: 2	the LORD your God in violation of his c, 1382
	29: 1	of the c the LORD commanded Moses 1382
	29: 1	in addition to the c he had made with them 1382
	29: 9	Carefully follow the terms of this c, 1382
	29:12	to enter into a c *with* the LORD your God, 1382
	29:12	a c the LORD is making with you this day 889S
	29:14	I am making this c, with its oath, 1382
	29:21	according to all the curses of the c written 1382
	29:25	"It is because this people abandoned the c 1382
	29:25	of their fathers, **the c** he made with them 889S
	31: 9	who carried the ark of the c of the LORD, 1382
	31:16	and break the c I made with them. 1382
	31:20	rejecting me and breaking my c. 1382
	31:25	the Levites who carried the ark of the c *of* 1382
	31:26	the Law and place it beside the ark of the c 1382
	33: 9	over your word and guarded your c. 1382
Jos	3: 3	the ark of the c of the LORD your God, 1382
	3: 6	"Take up the ark of the c and pass on ahead 1382
	3: 8	Tell the priests who carry the ark of the c: 1382
	3:11	of the c of the Lord of all the earth will go 1382
	3:14	the priests carrying the ark of the c went 1382
	3:17	The priests who carried the ark of the c 1382
	4: 7	before the ark of the c of the LORD. 1382
	4: 9	the ark of the c had stood. 1382
	4:18	up out of the river carrying the ark of the c 1382
	6: 6	"Take up the ark of the c of the LORD 1382
	6: 8	the ark of the LORD's c followed them. 1382
	7:11	Israel has sinned; they have violated my c, 1382
	7:15	He has violated the c of the LORD 1382
	8:33	on both sides of the ark of the c of 1382
	23:16	you violate the c of the LORD your God, 1382
	24:25	that day Joshua made a c for the people, 1382
Jdg	2: 1	I said, 'I will never break my c with you, 1382
	2: 2	and you shall not make a c with the people 1382
	2:20	the c that I laid down for their forefathers 1382
	20:27	the ark of the c of God was there, 1382
1Sa	4: 3	the ark of the LORD's c from Shiloh, 1382
	4: 4	and they brought back the ark of the c *of* 1382
	4: 4	were there with the ark of the c *of* God. 1382
	4: 5	When the ark of the LORD's c came into 1382
	18: 3	a c with David because he loved him 1382
	20: 8	for you have brought him into a c with you 1382
	20:16	Jonathan made a c with the house of David, 4162
	22: 8	No one tells me when my son **makes a c** 4162
	23:18	of them made a c before the LORD. 1382
2Sa	15:24	with him were carrying the ark of the c 1382
	23: 5	Has he not made with me an everlasting c, 1382
1Ki	3:15	the Lord's c and sacrificed burnt offerings 1382
	6:19	to set the ark of the c of the LORD there. 1382
	8: 1	up the ark of the LORD's c from Zion, 1382
	8: 6	the ark of the LORD's c to its place in 1382
	8: 9	the LORD **made a c** with the Israelites 4162
	8:21	the c of the LORD that he made 1382
	8:23	you who keep your c of love 1382
	11:11	not kept my c and my decrees, 1382
	19:10	The Israelites have rejected your c, 1382
	19:14	The Israelites have rejected your c, 1382
2Ki	11:12	a c with them and put them under oath at 1382
	11:12	a **copy of** the c and proclaimed him king. 6343
	11:17	then made a c between the LORD and 1382
	11:17	He also made a c between the king and NIH
2Ki	13:23	for them because of his c with Abraham, 1382
	17:15	the c he had made with their fathers, 1382
	17:35	the LORD made a c with the Israelites, 1382
	17:38	Do not forget the c I have made with you, 1382
	18:12	but had violated his c— 1382
	23: 2	the words of the Book of the C, 1382
	23: 3	the pillar and renewed the c in the presence 1382
	23: 3	thus confirming the words of the c written 1382
	23: 3	all the people pledged themselves to the c. 1382
	23:21	as it is written in this Book of the C." 1382
1Ch	15:25	a thousand went to bring up the ark of the c 1382
	15:26	the ark of the c of the LORD, 1382
	15:28	the ark of the c of the LORD with shouts, 1382
	15:29	the ark of the c of the LORD was entering 1382
	16: 6	before the ark of the c of God. 1382
	16:15	He remembers his c forever, 1382
	16:16	the c he made with Abraham, 889S
	16:17	to Israel as an everlasting c: 1382
	16:37	and his associates before the ark of the c *of* 1382
	17: 1	ark of the c of the LORD is under a tent." 1382
	22:19	so that you may bring the ark of the c *of* 1382
	28: 2	of rest for the ark of the c of the LORD, 1382
	28:18	and shelter the ark of the c of the LORD. 1382
2Ch	5: 2	up the ark of the LORD's c from Zion, 1382
	5: 7	the ark of the LORD's c to its place in 1382
	5:10	the LORD **made a c** with the Israelites 4162
	6:11	the c of the LORD that he made with 1382
	6:14	you who keep your c of love 1382
	13: 5	to David and his descendants forever by a c 1382
	15:12	They entered into a c to seek the LORD, 1382
	21: 7	of the c the LORD had made with David, 1382
	23: 1	He made a c with the commanders of units 1382
	23: 3	the whole assembly made a c with the king 1382
	23:11	a **copy** of the c and proclaimed him king. 6343
	23:16	then made a c that he and the people and 1382
	29:10	Now I intend to make a c with the LORD, 1382
	34:30	the words of the Book of the C, 1382
	34:31	in the presence of the LORD— 1382
	34:31	the words of the c written in this book. 1382
	34:32	in accordance with the c of God, 1382
Ezr	10: 3	Now let us make a c before our God 1382
Ne	1: 5	and awesome God, who keeps his c of love 1382
	9: 8	a c with him to give to his descendants 1382
	9:32	who keeps his c of love, 1382
	13:29	the c of the priesthood and of the Levites. 1382
Job	5:23	For you will have a c with the stones of 1382
	31: 1	a c with my eyes not to look lustfully at 1382
Ps	25:10	for those who keep the demands of his c. 1382
	25:14	he makes his c known to them. 1382
	44:17	not forgotten you or been false to your c. 1382
	50: 5	who made a c *with me* by sacrifice." 1382
	50:16	to recite my laws or take my c 1382
	55:20	he violates his c. 1382
	60: T	To [the tune of] "The Lily of the C." 6343
	74:20	Have regard for your c, 1382
	78:10	they did not keep God's c and refused 1382
	78:37	they were not faithful to his c. 1382
	80: T	To [the tune of] "The Lilies of the C." 6343
	89: 3	"I have made a c with my chosen one, 1382
	89:28	and my c with him will never fail. 1382
	89:34	I will not violate my c 1382
	89:39	You have renounced the c 1382
	103:18	with those who keep his c and remember 1382
	105: 8	He remembers his c forever, 1382
	105: 9	**the c** he made with Abraham, 889S
	105:10	to Israel as an everlasting c: 1382
	106:45	for their sake he remembered his c and out 1382
	111: 5	he remembers his c forever. 1382
	111: 9	he ordained his c forever— 1382
	132:12	if your sons keep my c and 1382
Pr	2:17	and ignored the c she *made before* God. 1382
Isa	24: 5	the statutes and broken the everlasting c. 1382
	28:15	"We have entered into a c with death, 1382
	28:18	Your c with death will be annulled; 1382
	42: 6	I will keep you and will make you to be a c 1382
	49: 8	I will keep you and will make you to be a c 1382
	54:10	be shaken nor my c of peace be removed," 1382
	55: 3	I will make an everlasting c with you, 1382
	56: 4	and hold fast to my c— 1382
	56: 6	and who hold fast to my c— 1382
	59:21	"As for me, this is my c with them," 1382
	61: 8	and make an everlasting c with them. 1382
Jer	3:16	'The ark of the c of the LORD.' 1382
	11: 2	"Listen to the terms of this c and tell them 1382
	11: 3	not obey the terms of this c— 1382
	11: 6	to the terms of this c and follow them. 1382
	11: 8	the c I had commanded them to follow but 1382
	11:10	the c I made with their forefathers. 1382
	14:21	Remember your c with us and do 1382
	22: 9	'Because they have forsaken the c of 1382
	31:31	"when I will make a new c with the house 1382
	31:32	be like the c I made with their forefathers 1382
	31:32	because they broke my c, 1382
	31:33	the c I will make with the house of Israel 1382
	32:40	I will make an everlasting c with them: 1382
	33:20	'If you can break my c with the day 1382
	33:20	with the day and my c *with* the night, 1382
	33:21	then my c with David my servant— 1382
	33:21	and my c with the Levites NIH
	33:25	not established my c with day and night 1382
	34: 8	after King Zedekiah had made a c with all 1382
	34:10	and people who entered into this c agreed 1382
	34:13	I made a c with your forefathers 1382
	34:18	You even made a c before me in the house 1382
	34:18	The men who have violated my c and have 1382
	34:18	not fulfilled the terms of the c they made 1382
	50: 5	the LORD in an everlasting c that will not 1382

Eze	16: 8	and entered into a **c** with you,	1382
	16:59	by breaking the **c**.	1382
	16:60	Yet I will remember the **c** I made with you	1382
	16:60	I will establish an everlasting **c** with you.	1382
	16:61	but not on the basis of my **c** with you.	1382
	16:62	So I will establish my **c** with you,	1382
	17:18	He despised the oath by breaking the **c**.	1382
	17:19	that he despised and my **c** that he broke.	1382
	20:37	and I will bring you into the bond of the **c**.	1382
	30: 5	Libya and the people of the **c** land will fall	1382
	34:25	a **c** *of* peace with them and rid the land	1382
	37:26	I will make a **c** *of* peace with them;	1382
	37:26	it will be an everlasting **c**.	1382
	44: 7	fat and blood, and you broke my **c**.	1382
Da	9: 4	and awesome God, who keeps his **c** of love	1382
	9:27	He will confirm a **c** with many	1382
	11:22	it and a prince of the **c** will be destroyed.	1382
	11:28	but his heart will be set against the holy **c**.	1382
	11:30	and vent his fury against the holy **c**.	1382
	11:30	to those who forsake the holy **c**.	1382
	11:32	With flattery he will corrupt those who have violated the **c**,	1382
Hos	2:18	a **c** for them with the beasts of the field and	1382
	6: 7	Like Adam, they have broken the **c**—	1382
	8: 1	the people have broken my **c** and rebelled	1382
Zec	9:11	because of the blood of my **c** with you,	1382
	11:10	the **c** I had made with all the nations.	1382
Mal	2: 4	so that my **c** with Levi may continue,"	1382
	2: 5	"My **c** was with him,	1382
	2: 5	a **c** of life and peace,	NIH
	2: 8	you have violated the **c** *with* Levi,"	1382
	2:10	Why do we profane the **c** *of* our fathers.	1382
	2:14	the wife of your **marriage c**.	1382
	3: 1	the messenger of the **c**, whom you desire,	1382
Mt	26:28	This is my blood of the **c**,	1347
Mk	14:24	"This is my blood of the **c**,	1347
Lk	1:72	to our fathers and to remember his holy **c**,	1347
	22:20	saying, "This cup is the new **c** in my blood,	1347
Ac	3:25	of the **c** God made with your fathers.	1347+1416
	7: 8	he gave Abraham the **c** of circumcision.	1347
Ro	11:27	And this is my **c** with them	1347
1Co	11:25	saying, "This cup is the new **c** in my blood;	1347
2Co	3: 6	as ministers of a new **c**—	1347
	3:14	when the old **c** is read.	1347
Gal	3:15	as no one can set aside or add to a human **c**	1347
	3:17	not set aside the **c** previously established	1347
	4:24	One **c** is from Mount Sinai	NIG
Heb	7:22	the guarantee of a better **c**.	1347
	8: 6	as the **c** of which he is mediator is superior	1347
	8: 7	had been nothing wrong with that first **c**,	NIG
	8: 8	a new **c** with the house of Israel and with	1347
	8: 9	be like the **c** I made with their forefathers	1347
	8: 9	they did not remain faithful to my **c**,	1347
	8:10	**c** *I* will **make** with the house of Israel	1347+1416
	8:13	By calling this "new,"	NIG
	9: 1	Now the first **c** had regulations for worship	NIG
	9: 4	and the gold-covered ark of the **c**.	1347
	9: 4	and the stone tablets of the **c**.	1347
	9:15	the mediator of a new **c**,	1347
	9:15	from the sins committed under the first **c**.	1347
	9:18	This is why even the first **c** was not put	NIG
	9:20	He said, "This is the blood of the **c**,	1347
	10:16	the **c** *I* will **make** with them after that time,	1347+1416
	10:29	the blood of the **c** that sanctified him,	1347
	12:24	to Jesus the mediator of a new **c**,	1347
	13:20	the blood of the eternal **c** brought back	1347
Rev	11:19	within his temple was seen the ark of his **c**.	1347

COVENANTED (2) [COVENANT]

2Ch	7:18	as *I* with David your father when I said,	4162
Hag	2: 5	'This is what *I* with you	4162

COVENANTS (3) [COVENANT]

Ro	9: 4	theirs the divine glory, the **c**,	1347
Gal	4:24	for the women represent two **c**,	1347
Eph	2:12	and foreigners to the **c** of the promise,	1347

COVER (98) [COVER-UP, COVERED, COVERING, COVERINGS, COVERS, GOLD-COVERED]

Ge	20:16	This is to **c the offense** against you	4064+6524
	37:26	if we kill our brother and **c** up his blood?	4059
Ex	10: 5	*They* will **c** the face of the ground so	4059
	21:33	and fails *to* **c** it and an ox or a donkey falls	4059
	25:17	"Make an **atonement c** of pure gold—	4114
	25:18	of hammered gold at the ends of the **c**.	4114
	25:19	make the cherubim of one piece with the **c**,	4114
	25:20	overshadowing the **c** with them.	4114
	25:20	looking toward the **c**.	4114
	25:21	the **c** on top of the ark and put in the ark	4114
	25:22	the **c** between the two cherubim that are	4114
	26:13	over the sides of the tabernacle so as to **c** it.	4059
	26:34	Put the **atonement c** on the ark of	4114
	30: 6	before the **atonement c** that is over	4114
	31: 7	the Testimony with the **atonement c** on it,	4114
	33:22	a cleft in the rock and **c** you with my hand	8503
	35:12	the ark with its poles and the **atonement c**	4114
	37: 6	He made the **atonement c** of pure gold—	4114
	37: 7	of hammered gold at the ends of the **c**.	4114
	37: 8	of one piece with the **c**.	4114
	37: 9	overshadowing the **c**.	4114
	37: 9	looking toward the **c**.	4114
	39:35	with its poles and the **atonement c**;	4114

Ex	40:20	the poles to the ark and put the **atonement c**	4114
Lev	13:45	**c** the lower part of his face and cry out,	6486
	16: 2	the curtain in front of the **atonement c** on	4114
	16: 2	I appear in the cloud over the **atonement c**.	4114
	16:13	of the incense will conceal the **atonement c**	4114
	16:14	on the front of the **atonement c;**	4059
	16:14	before the **atonement c**.	4114
	16:15	He shall sprinkle it on the **atonement c** and	4114
	17:13	be eaten must drain out the blood and **c** it	4059
Nu	4: 5	down the shielding curtain and **c** the ark of	4062+5989
	4: 6	*they are to* **c** this *with* hides of sea cows,	
	4: 8	**c** that with hides of sea cows	4059+4832
	4: 9	to take a blue cloth and **c** the lampstand	4059
	4:11	a blue cloth and **c** that with hides	4059+4832
	4:12	**c** that with hides of sea cows	4059+4832
	7:89	the two cherubim above the **atonement c** on	4114
	22: 5	*they* **c** the face of the land	4059
Dt	23:13	dig a hole and **c** up your excrement.	2256+4059+8740
Jdg	9:31	**Under c** he sent messengers to Abimelech,	928+9564
1Ki	18: 6	So they divided the land they *were* to **c**,	6296
Ne	4: 5	*Do not* **c** up their guilt or blot out their sins	4059
Job	14:17	*you will* **c** over my sin.	3260
	16:18	"O earth, *do not* **c** my blood;	4059
	21:26	and worms **c** them both.	4059
	24: 7	they have nothing to **c** themselves in	4064
	37: 8	The animals take **c;**	743
	38:34	to the clouds and **c** yourself *with* a flood	4059
Ps	10: 9	He lies in wait like a lion in **c;**	6108
	17:12	like a great lion crouching in **c**.	5041
	32: 5	to you and *did not* **c** up my iniquity.	4059
	83:16	**C** their faces *with* shame so	4848
	84: 6	the autumn rains also **c** it *with* pools.	6486
	91: 4	*He will* **c** you with his feathers,	6114
	104: 9	never again *will* they **c** the earth.	4059
Isa	8: 8	Its outspread wings will **c** the breadth	4850
	10:31	the people of Gebim take **c**.	6395
	11: 9	of the LORD as the waters **c** the sea.	4059
	14:11	and worms **c** you.	4833
	14:21	rise to inherit the land and **c** the earth	4848+7156
	54: 9	waters of Noah *would* never again **c**	6296+6584
	59: 6	*they* cannot **c** themselves	4059
	60: 6	Herds of camels *will* **c** your land,	4059
Jer	3:25	and *let* our disgrace **c** us.	4059
	14: 3	and despairing, *they* **c** their heads.	2902
	14: 4	the farmers are dismayed and **c** their heads.	2902
	46: 8	She says, 'I will rise and **c** the earth;	4059
	51:42	its roaring waves **c** *her*.	4059
Eze	12: 6	**C** your face so that you cannot see the land,	4059
	12:12	*He will* **c** his face so that he cannot see	4059
	13:10	they **c** it *with* whitewash.	3212
	13:11	therefore tell *those who* **c** it *with* whitewash	3212
	24: 7	where the dust *would* **c** it.	4059
	24:17	*do not* **c** the lower part of your face or eat	6486
	24:22	*You* will not **c** the lower part of your face	6486
	26:10	be so many that *they* will **c** you *with* dust.	4059
	26:19	over you and its vast waters **c** you,	4059
	32: 7	I will **c** the heavens	4059
	32: 7	I will **c** the sun with a cloud,	4059
	37: 6	and make flesh come upon you and **c** you	7965
Hos	2: 9	intended to **c** her nakedness.	4059
	10: 8	and thistles will grow up and **c** their altars.	6584
	10: 8	they will say to the mountains, "**C** us!"	4059
Mic	3: 7	They *will* all **c** their faces	6486
Hab	2:14	as the waters **c** the sea.	4059
	2:16	and disgrace will **c** your glory.	6584
Zec	5: 7	Then the **c** of lead was raised,	3971
	5: 8	and pushed the lead **c** down over its mouth.	74
Lk	23:30	and to the hills, "**C** us."	2821
1Co	11: 6	If a woman *does* not **c** her head,	2877
	11: 6	*she should* **c** her head.	2877
	11: 7	A man ought not *to* **c** his head,	2877
1Th	2: 5	nor *did we* **put on a mask to c** up greed	4733
Heb	9: 5	overshadowing the **atonement c**.	2663
Jas	5:20	from death and **c over** a multitude of sins.	2821
Rev	3:18	so *you can* **c** your shameful nakedness;	3590+5746

COVER-UP (1) [COVER]

1Pe	2:16	but *do not* use your freedom as a **c** for evil;	2127+2400

COVERED (101) [COVER]

Ge	7:19	under the entire heavens *were* **c**.	4059
	7:20	The waters rose and **c** the mountains to	4059
	9:23	in backward and **c** their father's nakedness.	4059
	24:65	So she took her veil and **c** herself.	4059
	27:16	*She* also **c** his hands and the smooth part	4252
	38:14	**c** herself *with* a veil to disguise herself,	4059
	38:15	for *she had* **c** her face.	4059
Ex	8: 6	and the frogs came up and **c** the land.	4059
	10:15	*They* **c** the ground until it was black.	4059
	10:22	total darkness **c** all Egypt for three days.	928+2118
	14:28	The water flowed back and **c** the chariots	4059
	15: 5	The deep waters *have* **c** them;	4059
	15:10	and the sea **c** them.	4059
	16:13	That evening quail came and **c** the camp,	4059
	19:18	Mount Sinai *was* **c with** smoke,	6939
	24:15	the cloud **c** it,	4059
	24:16	For six days the cloud **c** the mountain,	4059
	40:34	Then the cloud **c** the Tent of Meeting,	4059
Lev	13:13	and if the disease *has* **c** his whole body,	4059
Nu	7: 3	as their gifts before the LORD six **c** carts	7369
	9:15	was set up, the cloud **c** it.	4059

Nu	9:16	cloud **c** it, and at night it looked like fire.	4059
	16:42	suddenly the cloud **c** it and the glory of	4059
Jos	24: 7	he brought the sea over them and **c** them.	4059
Jdg	4:19	gave him a drink, and **c** him **up**.	4059
	6:39	the fleece dry and the ground **c with** dew."	6584
	6:40	all the ground was **c with** dew.	6584
2Sa	15:30	his head *was* **c** and he was barefoot.	2902
	15:30	All the people with him **c** their heads too	2902
	19: 4	The king **c** his face and cried aloud,	4286
1Ki	6:15	and **c** the floor of the temple with planks	7596
	6:21	Solomon **c** the inside of the temple	7596
	6:30	*He* also **c** the floors of both the inner	7596
	7: 7	and *he* **c** it with cedar from floor to ceiling.	6211
	20:27	while the Arameans **c** the countryside.	4848
2Ki	3:25	a stone on every good field until it *was* **c**.	4848
	18:16	which he *had* **c** the doors and doorposts	7596
	23:14	down the Asherah poles and **c** the sites	4848
2Ch	3: 5	He paneled the main hall with pine and **c** it	2902
	5: 8	the ark and **c** the ark and its carrying poles.	4059
	16:14	They laid him on a bier **c** *with* spices	4848
Est	6:12	with his head **c** in grief,	2902
	7: 8	*they* **c** Haman's face.	2902
Job	15:27	"Though his face *is* **c** with fat	2902
	29: 9	and **c** their mouths *with* their hands;	4200+8492
Ps	32: 1	are forgiven, *whose* sins are **c**.	4059
	34: 5	their faces *are* never **c with** shame.	2917
	44:15	and my face *is* **c** with shame	4059
	44:19	and made us a haunt for jackals and **c** us	4252
	65:13	The meadows *are* **c** with flocks and	4059
	71:13	to harm me *be* **c** with scorn and disgrace.	6486
	80:10	The mountains *were* **c** with its shade,	4059
	85: 2	of your people and **c** all their sins.	4059
	89:45	**c** him **with a mantle**	6486
	104: 6	You **c** it with the deep as with a garment;	4059
	106:11	The waters **c** their adversaries;	4059
	140: 9	*be* **c** with the trouble their lips have caused.	4059
Pr	7:16	*I have* **c** my bed *with* colored linens	5267+8048
	24:31	the ground *was* **c** with weeds,	4059
Isa	6: 2	With two wings *they* **c** their faces,	4059
	6: 2	with two *they* **c** their feet,	4059
	7:24	for the land will be **c with** briers and thorns.	3972
	14:19	you are **c** with the slain,	4229
	28: 8	the tables *are* **c** with vomit and there is not	4848
	29:10	*he has* **c** your heads (the seers).	4059
	30:22	with silver and your images *are* **c** with gold;	682
	34: 6	*it is* **c** with fat—	2014
	51:16	in your mouth and **c** you with the shadow	4059
Jer	48:37	and every waist is **c with** sackcloth.	6584
La	2: 1	**c** the Daughter of Zion **with the cloud**	6380
	3:43	"You have **c** yourself with anger	6114
	3:44	*You have* **c** yourself with a cloud so	6114
Eze	7:18	be **c** with shame and their heads will	448
	13:12	"Where is the whitewash *you* **c** it *with?*"	3212
	13:14	down the wall *you have* **c** with whitewash	3212
	13:15	and against those *who* **c** it *with* whitewash.	3212
	16: 8	over you and **c** your nakedness.	4059
	16:10	I dressed you in fine linen and **c** you	4059
	24: 8	so that it *would* not be **c**.	4059
	30:18	She *will be* **c** with clouds,	4059
	31:15	down to the grave *I* **c** the deep springs	4059
	37: 8	on them and skin **c** them,	7965
	41:16	including the threshold was **c with** wood.	6017+6017+8470
	41:16	and the windows *were* **c**.	4059
Da	9: 7	but this day we are **c** with shame—	4200+7156
	9: 8	our princes and our fathers are **c with** shame	4200+7156
Ob	1:10	you *will be* **c** with shame;	4059
Jnh	3: 6	**c** *himself* with sackcloth and sat down in	4059
	3: 8	But *let* man and beast *be* **c** with sackcloth.	4059
Mic	7:10	Then my enemy will see it and *will be* **c**	4059
Hab	2:19	It *is* **c** with gold and silver;	9530
	3: 3	His glory **c** the heavens	4059
Lk	5:12	a man came along who was **c** with leprosy.	4441
	16:20	a beggar named Lazarus, **c with** sores	1815
Jn	5: 2	by five **c colonnades**.	5119
Ac	7:57	At this *they* **c** their ears and,	5309
Ro	4: 7	are forgiven, whose sins are **c**.	2128
1Co	11: 4	with his head **c** dishonors his head.	2400+2848
Rev	4: 6	and *they* were **c with** eyes,	1154
	4: 8	and *was* **c with** eyes all around,	1154
	17: 3	that *was* **c with** blasphemous names	1154

COVERING (38) [COVER]

Ge	8:13	the **c** *from* the ark and saw that the surface	4832
Ex	22:27	his cloak is the only **c** he has for his body.	4064
	26:14	for the tent a **c** of ram skins dyed red,	4832
	26:14	and over that a **c** of hides of sea cows.	4832
	28:42	"Make linen undergarments as a **c** *for*	4059
	29:13	the **c** of the liver,	3866
	29:22	the **c** of the liver,	3866
	35:11	and its **c**, clasps, frames, crossbars, posts	4832
	36:19	for the tent a **c** *of* ram skins dyed red,	4832
	36:19	and over that a **c** *of* hides of sea cows.	4832
	39:34	the **c** *of* ram skins dyed red, the **covering**	4832
	39:34	the **c** of hides of sea cows and **covering**	4832
	40:19	the tabernacle and put the **c** over the tent,	4832
Lev	3: 4	and the **c** of the liver,	3866
	3:10	and the **c** of the liver,	3866
	3:15	and the **c** of the liver,	3866
	4: 9	and the **c** of the liver,	3866
	7: 4	and the **c** of the liver,	3866
	8:16	the **c** *of* the liver,	3866
	8:25	the **c** of the liver,	3866
	9:10	and the **c** of the liver from the sin offering,	3866
	9:19	the kidneys and the **c** *of* the liver—	3866

Nu	4:10	in a *c* of hides of sea cows and put it on	4832
	4:14	a *c* of hides of sea cows and put its poles	4062
	4:15	"After Aaron and his sons have finished *c*	4059
	4:25	its *c* and the outer covering of hides	4832
	4:25	and the outer *c* of hides of sea cows,	4832
Jdg	4:18	and she put a *c* over him.	8526
1Sa	19:13	*c* it with a garment	4059
2Sa	17:19	a *c* and spread it out over the opening of	5009
Ps	18:11	He made darkness his *c*,	6260
	105:39	He spread out a cloud as a *c*,	5009
Isa	50: 3	you will be like a cloud *c* the land.	4059
Eze	1:11	and two wings *c* its body.	4059
	1:23	and each had two wings *c* its body.	4059
	38: 9	you will be like a cloud *c* the land.	4059
Mal	2:16	a *man's c* himself *with* violence as well as	4059
1Co	11:15	For long hair is given to her as a *c*.	*4316*

COVERINGS (3) [COVER]

Ge	3: 7	and made *c* for themselves.	2514
Nu	3:25	for the care of the tabernacle and tent, its *c*,	4832
Pr	31:22	She makes *c* for her *bed*;	5267

COVERS (23) [COVER]

Ex	22:15	the money paid for the hire *c* the loss.	928+995
Lev	3: 3	the fat that *c* the inner parts or is connected	4059
	3: 9	the fat that *c* the inner parts or is connected	4059
	3:14	the fat that *c* the inner parts or is connected	4059
	4: 8	the fat that *c* the inner parts or is connected	4059
	7: 3	the fat tail and the fat that *c* the inner parts,	4059
	13:12	it *c* all the skin of the infected person	4059
Nu	22:11	that has come out of Egypt *c* the face of	4059
1Ki	1: 1	not keep warm even when they put *c*	955
Job	22:11	and why a flood of water *c* you.	4059
	23:17	by the thick darkness *that c* my face.	4059
	26: 9	*He c* the face of the full moon,	297
Ps	10:11	*he c* his face and never sees."	6259
	69: 7	and shame *c* my face.	4059
	147: 8	He *c* the sky with clouds;	4059
Pr	10:12	but love *c* over all wrongs.	4059
	17: 9	*He who c* an offense promotes love,	4059
Isa	25: 7	the sheet that *c* all nations;	5819
	60: 2	darkness *c* the earth and thick darkness is	4059
Jer	51:51	and shame *c* our faces,	4059
Eze	38:16	against my people Israel like a cloud *that c*	4059
2Co	3:15	a veil *c* their hearts.	2093+3023
1Pe	4: 8	because love *c* over a multitude of sins.	2821

COVES (1)

Jdg	5:17	on the coast and stayed in his *c*.	5153

COVET (9) [COVETED, COVETING, COVETOUS]

Ex	20:17	"You shall not *c* your neighbor's house.	2773
	20:17	*You shall* not *c* your neighbor's wife,	2773
	34:24	and no one will *c* your land when you go	2773
Dt	5:21	"You shall not *c* your neighbor's wife.	2773
	7:25	*Do* not *c* the silver and gold on them,	2773
Mic	2: 2	*They c* fields and seize them, and houses,	2773
Ro	7: 7	if the law had not said, "*Do* not *c*."	*2121*
	13: 9	Do not murder," "Do not steal," "*Do* not *c*,"	*2121*
Jas	4: 2	You kill and *c*,	*2420*

COVETED (2) [COVET]

Jos	7:21	*I c* them and took them.	2773
Ac	20:33	not *c* anyone's silver or gold or clothing.	*2121*

COVETING (1) [COVET]

Ro	7: 7	not have known **what** *c* really **was** if	*2123*

COVETOUS (1) [COVET]

Ro	7: 8	produced in me every kind of *c* **desire**.	*2123*

COW (4) [COWS, COWS']

Lev	22:28	not slaughter a *c* or a sheep and its young	8802
Isa	7:21	a man will keep alive a **young** *c*	1330+6320
	11: 7	The *c* will feed with the bear,	7239
Eze	4:15	bake your bread over *c* manure instead	1330

COWARDLY (1) [COWER]

Rev	21: 8	But the *c*, the unbelieving, the vile,	*1264*

COWER (1) [COWARDLY, COWERED, COWERING]

Dt	33:29	Your enemies *will c* before ˮou,	3950

COWERED (1) [COWER]

Job	9:13	even the cohorts of Rahab *c* at his feet.	8820

COWERING (1) [COWER]

Isa	51:14	The *c* **prisoners** will soon be set free;	7579

COWS (33) [COW]

Ge	32:15	forty *c* and ten bulls,	7239
	33:13	the ewes and *c* that are nursing their young.	1330
	41: 2	out of the river there came up seven *c*,	7239
	41: 3	After them, seven other *c*, ugly and gaunt,	7239
	41: 4	And the *c* that were ugly and gaunt ate up	7239
	41: 4	and gaunt ate up the seven sleek, fat *c*.	7239

Ge	41:18	out of the river there came up seven *c*,	7239
	41:19	After them, seven other *c* came up—	7239
	41:19	I had never seen such ugly *c* in all the land	2179S
	41:20	ugly *c* ate up the seven fat cows that came	7239
	41:20	ugly cows ate up the seven fat *c* that came	7239
	41:26	The seven good *c* are seven years,	7239
	41:27	The seven lean, ugly *c* that came	7239
Ex	25: 5	ram skins dyed red and hides of **sea c**;	9391
	26:14	and over that a covering of hides of **sea c**.	9391
	35: 7	ram skins dyed red and hides of **sea c**;	9391
	35:23	or hides of **sea c** brought them.	9391
	36:19	and over that a covering of hides of **sea c**.	9391
	39:34	of hides of **sea c** and the shielding curtain;	9391
Nu	4: 6	they are to cover this with hides of **sea c**,	9391
	4: 8	that with hides of **sea c** and put its poles	9391
	4:10	in a covering of hides of **sea c** and put it on	9391
	4:11	that with hides of **sea c** and put its poles	9391
	4:12	cover that with hides of **sea c** and put them	9391
	4:14	that with hides of **sea c** and put its poles in place.	9391
	4:25	and the outer covering of **hides of sea c**.	9391
1Sa	6: 7	with two *c* that have calved	7239
	6: 7	Hitch the *c* to the cart,	7239
	6:10	They took two such *c* and hitched them to	7239
	6:12	*c* went straight up toward Beth Shemesh,	7239
	6:14	up the wood of the cart and sacrificed the *c*	7239
Job	21:10	their *c* calve and do not miscarry.	7239
Am	4: 1	you *c* of Bashan on Mount Samaria,	7239

COWS' (1) [COW]

2Sa	17:29	from *c'* milk for David and his people	1330

COZ (KJV) See KOZ

COZBI (2)

Nu	25:15	to death was *C* daughter of Zur,	3944
	25:18	in the affair of Peor and their sister *C*,	3944

COZEBA (1)

1Ch	4:22	the men of *C*, and Joash and Saraph,	3943

CRACK (1) [CRACKED]

Na	3: 2	The *c* of whips, the clatter of wheels,	7754

CRACKED (5) [CRACK]

Jos	9: 4	with worn-out sacks and old wineskins, *c*	1324
	9:13	but see how *c they are*.	1324
Jdg	9:53	on his head and *c* his skull.	8368
Isa	30:13	*c* and bulging, that collapses suddenly,	5877+7288
Jer	14: 4	The ground *is c* because there is no rain in	3169

CRACKLING (2)

Ecc	7: 6	Like the *c* of thorns under the pot,	7754
Joel	2: 5	like a *c* fire consuming stubble,	7754

CRACKNELS (KJV) See CAKES

CRAFT (1) [CRAFTED, CRAFTINESS, CRAFTS, CRAFTSMAN, CRAFTSMAN'S, CRAFTSMANSHIP, CRAFTSMEN, CRAFTY]

1Ch	28:21	in any *c* will help you in all the work.	6275

CRAFTED (1) [CRAFT]

Nu	31:51	all the *c* articles.	5126

CRAFTINESS (3) [CRAFT]

Job	5:13	He catches the wise in their *c*,	6891
1Co	3:19	"He catches the wise in their *c*";	*4111*
Eph	4:14	and *c* of men in their deceitful scheming.	*4111*

CRAFTS (2) [CRAFT]

Ex	31: 3	ability and knowledge in all kinds of *c*—	4856
	35:31	ability and knowledge in all kinds of *c*—	4856

CRAFTSMAN (18) [CRAFT]

Ex	26: 1	into them by a **skilled c**.	3110
	26:31	into it by a **skilled c**.	3110
	28: 6	the work of a **skilled c**.	3110
	28:15	the work of a **skilled c**.	3110
	36: 8	into them by a **skilled c**.	3110
	36:35	into it by a **skilled c**.	3110
	38:23	a *c* and designer,	3093
	39: 3	the work of a **skilled c**.	3110
	39: 8	the work of a **skilled c**.	3110
1Ki	7:14	a man of Tyre and a *c* in bronze.	3086
Pr	8:30	Then I was the *c* at his side.	570
Isa	3: 3	skilled *c* and clever enchanter.	3093
	40:19	As for an idol, a *c* casts it,	3093
	40:20	He looks for a skilled *c* to set up an idol	3093
	41: 7	The *c* encourages the goldsmith,	3093
Jer	10: 3	and a *c* shapes it with his chisel.	3093
	10: 9	What the *c* and goldsmith have made is	3093
Hos	8: 6	This calf—a *c* has made it; it is not God.	3093

CRAFTSMAN'S (2) [CRAFT]

Dt	27:15	the work of a *c* hands—	3093
SS	7: 1	the work of a *c* hands.	588

CRAFTSMANSHIP (2) [CRAFT]

Ex	31: 5	and to engage in all kinds of *c*.	4856
	35:33	and to engage in all kinds of **artistic c**.	4742

CRAFTSMEN (23) [CRAFT]

Ex	31: 5	Also I have given skill to all the *c*	2682+4213
	35:35	with skill to do all kinds of work as *c*,	3093
	35:35	all of them **master** *c* and designers,	4856+6913
	36: 4	the **skilled** *c* who were doing all the work	2682
1Ki	5:18	The *c* of Solomon and Hiram and the men	1215
2Ki	24:14	and all the *c* and artisans—	3093
	24:16	and a thousand *c* and artisans.	3093
1Ch	4:14	It was called this because its people were *c*.	3093
	22:16	and iron—*c* beyond number.	NIH
	29: 5	and for all the work to be done by the *c*.	3093
2Ch	2: 7	in Judah and Jerusalem with my **skilled** *c*,	2682
	2:14	He will work with your *c* and with those	2682
Ne	11:35	in Lod and Ono, and in the Valley of the *C*.	3093
Isa	44:11	*c* are nothing but men.	3093
Jer	24: 1	the *c* and the artisans of Judah were carried	3093
	29: 2	the *c* and the artisans had gone into exile	3093
	52:15	the rest of the *c* and those who had gone	570
Eze	27: 9	Veteran *c* of Gebal were on board	2682
Hos	13: 2	all of them the work of *c*.	3093
Zec	1:20	Then the LORD showed me four *c*.	3093
	1:21	but **the** *c* have come to terrify them	465S
Ac	19:24	brought in no little business *for* the *c*.	*5493*
	19:38	and his fellow *c* have a grievance	*5493*

CRAFTY (8) [CRAFT]

Ge	3: 1	Now the serpent was more *c* than any of	6874
1Sa	23:22	They tell me he *is* very *c*.	6891+6891
Job	5:12	He thwarts the plans of the *c*,	6874
	15: 5	you adopt the tongue of the *c*.	6874
Pr	7:10	dressed like a prostitute and with *c* intent.	5915
	12: 2	but the LORD condemns a *c* man.	4659
	14:17	and a *c* man is hated.	4659
2Co	12:16	Yet, *c* **fellow** that I am,	*4112*

CRAG (3) [CRAGS]

Dt	32:13	and with oil from the flinty *c*,	7446
Job	39:28	a rocky *c* is his stronghold.	9094
Ps	78:16	of a **rocky** *c* and made water flow down	6152

CRAGS (6) [CRAG]

1Sa	24: 2	and his men near the *C* of the Wild Goats.	7446
Ps	104:18	the *c* are a refuge for the coneys.	6152
Pr	30:26	yet they make their home in the *c*;	6152
Isa	2:21	and to the overhanging *c* from dread of	6152
	57: 5	in the ravines and under the overhanging *c*.	6152
Am	6:12	Do horses run on the **rocky** *c*?	6152

CRANE (KJV) See SWIFT

CRASH (2)

Zep	1:10	and a loud *c* from the hills.	8691
Mt	7:27	that house, and it fell **with a great** *c*."	899+1639+3489+3836+4774

CRAVE (7) [CRAVED, CRAVES, CRAVING, CRAVINGS]

Nu	11: 4	with them *began* to *c* **other food**,	203+9294
Dt	12:20	and you *c* meat and say,	203
Pr	23: 3	*Do* not *c* his delicacies,	203
	23: 6	*do not c* his delicacies;	203
	31: 4	kings to drink wine, not for rulers to *c* beer,	197
Mic	7: 1	none of the early figs that I *c*.	203
1Pe	2: 2	Like newborn babies, *c* pure spiritual milk,	*2160*

CRAVED (4) [CRAVE]

Nu	11:34	the people who *had c* **other food**.	203
Ps	78:18	to the test by demanding the food they *c*.	5883
	78:29	for he had given them **what** they *c*.	9294
	78:30	before they turned from the food they *c*,	9294

CRAVES (3) [CRAVE]

Pr	13: 4	The sluggard *c* and gets nothing,	203
	21:10	The wicked man *c* evil;	203
	21:26	All day long *he c* for more,	203+9294

CRAVING (6) [CRAVE]

Job	20:20	"Surely he will have no respite from his *c*;	1061
Ps	106:14	*they* **gave in to** *their c*;	203+9294
Pr	10: 3	but he thwarts the *c* of the wicked.	2094
	13: 2	but the unfaithful have a *c for* violence.	5883
	21:25	The sluggard's *c* will be the death of him,	9294
Jer	2:24	sniffing the wind in her *c*—	205+5883

CRAVINGS (3) [CRAVE]

Ps	10: 3	He boasts of the *c* of his heart;	9294
Eph	2: 3	gratifying the *c* of our sinful nature	*2123*
1Jn	2:16	the *c* of sinful man,	*2123*

CRAWL (2) [CRAWLING]

Ge	3:14	*You will c* on your belly	2143
Mic	7:17	like *creatures that c on* the ground.	2323

CRAWLING (3) [CRAWL]

Lev	22: 5	or if he touches any c thing	9238
1Sa	14:11	"The Hebrews *are* c **out** of the holes	3655
Eze	8:10	of c things and detestable animals and all	8254

CREAM (2)

Job	20:17	the rivers flowing with honey and c.	2772
	29: 6	when my path was drenched with c and	2772

CREATE (11) [CREATED, CREATES, CREATING, CREATION, CREATOR]

Ps	51:10	C in me a pure heart, O God,	1343
Isa	4: 5	the LORD *will* c over all of Mount Zion	1343
	45: 7	I form the light and c darkness,	1343
	45: 7	I bring prosperity and c disaster;	1343
	45:18	*he did not* c it to be empty,	1343
	65:17	I *will* c new heavens and a new earth.	1343
	65:18	and rejoice forever in what I *will* c,	1343
	65:18	for I *will* c Jerusalem to be a delight	1343
Jer	31:22	The LORD *will* c a new thing on earth—	1343
Mal	2:10	*Did not* one God c us?	1343
Eph	2:15	*to* c in himself one new man out of the two,	3231

CREATED (47) [CREATE]

Ge	1: 1	In the beginning God c the heavens and	1343
	1:21	So God c the great creatures of the sea	1343
	1:27	So God c man in his own image,	1343
	1:27	in the image of God he c him;	1343
	1:27	male and female *he* c them.	1343
	2: 4	the heavens and the earth when they **were** c.	1343
	5: 1	When God c man,	1343
	5: 2	*He* c them male and female	1343
	5: 2	when they **were** c, he called them "man."	1343
	6: 7	"I will wipe mankind, whom I **have** c,	1343
Dt	4:32	from the day God c man on the earth;	1343
Ps	89:12	You c the north and the south;	1343
	89:47	For what futility *you have* c all men!	1343
	102:18	a people **not yet** c may praise the LORD:	1343
	104:30	When you send your Spirit, *they are* c,	1343
	139:13	For you c my inmost being;	7865
	148: 5	for he commanded and *they were* c.	1343
Isa	40:26	Who c all these?	1343
	41:20	that the Holy One of Israel *has* c it.	1343
	42: 5	*he who* c the heavens	1343
	43: 1	*he who* c you, O Jacob, he who formed you,	1343
	43: 7	whom *I* c for my glory,	1343
	45: 8	I, the LORD, *have* c it.	1343
	45:12	It is I who made the earth and c mankind	1343
	45:18	*he who* c the heavens, he is God;	1343
	48: 7	*They* **are** c now, and not long ago;	1343
	54:16	it is I *who* c the blacksmith who fans	1343
	54:16	And it is I *who have* c the destroyer	1343
	57:16	the breath of man that I *have* c.	6913
Eze	21:30	In the place where you **were** c,	1343
	28:13	on the day you **were** c they were prepared.	1343
	28:15	in your ways from the day you **were** c	1343
Mk	13:19	when God c the world, until now—	3231
Ro	1:25	and served c **things** rather than the	3232
1Co	11: 9	neither *was* man c for woman,	3231
Eph	2:10	c in Christ Jesus to do good works,	3231
	3: 9	in God, who c all things.	3231
	4:24	c to be like God in true righteousness	3231
Col	1:16	For by him all things *were* c:	3231
	1:16	all things *were* c by him and for him.	3231
1Ti	4: 3	which God c to be received	3232
	4: 4	For everything God c is good,	3233
Heb	12:27	that is, c **things**—	4472
Jas	1:18	be a kind of firstfruits *of* all he c.	3233
Rev	4:11	for you c all things,	3231
	4:11	and by your will *they were* c	3231
	10: 6	who c the heavens and all that is in them,	3231

CREATES (1) [CREATE]

Am	4:13	He who forms the mountains, c the wind,	1343

CREATING (2) [CREATE]

Ge	2: 3	from all the work *of* c that he had done.	1343
Isa	57:19	c praise on the lips of the mourners	1343

CREATION (25) [CREATE]

Hab	2:18	For he who makes it trusts in his own c;	3671
Mt	13:35	I will utter things hidden since the c of	2856
	25:34	the kingdom prepared for you since the c	2856
Mk	10: 6	the beginning *of* c God 'made them male	3232
	16:15	and preach the good news *to* all c.	3232
Jn	17:24	because you loved me before the c of	2856
Ro	1:20	c of the world God's invisible qualities—	3232
	8:19	The c waits in eager expectation for	3232
	8:20	For the c was subjected to frustration,	3232
	8:21	that the c itself will be liberated	3232
	8:22	that the whole c has been groaning as in	3232
	8:39	nor anything else in all c,	3232
2Co	5:17	if anyone is in Christ, he is a new c;	3232
Gal	6:15	what counts is a new c.	3232
Eph	1: 4	the c of the world to be holy and blameless	2856
Col	1:15	the firstborn *over* all c.	3232
Heb	4: 3	yet his work has been finished since the c	2856
	4:13	Nothing in all c is hidden	3232
	9:11	that is to say, not *a part of* this c.	3232
	9:26	to suffer many times since the c of	2856
1Pe	1:20	He was chosen before the c of the world,	2856
2Pe	3: 4	on as it has since the beginning *of* c."	3232

CREATOR (11) [CREATE]

Ge	14:19	God Most High, C *of* heaven and earth.	7865
	14:22	God Most High, C *of* heaven and earth,	7865
Dt	32: 6	Is he not your Father, your C,	7865
Ecc	12: 1	Remember your C in the days	1343
Isa	27:11	and their C shows them no favor.	3670
	40:28	the C of the ends of the earth.	1343
	43:15	your Holy One, Israel's C, your King."	1343
Mt	19: 4	at the beginning the C 'made them male	3231
Ro	1:25	and served created things rather than the C	3231
Col	3:10	in knowledge in the image *of* its C.	3231
1Pe	4:19	*to* their faithful C and continue to do good.	3234

CREATURE (37) [CREATURES]

Ge	1:28	the air and over every **living** c that moves	2651
	2:19	and whatever the man called each living c,	5883
	6:17	every c that has the breath of life in it.	NIH
	6:20	of animal and of every kind of c **that moves**	8254
	7: 4	of the earth every **living** c I have made."	3685
	7:14	every c that moves along the ground	8254
	8:17	Bring out every kind of living c that is	1414
	9: 2	upon every c that moves along the ground,	889S
	9:10	with every living c that was with you—	5883
	9:10	every **living** c *on* earth.	2651
	9:12	and every living c with you, a covenant "	5883
Lev	11:41	" 'Every c that moves about on	9238
	11:42	You are not to eat any c that moves about	9238
	11:44	Do not make yourselves unclean by any c	9238
	11:46	the water and every c that moves about on	5883
	17:11	For the life of a c is in the blood,	1414
	17:14	because the life of every c is its blood.	1414
	17:14	"You must not eat the blood of any c,	1414
	17:14	because the life of every c is its blood;	1414
Dt	4:18	or like any c **that moves** along the ground	8253
	14:20	But any **winged** c that is clean you may eat.	6416
Job	12:10	of every c and the breath of all mankind.	2644
	14:15	your hands have **made.**	5126
	41:33	a c without fear.	6913
Ps	136:25	and who gives food to every c.	1414
	145:21	Let every c praise his holy name for ever	1414
Isa	47: 8	"Now then, listen, you **wanton** c,	AIT
Eze	1:11	one touching the wing of **another** c on	408S
	1:15	I saw a wheel on the ground beside each c	2651
	38:20	every c that moves along the ground,	8254
Da	4:12	from it every c was fed.	10125
Col	1:23	and that has been proclaimed to every c	3232
Rev	4: 7	The first **living** c was like a lion,	2442
	5:13	Then I heard every c in heaven and	3233
	6: 3	I heard the second **living** c say, "Come!"	2442
	6: 5	I heard the third **living** c say, "Come!"	2442
	6: 7	the voice *of* the fourth **living** c say,	2442

CREATURES (82) [CREATURE]

Ge	1:20	"Let the water teem with living **c,**	5883
	1:21	the great c **of the sea** and every living	9490
	1:24	"Let the land produce living c according	5883
	1:24	livestock, c **that move** along the ground,	8254
	1:25	the c **that move** *along* the ground according	8254
	1:26	over all the c that move along the ground,	8254
	1:30	the birds of the air and all the c **that move**	8253
	6: 7	c **that move along the** ground,	8254
	6:19	to bring into the ark two of all living c,	1414
	7: 8	and of all c that move along the ground,	889S
	7:15	Pairs of all c that have the breath of life	1414
	7:21	all the c that swarm over the earth,	9238
	7:23	men and animals and the c **that move** along	8254
	8:17	and all the c that move along the ground—	8254
	8:19	the animals and all the c **that move** along	8254
	8:21	And never again will I destroy all living c,	2645
	9:15	and you and all living c of every kind.	5883
	9:16	and all living c of every kind on the earth."	5883
Lev	5: 2	c **that move along the** ground—	9238
	11: 9	" 'Of all **the** c living in the water of the seas	889S
	11:10	But all c in the seas or streams that do	NIH
	11:10	among all the other living c in the water—	5883
	11:21	some winged c that walk on all fours	9238
	11:23	But all other winged c	9238
	11:43	Do not defile yourselves by any of these c.	9238
	11:47	between **living** c that may be eaten	2651
Dt	14: 9	Of all **the** c living in the water,	889S
Ps	50:11	and the c *of* the field are mine.	2328
	74:14	and gave him as food to the c **of the desert.**	7470
	80:13	Boars from the forest ravage it and the c *of*	2328
	104:24	the earth is full of your c.	7871
	104:25	**teeming** with c beyond number—	8254
	148: 7	you **great sea** c and all ocean depths,	9490
	148:10	**small** c and flying birds,	8254
Pr	30:25	Ants are c of little strength, yet they store	6639
	30:26	coneys are c of little power,	6639
Isa	13:21	But **desert** c will lie there,	7470
	23:13	a place for **desert** c.	7470
	34:14	**Desert** c will meet with hyenas,	7470
	34:14	there the **night** c will also repose and find	4327
Jer	50:39	"So **desert** c and hyenas will live there,	7470
Eze	1: 5	like four **living** c.	2651
	1:13	the **living** c was like burning coals of fire	2651
	1:13	Fire moved back and forth among the c;	2651
	1:14	The c sped back and forth like flashes	2651
	1:15	As I looked at the **living** c,	2651
	1:17	of the four directions the c faced;	NIH
	1:17	the wheels did not turn about as the c went.	5527S

CREDITED (16) [CREDIT]

Eze	1:19	When the **living** c moved,	2651
	1:19	when the **living** c rose from the ground,	2651
	1:20	spirit of the **living** c was in the wheels.	2651
	1:21	When the c moved, they also moved;	4392S
	1:21	when **the** c stood still, they also stood still;	4392S
	1:21	and when **the** c rose from the ground,	4392S
	1:21	spirit of the **living** c was in the wheels.	2651
	1:22	the heads of the **living** c was what looked	2651
	1:24	When **the** c moved,	4392S
	3:13	the **living** c brushing against each other	2651
	10:15	These were the **living** c I had seen by	2651
	10:17	the spirit of the **living** c was in them.	2651
	10:20	the **living** c I had seen beneath the God	2651
	47: 9	Swarms of living c will live wherever	5883
Hos	2:18	and the birds of the air and the c **that move**	8254
Mic	7:17	like c that **crawl** on the ground.	AIT
Hab	1:14	like **sea** c that have no ruler.	8254
Zep	2:14	c of every kind.	2651
Jas	3: 7	reptiles and c **of** the sea are being tamed	1879
2Pe	2:12	They are like brute beasts, c **of instinct,**	5879
Rev	4: 6	around the throne, were four **living** c,	2442
	4: 8	Each of the four **living** c had six wings	2442
	4: 9	Whenever the **living** c give glory,	2442
	5: 6	*by* the four **living** c and the elders.	2442
	5: 8	the four **living** c and the twenty-four elders	2442
	5:11	They encircled the throne and the **living** c	2442
	5:14	The four **living** c said, "Amen,"	2442
	6: 1	Then I heard one of the four **living** c say	2442
	6: 6	like a voice among the four **living** c,	2442
	7:11	around the elders and the four **living** c.	2442
	8: 9	a third *of* the living c in the sea died,	3233
	14: 3	before the four **living** c and the elders.	2442
	15: 7	Then one of the four **living** c gave to	2442
	19: 4	and the four **living** c fell down	2442

CREDIT (6) [ACCREDITED, CREDITED, CREDITOR, CREDITORS, CREDITS]

Est	2:22	giving c to Mordecai.	928+9005
Lk	6:32	what c is that to you?	5921
	6:33	what c is that to you?	5921
	6:34	what c is that to you?	5921
Ro	4:24	to whom God will c righteousness—	3357
1Pe	2:20	how is it to your c if you receive a beating	3094

CREDITED (16) [CREDIT]

Ge	15: 6	and *he* c it to him as righteousness.	3108
Lev	7:18	*It will* not be c to the one who offered it,	3108
1Sa	18: 8	"They have c David *with* tens of thousands,	5989
Ps	106:31	This was c to him as righteousness	3108
Eze	18:20	of the righteous man will be c to him,	6584
Ro	4: 3	and *it was* c to him as righteousness."	3357
	4: 4	his wages *are* not c to him as a gift,	3357
	4: 5	his faith *is* c as righteousness.	3357
	4: 9	that Abraham's faith *was* c to him	3357
	4:10	Under what circumstances *was it* c?	3357
	4:11	that righteousness *might be* c to them.	3357
	4:22	This is why "*it was* c to him	3357
	4:23	The words "*it was* c to him" were written	3357
Gal	3: 6	and *it was* c to him as righteousness."	3357
Php	4:17	but I am looking for what may be c	4429
Jas	2:23	and *it was* c to him as righteousness,"	3357

CREDITOR (4) [CREDIT]

Dt	15: 2	Every c shall cancel the loan he has made	1251+2257+3338+5408
2Ki	4: 1	now his c is coming to take my two boys	5957
Ps	109:11	May a c seize all he has;	5957
Isa	24: 2	for debtor as for c.	5957

CREDITORS (1) [CREDIT]

Isa	50: 1	Or to which of my c did I sell you?	5957

CREDITS (1) [CREDIT]

Ro	4: 6	to whom God c righteousness apart	3357

CREPT (2)

1Sa	24: 4	Then David c **up** unnoticed and cut off	7756
Hab	3:16	decay c into my bones,	995

CRESCENS (1)

2Ti	4:10	C has gone to Galatia,	3206

CRESCENT (1)

Isa	3:18	bangles and headbands and c **necklaces,**	8448

CREST (2)

Est	6: 8	one with a royal c placed on its head.	4195
SS	4: 8	Descend from the c *of* Amana,	8031

CRETANS (2) [CRETE]

Ac	2:11	to Judaism); C and Arabs—	3205
Tit	1:12	"C are always liars, evil brutes,	3205

CRETE (5) [CRETANS]

Ac	27: 7	we sailed to the lee of C,	3207
	27:12	This was a harbor in C,	3207
	27:13	and sailed along the shore of C.	3207
	27:21	not to sail from C;	3207
Tit	1: 5	The reason I left you in C was	3207

CRETES, CRETIANS (KJV) See CRETANS

CREVICE (1) [CREVICES]
Jer 13: 4   now to Perath and hide it there in a **c** in   5932

CREVICES (2) [CREVICE]
Isa	7:19	the steep ravines and in the **c** in the rocks,	5932
Jer	16:16	on every mountain and hill and from the **c**	5932

CRIB (KJV) See MANGER

CRICKET (1)
Lev 11:22   katydid, **c** or grasshopper.   3005

CRIED (94) [CRY]
Ge	41:55	the people **c** to Pharaoh for food.	7590
	45: 1	and *he* **c** out, "Have everyone leave	7924
Ex	2:23	in their slavery and **c** out,	2410
	8:12	Moses **c** out to the LORD about	7590
	14:10	They were terrified and **c** out to	7590
	15:25	Then Moses **c** out to the LORD,	7590
	17: 4	Then Moses **c** out to the LORD,	7590
Nu	11: 2	When the people **c** out to Moses,	7590
	12:13	So Moses **c** out to the LORD, "O God,	7590
	16:22	Moses and Aaron fell facedown and **c** out,	606
	20:16	but when *we* **c** out to the LORD,	7590
Dt	26: 7	Then *we* **c** out to the LORD,	7590
Jos	24: 7	**c** to the LORD for help,	7590
Jdg	3: 9	But when they **c** out to the LORD,	2410
	3:15	Again the Israelites **c** out to the LORD,	2410
	4: 3	**c** to the LORD for help.	7590
	5:28	behind the lattice *she* **c** out,	3291
	6: 6	**c** out to the LORD for help.	2410
	6: 7	the Israelites **c** to the LORD because	2410
	10:10	Then the Israelites **c** out to the LORD,	2410
	10:12	**c** to me for help,	7590
	11:35	When he saw her, he tore his clothes and **c**,	606
	14:17	*She* **c** the whole seven days of the feast.	1134
	15:18	he was very thirsty, *he* **c** out to the LORD,	7924
	21: 3	"O LORD, the God of Israel," they **c**,	606
1Sa	5:10	the people of Ekron **c** out,	2410
	7: 9	He **c** out to the LORD on Israel's behalf,	2410
	12: 8	**c** to the LORD for help,	2410
	12:10	*They* **c** out to the LORD and said,	2410
	15:11	and *he* **c** out to the LORD all that night.	2410
	28:12	*she* **c** out at the top of her voice and said	2410
2Sa	19: 4	The king covered his face and **c** aloud,	2410
	22:42	*They* **c** for help, but there was no one	8775
1Ki	13: 2	*He* **c** out against the altar by the word of	7924
	13: 4	of God **c** out against the altar at Bethel,	7924
	13:21	*He* **c** out to the man of God who had come	7924
	17:20	Then *he* **c** out to the LORD,	7924
	17:21	on the boy three times and **c** to the LORD,	7924
	18:39	they fell prostrate and **c**, "The LORD—	606
	22:32	but when Jehoshaphat **c** out,	2410
2Ki	2:12	Elisha saw this and **c** out, "My father!	7590
	4: 1	from the company of the prophets **c** out	7590
	4:40	but as they began to eat it, they **c** out,	7590
	6: 5	"Oh, my lord," he **c** out,	7590
	6:26	a woman **c** to him, "Help me,	7590
	13:14	"My father! My father!" he **c**.	606
1Ch	4:10	Jabez **c** out to the God of Israel, "Oh,	7924
	5:20	*they* **c** out to him during the battle.	2410
2Ch	13:14	Then *they* **c** out to the LORD.	7590
	18:31	but Jehoshaphat **c** out,	2410
	32:20	and the prophet Isaiah son of Amoz **c** out	2410
Ne	9:27	they were oppressed they **c** out to you.	7590
	9:28	And when *they* **c** out to you again,	2410
Job	29:12	because I rescued the poor *who* **c** for help,	8775
Ps	18: 6	**c** to my God for help.	8775
	18:41	*They* **c** for help, but there was no one	8775
	22: 5	*They* **c** to you and were saved;	2410
	30: 8	to the Lord *I* **c** for mercy;	2858
	31:17	O LORD, for *I* have **c** out to you;	7924
	66:17	*I* **c** out to him with my mouth;	7924
	77: 1	**c** out to God for help;	7590+7754
	77: 1	*I* **c** out to God to hear me.	7754
	107: 6	*they* **c** out to the LORD in their trouble,	7590
	107:13	Then *they* **c** to the LORD in their trouble,	2410
	107:19	Then *they* **c** to the LORD in their trouble,	2410
	107:28	*they* **c** out to the LORD in their trouble,	7590
	118: 5	In my anguish *I* **c** to the LORD,	7924
	137: 7	"Tear it down," they **c**,	606
Isa	6: 5	"Woe to me!" *I* **c**.	606
	38:14	*I* **c** like a swift or thrush,	7627
Eze	11:13	I fell facedown and **c** out in a loud voice,	2410
Am	7: 2	*I* **c** out, "Sovereign LORD, forgive!	606
	7: 5	Then *I* **c** out, "Sovereign LORD,	606
Jnh	1: 5	All the sailors were afraid and each **c** out	2410
	1:14	Then *they* **c** to the LORD, "O LORD,	7924
Mt	14:26	"It's a ghost," they said, and **c** out in fear.	3189
	14:30	to sink, **c** out, "Lord, save me!"	3189+3306
	27:46	the ninth hour Jesus **c** out in a loud voice,	331
	27:50	*when* Jesus had **c** out again in a loud voice,	3189
Mk	1:23	by an evil spirit **c** out,	371
	3:11	they fell down before him and **c** out,	3189
	6:49	they thought he was a ghost. *They* **c** out,	371
	15:34	the ninth hour Jesus **c** out in a loud voice,	1066
Lk	4:33	*He* **c** out at the top of his voice,	371
	8:28	*he* **c** out and fell at his feet,	371
	23:18	With one voice *they* **c** out,	371
Jn	7:28	still teaching in the temple courts, **c** out,	3189
	12:44	Then Jesus **c** out,	3189
	20:16	toward him and **c** out in Aramaic,	3306
Ac	7:60	Then *he* fell on his knees and **c** out, "Lord,	3189+3489+5889
Rev	7:10	And *they* **c** out in a loud voice:	3189
	12: 2	She was pregnant and **c** out in pain	3189
	19: 4	And *they* **c**: "Amen, Hallelujah!"	3306
	19:17	*who* **c** in a loud voice to all the birds flying	3189

CRIES (26) [CRY]
Ge	4:10	Your brother's blood **c** out to me from	7590
Ex	22:27	When *he* **c** to me, I will hear,	7590
Nu	16:34	At their **c**, all the Israelites	7754
Job	30:24	on a broken man when *he* **c** for help	8780
	31:38	"if my land **c** out against me	2410
Ps	47: 1	shout to God with **c** of joy.	7754
Pr	1:21	at the head of the noisy streets *she* **c** out, in	7924
	8: 3	at the entrances, *she* **c** aloud:	8264
Isa	5: 7	for righteousness, but heard **c** of distress.	7591
	15: 5	My heart **c** out over Moab;	2410
	26:17	to give birth writhes and **c** out in her pain,	2410
	46: 7	Though *one* **c** out to it, it does not answer;	7590
	56:12	"Come," each one **c**, "let me get wine!	NIH
Jer	30: 5	" '**C** of fear are heard—terror, not peace.	7754
	46:12	your **c** will fill the earth.	7424
	48: 3	Listen to the **c** from Horonaim,	7591
	48: 3	**c** of great havoc and destruction.	NIH
	48: 5	on the road down to Horonaim anguished **c**	7591
Hos	8: 2	Israel **c** out to me, 'O our God,	2410
Am	1:14	that will consume her fortresses amid **war c**	9558
	2: 2	in great tumult amid **war c** and the blast of	9558
	5:16	and **c** of anguish in every public square.	606
Jn	1:15	*He* **c** out, saying, "This was he	3189
Ro	9:27	Isaiah **c** out concerning Israel:	3189
Heb	5: 7	and petitions with loud **c** and tears to	3199
Jas	5: 4	The **c** of the harvesters have reached	1068

CRIME (19) [CRIMES, CRIMINAL, CRIMINALS]
Ge	31:36	"What is my **c**?"	7322
Dt	19:15	to convict a man accused of any **c**	6411
	19:16	the stand to accuse a man of a **c**,	6240
	25: 2	with the number of lashes his **c** deserves,	8402
Jdg	9:24	the **c** against Jerub-Baal's seventy sons,	2805
	20:12	about this awful **c** that was committed	8288
1Sa	20: 1	What is my **c**?	6411
Ezr	6:11	And for *this* **c** his house is to be made a pile	AIT
Ps	69:27	Charge them with **c** upon crime;	6411
	69:27	Charge them with crime upon **c**;	6411
Ecc	8:11	When a sentence for a **c** is not quickly carried out,	5126+8288
Jer	37:18	"What **c** *have* I committed against you	2627
Hab	2:12	and establishes a town by **c**!	6406
Mt	27:23	What **c** has he committed?"	2805
Mk	15:14	What **c** has he committed?"	2805
Lk	23:22	What **c** has this man committed?	2805
Ac	18:14	about some misdemeanor or serious **c**,	4815
	24:20	these who are here should state what **c** they found in me	93
	28:18	not guilty of any **c** deserving death.	162

CRIMES (7) [CRIME]
Ecc	8:12	a hundred **c** and still lives a long time,	8273
Jer	18:23	Do not forgive their **c** or blot out their sins	6411
	41:11	with him heard about all the **c** Ishmael son	8288
Hos	6: 9	committing shameful **c**.	2365
	7: 1	the sins of Ephraim are exposed and the **c**	8288
Ac	25:18	with any *of* the **c** I had expected.	4505
Rev	18: 5	and God has remembered her **c**.	93

CRIMINAL (4) [CRIME]
Lk	23:40	But the other **c** rebuked him.	NIG
Jn	18:30	"If he were not a **c**," they replied,	2805+4472
2Ti	2: 9	even to the point of being chained like a **c**.	2806
1Pe	4:15	a murderer or thief or any other kind of **c**,	2804

CRIMINALS (4) [CRIME]
1Ki	1:21	I and my son Solomon will be treated as **c**."	2629
Lk	23:32	Two other men, both **c**,	2806
	23:33	there they crucified him, along with the **c**—	2806
	23:39	One *of* the **c** who hung there hurled insults	2806

CRIMSON (5)
2Ch	2: 7	and in purple, **c** and blue yarn	4147
	2:14	with purple and blue and **c** yarn	4147
	3:14	purple and **c** yarn and fine linen,	4147
Isa	1:18	they are red as **c**, they shall be like wool.	9355
	63: 1	from Bozrah, with his garments stained **c**?	2808

CRINGE (4) [CRINGING]
Ps	18:44	foreigners **c** before me.	3950
	66: 3	So great is your power that your enemies **c**	3950
	81:15	Those who hate the LORD *would* **c**	3950
Isa	10: 4	but *to* **c** among the captives or fall among	4156

CRINGING (1) [CRINGE]
2Sa 22:45   and foreigners come **c** to me;   3950

CRIPPLE (1) [CRIPPLED, CRIPPLES]
Ac 4: 9   to a **c** and are asked how he was healed,   476+822

CRIPPLED (15) [CRIPPLE]
Lev	21:19	no man with a **c** foot or hand,	8691
2Sa	4: 4	he fell and became **c**.	7174
	9: 3	he is **c** in both feet."	5783
	9:13	and he was **c** in both feet.	7177
Mal	1: 8	When you sacrifice **c** or diseased animals,	7177
	1:13	**c** or diseased animals and offer them	7177
Mt	15:30	the blind, the **c**, the mute and many others,	3245
	15:31	the **c** made well,	3245
	18: 8	or **c** than to have two hands or two feet	6000
Mk	9:45	for you to enter life **c** than to have two feet	6000
Lk	13:11	a woman was there *who had been* **c** by	819+2400
	14:13	you give a banquet, invite the poor, the **c**,	401
	14:21	the **c**, the blind and the lame.'	401
Ac	3: 2	Now a man **c** from birth was being carried	6000
	14: 8	In Lystra there sat a man **c** in his feet,	105

CRIPPLES (1) [CRIPPLE]
Ac 8: 7   and many paralytics and **c** were healed.   6000

CRISIS (1)
1Co 7:26   Because of the present **c**,   340

CRISPUS (2)
Ac	18: 8	**C**, the synagogue ruler,	3214
1Co	1:14	not baptize any of you except **C** and Gaius,	3214

CRITICAL (1) [CRITICISM]
1Sa 13: 6   of Israel saw that their situation was **c** and   7639

CRITICALLY (1) [CRITICISM]
1Sa 31: 3   they wounded him **c**.   4394

CRITICISM (1) [CRITICAL, CRITICALLY, CRITICIZED]
2Co 8:20   We want to avoid any **c** of   3699

CRITICIZED (2) [CRITICISM]
Jdg	8: 1	And *they* **c** him sharply.	8189
Ac	11: 2	the circumcised believers **c** him	1359

CROCUS (1)
Isa 35: 1   and blossom. Like the **c**,   2483

CROOKED (13)
Dt	32: 5	but a warped and **c** generation.	7350
2Sa	22:27	but to the **c** you show yourself shrewd.	6836
Ps	18:26	but to the **c** you show yourself shrewd.	6836
	125: 5	to **c** ways the LORD will banish with	6824
Pr	2:15	whose paths are **c** and who are devious	6836
	5: 6	her paths *are* **c**, but she knows it not.	5675
	8: 8	none of them is **c** or perverse;	7349
	10: 9	but *he who* takes **c** paths will be found out.	6835
Ecc	7:13	Who can straighten what *he has* made **c**?	6430
Isa	59: 8	*They* have turned them *into* **c** roads;	6835
La	3: 9	he has made my paths **c**.	6390
Lk	3: 5	The **c** roads shall become straight,	5021
Php	2:15	children of God without fault in a **c**	5021

CROP (17) [CROPS]
Ge	47:24	But when the **c** comes in,	9311
Lev	1:16	He is to remove the **c** with its contents	5263
	25:22	the old **c** and will continue to eat from it	9311
Isa	5: 2	Then he looked for a **c** of good grapes,	6913
Am	7: 1	and just as the second **c** was coming up.	4381
Hab	3:17	olive **c** fails and the fields produce no food,	5126
Mt	13: 8	where it produced a **c**—	2843
	13:23	He produces a **c**, yielding a hundred,	2844
	21:41	who will give him his share of the **c**	2843
Mk	4: 8	It came up, grew and produced a **c**,	2843
	4:20	hear the word, accept it, and produce a **c**—	2844
Lk	8: 8	It came up and yielded a **c**,	2843
	8:15	retain it, and by persevering produce a **c**.	2844
	12:16	of a certain rich man produced a good **c**.	2369
Jn	4:36	even now he harvests the **c** for eternal life,	2843
Heb	6: 7	on it and that produces a **c** useful to those	1083
Jas	5: 7	to yield its valuable **c** and how patient he is	2843

CROPS (43) [CROP]
Ge	4:12	it will no longer yield its **c** for you.	3946
	26:12	Isaac planted **c** in that land and	2445
Ex	23:10	to sow your fields and harvest the **c**,	9311
	23:16	with the firstfruits of the **c** you sow	5126
	23:16	when you gather in your **c** from the field.	5126
Lev	23:39	after you have gathered the **c** of the land,	9311
	25: 3	and gather their **c**.	9311
	25:15	the number of years left for harvesting **c**.	9311
	25:16	the number of **c**.	9311
	25:20	if we do not plant or harvest our **c**?"	9311
	26: 4	and the ground will yield its **c** and the trees	3292
	26:20	because your soil will not yield its **c**,	3292
Dt	7:13	the **c** of your land—	7262
	22: 9	not only the **c** you plant but also the fruit of	4852
	28: 4	and the **c** of your land and the young	7262
	28:11	the young of your livestock and the **c**	7262
	28:18	and the **c** of your land and the young	7262
	28:42	over all your trees and the **c** of your land.	7262
	28:51	the **c** of your land until you are destroyed.	7262
	30: 9	of your livestock and the **c** of your land.	7262

Jdg	6: 3	Whenever the Israelites **planted** *their* **c**,	2445
	6: 4	the **c** all the way to Gaza and did not spare	3292
2Sa	9:10	to farm the land for him and bring in the **c**,	NIH
Ne	10:35	the LORD each year the firstfruits of our **c**	141
	10:37	we will bring a tithe of our **c** to the Levites,	141
Job	31: 8	and may my **c** be uprooted.	7368
Ps	65:10	you soften it with showers and bless its **c**.	7542
	78:46	He gave their **c** to the grasshopper,	3292
Pr	3: 9	with the firstfruits of all your **c**;	9311
	10: 5	*He who* **gathers** **c** in summer is a wise son,	112
	28: 3	like a driving rain that leaves no **c**.	4312
Jer	5: 9	to live in or had vineyards, fields or **c**.	2446
Eze	34:27	and the ground will yield its **c**;	3292
	34:29	**land** renowned for its **c**,	4760
	36:30	the fruit of the trees and the **c** *of* the field,	9482
Hag	1:10	and the earth its **c**.	3292
Zec	8:12	the ground will produce its **c**,	3292
Mal	3:11	I will prevent pests from devouring your **c**,	141+2021+7262
Lk	12:17	I have no place to store my **c**.'	2843
Ac	14:17	by giving you rain from heaven and **c**	2845
2Ti	1: 6	be the first to receive a share *of* the **c**.	2843
Jas	5:18	and the earth produced its **c**.	2843
Rev	22: 2	bearing twelve **c** of fruit,	NIG

CROSS (85) [ACROSS, CROSSED, CROSSES, CROSSING, CROSSINGS]

Ex	30:14	All who **c** over,	6296
Nu	32: 5	*Do* not **make** us **c** the Jordan."	6296
	32:27	*will* **c** over to fight before the LORD,	6296
	32:29	**c** over the Jordan with you before	6296
	32:30	But if *they do* not **c** over with you armed,	6296
	32:32	We *will* **c** over before the LORD	6296
	33:51	'When you **c** the Jordan into Canaan,	6296
	34: 4	**c** south of Scorpion Pass,	6015
	35:10	'When you **c** the Jordan into Canaan,	6296
Dt	2:13	"Now get up and **c** the Zered Valley."	6296
	2:24	"Set out now and **c** the Arnon Gorge.	6296
	2:29	until *we* **c** the Jordan into the land	6296
	3:18	*must* **c** over ahead of your brother	6296
	3:27	since *you are* not going to **c** this Jordan.	6296
	4:21	and he solemnly swore that I *would* not **c**	6296
	4:22	I will not **c** the Jordan;	6296
	4:22	*about to* **c** over and take possession of	6296
	9: 1	You *are* now *about to* **c** the Jordan to go	6296
	11:31	You *are about to* **c** the Jordan to enter	6296
	12:10	But *you will* **c** the Jordan and settle in	6296
	30:13	"Who *will* **c** the sea to get it	6296
	31: 2	'You shall not **c** the Jordan.'	6296
	31: 3	The LORD your God himself *will* **c** over	6296
	31: 3	Joshua also *will* **c** over ahead of you,	6296
	34: 4	but *you will* not **c** over into it."	6296
Jos	1: 2	to **c** the Jordan River into the land I am	6296
	1:11	from now you *will* **c** the Jordan here to go	6296
	1:14	*must* **c** over ahead of your brothers.	6296
	3:14	the people broke camp to **c** the Jordan,	6296
Jdg	3:28	they allowed no one to **c** over.	6296
	12: 5	*"Let me* **c** over,"	6296
1Sa	14: 4	to **c** to reach the Philistine outpost was	6296
	14: 8	we *will* **c** over toward the men	6296
	30:10	to **c** the ravine.	6296
2Sa	17:16	**c** over without fail,	6296+6296
	17:21	"Set out and **c** the river at once;	6296
	19:31	down from Rogelim to **c** the Jordan with	6296
	19:33	**"C** over with me and stay with me	6296
	19:36	Your servant *will* **c** over the Jordan	6296
	19:37	*Let him* **c** over with my lord the king.	6296
	19:38	"Kimham *shall* **c** over with me,	6296
1Ki	2:37	The day you leave and **c** the Kidron Valley,	6296
Ps	104: 9	You set a boundary *they* cannot **c**;	6296
Isa	11:15	into seven streams so that *men can* **c** over	2005
	23: 6	**C** over to Tarshish;	6296
	23:12	"Up, **c** over *to* Cyprus;	6296
	51:10	the sea so that the redeemed *might* **c** over?	6296
Jer	2:10	**C** over *to* the coasts of Kittim and look,	6296
	5:22	an everlasting barrier *it* cannot **c**.	6296
	5:22	they may roar, but *they* cannot **c** it.	6296
	9:12	like a desert that no *one can* **c**?	6296
	41:10	and set out to **c** over to the Ammonites.	6296
Eze	33:28	so that no *one will* **c** them.	6296
	47: 5	but now it was a river that I could not **c**,	6296
	47: 5	a river that no *one could* **c**.	6296
Mt	8:18	he gave orders to **c** to the other side of	599
	10:38	not take his **c** and follow me is not worthy	5089
	16:24	he must deny himself and take up his **c**	5089
	27:32	and they forced him to carry the **c**.	5089
	27:40	Come down from the **c**,	5089
	27:42	Let him come down now from the **c**,	5089
Mk	8:34	he must deny himself and take up his **c**	5089
	15:21	and they forced him to carry the **c**.	5089
	15:30	come down from the **c** and save yourself!"	5089
	15:32	come down now from the **c**,	5089
Lk	9:23	take up his **c** daily and follow me.	5089
	14:27	And anyone who does not carry his **c**	5089
	16:26	nor can anyone **c** over from there to us.'	1385
	23:26	and put the **c** on him and made him carry it	5089
Jn	19:17	Carrying his own **c**,	5089
	19:19	a notice prepared and fastened to the **c**.	5089
	19:25	Near the **c** of Jesus stood his mother,	5089
Ac	2:23	**nailing** him to the **c**.	4699
1Co	1:17	lest the **c** of Christ be emptied of its power.	5089
	1:18	For the message *of* the **c** is foolishness	5089
Gal	5:11	the offense *of* the **c** has been abolished.	5089
	6:12	to avoid being persecuted *for* the **c**	5089
	6:14	May I never boast except in the **c**	5089
Eph	2:16	both of them to God through the **c**,	5089

Php	2: 8	obedient to death—even death on a **c**!	5089
	3:18	many live as enemies *of* the **c** of Christ.	5089
Col	1:20	peace through his blood, shed on the **c**.	5089
	2:14	he took it away, nailing it *to* the **c**.	5089
	2:15	triumphing over them by **the c**.	899S
Heb	12: 2	for the joy set before him endured the **c**,	5089

CROSS-EXAMINED (1) [EXAMINE]

| Ac | 12:19 | *he* **c** the guards and ordered that they | 373 |

CROSSBAR (2) [CROSSBARS]

| Ex | 26:28 | The center **c** is to extend from end to end at | 1378 |
| | 36:33 | They made the center **c** so that it extended | 1378 |

CROSSBARS (12) [CROSSBAR]

Ex	26:26	"Also make **c** *of* acacia wood:	1378
	26:29	and make gold rings to hold the **c**.	1378
	26:29	Also overlay the **c** with gold.	1378
	35:11	clasps, frames, **c**, posts and bases;	1378
	36:31	They also made **c** *of* acacia wood:	1378
	36:34	and made gold rings to hold the **c**.	1378
	36:34	They also overlaid the **c** with gold.	1378
	39:33	its clasps, frames, **c**, posts and bases;	1378
	40:18	inserted the **c** and set up the posts.	1378
Nu	3:36	its **c**, posts, bases, all its equipment,	1378
	4:31	to carry the frames of the tabernacle, its **c**,	1378
Jer	27: 2	"Make a yoke out of straps and **c** and put it	4574

CROSSED (58) [CROSS]

Ge	32:10	I had only my staff *when I* **c** this Jordan,	6296
	32:22	and his eleven sons and **c** the ford of	6296
Ex	38:26	from everyone who *had* **c** over	6296
Dt	2:13	So *we* **c** the valley.	6296
	2:14	the time we left Kadesh Barnea until *we* **c**	6296
	27: 2	When *you have* **c** the Jordan into the land	6296
	27: 3	the words of this law when you *have* **c** over	6296
	27: 4	And when you *have* **c** the Jordan,	6296
	27:12	When you *have* **c** the Jordan,	6296
Jos	3:16	So the people **c** over opposite Jericho.	6296
	4: 7	When it **c** the Jordan,	6296
	4:11	and as soon as all of them *had* **c**,	6296
	4:12	Gad and the half-tribe of Manasseh **c** over,	6296
	4:13	for battle **c** over before the LORD to	6296
	4:22	'Israel **c** the Jordan on dry ground.'	6296
	4:23	the Jordan before you until you *had* **c** over.	6296
	4:23	up before us until we *had* **c** over.	6296
	5: 1	before the Israelites until we *had* **c** over,	6296
	15: 3	**c** south of Scorpion Pass,	3655
	15:10	down to Beth Shemesh and **c** *to* Timnah.	6296
	16: 2	**c** over to the territory of the Arkites	6296
	18:13	From there it **c** to the south slope of Luz	6296
	24:11	*you* **c** the Jordan and came to Jericho.	6296
Jdg	6:33	and **c** over the Jordan and camped in	6296
	8: 4	came to the Jordan and **c** it.	6296
	10: 9	The Ammonites also **c** the Jordan to fight	6296
	11:29	*He* **c** Gilead and Manasseh,	6296
	12: 1	**c** over to Zaphon and said to Jephthah,	6296
	12: 3	I took my life in my hands and **c** over	6296
1Sa	13: 7	even **c** the Jordan to the land of Gad	6296
	26:13	Then David **c** over *to* the other side	6296
2Sa	2:29	*They* **c** the Jordan,	6296
	10:17	**c** the Jordan and went to Helam.	6296
	15:23	The king also **c** the Kidron Valley,	6296
	17:20	*"They* **c** over the brook."	6296
	17:22	and all the people with him set out and **c**	6296
	17:22	no one was left who *had* not **c** the Jordan.	6296
	17:24	and Absalom **c** the Jordan with all the men	6296
	19:18	*They* **c** at the ford to take	6296
	19:18	When Shimei son of Gera **c** the Jordan,	6296
	19:39	So all the people **c** the Jordan,	6296
	19:39	and then the king **c** over.	6296
	19:40	When the king **c** over to Gilgal,	6296
	19:40	Kimham **c** with him.	6296
2Ki	2: 8	and the two of them **c** over on dry ground.	6296
	2: 9	When they *had* **c**, Elijah said to Elisha,	6296
	2:14	and he **c** over.	6296
1Ch	12:15	It was they who **c** the Jordan in	6296
	19:17	he gathered all Israel and **c** the Jordan;	6296
Mt	9: 1	**c** over and came to his own town.	1385
	14:34	When they *had* **c** over,	1385
Mk	5:21	When Jesus *had* again **c** over by boat to	1385
	6:53	When they *had* **c** over,	1385
	8:13	into the boat and **c** to the other side.	599
Jn	5:24	*he* has **c** over from death to life.	3553
	6: 1	Jesus **c** to the far shore of the Sea	599
	18: 1	with his disciples and **c** the Kidron Valley,	4305
Ac	20:15	The day after that *we* **c** over to Samos,	4125

CROSSES (2) [CROSS]

| Ex | 30:13 | Each *one* who **c** over | 6296 |
| Jn | 19:31 | the bodies left on the **c** during the Sabbath, | 5089 |

CROSSING (16) [CROSS]

Ge	31:21	So he fled with all he had, and **c** the River,	6296
	48:14	though he was the younger, and **c** his arms,	8506
Dt	4:14	that *you are* **c** the Jordan to possess.	6296
	4:26	from the land that *you are* **c** the Jordan	6296
	6: 1	that *you are* **c** the Jordan to possess,	6296
	11: 8	in and take over the land that *you are* **c**	6296
	11:11	But the land you *are* **c** the Jordan	6296
	30:18	You will not live long in the land you *are* **c**	6296
	31:13	as you live in the land *you are* **c** the Jordan	6296
	32:47	the land you *are* **c** the Jordan to possess."	6296

Jos	3: 1	where they camped before **c** over.	6296
	3:17	until the whole nation had completed the **c**	6296
	4: 1	the whole nation had finished **c** the Jordan,	6296
2Sa	24: 1	After **c** the Jordan,	6296
Da	8: 5	**c** the whole earth without touching	6584+7156
Ac	21: 2	We found a ship **c** over to Phoenicia,	1385

CROSSINGS (1) [CROSS]

| Jer | 51:32 | the **river c** seized, the marshes set on fire, | 5045 |

CROSSROADS (2) [ROAD]

| Jer | 6:16 | "Stand at the **c** and look; | 2006 |
| Ob | 1:14 | not wait at the **c** to cut down their fugitives, | 7294 |

CROUCH (3) [CROUCHES, CROUCHING]

Nu	24: 9	Like a lion *they* **c** and lie down,	4156
Job	38:40	when *they* **c** in their dens or lie in wait in	8820
	39: 3	*They* **down** and bring forth their young;	4156

CROUCHES (1) [CROUCH]

| Ge | 49: 9 | Like a lion *he* **c** and lies down, | 4156 |

CROUCHING (2) [CROUCH]

| Ge | 4: 7 | sin *is* **c** at your door; | 8069 |
| Ps | 17:12 | like a great lion **c** in cover. | 3782 |

CROW (1) [CROWED, CROWS]

| Jn | 18:27 | and at that moment a rooster *began to* **c**. | 5888 |

CROWD (136) [CROWDED, CROWDING, CROWDS]

Ex	23: 2	"Do not follow the **c** in doing wrong.	8041
	23: 2	do not pervert justice by siding with the **c**,	8041
Jdg	6:31	Joash replied to the hostile **c** around him,	889+3972+6641
2Sa	6:19	to each person in the whole **c** of Israelites,	2162
2Ch	30:13	A very large **c** of people assembled	7736
	30:17	in the **c** had not consecrated themselves,	7736
Ezr	10: 1	a large **c** of Israelites—	7736
Job	31:34	so feared the **c** and so dreaded the contempt	2162
Ps	64: 2	from that **noisy c** of evildoers.	8095
Jer	9: 2	a **c** of unfaithful people.	6809
Eze	7:11	none of that **c**—no wealth, nothing of value.	2162
	7:12	for wrath is upon the whole **c**.	2162
	7:13	the vision concerning the whole **c** will not	2162
	7:14	for my wrath is upon the whole **c**,	2162
	23:42	"The noise of a carefree **c** was around her;	2162
Mt	8:18	When Jesus saw the **c** around him,	4063
	9: 8	When the **c** saw this,	4063
	9:23	and saw the flute players and the noisy **c**,	4063
	9:25	After the **c** had been put outside,	4063
	9:33	T'. ` was amazed and said,	4063
	11: 7	Jesus began to speak *to* the **c** about John:	4063
	12:46	While Jesus was still talking *to* the **c**,	4063
	13:34	Jesus spoke all these things *to* the **c**	4063
	13:36	Then he left the **c** and went into the house.	4063
	14:14	When Jesus landed and saw a large **c**,	4063
	14:22	while he dismissed the **c**.	4063
	15:10	Jesus called the **c** to him and said,	4063
	15:33	in this remote place to feed such a **c**?"	4063
	15:35	He told the **c** to sit down on the ground.	4063
	15:39	After Jesus had sent the **c** away,	4063
	17:14	When they came to the **c**,	4063
	20:29	a large **c** followed him.	4063
	20:31	The **c** rebuked them and told them to	4063
	21: 8	A very large **c** spread their cloaks on	4063
	21:46	the **c** because the people held that he was	4063
	26:47	With him was a large **c** armed with swords	4063
	26:55	At that time Jesus said *to* the **c**,	4063
	27:15	to release a prisoner chosen *by* the **c**.	4063
	27:17	So when **the c** had gathered,	899S
	27:20	and the elders persuaded the **c** to ask	4063
	27:24	and washed his hands in front of the **c**.	4063
Mk	2: 4	not get him to Jesus because of the **c**,	4063
	2:13	A large **c** came to him,	4063
	3: 7	and a large **c** from Galilee followed.	4436
	3: 9	Because of the **c** he told his disciples	4063
	3:20	and again a **c** gathered,	4063
	3:32	A **c** was sitting around him,	4063
	4: 1	The **c** that gathered around him was	4063
	4:36	Leaving the **c** behind, they took him along,	4063
	5:21	a large **c** gathered around him while he was	4063
	5:24	A large **c** followed and pressed	4063
	5:27	behind him in the **c** and touched his cloak,	4063
	5:30	He turned around in the **c** and asked,	4063
	6:34	When Jesus landed and saw a large **c**,	4063
	6:45	while he dismissed the **c**.	4063
	7:14	Again Jesus called the **c** to him and said,	4063
	7:17	After he had left the **c** and entered	4063
	7:33	After he took him aside, away from the **c**,	4063
	8: 1	During those days another large **c** gathered.	4063
	8: 6	He told the **c** to sit down on the ground.	4063
	8:34	the **c** to him along with his disciples	4063
	9:14	a large **c** around them and the teachers of	4063
	9:17	A man in the **c** answered, "Teacher,	4063
	9:25	When Jesus saw that a **c** was running to	4063
	10:46	together with a large **c**,	4063
	11:18	the whole **c** was amazed at his teaching.	4063
	12:12	But they were afraid of the **c**;	4063
	12:37	The large **c** listened to him with delight.	4063
	12:41	and watched the **c** putting their money into	4063
	14:43	With him was a **c** armed with swords	4063

Mk	15: 8	The c came up and asked Pilate to do	4063
	15:11	But the chief priests stirred up the c	4063
	15:15	Wanting to satisfy the c,	4063
Lk	3:10	"What should we do then?" the c asked.	4063
	4:30	But he walked right through the c and went	NIG
	5:19	not find a way to do this because of the c,	4063
	5:19	through the tiles into the middle of the c,	NIG
	5:29	and a large c of tax collectors	4063
	6:17	A large c of his disciples was there and	4063
	7: 9	and turning to the c following him,	4063
	7:11	and his disciples and a large c went along	4063
	7:12	And a large c from the town was with her.	4063
	7:24	Jesus began to speak to the c about John:	4063
	8: 4	While a large c was gathering	4063
	8:19	not able to get near him because of the c.	4063
	8:40	when Jesus returned, a c welcomed him,	4063
	9:12	"Send the c away so they can go to	4063
	9:13	unless we go and buy food for all this c."	3295
	9:37	a large c met him.	4063
	9:38	A man in the c called out, "Teacher,	4063
	11:14	and the c was amazed.	4063
	11:27	a woman in the c called out,	4063
	12: 1	when a c of many thousands had gathered,	4063
	12:13	Someone in the c said to him, "Teacher,	4063
	12:54	He said to the c:	4063
	18:36	When he heard the c going by,	4063
	19: 3	because of the c,	4063
	19:37	the whole c of disciples began joyfully	4436
	19:39	of the Pharisees in the c said to Jesus,	4063
	22: 6	over to them when no c was present.	4063
	22:47	While he was still speaking a c came up,	4063
	23: 4	to the chief priests and the c,	4063
Jn	5:13	for Jesus had slipped away into the c.	4063
	6: 2	and a great c of people followed him	4063
	6: 5	up and saw a great c coming toward him,	4063
	6:22	the c that had stayed on the opposite shore	4063
	6:24	Once the c realized that neither Jesus	4063
	7:20	"You are demon-possessed," the c answered	4063
	7:31	Still, many in the c put their faith in him.	4063
	7:32	the c whispering such things about him.	4063
	12: 9	Meanwhile a large c of Jews found out	4063
	12:12	The next day the great c that had come for	4063
	12:17	Now the c that was with him	4063
	12:29	The c that was there and heard it	4063
	12:34	The c spoke up, "We have heard	4063
Ac	2: 6	a c came together in bewilderment,	4436
	2:14	raised his voice and addressed the c:	899S
	14:11	When the c saw what Paul had done,	4063
	14:14	the city gates because he and the c wanted	4063
	14:14	and rushed out into the c, shouting:	4063
	14:18	they had difficulty keeping the c	4063
	14:19	and Iconium and won the c over.	4063
	16:22	The c joined in the attack against Paul	4063
	17: 5	in order to bring them out to the c.	1322
	17: 8	the c and the city officials were thrown	4063
	19:30	Paul wanted to appear before the c,	1322
	19:33	some of the c shouted instructions to him.	4063
	19:35	The city clerk quieted the c and said:	4063
	21:27	They stirred up the whole c and seized him,	4063
	21:32	and soldiers and ran down to the c.	899S
	21:34	The c shouted one thing and some another,	4063
	21:36	c that followed kept shouting,	3295+3836+4436
	21:40	on the steps and motioned to the c.	3295
	22:22	The c listened to Paul until he said this.	NIG
	24:12	up a c in the synagogues or anywhere else	4063
	24:18	There was no c with me,	4063

CROWDED (4) [CROWD]

Jdg	16:27	the temple was c with men and women;	4848
2Ki	10:21	They c into the temple of Baal	995
Jer	26: 9	the people c around Jeremiah in the house	7735
Da	3:27	governors and royal advisers c around	10359

CROWDING (4) [CROWD]

Mk	3: 9	to keep the people from c him.	2567
	5:31	"You see the people c against you,"	5315
Lk	5: 1	with the people c around him and listening	2130
	8:45	c and pressing against	5309

CROWDS (27) [CROWD]

Mt	4:25	Large c from Galilee, the Decapolis,	4063
	5: 1	Now when he saw the c,	4063
	7:28	the c were amazed at his teaching,	4063
	8: 1	large c followed him.	4063
	9:36	When he saw the c,	4063
	13: 2	Such large c gathered around him	4063
	14:13	the c followed him on foot from the towns	4063
	14:15	Send the c away,	4063
	15:30	Great c came to him, bringing the lame,	4063
	19: 2	Large c followed him,	4063
	21: 9	The c that went ahead of him and those	4063
	21:11	The c answered, "This is Jesus,	4063
	22:33	When the c heard this,	4063
	23: 1	Jesus said to the c and to his disciples:	4063
Mk	10: 1	Again c of people came to him,	4063
Lk	3: 7	to the c coming out to be baptized by him,	4063
	5:15	so that c of people came to hear him and	4063
	8:42	the c almost crushed him.	4063
	9:11	but the c learned about it and followed him.	4063
	9:18	he asked them, "Who do the c say I am?"	4063
	11:29	As the c increased, Jesus said,	4063
	14:25	Large c were traveling with Jesus,	4063
Jn	7:12	the c there was widespread whispering	4063
Ac	5:16	gathered also from the towns	4436
	8: 6	When the c heard Philip and saw	4063

Ac	13:45	When the Jews saw the c,	4063
	17:13	agitating the c and stirring them up.	4063

CROWED (3) [CROW]

Mt	26:74	Immediately a rooster c.	5888
Mk	14:72	Immediately the rooster c the second time.	5888
Lk	22:60	Just as he was speaking, the rooster c.	5888

CROWN (53) [CROWNED, CROWNS]

Jdg	9: 6	the pillar in Shechem to c Abimelech king.	4887
2Sa	1:10	And I took the c that was on his head and	5694
	12:30	He took the c from the head of their king—	6498
2Ki	11:12	the king's son and put the c on him;	5694
1Ch	20: 2	the c from the head of their king—	6498
2Ch	23:11	the king's son and put the c on him;	5694
Est	1:11	wearing her royal c,	4195
	2:17	So he set a royal c on her head	4195
	8:15	a large c of gold and a purple robe	6498
Job	19: 9	and removed the c from my head.	6498
	31:36	I would put it on like a c.	6498
Ps	21: 3	and placed a c of pure gold on his head.	6498
	65:11	You c the year with your bounty,	6497
	89:39	with your servant and have defiled his c in	5694
	132:18	but the c on his head will be resplendent."	5694
Pr	4: 9	and present you with a c of splendor."	6498
	10: 6	Blessings c the head of the righteous,	4200
	12: 4	wife of noble character is her husband's c,	6498
	14:24	The wealth of the wise is their c,	6498
	16:31	Gray hair is a c of splendor;	6498
	17: 6	Children's children are a c to the aged,	6498
	27:24	and a c is not secure for all generations.	5694
SS	3:11	and look at King Solomon wearing the c,	6498
	3:11	the c with which his mother crowned him	NIH
Isa	28: 5	the LORD Almighty will be a glorious c,	7619
	35:10	everlasting joy will c their heads.	6584
	51:11	everlasting joy will c their heads.	6584
	61: 3	to bestow on them a c of beauty instead	6996
	62: 3	be a c of splendor in the LORD's hand,	6498
Jer	2:16	the c of your head.	7721
La	5:16	The c has fallen from our head.	6498
Eze	16:12	earrings on your ears and a beautiful c	6498
	21:26	Take off the turban, remove the c.	5694
Zec	6:11	Take the silver and gold and make a c,	6498
	6:14	The c will be given to Heldai, Tobijah,	6498
	9:16	in his land like jewels in a c.	6498
Mt	27:29	then twisted together a c of thorns and set it	5109
Mk	15:17	then twisted together a c of thorns and set it	5109
Jn	19: 2	The soldiers twisted together a c of thorns	5109
	19: 5	When Jesus came out wearing the c	5109
1Co	9:25	They do it to get a c that will not last;	5109
	9:25	but we do it to get a c that will last forever.	NIG
Php	4: 1	my joy and c,	5109
1Th	2:19	the c in which we will glory in the presence	5109
2Ti	2: 5	he does not receive the victor's c	5110
	4: 8	the c of righteousness, which the Lord,	5109
Jas	1:12	the c of life that God has promised	5109
1Pe	5: 4	the c of glory that will never fade away.	5109
Rev	2:10	and I will give you the c of life.	5109
	3:11	so that no one will take your c.	5109
	6: 2	Its rider held a bow, and he was given a c,	5109
	12: 1	under her feet and a c of twelve stars	5109
	14:14	a son of man" with a c of gold on his head	5109

CROWNED (5) [CROWN]

Ps	8: 5	the heavenly beings and c him with glory	6497
Pr	14:18	but the prudent are c with knowledge.	4194
SS	3:11	the crown with which his mother c him on	6497
Heb	2: 7	you c him with glory and honor	5110
	2: 9	now c with glory and honor	5110

CROWNS (14) [CROWN]

Ps	68:21	the hairy c of those who go on in their sins.	7721
	103: 4	and c you with love and compassion,	6497
	149: 4	he c the humble with salvation.	6995
Pr	11:26	blessing c him who is willing to sell.	4200+8031
SS	7: 5	Your head c you like Mount Carmel.	6584
Isa	23: 8	the bestower of c,	6497
Jer	13:18	your glorious c will fall from your heads."	6498
Eze	23:42	of the woman and her sister and beautiful c	6498
Rev	4: 4	in white and had c of gold on their heads.	5109
	4:10	They lay their c before the throne and say:	5109
	9: 7	On their heads they wore something like c	5109
	12: 3	with seven heads and ten horns and seven c	1343
	13: 1	with ten c on his horns,	1343
	19:12	and on his head are many c.	1343

CROWS (8) [CROW]

Mt	26:34	"this very night, before the rooster c, you will disown me three times."	5888
	26:75	"Before the rooster c, you will disown me three times."	5888
Mk	13:35	or at midnight, or when the rooster c,	231
	14:30	before the rooster c twice you yourself will disown me three times."	5888
	14:72	"Before the rooster c twice you will disown me three times."	5888
Lk	22:34	Peter, before the rooster c today,	5888
	22:61	"Before the rooster c today,	5888
Jn	13:38	I tell you the truth, before the rooster c,	5888

CRUCIBLE (2)

Pr	17: 3	The c for silver and the furnace for gold,	5214
	27:21	The c for silver and the furnace for gold,	5214

CRUCIFIED (36) [CRUCIFY]

Mt	20:19	to be mocked and flogged and c."	5090
	26: 2	Son of Man will be handed over to be c."	5090
	27:26	and handed him over to be c.	5090
	27:35	When they had c him,	5090
	27:38	Two robbers were c with him,	5090
	27:44	the same way the robbers who were c with	5365
	28: 5	that you are looking for Jesus, who was c.	5090
Mk	15:15	and handed him over to be c.	5090
	15:24	And they c him.	5090
	15:25	It was the third hour when they c him.	5090
	15:27	They c two robbers with him,	5090
	15:32	Those c with him also heaped insults	5365
Lk	23:23	for Jesus the Nazarene, who was c.	5090
	23:23	they insistently demanded that he be c,	5090
	23:33	there they c him, along with	5090
	24: 7	be c and on the third day be raised again.' "	5090
	24:20	sentenced to death, and they c him;	5090
Jn	19:16	over to them to be c.	5090
	19:18	Here they c him, with	5090
	19:20	place where Jesus was c was near the city,	5090
	19:23	When the soldiers c Jesus,	5090
	19:32	of the first man who had been c with Jesus,	5365
	19:41	At the place where Jesus was c,	5090
Ac	2:36	God has made this Jesus, whom you c,	5090
	4:10	of Jesus Christ of Nazareth, whom you c	5090
Ro	6: 6	For we know that our old self was c with	5365
1Co	1:13	Was Paul c for you?	5090
	1:23	but we preach Christ c:	5090
	2: 2	with you except Jesus Christ and him c.	5090
	2: 8	they would not have c the Lord of glory.	5090
2Co	13: 4	For to be sure, he was c in weakness,	5090
Gal	2:20	I have been c with Christ	5365
	3: 1	Before your very eyes Jesus Christ was clearly portrayed as c.	5090
	5:24	Those who belong to Christ Jesus have c	5090
	6:14	through which the world has been c to me,	5090
Rev	11: 8	where also their Lord was c.	5090

CRUCIFY (15) [CRUCIFIED, CRUCIFYING]

Mt	23:34	Some of them you will kill and c;	5090
	27:22	They all answered, "C him!"	5090
	27:23	But they shouted all the louder, "C him!"	5090
	27:31	Then they led him away to c him.	5090
Mk	15:13	"C him!" they shouted.	5090
	15:14	But they shouted all the louder, "C him!"	5090
	15:20	Then they led him out to c him.	5090
Lk	23:21	But they kept shouting, "C him!	5090
	23:21	"Crucify him! C him!"	5090
Jn	19: 6	their officials saw him, they shouted, "C!	5090
	19: 6	they shouted, "Crucify! C!"	5090
	19: 6	"You take him and c him.	5090
	19:10	either to free you or to c you?"	5090
	19:15	Take him away! C him!"	5090
	19:15	"Shall I c your king?"	5090

CRUCIFYING (1) [CRUCIFY]

Heb	6: 6	c the Son of God all over again	416

CRUEL (16) [CRUELLY, CRUELTY]

Ge	49: 7	so fierce, and their fury, so c!	7996
Ex	6: 9	of their discouragement and c bondage.	7997
Dt	28:33	but c oppression all your days.	8368
Ps	71: 4	from the grasp of evil and c men.	2807
Pr	5: 9	to others and your years to one who is c,	426
	11:17	but a c man brings trouble on himself.	426
	12:10	but the kindest acts of the wicked are c.	426
		Anger is c and fury overwhelming,	427
Ecc	9:12	As fish are caught in a c net,	8273
Isa	13: 9	a c day, with wrath and fierce anger—	426
	14: 3	from suffering and turmoil and c bondage,	7997
	19: 4	over to the power of a c master,	7997
Jer	6:23	they are c and show no mercy.	426
	15:21	and redeem you from the grasp of the c."	6883
	30:14	and punished you as would the c,	426
	50:42	they are c and without mercy.	426

CRUELLY (1) [CRUEL]

Jdg	4: 3	and had c oppressed the Israelites	928+2622

CRUELTY (1) [CRUEL]

Na	3:19	for who has not felt your endless c?	8288

CRUMBLE (2) [CRUMBLED, CRUMBLES, CRUMBLING]

Lev	2: 6	C it and pour oil on it; it is a grain offering.	7326+7359
Eze	38:20	the cliffs will c and every wall will fall to	5877

CRUMBLED (1) [CRUMBLE]

Hab	3: 6	The ancient mountains c and	7207

CRUMBLES (1) [CRUMBLE]

Job	14:18	"But as a mountain erodes and c and as	5570

CRUMBLING (1) [CRUMBLE]

Job	15:28	houses c to rubble.	6963

CRUMBS (2)

Mt	15:27	the c that fall from their masters' table."	6033

Mk 7:28 under the table eat the children's **c**." 6033

CRUSE (KJV) See JUG, JAR

CRUSH (27) [CRUSHED, CRUSHES, CRUSHING]

Ge	3:15	he *will* **c** your head, and you will strike	8789
Nu	24:17	*He will* **c** the foreheads of Moab,	4730
Job	6: 9	that God would be willing *to* **c** me,	1917
	9:17	He *would* **c** me with a storm	8789
	19: 2	"How long will you torment me and **c** me	1917
	24:11	*They* **c** olives among the terraces;	7414
	39:15	unmindful that a foot *may* **c** them,	2318
	40:12	**c** the wicked where they stand.	2070
Ps	68:21	God *will* **c** the heads of his enemies,	4730
	72: 4	he *will* **c** the oppressor.	1917
	74: 8	*"We will* **c** them completely!"	3561
	89:23	*I will* **c** his foes before him and strike	4198
	94: 5	*They* **c** your people, O LORD;	1917
	110: 5	he *will* **c** kings on the day of his wrath.	4730
Pr	22:22	and do not **c** the needy in court,	1917
Isa	14:25	I *will* **c** the Assyrian in my land;	8689
	41:15	You will thresh the mountains and **c** them,	1990
	53:10	the LORD's will *to* **c** him and cause him	1917
Jer	50:17	*to* **c** his **bones** was Nebuchadnezzar king	6793
La	1:15	an army against me *to* **c** my young men.	8689
	3:34	To **c** underfoot all prisoners in the land,	1917
Da	2:40	so *it will* **c** and break all the others.	10182
	2:44	*It will* **c** all those kingdoms	10182
Am	2:13	I *will* **c** you as a cart crushes when loaded	6421
	4: 1	and **c** the needy and say to your husbands,	8368
Mic	6:15	you will **c** grapes but not drink the wine.	NIH
Ro	16:20	The God of peace *will* soon **c** Satan	5341

CRUSHED (45) [CRUSH]

Lev	2:14	offer **c** heads of new grain roasted in	1762
	2:16	the memorial portion of the **c grain** and	1762
	22:24	an animal whose testicles are bruised, **c**,	4198
Nu	11: 8	ground it in a handmill or **c** it in a mortar.	1870
Dt	9:21	Then *I* **c** it and ground it to powder as fine	4198
Jdg	5:26	She struck Sisera, *she* **c** his head,	4735
	10: 8	who that year shattered and **c** them.	8368
2Sa	22:38	"I pursued my enemies and **c** them;	9012
	22:39	*I* **c** them **completely;**	430+2256+4730
2Ch	14:13	*they* were **c** before the LORD	8689
	15: 6	One nation was *being* **c** by another	4198
	34: 7	the altars and the Asherah poles and **c**	4198
Job	4:19	who *are* **c** more readily than a moth!	1917
	5: 4	**c** in court without a defender.	1917
	16:12	he seized me by the neck and **c** me.	7207
	34:25	in the night and *they are* **c**.	1917
Ps	10:10	His victims are **c**, they collapse;	1920
	18:38	*I* **c** them so that they could not rise;	4730
	34:18	and saves *those who* are **c** in spirit.	1918
	38: 8	I am feeble and utterly **c**;	1920
	44: 2	*you* **c** the peoples	8317
	44:19	But *you* **c** us and made us a haunt	1920
	51: 8	let the bones *you* have **c** rejoice.	1920
	74:14	It was you *who* **c** the heads of Leviathan	8368
	89:10	You **c** Rahab like one of the slain;	1917
Pr	17:22	but a **c** spirit dries up the bones.	5779
	18:14	but a **c** spirit who can bear?	5779
Isa	21:10	O my people, **c** *on* the threshing floor,	4536
	23:12	O Virgin Daughter of Sidon, *now* **c**!	6943
	27: 9	to be like chalk stones **c to pieces,**	5879
	53: 5	*he* was **c** for our iniquities;	1917
Jer	5: 3	*you* **c** them, but they refused correction.	3983
	8:21	Since my people are **c**, I am crushed;	8691
	8:21	Since my people are crushed, *I am* **c**;	8689
	22:20	for all your allies are **c**.	8689
Eze	30: 8	I set fire to Egypt and all her helpers are **c**.	8689
Da	6:24	and **c** all their bones.	10182
	7: 7	*it* **c** and devoured its victims	10182
	7:19	the beast *that* **c** and devoured its victims	10182
Hab	3:13	*You* **c** the leader of the land of wickedness,	4730
Mal	1: 4	Edom may say, *"Though we have* been **c**,	8406
Mt	21:44	but *he* on whom it falls *will* be **c**."	3347
Lk	8:42	the crowds *almost* **c** him.	5231
	20:18	but *he* on whom it falls *will* be **c**."	3347
2Co	4: 8	on every side, but not **c**;	5102

CRUSHES (4) [CRUSH]

Ps	143: 3	*he* **c** me to the ground;	1917
Pr	15: 4	but a deceitful tongue **c** the spirit.	8691
	15:13	but heartache **c** the spirit.	5779
Am	2:13	I will crush you as a cart **c** when loaded	6421

CRUSHING (6) [CRUSH]

Nu	22:25	close to the wall, **c** Balaam's foot against it.	4315
Dt	23: 1	by **c** or cutting may enter the assembly of	1918
Ps	110: 6	the dead and **c** the rulers of the whole earth.	4730
Isa	3:15	by **c** my people and grinding the faces of	1917
Jer	14:17	suffered a grievous wound, a **c** blow.	2703+4394
Da	7:23	trampling it down and **c** it.	10182

CRUST (2) [ENCRUSTED]

1Sa	2:36	before him for a piece of silver and a **c**	3971
Pr	17: 1	Better a dry **c** with peace and quiet than	7326

CRUTCH (1)

2Sa	3:29	or leprosy or who leans on a **c** or who falls	7134

CRY (168) [CRIED, CRIES, CRYING]

Ge	27:34	a loud and bitter **c** and said to his father,	7591
Ex	2:23	and their **c** for help because	8784
	3: 9	now the **c** *of* the Israelites has reached me,	8784
	22:23	If you do and *they* **c** out to me,	7590+7590
	22:23	I will certainly hear their **c**.	7591
Lev	13:45	cover the lower part of his face and **c out,**	7924
Nu	20:16	he heard our **c** and sent an angel	7754
Dt	24:15	Otherwise *he may* **c** to the LORD	7924
	33: 7	"Hear, O LORD, the **c** of Judah;	7754
Jos	6:10	"*Do* not **give** a **war c,**	8131
Jdg	10:14	Go and **c** out to the gods you have chosen.	2410
1Sa	4:13	the whole town **sent up a c.**	2410
	8:18	*you will* **c** out for relief from	2410
	9:16	for their **c** has reached me."	7591
	17:20	shouting the **war c**.	4878
2Sa	22: 7	my **c** came to his ears.	8784
1Ki	8:28	Hear the **c** and the prayer	8262
	8:52	to them whenever they **c** out to you.	7924
	17:22	The LORD heard Elijah's **c**,	7754
	22:36	a **c** spread through the army:	8262
1Ch	16:35	**C** out, "Save us, O God our Savior,	606
2Ch	6:19	Hear the **c** and the prayer	8262
	13:12	the **battle c** against you.	9558
	13:15	and the men of Judah **raised the battle c.**	8131
	13:15	**sound** of their **battle c,**	8131
	20: 9	and *will* **c** out to you in our distress,	2410
Ne	9: 9	you heard their **c** at the Red Sea.	2411
Job	16:18	may my **c** never be laid to rest!	2411
	19: 7	"Though *I* **c**, 'I've been wronged!'	7590
	24:12	the souls of the wounded **c** for help,	8775
	27: 9	to his **c** when distress comes upon him?	7591
	30:20	"*I* **c** out to you, O God,	7775
	30:28	I stand up in the assembly and **c** for help.	8775
	34:28	They caused the **c** of the poor to come	7591
	34:28	so that he heard the **c** of the needy.	7591
	35: 9	"*Men* **c** out under a load of oppression;	2410
	35:12	when *men* **c** out because of the arrogance	7590
	36:13	he fetters them, *they* do not **c** for help.	8775
	38:41	for the raven when its young **c** out to God	8775
	39:25	shout of commanders and the **battle c**.	9558
Ps	3: 4	To the LORD *I* **c** aloud,	7924
	5: 2	Listen to my **c** for help,	7754+9384
	6: 9	The LORD has heard my **c** for mercy;	9382
	9:12	he does not ignore the **c** of the afflicted.	7591
	10:17	and you listen to their **c**,	NIH
	17: 1	listen to my **c**.	8262
	18: 6	my **c** came before him, into his ears.	8784
	22: 2	O my God, *I* **c** out by day,	7924
	22:24	from him but has listened to his **c for help.**	8775
	28: 2	Hear my **c** for mercy as I call to you	7754+9384
	28: 6	for he has heard my **c** for mercy.	7754+9384
	29: 9	And in his temple all **c**, "Glory!"	606
	31:22	Yet you heard my **c** for mercy	7754+9384
	34:15	and his ears are attentive to their **c**;	8784
	34:17	The righteous **c** out, and	7590
	39:12	O LORD, listen to my **c** for help;	8784
	40: 1	he turned to me and heard my **c**.	8784
	55:17	morning and noon *I* **c** out in distress,	2159
	57: 2	*I* **c** out to God Most High, to God,	7924
	61: 1	Hear my **c**, O God; listen to my prayer.	8262
	72:12	For he will deliver the needy *who* **c** out,	8775
	84: 2	and my flesh **c** out for the living God.	8264
	86: 6	listen to my **c** for mercy.	7754+9384
	88: 1	day and night *I* **c** out before you.	7590
	88: 2	turn your ear to my **c**.	8262
	88:13	**c** to you for help,	8775
	102: 1	let my **c** for help come to you.	8775
	106:44	of their distress when he heard their **c**;	8262
	116: 1	he heard my **c** for mercy.	9384
	119:147	I rise before dawn and **c** for help;	8775
	119:169	May my **c** come before you, O LORD;	8262
	130: 1	Out of the depths *I* **c** to you, O LORD;	7924
	130: 2	be attentive to my **c** for mercy.	7754+9384
	140: 6	Hear, O LORD, my **c** for mercy.	7754+9384
	142: 1	*I* **c** aloud to the LORD;	2410
	142: 1	*I* **c** to you, O LORD;	2410
	142: 5	I **c** to you, O LORD; I am in desperate need;	8262
	143: 1	hear my prayer, listen to my **c** for mercy;	9384
	144:14	no **c** of distress in our streets.	7424
	145:19	he hears their **c** and saves them.	8784
Pr	2: 3	and **c** aloud for understanding,	5989+7754
	21:13	If a man shuts his ears to the **c** *of* the poor,	2411
	21:13	he too *will* **c** out and not be answered.	7924
	30:15	"The leech has two daughters. 'Give! Give!' they **c**.	NIH
Isa	3: 7	But in that day *he will* **c** out,	606+4200+5951
	8: 9	**Raise the war c**, *you* nations,	8131
	10:30	**C** out, O Daughter of Gallim!	7412+7754
	15: 4	Heshbon and Elealeh **c** out,	2410
	15: 4	Therefore the armed men of Moab **c** out,	8131
	19:20	When *they* **c** out to the LORD because	7590
	24:11	In the streets they **c** out for wine;	7424
	30:19	How gracious he will be when you **c** for help!	2410+7754
	33: 7	their brave men **c** aloud in the streets;	7590
	40: 6	A voice says, "**C** out."	7924
	40: 6	And I said, "What *shall I* **c**?"	7924
	42: 2	He will not shout or **c** out,	9048
	42:13	with a shout *he* will **raise the battle c**	7658
	42:14	now, like a woman in childbirth, *I* **c** out,	7184
	57:13	When you **c** out for help,	2410
	58: 9	*you* will **c** for help, and he will say:	8775
	65:14	*My servants* will **c** out from anguish of heart	7590
Jer	3:21	A **c** is heard on the barren heights,	7754
	4: 5	**C** aloud and say: 'Gather together!	7924

Jer	4:16	raising a **war c** against the cities of Judah.	7754
	4:19	I have heard the battle **c**.	9558
	4:31	I hear a **c** as of a woman in labor,	7754
	4:31	the **c** of the Daughter of Zion gasping	2410
	8:19	the **c** of my people from a land far away:	8784
	11:11	Although *they* **c** out to me,	2410
	11:12	of Jerusalem will **c** out to the gods	2410
	12: 6	they have **raised** a loud **c** against you.	7924
	14: 2	and a **c** goes up *from* Jerusalem.	7424
	14:12	they fast, I will not listen to their **c**;	8262
	18:22	Let a **c** be heard from their houses	2411
	20: 8	*I* **c** out proclaiming violence	2410
	20:16	a **battle c** at noon.	9558
	22:20	"Go up to Lebanon and **c** out,	7590
	22:20	**c** out from Abarim,	7590
	25:36	Hear the **c** of the shepherds,	7591
	30:15	Why do you **c** out over your wound,	2410
	31: 6	be a day *when* watchmen **c** out on the hills	7924
	47: 2	The people *will* **c** out;	2410
	47: 2	" 'Ah, sword of the LORD,' [you **c**,]	NIH
	48: 4	her little ones *will* **c** out.	2411+9048
	48:20	Wail and **c** out!	2410
	48:31	for all Moab *I* **c** out,	2410
	48:34	"The sound of their **c** rises from Heshbon	2411
	49: 2	"when I will sound the **battle c**	9558
	49: 3	**C** out, O inhabitants of Rabbah!	7590
	49:21	their **c** will resound to the Red Sea.	7591+7754
	50:46	its **c** will resound among the nations.	2411
	51:54	"The sound of a **c** comes from Babylon,	2411
La	2:18	The hearts of the people **c** out to the Lord.	7590
	2:19	Arise, **c** out in the night,	8264
	3: 8	Even when I call out or **c** for help,	8775
	3:56	"Do not close your ears to my **c** for relief."	8784
	4:15	*men* **c** to them.	7924
Eze	6:11	and stamp your feet and **c** out "Alas!"	606
	21:12	**C** out and wail, son of man,	2410
	21:22	to sound the **battle c,**	9558
	27:28	when your seamen **c** out.	2411+7754
	27:30	They will raise their voice and **c** bitterly	2410
Hos	5: 8	**Raise the battle c** in Beth Aven;	8131
	7:14	not **c** out to me from their hearts but wail	2410
Joel	1:14	and **c** out to the LORD.	2410
Jnh	2: 2	and you listened to my **c**.	7754
Mic	3: 4	Then *they will* **c** out to the LORD,	2410
	4: 9	Why do you now **c** aloud—	8131+8275
Na	2: 8	they **c**, but no one turns back.	NIH
Hab	1: 2	Or **c** out to you, "Violence!"	2410
	2:11	The stones of the wall *will* **c** out,	2410
Zep	1:10	"a **c** will go up from the Fish Gate,	7591+7754
	1:14	**c** on the day of the LORD will be bitter,	7754
	1:16	and **battle c** against the fortified cities	9558
Mt	12:19	He will not quarrel or **c** out;	3198
	25: 6	"At midnight the **c** rang out:	3199
Mk	5: 5	in the hills he would **c** out and cut himself	3189
	15:37	With a loud **c**, Jesus breathed his last.	5889
	15:39	heard his **c** and saw how he died, he said,	3189
Lk	7:13	to her and he said, "Don't **c**."	3081
	7:32	we sang a dirge, and *you* did not **c**.'	3081
	18: 7	who **c** out to him day and night?	1066
	19:40	"if they keep quiet, the stones *will* **c** out."	3189
Ro	8:15	And by him we **c**, "Abba, Father."	3189
Gal	4: 6	break forth and **c** aloud;	1066
Rev	18:10	they will stand far off and **c**: " 'Woe!	3306
	18:16	and **c** out: " 'Woe! Woe,	3306
	18:19	and with weeping and mourning **c** out:	3189

CRYING (20) [CRY]

Ge	21:17	God heard the boy **c**,	7754
	21:17	God has heard the boy **c** as he lies there.	7754
Ex	2: 6	He was **c**, and she felt sorry for him.	1134
	3: 7	I have heard them **c** out because	7591
	5: 8	They are lazy; that is why they *are* **c** out,	7590
	14:15	"Why *are you* **c** out to me?	7590
Jdg	7:21	all the Midianites ran, **c** out as they fled.	8131
1Sa	7: 8	"Do not stop **c** out to the LORD our God	2410
Isa	22: 5	a day of battering down walls and of **c** out	8779
	65:19	and of **c** will be heard in it no more.	2411
Eze	9: 8	**c** out, "Ah, Sovereign LORD!	2410
Mt	15:22	**c** out, "Lord, Son of David,	3189+3306
	15:23	for *she* keeps **c** out after us."	3189
Mk	5:38	with people **c** and wailing loudly.	3081
Jn	20:11	but Mary stood outside the tomb **c**.	3081
	20:13	They asked her, "Woman, why *are you* **c**?"	3081
	20:15	"Woman," he said, "why *are you* **c**?	3081
Ac	9:39	**c** and showing him the robes	3081
Jas	5: 4	workmen who mowed your fields *are* **c** out	3189
Rev	21: 4	be no more death or mourning or **c** or pain,	3199

CRYSTAL (4)

Job	28:17	Neither gold nor **c** can compare with it,	2343
Rev	4: 6	like a sea of glass, clear as **c**.	3223
	21:11	like a jasper, **clear as c**.	3222
	22: 1	the river of the water of life, as clear as **c**,	3223

CUB (2) [CUBS]

Ge	49: 9	You are a lion's **c**, O Judah;	1594
Dt	33:22	About Dan he said: "Dan is a lion's **c**,	1594

CUBIT (37) [CUBITS]

Ex	25:10	a **c** and a half wide,	564
	25:10	and a **c** and a half high.	564
	25:17	a half cubits long and a **c** and a half wide.	564
	25:23	a **c** wide and a cubit and a half high.	564
	25:23	a cubit wide and a **c** and a half high.	564

Ex	26:13	The tent curtains will be a c longer on	564
	26:16	Each frame is to be ten cubits long and a c	564
	30: 2	It is to be square, a c long and a cubit wide,	564
	30: 2	It is to be square, a cubit long and a c wide,	564
	36:21	Each frame was ten cubits long and a c and	564
	37: 1	a c and a half wide,	564
	37: 1	and a c and a half high.	564
	37: 6	a half cubits long and a c and a half wide.	564
	37:10	two cubits long, a c wide,	564
	37:10	a cubit wide, and a c and a half high.	564
	37:25	It was square, a c long and a cubit wide,	564
	37:25	It was square, a cubit long and a c wide,	564
1Ki	7:24	gourds encircled it—ten to a c.	564
	7:31	that had a circular frame one c deep.	564
	7:31	and with its basework it measured a c and	564
	7:32	The diameter of each wheel was a c and	564
	7:35	a circular band half a c deep.	564
2Ch	3: 3	and twenty cubits wide (using the c of	564
	4: 3	figures of bulls encircled it—ten to a c.	564
Eze	40: 5	each of which was a c and a handbreadth.	564
	40:12	of each alcove was a wall one c high,	564
	40:42	each a c and a half long,	564
	40:42	a c and a half wide and a cubit high.	564
	40:42	a cubit and a half wide and a c high.	564
	43:13	that c being a cubit and a handbreadth:	564
	43:13	that cubit being a c and a handbreadth:	564
	43:13	Its gutter is a c deep and a cubit wide.	564
	43:13	Its gutter is a cubit deep and a c wide,	564
	43:14	and a c wide,	564
	43:14	and a c wide.	564
	43:17	a c and a gutter of a cubit all around.	564
	43:17	a cubit and a gutter of a c all around.	564

CUBITS (220) [CUBIT]

Ex	25:10	two and a half c long,	564
	25:17	a half c long and a cubit and a half wide.	564
	25:23	two c long, a cubit wide and a cubit and	564
	26: 2	twenty-eight c long and four cubits wide,	564
	26: 2	twenty-eight cubits long and four c wide.	564
	26: 8	thirty c long and four cubits wide,	564
	26: 8	thirty cubits long and four c wide.	564
	26:16	to be ten c long and a cubit and a half wide,	564
	27: 1	an altar of acacia wood, three c high;	564
	27: 1	five c long and five cubits wide.	564
	27: 1	five cubits long and five c wide.	564
	27: 9	be a hundred c long and is to have curtains	564
	27:11	be a hundred c long and is to have curtains,	NIH
	27:12	of the courtyard shall be fifty c wide	564
	27:13	The courtyard shall also be fifty c wide.	564
	27:14	Curtains fifteen c long are to be on one side	564
	27:15	and curtains fifteen c long are to be on	NIH
	27:16	provide a curtain twenty c long, of blue,	564
	27:18	be a hundred c long and fifty cubits wide,	564
	27:18	be a hundred cubits long and fifty c wide,	NIH
	27:18	of finely twisted linen five c high,	564
	30: 2	and two c high—	564
	36: 9	twenty-eight c long and four cubits wide,	564
	36: 9	twenty-eight cubits long and four c wide.	564
	36:15	thirty c long and four cubits wide,	564
	36:15	thirty cubits long and four c wide.	564
	36:21	Each frame was ten c long and a cubit and	564
	37: 1	two and a half c long,	564
	37: 6	a half c long and a cubit and a half wide.	564
	37:10	two c long, a cubit wide,	564
	37:25	and two c high—	564
	38: 1	of acacia wood, three c high;	564
	38: 1	five c long and five cubits wide.	564
	38: 1	five cubits long and five c wide.	564
	38: 9	The south side was a hundred c long	564
	38:11	also a hundred c long and had twenty posts	564
	38:12	The west end was fifty c wide	564
	38:13	toward the sunrise, was also fifty c wide.	564
	38:14	Curtains fifteen c long were on one side of	564
	38:15	and curtains fifteen c long were on	564
	38:18	It was twenty c long and,	564
	38:18	the curtains of the courtyard, five c high,	564
1Ki	6: 2	for the LORD was sixty c long,	564
	6: 3	that is twenty c,	564
	6: 3	and projected ten c from the front of	564
	6: 6	The lowest floor was five c wide,	564
	6: 6	the middle floor six c and	564
	6:16	He partitioned off twenty c at the rear of	564
	6:17	in front of this room was forty c long.	564
	6:20	The inner sanctuary was twenty c long,	564
	6:23	each ten c high.	564
	6:24	of the first cherub was five c long, and	564
	6:24	and the other wing five c—	564
	6:24	ten c from wing tip to wing tip.	564
	6:25	The second cherub also measured ten c,	564
	6:26	The height of each cherub was ten c.	564
	7: 2	of the Forest of Lebanon a hundred c long,	564
	7: 6	a colonnade fifty c long and thirty wide.	564
	7:10	some measuring ten c and some eight.	564
	7:15	each eighteen c high and twelve cubits	564
	7:15	each eighteen cubits high and twelve c	564
	7:16	each capital was five c high.	564
	7:19	in the shape of lilies, four c high.	564
	7:23	measuring ten c from rim to rim	564
	7:23	from rim to rim and five c high.	564
	7:23	a line of thirty c to measure around it.	564
	7:27	each was four c long,	564
	7:38	and measuring four c across.	564
2Ch	3: 3	the temple of God was sixty c long	564
	3: 3	and twenty c wide (using the cubit of	564
	3: 4	at the front of the temple was twenty c long	564

2Ch	3: 4	of the building and twenty c high.	NIH
	3: 8	twenty c long and twenty cubits wide.	564
	3: 8	twenty cubits long and twenty c wide.	564
	3:11	of the cherubim was twenty c.	564
	3:11	of the first cherub was five c long	564
	3:11	while its other wing, also five c long,	564
	3:12	of the second cherub was five c long	564
	3:12	and its other wing, also five c long,	564
	3:13	of these cherubim extended twenty c.	564
	3:15	which [together] were thirty-five c long,	564
	3:15	each with a capital on top measuring five c.	564
	4: 1	He made a bronze altar twenty c long,	564
	4: 1	twenty c wide and ten cubits high.	564
	4: 1	twenty cubits wide and ten c high.	564
	4: 2	measuring ten c from rim to rim	564
	4: 2	from rim to rim and five c high.	564
	4: 2	a line of thirty c to measure around it.	564
	6:13	he had made a bronze platform, five c long,	564
	6:13	five c wide and three cubits high,	564
	6:13	five cubits wide and three c high,	564
Jer	52:21	Each of the pillars was eighteen c high	564
	52:21	and twelve c in circumference;	564
	52:22	on top of the one pillar was five c high	564
Eze	40: 5	in the man's hand was six long c,	564
	40: 7	between the alcoves were five c thick.	564
	40: 9	it was eight c deep	564
	40: 9	and its jambs were two c thick.	564
	40:11	it was ten c and its length	564
	40:11	and its length was thirteen c.	564
	40:12	and the alcoves were six c square.	564
	40:13	the distance was twenty-five c	564
	40:14	of the gateway—sixty c.	564
	40:15	to the far end of its portico was fifty c.	564
	40:19	it was a hundred c on the east side as well	564
	40:21	It was fifty c long	564
	40:21	and twenty-five c wide.	564
	40:23	it was a hundred c.	564
	40:25	It was fifty c long	564
	40:25	and twenty-five c wide.	564
	40:27	it was a hundred c.	564
	40:29	It was fifty c long	564
	40:29	and twenty-five c wide.	564
	40:30	the inner court were twenty-five c wide	564
	40:30	and five c deep.)	564
	40:33	It was fifty c long	564
	40:33	and twenty-five c wide.	564
	40:36	It was fifty c long	564
	40:36	and twenty-five c wide.	564
	40:47	hundred c long and a hundred cubits wide.	564
	40:47	hundred cubits long and a hundred c wide.	564
	40:48	they were five c wide on either side.	564
	40:48	The width of the entrance was fourteen c	564
	40:48	and its projecting walls were three c wide	564
	40:49	The portico was twenty c wide,	564
	40:49	and twelve c from front to back.	564
	41: 1	width of the jambs was six c on each side.	564
	41: 2	The entrance was ten c wide,	564
	41: 2	on each side of it were five c wide.	564
	41: 2	it was forty c long and twenty cubits wide.	564
	41: 2	it was forty cubits long and twenty c wide.	564
	41: 3	each was two c wide.	564
	41: 3	The entrance was six c wide,	564
	41: 3	on each side of it were seven c wide.	564
	41: 4	it was twenty c,	564
	41: 4	and its width was twenty c across the end	564
	41: 5	it was six c thick,	564
	41: 5	around the temple was four c wide.	564
	41: 8	It was the length of the rod, six long c.	564
	41: 9	of the side rooms was five c thick.	564
	41:10	the [priests'] rooms was twenty c wide all	564
	41:11	the open area was five c wide all around.	564
	41:12	on the west side was seventy c wide.	564
	41:12	The wall of the building was five c thick all	564
	41:12	and its length was ninety c.	564
	41:13	it was a hundred c long,	564
	41:13	with its walls were also a hundred c long.	564
	41:14	was a hundred c.	564
	41:15	it was a hundred c.	564
	41:22	There was a wooden altar three c high	564
	41:22	and two c square;	564
	42: 2	a hundred c long and fifty cubits wide.	564
	42: 2	a hundred cubits long and fifty c wide.	564
	42: 3	In the section twenty c from the inner court	NIH
	42: 4	an inner passageway ten c wide and	564
	42: 4	and a hundred c long.	564
	42: 7	it extended in front of the rooms for fifty c.	564
	42: 8	to the outer court was fifty c long,	564
	42: 8	the sanctuary was a hundred c long.	564
	42:16	it was five hundred c.	564
	42:17	it was five hundred c by the measuring rod.	564
	42:18	it was five hundred c by the measuring rod.	564
	42:19	it was five hundred c by the measuring rod.	564
	42:20	five hundred c long	NIH
	42:20	and five hundred c wide,	NIH
	43:13	the altar in long c, that cubit being a cubit	564
	43:14	up to the lower ledge it is two c high and	564
	43:14	up to the larger ledge it is four c high and	564
	43:15	The altar hearth is four c high,	564
	43:16	twelve c long and twelve cubits wide.	NIH
	43:16	twelve cubits long and twelve c wide.	NIH
	43:17	fourteen c long and fourteen cubits wide,	NIH
	43:17	fourteen cubits long and fourteen c wide.	NIH
	45: 1	25,000 c long and 20,000 cubits wide;	NIH
	45: 1	25,000 cubits long and 20,000 c wide;	NIH
	45: 2	a section 500 c square is to be for	NIH
	45: 2	with 50 c around it for open land.	564
	45: 3	c long and 10,000 cubits wide.	NIH

Eze	45: 3	cubits long and 10,000 c wide.	NIH
	45: 5	An area 25,000 c long and 10,000	NIH
	45: 5	c wide will belong to the Levites,	NIH
	45: 6	c wide and 25,000 cubits long,	NIH
	45: 6	c long, adjoining the sacred portion;	NIH
	46:22	forty c long and thirty cubits wide;	NIH
	46:22	forty cubits long and thirty c wide;	NIH
	47: 3	a thousand c and then led me through water	564
	47: 4	He measured off another thousand c	NIH
	48: 8	It will be 25,000 c wide.	NIH
	48: 9	c long and 10,000 cubits wide.	NIH
	48: 9	cubits long and 10,000 c wide.	NIH
	48:10	It will be 25,000 c long on the north side,	NIH
	48:10	10,000 c wide on the west side, 10,000	NIH
	48:10	10,000 c wide on the east side and 25,000	NIH
	48:10	c long on the south side.	NIH
	48:13	c long and 10,000 cubits wide.	NIH
	48:13	cubits long and 10,000 c wide.	NIH
	48:13	c and its width 10,000 cubits.	NIH
	48:13	cubits and its width 10,000 c.	NIH
	48:15	5,000 c wide and 25,000 cubits long,	NIH
	48:15	5,000 cubits wide and 25,000 c long,	NIH
	48:16	the north side 4,500 c, the south side 4,500	NIH
	48:16	the south side 4,500 c, the east side 4,500	NIH
	48:16	c, and the west side 4,500 cubits.	NIH
	48:16	cubits, and the west side 4,500 c.	NIH
	48:17	The pastureland for the city will be 250 c	NIH
	48:17	250 c on the south, 250 cubits on the east,	NIH
	48:17	250 cubits on the south, 250 c on the east,	NIH
	48:17	and 250 c on the west.	NIH
	48:18	c on the east side and 10,000	NIH
	48:18	c on the west side.	NIH
	48:20	25,000 c on each side.	NIH
	48:21	c of the sacred portion to	NIH
	48:21	c to the western border.	NIH
	48:30	which is 4,500 c long,	NIH
	48:32	"On the east side, which is 4,500 c long,	NIH
	48:33	which measures 4,500 c,	NIH
	48:34	"On the west side, which is 4,500 c long,	NIH
	48:35	"The distance all around will be 18,000 c.	NIH
Rev	21:17	its wall and it was 144 c thick,	4388

CUBS (11) [CUB]

2Sa	17: 8	and as fierce as a wild bear robbed of her c.	8891
Job	4:11	and the c of the lioness are scattered.	1201
	38:32	or lead out the Bear with its c?	1201
Pr		Better to meet a bear robbed of her c than	408
Jer	51:38	they growl like lion c.	1596
Eze	19: 2	among the young lions and reared her c.	1594
	19: 3	She brought up one of her c,	1594
	19: 5	she took another of her c and made him	1594
Hos	13: 8	Like a bear robbed of her c,	8891
Na	2:11	the lion and lioness went, and the c,	793+1594
	2:12	The lion killed enough for his c	1596

CUCKOW (KJV) See GULL

CUCUMBERS (1)

Nu	11: 5	also the c, melons, leeks, onions and garlic.	7991

CUD (11)

Lev	11: 3	and that chews the c.	1742
	11: 4	" 'There are some that only chew the c	1742
	11: 4	The camel, though it chews the c,	1742
	11: 5	The coney, though it chews the c,	1742
	11: 6	The rabbit, though it chews the c,	1742
	11: 7	does not chew the c; it is unclean for you.	1742
	11:26	that does not chew the c is unclean for you;	1742
Dt	14: 6	in two and that chews the c.	1742
	14: 7	of those that chew the c or that have	1742
	14: 7	Although they chew the c,	1742
	14: 8	it does not chew the c.	1742

CULTIVATE (2) [CULTIVATED]

Dt	28:39	and c them but you will not drink the wine	6268
Ps	104:14	and plants for man to c—	6275

CULTIVATED (5) [CULTIVATE]

Isa	5: 6	neither pruned nor c,	6371
	7:25	As for all the hills once c by the hoe,	6371
Jer	13:21	over you those you c as your special allies?	4340
Eze	36:34	The desolate land will be c instead	6268
Ro	11:24	to nature were grafted into a c olive tree,	2814

CUMBERED (KJV) See DISTRACTED

CUMI (KJV) See KOUM

CUMMIN (4)

Isa	28:25	does he not sow caraway and scatter c?	4021
	28:27	nor is a cartwheel rolled over c;	4021
	28:27	and c with a stick.	4021
Mt	23:23	mint, dill and c.	3248

CUN (1)

1Ch	18: 8	From Tebah and C,	3923

CUNNING (4)

Ps	64: 6	Surely the mind and heart of man are c.	6678
	83: 3	With c they conspire against your people;	6891

2Co 11: 3 as Eve was deceived by the serpent's **c**, 4111
Eph 4:14 by every wind of teaching and by the **c** 3235

CUP (65) [CUPS]
Ge 40:11 Pharaoh's **c** was in my hand, 3926
    40:11 squeezed them into Pharaoh's **c** and put 3926
    40:11 into Pharaoh's cup and put the **c** 3926
    40:13 and you will put Pharaoh's **c** in his hand, 3926
    40:21 so that he once again put the **c** 3926
    44: 2 Then put my **c**, the silver one, 1483
    44: 5 Isn't this **the c** my master drinks from and 889S
    44:12 And the **c** was found in Benjamin's sack. 1483
    44:16 and the one who was found to have the **c**." 1483
    44:17 to have the **c** will become my slave. 1483
2Sa 12: 3 drank from his **c** and even slept in his arms. 3926
1Ki 7:26 and its rim was like the rim of a **c**, 3926
2Ch 4: 5 and its rim was like the rim of a **c**, 3926
Ps 16: 5 you have assigned me my portion and my **c**; 3926
    23: 5 with oil; my **c** overflows. 3926
    75: 8 a **c** full of foaming wine mixed with spices; 3926
    116:13 up the **c** of salvation and call on the name 3926
Pr 23:31 when it sparkles in the **c**, 3926
Isa 51:17 the hand of the LORD the **c** of his wrath, 3926
    51:22 of your hand the **c** that made you stagger; 3926
    51:22 from that **c**, the goblet of my wrath, NIH
Jer 25:15 from my hand this **c** filled with the wine 3926
    25:17 the **c** from the LORD's hand and made all 3926
    25:28 if they refuse to take the **c** from your hand 3926
    49:12 not deserve to drink the **c** must drink it, 3926
    51: 7 a gold **c** in the LORD's hand; 3926
La 4:21 But to you also the **c** will be passed; 3926
Eze 23:31 so I will put her **c** into your hand. 3926
    23:32 "You will drink your sister's **c**, 3926
    23:32 a **c** large and deep; NIH
    23:33 the **c** of ruin and desolation, 3926
    23:33 the **c** of your sister Samaria. 3926
Hab 2:16 **c** from the LORD's right hand is coming
                around to you, 3926
Zec 12: 2 to make Jerusalem a **c** that sends all 6195
Mt 10:42 And if anyone gives even a **c** of cold water 4539
    20:22 "Can you drink the **c** I am going to drink?" 4539
    20:23 "You will indeed drink from my **c**, 4539
    23:25 You clean the outside of the **c** and dish, 4539
    23:26 First clean the inside of the **c** and dish, 4539
    26:27 Then he took the **c**, gave thanks 4539
    26:39 may this **c** be taken from me. 4539
    26:42 for this **c** to be taken away unless I drink it, NIG
Mk 9:41 anyone who **gives** you a **c** of water 4539+4540
    10:38 "Can you drink the **c** I drink or be baptized 4539
    10:39 the **c** I drink and be baptized with 4539
    14:23 Then he took the **c**, gave thanks 4539
    14:36 Take this **c** from me. 4539
Lk 11:39 you Pharisees clean the outside of the **c** 4539
    22:17 After taking the **c**, he gave thanks and said, 4539
    22:20 after the supper he took the **c**, saying, 4539
    22:20 "This **c** is the new covenant in my blood, 4539
    22:42 if you are willing, take this **c** from me; 4539
Jn 18:11 not drink the **c** the Father has given me?" 4539
1Co 10:16 Is not the **c** of thanksgiving 4539
    10:21 You cannot drink the **c** of the Lord and 4539
    10:21 of the Lord and the **c** of demons too; 4539
    11:25 In the same way, after supper he took the **c**, 4539
    11:25 "This **c** is the new covenant in my blood; 4539
    11:26 whenever you eat this bread and drink this **c** 4539
    11:27 whoever eats the bread or drinks the **c** of 4539
    11:28 of the bread and drinks of the **c**. 4539
Rev 14:10 into the **c** of his wrath. 4539
    16:19 and gave her the **c** filled with the wine of 4539
    17: 4 She held a golden **c** in her hand, 4539
    18: 6 Mix her a double portion from her own **c**. 4539

CUPBEARER (10) [CUPBEARERS]
Ge 40: 1 the **c** and the baker of the king 5482
    40: 2 the chief **c** and the chief baker, 5482
    40: 5 the **c** and the baker of the king of Egypt, 5482
    40: 9 So the chief **c** told Joseph his dream. 5482
    40:13 just as you used to do when you were his **c**, 5482
    40:20 the heads of the chief **c** and the chief baker 5482
    40:21 He restored the chief **c** to his position, 5482
    40:23 The chief **c**, however, did not remember 5482
    41: 9 Then the chief **c** said to Pharaoh, 5482
Ne 1:11 I was **c** to the king. 5482

CUPBEARERS (2) [CUPBEARER]
1Ki 10: 5 the attending servants in their robes, his **c**, 5482
2Ch 9: 4 the **c** in their robes and 5482

CUPS (8) [CUP]
Ex 25:31 its flowerlike **c**, buds and blossoms shall be 1483
    25:33 Three **c** shaped like almond flowers 1483
    25:34 the lampstand there are to be four **c** shaped 1483
    37:17 its flowerlike **c**, buds and blossoms were 1483
    37:19 Three **c** shaped like almond flowers 1483
    37:20 And on the lampstand were four **c** shaped 1483
Jer 35: 5 Then I set bowls full of wine and some **c** 3926
Mk 7: 4 such as the washing of **c**, 4539

CURDLE (1) [CURDS]
Job 10:10 not pour me out like milk and **c** me 7884

CURDLED (1) [CURDS]
Jdg 5:25 for nobles she brought him **c** milk. 2772

CURDS (7) [CURDLE, CURDLED]
Ge 18: 8 then brought some **c** and milk and the calf 2772
Dt 32:14 with **c** and milk from herd and flock and 2772
2Sa 17:29 and **c**, sheep, and cheese from cows' milk 2772
Isa 7:15 He will eat **c** and honey 2772
    7:22 he will have **c** to eat. 2772
    7:22 All who remain in the land will eat **c** 2772
Eze 34: 3 You eat the **c**, 2693

CURE (8) [CURED]
2Ki 5: 3 He would **c** him of his leprosy." 665
    5: 6 so that you may **c** him of his leprosy." 665
    5:11 over the spot and **c** me of my leprosy. 665
Jer 3:22 I will **c** you of backsliding." 8324
    17: 9 above all things and **beyond c**. 631
    30:15 your pain that has **no c**? 631
Hos 5:13 But he is not able to **c** you, 8324
Lk 9: 1 to drive out all demons and to **c** diseases, 2543

CURED (14) [CURE]
Dt 28:27 from which you cannot **be c**. 8324
    28:35 and legs with painful boils that cannot **be c**, 8324
2Ki 5: 7 to me to **be c** of his leprosy? 665
Mt 8: 3 Immediately he was **c** of his leprosy. 2751
    11: 5 those who have leprosy are **c**, 2751
Mk 1:42 the leprosy left him and he was **c**. 2751
Lk 6:18 Those troubled by evil spirits were **c**. 2543
    7:21 very time Jesus **c** many who had diseases, 2543
    7:22 those who have leprosy are **c**, 2751
    8: 2 also some women who had been **c** 1639+2543
    8:36 how the demon-possessed man had been **c**. 5392
Jn 5: 9 At once the man was **c**; 5618
Ac 19:12 and their illnesses were **c** and 557
    28: 9 of the sick on the island came and were **c**. 2543

CURRENT (1) [CURRENTS]
Ge 23:16 **according to the weight c** among the
                merchants. 6296

CURRENTS (1) [CURRENT]
Jnh 2: 3 and the **c** swirled about me; 5643

CURRY (1)
Pr 19: 6 Many **c favor with** a ruler, 2704+7156

CURSE (87) [ACCURSED, CURSED, CURSES, CURSING]
Ge 4:11 Now you are **under a c** and driven from 826
    8:21 "Never again **will I c** the ground because 7837
    12: 3 and whoever curses you **I will c**; 826
    27:12 down a **c** on myself rather than a blessing." 7839
    27:13 "My son, let the **c** fall on me. 7839
    27:29 May those **who c** be cursed 826
Ex 22:28 "Do not blaspheme God or **c** the ruler 826
Lev 19:14 not **c** the deaf or put a stumbling block 7837
    24:11 the Name with a **c**; 7837
Nu 5:18 the bitter water that **brings a c**. 826
    5:19 may this bitter water that **brings a c** 826
    5:21 to put the woman under this **c** of the oath— 460
    5:21 "may the LORD cause your people to **c** 460
    5:22 that **brings a c** enter your body so 826
    5:24 the bitter water that **brings a c**, 826
    5:27 to drink the water that **brings a c**, it will go 826
    22: 6 Now come and **put a c** on these people, 826
    22: 6 and those you **c** are cursed." 826
    22:11 Now come and **put a c** on them for me. 7686
    22:12 You must not **put a c** on those people, 7686
    22:17 Come and **put a c** on these people for me." 7686
    23: 7 'Come,' he said, '**c** Jacob for me; 826
    23: 8 can I **c** those whom God has not cursed? 7686
    23:11 I brought you to **c** my enemies, 7686
    23:13 And from there, **c** them for me." 7686
    23:25 "Neither **c** them at all nor bless them 7686+7686
    23:27 to let you **c** them for me from there." 7686
    24: 9 be blessed and those who **c** you be cursed!" 826
    24:10 "I summoned you to **c** my enemies, 7686
Dt 11:26 before you today a blessing and a **c**— 7839
    11:28 the **c** if you disobey the commands of 7839
    21:23 on a tree is **under** God's **c**. 7839
    23: 4 in Aram Naharaim to **pronounce a c** on 7837
    23: 5 to Balaam but turned the **c** into a blessing 7839
Jos 9:23 You are now **under a c**: 826
    24: 9 for Balaam son of Beor to **put a c** on you. 7837
Jdg 5:23 '**C** Meroz,' said the angel of the LORD. 826
    5:23 '**C** its people bitterly, 826+826
    9:57 The **c** of Jotham son of Jerub-Baal came 7839
    17: 2 and about which I heard you **utter a c**— 457
2Sa 16: 9 "Why should this dead dog **c** my lord 7837
    16:10 '**C** David,' who can ask, 7837
    16:11 let him **c**, for the LORD has told him to. 7837
2Ki 2:24 and **called down a c** on them in the name 7837
Ne 10:29 and bind themselves with a **c** and an oath 460
    13: 2 but had hired Balaam to **call a c** down 7837
    13: 2 however, turned the **c** into a blessing.) 7839
Job 1:11 and he will surely **c** you to your face." 1385
    2: 5 and he will surely **c** you to your face." 1385
    2: 9 C God and die!" 1385
    3: 8 May those who **c** days curse that day, 826
    3: 8 May those who curse days **c** that day, 7686
    31:30 to sin by invoking a **c** against his life— 460
Ps 62: 4 but in their hearts they **c**. 7837
    102: 8 rail against me **use** my **name as a c**. 928+8678

CURSED (64) [CURSE]
Ge 3:14 "C are you above all the livestock and all 826
    3:17 "C is the ground because of you; 826
    5:29 by the ground the LORD has **c**." 826
    9:25 he said, "C be Canaan." 826
    27:29 May those who curse you **be c** 826
    49: 7 C be their anger, so fierce, and their fury, 826
Lev 20: 9 He has **c** his father or his mother, 7837
Nu 22: 6 and those you curse are **c**." 826
    23: 8 can I curse those whom God has not **c**? 7686
    24: 9 be blessed and those who curse you be **c**!" 826
Dt 27:15 "C is the man who carves an image or casts 826
    27:16 "C is the man who dishonors his father 826
    27:17 "C is the man who moves his neighbor's
                boundary stone." 826
    27:18 "C is the man who leads the blind astray 826
    27:19 "C is the man who withholds justice from 826
    27:20 "C is the man who sleeps with his father's
                wife, 826
    27:21 "C is the man who has sexual relations 826
    27:22 "C is the man who sleeps with his sister, 826
    27:23 "C is the man who sleeps with his
                mother-in-law." 826
    27:24 "C is the man who kills his neighbor 826
    27:25 "C is the man who accepts a bribe to kill 826
    27:26 "C is the man who does not uphold 826
    28:16 You will **be c** in the city and cursed in 826
    28:16 be cursed in the city and **c** in the country. 826
    28:17 and your kneading trough will **be c**. 826
    28:18 The fruit of your womb will **be c**, 826
    28:19 You will **be c** when you come in 826
    28:19 when you come in and **c** when you go out. 826
Jos 6:26 "C before the LORD is the man who 826
Jdg 9:27 and drinking, they **c** Abimelech. 7837
    21:18 'C be anyone who gives a wife to 826
1Sa 14:24 'C be any man who eats food 826
    14:28 'C be any man who eats food today!' 826
    17:43 And the Philistine **c** David by his gods. 7837
    26:19 may they be **c** before the LORD! 826
2Sa 16: 5 and he **c** as he came out. 7837
    16: 7 As he **c**, Shimei said, "Get out, get out, 7837
    19:21 He **c** the LORD's anointed." 7837
1Ki 21:10 that he has **c** both God and the king. 1385
    21:13 "Naboth has **c** both God and the king." 1385
2Ki 9:34 "Take care of that **c** woman," he said, 826
Job 1: 5 and **c** God in their hearts. 1385
    3: 1 Job opened his mouth and **c** the day 7837
    5: 3 but suddenly his house was **c**. 7686
    24:18 their portion of the land is **c**, 7837
Ps 119:21 who are **c** and who stray 826
Ecc 7:22 that many times you yourself have **c** others. 7837
Jer 11: 3 'C is the man who does not obey 826
    17: 5 "C is the one who trusts in man, 826
    20:14 C be the day I was born! 826
    20:15 C be the man who brought my father 826
Mal 1:14 "C is the cheat who has 826
    2: 2 Yes, I have already **c** them, 826
Mt 25:41 'Depart from me, you who are **c**, 2933
Mk 11:21 The fig tree you **c** has withered!" 2933
Ro 9: 3 that I myself were **c** and cut off from Christ 353
1Co 4:12 When we are **c**, we bless; 3366
    12: 3 "Jesus be **c**," and no one can say, 353
Gal 3:10 "C is everyone who does not continue 2129
    3:13 "C is everyone who is hung on a tree." 2129
Heb 6: 8 and is in danger of **being c**. 2932
Rev 16: 9 by the intense heat and they **c** the name 1059
    16:11 and **c** the God of heaven because 1059
    16:21 and they **c** God on account of the plague 1059

CURSES (32) [CURSE]
Ge 12: 3 and whoever **c** you I will curse; 7837
Ex 21:17 "Anyone who **c** his father or mother must 7837

Ps 109:17 He loved to pronounce a **c**— 7839
    109:28 They may **c**, but you will bless; 7837
Pr 3:33 LORD's **c** is on the house of the wicked, 4423
    11:26 People **c** the man who hoards grain, 7686
    24:24 an undeserved **c** does not come to rest. 7839
    26: 2 it will be taken as a **c**. 7839
    27:14 "There are those who **c** their fathers and do 7837
    30:10 or he will **c** you, and you will pay for it. 7837
    30:11 or the rich in your bedroom, 7837
Ecc 10:20 will **c** their king and their God. 7837
Isa 8:21 Therefore a **c** consumes the earth; 460
    24: 6 to my chosen ones as a **c**; 8652
    65:15 the **c** the land lies parched and the pastures 460
Jer 23:10 in Babylon will use this **c**: 7839
    29:22 "A **c** on him who is lax in doing 826
    48:10 A **c** on him who keeps his sword 826
    48:10 and may your **c** be on them! 9297
La 3:65 the **c** that is going out over the whole land; 460
Zec 5: 3 "I will send a **c** upon you, 4423
Mal 2: 2 and I will **c** your blessings. 826
    3: 9 You are under a **c**— 826+4423
    4: 6 and strike the land with a **c**." 3051
Lk 6:28 bless those who **c** you, 2933
Jn 7:49 there is a **c** on them." 2063
Ro 12:14 bless and do not **c**. 2933
1Co 16:22 does not love the Lord—a **c** be on him. 353
Gal 3:10 the law are under a **c**, for it is written: 2932
    3:13 the **c** of the law by becoming a curse for us, 2932
    3:13 the curse of the law by becoming a **c** for us, 2932
Jas 3: 9 and with it we **c** men, 2933
Rev 22: 3 No longer will there be any **c**. 2873

Lev	20: 9	" 'If anyone c his father or mother,	7837
	24:15	Say to the Israelites: 'If anyone c his God,	7837
Nu	5:23	" 'The priest is to write these c on a scroll	460
Dt	11:29	and on Mount Ebal the c.	7839
	27:13	on Mount Ebal to **pronounce c:**	7839
	28:15	all these c will come upon you	7839
	28:20	The LORD will send on you c,	4423
	28:45	All these c will come upon you.	7839
	29:20	All the c written in this book will fall	460
	29:21	the c of the covenant written in this Book	460
	29:27	so that he brought on it all the c written	7839
	30: 1	and c I have set before you come upon you	7839
	30: 7	The LORD your God will put all these c	460
	30:19	before you life and death, blessings and c.	7839
Jos	8:34	the blessings and the c—	7839
1Ki	2: 8	who **called down** bitter c on me	7837+7839
2Ch	34:24	the c written in the book that has been read	460
Ne	13:25	I rebuked them and **called c down**	7837
Ps	10: 7	His mouth is full of c and lies and threats;	460
	37:22	but *those* he c will be cut off.	7837
	59:12	For the c and lies they utter,	460
Pr	20:20	If a *man* c his father or mother,	7837
	28:27	to them receives many c.	4423
Jer	11: 8	I brought on them all the c of the covenant	1821
	15:10	yet everyone c me.	7837
Da	9:11	the c and sworn judgments written in	460
Mt	15: 4	and 'Anyone who c his father or mother'	2800
	26:74	Then he began *to* **call down** c on himself	2874
Mk	7:10	'Anyone who c his father or mother must	2800
	14:71	He began *to* **call down** c on himself,	354

CURSING (18) [CURSE]

2Sa	16:10	If *he is* c because the LORD said to him,	7837
	16:12	with good for the c I am receiving today."	7839
	16:13	c as he went and throwing stones at him	7837
Ps	109:18	He wore c as his garment;	7839
Ecc	7:21	or you may hear your servant c you—	7837
Jer	24: 9	an object of ridicule and c,	7839
	25:18	and an object of horror and scorn and c,	7839
	26: 6	an **object of** c among all the nations of	7839
	29:18	of the earth and an **object of** c and horror,	460
	42:18	You will be an **object of** c and horror,	460
	44: 8	an **object of** c and reproach among all	7839
	44:12	They will become an **object of** c	460
	44:22	your land became an **object of** c and	7839
	49:13	of reproach and of c;	7839
Hos	4: 2	There is only c, lying and murder,	457
Zec	8:13	As you have been an **object of** c among	7839
Ro	3:14	"Their mouths are full *of* c and bitterness."	725
Jas	3:10	Out of the same mouth come praise and c.	2932

CURTAIN (62) [CURTAINS]

Ex	26: 4	of blue material along the edge of the end c	3749
	26: 4	do the same with the end c in the other set.	3749
	26: 5	on one c and fifty loops on the end curtain	3749
	26: 5	and fifty loops on the end c of the other set,	3749
	26: 9	the sixth c double at the front of the tent.	3749
	26:10	the end c in one set and also along the edge	3749
	26:10	along the edge of the end c *in* the other set.	3749
	26:12	the half c that is left over is to hang down	3749
	26:31	"Make a c of blue,	7267
	26:33	the c from the clasps and place the ark of	7267
	26:33	the ark of the Testimony behind the c.	7267
	26:33	The c will separate the Holy Place from	7267
	26:35	the table outside the c on the north side of	7267
	26:36	the entrance to the tent make a c of blue,	5009
	26:37	Make gold hooks for this c and five posts	5009
	27:16	provide a c twenty cubits long, of blue,	5009
	27:21	the c that is in front of the Testimony,	7267
	30: 6	Put the altar in front of the c that is before	7267
	35:12	and the atonement cover and the c	7267
	35:15	the c for the doorway at the entrance to	5009
	35:17	and the c for the entrance to the courtyard;	7267
	36:11	of blue material along the edge of the end c	3749
	36:11	and the same was done with the end c in	3749
	36:12	on one c and fifty loops on the end curtain	3749
	36:12	and fifty loops on the end c of the other set,	3749
	36:17	the end c in one set and also along the edge	3749
	36:17	along the edge of the end c in the other set.	3749
	36:35	They made the c of blue,	7267
	36:37	For the entrance to the tent they made a c	5009
	38:18	The c for the entrance to the courtyard was	5009
	38:27	the bases for the sanctuary and for the c—	7267
	39:34	of hides of sea cows and the shielding c;	7267
	39:38	and the c for the entrance to the tent;	5009
	39:40	and the c for the entrance to the courtyard;	5009
	40: 3	in it and shield the ark with the c.	7267
	40: 5	the Testimony and put the c *at* the entrance	5009
	40: 8	Set up the courtyard around it and put the c	5009
	40:21	into the tabernacle and hung the shielding c	7267
	40:22	of the tabernacle outside the c	7267
	40:26	in the Tent of Meeting in front of the c	7267
	40:28	up the c *at* the entrance to the tabernacle.	5009
	40:33	and altar and put up the c *at* the entrance to	5009
Lev	4: 6	in front of the c of the sanctuary.	7267
	4:17	the LORD seven times in front of the c.	7267
	16: 2	the Most Holy Place behind the c in front	7267
	16:12	and take them behind the c.	7267
	16:15	the people and take its blood behind the c	7267
	21:23	not go near the c or approach the altar,	7267
	24: 3	Outside the c of the Testimony in the Tent	7267
Nu	3:25	the c *at* the entrance to the Tent	5009
	3:26	the c *at* the entrance to the courtyard	5009
	3:31	the c, and everything related to their use.	5009
	4: 5	in and take down the shielding c and cover	7267

Nu	4:26	the c for the entrance,	5009
	18: 7	at the altar and inside the c.	7267
2Ch	3:14	He made the c of blue,	7267
Mt	27:51	that moment the c of the temple was torn	2925
Mk	15:38	The c of the temple was torn in two	2925
Lk	23:45	And the c of the temple was torn in two.	2925
Heb	6:19	It enters the inner sanctuary behind the c,	2925
	9: 3	Behind the second c was a room called	2925
	10:20	living way opened for us through the c,	2925

CURTAINS (36) [CURTAIN]

Ex	26: 1	with ten c of finely twisted linen and blue,	3749
	26: 2	All the c are to be the same size—	3749
	26: 3	Join five of the c together,	3749
	26: 6	and use them to fasten the c together so	3749
	26: 7	"Make c of goat hair for the tent over	3749
	26: 8	All eleven c are to be the same size—	3749
	26: 9	the c together into one set and the other six	3749
	26:12	As for the additional length of the tent c,	3749
	26:13	The tent c will be a cubit longer on	3749
	27: 9	be a hundred cubits long and is to have c	7846
	27:11	be a hundred cubits long and is to have c,	7846
	27:12	be fifty cubits wide and have c	7846
	27:14	C fifteen cubits long are to be on one side	7846
	27:15	and c fifteen cubits long are to be on	7846
	27:18	and fifty cubits wide, with c	NIH
	35:17	the c of the courtyard with its posts	7846
	36: 8	with ten c of finely twisted linen and blue,	3749
	36: 9	All the c were the same size—	3749
	36:10	They joined five of the c together and did	3749
	36:13	to fasten the *two sets* of c together so that	3749
	36:14	They made c of goat hair for the tent over	3749
	36:15	All eleven c were the same size—	3749
	36:16	They joined five of the c into one set and	3749
	38: 9	and had c of finely twisted linen,	7846
	38:12	and had c, with ten posts and ten bases,	7846
	38:14	C fifteen cubits long were on one side of	7846
	38:15	and c fifteen cubits long were on	7846
	38:16	All the c around the courtyard were	7846
	38:18	like the c of the courtyard, five cubits high,	7846
	39:40	the c of the courtyard with its posts	7846
Nu	3:26	the c of the courtyard, the curtain at	7846
	4:25	They are to carry the c of the tabernacle,	3749
	4:25	the c for the entrance to the Tent	5009
	4:26	the c of the courtyard surrounding	7846
SS	1: 5	like the **tent** c of Solomon.	3749
Isa	54: 2	stretch your tent c wide, do not hold back;	3749

CURVED (4)

Jos	15: 3	past Hezron up to Addar and c around	6015
	15:10	it c westward from Baalah to Mount Seir,	6015
	16: 6	the north it c eastward to Taanath Shiloh,	6015
	18:17	*It* then c north, went to En Shemesh,	9305

CUSH (27) [CUSHITE, CUSHITES]

Ge	2:13	it winds through the entire land of C.	3932
	10: 6	C, Mizraim, Put and Canaan.	3932
	10: 7	The sons of C:	3932
	10: 8	C was the father of Nimrod,	3932
1Ch	1: 8	sons of Ham: C, Mizraim, Put and Canaan.	3932
	1: 9	The sons of C:	3932
	1:10	C was the father of Nimrod,	3932
Est	1: 1	from India to C:	3932
	8: 9	from India to C.	3932
Job	28:19	The topaz of C cannot compare with it;	3932
Ps	7: T	to the LORD concerning C,	3933
	68:31	C will submit herself to God.	3932
	87: T	Philistia too, and Tyre, along with C—	3932
Isa	11:11	from Upper Egypt, from C, from Elam,	3932
	18: 1	of whirring wings along the rivers of C,	3932
	20: 3	as a sign and portent against Egypt and C,	3932
	20: 5	in C and boasted in Egypt will be afraid	3932
	43: 3	C and Seba in your stead.	3932
	45:14	of Egypt and the merchandise of C,	3932
Jer	46: 9	men of C and Put who carry shields,	3932
Eze	29:10	as far as the border of C.	3932
	30: 4	and anguish will come upon C.	3932
	30: 5	C and Put, Lydia and all Arabia,	3932
	30: 9	to frighten C out of her complacency.	3932
	38: 5	Persia, C and Put will be with them,	3932
Na	3: 9	C and Egypt were her boundless strength;	3932
Zep	3:10	beyond the rivers of C my worshipers,	3932

CUSHAN (1)

Hab	3: 7	I saw the tents of C in distress,	3936

CUSHAN-RISHATHAIM (2)

Jdg	3: 8	that he sold them into the hands of C king	3937
	3:10	The LORD gave C king of Aram into	3937

CUSHI (2)

Jer	36:14	the son of Shelemiah, the son of C,	3935
Zep	1: 1	that came to Zephaniah son of C, the son	3935

CUSHION (1)

Mk	4:38	Jesus was in the stern, sleeping on a c.	4676

CUSHITE (17) [CUSH]

Nu	12: 1	against Moses because of his C wife,	3934
	12: 1	for he had married a C.	3934
2Sa	18:21	Then Joab said to a C, "Go,	3934
	18:21	The C bowed down before Joab	3934

2Sa	18:22	please let me run behind the C."	3934
	18:23	by way of the plain and outran the C.	3934
	18:31	Then the C arrived and said,	3934
	18:32	The king asked the C,	3934
	18:32	The C replied, "May the enemies	3934
2Ki	19: 9	Tirhakah, the C king [of Egypt],	3932
2Ch	14: 9	Zerah the C marched out against them with	3934
Isa	20: 4	the Egyptian captives and C exiles, young	3932
	37: 9	Tirhakah, the C king [of Egypt],	3932
Jer	38: 7	But Ebed-Melech, a C,	3934
	38:10	the king commanded Ebed-Melech the C,	3934
	38:12	Ebed-Melech the C said to Jeremiah,	3934
	39:16	the C, 'This is what the LORD Almighty,	3934

CUSHITES (8) [CUSH]

2Ch	12: 3	and C that came with him from Egypt,	3934
	14:12	The LORD struck down the C before Asa	3934
	14:12	before Asa and Judah. The C fled,	3934
	14:13	a great number of C fell that they could	3934
	16: 8	Were not the C and Libyans a mighty army	3934
	21:16	and of the Arabs who lived near the C.	3934
Am	9: 7	the same to me as the C?"	1201+3934
Zep	2:12	"You too, O C, will be slain by my sword."	3934

CUSTODY (7)

Ge	40: 3	in c *in* the house of the captain of	5464
	40: 4	After they had been in c for some time,	5464
	40: 7	in c with him *in* his master's house,	5464
	42:17	And he put them all in c for three days.	5464
Lev	24:12	in c until the will of the LORD should	5464
Nu	15:34	and they kept him in c,	5464
1Ch	29: 8	the temple of the LORD in the c of Jehiel	3338

CUSTOM (19) [ACCUSTOMED, CUSTOMARY, CUSTOMS]

Ge	19:31	as is the c all over the earth.	2006
	29:26	not our c here to give the younger daughter in marriage before the older on.	4027+6913
Jdg	8:24	(**It was the c** of the Ishamaelites	3954
	11:39	From this comes the Israelite c	2976
1Ki	18:28	as was their c, until their blood flowed.	5477
2Ki	11:14	standing by the pillar, as the c was.	5477
Est	9:27	upon themselves *to* **establish the c**	7756
Job	1: 5	This *was* Job's regular c.	6913
Mt	27:15	Now *it was* the governor's c at the Feast	1665
Mk	10: 1	and as *was* his c, he taught them.	1665
	15: 6	Now it was the c at the Feast to release	NIG
Lk	1: 9	according to the c of the priesthood,	1621
	2:27	the child Jesus to do for him what the c of	1616
	2:42	went up to the Feast, according to the c.	1621
	4:16	went into the synagogue, as was his c.	1665
Jn	18:39	But it is your c for me to release	5311
Ac	15: 1	*according to* the c taught by Moses,	1621
	17: 2	As his c was, Paul went into the synagogue,	1665
	25:16	not the Roman c to hand over any man	1621

CUSTOMARY (6) [CUSTOM]

Jdg	14:10	as *was* c for bridegrooms.	6913
1Sa	20:25	He sat in his c place by the wall,	928+3869+7193+7193
Est	1:13	Since it was c *for* the king	1821+4027
Eze	24:17	the lower part of your face or eat the c food	NIH
	24:22	the lower part of your face or eat the c food	NIH
Mk	14:12	it was c to sacrifice the Passover lamb,	NIG

CUSTOMERS (2)

Eze	27:15	and many coastlands were your c;	3338+6088
	27:21	all the princes of Kedar were your c;	3338+6086

CUSTOMS (13) [CUSTOM]

Lev	18:30	and do not follow any of the detestable c	2978
	20:23	the c of the nations I am going to drive out	2978
2Ki	17:33	in accordance with the c of the nations	5477
Est	3: 8	of your kingdom whose c are different	2017
Ps	106:35	with the nations and adopted their c.	5126
Jer	10: 3	For the c of the peoples are worthless;	2978
Jn	19:40	in accordance with Jewish burial c.	1621
Ac	6:14	and change the c Moses handed down	1621
	16:21	by advocating c unlawful for us Romans	1621
	21:21	or live *according to* our c.	1621
	26: 3	with all the Jewish c and controversies.	1621
	28:17	against our people or against the c	1621
Gal	2:14	you force Gentiles *to* **follow Jewish c?**	2678

CUT (288) [CUTS, CUTTER, CUTTING, FRESH-CUT]

Ge	9:11	Never again *will* all life be c off by the waters of a flood;	4162
	15:10	c them in two and arranged	1439
	15:10	the birds, however, *he* did not c **in half.**	1439
	17:14	*will* be c off from his people;	4162
	22: 3	When *he* had c enough wood for the burnt offering,	1324
Ex	4:25	c off her son's foreskin	4162
	12:15	the seventh *must* be c off from Israel.	4162
	12:19	in it *must* be c off from the community	4162
	29:17	C the ram into pieces and wash	5983
	30:33	a priest *must* be c off from his people.' "	4162
	30:38	like it to enjoy its fragrance *must* be c **off**	4162
	31: 5	to c and set stones,	3098
	31:14	on that day *must* be c off from his people.	4162
	34:13	and c **down** their Asherah poles.	4162

Ex	35:33	to **c** and set stones,	3098
	39: 3	and **c** strands to be worked into the blue,	7915
Lev	1: 6	He is to skin the burnt offering and **c** it	5983
	1:12	*He is to* **c** it into pieces,	5983
	3: 9	entire fat tail **c off** close to the backbone,	6073
	7:20	that person *must* **be c off** from his people.	4162
	7:21	to the LORD, that person *must* **be c off**	4162
	7:25	the LORD *must* **be c off** from his people.	4162
	7:27	that person *must* **be c off**	4162
	8:20	*He* **c** the ram into pieces and burned	5983
	17: 4	he has shed blood and *must* **be c off**	4162
	17: 9	that man *must* **be c off** from his people.	4162
	17:10	and *will* **c** him **off** from his people.	4162
	17:14	anyone who eats it *must* **be c off.**"	4162
	18:29	such persons *must* **be c off**	4162
	19: 8	that person *must* **be c off** from his people.	4162
	19:27	'Do not **c** the **hair** at the sides of your head	5938
	19:28	" 'Do not **c** your bodies for the dead	5989+8582
	20: 3	and *I will* **c** him **off** from his people;	4162
	20: 5	and *will* **c off** from their people both him	4162
	20: 6	and *I will* **c** him **off** from his people.	4162
	20:17	*They* must **be c off** before the eyes	4162
	20:18	of them *must* **be c off** from their people.	4162
	21: 5	edges of their beards or **c** their bodies.	8581+8583
	22: 3	to the LORD, that person *must* **be c off**	4162
	22:24	to the LORD an animal whose testicles are bruised, crushed, torn or **c.**	4162
	23:29	not deny himself on that day *must* **be c off**	4162
	26:26	When I **c** your supply of bread,	8689
	26:30	**c down** your incense altars	4162
Nu	4:18	the Kohathite tribal clans *are* not **c off**	4162
	9:13	that person *must* **be c off** from his people	4162
	13:23	*they* **c off** a branch bearing a single cluster	4162
	13:24	of grapes the Israelites **c off** there.	4162
	15:30	that person *must* **be c off** from his people.	4162
	15:31	*must surely* **be c off;**	4162+4162
	19:13	That person *must* **be c off** from Israel.	4162
	19:20	he *must* **be c off** from the community,	4162
Dt	7: 5	**c down** their Asherah poles	1548
	12: 3	**c down** the idols of their gods	1548
	12:29	The LORD your God *will* **c off**	4162
	14: 1	*Do* not **c** yourselves or shave the front	1517
	19: 5	into the forest with his neighbor to **c** wood,	2634
	20:19	*Do* not **c** them **down.**	4162
	20:20	*you may* **c down** trees that you know are	4162
	25:12	*you shall* **c off** her hand.	7915
	25:18	and **c off** all who were lagging behind;	2386
Jos	3:13	its waters flowing downstream *will* **be c off**	4162
	3:16	(the Salt Sea) *was* completely **c off.**	4162
	4: 7	that the flow of the Jordan *was* **c off** before	4162
	4: 7	the waters of the Jordan *were* **c off.**	4162
	8:22	Israel **c** them **down,**	4162
	10:10	to Beth Horon and **c** them **down** all the way	5782
Jdg	1: 6	and **c off** his thumbs and big toes.	7915
	1: 7	and big toes **c off** have picked up scraps	7915
	6:25	down your father's altar to Baal and **c down**	4162
	6:26	of the Asherah pole that *you* **c down,**	4162
	6:28	with the Asherah pole beside it **c down** and	4162
	6:30	and **c down** the Asherah pole beside it."	4162
	9:48	He took an ax and **c off** some branches,	4162
	9:49	So all the men **c** branches	4162
	19:29	he took a knife and **c up** his concubine,	5983
	20: 6	**c** her **into pieces** and sent one piece	5983
	20:21	and **c down** twenty-two thousand Israelites	8845
	20:25	from Gibeah to oppose them, *they* **c down**	8845
	20:42	of the towns **c** them **down** there.	8845
	20:45	the Israelites **c down** five thousand men	6618
	21: 6	"Today one tribe *is* **c off** from Israel,"	1548
1Sa	2:31	when *I will* **c short** your strength and	1548
	2:33	not **c off** from my altar will be spared only	4162
	11: 7	He took a pair of oxen, **c** them **into pieces,**	5983
	17:46	I'll strike you down and **c off** your head.	6073
	17:51	*he* **c off** his head with the sword.	4162
	20:15	and *do* not ever **c off** your kindness	4162
	20:15	even when the LORD *has* **c off** every one	4162
	24: 4	Then David crept up unnoticed and **c off**	4162
	24: 5	for *having* **c off** a corner of his robe.	4162
	24:11	I **c off** the corner of your robe but did	4162
	24:21	that *you will* not **c off** my descendants	4162
	28: 9	He *has* **c off** the mediums and spiritists	4162
	31: 9	*They* **c off** Israel his head	4162
2Sa	4: 7	*they* **c off** his head.	6073
	4:12	*They* **c off** their hands and feet and hung	7915
	7: 9	and *I have* **c off** all your enemies from	4162
	10: 4	**c off** their garments in the middle at	4162
	14:26	the hand of the man *who is trying to* **c off**	9012
	14:26	Whenever he **c** *the hair* of his head—	1662
	14:26	he used to **c** *his* **hair** from time to time	1662
	16: 9	Let me go over and **c off** his head."	6073
	20:22	and *they* **c off** the head of Sheba son	4162
1Ki	3:25	"**C** the living child in two and give half	1615
	3:26	**C** him **in two!**"	1615
	5: 6	that cedars of Lebanon *be* **c** for me.	4162
	5:18	the men of Gebal **c** and prepared the timber	7180
	7: 9	were made of blocks of high-grade stone **c**	1607
	7:11	Above were high-grade stones, **c** to size,	1607
	9: 7	then *I will* **c off** Israel from the	4162
	14:10	*I will* **c off** from Jeroboam every last male	4162
	14:14	over Israel who *will* **c off** the family	4162
	15:13	Asa **c** the pole **down** and burned it in	1548
	18:23	and *let them* **c** it **into pieces** and put it on	5983
	18:33	**c** the bull **into pieces**	5983
	21:21	I will consume your descendants and **c off**	4162
2Ki	3:19	*You will* **c down** every good tree,	5877
	3:25	They stopped up all the springs and **c down**	5877
	4:39	*he* **c** them **up** into the pot of stew,	7114
	6: 4	to the Jordan and *began to* **c down** trees.	1615

2Ki	6: 6	Elisha **c** a stick and threw it there,	7892
	6:32	to **c off** my head?	6073
	9: 8	*I will* **c off** from Ahab every last male	4162
	10: 7	So *they* **c** them **down** with the sword.	5782
	18: 4	smashed the sacred stones and **c down**	4162
	19: 9	and there *I will* **have** him **c down** with	5877
	19:23	*I have* **c down** its tallest cedars,	4162
	19:37	and Sharezer **c** him **down** with the sword,	5782
	23:14	and **c down** the Asherah poles and covered	4162
1Ch	17: 8	and *I have* **c off** all your enemies from	4162
	19: 4	**c off** their garments in the middle at	4162
2Ch	2:10	the woodsmen *who* **c** the timber,	4162
	2:16	and we *will* **c** all the logs from Lebanon	4162
	14: 3	smashed the sacred stones and **c down**	1548
	15:16	Asa **c** the pole **down,**	4162
	16:14	in the tomb that *he had* **c out** for himself in	4125
	31: 1	smashed the sacred stones and **c down**	1548
	32:21	of his sons **c** him **down** with the sword,	5877
	34: 4	*he* **c to pieces** the incense altars that were	1548
	34: 7	the idols to powder and **c to pieces** all	1548
Job	6: 9	to let loose his hand and **c** me **off!**	1298
	14: 7	If *it is* **c down,** it will sprout again,	4162
	17: 1	My spirit is broken, my days *are* **c short,**	2403
	24:24	*they* are **c off** like heads of grain.	4909
	26:12	by his wisdom *he* **c** Rahab **to pieces.**	4730
	27: 8	the godless when *he is* **c off,**	1298
Ps	12: 3	*May* the LORD **c off** all flattering lips	2933
	31:22	"I am **c off** from your sight!"	1746
	34:16	to **c off** the memory of them from	4162
	37: 9	For evil men *will* **be c off,**	4162
	37:28	but those he curses *will* **be c off;**	4162
	37:28	the offspring of the wicked *will* **be c off;**	4162
	37:34	when the wicked **are c off,** you will see it.	4162
	37:38	the future of the wicked *will* **be c off.**	4162
	74: 5	They behaved like men wielding axes to **c**	NIH
	75:10	*I will* **c off** the horns of all the wicked,	1548
	80:16	Your vine **is c down,** it is burned with fire;	4065
	88: 5	who **are c off** from your care.	1615
	89:45	*You have* **c short** the days of his youth;	7918
	101: 8	*I will* **c off** every evildoer from the city	4162
	102:23	*he* **c short** my days.	7918
	109:13	May his descendants be **c off,**	4162
	109:15	that *he may* **c off** the memory of them from	4162
	118:10	in the name of the LORD *I* **c** them **off.**	4577
	118:11	in the name of the LORD *I* **c** them **off.**	4577
	118:12	in the name of the LORD *I* **c** them **off.**	4577
	129: 4	*he has* **c** me **free** *from* the cords of	7915
Pr	2:22	the wicked *will* **be c off** from the land,	4162
	10:27	but the years of the wicked *are* **c short.**	7918
	10:31	but a perverse tongue *will* **be c out.**	4162
	23:18	and your hope *will* not **be c off.**	4162
	24:14	and your hope *will* not **be c off.**	4162
Isa	5: 2	a watchtower in it and **c out** a winepress	2933
	6:13	when they are **c down,**	8961
	9:14	So the LORD *will* **c off** from Israel	4162
	10:34	*He will* **c down** the forest thickets with	5937
	11:13	and Judah's enemies *will* **be c off;**	4162
	14: 8	no *woodsman* comes to **c** us **down.**"	4162
	14:22	"I *will* **c off** from Babylon her name	4162
	15: 2	and every beard **c off.**	1757
	18: 5	*he will* **c off** the shoots	4162
	18: 5	and **c down** and take away	9372
	22:16	and who gave you permission *to* **c out**	2933
	22:25	and the load hanging on it *will* **be c down.**"	4162
	29:20	all who have an eye for evil *will* **be c down**	4162
	33:12	like **c** thornbushes they will be set ablaze."	4065
	37: 7	and there *I will* **have** him **c down** with	5877
	37:24	*I have* **c down** its tallest cedars,	4162
	37:38	and Sharezer **c** him **down** with the sword,	5782
	38:12	and *he has* **c** me **off** from the loom;	1298
	44:14	He **c down** cedars,	4162
	45: 2	**c down** gates of bronze and **c through** bars	1548
	48: 9	so as not to **c** you **off,**	4162
	48:19	their name *would* never **be c off**	4162
	51: 1	to the rock from which *you* **were c** and to	2933
	51: 9	Was it not you who **c** Rahab **to pieces,**	2933
	53: 8	For *he was* **c off** from the land of the living;	1615
	56: 5	an everlasting name that *will* not **be c off.**	4162
Jer	6: 6	"**C down** the trees and build siege ramps	4162
	7:29	**C off** your hair and throw it away;	1605
	9:21	*it has* **c off** the children from the streets	4162
	9:22	like **c grain** behind the reaper,	6658
	10: 3	*they* **c** a tree out of the forest,	2634
	11:19	*let us* **c** him **off** from the land of the living	1517
	16: 6	and no *one* will **c** himself	1517
	22: 7	and *they* will **c up** your fine cedar beams	4162
	34:18	like the calf *they* **c** in two and then walked	4162
	36:23	the king **c** them **off** with a scribe's knife	7973
	36:29	and **c off** both men and animals from it?"	8697
	41: 5	torn their clothes and **c themselves** came	1517
	46:22	like *men who* **c down** trees.	2634
	47: 4	to **c off** all survivors who could help Tyre	4162
	47: 5	how long *will* you **c yourselves?**	1517
	48:25	Moab's horn *is* **c off;**	1548
	48:37	and every beard **c off;**	1757
	50:16	**C off** from Babylon the sower,	4162
	51:13	the time for you to **be c off.**	1299
La	2: 3	In fierce anger he *has* **c off** every horn	1548
	3:54	and I thought *I was about to* **be c off.**	1615
Eze	4:16	of man, I *will* **c off** the supply of food	8689
	5:16	upon you and **c off** your supply of food.	8689
	6: 6	*I will* **c** them **off** from my people.	4162
	14:13	*to* **c off** its food supply and send famine	8689
	16: 4	the day you were born your cord *was* not **c,**	4162
	21: 3	from its scabbard and **c off** from you both	4162
	21: 4	Because *I am going to* **c off** the righteous	4162
	23:25	*They* will **c off** your noses and your ears,	6073

Eze	23:47	The mob will stone them and **c** them **down**	1345
	25: 7	*I will* **c** you **off** from the nations	4162
	25:16	against the Philistines, and *I will* **c off**	4162
	30:15	and **c off** the hordes of Thebes.	4162
	31:12	of foreign nations **c** it **down** and left it.	4162
	35: 7	and **c off** from it all who come and go.	4162
	37:11	our hope is gone; we **are c off.**'	1615
	39:10	to gather wood from the fields or **c** it from	2634
Da	2: 5	and interpret it, I *will* **have** you **c into**	10522
	2:34	you were watching, a rock **was c out,**	10140
	2:45	the meaning of the vision of the rock **c out**	10140
	3:29	Meshach and Abednego **be c into** pieces	10522
	4:14	'**C down** the tree and trim off its branches;	10134
	4:23	'**C down** the tree and destroy it,	10134
	9:26	the Anointed One *will* **be c off**	4162
Hos	6: 5	Therefore *I* **c** you **in pieces**	2933
Joel	1: 9	and drink offerings *are* **c off** from	4162
	1:16	the food **been c off** before our very eyes—	4162
Am	3:14	the horns of the altar *will* **be c off** and fall	1548
Ob	1: 9	in Esau's mountains *will* **be c down** in	4162
	1:14	at the crossroads to **c down** their fugitives,	4162
Na	1:12	*they* will **be c off** and pass away.	1605
	3:15	the sword *will* **c** you **down,**	4162
Zep	1: 3	of rubble when *I* **c off** man from the face	4162
	1: 4	*I will* **c off** from this place every remnant of	4162
	3: 6	"*I have* **c off** nations;	4162
	3: 7	Then her dwelling *would* not **be c off,**	4162
Zec	9: 6	*I will* **c off** the pride of the Philistines.	4162
	11: 2	the dense forest *has been* **c down!**	3718
Mal	2:12	*may* the LORD **c** him **off** from the tents	4162
Mt	3:10	not produce good fruit *will be* **c down**	1716
	5:30	**c** it **off** and throw it away.	1716
	7:19	not bear good fruit *is* **c down** and thrown	1716
	18: 8	**c** it **off** and throw it away.	1716
	21: 8	while others **c** branches from the trees	3164
	24:22	If those days *had* not *been* **c short,**	3143
	24:51	He *will* **c** him **to pieces** and assign him	1497
	27:60	in his own new tomb that *he had* **c out** of	3300
Mk	5: 5	in the hills he would cry out and **c** himself	2888
	9:43	If your hand causes you to sin, **c** it **off.**	644
	9:45	And if your foot causes you to sin, **c** it **off.**	644
	11: 8	while others spread branches *they* **c** in	3164
	13:20	If the Lord *had* not **c short** those days,	3143
	15:46	and placed it in a tomb **c out** of rock.	1639+3300
Lk	3: 9	not produce good fruit *will be* **c down**	1716
	12:46	*He will* **c** him **to pieces** and assign him	1497
	13: 7	**C** it **down!**	1716
	13: 9	If not, then **c** it **down.**' "	1716
	23:53	and placed it in a tomb **c in the rock,**	3292
Jn	18:26	of the man whose ear Peter *had* **c off,**	644
Ac	2:37	*they* were **c** to the heart and said to Peter	2920
	3:23	completely **c off** from among his people.'	2017
	18:18	*he* had his hair **c off** at Cenchrea because of	3025
	27:32	So the soldiers **c** the ropes that held	644
Ro	9: 3	that I myself were cursed and **c off** from	608
	11:22	Otherwise, you also *will* **be c off.**	1716
	11:24	if you *were* **c out** of an olive tree	1716
1Co	11: 6	*she* should *have* her hair **c off;**	3025
	11: 6	a woman *to have her* **hair c** or shaved off,	3025
2Co	11:12	the ground **from under** those	1716
Gal	5: 7	Who **c in on** you and kept you	1601

CUTHAH (2)

2Ki	17:24	**C,** Avva, Hamath and Sepharvaim	3940
	17:30	the men from **C** made Nergal,	3939

CUTS (4) [CUT]

Job	28: 4	Far from where people dwell he **c** a shaft,	7287
	38:25	Who **c** a channel for the torrents of rain,	7103
Ps	107:16	down gates of bronze and **c through** bars	1548
Jn	15: 2	He **c off** every branch in me	149

CUTTER (1) [CUT]

Ex	28:11	the two stones the way a gem **c** engraves	3093

CUTTING (11) [CUT]

Dt	23: 1	**c** may enter the assembly of the LORD.	4162+9163
2Ki	6: 5	As one of them was **c down** a tree,	5877
2Ch	2: 8	that your men are skilled in **c** timber there.	4162
Ps	78:31	**c down** the young men of Israel.	4156
Pr	26: 6	Like **c off** one's feet	7894
Jer	44: 7	on yourselves by **c off** from Judah the men	4162
Mt	26:51	servant of the high priest, **c off** his ear.	904
Mk	14:47	servant of the high priest, **c off** his ear.	904
Lk	22:50	servant of the high priest, **c off** his right ear.	904
Jn	18:10	the high priest's servant, **c off** his right ear.	644
Ac	27:40	**C loose** the anchors,	4311

CUZA (1)

Lk	8: 3	Joanna the wife of **C,** the manager of Herod's household;	5966

CYCLE (1)

Isa	29: 1	**c** of festivals **go on.**	5938

CYMBAL (1) [CYMBALS]

1Co	13: 1	a resounding gong or a clanging **c.**	3247

CYMBALS (16) [CYMBAL]

2Sa	6: 5	lyres, tambourines, sistrums and **c.**	7529
1Ch	13: 8	lyres, tambourines, **c** and trumpets.	5199
	15:16	musical instruments: lyres, harps and **c.**	5199

CYPRESS (5)

1Ch	15:19	and Ethan were to sound the bronze c;	5199
	15:28	of rams' horns and trumpets, and of c, and	5199
	16: 5	Asaph was to sound the c,	5199
	16:42	of the trumpets and c and for the playing of	5199
	25: 1	accompanied by harps, lyres and c.	5199
	25: 6	with c, lyres and harps,	5199
2Ch	5:12	dressed in fine linen and playing c,	5199
	5:13	c and other instruments,	5199
	29:25	in the temple of the LORD with c, harps	5199
Ezr	3:10	and the Levites (the sons of Asaph) with c,	5199
Ne	12:27	of thanksgiving and with the music of c,	5199
Ps	150: 5	praise him with the clash of c,	7529
	150: 5	praise him with resounding c.	7529

CYPRESS (5)

Ge	6:14	So make yourself an ark of c wood;	1729
Isa	41:19	the fir and the c together,	9309
	44:14	or perhaps took a c or oak.	9560
	60:13	the pine, the fir and the c together,	9309
Eze	27: 6	of c wood from the coasts	9309

CYPRUS (11)

Isa	23: 1	From the land of C word has come to them.	4183
	23:12	"Up, cross over to C;	4183
Eze	27: 6	from the coasts of C they made your deck,	4183
Ac	4:36	Joseph, a Levite from C,	3250
	11:19	as far as Phoenicia, C and Antioch, telling	3251
	11:20	however, men from C and Cyrene,	3250
	13: 4	to Seleucia and sailed from there to C.	3251
	15:39	Barnabas took Mark and sailed for C,	3251
	21: 3	After sighting C and passing to the south	3251
	21:16	He was a man from C and one of	3250
	27: 4	of C because the winds were against us.	3251

CYRENE (7)

Mt	27:32	they met a man from C, named Simon,	3254
Mk	15:21	A certain man from C, Simon,	3254
Lk	23:26	they seized Simon from C,	3254
Ac	2:10	Egypt and the parts of Libya near C;	3255
	6: 9	Jews of C and Alexandria as well as	3254
	11:20	however, men from Cyprus and C,	3254
	13: 1	Simeon called Niger, Lucius of C,	3254

CYRENIAN, CYRENIANS (KJV) See CYRENE

CYRENIUS (KJV) See QUIRINIUS

CYRUS (23)

2Ch	36:22	In the first year of C king of Persia,	3931
	36:22	of C king of Persia to make a proclamation	3931
	36:23	"This is what C king of Persia says:	3931
Ezr	1: 1	In the first year of C king of Persia,	3931
	1: 1	of C king of Persia to make a proclamation	3931
	1: 2	"This is what C king of Persia says:	3931
	1: 7	King C brought out the articles belonging	3931
	1: 8	C king of Persia had them brought	3931
	3: 7	as authorized by C king of Persia.	3931
	4: 3	as King C, the king of Persia,	3931
	4: 5	during the entire reign of C king of Persia	3931
	5:13	in the first year of C king of Babylon,	10350
	5:13	King C issued a decree	10350
	5:14	"Then King C gave them to	10350
	5:17	to see if King C did in fact issue a decree	10350
	6: 3	In the first year of King C, the king issued	10350
	6:14	of the God of Israel and the decrees of C,	10350
Isa	44:28	who says of C, 'He is my shepherd	3931
	45: 1	to C, whose right hand I take hold of	3931
	45:13	I will raise up C in my righteousness:	2084S
Da	1:21	until the first year of King C.	3931
	6:28	of Darius and the reign of C the Persian.	10350
	10: 1	In the third year of C king of Persia,	3931

D

DABAREH (KJV) See DABERATH

DABBESHETH (1)

Jos 19:11 Going west it ran to Maralah, touched D, 1833

DABERATH (3)

Jos	19:12	of Kisloth Tabor and went on to D and up	1829
	21:28	from the tribe of Issachar, Kishion, D,	1829
1Ch	6:72	of Issachar they received Kedesh, D,	1829

DAGGER (3)

2Sa	2:16	and thrust his d into his opponent's side,	2995
	20: 8	at his waist was a belt with a d in its sheath.	2995
	20:10	Amasa was not on his guard against the d	2995

DAGON (8) [BETH DAGON, DAGON'S]

Jdg	16:23	to offer a great sacrifice to D their god and	1837
1Sa	5: 2	into Dagon's temple and set it beside D.	1837
	5: 3	the next day, there was D, fallen on his face	1837
	5: 3	They took D and put him back in his place.	1837
	5: 4	when they rose, there was D, fallen	1837
	5: 5	to this day neither the priests of D	1837
	5: 7	upon us and upon D our god."	1837
1Ch	10:10	and hung up his head in the temple of D.	1837

DAGON'S (2) [DAGON]

1Sa	5: 2	Then they carried the ark into D temple	1837
	5: 5	nor any others who enter D temple	1837

DAILY (30) [DAY]

Nu	29: 6	to the monthly and d burnt offerings	9458
1Ki	4:22	Solomon's d provisions were	285+3427+4200
2Ch	8:13	the d requirement for offerings commanded by Moses	928+3427+3427
	31:16	to perform the d duties	928+2257+3427+3427
Ezr	6: 9	must be given them d without fail,	10089+10317+10317
Ne	11:23	which regulated their d activity.	928+3427+3427
	12:47	all Israel contributed the d portions for the singers and gatekeepers.	928+1821+3427+3427
Job	23:12	of his mouth more than my d bread.	2976
Ps	68:19	who d bears our burdens.	3427+3427
Pr	8:34	watching d at my doors,	3427+3427
	30: 7	but give me only my d bread.	2976+4312
Eze	43:25	to provide a male goat d for a sin offering;	2021+3427+4200
Da	1: 5	The king assigned them a d amount of food and wine	928+3427+3427
	8:11	it took away the d sacrifice from him,	9458
	8:12	and the d sacrifice were given over to it.	9458
	8:13	the vision concerning the d sacrifice,	9458
	11:31	and will abolish the d sacrifice.	9458
	12:11	the time that the d sacrifice is abolished	9458
Mt	6:11	Give us today our d bread.	2157
Lk	9:23	and take up his cross d and follow me.	2465+2848
	11: 3	Give us each day our d bread,	2157
Ac	2:47	the Lord added to their number d those who were being saved.	2465+2848
	6: 1	overlooked in the d distribution of food.	2766
	16: 5	in the faith and grew d in numbers.	2465+2848
	17:11	had discussions d in the lecture hall	2465+2848
2Co	11:28	I face d the pressure of my concern	2465+2848
1Th	4:12	so that your d life may win the respect	4344
Tit	3:14	that they may provide for d necessities	338+5970
Heb	3:13	But encourage one another d,	1667+2465+2848
Jas	2:15	or sister is without clothes and d food.	2390

DAINTY (KJV) See CHOICEST, DELICACIES, RICHES

DALAIAH (KJV) See DELAIAH

DALE (KJV) See VALLEY

DALMANUTHA (1)

Mk 8:10 and went to the region of D. 1236

DALMATIA (1)

2Ti 4:10 and Titus to D. 1237

DALPHON (1)

Est 9: 7 They also killed Parshandatha, D, Aspatha, 1943

DAM (1)

Pr 17:14 Starting a quarrel is like breaching a d; 4784

DAMAGE (4) [DAMAGED]

2Ki	12: 5	be used to repair whatever d is found in	981
	12: 7	"Why aren't you repairing the d done to	981
Ac	27:21	you would have spared yourselves this d	5615
Rev	6: 6	and do not d the oil and the wine!"	92

DAMAGED (1) [DAMAGE]

Lev 21:20 or running sores or d testicles. 5293

DAMARIS (1)

Ac 17:34 also a woman named D, 1240

DAMASCENES (1) [DAMASCUS]

2Co 11:32 of the D guarded in order to arrest me. 1241

DAMASCUS (59) [DAMASCENES]

Ge	14:15	pursuing them as far as Hobah, north of D.	1966
	15: 2	who will inherit my estate is Eliezer of D?"	1966
2Sa	8: 5	of D came to help Hadadezer king	1966
	8: 6	in the Aramean kingdom of D,	1966
1Ki	11:24	the rebels went to D,	1966
	15:18	the king of Aram, who was ruling in D.	1966
	19:15	and go to the Desert of D.	1966
	20:34	up your own market areas in D,	1966
2Ki	5:12	Are not Abana and Pharpar, the rivers of D,	1966
	8: 7	Elisha went to D,	1966
	8: 9	of all the finest wares of D.	1966
	14:28	how he recovered for Israel both D	1966
	16: 9	of Assyria complied by attacking D	1966
	16:10	to D to meet Tiglath-Pileser king	1877
	16:10	in D and sent to Uriah the priest a sketch of	1966
	16:11	the plans that King Ahaz had sent from D	1966
	16:12	king came back from D and saw the altar,	1966
1Ch	18: 5	of D came to help Hadadezer king	2008
	18: 6	in the Aramean kingdom of D,	2008
2Ch	16: 2	who was ruling in D.	2008
	24:23	They sent all the plunder to their king in D.	2008
	28: 5	as prisoners and brought them to D,	2008
	28:23	He offered sacrifices to the gods of D,	2008
SS	7: 4	the tower of Lebanon looking toward D.	1966
Isa	7: 8	for the head of Aram is D,	1966
	7: 8	and the head of D is only Rezin.	1966
	8: 4	of D and the plunder of Samaria will	1966
	10: 9	and Samaria like D?	1966
	17: 1	An oracle concerning D:	1966
	17: 1	D will no longer be a city but will become	1966
	17: 3	and royal power from D;	1966
Jer	49:23	Concerning D: "Hamath	1966
	49:24	D has become feeble, she has turned to flee	1966
	49:27	"I will set fire to the walls of D;	1966
Eze	27:18	" 'D, because of your many products	1966
	47:16	on the border between D and Hamath,	1966
	47:17	along the northern border of D,	1966
	47:18	between Hauran and D,	1966
	48: 1	and the northern border of D next	1966
Am	1: 3	"For three sins of D, even for four,	1966
	1: 5	I will break down the gate of D;	1966
	3:12	of their beds and in D on their couches."	1966
	5:27	I will send you into exile beyond D,"	1966
Zec	9: 1	the land of Hadrach and will rest upon D—	1966
Ac	9: 2	for letters to the synagogues in D,	1242
	9: 3	As he neared D on his journey,	1242
	9: 8	So they led him by the hand into D.	1242
	9:10	In D there was a disciple named Ananias.	1242
	9:19	with the disciples in D.	1242
	9:22	the Jews living in D by proving that Jesus is	1242
	9:27	in D he had preached fearlessly in the name	1242
	22: 5	from them to their brothers in D,	1242
	22: 6	"About noon as I came near D,	1242
	22:10	'Get up,' the Lord said, 'and go into D.	1242
	22:11	My companions led me by the hand into D,	1242
	26:12	"On one of these journeys I was going to D	1242
	26:20	First to those in D,	1242
2Co	11:32	In D the governor under King Aretas had	1242
Gal	1:17	into Arabia and later returned to D.	1242

DAMMIM See EPHES DAMMIM, PAS DAMMIM

DAMNATION (KJV) See CONDEMNED, CONDEMNATION, DESTRUCTION, JUDGMENT, PUNISHED SEVERELY, SIN

DAMPNESS (1)

SS 5: 2 my hair with the d of the night." 8268

DAMSEL (KJV) See CHILD, LITTLE GIRL, SERVANT GIRL, SLAVE GIRL, VIRGIN, YOUNG WOMAN

DAN (59) [DAN JAAN, DANITE, DANITES, LAISH, LESHEM, MAHANEH DAN]

Ge	14:14	and went in pursuit as far as D	1969
	30: 6	Because of this she named him D.	1968
	35:25	of Rachel's maidservant Bilhah: D and Naphtali.	1968
	46:23	The son of D: Hushim.	1968
	49:16	"D will provide justice for his people	1968
	49:17	D will be a serpent by the roadside,	1968
Ex	1: 4	D and Naphtali; Gad and Asher.	1968
	31: 6	of the tribe of D, to help him.	1968
	35:34	of the tribe of D, the ability to teach others.	1968
	38:23	of the tribe of D—	1968
Nu	1:12	from D, Ahiezer son of Ammishaddai.	1968
	1:38	From the descendants of D:	1968
	1:39	number from the tribe of D was 62,700.	1968
	2:25	be the divisions of the camp of D,	1968
	2:25	of D is Ahiezer son of Ammishaddai.	1968
	2:31	to the camp of D number 157,600.	1968
	7:66	the leader of the people of D,	1968
	10:25	the divisions of the camp of D set out,	1201+1968
	13:12	the tribe of D, Ammiel son of Gemalli;	1968
	26:42	the descendants of D by their clans:	1968
	26:42	These were the clans of D;	1968
	34:22	the leader from the tribe of D;	1201+1968
Dt	27:13	Gad, Asher, Zebulun, D and Naphtali.	1968
	33:22	About D he said:	1968
	33:22	About Dan he said: "D is a lion's cub,	1968
	34: 1	from Gilead to D,	1968
Jos	19:40	seventh lot came out for the tribe of D,	1201+1968
	19:47	They settled in Leshem and named it D	1969
	19:48	the inheritance of the tribe of D,	1201+1968
	21: 5	D and half of Manasseh.	1968
	21:23	from the tribe of D they received Eltekeh,	1968
Jdg	5:17	And D, why did he linger by the ships?	1968
	18:29	They named it D after their forefather Dan,	1969
	18:29	They named it Dan after their forefather D,	1968

Jdg	18:30	the tribe of **D** until the time of the captivity	1974
	20: 1	the Israelites from **D** to Beersheba and from	1969
1Sa	3:20	from **D** to Beersheba recognized	1969
2Sa	3:10	and Judah from **D** to Beersheba."	1969
	17:11	Let all Israel, from **D** to Beersheba—	1969
	24: 2	"Go throughout the tribes of Israel from **D**	1969
	24:15	and seventy thousand of the people from **D**	1969
1Ki	4:25	from **D** to Beersheba, lived in safety,	1969
	12:29	One he set up in Bethel, and the other in **D**.	1969
	12:30	the people went even as far as **D** to worship	1969
	15:20	He conquered Ijon, **D**,	1969
2Ki	10:29	of the golden calves at Bethel and **D**.	1969
1Ch	2: 2	**D**, Joseph, Benjamin, Naphtali, Gad	1968
	12:35	men of **D**, ready for battle—28,600;	1974
	21: 2	the Israelites from Beersheba to **D**.	1969
	27:22	over **D**: Azarel son of Jeroham.	1968
2Ch	2:14	from **D** and whose father was from Tyre.	1968
	16: 4	They conquered Ijon, **D**,	1969
	30: 5	from Beersheba to **D**,	1969
Jer	4:15	A voice is announcing from **D**,	1969
	8:16	of the enemy's horses is heard from **D**;	1969
Eze	48: 1	**D** will have one portion;	1968
	48: 2	it will border the territory of **D** from east	1968
	48:32	the gate of Benjamin and the gate of **D**.	1968
Am	8:14	or say, 'As surely as your god lives, O **D**,'	1969

DAN JAAN (1) [DAN]

2Sa	24: 6	and on to **D** and around toward Sidon.	1970

DANCE (7) [DANCED, DANCES, DANCING]

Job	21:11	their little ones **d** about.	8376
Ecc	3: 4	a time to mourn and a time to **d**,	8376
SS	6:13	the Shulammite as on the **d** of Mahanaim?	4703
Jer	31: 4	up your tambourines and go out to **d** with	4688
	31:13	Then maidens will **d** and be glad,	4688
Mt	11:17	and *you* did not **d**;	4004
Lk	7:32	and *you* did not **d**;	4004

DANCED (5) [DANCE]

1Sa	18: 7	As they **d**, they sang:	8471
2Sa	6:14	**d** before the LORD with all his might,	4159
1Ki	18:26	And *they* **d** around the altar they had made.	7174
Mt	14: 6	of Herodias **d** for them and pleased Herod	4004
Mk	6:22	the daughter of Herodias came in and **d**,	4004

DANCES (2) [DANCE]

1Sa	21:11	Isn't he the one they sing about in their **d**:	4703
	29: 5	the David they sang about in their **d**:	4703

DANCING (13) [DANCE]

Ex	15:20	with tambourines and **d**.	4703
	32:19	the camp and saw the calf and the **d**,	4703
Jdg	11:34	**d** to the sound of tambourines!	4703
	21:21	the girls of Shiloh come out to join in the **d**,	4703
	21:23	While the *girls were* **d**,	2565
1Sa	18: 6	to meet King Saul with singing and **d**,	4703
2Sa	6:16	when she saw King David leaping and **d**	4159
1Ch	15:29	she saw King David **d** and celebrating,	8376
Ps	30:11	You turned my wailing into **d**;	4688
	149: 3	Let them praise his name with **d**	4688
	150: 4	praise him with tambourine and **d**,	4688
La	5:15	our **d** has turned to mourning.	4688
Lk	15:25	he heard music and **d**.	5962

DANDLED (1)

Isa	66:12	be carried on her arm and **d** on her knees.	9130

DANGER (17) [DANGEROUS, DANGERS, ENDANGER, ENDANGERED, ENDANGERS]

1Sa	20:21	you are safe; there is no **d**.	1821
Pr	22: 3	A prudent man sees **d** and takes refuge,	8288
	27:12	The prudent see **d** and take refuge,	8288
Mt	5:22	will be in **d** of the fire of hell.	1944
Lk	8:23	and *they were* in great **d**.	3073
Ac	19:27	There is **d** not only that	3073
	19:40	we are in **d** of being charged with rioting	3073
Ro	8:35	or persecution or famine or nakedness or **d**	3074
2Co	11:26	I have been in **d** from rivers,	3074
	11:26	in **d** from bandits, in danger	3074
	11:26	in **d** from my own countrymen,	3074
	11:26	in danger from Gentiles,	3074
	11:26	in **d** in the city, in danger in the country,	3074
	11:26	in danger in the city, in **d** in the country,	3074
	11:26	in danger in the country, in **d** at sea;	3074
	11:26	and in **d** from false brothers.	3074
Heb	6: 8	and thistles is worthless and is in **d** of	1584

DANGEROUS (1) [DANGER]

Ac	27: 9	and sailing had already become **d** because	2195

DANGERS (1) [DANGER]

Ecc	12: 5	when men are afraid of heights and of **d** in	3152

DANGLES (1)

Job	28: 4	far from men he **d** and sways.	1938

DANIEL (76) [DANIEL'S]

1Ch	3: 1	the second, **D** the son of Abigail of Carmel;	1975

Ezr	8: 2	of the descendants of Ithamar, **D**;	1975
Ne	10: 6	**D**, Ginnethon, Baruch,	1975
Eze	14:14	Noah, **D** and Job—	1975
	14:20	even if Noah, **D** and Job were in it,	1975
	28: 3	Are you wiser than **D**?	1975
Da	1: 6	**D**, Hananiah, Mishael and Azariah.	1975
	1: 7	to **D**, the name Belteshazzar;	1975
	1: 8	But **D** resolved not to defile himself with	1975
	1: 9	to show favor and sympathy to **D**,	1975
	1:10	but the official told **D**,	1975
	1:11	**D** then said to the guard whom	1975
	1:11	the chief official had appointed over **D**,	1975
	1:17	And **D** could understand visions	1975
	1:19	and he found none equal to **D**, Hananiah,	1975
	1:21	And **D** remained there until the first year	1975
	2:13	for **D** and his friends to put them to death.	10181
	2:14	**D** spoke to him with wisdom and tact.	10181
	2:15	Arioch then explained the matter to **D**.	10181
	2:16	**D** went in to the king and asked for time,	10181
	2:17	Then **D** returned to his house and explained	10181
	2:19	the night the mystery was revealed to **D** in	10181
	2:19	Then **D** praised the God of heaven	10181
	2:24	Then **D** went to Arioch,	10181
	2:25	Arioch took **D** to the king at once and said,	10181
	2:26	king asked **D** (also called Belteshazzar),	10181
	2:27	**D** replied, "No wise man, enchanter,	10181
	2:46	before **D** and paid him honor and ordered	10181
	2:47	The king said to **D**,	10181
	2:48	Then the king placed **D** in a high position	10181
	2:49	**D** himself remained at the royal court.	10181
	4: 8	**D** came into my presence and I told him	10181
	4:19	Then **D** (also called Belteshazzar) was greatly perplexed	10181
	5:12	This man **D**, whom the king called Belteshazzar,	10181
	5:12	Call for **D**, and he will tell you what	10181
	5:13	So **D** was brought before the king,	10181
	5:13	and the king said to him, "Are you **D**,	10181
	5:17	Then **D** answered the king,	10181
	5:29	**D** was clothed in purple,	10181
	6: 2	one of whom was **D**.	10181
	6: 3	Now **D** so distinguished himself among	10181
	6: 4	to find grounds for charges against **D**	10181
	6: 5	against this man **D** unless it has something	10181
	6:10	Now when **D** learned that	10181
	6:11	and found **D** praying and asking God	10181
	6:13	Then they said to the king, "**D**,	10181
	6:14	to rescue **D** and made every effort	10181
	6:16	and they brought **D** and threw him into	10181
	6:16	The king said to **D**, "May your God,	10181
	6:20	he called to **D** in an anguished voice,	10181
	6:20	"**D**, servant of the living God,	10181
	6:21	**D** answered, "O king, live forever!	10181
	6:23	and gave orders to lift **D** out of the den.	10181
	6:23	And when **D** was lifted from the den,	10181
	6:24	the men who had falsely accused **D** were	10181
	6:26	and reverence the God of **D**.	10181
	6:27	He has rescued **D** from the power of	10181
	6:28	So **D** prospered during the reign of Darius	10181
	7: 1	**D** had a dream,	10181
	7: 2	**D** said: "In my vision at night	10181
	7:15	"I, **D**, was troubled in spirit,	10181
	7:28	I, **D**, was deeply troubled by my thoughts,	10181
	8: 1	I, **D**, had a vision,	1975
	8:15	**D**, was watching the vision and trying	1975
	8:27	**D**, was exhausted and lay ill	1975
	9: 2	I, **D**, understood from the Scriptures,	1975
	9:22	He instructed me and said to me, "**D**,	1975
	10: 1	to **D** (who was called Belteshazzar).	1975
	10: 2	At that time I, **D**, mourned for three weeks.	1975
	10: 7	I, **D**, was the only one who saw the vision;	1975
	10:11	He said, "**D**, you who are highly esteemed,	1975
	10:12	Then he continued, "Do not be afraid, **D**.	1975
	12: 4	**D**, close up and seal the words of the scroll	1975
	12: 5	Then I, **D**, looked, and there	1975
	12: 9	He replied, "Go your way, **D**,	1975
Mt	24:15	spoken of through the prophet **D**—	1248

DANIEL'S (2) [DANIEL]

Da	2:49	at **D** request the king appointed Shadrach,	10181
	6:17	so that **D** situation might not be changed.	10089+10181

DANITE (1) [DAN]

Lev	24:11	the daughter of Dibri the **D**.)	1968+4200+4751

DANITES (14) [DAN]

Jos	19:47	the **D** had difficulty taking possession	1201+1968
Jdg	1:34	The Amorites confined the **D** to	1201+1968
	13: 2	named Manoah, from the clan of the **D**,	1974
	18: 1	in those days the tribe of the **D** was seeking	1974
	18: 2	So the **D** sent five warriors from Zorah	1201+1968
	18:11	six hundred men from the clan of the **D**,	1974
	18:16	The six hundred **D**, armed for battle,	1201+1968
	18:22	and overtook the **D**.	1201+1968
	18:23	the **D** turned and said to Micah,	1201+1968
	18:25	The **D** answered, "Don't argue with us,	1201+1968
	18:26	So the **D** went their way, and Micah,	1201+1968
	18:28	The **D** rebuilt the city and settled there.	NIH
	18:30	the **D** set up for themselves the idols,	1201+1968
Eze	27:19	"**D** and Greeks from Uzal	1968

DANNAH (1)

Jos	15:49	**D**, Kiriath Sannah (that is, Debir),	1972

DAPPLED (2)

Zec	6: 3	and the fourth **d**—all of them powerful.	1353
	6: 6	the one with the **d** horses toward the south."	1353

DARDA (2)

1Ki	4:31	wiser than Heman, Calcol and **D**,	1997
1Ch	2: 6	Zimri, Ethan, Heman, Calcol and **D**—	1997

DARE (12) [DARED, DARES, DARING]

2Sa	3:11	Ish-Bosheth *did* not **d** to say another word	3523
Job	13:16	no godless man *would* **d** come before him!	AIT
Pr	29:24	he is put under oath and *d* not **testify**.	AIT
Jn	2:16	**How d** you turn my Father's house into	3590
	9:34	how **d** you lecture us!"	NIG
Ac	7:32	Moses trembled with fear and *did* not **d**	5528
	23: 4	"You **d** to insult God's high priest?"	NIG
Ro	5: 7	good man someone *might* possibly **d** to die.	5528
1Co	6: 1	*he* take it before the ungodly	5528
2Co	10:12	not **d** to classify or compare ourselves	5528
	11:21	I also **d** to boast about.	5528
Jude	1: 9	*did* not **d** to bring a slanderous accusation	5528

DARED (7) [DARE]

Est	7: 5	man who *has* **d** to do such a thing?"	4213+4848
Mt	22:46	no one **d** to ask him any more questions.	5528
Mk	12:34	no *one* **d** ask him any more questions.	5528
Lk	20:40	no *one* **d** to ask him any more questions.	5528
Jn	21:12	None of the disciples **d** ask him,	5528
Ac	5:13	No one else **d** join them,	5528
1Th	2: 2	of our God we **d** to tell you his gospel	4245

DARES (5) [DARE]

Ge	49: 9	who **d** to rouse him?	AIT
Nu	24: 9	who **d** to rouse them?	AIT
Job	41:14	Who **d** open the doors of his mouth.	AIT
La	4:14	that no *one* **d** to touch their garments.	3523
2Co	11:21	What anyone else **d** to boast about—	5528

DARICS (2)

1Ch	29: 7	and ten thousand **d** of gold,	163
Ezr	8:27	**d**, and two fine articles of polished bronze,	163

DARING (1) [DARE]

Job	32: 6	**not d** to tell you what I know.	3707

DARIUS (25)

Ezr	4: 5	and down to the reign of **D** king of Persia.	2003
	4:24	until the second year of the reign of **D** king	10184
	5: 5	a report could go to **D** and his written reply	10184
	5: 6	sent to King **D**.	10184
	5: 7	To King **D**: Cordial greetings.	10184
	6: 1	King **D** then issued an order,	10184
	6:12	I **D** have decreed it.	10184
	6:13	because of the decree King **D** had sent,	10184
	6:14	**D** and Artaxerxes, kings of Persia.	10184
	6:15	in the sixth year of the reign of King **D**.	10184
Ne	12:22	were recorded in the reign of **D** the Persian.	2003
Da	5:31	and **D** the Mede took over the kingdom,	10184
	6: 1	It pleased **D** to appoint 120 satraps to rule	10184
	6: 6	"O King **D**, live forever!	10184
	6: 9	So King **D** put the decree in writing.	10184
	6:25	Then King **D** wrote to all the peoples,	10184
	6:28	during the reign of **D** and the reign of Cyrus	10184
	9: 1	In the first year of **D** son of Xerxes (a Mede	2003
	11: 1	And in the first year of **D** the Mede,	2003
Hag	1: 1	In the second year of King **D**,	2003
	1:15	in the second year of King **D**.	2003
	2:10	in the second year of **D**,	2003
Zec	1: 1	the eighth month of the second year of **D**,	2003
	1: 7	in the second year of **D**,	2003
	7: 1	In the fourth year of King **D**,	2003

DARK (39) [DARK-COLORED, DARKEN, DARKENED, DARKENING, DARKENS, DARKER, DARKEST, DARKNESS, PITCH-DARK]

Dt	28:29	about like a blind man in the **d**.	696
2Sa	22:10	**d** clouds were under his feet.	6906
	22:12	the **d** rain clouds of the sky.	3128
1Ki	8:12	that he would dwell in a **d** cloud;	6906
2Ch	6: 1	that he would dwell in a **d** cloud;	6906
Job	3: 9	*May* its morning stars *become* **d**;	3124
	18: 6	The light in his tent *becomes* **d**;	3124
	22:11	why it is so **d** you cannot see,	3125
	24:16	In the **d**, men break into houses,	3125
	34:22	There is no **d** place, no deep shadow,	3125
Ps	18: 9	**d** clouds were under his feet.	6906
	18:11	the **d** rain clouds of the sky.	3128
	35: 6	may their path be **d** and slippery,	3125
	74:20	because haunts of violence fill the **d** places	4743
	105:28	He sent darkness and *made* the land **d**—	3124
	139:12	even the **d** will not be **d** to you;	3124
Pr	2:13	the straight paths to walk in **d** ways,	3125
	7: 9	as the **d** of night set in.	413+696
	31:15	She gets up while it is still **d**;	4326
Ecc	12: 2	the light and the moon and the stars *grow* **d**,	3124
SS	1: 5	**D** am I, yet lovely,	8839
	1: 5	**d** like the tents of Kedar,	NIH
	1: 6	Do not stare at me because I am **d**,	8842
Isa	50:10	Let him who walks in the **d**,	3128

Jer	4:28	and the heavens above *grow* d,	7722
Eze	30:18	D *will be* the day at Tahpanhes	3124
Mic	3: 6	and the day *will* go d for them.	7722
Mt	10:27	What I tell you in the d,	5028
Mk	1:35	**while it was still** d, Jesus got up,	1939
Lk	11:36	and no part of it d,	5027
	12: 3	What you have said in the d will be heard	5028
Jn	6:17	By now it was d,	5028
	12:35	The man who walks in the d does not know	5028
	20: 1	while it was still d,	5028
Ro	2:19	a light for those who are in the d,	5030
Eph	6:12	against the powers of this d world and	5030
2Pe	1:19	as to a light shining in a d place,	903
Rev	8:12	so that a third of them **turned** d.	3125
	9:17	Their breastplates were fiery red, **d blue**,	5610

DARK-COLORED (4) [DARK, COLORED]

Ge	30:32	every d lamb and every spotted	2569
	30:33	or any lamb that is not d,	2569
	30:35	that had white on them) and all the d lambs,	2569
	30:40	the streaked and d animals that belonged	2569

DARKEN (3) [DARK]

Eze	32: 7	I will cover the heavens and d their stars;	7722
	32: 8	the shining lights in the heavens I will d	7722
Am	8: 9	"I will make the sun go down at noon and d	3124

DARKENED (13) [DARK]

Job	6:16	*when* d by thawing ice and swollen	7722
Ps	69:23	*May* their eyes *be* d so they cannot see,	3124
SS	1: 6	because I *am* d by the sun.	8812
Isa	5:30	even the light *will be* d by the clouds.	3124
	13:10	The rising sun *will be* d and the moon will	3124
Joel	2:10	the sky trembles, the sun and moon *are* d,	7722
	3:15	The sun and moon *will be* d,	7722
Mt	24:29	*be* d, and the moon will not give its light;	5029
Mk	13:24	" 'the sun *will be* d,	5029
Ro	1:21	and their foolish hearts *were* d.	5029
	11:10	*May* their eyes *be* d so they cannot see,	5029
Eph	4:18	They are d in their understanding	5031
Rev	9: 2	The sun and sky *were* d by the smoke from	5029

DARKENING (1) [DARK]

Jer	13:16	before your feet stumble on the d hills.	5974

DARKENS (2) [DARK]

Job	38: 2	"Who is this *that* d my counsel with words	3124
Am	5: 8	into dawn and d day *into* night, who calls	3124

DARKER (1) [DARK]

Ge	49:12	His eyes will be d than wine,	2679

DARKEST (1) [DARK]

Ps	88: 6	in the d depths.	4743

DARKNESS (158) [DARK]

Ge	1: 2	d was over the surface of the deep,	3125
	1: 4	and he separated the light from the **d.**	3125
	1: 5	and the d he called "night."	3125
	1:18	and to separate light from d,	3125
	15:12	a thick and dreadful d came over him.	3128
	15:17	When the sun had set and d had fallen,	6602
Ex	10:21	the sky so that d will spread over Egypt—	3125
	10:21	d that can be felt."	3125
	10:22	**total** d covered all Egypt for three days. 696+3125
	14:20	Throughout the night the cloud brought d to	3125
	20:21	while Moses approached the **thick** d	6906
Dt	4:11	with black clouds and **deep** d.	6906
	5:22	the cloud and the **deep** d;	6906
	5:23	When you heard the voice out of the d,	3125
Jos	24: 7	he put d between you and the Egyptians;	4419
1Sa	2: 9	but the wicked will be silenced in d.	3125
2Sa	22:12	He made d his canopy around him—	3125
	22:29	the LORD turns my d into light.	3125
Job	3: 4	That day—may it turn to d;	3125
	3: 5	May d and deep shadow claim it once more;	3125
	3: 6	That night—may **thick** d seize it;	694
	5:14	D comes upon them in the daytime;	3125
	10:22	where even the light is like d."	694
	11:17	and d will become like morning.	9507
	12:22	of d and brings deep shadows into the light.	3125
	12:25	They grope in d with no light;	3125
	15:22	He despairs of escaping the d;	3125
	15:23	he knows the day of d is at hand.	3125
	15:30	He will not escape the d;	3125
	17:12	in the face of d they say, 'Light is near.'	3125
	17:13	if I spread out my bed in d,	3125
	18:18	into d and is banished from the world.	3125
	19: 8	he has shrouded my paths in d.	3125
	20:26	total d lies in wait for his treasures.	3125
	22:13	Does he judge through such d?	6906
	23:17	Yet I am not silenced by the d,	3125
	23:17	by the **thick** d that covers my face.	694
	24:17	For all of them, **deep** d is their morning;	7516
	24:17	they make friends with the terrors of d.	7516
	26:10	for a boundary between light and d.	3125
	28: 3	Man puts an end to the d;	3125
	28: 3	for ore in the blackest d.	694
	29: 3	and by his light I walked through d!	3125
	30:26	when I looked for light, then came d.	694
	37:19	up our case because of our d.	3125
	38: 9	and wrapped it in **thick** d,	6906

Job	38:19	And where does d reside?	3125
Ps	18:11	He made d his covering,	3125
	18:28	my God turns my d into light.	3125
	44:19	for jackals and covered us over with **deep** d.	7516
	82: 5	They walk about in d;	3128
	88:12	Are your wonders known in *the place of* d,	3125
	88:18	the d is my closest friend.	4743
	91: 6	nor the pestilence that stalks in the d,	694
	97: 2	Clouds and **thick** d surround him;	6906
	104:20	You bring d, it becomes night,	3125
	105:28	He sent d and made the land dark—	3125
	107:10	Some sat in d and the deepest gloom,	3125
	107:14	He brought them out of d and	3125
	112: 4	Even in d light dawns for the upright,	3125
	139:11	"Surely the d will hide me and	3125
	139:12	even the d will not be dark to you;	3125
	139:12	for d is as light to you.	3128
	143: 3	in d like those long dead.	4743
Pr	4:19	But the way of the wicked is like **deep** d;	3125
	20:20	his lamp will be snuffed out in **pitch** d.	854+3125
Ecc	2:13	just as light is better than d.	3125
	2:14	while the fool walks in the d;	3125
	5:17	All his days he eats in d,	3125
	6: 4	It comes without meaning, it departs in d,	3125
	6: 4	and in d its name is shrouded.	3125
	11: 8	But let him remember the days of d,	3125
Isa	5:20	who put d for light and light for darkness,	3125
	5:20	who put darkness for light and light for d,	3125
	5:30	he will see d and distress;	3125
	8:22	toward the earth and see only distress and d	3128
	8:22	and they will be thrust into **utter** d.	696
	9: 2	people walking in d have seen a great light;	3125
	29:15	who do their work in d and think,	4743
	29:18	and the eyes of the blind will see.	3125
	42: 7	from the dungeon those who sit in d.	3125
	42:16	I will turn the d into light before them	4743
	45: 3	I will give you the treasures of d,	3125
	45: 7	I form the light and create d,	3125
	45:19	from somewhere in a land of d;	3125
	47: 5	"Sit in silence, go into d,	3125
	49: 9	'Come out,' and to those in d, 'Be free!'	3125
	50: 3	with d and make sackcloth its covering."	7725
	58:10	then your light will rise in the d,	3125
	59: 9	We look for light, but all is d;	3125
	60: 2	d covers the earth and thick darkness	3125
	60: 2	and **thick** d is over the peoples;	6906
	61: 1	for the captives and **release from** d for	7223
Jer	2: 6	a land of drought and d,	7516
	2:31	a desert to Israel or a land of **great** d?	4420
	13:16	before he **brings** the d,	3124
	13:16	but he will turn it to **thick** d and change it	7516
	23:12	be banished to d and there they will fall.	696
La	3: 2	and made me walk in d rather than light;	3125
	3: 6	He has made me dwell in d	4743
Eze	8:12	of the house of Israel are doing in the d,	3125
	32: 8	I will bring d over your land,	3125
	34:12	on a day of clouds and d.	6906
Da	2:22	he knows what lies in d,	10286
Joel	2: 2	a day of d and gloom,	3125
	2:31	be turned to d and the moon to blood before	3125
Am	4:13	he who turns dawn to d,	6547
	5:18	That day will be d, not light.	3125
	5:20	Will not the day of the LORD be d,	3125
Mic	3: 6	without visions, and d, without divination.	3127
	7: 8	I sit in d, the LORD will be my light.	3125
Na	1: 8	he will pursue his foes into d.	3125
Zep	1:15	a day of d and gloom,	3125
Mt	4:16	people living in d have seen a great light;	5030
	6:23	your whole body will be **full of** d.	5027
	6:23	If then the light within you is d,	5030
	6:23	how great is that d!	5030
	8:12	into the d, where there will be weeping	5030
	22:13	and throw him outside, into the d,	5030
	25:30	that worthless servant outside, into the d,	5030
	27:45	the sixth hour until the ninth hour d came	5030
Mk	15:33	the sixth hour d came over the whole land	5030
Lk	1:79	on those living in d and in the shadow	5030
	11:34	they are bad, your body also is **full of** d.	5027
	11:35	then, that the light within you is not d.	5030
	22:53	But this is your hour—when d reigns."	5030
	23:44	and d came over the whole land until	5030
Jn	1: 5	The light shines in the d,	5028
	1: 5	but the d has not understood it.	5028
	3:19	the world, but men loved d instead of light	5030
	8:12	Whoever follows me will never walk in d,	5030
	12:35	before d overtakes you.	5028
	12:46	no one who believes in me should stay in d.	5028
Ac	2:20	be turned to d and the moon to blood before	5030
	13:11	Immediately mist and d came over him,	5030
	26:18	to open their eyes and turn them from d	5030
Ro	13:12	So let us put aside the deeds *of* d and put	5030
1Co	4: 5	to light what is hidden in d and will expose	5030
2Co	4: 6	God, who said, "Let light shine out of d,"	5030
	6:14	Or what fellowship can light have with d?	5030
Eph	5: 8	For you were once d,	5030
	5:11	to do with the fruitless deeds *of* d,	5030
Col	1:13	from the dominion *of* d and brought us into	5030
1Th	5: 4	not in d so that this day should surprise you	5030
	5: 5	We do not belong to the night or to the d.	5030
Heb	12:18	*to* d, gloom and storm;	1190
1Pe	2: 9	the praises of him who called you out of d	5030
2Pe	2:17	Blackest d is reserved for them.	5030
1Jn	1: 6	in him there is no d at all.	5028
	1: 6	with him yet walk in the d,	5030
	2: 8	in him and you, because the d is passing	5028
	2: 9	but hates his brother is still in the d.	5028
	2:11	in the d and walks around in the darkness;	5028

1Jn	2:11	in the darkness and walks around in the d;	5028
	2:11	because the d has blinded him.	5028
Jude	1: 6	these he has kept in d,	2432
	1:13	whom blackest d has been reserved forever.	5030
Rev	16:10	and his kingdom was plunged into d.	5031

DARKON (2)

Ezr	2:56	Jaala, D, Giddel,	2010
Ne	7:58	Jaala, D, Giddel,	2010

DARLING (9)

SS	1: 9	I liken you, my d, to a mare harnessed	8299
	1:15	How beautiful you are, my d!	8299
	2: 2	among thorns is my d among the maidens.	8299
	2:10	my d, my beautiful one, and come with me.	8299
	2:13	my d; my beautiful one, come with me."	8299
	4: 1	How beautiful you are, my d!	8299
	4: 7	All beautiful you are, my d;	8299
	5: 2	"Open to me, my sister, my d, my dove,	8299
	6: 4	You are beautiful, my d, as Tirzah,	8299

DART (3) [DARTING]

Job	41:21	and flames d from his mouth.	3655
	41:26	nor does the spear or the d or the javelin.	5025
Na	2: 4	they d about like lightning.	8132

DARTING (4) [DART]

Pr	7:23	like a bird d into a snare,	4554
	26: 2	Like a fluttering sparrow or a d swallow,	6414
Isa	14:29	its fruit will be a d, venomous serpent.	6414
	30: 6	of adders and d snakes,	6414

DARTS (KJV) See ARROWS, CLUB, JAVELINS, WEAPONS

DASH (7) [DASHED, DASHES]

Jdg	20:37	in ambush **made a** sudden d into Gibeah,	7320
2Ki	8:12	d their little children **to the ground**,	8187
Ps	2: 9	you will d them **to pieces** like pottery."	5879
Eze	23:34	you will d it *to* pieces	1751
Na	2: 5	They d to the city wall;	4554
Lk	19:44	d you **to the ground**,	1610
Rev	2:27	he will d them **to pieces** like pottery'—	5341

DASHED (7) [DASH]

2Ch	25:12	down so that all were d to pieces.	1324
Ps	119:116	let my hopes be d.	1017
Isa	13:16	Their infants *will* be d to pieces	8187
Hos	10:14	mothers were d to the ground,	8187
	13:16	little ones *will* be d to the ground,	8187
Na	3:10	Her infants were d to pieces at the head	8187
Ac	27:29	that *we would be* d against the rocks,	1738

DASHES (1) [DASH]

Ps	137: 9	he who seizes your infants and d them	5879

DATE (3) [DATES]

Eze	24: 2	record this d, this very date,	3427
	24: 2	record this date, this very d,	3427
Ac	21:26	to the temple to give notice of the d when	NIG

DATES (4) [DATE]

2Sa	6:19	a **cake of** d and a cake of raisins	882
1Ch	16: 3	a **cake of** d and a cake of raisins	882
Ac	1: 7	or d the Father has set by his own authority.	2789
1Th	5: 1	about times and d we do not need to write	2789

DATHAN (10)

Nu	16: 1	D and Abiram, sons of Eliab,	2018
	16:12	Then Moses summoned D and Abiram,	2018
	16:24	from the tents of Korah, D and Abiram.' "	2018
	16:25	Moses got up and went to D and Abiram,	2018
	16:27	from the tents of Korah D and Abiram.	2018
	16:27	D and Abiram had come out	2018
	26: 9	of Eliab were Nemuel, D and Abiram.	2018
	26: 9	The same D and Abiram were	2018
Dt	11: 6	and what he did to D and Abiram,	2018
Ps	106:17	The earth opened up and swallowed D;	2018

DAUB (KJV) See COVER

DAUGHTER (281) [DAUGHTER'S, DAUGHTER-IN-LAW, DAUGHTERS, DAUGHTERS-IN-LAW, GRANDDAUGHTER, GRANDDAUGHTERS]

Ge	11:29	she was the d of Haran,	1426
	19:31	One day the **older** d said to the younger,	AIT
	19:33	and the **older** d went in and lay with him.	AIT
	19:34	The next day the **older** d said to	AIT
	19:35	and the **younger** d went and lay with him.	AIT
	19:37	The **older** d had a son,	AIT
	19:38	The **younger** d also had a son,	AIT
	20:12	d of my father though not *of* my mother;	1426
	24:15	She *was* the d of Bethuel son of Milcah,	3528
	24:23	Then he asked, "Whose d are you?	1426
	24:24	She answered him, "I am the d *of* Bethuel,	1426

Ge	24:47	"I asked her, 'Whose **d** are you?'	1426
	24:47	"She said, 'The **d** of Bethuel son of Nahor,	1426
	25:20	when he married Rebekah **d** of Bethuel	1426
	26:34	he married Judith **d** of Beeri the Hittite,	1426
	26:34	and also Basemath **d** of Elon the Hittite,	1426
	28: 9	the sister of Nebaioth and **d** of Ishmael son	1426
	29: 6	here comes his **d** Rachel with the sheep."	1426
	29:10	When Jacob saw Rachel **d** of Laban,	1426
	29:18	in return for your younger **d** Rachel."	1426
	29:23	he took his **d** Leah and gave her to Jacob,	1426
	29:24	to his **d** as her maidservant.	1426
	29:26	not our custom here to give the **younger** d	AIT
	29:28	Laban gave him his **d** Rachel to be his wife.	1426
	29:29	to his **d** Rachel as her maidservant.	1426
	30:21	Some time later she gave birth to a **d**	1426
	34: 1	Now Dinah, the **d** Leah had borne to Jacob,	1426
	34: 3	His heart was drawn to Dinah **d** of Jacob,	1426
	34: 5	that his **d** Dinah had been defiled,	1426
	34: 7	in Israel by lying with Jacob's **d**—	1426
	34: 8	My son Shechem has his heart set on your **d**	1426
	34:19	because he was delighted with Jacob's **d**.	1426
	36: 2	Adah **d** of Elon the Hittite,	1426
	36: 2	the Hittite, and Oholibamah **d** of Anah	1426
	36: 3	also Basemath **d** of Ishmael and sister	1426
	36:14	The sons of Esau's wife Oholibamah **d**	1426
	36:18	from Esau's wife Oholibamah **d** of Anah.	1426
	36:25	Dishon and Oholibamah **d** of Anah.	1426
	36:39	and his wife's name was Mehetabel **d**	1426
	36:39	the **d** of Me-Zahab.	1426
	38: 2	the **d** of a Canaanite man named Shua.	1426
	38:12	long time Judah's wife, the **d** of Shua, died.	1426
	41:45	and gave him Asenath **d** of Potiphera,	1426
	41:50	two sons were born to Joseph by Asenath **d**	1426
	46:15	besides his **d** Dinah.	1426
	46:18	whom Laban had given to his Leah—	1426
	46:20	to Joseph by Asenath **d** of Potiphera,	1426
	46:25	whom Laban had given to his **d** Rachel—	1426
Ex	2: 5	Pharaoh's **d** went down to the Nile to bathe,	1426
	2: 7	Then his sister asked Pharaoh's **d**,	1426
	2: 9	Pharaoh's **d** said to her,	1426
	2:10	to Pharaoh's **d** and he became her son.	1426
	2:21	who gave his **d** Zipporah to Moses	1426
	6:23	**d** of Amminadab and sister of Nahshon,	1426
	20:10	neither you, nor your son or **d**,	1426
	21: 7	"If a man sells his **d** as a servant,	1426
	21: 9	he must grant her the rights of a **d**.	1426
	21:31	also applies if the bull gores a son or **d**.	1426
Lev	12: 5	If she gives birth to a **d**,	5922
	12: 6	of her purification for a son or **d** are over,	1426
	18: 9	your father's **d** or your mother's daughter,	1426
	18: 9	your father's daughter or your mother's **d**,	1426
	18:10	not have sexual relations with your son's **d**	1426
	18:10	or your daughter's **d**;	1426
	18:11	" 'Do not have sexual relations with the **d**	1426
	18:17	with both a woman and her **d**.	1426
	18:17	with either her son's **d**	1426
	18:17	or her daughter's **d**;	1426
	19:29	" 'Do not degrade your **d** by making her	1426
	20:17	the **d** of either his father or his mother,	1426
	21: 2	such as his mother or father, his son or **d**,	1426
	21: 9	a priest's **d** defiles herself by becoming	1426
	22:12	If a priest's **d** marries anyone other than	1426
	22:13	priest's **d** becomes a widow or is divorced,	1426
	24:11	the **d** of Dibri the Danite).	1426
Nu	25:15	to death was Cozbi **d** of Zur,	1426
	25:18	the **d** of a Midianite leader,	1426
	26:46	(Asher had a **d** named Serah.)	1426
	27: 8	turn his inheritance over to his **d**.	1426
	27: 9	If he has no **d**, give his inheritance	1426
	30:16	between a father and his young **d** still living	1426
	36: 8	Every **d** who inherits land	1426
Dt	5:14	neither you, nor your son or **d**,	1426
	13: 6	If your very own brother, or your son or **d**,	1426
	18:10	among you who sacrifices his son or **d** in	1426
	22:16	"I gave my **d** in marriage to this man,	1426
	22:17	'I did not find your **d** to be a virgin.'	1426
	27:22	the **d** of his father or the daughter	1426
	27:22	of his father or the **d** of his mother."	1426
	28:56	the husband she loves and her own son or **d**	1426
Jos	15:16	"I will give my **d** Acsah in marriage to	1426
	15:17	Caleb gave his **d** Acsah to him in marriage.	1426
Jdg	1:12	"I will give my **d** Acsah in marriage to	1426
	1:13	Caleb gave his **d** Acsah to him in marriage.	1426
	11:34	to meet him but his **d**,	1426
	11:34	Except for her he had neither son nor **d**.	1426
	11:35	and cried, "Oh! My **d**!	1426
	11:40	for four days to commemorate the **d**	1426
	19:24	Look, here is my virgin **d**,	1426
	21: 1	"Not one of us will give his **d** in marriage	1426
Ru	2: 2	Naomi said to her, "Go ahead, my **d**."	1426
	2: 8	So Boaz said to Ruth, "My **d**, listen to me.	1426
	2:22	"It will be good for you, my **d**,	1426
	3: 1	"My **d**, should I not try to find a home	1426
	3:10	"The LORD bless you, my **d**," he replied.	1426
	3:11	And now, my **d**, don't be afraid.	1426
	3:16	Naomi asked, "How did it go, my **d**?"	1426
	3:18	Then Naomi said, "Wait, my **d**,	1426
1Sa	14:49	The name of his older **d** was Merab,	1426
	14:50	His wife's name was Ahinoam **d**	1426
	17:25	He will also give him his **d** in marriage	1426
	18:17	"Here is my older **d** Merab.	1426
	18:19	when the time came for Merab, Saul's **d**,	1426
	18:20	Saul's **d** Michal was in love with David,	1426
	18:27	Saul gave him his **d** Michal in marriage.	1426
	18:28	and that his **d** Michal loved David,	1426
	25:44	But Saul had given his **d** Michal,	1426
2Sa	3: 3	of Maacah **d** of Talmai king of Geshur;	1426

2Sa	3: 7	a concubine named Rizpah **d** of Aiah,	1426
	3:13	into my presence unless you bring Michal **d**	1426
	6:16	Michal **d** of Saul watched from a window.	1426
	6:20	Michal **d** of Saul came out to meet him	1426
	6:23	And Michal **d** of Saul had no children to	1426
	11: 3	the **d** of Eliam and the wife of Uriah	1426
	12: 3	It was like a **d** to him.	1426
	14:27	Three sons and a **d** were born to Absalom.	1426
	17:25	the **d** of Nahash and sister of Zeruiah	1426
	21: 8	the two sons of Aiah's **d** Rizpah,	1426
	21: 8	with the five sons of Saul's **d** Merab,	1426
	21:10	Rizpah **d** of Aiah took sackcloth	1426
	21:11	David was told what Aiah's **d** Rizpah,	1426
1Ki	3: 1	of Egypt and married his **d**.	1426
	4:11	to Taphath (**d** of Solomon);	1426
	4:15	in Naphtali (he had married Basemath **d**	1426
	7: 8	a palace like this hall for Pharaoh's **d**,	1426
	9:16	and then gave it as a wedding gift to his **d**,	1426
	9:24	After Pharaoh's **d** had come up from	1426
	11: 1	Solomon, however, loved many foreign	
		women besides Pharaoh's **d**—	1426
	15: 2	His mother's name was Maacah **d**	1426
	15:10	His grandmother's name was Maacah **d**	1426
	16:31	also married Jezebel **d** of Ethbaal king of	1426
	22:42	His mother's name was Azubah **d**	1426
2Ki	8:18	for he married a **d** of Ahab.	1426
	9:34	"and bury her, for she was a king's **d**."	1426
	11: 2	of King Jehoram and sister of Ahaziah,	1426
	14: 9	'Give your **d** to my son in marriage.'	1426
	15:33	His mother's name was Jerusha **d**	1426
	18: 2	His mother's name was Abijah **d**	1426
	19:21	'The Virgin **D** of Zion despises you	1426
	19:21	**D** of Jerusalem tosses her head as you flee.	1426
	21:19	His mother's name was Meshullemeth **d**	1426
	22: 1	His mother's name was Jedidah **d**	1426
	23:10	to sacrifice his son or **d** in the fire	1426
	23:31	His mother's name was Hamutal **d**	1426
	23:36	His mother's name was Zebidah **d**	1426
	24: 8	His mother's name was Nehushta **d**	1426
	24:18	His mother's name was Hamutal **d**	1426
1Ch	1:50	and his wife's name was Mehetabel **d**	1426
	1:50	the **d** of Me-Zahab.	1426
	2: 3	the **d** of Shua.	1426
	2:21	Hezron lay with the **d** of Makir the father	1426
	2:35	Sheshan gave his **d** in marriage	1426
	2:49	Caleb's **d** was Acsah.	1426
	3: 2	of Maacah **d** of Talmai king of Geshur;	1426
	3: 5	These four were by Bathsheba **d**	1426
	4:18	the children of Pharaoh's **d** Bithiah,	1426
	7:24	His **d** was Sheerah,	1426
	15:29	Michal **d** of Saul watched from a window.	1426
2Ch	8:11	Solomon brought Pharaoh's **d** up from	1426
	11:18	who was the **d** of David's son Jerimoth and	1426
	11:18	the **d** of Jesse's son Eliab.	1426
	11:20	Then he married Maacah **d** of Absalom,	1426
	11:21	Rehoboam loved Maacah **d**	1426
	13: 2	a **d** of Uriel of Gibeah.	1426
	20:31	His mother's name was Azubah **d**	1426
	21: 6	for he married a **d** of Ahab.	1426
	22:11	But Jehosheba, the **d** of King Jehoram,	1426
	22:11	the **d** of King Jehoram and wife of	1426
	25:18	'Give your **d** to my son in marriage.'	1426
	27: 1	His mother's name was Jerusha **d**	1426
	29: 1	His mother's name was Abijah **d**	1426
Ezr	2:61	and Barzillai (a man who had married a **d**	1426
Ne	6:18	and his son Jehohanan had married the **d**	1426
	7:63	and Barzillai (a man who had married a **d**	1426
Est	2: 7	and Mordecai had taken her as his own **d**	1426
	2:15	the **d** of his uncle Abihail) to go to	1426
	9:29	So Queen Esther, **d** of Abihail,	1426
Job	42:14	The first **d** he named Jemimah,	NIH
Ps	9:14	the gates of the **D** of Zion and there rejoice	1426
	45:10	Listen, O **d**, consider and give ear:	1426
	45:12	The **D** of Tyre will come with a gift,	1426
	137: 8	O **D** of Babylon, doomed to destruction,	1426
SS	6: 9	is unique, the only of her mother,	2085S
	7: 1	beautiful your sandaled feet, O prince's **d**!	1426
Isa	1: 8	The **D** of Zion is left like a shelter in	1426
	10:30	Cry out, O **D** of Gallim!	1426
	10:32	at the mount of the **D** of Zion.	1426
	16: 1	to the mount of the **D** of Zion.	1426
	23:10	O **D** of Tarshish,	1426
	23:12	O Virgin **D** of Sidon, now crushed!	1426
	37:22	Virgin **D** of Zion despises and mocks you.	1426
	37:22	**D** of Jerusalem tosses her head as you flee.	1426
	47: 1	sit in the dust, Virgin **D** of Babylon;	1426
	47: 1	**D** of the Babylonians.	1426
	47: 5	go into darkness, **D** of the Babylonians.	1426
	52: 2	O captive **D** of Zion.	1426
	62:11	"Say to the **D** of Zion, 'See,	1426
Jer	4:31	the cry of the **D** of Zion gasping for breath,	1426
	6: 2	I will destroy the **D** of Zion,	1426
	6:23	in battle formation to attack you, O **D**	1426
	14:17	for my virgin **d**—	1426
	31:22	How long will you wander, O unfaithful **d**?	1426
	46:11	O Virgin **D** of Egypt.	1426
	46:24	The **D** of Egypt will be put to shame,	1426
	48:18	O inhabitants of the **D** of Dibon,	1426
	49: 4	O unfaithful **d**, you trust in your riches	1426
	50:42	in battle formation to attack you, O **D**	1426
	51:33	"The **D** of Babylon is like a threshing floor	1426
	52: 1	His mother's name was Hamutal **d**	1426
La	1: 6	All the splendor has departed from the **D**	1426
	1:15	the Lord has trampled the Virgin **D**	1426
	2: 1	the **D** of Zion with the cloud of his anger!	1426
	2: 2	down the strongholds of the **D** of Judah.	1426
	2: 4	like fire on the tent of the **D** of Zion.	1426

La	2: 5	and lamentation for the **D** of Judah.	1426
	2: 8	to tear down the wall around the **D** of Zion.	1426
	2:10	the **D** of Zion sit on the ground in silence;	1426
	2:13	O **D** of Jerusalem?	1426
	2:13	O Virgin **D** of Zion?	1426
	2:15	they scoff and shake their heads at the **D**	1426
	2:18	O wall of the **D** of Zion,	1426
	4:21	Rejoice and be glad, O **D** of Edom,	1426
	4:22	O **D** of Zion, your punishment will end;	1426
	4:22	But, O **D** of Edom,	1426
Eze	14:20	they could save neither son nor **d**.	1426
	16:44	"Like mother, like **d**."	1426
	16:45	You are a true **d** of your mother,	1426
	22:11	his own father's **d**.	1426
	44:25	son or **d**, brother or unmarried sister,	1426
Da	11: 6	The **d** of the king of the South will go to	1426
	11:17	in marriage in order to overthrow	1426
Hos	1: 3	So he married Gomer **d** of Diblaim,	1426
	1: 6	and gave birth to a **d**.	1426
Mic	1:13	You were the beginning of sin to the **D**	1426
	4: 8	O stronghold of the **D** of Zion,	1426
	4: 8	kingship will come to the **D** of Jerusalem."	1426
	4:10	Writhe in agony, O **D** of Zion,	1426
	4:13	"Rise and thresh, O **D** of Zion,	1426
	7: 6	a **d** rises up against her mother,	1426
Zep	3:14	Sing, O **D** of Zion; shout aloud, O Israel!	1426
	3:14	O **D** of Jerusalem!	1426
Zec	2: 7	you who live in the **D** of Babylon!"	1426
	2:10	"Shout and be glad, O **D** of Zion.	1426
	9: 9	Rejoice greatly, O **D** of Zion!	1426
	9: 9	Shout, **D** of Jerusalem!	1426
Mal	2:11	by marrying the **d** of a foreign god.	1426
Mt	9:18	"My **d** has just died.	2588
	9:22	"Take heart, **d**," he said,	2588
	10:35	a **d** against her mother,	2588
	10:37	or **d** more than me is not worthy of me;	2588
	14: 6	the **d** of Herodias danced for them	2588
	15:22	My **d** is suffering terribly	2588
	15:28	And her **d** was healed from that very hour.	2588
	21: 5	"Say to the **D** of Zion,	2588
Mk	5:23	"My **little d** is dying.	2589
	5:34	He said to her, "**D**,	2588
	5:35	"Your **d** is dead," they said.	2588
	6:22	the **d** of Herodias came in and danced,	2588
	7:25	a woman whose **little d** was possessed	2589
	7:26	to drive the demon out of her **d**.	2588
	7:29	the demon has left your **d**."	2588
Lk	2:36	the **d** of Phanuel, of the tribe of Asher.	2588
	8:42	because his only **d**,	2588
	8:48	Then he said to her, "**D**,	2588
	8:49	"Your **d** is dead," he said.	2588
	12:53	against **d** and daughter against mother,	2588
	12:53	against daughter and **d** against mother,	2588
	13:16	should not this woman, a **d** of Abraham,	2588
Jn	12:15	O **D** of Zion;	2588
Ac	7:21	Pharaoh's **d** took him and brought him up	2588
Heb	11:24	to be known as the son of Pharaoh's **d**.	2588

DAUGHTER'S (5) [DAUGHTER]

Ge	29:27	Finish **this** d bridal week;	AIT
Lev	18:10	or your **d** daughter;	1426
	18:17	either her son's daughter or her **d** daughter;	1426
Dt	22:17	But here is the proof of my **d** virginity."	1426
2Sa	14:27	The **d** name was Tamar,	2023S

DAUGHTER-IN-LAW (17) [DAUGHTER]

Ge	11:31	and his **d** Sarai, the wife of his son Abram,	3987
	38:11	Judah then said to his **d** Tamar,	3987
	38:16	Not realizing that she was his **d**,	3987
	38:24	"Your **d** Tamar is guilty of prostitution.	3987
Lev	18:15	" 'Do not have sexual relations with your **d**.	3987
	20:12	" 'If a man sleeps with his **d**,	3987
Ru	1:22	the Moabitess, her **d**, arriving in Bethlehem	3987
	2:20	Naomi said to her **d**.	3987
	2:22	Naomi said to Ruth her **d**,	3987
	4:15	For your **d**, who loves you	3987
1Sa	4:19	His **d**, the wife of Phinehas,	3987
1Ch	2: 4	Judah's **d**, bore him Perez and Zerah.	3987
Eze	22:11	another shamefully defiles his **d**,	3987
Mic	7: 6	a **d** against her mother-in-law—	3987
Mt	10:35	a **d** against her mother-in-law—	3811
Lk	12:53	mother-in-law against **d**	3811
	12:53	and **d** against mother-in-law."	3811

DAUGHTERS (214) [DAUGHTER]

Ge	5: 4	and had other sons and **d**.	1426
	5: 7	and had other sons and **d**.	1426
	5:10	and had other sons and **d**.	1426
	5:13	and had other sons and **d**.	1426
	5:16	and had other sons and **d**.	1426
	5:19	and had other sons and **d**.	1426
	5:22	and had other sons and **d**.	1426
	5:26	and had other sons and **d**.	1426
	5:30	and had other sons and **d**.	1426
	6: 1	in number on the earth and **d** were born	1426
	6: 2	saw that the **d** of men were beautiful,	1426
	6: 4	when the sons of God went to the **d** of men	1426
	11:11	and had other sons and **d**.	1426
	11:13	and had other sons and **d**.	1426
	11:15	and had other sons and **d**.	1426
	11:17	and had other sons and **d**.	1426
	11:19	and had other sons and **d**.	1426
	11:21	and had other sons and **d**.	1426
	11:23	and had other sons and **d**.	1426
	11:25	and had other sons and **d**.	1426

Ge 19: 8 I have two **d** who have never slept with 1426
    19:12 sons-in-law, sons or **d**, 1426
    19:14 who were pledged to marry his **d.** 1426
    19:15 and your two **d** who are here, 1426
    19:16 and of his two **d** and led them safely out of 1426
    19:30 Lot and his two **d** left Zoar and settled in 1426
    19:30 He and his two **d** lived in a cave. 1426
    19:36 of Lot's **d** became pregnant by their father. 1426
    24: 3 for my son from the **d** of the Canaanites, 1426
    24:13 the **d** of the townspeople are coming out 1426
    24:37 for my son from the **d** of the Canaanites, 1426
    28: 2 from among the **d** of Laban, 1426
    29:16 Now Laban had two **d**; 1426
    31:26 and you've carried off my **d** like captives 1426
    31:28 and my **d** good-by. 1426
    31:31 I thought you would take your **d** away 1426
    31:41 for you fourteen years for your two **d** 1426
    31:43 "The women are my **d,** 1426
    31:43 Yet what can I do today about these **d** 1426
    31:50 If you mistreat my **d** or 1426
    31:50 or if you take any wives besides my **d,** 1426
    31:55 and his **d** and blessed them. 1426
    34: 9 give us your **d** and take our daughters 1426
    34: 9 give us your daughters and take our **d** 1426
    34:16 Then we will give you our **d** 1426
    34:16 and take your **d** for ourselves. 1426
    34:21 We can marry their **d** 1426
    36: 6 Esau took his wives and sons and **d** and all 1426
    37:35 All his sons and **d** came to comfort him, 1426
    46: 7 to Egypt his sons and grandsons and his **d** 1426
    46:15 These sons and **d** of his were thirty-three 1426
Ex 2:16 Now a priest of Midian had seven **d,** 1426
    2:20 he asked his **d.** 1426
    3:22 which you will put on your sons and **d.** 1426
    6:25 Eleazar son of Aaron married one of the **d** 1426
    10: 9 with our sons and **d,** 1426
    21: 4 a wife and she bears him sons or **d,** 1426
    32: 2 your sons and your **d** are wearing, 1426
    34:16 when you choose some of their **d** as wives 1426
    34:16 and those **d** prostitute themselves 1426
Lev 10:14 and your sons and your **d** may eat the breast 1426
    26:29 of your sons and the flesh of your **d.** 1426
Nu 18:11 and your sons and **d** as your regular share. 1426
    18:19 and your sons and **d** as your regular share. 1426
    21:29 and his **d** as captives to Sihon king of 1426
    26:33 he had only **d,** whose names were Mahlah, 1426
    27: 1 The **d** of Zelophehad son of Hepher, 1426
    27: 1 The names of the **d** were Mahlah, Noah, 1426
    27: 7 "What Zelophehad's **d** are saying is right. 1426
    36: 2 of our brother Zelophehad to his **d.** 1426
    36: 6 the LORD commands for Zelophehad's **d:** 1426
    36:10 So Zelophehad's **d** did as the LORD 1426
    36:11 Zelophehad's **d**—Mahlah, 1426
Dt 7: 3 Do not give your **d** to their sons 1426
    7: 3 to their sons or take their **d** for your sons, 1426
    12:12 you, your sons and **d,** 1426
    12:18 you, your sons and **d,** 1426
    12:31 They even burn their sons and **d** in the fire 1426
    16:11 you, your sons and **d,** 1426
    16:14 you, your sons and **d,** 1426
    28:32 and **d** will be given to another nation, 1426
    28:41 You will have sons and **d** but you will 1426
    28:53 and **d** the LORD your God has given you. 1426
    32:19 because he was angered by his sons and **d.** 1426
Jos 7:24 the gold wedge, his sons and **d,** his cattle, 1426
    17: 3 had no sons but only **d,** 1426
    17: 6 the **d** of the tribe of Manasseh received 1426
Jdg 3: 6 They took their **d** in marriage 1426
    3: 6 and gave their own **d** to their sons, 1426
    12: 9 He had thirty sons and thirty **d.** 1426
    12: 9 He gave his **d** away in marriage NIH
    21: 7 not to give them any of our **d** in marriage? 1426
    21:18 We can't give them our **d** as wives, 1426
    21:22 since you did not give your **d** to them.' " NIH
Ru 1:11 But Naomi said, "Return home, my **d.** 1426
    1:12 Return home, my **d;** I am too old to have 1426
    1:13 No, my **d.** 1426
1Sa 1: 4 and to all her sons and **d.** 1426
    2:21 and gave birth to three sons and two **d.** 1426
    8:13 He will take your **d** to be perfumers 1426
    30: 3 and sons and **d** taken captive. 1426
    30: 6 in spirit because of his sons and **d.** 1426
2Sa 1:20 lest the **d** of the Philistines be glad, 1426
    1:20 lest the **d** of the uncircumcised rejoice. 1426
    1:24 "O **d** of Israel, weep for Saul, 1426
    5:13 and more sons and **d** were born to him. 1426
    13:18 of garment the virgin **d** of the king wore. 1426
    13:18 the lives of your sons and **d** and the lives 1426
2Ki 17:17 They sacrificed their sons and **d** in the fire. 1426
1Ch 2:34 Sheshan had no sons—only **d.** 1426
    4:27 Shimei had sixteen sons and six **d,** 1426
    7:15 who had only **d.** 1426
    14: 3 and became the father of more sons and **d.** 1426
    23:22 he had only **d.** 1426
    25: 5 God gave Heman fourteen sons and three **d.** 1426
2Ch 11:21 twenty-eight sons and sixty **d.** 1426
    13:21 and had twenty-two sons and sixteen **d.** 1426
    24: 3 and he had sons and **d.** 1426
    28: 8 from their kinsmen two hundred thousand 1426
            wives, sons and **d.** 1426
    29: 9 and why our sons and **d** and our wives are 1426
    31:18 and **d** of the whole community listed 1426
Ezr 9: 2 They have taken some of their **d** as wives 1426
    9:12 do not give your **d** in marriage to their sons 1426
    9:12 to their sons or take their **d** for your sons. 1426
Ne 3:12 the next section with the help of his **d.** 1426
    4:14 your sons and your **d,** 1426

Ne 5: 2 "We and our sons and **d** are numerous; 1426
    5: 5 yet we have to subject our sons and **d** 1426
    5: 5 Some of our **d** have already been enslaved, 1426
    10:28 and all their sons and **d** who are able 1426
    10:30 not to give our **d** in marriage to the peoples 1426
    10:30 to the peoples around us or take their **d** 1426
    13:25 not to give your **d** in marriage to their sons, 1426
    13:25 to take their **d** in marriage for your sons or 1426
Job 1: 2 He had seven sons and three **d,** 1426
    1:13 and **d** were feasting and drinking wine at 1426
    1:18 and **d** were feasting and drinking wine at 1426
    42:13 And he also had seven sons and three **d.** 1426
    42:15 as beautiful as Job's **d,** 1426
Ps 45: 9 **D** of kings are among your honored 1426
    106:37 They sacrificed their sons and their **d** 1426
    106:38 the blood of their sons and **d,** 1426
    144:12 and our **d** will be like pillars carved 1426
Pr 30:15 "The leech has two **d.** 'Give! Give!' 1426
SS 1: 5 Dark am I, yet lovely, **d** of Jerusalem, 1426
    2: 7 **D** of Jerusalem, I charge you by 1426
    3: 5 **D** of Jerusalem, I charge you by 1426
    3:10 its interior lovingly inlaid by the **d** 1426
    3:11 Come out, you **d** of Zion, 1426
    5: 8 O **d** of Jerusalem, I charge you— 1426
    5:16 this my friend, O **d** of Jerusalem. 1426
    8: 4 **D** of Jerusalem, I charge you: 1426
Isa 23: 4 I have neither reared sons nor brought up **d.** 1435
    32: 9 you **d** who feel secure, 1426
    32:11 shudder, you **d** who feel secure! NIH
    43: 6 Bring my sons from afar and my **d** from 1426
    49:22 and carry your **d** on their shoulders. 1426
    56: 5 and a name better than sons and **d;** 1426
    60: 4 and your **d** are carried on the arm. 1426
Jer 3:24 their flocks and herds, their sons and **d.** 1426
    5:17 devour your sons and **d;** 1426
    7:31 of Ben Hinnom to burn their sons and **d** in 1426
    9:20 Teach your **d** how to wail; 1426
    11:22 their sons and **d** by famine. 1426
    14:16 their sons or their **d.** 1426
    16: 2 not marry and have sons or **d** in this place." 1426
    16: 3 the LORD says about the sons and **d** born 1426
    19: 9 the flesh of their sons and **d,** 1426
    29: 6 Marry and have sons and **d;** 1426
    29: 6 for your sons and give your **d** in marriage, 1426
    29: 6 so that they too may have sons and **d.** 1426
    32:35 of Ben Hinnom to sacrifice their sons and **d** 1426
    35: 8 nor our sons and **d** have ever drunk wine 1426
    41:10 the king's **d** along with all 1426
    43: 6 king's **d** whom Nebuzaradan commander 1426
    48:46 your sons are taken into exile and your **d** 1426
Eze 13:17 the **d** of your people who prophesy out 1426
    14:16 they could not save their own sons or **d.** 1426
    14:18 they could not save their own sons or **d.** 1426
    14:22 sons and **d** who will be brought out of it. 1426
    16:20 and **d** whom you bore to me 1426
    16:27 the **d** of the Philistines, 1426
    16:46 who lived to the north of you with her **d;** 1426
    16:46 who lived to the south of you with her **d,** 1426
    16:48 and her **d** never did what you 1426
    16:48 and your **d** have done. 1426
    16:49 She and her **d** were arrogant, 1426
    16:53 the fortunes of Sodom and her **d** and 1426
    16:53 and of Samaria and her **d,** 1426
    16:55 with her **d** and Samaria with her daughters, 1426
    16:55 with her daughters and Samaria with her **d,** 1426
    16:55 and your sons and your **d** will return 1426
    16:57 by the **d** of Edom and all her neighbors and 1426
    16:57 of Edom and all her neighbors and the **d** of 1426
    16:61 I will give them to you as **d,** 1426
    23: 2 **d** of the same mother. 1426
    23: 4 and gave birth to sons and **d.** 1426
    23:10 took away her sons and **d** and killed her 1426
    23:25 They will take away your sons and **d,** 1426
    23:47 they will kill their sons and **d** and burn 1426
    24:21 and **d** you left behind will fall by the sword. 1426
    24:25 and their sons and **d** as well— 1426
    32:16 The **d** of the nations chant it; 1426
    32:18 both her and the **d** of mighty nations, 1426
Hos 4:13 Therefore your **d** turn to prostitution 1426
    4:14 "I will not punish your **d** when they turn 1426
Joel 2:28 Your sons and **d** will prophesy. 1426
Am 7:17 and your sons and **d** will fall by the sword. 1426
Lk 23:28 "**D** of Jerusalem, do not weep for me; 2588
Ac 2:17 Your sons and **d** will prophesy, 2588
    21: 9 He had four unmarried **d** who prophesied. 2588
2Co 6:18 and you will be my sons and **d,** 2588
1Pe 3: 6 You are her **d** if you do what is right and do 5451

DAUGHTERS-IN-LAW (5) [DAUGHTER]

Ru 1: 6 Naomi and her **d** prepared to return home 3987
    1: 7 With her two **d** she left the place 3987
    1: 8 Then Naomi said to her two **d,** "Go back, 3987
Hos 4:13 to prostitution and your **d** to adultery. 3987
    4:14 nor your **d** when they commit adultery, 3987

DAVID (1004) [DAVID'S]

Ru 4:17 He was the father of Jesse, the father of **D.** 1858
    4:22 and Jesse the father of **D.** 1858
1Sa 16:13 on the Spirit of the LORD came upon **D** 1858
    16:19 "Send me your son **D,** 1858
    16:20 a young goat and sent them with his son **D** 1858
    16:21 **D** came to Saul and entered his service. 1858
    16:21 and **D** became one of his armor-bearers. NIH
    16:22 saying, "Allow **D** to remain in my service, 1858

1Sa 16:23 **D** would take his harp and play. 1858
    17:12 Now **D** was the son of an Ephrathite 1858
    17:14 **D** was the youngest. 1858
    17:15 but **D** went back and forth from Saul 1858
    17:17 Now Jesse said to his son **D,** 1858
    17:20 Early in the morning **D** left the flock with 1858
    17:22 **D** left his things with the keeper 1858
    17:23 and **D** heard it. 1858
    17:26 **D** asked the men standing near him, 1858
    17:29 "Now what have I done?" said **D.** 1858
    17:31 What **D** said was overheard and reported 1858
    17:32 **D** said to Saul, "Let no one lose heart 1858
    17:34 But **D** said to Saul, "Your servant 1858
    17:37 Saul said to **D,** "Go, 1858
    17:38 Then Saul dressed **D** in his own tunic. 1858
    17:39 **D** fastened on his sword over the tunic 1858
    17:41 kept coming closer to **D.** 1858
    17:42 He looked **D** over and saw that he was only 1858
    17:43 He said to **D,** "Am I a dog, 1858
    17:43 And the Philistine cursed **D** by his gods. 1858
    17:45 **D** said to the Philistine, 1858
    17:48 **D** ran quickly toward the battle line 1858
    17:50 So **D** triumphed over the Philistine with 1858
    17:51 **D** ran and stood over him. 1858
    17:54 **D** took the Philistine's head and brought it 1858
    17:55 As Saul watched **D** going out to meet 1858
    17:57 as **D** returned from killing the Philistine, 1858
    17:57 with **D** still holding the Philistine's head. 2257S
    17:58 **D** said, "I am the son of your servant Jesse 1858
    18: 1 After **D** had finished talking with Saul, 2257S
    18: 1 Jonathan became one in spirit with **D,** 1858
    18: 2 From that day Saul kept **D** with him and 2084S
    18: 3 with **D** because he loved him as himself. 1858
    18: 4 the robe he was wearing and gave it to **D,** 1858
    18: 5 **D** did it so successfully that Saul gave him 1858
    18: 6 after **D** had killed the Philistine, 1858
    18: 7 and **D** his tens of thousands." 1858
    18: 8 "They have credited **D** with tens 1858
    18: 9 that time on Saul kept a jealous eye on **D.** 1858
    18:10 while **D** was playing the harp, 1858
    18:11 saying to himself, "I'll pin **D** to the wall." 1858
    18:11 But **D** eluded him twice. 1858
    18:12 Saul was afraid of **D,** 1858
    18:12 the LORD was with **D** but had left Saul. 2257S
    18:13 So he sent **D** away from him 2084S
    18:13 and **D** led the troops in their campaigns. NIH
    18:16 But all Israel and Judah loved **D,** 1858
    18:17 Saul said to **D,** "Here is my older daughter 1858
    18:18 But **D** said to Saul, "Who am I, 1858
    18:19 Saul's daughter, to be given to **D,** 1858
    18:20 Saul's daughter Michal was in love with **D,** 1858
    18:21 So Saul said to **D,** "Now you have 1858
    18:22 "Speak to **D** privately and say, 'Look, 1858
    18:23 They repeated these words to **D.** 1858
    18:23 But **D** said, "Do you think it is 1858
    18:24 Saul's servants told him what **D** had said, 1858
    18:25 "Say to **D,** 'The king wants no other price 1858
    18:25 Saul's plan was to have **D** fall by the hands 1858
    18:26 When the attendants told **D** these things, 1858
    18:27 **D** and his men went out 1858
    18:28 that the LORD was with **D** and 1858
    18:28 and that his daughter Michal loved **D,** 2084S
    18:30 **D** met with more success than the rest 1858
    19: 1 and all the attendants to kill **D.** 1858
    19: 1 But Jonathan was very fond of **D** 1858
    19: 4 of **D** to Saul his father and said to him, "Let 1858
    19: 4 not the king do wrong to his servant **D;** 1858
    19: 5 to an innocent man like **D** by killing him 1858
    19: 6 LORD lives, **D** will not be put to death." NIH
    19: 7 So Jonathan called **D** and told him 1858
    19: 7 and **D** was with Saul as before. 1858
    19: 8 and **D** went out and fought the Philistines. 1858
    19: 9 While **D** was playing the harp, 1858
    19:10 but **D** eluded him as Saul drove the spear 1858
    19:10 That night **D** made good his escape. 1858
    19:12 So Michal let **D** down through a window, 1858
    19:14 When Saul sent the men to capture **D,** 1858
    19:15 Then Saul sent the men back to see **D** 1858
    19:18 When **D** had fled and made his escape, 1858
    19:19 "**D** is in Naioth at Ramah"; 1858
    19:22 And he asked, "Where are Samuel and **D?**" 1858
    20: 1 Then **D** fled from Naioth at Ramah 1858
    20: 3 But **D** took an oath and said, 1858
    20: 4 Jonathan said to **D,** "Whatever you want me 1858
    20: 5 So **D** said, "Look, tomorrow is 1858
    20: 6 '**D** earnestly asked my permission to hurry 1858
    20:10 **D** asked, "Who will tell me 1858
    20:12 Then Jonathan said to **D:** 1858
    20:16 a covenant with the house of **D,** 1858
    20:17 And Jonathan had **D** reaffirm his oath out 1858
    20:18 Then Jonathan said to **D:** 2257S
    20:24 So **D** hid in the field, 1858
    20:26 to **D** to make him ceremonially unclean— 2085S
    20:28 "**D** earnestly asked me for permission to go 1858
    20:33 that his father would kill **D.** 1858
    20:34 at his father's shameful treatment of **D.** 1858
    20:35 to the field for his meeting with **D.** 1858
    20:39 only Jonathan and **D** knew. 1858
    20:41 **D** got up from the south side [of the stone] 1858
    20:41 but **D** wept the most. 1858
    20:42 Jonathan said to **D,** "Go in peace, 1858
    20:42 **D** left, and Jonathan went back to the town. NIH
    21: 1 **D** went to Nob, to Ahimelech the priest. 1858
    21: 2 **D** answered Ahimelech the priest, 1858
    21: 4 But the priest answered **D,** 1858
    21: 5 **D** replied, "Indeed women have been kept 1858
    21: 8 **D** asked Ahimelech, "Don't you have 1858

1Sa		
21: 9	D said, "There is none like it;	1858
21:10	That day D fled from Saul and went	1858
21:11	"Isn't this D, the king of the land?	1858
21:11	and D his tens of thousands'?"	1858
21:12	D took these words to heart	1858
22: 1	D left Gath and escaped to the cave	1858
22: 3	From there D went to Mizpah in Moab	1858
22: 4	and they stayed with him as long as D was	1858
22: 5	But the prophet Gad said to D,	1858
22: 5	So D left and went to the forest of Hereth.	1858
22: 6	that D and his men had been discovered.	1858
22:14	"Who of all your servants is as loyal as D,	1858
22:17	because they too have sided with D.	1858
22:20	escaped and fled to join D.	1858
22:21	He told D that Saul had killed the priests of	1858
22:22	Then D said to Abiathar:	1858
23: 1	When D was told, "Look,	1858
23: 4	Once again D inquired of the LORD,	1858
23: 5	So D and his men went to Keilah,	1858
23: 6	the ephod down with him when he fled to D	1858
23: 7	Saul was told that D had gone to Keilah,	1858
23: 7	for D has imprisoned himself by entering	NIH
23: 8	down to Keilah to besiege D and his men.	1858
23: 9	When D learned that Saul was plotting	1858
23:10	D said, "O LORD, God of Israel,	1858
23:12	Again D asked, "Will the citizens	1858
23:13	So D and his men,	1858
23:13	When Saul was told that D had escaped	1858
23:14	D stayed in the desert strongholds and in	1858
23:14	but God did not give D into his hands.	2257S
23:15	D was at Horesh in the Desert of Ziph,	1858
23:16	to D at Horesh and helped him find strength	1858
23:18	but D remained at Horesh.	1858
23:19	not D hiding among us in the strongholds	1858
23:22	Find out where D usually goes	2257S
23:24	D and his men were in the Desert of Maon,	1858
23:25	and when D was told about it,	1858
23:25	into the Desert of Maon in pursuit of D.	1858
23:26	and D and his men were on the other side,	1858
23:26	As Saul and his forces were closing in on D	1858
23:28	of D and went to meet the Philistines.	1858
23:29	And D went up from there and lived in	1858
24: 1	"D is in the Desert of En Gedi."	1858
24: 2	to look for D and his men near the Crags of	1858
24: 3	D and his men were far back in the cave.	1858
24: 4	Then D crept up unnoticed and cut off	1858
24: 5	D was conscience-stricken	1858
24: 7	With these words D rebuked his men	1858
24: 8	Then D went out of the cave and called out	1858
24: 8	D bowed down and prostrated himself	1858
24: 9	'D is bent on harming you'?	1858
24:16	When D finished saying this, Saul asked,	1858
24:16	Saul asked, "Is that your voice, D my son?"	1858
24:22	So D gave his oath to Saul.	1858
24:22	but D and his men went up to	1858
25: 1	D moved down into the Desert of Maon.	1858
25: 4	While D was in the desert,	1858
25: 8	and your son D whatever you can find	1858
25:10	"Who is this D?	1858
25:13	D said to his men, "Put on your swords!"	1858
25:13	and D put on his.	1858
25:13	About four hundred men went up with D,	1858
25:14	"D sent messengers from the desert	1858
25:20	there were D and his men descending	1858
25:21	D had just said, "It's been useless—	1858
25:22	May God deal with D,	1858
25:23	When Abigail saw D,	1858
25:23	down before D with her face to the ground.	1858
25:32	D said to Abigail, "Praise be to the LORD,	1858
25:35	Then D accepted from her	1858
25:39	When D heard that Nabal was dead,	1858
25:39	Then D sent word to Abigail,	1858
25:40	"D has sent us to you to take you	1858
25:43	D had also married Ahinoam of Jezreel,	1858
26: 1	"Is not D hiding on the hill of Hakilah,	1858
26: 2	to search there for D.	1858
26: 3	but D stayed in the desert.	1858
26: 5	Then D set out and went to the place	1858
26: 6	D then asked Ahimelech the Hittite	1858
26: 7	D and Abishai went to the army by night,	1858
26: 8	Abishai said to D,	1858
26: 9	But D said to Abishai, "Don't destroy him!	1858
26:12	So D took the spear and water jug	1858
26:13	Then D crossed over to the other side	1858
26:15	D said, "You're a man, aren't you?	1858
26:17	"Is that your voice, D my son?"	1858
26:17	D replied, "Yes it is, my lord the king."	1858
26:21	Come back, D my son.	1858
26:22	"Here is the king's spear," D answered.	1858
26:25	Then Saul said to D, "May you be blessed,	1858
26:25	"May you be blessed, my son D;	1858
26:25	So D went on his way,	1858
27: 1	But D thought to himself,	1858
27: 2	So D and the six hundred men with him left	1858
27: 3	D and his men settled in Gath with Achish.	1858
27: 3	and D had his two wives:	1858
27: 4	Saul was told that D had fled to Gath,	1858
27: 5	Then D said to Achish,	1858
27: 7	D lived in Philistine territory a year	1858
27: 8	Now D and his men went up and raided	1858
27: 9	Whenever D attacked an area,	1858
27:10	D would say, "Against the Negev of Judah"	1858
27:11	'This is what D did.' "	1858
27:12	Achish trusted D and said to himself,	1858
28: 1	Achish said to D,	1858
28: 2	D said, "Then you will see	1858
28:17	of your neighbors—to D.	1858

1Sa		
29: 2	D and his men were marching at the rear	1858
29: 3	Achish replied, "Is this not D,	1858
29: 5	the D they sang about in their dances:	1858
29: 5	and D his tens of thousands'?"	1858
29: 6	So Achish called D and said to him,	1858
29: 8	"But what have I done?" asked D.	1858
29:11	So D and his men got up early in	1858
30: 1	D and his men reached Ziklag on	1858
30: 3	When D and his men came to Ziklag,	1858
30: 4	So D and his men wept aloud	1858
30: 6	D was greatly distressed because	1858
30: 6	But D found strength in	1858
30: 7	Then D said to Abiathar the priest,	1858
30: 8	and D inquired of the LORD,	1858
30: 9	D and the six hundred men with him came	1858
30:10	But D and four hundred men continued	1858
30:11	in a field and brought him to D.	1858
30:13	D asked him, "To whom do you belong,	1858
30:15	D asked him, "Can you lead me down	1858
30:16	He led D down, and there they were,	2084S
30:17	D fought them from dusk until the evening	1858
30:18	D recovered everything	1858
30:19	D brought everything back.	1858
30:21	Then D came to the two hundred men	1858
30:21	They came out to meet D and the people	1858
30:21	As D and his men approached,	1858
30:23	D replied, "No, my brothers,	1858
30:25	D made this a statute and ordinance	NIH
30:26	When D arrived in Ziklag,	1858
30:31	and to those in all the other places where D	1858

2Sa		
1: 1	D returned from defeating the Amalekites	1858
1: 2	When he came to D,	1858
1: 3	"Where have you come from?" D asked	1858
1: 4	"What happened?" D asked.	1858
1: 5	Then D said to the young man	1858
1:11	Then D and all the men with him took hold	1858
1:13	D said to the young man who brought him	1858
1:14	D asked him, "Why were you not afraid	1858
1:15	Then D called one of his men and said,	1858
1:16	For D had said to him,	1858
1:17	D took up this lament concerning Saul	1858
2: 1	D inquired of the LORD.	1858
2: 1	D asked, "Where shall I go?"	1858
2: 2	So D went up there with his two wives,	1858
2: 3	D also took the men who were with him,	1858
2: 4	to Hebron and there they anointed D king	1858
2: 4	When D was told that it was the men	1858
2:10	The house of Judah, however, followed D.	1858
2:11	The length of time D was king in Hebron	1858
2:15	of Saul, and twelve for D.	1858
3: 1	the house of Saul and the house of D lasted	1858
3: 1	D grew stronger and stronger,	1858
3: 2	Sons were born to D in Hebron:	1858
3: 5	These were born to D in Hebron.	1858
3: 6	the house of Saul and the house of D,	1858
3: 8	I haven't handed you over to D.	1858
3: 9	for D what the LORD promised him	1858
3:12	on his behalf to say to D,	1858
3:13	"Good," said D.	NIH
3:14	Then D sent messengers to Ish-Bosheth son	1858
3:17	to make D your king.	1858
3:18	For the LORD promised D,	1858
3:18	'By my servant D I will rescue my people Israel	1858
3:19	to Hebron to tell D everything that Israel	1858
3:20	came to D at Hebron,	1858
3:20	D prepared a feast for him and his men.	1858
3:21	Then Abner said to D,	1858
3:21	D sent Abner away, and he went in peace.	1858
3:22	But Abner was no longer with D in Hebron,	1858
3:22	because D had sent him away,	NIH
3:26	Joab then left D and sent messengers	1858
3:26	But D did not know it.	1858
3:28	Later, when D heard about this, he said,	1858
3:31	D said to Joab and all the people with him,	1858
3:31	King D himself walked behind the bier.	1858
3:35	Then they all came and urged D	1858
3:35	but D took an oath, saying,	1858
4: 8	They brought the head of Ish-Bosheth to D	1858
4: 9	D answered Recab and his brother Baanah,	1858
4:12	So D gave an order to his men,	1858
5: 1	All the tribes of Israel came to D at Hebron	1858
5: 3	of Israel had come to King D at Hebron,	1858
5: 3	and they anointed D king over Israel.	1858
5: 4	D was thirty years old	1858
5: 6	The Jebusites said to D,	1858
5: 6	They thought, "D cannot get in here."	1858
5: 7	D captured the fortress of Zion,	1858
5: 7	the fortress of Zion, the City of D.	1858
5: 9	On that day, D said,	1858
5: 9	D then took up residence in the fortress	1858
5: 9	in the fortress and called it the City of D.	1858
5:11	Hiram king of Tyre sent messengers to D,	1858
5:11	and they built a palace for D.	1858
5:12	And D knew that the LORD	1858
5:13	D took more concubines and wives	1858
5:17	that D had been anointed king over Israel,	1858
5:17	but D heard about it and went down to	1858
5:19	so D inquired of the LORD,	1858
5:20	So D went to Baal Perazim,	1858
5:21	and D and his men carried them off.	1858
5:23	so D inquired of the LORD,	1858
5:25	So D did as the LORD commanded him,	1858
6: 1	D again brought together out	1858
6: 5	D and the whole house of Israel	1858
6: 8	Then D was angry because	1858
6: 9	D was afraid of the LORD that day	1858

2Sa		
6:10	the LORD to be with him in the City of D.	1858
6:12	Now King D was told,	1858
6:12	So D went down and brought up the ark	1858
6:12	the house of Obed-Edom to the City of D	1858
6:14	D, wearing a linen ephod,	1858
6:16	of the LORD was entering the City of D,	1858
6:16	when she saw King D leaping and dancing	1858
6:17	inside the tent that D had pitched for it,	1858
6:17	and D sacrificed burnt offerings	1858
6:20	D returned home to bless his household,	1858
6:21	D said to Michal, "It was before	1858
7: 5	"Go and tell my servant D, 'This is what	1858
7: 8	"Now then, tell my servant D,	1858
7:17	to D all the words of this entire revelation.	1858
7:18	King D went in and sat before the LORD,	1858
7:20	"What more can D say to you?	1858
7:26	And the house of your servant D will	1858
8: 1	D defeated the Philistines	1858
8: 2	D also defeated the Moabites.	NIH
8: 2	So the Moabites became subject to D	1858
8: 3	D fought Hadadezer son of Rehob,	1858
8: 4	D captured a thousand of his chariots,	1858
8: 5	D struck down twenty-two thousand	1858
8: 6	The LORD gave D victory wherever he went.	1858
8: 7	D took the gold shields that belonged to	1858
8: 8	King D took a great quantity of bronze.	1858
8: 9	of Hamath heard that D had defeated	1858
8:10	he sent his son Joram to King D	1858
8:11	King D dedicated these articles to	1858
8:13	And D became famous after he returned	1858
8:14	and all the Edomites became subject to D.	1858
8:14	The LORD gave D victory wherever he went.	1858
8:15	D reigned over all Israel,	1858
9: 1	D asked, "Is there anyone still left of	1858
9: 2	They called him to appear before D,	1858
9: 5	So King D had him brought from Lo Debar,	1858
9: 6	the son of Saul, came to D,	1858
9: 6	D said, "Mephibosheth!"	1858
9: 7	"Don't be afraid," D said to him,	1858
10: 2	D thought, "I will show kindness	1858
10: 2	So D sent a delegation	1858
10: 3	"Do you think D is honoring your father	1858
10: 3	Hasn't D sent them to you to explore	1858
10: 5	When D was told about this,	1858
10: 7	D sent Joab out with the entire army	1858
10:17	When D was told of this,	1858
10:17	to meet D and fought against him.	1858
10:18	and D killed seven hundred	1858
11: 1	D sent Joab out with the king's men and	1858
11: 1	But D remained in Jerusalem.	1858
11: 2	One evening D got up from his bed	1858
11: 3	and D sent someone to find out about her.	1858
11: 4	Then D sent messengers to get her.	1858
11: 5	The woman conceived and sent word to D,	1858
11: 6	So D sent this word to Joab:	1858
11: 6	And Joab sent him to D.	1858
11: 7	D asked him how Joab was,	1858
11: 8	Then D said to Uriah,	1858
11:10	When D was told,	1858
11:11	Uriah said to D, "The ark and Israel and	1858
11:12	Then D said to him,	1858
11:13	and D made him drunk.	NIH
11:14	In the morning D wrote a letter to Joab	1858
11:18	Joab sent D a full account of the battle.	1858
11:22	he told D everything Joab had sent him	1858
11:23	The messenger said to D,	1858
11:25	D told the messenger, "Say this to Joab:	1858
11:27	D had her brought to his house,	1858
11:27	thing D had done displeased the LORD.	1858
12: 1	The LORD sent Nathan to D.	1858
12: 5	D burned with anger against the man	1858
12: 7	Then Nathan said to D, "You are the man!	1858
12:13	Then D said to Nathan,	1858
12:15	the child that Uriah's wife had borne to D,	1858
12:16	D pleaded with God for the child.	1858
12:18	we spoke to D but he would not listen to us.	2257S
12:19	D noticed that his servants were whispering	1858
12:20	Then D got up from the ground.	1858
12:24	Then D comforted his wife Bathsheba,	1858
12:27	Joab then sent messengers to D, saying,	1858
12:29	So D mustered the entire army and went	1858
12:31	Then D and his entire army returned	1858
13: 1	Amnon son of D fell in love with Tamar,	1858
13: 1	the beautiful sister of Absalom son of D.	1858
13: 7	D sent word to Tamar at the palace:	1858
13:21	When King D heard all this, he was furious.	1858
13:30	the report came to D:	1858
13:37	But King D mourned for his son every day.	NIH
15:13	A messenger came and told D,	1858
15:14	Then D said to all his officials who were	1858
15:22	D said to Ittai, "Go ahead, march on."	1858
15:30	But D continued up the Mount of Olives,	1858
15:31	Now D had been told,	1858
15:31	So D prayed, "O LORD,	1858
15:32	When D arrived at the summit,	1858
15:33	D said to him, "If you go with me,	1858
16: 1	When D had gone a short distance beyond	1858
16: 5	As King D approached Bahurim,	1858
16: 6	He pelted D and all the king's officials	1858
16:10	'Curse D,' who can ask,	1858
16:11	D then said to Abishai and all his officials,	1858
16:13	So D and his men continued along the road	1858
16:23	how both D and Absalom regarded all	1858
17: 1	and set out tonight in pursuit of D.	1858
17:16	a message immediately and tell D, 'Do	1858
17:17	and they were to go and tell King D.	1858
17:21	of the well and went to inform King D.	1858

2Sa 17:22	So **D** and all the people with him set out	1858
17:24	**D** went to Mahanaim,	1858
17:27	When **D** came to Mahanaim,	1858
17:29	from cows' milk for **D** and his people	1858
18: 1	**D** mustered the men who were with him	1858
18: 2	**D** sent the troops out—	1858
18:24	While **D** was sitting between the inner	1858
19:11	King **D** sent this message to Zadok	1858
19:16	with the men of Judah to meet King **D.**	1858
19:22	**D** replied, "What do you and I have	1858
19:43	a greater claim on **D** than you have.	1858
20: 1	"We have no share in **D,**	1858
20: 2	of Israel deserted **D** to follow Sheba son	1858
20: 3	**D** returned to his palace in Jerusalem,	1858
20: 6	**D** said to Abishai,	1858
20:11	and whoever is for **D,** let him follow Joab!"	1858
20:21	up his hand against the king, against **D.**	1858
21: 1	During the reign of **D,**	1858
21: 1	so **D** sought the face of the LORD.	1858
21: 3	**D** asked the Gibeonites,	1858
21: 4	to do for you?" **D** asked.	NIH
21: 7	of the oath before the LORD between **D**	1858
21:11	**D** was told what Aiah's daughter Rizpah,	1858
21:13	**D** brought the bones of Saul	NIH
21:15	**D** went down with his men to fight against	1858
21:16	said he would kill **D.**	1858
21:22	and they fell at the hands of **D** and his men.	1858
22: 1	**D** sang to the LORD the words	1858
22:51	to **D** and his descendants forever."	1858
23: 1	These are the last words of **D:**	1858
23: 1	"The oracle of **D** son of Jesse,	1858
23: 9	he was with **D** when they taunted	1858
23:13	of the thirty chief men came down to **D** at	1858
23:14	At that time **D** was in the stronghold,	1858
23:15	**D** longed for water and said, "Oh,	1858
23:16	of Bethlehem and carried it back to **D.**	1858
23:17	**D** would not drink it.	NIH
23:23	And **D** put him in charge of his bodyguard.	1858
24: 1	and he incited **D** against them, saying,	1858
24:10	**D** was conscience-stricken	1858
24:11	Before **D** got up the next morning,	1858
24:12	and tell **D,** 'This is what the LORD says:	1858
24:13	So Gad went to **D** and said to him,	1858
24:14	**D** said to Gad, "I am in deep distress.	1858
24:17	When **D** saw the angel who was striking	1858
24:18	On that day Gad went to **D** and said to him,	1858
24:19	So **D** went up, as the LORD had commanded	1858
24:21	"To buy your threshing floor," **D** answered,	1858
24:22	Araunah said to **D,** "Let my lord the king	1858
24:24	So **D** bought the threshing floor and	1858
24:25	**D** built an altar to the LORD there	1858
1Ki 1: 1	King **D** was old and well advanced in years,	1858
1:13	Go in to King **D** and say to him,	1858
1:28	Then King **D** said, "Call in Bathsheba."	1858
1:31	said, "May my lord King **D** live forever!"	1858
1:32	King **D** said, "Call in Zadok the priest,	1858
1:37	the throne of my lord King **D!**"	1858
1:43	"Our servant King **D** has made Solomon king.	1858
1:47	to congratulate our lord King **D.**	1858
2: 1	When the time drew near for **D** to die,	1858
2:10	Then **D** rested with his fathers	1858
2:10	and was buried in the City of **D.**	1858
2:12	Solomon sat on the throne of his father **D,**	1858
2:24	the throne of my father **D** and has founded	1858
2:26	the Sovereign LORD before my father **D**	1858
2:32	of my father **D** he attacked two men	1858
2:33	But on **D** and his descendants,	1858
2:44	the wrong you did to my father **D.**	1858
3: 1	of **D** until he finished building his palace	1858
3: 3	according to the statutes of his father **D,**	1858
3: 6	my father **D,** because he was faithful to you	1858
3: 7	king in place of my father **D,**	1858
3:14	and commands as **D** your father did,	1858
5: 1	to succeed his father **D,**	NIH
5: 1	on friendly terms with **D.**	1858
5: 3	of the wars waged against my father **D**	1858
5: 5	as the LORD told my father **D,**	1858
5: 7	for he has given **D** a wise son to rule	1858
6:12	the promise I gave to **D** your father.	1858
7:51	in the things his father **D** had dedicated—	1858
8: 1	from Zion, the City of **D.**	1858
8:15	with his own mouth to my father **D.**	1858
8:16	I have chosen **D** to rule my people Israel.'	1858
8:17	"My father **D** had it in his heart to build	1858
8:18	But the LORD said to my father **D,**	1858
8:20	I have succeeded **D** my father and now I sit	1858
8:24	to your servant **D** my father;	1858
8:25	keep for your servant **D** my father	1858
8:66	for his servant **D** and his people Israel.	1858
9: 4	as **D** your father did, and do all	1858
9: 5	as I promised your father when I said,	1858
9:24	of **D** to the palace Solomon had built	1858
11: 4	as the heart of **D** his father had been.	1858
11: 6	as **D** his father had done.	1858
11:12	Nevertheless, for the sake of **D** your father,	1858
11:13	the sake of **D** my servant and for the sake	1858
11:15	Earlier when **D** was fighting with Edom,	1858
11:21	that **D** rested with his fathers and that Joab	1858
11:24	when **D** destroyed the forces [of Zobah];	1858
11:27	in the wall of the city of **D** his father.	1858
11:32	of my servant **D** and the city of Jerusalem,	1858
11:33	nor kept my statutes and laws as **D,**	1858
11:34	of his life for the sake of **D** my servant,	1858
11:36	that my servant may always have a lamp	1858
11:38	as **D** my servant did, I will be with you.	1858

1Ki 11:38	as the one I built for **D** and will give Israel	1858
11:43	and was buried in the city of **D** his father.	1858
12:16	"What share do we have in **D,**	1858
12:16	Look after your own house, O **D!**"	1858
12:19	in rebellion against the house of **D**	1858
12:20	of Judah remained loyal to the house of **D.**	1858
12:26	now likely revert to the house of **D.**	1858
13: 2	be born to the house of **D.**	1858
14: 8	from the house of **D** and gave it to you,	1858
14: 8	but you have not been like my servant **D,**	1858
14:31	and was buried with them in the City of **D.**	1858
15: 3	as the heart of **D** his forefather had been.	1858
15: 5	For **D** had done what was right in the eyes	1858
15: 8	and was buried in the City of **D.**	1858
15:11	as his father **D** had done.	1858
15:24	with them in the city of his father **D.**	1858
22:50	with them in the city of **D** his father.	1858
2Ki 8:19	Nevertheless, for the sake of his servant **D,**	1858
8:19	He had promised to maintain a lamp for **D**	2257S
8:24	and was buried with them in the City of **D.**	1858
9:28	in his tomb in the City of **D.**	1858
11:10	that had belonged to King **D** and that were	1858
12:21	with his fathers in the City of **D.**	1858
14: 3	but not as his father **D** had done.	1858
14:20	in the City of **D.**	1858
15: 7	and was buried near them in the City of **D.**	1858
15:38	and was buried with them in the City of **D.**	1858
16: 2	Unlike **D** his father, he did not do what	1858
16:20	and was buried with them in the City of **D.**	1858
17:21	he tore Israel away from the house of **D,**	1858
18: 3	just as his father **D** had done.	1858
19:34	my sake and for the sake of **D** my servant."	1858
20: 5	the God of your father **D,** says:	1858
20: 6	and for the sake of my servant **D.**' "	1858
21: 7	of which the LORD had said to **D** and	1858
22: 2	and walked in all the ways of his father **D,**	1858
1Ch 3: 1	the sixth Ozem and the seventh **D,**	1858
3: 1	These were the sons of **D** born to him	1858
3: 4	These six were born to **D** in Hebron,	2257S
3: 4	reigned in Jerusalem thirty-three years,	NIH
3: 9	All these were the sons of **D,**	1858
4:31	These were their towns until the reign of **D.**	1858
6:31	the men **D** put in charge of the music in	1858
7: 2	During the reign of **D,**	1858
9:22	to their positions of trust by **D** and Samuel	1858
10:14	and turned the kingdom over to **D** son	1858
11: 1	All Israel came together to **D** at Hebron	1858
11: 3	of Israel had come to King **D** at Hebron,	1858
11: 3	and they anointed **D** king over Israel,	1858
11: 4	**D** and all the Israelites marched	1858
11: 5	said to **D,** "You will not get in here."	1858
11: 5	**D** captured the fortress of Zion,	1858
11: 5	the fortress of Zion, the City of **D.**	1858
11: 6	**D** had said, "Whoever leads the attack on	1858
11: 7	**D** then took up residence in the fortress,	1858
11: 7	and so it was called the City of **D.**	1858
11: 9	And **D** became more and more powerful,	1858
11:13	He was with **D** at Pas Dammim when	1858
11:15	the thirty chiefs came down to **D** to the rock	1858
11:16	At that time **D** was in the stronghold,	1858
11:17	**D** longed for water and said, "Oh,	1858
11:18	of Bethlehem and carried it back to **D.**	1858
11:19	**D** would not drink it.	NIH
11:25	And **D** put him in charge of his bodyguard.	1858
12: 1	to **D** at Ziklag, while he was banished from	1858
12: 8	to **D** at his stronghold in the desert.	1858
12:16	and some men from Judah also came to **D**	1858
12:17	**D** went out to meet them and said to them,	1858
12:18	We are yours, O **D!**	1858
12:18	So **D** received them and made them leaders	1858
12:19	of Manasseh defected to **D** when he went	1858
12:20	When **D** went to Ziklag,	2257S
12:21	They helped **D** against raiding bands,	1858
12:22	Day after day men came to help **D,**	1858
12:23	to **D** at Hebron to turn Saul's kingdom over	1858
12:31	by name to come and make **D** king—	1858
12:33	to help **D** with undivided loyalty—	NIH
12:38	to Hebron fully determined to make **D** king	1858
12:38	also of one mind to make **D** king.	1858
12:39	The men spent three days there with **D,**	1858
13: 1	**D** conferred with each of his officers,	1858
13: 5	So **D** assembled all the Israelites,	1858
13: 6	**D** and all the Israelites with him went	1858
13: 8	**D** and all the Israelites were celebrating	1858
13:11	Then **D** was angry because	1858
13:12	**D** was afraid of God that day and asked,	1858
13:13	the ark to be with him in the City of **D.**	1858
14: 1	Hiram king of Tyre sent messengers to **D,**	1858
14: 2	And **D** knew that the LORD had	1858
14: 3	In Jerusalem **D** took more wives	1858
14: 8	that **D** had been anointed king	1858
14: 8	**D** heard about it and went out to meet them.	1858
14:10	so **D** inquired of God:	1858
14:11	So **D** and his men went up to Baal Perazim,	1858
14:12	and **D** gave orders to burn them in the fire.	1858
14:14	so **D** inquired of God again,	1858
14:16	So **D** did as God commanded him,	1858
15: 1	After **D** had constructed buildings	NIH
15: 1	for himself in the City of **D,**	1858
15: 2	Then **D** said, "No one but the Levites	1858
15: 3	**D** assembled all Israel in Jerusalem to bring	1858
15:11	Then **D** summoned Zadok and Abiathar	1858
15:16	**D** told the leaders of the Levites	1858
15:25	So **D** and the elders of Israel and	1858
15:27	Now **D** was clothed in a robe of fine linen,	1858
15:27	**D** also wore a linen ephod.	1858
15:29	of the LORD was entering the City of **D,**	1858

1Ch 15:29	she saw King **D** dancing and celebrating,	1858
16: 1	and set it inside the tent that **D** had pitched	1858
16: 2	After **D** had finished sacrificing	1858
16: 7	That day **D** first committed to Asaph	1858
16:37	**D** left Asaph and his associates before	NIH
16:39	**D** left Zadok the priest	NIH
16:43	and **D** returned home to bless his family.	1858
17: 1	After **D** was settled in his palace,	1858
17: 2	Nathan replied to **D,**	1858
17: 4	"Go and tell my servant **D,** 'This is what	1858
17: 7	"Now then, tell my servant **D,**	1858
17:15	to **D** all the words of this entire revelation.	1858
17:16	King **D** went in and sat before the LORD,	1858
17:18	"What more can **D** say to you	1858
17:24	And the house of your servant **D** will	1858
18: 1	**D** defeated the Philistines	1858
18: 2	**D** also defeated the Moabites,	1858
18: 3	**D** fought Hadadezer king of Zobah,	1858
18: 4	**D** captured a thousand of his chariots,	1858
18: 5	**D** struck down twenty-two thousand	1858
18: 6	The LORD gave **D** victory everywhere he went.	1858
18: 7	**D** took the gold shields carried by	1858
18: 8	**D** took a great quantity of bronze,	1858
18: 9	of Hamath heard that **D** had defeated	1858
18:10	he sent his son Hadoram to King **D**	1858
18:11	King **D** dedicated these articles to	1858
18:13	and all the Edomites became subject to **D.**	1858
18:13	The LORD gave **D** victory everywhere he went.	1858
18:14	**D** reigned over all Israel,	1858
19: 2	**D** thought, "I will show kindness	1858
19: 2	So **D** sent a delegation	1858
19: 3	"Do you think **D** is honoring your father	1858
19: 5	someone came and told **D** about the men,	1858
19: 8	**D** sent Joab out with the entire army	1858
19:17	When **D** was told of this,	1858
19:17	**D** formed his lines to meet the Arameans	1858
19:18	and **D** killed seven thousand	1858
19:19	with **D** and became subject to him.	1858
20: 1	but **D** remained in Jerusalem.	1858
20: 2	**D** took the crown from the head	1858
20: 3	**D** did this to all the Ammonite towns.	1858
20: 3	Then **D** and his entire army returned	1858
20: 8	and they fell at the hands of **D** and his men.	1858
21: 1	against Israel and incited **D** to take a census	1858
21: 2	So **D** said to Joab and the commanders of	1858
21: 5	the number of the fighting men to **D:**	1858
21: 8	Then **D** said to God,	1858
21:10	and tell **D,** 'This is what the LORD says:	1858
21:11	So Gad went to **D** and said to him,	1858
21:13	**D** said to Gad, "I am in deep distress.	1858
21:16	**D** looked up and saw the angel of	1858
21:16	Then **D** and the elders, clothed in sackcloth,	1858
21:17	**D** said to God,	1858
21:18	the LORD ordered Gad to tell **D** to go up	1858
21:19	So **D** went up in obedience to the word	1858
21:21	Then **D** approached, and	1858
21:21	down before **D** with his face to the ground.	1858
21:22	**D** said to him,	1858
21:23	Araunah said to **D,** "Take it!	1858
21:24	But King **D** replied to Araunah, "No,	1858
21:25	So **D** paid Araunah six hundred shekels	1858
21:26	**D** built an altar to the LORD there	1858
21:28	when **D** saw that	1858
21:30	**D** could not go before it to inquire of God,	1858
22: 1	Then **D** said, "The house of	1858
22: 2	So **D** gave orders to assemble	1858
22: 4	brought large numbers of them to **D.**	1858
22: 5	**D** said, "My son Solomon is young	1858
22: 5	So **D** made extensive preparations	1858
22: 7	**D** said to Solomon:	1858
22:17	Then **D** ordered all the leaders of Israel	1858
23: 1	When **D** was old and full of years,	1858
23: 4	**D** said, "Of these, twenty-four thousand are	NIH
23: 6	**D** divided the Levites	1858
23:25	For **D** had said, "Since the LORD,	1858
23:27	According to the last instructions of **D,**	1858
24: 3	**D** separated them into divisions	1858
24:31	in the presence of King **D** and of Zadok,	1858
25: 1	**D,** together with the commanders of	1858
26:26	for the things dedicated by King **D,**	1858
26:32	and King **D** put them in charge of	1858
27:18	Elihu, a brother of **D;**	1858
27:23	**D** did not take the number of	1858
27:24	in the book of the annals of King **D.**	1858
28: 1	**D** summoned all the officials of Israel	1858
28: 2	King **D** rose to his feet and said:	1858
28:11	Then **D** gave his son Solomon the plans for	1858
28:19	**D** said, "I have in writing from the hand of	NIH
28:20	**D** also said to Solomon his son,	1858
29: 1	Then King **D** said to the whole assembly:	1858
29: 9	the king also rejoiced greatly.	1858
29:10	**D** praised the LORD in the presence of	1858
29:20	Then **D** said to the whole assembly,	1858
29:22	Then they acknowledged Solomon son of **D**	1858
29:23	the LORD as king in place of his father **D.**	1858
29:26	**D** son of Jesse was king over all Israel.	1858
2Ch 1: 1	of **D** established himself firmly	1858
1: 4	Now **D** had brought up the ark of God	1858
1: 8	to **D** my father and have made me king	1858
1: 9	let your promise to my father **D**	1858
2: 3	for my father **D** when you sent him cedar	1858
2: 7	whom my father **D** provided.	1858
2:12	He has given King **D** a wise son,	1858
2:14	and with those of my lord, **D** your father.	1858
2:17	after the census his father **D** had taken;	1858

2Ch	3: 1	the LORD had appeared to his father **D**.	1858
	3: 1	the place provided by **D**.	1858
	5: 1	in the things his father **D** had dedicated—	1858
	5: 2	from Zion, the City of **D**.	1858
	6: 4	with his mouth to my father **D**.	1858
	6: 6	I have chosen **D** to rule my people Israel.'	1858
	6: 7	"My father **D** had it in his heart to build	1858
	6: 8	But the LORD said to my father **D**,	1858
	6:10	I have succeeded **D** my father and now I sit	1858
	6:15	to your servant **D** my father;	1858
	6:16	keep for your servant **D** my father	1858
	6:17	you promised your servant **D** come true.	1858
	6:42	the great love promised to **D** your servant."	1858
	7: 6	which King **D** had made for praising	1858
	7:10	the good things the LORD had done for **D**	1858
	7:17	if you walk before me as **D** your father did,	1858
	7:18	as I covenanted with **D** your father	1858
	8:11	the City of **D** to the palace he had built	1858
	8:11	not live in the palace of **D** king of Israel,	1858
	8:14	with the ordinance of his father **D**,	1858
	8:14	because this was what **D** the man	1858
	9:31	and was buried in the city of **D** his father.	1858
	10:16	"What share do we have in **D**,	1858
	10:16	Look after your own house, O **D**!"	1858
	10:19	in rebellion against the house of **D**	1858
	11:17	walking in the ways of **D** and Solomon	1858
	12:16	and was buried in the City of **D**.	1858
	13: 5	of Israel to **D** and his descendants forever	1858
	13: 6	an official of Solomon son of **D**,	1858
	14: 1	and was buried in the City of **D**.	1858
	16:14	for himself in the City of **D**.	1858
	17: 3	in the ways his father **D** had followed.	1858
	21: 1	and was buried with them in the City of **D**.	1858
	21: 7	the covenant the LORD had made with **D**,	1858
	21: 7	not willing to destroy the house of **D**.	1858
	21:12	the God of your father **D**, says:	1858
	21:20	and was buried in the City of **D**,	1858
	23: 3	concerning the descendants of **D**.	1858
	23: 9	that had belonged to King **D** and that were	1858
	23:18	to whom **D** had made assignments in	1858
	23:18	and singing, as **D** had ordered.	1858
	24:16	with the kings in the City of **D**,	1858
	24:25	So he died and was buried in the City of **D**,	1858
	27: 9	and was buried in the City of **D**.	1858
	28: 1	Unlike **D** his father, he did not do what	1858
	29: 2	just as his father **D** had done.	1858
	29:25	harps and lyres in the way prescribed by **D**	1858
	29:27	by trumpets and the instruments of King **D**	1858
	29:30	with the words of **D** and of Asaph the seer.	1858
	30:26	of **D** king of Israel there had been nothing	1858
	32: 5	the supporting terraces of the City of **D**.	1858
	32:30	down to the west side of the City of **D**.	1858
	33: 7	of which God had said to **D** and	1858
	33:14	of the City of **D**, west of the Gihon spring	1858
	34: 2	and walked in the ways of his father **D**,	1858
	34: 3	he began to seek the God of his father **D**.	1858
	35: 3	that Solomon son of **D** king of Israel built.	1858
	35: 4	to the directions written by **D** king of Israel	1858
	35:15	were in the places prescribed by **D**, Asaph,	1858
Ezr	3:10	as prescribed by **D** king of Israel.	1858
	8: 2	of the descendants of **D**,	1858
	8:20	that **D** and the officials had established	1858
Ne	3:15	as the steps going down from the City of **D**.	1858
	3:16	up to a point opposite the tombs of **D**,	1858
	12:24	as prescribed by **D** the man of God.	1858
	12:36	with musical instruments [prescribed by] **D**	1858
	12:37	up the steps of the City of **D** on the ascent	1858
	12:37	the wall and passed above the house of **D** to	1858
	12:45	the commands of **D** and his son Solomon.	1858
	12:46	For long ago, in the days of **D** and Asaph,	1858
Ps	3: T	A psalm of **D**.	1858
	4: T	A psalm of **D**.	1858
	5: T	A psalm of **D**.	1858
	6: T	A psalm of **D**.	1858
	7: T	A shiggaion of **D**,	1858
	8: T	A psalm of **D**.	1858
	9: T	A psalm of **D**.	1858
	11: T	For the director of music. Of **D**.	1858
	12: T	A psalm of **D**.	1858
	13: T	For the director of music. Of **D**.	1858
	14: T	For the director of music. Of **D**.	1858
	15: T	A psalm of **D**.	1858
	16: T	A miktam of **D**.	1858
	17: T	A prayer of **D**.	1858
	18: T	Of **D** the servant of the LORD.	1858
	18:50	to **D** and his descendants forever.	1858
	19: T	For the director of music. A psalm of **D**.	1858
	20: T	For the director of music. A psalm of **D**.	1858
	21: T	For the director of music. A psalm of **D**.	1858
	22: T	A psalm of **D**.	1858
	23: T	A psalm of **D**.	1858
	24: T	Of **D**. A psalm.	1858
	25: T	Of **D**.	1858
	26: T	Of **D**.	1858
	27: T	Of **D**.	1858
	28: T	Of **D**.	1858
	29: T	A psalm of **D**.	1858
	30: T	of the temple. Of **D**.	1858
	31: T	For the director of music. A psalm of **D**.	1858
	32: T	Of **D**. A maskil.	1858
	34: T	Of **D**. When he pretended to be	1858
	35: T	Of **D**.	1858
	36: T	Of **D** the servant of the LORD.	1858
	37: T	Of **D**.	1858
	38: T	A psalm of **D**. A petition.	1858
	39: T	For the director of music. Of **D**.	1858
	40: T	For the director of music. Of **D**. A psalm.	1858

Ps	41: T	For the director of music. A psalm of **D**.	1858
	51: T	A psalm of **D**.	1858
	51: T	to him after **D** had committed adultery	NIH
	52: T	A maskil of **D**.	1858
	52: T	"**D** has gone to the house of Ahimelech."	1858
	53: T	A maskil of **D**.	1858
	54: T	A maskil of **D**.	1858
	54: T	"Is not **D** hiding among us?"	1858
	55: T	A maskil of **D**.	1858
	56: T	on Distant Oaks." Of **D**.	1858
	57: T	"Do Not Destroy." Of **D**.	1858
	58: T	"Do Not Destroy." Of **D**.	1858
	59: T	"Do Not Destroy." Of **D**.	1858
	60: T	A miktam of **D**.	1858
	61: T	With stringed instruments. Of **D**.	1858
	62: T	A psalm of **D**.	1858
	63: T	A psalm of **D**.	1858
	64: T	For the director of music. A psalm of **D**.	1858
	65: T	A psalm of **D**.	1858
	68: T	For the director of music. Of **D**.	1858
	69: T	To [the tune of] "Lilies." Of **D**.	1858
	70: T	For the director of music. Of **D**. A petition.	1858
	72:20	This concludes the prayers of **D** son	1858
	78:70	He chose **D** his servant and took him from	1858
	78:72	**D** shepherded them with integrity of heart;	NIH
	86: T	A prayer of **D**.	1858
	89: 3	I have sworn to **D** my servant,	1858
	89:20	I have found **D** my servant;	1858
	89:35	and I will not lie to **D**—	1858
	89:49	in your faithfulness you swore to **D**?	1858
	101: T	Of **D**. A psalm.	1858
	103: T	Of **D**.	1858
	108: T	A song. A psalm of **D**.	1858
	109: T	For the director of music. Of **D**. A psalm.	1858
	110: T	Of **D**. A psalm.	1858
	122: T	A song of ascents. Of **D**.	1858
	122: 5	the thrones of the house of **D**.	1858
	124: T	A song of ascents. Of **D**.	1858
	131: T	A song of ascents. Of **D**.	1858
	132: 1	remember **D** and all	1858
	132:10	For the sake of **D** your servant,	1858
	132:11	The LORD swore an oath to **D**,	1858
	132:17	"Here I will make a horn grow for **D**	1858
	133: T	A song of ascents. Of **D**.	1858
	138: T	Of **D**.	1858
	139: T	For the director of music. Of **D**. A psalm.	1858
	140: T	For the director of music. A psalm of **D**.	1858
	141: T	A psalm of **D**.	1858
	142: T	A maskil of **D**.	1858
	143: T	A psalm of **D**.	1858
	144: T	Of **D**.	1858
	144:10	who delivers his servant **D** from	1858
	145: T	A psalm of praise. Of **D**.	1858
Pr	1: 1	The proverbs of Solomon son of **D**,	1858
Ecc	1: 1	The words of the Teacher, son of **D**,	1858
SS	4: 4	Your neck is like the tower of **D**,	1858
Isa	7: 2	Now the house of **D** was told,	1858
	7:13	Isaiah said, "Hear now, you house of **D**!	1858
	16: 5	one from the house of **D**—	1858
	22: 9	of **D** had many breaches in its defenses;	1858
	22:22	on his shoulder the key to the house of **D**;	1858
	29: 1	Ariel, Ariel, the city where **D** settled!	1858
	37:35	my sake and for the sake of **D** my servant!"	1858
	38: 5	the God of your father **D**, says:	1858
	55: 3	my faithful love promised to **D**.	1858
Jer	21:12	O house of **D**, this is what the LORD says:	1858
	22:30	the throne of **D** or rule anymore in Judah."	1858
	23: 5	I will raise up to **D** a righteous Branch,	1858
	30: 9	the LORD their God and **D** their king,	1858
	33:17	'**D** will never fail to have a man to sit on	1858
	33:21	then my covenant with **D** my servant—	1858
	33:21	can be broken and **D** will no longer have	2257S
	33:22	the descendants of **D** my servant and	1858
	33:26	the descendants of Jacob and **D** my servant	1858
	36:30	to sit on the throne of **D**;	1858
Eze	34:23	my servant **D**, and he will tend them;	1858
	34:24	my servant **D** will be prince among them.	1858
	37:24	" 'My servant **D** will be king over them,	1858
	37:25	**D** my servant will be their prince forever.	1858
Hos	3: 5	the LORD their God and **D** their king.	1858
Am	6: 5	You strum away on your harps like **D**	1858
Zec	12: 7	of **D** and of Jerusalem's inhabitants may	1858
	12: 8	that the feeblest among them will be like **D**,	1858
	12: 8	and the house of **D** will be like God,	1858
	12:10	"And I will pour out on the house of **D** and	1858
	12:12	the clan of the house of **D** and their wives,	1858
	13: 1	a fountain will be opened to the house of **D**	1858
Mt	1: 1	the genealogy of Jesus Christ the son of **D**,	1253
	1: 6	and Jesse the father of King **D**.	1253
	1: 6	**D** was the father of Solomon,	1253
	1:17	in all from Abraham to **D**,	1253
	1:17	fourteen from **D** to the exile to Babylon,	1253
	1:20	"Joseph son of **D**,	1253
	9:27	calling out, "Have mercy on us, Son of **D**!"	1253
	12: 3	"Haven't you read what **D** did when he	1253
	12:23	"Could this be the Son of **D**?"	1253
	15:22	"Lord, Son of **D**, have mercy on me!	1253
	20:30	"Lord, Son of **D**, have mercy on us!"	1253
	20:31	"Lord, Son of **D**, have mercy on us!"	1253
	21: 9	"Hosanna to the Son of **D**!"	1253
	21:15	"Hosanna to the Son of **D**,"	1253
	22:42	"The son of **D**," they replied.	1253
	22:43	He said to them, "How is it then that **D**,	1253
	22:45	**D** calls him 'Lord,' how can he be his son?"	1253
Mk	2:25	"Have you never read what **D** did when he	1253
	10:47	"Jesus, Son of **D**, have mercy on me!"	1253
	10:48	but he shouted all the more, "Son of **D**,	1253

Mk	11:10	the coming kingdom of our father **D**!"	1253
	12:35	the law say that the Christ is the son of **D**?	1253
	12:36	**D** himself, speaking by the Holy Spirit,	1253
	12:37	**D** himself calls him 'Lord.'	1253
Lk	1:27	a descendant of **D**.	1253
	1:32	the throne of his father **D**,	1253
	1:69	for us in the house of his servant **D**	1253
	2: 4	to Bethlehem the town of **D**,	1253
	2: 4	to the house and line of **D**.	1253
	2:11	in the town of **D** a Savior has been born	1253
	3:31	the son of Nathan, the son of **D**,	1253
	6: 3	"Have you never read what **D** did when he	1253
	18:38	He called out, "Jesus, Son of **D**,	1253
	18:39	but he shouted all the more, "Son of **D**,	1253
	20:41	that they say the Christ is the Son of **D**?	1253
	20:42	**D** himself declares in the Book of Psalms:	1253
	20:44	**D** calls him 'Lord.'	1253
Jn	7:42	the town where **D** lived?"	1253
Ac	1:16	through the mouth of **D** concerning Judas,	1253
	2:25	**D** said about him:	1253
	2:29	that the patriarch **D** died and was buried,	1253
	2:34	For **D** did not ascend to heaven,	1253
	4:25	the mouth of your servant, our father **D**:	1253
	7:45	It remained in the land until the time of **D**,	1253
	13:22	After removing Saul, he made **D** their king.	1253
	13:22	'I have found **D** son of Jesse a man	1253
	13:34	the holy and sure blessings promised to **D**.'	1253
	13:36	"For when **D** had served God's purpose	1253
Ro	1: 3	to his human nature was a descendant of **D**,	1253
	4: 6	**D** says the same thing when he speaks of	1253
	11: 9	**D** says: "May their table become a snare	1253
2Ti	2: 8	raised from the dead, descended from **D**.	1253
Heb	4: 7	when a long time later he spoke through **D**,	1253
	11:32	Jephthah, **D**, Samuel and the prophets,	1253
Rev	3: 7	who holds the key of **D**.	1253
	5: 5	the Root of **D**, has triumphed.	1253
	22:16	I am the Root and the Offspring of **D**,	1253

DAVID'S (85) [DAVID]

1Sa	17:28	When Eliab, **D** oldest brother,	2257S
	19:11	Saul sent men to **D** house to watch it and	1858
	19:11	But Michal, **D** wife, warned him,	1858
	20:15	of **D** enemies from the face of the earth."	1858
	20:16	the LORD call **D** enemies to account."	1858
	20:25	but **D** place was empty.	1858
	20:27	**D** place was empty again.	1858
	23: 3	But **D** men said to him,	1858
	25: 9	When **D** men arrived,	1858
	25: 9	they gave Nabal this message in **D** name.	1858
	25:10	Nabal answered **D** servants,	1858
	25:12	**D** men turned around and went back.	1858
	25:42	with **D** messengers and became his wife.	1858
	25:44	**D** wife, to Paltiel son of Laish,	1858
	26:17	Saul recognized **D** voice and said,	1858
	30: 5	**D** two wives had been captured—	1858
	30:20	saying, "This is **D** plunder."	1858
	30:22	and troublemakers among **D** followers said,	1858
2Sa	2:13	Joab son of Zeruiah and **D** men went out	1858
	2:17	the men of Israel were defeated by **D** men.	1858
	2:30	nineteen of **D** men were found missing.	1858
	2:31	But **D** men had killed three hundred	1858
	3: 5	Ithream the son of **D** wife Eglah.	1858
	3:10	of Saul and establish **D** throne over Israel	1858
	3:22	then **D** men and Joab returned from a raid	1858
	5: 8	and blind' who are **D** enemies."	1858
	8:18	and **D** sons were royal advisers.	1858
	9:11	So Mephibosheth ate at **D** table like one of	2257S
	10: 2	**D** men came to the land of the Ammonites,	1858
	10: 4	So Hanun seized **D** men,	1858
	10: 4	that they had become a stench in **D** nostrils,	1858
	11:13	At **D** invitation, he ate and drank with him,	1858
	11:17	some of the men in **D** army fell;	1858
	12:18	**D** servants were afraid to tell him that	1858
	12:30	and it was placed on **D** head.	1858
	13: 3	of Shimeah, **D** brother.	1858
	13:32	But Jonadab son of Shimeah, **D** brother,	1858
	15:12	**D** counselor, to come from Giloh.	1858
	15:37	So **D** friend Hushai arrived at Jerusalem	1858
	16: 6	the special guard were on **D** right and left.	2257S
	16:16	Then Hushai the Arkite, **D** friend,	1858
	18: 7	the army of Israel was defeated by **D** men,	1858
	18: 9	Now Absalom happened to meet **D** men.	1858
	20:26	and Ira the Jairite was **D** priest.	1858+4200
	21:17	Abishai son of Zeruiah came to **D** rescue;	2257S
	21:17	Then **D** men swore to him, saying,	1858
	21:21	Jonathan son of Shimeah, **D** brother,	1858
	23: 8	are the names of **D** mighty men:	1858+4200
	24: 11	to Gad the prophet, **D** seer;	1858+4200
1Ki	1: 8	**D** special guard did not join Adonijah.	1858+4200
	1:11	without our lord **D** knowing it?	1858
	1:38	on King **D** mule and escorted him to Gihon.	1858
	2:45	and **D** throne will remain secure before	1858
	11:39	I will humble **D** descendants because	1858
	15: 4	for **D** sake the LORD his God gave him	1858
1Ch	11:10	were the chiefs of **D** mighty men—	1858+4200
	11:11	this is the list of **D** mighty men:	1858+4200
	14:17	So **D** fame spread throughout every land,	1858
	18:17	and **D** sons were chief officials at	1858
	19: 2	When **D** men came to Hanun in the land of	1858
	19: 4	So Hanun seized **D** men, shaved them,	1858
	19: 4	that they had become a stench in **D** nostrils,	1858
	20: 2	and it was placed on **D** head.	1858
	20: 7	Jonathan son of Shimea, **D** brother,	1858
	21: 9	The LORD said to Gad, **D** seer,	1858
	26:31	of **D** reign a search was made in	1858
	27:31	officials in charge of King **D** property.	1858+4200

1Ch	27:32	Jonathan, **D** uncle, was a counselor,	1858
	29:24	as well as all of King **D** sons,	1858
	29:29	As for the events of King **D** reign,	1858
2Ch	11:18	who was the daughter of **D** son Jerimoth	1858
	13: 8	which is in the hands of **D** descendants.	1858
	29:26	the Levites stood ready with **D** instruments,	1858
	32:33	where the tombs of **D** descendants are.	1858
Ps	59: T	When Saul had sent men to watch **D** house	2021^S
Isa	9: 7	on **D** throne and over his kingdom,	1858
Jer	13:13	the kings who sit on **D** throne,	1858+4200
	17:25	then kings who sit on **D** throne will come	1858
	22: 2	O king of Judah, you who sit on **D** throne—	1858
	22: 4	kings who sit on **D** throne will come	1858+4200
	29:16	about the king who sits on **D** throne and all	1858
	33:15	a righteous Branch sprout from **D** line;	1858
Am	9:11	"In that day I will restore **D** fallen tent.	1858
Jn	7:42	that the Christ will come from **D** family and	*1253*
Ac	15:16	this I will return and rebuild **D** fallen tent.	*1253*

DAWN (33) [DAWNED, DAWNS]

Ge	19:15	With the coming of **d**, the angels urged Lot,	8840
Jdg	16: 2	saying, "At **d** we'll kill him."	240+1332+2021
	19:25	and at **d** they let her go.	8840
1Sa	14:36	by night and plunder them till **d**,	240+1332+2021
Ne	4:21	**first light of d** till the stars came out.	6590+8840
Job	3: 9	in vain and not see the first rays of **d**,	8840
	4:20	Between **d** and dusk they are broken	1332
	7: 4	The night drags on, and I toss till **d**.	5974
	38:12	or shown the **d** its place,	8840
	41:18	his eyes are like the rays of **d**.	8840
Ps	37: 6	like the **d**, the justice of your cause like	240
	57: 8	I will awaken the **d**.	8840
	108: 2	Awake, harp and lyre! I will awaken the **d**.	8840
	110: 3	the womb of the **d** you will receive the dew	5423
	119:147	I rise before **d** and cry for help;	5974
	139: 9	If I rise on the wings of the **d**,	8840
Pr	4:18	of the righteous is like the first gleam of **d**,	5586
SS	6:10	Who is this that appears like the **d**,	8840
Isa	8:20	they have no **light of d**.	8840
	14:12	O morning star, son of the **d**!	8840
	38:13	I waited patiently till **d**,	1332
	58: 8	Then your light will break forth like the **d**,	8840
	60: 3	and kings to the brightness of your **d**.	2437
	62: 1	till her righteousness shines out like the **d**,	5586
Da	6:19	At the first light of **d**,	10740
Joel	2: 2	Like **d** spreading across the mountains	8840
Am	4:13	he who turns **d** to darkness,	8840
	5: 8	into **d** and darkens day into night, who calls	1332
Jnh	4: 7	the next day God provided a worm,	8840
Mt	28: 1	*at* **d** on the first day of the week,	2216
Mk	13:35	or when the rooster crows, or **at d**.	4745
Jn	8: 2	*At* **d** he appeared again in the temple	*3986*
Ac	27:33	Just before **d** Paul urged them all to eat.	
			1181+2465+3516

DAWNED (5) [DAWN]

Ge	44: 3	*As* morning **d**, the men were sent	239
Dt	33: 2	from Sinai and **d** over them from Seir;	2436
Isa	9: 2	of the shadow of death a light *has* **d**.	5585
Mt	4:16	of the shadow of death a light *has* **d**."	*422*
Ac	12:12	*When* this had **d** on him,	*5328*

DAWNS (4) [DAWN]

Ps	65: 8	morning **d** and evening fades you call forth	
		songs of	4604
	112: 4	Even in darkness light **d** for the upright,	2436
Hos	10:15	When that **day d**,	8840
2Pe	1:19	until the day **d** and the morning star rises	*1419*

DAY (1419) [DAILY, DAY'S, DAYBREAK, DAYLIGHT, DAYS, DAYTIME, EVERYDAY, MIDDAY, SEVEN-DAY, THREE-DAY]

Ge	1: 5	God called the light "**d**,"	3427
	1: 5	and there was morning—the first **d**.	3427
	1: 8	and there was morning—the second **d**.	3427
	1:13	and there was morning—the third **d**.	3427
	1:14	of the sky to separate the **d** from the night,	3427
	1:16	the greater light to govern the **d** and	3427
	1:18	to govern the **d** and the night,	3427
	1:19	and there was morning—the fourth **d**.	3427
	1:23	and there was morning—the fifth **d**.	3427
	1:31	and there was morning—the sixth **d**.	3427
	2: 2	By the seventh **d** God had finished	3427
	2: 2	the seventh **d** he rested from all his work.	3427
	2: 3	the seventh **d** and made it holy,	3427
	3: 8	in the garden in the cool of the **d**,	3427
	7:11	on the seventeenth **d** of the second month—	3427
	7:11	on that **d** all the springs of	3427
	7:13	On that very **d** Noah and his sons, Shem,	3427
	8: 4	on the seventeenth **d** of the seventh month	3427
	8: 5	on the first **d** of the tenth month the tops of	NIH
	8:13	By the first **d** of the first month	NIH
	8:14	the twenty-seventh **d** of the second month	3427
	8:22	**d** and night will never cease."	3427
	15:18	On that **d** the LORD made a covenant	3427
	17:23	that very **d** Abraham took his son Ishmael	3427
	17:26	both circumcised on that same **d**.	3427
	18: 1	the entrance to his tent in the heat of the **d**.	3427
	19:31	**One** of the older daughter said to	2256
	19:34	The **next d** the older daughter said to	4740
	21: 8	on the **d** Isaac was weaned Abraham held	3427
	22: 4	On the third **d** Abraham looked up and saw	3427
	22:14	And to this **d** it is said,	3427

Ge	26:32	That **d** Isaac's servants came and told him	3427
	26:33	and to this **d** the name of the town	3427
	27: 2	now an old man and don't know the **d**	3427
	27:45	Why should I lose both of you *in* one **d**?"	3427
	30:35	That same **d** he removed all the male goats	3427
	31:22	On the third **d** Laban was told	3427
	31:39	from me for whatever was stolen by **d**	3427
	32:32	Therefore to this **d** the Israelites do not eat	3427
	33:13	If they are driven hard just one **d**,	3427
	33:16	that **d** Esau started on his way back to Seir.	3427
	35: 3	who answered me in the **d** of my distress	3427
	35:20	to this **d** that pillar marks Rachel's tomb.	3427
	39:10	though she spoke to Joseph **d** *after* day,	4200
	39:10	though she spoke to Joseph day after **d**,	3427
	39:11	One **d** he went into the house to attend	3427
	40:20	Now the third **d** was Pharaoh's birthday,	3427
	42:18	On the third **d**, Joseph said to them,	3427
	48:15	the God who has been my shepherd all my	
		life to this **d**,	3427
	48:20	He blessed them that **d** and said,	3427
Ex	2:11	One **d**, after Moses had grown up,	3427
	2:13	The next **d** he went out	3427
	5: 6	That same **d** Pharaoh gave this order to	3427
	5:13	the work required of you **for each d**,	
			928+1821+3427+3427
	5:19	of bricks required of you **for each d**."	
			928+1821+3427+3427
	8:22	" 'But on that **d** I will deal differently with	3427
	9: 6	And the **next d** the LORD did it:	4740
	9:18	from the **d** it was founded till now.	3427
	10: 6	the **d** they settled in this land till now.' "	3427
	10:13	an east wind blow across the land all that **d**	3427
	10:28	The **d** you see my face you will die."	3427
	12: 3	on the tenth **d** of this month each man is	NIH
	12: 6	of them until the fourteenth **d** of the month,	3427
	12:14	"This is a **d** you are to commemorate;	3427
	12:15	On the first **d** remove the yeast	3427
	12:15	from the first **d** through the seventh must	3427
	12:16	On the first **d** hold a sacred assembly,	3427
	12:16	and another one on the seventh **d**.	3427
	12:17	because it was on this very **d**	3427
	12:17	Celebrate this **d** as a lasting ordinance for	3427
	12:18	from the evening of the fourteenth **d** until	3427
	12:18	until the evening of the twenty-first **d**.	3427
	12:41	At the end of the 430 years, to the very **d**,	3427
	12:51	And on that very **d** the LORD brought	3427
	13: 3	"Commemorate this **d**,	3427
	13: 3	the **d** you came out of Egypt,	889^S
	13: 6	the seventh **d** hold a festival to the LORD.	3427
	13: 8	On that **d** tell your son,	3427
	13:21	**By d** the LORD went ahead of them in	3429
	13:21	so that they could travel **by d** or night.	3429
	13:22	the pillar of cloud **by d** nor the pillar of fire	3429
	14:30	That **d** the LORD saved Israel from	3427
	16: 1	on the fifteenth **d** of the second month	3427
	16: 4	to go out each **d** and gather enough for	NIH
	16: 4	and gather enough for **that d**.	3427+3427
	16: 5	On the sixth **d** they are	3427
	16:22	the sixth **d**, they gathered twice as much—	3427
	16:23	'Tomorrow is to be a **d of rest**,	8702
	16:26	but on the seventh **d**, the Sabbath,	3427
	16:27	of the people went out on the seventh **d**	3427
	16:29	the sixth **d** he gives you bread for two days.	3427
	16:29	to stay where he is on the seventh **d**;	3427
	16:30	So the people rested on the seventh **d**.	3427
	18:13	The **next d** Moses took his seat to serve	4740
	19: 1	on the very **d**—they came to the Desert of	3427
	19:11	and be ready by the third **d**,	3427
	19:11	because on that **d** the LORD will come	3427
	19:15	"Prepare yourselves for the third **d**.	3427
	19:16	the third **d** there was thunder and lightning,	3427
	20: 8	the Sabbath **d** by keeping it holy.	3427
	20:10	but the seventh **d** is a Sabbath to	3427
	20:11	but he rested on the seventh **d**.	3427
	20:11	the LORD blessed the Sabbath **d**	3427
	21:21	to be punished if the slave gets up after a **d**	3427
	22:30	but give them to me on the eighth **d**.	3427
	23:12	but on the seventh **d** do not work,	3427
	24:16	the seventh **d** the LORD called to Moses	3427
	29:36	Sacrifice a bull each **d** as a sin offering	3427
	29:38	to offer on the altar regularly each **d**:	3427
	31:14	on that **d** must be cut off from his people.	2023^S
	31:15	but the seventh **d** is a Sabbath of rest,	3427
	31:15	on the Sabbath **d** must be put to death.	3427
	31:17	on the seventh **d** he abstained from work	3427
	32: 6	So the **next d** the people rose early	4740
	32:28	and that **d** about three thousand of	3427
	32:29	and he has blessed you this **d**."	3427
	32:30	The **next d** Moses said to the people,	4740
	34:21	but on the seventh **d** you shall rest;	3427
	35: 2	but the seventh **d** shall be your holy day,	3427
	35: 2	but the seventh day shall be your holy **d**,	NIH
	35: 3	in any of your dwellings on the Sabbath **d**."	3427
	40: 2	on the first **d** *of* the first month.	3427
	40:17	So the tabernacle was set up on the first **d**	NIH
	40:37	until the **d** it lifted.	3427
	40:38	of the LORD was over the tabernacle **by d**,	3429
Lev	6: 5	on the **d** he presents his guilt offering.	3427
	6:20	to the LORD on the **d** he is anointed:	3427
	7:15	be eaten on the **d** it is offered;	3427
	7:16	sacrifice shall be eaten on the **d** he offers it,	3427
	7:16	over may be eaten on the **next d**.	4740
	7:17	of the sacrifice left over till the third **d** must	3427
	7:18	on the third **d**,	3427
	7:35	and his sons on the **d** they were presented	3427
	7:36	On the **d** they were anointed,	3427
	7:38	on Mount Sinai on the **d** he commanded	3427

Lev	8:35	at the entrance to the Tent of Meeting **d**	3429
	9: 1	On the eighth **d** Moses summoned Aaron	3427
	12: 3	the eighth **d** the boy is to be circumcised.	3427
	13: 5	the seventh **d** the priest is to examine him,	3427
	13: 6	On the seventh **d** the priest is	3427
	13:27	the seventh **d** the priest is to examine him,	3427
	13:32	On the seventh **d** the priest is to examine	3427
	13:34	On the seventh **d** the priest is to examine	3427
	13:51	On the seventh **d** he is to examine it,	3427
	14: 9	the seventh **d** he must shave off all his hair;	3427
	14:10	the eighth **d** he must bring two male lambs	3427
	14:23	"On the eighth **d** he must bring them	3427
	14:39	On the seventh **d** the priest shall return	3427
	15:14	On the eighth **d** he must take two doves	3427
	15:29	On the eighth **d** she must take two doves	3427
	16:29	On the tenth **d** of the seventh month	NIH
	16:30	on this **d** atonement will be made for you,	3427
	19: 6	on the **d** you sacrifice it or on the next day;	3427
	19: 6	on the day you sacrifice it or on the **next d**;	4740
	19: 6	over until the third **d** must be burned up.	3427
	19: 7	If any of it is eaten on the third **d**,	3427
	22:27	From the eighth **d** on,	3427
	22:28	or a sheep and its young on the same **d**.	3427
	22:30	It must be eaten that same **d**;	3427
	23: 3	but the seventh **d** is a Sabbath of rest,	3427
	23: 3	a **d** of sacred assembly.	NIH
	23: 5	on the fourteenth **d** of the first month.	NIH
	23: 6	On the fifteenth **d** of that month	3427
	23: 7	On the first **d** hold a sacred assembly	3427
	23: 8	on the seventh **d** hold a sacred assembly	3427
	23:11	to wave it on the **d after** the Sabbath.	4740
	23:12	On the **d** you wave the sheaf,	3427
	23:14	until the very **d** you bring this offering	3427
	23:15	" 'From the **d after** the Sabbath,	4740
	23:15	the **d** you brought the sheaf of	3427
	23:16	up to the **d after** the seventh Sabbath.	4740
	23:21	On that same **d** you are to proclaim	3427
	23:24	'On the first **d** of the seventh month you are	NIH
	23:24	to have a **d of rest**,	8702
	23:27	"The tenth **d** of this seventh month is	NIH
	23:27	this seventh month is the **D** of Atonement.	3427
	23:28	Do no work on that **d**,	3427
	23:28	because it is the **D** *of* Atonement,	3427
	23:29	not deny himself on that **d** must be cut off	3427
	23:30	among his people anyone who does any	
		work on that **d**.	3427
	23:32	the evening of the ninth **d** of the month	NIH
	23:34	'On the fifteenth **d** of the seventh month	3427
	23:35	The first **d** is a sacred assembly;	3427
	23:36	and on the eighth **d** hold a sacred assembly	3427
	23:37	and drink offerings required for **each d**.	
			928+3427+3427
	23:39	with the fifteenth **d** of the seventh month,	3427
	23:39	the first **d** is a day of rest,	3427
	23:39	the first day is a **d of rest**,	8702
	23:39	and the eighth **d** also is a day of rest.	3427
	23:39	and the eighth day also is a **d of rest**.	8702
	23:40	the first **d** you are to take choice fruit from	3427
	25: 9	on the tenth **d** of the seventh month;	NIH
	25: 9	on the **D** *of* Atonement sound the trumpet	3427
	27:23	on that **d** as something holy to the LORD.	3427
Nu	1: 1	of Sinai on the first **d** of the second month	NIH
	1:18	the whole community together on the first **d**	NIH
	6: 9	he must shave his head on the **d**	3427
	6: 9	of his cleansing—the seventh **d**.	3427
	6:10	on the eighth **d** he must bring two doves	3427
	6:11	That same **d** he is to consecrate his head.	3427
	7:11	"**Each d** one leader is to bring his offering	
			2021+2021+3427+4200+4200
	7:12	the first **d** was Nahshon son of Amminadab	3427
	7:18	On the second **d** Nethanel son of Zuar,	3427
	7:24	On the third **d**, Eliab son of Helon,	3427
	7:30	On the fourth **d** Elizur son of Shedeur,	3427
	7:36	the fifth **d** Shelumiel son of Zurishaddai,	3427
	7:42	On the sixth **d** Eliasaph son of Deuel,	3427
	7:48	the seventh **d** Elishama son of Ammihud,	3427
	7:54	On the eighth **d** Gamaliel son of Pedahzur,	3427
	7:60	On the ninth **d** Abidan son of Gideoni,	3427
	7:66	the tenth **d** Ahiezer son of Ammishaddai,	3427
	7:72	On the eleventh **d** Pagiel son of Ocran,	3427
	7:78	On the twelfth **d** Ahira son of Enan,	3427
	9: 3	on the fourteenth **d** of this month,	3427
	9: 3	of Sinai at twilight on the fourteenth **d** of	3427
	9: 6	not celebrate the Passover on that **d**	3427
	9: 6	they came to Moses and Aaron that same **d**	3427
	9:11	They are to celebrate it on the fourteenth **d**	3427
	9:15	On the **d** the tabernacle,	3427
	9:16	Whether **by d** or by night,	3429
	10:11	On the twentieth **d** of the second month of	NIH
	10:34	over them **by d** when they set out from	3429
	11:19	You will not eat it *for* just one **d**,	3427
	11:32	All that **d** and night and all the next day	3427
	11:32	All that day and night and all the next **d**	3427
	14:14	in a pillar of cloud **by d** and a pillar of fire	3429
	15:23	the **d** the LORD gave them and continuing	3427
	15:32	on the Sabbath **d**.	3427
	16:41	The **next d** the whole Israelite community	
		grumbled against Moses	4740
	17: 8	The **next d** Moses entered the Tent of	4740
	19:12	on the third **d** and on the seventh day;	3427
	19:12	on the third day and on the seventh **d**;	3427
	19:19	and on the seventh **d** he is to purify him.	3427
	22:30	which you have always ridden, to this **d**?	3427
	28: 3	as a regular burnt offering each **d**.	3427
	28: 9	" 'On the Sabbath **d**, make an offering	3427
	28:16	" 'On the fourteenth **d** of the first month	3427
	28:17	On the fifteenth **d** of this month there is to	3427

Nu	28:18	On the first **d** hold a sacred assembly	3427
	28:24	for the offering made by fire every **d**	3427
	28:25	On the seventh **d** hold a sacred assembly	3427
	28:26	" 'On the **d** of firstfruits,	3427
	29: 1	" 'On the first **d** of the seventh month hold	NIH
	29: 1	It is a **d** for you to sound the trumpets.	3427
	29: 7	the tenth **d** of this seventh month hold	NIH
	29:12	" 'On the fifteenth **d** of the seventh month,	3427
	29:17	the second **d** prepare twelve young bulls,	3427
	29:20	" 'On the third **d** prepare eleven bulls,	3427
	29:23	" 'On the fourth **d** prepare ten bulls,	3427
	29:26	" 'On the fifth **d** prepare nine bulls,	3427
	29:29	" 'On the sixth **d** prepare eight bulls,	3427
	29:32	" 'On the seventh **d** prepare seven bulls,	3427
	29:35	" 'On the eighth **d** hold an assembly	3427
	30:14	to her about it from **d** to day,	3427
	30:14	to her about it from day to **d**,	3427
	31:24	On the seventh **d** wash your clothes	3427
	32:10	The LORD's anger was aroused that **d**	3427
	33: 3	on the fifteenth **d** of the first month,	3427
	33: 3	the **d** after the Passover.	4740
	33:38	on the first **d** of the fifth month of	NIH
Dt	1: 3	on the first **d** of the eleventh month,	NIH
	1:33	in fire by night and in a cloud **by d,**	3429
	2:22	and have lived in their place to this **d**.	3427
	2:25	This very **d** I will begin to put the terror	3427
	3:14	to this **d** Bashan is called Havvoth Jair.)	3427
	4:10	Remember the **d** you stood before	3427
	4:15	the LORD spoke to you at Horeb out	3427
	4:26	and earth as witnesses against you this **d**	3427
	4:32	from the **d** God created man on the earth;	3427
	4:39	Acknowledge and take to heart this **d** that	3427
	5:12	"Observe the Sabbath **d** by keeping it holy,	3427
	5:14	but the seventh **d** is a Sabbath to	3427
	5:15	to observe the Sabbath **d**.	3427
	8:11	and his decrees that I am giving you this **d**.	3427
	9: 7	the **d** you left Egypt until you arrived here,	3427
	9:10	on the **d** of the assembly.	3427
	10: 4	out of the fire, on the **d** of the assembly.	3427
	16: 4	on the evening of the first **d** remain	3427
	16: 8	and on the seventh **d** hold an assembly to	3427
	18:16	the LORD your God at Horeb on the **d** of	3427
	21:23	Be sure to bury him that same **d**,	3427
	24:15	Pay him his wages each **d** before sunset,	3427
	26:16	LORD your God commands you this **d**	3427
	26:17	You have declared this **d** that	3427
	26:18	And the LORD has declared this **d**	3427
	27:11	the same **d** Moses commanded the people:	3427
	28:13	the LORD your God that I give you this **d**	3427
	28:29	**d after day** you will be oppressed	
			2021+3427+3972
	28:29	**day after d** you will be oppressed	
			2021+3427+3972
	28:32	for them **d after day,**	2021+3427+3972
	28:32	for them **day after d,**	2021+3427+3972
	28:66	filled with dread both night and **d,**	3429
	29: 4	But to this **d** the LORD has not given you	3427
	29:12	with you this **d** and sealing with an oath,	3427
	29:13	to confirm you this **d** as his people,	3427
	30:18	to you this **d** that you will certainly	3427
	30:19	This **d** I call heaven and earth as witnesses	3427
	31:14	"Now the **d** of your death is near.	3427
	31:17	On that **d** I will become angry with them	3427
	31:17	and on that **d** they will ask,	3427
	31:18	And I will certainly hide my face on that **d**	3427
	31:22	So Moses wrote down this song that **d**	3427
	32:35	their **d** of disaster is near	3427
	32:46	solemnly declared to you this **d,**	3427
	32:48	On that same **d** the LORD told Moses,	3427
	33:12	for he shields him all **d** *long*,	3427
	34: 6	to this **d** no one knows where his grave is.	3427
Jos	1: 8	meditate on it **d** and night,	3429
	4: 9	And they are there to this **d**.	3427
	4:14	That the LORD exalted Joshua in	3427
	4:19	On the tenth **d** of the first month	NIH
	5: 9	the place has been called Gilgal to this **d**.	3427
	5:10	On the evening of the fourteenth **d**	3427
	5:11	The **d** after the Passover, that very day,	4740
	5:11	The day after the Passover, that very **d**,	3427
	5:12	the **d** after they ate this food from the land;	4740
	6: 4	On the seventh **d**, march around the city	3427
	6:10	do not say a word until the **d** I tell you	3427
	6:14	So on the second **d** they marched around	3427
	6:15	On the seventh **d**, they got up	3427
	6:15	on that **d** they circled the city seven times.	3427
	6:25	and she lives among the Israelites to this **d**.	3427
	7:26	which remains to this **d**.	3427
	8:25	and women fell that **d**—	3427
	8:28	a desolate place to this **d**.	3427
	8:29	which remains to this **d**.	3427
	9:12	when we packed it at home on the **d** we left	3427
	9:17	and on the third **d** came to their cities:	3427
	9:27	That **d** he made the Gibeonites woodcutters	3427
	9:27	And that is what they are to this **d**.	3427
	10:12	the **d** the LORD gave the Amorites over	3427
	10:13	and delayed going down about a full **d**.	3427
	10:14	There has never been a **d** like it before or	3427
	10:14	a **d** when the LORD listened to a man.	NIH
	10:27	which are there to this **d**.	3427
	10:28	That Joshua took Makkedah.	3427
	10:32	and Joshua took it on the second **d**.	3427
	10:35	They captured it that same **d** and put it to	3427
	13:13	to live among the Israelites to this **d**.	3427
	14: 9	So on that **d** Moses swore to me,	3427
	14:11	as strong today as the **d** Moses sent me out;	3427
	14:12	that the LORD promised me that **d**.	3427
	15:18	**One d** when she came to Othniel,	2118+2256

Jos	15:63	to this **d** the Jebusites live there with	3427
	16:10	to this **d** the Canaanites live among	3427
	22: 3	For a long time now—to this very **d**—	3427
	22:17	Up to this very **d** we have	3427
	22:22	do not spare us this **d**.	3427
	22:24	that **some d** your descendants might say	4737
	23: 9	to this **d** no one has been able	3427
	24:15	for yourselves this **d** whom you will serve,	3427
	24:25	On that **d** Joshua made a covenant for	3427
Jdg	1:14	**One d** when she came to Othniel,	2118+2256
	1:21	to this **d** the Jebusites live there with	3427
	1:26	which is its name to this **d**.	3427
	3:30	That **d** Moab was made subject to Israel,	3427
	4:14	This is the **d** the LORD has given Sisera	3427
	4:23	On that **d** God subdued Jabin,	3427
	5: 1	On that **d** Deborah and Barak son	3427
	6:24	To this **d** it stands in Ophrah of	3427
	6:32	So that **d** they called Gideon "Jerub-Baal,"	3427
	6:38	Gideon rose early the **next d**,	4740
	9: 8	One of the trees went out to anoint a king	NIH
	9:42	The **next d** the people of Shechem went out	4740
	9:45	that **d** Abimelech pressed his attack against	3427
	10: 4	which to this **d** are called Havvoth Jair.	3427
	11:27	the dispute this **d** between the Israelites and	3427
	13: 7	be a Nazirite of God from birth until the **d**	3427
	13:10	The man who appeared to me the other **d**!"	3427
	14:15	On the fourth **d**, they said	3427
	14:17	So on the seventh **d** he finally told her,	3427
	14:18	Before sunset on the seventh **d** the men of	3427
	16: 1	**One d** Samson went to Gaza,	2256
	16:16	With such nagging she prodded him **d after**	
		day	2021+3427+3972
	16:16	With such nagging she prodded him **day**	
		after d	2021+3427+3972
	18:12	is called Mahaneh Dan to this **d**.	3427
	19: 5	On the fourth **d** they got up early	3427
	19: 8	On the morning of the fifth **d**,	3427
	19: 9	Spend the night here; the **d** is nearly over.	3427
	19:11	near Jebus and the **d** was almost gone,	3427
	19:30	the **d** the Israelites came up out of Egypt.	3427
	20:21	on the battlefield that **d**.	3427
	20:22	where they had stationed themselves the	
		first **d**.	3427
	20:24	near to Benjamin the second **d**.	3427
	20:26	They fasted that **d** until evening	3427
	20:30	up against the Benjamites on the third **d**	3427
	20:35	on that **d** the Israelites struck down 25,100	3427
	20:46	on that **d** twenty-five thousand Benjamite	
		swordsmen fell,	3427
	21: 4	Early the **next d** the people built an altar	4740
Ru	4: 4	**One d** Naomi her mother-in-law said to her,	2256
	4: 5	"On the **d** you buy the land from Naomi	3427
	4:14	to the LORD, who this **d** has not left you	3427
1Sa	1: 4	the **d** came for Elkanah to sacrifice,	3427
	2:34	they will both die on the same **d**.	3427
	4:12	That same **d** a Benjamite ran from	3427
	4:16	I fled from it this very **d**."	3427
	5: 3	the people of Ashdod rose early the **next d**,	4740
	5: 5	That is why to this **d** neither the priests	3427
	6:15	On that **d** the people	3427
	6:16	and then returned that same **d** to Ekron.	3427
	6:18	is a witness to this **d** in the field of Joshua	3427
	7: 6	that **d** they fasted and there they confessed,	3427
	7:10	But that **d** the LORD thundered	3427
	8: 8	from the **d** I brought them up out of Egypt	3427
	8: 8	up out of Egypt until this **d**,	3427
	8:18	When that **d** comes,	3427
	8:18	the LORD will not answer you in that **d**."	3427
	9:15	Now the **d** before Saul came,	3427
	9:24	And Saul dined with Samuel that **d**.	3427
	10: 9	and all these signs were fulfilled that **d**.	3427
	11:11	The **next d** Saul separated his men	4740
	11:11	until the heat of the **d**.	3427
	11:13	for this **d** the LORD has rescued Israel."	3427
	12: 2	from my youth until this **d**.	3427
	12: 5	and also his anointed is witness this **d**,	3427
	12:18	and that same **d** the LORD sent thunder	3427
	13:22	the **d** of the battle not a soldier with Saul	3427
	14: 1	One **d** Jonathan son of Saul said to	3427
	14:23	So the LORD rescued Israel that **d**,	3427
	14:24	the men of Israel were in distress that **d**,	3427
	14:31	That **d**, after the Israelites had struck down	3427
	14:37	But God did not answer him that **d**.	3427
	15:35	Until the **d** Samuel died,	3427
	16:13	that **d** on the Spirit of the LORD came	3427
	17:10	"This **d** I defy the ranks of Israel!"	3427
	17:46	This **d** the LORD will hand you over	3427
	18: 2	that **d** Saul kept David with him and did	3427
	18:10	The **next d** an evil spirit	4740
	19:24	He lay thus way all that **d** and night.	3427
	20: 5	until the evening of the **d after tomorrow**.	8958
	20:12	by this time the **d after** tomorrow!	8958
	20:19	The **d after tomorrow**,	8992
	20:26	Saul said nothing that **d**, for he thought,	3427
	20:27	But the **next d**,	4740
	20:27	the next day, the second **d** of the month,	NIH
	20:34	that second **d** of the month he did not eat,	3427
	21: 6	by hot bread on the **d** it was taken away.	3427
	21: 7	one of Saul's servants was there that **d**,	3427
	21:10	That **d** David fled from Saul and went	3427
	22:15	Was that **d** the first time I inquired of God	3427
	22:18	That **d** he killed eighty-five men who wore	3427
	22:22	That **d**, when Doeg the Edomite was there,	3427
	23:14	**D after day** Saul searched for him,	
			2021+3427+3972
	23:14	**Day after d** Saul searched for him,	
			2021+3427+3972

1Sa	24: 4	the **d** the LORD spoke of when he said	3427
	24:10	This **d** you have seen with your own eyes	3427
	25:16	Night and **d** they were a wall around us all	3429
	25:33	for keeping me from bloodshed this **d** and	3427
	27: 6	So on that **d** Achish gave him Ziklag,	3427
	28:20	for he had eaten nothing all that **d**	3427
	29: 3	and from the **d** he left Saul until now,	3427
	29: 6	From the **d** you came to me until now,	3427
	29: 8	against your servant from the **d** I came	3427
	30: 1	and his men reached Ziklag on the third **d**.	3427
	30:17	from dusk until the evening of the **next d**,	4740
	30:25	and ordinance for Israel from that **d** to this.	3427
	31: 6	and all his men died together that same **d**.	3427
	31: 8	The **next d**, when the Philistines came	4740
2Sa	1: 2	the third **d** a man arrived from Saul's camp,	3427
	2:17	The battle that **d** was very fierce,	3427
	3: 8	This very **d** I am loyal to the house	3427
	3:35	to eat something while it was still **d**;	3427
	3:37	that all the people and all Israel knew that	3427
	3:38	and a great man has fallen in Israel this **d**?	3427
	4: 3	and have lived there as aliens to this **d**.	3427
	4: 5	the **d** while he was taking his noonday rest.	3427
	4: 8	This **d** the LORD has avenged my lord	3427
	5: 8	On that **d**, David said,	3427
	6: 8	to this **d** that place is called Perez Uzzah.	3427
	6: 9	David was afraid of the LORD that **d**	3427
	6:23	of Saul had no children to the **d**	3427
	7: 6	a house from the **d** I brought the Israelites	3427
	7: 6	the Israelites up out of Egypt to this **d**.	3427
	11:12	David said to him, "Stay here one more **d**,	3427
	11:12	So Uriah remained in Jerusalem that **d** and	3427
	12:18	On the seventh **d** the child died.	3427
	13:32	since the **d** Amnon raped his sister Tamar.	3427
	13:37	King David mourned for his son every **d**.	3427
	18: 7	and the casualties that **d** were great—	3427
	18: 8	the forest claimed more lives that **d** than	3427
	18:18	it is called Absalom's Monument to this **d**.	3427
	19: 2	that **d** was turned into mourning,	3427
	19: 2	because on that **d** the troops heard it said,	3427
	19: 3	that **d** as men steal in who are ashamed	3427
	19:19	on the **d** my lord the king left Jerusalem.	3427
	19:22	This **d** you have become my adversaries!	3427
	19:24	or washed his clothes from the **d**	3427
	19:24	the king left until the **d** he returned safely.	3427
	20: 3	They were kept in confinement till the **d**	3427
	21:10	the air touch them **by d** or the wild animals	3429
	22:19	They confronted me in the **d**	3427
	23:10	about a great victory that **d**.	3427
	23:20	He also went down into a pit on a snowy **d**	3427
	24:18	that **d** Gad went to David and said to him,	3427
1Ki	2: 8	down bitter curses on me the **d** I went	3427
	2:37	The **d** you leave and cross	3427
	2:42	'On the **d** you leave to go anywhere else,	3427
	3: 6	a son to sit on his throne this very **d**.	3427
	3:18	The third **d** after my child was born,	3427
	8:16	**d** I brought my people Israel out of Egypt,	3427
	8:28	in your presence this **d**.	3427
	8:29	be open toward this temple night and **d**,	3429
	8:59	be near to the LORD our God **d** and night,	3429
	8:64	On that same **d** the king consecrated	3427
	8:66	the following **d** he sent the people away.	3427
	9:13	a name they have to this **d**.	3427
	9:21	as it is to this **d**.	3427
	10:12	or seen since that **d**.)	3427
	12:19	against the house of David to this **d**.	3427
	12:32	He instituted a festival on the fifteenth **d** of	3427
	12:33	On the fifteenth **d** of the eighth month,	3427
	13: 3	That same **d** the man of God gave a sign:	3427
	13:11	that the man of God had done there that **d**.	3427
	14:14	This is the **d**!	3427
	16:16	over Israel that very **d** there in the camp.	3427
	17:14	the **d** the LORD gives rain on the land.' "	3427
	17:15	So there was food **every d** for Elijah and for	3427
	20:29	and on the seventh **d** the battle was joined.	3427
	20:29	on the Aramean foot soldiers in one **d**.	3427
	21: 9	"Proclaim a **d** of **fasting** and seat Naboth	7427
	21:29	I will not bring this disaster in his **d**,	3427
	22:25	"You will find out on the **d** you go to hide	3427
	22:35	**All d long** the battle raged,	
			928+2021+2021+2085+3427
2Ki	2:22	water has remained wholesome to this **d**,	3427
	4: 8	One **d** Elisha went to Shunem.	3427
	4:11	One **d** when Elisha came,	3427
	4:18	and one **d** he went out to his father,	3427
	6:29	The next **d** I said to her,	3427
	7: 9	a **d** of good news and we are keeping it	3427
	8: 6	from the **d** she left the country until now."	3427
	8:15	But the **next d** he took a thick cloth,	4740
	8:22	To this **d** Edom has been in rebellion	3427
	10:27	people have used it for a latrine to this **d**.	3427
	13:23	To **this d** he has been unwilling	6964
	14: 7	calling it Joktheel, the name it has to this **d**.	3427
	15: 5	the king with leprosy until the **d** he died,	3427
	16: 6	into Elath and have lived there to this **d**.	3427
	17:34	To this **d** they persist	3427
	17:41	To this **d** their children	3427
	19: 3	This **d** is a day of distress and rebuke	3427
	19: 3	a **d** of distress and rebuke and disgrace,	3427
	19:37	**One d**, while he was worshiping in	2118+2256
	20: 5	On the third **d** from now you will go up to	3427
	20: 8	to the temple of the LORD on the third **d**?"	3427
	20:17	that your fathers have stored up until this **d**,	3427
	21:15	the **d** their forefathers came out of Egypt	3427
	21:15	of Egypt until this **d**."	3427
	25: 1	on the tenth **d** of the tenth month,	NIH
	25: 3	the ninth **d** of the [fourth] month the famine	NIH
	25: 8	On the seventh **d** of the fifth month,	NIH

2Ki	25:27	the twenty-seventh **d** of the twelfth month.	NIH
	25:30	**D by day** the king gave Jehoiachin a regular allowance	928+1821+2257+3427+3427
	25:30	**Day by d** the king gave Jehoiachin a regular allowance	928+1821+2257+3427+3427
1Ch	4:41	as is evident to this **d**.	3427
	4:43	and they have lived there to this **d**.	3427
	5:26	where they are to this **d**.	3427
	9:33	for the work **d** and night.	3429
	10: 8	The **next d**, when the Philistines came	4740
	11:22	He also went down into a pit on a snowy **d**	3427
	12:22	**D after day** men came to help David,	3427
	12:22	**Day after d** men came to help David,	3427
	13:11	to this **d** that place is called Perez Uzzah.	3427
	13:12	David was afraid of God that **d** and asked,	3427
	16: 7	That **d** David first committed to Asaph	3427
	16:23	proclaim his salvation **d** after day.	3427
	16:23	proclaim his salvation day after **d**.	3427
	17: 5	from the **d** I brought Israel up out of Egypt	3427
	17: 5	up out of Egypt to this **d**.	3427
	26:17	There were six Levites a **d** on the east,	3427
	26:17	four a **d** on the north,	NIH
	26:17	four a **d** on the south and two at a time at	3427
	29:21	The next **d** they made sacrifices to	3427
	29:22	in the presence of the LORD that **d**.	3427
2Ch	3: 2	on the second **d** of the second month in	NIH
	6: 5	the **d** I brought my people out of Egypt,	3427
	6:20	be open toward this temple **d** and night,	3429
	7: 9	On the eighth **d** they held an assembly,	3427
	7:10	On the twenty-third **d** of	3427
	8: 8	as it is to this **d**.	3427
	8:16	from the **d** the foundation of the temple of	3427
	9:20	of little value in Solomon's **d**.	3427
	10:19	against the house of David to this **d**.	3427
	18:24	"You will find out on the **d** you go to hide	3427
	18:34	**All d long** the battle raged,	928+2021+2021+2085+3427
	20:26	the fourth **d** they assembled in the Valley	3427
	20:26	the Valley of Beracah to this **d**.	3427
	21:10	To this **d** Edom has been in rebellion	3427
	26:21	until the **d** he died.	3427
	28: 6	In one **d** Pekah son of Remaliah killed	3427
	29:17	They began the consecration on the first **d**	NIH
	29:17	by the eighth **d** of the month they reached	3427
	29:17	on the sixteenth **d** of the first month.	3427
	30:15	on the fourteenth **d** of the second month.	NIH
	30:21	priests sang to the LORD **every d**,	928+3427+3427
	35: 1	on the fourteenth **d** of the first month.	NIH
	35:25	and to this **d** all the men	3427
Ezr	3: 4	offerings prescribed for **each d**,	928+3427+3427
	3: 6	the first **d** of the seventh month they began	3427
	5:16	From **that d** to the present it has been	10008S
	6:15	The temple was completed on the third **d** of	10317
	6:19	On the fourteenth **d** of the first month,	NIH
	7: 9	on the first **d** of the first month,	NIH
	7: 9	and he arrived in Jerusalem on the first **d** of	NIH
	8:31	the twelfth **d** of the first month we set out	NIH
	8:33	On the fourth **d**, in the house of our God,	3427
	9:15	We are left this **d** as a remnant.	3427
	10: 9	And on the twentieth **d** of the ninth month,	NIH
	10:13	this matter cannot be taken care of in a **d**	3427
	10:16	the first **d** of the tenth month they sat down	3427
	10:17	and by the first **d** of the first month	3427
Ne	1: 6	before you **d** and night for your servants,	3429
	4: 2	Will they finish in a **d**?	3427
	4: 9	to our God and posted a guard **d** and night	3429
	4:16	From that **d** on, half of my men did	3427
	4:22	as guards by night and workmen by **d**."	3427
	5:18	Each **d** one ox,	3427
	6:10	**One d** I went to the house of Shemaiah son	2256
	8: 2	So on the first **d** of the seventh month Ezra	3427
	8: 9	"This **d** is sacred to the LORD your God.	3427
	8:10	This **d** is sacred to our Lord.	3427
	8:11	saying, "Be still, for this is a sacred **d**.	3427
	8:13	On the second **d** of the month,	3427
	8:17	the days of Joshua son of Nun until that **d**,	3427
	8:18	**D after day**, from the first day to the last,	3427
	8:18	**Day after d**, from the first day to the last,	3427
	8:18	Day after day, from the first **d** to the last,	3427
	8:18	and on the eighth **d**,	3427
	9: 1	On the twenty-fourth **d** of the same month,	3427
	9: 3	the LORD their God *for* a quarter of the **d**,	3427
	9:10	which remains to this **d**.	3427
	9:12	**By d** you led them with a pillar of cloud,	3429
	9:19	**By d** the pillar of cloud did not cease	928+3429
	10:31	from them on the Sabbath or on any holy **d**.	3427
	12:43	And on that **d** they offered great sacrifices,	3427
	13: 1	that **d** the Book of Moses was read aloud in	3427
	13:15	against selling food on that **d**.	3427
	13:17	desecrating the Sabbath **d**?	3427
	13:19	be brought in on the Sabbath **d**.	3427
	13:22	in order to keep the Sabbath **d** holy.	3427
Est	1:10	On the seventh **d**, when King Xerxes was	3427
	1:18	This very **d** the Persian and Median women	3427
	2:11	**Every d** he walked back and forth near	2256+3427+3427+3972
	3: 4	**D after day** they spoke to him	3427
	3: 4	after **d** they spoke to him but he refused	3427
	3: 7	in the presence of Haman to **select a d**	3427+3427+4200+4946
	3:12	Then on the thirteenth **d** of the first month	3427
	3:13	on a single **d**, the thirteenth day	3427
	3:13	the thirteenth **d** of the twelfth month,	NIH
	3:14	so they would be ready for that **d**.	3427
	4:16	not eat or drink for three days, night or **d**,	3427
	5: 1	On the third **d** Esther put on her royal robes	3427
	5: 9	Haman went out that **d** happy and	3427

Est	7: 2	they were drinking wine on that second **d**,	3427
	8: 1	That same **d** King Xerxes gave Queen Esther	3427
	8: 9	on the twenty-third **d** of the third month,	NIH
	8:12	The **d** appointed for the Jews to do this	3427
	8:12	of King Xerxes was the thirteenth **d** of	NIH
	8:13	so that the Jews would be ready on that **d**	3427
	9: 1	On the thirteenth **d** of the twelfth month,	3427
	9: 1	On this **d** the enemies of the Jews	3427
	9:11	to the king that same **d**.	3427
	9:15	In Susa came together on the fourteenth **d**	3427
	9:17	on the thirteenth **d** of the month of Adar,	3427
	9:17	the fourteenth they rested and made it a **d**	3427
	9:18	on the fifteenth they rested and made it a **d**	3427
	9:19	the fourteenth of the month of Adar as a **d**	3427
	9:19	a **d** for giving presents to each other.	3427
	9:22	and their mourning into a **d** of celebration.	3427
Job	1: 6	One **d** the angels came	3427
	1:13	One **d** when Job's sons	3427
	2: 1	On another **d** the angels came	3427
	3: 1	Job opened his mouth and cursed the **d**	3427
	3: 3	"May the **d** of my birth perish,	3427
	3: 4	That **d**—may it turn to darkness;	3427
	3: 8	May those who curse days curse that **d**,	2084S
	3:16	an infant who never saw the **light of d**?	240
	15:23	he knows the **d** of darkness is at hand.	3427
	17:12	These men turn night into **d**,	3427
	20:28	rushing waters on the **d** of God's wrath.	3427
	21:30	evil man is spared from the **d** of calamity,	3427
	21:30	that he is delivered from the **d** of wrath?	3427
	24:16	but by **d** they shut themselves in;	3429
Ps	1: 2	and on his law he meditates **d** and night.	3429
	7:11	a God who expresses his wrath every **d**.	3429
	13: 2	with my thoughts and **every d** have sorrow	3429
	18:18	They confronted me in the **d**	3427
	19: 2	**D after day** they pour forth speech;	3427
	19: 2	**Day after d** they pour forth speech;	3427
	22: 2	O my God, I cry out by **d**,	3429
	25: 5	and my hope is in you all **d long**.	3427
	27: 5	For in the **d** of trouble he will keep me safe	3427
	32: 3	through my groaning all **d long**.	3427
	32: 4	**d** and night your hand was heavy upon me;	3429
	35:28	and of your praises all **d long**.	3427
	37:13	for he knows their **d** is coming.	3427
	38: 6	all **d long** I go about mourning.	3427
	38:12	all **d long** they plot deception.	3427
	42: 3	My tears have been my food **d** and night,	3429
	42: 3	while men say to me all **d**,	3427
	42: 8	**By d** the LORD directs his love,	3429
	42:10	saying to me all **d long**,	3427
	44: 8	In God we make our boast all **d long**,	3427
	44:15	My disgrace is before me all **d long**,	3427
	44:22	Yet for your sake we face death all **d long**;	3427
	46: 5	God will help her at **break of d**.	1332+7155
	50:15	and call upon me in the **d** *of* trouble;	3427
	52: 1	Why do you boast all **d long**,	3427
	55:10	**D** and night they prowl about on its walls;	3429
	56: 1	all **d long** they press their attack.	3427
	56: 2	My slanderers pursue me all **d long**;	3427
	56: 5	All **d long** they twist my words;	3427
	61: 8	to your name and fulfill my vows **d**	3427
	61: 8	and fulfill my vows day after **d**.	3427
	71: 8	declaring your splendor all **d long**.	3427
	71:15	of your salvation all **d long**,	3427
	71:17	to **this d** I declare your marvelous deeds.	2178S
	71:24	of your righteous acts all **d long**,	3427
	72:15	for him and bless him all **d long**.	3427
	73:14	All **d long** I have been plagued;	3427
	74:16	The **d** is yours, and yours also the night;	3427
	74:22	remember how fools mock you all **d long**.	3427
	78: 9	turned back on the **d** of battle;	3427
	78:14	He guided them with the cloud **by d** and	3429
	78:42	the **d** he redeemed them from the oppressor,	3427
	78:43	the **d** he displayed his miraculous signs	889S
	81: 3	on the **d** of our Feast;	3427
	84:10	Better is *one* **d** in your courts than	3427
	86: 3	O Lord, for I call to you all **d**.	3427
	86: 7	In the **d** of my trouble I will call to you,	3427
	88: 1	**d** and night I cry out before you.	3427
	88: 9	I call to you, O LORD, every **d**;	3427
	88:17	All **d long** they surround me like a flood;	3427
	89:16	They rejoice in your name all **d long**;	3427
	90: 4	A thousand years in your sight are like a **d** that has just gone by,	919+3427
	91: 5	nor the arrow that flies by **d**,	3429
	92: T	A psalm. A song. For the Sabbath **d**.	3427
	95: 8	as you did that **d** at Massah in the desert,	3427
	96: 2	proclaim his salvation **d** after day.	3427
	96: 2	proclaim his salvation day after **d**.	3427
	102: 8	All **d long** my enemies taunt me;	3427
	110: 3	Your troops will be willing on your **d**	3427
	110: 5	he will crush kings on the **d** of his wrath.	3427
	118:24	This is the **d** the LORD has made;	3427
	119:91	Your laws endure to this **d**,	3427
	119:97	I meditate on it all **d long**.	3427
	119:164	a **d** I praise you for your righteous laws.	3427
	121: 6	the sun will not harm you by **d**,	3429
	136: 8	the sun to govern the **d**,	3427
	137: 7	the Edomites did on the **d** Jerusalem fell.	3427
	139:12	the night will shine like the **d**,	3427
	140: 2	in their hearts and stir up war every **d**.	3427
	140: 7	who shields my head in the **d** of battle—	3427
	145: 2	Every **d** I will praise you	3427
	146: 4	on that very **d** their plans come to nothing.	3427
Pr	4:18	shining ever brighter till the full light of **d**.	3427
	7: 9	as the **d** was fading,	3427
	8:30	I was filled with delight **d** after day,	3427

Pr	8:30	I was filled with delight day after **d**,	3427
	11: 4	Wealth is worthless in the **d** of wrath,	3427
	16: 4	even the wicked for a **d** of disaster.	3427
	21:26	All **d long** he craves for more,	3427
	21:31	The horse is made ready for the **d** of battle,	3427
	25:20	a garment on a cold **d**,	3427
	27: 1	you do not know what a **d** may bring forth.	3427
	27:15	like a constant dripping on a rainy **d**;	3427
Ecc	7: 1	the **d** of death better than the day of birth.	3427
	7: 1	the day of death better than the **d** of birth.	3427
	8: 8	no one has power over the **d** of his death.	3427
	8:16	his eyes not seeing sleep **d** or night—	3427
SS	2:17	Until the **d** breaks and the shadows flee,	3427
	3:11	on the **d** of his wedding,	3427
	3:11	the **d** his heart rejoiced.	3427
	4: 6	Until the **d** breaks and the shadows flee,	3427
	8: 8	for our sister for the **d** she is spoken for?	3427
Isa	2:11	the LORD alone will be exalted in that **d**.	3427
	2:12	The LORD Almighty has a **d** in store	3427
	2:17	the LORD alone will be exalted in that **d**,	3427
	2:20	that **d** men will throw away to the rodents	3427
	3: 7	in that **d** he will cry out, "I have no remedy.	3427
	3:18	In that **d** the Lord will snatch away their finery:	3427
	4: 1	In that **d** seven women will take hold	3427
	4: 2	In that **d** the Branch of the LORD will	3427
	4: 5	of smoke by **d** and a glow of flaming fire	3429
	4: 6	a shelter and shade from the heat of the **d**,	3429
	5:30	that **d** they will roar over it like the roaring	3427
	7:18	that **d** the LORD will whistle for flies from	3427
	7:20	that **d** the Lord will use a razor hired from	3427
	7:21	that **d**, a man will keep alive a young cow	3427
	7:23	In that **d**, in every place where there were	3427
	9: 4	For as in the **d** of Midian's defeat,	3427
	9:14	both palm branch and reed *in* a single **d**;	3427
	10: 3	What will you do on the **d** of reckoning,	3427
	10:17	in a single **d** it will burn	3427
	10:20	In that **d** the remnant of Israel,	3427
	10:27	In that **d** their burden will be lifted	3427
	10:32	This **d** they will halt at Nob;	3427
	11:10	In that **d** the Root of Jesse will stand as	3427
	11:11	In that **d** the Lord will reach out his hand	3427
	12: 1	In that **d** you will say:	3427
	12: 4	In that **d** you will say:	3427
	13: 6	Wail, for the **d** of the LORD is near;	3427
	13: 9	See, the **d** of the LORD is coming—	3427
	13: 9	a cruel **d**, with wrath and fierce anger—	NIH
	13:13	in the **d** of his burning anger.	3427
	14: 3	On the **d** the LORD gives you relief	3427
	17: 4	"In that **d** the glory of Jacob will fade;	3427
	17: 7	In that **d** men will look to their Maker	3427
	17: 9	In that **d** their strong cities,	3427
	17:11	though on the **d** you set them out,	3427
	17:11	yet the harvest will be as nothing in the **d**	3427
	19:16	In that **d** the Egyptians will be like women.	3427
	19:18	In that **d** five cities in Egypt will speak	3427
	19:19	that **d** there will be an altar to the LORD in	3427
	19:21	that **d** they will acknowledge the LORD.	3427
	19:23	that **d** there will be a highway from Egypt	3427
	19:24	In that **d** Israel will be the third,	3427
	20: 6	In that **d** the people who live	3427
	21: 8	the lookout shouted, "**D after day**,	3429+9458
	21: 8	the lookout shouted, "**Day after d**,	3429+9458
	22: 5	has a **d** of tumult and trampling and terror	3427
	22: 5	a **d** of battering down walls and	NIH
	22: 8	And you looked in that **d** to the weapons in	3427
	22:12	called you on that **d** to weep and to wail,	3427
	22:14	"Till your dying **d** this sin will not	AIT
	22:20	"In that **d** I will summon my servant,	3427
	22:25	"In that **d**," declares the LORD Almighty,	3427
	24:21	In that **d** the LORD will punish the powers	3427
	25: 9	In that **d** they will say,	3427
	26: 1	In that **d** this song will be sung in the land	3427
	27: 1	In that **d**, the LORD will punish	3427
	27: 2	In that **d**—"Sing about a fruitful vineyard:	3427
	27: 3	I guard it **d** and night so	3427
	27: 8	as on a **d** the east wind blows.	3427
	27:12	In that **d** the LORD will thresh from	3427
	27:13	And in that **d** a great trumpet will sound.	3427
	28: 5	In that **d** the LORD Almighty will be	3427
	28:19	morning after morning, by **d** and by night,	3427
	29:18	In that **d** the deaf will hear the words of	3427
	30:23	In that **d** your cattle will graze	3427
	30:25	In the **d** of great slaughter,	3427
	31: 7	that **d** every one of you will reject the idols	3427
	34: 8	For the LORD has a **d** of vengeance,	3427
	34:10	It will not be quenched night and **d**;	3429
	37: 3	This **d** is a day of distress and rebuke	3427
	37: 3	a **d** of distress and rebuke and disgrace,	3427
	37:38	**One d**, while he was worshiping in	2118+2256
	38:12	**d** and night you made an end of me.	3427
	38:13	**d** and night you made an end of me.	3427
	39: 6	that your fathers have stored up until this **d**,	3427
	47: 9	on a single **d**:	3427
	49: 8	and in the **d** of salvation I will help you;	3427
	51:13	that you live in constant terror every **d**	3427
	52: 5	all **d long** my name is constantly blasphemed.	3427
	52: 6	therefore in that **d** they will know	3427
	58: 2	For **d** after day they seek me out;	3427
	58: 2	For day after **d** they seek me out;	3427
	58: 3	"Yet on the **d** of your fasting,	3427
	58: 5	only a **d** *for* a man to humble himself?	3427
	58: 5	a **d** acceptable to the LORD?	3427
	58:13	from doing as you please on my holy **d**,	3427
	58:13	and the LORD's holy **d** honorable,	NIH
	60:11	they will never be shut, **d** or night,	3429

Isa	60:19	The sun will no more be your light **by d,**	3429
	61: 2	the LORD's favor and the **d** of vengeance	3427
	62: 6	they will never be silent **d** or night.	3427
	63: 4	For the **d** of vengeance was in my heart,	3427
	65: 2	All **d** long I have held out my hands to	3427
	65: 5	a fire that keeps burning all **d.**	3427
	66: 8	be born in a **d** or a nation be brought forth	3427
Jer	3:25	from our youth till this **d** we have	3427
	4: 9	"In that **d,**" declares the LORD,	3427
	7:25	until now, **d after day,** again	3427
	7:25	until now, **day after d,** again	3427
	9: 1	I would weep **d** and night for the slain	3429
	12: 3	Set them apart for the **d** of slaughter!	3427
	14:17	with tears night and **d** without ceasing;	3429
	15: 9	Her sun will set while it is still **d;**	3429
	16:13	there you will serve other gods **d** and night,	3429
	17:16	you know I have not desired the **d**	3427
	17:17	you are my refuge in the **d** of disaster.	3427
	17:18	Bring on them the **d** of disaster.	3427
	17:21	a load and bring on the Sabbath **d** or bring it through	3427
	17:22	but keep the Sabbath **d** holy,	3427
	17:24	the Sabbath **d** holy by not doing any work	3427
	17:27	the Sabbath **d** holy by not carrying any load	3427
	17:27	the gates of Jerusalem on the Sabbath **d,**	3427
	18:17	and not my face in the **d** of their disaster."	3427
	20: 3	The **next d,** when Pashhur released him	4740
	20: 7	I am ridiculed all **d** long;	3427
	20: 8	and reproach all **d** long.	3427
	20:14	Cursed be the **d** I was born!	3427
	20:14	the **d** my mother bore me not be blessed!	3427
	25: 3	of Amon king of Judah until this very **d**—	3427
	27:22	until the **d** I come for them,'	3427
	30: 7	How awful that **d** will be!	3427
	30: 8	" 'In that **d,**' declares the LORD	3427
	31: 6	be a **d** when watchmen cry out on the hills	3427
	31:35	he who appoints the sun to shine **by d,**	3429
	32:20	in Egypt and have continued them to this **d,**	3427
	32:31	From the **d** it was built until now,	3427
	33:20	with the **d** and my covenant with the night,	3429
	33:20	and my covenant with the night, so that **d**	3429
	33:25	not established my covenant with **d**	3429
	35:14	To this **d** they do not drink wine,	3427
	36: 6	of the LORD on a **d** of fasting and read to	3427
	36:30	be thrown out and exposed to the heat **by d**	3427
	37:21	given bread from the street of the bakers	
		each d until	2021+3427+4200
	38:28	until the **d** Jerusalem was captured.	3427
	39: 2	And on the ninth **d** of the fourth month	NIH
	39:17	But I will rescue you on that **d,**	3427
	41: 4	The **d** after Gedaliah's assassination,	3427
	44:10	To this **d** they have not humbled	3427
	46:10	But that **d** belongs to the Lord,	3427
	46:10	**d** of vengeance, for vengeance on his foes.	3427
	46:21	for the **d** of disaster is coming upon them,	3427
	47: 4	the **d** has come to destroy all the Philistines	3427
	48:41	that the hearts of Moab's warriors will be	3427
	49:22	that the hearts of Edom's warriors will be	3427
	49:26	all her soldiers will be silenced in that **d,"**	3427
	50:27	For their **d** has come,	3427
	50:30	all her soldiers will be silenced in that **d,"**	3427
	50:31	"for your **d** has come,	3427
	51: 2	they will oppose her on every side in the **d**	3427
	52: 4	on the tenth **d** of the tenth month,	NIH
	52: 6	the ninth **d** of the fourth month the famine	NIH
	52:11	where he put him in prison till the **d**	3427
	52:12	On the tenth **d** of the fifth month,	NIH
	52:31	on the twenty-fifth **d** of the twelfth month.	NIH
	52:34	**D by day** the king	928+1821+3427+3427
	52:34	**Day by d** the king	928+1821+3427+3427
	52:34	till the **d** of his death.	3427
La	1:12	that the LORD brought on me in the **d**	3427
	1:13	He made me desolate, faint all the **d** long.	3427
	1:21	May you bring the **d** you have announced	3427
	2: 1	not remembered his footstool in the **d**	3427
	2: 7	in the house of the LORD as on the **d** of	3427
	2:16	This is the **d** we have waited for;	3427
	2:18	let your tears flow like a river **d** and night;	3429
	2:21	You have slain them in the **d** of your anger;	3427
	2:22	"As you summon to a feast **d,**	3427
	2:22	In the **d** of the LORD's anger	3427
	3: 3	against me again and again, all **d** long.	3427
	3:14	they mock me in song all **d** long.	3427
	3:62	and mutter against me all **d** long.	3427
Eze	1: 1	in the fourth month on the fifth **d,**	NIH
	1:28	of a rainbow in the clouds on a rainy **d,**	3427
	2: 3	in revolt against me to this very **d.**	3427
	4: 6	a **d** for each year.	3427
	4:10	of food to eat each **d** and eat it at set times.	3427
	7: 7	The time has come, the **d** is near;	3427
	7:10	"The **d** is here!	3427
	7:12	The time has come, the **d** has arrived.	3427
	7:19	not be able to save them in the **d** of	3427
	8: 1	in the sixth month on the fifth **d,**	NIH
	12: 7	**During the d** I brought out my things	
		packed	3429
	13: 5	that it will stand firm in the battle on the **d**	3427
	16: 4	the **d** you were born your cord was not cut,	3427
	16: 5	on the **d** you were born you were despised.	3427
	16:56	even mention your sister Sodom in the **d**	3427
	20: 1	in the fifth month on the tenth **d,**	NIH
	20: 5	On the **d** I chose Israel,	3427
	20: 6	On that **d** I swore to them	3427
	20:29	(It is called Bamah to this **d.**)	3427
	20:31	with all your idols to this **d.**	3427
	21:25	whose **d** has come,	3427
	21:29	whose **d** has come,	3427
	22:14	or your hands be strong in the **d** I deal	3427

Eze	22:24	that has had no rain or showers in the **d**	3427
	23:39	On the very **d** they sacrificed their children	3427
	24: 1	in the tenth month on the tenth **d,**	NIH
	24: 2	to Jerusalem this very **d.**	3427
	24:25	on the **d** I take away their stronghold,	3427
	24:26	on that **d** a fugitive will come to tell you	3427
	26: 1	on the first **d** of the month,	NIH
	26:18	coastlands tremble on the **d** of your fall;	3427
	27:27	of the sea on the **d** of your shipwreck.	3427
	28:13	the **d** you were created they were prepared.	3427
	28:15	in your ways from the **d** you were created	3427
	29: 1	in the tenth month on the twelfth **d,**	NIH
	29:17	in the first month on the first **d,**	NIH
	29:21	that I will make a horn grow for the house	3427
	30: 2	" 'Wail and say, "Alas for that **d!**"	3427
	30: 3	**d** is near, the day of the LORD is near—	3427
	30: 3	day is near, the **d** of the LORD is near—	3427
	30: 3	of clouds, a time of doom for the nations.	3427
	30: 9	that **d** messengers will go out from me	3427
	30: 9	Anguish will take hold of them on the **d**	3427
	30:18	the **d** at Tahpanhes when I break the yoke	3427
	30:20	in the first month on the seventh **d,**	NIH
	31: 1	in the third month on the first **d,**	NIH
	31:15	On the **d** it was brought down to	3427
	32: 1	in the twelfth month on the first **d,**	NIH
	32:10	On the **d** of your downfall each	3427
	32:17	on the fifteenth **d** of the month,	NIH
	33:21	in the tenth month on the fifth **d,**	NIH
	34:12	the places where they were scattered on a **d**	3427
	36:33	On the **d** I cleanse you from all your sins,	3427
	38:10	that thoughts will come into your mind	3427
	38:14	In that **d,** when my people Israel are living	3427
	38:18	This is what will happen in that **d:**	3427
	39: 8	This is the **d** I have spoken of.	3427
	39:11	" 'On that **d** I will give Gog a burial place	3427
	39:13	and the **d** I am glorified will be	3427
	39:13	be a memorable **d** for them,	NIH
	39:22	that **d** forward the house of Israel will know	3427
	40: 1	on that very **d** the hand of the LORD was	3427
	43:22	the second **d** you are to offer a male goat	3427
	43:27	from the eighth **d** on,	3427
	44:27	On the **d** he goes into the inner court of	3427
	45:18	the first month on the first **d** you are to take	NIH
	45:20	You are to do the same on the seventh **d** of	NIH
	45:21	the first month on the fourteenth **d** you are	3427
	45:22	On that **d** the prince is to provide a bull as	3427
	45:23	Every **d** during the seven days of	3427
	45:25	in the seventh month on the fifteenth **d,**	3427
	46: 1	the six working days, but on the Sabbath **d**	3427
	46: 1	the **d** of the New Moon it is to be opened.	3427
	46: 4	the Sabbath **d** is to be six male lambs and	3427
	46: 6	the **d** of the New Moon he is to offer	3427
	46:12	as he does on the Sabbath **d.**	3427
	46:13	" 'Every **d** you are to provide	2021+3427+4200
Da	6:10	Three times a **d** he got down on his knees	10317
	6:13	He still prays three times a **d.**"	10317
	9: 7	but this **d** we are covered with shame—	3427
	9:15	for yourself a name that endures to this **d,**	3427
	10: 4	On the twenty-fourth **d** of the first month,	NIH
	10:12	Since the first **d** that you set your mind	3427
Hos	1: 5	In that **d** I will break Israel's bow in	3427
	1:11	for great will be the **d** of Jezreel.	3427
	2: 3	as bare as on the **d** she was born;	3427
	2:15	as in the **d** she came up out of Egypt.	3427
	2:16	"In that **d,**" declares the LORD,	3427
	2:18	that **d** I will make a covenant for them with	3427
	2:21	"In that **d** I will respond,"	3427
	4: 5	You stumble **d** and night,	3427
	5: 9	be laid waste on the **d** of reckoning.	3427
	6: 2	on the third **d** he will restore us,	3427
	7: 5	On the **d** of the festival of our king	3427
	9: 5	on the **d** of your appointed feasts,	3427
	10:14	as Shalman devastated Beth Arbel on the **d**	3427
	10:15	When that **d dawns,**	8840
	12: 1	the east wind all **d** and multiplies lies	3427
Joel	one 1:15	Alas for that **d!**	3427
	1:15	For the **d** of the LORD is near;	3427
	2: 1	for the **d** of the LORD is coming.	3427
	2: 2	a **d** of darkness and gloom,	3427
	2: 2	a **d** of clouds and blackness.	3427
	2:11	The **d** of the LORD is great; it is dreadful.	3427
	2:31	of the great and dreadful **d** of the LORD.	3427
	3:14	the **d** of the LORD is near in the valley	3427
	3:18	that **d** the mountains will drip new wine,	3427
Am	1:14	on the **d** of battle,	3427
	1:14	amid violent winds on a stormy **d.**	3427
	2:16	bravest warriors will flee naked on that **d,"**	3427
	3:14	"On the **d** I punish Israel for her sins,	3427
	5: 8	and darkens into night, who calls for	3427
	5:18	to you who long for the **d** of the LORD!	3427
	5:18	Why do you long for the **d** of the LORD?	3427
	5:18	That **d** will be darkness, not light.	NIH
	5:20	Will not the **d** of the LORD be darkness,	3427
	6: 3	the evil **d** and bring near a reign of terror.	3427
	8: 3	"In that **d,**" declares the Sovereign LORD,	3427
	8: 9	"In that **d,**" declares the Sovereign LORD,	3427
	8:10	an only son and the end of it like a bitter **d.**	3427
	8:13	"In that **d** "the lovely young women	3427
	9:11	that **d** I will restore David's fallen tent.	3427
Ob	1: 8	"In that **d,**" declares the LORD,	3427
	1:11	On the **d** you stood aloof	3427
	1:12	on your brother in the **d** of his misfortune,	3427
	1:12	of Judah in the **d** of their destruction,	3427
	1:12	nor boast so much in the **d** of their trouble.	3427
	1:13	through the gates of my people in the **d**	3427
	1:13	in their calamity in the **d** of their disaster,	3427
	1:13	nor seize their wealth in the **d**	3427

Ob	1:14	nor hand over their survivors in the **d**	3427
	1:15	"The **d** of the LORD is near.	3427
Jnh	3: 4	On the first **d,** Jonah started into the city.	3427
	4: 7	at dawn the **next d** God provided a worm,	4740
Mic	2: 4	In that **d** men will ridicule you;	3427
	3: 6	and the **d** will go dark for them.	3427
	4: 6	"In that **d,**" declares the LORD,	3427
	4: 7	in Mount Zion from **that d** and forever.	6964
	5:10	"In that **d,**" declares the LORD,	3427
	7: 4	The **d** of your watchmen has come,	3427
	7: 4	the **d** God visits you.	NIH
	7:11	The **d** for building your walls will come,	3427
	7:11	the **d** for extending your boundaries.	3427
	7:12	In that **d** people will come to you	3427
Na	2: 3	the **d** they are made ready;	3427
	3:17	locusts that settle in the walls on a cold **d**—	3427
Hab	3: 2	Renew them in our **d,**	9102
	3:16	Yet I will wait patiently for the **d**	3427
Zep	1: 7	for the **d** of the LORD is near.	3427
	1: 8	On the **d** of the LORD's sacrifice	3427
	1: 9	that **d** I will punish all who avoid stepping	3427
	1:10	"On that **d,**" declares the LORD,	3427
	1:14	"The great **d** of the LORD is near—	3427
	1:14	cry on the **d** of the LORD will be bitter,	3427
	1:15	That **d** will be a day of wrath,	3427
	1:15	That day will be a **d** of wrath,	3427
	1:15	a **d** of distress and anguish,	3427
	1:15	a **d** of trouble and ruin,	3427
	1:15	a **d** of darkness and gloom,	3427
	1:15	a **d** of clouds and blackness,	3427
	1:16	a **d** of trumpet and battle cry against	3427
	1:18	on the **d** of the LORD's wrath.	3427
	2: 2	and that **d** sweeps on like chaff,	3427
	2: 2	before the **d** of the LORD's wrath comes	3427
	2: 3	perhaps you will be sheltered on the **d** of	3427
	3: 5	and every **new d** he does not fail,	240
	3: 8	"for the **d** I will stand up to testify.	3427
	3:11	that **d** you will not be put to shame for all	3427
	3:16	On that **d** they will say to Jerusalem,	3427
Hag	1: 1	on the first **d** of the sixth month,	3427
	1:15	on the twenty-fourth **d** of the sixth month in	3427
	2: 1	On the twenty-first **d** of the seventh month,	NIH
	2:10	On the twenty-fourth **d** of the ninth month,	NIH
	2:15	to this from this **d** on—	3427
	2:18	'From this **d** on,	3427
	2:18	from this twenty-fourth **d** of	3427
	2:18	give careful thought to the **d** when	3427
	2:19	" 'From this **d** on I will bless you.' "	3427
	2:20	a second time on the twenty-fourth **d** of	NIH
	2:23	" 'On that **d,**' declares the LORD	3427
Zec	1: 7	the twenty-fourth **d** of the eleventh month,	3427
	2:11	in that **d** and will become my people.	3427
	3: 9	the sin of this land in a single **d.**	3427
	3:10	that **d** each of you will invite his neighbor	3427
	4:10	"Who despises the **d** of small things?	3427
	6:10	Go the same **d** to the house of Josiah son	3427
	7: 1	on the fourth **d** of the ninth month,	NIH
	9:16	on that **d** as the flock of his people.	3427
	11:11	It was revoked on that **d,**	3427
	12: 3	On that **d,** when all the nations of	3427
	12: 4	that **d** I will strike every horse with panic	3427
	12: 6	"On that **d** I will make the leaders of Judah	3427
	12: 8	that **d** the LORD will shield those who live	3427
	12: 9	On that **d** I will set out to destroy all	3427
	12:11	On that **d** the weeping in Jerusalem will	3427
	13: 1	"On that **d** a fountain will be opened to	3427
	13: 2	that **d,** I will banish the names of the idols	3427
	13: 4	"On that **d** every prophet will be ashamed	3427
	14: 1	A **d** of the LORD is coming	3427
	14: 3	as he fights in the **d** of battle.	3427
	14: 4	On that **d** his feet will stand on the Mount	3427
	14: 6	On that **d** there will be no light,	3427
	14: 7	It will be a unique **d,**	3427
	14: 7	a **d** known to the LORD.	NIH
	14: 8	On that **d** living water will flow out	3427
	14: 9	On that **d** there will be one LORD,	3427
	14:13	that **d** men will be stricken by the LORD	3427
	14:20	On that **d** HOLY TO THE LORD will	3427
	14:21	that **d** there will no longer be a Canaanite in	3427
Mal	3: 2	But who can endure the **d** of his coming?	3427
	3:17	"in the **d** when I make	3427
	4: 1	the **d** is coming; it will burn like a furnace.	3427
	4: 1	that **d** that is coming will set them on fire,"	3427
	4: 3	under the soles of your feet on the **d**	3427
	4: 5	and dreadful **d** of the LORD comes.	3427
Mt	6:34	Each **d** has enough trouble of its own.	
	7:22	Many will say to me on that **d,** 'Lord, Lord,	2465
	10:15	and Gomorrah on the **d** of judgment than	2465
	11:22	and Sidon on the **d** of judgment than	2465
	11:23	it would have remained to this **d.**	4958
	11:24	be more bearable for Sodom on the **d**	2465
	12: 5	the priests in the temple desecrate the **d** and	NIG
	12:36	that men will have to give account on the **d**	2465
	13: 1	That same **d** Jesus went out of the house	
	16:21	be killed and on the third **d** be raised to life.	2465
	17:23	and on the third **d** he will be raised to life."	2465
	20: 2	He agreed to pay them a denarius for the **d**	2465
	20: 6	'Why have you been standing here all **d**	
		long doing nothing?'	2465
	20:12	of the work and the **heat of the d.'**	3014
	20:19	On the third **d** he will be raised to life!"	2465
	22:23	That same **d** the Sadducees,	2465
	22:46	and from that **d** on no one dared	2465
	24:36	"No one knows about that **d** or hour,	2465
	24:38	up to the **d** Noah entered the ark;	2465
	24:42	not know on what **d** your Lord will come.	2465
	24:50	The master of that servant will come on a **d**	2465

Mt	25:13	because you do not know the **d** or the hour. 2465
	26:17	On the first **d** of the Feast NIG
	26:29	until that **d** when I drink it anew with you 2465
	26:55	**Every d** I sat in the temple courts teaching, 2465+2848
	27: 8	the Field of Blood to this **d**. 4958
	27:62	The **next d**, the one after Preparation Day, 2069
	27:62	The next day, the one after **Preparation D**, 4187
	27:64	to be made secure until the third **d**. 2465
	28: 1	at dawn on the first **d** of the week, NIG
	28:15	among the Jews to this **very d**. 2465+4958
Mk	2:20	and on that **d** they will fast. 2465
	4:27	Night and **d**, whether he sleeps or gets up, 2465
	4:35	That **d** when evening came, 2465
	5: 5	Night and **d** among the tombs and in 2465
	6:35	By this time it was **late in the d**, 4498+6052
	11:12	The **next d** as they were leaving Bethany, 2069
	13:32	"No one knows about that **d** or hour, 2465
	14:12	On the first **d** of the Feast 2465
	14:25	of the vine until that **d** when I drink it anew 2465
	14:49	**Every d** I was with you, 2465+2848
	15:42	It was **Preparation D** (that is, 4187
	15:42	**d** before the Sabbath). 4640
	16: 2	Very early on the first **d** of the week, NIG
	16: 9	on the first **d** of the week, 4879
Lk	1:20	not able to speak until the **d** this happens, 2465
	1:59	On the eighth **d** they came to circumcise 2465
	2:21	On the eighth **d**, when it was time 2465
	2:37	the temple but worshiped night and **d**, 2465
	2:44	they traveled on for a **d**. 2465
	4:16	the Sabbath **d** he went into the synagogue, 2465
	5: 1	**One d** as Jesus was standing by the Lake of Gennesaret, 1181+1254
	5:17	**One d** as he was teaching, 2465
	6:23	"Rejoice in that **d** and leap for joy, 2465
	8:22	**One d** Jesus said to his disciples, 2465
	9:22	and he must be killed and on the third **d** 2465
	9:37	The **next d**, when they came down from 2465
	10:12	be more bearable on that **d** for Sodom than 2465
	10:35	The **next d** he took out two silver coins 892
	11: 1	**One d** Jesus was praying in a certain place. 1181+2779
	11: 3	Give us each **d** our daily bread. 2465
	12:46	The master of that servant will come on a **d** 2465
	13:16	on the Sabbath **d** from what bound her?" 2465
	13:32	and on the third **d** I will reach my goal.' NIG
	13:33	and tomorrow and the **next d**— 2400
	14: 5	that falls into a well on the Sabbath **d**, 2465
	16:19	and fine linen and lived in luxury every **d**. 2465
	17: 4	If he sins against you seven times in a **d**, 2465
	17:24	of Man in his **d** will be like the lightning, 2465
	17:27	in marriage up to the **d** Noah entered 2465
	17:29	But the **d** Lot left Sodom, 2465
	17:30	"It will be just like this on the **d** the Son 2465
	17:31	On that **d** no one who is on the roof 2465
	18: 7	who cry out to him **d** and night?" 2465
	18:33	On the third **d** he will rise again." 2465
	19:42	on this **d** what would bring you peace— 2465
	19:47	**Every d** he was teaching at the temple. 2465
	20: 1	**One d** as he was teaching the people in 2465
	21:34	that **d** will close on you unexpectedly like 2465
	21:37	**Each d** Jesus was teaching at the temple, 2465+3836
	22: 7	Then came the **d** of Unleavened Bread 2465
	22:53	**Every d** I was with you in 2465
	23:12	That **d** Herod and Pilate became friends— 2465
	23:54	It was Preparation **D**, 2465
	24: 1	On the **first d** of the week, 1651
	24: 7	and on the third **d** be raised again.' " 2465
	24:13	Now that same **d** two of them were going to 2465
	24:21	it is the third **d** since all this took place. 2465
	24:29	the **d** is almost over." 2465
	24:46	and rise from the dead on the third **d**, 2465
Jn	1:29	The **next d** John saw Jesus coming 2069
	1:35	The **next d** John was there again with two 2069
	1:39	and spent that **d** with him. 2465
	1:43	**next d** Jesus decided to leave for Galilee. 2069
	2: 1	On the third **d** a wedding took place at Cana 2465
	5: 9	The **d** on which this took place was 2465
	5:17	at his work to **this very d**, 785
	6:22	The **next d** the crowd that had stayed on 2069
	6:39	but raise them up at the last **d**. 2465
	6:40	and I will raise him up at the last **d**." 2465
	6:44	and I will raise him up at the last **d**. 2465
	6:54	and I will raise him up *at* the last **d**. 2465
	7:37	On the last and greatest **d** of the Feast, 2465
	8:56	at the thought of seeing my **d**; 2465
	9: 4	As long as it is **d**, 2465
	9:14	the **d** on which Jesus had made the mud 2465
	11: 9	A man who walks by **d** will not stumble, 2465
	11:24	in the resurrection at the last **d**." 2465
	11:53	from that **d** on they plotted to take his life. 2465
	12: 7	that she should save this perfume for the **d** 2465
	12:12	The **next d** the great crowd that had come 2069
	12:48	will condemn him at the last **d**. 2465
	14:20	On that **d** you will realize that I am 2465
	16:23	that **d** you will no longer ask me anything. 2465
	16:26	In that **d** you will ask in my name. 2465
	19:14	the **d** of Preparation of Passover Week, 4187
	19:31	Now it was the **d of Preparation**, 4187
	19:31	and the next **d** was to be a special Sabbath. 2465
	19:42	the Jewish **d of Preparation** and since 4187
	20: 1	Early on the first **d** of the week, NIG
	20:19	On the evening *of* that first **d** of the week, 2465
Ac	1: 2	until the **d** he was taken up to heaven, 2465
	2: 1	When the **d** of Pentecost came, 2465
	2:20	the coming of the great and glorious **d** of 2465

Ac	2:29	and his tomb is here to this **d**. 2465
	2:41	to their number that **d**. 2465
	2:46	Every **d** they continued to meet together in 2465
	3: 1	One Peter and John were going up to NIG
	3: 2	where he was put every **d** to beg 2465
	4: 3	they put them in jail until the **next d**. 892
	4: 5	The **next d** the rulers, 892
	5:42	**D after day**, in the temple courts and 2465+4246
	5:42	**Day after d**, in the temple courts and 2465+4246
	7:26	The **next d** Moses came 2465
	8: 1	that **d** a great persecution broke out against 2465
	9:24	**D** and night they kept close watch on 2465
	10: 3	One **d** at about three in the afternoon he had NIG
	10: 9	About noon the **following d** as they were 2069
	10:23	The **next d** Peter started out with them, 2069
	10:24	The **following d** he arrived in Caesarea. 2069
	10:40	the dead on the third **d** and caused him to 2465
	12:21	*On* the appointed **d** Herod, 2465
	14:20	The **next d** he and Barnabas left for Derbe. 2069
	16:11	and the **next d** on to Neapolis. 2079
	17:11	and examined the Scriptures every **d** to see 2465
	17:17	in the marketplace **d** by day 2465+2848+4246
	17:17	in the marketplace **day by d** 2465+2848+4246
	17:31	For he has set a **d** when he will judge 2465
	19:15	[One] the evil spirit answered them, NIG
	20: 7	On the first **d** of the week we came together NIG
	20: 7	because he intended to leave the **next d**, 2069
	20:15	The **next d** we set sail from there 2079
	20:15	The **d after** that we crossed over to Samos, 2283
	20:15	and on the following **d** arrived at Miletus. NIG
	20:16	if possible, by the **d** of Pentecost. 2465
	20:18	the first **d** I came into the province of Asia. 2465
	20:31	of you night and **d** with tears. 2465
	21: 1	The **next d** we went to Rhodes and NIG
	21: 7	the brothers and stayed with them *for* a **d**. 2465
	21: 8	Leaving the **next d**, 2069
	21:18	The **next d** Paul and the rest of us went 2079
	21:26	The **next d** Paul took the men 2465
	22:30	The **next d**, since the commander wanted 2069
	23: 1	to God in all good conscience to this **d**." 2465
	23:32	The **next d** they let the cavalry go on 2069
	25: 6	and the **next d** he convened the court 2069
	25:17	the court the next **d** and ordered the man to NIG
	25:23	The **next d** Agrippa and Bernice came 2069
	26: 7	as they earnestly serve God **d** and night. 2465
	26:22	But I have had God's help to this very **d**, 2465
	27: 3	The **next d** we landed at Sidon; NIG
	27:18	from the storm that the next **d** they began NIG
	27:19	On the third **d**, they threw the ship's NIG
	28:13	The **next d** the south wind came up, 1651+2465+3552
	28:13	on the **following d** we reached Puteoli. 1308
	28:23	They arranged to meet Paul on a certain **d**, 2465
Ro	2: 5	against yourself for the **d** of God's wrath, 2465
	2:16	on the **d** when God will judge men's secrets 2465
	8:36	"For your sake we face death all **d** *long;* 2465
	10:21	"All **d** long I have held out my hands to 2465
	11: 8	so that they could not hear, to this **very d**." 2465+4958
	13:12	night is nearly over; the **d** is almost here. 2465
	14: 5	One man considers one **d** more sacred than another; 2465
	14: 5	another man considers every **d** alike. 2465
	14: 6	He who regards one **d** as special, 2465
1Co	1: 8	so that you will be blameless on the **d** 2465
	3:13	because the **D** will bring it to light. 2465
	5: 5	be destroyed and his spirit saved on the **d** of 2465
	10: 8	and *in* one **d** twenty-three thousand 2465
	15: 4	that he was raised *on* the third **d** according 2465
	15:31	I die every **d**— 2465
	16: 2	On the first **d** of every week, NIG
2Co	1:14	of us just as we will boast of you in the **d** of 2465
	3:14	for to **this d** the same veil remains when 2465+3836+4958
	3:15	Even to **this d** when Moses is read, 4958
	4:16	inwardly we are being renewed **d** by day, 2465
	4:16	inwardly we are being renewed day by **d**. 2465
	6: 2	and in the **d** of salvation I helped you." 2465
	6: 2	now is the **d** of salvation. 2465
	11:25	a night and a **d** in the open sea, 3819
Eph	4:30	with whom you were sealed for the **d** 2465
	6:13	so that when the **d** of evil comes, 2465
Php	1: 5	in the gospel from the first **d** until now, 2465
	1: 6	on to completion until the **d** of Christ Jesus. 2465
	1:10	be pure and blameless until the **d** of Christ, 2465
	2:16	that I may boast on the **d** of Christ that I did 2465
	3: 5	circumcised on the **eighth d**, of the people 3892
Col	1: 6	among you since the **d** you heard it 2465
	1: 9	since the **d** we heard about you, 2465
	2:16	a New Moon celebration or a **Sabbath d**. 4879
1Th	3:10	Night and **d** we pray most earnestly 2465
	5: 2	that the **d** of the Lord will come like a thief 2465
	5: 4	that this **d** should surprise you like a thief. 2465
	5: 5	of the light and sons of the **d**. 2465
	5: 5	But since we belong to the **d**, 2465
2Th	1:10	on the **d** he comes to be glorified 2465
	2: 2	that the **d** of the Lord has already come. 2465
	2: 3	for [that **d** will not come] until NIG
	3: 8	On the contrary, we worked night and **d**, 2465
1Ti	5: 5	in God and continues night and **d** to pray 2465
2Ti	1: 3	as night and **d** I constantly remember you 2465
	1:12	I have entrusted to him for that **d**. 2465
	1:18	from the Lord on that **d**! 2465
	4: 8	will award to me on that **d**— 2465
Heb	4: 4	about the seventh **d** in these words: NIG
	4: 4	"And on the seventh **d** God rested 2465

Heb	4: 7	Therefore God again set a certain **d**, 2465
	4: 8	not have spoken later about another **d**. 2465
	7:27	not need to offer sacrifices **d after day** 2465+2848
	7:27	not need to offer sacrifices **day after d** 2465+2848
	10:11	**D after day** every priest stands 2465+2848
	10:11	**Day after d** every priest stands 2465+2848
	10:25	all the more as you see the **D** approaching. 2465
Jas	5: 5	You have fattened yourselves in the **d** 2465
1Pe	2:12	and glorify God on the **d** he visits us. 2465
2Pe	1:19	until the **d** dawns and the morning star rises 2465
	2: 8	living among them **d after day**, 2465
	2: 8	living among them **day after d**, 2465
	2: 9	the unrighteous for the **d** of judgment, 2465
	3: 7	for the **d** of judgment and destruction 2465
	3: 8	With the Lord a **d** is like a thousand years, 2465
	3: 8	and a thousand years are like a **d**. 2465
	3:10	But the **d** of the Lord will come like a thief. 2465
	3:12	to the **d** of God and speed its coming. 2465
	3:12	**That d** will bring about the destruction of 4005S
1Jn	4:17	so that we will have confidence on the **d** 2465
Jude	1: 6	for judgment on the great **D**. 2465
Rev	1:10	On the Lord's **D** I was in the Spirit, 2465
	4: 8	**D** and night they never stop saying: 2465
	6:17	For the great **d** of their wrath has come, 2465
	7:15	before the throne of God and serve him **d** 2465
	8:12	A third of the **d** was without light, 2465
	9:15	and **d** and month and year were released 2465
	12:10	who accuses them before our God **d** 2465
	14:11	There is no rest **d** or night 2465
	16:14	to gather them for the battle *on* the great **d** 2465
	18: 8	in one **d** her plagues will overtake her: 2465
	20:10	They will be tormented **d** and night for ever 2465
	21:25	On no **d** will its gates ever be shut, 2465

DAY'S (9) [DAY]

Nu	11:31	as far as a **d** walk in any direction. 3427
1Ki	8:59	according to **each d** need, 3427+3427
	19: 4	he himself went a **d** journey into the desert. 3427
1Ch	16:37	according to **each d** requirements. 928+2257+3427+3427
2Ch	8:14	the priests according to **each d** requirement. 928+3427+3427
Est	9:13	to carry out this **d** edict tomorrow also, 3427
Ac	1:12	a **Sabbath d** walk from the city. 1584+2400+3847+4879
Rev	6: 6	saying, "A quart of wheat *for* a **d** wages, 1324
	6: 6	and three quarts of barley *for* a **d** wages, 1324

DAYBREAK (14) [DAY]

Ge	32:24	and a man wrestled with him till **d**. 8840
	32:26	Then the man said, "Let me go, for it is **d**." 8840
Ex	14:27	and at **d** the sea went back to its place. 1332+7155
Jos	6:15	they got up at **d** and marched around 2021+6590+8840
Jdg	19:26	At **d** the woman went back to the house 1332+2021+7155
1Sa	9:26	about **d** and Samuel called to Saul on 2021+6590+8840
	25:34	to Nabal would have been left alive by **d**." 240+1332+2021
	25:36	So she told him nothing until **d**. 240+1332+2021
2Sa	2:32	and arrived at Hebron *by* **d**. 239
	17:22	By **d**, no one was left who had not crossed 240+1332+2021
Ne	8: 3	from **d** till noon as he faced the square 240
Lk	4:42	At **d** Jesus went out to a solitary place. 1181+2002+2465
	22:66	At **d** the council of the elders of the people, 1181+2465
Ac	5:21	At **d** they entered the temple courts, 3986

DAYLIGHT (17) [DAY, LIGHT]

Nu	25: 4	kill them and expose them in **broad d**. 9087
Jdg	19:26	fell down at the door and lay there until **d**. 240
2Sa	12:11	and he will lie with your wives **in broad d**. 2021+2021+2296+4200+6524+9087
	12:12	I will do this thing **in broad d** 2021+5584+9087
2Ki	7: 9	If we wait until **d**, 240+1332+2021
Job	3: 9	for **d** in vain and not see the first rays 240
	24:14	When **d** is gone, the murderer rises up 240
Jer	8: 9	But, alas, the **d** is fading, 3427
Am	8: 9	noon and darken the earth in **broad d**. 240+3427
Mt	10:27	What I tell you in the dark, speak in the **d**; 5890
Lk	12: 3	in the dark will be heard in the **d**, 5890
Jn	11: 9	"Are there not twelve hours *of* **d**? 2465
Ac	16:35	When it was **d**, 2465
	20:11	After talking until **d**, he left. 879
	27:29	from the stern and prayed for **d**. 2465
	27:39	When **d** came, they did not recognize 2465
2Pe	2:13	of pleasure is to carouse in **broad d**. 2465

DAYS (619) [DAY]

Ge	1:14	as signs to mark seasons and **d** and years, 3427
	3:14	on your belly and you will eat dust all the **d** 3427
	3:17	you will eat of it all the **d** *of* your life. 3427
	6: 3	his **d** will be a hundred and twenty years." 3427
	6: 4	The Nephilim were on the earth in those **d** 3427
	7: 4	Seven **d** from now I will send rain on 3427
	7: 4	now I will send rain on the earth for forty **d** 3427
	7:10	And after the seven **d** the floodwaters came 3427
	7:12	on the earth forty **d** and forty nights, 3427
	7:17	For forty **d** the flood kept coming on 3427
	7:24	the earth for a hundred and fifty **d**. 3427
	8: 3	the hundred and fifty **d** the water had gone 3427

Ref	Text	Strong's
Ge 8: 6	After forty **d** Noah opened	3427
8:10	He waited seven more **d** and again sent out	3427
8:12	He waited seven more **d** and sent	3427
17:12	among you who is eight **d** old must	3427
21: 4	When his son Isaac was eight **d** old,	3427
24:55	"Let the girl remain with us ten **d** or so;	3427
27:41	"The **d** of mourning for my father are near;	3427
29:20	like only a few **d** to him because of his love	3427
31:23	he pursued Jacob for seven **d** and caught up	3427
34:25	Three **d** later, while all of them were still	3427
37:34	and mourned for his son many **d**.	3427
40:12	"The three branches are three **d**.	3427
40:13	Within three **d** Pharaoh will lift	3427
40:18	"The three baskets are three **d**.	3427
40:19	Within three **d** Pharaoh will lift off your head	3427
42:17	And he put them all in custody for three **d**.	3427
49: 1	to you in **d** to come.	3427
50: 3	taking a full forty **d**,	3427
50: 3	the Egyptians mourned for him seventy **d**.	3427
50: 4	When the **d** of mourning had passed,	3427
Ex 7:25	Seven **d** passed after the LORD struck	3427
10:22	and total darkness covered all Egypt *for* three **d**.	3427
10:23	or leave his place *for* three **d**.	3427
12:15	*For* seven **d** you are to eat bread made	3427
12:16	Do no work at all on **these d**,	2157S
12:19	*For* seven **d** no yeast is to be found	3427
13: 6	*For* seven **d** eat bread made without yeast,	3427
13: 7	*during* those seven **d**;	3427
13:14	"*In* **d to come**, when your son asks you,	4737
15:22	*For* three **d** they traveled in the desert	3427
16: 5	as much as they gather on the **other d**.	3427+3427
16:26	Six **d** you are to gather it,	3427
16:29	the sixth day he gives you bread *for* two **d**.	3427
20: 9	Six **d** you shall labor and do all your work,	3427
20:11	*in* six **d** the LORD made the heavens and	3427
22:30	with their mothers *for* seven **d**,	3427
23:12	Six **d** do your work,	3427
23:15	*for* seven **d** eat bread made without yeast,	3427
24:16	*For* six **d** the cloud covered the mountain,	3427
24:18	on the mountain forty **d** and forty nights.	3427
29:30	in the Holy Place is to wear them seven **d**.	3427
29:35	taking seven **d** to ordain them.	3427
29:37	*For* seven **d** make atonement for the altar	3427
31:15	*For* six **d**, work is to be done,	3427
31:17	*in* six **d** the LORD made the heavens and	3427
34:18	*For* seven **d** eat bread made without yeast,	3427
34:21	"Six **d** you shall labor,	3427
34:28	Moses was there with the LORD forty **d**	3427
35: 2	*For* six **d**, work is to be done, but	3427
Lev 8:33	to the Tent of Meeting *for* seven **d**,	3427
8:33	the **d** of your ordination are completed,	3427
8:33	for your ordination will last seven **d**.	3427
8:35	of Meeting day and night *for* seven **d**	3427
12: 2	be ceremonially unclean *for* seven **d**,	3427
12: 4	Then the woman must wait thirty-three **d** to	3427
12: 4	until the **d** of her purification are over.	3427
12: 5	Then she must wait sixty-six **d** to	3427
12: 6	" 'When the **d** of her purification for a son	3427
13: 4	the infected person in isolation *for* seven **d**.	3427
13: 5	to keep him in isolation another seven **d**.	3427
13:21	priest is to put him in isolation *for* seven **d**.	3427
13:26	priest is to put him in isolation *for* seven **d**.	3427
13:31	the infected person in isolation *for* seven **d**.	3427
13:33	to keep him in isolation another seven **d**.	3427
13:50	and isolate the affected article *for* seven **d**.	3427
13:54	Then he is to isolate it *for* another seven **d**.	3427
14: 8	he must stay outside his tent *for* seven **d**.	3427
14:38	of the house and close it up *for* seven **d**.	3427
15:13	he is to count off seven **d**	3427
15:19	of her monthly period will last seven **d**,	3427
15:24	he will be unclean *for* seven **d**,	3427
15:25	a discharge of blood *for* many **d** at	3427
15:25	just as in the **d** *of* her period.	3427
15:28	she must count off seven **d**,	3427
22:27	it is to remain with its mother *for* seven **d**.	3427
23: 3	" 'There are six **d** when you may work,	3427
23: 6	*for* seven **d** you must eat bread made	3427
23: 8	*For* seven **d** present an offering made to	3427
23:16	Count off fifty **d** up to the day after	3427
23:34	and it lasts *for* seven **d**.	3427
23:36	*For* seven **d** present offerings made to	3427
23:39	the festival to the LORD *for* seven **d**;	3427
23:40	before the LORD your God *for* seven **d**.	3427
23:41	to the LORD *for* seven **d** each year.	3427
23:42	Live in booths *for* seven **d**:	3427
Nu 6:12	The previous **d** do not count,	3427
9:20	over the tabernacle only a few **d**;	3427
9:22	over the tabernacle *for* two **d** or a month or	3427
10:33	of the LORD and traveled for three **d**.	3427
10:33	*during* those three **d** to find them a place	3427
11:19	or *two* **d**, or five, ten or twenty days,	3427
11:19	or two days, or five, ten or twenty **d**,	3427
12:14	not have been in disgrace *for* seven **d**?	3427
12:14	Confine her outside the camp *for* seven **d**;	3427
12:15	was confined outside the camp *for* seven **d**,	3427
13:25	of forty **d** they returned from exploring	3427
14:34	of the forty **d** you explored the land—	3427
19:11	of anyone will be unclean *for* seven **d**.	3427
19:12	on the third and seventh **d**,	3427
19:14	in it will be unclean *for* seven **d**,	3427
19:16	will be unclean *for* seven **d**.	3427
19:19	on the third and seventh **d**,	3427
20:29	of Israel mourned for him thirty **d**.	3427
24:14	to your people in **d** to come."	3427
28:17	*for* seven **d** eat bread made without yeast.	3427

Ref	Text	Strong's
Nu 28:24	*for* seven **d** as an aroma pleasing to	3427
29:12	a festival to the LORD *for* seven **d**.	3427
31:19	stay outside the camp seven **d**.	3427
31:19	and seventh **d** you must purify yourselves	3427
33: 8	and when they had traveled *for* three **d** in	3427
Dt 1: 2	(It takes eleven **d** to go from Horeb	3427
1:46	And so you stayed in Kadesh many **d**—	3427
4:30	then in later **d** you will return to	3427
4:32	Ask now about the former **d**,	3427
5:13	Six **d** you shall labor and do all your work,	3427
5:33	and prosper and prolong your **d** in the land	3427
9: 9	on the mountain forty **d** and forty nights;	3427
9:11	At the end of the forty **d** and forty nights,	3427
9:18	the LORD *for* forty **d** and forty nights;	3427
9:25	the LORD those forty **d** and forty nights	3427
10:10	Now I had stayed on the mountain forty **d**	3427
11:21	so that your **d** and the days	3427
11:21	and the **d** *of* your children may be many in	3427
11:21	as many as the **d** that the heavens are above	3427
16: 3	but *for* seven **d** eat unleavened bread,	3427
16: 3	the **d** *of* your life you may remember	3427
16: 4	in all your land *for* seven **d**.	3427
16: 8	*For* six **d** eat unleavened bread and on	3427
16:13	the Feast of Tabernacles *for* seven **d**	3427
16:15	*For* seven **d** celebrate the Feast to	3427
17:19	and he is to read it all the **d** *of* his life so	3427
28:33	but cruel oppression all your **d**.	3427
31:29	In **d** to come, disaster will fall upon you	3427
32: 7	Remember the **d** of old;	3427
33:25	and your strength will equal your **d**.	3427
34: 8	for Moses in the plains of Moab thirty **d**,	3427
Jos 1: 5	be able to stand up against you all the **d**	3427
1:11	Three **d** from now you will cross	3427
2:16	Hide yourselves there three **d**	3427
2:22	into the hills and stayed there three **d**,	3427
3: 2	After three **d** the officers went throughout	3427
4:14	and they revered him all the **d** *of* his life,	3427
6: 3	Do this *for* six **d**.	3427
6:14	They did this *for* six **d**.	3427
9:16	Three **d** after they made the treaty with	3427
Jdg 5: 6	"In the **d** of Shamgar son of Anath,	3427
5: 6	in the **d** of Jael, the roads were abandoned;	3427
11:40	of Israel go out *for* four **d** to commemorate	3427
14:12	the answer *within* the seven **d** of the feast,	3427
14:14	*For* three **d** they could not give the answer.	3427
14:17	She cried the whole seven **d** of the feast.	3427
15:20	for twenty years in the **d** *of* the Philistines.	3427
17: 6	In those **d** Israel had no king,	3427
18: 1	In those **d** Israel had no king.	3427
18: 1	And in those **d** the tribe of the Danites	3427
19: 1	In those **d** Israel had no king.	3427
19: 4	so he remained with him three **d**,	3427
20:27	(In those **d** the ark of the covenant	3427
21:25	In those **d** Israel had no king;	3427
Ru 1: 1	In the **d** *when* the judges ruled,	3427
1Sa 1:11	to the LORD *for* all the **d** *of* his life,	3427
3: 1	In those **d** the word of the LORD was rare;	3427
7:15	as judge over Israel all the **d** *of* his life.	3427
9:20	As for the donkeys you lost three **d** ago,	3427
10: 8	but you must wait seven **d** until I come	3427
11: 3	"Give us seven **d** so we can send	3427
13: 8	He waited seven **d**, the time set by Samuel;	3427
14:52	All the **d** of Saul there was bitter war with	3427
17:16	*For* forty **d** the Philistine came forward every morning	3427
18:29	he remained his enemy the rest of his **d**.	3427
25:10	from their masters these **d**.	3427
25:38	About ten **d** later,	3427
27: 1	of these **d** I will be destroyed by the hand	3427
28: 1	In those **d** the Philistines gathered their	3427
30:12	or drunk any water *for* three **d**	3427
30:13	when I became ill three **d** ago.	3427
31:13	and they fasted seven **d**.	3427
2Sa 1: 1	the Amalekites and stayed in Ziklag two **d**.	3427
7:12	When your **d** are over and you rest	3427
14: 2	a woman who has spent many **d** grieving	3427
16:23	in those **d** the advice Ahithophel gave was	3427
20: 4	of Judah to come to me *within* three **d**,	3427
21: 9	they were put to death during the first **d** *of*	3427
24: 8	at the end of nine months and twenty **d**.	3427
24:13	Or three **d** of plague in your land?	3427
1Ki 8:65	before the LORD our God for seven **d**,	3427
8:65	for seven days and seven **d** more,	3427
8:65	fourteen **d** in all.	3427
10:21	of little value in Solomon's **d**.	3427
11:34	have made him ruler all the **d** *of* his life	3427
12: 5	"Go away for three **d** and then come back	3427
12:12	Three **d** later Jeroboam and all	3427
12:12	"Come back to me in three **d**."	3427
15: 5	of the LORD's commands all the **d**	3427
16:15	Zimri reigned in Tirzah seven **d**.	3427
19: 8	he traveled forty **d** and forty nights	3427
20:29	*For* seven **d** they camped opposite each other,	3427
21:29	but I will bring it on his house in the **d**	3427
2Ki 2:17	who searched *for* three **d** but did	3427
3: 9	After a roundabout march of seven **d**,	3427
10:32	In those **d** the LORD began to reduce	3427
15:37	(In those **d** the LORD began	3427
19:25	In **d** of old I planned it;	3427
20: 1	In those **d** Hezekiah became ill and was at	3427
23:22	since the **d** *of* the judges who led Israel,	3427
23:22	throughout the **d** *of* the kings of Israel and	3427
1Ch 4:41	in the **d** *of* Hezekiah king of Judah.	3427
7:22	Ephraim mourned for them many **d**,	3427
10:12	and they fasted seven **d**.	3427
12:39	The men spent three **d** there with David,	3427

Ref	Text	Strong's
1Ch 17:11	When your **d** are over and you go to be	3427
21:12	or three **d** of the sword of the LORD—	3427
21:12	**d** of plague in the land,	NIH
29:15	Our **d** on earth are like a shadow,	3427
2Ch 7: 8	*for* seven **d**, and all Israel with him—	3427
7: 9	the dedication of the altar *for* seven **d** and	3427
7: 9	and the festival *for* seven **d** more.	3427
10: 5	"Come back to me in three **d**."	3427
10:12	Three **d** later Jeroboam and all	3427
10:12	"Come back to me in three **d**."	3427
14: 1	and in his **d** the country was at peace	3427
15: 5	In those **d** it was not safe to travel about,	6961
20:25	so much plunder that it took three **d**	3427
26: 5	He sought God during the **d** *of* Zechariah,	3427
29:17	For eight more **d** they consecrated	3427
30:21	the Feast of Unleavened Bread *for* seven **d**	3427
30:22	the seven **d** they ate their assigned portion	3427
30:23	to celebrate the festival seven more **d**;	3427
30:23	another seven **d** they celebrated joyfully.	3427
30:26	since the **d** *of* Solomon son of David king	3427
32:24	In those **d** Hezekiah became ill and was at	3427
32:26	upon them during the **d** *of* Hezekiah.	3427
35:17	the Feast of Unleavened Bread *for* seven **d**.	3427
35:18	in Israel since the **d** *of* the prophet Samuel;	3427
36: 9	in Jerusalem three months and ten **d**	3427
Ezr 4: 7	And in the **d** of Artaxerxes king of Persia,	3427
6:22	*For* seven **d** they celebrated with joy	3427
8:15	and we camped there three **d**.	3427
8:32	where we rested three **d**.	3427
9: 7	From the **d** of our forefathers until now,	3427
10: 8	within three **d** would forfeit all his property,	3427
10: 9	Within the three **d**,	3427
Ne 1: 4	*For some* **d** I mourned and fasted	3427
2:11	and after staying there three **d**	3427
5:18	and every ten **d** an abundant supply of wine	3427
6:15	on the twenty-fifth of Elul, in fifty-two **d**.	3427
6:17	in those **d** the nobles	3427
8:17	the **d** *of* Joshua son of Nun until that day,	3427
8:18	They celebrated the feast *for* seven **d**,	3427
9:32	and all your people, from the **d** *of* the kings	3427
12: 7	of the priests and their associates in the **d**	3427
12:12	In the **d** *of* Joiakim.	3427
12:22	The family heads of the Levites in the **d**	3427
12:26	They served in the **d** *of* Joiakim son	3427
12:26	and in the **d** *of* Nehemiah the governor and	3427
12:46	For long ago, in the **d** *of* David and Asaph,	3427
12:47	in the **d** *of* Zerubbabel and of Nehemiah,	3427
13:15	In those **d** I saw men	3427
13:23	in those **d** I saw men	3427
Est 1: 4	a full 180 **d** he displayed the vast wealth	3427
1: 5	When these **d** were over,	3427
1: 5	the king gave a banquet, lasting seven **d**,	3427
4:11	But thirty **d** have passed since I was called	3427
4:16	Do not eat or drink for three **d**,	3427
9:21	the fourteenth and fifteenth **d** of the month	3427
9:22	to observe **the d** as days of feasting and joy	4392S
9:22	as **d** *of* feasting and joy and giving presents	3427
9:26	(Therefore these **d** were called Purim,	3427
9:27	without fail observe these two **d** every year,	3427
9:28	These **d** should be remembered	3427
9:28	And these **d** of Purim should never cease to	3427
9:31	to establish these **d** of Purim	3427
Job 2:13	with him *for* seven **d** and seven nights.	3427
3: 6	the **d** *of* the year nor be entered in any of	3427
3: 8	May those who curse **d** curse that day,	3427
7: 1	Are not his **d** like those of a hired man?	3427
7: 6	"My **d** are swifter than a weaver's shuttle,	3427
7:16	Let me alone; my **d** have no meaning.	3427
8: 9	and our **d** on earth are but a shadow.	3427
9:25	"My **d** are swifter than a runner;	3427
10: 5	Are your **d** like those of a mortal	3427
10:20	Are not my few **d** almost over?	3427
14: 1	"Man born of woman is of few **d** and full	3427
14: 5	Man's **d** are determined;	3427
14:14	All the **d** of my hard service I will wait	3427
15:20	All his **d** the wicked man suffers torment,	3427
17: 1	My spirit is broken, my **d** are cut short,	3427
17:11	My **d** have passed, my plans are shattered,	3427
24: 1	in vain for such **d**?	3427
29: 2	for the **d** when God watched over me,	3427
29: 4	Oh, for the **d** when I was in my prime,	3427
29:18	my **d** as numerous as the grains of sand.	3427
30:16	my life ebbs away; **d** *of* suffering grip me.	3427
30:27	**d** *of* suffering confront me.	3427
33:25	it is restored as in the **d** *of* his youth.	3427
36:11	of their **d** in prosperity and their years	3427
38:23	for **d** *of* war and battle?	3427
Ps 21: 4	length of **d**, for ever and ever.	3427
23: 6	and love will follow me all the **d**	4328
25:13	He *will* spend *his* **d** in prosperity,	3427
27: 4	in the house of the LORD all the **d**	3427
34:12	and desires to see *many* good **d**,	3427
37:18	The **d** of the blameless are known to	3427
37:19	in **d** *of* famine they will enjoy plenty.	3427
39: 4	my life's end and the number of my **d**;	3427
39: 5	You have made my **d** a mere handbreadth;	3427
44: 1	our fathers have told us what you did in their **d**,	3427
44: 1	in their days, in **d** long ago.	3427
49: 5	Why should I fear when evil **d** come,	3427
55:23	not live out half their **d**.	3427
61: 6	**d** of the king's *life*,	3427
72: 7	In his **d** the righteous will flourish,	3427
77: 5	I thought about the former **d**,	3427
78:33	So he ended their **d** in futility	3427
89:45	You have cut short the **d** *of* his youth;	3427
90: 9	All our **d** pass away under your wrath;	3427

Ref	Text	Code
Ps 90:10	The **length of** our d is seventy years—	3427+9102
90:12	Teach us to number our d aright,	3427
90:14	we may sing for joy and be glad all our d.	3427
90:15	for as many d as you have afflicted us,	3427
93: 5	holiness adorns your house for endless d,	3427
94:13	you grant him relief from d of trouble,	3427
102: 3	For my d vanish like smoke;	3427
102:11	My d are like the evening shadow;	3427
102:23	he cut short my d.	3427
102:24	O my God, in the midst of my d;	3427
103:15	As for man, his d are like grass,	3427
109: 8	May his d be few;	3427
128: 5	the LORD bless you from Zion all the d	3427
139:16	All the d ordained for me were written	3427
143: 5	I remember the d of long ago;	3427
144: 4	his d are like a fleeting shadow.	3427
Pr 9:11	For through me your d will be many,	3427
15:15	All the d of the oppressed are wretched,	3427
31:12	not harm, all the d of her life.	3427
31:25	she can laugh at the d to come.	3427
Ecc 2: 3	to do under heaven during the few d	3427
2:16	in d to come both will be forgotten.	3427
2:23	All his d his work is pain and grief;	3427
5:17	All his d he eats in darkness,	3427
5:18	the few d of life God has given him—	3427
5:20	He seldom reflects on the d of his life,	3427
6:12	during the few and meaningless d he passes	3427
7:10	"Why were the old d better than these?"	3427
8:13	and their d will not lengthen like a shadow.	3427
8:15	the d of the life God has given him under	3427
9: 9	all the d of this meaningless life	3427
9: 9	all your meaningless d.	3427
11: 1	for after many d you will find it again.	3427
11: 8	But let him remember the d of darkness,	3427
11: 9	and let your heart give you joy in the d	3427
12: 1	in the d of your youth, before the days	3427
12: 1	before the d of trouble come and	3427
Isa 1:26	I will restore your judges as in d of old,	8037
2: 2	In the last d the mountain of the LORD's	3427
13:22	and her d will not be prolonged.	3427
24:22	up in prison and be punished after many d.	3427
27: 6	In d to come Jacob will take root,	NIH
30: 8	d to come it may be an everlasting witness.	3427
30:26	like the light of seven full d,	3427
37:26	In d of old I planned it;	3427
38: 1	In those d Hezekiah became ill and was at	3427
38:20	with stringed instruments all the d	3427
43:13	Yes, and from ancient d I am he.	3427
51: 9	awake, as in d gone by,	3427
53:10	he will see his offspring and prolong his d,	3427
54: 9	"To me this is like the d of Noah,	3427
60:20	and your d of sorrow will end.	3427
63: 9	he lifted them up and carried them all the d	3427
63:11	Then his people recalled the d of old,	3427
63:11	the d of Moses and his people—	NIH
65:20	be it an infant who lives but a few d, or	3427
65:22	For as the d of a tree,	3427
65:22	so will be the d of my people;	3427
Jer 2:32	Yet my people have forgotten me, d	3427
3:16	In those d, when your numbers have increased greatly in the land,"	3427
3:18	the house of Judah will join	3427
5:18	"Yet even in those d," declares the LORD,	3427
7:32	So beware, the d are coming,	3427
9:25	the d are coming," declares the LORD,	3427
13: 6	Many d later the LORD said to me,	3427
16: 9	Before your eyes and in your d I will bring	3427
16:14	"However, the d are coming,"	3427
19: 6	So beware, the d are coming,	3427
20:18	to see trouble and sorrow and to end my d	3427
23: 5	"The d are coming," declares the LORD,	3427
23: 6	In his d Judah will be saved	3427
23: 7	"So then, the d are coming,"	3427
23:20	In d to come you will understand it clearly.	3427
26:18	"Micah of Moresheth prophesied in the d	3427
30: 3	The d are coming," declares the LORD,	3427
30:20	Their children will be as in d of old,	7710
30:24	In d to come you will understand this.	3427
31:27	"The d are coming," declares the LORD,	3427
31:29	"In those d people will no longer say,	3427
31:38	"The d are coming," declares the LORD,	3427
33:14	" 'The d are coming,' declares the LORD,	3427
33:15	" 'In those d and at that time I will make	3427
33:16	In those d Judah will be saved	3427
42: 7	Ten d later the word of the LORD came	3427
48:12	"But d are coming," declares the LORD,	3427
48:47	the fortunes of Moab in d to come,"	3427
49: 2	But the d are coming,"	3427
49:39	"Yet I will restore the fortunes of Elam in d	3427
50: 4	"In those d, at that time,"	3427
50:20	In those d, at that time,"	3427
51:52	"But d are coming," declares the LORD,	3427
La 1: 7	In the d of her affliction	3427
1: 7	the treasures that were hers in d of old,	3427
4:18	Our end was near, our d were numbered,	3427
5:21	renew our d as of old	3427
Eze 3:15	I sat among them for seven d—	3427
3:16	of seven d the word of the LORD came	3427
4: 4	to bear their sin for the number of d you lie	3427
4: 5	I have assigned you the same number of d	3427
4: 5	for 390 d you will bear the sin of the house	3427
4: 6	I have assigned you 40 d,	3427
4: 8	until you have finished the d of your siege.	3427
5: 2	You are to eat it during the 390 d you lie	3427
5: 2	When the d of your siege come to an end,	3427
12:22	'The d go by and every vision comes	3427
12:23	'The d are near when every vision will	3427
Eze 12:25	For in your d, you rebellious house,	3427
16:22	not remember the d of your youth,	3427
16:43	" 'Because you did not remember the d	3427
16:60	the covenant I made with you in the d	3427
22: 4	You have brought your d to a close,	3427
23:19	and more promiscuous as she recalled the d	3427
38: 8	After many d you will be called to arms.	3427
38:16	In d to come, O Gog,	3427
38:17	of in former d by my servants the prophets	3427
43:25	"For seven d you are to provide	3427
43:26	For seven d they are to make atonement for	3427
43:27	At the end of these d,	3427
44:26	After he is cleansed, he must wait seven d.	3427
45:21	a feast lasting seven d,	3427
45:23	During the seven d of the Feast he is	3427
45:25	" 'During the seven d of the Feast,	3427
46: 1	to be shut on the six working d,	3427
Da 1:12	"Please test your servants for ten d:	3427
1:14	he agreed to this and tested them for ten d.	3427
1:15	the end of the ten d they looked healthier	3427
2:28	what will happen in d to come.	10317
5:26	the d of your reign and brought it to an end.	NIH
6: 7	to any god or man during the next thirty d,	10317
6:12	during the next thirty d anyone who prays	10317
7: 9	and the Ancient of D took his seat.	10317
7:13	of D and was led into his presence.	10317
7:22	of D came and pronounced judgment	10317
8:27	was exhausted and lay ill for several d.	3427
10:13	Persian kingdom resisted me twenty-one d.	3427
11: 6	In those d she will be handed over,	6961
12:11	there will be 1,290 d.	3427
12:12	for and reaches the end of the 1,335 d.	3427
12:13	and then at the end of the d you will rise	3427
Hos 2:11	her **Sabbath** d—all her appointed feasts.	8701
2:13	for the d she burned incense to the Baals;	3427
2:15	There she will sing as in the d of her youth,	3427
3: 3	"You are to live with me many d;	3427
3: 4	the Israelites will live many d without king	3427
3: 5	and to his blessings in the last d.	3427
6: 2	After two d he will revive us;	3427
9: 5	on the festival of the LORD?	3427
9: 7	The d of punishment are coming,	3427
9: 7	the d of reckoning are at hand.	3427
9: 9	as in the d of Gibeah.	3427
10: 9	"Since the d of Gibeah, you have sinned,	3427
12: 9	as in the d of your appointed feasts.	3427
Joel 1: 2	in your d or in the days of your forefathers?	3427
1: 2	or in the d of your forefathers?	3427
2:29	I will pour out my Spirit in those d.	3427
3: 1	"In those d and at that time,	3427
Am 8:11	"The d are coming," declares	3427
9:13	"The d are coming," declares the LORD,	3427
Jnh 1:17	inside the fish three d and three nights.	3427
3: 3	a visit required three d.	3427
3: 4	"Forty more d and Nineveh will	3427
Mic 4: 1	In the last d the mountain of	3427
7:14	In Bashan and Gilead as in d long ago.	3427
7:15	"As in the d when you came out of Egypt,	3427
7:20	on oath to our fathers in d long ago.	3427
Hab 1: 5	to do something in your d that you would	3427
Zec 8:23	"In those d ten men from all languages	3427
14: 5	as you fled from the earthquake in the d	3427
Mal 3: 4	as in d gone by, as in former years.	3427
Mt 3: 1	In those d John the Baptist came,	2465
4: 2	After fasting forty d and forty nights,	2465
11:12	From the d of John the Baptist until now,	2465
12:40	For as Jonah was three d and three nights in	2465
12:40	of Man will be three d and three nights in	2465
15:32	with me three d and have nothing to eat.	2465
17: 1	After six d Jesus took with him Peter,	2465
23:30	'If we had lived in the d of our forefathers,	2465
24:19	How dreadful it will be in those d	2465
24:22	If those d had not been cut short,	2465
24:22	sake of the elect those d will be shortened.	2465
24:29	of those d " 'the sun will be darkened, and	2465
24:37	As it was in the d of Noah,	2465
24:38	For in the d before the flood,	2465
26: 2	the Passover is two d away—	2465
26:61	of God and rebuild it in three d.' "	2465
27:40	to destroy the temple and build it in three d,	2465
27:63	'After three d I will rise again.'	2465
Mk 1:13	and he was in the desert forty d,	2465
2: 1	A few d later, when Jesus again	1328+2465
2:26	**In the** d of Abiathar the high priest,	2093
8: 1	those d another large crowd gathered.	2465
8: 2	with me three d and have nothing to eat.	2465
8:31	be killed and after three d rise again.	2465
9: 2	After six d Jesus took Peter,	2465
9:31	and after three d he will rise."	2465
10:34	Three d later he will rise."	2465
13:17	How dreadful it will be in those d	2465
13:19	be of distress unequaled from	2465
13:20	If the Lord had not cut short those d,	2465
13:24	"But in those d, following that distress,	2465
14: 1	Feast of Unleavened Bread were only two d away,	2465
14:58	and in three d will build another,	2465
15:29	to destroy the temple and build it in three d,	2465
Lk 1:25	"In these d he has shown his favor	2465
1:75	and righteousness before him all our d.	2465
2: 1	In those d Caesar Augustus issued a decree	2465
2:46	After three d they found him in	2465
4: 2	for forty d he was tempted by the devil.	2465
4: 2	He ate nothing during those d,	2465
5:35	in those d they will fast."	2465
6:12	of those d Jesus went out to a mountainside	2465
9:28	About eight d after Jesus said this,	2465
Lk 13:14	"There are six d for work.	2465
13:14	So come and be healed on those d,	NIG
17:22	when you will long to see one of the d of	2465
17:26	"Just as it was in the d of Noah,	2465
17:26	so also will it be in the d of the Son of Man.	2465
17:28	"It was the same in the d of Lot.	2465
19:43	The d will come upon you	2465
21:23	How dreadful it will be in those d	2465
24:18	that have happened there in these d?"	2465
Jn 2:12	There they stayed for a few d.	2465
2:19	and I will raise it again in three d."	2465
2:20	and you are going to raise it in three d?"	2465
4:40	and he stayed two d.	2465
4:43	After the two d he left for Galilee.	2465
10:40	John had been baptizing in the early d.	4754
11: 6	he stayed where he was two more d.	2465
11:17	in the tomb for four d.	2465
11:39	for he has been there four d."	5479
12: 1	Six d before the Passover,	2465
Ac 1: 3	to them over a period of forty d and spoke	2465
1: 5	but in a few d you will be baptized with	2465
1:15	In those d Peter stood up among	2465
2:17	" 'In the last d, I will pour out my Spirit	2465
2:18	I will pour out my Spirit in those d,	2465
3:24	have foretold these d.	2465
5:37	the d of the census and led a band of people	2465
6: 1	In those d when the number	2465
7: 8	and circumcised him eight d after his birth.	2465
9: 9	For three d he was blind,	2465
9:19	Saul spent several d with the disciples	2465
9:23	After many d had gone by,	2465
10:30	"Four d ago I was in my house praying	2465
10:48	to stay with them for a few d.	2465
13:31	and for many d he was seen	2465
13:41	for I am going to do something in your d	2465
16:12	And we stayed there several d.	2465
16:18	She kept this up for many d.	2465
17: 2	on three **Sabbath** d he reasoned with them	4879
20: 6	and five d later joined the others at Troas,	2465
20: 6	where we stayed seven d.	2465
21: 4	we stayed with them seven d.	2465
21:10	After we had been there a number of d,	2465
21:26	when the d of purification would end and	2465
21:27	When the seven d were nearly over,	2465
24: 1	Five d later the high priest Ananias went	2465
24:11	that no more than twelve d ago I went up	2465
24:24	Several d later Felix came	2465
25: 1	Three d after arriving in the province,	2465
25: 6	After spending eight or ten d with them,	2465
25:13	A few d later King Agrippa	2465
25:14	Since they were spending many d there,	2465
27: 7	We made slow headway for many d	2465
27:20	for many d and the storm continued raging,	2465
27:33	"For the last fourteen d," he said,	4958
28: 7	and for three d entertained us hospitably.	2465
28:12	in at Syracuse and stayed there three d.	2465
28:17	Three d later he called together the leaders	2465
Gal 1:18	with Peter and stayed with him fifteen d.	2465
4:10	You are observing special d and months	2465
Eph 5:16	because the d are evil.	2465
Php 4:15	in the early d of your acquaintance with	NIG
2Ti 3: 1	There will be terrible times in the last d.	2465
Heb 1: 2	but in these last d he has spoken to us	2465
5: 7	During the d of Jesus' life on earth,	2465
7: 3	without beginning of d or end of life,	2465
10:32	Remember those earlier d	2465
11:30	around them for seven d.	2465
Jas 5: 3	You have hoarded wealth in the last d.	NIG
1Pe 3:10	and see good d must keep his tongue	2465
3:20	the d of Noah while the ark was being built.	2465
2Pe 3: 3	that in the last d scoffers will come,	2465
Rev 2:10	and you will suffer persecution for ten d.	2465
2:13	even in the d of Antipas,	2465
9: 6	During those d men will seek death,	2465
10: 7	in the d when the seventh angel is about	2465
11: 3	and they will prophesy for 1,260 d,	2465
11: 9	and a half d men from every people,	2465
11:11	after the three and a half d a breath of life	2465
12: 6	be taken care of for 1,260 d.	2465

DAYSMAN (KJV) See ARBITRATE

DAYSPRING (KJV) See DAWN, RISING SUN

DAYTIME (7) [DAY]

Ref	Text	Code
Ge 31:40	The heat consumed me in the d and	3427
Jdg 6:27	he did it at night rather than in the d.	3429
Job 5:14	Darkness comes upon them in the d;	3429
Eze 12: 4	pack your belongings for exile and in the d,	3429
12: 4	**During the** d, while they watch,	3429
Zec 14: 7	without d or nighttime—	3427
Ro 13:13	Let us behave decently, as in the d,	2465

DAZZLING (2)

Ref	Text	Code
Da 2:31	an enormous, d statue,	10228
Mk 9: 3	His clothes became d white,	5118

DEACON (1) [DEACONS]

Ref	Text	Code
1Ti 3:12	A d must be the husband of but one wife	1356

DEACONS (3) [DEACON]

Ref	Text	Code
Php 1: 1	together with the overseers and d:	1356

1Ti	3: 8	**D,** likewise, are to be men worthy	1356
	3:10	let them **serve as d.**	1354

DEAD (314) [DIE]

Ge	20: 3	"You *are* as good as d because of	4637
	23: 3	Then Abraham rose from beside his d **wife**	4637
	23: 4	for a burial site here so I can bury my d."	4637
	23: 6	Bury your d in the choicest of our tombs.	4637
	23: 6	for burying your d."	4637
	23: 8	"If you are willing to let me bury my d,	4637
	23:11	Bury your d."	4637
	23:13	from me so I can bury my d there."	4637
	23:15	Bury your d."	4637
	34:27	of Jacob came upon the d **bodies** and looted	2728
	42:38	his brother *is* d and he is the only one left.	4637
	44:20	His brother *is* d,	4637
	50:15	that their father *was* d,	4637
Ex	4:19	all the men who wanted to kill you *are* d."	4637
	12:30	there was not a house without *someone* d.	4637
	14:30	and Israel saw the Egyptians *lying* d on	4637
	21:34	and the d *animal* will be his.	4637
	21:35	both the money and the d *animal* equally.	4637
	21:36	and the d *animal* will be his.	4637
Lev	7:24	The fat of an *animal* found d or torn	5577
	11:31	when they *are* d will be unclean	4637
	14:51	the blood of the d bird and the fresh water,	8821
	17:15	who eats **anything found** d or torn	5577
	19:28	for the d or put tattoo marks on yourselves.	5883
	21:11	not enter a place where there is a d body.	4637
	22: 8	He must not eat **anything found** d or torn	5577
	26:30	and pile your d **bodies** on the lifeless forms	7007
Nu	3: 4	**fell** d before the LORD when they made	4637
	5: 2	because of a d **body.**	5883
	6: 6	he must not go near a d **body.**	5883
	6:11	by being in the presence of the d **body.**	5883
	9: 6	on account of a d **body,**	5883
	9: 7	because of a d **body,**	5883
	9:10	of a d **body** or are away on a journey,	5883
	16:48	He stood between the living and the d,	4637
	19:11	the d **body** of anyone will be unclean	4637
	19:13	Whoever touches the d **body** of anyone	4637
	20: 3	when our brothers **fell** d before	1588
Dt	14: 1	or shave the front of your heads for the d,	4637
	14:21	Do not eat anything you find **already** d.	5577
	18:11	a medium or spiritist or who consults the d.	4637
	25: 6	of the d brother so that his name will not	4637
	26:14	nor have I offered any of it to the d.	4637
Jos	1: 2	"Moses my servant *is* d.	4637
Jdg	3:25	they saw their lord fallen to the floor, d.	4637
	4:22	through his temple—d.	4637
	5:27	where he sank, there he fell—d.	8720
	9:55	the Israelites saw that Abimelech *was* d,	4637
Ru	1: 8	as you have shown to your d and to me.	4637
	2:20	to the living and the d."	4637
	4: 5	you acquire the d *man's* widow,	4637
	4: 5	in order to maintain the name of the d	4637
	4:10	in order to maintain the name of the d	4637
1Sa	4:17	Hophni and Phinehas, *are* d,	4637
	4:19	and her husband *were* d,	4637
	17:51	the Philistines saw that their hero *was* d,	4637
	17:52	Their d were strewn along	2728
	24:14	A d dog? A flea?	4637
	25:39	When David heard that Nabal *was* d,	4637
	28: 3	Now Samuel *was* d,	4637
	31: 5	the armor-bearer saw that Saul *was* d,	4637
	31: 8	when the Philistines came to strip the d,	2728
2Sa	1: 4	And Saul and his son Jonathan *are* d."	4637
	1: 5	that Saul and his son Jonathan *are* d?"	4637
	2: 7	for Saul your master *is* d,	4637
	4:10	when a man told me, 'Saul *is* d,'	4637
	9: 8	that you should notice a d dog like me?"	4637
	11:21	'Also, your servant Uriah the Hittite *is* d.' "	4637
	11:24	your servant Uriah the Hittite *is* d."	4637
	11:26	Uriah's wife heard that her husband *was* d,	4637
	12:18	to tell him that the child *was* d,	4637
	12:18	How can we tell him the child *is* d?	4637
	12:19	and he realized the child *was* d.	4637
	12:19	*"Is* the child d?"	4637
	12:19	"Yes," they replied, *"he is* d."	4637
	12:21	but now that the child *is* d,	4637
	12:23	But now that *he is* d, why should I fast?	4637
	13:32	only Amnon *is* d.	4637
	13:33	the report that all the king's sons *are* d.	4637
	13:33	Only Amnon *is* d."	4637
	14: 2	like a woman who has spent many days grieving for the d.	4637
	14: 5	my husband *is* d.	4637
	16: 9	"Why should this d dog curse my lord	4637
	18:20	because the king's son *is* d."	4637
	19: 6	and all of us *were* d.	4637
	23:10	but only to **strip the** d.	7320
1Ki	3:20	She put him by her breast and put her d son	4637
	3:21	and *he was* d!	4637
	3:22	the d *one* is yours."	4637
	3:22	The d *one* is yours; the living one is mine."	4637
	3:23	'My son is alive and your son *is* d,'	4637
	3:23	Your son *is* d and mine is alive.' "	4637
	11:15	who had gone up to bury the d,	2728
	11:21	the commander of the army *was* also d,	4637
	21:14	"Naboth has been stoned and *is* d."	4637
	21:15	He is no longer alive, but d."	4637
	21:16	When Ahab heard that Naboth *was* d,	4637
2Ki	4: 1	"Your servant my husband *is* d,	4637
	4:32	there was the boy lying d on his couch.	4637
	8: 5	the king how Elisha had restored the d	4637
	11: 1	of Ahaziah saw that her son *was* d,	4637

2Ki	19:35	there were all the d bodies!	4637
1Ch	10: 5	the armor-bearer saw that Saul *was* d,	4637
	10: 8	when the Philistines came to strip the d,	2728
	21:14	seventy thousand men of Israel **fell** d.	5877
2Ch	20:24	they saw only d **bodies** lying on the ground;	7007
	22:10	of Ahaziah saw that her son *was* d,	4637
Job	1:19	It collapsed on them and *they are* d,	4637
	26: 5	"The d are in deep anguish,	8327
Ps	6: 5	No one remembers you when he is d.	4638
	31:12	I am forgotten by them as though I *were* d;	4637
	79: 2	the d **bodies** *of* your servants as food to	5577
	79: 3	and there is no one to bury the d.	NIH
	88: 5	I am set apart with the d,	4637
	88:10	Do you show your wonders to the d?	4637
	88:10	Do *those who are* d rise up and praise you?	8327
	110: 6	heaping up the d and crushing the rulers of	1581
	115:17	It is not the d who praise the LORD,	4637
	143: 3	in darkness like *those* long d.	4637
Pr	2:18	and her paths to the **spirits of the** d.	8327
	9:18	But little do they know that the d are there,	8327
	21:16	to rest in the company of the d.	8327
Ecc	4: 2	And I declared that the d,	4637
	9: 3	and afterward they join the d.	4637
	9: 4	even a live dog is better off than a d lion!	4637
	9: 5	but the d know nothing;	4637
	10: 1	As d flies give perfume a bad smell,	4638
Isa	5:25	the d **bodies** are like refuse in the streets.	5577
	8:19	Why consult the d on behalf of the living?	4637
	19: 3	the idols and the **spirits of the** d,	356
	26:14	*They are now* d, they live no more;	4637
	26:19	But your d will live; their bodies will rise.	4637
	26:19	the earth will give birth to her d.	8327
	34: 3	their d **bodies** will send up a stench;	7007
	37:36	there were all the d **bodies!**	4637
	59:10	among the strong, we *are* like the d.	4637
	66:24	upon the d **bodies** *of* those who rebelled	7007
Jer	7:32	for they will bury the d in Topheth	NIH
	9:22	" 'The d **bodies** *of* men will lie like refuse	5577
	16: 4	and their d **bodies** will become food for	5577
	16: 7	to comfort those who mourn for the d—	4637
	19:11	They will bury the d in Topheth	NIH
	22:10	not weep for the d [king] or mourn his loss;	4637
	31:40	where d **bodies** and ashes are thrown,	7007
	33: 5	'They will be filled with the d **bodies** of	7007
	34:20	Their d **bodies** will become food for	5577
	41: 9	of Nethaniah filled it with the d.	2728
La	3: 6	in darkness like *those* long d.	4637
Eze	4:14	now I have never eaten **anything found** d	5577
	6: 5	I will lay the d **bodies** of the Israelites	7007
	11: 6	in this city and filled its streets with the d.	2728
	24:17	Groan quietly; do not mourn for the d.	4637
	44:25	not defile himself by going near a d person;	4637
	44:25	if the d person was his father or mother,	NIH
	44:31	**found** d or torn by wild animals."	5577
Am	1: 8	till the last of the Philistines is d,"	6
Na	3: 3	Many casualties, piles of d,	7007
Hag	2:13	with a d **body** touches one of these things,	5883
Mt	2:20	to take the child's life are d."	2569
	8:22	and let the d bury their own dead."	3738
	8:22	and let the dead bury their own d."	3738
	9:24	The girl *is* not d but asleep."	633
	10: 8	Heal the sick, raise the d,	3738
	11: 5	the deaf hear, the d are raised,	3738
	14: 2	he has risen from the d!	3738
	17: 9	the Son of Man has been raised from the d."	3738
	22:31	But about the resurrection of the d—	3738
	22:32	not the God *of* the d but of the living."	3738
	23:27	but on the inside are full of d men's bones	3738
	27:64	that he has been raised from the d.	3738
	28: 4	that they shook and became like d men.	3738
	28: 7	'He has risen from the d and is going ahead	3738
Mk	5:35	"Your daughter *is* d," they said.	633
	5:39	The child *is* not d but asleep."	633
	6:14	the Baptist has been raised from the d.	3738
	6:16	has been raised from the d!"	3738
	9: 9	until the Son of Man had risen from the d.	3738
	9:10	discussing what "rising from the d" meant.	3738
	9:26	like a corpse that many said, *"He's* d."	633
	12:25	When the d rise, they will neither marry nor	3738
	12:26	Now about the d rising—	3738
	12:27	He is not the God of the d,	3738
	15:44	to hear that *he was* already d.	2569
Lk	7:12	a d *person* was being carried out—	2569
	7:15	The d *man* sat up and began to talk,	3738
	7:22	the deaf hear, the d are raised,	3738
	8:49	"Your daughter *is* d," he said.	2569
	8:52	*"She is* not d but asleep."	633
	8:53	knowing that *she was* d.	633
	9: 7	that John had been raised from the d,	3738
	9:60	"Let the d bury their own dead,"	3738
	9:60	"Let the dead bury their own d,	3738
	10:30	leaving him **half** d.	2467
	15:24	this son of mine was d and is alive again;	3738
	15:32	because this brother of yours was d	3738
	16:30	'but if someone from the d goes to them,	3738
	16:31	even if someone rises from the d.' "	3738
	17:37	He replied, "Where there is a d body,	5393
	20:35	from the d will neither marry nor be given	3738
	20:37	even Moses showed that the d rise,	3738
	20:38	He is not the God of the d,	3738
	24: 5	for the living among the d?	3738
	24:46	The Christ will suffer and rise from the d	3738
Jn	2:22	After he was raised from the d,	3738
	5:21	the Father raises the d and gives them life,	3738
	5:25	now come when the d will hear the voice of	3738
	11:14	then he told them plainly, "Lazarus *is* d,	633
	11:39	Lord," said Martha, the sister *of the* d man,	5462

Jn	11:44	The d **man** came out,	2569
	12: 1	whom Jesus had raised from the d.	3738
	12: 9	whom he had raised from the d.	3738
	12:17	from the d continued to spread the word.	3738
	19:33	to Jesus and found that he was already d,	2569
	20: 9	that Jesus had to rise from the d.)	3738
	21:14	after he was raised from the d.	3738
Ac	2:24	**raised** him **from the** d,	482
	3:15	but God raised him from the d.	3738
	4: 2	in Jesus the resurrection of the d.	3738
	4:10	but whom God raised from the d,	3738
	5:10	the young men came in and, finding her d,	3738
	5:30	**raised Jesus from the—**	1586
	9:40	Turning toward the d **woman,** he said,	5393
	10:40	**raised** him **from the** d	1586
	10:41	with him after he rose from the d.	3738
	10:42	as judge *of* the living and the d.	3738
	13:30	But God raised him from the d.	3738
	13:34	The fact that God raised him from the d,	3738
	13:37	But the one whom God **raised from the** d	1586
	14:19	thinking he was d.	2569
	17: 3	the Christ had to suffer and rise from the d.	3738
	17:31	this to all men by raising him from the d."	3738
	17:32	about the resurrection of the d,	3738
	20: 9	from the third story and was picked up d.	3738
	23: 6	of my hope in the resurrection *of the* d."	3738
	24:21	the d that I am on trial before you today.' "	3738
	25:19	about a d **man** named Jesus who Paul claimed was alive.	2569
	26: 8	that God raises the d?	3738
	26:23	as the first to rise *from the* d,	3738
	28: 6	to swell up or suddenly fall d,	3738
Ro	1: 4	of God by his resurrection *from the* d:	3738
	4:17	*to the* d and calls things that are not as	3738
	4:19	fact that his body was **as good as** d—	2453+3739
	4:19	and that Sarah's womb was also d.	3740
	4:24	him who raised our Lord from the d.	3738
	6: 4	just as Christ was raised from the d through	3738
	6: 9	that since Christ was raised from the d,	3738
	6:11	count yourselves d to sin but alive to God	3738
	7: 4	to him who was raised from the d,	3738
	7: 8	For apart from law, sin is d.	3738
	8:10	your body is d because of sin,	3738
	8:11	of him who raised Jesus from the d is living	3738
	8:11	he who raised Christ from the d will	3738
	10: 7	(that is, to bring Christ up from the d).	3738
	10: 9	that God raised him from the d,	3738
	11:15	be but life from the d?	3738
	14: 9	that he might be the Lord *of* both the d and	3738
1Co	6:14	**raised** the Lord **from the** d,	1586
	15:12	that Christ has been raised from the d,	3738
	15:12	that there is no resurrection *of the* d?	3738
	15:13	If there is no resurrection *of the* d,	3738
	15:15	**raised** Christ **from the** d.	1586
	15:15	But he did not raise him if in fact the d are	3738
	15:16	For if the d are not raised,	3738
	15:20	Christ has indeed been raised from the d,	3738
	15:21	the resurrection *of the* d comes also	3738
	15:29	will those do who are baptized for the d?	3738
	15:29	If the d are not raised at all,	3738
	15:32	If the d are not raised,	3738
	15:35	someone may ask, "How are the d raised?	3738
	15:42	So will it be with the resurrection *of the* d.	3738
	15:52	the d will be raised imperishable,	3738
2Co	1: 9	who raises the d.	3738
	4:14	**raised** the Lord Jesus **from the** d	1586
Gal	1: 1	who raised him from the d—	3738
Eph	1:20	from the d and seated him at his right hand	3738
	2: 1	you were d in your transgressions and sins,	3738
	2: 5	even when we were d in transgressions—	3738
	5:14	"Wake up, O sleeper, rise from the d,	3738
Php	3:11	to attain to the resurrection from the d.	3738
Col	1:18	and the firstborn from among the d,	3738
	2:12	who raised him from the d.	3738
	2:13	When you were d in your sins and in	3738
1Th	1:10	whom he raised from the d—	3738
	4:16	and the d in Christ will rise first.	3738
1Ti	5: 6	the widow who lives for pleasure is d even	2569
2Ti	2: 8	Remember Jesus Christ, raised from the d,	3738
	4: 1	who will judge the living and the d,	3738
Heb	6: 2	the resurrection of the d,	3738
	11: 4	by faith he still speaks, *even though he is* d.	633
	11:12	so from this one man, and he as good as d,	3739
	11:19	that God could raise the d,	3738
	11:35	Women received back their d,	3738
	13:20	from the d our Lord Jesus.	3738
Jas	2:17	if it is not accompanied by action, is d.	3738
	2:26	As the body without the spirit is d,	3738
	2:26	so faith without deeds is d.	3738
1Pe	1: 3	the resurrection of Jesus Christ from the d,	3738
	1:21	from the d and glorified him,	3738
	4: 5	to judge the living and the d.	3738
	4: 6	even *to* those who are now d,	3738
Jude	:12	and uprooted—twice d.	633
Rev	1: 5	the firstborn *from* the d,	3738
	1:17	I fell at his feet as though d.	3738
	1:18	I am the Living One; I was d,	3738
	2:23	*I will* **strike** her children d.	650
	3: 1	a reputation of being alive, but you are d.	3738
	11:18	The time has come for judging the d,	3738
	14:13	Blessed are the d who die in the Lord from	3738
	16: 3	and it turned into blood like that of a d man,	3738
	20: 5	(The rest *of the* d did not come to life until	3738
	20:12	And I saw the d, great and small,	3738
	20:12	the d were judged according	3738
	20:13	The sea gave up the d that were in it,	3738
	20:13	and Hades gave up the d that were in them,	3738

DEADENED (1) [DIE]
Jn 12:40 and **d** their hearts, so they can neither see 4800

DEADLY (16) [DIE]
Ex	10:17	to take this **d** plague away from me."	4638
Dt	32:24	consuming pestilence and **d** plague;	5321
	32:33	the **d** poison of cobras.	425
Ps	7:13	He has prepared his **d** weapons;	4638
	64: 3	and aim their words like **d** arrows.	5253
	91: 3	and from the **d** pestilence.	2095
	144:10	from the **d** sword.	8273
Pr	21: 6	a fleeting vapor and a **d** snare.	4638
	26:18	a madman shooting firebrands or **d** arrows	4638
Jer	9: 8	Their tongue is a **d** arrow;	8821
	16: 4	"They will die of **d** diseases.	4926
Eze	5:16	at you with my **d** and destructive arrows	8273
	9: 2	each with a **d** weapon in his hand.	5150
Mk	16:18	and when they drink **d** poison,	2503+5516
2Co	1:10	He has delivered us from such a **d** peril,	2505
Jas	3: 8	It is a restless evil, full *of* **d** poison.	2504

DEAF (18)
Ex	4:11	Who makes him **d** or mute?	3094
Lev	19:14	" 'Do not curse the **d** or	3094
Dt	1:45	weeping and **turned a d ear** to you.	263+4202
Ps	28: 1	*do* not **turn a d ear** to me.	3087
	38:13	I am like a **d** *man*, who cannot hear,	3094
	39:12	be not **d** to my weeping.	3087
Pr	28: 9	If anyone turns a **d** ear *to* the law,	4946+9048
Isa	29:18	In that day the **d** will hear the words of	3094
	35: 5	be opened and the ears of the **d** unstopped.	3094
	42:18	"Hear, you **d**; look, you blind, and see!	3094
	42:19	and **d** like the messenger I send?	3094
	43: 8	who have ears but are **d**.	3094
Mic	7:16	and their ears *will* become **d**.	3087
Mt	11: 5	the **d** hear, the dead are raised,	3273
Mk	7:32	a *man* who was **d** and could hardly talk,	3273
	7:37	even makes the **d** hear and the mute speak."	3273
	9:25	"*You* **d** and mute spirit," he said,	3273
Lk	7:22	the **d** hear, the dead are raised,	3273

DEAL (51) [DEALER, DEALING, DEALINGS, DEALS, DEALT]
Ge	21:23	before God that *you* will not **d** falsely	9213
Ex	1:10	*we must* **d** shrewdly with them	2681
	8:22	" 'But on that day *I will* **d** differently	7111
Ru	1:17	May the LORD **d** with me,	6913
1Sa	3:17	May God **d** with you, be it ever so severely,	6913
	14:44	Saul said, "May God **d** with me,	6913
	20:13	*may* the LORD **d** with me,	6913
	24: 4	into your hands *for you to* **d** with	6913
	25:22	May God **d** with David,	6913
2Sa	3: 9	May God **d** with Abner,	6913
	3:22	a raid and brought with them a **great d**	8041
	3:35	"May God **d** with me, be it ever so severely,	6913
	19:13	May God **d** with me, be it ever so severely,	6913
1Ki	2: 6	**D** with him according to your wisdom,	6913
	2:23	"May God **d** with me, be it ever so severely,	6913
	8:39	**d** with each man according to all he does,	5989
	19: 2	"May the gods **d** with me,	6913
	20:10	"May the gods **d** with me,	6913
2Ki	6:31	He said, "May God **d** with me,	6913
2Ch	6:30	**d** with each man according to all he does,	5989
	12:15	of Iddo the seer *that* **d with genealogies?**	3509
	28: 8	They also took a **great d** of plunder,	8041
Ne	5: 7	a large meeting to **d with** them	6584
	9:24	to **d** with them as they pleased.	6913
Job	42: 8	and not **d** with you according to your folly.	6913
Ps	109:21	**d** well with me for your name's sake;	6213
	119:124	**D** with your servant according to your love	6213
Isa	10:11	not **d** with Jerusalem and her images	6913
	23:17	the LORD *will* **d with** Tyre.	7212
Jer	2: 8	*Those who* **d with** the law did not know me;	9530
	7: 5	and **d** with each other justly,	6913+6913
	18:23	**d** with them in the time of your anger.	6913
	24: 8	'so *will I* **d** with Zedekiah king of Judah,	5989
	32: 5	where he will remain until I **d** with him,	7212
La	1:22	**d** with them as you have dealt with me	6618
Eze	7:27	*I will* **d** with them according	6913
	8:18	Therefore *I will* **d** with them in anger;	6913
	16:59	*I will* **d** with you as you deserve,	6913
	20:44	when I **d** with you for my name's sake and	6913
	22:14	or your hands be strong in the day I **d**	6913
	23:25	and *they will* **d** with you in fury.	6913
	23:29	*They will* **d** with you in hatred	6913
	25:14	and *they will* **d** with Edom in accordance	6913
	31:11	for *him to* **d** with according to its wickedness.	6913+6913
Zep	3:19	At that time I *will* **d**	6913
Zec	8:11	But now I will not **d** with the remnant	NIH
Mt	27:19	a **great d** today in a dream because of him."	4498
Mk	5:26	She had suffered a **great d** under the care	4498
Ac	16:16	She earned a **great d** of money	4498
2Ti	4:14	the metalworker did me a **great d** of harm.	4498
Heb	5: 2	*to* **d** gently with those who are ignorant	3584

DEALER (1) [DEAL]
Ac 16:14 a **d in** purple cloth from the city 4527

DEALING (4) [DEAL]
2Sa	7:19	Is this your **usual way of d** *with* man,	9368
Ezr	10:17	of the first month they finished **d with** all	928
Lk	16: 8	in **d** with their own kind than are the people	NIG

DEALINGS (1) [DEAL]
1Sa 25: 3 a Calebite, was surly and mean in his **d**. 5095

DEALS (3) [DEAL]
Dt	25:16	anyone *who* **d** dishonestly.	6913
Jer	5: 1	but one person *who* **d** honestly and seeks	6913
1Th	2:11	that we dealt with each of you as a father **d**	NIG

DEALT (9) [DEAL]
Ex	10: 2	and grandchildren how *I* **d** harshly with	6618
1Sa	6:19	of the heavy blow the LORD *had* **d** them,	5782
2Sa	22:21	"The LORD *has* **d** with me according	1694
Ps	18:20	The LORD *has* **d** with me according	1694
Isa	10:11	with Jerusalem and her images as *I* **d**	6913
La	1:22	with them as *you have* **d** with me because	6618
Eze	39:24	*I* **d** with them according	6913
Ac	7:19	He **d** treacherously with our people	2947
1Th	2:11	For you know that we **d** with each of you as	NIG

DEAR (62) [DEARER, DEARLY]
2Sa	1:26	you were very **d** to me.	5838
Ps	102:14	For her stones *are* **d** to your servants;	8354
Jer	31:20	Is not Ephraim my **d** son,	3692
Jn	2: 4	"**D** woman, why do you involve me?"	1222
	19:26	he said to his mother, "**D** woman,	1222
Ac	15:25	with our **d** friends Barnabas and Paul—	28
Ro	16: 5	Greet my **d friend** Epenetus,	28
	16: 9	and my **d friend** Stachys.	28
	16:12	Greet my **d friend** Persis,	28
1Co	4:14	but to warn you, as my **d** children.	28
	10:14	Therefore, my **d friends**, flee from idolatry.	28
	15:58	Therefore, my **d** brothers, stand firm.	28
2Co	7: 1	Since we have these promises, **d friends**,	28
	12:19	and everything we do, **d friends**,	28
Gal	4:19	My **d** children, for whom I am again in	5451
Eph	6:21	the **d** brother and faithful servant in	28
Php	2:12	my **d friends**, as you have always obeyed—	28
	4: 1	in the Lord, **d friends**!	28
Col	1: 7	Epaphras, our **d** fellow servant,	28
	4: 7	He is a **d** brother,	28
	4: 9	Onesimus, our faithful and **d** brother,	28
	4:14	Our **d friend** Luke, the doctor,	28
1Th	2: 8	because you had become **so d** to us.	28
1Ti	6: 2	and **d** to them.	28
2Ti	1: 2	*To* Timothy, my **d** son:	28
Phm	1: 1	*To* Philemon our **d friend**	28
	1:16	but better than a slave, as a **d** brother.	28
	1:16	He is very **d** to me but even dearer to you,	NIG
Heb	6: 9	Even though we speak like this, **d friends**,	28
Jas	1:16	Don't be deceived, my **d** brothers.	28
	1:19	My **d** brothers, take note of this:	28
	2: 5	Listen, my **d** brothers:	28
1Pe	2:11	**D friends**, I urge you,	28
	4:12	**D friends**, do not be surprised at	28
2Pe	3: 1	**D friends**, this is now my second letter	28
	3: 8	But do not forget this one thing, **d friends**:	28
	3:14	**d friends**, since you are looking forward	28
	3:15	as our **d** brother Paul also wrote you with	28
	3:17	**d friends**, since you already know this,	28
1Jn	2: 1	My **d** children, I write this to you so	5448
	2: 7	**D friends**, I am not writing you	28
	2:12	I write to you, **d children**,	5448
	2:13	I write to you, **d children**,	4086
	2:18	**D children**, this is the last hour;	4086
	2:28	And now, **d children**, continue in him,	5448
	3: 2	**D friends**, now we are children of God,	28
	3: 7	**D children**, do not let anyone lead you astray.	5448
	3:18	**D children**, let us not love with words	5448
	3:21	**D friends**, if our hearts do not condemn us,	28
	4: 1	**D friends**, do not believe every spirit,	28
	4: 4	**d children**, are from God	5448
	4: 7	**D friends**, let us love one another,	28
	4:11	**D friends**, since God so loved us,	28
	5:21	**D children**, keep yourselves from idols.	5448
2Jn	1: 5	And now, **d lady**, I am not writing you	3257
3Jn	1: 1	The elder, *To* my **d friend** Gaius,	28
	1: 2	**D friend**, I pray that you may enjoy	28
	1: 5	**D friend**, you are faithful	28
	1:11	**D friend**, do not imitate what is evil	28
Jude	1: 3	**D friends**, although I was very eager	28
	1:17	But, **d friends**, remember what the apostles	28
	1:20	But you, **d friends**, build yourselves up	28

DEARER (1) [DEAR]
Phm 1:16 He is very dear to me but even **d** to you, NIG

DEARLY (3) [DEAR]
Hos	4:18	their rulers **d** love shameful ways.	170
Eph	5: 1	as **d** loved children	28
Col	3:12	as God's chosen people, holy and **d** loved,	5073

DEARTH (KJV) See DROUGHT, FAMINE

DEATH (450) [DIE]
Ge	24:67	Isaac was comforted **after** his mother's **d**.	AIT
	25:11	After Abraham's **d**, God blessed his son Isaac,	4638
	26:11	**surely be put to d**."	4637+4637
	27: 2	and don't know the day of my **d**.	4638
Ge	38: 7	so the LORD **put** him to **d**.	4637
	38:10	so *he* **put** him to **d** also.	4637
	38:24	"Bring her out and *have* her **burned to d**!"	8596
	42:37	**put** both of my sons to **d**	4637
Ex	16: 3	to starve this entire assembly *to* **d**."	4637
	19:12	**surely be put to d**.	4637+4637
	21:12	**surely be put to d**.	4637+4637
	21:14	from my altar and *put* him to **d**.	4637
	21:15	**must be put to d**.	4637+4637
	21:16	**must be put to d**.	4637+4637
	21:17	**must be put to d**.	4637+4637
	21:28	"If a bull gores a man or a woman *to* **d**,	4637
	21:28	**must be stoned to d**,	6232+6232
	21:29	and the owner also *must* **be put to d**.	4637
	22:19	**must be put to d**.	4637+4637
	23: 7	**put** an innocent or honest person *to* **d**,	2222
	31:14	**must be put to d**;	4637+4637
	31:15	**must be put to d**.	4637+4637
	35: 2	on it *must* **be put to d**.	4637
Lev	16: 1	The LORD spoke to Moses after the **d** *of*	4638
	19:20	Yet *they are* not *to* **be put to d**,	4637
	20: 2	**must be put to d**;	4637
	20: 4	to Molech and they fail to **put** him to **d**,	4637
	20:10	**must be put to d**.	4637+4637
	20:11	**must be put to d**;	4637+4637
	20:12	**must be put to d**;	4637+4637
	20:13	**must be put to d**,	4637+4637
	20:15	**must be put to d**,	4637+4637
	20:16	**must be put to d**;	4637+4637
	20:27	**must be put to d**.	4637+4637
	24:16	**must be put to d**.	4637+4637
	24:16	**must be put to d**;	4637+4637
	24:17	**must be put to d**.	4637+4637
	24:21	but whoever kills a man *must* **be put to d**.	4637
	27:29	**must be put to d**.	4637+4637
Nu	1:51	near it *shall* **be put to d**.	4637
	3:10	the sanctuary *was* to **be put to d**."	4637
	3:38	the sanctuary *was* to **be put to d**.	4637
	11:15	**put** me to **d** right now—	2222+2222
	14:15	**put** these people to **d**	4637
	15:36	the camp and stoned him *to* **d**,	4637
	16:29	If these men die a natural **d**	4638
	18: 7	near the sanctuary *must* **be put to d**."	4637
	19:16	or *someone who has* **died a natural d**,	4637
	19:18	or *someone who has* **died a natural d**.	4637
	23:10	Let me die the **d** *of* the righteous,	4638
	25: 5	"Each *of you must* **put** to **d** those	2222
	25:15	Midianite woman who **was put to d** was Cozbi	5782
	35:16	**shall be put to d**.	4637+4637
	35:17	**shall be put to d**.	4637+4637
	35:18	**shall be put to d**.	4637+4637
	35:19	the murderer **to d**;	4637
	35:19	when he meets him, he *shall* **put** him **to d**.	4637
	35:21	**shall be put to d**;	4637+4637
	35:21	**put** the murderer *to* **d**	4637
	35:25	He must stay there until the **d** *of*	4637
	35:28	of refuge until the **d** *of* the high priest;	4638
	35:28	after the **d** *of* the high priest may he return	4638
	35:30	*to be* **put to d** as a murderer only on	8357
	35:30	But no one *is to* **be put to d** on	4637
	35:31	*must surely* **be put to d**.	4637+4637
	35:32	and live on his own land before the **d** *of*	4638
Dt	9:28	he brought them out to **put** them **to d** in	4637
	13: 5	That prophet or dreamer *must* **be put to d**,	4637
	13: 9	**must certainly put** him to **d**.	2222+2222
	13: 9	be the first in **putting** him **to d**,	4637
	13:10	Stone him **to d**,	4637
	17: 5	to your city gate and stone that person *to* **d**,	4637
	17: 6	or three witnesses a man *shall* **be put to d**,	4637
	17: 6	but no *one shall* **be put to d** on	4637
	17: 7	be the first in **putting** him **to d**,	4637
	17:12	to the LORD your God *must* **be put to d**.	4637
	18:20	*must be put to* **d**.	4637
	19: 6	even though he is not deserving of **d**,	4638
	21:21	the men of his town shall stone him *to* **d**.	4637
	21:22	a man guilty of a capital offense **is put to d**	4637
	22:21	the men of her town shall stone her *to* **d**.	4637
	22:24	the gate of that town and stone them *to* **d**—	4637
	22:26	she has committed no sin deserving **d**.	4638
	24:16	not **be put to d** for their children,	4637
	24:16	nor children **put to d** for their fathers;	4637
	30:15	before you today life and prosperity, **d**	4638
	30:19	that I have set before you life and **d**,	4638
	31:14	"Now the day of your **d** is near.	4637
	31:29	For I know that after my **d** you are sure	4638
	32:22	one that burns to the **realm of d** below.	8619
	32:39	I **put** to **d** and I bring to life,	4637
	33: 1	on the Israelites before his **d**.	4638
Jos	1: 1	the **d** *of* Moses the servant of the LORD,	4637
	1:18	*will* **be put to d**.	4637
	2:13	and that you will save us from **d**."	4638
	11:17	**putting** them to **d**.	4637
	20: 6	until the **d** *of* the high priest who is serving	4638
Jdg	1: 1	After the **d** *of* Joshua,	4638
	6:31	Whoever fights for him *shall* **be put to d**	4637
	13: 7	of God from birth until the day of his **d**.'	4638
	14:15	**burn** you and your father's household *to* **d**.	836+928+2021+8596
	15: 6	**burned** her and her father *to* **d**.	836+928+2021+8596
	16:16	after day until he was tired of **d**.	4637
	20:13	so that *we may* **put** them *to* **d** and purge	4637
	21: 5	**certainly be put to d**.	4637+4637
Ru	1:17	if anything but **d** separates you and me."	4638
	2:11	for your mother-in-law since the **d**	4638

| 2Co | 13: 3 | He is not weak in **d** with you, | 1650 |

1Sa
2: 6	"The LORD brings **d** and makes alive;	4637
2:25	it was the LORD's will to **put** them **to d.**	4637
5:11	For **d** had filled the city with panic;	4638
6:19	**putting** seventy of them **to d**	5782
11:12	to us and *we will* **put** them **to d.**"	4637
11:13	Saul said, "No one *shall* **be put to d** today;	4637
14:45	and *he was* not **put to d.**	4637
15: 3	**put to d** men and women,	4637
15:32	"Surely the bitterness of **d** is past."	4638
15:33	And Samuel **put** Agag **to d** before	9119
19: 6	LORD lives, David *will* not **be put to d.**"	4637
20: 3	there is only a step between me and **d.**"	4638
20:32	"Why *should he* **be put to d?**	4637
22:22	for the **d** *of* your father's whole family.	5883
28: 9	a trap for my life to **bring about** my **d?**"	4637

2Sa
1: 1	After the **d** *of* Saul,	4638
1: 9	I am in the **throes of d,** but I'm still alive.'	8688
1:23	and in **d** they were not parted.	4638
4:10	I seized him and **put** him **to d** in Ziklag.	2222
6:23	of Saul had no children to the day of her **d.**	4638
8: 2	Every two lengths of them *were* **put to d,**	4637
13:39	he was consoled concerning Amnon's **d.**	4637
14: 7	so that *we may* **put** him **to d** for the life	4637
14:32	*let him* **put** me **to d.**"	4637
15:21	whether it means life or **d,**	4638
17: 3	The **d** of the man you seek will mean	NIH
19:21	"Shouldn't Shimei **be put to d** for this?	4637
19:22	*Should* anyone **be put to d** in Israel today?	4637
19:28	but **d** from my lord the king,	4637
20: 3	in confinement till the day of their **d,**	4637
21: 1	**put** the Gibeonites **to d.**"	4637
21: 4	**put** anyone in Israel *to* **d.**"	4637
21: 9	they *were* **put to d** during the first days of	4637
22: 5	"The waves of **d** swirled about me;	4638
22: 6	the snares of **d** confronted me.	4638

1Ki
1:51	**put** his servant **to d**	4637
2: 8	*'I will* not **put** you **to d** by the sword.'	4637
2:24	Adonijah *shall* **be put to d** today!"	4637
2:26	but *I will* not **put** you **to d** now;	4637
3:11	the **d** *of* your enemies but for discernment	5883
11:40	and stayed there until Solomon's **d.**	4638
12:18	but all Israel stoned him **to d.**	4637
18: 9	over to Ahab to be **put to d?**	4637
19:10	**put** your prophets **to d**	2222
19:14	**put** your prophets **to d**	2222
19:17	Jehu *will* **put to d** any who escape	4637
19:17	and Elisha *will* **put to d** any who escape	4637
21:10	Then take him out and stone him *to* **d.**"	4637
21:13	the city and stoned him *to* **d**	4637
21:15	that Naboth had been stoned *to* **d,**	4637
22:20	and **going to** *his* **d** there?'	5877

2Ki
1: 1	Ahab's **d,** Moab rebelled against Israel.	4638
2:21	Never again will it cause **d** or make	4638
4:40	"O man of God, there is **d** in the pot!"	4638
11: 8	Anyone who approaches your ranks *must* **be put to d.**	4637
11:15	*"She must* not **be put to d** in the temple of	4637
11:16	and there *she* **was put to d.**	4637
14: 6	**put** the sons of the assassins **to d,**	4637
14: 6	not **be put to d** for their children,	4637
14: 6	nor children **put to d** for their fathers;	4637
14:17	after the **d** *of* Jehoash son of Jehoahaz king	4638
16: 9	to Kir and **put** Rezin **to d.**	4637
18:32	Choose life and not **d!**	4637
19:35	of the LORD went out and **put to d**	5782
20: 1	and was at the point of **d.**	4637

1Ch
2: 3	so the LORD **put** him **to d.**	4637
10:14	So the LORD **put** him **to d** and turned	4637
22: 5	So David made extensive preparations before his **d.**	4638

2Ch
1:11	nor for the **d** *of* your enemies,	5883
10:18	but the Israelites stoned him *to* **d.**	4637
15:13	the God of Israel, *were to* **be put to d,**	4637
18:19	and **going to** *his* **d** there?'	5877
22: 4	his father's **d** they became his advisers,	4638
22: 9	He was brought to Jehu and **put to d.**	4637
23: 7	the temple *must* **be put to d.**	4637
23:14	"Do not **put** her **to d** *at* the temple of	4637
23:15	and there *they* **put** her **to d.**	4637
24:17	After the **d** *of* Jehoiada,	4638
24:21	order of the king *they* **stoned** him *to* **d**	74+8083
25: 4	**put** their sons **to d,**	4637
25: 4	*to* **d** for their children, nor children put	4637
25: 4	nor children *put to* **d** for their fathers;	4637
25:25	after the **d** *of* Jehoash son of Jehoahaz king	4638
28:22	and was at the point of **d.**	4637

Ezr
7:26	of the king must surely be punished by **d,**	10409

Est
4:11	that he *be* **put to d.**	4637
9:15	*they* **put to d** in Susa three hundred men,	2222

Job
3:21	to those who long for **d** that does not come,	4638
5:20	In famine he will ransom you from **d,**	4638
7:15	so that I prefer strangling and **d,**	4638
9:23	When a scourge **brings** sudden **d,**	4637
17:16	Will it go down to the gates of **d?**	8619
26: 6	**D** is naked before God;	8619
28:22	Destruction and **D** say,	4638
30:23	I know you will bring me down to **d,**	4637
33:22	and his life to the **messengers of d.**	4637
38:17	Have the gates of **d** been shown to you?	8619
38:17	the gates of the **shadow of d?**	7516

Ps
9: T	To [the tune of] "The **D** of the Son."	4637
9:13	and lift me up from the gates of **d,**	4638
13: 3	Give light to my eyes, or I will sleep in **d;**	4638
18: 4	The cords of **d** entangled me;	4638
18: 5	the snares of **d** confronted me.	4638
22:15	you lay me in the dust of **d.**	4638
23: 4	through the valley of the **shadow of d,**	7516

Ps
33:19	to deliver them from **d** and keep them alive	4638
44:22	Yet for your sake *we* **face d** all day long;	2222
49:14	and **d** will feed on them.	4638
55: 4	the terrors of **d** assail me.	4638
55:15	Let **d** take my enemies by surprise;	4638
56:13	from **d** and my feet from stumbling,	4638
68:20	from the Sovereign LORD comes escape from **d.**	4638
72:13	and the needy and save the needy from **d.**	5883
78:31	*he* **put to d** the sturdiest among them,	2222
78:50	he did not spare them from **d** but gave them	4638
88:15	and **close to d;**	1588
89:48	What man can live and not see **d,**	4638
90: 5	You sweep men away in the **sleep of d;**	9104
94:17	in the **silence of d.**	1872
94:21	and condemn the innocent to **d.**	1947
102:20	and release those condemned to **d.**"	9456
107:18	and drew near the gates of **d.**	4638
109:16	but hounded to **d** the poor and the needy	4637
116: 3	The cords of **d** entangled me,	4638
116: 8	O LORD, have delivered my soul from **d,**	4638
116:15	Precious in the sight of the LORD is the **d**	4638
118:18	but he has not given me over to **d.**	4638
141: 8	**give** me **over to d.**	6867

Pr
2:18	to **d** and her paths to the spirits of the dead.	4638
5: 5	Her feet go down to **d;**	4638
7:27	leading down to the chambers of **d.**	4638
8:36	all who hate me love **d.**"	4638
10: 2	but righteousness delivers from **d.**	4638
11: 4	but righteousness delivers from **d.**	4638
11:19	but he who pursues evil goes to his **d.**	4638
13:14	turning a man from the snares of **d.**	4638
14:12	but in the end it leads to **d.**	4638
14:32	turning a man from the snares of **d.**	4638
14:32	but even in **d** the righteous have a refuge.	4638
15:11	**D** and Destruction lie open before	8619
16:14	A king's wrath is a messenger of **d,**	4638
16:25	but in the end it leads to **d.**	4638
18:21	The tongue has the power of life and **d,**	4638
19:18	do not be a willing party to his **d.**	4637
21:25	sluggard's craving *will be* the **d** *of* him,	4637
23:14	with the rod and save his soul from **d.**	8619
24:11	Rescue those being led away to **d;**	4638
27:20	**D** and Destruction are never satisfied,	8619
28:17	the guilt of murder will be a fugitive till **d;**	1014

Ecc
7: 1	and the day of **d** better than the day of birth.	4638
7: 2	for **d** is the destiny of every man;	2085S
7:26	I find more bitter than **d** the woman who is	4638
8: 8	so no one has power over the day of his **d.**	4638

SS
8: 6	for love is as strong as **d,**	4638

Isa
9: 2	land of the **shadow of d** a light has dawned.	7516
25: 8	he will swallow up **d** forever.	4638
28:15	"We have entered into a covenant with **d,**	4638
28:18	Your covenant with **d** will be annulled;	4638
37:36	of the LORD went out and **put to d**	5782
38: 1	and was at the point of **d.**	4637
38:10	of **d** and be robbed of the rest of my years?"	8619
38:18	**d** cannot sing your praise;	4638
53: 9	and with the rich in his **d,**	4638
53:12	because he poured out his life unto **d,**	4638
57: 2	they find rest as they **lie in d.**	5435
65:15	the Sovereign LORD *will* **put** you **to d,**	4637

Jer
8: 3	of this evil nation will prefer **d** to life,	4638
9:21	**D** has climbed in through our windows	4638
15: 2	" 'Those destined for **d,** to death;	4638
15: 2	" 'Those destined for death, to **d;**	4638
18:21	let their men be **put to d,**	2222+4638
21: 8	before you the way of life and the way of **d.**	4638
26:11	"This man should be sentenced to **d**	4638
26:15	however, that if you **put** me **to d,**	4637
26:16	"This man should not be sentenced to **d!**	4638
26:19	or anyone else in Judah **put** him **to d?**	4637+4637
26:21	the king sought to **put** him **to d,**	4637
26:24	over to the people to be **put to d.**	4637
29:21	of Babylon, and *he will* **put** them **to d**	5782
38: 4	"This man *should* **be put to d.**	4637
38: 9	to **d** when there is no longer any bread in	4637
43:11	bringing **d** to those destined for death,	4638
43:11	bringing death to those destined for **d,**	4638
52:11	in prison till the day of his **d.**	4638
52:34	till the day of his **d.**	4638

La
1:20	inside, there is only **d.**	4638

Eze
18:13	**surely be put to d**	4637+4637
18:23	Do I take any pleasure in the **d** *of*	4638
18:32	For I take no pleasure in the **d** *of* anyone,	4638
28: 8	and you will die a violent **d** in the heart of	4926
28:10	You will die the **d** of the uncircumcised at	4638
31:14	they are all destined for **d,**	4638
33:11	I take no pleasure in the **d** of the wicked,	4638

Da
2:13	**put** the wise men **to d,**	10625
2:13	for Daniel and his friends to **put** them **to d.**	10625
2:14	had gone out to **put to d** the wise men	10625
5:19	Those the king wanted to put to **d,**	NIH
5:19	*he* **put to d;**	10625

Hos
13:14	I will redeem them from **d.**	4638
13:14	Where, O **d,** are your plagues?	4638

Hab
2: 5	as the grave and like **d** is never satisfied,	4638

Mt
2:15	where he stayed until the **d** of Herod.	5463
4:16	land of the **shadow of d** a light has dawned.	2505
10:21	"Brother will betray brother to **d,**	2505
10:21	and *have* them **put to d.**'	2506
15: 4	or mother *must* **be put to d.**'	2505+5462
16:28	some who are standing here will not taste **d**	2505
20:18	They will condemn him to **d**	2505
24: 9	over to be persecuted and **put to d,**	650
26:38	with sorrow to the point of **d.**	2505
26:59	so that *they could* **put** him **to d.**	2506

Mt
26:66	"He is worthy *of* **d,**" they answered.	2505
27: 1	to the decision *to* **put** Jesus **to d.**	2506

Mk
7:10	or mother *must be* **put to d.**'	2505+5462
9: 1	some who are standing here will not taste **d**	2505
10:33	condemn him *to* **d** and will hand him over	2505
13:12	"Brother will betray brother to **d,**	2505
13:12	and *have* them **put to d.**	2506
14:34	with sorrow to the point *of* **d,"**	2505
14:55	so that they could **put** him **to d,**	2506
14:64	They all condemned him as worthy *of* **d.**	2505

Lk
1:79	in darkness and in the shadow *of* **d,**	2505
9:27	some who are standing here will not taste **d**	2505
15:17	and here I *am* **starving to d!**	660+3350
21:16	**put** some of you **to d.**	2506
22:33	to go with you to prison and to **d.**"	2505
23:15	he has done nothing to deserve **d.**	2505
23:22	**grounds for the d penalty,**	165+2505
24:20	be sentenced to **d,** and they crucified him;	2505

Jn
4:47	who was close to **d.**	633
5:24	he has crossed over from **d** to life.	2505
8:51	he will never see **d.**"	2505
8:52	he will never taste **d.**"	2505
11: 4	Jesus said, "This sickness will not end in **d.**	2505
11:13	Jesus had been speaking of his **d,**	2505
12:33	to show the kind of **d** he was going to die.	2505
18:32	of **d** he was going to die would be fulfilled.	2505
21:19	of **d** by which Peter would glorify God.	2505

Ac
2:23	**put** him **to d** by nailing him to the cross.	359
2:24	freeing him from the agony *of* **d,**	2505
2:24	because it was impossible for **d**	899S
5:33	and wanted *to* **put** them **to d.**	359
7: 4	After the **d** of his father,	633
8: 1	Saul was there, giving approval *to* his **d.**	358
12: 2	**put to d** with the sword.	359
13:28	found no proper ground *for* a **d** sentence,	2505
22: 4	the followers of this Way to their **d,**	2505
23:29	that deserved **d** or imprisonment.	2505
25:11	I am guilty of doing anything deserving **d,**	2505
25:25	*of* **d,** but because he made his appeal to	2505
26:10	and *when* they *were* **put to d,**	359
26:31	not doing anything that deserves **d**	2505
28:18	not guilty of any crime deserving **d.**	2505

Ro
1:32	that those who do such things deserve **d,**	2505
4:25	over to **d** for our sins and was raised to life	NIG
5:10	we were reconciled to him through the **d**	2505
5:12	and **d** through sin, and	2505
5:12	and in this way **d** came to all men,	2505
5:14	**d** reigned from the time of Adam to	2505
5:17	**d** reigned through that one man,	2505
5:21	just as sin reigned in **d,**	2505
6: 3	into Christ Jesus were baptized into his **d?**	2505
6: 4	with him through baptism into **d** in order	2505
6: 5	with him like this in his **d,**	2505
6: 9	**d** no longer has mastery over him.	2505
6:10	**The d** he died, he died to sin once for all;	4005S
6:13	those who have been brought from **d** to life;	3738
6:16	which leads to **d,** or to obedience,	2505
6:21	Those things result in **d!**	2505
6:23	For the wages of sin is **d,**	2505
7: 5	so that we bore fruit *for* **d.**	2505
7:10	to bring life actually brought **d.**	2505
7:11	through the commandment **put** me **to d.**	650
7:13	which is good, then, become **d** to me?	2505
7:13	it produced **d** in me through what was good,	2505
7:24	Who will rescue me from this body *of* **d?**	2505
8: 2	from the law of sin and **d.**	2505
8: 6	The mind of sinful man is **d,**	2505
8:13	by the Spirit *you* **put to d** the misdeeds of	2506
8:36	"For your sake *we* **face d** all day long;	2506
8:38	For I am convinced that neither **d** nor life,	2505

1Co
11:26	or the world or life or **d** or the present or	2505
11:26	you proclaim the Lord's **d** until he comes.	2505
15:21	For since **d** came through a man,	2505
15:26	The last enemy to be destroyed is **d.**	2505
15:54	"**D** has been swallowed up in victory."	2505
15:55	Where, O **d,** is your victory?	2505
15:55	Where, O **d,** is your sting?"	2505
15:56	The sting *of* **d** is sin,	2505

2Co
1: 9	in our hearts we felt the sentence of **d.**	2505
2:16	To the one we are the smell of **d;**	2505
3: 7	Now if the ministry that brought **d,**	2505
4:10	We always carry around in our body the **d**	3740
4:11	given over to **d** for Jesus' sake,	2505
4:12	**d** is at work in us, but life is at work in you.	2505
7:10	but worldly sorrow brings **d.**	2505
11:23	and been **exposed to d** again and again.	2505

Eph
2:16	by which he **put to d** their hostility.	650

Php
1:20	whether by life or by **d.**	2505
2: 8	and became obedient to **d—**	2505
2: 8	even **d** on a cross!	2505
3:10	becoming like him in his **d,**	2505

Col
1:22	through **d** to present you holy in his sight,	2505
3: 5	**Put to d,** therefore, whatever belongs	3739

2Ti
1:10	who has destroyed **d** and has brought life	2505

Heb
2: 9	and honor because he suffered **d,**	2505
2: 9	so that by the grace of God he might taste **d**	2505
2:14	by his **d** he might destroy him who holds	2505
2:14	the power *of* **d**—that is, the devil—	2505
2:15	in slavery by their fear of **d.**	2505
5: 7	to the one who could save him from **d,**	2505
6: 1	of repentance from acts that lead to **d,**	3738
7:23	since **d** prevented them from continuing	2505
9:14	from acts that lead to **d,**	3738
9:16	to prove the **d** of the one who made it,	2505
11: 5	so that *he did* not experience **d;**	2505
11:19	he did receive Isaac back **from d.**	3854S
11:37	*they were* **put to d** by the sword.	633+1877+5840

Jas	1:15	sin, when it is full-grown, gives birth to **d**.	2505
	5:20	of his way will save him from **d** and cover	2505
1Pe	3:18	He was **put to d** in the body but made alive	2506
1Jn	3:14	We know that we have passed from **d**	2505
	3:14	Anyone who does not love remains in **d**.	2505
	5:16	a sin that does not lead to **d**,	2505
	5:16	to those whose sin does not lead to **d**.	2505
	5:16	There is a sin that leads to **d**.	2505
	5:17	and there is sin that does not lead to **d**.	2505
Rev	1:18	And I hold the keys of **d** and Hades.	2505
	2:10	Be faithful, even to the point of **d**,	2505
	2:11	not be hurt at all by the second **d**.	2505
	2:13	who was **put to d** in your city—	650
	6: 8	Its rider was named **D**,	2505
	9: 6	During those days men will seek **d**,	2505
	9: 6	they will long to die, but **d** will elude them.	2505
	12:11	so much as to shrink from **d**.	2505
	18: 8	**d**, mourning and famine.	2505
	20: 6	The second **d** has no power over them,	2505
	20:13	and **d** and Hades gave up the dead that were	2505
	20:14	Then **d** and Hades were thrown into	2505
	20:14	The lake of fire is the second **d**.	2505
	21: 4	There will be no more **d** or mourning	2505
	21: 8	This is the second **d**."	2505

DEATH'S (1) [DIE]

Job	18:13	**d** firstborn devours his limbs.	4638

DEATHLY (2) [DIE]

Jer	30: 6	every face turned **d** pale?	3766
Da	10: 8	my face turned **d** pale and I was helpless.	5422

DEATHS (1) [DIE]

1Sa	4:21	the **d** of her father-in-law and her husband.	NIH

DEBAR See LO DEBAR

DEBASE (KJV) See DESCENDED

DEBATE (2) [DEBATED, DEBATING]

Ac	15: 2	and Barnabas into sharp dispute and **d**	2428
	18:28	he vigorously refuted the Jews in public **d**,	NIG

DEBATED (1) [DEBATE]

Ac	9:29	He talked and **d** with the Grecian Jews,	5184

DEBATING (1) [DEBATE]

Mk	12:28	of the law came and heard them **d**.	5184

DEBAUCHERY (5)

Ro	13:13	not in sexual immorality and **d**,	816
2Co	12:21	and **d** in which they have indulged.	816
Gal	5:19	sexual immorality, impurity and **d**;	816
Eph	5:18	Do not get drunk on wine, which leads to **d**.	861
1Pe	4: 3	living in **d**, lust, drunkenness, orgies,	816

DEBIR (12) [KIRIATH SANNAH]

Jos	10: 3	Japhia king of Lachish and **D** king	1809
	10:38	with him turned around and attacked **D**.	1810
	10:39	They did to **D** and its king as they had done	1810
	11:21	from Hebron, **D** and Anab,	1810
	12:13	the king of **D** one the king of Geder one	1810
	13:26	and from Mahanaim to the territory of **D**;	1810
	15: 7	then went up to **D** from the Valley of Achor	1810
	15:15	in **D** (formerly called Kiriath Sepher).	1810
	15:49	Dannah, Kiriath Sannah (that is, **D**),	1810
	21:15	Holon, **D**,	1810
Jdg	1:11	in **D** (formerly called Kiriath Sepher).	1810
1Ch	6:58	Hilen, **D**,	1810

DEBORAH (11)

Ge	35: 8	Now **D**, Rebekah's nurse,	1806
Jdg	4: 4	**D**, a prophetess, the wife of Lappidoth,	1806
	4: 5	the Palm of **D** between Ramah and Bethel	1806
	4: 9	"Very well," **D** said, "I will go with you.	NIH
	4: 9	So **D** went with Barak to Kedesh,	1806
	4:10	and **D** also went with him.	1806
	4:14	Then **D** said to Barak, "Go!	1806
	5: 1	On that day **D** and Barak son	1806
	5: 7	**D**, arose, arose a mother in Israel.	1806
	5:12	'Wake up, wake up, **D**!	1806
	5:15	The princes of Issachar were with **D**;	1806

DEBT (11) [DEBTOR, DEBTORS, DEBTS]

Dt	15: 3	must cancel any **d** your brother owes you.	9023
	24: 6	take a pair of millstones—not even the upper one—as **security for a d**,	2471
1Sa	22: 2	in distress or in **d** or discontented	4200+5957
Job	24: 9	the infant of the poor is **seized for a d**,	2471
Mt	18:25	and all that he had be sold to **repay the d**.	625
	18:27	canceled the **d** and let him go.	1245
	18:30	into prison until he could pay the **d**.	4053
	18:32	that **d** of yours because you begged me to.	4051
Lk	7:43	the one who had the bigger **d** canceled."	NIG
Ro	13: 8	Let no **d remain outstanding**, except	4053
	13: 8	except the continuing **d** to love one another,	NIG

DEBTOR (1) [DEBT]

Isa	24: 2	for **d** as for creditor.	928+5957

DEBTORS (3) [DEBT]

Hab	2: 7	Will not your **d** suddenly arise?	5967
Mt	6:12	as we also have forgiven our **d**.	4050
Lk	16: 5	"So he called in each one of his master's **d**.	5971

DEBTS (9) [DEBT]

Dt	15: 1	every seven years you must cancel **d**.	6913+9024
	15: 2	LORD's **time for canceling d** has been proclaimed.	9024
	15: 9	the year for **canceling d**, is near,"	9024
	31:10	in the year for **canceling d**,	9024
2Ki	4: 7	"Go, sell the oil and pay your **d**.	5963
Ne	10:31	the land and will cancel all **d**.	3338+5391
Pr	22:26	in pledge or puts up security for **d**;	5391
Mt	6:12	Forgive us our **d**,	4052
Lk	7:42	so he canceled the **d** of both.	NIG

DECAPOLIS (3)

Mt	4:25	Large crowds from Galilee, the **D**,	1279
Mk	5:20	in the **D** how much Jesus had done for him.	1279
	7:31	of Galilee and into the region of the **D**.	1279

DECAY (12) [DECAYED]

Ps	16:10	nor will you let your Holy One see **d**.	8846
	49: 9	that he should live on forever and not see **d**.	8846
	49:14	their forms will **d** in the grave,	1162
Pr	12: 4	but a disgraceful wife is like **d** in his bones.	8373
Isa	5:24	so their roots will **d**	5215
Hab	3:16	**d** crept into my bones,	8373
Ac	2:27	nor will you let your Holy One see **d**.	1426
	2:31	nor did his body see **d**.	1426
	13:34	God raised him from the dead, never to **d**,	1426+1650+5715
	13:35	" 'You will not let your Holy One see **d**.'	1426
	13:37	from the dead did not see **d**.	1426
Ro	8:21	to **d** and brought into the glorious freedom	5785

DECAYED (2) [DECAY]

Jer	49: 7	Has their wisdom **d**?	6244
Ac	13:36	with his fathers and his body **d**.	1426+3972

DECEASED (KJV) See DEPARTED
SPIRITS, DIED

DECEIT (32) [DECEIVE]

Job	15:35	their womb fashions **d**."	5327
	27: 4	and my tongue will utter no **d**.	8245
	31: 5	in falsehood or my foot has hurried after **d**	5327
Ps	5: 9	with their tongue they **speak d**.	2744
	32: 2	against him and in whose spirit is no **d**.	8245
	50:19	for evil and harness your tongue to **d**.	5327
	52: 2	like a sharpened razor, you who practice **d**.	8245
	101: 7	No one who practices **d** will dwell	8245
Pr	6:14	who plots evil with **d** in his heart;	9337
	12:20	There is **d** in the hearts	5327
	26:24	but in his heart he harbors **d**.	5327
Isa	5:18	along with cords of **d**,	8736
	30:12	relied on oppression and depended on **d**,	4279
	53: 9	nor was any **d** in his mouth.	5327
Jer	5:27	their houses are full of **d**;	5327
	6:13	prophets and priests alike, all practice **d**.	9214
	8: 5	They cling to **d**; they refuse to return.	9567
	8:10	prophets and priests alike, all practice **d**.	9214
	9: 6	in their **d** they refuse to acknowledge me,"	5327
	9: 8	it speaks with **d**.	5327
Da	8:25	He will cause **d** to prosper,	5327
Hos	7: 1	They practice **d**, thieves break into houses,	9214
	11:12	the house of Israel with **d**.	5327
Zep	1: 9	of their gods with violence and **d**.	5327
	3:13	nor will **d** be found in their mouths.	4383+9567
Zec	10: 2	The idols speak **d**, diviners see visions	224
Mk	7:22	malice, **d**, lewdness, envy, slander,	1515
Ac	13:10	You are full of all kinds of **d** and trickery.	1515
Ro	1:29	murder, strife, **d** and malice.	1515
	3:13	their tongues **practice d**."	1514
1Pe	2: 1	rid yourselves of all malice and all **d**,	1515
	2:22	and no **d** was found in his mouth."	1515

DECEITFUL (26) [DECEIVE]

Job	11:11	Surely he recognizes **d** men;	8736
Ps	5: 6	bloodthirsty and **d** men the LORD abhors.	5327
	17: 1	it does not rise from **d** lips.	5327
	26: 4	I do not sit with **d** men,	8736
	36: 3	The words of his mouth are wicked and **d**;	5327
	43: 1	rescue me from **d** and wicked men.	5327
	52: 4	O you **d** tongue!	5327
	55:23	and **d** men will not live out half their days.	5327
	109: 2	and **d** men have opened their mouths	5327
	119:29	Keep me from **d** ways;	9214
	120: 2	from lying lips and from **d** tongues.	8245
	120: 3	and what more besides, O **d** tongue?	8245
	144: 8	whose right hands are **d**.	9214
	144:11	whose right hands are **d**.	9214
Pr	12: 5	but the advice of the wicked is **d**.	5327
	14:25	but a false witness is **d**.	5327
	15: 4	but a **d** tongue crushes the spirit.	6157
	17:20	he whose tongue is **d** falls into trouble.	2200
Isa	30: 9	These are rebellious people, **d** children,	3952
Jer	17: 9	heart is **d** above all things and beyond cure.	6815
Hos	10: 2	Their heart is **d**,	2744
2Co	11:13	such men are false apostles, **d** workmen,	1513

DEBTOR (1) [DEBT]

Isa	24: 2	for **d** as for creditor.	928+5957

Eph	4:14	and craftiness of men in their **d** scheming.	4415
	4:22	which is being corrupted by its **d** desires;	573
1Pe	3:10	from evil and his lips from **d** speech.	1515
Rev	21:27	anyone who does what is shameful or **d**,	6022

DECEITFULLY (6) [DECEIVE]

Ge	27:35	"Your brother came **d**	928+5327
	34:13	Jacob's sons replied **d** as they spoke	928+5327
Ex	8:29	not **act d** again by not letting the people go	9438
Job	13: 7	Will you speak **d** for him?	8245
Da	11:23	he will act **d**,	5327
Mic	6:12	and their tongues speak **d**.	8245

DECEITFULNESS (4) [DECEIVE]

Ps	119:118	for their **d** is in vain.	9567
Mt	13:22	of this life and the **d** of wealth choke it,	573
Mk	4:19	the **d** of wealth and the desires	573
Heb	3:13	none of you may be hardened by sin's **d**.	573

DECEIVE (32) [DECEIT, DECEITFUL, DECEITFULLY, DECEITFULNESS, DECEIVED, DECEIVER, DECEIVERS, DECEIVES, DECEIVING, DECEPTION, DECEPTIVE, DECEPTIVELY]

Ge	31:27	Why did you run off secretly and **d** me?	1704
Lev	19:11	" 'Do not **d** one another.	9213
Jos	9:22	"Why did you **d** us by saying,	8228
1Sa	19:17	"Why did you **d** me like this	8228
2Sa	3:25	to **d** you and observe your movements	7331
2Ki	18:29	Do not let Hezekiah **d** you.	5958
	19:10	let the god you depend on **d**	5958
2Ch	32:15	not let Hezekiah **d** you and mislead you	5958
Job	13: 9	Could you **d** him	9438
	13: 9	as you might **d** men?	9438
	15:31	not **d himself** by trusting what is worthless,	9494
Pr	14: 5	A truthful witness does not **d**,	3941
	24:28	or use your lips to **d**.	7331
Isa	36:14	Do not let Hezekiah **d** you.	5958
	37:10	the god you depend on **d** you when he says,	5958
Jer	29: 8	the prophets and diviners among you **d** you.	5958
	37: 9	Do not **d** yourselves, thinking,	5958
Ob	1: 7	your friends will **d** and overpower you;	5958
Zec	13: 4	on a prophet's garment of hair in order to **d**.	3950
Mt	24: 5	'I am the Christ,' and will **d** many.	4414
	24:11	and **d** many people.	4414
	24:24	and perform great signs and miracles to **d**	4414
Mk	13: 6	claiming, 'I am he,' and will **d** many.	4414
	13:22	and perform signs and miracles to **d**	675
Ro	16:18	By smooth talk and flattery they **d**	1987
1Co	3:18	Do not **d** yourselves.	1987
	3:18	I tell you this so that no one may **d** you	4165
Eph	5: 6	Let no one **d** you with empty words,	572
Col	2: 4	Don't let anyone **d** you in any way,	1987
2Th	2: 3	and so **d** yourselves.	4165
Jas	1:22	we **d** ourselves and the truth is not in us.	4414
1Jn	1: 8	to **d** the nations in the four corners of	4414
Rev	20: 8		4414

DECEIVED (29) [DECEIVE]

Ge	3:13	The woman said, "The serpent **d** me,	5958
	27:36	He has **d** me these two times:	6810
	29:25	Why have you **d** me?"	8228
	31:20	Jacob **d** Laban the Aramean by	1704+4213
	31:26	"What have you done? You've **d** me,	1704+4222
Nu	25:18	when they **d** you in the affair	928+5792+5793
1Sa	28:12	"Why have you **d** me?	8228
Job	12:16	both **d** and deceiver are his.	8704
Isa	19:13	the leaders of Memphis are **d**;	5958
Jer	4:10	how **completely** you have **d**	5958+5958
	20: 7	O LORD, you **d** me, and I was deceived;	7331
	20: 7	O LORD, you deceived me, and I was **d**;	7331
	20:10	saying, "Perhaps he will be **d**;	7331
	49:16	and the pride of your heart have **d** you,	5958
Hos	7:11	**easily d** and senseless—	7331
Ob	1: 3	The pride of your heart has **d** you,	5958
Lk	21: 8	He replied: "Watch out that you are not **d**.	4414
Jn	7:47	"You mean he has **d** you also?"	4414
Ro	7:11	by the commandment, **d** me, and through	1987
1Co	6: 9	Do not be **d**: Neither the sexually immoral	4414
2Co	11: 3	But I am afraid that just as Eve was **d** by	1987
Gal	6: 7	Do not be **d**: God cannot be mocked.	4414
1Ti	2:14	And Adam was not the one **d**;	572
	2:14	the woman who was **d** and became a sinner.	1987
2Ti	3:13	deceiving and being **d**.	4414
Tit	3: 3	**d** and enslaved by all kinds of passions	4414
Jas	1:16	Don't be **d**, my dear brothers.	4414
Rev	13:14	he **d** the inhabitants of the earth.	4414
	20:10	And the devil, who **d** them,	4414

DECEIVER (5) [DECEIVE]

Job	12:16	both deceived and **d** are his.	8706
Jer	9: 4	For every brother is a **d**,	6810+6810
Mic	2:11	If a liar and **d** comes and says,	9214
Mt	27:63	that while he was still alive that **d** said,	4418
2Jn	1: 7	Any such person is the **d** and the antichrist.	4418

DECEIVERS (3) [DECEIVE]

Ps	49: 5	when wicked **d** surround me—	6812
Tit	1:10	mere talkers and **d**,	5855
2Jn	1: 7	Many **d**, who do	4418

DECEIVES (8) [DECEIVE]

Pr	26:19	is a man *who* d his neighbor and says,	8228
Jer	9: 5	Friend d friend, and no one speaks	9438
Mt	24: 4	"Watch out that no one d you.	4414
Mk	13: 5	"Watch out that no one d you.	4414
Jn	7:12	Others replied, "No, he d the people."	4414
Gal	6: 3	when he is nothing, *he* d himself.	5854
2Th	2:10	of evil that d those who are perishing.	573
Jas	1:26	he d himself and his religion is worthless,	572

DECEIVING (4) [DECEIVE]

Lev	6: 2	to the LORD *by* d his neighbor	3950
1Ti	4: 1	and follow d spirits and things taught	4418
2Ti	3:13	d and being deceived.	4414
Rev	20: 3	to keep *him* from d the nations anymore	4414

DECENCY (1) [DECENTLY]

1Ti	2: 9	with d and propriety,	133

DECENTLY (1) [DECENCY]

Ro	13:13	Let us behave d, as in the daytime,	2361

DECEPTION (9) [DECEIVE]

Ps	12: 2	flattering lips speak with d.	2256+4213+4213
	38:12	all day long they plot d.	5327
Pr	14: 8	but the folly of fools is d.	5327
	26:26	His malice may be concealed by d,	5396
Jer	3:23	on the hills and mountains is a d;	9214
	9: 6	You live in the midst of d;	5327
Hos	10:13	you have eaten the fruit of d.	3951
Mt	27:64	This last d will be worse than the first."	4415
2Co	4: 2	we do not use d,	1877+4111+4344

DECEPTIVE (8) [DECEIVE]

Pr	11:18	The wicked man earns d wages,	9214
	23: 3	for that food is d.	3942
	31:30	Charm is d, and beauty is fleeting.	9214
Jer	7: 4	Do not trust in d words and say,	9214
	7: 8	in d words that are worthless.	9214
	15:18	Will you be to me like a d brook,	423
Mic	1:14	The town of Aczib will prove d to the kings	423
Col	2: 8	through hollow and d philosophy,	573

DECEPTIVELY (1) [DECEIVE]

2Ki	10:19	Jehu was acting d in order to destroy	928+6817

DECIDE (16) [DECIDED, DECISION, DECISIONS]

Ex	18:16	and *I* d between the parties	9149
	18:22	the simple cases *they can* d themselves.	9149
	33: 5	and *I will* d what to do with you.' "	3359
Dt	21: 5	and to d all cases of dispute	2118+6584+7023
	25: 1	to take it to court and *the judges will* d	9149
Jdg	11:27	d *the dispute* this day between the Israelites	9149
1Sa	24:15	the LORD be our judge and d between us.	9149
2Sa	24:13	think it over and d how I should answer	8011
1Ch	21:12	d how I should answer	8011
Job	22:28	What *you* d on will be done,	1615
	34:33	You *must* d, not I;	1047
Isa	11: 3	or d by what he hears with his ears;	3519
Eze	44:24	the priests are to serve as judges and d it	9149
Jn	19:24	"*Let's* d by lot who will get it."	3275
Ac	4:21	*They* could not d how to punish them,	2351
	24:22	he said, "*I will* d your case."	1336

DECIDED (29) [DECIDE]

Ge	41:32	that the matter *has been firmly* d by God,	3922
Ex	18:26	but the simple ones *they* d themselves.	9149
Jdg	4: 5	to her to have their *disputes* d.	5477
2Ch	24: 2	Joash d to restore the temple	2118+4213+6640
	30: 2	in Jerusalem to celebrate the Passover in	3619
	30: 5	*They* d to send a proclamation	1821+6641
Est	7: 7	Haman, realizing that the king *had already* d his fate,	3983
Jer	4:28	*I have* d and will not turn back."	2372
Da	2: 5	"This is what I have firmly d:	10418
	2: 8	that this is what I have firmly d:	10418
Zep	3: 8	I have d to assemble the nations,	5477
Mt	27: 7	So they d to use the money to buy	3284+5206
Lk	23:24	So Pilate d to grant their demand.	2137
Jn	1:43	The next day Jesus d to leave for Galilee.	2527
	9:22	for already the Jews *had* d	5338
Ac	3:13	*though he had* d to let him go.	3212
	4:28	and will *had* d beforehand should happen.	4633
	7:23	he d to visit his fellow Israelites.	326+2093+2840+3836
	11:29	d to provide help for the brothers living	3988
	15:22	d to choose some of their own men	1506
	19:21	Paul d to go to Jerusalem,	5502
	20: 3	he d to go back through Macedonia.	1181+1191
	20:16	Paul *had* d to sail past Ephesus	3212
	25:25	to the Emperor *I* d to send him to Rome.	3212
	27: 1	When *it was* d that we should sail	3212
	27:12	the majority d that we should sail on,	1087+5502
	27:39	where *they* d to run the ship aground	1086
2Co	9: 7	Each man should give what he has d	4576
Tit	3:12	because *I have* d to winter there.	3212

DECIMATED (1)

2Sa	21: 5	plotted against us so that *we have* been d	9012

DECISION (15) [DECIDE]

Ex	28:29	over his heart on the breastpiece of d as	5477
2Sa	15: 2	to be placed before the king for a d,	5477
Ezr	5:17	let the king send us his d in this matter.	10668
	10: 8	in accordance with the d *of* the officials	6783
Pr	16:33	but its every d is from the LORD.	5477
Isa	16: 3	"Give us counsel, render a d.	7131
Da	4:17	" 'The d is announced by messengers,	10601
Joel	3:14	Multitudes, multitudes in the valley of d!	3025
	3:14	day of the LORD is near in the valley of d.	3025
Mt	27: 1	the elders of the people came to the d	3284+5206
Mk	15: 1	and the whole Sanhedrin, reached a d.	5206
Lk	23:51	not consented *to* their d and action.	1087
Jn	1:13	nor of human d or a husband's will,	2525
Ac	21:25	to them *our* d that they should abstain	3212
	25:21	to be held over for the Emperor's d,	1338

DECISIONS (10) [DECIDE]

Ex	28:15	"Fashion a breastpiece for **making** d—	5477
	28:30	the **means of making** d *for* the Israelites	5477
Nu	27:21	who will obtain d for him by inquiring of	8626
Dt	17:10	according to the d they give you at	1821
	17:11	and the d they give you.	5477
Isa	11: 4	with justice he will **give** d for the poor of	3519
	28: 7	they stumble when **rendering** d.	7133
	58: 2	for just d and seem eager for God to come	5477
Jn	8:16	But if I do judge, my d are right,	3213
Ac	16: 4	they delivered the d reached by the apostles	3212

DECK (2) [DECKED, DECKS]

Eze	27: 6	the coasts of Cyprus they made your d,	7983
Jnh	1: 5	But Jonah had gone **below** d,	2021+3752+6208

DECKED (1) [DECK]

Hos	2:13	she d herself *with* rings and jewelry,	6335

DECKEDST, DECKEST (KJV) See
DRESS, MAKE GAUDY, PUT ON

DECKS (1) [DECK]

Ge	6:16	middle and **upper** d.	AIT

DECLARE (46) [DECLARED, DECLARES, DECLARING]

Ex	22: 9	the judges d **guilty** must pay back double	8399
Dt	5: 1	Hear, O Israel, the decrees and laws I d	1819
	5: 5	and you to d to you the word of the LORD	5583
	21: 7	and *they shall* d: "Our hands did not shed	6699
	26: 3	"*I* d today to the LORD your God	5583
	26: 5	*you shall* d before the LORD your God:	6699
	30:18	*I* d to you this day that you will certainly	5583
	32:40	I lift my hand to heaven and d:	606
1Ki	1:36	the God of my lord the king, so d it.	606
	8:32	D the innocent **not guilty**,	7405
2Ki	9: 3	the flask and pour the oil on his head and d,	606
1Ch	16:24	D his glory among the nations,	6218
	17:10	" '*I* d to you that the LORD will build	5583
2Ch	6:23	D the innocent **not guilty**	7405
Job	34:34	"Men of understanding d,	NIH
Ps	5:10	D them **guilty**, O God!	870
	9:14	that *I may* d your praises in the gates of	6218
	19: 1	The heavens d the glory of God;	6218
	22:22	*I will* d your name to my brothers;	6218
	40: 5	they would be too many to d.	6218
	51:15	and my mouth *will* d your praise.	5583
	71:17	and to this day *I* d your marvelous deeds.	5583
	71:18	till *I* d your power to the next generation,	5583
	75: 9	As for me, *I will* d this forever;	5583
	89: 2	*I will* d that your love stands firm forever,	606
	96: 3	D his glory among the nations,	6218
	106: 2	Or d or fully d his praise?	9048
Isa	41:22	Or d *to* us the things to come,	9048
	42: 9	and new things I d;	5583
	44: 7	*Let him* d and lay out	5583
	45:19	I d what is right.	5583
	45:21	D what is to be, present it—	5583
	58: 1	D to my people their rebellion and to	5583
Jer	23:31	against the prophets who wag their own tongues and d,	5535
Eze	38:19	In my zeal and fiery wrath *I* d that at	1819
Da	4:17	the holy ones d the verdict,	10397
Joel	1:14	D a **holy** fast; call a sacred assembly.	7727
	2:15	Blow the trumpet in Zion, d a **holy** fast,	7727
Mic	3: 8	to d to Jacob his transgression,	5583
Ac	20:26	*I* d to you today that I am innocent of	3458
1Co	15:50	*I* d to you, brothers,	5774
Gal	5: 3	Again *I* d to every man who lets himself	3458
Eph	6:20	Pray that I **may** d it fearlessly, as I should.	3281
Heb	2:12	"*I will* d your name to my brothers;	550
1Pe	2: 9	that *you may* d the praises	1972
1Jn	1: 5	the message we have heard from him and d	334

DECLARED (50) [DECLARE]

Nu	14:17	just as *you have* d:	1819
Dt	4:13	*He* d to you his covenant,	5583
	26:17	*You have* d this day that	606
	26:18	And the LORD *has* d this day	606
	26:19	He *has* d that he will set you in praise,	NIH
	32:46	to heart all the words I *have* **solemnly** d	6386
1Ki	1:24	d that Adonijah shall be king after you,	606
	8:53	just as *you* d through your servant Moses	1819

DECLARES (371) [DECLARE]

Ge	22:16	"I swear by myself, d the LORD,	5536
Ex	21: 5	"But if the servant d, 'I love my master	606+606
Nu	14:28	'As surely as I live, d the LORD,	5536
1Sa	2:30	the LORD, the God of Israel, d:	5536
	2:30	But now the LORD d: 'Far be it from me!	5536
2Sa	7:11	" 'The LORD d to you that	5583
2Ki	9:26	and the blood of his sons, d the LORD,	5536
	9:26	for it on this plot of ground, d the LORD.'	5536
	19:33	he will not enter this city, d the LORD.	5536
	22:19	I have heard you, d the LORD.	5536
2Ch	34:27	I have heard you, d the LORD.	5536
Isa	1:24	the Mighty One of Israel, d:	5536
	3:15	d the Lord, the LORD Almighty.	5536
	14:22	d the LORD Almighty.	5536
	14:22	and descendants," d the LORD.	5536
	14:23	d the LORD Almighty.	5536
	17: 3	d the LORD Almighty.	5536
	17: 6	d the LORD, the God of Israel.	5536
	19: 4	d the Lord, the LORD Almighty.	5536
	22:25	"In that day," d the LORD Almighty,	5536
	30: 1	d the LORD, "to those who carry out plans	5536
	31: 9	d the LORD, whose fire is in Zion,	5536
	37:34	he will not enter this city," d the LORD.	5536
	41:14	for I myself will help you," d the LORD,	5536
	43:10	"You are my witnesses," d the LORD,	5536
	43:12	You are my witnesses," d the LORD,	5536
	49:18	As surely as I live," d the LORD,	5536
	52: 5	d the LORD.	5536
	52: 5	and those who rule them mock," d	5536
	54:17	and this is their vindication from me," d	5536
	55: 8	neither are your ways my ways," d the LORD.	5536
	56: 8	The Sovereign LORD d—	5536
	59:20	in Jacob who repent of their sins," d	5536
	66: 2	d the LORD.	5536
	66:17	they will meet their end together," d	5536
	66:22	that I make will endure before me," d	5536
Jer	1: 8	for I am with you and will rescue you," d	5536
	1:15	of the northern kingdoms," d the LORD.	5536
	1:19	for I am with you and will rescue you," d	5536
	2: 3	and disaster overtook them,' " d	5536
	2: 9	against you again," d the LORD.	5536
	2:12	and shudder with great horror," d	5536
	2:19	d the Lord, the LORD Almighty.	5536
	2:22	d the Sovereign LORD.	5536
	2:29	against me," d the LORD.	5536
	3: 1	d the LORD.	5536
	3:10	but only in pretense," d the LORD.	5536
	3:12	" 'Return, faithless Israel,' d the LORD,	5536
	3:12	d the LORD, 'I will not be angry forever.	5536
	3:13	and have not obeyed me," d the LORD.	5536
	3:14	"Return, faithless people," d the LORD,	5536
	3:16	d the LORD, "men will no longer say,	5536
	3:20	O house of Israel," d the LORD.	5536
	4: 1	O Israel, return to me," d the LORD.	5536
	4: 9	"In that day," d the LORD,	5536
	4:17	she has rebelled against me,' " d the LORD.	5536
	5: 9	d the LORD.	5536
	5:11	to me," d the LORD.	5536
	5:18	"Yet even in those days," d the LORD,	5536
	5:22	d the LORD.	5536

Jer	5:29	**d** the LORD.	5536
	6:12	against those who live in the land," **d**	5536
	7:11	**d** the LORD.	5536
	7:13	**d** the LORD, I spoke to you again	5536
	7:19	**d** the LORD.	5536
	7:30	of Judah have done evil in my eyes, **d**	5536
	7:32	the days are coming, **d** the LORD,	5536
	8: 1	" 'At that time, **d** the LORD,	5536
	8: 3	**d** the LORD Almighty.'	5536
	8:13	'I will take away their harvest, **d** the LORD.	5536
	8:17	and they will bite you," **d** the LORD.	5536
	9: 3	not acknowledge me," **d** the LORD.	5536
	9: 6	to acknowledge me," **d** the LORD.	5536
	9: 9	**d** the LORD.	5536
	9:22	Say, "This is what the LORD **d:**	5536
	9:24	for in these I delight," **d** the LORD.	5536
	9:25	"The days are coming," **d** the LORD,	5536
	12:17	and destroy it," **d** the LORD.	5536
	13:11	and the whole house of Judah to me,' **d**	5536
	13:14	fathers and sons alike, **d** the LORD.	5536
	13:25	the portion I have decreed for you," **d**	5536
	15: 3	of destroyers against them," **d** the LORD,	5536
	15: 6	You have rejected me," **d** the LORD.	5536
	15: 9	to the sword before their enemies," **d**	5536
	15:20	to rescue and save you," **d** the LORD.	5536
	16: 5	from this people," **d** the LORD.	5536
	16:11	**d** the LORD, 'and followed other gods	5536
	16:14	the days are coming," **d** the LORD.	5536
	16:16	"and they will catch them.	5536
	17:24	**d** the LORD, and bring no load through	5536
	18: 6	**d** the LORD.	5536
	19: 6	the days are coming, **d** the LORD,	5536
	19:12	to this place and to those who live here, **d**	5536
	21: 7	After that, **d** the LORD.	5536
	21:10	to do this city harm and not good, **d**	5536
	21:13	above this valley on the rocky plateau, **d**	5536
	21:14	as your deeds deserve, **d** the LORD.	5536
	22: 5	But if you do not obey these commands, **d**	5536
	22:16	**d** the LORD.	5536
	22:24	"As surely as I live," **d** the LORD,	5536
	23: 1	**d** the LORD.	5536
	23: 2	for the evil you have done," **d** the LORD.	5536
	23: 4	nor will any be missing," **d** the LORD.	5536
	23: 5	"The days are coming," **d** the LORD,	5536
	23: 7	the days are coming," **d** the LORD,	5536
	23:11	in my temple I find their wickedness," **d**	5536
	23:12	the year they are punished," **d** the LORD.	5536
	23:23	"Am I only a God nearby," **d** the LORD,	5536
	23:24	**d** the LORD.	5536
	23:24	**d** the LORD.	5536
	23:28	**d** the LORD.	5536
	23:29	"Is not my word like fire," **d** the LORD,	5536
	23:30	"Therefore," **d** the LORD,	5536
	23:31	**d** the LORD, "I am against	5536
	23:31	and yet declare, 'The LORD **d.**'	5536
	23:32	who prophesy false dreams," **d** the LORD.	5536
	23:32	not benefit these people in the least," **d**	5536
	23:33	I will forsake you, **d** the LORD.'	5536
	25: 7	you did not listen to me," **d** the LORD.	5536
	25: 9	**d** the LORD, "and I will bring them	5536
	25:12	for their guilt," **d** the LORD,	5536
	25:29	**d** the LORD Almighty.'	5536
	25:31	the wicked to the sword,' " **d** the LORD.	5536
	27: 8	**d** the LORD, until I destroy it by his hand.	5536
	27:11	to till it and to live there, **d** the LORD." ' "	5536
	27:15	'I have not sent them,' **d** the LORD.	5536
	27:22	the day I come for them,' **d** the LORD.	5536
	28: 4	to Babylon,' **d** the LORD, 'for I will break	5536
	29: 9	I have not sent them," **d** the LORD.	5536
	29:11	**d** the LORD, "plans to prosper you and	5536
	29:14	I will be found by you," **d** the LORD,	5536
	29:14	where I have banished you," **d** the LORD,	5536
	29:19	For they have not listened to my words," **d**	5536
	29:19	And you exiles have not listened either," **d**	5536
	29:23	and am a witness to it," **d** the LORD.	5536
	29:32	the good things I will do for my people, **d**	5536
	30: 3	The days are coming,' **d** the LORD,	5536
	30: 8	" 'In that day,' **d** the LORD Almighty,	5536
	30:10	O Israel,' **d** the LORD.	5536
	30:11	with you and will save you,' **d** the LORD.	5536
	30:17	and heal your wounds,' **d** the LORD,	5536
	30:21	**d** the LORD.	5536
	31: 1	"At that time," **d** the LORD,	5536
	31:14	be filled with my bounty," **d** the LORD.	5536
	31:16	for your work will be rewarded," **d**	5536
	31:17	So there is hope for your future," **d**	5536
	31:20	I have great compassion for him," **d**	5536
	31:27	"The days are coming," **d** the LORD,	5536
	31:28	to build and to plant," **d** the LORD,	5536
	31:31	"The time is coming," **d** the LORD,	5536
	31:32	though I was a husband to them," **d**	5536
	31:33	with the house of Israel after that time," **d**	5536
	31:34	from the least of them to the greatest," **d**	5536
	31:36	if these decrees vanish from my sight," **d**	5536
	31:37	of Israel because of all they have done," **d**	5536
	31:38	"The days are coming," **d** the LORD,	5536
	32: 5	until I deal with him, **d** the LORD.	5536
	32:30	with what their hands have made, **d**	5536
	32:44	because I will restore their fortunes, **d**	5536
	33:14	" 'The days are coming,' **d** the LORD,	5536
	34: 5	I myself make this promise, **d** the LORD.' "	5536
	34:17	So I now proclaim 'freedom' for you, **d**	5536
	34:22	I am going to give the order, **d** the LORD,	5536
	35:13	**d** the LORD.	5536
	39:17	I will rescue you on that day, **d** the LORD;	5536
	39:18	because you trust in me, **d** the LORD.' "	5536
	42:11	Do not be afraid of him, **d** the LORD,	5536

Jer	44:29	that I will punish you in this place,' **d**	5536
	45: 5	For I will bring disaster on all people, **d**	5536
	46: 5	and there is terror on every side," **d**	5536
	46:18	"As surely as I live," **d** the King,	5536
	46:23	**d** the LORD, "dense though it be.	5536
	46:26	be inhabited as in times past," **d**	5536
	46:28	for I am with you," **d** the LORD.	5536
	48:12	But days are coming," **d** the LORD,	5536
	48:15	down in the slaughter," **d** the King,	5536
	48:25	her arm is broken," **d** the LORD.	5536
	48:30	but it is futile," **d** the LORD,	5536
	48:35	and burn incense to their gods," **d**	5536
	48:38	like a jar that no one wants," **d** the LORD.	5536
	48:43	O people of Moab," **d** the LORD.	5536
	48:44	the year of her punishment," **d** the LORD.	5536
	48:47	of Moab in days to come," **d** the LORD.	5536
	49: 2	But the days are coming," **d** the LORD,	5536
	49: 5	**d** the Lord, the LORD Almighty.	5536
	49: 6	of the Ammonites," **d** the LORD.	5536
	49:13	I swear by myself," **d** the LORD,	5536
	49:16	I will bring you down," **d** the LORD.	5536
	49:26	**d** the LORD Almighty.	5536
	49:30	you who live in Hazor," **d** the LORD.	5536
	49:31	which lives in confidence," **d** the LORD.	5536
	49:32	on them from every side," **d** the LORD.	5536
	49:37	even my fierce anger," **d** the LORD.	5536
	49:38	and destroy her king and officials," **d**	5536
	49:39	of Elam in days to come," **d** the LORD.	5536
	50: 4	"In those days, at that time," **d** the LORD,	5536
	50:10	all who plunder her will have their fill," **d**	5536
	50:20	In those days, at that time," **d** the LORD,	5536
	50:21	and completely destroy them," **d**	5536
	50:30	be silenced in that day," **d** the LORD.	5536
	50:31	**d** the Lord, the LORD Almighty,	5536
	50:35	against the Babylonians!" **d** the LORD—	5536
	50:40	**d** the LORD, "so no one will live there;	5536
	51:24	the wrong they have done in Zion," **d**	5536
	51:25	the whole earth," **d** the LORD.	5536
	51:26	be desolate forever," **d** the LORD.	5536
	51:39	then sleep forever and not awake," **d**	5536
	51:48	of the north destroyers will attack her," **d**	5536
	51:52	"But days are coming," **d** the LORD,	5536
	51:53	against her," **d** the LORD.	5536
	51:57	they will sleep forever and not awake," **d**	5536
Eze	5:11	**d** the Sovereign LORD.	5536
	11: 8	**d** the Sovereign LORD.	5536
	11:21	**d** the Sovereign LORD."	5536
	12:25	**d** the Sovereign LORD.' "	5536
	12:28	**d** the Sovereign LORD.' "	5536
	13: 6	They say, "The LORD **d,**"	5536
	13: 7	"The LORD **d,**" though I have not spoken?	5536
	13: 8	I am against you, **d** the Sovereign LORD.	5536
	13:16	**d** the Sovereign LORD.' "	5536
	14:11	**d** the Sovereign LORD.' "	5536
	14:14	**d** the Sovereign LORD.	5536
	14:16	**d** the Sovereign LORD.	5536
	14:18	**d** the Sovereign LORD.	5536
	14:20	**d** the Sovereign LORD, even if Noah,	5536
	14:23	**d** the Sovereign LORD."	5536
	15: 8	**d** the Sovereign LORD."	5536
	16: 8	**d** the Sovereign LORD.	5536
	16:14	**d** the Sovereign LORD.	5536
	16:19	**d** the Sovereign LORD.	5536
	16:23	Woe to you, **d** the Sovereign LORD.	5536
	16:30	**d** the Sovereign LORD,	5536
	16:43	**d** the Sovereign LORD.	5536
	16:48	As surely as I live, **d** the Sovereign LORD,	5536
	16:58	and your detestable practices, **d**	5536
	16:63	**d** the Sovereign LORD.' "	5536
	17:16	surely as I live, **d** the Sovereign LORD,	5536
	18: 3	surely as I live, **d** the Sovereign LORD,	5536
	18: 9	he will surely live, **d** the Sovereign LORD.	5536
	18:23	**d** the Sovereign LORD.	5536
	18:30	**d** the Sovereign LORD.	5536
	18:32	**d** the Sovereign LORD.	5536
	20: 3	**d** the Sovereign LORD.'	5536
	20:31	As surely as I live, **d** the Sovereign LORD,	5536
	20:33	As surely as I live, **d** the Sovereign LORD,	5536
	20:36	**d** the Sovereign LORD.	5536
	20:40	**d** the Sovereign LORD,	5536
	20:44	**d** the Sovereign LORD."	5536
	21: 7	**d** the Sovereign LORD."	5536
	21:13	**d** the Sovereign LORD.'	5536
	22:12	**d** the Sovereign LORD.	5536
	22:31	**d** the Sovereign LORD."	5536
	23:34	I have spoken, **d** the Sovereign LORD.	5536
	24:14	**d** the Sovereign LORD.' "	5536
	25:14	**d** the Sovereign LORD.' "	5536
	26: 5	for I have spoken, **d** the Sovereign LORD.	5536
	26:14	**d** the Sovereign LORD.	5536
	26:21	**d** the Sovereign LORD."	5536
	28:10	I have spoken, **d** the Sovereign LORD.' "	5536
	29:20	**d** the Sovereign LORD.	5536
	30: 6	**d** the Sovereign LORD.	5536
	31:18	**d** the Sovereign LORD.' "	5536
	32: 8	**d** the Sovereign LORD.	5536
	32:14	**d** the Sovereign LORD.	5536
	32:16	**d** the Sovereign LORD."	5536
	32:31	**d** the Sovereign LORD.	5536
	32:32	**d** the Sovereign LORD.	5536
	33:11	**d** the Sovereign LORD,	5536
	34: 8	**d** the Sovereign LORD,	5536
	34:15	**d** the Sovereign LORD.	5536
	34:30	are my people, **d** the Sovereign LORD.	5536
	34:31	**d** the Sovereign LORD."	5536
	35: 6	**d** the Sovereign LORD,	5536
	35:11	**d** the Sovereign LORD,	5536

Eze	36:14	**d** the Sovereign LORD.	5536
	36:15	**d** the Sovereign LORD.' "	5536
	36:23	**d** the Sovereign LORD.	5536
	36:32	**d** the Sovereign LORD.	5536
	37:14	and I have done it, **d** the LORD.' "	5536
	38:18	**d** the Sovereign LORD.	5536
	38:21	**d** the Sovereign LORD.	5536
	39: 5	for I have spoken, **d** the Sovereign LORD.	5536
	39: 8	**d** the Sovereign LORD.	5536
	39:10	**d** the Sovereign LORD.	5536
	39:13	**d** the Sovereign LORD.	5536
	39:20	**d** the Sovereign LORD.	5536
	39:29	**d** the Sovereign LORD."	5536
	43:19	**d** the Sovereign LORD.	5536
	43:27	I will accept you, **d** the Sovereign LORD."	5536
	44:12	**d** the Sovereign LORD.	5536
	44:15	**d** the Sovereign LORD.	5536
	44:27	**d** the Sovereign LORD.	5536
	45: 9	**d** the Sovereign LORD.	5536
	45:15	**d** the Sovereign LORD.	5536
	47:23	**d** the Sovereign LORD.	5536
	48:29	**d** the Sovereign LORD.	5536
Hos	2:13	but me she forgot," **d** the LORD.	5536
	2:16	"In that day," **d** the LORD,	5536
	2:21	that day I will respond," **d** the LORD—	5536
	11:11	in their homes," **d** the LORD.	5536
Joel	2:12	"Even now," **d** the LORD,	5536
Am	2:11	**d** the LORD.	5536
	2:16	on that day," **d** the LORD.	5536
	3:10	**d** the LORD, "who hoard plunder and loot	5536
	3:13	**d** the Lord, the LORD God Almighty.	5536
	3:15	and the mansions will be demolished," **d**	5536
	4: 3	and you will be cast out toward Harmon," **d**	5536
	4: 5	**d** the Sovereign LORD.	5536
	4: 6	yet you have not returned to me," **d**	5536
	4: 8	yet you have not returned to me," **d**	5536
	4: 9	yet you have not returned to me," **d**	5536
	4:10	yet you have not returned to me," **d**	5536
	4:11	the fire, yet you have not returned to me," **d**	5536
	6: 8	the LORD God Almighty **d:**	5536
	6:14	For the LORD God Almighty **d,**	5536
	8: 3	"In that day," **d** the Sovereign LORD,	5536
	8: 9	"In that day," **d** the Sovereign LORD,	5536
	8:11	**d** the Sovereign LORD,	5536
	9: 7	**d** the LORD.	5536
	9: 8	not totally destroy the house of Jacob," **d**	5536
	9:12	**d** the LORD, who will do these things.	5536
	9:13	"The days are coming," **d** the LORD,	5536
Ob	1: 4	from there I will bring you down," **d**	5536
	1: 8	"In that day," **d** the LORD,	5536
Mic	4: 6	"In that day," **d** the LORD,	5536
	5:10	"In that day," **d** the LORD,	5536
Na	2:13	**d** the LORD Almighty.	5536
	3: 5	**d** the LORD Almighty.	5536
Zep	1: 2	from the face of the earth," **d** the LORD.	5536
	1: 3	from the face of the earth," **d** the LORD.	5536
	1:10	"On that day," **d** the LORD,	5536
	2: 9	as surely as I live," **d** the LORD Almighty,	5536
	3: 8	Therefore wait for me," **d** the LORD,	5536
Hag	1: 9	**d** the LORD Almighty.	5536
	1:13	"I am with you," **d** the LORD.	5536
	2: 4	be strong, O Zerubbabel,' **d** the LORD.	5536
	2: 4	all you people of the land,' **d** the LORD,	5536
	2: 4	I am with you,' **d** the LORD Almighty.	5536
	2: 8	**d** the LORD Almighty.	5536
	2: 9	**d** the LORD Almighty."	5536
	2:14	and this nation in my sight,' **d** the LORD.	5536
	2:17	yet you did not turn to me,' **d** the LORD.	5536
	2:23	" 'On that day,' **d** the LORD Almighty,	5536
	2:23	**d** the LORD, 'and I will make you	5536
	2:23	**d** the LORD Almighty."	5536
Zec	1: 3	'Return to me,' **d** the LORD Almighty,	5536
	1: 4	or pay attention to me, **d** the LORD.	5536
	1:16	**d** the LORD Almighty.	5536
	2: 5	of fire around it,' **d** the LORD, 'and I will	5536
	2: 6	from the land of the north," **d** the LORD,	5536
	2: 6	to the four winds of heaven," **d** the LORD.	5536
	2:10	and I will live among you," **d** the LORD.	5536
	3:10	**d** the LORD Almighty."	5536
	5: 4	The LORD Almighty **d,** 'I will send it out,	5536
	8: 6	**d** the LORD Almighty.	5536
	8:11	**d** the LORD Almighty.	5536
	8:17	I hate all this," **d** the LORD.	5536
	10:12	in his name they will walk," **d** the LORD.	5536
	11: 6	on the people of the land," **d** the LORD.	5536
	12: 1	the spirit of man within him, **d:**	5536
	12: 4	and its rider with madness," **d** the LORD.	5536
	13: 2	**d** the LORD Almighty.	5536
	13: 7	**d** the LORD Almighty.	5536
	13: 8	In the whole land," **d** the LORD,	5536
Lk	20:42	David himself **d** in the Book of Psalms:	3306
Ro	2:16	as my gospel **d.**	NIG
Gal	3:22	But the Scripture **d** that the whole world is	NIG
Heb	8: 8	"The time is coming, the Lord,	3306
	8: 9	and I turned away from them, **d** the Lord.	3306
	8:10	with the house of Israel after that time, **d**	3306

DECLARING (3) [DECLARE]

Ps	71: 8	**d** your splendor all day long.	NIH
Jer	50:28	the fugitives and refugees from Babylon **d**	5583
Ac	2:11	we hear them **d** the wonders of God	3281

DECLINED (1)

| Ac | 18:20 | to spend more time with them, *he* **d.** | 2153+4024 |

DECORATE (2) [DECORATED, DECORATES, DECORATING, DECORATIONS]

1Ki	7:18	in two rows encircling each network to **d**	4059
Mt	23:29	You build tombs for the prophets and **d**	*3175*

DECORATED (9) [DECORATE]

2Ki	25:17	and was **d** with a network and pomegranates	6584
2Ch	3: 5	and **d** it with palm tree and chain designs.	6590
SS	5:14	like polished ivory **d** with sapphires.	6634
Jer	52:22	was **d** with a network and pomegranates	6584
Eze	40:22	the projecting walls were **d** with palm trees.	448
	40:31	palm trees **d** its jambs,	448
	40:34	palm trees **d** the jambs on either side,	448
	40:37	palm trees **d** the jambs on either side,	448
Rev	21:19	The foundations of the city walls were **d**	*3175*

DECORATES (1) [DECORATE]

Jer	22:14	panels it with cedar and **d** it in red.	5417

DECORATING (4) [DECORATE]

1Ki	7:41	of network **d** the two bowl-shaped capitals	4059
	7:42	**d** the bowl-shaped capitals on top of	4059
2Ch	4:12	of network **d** the two bowl-shaped capitals	4059
	4:13	**d** the bowl-shaped capitals on top of	4059

DECORATIONS (2) [DECORATE]

Eze	40:22	its portico and its **palm tree d** had	9474
	40:26	it had **palm tree d** on the faces of	9474

DECREASE (2) [DECREASED]

Lev	25:16	you are to **d** the price,	5070
Jer	29: 6	Increase in number there; do not **d.**	5070

DECREASED (2) [DECREASE]

Ps	107:39	Then their **numbers d,**	5070
Jer	30:19	and they will not be **d;**	5070

DECREE (41) [DECREED, DECREES]

Ex	15:25	the LORD made a **d** and a law for them,	2976
1Ch	16:17	He confirmed it to Jacob as a **d,**	2976
Ezr	5:13	King Cyrus issued a **d** to rebuild this house	10302
	5:17	to see if King Cyrus did in fact issue a **d**	10302
	6: 3	the king issued a **d** concerning the temple	10302
	6: 8	I hereby **d** what you are to do	10302+10682
	6:11	I **d** that if anyone changes this edict,	10302+10682
	6:12	or people who lifts a hand to change this **d**	NIH
	6:13	because of the **d** King Darius had sent,	NIH
	7:13	I **d** that any of the Israelites in my kingdom,	10302+10682
Est	1:19	let him issue a royal **d** and let it be written	1821
	3: 9	let a **d** be issued to destroy them,	4180
	8: 8	Now write another **d** in the king's name	NIH
	9:32	Esther's **d** confirmed these regulations	4411
Job	23:14	He carries out his **d** against me,	2976
	28:26	when he made a **d** for the rain and a path	2976
Ps	2: 7	I will proclaim the **d** of the LORD:	2976
	7: 6	Awake, my God; **d** justice.	7422
	81: 4	this is a **d** for Israel,	2976
	105:10	He confirmed it to Jacob as a **d,**	2976
	148: 6	he gave a **d** that will never pass away.	2976
Jer	51:12	his **d** against the people of Babylon.	1819
Da	2:13	**d** was issued to put the wise men to death,	10186
	2:15	"Why did the king issue such a harsh **d?**"	10186
	3:10	You have issued a **d,** O king,	10302
	3:29	I **d** that the people of any nation	10302+10682
	4:24	and this is the **d** the Most High has issued	10141
	6: 7	and enforce the **d** that anyone who prays	10057
	6: 8	the **d** and put it in writing so that it cannot	10057
	6: 9	So King Darius put the **d** in writing.	10057
	6:10	that the **d** had been published,	10375
	6:12	the king and spoke to him about his royal **d**	10057
	6:12	"Did you not publish a **d** that during	10057
	6:12	The king answered, "The **d** stands—	10418
	6:13	O king, or to the **d** you put in writing.	10057
	6:15	of the Medes and Persians no **d** or edict that	10057
	6:26	"I issue a **d** that in every part	10302
	9:25	the **d** to restore and rebuild Jerusalem until	1821
Jnh	3: 7	"By the **d** of the king and his nobles:	3248
Lk	2: 1	In those days Caesar Augustus issued a **d**	*1504*
Ro	1:32	Although they know God's **righteous d**	*1468*

DECREED (24) [DECREE]

1Ki	22:23	The LORD has **d** disaster for you."	1819
2Ki	8: 1	the LORD has **d** a famine in the land	7924
2Ch	18:22	The LORD has **d** disaster for you."	1819
Ezr	6:12	I Darius have **d** it.	10302+10682
Est	2: 1	and what she had done and what he had **d**	1615
	9:31	Mordecai the Jew and Queen Esther had **d**	7756
Job	14: 5	you have **d** the number of his months	907
Ps	78: 5	He **d** statutes for Jacob and established	7756
Isa	10:22	Destruction has been **d,**	3076
	10:23	the destruction **d** upon the whole land.	3076
	28:22	of the destruction **d** against the whole land.	3076
Jer	11:17	who planted you, has **d** disaster for you,	1819
	13:25	the portion I have **d** for you,"	4496
	16:10	the LORD **d** such a great disaster	1819
	40: 2	"The LORD your God **d** this disaster	1819
La	1:17	The LORD has **d** for Jacob	7422

La	2:17	which he **d** long ago.	7422
	3:37	and have it happen if the Lord has not **d** it?	7422
Da	4:31	"This is what is **d** for you,	10042
	9:24	"Seventy 'sevens' are **d** for your people	3155
	9:26	and desolations have been **d.**	3076
	9:27	the end that is **d** is poured out on him."	3076
Na	2: 7	It is **d** that [the city] be exiled	5893
Lk	22:22	The Son of Man will go as it has been **d,**	*3988*

DECREES (132) [DECREE]

Ge	26: 5	my commands, my **d** and my laws."	2978
Ex	15:26	to his commands and keep all his **d,**	2976
	18:16	and inform them of God's **d** and laws."	2976
	18:20	Teach them the **d** and laws,	2976
Lev	10:11	and you must teach the Israelites all the **d**	2976
	18: 4	and be careful to follow my **d.**	2978
	18: 5	Keep my **d** and laws,	2978
	18:26	But you must keep my **d** and my laws.	2978
	19:19	" 'Keep my **d.**	2978
	19:37	" 'Keep all my **d** and all my laws	2978
	20: 8	Keep my **d** and follow them.	2978
	20:22	" 'Keep all my **d** and follow them,	2978
	25:18	" 'Follow my **d** and be careful	2978
	26: 3	" 'If you follow my **d** and are careful	2978
	26:15	and if you reject my **d** and abhor my laws	2978
	26:43	and abhorred my **d.**	2978
	26:46	These are the **d,** the laws and	2976
Dt	4: 1	the **d** and laws I am about to teach you.	2976
	4: 5	I have taught you **d** and laws as	2976
	4: 6	who will hear about all these **d** and say,	2976
	4: 8	as to have such righteous **d** and laws	2976
	4:14	the **d** and laws you are to follow in the land	2976
	4:40	Keep his **d** and commands,	2976
	4:45	**d** and laws Moses gave them	2976
	5: 1	Hear, O Israel, the **d** and laws I declare	2976
	5:31	**d** and laws you are to teach them to follow	2976
	6: 1	the commands, **d** and laws	2976
	6: 2	as long as you live by keeping all his **d**	2978
	6:17	and the stipulations and **d** he has given you.	2976
	6:20	the meaning of the stipulations, **d** and laws	2976
	6:24	to obey all these **d** and to fear	2976
	7:11	**d** and laws I give you today.	2976
	8:11	and his **d** that I am giving you this day.	2978
	10:13	to observe the LORD's commands and **d**	2978
	11: 1	his **d,** his laws and his commands always.	2978
	11:32	be sure that you obey all the **d**	2976
	12: 1	the **d** and laws you must be careful	2976
	16:12	and follow carefully these **d.**	2976
	17:19	the words of this law and these **d**	2978
	26:16	to follow these **d** and laws;	2976
	26:17	that you will keep his **d,**	2976
	27:10	and follow his commands and **d**	2978
	28:15	and **d** I am giving you today,	2978
	28:45	the commands and **d** he gave you.	2978
	30:10	and **d** that are written in this Book of	2978
	30:16	and to keep his commands, **d** and laws;	2978
Jos	24:25	at Shechem he drew up for them **d**	2976
2Sa	22:23	I have not turned away from his **d.**	2978
1Ki	2: 3	keep his **d** and commands,	2978
	6:12	if you follow my **d,**	2978
	8:58	**d** and regulations he gave our fathers.	2976
	8:61	to live by his **d** and obey his commands,	2976
	9: 4	and do all I command and observe my **d**	2976
	9: 6	the commands and **d** I have given you	2978
	11:11	not kept my covenant and my **d,**	2978
2Ki	17:13	Observe my commands and **d,**	2978
	17:15	They rejected his **d**	2976
	17:34	nor adhere to the **d** and ordinances,	2978
	17:37	You must always be careful to keep the **d**	2976
	23: 3	and keep his commands, regulations and **d**	2978
1Ch	22:13	the **d** and laws that the LORD gave Moses	2976
	29:19	requirements and **d** and to do everything	2976
2Ch	7:17	and observe my **d** and laws,	2976
	7:19	"But if you turn away and forsake the **d**	2978
	19:10	commands, **d** or ordinances—	2976
	33: 8	**d** and ordinances given through Moses."	2976
	34:31	and keep his commands, regulations and **d**	2976
Ezr	6:14	the command of the God of Israel and the **d**	10302
	7:10	and to teaching its **d** and laws in Israel.	2976
	7:11	in matters concerning the commands and **d**	2976
Ne	1: 7	**d** and laws you gave your servant Moses.	2976
	9:13	and **d** and commands that are good,	2976
	9:14	and laws through your servant Moses.	2978
	10:29	regulations and **d** of the LORD our Lord.	2976
Ps	18:22	I have not turned away from his **d,**	2978
	44: 4	who decrees victories for Jacob.	7422
	89:31	if they violate my **d** and fail	2978
	94:20	one that brings on misery by its **d?**	2976
	99: 7	and the **d** he gave them.	2706
	119: 5	my ways were steadfast in obeying your **d!**	2976
	119: 8	I will obey your **d;**	2976
	119:12	teach me your **d.**	2976
	119:16	I delight in your **d**	2978
	119:23	your servant will meditate on your **d.**	2976
	119:26	teach me your **d.**	2976
	119:33	Teach me, O LORD, to follow your **d;**	2976
	119:48	which I love, and I meditate on your **d.**	2976
	119:54	Your **d** are the theme	2978
	119:64	teach me your **d.**	2976
	119:68	teach me your **d.**	2976
	119:71	to be afflicted so that I might learn your **d.**	2976
	119:80	May my heart be blameless toward your **d,**	2976
	119:83	I do not forget your **d.**	2976
	119:112	My heart is set on keeping your **d** to	2976
	119:117	I will always have regard for your **d;**	2976
	119:118	You reject all who stray from your **d,**	2976

Ps	119:124	to your love and teach me your **d.**	2976
	119:135	upon your servant and teach me your **d.**	2976
	119:145	O LORD, and I will obey your **d.**	2976
	119:155	for they do not seek out your **d.**	2976
	119:171	for you teach me your **d.**	2976
	147:19	his laws and **d** to Israel.	2976
Pr	31: 5	lest they drink and forget what the law **d,**	2976
Isa	10: 1	to those who issue oppressive **d,**	4180+4180
Jer	31:35	who **d** the moon and stars to shine by night,	2978
	31:36	"Only if these **d** vanish from my sight,"	2976
	44:10	and the **d** I set before you and your fathers.	2978
	44:23	not obeyed him or followed his law or his **d**	2978
Eze	5: 6	and **d** more than the nations and countries	2978
	5: 7	around you and have not followed my **d**	2978
	11:12	not followed my **d** or kept my laws	2978
	11:20	Then they will follow my **d** and be careful	2978
	18: 9	He follows my **d** and faithfully keeps	2978
	18:17	He keeps my laws and follows my **d.**	2978
	18:19	and has been careful to keep all my **d,**	2978
	18:21	and keeps all my **d** and does what is just	2978
	20:11	I gave them my **d** and made known	2978
	20:13	not follow my **d** but rejected my laws—	2978
	20:16	and did not follow my **d**	2978
	20:19	follow my **d** and be careful	2978
	20:21	They did not follow my **d,**	2978
	20:24	not obeyed my laws but had rejected my **d**	2978
	33:15	follows the **d** that give life,	2978
	36:27	in you and move you to follow my **d** and	2978
	37:24	and be careful to keep my **d.**	2978
	44:24	and my **d** for all my appointed feasts,	2978
Am	2: 4	of the LORD and have not kept his **d,**	2976
Zec	1: 6	But did not my words and my **d,**	2976
Mal	3: 7	from my **d** and have not kept them.	2976
	4: 4	the **d** and laws I gave him at Horeb	2976
Ac	17: 7	They are all defying Caesar's **d,**	*1504*

DEDAN (10) [DEDANITES]

Ge	10: 7	The sons of Raamah: Sheba and **D.**	1847
	25: 3	Jokshan was the father of Sheba and **D;**	1847
	25: 3	the descendants of **D** were the Asshurites.	1847
1Ch	1: 9	The sons of Raamah: Sheba and **D.**	1847
	1:32	The sons of Jokshan: Sheba and **D.**	1847
Jer	25:23	**D,** Tema, Buz and all who are	1847
	49: 8	hide in deep caves, you who live in **D,**	1847
Eze	25:13	and from Teman to **D** they will fall by	1847
	27:20	" '**D** traded in saddle blankets with you.	1847
	38:13	Sheba and **D** and the merchants of Tarshish	1847

DEDANITES (1) [DEDAN]

Isa	21:13	You caravans of **D,**	1848

DEDICATE (7) [DEDICATED, DEDICATES, DEDICATION]

Lev	27: 2	a special vow to **d** persons to the LORD	NIH
	27:26	however, may **d** the firstborn of an animal,	7727
Nu	6:12	He must **d** himself to the LORD for	5693
Dt	20: 5	in battle and someone else may **d** it.	2852
2Ch	2: 4	the Name of the LORD my God and to **d** it	7727
Pr	20:25	a man to **d** something rashly and only later	7731
Eze	43:26	thus they will **d** it.	3338+4848

DEDICATED (30) [DEDICATE]

Lev	21:12	because he has been **d** by the anointing oil	5694
Nu	6: 9	thus defiling the hair he has **d,**	5694
	6:18	Nazirite must shave off the hair that he **d.**	5694
	18: 6	**d** to the LORD to do the work at the Tent	5989
Dt	20: 5	a new house and not **d** it?	2852
2Sa	8:11	King David **d** these articles to the LORD,	7727
	8:12	He also **d** the plunder taken	NIH
1Ki	7:51	things his father David had **d**—	7731
	8:63	the king and all the Israelites **d** the temple	2852
	15:15	and the articles that he and his father had **d.**	7731
2Ki	12:18	of Judah took all the sacred objects **d**	7727
	12:18	**gifts** he himself had **d**	7731
	23:11	the horses that the kings of Judah had **d** to	5989
	23:11	then burned the **chariots d** to the sun.	AIT
1Ch	18:11	King David **d** these articles to the LORD,	7727
	26:20	of God and the treasuries for the **d things.**	7731
	26:26	of all the treasuries for the things **d**	7727
	26:27	in battle they **d** for the repair of the temple	7727
	26:28	And everything **d** by Samuel the seer and	7727
	26:28	and all the other **d** things were in the care	7727
	28:12	and for the treasuries for the **d things.**	7731
2Ch	5: 1	**things** his father David had **d**—	7731
	7: 5	So the king and all the people **d** the temple	2852
	15:18	and the articles that he and his father had **d.**	7731
	29:31	"You have now **d** yourselves to the LORD.	3338+4848
	31: 6	the holy things **d** to the LORD their God,	7727
	31:12	tithes and **d** gifts.	7731
Ne	3: 1	They **d** it and set its doors in place,	7727
	3: 1	as the Tower of the Hundred, which they **d,**	7727
Lk	21: 5	and with **gifts d** to God.	*356*

DEDICATES (7) [DEDICATE]

Lev	27:14	" 'If a man **d** his house as something holy	7727
	27:15	his house redeems it,	7727
	27:16	" 'If a man **d** to the LORD part	7727
	27:17	If he **d** his field during the Year of Jubilee,	7727
	27:18	But if he **d** his field after the Jubilee,	7727
	27:19	the man who **d** the field wishes to redeem it,	7727
	27:22	a man **d** to the LORD a field he has bought,	7727

DEDICATION (15) [DEDICATE]

Nu	6:19	the Nazirite has shaved off the hair of his **d**,	5694
	7:10	the leaders brought their offerings for its **d**	2853
	7:11	to bring his offering for the **d** of the altar."	2853
	7:84	**offerings** of the Israelite leaders **for the d**	2853
	7:88	These were the **offerings for the d** of	2853
2Ch	7: 9	for they had celebrated the **d** of the altar	2853
Ezr	6:16	celebrated the **d** of the house of God	10273
	6:17	For the **d** of this house of God they offered	10273
Ne	12:27	At the **d** of the wall of Jerusalem,	2853
	12:27	the **d** with songs of thanksgiving and with	2853
Ps	30: T	For the **d** of the temple.	2853
Da	3: 2	to the **d** of the image he had set up.	10273
	3: 3	for the **d** of the image	10273
Jn	10:22	Then came the **Feast of D** at Jerusalem.	1589
1Ti	5:11	their **sensual desires overcome their d** to	2952

DEED (12) [DEEDED, DEEDS]

Dt	17: 5	the man or woman who has done this evil **d**	1821
Ecc	3:17	a time for every **d."**	5126
	12:14	For God will bring every **d** into judgment,	5126
Jer	32:10	I signed and sealed the **d**, had it witnessed,	6219
	32:11	I took the **d** of purchase	6219
	32:12	and I gave this **d** to Baruch son of Neriah,	6219
	32:12	of the witnesses who had signed the **d** and	6219
	32:14	both the sealed and unsealed copies of the **d**	6219
	32:16	the **d** of purchase to Baruch son of Neriah,	6219
Lk	24:19	powerful in word and **d** before God and all	2240
Col	3:17	whatever you do, whether in word or **d**,	2240
2Th	2:17	and strengthen you in every good **d**	2240

DEEDED (2) [DEED]

Ge	23:17	within the borders of the field—was **d**	7756
	23:20	in it were **d** to Abraham by the Hittites as	7756

DEEDS (110) [DEED]

Dt	3:24	in heaven or on earth who can do the **d**	5126
	4:34	or by great and **awesome d,**	4616
	34:12	or performed the awesome **d** that Moses did	1524
1Sa	2: 3	and by him **d** are weighed.	6613
	2:23	the people about these wicked **d** of yours.	1821
	24:13	'From evildoers come **evil d,'**	8400
2Sa	3:39	the evildoer according to his **evil d!"**	8288
1Ch	16:24	his marvelous **d** among all peoples.	AIT
Ezr	9:13	a result of our evil **d** and our great guilt,	5126
Ne	6:19	they kept reporting to me his **good d** and	3208
Job	34:25	Because he takes note of their **d,**	5042
Ps	14: 1	They are corrupt, their **d** are vile;	6613
	17: 4	As for the **d** of men—	7190
	26: 7	and telling of all your **wonderful d.**	AIT
	28: 4	for their **d** and for their evil work;	7189
	45: 4	let your right hand display **awesome d.**	AIT
	65: 5	with **awesome d** of righteousness,	3707
	66: 3	Say to God, "How awesome are your **d!**	5126
	71:17	and to this day I declare your **marvelous d.**	AIT
	72:18	who alone does **marvelous d.**	AIT
	73:28	I will tell of all your **d.**	4856
	75: 1	men tell of your **wonderful d.**	AIT
	77:11	I will remember the **d** of the LORD;	5095
	77:12	and consider all your **mighty d.**	6613
	78: 4	the next generation the **praiseworthy d** of	9335
	78: 7	in God and would not forget his **d**	5095
	86: 8	no **d** can compare with yours.	5126
	86:10	For you are great and do **marvelous d;**	AIT
	88:12	or your **righteous d** in the land of oblivion?	7407
	90:16	May your **d** be shown to your servants,	7189
	92: 4	you make me glad by your **d,** O LORD;	7189
	96: 3	his **marvelous d** among all peoples.	AIT
	101: 3	The **d** of faithless men I hate;	6913
	103: 7	his **d** to the people of Israel;	6613
	106:22	miracles in the land of Ham and **awesome d**	AIT
	106:29	the LORD to anger by their **wicked d,**	5095
	106:39	by their **d** they prostituted themselves.	5095
	107: 8	for his unfailing love and his **wonderful d**	AIT
	107:15	for his unfailing love and his **wonderful d**	AIT
	107:21	for his unfailing love and his **wonderful d**	AIT
	107:24	his **wonderful d** in the deep.	AIT
	107:31	for his unfailing love and his **wonderful d**	AIT
	111: 3	Glorious and majestic are his **d,**	7189
	141: 4	in wicked **d** with men who are evildoers;	6613
	141: 5	against the **d of evildoers;**	8288
	145: 6	and I will proclaim your **great d.**	1525
Pr	5:22	The **evil d** of a wicked man ensnare him;	6411
	8:22	before his **d** of old;	5148
Isa	1:16	Take your evil **d** out of my sight!	5095
	3: 8	their words and **d** are against the LORD,	5095
	3:10	for they will enjoy the fruit of their **d.**	5095
	5:12	but they have no regard for the **d** of	7189
	32: 8	and by **noble d** he stands.	AIT
	41:29	Their **d** amount to nothing;	5126
	59: 6	Their **d** are evil deeds,	5126
	59: 6	Their deeds are evil **d,**	5126
	63: 7	**d** for which he is to be **praised,**	AIT
	65: 7	the full payment for their former **d."**	7190
Jer	5:28	Their evil **d** have no limit;	1821
	17:10	according to what his **d deserve."**	5095
	21:14	I will punish you as your **d deserve,**	5095
	23:22	from their evil ways and from their evil **d.**	5095
	25:14	I will repay them according to their **d** and	7189
	32:19	and mighty are your **d,**	6614
	32:19	to his conduct and as his **d deserve.**	5095
	32:44	and **d** will be signed,	6219
	48: 10	Since you trust in your **d** and riches,	5126
	50:29	Repay her for her **d;**	7189

Eze	22:28	Her prophets whitewash these **d** for them	NIH
	36:31	Then you will remember your evil ways and wicked **d,**	5095
Hos	4: 9	for their ways and repay them for their **d.**	5095
	5: 4	"Their **d** do not permit them to return	5095
	7: 2	not realize that I remember all their **evil d.**	8288
	9:15	Because of their sinful **d,**	5095
	12: 2	and repay him according to his **d.**	5095
Ob	1:15	your **d** will return upon your own head.	1691
Mic	7:13	as the result of their **d.**	5095
Hab	3: 2	I stand in awe of your **d,** O LORD.	7189
Mt	5:16	that they may see your good **d**	2240
Lk	1:51	He has performed **mighty d** with his arm;	3197
	23:41	for we are getting what our **d** deserve.	4556
Jn	3:19	of light because their **d** were evil.	2240
	3:20	the light for fear that his **d** will be exposed.	2240
Ac	19:18	and openly confessed their evil **d.**	4552
	26:20	and prove their repentance by their **d.**	2240
Ro	13:12	So let us put aside the **d** of darkness and put	2240
Eph	5:11	Have nothing to do with the fruitless **d**	2240
1Ti	2:10	but with good **d,**	2240
	5:10	and is well known for her good **d,**	2240
	5:10	and devoting herself to all kinds of good **d.**	2240
	5:25	In the same way, good **d** are obvious,	2240
	6:18	to be rich in good **d,**	2240
Heb	10:24	on toward love and good **d.**	2240
Jas	2:14	if a man claims to have faith but has no **d?**	2240
	2:18	"You have faith; I have **d."**	2240
	2:18	Show me your faith without **d,**	2240
	2:20	that faith without **d** is useless?	2240
	2:26	so faith without **d** is dead.	2240
	3:13	by **d** done in the humility that comes	2240
1Pe	2:12	they may see your good **d** and glorify God	2240
2Pe	2: 8	by the lawless **d** he saw and heard)—	2240
Rev	2: 2	I know your **d,** your hard work and	2240
	2:19	I know your **d,** your love and faith,	2240
	2:23	repay each of you according to your **d.**	2240
	3: 1	I know your **d;** you have a reputation	2240
	3: 2	for I have not found your **d** complete in	2240
	3: 8	I know your **d.**	2240
	3:15	I know your **d,** that you are neither cold	2240
	14:13	for their **d** will follow them."	2240
	15: 3	"Great and marvelous are your **d,**	2240

DEEP (107) [ANKLE-DEEP, DEEPER, DEEPEST, DEEPLY, DEEPS, DEPTH, DEPTHS]

Ge	1: 2	darkness was over the surface of the **d,**	9333
	2:21	the man to fall into a **d sleep;**	9554
	7:11	the springs of the great **d** burst forth,	9333
	8: 2	Now the springs of the **d** and the floodgates	9333
	15:12	Abram fell into a **d sleep,**	9554
	49:25	blessings of the **d** that lies below,	9333
Ex	15: 5	The **d waters** have covered them;	9333
	15: 8	**d waters** congealed in the heart of the sea.	9333
Lev	13: 3	the sore appears to be more than skin **d,**	6678
	13: 4	to be more than skin **d** and the hair in it has	6678
	13:20	and if it appears to be more than skin **d** and	9166
	13:21	not more than skin **d** and has faded,	9166
	13:25	and it appears to be more than skin **d,**	6678
	13:26	in the spot and if it is not more than skin **d**	9166
	13:30	and if it appears to be more than skin **d** and	6678
	13:31	it does not seem to be more than skin **d**	6678
	13:32	not appear to be more than skin **d,**	6678
	13:34	and appear to be no more than skin **d,**	6678
Dt	4:11	with black clouds and **d darkness.**	6906
	5:22	the cloud and the **d darkness;**	6906
	33:13	above and with the **d waters** that lie below;	9333
1Sa	26:12	the LORD had put them into a **d sleep.**	9554
2Sa	22:17	he drew me out of **d waters.**	8041
	24:14	David said to Gad, "I am in **d distress.**	4394
1Ki	7:31	that had a circular frame one cubit **d**	2025+5087
	7:35	a circular band half a cubit **d.**	7757
	18:27	Perhaps he is in **d thought,** or busy,	8488
1Ch	21:13	David said to Gad, "I am in **d distress.**	4394
Job	3: 5	and **d shadow** claim it once more;	7516
	4:13	when **d sleep** falls on men,	9554
	7:12	Am I the sea, or the **monster of the d,**	9490
	10:21	to the land of gloom and **d shadow,**	7516
	10:22	of **d shadow** and disorder,	7516
	12:22	He reveals the **d things** of darkness	6678
	12:22	and brings **d shadows** into	7516
	16:16	**d shadows** ring my eyes;	7516
	24:17	For all of them, **d darkness** is their morning	7516
	26: 5	"The dead are in **d anguish,**	2655
	28:14	The **d** says, 'It is not in me';	9333
	33:15	when **d sleep** falls on men as they slumber	9554
	34:22	There is no dark place, no **d shadow,**	7516
	38:16	the sea or walked in the recesses of the **d?**	9333
	38:30	when the surface of the **d** is frozen?	9333
	41:32	one would think the **d** had white hair.	9333
Ps	18:16	he drew me out of **d waters.**	8041
	33: 7	he puts the **d** into storehouses.	9333
	36: 6	your justice like the great **d.**	9333
	42: 7	**D** calls to deep in the roar	9333
	42: 7	to **d** in the roar of your waterfalls;	9333
	44:19	and covered us over with **d darkness.**	7516
	69: 2	I have come into the **d waters;**	5099
	69:14	from those who hate me, from the **d waters.**	5099
	104: 6	You covered it with the **d** as with	9333
	107:24	his wonderful deeds in the **d.**	5185
Pr	4:19	the way of the wicked is like **d darkness;**	696
	7:18	Come, let's **drink d** of love till morning;	8115
	8:27	the horizon on the face of the **d,**	9333
	8:28	and fixed securely the fountains of the **d,**	9333

Pr	18: 4	The words of a man's mouth are **d waters,**	6678
	19:15	Laziness brings on **d sleep,**	9554
	20: 5	The purposes of a man's heart are **d waters,**	6678
	22:14	The mouth of an adulteress is a **d pit;**	6678
	23:27	a prostitute is a **d pit** and a wayward wife is	6678
	25: 3	As the heavens are high and the earth is **d,**	6679
Isa	29:10	over you a **d sleep:**	8120+9554
	30:33	Its fire pit has been made **d** and wide,	6676
	44:27	who says to the **watery d,**	7425
	51:10	the waters of the great **d,**	9333
	54: 7	with **d compassion** I will bring you back.	1524
	54: 8	for brightness, but we walk in **d shadows.**	696
Jer	13:16	to thick darkness and change it to **d gloom.**	6906
	49: 8	Turn and flee, hide in **d caves,**	6676
	49:30	Stay in **d caves,** you who live in Hazor,"	6676
La	2:13	Your wound is as **d** as the sea.	1524
Eze	23:32	a cup large and **d;**	6678
	31: 4	**d springs** made it grow tall;	9333
	31:15	down to the grave I covered the **d springs**	9333
	40: 7	it was one rod **d.**	8145
	40: 7	the portico facing the temple was one rod **d.**	NIH
	40: 9	it was eight cubits **d**	6678
	40:30	and five cubits **d.)**	8145
	43:13	Its gutter is a cubit **d** and a cubit wide,	NIH
	47: 5	**d enough to swim in—**	8467
Da	2:22	He reveals **d** and hidden things;	10555
	8:18	I was in a **d sleep,**	8101
	10: 9	I fell into a **d sleep,**	8101
Hos	5: 2	The rebels are **d** in slaughter.	6676
	9: 9	They have sunk **d** into corruption,	6676
Am	1: 4	up the great **d** and devoured the land.	9333
Jnh	1: 5	he lay down and **fell into a d sleep.**	8101
	2: 3	You hurled me into the **d,**	5185
	2: 5	the **d** surrounded me;	9333
Hab	3:10	the **d** roared and lifted its waves on high.	9333
Mk	7:34	up to heaven and **with a d sigh** said to him,	5100
Lk	5: 4	he said to Simon, "Put out into **d water,**	958
	6:48	who dug **down** and laid the foundation	959
Jn	4:11	to draw with and the well is **d.**	960
Ac	20: 9	into a **d sleep** as Paul talked on and on.	960
	27:28	**a hundred and twenty feet d.**	1633+3976
	27:28	and found it was **ninety feet d.**	1278+3976
Ro	10: 7	"or 'Who will descend into the **d?' "**	12
1Co	2:10	even the **d things** of God.	958
2Co	7: 7	your **d sorrow,** your ardent concern for me,	3851
Eph	3:18	how wide and long and high and **d** is	958
1Th	1: 5	with the Holy Spirit and with **d conviction.**	4498
1Ti	3: 9	They must keep hold of the **d truths** of	3696
Rev	2:24	learned Satan's so-called **d secrets**	960

DEEPER (2) [DEEP]

Lev	14:37	that appear to be **d** than the surface of	9166
Job	11: 8	They are **d** than the depths of the grave—	6678

DEEPEST (4) [DEEP]

Job	10:22	to the land of **d night,**	694+4017+6547
Ps	107:10	Some sat in darkness and the **d gloom,**	7516
	107:14	the **d gloom** and broke away their chains.	7516
Isa	7:11	in the **d depths** or in the highest heights."	6676

DEEPLY (12) [DEEP]

Ge	43:30	**D moved** at the sight of his brother,	4023+8171
1Sa	1:15	"I am a woman who is **d troubled.**	7997+8120
Isa	66:11	you will **drink d** and delight	5209
Da	7:28	I, Daniel, was **d troubled** by my thoughts,	10678
Mk	3: 5	**d distressed** at their stubborn hearts,	5200
	8:12	He **sighed d** and said, "Why	417+3836+4460
	14:33	he began to be **d distressed** and troubled.	1701
Jn	11:33	he was **d moved** in spirit and troubled.	1839
	11:38	Jesus, once more **d moved,**	1839
Ac	8: 2	Godly men buried Stephen and **mourned d**	3157+3489+4472
1Pe	1:22	love one another **d,** from the heart.	1757
	4: 8	Above all, love each other **d,**	1756

DEEPS (1) [DEEP]

Pr	3:20	by his knowledge the **d** were divided,	9333

DEER (14)

Dt	12:15	as if it were gazelle or **d,**	385
	12:22	Eat them as you would gazelle or **d.**	385
	14: 5	the **d,** the gazelle, the roe deer,	385
	14: 5	the gazelle, the **roe d,** the wild goat,	3502
	15:22	as if it were gazelle or **d,**	385
2Sa	22:34	He makes my feet like the feet of a **d;**	387
1Ki	4:23	as well as **d,** gazelles,	385
Ps	18:33	He makes my feet like the feet of a **d;**	387
	42: 1	As the **d** pants for streams of water,	385
Pr	5:19	A loving doe, a graceful **d—**	3607
	7:22	like a **d** stepping into a noose	385
Isa	35: 6	Then will the lame leap like a **d,**	385
La	1: 6	Her princes are like **d** that find no pasture;	385
Hab	3:19	he makes my feet like the feet of a **d,**	387

DEFAMED (1)

Isa	48:11	How can I let myself be **d?**	2725

DEFEAT (9) [DEFEATED, DEFEATING]

Ex	32:18	it is not the sound of **d;**	2711
Nu	14:45	be able to **d** them and drive them out of	5782
Jdg	2:15	of the LORD was against them to **d** them,	8288
1Sa	4: 3	"Why did the LORD bring **d** upon us today	5597

2Ki	13:19	But now *you* will **d** it only three times."	5782
Ps	92:11	My eyes have seen the **d** of my adversaries;	NIH
Isa	9: 4	For as in the day of Midian's **d**,	NIH
Jer	37:10	to **d** the entire Babylonian army	5782
Heb	7: 1	He met Abraham returning from the **d** of	3158

DEFEATED (53) [DEFEAT]

Ge	14: 5	and **d** the Rephaites in Ashteroth Karnaim,	5782
	36:35	who **d** Midian in the country of Moab,	5782
Lev	26:17	so that *you* will be **d** by your enemies,	5597
Nu	14:42	*You* will be **d** by your enemies.	5597
Dt	1: 4	after he had **d** Sihon king of the Amorites,	5782
	1: 4	and at Edrei had **d** Og king of Bashan,	NIH
	1:42	*You* will be **d** by your enemies.' "	5597
	4:46	and was **d** by Moses and the Israelites	5782
	7: 2	over to you and *you* have **d** them,	5782
	28: 7	up against you *will* be **d** before you.	5597
	28:25	The LORD will cause you *to* be **d**	5597
	29: 7	but *we* **d** them,	5782
Jos	10:10	who **d** them in a great victory at Gibeon,	5782
	10:33	but Joshua **d** him and his army—	5782
	11: 8	*They* **d** them and pursued them all the way	5782
	12: 1	of the land whom the Israelites had **d**	5782
	13:12	Moses had **d** them and taken over their land.	5782
	13:21	Moses had **d** him and the Midianite chiefs,	5782
Jdg	1:10	and **d** Sheshai, Ahiman	5782
	11:21	and *they* **d** them.	5782
	20:35	The LORD **d** Benjamin before Israel,	5597
1Sa	4: 2	Israel was **d** by the Philistines,	5597
	4:10	and the Israelites were **d** and every man fled	5597
	14:48	He fought valiantly and **d** the Amalekites,	5782
2Sa	2:17	the men of Israel were **d** by David's men,	5597
	5:20	and there he **d** them.	5782
	8: 1	David **d** the Philistines and subdued them,	5782
	8: 2	David also **d** the Moabites.	5782
	8: 9	of Hamath heard that David had **d**	5782
	10:19	of Hadadezer saw that *they* had **been d**	5597
	18: 7	the army of Israel was **d** by David's men,	5597
1Ki	8:33	"When your people Israel *have* been **d** by	5597
2Ki	13:19	then *you would have* **d** Aram	5782
	13:25	Three times Jehoash **d** him,	5782
	14: 7	the *one who* **d** ten thousand Edomites in	5782
	14:10	*You have* indeed **d** Edom and	5782+5782
	18: 8	he **d** the Philistines,	5782
1Ch	1:46	who **d** Midian in the country of Moab,	5782
	5:10	*who were* **d** at their hands,	5877
	14:11	and there *he* **d** them.	5782
	18: 1	David **d** the Philistines and subdued them,	5782
	18: 2	David also **d** the Moabites.	5782
	18: 9	of Hamath heard that David had **d**	5782
	19:19	of Hadadezer saw that *they* had been **d**	5597
2Ch	6:24	"When your people Israel *have* been **d** by	5597
	20:22	and *they* were **d**.	5597
	25:19	You say to yourself that *you* have **d** Edom,	5782
	28: 5	The Arameans **d** him and took many	5782
	28:23	who had **d** him;	5782
Jer	46: 2	of Egypt, which was **d** at Carchemish on	5782
	46: 5	they are retreating, their warriors are **d**.	4198
Da	11:11	army, but it *will* be **d**.	928+3338+5989
1Co	6: 7	lawsuits among you means you have been completely **d** already.	2488

DEFEATING (5) [DEFEAT]

Ge	14:17	After Abram returned from **d** Kedorlaomer	5782
Jdg	20:32	"We *are* **d** them as before,"	5597
	20:39	"We *are* **d** them as in the first battle."	5597+5597
2Sa	1: 1	David returned from **d** the Amalekites	5782
Da	7:21	against the saints and **d** them,	10321

DEFECT (58) [DEFECTED, DEFECTS]

Ex	12: 5	be year-old males without **d**,	9459
	29: 1	Take a young bull and two rams **without d**.	9459
Lev	1: 3	he is to offer a male **without d**.	9459
	1:10	he is to offer a male **without d**.	9459
	3: 1	before the LORD an animal **without d**.	9459
	3: 6	he is to offer a male or female **without d**.	9459
	4: 3	a young bull **without d** as a sin offering for	9459
	4:23	as his offering a male goat **without d**.	9459
	4:28	a female goat **without d**.	9459
	4:32	he is to bring a female **without d**.	9459
	5:15	one **without d** and of the proper value	9459
	5:18	one **without d** and of the proper value.	9459
	6: 6	one **without d** and of the proper value.	9459
	9: 2	*both* **without d**, and present them before	9459
	9: 3	both a year old and **without d**—	9459
	14:10	each **without d**, along with three-tenths of	9459
	21:17	of your descendants who has a **d** may come	4583
	21:18	No man who has any **d** may come near:	4583
	21:20	or who has any eye **d**,	9319
	21:21	the priest who has any **d** is to come near	4583
	21:21	He has a **d**;	4583
	21:23	yet because of his **d**,	4583
	22:19	you must present a male **without d** from	9459
	22:20	Do not bring anything with a **d**,	4583
	22:21	be **without d** or defect to be acceptable.	9459
	23:12	to the LORD a lamb a year old **without d**,	9459
	23:18	each a year old and **without d**,	9459
Nu	6:14	a year-old male lamb **without d** for	9459
	6:14	a year-old ewe lamb **without d** for	9459
	6:14	a ram **without d** for a fellowship offering,	9459
	19: 2	a red heifer **without d** or blemish and	9459
	28: 3	two lambs a year old **without d**,	9459
	28: 9	of two lambs a year old **without d**,	9459
	28:11	a year old, *all* **without d**.	9459
	28:19	a year old, *all* **without d**.	9459

Nu	28:31	Be sure the animals are **without d**.	9459
	29: 2	male lambs a year old, *all* **without d**.	9459
	29: 8	male lambs a year old, *all* **without d**.	9459
	29:13	male lambs a year old, *all* **without d**.	9459
	29:17	male lambs a year old, *all* **without d**.	9459
	29:20	male lambs a year old, *all* **without d**.	9459
	29:23	male lambs a year old, *all* **without d**.	9459
	29:26	male lambs a year old, *all* **without d**.	9459
	29:29	male lambs a year old, *all* **without d**.	9459
	29:32	male lambs a year old, *all* **without d**.	9459
	29:36	male lambs a year old, *all* **without d**.	9459
Dt	15:21	If an animal has a **d**, is lame or blind,	4583
	17: 1	an ox or a sheep that has any **d** or flaw in it,	4583
Eze	43:22	a male goat **without d** for a sin offering;	9459
	43:23	and a ram from the flock, both **without d**.	9459
	43:25	and a ram from the flock, *both* **without d**.	9459
	45:18	to take a young bull **without d** and purify	9459
	45:23	and seven rams **without d** as	9459
	46: 4	and a ram, *all* **without d**.	9459
	46: 6	six lambs and a ram, *all* **without d**.	9459
	46:13	to provide a year-old lamb **without d** for	9459
Da	1: 4	young men without any **physical d**,	4583
1Pe	1:19	a lamb **without** blemish or **d**.	834

DEFECTED (3) [DEFECT]

1Ch	12: 8	Some Gadites **d** to David at his stronghold	976
	12:19	of Manasseh **d** to David when he went with	5877
	12:20	these were *the men* of Manasseh *who* **d**	5877

DEFECTS (1) [DEFECT]

Lev	22:25	because they are deformed and have **d**.' "	4583

DEFEND (23) [DEFENDED, DEFENDER, DEFENDERS, DEFENDING, DEFENDS, DEFENSE, DEFENSES]

Jdg	6:31	he can **d** himself when someone breaks	8189
2Ki	19:34	*I will* **d** this city and save it,	1713
	20: 6	*I will* **d** this city for my sake and for	1713
Job	13:15	I *will* surely **d** my ways to his face.	3519
Ps	72: 4	He will **d** the afflicted among the people	9149
	74:22	Rise up, O God, and **d** your cause;	8189
	82: 2	"How long will you **d** the unjust	9149
	82: 3	**D** *the* cause *of* the weak and fatherless;	9149
	119:154	**D** my cause and redeem me;	8189
Pr	31: 9	**d** the rights *of* the poor and needy."	1906
Ecc	4:12	two *can* **d** themselves.	5584+6641
Isa	1:17	**D** *the* cause *of* the fatherless,	9149
	1:23	They *do* not **d** the cause *of* the fatherless;	9149
	37:35	"I *will* **d** this city and save it,	1713
	38: 6	*I will* **d** this city.	1713
Jer	5:28	they *do* not **d** the rights of the poor.	9149
	50:34	He *will* vigorously **d** their cause so	8189+8189
	51:36	"See, I *will* **d** your cause and avenge you;	8189
Da	3:16	we do not need to **d** ourselves *before* you	10601+10754
Zec	9: 8	But *I will* **d** my house	2837
Lk	12:11	about how *you will* **d** yourselves	664
	21:14	how *you will* **d** yourselves.	664
Ac	25:16	and has had an opportunity to **d** himself	665

DEFENDED (3) [DEFEND]

2Sa	23:12	He **d** it and struck the Philistines down,	5911
1Ch	11:14	*They* **d** it and struck the Philistines down,	5911
Jer	22:16	He **d** the cause of the poor and needy,	1906

DEFENDER (6) [DEFEND]

Ex	22: 2	the **d** is not guilty of bloodshed;	2257S
Job	31:35	crushed in court without a **d**.	5911
Ps	68: 5	A father to the fatherless, a **d** *of* widows,	1908
Pr	23:11	for their **D** is strong;	1457
Isa	19:20	he will send them a savior and **d**,	8189
	29:21	who ensnare the **d** in court and	3519

DEFENDERS (1) [DEFEND]

2Sa	11:16	where he knew the **strongest d** were.	408+2657

DEFENDING (5) [DEFEND]

2Ki	9:14	and all Israel had been **d** Ramoth Gilead	9068
Ps	10:18	**d** the fatherless and the oppressed,	9149
Ro	2:15	now even **d** them.)	664
2Co	12:19	that *we have been* **d** ourselves to you?	664
Php	1: 7	in chains or **d** and confirming the gospel,	665

DEFENDS (3) [DEFEND]

Dt	10:18	He **d** the cause of the fatherless and	6913
	33: 7	With his own hands he **d** his **cause**.	8189
Isa	51:22	your God, *who* **d** his people:	8189

DEFENSE (17) [DEFEND]

2Ch	11: 5	in Jerusalem and built up towns for **d**	5190
Job	31:35	I sign now my —	NIH
Ps	35:23	Awake, and rise to my **d!**	5477
Jer	41: 9	of his **d against** Baasha king of Israel.	4946+7156
Na	3: 8	The river was her **d**, the waters her wall.	2658
Ac	7:24	so he went to *his* **d** and avenged him	310
	19:33	in order to make *his* **d** before the people.	664+2527
	22: 1	"Brothers and fathers, listen now to my **d**."	665
	24:10	so I *gladly* make my **d**.	664
	25: 8	Then Paul made *his* **d**:	664
	26: 1	with his hand and began his **d**:	664

Ac	26: 2	as *I* make my **d** against all the accusations	664
	26:24	At this point Festus interrupted Paul's **d**,	664
1Co	9: 3	This is my **d** to those who sit in judgment	665
Php	1:16	that I am put here for the **d** of the gospel.	665
2Ti	4:16	At my first **d**, no one came to my support,	665
1Jn	2: 1	**one who speaks** to the Father in *our* **d**—	4156

DEFENSES (8) [DEFEND]

2Ch	11:11	He strengthened their **d**	5193
	26:15	for use on the towers and on the **corner d**	7157
Job	13:12	your **d** are defenses of clay.	1462
	13:12	your defenses are **d** of clay.	1462
Isa	22: 8	the **d** of Judah are stripped away.	5009
	22: 9	of David had many **breaches in** its **d**;	1323
Joel	2: 8	through **d** without breaking ranks.	8939
Na	3:14	for the siege, strengthen your **d!**	4448

DEFERENCE (1) [DEFERRED]

2Ki	16:18	in **d** to the king of Assyria.	4946+7156

DEFERRED (1) [DEFERENCE]

Pr	13:12	Hope **d** makes the heart sick,	5432

DEFIANCE (1) [DEFY]

1Sa	17:23	from his lines and shouted his usual **d**,	1821

DEFIANT (1) [DEFY]

Pr	7:11	(She is loud and **d**,	6253

DEFIANTLY (2) [DEFY]

Nu	15:30	" 'But anyone who **sins d**,	928+3338+6913+8123
Job	15:26	**d** charging against him with a thick,	928+7418

DEFIED (9) [DEFY]

1Sa	17:36	he has **d** the armies of the living God.	3070
	17:45	whom *you have* **d**.	3070
1Ki	13:21	'You have **d** the word of the LORD	5286
	13:26	"It is the man of God who **d** the word of	5286
Isa	65: 7	on the mountains and **d** me on the hills,	3070
Jer	48:26	"Make her drunk, for *she* has **d** the LORD.	1540+6584
	48:42	be destroyed as a nation because *she* **d**	1540+6584
	50:29	For *she* has **d** the LORD,	2326
Da	3:28	**d** the king's command and were willing	10731

DEFIES (1) [DEFY]

Pr	18: 1	*he* **d** all sound judgment.	1679

DEFILE (32) [DEFILED, DEFILEMENT, DEFILES, DEFILING]

Ex	20:25	for *you* will **d** it if you use a tool on it.	2725
Lev	11:43	not **d** yourselves by any of these creatures.	9210
	18:20	with your neighbor's wife and **d** yourself	3237
	18:23	with an animal and **d** yourself with it.	3237
	18:24	not **d** yourselves in any of these ways,	3237
	18:30	before you came and *do* not **d** yourselves	3237
	20:25	*Do* not **d** yourselves by any animal or bird	9210
	21: 4	and so **d** himself.	2725
	21:15	not **d** his offspring among his people.	2725
Nu	5: 3	the camp so *they will* not **d** their camp,	3237
	18:32	then *you will* not **d** the holy offerings of	2725
	35:34	*Do* not **d** the land where you live and	3237
2Ki	23:16	from them and burned on the altar to **d** it,	3237
Isa	30:22	Then *you will* **d** your idols overlaid	3237
Eze	7:21	and *they will* **d** it.	2725
	9: 7	"**D** the temple and fill the courts with	3237
	14:11	nor *will they* **d** themselves anymore	3237
	18: 6	He does not **d** his neighbor's wife or lie	3237
	18:15	He does not **d** his neighbor's wife.	3237
	20: 7	*do* not **d** yourselves with the idols of Egypt.	3237
	20:18	or keep their laws or **d** yourselves	3237
	20:30	*Will* you **d** yourselves	3237
	20:31	to **d** yourselves with all your idols	3237
	37:23	They *will* no longer **d** themselves	3237
	43: 7	of Israel *will* never again **d** my holy name—	3237
	44:25	not **d** *himself* by going near a dead person;	3237
	44:25	then *he may* **d** himself.	3237
Da	1: 8	to **d** himself with the royal food and wine,	1458
	1: 8	for permission not *to* **d** himself this way.	1458
Heb	12:15	up to cause trouble and **d** many.	3620
Rev	14: 4	These are those who *did* not **d** *themselves*	3662

DEFILED (70) [DEFILE]

Ge	34: 5	that his daughter Dinah *had been* **d**,	3237
	34:13	Because their sister Dinah *had been* **d**,	3237
	34:27	the city where their sister *had been* **d**.	3237
	49: 4	onto my couch and **d** it.	2725
Lev	18:24	to drive out before you **became d**.	3237
	18:25	Even the land *was* **d**;	3237
	18:27	and the land **became d**.	3237
	19:31	for *you will* be **d** by them.	3237
	20: 3	to Molech, *he* has **d** my sanctuary	3237
	21: 7	not marry women **d** *by* prostitution	2729
	21:14	or a *woman* **d** *by* prostitution	2729
	22: 4	also be unclean if he touches something **d**	3238
Nu	5:20	and *you have* **d** yourself by sleeping with	3237
	5:27	If *she has* **d herself** and been unfaithful	3237
	5:28	not **d herself** and is free from impurity,	3237
	6:12	because *he became* **d** during his separation.	3237

Nu	19:20	he has **d** the sanctuary of the LORD.	3237
Dt	22: 9	but also the fruit of the vineyard *will be* **d.**	7727
	24: 4	to marry her again after *she has* **been d.**	3237
Jos	22:19	If the land you possess is **d,**	3238
2Sa	1:21	For there the shield of the mighty **was d.**	1718
2Ki	23:19	and **d** all the shrines at the high places that	6913S
1Ch	5: 1	but when he **d** his father's marriage bed,	2725
Ne	7:64	because they **d** the priestly office and	1459
Job	31: 7	or if my hands *have been* **d,**	1815+4583
Ps	74: 7	they **d** the dwelling place of your Name.	2725
	79: 1	*they have* **d** your holy temple,	3237
	89:39	with your servant and *have* **d** his crown in	2725
	106:39	*They* **d** *themselves* by what they did;	3237
Isa	24: 5	The earth *is* **d** by its people;	2866
	52: 1	and **d** will not enter you again.	3238
Jer	2: 7	But you came and **d** my land	3237
	2:23	"How can you say, '*I am* not **d**;'	3237
	3: 1	*Would* not the land be **completely d?**	2866+2866
	3: 2	*You have* **d** the land with your prostitution	2866
	3: 9	she **d** the land and committed adultery	2866
	7:30	the house that bears my Name and *have* **d** it.	3237
	16:18	because *they have* **d** my land with	2725
	19:13	the kings of Judah will be **d** like this place,	3238
	32:34	in the house that bears my Name and **d** it.	3237
La	4:14	*They are so* **d** with blood that no one dares	1458
Eze	4:13	of Israel will eat **d** food among the nations	3238
	4:14	*I have* never **d** myself.	3237
	5:11	because *you have* **d** my sanctuary	3237
	20:26	*I let them* become **d** through their gifts—	3237
	20:43	by which *you have* **d** yourselves,	3237
	22: 4	the blood you have shed and *have* become **d**	3237
	22:16	*you have* **been d** in the eyes of the nations,	2725
	23: 7	the elite of the Assyrians and **d** herself	3237
	23:13	I saw that *she too* **d** herself;	3237
	23:17	and in their lust *they* **d** her.	3237
	23:17	After *she had been* **d** by them,	3237
	23:30	the nations and **d** yourself with their idols.	3237
	23:38	At that same time *they* **d** my sanctuary	3237
	36:17	*they* **d** it by their conduct and their actions.	3237
	36:18	and because *they had* **d** it with their idols.	3237
	43: 8	*they* **d** my holy name	3237
Hos	6:10	to prostitution and Israel *is* **d.**	3237
Mic	2:10	because *it is* **d,** it is ruined,	3237
	4:11	They say, "Let her be **d,**	2866
Zep	3: 1	to the city of oppressors, rebellious and **d!**	1458
Hag	2:13	"If a *person is* **d** by contact with a dead body	3238
	2:13	*does it become* **d?"**	3237
	2:13	"Yes," the priests replied, "it becomes **d."**	3237
	2:14	and whatever they offer there is **d.**	3238
Mal	1: 7	"You place **d** food on my altar.	1458
	1: 7	"But you ask, 'How *have we* **d** you?'	1458
	1:12	'It *is* **d,'** and of its food,	1458
Ac	21:28	into the temple area and **d** this holy place."	3124
1Co	8: 7	and since their conscience is weak, *it is* **d.**	3662

DEFILEMENT (1) [DEFILE]

2Ch	29: 5	Remove *all* **d** from the sanctuary.	5614

DEFILES (7) [DEFILE]

Lev	21: 9	a priest's daughter **d herself** by becoming	2725
Nu	5:29	and **d herself** while married to her husband,	3237
	19:13	and fails to purify himself **d** the LORD's	3237
Eze	18:11	He **d** his neighbor's wife.	3237
	22: 3	in her midst and **d** herself by making idols,	3237
	22:11	another shamefully **d** his daughter-in-law,	3237
	33:26	and each of you **d** his neighbor's wife.	3237

DEFILING (3) [DEFILE]

Lev	15:31	for **d** my dwelling place,	3237
Nu	6: 9	thus **d** the hair he has dedicated,	3237
2Ch	36:14	and **d** the temple of the LORD,	3237

DEFINITE (2) [DEFINITELY]

1Sa	23:23	and come back to me with **d information.**	3922
Ac	25:26	But I have nothing **d** to write	855

DEFINITELY (2) [DEFINITE]

1Sa	23:10	servant *has* **heard d** that Saul plans	9048+9048
	26: 4	and learned that Saul had **d** arrived.	448+3922

DEFORMED (3) [FORM]

Lev	21:18	or lame, disfigured or **d;**	8594
	22:23	an ox or a sheep *that is* **d** or stunted,	8594
	22:25	because they are **d** and have defects.'"	5426

DEFRAUD (5) [FRAUD]

Lev	19:13	"'Do not **d** your neighbor or rob him.	6943
Hos	12: 7	he loves to **d.**	6943
Mic	2: 2	*They* **d** a man of his home,	6943
Mal	3: 5	against *those who* **d** laborers *of* their wages,	6943
Mk	10:19	*do not* **d,** honor your father and mother.'"	691

DEFY (3) [DEFIANCE, DEFIANT, DEFIANTLY, DEFIED, DEFIES, DEFYING]

1Sa	17:10	"This day I **d** the ranks of Israel!"	3070
	17:25	He comes out to **d** Israel.	3070
	17:26	that *he should* **d** the armies of	3070

DEFYING (2) [DEFY]

Isa	3: 8	**d** his glorious presence.	5286
Ac	17: 7	They *are all* **d** Caesar's decrees,	595+4556

DEGENERATE (KJV) See CORRUPT

DEGRADE (1) [DEGRADED, DEGRADING]

Lev	19:29	"'Do not **d** your daughter by making her	2725

DEGRADED (2) [DEGRADE]

Dt	25: 3	your brother *will be* **d** in your eyes.	7829
Eze	16:25	and **d** your beauty,	9493

DEGRADING (1) [DEGRADE]

Ro	1:24	to sexual impurity *for* the **d of** their bodies	869

DEGREE (KJV) See CIRCUMSTANCES, EXALTED, HIGHBORN, HUMBLE, LOWBORN, RANK, STANDING

DEHAVITES (KJV) See OF (Ezr 4:9)

DEITY (1)

Col	2: 9	For in Christ all the fullness of the **D** lives	2540

DEJECTED (2)

Ge	40: 6	he saw that they *were* **d.**	2407
Isa	19:10	The workers in cloth will be **d,**	1917

DEKAR (KJV) See BEN-DEKER

DELAIAH (7)

1Ch	3:24	Pelaiah, Akkub, Johanan, **D** and Anani—	1933
	24:18	the twenty-third to **D** and the twenty-fourth	1934
Ezr	2:60	The descendants of **D,**	1933
Ne	6:10	to the house of Shemaiah son of **D,**	1933
	7:62	the descendants of **D,**	1933
Jer	36:12	Elishama the secretary, **D** son of Shemaiah,	1934
	36:25	**D** and Gemariah urged the king not to burn	1934

DELAY (15) [DELAYED]

Ge	45: 9	Come down to me; don't **d.**	6641
2Ki	9: 3	Then open the door and run; don't **d!"**	2675
Ps	40:17	O my God, *do not* **d.**	336
	70: 5	O LORD, *do not* **d.**	336
	119:60	and not **d** to obey your commands.	4538
Ecc	5: 4	*do not* **d** in fulfilling it.	336
Isa	48: 9	For my own name's sake *I* **d** my wrath,	799
Jer	4: 6	Flee for safety without **d!**	6641
Eze	12:25	and it shall be fulfilled without **d.**	5432
Da	9:19	For your sake, O my God, *do not* **d,**	336
Hab	2: 3	it will certainly come and *will not* **d.**	336
Mk	1:20	Without **d** he called them,	2317
Ac	25:17	I did not **d** the case,	332+4472
Heb	10:37	and *will not* **d.**	5988
Rev	10: 6	and said, "There will be no more **d!**	5989

DELAYED (6) [DELAY]

Ge	43:10	As it is, if *we had* not **d,**	4538
Jos	10:13	and **d** going down about a full day.	237+4202
Jdg	5:28	Why *is* the clatter of his chariots **d?'**	336
Isa	46:13	and my salvation *will* not be **d.**	336
Eze	12:28	None of my words *will* be **d** any longer;	5432
1Ti	3:15	if *I am* **d,** you will know how people ought	1094

DELEGATION (5)

Jos	9: 4	*as a* **d** whose donkeys were loaded	7493
2Sa	10: 2	So David sent a **d** to express his	928+3338+6269
1Ch	19: 2	So David sent a **d** to express his sympathy	4855
Lk	14:32	a **d** while the other is still a long way off	4561
	19:14	"But his subjects hated him and sent a **d**	4561

DELIBERATELY (3)

Ex	21:14	a man schemes and kills another man **d,**	928+6893
Heb	10:26	If we **d** keep on sinning	1731
2Pe	3: 5	But they **d** forget that long ago	2527

DELICACIES (6) [DELICATE]

Ge	49:20	he will provide **d** *fit for* a king.	5052
Ps	141: 4	let me not eat of their **d.**	4982
Pr	23: 3	Do not crave his **d,**	4761
	23: 6	do not crave his **d.**	4761
Jer	51:34	and filled his stomach with our **d.**	6358
La	4: 5	Those who once ate **d** are destitute in	5052

DELICACY (1) [DELICATE]

SS	7:13	and at our door is every **d,**	4458

DELICATE (2) [DELICACIES, DELICACY]

Isa	47: 1	No more will you be called tender or **d.**	6697
Jer	6: 2	so beautiful and **d.**	6695

DELICIOUS (1)

Pr	9:17	food eaten in secret *is* **d!"**	5838

DELIGHT (69) [DELIGHTED, DELIGHTFUL, DELIGHTING, DELIGHTS]

Lev	26:31	and *I will* take no **d** in the pleasing aroma	8193

Dt	30: 9	The LORD *will* again **d** in you	8464
1Sa	2: 1	for *I* **d** in your deliverance.	8523
	15:22	"Does the LORD **d** in burnt offerings	2914
Ne	1:11	and to the prayer of your servants who **d**	2913
Job	22:26	then *you will* **find d** in the Almighty	6695
	27:10	*Will he* **find d** in the Almighty?	6695
Ps	1: 2	But his **d** is in the law of the LORD,	2914
	16: 3	the glorious ones in whom is all my **d.**	2914
	35: 9	in the LORD and **d** in his salvation.	8464
	35:27	May *those who* **d in** my vindication shout	2913
	37: 4	**D yourself** in the LORD	6695
	43: 4	to God, my joy and my **d.**	1637
	51: 6	*You do* not **d** in sacrifice,	2911
	51:19	whole burnt offerings *to* **d** you;	2911
	62: 4	*they* **take d** in lies.	8354
	68:30	Scatter the nations *who* **d in** war.	2911
	111: 2	they are pondered by all *who* **d** in them.	2913
	112: 1	*who* **finds** great **d** in his commands.	2911
	119:16	*I* **d** in your decrees;	9130
	119:24	Your statutes are my **d;**	9141
	119:35	for there *I* **find d.**	2911
	119:47	for *I* **d** in your commands	9130
	119:70	but I **d** *in your* law.	9130
	119:77	for your law is my **d.**	9141
	119:92	If your law had not been my **d,**	9141
	119:143	but your commands are my **d.**	9141
	119:174	O LORD, and your law is my **d.**	9141
	147:10	nor *his* **d** in the legs of a man;	8354
	149: 4	For the LORD **takes d** in his people;	8354
Pr	1:22	How long *will* mockers **d** in mockery	2773
	2:14	*who* **d in** doing wrong and rejoice in	8524
	8:30	I was **filled with d** day after day,	9141
	11: 1	but accurate weights are his **d.**	8356
	29:17	he will bring **d** to your soul.	5052
Ecc	2:10	My heart *took* **d** in all my work,	8524
SS	1: 4	We rejoice and **d** in you;	8523
	2: 3	*I* **d** to sit in his shade,	2773
Isa	5: 7	the men of Judah are the garden of his **d.**	9141
	11: 3	and he *will* **d** in the fear of the LORD.	8193
	13:17	not care for silver and *have* no **d** in gold.	2911
	32:14	the **d** of donkeys, a pasture for flocks,	5375
	42: 1	my chosen one in whom I **d;**	8354
	55: 2	and your soul *will* **d** in the richest of fare.	6695
	58:13	a **d** and the LORD's holy day honorable,	6696
	61:10	*I* **d** greatly in the LORD;	8464+8464
	62: 4	for the LORD *will* **take d** in you,	2911
	65:18	for I will create Jerusalem to be a **d**	1638
	65:19	over Jerusalem and **take d** in my people;	8464
	66: 3	and their souls **d** in their abominations;	2911
	66:11	and **d** in her overflowing abundance."	6695
Jer	9:24	for in these *I* **d,"** declares the LORD.	2911
	15:16	they were my joy and my heart's **d,**	8525
	31:20	the child in whom I **d?**	9141
	49:25	the town in which I **d?**	5375
Eze	24:16	to take away from you the **d** of your eyes.	4718
	24:21	the **d** of your eyes,	4718
	24:25	the **d** of their eyes, their heart's desire,	4718
Hos	7: 3	"They **d** the king with their wickedness,	8523
Mic	1:16	for the children in whom you **d;**	9503
	7:18	not stay angry forever but **d** to show mercy.	2911
Zep	3:17	He will **take great d** in you,	928+8464+8525
Mt	12:18	the one I love, in whom I **d;**	2305
Mk	12:37	The large crowd listened to him with **d.**	2452
Lk	1:14	He will be a joy and **d** to you,	21
Ro	7:22	For in my inner being *I* **d** in God's law;	5310
1Co	13: 6	Love *does* not **d** in evil but rejoices with	5897
2Co	12:10	*I* **d** in weaknesses, in insults, in hardships,	2305
Col	2: 5	I am present with you in spirit and **d** to see	5897

DELIGHTED (15) [DELIGHT]

Ge	34:19	because *he was* **d** with Jacob's daughter.	2911
Ex	18: 9	Jethro *was* **d** to hear about all	2525
Dt	30: 9	just as *he* **d** in your fathers.	8464
2Sa	22:20	he rescued me because *he* **d** in me.	2911
1Ki	10: 9	who *has* **d** in you and placed you on	2911
2Ch	9: 8	who *has* **d** in you and placed you	2911
Est	5:14	This suggestion **d** Haman,	3512
Ps	22:20	he rescued me because *he* **d** in me.	2911
Isa	1:29	of the sacred oaks *in* which *you have* **d;**	2773
Mk	14:11	They *were* **d** to hear this and promised	5897
Lk	13:17	but the people *were* **d** with all	5897
	22: 5	*They were* **d** and agreed to give him money.	5897
2Co	7:13	*we were* especially **d** to see how	4359+5897
1Th	2: 8	so much that *we were* **d** to share with you	2305
2Th	2:12	the truth but *have* **d** in wickedness.	2305

DELIGHTFUL (4) [DELIGHT]

Ps	16: 6	surely I have a **d** inheritance.	9182
SS	1: 2	for your love is more **d** than wine.	3202
	4:10	How **d** *is* your love, my sister, my bride!	3636
Mal	3:12	for yours will be a **d** land,"	2914

DELIGHTING (1) [DELIGHT]

Pr	8:31	in his whole world and **d** in mankind.	9141

DELIGHTS (21) [DELIGHT]

Est	6: 6	be done for the man the king **d** to honor?"	2911
	6: 7	"For the man the king **d** to honor,	2911
	6: 9	Let them robe the man the king **d** to honor,	2911
	6: 9	'This is what is done for the man the king **d**	2911
	6:11	"This is what is done for the man the king **d**	2911
Ps	22: 8	Let him deliver him, since *he* **d** in him."	2911
	35:27	who **d** in the well-being of his servant."	2913
	36: 8	you give them drink from your river of **d.**	6358

Ps	37:23	If the LORD **d** in a man's way,	2911
	147:11	the LORD **d** in those who fear him,	8354
Pr	3:12	as a father the son he **d** in.	8354
	10:23	but a man of understanding **d** in wisdom.	NIH
	11:20	but he **d** in those whose ways are blameless.	8356
	12:22	but he **d** in men who are truthful.	8356
	14:35	A king **d** in a wise servant,	8356
	15:21	Folly **d** a man who lacks judgment,	8525
	18:2	but **d** in airing his own opinions.	NIH
	23:24	he who has a wise son **d** in him.	8523
Ecc	2:8	the **d of the heart** of man.	9503
SS	7:6	O love, with your **d**!	9503
Col	2:18	not let anyone who **d** in false humility and	2527

DELILAH (7)

Jdg	16:4	in the Valley of Sorek whose name was **D**.	1935
	16:6	So **D** said to Samson,	1935
	16:10	Then **D** said to Samson,	1935
	16:12	**D** took new ropes and tied him with them.	1935
	16:13	**D** then said to Samson, "Until now,	1935
	16:13	**D** took the seven braids of his head,	NIH
	16:18	**D** saw that he had told her everything,	1935

DELIVER (79) [DELIVERANCE, DELIVERED, DELIVERER, DELIVERERS, DELIVERING, DELIVERS, DELIVERY]

Nu	21:2	"If you will **d** these people into our hands,	5989+5989
Dt	1:27	so he brought us out of Egypt to **d** us into	5989
	2:31	**d** Sihon and his country over	5989
	7:23	the LORD your God will **d** them over	5989
	23:14	to protect you and to **d** your enemies	5989
	31:5	The LORD will **d** them to you,	5989
	32:39	and no one can **d** out of my hand.	5911
Jos	7:7	across the Jordan to **d** us into the hands of	5989
	8:18	for into your hand I will **d** the city."	5989
Jdg	7:2	for me to **d** Midian into their hands.	5989
1Sa	4:8	Who will **d** us from the hand	5911
	7:3	and he will **d** you out of the hand of	5911
	9:16	he will **d** my people from the hand of	3828
	12:10	now **d** us from the hands of our enemies,	5911
	17:37	the lion and the paw of the bear will **d** me	5911
	26:24	so may the LORD value my life and **d** me	5911
2Sa	14:16	Perhaps the king will agree to **d** his servant	5911
1Ki	20:28	I will **d** this vast army into your hands,	5989
2Ki	17:39	it is he who will **d** you from the hand	5911
	18:29	He cannot **d** you from my hand.	5911
	18:30	'The LORD will **surely d** us;	5911+5911
	18:32	'The LORD will **d** us.'	5911
	18:35	the LORD **d** Jerusalem from my hand?"	5911
	19:3	of birth and there is no strength to **d** them.	4256
	19:12	by my forefathers **d** them:	5911
	19:19	O LORD our God, **d** us from his hand,	3828
	20:6	And I will **d** you and this city from	5911
1Ch	16:35	gather us and **d** us from the nations,	5911
2Ch	32:13	of those nations ever able to **d** their land	5911
	32:14	then can your god **d** you from my hand?	5911
	32:15	to **d** his people from my hand or the hand	5911
	32:15	How much less will your god **d** you	5911
Ezr	7:19	**D** to the God of Jerusalem all	10719
Job	6:23	**d** me from the hand of the enemy,	4880
	22:30	He will **d** even one who is not innocent,	4880
Ps	3:2	"God will not **d** him."	3802
	3:7	**D** me, O my God!	3828
	6:4	Turn, O LORD, and **d** me;	2740
	7:1	save and **d** me from all who pursue me,	5911
	22:8	Let him **d** him, since he delights in him."	5911
	22:20	**D** my life from the sword,	5911
	31:1	**d** me in your righteousness.	7117
	31:15	**d** me from my enemies and	5911
	33:19	to **d** them from death and keep them alive	5911
	50:15	I will **d** you, and you will honor me."	2740
	59:1	**D** me from my enemies, O God;	5911
	59:2	**D** me from evildoers and save me	5911
	69:14	**d** me from those who hate me,	5911
	71:2	Rescue me and **d** me in your righteousness;	7117
	71:4	**D** me, O my God,	7117
	72:12	For he will **d** the needy who cry out,	5911
	79:9	**d** us and forgive our sins	5911
	82:4	**d** them from the hand of the wicked.	5911
	91:15	I will **d** him and honor him.	2740
	109:21	out of the goodness of your love, **d** me.	5911
	119:153	Look upon my suffering and **d** me,	2740
	119:170	**d** me according to your promise.	5911
	144:7	**d** me and rescue me from	7198
	144:11	**D** me and rescue me from the hands	7198
Pr	20:22	Wait for the LORD, and he will **d** you.	3828
Isa	31:5	he will shield it and **d** it,	5911
	36:14	He cannot **d** you!	5911
	36:15	'The LORD will **surely d** us;	5911+5911
	36:18	'The LORD will **d** us.'	5911
	36:20	the LORD **d** Jerusalem from my hand?"	5911
	37:3	of birth and there is no strength to **d** them.	4256
	37:12	by my forefathers **d** them—	5911
	37:20	O LORD our God, **d** us from his hand,	3828
	38:6	And I will **d** you and this city from	5911
	43:13	No one can **d** out of my hand.	5911
Jer	15:11	"Surely I will **d** you for a good purpose;	9223
	42:11	with you and will save you and **d** you	5911
Am	6:8	I will **d** up the city and everything in it."	6037
Mic	5:6	He will **d** us from the Assyrian	5911
Hab	2:9	You came out to **d** your people,	3829
Mt	6:13	but **d** us from the evil one.'	4861
Lk	21:12	They will **d** you to synagogues	4140
2Co	1:10	and he will **d** us.	4861

2Co	1:10	that he will continue to **d** us,	4861

DELIVERANCE (19) [DELIVER]

Ge	45:7	on earth and to save your lives by a great **d**.	7129
	49:18	"I look for your **d**, O LORD.	3802
Ex	14:13	the **d** the LORD will bring you today.	3802
Jdg	13:5	and he will begin the **d** of Israel from	3828
1Sa	2:1	for I delight in your **d**.	3802
	14:45	he who has brought about this great **d**	3802
2Ch	12:7	not destroy them but will soon give them **d**.	7129
	20:17	and see the **d** the LORD will give you,	3802
Est	4:14	relief and **d** for the Jews will arise	2208
Job	13:16	Indeed, this will turn out for my **d**,	3802
Ps	3:8	From the LORD comes **d**.	3802
	32:7	and surround me with songs of **d**.	7119
	33:17	A horse is a vain hope for **d**;	9591
	78:22	they did not believe in God or trust in his **d**.	3802
Isa	20:6	to for help and **d** from the king of Assyria!	5911
	59:11	for **d**, but it is far away.	3802
Joel	2:32	and in Jerusalem there will be **d**,	7129
Ob	1:17	But on Mount Zion will be **d**;	7129
Php	1:19	will turn out for my **d**.	5401

DELIVERED (71) [DELIVER]

Ge	14:20	who **d** your enemies into your hand."	4481
	48:16	the Angel who has **d** me from all harm—	1457
Dt	2:33	the LORD our God **d** him over to us	5989
	7:2	the LORD your God has **d** them over	5989
Jos	6:2	"See, I have **d** Jericho into your hands,	5989
	8:1	I have **d** into your hands the king of Ai,	5989
	24:10	and I **d** you out of his hand.	5911
Jdg	13:1	so the LORD **d** them into the hands of	5989
	16:23	saying, "Our god has **d** Samson, our enemy,	5989
	16:24	"Our god has **d** our enemy into our hands,	5989
1Sa	7:14	and Israel **d** the neighboring territory from	5911
	10:18	of Egypt, and I **d** you from the power	5911
	11:9	tomorrow, you will be **d**.' "	9591
	12:11	and he **d** you from the hands	5911
	17:37	The LORD who **d** me from the paw of	5911
	24:10	with your own eyes how the LORD **d** you	5989
	24:18	the LORD **d** me into your hands,	6037
	26:8	"Today God has **d** your enemy	6037
	26:23	The LORD **d** you into my hands today,	5989
2Sa	3:9	who has **d** me out of all trouble,	7009
	12:7	and I **d** you from the hand of Saul.	5911
	18:19	the king that the LORD has **d** him from	9149
	18:28	He has **d** up the men who lifted their hands	6037
	18:31	The LORD has **d** you today	9149
	19:9	king **d** us from the hand of our enemies;	5911
	22:1	of this song when the LORD **d** him from	5911
	22:44	"You have **d** me from the attacks	7117
1Ki	1:29	who has **d** me out of every trouble,	7009
	9:28	which they **d** to King Solomon.	995
2Ki	17:13	and that I **d** to you through my servants	8938
	18:33	the god of any nation ever **d** his land	5911+5911
	19:11	And will you be **d**?	5911
2Ch	8:18	which they **d** to King Solomon.	995
	13:16	and God **d** them into their hands.	5989
	16:8	he **d** them into your hand.	5989
	24:24	the LORD **d** into their hands	5989
Ezr	8:36	also **d** the king's orders to the royal satraps	5989
Ne	9:28	and in your compassion you **d** them time	5911
Est	1:12	the attendants **d** the king's command,	928+3338
Job	21:30	that he is **d** from the day of wrath?	3297
	22:30	who will be **d** through the cleanness	4880
	23:7	and I would be **d** forever from my judge.	7117
Ps	18:18	of this song when the LORD **d** him from	5911
	18:43	You have **d** me from the attacks of	7117
	22:4	they trusted and you **d** them.	7117
	34:4	he **d** me from all my fears.	5911
	54:7	For he has **d** me from all my troubles,	5911
	56:13	For you have **d** me from death and my feet	5911
	60:5	that those you love may be **d**.	2740
	86:13	you have **d** me from the depths of	5911
	106:43	Many times he **d** them,	5911
	107:6	and he **d** them from their distress.	5911
	108:6	that those you love may be **d**.	2740
	116:8	you, O LORD, have **d** my soul from death,	2740
	119:117	Uphold me, and I will be **d**;	3828
Isa	36:18	Has the god of any nation ever **d** his land	5911
	37:11	And will you be **d**?	5911
Eze	35:5	an ancient hostility and **d** the Israelites over	5599
Da	3:28	And the Lord **d** Jehoiakim king of Judah	5989
	11:41	Moab and the leaders of Ammon will be **d**	4880
	12:1	found written in the book—will be **d**.	4880
Lk	24:7	'The Son of Man must be **d** into the hands	4140
Ac	12:21	sat on his throne and **d** a public address to	1319
	15:30	the church together and **d** the letter.	2113
	16:4	they **d** the decisions reached by the apostles	4140
	23:33	they **d** the letter to the governor	347
Ro	4:25	He was **d** over to death for our sins	4140
2Co	1:10	He has **d** us from such a deadly peril,	4861
2Th	3:2	that we may be **d** from wicked and evil men,	4861
2Ti	4:17	And I was **d** from the lion's mouth.	4861
Jude	1:5	that the Lord **d** his people out of Egypt,	5392

DELIVERER (11) [DELIVER]

Jdg	3:9	he raised up for them a **d**,	4635
	3:15	and he gave them a **d**—	4635
2Sa	22:2	LORD is my rock, my fortress and my **d**;	7117
2Ki	13:5	The LORD provided a **d** for Israel,	4635
Ps	18:2	LORD is my rock, my fortress and my **d**;	7117
	40:17	You are my help and my **d**;	7117
	70:5	You are my help and my **d**;	7117
	140:7	O Sovereign LORD, my strong **d**,	3802

Ps	144:2	my stronghold and my **d**, my shield,	7117
Ac	7:35	to be their ruler and **d** by God himself,	3392
Ro	11:26	"The **d** will come from Zion;	4861

DELIVERERS (2) [DELIVER]

Ne	9:27	in your great compassion you gave them **d**,	4635
Ob	1:21	**D** will go up on Mount Zion to govern	4635

DELIVERING (2) [DELIVER]

1Sa	14:48	Amalekites, **d** Israel from the hands	5911
	24:15	may he vindicate me by **d** me	NIH

DELIVERS (15) [DELIVER]

Dt	20:13	the LORD your God **d** it into your hand,	5989
	21:10	and the LORD your God **d** them	5989
Job	36:15	But those who suffer he **d** in their suffering;	2740
Ps	34:7	and he **d** them.	2740
	34:17	he **d** them from all their troubles.	5911
	34:19	but the LORD **d** him from them all;	5911
	37:40	The LORD helps them and **d** them;	7117
	37:40	he **d** them from the wicked and saves them,	7117
	41:1	the LORD **d** him in times of trouble.	4880
	97:10	and **d** them from the hand of the wicked.	5911
	144:10	who **d** his servant David from	7198
Pr	10:2	but righteousness **d** from death.	5911
	11:4	but righteousness **d** from death.	5911
	11:6	The righteousness of the upright **d** them,	5911
Isa	66:7	before the pains come upon her, she **d**	4880

DELIVERY (4) [DELIVER]

Ex	1:16	and observe them on the **d** stool, if it is	78
1Sa	4:19	pregnant and **near the time of d**.	3528
Isa	66:9	to the moment of birth and not **give d**?"	3528
	66:9	up the womb when I **bring to d**?"	3528

DELUDED (2) [DELUSION]

Isa	44:20	He feeds on ashes, a **d** heart misleads him;	9438
Rev	19:20	With these signs he had **d** those who had received the mark of the beast	4414

DELUGED (1)

2Pe	3:6	the world of that time was **d** and destroyed.	2885+5623

DELUSION (1) [DELUDED, DELUSIONS]

2Th	2:11	a powerful **d** so that they will believe the lie	4415

DELUSIONS (3) [DELUSION]

Ps	4:2	long will you love **d** and seek false gods?	8198
Jer	14:14	idolatries and the **d** of their own minds.	9567
	23:26	who prophesy the **d** of their own minds?	9567

DEMAND (15) [DEMANDED, DEMANDING, DEMANDS]

Ge	9:5	lifeblood I will surely **d** an accounting.	2011
	9:5	I will **d** an accounting from every animal	2011
	9:5	I will **d** an accounting for the life	2011
Dt	23:21	the LORD your God will **certainly d** it	2011+2011
2Sa	3:13	But I **d** one thing of you:	8626
	4:11	not now **d** his blood from your hand and rid	1335
	21:4	to **d** silver or gold from Saul or his family,	NIH
1Ki	20:6	'I sent to **d** your silver and gold,	606
	20:9	but this **d** I cannot meet.' "	1821
2Ki	18:14	and I will pay whatever you **d** of me."	5989
Ne	5:18	we will not **d** anything more from them.	1335
Job	17:3	"Give me, O God, the pledge you **d**.	6640
Lk	6:30	do not **d** it **back**.	555
1Co	1:22	Jews **d** miraculous signs and Greeks look	160

DEMANDED (18) [DEMAND]

Ge	31:39	And you **d** payment from me	1335
Ex	21:30	However, if payment is **d** of him,	8883
	21:30	by paying whatever is **d**.	8883
Jdg	6:30	The men of the town **d** of Joash,	606
1Ki	20:9	'Your servant will do all you **d**	8938
2Ki	23:35	He summoned his officers and **d** of them,	606
	23:35	the silver and gold he **d**.	6584+7023
Ne	5:18	I never **d** the food allotted to the governor,	2471
Job	22:6	You **d** security from your brothers	1335
Ps	137:3	our tormentors **d** songs of joy;	NIH
Mt	3306	'Pay back what you owe me!' he **d**.	3306
Lk	12:20	This very night your life will be **d** from	555
	12:48	much will be **d**;	2426
	22:64	They blindfolded him and **d**, "Prophesy!	2089
	23:23	But with loud shouts they insistently **d** that	160
Jn	8:25	Then the Jews **d** of him,	646
	9:10	then were your eyes opened?" they **d**.	3306
	18:22	"Is this the way you answer the high priest?" he **d**.	3306

DEMANDING (3) [DEMAND]

2Sa	3:13	**d**, "Give me my wife Michal.	606
Ps	78:18	They willfully put God to the test by **d**	8626
2Co	13:3	since you are **d** proof	2426

DEMANDS (6) [DEMAND]

Ex	21:22	be fined whatever the woman's husband **d**	8883
1Ki	20:8	"Don't listen to him or **agree to** his **d**."	14

Ne 5:18 because the **d** were heavy on these people. 6275
Ps 25:10 for those who keep the **d** of his covenant. 6343
Isa 43:23 with grain offerings nor wearied you with **d** NIH
Mic 7: 3 the ruler **d** gifts, the judge accepts bribes, 8626

DEMAS (3)

Col 4:14 the doctor, and **D** send greetings. *1318*
2Ti 4:10 for **D**, because he loved this world, *1318*
Phm 1:24 And so do Mark, Aristarchus, **D** and Luke, *1318*

DEMETRIUS (3)

Ac 19:24 A silversmith named **D**, *1320*
    19:38 **D** and his fellow craftsmen have *1320*
3Jn 1:12 **D** is well spoken of by everyone— *1320*

DEMOLISH (11) [DEMOLISHED]

Ex 23:24 *You* **must d** them 2238+2238
Nu 33:52 and **d** all their high places. 9012
Jer 43:13 in Egypt he will **d** the sacred pillars 8689
Eze 26: 9 against your walls and **d** your towers 5997
    26:12 down your walls and **d** your fine houses 5997
Hos 10: 2 The LORD *will* **d** their altars 6904
Mic 5:10 from among you and **d** your chariots. 6
    5:14 and **d** your cities. 9012
Mal 1: 4 "They may build, but I *will* **d**. 2238
2Co 10: 4 they have divine power to **d** strongholds. 2746
    10: 5 *We* **d** arguments and every pretension 2747

DEMOLISHED (11) [DEMOLISH]

Nu 21:30 *We have* **d** them as far as Nophah, 9037
Jdg 6:28 there was Baal's altar, **d**, 5997
2Ki 10:27 *They* **d** the sacred stone of Baal and tore 5997
    23:15 even that altar and high place *he* **d**. 5997
2Ch 33: 3 the high places his father Hezekiah *had* **d**; 5997
Jer 31:40 The city will never again be uprooted or **d**." 2238
Eze 6: 4 Your altars *will* **be d** 9037
    6: 6 be laid waste and the high places **d**, 9037
Am 3:15 be destroyed and the mansions *will be* **d**," 6066
Zep 1:13 be plundered, their houses **d**, 9039
    3: 6 their strongholds **are d**. 9037

DEMON (16) [DEMONS, DEMON-POSSESSED, DEMON-POSSESSION]

Mt 9:33 And when the **d** was driven out, *1228*
    11:18 and they say, 'He has a **d**.' *1228*
    17:18 Jesus rebuked the **d**, *1228*
Mk 7:26 She begged Jesus to drive the **d** out *1228*
    7:29 the **d** has left your daughter." *1228*
    7:30 and the **d** gone. *1228*
Lk 4:33 a man possessed by a **d**, *1228*
    4:35 the **d** threw the man down before them all *1228*
    7:33 and you say, 'He has a **d**.' *1228*
    8:29 had been driven by the **d** *1228*
    9:42 **d** threw him to the ground in a convulsion. *1228*
    11:14 Jesus was driving out a **d** that was mute. *1228*
    11:14 When the **d** left, *1228*
Jn 8:49 "I am not possessed by a **d**," said Jesus, *1228*
    10:21 not the sayings *of* a **man possessed by a d**. *1227*
    10:21 Can a **d** open the eyes of the blind?" *1228*

DEMON-POSSESSED (16) [DEMON, POSSESS]

Mt 4:24 those suffering severe pain, the **d**, *1227*
    8:16 many *who were* **d** were brought to him, *1227*
    8:28 two **d** men coming from the tombs met him. *1227*
    8:33 including what had happened to the **d** *men*. *1227*
    9:32 a man *who was* **d** and could *1227*
    12:22 a **d** *man* who was blind and mute, *1227*
Mk 1:32 to Jesus all the sick and **d**. *1227*
    5:16 the people what had happened *to the* **d** man *1227*
    5:18 man *who had been* **d** begged to go with him. *1227*
Lk 8:27 he was met by a **d** man from the town. 1228+2400
    8:36 the people how the **d** *man* had been cured. *1227*
Jn 7:20 *"You are* **d**," the crowd answered. 1228+2400
    8:48 saying that you are a Samaritan and **d**? 1228+2400
    8:52 "Now we know that *you* are **d**! 1228+2400
    10:20 *"He is* **d** and raving mad." 1228+2400
Ac 19:13 of the Lord Jesus over those who *were* **d**. 2400+3836+3836+4460+4505

DEMON-POSSESSION (1) [DEMON, POSSESS]

Mt 15:22 **suffering** terribly **from d**." *1227*

DEMONS (49) [DEMON]

Dt 32:17 They sacrificed to **d**, which are not God— 8717
Ps 106:37 and their daughters to **d**. 8717
Mt 7:22 and in your name drive out **d** *1228*
    8:31 The **d** begged Jesus, "If you drive us out, *1230*
    9:34 the prince *of* **d** that he drives out demons." *1228*
    9:34 the prince of demons that he drives out **d**." *1228*
    10: 8 cleanse those who have leprosy, drive out **d**. *1228*
    12:24 "It is only by Beelzebub, the prince of **d**, *1228*
    12:24 that this fellow drives out **d**." *1228*
    12:27 And if I drive out **d** by Beelzebub, *1228*
    12:28 But if I drive out **d** by the Spirit of God, *1228*
Mk 1:34 He also drove out many **d**, *1228*
    1:34 the **d** speak because they knew who he was. *1228*
    1:39 in their synagogues and driving out **d**. *1228*
    3:15 and to have authority to drive out **d**. *1228*

Mk 3:22 the prince *of* **d** he is driving out demons." *1228*
    3:22 the prince of demons he is driving out **d**." *1228*
    5:12 The **d** begged Jesus, "Send us among *NIG*
    5:15 **possessed** by the legion of **d**, *1227*
    6:13 They drove out many **d** *1228*
    9:38 "we saw a man driving out **d** in your name *1228*
    16: 9 out of whom he had driven seven **d**. *1228*
    16:17 In my name they will drive out **d**; *1228*
Lk 4:41 Moreover, **d** came out of many people, *1228*
    8: 2 from whom seven **d** had come out; *1228*
    8:30 because many **d** had gone into him. *1228*
    8:32 The **d** begged Jesus to let them go *NIG*
    8:33 When the **d** came out of the man, *1228*
    8:35 the man from whom the **d** had gone out, *1228*
    8:38 the **d** had gone out begged to go with him, *1228*
    9: 1 to drive out all **d** and to cure diseases, *1228*
    9:49 "we saw a man driving out **d** in your name *1228*
    10:17 even the **d** submit to us in your name." *1228*
    11:15 the prince *of* **d**, he is driving out demons." *1228*
    11:15 the prince of demons, he is driving out **d**." *1228*
    11:18 because you claim that I drive out **d** *1228*
    11:19 Now if I drive out **d** by Beelzebub, *1228*
    11:20 But if I drive out **d** by the finger of God, *1228*
    13:32 'I will drive out **d** and heal people today *1228*
Ro 8:38 neither angels nor **d**, *794*
1Co 10:20 the sacrifices of pagans are offered *to* **d**, *1228*
    10:20 I do not want you to be participants *with* **d**. *1228*
    10:21 the cup of the Lord and the cup *of* **d** too; *1228*
    10:21 in both the Lord's table and the table *of* **d**. *1228*
1Ti 4: 1 and things taught *by* **d**. *1228*
Jas 2:19 Even the **d** believe that—and shudder. *1228*
Rev 9:20 they did not stop worshiping **d**, *1228*
    16:14 *of* **d** performing miraculous signs, *1228*
    18: 2 She has become a home *for* **d** and a haunt *1228*

DEMONSTRATE (2) [DEMONSTRATES, DEMONSTRATION]

Ro 3:25 He did this to **d** his justice, *1893*
    3:26 he did it to **d** his justice at the present time, *1893*

DEMONSTRATES (1) [DEMONSTRATE]

Ro 5: 8 But God **d** his own love for us in this: *5319*

DEMONSTRATION (1) [DEMONSTRATE]

1Co 2: 4 but with a **d** of the Spirit's power, *618*

DEN (16) [DENS]

Jer 7:11 become a **d** *of* robbers to you? 5117
Da 6: 7 O king, shall be thrown into the lions' **d**. 10129
    6:12 O king, would be thrown into the lions' **d**?" 10129
    6:16 and threw him into the lions' **d**. 10129
    6:17 and placed over the mouth of the **d**, 10129
    6:19 the king got up and hurried to the lions' **d**. 10129
    6:20 When he came near the **d**, 10129
    6:23 and gave orders to lift Daniel out of the **d**. 10129
    6:23 And when Daniel was lifted from the **d**, 10129
    6:24 in and thrown into the lions' **d**, 10129
    6:24 And before they reached the floor of the **d**, 10129
Am 3: 4 in his **d** when he has caught nothing? 5104
Na 2:11 Where now is the lions' **d**, 5061
Mt 21:13 but you are making it a '**d** of robbers.' " 5068
Mk 11:17 But you have made it 'a **d** of robbers.' " 5068
Lk 19:46 but you have made it 'a **d** of robbers.' " 5068

DENARII (2) [DENARIUS]

Mt 18:28 fellow servants who owed him a hundred **d**. *1324*
Lk 7:41 One owed him five hundred **d**, *1324*

DENARIUS (7) [DENARII]

Mt 20: 2 to pay them a **d** for the day and sent them *1324*
    20: 9 and each received a **d**. *1324*
    20:10 But each one of them also received a **d**. *1324*
    20:13 Didn't you agree to work for a **d**? *1324*
    22:19 They brought him a **d**, *1324*
Mk 12:15 "Bring me a **d** and let me look at it." *1324*
Lk 20:24 "Show me a **d**. *1324*

DENIED (17) [DENY]

Job 6:10 that *I* had not **d** the words of the Holy One. 3948
    27: 2 who has **d** me justice, the Almighty, 6073
    31:13 "If *I* have **d** justice *to* my menservants 4415
    31:16 "If *I* have **d** the desires of the poor or let 4979
    38:15 The wicked **are d** their light, 4979
Ecc 2:10 I **d** *myself* nothing my eyes desired; 724
    5: 8 and justice and rights **d**, 1609
Mt 26:70 But he **d** it before them all. 766
    26:72 *He* **d** it again, with an oath: "I don't know 766
Mk 14:68 But he **d** it. "I don't know 766
    14:70 Again he **d** it. 766
Lk 8:45 *When* they all **d** it, Peter said, "Master, 766
    22:57 But he **d** it. 766
Jn 18:25 He **d** it, saying, "I am not." 766
    18:27 Again Peter **d** it, and at that moment 766
1Ti 5: 8 he has **d** the faith and is worse than 766
Rev 3: 8 kept my word and *have* not **d** my name. 766

DENIES (4) [DENY]

Job 34: 5 'I am innocent, but God **d** me justice. 6073
1Jn 2:22 It is the man who **d** that Jesus is the Christ. 766
    2:22 he **d** the Father and the Son. 766
    2:23 No one who **d** the Son has the Father; 766

DENOUNCE (5) [DENOUNCED, DENOUNCES]

Nu 5:21 and **d** you when he causes your thigh 8652
    23: 7 for me; come, **d** Israel.' 2404
    23: 8 How *can I* **d** those whom the LORD has 2404
Pr 24:24 peoples will curse him and nations **d** him. 2404
Mt 11:20 Then Jesus began *to* **d** the cities *3943*

DENOUNCED (3) [DENOUNCE]

Nu 23: 8 the LORD *has* not **d**? 2404
Da 3: 8 and **d** the Jews. 10030+10642
1Co 10:30 why *am I* **d** because *1059*

DENOUNCES (2) [DENOUNCE]

Job 17: 5 If a *man* **d** his friends for reward, 5583
    21:31 Who **d** his conduct to his face? 5583

DENS (6) [DEN]

Job 37: 8 they remain in their **d**. 5104
    38:40 when they crouch in their **d** or lie in wait in 5104
Ps 104:22 they return and lie down in their **d**. 5104
SS 4: 8 from the lions' **d** and the mountain haunts 5104
Mic 7:17 They will come trembling out of their **d**; 4995
Na 2:12 filling his lairs with the kill and his **d** with 5104

DENSE (6)

Ge 19:28 and he saw **d** smoke rising *from* the land, 7798
Ex 8:24 **D** swarms of flies poured 3878
    19: 9 "I am going to come to you in a **d** cloud, 6051
Isa 30:27 with burning anger and *d* clouds of smoke; 3880
Jer 46:23 declares the LORD, "**d** though *it be*. 2983+4202
Zec 11: 2 the **d** forest has been cut down! 1293

DENY (20) [DENIED, DENIES, DENYING]

Ex 23: 6 *"Do* not **d** justice to your poor people 5742
Lev 16:29 the seventh month *you* **must d** yourselves 6700
    16:31 and *you* **must d** yourselves; 6700
    23:27 Hold a sacred assembly and **d** yourselves, 6700
    23:29 not **d** *himself* on that day must be cut off 6700
    23:32 and *you* **must d** yourselves. 6700
Nu 29: 7 *You* **must d** yourselves and do no work. 6700
    30:13 or any sworn pledge to **d** herself. 6700
Job 27: 5 till I die, I *will* not **d** my integrity. 6073
Isa 5:23 but **d** justice to the innocent. 6073
La 3:35 to **d** a man his rights before the Most High, 5742
Am 2: 7 as upon the dust of the ground *and* justice 5742
Mt 16:24 he must **d** himself and take up his cross 565
Mk 8:34 he must **d** himself and take up his cross 565
Lk 9:23 after me, *he* must **d** himself and take 766
    22:34 *you will* **d** three times that you know me." 565
Ac 4:16 and we cannot **d** it. 766
Tit 1:16 but by their actions *they* **d** him. 766
Jas 3:14 not boast about it or **d** the **truth**. 237+2848+6017
Jude 1: 4 and **d** Jesus Christ our only Sovereign 766

DENYING (3) [DENY]

Eze 22:29 and mistreat the alien, **d** them justice. 4202
2Ti 3: 5 having a form of godliness but **d** its power. 766
2Pe 2: 1 **d** the sovereign Lord who bought them— 766

DEPART (12) [DEPARTED, DEPARTING, DEPARTS, DEPARTURE]

Ge 49:10 The scepter *will* not **d** from Judah, 6073
Jos 1: 8 *Do not* let this Book of the Law **d** 4631
2Sa 12:10 the sword *will* never **d** from your house, 6073
Job 1:21 and naked *I will* **d**. 8740
Ps 39:13 that I may rejoice again before *I* **d** 2143
Isa 49:17 and those who laid you waste **d** from you. 3655
    52:11 **D**, depart, go out from there! 6073
    52:11 Depart, **d**, go out from there! 6073
    59:21 in your mouth *will* not **d** from your mouth, 4631
Jer   so will he wrap Egypt around himself and **d** 3655
Mt 25:41 he will say to those on his left, '**D** from me, *4513*
Php 1:23 I desire to **d** and be with Christ, *386*

DEPARTED (11) [DEPART]

Jos 2:21 So she sent them away and *they* **d**. 2143
1Sa 4:21 saying, "The glory *has* **d** from Israel"— 1655
    4:22 She said, "The glory *has* **d** from Israel, 1655
    16:14 the Spirit of the LORD *had* **d** from Saul, 6073
Job 23:12 *I have* not **d** *from* the commands of his lips; 4631
Ps 119:102 *I have* not **d** from your laws, 6073
Isa 14: 9 it rouses the **spirits of the d** to greet you— 8327
    26:14 *those* **d** spirits do not rise. 8327
La 1: 6 All the splendor *has* **d** from the Daughter 3655
Eze 10:18 of the LORD **d** from over the threshold of 3655
Jn 4:50 The man took Jesus at his word and **d**. *4513*

DEPARTING (1) [DEPART]

Hos 1: 2 the vilest adultery *in* **d** from the LORD." 339+4946

DEPARTS (4) [DEPART]

Ps 146: 4 their spirit **d**, they return to the ground; 3655
Ecc 5:15 as he comes, so he **d**. 8740
    5:16 As a man comes, so *he* **d**, 2143
    6: 4 *it* **d** in darkness, and in darkness 2143

DEPARTURE (6) [DEPART]

Dt 16: 3 the time of your **d** from Egypt. 3655

Dt 16: 6 on the anniversary of your **d** from Egypt. 3655
SS 5: 6 My heart sank at his **d.** 1818
Lk 9:31 They spoke about his **d,** 2016
2Ti 4: 6 and the time has come *for* my **d.** 385
2Pe 1:15 that after my **d** you will always be able 2016

DEPEND (6) [DEPENDED, DEPENDENT, DEPENDING, DEPENDS]

2Ki 18:21 Such is Pharaoh king of Egypt to all who **d** 1053
    19:10 Do not let the god you **d** on deceive you 1053
Ps 62: 7 My salvation and my honor **d on** God; 6584
Isa 36: 6 Such is Pharaoh king of Egypt to all who **d** 1053
    37:10 **let** the god you **d** 1053
Ro 9:16 therefore, **d** on man's desire or effort, NIG

DEPENDED (3) [DEPEND]

Isa 30:12 relied on oppression and **d** on deceit, 9128
Hos 10:13 Because *you have* **d** on your own strength 1053
Ac 12:20 because they **d** on the king's country NIG

DEPENDENT (2) [DEPEND]

Lev 21: 3 or an unmarried sister who is **d** on him 7940
1Th 4:12 so that *you will* not **be d on** anybody. 2400+5970

DEPENDING (8) [DEPEND]

2Ki 18:20 On whom *are you* **d,** 1053
    18:21 Look now, *you are* **d** on Egypt, 1053
    18:22 *"We are* **d** on the LORD our God"— 1053
    18:24 though *you are* **d** on Egypt for chariots 1053
Isa 36: 5 On whom *are you* **d,** 1053
    36: 6 Look now, *you are* **d** on Egypt, 1053
    36: 7 *"We are* **d** on the LORD our God"— 1053
    36: 9 though *you are* **d** on Egypt for chariots 1053

DEPENDS (5) [DEPEND]

Jer 17: 5 the one who trusts in man, *who* **d** on flesh 8492
Ro 12:18 If it is possible, *as far as* **it d on** you, 1666+3836+5148
Gal 3:18 For if the inheritance **d** on the law, 1666
    3:18 then it no longer **d on** a promise; 1666
Col 2: 8 which **d** on human tradition and 2848

DEPLOYED (5)

1Sa 4: 2 The Philistines **d** *their forces* 6885
2Sa 10: 9 the best troops in Israel and **d** them against 6885
    10:10 of Abishai his brother and **d** them against 6885
1Ch 19:10 the best troops in Israel and **d** them against 6885
    19:11 and *they were* **d** against the Ammonites. 6885

DEPORTED (11)

2Ki 15:29 and **d** the people to Assyria. 1655
    16: 9 *He* **d** its inhabitants to Kir and put Rezin 1655
    17: 6 the king of Assyria captured Samaria and **d** 1655
    17:26 "The people *you* **d** and resettled in 1655
    18:11 The king of Assyria **d** Israel to Assyria 1655
    24:16 The king of Babylon also **d** to Babylon 995+1583
1Ch 6:15 Jehozadak *was* **d** when 2143
    8: 6 of those living in Geba and *were* **d** 1655
    8: 7 who **d** them and who was the father 1655
Ezr 4:10 and honorable Ashurbanipal **d** and settled 10144
    5:12 who destroyed this temple and **d** the people 10144

DEPOSE (1) [DEPOSED, DEPOSES]

Isa 22:19 *I will* **d** you from your office, 2074

DEPOSED (3) [DEPOSE]

1Ki 15:13 He even **d** his grandmother Maacah 6073
2Ch 15:16 King Asa also **d** his grandmother Maacah 6073
Da 5:20 he was **d** from his royal throne and stripped 10474

DEPOSES (1) [DEPOSE]

Da 2:21 he sets up kings and **d** them. 10528

DEPOSIT (10) [DEPOSITED]

Ezr 5:15 'Take these articles and go and **d** them in 10474
Eze 24: 6 whose **d** will not go away! 2689
    24:11 be melted and its **d** burned away. 2689
    24:12 its heavy **d** has not been removed, 2689
Mt 25:27 you should have put my money on **d** with NIG
Lk 19:23 Why then didn't you put my money on **d,** 5544
2Co 1:22 and put his Spirit in our hearts as a **d,** 775
    5: 5 the Spirit as a **d, guaranteeing** what is 775
Eph 1:14 who is a **d guaranteeing** our inheritance 775
2Ti 1:14 the good **d** that was **entrusted** to you— 4146

DEPOSITED (2) [DEPOSIT]

1Sa 10:25 He wrote them down on a scroll and **d** it 5663
Ezr 6: 5 they *are to be* **d** in the house of God. 10474

DEPRAVED (5) [DEPRAVITY]

Eze 16:47 ways *you* soon *became* more **d** than they. 8845
    23:11 prostitution *she was* more **d** than her sister. 8845
Ro 1:28 he gave them over to a **d** mind, 99
Php 2:15 without fault in a crooked and **d** generation, 1406
2Ti 3: 8 men oppose the truth—men of **d** minds, 2967

DEPRAVITY (2) [DEPRAVED]

Ro 1:29 of wickedness, evil, greed and **d.** 2798

2Pe 2:19 while they themselves are slaves *of* **d**— 5785

DEPRESSIONS (1)

Lev 14:37 if it has greenish or reddish **d** that appear to 9206

DEPRIVE (13) [DEPRIVED, DEPRIVES, DEPRIVING]

Ex 21:10 he must not **d** the first one *of* her food, 1757
Dt 24:17 not **d** the alien or the fatherless *of* justice, 5742
Pr 18: 5 be partial to the wicked or to **d** the innocent 5742
    31: 5 and **d** all the oppressed *of* their rights. 9101
Isa 10: 2 to **d** the poor of their rights 5742
    29:21 and with false testimony **d** the innocent 5742
La 3:36 to **d** a man *of* justice— 6430
Eze 36:12 **d** them *of* their **children.** 8897
    36:13 **d** your nation *of* its **children,"** 8897
Am 5:12 **d** the poor *of* justice 5742
Mal 3: 5 and **d** aliens *of* justice, 5742
1Co 7: 5 not **d** each other except by mutual consent 691
    9:15 I would rather die than have anyone **d** me 3033

DEPRIVED (5) [DEPRIVE]

Ge 42:36 **d** me of my **children.** 8897
Jer 5:25 your sins *have* **d** you of good. 4979
La 3:17 *I have been* **d** of peace; 2396
Mic 7:16 **d** of all their power. 4946
Ac 8:33 In his humiliation he *was* **d** of justice." 149

DEPRIVES (1) [DEPRIVE]

Job 12:24 *He* **d** the leaders of the earth *of* their reason; 6073

DEPRIVING (1) [DEPRIVE]

Ecc 4: 8 "and why *am* I **d** myself of enjoyment?" 2893

DEPTH (6) [DEEP]

Ge 7:20 covered the mountains to a **d** 2025+4200+5087
La 3:60 You have seen the **d** *of* their vengeance, 3972
Ro 8:39 neither height nor **d,** 958
    11:33 the **d** of the riches of the wisdom 958
2Co 2: 4 not to grieve you but to let you know the **d** 4359
Php 1: 9 and more in knowledge and **d** of insight, 4246

DEPTHS (39) [DEEP]

Ex 15: 5 they sank to the **d** like a stone. 5185
Ne 9:11 but you hurled their pursuers into the **d,**— 5185
Job 11: 8 They are deeper than the **d of the grave**— 8619
    36:30 bathing the **d** *of* the sea. 9247
    41:31 He makes the **d** churn like a boiling caldron 5185
Ps 30: 1 lifted me out of the **d** 1926
    63: 9 they will go down to the **d** *of* the earth. 9397
    68:22 I will bring them from the **d** *of* the sea, 5185
    69: 2 I sink in the miry **d,** 5185
    69:15 or the **d** swallow me up or 5185
    71:20 from the **d** of the earth you will again bring 9333
    77:16 the very **d** were convulsed. 9333
    86:13 you have delivered me from the **d** of 9397
    88: 6 in the darkest **d.** 5185
    95: 4 In his hand are the **d** *of* the earth, 4736
    106: 9 he led them through the **d** as through 9333
    107:26 up to the heavens and went down to the **d;** 9333
    130: 1 Out of the **d** I cry to you, O LORD; 5099
    135: 6 in the seas and all their **d.** 9333
    139: 8 if I make my bed in the **d,** you are there. 8619
    139:15 I was woven together in the **d** *of* the earth, 9397
    148: 7 you great sea creatures and all **ocean d,** 9333
Pr 9:18 that her guests are in the **d** of the grave. 6679
Isa 7:11 in the deepest **d** or in the highest heights." 8619
    14:15 to the **d** *of* the pit. 3752
    29:15 Woe to those *who* **go to great d** 6676
    51:10 who made a road in the **d** *of* the sea so that 5099
    63:13 who led them through the **d?** 9333
La 3:55 O LORD, from the **d** *of* the pit. 9397
Eze 26:19 and when I bring the **ocean d** over you 9333
    27:34 Now you are shattered by the sea in the **d** 5099
    32:23 in the **d** *of* the pit and her army lies 3752
Am 9: 2 they dig down to the **d of the grave,** 8619
Jnh 2: 2 From the **d** *of* the grave I called for help, 1061
Mic 7:19 and hurl all our iniquities into the **d** *of* 5185
Zec 10:11 and all the **d** *of* the Nile will dry up. 5185
Mt 11:23 No, you will go down to the **d.** 87
    18: 6 around his neck and to be drowned in the **d** 4283
Lk 10:15 No, you will go down to the **d.** 87

DEPUTED (KJV) See REPRESENTATIVE

DEPUTY (2)

Jdg 9:28 and isn't Zebul his **d?** 7224
1Ki 22:47 There was then no king in Edom; a **d** ruled. 5893

DERBE (4)

Ac 14: 6 the Lycaonian cities of Lystra and **D** and to 1292
    14:20 The next day he and Barnabas left for **D.** 1292
    16: 1 He came to **D** and then to Lystra, 1292
    20: 4 Gaius *from* **D,** Timothy also, 1291

DERIDE (1) [DERIDES, DERISION]

Hab 1:10 They **d** kings and scoff at rulers. 7840

DERIDED (KJV) See SNEERED

DERIDES (1) [DERIDE]

Pr 11:12 A man who lacks judgment **d** his neighbor, 996

DERISION (5) [DERIDE]

Job 27:23 **claps** its hands in **d** 8562
Ps 44:13 the scorn and **d** of those around us. 7841
    79: 4 of scorn and **d** to those around us. 7841
Eze 23:32 it will bring scorn and **d,** 4353
Mic 6:16 over to ruin and your people to **d;** 9240

DERIVES (1)

Eph 3:15 in heaven and on earth **d** *its* **name.** 3951

DESCEND (7) [DESCENDANT, DESCENDANTS, DESCENDED, DESCENDING, DESCENDS, DESCENT]

Dt 32: 2 like rain and my words **d** like dew, 5688
Job 17:16 *Will we* **d** together into the dust?" 5737
Ps 49:17 his splendor *will* not **d** with him. 3718
SS 4: 8 **D** from the crest of Amana, 8801
Isa 5:14 into it *will* **d** their nobles and masses 3718
    14:19 *those who* **d** to the stones of the pit. 3718
Ro 10: 7 "or 'Who *will* **d** into the deep?'" 2849

DESCENDANT (25) [DESCEND]

Lev 6:18 Any male **d** of Aaron may eat it. 1201
    21:21 No **d** of Aaron 2446
    22: 4 a **d** *of* Aaron has an infectious skin disease 408+2446+4946
Nu 16:40 a **d** *of* Aaron should come to burn incense 2446
    26:59 Amram's wife was Jochebed, a **d** *of* Levi, 1426
    32:41 Jair, a **d** *of* Manasseh, 1201
Dt 3:14 Jair, a **d** *of* Manasseh, 1201
2Sa 14: 7 leaving my husband neither name nor **d** on 8642
1Ch 7:14 Asriel *was* his **d** 3528
    7:15 Another **d** was named Zelophehad, NIH
    9: 4 the son of Bani, a **d** *of* Perez son of Judah. 1201
    24: 3 a **d** *of* Eleazar and Ahimelech a descendant 1201
    24: 3 a descendant of Eleazar and Ahimelech a **d** 1201
    26:24 Shubael, a **d** *of* Gershom son of Moses, 1201
    27: 3 He was a **d** *of* Perez and chief of all 1201
2Ch 20:14 a Levite and **d** *of* Asaph, 1201
Ezr 5: 1 Zechariah the prophet, a **d** *of* Iddo, 10120
    6:14 Zechariah, a **d** *of* Iddo. 10120
Ne 11: 4 the son of Mahalalel, a **d** *of* Perez; 1201
    11: 5 the son of Zechariah, a **d** *of* Shelah. 1201
Jer 33:21 and David will no longer have a **d** to reign 1201
Lk 1: 5 his wife Elizabeth was also a **d** *of* Aaron. 1666+2588+3836
    1:27 a man named Joseph, a **d** *of* David. 1666+3875
Ro 1: 3 as to his human nature was a **d** *of* David, 5065
    11: 1 I am an Israelite myself, a **d** *of* Abraham, 5065

DESCENDANTS (364) [DESCEND]

Ge 9: 9 with you and with your **d** after you 2446
    15:13 for certain that your **d** will be strangers in 2446
    15:16 In the fourth generation your **d** will come NIH
    15:18 "To your **d** I give this land, 2446
    16:10 "I will so increase your **d** that they will 2446
    17: 7 between me and you and your **d** after you 2446
    17: 7 to be your God and the God of your **d** 2446
    17: 8 an everlasting possession to you and your **d** 2446
    17: 9 you and your **d** after you for the generations 2446
    17:10 and your **d** after you, the covenant you are 2446
    17:19 an everlasting covenant for his **d** after him. 2446
    21:23 with me or my children or my **d.** 5781
    22:17 and make your **d** as numerous as the stars 2446
    22:17 Your **d** will take possession of the cities 2446
    25: 3 the **d** *of* Dedan were the Asshurites, 1201
    25: 4 All these were **d** *of* Keturah. 1201
    25:18 His **d** settled in the area from Havilah NIH
    26: 3 to you and your **d** I will give all these lands 2446
    26: 4 I will make your **d** as numerous as the stars 2446
    26:24 and will increase the number of your **d** for 2446
    28: 4 and your **d** the blessing given to Abraham, 2446
    28:13 and your **d** the land on which you are lying. 2446
    28:14 Your **d** will be like the dust of the earth, 2446
    32:12 and will make your **d** like the sand of 2446
    35:12 I will give this land to your **d** after you." 2446
    36:15 These were the chiefs among Esau's **d:** 1201
    46: 8 of Israel (Jacob and his **d**) who went 3655+3751
    46:26 *those who were* his **direct d,** 3655+3751
    48: 4 as an everlasting possession to your **d** 2446
    48:19 and his **d** will become a group of nations." 2446
Ex 1: 5 The **d** of Jacob numbered seventy in all; 3655+3751+5883
    12:24 as a lasting ordinance for you and your **d.** 1201
    28:43 be a lasting ordinance for Aaron and his **d.** 2446
    29:29 to his **d** so that they can be anointed 1201
    30:21 a lasting ordinance for Aaron and his **d** for 2446
    32:13 'I will make your **d** as numerous as 2446
    32:13 I will give your **d** all this land I promised 2446
    33: 1 saying, 'I will give it to your **d.'** 2446
Lev 21:17 of your **d** who has a defect may come near 2446
    22: 3 if any of your **d** is ceremonially unclean 2446
    23:43 so your **d** will know that I had 1887
    25:30 to the buyer and his **d.** 1887
Nu 1:20 the **d** *of* Reuben the firstborn son of Israel: 1201
    1:22 From the **d** *of* Simeon: 1201
    1:24 From the **d** *of* Gad: 1201
    1:26 From the **d** *of* Judah: 1201
    1:28 From the **d** *of* Issachar: 1201

Nu	1:30	From the **d** of Zebulun:	1201
	1:32	From the **d** of Ephraim:	1201
	1:34	From the **d** of Manasseh:	1201
	1:36	From the **d** of Benjamin:	1201
	1:38	From the **d** of Dan:	1201
	1:40	From the **d** of Asher:	1201
	1:42	From the **d** of Naphtali:	1201
	9:10	'When any of you or your **d** are unclean	1887
	13:22	Sheshai and Talmai, the **d** of Anak, lived.	3535
	13:28	We even saw **d** of Anak there.	3535
	13:33	(the **d** of Anak come from the Nephilim).	1201
	14:24	and his **d** will inherit it.	2446
	25:13	He and his **d** will have a covenant of	2446
	26: 5	The **d** of Reuben, the firstborn son	1201
	26:12	The **d** of Simeon by their clans were:	1201
	26:15	The **d** of Gad by their clans were:	1201
	26:20	The **d** of Judah by their clans were:	1201
	26:21	The **d** of Perez were:	1201
	26:23	The **d** of Issachar by their clans were:	1201
	26:26	The **d** of Zebulun by their clans were:	1201
	26:28	The **d** of Joseph by their clans	1201
	26:29	The **d** of Manasseh:	1201
	26:30	These were the **d** of Gilead:	1201
	26:35	the **d** of Ephraim by their clans:	1201
	26:36	These were the **d** of Shuthelah:	1201
	26:37	These were the **d** of Joseph by their clans.	1201
	26:38	The **d** of Benjamin by their clans were:	1201
	26:40	The **d** of Bela through Ard	1201
	26:42	These were the **d** of Dan by their clans:	1201
	26:44	The **d** of Asher by their clans were:	1201
	26:45	and through the **d** of Beriah:	1201
	26:48	The **d** of Naphtali by their clans were:	1201
	32:39	The **d** of Makir son of Manasseh went	1201
	32:40	the **d** of Manasseh, and they settled there.	1201
	36: 1	from the clans of the **d** of Joseph,	1201
	36: 5	of the **d** of Joseph is saying is right.	1201
	36:12	within the clans of the **d** of Manasseh son	1201
Dt	1: 8	and to their **d** after them."	2446
	1:36	and his **d** the land he set his feet on,	1201
	2: 4	the territory of your brothers the **d** of Esau,	1201
	2: 8	we went on past our brothers the **d** of Esau,	1201
	2: 9	I have given Ar to the **d** of Lot as	1201
	2:12	but the **d** of Esau drove them out.	1201
	2:19	I have given it as a possession to the **d**	1201
	2:22	The LORD had done the same for the **d**	1201
	2:29	as the **d** of Esau, who live in Seir, and	1201
	4:37	and chose their **d** after them,	2446
	10:15	their **d**, above all the nations, as it is today.	2446
	11: 9	to give to them and their **d**,	2446
	17:20	Then he and his **d** will reign a long time	1201
	18: 5	and their **d** out of all your tribes to stand	1201
	23: 2	nor any of **his d** may enter the assembly of	2257S
	23: 3	or any of **his d** may enter the assembly of	2157S
	28:46	and a wonder to you and your **d** forever.	1201
	28:59	on you and your **d**,	2446
	30: 6	and the hearts of your **d**,	2446
	31:21	because it will not be forgotten by their **d**.	2446
	34: 4	'I will give it to your **d**.'	2446
Jos	4:21	"In the future when your **d** ask their fathers,	1201
	13:29	to half the family of the **d** of Manasseh,	1201
	13:31	for the **d** of Makir son of Manasseh—	1201
	15:14	and Talmai—**d** of Anak.	3535
	16: 4	Manasseh and Ephraim, the **d** of Joseph,	1201
	17: 2	the other male **d** of Manasseh son	1201
	17: 6	of Gilead belonged to the rest of the **d**	1201
	21: 4	The Levites who were **d** of Aaron	1201
	21: 5	of Kohath's **d** were allotted ten towns	1201
	21: 6	The **d** of Gershon were allotted thirteen towns	1201
	21: 7	The **d** of Merari, clan by clan,	1201
	21:10	(these towns were assigned to the **d**	1201
	21:13	the **d** of Aaron the priest they gave Hebron	1201
	21:19	the **d** of Aaron, were thirteen,	1201
	22:24	that some day your **d** might say to ours,	1201
	22:25	So your **d** might cause ours to stop fearing	1201
	22:27	in the future your **d** will not be able to say	1201
	22:28	'If they ever say this to us, or to our **d**,	1887
	24: 3	throughout Canaan and gave him many **d**.	2446
	24:32	This became the inheritance of Joseph's **d**.	1201
Jdg	1:16	The **d** of Moses' father-in-law, the Kenite,	1201
	3: 2	(he did this only to teach warfare to the **d**	1887
	4:11	the **d** of Hobab, Moses' brother-in-law,	1201
1Sa	2:33	all your **d** will die in the prime of life.	1074+5270
	20:42	and between your **d**	2446
	20:42	and my **d** forever.' "	2446
	24:21	the LORD that you will not cut off my **d**	2446
2Sa	19:28	All my grandfather's **d** deserved nothing	1074
	21: 6	let seven of his male **d** be given to us to	1201
	21:16	And Ishbi-Benob, one of the **d** of Rapha,	3535
	21:18	one of the **d** of Rapha.	3535
	21:22	These four were **d** of Rapha in Gath,	3528
	22:51	to David and his **d** forever."	2446
1Ki	2: 4	'If your **d** watch how they live,	1201
	2:33	on the head of Joab and his **d** forever.	2446
	2:33	But on David and his **d**,	2446
	9:21	their **d** remaining in the land,	1201
	11:39	I will humble David's **d** because of this,	2446
	11:21	I will consume your **d** and cut off	339
2Ki	5:27	to you and to your **d** forever."	2446
	8:19	a lamp for David and his **d** forever.	1201
	10:30	your **d** will sit on the throne of Israel to	1201
	15:12	"Your **d** will sit on the throne of Israel to	1201
	17:34	and commands that the LORD gave the **d**	1201
	20:18	And some of your **d**,	1201
1Ch	1:29	These were their **d**:	9352
	1:33	All these were **d** of Keturah.	1201
	2:23	All these were **d** of Makir the father	1201

1Ch	2:33	These were the **d** of Jerahmeel.	1201
	2:50	These were the **d** of Caleb.	1201
	2:52	The **d** of Shobal the father	1201
	2:54	The **d** of Salma:	1201
	3:17	The **d** of Jehoiachin the captive:	1201
	3:21	The **d** of Hananiah:	1201
	3:22	The **d** of Shecaniah:	1201
	4: 1	The **d** of Judah:	1201
	4: 4	These were the **d** of Hur,	1201
	4: 6	These were the **d** of Naarah.	1201
	4:20	The **d** of Ishi: Zoheth and Ben-Zoheth.	1201
	4:24	The **d** of Simeon:	1201
	4:26	The **d** of Mishma:	1201
	5: 4	The **d** of Joel:	1201
	6:22	the **d** of Kohath:	1201
	6:25	The **d** of Elkanah: Amasai, Ahimoth,	1201
	6:29	The **d** of Merari:	1201
	6:49	But Aaron and his **d** were	1201
	6:50	These were the **d** of Aaron:	1201
	6:54	to the **d** of Aaron who were from	1201
	6:57	the **d** of Aaron were given Hebron (a city	1201
	6:61	of Kohath's **d** were allotted ten towns from	1201
	6:62	the **d** of Gershon, clan by clan,	1201
	6:63	The **d** of Merari, clan by clan,	1201
	7: 2	the **d** of Tola listed as fighting men	NIH
	7:12	The Shuppites and Huppites were the **d**	1201
	7:12	and the Hushites the **d** of Aher.	1201
	7:13	the **d** of Bilhah.	1201
	7:14	The **d** of Manasseh:	1201
	7:20	The **d** of Ephraim:	1201
	7:29	The **d** of Joseph son of Israel lived	1201
	7:40	All these were **d** of Asher—	1201
	8: 6	These were the **d** of Ehud,	1201
	8:40	All these were the **d** of Benjamin.	1201
	9:23	They and their **d** were in charge of guarding	1201
	15: 4	He called together the the **d** of Aaron and	1201
	15: 5	From the **d** of Kohath, Uriel the leader	1201
	15: 6	from the **d** of Merari, Asaiah the leader	1201
	15: 7	from the **d** of Gershon, Joel the leader	1201
	15: 8	the **d** of Elizaphan, Shemaiah the leader	1201
	15: 9	from the **d** of Hebron, Eliel the leader	1201
	15:10	from the **d** of Uzziel,	1201
	16:13	O **d** of Israel his servant,	2446
	20: 4	one of the **d** of the Rephaites,	3535
	20: 6	These were **d** of Rapha in Gath,	3528
	23:13	Aaron was set apart, he and his **d** forever,	1201
	23:16	The **d** of Gershom: Shubael was the first.	1201
	23:17	The **d** of Eliezer: Rehabiah was the first.	1201
	23:24	the **d** of Levi by their families—	1201
	23:28	of the Levites was to help Aaron's **d** in	1201
	23:32	under their brothers the **d** of Aaron,	1201
	24: 4	among Eleazar's **d** than among Ithamar's,	1201
	24: 4	sixteen heads of families from Eleazar's **d**	1201
	24: 4	of families from Ithamar's **d**.	1201
	24: 5	among the **d** of both Eleazar and Ithamar.	1201
	24:20	As for the rest of the **d** of Levi:	1201
	24:31	just as their brothers the **d** of Aaron did,	1201
	26: 8	All these were **d** of Obed-Edom;	1201
	26: 8	**d** of Obed-Edom, 62 in all.	NIH
	26:19	the divisions of the gatekeepers who were **d**	1201
	26:21	The **d** of Ladan,	1201
	28: 8	on as an inheritance to your **d** forever.	1201
2Ch	8: 8	their **d** remaining in the land,	1201
	13: 5	to David and his **d** forever by a covenant	1201
	13: 8	which is in the hands of David's **d**.	1201
	20: 7	to the **d** of Abraham your friend?	2446
	21: 7	a lamp for him and his **d** forever.	1201
	23: 3	as the LORD promised concerning the **d**	1201
	26:18	That is for the priests, the **d** of Aaron,	1201
	29:13	from the **d** of Elizaphan, Shimri and Jeiel;	1201
	29:13	from the **d** of Asaph,	1201
	29:14	from the **d** of Heman, Jehiel and Shimei;	1201
	29:14	from the **d** of Jeduthun,	1201
	29:21	the **d** of Aaron,	1201
	31:19	As for the priests, the **d** of Aaron,	1201
	32:33	the hill where the tombs of David's **d** are.	1201
	35:14	because the priests, the **d** of Aaron,	1201
	35:15	The musicians, the **d** of Asaph,	1201
Ezr	2: 3	the **d** of Parosh 2,172	1201
	2:36	the **d** of Jedaiah (through the family	1201
	2:40	the **d** of Jeshua and Kadmiel (through	1201
	2:41	The singers: the **d** of Asaph 128	1201
	2:42	the **d** of Shallum, Ater, Talmon, Akkub,	1201
	2:43	the **d** of Ziha, Hasupha, Tabbaoth,	1201
	2:55	The **d** of the servants of Solomon:	1201
	2:55	the **d** of Sotai, Hassophereth, Peruda,	1201
	2:58	and the **d** of the servants of Solomon 392	1201
	2:60	The **d** of Delaiah, Tobiah and Nekoda 652	1201
	2:61	The **d** of Hobaiah,	1201
	3: 9	and Kadmiel and his sons (**d** of Hodaviah)	1201
	8: 2	of the **d** of Phinehas, Gershom;	1201
	8: 2	of the **d** of Ithamar, Daniel;	1201
	8: 2	of the **d** of David;	1201
	8: 3	of the **d** of Shecaniah;	1201
	8: 3	of the **d** of Parosh, Zechariah;	1201
	8: 4	of the **d** of Pahath-Moab, Eliehoenai son	1201
	8: 5	the **d** of Zattu, Shecaniah son of Jahaziel;	1201
	8: 6	of the **d** of Adin, Ebed son of Jonathan, and	1201
	8: 7	of the **d** of Elam, Jeshaiah son of Athaliah;	1201
	8: 8	of the **d** of Shephatiah, Zebadiah son	1201
	8: 9	of the **d** of Joab, Obadiah son of Jehiel, and	1201
	8:10	the **d** of Bani, Shelomith son of Josiphiah,	1201
	8:11	the **d** of Bebai, Zechariah son of Bebai, and	1201
	8:12	the **d** of Azgad, Johanan son of Hakkatan;	1201
	8:13	of the **d** of Adonikam,	1201
	8:14	of the **d** of Bigvai,	1201
	8:18	from the **d** of Mahli son of Levi,	1201

Ezr	8:19	with Jeshaiah from the **d** of Merari,	1201
	10: 2	one of the **d** of Elam, said to Ezra,	1201
	10:18	Among the **d** of the priests,	1201
	10:18	From the **d** of Jeshua son of Jozadak,	1201
	10:20	From the **d** of Immer:	1201
	10:21	From the **d** of Harim:	1201
	10:22	From the **d** of Pashhur:	1201
	10:25	From the **d** of Parosh:	1201
	10:26	From the **d** of Elam:	1201
	10:27	From the **d** of Zattu:	1201
	10:28	From the **d** of Bebai:	1201
	10:29	From the **d** of Bani:	1201
	10:30	From the **d** of Pahath-Moab:	1201
	10:31	From the **d** of Harim:	1201
	10:33	From the **d** of Hashum:	1201
	10:34	From the **d** of Bani: Maadai, Amram, Uel,	1201
	10:38	From the **d** of Binnui: Shimei,	1201
	10:43	From the **d** of Nebo:	1201
Ne	7: 8	the **d** of Parosh 2,172	1201
	7:39	the **d** of Jedaiah (through the family	1201
	7:43	the **d** of Jeshua (through Kadmiel through	1201
	7:44	The singers: the **d** of Asaph 148	1201
	7:45	the **d** of Shallum, Ater, Talmon, Akkub,	1201
	7:46	the **d** of Ziha, Hasupha, Tabbaoth,	1201
	7:57	The **d** of the servants of Solomon:	1201
	7:57	the **d** of Sotai, Sophereth, Perida,	1201
	7:60	and the **d** of the servants of Solomon 392	1201
	7:62	the **d** of Delaiah, Tobiah and Nekoda 642	1201
	7:63	the **d** of Hobaiah,	1201
	9: 8	to give to his **d** the land of the Canaanites,	2446
	11: 3	and **d** of Solomon's servants lived in	1201
	11: 4	From the **d** of Judah:	1201
	11: 6	The **d** of Perez who lived	1201
	11: 7	From the **d** of Benjamin:	1201
	11:22	Uzzi was one of Asaph's **d**,	1201
	11:24	one of the **d** of Zerah son of Judah,	1201
	11:31	The **d** of the Benjamites from Geba lived	1201
	12:23	the **d** of Levi up to the time of Johanan son	1201
	12:47	the Levites set aside the portion for the **d**	1201
Est	9:27	to establish the custom that they and their **d**	2446
	9:28	the memory of them die out among their **d**.	2446
	9:31	for themselves and their **d** in regard	2446
Job	5:25	and your **d** like the grass of the earth.	7368
	18:19	He has no offspring or **d** among his people,	5781
	18:50	to David and his **d** forever.	2446
Ps	21:10	You will destroy their **d** from the earth,	7262
	22:23	All you **d** of Jacob, honor him!	2446
	22:23	Revere him, all you **d** of Israel!	2446
	25:13	and his **d** will inherit the land.	2446
	77:15	the **d** of Jacob and Joseph.	1201
	83: 8	to lend strength to the **d** of Lot.	1201
	102:28	their **d** will be established before you."	2446
	105: 6	O **d** of Abraham his servant,	2446
	106:27	make their **d** fall among the nations	2446
	109:13	May his **d** be cut off,	344
	132:11	"One of your own **d** I will place on your throne—	1061+7262
Isa	14:22	her offspring and **d**," declares the LORD.	5781
	39: 7	And some of your **d**,	1201
	41: 8	you **d** of Abraham my friend,	2446
	44: 3	and my blessing on your **d**.	7368
	45:19	I have not said to Jacob's **d**,	2446
	45:25	But in the LORD all the **d** of Israel will	2446
	48:19	Your **d** would have been like the sand,	2446
	53: 8	And who can speak of his **d**?	1887
	54: 3	your **d** will dispossess nations and settle	2446
	59:21	or from the mouths of their **d** from this time	2446
	61: 9	Their **d** will be known among the nations	2446
	65: 9	I will bring forth **d** from Jacob,	2446
	65:23	they and their **d** with them.	7368
	66:22	"so will your name and **d** endure.	2446
Jer	22: 8	who brought the **d** of Israel up out of	2446
	29:32	the Nehelamite and his **d**.	2446
	30:10	your **d** from the land of their exile.	2446
	31:36	the **d** of Israel ever cease to be a nation	2446
	31:37	be searched out will I reject all the **d**	2446
	33:22	I will make the **d** of David my servant and	2446
	33:26	the **d** of Jacob and David my servant	2446
	33:26	of his sons to rule over the **d** of Abraham,	2446
	35: 6	nor your **d** must ever drink wine.	1201
	35:16	The **d** of Jonadab son	1201
	46:27	your **d** from the land of their exile.	2446
Eze	20: 5	with uplifted hand to the **d** of the house	2446
	44:15	who are Levites and **d** of Zadok	1201
	46:16	it will also belong to his **d**;	1201
Da	11: 4	It will not go to his **d**,	344
Na	1:14	"You will have no **d** to bear your name.	2445
Mal	2: 3	"Because of you I will rebuke your **d**;	2446
	3: 6	So you, O **d** of Jacob, are not destroyed.	1201
Mt	23:31	the **d** of those who murdered the prophets.	5626
Lk	1:55	to Abraham and his **d** forever,	5065
Jn	8:33	"We are Abraham's **d**	5065
	8:37	I know you are Abraham's **d**.	5065
Ac	2:30	he would place one of his **d** on his throne. 2843+3836+4019	
	7: 5	and his **d** after him would possess the land,	5065
	7: 6	'Your **d** will be strangers in a country	5065
	8:33	Who can speak of his **d**?	1155
	13:23	"From this man's **d** God has brought	5065
Ro	9: 7	Nor because they are his **d** are they all Abraham's children.	5065
	9:29	"Unless the Lord Almighty had left us **d**,	5065
2Co	11:22	Are they Abraham's **d**?	5065
Heb	2:16	it is not angels he helps, but Abraham's **d**.	5065
	6:14	bless you and **give** you **many d**."	4437+4437
	7: 5	the **d** of Levi who become priests to collect	5626
	11:12	**came** **d** as numerous as the stars in the sky	1164

DESCENDED (24) [DESCEND]

Ge	36:16	These were the **chiefs** d *from* Eliphaz	AIT
	36:17	These were the **chiefs** d *from* Reuel	AIT
	36:18	These were the **chiefs** d *from* Esau's wife	AIT
	36:40	These were the **chiefs** d *from* Esau,	AIT
Ex	19:18	because the LORD d on it in fire.	3718
	19:20	The LORD d to the top of Mount Sinai	3718
Jos	16: 3	d westward to the territory of	3718
2Sa	21:20	He also **was** d from Rapha.	3528
1Ki	18:31	one for each of the tribes d *from* Jacob,	1201
1Ch	2:53	From these d the Zorathites and Eshtaolites.	3655
	20: 6	He also **was** d from Rapha.	3528
2Ch	34:12	Levites d from Merari,	1201
	34:12	and Zechariah and Meshullam, d	1201
Ezr	2:59	that their families were d from Israel:	2446
Ne	7:61	that their families were d from Israel:	2446
	10:38	A priest d *from* Aaron is to accompany	1201
Isa	57: 9	*you* d to the grave itself!	9164
Lk	3:22	the Holy Spirit d on him in bodily form like	2849
Ro	9: 6	For not all who are d **from** Israel are Israel.	1666
Eph	4: 9	that *he* also d to the lower,	2849
	4:10	He who d is the very one who ascended	2849
2Ti	2: 8	raised from the dead, d *from* David.	1666+5065
Heb	7: 5	their brothers *are* d **from** Abraham.	2002+4019
	7:14	For it is clear that our Lord d **from** Judah,	422

DESCENDING (7) [DESCEND]

Ge	28:12	the angels of God were ascending and d	3718
1Sa	25:20	there were David and his men d toward her,	3718
SS	4: 1	like a flock of goats d from Mount Gilead.	1683
	6: 5	like a flock of goats d from Gilead.	1683
Mt	3:16	the Spirit of God like a dove and lighting	2849
Mk	1:10	and the Spirit d on him like a dove.	2849
Jn	1:51	and the angels of God ascending and d on	2849

DESCENDS (1) [DESCEND]

Isa	34: 5	see, it d in judgment on Edom,	3718

DESCENT (7) [DESCEND]

Ge	10:32	according to their **lines of** d,	9352
Ne	9: 2	of Israelite d had separated themselves	2446
	13: 3	from Israel all who were **of foreign** d.	6850
Eze	44:22	they may marry only virgins of Israelite d	2446
Da	11: 1	(a Mede by d), who was made ruler over	2446
Jn	1:13	children born not of **natural** d,	135
Heb	7: 6	however, *did* not **trace** *his* d from Levi,	1156

DESCRIBE (2) [DESCRIBED, DESCRIBES, DESCRIPTION, DESCRIPTIONS]

Eze	43:10	d the temple *to* the people of Israel,	5583
Mk	4:30	or what parable shall we use to d it?	NIG

DESCRIBED (5) [DESCRIBE]

1Ki	4:33	*He* d plant life, from the cedar	1819
Ac	12:17	and d how the Lord had brought him out	1455
	15:14	Simon *has* d to us how God	2007
Rev	22:19	to them, God will add to him the plagues d	1211
	22:19	which *are* d in this book.	1211

DESCRIBES (1) [DESCRIBE]

Ro	10: 5	Moses d in this way the righteousness	1211

DESCRIPTION (3) [DESCRIBE]

Jos	18: 4	a survey of the land and *to* **write a** d of it,	4180
	18: 8	and make a survey of the land and **write a** d	4180
	18: 9	*They* **wrote** its d on a scroll, town by town,	4180

DESCRIPTIONS (1) [DESCRIBE]

Jos	18: 6	After you *have* **written** d of the seven parts	4180

DESCRY (KJV) See SPY OUT

DESECRATE (10) [DESECRATED, DESECRATES, DESECRATING]

Lev	21:12	nor leave the sanctuary of his God or d it,	2725
	21:23	and so d my sanctuary.	2725
	22:15	The priests *must* not d the sacred offerings	2725
Dt	21:23	*You* **must** not d the land	3237
Eze	7:22	and *they will* d my treasured place;	2725
	7:22	robbers will enter it and d it.	2725
	24:21	I *am about to* d my sanctuary—	2725
Da	11:31	up *to* d the temple fortress and will abolish	2725
Mt	12: 5	the temple d the day and yet are innocent?	1014
Ac	24: 6	and even tried *to* d the temple;	1014

DESECRATED (17) [DESECRATE]

Lev	19: 8	because *he has* d what is holy to	2725
2Ki	23: 8	the priests from the towns of Judah and d	3237
	23:10	*He* d Topheth, which was in the Valley	3237
	23:13	also d the high places that were east	3237
Ps	106:38	and the land *was* d by their blood.	2866
Isa	47: 6	with my people and d my inheritance;	2725
Eze	7:24	and their sanctuaries *will* be d.	2725
	20:13	and *they* utterly d my Sabbaths.	2725
	20:16	not follow my decrees and d my Sabbaths,	2725
	20:21	and *they* d my Sabbaths,	2725
	20:24	and d my Sabbaths,	2725
	22: 8	and d my Sabbaths,	2725
	23:38	and d my Sabbaths.	2725

Eze	23:39	they entered my sanctuary and d it.	2725
	25: 3	over my sanctuary when *it* **was** d and over	2725
	28:18	dishonest trade you *have* d your sanctuaries.	2725
Mal	2:11	Judah *has* d the sanctuary the LORD loves,	2725

DESECRATES (1) [DESECRATE]

Ex	31:14	*Anyone who* d it must be put to death;	2725

DESECRATING (5) [DESECRATE]

Ne	13:17	d the Sabbath day?	2725
	13:18	up more wrath against Israel by d	2725
Isa	56: 2	who keeps the Sabbath without d it,	2725
	56: 6	the Sabbath without d it and who hold fast	2725
Eze	44: 7	d my temple while you offered me food,	2725

DESERT (312) [DESERTED, DESERTING, DESERTS]

Ge	14: 6	as far as El Paran near the d.	4497
	16: 7	near a spring in the d;	4497
	21:14	She went on her way and wandered in the d	4497
	21:20	He lived in the d and became an archer.	4497
	21:21	While he was living in the D *of* Paran,	4497
	36:24	in the d while he was grazing the donkeys	4497
	37:22	Throw him into this cistern here in the d,	4497
Ex	3: 1	and he led the flock to the far side of the d	4497
	3:18	Let us take a three-day journey into the d	4497
	4:27	"Go into the d to meet Moses."	4497
	5: 1	a festival to me in the d.'"	4497
	5: 3	into the d to offer sacrifices to	4497
	7:16	so that they may worship me in the d.	4497
	8:27	We must take a three-day journey into the d	4497
	8:28	to the LORD our God in the d,	4497
	13:18	So God led the people around by the d road	4497
	13:20	at Etham on the edge of the d.	4497
	14: 3	hemmed in by the d.'	4497
	14:11	in Egypt that you brought us to the d	4497
	14:12	to serve the Egyptians than to die in the d!"	4497
	15:22	from the Red Sea and they went into the D	4497
	15:22	For three days they traveled in the d	4497
	16: 1	from Elim and came to the D *of* Sin,	4497
	16: 2	In the d the whole community grumbled	4497
	16: 3	into this d to starve this entire assembly	4497
	16:10	they looked toward the d,	4497
	16:14	on the ground appeared on the d floor.	4497
	16:32	the d when I brought you out of Egypt.'"	4497
	17: 1	from the D *of* Sin,	4497
	18: 5	came to him in the d,	4497
	19: 1	they came to the D *of* Sinai.	4497
	19: 2	they entered the D *of* Sinai,	4497
	19: 2	and Israel camped there in the d in front of	4497
	23:31	and from the d to the River.	4497
Lev	7:38	in the D *of* Sinai.	4497
	11:18	the white owl, the d **owl**, the osprey,	7684
	16:10	by sending it into the d as a scapegoat.	4497
	16:21	into the d in the care of a man appointed for	4497
	16:22	and the man shall release it in the d.	4497
Nu	1: 1	in the Tent of Meeting in the D *of* Sinai on	4497
	1:19	And so he counted them in the D *of* Sinai:	4497
	3: 4	with unauthorized fire before him in the D	4497
	3:14	The LORD said to Moses in the D	4497
	9: 1	in the D *of* Sinai in the first month of	4497
	9: 5	and they did so in the D *of* Sinai at twilight	4497
	10:12	from the D *of* Sinai and traveled from place	4497
	10:12	the cloud came to rest in the D *of* Paran.	4497
	10:31	You know where we should camp in the d,	4497
	12:16	and encamped in the D *of* Paran.	4497
	13: 3	from the D *of* Paran.	4497
	13:21	up and explored the land from the D *of* Zin	4497
	13:26	at Kadesh in the D *of* Paran.	4497
	14: 2	Or in this d!	4497
	14:16	so he slaughtered them in the d.'	4497
	14:22	and in the d but who disobeyed me	4497
	14:25	and set out toward the d along the route to	4497
	14:29	in this d your bodies will fall!	4497
	14:32	But you—your bodies will fall in this d.	4497
	14:33	until the last of your bodies lies in the d.	4497
	14:35	They will meet their end in this d;	4497
	15:32	While the Israelites were in the d,	4497
	16:13	with milk and honey to kill us in the d?	4497
	20: 1	at the D *of* Zin,	4497
	20: 4	the LORD's community into this d,	4497
	21: 5	up out of Egypt to die in the d?	4497
	21:11	in the d that faces Moab toward the sunrise.	4497
	21:13	in the d extending into Amorite territory.	4497
	21:18	Then they went from the d to Mattanah,	4497
	21:23	and marched out into the d against Israel.	4497
	24: 1	but turned his face toward the d.	4497
	26:64	when they counted the Israelites in the D	4497
	26:65	surely die in the d,	4497
	27: 3	"Our father died in the d,	4497
	27:14	at the waters in the D *of* Zin,	4497
	27:14	in the D *of* Zin.)	4497
	32:13	in the d forty years,	4497
	32:15	he will again leave all this people in the d,	4497
	33: 6	on the edge of the d.	4497
	33: 8	and passed through the sea into the d,	4497
	33: 8	for three days in the D *of* Etham,	4497
	33:11	They left the Red Sea and camped in the D	4497
	33:12	the D *of* Sin and camped at Dophkah.	4497
	33:15	They left Rephidim and camped in the D	4497
	33:16	They left the D *of* Sinai and camped	4497
	33:36	in the D *of* Zin.	4497
	34: 3	of the D *of* Zin along the border of Edom.	4497
Dt	1: 1	to all Israel in the d east of the Jordan—	4497

Dt	1:19	that vast and dreadful d that you have seen,	4497
	1:31	and in the d. There you saw	4497
	1:40	turn around and set out toward the d along	4497
	2: 1	toward the d along the route to the Red Sea,	4497
	2: 7	over your journey through this vast d.	4497
	2: 8	and traveled along the d road of Moab.	4497
	2:26	From the d *of* Kedemoth I sent messengers	4497
	4:43	Bezer in the d plateau, for the Reubenites;	4497
	8: 2	the way in the d these forty years,	4497
	8:15	He led you through the vast and dreadful d,	4497
	8:16	He gave you manna to eat in the d,	4497
	9: 7	the LORD your God to anger in the d.	4497
	9:28	to put them to death in the d.'	4497
	11: 5	in the d until you arrived at this place,	4497
	11:24	Your territory will extend from the d	4497
	14:17	the d **owl**, the osprey, the cormorant,	7684
	29: 5	the forty years that I led you through the d,	4497
	32:10	In a d land he found him,	4497
	32:51	at the waters of Meribah Kadesh in the D	4497
Jos	1: 4	the d to Lebanon, and from the great river,	4497
	5: 4	in the d on the way after leaving Egypt.	4497
	5: 5	the people born in the d during the journey	4497
	5: 6	the d forty years until all the men who were	4497
	8:15	and they fled toward the d.	4497
	8:20	toward the d had turned back	4497
	8:24	and in the d where they had chased them,	4497
	12: 8	the mountain slopes, the d and the Negev—	4497
	14:10	while Israel moved about in the d.	4497
	15: 1	to the D *of* Zin in the extreme south.	4497
	15:61	in the d: Beth Arabah, Middin, Secacah,	4497
	16: 1	and went up from there through the d into	4497
	18:12	coming out at the d of Beth Aven.	4497
	20: 8	of Jericho they designated Bezer in the d on	4497
	24: 7	Then you lived in the d for a long time.	4497
Jdg	1:16	to live among the people of the D *of* Judah	4497
	8: 7	I will tear your flesh with d thorns	4497
	8:16	by punishing them with d thorns and briers.	4497
	11:16	Israel went through the d to the Red Sea	4497
	11:18	"Next they traveled through the d,	4497
	11:22	to the Jabbok and from the d to the Jordan.	4497
	20:42	the Israelites in the direction of the d,	4497
	20:45	As they turned and fled toward the d to	4497
	20:47	and fled into the d to the rock of Rimmon,	4497
1Sa	4: 1	with all kinds of plagues in the d.	4497
	13:18	the Valley of Zeboim facing the d.	4497
	17:28	with whom did you leave those few sheep in the d?	4497
	23:14	David stayed in the d strongholds and in	4497
	23:14	and in the hills of the D *of* Ziph.	4497
	23:15	David was at Horesh in the D *of* Ziph,	4497
	23:24	David and his men were in the D *of* Maon,	4497
	23:25	to the rock and stayed in the D *of* Maon.	4497
	23:25	into the D *of* Maon in pursuit of David.	4497
	24: 1	"David is in the D *of* En Gedi."	4497
	25: 1	David moved down into the D *of* Maon.	4497
	25: 4	While David was in the d,	4497
	25:14	from the d to give our master his greetings,	4497
	25:21	in the d so that nothing of his was missing.	4497
	26: 2	So Saul went down to the D *of* Ziph,	4497
	26: 3	but David stayed in the d.	4497
2Sa	15:23	and all the people moved on toward the d.	4497
	15:28	at the fords in the d until word comes	4497
	16: 2	to refresh those who become exhausted in the d."	4497
	17:16	not spend the night at the fords in the d;	4497
	17:29	and tired and thirsty in the d."	4497
1Ki	2:34	and he was buried on his own land in the d.	4497
	9:18	and Tadmor in the d, within his land,	4497
	19: 4	he himself went a day's journey into the d.	4497
	19:15	and go to the D *of* Damascus.	4497
2Ki	3: 8	"Through the D *of* Edom," he answered.	4497
1Ch	5: 9	of the d that extends to the Euphrates River,	4497
	6:78	of Jericho they received Bezer in the d,	4497
	12: 8	to David at his stronghold in the d.	4497
	21:29	which Moses had made in the d,	4497
2Ch	1: 3	the LORD's servant had made in the d.	4497
	8: 4	in the d and all the store cities he had built	4497
	20:16	at the end of the gorge in the D *of* Jeruel.	4497
	20:20	in the morning they left for the D *of* Tekoa.	4497
	20:24	to the place that overlooks the d and looked	4497
	24: 9	of God had required of Israel in the d.	4497
Ne	9:17	Therefore *you* did not d them,	6440
	9:19	not abandon them in the d.	4497
	9:21	For forty years you sustained them in the d;	4497
Job	1:19	in from the d and struck the four corners of	4497
	24: 5	Like wild donkeys in the d,	4497
	38:26	a d with no one in it,	4497
Ps	29: 8	The voice of the LORD shakes the d;	4497
	29: 8	the LORD shakes the D *of* Kadesh.	4497
	55: 7	I would flee far away and stay in the d;	4497
	63: T	When he was in the D *of* Judah.	4497
	65:12	The grasslands of the d overflow;	4497
	72: 9	The d tribes will bow before him	7470
	74:14	as food to the **creatures of the** d.	7470
	75: 6	the east or the west or from the d can exalt	4497
	78:15	the d and gave them water as abundant as	4497
	78:17	rebelling against the Most High.	7480
	78:19	saying, "Can God spread a table in the d?	4497
	78:40	in the d and grieved him in the wasteland!	4497
	78:52	he led them like sheep toward the d.	4497
	95: 8	as you did that day at Massah in the d,	4497
	102: 6	I am like a d owl,	4497
	105:41	like a river it flowed in the d.	7480
	106: 9	through the depths as through a d.	4497
	106:14	In the d they gave in to their craving;	4497
	106:26	that he would make them fall in the d,	4497

Ps 107: 4 Some wandered in d wastelands, 4497
107:33 He turned rivers into a d, 4497
107:35 He turned the d into pools of water and 4497
136:16 to him who led his people through the d, 4497
Pr 21:19 Better to live in a d than with 824+4497
SS 3: 6 up from the d like a column of smoke, 4497
8: 5 Who is this coming up from the d leaning 4497
Isa 13:21 But d creatures will lie there, 7470
14:17 the man who made the world a d, 4497
16: 1 from Sela, across the d, 4497
16: 8 and spread toward the d. 4497
21: 1 An oracle concerning the D by the Sea: 4497
21: 1 an invader comes from the d, 4497
23:13 a place for d creatures; 7470
25: 5 and like the heat of the d. 7481
27:10 forsaken like the d; 4497
32: 2 in the d and the shadow of a great rock in 7481
32:15 and the d becomes a fertile field, 4497
32:16 in the d and righteousness live in 4497
34:11 The d owl and screech owl will possess it; 7684
34:14 D creatures will meet with hyenas, 7470
35: 1 The d and the parched land will be glad; 4497
35: 6 in the wilderness and streams in the d. 6858
40: 3 "In the d prepare the way for the LORD; 4497
41:18 I will turn the d into pools of water, 4497
41:19 I will put in the d the cedar and the acacia, 4497
42:11 Let the d and its towns raise their voices; 4497
43:19 a way in the d and streams in the wasteland. 4497
43:20 in the d and streams in the wasteland, 4497
49:10 the d heat or the sun beat upon them. 9220
50: 2 I turn rivers into a d; 4497
64:10 Your sacred cities have become a d; 4497
64:10 even Zion is a d, Jerusalem a desolation. 4497
Jer 2: 2 and followed me through the d, 4497
2:24 a wild donkey accustomed to the d, sniffing 4497
2:31 a d to Israel or a land of great darkness? 4497
3: 2 sat like a nomad in the d. 4497
4:11 in the d blows toward my people, but not 4497
4:26 I looked, and the fruitful land was a d; 4497
5: 6 a wolf from the d will ravage them, 6858
9: 2 in the d a lodging place for travelers, so 4497
9:10 up a lament concerning the d pastures. 4497
9:12 the land been ruined and laid waste like a d 4497
9:26 and all who live in the d in distant places. 4497
12:12 the d destroyers will swarm, for the sword 4497
13:24 like chaff driven by the d wind. 4497
17: 6 in the parched places of the d, 4497
17:11 his life is half gone, they will d him, 6440
22: 6 I will surely make you like a d, 4497
23:10 and the pastures in the d are withered. 4497
25:24 of the foreign people who live in the d; 4497
31: 2 the sword will find favor in the d; 4497
48: 6 become like a bush in the d. 4497
50:12 a wilderness, a dry land, a d. 6858
50:39 "So d creatures and hyenas will live there, 7470
51:43 a dry and d land, a land where no one lives, 6858
La 4: 3 like ostriches in the d. 4497
4:19 and lay in wait for us in the d. 4497
5: 9 of our lives because of the sword in the d. 4497
Eze 6:14 a desolate waste from the d to Diblah— 4497
19:13 Now it is planted in the d, 4497
20:10 of Egypt and brought them into the d. 4497
20:13 of Israel rebelled against me in the d. 4497
20:13 on them and destroy them in the d. 4497
20:15 to them in the d that I would not bring them 4497
20:17 or put an end to them in the d. 4497
20:18 I said to their children in the d, 4497
20:21 and spend my anger against them in the d. 4497
20:23 to them in the d that I would disperse them 4497
20:35 I will bring you into the d of the nations 4497
20:36 As I judged your fathers in the d of 4497
23:42 from the d along with men from the rabble, 4497
29: 5 I will leave you in the d. 4497
34:25 of wild beasts so that they may live in the d 4497
Hos 2: 3 I will make her like a d, 4497
2:14 I will lead her into the d and speak tenderly 4497
9:10 it was like finding grapes in the d; 4497
13: 5 I cared for you in the d, 4497
13:15 blowing in from the d; 4497
Joel 2: 3 a d waste—nothing escapes them. 4497
3:19 Egypt will be desolate, Edom a d waste, 4497
Am 2:10 the d to give you the land of the Amorites. 4497
5:25 and offerings forty years in the d, 4497
Hab 1: 9 like a d wind and gather prisoners like sand. 7708
Zep 2:13 and dry as the d. 4497
2:14 The d owl and the screech owl will roost 7684
Mal 1: 3 and left his inheritance to the d jackals." 4497
Mt 3: 1 preaching in the D of Judea 2245
3: 3 "A voice of one calling in the d, 2245
4: 1 Then Jesus was led by the Spirit into the d 2245
11: 7 "What did you go out into the d to see? 2245
24:26 anyone tells you, 'There he is, out in the d,' 2245
Mk 1: 3 "a voice of one calling in the d, 2245
1: 4 in the d region and preaching a baptism 2245
1:12 At once the Spirit sent him out into the d, 2245
1:13 and he was in the d forty days 2245
Lk 1:80 in the d until he appeared publicly to Israel. 2245
3: 2 to John son of Zechariah in the d. 2245
3: 4 "A voice of one calling in the d, 2245
4: 1 and was led by the Spirit into the d, 2245
7:24 What did you go out into the d to see? 2245
Jn 1:23 "I am the voice of one calling in the d, 2245
3:14 Just as Moses lifted up the snake in the d, 2245
6:31 Our forefathers ate the manna in the d; 2245
6:49 Your forefathers ate the manna in the d, 2245
11:54 Instead he withdrew to a region near the d, 2245
Ac 7:30 a burning bush in the d near Mount Sinai. 2245

Ac 7:36 at the Red Sea and for forty years in the d. 2245
7:38 He was in the assembly in the d, 2245
7:42 and offerings forty years in the d, 2245
7:44 of the Testimony with them in the d. 2245
8:26 to the road—the d road— 2245
13:18 for about forty years in the d, 2245
21:38 into the d some time ago?" 2245
1Co 10: 5 their bodies were scattered over the d. 2245
Heb 3: 8 during the time of testing in the d, 2245
3:17 whose bodies fell in the d? 2245
Rev 12: 6 the d to a place prepared for her by God, 2245
12:14 to the place prepared for her in the d, 2245
17: 3 angel carried me away in the Spirit into a d. 2245

DESERTED (34) [DESERT]

Lev 26:22 in number that your roads will be d. 9037
26:43 be d by them and will enjoy its sabbaths 6440
Dt 32:18 You d the Rock, who fathered you; 8861
Jos 22: 3 not d your brothers but have carried out 6440
2Sa 20: 2 Israel d David to follow Sheba 339+4946+6590
Ezr 9: 9 our God has not d us in our bondage. 6440
Ps 69:25 May their place be d; 9037
Isa 6:11 the houses are left d and the fields ruined 132+401+4946
17: 2 cities of Aroer will be d and left to flocks, 6440
32:14 the noisy city d; 6440
33: 8 The highways are d, 9037
54: 6 as if you were a wife d and distressed 6440
62: 4 No longer will they call you D, 6440
62:12 the City No Longer D. 6440
Jer 2:15 his towns are burned and d. 1172+3782+4946
4:29 All the towns are d; no one lives in them. 6440
26: 9 this city will be desolate and d?" 401+3782+4946
33:10 and the streets of Jerusalem that are d, 4497
38:22 your friends have d you.' 294+6047
44: 2 Today they lie d and in ruins 401+3782
La 1: 1 How d lies the city, once so full of people! 970
Eze 14: 5 who have all d me for their idols.' 2319
36: 4 and the d towns that have been plundered 6440
Hos 4:10 but not increase, because they have d 6440
Am 5: 2 never to rise again, d in her own land, 5759
Zep 3: 6 I have left their streets d, 2990
Zec 9: 5 and Ashkelon will be d. 3782+4202
Mt 26:56 Then all the disciples d him and fled. 918
Mk 14:50 Then everyone d him and fled. 918
Ac 1:20 "'May his place be d; 2245
15:38 because he had d them in Pamphylia 918
2Ti 1:15 in the province of Asia has d me, 695
4:10 has d me and has gone to Thessalonica. 1593
4:16 but everyone d me. 1593

DESERTING (3) [DESERT]

Jer 37:13 "You are d to the Babylonians!" 5877
37:14 "I am not d to the Babylonians." 5877
Gal 1: 6 I am astonished that you are so quickly d 608+3572
the one who called you

DESERTS (8) [DESERT]

1Ch 12:19 "It will cost us our heads if he d 5877
Pr 19: 4 but a poor man's friend d him. 7233
Isa 48:21 not thirst when he led them through the d; 2999
51: 3 he will make her d like Eden, 4497
Jer 2: 6 through a land of d and rifts, 6858
14: 5 the doe in the field d her newborn fawn 6440
Zec 11:17 who d the flock! 6440
Heb 11:38 They wandered in d and mountains, 2244

DESERVE (30) [DESERVED, DESERVES, DESERVING]

Ge 40:15 to d being put in a dungeon." AIT
Lev 26:21 seven times over, as your sins d. 3869
Jdg 20:10 it can give them what they d for 3869
1Sa 26:16 LORD lives, you and your men d to die, 1201
1Ki 2:26 You d to die, 408
Ps 28: 4 and bring back upon them what they d. 1691
94: 2 pay back to the proud what they d. 1691
103:10 he does not treat us as our sins d 5646
Pr 3:27 Do not withhold good from those who d it, 1251
Ecc 8:14 righteous men who get what the wicked d, 3869+5126
8:14 and wicked men who get what the righteous d. 3869+5126
Isa 66: 6 LORD repaying his enemies all they d. 1691
Jer 14:16 on them the calamity they d. AIT
17:10 according to what his deeds d." 7262
21:14 I will punish you according to your deeds d, 7262
32:19 according to his conduct and as his deeds d. 7262
49:12 not d to drink the cup must drink it, 5477
La 3:64 Pay them back what they d, O LORD, 1691
Eze 16:59 I will deal with you as you d, 6913
Zec 1: 6 what our ways and practices d, 3869
Mt 8: 8 not d to have you come under my roof 1639+2653
22: 8 but those I invited did not d to come. 545+1639
Lk 7: 6 "Lord, don't trouble yourself, for I do not d 1639+2653
to have you come
23:15 he has done nothing to d death. 545
23:41 for we are getting what our deeds d. 545
Ro 1:32 that those who do such things d death, 545+1639
16:18 Such men d recognition. AIT
2Co 11:15 Their end will be what their actions d. 2240+2848
Rev 16: 6 given them blood to drink as they d." 545+1639

DESERVED (5) [DESERVE]

2Sa 19:28 All my grandfather's descendants d nothing 408
Ezr 9:13 punished us less than our sins have d 4946
Job 33:27 but I did not get what I d. 8750
Ac 23:29 against him that d death or imprisonment. 545
Ro 3: 8 Their condemnation is d. 1899

DESERVES (14) [DESERVE]

Nu 35:31 who d to die. 8401
Dt 25: 2 If the guilty man d to be beaten, 1201
25: 2 with the number of lashes his crime d, 1896+3869
Jdg 9:16 and if you have treated him as he d— 1691+3338
2Sa 12: 5 the man who did this d to die! 1201
Job 34:11 he brings upon them what his conduct d. 3869
Jer 51: 6 he will pay her what she d. 1691
Lk 7: 4 "This man d to have you do this, 545+1639
10: 7 for the worker d his wages. 545
Ac 26:31 not doing anything that d death 545
1Ti 1:15 a trustworthy saying that d full acceptance: 545
4: 9 a trustworthy saying that d full acceptance 545
5:18 and "The worker d his wages." 545
Heb 10:29 a man d to be punished who has trampled 546

DESERVING (7) [DESERVE]

Dt 19: 6 kill him even though he is not d of death, 5477
22:26 she has committed no sin d death. AIT
Mt 10:13 If the home is d, let your peace rest on it; 545
Lk 12:48 and does things d punishment will 545
Ac 25:11 I am guilty of doing anything d death, 545
25:25 I found he had done nothing d of death, 545
28:18 not guilty of any crime d death. NIG

DESIGN (7) [DESIGNED, DESIGNER, DESIGNERS, DESIGNS]

1Ki 7: 8 set farther back, was similar in d. 5126
2Ch 2:14 of engraving and can execute any d given 4742
24:13 of God according to its original d 5504
Eze 43:11 make known to them the d of the temple— 7451
43:11 its whole d and all its regulations and laws. 7451
43:11 to its d and follow all its regulations. 7451
Ac 17:29 an image made by man's d and skill. 1927

DESIGNATE (3) [DESIGNATED, DESIGNATING]

Ex 21:13 he is to flee to a place I will d. 8492
Dt 23:12 D a place outside the camp 2118
Jos 20: 2 "Tell the Israelites to d the cities of refuge, 5989

DESIGNATED (14) [DESIGNATE]

Jos 20: 8 of the Jordan of Jericho they d Bezer in 5989
20: 9 to these d cities and not be killed by 4597
2Sa 24:15 that morning until the end of the time d, 4595
1Ch 12:31 d by name to come and make David king— 5918
16:41 and the rest of those chosen and d by name 5918
28:14 He d the weight of gold for all NIH
2Ch 28:15 The men d by name took the prisoners, 5918
31:19 men were d by name to distribute portions 5918
Ezr 10:16 and all of them d by name. NIH
Ne 13:31 for contributions of wood at d times, 2374
Est 9:31 of Purim at their d times, 2375
Eze 43:21 for the sin offering and burn it in the d part 5152
Lk 6:13 whom he also d apostles: 3951
Heb 5:10 d by God to be high priest in the order 4641

DESIGNATING (1) [DESIGNATE]

Mk 3:14 He appointed twelve—d them apostles— 3951

DESIGNED (1) [DESIGN]

2Ch 26:15 In Jerusalem he made machines d 4742

DESIGNER (1) [DESIGN]

Ex 38:23 a craftsman and d, 3110

DESIGNERS (2) [DESIGN]

Ex 35:35 d, embroiderers in blue, 3110
35:35 all of them master craftsmen and d. 3110+4742

DESIGNS (3) [DESIGN]

Ex 31: 4 to make artistic d for work in gold, 4742
35:32 to make artistic d for work in gold, 4742
2Ch 3: 5 palm tree and chain d. 9474

DESIRABLE (3) [DESIRE]

Ge 3: 6 and also d for gaining wisdom, 2773
Pr 22: 1 A good name is more d than great riches; 1047
Jer 3:19 like sons and give you a d land, 2775

DESIRE (56) [DESIRABLE, DESIRED, DESIRES]

Ge 3:16 Your d will be for your husband, 9592
Dt 5:21 not set your d on your neighbor's house 203
1Sa 9:20 And to whom is all the d of Israel turned, 2775
2Sa 19:38 anything you d from me I will do for you." 1047
23: 5 and grant me my every d? 2914
1Ch 29:18 keep this d in the hearts 3671+4742
2Ch 1:11 "Since this is your heart's d and you have 6640
9: 8 for Israel and his d to uphold them forever, NIH
Job 13: 3 But I d to speak to the Almighty and 2911

Job	21:14	*We* **have** no **d** to know your ways.	2911
Ps	10:17	You hear, O LORD, the **d** of the afflicted;	9294
	20: 4	May he give you the **d** of your heart	3869
	21: 2	You have granted him the **d** of his heart	9294
	27:12	Do not turn me over to the **d** of my foes,	5883
	40: 6	Sacrifice and offering *you did* not **d**,	2911
	40: 8	*I* **d** to do your will, O my God;	2911
	40:14	may *all who* **d** my ruin be turned back	2913
	41: 2	and not surrender him to the **d** of his foes.	5883
	51: 6	Surely *you* **d** truth in the inner parts;	2911
	70: 2	may *all who* **d** my ruin be turned back	2913
	73:25	And earth has nothing *I* **d** besides you.	2911
Pr	3:15	nothing you **d** can compare with her.	2914
	8:11	and nothing you **d** can compare with her.	2914
	10:24	*what* the righteous **d** will be granted.	9294
	11:23	The **d** of the righteous ends only in good,	9294
	12:12	The wicked **d** the plunder of evil men,	2773
	17:16	since he has no **d** to get wisdom?	4213
	24: 1	*do not* **d** their company;	203
Ecc	12: 5	along and **d** no longer is stirred.	37
SS	6:12	my **d** set me among the royal chariots	5883
	7:10	I belong to my lover, and his **d** is for me.	9592
Isa	26: 8	and renown are the **d** of our hearts.	9294
	53: 2	in his appearance that *we should* **d** him.	2773
	55:11	to me empty, but will accomplish what *I* **d**	2911
Eze	24:25	the delight of their eyes, their heart's **d**,	5362
Hos	6: 6	For *I* **d** mercy, not sacrifice,	2911
Mic	7: 3	the powerful dictate what they **d**—	2094
Mal	3: 1	whom you **d**, will come,"	2913
Mt	9:13	'*I* **d** mercy, not sacrifice.'	2527
	12: 7	'*I* **d** mercy, not sacrifice.'	2527
Jn	8:44	and you want to carry out your father's **d**.	2123
Ro	7: 8	produced in me every kind of **covetous d**.	2123
	7:18	For I have the **d** to do what is good,	2527
	9:16	therefore, depend on man's **d** or effort,	2527
	10: 1	my heart's **d** and prayer to God for	2306
1Co	12:31	But eagerly **d** the greater gifts.	2420
	14: 1	of love and eagerly **d** spiritual gifts,	2420
2Co	8:10	to give but also *to* **have** the **d** to do so.	2527
	8:13	Our **d** is not that others might be relieved	NIG
Php	1:23	*I* **d** to depart and be with Christ,	2123+2400
Heb	10: 5	"Sacrifice and offering *you did* not **d**,	2527
	10: 8	and sin offerings *you did* not **d**,	2527
	13:18	a clear conscience and **d** to live honorably	2527
Jas	1:14	by his own **evil d**, he is dragged away	2123
	1:15	after **d** has conceived, it gives birth to sin;	2123
2Pe	2:10	of those who follow the corrupt **d** of	2123

DESIRED (13) [DESIRE]

1Ki	9: 1	and had achieved all he had **d** to do,	2911+3139
	9:19	whatever he **d** to build in Jerusalem,	3137+3139
	10:13	the queen of Sheba all she **d** and asked for,	2914
2Ch	8: 6	whatever he **d** to build in Jerusalem,	3137+3139
	9:12	the queen of Sheba all she **d** and asked for;	2914
Ps	107:30	and he guided them to their **d** haven.	2914
	132:13	he has **d** it for his dwelling;	203
	132:14	here I will sit enthroned, for *I have* **d** it—	203
Ecc	2:10	I denied myself nothing my eyes **d**;	8626
Jer	17:16	you know *I have* not **d** the day of despair.	203
Da	11:37	for the gods of his fathers or for the *one* **d**	2775
Hag	2: 7	and the **d** of all nations will come,	2775
Lk	22:15	"*I have* eagerly **d** to eat this Passover	2121+2123

DESIRES (49) [DESIRE]

Ge	4: 7	it **d** to have you, but you must master it."	9592
	41:16	the answer he **d**."	8934
2Sa	3:21	that you may rule over all that your heart **d**.	203
1Ki	11:37	and you will rule over all that your heart **d**;	203
Job	17:11	and so are the **d** of my heart.	4626
	31:16	"If I have denied the **d** of the poor or let	2914
Ps	34:12	Whoever of you loves life and **d**	170
	37: 4	and he will give you the **d** of your heart.	5399
	103: 5	who satisfies your **d** with good things so	6344
	140: 8	do not grant the wicked their **d**, O LORD;	4397
	145:16	and satisfy the **d** of every living thing.	8356
	145:19	He fulfills the **d** of those who fear him;	8356
Pr	11: 6	but the unfaithful are trapped by **evil d**.	2094
	13: 4	but the **d** of the diligent are fully satisfied.	5883
	19:22	*What* a man **d** is unfailing love;	9294
Ecc	6: 2	so that he lacks nothing his heart **d**,	203
SS	2: 7	Do not arouse or awaken love until *it so* **d**.	2911
	3: 5	Do not arouse or awaken love until *it so* **d**.	2911
	8: 4	Do not arouse or awaken love until *it so* **d**.	2911
Hab	2: 4	his **d** are not upright—	5883
Mk	4:19	of wealth and the **d** for other things come in	2123
Ro	1:24	over in the **sinful d** of their hearts	2123
	6:12	so that you obey its **evil d**.	2123
	8: 5	on what that nature **d**;	NIG
	8: 5	on what the Spirit **d**.	NIG
	13:14	and do not think about how to gratify the **d**	2123
Gal	5:16	not gratify the **d** of the sinful nature.	2123
	5:17	For the sinful nature **d** what is contrary to	2121
	5:24	the sinful nature with its passions and **d**.	2123
Eph	2: 3	of our sinful nature and following its **d**	2525
	4:22	which is being corrupted by its deceitful **d**;	2123
Col	3: 5	lust, evil and greed, which is idolatry.	2123
1Ti	3: 1	he **d** a noble task.	2121
	5:11	**sensual d** overcome their dedication to	2952
	6: 9	a trap and into many foolish and harmful **d**	2123
2Ti	2:22	Flee the **evil d** of youth,	2123
	3: 6	and are swayed by all kinds of **evil d**,	2123
	4: 3	Instead, to suit their own **d**,	2123
Jas	1:20	about the righteous life that God **d**.	NIG
	4: 1	Don't they come from your **d** that battle	2454
1Pe	1:14	do not conform *to* the **evil d** you had	2123

1Pe	2:11	to abstain from sinful **d**,	2123
	4: 2	of his earthly life *for* **evil human d**,	2123
2Pe	1: 4	in the world caused by **evil d**.	2123
	2:18	to the **lustful d** of sinful human nature,	816+2123
	3: 3	scoffing and following their own **evil d**.	2123
1Jn	2:17	The world and its **d** pass away,	2123
Jude	1:16	they follow their own **evil d**;	2123
	1:18	there will be scoffers who will follow their own ungodly **d**."	2123

DESOLATE (83) [DESOLATION, DESOLATIONS]

Ge	47:19	and that the land *may* not become **d**."	9037
Ex	23:29	because the land would become **d** and	9039
Lev	26:34	that *it* lies **d** and you are in the country	9037
	26:35	All the time *that it* lies **d**,	9037
	26:43	and will enjoy its sabbaths while *it* lies **d**	9037
Jos	8:28	a **d** place to this day.	9039
2Sa	13:20	in her brother Absalom's house, a **d** *woman.*	9037
Job	30: 3	the parched land in **d** wastelands at night.	8739
	38:27	to satisfy a **d** wasteland and make it sprout	8739
Isa	1: 7	Your country is **d**, your cities burned	9039
	5: 9	"Surely the great houses will become **d**,	9014
	13: 9	the land and destroy the sinners within it.	9014
	24:10	The ruined city *lies* **d**;	8689
	27:10	The fortified city stands **d**,	970
	34:10	to generation *it will lie* **d**;	2990
	49: 8	the land and to reassign its **d** inheritances,	9037
	49:19	"Though you were ruined and made **d**	9037
	54: 1	of the **d** *woman* than of her who has	9037
	54: 3	and settle in their **d** cities.	9037
	62: 4	or name your land **D**.	9039
Jer	6: 8	and make your land so no one can live	9039
	7:34	for the land will become **d**.	2999
	9:10	*They are* **d** and untraveled.	5898
	10:22	It will make the towns of Judah **d**,	9039
	12:10	into a **d** wasteland.	9039
	12:11	parched and **d** before me;	9038
	25:11	a **d** wasteland, and these nations will serve	2999
	25:12	"and will make it **d** forever.	9039
	25:38	and their land will become **d** because of	9014
	26: 9	and this city *will be* **d** and deserted?"	2990
	42:43	'It is a **d waste**, without men or animals,	9039
	33:10	'You say about this place, "It is a **d waste**,	2992
	33:12	and without men or animals—	2992
	44: 6	and made them the **d** ruins they are today.	2999
	44:22	and a **d** waste without inhabitants,	2999
	48: 9	her towns will become **d**,	9014
	49:33	a **d** place forever.	9039
	50:13	not be inhabited but will be completely **d**.	9039
	50:23	How **d** is Babylon among the nations!	9014
	51:26	for you will be **d** forever,"	9039
	51:43	Her towns will be **d**, a dry and desert land,	9014
	51:62	it will be **d** forever."	9039
La	1: 4	All her gateways are **d**, her priests groan,	9037
	1:13	He made me **d**, faint all the day long.	9037
	5:18	which *lies* **d**, with jackals prowling over it.	9037
Eze	6:14	and make the land a **d** waste from the desert	9039
	12:20	be laid waste and the land will be **d**.	9039
	14:15	and they leave it childless and it becomes **d**	9039
	14:16	but the land would be **d**.	9039
	15: 8	I will make the land **d**	9039
	26:19	When I make you a **d** city,	2990
	29: 9	Egypt will become a **d** wasteland.	9039
	29:10	of Egypt a ruin and a **d** waste from Migdol	9039
	29:12	of Egypt among devastated lands,	9039
	29:12	and her cities will lie **d** forty years	9039
	30: 7	" '*They will be* **d** among desolate lands,	9037
	30: 7	" '*They will be* desolate among **d** lands,	9039
	32:15	When I make Egypt **d** and strip the land	9039
	33:28	I will make the land a **d** waste,	9039
	33:28	and the mountains of Israel *will become* **d**	9037
	33:29	when I have made the land a **d** waste	9039
	35: 3	against you and make you a **d** waste.	9039
	35: 4	into ruins and you will be **d**.	9039
	35: 7	a **d** waste and cut off from it all who come	9040
	35: 9	I will make you **d** forever;	9039
	35:14	the whole earth rejoices, I will make you **d**.	9039
	35:15	of the house of Israel became **d**,	9037
	35:15	You will be **d**, O Mount Seir,	9039
	36: 4	the ravines and valleys, to the **d** ruins and	9037
	36:34	The **d** land will be cultivated instead	9037
	36:34	be cultivated instead of lying **d** in the sight	9039
	36:35	that were lying in ruins, and destroyed,	9037
	36:36	and have replanted what *was* **d**.	9037
	38: 8	which had long been **d**.	2999
Da	9:17	look with favor on your **d** sanctuary.	9038
Joel	3:19	But Egypt will be **d**, Edom a desert waste,	9039
Mic	7:13	The earth will become **d** because	9039
Zep	2:13	leaving Nineveh **utterly d** and dry as	9039
Zec	7:14	The land **was left so d** behind them	9037
	7:14	how they made the pleasant land **d**.' "	9014
Mt	23:38	Look, your house is left to you **d**.	2245
Lk	13:35	Look, your house is left to you **d**.	2245
Gal	4:27	of the **d** *woman* than of her who has	2245

DESOLATION (14) [DESOLATE]

2Ch	36:21	all the time of its **d** it rested,	9014
Isa	17: 9	And all will be **d**.	9039
	34:11	of chaos and the plumb line of **d**.	983
	64:10	even Zion is a desert, Jerusalem a **d**	9039
Eze	23:33	the cup of ruin and **d**.	9039
Da	8:13	the rebellion *that* **causes d**,	9037
	9: 2	**d** of Jerusalem would last seventy years.	2999
	9:18	open your eyes and see the **d** of the city	9037

Da	9:27	set up an abomination *that* **causes d**,	9037
	11:31	set up the abomination *that* **causes d**.	9037
	12:11	and the abomination *that* **causes d** is set up,	9037
Mt	24:15	'the abomination *that* **causes d**,' spoken of	2247
Mk	13:14	'the abomination *that causes* **d**' standing	2247
Lk	21:20	you will know that its **d** is near.	2247

DESOLATIONS (2) [DESOLATE]

Ps	46: 8	the **d** he has brought on the earth.	9014
Da	9:26	and **d** have been decreed.	9037

DESPAIR (12) [DESPAIRED, DESPAIRING, DESPAIRS]

1Sa	4:20	"Don't **d**; you have given birth to a son."	3707
Job	9:23	he mocks the **d** of the innocent.	5000
Ps	88:15	I have suffered your terrors and *am* in **d**.	7041
Ecc	2:20	to **d** over all my toilsome labor under	3286
Isa	19: 9	Those who work with combed flax *will* **d**,	1017
	61: 3	a garment of praise instead of a spirit of **d**.	3910
Jer	17:16	you know I have not desired the day of **d**.	631
Eze	4:16	in anxiety and drink rationed water in **d**,	9041
	7:27	the prince will be clothed with **d**,	9039
	12:19	in anxiety and drink their water in **d**,	9041
Joel	1:11	**D**, you farmers, wail, you vine growers;	1017
2Co	4: 8	perplexed, but not in **d**;	*1989*

DESPAIRED (1) [DESPAIR]

2Co	1: 8	so that we **d** even of life.	*1989*

DESPAIRING (4) [DESPAIR]

Dt	28:65	eyes weary with longing, and a **d** heart.	1792
Job	6:14	"A **d** *man* should have the devotion	4988
	6:26	and treat the words of a **d** *man* as wind?	3286
Jer	14: 3	dismayed and **d**, they cover their heads.	4007

DESPAIRS (1) [DESPAIR]

Job	15:22	*He* **d** of escaping the darkness;	586+4202

DESPERATE (4)

2Sa	12:18	He may do **something d**."	8288
Ps	60: 3	You have shown your people **d times**;	7997
	79: 8	for we are in **d** need.	4394
	142: 6	Listen to my cry, for I am in **d** need;	4394

DESPISE (34) [DESPISED, DESPISES]

Ge	16: 4	*she began to* **d** her mistress.	928+6524+7837
1Sa	2:30	but *those who* **d** me will be disdained.	1022
2Sa	12: 9	Why *did you* **d** the word of the LORD	1022
Est	1:17	and so they *will* **d** their husbands	1022+6524
Job	5:17	so *do not* **d** the discipline of the Almighty.	4415
	7:16	*I* **d** my life; I would not live forever.	4415
	9:21	*I* **d** my own life.	4415
	36: 5	"God is mighty, but *does* not **d** men;	4415
	42: 6	Therefore *I* **d** *myself* and repent in dust	4415
Ps	51:17	O God, *you* will not **d**.	1022
	69:33	and *does* not **d** his captive people.	1022
	73:20	O Lord, *you will* **d** them as fantasies.	1022
	102:17	*he will* not **d** their plea.	1022
Pr	1: 7	but fools **d** wisdom and discipline.	1022
	3:11	*do not* **d** the LORD's discipline and do	4415
	6:30	*Men do* not **d** a thief if he steals	996
	23:22	*and do not* **d** your mother when she is old.	996
SS	8: 1	I would kiss you, and no *one would* **d** me.	996
Isa	60:14	all *who* **d** you will bow down at your feet	5540
Jer		Your lovers will **d** you; they seek your life.	4415
	14:19	*Do you* **d** Zion?	1718
	14:21	For the sake of your name *do not* **d** us;	5540
	23:17	They keep saying to *those who* **d** me,	5540
	33:24	So *they* **d** my people	5540
La	1: 8	All who honored her **d** her,	2361
Eze	16:57	all those around you who **d** you.	8764
Am	5:10	in court and **d** him who tells the truth.	9493
	5:21	"I hate, *I* **d** your religious feasts;	4415
Mic	3: 9	who **d** justice and distort all that is right;	9493
Mt	6:24	be devoted to the one and **d** the other.	2969
Lk	16:13	be devoted to the one and **d** the other.	2969
1Co	11:22	Or *do you* **d** the church of God	2969
Tit	2:15	*Do not let* anyone **d** you.	4368
2Pe	2:10	of the sinful nature and **d** authority.	2969

DESPISED (37) [DESPISE]

Ge	25:34	So Esau **d** his birthright.	1022
Nu	15:31	Because *he has* **d** the LORD's word	1022
1Sa	10:27	*They* **d** him and brought him no gifts.	1022
	15: 9	*that was* **d** and weak they totally destroyed.	1022
	17:42	ruddy and handsome, and *he* **d** him.	1022
2Sa	6:16	*she* **d** him in her heart.	1022
	12:10	because *you* **d** me and took the wife	1022
1Ch	15:29	*she* **d** him in her heart.	1022
2Ch	36:16	**d** his words and scoffed at his prophets	1022
Ne	4: 4	Hear us, O our God, for we are **d**.	999
Ps	22: 6	scorned by men and **d** *by* the people.	1022
	22:24	For *he has* not **d** or disdained the suffering	1022
	53: 5	you put them to shame, for God **d** them.	4415
	106:24	Then *they* **d** the pleasant land;	4415
	107:11	of God and **d** the counsel of the Most High.	5540
	119:141	Though I am lowly and **d**,	1022
Pr	12: 8	but men with warped minds are **d**.	997
Ecc	9:16	But the poor man's wisdom **is d**,	1022
Isa	16:14	and all her many people *will* be **d**,	7829
	33: 8	The treaty is broken, its witnesses *are* **d**,	4415

Isa	49: 7	to him *who was* d and abhorred by	1022
	53: 3	*He was* d and rejected by men,	1022
	53: 3	from whom men hide their faces *he was* d,	1022
Jer	22:28	*Is* this man Jehoiachin a d, broken pot,	1022
	49:15	among the nations, d among men.	1022
La	1:11	"Look, O LORD, and consider, for I am d."	2361
Eze	16: 5	for on the day you were born you were d.	1719
	16:45	*who* d her husband and her children;	1718
	16:45	who d their husbands and their children.	1718
	16:59	because *you have* d my oath by breaking	1022
	17:16	whose oath *he* d and whose treaty he broke.	1022
	17:18	*He* d the oath by breaking the covenant.	1022
	17:19	that *he* d and my covenant that he broke.	1022
	22: 8	*You have* d my holy things	1022
Ob	1: 2	you *will* be utterly d.	1022
Mal	2: 9	to be d and humiliated before all	1022
1Co	1:28	of this world and the d *things*—	2024

DESPISES (11) [DESPISE]

Ge	16: 5	knows she is pregnant, she d *me*.	928+6524+7837
2Ki	19:21	" 'The Virgin Daughter of Zion d you	996
Ps	15: 4	*who* d a vile man but honors those who fear the LORD,	928+1022+6524
Pr	14: 2	but he whose ways are devious d him.	1022
	14:21	*He who* d his neighbor sins,	996
	15:20	but a foolish man d his mother.	1022
	15:32	He who ignores discipline d himself,	4415
Isa	37:22	Virgin Daughter of Zion d and mocks you.	996
Eze	21:10	The sword d every such stick.	4415
	21:13	which the sword d, does not continue?	4415
Zec	4:10	"Who d the day of small things?	996

DESPITE (9)

Ezr	3: 3	**D** their fear of the peoples around them,	3954
Ps	33:17	d all its great strength it cannot save.	928
	49:12	But man, d his riches, does not endure;	928
Ecc	7:	**D** all his efforts to search it out,	928+4200+8611
Isa	25:11	God will bring down their pride d	6640
Eze	21:29	**D** false visions concerning you	928
	32:29	d their power, they are laid	928
	32:30	they went down with the slain in disgrace d	928
Hos	7:10	but d all this he does not return to	928

DESPITE (KJV) See also INSULTED, MALICE

DESPOIL (1) [SPOIL]

Jer	30:16	who make spoil of you I will d.	1020+4200+5989

DESTINATION (1)

2Sa	16:14	with him arrived at their d exhausted.	NIH

DESTINE (1) [DESTINED, DESTINY, PREDESTINED]

Isa	65:12	*I will* d you for the sword,	4948

DESTINED (13) [DESTINE]

Ps	49:14	Like sheep *they are* d for the grave,	9286
Isa	9: 5	in blood will be d for burning,	4200
Jer	15: 2	" 'Those d for death, to death;	4200
	43:11	bringing death to those d for death,	4200
	43:11	captivity to those d for captivity,	4200
	43:11	and the sword to those d for the sword.	4200
Eze	31:14	they are all d for death, for the earth below,	5989
Lk	2:34	"This child *is* d to cause the falling	3023
1Co	2: 7	that God d for our glory before time began.	4633
Col	2:22	These are all d to perish with use,	NIG
1Th	3: 3	You know quite well that *we were* d	3023
Heb	9:27	Just as man is d to die once,	641
1Pe	2: 8	which is also what *they were* d for.	5502

DESTINY (7) [DESTINE]

Job	8:13	Such is the d *of* all who forget God;	784
Ps	73:17	then I understood their **final** d.	344
Ecc	7: 2	for death is the d of every man;	6067
	9: 2	All share a common d—	5247
	9: 3	The same d overtakes all.	5247
Isa	65:11	and fill bowls of mixed wine for **D**,	4972
Php	3:19	Their d is destruction,	5465

DESTITUTE (8)

Ge	45:11	and all who belong to you *will become* d.'	3769
Job	20:19	the poor and left them d;	6440
Ps	102:17	He will respond to the prayer of the d;	6899
Pr	31: 8	for the rights of all *who* are d.	1201+2710
Isa	3:26	d, she will sit on the ground.	5927
La	1:16	My children are d because	9037
	4: 5	Those who once ate delicacies *are* d in	9037
Heb	11:37	d, persecuted and mistreated—	5728

DESTROY (247) [DESTROYED, DESTROYER, DESTROYERS, DESTROYING, DESTROYS, DESTRUCTION, DESTRUCTIVE]

Ge	6:13	surely *going to* d both them and the earth.	8845
	6:17	on the earth to d all life under the heavens,	8845
	8:21	And never again *will I* d all living creatures,	5782
	9:11	never again will there be a flood to d	8845
	9:15	the waters become a flood to d all life.	8845
Ge	18:28	*Will you* d the whole city because	8845
	18:28	he said, "I will not d it."	8845
	18:31	"For the sake of twenty, I will not d it."	8845
	18:32	"For the sake of ten, I will not d it."	8845
	19:13	because we *are going to* d this place.	8845
	19:13	so great that he has sent us to d it."	8845
	19:14	The LORD *is about to* d the city!"	8845
	20: 4	"Lord, *will you* d an innocent nation?	2222
Ex	15: 9	and my hand *will* d them.'	3769
	32:10	against them and that I *may* d them.	3983
	33: 3	a stiff-necked people and I *might* d you on	3983
	33: 5	I *might* d you.	3983
Lev	23:30	I *will* d from his people	6
	26:16	and fever that *will* d your sight	3983
	26:22	d your cattle and make you so few	4162
	26:30	I *will* d your high places,	9012
	26:44	so as to d them **completely,**	3983
Nu	14:12	down with a plague and d them,	3769
	21: 2	*we will* **totally** d their cities."	3049
	24:19	of Jacob and d the survivors of the city."	6
	33:52	**D** all their carved images	8845
Dt	1:27	into the hands of the Amorites to d us.	9012
	4:31	not abandon or d you or forget the covenant	8845
	6:15	and *he will* d you from the face of the land.	8845
	7: 2	**must** d them **totally.**	3049+3049
	7: 4	against you and *will* quickly d you.	9012
	7:16	*You must* d all the peoples	430
	7:24	you *will* d them.	9012
	9: 3	He *will* d them;	9012
	9: 8	so that he was angry enough to d you	9012
	9:14	that I *may* d them and blot out their name	9012
	9:19	for he was angry enough with you to d you.	9012
	9:20	with Aaron to d him,	9012
	9:25	the LORD had said he would d you.	9012
	9:26	*do not* d your people,	8845
	10:10	It was not his will *to* d you.	8845
	12: 2	**D** completely all the places on	6+6
	13:15	**D** it **completely,** both its people	3049
	20:17	**Completely** d them—	3049+3049
	20:19	*do not* d its trees by putting an ax to them,	8845
	28:63	so it will please him to ruin and d you.	9012
	31: 3	He *will* d these nations before you,	9012
	33:27	before you, saying, **'D** him!'	9012
Jos	7: 7	into the hands of the Amorites to d us?	6
	7:12	with you anymore unless you d whatever	9012
	11:20	so that he *might* d them **totally,**	3049
1Sa	15: 3	the Amalekites and **totally** d everything	3049
	15: 6	the Amalekites so that I *do* not d you along	3578
	15: 9	*to* d **completely,** but everything	3049
	15:18	and **completely** d those wicked people,	3049
	23:10	to Keilah and d the town on account of me.	8845
	26: 9	But David said to Abishai, "Don't d him!	8845
	26:15	Someone came to d your lord the king.	8845
2Sa	1:14	not afraid to lift your hand to d	8845
	11:25	Press the attack against the city and d it.'	2238
	20:19	You are trying to d a city that is a mother	4637
	20:20	"Far be it from me to swallow up or d!	8845
	24:16	angel stretched out his hand to d Jerusalem,	8845
2Ki	8:19	the LORD was not willing to d Judah.	8845
	9: 7	*to* d the house of Ahab your master,	5782
	10:19	in order to d the ministers of Baal.	6
	11: 1	she proceeded *to* d the whole royal family.	6
	13:17	"You will completely d the Arameans	5782
	13:23	*to* d them or banish them	8845
	18:25	to attack and d this place without word	8845
	18:25	to march against this country and d it.' "	8845
	24: 2	He sent them to d Judah,	6
1Ch	21:15	And God sent an angel to d Jerusalem,	8845
2Ch	12: 7	I *will* not d them	8845
	20:10	from them and *did* not d them.	9012
	20:23	from Mount Seir to d and annihilate them.	3049
	20:23	they helped to d one another.	8845
	20:37	the LORD *will* d what you have made."	7287
	21: 7	the LORD was not willing to d the house	8845
	22: 7	the LORD had anointed to d the house	4162
	22:10	she proceeded *to* d the whole royal family	1818
	25:16	"I know that God has determined to d you,	8845
	35:21	who is with me, or *he will* d you."	8845
Ezr	6:12	to change this decree or to d this temple	10243
	9:14	not be angry enough with us *to* d us,	3983
Est	3: 9	for a way to d all Mordecai's people,	9012
	3: 9	let a decree be issued to d them,	6
	3:13	with the order to d, kill and annihilate all	9012
	8: 5	to d the Jews in all the king's provinces.	6
	8:11	to d, kill and annihilate any armed force	9012
	9:24	against the Jews to d them and had cast	6
Job	10: 8	*Will you* now turn and d me?	1180
	14:19	so *you* d man's hope.	6
Ps	5: 6	*You* d those who tell lies;	6
	21:10	*You will* d their descendants from	7551
	54: 5	in your faithfulness d them.	7551
	57: T	[To the tune of] *"Do Not D."*	8845
	58: T	[To the tune of] *"Do Not D."*	8845
	59: T	[To the tune of] *"Do Not D."*	8845
	69: 4	*those who* seek to d me.	7551
	73:27	*you* d all who are unfaithful to you.	7551
	74:11	from the folds of your garment and d them!	3983
	75: T	[To the tune of] *"Do Not D."*	8845
	78:38	and *did* not d them.	8845
	83: 4	they say, "let us d them as a nation,	3948
	94:23	and d them for their wickedness,	7551
	94:23	the LORD our God *will* d them.	7551
	106:23	So he said he would d them—	9012
	106:34	*They did* not d the peoples as	9012
	119:95	The wicked are waiting to d me,	6
	143:12	d all my foes, for I am your servant.	6
	145:20	but all the wicked he *will* d.	9012
Pr	1:32	and the complacency of fools *will* d them;	6
Ecc	5: 6	be angry at what you say and d the work	2472
	7:16	be overwise—why d **yourself?**	9037
Isa	10: 7	his purpose is to d,	9012
	10:18	and fertile fields *it will* completely d,	3983
	11: 9	nor d on all my holy mountain,	8845
	13: 5	to d the whole country.	2472
	13: 9	the land desolate and d the sinners within it.	9012
	14:30	But your root *I will* d by famine;	4637
	25: 7	On this mountain he *will* d the shroud	1180
	32: 7	he makes up evil schemes to d the poor	2472
	34: 2	He *will* **totally** d them,	3049
	36:10	have I come to attack and d this land	8845
	36:10	to march against this country and d it.' "	8845
	65: 8	'Don't d it, there is yet some good in it,'	8845
	65: 8	*I will* not d them all.	8845
	65:25	nor d on all my holy mountain,"	8845
Jer	1:10	to d and overthrow, to build and to plant."	6
	4:27	though *I will* not d it **completely.**	3986+6913
	5:10	but *do not* d them **completely.**	3986+6913
	5:17	the sword *they will* d the fortified cities	8406
	5:18	"I will not d you **completely.**	3986+6913
	6: 2	*I will* d the Daughter of Zion,	1950
	6: 5	let us attack at night and d her fortresses!"	8845
	11:19	saying, "Let us d the tree and its fruit;	8845
	12:17	I will completely uproot and d it,"	6
	14:12	Instead, *I will* d them with the sword,	3983
	15: 3	and the beasts of the earth to devour and d.	8845
	15: 6	So I will lay hands on you and d you;	8845
	17:18	d them *with* double destruction.	8689
	21:10	and *he will* d it with fire.'	8596
	25: 9	*I will* **completely** d them	3049
	27: 8	until I d it by his hand.	9462
	30:11	Though *I* **completely** d all the nations	3986+6913
	30:11	*I will* not **completely** d you.	3986+6913
	31:28	and to overthrow, d and bring disaster,	6
	36:29	and d this land and cut off both men	8845
	44: 8	*You will* d yourselves	4162
	44:11	to bring disaster on you and to d all Judah.	4162
	46: 8	*I will* d cities and their people.'	6
	46:28	"Though *I* **completely** d all the nations	3986+6913
	46:28	*I will* not **completely** d you.	3986+6913
	47: 4	the day has come to d all the Philistines and	8720
	47: 4	The LORD *is about to* d the Philistines,	8720
	49:20	he will **completely** d their pasture	9037
	49:20	attack Kedar and d the people of the East.	8720
	49:38	I will set my throne in Elam and d her king	6
	50:21	Pursue, kill and **completely** d them,"	3049
	50:26	**Completely** d her and leave her no	3049
	50:45	he will **completely** d their pasture	9037
	51: 3	**completely** d her army.	3049
	51:11	because his purpose is to d Babylon.	8845
	51:20	with you I d kingdoms,	8845
	51:25	you who d the whole earth,"	8845
	51:55	The LORD *will* d Babylon;	8720
	51:62	you have said you will d this place,	4162
La	3:66	in anger and d them from under the heavens	9012
Eze	5:16	I will shoot to d you.	8845
	6: 3	and I *will* d your high places.	6
	9: 8	*Are you going to* d the entire remnant	8845
	11:13	*Will you* **completely** d the remnant	3986+6913
	14: 9	and d him from among my people Israel.	9012
	16:39	and d your lofty shrines.	5997
	17:17	and siege works erected to d many lives.	4162
	20:13	on them and d them in the desert.	3983
	20:17	on them with pity and *did not* d them or put	8845
	22:30	of the land so I *would not have* to d it,	8845
	25: 7	*I will* d you, and you will know that	9012
	25:15	with ancient hostility sought to d Judah,	5422
	25:16	the Kerethites and d those remaining along	6
	26: 4	*They will* d the walls of Tyre and pull	8845
	30:11	will be brought in to d the land.	8845
	30:13	" 'I will d the idols and put an end to	6
	32:13	*I will* d all her cattle from	8845
	34:16	but the sleek and the strong *I will* d.	9012
	43: 3	to d the city and like the visions I had seen	8845
Da	4:23	'Cut down the tree and d it,	10243
	8:24	*He will* d the mighty men and	8845
	8:25	*he will* d many and take his stand against	8845
	9:26	the ruler who will come will d the city and	8845
	11:16	and will have the **power to d** it.	3986
	11:26	the king's provisions *will try to* d him;	8689
	11:44	in a great rage to d and annihilate many.	9012
Hos	4: 5	So *I will* d your mother,	1950
	10: 2	and d their sacred stones.	8720
	11: 6	*will* d the bars of their gates and put	3983
Am	1: 5	*I will* d the king who is in the Valley	4162
	1: 8	*I will* d the king of Ashdod and	4162
	2: 3	*I will* d her ruler and kill all her officials	4162
	3:14	*I will* d the altars of Bethel;	7212
	9: 8	*I will* d it from the face of the earth—	9012
	9: 8	yet *I will* not **totally** d the house	9012+9012
Ob	1: 8	"*will I* not d the wise men of Edom,	1950
Mic	1: 7	*I will* d all her images.	8492+9039
	5:10	"I will d your horses from among you	4162
	5:11	*I will* d the cities of your land and tear	4162
	5:12	*I will* d your witchcraft	4162
	5:13	*I will* d your carved images	4162
	6:13	Therefore, I have begun to d you,	5782
Na	1:14	*I will* d the carved images and cast idols	4162
Zep	2: 5	"I will d you, and none will be left."	6
	2:13	against the north and d Assyria,	6
Zec	5: 4	It will remain in his house and d it,	3983
	9: 4	and d her power on the sea,	5782
	9:15	*They will* d and overcome	430
	12: 9	On that day I will set out to d all the nations	9012
Mt	6:19	where moth and rust d,	906

Mt	6:20	where moth and rust *do* not **d**,	906
	10:28	of the One who can **d** both soul and body	660
	26:61	*to* **d** the temple of God and rebuild it	2907
Mk	1:24	Have you come *to* **d** us?	660
	14:58	'I *will* **d** this man-made temple and	2907
	15:29	*to* **d** the temple and build it in three days,	2907
Lk	4:34	Have you come *to* **d** us?	660
	6: 9	to save life or *to* **d** it?"	660
	9:54	to call fire down from heaven *to* **d** them?"	384
Jn	2:19	Jesus answered them, "**D** this temple,	3395
	10:10	thief comes only to steal and kill and **d**;	660
Ac	6:14	that this Jesus of Nazareth *will* **d** this place	2907
	8: 3	But Saul **began** *to* **d** the church.	3381
Ro	14:15	*Do* not by your eating **d** your brother	660
	14:20	not **d** the work of God for the sake of food.	2907
1Co	1:19	"I *will* **d** the wisdom of the wise;	660
	3:17	destroys God's temple, God *will* **d** him;	5780
	6:13	but God *will* **d** them both.	2934
Gal	1:13	the church of God and *tried to* **d** it.	4514
	1:23	now preaching the faith he once *tried to* **d**."	4514
2Th	2: 8	with the breath of his mouth and **d** by	2934
2Ti	2:18	and *they* **d** the faith of some.	426
Heb	2:14	that by his death he might **d** him who holds	2934
Jas	4:12	the one who is able to save and **d**.	660
1Jn	3: 8	of God appeared was to **d** the devil's work.	3395
Jude	1:10	these are the very things that **d** them.	5780
Rev	11:18	and for destroying those who **d** the earth."	1425

DESTROYED (216) [DESTROY]

Ge	13:10	(This was before the LORD **d** Sodom	8845
	19:29	So when God **d** the cities of the plain,	8845
	34:30	I and my household *will* **be d**."	9012
Ex	9:31	(The flax and barley were **d**,	5782
	9:32	The wheat and spelt, however, were not **d**,	5782
	22:20	the LORD *must* **be d**.	3049
Lev	10: 6	for those the LORD has **d** by fire.	8596
Nu	21: 3	They **completely d** them and their towns;	3049
	21:29	*You are* **d**, O people of Chemosh!	6
	21:30	Heshbon *is* **d** all the way to Dibon.	6
	24:22	be **d** when Asshur takes you captive."	1278
Dt	2:12	They **d** the Horites before them	9012
	2:21	The LORD **d** them from before	9012
	2:22	when he **d** the Horites from before them.	9012
	2:23	from Caphtor **d** them and settled	9012
	2:34	and **completely d** them—	3049
	3: 6	We **completely d** them,	3049
	4: 3	The LORD your God **d** from	9012
	4:26	but *will* **certainly be d**.	9012+9012
	7:23	into great confusion until they **are d**.	9012
	8:19	that *you will* **surely be d**.	6+6
	8:20	Like the nations the LORD **d** before you,	6
	8:20	so *you will* **be d** for not obeying	6
	12:30	and after they have **been d** before you,	9012
	19: 1	When the LORD your God has **d**	4162
	28:20	until *you are* **d** and come to sudden ruin	9012
	28:21	with diseases until he has **d** you from	3983
	28:24	down from the skies until *you are* **d**	9012
	28:45	and overtake you until *you are* **d**,	9012
	28:48	on your neck until he has **d** you.	9012
	28:51	and the crops of your land until *you are* **d**.	9012
	28:61	until *you are* **d**.	9012
	30:18	that *you will* **certainly be d**.	6+6
	31: 4	whom he **d** along with their land.	9012
	31:17	and they will **be d**.	430
Jos	2:10	whom you **completely d**.	3049
	6:21	**devoted** the city to the LORD and **d**	3049
	7:15	with the devoted things *shall* be **d** by fire,	8596
	8:26	until he had **d** all who lived in Ai.	3049
	10: 1	that Joshua had taken Ai and **totally d** it,	3049
	10:20	and the Israelites **d** them completely—	
			1524+4394+4804+5782
	10:28	the sword and **totally d** everyone in it.	3049
	10:35	the sword and **totally d** everyone in it,	3049
	10:37	*they* **totally d** it and everyone in it.	3049
	10:39	Everyone in it *they* **totally d**.	3049
	10:40	He **totally d** all who breathed,	3049
	11:11	They **totally d** them,	3049
	11:12	He **totally d** them,	3049
	11:14	the sword until they **completely d** them,	9012
	11:21	that time Joshua went and **d** the Anakites	4162
	11:21	Joshua **totally d** them and their towns.	3049
	23:15	until he has **d** you from this good land	9012
	24: 8	I **d** them from before you,	9012
Jdg	1:17	and *they* **totally d** the city.	3049
	4:24	the Canaanite king, until *they* **d** him.	4162
	9:45	Then he **d** the city and scattered salt over it.	5997
	21:16	"With the women of Benjamin **d**,	6
1Sa	15: 8	and all his people he **totally d** with	3049
	15: 9	and weak *they* **totally d**.	3049
	15:15	but *we* **totally d** the rest."	3049
	15:20	I **completely d** the Amalekites	3049
	27: 1	"One of these days I *will* **be d** by the hand	6200
	30: 3	they found *it* **d** by fire and their wives	8596
2Sa	11: 1	They **d** the Ammonites	8845
	14:11	so that my son *will* not **be d**."	9012
	21: 5	for the man who **d** us and plotted against us	3983
	22:38	I did not turn back till they were **d**.	3983
	22:41	and I **d** my foes.	7551
1Ki	11:16	until they had all the men in Edom.	4162
	11:24	of a band of rebels when David the forces	2222
	15:29	but **d** them all, according to the word of	9012
	16: 7	and also because he **d** it.	5782
	16:12	So Zimri **d** the whole family of Baasha,	9012
	22:11	the Arameans until they are **d**.' "	3983
2Ki	3:25	*They* **d** the towns,	2238

2Ki	10:17	he **d** them, according to the word of	9012
	10:28	So Jehu **d** Baal worship in Israel.	9012
	13: 7	of Aram had **d** the rest and made them like	6
	13:19	and **completely d** it.	3983+6330
	19:12	that were **d** by my forefathers deliver them:	8845
	19:18	into the fire and **d** them,	6
	21: 3	the high places his father Hezekiah had **d**;	6
	21: 9	the LORD had **d** before the Israelites.	9012
1Ch	4:41	and **completely d** them,	3049
	5:25	whom God had **d** before them.	9012
2Ch	8: 8	whom the Israelites had not **d**—	3983
	12:12	and he was not totally **d**.	8845
	14:14	They **d** all the villages around Gerar,	5782
	18:10	the Arameans until they are **d**.' "	3983
	31: 1	They **d** the high places and the altars	5997
	31: 1	After they had **d** all of them,	3983
	32:14	that my fathers **d** has been able	3049
	33: 9	the LORD had **d** before the Israelites.	9012
	36:19	the palaces and everything of value there.	8845
Ezr	4:15	That is why this city was **d**.	10281
	5:12	who **d** this temple and deported the people	10520
Ne	2: 3	and its gates have **been d** by fire?	430
	2:13	and its gates, which had been **d** by fire.	430
Est	9: 6	the Jews killed and **d** five hundred men.	6
	9:12	and **d** five hundred men and the ten sons	6
Job	4: 7	were the upright *ever* **d**?	3948
	4: 9	At the breath of God *they are* **d**;	6
	19:26	And after my skin has been **d**,	5937
	22:20	'Surely our foes are **d**,	3948
Ps	2:12	lest he be angry and *you be* **d** in your way,	6
	9: 5	You have rebuked the nations and **d**	6
	11: 3	When the foundations *are being* **d**,	2238
	18:37	I did not turn back till they were **d**.	3983
	18:40	and I **d** my foes.	7551
	37:38	But all sinners *will* **be d**;	9012
	48: 7	*You* **d** them like ships of Tarshish shattered	8689
	63: 9	They who seek my life will be **d**;	8739
	73:19	How suddenly are they **d**,	9014
	78:47	He **d** their vines with hail	2222
	79: 7	and **d** his homeland.	9037
	88:16	your terrors have **d** me.	7551
	92: 7	they *will* **be** forever **d**.	9012
	105:16	on the land and **d** all their supplies of food;	8689
Pr	6:15	he *will* suddenly **be d**—without remedy.	8689
	11: 3	but the unfaithful *are* **d** by their duplicity.	8720
	11:11	but by the mouth of the wicked *it is* **d**.	2238
	14:11	The house of the wicked *will* **be d**,	9012
	21:28	whoever listens to him *will be* **d** forever.	1818
	22: 8	and the rod of his fury *will* **be d**.	3983
	29: 1	after many rebukes *will* suddenly **be d**—	8689
Isa	5: 5	I will take away its hedge, and it will **be d**;	1278
	14:20	for *you have* **d** your land	8845
	15: 1	Ar in Moab is ruined, **d** in a night!	8720
	15: 1	Kir in Moab is ruined, **d** in a night!	8720
	23: 1	Tyre *is* **d** and left without house or harbor.	8720
	23:11	that her fortresses be **d**.	9012
	23:14	your fortress *is* **d**!	8720
	33: 1	O destroyer, you *who have* not **been d**!	8720
	33: 1	When you stop destroying, *you will* **be d**;	8720
	34: 5	the people I have **totally d**.	3051
	37:12	Did the gods of the nations that were **d**	8845
	37:19	into the fire and **d** them,	6
	48:19	their name would never be cut off nor **d**	9012
	55:13	an everlasting sign, *which* will not **be d**."	4162
Jer	4:20	In an instant my tents are **d**,	8720
	9:16	with the sword until I have **d** them."	3983
	10:20	My tent *is* **d**; all its ropes are snapped.	8720
	10:25	and **d** his homeland.	9037
	18: 7	torn down and **d**,	6
	24:10	and plague against them until they are **d**	9462
	44:27	by sword and famine until they are all **d**.	3983
	48: 8	The valley will be ruined and the plateau **d**,	9012
	48:15	Moab *will* **be d** and her towns invaded;	8720
	48:20	Announce by the Arnon that Moab is **d**.	8720
	48:42	Moab *will* **be d** as a nation	9012
	48:46	The people of Chemosh *are* **d**;	6
	49: 3	"Wail, O Heshbon, for Ai is **d**!	8720
	51: 6	*Do* not **be d** because of her sins.	1959
La	2: 5	up all her palaces and **d** her strongholds.	8845
	2: 6	he has **d** his place of meeting.	8845
	2: 9	their bars he has broken and **d**.	6
	2:11	on the ground because my people are **d**,	8691
	2:22	for and reared, my enemy has **d**."	3983
	3:48	from my eyes because my people are **d**.	8691
	4:10	when my people were **d**.	8691
Eze	13:14	When it falls, *you will* **be d** in it;	3983
	26:17	" 'How *you are* **d**, O city of renown,	6
	36:35	that were lying in ruins, desolate and **d**,	2238
	36:36	that I the LORD have rebuilt what was **d**	2238
	43: 8	So I **d** them in my anger.	430
Da	2:44	up a kingdom that *will* never **be d**,	10243
	6:26	his kingdom *will* not **be d**,	10243
	7:11	until the beast was slain and its body **d**	10005
	7:14	his kingdom is one that *will* never **be d**.	10243
	7:26	and **completely d** forever.	10005+10221+10722
	8:24	Yet he *will* **be d**, but not by human power.	8689
	11:20	In a few years, however, he *will* **be d**,	8689
	11:22	and a prince of the covenant *will* **be d**.	8689
Hos	4: 6	my people are **d** from lack of knowledge.	1950
	10: 8	The high places of wickedness *will* **be d**—	9012
	10:15	king of Israel *will* be **completely d**.	1950+1950
	13: 9	"*You are* **d**, O Israel,	8845
Joel	1:10	the grain is **d**, the new wine is dried up,	8720
	1:11	because harvest of the field is **d**.	6
Am	2: 9	"I **d** the Amorite before them,	9012
	2: 9	I **d** his fruit above and his roots below.	9012
	3:15	*be* **d** and the mansions will be demolished,"	6

Am	7: 9	"The high places of Isaac *will* **be d** and	9037
Ob	1:10	*you will* **be d** forever.	4162
Mic	5: 9	and all your foes *will* **be d**.	4162
Na	1:15	they *will* **be** completely **d**.	4162
Hab	2: 8	you have **d** lands and cities and everyone	2805
	2:17	you have **d** lands and cities and everyone	2805
Zep	3: 6	Their cities are **d**;	7400
Zec	11: 3	their rich pastures are **d**!	8720
	14:11	It will be inhabited; never again will it be **d**.	3051
Mal	3: 6	So you, O descendants of Jacob, *are* not **d**.	3983
Mt	22: 7	He sent his army and **d** those murderers	660
Lk	17:27	Then the flood came and **d** them all.	660
	17:29	down from heaven and **d** them all.	660
Ac	27:22	only the ship will be **d**.	NIG
1Co	5: 5	be **d** and his spirit saved on the day of	3897
	8:11	*is* **d** by your knowledge.	660
	15:24	the Father after he has **d** all dominion,	2934
	15:26	The last enemy *to be* **d** is death.	2934
2Co	4: 9	struck down, but not **d**.	660
	5: 1	that if the earthly tent we live in *is* **d**,	2907
Gal	2:18	If I rebuild what *I* **d**,	2907
	5:15	watch out or *you will* **be d** by each other.	384
Eph	2:14	who has made the two one and has **d**	3395
Php	1:28	This is a sign to them that they will be **d**,	724
2Ti	1:10	*who has* **d** death and has brought life	2934
Heb	10:39	not of those who shrink back and are **d**,	724+1650
Jas	1:11	its blossom falls and its beauty *is* **d**.	660
2Pe	2:12	born only to be caught and **d**,	5785
	3: 6	the world of that time *was* deluged and **d**.	660
	3:10	the elements *will be* **d** by fire,	3395
	3:11	Since everything *will be* **d** in this way,	3395
Jude	1: 5	but later **d** those who did not believe.	660
	1:11	*they have* **been d** in Korah's rebellion.	660
Rev	8: 9	and a third of the ships were **d**.	1425

DESTROYER (12) [DESTROY]

Ex	12:23	not permit the **d** to enter your houses	5422
Isa	16: 4	be their shelter from the **d**."	8720
	33: 1	Woe to you, O **d**,	8720
	54:16	And it is I who have created the **d**	5422
Jer	4: 7	a **d** *of* nations has set out.	5422
	6:26	for suddenly the **d** will come upon us.	8720
	15: 8	a **d** against the mothers of their young men;	8720
	48: 8	The **d** will come against every town,	8720
	48:32	The **d** has fallen on your ripened fruit.	8720
	51: 1	up the spirit of a **d** against Babylon and	5422
	51:56	A **d** will come against Babylon;	8720
Heb	11:28	that the **d** of the firstborn would not touch	3905

DESTROYERS (6) [DESTROY]

Jer	12:12	in the desert **d** will swarm, for the sword of	8720
	15: 3	"I will send four kinds of **d** against them,"	NIH
	22: 7	I will send **d** against you,	5422
	51:48	for out of the north **d** will attack her,"	8720
	51:53	I will send **d** against her,"	8720
Na	2: 2	though **d** have laid them waste	1327

DESTROYING (20) [DESTROY]

Dt	3: 6	**d** every city—men, women and children.	3049
1Sa	5: 6	of the tumors and the rats that were **d**	8845
2Ki	19:11	to all the countries, **d** them **completely**.	3049
1Ch	21:15	and said to the angel who *was* **d** the people,	8845
Est	9: 5	killing and **d** them,	12
Job	30:13	they succeed in **d** me—	2095
Ps	52: 7	and grew strong by **d** others!"	2095
	78:49	a band of **d** angels.	8273
	106:23	before him to keep his wrath from **d** them.	8845
Isa	33: 1	When you stop **d**, you will be destroyed;	8720
	37:11	to all the countries, **d** them **completely**.	3049
Jer	13:14	or compassion *to* keep me from **d** them.' "	8845
	23: 1	to the shepherds *who are* **d** and scattering	6
	25:36	for the LORD *is* **d** their pasture.	8720
	51:25	"I am against you, O **d** mountain,	8845
La	2: 8	and did not withhold his hand from **d**.	1180
Hab	1:17	**d** nations without mercy?	2222
Lk	9:39	It scarcely ever leaves him and is **d** him.	5341
1Co	10:10	and were killed by the **d** angel.	3904
Rev	11:18	and *for* **d** those who destroy the earth."	1425

DESTROYS (13) [DESTROY]

Ex	21:26	or maidservant in the eye and **d** it,	8845
Job	9:22	'He **d** both the blameless and the wicked.'	3983
	12:23	He makes nations great, and **d** them;	6
Ps	91: 6	nor the plague that **d** at midday.	8720
Pr	6:32	whoever does so **d** himself.	8845
	11: 9	With his mouth the godless **d** his neighbor,	8845
	18: 9	in his work is brother to one who **d**.	1251+5422
	28:24	he is partner to him who **d**.	5422
Ecc	9:18	but one sinner **d** much good.	6
Jer	48:18	*he who* **d** Moab will come up against you	8720
Zep	2:11	be awesome to them when he **d** all the gods	8135
Lk	1:25	where no thief comes near and no moth **d**.	1425
1Co	3:17	If anyone **d** God's temple,	5780

DESTRUCTION (96) [DESTROY]

Lev	27:29	" 'No person **devoted** *to* **d** may	3049+3051
Nu	32:15	and *you will* **be** the **cause** of their **d**."	8845
Dt	7:10	to their face by **d**;	6
	7:26	like it, will be **set apart** for **d**.	3051
	7:26	for it is **set apart** for **d**.	3051
	29:23	be like the **d** of Sodom and Gomorrah,	4550
	30:15	and prosperity, death and **d**.	8273
Jos	6:18	**bring about** *your own* **d**	3049
	6:18	of Israel liable to **d** and bring trouble on it.	3051

Jos	7:12	because they have been made liable to d.	3051
	7:12	among you is **devoted to d.**	3051
2Sa	14:11	the avenger of blood from adding to the d,	8845
	22: 5	The torrents of d overwhelmed me.	1175
1Ki	13:34	to its downfall and to its d from the face of	9012
Est	4: 7	into the royal treasury for the d of the Jews.	6
	7: 4	For I and my people have been sold for d	9012
	8: 6	How can I bear to see the d of my family?"	13
	9: 2	to attack those seeking their d.	8288
	9:24	for their ruin and d.	6
Job	5:21	and need not fear when d comes.	8719
	5:22	You will laugh at d and famine,	8719
	21:20	Let his own eyes see his d;	3957
	26: 6	before God; D lies uncovered.	11
	28:22	**D** and Death say, 'Only a rumor of it	11
	31:12	It is a fire that burns to **D**;	11
	31:23	For I dreaded d from God,	369
Ps	5: 9	their heart is filled with d.	2095
	18: 4	the torrents of d overwhelmed me.	1175
	30: 9	"What gain is there in my **d,**	1947
	52: 2	Your tongue plots d;	2095
	74: 3	d the enemy has **brought**	8317
	88:11	your faithfulness in **D?**	11
	137: 8	O Daughter of Babylon, **doomed to d,**	8720
Pr	15:11	Death and **D** lie open before the LORD—	11
	16:18	Pride goes before d,	8691
	17:19	he who builds a high gate invites d.	8691
	24:22	those two will send sudden d upon them,	369
	27:20	Death and **D** are never satisfied,	9
Isa	10:22	**D** has been decreed,	4001
	10:23	the d decreed upon the whole land.	3986
	10:25	and my wrath will be directed to their d."	9318
	13: 6	it will come like d from the Almighty.	8719
	14:23	I will sweep her with the broom of d,"	9012
	15: 5	the road to Horonaim they lament their d.	8691
	16: 4	and d will cease;	8719
	19:18	One of them will be called the City of **D.**	2239
	22: 4	to console me over the d of my people."	8719
	28:22	of the d decreed against the whole land.	3986
	30:28	He shakes the nations in the sieve of d;	8736
	38:17	In your love you kept me from the pit of d;	1172
	43:28	and I will consign Jacob to d and Israel	3051
	51:13	who is bent on d?	8845
	51:19	ruin and d, famine and sword—	8691
	59: 7	ruin and d mark their ways.	8691
	60:18	nor ruin or d within your borders,	8691
Jer	4: 6	from the north, even terrible d."	8691
	6: 1	of the north, even terrible d.	8691
	6:19	Violence and d resound in her;	8719
	15: 7	I will bring bereavement and d	6
	17:18	destroy them with double d.	8695
	20: 8	I cry out proclaiming violence and d.	8719
	48: 3	cries of great havoc and d.	8691
	48: 5	over the d are heard.	8691
	50:22	the noise of great d!	8691
	51:54	of great d from the land of the Babylonians.	8691
La	1: 7	at her and laughed at her d.	5404
	3:47	and pitfalls, ruin and d."	8691
Eze	21:31	over to brutal men, men skilled in d.	5422
	32: 9	of many peoples when I bring about your d	8691
Hos	7:13	**D** to them, because they have rebelled	8719
	8: 4	for themselves to their own **d.**	4162
	9: 6	Even if they escape from d,	8719
	13:14	Where, O grave, is your d?	7776
Joel	1:15	it will come like d from the Almighty.	8719
Am	9: 8	he flashes d on the stronghold and brings	8719
Ob	1:12	the people of Judah in the day of their d,	6
Jnh	3:10	upon them the d he had threatened.	8288
Hab	1: 3	**D** and violence are before me;	8719
	2:17	and your d of animals will terrify you.	8719
Mt	7:13	and broad is the road that leads to d,	724
Lk	6:49	it collapsed and its d was complete."	4837
Jn	17:12	been lost except the one **doomed to d**	724
Ro	9:22	of his wrath—prepared for d?	724
Gal	6: 8	from that nature will reap d;	5785
Php	3:19	Their destiny is d,	724
1Th	5: 3	d will come on them suddenly,	3897
2Th	1: 9	be punished with everlasting d and shut out	3897
	2: 3	the man **doomed to d.**	724
1Ti	6: 9	that plunge men into ruin and d.	724
2Pe	2: 1	bringing swift d on themselves.	724
	2: 3	and their d has not been sleeping.	724
	3: 7	the day of judgment and d of ungodly men.	724
	3:12	That day will bring about the d of	3395
	3:16	Scriptures, to their own d.	724
Rev	17: 8	up out of the Abyss and go to his d.	724
	17:11	to the seven and is going to his d.	724

DESTRUCTIVE (9) [DESTROY]

Ex	12:13	No d plague will touch you	5422
Lev	13:51	it is a d mildew; the article is unclean.	4421
	13:52	because the mildew is d;	4421
	14:44	it is a d mildew; the house is unclean.	4421
Ps	55:11	**D** forces are at work in the city;	2095
Isa	28: 2	Like a hailstorm and a d wind,	7776
Eze	5:16	with my deadly and d arrows of famine,	5422
	13:13	and torrents of rain will fall with d fury.	3986
2Pe	2: 1	They will secretly introduce d heresies,	724

DETACHMENT (4) [DETACHMENTS]

1Sa	13:23	a d of Philistines had gone out to the pass	5163
Jn	18: 3	guiding a d of soldiers and some officials	5061
	18:12	Then the d of soldiers with its commander	5061
Ac	23:23	"Get ready a d of two hundred soldiers,	NIG

DETACHMENTS (1) [DETACHMENT]

| 1Sa | 13:17 | from the Philistine camp in three d. | 8031 |

DETAIL (3) [DETAILED, DETAILS]

Ac	21:19	and reported in d what God had done	1651+1667
Col	2:18	**goes into great d about** what he has seen,	1836
Heb	9: 5	we cannot discuss these things in d now.	3538

DETAILED (1) [DETAIL]

| 2Ki | 16:10 | with d plans for its construction. | 3972 |

DETAILS (3) [DETAIL]

1Ki	6:38	in all its d according to its specifications.	1821
1Ch	28:19	and he gave me understanding in all the d	4856
	29:30	together with the d of his reign and power,	3972

DETAIN (2) [DETAINED]

| Ge | 24:56 | But he said to them, "Do not d me, | 336 |
| Jdg | 13:16 | "Even though you d me, | 6806 |

DETAINED (2) [DETAIN]

| 1Sa | 21: 7 | d before the LORD; | 6806 |
| Da | 10:13 | I was d there with the king of Persia. | 3855 |

DETECT (3)

Job	39:29	his eyes d it from afar.	5564
Ps	36: 2	to d or hate his sin.	5162
Ob	1: 7	but you will not d it.	9312

DETER (1) [DETRIMENT]

| Mt | 3:14 | But John tried to d him, saying, | 1361 |

DETERMINATE (KJV) See SET

DETERMINE (8) [DETERMINED, DETERMINES]

Ex	12: 4	d the **amount** of lamb **needed**	4082
	22: 8	to d whether he has laid his hands on	NIH
Lev	13: 8	to d when something is clean or unclean.	3723
	25:27	he is to d the value for the years	3108
	27:18	the priest will d the value according to	3108
	27:23	the priest will d its value up to the Year	3108
Ne	10:34	to d when each of our families is to bring to	NIH
Da	11:17	He will d to come with the might	7156+8492

DETERMINED (33) [DETERMINE]

Jos	17:12	the Canaanites were d to live in that region.	3283
Jdg	1:27	the Canaanites were d to live in that land.	3283
	1:35	And the Amorites were d also to hold out	3283
Ru	1:18	When Naomi realized that Ruth was d to go	599
1Sa	20: 7	you can be sure that he is d to harm me.	3983
	20: 9	the least inkling that my father was d	3983
2Sa	17:14	For the LORD had d to frustrate	7422
1Ki	7:47	the weight of the bronze was not d.	2983
	20:42	a man I had d should die.	3051
2Ki	12:11	When the amount had been d,	9419
1Ch	12:38	**fully** d to make David king	928+4222+8969
2Ch	4:18	that the weight of the bronze was not d.	2983
	25:16	"I know that God has d to destroy you,	3619
Job	14: 5	Man's days are d;	3076
Ecc	7:23	"I am d to be **wise"**—but this was beyond me.	AIT
Isa	14:26	This is the plan d for the whole world;	3619
Jer	21:10	I have d to do this city harm and not good,	7156+8492
	42:15	'If you are d to go to Egypt	7156+8492+8492
	42:17	All who are d to go to Egypt	7156+8492
	44:11	I am d to bring disaster on you and	7156+8492
	44:12	the remnant of Judah who were d to go	7156+8492
La	2: 8	The LORD d to tear down the wall around	3108
Da	6:14	he was d to rescue Daniel	10104+10682
	11:36	for what has **been** d must take place.	3076
Hos	11: 7	My people are d to turn from me.	9428
Hab	2:13	Has not the LORD Almighty d that	907+4946
Zec	1: 6	just as he d to do.' "	2372
	8:14	"Just as I had d to bring disaster upon you	2372
	8:15	"so now I have d to do good again	2372
Jn	8:40	As it is, you are d to kill me,	2426
Ac	5:28	with your teaching and are d	1089
	17:26	and he d the times set for them and	3988
1Co	15:38	But God gives it a body as he has d,	2527

DETERMINES (3) [DETERMINE]

Ps	147: 4	He d the number of the stars	4948
Pr	16: 9	but the LORD d his steps.	3922
1Co	12:11	and he gives them to each one, just as he d.	1089

DETEST (17) [DETESTABLE, DETESTED, DETESTS]

Lev	11:10	you are to d.	9211
	11:11	And since you are to d them,	9211
	11:11	and you must d their carcasses.	9210
	11:13	" 'These are the birds you are to d and	9210
	11:23	that have four legs you are to d.	9211
Nu	21: 5	And we d this miserable food!"	7762
Dt	7:26	Utterly abhor and d it,	9493+9493
Job	9:31	so that even my clothes would d me.	9493
	19:19	All my intimate friends d me;	9493

Job	30:10	They d me and keep their distance;	9493
Pr	8: 7	for my lips d wickedness.	9359
	13:19	but fools d turning from evil.	9359
	16:12	Kings d wrongdoing, for	9359
	24: 9	and men d a mocker.	9359
	29:27	The righteous d the dishonest;	9359
	29:27	the wicked d the upright.	9359
Am	6: 8	the pride of Jacob and d his fortresses;	8533

DETESTABLE (111) [DETEST]

Ge	43:32	for that is d to Egyptians.	9359
	46:34	for all shepherds are d to the Egyptians."	9359
Ex	8:26	the LORD our God would be d to	9359
	8:26	if we offer sacrifices that are d in their eyes,	9359
Lev	7:21	an unclean animal or any unclean, d thing—	9211
	11:12	that does not have fins and scales is to be d	9211
	11:13	to detest and not eat because they are d;	9211
	11:20	that walk on all fours are to be d to you.	9211
	11:41	that moves about on the ground is d;	9211
	11:42	on many feet; it is d.	9211
	18:22	with a woman; that is d.	9359
	18:26	not do any of these d things,	9359
	18:29	" 'Everyone who does any of these d things	9359
	18:30	and do not follow any of the d customs	9359
	20:13	both of them have done what is d.	9359
Dt	7:25	for it is d to the LORD your God.	9359
	7:26	not bring a d thing into your house or you,	9359
	12:31	of d things the LORD hates.	9359
	13:14	that this d thing has been done among you,	9359
	14: 3	Do not eat any d thing.	9359
	17: 1	for that would be d to him.	9359
	17: 4	that this d thing has been done in Israel,	9359
	18: 9	to imitate the d ways of the nations there.	9359
	18:12	Anyone who does these things is d to	9359
	18:12	and because of these d practices	9359
	20:18	to follow all the d things they do	9359
	24: 4	That would be d in the eyes of the LORD.	9359
	27:15	a thing d to the LORD,	9359
	29:17	among them their d images and idols	9199
	32:16	and angered him with their d idols.	9359
1Ki	11: 5	and Molech the d god of the Ammonites.	9199
	11: 7	a high place for Chemosh the d god	9199
	11: 7	for Molech the d god of the Ammonites.	9199
	14:24	the people engaged in all the d practices of	9359
2Ki	16: 3	following the d ways of the nations	9359
	21: 2	following the d practices of the nations	9359
	21:11	of Judah has committed these d sins.	9359
	23:13	Molech the d god of the people of Ammon.	9359
	23:24	the idols and all the other d things seen	9199
2Ch	15: 8	the d idols from the whole land of Judah	9199
	28: 3	following the d ways of the nations	9359
	33: 2	following the d practices of the nations	9359
	34:33	the d idols from all the territory belonging	9199
	36: 8	the d things he did and all that was found	9199
	36:14	following all the d practices of the nations	9359
Ezr	9: 1	with their d practices,	9359
	9:11	By their d practices they have filled it	9359
	9:14	the peoples who commit such d practices?	9359
Pr	6:16	seven that are d to him:	9359
	21:27	The sacrifice of the wicked is d—	9359
	28: 9	even his prayers are d.	9359
Isa	1:13	Your incense is d to me.	9359
	41:24	he who chooses you is d.	9359
	44: 19	Shall I make a d thing from what is left?	9359
Jer	2: 7	and made my inheritance d.	9359
	4: 1	"If you put your d idols out of my sight	9199
	7:10	safe to do all these d things?	9359
	7:30	They have set up their d idols in the house	9199
	13:27	I have seen your d acts on the hills and in	9199
	16:18	with their d idols."	9359
	32:35	that they should do such a d thing and	9359
	44: 4	'Do not do this d thing that I hate!'	9359
	44:22	and the d things you did,	9359
Eze	5: 9	Because of all your d idols,	9359
	5:11	with all your vile images and d practices,	9359
	6: 9	and for all their d practices.	9359
	6:11	because of all the wicked and d practices	9359
	7: 3	and repay you for all your d practices.	9359
	7: 4	for your conduct and the d practices	9359
	7: 8	and repay you for all your d practices	9359
	7: 9	with your conduct and the d practices	9359
	7:20	to make their d idols and vile images.	9359
	8: 6	the utterly d things the house	9359
	8: 6	things that are even more d."	9359
	8: 9	and d things they are doing here.	9359
	8:10	and d animals and all the idols of the house	9211
	8:13	things that are even more d."	9359
	8:15	things that are even more d	9359
	8:17	to do the d things they are doing here?	9359
	9: 4	over all the d things that are done in it."	9359
	11:18	and remove all its vile images and d idols.	9199
	11:21	to their vile images and d idols,	9359
	12:16	they may acknowledge all their d practices.	9359
	14: 6	and renounce all your d practices!	9359
	16: 2	confront Jerusalem with her d practices	9359
	16:22	In all your d practices	9359
	16:36	and because of all your d idols,	9199
	16:43	to all your other d practices?	9359
	16:47	in their ways and copied their d practices,	9359
	16:50	They were haughty and did d things	9359
	16:51	You have done more d things than they,	9359
	16:58	of your lewdness and your d practices,	9359
	18:12	He does d things.	9359
	18:13	Because he has done all these d things,	9359
	18:24	and commits sin and does the same d things	9359
	20: 4	Then confront them with the d practices	9359

Eze	22: 2	Then confront her with all her **d** practices	9359
	22:11	a **d** offense with his neighbor's wife,	9359
	23:36	Then confront them with their **d** practices,	9359
	33:26	You rely on your sword, you do **d** things,	9359
	33:29	because of all the **d** things they have done.'	9359
	36:31	for your sins and **d** practices.	9359
	43: 8	defiled my holy name by their **d** practices.	9359
	44: 6	Enough of your **d** practices,	9359
	44: 7	In addition to all your other **d** practices,	9359
	44:13	the shame of their **d** practices.	9359
Mal	2:11	A **d** thing has been committed in Israel and	9359
Lk	16:15	What is highly valued among men is **d**	1007
Tit	1:16	They are **d**, disobedient and unfit	1008
1Pe	4: 3	orgies, carousing and **d** idolatry.	116
Rev	18: 2	a haunt for every unclean and **d** bird.	3631

DETESTED (1) [DETEST]
Zec	11: 8	The flock **d** me,	1041

DETESTS (13) [DETEST]
Dt	22: 5	LORD your God **d** anyone who does this.	9359
	23:18	because the LORD your God **d** them both.	9359
	25:16	the LORD your God **d** anyone who does	
		these things,	9359
Pr	3:32	for the LORD **d** a perverse man but takes	9359
	11:20	The LORD **d** men of perverse heart	9359
	12:22	The LORD **d** lying lips,	9359
	15: 8	The LORD **d** the sacrifice of the wicked,	9359
	15: 9	The LORD **d** the way of the wicked	9359
	15:26	The LORD **d** the thoughts of the wicked,	9359
	16: 5	The LORD **d** all the proud of heart.	9359
	17:15	the LORD **d** them both.	9359
	20:10	differing measures—the LORD **d** them both.	9359
	20:23	The LORD **d** differing weights,	9359

DETHRONED (1) [THRONE]
2Ch	36: 3	of Egypt **d** him in Jerusalem and imposed	6073

DETRIMENT (1) [DETER]
Ezr	4:22	to the **d** of the royal interests?	10472

DEUEL (5)
Nu	1:14	from Gad, Eliasaph son of **D**;	1979
	2:14	of the people of Gad is Eliasaph son of **D**.	1979
	7:42	On the sixth day Eliasaph son of **D**,	1979
	7:47	This was the offering of Eliasaph son of **D**.	1979
	10:20	and Eliasaph son of **D** was over the division	1979

DEVASTATE (6) [DEVASTATED, DEVASTATION]
Jos	22:33	to war against them to **d** the country where	8845
Job	12:15	if he lets them loose, they **d** the land.	2200
Isa	24: 1	to lay waste the earth and **d** it;	1191
Jer	19: 8	I will **d** this city and make it an object	9014
	51: 2	to winnow her and to **d** her land;	1327
Hos	11: 9	nor will I turn and **d** Ephraim.	8845

DEVASTATED (11) [DEVASTATE]
Jdg	11:33	He **d** twenty towns from	1524+4394+4804+5782
Job	16: 7	you have **d** my entire household.	9037
Ps	78:45	and frogs that **d** them.	8845
Isa	61: 4	and restore the places long **d**;	9037
	61: 4	that have been **d** for generations.	9037
Jer	4:30	What are you doing, O **d** one?	8720
Eze	6: 6	so that your altars will be laid waste and **d**,	870
	19: 7	down their strongholds and **d** their towns.	2990
	29:12	the land of Egypt desolate among **d** lands,	9037
Hos	10:14	so that all your fortresses will be **d**—	8720
	10:14	Shalman **d** Beth Arbel on the day of battle,	8720

DEVASTATION (2) [DEVASTATE]
1Sa	5: 6	he brought **d** upon them and afflicted them	9037
Da	8:24	He will cause astounding **d**	8845

DEVELOPED (2) [DEVELOPS]
Eze	16: 7	up and **d** and became the most beautiful	1540
Jn	3:25	An argument **d** between some	1181

DEVELOPS (1) [DEVELOPED]
Jas	1: 3	that the testing of your faith **d** perseverance.	2981

DEVIATE (1)
2Ch	8:15	They did not **d** from the king's commands to	6073

DEVICES (1) [DEVISE]
Ps	81:12	to follow their own **d**.	4600

DEVIL (33) [DEVIL'S]
Mt	4: 1	into the desert to be tempted by the **d**.	1333
	4: 5	Then the **d** took him to the holy city	1333
	4: 8	the **d** took him to a very high mountain	1333
	4:11	Then the **d** left him,	1333
	13:39	and the enemy who sows them is the **d**.	1333
	25:41	into the eternal fire prepared for the **d**	1333
Lk	4: 2	for forty days he was tempted by the **d**.	1333
	4: 3	**d** said to him, "If you are the Son of God,	1333
	4: 5	The **d** led him up to a high place	1333
	4: 9	The **d** led him to Jerusalem	NIG

Lk	4:13	When the **d** had finished all this tempting,	1333
	8:12	then the **d** comes and takes away the word	1333
Jn	6:70	Yet one of you is a **d**!"	1333
	8:44	You belong to your father, the **d**,	1333
	13: 2	the **d** had already prompted Judas Iscariot,	1333
Ac	10:38	under the power of the **d**,	1333
	13:10	a child of the **d** and an enemy of everything	1333
Eph	4:27	and do not give the **d** a foothold.	1333
1Ti	3: 6	and fall under the same judgment as the **d**.	1333
2Ti	2:26	and escape from the trap of the **d**,	1333
Heb	2:14	holds the power of death—that is, the **d**—	1333
Jas	3:15	but is earthly, unspiritual, of the **d**.	1229
	4: 7	Resist the **d**, and he will flee from you.	1333
1Pe	5: 8	Your enemy the **d** prowls around like	1333
1Jn	3: 8	He who does what is sinful is of the **d**,	1333
	3: 8	the **d** has been sinning from the beginning.	1333
	3:10	and who the children of the **d** are:	1333
Jude	1: 9	when he was disputing with the **d** about	1333
Rev	2:10	**d** will put some of you in prison to test you,	1333
	12: 9	that ancient serpent called the **d**, or Satan,	1333
	12:12	because the **d** has gone down to you	1333
	20: 2	that ancient serpent, who is the **d**, or Satan,	1333
	20:10	And the **d**, who deceived them,	1333

DEVIL'S (3) [DEVIL]
Eph	6:11	take your stand against the **d** schemes.	1333
1Ti	3: 7	not fall into disgrace and into the **d** trap.	1333
1Jn	3: 8	of God appeared was to destroy the **d** work.	1333

DEVILS (KJV) See DEMONS, GOAT IDOLS

DEVIOUS (3) [DEVISE]
Pr	2:15	whose paths are crooked and who are **d**	4279
	14: 2	but he whose ways are **d** despises him.	4279
	21: 8	The way of the guilty is **d**,	2203

DEVISE (7) [DEVICES, DEVISED, DEVISES, DEVISING]
Ps	21:11	against you and **d** wicked schemes,	3108
	35:20	but **d** false accusations	3108
	58: 2	No, in your heart you **d** injustice,	7188
	119:150	Those who **d** wicked schemes are near,	8103
	140: 2	who **d** evil plans in their hearts and stir	8103
Isa	8:10	**D** your strategy, but it will be thwarted;	6418
Eze	38:10	and you will **d** an evil scheme.	3108

DEVISED (8) [DEVISE]
2Sa	14:13	then have you **d** a thing like this against	3108
Est	8: 3	which he had **d** against the Jews.	3108
	8: 5	**d** and wrote to destroy the Jews in all	4742
	9:25	that the evil scheme Haman had **d** against	3108
Ps	64: 6	"We have **d** a perfect plan!"	2924
Jer	49:30	he has **d** a plan against you.	3108
Da	11:25	to stand because of the plots **d** against him.	3108
Mt	28:12	with the elders and **d** a plan,	3284+5206

DEVISES (3) [DEVISE]
2Sa	14:14	he **d** ways so that a banished person may	3108
Ps	10: 2	who are caught in the schemes he **d**.	3108
Pr	6:18	a heart that **d** wicked schemes,	3086

DEVISING (1) [DEVISE]
Jer	18:11	a disaster for you and **d** a plan against you.	3108

DEVOTE (11) [DEVOTED, DEVOTES, DEVOTING, DEVOTION, DEVOUT]
1Ch	22:19	Now **d** your heart and soul to seeking	5989
2Ch	31: 4	and Levites so they could **d** themselves to	2616
Job	11:13	"Yet if you **d** your heart to him	3922
Jer	30:21	for who is he who will **d** himself to	6842
Mic	4:13	You will **d** their ill-gotten gains to	3049
1Co	7: 5	so that you may **d** yourselves to prayer.	5390
Col	4: 2	**D** yourselves to prayer,	4674
1Ti	1: 4	nor to **d** themselves to myths	4668
	4:13	**d** yourself to the public reading	4668
Tit	3: 8	in God may be careful to **d** themselves	4613
	3:14	Our people must learn to **d** themselves to	4613

DEVOTED (35) [DEVOTE]
Lev	27:21	like a field **d** to the LORD.	3051
	27:28	everything so **d** is most holy to the LORD.	3051
	27:29	" 'No person **d** to destruction may	3049+3051
Nu	18:14	in Israel that is **d** to the LORD is yours.	3051
Jos	6:17	The city and all that is in it are to be **d** to	3051
	6:18	But keep away from the **d** things,	3051
	6:21	**d** the city to the LORD and destroyed	3049
	7: 1	in regard to the **d** things;	3051
	7:11	They have taken some of the **d** things,	3051
	7:12	among you is **d** to destruction.	3051
	7:13	That which is **d** is among you, O Israel.	3051
	7:15	with the **d** things shall be destroyed by fire,	3051
	22:20	the **d** things, did not wrath come upon	3051
1Sa	15:21	the best of what was **d** to God,	3051
1Ki	11: 4	not fully **d** to the LORD his God,	8969
	15: 3	not fully **d** to the LORD his God,	8969
1Ch	2: 7	by violating the ban on **d** things.	3051
2Ch	17: 6	His heart was **d** to the ways of the LORD;	1467
Ezr	7:10	For Ezra had **d** himself to the study	3922
Ne	5:16	I **d** myself to the work on this wall.	2616
Ps	86: 2	Guard my life, for I am **d** to you.	2883

Ecc	1:13	I **d** myself to study and to explore	5989
Eze	11:21	But as for those whose hearts are **d** to	2143
	20:16	For their hearts were **d** to their idols.	339+2143
	44:29	in Israel **d** to the LORD will belong	3051
Mt	6:24	or he will be **d** to the one and despise	504
	15: 5	from me is a gift **d** to God,'	6067
Mk	7:11	Corban' (that is, a gift **d** to God),	1565
Lk	16:13	or he will be **d** to the one and despise	504
Ac	2:42	They **d** themselves to the apostles'	1639+4674
	18: 5	Paul **d** himself exclusively to preaching,	5309
Ro	12:10	Be **d** to one another in brotherly love.	5816
1Co	7:34	Her aim is to be **d** to the Lord in both body	41
	16:15	and they have **d** themselves to the service of	5435
2Co	7:12	for yourselves how **d** to us you are.	5082

DEVOTES (1) [DEVOTE]
Lev	27:28	" 'But nothing that a man owns and **d** to	3049

DEVOTING (1) [DEVOTE]
1Ti	5:10	and **d** herself to all kinds of good deeds.	2051

DEVOTION (13) [DEVOTE]
2Ki	20: 3	and with wholehearted **d**	4222+8969
1Ch	28: 9	and serve him with wholehearted **d**	4213+8969
	29: 3	in my **d** to the temple of my God I	8354
	29:19	the wholehearted **d** to keep your	
		commands,	4222+8969
2Ch	32:32	and his acts of **d** are written in the vision	2876
	35:26	of Josiah's reign and his acts of **d**,	2876
Job	6:14	"A despairing man should have the **d**	2876
	15: 4	But you even undermine piety and hinder **d**	8491
Isa	38: 3	and with wholehearted **d**	4213+8969
Jer	2: 2	" 'I remember the **d** of your youth,	2876
Eze	33:31	With their mouths they express **d**,	6313
1Co	7:35	in a right way in undivided **d** to the Lord.	2339
2Co	11: 3	be led astray from your sincere and pure **d**	605

DEVOUR (53) [DEVOURED, DEVOURING, DEVOURS]
Ex	10: 5	They will **d** what little you have left after	430
	10:12	over the land and **d** everything growing in	430
Lev	26:38	the land of your enemies will **d** you.	430
Nu	24: 8	They **d** hostile nations	430
Dt	28:38	because locusts will **d** it.	2887
	28:51	They will **d** the young of your livestock	430
	32:22	It will **d** the earth and its harvests	430
2Sa	2:26	"Must the sword **d** forever?	430
1Ki	21:23	'Dogs will **d** Jezebel by the wall	430
2Ki	9:10	dogs will **d** her on the plot of ground	430
	9:36	at Jezreel dogs will **d** Jezebel's flesh.	430
2Ch	7:13	or command locusts to **d** the land or send	430
Job	20:21	Nothing is left for him to **d**;	430
	20:26	and **d** what is left in his tent.	8286
Ps	14: 4	those who **d** my people as men eat bread	430
	27: 2	evil men advance against me to **d** my flesh,	430
	53: 4	those who **d** my people as men eat bread	430
Pr	30:14	with knives to **d** the poor from the earth,	430
Isa	9:20	On the right they will **d**,	1616
	31: 8	a sword, not of mortals, will **d** them.	430
	51: 8	the worm will **d** them like wool.	430
	56: 9	come and **d**, all you beasts of the forest!	430
Jer	5:17	They will **d** your harvests and food,	430
	5:17	**d** your sons and daughters;	430
	5:17	they will **d** your flocks and herds,	430
	5:17	**d** your vines and fig trees.	430
	8:16	to **d** the land and everything in it,	430
	12: 9	bring them to **d**.	430
	12:12	of the LORD will **d** from one end of	430
	15: 3	and the beasts of the earth to **d** and destroy.	430
	30:16	" 'But all who **d** you will be devoured;	430
	46:10	The sword will **d** till it is satisfied,	430
	50:17	The first to **d** him was the king of Assyria;	430
Eze	22:25	they **d** people, take treasures	430
	34:28	nor will wild animals **d** them.	430
	35:12	and have been given over to us to **d**."	433
	36:13	Because people say to you, "You **d** men	430
	36:14	therefore you will no longer **d** men	430
Da	7:23	from all the other kingdoms and will **d**	10030
Hos	2:12	and wild animals will **d** them.	430
	5: 7	their New Moon festivals will **d** them	430
	7: 7	they **d** their rulers.	430
	13: 8	Like a lion I will **d** them;	430
Am	5: 6	it will **d**, and Bethel will have no one	430
Na	2:13	and the sword will **d** your young lions.	430
	3:15	There the fire will **d** you,	430
Hab	1: 8	They fly like a vulture swooping to **d**;	430
	3:14	though about to **d** the wretched who were	430
Zec	11: 1	O Lebanon, so that fire may **d** your cedars!	430
Mk	12:40	They **d** widows' houses and for	2983
Lk	20:47	They **d** widows' houses and for	2983
1Pe	5: 8	a roaring lion looking for someone to **d**.	2927
Rev	12: 4	so that he might **d** her child the moment it	
		was born.	2983

DEVOURED (29) [DEVOUR]
Ge	37:20	and say that a ferocious animal **d** him.	430
	37:33	Some ferocious animal has **d** him.	430
Ex	10:15	They **d** all that was left after the hail—	430
Nu	26:10	whose followers died when the fire **d**	430
Job	31:39	if I have **d** its yield without payment	430
Ps	44:11	up to be **d** like sheep and have scattered us	4407
	78:45	He sent swarms of flies that **d** them,	430
	79: 7	for they have **d** Jacob	430

Isa 1:20 *you will* **be d** *by the sword."* 430
    9:12 and Philistines from the west *have* **d** Israel 430
  49:19 and *those who* **d** you will be far away. 1180
Jer 2: 3 all *who* **d** her were held guilty, 430
   2:30 Your sword *has* **d** your prophets like 430
  10:25 For *they have* **d** Jacob; 430
  10:25 *they have* **d** him completely 430
  30:16 " 'But all who devour you *will* **be d;** 430
  50: 7 Whoever found them **d** them; 430
  51:34 "Nebuchadnezzar king of Babylon *has* **d** us, 430
Eze 7:15 in the city *will* **be d** by famine and plague. 430
  19: 3 He learned to tear the prey and **d** men. 430
  19: 6 He learned to tear the prey and *he* **d** men. 430
  33:27 to the wild animals *to be* **d,** 430
Da 7: 7 it crushed and **d** its victims 10030
   7:19 the beast that crushed and **d** its victims 10030
Joel 1:19 for fire *has* **d** the open pastures 430
   1:20 of water have dried up and fire *has* **d** 430
Am 4: 9 Locusts **d** your fig and olive trees, 430
   7: 4 it dried up the great deep and **d** the land. 430
Rev 20: 9 fire came down from heaven and **d** them. *2983*

DEVOURING (4) [DEVOUR]

Dt 9: 3 across ahead of you like a **d** fire. 430
Isa 29: 6 and tempest and flames of a **d** fire. 430
Mal 3:11 I will prevent pests from **d** your crops, 8845
Gal 5:15 If *you keep on* biting and **d** each other, *2983*

DEVOURS (12) [DEVOUR]

Ge 49:27 in the morning *he* **d** the prey, 430
Nu 13:32 "The land we explored **d** those living in it. 430
  23:24 a lion that does not rest till *he* **d** his prey 430
Dt 32:42 while my sword **d** flesh; 430
2Sa 11:25 the sword **d** one as well as another. 430
Job 18:13 death's firstborn **d** his limbs. 430
  22:20 and fire **d** their wealth.' 430
Ps 50: 3 a fire **d** before him, 430
Pr 21:20 but a foolish man **d** all he has. 1180
Jer 46:14 for the sword **d** those around you.' 430
Joel 2: 3 Before them fire **d,** 430
Rev 11: 5 from their mouths and **d** their enemies. *2983*

DEVOUT (7) [DEVOTE]

1Ki 18: 3 (Obadiah was a **d** believer in the LORD. 4394
Isa 57: 1 **d** men are taken away, 2876
Lk 2:25 who was righteous and **d.** 2327
Ac 10: 2 and all his family were **d** and God-fearing; 2356
  10: 7 of his servants and a **d** soldier who was one 2356
  13:43 and **d** converts to Judaism followed Paul 4936
  22:12 He was a **d** observer of the law 2327

DEW (36)

Ge 27:28 of heaven's **d** and of earth's richness— 3228
  27:39 away from the **d** *of* heaven above. 3228
Ex 16:13 the morning there was a layer of **d** around 3228
  16:14 When the **d** was gone, 3228
Nu 11: 9 When the **d** settled on the camp at night, 3228
Dt 32: 2 like rain and my words descend like **d,** 3228
  33:13 the precious **d** from heaven above and with 3228
  33:28 where the heavens drop **d.** 3228
Jdg 6:37 If there is **d** only on the fleece and all 3228
   6:38 he squeezed the fleece and wrung out the **d** 3228
   6:39 and the ground covered with **d.**" 3228
   6:40 all the ground was covered with **d.** 3228
2Sa 1:21 may you have neither **d** nor rain, 3228
  17:12 and we will fall on him as **d** settles on 3228
1Ki 17: 1 there will be neither **d** nor rain in 3228
Job 29:19 and the **d** will lie all night on my branches. 3228
  38:28 Who fathers the drops of **d?** 3228
Ps 110: 3 of the dawn you will receive the **d** 3228
  133: 3 It is as if the **d** of Hermon were falling 3228
Pr 3:20 and the clouds let drop the **d.** 3228
  19:12 but his favor is like **d** on the grass. 3228
SS 5: 2 My head is drenched with **d,** 3228
Isa 18: 4 like a cloud of **d** in the heat of harvest." 3228
  26:19 Your **d** is like the dew of the morning; 3228
  26:19 Your dew is like the **d** *of* the morning; 3228
Da 4:15 be drenched with the **d** *of* heaven, 10299
   4:23 Let him be drenched with the **d** *of* heaven; 10299
   4:25 and be drenched with the **d** *of* heaven. 10299
   4:33 with the **d** of heaven until his hair grew 10299
   5:21 and his body was drenched with the **d** 10299
Hos 6: 4 like the early **d** that disappears, 3228
  13: 3 like the early **d** that disappears, 3228
  14: 5 I will be like the **d** to Israel; 3228
Mic 5: 7 be in the midst of many peoples like **d** from 3228
Hag 1:10 of you the heavens have withheld their **d** 3228
Zec 8:12 and the heavens will drop their **d.** 3228

DIADEM (4)

Ex 29: 6 on his head and attach the sacred **d** to 5694
  39:30 They made the plate, the sacred **d,** 5694
Lev 8: 9 the sacred **d,** on the front of it, 5694
Isa 62: 3 a royal **d** in the hand of your God. 7565

DIAMETER (1)

1Ki 7:32 The **d** *of* each wheel was a cubit and a half. 7757

DIAMOND   (KJV) See EMERALD, FLINT

DIANA   (KJV) See ARTEMIS

DIBLAH (1)

Eze 6:14 a desolate waste from the desert to **D—** 1812

DIBLAIM (1)

Hos 1: 3 So he married Gomer daughter of **D,** 1813

DIBLATH   (KJV) See DIBLAH

DIBLATHAIM   See ALMON DIBLATHAIM, BETH DIBLATHAIM

DIBON (9) [DIBON GAD]

Nu 21:30 Heshbon is destroyed all the way to **D.** 1897
  32: 3 **D,** Jazer, Nimrah, Heshbon, Elealeh, 1897
  32:34 The Gadites built up **D,** Ataroth, Aroer, 1897
Jos 13: 9 the whole plateau of Medeba as far as **D,** 1897
  13:17 including **D,** Bamoth Baal, 1897
Ne 11:25 in **D** and its settlements, 1897
Isa 15: 2 **D** goes up to its temple, 1897
Jer 48:18 O inhabitants of the Daughter of **D,** 1897
  48:22 to **D,** Nebo and Beth Diblathaim, 1897

DIBON GAD (2) [DIBON, GAD]

Nu 33:45 They left Iyim and camped at **D.** 1898
  33:46 They left **D** and camped 1898

DIBRI (1)

Lev 24:11 Shelomith, the daughter of **D** the Danite.) 1828

DICTATE (2) [DICTATED, DICTATING, DICTATION, EDICT]

Jer 36:17 Did Jeremiah **d** it?" 4946+7023
Mic 7: 3 the powerful **d** what they desire— 1819

DICTATED (4) [DICTATE]

Jer 36: 4 and while Jeremiah **d** all the words 4946+7023
  36: 6 of the LORD that you wrote as I **d.** 4946+7023
  36:18 Baruch replied, "he **d** all these words to me, 4946+7023+7924
  36:32 and as Jeremiah **d,** Baruch wrote 7023

DICTATING (1) [DICTATE]

Jer 45: 1 written on a scroll the words Jeremiah was then **d:** 4946+7023

DICTATION (1) [DICTATE]

Jer 36:27 Baruch had written *at* Jeremiah's **d,** 4946+7023

DID (1316) [DO]

Ge 3: 1 He said to the woman, "**D** God really *say,* AIT
   3: 3 but God **d** *say,* "You must not eat AIT
   4: 5 **d** not **look with favor.** AIT
   6:22 Noah **d** everything just as God commanded 6913
   7: 5 And Noah **d** all that the LORD commanded 6913
   8:12 but this time *it* **d** not **return** to him. AIT
  12:19 Why **d** you *say,* 'She is my sister,' AIT
  15:10 *he* **d** not **cut in half.** AIT
  18:13 "Why **d** Sarah **laugh** and say, AIT
  18:15 so she lied and said, "I **d** not **laugh.**" AIT
  18:15 But he said, "Yes, *you* **d laugh.**" AIT
  19: 3 But he insisted so strongly that *they* **d** go AIT
  20: 5 **D** he not **say** to me, 'She is my sister,' AIT
  20: 6 I know *you* **d** this with a clear conscience, 6913
  20: 6 That is why *I* **d** not **let** you touch her. AIT
  21: 1 LORD **d** for Sarah what he had promised. 6913
  21:26 You **d** not **tell** me, AIT
  26: 9 Why **d** you *say,* 'She is my sister'?" AIT
  26:29 just as *we* **d** not **molest** you AIT
  27:20 "How **d** *you* **find** it so quickly, my son?" AIT
  27:23 *He* **d** not **recognize** him, AIT
  27:45 with you and forgets what *you* **d** to him, 6913
  28:28 And Jacob **d** so. 6913
  30:40 and **d** not **put** them with Laban's animals. AIT
  31:27 Why **d** you **run off** secretly AIT
  31:30 But why **d** you **steal** my gods?" AIT
  31:32 Now Jacob **d** not **know** AIT
  31:39 *I* **d** not **bring** you animals torn AIT
  38:10 What *he* **d** was wicked in 6913
  38:20 but *he* **d** not **find** her. AIT
  38:23 After all, *I* **d** send her this young goat, AIT
  38:26 And *he* **d** not **sleep with** her again. AIT
  39: 3 in everything he **d,** 6913
  39: 6 in charge, *he* **d** not **concern** *himself* AIT
  39:23 and gave him success in whatever he **d.** 6913
  40:23 **d** not **remember** Joseph; he forgot him. AIT
  42: 4 But Jacob **d** not **send** Benjamin, AIT
  42: 8 they **d** not **recognize** him. AIT
  42:23 They **d** not **realize** AIT
  43: 6 **d** *you* **bring** *this* **trouble** AIT
  43:17 The man **d** as Joseph told him and took 6913
  44: 2 And *he* **d** as Joseph said. 6913
  45:21 So the sons of Israel **d** this. 6913
  45:26 Jacob was stunned; *he* **d** not **believe** them. AIT
  46:34 just as our fathers **d.'** NIH
  47:22 *he* **d** not **buy** the land of the priests, AIT
  47:22 That is why *they* **d** not **sell** their land. AIT

Ge 47:26 of the priests that **d** not **become** Pharaoh's. AIT
  50:12 Jacob's sons **d** as he had commanded them: 6913
  50:15 and pays us back for all the wrongs *we* **d** 1694
Ex 1: 8 a new king, who **d** not **know about** Joseph, AIT
   1:17 feared God and **d** not **do** what the king AIT
   2:14 "What I **d** must have become known." NIH
   2:20 "Why **d** you **leave** him? AIT
   3: 2 the bush was on fire *it* **d** not **burn up.** AIT
   4: 1 'The LORD **d** not **appear** to you'?" AIT
   6: 3 **d** not **make myself known** AIT
   6: 9 but *they* **d** not **listen** to him because AIT
   7: 6 Moses and Aaron **d** just as the LORD 6913
   7:10 and Aaron went to Pharaoh and **d** just as 6913
   7:11 also **d** the same things by their secret arts: 6913
   7:20 Moses and Aaron **d** just as the LORD 6913
   7:22 the Egyptian magicians **d** the same things 6913
   7:23 and **d** not **take** even this *to* heart. AIT
   8:13 And the LORD **d** what Moses asked. 6913
   8:17 *They* **d** this, and when Aaron 6913
   8:24 And the LORD **d** this. 6913
   8:31 and the LORD **d** what Moses asked: 6913
   9: 6 And the next day the LORD **d** it: 6913
   9:26 The only place *it* **d** not **hail** was the land 2118
  12:28 The Israelites **d** just what the LORD 6913
  12:35 The Israelites **d** as Moses instructed 6913
  12:39 and **d** not **have time** to prepare food AIT
  12:50 All the Israelites **d** just what the LORD 6913
  13: 8 'I **d** this because of what the LORD **d** 6913
  13:17 God **d** not **lead** them *on* the road through AIT
  14: 4 So the Israelites **d** this. 6913
  16:15 For *they* **d** not **know** what it was. AIT
  16:17 The Israelites **d** as they were told; 6913
  16:18 **d** not **have too much,** AIT
  16:18 **d** not **have too little.** AIT
  16:24 and *it* **d** not **stink** or get maggots in it. AIT
  17: 3 **d** *you* **bring** us up AIT
  17: 6 So Moses **d** this in the sight of the elders 6913
  18:11 for he **d** this to those who had treated Israel NIH
  18:24 and **d** everything he said. 6913
  19: 4 'You yourselves have seen what *I* **d** 6913
  21:36 **d** not **keep** it **penned up,** AIT
  22:11 that the neighbor *d* not **lay** hands on AIT
  24:11 But God **d** not **raise** his hand AIT
  32:14 Then the LORD **relented and d** not bring 5714
  32:21 "What **d** these people **d** to you, AIT
  32:28 The Levites **d** as Moses commanded, 6913
  32:35 with a plague because of what *they* **d** with 6913
  33:11 of Nun **d** not **leave** the tent. AIT
  36:10 and **d** the same *with* 285+285+448+2489S
  39:32 The Israelites **d** everything just as the LORD 6913
  40:16 Moses **d** everything just as the LORD 6913
  40:37 the cloud **d** not **lift,** they did not set out— AIT
  40:37 *they* **d** not **set out**—until the day it lifted. AIT
Lev 4:20 with this bull just as *he* **d** with the bull for 6913
   6: 7 of these things he **d** that made him guilty." 6913
   8: 4 Moses **d** as the LORD commanded him, 6913
   8:36 So Aaron and his sons **d** everything 6913
   9:15 and offered it for a sin offering as he **d** with NIH
  10: 7 So *they* **d** as Moses said. 6913
  16:15 and do with it as *he* **d** with the bull's blood: 6913
  20:23 *they* **d** all these things, I abhorred them. 6913
  24:23 The Israelites **d** as the LORD 6913
  26:35 the land will have the rest *it* **d** not **have** AIT
Nu 1:54 The Israelites **d** all this just as the LORD 6913
   2:34 So the Israelites **d** everything the LORD 6913
   5: 4 The Israelites **d** this; 6913
   5: 4 They **d** just as the LORD 6913
   7: 9 But Moses *d* not **give** any to the Kohathites, AIT
   8: 3 Aaron **d** so; he set up the 6913
   8:20 Aaron and the whole Israelite community **d** 6913
   8:22 *They* **d** with the Levites just as 6913
   9: 5 and *they* **d** so in the Desert of Sinai 906+2021+6913+7175S
   9: 5 The Israelites **d** everything just as the LORD 6913
   9:13 from his people because *he* **d** not **present** AIT
   9:19 the LORD's order and **d** not **set out.** AIT
  11:12 **D** I **conceive** all these people? AIT
  11:12 **D** I **give** them **birth?** AIT
  11:20 saying, "Why **d** *we* ever **leave** Egypt?" ' " AIT
  11:25 **d** not **do so again.** AIT
  11:26 but **d** not **go out** to the Tent. AIT
  12:15 and the people **d** not **move on** AIT
  16:47 So Aaron **d** as Moses said, 4374S
  17:11 Moses **d** just as the LORD commanded 6913
  20: 4 Why **d** *you* **bring** the LORD's community AIT
  20: 5 **d** *you* **bring** us up AIT
  20:12 "Because *you* **d** not **trust** in me enough AIT
  20:27 Moses **d** as the LORD commanded: 6913
  21:34 Do to him what *you* **d** to Sihon king of 6913
  22:19 Now stay here tonight as the others **d,** NIH
  22:34 *I* **d** not **realize** you were standing in AIT
  22:37 "**D** I not **send** you an **urgent** AIT
  23: 2 Balak **d** as Balaam said, 6913
  23:17 "What **d** the LORD **say?"** AIT
  23:26 "**D** I not **tell** you I must do whatever AIT
  23:30 Balak **d** as Balaam had said, 6913
  24: 1 he **d** not **resort to** sorcery as at other times, AIT
  24:12 "**D** I not **tell** the messengers you sent me, AIT
  25:11 *I* **d** not **put an end** to them. AIT
  26:11 The line of Korah, however, **d** not **die out.** AIT
  27:22 Moses **d** as the LORD commanded him. 6913
  31:31 So Moses and Eleazar the priest **d** as 6913
  32: 8 This is what your fathers **d** 6913
  35:23 not his enemy and *he* **d** not **intend** AIT
  36:10 So Zelophehad's daughters **d** as the LORD 6913
Dt 1:30 will fight for you, as *he* **d** for you in Egypt, 6913

Dt	1:32	you *d* not **trust** in the LORD your God,
	2:12	just as Israel **d** in the land
	2:29	who live in Ar, **d** for us—
	2:37	*you d* not **encroach** on any of the land of
	3: 2	Do to him what *you d* to Sihon king of
	3: 4	not one of the sixty cities that *we d* not **take**
	4: 3	with your own eyes what the LORD **d**
	4:34	the things the LORD your God **d** for you
	5: 5	of the fire and *d* not **go up** the mountain.)
	6:10	flourishing cities *you d* not **build**,
	6:11	of good things *you d* not **provide**,
	6:11	wells *you d* not **dig**,
	6:11	and olive groves *you d* not **plant**—
	6:16	Do not test the LORD your God as *you d*
	7: 7	*d* not **set** his **affection**
	7:18	the LORD your God **d** to Pharaoh and
	8: 4	Your clothes *d* not **wear out**
	8: 4	not wear out and your feet *d* not **swell**
	9:23	*You d* not **trust** him or obey him.
	10:10	as I **d** the first time,
	11: 3	the signs he performed and the **things** he **d**
	11: 4	what *he* **d** to the Egyptian army,
	11: 5	It was not your children who saw what *he* **d**
	11: 6	and what *he* **d** to Dathan and Abiram,
	19: 6	since he **d** it to his neighbor
	21: 7	"Our hands *d* not **shed** this blood,
	21: 7	nor *d* our eyes **see** it done.
	22:14	*I d* not **find** proof of her virginity,"
	22:17	'*I d* not **find** your daughter to be a virgin.'
	22:24	*d* not **scream for help**,
	23: 4	*d* not **come to meet**
	24: 9	Remember what the LORD your God **d**
	25:17	Remember what the Amalekites **d** to you
	28:45	because *you d* not **obey**
	28:47	Because *you d* not **serve**
	28:62	because *you d* not **obey**
	29: 2	Your eyes have seen all that the LORD **d**
	29: 5	your clothes *d* not **wear out**,
	29: 5	nor the sandals on your feet.
	29: 6	I **d** this so that you might know that I am
	29:26	gods *they d* not **know**,
	31: 4	And the LORD will do to them what *he* **d**
	32:17	gods your fathers *d* not **fear**.
	32:51	not **uphold** my **holiness**
	33: 9	*He d* not **recognize** his brothers
	34: 9	So the Israelites listened to him and **d** what
	34:11	who **d** all those miraculous signs
	34:12	that Moses **d** in the sight of all Israel.
Jos	2: 4	*I d* not **know** where they had come from.
	2:10	and what *you* **d** to Sihon and Og,
	4: 8	the Israelites **d** as Joshua commanded them.
	4:23	The LORD your God **d** to the Jordan
	4:24	He **d** this so that all the peoples of
	5: 4	Now this is why he **d so:**
	5:15	And Joshua **d so.**
	6:14	*They* **d** this for six days.
	7: 6	The elders of Israel **d** the same,
	7: 7	*d you* ever **bring** this people **across**
	8: 2	You shall do to Ai and its king as *you* **d**
	8: 5	as they **d** before, we will flee from them.
	8: 6	from us as they **d** before.'
	8:14	But he **d** not **know** that
	8:17	in Ai or Bethel who *d* not **go** after Israel.
	8:19	As soon as he **d** this,
	8:26	For Joshua *d* not **draw back** the hand
	8:27	But Israel *d* **carry off** for themselves
	8:35	that Joshua *d* not **read** to
	9: 9	all that *he* **d** in Egypt,
	9:10	and all that *he* **d** to the two kings of
	9:14	but *d* not **inquire** of the LORD.
	9:18	But the Israelites *d* not **attack** them,
	9:22	"Why *d you* **deceive** us by saying,
	9:24	and that is why *we* **d** this.
	9:26	and *they d* not **kill** them.
	10:28	And he **d** to the king of Makkedah
	10:30	And he **d** to its king as he had done to
	10:39	*They* **d** to Debir and its king
	11: 9	Joshua **d** to them as the LORD had directed:
	11:13	Yet Israel *d* not **burn** any of the cities built
	11:15	and Joshua **d** it;
	11:22	Gath and Ashdod *d any* **survive.**
	13:13	But the Israelites *d* not **drive out** the people
	16:10	*They d* not **dislodge** the Canaanites living
	17:13	*d* not **drive** them **out completely.**
	22:20	*d* not **wrath come** upon
	22:24	*We d* it for fear that some day
	24: 5	I afflicted the Egyptians by what *I* **d** there,
	24: 7	You saw with your own eyes what *I* **d** to
	24:11	as **d** also the Amorites, Perizzites,
	24:12	You **d** not do it with your own sword
	24:13	on which *you d* not **toil** and cities you did
	24:13	not toil and cities *you d* not **build;**
	24:13	and olive groves that *you d* not **plant.'**
Jdg	1: 7	Now God has paid me back for what *I* **d**
	1:27	But Manasseh *d* not **drive out** the people
	1:29	Nor *d* Ephraim **drive out**
	1:30	Neither *d* Zebulun **drive out**
	1:30	but they **d** subject them to forced labor.
	1:31	Nor *d* Asher **drive out** those living in Acco
	1:33	Neither *d* Naphtali **drive out** those living
	2:11	Then the Israelites **d** evil in the eyes of
	2:22	and walk in it as their forefathers **d."**
	2:23	*d* not **drive** them **out**
	3: 2	(he **d** this only to teach warfare to
	3: 7	The Israelites **d** evil in the eyes of
	3:12	Once again the Israelites **d** evil in the eyes
	3:12	and because *they* **d** this evil

Dt	1:32		AIT
	2:12		6913
	2:29		AIT
	2:37		AIT
	3: 2		6913
	3: 4		AIT
	4: 3		6913
	4:34		6913
	5: 5		AIT
	6:10		AIT
	6:11		AIT
	6:11		AIT
	6:11		AIT
	6:16		5814S
	7: 7		AIT
	7:18		6913
	8: 4		AIT
	8: 4		AIT
	9:23		AIT
	10:10		NIH
	11: 3		5126
	11: 4		AIT
	11: 5		6913
	11: 6		6913
	19: 6		NIH
	21: 7		AIT
	21: 7		AIT
	22:14		AIT
	22:17		AIT
	22:24		AIT
	23: 4		AIT
	24: 9		6913
	25:17		6913
	28:45		AIT
	28:47		AIT
	28:62		AIT
	29: 2		6913
	29: 5		AIT
	29: 5		1162S
	29: 6		NIH
	29:26		AIT
	31: 4		6913
	32:17		AIT
	32:51		AIT
	33: 9		AIT
	34: 9		6913
	34:11		NIH
	34:12		6913

Jdg	3:22	*d* not **pull** the sword **out,**
	3:25	when he *d* not **open** the doors of the room,
	4: 1	the Israelites once again **d** evil in the eyes
	5:16	Why *d you* **stay** among the campfires
	5:17	And Dan, why *d he* **linger** by the ships?
	5:18	so **d** Naphtali on the heights of the field.
	5:23	because *they d* not **come** to help the LORD,
	6: 1	Again the Israelites **d** evil in the eyes of
	6: 4	and *d* not **spare** a living thing for Israel,
	6:13	'*D* not the LORD **bring us up**
	6:20	And Gideon **d so.**
	6:27	So Gideon took ten of his servants and **d** as
	6:27	he **d** it at night rather than in the daytime.
	6:29	They asked each other, "Who **d** this?"
	6:29	they were told, "Gideon son of Joash **d** it."
	6:40	That night God **d so.**
	8:18	"What kind of men *d you* **kill** at Tabor?"
	8:20	But Jether *d* not **draw** his sword,
	8:28	the Israelites and *d* not **raise** its head again.
	8:34	and *d* not **remember** the LORD their God,
	9:24	God **d** this in order that the crime
	10: 6	Again the Israelites **d** evil in the eyes of
	10:12	*d I* not **save** you from their hands?
	11:15	Israel *d* not **take** the land of Moab or
	11:18	*They d* not **enter** the territory of Moab,
	11:20	*d* not **trust** Israel to pass
	11:25	*D* he ever **quarrel** with Israel or fight
	11:39	she returned to her father and *he* **d** to her
	12: 1	"Why *d you* **go** to fight the Ammonites
	13: 1	Again the Israelites **d** evil in the eyes of
	13:16	(Manoah *d* not **realize** that it was the angel
	13:19	And the LORD **d** an amazing thing
	13:21	*d* not **show** himself **again**
	14: 4	(His parents *d* not **know** that this was from
	14: 9	But *he d* not **tell** them that he had taken
	14:15	*D you* **invite** us here to rob us?"
	15: 6	When the Philistines asked, "Who **d** this?"
	15:10	they answered, "to do to him as *he* **d** to us."
	15:11	"I merely **d** them what they did to me."
	15:11	"I merely did to them what *they* **d** to me."
	16:20	he *d* not **know** that the LORD had left him.
	17: 6	everyone **d** as he saw fit.
	18: 8	"How *d you* **find** things?"
	19:17	Where *d you* **come** from?"
	20:34	so heavy that the Benjamites *d* not **realize**
	21:22	*we d* not **get** wives for them during the war,
	21:22	you *d* not **give** your daughters to them.' "
	21:23	So that is what the Benjamites **d.**
	21:25	everyone **d** as he saw fit.
Ru	2:11	to live with a people *you d* not **know** before.
	2:19	"Where *d you* **glean** today?
	2:19	Where *d you* **work?**
	3: 6	and **d** everything her mother-in-law told her
	3:15	When *she d so,*
	3:16	Naomi asked, **"How d it go,** my daughter?"
	4: 2	"Sit here," and *they* **d so.**
1Sa	1:22	Hannah *d* not **go.**
	2:25	*d* not **listen** to their father's rebuke,
	2:27	'*D I* not **clearly reveal myself**
	3: 5	But Eli said, "*I d* not **call;**
	3: 6	"My son," Eli said, "*I d* not **call;**
	3: 7	Now Samuel *d* not yet **know** the LORD:
	4: 3	*d* the LORD **bring defeat upon**
	4:20	But *she d* not **respond** or pay any attention.
	5:12	Those who *d* not **die** were afflicted
	6: 6	harden your hearts as the Egyptians and Pharaoh **d?**
	6: 6	*d* *they* not **send** the Israelites **out**
	6: 9	So they **d** this.
	6:12	*they d* not **turn** to the right or to the left.
	7:13	and *d* not **invade** Israelite territory again.
	8: 3	But his sons *d* not **walk** in his ways.
	9: 4	but *they d* not **find** them.
	9: 4	but *they d* not **find** them.
	9:27	and the servant **d so—**
	10:16	he *d* not **tell** his uncle what Samuel had said
	12:17	an evil thing *you d* in the eyes of
	13: 8	but Samuel *d* not **come** to Gilgal,
	13:11	and that *you d* not **come** at the set time,
	14: 1	But he *d* not **tell** his father.
	14:17	When *they,* **d** it was Jonathan
	14:37	But God *d* not **answer** him that day.
	14:45	for he **d** this today with God's help."
	15: 2	the Amalekites for what *they* **d** to Israel
	15:17	*d you* not **become** the head of the tribes
	15:19	Why *d you* not **obey** the LORD?
	15:19	Why *d you* **pounce** on the plunder
	15:20	"But *I d* **obey** the LORD," Saul said.
	15:35	*d* not go to see
	16: 4	Samuel **d** what the LORD said.
	17:28	with whom *d you* **leave** those few sheep
	18: 2	with him and *d* not **let** him return
	18: 5	David **d** it so successfully
	18:10	as he usually **d.**
	18:14	In everything he **d** he had great success,
	18:30	and as often as they **d,**
	19:17	"Why *d you* **deceive** me like this
	20:34	that second day of the month he *d* not **eat,**
	22:17	yet *they d* not **tell** me."
	23:13	he *d* not **go** there.
	23:14	but God *d* not **give** David into his hands.
	24: 7	and *d* not **allow** them to attack Saul.
	24: 7	the corner of your robe but *d* not **kill** you.
	24:18	now told me of the good *you d* to me;
	24:18	but *you d* not **kill** me.
	25: 7	*we d* not **mistreat** them,

Jdg	3:22	AIT
	3:25	AIT
	4: 1	6913
	5:16	AIT
	5:17	AIT
	5:18	NIH
	5:23	AIT
	6: 1	6913
	6: 4	AIT
	6:13	AIT
	6:20	6913
	6:27	6913
	6:27	6913
	6:29	6913
	6:29	6913
	6:40	6913
	8:18	AIT
	8:20	AIT
	8:28	AIT
	8:34	AIT
	9:24	NIH
	10: 6	6913
	10:12	AIT
	11:15	AIT
	11:18	AIT
	11:20	AIT
	11:25	AIT
	11:39	6913
	12: 1	AIT
	13: 1	6913
	13:16	AIT
	13:19	6913
	13:21	AIT
	14: 4	AIT
	14: 9	AIT
	14:15	AIT
	15: 6	6913
	15:10	6913
	15:11	6913
	15:11	6913
	16:20	AIT
	17: 6	6913
	18: 8	NIH
	19:17	AIT
	20:34	AIT
	21:22	AIT
	21:22	AIT
	21:23	6913
	21:25	6913
Ru	2:11	AIT
	2:19	AIT
	2:19	AIT
	3: 6	6913
	3:15	296S
	3:16	905+4769
	4: 2	3782S
1Sa	1:22	AIT
	2:25	AIT
	2:27	AIT
	3: 5	AIT
	3: 6	AIT
	3: 7	AIT
	4: 3	AIT
	4:20	AIT
	5:12	AIT
	6: 6	906+3877+4213+4392S
	6: 6	AIT
	6: 9	6913
	6:12	AIT
	7:13	AIT
	8: 3	AIT
	9: 4	AIT
	9: 4	AIT
	9:27	6296S
	10:16	AIT
	12:17	6913
	13: 8	AIT
	13:11	AIT
	14: 1	AIT
	14:17	7212S
	14:37	AIT
	14:45	6913
	15: 2	6913
	15:17	NIH
	15:19	AIT
	15:19	AIT
	15:20	AIT
	15:35	AIT
	16: 4	6913
	17:28	AIT
	18: 2	AIT
	18: 5	3655S
	18:10	928+3427+3427+3869
	18:14	2006
	18:30	3655S
	19:17	AIT
	20:34	AIT
	22:17	AIT
	23:13	AIT
	23:14	AIT
	24: 7	AIT
	24: 7	AIT
	24:18	6913
	24:18	AIT
	25: 7	AIT

1Sa	25:15	They *d* not **mistreat** us,
	25:19	But *she d* not **tell** her husband Nabal.
	25:25	*I d* not **see** the men my master sent.
	26:12	nor *d anyone* **wake up.**
	26:16	because *you d* not **guard** your master,
	27: 9	*d* not **leave** a man or woman **alive,**
	27:10	"Where *d you* **go raiding** today?"
	27:11	*d* not **leave** a man or woman **alive**
	27:11	'This is what David **d.' "**
	28: 6	but the LORD *d* not **answer** him by dreams
	28:18	Because *you d* not **obey** the LORD
	28:21	in my hands and **d** what you told me to do.
	30:22	"Because *they d* not **go out** with us,
2Sa	1:22	the bow of Jonathan *d* not **turn** back,
	1:22	the sword of Saul *d* not **return** unsatisfied.
	2:28	nor *d they* fight **anymore.**
	3: 7	"Why *d you* **sleep with**
	3:11	Ish-Bosheth *d* not **dare** to say another word
	3:24	*d you* **let** him go?
	3:26	But David *d* not **know** it.
	3:36	indeed, everything the king **d** pleased them.
	5:25	So David **d** as the LORD commanded him,
	7: 7	*d I* ever **say** to any
	7:10	as they **d** at the beginning
	11: 9	and *d* not **go down** to his house.
	11:10	David was told, "Uriah *d* not **go home,"**
	11:13	he *d* not **go** home.
	11:20	*d you* **get so close**
	11:21	*d you* **get so close**
	12: 5	the man who **d** this deserves to die!
	12: 6	because he **d** such a thing and had no pity."
	12: 9	Why *d you* **despise** the word of the LORD
	12:12	You **d** it in secret,
	12:31	*He* **d** this to all the Ammonite towns.
	13:29	So Absalom's men **d**
	14:20	Your servant Joab **d** this to change
	14:24	to his own house and *d* not **see** the face of
	14:31	Then Joab *d* **go** to Absalom's house
	19:19	not remember how your servant **d wrong** on
	19:41	*d* our brothers, the men of Judah, **steal** the king **away**
	19:42	"We **d** this because the king is closely
	20: 3	but *d* not **lie** with them.
	20: 6	will do us more harm than Absalom **d.**
	21:10	*she d* not **let** the birds of
	21:14	and **d** everything the king commanded.
	22:38	*I d* not **turn back** till they were destroyed.
	22:42	to the LORD, but he *d* not **answer.**
	22:44	People *I d* not **know** are subject to me,
1Ki	1: 8	Shimei and Rei and David's special guard **d**
	1:10	but he *d* not **invite** Nathan the prophet
	1:13	*d you* not **swear** to me your servant:
	1:26	and your servant Solomon he *d* not **invite.**
	2: 5	what Joab son of Zeruiah **d** to me—
	2: 5	what he **d** to the two commanders
	2:42	"*D I* not **make** you **swear**
	2:43	then *d you* not **keep** your oath to the LORD
	2:44	the wrong *you d* to my father David.
	3:14	and commands as David your father **d,**
	7:14	He came to King Solomon and **d** all
	7:18	*He* **d** the same for each capital.
	8:18	*you d* **well** to have this in your heart.
	9: 4	as David your father **d,**
	9:22	But Solomon *d* not **make slaves** of any of
	9:23	550 officials supervising the men who **d**
	10: 7	But *I d* not **believe** these things
	11: 6	Solomon **d** evil in the eyes of the LORD;
	11: 6	*d* not follow the LORD **completely,**
	11: 8	*He* **d** the same for all his foreign wives,
	11:10	Solomon *d* not **keep** the LORD's command.
	11:28	how well the young man **d** his work,
	11:33	and laws as David, Solomon's father, **d.**
	11:38	as David my servant **d,** I will be with you.
	11:41	all he **d** and the wisdom he displayed—
	12:15	So the king *d* not **listen** to the people,
	12:32	This he **d** in Bethel,
	13:10	So he took another road and *d* not **return** by
	13:12	"Which way *d he* **go?"**
	13:27	"Saddle the donkey for me," and *they* **d so.**
	13:33	this, Jeroboam *d* not **change** his evil ways,
	14: 4	So Jeroboam's wife **d** what he said
	14:22	Judah **d** evil in the eyes of the LORD.
	14:29	events of Rehoboam's reign, and all he **d,**
	15: 7	other events of Abijah's reign, and all he **d,**
	15:11	Asa **d** what was right in the eyes of
	15:14	Although he *d* not **remove** the high places,
	15:23	all he **d** and the cities he built,
	15:26	*He* **d** evil in the eyes of the LORD,
	15:29	*He* **d** not **leave** Jeroboam anyone
	15:31	other events of Nadab's reign, and all he **d,**
	15:34	*He* **d** evil in the eyes of the LORD,
	16: 5	what he **d** and his achievements,
	16: 7	provoking him to anger by the **things** he **d,**
	16:11	*He d* not **spare** a single male,
	16:14	other events of Elah's reign, and all he **d,**
	16:25	But Omri **d** evil in the eyes of the LORD
	16:27	what he **d** and the things he achieved,
	16:30	Ahab son of Omri **d** more evil in the eyes
	16:33	an Asherah pole and **d** more to provoke
	16:33	to anger than all the kings of Israel
	17: 5	So he **d** what the LORD had told him.
	17:15	She went away and **d** as Elijah had told her.
	17:16	not used up and the jug of oil *d* not **run dry,**
	17:18	*D you* **come** to remind me of my sin
	18:13	what *I* **d** while Jezebel was killing
	18:34	"Do it again," he said, and *they* **d** it **again.**

1Sa	25:15	AIT
	25:19	AIT
	25:25	AIT
	26:12	AIT
	26:16	AIT
	27: 9	AIT
	27:10	AIT
	27:11	AIT
	27:11	6913
	28: 6	AIT
	28:18	AIT
	28:21	9048
	30:22	AIT
2Sa	1:22	AIT
	1:22	AIT
	2:28	AIT
	3: 7	AIT
	3:11	AIT
	3:24	AIT
	3:26	AIT
	3:36	6913
	5:25	6913
	7: 7	AIT
	7:10	NIH
	11: 9	AIT
	11:10	AIT
	11:13	AIT
	11:20	AIT
	11:21	AIT
	12: 5	6913
	12: 6	6913
	12: 9	AIT
	12:12	6913
	12:31	6913
	13:29	6913
	14:20	6913
	14:24	AIT
	14:31	AIT
	19:19	6390
	19:41	AIT
	19:42	NIH
	20: 3	AIT
	20: 6	NIH
	21:10	AIT
	21:14	6913
	22:38	AIT
	22:42	AIT
	22:44	AIT
1Ki	1: 8	2118
	1:10	AIT
	1:13	AIT
	1:26	AIT
	2: 5	6913
	2: 5	6913
	2:42	AIT
	2:43	6913
	2:44	6913
	3:14	2143S
	7:14	6913
	7:18	6913
	8:18	3201
	9: 4	2143S
	9:22	AIT
	9:23	6913
	10: 7	AIT
	11: 6	6913
	11: 6	4848
	11: 8	6913
	11:10	AIT
	11:28	6913
	11:33	NIH
	11:38	6913
	11:41	6913
	12:15	AIT
	12:32	6913
	13:10	AIT
	13:12	AIT
	13:27	2502S
	13:33	AIT
	14: 4	6913
	14:22	6913
	14:29	6913
	15: 7	6913
	15:11	6913
	15:14	AIT
	15:23	6913
	15:26	6913
	15:29	6913
	15:31	6913
	15:34	6913
	16: 5	6913
	16: 7	3338+5126
	16:11	AIT
	16:14	6913
	16:25	6913
	16:27	6913
	16:30	6913
	16:33	6913
	16:33	NIH
	17: 5	6913
	17:15	6913
	17:16	AIT
	17:18	AIT
	18:13	6913
	18:34	9101

1Ki	18:34	**d** it the third time.	8992
	20: 7	my silver and my gold, I **d** not **refuse** him."	AIT
	20:34	as my father **d** in Samaria."	8492S
	21:11	and nobles who lived in Naboth's city **d**	6913
	22:24	**d** the spirit from the LORD **go**	AIT
	22:39	events of Ahab's reign, including all he **d,**	6913
	22:43	of his father Asa and **d** not **stray** from them;	AIT
	22:43	he **d** what was right in the eyes of	6913
	22:52	He **d** evil in the eyes of the LORD,	6913
2Ki	1:18	events of Ahaziah's reign, and what he **d,**	6913
	2:17	for three days but **d** not **find** him.	AIT
	3: 2	He **d** evil in the eyes of the LORD,	6913
	3: 3	he **d** not **turn away** from them.	AIT
	3:14	**d** not **have respect for**	AIT
	4:28	"**D** I ask you for a son, my lord?"	AIT
	4:36	And he **d.**	7924S
	6: 6	"Where **d** it **fall?"**	AIT
	8:14	"What **d** Elisha **say** to you?"	AIT
	8:18	He **d** evil in the eyes of the LORD.	6913
	8:23	events of Jehoram's reign, and all he **d,**	6913
	8:27	the ways of the house of Ahab and **d** evil in	6913
	9:11	Why **d** this madman **come** to you?"	AIT
	10:15	So he **d,** and Jehu helped him	2257+3338+5989S
	10:29	he **d** not **turn away** from the sins	AIT
	10:31	He **d** not **turn away** from the sins	AIT
	10:34	for the other events of Jehu's reign, all he **d,**	6913
	11: 9	of units of a hundred **d** just as Jehoiada	6913
	12: 2	Joash **d** what was right in the eyes of	6913
	12:15	**d** not **require an accounting**	AIT
	12:19	of the reign of Joash, and all he **d,**	6913
	13: 2	He **d** evil in the eyes of the LORD	6913
	13: 2	and he **d** not **turn away** from them.	AIT
	13: 6	But they **d** not **turn away** from the sins of	AIT
	13: 8	all he **d** and his achievements,	6913
	13:11	He **d** evil in the eyes of the LORD and did	6913
	13:11	of the LORD and **d** not **turn away**	AIT
	13:12	all he **d** and his achievements,	6913
	13:15	"Get a bow and some arrows," and he **d so.**	2256+2932+4374+8008S
	14: 3	He **d** what was right in the eyes of	6913
	14: 6	**d** not **put** the sons of the assassins **to death,**	AIT
	14:15	what he **d** and his achievements,	6913
	14:24	He **d** evil in the eyes of the LORD and did	6913
	14:24	the eyes of the LORD and **d** not **turn away**	AIT
	14:28	other events of Jeroboam's reign, all he **d,**	6913
	15: 3	He **d** what was right in the eyes of	6913
	15: 6	events of Azariah's reign, and all he **d,**	6913
	15: 9	He **d** evil in the eyes of the LORD,	6913
	15: 9	He **d** not **turn away** from the sins	AIT
	15:18	He **d** evil in the eyes of the LORD.	6913
	15:18	During his entire reign he **d** not **turn away**	AIT
	15:21	events of Menahem's reign, and all he **d,**	6913
	15:24	Pekahiah **d** evil in the eyes of the LORD.	6913
	15:24	He **d** not **turn away** from the sins	AIT
	15:26	events of Pekahiah's reign, and all he **d,**	6913
	15:28	He **d** evil in the eyes of the LORD.	6913
	15:28	He **d** not **turn away** from the sins	AIT
	15:31	other events of Pekah's reign, and all he **d,**	6913
	15:34	He **d** what was right in the eyes of	6913
	15:36	events of Jotham's reign, and what he **d,**	6913
	16: 2	he **d** not **do** what was right in the eyes of	AIT
	16:16	the priest **d** just as King Ahaz had ordered.	6913
	16:19	events of the reign of Ahaz, and what he **d,**	6913
	17: 2	He **d** evil in the eyes of the LORD,	6913
	17: 9	The Israelites **secretly d** things against	2901
	17:11	They **d** wicked things that provoked	6913
	17:14	who **d** not **trust** in the LORD their God.	AIT
	17:15	and they **d** the things	NIH
	17:19	and even Judah **d** not **keep** the commands of	AIT
	17:22	the sins of Jeroboam and **d** not **turn away**	AIT
	17:25	they **d** not **worship** the LORD;	AIT
	17:41	to do as their fathers **d.**	6913
	18: 3	He **d** what was right in the eyes of	6913
	18: 6	He held fast to the LORD and **d** not **cease**	AIT
	18: 7	the king of Assyria and **d** not **serve** him.	AIT
	19:12	**D** the gods of the nations that were destroyed by my forefathers **deliver**	AIT
	20: 7	They **d so** and applied it to the boil,	4374S
	20:13	that Hezekiah **d** not **show** them.	AIT
	20:14	"What **d** those men **say,**	AIT
	20:14	and where **d** they **come** from?"	AIT
	20:15	"What **d** they **see** in your palace?"	AIT
	20:15	that I **d** not **show** them."	AIT
	21: 2	He **d** evil in the eyes of the LORD,	6913
	21: 6	He **d** much evil in the eyes of the LORD,	6913
	21: 9	But the people **d** not **listen.**	AIT
	21: 9	so that they **d** more evil than the nations	6913
	21:16	to commit, so that they **d** evil in the eyes of	6913
	21:17	events of Manasseh's reign, and all he **d,**	6913
	21:20	He **d** evil in the eyes of the LORD.	6913
	21:22	and **d** not **walk** in the way of the LORD.	AIT
	21:25	events of Amon's reign, and what he **d,**	6913
	22: 2	He **d** what was right in the eyes of	6913
	23: 5	He **d** away with the pagan priests appointed	8697
	23: 7	and where women **d** weaving	755+1428
	23: 9	of the high places **d** not **serve** at the altar of	AIT
	23:24	This he **d** to fulfill the requirements of	6913
	23:25	like him who turned to the LORD as he **d**—	NIH
	23:26	the LORD **d** not **turn away** from the heat	AIT
	23:28	other events of Josiah's reign, and all he **d,**	6913
	23:32	He **d** evil in the eyes of the LORD.	6913
	23:37	and he **d** evil in the eyes of the LORD,	6913
	24: 5	events of Jehoiakim's reign, and all he **d,**	6913
	24: 7	The king of Egypt **d** not **march out**	AIT
	24: 9	He **d** evil in the eyes of the LORD,	6913
	24:19	He **d** evil in the eyes of the LORD,	6913
1Ch	4:27	but his brothers **d** not have many children;	NIH

1Ch	4:27	**d** not **become** as **numerous**	AIT
	10:13	he **d** not **keep** the word of the LORD and	AIT
	10:14	and **d** not **inquire** of the LORD.	AIT
	12:19	(He and his men **d** not **help** the Philistines	AIT
	13: 3	for we **d** not **inquire** of it during the reign	AIT
	13:13	He **d** not **take** the ark to be with him in	AIT
	14:11	So David **d** as God commanded him,	6913
	15:13	**d** not **bring** it up the first time that	AIT
	15:13	We **d** not **inquire** of him about how to do it	AIT
	17: 6	**d** I ever **say** to any	AIT
	17: 9	as they **d** at the beginning	NIH
	20: 3	David **d** this to all the Ammonite towns.	6913
	21: 6	**d** not **include** Levi and Benjamin in the **numbering,**	AIT
	23:11	but Jeush and Beriah **d** not **have many** sons;	AIT
	24: 2	Nadab and Abihu died before their father **d,**	NIH
	24:31	the descendants of Aaron **d,**	NIH
	27:23	David **d** not **take** the number of	AIT
	27:24	to count the men but **d** not **finish.**	AIT
2Ch	2: 3	"Send me cedar logs as you **d**	6913
	6: 8	you **d** well to have this in your heart.	3201
	7: 6	as **d** the Levites with	NIH
	7:17	you walk before me as David your father **d,**	2143S
	8: 9	But Solomon **d** not **make** slaves of	AIT
	8:15	They **d** not **deviate** from	AIT
	9: 6	But I **d** not **believe** what they said	AIT
	10:15	So the king **d** not **listen** to the people,	AIT
	12:14	He **d** evil because he had not set his heart	6913
	13:20	Jeroboam **d** not **regain** power during	AIT
	13:22	what he **d** and what he said,	2006
	14: 2	Asa **d** what was good and right in the eyes	6913
	15:17	Although he **d** not **remove** the high places	AIT
	16:12	even in his illness he **d** not **seek help** from	AIT
	17: 3	He **d** not **consult** the Baals	AIT
	17:10	that they **d** not **make war** with Jehoshaphat.	AIT
	18:23	**d** the spirit from the LORD **go**	AIT
	20: 7	**d** you not **drive out**	AIT
	20:10	from them and **d** not **destroy** them.	AIT
	20:32	of his father Asa and **d** not **stray** from them;	AIT
	20:32	he **d** what was right in the eyes of	6913
	21: 6	He **d** evil in the eyes of the LORD.	6913
	21:13	just as the house of Ahab **d.**	2388S
	22: 4	He **d** evil in the eyes of the LORD,	6913
	23: 8	The Levites and all the men of Judah **d** just	6913
	24: 2	Joash **d** what was right in the eyes of	6913
	24: 5	**d** not **act at once.**	AIT
	24:11	They **d** this regularly and collected	6913
	24:22	King Joash **d** not **remember**	AIT
	25: 2	He **d** what was right in the eyes of	6913
	25: 4	**d** not **put** their sons **to death,**	AIT
	26: 4	He **d** what was right in the eyes of	6913
	27: 2	He **d** what was right in the eyes of	6913
	27: 2	but unlike him he **d** not **enter** the temple of	AIT
	27: 3	and extensive **work** on the wall at the hill	1215
	27: 7	and the other **things** he **d,**	2006
	28: 1	he **d** not **do** what was right in the eyes of	AIT
	28:21	but that **d** not help him.	NIH
	29: 2	He **d** what was right in the eyes of	6913
	29: 6	they **d** evil in the eyes of	6913
	29: 7	They **d** not **burn** incense	AIT
	31:20	This is what Hezekiah **d** throughout Judah,	6913
	32:17	**D** not Hezekiah himself **remove**	AIT
	32:17	of the other lands **d** not **rescue** their people	AIT
	32:19	about the God of Jerusalem as they **d** about	NIH
	32:25	and he **d** not **respond** to	AIT
	32:26	as **d** the people of Jerusalem;	NIH
	32:26	the LORD's wrath **d** not **come** upon them	AIT
	33: 2	He **d** evil in the eyes of the LORD,	6913
	33: 6	He **d** much evil in the eyes of the LORD,	6913
	33: 9	so that they **d** more evil than the nations	6913
	33:22	He **d** evil in the eyes of the LORD,	6913
	33:23	he **d** not **humble himself** before the LORD;	AIT
	34: 2	He **d** what was right in the eyes of	6913
	34:12	The men **d** the work faithfully.	6913
	34:32	of Jerusalem **d** this in accordance with	6913
	34:33	they **d** not **fail** to follow the LORD,	AIT
	35:12	They **d** the same with the cattle.	NIH
	35:15	**d** not **need to leave**	AIT
	35:18	a Passover as **d** Josiah,	6913
	36: 5	He **d** evil in the eyes of the LORD his God.	6913
	36: 8	the detestable things he **d** and all	6913
	36: 9	He **d** evil in the eyes of the LORD	6913
	36:12	He **d** evil in the eyes of the LORD his God	6913
	36:12	and **d** not **humble himself** before Jeremiah	
Ezr	5:17	to see if King Cyrus **d** in fact **issue** a decree	AIT
	10:16	So the exiles **d** as was proposed.	6913
Ne	2:16	The officials **d** not **know** where I had gone	AIT
	4:16	half of my men **d** the work,	6913
	4:17	Those who carried materials **d** their work	6913
	5:13	And the people **d** as they had promised.	6913
	5:15	of reverence for God I **d** not **act** like that.	AIT
	5:16	we **d** not **acquire** any land.	AIT
	9:16	and **d** not **obey** your commands.	AIT
	9:17	Therefore you **d** not **desert** him,	AIT
	9:19	great compassion you **d** not **abandon** them	AIT
	9:19	the pillar of cloud **d** not **cease** to guide them	AIT
	9:20	You **d** not **withhold** your manna	AIT
	9:21	their clothes **d** not **wear out**	AIT
	9:21	their feet became **swollen.**	AIT
	9:28	they again **d** what was evil in your sight.	6913
	9:31	in your great mercy you **d** not **put** an end	AIT
	9:33	while we **d wrong.**	8399
	9:34	and our fathers **d** not **follow** your law;	AIT
	9:34	they **d** not **pay attention**	AIT
	9:35	they **d** not **serve** you or turn	AIT
	12:40	so **d** I, together with half the officials,	NIH
	12:45	as **d** also the singers and gatekeepers,	NIH

Ne	13:24	and **d** not **know** how to speak the language	AIT
Est	1:21	so the king **d** as Memucan proposed.	6913
	9: 5	and they **d** what they pleased	6913
	9:10	they **d** not **lay** their hands on the plunder.	AIT
	9:15	they **d** not **lay** their hands on the plunder.	AIT
	9:16	but **d** not **lay** their hands on the plunder.	AIT
Job	1:22	Job **d** not **sin** by charging God	AIT
	2:10	In all this, Job **d** not **sin** in what he said.	AIT
	3:10	for it **d** not **shut** the doors of the womb	AIT
	3:11	"Why **d** I not **perish** at birth,	AIT
	10:10	**D** you not **pour** me out	AIT
	10:18	**d** you **bring** me out	AIT
	20:19	he has seized houses he **d** not **build.**	AIT
	31:15	**D** not he who made me in the womb **make**	AIT
	31:15	**D** not the same one **form**	AIT
	31:20	and his heart **d** not **bless** me	AIT
	33:27	**d** not **get what** I deserved.	AIT
	39:17	for God **d** not **endow** her with wisdom	AIT
	42: 3	of things I **d** not **understand,**	AIT
	42: 9	and Zophar the Naamathite **d** what	6913
Ps	18:37	I **d** not **turn back** till they were destroyed.	AIT
	18:41	to the LORD, but he **d** not **answer.**	AIT
	18:43	people I **d** not **know** are subject to me.	AIT
	30: 1	**d** not **let** my enemies **gloat**	AIT
	32: 5	to you and **d** not **cover up** my iniquity.	AIT
	40: 6	Sacrifice and offering you **d** not **desire,**	AIT
	40: 6	and sin offerings you **d** not **require.**	AIT
	44: 1	our fathers have told us what you **d**	7188
	44: 3	**d** their arm **bring** them **victory,**	AIT
	52: 7	man who **d** not **make** God his stronghold	AIT
	69: 4	I am forced to restore what I **d** not **steal.**	AIT
	78:10	they **d** not **keep** God's covenant and refused	AIT
	78:12	He **d** miracles in the sight of their fathers in	6913
	78:22	for they **d** not **believe** in God or trust	AIT
	78:32	in spite of his wonders, they **d** not **believe.**	AIT
	78:38	and **d** not **destroy** them.	AIT
	78:38	and **d** not **stir up** his full wrath.	AIT
	78:42	They **d** not **remember** his power—	AIT
	78:50	he **d** not **spare** them from death	AIT
	78:56	they **d** not **keep** his statutes.	AIT
	78:67	he **d** not **choose** the tribe of Ephraim;	AIT
	81: 5	we heard a language we **d** not **understand.**	AIT
	83: 9	Do to them as you **d** to Midian,	NIH
	83: 9	as you **d** to Sisera and Jabin at	NIH
	95: 8	not harden your hearts as you **d** at Meribah,	NIH
	95: 8	as you **d** that day at Massah in the desert,	NIH
	95: 9	though they had seen what I **d.**	7189
	106: 6	We have sinned, even as our fathers **d;**	NIH
	106: 7	they **d** not **remember** your many kindnesses	AIT
	106:13	and **d** not **wait** for his counsel.	AIT
	106:24	they **d** not **believe** his promise.	AIT
	106:25	They grumbled in their tents and **d** not **obey**	AIT
	106:34	They **d** not **destroy** the peoples as	AIT
	106:39	They defiled themselves by **what** they **d;**	5126
	107:11	**d** not **let** their herds **diminish.**	AIT
	137: 7	the Edomites **d** on the day Jerusalem fell.	NIH
Pr	1:29	and **d** not **choose** to fear the LORD,	AIT
	24:29	I'll pay that man back for what he **d."**	7189
Ecc	8:10	in the city where they **d** this.	6913
SS	3: 1	I looked for him but **d** not **find** him.	AIT
	3: 2	So I looked for him but **d** not **find** him.	AIT
	5: 6	I looked for him but **d** not **find** him.	AIT
	5: 6	I called him but he **d** not **answer.**	AIT
	6: 1	Which way **d** your lover **turn,**	AIT
Isa	5: 4	why **d** it **yield** only bad?	AIT
	10: 3	and lift up a club against you, as Egypt **d.**	NIH
	10:26	as he **d** in Egypt.	NIH
	20: 2	he **d** so, going around stripped and barefoot.	6913
	22: 2	nor **d** they **die** in battle.	AIT
	22:11	but you **d** not **look** to the One who made it,	AIT
	28:21	The LORD will rise up as he **d**	NIH
	29:16	"He **d** not **make me"?**	AIT
	37:12	**D** the gods of the nations that were destroyed by my forefathers **deliver**	AIT
	39: 2	that Hezekiah **d** not **show** them.	AIT
	39: 3	"What **d** those men **say,**	AIT
	39: 3	and where **d** they **come** from?"	AIT
	39: 4	"What **d** they **see** in your palace?"	AIT
	39: 4	that I **d** not **show** them."	AIT
	40:14	**d** the LORD **consult**	AIT
	42:24	they **d** not **obey** his law.	AIT
	42:25	yet they **d** not **understand;**	AIT
	42:25	but they **d** not **take** it to heart.	AIT
	44: 8	**D** I not **proclaim** it	AIT
	45:18	he **d** not **create** it to be empty,	AIT
	47: 7	But you **d** not **consider** these things	AIT
	48: 5	that you could not say, 'My idols **d** them;	6913
	48:21	They **d** not **thirst** when he led them through	AIT
	50: 1	Or to which of my creditors **d** I **sell** you?	AIT
	50: 6	I **d** not **hide** my face from mocking	AIT
	53: 7	yet he **d** not **open** his mouth;	AIT
	53: 7	so he **d** not **open** his mouth.	AIT
	57:10	and so you **d** not **faint.**	AIT
	63:13	they **d** not **stumble;**	AIT
	64: 3	when you **d** awesome things that we did	6913
	64: 3	that we **d** not **expect,**	AIT
	65: 1	"I revealed myself to those who **d** not **ask**	AIT
	65: 1	I was found by those who **d** not **seek** me.	AIT
	65: 1	To a nation that **d** not **call** on my name,	AIT
	65:12	for I called but you **d** not **answer,**	AIT
	65:12	I spoke but you **d** not **listen.**	AIT
	66: 4	You **d** evil in my sight	6913
	66: 4	They **d** evil in my sight	6913
Jer	2: 5	"What fault **d** your fathers **find** in me,	AIT
	2: 6	They **d** not **ask,** 'Where is the LORD,	AIT
	2: 8	priests **d** not **ask,** 'Where is the LORD?'	AIT
	2: 8	Those who deal with the law **d** not **know** me	AIT

Jer	2:21	*d* you **turn** against me **into** a corrupt	AIT
	2:30	*they d* not **respond to** correction.	AIT
	2:34	though *you d* not **catch** them breaking in.	AIT
	3: 7	to me but *she d* not,	8740^S
	3:10	her unfaithful sister Judah *d* not **return**	AIT
	7:12	and see what *I d* to it because of	6913
	7:13	but *you d* not **listen;**	AIT
	7:13	I called you, but *you d* not **answer.**	AIT
	7:14	what *I d* to Shiloh I will now do to	6913
	7:15	just as *I d* all your brothers,	8959^S
	7:22	*d* not *just* **give** them **commands**	AIT
	7:24	But *they d* not **listen** to me or pay attention.	AIT
	7:26	*they d* not **listen** to me or pay attention.	AIT
	7:26	and *d* more **evil** than their forefathers.'	8317
	7:31	something *I d* not **command,**	AIT
	7:31	nor *d it* **enter** my mind.	AIT
	10:11	who *d* not **make** the heavens and the earth,	AIT
	11: 8	But *they d* not **listen** or pay attention;	AIT
	11: 8	to follow but that *they d* not **keep.'** "	AIT
	11:19	*I d* not **realize** that they had plotted	AIT
	14:15	*I d* not **send** them, yet they are saying,	AIT
	15: 4	of Hezekiah king of Judah *d* in Jerusalem.	6913
	16:11	They forsook me and *d* not **keep** my law.	AIT
	16:19	worthless idols *that d* them no **good.**	3603
	17:11	that hatches eggs *it d* not **lay** is	AIT
	17:23	Yet *they d* not **listen** or pay attention;	AIT
	19: 5	something *I d* not **command** or mention,	AIT
	19: 5	nor *d it* **enter** my mind.	AIT
	20:17	For *he d* not **kill** me in the womb,	AIT
	20:18	*d I* ever **come out**	AIT
	22:15	*D* not your father **have food**	AIT
	22:15	*He d* what was right and just,	6913
	23:21	*I d* not **send** these prophets,	AIT
	23:21	*I d* not **speak** to them,	AIT
	23:32	yet *I d* not **send** or appoint them.	AIT
	25: 7	"But *you d* not **listen** to me,"	AIT
	26:19	"*D* Hezekiah king of Judah or anyone else in Judah **put him to death?**	AIT
	26:19	*D* not Hezekiah **fear** the LORD	AIT
	26:19	*d* not the LORD **relent,** so that he *did not* **bring** the disaster	AIT
	26:19	**relent,** so that he *d* not **bring** the disaster	AIT
	26:20	and this land as Jeremiah *d.*	NIH
	27:20	of Babylon *d* not **take away**	AIT
	29:16	your countrymen who *d* not **go** with you	AIT
	29:23	which *I d* not **tell** them to do.	AIT
	29:31	even though *I d* not **send** him,	AIT
	32:23	but *they d* not **obey** you or follow your law;	AIT
	32:23	*they d* not do what you commanded them	AIT
	32:35	nor *d it* **enter** my mind,	AIT
	34:14	*d* not **listen** to me or pay attention to me.	AIT
	34:15	Recently you repented and *d* what is right	6913
	35:17	I spoke to them, but *they d* not **listen;**	AIT
	35:17	I called to them, but *they d* not **answer.'** "	AIT
	36: 8	of Neriah *d* everything Jeremiah	6913
	36:17	how *d you* **come to write** all this?	AIT
	36:17	"*D* Jeremiah dictate it?"	NIH
	36:24	nor *d they* **tear** their clothes.	AIT
	36:29	that scroll and said, "Why *d you* **write** on it	6913
	38:12	to pad the ropes." Jeremiah *d* so,	6913
	38:15	Even if *I d* **give** you **counsel,**	AIT
	38:27	All the officials *d* **come** to Jeremiah	AIT
	40: 3	against the LORD and *d* not **obey** him.	AIT
	40:14	of Ahikam *d* not **believe** them.	AIT
	41: 8	So he let them alone and *d* not **kill** them	AIT
	44: 5	But *they d* not **listen** or pay attention;	AIT
	44: 5	*they d* not **turn** from their wickedness	AIT
	44:17	our kings and our officials in the towns	6913
	44:19	*d* not our husbands **know**	NIH
	44:21	"*D* not the LORD **remember**	AIT
	44:22	and the detestable things *you d,*	6913
	48:11	So she tastes as she *d,*	6641^S
	52: 2	*He d* **evil** in the eyes of the LORD,	6913
La	1: 9	*she d* not **consider** her future.	AIT
	2: 8	and *d* not **withhold** his hand	AIT
	2:14	*they d* not **expose** your sin	AIT
	4:12	The kings of the earth *d* not **believe,**	AIT
	4:12	nor *d* any of the world's people,	NIH
Eze	1: 9	*they d* not **turn** as they moved.	AIT
	1:17	the wheels *d* not **turn about** as	AIT
	3:20	*you d* not **warn** him, he will die for his sin.	AIT
	3:20	The righteous things *he d* will not	6913
	6:10	*I d* not **threaten** in vain	AIT
	10:11	the wheels *d* not **turn about** as	AIT
	10:16	the wheels *d* not **leave** their side.	AIT
	12: 7	So *I d* as I was commanded.	6913
	12: 9	*d* not that rebellious house of Israel **ask**	AIT
	16:22	and your prostitution *you d* not **remember**	AIT
	16:43	" 'Because *you d* not **remember** the days	AIT
	16:43	*D you* not **add** lewdness	AIT
	16:48	and her daughters never *d* what you	6913
	16:49	*they d* not **help** the poor and needy.	AIT
	16:50	They were haughty and *d* detestable things	6913
	16:50	*I d* **away** with them as you have seen.	6073
	16:51	Samaria did not **commit** half the sins you did.	AIT
	16:51	Samaria did not commit half the sins you *d.*	NIH
	17:18	in pledge and yet *d* all these things,	AIT
	18:18	robbed his brother and *d* what was wrong	6913
	20: 8	*d* not **get rid of**	AIT
	20: 8	nor *d they* **forsake** the idols of Egypt.	AIT
	20: 9	of my name *I d* what would keep it	6913
	20:13	*They d* not **follow** my decrees,	AIT
	20:14	of my name *I d* what would keep it	6913
	20:16	and *d* not **follow** my decrees	AIT
	20:17	on them with pity and *d* not **destroy** them	AIT
	20:21	*They d* not **follow** my decrees,	AIT
	20:22	of my name *I d* what would keep it	6913
Eze	20:30	the way your fathers *d* and lust	NIH
	23: 8	*She d* not **give up** the prostitution she began	AIT
	23:39	That is what *they d* in my house.	6913
	24: 7	*she d* not **pour** it on the ground,	AIT
	24:18	The next morning *I d* as	6913
	27:12	" 'Tarshish *d* **business with** you because	6086
	27:16	" 'Aram *d* **business with** you because	6086
	27:18	*d* **business with** you in wine from Helbon	6086
	27:21	*they d* **business with** you in lambs,	6086
	29:20	for his efforts because *he and his army d* it	6913
	33: 5	of the trumpet but *d* not **take warning,**	AIT
	34: 8	and because my shepherds *d* not **search for**	AIT
	35: 6	Since *you d* not **hate** bloodshed,	AIT
	40:36	as *d* its alcoves,	NIH
	48:11	and not **go astray** as the Levites did when	AIT
	48:11	and did not go astray as the Levites *d* when	9494^S
Da	2:15	"Why *d* the king issue such	NIH
	5:23	But *you d* not **honor** the God who holds	AIT
	6:12	"*D you* not **publish** a decree that during	AIT
	8: 4	*He d* as he pleased and became great.	6913
	8:12	It prospered in everything *it d,*	6913
	9:14	The LORD *d* not **hesitate** to bring	9193
	10: 7	the men with me *d* not **see** it,	AIT
	11:24	nor his forefathers *d.*	6913
	12: 8	I heard, but *I d* not **understand.**	6913
Hos	10: 3	"We have no king because *we d* not **revere**	AIT
	10: 9	*D* not war **overtake** the evildoers	AIT
	11: 3	*they d* not **realize** it was I who healed them.	AIT
Am	4: 8	for water but *d* not **get enough** to drink,	AIT
	4:10	"I sent plagues among you as I *d* to Egypt.	NIH
	5:25	"*D you* bring me sacrifices	AIT
	6:13	"*D we* not **take** Karnaim	AIT
	9: 7	"*D I* not **bring** Israel **up**	AIT
Jnh	1:13	*d* their best to **row**	AIT
	3:10	When God saw **what** they *d* and	5126
	3:10	he had compassion and *d* not **bring**	AIT
	4:10	though *you d* not **tend** it or make it grow.	AIT
Hab	1: 3	*D* you rage against the sea when you rode	NIH
Zep	3: 7	to act corruptly in all they *d.*	6613
Hag	2:17	mildew and hail, yet *you d* not **turn** to me,'	NIH
Zec	1: 6	*d* not my words and my decrees, which I commanded my servants the prophets, **overtake** your forefathers?	AIT
	7:13	" 'When I called, *they d* not **listen;**	AIT
	8:11	with the remnant of this people as *I d* in the	NIH
Mal	2:10	*D* not one God **create** us?	AIT
	3:14	What *d* we gain by carrying out his	NIH
Mt	1:19	a righteous man and *d* not want	NIG
	1:24	*he d* what the angel of the Lord	4472
	7:22	Lord, *d we* not **prophesy** in your name,	AIT
	7:25	yet *it d* not **fall,**	AIT
	9:19	and so *d* his disciples.	NIG
	10:34	*I d* not **come** to bring peace, but a sword.	AIT
	11: 7	"What *d you* **go out** into the desert to see?	AIT
	11: 8	If not, what *d you* **go out** to see?	AIT
	11: 9	Then what *d you* **go out** to see?	AIT
	11:17	and *you d* not **dance;**	AIT
	11:17	we sang a dirge, and *you d* not **mourn.'**	AIT
	11:20	because *they d* not **repent.**	AIT
	12: 3	"Haven't you read what David *d* when he	4472
	13: 5	where *it d* not **have** much soil.	AIT
	13:17	to see what you see but *d* not **see** it,	AIT
	13:17	and to hear what you hear but *d* not **hear** it.	AIT
	13:27	Where then *d* the weeds come from?'	NIG
	13:28	" 'An enemy *d* this,' he replied.	4472
	13:34	*he d* not **say** anything to them without using	AIT
	13:54	"Where *d* this man get this wisdom	NIG
	13:56	then *d* this man get all these things?"	NIG
	13:58	And *he d* not **do** many miracles there	AIT
	14:31	he said, "why *d you* **doubt?**"	AIT
	15:23	Jesus *d* not **answer** a word.	AIT
	17:12	and *they d* not **recognize** him,	AIT
	18:13	about the ninety-nine that *d* not **wander off.**	AIT
	19: 7	"*d* Moses **command** that a man give his wife a certificate of divorce	AIT
	20: 5	and the ninth hour and *d* the same thing.	4472
	20:28	as the Son of Man *d* not **come** to be served,	4472
	21: 6	and *d* as Jesus had instructed them.	4472
	21:15	the law saw the wonderful things *he d* and	4472
	21:20	*d* the fig tree **wither**	AIT
	21:25	John's baptism—where *d* it come from?	NIG
	21:30	He answered, 'I will, sir,' but *he d* not **go.**	AIT
	21:31	of the two *d* what his father wanted?"	4472
	21:32	and *you d* not **believe** him,	AIT
	21:32	but the tax collectors and the prostitutes *d.*	4409^S
	21:32	*you d* not **repent** and believe him.	AIT
	22: 8	but those I invited *d* not **deserve** to come.	AIT
	22:12	'how *d you* **get in** here	AIT
	25: 3	but *d* not **take** any oil with them.	AIT
	25:37	when *d we* **see** you hungry and feed you,	AIT
	25:38	When *d we* **see** you a stranger and invite you	AIT
	25:39	When *d we* **see** you sick or in prison and go	AIT
	25:40	whatever *you d* for one of the least	4472
	25:40	*you d* for me.'	4472
	25:43	*d* not **invite** me **in,**	AIT
	25:43	I needed clothes and *you d* not **clothe** me,	AIT
	25:43	in prison and *you d* not **look after** me.'	AIT
	25:44	when *d we* **see** you hungry or thirsty or	AIT
	25:44	and *d* not **help** you?'	AIT
	25:45	whatever *you d* not **do** for one of the least	AIT
	25:45	*you d* for me.'	AIT
	26:12	*she d* it to prepare me for burial.	4472
	26:19	the disciples *d* as Jesus had directed them	4472
	26:55	and *d* not **arrest** me.	AIT
	26:60	But *they d* not **find** any,	AIT
	28:15	the money and *d* as they were instructed.	4472
Mk	2:25	"Have you never read what David *d*	4472
Mk	4: 5	where *it d* not **have** much soil.	AIT
	4: 7	so that *they d* not **bear** grain.	AIT
	4:34	*He d* not **say** anything to them without using	AIT
	5:19	Jesus *d* not **let** him, but said,	AIT
	5:37	*He d* not **let** anyone follow him except	AIT
	6: 2	"Where *d* this man get these things?"	NIG
	6:17	*He d* this because of Herodias,	NIG
	6:26	*he d* not **want** to refuse her.	AIT
	6:31	that they *d* not even have a chance to eat,	NIG
	7:24	a house and *d* not **want** anyone to know it;	AIT
	7:36	But the more *he d* so,	1403^S
	8: 6	and *they d* so.	4192^S
	8:19	many basketfuls of pieces *d you* **pick up?**"	AIT
	8:20	many basketfuls of pieces *d you* **pick up?**"	AIT
	9: 6	(*He d* not **know** what to say,	AIT
	9:30	Jesus *d* not **want** anyone to know	AIT
	9:32	But they *d* **not understand** what he meant	AIT
	10: 3	"What *d* Moses **command** you?" he replied.	AIT
	10:45	the Son of Man *d* not **come** to be served,	AIT
	14: 8	*She d* what she could.	4472
	14:40	*They d* not **know** what to say to him.	AIT
	14:49	and *you d* not **arrest** me.	AIT
	14:55	but *they d* not **find** any.	AIT
	14:56	but their statements *d* not agree.	1639
	14:59	Yet even then their testimony *d* not agree.	1639
	15: 8	to do for them what he usually *d.*	NIG
	15:23	but he *d* not **take** it.	AIT
	16:11	*they d* not **believe** it.	AIT
	16:13	but *they d* not **believe** them either.	AIT
Lk	1:20	because *you d* not **believe** my words,	AIT
	2:45	When *they d* not **find** him,	AIT
	2:50	they *d* not **understand** what he was saying	AIT
	4:23	that *you d* in Capernaum.' "	1181
	6: 3	"Have you never read what David *d*	4472
	6:10	"Stretch out your hand." He *d* so,	4472
	7: 7	*d* not even **consider** myself **worthy**	AIT
	7:24	"What *d you* **go out** into the desert to see?	AIT
	7:25	If not, what *d you* **go out** to see?	AIT
	7:26	But what *d you* **go out** to see?	AIT
	7:32	and *you d* not **dance;**	AIT
	7:32	we sang a dirge, and *you d* not **cry.'**	AIT
	7:44	*You d* not **give** me any water for my feet,	AIT
	7:45	*You d* not **give** me a kiss, but this woman,	AIT
	7:46	*d* not **put** oil on my head,	AIT
	8:51	*he d* not **let** anyone go in	AIT
	9:15	The disciples *d* so,	4472
	9:33	(*He d* not **know** what he was saying.)	AIT
	9:43	at all that Jesus *d,*	4472
	9:45	But they *d* not **understand** what this meant.	AIT
	9:45	so that *they d* not **grasp** it,	AIT
	9:53	but the *people* there *d* not **welcome** him,	AIT
	10:24	to see what you see but *d* not **see** it,	AIT
	10:24	and to hear what you hear but *d* not **hear** it."	AIT
	11:38	that Jesus *d* not first **wash** before the meal,	AIT
	11:40	*D* not the one who made the outside **make**	AIT
	11:48	of what your forefathers *d;*	2240
	13: 6	but *d* not **find** any.	AIT
	17: 9	the servant because *he d* what he was told	4472
	18:34	The disciples *d* not **understand** any of this.	AIT
	18:34	*they d* not **know** what he was talking about.	AIT
	19:21	You take out what *you d* not **put in**	AIT
	19:21	not put in and reap what *you d* not **sow.'**	AIT
	19:22	You knew, *d you,* that I am a hard man,	NIG
	19:22	taking out what *I d* not **put in,**	AIT
	19:22	and reaping what *I d* not **sow?**	AIT
	19:27	of mine who *d* not **want** me to be king	AIT
	19:44	because *you d* not **recognize** the time	AIT
	22:35	bag or sandals, *d you* **lack** anything?"	AIT
	22:53	and *you d* not **lay** a hand on me.	AIT
	24: 3	*they d* not **find** the body of the Lord Jesus.	AIT
	24:11	But *they d* not **believe** the women,	AIT
	24:24	but him *they d* not **see.**"	AIT
	24:26	*D* not the Christ **have** to suffer these things	AIT
	24:41	*while* they still *d* not **believe** it because	AIT
Jn	1:10	the world *d* not **recognize** him.	AIT
	1:11	but his own *d* not **receive** him.	AIT
	1:20	*d* not fail to **confess,**	AIT
	1:31	I myself *d* not **know** him,	AIT
	1:41	The first thing Andrew *d* was	NIG
	2: 8	of the banquet." They *d* so,	5770^S
	2: 9	*He d* not **realize** where it had come from,	AIT
	2:25	*He d* not **need** man's testimony about man,	AIT
	3:17	For God *d* not **send** his Son into the world	AIT
	4:12	*d* also his sons and his flocks and herds?"	NIG
	4:29	a man who told me everything *I* ever *d.*	4472
	4:39	"He told me everything *I* ever *d.*"	4472
	6:11	He *d* the same with the fish.	NIG
	6:14	the miraculous sign that Jesus *d,*	4472
	6:25	"Rabbi, when *d you* **get** here?"	AIT
	6:64	the beginning which of them *d* not **believe**	AIT
	7: 5	even his own brothers *d* not **believe** in him.	AIT
	7:14	the Feast *d* Jesus **go up** to the temple courts	AIT
	7:15	*d* this man **get** such **learning**	AIT
	7:21	Jesus said to them, "I *d* one miracle,	4472
	7:22	(though actually *it d* not **come** from Moses,	AIT
	7:36	What *d he* **mean** when he said,	AIT
	8:27	*They d* not **understand**	AIT
	8:39	"then you would do the things Abraham *d.*	NIG
	8:40	Abraham *d* not **do** such things.	AIT
	8:52	Abraham died and so *d* the prophets,	NIG
	8:53	He died, and so *d* the prophets.	NIG
	8:55	If I said I *d* not, I would be a liar like you,	NIG
	9:18	The Jews still *d* not **believe**	AIT
	9:26	they asked him, "What *d he* do to you?	AIT
	9:26	How *d he* **open** your eyes?"	AIT
	9:27	and *you d* not **listen.**	AIT
	10: 6	*d* not **understand** what he was telling them.	AIT

Jn	10: 8	but the sheep *d* not **listen** *to* them.	*AIT*
	10:25	Jesus answered, "I *d* **tell** you,	*AIT*
	11:40	"*D* I not **tell** you that if you believed,	*AIT*
	11:45	and had seen what Jesus *d*,	*4472*
	11:51	but *she* **d** not **say** this on his own,	*AIT*
	12: 6	He *d* not **say** this because he cared about	*AIT*
	12:16	At first his disciples *d* not **understand** all	*AIT*
		this.	
	12:16	after Jesus was glorified *d* they **realize**	*AIT*
	12:47	For I *d* not **come** to judge the world,	*AIT*
	12:49	For I *d* not **speak** of my own accord,	*AIT*
	15:16	You *d* not **choose** me,	*AIT*
	15:24	not done among them what no one else *d*,	*4472*
	16: 4	I *d* not **tell** you this at first	*AIT*
	18:23	if I spoke the truth, why *d you* **strike** me?"	*AIT*
	18:28	the Jews *d* not **enter** the palace;	*AIT*
	18:34	"or *d* others **talk** to you about me?"	*AIT*
	19:24	So this is what the soldiers **d**.	*4472*
	19:31	Because the Jews *d* not want the bodies left	*NIG*
	19:33	they *d* not **break** his legs.	*AIT*
	20: 5	of linen lying there but *d* not **go in**.	*AIT*
	20: 9	(They still *d* not **understand** from Scripture	*AIT*
	20:14	but *she* **d** not **realize** that it was Jesus.	*AIT*
	20:30	Jesus *d* many other miraculous signs in	*4472*
	21: 4	the disciples *d* not **realize** that it was Jesus.	*AIT*
	21: 6	When *they* **d**, they were unable to haul	*965S*
	21:13	and *d* the same with the fish.	*NIG*
	21:23	But Jesus *d* not **say** that he would not die;	*AIT*
	21:25	Jesus *d* many other things as well.	*4472*
Ac	2:22	which God *d* among you through him,	*4472*
	2:31	nor *d* his body see decay.	*AIT*
	2:34	For David *d* not **ascend** to heaven,	*AIT*
	3: 4	Peter looked straight at him, as *d* John.	*NIG*
	3:17	as *d* your leaders.	*NIG*
	4: 7	or what name *d* you **do** this?"	*AIT*
	4:28	They *d* what your power	*4472*
	5:22	the officers *d* not **find** them there.	*NIG*
	5:26	They *d* not use force,	*NIG*
	6: 8	*d* great wonders and miraculous signs	*4472*
	7:25	but they *d* not.	*5317S*
	7:32	Moses trembled with fear and *d* not **dare**	*AIT*
	7:36	He led them out of Egypt and *d* **wonders**	*4472*
	7:42	" '*D* you **bring** me sacrifices	*AIT*
	7:52	a prophet your fathers *d* not **persecute**?	*AIT*
	8: 6	and saw the miraculous signs *he* **d**,	*4472*
	8:32	so *he* **d** not **open** his mouth.	*AIT*
	8:32	and the eunuch *d* not **see** him again,	*AIT*
	9: 7	they heard the sound but *d* not **see** anyone.	*AIT*
	9: 9	and *d* not **eat** or drink anything.	*AIT*
	10:39	"We are witnesses of everything *he* **d** in	*4472*
	11:30	This *they* **d**, sending their gift to the elders	*4472*
	12: 8	And Peter *d* so.	*4472*
	12:19	for him and *d* not **find** him,	*AIT*
	12:23	because Herod *d* not **give** praise to God,	*AIT*
	13:27	and their rulers *d* not **recognize** Jesus,	*AIT*
	13:37	from the dead *d* not **see** decay.	*AIT*
	15: 8	just as he *d* to us.	*NIG*
	15:38	Paul *d* not **think it wise** to take him,	*AIT*
	17: 4	as *d* a large number of God-fearing Greeks	*NIG*
	17: 6	But when they *d* not **find** them,	*AIT*
	17:12	as *d* also a number	*NIG*
	17:27	God *d* this so that men would seek him	*NIG*
	19: 2	"*D* you **receive** the Holy Spirit	*AIT*
	19: 3	**baptism** *d you* **receive?**"	*AIT*
	19:11	God *d* extraordinary miracles through Paul,	*4472*
	19:32	*d* not even know why they were there.	*NIG*
	20:35	In everything I *d*, I showed you that	*NIG*
	22: 9	but *they* **d** not **understand** the voice	*AIT*
	23: 5	I *d* not **realize** that he was the high priest;	*AIT*
	24:12	My accusers *d* not **find** me arguing	*AIT*
	25:17	*d* not **delay** the case, but convened the court	*AIT*
		the next day and **ordered**	
	25:18	*they* **d** not **charge** him with any of	*AIT*
	26:10	And that is just what I *d* in Jerusalem.	*4472*
	27: 7	*d* not **allow us to hold** our course,	*AIT*
	27:39	*they* **d** not **recognize** the land,	*AIT*
Ro	1:28	*d* not **think it worthwhile**	*AIT*
	3: 3	What if some *d* not **have faith?**	*AIT*
	3:25	He *d* this to demonstrate his justice,	*NIG*
	3:26	he *d* it to demonstrate his justice at	*NIG*
	4:20	Yet he *d* not **waver**	*AIT*
	5:14	even for those who *d* not **sin** by breaking	*AIT*
	5:14	a command, as *d* Adam, who was a pattern	*NIG*
	5:15	*d* God's grace and the gift that came by the	*AIT*
		grace of the one man, Jesus Christ, **overflow**	
	6:21	What benefit *d* you **reap** at that time from	*AIT*
	7:13	*D* that which is good, then, **become**	*AIT*
	8: 3	God *d* by sending his own Son in	*NIG*
	8:15	For *you* **d** not **receive** a spirit	*AIT*
	8:32	He who *d* not **spare** his own Son,	*AIT*
	9:20	'Why *d you* **make** me like this?' "	*AIT*
	9:23	What if he *d* this to make the riches	*NIG*
	9:30	Gentiles, who *d* not **pursue** righteousness,	*AIT*
	10: 3	*Since they* **d not know** the righteousness	*AIT*
	10: 3	*they* **d** not **submit** to God's righteousness.	*AIT*
	10:18	But I ask: *D they* not **hear?**	*AIT*
	10:18	Of course they *d*:	*NIG*
	10:19	*D* Israel not **understand?**	*AIT*
	10:20	"I was found by those who *d* not **seek** me;	*AIT*
	10:20	to those who *d* not **ask for** me."	*AIT*
	11: 1	I ask then: *D* God **reject** his people?	*AIT*
	11: 2	God *d* not **reject** his people,	*AIT*
	11: 7	so earnestly it *d* not **obtain**,	*AIT*
	11: 7	but the elect **d**.	*NIG*
	11:11	*D they* **stumble** so as to fall	*AIT*
	11:21	For if God *d* not **spare** the natural branches,	*AIT*
	15: 3	For even Christ *d* not **please** himself but,	*AIT*

1Co	1:14	I am thankful that *I d* not **baptize** any	*AIT*
	1:17	For Christ *d* not **send** me to baptize,	*AIT*
	1:21	through its wisdom *d* not **know** him,	*AIT*
	2: 1	I *d* not **come** with eloquence	*AIT*
	4: 7	What do you have that *you* **d** not **receive?**	*AIT*
	4: 7	And if *you* **d** **receive** it,	*AIT*
	4: 7	why do you boast as though you *d* not?	*NIG*
	5: 2	of your fellowship the man who *d* this?	*4556*
	5: 3	on the one who **d** this,	*2981*
	7:30	as if they *d* not;	*NIG*
	9:12	But *we* **d** not **use** this right.	*AIT*
	10: 6	on evil things as they **d**.	*2121S*
	10: 8	as some of them **d—**	*4519S*
	10: 9	as some of them **d—**	*4279S*
	10:10	And do not grumble, as some of them **d—**	*1197S*
	11: 8	For man *d* not **come** from woman,	*AIT*
	14:36	*D* the word of God **originate**	*AIT*
	15:15	But he *d* not **raise** him if in fact the dead are	*AIT*
	15:46	The spiritual *d* not come first,	*NIG*
2Co	1:17	When I planned this, *d I* **do** it lightly?	*AIT*
	1:23	to spare you that I *d* not **return** to Corinth.	*AIT*
	2: 3	I wrote **as I** *d* so that when I came	*899+4047*
	2:13	*because* **I d** not **find** my brother Titus there.	*AIT*
	7: 8	Though *I d* **regret** it—	*AIT*
	7:12	not on account of the one who *d* the **wrong**	*92*
	8: 5	And they *d* not do as we expected,	*NIG*
	8:15	*d* not **have too much**,	*AIT*
	8:15	*d* not **have too little.**"	*AIT*
	10:14	for *we* **d** **get** as far as you with the gospel	*AIT*
	12:17	*D* I **exploit** you through any of	*AIT*
	12:18	Titus *d* not **exploit** you, did he?	*AIT*
	12:18	Titus did not exploit you, *d* he?	*NIG*
	12:18	*D* we not **act** in the same spirit and follow	*AIT*
Gal	1:12	I *d* not **receive** it from any man,	*AIT*
	1:16	I *d* not **consult** any man,	*AIT*
	1:17	nor *d I* **go up** to Jerusalem	*AIT*
	2: 2	But I *d* this privately to those who seemed	*NIG*
	2: 5	*We* **d** not **give in** to them for a moment,	*AIT*
	3: 2	*D* you **receive** the Spirit by observing	*AIT*
	4: 8	Formerly, *when you d* not **know** God,	*AIT*
	4:14	*d* not **treat** me **with contempt** or scorn.	*AIT*
	5:21	I warn you, *as I d* **before**,	*4625S*
Eph	4:20	*d* not **come** to **know**	*AIT*
Php	2: 6	*d* not **consider** equality with God something	*AIT*
	2:16	the day of Christ that *I d* not **run** or labor	*AIT*
1Th	2: 5	nor *d* we put on a mask to cover up greed—	*NIG*
	2:18	certainly I, Paul, *d*, again and again—	*NIG*
	4: 7	For God *d* not **call** us to be impure,	*AIT*
	5: 9	For God *d* not **appoint** us to suffer wrath	*AIT*
2Th	3: 8	nor *d we* **eat** anyone's food without paying	*AIT*
	3: 9	We *d* this, not because we do not have	*NIG*
2Ti	1: 3	whom I serve, as my forefathers *d*,	*NIG*
	1: 7	For God *d* not **give** us a spirit of timidity,	*AIT*
	4:14	the metalworker *d* me a great deal of harm.	*1892*
Phm	1:14	But I *d* not **want** to do anything	*AIT*
Heb	1: 5	For to which of the angels *d* God ever **say**,	*AIT*
	1:13	To which of the angels *d* God ever **say**,	*AIT*
	3: 8	do not harden your hearts as you *d* in	*AIT*
	3: 9	and for forty years saw what I **d**.	*2240+3836*
	3:15	do not harden your hearts as you *d* in	*NIG*
	3:18	And to whom *d* God **swear**	*AIT*
	4: 2	gospel preached to us, just as they *d*;	*NIG*
	4: 2	*d* not **combine** it with	*AIT*
	4: 6	the gospel preached to them *d* not **go in**,	*NIG*
	4:10	just as God *d* from his.	*NIG*
	5: 5	*d* not **take** upon himself the **glory**	*AIT*
	6:18	God *d* this so that,	*NIG*
	7: 6	*d* not **trace** *his* **descent**	*AIT*
	8: 9	*d* not **remain faithful** to	*AIT*
	9:12	He *d* not **enter** by means of the blood	*AIT*
	9:24	For Christ *d* not **enter** a man-made	*AIT*
	9:25	Nor *d* he enter heaven to offer himself	*NIG*
	10: 5	"Sacrifice and offering *you* **d** not **desire**,	*AIT*
	10: 8	and sin offerings *you* **d** not **desire**,	*AIT*
	11: 4	a better sacrifice than Cain **d**.	*NIG*
	11: 5	*d* not **experience death**;	*AIT*
	11: 8	*though he* **d** not **know** where he was going.	*AIT*
	11: 9	he lived in tents, as *d* Isaac and Jacob,	*NIG*
	11:13	*They* **d** not **receive** the things promised;	*AIT*
	11:19	*he* **d** **receive** Isaac back from death.	*AIT*
	12:25	If they *d* not **escape**	*AIT*
Jas	2:21	for what he *d* when he offered his son Isaac	*2240*
	2:22	his faith was made complete by what he **d**.	*2240*
	2:25	for what she *d* when she gave lodging to	*2240*
	5:17	and it *d* not **rain** on the land for three and	*AIT*
1Pe	2:23	he *d* not **retaliate**;	*AIT*
2Pe	1:16	*We* **d** not **follow** cleverly invented stories	*AIT*
	2: 4	if God *d* not **spare** angels when they sinned,	*AIT*
	2: 5	if he *d* not **spare** the ancient world	*AIT*
1Jn	2: 6	to live in him must walk as Jesus **d**.	*4344S*
	2:19	*d* not really **belong to**	*AIT*
	3: 1	not know us is that *it d* not **know** him.	*AIT*
	3:12	And why *d* he **murder** him?	*AIT*
	5: 6	He *d* not come by water only,	*NIG*
Jude	1: 6	the angels who *d* not **keep** their positions	*AIT*
	1: 9	*d* not **dare** to bring a slanderous accusation	*AIT*
Rev	2: 5	Repent and do the things you *d* at first.	*NIG*
	2:13	*You* **d** not **renounce** your faith in me,	*AIT*
	2:19	that you are now doing more than you *d*	*NIG*
	7:13	and where *d they* **come** from?"	*AIT*
	9: 4	but only those people who *d* not **have**	*AIT*
	9:20	not killed by these plagues still *d* not **repent**	*AIT*
	9:20	*they* **d** not stop **worshiping** demons,	*AIT*
	9:21	Nor *d* they **repent** of their murders,	*AIT*
	12:11	*they* **d** not **love** their lives so much as	*AIT*
	14: 4	These are those who *d* not **defile** *themselves*	*AIT*

Rev	20: 5	*d* not **come to life**	*AIT*
	21:22	I *d* not **see** a temple in the city,	*AIT*

DIDN'T (44) [DO, NOT]

Ge	12:18	"Why *d* you tell me she was your wife?	*4202*
	20: 5	and *d* she also **say**, 'He is my brother'?	*AIT*
	29:25	I served you for Rachel, *d* I?	*4202*
	31:27	Why *d* you tell me,	*4202*
	31:28	You *d* even let me kiss my grandchildren	*4202*
	38:22	"I *d* find her.	*4202*
	38:23	but you *d* find her."	*4202*
	42:22	"*D* I tell you not to sin against the boy?	*4202*
Ex	5:14	"Why *d* you meet your quota	*4202*
	14:12	*D* we say to you in Egypt, 'Leave us alone;	*4202*
Lev	10:17	"Why *d* you eat the sin offering in	*4202*
Nu	22:37	Why *d* you come to me?	*4202*
Jdg	8: 1	Why *d* you call us when you went	*1194*
	11: 7	"*D* you hate me and drive me	*4202*
	11:26	Why *d* you retake them during that time?	*4202*
	12: 2	*d* you save me out of their hands.	*4202*
	13: 6	I *d* ask him where he came from,	*4202*
	13: 6	and he *d* tell me his name.	*4202*
1Sa	26:15	Why *d* you guard your lord the king?	*4202*
2Sa	11:10	Why *d* you go home?"	*4202*
	11:20	*D* you know they would shoot arrows from	*4202*
	11:21	*D* a woman throw an upper millstone	*4202*
	16:17	Why *d* you go with your friend?"	*4202*
	18:11	Why *d* you strike him to	*4202*
	19:25	"Why *d* you go with me, Mephibosheth?"	*4202*
1Ki	22:18	"*D* I tell you that he never prophesies	*4202*
2Ki	2:18	he said to them, "*D* I tell you not to go?"	*4202*
	4:28	"*D* I tell you, 'Don't raise my hopes'?	*4202*
	5:25	"Your servant *d* go anywhere,"	*AIT*
2Ch	13: 9	But *d* you drive out the priests of	*4202*
	18:17	"*D* I tell you that he never prophesies	*4202*
Ne	13:18	*D* your forefathers do the same things,	*4202*
Mt	13:27	'Sir, *d* you sow good seed in your field?	*4049*
	16: 7	"It is because we *d* bring any bread."	*4024*
	20:13	*D* you agree to work for a denarius?	*4049*
	21:25	he will ask, 'Then why *d* you believe him?'	*4024*
Mk	11:31	he will ask, 'Then why *d* you believe him?'	*4024*
Lk	2:49	"*D* you know I had to be	*4024*
	19:23	Why then *d* you put my money on deposit,	*4024*
	20: 5	he will ask, 'Why *d* you believe him?'	*4024*
	24:23	but *d* find his body.	*3590*
Jn	7:45	"Why *d* you bring him in?"	*4024*
	18:26	"*D* I see you with him in the olive grove?"	*4024*
Ac	5: 4	*D* it belong to you before it was sold?	*4049*

DIDYMUS (3)

Jn	11:16	Then Thomas (called **D**) said to the rest of	*1441*
	20:24	Now Thomas (called **D**),	*1441*
	21: 2	Thomas (called **D**), Nathanael from Cana	*1441*

DIE (300) [DEAD, DEADENED, DEADLY, DEATH, DEATH'S, DEATHLY, DEATHS, DIED, DIES, DYING]

Ge	2:17	when you eat of it *you will* **surely d**."	*4637+4637*
	3: 3	and you must not touch it, or *you will* **d**.' "	*4637*
	3: 4	*"You will not surely* **d**,"	*4637+4637*
	19:19	this disaster will overtake me, and *I'll* **d**.	*4637*
	20: 7	be sure that you and all yours *will* **d**."	*4637+4637*
	21:16	for she thought, "I cannot watch the boy **d**."	*4638*
	25:32	"Look, I am about to **d**," Esau said.	*4637*
	27: 4	I may give you my blessing before *I* **d**."	*4637*
	27: 7	in the presence of the LORD before *I* **d**.'	*4638*
	30: 1	"Give me children, or *I'll* **d!**"	*4637*
	33:13	all the animals will **d**.	*4637*
	38:11	For he thought, "He may **d** too,	*4637*
	42: 2	so that we may live and not **d**."	*4637*
	42:20	be verified and that *you may* not **d**."	*4637*
	43: 8	and our children may live and not **d**.	*4637*
	44: 9	to have it, *he will* **d**;	*4637*
	44:22	if he leaves, his father *will* **d**.'	*4637*
	44:31	that the boy isn't there, *he will* **d**.	*4637*
	45:28	I will go and see him before *I* **d**."	*4637*
	46:30	"Now *I am ready to* **d**,	*4637*
	47:15	Why *should we* **d** before your eyes?	*4637*
	47:19	Give us seed so that we may live and not **d**,	*4637*
	47:29	When the time drew near for Israel to **d**,	*4637*
	48:21	Israel said to Joseph, "*I am about to* **d**,	*4637*
	50: 5	"*I am about to* **d**.	*4637*
	50:24	"*I am about to* **d**.	*4637*
Ex	7:18	The fish in the Nile *will* **d**,	*4637*
	9: 4	to the Israelites *will* **d**.' "	*4637*
	9:19	and *they will* **d**.' "	*4637*
	10:28	The day you see my face *you will* **d**."	*4637*
	11: 5	Every firstborn son in Egypt *will* **d**,	*4637*
	12:33	"For otherwise," they said, "we *will all* **d!**"	*4637*
	14:11	that you brought us to the desert to **d**?	*4637*
	14:12	for us to serve the Egyptians than *to* **d** in	*4637*
	17: 3	**make** us and our children and livestock **d**."	*4637*
	20:19	do not have God speak to us or *we will* **d**."	*4637*
	21:18	and *he does* not **d** but is confined to bed,	*4637*
	28:35	so that *he will* not **d**.	*4637*
	28:43	so that they will not incur guilt and **d**.	*4637*
	30:20	with water so that *they will* not **d**.	*4637*
	30:21	and feet so that *they will* not **d**.	*4637*
Lev	8:35	so *you will* not **d**;	*4637*
	10: 6	or *you will* **d** and the LORD will	*4637*
	10: 7	to the Tent of Meeting or *you will* **d**,	*4637*
	10: 9	or *you will* **d**.	*4637*
	15:31	so *they will* not **d** in their uncleanness	*4637*
	16: 2	or else *he will* **d**,	*4637*

Lev	16:13	so that *he* will not **d.** 4637
	20:20	*they will* **d** childless. 4637
	21: 1	for any of his people who **d,** 5883
	22: 9	not become guilty and **d** for treating them 4637
Nu	4:15	not touch the holy things or *they will* **d.** 4637
	4:19	and not **d** when they come near 4637
	4:20	even for a moment, or *they will* **d."** 4637
	14:35	here *they will* **d."** 4637
	15:35	the Lord said to Moses, "The man **must d.** 4637+4637
	16:29	If these men **d** a natural death 4637
	17:10	so that *they will* not **d."** 4637
	17:12	The Israelites said to Moses, *"We will* **d!** 1588
	17:13	near the tabernacle of the Lord *will* **d.** 4637
	17:13	Are we all *going to* **d?"** 1588
	18: 3	or both they and you *will* **d.** 4637
	18:22	the consequences of their sin and *will* **d.** 4637
	18:32	and *you will* not **d.'"** 4637
	20: 4	that we and our livestock *should* **d** here? 4637
	20:26	*he will* **d."** 4637
	21: 5	up out of Egypt to **d** in the desert? 4637
	23:10	*Let me* **d** the death of the righteous, 4637
	26:11	The line of Korah, however, *did not* **d out.** 4637
	26:65	the Lord had told those Israelites they would **surely d** in the desert, 4637+4637
	35:12	that a person accused of murder *may not* **d** 4637
	35:31	who deserves to **d.** 4637
Dt	4:22	I *will* **d** in this land; 4637
	5:25	But now, why *should we* **d?** 4637
	5:25	and we *will* **d** if we hear the voice of 4637
	18:16	or we *will* **d."** 4637
	19:12	hand him over to the avenger of blood *to* **d.** 4637
	20: 5	or *he may* **d** in battle 4637
	20: 6	or *he may* **d** in battle 4637
	20: 7	or *he may* **d** in battle 4637
	22:22	with her and the woman *must* **d.** 4637
	22:25	only the man who has done this *shall* **d.** 4637
	24: 7	the kidnapper *must* **d.** 4637
	24:16	each *is to* **d** for his own sin. 4637
	31:27	how much more will you rebel after I **d!** 4638
	32:50	that you have climbed *you will* **d** and 4637
	33: 6	"Let Reuben live and not **d,** 4637
Jdg	6:23	*You are* not *going to* **d."** 4637
	6:30	*He must* **d,** because he has broken 4637
	13:22	*"We are* **doomed to d!"** 4637+4637
	15:18	now **d** of thirst and fall into the hands of 4637
	16:30	*"Let me* **d** with the Philistines!" 4637
Ru	1:17	Where *you* **d** I will die, 4637
	1:17	Where you die *I will* **d,** 4637
1Sa	2:33	and all your descendants *will* **d** in 4637
	2:34	they *will* both **d** on the same day. 4637
	5:12	Those who *did not* **d** were afflicted 4637
	12:19	for your servants so that *we will* not **d,** 4637
	14:39	with my son Jonathan, *he must* **d."** 4637+4637
	14:43	And now *must I* **d?"** 4637
	14:44	be it ever so severely, if *you do* not **d,** 4637+4637
	14:45	the men said to Saul, "Should Jonathan **d—** 4637
	20: 2	*"You are* not *going to* **d!** 4637
	20:31	for he *must* **d!"** 1201+4638
	22:16	But the king said, *"You will* **surely d,** 4637+4637
	26:10	either his time will come and *he will* **d,** 4637
	26:16	you and your men deserve to **d,** 4637
2Sa	3:33	"Should Abner have died as the lawless **d?** 4638
	11:15	from him so he will be struck down and **d."** 4637
	12: 5	the man who did this deserves to **d!** 4638
	12:13	*You are* not *going to* **d.** 4637
	12:14	the son born to you *will* **d."** 4637+4637
	14:14	cannot be recovered, so *we* **must d.** 4637+4637
	18: 3	Even if half of us **d,** they won't care; 4637
	19:23	the king said to Shimei, *"You shall* not **d."** 4637
	19:37	that I *may* **d** in my own town near the tomb 4637
1Ki	1:52	but if evil is found in him, *he will* **d."** 4637
	2: 1	When the time drew near for David to **d,** 4637
	2:26	You deserve to **d,** 4638
	2:30	But he answered, "No, *I will* **d** here." 4637
	2:37	you can be sure *you will* **d;** 4637+4637
	2:42	you can be sure *you will* **d'?** 4637+4637
	13:31	he said to his sons, "When I **d,** 4637
	14:11	to Jeroboam *who* **d** in the city, 4637
	14:11	the birds of the air will feed on those *who* **d** 4637
	14:12	the boy *will* **d.** 4637
	16: 4	to Baasha *who* **d** in the city, 4637
	16: 4	the birds of the air will feed on those *who* **d** 4637
	17:12	that we may eat it—and **d."** 4637
	17:20	**causing** her son to **d?"** 4637
	19: 4	down under it and prayed that he *might* **d.** 4637
	20:42	a man I had **determined should d.** 3051
	21:24	to Ahab *who* **d** in the city, 4637
	21:24	the birds of the air will feed on those *who* **d** 4637
2Ki	1: 4	*You will* **certainly d!' "** 4637+4637
	1: 6	*You will* **certainly d!' ' "** 4637+4637
	1:16	*You will* **certainly d!"** 4637+4637
	7: 3	"Why stay here until we **d?** 4637
	7: 4	a famine is there, and *we will* **d.** 4637
	7: 4	And if we stay here, *we will* **d.** 4637
	7: 4	if they kill us, then *we* **d."** 4637
	8:10	to me that he will **in fact d."** 4637+4637
	14: 6	each *is to* **d** for his own sins." 4637
	20: 1	because *you are going to* **d;** 4637
2Ch	25: 4	each *is to* **d** for his own sins." 4637
	32:11	to let you **d** of hunger and thirst. 4637
Est	9:28	of them **d** out among their descendants. 6066
Job	2: 9	Curse God and **d!"** 4637
	3:11	and **d** as I came from the womb? 1588
	4:21	so that *they* **d** without wisdom?' 4637
	12: 2	and wisdom *will* **d** with you! 4637
	13:19	If so, I will be silent and **d.** 1588

Job	14: 8	in the ground and its stump **d** in the soil, 4637
	27: 5	till I **d,** I will not deny my integrity. 1588
	29:18	"I thought, 'I will **d** in my own house, 1588
	34:20	*They* **d** in an instant, 4637
	36:12	by the sword and **d** without knowledge. 1588
	36:14	They **d** in their youth, 4637
Ps	37: 2	like green plants *they will* soon **d away.** 5570
	41: 5	"When *will he* **d** and his name perish?" 4637
	49:10	For all can see that wise men **d;** 4637
	79:11	of your arm preserve those condemned to **d.** 9456
	82: 7	But *you will* **d** like mere men; 4637
	104:29	*they* **d** and return to the dust. 1588
	105:29	**causing** their fish **to d.** 4637
	118:17	*I will* not **d** but live, 4637
Pr	5:23	He will **d** for lack of discipline. 4637
	10:21	but fools **d** for lack of judgment. 4637
	15:10	he who hates correction *will* **d.** 4637
	19:16	of his ways *will* **d.** 4637
	23:13	you punish him with the rod, *he will* not **d.** 4637
Ecc	2:16	Like the fool, the wise man too *must* **d!** 4637
	3: 2	a time to be born and a time to **d,** 4637
	7:17	why **d** before your time? 4637
	9: 5	For the living know that *they will* **d,** 4637
Isa	5:13	their men of rank will **d** *of* hunger 4637
	22: 2	nor *did they* **d** in battle. 4637
	22:13	you say, "for tomorrow *we* **d!"** 4637
	22:18	There *you will* **d** 4637
	38: 1	because you *are going to* **d;** 4637
	50: 2	their fish rot for lack of water and **d** 4637
	51: 6	a garment and its inhabitants **d** like flies. 4637
	51:14	*they will* not **d** in their dungeon, 4637
	59: 5	Whoever eats their eggs *will* **d,** 4637
	66:24	their worm *will* not **d,** 4637
Jer	11:21	the Lord or *you will* **d** by our hands'— 4637
	11:22	Their young men *will* **d** by the sword, 4637
	16: 4	"They *will* **d** *of* deadly diseases. 4637
	16: 6	"Both high and low *will* **d** in this land. 4637
	20: 6	There *you will* **d** and be buried, 4637
	21: 6	and *they will* **d** of a terrible plague. 4637
	21: 9	Whoever stays in this city *will* **d** by 4637
	22:12	*He will* **d** in the place 4637
	22:26	and there *you both will* **d.** 4637
	26: 8	seized him and said, *"You* **must d!** 4637+4637
	27:13	Why *will* you and your people **d** by 4637
	28:16	This very year you *are going to* **d,** 4637
	31:30	Instead, everyone *will* **d** for his own sin; 4637
	34: 4	*You will* not **d** by the sword; 4637
	34: 5	*you will* **d** peacefully. 4637
	37:20	or *I will* **d** there." 4637
	38: 2	'Whoever stays in this city *will* **d** by 4637
	38:24	or *you may* **d.** 4637
	38:26	to Jonathan's house to **d** there.' " 4637
	42:16	and there *you will* **d.** 4637
	42:17	to settle there *will* **d** by the sword, famine 4637
	42:22	*You will* **d** by the sword, 9462
	44:12	by the sword or **d** from famine. 4637
	44:12	*they will* **d** by sword or famine. 4637
La	4: 9	better off than *those who* **d** of famine; 2728
Eze	3:18	*'You will* **surely d,'** 4637+4637
	3:18	that wicked man *will* **d** for his sin, 4637
	3:19	he *will* **d** for his sin; 4637
	3:20	a stumbling block before him, he *will* **d.** 4637
	3:20	you did not warn him, *he will* **d** for his sin. 4637
	5:12	A third of your people *will* **d** of the plague 4637
	6:12	He that is far away *will* **d** of the plague, 4637
	6:12	and he that survives and is spared *will* **d** 4637
	7:15	those in the country *will* **d** by the sword, 4637
	12:13	but he will not see it, and there *he will* **d.** 4637
	17:16	*he shall* **d** in Babylon. 4637
	18: 4	The soul who sins is the one *who will* **d.** 4637
	18:17	He *will* not **d** for his father's sin; 4637
	18:18	But his father *will* **d** for his own sin, 4637
	18:20	The soul who sins is the one *who will* **d.** 4637
	18:21	*he will* not **d.** 4637
	18:24	of the sins he has committed, *he will* **d.** 4637
	18:26	*he will* **d** for it; 4637
	18:26	of the sin he has committed *he will* **d.** 4637
	18:28	*he will* not **d.** 4637
	18:31	Why *will you* **d,** O house of Israel? 4637
	28: 8	and *you will* **d** a violent death in the heart 4637
	28:10	*You will* **d** the death of the uncircumcised 4637
	33: 8	'O wicked man, *you will* **surely d,'** 4637+4637
	33: 8	that wicked man *will* **d** for his sin, 4637
	33: 9	he *will* **d** for his sin, 4637
	33:11	Why *will you* **d,** O house of Israel?' 4637
	33:13	he *will* **d** for the evil he has done. 4637
	33:14	*'You will* **surely d,'** but he 4637+4637
	33:15	*he will* not **d.** 4637
	33:18	*he will* **d** for it. 4637
	33:27	and those in strongholds and caves *will* **d** 4637
Am	6: 9	*they* too *will* **d.** 4637
	7:11	" 'Jeroboam *will* **d** by the sword, 4637
	7:17	and you yourself *will* **d** in 4637
	9:10	All the sinners among my people *will* **d** by 4637
Jnh	1:14	not *let us* **d** for taking this man's life. 6
	4: 3	for it is better for me to **d** than to live." 4638
	4: 8	He wanted to **d,** and said, 4638
	4: 8	"It would be better for me to **d** than 4638
	4: 9	"I am angry enough to **d."** 4638
Hab	1:12	My God, my Holy One, *we will* not **d.** 4637
Zec	11: 9	*Let the dying* **d,** and the perishing perish. 4637
	13: 3	will say to him, *'You must* **d,** 2649+4202
Mt	26:35	"Even if I have to **d** with you, 633
	26:52	"for all who draw the sword *will* **d** by 660
Mk	9:48	where " 'their worm *does* not **d,** 5462
	14:31	"Even if I have *to* **d** with you, 5271

Lk	2:26	he *would* not **d** before he had seen the Lord's Christ. 2505+3972
	7: 2	was sick and about to **d.** 5462
	13:33	surely no prophet can **d** outside Jerusalem! 660
	20:36	and they can no longer **d;** 633
Jn	6:50	which a man may eat and not **d.** 633
	8:21	and *you will* **d** in your sins." 633
	8:24	I told you that *you would* **d** in your sins; 633
	8:24	*you will* indeed **d** in your sins." 633
	11:16	"Let us also go, that *we may* **d** with him." 633
	11:26	and believes in me *will never* **d.** 633
	11:50	for you that one man **d** for the people than 633
	11:51	that year he prophesied that Jesus *would* **d** 633
	12:33	the kind of death he was going to **d.** 633
	18:32	the kind of death he was going to **d** 633
	19: 7	and according to that law he *must* **d,** 633
	21:23	the brothers that this disciple *would* not **d.** 633
	21:23	but Jesus did not say that *he would* not **d;** 633
Ac	7:19	so that *they would* **d.** 2441+3590
	21:13	but also *to* **d** in Jerusalem for the name of 633
	25:11	I do not refuse *to* **d.** 633
Ro	5: 7	Very rarely *will* anyone **d** for a righteous 633
	5: 7	for a good man someone might possibly dare *to* **d.** 633
	6: 9	*he cannot* **d** again; 633
	8:13	according to the sinful nature, you will **d;** 633
	14: 8	and if *we* **d,** we die to the Lord. 633
	14: 8	and if we die, *we* **d** to the Lord. 633
	14: 8	So, whether *we* live or **d,** 633
1Co	4: 9	like men **condemned to d** in the arena. 2119
	9:15	I *would* rather **d** than have anyone deprive me of this boast. 633
	15:22	For as in Adam all **d,** so in Christ all will be made alive. 633
	15:31	*I* **d** every day—I mean that, brothers— 633
	15:32	"Let us eat and drink, for tomorrow *we* **d."** 633
2Co	7: 3	in our hearts that we *would* live or **d** with 5271
Php	1:21	For to me, to live is Christ and *to* **d** is gain. 633
Heb	7: 8	the tenth is collected by men who **d;** 633
	9:27	Just as man is destined *to* **d** once, 633
1Pe	2:24	so that we might **d** to sins and live 614
Rev	3: 2	Strengthen what remains and is about to **d,** 633
	9: 6	they will long *to* **d,** but death will elude them 633
	11: 5	anyone who wants to harm them must **d.** 650
	14:13	the dead who **d** in the Lord from now on." 633

DIED (257) [DIE]

Ge	5: 5	Adam lived 930 years, and then *he* **d.** 4637
	5: 8	Seth lived 912 years, and then *he* **d.** 4637
	5:11	Enosh lived 905 years, and then *he* **d.** 4637
	5:14	Kenan lived 910 years, and then *he* **d.** 4637
	5:17	Mahalalel lived 895 years, and then *he* **d.** 4637
	5:20	Jared lived 962 years, and then *he* **d.** 4637
	5:27	Methuselah lived 969 years, and then *he* **d.** 4637
	5:31	Lamech lived 777 years, and then *he* **d.** 4637
	7:22	that had the breath of life in its nostrils **d.** 4637
	9:29	Noah lived 950 years, and then *he* **d.** 4637
	11:28	Haran **d** in Ur of the Chaldeans, 4637
	11:32	Terah lived 205 years, and **d** in Haran. 4637
	23: 2	She **d** at Kiriath Arba (that is, Hebron), 4637
	25: 8	and **d** at a good old age, an old man and full 4637
	25:17	He breathed his last and **d.** 4637
	26:18	had stopped up after Abraham **d,** 4638
	35: 8	Deborah, Rebekah's nurse, **d** and 4637
	35:19	So Rachel **d** and was buried on the way 4637
	35:29	and **d** and was gathered to his people, 4637
	36:33	When Bela **d,** Jobab son of Zerah 4637
	36:34	When Jobab **d,** Husham from the land of 4637
	36:35	When Husham **d,** Hadad son of Bedad, 4637
	36:36	When Hadad **d,** Samlah 4637
	36:37	When Samlah **d,** Shaul from Rehoboth on 4637
	36:38	When Shaul **d,** Baal-Hanan son 4637
	36:39	When Baal-Hanan son of Acbor **d,** 4637
	38:12	the daughter of Shua, **d.** 4637
	46:12	Perez and Zerah (but Er and Onan *had* **d** in 4637
	48: 7	to my sorrow Rachel **d** in the land 4637
	50:16	"Your father left these instructions before he **d:** 4638
	50:26	So Joseph **d** at the age of a hundred and ten. 4637
Ex	1: 6	and all that generation **d,** 4637
	2:23	the king of Egypt **d.** 4637
	7:21	The fish in the Nile **d,** 4637
	8:13	The frogs **d** in the houses, 4637
	9: 6	All the livestock of the Egyptians **d,** 4637
	9: 6	not one animal belonging to the Israelites **d.** 4637
	9: 7	of the animals of the Israelites *had* **d,** 4637
	16: 3	"If only we *had* **d** by the Lord's hand 4637
	32:28	about three thousand of the people **d.** 5877
Lev	10: 2	and *they* **d** before the Lord. 4637
	16: 1	the death of the two sons of Aaron *who* **d** 4637
Nu	11: 2	to the Lord and the fire **d down.** 9205
	14: 2	"If only *we had* **d** in Egypt! 4637
	14:37	*were* **struck down and d** of a plague 4637
	16:49	But 14,700 *people* **d** from the plague, 4637
	16:49	in addition to those *who had* **d** because 4637
	19:16	or *someone who has* **d a natural death** 4637
	19:18	or someone who has **d a natural death.** 4637
	20: 1	There Miriam **d** and was buried. 4637
	20: 3	"If only *we had* **d** when our brothers fell 1588
	20:28	And Aaron **d** there on top of the mountain. 4637
	20:29	whole community learned that Aaron *had* **d,** 1588
	21: 6	they bit the people and many Israelites **d;** 4637
	25: 9	those *who* **d** in the plague numbered 24,000. 4637
	26:10	whose followers **d** when the fire devoured 4637
	26:19	but *they* **d** in Canaan. 4637
	26:61	and Abihu **d** when they made an offering 4637

Nu	27: 3	"Our father **d** in the desert.	4637
	27: 3	but *he* **d** for his own sin and left no sons.	4637
	33:38	where *he* **d** on the first day of	4637
	33:39	and twenty-three years old when he **d**	4637
Dt	2:16	among the people had **d,**	4637
	10: 6	There Aaron **d** and was buried,	4637
	32:50	just as your brother Aaron **d** on Mount Hor	4637
	34: 5	the servant of the LORD **d** there in Moab,	4637
	34: 7	a hundred and twenty years old when he **d,**	4637
Jos	5: 4	**d** in the desert on the way	4637
	5: 6	of military age when they left Egypt had **d,**	9462
	10:11	and more of them **d** from	4637
	22:20	He was not the only one *who* **d** for his sin.'	1588
	24:29	**d** at the age of a hundred and ten.	4637
	24:33	And Eleazar son of Aaron **d** and was buried	4637
Jdg	1: 7	Jerusalem, and *he* **d** there.	4637
	2: 8	**d** at the age of a hundred and ten.	4637
	2:19	But when the judge **d,**	4638
	2:21	of the nations Joshua left when *he* **d.**	4637
	3:11	until Othniel son of Kenaz **d.**	4637
	4: 1	After Ehud, the Israelites once again did evil in the eyes of the LORD.	4637
	4:21	into the ground, and *he* **d.**	4637
	8:32	of Joash **d** at a good old age and was buried	4637
	8:33	No sooner had Gideon **d** than	4637
	9:49	about a thousand men and women, also **d.**	4637
	9:54	So his servant ran him through, and *he* **d.**	4637
	10: 2	then *he* **d,** and was buried in Shamir.	4637
	10: 5	When Jair **d,** he was buried in Kamon.	4637
	12: 7	Then Jephthah the Gileadite **d,**	4637
	12:10	Ibzan **d,** and was buried in Bethlehem.	4637
	12:12	Then Elon **d,** and was buried in Aijalon in	4637
	12:15	Then Abdon son of Hillel **d,**	4637
	16:30	Thus he killed many more when he **d** than	4638
	20: 5	They raped my concubine, and *she* **d.**	4637
Ru	1: 3	Now Elimelech, Naomi's husband, **d,**	4637
	1: 5	both Mahlon and Kilion also **d,**	4637
1Sa	4:11	Hophni and Phinehas, **d.**	4637
	4:18	His neck was broken and *he* **d,**	4637
	15:35	Until the day Samuel **d,**	4638
	25: 1	Now Samuel **d,** and all Israel assembled	4637
	25:38	the LORD struck Nabal and *he* **d.**	4637
	31: 5	he too fell on his sword and **d** with him.	4637
	31: 6	and all his men **d** together that same day.	4637
	31: 7	and that Saul and his sons had **d,**	4637
2Sa	1: 4	Many of them fell and **d.**	4637
	1:15	So he struck him down, and *he* **d.**	4637
	2:23	He fell there and **d** on the spot.	4637
	2:23	to the place where Asahel had fallen and **d.**	4637
	3:27	Joab stabbed him in the stomach, and *he* **d.**	4637
	3:33	"Should Abner *have* **d** as the lawless die?	4637
	4: 1	of Saul heard that Abner had **d** in Hebron,	4637
	6: 7	down and *he* **d** there beside the ark of God.	4637
	10: 1	the king of the Ammonites **d,**	4637
	10:18	and *he* **d** there.	4637
	11:17	moreover, Uriah the Hittite **d.**	4637
	11:21	so that *he* **d** in Thebez?	4637
	11:24	and some of the king's men **d.**	4637
	12:18	On the seventh day the child **d.**	4637
	17:23	So *he* **d** and was buried in his father's tomb.	4637
	18:33	If only I had **d** instead of you—	4637
	19:10	*has* **d** in battle.	4637
	20:10	Without being stabbed again, Amasa **d.**	4637
	24:15	of the people from Dan to Beersheba **d.**	4637
1Ki	2:25	and he struck down Adonijah and *he* **d.**	4637
	3:19	"During the night this woman's son **d**	4637
	14:17	over the threshold of the house, the boy **d**	4637
	16:18	palace on fire around him. So *he* **d,**	4637
	16:22	So Tibni **d** and Omri became king.	4637
	22:35	and that evening *he* **d.**	4637
	22:37	So the king **d** and was brought to Samaria,	4637
2Ki	1:17	So *he* **d,** according to the word of	4637
	3: 5	But after Ahab **d,**	4638
	4:20	and then *he* **d.**	4637
	7:17	in the gateway, and *he* **d,** just as the man	4637
	7:20	in the gateway, and *he* **d.**	4637
	8:15	so that *he* **d.**	4637
	9:27	but he escaped to Megiddo and **d** there.	4637
	12:21	*He* **d** and was buried with his fathers in	4637
	13:14	from the illness from which *he* **d.**	4637
	13:20	Elisha **d** and was buried.	4637
	13:24	Hazael king of Aram **d,**	4637
	15: 5	the king with leprosy until the day he **d,**	4637
	23:34	and there *he* **d.**	4637
1Ch	1:44	When Bela **d,** Jobab son of Zerah	4637
	1:45	When Jobab **d,** Husham from the land of	4637
	1:46	When Husham **d,** Hadad son of Bedad,	4637
	1:47	When Hadad **d,** Samlah	4637
	1:48	When Samlah **d,** Shaul from Rehoboth on	4637
	1:49	When Shaul **d,** Baal-Hanan son	4637
	1:50	When Baal-Hanan **d,** Hadad succeeded him	4637
	1:51	Hadad also **d.**	4637
	2:19	When Azubah **d,** Caleb married Ephrath,	4637
	2:24	After Hezron **d** in Caleb Ephrathah,	4638
	2:30	Seled **d** without children.	4637
	2:32	Jether **d** without children.	4637
	10: 5	he too fell on his sword and **d.**	4637
	10: 6	So Saul and his three sons **d.**	4637
	10: 6	and all his house **d** together.	4637
	10: 7	and that Saul and his sons had **d,**	4637
	10:13	Saul **d** because he was unfaithful to	4637
	13:10	So *he* **d** there before God.	4637
	19: 1	Nahash king of the Ammonites **d,**	4637
	23:22	Eleazar **d** without having sons:	4637
	24: 2	Nadab and Abihu **d** before their father did,	4637
	29:28	*He* **d** at a good old age,	4637
2Ch	13:20	And the LORD struck him down and *he* **d.**	4637

2Ch	16:13	in the forty-first year of his reign Asa **d**	4637
	18:34	Then at sunset *he* **d.**	4637
	21:19	and *he* **d** in great pain.	4637
	24:15	and *he* **d** at the age of a hundred and thirty.	4637
	24:25	*he* **d** and was buried in the City of David,	4637
	26:21	King Uzziah had leprosy until the day he **d.**	4638
	32:33	of Jerusalem honored him when he **d.**	4637
	35:24	and brought him to Jerusalem, where *he* **d.**	4637
Est	2: 7	when her father and mother **d.**	4638
Job	10:18	*I wish I had* **d** before any eye saw me.	1588
	42:17	And so he **d,** old and full of years.	4637
Ps	118:12	but *they* **d** out as quickly as burning thorns;	1980
Ecc	4: 2	I declared that the dead, who had already **d,**	4637
Isa	6: 1	In the year that King Uzziah **d,**	4638
	14:28	This oracle came in the year King Ahaz **d:**	4638
Jer	28:17	Hananiah the prophet **d.**	4637
Eze	11:13	Pelatiah son of Benaiah **d.**	4637
	13:19	have killed those who *should* not *have* **d**	4637
	24:18	and in the evening my wife **d.**	4637
Hos	13: 1	he became guilty of Baal worship and **d.**	4637
Jnh	4:10	It sprang up overnight and **d** overnight.	6
Mt	2:19	*After* Herod **d,** an angel of the Lord	5462
	8:32	down the steep bank into the lake and **d** in	633
	9:18	"My daughter *has* just **d.**	5462
	14:32	the wind **d down.**	3156
	22:25	The first one married and **d,**	5462
	22:27	Finally, the woman **d.**	633
	27:52	of many holy people who *had* **d** were raised	3121
Mk	4:39	wind **d down** and it was completely calm.	3156
	6:51	and the wind **d down.**	3156
	12:20	and **d** without leaving any children.	633
	12:21	but *he* also **d,** leaving no child.	633
	12:22	Last of all, the woman **d** too.	633
	15:39	heard his cry and saw how he **d,** he said,	1743
	15:44	he asked him if Jesus *had* already **d.**	633
Lk	13: 4	Or those eighteen who **d** when the tower	650
	16:22	the beggar **d** and the angels carried him	633
	16:22	The rich man also **d** and was buried.	633
	20:29	a woman and **d** childless.	633
	20:31	and in the same way the seven **d,**	633
	20:32	Finally, the woman **d** too.	633
Jn	6:49	the manna in the desert, yet *they* **d.**	633
	6:58	Your forefathers ate manna and **d,**	633
	8:52	Abraham **d** and so did the prophets,	633
	8:53	He **d,** and so did the prophets.	633
	11:21	my brother would not *have* **d.**	633
	11:32	my brother would not *have* **d.**	633
	18:14	that it would be good *if* one man **d** for	633
Ac	2:29	that the patriarch David **d** and was buried,	5462
	5: 5	*he* fell down and **d.**	1775
	5:10	that moment she fell down at his feet and **d.**	1775
	7:15	where he and our fathers **d.**	5462
	9:37	About that time she became sick and **d,**	633
	12:23	and he was eaten by worms and **d.**	1775
Ro	5: 6	Christ **d** for the ungodly.	633
	5: 8	While we were still sinners, Christ **d** for us.	633
	5:15	the many **d** by the trespass of the one man,	633
	6: 2	We **d** to sin; how can we live in it	633
	6: 7	anyone who *has* **d** has been freed from sin.	633
	6: 8	Now if *we* **d** with Christ,	633
	6:10	The death *he* **d,** he died to sin once for all;	633
	6:10	The death he died, *he* **d** to sin once for all;	633
	7: 4	you also **d** to the law through the body	2506
	7: 9	sin sprang to life and I **d.**	633
	8:34	that condemns? Christ Jesus, who **d**—	633
	14: 9	Christ **d** and returned to life so	633
	14:15	your brother for whom Christ **d.**	633
1Co	8:11	So this weak brother, for whom Christ **d,**	633
	10: 8	in one day twenty-three thousand of them **d.**	4406
	15: 3	that Christ **d** for our sins according to	633
2Co	5:14	because we are convinced that one **d** for all,	633
	5:14	and therefore all **d.**	633
	5:15	And *he* **d** for all, that those who live	633
	5:15	for themselves but for him who **d** for them	633
Gal	2:19	I **d** to the law so that I might live for God.	633
	2:21	Christ **d** for nothing!"	633
Php	2:27	Indeed he was ill, and almost **d.**	2505
	2:30	because he almost **d** for the work of Christ,	2505
Col	2:20	Since *you* **d** with Christ to the basic	633
	3: 3	For *you* **d,** and your life is now hidden	633
1Th	4:14	We believe that Jesus **d** and rose again and	633
	5:10	He **d** for us so that, whether we are awake or	633
2Ti	2:11	If *we* **d** with him, we will also live with him	5271
Heb	9:15	*that he has* **d** as a ransom to set them free from the sins	1181+2505
	9:17	because a will is in force only when somebody has **d;**	2093+3738
	10:28	**d** without mercy on the testimony of two	633
	11:13	still living by faith when *they* **d.**	633
1Pe	3:18	For Christ **d** for sins once for all,	633
2Pe	3: 4	Ever since our fathers **d,**	3121
Rev	2: 8	who **d** and came to life again.	1181+3738
	8: 9	a third of the living creatures in the sea **d,**	633
	8:11	and many people **d** from the waters	633
	16: 3	and every living thing in the sea **d.**	633

DIES (43) [DIE]

Ge	27:10	he may give you his blessing before he **d.**	4638
Ex	21:20	with a rod and the slave **d** as a direct result,	4637
	21:35	the bull of another and *it* **d,**	4637
	22: 2	in and is struck so that *he* **d,** the defender is	4637
	22:10	to his neighbor for safekeeping and *it* **d**	4637
	22:14	and it is injured or **d** while the owner is	4637
Lev	11:32	of them **d** and falls on something,	4637
	11:39	an animal that you are allowed to eat **d,**	4637
Nu	6: 7	or mother or brother or sister **d,**	4637

Nu	6: 9	" 'If someone **d** suddenly in his presence,	4637
	19:14	the law that applies when a person **d** in	4637
	27: 8	'If a man **d** and leaves no son,	4637
	35:16	an iron object so that *he* **d,** he is a murderer;	4637
	35:17	and he strikes someone so that *he* **d,**	4637
	35:18	and he hits someone so that *he* **d,**	4637
	35:20	at him intentionally so that *he* **d**	4637
	35:21	that *he* **d,** that person shall be put to death;	4637
	35:23	a stone on him that could kill him, and *he* **d,**	4637
Dt	24: 3	sends her from his house, or if *he* **d,**	4637
	25: 5	and one of them **d** without a son,	4637
Job	14:10	But man **d** and is laid low;	4637
	14:14	If a man **d,** will he live again?	4637
	21:23	One man **d** in full vigor,	4637
	21:25	Another man **d** in bitterness of soul,	4637
Ps	49:17	he will take nothing with him when he **d,**	4638
Pr	11: 7	When a wicked man **d,** his hope perishes;	4638
	26:20	without gossip a quarrel **d down.**	9284
Ecc	3:19	As one **d,** so dies the other.	4638
	3:19	As one dies, so **d** the other.	4638
Isa	65:20	*he who* **d** at a hundred will be thought	4637
Jer	38:10	the prophet out of the cistern before he **d.**"	4637
Mt	22:24	that if a man **d** without having children,	633
Mk	12:19	that if a man's brother **d** and leaves a wife	633
Lk	20:28	that if a man's brother **d** and leaves a wife	633
Jn	4:49	"Sir, come down before my child **d.**"	633
	11:25	believes in me will live, even though he **d;**	633
	12:24	a kernel of wheat falls to the ground and **d,**	633
	12:24	But if it **d,** it produces many seeds.	633
Ro	7: 2	but if her husband **d,** she is released	633
	7: 3	But if her husband **d,** she is released	633
	14: 7	and none of us **d** to himself alone.	633
1Co	7:39	But if her husband **d,** she is free to marry	3121
	15:36	you sow does not come to life unless *it* **d.**	633

DIFFERENCE (7) [DIFFERENT]

2Sa	19:35	*Can I* tell the **d** between what is good	3359
2Ch	12: 8	so that *they may* learn the **d** between	3359
Eze	22:26	that there is no **d** between the unclean and	1068
	44:23	They are to teach my people the **d** between	1068
Ro	3:22	to all who believe. There is no **d,**	1405
	10:12	there is no **d** between Jew and Gentile—	1405
Gal	2: 6	whatever they were makes no **d** to me;	1422

DIFFERENCES (1) [DIFFERENT]

1Co	11:19	No doubt there have to be **d** among you	146

DIFFERENT (25) [DIFFERENCE, DIFFERENCES, DIFFERENTLY, DIFFERING, DIFFERS]

Lev	19:19	" 'Do not mate **d** kinds *of* animals.	3977
Nu	14:24	But because my servant Caleb has a **d** spirit	337
1Sa	10: 6	and you will be changed into a **d** person.	337
Est	1: 7	each one **d** from the other,	9101
	3: 8	of your kingdom whose customs *are* **d**	9101
Da	7: 3	Four great beasts, each **d** from the others,	10731
	7: 7	It *was* **d** from all the former beasts,	10731
	7:19	which was **d** from all the others	10731
	7:23	*It will be* **d** from all the other kingdoms	10731
	7:24	**d** from the earlier ones;	10731
	11:29	but this time the outcome will be **d**	3869+4202
Mk	16:12	Afterward Jesus appeared in a **d** form	2283
Ro	12: 6	We have **d** gifts, according to the grace	1427
1Co	4: 7	For who makes you **d** from anyone else?	1359
	12: 4	There are **d** kinds of gifts,	1348
	12: 5	There are **d** kinds of service,	1348
	12: 6	There are **d** kinds of working,	1348
	12:10	to another speaking in **d** kinds of tongues,	NIG
	12:28	and those speaking in **d** kinds of tongues.	NIG
2Co	11: 4	a **d** spirit *from* the one you received,	2283
	11: 4	or a **d** gospel *from* the one you accepted,	2283
Gal	1: 6	of Christ and are turning to a **d** gospel—	2283
	4: 1	*he is* no **d** *from* a slave,	1422
Heb	7:13	belonged to a **d** tribe,	2283
Jas	2:25	and sent them off *in* a **d** direction?	2283

DIFFERENTLY (2) [DIFFERENT]

Ex	8:22	on that day *I will* deal **d** *with* the land	7111
Php	3:15	And if on some point you think **d,**	2284

DIFFERING (5) [DIFFERENT]

Dt	25:13	Do not have two **d** weights in your bag—	74+74+2256
	25:14	Do not have two **d** measures in your house—	406+406+2256
Pr	20:10	**D** weights and differing measures—	74+74+2256
	20:10	Differing weights and **d** measures—	406+406+2256
	20:23	The LORD detests **d** weights,	74+74+2256

DIFFERS (1) [DIFFERENT]

1Co	15:41	and star **d** from star in splendor.	1422

DIFFICULT (13) [DIFFICULTIES, DIFFICULTY]

Ge	47: 9	My years have been few and **d,**	8273
Ex	18:22	but have them bring every *case* to you;	1524
	18:26	The **d** cases they brought to Moses,	7997
Dt	17: 8	before your courts *that are* too **d** for you	7098
	30:11	not too **d** for you or beyond your reach.	7098
2Ki	2:10	"You have asked a **d** *thing,*" Elijah said,	7996

Eze	3: 5	and **d** language, but to the house of Israel—	3878
	3: 6	of obscure speech and **d** language,	3878
Da	2:11	What the king asks is **too d.**	10330
	4: 9	and no mystery is *too d* for you.	10048
	5:12	explain riddles and solve **d problems.**	10626
	5:16	and to solve **d problems.**	10626
Ac	15:19	that *we should* not **make it d** for	*4214*

DIFFICULTIES (3) [DIFFICULT]

Dt	31:17	Many disasters and **d** will come upon them,	7650
	31:21	And when many disasters and **d** come	7650
2Co	12:10	in hardships, in persecutions, *in* **d.**	*5103*

DIFFICULTY (7) [DIFFICULT]

Ge	35:16	Rachel began to give birth and *had* **great d.**	7996
	35:17	as she *was* **having great d** in childbirth,	7996
Ex	14:25	so that they had **d** driving.	3881
Jos	19:47	Danites **had d taking possession of**	3655+4946
Ac	14:18	they had **d** keeping the crowd from	3660
	27: 7	and had **d** arriving off Cnidus.	3660
	27: 8	We moved along the coast **with d** and came	3660

DIG (10) [DIGGING, DIGS, DUG, GRAVEDIGGERS]

Dt	6:11	wells *you did* not **d,**	2933
	8: 9	the rocks are iron and *you can* **d** copper out	2933
	23:13	your equipment have **something to d with,**	3845
	23:13	**d** a hole and cover up your excrement.	2916
Ps	119:85	The arrogant **d** pitfalls for me,	4125
Eze	8: 8	"Son of man, now **d** into the wall."	3168
	12: 5	**d** through the wall	3168
Am	9: 2	*they* **d** down to the depths of the grave,	3168
Lk	13: 8	and *I'll* **d** around it and fertilize it.	4999
	16: 3	I'm not strong enough *to* **d,**	4999

DIGGING (1) [DIG]

Mk	2: 4	*after* **d** through it,	*2021*

DIGNITARIES (3) [DIGNITY]

Ge	50: 7	the **d** *of* his court and all the dignitaries	2418
	50: 7	the dignitaries of his court and all the **d**	2418
Isa	43:28	So I will disgrace the **d** *of* your temple,	8569

DIGNITY (4) [DIGNITARIES]

Ex	28: 2	to give him **d** and honor.	3883
	28:40	to give them **d** and honor.	3883
Job	30:15	my **d** is driven away as by the wind,	5619
Pr	31:25	She is clothed with strength and **d;**	2077

DIGS (4) [DIG]

Ex	21:33	a pit or **d** one and fails to cover it and an ox	4125
Ps	7:15	*He who* **d** a hole and scoops it out falls into	4125
Pr	26:27	If a *man* **d** a pit, he will fall into it;	4125
Ecc	10: 8	*Whoever* **d** a pit may fall into it;	2916

DIKLAH (2)

Ge	10:27	Hadoram, Uzal, **D,**	1989
1Ch	1:21	Hadoram, Uzal, **D,**	1989

DILEAN (1)

Jos	15:38	**D,** Mizpah, Joktheel,	1939

DILIGENCE (6) [DILIGENT]

Ezr	5: 8	on *with* **d** and is making rapid progress	10056
	6:12	Let it be carried out **with d.**	10056
	6:13	and their associates carried it out **with d.**	10056
	7:21	to provide **with d** whatever Ezra the priest,	10056
	7:23	be done **with d** for the temple of the God	10012
Heb	6:11	of you to show this same **d** to the very end,	*5082*

DILIGENT (7) [DILIGENCE, DILIGENTLY]

2Ch	24:13	The men in charge of the work *were* **d,**	6913
Pr	10: 4	but **d** hands bring wealth.	3026
	12:24	**D** hands will rule,	3026
	12:27	but the **d** man prizes his possessions.	3026
	13: 4	but the desires of the **d** are fully satisfied.	3026
	21: 5	the **d** lead to profit as surely as haste leads	3026
1Ti	4:15	**Be d** in these matters;	*1639*

DILIGENTLY (3) [DILIGENT]

Zec	6:15	if *you* **d** obey the LORD your God."	
			928+7754+9048+9048
Jn	5:39	*You* **d study** the Scriptures	*2236*
Ro	12: 8	if it is leadership, let him govern **d;**	*1877+5082*

DILL (1)

Mt	23:23	mint, **d** and cummin.	*464*

DILUTED (1)

Isa	1:22	your choice wine *is* **d** with water.	4543

DIM (4)

Job	17: 7	My eyes *have* **grown d** with grief;	3908
Ps	88: 9	my eyes *are* **d** with grief.	1790
Ecc	12: 3	those looking through the windows *grow* **d;**	3124
La	5:17	because of these things our eyes *grow* **d**	3124

DIMENSIONS (2)

Job	38: 5	Who marked off its **d?**	4924
Eze	42:11	with similar exits and **d.**	5477

DIMINISH (1)

Ps	107:38	and *he did* not **let** their herds **d.**	5070

DIMNAH (1)

Jos	21:35	**D** and Nahalal, together	1962

DIMON (1) [DIMON'S]

Isa	15: 9	but I will bring still more upon **D—**	1904

DIMON'S (1) [DIMON]

Isa	15: 9	**D** waters are full of blood,	1904

DIMONAH (1)

Jos	15:22	Kinah, **D,** Adadah,	1905

DIN (1)

Jer	51:55	he will silence her **noisy d.**	1524+7754

DINAH (7) [DINAH'S]

Ge	30:21	to a daughter and named her **D.**	1909
	34: 1	Now **D,** the daughter Leah had borne	1909
	34: 3	His heart was drawn to **D** daughter	1909
	34: 5	that his daughter **D** had been defiled,	1909
	34:13	Because their sister **D** had been defiled,	1909
	34:26	and took **D** from Shechem's house and left.	1909
	46:15	besides his daughter **D.**	1909

DINAH'S (2) [DINAH]

Ge	34:11	Shechem said to **D** father and brothers,	2023S
	34:25	Simeon and Levi, **D** brothers,	1909

DINAITES (KJV) See JUDGES

DINE (4) [DINED, DINNER]

1Sa	20: 5	*am* supposed to **d** with the king;	430+3782+3782
Est	7: 1	and Haman went to **d** with Queen Esther,	9272
Pr	23: 1	When you sit to **d** with a ruler,	4310
Am	6: 4	*You* **d on** choice lambs and fattened calves.	430

DINED (1) [DINE]

1Sa	9:24	And Saul **d** with Samuel that day.	430

DINHABAH (2)

Ge	36:32	His city was named **D.**	1973
1Ch	1:43	Bela son of Beor, whose city was named **D.**	1973

DINNER (11) [DINE]

Ge	43:16	slaughter an animal and prepare **d;**	NIH
Est	5:14	go with the king to the **d** and be happy."	5492
Mt	9:10	*While Jesus was* **having d**	*367*
	14: 9	but because of his oaths and his **d guests,**	5263
	22: 4	that I have prepared my **d:**	756
Mk	2:15	While Jesus was *having* **d** at Levi's house,	2879
	6:22	she pleased Herod and his **d guests.**	5263
	6:26	but because of his oaths and his **d guests,**	367
Lk	7:36	of the Pharisees invited Jesus to **have d**	2266
	14:12	"When you give a luncheon or **d,**	1270
Jn	12: 2	Here a **d** was given in Jesus' honor.	1270

DIONYSIUS (1)

Ac	17:34	Among them was **D,** a member of	*1477*

DIOTREPHES (1)

3Jn	1: 9	I wrote to the church, but **D,**	*1485*

DIP (9) [DIPPED, DIPPING, DIPS]

Ex	12:22	**d** it into the blood in the basin and put some	3188
Lev	4: 6	He *is to* **d** his finger into the blood	3188
	4:17	He *shall* **d** his finger into the blood	3188
	14: 6	He is then to take the live bird and **d** it,	3188
	14:16	his right forefinger into the oil	3188
	14:51	**d** them into the blood of the dead bird and	3188
Nu	19:18	**d** it in the water and sprinkle the tent	3188
Ru	2:14	and **d** it in the wine vinegar."	3188
Lk	16:24	and send Lazarus to **d** the tip of his finger	970

DIPPED (7) [DIP]

Ge	37:31	slaughtered a goat and **d** the robe in	3188
Lev	9: 9	and *he* **d** his finger into the blood and put it	3188
1Sa	14:27	of the staff that was in his hand and **d** it into	3188
2Ki	5:14	and **d** *himself* in the Jordan seven times,	3188
Mt	26:23	"The one who *has* **d** his hand into the bowl	1835
Jn	13:26	of bread when I *have* **d** it in the dish."	970
Rev	19:13	He is dressed in a robe **d** in blood,	970

DIPPING (1) [DIP]

Jn	13:26	Then, **d** the piece of bread,	970

DIPS (1) [DIP]

Mk	14:20	"one who **d** bread into the bowl with me.	1835

DIRE (2)

Dt	28:48	in nakedness and **d** poverty,	3972
Isa	21: 2	A **d** vision has been shown to me:	7997

DIRECT (12) [DIRECTED, DIRECTING, DIRECTION, DIRECTIONS, DIRECTIVES, DIRECTLY, DIRECTOR, DIRECTORS, DIRECTS]

Ge	18:19	so that *he will* **d** his children	7422
	46:26	*those who were* his **d descendants,**	3655+3751
Ex	21:20	a rod and the slave dies **as a d result,**	3338+9393
Dt	17:10	Be careful to do everything *they* **d** you	3723
2Ch	34:12	to **d** them were Jahath and Obadiah,	5904
Ps	119:35	**D** me in the path of your commands,	2005
	119:133	**D** my footsteps according to your word;	3922
Jer	10:23	it is not for man *to* **d** his steps.	3922
Eze	23:25	*I will* **d** my jealous anger against you,	5989
	26: 9	*He will* **d** the blows of his battering rams	5989
2Th	3: 5	*May* the Lord **d** your hearts into God's love	*2985*
1Ti	5:17	The elders who **d** the affairs of the church	*4613*

DIRECTED (25) [DIRECT]

Ge	24:51	as the LORD *has* **d.**"	1819
	45:19	"You **are** also **d** to tell them, 'Do this:	7422
	47:11	the district of Rameses, as Pharaoh **d.**	7422
	50: 2	Then Joseph **d** the physicians in his service	7422
Nu	16:40	as the LORD **d** him through Moses.	1819
Dt	2: 1	as the LORD *had* **d** me.	1819
	4:14	the LORD **d** me at that time to teach you	7422
	6: 1	the LORD your God **d** me to teach you	7422
Jos	4:10	just as Moses *had* **d** Joshua.	7422
	4:12	as Moses *had* **d** them.	1819
	11: 9	Joshua did to them as the LORD *had* **d:**	606
	11:23	just as the LORD *had* **d** Moses,	1819
1Sa	13:14	loaded up and set out, just as Jesse *had* **d.**	7422
1Ki	5:16	the project and **d** the workmen.	8097
	21:11	as Jezebel **d** in the letters she had written	8938
Job	21: 4	"Is my complaint **d** to man?	4200
Pr	20:24	A man's steps are **d** by the LORD.	4946
Isa	10:25	and my wrath will be **d** to	6584
Jer	13: 2	So I bought a belt, as the LORD **d,**	1821
Mt	14:19	*he* **d** the people to sit down on the grass.	*3027*
Mk	6:39	Then Jesus **d** them to have all the people sit	*2199*
Ac	7:44	It had been made as God **d** Moses,	*1411*
	22:24	*He* **d** that he be flogged and questioned	*3306*
Tit	1: 5	appoint elders in every town, as I **d** you.	*1411*

DIRECTING (1) [DIRECT]

1Ch	15:21	**d** according to sheminith.	5904

DIRECTION (24) [DIRECT]

Ex	38:21	by the Levites under the **d** *of* Ithamar son	3338
Nu	4:27	be done under the **d** *of* Aaron and his sons.	7023
	4:28	to be under the **d** *of* Ithamar son of Aaron,	3338
	4:33	of Meeting under the **d** *of* Ithamar son	3338
	7: 8	They were all under the **d** *of* Ithamar son	3338
	11:31	as far as a day's walk **in any d.**	2256+3907+3907
Dt	28: 7	They will come at you from one **d** but flee	2006
	28:25	You will come at them from one **d** but flee	2006
Jos	8:20	no chance to escape **in any d,**	2178+2178+2256
Jdg	9:37	and a company is coming from the **d** *of*	2006
	20:42	So they fled before the Israelites in the **d** *of*	2006
2Sa	13:34	"I see men in the **d** *of* Horonaim,	2006
1Ki	18: 6	Ahab going in one **d** and Obadiah	2006
2Ki	3:21	water flowing from the **d** *of* Edom!	2006
2Ch	26:11	and Maaseiah the officer under the **d**	3338
	34: 4	**Under** his **d** the altars of the Baals	4200+7156
Ezr	5: 8	and is making rapid progress under their **d.**	10311
Ne	12:38	in the **opposite d.**	4578
	12:42	The choirs sang under the **d** *of* Jezrahiah.	7224
Job	37:12	At his **d** they swirl around over the face of	9374
Pr	7: 8	walking along in the **d** *of* her house	2006
Eze	9: 2	And I saw six men coming from the **d** *of*	2006
	10:11	The cherubim went in whatever **d**	5226
Jas	2:25	and sent them off *in* a different **d?**	*3847*

DIRECTIONS (7) [DIRECT]

Ge	46:28	ahead of him to Joseph to **get d** to Goshen.	3723
1Sa	14:16	the army melting away **in all d.**	2151
2Ch	35: 4	to the **d written** by David king of Israel and	4181
Eze	1:17	in any one of the four **d** the creatures faced;	8063
	10:11	in any one of the four **d** the cherubim faced;	8063
Ac	21:30	and the people came running from all **d.**	NIG
1Co	11:34	And when I come *I will* **give** further **d.**	*1411*

DIRECTIVES (1) [DIRECT]

1Co	11:17	In the following **d** I have no praise for you,	*4133*

DIRECTLY (7) [DIRECT]

Ge	30:38	be **d** in front of the flocks	4200+5790
Ex	14: 2	sea, **d** opposite Baal Zephon.	4200+5790+7156
Lev	25:12	eat only what is taken **d** from the fields.	4946
Ne	12:37	At the Fountain Gate they continued **d** up	5584
Pr	4:25	**fix** your gaze before you.	3837
Lk	20:17	Jesus **looked d** at them and asked,	*1838*
Ac	14: 9	Paul **looked d** at him,	*867*

DIRECTOR (58) [DIRECT]

Ne	11:17	the **d** who led in thanksgiving and prayer;	8031

Ps	4: T	For the **d of music.**	5904
	5: T	For the **d of music.**	5904
	6: T	For the **d of music.**	5904
	8: T	For the **d of music.**	5904
	9: T	For the **d of music.**	5904
	11: T	For the **d of music.** Of David.	5904
	12: T	For the **d of music.**	5904
	13: T	For the **d of music.** A psalm of David.	5904
	14: T	For the **d of music.** Of David.	5904
	18: T	For the **d of music.**	5904
	19: T	For the **d of music.** A psalm of David.	5904
	20: T	For the **d of music.** A psalm of David.	5904
	21: T	For the **d of music.** A psalm of David.	5904
	22: T	For the **d of music.**	5904
	31: T	For the **d of music.** A psalm of David.	5904
	36: T	For the **d of music.**	5904
	39: T	For the **d of music.**	5904
	40: T	For the **d of music.** Of David. A psalm.	5904
	41: T	For the **d of music.** A psalm of David.	5904
	42: T	For the **d of music.**	5904
	44: T	For the **d of music.**	5904
	45: T	For the **d of music.**	5904
	46: T	For the **d of music.**	5904
	47: T	For the **d of music.**	5904
	49: T	For the **d of music.**	5904
	51: T	For the **d of music.**	5904
	52: T	For the **d of music.**	5904
	53: T	For the **d of music.**	5904
	54: T	For the **d of music.**	5904
	55: T	For the **d of music.**	5904
	56: T	For the **d of music.**	5904
	57: T	For the **d of music.**	5904
	58: T	For the **d of music.**	5904
	59: T	For the **d of music.**	5904
	60: T	For the **d of music.**	5904
	61: T	For the **d of music.**	5904
	62: T	For the **d of music.**	5904
	64: T	For the **d of music.** A psalm of David.	5904
	65: T	For the **d of music.**	5904
	66: T	For the **d of music.** A song. A psalm.	5904
	67: T	For the **d of music.**	5904
	68: T	For the **d of music.**	5904
	69: T	For the **d of music.**	5904
	70: T	For the **d of music.** Of David. A petition.	5904
	75: T	For the **d of music.**	5904
	76: T	For the **d of music.**	5904
	77: T	For the **d of music.**	5904
	80: T	For the **d of music.**	5904
	81: T	For the **d of music.**	5904
	84: T	For the **d of music.**	5904
	85: T	For the **d of music.**	5904
	88: T	For the **d of music.**	5904
	109: T	For the **d of music.** Of David. A psalm.	5904
	139: T	For the **d of music.** A psalm.	5904
	140: T	For the **d of music.** A psalm of David.	5904
Hab	3:19	For the **d of music.**	5904
Ro	16:23	who is the city's **d of public works,**	3874

DIRECTORS (1) [DIRECT]

Ne	12:46	there had been **d** for the singers and for	8031

DIRECTS (4) [DIRECT]

Jdg	20: 9	We'll go up against it **as** the lot **d.**	928
Ps	42: 8	By day the LORD **d** his love,	7422
Pr	21: 1	he **d** it like	5742
Isa	48:17	who **d** you in the way you should go.	2005

DIRGE (2)

Mt	11:17	we **sang a d**, and you did not mourn.'	2577
Lk	7:32	we **sang a d**, and you did not cry.'	2577

DIRT (3)

2Sa	16:13	at him and showering him with **d.**	6760
Zec	9: 3	and gold like the **d** of the streets.	3226
1Pe	3:21	not the removal of **d** from the body but	4866

DISABLED (2) [ABLE]

Jn	5: 3	a great number of **d** people used to lie—	820
Heb	12:13	so that the lame may not be **d,**	1762

DISAGREED (1) [AGREE, DISAGREEMENT]

Ac	28:25	They **d** among themselves and began	851+1639

DISAGREEMENT (1) [AGREE, DISAGREED]

Ac	15:39	a sharp **d** that they parted company.	4237

DISALLOW (KJV) See FORBID

DISANNUL, DISANNULLED (KJV) See DISCREDIT, THWART, SET ASIDE

DISAPPEAR (10) [DISAPPEARED, DISAPPEARS]

Nu	27: 4	Why should our father's name **d**	1757
Ru	4:10	not **d** from among his family or from	4162
Isa	2:18	and the idols will totally **d.**	2736
	17: 3	The fortified city will **d** from Ephraim,	8697

Isa	29:20	the mockers will **d**, and all who have	3983
Mt	5:18	until heaven and earth **d,**	4216
	5:18	will by any means **d** from the Law	4216
Lk	16:17	It is easier for heaven and earth to **d** than	4216
Heb	8:13	what is obsolete and aging will soon **d.**	907
2Pe	3:10	The heavens will **d** with a roar;	4216

DISAPPEARED (3) [DISAPPEAR]

Jdg	6:21	And the angel of the LORD **d.**	2143+4946+6524
1Ki	20:40	and there, the man **d.**"	401
Lk	24:31	and he **d** from their sight.	908+1181

DISAPPEARS (4) [DISAPPEAR]

Job	14:11	As water **d** from the sea or	261
Hos	6: 4	like the early dew that **d.**	2143
	13: 3	like the early dew that **d,**	2143
1Co	13:10	when perfection comes, the imperfect **d.**	2934

DISAPPOINT (1) [DISAPPOINTED]

Ro	5: 5	And hope does not **d** us,	2875

DISAPPOINTED (4) [DISAPPOINT]

Job	6:20	they arrive there, only to be **d.**	2917
Ps	22: 5	in you they trusted and were not **d.**	1017
Isa	49:23	those who hope in me will not be **d.**"	1017
Jer	2:36	be **d** by Egypt as you were by Assyria.	1017

DISAPPROVE (1)

Pr	24:18	and **d** and turn his wrath away from him.	928+6524+8317

DISARMED (1) [DISARMS]

Col	2:15	And having **d** the powers and authorities,	588

DISARMS (1) [DISARMED]

Job	12:21	contempt on nobles and **d** the mighty.	4653+8332

DISASTER (119) [DISASTERS, DISASTROUS]

Ge	19:19	this **d** will overtake me, and I'll die.	8288
Ex	32:12	relent and do not bring **d** on your people.	8288
	32:14	on his people the **d** he had threatened.	8288
Dt	28:61	and **d** not recorded in this Book of the Law,	4804
	29:19	This will bring **d** on the watered land	6200
	29:21	from all the tribes of Israel for **d,**	8288
	31:29	**d** will fall upon you	8288
	32:35	their day of **d** is near and their doom rushes	369
Jos	24:20	he will turn and bring **d** on you and make	8317
Jdg	20:34	not realize how near **d** was.	8288
	20:41	they realized that **d** had come upon them.	8288
1Sa	6: 9	the LORD has brought this great **d** on us.	8288
	25:17	because **d** is hanging over our master	8288
2Sa	17:14	of Ahithophel in order to bring **d**	8288
	22:19	They confronted me in the day of my **d,**	369
1Ki	5: 4	and there is no adversary or **d.**	7004+8273
	8:37	whatever **d** or disease may come,	5596
	9: 9	the LORD brought all this **d** on them.' "	8288
	14:10	to bring **d** on the house of Jeroboam.	8288
	21:21	'I am going to bring **d** on you.	8288
	21:29	I will not bring this **d** in his day,	8288
	22:23	The LORD has decreed **d** for you."	8288
2Ki	6:33	[the king] said, "This **d** is from the LORD.	8288
	21:12	to bring such **d** on Jerusalem and Judah that	8288
	22:16	to bring **d** on this place and its people,	8288
	22:20	Your eyes will not see all the **d** I am going	8288
2Ch	6:28	whatever **d** or disease may come,	5596
	7:22	that is why he brought all this **d** on them.' "	8288
	18:22	The LORD has decreed **d** for you."	8288
	34:24	to bring **d** on this place and its people—	8288
	34:28	Your eyes will not see all the **d** I am going	8288
Est	8: 6	how can I bear to see **d** fall on my people?	8288
Job	18:12	**d** is ready for him when he falls.	369
	31: 3	**d** for those who do wrong?	5798
Ps	18:18	They confronted me in the day of my **d,**	369
	37:19	In times of **d** they will not wither;	8288
	57: 1	of your wings until the **d** has passed.	2095
	91:10	no **d** will come near your tent.	5596
	140:11	may **d** hunt down men of violence.	8273
Pr	1:26	I in turn will laugh at your **d;**	369
	1:27	when **d** sweeps over you like a whirlwind,	369
	3:25	of sudden **d** or of the ruin that overtakes	7065
	6:15	Therefore **d** will overtake him in an instant;	369
	16: 4	even the wicked for a day of **d.**	8288
	17: 5	over **d** will not go unpunished.	369
	27:10	when **d** strikes you—	369
Ecc	11: 2	not know what **d** may come upon the land.	8288
Isa	3: 9	They have brought **d** upon themselves.	8288
	3:11	**D** is upon them!	8273
	10: 3	when **d** comes from afar?	8739
	31: 2	Yet he too is wise and can bring **d;**	8273
	45: 7	I bring prosperity and create **d;**	8273
	47:11	**D** will come upon you,	8288
Jer	1:14	"From the north **d** will be poured out	8288
	2: 3	and **d** overtook them,' "	8288
	4: 6	For I am bringing **d** from the north,	8288
	4:15	proclaiming **d** from the hills of Ephraim.	224
	4:20	**D** follows disaster; the whole land lies in ruins.	8691
	4:20	Disaster follows **d;** the whole land lies in ruins.	8691
	6: 1	For **d** looms out of the north,	8288

Jer	6:19	I am bringing **d** on this people,	8288
	11:11	on them a **d** they cannot escape.	8288
	11:12	not help them at all when **d** strikes.	8288
	11:17	who planted you, has decreed **d** for you,	8288
	11:23	because I will bring **d** on the men	8288
	15:11	with you in times of **d** and times of distress.	8288
	16:10	the LORD decreed such a great **d**	8288
	17:17	you are my refuge in the day of **d.**	8288
	17:18	Bring on them the day of **d;**	8288
	18: 8	and not inflict on it the **d** I had planned.	8288
	18:11	a **d** for you and devising a plan against you.	8288
	18:17	and not my face in the day of their **d.**"	369
	19: 3	to bring a **d** on this place that will make	8288
	19:15	the villages around it every **d** I pronounced	8288
	23:12	I will bring **d** on them in	8288
	25:29	to bring **d** on the city that bears my Name,	8317
	25:32	**D** is spreading from nation to nation;	8288
	26: 3	and not bring on them the **d** I was planning	8288
	26:13	and not bring the **d** he has pronounced	8288
	26:19	that he did not bring the **d** he pronounced	8288
	26:19	about to bring a terrible **d** on ourselves!"	8288
	28: 8	**d** and plague against many countries	8288
	31:28	and to overthrow, destroy and bring **d,**	8317
	32:23	So you brought all this **d** upon them.	8288
	35:17	in Jerusalem every **d** I pronounced	8288
	36: 3	about every **d** I plan to inflict on them, each	8288
	36:31	the people of Judah every **d** I pronounced	8288
	39:16	against this city through a **d,**	8288
	40: 2	"The LORD your God decreed this **d**	8288
	42:10	for I am grieved over the **d** I have inflicted	8288
	42:17	or escape the **d** I will bring on them.'	8288
	44: 2	You saw the great **d** I brought on Jerusalem	8288
	44: 7	Why bring such great **d** on yourselves	8288
	44:11	to bring **d** on you and to destroy all Judah.	8288
	44:23	this **d** has come upon you, as you now see."	8288
	45: 5	For I will bring **d** on all people,	8288
	46:21	for the day of **d** is coming upon them,	369
	49: 8	for I will bring **d** on Esau at	369
	49:32	and will bring **d** on them from every side,"	369
	49:37	I will bring **d** upon them,	8288
	51: 2	on every side in the day of her **d.**	8288
	51:64	to rise no more because of the **d** I will bring	8288
Eze	7: 5	"This is what the Sovereign LORD says: **D!**	8288
	7: 5	An unheard-of **d** is coming.	8288
	14:22	be consoled regarding the **d** I have brought	8288
	14:22	every **d** I have brought upon it.	889S
Da	9:12	by bringing upon us great **d.**	8288
	9:13	all this **d** has come upon us,	8288
	9:14	The LORD did not hesitate to bring the **d**	8288
Am	3: 6	When **d** comes to a city,	8288
	9:10	'**D** will not overtake or meet us.'	8288
Ob	1: 5	Oh, what a **d** awaits you—	1950
	1:13	the gates of my people in the day of their **d,**	369
	1:13	in their calamity in the day of their **d,**	369
	1:13	nor seize their wealth in the day of their **d.**	369
Mic	1:12	because **d** has come from the LORD,	8273
	2: 3	"I am planning **d** against this people,	8288
	3:11	No **d** will come upon us."	8288
Zec	8:14	as I had determined to bring **d** upon you	8317

DISASTERS (5) [DISASTER]

Dt	28:59	harsh and prolonged **d,**	4804
	31:17	Many **d** and difficulties will come	8288
	31:17	'Have not these **d** come upon us	8288
	31:21	And when many **d** and difficulties come	8288
Jer	51:60	on a scroll about all the **d** that would come	8288

DISASTROUS (1) [DISASTER]

Ac	27:10	voyage is going to be **d** and bring great loss to ship and cargo,	3552+5615

DISCARD (1) [DISCARDED]

Ps	119:119	the wicked of the earth you **d** like dross;	8697

DISCARDED (1) [DISCARD]

Ps	102:26	and they will be **d.**	2736

DISCERN (6) [DISCERNED, DISCERNING, DISCERNMENT]

Dt	32:29	and **d** what their end will be!	1067
Job	6:30	Can my mouth not **d** malice?	1067
	34: 4	Let us **d** for ourselves what is right;	1047
Ps	19:12	Who can **d** his errors?	1067
	139: 3	You **d** my going out and my lying down;	2431
Php	1:10	be able to **d** what is best and may be pure	1507

DISCERNED (1) [DISCERN]

1Co	2:14	because they are spiritually **d.**	373

DISCERNING (19) [DISCERN]

Ge	41:33	for a **d** and wise man and put him in charge	1067
	41:39	there is no one so **d** and wise as you.	1067
2Sa	14:17	the king is like an angel of God in **d** good	9048
1Ki	3: 9	a **d** heart to govern your people and	9048
	3:12	I will give you a wise and **d** heart,	1067
Pr	1: 5	and let the **d** get guidance—	1067
	8: 9	To the **d** all of them are right;	1067
	10:13	Wisdom is found on the lips of the **d,**	1067
	14: 6	but knowledge comes easily to the **d.**	1067
	14:33	the **d** and even among fools she lets herself	1067
	15:14	The **d** heart seeks knowledge,	1067
	16:21	The wise in heart are called **d,**	1067

Pr	17:24	A **d** *man* keeps wisdom in view,	1067
	17:28	and **d** if he holds his tongue.	1067
	18:15	The heart of the **d** acquires knowledge;	1067
	19:25	rebuke a *man*, and he will gain knowledge	1067
	28: 7	He who keeps the law *is* a **d** son,	1067
Da	2:21	to the wise and knowledge to the **d**.	10100+10313
Hos	14: 9	Who *is* **d**? He will understand them.	1067

DISCERNMENT (8) [DISCERN]

Dt	32:28	there is no **d** in them.	9312
1Ki	3:11	for the death of your enemies but for **d**	1067
2Ch	2:12	endowed with intelligence and **d**,	1069
Job	12:20	of trusted advisers and takes away the **d**	3248
Ps	119:125	me **d** that I may understand your	1067
Pr	3:21	My son, preserve sound judgment and **d**,	4659
	17:10	A rebuke impresses a *man* of **d** more than	1067
	28:11	but a poor man *who has* **d** sees through him.	1067

DISCHARGE (21) [DISCHARGED, DISCHARGING]

Lev	15: 2	'When any man has a bodily **d**,	2307
	15: 2	a bodily discharge, the **d** is unclean.	2308
	15: 3	how his **d** will bring about uncleanness:	2308
	15: 4	the *man with a* **d** lies on will be unclean,	2307
	15: 6	anything the *man with a* **d** sat on	2307
	15: 7	the *man who has a* **d** must wash his clothes	2307
	15: 8	*with the* **d** spits on someone who is clean,	2307
	15:11	*with a* **d** touches without rinsing his hands	2307
	15:13	" 'When a man is cleansed from his **d**,	2308
	15:15	the LORD for the man because of his **d**.	2308
	15:25	woman *has a* **d** *of* blood for many days	2307+2308
	15:25	or *has a* **d** that continues beyond her period,	2307
	15:25	be unclean as long as she has the **d**,	2308+3240
	15:26	on while her **d** continues will be unclean,	2308
	15:28	" 'When she is cleansed from her **d**,	2308
	15:30	the LORD for the uncleanness of her **d**.	2308
	15:32	the regulations for a *man with a* **d**,	2307
	15:25	for a man or a woman *with a* **d**,	2307+2308
	22: 4	an infectious skin disease or a **bodily d**,	2307
Nu	5: 2	an infectious skin disease or a **d**	2307
2Ti	4: 5	**d** all the duties of your ministry.	4442

DISCHARGED (1) [DISCHARGE]

Ecc	8: 8	As no one is **d** in time of war,	5449

DISCHARGING (1) [DISCHARGE]

1Co	9:17	I am simply **d** the trust committed to me.	NIG

DISCIPLE (29) [DISCIPLES, DISCIPLES']

Isa	19:11	a **d** *of* the ancient kings"?	1201
Mt	8:21	Another **d** said to him, "Lord,	3412
	10:42	of these little ones because he is my **d**,	3412
	27:57	who *had* himself **become a d** of Jesus.	3411
Lk	14:26	he cannot be my **d**.	3412
	14:27	and follow me cannot be my **d**.	3412
	14:33	up everything he has cannot be my **d**.	3412
Jn	9:28	"You are his fellow's **d**!	3412
	13:23	One of them, the **d** whom Jesus loved,	NIG
	13:24	Simon Peter motioned to this **d** and said,	NIG
	18:15	and another **d** were following Jesus.	3412
	18:15	this **d** was known to the high priest,	3412
	18:16	The other **d**, who was known to	3412
	19:26	and the **d** whom he loved standing nearby,	3412
	19:27	and *to* the **d**, "Here is your mother."	3412
	19:27	this **d** took her into his home.	3412
	19:38	Now Joseph was a **d** of Jesus,	3412
	20: 2	to Simon Peter and the other **d**,	3412
	20: 3	Peter and the other **d** started for the tomb.	3412
	20: 4	but the other **d** outran Peter and reached	3412
	20: 8	Finally the other **d**, who had reached	3412
	21: 7	Then the **d** whom Jesus loved said to Peter,	3412
	21:20	**d** whom Jesus loved was following them.	3412
	21:23	the brothers that this **d** would not die.	3412
	21:24	This is the **d** who testifies to these things	3412
Ac	9:10	In Damascus there was a **d** named Ananias.	3412
	9:26	not believing that he really was a **d**.	3412
	9:36	In Joppa there was a **d** named Tabitha	3413
	16: 1	where a **d** named Timothy lived,	3412

DISCIPLES (266) [DISCIPLE]

Isa	8:16	and seal up the law among my **d**.	4341
Mt	5: 1	His **d** came to him,	3412
	8:23	he got into the boat and his **d** followed him.	3412
	8:25	The **d** went and woke him, saying, "Lord,	NIG
	9:10	and ate with him and his **d**.	3412
	9:11	they asked his **d**,	3412
	9:14	Then John's **d** came and asked him,	3412
	9:14	but your **d** do not fast?"	3412
	9:19	and so did his **d**.	3412
	9:37	Then he said *to* his **d**, "The harvest is	3412
	10: 1	He called his twelve **d** to him	3412
	11: 1	After Jesus had finished instructing his twelve **d**,	3412
	11: 2	what Christ was doing, he sent his **d**	3412
	11: 7	As **John's d** were leaving,	4047S
	12: 1	His **d** were hungry and began	3412
	12: 2	Your **d** are doing what is unlawful on	3412
	12:49	Pointing to his **d**, he said,	3412
	13:10	The **d** came to him and asked,	3412
	13:36	His **d** came to him and said,	3412
	14:12	John's **d** came and took his body	3412
	14:15	the **d** came to him and said,	3412
	14:19	Then he gave them *to* the **d**,	3412

Mt	14:19	and the **d** gave them to the people.	3412
	14:20	and the **d** picked up twelve basketfuls	NIG
	14:22	the **d** get into the boat and go on ahead	3412
	14:26	When the **d** saw him walking on the lake,	3412
	15: 2	"Why do your **d** break the tradition of	3412
	15:12	Then the **d** came to him and asked,	3412
	15:23	So his **d** came to him and urged him,	3412
	15:32	Jesus called his **d** to him and said,	3412
	15:33	His **d** answered, "Where could we get	3412
	15:36	he broke them and gave them *to* the **d**,	3412
	16: 5	Afterward the **d** picked up seven basketfuls	NIG
	16: 5	the **d** forgot to take bread.	3412
	16:13	he asked his **d**, "Who do people say	3412
	16:20	Then he warned his **d** not to tell anyone	3412
	16:21	that time on Jesus began to explain *to* his **d**	3412
	16:24	Then Jesus said *to* his **d**,	3412
	17: 6	When the **d** heard this, they fell facedown	3412
	17:10	The **d** asked him, "Why then do the	3412
	17:13	Then the **d** understood that he was talking	3412
	17:16	I brought him *to* your **d**,	3412
	17:19	the **d** came to Jesus in private and asked,	3412
	17:23	And the **d** were filled with grief.	NIG
	17:24	**Jesus and his d** arrived in Capernaum,	899S
	18: 1	At that time the **d** came to Jesus and asked,	3412
	19:10	The **d** said to him,	3412
	19:13	But the **d** rebuked those who brought them.	3412
	19:23	Then Jesus said *to* his **d**,	3412
	19:25	When the **d** heard this,	3412
	20:17	he took the twelve **d** aside and said to them,	3412
	20:29	As **Jesus and his d** were leaving Jericho,	899S
	21: 1	Jesus sent two **d**,	3412
	21: 6	The **d** went and did as Jesus had instructed	3412
	21:20	When the **d** saw this, they were amazed.	3412
	22:16	They sent their **d** to him along with	3412
	23: 1	Then Jesus said to the crowds and *to* his **d**:	3412
	24: 1	and was walking away when his **d** came up	3412
	24: 3	the **d** came to him privately.	3412
	26: 1	all these things, he said *to* his **d**,	3412
	26: 8	When the **d** saw this, they were indignant.	3412
	26:17	the **d** came to Jesus and asked,	3412
	26:18	the Passover with my **d** at your house.' "	3412
	26:19	So the **d** did as Jesus had directed them	3412
	26:26	and gave it *to* his **d**, saying, "Take and eat;	3412
	26:35	And all the other **d** said the same.	3412
	26:36	with **his d** to a place called Gethsemane,	899S
	26:40	to his **d** and found them sleeping.	3412
	26:45	Then he returned to the **d** and said to them,	3412
	26:56	Then all the **d** deserted him and fled.	3412
	27:64	his **d** may come and steal the body and tell	3412
	28: 7	Then go quickly and tell his **d**:	3412
	28: 8	and ran to tell his **d**.	3412
	28:13	'His **d** came during the night	3412
	28:16	Then the eleven **d** went to Galilee,	3412
	28:19	Therefore go and **make d** of all nations,	3411
Mk	2:15	with him and his **d**,	3412
	2:16	they asked his **d**: "Why does he eat	3412
	2:18	John's **d** and the Pharisees were fasting.	3412
	2:18	"How is it that John's **d** and the disciples of	3412
	2:18	"How is it that John's **disciples** and the **d** of	3412
	2:23	and as his **d** walked along,	3412
	3: 7	Jesus withdrew with his **d** to the lake,	3412
	3: 9	Because of the crowd he told his **d** to have	3412
	3:20	that **he and his d** were not even able to eat.	899
	4:34	But when he was alone *with* his own **d**,	3412
	4:35	he said *to* **his d**, "Let us go over	899S
	4:38	The **d** woke him and said to him, "Teacher,	NIG
	4:40	He said *to* **his d**, "Why are you so afraid?	899S
	5:31	his **d** answered, "and yet you can ask,	3412
	5:40	and mother and the **d** who were with him,	NIG
	6: 1	accompanied by his **d**.	3412
	6:29	John's **d** came and took his body and laid it	3412
	6:35	so his **d** came to him.	3412
	6:41	Then he gave them *to* his **d** to set before	3412
	6:43	and the **d** picked up twelve basketfuls	NIG
	6:45	Immediately Jesus made his **d** get into	3412
	6:48	He saw the **d** straining at the oars,	899S
	7: 2	saw some *of* his **d** eating food with hands	3412
	7: 5	"Why don't your **d** live according to	3412
	7:17	his **d** asked him about this parable.	3412
	8: 1	Jesus called his **d** to him and said,	3412
	8: 4	His **d** answered, "But where	3412
	8: 6	he broke them and gave them *to* his **d**	3412
	8: 7	he gave thanks for them also and told the **d**	NIG
	8: 8	Afterward the **d** picked up seven basketfuls	NIG
	8:10	he got into the boat with his **d** and went to	3412
	8:14	The **d** had forgotten to bring bread,	NIG
	8:27	Jesus and his **d** went on to the villages	3412
	8:33	But when Jesus turned and looked at his **d**,	3412
	8:34	the crowd to him along with his **d** and said:	3412
	9:14	When they came to the other **d**,	3412
	9:18	I asked your **d** to drive out the spirit,	3412
	9:28	his **d** asked him privately,	3412
	9:31	because he was teaching his **d**.	3412
	10:10	the **d** asked Jesus about this.	3412
	10:13	but the **d** rebuked them.	3412
	10:23	Jesus looked around and said *to* his **d**,	3412
	10:24	The **d** were amazed at his words.	3412
	10:26	The **d** were even more amazed,	1254+3836S
	10:32	and the **d** were astonished.	NIG
	10:46	As Jesus and his **d**,	3412
	11: 1	Jesus sent two *of* his **d**,	3412
	11:14	And his **d** heard him say it.	3412
	12:43	Calling his **d** to him, Jesus said,	3412
	13: 1	one *of* his **d** said to him, "Look, Teacher!	3412
	14:12	Jesus' **d** asked him, "Where do you want	3412
	14:13	So he sent two *of* his **d**, telling them,	3412
	14:14	where I may eat the Passover with my **d**?'	3412

Mk	14:16	the **d** left, went into the city	3412
	14:22	and gave it *to* **his d**, saying, "Take it;	899S
	14:32	and Jesus said *to* **his d**,	3412
	14:37	to his **d** and found them sleeping.	NIG
	16: 7	But go, tell his **d** and Peter,	3412
	16:20	**the d** went out and preached everywhere,	1697S
Lk	5:30	to their sect complained to his **d**,	3412
	5:33	"John's **d** often fast and pray,	3412
	5:33	and so do the **d** of the Pharisees,	NIG
	6: 1	his **d** began to pick some heads of grain,	3412
	6:13	he called his **d** to him and chose twelve	3412
	6:17	*of* his **d** was there and a great number	3412
	6:20	Looking at his **d**, he said:	3412
	7:11	and his **d** and a large crowd went along	3412
	7:18	John's **d** told him about all these things.	3412
	8: 9	His **d** asked him what this parable meant.	3412
	8:22	One day Jesus said to **his d**,	899S
	8:24	The **d** went and woke him, saying, "Master,	NIG
	8:25	"Where is your faith?" he asked his **d**.	899S
	9:14	But he said to his **d**, "Have them sit	3412
	9:15	The **d** did so, and everybody sat down.	NIG
	9:16	Then he gave them *to* the **d** to set before	3412
	9:17	and the **d** picked up twelve basketfuls	NIG
	9:18	in private and his **d** were with him,	3412
	9:36	The **d** kept this to themselves,	899S
	9:40	I begged your **d** to drive it out,	3412
	9:43	he said to his **d**,	3412
	9:46	among **the d** as to which of them would be	899S
	9:54	When the **d** James and John saw this,	3412
	10:23	Then he turned to his **d** and said privately,	3412
	10:38	As **Jesus and his d** were on their way,	899S
	11: 1	When he finished, one *of* his **d** said to him,	3412
	11: 1	teach us to pray, just as John taught his **d**."	3412
	12: 1	Jesus began to speak first to his **d**, saying:	3412
	12:22	Then Jesus said to his **d**:	3412
	16: 1	Jesus told his **d**: "There was a rich man	3412
	17: 1	Jesus said to his **d**: "Things that	3412
	17:22	Then he said to his **d**, "The time is coming	3412
	18: 1	Then Jesus told **his d** a parable to show	899S
	18:15	When the **d** saw this, they rebuked them.	3412
	18:34	The **d** did not understand any of this.	899S
	19:29	he sent two *of* his **d**, saying to them,	3412
	19:37	the whole crowd *of* **d** began joyfully	3412
	19:39	"Teacher, rebuke your **d**!"	3412
	20:45	people were listening, Jesus said *to* his **d**,	3412
	21: 5	Some of his **d** were remarking about how	NIG
	22:11	where I may eat the Passover with my **d**?'	3412
	22:38	The **d** said, "See, Lord,	1254+3836S
	22:39	and his **d** followed him.	3412
	22:45	from prayer and went back to the **d**,	3412
Jn	1:35	John was there again with two of his **d**.	3412
	1:37	When the two **d** heard him say this,	3412
	2: 2	and Jesus and his **d** had also been invited to	3412
	2:11	and his **d** put their faith in him.	3412
	2:12	with his mother and brothers and his **d**.	3412
	2:17	His **d** remembered that it is written:	3412
	2:22	his **d** recalled what he had said.	3412
	3:22	Jesus and his **d** went out into	3412
	3:25	between some of John's **d** and a certain Jew	3412
	4: 1	and baptizing more **d** than John,	3412
	4: 2	not Jesus who baptized, but his **d**.	3412
	4: 8	(His **d** had gone into the town to buy food.)	3412
	4:27	Just then his **d** returned and were surprised	3412
	4:31	Meanwhile his **d** urged him, "Rabbi,	3412
	4:33	Then his **d** said to each other,	3412
	6: 3	on a mountainside and sat down with his **d**.	3412
	6: 8	Another of his **d**, Andrew,	3412
	6:12	he said *to* his **d**, "Gather the pieces	3412
	6:16	evening came, his **d** went down to the lake,	3412
	6:22	and that Jesus had not entered it *with* his **d**,	3412
	6:24	that neither Jesus nor his **d** were there,	3412
	6:60	On hearing it, many of his **d** said,	3412
	6:61	that his **d** were grumbling about this,	3412
	6:66	From this time many of his **d** turned back	3412
	7: 3	so that your **d** may see the miracles you do.	3412
	8:31	hold to my teaching, you are really my **d**.	3412
	9: 2	His **d** asked him, "Rabbi, who sinned,	3412
	9:27	Do you want to become his **d**, too?"	3412
	9:28	We are **d** of Moses!	3412
	11: 7	he said *to* his **d**, "Let us go back to Judea."	3412
	11:12	His **d** replied, "Lord, if he sleeps,	3412
	11:13	but **his d** thought he meant natural sleep.	1697S
	11:16	said *to* **the rest of** the **d**,	5209
	11:54	where he stayed with his **d**.	3412
	12: 4	But one of his **d**, Judas Iscariot,	3412
	12:16	At first his **d** did not understand all this.	3412
	13:22	His **d** stared at one another,	3412
	13:35	all men will know that you are my **d**,	3412
	15: 8	showing yourselves to be my **d**.	3412
	16:17	Some of his **d** said to one another,	3412
	16:29	Then Jesus' **d** said,	3412
	18: 1	with his **d** and crossed the Kidron Valley.	3412
	18: 1	and he and his **d** went into it.	3412
	18: 2	Jesus had often met there with his **d**.	3412
	18:17	"You are not one of his **d**, are you?"	3412
	18:19	the high priest questioned Jesus about his **d**	3412
	18:25	he was asked, "You are not one of his **d**,	3412
	20:10	Then the **d** went back to their homes,	3412
	20:18	Mary Magdalene went *to* the **d** with	3412
	20:19	when the **d** were together,	3412
	20:20	The **d** were overjoyed when they saw	3412
	20:24	was not with **the d** when Jesus came.	899S
	20:25	other **d** told him, "We have seen the Lord!"	3412
	20:26	A week later his **d** were in the house again,	3412
	20:30	miraculous signs in the presence of his **d**,	3412
	21: 1	Afterward Jesus appeared again *to* his **d**,	3412
	21: 2	and two other **d** were together.	3412

Jn	21: 4	but the **d** did not realize that it was Jesus.	3412
	21: 8	The other **d** followed in the boat,	3412
	21:12	None of the **d** dared ask him,	3412
	21:14	now the third time Jesus appeared to his **d**	3412
Ac	6: 1	when the number of **d** was increasing,	3412
	6: 2	So the Twelve gathered all the **d** together	3412+3836
	6: 7	number of **d** in Jerusalem increased rapidly,	3412
	9: 1	murderous threats against the Lord's **d**.	3412
	9:19	Saul spent several days with the **d**	3412
	9:26	he tried to join the **d**,	3412
	9:38	when the **d** heard that Peter was in Lydda,	3412
	11:26	The **d** were called Christians first	3412
	11:29	The **d**, each according to his ability,	3412
	13:52	And the **d** were filled with joy and with	3412
	14:20	But after the **d** had gathered around him,	3412
	14:21	won a large number of **d**.	3411
	14:22	the **d** and encouraging them to remain true	3412
	14:28	they stayed there a long time with the **d**.	3412
	15:10	on the necks of the **d** a yoke that neither we	3412
	18:23	strengthening all the **d**.	3412
	18:27	and wrote to the **d** there to welcome him.	3412
	19: 1	There he found some **d**	3412
	19: 9	the **d** with him and had discussions daily in	3412
	19:30	but the **d** would not let him.	3412
	20: 1	Paul sent for the **d** and,	3412
	20:30	in order to draw away **d** after them.	3412
	21: 4	Finding the **d** there, he stayed with them	3412
	21: 5	All the **d** and their wives	NIG
	21:16	of the **d** from Caesarea accompanied us	3412
	21:16	a man from Cyprus and one of the early **d**.	3412

DISCIPLES' (1) [DISCIPLE]

Jn	13: 5	into a basin and began to wash his **d'** feet,	3412

DISCIPLINE (36) [DISCIPLINED, DISCIPLINES, SELF-DISCIPLINE]

Dt	4:36	From heaven he made you hear his voice to	
		d you.	3579
	11: 2	not the ones who saw and experienced the **d**	4592
	21:18	not listen to them when they **d** him,	3579
Job	5:17	so do not despise the **d** of the Almighty.	4592
Ps	6: 1	do not rebuke me in your anger or **d** me	3579
	38: 1	do not rebuke me in your anger or **d** me	3579
	39:11	You rebuke and **d** men for their sin;	3579
	94:12	Blessed is the man you **d**, O Lord,	3579
Pr	1: 2	for attaining wisdom and **d**;	4592
	1: 7	but fools despise wisdom and **d**.	4592
	3:11	do not despise the Lord's **d** and do	4592
	5:12	You will say, "How I hated **d**!	4592
	5:23	He will die for lack of **d**,	4592
	6:23	and the corrections of **d** are the way to life,	4592
	10:17	He who heeds **d** shows the way to life,	4592
	12: 1	Whoever loves **d** loves knowledge,	4592
	13:18	He who ignores **d** comes to poverty	4592
	13:24	but he who loves him is careful to **d** him.	4592
	15: 5	A fool spurns his father's **d**,	4592
	15:10	Stern **d** awaits him who leaves the path;	4592
	15:32	He who ignores **d** despises himself,	4592
	19:18	**D** your son, for in that there is hope;	3579
	22:15	but the rod of **d** will drive it far from him.	4592
	23:13	Do not withhold **d** from a child.	4592
	23:23	get wisdom, **d** and understanding.	4592
	29:17	**D** your son, and he will give you peace;	3579
Jer	17:23	and would not listen or respond to **d**.	4592
	30:11	I will **d** you but only with justice;	3579
	32:33	they would not listen or respond to **d**.	4592
	46:28	I will **d** you but only with justice;	3579
Hos	5: 2	I will **d** all of them.	4592
Heb	12: 5	"My son, do not make light of the Lord's **d**,	4082
	12: 7	Endure hardship as **d**;	4082
	12: 8	(and everyone undergoes **d**),	4005S
	12:11	No **d** seems pleasant at the time,	4082
Rev	3:19	Those whom I love I rebuke and **d**.	4084

DISCIPLINED (10) [DISCIPLINE]

Pr	1: 3	a **d** and prudent life, doing what is right	4592
Isa	26:16	when you **d** them,	4592
Jer	31:18	'You **d** me like an unruly calf,	3579
	31:18	and I have been **d**.	3579
1Co	11:32	we are being **d** so that we will not	4084
Tit	1: 8	who is self-controlled, upright, holy and **d**.	1604
Heb	12: 7	For what son is not **d** by his father?	4084
	12: 8	not **d** (and everyone undergoes discipline),	4082
	12: 9	we have all had human fathers who **d** us	4083
	12:10	Our fathers **d** us for a little while	4084

DISCIPLINES (6) [DISCIPLINE]

Dt	8: 5	then in your heart that as a man **d** his son,	3579
	8: 5	so the Lord your God **d** you.	3579
Ps	94:10	Does he who **d** nations not punish?	3579
Pr	3:12	because the Lord **d** those he loves,	3519
Heb	12: 6	because the Lord **d** those he loves,	4084
	12:10	but God **d** us for our good,	NIG

DISCLOSE (2) [DISCLOSED]

Job	11: 6	and **d** to you the secrets of wisdom,	5583
Isa	26:21	The earth will **d** the blood shed upon her;	1655

DISCLOSED (6) [DISCLOSE]

Mt	10:26	nothing concealed that will not be **d**,	636
Mk	4:22	For whatever is hidden is meant to be **d**,	5746
Lk	8:17	there is nothing hidden that will not be **d**,	5745

Lk	12: 2	nothing concealed that will not be **d**,	636
Col	1:26	but is now **d** to the saints,	5746
Heb	9: 8	into the Most Holy Place had not yet been **d**	5746

DISCOMFITED, DISCOMFITURE (KJV)
See BEAT, CONFUSION, FORCED LABOR, OVERCAME, PANIC, ROUTED, ROUTING

DISCOMFORT (1)

Jnh	4: 6	to give shade for his head to ease his **d**,	8288

DISCONTENTED (1)

1Sa	22: 2	or in debt or **d** gathered around him,	5253+5883

DISCORD (2)

Est	1:18	There will be no end of disrespect and **d**.	7912
Gal	5:20	hatred, **d**, jealousy, fits of rage,	2251

DISCOURAGE (2) [DISCOURAGED, DISCOURAGEMENT, DISCOURAGING]

Nu	32: 7	Why do you **d** the Israelites from going	
		over into the land	4213+5648
Ezr	4: 4	the peoples around them set out to **d**	3338+8332

DISCOURAGED (15) [DISCOURAGE]

Nu	32: 9	they **d** the Israelites from entering the land	
			4213+5648
Dt	1:21	Do not be afraid; do not be **d**."	3169
	31: 8	Do not be afraid; do not be **d**."	3169
Jos	1: 9	Do not be terrified; do not be **d**,	3169
	8: 1	Do not be afraid; do not be **d**.	3169
	10:25	Do not be afraid; do not be **d**.	3169
1Ch	22:13	Do not be afraid or **d**.	3169
	28:20	Do not be afraid or **d**, for the Lord God,	3169
2Ch	20:15	not be afraid or **d** because of this vast army.	3169
	20:17	Do not be afraid; do not be **d**.	3169
	32: 7	Do not be afraid or **d** because of the king	3169
Job	4: 5	now trouble comes to you, and you are **d**;	4206
Isa	42: 4	not falter or be **d** till he establishes justice	8368
Eph	3:13	to be **d** because of my sufferings for you,	1591
Col	3:21	or they will become **d**.	126

DISCOURAGEMENT (1) [DISCOURAGE]

Ex	6: 9	because of their **d** and cruel bondage.	7919+8120

DISCOURAGING (1) [DISCOURAGE]

Jer	38: 4	He is **d** the soldiers who are left	3338+8332

DISCOURSE (2) [DISCOURSED]

Job	27: 1	And Job continued his **d**:	5442
	29: 1	Job continued his **d**:	5442

DISCOURSED (1) [DISCOURSE]

Ac	24:25	As Paul **d** on righteousness,	1363

DISCOVER (5) [DISCOVERED]

Ecc	7:14	a man cannot **d** anything about his future.	5162
	7:24	and most profound—who can **d** it?	5162
	7:27	to another to **d** the scheme of things—	5162
	8:17	man cannot **d** its meaning.	5162
2Co	13: 6	And I trust that you will **d** that we have	1182

DISCOVERED (12) [DISCOVER]

Ge	26:19	the valley and **d** a well of fresh water there.	5162
	36:24	This is the Anah who **d** the hot springs in	5162
Dt	22:28	to be married and rapes her and they are **d**,	5162
Jdg	16: 9	So the secret of his strength was not **d**.	3359
	21: 8	They **d** that no one from Jabesh Gilead	2180
Ru	3: 8	he turned and **d** a woman lying at his feet.	2180
1Sa	22: 6	that David and his men had been **d**.	3359
2Ki	17: 4	king of Assyria **d** that Hoshea was a traitor,	5162
	23:24	the priest had **d** in the temple of the Lord.	5162
Ps	44:21	would not God have **d** it,	2983
Ecc	7:27	says the Teacher, "this is what I have **d**:	5162
Ro	4: 1	our forefather, **d** in this matter?	2351

DISCREDIT (2) [DISCREDITED]

Ne	6:13	they would give me a bad name to **d** me.	3070
Job	40: 8	"Would you **d** my justice?	7296

DISCREDITED (2) [DISCREDIT]

Ac	19:27	temple of the great goddess Artemis will be	
		d,	1650+3357+4029
2Co	6: 3	so that our ministry will not be **d**.	3699

DISCREETLY (1) [DISCRETION]

Pr	26:16	than seven men who answer **d**.	3248

DISCRETION (6) [DISCREETLY]

1Ch	22:12	the Lord give you **d** and understanding	8507
Pr	1: 4	knowledge and **d** to the young—	4659
	2:11	**D** will protect you,	4659
	5: 2	that you may maintain **d**	4659
	8:12	I possess knowledge and **d**.	4659

Pr	11:22	a beautiful woman who shows no **d**.	3248

DISCRIMINATED (1)

Jas	2: 4	not **d** among yourselves and become judges	1359

DISCUSS (2) [DISCUSSED, DISCUSSING, DISCUSSION, DISCUSSIONS]

Lk	6:11	to **d** with one another what they might do	1362
Heb	9: 5	But we cannot **d** these things in detail now.	3306

DISCUSSED (9) [DISCUSS]

1Sa	20:23	And about the matter you and I **d**—	1819
Mt	16: 7	They **d** this among themselves and said,	1368
	21:25	They **d** it among themselves and said,	1368
Mk	8:16	They **d** this with one another and said,	1368
	11:31	They **d** it among themselves and said,	1368
Lk	20: 5	They **d** it among themselves and said,	5199
	22: 4	and **d** with them how he might betray Jesus.	5196
	24:15	and **d** these things with each other,	5184
Ac	25:14	Festus **d** Paul's case with the king.	423

DISCUSSING (2) [DISCUSS]

Mk	9:10	**d** what "rising from the dead" meant.	5184
Lk	24:17	"What are you **d** together	506

DISCUSSION (3) [DISCUSS]

Mt	16: 8	Aware of their **d**, Jesus asked,	NIG
Mk	8:17	Aware of their **d**, Jesus asked them:	NIG
Ac	15: 7	After much **d**, Peter got up	2428

DISCUSSIONS (1) [DISCUSS]

Ac	19: 9	with him and had **d** daily in the lecture hall	1363

DISDAINED (4) [DISDAINFUL]

1Sa	2:30	but those who despise me will be **d**.	7837
Job	30: 1	whose fathers I would have **d** to put	4415
Ps	22:24	For he has not despised or **d** the suffering	9210
Jer	30:19	and they will not be **d**.	7592

DISDAINFUL (1) [DISDAINED]

Pr	30:13	whose glances are so **d**;	5951

DISEASE (39) [DISEASED, DISEASES]

Lev	13: 2	that may become an infectious **skin d**,	7669
	13: 3	it is an infectious **skin d**.	7669
	13: 8	it is an **infectious d**.	7669
	13: 9	"When anyone has an infectious **skin d**,	7669
	13:11	it is a chronic **skin d** and	7669
	13:12	"If the **d** breaks out all over his skin and,	7669
	13:13	and if the **d** has covered his whole body,	7669
	13:15	he has an **infectious d**.	7669
	13:20	It is an infectious **skin d** that has broken out	7669
	13:25	it is an **infectious d** that has broken out in	7669
	13:25	it is an infectious **skin d**.	7669
	13:27	it is an infectious **skin d**.	7669
	13:30	an **infectious d** of the head or chin.	7669
	13:42	an **infectious d** breaking out on his head	7669
	13:43	like an **infectious skin d**,	7669
	13:45	an infectious **d** must wear torn clothes,	7665
	14: 3	of his infectious **skin d**,	7669
	14: 7	the **infectious d** and pronounce him clean.	7669
	14:32	an infectious **skin d** and who cannot afford	7669
	14:54	the regulations for any infectious **skin d**,	7669
	22: 4	has an infectious **skin d** or a bodily	7665
Nu	5: 2	anyone who **has an infectious skin d**	7665
Dt	7:15	The Lord will keep you free from every **d**	2716
	28:22	The Lord will strike you with **wasting d**,	8831
1Ki	8:37	whatever disaster or **d** may come,	4701
2Ch	6:28	whatever disaster or **d** may come,	4701
	16:12	of his reign Asa was **afflicted with a d**	2688
	16:12	Though his **d** was severe,	2716
	21:15	be very ill with a lingering **d** of the bowels	4700
	21:15	the **d** causes your bowels to come out.' "	2716
	21:18	with an incurable **d** of the bowels.	2716
	21:19	his bowels came out because of the **d**,	2716
Ps	41: 8	"A vile **d** has beset him;	1821
	106:15	but sent a **wasting d** upon them.	8137
Isa	10:16	a **wasting d** upon his sturdy warriors;	8137
	17:11	in the day of **d** and incurable pain.	5710
Mt	4:23	and healing every **d** and sickness among	3798
	9:35	of the kingdom and healing every **d**	3798
	10: 1	to drive out evil spirits and to heal every **d**	3798

DISEASED (6) [DISEASE]

Lev	13:33	he must be shaved except for the **d** area,	5999
	13:44	the man is **d** and is unclean.	7665
	14: 2	"These are the regulations for the **d** person	7665
1Ki	15:23	In his old age, however, his feet became **d**.	2703
Mal	1: 8	When you sacrifice crippled or **d** animals,	2703
	1:13	or **d** animals and offer them as sacrifices,	2703

DISEASES (19) [DISEASE]

Ge	12:17	the Lord inflicted serious **d** on Pharaoh	5596
Ex	15:26	not bring on you any of the **d** I brought on	4701
Lev	14:57	**infectious skin d** and mildew.	7669
	26:16	upon you sudden terror, **wasting d**	8831
Dt	7:15	not inflict on you the horrible **d** you knew	4504
	24: 8	of leprous **d** be very careful to do exactly as	5596
	28:21	with **d** until he has destroyed you from	1822

Dt	28:60	He will bring upon you all the **d** *of* Egypt	4504
	29:22	that have fallen on the land and the **d**	9377
Ps	103: 3	and heals all your **d**,	9377
Jer	16: 4	"They will die of deadly **d**,	9377
Mt	4:24	to him all who were ill *with* various **d**,	3798
	8:17	up our infirmities and carried our **d**."	3798
Mk	1:34	Jesus healed many who had various **d**.	2809+3798
	3:10	with **d** were pushing forward to touch him.	3465
Lk	6:18	to hear him and to be healed of their **d**.	3798
	7:21	very time Jesus cured many who had **d**,	3798
	8: 2	of evil spirits and **d**:	819
	9: 1	to drive out all demons and to cure **d**,	3798

DISFIGURE (1) [DISFIGURED]

Mt	6:16	for *they* **d** their faces	906

DISFIGURED (2) [DISFIGURE]

Lev	21:18	no man who is blind or lame, **d**	3050
Isa	52:14	his appearance *was* so **d** beyond that	5425

DISGRACE (61) [DISGRACED, DISGRACEFUL, DISGRACES]

Ge	30:23	"God has taken away my **d**."	3075
	34:14	That would be a **d** to us.	3075
Lev	20:17	and they have sexual relations, it is a **d**.	2875
Nu	12:14	not *have* been in **d** for seven days?	4007
1Sa	1: 2	of you and so bring **d** on all Israel."	3075
	17:26	and removes this **d** from Israel?	3075
2Sa	13:13	Where could I get rid of my **d**?	3075
2Ki	19: 3	a day of distress and rebuke and **d**,	5541
2Ch	32:21	So he withdrew to his own land in **d**.	1425+7156
Ne	1: 3	in the province are in great trouble and **d**.	3075
	2:17	and we will no longer be in **d**."	3075
Ps	6:10	they will turn back *in* sudden **d**.	1017
	35:26	over me be clothed with shame and **d**.	4009
	40:14	be turned back in **d**.	4007
	44:15	My **d** is before me all day long,	4009
	52: 1	you who are a **d** *in the eyes of* God?	2875
	70: 2	be turned back in **d**.	4007
	71:13	to harm me be covered with scorn and **d**.	4009
	74:21	Do not let the oppressed retreat in **d**;	4007
	83:17	may they perish in **d**.	2917
	109:29	with **d** and wrapped with shame as in a cloak.	4009
	119:39	Take away the **d** I dread,	3075
Pr	6:33	Blows and **d** are his lot,	7830
	11: 2	When pride comes, then comes **d**,	7830
	13: 5	but the wicked bring shame and **d**.	2917
	14:34	but sin is a **d** *to* any people.	2875
	18: 3	so does contempt, and with shame comes **d**.	3075
	19:26	a son who brings shame and **d**.	2917
Isa	4: 1	Take away our **d**!"	3075
	22:18	you **d** *to* your master's house!	7830
	25: 8	he will remove the **d** *of* his people from all	3075
	30: 3	Egypt's shade will bring you **d**.	4009
	30: 5	but only shame and **d**."	3075
	37: 3	a day of distress and rebuke and **d**,	5541
	43:28	So I *will* **d** the dignitaries of your temple,	2725
	45:16	they will go off into **d** together.	4009
	54: 4	*Do* not *fear* **d**; you will not be humiliated.	4007
	61: 7	of **d** they will rejoice in their inheritance;	4009
Jer	3:25	and let our **d** cover us.	4009
	23:40	I will bring upon you everlasting **d**—	3075
	31:19	and humiliated because I bore the **d**	3075
La	3:30	and let him be filled with **d**.	3075
	5: 1	look, and see our **d**.	3075
Eze	16:52	Bear your **d**, for you have furnished some justification for	4009
	16:52	So then, be ashamed and bear your **d**,	4009
	16:54	that you may bear your **d** and be ashamed	4009
	28:16	I drove you in **d** from the mount of God,	2725
	32:30	with the slain in **d** despite the terror caused	1017
	36:30	so that you will no longer suffer **d** among	3075
Hos	2: 5	and has conceived them in **d**.	1017
Mic	2: 6	**d** will not overtake us.	4009
Hab	2:16	and **d** will cover your glory.	7814
Mt	1:19	**expose** her **to public d**,	1258
Lk	1:25	and taken away my **d** among the people."	3945
Ac	5:41	*of* suffering **d** for the Name.	869
1Co	11: 6	if it is a **d** for a woman to have her hair cut	156
	11:14	if a man has long hair, it is a **d** to him,	871
1Ti	3: 7	not fall into **d** and into the devil's trap.	3944
Heb	6: 6	**subjecting** him **to public d**,	4136
	11:26	He regarded **d** for the sake of Christ as	3944
	13:13	bearing the **d** he bore.	3944

DISGRACED (24) [DISGRACE]

2Sa	13:22	because *he had* **d** his sister Tamar.	6700
Ezr	9: 6	"O my God, I am too ashamed and **d** to lift	4007
Ps	35: 4	*May* those who seek my life *be* **d** and put	1017
	69: 6	in you not *be* **d** because of me, O Lord,	1017
	69:19	how I am scorned, **d** and shamed;	1425
Isa	1:29	*you will be* **d** because of the gardens	2917
	41:11	against you will surely be ashamed and **d**;	4007
	45:16	of idols will be put to shame and **d**,	4007
	45:17	you will never be put to shame or **d**,	4007
	50: 7	*I will* not *be* **d**.	4007
Jer	2:26	"As a thief is **d** when he is caught,	1425
	2:26	so the house of Israel is **d**—	1017
	15: 9	*she will be* **d** and humiliated.	1017
	20:11	They will fail and *be* thoroughly **d**;	1017
	22:22	Then you will be ashamed and **d** because	4007
	48: 1	Kiriathaim *will be* **d** and captured;	1017
	48: 1	the stronghold *will be* **d** and shattered.	1017
	48:20	Moab *is* **d**, for she is shattered.	1017

Jer	50:12	she who gave you birth *will be* **d**.	2917
	51:47	*be* **d** and her slain will all lie fallen	1017
	51:51	"We are **d**, for we have been insulted	1017
Eze	36:32	Be ashamed and **d** for your conduct,	2917
Hos	10: 6	Ephraim *will be* **d**;	1423+4374
Mic	3: 7	be ashamed and the diviners **d**.	2917

DISGRACEFUL (11) [DISGRACE]

Ge	34: 7	because Shechem had done a **d** thing	5576
Dt	22:21	a **d** thing in Israel by being promiscuous	5576
Jos	7:15	of the LORD and has done a **d** thing	5576
Jdg	19:23	don't do this **d** thing.	5576
	19:24	But to this man, don't do such a **d** thing."	5576
	20: 6	because they committed this lewd and **d** act	5576
Pr	10: 5	he who sleeps during harvest *is* a **d** son.	1017
	12: 4	but a **d** wife is like decay in his bones.	1017
	17: 2	A wise servant will rule over a **d** son,	1017
Hos	4: 7	they exchanged their Glory for *something* **d**.	7830
1Co	14:35	it is **d** for a woman to speak in the church.	156

DISGRACES (3) [DISGRACE]

Lev	21: 9	she **d** her father;	2725
Pr	28: 7	but a companion of gluttons **d** his father.	4007
	29:15	but a child left to himself **d** his mother.	1017

DISGUISE (4) [DISGUISED, DISGUISES]

Ge	38:14	covered herself with a veil *to* **d** herself,	6634
1Ki	14: 2	**d** yourself, so you won't be recognized as	9101
	22:30	"I will enter the battle in **d**,	2924
2Ch	18:29	"I will enter the battle in **d**,	2924

DISGUISED (5) [DISGUISE]

1Sa	28: 8	So Saul **d** himself, putting on other clothes,	2924
1Ki	20:38	*He* **d** himself with his headband down	2924
	22:30	So the king of Israel **d** himself and went	2924
2Ch	18:29	So the king of Israel **d** himself and went	2924
	35:22	but **d** himself to engage him in battle.	2924

DISGUISES (1) [DISGUISE]

Pr	26:24	A malicious man **d** himself with his lips,	5795

DISGUST (4) [DISGUSTED]

Eze	23:17	**turned away** from them in **d**.	3697
	23:18	**turned away** from her in **d**,	3697
	23:22	**turned away** from them in **d**,	5936
	23:28	**turned away** from them in **d**.	5936

DISGUSTED (1) [DISGUST]

Ge	27:46	"I'm **d** with living because	7762

DISH (22) [DISHES]

Nu	7:14	one gold **d** weighing ten shekels, filled	4090
	7:20	one gold **d** weighing ten shekels, filled	4090
	7:26	one gold **d** weighing ten shekels, filled	4090
	7:32	one gold **d** weighing ten shekels, filled	4090
	7:38	one gold **d** weighing ten shekels, filled	4090
	7:44	one gold **d** weighing ten shekels, filled	4090
	7:50	one gold **d** weighing ten shekels, filled	4090
	7:56	one gold **d** weighing ten shekels, filled	4090
	7:62	one gold **d** weighing ten shekels, filled	4090
	7:68	one gold **d** weighing ten shekels, filled	4090
	7:74	one gold **d** weighing ten shekels, filled	4090
	7:80	one gold **d** weighing ten shekels, filled	4090
2Ki	21:13	I will wipe out Jerusalem as one wipes a **d**,	7505
1Ch	28:17	weight of gold for **each** gold **d**;	2256+4094+4094
	28:17	of silver for **each** silver **d**;	2256+4094+4094
Pr	19:24	The sluggard buries his hand in the **d**;	7505
	26:15	The sluggard buries his hand in the **d**;	7505
Mt	23:25	You clean the outside of the cup and **d**,	4243
	23:26	First clean the inside of the cup and **d**,	4243
Lk	11:39	clean the outside *of* the cup and **d**,	4402
	11:41	But give what is inside [the **d**] to the poor,	NIG
Jn	13:26	of bread when I have dipped it in the **d**."	NIG

DISHAN (5)

Ge	36:21	Dishon, Ezer and **D**. These sons of Seir	1915
	36:28	The sons of **D**: Uz and Aran.	1915
	36:30	Dishon, Ezer and **D**. These were the Horite chiefs,	1915
1Ch	1:38	Shobal, Zibeon, Anah, Dishon, Ezer and **D**.	1915
	1:42	The sons of **D**: Uz and Aran.	1914

DISHEARTENED (3) [HEART]

Dt	20: 8	so that his brothers *will* not *become* **d** too."	906+4222+5022
Jer	49:23	*They are* **d**, troubled like the restless sea.	4570
Eze	13:22	Because you **d** the righteous with your lies,	3874+4213

DISHES (15) [DISH]

Ex	25:29	And make its plates and **d** of pure gold,	4090
	37:16	its plates and **d** and bowls and its pitchers	4090
Nu	4: 7	**d** and bowls, and the jars	4090
	7:84	and twelve gold **d**.	4090
	7:85	the silver **d** weighed two thousand four hundred shekels,	3998
	7:86	The twelve gold **d** filled	4090
	7:86	the gold **d** weighed a hundred and twenty shekels,	4090
1Ki	7:50	sprinkling bowls, **d** and censers;	4090

2Ki	25:14	**d** and all the bronze articles used in	4090
2Ch	4:22	sprinkling bowls, **d** and censers;	4090
	24:14	also **d** and other objects of gold and silver.	4090
Ezr	1: 9	gold **d** 30 silver dishes 1,000	113
	1: 9	gold dishes 30 silver **d** 1,000	113
Jer	52:18	**d** and all the bronze articles used in	4090
	52:19	**d** and bowls used for drink offerings—	4090

DISHES (Anglicized) See also BASINS

DISHON (7)

Ge	36:21	**D**, Ezer and Dishan. These sons of Seir	1914
	36:25	**D** and Oholibamah daughter of Anah.	1914
	36:26	The sons of **D**:	1914
	36:30	**D**, Ezer and Dishan. These were the Horite chiefs,	1914
1Ch	1:38	Lotan, Shobal, Zibeon, Anah, **D**,	1914
	1:41	The son of Anah: **D**.	1914
	1:41	The sons of **D**:	1914

DISHONEST (18) [DISHONESTLY]

Ex	18:21	trustworthy men who hate **d** gain—	1299
Lev	19:35	not use **d** standards when measuring length,	6404
1Sa	8: 3	after **d** gain and accepted bribes	1299
Pr	11: 1	The LORD abhors **d** scales,	5327
	13:11	**D** money dwindles away,	2039
	20:23	and **d** scales do not please him.	5327
	29:27	The righteous detest the **d**;	6404
Jer	22:17	and your heart are set only on **d** gain,	1299
Eze	28:18	**d** trade you have desecrated your sanctuaries.	6404
Hos	12: 7	merchant uses **d** scales; he loves to defraud.	5327
Am	8: 5	the price and cheating with **d** scales,	5327
Mic	6:11	Shall I acquit a man with **d** scales,	8400
Lk	16: 8	"The master commended the **d** manager	94
	16:10	and whoever is **d** with very little will also	96
	16:10	with very little will also be **d** with much.	96
1Ti	3: 8	and not **pursuing d** gain.	153
Tit	1: 7	not violent, not **pursuing d** gain.	153
	1:11	and that for the sake of **d** gain.	156

DISHONESTLY (1) [DISHONEST]

Dt	25:16	anyone who deals **d**.	6404

DISHONOR (16) [DISHONORED, DISHONORS]

Lev	18: 7	**d** your father **by having sexual relations with** your mother.	1655+6872
	18: 8	that would **d** your father.	6872
	18:10	that would **d** you.	6872
	18:14	**d** your father's brother **by** approaching his wife **to have sexual relations**;	1655+6872
	18:16	that would **d** your brother.	6872
	20:19	for *that would* **d** a close relative;	6867
Dt	22:30	he must not **d** his father's **bed**.	1655+4053
Pr	30: 9	and so **d** the name of my God.	9530
Jer	14:21	*do* not **d** your glorious throne.	5571
	20:11	their **d** will never be forgotten.	4009
La	2: 2	and its princes down to the ground *in* **d**.	2725
Eze	22:10	In you are *those who* **d** their fathers' **bed**;	1655+6872
Jn	8:49	"but I honor my Father and you **d** me.	869
Ro	2:23	*do* you **d** God by breaking the law?	869
1Co	15:43	it is sown in **d**, it is raised in glory;	871
2Co	6: 8	glory and **d**, bad report and good report;	871

DISHONORED (7) [DISHONOR]

Lev	20:11	he has **d** his father.	1655+6872
	20:17	He has **d** his sister and will	1655+6872
	20:20	If a man sleeps with his aunt, *he has* **d** his uncle.	1655+6872
	20:21	*he has* **d** his brother.	1655+6872
Dt	21:14	since *you have* **d** her.	6700
Ezr	4:14	and it is not proper for us to see the king **d**,	10571
1Co	4:10	You are honored, we are **d**!	872

DISHONORS (6) [DISHONOR]

Dt	27:16	the man *who* **d** his father or his mother."	7829
	27:20	for he **d** his father's **bed**."	1655+4053
Job	20: 3	I hear a rebuke that **d** me,	4009
Mic	7: 6	For a son **d** his father,	5571
1Co	11: 4	with his head covered **d** his head.	2875
	11: 5	with her head uncovered **d** her head—	2875

DISILLUSIONMENT (1)

Ps	7:14	and conceives trouble gives birth to **d**.	9214

DISLIKES (3)

Dt	22:13	a wife and, after lying with her, **d** her	8533
	22:16	but he **d** her.	8533
	24: 3	and her second husband **d** her	8533

DISLODGE (3)

Jos	15:63	Judah could not **d** the Jebusites,	3769
	16:10	not **d** the Canaanites living in Gezer;	3769
Jdg	1:21	however, failed to **d** the Jebusites,	3769

DISLOYAL (1)

Ps	78:57	Like their fathers *they were* **d** and faithless,	6047

DISMAY (3) [DISMAYED]
Job	41:22	**d** goes before him.	1791
Ps	35: 4	be turned back in **d**.	2917
	116:11	And in my **d** I said, "All men are liars."	2905

DISMAYED (18) [DISMAY]
1Sa	17:11	and all the Israelites were **d** and terrified.	3169
2Ki	19:26	drained of power, are **d** and put to shame.	3169
Job	4: 5	it strikes you, and you are **d**	987
	32:15	"They are **d** and have no more to say;	3169
Ps	6:10	All my enemies will be ashamed and **d**;	987+4394
	30: 7	but when you hid your face, I was **d**.	987
	83:17	May they ever be ashamed and **d**;	987
	143: 4	my heart within me is **d**.	9037
Isa	28:16	the one who trusts will never be **d**.	2591
	37:27	drained of power, are **d** and put to shame.	3169
	41:10	do not be **d**, for I am your God.	9283
	41:23	so that we will be **d** and filled with fear.	9283
Jer	8: 9	they will be **d** and trapped.	3169
	14: 3	**d** and despairing, they cover their heads.	1017
	14: 4	the farmers are **d** and cover their heads.	1017
	30:10	do not be **d**, O Israel,' declares the LORD.	3169
	46:27	do not be **d**, O Israel.	3169
	49:23	"Hamath and Arpad are **d**,	1017

DISMISS (1) [DISMISSED]
Lk	2:29	you now **d** your servant in peace.	668

DISMISSED (9) [DISMISS]
Jdg	2: 6	After Joshua had **d** the Israelites,	8938
1Sa	10:25	Then Samuel **d** the people,	8938
2Ch	25:10	So Amaziah **d** the troops who had come	976
Mt	14:22	while he **d** the crowd.	668
	14:23	After he had **d** them,	668
Mk	6:45	while he **d** the crowd.	668
Ac	13:43	When the congregation was **d**,	3395
	19:41	After he had said this, he **d** the assembly.	668
	23:22	The commander **d** the young man	668

DISOBEDIENCE (9) [DISOBEY]
Jos	22:22	If this has been in rebellion or **d** to	5086
Jer	43: 7	So they entered Egypt in **d** to the LORD	
			928+4202+7754+9048
Ro	5:19	For just as through the **d** of the one man	4157
	11:30	received mercy as a result of their **d**,	577
	11:32	to **d** so that he may have mercy on them all.	577
2Co	10: 6	we will be ready to punish every act of **d**,	4157
Heb	2: 2	and **d** received its just punishment,	4157
	4: 6	did not go in, because of their **d**.	577
	4:11	by following their example of **d**.	577

DISOBEDIENT (14) [DISOBEY]
Ne	9:26	"But they were **d** and rebelled against you;	5286
Lk	1:17	to their children and the **d** to the wisdom of	579
Ac	26:19	I was not **d** to the vision from heaven.	579
Ro	10:21	to a **d** and obstinate people."	578
	11:30	as you who were at one time **d** to God have	578
	11:31	now become **d** in order that they too may	578
Eph	2: 2	now at work in those who are **d**.	577
	5: 6	God's wrath comes on those who are **d**.	577
	5:12	even to mention what the **d** do in secret.	NIG
2Ti	3: 2	boastful, proud, abusive, **d** to their parents,	579
Tit	1: 6	not open to the charge of being wild and **d**.	538
	1:16	**d** and unfit for doing anything good.	579
	3: 3	At one time we too were foolish, **d**,	579
Heb	11:31	was not killed with those who were **d**.	578

DISOBEY (6) [DISOBEDIENCE, DISOBEDIENT, DISOBEYED, DISOBEYING, DISOBEYS]
Dt	11:28	the curse if you **d** the commands of	4202+9048
2Ch	24:20	'Why do you **d** the LORD's commands?	6296
Est	3: 3	"Why do you **d** the king's command?"	6296
Jer	42:13	so **d** the LORD your God,	928+1194+7754+9048
Ro	1:30	they **d** their parents;	579
1Pe	2: 8	because they **d** the message—	578

DISOBEYED (9) [DISOBEY]
Nu	14:22	but who **d** me and tested me ten times—	928+4202+7754+9048
	27:14	both of you **d** my command to honor me	5286
Jdg	2: 2	Yet you have **d** me.	928+4202+7754+9048
Ne	9:29	and **d** your commands.	4202+9048
Isa	24: 5	they have **d** the laws,	6296
Jer	43: 4	the army officers and all the people **d**	4202+9048
Lk	15:29	for you and never **d** your orders.	4216
Heb	3:18	if not to those who **d**?	578
1Pe	3:20	who **d** long ago when God waited patiently	578

DISOBEYING (1) [DISOBEY]
Nu	14:41	"Why are you **d** the LORD's command?	6296

DISOBEYS (1) [DISOBEY]
Eze	33:12	not save him when he **d**,	7322

DISORDER (4)
Job	10:22	of deep shadow and **d**,	4202+6043
1Co	14:33	For God is not a God of **d** but of peace.	189
2Co	12:20	factions, slander, gossip, arrogance and **d**.	189

Jas	3:16	there you find **d** and every evil practice.	189

DISOWN (13) [DISOWNED, DISOWNS]
Pr	30: 9	I may have too much and **d** you and say,	3950
Mt	10:33	I will **d** him before my Father in heaven.	766
	26:34	rooster crows, you will **d** me three times."	565
	26:35	I will never **d** you."	565
	26:75	rooster crows, you will **d** me three times."	565
Mk	14:30	before the rooster crows twice you yourself will **d** me three times."	565
	14:31	I will never **d** you."	565
	14:72	"Before the rooster crows twice you will **d** me three times."	565
Lk	22:61	"Before rooster crows today, you will **d** me three times."	565
Jn	13:38	rooster crows, you will **d** me three times!	766
2Ti	2:12	If we **d** him, he will also disown us;	766
	2:12	If we disown him, he will also **d** us;	766
	2:13	for he cannot **d** himself.	766

DISOWNED (3) [DISOWN]
Lk	12: 9	before men will be **d** before the angels	766
Ac	3:13	and you **d** him before Pilate.	766
	3:14	You **d** the Holy and Righteous One	766

DISOWNS (3) [DISOWN]
Job	8:18	that place **d** it and says, 'I never saw you.'	3950
Mt	10:33	But whoever **d** me before men,	766
Lk	12: 9	But he who **d** me before men will	766

DISPATCH (1) [DISPATCHED, DISPATCHES]
Isa	10: 6	I **d** him against a people who anger me,	7422

DISPATCHED (1) [DISPATCH]
1Ki	20:17	Ben-Hadad had **d** scouts, who reported,	8938

DISPATCHES (4) [DISPATCH]
Est	1:22	He sent **d** to all parts of the kingdom,	6219
	3:13	**D** were sent by couriers to all	6219
	8: 5	be written overruling the **d** that Haman son	6219
	8:10	sealed the **d** with the king's signet ring,	6219

DISPENSATION (KJV) See ADMINISTRATION, COMMISSION, TRUST

DISPENSES (1)
Zep	3: 5	Morning by morning he **d** his justice,	5989

DISPERSE (7) [DISPERSED, DISPERSES, DISPERSING]
Ge	49: 7	I will scatter them in Jacob and **d** them.	7046
Eze	12:15	when I **d** them among the nations	7046
	20:23	to them in the desert that I would **d** them	7046
	22:15	I will **d** you among the nations	7046
	29:12	And I will **d** the Egyptians among	7046
	30:23	I will **d** the Egyptians among the nations	7046
	30:26	I will **d** the Egyptians among the nations	7046

DISPERSED (6) [DISPERSE]
2Sa	20:22	and his men **d** from the city,	7046
1Ki	1:49	all Adonijah's guests rose in alarm and **d**.	2006+2143+4200
Est	3: 8	"There is a certain people **d** and scattered	7061
Job	38:24	to the place where the lightning is **d**,	2745
Eze	36:19	I **d** them among the nations,	7046
Ac	5:36	He was killed, all his followers were **d**,	1370

DISPERSES (2) [DISPERSE]
Dt	30: 1	the LORD your God **d** you among	5615
Job	12:23	he enlarges nations, and **d** them.	5697

DISPERSING (1) [DISPERSE]
2Ch	11:23	**d** some of his sons throughout the districts	7287

DISPLACES (1)
Pr	30:23	and a maidservant who **d** her mistress.	3769

DISPLAY (13) [DISPLAYED, DISPLAYS]
Dt	22:17	Then her parents shall **d** the cloth before	7298
Est	1:11	to **d** her beauty to the people and nobles,	8011
Job	10:16	again your **awesome power** against me.	7098
Ps	19: 2	night after night they **d** knowledge.	2555
	45: 4	let your right hand **d** awesome deeds.	3723
	77:14	you **d** your power among the peoples.	3359
Isa	49: 3	Israel, in whom I will **d** my splendor."	6995
	60:21	for the **d** of my **splendor**.	6995
	61: 3	of the LORD for the **d** of his splendor.	6995
Eze	39:21	"I will **d** my glory among the nations,	5989
Ro	9:17	that I might **d** my power in you and	1892
1Co	4: 9	**put** us apostles on **d**	617
1Ti	1:16	Christ Jesus might **d** his unlimited patience	1892

DISPLAYED (8) [DISPLAY]
Ex	14:31	saw the great power the LORD **d** against	6913
Nu	14:17	"Now may the Lord's strength be **d**,	1540

1Ki	11:41	all he did and the wisdom he **d**—	NIH
Est	1: 4	For a full 180 days he **d** the vast wealth	8011
Job	26: 3	And what great insight you have **d**!	3359
Ps	78:43	the day he **d** his miraculous signs in Egypt,	8492
Jn	9: 3	that the work of God might be **d** in his life.	5746
2Th	2: 9	be in accordance with the work of Satan **d**	NIG

DISPLAYS (2) [DISPLAY]
Pr	14:29	but a quick-tempered man **d** folly.	8123
Isa	44:23	he **d** his glory in Israel.	6995

DISPLEASE (3) [DISPLEASED, DISPLEASES, DISPLEASING, DISPLEASURE]
Nu	11:11	What have I done to **d** you that you put the burden	928+2834+4202+5162+6524
1Sa	29: 7	do nothing to **d** the Philistine rulers."	928+6524+8273
1Th	2:15	They **d** God and are hostile to all men	743+3590

DISPLEASED (7) [DISPLEASE]
Ge	48:17	on Ephraim's head he was **d**;	928+6524+8317
Nu	22:34	Now if you are **d**, I will go back.	928+6524+8317
1Sa	8: 6	this **d** Samuel; so he prayed to the LORD.	928+6524+8317
2Sa	11:27	the thing David had done **d** the LORD.	928+6524+8317
Ne	13: 8	I was greatly **d** and threw all	8317
Isa	59:15	was **d** that there was no justice.	928+6524+8317
Jnh	4: 1	But Jonah was greatly **d** and became angry.	8288+8317

DISPLEASES (2) [DISPLEASE]
Isa	65:12	in my sight and chose what **d** me."	2911+4202
	66: 4	in my sight and chose what **d** me."	2911+4202

DISPLEASING (2) [DISPLEASE]
Ge	28: 8	how **d** the Canaanite women were to his father	928+6524+8273
Dt	24: 1	If a man marries a woman who becomes **d** to him	928+2834+4202+5162+6524

DISPLEASURE (1) [DISPLEASE]
Ps	85: 4	and put away your **d** toward us.	4088

DISPOSAL (2) [DISPOSED]
Mt	26:53	at once **put at** my **d** more than twelve legions of angels?	4225
Ac	5: 4	it was sold, wasn't the money at your **d**?	2026

DISPOSED (5) [DISPOSAL]
Ex	3:21	the Egyptians **favorably d toward** this people,	928+2834+6524
	11: 3	the Egyptians **favorably d toward** the people,	928+2834+6524
	12:36	the Egyptians **favorably d toward** the people,	928+2834+6524
Dt	31:21	I know what they are **d** to do,	3671
1Sa	20:12	If he is **favorably d** toward you,	3201

DISPOSSESS (5) [DISPOSSESSING]
Dt	9: 1	and **d** nations greater and stronger than you,	3769
	11:23	and you will **d** nations larger	3769
	12:29	the nations you are about to invade and **d**.	3769
	18:14	The nations you will **d** listen	3769
Isa	54: 3	your descendants will **d** nations and settle	3769

DISPOSSESSED (KJV) See DRIVEN OUT, DROVE OUT

DISPOSSESSING (2) [DISPOSSESS]
Dt	12: 2	the nations you are **d** worship their gods.	3769
Eze	45: 9	Stop **d** my people,	1766

DISPUTABLE (1) [DISPUTE]
Ro	14: 1	without passing judgment on **d** matters.	1369

DISPUTE (18) [DISPUTABLE, DISPUTED, DISPUTES, DISPUTING]
Ex	18:16	Whenever they have a **d**,	1821
	24:14	anyone involved in a **d** can go to them."	1821
Dt	19:17	the two men involved in the **d** must stand in	8190
	21: 5	of the LORD and to decide all **cases** of **d**	8190
	25: 1	When men have a **d**,	8190
Jdg	11:27	**decide** the **d** this day between the Israelites	9149
Job	9: 3	Though one wished to **d** with him,	8189
	9:14	"How then can I **d** with him?	6699
Pr	17:14	so drop the matter before a **d** breaks out.	8190
Eze	44:24	" 'In any **d**, the priests are to serve	8190
Lk	22:24	Also a **d** arose among them as to which	5808
Ac	15: 2	and Barnabas into sharp **d** and debate	5087
	17:18	and Stoic philosophers began to **d** with him.	5202
	23: 7	a **d** broke out between the Pharisees and	5087
	23:10	The **d** became so violent that	5087
	25:19	they had some **points** of **d** with him	2427
1Co	6: 1	If any of you has a **d** with another,	4547
	6: 5	among you wise enough to **judge** a **d**	1359

DISPUTED (1) [DISPUTE]
Ge 26:20 because *they* d with him.   6921

DISPUTES (10) [DISPUTE]
Ex	18:19	before God and bring their d to him.	1821
Dt	1:12	and your burdens and your d all by myself?	8190
	1:16	Hear the d between your brothers	NIH
Jdg	4:5	to her to have their d decided.	5477
2Ch	19:8	the law of the LORD and to settle d.	8190
Pr	18:18	Casting the lot settles d	4506
	18:19	and d are like the barred gates of a citadel.	4506
Isa	2:4	between the nations and *will* settle d	3519
Mic	4:3	between many peoples and *will* settle d	3519
1Co	6:4	if you have d about such matters,	3215

DISPUTING (2) [DISPUTE]
1Ti	2:8	without anger or d.	1369
Jude	1:9	when *he* d with the devil about the body of Moses,	1359+1363

DISQUALIFIED (1) [DISQUALIFY]
1Co 9:27 I myself will not be d for the prize.   99

DISQUALIFY (1) [DISQUALIFIED]
Col 2:18 d you **for the prize.**   2857

DISQUIETING (1)
Job 4:13 Amid d dreams in the night,   8546

DISREGARDED (2) [DISREGARDING]
Ezr	9:10	For *we have* d the commands	6440
Isa	40:27	my cause *is* d by my God"?	6296

DISREGARDING (1) [DISREGARDED]
Am 1:9 d a treaty of brotherhood,   2349+4202

DISREPUTE (1)
2Pe 2:2 **bring** the way of truth **into** d.   1059

DISRESPECT (1)
Est 1:18 There will be no end of d and discord.   1025

DISROBING (1)
2Sa 6:20 d in the sight of the slave girls   1655

DISSEMBLED, DISSIMULATION (KJV)
See LIED, FATAL MISTAKE, JOINED IN HYPOCRISY

DISSENSION (8) [DISSENSIONS]
Pr	6:14	he always stirs up d.	4506
	6:19	and a man who stirs up d among brothers.	4506
	10:12	Hatred stirs up d,	4506
	15:18	A hot-tempered man stirs up d,	4506
	16:28	A perverse man stirs up d,	4506
	28:25	A greedy man stirs up d,	4506
	29:22	An angry man stirs up d,	4506
Ro	13:13	not *in* d and jealousy.	2251

DISSENSIONS (1) [DISSENSION]
Gal 5:20 jealousy, fits of rage, selfish ambition, d,   1496

DISSIPATION (2)
Lk	21:34	be weighed down with d,	3190
1Pe	4:4	with them into the same flood *of* d,	861

DISSOLVED (1)
Isa 34:4 the heavens *will* be d and the sky rolled up   5245

DISSUADE (2) [DISSUADED]
Eze	3:18	or speak out to d him from his evil ways	2302
	33:8	not speak out to d him from his ways,	2302

DISSUADED (1) [DISSUADE]
Ac 21:14 *When* he *would* not *be* d,   4275

DISTAFF (1)
Pr 31:19 In her hand she holds the d and grasps   3969

DISTANCE (50) [DISTANT]
Ge	22:4	up and saw the place in the d.	8158
	35:16	While they were still **some** d from Ephrath,	824+2021+3896
	36:6	a land **some** d **from** his brother Jacob.	4946+7156
	37:18	But they saw him in the d,	8158
	48:7	a **little** d **from** Ephrath.	824+3896
Ex	2:4	at a d to see what would happen to him.	8158
	20:18	They stayed at a d	8158
	20:21	The people remained at a d,	8158
	24:1	You are to worship at a d,	8158
	33:7	outside the camp **some** d **away,**	4946+8178
Nu	2:2	to camp around the Tent of Meeting **some** d	5584
	16:37	and scatter the coals **some** d **away,** for	2134
Dt	19:6	overtake him if the d is too great,	2006
	20:15	cities that are **at a** d from you	4394+8158
	21:2	and judges shall go out and **measure** *the* d	4499
	32:52	you will see the land only from a d;	5584
Jos	3:4	a d of about a thousand yards between you	8158
	3:16	It piled up in a heap a great d **away,**	8178
Jdg	18:22	they *had* gone some d from Micah's house,	8178
1Sa	26:13	stood on top of the hill **some** d **away;**	4946+8158
2Sa	11:10	"Haven't you just come from a d?	2006
	15:17	and they halted at a place **some** d **away.**	5305
	16:1	When David had gone a **short** d beyond	5071
	18:13	you *would have* **kept** *your* d *from* me."	
	19:36	over the Jordan with the king for a **short** d,	3656+4946+5584 5071
2Ki	2:7	of the prophets went and stood at a d,	8158
	4:25	When he saw her in the d,	5584
	5:19	After Naaman had traveled **some** d,	824+3896
Job	2:12	When they saw him from a d,	8158
	30:10	They detest me and **keep** *their* d;	8178
Isa	59:14	and righteousness stands at a d;	8158
Eze	40:3	the d was twenty-five cubits	8145
	40:15	The d from the entrance of the gateway to	NIH
	40:19	Then he measured the d from the inside of	8145
	48:35	"The d all around will be 18,000 cubits.	NIH
Mt	8:30	**Some** d from them a large herd	3426
	14:24	but the boat was already a considerable d	5084
	26:58	But Peter followed him at a d,	3427
	27:55	women were there, watching from a d.	3427
Mk	5:6	When he saw Jesus from a d,	3427
	8:3	some of them have come a **long** d."	3427
	11:13	Seeing in the d a fig tree in leaf,	3427
	14:54	Peter followed him at a d,	3427
	15:40	Some women were watching from a d.	3427
Lk	17:12	They stood **at a** d	4523
	18:13	"But the tax collector stood **at a** d.	3427
	22:54	Peter followed him **at a** d.	3427
	23:49	stood at a d, watching these things.	3427
Heb	11:13	and welcomed them **from a** d.	4523
Rev	14:20	as high as the horses' bridles **for a** d of	608

DISTANT (37) [DISTANCE]
Dt	14:24	But if that place *is* too d	2006+2021+8049
	29:22	from d lands will see the calamities	8158
	30:4	to the **most** d land *under* the heavens,	7895
Jos	9:6	"We have come from a d country;	8158
	9:9	from a very d country because of the fame	8158
1Ki	8:41	from a d land because of your name—	8158
2Ki	20:14	"From a d land," Hezekiah replied.	8158
2Ch	6:32	from a d land because of your great name	8158
Est	10:1	throughout the empire, to its d **shores.**	362+3542
Ps	56:T	To [the tune of] "A Dove on D Oaks."	8158
	72:10	and of d **shores** will bring tribute to him;	362
	97:1	let the d **shores** rejoice.	8041
Pr	25:25	to a weary soul is good news from a d land.	5305
Isa	5:26	He lifts up a banner for the d nations,	4946+8158
	7:18	the d streams of Egypt and for bees from	7895
	8:9	Listen, all you d lands.	5305
	39:3	"From a d land," Hezekiah replied.	8158
	45:21	who declared it from the d **past?**	255
	49:1	hear this, you d nations:	4946+8158
	66:19	and Greece, and to the d islands that have	8158
Jer	4:16	'A besieging army is coming from a d land,	5305
	5:15	"I am bringing a d nation against you	4946+5305
	6:20	or sweet calamus from a d land?	5305
	9:26	and all who live in the desert in d places.	7899
	18:14	Do its cool waters from d **sources** ever cease	2424
	25:23	Tema, Buz and all who are in d **places;**	6991+7899
	30:10	'I will surely save you out of a d **place,**	8158
	31:10	proclaim it in d coastlands:	4946+5305
	46:27	I will surely save you out of a d **place,**	8158
	49:32	those who are in d **places**	6991+7899
	51:50	Remember the LORD in a d *land,*	8158
Eze	12:27	and he prophesies about the d **future.'**	8158
Da	4:22	and your dominion extends to d **parts** *of*	10509
	8:26	for it concerns the d **future."**	3427+8041
Zec	10:9	yet in d **lands** they will remember me.	5305
Lk	15:13	a d country and there squandered his wealth	3431
	19:12	a d country to have himself appointed king	3431

DISTILL (1)
Job 36:27 *which* d as rain to the streams;   2423

DISTINCTION (7) [DISTINCTLY]
Ex	8:23	a d between my people and your people.	7151
	9:4	But the LORD *will* **make** a d between	7111
	11:7	that the LORD **makes** a d between Egypt	7111
Lev	20:25	therefore **make** a d between clean	976
Mal	3:18	the d **between** the righteous and the wicked,	1068
Ac	15:9	*He* **made** no d between us and them,	1359
1Co	14:7	unless there is a d in the notes?	1405

DISTINCTLY (1) [DISTINCTION]
Ac 10:3 He d saw an angel of God,   5747

DISTINGUISH (8) [DISTINGUISHED, DISTINGUISHING]
Ex	33:16	What else *will* d me and your people	7111
Lev	10:10	You **must** d between the holy and the common,	976
	11:47	You **must** d between the unclean and the clean,	976
1Ki	3:9	and to d between right and wrong.	1067
Ezr	3:13	No one *could* d the sound of the shouts	5795
Eze	22:26	not d between the holy and the common;	976
	44:23	show them **how to** d between	3359
Heb	5:14	to d good **from** evil.	1360

DISTINGUISHED (4) [DISTINGUISH]
Nu	22:15	more numerous and more d than the first.	3877
2Sa	6:20	How the king of Israel *has* d himself today,	3877
Da	6:3	so d himself among the administrators and	10488
Lk	14:8	a **person more** d **than** you may have been invited.	1952

DISTINGUISHING (2) [DISTINGUISH]
1Co	12:10	to another d between spirits,	1360
2Th	3:17	which is **the** d mark in all my letters.	4956

DISTORT (5) [DISTORTED]
Jer	23:36	and so *you* d the words of the living God,	2200
Mic	3:9	who despise justice and d all that is right;	6835
Ac	20:30	and d **the truth** in order	1406+3281
2Co	4:2	nor *do we* d the word of God.	1516
2Pe	3:16	which ignorant and unstable people d,	5137

DISTORTED (1) [DISTORT]
Eze 27:35 with horror and their faces *are* d **with fear.**   8307

DISTRACTED (1)
Lk 10:40 But Martha *was* d by all the preparations   4352

DISTRAUGHT (1)
Ps 55:2 My thoughts trouble me and *I am* d   2101

DISTRESS (84) [DISTRESSED, DISTRESSES, DISTRESSING]
Ge	32:7	and d Jacob divided the people who were	7674
	35:3	who answered me in the day of my d	7650
	42:21	that's why this d has come upon us."	7650
Dt	4:30	in d and all these things have happened	7639
	28:57	in the d that your enemy will inflict on you	5186
Jdg	2:15	They *were* in great d.	7674
	10:9	and Israel *was* in great d.	7674
1Sa	2:32	and you will see d in my dwelling.	7639
	14:24	Now the men of Israel *were* in d that day,	5601
	22:2	in d or in debt or discontented gathered	5186
	28:15	"I am in great d," Saul said.	7639
2Sa	16:12	that the LORD will see my d and repay me	6715
	22:7	In my d I called to the LORD;	7639
	24:14	David said to Gad, "I am in deep d.	7639
2Ki	4:27	She *is* **in bitter** d,	5352
	19:3	a day of d and rebuke and disgrace,	7650
1Ch	21:13	David said to Gad, "I am in deep d.	7639
2Ch	15:4	But in their d they turned to the LORD,	7639
	15:6	with every kind of d.	7650
	20:9	and will cry out to you in our d,	7650
	33:12	In his d he sought the favor of	7674
Ne	9:37	We are in great d.	7650
Est	4:4	she *was* in great d.	2655
	7:4	because no such d would justify disturbing	7639
Job	15:24	D and anguish fill him with terror;	7639
	20:22	d *will* overtake him;	7674
	27:9	Does God listen to his cry when d comes	7650
	30:24	when he cries for help in his d.	7085
	33:19	a bed of pain with constant d *in* his bones,	8190
	36:16	from the jaws of d to a spacious place free	7639
	36:19	so you would not be in d?	7639
Ps	4:1	Give me relief from my d;	7639
	18:6	In my d I called to the LORD;	7639
	20:1	the LORD answer you when you are in d;	7650
	25:18	and my d and take away all my sins.	6662
	31:9	O LORD, for I am in d;	7639
	35:26	over my d be put to shame and confusion;	8288
	55:17	Evening, morning and noon I cry out in d,	8488
	57:6	I *was* **bowed down in** d.	4104
	69:29	I am in pain and d;	6714
	77:2	When I was *in* d, I sought the Lord;	7650
	81:7	In your d you called and I rescued you,	7650
	102:2	me when I am in d.	7639
	106:44	of their d when he heard their cry;	7639
	107:6	and he delivered them from their d.	5188
	107:13	and he saved them from their d.	5188
	107:19	and he saved them from their d.	5188
	107:28	and he brought them out of their d.	5188
	119:143	Trouble and d have come upon me,	5186
	120:1	I call on the LORD in my d,	7650
	144:14	no **cry of** d in our streets.	7424
Pr	1:27	when d and trouble overwhelm you.	7650
Isa	5:7	for righteousness, but heard **cries of** d.	7591
	5:30	he will see darkness and d;	7639
	8:22	the earth and see only d and darkness	7650
	9:1	be no more gloom for those who were *in* d.	4608
	25:4	a refuge for the needy in his d,	7639
	26:16	LORD, they came to you in their d;	7639
	30:6	Through a land of hardship and d,	7442
	33:2	our salvation in time of d.	7650
	37:3	a day of d and rebuke and disgrace.	7650
	63:9	In all their d he too was distressed,	7650
Jer	10:18	*I will* **bring** d on them so that they may	7674
	11:14	when they call to me in the time of their d.	8288
	14:8	O Hope of Israel, its Savior in times of d,	7650
	15:11	with you in times of disaster and times of d.	7650
	16:19	my refuge in time of d,	7650
La	1:3	in the midst of her d.	5210
	1:21	All my enemies have heard of my d;	8288

Eze 30:16 Memphis will be in constant **d.** 7639
Da 12: 1 a time of **d** such as has not happened from 7650
Jnh 2: 2 He said: "In my **d** I called to the LORD, 7650
Hab 3: 7 I saw the tents of Cushan in **d**, 224
Zep 1:15 a day of **d** and anguish, 7650
    1:17 I will **bring d** on the people 7674
Mt 24:21 For then there will be great **d.** 2568
    24:29 after the **d** of those days " 'the sun will 2568
Mk 13:19 be days of **d** unequaled from the beginning, 2568
    13:24 "But in those days, following that **d**, 2568
Lk 21:23 There will be great **d** in the land and wrath 340
Ro 2: 9 There will be trouble and **d** 5103
2Co 2: 4 For I wrote you out of great **d** and anguish 2568
1Th 3: 7 in all our **d** 340
Jas 1:27 to look after orphans and widows in their **d** 2568

DISTRESSED (24) [DISTRESS]
Ge 21:11 The matter **d** Abraham greatly 928+6524+8317
    21:12 Do not be so **d** about the boy and your
        maidservant. 928+6524+8317
    42:21 We saw how **d** he was when he pleaded 7650
    45: 5 be **d** and do not be angry with yourselves 6772
1Sa 30: 6 David was greatly **d** because 7674
Ezr 10: 9 greatly **d** by the occasion and because of 8283
Job 6:20 They are **d**, because they had been confident 1017
Isa 8:21 **D** and hungry, they will roam through 7996
    54: 6 as if you were a wife deserted and **d** 6772
    63: 9 In all their distress he too was **d**, 7639
La 1:20 "See, O LORD, how **d** I am! 7639
Da 6:14 When the king heard this, he was greatly **d**; 10091
Mt 14: 9 The king was **d**, but because of his oaths 3382
    18:31 they were greatly **d** and went 3382
Mk 3: 5 deeply **d** at their stubborn hearts, 5200
    6:26 The king was greatly **d**, 4337
    14:33 and he began to be deeply **d** and troubled. 1701
Lk 12:50 and how **d** I am until it is completed! 5309
Ac 17:16 he was greatly **d** to see that 4236
Ro 14:15 If your brother is **d** because 3382
2Co 1: 6 If we are **d**, it is for your comfort 2567
    2: 3 so that when I came I should not be **d** 2400+3383
Php 2:26 and is **d** because you heard he was ill. 86
2Pe 2: 7 who was **d** by the filthy lives of lawless men 2930

DISTRESSES (2) [DISTRESS]
1Sa 10:19 of all your calamities and **d.** 7650
2Co 6: 4 in troubles, hardships and **d**; 5103

DISTRESSING (1) [DISTRESS]
Ex 33: 4 When the people heard these **d** words, 8273

DISTRIBUTE (7) [DISTRIBUTED, DISTRIBUTES, DISTRIBUTING, DISTRIBUTION]
Nu 33:54 **D** the land by lot, according to your clans. 5706
    33:54 **D** it according to your ancestral tribes. 5706
2Ch 31:19 men were designated by name to **d** portions 5989
Eze 47:21 **d** this land among yourselves according 2745
Da 11:24 He will **d** plunder, 1029
    11:39 over many people and will **d** the land at 2745
Mk 8: 7 also and told the disciples to **d** them. 4192

DISTRIBUTED (10) [DISTRIBUTE]
Nu 26:55 Be sure that the land is **d** by lot. 2745
    26:56 Each inheritance is to be **d** by lot among 2745
Jos 18:10 and there he **d** the land to the Israelites 2745
1Ch 6:60 which were **d** among the Kohathite clans, 928
2Ch 31:16 they to the males three years old NIH
    31:17 And they **d** to the priests enrolled NIH
Est 2:18 throughout the provinces and **d** gifts 5989
Jn 6:11 and to those who were seated as much 1443
Ac 4:35 and it was **d** to anyone as he had need. 1344
Heb 2: 4 and **gifts** of the Holy Spirit **d** 3536

DISTRIBUTES (1) [DISTRIBUTE]
Isa 34:17 his hand **d** them by measure. 2745

DISTRIBUTING (3) [DISTRIBUTE]
2Ch 31:14 **d** the contributions made to the LORD and 5989
    31:15 **d** to their fellow priests according 5989
Ne 13:13 for **d** the **supplies** to their brothers. 2745

DISTRIBUTION (1) [DISTRIBUTE]
Ac 6: 1 overlooked in the daily **d** of food. 1355

DISTRICT (23) [DISTRICTS, HALF-DISTRICT]
Ge 47:11 the **d** of Rameses, as Pharaoh directed. 824
1Sa 9: 4 They went on into the **d** of Shaalim, 824
    9: 5 When they reached the **d** of Zuph, 824
1Ki 4: 7 also had twelve **d** governors over all Israel, 5893
    4: 5 in charge of the **d** officers; 5893
    4:13 as well as the **d** of Argob in Bashan 2475
    4:19 He was the only governor over the **d**. 824
    4:27 The **d** officers, each in his month, 5893
2Ki 22:14 She lived in Jerusalem, in the **Second D**. 5467
2Ch 34:22 She lived in Jerusalem, in the **Second D**. 5467
Ezr 5: 8 king should know that we went to the **d** 10406
Ne 3:14 ruler of the **d** of Beth Hakkerem. 7135
    3:15 ruler of the **d** of Mizpah. 7135
    3:17 Hashabiah, ruler of half the **d** of Keilah, 7135

Ne 3:17 carried out repairs for his **d**. 7135
    11: 9 was over the **Second D** of the city. 5467
Ecc 5: 8 If you see the poor oppressed in a **d**, 4519
Eze 45: 1 of the land as a **sacred d**, 25,000 cubits long AIT
    45: 3 In the sacred **d**, measure off 4500
    45: 7 by the sacred **d** and the property of the city. 9556
Zep 1:11 Wail, you who live in the **market d**; 4847
Mt 2:22 he withdrew to the **d** of Galilee. 3538
Ac 16:12 the leading city of that **d** of Macedonia. 3535

DISTRICTS (5) [DISTRICT]
Jdg 5:15 the **d** of Reuben there was much searching 7106
    5:16 the **d** of Reuben there was much searching 7106
1Ch 27:25 of the storehouses in the **outlying d**, 8441
2Ch 11:13 The priests and Levites from all their **d** 1473
    11:23 throughout the **d** of Judah and Benjamin, 824

DISTURB (1) [DISTURBANCE, DISTURBED, DISTURBING]
2Ki 23:18 "Don't let anyone **d** his bones." 5675

DISTURBANCE (2) [DISTURB]
Ac 19:23 About that time there arose a **great d** about 3900+4024+5431
    24:18 nor was I involved in any **d.** 2573

DISTURBED (14) [DISTURB]
1Sa 28:15 "Why have you **d** me by bringing me up?" 8074
2Sa 7:10 a home of their own and no longer be **d**. 8074
1Ch 17: 9 a home of their own and no longer be **d**. 8074
Ne 2:10 they were very much **d** 8288+8317
Job 20: 2 to answer because I am greatly **d**. 2591
Ps 42: 5 Why so **d** within me? 2159
    42:11 Why so **d** within me? 2159
    43: 5 Why so **d** within me? 2159
Isa 31: 4 he is not frightened by their shouts or **d** 6700
La 1:20 and in my heart I am **d**, 2200
Da 7:15 that passed through my mind **d** me. 10097
Mt 2: 3 When King Herod heard this he was **d**, 5429
Ac 4: 2 They were greatly **d** because 1387
    15:24 without our authorization and **d** you, 5429

DISTURBING (1) [DISTURB]
Est 7: 4 no such distress would justify **d** the king." 5691

DITCHES (1)
2Ki 3:16 Make this valley **full of d.** 1463+1463

DIVERS, DIVERSE (KJV) See
COLORFUL, DIFFERENT, EMBROIDERED, KINDS, RICHLY ORNAMENTED, SOME, SWARMS, VARIED

DIVIDE (23) [DIVIDED, DIVIDES, DIVIDING, DIVISION, DIVISIONS, DIVISIVE, SUBDIVISION, SUBDIVISIONS]
Ex 14:16 and stretch out your hand over the sea to **d** 1324
    15: 9 I will **d** the spoils; 2745
    21:35 **d** both the money and the dead animal
        equally. 2936
Nu 31:27 **D** the spoils between the soldiers 2936
Dt 19: 3 Build roads to them and **d** into three 8992
    31: 7 **d** it among them as their **inheritance**. 5706
Jos 13: 7 and **d** it as an inheritance among 2745
    18: 5 You are to **d** the land into seven parts. 2745
    22: 8 and **d** with your brothers the plunder 2745
2Sa 19:29 I order you and Ziba to **d** the fields." 2745
Job 27:17 and the innocent will **d** his silver. 2745
    41: 6 Will they **d** him **up** among the merchants? 2936
Ps 22:18 They **d** my garments among them 2745
    68:12 in the camps men **d** the plunder. 2745
Isa 7: 6 let us tear it apart and **d** it among ourselves, 1324
    53:12 and he will **d** the spoils with the strong, 2745
Eze 5: 1 Then take a set of scales and **d** up the hair. 2745
    47:13 **d** the land **for an inheritance** 5706
    47:14 You are to **d** it equally among you. 5706
Mic 2: 5 in the assembly of the LORD to **d** the land 8959
Lk 12:13 tell my brother to **d** the inheritance 3532
    22:17 "Take this and **d** it among you. 1374
Jude 1:19 These are the men who **d** you, 626

DIVIDED (58) [DIVIDE]
Ge 10:25 because in his time the earth was **d**; 7103
    14:15 the night Abram **d** his men to attack them 2745
    32: 7 and distress Jacob **d** the people who were 2936
    33: 1 so he **d** the children among Leah, 2936
Ex 14:21 The waters were **d**, 1324
Lev 11: 3 a split hoof **completely d** and that chews
        the cud. 9117+9118
    11: 7 it has a split hoof **completely d**, 9117+9118
    11:26 a split hoof not **completely d** or 9117+9118
Dt 14: 6 a split hoof **d** in two and that chews 9117+9118
    14: 7 a split hoof **completely d** you may not eat 9117
    32: 8 when he **d** all mankind, 7233
Jos 14: 5 So the Israelites **d** the land, 2745
Jdg 9:43 **d** them into three companies and set 2936
1Ki 18: 6 So they **d** the land to cover, 2745

2Ki 2: 8 The water **d** to the right and to the left, 2936
    2:14 it **d** to the right and to the left, 2936
1Ch 1:19 because in his time the earth was **d**; 7103
    23: 6 David **d** the Levites into groups 2745
    24: 4 and they were **d** accordingly: 2745
    24: 5 They **d** them impartially by drawing lots. 2745
Ne 9:11 You **d** the sea before them, 1324
Ps 78:13 He **d** the sea and led them through; 1324
  136:13 to him who **d** the Red Sea asunder 1615
Pr 18: 2 by his knowledge the deeps were **d**, 1324
Isa 18: 2 whose land is **d** by rivers. 1021
    18: 7 whose land is **d** by rivers— 1021
    33:23 Then an abundance of spoils will be **d** 2745
    63:12 who **d** the waters before them, 1324
Eze 37:22 be two nations and no longer be **d** into two kingdoms. 2936
Da 2:41 so this will be a **d** kingdom; 10583
    5:28 Your kingdom is **d** and given to the Medes 10592
Joel 3: 2 among the nations and **d** up my land. 2745
Am 7:17 be measured and **d** up. 2745
Mic 2: 4 my people's possession is **d** up. 4614
Zec 14: 1 when your plunder will be **d** among you. 2745
Mt 12:25 "Every kingdom **d** against itself will 3532
    12:25 or household **d** against itself will not stand. 3532
    12:26 he is **d** against himself. 3532
    27:35 they **d** up his clothes by casting lots. 1374
Mk 3:24 If a kingdom is **d** against itself, 3532
    3:25 If a house is **d** against itself, 3532
    3:26 And if Satan opposes himself and is **d**, 3532
    6:41 He also **d** the two fish among them all. 3532
Lk 11:17 "Any kingdom **d** against itself will 1374
    11:17 and a house **d** against itself will fall. NIG
    11:18 If Satan is **d** against himself, 1374
    12:52 be five in one family **d** against each other, 1374
    12:53 They will be **d**, father against son 1374
    15:12 So he **d** his property **between** them. 1349
    23:34 And they **d** up his clothes by casting lots. 1374
Jn 7:43 Thus the people were **d** because of Jesus. 5388
    9:16 So they were **d**. 5388
    10:19 At these words the Jews were again **d**. 5388
    19:24 "They **d** my garments **among** them 1374
Ac 14: 4 The people of the city were **d**; 5387
    23: 7 and the assembly was **d**. 5387
1Co 1:13 Is Christ **d**? Was Paul crucified for you? 3532
    7:34 and his interests are **d**. 3532

DIVIDES (2) [DIVIDE]
Ge 49:27 in the evening he **d** the plunder." 2745
Lk 11:22 the man trusted and **d** up the spoils. 1344

DIVIDING (9) [DIVIDE]
Jos 19:49 When they had finished **d** the land 5706
    19:51 And so they finished **d** the land. 2745
Jdg 5:30 'Are they not finding and **d** the spoils: 2745
    7:16 **D** the three hundred men 2936
Isa 9: 3 as men rejoice when **d** the plunder. 2745
Mk 15:24 **D** up his clothes, 1374
Jn 19:23 **d** them **into four shares**, 3538+4472
Eph 2:14 the **d** wall of hostility, 3546
Heb 4:12 it penetrates even to **d** soul and spirit, 3536

DIVINATION (16) [DIVINATIONS, DIVINE, DIVINER, DIVINERS]
Ge 30:27 I have **learned** by **d** that 5727
    44: 5 from and also **uses for d**? 5727+5727
    44:15 **find things out by d**?" 5727+5727
Lev 19:26 " 'Do not **practice d** or sorcery. 5727
Nu 22: 7 taking with them the **fee for d**. 7877
    23:23 no **d** against Israel. 7877
Dt 18:10 who **practices d** or sorcery, 7876+7877
    18:14 to those who practice sorcery or **d**, 7876
Jos 13:22 of Beor, who **practiced d**. 7876
1Sa 15:23 For rebellion is like the sin of **d**, 7877
2Ki 17:17 They **practiced d** and sorcery 7876+7877
    21: 6 practiced sorcery and **d**, 5727
2Ch 33: 6 practiced sorcery, **d** and witchcraft, 5727
Isa 2: 6 they **practice d** like the Philistines 6726
Eze 13:23 therefore you will no longer see false
        visions or **practice d.** 7876+7877
Mic 3: 6 without visions, and darkness, without **d.** 7876

DIVINATIONS (7) [DIVINATION]
Jer 14:14 to you false visions, **d**, idolatries and 7877
Eze 12:24 or flattering **d** among the people of Israel. 5241
    13: 6 Their visions are false and their **d** a lie. 7877
    13: 7 not seen false visions and uttered lying **d** 5241
    13: 9 and **utter** lying **d**. 7876
    21:29 concerning you and lying **d** about you, 7876
    22:28 for them by false visions and lying **d.** 7876

DIVINE (9) [DIVINATION]
Isa 35: 4 with **d** retribution he will come 466
Ac 8:10 the **d** power known as the Great Power." 2536
    17:29 the **d** being is like gold or silver or stone— 2521
    19:27 will be robbed of her **d** majesty." 3484
Ro 1:20 his eternal power and **d** nature— 2522
    9: 4 theirs the **d** glory, the covenants, NIG
2Co 10: 4 they have **d** power to demolish strongholds. 2536
2Pe 1: 3 His **d** power has given us everything we
        need for life and godliness 2521
    1: 4 you may participate in the **d** nature and 2521

DIVINER (1) [DIVINATION]
Da 2:27 magician or **d** can explain to the king 10140

DIVINERS (9) [DIVINATION]

1Sa	6: 2	for the priests and the **d** and said,	7876
Isa	44:25	of false prophets and makes fools of **d**,	7876
Jer	27: 9	So do not listen to your prophets, your **d**,	7876
	29: 8	the prophets and **d** among you deceive you.	7876
Da	4: 7	enchanters, astrologers and **d** came,	10140
	5: 7	astrologers and **d** to be brought and said	10140
	5:11	enchanters, astrologers and **d**.	10140
Mic	3: 7	be ashamed and the **d** disgraced.	7876
Zec	10: 2	**d** see visions that lie;	7876

DIVISION (43) [DIVIDE]

Nu	2: 4	His **d** numbers 74,600.	7372
	2: 6	His **d** numbers 54,400.	7372
	2: 8	His **d** numbers 57,400.	7372
	2:11	His **d** numbers 46,500.	7372
	2:13	His **d** numbers 59,300.	7372
	2:15	His **d** numbers 45,650.	7372
	2:19	His **d** numbers 40,500.	7372
	2:21	His **d** numbers 32,200.	7372
	2:23	His **d** numbers 35,400.	7372
	2:26	His **d** numbers 62,700.	7372
	2:28	His **d** numbers 41,500.	7372
	2:30	His **d** numbers 53,400.	7372
	10:15	Nethanel son of Zuar was over the **d** of	7372
	10:16	and Eliab son of Helon was over the **d** of	7372
	10:19	of Zurishaddai was over the **d** of the tribe	7372
	10:20	of Deuel was over the **d** of the tribe of Gad.	7372
	10:23	Gamaliel son of Pedahzur was over the **d**	7372
	10:24	and Abidan son of Gideoni was over the **d**	7372
	10:26	Pagiel son of Ocran was over the **d** of	7372
	10:27	and Ahira son of Enan was over the **d** of	7372
Jos	22:14	of a family **d** among the Israelite clans.	1074
1Ch	27: 1	Each **d** consisted of 24,000 men.	4713
	27: 2	In charge of the first **d**, for the first month,	4713
	27: 2	There were 24,000 men in his **d**.	4713
	27: 4	of the **d** for the second month was Dodai	4713
	27: 4	Mikloth was the leader of his **d**.	4713
	27: 4	There were 24,000 men in his **d**.	4713
	27: 5	and there were 24,000 men in his **d**.	4713
	27: 6	His son Ammizabad was in charge of his **d**.	4713
	27: 7	There were 24,000 men in his **d**.	4713
	27: 8	There were 24,000 men in his **d**.	4713
	27: 9	There were 24,000 men in his **d**.	4713
	27:10	There were 24,000 men in his **d**.	4713
	27:11	There were 24,000 men in his **d**.	4713
	27:12	There were 24,000 men in his **d**.	4713
	27:13	There were 24,000 men in his **d**.	4713
	27:14	There were 24,000 men in his **d**.	4713
	27:15	There were 24,000 men in his **d**.	4713
Ezr	10:16	one from each family **d**,	1074
Lk	1: 5	who belonged to the **priestly d** of Abijah;	2389
	1: 8	Once when Zechariah's **d** was on duty	2389
	12:51	No, I tell you, but **d**.	1375
1Co	12:25	so that there should be no **d** in the body,	5388

DIVISIONS (51) [DIVIDE]

Ge	36:30	according to their **d**, in the land of Seir.	477
Ex	6:26	the Israelites out of Egypt by their **d**."	7372
	7: 4	of judgment I will bring out my **d**,	7372
	12:17	on this very day that I brought your **d** out	7372
	12:41	all the LORD's **d** left Egypt.	7372
	12:51	the Israelites out of Egypt by their **d**.	7372
Nu	1: 3	You and Aaron are to number by their **d** all	7372
	1:52	The Israelites are to set up their tents by **d**,	7372
	2: 3	the **d** of the camp of Judah are to encamp	7372
	2: 9	according to their **d**, number 186,400.	7372
	2:10	On the south will be the **d** of the camp	7372
	2:16	according to their **d**, number 151,450.	7372
	2:18	On the west will be the **d** of the camp	7372
	2:24	according to their **d**, number 108,100.	7372
	2:25	the north will be the **d** of the camp of Dan,	7372
	2:32	All those in the camps, by their **d**,	7372
	10:14	The **d** of the camp of Judah went first,	7372
	10:18	The **d** of the camp of Reuben went next,	7372
	10:22	The **d** of the camp of Ephraim went next,	7372
	10:25	the **d** of the camp of Dan set out,	7372
	10:28	march for the Israelite **d** as they set out.	7372
	33: 1	when they came out of Egypt by **d** under	7372
Jos	11:23	to Israel according to their tribal **d**.	4713
	12: 7	of Israel according to their tribal **d**—	4713
	18:10	to the Israelites according to their tribal **d**.	4713
1Sa	11:11	The next day Saul separated his men into three **d**;	8031
1Ch	24: 1	These were the **d** of the sons of Aaron:	4713
	24: 3	David **separated** them into **d**	2745
	26: 1	The **d** of the gatekeepers:	4713
	26:12	These **d** of the gatekeepers,	4713
	26:19	These were the **d** of	4713
	27: 1	in all that concerned the **army d** that were	4713
	28: 1	over the tribes, the commanders of the **d** in	4713
	28:13	He gave him instructions for the **d** of	4713
	28:21	The **d** of the priests and Levites are ready	4713
2Ch	5:11	regardless of their **d**.	4713
	8:14	the **d** of the priests for their duties,	4713
	8:14	He also appointed the gatekeepers by **d** for	4713
	23: 8	the priest had not released any of the **d**.	4713
	26:11	to go out by **d** according to their numbers	1522
	31: 2	the priests and Levites into **d**—	4713
	31:15	to their fellow priests according to their **d**,	4713
	31:16	to their responsibilities and their **d**.	4713
	31:17	to their responsibilities and their **d**.	4713
	35: 4	Prepare yourselves by families in your **d**,	4713
	35:10	in their places with the Levites in their **d** as	4713
Ezr	6:18	the priests in their **d** and the Levites	10585

Ne	11:36	of the **d** of the Levites of Judah settled	4713
Ro	16:17	for those who cause **d** and put obstacles	1496
1Co	1:10	with one another so that there may be no **d**	5388
	11:18	there are **d** among you,	5388

DIVISIVE (1) [DIVIDE]

| Tit | 3:10 | Warn a **d** person once, | 148 |

DIVORCE (18) [DIVORCED, DIVORCES]

Dt	22:19	he must not **d** her as long as he lives.	8938
	22:29	He can never **d** her as long as he lives.	8938
	24: 1	and he writes her a certificate of **d**,	4135
	24: 3	and writes her a certificate of **d**,	4135
Isa	50: 1	"Where is your mother's certificate of **d**	4135
Jer	3: 8	I gave faithless Israel her certificate of **d**	4135
Mal	2:16	"I hate **d**," says the LORD God of Israel,	8938
Mt	1:19	he had in mind to **d** her quietly.	668
	5:31	must give her a **certificate of d.'**	687
	19: 3	"Is it lawful for a man to **d** his wife for any	668
	19: 7	that a man give his wife a certificate of **d**	687
	19: 8	"Moses permitted you to **d** your wives	668
Mk	10: 2	"Is it lawful for a man to **d** his wife?"	668
	10: 4	a certificate of **d** and send her away."	687
1Co	7:11	And a husband **must** not **d** his wife.	918
	7:12	he **must** not **d** her.	918
	7:13	she **must** not **d** him.	918
	7:27	Are you married? Do not seek a **d**.	3386

DIVORCED (9) [DIVORCE]

Lev	21: 7	by prostitution or **d** from their husbands,	1763
	21:14	He must not marry a widow, a **d** woman,	1763
	22:13	priest's daughter becomes a widow or is **d**,	1763
Nu	30: 9	a widow or **d** woman will be binding on her.	1763
Dt	24: 4	then her first husband, who **d** her, is	8938
1Ch	8: 8	after he had **d** his wives Hushim and Baara.	8938
Eze	44:22	They must not marry widows or **d** women;	1763
Mt	5:32	the **d** woman commits adultery.	668
Lk	16:18	a **d** woman commits adultery.	467+608+668

DIVORCES (7) [DIVORCE]

Jer	3: 1	"If a man **d** his wife and she leaves him	8938
Mt	5:31	'Anyone who **d** his wife must give her	668
	5:32	But I tell you that anyone who **d** his wife,	668
	19: 9	I tell you that anyone who **d** his wife,	668
Mk	10:11	"Anyone who **d** his wife and marries	668
	10:12	she **d** her husband and marries another man,	668
Lk	16:18	"Anyone who **d** his wife and marries	668

DIZAHAB (1)

| Dt | 1: 1 | Laban, Hazeroth and **D**. | 1903 |

DIZZINESS (1)

| Isa | 19:14 | LORD has poured into them a spirit of **d**; | 6413 |

DO (2715) [DID, DIDN'T, DO-NOTHING, DOES, DOESN'T, DOING, DONE, DON'T]

Ge	4: 7	If you **d** what is right,	3512
	4: 7	**d** not **do** what is right,	AIT
	4: 7	But if you do not **d** what is right,	3512
	11: 6	to **d** this, then nothing they plan to do will	6913
	11: 6	to **d** will be impossible for them.	6913
	15: 1	"**D** not be **afraid**, Abram.	AIT
	16: 6	"**D** with her whatever you think best."	6913
	18: 3	my lord, **d** not **pass** your servant by.	AIT
	18: 5	they answered, "**d** as you say."	6913
	18:17	from Abraham what I **am about to d**?	6913
	18:25	Far be it from you to **d** such a thing—	6913
	18:25	not the Judge of all the earth **d** right?"	6913
	18:29	"For the sake of forty, I **will** not **d** it."	6913
	18:30	"I **will** not **d** it if I find thirty there."	6913
	19: 7	Don't **d** this **wicked** thing.	8317
	19: 8	and you can **d** what you like with them.	6913
	19: 8	But don't **d** anything to these men,	6913
	19:12	"**D** you have anyone else here—	NIH
	19:22	I cannot **d** anything until you reach it."	6913
	20: 7	But if you **d** not **return** her,	AIT
	21:12	"**D** not be so **distressed**	AIT
	21:17	**D** not be **afraid**;	AIT
	21:22	"God is with you in everything you **d**.	6913
	22:12	"**D** not **lay** a hand on the boy," he said.	AIT
	22:12	"**D** not **do** anything to him.	AIT
	22:12	"**Do** not **d** anything to him.	6913
	24: 6	**d** not **take** my son back	AIT
	24: 8	**d** not **take** my son back	AIT
	24:56	But he said to them, "**D** not **detain** me,	AIT
	26: 2	"**D** not **go down** to Egypt;	AIT
	26:24	**D** not be **afraid**, for I am with you;	AIT
	26:29	that **you will d** us no harm,	6913
	27: 8	listen carefully and **d** what I tell you:	NIH
	27:13	Just **d** what I say; go and get them for me."	9048
	27:37	So what **can I possibly d** for you,	6913
	27:38	"**D** you have only one blessing, my father?"	NIH
	27:43	Now then, my son, **d** what I say:	9048
	28: 1	"**D** not **marry** a Canaanite woman.	AIT
	28: 6	"**D** not **marry** a Canaanite woman,"	AIT
	29: 5	He said to them, "**D** you **know** Laban,	AIT
	30:30	**may I d** something for my own household?"	6913
	30:31	"But if **you will d** this one thing for me,	6913
	31:14	**D** we still **have** any share in the inheritance	AIT
	31:16	So **d** whatever God has told you."	6913
	31:43	Yet what **can I d** today	6913
	32:17	'To whom **d** you belong,	NIH

Ge	32:29	But he replied, "Why **d** you **ask** my name?"	AIT
	32:32	Therefore to this day the Israelites **d** not **eat**	AIT
	33: 8	"What **d** you mean	NIH
	33:15	"But why **d** that?"	NIH
	34:14	"We can't **d** such a thing;	6913
	37: 8	"**D** you **intend to reign**	AIT
	39: 9	then **could I d** such a wicked thing and sin	6913
	40: 8	"**D** not interpretations belong to God?	NIH
	40:13	to **d** when you were his cupbearer.	5477
	41:16	"I cannot **d** it," Joseph replied to Pharaoh,	NIH
	41:25	to Pharaoh **what he is about to d**.	6913
	41:28	God has shown Pharaoh what **he is about to d**.	6913
	41:32	and God **will d** it soon.	6913
	41:55	"Go to Joseph and **d** what he tells you."	6913
	42: 1	**d** you just keep **looking at each other?**"	AIT
	42: 7	"Where **d** you **come** from?"	AIT
	42:18	"**D** this and you will live, for I fear God:	6913
	42:20	This they **proceeded to d**.	6913
	42:37	**d** not **bring** him back	AIT
	43: 7	'**D** you **have** another brother?'	AIT
	43: 9	**d** not **bring** him back	AIT
	43:11	"If it must be, then **d** this:	6913
	44: 7	from your servants to **d** anything like that!	6913
	44:17	"Far be it from me to **d** such a thing!	6913
	44:18	**D** not be **angry** with your servant,	AIT
	44:19	'**D** you **have** a father or a brother?'	AIT
	44:32	**d** not **bring** him back	AIT
	44:34	**D** not **let me see**	AIT
	45: 5	**d** not be **distressed** and do not be angry	AIT
	45: 5	do not be distressed and **d** not be **angry**	AIT
	45:17	"Tell your brothers, '**D** this:	6913
	45:19	"You are also directed to tell them, '**D** this:	6913
	46: 3	"**D** not be **afraid** to go down to Egypt,	AIT
	47: 9	and **they d** not **equal** the years of	AIT
	47:29	**D** not **bury** me in Egypt,	AIT
	47:30	"I **will d** as you say," he said.	6913
	50: 6	**made** you **swear to d**."	AIT
Ex	1:17	not **d** what the king of Egypt had told them	6913
	1:17	the king of Egypt had told them to **d**;	NIH
	3: 5	"**D** not **come** any **closer**,"	AIT
	4: 1	"What if they **d** not **believe** me or listen	AIT
	4: 8	"If they **d** not **believe** you or pay attention	AIT
	4: 9	But if they **d** not **believe** these two signs	AIT
	4:13	"O Lord, please send someone else to **d** it."	NIH
	4:15	of you speak and will teach you what to **d**.	6913
	4:21	wonders I have given you the power to **d**.	NIH
	5: 2	**I d** not **know** the LORD and I will	AIT
	6: 1	you will see what **I will d** to Pharaoh:	6913
	8:21	**d** not **let** my people go,	AIT
	9: 5	"Tomorrow the LORD **will d** this in	6913
	9:30	that you and your officials still **d** not **fear**	AIT
	10: 7	**D** you not yet **realize**	AIT
	10:28	Make sure **you d** not **appear**	AIT
	12: 9	**D** not **eat** the meat raw or cooked in water,	AIT
	12:10	**D** not **leave** any of it till morning;	AIT
	12:16	**D** no work at all on these days,	6913
	12:16	that is all you **may d**.	6913
	12:46	**D** not **break** any of the bones.	AIT
	13: 8	'I **d** this because of what the LORD did	NIH
	13:13	but if you **d** not **redeem** it, break its neck.	AIT
	14:13	"**D** not be **afraid**.	AIT
	15:26	of the LORD your God and **d** what is right	6913
	17: 2	"Why **d** you **quarrel** with me?	AIT
	17: 2	**d** you **put** the LORD **to the test?**"	AIT
	17: 4	"What am **I** to **d** with these people?"	6913
	18:14	**d** you alone **sit as judge**,	AIT
	18:23	If **you d** this and God so commands,	6913
	19:12	'**We will d** everything	6913
	19:12	that you **d** not **go up** the mountain or touch	AIT
	19:21	**d** not **force their way through**	AIT
	20: 9	and **d** all your work,	6913
	20:10	On it you shall not **d** any work,	6913
	20:19	**d** not **make God speak**	AIT
	20:20	Moses said to the people, "**D** not be **afraid**.	AIT
	20:23	**D** not **make** any gods to be alongside me;	AIT
	20:23	**d** not **make** for yourselves gods of silver	AIT
	20:25	**d** not **build** it with dressed stones,	AIT
	20:26	And **d** not **go up** to my altar on steps,	AIT
	21: 5	**d** not **want to go**	AIT
	21: 7	she is not to go free as menservants **d**.	3655S
	21:13	if he **does** not **d** it **intentionally**,	7399
	22:18	"**D** not **allow** a sorceress **to live**.	AIT
	22:21	"**D** not **mistreat** an alien or oppress him,	AIT
	22:22	"**D** not **take advantage** of a widow or	AIT
	22:23	If you **d** and they cry out to me,	6700+6700S
	22:25	**d** not be like a moneylender;	AIT
	22:28	"**D** not **blaspheme** God or curse the ruler	AIT
	22:29	"**D** not **hold back** offerings	AIT
	22:30	**D** the same with your cattle and your sheep.	6913
	22:31	So **d** not **eat** the meat of an animal torn	AIT
	23: 1	"**D** not **spread** false reports.	AIT
	23: 1	**D** not **help** a wicked man by being	AIT
	23: 2	"**D** not **follow** the crowd in doing wrong.	AIT
	23: 2	**d** not **pervert** justice by siding with	AIT
	23: 3	and **d** not **show favoritism** to a poor man	AIT
	23: 5	**d** not leave it there;	2532
	23: 6	"**D** not **deny** justice to your poor people	AIT
	23: 7	Have nothing to **d** with a false charge	8178
	23: 7	**d** not **put** an innocent or honest person **to death**,	AIT
	23: 8	"**D** not **accept** a bribe,	AIT
	23: 9	"**D** not **oppress** an alien,	AIT
	23:11	**D** the same with your vineyard	6913
	23:12	"Six days of **your work**,	6913
	23:12	but on the seventh day **d** not **work**,	8697
	23:13	"Be **careful** to **d** everything I have said	9068

Ex	23:13	D not **invoke** the names of other gods;	AIT
	23:13	d not *let them* **be heard**	AIT
	23:15	**D** this at the appointed time in the month	NIH
	23:18	"D not **offer** the blood of a sacrifice to me	AIT
	23:19	"D not **cook** a young goat in its mother's	AIT
	23:21	D not **rebel** against him;	AIT
	23:22	to what he says and **d** all that I say,	6913
	23:24	D not **bow down** before their gods	AIT
	23:32	D not **make** a covenant with them or	AIT
	23:33	D not *let them* **live**	AIT
	24: 3	the LORD has said we will **d**."	6913
	24: 7	"We will **d** everything the LORD has said;	6913
	26: 3	and **d the same** *with* the other five.	2489S
	26: 4	and **d** the same with the end curtain in	6913
	29: 1	"This is what *you are to* **d**	6913
	29:35	"**D** for Aaron and his sons everything I have commanded you,	6913
	30: 9	D not **offer** on this altar any other incense	AIT
	30: 9	and *d* not **pour** a drink offering on it.	AIT
	30:32	D not **pour** it on men's bodies and do	AIT
	30:32	*d* not **make** any oil with the same formula.	AIT
	30:37	D not **make** any incense with this formula	AIT
	32:12	**relent** and d not **bring** disaster	5714
	32:21	"What *did* these people *d* to you,	6913
	32:22	"D not **be angry**, my lord," Aaron answered.	AIT
	32:22	and I will decide what *to* **d** with you.' "	6913
	33: 5	and I will **d** with you.' "	6913
	33:15	*d* not **send** us **up**	AIT
	33:17	"I will **d** the very thing you have asked,	6913
	34:10	all your people I will **d** wonders never	6913
	34:10	the LORD, will **d** for you.	6913
	34:14	D not **worship** any other god, for the LORD,	AIT
	34:16	they will **lead** your sons to **d the same**.	339+466+2177+2388S
	34:17	"D not **make** cast idols.	AIT
	34:18	**D** this at the appointed time in the month	NIH
	34:20	but if *you* **d** not **redeem** it, break its neck.	AIT
	34:25	"D not **offer** the blood of a sacrifice to me	AIT
	34:25	*d* not *let* any of the sacrifice from the Passover Feast **remain** until morning.	AIT
	34:26	"D not **cook** a young goat in its mother's	AIT
	35: 1	the LORD has commanded you to **d**:	6913
	35: 3	D not **light** a fire in any of your dwellings	AIT
	35:29	through Moses had commanded them to **d**.	6913
	35:35	He has filled them with skill to **d** all kinds	6913
	36: 1	the sanctuary *are to* **d** *the* **work** just as	6913
	36: 2	and who was willing to come and **d**	6913
	36: 7	to **d** all the work.	6913
Lev	2:13	D not **leave** the salt of the covenant	AIT
	4:20	and **d** with this bull just as he did with	6913
	5: 4	**d** anything, whether **good**	3512
	5:16	for what *he has* **failed to d** in regard to	2627
	6: 3	he commits any such sin that people *may* **d**	6913
	7:23	'D not **eat** any of the fat of cattle,	AIT
	8:33	D not **leave** the entrance to the Tent	AIT
	8:35	and night for seven days and **d** what	9068
	9: 6	the LORD has commanded you *to* **d**,	6913
	10: 6	"D not *let* your hair **become unkempt**,	AIT
	10: 6	and *d* not **tear** your clothes,	AIT
	10: 7	D not **leave** the entrance to the Tent	AIT
	11:10	or streams that **d** not have fins and scales—	NIH
	11:43	D not **defile** yourselves by any	AIT
	11:43	D not **make yourselves unclean**	AIT
	11:44	D not **make yourselves unclean**	AIT
	16:15	and take its blood behind the curtain and **d**	6913
	16:16	*to* **d** the same for the Tent of Meeting,	6913
	16:29	and not **d** any work—	6913
	18: 3	*You must* not **d** as they do in Egypt,	6913
	18: 3	You must not do as they **d** *in* Egypt,	5126
	18: 3	and *you must* not **d** as they do in the land	6913
	18: 3	and you must not do as they **d** *in* the land	5126
	18: 3	D not **follow** their practices.	AIT
	18: 7	" 'D not **dishonor** your father **by having sexual relations** with your mother.	AIT
	18: 7	*d* not **have relations with** her.	AIT
	18: 8	" 'D not **have sexual relations with**	AIT
	18: 9	" 'D not **have sexual relations with**	AIT
	18:10	" 'D not **have sexual relations with**	AIT
	18:11	" 'D not **have sexual relations with**	AIT
	18:12	" 'D not **have sexual relations with**	AIT
	18:13	" 'D not **have sexual relations with**	AIT
	18:14	" 'D not **dishonor** your father's brother **by** approaching his wife **to have sexual relations;**	AIT
	18:15	" 'D not **have sexual relations with**	AIT
	18:15	*d* not **have relations with**	AIT
	18:16	" 'D not **have sexual relations with**	AIT
	18:17	" 'D not **have sexual relations with**	AIT
	18:17	D not **have sexual relations with**	AIT
	18:18	" 'D not **take** your wife's sister as	AIT
	18:19	" 'D not **approach** a woman	AIT
	18:20	" 'D not **have sexual relations**	AIT
	18:21	" 'D not **give** any of your children to	AIT
	18:22	" 'D not **lie with** a man as one lies with a woman;	AIT
	18:23	" 'D not **have sexual relations**	AIT
	18:24	" 'D not **defile yourselves**	AIT
	18:26	the aliens living among you *must* not **d** any	6913
	18:30	and *d* not **follow** any of the detestable	AIT
	18:30	*d* not **defile yourselves**	AIT
	19: 4	" 'D not **turn** to idols or make gods	AIT
	19: 9	*d* not **reap** *to* the very edges of your field	AIT
	19:10	D not **go over** your vineyard **a second time**	AIT
	19:11	" 'D not **steal**.	AIT
	19:11	" 'D not **lie**.	AIT
	19:11	" 'D not **deceive** one another.	AIT
	19:12	" 'D not **swear** falsely by my name and	AIT
	19:13	" 'D not **defraud** your neighbor or rob him.	AIT

Lev	19:13	" 'D not **hold back** the wages of a hired man **overnight**.	AIT
	19:14	" 'D not **curse** the deaf or put	AIT
	19:15	" 'D not **pervert** justice;	AIT
	19:15	*d* not **show partiality** *to* the poor	AIT
	19:16	" 'D not **go about** spreading slander	AIT
	19:16	" 'D not **do anything that endangers** your neighbor's **life**.	AIT
	19:16	" 'D not **d anything that endangers** your neighbor's **life**.	1947+6584+6641
	19:17	" 'D not **hate** your brother in your heart.	AIT
	19:18	" 'D not **seek revenge** or bear a grudge	AIT
	19:19	" 'D not **mate** different kinds of animals.	AIT
	19:19	" 'D not **plant** your field **with** two kinds of **seed**.	AIT
	19:19	" 'D not **wear** clothing woven of two kinds	AIT
	19:26	" 'D not **eat** any meat with the blood still	AIT
	19:26	" 'D not **practice divination**	AIT
	19:27	" 'D not **cut the hair**	AIT
	19:28	" 'D not **cut** your bodies for the dead	AIT
	19:29	" 'D not **degrade** your daughter	AIT
	19:31	" 'D not **turn** to mediums	AIT
	19:33	*d* not **mistreat** him.	AIT
	19:35	" 'D not **use** dishonest standards	AIT
	20:19	" 'D not **have sexual relations with**	AIT
	20:25	D not **defile** yourselves by any animal	AIT
	22: 9	so that they *d* not **become guilty** and die	AIT
	22:20	D not **bring** anything with a defect,	AIT
	22:22	D not **offer** to the LORD the blind,	AIT
	22:22	D not **place** any of these on the altar as	AIT
	22:24	*You must* not **d** this in your own land,	6913
	22:28	D not **slaughter** a cow or a sheep	AIT
	22:32	D not **profane** my holy name.	AIT
	23: 3	*You are* not to **d** any work;	6913
	23: 7	a sacred assembly and **d** no regular work.	6913
	23: 8	a sacred assembly and **d** no regular work.' "	6913
	23:21	a sacred assembly and **d** no regular work.	6913
	23:22	*d* not **reap** *to* the very edges of your field	AIT
	23:25	**D** no regular work,	6913
	23:28	**D** no work on that day,	6913
	23:31	*You shall* **d** no work at all.	6913
	23:35	**d** no regular work.	6913
	23:36	**d** no regular work.	6913
	25: 4	D not **sow** your fields	AIT
	25: 5	D not **reap** what grows of itself or harvest	AIT
	25:11	*d* not **sow** and do not reap what grows	AIT
	25:11	not sow and *d* not **reap** what grows of itself	AIT
	25:14	D not **take advantage of** each other.	AIT
	25:17	D not **take advantage of** each other,	AIT
	25:20	if *we d* not **plant** or harvest our crops?"	AIT
	25:36	D not **take** interest of any kind from him,	AIT
	25:39	*d* not **make** him **work** as a slave.	AIT
	25:43	D not **rule** over them ruthlessly,	AIT
	26: 1	" 'D not **make** idols or set up an image or	AIT
	26: 1	and *d* not **place** a carved stone in your land	AIT
	26:16	then I *will* **d** this to you:	6913
	26:23	*d* not **accept** my **correction**	AIT
	26:27	" 'If in spite of this *you still d* not **listen**	AIT
Nu	1:51	the Levites *shall* **d** it.	7756S
	4:15	to come to **d** *the* **carrying**.	AIT
	4:19	**d** this for them:	6913
	4:26	The Gershonites *are to* **d** all that needs to	6268
	4:47	of age who came to **d** the work of serving	6268
	6:12	The previous days *d* not **count**,	5877
	8: 7	To purify them, **d** this:	6913
	8:11	so that they may be ready to **d** the work of	6268
	8:15	they are to come to **d** *their* **work** at the Tent	6268
	8:19	as gifts to Aaron and his sons to **d** the work	6268
	8:22	the Levites came to **d** their **work** at the Tent	6268
	8:26	but *they themselves must* not **d** the work.	6268
	9:14	to celebrate the LORD's Passover *must* **d**	6913
	10:31	But Moses said, "Please *d* not **leave** us.	AIT
	11:12	Why *d you* **tell** me to carry them	AIT
	11:15	*d* not *let* me **face** my own ruin."	AIT
	11:25	but *they* did *d* not **d** *so* **again**.	3578
	12:11	*d* not **hold** against us the sin we have	AIT
	12:12	D not *let her* **be** like a stillborn infant	AIT
	13:19	What kind of land *d* they **live** in?	AIT
	13:19	What kind of towns *d* they **live** in?	AIT
	13:20	**D** your **best** to bring back some of the fruit	2616
	13:30	for *we can* certainly **d** it."	3523+3523
	14: 9	Only *d* not **rebel** against the LORD.	AIT
	14: 9	*d* not **be afraid** of the people of the land,	AIT
	14: 9	D not **be afraid** of them."	AIT
	14:28	I *will* **d** to you the very things	6913
	14:35	and I *will* surely **d** these things	6913
	14:42	D not **go up**,	AIT
	15:12	**D** this for each one,	6913
	15:13	" 'Everyone who is native-born *must* **d** these things	6913
	15:14	he *must* **d** exactly as you do.	6913
	15:14	he must do exactly as *you* **d**.	6913
	16: 3	Why then *d you* **set yourselves** above	AIT
	16: 6	Korah, and all your followers *are to* **d** this:	6913
	16: 9	and brought you near himself to **d** the work	6268
	16:15	"D not **accept** their offering.	AIT
	16:26	D not **touch** anything belonging to them,	AIT
	16:28	the LORD has sent me to **d** all these things	6913
	18: 6	dedicated to the LORD to **d** the work at	6268
	18:21	in return for the work they **d** while serving	6268
	18:23	It is the Levites *who are to* **d** the work at	6268
	21:34	"D not **be afraid** of him,	AIT
	21:34	**D** to him what you did to Sihon king of	6913
	22:12	God said to Balaam, "D not **go** with them.	AIT
	22:16	D not *let anything* **keep**	AIT
	22:17	and **d** whatever you say.	6913
	22:18	not **d** anything great or small to go beyond	6913

Nu	22:20	go with them, but **d** only what I tell you."	6913
	23: 9	*d* not **consider themselves**	AIT
	23:26	"Did I not tell you I *must* **d** whatever	6913
	24:13	I could not **d** anything of my own accord,	6913
	24:14	let me warn you of what this people *will* **d**	6913
	28:18	a sacred assembly and **d** no regular work.	6913
	28:25	a sacred assembly and **d** no regular work.	6913
	28:26	a sacred assembly and **d** no regular work.	6913
	29: 1	a sacred assembly and **d** no work.	6913
	29: 7	You must deny yourselves and **d** no work.	6913
	29:12	a sacred assembly and **d** no work.	6913
	29:35	an assembly and **d** no regular work.	6913
	30: 2	but *must* **d** everything he said.	6913
	32: 5	D not **make** us **cross**	AIT
	32: 7	Why *d you* **discourage** the Israelites	AIT
	32:20	Moses said to them, "If *you will* **d** this—	6913
	32:23	"But if *you* fail to **d** this,	6913
	32:24	but **d** what you have promised."	6913
	32:25	"We your servants *will* **d**	6913
	32:30	if *they* **d** not **cross over** with you armed,	AIT
	32:31	"Your servants *will* **d** what	6913
	33:55	if *you* **d** not **drive out** the inhabitants of	AIT
	33:56	And then I *will* **d** to you what I plan to do	6913
	33:56	I will do to you what I plan to **d** to them.' "	6913
	35:31	" 'D not **accept** a ransom for the life of	AIT
	35:32	" 'D not **accept** a ransom for anyone	AIT
	35:33	" 'D not **pollute** the land where you are.	AIT
	35:34	D not **defile** the land where you live and	AIT
Dt	1:14	"What you propose to **d** is good."	6913
	1:17	D not **show partiality**	AIT
	1:17	D not **be afraid** of any man,	AIT
	1:18	I told you everything *you were to* **d**.	6913
	1:21	D not **be afraid**; do not be discouraged."	AIT
	1:21	Do not be afraid; *d* not **be discouraged**."	AIT
	1:29	Then I said to you, "D not **be terrified**;	AIT
	1:29	*d* not **be afraid** of them.	AIT
	1:39	your children who *d* not yet **know** good	AIT
	1:42	"Tell them, 'D not **go up** and fight,	AIT
	2: 5	D not **provoke** them **to war,**	AIT
	2: 9	"D not **harass** the Moabites or provoke them to war,	AIT
	2:19	*d* not **harass** them or provoke them to war,	AIT
	3: 2	"D not **be afraid** of him,	AIT
	3: 2	**D** to him what you did to Sihon king of	6913
	3:21	The LORD *will* **d** the same to all	6913
	3:22	D not **be afraid** of them;	AIT
	3:24	in heaven or on earth who *can* **d** the deeds	6913
	3:24	the deeds and mighty works you **d**?	NIH
	3:26	"D not **speak** to me anymore	AIT
	4: 2	D not **add** to what I command you and do	AIT
	4: 2	to what I command you and *d* not **subtract**	AIT
	4: 9	so that *you d* not **forget**	AIT
	4:16	so that *you d* not **become corrupt** and make	AIT
	4:19	*d* not **be enticed** *into* bowing down to them	AIT
	4:23	*d* not **make** for yourselves an idol in the form of anything	AIT
	5:13	and **d** all your work,	6913
	5:14	On it *you shall* not **d** any work,	6913
	5:14	and maidservant may rest, as *you* **d**.	NIH
	5:32	So be careful to **d** what	6913
	5:32	*d* not **turn aside** *to* the right or to the left.	AIT
	6:12	that *you d* not **forget** the LORD,	AIT
	6:14	D not **follow** other gods,	AIT
	6:16	D not **test** the LORD your God as you did	AIT
	6:18	**D** what is right and good in	6913
	7: 3	D not **intermarry** with them.	AIT
	7: 3	D not **give** your daughters to their sons	AIT
	7: 5	This is what *you are to* **d** to them:	6913
	7:16	D not **look** on them **with pity**	AIT
	7:16	with pity and *d* not **serve** their gods,	AIT
	7:18	But *d* not **be afraid** of them;	AIT
	7:19	The LORD your God *will* **d** the same	6913
	7:21	D not **be terrified** by them,	AIT
	7:25	D not **covet** the silver and gold on them,	AIT
	7:25	and *d* not **take** it for yourselves,	AIT
	7:26	D not **bring** a detestable thing	AIT
	8:11	Be careful that *you d* not **forget**	AIT
	9: 4	*d* not **say** to yourself,	AIT
	9:26	*d* not **destroy** your people,	AIT
	10: 8	as they still **d** today.	NIH
	10:16	and *d* not **be stiff-necked** any longer.	AIT
	12: 8	*You are* not *to* **d** as we do here today,	6913
	12: 8	You are not to do as *we* **d** here today,	6913
	12:23	But be sure you *d* not **eat** the blood,	AIT
	12:25	D not **eat** it, so that it may go well	AIT
	12:30	"How *d* these nations **serve** their gods?	AIT
	12:30	We *will* **d** the same."	6913
	12:31	*they* **d** all kinds of detestable things	6913
	12:32	See that *you* **d** all I command you;	6913
	12:32	*d* not **add** to it or take away from it.	AIT
	13: 8	*d* not **yield** to him or listen to him.	AIT
	13: 8	D not **spare** him or shield him.	AIT
	13:11	among you *will* **d** such an evil thing again.	6913
	14: 1	D not **cut yourselves** or shave the front	AIT
	14: 3	D not **eat** any detestable thing.	AIT
	14: 7	*d* not **have** a **split** hoof;	AIT
	14:19	*d* not **eat** them.	AIT
	14:21	D not **eat** anything you find already dead.	AIT
	14:21	D not **cook** a young goat in its mother's	AIT
	14:27	And *d* not **neglect** the Levites living	AIT
	15: 7	*d* not **be hardhearted** or tightfisted	AIT
	15: 9	*d* not **show ill will**	AIT
	15:10	to him and **d** so without a grudging heart;	5989S
	15:13	*d* not **send** him away empty-handed.	AIT
	15:16	I *d* not **want** to **leave**	AIT
	15:17	**D** the same for your maidservant.	6913
	15:18	D not **consider** it a hardship	AIT

Dt	15:18	God will bless you in everything *you* d.	6913
	15:19	*D* not **put** the firstborn of your oxen **to work,**	AIT
	15:19	and *d* not **shear** the firstborn of your sheep.	AIT
	16: 3	*D* not **eat** it with bread made with yeast,	AIT
	16: 4	*D* not **let** any of the meat you sacrifice on the evening of the first day **remain**	AIT
	16: 8	to the LORD your God and *d* no work.	6913
	16:19	*D* not **pervert** justice or show partiality.	AIT
	16:19	*D* not **accept** a bribe.	AIT
	16:21	*D* not **set up** any wooden Asherah pole	AIT
	16:22	and *d* not **erect** a sacred stone,	AIT
	17: 1	*D* not **sacrifice** to the LORD your God	AIT
	17:10	Be careful to *d* everything they direct you	6913
	17:10	to do everything they direct you to *d*.	NIH
	17:11	*D* not **turn aside** from what they tell you,	AIT
	17:15	*D* not **place** a foreigner over you,	AIT
	18: 9	*d* not **learn** to imitate the detestable ways	AIT
	18:14	not **permitted** you to *d* so.	5989
	18:22	*D* not **be afraid** of him.	AIT
	19:10	**D** this so that innocent blood will not	NIH
	19:14	*d* not **move** your neighbor's boundary stone	AIT
	19:19	*d* to him as he intended to do to his brother.	6913
	19:19	do to him as he intended to *d* to his brother.	6913
	20: 1	*d* not **be afraid** of them,	AIT
	20: 3	*D* not **be fainthearted** or afraid;	AIT
	20: 3	*d* not **be terrified** or give way to panic	AIT
	20:15	at a distance from you and *d* not belong to	NIH
	20:16	*d* not **leave alive** anything that breathes.	AIT
	20:18	to follow all the detestable things *they* **d**	6913
	20:19	*d* not **destroy** its trees by putting an ax	AIT
	20:19	*D* not **cut** them **down.**	AIT
	21: 8	and *d* not **hold** your people guilty of	AIT
	22: 1	*d* not **ignore** it but be sure to take it back	AIT
	22: 2	near you or if *you d* not **know** who he is,	AIT
	22: 3	**D** the same if you find your brother's donkey	6913
	22: 3	*D* not **ignore** it.	AIT
	22: 4	*d* not **ignore** it.	AIT
	22: 6	*d* not **take** the mother with the young.	AIT
	22: 9	*D* not **plant** two kinds of **seed**	AIT
	22: 9	if you **d**, not only the crops you plant but	NIH
	22:10	*D* not **plow** with an ox and	AIT
	22:11	*D* not **wear clothes** of wool and linen	AIT
	22:26	**D** nothing to the girl;	6913
	23: 6	*D* not **seek** a treaty of friendship with them	AIT
	23: 7	*D* not **abhor** an Edomite,	AIT
	23: 7	*D* not **abhor** an Egyptian,	AIT
	23:15	*d* not **hand** him **over**	AIT
	23:16	*D* not **oppress** him.	AIT
	23:19	*D* not **charge** your brother **interest,**	AIT
	23:21	*d* not **be slow** to pay it,	AIT
	23:23	be sure *to* **d,**	6913
	23:24	but *d* not **put** any in your basket.	AIT
	24: 4	*D* not **bring sin** upon the land	AIT
	24: 6	*D* not **take** a pair of millstones—not even the upper one—**as security for a debt,**	AIT
	24: 8	be very careful to *d* exactly as the priests,	6913
	24:10	*d* not **go into** his house	AIT
	24:12	*d* not **go to sleep** with his pledge in your	AIT
	24:14	*D* not **take advantage** *of* a hired man	AIT
	24:17	*D* not **deprive** the alien or the fatherless	AIT
	24:18	That is why I command you to *d* this.	6913
	24:19	*d* not **go back** to get it.	AIT
	24:20	*d* not **go over the branches a second time.**	AIT
	24:21	*d* not **go over the vines again.**	AIT
	24:22	That is why I command you to *d* this.	6913
	25: 4	*D* not **muzzle** an ox while it is treading out	6913
	25: 8	"*I d* not **want** to marry her,"	AIT
	25:13	*D* not **have** two differing weights	AIT
	25:14	*D* not **have** two differing measures	AIT
	25:19	*D* not **forget!**	AIT
	27: 5	*D* not **use** any iron tool upon them.	AIT
	28:14	*D* not **turn aside** from any of the commands	AIT
	28:15	if *you d* not **obey** the LORD your God	AIT
	28:15	*d* not carefully **follow** all his commands	AIT
	28:29	be unsuccessful in **everything** you **d;**	2006
	28:33	that *you d* not **know** will eat what your land	AIT
	28:58	If *you d* not **carefully** follow all	AIT
	28:58	and *d* not **revere** this glorious	AIT
	29: 9	that you may prosper in everything *you* **d.**	6913
	31: 4	the LORD *will* **d** to them what he did	6913
	31: 5	and *you* must **d** them all	6913
	31: 6	*D* not **be afraid** or terrified because	AIT
	31: 8	*D* not **be afraid;** do not **be discouraged."**	AIT
	31: 8	Do not **be afraid;** *d* not **be discouraged."**	AIT
	31:13	Their children, who *d* not **know** this law,	AIT
	31:21	I know what they are disposed to **d,**	6913
	31:29	because *you* will **d** evil in the sight of	6913
	34:11	and wonders the LORD sent him to **d**	6913
Jos	1: 7	*d* not **turn** from it to the right or to the left,	AIT
	1: 8	*D* not **let** this Book of the Law **depart**	AIT
	1: 8	be careful to **d** everything written in it.	6913
	1: 9	*D* not **be terrified?**	AIT
	1: 9	Do not be terrified; *d* not **be discouraged,**	AIT
	1:16	"Whatever you have commanded us *we will* **d,**	6913
	3: 4	*d* not **go near** it."	AIT
	3: 5	the LORD *will* **d** amazing things	6913
	4: 6	'What **d** these stones **mean?'**	NIH
	4:21	'What **d** these stones mean?"	NIH
	6: 3	**D** this for six days.	6913
	6:10	"*D* not **give** a war **cry,**	AIT
	6:10	*d* not **raise** your voices,	AIT
	6:10	*d* not **say** a word until the day I tell you	AIT
	7: 3	to take it and *d* not **weary** all the people,	AIT
	7: 9	What then *will you* **d**	6913

Jos	7:19	*d* not **hide** it from me."	AIT
	8: 1	LORD said to Joshua, "*D* not **be afraid;**	AIT
	8: 1	*d* not **be discouraged.**	AIT
	8: 2	*You shall* **d** to Ai and its king as you did	6913
	8: 8	**D** what the LORD has commanded.	6913
	9: 8	and where *d you* **come** from?"	AIT
	9:20	This is what *we will* **d** to them:	6913
	9:25	**D** to us whatever seems good and right	6913
	10: 6	"*D* not **abandon** your servants.	AIT
	10: 8	"*D* not **be afraid** of them;	AIT
	10:25	Joshua said to them, "*D* not **be afraid;**	AIT
	10:25	*d* not **be discouraged.**	AIT
	10:25	This is what the LORD *will* **d** to all	6913
	11: 6	"*D* not **be afraid** of them,	AIT
	15:18	Caleb asked her, "What can I **d** for you?"	4200
	15:19	She replied, **"D** me a special favor.	5989
	16:10	but are required to **d** forced labor.	6268
	18: 7	however, *d* not **get** a portion among you,	NIH
	22:19	But *d* not **rebel** against the LORD or	AIT
	22:22	*d* not **spare** us this day.	AIT
	22:24	'What **d** you have to do with the LORD,	NIH
	22:24	'What **d** you **have to** d with the LORD,	4200
	23: 7	*D* not **associate with** these nations	AIT
	23: 7	*d* not **invoke** the names of their gods	AIT
	24:12	not **d** it with your own sword and bow.	NIH
Jdg	1:14	Caleb asked her, "What can I **d** for you?"	4200
	1:15	She replied, **"D** me a special favor.	2035
	6:10	*d* not **worship** the gods of the Amorites,	AIT
	6:18	Please *d* not **go away** until I come back	AIT
	6:23	*D* not **be afraid.**	AIT
	6:39	"*D* not **be angry** with me.	AIT
	7:17	**d** exactly as I do.	6913
	7:17	do exactly as *I* **d.**	6913
	8: 3	What was I able to *d* compared to you?"	6913
	8: 6	"**D** you already have the hands of Zebah	NIH
	8:15	"**D** you already have the hands of Zebah	NIH
	8:21	"Come, **d** it yourself.	7003S
	8:24	And he said, "*I d* **have** one **request,**	AIT
	9:33	**d** whatever your hand finds to do."	6913
	9:33	do whatever your hand finds to **d."**	NIH
	9:48	**D** what you have seen me **do!"**	6913
	9:48	Do what you have seen me **d!"**	6913
	10:15	**D** with us whatever you think best,	6913
	11: 7	Why *d you* **come** to me now,	AIT
	11:10	*we will* certainly **d** as you say."	6913
	11:12	"What **d** you have against us	NIH
	11:36	**D** to me just as you promised;	6913
	13: 4	and that *you d* not **eat** anything unclean,	AIT
	13: 7	and *d* not **eat** anything unclean,	AIT
	13:13	"Your wife *must* **d** all that I have told her.	9068
	13:14	She must **d** everything I have commanded her."	9068
	13:18	He replied, "Why *d you* **ask** my name?	AIT
	15:10	"to **d** to him as he did to us."	AIT
	18: 9	**Aren't** you *going to* **d something?**	3120
	18:14	"*D* **you know** that one of these houses has	AIT
	18:14	Now you know what to **d."**	6913
	18:24	What else **d** I have?	NIH
	19:23	don't **d** this disgraceful thing.	6913
	19:24	and **d** to them whatever you wish.	6913
	19:24	don't **d** such a disgraceful thing."	6913
	19:30	Tell us what to **d!"**	NIH
	20: 9	But now this is what *we'll* **d** to Gibeah:	6913
	21:11	"This is what *you* are to **d,"** they said.	6913
	21:22	'**D** us **a kindness** by helping them,	2858
Ru	2:13	though I *d* not **have** the standing of one	AIT
	3: 4	He will tell you what to **d."**	6913
	3: 5	"*I will* **d** whatever you say,"	6913
	3: 6	everything her mother-in-law told her to **d.**	NIH
	3:11	*I will* **d** for you all you ask.	6913
	3:13	as surely as the LORD lives I *will* **d** it.	1457S
	4: 4	If you will redeem it, **d** so.	1457S
	4: 4	no one **has the right to d** it	1457S
	4: 6	I cannot **d** it."	1457S
1Sa	1:16	*D* not **take** your servant for	AIT
	1:23	"**D** what seems best to you,"	6913
	2: 3	"*D* not **keep talking** so proudly	AIT
	2:23	"Why *d you* **do** such things?"	AIT
	2:23	"Why do you **d** such things?"	6913
	2:29	Why *d you* **scorn** my sacrifice and offering	AIT
	2:29	Why *d you* **honor** your sons more than me	AIT
	2:33	that I *d* not **cut off** from my altar will	AIT
	2:35	who *will* **d** according to what is in my heart	6913
	3:11	"See, I *am* about to **d** something in Israel	6913
	3:17	"*D* not **hide** it from me.	AIT
	3:18	let him **d** what is good in his eyes."	6913
	5: 8	"What *shall we* **d** with the ark of the god	6913
	6: 2	"What *shall we* **d** with the ark of	6913
	6: 3	*d* not **send** it **away**	AIT
	6: 6	Why *d you* **harden** your hearts as	AIT
	7: 8	"*D* not **stop** crying out to	AIT
	8: 5	and your sons *d* not **walk** in your ways;	AIT
	8: 9	what the king who will reign over them will **d."**	5477S
	8:11	what the king who will reign over you will **d:**	5477S
	9: 7	What **d** we have?"	NIH
	9:20	*d* not **worry** about them;	AIT
	9:21	Why *d you* **say** such a thing to me?"	AIT
	10: 2	"What *shall I* **d** about my son?" '	6913
	10: 7	**d** whatever your hand finds to do,	6913
	10: 7	do whatever your hand finds to **d,**	NIH
	10: 8	to you and tell you what *you are to* **d."**	6913
	10:24	"*D you* see the man the LORD has chosen?"	6913
	11:10	and *you can* **d** to us whatever seems good	6913
	12:14	and *d* not **rebel** against his commands, and	AIT
	12:15	But if *you d* not **obey** the LORD,	AIT

1Sa	12:16	*about to* **d** before your eyes!	6913
	12:20	"*D* not **be afraid,"** Samuel replied.	AIT
	12:20	yet *d* not **turn away** from the LORD,	AIT
	12:21	*D* not **turn away** after useless idols.	AIT
	12:21	They can **d** you no **good,**	3603
	14: 7	"**D** all that you have in mind,"	6913
	14:34	*D* not **sin** against the LORD by eating meat	AIT
	14:36	"**D** whatever seems best to you,"	6913
	14:40	"**D** what seems best to you,"	6913
	14:44	be it ever so severely, if *you d* not **die,**	AIT
	15: 3	*D* not **spare** them;	AIT
	15: 6	the Amalekites so that *I d* not **destroy** you	AIT
	15:19	on the plunder and **d** evil in the eyes of	6913
	16: 3	and I will show you what to **d.**	6913
	16: 4	They asked, "*D* you **come** in peace?"	AIT
	16: 7	*D* not **consider** his appearance or his height,	AIT
	17: 8	"Why *d you* **come out** and line up	AIT
	17:25	*D you* **see** how this man keeps coming out?	AIT
	18: 5	Whatever Saul sent him to **d,**	6913
	18:17	Let the Philistines **d** that!	928+2118+2257+3338S
	18:23	"*D* you think *it is a* **small**	AIT
	19: 4	not the king **d wrong** to his servant David;	2627
	19: 5	Why then *would you* **d** wrong to	2627
	20: 2	Look, my father doesn't **d** anything,	6913
	20: 4	"Whatever you want me to **d,**	NIH
	20: 4	*I'll* **d** for you."	6913
	20:13	*d* not **let you know**	AIT
	20:15	*d* not ever **cut off** your kindness	AIT
	21: 3	*d* you **have on hand?**	AIT
	22: 3	with you until I learn what God *will* **d**	6913
	22: 5	"*D* not **stay** in the stronghold.	AIT
	23:20	down whenever it pleases you to **d** so,	3718S
	24: 6	that *I should* **d** such a thing to my master,	6913
	24: 9	"Why *d you* **listen** when men say,	AIT
	25:17	Now think it over and see what *you can* **d,**	6913
	26:20	*d* not **let** my blood **fall** to the ground	AIT
	26:25	*you will* **d great things** and	6913+6913
	27: 1	The best thing I can **d** is to escape to	NIH
	28: 2	for yourself what your servant *can* **d."**	6913
	28:13	What *d you* **see?"**	AIT
	28:15	I have called on you to tell me what *to* **d."**	6913
	28:16	Samuel said, "Why *d you* **consult** me,	AIT
	28:21	in my hands and did what you told me to **d.**	6913
	29: 7	*d* nothing to displease the Philistine rulers."	6913
	30:13	David asked him, "To whom *d* you belong,	NIH
	30:13	and where *d you* **come** from?"	NIH
	30:23	*you must* not **d** that with what	6913
	31: 4	and would not **d** it;	NIH
2Sa	1: 5	"How *d you* **know** that Saul	AIT
	1: 7	and I said, '**What can I** d?'	2180
	2:14	**"All right,** *let them* **d** it,"	7756S
	3: 9	if *I d* not **do** for David what	AIT
	3: 9	if *I do* not **d** for David what	6913
	3:13	Do not **come into** my **presence**	AIT
	3:18	Now **d** it!	6913
	3:19	the whole house of Benjamin **wanted to** d.	928+3202+6524
	3:38	"*D you* not **realize** that a prince and	AIT
	5:23	"*D* not **go straight up,**	AIT
	7: 3	go ahead and **d** it,	6913
	7:25	**D** as you promised,	6913
	9:11	"Your servant *will* **d** whatever my lord	6913
	9:11	the king commands his servant to **d."**	NIH
	10: 3	"*D* you think David is honoring your father	NIH
	10:12	The LORD *will* **d** what is good	6913
	11:11	as you live, *I will* not **d** such a thing!"	6913
	12:12	but *I will* **d** this thing in broad daylight	6913
	12:18	He *may* **d** something desperate."	6913
	13: 2	for him to **d** anything to her.	6913
	13: 4	He asked Amnon, "Why *d you,*	NIH
	13:12	Don't **d** this wicked thing.	6913
	13:15	perhaps he *will* **d** what his servant asks.	6913
	14:18	"*D* not **keep** from me the answer	AIT
	14:19	to **d** this and who put all these words into	NIH
	14:21	"Very well, *I will* **d** it.	6913
	15:15	"Your servants are **ready to d** whatever our lord the king chooses."	2180
	15:20	**d** not **know** where I am going?	889+2143+2143+6584
	15:26	*let him* **d** to me whatever seems good	6913
	16:10	"What **d** you and I have in common,	NIH
	16:10	who can ask, 'Why *d you* **do** this?' "	AIT
	16:10	who can ask, 'Why do you **d** this?' "	6913
	16:20	What *should we* **d?"**	6913
	17: 6	*Should we* **d** what he says?	6913
	17:15	and the elders of Israel to **d** such and such,	NIH
	17:15	but I have advised them to **d** so and so.	NIH
	17: 9	'*D* not **spend** the night at the fords in	AIT
	18: 4	"*I will* **d** whatever seems best to you."	6913
	18:20	but *you must* not **d** so today,	1413S
	18:22	*d you* **want to go?**	AIT
	19:10	So why *d you* **say nothing** *about* bringing	AIT
	19:18	over and to **d** whatever he wished.	6913
	19:19	*D* not **remember** how your servant did wrong	AIT
	19:22	"What **d** you and I have in common,	NIH
	19:22	*D I* not **know** that today I am king	AIT
	19:27	so **d** whatever pleases you.	6913
	19:28	So what right **d** I have	NIH
	19:37	**D** for him whatever pleases you."	6913
	19:38	and *I will* **d** for him whatever pleases you,	6913
	19:38	And anything you desire from me *I will* **d**	6913
	19:43	*d you* **treat** us **with contempt?**	AIT
	20: 6	*will* **d** us more **harm** than Absalom did.	8317
	20:19	*d you* want to **swallow up**	AIT
	21: 3	"What *shall I* **d** for you?	6913
	21: 4	nor **d** we have the right to put anyone	NIH

2Sa	21: 4	"What d you **want** me to do for you?"	AIT
	21: 4	"What do you want *me* to **d** for you?"	6913
	22:37	so that my ankles d not **turn.**	AIT
	23:17	"Far be it from me, O LORD, *to* **d** this!"	6913
	24: 3	the king want to **d** such a thing?"	NIH
	24:14	d not *let me* **fall** into the hands	AIT
1Ki	1: 6	"Why d you **behave** as you do?"	AIT
	1: 6	"Why do you behave as you **d?"**	NIH
	1:18	my lord the king, d not **know** about it.	AIT
	2: 3	so that you may prosper in all *you* **d**	6913
	2: 6	d not *let* his gray head **go down**	AIT
	2: 9	d not **consider** him **innocent.**	AIT
	2: 9	you will know what *to* **d** to him.	6913
	2:13	"D you **come** peacefully?"	AIT
	2:16	D not **refuse** me."	AIT
	2:20	"D not **refuse** me."	AIT
	2:22	"Why **d** you **request** Abishag	AIT
	2:31	king commanded Benaiah, "**D** as he says.	6913
	2:36	but d not **go** anywhere else.	AIT
	2:38	Your servant *will* **d** as my lord	6913
	3: 7	and d not **know** how to carry out my duties.	AIT
	3:12	I *will* **d** what you have asked.	6913
	3:27	D not **kill** him; she is his mother."	AIT
	5: 8	and *will* **d** all you want in providing	6913
	5:11	*to* **d** this for Hiram year after year.	5989S
	8:25	if only your sons are careful in **all** they **d**	2006
	8:43	and **d** whatever the foreigner asks of you,	6913
	8:43	as **d** your own people Israel,	NIH
	9: 1	and had achieved all he had desired to **d,**	6913
	9: 4	and **d** all I **command**	6913
	9: 6	from me and d not **observe** the commands	AIT
	11:12	I *will* **d** it during your lifetime.	6913
	11:22	Hadad replied, "but d **let me go!"**	8938+8938
	11:33	I will **d** this because they have forsaken me	NIH
	11:38	If *you* **d** whatever I command you	9048
	11:38	in my ways and **d** what is right in my eyes	6913
	12:16	"What share do we **have** in David,	NIH
	12:24	D not **go up** to fight against your brothers.	AIT
	17:13	Go home and **d** as you have said.	6913
	17:18	"What *d* you have against me, man of God?	NIH
	18:25	but *d* not **light** the fire."	AIT
	18:34	"**D** it again," he said, and they did it again.	9101
	18:34	"**D** it a third time,"	8992
	19: 2	if by this time tomorrow *I* **d** not **make** your life	AIT
	20: 9	'Your servant *will* **d** all you demanded	6913
	20:13	'*D* you **see** this vast army?	AIT
	20:14	"But who *will* **d** this?"	928
	20:14	of the provincial commanders *will* **d** it.' "	928
	20:24	**D** this: Remove all the kings from their	6913
	21:20	"because you have sold yourself to **d** evil in	6913
	21:25	who sold himself to **d** evil in the eyes of	6913
	22:22	"'Go and **d** it.'	6913
	22:31	"*D* not **fight** with anyone, small or great,	AIT
2Ki	1:15	*d* not *be* **afraid** of him."	AIT
	2: 3	"*D* you **know** that the LORD is going	AIT
	2: 3	Elisha replied, "but *d* **not speak** *of* it."	AIT
	2: 5	"*D* you **know** that the LORD is going	AIT
	2: 5	I know," he replied, "but *d* **not speak** *of* it."	AIT
	2: 9	what *can I* **d** for you before I am taken	6913
	2:16	"No," Elisha replied, "*d* **not send** them."	AIT
	3:13	"What *d* we have to do with each other?	NIH
	3:13	"What do we **have** to **d** with each other?	2256+4200+4200
	4: 2	Tell me, what **d** you have in your house?"	NIH
	4:29	If you meet anyone, *d* not **greet** him,	AIT
	4:29	and if anyone greets you, *d* not **answer.**	AIT
	5:13	prophet had told you to **d** some great thing,	NIH
	6:15	"Oh, my lord, what *shall* we **d?"**	6913
	6:22	"*D* not **kill** them," he answered,	AIT
	8: 2	The woman proceeded *to* **d** as the man	6913
	8:12	"Because I know the harm *you will* **d** to	6913
	9:17	'*D* you **come** in peace?' "	NIH
	9:18	'*D* you **come** in peace?' "	NIH
	9:18	"What do you have to do with peace?"	NIH
	9:18	"What do you **have** to **d** with peace?"	4200
	9:19	'*D* you **come** in peace?' "	NIH
	9:19	"What do you have to do with peace?	NIH
	9:19	"What do you **have** to **d** with peace?	4200
	10: 5	and *we will* **d** anything you say.	6913
	10: 5	you **d** whatever you think best."	6913
	10:30	to the house of Ahab all I had in mind to **d,**	NIH
	11: 5	saying, "This is what *you are to* **d:**	6913
	16: 2	he did not **d** what was right in the eyes of	6913
	17:12	"You *shall* not **d** this."	6913
	17:15	"*D* not **do** as they do,"	AIT
	17:15	"*Do* not **d** as they do,"	6913
	17:15	"Do not **do** as they **d,"**	NIH
	17:15	the LORD had forbidden them to **d.**	NIH
	17:17	and sorcery and sold themselves to **d** evil in	6913
	17:26	in the towns of Samaria *d* not **know** what	AIT
	17:26	the people *d* not **know** what he requires."	AIT
	17:35	"*D* not **worship** any other gods or bow	AIT
	17:37	D not **worship** other gods.	AIT
	17:38	D not **forget** the covenant I have made	AIT
	17:38	and *d* not **worship** other gods.	AIT
	17:41	and grandchildren *continue to* **d**	6913
	18:29	D not *let* Hezekiah **deceive**	AIT
	18:30	D not *let* Hezekiah **persuade** you **to trust**	AIT
	18:31	"D not **listen** to Hezekiah.	AIT
	18:32	"D not **listen** to Hezekiah.	AIT
	18:36	"D not **answer** him."	AIT
	19: 6	D not *be* **afraid** of what you have heard—	AIT
	19:10	D not *let* the god you depend on **deceive**	AIT
	20: 9	the LORD *will* **d** what he has promised:	6913
	21: 8	*to* **d** everything I commanded them	6913
	23:35	In order to **d** so,	5989S

2Ki	25:24	"*D* not *be* **afraid** of	AIT
1Ch	10: 4	and would not **d** it;	NIH
	11:19	"God forbid that I *should* **d** this!"	6913
	12:32	the times and knew what Israel *should* **d**—	6913
	13: 4	The whole assembly agreed to **d** this,	6913
	14:14	"*D* not **go** straight up,	NIH
	15:13	We did not inquire of him about how to **d** it	NIH
	16:22	"*D* not **touch** my anointed ones;	AIT
	16:22	*d* my prophets no **harm."**	AIT
	17: 2	"Whatever you have in mind, **d** it,	6913
	17:23	**D** as you promised,	6913
	19: 3	"**D** you think David is honoring your father	NIH
	19:13	The LORD *will* **d** what is good	6913
	21: 3	Why *does* my lord **want** to **d** this?	1335
	21:13	*d* not *let me* **fall** into the hands	AIT
	21:13	but **d** not let this plague remain	AIT
	21:23	the king **d** whatever pleases him.	6913
	22:13	D not *be* **afraid** or discouraged.	AIT
	23:30	They were to **d** the same in the evening	NIH
	26: 8	with the strength to **d** the **work**—	NIH
	28:10	Be strong and **d** *the* **work."**	6913
	28:20	"Be strong and courageous, and **d** *the* **work.**	6913
	28:20	D not *be* **afraid** or discouraged,	AIT
	29:19	and decrees and to **d** everything to build	6913
2Ch	6:16	in **all** they **d** to walk before me according	2006
	6:33	and **d** whatever the foreigner asks of you,	6913
	6:33	as **d** your own people Israel,	NIH
	6:42	*d* not **reject** your anointed one.	AIT
	7:11	in mind to **d** in the temple of the LORD	6913
	7:17	and **d** all I **command,**	6913
	10:16	"What share **d** we have in David,	NIH
	11: 4	*D* not **go up** to fight against your brothers.	AIT
	13: 9	as the peoples of other lands **d?**	NIH
	13:12	*d* not **fight** against the LORD,	AIT
	14:11	*d* not *let* man **prevail**	AIT
	15: 7	But as for you, be strong and *d* not **give up,**	AIT
	18:21	'Go and **d** it.'	6913
	18:30	"*D* not **fight** with anyone, small or great,	AIT
	19: 6	"Consider carefully what you **d,**	6913
	19:10	**D** this, and you will not sin.	6913
	19:11	may the LORD be with those who **d** well."	NIH
	20:12	We **d** not **know** what to do,	AIT
	20:12	We do not know what to **d,**	6913
	20:15	'*D* not *be* **afraid** or discouraged because	AIT
	20:17	D not *be* **afraid;** do not be discouraged.	AIT
	20:17	Do not be afraid; *d* not *be* **discouraged.**	AIT
	23: 4	Now this is what *you are to* **d:**	6913
	23:14	*d* not **put** her to **death**	AIT
	24: 5	**D** it **now."**	4554
	24:20	'Why **d** you **disobey**	AIT
	25:15	"Why *d* you **consult** this people's gods,	AIT
	28: 1	he did not **d** what was right in the eyes of	6913
	28:13	*D* you **intend** to add to our sin and guilt?"	AIT
	29:11	My sons, *d* not *be* **negligent** now,	AIT
	30: 7	D not *be* **like** your fathers and brothers,	AIT
	30: 8	D not *be* **stiff-necked,** as your fathers were;	AIT
	32: 7	D not *be* **afraid** or discouraged because of	AIT
	32:13	"*D* you not **know** what I	AIT
	32:15	*d* not *let* Hezekiah **deceive**	AIT
	32:15	D not **believe** him,	AIT
	33: 8	to **d** everything I commanded them	6913
Ezr	6: 7	"*D* not **interfere** with the work	AIT
	6: 8	*to* **d** for these elders of the Jews in	10522
	7:18	then **d** whatever seems best with the rest of	10522
	7:25	you are to teach any who *d* not **know** them.	NIH
	9:12	*d* not **give** your daughters **in marriage**	AIT
	9:12	D not **seek** a treaty of friendship with them	AIT
	10: 4	so take courage and **d** it."	6913
	10: 5	under oath to **d** what had been suggested	6913
	10:11	the God of your fathers, and **d** his will.	6913
	10:12	We *must* **d** as you say.	6913
Ne	2:12	in my heart to **d** for Jerusalem.	6913
	4: 5	D not **cover up** their guilt	AIT
	5:12	We will **d** as you say."	6913
	5:12	an oath to **d** what they had promised.	6913
	7: 2	and feared God more than most men **d.**	NIH
	8: 9	D not **mourn** or weep."	AIT
	8:10	D not **grieve,** for the joy of	AIT
	8:11	D not **grieve."**	AIT
	9:32	*d* not *let* all this hardship *seem* **trifling**	AIT
	13:14	and *d* not **blot out** what I have	6913
	13:18	Didn't your forefathers **d** the same things,	6913
	13:21	*d* you **spend** the night	AIT
	13:21	you **d** this again, I will lay hands on you."	9101
Est	2:10	Mordecai had forbidden her to **d** so.	5583S
	2:20	as Mordecai had told her to **d,**	NIH
	3: 3	"Why *d* you **disobey** the king's command?"	AIT
	3: 8	of all other people and who *d* not **obey**	AIT
	3:11	"and **d** with the people as you please."	6913
	4:13	"*D* not **think** that because you are in	AIT
	4:16	D not **eat** or drink for three days,	AIT
	4:16	I and my maids will fast as you **d.**	NIH
	5: 5	"so that we **may d** what Esther asks."	6913
	6:10	the horse and **d** just as you have suggested	6913
	6:10	D not **neglect** anything you have recommended."	AIT
	7: 5	the man who has dared to **d** such a thing?"	6913
	8: 5	with favor and thinks it the right thing to **d,**	NIH
	8:12	for the Jews to **d** this in all the provinces	NIH
Job	1:12	but on the man himself *d* not **lay** a finger."	AIT
	5:17	*d* not **despise** the discipline of the Almighty.	AIT
	6:11	"What strength **d** I have,	NIH
	6:12	**D** I have the strength of stone?	NIH
	6:13	**D** I have any power to help myself,	NIH
	6:25	*d* your arguments **prove?**	AIT
	6:26	*D* you **mean** to correct what I say,	AIT
	6:29	Relent, *d* not *be* **unjust;**	AIT

Job	7:21	Why *d* you not **pardon** my offenses	AIT
	9:16	*I* **d** not **believe** he would give me	AIT
	10: 2	I will say to God: *D* not **condemn** me,	AIT
	10: 4	**D** you have eyes of flesh?	NIH
	10: 4	*D* you **see** as a mortal sees?	AIT
	11: 8	what *can you* **d?**	7188
	13:14	*d I* **put** myself **in jeopardy**	AIT
	13:24	Why *d* you **hide** your face	AIT
	14: 3	*D* you **fix** your eye on such a one?	AIT
	15: 8	*D* you **listen in** on God's council?	AIT
	15: 8	*D* you **limit** wisdom to yourself?	AIT
	15: 9	What *d* you **know** that we do not know?	AIT
	15: 9	What do you know that *we* **d** not **know?**	AIT
	15: 9	What **insights** *d* you **have** that we **d**	AIT
	15: 9	What insights do you have that we **d**	NIH
	15:12	and why *d* your eyes **flash,**	AIT
	16:18	"O earth, *d* not **cover** my blood;	AIT
	19:22	Why *d* you **pursue** me as God does?	AIT
	21: 7	*d* the wicked **live on,**	AIT
	21:10	their cows calve and *d* not **miscarry.**	AIT
	22:17	What *can* the Almighty **d** to us?'	7188
	23: 8	if I go to the west, *I* **d** not **find** him.	AIT
	23: 9	he is at work in the north, *I* **d** not **see** him;	AIT
	24:13	*who* **d** not **know** its ways or stay in its paths.	AIT
	24:16	**want** nothing *to* **d** with the light.	3359
	26: 8	the clouds *d* not **burst** under their weight.	AIT
	27:19	but *will* **d** so no more;	665
	28: 8	*d* not **set foot on** it,	AIT
	30:10	*they* **d** not **hesitate** to spit in my face.	AIT
	30:20	O God, but *you* **d** not **answer,**	AIT
	31: 3	disaster for *those who* **d** wrong?	7188
	31:14	what *will I* **d** when God confronts me?	6913
	31:23	of his splendor I could not **d** such things.	3523
	31:33	if I have concealed my sin as men **d,**	NIH
	32:13	D not **say,** 'We have found wisdom;	AIT
	33:13	Why *d* you **complain** to him	AIT
	34:10	Far be it from God to **d** evil,	NIH
	34:10	from the Almighty to **d** wrong.	NIH
	34:12	It is unthinkable that God *would* **d** wrong,	8399
	34:32	I have done wrong, *I will* not **d** so **again.'**	3578
	35: 3	"*D* you **think** this is just?	AIT
	35: 3	and what *d I* **gain** by not sinning?'	AIT
	35: 6	what *does that* **d** to him?	6913
	35: 7	you are righteous, what *d* you **give** to him,	AIT
	35:14	when you say that *you* **d** not **see** him,	AIT
	36:12	But if *they* **d** not **listen,**	AIT
	36:13	*d* not **cry for help.**	AIT
	36:18	*d* not *let* a large bribe **turn** you **aside.**	AIT
	36:20	D not **long for** the night,	AIT
	37:12	to **d** whatever he commands them.	7188
	37:15	*D* you **know** how God controls the clouds	AIT
	37:16	*D* you **know** how the clouds hang poised,	AIT
	38:20	*D* you **know** the paths to their dwellings?	AIT
	38:33	*D* you **know** the laws of the heavens?	AIT
	38:35	*D* you **send** the lightning bolts on their way?	AIT
	38:35	*D* they **report** to you, 'Here we are'?	AIT
	38:39	"*D* you **hunt** the prey for the lioness	AIT
	39: 1	"*D* you **know** when the mountain goats	AIT
	39: 1	*D* you **watch** when the doe bears her fawn?	AIT
	39: 2	*D* you **count** the months till they bear?	AIT
	39: 2	*D* you **know** the time they give birth?	AIT
	39: 4	they leave and *d* not **return.**	AIT
	39:19	"*D* you **give** the horse his strength	AIT
	39:20	*D* you **make** him **leap**	AIT
	40: 9	**D** you have an arm like God's,	NIH
	41: 8	the struggle and never *d* **it again!**	3578
	41:28	*d* not **make** him **flee;**	AIT
	42: 2	"I know that *you can* **d** all things;	3523
Ps	2: 1	Why *d* the nations **conspire** and	AIT
	4: 4	In your anger *d* not **sin;**	AIT
	5: 5	you hate all *who* **d** wrong.	7188
	6: 1	*d* not **rebuke** me in your anger	AIT
	6: 8	Away from me, all you *who* **d** evil,	7188
	10: 1	O LORD, *d* you **stand** far off?	AIT
	10: 1	Why *d* you **hide** yourself in times	AIT
	10:12	D not **forget** the helpless.	AIT
	10:14	But you, O God, *d* **see** trouble and grief;	AIT
	11: 3	what *can* the righteous **d?"**	7188
	14: 4	as men eat bread and *who* **d** not **call on**	AIT
	18:36	so that my ankles *d* not **turn.**	AIT
	22: 2	I cry out by day, but *you* **d** not **answer,**	AIT
	22:11	D not *be* **far** from me,	AIT
	25: 2	D not *let me be* **put to shame,**	AIT
	26: 4	*I* **d** not **sit** with deceitful men,	AIT
	26: 4	nor *d I* **consort** with hypocrites;	AIT
	26: 9	D not **take away** my soul along with sinners,	AIT
	27: 9	D not **hide** your face from me,	AIT
	27: 9	*d* not **turn** your servant **away**	AIT
	27: 9	D not **reject** me or forsake me,	AIT
	27:12	D not **turn** me **over**	AIT
	28: 1	*d* not **turn a deaf ear.**	AIT
	28: 3	D not **drag** me **away**	AIT
	28: 3	with *those who* **d** evil,	7188
	32: 9	D not *be* **like** the horse or the mule,	AIT
	33:15	who considers everything they **d.**	5126
	34:14	Turn from evil and **d** good;	6913
	34:16	of the LORD is against *those who* **d** evil,	6913
	35:20	*They d* not **speak** peaceably,	AIT
	35:22	D not *be* **far** from me, O Lord.	AIT
	35:24	*d* not *let them* **gloat**	AIT
	35:25	D not *let them* **think,**	AIT
	36: 3	he has ceased to be wise and to **d** good.	3512
	37: 1	D not **fret** because of evil men or	AIT
	37: 1	or be envious of *those who* **d** wrong;	6913
	37: 3	Trust in the LORD and **d** good;	6913
	37: 5	trust in him and he *will* **d** this:	6913

Ps	37: 7	*d* not **fret** when men succeed in their ways,	AIT
	37: 8	*d* not **fret**—it leads only to evil.	AIT
	37:21	The wicked borrow and *d* not **repay**,	AIT
	37:27	Turn from evil and **d** good;	6913
	37:31	his feet *d* not **slip**.	AIT
	38: 1	*d* not **rebuke** me in your anger	AIT
	38:16	"*D* not let them **gloat**	AIT
	38:21	O LORD, *d* not **forsake** me;	AIT
	39: 7	"But now, Lord, what *d* **I look for?**	AIT
	39: 8	*d* not **make** me the scorn of fools.	AIT
	40: 8	I desire to **d** your will, O my God;	6913
	40: 9	I *d* not **seal** my lips, as you know,	AIT
	40:10	I *d* not **hide** your righteousness in my heart;	AIT
	40:10	I *d* not **conceal** your love and your truth	AIT
	40:11	*D* not **withhold** your mercy from me,	AIT
	40:17	O my God, *d* not **delay**.	AIT
	44: 6	I *d* not **trust** in my bow,	AIT
	44:23	Why *d* you **sleep?**	AIT
	44:23	*D* not **reject** us forever.	AIT
	44:24	Why *d* you **hide** your face	AIT
	49:16	*D* not **be overawed** when a man grows rich,	AIT
	50: 8	I *d* not **rebuke** you for your sacrifices	AIT
	50:13	*D* I **eat** the flesh of bulls or drink the blood	AIT
	51:11	*D* not **cast** me from your presence	AIT
	51:16	*You d* not **delight in** sacrifice,	AIT
	51:16	*d* not **take pleasure in** burnt offerings.	AIT
	52: 1	Why *d* you **boast** of evil, you mighty man?	AIT
	52: 1	Why *d* you **boast** all day long,	NIH
	53: 4	as men eat bread and *who d* not **call on**	AIT
	55: 1	O God, *d* not **ignore** my plea;	AIT
	56: 4	What *can* mortal man **d** to me?	6913
	56:11	What *can* man **d** to me?	6913
	57: T	[To the tune of] "*D* Not **Destroy.**"	AIT
	58: T	[To the tune of] "*D* Not **Destroy.**"	AIT
	58: 1	*D* you rulers indeed **speak**	AIT
	58: 1	*D* you **judge** uprightly among men?	AIT
	59: T	[To the tune of] "*D* Not **Destroy.**"	AIT
	59: 1	But *d* not **kill** them, O Lord our shield,	AIT
	62:10	*D* not **trust** in extortion or take pride	AIT
	62:10	*d* not **set** your heart on them.	AIT
	69:14	*d* not *let me* **sink;**	AIT
	69:15	*D* not **let** the floodwaters **engulf**	AIT
	69:17	*D* not **hide** your face from your servant;	AIT
	69:27	*d* not **let** them **share**	AIT
	70: 5	O LORD, *d* not **delay**.	AIT
	71: 9	*D* not **cast** me **away**	AIT
	71: 9	*d* not **forsake** me when my strength is gone.	AIT
	71:18	*d* not **forsake** me, O God,	AIT
	74:11	Why *d* you **hold back** your hand,	AIT
	74:19	*D* not **hand over** the life of your dove	AIT
	74:19	*d* not **forget** the lives of your afflicted	AIT
	74:21	*D* not **let** the oppressed **retreat**	AIT
	74:23	*D* not **ignore** the clamor of your adversaries,	AIT
	75: T	[To the tune of] "*D* Not **Destroy.**"	AIT
	75: 4	'*D* not **lift up** your horns.	AIT
	75: 5	*D* not **lift** your horns against heaven';	AIT
	75: 5	*d* not **speak** with outstretched neck.' "	AIT
	79: 6	the nations that *d* not **acknowledge** you, on	AIT
	79: 6	on the kingdoms that *d* not **call**	AIT
	79: 8	*D* not **hold** against us the sins of	AIT
	83: 1	O God, **d** not keep silent;	NIH
	83: 9	**D** to them as you did to Midian,	6913
	86:10	For you are great and **d** marvelous deeds;	6913
	88:10	*D* you **show** your wonders to the dead?	AIT
	88:10	*D* those who are dead **rise up**	AIT
	88:14	*d* you **reject** me and hide your face	AIT
	89:30	and *d* not **follow** my statutes,	AIT
	92: 6	fools *d* not **understand**,	AIT
	95: 8	*d* not **harden** your hearts as you did	AIT
	101: 4	I *will* have nothing to **d** with evil.	3359
	102: 2	*D* not **hide** your face from me when I am	AIT
	102:24	"*D* not **take me away**,	AIT
	103:20	you mighty ones *who* **d** his bidding,	6913
	103:21	you his servants *who* **d** his will.	6913
	105:15	"*D* not **touch** my anointed ones;	AIT
	105:15	*d* my prophets no **harm**."	8317
	106: 3	who constantly **d** what is right.	6913
	109: 1	O God, whom I praise, *d* not *remain* **silent,**	AIT
	115: 2	Why *d* the nations **say,**	AIT
	118: 6	What *can* man **d** to me?	6913
	119: 3	They **d** nothing wrong;	7188
	119: 8	*d* not utterly **forsake** me.	AIT
	119:10	*d* not **let** me **stray**	AIT
	119:17	**D good** to your servant, and I will live;	1694
	119:19	*d* not **hide** your commands from me.	AIT
	119:31	*d* not **let** me **be put to shame**.	AIT
	119:43	*D* not **snatch** the word of truth	AIT
	119:51	but *I* **d** not **turn** from your law.	AIT
	119:65	*D* good to your servant according	6913
	119:68	You are good, and *what you* **d** *is* **good;**	3512
	119:83	*I* **d** not **forget** your decrees.	AIT
	119:116	*d* not **let** my hopes **be dashed**.	AIT
	119:121	*d* not **leave** me to my oppressors.	AIT
	119:132	you *always* **d** to those who love your name.	5477
	119:141	*I* **d** not **forget** your precepts.	AIT
	119:155	for *they* **d** not **seek out** your decrees.	AIT
	119:158	for *they* **d** not **obey** your word.	AIT
	120: 3	What *will he* **d** to you,	5989
	125: 3	**use** their hands to **d** evil.	8938
	125: 4	**D good**, O LORD, to those who are good,	3512
	131: 1	*I* **d** not **concern** *myself* with great matters	AIT
	132:10	*d* not **reject** your anointed one.	AIT
	137: 6	of my mouth if *I* **d** not **remember** you,	AIT
	137: 6	*I* **d** not **consider** Jerusalem my highest joy.	AIT
	138: 8	*d* not **abandon** the works of your hands.	AIT
	139:21	*D I* not **hate** those who hate you,	AIT
	140: 8	*d* not **grant** the wicked their desires,	AIT
Ps	140: 8	*d* not **let** their plans **succeed**,	AIT
	141: 8	*d* not **give** me **over to death.**	AIT
	143: 2	*D* not **bring** your servant into judgment,	AIT
	143: 7	*D* not **hide** your face from me or I will be	AIT
	143:10	Teach me to **d** your will,	6913
	146: 3	*D* not **put** your **trust** in mortal men,	AIT
	147:20	*they* **d** not **know** his laws.	AIT
	148: 8	stormy winds *that* **d** his bidding,	6913
Pr	1: 8	and *d* not **forsake** your mother's teaching.	AIT
	1:10	if sinners entice you, *d* not **give in** *to* them.	AIT
	1:15	*d* not **go along** with them,	AIT
	1:15	*d* not **set foot** on their paths;	AIT
	3: 1	My son, *d* not **forget** my teaching,	AIT
	3: 7	*D* not **be wise** in your own eyes;	AIT
	3:11	*d* not **despise** the LORD's discipline and do	AIT
	3:11	and *d* not **resent** his rebuke,	AIT
	3:21	*d* not **let** them **out** of your sight;	AIT
	3:27	*D* not **withhold** good	AIT
	3:28	*D* not **say** to your neighbor,	AIT
	3:29	*D* not **plot** harm against your neighbor,	AIT
	3:30	*D* not **accuse** a man for no reason—	AIT
	3:31	*D* not **envy** a violent man or choose any	AIT
	4: 2	so *d* not **forsake** my teaching.	AIT
	4: 5	*d* not **forget** my words or swerve	AIT
	4: 6	*D* not **forsake** wisdom,	AIT
	4:13	*d* not **let it go;**	AIT
	4:14	*D* not **set foot** on the path of the wicked	AIT
	4:15	Avoid it, *d* not **travel** on it;	AIT
	4:16	For they cannot sleep till *they* **d** evil;	8317
	4:19	*they* **d** not **know** what makes them stumble.	AIT
	4:21	*D* not **let** *them* **out** of your sight,	AIT
	4:27	*D* not **swerve** to the right or the left;	AIT
	5: 7	*d* not **turn aside** from what I say.	AIT
	5: 8	*d* not **go near** the door of her house,	AIT
	6: 3	then **d** this, my son, to free yourself;	6913
	6:20	and *d* not **forsake** your mother's teaching.	AIT
	6:25	*D* not **lust** in your heart **after**	AIT
	6:30	Men *d* not **despise** a thief if he steals	AIT
	7:25	*D* not **let** your heart **turn**	AIT
	8:33	*d* not **ignore** it.	AIT
	9: 8	*D* not **rebuke** a mocker or he will hate you;	AIT
	9:18	little *d* they **know** that the dead are there,	AIT
	10:29	but it is the ruin of *those who* **d** evil.	7188
	14:22	*D* not those who plot evil **go astray?**	AIT
	16: 3	Commit to the LORD **whatever** you **d,**	5126
	19: 7	how much more *d* his friends **avoid** him!	AIT
	19:18	*d* not **be a willing party**	AIT
	19:19	*you* will have to **d** it **again.**	3578+6388
	20:13	*D* not **love** sleep or you will grow poor;	AIT
	20:22	*D* not **say,** "I'll pay you back	AIT
	20:23	and dishonest scales *d* not please him.	NIH
	21: 3	*To* **d** what is right	6913
	21: 7	for they refuse to **d** what is right.	6913
	22:22	*D* not **exploit** the poor	AIT
	22:22	because they are poor and *d* not **crush**	AIT
	22:24	*D* not **make friends** with a hot-tempered man,	AIT
	22:24	*d* not **associate** with one easily angered,	AIT
	22:26	*D* not **be** a man who strikes hands in pledge	AIT
	22:28	*D* not **move** an ancient boundary stone set	AIT
	22:29	*D you* see a man skilled in his work?	AIT
	23: 3	*D* not **crave** his delicacies,	AIT
	23: 4	*D* not **wear** *yourself* **out**	AIT
	23: 6	*D* not **eat** the food of a stingy man,	AIT
	23: 6	*d* not **crave** his delicacies,	AIT
	23: 9	*D* not **speak** to a fool,	AIT
	23:10	*D* not **move** an ancient boundary stone	AIT
	23:13	*D* not **withhold** discipline from a child;	AIT
	23:17	*D* not **let** your heart **envy**	AIT
	23:20	*D* not **join** those who drink too much wine	AIT
	23:22	*d* not **despise** your mother when she is old.	AIT
	23:23	Buy the truth and *d* not **sell** it;	AIT
	23:31	*D* not **gaze** at wine when it is red,	AIT
	24: 1	*D* not **envy** wicked men,	AIT
	24: 1	*d* not **desire** their company;	AIT
	24:15	*D* not **lie in wait**	AIT
	24:15	*d* not **raid** his dwelling place;	AIT
	24:17	*D* not **gloat** when your enemy falls;	AIT
	24:17	*d* not **let** your heart **rejoice,**	AIT
	24:19	*D* not **fret** because of evil men or	AIT
	24:21	my son, and *d* not **join** with the rebellious,	AIT
	24:28	*D* not **testify** against your neighbor	AIT
	24:29	*D* not **say,** "I'll do to him as he has done	AIT
	24:29	"I'll **d** to him as he has done to me;	6913
	25: 6	*D* not **exalt yourself**	AIT
	25: 6	and *d* not **claim** a place among great men;	AIT
	25: 8	*d* not **bring** hastily to court,	AIT
	25: 8	for what *will you* **d** in the end	6913
	25: 9	*d* not **betray** another man's confidence,	AIT
	26: 4	*D* not **answer** a fool according to his folly,	AIT
	26:12	*D you* see a man wise in his own eyes?	AIT
	26:25	his speech is charming, *d* not **believe** him,	AIT
	27: 1	*D* not **boast** about tomorrow,	AIT
	27: 1	*you d* not **know** what a day may bring forth.	AIT
	27:10	*D* not **forsake** your friend and the friend	AIT
	27:10	and *d* not **go** *to* your brother's house	AIT
	27:24	for riches *d* not **endure** forever,	NIH
	28: 5	Evil men *d* not **understand** justice,	AIT
	28:21	a man *will* **d** wrong for a piece of bread.	7321
	29:20	*D you* see a man who speaks in haste?	AIT
	30: 2	I *d* not have a man's understanding.	NIH
	30: 6	*D* not **add** to his words,	AIT
	30: 7	*d* not **refuse** me before I die;	AIT
	30:10	"*D* not **slander** a servant to his master,	AIT
	30:11	and *d* not **bless** their mothers;	AIT
	30:18	four *that I* **d** not **understand:**	AIT
	31: 3	*d* not **spend** your strength on women,	AIT
Pr	31:29	"Many women **d** noble things,	6913
Ecc	2: 3	to see what was worthwhile for men *to* **d**	6913
	2:12	king's successor **d** than what has already been done?	NIH
	2:15	What then **d** I gain by being wise?"	NIH
	2:21	For a man *may* **d** his work with wisdom,	3780
	2:24	A man can **d** nothing better than to eat	NIH
	3:12	to be happy and **d** good while they live.	6913
	5: 1	who **d** not **know** that they do wrong.	AIT
	5: 1	who do not know that they **d** wrong.	6913
	5: 2	*D* not **be** **quick** with your mouth,	AIT
	5: 2	*d* not **be** **hasty** in your heart	AIT
	5: 4	*d* not **delay** in fulfilling it.	AIT
	5: 6	*D* not **let** your mouth lead you into sin.	AIT
	5: 6	And *d* not **protest** to	AIT
	5: 8	*d* not **be surprised** at such things;	AIT
	5:11	so **d** those who consume them.	8045S
	6: 6	*D* not all **go** to the same place?	AIT
	7: 9	*D* not **be quickly provoked**	AIT
	7:10	*D* not **say,** "Why were	AIT
	7:16	*D* not **be overrighteous,** neither be overwise	AIT
	7:17	*D* not **be overwicked,** and do not be a fool	AIT
	7:17	Do not be overwicked, and *d* not **be** a fool	AIT
	7:21	*D* not pay **attention**	AIT
	8: 3	*D* not **be in a hurry**	AIT
	8: 3	*D* not **stand up** for a bad cause,	AIT
	8: 3	for *he will* **d** whatever he pleases.	6913
	8:11	with schemes to **d** wrong.	6913
	8:13	Yet because the wicked *d* not **fear God**,	NIH
	9: 1	and what they **d** are in God's hands,	6271
	9: 2	and *those who* **d** not.	2284S
	9: 7	for it is now that God favors what you **d.**	5126
	9:10	Whatever your hand finds to **d,**	6913
	9:10	**d** it with all your might, for in the grave,	6913
	10: 4	*d* not **leave your post;**	AIT
	10:20	*D* not **revile** the king even	AIT
	11: 2	for *you* **d** not **know** what disaster may come	AIT
	11: 5	As you *d* not **know** the path of the wind,	AIT
	11: 6	for you *d* not **know** which will succeed,	AIT
	11: 6	or whether both will **d** equally well.	NIH
SS	1: 6	*D* not **stare** *at* me because I am dark,	AIT
	1: 8	If *you* **d** not **know,**	AIT
	2: 7	*D* not **arouse** or awaken love until it	AIT
	3: 5	*D* not **arouse** or awaken love until it	AIT
	8: 4	*D* not **arouse** or awaken love until it	AIT
	8: 8	What *shall we* **d** for our sister for	6913
Isa	1: 3	my people *d* not **understand."**	AIT
	1: 5	Why *d you* **persist** *in* rebellion?	AIT
	1:17	learn to **d** right!	3512
	1:23	*d* not **defend the cause** of the fatherless	AIT
	2: 9	*d* not **forgive** them.	AIT
	3: 7	*d* not **make** me the leader of the people."	AIT
	3: 9	*they* **d** not **hide** it.	AIT
	3:15	What **d** you mean by crushing my people	NIH
	5: 5	Now I will tell you what I *am going to* **d**	6913
	7: 4	*D* not **lose heart** because	AIT
	7: 9	*d* not **stand firm** in *your* **faith,**	AIT
	8:12	"*D* not **call** conspiracy everything	AIT
	8:12	*d* not **fear** what they fear,	AIT
	8:12	and *d* not **dread** it.	AIT
	8:20	If *they* **d** not **speak** according to this word,	AIT
	10: 3	What *will* you **d** on the day of reckoning	6913
	10:24	*d* not **be afraid** of the Assyrians,	AIT
	13:17	who *d* not **care** for silver	AIT
	14:29	*D* not **rejoice,** all you Philistines, that	AIT
	16: 3	*d* not **betray** the refugees.	AIT
	19:15	There is nothing Egypt *can* **d—**	6913
	22: 4	*D* not **try** to console me over	AIT
	24: 9	No longer *d* they **drink** wine with a song;	AIT
	26:10	*they* **d** not **learn** righteousness;	AIT
	26:11	your hand is lifted high, but *they* **d** not **see** it.	AIT
	26:13	but your name alone **d** we **honor.**	AIT
	26:14	those departed spirits *d* not **rise.**	AIT
	28:10	For it is: **D** and do, do and do, rule on rule,	7422
	28:10	For it is: Do and **d,** do and do, rule on rule,	7422
	28:10	For it is: Do and do, **d** and do, rule on rule,	7422
	28:10	For it is: Do and do, do and **d,** rule on rule,	7422
	28:13	**D** and do, do and do, rule on rule,	7422
	28:13	Do and **d,** do and do, rule on rule,	7422
	28:13	Do and do, **d** and do, rule on rule,	7422
	28:13	Do and do, do and **d,** rule on rule,	7422
	28:21	to **d** his work, his strange work,	6913
	28:28	his horses *d* not **grind** it.	AIT
	29:15	who **d** their work in darkness and think,	2118
	31: 1	but *d* not **look** to the Holy One of Israel,	AIT
	31: 4	down to **d** battle on Mount Zion and	7371
	35: 4	"Be strong, *d* not **fear;**	AIT
	36:14	*D* not **let** Hezekiah **deceive**	AIT
	36:15	*D* not **let** Hezekiah **persuade** you **to trust**	AIT
	36:16	"*D* not **listen** to Hezekiah.	AIT
	36:18	"*D* not **let** Hezekiah **mislead**	AIT
	36:21	"*D* not **answer** him."	AIT
	37: 6	*D* not **be afraid** of what you have heard—	AIT
	37:10	*D* not **let** the god you **depend**	AIT
	38: 7	the LORD *will* **d** what he has promised:	6913
	40: 9	lift it up, *d* not **be afraid;**	AIT
	40:21	*D* you not **know?**	AIT
	40:24	no sooner *d* they **take root** in the ground,	AIT
	40:27	Why *d* you **say,** O Jacob, and complain,	AIT
	40:28	*D* you not **know?**	AIT
	41:10	So *d* not **fear,** for I am with you;	AIT
	41:10	*d* not **be dismayed,** for I am your God.	AIT
	41:13	*D* not **fear;** I will help you.	AIT
	41:14	*D* not **be afraid,** O worm Jacob,	AIT
	41:23	**D** something, whether **good**	3512
	42:16	These are the things *I will* **d;**	6913

Isa 43: 5 *D* not be **afraid**, for I am with you; — AIT
43: 6 '*D* not **hold** them **back**.' — AIT
43:18 *d* not **dwell** on the past. — AIT
43:19 Now it springs up; *d* you not **perceive** it? — AIT
44: 2 *D* not be **afraid**, O Jacob, my servant, — AIT
44: 8 *D* not **tremble**, do not be afraid. — AIT
44: 8 Do not tremble, *d* not be **afraid**. — AIT
44: 4 though *you d* not **acknowledge** me. — AIT
45: 7 I, the LORD, *d* all these things. — 6913
45:11 *d* you **question** me about my children, — AIT
46:10 and *I will d* all that I please. — 6913
46:11 what I have planned, that *will I* **d**. — 6913
47:15 That is all *they can* **d** for you— — 2118
48: 8 Well *d I* **know** how treacherous you are; — AIT
48:11 my own sake, for my own sake, *I* **d** this. — 6913
50: 2 **D** I lack the strength to rescue you? — NIH
51: 7 *D* not **fear** the reproach of men or — AIT
52: 5 "And now what **d** I have here?" — NIH
54: 2 *d* not **hold back**; — AIT
54: 4 *D* not be **afraid**; you will not suffer shame. — AIT
54: 4 *D* not **fear disgrace**. — AIT
55: 5 and nations *that d* not **know** you will hasten — AIT
55:10 and *d* not **return** to it without watering — AIT
56: 1 "Maintain justice and **d** what is right, — 6913
57: 4 At whom *d you* **sneer** — AIT
57:11 that *you d* not **fear** me? — AIT
58: 1 "Shout it aloud, *d* not **hold back**. — AIT
58: 3 *you* **d** as you please — 5162
58: 4 as *you* **d** today and expect your voice to — NIH
58: 9 "If *you* **d away with** the yoke of oppression, — 4946+6073+9348
59: 8 The way of peace *they d* not **know**; — AIT
60:22 in its time *I will* **d** this **swiftly**." — 2590
63:17 *d you* **make** us **wander** — AIT
63:17 and harden our hearts so we **d** — NIH
64: 5 to the help of those who gladly **d** right, — 6913
64: 9 *D* not be **angry** beyond measure, O LORD; — AIT
64: 9 *d* not **remember** our sins forever. — AIT
65: 8 so *will I* **d** in behalf of my servants; — 6913
65:16 a blessing in the land *will* **d** so by the God — 1385ˢ
66: 9 *D* I **bring** to the moment of birth — AIT
66: 9 "*D* I **close** up the womb when I bring — AIT
Jer 1: 6 I said, "I *d* not **know** how to speak; — AIT
1: 7 But the LORD said to me, "*D* not **say**, — AIT
1: 8 *D* not be **afraid** of them, — AIT
1:11 "What *d you* **see**, Jeremiah?" — AIT
1:13 "What *d you* **see**?" — AIT
1:17 *D* not be **terrified** by them, — AIT
2:25 **D** not **run** until your feet are bare — 4979
2:29 "Why *d you* **bring charges** against me? — AIT
2:31 Why *d* my people **say**, — AIT
2:36 Why *d you* **go about** so much, — AIT
3: 5 but *you* **d** all the evil you can." — 6913
4: 3 up your unplowed ground and *d* not **sow** — AIT
4:22 "My people are fools; *they d* not **know** me. — AIT
4:22 they know not how to **d** **good**?" — 3512
5: 3 O LORD, *d* not your eyes look for truth? — NIH
5: 4 for *they d* not **know** the way of the LORD, — AIT
5:10 *d* not **destroy** them **completely**. — AIT
5:10 these people *d* not belong to the LORD. — NIH
5:12 they said, "He will **d** nothing!" — NIH
5:15 a people whose language *you d* not **know**, — AIT
5:15 whose speech *you d* not **understand**. — AIT
5:21 who have eyes but *d* not **see**, — AIT
5:21 who have ears but *d* not **hear**: — AIT
5:24 *They d* not **say** to themselves, — AIT
5:28 *they d* not **plead** the case of the fatherless — AIT
5:28 *they d* not **defend** the rights of the poor. — AIT
5:31 But what *will you* **d** in the end? — 6913
6:15 *d* not even **know how** — AIT
6:20 **What d** I **care about** incense from Sheba — 2296+3276+4200+4200+4537
6:20 your sacrifices *d* not **please** me." — AIT
6:25 *D* not **go out** to the fields or walk on — AIT
7: 4 *D* not **trust** in deceptive words and say, — AIT
7: 6 if *you d* not **oppress** the alien, — AIT
7: 6 or the widow and *d* not **shed** innocent blood — AIT
7: 6 and if *you d* not **follow** other gods — AIT
7:10 safe to **d** all these detestable things? — 6913
7:14 *now* to the house that bears my Name, — 6913
7:16 "So *d* not **pray** for this people — AIT
7:16 *d* not **plead** with me, — AIT
7:17 *D* you not **see** what they are doing in — AIT
8: 4 *d* they not **get up**? — AIT
8: 6 but *they d* not **say** what is right. — AIT
8: 7 But my people *d* not **know** the requirements — AIT
8: 9 what kind of wisdom **d** they have? — NIH
8:12 *d* not even **know how** to blush. — AIT
9: 3 *they d* not **acknowledge** me," — AIT
9: 4 *d* not **trust** your brothers. — AIT
9: 7 for what else *can I* **d** because of the sin — 6913
10: 2 "*D* not **learn** the ways of the nations or — AIT
10: 5 *D* not **fear** them; — AIT
10: 5 *they can* **d** no **harm** — 8317
10: 5 nor *can they* **d** *any* **good**." — 3512
10:21 and *d* not **inquire** of the LORD; — AIT
10:21 so *they d* not **prosper** — AIT
10:25 on the nations that *d* not **acknowledge** you, — AIT
10:25 the peoples who *d* not **call** on your name. — AIT
11: 4 and **d** everything I command you, — 6913
11:14 *D* not **pray** for this people — AIT
11:21 '*D* not **prophesy** in the name of the LORD — AIT
12: 1 *d* all the faithless **live at ease**? — AIT
12: 6 *D* not **trust** them, — AIT
13: 1 *d* not **let** it **touch** water." — AIT
13:15 Hear and pay attention, *d* not be **arrogant**, — AIT
13:17 But if *you d* not **listen**, — AIT

Jer 13:23 Neither can you **d** good who are accustomed to doing evil. — 3512
14: 7 **d** something for the sake of your name. — 6913
14: 9 *d* not **forsake** us! — AIT
14:10 *they d* not **restrain** their feet. — AIT
14:11 *D* not **pray** for the well-being of this people. — AIT
14:19 *D* you **despise** Zion? — AIT
14:21 For the sake of your name *d* not **despise** us; — AIT
14:21 *d* not **dishonor** your glorious throne. — AIT
14:21 with us and *d* not **break** it. — AIT
14:22 *D* any of the worthless idols of the nations **bring rain**? — AIT
14:22 *D* the skies *themselves* **send down** — AIT
15:14 to your enemies in a land *you d* not **know**, — AIT
15:15 *d* not **take** me **away**; — AIT
16: 5 "*D* not **enter** a house where there is — AIT
16: 5 *d* not **go** to mourn or show sympathy, — AIT
16: 8 "And *d* not **enter** a house — AIT
16:20 *D* men **make** their own gods? — AIT
17: 4 to your enemies in a land *you d* not **know**, — AIT
17:17 *D* not be a **terror** to me; — AIT
17:22 *D* not **bring** a load **out** — AIT
17:22 a load out of your houses or **d** any work on — 6913
17:27 But if *you d* not **obey** me to keep — AIT
18: 6 can I not **d** with you as this potter does?" — 6913
18:10 **good** I had intended to **d** — 3208+3512
18:14 *D* its cool waters from distant sources *ever* **cease** — AIT
18:23 *D* not **forgive** their crimes — AIT
19:12 This is what *I will* **d** to this place and — 6913
21:10 I have determined to **d** this city harm and — NIH
22: 3 **D** what is just and right. — 6913
22: 3 **D** no **wrong** or violence to the alien, — 3561
22: 3 and *d* not **shed** innocent blood in this place. — AIT
22: 5 But if *you d* not **obey** these commands, — AIT
22:10 *D* not **weep** for the dead [king] — AIT
22:28 cast into a land *they d* not **know**? — AIT
23: 5 and **d** what is just and right in the land. — 6913
23:16 "*D* not **listen** to what the prophets — AIT
23:24 "*D* not I **fill** heaven and earth?" — AIT
23:28 what *has* straw to **d** with grain?" — 4200
23:32 *d* not **benefit** these people **in the least**," — AIT
24: 3 the LORD asked me, "What *d you* **see**, — AIT
25: 6 *D* not **follow** other gods to serve — AIT
25: 6 *d* not **provoke** me to **anger** — AIT
26: 2 *d* not **omit** a word. — AIT
26: 4 *you d* not **listen** to me and follow my law, — AIT
26: 5 and if *you d* not **listen** to the words — AIT
26: 9 Why *d you* **prophesy** in the LORD's name — AIT
26:14 **d** with me whatever you think is good — 6913
27: 9 So *d* not **listen** to your prophets, — AIT
27:14 *D* not **listen** to the words of the prophets — AIT
27:16 *D* not **listen** to the prophets who say, — AIT
27:17 *D* not **listen** to them. — AIT
28: 6 *May* the LORD **d** so! — 6913
29: 6 Increase in number there; *d* not **decrease**. — AIT
29: 8 "*D* not *let* the prophets and diviners among you **deceive** you. — AIT
29: 8 *D* not **listen** to the dreams — AIT
29:23 which I did not tell them to **d**. — NIH
29:32 the good things I *will* **d** for my people, — 6913
30: 6 Then why *d I* **see** every strong man — AIT
30:10 " 'So *d* not **fear**, O Jacob my servant, — AIT
30:10 *d* not be **dismayed**, O Israel.' — AIT
30:15 Why *d you* **cry out** over your wound, — AIT
32: 3 saying, "Why *d you* **prophesy** as you do? — AIT
32: 3 saying, "Why *d you* prophesy as you do? — NIH
32:23 *they did* not **d** what you commanded them — 6913
32:23 not do what you commanded them to **d**. — 6913
32:35 that they *should* **d** such a detestable thing — 6913
33: 3 and unsearchable things *you d* not **know**.' — 6913
33: 9 on earth that hear of all the good things I **d** — 6913
33:15 he *will* **d** what is just and right in the land." — 6913
35: 6 But they replied, "*We d* not **drink** wine, — AIT
35:14 To this day *they d* not **drink** wine, — AIT
35:15 *d* not **follow** other gods to serve them. — AIT
36: 8 the prophet told him to **d**; — NIH
37: 9 *D* not **deceive** yourselves, thinking, — AIT
37:20 *D* not **send** me **back** — AIT
38: 5 "The king *can* **d** nothing to oppose you." — 3523
38:14 "*D* not **hide** anything from me." — AIT
38:24 "*D* not *let* anyone **know** — AIT
38:25 *d* not **hide** it from us or we will kill you,' — AIT
39:12 but **d** for him whatever he asks." — 6913
40: 4 but if *you d* not want to, then don't come. — NIH
40: 9 "*D* not be **afraid** to serve the Babylonians," — AIT
40:16 "Don't **d** such a thing!" — 6913
42: 3 where we should **d** and what *we should* **d**." — 6913
42: 5 against us if *we d* not **act** in accordance — AIT
42:11 *D* not be **afraid** of the king of Babylon, — AIT
42:11 *D* not be **afraid** of him, — AIT
42:15 to go to Egypt and *you d* **go** to settle there, — AIT
42:19 *D* not **go** to Egypt.' — AIT
42:20 tell us everything he says and *we will* **d** it.' — 6913
44: 4 '*D* not **do** this detestable thing that I hate!' — AIT
44: 4 '*Do* not **d** this detestable thing that I hate!' — 6913
44:17 *We will* **certainly d** everything we said we would: — 6913+6913
44:25 *Go* ahead then, **d** what you promised! — 6913+6913
46: 5 What *d I* **see**? — AIT
46:27 "*D* not **fear**, O Jacob my servant, — AIT
46:27 *d* not be **dismayed**, O Israel. — AIT
46:28 *D* not **fear**, O Jacob my servant, — AIT
49: 1 Why *d* Molech **live** in its towns? — AIT
49: 4 Why *d you* **boast** of your valleys, — AIT
49:12 "If those who *d* not **deserve** to drink — NIH
49:36 be a nation where Elam's exiles *d* not **go**. — AIT

Jer 50: 9 like skilled warriors *who d* not **return** empty-handed. — AIT
50:15 **d** to her as she has done to others. — 6913
50:21 "*D* everything I have **commanded** you. — 6913
50:25 to **d** in the land of the Babylonians. — NIH
50:29 **d** to her as she has done. — 6913
51: 3 *D* not **spare** her young men; — AIT
51: 6 *D* not be **destroyed** because of her sins. — AIT
51:46 *D* not **lose heart** or be afraid — AIT
51:50 leave and *d* not **linger**! — AIT
La 3:56 "*D* not **close** your ears to my cry for relief." — AIT
3:57 and you said, "*D* not **fear**." — AIT
5:20 Why *d you* always **forget** us? — AIT
5:20 Why *d you* **forsake** us so long? — AIT
Eze 2: 6 *d* not be **afraid** of them or their words. — AIT
2: 6 *D* not be **afraid**, — AIT
2: 6 *D* not be **afraid** of what they say — AIT
2: 8 *D* not **rebel** like that rebellious house; — AIT
3: 9 *D* not be **afraid** *of* them or terrified — AIT
3:18 and *you d* not **warn** him or speak out — AIT
3:19 if *you d* **warn** the wicked man and he does — AIT
3:21 if *you d* **warn** the righteous man not to sin — AIT
5: 9 *I will* **d** to you what I have never done — 6913
5: 9 before and *will* never **d** again. — 6913
8: 6 *d* you **see** what they are doing— — AIT
8:15 He said to me, "*D* you **see** this, son of man? — AIT
8:17 a trivial matter for the house of Judah to **d** — 6913
9: 6 but *d* not **touch** anyone who has the mark. — AIT
12: 2 They have eyes to see but *d* not **see** and ears — AIT
12: 2 not see and ears to hear but *d* not **hear**, — AIT
14: 5 I will **d** this to recapture the hearts of — NIH
15: 3 *D* they **make** pegs from it to hang things on? — AIT
16: 5 or had compassion enough to **d** any — 6913
16:30 when you **d** all these things, — 6913
17:12 '*D* you not **know** what these things mean?' — AIT
17:24 and *I will* **d** it.' " — 6913
18: 2 "**What d** you **people mean** — 4013+4200+4537
18:14 *he does* not **d** such things: — 6913
18:23 *D* I **take** any **pleasure in** the death of — AIT
20: 7 *d* not **defile** yourselves — AIT
20:18 "*D* not **follow** the statutes of your fathers — AIT
21:24 revealing your sins in all *that* you **d**— — 6613
22:14 I the LORD have spoken, and *I will* **d** it. — 6913
22:26 Her priests **d** **violence** *to* my law — 2803
22:26 *they d* not **distinguish** between the holy and — AIT
24:16 *d* not **lament** or weep or shed any tears. — AIT
24:17 Groan quietly; **d** not **mourn** for the dead. — 6913
24:17 *d* not **cover** the lower part of your face — AIT
24:19 "Won't you tell us what these things *have* **to d with** us?" — 4200
24:22 And *you will* **d** as I have done. — 6913
24:24 *you will* **d** just as he has done. — 6913
32:27 *D* they not **lie** with — AIT
33: 8 and *you d* not **speak out** to dissuade him — AIT
33: 9 But if *you d* **warn** the wicked man to turn — AIT
33: 9 to turn from his ways and *he does* not **d** so, — 2006+4946+8740ˢ
33:26 *you* **d** detestable things, — 6913
33:31 My people come to you, as they usually **d**, — 4427ˢ
33:31 *d* not **put** them **into practice**. — AIT
33:32 *d* not **put** them **into practice**. — AIT
34: 3 *d* not **take care** of the flock. — AIT
36:22 that I *am going to* **d** these things, — 6913
36:36 and *I will* **d** it.' — 6913
36:37 to the plea of the house of Israel and **d** this — 6913
44:19 so that *they d* not **consecrate** the people — AIT
45: 9 and oppression and **d** what is just and right. — 6913
45:20 *You are to* **d** the same on the seventh day — 6913
47: 6 He asked me, "Son of man, *d you* **see** this?" — AIT
Da 2: 5 If *you d* not **tell** me what my dream was — AIT
2: 9 If *you d* not **tell** me the dream, — AIT
2:10 on earth who can **d** what the king asks! — 10252ˢ
2:11 and they *d* not **live** among men." — 10029
2:24 "*D* not **execute** the wise men of Babylon. — AIT
3: 4 "This is what you are **commanded** to **d**, — NIH
3:14 that *you d* not **serve** my gods or worship — AIT
3:15 But if *you d* not **worship** it, — AIT
3:16 *we d* not **need** to defend ourselves — AIT
4:19 *d* not *let* the dream or its meaning **alarm** — AIT
6: 4 they were unable to **d** so. — 10353+10544+10708ˢ
6: 5 unless it has **something** to **d** with the law — 10089
9:18 We *d* not **make** requests of you — AIT
9:19 For your sake, O my God, *d* not **delay**, — AIT
10:12 he continued, "*D* not be **afraid**, Daniel. — AIT
10:19 "*D* not be **afraid**, O man highly esteemed," — AIT
10:20 "*D* you **know** why I have come to you? — AIT
11: 3 with great power and **d** as he pleases. — 6913
11:16 The invader *will* **d** as he pleases; — 6913
11:36 "The king *will* **d** as he pleases. — 6913
Hos 4:15 "*D* not **go** to Gilgal; — AIT
4:15 *d* not **go up** to Beth Aven. — AIT
4:15 And *d* not **swear**, — AIT
5: 4 "Their deeds *d* not **permit** them to return — AIT
5: 4 *they d* not **acknowledge** the LORD. — AIT
6: 4 "What *can I* **d** with you, Ephraim? — 6913
6: 4 What *can I* **d** with you, Judah? — 6913
6: 9 so **d** bands of priests; — NIH
7: 2 but they *d* not **realize** — AIT
7:14 *They d* not **cry out** to me from their hearts — AIT
7:16 *They d* not **turn** *to* the Most High; — AIT
9: 1 *D* not **rejoice**, O Israel; — AIT
9: 1 *d* not be **jubilant** like the other nations. — AIT
9: 5 What *will you* **d** on the day — 6913
10: 3 if we had a king, what *could he* **d** for us?" — 6913
12:11 *D* they **sacrifice** bulls in Gilgal? — AIT
14: 8 *have* I to **d** with idols? — 4200
Joel 2: 8 *They* **d** not **jostle** each other; — AIT

Ref	Text	Code
Joel 2:17	D not **make** your inheritance an object	AIT
Am 3:3	D two **walk** together unless they have	AIT
3:3	unless they have agreed to **d** so?	NIH
3:6	d not the people **tremble**?	AIT
3:10	"They d not **know how** to do right,"	AIT
3:10	"They do not know how to **d** right,"	6913
4:5	for this is what you love to **d**,"	NIH
4:12	"Therefore this is what I will **d** to you,	6913
4:12	Israel, and because I will **d** this to you,	6913
5:5	d not **seek** Bethel,	AIT
5:5	d not **go** to Gilgal,	AIT
5:5	d not **journey** to Beersheba.	AIT
5:18	Why d you **long for** the day of	AIT
6:6	you d not **grieve** over the ruin of Joseph.	AIT
6:12	D horses **run** on the rocky crags?	AIT
7:8	And the LORD asked me, "What d you **see**,	AIT
7:12	and d your **prophesying** there.	AIT
7:16	You say, " 'D not **prophesy** against Israel,	AIT
8:2	"What d you **see**, Amos?"	AIT
8:4	you who trample the needy and **d** away with the poor of the land,	8697
9:12	who will **d** these things.	6913
Jnh 1:8	What d you **do**?	NIH
1:8	What do you **d**?	4856
1:8	Where d you **come** from?	AIT
1:11	"What **should** we **d** to you to make	6913
1:14	d not **let** us **die**	AIT
1:14	D not **keep** us **accountable**	AIT
3:7	D not let any man or beast, herd or flock, **taste** anything;	AIT
3:7	d not let them **eat** or drink.	AIT
4:9	"D you **have a right**	AIT
4:9	"I **d**," he said.	3512S
Mic 2:1	because it is in their power to **d** it.	NIH
2:6	"D not **prophesy**," their prophets say.	AIT
2:6	"D not **prophesy** about these things;	AIT
2:7	Does he d such things?"	5095
2:7	"Do not my words **do good**	AIT
2:7	"Do not my words **d good**	3512
4:9	d you now **cry aloud**—	AIT
4:12	they d not **know** the thoughts of the LORD;	AIT
4:12	they d not **understand** his plan,	AIT
5:7	which d not **wait** for man or linger	AIT
7:5	D not **trust** a neighbor;	AIT
7:8	D not **gloat** over me, my enemy!	AIT
7:18	You d not **stay** angry forever but delight	AIT
Hab 1:2	must I call for help, but you d not **listen**?	AIT
1:2	but you d not **save**?	AIT
1:3	d you **make** me **look**	AIT
1:3	Why d you **tolerate** wrong?	AIT
1:5	For I am going to **d** something in your days	7188
1:13	Why then d you **tolerate** the treacherous?	AIT
Zep 1:12	'The LORD will d nothing, either **good**	AIT
2:3	you who d what he commands.	7188
3:4	the sanctuary and **d** violence to the law.	2803
3:13	The remnant of Israel will **d** no wrong;	6913
3:16	"D not **fear**, O Zion;	AIT
3:16	d not let your hands **hang limp**.	AIT
Hag 2:5	D not **fear**.'	AIT
2:14	'Whatever they **d** and whatever they offer there is defiled.	3338+5126
Zec 1:4	D not be like your forefathers,	AIT
1:5	And the prophets, d they **live** forever?	AIT
1:6	just as he determined to **d**.' "	6913
1:21	I asked, "What are these coming to **d**?"	6913
4:2	He asked me, "What d you **see**?"	AIT
4:5	"D you not **know** what these are?"	AIT
4:13	"D you not **know** what these are?"	AIT
5:2	He asked me, "What d you **see**?"	AIT
7:10	D not **oppress** the widow or the fatherless,	AIT
7:10	In your hearts d not **think** evil of each other.'	AIT
8:13	D not be **afraid**,	AIT
8:15	"so now I have determined to **d good** again	3512
8:15	D not be **afraid**.	AIT
8:16	These are the things you are to **d**:	6913
8:17	d not **plot** evil against	AIT
8:17	and d not **love** to swear falsely.	AIT
11:5	Their own shepherds d not **spare** them.	AIT
14:17	of the peoples of the earth d not **go up**	AIT
14:18	If the Egyptian people d not **go up**	AIT
14:18	on the nations that d not **go up** to celebrate	AIT
14:19	the nations that d not **go up** to celebrate	AIT
Mal 2:2	If you d not **listen**,	AIT
2:2	and if you d not **set** your heart	AIT
2:10	Why d we **profane** the covenant	AIT
2:13	Another thing you **d**:	6913
2:15	and d not **break faith** with the wife	AIT
2:16	and d not **break faith**.	AIT
2:17	"All who d evil are good in the eyes of	6913
3:5	but d not **fear** me,"	AIT
3:6	"I the LORD d not **change**.	AIT
3:8	"But you ask, 'How d we **rob** you?'	AIT
3:18	and those who d not.	6268S
4:3	on the day when I d these things,"	6913
Mt 1:20	d not be **afraid** to take Mary home	AIT
3:9	And d not **think** you can say to yourselves,	AIT
3:14	and d you **come** to me?"	AIT
3:15	for us to **d** this to fulfill all righteousness."	NIG
4:7	'D not **put** the Lord your God to the test.' "	AIT
5:15	Neither d people **light** a lamp and put it	AIT
5:17	"D not **think** that I have come to abolish	AIT
5:19	and teaches others to **d** the same will	NIG
5:21	to the people long ago, 'D not **murder**,	AIT
5:25	D it while you are still with him on	NIG
5:27	'D not **commit adultery**.'	AIT
5:33	'D not **break** your **oath**,	AIT
5:34	But I tell you, D not **swear** at all:	AIT
Mt 5:36	And d not **swear** by your head,	AIT
5:39	But I tell you, D not **resist** an evil person.	AIT
5:42	d not **turn away** from the one who wants	AIT
5:47	D not even pagans **do** that?	AIT
5:47	Do not even pagans **d** that?	4472
6:1	not to **d** your 'acts of righteousness'	4472
6:1	If you **d**, you will have no reward	1145+3590S
6:2	d not **announce** it **with trumpets**,	AIT
6:2	the hypocrites **d** in the synagogues and on	4472
6:3	d not let your left hand **know**	AIT
6:5	when you pray, d not **be** like the hypocrites,	AIT
6:7	d not **keep on babbling**	AIT
6:8	D not be **like** them,	AIT
6:15	But if you d not **forgive** men their sins,	AIT
6:16	d not look **somber** as the hypocrites do,	AIT
6:16	do not look somber as the hypocrites **d**,	NIG
6:19	"D not **store up** for yourselves treasures	AIT
6:20	where moth and rust d not **destroy**,	AIT
6:20	and where thieves d not **break in** and steal.	AIT
6:25	I tell you, d not **worry** about your life,	AIT
6:26	they d not **sow** or reap or store away	AIT
6:28	"And why d you **worry** about clothes?	AIT
6:28	They d not **labor** or spin.	AIT
6:31	d not **worry**, saying, 'What shall we eat?'	AIT
6:34	Therefore d not **worry** about tomorrow,	AIT
7:1	"D not **judge**, or you too will be judged.	AIT
7:3	"Why d you **look** at the speck of sawdust	AIT
7:6	"D not **give** dogs what is sacred;	AIT
7:6	d not **throw** your pearls to pigs.	AIT
7:6	If you **d**, they may trample them	3607
7:12	**d** to others what you would have them do	4472
7:12	do to others what you would have **them d**	4472
7:16	D people **pick** grapes from thornbushes,	AIT
8:8	I d not **deserve** to have you come	AIT
8:9	I say to my servant, '**D this**,'	4472
8:29	**"What d you want with** us,	2779+5515
9:4	d you **entertain** evil thoughts	AIT
9:14	but your disciples d not **fast**?"	AIT
9:17	Neither d men **pour** new wine	AIT
9:17	If they **d**, the skins will burst;	1145+3590S
9:28	"D you **believe** that I am able to do this?"	AIT
9:28	"Do you believe that I am able to **d** this?"	4472
10:5	"D not **go** among the Gentiles	AIT
10:9	D not **take along** any gold or silver	AIT
10:19	d not **worry about** what to say or how	AIT
10:26	d not be **afraid** of them.	AIT
10:28	D not be **afraid** of those who kill the body	AIT
10:34	"D not **suppose** that I have come	AIT
12:4	which was not lawful for them to **d**,	2266S
12:12	it is lawful to **d** good on the Sabbath."	4472
12:27	d your people **drive** them **out**?	AIT
13:10	"Why d you **speak** to the people	AIT
13:13	"Though seeing, they d not **see**;	AIT
13:13	d not **hear** or understand.	AIT
13:28	'D you **want** us to go and pull them up?'	AIT
13:41	that causes sin and all who **d** evil.	4472
13:58	And he did not **d** many miracles there	4472
14:16	Jesus replied, "They d not **need** to go away.	AIT
15:2	"Why d your disciples **break** the tradition	AIT
15:3	"And why d you **break** the command of God	AIT
15:12	"D you **know** that the Pharisees	AIT
15:32	I d not **want** to send them away hungry,	AIT
15:34	"How many loaves d you **have**?"	AIT
16:9	D you still not **understand**?	AIT
16:13	"Who d people **say** the Son of Man is?"	AIT
16:15	"Who d you **say** I am?"	AIT
16:23	d not **have in mind** the things of God,	AIT
17:10	"Why then d the teachers of the law **say**	AIT
17:25	"What d you **think**, Simon?"	AIT
17:25	d the kings of the earth **collect** duty	AIT
18:10	d not **look down on** one of these little ones.	AIT
18:12	"What d you **think**?	AIT
19:14	and d not **hinder** them,	AIT
19:16	what good thing **must I d**	4472
19:17	"Why d you **ask** me about what is good?"	AIT
19:18	Jesus replied, " 'D not **murder**,	AIT
19:18	d not **commit adultery**,	AIT
19:18	d not **steal**, do not give false testimony,	AIT
19:18	d not **give false testimony**,	AIT
19:20	"What d I still **lack**?"	AIT
20:15	to **d** what I want with my own money?	4472
20:32	"What d you **want** me to do for you?"	AIT
20:32	"What do you want me to **d** for you?"	4472
21:16	D you **hear** what these children are saying?"	AIT
21:21	if you have faith and d not **doubt**,	AIT
21:21	not only can you **d** what was done to	4472
21:28	"What d you **think**?	AIT
21:40	what will he **d** to those tenants?"	4472
22:29	"You are in error because you d not **know**	AIT
22:42	"What d you **think** about the Christ?	AIT
23:3	and d everything they tell you.	4472
23:3	But d not **do** what they do,	AIT
23:3	But do not **d** what they do,	4472
23:3	But do not do what they **d**,	2240
23:3	for they d not **practice** what they preach.	2240
23:5	"Everything they **d** is done for men to see:	AIT
23:9	And d not **call** anyone on earth 'father,'	AIT
23:13	You yourselves d not **enter**,	AIT
24:2	"D you **see** all these things?"	AIT
24:23	d not **believe** it.	AIT
24:26	out in the desert,' d not **go out**;	AIT
24:26	in the inner rooms,' d not **believe** it.	AIT
24:42	because you d not **know**	AIT
24:44	at an hour when you d not **expect** him.	AIT
25:13	because you d not **know** the day or the hour.	AIT
25:45	whatever you did not **d** for one of the least	4472
25:45	you did not **d** for me.'	4472
Mt 26:17	"Where d you **want** us	AIT
26:50	d what you **came for**."	AIT
26:53	D you **think** I cannot call on my Father,	AIT
26:65	Why d we **need** any more witnesses?	AIT
26:66	What d you **think**?"	AIT
27:17	"Which one d you **want** me to release	AIT
27:19	"Don't have anything to **d** with	NIG
27:21	the two d you **want** me to release to you?"	AIT
27:22	"What shall I **d**, then, **with**	4472
28:5	"D not be **afraid**,	AIT
28:10	Then Jesus said to them, "D not be **afraid**.	AIT
Mk 1:24	**"What d you want with**	2779+5515
3:4	to **d** good or to do evil,	4472
3:4	to do good or to **d evil**,	2803
4:21	D you **bring** in a lamp to put it under a bowl	AIT
4:40	D you still **have** no faith?"	AIT
5:7	**"What d you want with**	2779+5515
6:5	He could not **d** any miracles there,	4472
6:38	"How many loaves d you **have**?"	AIT
7:3	(The Pharisees and all the Jews d not **eat**	AIT
7:4	from the marketplace they d not **eat**	AIT
7:12	then you no longer let him **d** anything	4472
7:13	And you **d** many things like that."	4472
8:5	"How many loaves d you **have**?"	AIT
8:17	D you still not **see**	AIT
8:18	D you have eyes but fail to **see**,	AIT
8:21	"D you still not **understand**?"	AIT
8:23	Jesus asked, "D you **see** anything?"	AIT
8:27	"Who d people **say** I am?"	AIT
8:29	"Who d you **say** I am?"	AIT
8:33	d not **have in mind**	AIT
9:11	d the teachers of the law **say**	AIT
9:22	But if you can **d** anything,	1538
9:24	the boy's father exclaimed, "I d **believe**;	AIT
9:39	"D not **stop** him," Jesus said.	AIT
10:14	and d not **hinder** them,	AIT
10:17	"what **must I d** to inherit eternal life?"	4472
10:18	"Why d you **call** me good?"	AIT
10:19	'D not **murder**, do not commit adultery,	AIT
10:19	d not **commit adultery**,	AIT
10:19	d not **steal**, do not give false testimony,	AIT
10:19	d not **give false testimony**,	AIT
10:19	do not give false testimony, d not **defraud**,	AIT
10:35	to **d** for us whatever we ask."	4472
10:36	"What d you **want** me to do for you?"	AIT
10:36	"What do you want me to **d** for you?"	4472
10:51	"What d you **want** me to do for you?"	AIT
10:51	"What do you want me to **d** for you?"	4472
11:28	"And who gave you authority to **d** this?"	4472
12:9	then will the owner of the vineyard **d**?	4472
12:24	because you d not **know** the Scriptures or	AIT
13:2	"D you **see** all these great buildings?"	AIT
13:7	d not be **alarmed**.	AIT
13:11	d not **worry** beforehand about	AIT
13:21	d not **believe** it.	AIT
13:33	You d not **know** when that time will come.	AIT
13:35	because you d not **know** when the owner of	AIT
13:36	d not let him find you sleeping.	NIG
14:12	"Where d you **want** us to go	AIT
14:63	"Why d we **need** any more witnesses?"	AIT
14:64	What d you **think**?"	AIT
15:8	The crowd came up and asked Pilate to **d**	4472
15:9	"D you **want** me to release to you the king	AIT
15:12	"What shall I **d**, then, **with**	4472
Lk 1:13	"D not be **afraid**, Zechariah;	AIT
1:30	But the angel said to her, "D not be **afraid**,	AIT
2:10	But the angel said to them, "D not be **afraid**.	AIT
2:27	the parents brought in the child Jesus to **d**	4472
3:8	And d not **begin** to say to yourselves,	AIT
3:10	"What should we **d** then?" the crowd asked.	4472
3:11	the one who has food should **d** the same."	4472
3:12	they asked, "what should we **d**?"	4472
3:14	"And what should we **d**?"	4472
4:12	'D not put the Lord your God **to the test**.' "	AIT
4:23	D here in your hometown what we have heard that you did in Capernaum.' "	4472
4:34	What d you **want with**	2779+5515
5:19	When they could not find a way to **d** this	1662S
5:30	"Why d you **eat and drink**	AIT
5:33	and so **d** the disciples of the Pharisees	3931
6:9	to **d** good or to do evil,	16
6:9	to do good or to **d evil**,	2803
6:11	with one another what they might **d**	4472
6:27	**d good** to those who hate you,	4472
6:29	d not **stop** him from taking	AIT
6:30	d not **demand** it back.	AIT
6:31	D to others as you would have them do	4472
6:31	to others as you would have them **d** to you.	4472
6:33	And if you **d good** to those who are good	16
6:33	Even 'sinners' **d** that.	4472
6:35	But love your enemies, **d good** to them,	16
6:37	"D not **judge**, and you will not be judged.	AIT
6:37	D not **condemn**, and you will not	AIT
6:41	"Why d you **look** at the speck of sawdust	AIT
6:44	People d not **pick** figs from thornbushes,	AIT
6:46	"Why d you **call** me, 'Lord, Lord,'	AIT
6:46	'Lord, Lord,' and d not **do** what I say?	AIT
6:46	'Lord, Lord,' and do not **d** what I say?	4472
7:4	"This man deserves to have you **d** this,	4218
7:6	for I d not **deserve** to have you	AIT
7:8	I say to my servant, '**D this**,'	4472
7:44	"D you **see** this woman?	AIT
8:14	riches and pleasures, and they d not **mature**.	AIT
8:28	**"What d you want with**	2779+5515
9:5	If people d not **welcome** you,	AIT
9:18	"Who d the crowds **say** I am?"	AIT

Lk	9:20	"Who *d* you **say** I am?"	AIT
	9:50	"*D* not **stop** him," Jesus said,	AIT
	9:54	*d* you **want** us to call fire down	AIT
	10: 4	*D* not **take** a purse or bag or sandals;	AIT
	10: 4	and *d* not **greet** anyone on the road.	AIT
	10: 7	*D* not **move around** from house to house.	AIT
	10:20	*d* not **rejoice** that the spirits submit to you,	AIT
	10:25	"what **must** I *d* to inherit eternal life?"	4472
	10:26	"How *d* you **read** it?"	AIT
	10:28	**"D** this and you will live."	4472
	10:36	of these three *d* you **think** was a neighbor to	AIT
	10:37	Jesus told him, "Go and *d* likewise."	4472
	10:40	that my sister has left me *to* **d** the work	1354
	11:19	*d* your followers **drive** them **out?**	AIT
	12: 4	*d* not **be afraid** of those who kill the body	AIT
	12: 4	the body and after that can *d* no more.	4472
	12:11	*d* not **worry** about how you will defend	AIT
	12:17	He thought to himself, 'What **shall** I *d?*	4472
	12:18	"Then he said, 'This is what *I'll* **d.**	4472
	12:22	*d* not **worry** about your life,	AIT
	12:24	Consider the ravens: They *d* not **sow** or reap,	AIT
	12:26	you **cannot** *d* this very little thing,	1538+4028
	12:26	why *d* you **worry** about the rest?	AIT
	12:27	They *d* not **labor** or spin.	AIT
	12:29	*d* not **set** your **heart on** what you will eat	AIT
	12:29	*d* not **worry** about it.	AIT
	12:32	"*D* not **be afraid**, little flock,	AIT
	12:40	at an hour when you *d* not **expect** him."	AIT
	12:47	not *d* what his master wants will be beaten	4472
	12:51	*D* you **think** I came to bring peace on earth?	AIT
	13: 2	Jesus answered, "*D* you **think**	AIT
	13: 4	*d* you **think** they were more guilty than all	AIT
	14: 8	*d* not **take** the place of honor,	AIT
	14:12	*d* not **invite** your friends,	AIT
	14:12	if you *d*, they may invite you back and	3607
	15: 7	over ninety-nine righteous persons who *d* not **need** to repent.	AIT
	16: 3	'What **shall** I *d* now?	4472
	16: 4	I know what *I'll* **d** so that,	4472
	16: 5	'How much *d* you **owe** my master?'	AIT
	16: 7	'And how much *d* you **owe?'**	AIT
	16:31	'If they *d* not **listen** *to* Moses and	AIT
	17: 9	because he did what he *was* **told to d?**	1411
	17:10	you have done everything you *were* **told to d,**	1411
	17:23	*D* not **go running off after** them,	AIT
	18:16	and *d* not **hinder** them,	AIT
	18:18	what **must** I *d* to inherit eternal life?"	4472
	18:19	"Why *d* you **call** me good?"	AIT
	18:20	'*D* not **commit adultery,**	AIT
	18:20	'Do not commit adultery, *d* not **murder,**	AIT
	18:20	*d* not **steal,** do not give false testimony,	AIT
	18:20	*d* not **give false testimony,**	AIT
	18:41	"What *d* you **want** me to do for you?"	AIT
	18:41	"What do you want me to *d* for you?"	4472
	19:48	Yet they could not find any way *to* **d** it,	4472
	20:13	'What **shall** I *d?*	4472
	20:15	then *will* the owner of the vineyard **d**	4472
	20:21	that you *d* not **show partiality** but teach	AIT
	21: 8	*D* not **follow** them.	AIT
	21: 9	*d* not **be frightened.**	AIT
	22: 9	"Where *d* you **want** us to prepare for it?"	AIT
	22:19	*d* this in remembrance of me."	4472
	22:23	of them it might be who would *d* this.	4556
	22:71	"Why *d* we **need** any more testimony?"	AIT
	23:28	Daughters of Jerusalem, *d* not **weep** for me;	AIT
	23:31	if *men* **d** these things when the tree is green,	4472
	23:34	for they *d* not **know** what they are doing."	AIT
	24: 5	"Why *d* you **look for** the living among	AIT
	24:18	to Jerusalem and *d* not **know** the things	AIT
	24:38	and why *d* doubts **rise** in your minds?	AIT
	24:41	"*D* you **have** anything here to eat?"	AIT
Jn	1:22	What *d* you **say** about yourself?"	AIT
	1:25	"Why then *d* you **baptize** if you are not	AIT
	1:26	"but among you stands one you *d* not **know.**	AIT
	1:38	"What *d* you **want?"**	AIT
	1:48	"How *d* you **know** me?"	AIT
	2: 4	Dear woman, **why** *d* you **involve** me?	2779+5515
	2: 5	"*D* whatever he tells you."	4472
	2:18	to prove your authority *to* **d** all this?"	4472
	3:10	"and *d* you not **understand** these things?	AIT
	3:11	still you people *d* not **accept** our testimony.	AIT
	3:12	of earthly things and you *d* not **believe;**	AIT
	4: 9	(For Jews *d* not **associate with** Samaritans.)	AIT
	4:22	Samaritans worship what you *d* not **know;**	AIT
	4:22	we worship what *we* **d know,**	AIT
	4:27	But no one asked, "What *d* you **want?"**	AIT
	4:34	"is to *d* the will of him who sent me and	4472
	4:35	*D* you not **say,** 'Four months more	AIT
	5: 6	he asked him, "*D* you **want** to get well?"	AIT
	5:19	the Son can *d* nothing by himself;	4472
	5:19	he can *d* only what he sees his Father doing,	NIG
	5:28	"*D* not **be amazed** at this,	AIT
	5:30	By myself I can *d* nothing;	4472
	5:38	for you *d* not **believe** the one he sent.	AIT
	5:41	"I *d* not **accept** praise from men,	AIT
	5:42	I know that you *d* not **have** the love of God	AIT
	5:43	and you *d* not **accept** me;	AIT
	5:45	"But *d* not **think** I will accuse you before	AIT
	5:47	But since you *d* not **believe** what he wrote,	AIT
	6: 6	in mind what he was going to *d.*	4472
	6:27	*D* not **work for** food that spoils, but **for**	AIT
	6:28	"What **must** we *d* to do	4472
	6:28	to *d* the works God requires?"	2237
	6:30	What *will* you **d?**	2237
	6:36	and still you *d* not **believe.**	AIT
	6:38	down from heaven not to *d* my will but	4472

Jn	6:38	from heaven not to do my will but to *d*	NIG
	6:64	there are some of you who *d* not **believe."**	AIT
	6:67	"You *d* not **want** to leave too, do you?"	AIT
	6:67	"You do not want to leave too, *d* you?"	NIG
	7: 3	disciples may see the miracles you *d.*	4472
	7:17	If anyone chooses *to* **d** God's will,	4472
	7:28	You *d* not **know** him,	AIT
	7:31	*will* he **d** more miraculous signs than this man?"	4472
	8: 5	Now what *d* you **say?"**	AIT
	8:11	neither *d* I **condemn** you," Jesus declared.	AIT
	8:16	But if I *d* **judge,** my decisions are right,	AIT
	8:19	"You *d* not **know** me or my Father,"	AIT
	8:24	if you *d* not **believe** that I am	AIT
	8:28	and that I *d* nothing on my own	4472
	8:29	for I always *d* what pleases him."	4472
	8:38	and you *d* what you have heard	4472
	8:39	"then *you would* **d** the things Abraham did.	4472
	8:40	Abraham did not *d* such things.	4472
	8:45	I tell the truth, you *d* not **believe** me!	AIT
	8:47	The reason you *d* not **hear** is that you do	AIT
	8:47	not hear is that you *d* not **belong to** God."	AIT
	8:53	Who *d* you **think** you are?"	4472+4932+5515
	8:55	Though *you* **d** not **know** him, I know him.	AIT
	8:55	but *I* **d know** him and keep his word.	AIT
	9: 4	we must *d* the work of him who sent me.	2237
	9:16	can a sinner *d* such miraculous signs?"	AIT
	9:25	One thing I *d* **know.**	AIT
	9:26	they asked him, "What *did* he **d** to you?	4472
	9:27	Why *d* you **want** to hear it again?	AIT
	9:27	*D* you **want** to become his disciples, too?"	AIT
	9:33	he could *d* nothing."	4472
	9:35	"*D* you **believe** in the Son of Man?"	AIT
	10: 5	from him because *they* **d** not **recognize**	AIT
	10:25	"I did tell you, but *you* **d** not **believe.**	AIT
	10:25	The miracles I *d* in my Father's name speak	4472
	10:26	but you *d* not **believe** because you are	AIT
	10:32	For which of these *d* you **stone** me?"	AIT
	10:36	Why then *d* you **accuse** me of blasphemy	AIT
	10:37	*D* not **believe** me	AIT
	10:37	unless I *d* what my Father does.	4472
	10:38	But if I *d* it, even though you do not believe	4472
	10:38	I do it, even though you *d* not **believe** me,	AIT
	11:26	*D* you **believe** this?"	AIT
	11:50	You *d* not **realize** that it is better for you	AIT
	11:56	"What *d* you **think?**	AIT
	12:15	"*D* not **be afraid,** O Daughter of Zion;	AIT
	12:47	I *d* not **judge** him.	AIT
	13: 7	"You *d* not **realize** now what I am doing,	AIT
	13:12	"*D* you **understand** what I have done	AIT
	13:15	that you *should* **d** as I have done for you.	4472
	13:17	you will be blessed if *you* **d** them.	4472
	13:27	"What you are about to *d,* do quickly,"	4472
	13:27	"What you are about to do, *d* quickly,"	4472
	14: 1	"*D* not **let** your hearts *be* **troubled.**	AIT
	14: 7	you *d* **know** him and have seen him."	4472
	14:12	in me *will* **d** what I have been doing.	4472
	14:12	He *will* **d** even greater things than these,	4472
	14:13	I *will* **d** whatever you ask in my name,	4472
	14:14	and I *will* **d** it.	4472
	14:22	why *d* you **intend** to show yourself to us	AIT
	14:27	I *d* not **give** to you as the world gives.	AIT
	14:27	*D* not **let** your hearts *be* **troubled**	AIT
	14:27	be troubled and *d* not **be afraid.**	AIT
	14:31	I *d* exactly what my Father has commanded me.	4472
	15: 5	apart from me you can *d* nothing.	4472
	15:14	if you *d* what I command.	4472
	15:19	As it is, you *d* not **belong to** the world,	AIT
	15:21	for they *d* not **know** the One who sent me.	AIT
	16: 3	They *will* **d** such things because they have	4472
	16: 3	because *men* **d** not **believe** in me;	AIT
	16:30	and that you *d* not even **need**	AIT
	17: 4	by completing the work you gave me to *d.*	4472
	18:39	*D* you **want** me to release 'the king of	AIT
	19: 9	"Where *d* you **come from?"**	AIT
	19:10	"*D* you **refuse** *to* **speak**	AIT
	19:21	"*D* not **write** 'The King of the Jews,'	AIT
	20:17	"*D* not **hold on to** me,	AIT
	20:23	if you *d* not **forgive** them,	AIT
	21:15	*d* you **truly love** me more than these?"	AIT
	21:16	"Simon son of John, *d* you **truly love** me?"	AIT
	21:17	"Simon son of John, *d* you **love** me?"	AIT
	21:17	"*D* you **love** me?"	AIT
	21:18	and lead you where *you* **d** not **want** to go."	AIT
Ac	1: 1	about all that Jesus began *to* **d** and to teach	4472
	1: 4	"*D* not **leave** Jerusalem,	AIT
	1:11	"why *d* you **stand** here looking into	AIT
	2:37	"Brothers, what **shall** we *d?"**	4472
	3: 6	Peter said, "Silver or gold I *d* not **have,**	AIT
	3:12	Why *d* you **stare at** us as if	AIT
	4: 7	or what name *did* you **d** this?"	4472
	4:16	"What *are* we **going to d** with these men?"	4472
	4:25	'Why *d* the nations **rage** and	AIT
	5:35	consider carefully what you intend *to* **d**	4556
	7:26	why *d* you **want** to **hurt** each other?'	AIT
	7:28	*D* you **want** to kill me as you killed	AIT
	7:60	"Lord, *d* not **hold** this sin against them."	AIT
	8:30	"*D* you **understand** what you are reading?"	AIT
	9: 4	"Saul, Saul, why *d* you **persecute** me?"	AIT
	9: 6	and you will be told what you must *d.*	4472
	10:15	"*D* not **call** anything **impure**	AIT
	10:20	*D* not **hesitate** to go with them,	AIT
	11: 9	and *d* what is right,	2237
	11: 9	'*D* not **call** anything **impure**	AIT
	13:22	he *will* **d** everything I want him to do.'	4472
	13:22	he will do everything I want him to *d.'*	NIG

Ac	13:25	'Who *d* you **think** I am?	AIT
	13:41	for I *am going to* **d** something in your days	2237
	13:46	and *d* not **consider** yourselves worthy	AIT
	14: 3	by enabling them to *d* miraculous signs	1181
	15:10	*d* you try *to* **test** God	AIT
	15:29	You *will* **d** well to avoid these things.	4556
	16:30	"Sirs, what must I *d* to be saved?"	4472
	16:37	*d* they **want** to **get rid of** us quietly?"	AIT
	18: 9	"*D* not **be afraid,**	AIT
	18: 9	keep on speaking, *d* not **be silent.**	AIT
	19:36	to be quiet and not *d* anything rash.	4556
	21:22	**What shall we d?**	1639+4036+5515
	21:23	so *d* what we tell you.	4472
	21:37	"*D* you **speak** Greek?"	AIT
	22: 7	Why *d* you **persecute** me?	AIT
	22:10	" 'What **shall** I *d,* Lord?"	4472
	22:10	that you have been assigned *to* **d.'**	4472
	22:26	"What are you going to *d?"**	4472
	23: 5	'*D* not **speak** evil **about** the ruler	AIT
	23:29	that the accusation had to *d* with questions	4309
	25: 9	Festus, wishing *to* **d** the Jews a favor,	2960
	25:11	I *d* not **refuse** to die.	AIT
	26: 9	"I too was convinced that I ought *to* **d** all	4556
	26:14	'Saul, Saul, why *d* you **persecute** me?	AIT
	26:27	King Agrippa, *d* you **believe** the prophets?	AIT
	26:27	I know you *d."*	4409S
	26:28	"*D* you **think** that in such a short time	NIG
	27:24	'*D* not **be afraid,** Paul.	AIT
Ro	1:13	I *d* not **want** you to be unaware, brothers,	AIT
	1:28	*to* **d** what ought not to be done.	4472
	1:32	that those who *d* such things deserve death,	4556
	1:32	not only *continue to* **d** these very things,	4472
	2: 1	you who pass judgment *d* the same things.	4556
	2: 2	against those who *d* such things is based	4556
	2: 3	on them and yet *d* the same things,	4472
	2: 3	*d* you **think** you will escape God's judgment?	AIT
	2: 4	*d* you **show contempt for**	AIT
	2:14	when Gentiles, who *d* not **have** the law,	AIT
	2:14	*d* by nature things required by the law,	4472
	2:14	*even though they* **d** not **have** the law,	4472
	2:21	who teach others, *d* you not **teach** yourself?	AIT
	2:21	against stealing, *d* you **steal?**	AIT
	2:22	*d* you **commit adultery?**	AIT
	2:22	You who abhor idols, *d* you **rob temples?**	AIT
	2:23	*d* you **dishonor** God by breaking the law?	AIT
	3: 8	"*Let us* **d** evil that good may result"?	4472
	3:17	and the way of peace they *d* not **know."**	AIT
	3:31	*D* we, then, **nullify** the law by this faith?	AIT
	4:21	*to* **d** what he had promised.	4472
	6:12	*d* not **let** sin **reign** in your mortal body	AIT
	6:13	*D* not **offer** the parts of your body to sin,	AIT
	7: 1	*D* you **not know,** brothers—	AIT
	7: 7	if the law had not said, "*D* not **covet."**	AIT
	7:15	I *d* not **understand** what I do.	AIT
	7:15	I do not understand what I *d.*	2981
	7:15	For what I want to do I *d* not **do,**	NIG
	7:15	For what I want to do I *d* not **do,**	AIT
	7:15	For what I want to do I *do* not **do,**	4556
	7:15	but what I hate I *d.*	4472
	7:16	And if I *d* what I do not want to do,	4472
	7:16	And if I do what I do not want to *d,*	AIT
	7:16	And if I do what I do not want to *d,*	NIG
	7:17	As it is, it is no longer myself who *d* it,	2981
	7:18	For I have the desire *to* **d** what is good,	NIG
	7:19	For what I *d* is not the good I want to do;	4472
	7:19	For what I do is not the good I want to *d;*	NIG
	7:19	no, the evil I *d* not **want** to do—	AIT
	7:19	no, the evil I do not want to *d—*	NIG
	7:20	Now if I *d* what I do not want to do,	4472
	7:20	Now if I do what I *d* not **want** to do,	AIT
	7:20	Now if I do what I do not want to *d,*	NIG
	7:20	it is no longer I who *d* it,	2981
	7:21	When I want to *d* good,	4472
	8: 3	For what the law was powerless *to* **d** in	NIG
	8: 4	who *d* not **live** according to	NIG
	8: 7	nor can it *d* so.	NIG
	8:25	But if we hope for what *we* **d** not yet **have,**	AIT
	8:26	*We* **d** not **know** what we ought to pray for,	AIT
	10: 6	"*D* not **say** in your heart,	AIT
	11:18	*d* not **boast over** those branches.	AIT
	11:18	If you *d,* consider this:	NIG
	11:18	You *d* not **support** the root,	AIT
	11:20	*D* not **be arrogant,** but be afraid.	AIT
	11:23	And if they *d* not **persist in** unbelief,	AIT
	11:25	I *d* not **want** you to be ignorant	AIT
	12: 2	*D* not **conform** *any longer* **to the pattern of**	AIT
	12: 3	*D* not **think** of yourself more **highly**	AIT
	12: 4	and these members *d* not all have	AIT
	12: 8	it is showing mercy, let him *d* it cheerfully.	NIG
	12:14	bless and *d* not **curse.**	AIT
	12:16	*D* not **be proud.**	AIT
	12:16	*D* not **be conceited.**	AIT
	12:17	*D* not **repay** anyone evil for evil.	AIT
	12:17	to *d* what is right in the eyes of everybody.	NIG
	12:19	*D* not **take revenge,** my friends,	AIT
	12:21	*D* not **be overcome** by evil,	AIT
	13: 2	and those who *d* so will bring judgment	468S
	13: 3	rulers hold no terror *for* those who *d* right,	2240
	13: 3	but *for* those who **wrong.**	NIG
	13: 3	*D* you **want** to be free from fear of the one	AIT
	13: 3	*d* what is right and he will commend you.	4472
	13: 4	For he is God's servant to *d* you good.	NIG
	13: 4	But if you *d* **wrong,** be afraid,	4472
	13: 9	"*D* not **commit adultery,"**	AIT
	13: 9	"*D* not **murder,"**	AIT
	13: 9	"*D* not **steal,"**	AIT

Ro	13: 9	"Do not steal," "D not **covet**,"	AIT
	13:11	And **d** this, understanding the present time.	NIG
	13:14	and **d** not **think about** how to gratify	AIT
	14:10	You, then, why **d** you **judge** your brother?	AIT
	14:10	**d** you **look down on**	AIT
	14:15	**D** not by your eating **destroy**	AIT
	14:16	**D** not *allow* what you consider good *to be* **spoken of as evil.**	AIT
	14:19	therefore make every effort to **d** what leads	NIG
	14:20	**D** not **destroy** the work of God for the sake	AIT
	14:21	or drink wine or to **d** anything else	NIG
	15:24	I plan to **d** so when I go to Spain.	NIG
	15:27	They were pleased to **d** it,	NIG
	16:21	**sends** *his* **greetings to** you, as **d**	AIT
1Co	1: 7	Therefore you **d** not **lack** any spiritual gift	AIT
	2: 6	*We* **d**, however, **speak** a message of wisdom	AIT
	3:18	**D** not **deceive** yourselves.	AIT
	4: 3	indeed, *I* **d** not even **judge** myself.	AIT
	4: 6	"**D** not go beyond what is written."	NIG
	4: 7	What *d* you **have** that you did not receive?	AIT
	4: 7	why *d* you **boast** as though you did not?	AIT
	4:15	you **d** not have many fathers,	NIG
	4:21	What *d* you **prefer?**	AIT
	5:11	**With** such a man *d* not even **eat.**	AIT
	6: 2	*D* you not **know** that the saints will judge	AIT
	6: 3	*D* you not **know** that we will judge angels?	AIT
	6: 8	Instead, *you* yourselves cheat and **d wrong,**	92
	6: 8	and *you* **d** this to your brothers.	NIG
	6: 9	*D* you not **know** that the wicked will	AIT
	6: 9	*D* not be **deceived:**	AIT
	6:15	*D* you not **know** that the wicked will not	AIT
	6:16	*D* you not **know** that he who unites himself	AIT
	6:19	*D* you not **know** that your body is a temple	AIT
	7: 5	*D* not **deprive** each other except	AIT
	7:15	But if the unbeliever leaves, *let him do* **so.**	6004S
	7:16	How *d* you **know**, wife,	AIT
	7:16	Or, how *d* you **know**, husband,	AIT
	7:21	if you can gain your freedom, **d so.**	3437+5968
	7:23	*d* not **become** slaves of men.	AIT
	7:27	Are you married? *D* not **seek** a divorce.	AIT
	7:27	Are you unmarried? *D* not **look for** a wife.	AIT
	7:28	But if you *d* **marry,** you have not sinned;	AIT
	7:36	he should **d** as he wants.	4472
	8: 8	we are no worse if *we* **d** not **eat,**	AIT
	8: 8	and no better if *we* **d.**	2266S
	9: 5	as **d** the other apostles and	NIG
	9: 8	*D* I **say** this merely from a human point	AIT
	9: 9	"**D** not **muzzle** an ox while it is treading out	AIT
	9:10	to **d** so in the hope of sharing in the harvest.	NIG
	9:15	in the hope that you *will* **d** such things	1181
	9:16	Woe to me if *I* **d** not **preach the gospel!**	AIT
	9:23	*I* **d** all this for the sake of the gospel,	4472
	9:24	*D* you not **know** that in a race all	AIT
	9:25	They **d** it to get a crown that will not last;	NIG
	9:25	we **d** it to get a crown that will last forever.	NIG
	9:26	*I* **d** not **run** like a man running aimlessly;	AIT
	9:26	*I* **d** not **fight** like a man beating the air.	AIT
	10: 1	*I* **d** not **want** you to be ignorant of the fact,	AIT
	10: 7	*D* not be **idolaters**, as some of them were;	AIT
	10:10	And *d* not **grumble**, as some of them did—	AIT
	10:18	*D* not those who eat the sacrifices **participate** in the altar?	AIT
	10:19	*D* I **mean** then that a sacrifice offered to	AIT
	10:20	and *I* **d** not **want** you to be participants	AIT
	10:28	then **d** not **eat** it.	AIT
	10:31	or drink or whatever *you* **d,**	4472
	10:31	**d** it all for the glory of God.	4472
	10:32	**D** not cause anyone to stumble,	1181
	11:16	nor **d** the churches of God.	NIG
	11:17	for your meetings **d** more harm than good.	NIG
	11:22	Or *d* you **despise** the church of God	AIT
	11:24	**d** this in remembrance of me."	4472
	11:25	**d** this, whenever you drink it,	4472
	12: 1	brothers, *I* **d** not **want** you to be ignorant.	AIT
	12:15	*I* **d** not **belong to the body,"**	1639
	12:16	*I* **d** not **belong to the body,"**	1639
	12:29	**D** all work miracles?	NIG
	12:30	**D** all have gifts of healing?	NIG
	12:30	**D** all speak in tongues?	NIG
	12:30	**D** all interpret?	NIG
	14:11	It then *I* **d** not **grasp the meaning**	AIT
	14:15	So what *shall* I **d?**	1639
	14:16	among **those who** *d* not **understand**	2626
	14:23	and **some who** *d* not **understand**	2626
	14:39	and *d* not **forbid** speaking in tongues.	AIT
	15: 9	For I am the least of the apostles and *I* **d** not	1639
	15:29	what *will* those **d** who are baptized for	4472
	15:30	why *d* we **endanger** ourselves every hour?	AIT
	15:33	**D** not be **misled:**	AIT
	15:37	*you* **d** not **plant** the body that will be,	AIT
	16: 1	**D** what I told the Galatian churches to do.	4472
	16: 1	Do what I told the Galatian churches to **d.**	NIG
	16: 7	*I* **d** not **want** to see you now and make only	AIT
	16:14	**D** everything in love.	1181
2Co	1: 8	*We* **d** not **want** you to be uninformed,	AIT
	1:13	*we* **d** not **write** you anything you cannot read	AIT
	1:17	When I planned this, *did I* **d** it lightly?	5968
	1:17	Or *d* I **make** *my* **plans** in a worldly manner	AIT
	2:17	*we* **d** not peddle the word of God for profit.	1639
	3: 1	Or *d* we **need**, like some people,	AIT
	4: 1	*we* **d** not **lose heart.**	AIT
	4: 2	we **d** not **use deception,**	AIT
	4: 2	nor *d* we **distort** the word of God.	AIT
	4: 5	For *we* **d** not **preach** ourselves,	AIT
	4:16	Therefore *we* **d** not **lose heart.**	AIT
	5: 4	because *we* **d** not **wish** to be unclothed but	AITS
	5:16	*we* **d** so no longer.	1182S

2Co	6:14	*D* not **be** yoked together with unbelievers.	AIT
	6:14	For what **d** righteousness	NIG
	7: 3	*I* **d** not **say** this to condemn you;	AIT
	7: 8	*I* **d** not **regret** it.	AIT
	8:10	to give but also to have the desire to **d** so.	NIG
	8:11	to **d** it may be matched by your completion	NIG
	8:21	For we are taking pains to **d** what is right,	NIG
	10: 3	*we* **d** not **wage war** as the world does.	AIT
	10: 9	*I* **d** not **dare** to classify	AIT
	10:12	*We* **d** not **dare** to classify	AIT
	10:15	Neither *d* we go beyond our limits	AIT
	10:16	*d* not *want* to **boast about**	AIT
	11: 5	But *I* **d** not **think** I am in the least inferior	AIT
	11: 6	but *I* **d** have knowledge.	NIG
	11: 9	and will *continue* to **d** so.	5498S
	11:11	Because *I* **d** not **love** you?	AIT
	11:11	God knows *I* **d!**	NIG
	11:16	But if you **d,**	1145+3590S
	11:16	so that I *may* **d** a little **boasting.**	AIT
	11:29	Who is weak, and *I* **d** not **feel weak?**	AIT
	11:29	and I *d* not inwardly **burn?**	AIT
	12: 2	in the body or out of the body *I* **d** not **know**	AIT
	12: 3	the body *I* **d** not **know**, but God knows—	AIT
	12: 6	of me than is warranted by what I **d** or say.	1063S
	12:19	and everything we **d,** dear friends,	NIG
	13: 5	*D* you not **realize** that Christ Jesus is	AIT
	13: 7	to God that you *will* **d** not anything wrong.	4472
	13: 7	the test but that you *will* **d** what is right	4472
	13: 8	For *we* **cannot d** anything against the truth,	1538+4024
Gal	2:10	the very thing I was eager *to* **d.**	4472
	2:21	*I* **d** not **set aside** the grace of God,	AIT
	3:10	not continue *to* **d** everything written in	4472
	3:17	by God and thus **d away with** the promise.	2934
	4: 9	*D* you wish to be enslaved by them all	AIT
	5: 1	*d* not *let yourselves* be **burdened**	AIT
	5:13	But **d** not use your freedom to indulge	NIG
	5:17	so that you *d* not **do** what you want.	AIT
	5:17	so that *you* do not **d** what you want.	4472
	6: 7	**D** not be **deceived:** God cannot be mocked.	AIT
	6: 9	a harvest *if we* **d** not **give up.**	AIT
	6:10	let *us* **d** good to all people,	2237
Eph	2:10	created in Christ Jesus to **d** good works,	NIG
	2:10	God prepared in advance for *us to* **d.**	4344
	3:20	to **d** immeasurably more than all we ask	4472
	4:17	you must no longer live as the Gentiles **d,**	NIG
	4:26	"In your anger *d* not **sin":**	AIT
	4:26	**D** not **let** the sun **go down**	AIT
	4:27	and *d* not **give** the devil a foothold.	AIT
	4:29	**D** not *let* any unwholesome talk **come out**	AIT
	4:30	And *d* not **grieve** the Holy Spirit of God,	AIT
	5: 7	Therefore *d* not be **partners** with them.	AIT
	5:11	**Have nothing to d with** the fruitless deeds	5170
	5:12	to mention what the disobedient **d** in secret.	1181
	5:17	Therefore *d* not be **foolish,**	AIT
	5:18	**D** not **get drunk** on wine,	AIT
	6: 4	Fathers, *d* not **exasperate** your children;	AIT
	6: 9	**D** not **threaten** them,	AIT
Php	1:16	The latter **d** so in love,	NIG
	1:22	*I* **d** not **know!**	AIT
	2: 3	**D** nothing out of selfish ambition	NIG
	2:14	**D** everything without complaining	4472
	3: 2	those men who **d** evil,	2239
	3:13	*I* **d** not **consider** myself yet	AIT
	3:13	But one thing *I* **d;**	NIG
	4: 6	**D** not be **anxious about**	AIT
	4:13	*I* can **d** everything through him who gives	2710
Col	2:16	*d* not *let* anyone **judge** you by what	AIT
	2:18	**D** not *let* anyone who delights in false humility and the worship of angels **disqualify** you **for the prize.**	AIT
	2:20	*d* you **submit** to its **rules:**	AIT
	2:21	"**D** not **handle!**	AIT
	2:21	**D** not **taste!**	AIT
	2:21	**D** not **touch!"?**	AIT
	3: 9	**D** not **lie** to each other,	AIT
	3:17	And whatever *you* **d,**	4472
	3:17	**d** it all in the name of the Lord Jesus,	NIG
	3:19	love your wives and *d* not be **harsh**	AIT
	3:21	Fathers, *d* not **embitter** your children,	AIT
	3:22	and **d** it, not only when their eye is on you	NIG
	3:23	Whatever *you* **d,** work at it	4472
1Th	1: 8	*we* **d** not **need** to say anything about it,	AIT
	4: 1	**d** this more and more.	3437+4355
	4: 5	who **d** not **know** God;	AIT
	4: 9	about brotherly love *we* **d** not **need** to write	AIT
	4:10	you **d** love all the brothers	AIT
	4:10	**d** so more and more.	3437+4355
	4:13	*we* **d** not **want** you to be ignorant	AIT
	5: 1	about times and dates *we* **d** not **need** to write	AIT
	5: 5	*d* not **belong to** the night or to	AIT
	5:19	**D** not **put out** the Spirit's fire;	AIT
	5:20	*d* not **treat** prophecies **with contempt.**	AIT
	5:24	and he *will* **d** it.	4472
2Th	1: 8	He will punish those who *d* not **know** God	AIT
	1: 8	and *d* not **obey** the gospel of our Lord Jesus.	AIT
	2: 7	now holds it back will continue to **d** so	NIG
	3: 4	*to* **d** the things we command.	4472
	3: 9	*we* **d** not **have** the right to such help,	AIT
	3:14	*D* not **associate with** him,	AIT
	3:15	Yet *d* not **regard** him as an enemy,	AIT
1Ti	1: 7	but *they* **d** not **know** what they are talking	AIT
	2:12	*I* **d** not **permit** a woman to teach or	AIT
	4: 7	*Have* **nothing to d** with godless myths	4148
	4:14	**D** not **neglect** your gift,	AIT

1Ti	4:16	Persevere in them, because *if you* **d,**	4472
	5: 1	*D* not **rebuke** an older man **harshly,**	AIT
	5:11	*d* not put them **on such a list.**	AIT
	5:13	And not only *d* they become idlers,	NIG
	5:18	"**D** not **muzzle** the ox while it is treading	AIT
	5:19	**D** not **entertain** an accusation against	AIT
	5:21	and *to* **d** nothing out of favoritism.	4472
	5:22	**D** not be hasty in the **laying on of**	AIT
	5:22	and *d* not **share** in the sins of others.	AIT
	6:18	Command them *to* **d good,**	14
2Ti	1: 8	*d* not *be* **ashamed** to testify about our Lord,	AIT
	2:15	**D** *your* **best** to present yourself to God	5079
	2:21	and prepared **to d** any good work.	1650
	2:23	**Don't have anything to d with** foolish	4148
	2:26	who has taken them captive to **d** his will.	1650
	3: 5	**Have nothing to d with** them.	706
	4: 5	**d** the work of an evangelist,	4472
	4: 9	**D** *your* **best** to come to me quickly,	5079
	4:21	**D** *your* **best** to get here before winter.	5079
	4:21	Eubulus greets you, and so **d** Pudens,	NIG
Tit	1:15	who are corrupted and **d** not believe,	NIG
	2:14	eager *to* **d** what is good.	2240
	2:15	**D** not *let* anyone **despise** you.	AIT
	3: 1	to be ready to **d** whatever is good,	2240
	3:10	After that, *have* **nothing to d with** him.	4148
	3:12	**d** *your* **best** to come to me at Nicopolis,	5079
	3:13	**D** everything you can to **help** Zenas the lawyer and Apollos **on** *their* **way**	AIT
Phm	1: 8	be bold and order you to **d** what you ought	NIG
	1: 8	to do **what you ought to d,**	465+3836
	1:14	to **d** anything without your consent,	4472
	1:14	so that any favor you **d** will be spontaneous	NIG
	1:20	*I* **d wish,** brother, *that I may have* some **benefit** from you	AIT
	1:21	that *you will* **d** even more than I ask.	4472
	1:24	And so **d** Mark, Aristarchus,	NIG
Heb	2: 1	so that *we* **d** not **drift away.**	AIT
	2: 8	at present *we* **d** not **see** everything subject	AIT
	3: 8	*d* not **harden** your hearts as you did in	AIT
	3:15	*d* not **harden** your hearts as you did in	AIT
	4: 7	*d* not **harden** your hearts."	AIT
	4:15	For *we* **d** not **have** a high priest who is	AIT
	6: 3	And God permitting, *we will* **d** so.	4472
	6:12	*We* **d** not want you to become lazy,	NIG
	8: 1	*We* **d have** such a high priest,	AIT
	9:26	at the end of the ages to **d away** with sin by	120
	10: 7	I have come to **d** your will, O God.' "	4472
	10: 9	"Here I am, I have come to **d** your will."	4472
	10:29	How much more severely *d* you **think**	AIT
	10:35	So **d** not **throw away** your confidence;	AIT
	11: 1	for and certain of what *we* **d** not **see.**	AIT
	11:29	but *when* the Egyptians **tried to d** so,	3284+4272
	11:32	*I* **d** not **have** time to tell about Gideon,	AIT
	12: 5	*d* not **make light of** the Lord's discipline,	AIT
	12: 5	and *d* not **lose heart** when he rebukes you,	AIT
	12:25	to it that *you* **d** not **refuse** him who speaks.	AIT
	13: 2	**D** not **forget** to entertain strangers,	AIT
	13: 6	What *can* man **d** to me?"	4472
	13: 9	**D** not be **carried away**	AIT
	13:14	For here *we* **d** not **have** an enduring city,	AIT
	13:16	And *d* not **forget** to do good and to share	AIT
	13:16	And do not forget to **d** good and to share	2343
Jas	1:22	**D** not merely listen to the word,	NIG
	1:22	**D** what it says.	1181+4475
	1:23	the word but does not **d** what it says is like	4475
	1:25	and continues to **d** this,	NIG
	2:11	"**D** not **commit adultery,"**	AIT
	2:11	also said, "**D** not **murder."**	AIT
	2:11	*d* not **commit adultery**	AIT
	2:11	not commit adultery but *d* **commit murder,**	AIT
	2:18	and I will show you my faith by what I **d.**	2240
	2:20	*d* you **want** evidence that faith	AIT
	3:14	*d* not **boast** about it or deny the truth.	AIT
	4: 2	*You* **d** not **have,**	AIT
	4: 2	because you *d* not **ask** God.	AIT
	4: 3	When you ask, *you* **d** not **receive,**	AIT
	4: 5	Or *d* you **think** Scripture says	AIT
	4:11	Brothers, *d* not **slander** one another.	AIT
	4:14	you *d* not even **know** what will happen tomorrow.	AIT
	4:15	we will live and **d** this or that."	4472
	4:17	the good *he ought to* **d** and doesn't do it,	4472
	4:17	the good he ought to do and doesn't **d** it,	4472
	5:12	*d* not **swear**—not by heaven	AIT
1Pe	1: 8	and *even though you* **d** not **see** him now,	AIT
	1:14	*d* not **conform** to the evil desires you had	AIT
	1:15	so be holy in all you **d;**	419
	2: 7	But to those who **d** not believe,	NIG
	2:14	by him to **punish** *those who* **d wrong**	2804
	2:14	and to commend *those who* **d right.**	18
	2:16	*d* not *use* your freedom as a **cover-up**	AIT
	3: 1	if any of them *d* **not believe** the word,	578
	3: 6	*if you* **d** what is right and do not give way	16
	3: 6	*d* not give way to **fear.**	AIT
	3: 9	**D** not **repay** evil with evil or insult	AIT
	3:11	He must turn from evil and **d good;**	4472
	3:12	the face of the Lord is against **those who d** evil."	4472
	3:13	to harm you if you are eager to **d** good?	NIG
	3:14	"**D** not **fear** what they fear;	AIT
	3:14	*d* not be **frightened."**	AIT
	3:15	But **d** this with gentleness and respect,	NIG
	4: 3	in the past doing what pagans choose to **d**—	NIG
	4: 4	that *you* **d** not **plunge** with them into	AIT
	4:11	he should **d** it as one speaking	NIG
	4:11	he should **d** it with the strength God	NIG
	4:12	*d* not be **surprised** at the painful trial	AIT

1Pe	4:16	you suffer as a Christian, *d* not **be ashamed**,	AIT
	4:17	the outcome be *for* those who *d* **not obey**	AIT
	4:19	and continue to **d** good.	17
2Pe	1:10	For *if you* **d** these things,	4472
	1:19	and you *will* **d** well to pay attention to it,	4472
	2:11	*d* not **bring** slanderous accusations	AIT
	2:12	in matters *they* **d** **not understand**.	AIT
	3: 8	*d* not **forget** this one thing, dear friends:	AIT
	3:16	as they **d** the other Scriptures,	NIG
1Jn	1: 6	we lie and *d* not **live by** the truth.	
	2: 4	but *does* not **d** what he commands is a liar,	5498
	2:15	*D* not **love** the world or anything in	AIT
	2:21	*I* **d** not **write** to you because you do	AIT
	2:21	to you because *you* **d** not **know** the truth,	AIT
	2:21	but because *you* **d** not **understand.**	AIT
	2:27	and *you* **d** not **need** anyone to teach you.	AIT
	3: 7	*d* not **let** anyone **lead** you **astray.**	AIT
	3:10	Anyone who *does* not **d** what is right is not	4472
	3:12	*D* not **be like Cain,**	NIG
	3:13	*D* not *be* **surprised,** my brothers.	AIT
	3:21	Dear friends, if our hearts **d** not **condemn** us,	AIT
	3:22	and **d** what pleases him.	4472
	4: 1	Dear friends, *d* not **believe** every spirit,	AIT
	4:18	because fear has to **d** with punishment.	NIG
2Jn	1: 7	who *d* not **acknowledge** Jesus Christ	AIT
	1: 8	that *you* **d** not **lose** what you have worked	AIT
	1:10	*d* not **take** him into your house	AIT
	1:12	but *I* **d** not **want** to use paper and ink.	AIT
3Jn	1: 6	*You will* **d** well to send them on their way	4472
	1: 9	*will* **have** nothing to **d** with us.	AIT
	1:10	to **d** so and puts them out of the church.	NIG
	1:11	*d* not **imitate** what is evil but what is good.	AIT
	1:13	but *I* **d** not **want** to do so with pen and ink.	AIT
	1:13	but I do not want *to* **d** so with pen and ink.	1211S
Jude	1:10	against whatever *they* **d** not **understand,**	AIT
	1:10	what things *they* **d** **understand** by instinct,	AIT
	1:19	and *d* not **have the Spirit.**	AIT
Rev	1:17	"*D* not *be* **afraid.**	AIT
	2: 5	Repent and **d** the things you did at first.	4472
	2: 5	If *you* **d** not **repent,**	AIT
	2:10	*D* not *be* **afraid of** what you are about to suffer.	AIT
	2:24	to you who *d* not **hold to** her teaching	AIT
	3: 3	But if *you* **d** not **wake up,**	AIT
	3:17	I have acquired wealth and *d* not **need**	AIT
	3:17	*you* **d** not **realize** that you are wretched,	AIT
	5: 5	one of the elders said to me, "*D* not **weep!**	AIT
	6: 6	and *d* not **damage** the oil and the wine!"	AIT
	7: 3	"**D** not **harm** the land or the sea or the trees	92
	10: 4	*d* not **write** it **down.**"	AIT
	11: 2	exclude the outer court; *d* not **measure** it,	AIT
	13:14	of the signs he was given power *to* **d**	4472
	19:10	But he said to me, "*D* not **do it!**	AIT
	19:10	But he said to me, "*Do* not **d it!**	3972S
	22: 9	But he said to me, "*D* not **do it!**	AIT
	22: 9	But he said to me, "*Do* not **d it!**	3972S
	22:10	"*D* not **seal up** the words of the prophecy	AIT
	22:11	Let him who does wrong continue *to* **d** **wrong;**	92
	22:11	let him who does right continue *to* **d** right;	4472

DO-NOTHING (1) [DO, NOTHING]

Isa	30: 7	Therefore I call her Rahab the **D.**	8700

DOCTOR (4) [DOCTORS]

Mt	9:12	"It is not the healthy who need a **d,**	2620
Mk	2:17	"It is not the healthy who need a **d,**	2620
Lk	5:31	"It is not the healthy who need a **d,**	2620
Col	4:14	Our dear friend Luke, the **d,**	2620

DOCTORS (1) [DOCTOR]

Mk	5:26	a great deal under the care *of* many **d**	2620

DOCTRINE (5) [DOCTRINES]

1Ti	1:10	for whatever else is contrary *to* the sound **d**	1436
	4:16	Watch your life and **d** closely.	1436
2Ti	4: 3	when men will not put up with sound **d.**	1436
Tit	1: 9	so that he can encourage others by sound **d**	1436
	2: 1	in accord *with* sound **d.**	1436

DOCTRINES (2) [DOCTRINE]

1Ti	1: 3	not *to* **teach false d** any longer	2281
	6: 3	If anyone **teaches false d** and does	2281

DOCUMENT (1) [DOCUMENTS]

Est	8: 8	for no **d** written in the king's name	4181

DOCUMENTS (1) [DOCUMENT]

Jer	32:14	Take these **d,** both the sealed	6219

DODAI (3)

2Sa	23: 9	to him was Eleazar son of **D** the Ahohite.	1862
1Ch	11:12	to him was Eleazar son of **D** the Ahohite,	1862
	27: 4	of the division for the second month was **D**	1862

DODAVAHU (1)

2Ch	20:37	Eliezer son of **D** of Mareshah prophesied	1845

DODO (3)

Jdg	10: 1	the son of **D,** rose to save Israel.	1861
2Sa	23:24	Elhanan son of **D** *from* Bethlehem,	1861
1Ch	11:26	Elhanan son of **D** from Bethlehem,	1861

DOE (5) [DOES]

Ge	49:21	a **d** set free that bears beautiful fawns.	387
Job	39: 1	Do you watch when the **d** bears her fawn?	387
Ps	22: T	To [the tune of] "The **D** *of* the Morning."	387
Pr	5:19	A loving **d,** a graceful deer—	387
Jer	14: 5	the **d** in the field deserts her newborn fawn	387

DOEG (6)

1Sa	21: 7	he was **D** the Edomite,	1795
	22: 9	But **D** the Edomite,	1795
	22:18	The king then ordered **D,**	1795
	22:18	So **D** the Edomite turned	1795
	22:22	"That day, when **D** the Edomite was there,	1795
Ps	52: T	When **D** the Edomite had gone to Saul	1795

DOES (582) [DO, DOE]

Ge	31:15	*D* he not **regard** *us as* foreigners?	AIT
	39: 8	"my master *d* not **concern** *himself*	AIT
	44: 7	"Why *d* my lord **say** such things?	AIT
Ex	4: 3	why the bush *d* not **burn up.**"	AIT
	8:29	*d* not **act** deceitfully	AIT
	11: 1	and when he **d,** he will drive you out	8938S
	12:26	'What **d** this ceremony mean to you?'	NIH
	13:14	'What **d** this mean?'	NIH
	21: 8	If she *d* not **please** the master	AIT
	21:11	If *he* **d** not **provide** her with these three	AIT
	21:13	*d* not **do** it intentionally,	AIT
	21:18	with his fist and *he* **d** not **die** but is confined	AIT
	31:14	whoever *d* any work on that day must	6913
	31:15	Whoever **d** any work on	6913
	33:15	"If your Presence *d* not **go** with us,	AIT
	34: 7	*d* not **leave the guilty unpunished;**	AIT
	35: 2	Whoever *d* any work on it must be put	6913
Lev	4: 2	and **d** what is forbidden in any of	6913
	4:13	and **d** what is forbidden in any of	6913
	4:22	and **d** what is forbidden in any of	6913
	4:27	and **d** what is forbidden in any of	6913
	5: 1	'If a person sins because *he* **d** not **speak up**	AIT
	5:17	a person sins and **d** what is forbidden in any	6913
	5:17	even though *he* **d** not **know** it,	AIT
	11: 4	*d* not **have a split** hoof;	AIT
	11: 5	*d* not **have a split** hoof;	AIT
	11: 6	*d* not **have a split** hoof;	AIT
	11: 7	but *d* not **chew** the cud; it is unclean for you.	AIT
	11:12	the water that **d** not **have** fins and scales is	NIH
	11:26	*that* **d** not **chew** the cud is unclean for you;	AIT
	13: 4	but **d** not appear to be more than skin deep	NIH
	13: 7	But if the rash **d** **spread** in his skin	AIT
	13:31	it **d** not seem to be more than skin deep	NIH
	13:32	and there is no yellow hair in it and it **d**	NIH
	13:35	But if the itch **d** **spread** in the skin	AIT
	13:36	*d* not **need** to look for yellow hair	AIT
	17: 9	and *d* not **bring** it to the entrance to the Tent	AIT
	17:16	*he* **d** not **wash** his clothes and bathe himself,	AIT
	18:29	"Everyone who **d** any of these	6913
	23:29	Anyone who *d* not **deny himself** on	AIT
	23:30	among his people anyone who **d** any work	6913
	25:28	if he *d* not **acquire** the means to repay him,	AIT
	25:53	to it that his owner *d* not **rule over**	AIT
	27:20	If, however, he *d* not **redeem** the field,	AIT
	27:27	If he *d* not **redeem** *it,*	AIT
	27:33	If *he* **d** **make a substitution,**	AIT
Nu	5:17	and it *d* **flow** with milk and honey!	AIT
	14:18	*d* not **leave the guilty unpunished;**	AIT
	19:12	But if *he* **d** not **purify** himself on the third	AIT
	19:20	person who is unclean *d* not **purify himself,**	AIT
	23:19	*D* he **speak** and then not act?	AIT
	23:19	*D* he **promise** and not fulfill?	AIT
	23:24	a lion *that* **d** not **rest** till he devours his prey	AIT
	24:23	"Ah, who can live when God **d** this?	8492
	30:11	but says nothing to her and *d* not **forbid** her,	AIT
Dt	8: 3	that man *d* not **live** on bread alone but	AIT
	10:12	what the LORD your God *d* **ask** of you	AIT
	14: 8	it **d** not **chew** the cud.	NIH
	14:10	that **d** not **have** fins and scales you may	NIH
	18:12	Anyone *who* **d** these things is detestable to	6913
	18:19	If anyone *d* not **listen** to my words that	AIT
	18:22	in the name of the LORD *d* not **take place**	AIT
	21:15	the son of the wife *he* **d** not **love,**	AIT
	21:16	the son of the wife *he* **d** **not love.**	AIT
	21:18	and rebellious son who *d* not **obey** his father	AIT
	22: 2	The brother **d** not live near you or if you do	NIH
	22: 5	LORD your God detests anyone *who* **d** this.	6913
	25: 7	man *d* not **want** to marry his brother's wife,	AIT
	25:16	LORD your God detests anyone *who* **d** these	6913
	27:26	"Cursed is the man *who* **d** not **uphold**	AIT
	32: 4	A faithful God who **d** no wrong,	NIH
Jos	1:18	and *d* not **obey** your words,	AIT
	5:14	"What message **d** my Lord **have**	6219
1Sa	6: 9	But if it **d** not,	NIH
	11: 7	of anyone who *d* not **follow** Saul	AIT
	15:22	"*D* the LORD delight in burnt offerings	NIH
	15:29	He who is the Glory of Israel *d* not **lie**	NIH
	16: 7	The LORD *d* not **look** at the things man looks	NIH
	22: 8	as he **d** today."	NIH
	22:13	as he **d** today?"	NIH
	24:19	*d he* **let** him **get away**	AIT
	28:14	"What **d** he look like?"	NIH
2Sa	7:14	When he **d** wrong, I will punish him	6390
2Sa	14:13	*d* he not convict himself,	NIH
	14:14	But God *d* not **take away** life;	AIT
	24: 3	*d* my lord the king **want**	AIT
1Ki	2:23	be it ever so severely, if Adonijah *d* not pay	NIH
	8:39	deal with each man according to all he **d,**	2006
	8:41	"As for the foreigner who *d* not **belong**	NIH
	8:46	for there is no one who *d* not **sin**—	AIT
2Ki	5: 7	Why *d* this fellow **send** someone to me to	AIT
	6:27	"If the LORD *d* not **help** you,	AIT
1Ch	21: 3	*Why d* my lord **want to** do this?	AIT
2Ch	6:30	deal with each man according to all he **d,**	2006
	6:32	"As for the foreigner who *d* not **belong**	NIH
	6:36	for there is no one who *d* not **sin**—	AIT
Ezr	7:26	Whoever *d* not **obey** the law of your God	AIT
Ne	2: 2	"Why *d* your face look so sad when you are	NIH
	5:13	every man who *d* not **keep** this promise.	AIT
Job	1: 9	"*D* Job **fear** God for nothing?" Satan replied.	AIT
	3:21	who long for death that *d* not **come,**	NIH
	5: 6	For hardship *d* not **spring** from the soil,	AIT
	5: 6	nor *d* trouble **sprout** from the ground.	AIT
	6: 5	*D* a wild donkey **bray**	AIT
	7: 1	"*D* not man have hard service on earth?	NIH
	7: 9	down to the grave *d* not **return.**	AIT
	8: 3	*D* God **pervert** justice?	AIT
	8: 3	*D* the Almighty **pervert**	AIT
	8:15	he clings to it, but *it d* not **hold.**	AIT
	8:20	"Surely God *d* not **reject** a blameless man	AIT
	9: 7	He speaks to the sun and *it d* not **shine;**	AIT
	9:13	God *d* not **restrain** his anger;	AIT
	10: 3	*D* it please you to oppress me,	NIH
	11:11	*d* he not **take note?**	AIT
	12: 3	Who *d* not **know** all these things?	NIH
	12: 9	Which of all these *d* not **know** that the hand	AIT
	12:11	*D* not the ear **test** words	AIT
	12:12	*D* not long life bring understanding?	NIH
	14: 2	like a fleeting shadow, *he* **d** not **endure.**	AIT
	14:12	so man lies down and *d* not **rise;**	AIT
	14:21	If his sons are honored, *he* **d** not **know** it;	AIT
	14:21	if they are brought low, *he* **d** not **see** it.	AIT
	16: 6	and if I refrain, *it d* not **go away.**	AIT
	19:16	I summon my servant, but *he d* not **answer,**	AIT
	19:22	Why do you pursue me as God *d?*	NIH
	21:17	How often *d* calamity **come** upon them,	AIT
	21:21	For what *d* he **care** about the family	NIH
	22:13	Yet you say, 'What *d* God **know?**	AIT
	22:13	*D* he **judge** through such darkness?	AIT
	22:14	so *he d* not **see** us as he goes about in	AIT
	23:13	He *d* whatever he pleases.	6913
	24: 1	*d* the Almighty not **set** times for judgment?	AIT
	25: 3	*d* his light not **rise?**	AIT
	27: 9	*D* God **listen** to his cry	AIT
	28:12	Where *d* understanding dwell?	NIH
	28:13	Man *d* not **comprehend** its worth;	AIT
	28:20	"Where then *d* wisdom **come** from?	NIH
	28:20	Where *d* understanding dwell?	NIH
	31: 4	*D* he not **see** my ways	AIT
	33:14	For God *d* **speak**—	AIT
	33:29	"God *d* all these things to a man—	7188
	34:19	to princes and *d* not **favor** the rich over	AIT
	35: 6	If you sin, how *d* that **affect** him?	AIT
	35: 6	your sins are many, what *d* that **do** to him?	AIT
	35: 7	or what *d* he **receive** from your hand?	AIT
	35:12	He *d* not **answer** when men cry out because	AIT
	35:13	God *d* not **listen** to their empty plea;	AIT
	35:15	*d* not **take** the least **notice**	AIT
	36: 5	"God is mighty, but *d* not **despise** men;	AIT
	36: 6	*d* not **keep** the wicked **alive**	AIT
	36: 7	He *d* not **take** his eyes off the righteous;	AIT
	37: 5	he **d** great things beyond our understanding.	6913
	37:23	and great righteousness, *he* **d** not **oppress.**	AIT
	37:24	*d* he not **have regard for**	AIT
	38:19	And where *d* darkness reside?	NIH
	38:28	*D* the rain **have** a father?	AIT
	39: 7	*he* **d** not **hear** a driver's shout.	AIT
	39:22	*he* **d** not **shy away** from the sword.	AIT
	39:26	"*D* the hawk **take flight**	AIT
	39:27	*D* the eagle **soar** at your command	AIT
	41:26	nor *d* the spear or the dart or the javelin.	NIH
Ps	1: 1	the man who *d* not **walk** in the counsel of	AIT
	1: 3	in season and whose leaf *d* not **wither.**	AIT
	1: 3	Whatever *he* **d** prospers.	6913
	7:12	*he* **d** not **relent,** he will sharpen his sword;	AIT
	9:12	*he* **d** not **ignore** the cry of the afflicted.	AIT
	10: 4	In his pride the wicked *d* not **seek** him;	AIT
	10:13	*d* the wicked man **revile**	AIT
	10:13	Why *d* he **say** to himself,	AIT
	14: 1	there is no *one who* **d** good.	6913
	14: 3	there is no *one who* **d** good, not even one.	6913
	15: 2	and *who* **d** what is righteous,	7188
	15: 3	*who* **d** his neighbor no wrong,	6913
	15: 5	without usury and *d* not **accept** a bribe	6913
	15: 5	He who *d* these things will never be shaken.	6913
	17: 1	it *d* not **rise** from deceitful lips.	NIH
	24: 4	who *d* not **lift up** his soul to an idol	AIT
	32: 2	the man whose sin the LORD *d* not **count**	AIT
	33: 4	he is faithful in all he **d.**	5126
	36: 4	and *d* not **reject** what is wrong.	AIT
	38:14	I have become like a man who *d* not **hear,**	AIT
	40: 4	who *d* not **look** to the proud,	AIT
	41:11	for my enemy *d* not **triumph** over me.	AIT
	44: 6	do not **bring** me **victory;**	AIT
	49:12	But man, despite his riches, *d* not **endure;**	AIT
	53: 1	there is no *one who* **d** good.	6913
	53: 3	there is no *one who* **d** good, not even one.	6913
	69:33	and *d* not **despise** his captive people.	AIT
	72:18	*who* alone **d** marvelous deeds.	6913

Ps 73:11 **D** the Most High have knowledge?" NIH
74: 1 Why *d* your anger **smolder** against AIT
78:39 a passing breeze *that d* not **return.** AIT
84:11 no good thing *d* he **withhold** AIT
92: 6 The senseless man *d* not **know,** AIT
94: 7 They say, "The LORD *d* not **see;** AIT
94: 9 *D* he who implanted the ear not **hear?** AIT
94: 9 *D* he who formed the eye not **see?** AIT
94:10 *D* he who disciplines nations not **punish?** AIT
94:10 *D* he who teaches man lack knowledge? NIH
103:10 he *d* not **treat** us as our sins deserve AIT
115: 3 he *d* whatever pleases him. 6913
121: 1 where *d* my help **come** from? AIT
135: 6 The LORD *d* whatever pleases him, 6913
136: 4 to him who alone *d* great wonders, 6913
Pr 6:32 whoever *d* so destroys himself. 6913
8: 1 *D* not wisdom **call out?** AIT
8: 1 *D* not understanding **raise** her voice? AIT
10: 3 *d* not let the righteous go **hungry** AIT
12:27 The lazy man *d* not **roast** his game, AIT
13: 1 but a mocker *d* not **listen** *to* rebuke. AIT
14: 5 A truthful witness *d* not **deceive,** AIT
14:17 A quick-tempered man *d* foolish things, 6913
17:20 A man of perverse heart *d* not **prosper;** AIT
18: 3 When wickedness comes, so *d* contempt, 995S
20: 4 A sluggard *d* not **plow** in season; AIT
20:16 in pledge if he *d* it for a wayward woman. NIH
24:12 *d* not he who weighs the heart **perceive** AIT
24:12 *D* not he who guards your life **know** AIT
25:14 boasts of **gifts** he *d* not **give.** 5522+9214
26: 2 an undeserved curse *d* not **come to rest.** AIT
27:13 in pledge if he *d* it for a wayward woman. NIH
28:13 He who conceals his sins *d* not **prosper,** AIT
29:16 When the wicked thrive, so *d* sin, 8049S
31:18 and her lamp *d* not **go out** at night. AIT
31:27 the affairs of her household and *d* not **eat** AIT
Ecc 1: 3 What *d* man gain from all his labor NIH
2: 2 *d* pleasure **accomplish?"** AIT
2:22 What *d* a man **get** for all the toil AIT
2:23 even at night his mind *d* not **rest.** AIT
3: 9 What *d* the worker gain from his toil? NIH
3:14 that everything God *d* will endure forever; 6913
3:14 God *d* it so that men will revere him. 6913
5:16 so he departs, and what *d* he gain, NIH
6: 2 but God *d* not **enable** him to enjoy them, AIT
6: 3 and *d* not **receive** proper burial, AIT
6: 5 it has more rest than *d* that man— NIH
6: 8 What *d* a poor man gain by knowing how NIH
6:11 and how *d* that profit anyone? NIH
7:20 on earth who *d* what is right and never sins. 6913
9:11 or the battle to the strong, nor *d* food come NIH
10:15 he *d* not **know** the way to town. AIT
SS 2: 7 I charge you by the gazelles and by the *d* of 387
3: 5 I charge you by the gazelles and by the *d* of 387
Isa 1: 3 but Israel *d* not **know,** AIT
1:23 the widow's case *d* not **come** before them. AIT
10:15 *D* the ax **raise itself** AIT
19:14 they make Egypt stagger in all *that* she *d,* 5126
28:24 *d* he plow continually? NIH
28:24 *D* he keep on **breaking up** AIT
28:25 *d* he not **sow** caraway and scatter cummin? AIT
28:25 *D* he not **plant** wheat in its place, AIT
28:28 *d* not **go on threshing** AIT
31: 2 he *d* not **take** back his words. AIT
45: 9 *D* the clay **say** to the potter, AIT
45: 9 *D* your work say, 'He has no hands'? NIH
46: 7 Though one cries out to it, *it d* not **answer;** AIT
54:15 If *anyone d* **attack** you, AIT
55: 2 and your labor on what *d* not satisfy? NIH
56: 2 Blessed is the man *who d* this, 6913
58: 2 as if they were a nation that *d* what is right 6913
59: 9 and righteousness *d* not **reach** us. AIT
63:16 though Abraham *d* not **know** us AIT
65:20 an old man who *d* not **live out** his years; AIT
Jer 2:32 *D* a maiden **forget** her jewelry, AIT
8: 4 When a man turns away, *d* he not **return?** AIT
8: 5 Why *d* Jerusalem **always** turn away? 5904
11: 3 'Cursed is the man who *d* not **obey** the
terms of this covenant— AIT
12: 1 Why *d* the way of the wicked **prosper?** AIT
12:17 But if any nation *d* not **listen,** AIT
14:10 So the LORD *d* not **accept** them; AIT
14:22 for you are the *one who d* all this. 6913
17: 8 *It d* not **fear** when heat comes; AIT
18: 6 can I not do with you as this potter *d?"* NIH
18:10 it *d* evil in my sight and does not obey me, 6913
18:10 if it does evil in my sight and *d* not **obey**
me, AIT
18:14 *D* the snow of Lebanon *ever* **vanish** AIT
22:15 *"D* it make you a **king** AIT
La 3:33 *d* not willingly **bring affliction** AIT
Eze 3:19 and he *d* not **turn** from his wickedness or AIT
3:20 from his righteousness and *d* evil, 6913
3:21 not to sin and he *d* not **sin,** AIT
8:12 They say, 'The LORD *d* not **see** us; AIT
9: 9 the LORD *d* not **see.'** AIT
17:15 Will he who *d* such things escape? 6913
18: 5 a righteous man *who d* what is just and
right. 6913
18: 6 He *d* not **eat** at the mountain shrines or look AIT
18: 6 He *d* not **defile** his neighbor's wife or lie AIT
18: 7 He *d* not **oppress** anyone, AIT
18: 7 He *d* not **commit robbery** but gives his
food to the hungry AIT
18: 8 He *d* not **lend** at usury AIT
18:10 or *d* any of these other things 6913
18:12 He *d* not **return** what he took in pledge. AIT

Eze 18:12 He *d* detestable things. 6913
18:14 he *d* not **do** such things: AIT
18:15 "He *d* not **eat** at the mountain shrines AIT
18:15 He *d* not **defile** his neighbor's wife. AIT
18:16 He *d* not **oppress** anyone or require a
pledge AIT
18:16 He *d* not **commit robbery** but gives his
food to the hungry AIT
18:19 *d* the son not **share** AIT
18:21 and keeps all my decrees and *d* what is just 6913
18:24 and *d* the same detestable things 6913
18:24 detestable things the wicked man *d,* 6913
18:27 and *d* what is just and right, 6913
21:13 which the sword despises, *d* not **continue?** AIT
33: 4 *d* not **take warning** and the sword comes AIT
33: 6 and *d* not **blow** the trumpet to warn AIT
33: 9 to turn from his ways and *he d* not **do so,** AIT
33:13 in his righteousness and *d* evil, none of 6913
33:14 from his sin and *d* what is just and right— 6913
33:15 and *d* no evil, he will surely live; 6913
33:18 from his righteousness and *d* evil, AIT
33:19 from his wickedness and *d* what is just 6913
46:12 or his fellowship offerings as *he d* on 6913
Da 3: 6 Whoever *d* not **fall down** AIT
3:11 and that whoever *d* not **fall down** AIT
3:18 But even if he *d* not, we want you to know, NIH
4:35 He *d* as he pleases with the powers 10522
4:37 because everything he *d* is right 10434
8:24 and will succeed in whatever he *d.* 6913
9:14 God is righteous in everything he *d;* 6913
Hos 7: 9 but he *d* not **realize** it. AIT
7: 9 but he *d* not **notice.** AIT
7:10 but despite all this *he d* not **return** to AIT
13:13 he *d* not **come** to the opening of the womb. AIT
Am 3: 4 *D* a lion **roar** in the thicket AIT
3: 4 *D* he **growl** in his den AIT
3: 5 *D* a bird **fall** into a trap on the ground AIT
3: 5 *D* a trap **spring up** AIT
3: 7 Surely the Sovereign LORD *d* nothing 6913
6:12 *D* one **plow** there with oxen? AIT
Mic 2: 7 *D* he **do** such things?" NIH
2: 7 if *he d* not, they prepare to wage war 5989
6: 8 And what *d* the LORD **require** of you? AIT
Hab 3:17 Though the fig tree *d* not **bud** AIT
Zep 3: 2 She *d* not **trust** in the LORD, AIT
3: 2 she *d* not **draw near** to her God. AIT
3: 5 he *d* no wrong. 6913
3: 5 and every new day *he d* not **fail,** AIT
Hag 2: 3 How *d* it **look** to you now? AIT
2: 3 *D* it not seem to you like nothing? NIH
2:12 *d* it become **consecrated?** " AIT
2:13 *d* it become **defiled?"** AIT
Mal 2:12 As for the man who *d* this, 6913
Mt 3:10 that *d* not **produce** good fruit will be cut AIT
4: 4 'Man *d* not **live** on bread alone,' AIT
7:19 Every tree that *d* not **bear** good fruit is cut AIT
7:21 but only he who *d* the will 4472
7:26 *d* not **put** them **into practice** AIT
8: 9 I say to my servant, 'Do this,' and *he d* it." 4472
9:11 "Why *d* your teacher **eat** with tax collectors AIT
10:38 and anyone who *d* not **take** his cross AIT
11: 6 the man who *d* not **fall away** on account AIT
12:30 and he who *d* not **gather** with me scatters. AIT
12:43 and *d* not **find** it. AIT
12:50 For whoever *d* the will of my Father 4472
13:12 Whoever *d* not **have,** AIT
13:19 about the kingdom and *d* not **understand** it, AIT
15:11 *d* not **make** him **'unclean,'** AIT
15:20 *d* not **make** him **'unclean.' "** AIT
17:25 "Yes, he *d,*" he replied. NIG
24:50 on a day when *he d* not **expect** him and at AIT
25:29 Whoever *d* not **have,** AIT
Mk 2: 7 "Why *d* this fellow **talk** like that? AIT
2:16 "Why *d* he **eat** with tax collectors AIT
2:21 If he *d,* the new piece will pull away from
the old, 1254+1623+3590
2:22 If he *d,* the wine will burst the skins, 1254+1623+3590
3:35 Whoever *d* God's will is my brother 4472
4:25 whoever *d* not **have,** AIT
4:27 though he *d* not **know** how. AIT
6: 2 that he even *d* miracles! 1181
8:12 *d* this generation **ask** for AIT
9:12 Elijah *d* **come** first, and restores all things. AIT
9:37 whoever welcomes me not **welcome** me AIT
9:39 "No one who *d* a miracle in my name can 4472
9:48 where " 'their worm *d* not **die,** AIT
11:23 and *d* not **doubt** in his heart but believes AIT
13:14 where *it d* not **belong—** AIT
16:16 whoever *d* not **believe** will be condemned. AIT
Lk 3: 9 *that d* not **produce** good fruit will be cut AIT
4: 4 'Man *d* not **live** on bread alone.' " AIT
5:36 If he *d,* he will have torn the new garment, 1145+3590S
5:37 If he *d,* the new wine will burst the skins, 1145+3590S
6:43 nor *d* a bad tree **bear** good fruit. AIT
6:49 *d* not **put** them **into practice** AIT
7: 8 I say to my servant, 'Do this,' and *he d* it." 4472
7:23 the man who *d* not **fall away** on account AIT
8:18 whoever *d* not **have,** AIT
11:23 and he who *d* not **gather** with me, scatters. AIT
11:24 and *d* not **find** it. AIT
12:15 a man's life *d* not **consist** in the abundance AIT
12:46 on a day when *he d* not **expect** him and at AIT
12:47 and *d* not **get ready** or does AIT
12:47 or *d* not **do** what his master wants will AIT

Lk 12:48 But the one who *d* not **know** AIT
12:48 and *d* things deserving punishment will 4472
12:54 'It's going to rain,' and *it d.* 1181+4048S
14:26 to me and *d* not **hate** his father and mother, AIT
14:27 And anyone who *d* not **carry** his cross AIT
14:33 any of you who *d* not **give up** AIT
15: 4 *D* he not **leave** the ninety-nine in AIT
15: 8 *D* she not **light** a lamp, AIT
17:20 "The kingdom of God *d* not **come** AIT
24:39 a ghost *d* not **have** flesh and bones, AIT
Jn 3:18 whoever *d* not **believe** stands condemned
already AIT
3:20 Everyone who *d* evil hates the light, 4556
5:19 whatever the Father *d* the Son also does. 4472
5:19 whatever the Father does the Son also *d.* 4472
5:20 the Son and shows him all he *d.* 4472
5:23 He who *d* not **honor** the Son does not honor AIT
5:23 He who does not honor the Son *d* not **honor** AIT
5:38 nor *d* his word **dwell** in you, AIT
6:61 Jesus said to them, "*D* this **offend** you? AIT
7: 7 because I testify that what it *d* is evil. 2240
7:18 on his own *d* so to gain honor for himself, NIG
7:35 "Where *d* this man **intend** to go AIT
7:42 *D* not the Scripture **say** AIT
7:46 "No one ever spoke the way this man *d,"* NIG
7:51 "*D* our law **condemn** anyone without first AIT
7:52 that a prophet *d* not **come** out of Galilee." AIT
8:41 You are doing the things your own father *d.* " NIG
9:16 for he *d* not **keep** the Sabbath." AIT
9:31 We know that God *d* not **listen** to sinners. AIT
9:31 He listens to the godly man who *d* his will. 4472
10: 1 the man who *d* not **enter** the sheep pen by AIT
10:37 unless I do what my Father *d.* NIG
12:35 The man who walks in the dark *d* not **know** AIT
12:44 he *d* not **believe** in me only, AIT
12:47 but *d* not **keep** them, AIT
12:48 and *d* not **accept** my words; AIT
13:19 *it d* **happen** you will believe that I am He. AIT
14:24 He who *d* not **love** me will AIT
14:29 so that when *it d* **happen** you will believe. AIT
15: 2 *that d* **bear** fruit he prunes so that it will be AIT
15: 6 If anyone *d* not **remain** in me, AIT
15:15 a servant *d* not **know** his master's business. AIT
16:17 "What *d* he **mean** by saying, AIT
16:18 "What *d* he **mean** by 'a little while'? AIT
17:25 though the world *d* not **know** you, AIT
Ac 2:12 "What *d* this **mean?"** AIT
3:12 "Men of Israel, why *d* this **surprise** you? AIT
3:23 Anyone who *d* not **listen** to him will AIT
7:48 the Most High *d* not **live** in houses made AIT
10:34 that God *d* not **show favoritism.** AIT
13:40 the prophets have said *d* not **happen to** you: AIT
15:17 says the Lord, *who d* these things' 4472
17:24 and *d* not **live** in temples built by hands. AIT
Ro 2: 9 for every human being who *d* evil: 2981
2:10 honor and peace *for* everyone who *d* good: 2237
2:11 For God *d* not **show favoritism.** AIT
3:12 there is no one who *d* good, not even one." 4472
4: 3 What *d* the Scripture **say?** AIT
4: 5 to the man who *d* not **work** AIT
5: 5 And hope *d* not **disappoint** us, AIT
7:20 but it is sin living in me that *d* it. NIG
8: 7 *It d* not **submit** to God's law, AIT
8: 9 if anyone *d* not **have** the Spirit of Christ, AIT
8: 9 he *d* not **belong to** Christ. 1639
9:16 It *d* not, therefore, depend on man's desire NIG
9:19 "Then why *d* God still **blame** us? AIT
9:21 *D* not the potter **have** the right AIT
10: 5 "The man who *d* these things will live 4472
10: 8 But what *d* it **say?** AIT
13: 4 for he *d* not **bear** the sword for nothing. AIT
13:10 Love *d* no harm to its neighbor. 2237
14: 3 not look down on him who *d* not, NIG
14: 3 and the man who *d* not **eat** everything must AIT
14: 3 not condemn the man who *d,* NIG
14: 6 one day as special, *d* so to the Lord. 5858S
14: 6 who abstains, *d* so to the Lord and gives
thanks to God. 2266+4024S
14:22 the man who *d* not **condemn** himself AIT
14:23 everything that *d* not come from faith is sin. NIG
1Co 2:14 the Spirit *d* not **accept** the things that come AIT
4: 4 but that *d* not **make** *me* innocent. AIT
5: 1 a kind that *d* not occur even among pagans: NIG
7: 4 The wife's body *d* not **belong to** her alone AIT
7: 4 *d* not **belong to** him alone but also to AIT
7:11 But if *she d,* she must remain unmarried 6004S
7:37 this *man* also *d* the right thing. 4472
7:38 So then, he who marries the virgin *d* right, 4472
7:38 he who *d* not **marry** her does even better. AIT
7:38 he who does not marry her *d* even better. 4472
8: 2 The man who thinks he knows something *d*
not yet **know** AIT
8: 8 food *d* not **bring** us **near** to God; AIT
8: 9 the exercise of your freedom *d* not **become** AIT
9: 7 a vineyard and *d* not **eat** of its grapes? AIT
9: 7 Who tends a flock and *d* not **drink** of AIT
11: 6 If a woman *d* not **cover** her head, AIT
11:14 *D* not the very nature of things **teach** AIT
13: 4 *It d* not **envy,** it does not boast, AIT
13: 4 It does not envy, it *d* not **boast,** AIT
13: 6 Love *d* not **delight** in evil but rejoices with AIT
14: 2 in a tongue *d* not **speak** to men but to God. AIT
14: 8 if the trumpet *d* not **sound** a clear call, AIT
14:16 since he *d* not **know** what you are saying? AIT
14:24 someone who *d* not **understand** 2626
15:27 that this *d* not include God himself, NIG
15:36 *d* not **come to life** unless it dies. AIT

1Co	15:50	nor *d* the perishable **inherit**	AIT
	16:19	so *d* the church that meets at their house.	NIG
	16:22	If anyone *d* not **love the Lord**—	AIT
2Co	6:15	What *d* a believer have in common with	NIG
	8:12	not according to what *he d* not **have.**	AIT
	10: 3	we do not wage war **as** the world *d*.	2848
	11:18	**in the way** the world *d*,	2848
Gal	2: 6	*d* not **judge by external appearance**—	AIT
	2:17	**d that mean that** Christ promotes sin?	727
	3: 5	*D* God give you his Spirit	AIT
	3:10	"Cursed is everyone who *d* not **continue**	AIT
	3:12	man who *d* these things will live by them."	4472
	3:16	The Scripture *d* not **say** "and to seeds,"	AIT
	3:17	*d* not **set aside** the covenant	AIT
	3:20	however, *d* not represent just one party;	NIG
	4:30	But what *d* the Scripture **say**?	AIT
	5: 8	That kind of persuasion *d* not come from	NIG
Eph	4: 9	(What *d* "he ascended" **mean** except that he	AIT
	4:16	as each part *d* its work.	NIG
	5:29	just as Christ *d* the church—	NIG
	6: 8	for whatever good *he d*,	4472
Php	1:18	But **what** *d* it matter?	1142+5515
Col	3:25	Anyone who *d* **wrong** will be repaid	92
	4:10	as *d* Mark, the cousin of Barnabas.	NIG
1Th	2: 3	the appeal we make *d* not spring from error	NIG
	3:12	just as ours *d* for you.	NIG
	4: 8	he who rejects this instruction *d* not **reject** man but God,	AIT
2Th	3: 6	and *d* not **live** according to the teaching	AIT
	3:14	If anyone *d* not **obey** our instruction	AIT
1Ti	3: 5	(If anyone *d* not **know** how to manage	AIT
	5: 8	*d* not **provide** for his relatives,	AIT
	6: 3	and *d* not **agree** to the sound instruction	AIT
2Ti	2: 5	*he d* not **receive the victor's crown**	AIT
	2:15	a workman *who d* **not need to be ashamed**	454
Tit	1: 2	which God, who *d* **not lie,**	AIT
Heb	7:27	he *d* not **need** to offer sacrifices day	AIT
Jas	1: 8	unstable in all he *d*.	NIG
	1:13	nor *d* he **tempt** anyone;	AIT
	1:17	who *d* not **change** like shifting shadows.	AIT
	1:20	for man's anger *d* not **bring about**	AIT
	1:23	to the word but *d* not do what it says is like	NIG
	1:25	he will be blessed in what he *d*.	4474
	1:26	*d* not **keep a tight rein on** his tongue,	4474
	2:16	but *d* nothing about his physical needs,	1443
	2:24	that a person is justified by **what he** *d* and	2240
	3:15	Such "wisdom" *d* not **come down**	AIT
1Pe	4: 2	*he d* not **live** the rest of his earthly life	AIT
	5:13	and so *d* my son Mark.	NIG
2Pe	1: 9	But **if** anyone *d* not **have** them,	AIT
1Jn	2: 1	But if anybody *d* **sin,** we have someone who	AIT
	2: 4	but *d* not **do** what he commands is a liar,	AIT
	2:11	*he d* not **know** where he is going,	AIT
	2:16	**what he has and**—	1050
	2:17	man who *d* the will of God lives forever.	4472
	2:24	If it *d*, you also will remain in the Son	1877+3531+5148S
	2:29	everyone who *d* what is right has been born	4472
	3: 1	The reason the world *d* not **know** us is	AIT
	3: 7	He who *d* what is right is righteous,	4472
	3: 8	He who *d* what is sinful is of the devil,	4472
	3:10	Anyone who *d* not **do** what is right is not	AIT
	3:10	nor is anyone who *d* not **love** his brother.	AIT
	3:14	Anyone who *d* not **love** remains in death.	AIT
	4: 3	that *d* not **acknowledge** Jesus is not	AIT
	4: 6	but whoever is not from God *d* not **listen**	AIT
	4: 8	Whoever *d* not **love** does not know God,	AIT
	4: 8	Whoever does not love *d* not **know** God,	AIT
	4:20	For anyone who *d* not **love** his brother,	AIT
	5:10	Anyone who *d* not **believe** God has made him out to be a liar,	AIT
	5:12	he who *d* not **have** the Son of God does	AIT
	5:12	not have the Son of God *d* not **have** life.	AIT
	5:16	a sin that *d* not lead to death.	NIG
	5:16	to those whose sin *d* not lead to death.	NIG
	5:17	and there is sin that *d* not lead to death.	NIG
	5:18	*d* not **continue** to **sin;**	AIT
2Jn	1: 9	Anyone who runs ahead and *d* not **continue**	AIT
	1: 9	in the teaching of Christ *d* not **have** God;	AIT
	1:10	to you and *d* not **bring** this teaching,	AIT
3Jn	1:11	Anyone who *d* **what is good** is from God.	16
	1:11	Anyone who *d* **what is evil** has	2803
Rev	2:26	To him who overcomes and *d* my will to	5498
	17:10	*he d* **come,** he must remain for a little while.	AIT
	21:23	The city *d* not **need** the sun or the moon	AIT
	21:27	nor will anyone who *d* what is shameful	4472
	22:11	Let him who *d* **wrong** continue to do wrong;	92
	22:11	let him who *d* **right** continue to do right;	AIT

DOESN'T (9) [DO]

1Sa	20: 2	Look, my father *d* do anything,	4202
1Ki	18:12	If I go and tell Ahab and he *d* find you,	4202
Mt	17:24	"*D* your teacher pay the temple tax?"	4024
Mk	7:19	it *d* go into his heart but into his stomach,	4024
Lk	13:15	*D* each of you on the Sabbath untie his ox	4024
Ac	19:35	"Men of Ephesus, *d* all the world know that	4024
1Co	9: 8	*D* the Law say the same thing?	4024
	9:10	Surely he says this for us, *d* he?	3590
Jas	4:17	the good he ought to do and *d* do it,	3590

DOG (12) [DOG'S, DOGS]

Ex	11: 7	But among the Israelites not a *d* will bark	3978
Jdg	7: 5	a *d* from those who kneel down to drink."	3978
1Sa	17:43	He said to David, "Am I a *d*,	3978
	24:14	A dead *d*? A flea?	3978

2Sa	9: 8	that you should notice a dead *d* like me?"	3978
	16: 9	"Why should this dead *d* curse my lord	3978
2Ki	8:13	"How could your servant, a mere *d*,	3978
Job	18:11	on every side and *d* his every step.	7046
Pr	26:11	As a *d* returns to its vomit,	3978
	26:17	Like one who seizes a *d* by the ears	3978
Ecc	9: 4	even a live *d* is better off than a dead lion!	3978
2Pe	2:22	"A *d* returns to its vomit," and,	3264

DOG'S (2) [DOG]

2Sa	3: 8	"Am I a *d* head—on Judah's side?	3978
Isa	66: 3	like one who breaks a *d* neck;	3978

DOGS (27) [DOG]

Ex	22:31	throw it to the **d.**	3978
1Ki	14:11	*D* will eat those belonging to Jeroboam	3978
	16: 4	*D* will eat those belonging to Baasha	3978
	21:19	where *d* licked up Naboth's blood,	3978
	21:19	*d* will lick up your blood—yes, yours!'"	3978
	21:23	'*D* will devour Jezebel by the wall	3978
	21:24	"*D* will eat those belonging to Ahab	3978
	22:38	and the *d* licked up his blood,	3978
2Ki	9:10	*d* will devour her on the plot of ground	3978
	9:36	at Jezreel *d* will devour Jezebel's flesh.	3978
Job	30: 1	to put with my sheep *d*.	3978
Ps	22:16	*D* have surrounded me;	3978
	22:20	my precious life from the power of the *d*.	3978
	59: 6	snarling like *d*, and prowl about the city.	3978
	59:14	snarling like *d*, and prowl about the city.	3978
	68:23	the tongues of your *d* have their share."	3978
Isa	56:10	they are all mute *d*, they cannot bark;	3978
	56:11	They are *d* **with** mighty appetites;	3978
Jer	15: 3	to kill and the *d* to drag away and the birds	3978
Mt	7: 6	"Do not give *d* what is sacred;	3264
	15:26	the children's bread and toss it *to their* **d.**"	3249
	15:27	"but even the *d* eat the crumbs that fall	3249
Mk	7:27	the children's bread and toss it *to their* **d.**"	3249
	7:28	"but even the *d* under the table eat	3249
Lk	16:21	Even the *d* came and licked his sores.	3264
Php	3: 2	Watch out for those *d*, those men who do evil,	3264
Rev	22:15	Outside are the *d*, those who practice magic arts,	3264

DOING (183) [DO]

Ge	2: 2	the work he had been *d*,	6913
	18:19	of the LORD by *d* what is right and just,	6913
	20:10	"What was your reason for *d* this?"	6913
	31:12	for I have seen all that Laban *has been* **d**	6913
	34:19	lost no time in *d* what they said,	6913
Ex	18:14	that Moses *was d* for the people,	6913
	18:14	"What is this you *are d* for the people?	6913
	18:17	"What you *are d* is not good.	6913
	23: 2	"Do not follow the crowd in *d* **wrong.**	AIT
	36: 4	So all the skilled craftsmen who *were d* all	6913
	36: 5	for *d* the work the LORD commanded to	6275
Nu	3: 7	of Meeting *d* the work of the tabernacle.	6268
	3: 8	**fulfilling** the obligations of the Israelites **by** *d* the work	6268
	4:27	whether carrying or *d* other **work,**	6275
	22:30	Have I been in the habit of *d* this to you?"	6913
Dt	4:25	*d* evil in the eyes of the LORD your God	6913
	9:18	the sin you had committed, *d* what was evil	6913
	12:25	because *you will be d* what is right in	6913
	12:28	*be d* what is good and right in the eyes of	6913
	13:18	and *d* what is right in his eyes.	6913
	17: 2	the LORD gives you is found **d** evil in	6913
Jos	2:14	"If you don't tell what we are *d*,	1821
	2:20	But if you tell what we are *d*,	1821
	7:10	What *are you d* **down** on your face?	AIT
	10: 1	*d* to Ai and its king as he had done	6913
Jdg	11:27	but you are *d* me wrong by waging war	6913
	18: 3	What *are you d* in this place?	6913
	18:18	the priest said to them, "What *are you d*?"	6913
1Sa	2:22	heard about everything his sons *were d*	6913
	8: 8	so they are *d* to you.	6913
	12:25	Yet if *you* **persist in** *d* **evil,**	8317+8317
	25:39	He has kept his servant from *d* wrong	NIH
2Sa	3:25	and find out everything you are **d.**"	6913
	8:15	*d* what was just and right for all his people.	6913
	12: 9	of the LORD by *d* what is evil in his eyes?	6913
	12:14	by *d* this you have made the enemies of	NIH
1Ki	12:24	every one of you, for this is my *d*.'"	907+4946
	14: 8	*d* only what was right in my eyes.	6913
	16:19	*d* evil in the eyes of the LORD	6913
	19: 9	"**What are you d** here, Elijah?"	3870+4200+4537
	19:13	a voice said to him, "**What are you d** here,	3870+4200+4537
	22: 3	and yet we are *d* **nothing** to retake it from	3120
2Ki	7: 9	they said to each other, "We're not *d* right.	6913
1Ch	18:14	*d* what was just and right for all his people.	6913
	21: 8	"I have sinned greatly by *d* this.	6913
	21:15	But as the angel *was d* so,	8845S
2Ch	11: 4	every one of you, for this is my *d*.'"	907+4946
	22: 3	for his mother encouraged him in *d* **wrong.**	8399
	31: 7	They began *d* this in the third month	2021+3569+6894S
	31:20	*d* what was good and right and faithful	6913
	34:16	"Your officials are *d* everything	6913
	35: 6	*d* what the LORD commanded	6913
Ne	2:16	not know where I had gone or what I *was d*,	6913
	2:16	or officials or any others *who would be d*	6913
	2:19	"What is this you *are d*?"	6913
	4: 2	he said, "What are those feeble Jews *d*?	6913
	5: 9	I continued, "What you *are d* is not right.	6913

Ne	6:13	so that I would commit a sin by *d* this,	6913
	13:17	"What is this wicked thing you *are d*—	6913
	13:27	you too *are d* all this terrible wickedness	6913
Est	9:23	*d* what Mordecai had written to them.	NIH
Job	9:12	Who can say to him, 'What *are you d*?'	6913
Ps	109:16	For he never thought of *d* a kindness,	6913
Pr	1: 3	*d what is* **right** and just and fair;	AIT
	2:14	in *d* wrong and rejoice in the perverseness	6913
	25:22	**In** *d* **this,** you will heap burning coals	3954
Ecc	8: 4	who can say to him, "What *are you d*?"	6913
Isa	1:16	of my sight! Stop *d* wrong,	8317
	22:16	**What are you** *d* here	3870+4200+4537
	26:10	of uprightness *they go on* **d** evil and regard	6401
	38:19	they praise you, as I am *d* today;	NIH
	43:19	See, I am *d* a new thing!	6913
	54:15	it will not be my *d*;	907+4946
	56: 2	and keeps his hand from *d* any evil.	6913
	58:13	and from *d* as you please on my holy day,	6913
	58:13	not *d* as you please or speaking idle words,	5162
Jer	4:22	They are skilled in *d* evil;	8317
	4:30	What *are you d*, O devastated one?	6913
	7:13	While you *were d* all these things,	6913
	7:17	Do you not see what they *are d* in the towns	6913
	11:15	"**What is** my beloved *d*	4200+4537
	11:18	that time he showed me **what** they were **d.**	5095
	13:23	Neither can you do good who are accustomed to *d* evil.	8317
	17:24	the Sabbath day holy by not *d* any work	6913
	32:40	I will never stop *d* good *to* them,	3512
	32:41	I will rejoice in *d* them good	3201
	38:20	"Obey the LORD by *d* what I tell you.	NIH
	48:10	on *him who is* lax in *d* the LORD's work!	6913
Eze	8: 6	"Son of man, do you see what they *are d*—	6913
	8: 6	the house of Israel *is* **d** here,	6913
	8: 9	and detestable things they *are d* here?	6913
	8:12	of the house of Israel *are d* in the darkness,	6913
	8:13	"You will see them *d* things that are	6913
	8:17	to do the detestable things *they are* **d** here?	6913
	12: 9	'What *are you d*?'	6913
	18:12	He withholds his hand from *d* wrong	6404
	25:12	of Judah and became very guilty *by d* so,	5933
	33:19	he will live by *d* so.	2157S
	36:32	to know that I am not *d* this for your sake,	6913
Da	4:27	Renounce your sins by *d* what is right,	NIH
Mic	7: 3	Both hands are skilled in *d* evil;	NIH
Mt	5:46	*Are* not even the tax collectors *d* that?	4472
	5:47	what *are you d* more than others?	4472
	6: 3	do not let your left hand know what your right hand is *d*,	4472
	11: 2	John heard in prison what Christ was *d*,	2240
	12: 2	Your disciples *are d* what is unlawful on	4472
	20: 3	in the marketplace *d* **nothing.**	734
	20: 6	'Why have you been standing here all day long *d* **nothing?**"	734
	21:23	"By what authority *are you d* these things?"	4472
	21:24	by what authority *I am d* these things.	4472
	21:27	by what authority *I am d* these things.	4472
	24:46	for that servant whose master finds him *d*	4472
Mk	2:24	why *are they d* what is unlawful on	4472
	3: 8	When they heard all he was *d*,	4472
	11: 3	If anyone asks, 'Why *are you d* this?'	4472
	11: 5	"What *are you d*, untying that colt?"	4472
	11:28	"By what authority *are you d* these things?"	4472
	11:29	by what authority *I am d* these things.	4472
	11:33	by what authority *I am d* these things."	4472
Lk	6: 2	"Why *are you d* what is unlawful on	4472
	12:43	for that servant whom the master finds *d* so	4472
	13:17	with all the wonderful things he was *d*.	1181
	20: 2	by what authority *you are d* these things,"	4472
	20: 8	by what authority *I am d* these things."	4472
	23:34	for they do not know what *they are* **d.**"	4472
Jn	2:23	the miraculous signs he was *d* and believed	4472
	3: 2	the miraculous signs you *are d* if God were	4472
	5:16	Jesus *was d* these things on the Sabbath,	4472
	5:19	he can do only what he sees his Father *d*,	4472
	5:36	and which *I am d*,	4472
	7: 4	Since *you are d* these things,	4472
	7:51	to find out what he is *d*?"	4472
	8:41	You *are d* the things your own father does."	4472
	13: 7	"You do not realize now what I am *d*,	4472
	14:10	living in me, who *is* **d** his work.	4472
	14:12	in me will do what I *have been* **d.**	4472
Ac	5: 4	What made you think of *d* such a thing?	NIG
	9:36	who was always *d* good and helping	2240
	10:38	around *d* good and healing all who were	2308
	12: 9	the angel was *d* was really happening;	NIG
	14:15	why *are you d* this?	4472
	15:36	of the Lord and see how they *are d*."	2400
	17:21	foreigners who lived there spent their time *d* nothing	1650
	19:14	a Jewish chief priest, were *d* this.	4472
	24:18	in the temple courts *d* this.	NIG
	25:11	I am guilty of *d* anything deserving death,	4556
	26:31	not *d* anything that deserves death	4556
Ro	1:13	(but have been prevented from *d* so	NIG
	1:30	they invent ways of *d* evil;	NIG
	2: 7	by persistence in *d* good seek glory,	2240
	7:19	this I keep on *d*.	4556
	12:20	**In** *d* **this,** you will heap burning coals	4472
2Co	11: 1	but *you are already* **d** that.	462S
	11:12	And I will keep on *d* what I am doing	4472
	11:12	And I will keep on doing what *I am* **d**	4472
Gal	6: 9	Let us not become weary in *d* good,	4472
Eph	4:28	something useful with his own hands,	2237
	6: 6	*d* the will of God from your heart.	4472
	6:21	also may know how I am and what *I am* **d.**	4556
Col	1: 6	just as it has been *d* among you since	NIG

1Th	5:11	just as in fact *you are* **d.**	4472
2Th	3: 4	in the Lord that *you are* **d** and will continue	4472
	3:13	you, brothers, never tire of **d what is right.**	2818
1Ti	6:21	and in so **d** have wandered from the faith.	NIG
Tit	1:16	disobedient and unfit for **d** anything good.	2240
	2: 7	an example *by* **d** what is good.	2240
	3: 8	to devote themselves to **d** what is good.	2240
	3:14	to devote themselves to **d** what is good,	2240
Heb	10:25	as some are in the habit of **d,**	4472
	13: 2	by so **d** some people have entertained angels	4047S
	13:21	with everything good for **d** his will,	4472
Jas	1:25	not forgetting what he has heard, but **d** it—	4475
	2: 8	*you are* **d** right.	4472
1Pe	2:12	though they accuse you of **d wrong,**	2804
	2:15	that *by* **d good** you should silence	16
	2:20	a beating *for* **d wrong** and endure it?	279
	2:20	if you suffer *for* **d good** and you endure it,	16
	3:17	to suffer *for* **d good** than for doing evil.	16
	3:17	to suffer for doing good than *for* **d evil.**	2803
	4: 3	in the past **d** what pagans choose to do—	2981
3Jn	1: 5	you are faithful in what *you are* **d** for	2237
	1:10	I will call attention to what *he is* **d,**	4472
Rev	2:19	and that you are now **d** more than you did	2240

DOLE (1)

Lev	26:26	and *they will* **d out** the bread by weight.	8740

DOLEFUL (KJV) See MOURNFUL

DOMAIN (2) [DOMINION]

Dt	33:20	"Blessed is he who enlarges Gad's **d!**	NIH
Eze	27: 4	Your **d** was on the high seas;	1473

DOMINION (18) [DOMAIN]

Job	25: 2	"**D** and awe belong to God;	5440
	38:33	Can you set up [God's] **d** over the earth?	5428
Ps	22:28	for **d** belongs to the LORD and he rules	4867
	103:22	all his works everywhere in his **d.**	4939
	114: 2	Judah became God's sanctuary, Israel his **d.**	4939
	145:13	and your **d** endures through all generations.	4939
Da	2:37	of heaven has given you **d** and power	10424
	4: 3	his **d** endures from generation	10717
	4:22	your **d** extends to distant parts of the earth.	10717
	4:34	His **d** is an eternal dominion;	10717
	4:34	His dominion is an eternal **d;**	10717
	6:26	his **d** will never end.	10717
	7:14	His **d** is an everlasting dominion that will	10717
	7:14	His dominion is an everlasting **d** that will	10717
Mic	4: 8	the former **d** will be restored to you;	4939
1Co	15:24	the Father after he has destroyed all **d,**	794
Eph	1:21	and authority, power and **d,** and every title	3262
Col	1:13	from the **d** of darkness and brought us into	2026

DOMINIONS (KJV) See RULERS

DON'T (213) [DO, NOT]

Ge	4: 9	"I **d** know," he replied.	4202
	19: 7	**D** do this wicked thing.	440
	19: 8	But **d** do anything to these men,	440
	19:17	**D** look back, and don't stop anywhere in	440
	19:17	and **d** stop anywhere in the plain!	440
	21:26	"I **d** know who has done this.	4202
	27: 2	"I am now an old man and **d** know the day	4202
	30:31	"**D** give me anything," Jacob replied.	4202
	31:35	Rachel said to her father, "**D** be angry,	440
	35:17	"**D** be afraid, for you have another son."	440
	37:22	"**D** shed any blood.	440
	37:22	but **d** lay a hand on him."	440
	43:22	We **d** know who put our silver	4202
	43:23	"**D** be afraid.	440
	44:15	**D** you know that a man	NIG
	45: 9	Come down to me; **d** delay.	440
	45:24	"**D** quarrel on the way!"	440
	50:19	But Joseph said to them, "**D** be afraid.	440
	50:21	So then, **d** be afraid.	440
Ex	5: 8	**d** reduce the quota.	4202
	9:28	you **d** have to stay any longer."	4202
	32: 1	we **d** know what has happened to him."	4202
	32:23	we **d** know what has happened to him.'	4202
Jos	2: 5	I **d** know which way they went.	4202
	2:14	"If you **d** tell what we are doing,	4202
	8: 4	**D** go very far from it.	440
	10:19	But **d** stop!	440
	10:19	the rear and **d** let them reach their cities,	440
Jdg	4: 8	but if you **d** go with me, I won't go.	4202
	4:18	**D** be afraid."	440
	14:16	You **d** really love me.	4202
	15:11	"**D** you realize that the Philistines are rulers	4202
	18: 9	**D** hesitate to go there and take it over.	440
	18:19	**D say a word.**	3338+6584+7023+8492
	18:25	The Danites answered, "**D** argue with us,	440
	19:19	We **d** need anything."	401
	19:20	Only **d** spend the night in the square."	440
	19:23	"No, my friends, **d** be so vile.	440
	19:23	**d** do this disgraceful thing.	440
	19:24	**d** do such a disgraceful thing."	4202
Ru	1:16	"**D** urge me to leave you or to turn back	440
	1:20	"**D** call me Naomi," she told them.	440
	2: 8	**D** go and glean in another field	440
	2: 8	in another field and **d** go away from here.	4202
	2:15	among the sheaves, **d** embarrass her.	4202
	2:16	and **d** rebuke her."	4202
	3: 3	but **d** let him know you are there	440

Ru	3:11	And now, my daughter, **d** be afraid.	440
	3:14	"**D** let it be known that a woman came to	440
	3:17	of barley, saying, '**D** go back	440
1Sa	1: 8	Why **d** you eat?	4202
	1: 8	**D** I mean more to you than ten sons?"	4202
	2:16	if you **d,** I'll take it by force."	4202
	17:55	"As surely as you live, O king, I **d** know."	561
	19:11	"If you **d** run for your life tonight,	401
	20:30	**D** I know that you have sided with the son	4202
	20:38	"Hurry! Go quickly! **D** stop!"	440
	21: 4	"I **d** have any ordinary bread on hand;	401
	21: 8	"**D** you have a spear or a sword here?	403
	22:23	Stay with me; **d** be afraid;	440
	23:17	"**D** be afraid," he said.	440
	26: 9	But David said to Abishai, "**D** destroy him!	440
	28:13	The king said to her, "**D** be afraid.	440
	29: 6	but the rulers **d** approve of you.	4202
2Sa	2:26	**D** you realize that this will end	4202
	9: 7	"**D** be afraid," David said to him,	440
	11:25	'**D** let this upset you;	440
	13:12	"**D,** my brother!"	440
	13:12	"**D** force me.	440
	13:12	**D** do this wicked thing.	440
	13:20	**D** take this thing to heart."	440
	13:28	**D** be afraid.	440
	14: 2	and **d** use any cosmetic lotions.	440
	18:22	You **d** have any news that will bring you	401
	18:29	your servant, but I **d** know what it was."	4202
	19: 7	I swear by the LORD that if you **d** go out,	401
1Ki	3:26	**D** kill him!"	440
	17:12	she replied, "I **d** have any bread—	561
	17:13	Elijah said to her, "**D** be afraid.	440
	18:12	I **d** know where the Spirit of	4202
	18:40	**D** let anyone get away!"	440
	20: 8	"**D** listen to him or agree to his demands."	440
	22: 3	"**D** you know that Ramoth Gilead belongs	2022
2Ki	4: 3	**D** ask for just a few.	440
	4:16	"**D** mislead your servant, O man of God!"	440
	4:24	**d** slow down for me unless I tell you."	440
	4:28	"Didn't I tell you, '**D** raise my hopes'?"	4202
	6:16	"**D** be afraid," the prophet answered.	440
	6:32	to the elders, "**D** you see	2022
	9: 3	Then open the door and run; **d** delay!"	4202
	9:15	**d** let anyone slip out of the city to go	440
	18:26	**D** speak to us in Hebrew in the hearing of	440
	23:18	"**D** let anyone disturb his bones."	440
2Ch	13: 5	**D** you know that the LORD,	4202
Ne	4:14	"**D** be afraid of them.	440
Pr	23:35	They beat me, but I **d** feel it!	1153
Isa	7: 4	'Be careful, keep calm and **d** be afraid.	440
	29:12	he will answer, "I **d** know how to read."	4202
	36:11	**D** speak to us in Hebrew in the hearing of	440
	65: 5	**d** come near me,	440
	65: 8	'**D** destroy it, there is yet some good in it,'	440
Jer	13:12	'**D** we know that every wineskin should	4202
	36:19	**D** let anyone know where you are."	440
	39:12	**d** harm him but do	440
	40: 4	but if you do not want to, then **d** come.	2532
	40:14	"**D** you know that Baalis king of	2022
	40:16	"**D** do such a thing!	440
	41: 8	But ten of them said to Ishmael, "**D** kill us!	440
La	4:15	"**D** touch us!"	440
Da	5:10	"**D** be alarmed!	10031
	5:10	**D** look so pale!	10031
Am	7:13	**D** prophesy anymore at Bethel,	4202
Mt	8: 4	"See that you **d** tell **anyone.**	3594
	10:31	So **d** be afraid;	3590
	14:27	**D** be afraid."	3590
	15: 2	They **d** wash their hands before they eat!"	4024
	15:17	"**D** you see that whatever enters	4024
	16: 9	**D** you remember the five loaves for	4028
	16:11	How is it you **d** understand that I was	4024
	17: 7	"**D** be afraid."	3590
	17: 9	"**D** tell **anyone** what you have seen,	3594
	20:15	**D** I have the right to do what I want	4024
	20:22	"You **d** know what you are asking,"	4024
	21:27	So they answered Jesus, "We **d** know."	4024
	25:12	'I tell you the truth, I **d** know you.'	4024
	26:70	"I **d** know what you're talking about,"	4024
	26:72	"I **d** know the man!"	4024
	26:74	"I **d** know the man!"	4024
	27:13	"**D** you hear the testimony they are bringing	4202
	27:19	"**D** have **anything** to do with	3594
Mk	1:44	"See that you **d** tell **this** to anyone.	3594
	4:13	"**D** you understand this parable?	4024
	4:21	Instead, **d** you put it on its stand?	4024
	4:38	"Teacher, **d** you care if we drown?"	4024
	5:36	"**D** be afraid; just believe."	3590
	6:50	**D** be afraid."	3590
	7: 5	"Why **d** your disciples live according to	4024
	7:18	"**D** you see that nothing that enters a man	4024
	8:18	And **d** you remember?	4024
	8:26	saying, "**D** go into the village.	3593
	10:38	"You **d** know what you are asking,"	4024
	11:33	So they answered Jesus, "We **d** know."	4024
	14:68	"I **d** know or understand what you're talking	4046
	14:71	"I **d** know this man you're talking about."	4024
	16: 6	"**D** be alarmed," he said.	3590
Lk	3:13	"**D** collect any more than you are required	3594
	3:14	He replied, "**D** extort money	3594
	3:14	"Don't extort money and **d** accuse people falsely—	3593
	5:10	Then Jesus said to Simon, "**D** be afraid;	3590
	5:14	Then Jesus ordered him, "**D** tell **anyone,**	3594
	7: 6	"Lord, **d** trouble yourself,	3590
	7:13	to her and he said, "**D** cry."	3590

Lk	8:28	I beg you, **d** torture me!"	3590
	8:49	"**D** bother the teacher **any more.**"	3600
	8:50	Jesus said to Jairus, "**D** be afraid;	3590
	10:40	**d** you care that my sister has left me to do	3590
	11: 7	the one inside answers, '**D** bother me.	3590
	12: 7	of your head are all numbered. **D** be afraid;	3590
	12:56	How is it that you **d** know how	4024
	12:57	"Why **d** you judge for yourselves	4024
	13:25	'I **d** know you or where you come from.'	4024
	13:27	'I **d** know you or where you come from.	4024
	18: 4	though I **d** fear God or care about men,	4024
	19:14	'We **d** want this man to be our king.'	4024
	20: 7	"We **d** know where it was from."	3590
	22:36	and if you **d** have a sword,	3590
	22:57	"Woman, I **d** know him," he said.	4024
	22:60	I **d** know what you're talking about!"	4024
	23:40	"**D** you fear God," he said.	4024
Jn	6:20	But he said to them, "It is I; **d** be afraid."	3590
	8:46	why **d** you believe me?	4024
	9:12	"I **d** know," he said.	4024
	9:21	or who opened his eyes, we **d** know.	4024
	9:25	"Whether he is a sinner or not, I **d** know.	4024
	9:29	we **d** even know where he comes from."	4024
	9:30	You **d** know where he comes from,	4024
	14: 5	"Lord, we **d** know where you are going,	4024
	14: 9	Jesus answered: "**D** you know me, Philip,	4024
	14:10	**D** you believe that I am in the Father,	4024
	16:18	We **d** understand what he is saying."	4024
	19:10	"**D** you realize I have power either	4024
	20: 2	and we **d** know where they have put him!"	4024
	20:13	"and I **d** know where they have put him."	4024
Ac	7:40	we **d** know what has happened to him!'	4024
	16:28	But Paul shouted, "**D** harm yourself!	3594
	20:10	"**D** be alarmed," he said.	3590
	23:21	**D** give in to them,	3590
	23:22	"**D** tell **anyone** that you have reported this	3594
Ro	6: 3	Or **d** *you* know that all	51
	6:16	**D** you know that when you offer yourselves	4024
	11: 2	**D** you know what the Scripture says in	4024
1Co	1:16	I **d** remember if I baptized anyone else.)	4024
	3:16	**D** you know that you yourselves are God's temple	4024
	5: 6	**D** you know that a little yeast works	4024
	7:21	**D** let it trouble you—	3590
	9: 4	**D** we have the right to food and drink?	3590+4024
	9: 5	**D** we have the right to take a believing wife	3590+4024
	9:13	**D** you know that those who work in	4024
	10:12	be careful that you **d** fall!	3590
	11:22	**D** you have homes to eat and drink in?	3590+4024
	12:21	"I **d** need you!"	4024
	12:21	"I **d** need you!"	4024
2Th	2: 3	**D** let anyone deceive you in any way,	3590
	2: 5	**D** you remember that when I was	3590
1Ti	4:12	**D** let **anyone** look down on you	3594
2Ti	2:23	**D** have anything to do with	4148
Jas	1:16	**D** be deceived, my dear brothers.	3590
	2: 1	**d** show favoritism.	3590
	4: 1	**D** they come from your desires that battle	4024
	4: 2	You want something but **d** get it.	4024
	4: 4	**d** you know that friendship with	4024
	5: 9	**D** grumble against each other, brothers,	3590

DONATED (1)

Ezr	8:25	and all Israel present there *had* **d** for the house of our God.	8123

DONE (549) [DO]

Ge	2: 3	from all the work of creating that he *had* **d.**	6913
	3:13	"What is this *you have* **d?**"	6913
	3:14	"Because *you have* **d** this,	6913
	4:10	The LORD said, "What *have you* **d?**	6913
	8:21	as *I have* **d.**	6913
	9:24	and found out what his youngest son *had* **d**	6913
	12:18	"What *have you* **d** to me?"	6913
	18:21	down and see if *what they have* **d** is as bad	6913
	20: 5	*I have* **d** this with a clear conscience	6913
	20: 9	"What *have you* **d** to us?	6913
	20: 9	You *have* **d** things to me that should not	6913
	20: 9	to me *that should* not *be* **d.**"	6913
	21:26	"I *don't* know who *has* **d** this.	6913
	22:16	that because *you have* **d** this and have	6913
	24:66	Then the servant told Isaac all *he had* **d.**	6913
	26:10	"What is this *you have* **d** to us?	6913
	27:19	*I have* **d** as you told me.	6913
	28:15	until *I have* **d** what I have promised you."	6913
	29:25	"What is this *you have* **d** to me?	6913
	30:26	You know how much work I've **d** *for* you."	6268
	31:26	Laban said to Jacob, "What *have you* **d?**	6913
	31:28	*You have* **d** a foolish thing.	6913
	34: 7	because Shechem *had* **d** a disgraceful thing	6913
	34: 7	a *thing that should* not *be* **d.**	6913
	39:22	for all that *was* **d** there.	6913
	40:15	and even here I *have* **d** nothing	6913
	41:21	no one could tell that they *had* **d** so;	448+995+7931S
	42:25	After this *was* **d** for them,	6913
	42:28	"What is this that God *has* **d** to us?"	6913
	44: 5	This is a wicked thing *you have* **d.**'"	6913
	44:15	"What is this *you have* **d?**	6913
	45: 4	When *they had* **d** so, he said,	5602S
	50:20	to accomplish what is now being **d,**	NIH
Ex	1:18	"Why *have you* **d** this?	6913
	3:16	over you and have seen what *has been* **d**	6913
	14: 5	"What *have we* **d?**	6913

Ex	14:11	What *have you* **d** to us by bringing us out	6913
	18: 1	heard of everything God *had* **d** for Moses	6913
	18: 8	about everything the LORD *had* **d**	6913
	18: 9	the LORD *had* **d** for Israel in rescuing them	6913
	31:15	For six days, work *is to be* **d**,	6913
	34:10	before **d** in any nation in all the world.	1343
	35: 2	For six days, work *is to be* **d**.	6913
	36: 5	the work the LORD commanded to *be* **d**."	6913
	36:11	and the same *was* **d** with the end curtain in	6913
	39:42	The Israelites *had* **d** all the work just as	6913
	39:43	the work and saw that *they had* **d** it just as	6913
Lev	8: 5	the LORD *has* commanded to *be* **d**."	6913
	8:34	What *has been* **d** today was commanded by	6913
	16:34	And *it was* **d**, as the LORD commanded	6913
	18:27	for all these things *were* **d** by	6913
	20:12	What *they have* **d** is a perversion;	6913
	20:13	both of them *have* **d** what is detestable.	6913
	24:19	whatever *he has* **d** must be done to him:	6913
	24:19	whatever *he has* done *must be* **d** to him.	6913
Nu	4:26	that *needs to be* **d** with these things.	6913
	4:27	*is to be* **d** under the direction of Aaron	2118
	11:11	What *have I* **d** to **displease** you	AIT
	15:24	and if *this is* **d** unintentionally without	6913
	15:34	it was not clear what *should be* **d** to him.	6913
	22: 2	of Zippor saw all that Israel *had* **d** to	6913
	22:28	"What *have I* **d** to you	6913
	23:11	"What *have you* **d** to me?	6913
	23:11	*you have* **d** nothing but bless them!"	1385+1385
	23:23	'See what God *has* **d**!'	7188
	32:13	whole generation of those *who had* **d** evil in	
		his sight was gone.	6913
Dt	2:22	The LORD *had* **d** the same for	6913
	2:30	as he has now **d**.	NIH
	3: 6	as *we had* **d** with Sihon king of Heshbon,	6913
	3:21	that the LORD your God *has* **d**	6913
	11: 7	the LORD *has* **d**.	6913
	13:14	that this detestable thing *has been* **d**	6913
	15: 2	This is how it is to be **d**.	NIH
	17: 4	this detestable thing *has been* **d** in Israel,	6913
	17: 5	the man or woman *who has* **d** this evil deed	6913
	19:20	an evil thing *be* among you.	6913
	21: 7	nor did our eyes see it **d**.	NIH
	21: 9	since *you have* **d** what is right in the eyes of	6913
	22:21	*She has* **d** a disgraceful thing in Israel	6913
	22:25	the man who *has* **d** this shall die.	6640+8886ˢ
	25: 9	"This is what *is* **d** to the man who will	6913
	26:14	*I have* **d** everything you commanded me.	6913
	28:20	of the evil you have **d** in forsaking him.	5095
	29:24	"Why *has* the LORD **d** this to this land?	6213
	32:27	the LORD *has* not **d** all this.' "	7188
Jos	1:15	as he has **d** for you,	NIH
	4:10	the LORD had commanded Joshua *was* **d**	9462
	4:23	the Jordan just what *he had* **d** to the Red Sea	6913
	6:23	young men who *had* **d** the **spying** went in	AIT
	7:15	of the LORD and *has* **d** a disgraceful thing	6913
	7:19	Tell me what *you have* **d**;	6913
	7:20	This is what *I have* **d**:	6913
	9: 3	of Gibeon heard what Joshua *had* **d**	6913
	10: 1	to Ai and its king as *he had* **d** to Jericho	6913
	10:28	to the king of Makkedah as *he had* **d** to the	
		king of Jericho.	6913
	10:30	And he did to its king as *he had* **d** to the	
		king of Jericho.	6913
	10:32	just as *he had* **d** to Libnah	6913
	10:35	just as *they had* **d** to Lachish.	6913
	10:39	to Debir and its king as *they had* **d** to	
		Libnah	6913
	22: 2	"You *have* **d** all that Moses the servant of	9068
	23: 3	the LORD your God *has* **d**	6913
	24:31	the LORD *had* **d** for Israel.	6913
Jdg	2: 2	Why *have you* **d** this?	6913
	2: 7	the great things the LORD *had* **d** for Israel.	6913
	2:10	the LORD nor what *he had* **d** for Israel.	6913
	8:35	for all the good things *he had* **d** for them.	6913
	9:56	the wickedness that Abimelech *had* **d**	6913
	14: 6	nor his mother what *he had* **d**.	6913
	15:11	What *have you* **d** to us?"	6913
	18: 4	He told them what Micah *had* **d** for him,	6913
	19:30	"Such a thing has never been seen or **d**,	2118
	20:10	for all this vileness in Israel."	6913
	20:30	**as** they had **d** before.	928+3869+7193+7193
Ru	2:11	"I've been told all about what *you have* **d**	6913
	2:12	the LORD repay you for *what* you have **d**,	7189
	3:16	she told her everything Boaz *had* **d** for her	6913
1Sa	2:32	Although **good** *will be* **d** to Israel,	3512
	8: 8	As *they have* **d** from the day I brought them	6913
	11: 7	"This is what *will be* **d** to the oxen	6913
	12: 3	If I have **d** any of these,	NIH
	12:20	"You *have* **d** all this evil;	6913
	12:24	**great things** he has **d**	1540
	13:11	"What *have you* **d**?"	6913
	14:35	it was the first time *he had* **d** this.	
		1215+3378+4200+4640ˢ	
	14:43	"Tell me what *you have* **d**."	6913
	17:26	"What *will be* **d** for	6913
	17:27	"This is what *will be* **d** for	6913
	17:29	"Now what *have I* **d**?"	6213
	19: 4	**what** he has **d** has benefited you greatly.	5126
	19:18	at Ramah and told him all that Saul *had* **d**	6913
	20: 1	"What *have I* **d**?	6213
	20:32	What *has he* **d**?"	6213
	24:12	**avenge** the **wrongs** you have **d**	AIT
	25:30	When the LORD *has* **d**	6913
	26:16	What *you have* **d** is not good.	6913
	26:18	What *have I* **d**,	6213
	26:19	If, however, men have **d** it,	NIH
	28: 9	"Surely you know what Saul *has* **d**.	6213

1Sa	28:17	The LORD *has* **d** what he predicted	6213
	28:18	the LORD *has* **d** this to you today.	6213
	29: 8	"But what *have I* **d**?"	6213
	31:11	of what the Philistines *had* **d** to Saul,	6213
2Sa	2: 6	the same favor because *you have* **d** this.	6213
	3:24	"What *have you* **d**?	6213
	7:11	and have **d** ever since	NIH
	7:21	*you have* **d** this great thing	6213
	8:11	as *he had* **d** with the silver and gold	7727ˢ
	11:27	thing David *had* **d** displeased the LORD.	6213
	13:12	Such a thing *should* not *be* **d** in Israel!	6213
	13:16	greater wrong than what *you have already* **d**	6213
	21:11	Saul's concubine, *had*, **d**,	6213
	22:22	not *d* **evil** by turning from my God.	8399
	24:10	"I have sinned greatly in what *I have* **d**.	6213
	24:10	**d** a very **foolish** thing."	6118
	24:17	"I am the one who has sinned and **d** **wrong**.	6390
	24:17	What *have they* **d**?	6213
1Ki	1:27	*Is* this something my lord the king *has* **d**	2118
	7:51	work King Solomon *had* **d** for the temple	6913
	8:25	to walk before me as *you have* **d**.'	2143ˢ
	8:32	down on his own head what *he has* **d**.	2006
	8:47	**we have** **d** **wrong**, we have acted wickedly';	6390
	8:66	for all the good things the LORD *had* **d**	6213
	9: 8	the LORD *d* such a thing to this land and	6213
	11: 6	as David his father had **d**.	NIH
	11:33	nor *d* what is right in my eyes,	6213
	13:11	the man of God *had* **d** there that day.	5126+6913
	14: 9	You have **d** more evil than all who lived	6213
	14:22	stirred up his jealous anger more than their	
		fathers *had* **d**.	6213
	15: 3	He committed all the sins his father *had* **d**	6213
	15: 5	For David *had* **d** what was right in the eyes	6213
	15:11	as his father David had **d**.	NIH
	16: 7	because of all the evil *he had* **d**	6213
	18: 9	"What *have I* **d** **wrong**," asked Obadiah,	2627
	18:36	and *have* **d** all these things	6213
	19: 1	Ahab told Jezebel everything Elijah *had* **d**	6213
	19:20	"What *have I* **d** to you?"	6213
	20:22	and see what *must be* **d**,	6213
	22:53	to anger, just as his father *had* **d**.	6213
2Ki	1:16	Because you have **d** this,	NIH
	3: 2	but not as his father and mother had **d**.	NIH
	4:13	Now what *can be* **d** for you?	6213
	4:14	"What *can be* **d** for her?"	6213
	5:13	*would you* not *have* **d** it?	6213
	7:12	"I will tell you what the Arameans *have* **d**.	6213
	8: 4	about all the great things Elisha *has* **d**."	6213
	8:18	as the house of Ahab *had* **d**,	6213
	8:27	as the house of Ahab had **d**,	NIH
	10:10	The LORD *has* **d** what he promised	6213
	10:30	"Because *you have* **d** well	3201
	10:30	and *have* **d** to the house of Ahab all I had	6213
	12: 7	"Why aren't you repairing the **damage** *d to*	AIT
	14: 3	but not as his father David had **d**.	NIH
	15: 3	just as his father Amaziah *had* **d**.	6213
	15: 9	as his fathers *had* **d**.	6213
	15:34	just as his father Uzziah *had* **d**.	6213
	17: 4	as he had **d** year by year.	NIH
	17:11	before them had **d**.	NIH
	18: 3	just as his father David had **d**.	6213
	18:14	"I have **d** **wrong**.	2627
	19:11	of Assyria *have* **d** to all the countries,	6213
	20: 3	and *have* **d** what is good in your eyes."	6213
	21: 3	as Ahab king of Israel *had* **d**.	6213
	21:11	*He has* **d** more **evil** than	8317
	21:15	because *they have* **d** evil in my eyes	6213
	21:20	as his father Manasseh *had* **d**.	6213
	23:17	of Bethel the very things *you have* **d** to it."	6213
	23:19	Just as *he had* **d** at Bethel.	5126+6913
	23:26	*d* to **provoke** him **to anger**.	AIT
	23:32	just as his fathers *had* **d**.	6213
	23:37	just as his fathers *had* **d**.	6213
	24: 3	of the sins of Manasseh and all *he had* **d**,	6213
	24: 9	just as his father *had* **d**.	6213
	24:19	just as Jehoiakim *had* **d**.	6213
1Ch	6:49	of incense in connection with all that was **d**	4856
	10:11	of everything the Philistines *had* **d** to Saul,	6213
	16: 8	among the nations what *he has* **d**.	6613
	16:12	Remember the wonders *he has* **d**,	6213
	17:10	and *have* **d** ever since	NIH
	17:19	*you have* **d** this great thing	6213
	18:11	as he had **d** with the silver	NIH
	21: 8	**d** a very **foolish** thing."	6118
	21:17	I am the one who has sinned and **d** **wrong**.	
		8317+8317	
	21:17	What *have they* **d**?	6213
	28: 7	as is being *d* at this time."	6213
	29: 5	all the work to be **d** by the craftsmen.	928+3338
2Ch	5: 1	the work Solomon *had* **d** for the temple of	6213
	6:16	as *you have* **d**.'	2143ˢ
	6:23	down on his own head what *he has* **d**.	2006
	6:37	**we have** **d** **wrong** and acted wickedly';	6390
	7:10	the good things the LORD *had* **d** for David	6213
	7:21	the LORD **d** such a thing to this land and	6213
	16: 9	*You have* **d** a **foolish** thing,	6118
	21: 6	as the house of Ahab *had* **d**,	6213
	22: 4	as the house of Ahab *had* **d**,	NIH
	24:16	because of the good *he had* **d** in Israel	6213
	25:16	because *you have* **d** this and have	6213
	26: 4	just as his father Amaziah *had* **d**,	6213
	27: 2	just as his father Uzziah *had* **d**,	6213
	29: 2	just as his father David *had* **d**,	6213
	29:36	because God *had* **d** it so quickly.	2118
	31:11	and *this was* **d**.	3922ˢ
	32: 1	After *all* that Hezekiah had so faithfully **d**,	1821
	32:13	and my fathers *have* **d** to all the peoples of	6213

2Ch	33:22	as his father Manasseh *had* **d**.	6213
Ezr	7:23	*let it be* **d** with diligence for the temple of	10522
	9: 1	After these things had been **d**,	3983
	10: 3	*Let it be* **d** according to the Law.	6213
Ne	5:19	for all *I have* **d** for these people.	6213
	6:14	O my God, because of what they have **d**;	5126
	6:16	that this work *had been* **d** with the help	6213
	13: 7	about the evil thing Eliashib *had* **d**	6213
	13:14	not blot out what *I have* so faithfully **d** for	6213
Est	1:15	what *must be* **d** to Queen Vashti?"	6213
	1:16	"Queen Vashti has **d** **wrong**,	6390
	2: 1	what *she had* **d** and what he had decreed	6213
	2:20	as *she had* **d** when he was bringing her up.	2118
	4: 1	Mordecai learned of all that *had been* **d**,	6213
	4:16	When this is **d**, I will go to the king,	NIH
	6: 3	"Nothing *has been* **d** for him,"	6213
	6: 6	*be* **d** for the man the king delights	6213
	6: 9	'This is what *is* **d** for the man	6213
	6:11	"This is what *is* **d** for the man	6213
	9:12	What *have they* **d** in the rest of	6213
	9:14	So the king commanded that this *be* **d**.	6213
Job	7:20	If I have sinned, what *have I* **d** to you,	7188
	12: 9	that the hand of the LORD *has* **d** this?	6213
	21:31	Who repays him for what *he has* **d**?	6213
	22:28	What you decide on *will be* **d**,	7756
	34:11	He repays a man for **what** he has **d**;	7189
	34:32	if *I have* **d** **wrong**, I will not do so again.'	7188
	36: 9	he tells them **what** they have **d**—	7189
	36:23	or said to him, 'You *have* **d** **wrong**'?	7188
Ps	7: 3	if *I have* **d** this and there is guilt	6213
	7: 4	if *I have* **d** evil *to* him who is at peace	1694
	9:11	proclaim among the nations **what** he has **d**.	6613
	18:21	not *d* **evil** by turning from my God.	8399
	22:31	for *he has* **d** it.	6213
	28: 4	**what** their hands have **d**	5126
	28: 5	**what** his hands have **d**,	5126
	39: 9	for you are the *one* who has **d** this.	6213
	40: 5	are the wonders *you have* **d**.	6213
	50:21	These things *you have* **d** and I kept silent;	6213
	51: 4	have I sinned and **d** what is evil	6213
	52: 9	for *what you have* **d**.	6213
	59: 4	I have **d** no **wrong**,	NIH
	62:12	according to **what** he has **d**.	5126
	64: 9	works of God and ponder **what** he has **d**.	6213
	66: 5	Come and see **what** God has **d**,	5149
	66:16	let me tell you what *he has* **d** for me.	6213
	68:28	O God, as *you have* **d** before.	7188
	71:19	O God, *you* who *have* **d** great things.	6213
	78: 4	his power, and the wonders *he has* **d**.	6213
	78:11	They forgot **what** he had **d**,	6613
	98: 1	for *he has* **d** marvelous things;	6213
	99: 4	in Jacob you *have* **d** what is just and right.	6213
	105: 1	among the nations **what** he has **d**.	6613
	105: 5	Remember the wonders *he has* **d**,	6213
	106: 6	**we have** **d** **wrong** and acted wickedly.	6390
	106:13	But they soon forgot **what** he had **d** and did	5126
	106:21	*who had* **d** great things in Egypt,	6213
	109:27	that you, O LORD, *have* **d** it.	6213
	111: 8	**d** in faithfulness and uprightness.	6213
	118:15	LORD's right hand *has* **d** mighty things!	6213
	118:16	the LORD's right hand *has* **d** mighty things!"	6213
	118:17	**what** the LORD has **d**.	5126
	118:23	the LORD *has* **d** this,	2118
	119:121	*I have* **d** what is righteous and just;	6213
	126: 2	"The LORD *has* **d** great things for them."	6213
	126: 3	The LORD *has* **d** great things for us,	6213
	137: 8	for *what you have* **d** to us—	1694
	143: 5	**what** your hands have **d**.	5126
	147:20	*He has* **d** this for no other nation;	6213
Pr	19:17	and he will reward him for **what** he has **d**.	1691
	21:15	*When* justice is **d**, it brings joy	6213
	24:12	according to **what** he has **d**?	7189
	24:29	"I'll do to him as *he has* **d** to me;	6213
	30:20	'I've **d** nothing **wrong**.'	7188
Ecc	1: 9	what *has been* **d** will be done again;	6213
	1: 9	what has been done *will be* **d** *again;*	6213
	1:13	and to explore by wisdom all that is **d**	6213
	1:14	I have seen all the things that *are* **d** under	6213
	2:11	when I surveyed all that my hands *had* **d**	6213
	2:12	What more can king's successor do than	
		what *has already been* **d**?	6213
	2:17	that *is* **d** under the sun was grievous to me.	6213
	3:11	yet they cannot fathom what God *has* **d**	6213
	4: 3	has not seen the evil that *is* **d** under	5126+6913
	7:13	Consider **what** God has **d**:	5126
	8: 9	as I applied my mind to everything **d** under	6213
	8:17	then I saw all **that** God has **d**.	5126
Isa	5: 4	**what** their hands have **d**.	1691
	5: 4	What more *could have been* **d**	6213
	5: 4	for my vineyard than *I have* **d** for it?	6213
	10:13	" 'By the strength of my hand *I have* **d** this,	6213
	12: 4	among the nations **what** he has **d**,	6613
	12: 5	for *he has* **d** glorious things;	6213
	25: 1	in perfect faithfulness *you have* **d**	
		marvelous things,	6213
	26:12	all that we have accomplished *you have* **d**.	7188
	33:13	You who are far away, hear what *I have* **d**;	6213
	37:11	of Assyria *have* **d** to all the countries,	6213
	38: 3	and *have* **d** what is good in your eyes."	6213
	38:15	and he himself *has* **d** this.	6213
	41: 4	Who has **d** this and carried it through,	7188
	41:20	that the hand of the LORD *has* **d** this,	6213
	44:23	O heavens, for the LORD *has* **d** this;	6213
	53: 9	though *he had* **d** no violence,	6213
	59:18	According to **what** they have **d**,	1692
	63: 7	according to all the LORD *has* **d** *for* us—	1694

Isa	63: 7	the many good things he has **d** for the house	1694
Jer	2:23	consider what you have **d**.	6913
	3: 6	"Have you seen what faithless Israel has **d**?	6913
	3: 7	that after she had **d** all this she would return	6913
	4: 4	like fire because of the evil you have **d**—	5095
	5:13	so let what they say be **d** to them."	6913
	5:19	'Why has the LORD our God **d** all this	6913
	7:30	" 'The people of Judah have **d** evil	6913
	8: 6	saying, "What have I **d**?"	6913
	11:17	of Israel and the house of Judah have **d** evil	6913
	16:10	What wrong have we **d**?	NIH
	18:13	A most horrible thing has been **d**	6913
	21:12	like fire because of the evil you have **d**—	5095
	22: 8	'Why has the LORD **d** such a thing	6913
	23: 2	on you for the evil you have **d**,"	5095
	26: 3	because of the evil they have **d**.	5095
	29:23	of Israel because of all they have **d**,"	6913
	30:15	and many sins I have **d** these things to you.	6913
	31:37	of Israel because of all they have **d**,"	6913
	32:30	of Israel and Judah have **d** nothing but evil	6913
	32:30	indeed, the people of Israel have **d** nothing	NIH
	32:32	by all the evil they have **d**—	6913
	35:18	and have **d** everything he ordered.'	6913
	38: 9	in all they have **d** to Jeremiah the prophet.	6913
	40: 3	he has **d** just as he said he would.	6913
	44: 3	because of the evil they have **d**.	6913
	50:15	do to her as she has **d** to others.	6913
	50:29	do to her as she has **d**.	6913
	51:10	what the LORD our God has **d**.'	5126
	51:24	in Babylonia for all the wrong they have **d**	6913
	51:35	May the violence to our flesh be	NIH
	52: 2	just as Jehoiakim had **d**.	6913
La	1:21	they rejoice at what you have **d**.	6913
	2:17	The LORD has **d** what he planned;	6913
	3:59	O LORD, the wrong **d** to me.	6432
	3:64	what their hands have **d**.	5126
Eze	5: 9	I will do to you what I have never **d** before	6913
	6: 9	for the evil they have **d** and	6913
	9: 4	over all the detestable things that are **d**	6913
	9:10	bring down on their own heads what they have **d**."	2006
	9:11	saying, "I have **d** as you commanded."	6913
	11:21	down on their own heads what they have **d**,	2006
	12:11	"As I have **d**, so it will be done to them.	6913
	12:11	"As I have **d**, so it will be **d** to them.	6913
	14:23	that I have **d** nothing in it without cause,	6913
	16:43	down on your head what you have **d**,	2006
	16:48	and your daughters have **d**.	6913
	16:51	You have **d** more detestable things than they,	8049
	16:51	by all these things you have **d**.	6913
	16:54	of all you have **d** in giving them comfort.	6913
	16:63	for you for all you have **d**,	6913
	18:11	(though the father has **d** none of them):	6913
	18:13	Because he has **d** all these detestable things,	6913
	18:19	Since the son has **d** what is just and right	6913
	18:22	of the righteous things he has **d**, he will live.	6913
	18:24	None of the righteous things he has **d** will	6913
	20:43	for all the evil you have **d**.	6913
	21:24	you have **d** this, you will be taken captive.	2349S
	22:31	down on their own heads all they have **d**,	2006
	23:38	They have also **d** this to me:	6913
	24:22	And you will do as I have **d**.	6913
	24:24	you will do just as he has **d**.	6913
	33:13	none of the righteous things he has **d** will	NIH
	33:13	he will die for the evil he has **d**.	6913
	33:16	He has **d** what is just and right;	6913
	33:29	of all the detestable things they have **d**.'	6913
	37:14	and I have **d** it, declares the LORD.' "	6913
	43:11	and if they are ashamed of all they have **d**,	6913
	44:14	the temple and all the work that is to be **d**	6913
Da	4:35	"What have you **d**?"	10522
	6:10	just as he had **d** before.	10522
	6:22	Nor have I ever **d** any wrong before you,	10522
	9: 5	we have sinned and **d** wrong.	6390
	9:12	the whole heaven nothing has ever been **d**	6913
	9:12	like what has been **d** to Jerusalem.	6913
	9:15	we have sinned, we have **d** wrong.	8399
Joel	2:20	Surely he has **d** great things.	6913
	2:21	Surely the LORD has **d** great things.	6913
	3: 4	for something I have **d**?	1691
	3: 4	on your own heads what you have **d**.	1691
	3: 7	on your own heads what you have **d**.	1691
	3:19	of violence **d** to the people of Judah,	AIT
Am	8: 7	"I will never forget anything they have **d**.	5126
Ob	1:15	As you have **d**, it will be done to you;	6913
	1:15	As you have **d**, it will be **d** to you;	6913
Jnh	1:10	"What have you **d**?"	6213
	1:14	for you, O LORD, have **d** as you pleased."	6913
Mic	3: 4	from them because of the evil they have **d**.	5095
	6: 3	"My people, what have I **d** to you?	6913
Hab	2:17	The violence you have **d**	NIH
Zep	3:11	to shame for all the wrongs you have **d**	6613
Zec	1: 6	'The LORD Almighty has **d**	6913
	7: 3	as I have **d** for so many years?"	6913
Mt	6: 4	your Father, who sees what is **d** in secret,	NIG
	6: 6	your Father, who sees what is **d** in secret,	NIG
	6:10	your will be **d** on earth as it is in heaven.	1181
	6:18	your Father, who sees what is **d** in secret,	NIG
	8:13	It will be **d** just as you believed it would."	1181
	9:29	"According to your faith will it be **d**	1181
	16:27	according to what he has **d**.	4552
	17:12	but have **d** to him everything they wished.	4472
	18:19	be **d** for you by my Father in heaven.	1181
	21:21	only can you do what was **d** to the fig tree,	NIG
	21:21	and it will be **d**.	1181
	21:42	the Lord has **d** this,	1181

Mt	23: 5	"Everything they do is **d** for men to see:	4472
	25:21	"His master replied, 'Well **d**,	2292
	25:23	"His master replied, 'Well **d**,	2292
	26:10	She has **d** a beautiful thing to me.	2237
	26:13	what she has **d** will also be told,	4472
	26:42	may your will be **d**."	1181
Mk	5:19	and tell them how much the Lord has **d**	4472
	5:20	in the Decapolis how much Jesus had **d**	4472
	5:32	around to see who had **d** it.	4472
	6:30	and reported to him all they had **d**	4472
	7:37	"He has **d** everything well," they said.	4472
	9:13	they have to him everything they wished,	4472
	11:23	it will be **d** for him.	NIG
	12:11	the Lord has **d** this,	1181
	14: 6	She has **d** a beautiful thing to me.	2237
	14: 9	what she has **d** will also be told,	4472
Lk	1:25	"The Lord has **d** this for me," she said.	4472
	1:49	the Mighty One has **d** great things for me—	4472
	2:39	and Mary had **d** everything required by	5464
	3:19	and all the other evil things he had **d**,	4472
	5: 6	When they had **d** so,	4472
	8:39	"Return home and tell how much God has **d**	4472
	8:39	over town how much Jesus had **d** for him.	4472
	9:10	they reported to Jesus what they had **d**.	4472
	14:22	'what you ordered has been **d**,	1181
	17:10	you have **d** everything you were told to do,	4472
	17:10	we have only **d** our duty.' "	4472
	19:17	" 'Well **d**, my good servant!'	2301
	22:42	yet not my will, but yours be **d**."	1181
	23:15	he has **d** nothing to deserve death.	1639+4556
	23:41	But this man has **d** nothing wrong."	4556
Jn	3:21	that what he has **d** has been done	2240
	3:21	that what he has **d** has been done	1639+4556
	4:38	Others have **d** the hard work,	AIT
	4:45	They had seen all that he had **d** in Jerusalem	4472
	5:29	those who have **d** good will rise to live,	4472
	5:29	to live, and those who have **d** evil will rise	4556
	11:46	and told them what Jesus had **d**.	4472
	12:16	about him and that they had **d** these things	4472
	12:37	after Jesus had **d** all these miraculous signs	4472
	13:12	"Do you understand what I have **d** for you?"	4472
	13:15	an example that you should do as I have **d**	4472
	15:24	not **d** among them what no one else did,	4472
	18:35	What is it you have **d**?"	4472
Ac	2:43	and miraculous signs were **d** by	1181
	4:16	in Jerusalem knows they have **d**	1181
	9:13	about this man and all the harm he has **d**	4472
	14:11	When the crowd saw what Paul had **d**,	4472
	14:27	that God had **d** through them and	4472
	15: 4	they reported everything God had **d**	4472
	15:12	miraculous signs and wonders God had **d**	4472
	21:14	"The Lord's will be **d**."	1181
	21:19	what God had **d** among the Gentiles	4472
	21:33	asked who he was and what he had **d**.	1639+4472
	25: 5	if he has **d** anything wrong."	1639
	25: 8	"I have **d** nothing wrong against the law of	279
	25:10	I have not **d** any wrong to the Jews,	92
	25:25	I found he had **d** nothing deserving of death,	4556
	26:26	because it was not **d** in a corner.	4556
	28:17	"My brothers, although I have **d** nothing	4472
Ro	1:28	to do what ought not to be **d**."	2763
	2: 6	each person according to what he has **d**."	2240
	6: 6	so that the body of sin might be **d** away with,	2934
	9:11	the twins were born or had **d** anything good	4556
	15:18	to obey God by what I have said and **d**—	2240
1Co	14:26	these must be **d** for the strengthening of	1181
	14:40	But everything should be **d** in a fitting	1181
	15:28	When he has **d** this,	5718S
2Co	1:12	We have **d** so not according	NIG
	5:10	for the things **d** while in the body,	4556
	7:11	readiness to see justice **d**.	1689
	10:15	beyond our limits by boasting of work **d** by	1877
	10:16	not want to boast about work already **d**	2289
	12: 12	were **d** among you with great perseverance.	2981
Gal	4:12	You have **d** me no wrong.	92
	4:15	I can testify that, if you could have **d** so,	1543
Eph	2:11	in the body by the hands	5935
	6:13	and after you have **d** everything, to stand.	2981
Col	2:11	not with a circumcision **d** by the hands of men	942
	2:11	but with the circumcision **d** by Christ,	NIG
2Ti	1: 9	because of anything we have **d** but because	2240
	4:14	The Lord will repay him for what he has **d**.	2240
Tit	3: 5	not because of righteous things we had **d**,	4472
Phm	1:18	If he has **d** you any wrong	92
Heb	10:36	so that when you have **d** the will of God,	4472
Jas	3:13	by deeds **d** in the humility that comes	NIG
1Pe	4: 1	in his body is **d** with sin.	4264
2Pe	2:13	with harm for the harm they have **d**.	92
Jude	1:15	**d** in the ungodly way,	814
Rev	16:11	they refused to repent of what they had **d**.	2240
	16:17	from the throne, saying, "It is **d**!"	1181
	18: 6	pay her back double for what she has **d**.	2240
	20:12	to what they had **d** as recorded in the books.	2240
	20:13	according to what he had **d**.	2240
	21: 6	He said to me: "It is **d**.	1181
	22:12	to everyone according to what he has **d**.	2240

DONKEY (74) [DONKEY'S, DONKEYS, DONKEYS']

Ge	16:12	He will be a **wild d** of a man;	7230
	22: 3	up and saddled his **d**.	2789
	22: 5	the **d** while I and the boy go over there.	2789
	42:27	to get feed for his **d**,	2789
	49:11	He will tether his **d** to a vine,	6554

Ge	49:14	"Issachar is a rawboned **d** lying down	2789
Ex	4:20	put them on a **d** and started back to Egypt.	2789
	13:13	Redeem with a lamb every firstborn **d**,	2789
	20:17	his ox or **d**, or anything that belongs	2789
	21:33	and fails to cover it and an ox or a **d** falls	2789
	22: 4	whether ox or **d** or sheep—	2789
	22: 9	a **d**, a sheep, a garment,	2789
	22:10	"If a man gives a **d**, an ox,	2789
	23: 4	across your enemy's ox or **d** wandering off,	2789
	23: 5	the **d** of someone who hates you fallen	2789
	23:12	so that your ox and your **d** may rest and	2789
	34:20	Redeem the firstborn **d** with a lamb,	2789
Nu	16:15	I have not taken so much as a **d** from them,	2789
	22:21	saddled his **d** and went with the princes	912
	22:22	Balaam was riding on his **d**,	912
	22:23	the **d** saw the angel of the LORD standing	912
	22:25	When the **d** saw the angel of the LORD,	912
	22:27	When the **d** saw the angel of the LORD,	912
	22:29	Balaam answered the **d**,	912
	22:30	The **d** said to Balaam,	912
	22:30	"Am I not your own **d**,	912
	22:32	"Why have you beaten your **d** these three times?	912
	22:33	The **d** saw me and turned away	912
Dt	5:14	nor your ox, your **d** or any of your animals,	2789
	5:21	his manservant or maidservant, his ox or **d**,	2789
	22: 3	Do the same if you find your brother's **d**	2789
	22: 4	If you see your brother's **d** or his ox fallen	2789
	22:10	with an ox and a **d** yoked together.	2789
	28:31	Your **d** will be forcibly taken from you	2789
Jos	15:18	When she got off her **d**, Caleb asked her,	2789
Jdg	1:14	When she got off her **d**, Caleb asked her,	2789
	15:15	Finding a fresh jawbone of a **d**,	2789
	19:28	man put her on his **d** and set out for home.	2789
1Sa	12: 3	Whose **d** have I taken?	2789
	16:20	So Jesse took a **d** loaded with bread,	2789
	25:20	As she came riding her **d** into	2789
	25:23	she quickly got off her **d** and bowed down	2789
	25:42	Abigail quickly got on a **d** and,	2789
2Sa	17:23	he saddled his **d** and set out for his house	2789
	19:26	'I will have my **d** saddled and will ride	2789
1Ki	2:40	he saddled his **d** and went to Achish at Gath	2789
	13:13	he said to his sons, "Saddle the **d** for me."	2789
	13:13	And when they had saddled the **d** for him,	2789
	13:23	the prophet who had brought him back saddled his **d**	2789
	13:24	both the **d** and the lion standing beside it.	2789
	13:27	"Saddle the **d** for me," and they did so.	2789
	13:28	with the **d** and the lion standing beside it.	2789
	13:28	the body nor mauled the **d**.	2789
	13:29	laid it on the **d**,	2789
2Ki	4:22	"Please send me one of the servants and a **d**	912
	4:24	She saddled the **d** and said to her servant,	912
Job	6: 5	Does a **wild d** bray when it has grass,	7230
	24: 3	They drive away the orphan's **d** and take	2789
	39: 5	"Who let the **wild d** go free?	7230
Pr	26: 3	A whip for the horse, a halter for the **d**,	2789
Isa	1: 3	the **d** his owner's manger,	2789
Jer	2:24	a **wild d** accustomed to the desert, sniffing	7241
	22:19	He will have the burial of a **d**—	2789
Hos	8: 9	to Assyria like a **wild d** wandering alone.	7230
Zec	9: 9	gentle and riding on a **d**, on a colt,	2789
	9: 9	on a colt, the foal of a **d**.	912
Mt	21: 2	and at once you will find a **d** tied there,	3952
	21: 5	gentle and riding on a **d**, on a colt,	3952
	21: 5	on a colt, the foal of a **d**.' "	5689
	21: 7	They brought the **d** and the colt,	3952
Lk	10:34	Then he put the man on his own **d**,	3229
	13:15	the Sabbath untie his ox or **d** from the stall	3952
Jn	12:14	Jesus found a **young d** and sat upon it,	3942
2Pe	2:16	for his wrongdoing by a **d**—a beast	5689

DONKEY'S (6) [DONKEY]

Nu	22:28	Then the LORD opened the **d** mouth,	912
Jdg	15:16	a **d** jawbone I have made donkeys of them.	2789
	15:16	a **d** jawbone I have killed a thousand men."	2789
2Ki	6:25	so long that a **d** head sold for eighty shekels	2789
Job	11:12	a **wild d** colt can be born a man.	7230
Jn	12:15	your king is coming, seated on a **d** colt."	3952

DONKEYS (71) [DONKEY]

Ge	12:16	**male** and female **d**,	2789
	24:35	and camels and **d**.	2789
	30:43	and camels and **d**.	2789
	32: 5	I have cattle and **d**, sheep and goats,	2789
	32:15	and twenty **female d** and ten male donkeys.	912
	32:15	and twenty female donkeys and ten **male d**.	6555
	34:28	They seized their flocks and herds and **d**	2789
	36:24	in the desert while he was grazing the **d**	2789
	42:26	they loaded their grain on their **d** and left.	2789
	43:18	and seize us as slaves and take our **d**."	2789
	43:24	and provided fodder for their **d**.	2789
	44: 3	on their way with their **d**.	2789
	44:13	Then they all loaded their **d** and returned to	2789
	45:23	ten **d** loaded with the best things of Egypt,	2789
	45:23	and ten **female d** loaded with grain	912
	47:17	their sheep and goats, their cattle and **d**.	2789
Ex	9: 3	on your horses and **d** and camels and	2789
Nu	31:28	whether persons, cattle, **d**, sheep or goats.	2789
	31:30	cattle, **d**, sheep, goats or other animals.	2789
	31:34	61,000 **d**	2789
	31:39	of which the tribute for the LORD was 61;	2789
	31:45	30,500 **d**	2789
Jos	6:21	young and old, cattle, sheep and **d**.	2789
	7:24	**d** and sheep, his tent and all that he had,	2789

Jos	9: 4	as a delegation whose *d* were loaded	2789
Jdg	5:10	"You who ride on white *d*,	912
	6: 4	neither sheep nor cattle nor *d*.	2789
	10: 4	He had thirty sons, who rode thirty *d*.	6555
	12:14	who rode on seventy *d*,	6555
	15:16	"With a donkey's jawbone I have made	
		of them.	2789+2789
	19: 3	He had with him his servant and two *d*.	2789
	19:10	with his two saddled *d* and his concubine.	2789
	19:19	both straw and fodder for our *d* and bread	2789
	19:21	So he took him into his house and fed his *d*.	2789
1Sa	8:16	the best of your cattle and *d* he will take	2789
	9: 3	*d* belonging to Saul's father Kish were lost,	912
	9: 3	with you and go and look for the *d*."	912
	9: 4	but the *d* were not there.	NIH
	9: 5	or my father will stop thinking about the *d*	912
	9:20	As for the *d* you lost three days ago,	912
	10: 2	*d* you set out to look for have been found.	912
	10:14	"Looking for the *d*," he said.	912
	10:16	"He assured us that the *d* had been found."	912
	15: 3	cattle and sheep, camels and *d*.' "	2789
	22:19	and its cattle, *d* and sheep.	2789
	25:18	and loaded them on *d*.	2789
	27:	but took sheep and cattle, *d* and camels,	2789
2Sa	16: 1	He had a string of *d* saddled and loaded	2789
	16: 2	*d* are for the king's household to ride on,	2789
2Ki	7: 7	and their horses and *d*,	2789
	7:10	only tethered horses and *d*,	2789
1Ch	5:21	and two thousand *d*.	2789
	12:40	and Naphtali came bringing food on *d*,	2789
	27:30	the Meronothite was in charge of the *d*.	912
2Ch	28:15	All those who were weak they put on *d*,	2789
Ezr	2:67	435 camels and 6,720 *d*.	2789
Ne	7:69	435 camels and 6,720 *d*.	2789
	13:15	and bringing in grain and loading it on *d*,	2789
Job	1: 3	of oxen and five hundred *d*,	912
	1:14	and the *d* were grazing nearby,	912
	24: 5	Like **wild** *d* in the desert,	7230
	42:12	a thousand yoke of oxen and a thousand *d*.	912
Ps	104:11	the **wild** *d* quench their thirst.	7230
Isa	21: 7	riders on *d* or riders on camels,	2789
	30:24	and *d* that work the soil will eat fodder	6555
	32:14	the delight of *d*, a pasture for flocks,	7230
	32:20	and letting your cattle and *d* range free.	2789
Jer	14: 6	**Wild** *d* stand on the barren heights	7230
Eze	23:20	like those of *d* and whose emission was like	2789
Da	5:21	with the **wild** *d* and ate grass like cattle;	10570
Zec	14:15	the camels and *d*,	2789

DONKEYS' (1) [DONKEY]

Isa	30: 6	the envoys carry their riches on *d'* backs,	6555

DOOM (7) [DOOMED]

Dt	32:35	of disaster is near and their *d* rushes	6969
Eze	7: 7	*D* has come upon you—	7619
	7:10	*D* has burst forth, the rod has budded,	7619
	22: 3	on herself *d* by shedding blood in her midst	6961
	30: 3	a day of clouds, a time of *d* for the nations.	NIH
	30: 9	of them on the day of Egypt's *d*,	NIH
Rev	18:10	In one hour your *d* has come!'	3213

DOOMED (7) [DOOM]

Jdg	13:22	"We are *d* to die!"	4637+4637
2Ki	7:13	be like all these Israelites who *are* *d*.	9462
Ps	137: 8	O Daughter of Babylon, *d* to destruction,	8720
Isa	65:23	in vain or bear children *d* to misfortune;	4200
Jer	8:14	For the LORD our God *has* *d* us **to perish**	1959
Jn	17:12	the one *d* to destruction	724
2Th	2: 3	the man *d* to destruction.	724

DOOR (71) [DOORFRAME, DOORFRAMES, DOORKEEPER, DOORKEEPERS, DOORPOST, DOORPOSTS, DOORS, DOORWAY, DOORWAYS]

Ge	4: 7	sin is crouching at your *d*;	7339
	6:16	a *d* in the side of the ark and make lower,	7339
	19: 6	to meet them and shut the *d* behind him	1946
	19: 9	and moved forward to break down the *d*.	1946
	19:10	into the house and shut the *d*.	1946
	19:11	Then they struck the men who were at the *d*	7339
	19:11	so that they could not find the *d*.	7339
Ex	12:22	of you shall go out the *d* *of* his house	7339
	21: 6	the *d* or the doorpost and pierce his ear with	1946
Dt	15:17	and push it through his ear lobe into the *d*,	1946
	22:21	be brought to the *d* *of* her father's house	7339
Jdg	11:31	whatever comes out of the *d* *of* my house	1946
	19:22	Pounding on the *d*,	1946
	19:26	down at the *d* and lay there until daylight.	7339
	19:27	the morning and opened the *d* *of* the house	1946
2Sa	13:17	"Get this woman out of here and bolt the *d*	1946
	13:18	So his servant put her out and bolted the *d*.	1946
1Ki	14: 6	the sound of her footsteps at the *d*,	7339
2Ki	4: 4	Then go inside and shut the *d* behind you	1946
	4: 5	She left him and afterward shut the *d*.	1946
	4:21	then shut the *d* and went out.	NIH
	4:33	shut the *d* on the two of them and prayed to	1946
	5: 9	and stopped at the *d* of Elisha's house.	7339
	6:32	shut the *d* and hold it shut against him.	1946
	9: 3	Then open the *d* and run; don't delay!"	1946
	9:10	Then he opened the *d* and ran.	1946
Job	31: 9	or if I have lurked at my neighbor's *d*,	7339
	31:32	for my *d* was always open to the traveler—	1946

Ps	141: 3	keep watch over the *d* *of* my lips.	1923
Pr	5: 8	do not go near the *d* *of* her house,	7339
	9:14	She sits at the *d* *of* her house,	7339
	26:14	As a *d* turns on its hinges,	1946
SS	7:13	and at our *d* is every delicacy,	7339
	8: 9	If she is a *d*, we will enclose her	1946
Eze	41:24	Each *d* had two leaves—	1946
	41:24	two hinged leaves for each *d*.	1946
	42: 2	The building whose *d* faced north was	7339
Hos	2:15	will make the Valley of Achor a *d* *of* hope.	7339
Mt	6: 6	close the *d* and pray to your Father,	2598
	7: 7	knock and the *d* will be opened to you.	NIG
	7: 8	to him who knocks, the *d* will be opened.	NIG
	24:33	you know that it is near, right at the *d*.	2598
	25:10	And the *d* was shut.	2598
	25:11	'Open the *d* for us!'	NIG
Mk	1:33	The whole town gathered at the *d*,	2598
	2: 2	not even outside the *d*,	2598
	13:29	you know that it is near, right at the *d*.	2598
	13:34	and tells the **one** **at the** *d* to keep watch.	2601
Lk	11: 7	The *d* is already locked,	2598
	11: 9	knock and the *d* will be opened to you.	NIG
	11:10	to him who knocks, the *d* will be opened.	NIG
	12:36	they can immediately open the *d* for him.	NIG
	13:24	to enter through the narrow *d*,	2598
	13:25	of the house gets up and closes the *d*,	2598
	13:25	'Sir, open the *d* for us.'	2598
Jn	18:16	but Peter had to wait outside at the *d*.	2598
	18:17	the girl *at* the *d* asked Peter.	2601
Ac	5: 9	men who buried your husband are at the *d*,	2598
	12:13	to answer the *d*.	NIG
	12:14	"Peter is at the *d*!"	4784
	12:16	and when they opened the *d* and saw him,	NIG
	14:27	through them and how he had opened the *d*	2598
	18: 7	The synagogue and went **next** *d* to the house	5327
1Co	16: 9	a great *d* for effective work has opened	2598
2Co	2:12	and found that the Lord had opened a *d*	2598
Col	4: 3	that God may open a *d* for our message,	2598
Jas	5: 9	The Judge is standing at the *d*!	2598
Rev	3: 8	before you an open *d* that no one can shut.	2598
	3:20	I stand at the *d* and knock.	2598
	3:20	If anyone hears my voice and opens the *d*,	2598
	4: 1	before me was a *d* standing open in heaven.	2598

DOORFRAME (3) [DOOR, FRAME]

Ex	12:22	on the top and on both sides of the *d*.	4647
	12:23	the top and sides of the *d* and will pass over	4647
Eze	41:21	The outer sanctuary had a rectangular *d*,	4647

DOORFRAMES (4) [DOOR, FRAME]

Ex	12:	on the sides and tops of the *d* of the houses	4647
Dt	6: 9	on the *d* of your houses and on your gates.	4647
	11:20	on the *d* of your houses and on your gates,	4647
2Ch	3: 7	He overlaid the ceiling beams, *d*,	6197

DOORKEEPER (2) [DOOR, KEEP]

Ps	84:10	be a *d* in the house of my God than dwell in	6214
Jer	35: 4	of Maaseiah son of Shallum the *d*.	6197+9068

DOORKEEPERS (9) [DOOR, KEEP]

2Ki	22: 4	the *d* have collected from the people.	6197+9068
	23: 4	and the *d* to remove from the temple	6197+9068
	25:18	the priest next in rank and the three *d*.	6197+9068
1Ch	15:23	Berekiah and Elkanah were to be *d* for	8788
	15:24	Obed-Edom and Jehiah were also to be *d*.	8788
2Ch	23:19	He also stationed *d* at the gates of	8788
	34:	Levites *who were* the *d* had collected	6197+9068
	34:13	the Levites were secretaries, scribes and *d*.	8788
Jer	52:24	the priest next in rank and the three *d*.	6197+9068

DOORPOST (2) [DOOR, POST]

Ex	21: 6	to the door or the *d* and pierce his ear with	4647
1Sa	1: 9	on a chair by the *d* *of* the LORD's temple.	4647

DOORPOSTS (6) [DOOR, POST]

2Ki	18:16	with which he had covered the doors and *d*	595
Isa	6: 4	of their voices the *d* and thresholds shook	564
	57: 8	your *d* you have put your pagan symbols.	4647
Eze	43: 8	and their *d* beside my doorposts,	4647
	43: 8	and their doorposts beside my *d*,	4647
	45:19	of the sin offering and put it on the *d* *of*	4647

DOORS (59) [DOOR]

Jdg	3:23	he shut the *d* *of* the upper room behind him	1946
	3:24	and found the *d* *of* the upper room locked.	1946
	3:25	when he did not open the *d* *of* the room,	1946
	16: 3	up and took hold of the *d* *of* the city gate,	1946
1Sa	3:15	down until morning and then opened the *d*	1946
	21:13	like a madman, making marks on the *d* *of*	1946
1Ki	6:31	of the inner sanctuary he made *d*	1946
	6:32	the two olive wood *d* he carved cherubim,	1946
	6:34	He also made two pine *d*,	1946
	7:50	and the gold sockets for the *d* *of*	1946
	7:50	also for the *d* *of* the main hall of the temple.	1946
2Ki	18:16	the gold with which he had covered the *d*	1946
1Ch	22: 3	to make nails for the *d* *of* the gateways and	1946
2Ch	3: 7	walls and *d* of the temple with gold,	1946
	4: 9	and the large court and the *d* for the court,	1946
	4: 9	and overlaid the *d* with bronze.	1946
	4:22	and the gold *d* *of* the temple:	7339
	4:22	the inner *d* to the Most Holy Place and	1946
	4:22	Most Holy Place and the *d* of the main hall.	1946

2Ch	23: 4	on the Sabbath are to keep watch at the *d*,	6197
	28:24	He shut the *d* *of* the LORD's temple	1946
	29: 3	the *d* of the temple of the LORD	1946
	29: 7	the *d* of the portico and put out the lamps.	1946
Ne	3: 1	They dedicated it and set its *d* in place,	1946
	3: 3	They laid its beams and put its *d* and bolts	1946
	3: 6	They laid its beams and put its *d* and bolts	1946
	3:13	and put its *d* and bolts and bars in place.	1946
	3:14	He rebuilt it and put its *d* and bolts and bars	1946
	3:15	roofing it over and putting its *d* and bolts	1946
	6: 1	though up to that time I had not set the *d* in	1946
	6:10	and let us close the temple *d*,	1946
	7: 1	the wall had been rebuilt and I had set the *d*	1946
	7: 3	have them shut the *d* and bar them.	1946
	13:19	I ordered the *d* to be shut and not opened	1946
Job	3:10	for it did not shut the *d* *of* the womb on me	1946
	38: 8	up the sea behind *d* when it burst forth from	1946
	38:10	when I fixed limits for it and set its *d*	1946
	41:14	Who dares open the *d* *of* his mouth,	1946
Ps	24: 7	be lifted up, you ancient *d*,	7339
	24: 9	lift them up, you ancient *d*,	7339
	78:23	above and opened the *d* *of* the heavens;	1946
Pr	8:34	watching daily at my *d*,	1946
Ecc	12: 4	the *d* to the street are closed and the sound	1946
Isa	26:20	enter your rooms and shut the *d*	1946
	45: 1	to open *d* before him so that gates will not	1946
	57: 8	Behind your *d* and your doorposts you have	
		put your pagan symbols.	1946
Eze	26: 2	and its *d* have swung open to me;	NIH
	33:30	by the walls and at the *d* of the houses,	7339
	41:23	and the Most Holy Place had double *d*.	1946
	41:25	And on the *d* *of* the out sanctuary	1946
	42: 4	Their *d* were on the north.	7339
Zec	11: 1	Open your *d*, O Lebanon,	1946
Mal	1:10	that one of you would shut the temple *d*,	1946
Jn	20:19	with the *d* locked for fear of the Jews,	2598
	20:26	Though the *d* were locked,	2598
Ac	5:19	an angel of the Lord opened the *d* of the jail	2598
	5:23	with the guards standing at the *d*;	2598
	16:26	At once all the prison *d* flew open,	2598
	16:27	and when he saw the prison *d* open,	2598

DOORWAY (13) [DOOR, WAY]

Ex	12:23	of the doorframe and will pass over that *d*,	7339
	35:15	for the *d* at the entrance to the tabernacle;	7339
Lev	14:38	the priest shall go out the *d* *of* the house	7339
Jdg	19:27	"Stand in the *d* *of* the tent," he told her.	7339
	19:27	fallen in the *d* *of* the house,	7339
2Ki	4:15	So he called her, and she stood in the *d*.	7339
Est	2:21	of the king's officers who guarded the *d*,	6197
	6: 2	of the king's officers who guarded the *d*,	6197
Pr	8:34	waiting at my *d*.	4647+7339
Eze	8: 8	So I dug into the wall and saw a *d* there.	7339
	40:38	A room with a *d* was by the portico in each	7339
	42:12	a *d* at the beginning of the passageway	7339
Mk	11:	a colt outside in the street, tied at a *d*.	2598

DOORWAYS (4) [DOOR, WAY]

1Ki	7: 5	All the *d* had rectangular frames;	4647+7339
Eze	42:11	Similar to the *d* on the north	7339
	42:12	were the *d* of the rooms on the south.	7339
Zep	2:14	rubble will be in the *d*,	6197

DOPHKAH (2)

Nu	33:12	the Desert of Sin and camped at *D*.	1986
	33:13	They left *D* and camped at Alush.	1986

DOR (4) [HAMMOTH DOR, NAPHOTH DOR]

Jos	12:23	the king of *D* (in Naphoth Dor) one	1888
	17:11	Ibleam and the people of *D*, Endor,	1799
Jdg	1:27	the people of Beth Shan or Taanach or *D*	1888
1Ch	7:29	Taanach, Megiddo and *D*,	1888

DORCAS (2) [TABITHA]

Ac	9:36	Tabitha (which, when translated, is *D*),	*1520*
	9:39	that *D* had made while she was still	*1520*

DOTED (KJV) See LUSTED AFTER

DOTHAN (3)

Ge	37:17	"I heard them say, 'Let's go to *D*.' "	2019
	37:17	after his brothers and found them near *D*.	2019
2Ki	6:13	The report came back: "He is in *D*."	2019

DOUBLE (24) [DOUBLE-EDGED, DOUBLE-MINDED, DOUBLE-PRONGED, DOUBLY]

Ge	43:12	Take *d* the amount of silver with you,	5467
	43:15	So the men took the gifts and *d* the amount	5467
Ex	22: 4	he must pay back *d*.	9109
	22: 7	the thief, if he is caught, must pay back *d*.	9109
	22: 9	the judges declare guilty must pay back *d*	9109
	26: 9	**Fold** the sixth curtain in	4100
	26:24	be *d* from the bottom all the way to the top,	9339
	28:16	and a span wide—and folded *d*.	4100
	36:29	At these two corners the frames were *d*	9339
	39: 9	and a span wide—and **folded** *d*.	4100
Dt	21: 7	as the firstborn by giving him a *d* share	9109
1Sa	1: 5	But to Hannah he gave a *d* portion	678
2Ki	2: 9	"Let me inherit a *d* portion of your spirit,"	9109
Isa	40: 2	from the LORD's hand *d* for all her sins.	4101

Isa	51:19	These **d** calamities have come upon you—	9109
	61: 7	Instead of their shame my people will	
		receive a **d portion,**	5467
	61: 7	and so they will inherit a **d portion**	5467
Jer	16:18	I will repay them **d** for their wickedness	5467
	17:18	destroy them with **d** destruction.	5467
Eze	41:23	and the Most Holy Place had **d** doors.	9109
Hos	10:10	to put them in bonds for their **d** sin.	9109
1Ti	5:17	of the church well are worthy *of* **d** honor,	1486
Rev	18: 6	**pay** her **back d** for what she has done.	*1486+1488*
	18: 6	Mix her a **d** *portion* from her own cup.	*1486*

DOUBLE-EDGED (6) [DOUBLE, EDGE]

Jdg	3:16	Now Ehud had made a **d** sword	7023+9109
Ps	149: 6	and a sword in their hands,	7092
Pr	5: 4	sharp as a **d** sword.	7023
Heb	4:12	Sharper than any **d** sword,	1492
Rev	1:16	and out of his mouth came a sharp **d** sword.	1492
	2:12	of him who has the sharp, **d** sword.	1492

DOUBLE-MINDED (3) [DOUBLE, MIND]

Ps	119:113	I hate **d** men, but I love your law.	6189
Jas	1: 8	he is a **d** man, unstable in all he does.	1500
	4: 8	you sinners, and purify your hearts, you **d.**	1500

DOUBLE-PRONGED (1) [DOUBLE]

Eze	40:43	And **d** hooks, each a handbreadth long,	9191

DOUBLY (1) [DOUBLE]

1Ch	11:21	He was **d** honored above the Three	
			928+2021+9109

DOUBT (8) [DOUBTED, DOUBTING, DOUBTLESS, DOUBTS]

Mt	14:31	he said, "why did you **d**?"	1491
	21:21	if you have faith and *do* not **d,**	1359
Mk	11:23	and *does* not **d** in his heart but believes	1359
Ac	12:11	"Now I know *without* a **d** that	242
1Co	11:19	No **d** there have to be differences	NIG
Heb	7: 7	And without **d** the lesser person is blessed	517
Jas	1: 6	when he asks, he must believe and not **d,**	1359
Jude	1:22	Be merciful to those who **d;**	1359

DOUBTED (1) [DOUBT]

Mt	28:17	they worshiped him; but some **d.**	1491

DOUBTING (1) [DOUBT]

Jn	20:27	Stop **d** and believe."	603+1181

DOUBTLESS (1) [DOUBT]

Job	12: 2	"**D** you are the people,	597

DOUBTS (3) [DOUBT]

Lk	24:38	and why do **d** rise in your minds?	1369
Ro	14:23	the man who *has* **d** is condemned if he eats,	1359
Jas	1: 6	because he who **d** is like a wave of the sea,	1359

DOUGH (11)

Ex	12:34	So the people took their **d** before	1302
	12:39	*With* the **d** they had brought from Egypt,	1302
	12:39	The **d** was without yeast	NIH
2Sa	13: 8	She took some **d,** kneaded it,	1302
Jer	7:18	and the women knead the **d** and make cakes	1302
Hos	7: 4	from the kneading of the **d** till it rises.	1302
Mt	13:33	until it **worked** all **through the d."**	2435
Lk	13:21	until it **worked** all **through the d."**	2435
Ro	11:16	of the **d** offered as firstfruits is holy, then	NIG
1Co	5: 6	works through the whole **batch of d?**	5878
Gal	5: 9	works through the whole **batch of d."**	5878

DOVE (24) [DOVES]

Ge	8: 8	a **d** to see if the water had receded from	3433
	8: 9	But the **d** could find no place to set its feet	3433
	8: 9	He reached out his hand and took **the d**	2023S
	8:10	and again sent out the **d** from the ark.	3433
	8:11	When the **d** returned to him in the evening,	3433
	8:12	and sent the **d** out again,	3433
	15: 9	along with a **d** and a young pigeon."	9367
Lev	1:14	he is to offer a **d** or a young pigeon	9367
	12: 6	a burnt offering and a young pigeon or a **d**	9367
Ps	55: 6	I said, "Oh, that I had the wings of a **d!**	3433
	56: T	To [the tune of] "A **D** on Distant Oaks."	3433
	68:13	wings of [my] **d** are sheathed with silver,	3433
	74:19	over the life of your **d** to wild beasts;	9367
SS	2:14	My **d** in the clefts of the rock,	3433
	5: 2	"Open to me, my sister, my darling, my **d,**	3433
	6: 9	but my **d,** my perfect one, is unique,	3433
Isa	38:14	I moaned like a mourning **d.**	3433
Jer	8: 7	and the **d,** the swift and the thrush observe	9367
	48:28	Be like a **d** that makes its nest at the mouth	3433
Hos	7:11	"Ephraim is like a **d,**	3433
Mt	3:16	of God descending like a **d** and lighting	4361
Mk	1:10	and the Spirit descending on him like a **d.**	4361
Lk	3:22	on him in bodily form like a **d.**	4361
Jn	1:32	the Spirit come down from heaven as a **d**	4361

DOVES (23) [DOVE]

Lev	5: 7	he is to bring two **d** or two young pigeons	9367
	5:11	" 'If, however, he cannot afford two **d**	9367

Lev	12: 8	she is to bring two **d** or two young pigeons,	9367
	14:22	and two **d** or two young pigeons,	9367
	14:30	Then he shall sacrifice the **d** or	9367
	15:14	On the eighth day he must take two **d**	9367
	15:29	On the eighth day she must take two **d**	9367
Nu	6:10	Then on the eighth day he must bring two **d**	9367
SS	1:15	Your eyes are **d.**	3433
	2:12	the cooing of **d** is heard in our land.	9367
	4: 1	Your eyes behind your veil are **d.**	3433
	5:12	His eyes are like **d** by the water streams,	3433
Isa	59:11	we moan mournfully like **d.**	3433
	60: 8	like **d** to their nests?	3433
Eze	7:16	moaning like **d** *of* the valleys,	3433
Hos	11:11	like **d** from Assyria.	3433
Na	2: 7	Its slave girls moan like **d** and beat	3433
Mt	10:16	as shrewd as snakes and as innocent as **d.**	4361
	21:12	and the benches of those selling **d.**	4361
Mk	11:15	and the benches of those selling **d,**	4361
Lk	2:24	"a pair *of* **d** or two young pigeons."	5583
Jn	2:14	sheep and **d,** and others sitting	4361
	2:16	To those who sold **d** he said,	4361

DOWN (1207) [DOWNCAST, DOWNFALL, DOWNHEARTED, DOWNPOUR, DOWNSTAIRS, DOWNSTREAM]

Ge	8: 3	and fifty days the water *had* gone **d,**	2893
	11: 5	But the LORD came **d** to see the city and	3718
	11: 7	*let us* go **d** and confuse their language	3718
	12:10	and Abram went **d** to Egypt to live there for	3718
	15:11	Then birds of prey came **d** on the carcasses,	3718
	18:16	they looked **d** toward Sodom,	9207
	18:21	that *I* will go **d** and see	3718
	19: 1	up to meet them and bowed **d** *with* his face	2556
	19: 9	and moved forward to break **d** the door.	8689
	19:24	Then the LORD rained **d** burning sulfur	4763
	19:28	He looked **d** toward Sodom and Gomorrah,	9207
	19:33	He was not aware of it when she lay **d** or	8886
	19:35	of it when she lay **d** or when she got up.	8886
	21:16	Then she went off and sat **d** nearby,	3782
	23: 7	and bowed **d** before the people of the land,	2556
	23:12	Again Abraham bowed **d** before the people	2556
	24:11	had the camels kneel **d**	1384
	24:14	'Please let **d** your jar that I may have	5742
	24:16	*She* went **d** to the spring,	3718
	24:26	the man bowed **d** and worshiped the LORD,	7702
	24:45	*She* went **d** to the spring and drew water,	3718
	24:48	and *I* bowed **d** and worshiped the LORD.	7702
	24:52	he bowed **d** to the ground before the LORD.	2556
	24:64	*She* got **d** from her camel	5877
	26: 2	"*Do* not go **d** to Egypt;	3718
	26: 8	Abimelech king of the Philistines looked **d**	9207
	27:12	be tricking him and *would* bring **d** a curse	995
	27:29	May nations serve you and peoples bow **d**	2556
	27:29	*may* the sons of your mother bow **d** to you.	2556
	28:11	under his head and lay **d** to sleep.	8886
	31:36	that *you* hunt me **d**?	1944
	33: 3	He himself went on ahead and bowed **d** to	2556
	33: 6	and their children approached and bowed **d.**	2556
	33: 7	Leah and her children came and bowed **d.**	2556
	33: 7	and *they* too bowed **d.**	2556
	37: 7	around mine and bowed **d** to it."	2556
	37: 9	and moon and eleven stars *were* bowing **d**	2556
	37:10	and your brothers actually come and bow **d**	2556
	37:25	As *they* sat **d** to eat their meal,	3782
	37:25	and they were on their way to take them **d**	3718
	37:35	"in mourning *will I* go **d** to the grave	3718
	38: 1	Judah left his brothers and went **d** to stay	3718
	38:14	and then sat **d** at the entrance to Enaim,	3782
	39: 1	Now Joseph *had* been taken **d** to Egypt.	3718
	42: 2	Go **d** there and buy some for us,	3718
	42: 3	of Joseph's brothers went **d** to buy grain	3718
	42: 6	*they* bowed **d** to him *with* their faces to	2556
	42:38	"My son *will* not go **d** there with you;	3718
	42:38	bring my gray head **d**	3718
	43: 4	*we will* go **d** and buy food for you.	3718
	43: 5	if you will not send him, *we will* not go **d,**	3718
	43: 7	'Bring your brother **d** here'?	3718
	43:11	in your bags and take them **d** to the man *as*	3718
	43:15	They hurried **d** *to* Egypt	3718
	43:20	"we came **d** here the first time to buy food.	
			3718+3718
	43:26	and *they* bowed **d** before him to the ground.	2556
	44:21	'Bring him **d** to me so I can see him	3718
	44:23	your youngest brother *comes* **d** with you,	3718
	44:26	But we said, 'We cannot go **d.**	3718
	44:29	bring my gray head **d**	3718
	44:31	bring the gray head of our father **d**	3718
	45: 9	Come **d** to me; don't delay.	3718
	45:13	And bring my father **d** here quickly."	3718
	46: 3	"Do not be afraid to go **d** to Egypt,	3718
	46: 4	I *will* go **d** to Egypt with you,	3718
	48:12	and bowed **d** *with* his face to the ground.	2556
	49: 8	your father's sons *will* bow **d** to you.	2556
	49: 9	Like a lion he crouches and lies **d,**	8069
	49:14	"Issachar is a rawboned donkey lying **d**	8069
	50:18	and threw *themselves* **d** before him.	5877
Ex	2: 5	Then Pharaoh's daughter went **d** to the Nile	3718
	2:15	where *he* sat **d** by a well.	3782
	3: 8	So *I* have come **d** to rescue them from	3718
	4:31	*they* bowed **d** and worshiped.	7702
	7: 9	and throw it **d** before Pharaoh,'	8959
	7:10	Aaron threw his staff **d** in front of Pharaoh	8959
	7:12	Each one threw **d** his staff and it became	8959
	9:23	and lightning flashed **d** to the ground.	2143
	9:25	it beat **d** everything growing in the fields	5782

Ex	9:33	the rain no *longer* poured **d** on the land.	5988
	10:14	and settled **d** in every area of the country	5663
	11: 8	bowing **d** before me and saying, 'Go,	2556
	12:12	and strike **d** every firstborn—	5782
	12:23	the LORD goes through the land to strike **d**	5597
	12:23	to enter your houses and strike you **d.**	5597
	12:27	and spared our homes when he struck **d**	5597
	12:27	Then the people bowed **d** and worshiped.	7702
	12:29	the LORD struck **d** all the firstborn	5782
	14:24	the LORD looked **d** from the pillar of fire	9207
	15: 7	the greatness of your majesty *you* threw **d**	2238
	16: 4	"I *will* rain **d** bread from heaven for you.	4763
	18: 7	to meet his father-in-law and bowed **d**	2556
	19:11	the LORD *will* come **d** on Mount Sinai in	3718
	19:14	After Moses *had* gone **d** the mountain to	3718
	19:21	"Go **d** and warn the people lest they do	3718
	19:24	"Go **d** and bring Aaron up with you.	3718
	19:25	Moses went **d** to the people and told them.	3718
	20: 5	not bow **d** to them or worship them;	2556
	23: 5	of someone who hates you fallen **d**	8069
	23:24	not bow **d** before their gods or worship	2556
	24: 4	Moses then wrote **d** everything	4180
	26:12	that is left over *is to* hang **d** at the rear of	6243
	32: 1	that Moses was so long in coming **d** from	3718
	32: 6	Afterward *they* sat **d** to eat and drink	3782
	32: 7	Then the LORD said to Moses, "Go **d,**	3718
	32: 8	They have bowed **d** to it and sacrificed to it	2556
	32:15	Moses turned and went **d** the mountain with	3718
	33: 9	the pillar of cloud *would* come **d** and stay at	3718
	34: 5	Then the LORD came **d** in the cloud	3718
	34:13	Break **d** their altars.	5997
	34:13	sacred stones and cut **d** their Asherah poles	4162
	34:27	"Write **d** these words,	4180
	34:29	When Moses came **d** from Mount Sinai	3718
Lev	9:22	and the fellowship offering, *he* stepped **d.**	3718
	14:45	It must be torn **d**—	5997
	22: 7	When the sun goes **d,** he will be clean,	995
	26: 1	a carved stone in your land to bow **d**	2556
	26: 6	and *you will* lie **d**	8886
	26:19	*I will* break **d** your stubborn pride	8689
	26:30	cut **d** your incense altars	4162
Nu	1:51	the Levites *are to* take it **d,**	3718
	3:13	When I struck **d** all the firstborn in Egypt,	5782
	4: 5	Aaron and his sons are to go in and take **d**	3718
	8:17	When I struck **d** all the firstborn in Egypt,	5782
	10:17	Then the tabernacle *was* taken **d,**	3718
	11: 2	he prayed to the LORD and the fire died **d.**	9205
	11: 9	the manna also came **d.**	3718
	11:17	*I will* come **d** and speak with you there,	3718
	11:25	the LORD came **d** in the cloud and spoke	3718
	11:31	*It* brought them **d** all around the camp to	5759
	12: 5	the LORD came **d** in a pillar of cloud;	3718
	14:12	*I will* strike them **d** with a plague	5782
	14:37	*were* struck **d** and died of a plague	4637
	14:45	that hill country came **d** and attacked them	3718
	14:45	down and attacked them and beat them **d**	4198
	16:30	and *they* go **d** alive into the grave,	3718
	16:33	They went **d** alive into the grave,	3718
	20:15	Our forefathers went **d** into Egypt,	3718
	20:28	and Eleazar came **d** from the mountain,	3718
	21:35	So *they* struck him **d,**	5782
	22:27	she lay **d** under Balaam,	8069
	24: 9	Like a lion they crouch and lie **d,**	8886
	25: 2	and bowed **d** before these gods.	2556
	33: 4	whom the LORD *had* struck **d** among them;	5782
	34:11	The boundary *will* go **d** from Shepham	3718
	34:12	the boundary *will* go **d** along the Jordan	3718
Dt	1:25	*they* brought it **d** to us and reported,	3718
	1:44	and beat you **d** from Seir all the way	5782
	2:33	over to us and *we* struck him **d,**	5782
	3: 3	*We* struck them **d,** leaving no survivors.	5782
	3:16	the territory extending from Gilead **d** to	6330
	4:19	do not be enticed into bowing **d** to them	2556
	5: 9	not bow **d** to them or worship them;	2556
	6: 7	when you lie **d** and when you get up.	8886
	7: 5	Break **d** their altars,	5997
	7: 5	cut **d** their Asherah poles	1548
	8:12	when you build fine houses and settle **d,**	3782
	8:19	and worship and bow **d** to them,	2556
	9:12	LORD told me, "Go **d** from here at once,	3718
	9:15	So I turned and went **d** from the mountain	3718
	9:21	into a stream that flowed **d** the mountain.	3718
	10: 5	Then I came back **d** the mountain and put	3718
	10:22	Your forefathers who went **d**	3718
	11:16	and worship other gods and bow **d** to them.	2556
	11:19	when you lie **d** and when you get up.	8886
	12: 3	Break **d** their altars,	5997
	12: 3	cut **d** the idols of their gods,	1548
	16: 6	when the sun goes **d,**	995
	17: 3	bowing **d** to them or to the sun or the moon	2556
	20:19	*Do* not cut them **d.**	4162
	20:20	*you may* cut **d** trees that you know are	4162
	21: 4	and lead her **d** to a valley that has	3718
	23: 2	even **d** to the tenth generation.	NIH
	23: 3	even **d** to the tenth generation.	NIH
	25: 2	the judge *shall* make him lie **d**	5877
	26: 4	from your hands and set it **d** in front of	5663
	26: 5	and *he* went **d** into Egypt with a few people	3718
	26:10	before the LORD your God and bow **d**	2556
	26:15	Look **d** from heaven,	9207
	28:24	*it will* come **d** from the skies	3718
	28:49	like an eagle swooping **d,**	1797
	28:52	in which you trust fall **d.**	3718
	29:26	and worshiped other gods and bowed **d**	2556
	30:17	*to* bow **d** to other gods and worship them,	2556
	31: 9	So Moses wrote **d** this law and gave it to	4180
	31:19	"Now write **d** for yourselves this song	4180

Ref	Text	No.
Dt 31:22	So Moses **wrote** d this song that day	4180
33: 3	At your feet they all **bow** d,	9413
33:29	and you *will* **trample** d their high places."	2005
Jos 2: 8	Before the spies **lay** d for the night,	8886
2:15	So *she* **let** them d by a rope through	3718
2:18	the window through which *you* let us d,	3718
2:23	*They* **went** d out of the hills,	3718
3:16	while the water flowing d to the Sea of	3718
4: 3	to carry them over with you and **put** them d	5663
4: 8	where *they* **put** them d.	5663
7: 5	as the stone quarries and **struck** them d on	5782
7:10	What *are* you **doing** d on your face?	5877
8:22	Israel **cut** them d,	5782
8:29	take his body from the tree and **throw** it d	8959
10:10	to Beth Horon and **cut** them d all the way	5782
10:11	Israel on the **road** d *from* Beth Horon	4618
10:11	**hurled** large hailstones d	8959
10:13	the middle of the sky and delayed **going** d	995
10:27	the order and *they* **took** them d from	3718
11:17	and **struck** them d,	5782
15: 1	extended d to the territory of Edom,	448
15: 9	of Mount Ephron and **went** d *toward* Baalah	9305
15:10	**continued** d to Beth Shemesh and crossed	3718
16: 7	Then *it* **went** d from Janoah to Ataroth	3718
18:13	and **went** d to Ataroth Addar on	3718
18:16	The boundary **went** d to the foot of	3718
18:16	*It* **continued** d the Hinnom Valley along	3718
18:17	and **ran** d to the Stone of Bohan son	3718
18:18	the northern slope of Beth Arabah and on d	3718
23: 7	You must not serve them nor **bow** d to them.	2556
23:16	go and serve other gods and **bow** d to them,	2556
24: 4	but Jacob and his sons **went** d to Egypt.	3718
Jdg 1: 4	and *they* **struck** d ten thousand men	5782
1: 9	the men of Judah **went** d to fight against	3718
1:34	not allowing them to **come** d into the plain.	3718
2: 2	but *you shall* **break** d their altars.'	5997
2:20	that *I* **laid** d for their forefathers and has	7422
3:27	Israelites **went** d with him from the hills,	3718
3:28	So *they* followed him d and,	3718
3:29	At that time *they* **struck** d	5782
3:31	*who* **struck** d six hundred Philistines with	5782
4:14	So Barak **went** d Mount Tabor,	3718
5: 4	the clouds **poured** d water.	5752
5:11	"Then the people of the LORD **went** d to	3718
5:13	the men who were left **came** d to the nobles;	3718
5:14	From Makir captains **came** d,	3718
6:11	the LORD came and **sat** d under the oak	3782
6:16	and *you will* **strike** d all	5782
6:25	**Tear** d your father's altar to Baal and cut	2238
6:25	down your father's altar to Baal and **cut** d	4162
6:26	of the Asherah pole that you **cut** d,	4162
6:28	with the Asherah pole beside it **cut** d and	4162
6:30	because he has **broken** d Baal's altar and	5997
6:30	and **cut** d the Asherah pole beside it."	4162
6:31	when *someone* **breaks** d his altar."	5997
6:32	because he **broke** d Baal's altar.	5997
7: 4	**Take** them d to the water,	3718
7: 5	So Gideon **took** the men d to the water.	3718
7: 5	a dog from those who kneel d to drink."	4156
7: 6	All the rest **got** d on their knees to drink.	4156
7: 9	"Get up, **go** d against the camp,	3718
7:10	**go** d to the camp with your servant Purah	3718
7:11	and Purah his servant **went** d to the outposts	3718
7:24	"**Come** d against the Midianites and seize	3718
8: 9	I will **tear** d this tower."	5997
8:14	the young man **wrote** d for him the names	4180
8:17	He also **pulled** d the tower of Peniel	5997
9:36	people *are* **coming** d from the tops of	3718
9:37	"Look, people *are* **coming** d from the center	3718
9:44	upon those in the fields and **struck** them d.	5782
12: 1	to **burn** d your house over your head."	836+928+2021+8596
12: 4	The Gileadites **struck** them d because	5782
14: 1	Samson **went** d to Timnah and saw there	3718
14: 5	Samson **went** d to Timnah together	3718
14: 7	Then *he* **went** d and talked with the woman,	3718
14:10	Now his father **went** d to see the woman.	3718
14:19	He **went** d to Ashkelon,	3718
14:19	**struck** d thirty of their men,	5782
15: 8	Then *he* **went** d and stayed in a cave in	3718
15:11	from Judah **went** d to the cave in the rock	3718
15:15	he grabbed it and **struck** d a thousand men.	5782
16:21	gouged out his eyes and **took** him d	3718
16:30	and d **came** the temple on the rulers and all	5877
16:31	and his father's whole family **went** d	3718
18:27	with the sword, and **burned** d their city.	836+928+2021+8596
19: 6	two of them **sat** d to eat and drink together.	3782
19:26	**fell** d at the door and lay there	5877
20:21	and **cut** d twenty-two thousand Israelites	8845
20:25	from Gibeah to oppose them, *they* **cut** d	8845
20:35	on that day the Israelites **struck** d 25,100	8845
20:42	of the towns **cut** them d there.	8845
20:45	the Israelites **cut** d five thousand men	6618
20:45	as Gidom and **struck** d two thousand more.	5782
Ru 2:10	she bowed with her face to the ground.	5877
2:14	When *she* **sat** d with the harvesters,	3782
3: 2	Then **go** d to the threshing floor,	3718
3: 4	When he **lies** d,	8886
3: 4	Then go and uncover his feet and **lie** d.	8886
3: 6	So *she* **went** d to the threshing floor	3718
3: 7	over to **lie** d at the far end of the grain pile.	8886
3: 7	uncovered his feet and **lay** d.	8886
4: 1	"Come over here, my friend, and **sit** d."	3782
4: 1	So he went over and **sat** d.	3782
1Sa 2: 6	he **brings** d to the grave and raises up.	3718
2:36	and **bow** d before him for a piece of silver	2556

Ref	Text	No.
1Sa 3: 2	was **lying** d in his usual place.	8886
3: 3	and Samuel *was* **lying** d in the temple of	8886
3: 5	Eli said, "I did not call; go back and **lie** d."	8886
3: 5	So he went and **lay** d.	8886
3: 6	go back and **lie** d."	8886
3: 9	So Eli told Samuel, "Go and **lie** d,	8886
3: 9	So Samuel went and **lay** d in his place.	8886
3:15	Samuel **lay** d until morning and	8886
6:15	The Levites **took** d the ark of the LORD,	3718
6:19	But God **struck** d some of the men	5782
6:21	**Come** d and take it up to your place."	3718
9:25	After *they* **came** d from the high place to	3718
9:27	*they were* **going** d to the edge of the town,	3718
10: 5	of prophets **coming** d from the high place	3718
10: 8	"**Go** d ahead of me *to* Gilgal.	3718
10: 8	I *will* surely **come** d to you	3718
10:25	He **wrote** them d on a scroll and deposited it before the LORD.	4180
13:12	the Philistines *will* **come** d against me	3718
13:20	So all Israel **went** d *to* the Philistines	3718
14:31	the Israelites *had* **struck** d the Philistines	5782
14:36	"Let us **go** d after the Philistines by night	3718
14:37	"Shall I **go** d after the Philistines?	3718
15:12	and has turned and gone on d to Gilgal."	3718
16:11	we will not **sit** d until he arrives."	6015
17: 8	Choose a man and have him **come** d to me.	3718
17:28	"Why *have* you **come** d here?	3718
17:28	you **came** d only to watch the battle."	3718
17:46	I'll **strike** you d and cut off your head.	5782
17:50	without a sword in his hand *he* **struck** d	5782
19:12	So Michal **let** David d through a window,	3718
20:24	the king **sat** d to eat.	3782
20:41	and bowed d before Jonathan three times,	5877
21:13	the gate and letting saliva **run** d his beard.	3381
22: 1	*they* **went** d to him there.	3718
22:18	"You turn and **strike** d the priests."	7003
22:18	The Edomite turned and **struck** them d.	7003
23: 4	"**Go** d *to* Keilah,	3718
23: 6	of Ahimelech *had* **brought** the ephod d	3718
23: 8	to **go** d *to* Keilah to besiege David	3718
23:11	*Will* Saul **come** d,	3718
23:20	**come** d whenever it pleases you to do so,	3718
23:23	in the area, *I will* **track** him d among all	2924
23:25	he **went** d *to* the rock and stayed in	3718
24: 8	David **bowed** d and prostrated himself	7702
24:11	but you *are* **hunting** me d to take my life.	7399
25: 1	David **moved** d into the Desert of Maon.	3718
25:23	and bowed d before David with her face to	5877
25:39	**brought** Nabal's wrongdoing d	8740
25:41	*She* **bowed** d with her face to the ground	2556
26: 2	So Saul **went** d to the Desert of Ziph,	3718
26: 5	the commander of the army, *had* **lain** d.	8886
26: 6	"Who will **go** d into the camp with me	3718
28:14	and he **bowed** d and prostrated himself	7702
30:15	"Can you **lead** me d to this raiding party?"	3718
30:15	and *I will* **take** you d to them."	3718
30:16	He led David d, and there they were,	3718
30:24	to be the same as that of him *who* **went** d to	3718
31:12	*They* **took** d the bodies of Saul and his sons	4374
2Sa 1:15	of his men and said, "Go, **strike** him d!"	7003
1:15	So he **struck** him d, and he died.	5782
2:13	One group **sat** d on one side of the pool	3782
2:16	and they **fell** d together.	5307
2:22	Why should I strike you d?	824+2025
5:17	but David heard about it and **went** d to	3718
5:25	and he **struck** d the Philistines all the way	5782
6: 7	therefore God **struck** him d	5782
6:12	So David **went** d and brought up the ark	2143
8: 2	He made them **lie** d on the ground	8886
8: 2	David **struck** d twenty-two thousand	5782
8:13	from **striking** d eighteen thousand Edomites	5782
9: 6	he **bowed** d to pay him honor.	5877+6584+7156
9: 8	Mephibosheth **bowed** d and said,	2556
10:18	He also **struck** d Shobach the commander	5782
11: 8	"**Go** d to your house and wash your feet."	3718
11: 9	and *did not* **go** d to his house.	3718
11:15	from him so he will be **struck** d and die."	5782
12: 9	*You* **struck** d Uriah the Hittite with	5782
13: 6	So Amnon **lay** d and pretended to be ill.	8886
13: 8	who was **lying** d.	8886
13:28	'Strike Amnon d,' then kill him.	5782
13:30	"Absalom *has* **struck** d all the king's sons;	5782
13:31	tore his clothes and **lay** d on the ground;	8886
13:34	**coming** d the side of the hill.	4946
14: 7	over the one who **struck** his brother d, so	5782
14:33	and **bowed** d with his face to the ground	2556
15: 5	whenever anyone approached him to **bow** d	2556
15:24	They **set** d the ark of God,	3668
17: 2	I would **strike** d only the king	5782
17:13	and we will **drag** it d to the valley until	6079
17:18	and *they* **climbed** d into it.	3718
18:21	The Cushite **bowed** d before Joab	2556
18:26	and he called d to the gatekeeper, "Look,	448
18:28	He **bowed** d before the king with his face to	2556
19:16	**hurried** d with the men of Judah	3718
19:20	of the whole house of Joseph to **come** d	3718
19:24	also **went** d to meet the king.	3718
19:31	the Gileadite also **came** d from Rogelim	3718
20:15	they were battering the wall to **bring** it d,	5877
21:10	till the rain **poured** d from the heavens on	5988
21:12	after they **struck** Saul d on Gilboa	5782
21:15	David **went** d with his men to fight against	3718
21:17	he **struck** the Philistine d and killed him.	5782
22:10	He parted the heavens and **came** d;	3718
22:36	"You **reached** d from on high and took hold	8938
22:36	you **stoop** d to make me great.	6700
23:10	but he stood his ground and **struck** d	5782

Ref	Text	No.
2Sa 23:12	**struck** the Philistines d,	5782
23:13	of the thirty chief men came d to David at	3718
23:20	He **struck** d two of Moab's best men.	5782
23:20	He also **went** d into a pit on a snowy day	3718
23:21	And he **struck** d a huge Egyptian.	5782
24:17	the angel who *was* **striking** d the people,	5782
24:20	and **bowed** d before the king with his face to the ground.	2556
1Ki 1:25	Today he has **gone** d	3718
1:33	on my own mule and **take** him d to Gihon.	3718
1:38	and the Pelethites **went** d and put Solomon	3718
1:53	and *they* **brought** him d from the altar.	3718
1:53	And Adonijah came and **bowed** d	2556
2: 6	**let** his gray head go d	3718
2: 8	**called** d bitter curses	7837+7839
2: 8	When he **came** d to meet me at the Jordan,	3718
2: 9	**Bring** his gray head d	3718
2:19	**bowed** d to her and sat down on his throne.	2556
2:19	bowed down to her and **sat** d on his throne.	3782
2:19	and *she* **sat** d at his right hand.	3782
2:25	and he **struck** d Adonijah and he died.	7003
2:29	of Jehoiada, "Go, **strike** him d!"	7003
2:31	**Strike** him d and bury him,	7003
2:34	of Jehoiada went up and **struck** d Joab	7003
2:46	and he went out and **struck** Shimei d	7003
5: 9	My men *will* **haul** them d from Lebanon	3718
8:32	condemning the guilty and **bringing** d	5989
11:15	*had* **struck** d all the men in Edom.	5782
13:24	and his body was **thrown** d on the road,	8959
13:25	saw the body **thrown** d there,	8959
13:28	and found the body **thrown** d on the road,	8959
15:13	Asa **cut** the pole d and burned it in	4162
15:27	and he **struck** him d at Gibbethon,	5782
16:10	**struck** him d and killed him in	5782
17:23	the child and **carried** him d from the room	3718
18: 7	**bowed** d to the ground,	5877+6584+7156
18:40	and Elijah had them **brought** d to	3718
18:42	**bent** d to the ground and put his face	1566
18:44	'Hitch up your chariot and **go** d before	3718
19: 4	**sat** d under it and prayed that he might die.	3782
19: 5	he **lay** d under the tree and fell asleep.	8886
19: 6	He ate and drank and then **lay** d again.	8886
19:10	**broken** d your altars,	2238
19:14	**broken** d your altars,	2238
19:18	all whose knees *have* not **bowed** d to Baal	4156
20:20	and each one **struck** d his opponent.	5782
20:38	He disguised himself with his headband d	NIH
21:16	he got up and **went** d to take possession	3718
21:18	"**Go** d to meet Ahab king of Israel,	3718
22: 2	of Judah **went** d to see the king of Israel.	3718
2Ki 1: 9	"Man of God, the king says, '**Come** d!' "	3718
1:10	*may* fire **come** d from heaven	3718
1:11	'**Come** d at once!' "	3718
1:12	"*may* fire **come** d from heaven	3718
1:15	"**Go** d with him; do not be afraid of him."	3718
1:15	So Elijah got up and **went** d with him to	3718
2: 2	So *they* **went** d to Bethel.	3718
2:16	up and **set** him d on some mountain or	8959
2:24	and **called** d a curse *on* them in the name	7837
3:12	and the king of Edom **went** d to him.	3718
3:19	You will **cut** d every good tree,	5877
3:25	They stopped up all the springs and **cut** d	5877
4:11	he went up to his room and **lay** d there.	8886
4:24	don't **slow** d for me unless I tell you."	4200+6806+8206
5:14	So *he* **went** d and dipped himself in	3718
5:18	of Rimmon to **bow** d and he is leaning	2556
5:18	when I **bow** d *in* the temple of Rimmon,	2556
5:21	he **got** d from the chariot to meet him.	5877
5:26	not my spirit with you when the man **got** d	2200
6: 4	They went to the Jordan and **began** to **cut** d	1615
6: 5	As one of them was **cutting** d a tree,	5877
6: 9	because the Arameans *are* **going** d there."	5741
6:18	As the enemy **came** d toward him,	3718
6:33	the messenger **came** d to him.	3718
7:17	of God had foretold when the king **came** d	3718
8:29	of Judah **went** d to Jezreel to see Joram son	3718
9:16	and Ahaziah king of Judah *had* **gone** d	3718
9:24	and he **slumped** d in his chariot.	4156
9:32	Two or three eunuchs **looked** d at him.	9207
9:33	"**Throw** her d!"	9023
9:33	So *they* **threw** her d,	9023
10:13	and we have **come** d to greet the families of	3718
10:25	So *they* **cut** them d with the sword.	5782
10:27	of Baal and **tore** d the temple of Baal,	5997
11:18	to the temple of Baal and **tore** it d.	5997
11:19	and *together* they **brought** the king d from	3718
12:20	on the **road** d to Silla.	3718
13:14	Jehoash king of Israel **went** d to see him	3718
14:13	Then Jehoash went to Jerusalem and **broke** d the wall	7287
17:16	*They* **bowed** d to all the starry hosts,	2556
17:35	"Do not worship any other gods or **bow** d	2556
17:36	To him *you shall* **bow** d and	2556
18: 4	smashed the sacred stones and **cut** d	4162
19: 7	and there *I will* **have** him **cut** d with	5877
19:23	*I have* **cut** d its tallest cedars,	4162
19:37	and Sharezer **cut** him d with the sword,	5782
20:11	ten steps it *had* **gone** d on the stairway	345+3718
21: 3	*He* **bowed** d to all the starry hosts	2556
21:13	wiping it and turning it **upside** d.	6584+7156
21:21	and **bowed** d to them.	2556
23: 7	*He* also **tore** d the quarters of	5997
23: 8	*He* **broke** d the shrines at the gates—	5997
23:12	*He* **pulled** d the altars the kings	5997
23:14	Josiah smashed the sacred stones and **cut** d	4162

2Ki	25: 9	Every important building *he* **burned d.**	
			836+928+2021+8596
	25:10	**broke d** the walls around Jerusalem.	5597
	25:24	"**Settle d** in the land and serve the king	3782
1Ch	6:32	according to the **regulations laid d**	AIT
	7:21	when *they* **went d** to seize their livestock.	3718
	11:14	**struck** the Philistines **d,**	5782
	11:15	Three of the thirty chiefs **came d** to David	3718
	11:22	He **struck d** two of Moab's best men.	5782
	11:22	He also **went d** into a pit on a snowy day	3718
	11:23	And he **struck d** an Egyptian	5782
	13:10	and *he* **struck him d**	5782
	14:16	and *they* **struck d** the Philistine army,	5782
	18: 5	David **struck d** twenty-two thousand	5782
	18:12	Abishai son of Zeruiah **struck d**	5782
	21:21	and **bowed d** before David with his face to	2556
2Ch	2:16	**float** them in rafts by sea *d* to Joppa.	AIT
	6:13	He stood on the platform and then **knelt d**	
			1384+1386+6584
	6:23	repaying the guilty by **bringing d**	5989
	7: 1	fire **came d** from heaven and consumed	3718
	7: 3	the Israelites saw the fire **coming d** and	3718
	13:20	And the LORD **struck** him *d* and he died.	5597
	14: 3	smashed the sacred stones and **cut d**	1548
	14:12	The LORD **struck d** the Cushites	5597
	15:16	Asa **cut** the pole **d,**	4162
	18: 2	Some years later *he* **went d** to visit Ahab	3718
	18:29	Tomorrow **march d** against them.	3718
	20:16	They will **march d** against them.	3718
	20:18	of Judah and Jerusalem **fell d** in worship	5877
	22: 6	of Judah **went d** to Jezreel to see Joram son	3718
	23:17	to the temple of Baal and **tore** it **d.**	5997
	23:20	and **brought** the king *d* from the temple of	3718
	25:12	threw them *d* so that all were dashed	4946+8031
	25:14	**bowed d** to them and burned sacrifices	2556
	25:16	Why **be struck d?**"	5782
	25:23	and **broke** the wall of Jerusalem from	7287
	26: 6	against the Philistines and **broke d** the walls	7287
	29:29	and everyone present with him **knelt d**	4156
	31: 1	smashed the sacred stones and **cut d**	1548
	32:21	some of his sons **cut** him *d* with the sword.	5877
	32:30	spring and channeled the water *d*	4200+4752
	33: 3	*He* **bowed d** to all the starry hosts	2556
	34: 4	the altars of the Baals *were* **torn d;**	5997
	34: 7	*he* **tore d** the altars and the Asherah poles	5997
	36:19	They set fire to God's temple and **broke d**	5997
Ezr	4: 5	and *d* to the reign of Darius king of Persia.	6330
	5:10	so that *we could* **write d** the names	10374
	9: 3	from my head and beard and **sat d**	3782
	10: 1	and **throwing himself d** before the house	5877
	10:16	of the tenth month *they* **sat d** to investigate	3782
Ne	1: 3	The wall of Jerusalem *is* **broken d,**	7287
	1: 4	I **sat d** and wept.	3782
	2:13	which *had been* **broken d,** and its gates,	7287
	3:15	as the steps **going d** from the City of David.	3718
	4: 3	*he would* **break d** their wall of stones!"	7287
	6: 3	on a great project and cannot **go d.**	3718
	6: 3	the work stop while I leave it and **go d**	3718
	8: 6	Then *they* **bowed d** and worshiped	7702
	9:13	"You **came d** on Mount Sinai;	3718
	13: 2	but had hired Balaam **to call a curse d**	7837
	13:25	I rebuked them and **called curses d**	7837
Est	3: 2	the royal officials at the king's gate **knelt d**	4156
	3: 2	But Mordecai *would not* **kneel d**	4156
	3: 5	that Mordecai *would* not **kneel d**	4156
	3:15	The king and Haman **sat d** to drink,	3782
	9: 5	The Jews **struck d** all their enemies *with*	
		the sword,	4804+5782
	9:32	and *it was* **written d** in the records.	4180
Job	1:17	and **swept d** on your camels	7320
	3:13	For now *I would be* **lying d** in peace;	8886
	7: 4	When *I* **lie d** I think,	8886
	7: 9	*he who* **goes d** *to* the grave does not return.	3718
	7:21	For I *will* soon **lie d** in the dust;	8886
	9:26	like eagles **swooping d** on their prey.	3216
	11:19	*You will* **lie d,**	8069
	12:14	What *he* **tears d** cannot be rebuilt;	2238
	13:26	For *you* **write d** bitter things against me	4180
	14: 7	If *it is* **cut d,** it will sprout again,	4162
	14:12	so man **lies d** and does not rise;	8886
	17:16	*Will it* **go d** *to* the gates of death?	3718
	18: 7	his own schemes **throw** him *d*.	8959
	19:10	*He* **tears** me *d* on every side till I am gone;	5997
	20:23	against him and **rain d** his blows upon him.	4763
	21:13	in prosperity and **go d** *to* the grave	5737
	27:19	*He* **lies d** wealthy, but will do so no more;	8886
	30:23	I know *you will* **bring** me *d to* death,	8740
	33:24	'Spare him from **going d** *to* the pit;	3718
	33:28	He redeemed my soul from **going d** *to*	6296
	36:28	the clouds **pour d** *their* moisture	5688
	39: 3	*They* **crouch d** and bring forth their young;	4156
	41: 1	a fishhook or **tie d** his tongue with a rope?	9205
	41: 9	*He* **looks d** on all that are haughty;	8011
Ps	3: 5	I **lie d** and sleep;	8886
	4: 8	*I will* **lie d** and sleep in peace,	8886
	5: 7	in reverence *will I* **bow d**	2556
	7:16	his violence **comes d** on his own head.	3718
	10: 2	In his arrogance the wicked man **hunts d**	1944
	14: 2	The LORD **looks d** from heaven on	9207
	17:11	*They* have **tracked** me **d,**	892
	17:13	O LORD, confront them, **bring** them **d;**	4156
	18: 9	He parted the heavens and **came d;**	3718
	18:16	*He* **reached d** from on high and took hold	8938
	18:35	you **stoop d** to make me great.	6708
	22:27	the families of the nations *will* **bow d**	2556
	22:29	all *who* **go d** *to* the dust will kneel	3718
	23: 2	*He* **makes** me **lie d** in green pastures,	8069
	28: 1	be like *those who* have **gone d** *to* the pit.	3718

Ps	28: 5	*he will* **tear** them *d* and never build them	2238
	30: 3	you spared me from **going d** *into* the pit.	3718
	30: 9	in my **going d** into the pit?	3718
	33:13	the LORD **looks d** and sees all mankind;	5564
	36:12	**thrown d,** not able to rise!	1890
	37:14	the bow to **bring d** the poor and needy,	5877
	38: 2	and your hand *has* **come d** upon me.	5737
	38: 6	*I am* **bowed d** and brought very low;	6390
	44:25	We *are* **brought d** to the dust;	8863
	52: 5	**bring** you *d* to everlasting **ruin:**	5997
	53: 2	God **looks d** from heaven on the sons	9207
	55: 3	for *they* **bring d** suffering upon me	4572
	55:15	*let them* **go d** alive to the grave;	3718
	55:23	*will* **bring d** the wicked into the pit	3718
	56: 7	in your anger, O God, **bring d** the nations.	3718
	57: 6	I *was* **bowed d** in distress.	4104
	59:11	and **bring** them **d.**	3718
	60: 1	and **struck d** twelve thousand Edomites in	5782
	60:12	and *he will* **trample d** our enemies.	1008
	62: 3	*Would* all of you **throw** him **d—**	8357
	63: 9	*they will* **go d** to the depths of the earth.	995
	64: 7	suddenly they will be **struck d.**	4804
	66: 4	All the earth **bows d** to you;	2556
	68: 8	the heavens **poured d rain,** before God,	5752
	72:11	All kings *will* **bow d** to him	2556
	73:18	*you* cast them *d* to ruin.	5877
	75: 7	*He* **brings** one *d,* he exalts another.	9164
	75: 8	and all the wicked of the earth **drink** it *d*	5172
	77:17	The clouds **poured d** water,	2442
	78:16	of a rocky crag and **made** water **flow d**	3718
	78:24	*He* **rained d** manna for the people to eat,	4763
	78:27	*He* **rained** meat *d* on them like dust,	4763
	78:28	*He* **made** them **come d** inside their camp,	5877
	78:31	**cutting d** the young men of Israel.	4156
	78:51	*He* **struck d** all the firstborn of Egypt,	5782
	80:12	Why *have you* **broken d** its walls so	7287
	80:14	**Look d** from heaven and see!	5564
	80:16	Your vine *is* **cut d,** it is burned with fire;	4065
	81: 9	*you* shall not **bow d** *to* an alien god.	2556
	85:11	and righteousness **looks d** from heaven.	9207
	88: 4	I am counted among *those who* **go d** *to*	3718
	89:23	I will crush his foes before him and **strike d**	5597
	95: 6	Come, *let us* **bow d** in worship,	4156
	102:19	"The LORD **looked d** from his sanctuary	9207
	104: 8	*they* **went d** *into* the valleys,	3718
	104:19	and the sun knows when to **go d.**	4427
	104:22	*they* return and **lie d** in their dens.	8069
	105:16	He **called d** famine on the land	7924
	105:33	*he* **struck d** their vines and fig trees	5782
	105:36	*he* **struck d** all the firstborn in their land,	5782
	107:16	for *he* **breaks d** gates of bronze and cuts	8689
	107:26	They mounted up to the heavens and **went d**	3718
	108:13	and *he will* **trample d** our enemies.	1008
	113: 6	who **stoops d** to look on the heavens and	9164
	115:17	*those who* **go d** *to* silence;	3718
	119: 4	You *have* **laid d** precepts that are to	7422
	119:138	The statutes *you have* **laid d** are righteous;	7422
	133: 2	**running d** on the beard,	3718
	133: 2	running *d* on Aaron's beard,	NIH
	133: 2	*d* upon the collar of his robes.	3718
	135: 8	He **struck d** the firstborn of Egypt,	5782
	135:10	He **struck d** many nations	5782
	136:10	to *him who* **struck d** the firstborn	5782
	136:17	*who* **struck d** great kings,	5782
	137: 7	"Tear it **d,**" they cried,	6867
	137: 7	they cried, "**tear** it *d* to its foundations!"	6867
	138: 2	*I will* **bow d** toward your holy temple	2556
	139: 3	and my **lying d;**	8061
	140:11	*may* disaster **hunt d** men of violence.	
			4200+4511+7421
	141: 6	their rulers *will* **be thrown d** from the cliffs,	9023
	143: 7	from me or I will be like *those who* **go d** *to*	3718
	144: 5	Part your heavens, O LORD, and **come d;**	3718
	144: 7	**Reach d** your hand from on high;	8938
	145:14	and lifts up all who **are bowed d.**	4104
	146: 8	the LORD lifts up *those who* **are bowed d,**	4104
	147:17	*He* **hurls d** his hail like pebbles.	8959
Pr	1:12	and whole, like *those who* **go d** *to* the pit;	3718
	2:18	For her house **leads d** to death	8755
	3:24	when you **lie d,** you will not be afraid;	8886
	3:24	when you **lie d,** your sleep will be sweet.	8886
	5: 5	Her feet **go d** *to* death;	3718
	7: 8	*He was* **going d** the street near her corner,	6296
	7:26	Many are the victims *she has* **brought d;**	5877
	7:27	**leading d** to the chambers of death.	3718
	11: 5	but the wicked *are* **brought d**	5877
	12:25	An anxious heart **weighs** a man **d,**	8817
	14: 1	The foolish one **tears** hers **d.**	2238
	14:19	Evil men *will* **bow d** in the presence of	8820
	14:32	calamity comes, the wicked **are brought d,**	1890
	15:24	for the wise to keep him from **going d** *to*	4752
	15:25	The LORD **tears d** the proud man's house	5815
	16:29	and leads him **d** a path that is not good.	928
	18: 8	they **go d** *to* a man's inmost parts.	3718
	19:28	and the mouth of the wicked **gulps d** evil.	1180
	21:22	of the mighty and **pulls d** the stronghold	3718
	23:31	*when* it goes **d** smoothly!	2143
	24:16	but the wicked *are* **brought d** by calamity.	4173
	25:28	Like a city whose walls *are* **broken d** is	7287
	26:20	without gossip a quarrel **dies d.**	9284
	26:22	they **go d** *to* a man's inmost parts.	3718
	29: 4	but one who is greedy for bribes **tears** it **d.**	2238
	30: 4	Who has gone up to heaven and **come d?**	3718
Ecc	3: 3	a time to **tear d** and a time to build,	7287
	3:21	and if the spirit of the animal **goes d** *into*	
		the earth?	3718+4200+4752
	4:10	If one **falls d,** his friend can help him up.	5877

Ecc	4:11	if two **lie d** *together,* they will keep warm.	8886
SS	4:15	a well of flowing water **streaming d**	5688
	6: 2	My lover *has* **gone d** to his garden,	3718
	6:11	*I* **went d** to the grove of nut trees to look at	3718
Isa	2: 8	*they* **bow d** to the work of their hands,	2556
	5: 5	I *will* **break d** its wall,	7287
	5:24	of fire lick up straw and as dry grass **sinks d**	8332
	5:25	his hand is raised and *he* **strikes** them **d.**	5782
	6:13	and oak leave stumps when they are **cut d,**	8961
	9:10	"The bricks *have* **fallen d,**	5307
	10: 6	**trample** them *d* like mud in the streets	5330+8492
	10:19	be so few that a child *could* **write** them **d.**	4180
	10:20	no longer rely *on him who* **struck** them **d,**	5782
	10:26	he **struck d** Midian at the rock of Oreb;	4804
	10:34	*He will* **cut d** the forest thickets with	5937
	11: 6	the leopard *will* **lie d** with the goat,	8069
	11: 7	their young *will* **lie d** together,	8069
	11:14	*They will* **swoop d** on the slopes of Philistia	6414
	13:18	Their bows *will* **strike d** the young men;	8187
	14: 6	*which* in anger **struck d** peoples	5782
	14: 8	no woodsman comes to **cut us d.**"	4162
	14:11	All your pomp *has* **been brought d** *to*	3718
	14:12	*You have* **been cast d** to the earth,	1548
	14:15	But *you* are **brought d** to the grave,	3718
	14:25	on my mountains I *will* **trample** him **d.**	1008
	14:30	and the needy *will* **lie d** in safety.	8069
	16: 8	The rulers of the nations *have* **trampled d**	2150
	17: 2	*which will* **lie d,**	8069
	18: 5	and **cut d** and take away	9372
	22: 5	of **battering d** walls and of crying out to	7982
	22:10	and **tore d** houses to strengthen the wall.	5997
	22:25	and the load hanging on it *will* **be cut d.**"	4162
	25:10	as straw *is* **trampled d** in the manure.	1889
	25:11	God *will* **bring d** their pride despite	9164
	25:12	*He will* **bring d** your high fortified walls	8820
	25:12	he *will* **bring** them **d** to the ground,	5595
	26: 5	he levels it to the ground and **casts** it **d** to	5595
	26: 6	Feet **trample** it **d—**	8252
	27: 7	Has [the LORD] struck her as he **struck d**	4804
	27:10	there the calves graze, there *they* **lie d;**	8069
	28:18	you will be **beaten d** by it.	5330
	29:16	You **turn** things **upside d.**	2201
	29:20	all who have an eye for evil *will* **be cut d—**	4162
	30: 2	who **go d** to Egypt without consulting me;	3718
	30:30	and will make them see his arm **coming d**	5738
	30:31	with his scepter *he will* **strike** them **d.**	5782
	31: 1	Woe to those *who* **go d** to Egypt for help,	3718
	31: 4	so the LORD Almighty *will* **come d**	3718
	37: 7	and there *I will* **have** him **cut d** with	5877
	37:24	*I have* **cut d** its tallest cedars,	4162
	37:38	and Sharezer **cut** him *d* with the sword,	5782
	38: 8	the sun go back the ten steps *it has* **gone d**	3718
	38: 8	the ten steps *it had* **gone d.**	3718
	38:12	shepherd's tent my house *has* **been pulled d**	5825
	38:18	*those who* **go d** *to* the pit cannot hope	3718
	41: 7	*He* **nails d** the idol so it will not topple.	
			928+2616+5021
	42:10	you *who* **go d** *to* the sea, and all that is in it,	3718
	43:14	to Babylon and **bring d** as fugitives all	3718
	44:11	*be* **brought d** to terror and infamy.	7064
	44:14	He **cut d** cedars,	4162
	44:15	he makes an idol and **bows d** to it.	6032
	44:17	he **bows d** to it and worships.	6032
	44:19	*Shall I* **bow d** to a block of wood?"	6032
	45: 2	I *will* **break d** gates of bronze and cut	8689
	45: 8	"You heavens above, **rain d** righteousness;	8319
	45: 8	*let* the clouds **shower** it **d.**	5688
	45:14	*they will* **bow d** before you and plead	2556
	46: 1	Bel **bows d,** Nebo stoops low;	4156
	46: 2	They stoop and **bow d** together;	4156
	46: 6	and *they* **bow d** and worship it.	6032
	47: 1	"**Go d,** sit in the dust,	3718
	49: 7	princes will see and **bow d,**	2556
	49:23	*They will* **bow d** before you	2556
	50:11	*You will* **lie d** in torment.	8886
	52: 4	"At first my people **went d** *to* Egypt to live;	3718
	55:10	the rain and the snow **come d** from heaven,	3718
	60:14	all who despise you *will* **bow d** at your feet	2556
	63: 3	in my anger and **trod** them *d* in my wrath;	8252
	63:14	like cattle *that* **go d** *to* the plain,	3718
	63:15	**Look d** from heaven and see	5564
	63:18	but now our enemies *have* **trampled d**	1008
	64: 1	you would rend the heavens and **come d,**	3718
	64: 2	come *d* to make your name known	NIH
	64: 3	*you* **came d,** and the mountains trembled	3718
	65:12	and you *will* all **bend d** for the slaughter;	4156
	66:15	he *will* **bring d** his anger with fury,	8740
	66:23	all mankind will come and **bow d**	2556
Jer	1: 3	and *d* to the fifth month of the eleventh year of	
		Zedekiah	6330+9462
	1:10	and kingdoms to uproot and **tear d,**	5997
	2:20	and under every spreading tree you **lay d,**	7579
	3:25	*Let us* **lie d** in our shame,	8886
	5: 1	"**Go up and d** the streets of Jerusalem,	8763
	6: 6	"**Cut d** the trees and build siege ramps	3772
	6:11	and the old, *those* **weighed d** *with* years.	4849
	6:15	*they will* **be brought d**	4173
	8: 4	" 'When *men* **fall d,** do they not get up?	5877
	8:12	*they will* **be brought d**	4173
	12:10	and **trample d** my field;	1008
	13:18	"**Come d** from your thrones,	9164
	14:22	*Do* the skies *themselves* **send d** showers?	5989
	15: 8	suddenly *I will* **bring d** on them anguish	5877
	16: 8	a house where there is feasting and **sit d**	3782
	16:16	and *they* will be greedy the wicked **hunt d**	7421
	18: 2	"**Go d** *to* the potter's house,	3718
	18: 3	So *I* **went d** *to* the potter's house,	3718

Jer 18: 7 torn d and destroyed,   5997
21: 6 *I will* strike d those who live in this city—   5782
22: 1 "Go d *to* the palace of the king of Judah   3718
23:19 a whirlwind **swirling** d on the heads of   2565
24: 6 I will build them up and not **tear** them d;   2238
25:29 for *I am* **calling** d a sword   7924
26:23 who had him **struck** d with a sword   5782
29: 5 "Build houses and **settle** d;   3782
29:28 Therefore build houses and **settle** d;   3782
30:23 a driving wind **swirling** d on the heads of   2565
31:28 over them to uproot and **tear** d,   5997
32:29 *they will* **burn** it d,   8596
33: 4 of Judah that *have* **been torn** d to be used   5997
34: 2 and *he will* **burn** it d.   836+928+2021+8596
34:22 take it and **burn** it d.   836+928+2021+8596
36:12 he went d to the secretary's room in   3718
36:15 They said to him, "Sit d, please,   3782
37: 8 they will capture it and **burn** it d.'   836+928+2021+8596
37:10 they would come out and **burn** this city d."   836+928+2021+8596
38: 6 and Jeremiah **sank** d into the mud.   3190
38:11 and **let** them d with ropes to Jeremiah in   8938
38:17 and this city *will* not **be burned** d;   836+928+2021+8596
38:18 the Babylonians and *they will* **burn** it d;   836+928+2021+8596
38:23 and this city *will* **be burned** d."   836+2021+8596
39: 8 and the houses of the people and **broke** d   5997
40: 9 "**Settle** d in the land and serve the king   3782
41: 2 with him got up and **struck** d Gedaliah son   5782
42:10 I will build you up and not **tear** you d;   2238
43:13 and *will* **burn** the temples of the gods   836+928+2021+8596
46:12 both *will* **fall** d together."   5877
46:15 for the LORD *will* **push** them d.   2074
46:22 like men *who* **cut** d trees.   2634
46:23 They will **chop** d her forest,"   4162
48: 5 on the **road** d *to* Horonaim anguished cries   4618
48:15 her finest young men *will* **go** d in   3718
48:18 "Come d from your glory and sit on   3718
48:40 An eagle is **swooping** d,   1797
49:16 from there *I will* **bring** you d,"   3718
49:22 An eagle will soar and **swoop** d,   1797
50:15 her towers fall, her walls are **torn** d.   2238
50:27 let them **go** d to the slaughter!   3718
51: 4 *They will* **fall** d slain in Babylon,   5877
51:40 "*I will* **bring** them d like lambs to   3718
52:13 Every important building *he* **burned** d.   836+928+2021+8596
52:14 of the imperial guard **broke** d all the walls   5997
La 1:13 **sent** it d into my bones.   8959
2: 1 *He has* **hurled** d the splendor of Israel   8959
2: 2 in his wrath *he has* **torn** d the strongholds   2238
2: 2 **brought** her kingdom and its princes d   5595
2: 8 The LORD determined to **tear** d the wall   8845
3: 7 he has **weighed** me d with chains.   3877
3:50 The LORD **looks** d from heaven and sees.   9207
Eze 1:27 that from there d he looked like fire;   4200+4752
4: 6 "After you have finished this, **lie** d again,   8886
6: 6 your incense altars **broken** d,   1548
8: 2 From what appeared to be his waist d   4200+4752
8:16 they *were* **bowing** d to the sun in the east.   2556
9:10 but *I will* **bring** d   5989
11:21 *I will* **bring** d   5989
13:11 and I will send hailstones **hurtling** d,   5877
13:14 *I will* **tear** d the wall you have covered   2238
14: 1 of the elders of Israel came to me and **sat** d   3782
16:39 and *they will* **tear** d your mounds   2238
16:41 *They will* **burn** d your houses   836+928+2021+8596
16:43 I *will* surely **bring** d   5989
17:19 *I will* **bring** d on his head my oath   5989
17:24 the LORD **bring** d the tall tree and make   9164
19: 2 She **lay** d among the young lions   8069
19: 7 *He* **broke** d their strongholds   1548
20: 1 and *they* **sat** d in front of me.   3782
22:31 with my fiery anger, **bringing** d   5989
23:47 The mob will stone them and **cut** them d   1345
23:47 **burn** d their houses.   836+928+2021+8596
26: 4 the walls of Tyre and **pull** d her towers;   2238
26:12 *they will* **break** d your walls   2238
26:16 of the coast *will* **step** d from their thrones   3718
26:20 then *I will* **bring** you d with those who go   3718
26:20 down with *those who* **go** d to the pit,   3718
26:20 with *those who* **go** d to the pit,   3718
27:34 all your company *have* **gone** d with you.   5877
28: 8 *They will* **bring** you d to the pit,   3718
30: 4 and her foundations **torn** d.   2238
31: 7 for its roots *went* d to abundant waters.   AIT
31:12 the most ruthless of foreign nations **cut** it d   4162
31:14 with *those who* **go** d to the pit.   3718
31:15 On the day it *was* **brought** d to   3718
31:16 the sound of its fall when I **brought** it d to   3718
31:16 to the grave with *those who* **go** d to the pit.   3718
31:17 had also **gone** d to the grave with it,   3718
31:18 will **be brought** d with the trees of Eden to   3718
32:15 when I **strike** d all who live there,   5782
32:18 with *those who* **go** d to the pit.   3718
32:19 **Go** d and be laid among the uncircumcised.   3718
32:21 'They *have* **come** d and they lie with   3718
32:24 the land of the living **went** d uncircumcised   3718
32:24 They bear their shame with *those who* **go** d   3718
32:25 they bear their shame with *those who* **go** d   3718
32:27 who **went** d to the grave   3718
32:29 with *those who* **go** d to the pit.   3718
32:30 *they* **went** d with the slain in disgrace   3718

Eze 32:30 and bear their shame with *those who* **go** d   3718
33:10 "Our offenses and sins **weigh** us d,   6584
34:14 There *they will* **lie** d   8069
34:15 and have them **lie** d,   8069
34:26 *I will* **send** d showers in season;   3718
38:22 *I will* **pour** d torrents of rain,   4763
43:11 **Write** these d before them so that they may   4180
47: 1 The water *was* **coming** d from under   3718
47: 8 toward the eastern region and **goes** d into   3718
Da 3: 5 *you must* **fall** d and worship the image   10484
3: 6 not **fall** d and worship will immediately   10484
3: 7 nations and men of every language **fell** d   10484
3:10 pipes and all kinds of music *must* **fall** d   10484
3:11 not **fall** d and worship will be thrown   10484
3:15 *to* **fall** d and worship the image I made,   10484
4:13 a holy one, **coming** d from heaven.   10474
4:14 'Cut d the tree and trim off its branches;   10134
4:23 **coming** d from heaven and saying,   10474
4:23 'Cut d the tree and destroy it,   10134
6:10 Three times a day he got d on his knees   10121
7: 1 *He* **wrote** d the substance of his dream.   10374
7:23 **trampling** it d and crushing it.   10165
8:10 **threw** some of the starry host d   5877
Hos 2:18 so that all *may* **lie** d in safety.   8886
7:12 *I will* **pull** them d like birds of the air.   3718
11: 4 from their neck and **bent** d to feed them.   5742
14: 5 a cedar of Lebanon he will **send** d his roots;   5782
Joel 1:17 the granaries *have* **been broken** d,   2238
3: 2 I will gather all nations and **bring** them d to   3718
3:11 **Bring** d your warriors, O LORD!   5737
Am 1: 5 *I will* **break** the gate of Damascus;   8689
2: 2 Moab *will* **go** d   4637
2: 8 *They* **lie** d beside every altar   5742
3:11 *he will* **pull** d your strongholds   3718
3:15 *I will* **tear** d the winter house along with   5782
6: 2 and then **go** d *to* Gath in Philistia.   3718
8: 9 make the sun **go** d   995
9: 1 **Bring** them d on the heads of all the people;   1298
9: 2 *they* **dig** d to the depths of the grave,   3168
9: 2 from there *I will* **bring** them d.   3718
9: 3 there *I will* **hunt** them d and seize them.   2924
Ob 1: 3 'Who *can* **bring** me d to the ground?'   3718
1: 4 from there *I will* **bring** you d,"   3718
1: 9 in Esau's mountains *will* **be cut** d in   4162
1:12 You should not **look** d on your brother in   8011
1:13 nor **look** d on them in their calamity in   8011
1:14 at the crossroads to **cut** d their fugitives,   4162
Jnh 1: 3 *He* **went** d *to* Joppa,   3718
1: 5 where *he* **lay** d and fell into a deep sleep.   8886
1:11 to you *to make* the sea **calm** d for us?"   9284
2: 6 To the roots of the mountains *I* **sank** d;   3718
4: 5 covered himself with sackcloth and **sat** d in   3782
4: 5 Jonah went out and **sat** d at a place east of   3782
Mic 1: 4 *he* **comes** d and treads the high places of   3718
1: 4 like water rushing d a slope.   928
5:11 the cities of your land and **tear** d   2238
5:13 *you will* no longer **bow** d to the work   2556
6: 6 before the LORD and **bow** d before   4104
Na 3:15 the sword *will* **cut** you d and,   4162
3:18 your nobles **lie** d to rest.   8905
Hab 2: 2 "**Write** d the revelation and make it plain   4180
Zep 1: 5 **bow** d on the roofs *to* **worship**   2556
1: 5 those *who* **bow** d and swear by the LORD   2556
2: 7 the evening *they will* **lie** d in the houses   8069
2:14 Flocks and herds *will* **lie** d there,   8069
3:13 They will eat and **lie** d   8069
Hag 1: 8 the mountains and **bring** d timber and build   995
Zec 1:21 to terrify them and **throw** d these horns of   3343
5: 8 **pushed** the lead cover d   8959
10:11 Assyria's pride *will* **be brought** d   3718
11: 2 the dense forest *has* **been cut** d!   3718
13: 8 "two-thirds *will* **be struck** d and perish;   4162
Mal 4: 3 Then *you will* **trample** d the wicked;   6748
Mt 2:11 and they **bowed** d and worshiped him.   4406
3:10 not produce good fruit *will* **be cut** d   1716
4: 6 he said, "throw yourself d.   3004
4: 9 "if you will **bow** d and worship me."   4406
5: 1 he went up on a mountainside and **sat** d.   2767
7:19 not bear good fruit *is* **cut** d and thrown   1716
7:25 The rain **came** d, the streams rose,   2849
7:27 The rain **came** d, the streams rose,   2849
8: 1 *When* he **came** d from the mountainside,   2849
8:32 the whole herd rushed d the steep bank into   2848
11:23 No, *you will* **go** d to the depths.   2849
13:47 of heaven is like a net that *was* **let** d into   965
13:48 Then they **sat** d and collected the good fish   2767
14:19 he directed the people to **sit** d on the grass.   369
14:29 Then Peter **got** d out of the boat,   2849
14:32 they climbed into the boat, the wind **died** d.   3156
15:29 *he* went up on a mountainside and **sat** d.   2764
15:35 He told the crowd *to* **sit** d on the ground.   404
17: 9 *As they were* **coming** d the mountain,   2849
18:10 not **look** d on one of these little ones.   2969
20:20 **kneeling** d, asked a favor of him.   4686
22:26 **right** on d to the seventh.   2401
24: 2 every one *will* **be thrown** d."   2907
24:17 no one on the roof of his house **go** d   2849
26:58 *He* entered and **sat** d with the guards to see   2764
26:74 *to* **call** d curses on himself and he swore   2874
27:36 **sitting** d, they kept watch over him there.   2764
27:40 **Come** d from the cross,   2849
27:42 *Let him* **come** d now from the cross,   2849
28: 2 angel of the Lord **came** d from heaven and,   2849
Mk 1: 7 not worthy to **stoop** d and untie.   3252
3:11 *they* **fell** d before him and cried,   4700
3:22 of the law who **came** d from Jerusalem said,   2849
4:39 the wind **died** d and it was completely calm.   3156

Mk 5:13 rushed d the steep bank into the lake   2848
6:39 have all the people **sit** d   369
6:40 *they* **sat** d in groups of hundreds and fifties.   404
6:51 and the wind **died** d.   3156
7:13 by your tradition that *you have* **handed** d.   4140
7:31 d to the Sea of Galilee and into the region   NIG
8: 6 He told the crowd *to* **sit** d on the ground.   404
9: 9 *As they were* **coming** d the mountain,   2849
9:35 **Sitting** d, Jesus called the Twelve   2767
12:41 Jesus **sat** d opposite the place where   2767
13: 2 every one *will be* **thrown** d."   2907
13:15 *Let* no one on the roof of his house **go** d   2849
14:71 He began *to* **call** d curses on himself,   354
14:72 And he **broke** d and wept.   2095
15:30 **come** d from the cross and save yourself!"   2849
15:32 **come** d now from the cross,   2849
15:36 Let's see if Elijah comes *to* **take** him d,"   2747
15:46 **took** d the body, wrapped it in the linen,   2747
Lk 1: 2 as *they were* **handed** d to us by those who   4140
1:52 *He has* **brought** d rulers from their thrones   2747
2:51 Then *he* **went** d to Nazareth with them   2849
3: 9 not produce good fruit *will be* **cut** d   1716
4: 9 he said, "throw yourself d from here.   3004
4:20 gave it back to the attendant and **sat** d.   2767
4:29 **throw** him d the cliff.   2889
4:31 Then *he* **went** d *to* Capernaum,   2982
4:35 the demon **threw** the man d before them all   4849
5: 3 Then he **sat** d and taught the people from   2767
5: 4 and **let** d the nets for a catch."   5899
5: 5 you say so, *I will* **let** d the nets."   5899
6:17 He **went** d with them and stood on   2849
6:38 A good measure, **pressed** d,   4390
6:48 who dug d deep and laid the foundation   959
8:23 A squall **came** d on the lake,   2849
8:33 and the herd rushed d the steep bank into   2848
9:14 "Have them **sit** d in groups of   2884
9:15 The disciples did so, and everybody **sat** d.   2884
9:37 *when* they **came** d from the mountain,   2982
9:54 to call fire d from heaven to destroy them?"   2849
10:15 No, *you will* **go** d to the depths.   2849
10:30 man *was* **going** d from Jerusalem to Jericho,   2849
10:31 A priest happened *to be* **going** d   2849
11:46 because *you* **load** people d   5844
12:18 *I will* **tear** d my barns   2747
13: 7 Cut it d!   1716
13: 9 If not, then **cut** it d.' "   1716
14:28 Will he not first **sit** d and estimate the cost   2767
14:31 Will he not first **sit** d and consider   2767
16: 6 **sit** d quickly, and make it four hundred.'   2767
17: 7 'Come along now and **sit** d to eat'?   404
17:29 fire and sulfur rained d from heaven   608
17:31 *should* **go** d to get them.   2849
18: 9 of their own righteousness and **looked** d on   2024
19: 5 "Zacchaeus, **come** d immediately.   2849
19: 6 *he* **came** d at once and welcomed him gladly.   2849
19:37 **place where the road goes** d   2853
21: 6 every one of them *will be* **thrown** d."   2907
21:34 or your hearts *will be* **weighed** d   976
22:41 **knelt** d and prayed,   1205+5502
22:55 of the courtyard and *had* **sat** d together,   5154
22:55 Peter **sat** d with them.   2764
23:53 Then he **took** it d,   2747
24: 5 the women **bowed** d with their faces to   3111
Jn 1:32 the Spirit **come** d from heaven as a dove   2849
1:33 on whom you see the Spirit **come** d   2849
2:12 After this *he* **went** d to Capernaum   2849
4: 6 **sat** d by the well.   2757
4:49 "Sir, **come** d before my child dies."   2849
5: 7 someone else **goes** d ahead of me."   2849
6: 3 a mountainside and **sat** d with his disciples.   2764
6:10 Jesus said, "Have the people **sit** d."   404
6:10 and the men **sat** d,   404
6:16 his disciples **went** d to the lake,   2849
6:33 For the bread of God is he who **comes** d   2849
6:38 For *I have* **come** d from heaven not   2849
6:41 "I am the bread that **came** d from heaven."   2849
6:42 can he now say, '*I came* d from heaven'?"   2849
6:50 here is the bread that **comes** d from heaven,   2849
6:51 the living bread that **came** d from heaven.   2849
6:58 This is the bread that **came** d from heaven.   2849
8: 2 and *he* **sat** d to teach them.   2764
8: 6 But Jesus bent d and started to write on   3004
8: 8 Again *he* **stooped** d and wrote on   2893
10:11 good shepherd **lays** d his life for the sheep.   5502
10:15 and *I* **lay** d my life for the sheep.   5502
10:17 that *I* **lay** d my life—   5502
10:18 but *I* **lay** it d of my own accord.   5502
10:18 I have authority *to* **lay** it d and authority   5502
13:37 *I will* **lay** d my life for you."   5502
13:38 "Will *you* really **lay** d your life for me?   5502
15:13 that he **lay** d his life for his friends.   5502
19:13 he brought Jesus out and **sat** d on   2767
19:31 the legs broken and the bodies **taken** d.   149
21:24 to these things and who **wrote** them d,   1211
21:25 If every one of them *were* **written** d,   1211
Ac 5: 5 he **fell** d and died.   4406
5:10 At that moment *she* **fell** d at his feet   4406
6:14 and change the customs Moses **handed** d   4140
7:15 Then Jacob **went** d to Egypt,   2849
7:34 I have heard their groaning and *have* **come** d to set them free.   2849
8: 5 Philip **went** d to a city in Samaria   2982
8:26 that **goes** d from Jerusalem to Gaza."   2849
8:38 Then both Philip and the eunuch **went** d   2849
9:30 *they* **took** him d to Caesarea   2864
9:40 then *he* **got** d on his knees and prayed.   5502

Ac	10:11	like a large sheet *being let d* to earth	2768
	10:21	Peter went **d** and said to the men,	2849
	11: 5	like a large sheet *being* **let d** from heaven	2768
	11: 5	and it came **d** to where I was.	2849
	11:27	During this time some prophets **came d**	2982
	12:23	an angel of the Lord **struck** him **d,**	4250
	13: 4	went **d** to Seleucia and sailed from there	2982
	13:14	the synagogue and **sat d.**	2767
	13:29	they **took** him **d** from the tree and laid him	2747
	14:11	"The gods *have* **come d** to us	2849
	14:25	*they* went **d** to Attalia.	2849
	15: 1	Some men **came d** from Judea to Antioch	2982
	15:30	The men were sent off and **went d**	2982
	16: 8	they passed by Mysia and **went d** to Troas.	2849
	16:13	We **sat d** and began to speak to	2767
	18:22	up and greeted the church and then **went d**	2849
	20:10	Paul **went d,** threw himself on	2849
	20:36	he **knelt d** with all of them and prayed.	
			1205+3836+5502
	21:10	prophet named Agabus **came d** from Judea.	2982
	21:32	and soldiers and **ran d** to the crowd.	2963
	23:10	to **go d** and take him away from them	2849
	24: 1	the high priest Ananias **went d** to Caesarea	2849
	25: 6	*he* **went d** to Caesarea,	2849
	25: 7	the Jews *who had* **come d**	2849
	27:14	swept **d** from the island.	2848
	27:30	the sailors **let** the lifeboat **d** into the sea,	5899
Ro	10: 6	*to bring* Christ **d)**	2864
	11: 3	they have killed your prophets and **torn d**	2940
	14: 3	not **look d** on him who does not,	2024
	14:10	Or why *do* you **look d** on your brother?	2024
	16:22	I, Tertius, who **wrote** this letter,	1211
1Co	7:17	the rule I lay **d** in all the churches.	1411
	10: 7	"The people **sat d** to eat and drink and got	2767
	10:11	examples and *were* **written d** as warnings	1211
	14:25	So he will **fall d** and worship God,	4406
	14:30	to someone *who is* **sitting d,**	2764
2Co	4: 9	**struck d,** but not destroyed.	2850
	10: 8	up rather than **pulling** you **d,**	2746
	13:10	not for **tearing** you **d.**	2746
Eph	4:26	the sun **go d** while you are still angry,	2115
1Th	4:16	the Lord himself *will* **come d** from heaven,	2849
2Th	3:12	to **settle d** and earn the bread they eat.	2484+3552
1Ti	4:12	Don't *let* anyone **look d** on you	2969
2Ti	3: 6	who are **loaded d** with sins and are swayed	5397
Heb	1: 3	he **sat d** at the right hand of the Majesty	2767
	8: 1	We do have such a high priest, who **sat d** at	2767
	10:12	he **sat d** at the right hand of God.	2767
	12: 2	**sat d** at the right hand of the throne of God.	2767
Jas	1:17	**coming d** from the Father of	2849
	3:15	not **come d** from heaven but is earthly,	2982
	1:18	**handed d** to you **from** your **forefathers,**	4261
1Pe			
1Jn	3:16	Jesus Christ **laid d** his life for us.	5502
	3:16	*to* **lay d** our lives for our brothers.	5502
Rev	1:13	a robe reaching **d** to his **feet**	4468
	3: 9	and **fall d** at your feet and acknowledge	4686
	3:12	which *is* **coming d** out of heaven	2849
	3:21	just as I overcame and **sat d** with my Father	2767
	4:10	the twenty-four elders **fall d** before him	4406
	5: 8	and the twenty-four elders **fell d** before	4406
	5:14	and the elders **fell d** and worshiped.	4406
	7:11	*They* **fell d** on their faces before	4406
	8: 7	and it was hurled **d** upon the earth.	1650
	9: 3	of the smoke locusts came **d** upon the earth	1650
	10: 1	Then I saw another mighty angel **coming d**	2849
	10: 4	and *do not* **write** it **d."**	1211
	12: 9	The great dragon *was* **hurled d—**	965
	12:10	*has been* **hurled d.**	965
	12:12	because the devil *has* **gone d** to you!	2849
	13:13	*to* **come d** from heaven to earth in full view	2849
	18: 1	After this I saw another angel **coming d**	2849
	18:21	the great city of Babylon *will be* **thrown d,**	965
	19: 4	and the four living creatures **fell d**	4406
	19:15	a sharp sword with which to **strike d**	4250
	20: 1	And I saw an angel **coming d** out of heaven,	2849
	20: 9	But fire **came d** from heaven	2849
	21: 2	**coming d** out of heaven from God,	2849
	21: 5	Then he said, "**Write** this **d,**	1211
	21:10	**coming d** out of heaven from God.	2849
	22: 2	**d** the middle of the great street of the city.	1877
	22: 8	I **fell d** to worship at the feet of the angel	4406

DOWNCAST (11) [DOWN, CAST]

Ge	4: 5	So Cain was very angry, and his face *was* **d.**	5877
	4: 6	Why *is* your face **d?**	5877
1Sa	1:18	and her face *was* no longer **d.**	2118+4200
Job	22:29	then he will save the **d.**	6524+3552
Ps	42: 5	Why *are* you **d,** O my soul?	8863
	42: 6	My soul *is* **d** within me;	8863
	42:11	Why *are* you **d,** O my soul,	8863
	43: 5	Why *are* you **d,** O my soul,	8863
La	3:20	and my soul *is* **d** within me.	8820
Lk	24:17	They stood still, their faces **d.**	5034
2Co	7: 6	But God, who comforts the **d,**	5424

DOWNFALL (16) [DOWN, FALL]

1Ki	13:34	the house of Jeroboam that **led** to its **d** and	3948
2Ki	14:10	Why ask for trouble and *cause* your own **d**	5877
2Ch	22: 7	God brought about Ahaziah's **d.**	9313
	25:19	Why ask for trouble and *cause* your own **d**	5877
	26:16	his pride led to his **d.**	8845
	28:23	But these were his **d** and the downfall	4173
	28:23	But they were his downfall and the **d**	NIH
Est	6:13	before whom your **d** has started,	5877
Ps	5:10	*Let* their intrigues *be their* **d.**	5877

Pr	18:12	Before his **d** a man's heart is proud,	8691
	29:16	but the righteous will see their **d.**	5147
Jer	48: 2	in Heshbon men will plot her **d:**	8288
Eze	18:30	then sin will not be your **d.**	4842
	32:10	On the day of your **d** each	5147
Hos	7:10	Your sins *have been* your **d!**	4173
Mic	7:10	My eyes will see her **d;**	NIH

DOWNHEARTED (1) [DOWN, HEART]

1Sa	1: 8	Why *are* you **d?**	4222+8317

DOWNPOUR (2) [DOWN, POUR]

Job	37: 6	to the rain shower, 'Be a mighty **d.'**	1773+4764
Isa	28: 2	like a driving rain and a **flooding d,**	3888+8851

DOWNSITTING (KJV) See SIT

DOWNSTAIRS (1) [DOWN, STAIRS]

Ac	10:20	So get up and **go d.**	2849

DOWNSTREAM (1) [DOWN, STREAM]

Jos	3:13	in the Jordan, its waters flowing **d** will be	
		cut off	2025+4200+4946+5087

DOWNWARD (KJV) See BELOW, DOWN

DOWRY (KJV) See BRIDE-PRICE, GIFT, PRICE FOR THE BRIDE

DRACHMAS (5) [FOUR-DRACHMA, TWO-DRACHMA]

Ezr	2:69	for this work 61,000 **d** of gold, 5,000 minas	2007
Ne	7:70	The governor gave to the treasury 1,000 **d**	2007
	7:71	20,000 **d** of gold and 2,200 minas of silver.	2007
	7:72	the rest of the people was 20,000 **d** of gold,	2007
Ac	19:19	the total came to fifty thousand **d.**	736

DRAG (8) [DRAGGED, DRAGGING, DRAGS]

2Sa	17:13	and *we will* **d** it **down** to the valley until not	6079
Job	36:20	to **d** people *away from* their homes.	6590
Ps	28: 3	*Do not* **d** me *away* with the wicked,	5432
Pr	21: 7	violence of the wicked *will* **d** them *away,*	1760
Jer	12: 3	**D** them *off* like sheep to be butchered!	5998
	15: 3	to kill and the dogs to **d** away and the birds	6079
Eze	39: 2	I will turn you around and **d** you *along.*	9255
Lk	12:58	or he *may* **d** you *off* to the judge,	2955

DRAGGED (14) [DRAG]

2Sa	20:12	he **d** him from the road *into* a field	6015
Jer	22:19	**d** *away* and thrown outside the gates	6079
	49:20	The young of the flock *will be* **d** *away;*	6079
	50:45	The young of the flock *will be* **d** *away;*	6079
La	3:11	he **d** me *from* the path and mangled me	6073
Eze	32:20	*let* her be **d** *off* with all her hordes.	5432
Jn	21:11	Simon Peter climbed aboard and **d**	1816
Ac	7:58	**d** him out of the city and began	1675
	8: 3	he **d** *off* men and women and put them	5359
	14:19	*They* stoned Paul and **d** him outside	5359
	16:19	they seized Paul and Silas and **d** them into	1816
	17: 6	they **d** Jason and some other brothers	5359
	21:30	Seizing Paul, *they* **d** him from the temple,	1816
Jas	1:14	he is **d** *away* and enticed.	1999

DRAGGING (1) [DRAG]

Jas	2: 6	not the ones who *are* **d** you into court?	1816

DRAGNET (2) [NET]

Hab	1:15	he gathers them up in his **d;**	4823
	1:16	to his net and burns incense to his **d,**	4823

DRAGON (14)

Rev	12: 3	an enormous red **d** with seven heads	1532
	12: 4	The **d** stood in front of the woman who was	1532
	12: 7	and his angels fought against the **d,**	1532
	12: 7	and the **d** and his angels fought back.	1532
	12: 9	The great **d** was hurled down—	1532
	12:13	When the **d** saw that he had been hurled to	1532
	12:16	that the **d** had spewed out of his mouth.	1532
	12:17	Then the **d** was enraged at the woman	1532
	13: 1	And the **d** stood on the shore of the sea.	NIG
	13: 2	The **d** gave the beast his power	1532
	13: 4	the **d** because he had given authority to	1532
	13:11	but he spoke like a **d.**	1532
	16:13	they came out of the mouth *of* the **d,**	1532
	20: 2	He seized the **d,** that ancient serpent,	1532

DRAGONS (KJV) See JACKAL WELL, SERPENT

DRAGS (4) [DRAG]

Job	7: 4	The night **d** on, and I toss till dawn.	4499
	24:22	But God **d** *away* the mighty by his power;	5432
Ps	10: 9	he catches the helpless and **d** them *off*	5432
Ecc	12: 5	and the grasshopper **d** *himself* along	6022

DRAIN (3) [DRAINED, DRAINING]

Lev	17:13	be eaten *must* **d** *out* the blood and cover it	9161
	26:16	and **d** *away* your life.	1853
Eze	23:34	You will drink it and **d** it **dry;**	5172

DRAINED (5) [DRAIN]

Lev	1:15	its blood *shall* be **d** out on the side of	5172
	5: 9	of the blood *must* be **d** out at the base of	5172
2Ki	19:26	Their people, **d** *of* power,	7920
Isa	37:27	Their people, **d** *of* power,	7920
	51:17	*you who have* **d** to its dregs the goblet	5172+9272

DRAINING (1) [DRAIN]

Na	2: 8	and its water *is* **d** away.	5674

DRAMS (KJV) See DARICS, DRACHMAS

DRANK (40) [DRINK]

Ge	9:21	When *he* **d** some of its wine,	9272
	24:46	So I **d,** and she watered the camels also.	9272
	24:54	and the men who were with him ate and **d**	9272
	25:34	He ate and **d,** and then got up and left.	9272
	26:30	and they ate and **d.**	9272
	27:25	and he brought some wine and he **d.**	9272
	43:34	So they feasted and **d** freely with him.	8910
Ex	24:11	they saw God, and they ate and **d.**	9272
Nu	20:11	and the community and their livestock **d.**	9272
Dt	9: 9	I ate no bread and **d** no water.	9272
	9:18	I ate no bread and **d** no water,	9272
	29: 6	and **d** no wine or other fermented drink.	9272
	32:14	*You* **d** the foaming blood of the grape.	9272
	32:38	the fat of their sacrifices and **d** the wine	9272
Jdg	15:19	When Samson **d,** his strength returned	9272
2Sa	11:13	he ate and **d** with him,	9272
	12: 3	**d** from his cup and even slept in his arms.	9272
1Ki	4:20	they ate, *they* **d** and they were happy.	9272
	13:19	returned with him and ate and **d** in his house.	9272
	13:22	and **d** water in the place where he told you	9272
	17: 6	and he **d** from the brook.	9272
	19: 6	He ate and **d** and then lay down again.	9272
	19: 8	So he got up and ate and **d.**	9272
2Ki	7: 8	They ate and **d,** and carried away silver,	9272
	9:34	Jehu went in and ate and **d.**	9272
1Ch	29:22	and **d** with great joy in the presence of	9272
Ezr	10: 6	he ate no food and **d** no water,	9272
Job	29:23	and **d** in my words as the spring rain.	7023+7196
Jer	51: 7	The nations **d** her wine;	9272
Da	5: 1	for a thousand of his nobles and **d** wine	10748
	5: 3	his wives and his concubines **d** from them.	10748
	5: 4	*As they* **d** the wine,	10748
	5:23	and your concubines **d** wine from them.	10748
Ob	1:16	Just as *you* **d** on my holy hill,	9272
		and *they* all **d** from it.	
Mk	14:23	and *they* all **d** from it.	4403
Lk	13:26	you will say, 'We ate and **d** with you,	4403
Jn	4:12	who gave us the well and **d** from it himself,	4403
Ac	10:41	and **d** with him after he rose from the dead.	5228
1Co	10: 4	and **d** the same spiritual drink;	4403
	10: 4	for *they* **d** from the spiritual rock	4403

DRAUGHT (KJV) See CATCH, LATRINE, OUT OF BODY

DRAW (48) [DRAWING, DRAWN, DRAWS, DREW]

Ge	24:11	the time the *women* go out *to* **d** water.	8612
	24:13	the townspeople are coming out to **d** water.	8612
	24:19	she said, "I'll **d** water for your camels too,	8612
	24:20	ran back to the well to **d** *more* water,	8612
	24:43	if a maiden comes out to **d** water and I say	8612
	24:44	and I'll **d** water for your camels too,"	8612
Ex	2:16	and they came *to* **d** water and fill	1926
		I will **d** my sword	8197
Lev	26:33	and *will* **d** *out* my sword and pursue you.	8197
Nu	5:15	reminder offering *to* **d** **attention** *to* guilt.	2349
Jos	8:26	not **d** *back* the hand that held out his javelin	8740
Jdg	8:20	But Jether *did* not **d** his sword,	8990
	9:54	"**D** your sword and kill me,	8990
	20:32	Let's retreat and **d** them *away* from the city	5998
1Sa	9:11	they met some girls coming out to **d** water,	8612
	31: 4	"**D** your sword and run me through,	8990
1Ch	10: 4	"**D** your sword and run me through,	8990
Job	37:19	*we cannot* **d** *up* our case because	6885
Ps	37:14	The wicked **d** the sword and bend the bow	7337
	58: 7	*when they* **d** the bow,	2005
	144:11	our oxen *will* **d** **heavy loads.**	6022
Isa	5:18	Woe *to those who* **d** sin along with cords	5432
	12: 3	With joy you will **d** water from the wells	8612
Jer	46: 9	men of Lydia *who* **d** the bow.	2005
	50:14	all you *who* **d** the bow.	2005
	50:29	all *those who* **d** the bow.	2005
Eze	5: 2	in front of you and **d** the city of Jerusalem	2980
	21: 3	*I will* **d** my sword from its scabbard	3655
	28: 7	*they will* **d** their swords	8197
	30:11	*They will* **d** their swords against Egypt	8197
	40:46	who are the only Levites who may **d** near to	7929
	45: 4	in the sanctuary and who **d** near to minister	7929
Joel	3: 9	*Let* all the fighting men **d** near and attack.	5602
Na	3:14	**D** water for the siege,	8612
Zep	3: 2	she *does* not **d** near to her God.	7928
Hag	2:16	to a wine vat to **d** fifty measures,	3106
Mt	26:52	all who **d** the sword will die by the sword.	3284
Lk	1: 1	Many have undertaken *to* **d** *up* an account	421

Jn	2: 8	"Now *d* some *out* and take it to the master	533
	4: 7	a Samaritan woman came *to* **d** water,	533
	4:11	"you have nothing **to d** with and	534
	4:15	and have to keep coming here *to* **d water."**	533
	12:32	*will* **d** all men to myself."	1816
Ac	20:30	in order to **d** away disciples after them.	685
Gal	2:12	*he began to* **d back** and separate himself	5713
Heb	7:19	by which *we* **d** near to God.	1581
	10: 1	make perfect those who **d near** to worship.	4665
	10:22	let *us* **d** near to God with a sincere heart	4665

DRAWING (3) [DRAW]

1Sa	17:21	Israel and the Philistines *were* **d** up	6885
1Ch	24: 5	They divided them impartially by **d lots,**	1598
Lk	21:28	because your redemption *is* **d near."**	1581

DRAWN (24) [DRAW]

Ge	34: 3	His heart *was* **d** to Dinah daughter of Jacob,	1815
Nu	22:23	in the road with **d** sword in his hand,	8990
	22:31	in the road with his sword **d.**	8990
Dt	30:17	and if *you* **are d** away to bow down	5615
Jos	5:13	in front of him with a **d** sword in his hand.	8990
Jdg	20:31	meet them and *were* **d** away from the city.	5998
1Ch	21:16	with a **d** sword in his hand extended	8990
Job	19: 6	that God has wronged me and **d** his net	5938
Ps	3: 6	of thousands **d** up against me on every side.	8883
	21:12	when you aim at them with **d bow.**	4798
	55:21	yet they are **d swords.**	7347
	141: 4	Let not my heart *be* **d** to what is evil,	5742
Isa	21:15	from the **d** sword,	5759
	50: 5	*I have* not **d back.**	294+6047
Jer	31: 3	*I have* **d** you with loving-kindness.	5432
Eze	5: 2	For *I will* pursue them *with* **d** sword.	8197
	5: 2	to the winds and pursue *with* **d** sword.	8197
	12:14	and *I will* pursue them *with* **d** sword.	8197
	21: 5	that I the LORD *have* **d** my sword	3655
	21:28	" 'A sword, a sword, **d** for the slaughter,	7337
	32:20	The sword **is d;**	5989
Joel	2: 5	like a mighty army **d** up *for* battle.	6885
Mic	5: 6	the land of Nimrod with **d sword.**	7347
Jn	2: 9	the servants who *had* **d** the water knew.	533

DRAWS (7) [DRAW]

Job	33:22	His soul **d** near to the pit,	7928
	36:27	*"He* **d** up the drops of water,	1758
Ps	88: 3	of trouble and my life **d** near the grave.	5595
Pr	20: 5	but a man of understanding **d** them *out.*	1926
Isa	51: 5	My righteousness *d* near speedily,	AIT
Jn	4:36	Even now the reaper **d** his wages,	3284
	6:44	to me unless the Father who sent me **d** him,	1816

DREAD (22) [DREADED, DREADFUL, DREADS]

Ge	9: 2	and **d** *of* you will fall upon all the beasts of	3145
Ex	1:12	so the Egyptians *came to* **d** the Israelites	7762
	15:16	terror and **d** will fall upon them.	7065
Nu	22: 3	Moab *was* **filled with d** because of	7762
Dt	28:66	**filled with d** both night and day,	7064
2Ch	29: 8	an **object of d** and horror and scorn,	2317
Job	9:28	*I still* **d** all my sufferings,	3336
	13:11	Would not the **d** *of* him fall on you?	7065
Ps	14: 5	There they are, **overwhelmed with d,**	7064+7065
	31:11	I am a **d** to my friends—	7065
	53: 5	they were, **overwhelmed with d,**	7064+7065
	53: 5	where there was nothing to **d.**	7065
	105:38	because of *d* of Israel had fallen on them.	7065
	119:39	Take away the disgrace *I* **d,**	3336
Isa	2:10	hide in the ground from **d** *of* the LORD	7065
	2:19	the rocks and to holes in the ground from **d**	7065
	2:21	and to the overhanging crags from **d** *of*	7065
	7:16	of the two kings you **d** will be laid waste.	7762
	8:12	do not fear what they fear, and *do* not **d** it.	6907
	8:13	he is the *one* you are to **d,**	6907
	66: 4	and will bring upon them *what* they **d.**	4475
Jer	42:16	and the famine you **d** will follow you	1793

DREADED (8) [DREAD]

Dt	28:60	the diseases of Egypt that *you* **d,**	3336
	32:27	but *I* **d** the taunt of the enemy, lest	1593
Job	3:25	what *I* **d** has happened to me.	3336
	31:23	For I **d** destruction from God,	7065
	31:34	so feared the crowd and so **d** the contempt	3169
Isa	57:11	*so* **d** and feared that you have been false	1793
Da	5:19	and nations and men of every language **d**	10227
Hab	1: 7	They are a feared and **d** *people;*	3707

DREADFUL (12) [DREAD]

Ge	15:12	and a thick and **d** darkness came over him.	399
Dt	1:19	that vast and **d** desert that you have seen,	3707
	8:15	He led you through the vast and **d** desert,	3707
Job	6:21	you *see* **something d** and are afraid.	3170
Eze	14:21	against Jerusalem my four **d** judgments—	8273
Joel	2:11	The day of the LORD is great; it is **d.**	3707+4394
	2:31	coming of the great and **d** day of the LORD.	3707
Mal	4: 5	that great and **d** day of the LORD comes.	3707
Mt	24:19	**How d** it will be in those days	4026
Mk	13:17	**How d** it will be in those days	4026
Lk	21:23	**How d** it will be in those days	4026
Heb	10:31	It is a **d** *thing* to fall into the hands of	5829

DREADS (1) [DREAD]

| Pr | 10:24 | *What* the wicked **d** will overtake him; | 4475 |

DREAM (77) [DREAMED, DREAMER, DREAMERS, DREAMING, DREAMS]

Ge	20: 3	in a **d** one night and said to him, "You are	2706
	20: 6	Then God said to him in the **d,** "Yes,	2706
	28:12	*He* had a **d** in which he saw	2731
	31:10	a **d** in which I looked up and saw that	2706
	31:11	The angel of God said to me in the **d,**	2706
	31:24	to Laban the Aramean in a **d** *at* night	2731
	37: 5	Joseph **had a d,**	2706+2731
	37: 6	said to them, "Listen to this **d / had:**	2706+2731
	37: 8	because of his **d** and what he had said.	2706
	37: 9	Then *he* had another **d,**	2706+2731
	37: 9	"Listen," he said, "*I* had another **d,**	2706+2731
	37:10	"What is this *d* you had?"	2706+2731
	40: 5	**had a d** the same night,	2706+2731
	40: 5	and each had a meaning of its own.	2706
	40: 9	So the chief cupbearer told Joseph his **d.**	2706
	40: 9	"In my **d** I saw a vine in front of me,	2706
	40:16	he said to Joseph, "I too had a **d:**	2706
	41: 1	Pharaoh had a **d:**	2731
	41: 5	He fell asleep again and **had a second d:**	2731
	41: 7	Then Pharaoh woke up; it had been a **d.**	2706
	41:11	Each of us **had a d** the same night,	2706+2731
	41:11	and each had a meaning of its own.	2706
	41:12	giving each man the interpretation of his **d.**	2706
	41:15	Pharaoh said to Joseph, "*I* **had a d,**	2706+2731
	41:15	that when you hear a **d** you can interpret it."	2706
	41:17	"In my **d** I was standing on the bank of	2706
	41:26	it is one and the same **d.**	2706
	41:32	the **d** was given to Pharaoh in two forms is	2706
Jdg	7:13	as a man was telling a friend his **d.**	2706
	7:13	"*I had a* **d,"** he was saying.	2706+2731
	7:15	the **d** and its interpretation,	2706
1Ki	3: 5	to Solomon during the night in a **d,**	2706
	3:15	and he realized it had been a **d.**	2706
Job	20: 8	Like a **d** he flies away,	2706
	33:15	In a **d,** in a vision of the night,	2706
Ps	73:20	As a **d** when one awakes,	2706
Ecc	5: 3	As a **d** comes when there are many cares,	2706
Isa	29: 7	will be as it is with a **d,**	2706
	56:10	they lie around and **d,** they love to sleep.	2111
Jer	23:25	They say, "*I* **had a d!**	2731
	23:25	*I* **had a d!"**	2731
	23:28	Let the prophet who has a **d** tell his dream,	2731
	23:28	Let the prophet who has a dream tell his **d,**	2706
Da	2: 3	"*I have* **had a d** that troubles me	2706+2731
	2: 4	Tell your servants the **d,**	10267
	2: 5	not tell me what my **d** was and interpret it,	10267
	2: 6	But if you tell me the **d** and explain it,	10267
	2: 6	So tell me the **d** and interpret it for me."	10267
	2: 7	"Let the king tell his servants the **d,**	10267
	2: 9	If you do not tell me the **d,**	10267
	2: 9	So then, tell me the **d,**	10267
	2:16	so that he might interpret the **d** for him.	NIH
	2:23	of you, you have made known to us the **d**	10418S
	2:24	and I will interpret his **d** for him."	NIH
	2:25	the king what his **d** means."	NIH
	2:26	Are you able to tell me what I saw in my **d**	10267
	2:28	Your **d** and the visions that passed	10267
	2:36	"This was the **d,**	10267
	2:45	The **d** is true and	10267
	4: 5	I had a **d** that made me afraid.	10267
	4: 6	be brought before me to interpret the **d**	10267
	4: 7	I told them the **d,**	10267
	4: 8	into my presence and I told him the **d.**	10267
	4: 9	Here is my **d;** interpret it for me.	10256+10267
	4:18	"This is the **d** that I, King Nebuchadnezzar,	10267
	4:19	do not let the **d** or its meaning alarm you."	10267
	4:19	if only the **d** applied to your enemies	10267
	7: 1	Daniel had a **d,**	10267
	7: 1	He wrote down the substance of his **d.**	10267
Joel	2:28	your old men *will* **d** dreams,	2731
Mt	1:20	of the Lord appeared to him in a **d** and said,	3941
	2:12	And having been warned in a **d** not	3941
	2:13	of the Lord appeared to Joseph in a **d.**	3941
	2:19	the Lord appeared in a **d** to Joseph in Egypt	3941
	2:22	Having been warned in a **d,**	3941
	27:19	for I have suffered a great deal today in a **d**	3941
Ac	2:17	your old men *will* **d** dreams.	1965

DREAMED (2) [DREAM]

| Ps | 126: 1 | we were like *men who* **d.** | 2731 |
| Da | 2: 2 | and astrologers to tell him *what* he had **d.** | 2706 |

DREAMER (3) [DREAM]

Ge	37:19	"Here comes that **d!"** they said	1251+2021+2706
Dt	13: 3	you must not listen to the words of that	
		prophet or **d.**	2706+2731
	13: 5	That prophet or **d** must be put to death	2706+2731

DREAMERS (1) [DREAM]

| Jude | 1: 8 | these **d** pollute their own bodies, | 1965 |

DREAMING (1) [DREAM]

| Ecc | 5: 7 | Much **d** and many words are meaningless. | 2706 |

DREAMS (26) [DREAM]

Ge	37:20	Then we'll see what comes of his **d."**	2706
	40: 8	*"We both had* **d,"** they answered,	2706+2731
	40: 8	Tell me your **d."**	NIH
	41: 8	Pharaoh told them his **d,**	2706
	41:12	We told him our **d,**	2706
	41:22	"In my **d** I also saw seven heads of grain,	2706

Ge	41:25	"The **d** of Pharaoh are one and the same.	2706
	42: 9	Then he remembered his **d** about them	2706+2731
Nu	12: 6	I speak to him in **d.**	2706
Dt	13: 1	If a prophet, or *one who* **foretells by d**	2706+2731
1Sa	28: 6	not answer him by **d** or Urim or prophets.	2706
	28:15	either by prophets or by **d.**	2706
Job	4:13	Amid disquieting **d** in the night,	2612
	7:14	then you frighten me with **d** and terrify me	2706
Isa	29: 8	as *when* a hungry man **d** that he is eating,	2731
	29: 8	as *when* a thirsty man *that* he is drinking,	2731
Jer	23:27	**d** they tell one another will make my	
		people forget my name,	2706
	23:32	I am against those who prophesy false **d,"**	2706
	27: 9	your diviners, your **interpreters of d,**	2706
	29: 8	**d** you **encourage** them **to have.**	2706+2731
Da	1:17	And Daniel could understand visions and **d**	2706
	2: 1	Nebuchadnezzar **had d;**	2706+2731
	5:12	and also the ability to interpret **d,**	10267
Joel	2:28	your old men will dream **d,**	2706
Zec	10: 2	they tell **d** that are false,	2706
Ac	2:17	your old *men* will dream **d.**	1966

DREGS (4)

Ps	75: 8	of the earth drink it down to its very **d.**	9069
Isa	51:17	*you who have* **drained to** its **d** the goblet	5172+9272
Jer	48:11	like wine left on its **d,**	9069
Zep	1:12	who are like wine left on its **d,** who think,	9069

DRENCH (4) [DRENCHED]

Ps	6: 6	with weeping and **d** my couch with tears.	4998
	65:10	You **d** its furrows and level its ridges;	8115
Isa	16: 9	O Heshbon, O Elealeh, *I* **d** you *with* tears!	8115
Eze	32: 6	*I will* **d** the land with your flowing blood	9197

DRENCHED (9) [DRENCH]

Job	24: 8	*They are* **d** by mountain rains and hug	8182
	29: 6	when my path *was* **d** with cream and	8175
SS	5: 2	My head *is* **d** with dew,	4848
Isa	34: 7	Their land *will* *be* **d** with blood,	8115
Da	4:15	" '*Let him* **be d** with the dew of heaven,	10607
	4:23	*Let him* **be d** with the dew of heaven;	10607
	4:25	like cattle and *be* **d** with the dew of heaven.	10607
	4:33	His body *was* **d** with the dew of heaven	10607
	5:21	and his body *was* **d** with the dew of heaven,	10607

DRESS (13) [DRESSED, DRESSING, WELL-DRESSED]

Ex	29: 5	the garments and **d** Aaron *with* the tunic,	4252
	29: 8	Bring his sons and **d** them *in* tunics	4252
	40:13	Then **d** Aaron in the sacred garments,	4252
	40:14	Bring his sons and **d** them *in* tunics.	4252
2Sa	14: 2	**D** in mourning clothes,	4252
Jer	4:30	Why *d yourself in* scarlet and put	4252
	6:14	*They* **d** the wound of my people as	8324
	8:11	*They* **d** the wound of my people as	8324
Eze	16:10	an **embroidered d** and put leather sandals	8391
	23:12	warriors *in* full **d,** mounted horsemen,	4229
Lk	12:37	he will *himself* **d to serve,**	4322
Jn	21:18	and someone else *will* **d** you and lead you	2439
1Ti	2: 9	I also want women *to* **d** modestly,	3175

DRESSED (43) [DRESS]

Ge	41:42	He **d** him *in* robes of fine linen and put	4252
Ex	20:25	do not build it with **d stones,**	1607
1Sa	17:38	Then Saul **d** David in his own tunic.	4252
	25:18	five **d** sheep, five seahs of roasted grain,	6913
1Ki	5:17	a foundation of **d** stone for the temple.	1607
	6: 7	only blocks **d** *at* the quarry were used,	8969
	6:36	of three courses of **d** stone and one course	1607
	7:12	of three courses of **d stone** and one course	1607
	22:10	**D** in their royal robes,	4252
2Ki	12:12	and **d** stone for the repair of the temple of	4732
	12:12	and **d** stone to repair the temple.	4732
1Ch	22: 2	to prepare **d** stone for building the house	1607
2Ch	5:12	**d** *in* fine linen and playing cymbals,	4252
	18: 9	**D** in their royal robes,	4252
	34:11	and builders to purchase **d** stone,	4732
Pr	7:10	**d** *like* a prostitute with crafty intent.	8884
Isa	9:10	but we will rebuild with **d stone;**	1607
Jer	10: 9	and goldsmith have made is then **d** *in* blue	4230
Eze	16:10	*I* **d** you in fine linen and covered you	2502
	40:42	There were also four tables of **d** stone for	1607
Da	10: 5	and there before me was a man *d* in linen,	4229
Zec	3: 3	Now Joshua was **d** in filthy clothes,	4252
Mt	6:29	not even Solomon in all his splendor *was* **d**	4314
	11: 8	A man *d* in fine clothes?	314
Mk	5:15	sitting there, **d** and in his right mind;	2667
	16: 5	a young man **d** in a white robe sitting on	4314
Lk	7:25	A man *d* in fine clothes?	314
	8:35	**d** and in his right mind;	2667
	12:27	not even Solomon in all his splendor *was* **d**	4314
	12:35	"Be **d** ready for service	3836+4019+4322
	16:19	"There was a rich man *who was* **d in** purple	1898
Jn	21:18	when you were younger *you* **d** yourself	2439
Ac	1:10	when suddenly two men **d** in white stood	2264
Rev	1:13	**d** in a robe reaching down to his feet and	1907
	3: 4	They will walk with me, **d** in white,	NIG
	3: 5	like them, *be* **d** in white.	2668+4314
	4: 4	*They were* **d** in white and had crowns	2668+4314
	15: 6	*They were* **d** in clean, shining linen	1907
	17: 4	The woman was **d** *in* purple and scarlet,	4314
	18:16	Woe, O great city, **d** *in* fine linen,	4314

Rev	19:13	He is **d** in a robe dipped in blood,	4314
	19:14	riding on white horses and **d** in fine linen,	1907
	21: 2	as a bride **beautifully d** for her husband.	3175

DRESSING (1) [DRESS]

| Lk | 23:11 | **D** him **in** an elegant robe, | 4314 |

DREW (37) [DRAW]

Ge	14: 8	**d** up their battle **lines**	6885
	24:20	and **d** enough for all his camels.	8612
	24:45	She went down to the spring and **d water,**	8612
	38:29	But when he **d** back his hand,	8740
	47:29	When the time **d near** for Israel to die,	7928
	49:33	he **d** his feet **up** into the bed,	665
Ex	2:10	saying, "*I* **d** him out of the water."	5406
	2:19	He even **d water** for us and watered the flock."	1926+1926
Jos	24:25	at Shechem he **d up** for them decrees	8492
Jdg	3:21	**d** the sword from his right thigh	4374
	20:24	Then the Israelites **d near** to Benjamin	7928
1Sa	7: 6	they **d** water and poured it out before	8612
	7:10	the Philistines **d near** to engage Israel	5602
	17: 2	**d up** their battle **line**	6885
	17:51	of the Philistine's sword and **d** it from	8990
2Sa	10: 8	The Ammonites came out and **d up**	6885
	22:17	he **d** me **out** of deep waters.	5406
	23:16	**d** water from the well near the gate	8612
1Ki	1: 1	When the time **d near** for David to die,	7928
	22:34	But someone **d** his bow at random and hit	5432
2Ki	9:24	Jehu **d** his bow and shot Joram	928+3338+4848
1Ch	11:18	**d** water from the well near the gate	8612
	19: 9	The Ammonites came out and **d up**	6885
2Ch	13: 3	**d up** a battle **line**	6885
	18:31	God **d** them **away** from him,	6077
	18:33	But someone **d** his bow at random and hit	5432
Ps	18:16	he **d** me **out** of deep waters.	5406
	107:18	They loathed half all food and **d near** the gates	5595
Isa	43:17	who **d out** the chariots and horses,	3655
La	3:12	He **d** his bow and made me the target	2005
Mt	26:51	**d** it **out** and struck the servant of	685
Mk	14:47	they **d** his sword and struck the servant of	5060
Jn	18: 6	they **d** back and fell to the ground.	599
	18:10	**d** it and struck the high priest's servant,	1816
Ac	7:17	"As the time **d near** for God	1581
	16:27	he **d** his sword and was about to kill himself	5060
	23:19	**d** him aside and asked,	432

DRIED (27) [DRY]

Ge	8: 7	until the water had **d** up from the earth.	3312
	8:13	the water had **d** up from the earth.	2990
Jos	2:10	the LORD **d up** the water of the Red Sea	3312
	4:23	For the LORD your God **d up** the Jordan	3312
	4:23	to the Red Sea when he **d** it **up** before us	3312
	5: 1	how the LORD had **d up** the Jordan before	3312
Jdg	16: 7	that have not been **d,**	2990
	16: 8	that had not been **d,**	2990
1Ki	17: 7	Some time later the brook **d up**	3312
2Ki	19:24	With the soles of my feet I have **d up** all	2990
Ps	22:15	My strength is **d up** like a potsherd,	3312
	74:15	you **d up** the ever flowing rivers.	3312
	106: 9	He rebuked the Red Sea, and it **d up;**	2990
Isa	15: 6	The waters of Nimrim are **d up**	5457
	37:25	With the soles of my feet I have **d up** all	2990
	51:10	Was it not you who **d up** the sea,	2990
Jer	48:34	for even the waters of Nimrim are **d up.**	5457
Eze	37:11	'Our bones are **d up** and our hope is gone;	3312
Joel	1:10	The fields are ruined, the ground is **d up;**	62
	1:10	the new wine is **d up,** the oil fails.	3312
	1:12	vine is **d up** and the fig tree is withered;	3312
	1:12	of the field—are **d up,**	3312
	1:17	for the grain has **d up.**	3312
	1:20	of water have **d up** and fire has devoured	3312
Am	4: 7	another had none and **d up.**	3312
	7: 4	it **d up** the great deep and devoured	430
Rev	16:12	and its water was **d up** to prepare the way	3830

DRIES (4) [DRY]

Pr	17:22	but a crushed spirit **d up** the bones.	3312
Isa	24: 4	The earth **d up** and withers,	62
	24: 7	The new wine **d up** and the vine withers;	62
Na	1: 4	He rebukes the sea and **d** it **up;**	3312

DRIFT (1)

| Heb | 2: 1 | so that we do not **d away.** | 4184 |

DRINK (320) [DRANK, DRINKERS, DRINKING, DRINKS, DRUNK, DRUNKARD, DRUNKARD'S, DRUNKARDS, DRUNKEN, DRUNKENNESS]

Ge	19:32	**get** our father **to d** wine	9197
	19:33	**got** their father **to d** wine,	9197
	19:34	*Let's* **get** him **to d** wine again tonight,	9197
	19:35	**got** their father **to d** wine that night also,	9197
	21:19	**gave** the boy a **d.**	9197
	24:14	that *I* may **have** a **d,'** and she says, 'Drink,	9272
	24:14	*and*, I'll water your camels too'—	9272
	24:18	"**D,** my lord," she said,	9272
	24:18	the jar to her hands and **gave** him a **d.**	9197
	24:19	After *she* had **given** him a **d,** she said,	9197
	24:43	to her, "Please **let** me a little water	9197

Ge	24:44	if she says to me, "**D,** and I'll draw water	9272
	24:45	and I said to her, 'Please **give** me a **d.'**	9197
	24:46	'**D,** and I'll water your camels too.'	9272
	30:38	in front of the flocks when they came to **d.**	9272
	30:38	the flocks were in heat and came to **d,**	9272
	35:14	and he poured out a **d offering** on it;	5821
Ex	7:18	not be able to **d** its water.' "	9272
	7:21	that the Egyptians could not **d** its water.	9272
	7:24	they could not **d** the water of the river.	9272
	15:23	not **d** its water because it was bitter.	9272
	15:24	saying, "What *are we to* **d?**"	9272
	17: 1	but there was no water *for* the people to **d.**	9272
	17: 2	"**Give** us water to **d.**"	9272
	17: 6	of it *for* the people to **d.**"	9272
	29:40	a quarter of a hin of wine as a **d offering.**	5821
	29:41	the same grain offering and its **d offering**	5821
	30: 9	and do not pour a **d offering** on it.	5821
	32: 6	down to eat and **d** and got up to indulge	9272
	32:20	on the water and **made** the Israelites **d** it.	9197
	37:16	**pouring** out of **d offerings.**	5818
Lev	10: 9	"You and your sons *are* not *to* **d** wine	9272
	10: 9	or other **fermented d** whenever you go into	8911
	23:13	its **d offering** of a quarter of a hin of wine.	5821
	23:18	with their grain offerings and **d offerings**—	5821
	23:37	and **d offerings** required for each day.	5821
Nu	4: 7	and the jars for **d offerings;**	5821
	5:24	He shall **have** the woman **d** the bitter water	9197
	5:26	he is to **have** the woman **d** the water.	9197
	5:27	when she is **made** to **d** the water that brings	9197
	6: 3	from wine and other **fermented d** and must	8911
	6: 3	and *must* not **d** vinegar made from wine or	9272
	6: 3	from wine or from other **fermented d.**	8911
	6: 3	not **d** grape juice or eat grapes or raisins.	9272
	6:15	with their grain offerings and **d offerings,**	5821
	6:17	with its grain offering and **d offering.**	5821
	6:20	After that, the Nazirite *may* **d** wine.	9272
	15: 5	a quarter of a hin of wine as a **d offering.**	5821
	15: 7	and a third of a hin of wine as a **d offering.**	5821
	15:10	bring half a hin of wine as a **d offering.**	5821
	15:24	and **d offering,** and a male goat for	5821
	20: 5	And there is no water to **d!**"	9272
	20: 8	so they and their livestock *can* **d.**"	9197
	20:17	or **d** water from any well.	9272
	20:19	if we or our livestock **d** any of your water,	9272
	21:22	or **d** water from any well.	9272
	28: 7	The accompanying **d offering** is to be	5821
	28: 7	of a hin of **fermented d** with each lamb.	8911
	28: 7	Pour out the **d offering** to the LORD at	5821
	28: 8	and **d offering** that you prepare in	5821
	28: 9	with its **d offering** and a grain offering	5821
	28:10	and its **d offering.**	5821
	28:14	With each bull there is to be a **d offering**	5821
	28:15	with its **d offering,**	5821
	28:24	and its **d offering.**	5821
	28:31	with their **d offerings,**	5821
	29: 6	with their grain offerings and **d offerings**	5821
	29:11	and their **d offerings.**	5821
	29:16	with its grain offering and **d offering.**	5821
	29:18	and **d offerings** according to	5821
	29:19	and their **d offerings.**	5821
	29:21	and **d offerings** according to	5821
	29:22	with its grain offering and **d offering.**	5821
	29:24	and **d offerings** according to	5821
	29:25	with its grain offering and **d offering.**	5821
	29:27	with its grain offering and **d offering.**	5821
	29:28	with its grain offering and **d offering.**	5821
	29:30	and **d offerings** according to	5821
	29:31	with its grain offering and **d offering.**	5821
	29:33	and **d offerings** according to	5821
	29:34	with its grain offering and **d offering.**	5821
	29:37	and **d offerings** according to	5821
	29:38	with its grain offering and **d offering.**	5821
	29:39	**d offerings** and fellowship offerings.' "	5821
Dt	2: 6	for the food you eat and the water you **d.'** "	9272
	2:28	and water *to* **d** for their price in silver.	9272
	14:26	cattle, sheep, wine or other **fermented d,**	8911
	28:39	and cultivate them but *you* will not **d**	9272
	29: 6	and drank no wine or other **fermented d.**	8911
	32:38	and drank the wine of their **d offerings?**	5816
Jdg	4:19	She opened a skin of milk, **gave** him a **d,**	9197
	7: 5	from those who kneel down to **d.**"	9272
	7: 6	All the rest got down on their knees to **d.**	9272
	13: 4	Now see to it that *you* **d** no wine	9272
	13: 4	that you drink no wine or other **fermented d** nor eat anything unclean.	8911
	13: 7	**d** no wine or other **fermented** drink and do	9272
	13: 7	drink no wine or other **fermented d** and do	8911
	13:14	nor **d** any wine or other fermented drink	9272
	13:14	nor drink any wine or other **fermented d**	8911
	19: 6	two of them sat down to eat and **d** together.	9272
	19:21	they had something to eat and **d.**	9272
Ru	2: 9	go and **get** a **d** from the water jars	9272
1Sa	30:11	They **gave** him water *to* **d** and food	9197
2Sa	11:11	How could I go to my house to eat and **d**	9272
	23:15	that someone *would* **get** me a **d** *of* water	9197
	23:16	But he refused to **d** it;	9272
	23:17	And David would not **d** it.	9272
1Ki	13: 8	nor would I eat bread or **d** water here.	9272
	13: 9	not eat bread or **d** water or return by	9272
	13:16	nor can I eat bread or **d** water with you	9272
	13:17	not eat bread or **d** water there or return by	9272
	13:18	so that he may eat bread and **d** water.' "	9272
	13:22	the place where he told you not to eat or **d.**	9272
	17: 4	You **d** from the brook,	9272
	17:10	a little water in a jar so *I* may **have** a **d?**"	9197
	18:41	And Elijah said to Ahab, "Go, eat and **d,**	9272

1Ki	18:42	So Ahab went off to eat and **d,**	9272
2Ki	3:17	your cattle and your other animals *will* **d.**	9272
	6:22	so that they may eat and **d** and then go back	9272
	16:13	poured out his **d offering,**	5821
	16:15	their grain offering and their **d offering.**	5821
	18:27	and **d** their own urine?"	9272
	18:31	from his own vine and fig tree and **d** water	9272
1Ch	11:17	that someone *would* **get** me a **d** *of* water	9197
	11:18	But he refused to **d** it;	9272
	11:19	"Should I **d** the blood these men who	9272
	11:19	David would not **d** it.	9272
	29:21	together with their **d offerings,**	5821
2Ch	28:15	food and **d,** and healing balm.	9197
	29:35	the fellowship offerings and the **d offerings**	5821
Ezr	3: 7	and gave food and **d** and oil to the people	5492
	7:17	with their grain offering and **d offerings,**	10483
Ne	8:12	Then all the people went away to eat and **d,**	9272
Est	1: 8	was allowed to **d** in his own way,	9276
	3:15	The king and Haman sat down to **d,**	9272
	4:16	Do not eat or **d** for three days, night or day.	9272
Job	1: 4	to eat and **d** with them.	9272
	21:20	let him **d** of the wrath of the Almighty.	9272
Ps	36: 8	you give them **d** *from* your river	9197
	50:13	the flesh of bulls or **d** the blood of goats?	9272
	73:10	to them and **d up** waters in abundance.	5172
	75: 8	all the wicked of the earth **d** it **down**	5172
	78:44	*they* could not **d** *from* their streams.	9272
	80: 5	you have **made** them **d** tears by the bowlful.	9197
	102: 9	For I eat ashes as my food and mingle my **d**	9198
	110: 7	He will **d** from a brook beside the way;	9272
Pr	4:17	of wickedness and **d** the wine of violence.	9272
	5:15	**D** water from your own cistern,	9272
	7:18	Come, *let's* **d** deep of love till morning;	8115
	9: 5	eat my food and **d** the wine I have mixed.	9272
	23: 7	"Eat and **d,**" he says to you,	9272
	23:20	Do not join *those who* **d too much** wine	6010
	23:35	will I wake up so I can find another **d?**"	5647S
	25:21	**give** him water to **d.**	9197
	31: 4	not for kings *to* **d** wine,	9272
	31: 5	lest *they* **d** and forget what the law decrees,	9272
	31: 7	*let them* **d** and forget their poverty	9272
Ecc	2:24	and **d** and find satisfaction in his work.	9272
	3:13	That everyone may eat and **d,**	9272
	5:18	a man to eat and **d,** and to find satisfaction	9272
	8:15	under the sun than to eat and **d** and be glad.	9272
	9: 7	and **d** your wine with a joyful heart,	9272
SS	5: 1	Eat, O friends, and **d;**	9272
	5: 1	**d** your **fill,** O lovers.	8910
	8: 2	**give** you spiced wine to **d,**	9197
Isa	21: 5	they spread the rugs, they eat, they **d!**	9272
	22:13	"Let us eat and **d,**" you say,	9272
	24: 9	No longer *do they* **d** wine with a song;	9272
	36:12	and **d** their own urine?	9272
	36:16	from his own vine and fig tree and **d** water	9272
	43:20	to **give d** *to* my people, my chosen,	9197
	51:22	you will never **d** again.	9272
	56:12	Let us **d** our **fill** *of* beer!	6010
	57: 6	to them you have poured out **d offerings**	5821
	60:16	You will **d** the milk of nations and	3567
	62: 8	and never again *will* foreigners **d**	9272
	62: 9	and those who gather the grapes *will* **d** it	9272
	65:13	my servants *will* **d,** but you will go thirsty;	9272
	66:11	*you will* **d deeply** and delight	5209
Jer	2:18	Now why go to Egypt to **d** water from	9272
	2:18	And why go to Assyria to **d** water from	9272
	7:18	They pour out **d offerings** to other gods	5821
	8:14	**given** us poisoned water to **d,**	9197
	9:15	and **d** poisoned water.	9197
	16: 7	nor *will anyone* **give** them a **d**	3926+9197
	16: 8	and sit down to eat and **d.**	9272
	19:13	and poured out **d offerings** to other gods.' "	5821
	22:15	Did not your father have food and **d?**	9272
	23:15	and **d** poisoned water,	9197
	25:15	**make** all the nations to whom I send you **d**	9197
	25:16	When *they* **d** it,	9272
	25:17	**made** all the nations to whom he sent me **d**	9197
	25:26	the king of Sheshach *will* **d** it too.	9272
	25:27	**D,** get drunk and vomit,	9272
	25:28	to take the cup from your hand and **d,**	9272
	25:28	*You* **must d** it!	9272+9272
	32:29	by pouring out **d offerings** to other gods.	5821
	35: 2	**give** them wine to **d.**"	9197
	35: 5	and said to them, "**D** some wine."	9272
	35: 6	But they replied, "We do not **d** wine,	9272
	35: 6	nor your descendants *must ever* **d** wine.	9272
	35:14	to **d** wine and this command has been kept.	9272
	35:14	To this day they do not **d** wine,	9272
	44:17	and will pour out **d offerings** to her,	5821
	44:18	and pouring out **d offerings** to her,	5821
	44:19	and poured out **d offerings** to her,	5821
	44:19	like her image and pouring out **d offerings**	5821
	44:25	to burn incense and pour out **d offerings** to	5821
	49:12	not deserve to **d** the cup must drink it,	9272
	49:12	not deserve to drink the cup **must d** it,	9272+9272
	49:12	You will not go unpunished, but **must d** it.	9272+9272
	52:19	**bowls** used for **d offerings**—	4984
La	5: 4	We must buy the water we **d;**	9272
Eze	4:11	of a hin of water and **d** it at set times.	9272
	4:16	in anxiety and rationed water in despair,	9272
	12:18	and shudder in fear *as you* **d** your water.	9272
	12:19	in anxiety and **d** their water in despair,	9272
	20:28	and poured out their **d offerings.**	5821
	23:32	"You will **d** your sister's cup,	9272
	23:34	You will **d** it and drain it dry;	9272
	25: 4	they will eat your fruit and **d** your milk.	9272
	34:18	Is it not enough for *you* to **d** clear water?	9272

Eze	34:19	and **d** what you have muddied	9272
	39:17	There you will eat flesh and **d** blood.	9272
	39:18	You will eat the flesh of mighty men and **d**	9272
	39:19	till you are glutted and **d** blood	9272
	44:21	*to* **d** wine when he enters the inner court.	9272
	45:17	grain offerings and **d** offerings at	5821
Da	1:10	who has assigned your food and **d**.	5492
	1:12	but vegetables to eat and water *to* **d**.	9272
	1:16	to **d** and gave them vegetables instead.	5492
	5: 2	and his concubines *might* **d** from them.	10748
Hos	2: 5	my wool and my linen, my oil and my **d.**'	9198
Joel	1: 9	Grain offerings and **d** offerings are cut off	5821
	1:13	and **d** offerings are withheld from	5821
	2:14	and **d** offerings for the LORD your God.	5821
	3: 3	they sold girls for wine that *they might* **d**.	9272
Am	2: 8	In the house of their god *they* **d** wine taken	9272
	2:12	"But *you* **made** the Nazirites **d** wine	9197
	4: 8	for water but did not get enough *to* **d**,	9272
	5:11	*you will* not **d** their wine.	9272
	6: 6	You **d** wine by the bowlful and use	9272
	9:14	They will plant vineyards and **d** their wine;	9272
Ob	1:16	so all the nations *will* **d** continually;	9272
	1:16	they will **d** and drink and be as	9272
	1:16	and **d** and be as if they had never been.	4363
Jnh	3: 7	do not let them eat or **d**	9272
Mic	6:15	you will crush grapes but not **d** the wine.	9272
Hab	2:15	"Woe to *him who* **gives** **d** to his neighbors,	9197
	2:16	**D** and be exposed!	9272
Zep	1:13	they will plant vineyards but not **d**	9272
Hag	1: 6	You **d**, but never have your fill.	9272
Zec	9:15	They will **d** and roar as with wine;	9272
Mt	6:25	what you will eat or **d**;	4403
	6:31	or 'What *shall* we **d**?'	4403
	20:22	"Can you **d** the cup I am going to drink?"	4403
	20:22	"Can you drink the cup I am going to **d**?"	4403
	20:23	*"You will* indeed **d** from my cup,	4403
	24:49	to beat his fellow servants and to eat and **d**	4403
	25:35	**gave** me something to **d**,	4540
	25:37	**give** you something to **d**?	4540
	25:42	**gave** me nothing to **d**,	4540
	26:27	saying, "**D** from it, all of you.	4403
	26:29	*I will* not **d** of this fruit of the vine from	4403
	26:29	until that day when *I* **d** it anew with you	4403
	26:42	for this cup to be taken away unless *I* **d** it,	4403
	27:34	There they offered Jesus wine *to* **d**,	4403
	27:34	but after tasting it, he refused *to* **d**.	4403
	27:48	offered it to Jesus *to* **d**.	4540
Mk	10:38	"Can you **d** the cup I drink or be baptized	4403
	10:38	"Can you drink the cup I **d** or be baptized	4403
	10:39	*"You will* **d** the cup I drink and be baptized	4403
	10:39	"You will drink the cup I **d** and be baptized	4403
	14:25	*I will* not **d** again of the fruit of the vine	4403
	14:25	when *I* **d** it anew in the kingdom of God."	4403
	15:36	offered it to Jesus *to* **d**.	4540
	16:18	and when *they* **d** deadly poison,	4403
Lk	1:15	to take wine or other **fermented** **d**,	4975
	5:30	"Why do you eat and **d** with tax collectors	4403
	12:19	Take life easy; eat, **d** and be merry." '	4403
	12:29	on what you will eat or **d**;	4403
	12:45	and maidservants and *to* eat and **d**;	4403
	17: 8	and wait on me while *I* eat and **d**;	4403
	17: 8	after that *you may* eat and **d**'?	4403
	22:18	*I* will not **d** again of the fruit of the vine until	4403
	22:30	and **d** at my table in my kingdom and sit	4403
Jn	2:10	guests *have* **had too much** to **d**;	3499
	4: 7	Jesus said to her, "Will you give me a **d**?"	4403
	4: 9	How can you ask me for a **d**?"	4403
	4:10	of God and who it is that asks you for a **d**,	4403
	6:53	the flesh of the Son of Man and his blood,	4403
	6:55	and my blood is real **d**.	4530
	7:37	let him come to me and **d**.	4403
	18:11	not **d** the cup the Father has given me?"	4403
	19:30	When he had received the **d**, Jesus said,	NIG
Ac	9: 9	and did not eat or **d** anything.	4403
	23:12	not to eat or **d** until they had killed Paul.	4403
	23:21	not to eat or **d** until they have killed him.	4403
Ro	12:20	**give** him something to **d**.	4540
	14:21	to eat meat or **d** wine or to do anything else	4403
1Co	9: 4	Don't we have the right to food and **d**?	4403
	9: 7	Who tends a flock and *does* not **d** of	2266
	10: 4	and drank the same spiritual **d**;	4503
	10: 7	"The people sat down to eat and **d** and got	4403
	10:21	You cannot **d** the cup of the Lord and	4403
	10:31	whether you eat or **d** or whatever you do,	4403
	11:22	Don't you have homes to eat and **d** in?	4403
	11:25	do this, whenever *you* **d** it,	4403
	11:26	whenever you eat this bread and **d** this cup,	4403
	12:13	we were all **given** the one Spirit *to* **d**.	4540
	15:32	the dead are not raised, *"Let us* eat and **d**,	4403
Php	2:17	**poured out** like a **d** offering	5064
Col	2:16	by what you eat or **d**,	4530
2Ti	4: 6	**poured out** like a **d** offering,	5064
Heb	9:10	**d** and various ceremonial washings—	4503
Rev	14: 8	**made** all the nations **d**	4540
	14:10	too, *will* **d** of the wine of God's fury,	4403
	16: 6	and you have given them blood *to* **d**	4403
	21: 6	To him who is thirsty I will give to **d**	NIG

DRINKERS (2) [DRINK]

Isa	24: 9	the beer is bitter to its **d**.	9272
Joel	1: 5	Wail, all you **d** *of* wine;	9272

DRINKING (39) [DRINK]

Ge	24:19	until they have finished **d**."	9272
	24:22	When the camels had finished **d**,	9272

Ex	7:24	along the Nile to *get* **d** water,	9272
	34:28	without eating bread or **d** water.	9272
Jdg	19: 4	eating and **d**, and sleeping there.	9272
Ru	3: 3	until he has finished eating and **d**.	9272
	3: 7	When Boaz had finished eating and **d**	9272
1Sa	1: 9	Once when they had finished eating and **d**	9272
	1:15	I have not *been* **d** wine or beer;	9272
	30:16	**d** and reveling because of the great amount	9272
2Sa	13:28	in high spirits from **d** wine and I say to you,	NIH
1Ki	13:23	Right now they are eating and **d** with him	9272
	13:23	the man of God had finished eating and **d**,	9272
	20:12	while he and the kings *were* **d** in their tents,	9272
2Ki	6:23	and after they had finished eating and **d**,	9272
1Ch	12:39	with David, eating and **d**,	9272
Est	5: 6	As they were **d** wine,	9272
	7: 2	and as they were **d** wine on that second day,	5492
Job	1:13	and daughters were feasting and **d** wine at	9272
	1:18	and daughters were feasting and **d** wine at	9272
Pr	26: 6	Like cutting off one's feet or **d** violence is	9272
Isa	5:22	at wine and champions at mixing drinks,	9272
	22:13	eating of meat and **d** *of* wine!	9272
	29: 8	as when a thirsty man dreams that *he is* **d**,	9272
Da	5: 2	While Belshazzar **d** his wine,	10302
Zec	7: 6	And when you were eating and **d**,	9272
Mt	11:18	For John came neither eating nor **d**,	4403
	11:19	The Son of Man came eating and **d**,	4403
	24:38	people were eating and **d**,	4403
Lk	5:33	but yours *go on* eating and **d**."	4403
	5:39	no one *after* **d** old wine wants the new,	4403
	7:33	nor **d** wine, and you say, 'He has	4403
	7:34	The Son of Man came eating and **d**,	4403
	10: 7	eating and **d** whatever they give you,	4403
	17:27	*People were* eating, **d**,	4403
	17:28	People were eating and **d**,	4403
Ro	14:17	of God is not a matter of eating and **d**,	4530
1Ti	5:23	Stop **d** only water,	5621

DRINKS (22) [DRINK]

Ge	44: 5	the cup my master **d** from and also uses	9272
Nu	23:24	till he devours his prey and **d** the blood	9272
Dt	11:11	a land of mountains and valleys that **d** rain	9272
2Sa	19:35	Can your servant taste what he eats and **d**?	9272
Ne	8:10	"Go and enjoy choice food and sweet **d**,	9272
Job	6: 4	my spirit **d** in their poison;	9272
	15:16	who **d** up evil like water!	9272
	34: 7	who **d** scorn like water?	9272
Isa	5:11	in the morning to run after their **d**,	8911
	5:22	and champions at mixing **d**,	8911
	44:12	he **d** no water and grows faint.	9272
Hos	4:18	Even when their **d** are gone,	6011
Am	4: 1	"Bring us *some* **d**!"	9272
Jn	4:13	"Everyone who **d** this water will be thirsty	4403
	4:14	but whoever **d** the water I give him will never thirst.	4403
	6:54	and **d** my blood has eternal life,	4403
	6:56	and **d** my blood remains in me,	4403
1Co	11:27	whoever eats the bread or **d** the cup of	4403
	11:28	before he eats of the bread and **d** of the cup.	4403
	11:29	and **d** without recognizing the body of	4403
	11:29	of the Lord eats and **d** judgment on himself.	4403
Heb	6: 7	Land that **d** in the rain often falling on it	4403

DRIP (3) [DRIPPED, DRIPPING]

Pr	5: 3	For the lips of an adulteress **d** honey,	5752
Joel	3:18	that day the mountains *will* **d** new wine,	5752
Am	9:13	New wine *will* **d** from the mountains	5752

DRIPPED (1) [DRIP]

SS	5: 5	and my hands **d** *with* myrrh,	5752

DRIPPING (3) [DRIP]

Pr	19:13	quarrelsome wife is like a **constant** **d**.	1942+3265
	27:15	quarrelsome wife is like a **constant** **d**	1942+3265
SS	5:13	His lips are like lilies **d** *with* myrrh.	5752

DRIVE (89) [DRIVEN, DRIVER, DRIVER'S, DRIVERS, DRIVES, DRIVING, DROVE]

Ex	6: 1	of my mighty hand *he will* **d** them out	1763
	11: 1	he will **d** you out completely.	1763+1763
	23:28	the hornet ahead of you *to* **d** the Hivites,	1763
	23:29	But *I will* not **d** them out in a single year,	1763
	23:30	by little *I will* **d** them out before you,	1763
	23:31	and *you will* **d** them out before you.	1763
	33: 2	I will send an angel before you and **d** out	1763
	34:11	*I will* **d** out before you the Amorites.	1763
	34:24	*I will* **d** out nations before you	3769
Lev	18:24	how the nations that I *am going to* **d** out	8938
	20:23	the nations I *am going to* **d** out before you.	8938
Nu	22: 6	be able to defeat them and **d** them **out** of	1763
	22:11	be able to fight them and **d** them **away.' "**	1763
	33:52	**d** out all the inhabitants of the land	3769
	33:55	" 'But if *you do* not **d** out the inhabitants of	3769
Dt	4:27	to which the LORD *will* **d** you.	5627
	4:38	to **d** out before you nations greater	3769
	7:17	How can we **d** them out?"	3769
	7:22	The LORD your God *will* **d** out those nations	5970
	9: 3	And *you will* **d** them **out**	3769
	9: 4	that the LORD *is going to* **d** them **out**	3769
	9: 5	the LORD your God *will* **d** them **out**	3769
	11:23	the LORD *will* **d** out all these nations	3769
	18:12	LORD your God *will* **d** out those nations	3769
	28:34	The sights you see will **d** you **mad.**	8713

Dt	28:36	The LORD *will* **d** you and the king	2143
	28:37	the nations where the LORD *will* **d** you.	5627
	33:27	He will **d** out your enemy before you,	1763
Jos	3:10	that *he* will **certainly** **d** out before you	3769+3769
	13: 6	I myself *will* **d** them **out** before	3769
	13:13	But the Israelites *did* not **d** out the people	3769
	14:12	*I will* **d** them **out** just as he said."	3769
	17:13	**d** them **out** completely,	3769+3769
	17:18	*you can* **d** them **out.**"	3769
	23: 5	The LORD your God himself *will* **d** them **out**	2074
	23:13	LORD your God will no longer **d** out these nations	3769
Jdg	1:19	but *they* were unable to **d** the people **from**	3769
	1:27	But Manasseh *did* not **d** out the people	3769
	1:29	Nor did Ephraim **d** out the Canaanites	3769
	1:30	Neither *did* Zebulun **d** out the Canaanites	3769
	1:31	Nor *did* Asher **d** out those living in Acco	3769
	1:33	Neither *did* Naphtali **d** out those living	3769
	2: 3	that *I* will not **d** them out before you;	1763
	2:21	I will no longer **d** out before them any of	3769
	2:23	not **d** them **out** at once by giving them into	3769
	11: 7	and **d** me from my father's house?	1763
2Ch	13: 9	But didn't *you* **d** out the priests of	5615
	20: 7	not **d** the inhabitants of this land	3769
	20:11	to **d** us **out** of the possession you gave us	1763
Job	24: 3	*They* **d** away the orphan's donkey and take	5627
	30:22	You snatch me up and **d** me before	8206
Ps	36:11	nor the hand of the wicked **d** me **away.**	5653
Pr	22:10	**D** out the mocker, and out goes strife;	1763
	22:15	rod of discipline *will* **d** it **far** from him.	8178
Isa	22:23	*I will* **d** him like a peg into a firm place;	9546
Jer	22:22	**d** all your shepherds **away**,	8286
	29:18	among all the nations where *I* **d** them.	5615
	46: 9	**D** furiously, O charioteers!	2147
	49: 2	Israel *will* **d** out those who drove her out,"	3769
Eze	4:13	among the nations where I *will* **d** them."	5615
	8: 6	that *will* **d** me far from my sanctuary?	8178
	11: 7	but *I will* **d** you **out** of it.	3655
	11: 9	*I will* **d** you **out** of the city and hand you	3655
Hos	9:15	*I will* **d** them out of my house.	1763
	10:11	*I will* **d** Ephraim, Judah must plow,	8206
Joel	2:20	the northern army **far**	8178
Mic	2: 9	*You* **d** the women of my people	1763
Mt	7:22	and in your name **d** out demons	1675
	8:31	"If *you* **d** us **out**,	1675
	10: 1	to **d** out evil spirits and	1675
	10: 8	cleanse those who have leprosy, **d** out demons.	1675
	12:27	And if *I* **d** out demons by Beelzebub,	1675
	12:27	by whom *do your* people **d** them out?	1675
	12:28	But if *I* **d** out demons by the Spirit of God,	1675
	17:19	"Why couldn't we **d** it **out?**"	1675
Mk	3:15	and to have authority *to* **d** out demons.	1675
	3:23	"How can Satan **d** out Satan?	1675
	7:26	She begged Jesus to **d** the demon **out**	1675
	9:18	I asked your disciples to **d** out the spirit,	1675
	9:28	"Why couldn't we **d** it **out?**"	1675
	16:17	In my name *they will* **d** out demons;	1675
Lk	9: 1	*to* **d** out all demons and to cure diseases,	2093
	9:40	I begged your disciples to **d** it **out,**	1675
	11:18	because you claim that I **d** out demons	1675
	11:19	Now if *I* **d** out demons by Beelzebub,	1675
	11:19	by whom *do your* followers **d** them out?	1675
	11:20	But if *I* **d** out demons by the finger of God,	1675
	13:32	*'I will* **d** out demons	1675
Jn	6:37	to me *I* will never **d** away.	1675

DRIVEN (49) [DRIVE]

Ge	4:11	Now you are under a curse and **d** from	4946
	33:13	If they *are* **d** hard just one day,	1985
Ex	10:11	Then Moses and Aaron *were* **d** out	1763
	12:39	without yeast because *they had* **been** **d** out	1763
Nu	32:21	until he *has* **d** his enemies out before him—	3769
Dt	9: 4	After the LORD your God has **d** them **out**	2074
	12:29	But when *you have* **d** them **out** and settled	3769
	19: 1	and when *you have* **d** them **out** and settled	3769
Jos	8:15	**let themselves** be **d** back before them,	5595
		"The LORD *had* **d** out before you great	3769
Jdg	11:23	*has* **d** the Amorites **out**	3769
1Sa	26:19	*They have* now **d** me from my share in	1763
1Ki	14:24	of the nations the LORD *had* **d** out before	3769
2Ki	16: 3	of the nations the LORD *had* **d** out before	3769
	17: 8	of the nations the LORD *had* **d** out before	3769
	17:11	the LORD *had* **d** out before them had done.	1655
	21: 2	of the nations the LORD *had* **d** out before	3769
2Ch	28: 3	of the nations the LORD *had* **d** out before	3769
	33: 2	of the nations the LORD *had* **d** out before	3769
Job	6:13	now that success *has* **been** **d** from me?	5615
	18:18	He *is* **d** from light into darkness	2074
	30: 8	*they were* **d** out of the land.	5777
	30:15	my dignity *is* **d** **away** as *by* the wind,	8103
Ps	109:10	*may they* be **d** from their ruined homes.	1763
Isa	17:13	**d** before the wind like chaff on the hills,	8103
	22:25	peg into the firm place will give way;	9546
	59:14	So justice *is* **d** **back**,	294+6047
Jer	13:24	scatter you like chaff **d** by the desert wind.	6296
	23: 2	and **d** them **away** and have	5615
	23: 3	of all the countries where *I have* **d** them	5615
	49: 5	"Every one of *you* will be **d** **away**,	5615
La	3: 2	He has **d** me **away** and made me walk	5627
Eze	34:21	until *you have* **d** them **away**,	7046
Da	4:25	be **d** away from people and will live with	10304
	4:32	be **d** away from people and will live with	10304
	4:33	He was **d** away from people and ate grass	10304
	5:21	He was **d** **away** from people and given	10304
Am	9: 4	Though *they are* **d** into exile	2143

Mic	4: 7	those **d** away a strong nation.	2133
Mt	9:33	And when the demon was **d** out,	1675
Mk	16: 9	out of whom he had **d** seven demons.	1675
Lk	8:29	he had broken his chains and had been **d** by	1785
Jn	12:31	now the prince of this world will be **d** out.	1675
Ac	27:15	so we gave way to it and were **d** along.	5770
	27:17	let the ship be **d** along.	5770
	27:27	the fourteenth night we were still being **d**	1422
	28: 3	a viper, **d** out by the heat,	2002
Jas	3: 4	they are so large and are **d** by strong winds,	1785
2Pe	2:17	without water and mists **d** by a storm.	1785

DRIVER (3) [DRIVE]

1Ki	22:34	The king told his chariot **d**,	8208
2Ch	18:33	The king told the chariot **d**,	8208
Jer	51:21	with you I shatter chariot and **d**,	8206

DRIVER'S (2) [DRIVE]

Job	3:18	they no longer hear the **slave d** shout.	5601
	39: 7	he does not hear a **d** shout.	5601

DRIVERS (7) [DRIVE]

Ex	3: 7	because of their **slave d**,	5601
	5: 6	to the **slave d** and foremen in charge of	5601
	5:10	Then the **slave d** and the foremen went out	5601
	5:13	The **slave d** kept pressing them, saying,	5601
	5:14	by Pharaoh's **slave d** were beaten	5601
2Ki	7:14	He commanded the **d**,	NIH
Hag	2:22	I will overthrow chariots and their **d**;	8206

DRIVES (12) [DRIVE]

Dt	7: 1	and **d** out before you many nations—	5970
2Ki	9:20	he **d** like a madman."	5627
Pr	16:26	his hunger **d** him on.	436
	19:26	and **d** out his mother is	1368
	20:26	he **d** the threshing wheel over them.	8740
Isa	27: 8	with his fierce blast he **d** her out,	2048
	28:28	**d** the wheels of his threshing cart over	2169
	59:19	that the breath of the LORD **d** along.	5674
Mt	9:34	of demons that he **d** out demons."	1675
	12:24	that this fellow **d** out demons."	1675
	12:26	If Satan **d** out Satan,	1675
1Jn	4:18	But perfect love **d** out fear,	965

DRIVING (24) [DRIVE]

Ge	4:14	Today you are **d** me from the land,	1763
Ex	14:25	so that they had difficulty **d**.	5627
2Sa	7:23	and awesome wonders by **d** out nations	1763
1Ki	19:19	and he himself was **d** the twelfth pair.	928
2Ki	9:20	The **d** is like that of Jehu son of Nimshi—	4952
	16: 6	of Aram recovered Elath for Aram by **d** out	5970
1Ch	17:21	by **d** out nations from before your people,	1763
Job	37: 9	the cold from the **d** winds.	4668
Ps	35: 5	with the angel of the LORD **d** them away;	1890
Pr	28: 3	like a **d** rain that leaves no crops.	6085
Isa	25: 4	the ruthless is like a **storm d** against a wall	AIT
	28: 2	like a **d** rain and a flooding downpour,	2443+4784
Jer	30:23	a **d** wind swirling down on the heads of	1760
Eze	46:18	**d** them off their property.	3561
Mk	1:39	in their synagogues and **d** out demons.	1675
	3:22	the prince of demons he is **d** out demons."	1675
	9:38	"we saw a man **d** out demons in your name	1675
	11:15	and began **d** out those who were buying	1675
Lk	9:49	"we saw a man **d** out demons in your name	1675
	11:14	Jesus was **d** out a demon that was mute.	1675
	11:15	the prince of demons, he is **d** out demons."	1675
	19:45	and began **d** out those who were selling.	1675
Ac	19:13	around **d** out evil spirits tried to invoke	2020
	26:24	"Your great learning is **d** you insane."	4365

DROMEDARIES, DROMEDARY (KJV)
See CAMELS, CAMEL

DROP (11) [DROPPED, DROPPING, DROPS]

Dt	28:40	because the olives will **d** off.	5970
	33:28	where the heavens **d** dew.	6903
Pr	3:20	and the clouds let **d** the dew.	8319
	17:14	so **d** the matter before a dispute breaks out.	5759
SS	4:11	Your lips **d** sweetness as the honeycomb,	5752
Isa	33: 9	and Bashan and Carmel **d** their leaves.	5850
	40:15	Surely the nations are like a **d** in a bucket;	5254
Eze	20:28	your left hand and make your arrows **d**	5877
Zec	8:12	and the heavens will **d** their dew.	5989
Lk	16:17	for the least stroke of a pen to **d** out of	4406
Rev	6:13	as late figs **d** from a fig tree when shaken	965

DROPPED (4) [DROP]

Jdg	9:53	a woman **d** an upper millstone on his head	8959
	15:14	and the bindings **d** from his hands.	5022
2Sa	20: 8	he stepped forward, it **d** out of its sheath.	5877
Ac	27:29	they **d** four anchors from the stern	4849

DROPPING (1) [DROP]

2Ch	24:10	**d** them into the chest until it was full.	8959

DROPS (4) [DROP]

Nu	35:23	**d** a stone on him that could kill him,	5877
Job	36:27	"He draws up the **d** of water,	5754
	38:28	Who fathers the **d** of dew?	103

Lk	22:44	and his sweat was like **d** of blood falling to	2584

DROPSY (1)

Lk	14: 2	in front of him was a man **suffering from d**.	5622

DROSS (7)

Ps	119:119	the wicked of the earth you discard like **d**;	6092
Pr	25: 4	Remove the **d** from the silver,	6092
Isa	1:22	Your silver has become **d**,	6092
	1:25	I will thoroughly purge away your **d**	6092
Eze	22:18	the house of Israel has become **d** to me;	6092
	22:18	They are but the **d** of silver.	6092
	22:19	'Because you have all become **d**,	6092

DROUGHT (8)

Dt	28:22	with scorching heat and **d**,	2996
Job	12:15	If he holds back the waters, there is **d**;	3312
	24:19	heat and **d** snatch away the melted snow,	7480
Jer	2: 6	a land of **d** and darkness,	7480
	14: 1	the LORD to Jeremiah concerning the **d**:	1314
	17: 8	in a year of **d** and never fails to bear fruit."	1316
	50:38	A **d** on her waters!	2996
Hag	1:11	for a **d** on the fields and the mountains,	2996

DROVE (43) [DRIVE]

Ge	3:24	After he **d** the man out,	1763
	15:11	but Abram **d** them away.	5959
	31:18	**d** all his livestock ahead	5627
Ex	2:17	along and **d** them away,	1763
	14:21	and all that night the LORD **d** the sea back	2143
Nu	11:31	the LORD and **d** quail in from the sea.	1577
	21:32	and **d** out the Amorites who were there.	3769
	25: 8	He **d** the spear through both of them—	1991
	32:39	and **d** out the Amorites who were there.	3769
Dt	2:12	but the descendants of Esau **d** them out.	3769
	2:21	who **d** them out and settled in their place.	3769
	2:22	They **d** them out and have lived	3769
Jos	15:14	From Hebron Caleb **d** out	3769
	24:12	which **d** them out before you—	1763
	24:18	the LORD **d** out before us all the nations,	1763
Jdg	1:20	who **d** from it the three sons of Anak.	3769
	1:28	**d** them out completely.	3769+3769
	4:21	She **d** the peg through his temple into	9546
	6: 9	I **d** them from before you	1763
	9:41	and Zebul **d** Gaal and his brothers out	1763
	11: 2	they **d** Jephthah away.	1763
1Sa	19:10	but David eluded him as Saul **d** the spear	5782
	30:20	and his men **d** them ahead of	1763
2Sa	11:23	but we **d** them back to the entrance to	2118+6584
1Ki	21:26	like the Amorites the LORD **d** out	3769
1Ch	8:13	in Aijalon and who **d** out the inhabitants	1368
Ne	13:28	And I **d** him away from me.	1368
Ps	34: T	who **d** him away, and he left.	1763
	44: 2	With your hand you **d** out the nations	3769
	78:55	He **d** out nations before them	1763
	80: 8	you **d** out the nations and planted it.	1763
Jer	49: 2	Israel will drive out those who **d** her out,"	3769
Eze	31:10	I **d** you in disgrace from the mount of God,	2725
	29:18	of Babylon his army in a hard campaign	6268
Mt	8:16	and he **d** out the spirits with a word	1675
	21:12	and **d** out all who were buying	1675
Mk	1:34	He also **d** out many demons,	1675
	6:13	They **d** out many demons	1675
Lk	4:29	They got up, **d** him out of the town,	1675
Jn	2:15	and **d** all from the temple area,	1675
Ac	7:45	from the nations God **d** out before them.	2034
2Co	12:11	but you **d** me to it.	337
1Th	2:15	and the prophets and also **d** us out.	1691

DROVES (4)

Ge	33: 8	"What do you mean by all these **d** I met?"	4722
	33:14	along slowly at the pace of the **d** before me	4856
Ex	12:38	as well as large **d** of livestock,	5238
2Ch	14:15	and carried off **d** of sheep and goats	4200+8044

DROWN (3) [DROWNED]

Mt	8:25	We're going to **d**!"	660
Mk	4:38	"Teacher, don't you care if we **d**?"	660
Lk	8:24	saying, "Master, Master, we're going to **d**!"	660

DROWNED (6) [DROWN]

Ex	15: 4	of Pharaoh's officers are **d** in the Red Sea.	3190
Job	10:15	I am full of shame and **d** in my affliction.	8116
Mt	18: 6	around his neck and to be **d** in the depths	2931
Mk	5:13	the steep bank into the lake and were **d**.	4464
Lk	8:33	the steep bank into the lake and was **d**.	678
Heb	11:29	the Egyptians tried to do so, they were **d**.	2927

DROWSINESS (1) [DROWSY]

Pr	23:21	and **d** clothes them in rags.	5671

DROWSY (1) [DROWSINESS]

Mt	25: 5	and they all became **d** and fell asleep.	3818

DRUNK (38) [DRINK]

Ge	9:21	he became **d** and lay uncovered	8910
Lev	11:34	that could be **d** from it is unclean.	9272
Dt	32:42	I will make my arrows **d** with blood,	8910
1Sa	1:13	Eli thought she was **d**	8893
	1:14	"How long will you **keep on getting d**?	8910

1Sa	25:36	He was in high spirits and very **d**.	8893
	30:12	not eaten any food or **d** any water	9272
2Sa	11:13	and David made him **d**.	8910
1Ki	16: 9	getting **d** in the home of Arza,	8893+9272
	20:16	with him were in their tents getting **d**.	8893+9272
2Ki	19:24	I have dug wells in foreign lands and **d**	9272
SS	5: 1	I have **d** my wine and my milk.	9272
Isa	29: 9	be **d**, but not from wine, stagger,	8910
	34: 5	My sword has **d** its fill in the heavens;	8115
	37:25	I have dug wells in foreign lands and **d**	9272
	49:26	they will be **d** on their own blood,	8910
	51:17	you who have **d** from the hand of	9272
	51:21	made **d**, but not with wine.	8912
	63: 6	in my wrath I made them **d**	8910
Jer	25:27	Drink, get **d** and vomit,	8910
	35: 8	and daughters have ever **d** wine	9272
	48:26	"Make her **d**, for she has defied the LORD.	8910
	51: 7	made the whole earth **d**.	8910
	51:39	make them **d**, so that they shout	8910
	51:57	make her officials and wise men **d**,	8910
La	4:21	you will be **d** and stripped naked.	8910
Eze	39:19	and drink blood till you are **d**.	8913
Na	1:10	They will be entangled among thorns and **d**	6010
	3:11	You too will become **d**;	8910
Hab	2:15	pouring it from the wineskin till they are **d**,	8910
Lk	12:45	and to eat and drink and get **d**.	3499
Ac	2:15	These men are not **d**, as you suppose.	3501
1Co	11:21	One remains hungry, another gets **d**.	3501
Eph	5:18	Do not get **d** on wine,	3499
1Th	5: 7	and those who get **d**, get drunk at night.	3499
	5: 7	and those who get drunk, get **d** at night.	3501
Rev	17: 6	I saw that the woman was **d** with the blood	3501
	18: 3	the nations have **d** the maddening wine	4540

DRUNKARD (6) [DRINK]

Dt	21:20	He is a profligate and a **d**."	6010
Isa	19:14	as a **d** staggers around in his vomit.	8893
	24:20	The earth reels like a **d**,	8893
Mt	11:19	and they say, 'Here is a glutton and a **d**,	3884
Lk	7:34	and you say, 'Here is a glutton and a **d**,	3884
1Co	5:11	an idolater or a slanderer, a **d** or a swindler.	3500

DRUNKARD'S (1) [DRINK]

Pr	26: 9	a **d** hand is a proverb in the mouth of a fool.	8893

DRUNKARDS (8) [DRINK]

Job	12:25	he makes them stagger like **d**.	8893
Ps	69:12	and I am the song of the **d**.	8911+9272
Pr	23:21	for **d** and gluttons become poor,	6010
Isa	28: 1	the pride of Ephraim's **d**,	8893
	28: 3	That wreath, the pride of Ephraim's **d**,	8893
Joel	1: 5	Wake up, you **d**, and weep!	8893
Mt	24:49	and to eat and drink with **d**.	3501
1Co	6:10	nor the greedy nor **d** nor slanderers	3500

DRUNKEN (2) [DRINK]

Ps	107:27	They reeled and staggered like **d** men;	8893
Jer	23: 9	I am like a **d** man,	8893

DRUNKENNESS (9) [DRINK]

Ecc	10:17	for strength and not for **d**.	9275
Jer	13:13	to fill with **d** all who live in this land,	8913
Eze	23:33	You will be filled with **d** and sorrow,	8913
Lk	21:34	**d** and the anxieties of life,	3494
Ro	13:13	as in the daytime, not in orgies and **d**,	3494
Gal	5:21	**d**, orgies, and the like.	3494
1Ti	3: 3	not given to **d**, not violent but gentle,	4232
Tit	1: 7	not quick-tempered, not given to **d**,	4232
1Pe	4: 3	living in debauchery, lust, **d**, orgies,	3886

DRUSILLA (1)

Ac	24:24	Felix came with his wife **D**,	1537

DRY (77) [DRIED, DRIES, DRYING]

Ge	1: 9	and let **d** ground appear.	3317
	1:10	God called the **d** ground "land,"	3317
	7:22	Everything on **d** land that had the breath	3000
	8:13	that the surface of the ground was **d**.	2990
	8:14	the earth was completely **d**.	3312
Ex	4: 9	from the Nile and pour it on the **d** ground.	3317
	14:16	through the sea on **d** ground.	3317
	14:21	and turned it into **d** land.	3000
	14:22	Israelites went through the sea on **d** ground,	3317
	14:29	Israelites went through the sea on **d** ground,	3317
	15:19	through the sea on **d** ground.	3317
Lev	7:10	whether mixed with oil or **d**,	2992
Dt	29:19	on the watered land as well as the **d**.	7534
Jos	3:17	of the LORD stood firm on **d** ground in	3000
	3:17	the crossing on **d** ground.	3000
	4:18	on the **d** ground than the waters of	3000
	4:22	'Israel crossed the Jordan on **d** ground.'	3000
	9: 5	All the bread of their food supply was **d**	3312
	9:12	But now see how **d** and moldy it is.	3312
Jdg	6:37	If there is dew only on the fleece and all the ground is **d**,	2996
	6:39	the fleece and the ground covered	2996
	6:40	Only the fleece was **d**;	2996
1Ki	17:14	be used up and the jug of oil will not run **d**	2893
	17:16	not used up and the jug of oil did not run **d**,	2893
2Ki	2: 8	the two of them crossed over on **d** ground.	3000
Ne	9:11	so that they passed through it on **d** ground,	3317
Job	6:17	but that cease to flow in the **d** season,	2427

Job	13:25	Will you chase after **d** chaff?	3313
	14:11	or a riverbed becomes parched and **d**,	3312
	18:16	His roots **d** up below	3312
	30: 6	to live in the **d** stream beds,	6877
Ps	58: 9	whether they be green or **d**—	3019
	63: 1	a **d** and weary land where there is no water.	7480
	66: 6	He turned the sea into **d** land,	3317
	90: 6	by evening *it is* **d** and withered.	4908
	95: 5	and his hands formed the **d** land.	3318
Pr	17: 1	Better a **d** crust with peace and quiet than	2992
Isa	5:24	and as **d** grass sinks down in the flames,	3143
	11:15	The Lord *will* **d up** the gulf of	2990
	19: 5	The waters of the river *will* **d up**,	5980
	19: 5	and the riverbed will be parched and **d**.	3312
	19: 6	the streams of Egypt will dwindle and **d up**.	2990
	27:11	When its twigs *are* **d**,	3312
	42:15	and hills and **d up** all their vegetation;	3312
	42:15	I will turn rivers into islands and **d up**	3312
	44: 3	and streams on the **d** ground;	3317
	44:27	'*Be* **d**, and I will dry up your streams,'	2990
	44:27	'Be dry, and *I will* **d up** your streams,'	3312
	50: 2	By a mere rebuke *I* **d up** the sea,	2990
	53: 2	and like a root out of **d** ground,	7480
	56: 3	"I am only a **d** tree."	3313
Jer	2:25	until your feet are bare and your throat is **d**.	7535
	50:12	a wilderness, a **d** land, a desert.	7480
	50:38	They will **d up**.	3312
	51:36	*I will* **d up** her sea	2990
	51:36	I will dry up her sea and **make** her springs **d**	3312
	51:43	a **d** and desert land,	7480
La	4: 8	it has become as **d** as a stick.	3313
Eze	17:24	*I* **d up** the green tree and make	3312
	17:24	the green tree and make the **d** tree flourish.	3313
	19:13	in a **d** and thirsty land.	7480
	20:47	both green and **d**.	3313
	23:34	You will drink it and **drain** it **d**;	5172
	30:12	*I will* **d up** the streams of the Nile	3000+5989
	37: 2	bones *that* were very **d**.	3313
	37: 4	'**D** bones, hear the word of the Lord!'	3313
Hos	9:14	that miscarry and breasts *that are* **d**.	7546
	13:15	his spring will fail and his well **d up**.	2990
Am	1: 2	the pastures of the shepherds **d up**,	62
Jnh	2:10	and it vomited Jonah onto **d** land.	3317
Na	1: 4	**makes** all the rivers **run d**.	2990
	1:10	they will be consumed like **d** stubble.	3313
Zep	2:13	leaving Nineveh utterly desolate and **d** as	7480
Hag	2: 6	the sea and the **d** land.	3000
Zec	10:11	and all the depths of the Nile *will* **d up**.	3312
Lk	23:31	what will happen when it is **d**?"	3831
Heb	11:29	through the Red Sea as on **d** land;	3831

DRYING (1) [DRY]

Jn	13: 5	**d** them with the towel that was wrapped	1726

DRYSHOD (KJV) See IN SANDALS

DUE (20) [DULY]

Lev	19:20	there must be **d** punishment.	1334
Dt	18: 3	This is the **share** **d** the priests from	AIT
	32:35	In **d** time their foot will slip;	6961
1Ch	16:29	to the Lord the **glory** **d** his name.	AIT
2Ch	24: 5	the money **d** annually from all Israel,	
			928+1896+4946+9102+9102
	31: 4	to give the **portion** **d** the priests and Levites	AIT
Job	36:17	But now you are laden with the **judgment** **d**	AIT
Ps	29: 2	to the Lord the **glory** **d** his name;	AIT
	90:11	as great as the **fear** *that is* **d** you.	AIT
	96: 8	to the Lord the **glory** **d** his name;	AIT
Pr	11:31	If the righteous **receive** *their* **d** on earth,	8966
Isa	49: 4	Yet *what* is **d** me is in the Lord's hand,	5477
	59:18	he will repay the islands their **d**.	1691
Jer	10: 7	This is your **d**.	3278
Mal	1: 6	If I am a father, where is the **honor** **d** me?	AIT
	1: 6	where is the **respect** **d** me?"	AIT
Ro	1:27	and received in themselves the **d** penalty	1256
2Co	5:10	that each one may receive what is **d** him for	NIG
Eph	4:18	in them **d** to the hardening of their hearts.	1328
1Pe	5: 6	that he may lift you up in **d** time.	2789

DUG (32) [DIG]

Ge	21:30	as a witness that *I* **d** this well."	2916
	26:15	the wells that his father's servants *had* **d** in	2916
	26:18	Isaac reopened the wells that *had been* **d** in	2916
	26:19	Isaac's servants **d** in the valley	2916
	26:21	Then *they* **d** another well,	2916
	26:22	on from there and **d** another well,	2916
	26:25	and there his servants **d** a well.	4125
	26:32	and told him about the well *they had* **d**.	2916
	50: 5	bury me in the tomb *I* **d** for myself in	4125
Ex	7:24	And all the Egyptians **d** along the Nile	2916
Nu	21:18	the well that the princes **d**, that the nobles	2916
1Ki	18:32	and he **d** a trench around it large enough	6913
2Ki	19:24	I have **d** wells in foreign lands and drunk	7769
2Ch	26:10	in the desert and **d** many cisterns,	2933
Ne	9:25	wells *already* **d**, vineyards,	2933
Ps	9:15	nations have fallen into the pit *they have* **d**;	6913
	35: 7	for me without cause and without cause **d**	2916
	57: 6	*They* **d** a pit in my path—	4125
	94:13	till a pit is **d** for the wicked.	4125
Isa	5: 2	He **d** it up and cleared it of stones	6466
	37:25	I have **d** wells in foreign lands and drunk	7769
Jer	2:13	and *have* **d** their own cisterns,	2933
	13: 7	to Perath and **d up** the belt and took it from	2916
	18:20	Yet *they have* **d** a pit for me.	4125

Jer	18:22	for *they have* **d** a pit to capture me	4125
Eze	8: 8	*I* **d** into the wall and saw a doorway there.	3168
	12: 7	Then in the evening *I* **d** through the wall	3168
	12:12	and a hole *will be* **d** in the wall for him	3168
Mt	21:33	**d** a winepress in it and built a watchtower.	4002
	25:18	**d** a hole in the ground	4002
Mk	12: 1	**d** a pit for the winepress and built	4002
Lk	6:48	who **d** down deep and laid the foundation	4999

DUKE, DUKES (KJV) See CHIEF, CHIEFS

DULCIMER (KJV) See PIPES

DULL (8)

Lev	13:39	and if the spots are **d** white,	3910
Ecc	10:10	If the ax *is* **d** and its edge unsharpened,	7733
Isa	6:10	**make** their ears **d** and close their eyes.	3877
	59:	nor his ear too **d** to hear.	3877
La	4: 1	the fine gold *become* **d**!	9096
Mt	15:16	"Are you still so **d**?" Jesus asked them.	852
Mk	7:18	"Are you so **d**?"	852
2Co	3:14	But their minds *were* **made d**,	4800

DULY (1) [DUE]

Gal	3:15	*that has been* **d** established,	*3263*

DUMAH (4)

Ge	25:14	Mishma, **D**, Massa,	1874
Jos	15:52	Arab, **D**, Eshan,	1873
1Ch	1:30	Mishma, **D**, Massa, Hadad, Tema,	1874
Isa	21:11	An oracle concerning **D**:	1874

DUMB (KJV) See CANNOT SPEAK,
COULD NOT TALK, LIFELESS, MUTE,
ROBBED OF SPEECH, SILENT,
SPEECHLESS, WITHOUT SPEECH

DUMPED (1)

Lev	14:41	and the material that is scraped off **d** into	9161

DUNG (6)

1Ki	14:10	up the house of Jeroboam as one burns **d**,	1672
Ne	2:13	toward the Jackal Well and the **D** Gate,	883
	3:13	of the wall as far as the **D** Gate,	883
	3:14	The **D** Gate was repaired by Malkijah son	883
	12:31	toward the **D** Gate.	883
Job	20: 7	he will perish forever, like his own **d**;	1645

DUNGEON (7) [DUNGEONS]

Ge	40:15	to deserve being put in a **d**."	1014
	41:14	and he was quickly brought from the **d**.	1014
Ex	12:29	who was in the **d**,	1014+1074
Isa	24:22	like prisoners bound in a **d**;	1014
	42: 7	and to release from the **d** those who sit	1074+3975
	51:14	they will not die in their **d**,	8846
Jer	37:16	Jeremiah was put into a vaulted cell in a **d**,	
			1014+1074

DUNGEONS (1) [DUNGEON]

2Pe	2: 4	into gloomy **d** to be held for judgment;	4987

DUNGHILL (KJV) See ASH HEAP,
MANURE PILE, PILE OF RUBBLE,

DUPLICITY (2)

Pr	11: 3	but the unfaithful are destroyed by their **d**,	6157
Lk	20:23	He saw through their **d** and said to them,	*4111*

DURA (1)

Da	3: 1	the plain of **D** in the province of Babylon.	10164

DURETH (KJV) See LASTS

DURING (133)

Ge	14:15	*D* the **night** Abram divided his men	AIT
	30:14	*D* wheat harvest, Reuben went out into	928+3427
	41:34	of Egypt **d** the seven years of abundance.	928
	41:36	to be used **d** the seven years of famine	4200
	41:47	**D** the seven years of abundance	928
Ex	2:23	**D** that long period, the king of Egypt died.	928
	12:30	and all the Egyptians got up **d** the **night**,	AIT
	12:31	*D* the **night** Pharaoh summoned Moses	AIT
	13: 7	Eat unleavened bread **d** those seven **days**;	AIT
	14:24	**D** the last watch of the night	928
	23:11	but **d** the seventh year let	NIH
	34:21	even **d** the plowing season	928
	40:38	of all the house of Israel **d** all their travels.	928
Lev	12: 2	just as she is unclean **d** her monthly period.	3427
	12: 5	unclean, as **d** her period.	NIH
	15:20	" 'Anything she lies on **d** her period will	928
	15:26	unclean, as is her bed **d** her monthly period,	NIH
	15:26	unclean, as **d** her period.	NIH
	18:19	to have sexual relations **d** the uncleanness	928
	20:18	with a woman **d** her monthly period	NIH
	25: 6	the land yields **d** the sabbath year will	NIH
	25:22	While you plant the eighth year,	NIH

Lev	25:29	**D** that time he may redeem it.	3427
	26:35	the land will have the rest it did not have **d**	928
	27:17	he dedicates his field **d** the Year of Jubilee,	4946
Nu	3: 4	and Ithamar served as priests **d** the lifetime	6584
	6: 5	" '**D** the entire **period** *of* his vow	AIT
	6:12	because he became defiled **d** his separation.	NIH
	10:33	before them **d** those three **days** to find them	AIT
	28:14	to be made at each **new moon** **d** the year.	AIT
	28:26	to the Lord an offering of new grain **d**	928
Dt	8: 4	not swell **d** these forty **years**.	AIT
	28:53	that your enemy will inflict on you **d**	928
	28:55	on you **d** the siege of all your cities.	928
	28:57	to eat them secretly **d** the siege and in	928
	29: 5	**D** the forty **years** that I led you through	AIT
	31:10	**d** the Feast of Tabernacles,	928
Jos	3:15	the Jordan is at flood stage all **d** harvest.	3427
	5: 5	the people born in the desert **d** the journey	928
Jdg	7: 9	**D** that night the Lord said to Gideon,	928
	8:28	**D** Gideon's lifetime, the land enjoyed peace	928
	9:32	**d** the **night** you and your men should come	AIT
	11:26	Why didn't you retake them **d** that time?	928
	16: 2	They made no move **d** the night, saying,	3972
	20: 5	**D** the **night** the men of Gibeah came	AIT
	21:22	we did not get wives for them **d** the war,	928
1Sa	11:11	**d** the last watch of the night they broke into	928
	29: 4	or he will turn against us **d** the fighting.	928
2Sa	3: 6	**D** the war between the house of Saul and	928
	18:18	**d** his lifetime Absalom had taken a pillar	928
	19:32	He had provided for the king **d** his stay	928
	21: 1	**D** the reign of David, there was a famine	928
	21: 9	they were put to death **d** the first days of	928
	23:13	**D** harvest time, three of the thirty chief men	448
1Ki	3: 5	to Solomon **d** the **night** in a dream,	AIT
	3:19	"*D* the **night** this woman's son died	AIT
	4:25	**D** Solomon's lifetime Judah and Israel,	3972
	9:10	**d** which Solomon built these two buildings	AIT
	11:12	I will not do it **d** your lifetime.	928
	12: 6	elders who had served his father Solomon **d**	928
2Ki	15:18	**D** his entire **reign** he did not turn away from	AIT
	24: 1	**D** Jehoiakim's reign, Nebuchadnezzar king	928
1Ch	5:10	**D** Saul's reign they waged war against	928
	5:17	in the genealogical records **d** the reigns	928
	5:20	because they cried out to him **d** the battle.	928
	7: 2	**D** the reign of David,	928
	13: 3	we did not inquire of it **d** the reign of Saul."	928
	22: 9	and I will grant Israel peace and quiet **d**	928
2Ch	8: 1	**d** which Solomon built the temple of	AIT
	10: 6	elders who had served his father Solomon **d**	928
	11:17	the ways of David and Solomon **d** this time.	4200
	13:20	Jeroboam did not regain power **d** the time	928
	14: 6	No one was at war with him **d** those years,	928
	26: 5	He sought God **d** the days of Zechariah,	928
	32:26	upon them **d** the days of Hezekiah.	928
Ezr	4: 5	and frustrate their plans **d** the entire reign	NIH
	7: 1	**d** the reign of Artaxerxes king of Persia,	928
	8: 1	up with me from Babylon **d** the reign	928
Ne	2:12	I set out **d** the **night** with a few men.	AIT
	5: 3	our vineyards and our homes to get grain **d**	928
	8:14	in booths **d** the feast of the seventh month	928
Est	1: 1	This is what happened **d** the time	928
	2:21	**D** the time Mordecai was sitting at	928
Pr	10: 5	but he who sleeps **d** harvest is	928
Ecc	2: 3	for men to do under heaven **d** the few days	NIH
	5:18	in his toilsome labor under the sun **d**	NIH
	6:12	**d** the few and meaningless days he passes	NIH
Isa	1: 1	that Isaiah son of Amoz saw **d** the reigns	928
	49:20	The **children** *born d* your bereavement will	AIT
Jer	3: 6	**D** the reign of King Josiah,	928
	19: 9	and they will eat one another's flesh **d**	928
	35: 1	that came to Jeremiah from the Lord **d**	928
	49: 9	If thieves came **d** the night,	928
Eze	4: 5	to eat it **d** the 390 days you lie on your side.	5031
	12: 4	**D** the daytime, while they watch,	3429
	12: 7	**D** the day I brought out my things packed	3429
	18: 6	or lie with a woman **d** her **period**.	AIT
	22:10	in you are those who violate women **d**	NIH
	23: 8	when **d** her youth men slept with her,	928
	36:38	as the flocks for offerings at Jerusalem **d**	928
	45:21	**d** which you shall eat bread made	NIH
	45:23	**D** the seven days of the Feast,	AIT
	45:25	" '**D** the seven days of the Feast,	928
Da	2:19	**D** the night the mystery was revealed	10168
	6: 7	that anyone who prays to any god or man **d**	10527
	6:12	"Did you not publish a decree that **d**	10527
	6:28	So Daniel prospered **d** the reign of Darius	10089
Hos	1: 1	to Hosea son of Beeri **d** the reigns	928
	1: 1	and the reign of Jeroboam son	928
Mic	1: 1	of Moresheth **d** the reigns of Jotham, Ahaz	928
Zep	1: 1	**d** the reign of Josiah son of Amon king	928
Zec	1: 8	**D** the night I had a vision—	NIH
Mt	1: 1	**d** the time of King Herod,	1877
	2:14	the child and his mother **d** *the* **night** and left	*AIT*
	14:25	**d** the **fourth watch** of the night	*AIT*
	26: 5	"But not **d** the Feast," they said,	1877
	28:13	'His disciples came **d** the **night**	*AIT*
Mk	1: 1	**D** those days another large crowd gathered.	1877
	14: 2	"But not **d** the Feast," they said,	1877
Lk	3: 2	**d** the high priesthood of Annas	2093
	4: 2	He ate nothing **d** those days,	1877
Jn	19:31	the bodies left on the crosses **d** the Sabbath,	1877
Ac	1: 1	But **d** the night an angel of the Lord opened	1328
	11:27	**D** this time some prophets came down	1877
	11:28	(This happened **d** the reign of Claudius.)	2093
	12: 3	This happened **d** the Feast	2465
	13:17	the people prosper **d** their stay in Egypt,	1877
	16: 9	**D** the night Paul had a vision of a man	1328
	23:31	with them **d** the night and brought him	1328

Heb	3: 8	d the time of testing in the desert,	2848
	5: 7	D the days of Jesus' life on earth,	1877
Rev	9: 6	D those days men will seek death,	1877
	11: 6	not rain d **the time** they are prophesying;	AIT

DURST (KJV) See DARE, DARED, DARING

DUSK (10)

Jos	2: 5	At d, when it was time to close	3125
1Sa	30:17	David fought them from d until the evening	5974
2Ki	7: 5	At d they got up and went to the camp of	5974
	7: 7	and fled in the d and abandoned their tents	5974
Job	4:20	Between dawn and d they are broken	6847
	24:15	The eye of the adulterer watches for d;	5974
Eze	12: 6	and carry them out at d.	6602
	12: 7	I took my belongings out at d,	6602
	12:12	on his shoulder at d and leave,	6602
Hab	1: 8	fiercer than wolves at d.	6847

DUST (109)

Ge	2: 7	the LORD God formed the man from the d	6760
	3:14	on your belly and you will eat d all the days	6760
	3:19	for d you are and to dust you will return.	6760
	3:19	for dust you are and to d you will return."	6760
	13:16	I will make your offspring like the d of	6760
	13:16	so that if anyone could count the d,	6760
	18:27	though I am nothing but d and ashes,	6760
	28:14	Your descendants will be like the d of	6760
Ex	8:16	'Stretch out your staff and strike the d of	6760
	8:16	the land of Egypt the d will become gnats."	NIH
	8:17	the staff and struck the d of the ground,	6760
	8:17	All the d throughout the land	6760
	9: 9	It will become **fine** d over the whole land	85
Nu	5:17	and put some d from the tabernacle floor	6760
	23:10	Who can count the d of Jacob or number	6760
Dt	9:21	as fine as d and threw the dust into a stream	6760
	9:21	as fine as dust and threw the d into a stream	6760
	28:24	the rain of your country into d and powder;	6760
	32:24	the venom of vipers that glide in the d.	6760
Jos	7: 6	and sprinkled d on their heads.	6760
1Sa	2: 8	the poor from the d and lifts the needy from	6760
	4:12	his clothes torn and d on his head.	141
2Sa	1: 2	with his clothes torn and with d	141
	15:32	his robe torn and d on his head.	141
	22:43	I beat them as fine as the d of the earth;	6760
1Ki	16: 2	up from the d and made you leader	6760
	20:10	be it ever so scarce, if enough d remains	6760
2Ki	13: 7	and made them like the d at threshing time.	6760
	23: 6	He ground it to powder and scattered the d	6760
2Ch	1: 9	over a people who are as numerous as the d of	6760
Ne	9: 1	fasting and wearing sackcloth and having d	141
Job	2:12	and they tore their robes and sprinkled d	6760
	4:19	whose foundations are in the d,	6760
	7:21	For I will soon lie down in the d;	6760
	10: 9	Will you now turn me to d again?	6760
	16:15	over my skin and buried my brow in the d.	6760
	17:16	Will we descend together into the d?"	6760
	20:11	with him in the d.	6760
	21:26	Side by side they lie in the d,	6760
	22:24	and assign your nuggets to the d,	6760
	27:16	Though he heaps up silver like d	6760
	28: 6	and its d contains nuggets of gold.	6760
	30:19	and I am reduced to d and ashes.	6760
	34:15	and man would return to d.	6760
	38:38	when the d becomes hard and the clods	6760
	40:13	Bury them all in the d together;	6760
	42: 6	Therefore I despise myself and repent in d	6760
Ps	7: 5	to the ground and make me sleep in the d.	6760
	18:42	I beat them as fine as d borne on the wind;	6760
	22:15	you lay me in the d of death.	6760
	22:29	down to the d will kneel before him—	6760
	30: 9	Will the d praise you?	6760
	44:25	We are brought down to the d;	6760
	72: 9	before him and his enemies will lick the d.	6760
	78:27	He rained meat down on them like d,	6760
	89:39	and have defiled his crown in the d.	824
	90: 3	You turn men back to d, saying,	1919
	90: 3	saying, "Return to d, O sons of men."	NIH
	102:14	her very d moves them to pity.	6760
	103:14	he remembers that we are d.	6760
	104:29	they die and return to the d.	6760
	113: 7	the poor from the d and lifts the needy from	6760
	119:25	I am laid low in the d;	6760
Pr	8:26	or its fields or any of the d of the world.	6760
Ecc	3:20	all come from d, and to dust all return.	6760
	3:20	all come from dust, and to d all return.	6760
	12: 7	the d returns to the ground it came from,	6760
Isa	5:24	and their flowers blow away like d;	85
	25:12	down to the ground, to the d.	6760
	26: 5	to the ground and casts it down to the d.	6760
	26:19	You who dwell in the d,	6760
	29: 4	your speech will mumble out of the d.	6760
	29: 4	out of the d your speech will whisper.	6760
	29: 5	like fine d, the ruthless hordes	85
	34: 7	and the d will be soaked with fat.	6760
	34: 9	her d into burning sulfur;	6760
	40:12	Who has held the d of the earth in a basket,	6760
	40:15	they are regarded as d on the scales;	8836
	40:15	the islands as though they were fine d.	NIH
	41: 2	He turns them to d with his sword,	6760
	47: 1	"Go down, sit in the d,	6760
	49:23	they will lick the d at your feet.	6760
	52: 2	Shake off your d;	6760
	65:25	but d will be the serpent's food.	6760
Jer	17:13	in the d because they have forsaken	824

Jer	25:34	roll in the d, you leaders of the flock.	NIH
La	2:10	they have sprinkled d on their heads	6760
	2:21	and old lie together in the d of the streets;	824
	3:16	he has trampled me in the d.	709
	3:29	Let him bury his face in the d—	6760
Eze	24: 7	where the d would cover it.	6760
	26:10	be so many that they will cover you with d.	85
	27:30	they will sprinkle d on their heads and roll	6760
Da	12: 2	Multitudes who sleep in the d of	6760
Am	2: 7	upon the d of the ground and deny justice	6760
Jnh	3: 6	with sackcloth and sat down in the d.	709
Mic	1:10	In Beth Ophrah roll in the d.	6760
	7:17	They will lick the d like a snake,	6760
Na	1: 3	and clouds are the d of his feet.	85
Zep	1:17	be poured out like d and their entrails	6760
Zec	9: 3	she has heaped up silver like d,	6760
Mt	10:14	shake the d off your feet when you leave	3155
Mk	6:11	shake the d off your feet when you leave	5967
Lk	9: 5	shake the d off your feet when you leave	3155
	10:11	'Even the d of your town that sticks	3155
Ac	13:51	the d from their feet in protest against them	3155
	22:23	and throwing off their cloaks and flinging d	3155
1Co	15:47	The first man was of the d of the earth,	5954
Rev	18:19	They will throw d on their heads,	5967

DUTIES (25) [DUTY]

Ge	39:11	into the house to attend to his d,	4856
Ex	18:20	to live and the d they are to perform.	5126
Nu	3: 7	They are to perform d for him and for	5466
	4:28	Their d are to be under the direction	5466
	8:26	in performing their d at the Tent	5466
	18: 3	and are to perform all the d of the Tent,	5466
1Ki	3: 7	and do not know how to **carry out** my d.	995+2256+3655
1Ch	6:32	They performed their d according to	6275
	6:48	to all the other d of the tabernacle,	6275
	9:25	from time to time and **share their** d	465+6640
	9:33	were exempt from other d	7080
	23:28	and the performance of other d at the house	6275
	25: 8	cast lots for their d.	5466
	26:12	had d for ministering in the temple of	5466
	26:29	and his sons were assigned d away from	4856
2Ch	8:14	the divisions of the priests for their d,	6275
	31: 2	each of them according to their d as priests	6275
	31:16	to perform the daily d of their various tasks,	1821
	35: 2	the priests to their d and encouraged them	5466
Ne	10:33	and for all the d of the house of our God.	4856
	13:30	and assigned them d, each to his own task.	5466
Eze	44:14	the d of the temple and all the work that is	5466
	44:15	and who faithfully carried out the d	5466
2Ti	4: 5	discharge all the d of your ministry.	NIG
Heb	10:11	**performs** his **religious** d;	3310

DUTY (32) [DUTIES]

Ge	38: 8	**fulfill** your d to her **as a brother-in-law**	3302
Nu	4:31	This is their d as they perform service at	5466
Dt	24: 5	not be sent to war or have any other d laid	1821
	25: 5	**fulfill the** d of a brother-in-law	3302
	25: 7	**fulfill the** d of a brother-in-law	3302
1Ki	14:27	to the commanders of the guard on d at	9068
2Ki	11: 5	the three companies that are **going on** d on	995
	11: 7	that normally **go off** Sabbath d are all	3655
	11: 9	those who were going on d on the Sabbath	995
	11: 9	and those who were going off d—	3655
1Ch	23:28	The d of the Levites was	5096
	27: 1	that were on d month by month	995+2256+3655
2Ch	12:10	to the commanders of the guard on d at	9068
	23: 4	and Levites who are going on d on	995
	23: 6	the priests and Levites on d;	9250
	23: 8	those who were going on d on the Sabbath	995
	23: 8	and those who were going off d—	3655
Ezr	4:13	no more taxes, tribute or d will be paid,	10208
	4:20	and taxes, tribute and d were paid to them.	10208
	7:24	tribute or d on any of the priests, Levites,	10208
Ne	7: 3	While the gatekeepers are still on d,	6641
Ecc	12:13	for this is the whole [d] of man.	NIH
Jer	32: 7	**as nearest relative** it is your right and d	1460
Eze	44: 8	Instead of carrying out your d in regard	5466
	45:17	It will be **the** d of the prince to provide	6584
Mt	17:25	the kings of the earth collect d and taxes—	5465
Lk	17: 9	Once when Zechariah's division was on d	NIG
	17:10	we have only done our d.' "	4005+4053+4472
Jn	18:16	the **girl on** d there and brought Peter in.	2601
Ac	23: 1	I have **fulfilled** my d to God	4488
Ro	15:16	the **priestly** d of proclaiming the gospel	2646
1Co	7: 3	The husband should fulfill his marital d	4051

DWARFED (1)

Lev	21:20	or who is hunchbacked or d,	1987

DWELL (79) [DWELLERS, DWELLING, DWELLINGS, DWELLS, DWELT, TENT-DWELLING]

Ex	25: 8	and I will d among them.	8905
	29:45	Then I will d among the Israelites and	8905
	29:46	of Egypt so that I might d among them.	8905
Nu	5: 3	where I d among them.	8905
	35:34	the land where you live and where I d,	8905
	35:34	for I, the LORD, d among the Israelites.' "	8905
2Sa	7: 5	the one to build me a house to d in?	3782
1Ki	8:12	"The LORD has said that he would d in	8905
	8:13	a place for you to d forever."	3782
	8:27	"But will God really d on earth?	3782

1Ch	17: 4	not the one to build me a house to d in.	3782
	23:25	and has come to d in Jerusalem forever,	8905
2Ch	6: 1	"The LORD has said that he would d in	8905
	6: 2	a place for you to d forever."	3782
	6:18	"But will God really d on earth with men?	3782
Ezr	6:12	who has caused his Name to d there,	10709
Job	11:14	allow no evil to d	8905
	17: 2	my eyes must d on their hostility.	4328
	28: 4	Far from where people d he cuts a shaft,	1591
	28:12	Where does understanding d?	5226
	28:20	Where does understanding d?	5226
Ps	4: 8	O LORD, **make** me d in safety.	3782
	5: 4	with you the wicked cannot d.	1591
	15: 1	LORD, who may d in your sanctuary?	1591
	23: 6	and I will d in the house of	8740
	27: 4	that I may d in the house of the LORD all	3782
	37: 3	d in the land and enjoy safe pasture.	8905
	37:27	then you will d in the land forever.	8905
	37:29	the righteous will inherit the land and d	8905
	39:12	For I d with you as an alien, a stranger,	6640
	43: 3	to the **place where** you d.	5438
	61: 4	to d in your tent forever and take refuge in	1591
	68:16	where the LORD himself will d forever?	8905
	68:18	that you, O LORD God, might d there.	8905
	69:25	let there be no one to d in their tents.	3782
	69:36	and those who love his name will d there.	8905
	84: 4	Blessed are those who d in your house;	3782
	84:10	a doorkeeper in the house of my God than d	1884
	85: 9	that his glory may d in our land.	8905
	101: 6	that they may d with me;	3782
	101: 7	No one who practices deceit will d	3782
	120: 5	Woe to me that I d in Meshech,	1591
	143: 3	he makes me d in darkness	3782
Pr	8:12	"I, wisdom, d together with prudence;	8905
SS	8:13	You who d in the gardens with friends	3782
Isa	5: 7	righteousness used to d in her—	4328
	13:21	there the owls will d,	8905
	26: 5	He humbles those who d on high,	3782
	26:19	You who d in the dust,	8905
	32:16	Justice will d in the desert	8905
	33:14	"Who of us can d with the consuming fire?	1591
	33:14	Who of us can d with everlasting burning?"	1591
	33:16	this is the man who will d on the heights,	8905
	33:24	sins of those who d there will be forgiven.	3782
	34:17	and there from generation to generation.	8905
	38:11	or be with those who now d in this world.	3782
	43:18	do not d on the past.	1067
	44:13	that it may d in a shrine,	3782
	65:21	They will build houses and d in them;	3782
Jer	17: 6	He will d in the parched places of	8905
	47: 2	all who d in the land will wail	3782
	48:28	Abandon your towns and d among	8905
	49:18	no man will d in it.	1591
	49:33	no man will d in it."	1591
	50:39	and there the owl will d.	3782
	50:40	no man will d in it.	1591
La	3: 6	He has **made** me d in darkness	3782
Eze	7: 7	you who d in the land.	8905
	26:20	I will **make** you d in the earth below,	3782
Hos	3: 4	Men will d again in his shade.	3782
Joel	3:17	the LORD your God, d in Zion.	8905
Zep	2: 6	The land by the sea, where the Kerethites d,	5661
Zec	8: 3	"I will return to Zion and d in Jerusalem.	8905
Jn	5:38	nor does his word d in you,	2400+3531
Ac	1:20	let there be no one to d in it,' and,	2997
Eph	3:17	Christ may d in your hearts through faith.	2997
Col	1:19	to have all his fullness d in him,	2997
	3:16	Let the word of Christ d in you richly	1940
Rev	12:12	you heavens and you who d in them!	5012

DWELLERS (1) [DWELL]

Isa	5: 3	"Now you d in Jerusalem and men	3782

DWELLING (72) [DWELL]

Ge	27:39	"Your d will be away from the earth's	4632
Ex	15:13	guide them to your holy d.	5659
	15:17	the place, O LORD, you made for your d,	3782
Lev	15:31	for defiling my d place,	5438
	26:11	I will put my d place among you,	5438
Nu	24: 5	O Jacob, your d places, O Israel!	5438
	24:21	"Your d place is secure,	4632
Dt	12: 5	to put his Name there for his d.	8905
	12:11	the LORD your God will choose as a d	8905
	14:23	at the place he will choose as a d	8905
	16: 2	at the place the LORD will choose as a d	8905
	16: 6	except in the place he will choose as a d	8905
	16:11	at the place he will choose as a d	8905
	26: 2	the LORD your God will choose as a d	8905
	26:15	your holy d place,	5061
1Sa	2:29	and offering that I prescribed for my d?	5061
	2:32	and you will see distress in my d.	5061
2Sa	6:17	from place to place with a tent as my d.	5438
	15:25	and let me see it and his d place again.	5659
1Ki	8:30	Hear from heaven, your d place.	3782
	8:39	then hear from heaven, your d place.	3782
	8:43	from heaven, your d place, and do whatever	3782
	8:49	from heaven, your d place, hear their prayer	3782
1Ch	9:19	for guarding the entrance to the d of	4722
	16:27	strength and joy in his d place.	5226
	17: 5	from one d place to another.	5438
2Ch	6:21	Hear from heaven, your d place;	3782
	6:30	then hear from heaven, your d place.	3782
	6:33	from heaven, your d place, and do whatever	3782
	6:39	from heaven, your d place, hear their prayer	3782
	29: 6	from the LORD's d place	5438

2Ch	30:27	his holy **d** place.	5061
	31: 2	at the gates of the LORD's **d**.	4722
	36:15	on his people and on his **d** place.	5061
Ezr	7:15	whose **d** is in Jerusalem,	10445
Ne	1: 9	to the place I have chosen as a **d**	8905
Job	18:15	burning sulfur is scattered over his **d**.	5659
	18:21	Surely such is the **d** of an evil man;	5438
	23: 3	if only I could go to his **d**!	9414
Ps	27: 5	of trouble he will keep me safe in his **d**;	6108
	31:20	in your **d** you keep them safe	6109
	33:14	from his **d** place he watches all who live	3782
	68: 5	a defender of widows, is God in his holy **d**.	5061
	74: 7	they defiled the **d** place of your Name.	5438
	76: 2	His tent is in Salem, his **d** place in Zion.	5104
	84: 1	How lovely is your **d** place,	5438
	90: 1	you have been our **d** place	5061
	91: 9	If you make the Most High your **d**—	5061
	132: 5	a **d** for the Mighty One of Jacob."	5438
	132: 7	"Let us go to his **d** place;	5438
	132:13	he has desired it for his **d**:	4632
Pr	24:15	do not raid his **d** place;	8070
Isa	18: 4	and will look on from my **d** place,	4806
	26:21	the LORD is coming out of his **d** to punish	5226
	32:18	My people will live in peaceful **d** places,	5659
Jer	7:12	to the place in Shiloh where I first made a **d**	8905
	25:30	from his holy **d** and roar mightily	5061
	31:23	'The LORD bless you, O righteous **d**,	5659
La	2: 6	He has laid waste his **d** like a garden;	8226
Eze	3:12	of the LORD be praised in his **d** place!—	5226
	37:27	My **d** place will be with them;	5438
Mic	1: 3	The LORD is coming from his **d** place;	5226
Hab	1: 6	across the whole earth to seize **d** places	5438
Zep	3: 7	Then her **d** would not be cut off,	5061
Zec	2:13	he has roused himself from his holy **d**."	5061
Jn	1:14	The Word became flesh and made his **d**	5012
Ac	7:46	and asked that he might provide a **d** place	5013
2Co	5: 2	longing to be clothed with our heavenly **d**,	3863
	5: 4	but to be clothed with our heavenly **d**,	NIG
Eph	2:22	a **d** in which God lives by his Spirit.	2999
Rev	13: 6	and to slander his name and his **d** place	5008
	21: 3	"Now the **d** of God is with men,	5008

DWELLINGS (13) [DWELL]

Ex	35: 3	a fire in any of your **d** on the Sabbath day."	4632
1Ch	4:41	They attacked the Hamites in their **d** and	185
	5:10	they occupied the **d** of the Hagrites	185
Job	38:20	Do you know the paths to their **d**?	1074
Ps	49:11	their **d** for endless generations,	5438
	87: 2	of Zion more than all the **d** of Jacob.	5438
Isa	58:12	Restorer of Streets with **D**.	3782
Jer	30:18	and have compassion on his **d**;	5438
	51:30	Her **d** are set on fire;	5438
La	2: 2	the Lord has swallowed up all the **d**	5661
Hab	3: 7	the **d** of Midian in anguish.	3749
Zec	12: 7	"The LORD will save the **d** of Judah first,	185
Lk	16: 9	you will be welcomed into eternal **d**.	5008

DWELLS (12) [DWELL]

Job	28:23	the way to it and he alone knows where it **d**,	5226
	39:28	He **d** on a cliff and stays there at night;	8905
Ps	26: 8	O LORD, the place where your glory **d**.	5438
	46: 4	where the Most High **d**.	5438
	91: 1	He who **d** in the shelter of the Most High	3782
	135:21	to him who **d** in Jerusalem.	8905
Isa	8:18	who **d** on Mount Zion.	8905
	33: 5	The LORD is exalted, for he **d** on high;	8905
La	1: 3	She **d** among the nations;	3782
Da	2:22	and light **d** with him.	10742
Joel	3:21	The LORD **d** in Zion!	8905
Mt	23:21	by it and by the one who **d** in it.	2997

DWELT (6) [DWELL]

Dt	33:16	the favor of him who **d** in the burning bush.	8905
2Sa	7: 6	not **d** in a house from the day I brought	3782
1Ch	17: 5	I have not **d** in a house from	3782
Job	29:25	I **d** as a king among his troops;	8905
Ps	74: 2	Mount Zion, where you **d**.	8905
	94:17	I would soon have **d** in the silence of death.	8905

DWINDLE (1) [DWINDLES]

Isa	19: 6	the streams of Egypt will **d** and dry up.	1937

DWINDLES (1) [DWINDLE]

Pr	13:11	Dishonest money **d** away,	5070

DYED (6)

Ex	25: 5	ram skins **d** red and hides of sea cows;	131
	26:14	for the tent a covering of ram skins **d** red,	131
	35: 7	ram skins **d** red and hides of sea cows;	131
	35:23	ram skins **d** red or hides of sea cows	131
	36:19	for the tent a covering of ram skins **d** red,	131
	39:34	of ram skins **d** red, the covering of hides	131

DYING (15) [DIE]

Ge	35:18	for she was **d**—she named her son Ben-Oni.	4637
1Sa	4:20	As she was **d**, the women attending her	4637
2Ch	24:22	who said as he lay **d**,	4638
Job	11:20	their hope will become a **d** gasp."	5883
	24:12	The groans of the **d** rise from the city,	4637
	29:13	The man who was **d** blessed me;	6
Isa	22:14	"Till your **d** day this sin will not be atoned	4637
Hos	4: 3	of the air and the fish of the sea are **d**.	665

Zec	11: 9	Let the **d** die, and the perishing perish.	4637
Mk	5:23	"My little daughter is **d**.	2275
Lk	8:42	a girl of about twelve, was **d**.	633
Jn	11:37	the blind man have kept this man from **d**?"	633
Ro	7: 6	But now, by **d** to what once bound us,	633
2Co	6: 9	**d**, and yet we live on;	633
Heb	11:21	By faith Jacob, when he was **d**,	633

DYNASTY (3)

1Sa	25:28	the LORD will certainly make a lasting **d**	1074
1Ki	2:24	of my father David and has founded a **d**	1074
	11:38	a **d** as enduring as the one I built for David	1074

DYSENTERY (1)

Ac	28: 8	suffering from fever and **d**.	1548

E

EACH (628)

Ge	1:24	and wild animals, **e** according to its kind."	NIH
	2:19	whatever the man called **e** living creature,	2257
	9: 5	And from **e** man, too,	278+408+2257
	10: 5	**e** with its own language.)	408
	11: 3	They said to **e** other, "Come,	408
	11: 7	so they will not understand **e** other."	408
	15: 9	a goat and a ram, **e** three years old,	NIH
	15:10	and arranged the halves opposite **e** other;	408
	25:22	The babies **jostled e** other within her,	8368
	26:31	the men swore an oath to **e** other.	408
	31:49	and me when we are away from **e** other.	408
	32:16	care of his servants, **e** herd by itself,	6373+6373
	37:19	they said to **e** other.	408
	40: 5	**e** of the two men—	408
	40: 5	and **e** dream had a meaning of its own.	408
	41:11	**E** of us had a dream the same night,	638+2085+2256
	41:11	and **e** dream had a meaning of its own.	408
	41:12	giving **e** man the interpretation	AIT
	41:48	In **e** city he put the food grown in	2021
	42: 1	"Why do you just keep **looking at e** other?"	8011
	42:25	to put **e** man's silver back in his sack,	408
	42:28	and they turned to **e** other trembling	408
	42:35	in **e** man's sack was his pouch of silver!	408
	43:21	for the night we opened our sacks and **e**	408
	43:33	and they looked at **e** other in astonishment.	408
	44: 1	put **e** man's silver in the mouth of his sack.	AIT
	44:11	**E** of them quickly lowered his sack to	408
	45:22	To **e** of them he gave new clothing,	3972
	49:28	giving **e** the blessing appropriate to him.	408
Ex	1: 1	**e** with his family:	408
	5:13	the work required of you for **e** day,	928+1821+3427+3427
	5:19	number of bricks required of you for **e** day."	928+1821+3427+3427
	7:12	**E** one threw down his staff and it became	408
	12: 3	that on the tenth day of this month **e** man is	AIT
	12: 3	one for **e** household.	2021
	12: 4	in accordance with what **e** person will eat.	408
	13:15	and redeem **e** of my firstborn sons.'	3972
	16: 4	to go out **e** day and gather enough for	NIH
	16:15	the Israelites saw it, they said to **e** other,	408
	16:16	'**E** one is to gather as much as he needs.	408
	16:16	for **e** person you have in your tent.'"	1653+5031
	16:18	**E** one gathered as much as he needed.	408
	16:21	**E** morning everyone gathered as much as he needed.	928+928+1332+1332+2021+2021
	16:22	two omers for **e** person—	285
	18: 7	They greeted **e** other and then went into	408
	25: 2	from **e** man whose heart prompts him	3972
	25:20	The cherubim are to face **e** other,	408
	26: 5	with the loops opposite **e** other.	851
	26:16	**E** frame is to be ten cubits long and a cubit	285
	26:17	with two projections set parallel to **e** other.	851
	26:19	two bases for **e** frame,	285
	26:19	one under **e** projection.	9109
	26:21	and forty silver bases—two under **e** frame.	285
	26:25	two under **e** frame.	285
	27: 2	Make a horn at **e** of the four corners,	NIH
	27: 4	a bronze ring at **e** of the four corners of	NIH
	28:21	one for **e** of the names of the sons of Israel,	NIH
	28:21	**e** engraved like a seal with the name of one	408
	29:36	Sacrifice a bull **e** day as a sin offering	4200
	29:38	to offer on the altar regularly **e** day:	4200
	30:12	**e** one must pay the LORD a ransom	408
	30:13	**E** one who crosses over	3972
	32:27	'**E** man strap a sword to his side.	408
	32:27	**e** killing his brother and friend	408
	33:10	**e** at the entrance to his tent.	408
	34:24	up three times **e** year to appear before	2021
	36:12	with the loops opposite **e** other.	285
	36:21	**E** frame was ten cubits long and a cubit and	285
	36:22	with two projections set parallel to **e** other.	285
	36:24	two bases for **e** frame,	285
	36:24	one under **e** projection.	9109
	36:26	and forty silver bases—two under **e** frame.	285
	36:30	two under **e** frame.	285

Ex	37: 9	The cherubim faced **e** other,	408
	38: 2	They made a horn at **e** of the four corners,	NIH
	38:27	one talent for **e** base.	2021
	39:14	one for **e** of the names of the sons of Israel,	NIH
	39:14	**e** engraved like a seal with the name of one	408
Lev	7:14	He is to bring one of **e** kind as an offering,	3972
	14:10	**e** without defect, along with three-tenths of	NIH
	19: 3	"'**E** of you must respect his mother	408
	23:18	**e** a year old and without defect,	NIH
	23:19	**e** a year old, for a fellowship offering.	NIH
	23:37	offerings required for **e** day.	928+3427+3427
	23:41	to the LORD for seven days **e** year.	928
	24: 5	using two-tenths of an ephah for **e** loaf.	285
	24: 6	Set them in two rows, six in **e** row,	2021
	24: 7	Along **e** row put some pure incense as	2021
	25:10	**e** one of you is to return	408
	25:10	to return to his family property and **e**	408
	25:14	do not take advantage of **e** other.	408
	25:17	Do not take advantage of **e** other,	408
Nu	1: 4	One man from **e** tribe,	2021
	1: 4	**e** the head of his family, is to help you.	408
	1:44	**e** one representing his family.	408+408
	1:52	**e** man in his own camp	AIT
	2: 2	**e** man under his standard with the banners	AIT
	2:17	**e** in his own place under his standard.	408
	2:34	**e** with his clan and family.	408
	3:47	collect five shekels for **e** one,	1653
	4:19	and assign to **e** man his work and what he is	408
	4:32	Assign to **e** man the specific things he	928+9005
	4:49	**e** was assigned his work and told what	408+408
	5:10	**E** man's sacred gifts are his own,	AIT
	7: 3	ox from **e** leader and a cart from every two.	285
	7: 5	to the Levites as **e** man's work requires."	AIT
	7:11	"**E** day one leader is to bring his offering	2021+2021+3427+3427+4200+4200
	7:13	**e** filled with fine flour mixed with oil as	9109
	7:19	**e** filled with fine flour mixed with oil as	9109
	7:25	**e** filled with fine flour mixed with oil as	9109
	7:31	**e** filled with fine flour mixed with oil as	9109
	7:37	**e** filled with fine flour mixed with oil as	9109
	7:43	**e** filled with fine flour mixed with oil as	9109
	7:49	**e** filled with fine flour mixed with oil as	9109
	7:55	**e** filled with fine flour mixed with oil as	9109
	7:61	**e** filled with fine flour mixed with oil as	9109
	7:67	**e** filled with fine flour mixed with oil as	9109
	7:73	**e** filled with fine flour mixed with oil as	9109
	7:79	**e** filled with fine flour mixed with oil as	9109
	7:85	**E** silver plate weighed a hundred	285
	7:85	and **e** sprinkling bowl seventy shekels.	285
	7:86	with incense weighed ten shekels **e**,	2021+4090S
	11:10	**e** at the entrance to his tent.	408
	13: 2	From **e** ancestral tribe send one	3972
	14: 4	And they said to **e** other,	408
	14:34	for **e** of the forty days you explored	3427S
	15: 5	With **e** lamb for the burnt offering or	285
	15:11	**E** bull or ram, each lamb or young goat,	285
	15:11	Each bull or ram, **e** lamb or young goat,	2021
	15:12	Do this for **e** one,	285
	15:38	with a blue cord on **e** tassel.	2021
	16:17	**E** man is to take his censer and put incense	AIT
	16:18	So **e** man took his censer,	AIT
	17: 2	from the leader of **e** of their ancestral tribes.	3972
	17: 2	Write the name of **e** man on his staff.	AIT
	17: 3	one staff for the head of **e** ancestral tribe.	4392S
	17: 6	for the leader of **e** of their ancestral tribes,	NIH
	17: 9	and **e** man took his own staff.	AIT
	23: 2	of them offered a bull and a ram on **e** altar.	2021
	23: 4	on **e** altar I have offered a bull and a ram."	2021
	23:14	and offered a bull and a ram on **e** altar.	2021
	23:30	and offered a bull and a ram on **e** altar.	2021
	25: 5	"**E** of you must put to death those	408
	26:54	**e** is to receive its inheritance according to	408
	26:55	What **e** group inherits will be	NIH
	26:56	**E** inheritance is to be distributed by lot	2257
	28: 3	as a regular burnt offering **e** day.	2021
	28: 7	of a hin of fermented drink with **e** lamb.	285
	28:12	With **e** bull there is to be a grain offering	285
	28:13	and with **e** lamb,	285
	28:14	With **e** bull there is to be a drink offering	2021
	28:14	and with **e** lamb, a quarter of a hin.	2021
	28:14	to be made at **e** new moon during the year.	NIH
	28:20	With **e** bull prepare a grain offering	2021
	28:21	and with **e** of the seven lambs, one-tenth.	285
	28:28	With **e** bull there is to be a grain offering	285
	28:29	and with **e** of the seven lambs, one-tenth.	285
	29: 4	and with **e** of the seven lambs, one-tenth.	285
	29:10	and with **e** of the seven lambs, one-tenth.	285
	29:14	With **e** of the thirteen bulls prepare	285
	29:14	with **e** of the two rams, two-tenths;	285
	29:15	and with **e** of the fourteen lambs, one-tenth.	285
	31: 4	Send into battle a thousand men from **e** of	3972
	31: 5	a thousand from **e** tribe,	2021
	31: 6	a thousand from **e** tribe,	2021
	31:50	an offering to the LORD the gold articles **e**	408
	31:53	**E** soldier had taken plunder for himself.	408
	34:18	And appoint one leader from **e** tribe	285
	35: 8	in proportion to the inheritance of **e** tribe:	408
	36: 9	for **e** Israelite tribe is to keep	408
Dt	1:13	understanding and respected men from **e**	NIH
	1:23	one man from **e** tribe.	2021
	3:20	**e** of you may go back to	408
	14:22	of all that your fields produce **e** year.	9102+9102
	15:20	**E** year you and your family are to eat them	928+9102+9102
	16:17	**E** of you must bring a gift in proportion to	408
	16:18	Appoint judges and officials for **e**	NIH
	24:15	Pay him his wages **e** day before sunset,	928

Dt	24:16	e is to die for his own sin.	408
Jos	3:12	one from e tribe.	2021
	4: 2	one from e tribe,	NIH
	4: 4	one from e tribe,	NIH
	4: 5	E of you is to take up a stone	408
	18: 4	Appoint three men from e tribe.	2021
	18: 4	according to the inheritance of e.	4392
	21:42	E of these **towns** had pasturelands	
		surrounding it;	6551+6551
	22:14	one for e of the tribes of Israel,	3972
	22:14	e the head of a family division among	408
	24:28	e to his own inheritance.	408
Jdg	1:18	e city with its territory.	NIH
	2: 6	e to his own inheritance.	408
	5:30	a girl or two for e man,	8031
	6:29	They asked e other, "Who did this?"	408
	7: 7	e to his own place."	408
	7:21	e man held his position around the camp,	AIT
	7:22	throughout the camp to turn on e other	2084
	8:18	"e man with the bearing of a prince."	AIT
	8:24	that e of you give me an earring	408
	8:25	e man threw a ring from his plunder onto it.	AIT
	10:18	of the people of Gilead said to e other,	408
	11:40	e year the young women	2025+3427+3427+4946
	16: 5	E one of us will give you eleven hundred	
		shekels of silver."	408
	20: 6	into pieces and sent one piece to e region	3972
	20:16	e of whom could sling a stone at a hair and	3972
	21:21	and e of you seize a wife from the girls	408
	21:23	e man caught one and carried her off	4200+5031ˢ
	21:24	e to his own inheritance.	408
Ru	1: 8	"Go back, e of you, to your mother's home.	851
	1: 9	The LORD grant that e of you will find rest	851
1Sa	2:19	E year his mother made him a little robe	
			2025+3427+3427+4946
	6:17	one e for Ashdod, Gaza, Ashkelon,	AIT
	10:11	they asked e other,	408
	10:25	e to his own home.	408
	14: 4	On e **side** of the pass	2021+2021+2296+2296
			+4946+4946+4946+4946+6298+6298
	14:20	striking e other with their swords.	408
	14:34	'E of you bring me your cattle and sheep,	408
	17:10	Give me a man and let us fight e **other.**"	3480
	17:21	up their lines **facing** e **other.**	5120+7925
	20:41	they kissed e other and wept together—	408
	20:42	we have sworn friendship with e **other**	5646+9109
	27: 3	E man had his family with him,	AIT
	30: 6	e one was bitter in spirit because of his sons	3972
	30:22	e man may take his wife and children	AIT
2Sa	2: 3	e with his family,	408
	2:16	Then e man grabbed his opponent by	AIT
	6:19	to e person in the whole crowd of Israelites,	3972
	10: 4	shaved off half of e **man's** beard,	AIT
	14: 6	They got into a fight with e **other** in	2157+9109ˢ
	18: 5	concerning Absalom to e of	3972
	19: 9	the people were all **arguing with** e **other,**	1906
	20:22	e returning to his home.	408
	21:20	with six fingers on e hand and six toes	2257
	21:20	on each hand and six toes on e foot—	2257
1Ki	4: 7	E one had to provide supplies	2021
	4:25	e man under his own vine and fig tree.	AIT
	4:27	The district officers, e in his month,	408
	6:10	The height of e was five cubits,	2257
	6:23	e ten cubits high.	2257
	6:26	The height of e cherub was ten cubits.	285
	6:27	and their wings touched e other in	4053ˢ
	6:34	e having two leaves that turned in sockets.	285
	7: 4	in sets of three, **facing** e **other.**	448+4691+4691
	7: 5	in sets of three, **facing** e **other.**	448+4691+4691
	7:15	e eighteen cubits high and twelve cubits	285
	7:16	e capital was five cubits high.	285
	7:17	seven for e capital.	285
	7:18	in two rows encircling e network	285
	7:18	He did the same for e capital.	9108
	7:27	e was four cubits long,	285
	7:30	E stand had four bronze wheels	285
	7:30	and e had a basin resting on four supports,	2157
	7:30	cast with wreaths on e side.	408
	7:32	The diameter of e wheel was a cubit and	285
	7:34	E stand had four handles,	285
	7:34	one on e corner, projecting from the stand.	752ˢ
	7:38	e holding forty baths	285
	7:38	one basin to go on e of the ten stands.	285
	7:42	of pomegranates for e network, decorating	285
	8:38	e one aware of the afflictions	408
	8:39	deal with e man according to all he does,	2021
	8:59	according to e **day's** need,	3427+3427
	10:16	of gold went into e shield.	285
	10:17	with three minas of gold in e shield.	285
	10:19	with a lion standing beside e of them.	9109
	10:20	one at either end of e step.	NIH
	18: 4	fifty in e, and had supplied them with food	NIH
	18:13	in two caves, fifty in e, and supplied them	NIH
	18:31	one for e of the tribes descended	3869+5031
	20:10	in Samaria to give e of my men a handful."	3972
	20:20	and e one struck down his opponent.	408
	20:29	seven days they camped opposite e other,	465
	22:17	Let e one go home in peace.' "	408
2Ki	3:13	"What do we have to do with e other?	3870ˢ
	3:23	and slaughtered e other.	408
	3:25	and e man threw a stone	AIT
	4: 4	Pour oil into all the jars, and as e is filled,	2021
	6: 2	where e of us can get a pole;	408
	7: 3	they said to e other,	408
	7: 9	they said to e other, "We're not doing right.	408
	9:21	e in his own chariot, to meet Jehu.	408
	11: 8	e man with his weapon in his hand.	AIT

2Ki	11: 9	E one took his men—	408
	11:11	The guards, e with his weapon in his hand,	408
	14: 6	e is to die for his own sins."	408
	14:11	Amaziah king of Judah **faced** e **other**	7156+8011
	17:29	e **national group** made its own gods	1580+1580
	25:17	E pillar was twenty-seven feet high.	285
1Ch	9:27	charge of the key for opening it e **morning.**	
			1332+1332+2021+2021+4200+4200
	13: 1	David conferred with e of his officers,	3972
	16: 3	of raisins to e Israelite man and woman.	3972
	16:37	according to e **day's** requirements.	
			928+2257+3427+3427
	16:43	all the people left, e for his own home,	408
	20: 6	with six fingers on e hand and six toes	NIH
	20: 6	on each hand and six toes on e foot—	NIH
	26:13	Lots were cast for e **gate,**	2256+9133+9133
	27: 1	E division consisted of 24,000 men.	285
	28:15	the weight for e **lampstand** and its lamps;	
			2256+4963+4963
	28:15	the weight of silver for e silver **lampstand**	
			4963+4963
	28:15	according to the use of e **lampstand;**	
			2256+4963+4963
	28:16	of gold for e **table** for consecrated bread;	
			2256+8947+8947
	28:17	weight of gold for e **gold dish;**	2256+4094+4094
	28:17	weight of silver for e silver **dish**	2256+4094+4094
2Ch	3:15	e with a capital on top measuring five cubits	2257
	4:13	of pomegranates for e network, decorating	285
	6:29	e one aware of his afflictions and pains,	408
	6:30	deal with e man according to all he does,	2021
	8:14	according to e **day's** requirement	928+3427+3427
	9:15	of hammered gold went into e shield.	285
	9:16	of gold in e shield.	285
	9:18	with a lion standing beside e of them.	9109
	9:19	one at either end of e step.	NIH
	18:16	Let e one go home in peace.' "	408
	19: 5	in e of the fortified cities of Judah.	3972
	23: 7	e man with his weapons in his hand.	AIT
	23: 8	E one took his men—	408
	23:10	e with his weapon in his hand,	408
	25: 4	e is to die for his own sins."	408
	25:21	Amaziah king of Judah **faced** e **other**	7156+8011
	31: 2	e of them according to their duties	408
	35: 5	with a group of Levites for e **subdivision** of	AIT
	35:15	The gatekeepers at e **gate**	2256+9133+9133
Ezr	2: 1	e to his own town,	408
	3: 4	offerings prescribed for e **day.**	928+3427+3427
	6:17	one for e of the tribes of Israel.	10433
	10:14	the elders and judges of e **town,**	2256+6551+6551
	10:16	one from e family division,	4392
	10:19	for their guilt they e presented a ram from	NIH
Ne	3:28	e in front of his own house.	408
	4:15	e to his own work.	408
	4:18	and e of the builders wore his sword	408
	4:19	and we are widely separated from e other	408
	4:23	e had his weapon,	408
	5:18	E day one ox,	285
	6: 4	and e time I gave them the same answer.	NIH
	7: 6	e to his own town,	408
	10:32	a shekel e year for the service of the house	2021
	10:34	to determine when e of our families is	NIH
	10:34	at set times e **year** a contribution	928+9102+9102
	10:35	of the LORD e **year** the firstfruits	928+9102+9102
	11: 3	e on his own property in the various towns,	408
	11:20	e on his ancestral property.	408
	13:30	and assigned them duties, e to his own task.	408
Est	1: 7	e one different from the other,	AIT
	1: 8	the king's command e guest was allowed	NIH
	1: 8	to serve e **man** what he wished.	AIT
	1:22	to e **province** in its own script	2256+4519+4519
	1:22	to e **people** in its own language,	2256+6639+6639
	1:22	in e people's tongue that every man should	2257
	3:12	the script of e **province** and	2256+4519+4519
	3:12	of e **people** all Haman's orders	2256+6639+6639
	8: 9	in the script of e **province**	2256+4519+4519
	8: 9	and the language of e **people**	2256+6639+6639
	9:19	a day for giving presents to e other.	408
Job	1: 5	a burnt offering for e of them,	3972
	9:32	that we might confront e **other** in court.	3481
	41:16	e is so close to the next	285
	42:11	and e one gave him a piece of silver and	408
Ps	39: 5	E man's life is but a breath.	3972
	39:11	e man is but a breath.	3972
	62:12	Surely you will reward e **person** according	AIT
	64: 5	They encourage e **other** in evil plans,	4564ˢ
	84: 7	till e **appears** before God in Zion.	AIT
	85:10	righteousness and peace **kiss** e **other.**	AIT
	147: 4	the number of the stars and calls them e	3972
Pr	14:10	E **heart** knows its own bitterness,	AIT
	24:12	Will he not repay e **person** according	AIT
SS	3: 8	e with his sword at his side,	408
	4: 2	E has its twin; not one of them is alone.	3972
	6: 6	E has its twin, not one of them is alone.	3972
	8:11	E was to bring for its fruit	408
Isa	3: 5	People **will oppress** e **other**—	5601
	6: 2	Above him were seraphs, e with six wings:	285
	9:20	E will feed on the flesh	408
	13: 8	They will look aghast at e other,	408
	13:14	e will return to his own people,	408
	13:14	e will flee to his native land.	408
	14:18	e in his own tomb.	408
	32: 2	E **man** will be like a shelter from the wind	AIT
	34:14	and wild goats will bleat to e **other;**	8276ˢ
	34:15	also the falcons will gather, e with its mate.	851
	40:26	and calls them e by name.	3972
	41: 6	e helps the other and says to his brother,	408

Isa	47:15	E of them goes on in his error;	408
	50: 8	Let us face e **other!**	3480
	53: 6	e of us has turned to his own way;	408
	56:11	e seeks his own gain.	408
	56:12	"Come," e one cries, "let me get wine!	NIH
	58: 4	and in **striking** e **other** with wicked fists.	AIT
Jer	5: 8	e neighing for another man's wife.	408
	6: 3	e tending his own portion."	408
	7: 5	and deal with e other justly,	408
	8: 6	E pursues his own course like	3972
	9: 8	With his mouth e **speaks** cordially	AIT
	12:15	and will bring e of them back	408
	16:12	how e of you is following the stubbornness	408
	18:11	So turn from your evil ways, e one of you,	408
	18:12	e of us will follow the stubbornness	408
	22: 7	e **man** with his weapons,	AIT
	23:35	This is what e of you keeps on saying	408
	25: 5	They said, "Turn now, e of you,	408
	26: 3	Perhaps they will listen and e will turn	408
	34:14	'Every seventh year e of you must free any	408
	34:15	E of you proclaimed freedom	408
	34:16	e of you has taken back the male	408
	35:15	"E of you must turn	408
	36: 3	e of them will turn from his wicked way;	408
	36: 7	e will turn from his wicked ways,	408
	36:16	they looked at e other in fear and said	408
	37:21	the street of the bakers e **day**	2021+3427+4200
	46:16	they will fall over e other.	408
	51: 9	let us leave her and e go to his own land,	408
	52:21	E of the pillars was eighteen cubits high	285
	52:21	e was four fingers thick, and hollow.	2257
Eze	1: 6	e of them had four faces and four wings.	285
	1: 9	E one went straight ahead;	408
	1:10	E of the four had the face of a man,	4392
	1:10	on the right side e had the face of a lion,	5527
	1:10	e also had the face of an eagle.	5527
	1:11	e had two wings,	408
	1:12	E one went straight ahead.	408
	1:15	a wheel on the ground beside e creature	2021
	1:16	E appeared to be made like	2157
	1:23	and e had two wings covering its body.	408
	3:13	the living creatures brushing against e other	851
	4: 6	a day for e year.	2021
	4:10	of food to eat e day and eat it at set times.	2021
	4:17	They will be appalled at the sight of e other	408
	7:16	e because of his sins.	408
	8:11	E had a censer in his hand,	408
	8:12	e at the shrine of his own idol?	408
	9: 1	e with a weapon in his hand."	408
	9: 2	e with a deadly weapon in his hand.	408
	10: 9	one beside e of the cherubim;	285
	10:10	e **was** like a wheel intersecting a wheel.	AIT
	10:14	E of the cherubim had four faces:	285
	10:21	E had four faces and four wings,	285
	10:22	E one went straight ahead.	408
	18:30	e one according to his ways,	408
	20: 7	And I said to them, "E of you,	408
	22: 9	how e of the princes of Israel who are	408
	32:10	On the day of your downfall e	408
	33:20	But I will judge e of you according	408
	33:26	and e of you defiles his neighbor's wife.	408
	33:30	saying to e other,	2522
	40: 5	e of which was a cubit and a handbreadth.	NIH
	40:10	the east gate were three alcoves on e side;	
			2256+4946+4946+7024+7024
	40:10	of the projecting walls on e side had	
			2256+4946+4946+7024+7024
	40:12	of e alcove was a wall one cubit high,	2021
	40:21	Its alcoves—three on e side—	
			2256+4946+4946+7024+7024
	40:26	the faces of the projecting walls on e side.	
			2256+4946+4946+7024+7024
	40:38	with a doorway was by the portico in e of	NIH
	40:39	of the gateway were two tables on e side,	
			2256+4946+4946+7024+7024
	40:42	e a cubit and a half long,	NIH
	40:43	e a handbreadth long,	NIH
	40:49	and there were pillars on e side of the	
		jambs.	2256+4946+4946+7024+7024
	41: 1	width of the jambs was six cubits on e side.	
			2256+4946+4946+7024+7024
	41: 2	and the projecting walls on e side	
			2256+4946+4946+7024+7024
	41: 3	e was two cubits wide.	NIH
	41: 3	on e side of it were seven cubits wide.	NIH
	41: 5	it was six cubits thick, and e side room	2021
	41: 6	one above another, thirty on e level.	AIT
	41: 7	wider **at** e **successive level.**	
			2025+2025+4200+4200+5087+5087
	41:15	including its galleries on e side;	
			2256+4946+4946+7024+7024
	41:18	E cherub had two faces:	2021
	41:24	E door had two leaves—	9109ˢ
	41:24	two hinged leaves for e door.	285
	41:26	with palm trees carved **on** e **side.**	
			2256+4946+4946+7024+7024
	45: 7	the land **bordering** e **side** of the area	
		formed	2256+2296+2296+4946+4946ˢ
	45:13	an ephah from e homer of wheat and a sixth	NIH
	45:13	a sixth of an ephah from e homer of barley.	NIH
	45:14	a tenth of a bath from e cor (which consists	2021
	45:24	as a grain offering an ephah for e bull and	2021
	45:24	for each bull and an ephah for e ram,	2021
	45:24	along with a hin of oil for e ephah.	2021
	46: 5	along with a hin of oil for e ephah.	2021
	46: 7	along with a hin of oil with e ephah.	2021
	46: 9	e is to **go out**	AIT

Eze	46:11	along with a hin of oil for e ephah.	2021
	46:21	and I saw in e corner another court.	
			928+928+5243+5243
	46:22	e of the courts in the four corners was	AIT
	46:23	e of the four courts	AIT
	47: 7	I saw a great number of trees on e side of	
			2256+2296+2296+4946+4946S
	48:20	25,000 cubits on e side.	928
Da	7: 3	e different from the others,	10154
	11:27	at the same table and lie to e other,	AIT
Joel	2: 8	They do not jostle e other;	408
	2: 8	e marches straight ahead.	1505S
Am	4: 3	You will e go straight out through breaks in	851
Jnh	1: 5	All the sailors were afraid and e cried out	408
	1: 7	Then the sailors said to e other, "Come,	408
Mic	7: 2	e hunts his brother with a net.	408
Hag	1: 9	while e of you is busy with his own house.	408
	2:22	e by the sword of his brother.	408
Zec	3:10	that day e of you will invite his neighbor	408
	7:10	In your hearts do not think evil of e other.'	408
	8: 4	e with cane in hand because of his age.	408
	8:16	Speak the truth to e other,	408
	11:12	The land will mourn, e clan by itself,	5476+5476
	14:13	E man will seize the hand of another,	AIT
	14:13	and they will attack e other.	2084
Mal	3:16	the LORD talked with e other,	408
Mt	6:34	E day has enough trouble of its own.	3836
	16:27	and then he will reward e person according	1667
	18:35	how my heavenly Father will treat e of you	1667
	20: 9	the eleventh hour came and e received	324
	20:10	e one of them also received a denarius.	324+3836
	21:38	the tenants saw the son, they said to e other,	1571
	24:10	the faith and will betray and hate e other,	253
	25:15	e according to his ability.	1667
Mk	1:27	so amazed that they asked e other,	1571
	4:41	They were terrified and asked e other,	253
	9:50	and be at peace with e other."	253
	10:26	and said to e other,	1571
	13:34	e with his assigned task,	1667
	15:24	they cast lots to see what e would get.	5515
	16: 3	and they asked e other,	1571
Lk	4:36	the people were amazed and said to e other,	253
	4:40	and laying his hands on e one,	1667
	6:44	E tree is recognized by its own fruit.	1667
	7:32	the marketplace and calling out to e other:	253
	9:14	down in groups of about fifty e."	324
	11: 3	Give us e day our daily bread.	2848
	12:52	in one family divided against e other,	NIG
	13:15	Doesn't e of you on	1667
	16: 5	he called in e one of his master's debtors.	1667
	21:37	E day Jesus was teaching at the temple,	
			2465+3836
	21:37	and e evening he went out to spend	3816+3836
	24:14	They were talking with e other	253
	24:15	and discussed these things with e other,	NIG
	24:32	They asked e other,	253
Jn	2: 6	e holding from twenty to thirty gallons.	NIG
	4:33	Then his disciples said to e other,	253
	6: 7	not buy enough bread for e one to have	1667
	7:53	Then e went to his own home.	1667
	15:12	Love e other as I have loved you.	253
	15:17	This is my command: Love e other.	253
	16:32	e to his own home.	1667
	19:18	one on e side and Jesus in the middle.	
			1949+1949+2779
	19:23	one for e of them,	1667
Ac	2: 3	tongues of fire that separated and came to	
		rest on e of them.	1651+1667
	2: 6	because e one heard them speaking	1667
	2: 8	then how is it that e of us hears them	1667
	3:26	to you to bless you by turning e of you	1667
	7:26	why do you want to hurt e other?'	253
	11:29	The disciples, e according to his ability,	1667
	12: 4	by four squads of four soldiers e.	NIG
	14:23	for them in e church and,	2848
	17:27	though he is not far from e one of us.	1667
	20:31	three years I never stopped warning e	1651+1667
	21: 6	After saying good-by to e other,	253
	21:26	offering would be made for e of them.	1651+1667
	28: 4	they said to e other,	253
Ro	1:12	be mutually encouraged by e other's faith.	253
	2: 6	to e person according to what he has done."	1667
	12: 4	Just as e of us has one body	NIG
	12: 5	and e member belongs to all the others.	1651
	14: 5	E one should be fully convinced	1667
	14:12	e of us will give an account of himself	1667
	15: 2	E of us should please his neighbor	1667
1Co	3: 5	as the Lord has assigned to e his task.	1667
	3: 8	and e will be rewarded according	1667
	3:10	But e one should be careful how he builds.	1667
	3:13	fire will test the quality of e man's work.	1667
	4: 5	that time e will receive his praise from God.	1667
	7: 2	e man should have his own wife,	1667
	7: 2	and e woman her own husband.	1667
	7: 5	Do not deprive e other except	253
	7: 7	But e man has his own gift from God;	1667
	7:17	e one should retain the place in life that	1667
	7:20	E one should remain in the situation	1667
	7:24	Brothers, as responsible to God,	1667
	11:21	e of you goes ahead without waiting	1667
	11:33	wait for e other.	253
	12: 7	Now to e one the manifestation of	1667
	12:11	and he gives them to e one,	1667
	12:25	parts should have equal concern for e other.	253
	12:27	and e one of you is a part of it.	3517S
	15:23	But e in his own turn:	1667
	15:38	to e kind of seed he gives its own body.	1667

1Co	16: 2	e one of you should set aside a sum	1667
2Co	5:10	that e one may receive what is due him for	1667
	9: 7	E man should give what he has decided	1667
Gal	5:15	on biting and devouring e other,	253
	5:15	or you will be destroyed by e other.	253
	5:17	They are in conflict with e other,	253
	5:26	provoking and envying e other.	253
	6: 2	Carry e other's burdens,	253
	6: 4	E one should test his own actions.	1667
	6: 5	for e one should carry his own load.	1667
Eph	4: 7	But to e one of us grace has been given	1651+1667
	4:16	as e part does its work.	1667
	4:25	Therefore e of you must put off falsehood	1667
	4:32	to one another, forgiving e other, just as	4932
	5:33	e one of you also must love his wife	1667
Php	2: 4	E of you should look not only to your own	1667
	4: 2	with Syntyche to agree with e other in	NIG
Col	3: 9	Do not lie to e other,	253
	3:13	Bear with e other and forgive	253
1Th	2:11	you know that we dealt with e of you	1651+1667
	3:12	for e other and for everyone else,	253
	4: 4	that e of you should learn	1667
	4: 9	by God to love e other,	253
	4:18	encourage e other with these words.	253
	5:11	encourage one another and build e other up,	
			1651+1651+3836
	5:13	Live in peace with e other.	4932
	5:15	to be kind to e other and to everyone else.	253
2Th	1: 3	of you has for e other is increasing.	253
Heb	6:11	We want e of you to show this same	1667
	11:21	blessed e of Joseph's sons,	1667
	13: 1	Keep on loving e other as brothers.	5789
Jas	1:14	but e one is tempted when,	1667
	5: 9	Don't grumble against e other, brothers,	253
	5:16	Therefore confess your sins to e other	253
	5:16	for e other so that you may be healed.	253
1Pe	1:17	Father who judges e man's work impartially	1667
	4: 8	Above all, love e other deeply,	4932
	4:10	E one should use whatever gift he has	
		received	1667
Rev	2:23	and I will repay e of you according	1667
	4: 8	E of the four living creatures had six wings	
			1651+1651+2848
	5: 8	E one had a harp	1667
	6: 4	the earth and to make men slay e other.	253
	6:11	Then e of them was given a white robe,	1667
	11:10	and will celebrate by sending e other gifts,	253
	13: 1	and on e head a blasphemous name.	3836
	16:21	of about a hundred pounds fell upon men.	NIG
	20:13	and e person was judged according	1667
	21:21	e gate made of a single pearl.	324+1651+1667
	22: 2	On e side of the river stood the tree of life,	
			1696+1949+2779

EAGER (21) [EAGERLY, EAGERNESS]

2Ch	26:20	Indeed, he himself was e to leave,	1894
Ps	56: 6	they watch my steps, e to take my life.	7747
Pr	28:20	one e to get rich will not go unpunished.	237
	28:22	A stingy man is e to get rich	987
	31:13	and flax and works with e hands.	2914
Isa	58: 2	they seem e to know my ways,	2911
	58: 2	and seem e for God to come near them.	2911
Zep	3: 7	But they were still e to act corruptly	8899
Ro	1:15	That is why I am so e to preach the gospel	4609
	8:19	The creation waits in e expectation for	638
1Co	14:12	Since you are e to have spiritual gifts,	2421
	14:39	Therefore, my brothers, be e to prophesy,	2420
2Co	8:11	so that your e willingness to do it may	4608
Gal	2:10	the very thing I was e to do.	5079
Php	2:28	Therefore I am all the more e to send him,	5081
1Ti	6:10	Some people, e for money,	3977
Tit	2:14	e to do what is good.	2421
1Pe	3:13	Who is going to harm you if you are e	2421
	5: 2	not greedy for money, but e to serve;	4610
2Pe	1:10	be all the more e to make your calling	5079
Jude	1: 3	although I was very e to write to you about	5082

EAGERLY (11) [EAGER]

2Ch	15:15	They sought God e,	928+3972+8356
Job	7: 2	or a hired man waiting e for his wages.	7747
Ps	78:34	they e turned to him again.	8838
Lk	22:15	"I have e desired to eat this Passover	2121+2123
Ro	8:23	as we wait e for our adoption as sons,	587
1Co	1: 7	not lack any spiritual gift as you e wait for	587
	12:31	But e desire the greater gifts.	2420
	14: 1	the way of love and e desire spiritual gifts,	2420
Gal	5: 5	e await through the Spirit the righteousness	
		for which we hope.	587
Php	1:20	I expect and hope that I will in no way	638
	3:20	And we e await a Savior from there,	587

EAGERNESS (4) [EAGER]

Ac	17:11	for they received the message with great e	4608
2Co	7:11	what e to clear yourselves,	665
	8:19	to honor the Lord himself and to show our e	4608
	9: 2	For I know your e to help,	4608

EAGLE (20) [EAGLE'S, EAGLES, EAGLES']

Lev	11:13	the e, the vulture, the black vulture,	5979
Dt	14:12	the e, the vulture, the black vulture,	5979
	28:49	like an e swooping down,	5979
	32:11	like an e that stirs up its nest and hovers	5979
Job	39:27	Does the e soar at your command	5979
Pr	23: 5	and fly off to the sky like an e.	5979

Pr	30:19	the way of an e in the sky,	5979
Jer	48:40	An e is swooping down,	5979
	49:22	An e will soar and swoop down,	5979
Eze	1:10	each also had the face of an e.	5979
	10:14	and the fourth the face of an e.	5979
	17: 3	A great e with powerful wings,	5979
	17: 7	" 'But there was another great e	5979
Da	4:33	of an e and his nails like the claws of a bird.	10495
	7: 4	and it had the wings of an e.	10495
Hos	8: 1	is over the house of the LORD	5979
Ob	1: 4	the e and make your nest among the stars,	5979
Rev	4: 7	the fourth was like a flying e.	108
	8:13	an e that was flying in midair call out in	108
	12:14	the two wings of a great e,	108

EAGLE'S (2) [EAGLE]

Ps	103: 5	so that your youth is renewed like the e.	5979
Jer	49:16	you build your nest as high as the e,	5979

EAGLES (5) [EAGLE]

2Sa	1:23	They were swifter than e,	5979
Job	9:26	like e swooping down on their prey.	5979
Isa	40:31	They will soar on wings like e;	5979
Jer	4:13	his horses are swifter than e.	5979
La	4:19	Our pursuers were swifter than e in	5979

EAGLES' (1) [EAGLE]

Ex	19: 4	on e' wings and brought you to myself.	5979

EAR (56) [EARS]

Ex	21: 6	to the door or the doorpost and pierce his e	265
Lev	8:23	and put it on the lobe of Aaron's right e,	265
	14:14	of the right e of the one to be cleansed,	265
	14:17	in his palm on the lobe of the right e of	265
	14:25	of the right e of the one to be cleansed,	265
	14:28	of the right e of the one to be cleansed,	265
Dt	1:45	and turned a deaf e to you.	263+4202
	15:17	an awl and push it through his e lobe into	265
2Ki	19:16	Give e, O LORD, and hear;	265+5742
Ne	1: 6	let your e be attentive and your eyes open	265
	1:11	let your e be attentive to the prayer	265
Job	12:11	the e test words as the tongue tastes food?	265
	34: 3	the e tests words as the tongue tastes food.	265
Ps	5: 1	Give e to my words, O LORD,	263
	17: 1	Give e to my prayer—	263
	17: 6	give e to me and hear my prayer.	265+5742
	28: 1	do not turn a deaf e to me.	3087
	31: 2	Turn your e to me,	265
	45:10	Listen, O daughter, consider and give e:	265+5742
	49: 4	I will turn my e to a proverb;	265
	71: 2	turn your e to me and save me.	265
	88: 2	turn your e to my cry.	265
	94: 9	Does he who implanted the e not hear?	265
	102: 2	Turn your e to me;	265
	116: 2	Because he turned his e to me,	265
Pr	2: 2	turning your e to wisdom	265
	25:12	a wise man's rebuke to a listening e.	265
	28: 9	If anyone turns a deaf e to the law,	265
Ecc	1: 8	nor the e its fill of hearing.	265
Isa	37:17	Give e, O LORD, and hear;	265+5742
	48: 8	from of old your e has not been open.	265
	50: 4	wakens my e to listen like one being taught.	265
	55: 3	Give e and come to me;	265+5742
	59: 1	nor his e too dull to hear.	265
	64: 4	no e has perceived.	263
Da	9:18	Give e, O God, and hear;	265+5742
Am	3:12	or a piece of an e,	265
Mt	10:27	what is whispered in your e,	4044
	26:51	servant of the high priest, cutting off his e.	6065
Mk	14:47	servant of the high priest, cutting off his e.	6064
Lk	12: 3	the e in the inner rooms will be proclaimed	4044
	22:50	of the high priest, cutting off his e.	4044
	22:51	he touched the man's e and healed him.	6065
Jn	18:10	high priest's servant, cutting off his right e.	6064
	18:26	of the man whose e Peter had cut off,	6065
1Co	2: 9	"No eye has seen, no e has heard,	4044
	12:16	And if the e should say,	4044
	12:17	If the whole body were an e,	198
Rev	2: 7	He who has an e, let him hear	4044
	2:11	He who has an e, let him hear	4044
	2:17	He who has an e, let him hear	4044
	2:29	He who has an e, let him hear	4044
	3: 6	He who has an e, let him hear	4044
	3:13	He who has an e, let him hear	4044
	3:22	He who has an e, let him hear	4044
	13: 9	He who has an e, let him hear	4044

[IN THE] EAR (Anglicized) See HEADED

EARED, EARING (KJV) PLOW, PLOWED

EARLIER (18) [EARLY]

Ge	13: 3	and Ai where his tent had been e	928+2021+9378
	26: 1	besides the e famine of Abraham's time—	8037
Ru	3:10	that which you showed e:	8037
	4: 7	(Now in e times in Israel,	7156
1Ki	11:15	E when David was fighting with Edom,	2118
1Ch	9:20	In e times Phinehas son of Eleazar	4200+7156
Ne	5:15	But the e governors—	8037
Da	7:24	different from the e ones;	10623
	9:21	Gabriel, the man I had seen in the e vision,	
			928+2021+9378

Zec	1: 4	to whom the e prophets proclaimed:	8037
	7: 7	through the e prophets when Jerusalem	8037
	7:12	by his Spirit through the e prophets.	8037
Jn	7:50	who had gone to Jesus e and who was one	4728
	19:39	the man who e had visited Jesus at night.	4754
2Co	8: 6	since *he had* e **made a beginning,**	4599
	12:21	be grieved over many who *have* **sinned** e	4579
	13: 2	not spare those who **sinned** e or any of	4579
Heb	10:32	Remember those e days	4728

EARLIEST (1) [EARLY]

Ac	15:21	in every city from the e times and is read in	792

EARLY (69) [EARLIER, EARLIEST]

Ge	19: 2	then go on your way e **in the morning."**	8899
	19:27	E the next morning Abraham **got up**	8899
	20: 8	E the next morning Abimelech summoned	
		all his officials,	8899
	21:14	E the next morning Abraham took some	8899
	22: 3	E the next morning Abraham **got up**	8899
	26:31	E the next morning the men swore an oath	8899
	28:18	E the next morning Jacob took	8899
	31:55	E the next morning Laban kissed his	
		grandchildren and his daughters	8899
Ex	2:18	"Why have you returned *so* e today?"	4554
	8:20	**"Get up** e **in the morning**	8899
	9:13	**"Get up** e **in the morning,**	8899
	24: 4	*He* **got up** e the next morning and built	8899
	32: 6	So the next day the people **rose** e	8899
	34: 4	the first ones and went up Mount Sinai e in	8899
Nu	14:40	E the next morning they went up toward	8899
Jos	3: 1	E in the morning Joshua and all	8899
	6:12	Joshua **got up** e the next morning and	8899
	7:16	E the next morning Joshua had Israel come	
		forward by tribes,	8899
	8:10	E the next morning Joshua mustered his	
		men,	8899
	8:14	of the city hurried out e **in the morning**	8899
Jdg	6:38	Gideon **rose** e the next day;	8899
	7: 1	E **in the morning,** Jerub-Baal	8899
	19: 5	On the fourth day *they* **got up** e	8899
	19: 9	E tomorrow **morning** *you can* **get up**	8899
	21: 4	and that the people built an altar	8899
1Sa	1:19	E the next morning *they* **arose**	8899
	5: 3	the people of Ashdod **rose** e the next day,	8899
	15:12	E in the morning Samuel **got up**	8899
	17:20	E in the morning David left the flock with	8899
	29:10	Now **get up** e,	8899
	29:11	and his men **got up** e **in the morning**	8899
2Sa	15: 2	He *would* **get up** e and stand by the side of	8899
2Ki	3:22	When *they* **got up** e in the morning,	8899
	6:15	up and went out e **the next morning,**	8899
2Ch	17: 3	because in his e years he walked in	8037
	20:20	E in the morning they left for the Desert	8899
	29:20	E **the next morning** King Hezekiah	8899
Job	1: 5	E in the morning he would sacrifice	8899
Ps	127: 2	In vain you rise e and stay up late,	8899
Pr	27:14	If a man loudly blesses his neighbor e in	8899
SS	2:13	The fig tree forms its e **fruit;**	7001
	7:12	*Let us go* e to the vineyards to see if	8899
Isa	5:11	to *those who* **rise** e in the morning to run	8899
Jer	24: 2	like those that **ripen** e;	1136
	26: 1	E *in the reign* of Jehoiakim son	928+8040
	27: 1	E *in the reign* of Zedekiah son	928+8040
	28: 1	e *in the reign* of Zedekiah king of Judah	928+8040
	28: 8	From e **times** the prophets who preceded	6409
	49:34	e *in the reign* of Zedekiah king of Judah:	8040
Hos	6: 4	like the dew that disappears.	8899
	9:10	it was like seeing the e **fruit** on the fig tree.	1136
	13: 3	like the dew that disappears.	8899
Mic	7: 1	none of the e **figs** that I crave.	1136
Mt	20: 1	a landowner who went out e **in the**	
		morning	275+4745
	21:18	E **in the morning,** as he was on his way	4745
	27: 1	E **in the morning,** all the chief priests	4746
Mk	1:35	Very e **in the morning,**	4745
	15: 1	Very e **in the morning,**	2317+4745
	16: 2	Very e on the first day of the week,	4745
	16: 9	When Jesus rose e on the first day of	4745
Lk	21:38	the people **came** e in the morning	3983
	24: 1	**very** e **in the morning,**	960+3986
	24:22	They went to the tomb e this **morning**	3984
Jn	10:40	John had been baptizing **in the** e **days.**	4754
	18:28	By now it was e **morning,**	4745
	20: 1	E on the first day of the week,	4745
	21: 4	E **in the morning,** Jesus stood on the shore,	1181+4746
Ac	21:16	from Cyprus and one of the e disciples.	792
Php	4:15	in the e days of your acquaintance with	794

EARN (5) [EARNED, EARNERS, EARNINGS, EARNS]

Dt	23:19	or food or anything else that *may* e **interest.**	5967
Am	7:12	E your bread there	430
Hag	1: 6	You e wages, only to put them in a purse	
		with holes in it.	8509+8509
2Th	3:12	settle down and e the bread they eat.	2237
Rev	18:17	and all who e *their* living from the sea,	2237

EARNED (4) [EARN]

Pr	31:31	Give her the **reward** she has e,	3338+7262
Lk	19:16	'Sir, your mina *has* e ten **more.'**	4664
	19:18	'Sir, your mina *has* e five **more.'**	4472
Ac	16:16	She e a great deal of money for her owners	4218

EARNERS (1) [EARN]

Isa	19:10	and all the wage e will be sick at heart.	6913

EARNEST (2) [EARNESTNESS, EARNESTLY]

Pr	27: 9	of one's friend springs from his e counsel.	5883
Rev	3:19	So *be* e, and repent.	2418

EARNESTLY (13) [EARNEST]

1Sa	20: 6	'David e **asked** my **permission** to hurry to	
		Bethlehem,	8626+8626
	20:28	e **asked** me **for permission**	8626+8626
Ps	63: 1	O God, you are my God, e *I* seek you;	8838
Hos	5:15	in their misery *they will* e **seek** me."	8838
Mk	5:23	and pleaded e with him,	4498
Lk	7: 4	they pleaded e with him,	5081
	22:44	And being in anguish, he prayed *more* e,	1757
Ac	12: 5	the church was e praying to God for him.	1757
	26: 7	to see fulfilled as they e serve God day	1755+1877
Ro	11: 7	What Israel **sought** so e it did not obtain,	2118
1Th	3:10	Night and day we pray **most** e	5655
Heb	11: 7	and that he rewards those who e **seek** him.	1699
Jas	5:17	*He* **prayed** e that it would not rain,	4666+4667

EARNESTNESS (4) [EARNEST]

Dt	18: 6	all e to the place the LORD will choose,	205+5883
2Co	7:11	what e, what eagerness to clear yourselves,	5082
	8: 7	*in* complete e and in your love for us—	5082
	8: 8	of your love by comparing it with the e	5082

EARNINGS (3) [EARN]

Dt	23:18	not bring the e *of* a female prostitute or of	924
Pr	31:16	out of her e she plants a vineyard.	4090+7262
Isa	23:18	Yet her profit and her e will be set apart for	924

EARNS (1) [EARN]

Pr	11:18	The wicked man e deceptive wages,	6913

EARRING (2) [EARRINGS]

Jdg	8:24	you give me an e *from* your share of	5690
Pr	25:12	an e *of* gold or an ornament of fine gold is	5690

EARRINGS (9) [EARRING]

Ex	32: 2	"Take off the gold e that your wives,	5690
	32: 3	So all the people took off their e	5690
	35:22	brooches, e, rings and ornaments.	5690
Nu	31:50	bracelets, signet rings, e and necklaces—	6316
Jdg	8:24	of the Ishmaelites to wear gold e.)	5690
SS	1:10	Your cheeks are beautiful with e,	9366
	1:11	We will make you e *of* gold,	9366
Isa	3:19	the e and bracelets and veils,	5755
Eze	16:12	e on your ears and a beautiful crown	6316

EARS (84) [EAR]

Ge	35: 4	and the rings in their e,	265
Ex	29:20	of the right e *of* Aaron and his sons,	265
Lev	8:24	of the blood on the lobes of their right e,	265
Dt	29: 4	that understands or eyes that see or e	265
1Sa	3:11	that will make the e *of* everyone who hears	265
	15:14	then is this bleating of sheep in my e?	265
2Sa	7:22	as we have heard with our own e.	265
	22: 7	my cry came to his e.	265
2Ki	19:28	and your insolence has reached my e,	265
	21:12	and Judah that the e *of* everyone who hears	265
1Ch	17:20	as we have heard with our own e.	265
2Ch	6:40	may your eyes be open and your e attentive	265
	7:15	and my e attentive to the prayers offered	265
Job	4:12	my e caught a whisper of it.	265
	13: 1	my e have heard and understood it.	265
	13:17	let your e take in what I say.	265
	15:21	Terrifying sounds fill his e;	265
	28:22	'Only a rumor of it has reached our e.'	265
	29:22	my words fell gently on their e.	NIH
	33:16	in their e and terrify them with warnings,	265
	42: 5	My e had heard of you but	265
Ps	18: 6	my cry came before him, into his e.	265
	34:15	on the righteous and his e are attentive	265
	40: 6	but my e you have pierced;	265
	44: 1	We have heard with our e, O God;	265
	58: 4	like that of a cobra that has stopped its e,	265
	92:11	my e have heard the	265
	115: 6	they have e, but cannot hear, noses,	265
	130: 2	Let your e be attentive to my cry for mercy.	265
	135:17	they have e, but cannot hear,	265
Pr	18:15	the e of the wise seek it out.	265
	20:12	E that hear and eyes that see—	265
	21:13	If a man shuts his e to the cry of the poor,	265
	23:12	Apply your heart to instruction and your e	265
	26:17	a dog by the e is a passer-by who meddles	265
Isa	6:10	make their e dull and close their eyes.	265
	6:10	hear with their e,	265
	11: 3	or decide by what he hears with his e;	265
	30:21	your e will hear a voice behind you, saying,	265
	32: 3	and the e *of* those who hear will listen.	265
	33:15	who stops his e against plots of murder	265
	35: 5	the eyes of the blind be opened and the e *of*	265
	37:29	because your insolence has reached my e,	265
	42:20	your e are open, but you hear nothing."	265
	43: 8	who have e but are deaf.	265
	50: 5	The Sovereign LORD has opened my e,	265
Jer	5:21	who have e but do not hear:	265

Jer	6:10	Their e are closed so they cannot hear.	265
	9:20	open your e to the words of his mouth.	265
	19: 3	that will make the e of everyone who hears	265
	26:11	You have heard it with your own e!"	265
La	3:56	"Do not close your e to my cry for relief."	265
Eze	8:18	Although they shout in my e,	265
	12: 2	but do not see and e to hear but do not hear,	265
	16:12	earrings on your e and a beautiful crown	265
	23:25	They will cut off your noses and your e,	265
	40: 4	look with your eyes and hear with your e	265
Mic	7:16	their e will become deaf.	265
Zec	7:11	and stopped up their e.	265
Mt	11:15	He who has e, let him hear."	4044
	13: 9	He who has e, let him hear."	4044
	13:15	they hardly hear *with* their e,	4044
	13:15	hear *with* their e,	4044
	13:16	and your e because they hear.	4044
	13:43	He who has e, let him hear."	4044
Mk	4: 9	Then Jesus said, "He who has e to hear,	4044
	4:23	If anyone has e to hear, let him hear."	4044
	7:33	Jesus put his fingers into the man's e.	4044
	7:35	At this, the man's e were opened,	198
	8:18	and e but fail to hear?	4044
Lk	1:44	as the sound of your greeting reached my e,	4044
	8: 8	"He who has e to hear, let him hear."	4044
	14:35	He who has e to hear, let him hear."	4044
Ac	7:51	with uncircumcised hearts and e!	4044
	7:57	At this they covered their e and,	4044
	11:22	News of this reached the e of the church	4044
	17:20	to our e, and we want	198
	28:27	they hardly hear *with* their e,	4044
	28:27	hear *with* their e,	4044
Ro	11: 8	not see and e so that they could not hear,	4044
2Ti	4: 3	to say **what** their itching e **want to hear.**	198
	4: 4	They will turn their e away from the truth	198
Jas	5: 4	of the harvesters have reached the e of	4044
1Pe	3:12	on the righteous and his e are attentive	4044

EARS OF CORN (Anglicized) See HEADS OF GRAIN

EARTH (738) [EARTH'S, EARTHEN, EARTHLY]

Ge	1: 1	God created the heavens and the e.	824
	1: 2	Now the e was formless and empty,	824
	1:15	of the sky to give light on the e."	824
	1:17	of the sky to give light on the e,	824
	1:20	above the e across the expanse of the sky."	824
	1:22	and let the birds increase on the e."	824
	1:26	over the livestock, over all the e,	824
	1:28	fill the e and subdue it.	824
	1:29	of the whole e and every tree that has fruit	824
	1:30	to all the beasts of the e and all the birds of	824
	2: 1	Thus the heavens and the e were completed	824
	2: 4	This is the account of the heavens and the e	824
	2: 4	When the LORD God made the e and	824
	2: 5	of the field had yet appeared on the e	824
	2: 5	not sent rain on the e and there was no man	824
	2: 6	but streams came up from the e and watered	824
	4:12	You will be a restless wanderer on the e."	824
	4:14	I will be a restless wanderer on the e,	824
	6: 1	in number on the e and daughters were born	141
	6: 4	Nephilim were on the e in those days—	824
	6: 5	on the e had become,	824
	6: 6	that he had made man on the e,	824
	6: 7	whom I have created, from the face of the e	141
	6:11	Now the e was corrupt in God's sight	824
	6:12	God saw how corrupt the e had become,	824
	6:12	the people on e had corrupted their ways.	824
	6:13	e is filled with violence because of them.	824
	6:13	surely going to destroy both them and the e.	824
	6:17	the e to destroy all life under the heavens,	824
	6:17	Everything on e will perish.	824
	7: 3	to keep their various kinds alive throughout	
		the e.	824
	7: 4	now I will send rain on the e for forty days	824
	7: 4	of the e every living creature I have made."	141
	7: 6	when the floodwaters came on the e.	824
	7:10	the floodwaters came on the e.	824
	7:12	on the e forty days and forty nights.	824
	7:17	the flood kept coming on the e,	824
	7:17	the ark high above the e.	824
	7:18	and increased greatly on the e,	824
	7:19	They rose greatly on the e,	824
	7:21	that moved on the e perished—	824
	7:21	all the creatures that swarm over the e,	824
	7:23	on the face of the e was wiped out;	141
	7:23	the birds of the air were wiped from the e.	824
	7:24	The waters flooded the e for a hundred	824
	8: 1	and he sent a wind over the e,	824
	8: 3	The water receded steadily from the e.	824
	8: 7	until the water had dried up from the e.	824
	8: 9	over all the surface of the e;	824
	8:11	that the water had receded from the e.	824
	8:13	the water had dried up from the e.	824
	8:14	the second month the e was completely dry.	824
	8:17	so they can multiply on the e and be fruitful	824
	8:19	everything that moves on the e—	824
	8:22	"As long as the e endures,	824
	9: 1	and increase in number and fill the e.	824
	9: 2	upon all the beasts of the e and all the birds	824
	9: 7	multiply on the e and increase upon it."	824
	9:10	every living creature on e.	824
	9:11	be a flood to destroy the e."	824
	9:13	sign of the covenant between me and the e.	824

Ge 9:14 the e and the rainbow appears in the clouds, 824
9:16 of every kind on the e." 824
9:17 between me and all life on the e." 824
9:19 the people who were scattered over the e. 824
10:8 who grew to be a mighty warrior on the e. 824
10:25 because in his time the e was divided; 824
10:32 the nations spread out over the e after 824
11:4 be scattered over the face of the whole e." 824
11:8 from there over all the e, 824
11:9 over the face of the whole e. 824
12:3 and all peoples on e will be blessed 141
13:16 like the dust of the e, 824
14:19 Creator of heaven and e, 824
14:22 God Most High, Creator of heaven and e, 824
18:18 and all nations on e will be blessed 824
18:25 Will not the Judge of all the e do right?" 824
19:31 as is the custom all over the e. 824
22:18 through your offspring all nations on e will 824
24:3 the God of heaven and the God of e, 824
26:4 through your offspring all nations on e will 824
26:15 stopped up, filling them with e. 6760
28:12 in which he saw a stairway resting on the e, 824
28:14 be like the dust of the e, 824
28:14 on e will be blessed through you 141
45:7 of you to preserve for you a remnant on e 824
48:16 and may they increase greatly upon the e." 824
Ex 9:14 that there is no one like me in all the e. 824
9:15 that would have wiped you off the e. 824
9:16 be proclaimed in all the e. 824
9:29 you may know that the e is the LORD's. 824
15:12 and the e swallowed them. 824
19:5 Although the whole e is mine, 824
20:4 or on the e beneath or in the waters below. 824
20:11 the LORD made the heavens and the e, 824
20:24 " 'Make an altar of e for me and sacrifice 141
31:17 the LORD made the heavens and the e, 824
32:12 and to wipe them off the face of the e'? 141
33:16 the other people on the face of the e?" 141
Lev 17:13 the blood and cover it with e, 6760
Nu 12:3 on the face of the e.) 141
14:21 as the glory of the LORD fills the whole e, 824
16:30 e opens its mouth and swallows them, 141
16:32 e opened its mouth and swallowed them, 824
16:33 the e closed over them, 824
16:34 "The e is going to swallow us too!" 824
26:10 The e opened its mouth 824
Dt 3:24 in heaven or on e who can do the deeds 824
4:17 or like any animal on e or any bird that flies 824
4:26 and e as witnesses against you this day 824
4:32 from the day God created man on the e; 824
4:36 On e he showed you his great fire, 824
4:39 in heaven above and on the e below. 824
5:8 or on the e beneath or in the waters below. 824
7:6 of all the peoples on the face of the e to 141
10:14 the e and everything in it. 824
11:6 the e opened its mouth right in the middle 824
11:21 as the days that the heavens are above the e. 824
14:2 Out of all the peoples on the face of the e, 141
28:1 above all the nations on e. 824
28:10 the peoples on e will see that you are called 824
28:25 a thing of horror to all the kingdoms on e. 824
28:26 the birds of the air and the beasts of the e, 824
28:49 from the ends of the e, 824
28:64 from one end of the e to the other. 824
30:19 This day I call heaven and e as witnesses 824
31:28 in their hearing and call heaven and e 824
32:1 hear, O e, the words of my mouth. 824
32:22 It will devour the e and its harvests 824
33:16 with the best gifts of the e and its fullness 824
33:17 even those at the ends of the e. 824
Jos 2:11 in heaven above and on the e below. 824
3:11 the covenant of the Lord of all the e will go 824
3:13 the Lord of all the e— 824
4:24 that all the peoples of the e might know that 824
7:9 and wipe out our name from the e. 824
23:14 "Now I am about to go the way of all the e. 824
Jdg 5:4 the e shook, the heavens poured, 824
1Sa 2:8 the foundations of the e are the LORD's; 824
2:10 the LORD will judge the ends of the e. 824
17:46 the birds of the air and the beasts of the e, 824
20:15 of David's enemies from the face of the e." 141
20:31 As long as the son of Jesse lives on this e, 141
2Sa 4:11 from your hand and rid the e of you!" 824
7:9 like the names of the greatest men of the e. 824
7:23 the one nation on e that God went out 824
14:7 nor descendant on the face of the e." 141
22:8 "The e trembled and quaked, 824
22:16 the e laid bare at the rebuke of the LORD, 9315
22:43 I beat them as fine as the dust of the e; 824
23:4 after rain that brings the grass from the e.' 824
1Ki 2:2 "I am about to go the way of all the e," 824
8:23 like you in heaven above or on e below— 824
8:27 "But will God really dwell on e? 824
8:43 of the e may know your name and fear you, 824
8:60 the e may know that the LORD is God and 824
10:23 the other kings of the e. 824
13:34 and to its destruction from the face of the e. 141
2Ki 5:17 as much e as a pair of mules can carry, 141
19:15 over all the kingdoms of the e. 824
19:15 You have made heaven and e. 824
19:19 so that all kingdoms on e may know 824
1Ch 1:10 who grew to be a mighty warrior on e. 824
1:19 because in his time the e was divided; 824
16:14 his judgments are in all the e. 824
16:23 Sing to the LORD, all the e; 824
16:30 Tremble before him, all the e! 824
16:31 Let the heavens rejoice, let the e be glad; 824

1Ch 16:33 for he comes to judge the e. 824
17:8 like the names of the greatest men of the e. 824
17:21 the one nation on e whose God went out 824
21:16 the LORD standing between heaven and e, 824
22:8 because you have shed much blood on the e 824
29:11 for everything in heaven and e is yours. 824
29:15 Our days on e are like a shadow, 824
2Ch 1:9 as numerous as the dust of the e, 824
2:12 the God of Israel, who made heaven and e! 824
6:14 there is no God like you in heaven or on e— 824
6:18 "But will God really dwell on e with men? 824
6:33 of the e may know your name and fear you, 824
9:22 the other kings of the e. 824
9:23 the e sought audience with Solomon to hear 824
16:9 of the LORD range throughout the e 824
36:23 of the e and he has appointed me to build 824
Ezr 1:2 of the e and he has appointed me to build 824
5:11 the servants of the God of heaven and e, 10075
Ne 9:6 the e and all that is on it, 824
Job 1:7 through the e and going back and forth 824
1:8 There is no one on e like him; 824
2:2 through the e and going back and forth 824
2:3 There is no one on e like him; 824
3:14 with kings and counselors of the e, 824
5:10 He bestows rain on the e; 824
5:22 and need not fear the beasts of the e, 824
5:25 your descendants like the grass of the e. 824
7:1 "Does not man have hard service on e? 824
8:9 our days on e are but a shadow. 824
9:6 He shakes the e from its place 824
11:9 Their measure is longer than the e 824
12:8 or speak to the e, 824
12:24 the leaders of the e of their reason; 824
16:18 "O e, do not cover my blood; 824
18:4 is the e to be abandoned for your sake? 824
18:17 The memory of him perishes from the e; 824
19:25 and that in the end he will stand upon the e. 6760
20:4 ever since man was placed on the e, 824
20:27 the e will rise up against him. 824
26:7 he suspends the e over nothing. 824
28:2 Iron is taken from the e, 6760
28:5 The e, from which food comes, 824
28:24 the ends of the e and sees everything under 824
34:13 Who appointed him over the e? 824
35:11 the beasts of the e and makes us wiser than 824
37:3 and sends it to the ends of the e. 824
37:6 He says to the snow, 'Fall on the e,' 824
37:12 around over the face of the whole e 824+9315
37:13 or to water his e and show his love. 824
38:13 the beasts of the e be shaken the wicked out 824
38:14 The e takes shape like clay under a seal; NIH
38:18 the vast expanses of the e? 824
38:24 The east winds are scattered over the e? 824
38:33 you set up [God's] dominion over the e? 824
38:38 and the clods of e stick together? 8073
41:33 Nothing on e is his equal— 6760
Ps 2:2 The kings of the e take their stand and 824
2:8 the ends of the e your possession. 824
2:10 be warned, you rulers of the e. 824
8:1 how majestic is your name in all the e! 824
8:9 how majestic is your name in all the e! 824
10:18 who is of the e, may terrify no more. 824
18:7 The e trembled and quaked, 824
18:15 and the foundations of the e laid bare 9315
19:4 Their voice goes out into all the e, 824
21:10 from the e, their posterity 824
22:27 the ends of the e will remember and turn to 824
22:29 All the rich of the e will feast and worship; 824
24:1 The e is the LORD's, and everything in it, 824
33:5 the e is full of his unfailing love. 824
33:8 Let all the e fear the LORD; 824
33:14 from his dwelling place he watches all who
live on e— 824
34:16 to cut off the memory of them from the e. 824
46:2 e give way and the mountains fall into 824
46:6 he lifts his voice, the e melts. 824
46:8 the desolations he has brought on the e. 824
46:9 He makes wars cease to the ends of the e; 824
46:10 I will be exalted in the e." 824
47:2 the great King over all the e! 824
47:7 For God is the King of all the e; 824
47:9 for the kings of the e belong to God; 824
48:2 the joy of the whole e. 824
48:10 your praise reaches to the ends of the e; 824
50:1 the e from the rising of the sun to the place 824
50:4 He summons the heavens above, and the e, 824
57:5 let your glory be over all the e. 824
57:11 let your glory be over all the e. 824
58:2 and your hands mete out violence on the e. 824
58:11 surely there is a God who judges the e." 824
59:13 the ends of the e that God rules over Jacob. 824
61:2 From the ends of the e I call to you, 824
63:9 they will go down to the depths of the e. 824
65:5 the ends of the e and of the farthest seas, 824
66:1 Shout with joy to God, all the e! 824
66:4 All the e bows down to you; 824
67:2 that your ways may be known on e, 824
67:4 and guide the nations of the e. 824
67:7 and all the ends of the e will fear him. 824
68:8 the e shook, the heavens poured down rain, 824
68:32 Sing to God, O kingdoms of the e, 824
69:34 Let heaven and e praise him, 824
71:20 the depths of the e you will again bring me up. 824
72:6 like showers watering the e. 824
72:8 and from the River to the ends of the e. 824
72:19 may the whole e be filled with his glory. 824
73:9 and their tongues take possession of the e. 824

Ps 73:25 And e has nothing I desire besides you. 824
74:12 you bring salvation upon the e. 824
74:17 the boundaries of the e; 824
75:3 When the e and all its people quake, 824
75:8 and all the wicked of the e drink it down 824
76:12 he is feared by the kings of the e. 824
77:18 the e trembled and quaked. 824
78:69 like the e that he established forever. 824
79:2 flesh of your saints to the beasts of the e. 824
82:5 all the foundations of the e are shaken. 824
82:8 Rise up, O God, judge the e, 824
83:18 you alone are the Most High over all the e. 824
85:11 Faithfulness springs forth from the e, 824
89:11 heavens are yours, and yours also the e; 824
89:27 the most exalted of the kings of the e. 824
90:2 or you brought forth the e and the world, 824
94:2 Rise up, O Judge of the e; 824
95:4 In his hand are the depths of the e, 824
96:1 sing to the LORD, all the e. 824
96:9 tremble before him, all the e. 824
96:11 Let the heavens rejoice, let the e be glad; 824
96:13 for he comes, he comes to judge the e. 824
97:1 The LORD reigns, let the e be glad; 824
97:4 the e sees and trembles. 824
97:5 before the Lord of all the e. 824
97:9 are the Most High over all the e; 824
98:3 of the e have seen the salvation of our God. 824
98:4 Shout for joy to the LORD, all the e, 824
98:9 for he comes to judge the e. 824
99:1 between the cherubim, let the e shake. 824
100:1 Shout for joy to the LORD, all the e. 824
102:15 all the kings of the e will revere your glory. 824
102:19 from heaven he viewed the e, 824
102:25 the foundations of the e, 824
103:11 For as high as the heavens are above the e, 824
104:5 He set the e on its foundations; 824
104:9 never again will they cover the e. 824
104:13 the e is satisfied by the fruit of his work. 824
104:14 bringing forth food from the e: 824
104:24 the e is full of your creatures. 824
104:30 and you renew the face of the e. 141
104:32 he who looks at the e, 824
104:35 But may sinners vanish from the e and 824
105:7 his judgments are in all the e. 824
106:17 The e opened up and swallowed Dathan; 824
108:5 and let your glory be over all the e. 824
109:15 the memory of them from the e. 824
110:6 and crushing the rulers of the whole e. 824
113:6 down to look on the heavens and the e? 824
114:7 Tremble, O e, at the presence of the Lord, 824
115:15 the Maker of heaven and e. 824
115:16 but the e he has given to man. 824
119:19 I am a stranger on e; 824
119:64 The e is filled with your love, O LORD; 824
119:87 They almost wiped me from the e, 824
119:90 you established the e, and it endures. 824
119:119 the wicked of the e you discard like dross; 824
121:2 the Maker of heaven and e. 824
124:8 the Maker of heaven and e. 824
134:3 the Maker of heaven and e. 824
135:6 in the heavens and on the e, 824
135:7 from the ends of the e; 824
136:6 who spread out the e upon the waters, 824
138:4 May all the kings of the e praise you, 824
139:15 I was woven together in the depths of the e, 824
141:7 "As one plows and breaks up the e, 824
146:6 and e, the sea, and everything in them— 824
147:8 the e with rain and makes grass grow on 824
147:15 He sends his command to the e; 824
148:7 Praise the LORD from the e, 824
148:11 kings of the e and all nations, 824
148:11 you princes and all rulers on e, 824
148:13 his splendor is above the e and the heavens. 824
Pr 8:16 and all nobles who rule on e. 824
8:26 before he made the e or its fields or any of 824
8:29 he marked out the foundations of the e, 824
11:31 If the righteous receive their due on e, 824
17:24 a fool's eyes wander to the ends of the e. 824
25:3 As the heavens are high and the e is deep, 824
30:4 Who has established all the ends of the e? 824
30:14 with knives to devour the poor from the e, 824
30:21 "Under three things the e trembles, 824
30:24 "Four things on e are small, 824
Ecc 1:4 but the e remains forever. 824
3:21 of the animal goes down into the e?" 824
5:2 God is in heaven and you are on e, 824
7:20 a righteous man on e who does what is right 824
8:14 meaningless that occurs on e— 824
8:16 and to observe man's labor on e— 824
11:3 they pour rain upon the e. 824
SS 2:12 Flowers appear on the e; 824
Isa 1:2 Listen, O e! 824
2:19 when he rises to shake the e. 824
2:21 when he rises to shake the e. 824
5:26 he whistles for those at the ends of the e. 824
6:3 the whole e is full of his glory." 824
8:22 the e and see only distress and darkness 824
11:4 for the poor of the e. 824
11:4 He will strike the e with the rod 824
11:9 for the e will be full of the knowledge of 824
11:12 of Judah from the four quarters of the e. 824
13:13 the e will shake from its place at the wrath 824
14:12 You have been cast down to the e, 824
14:16 the e and made kingdoms tremble, 824
14:21 the land and cover the e with their cities. 9315
18:3 you who live on the e, 824
19:24 a blessing on the e. 824

Isa	23: 8	whose traders are renowned in the e?	824
	23: 9	to humble all who are renowned on the e.	824
	23:17	with all the kingdoms on the face of the e.	141
	24: 1	the LORD is going to lay waste the e	824
	24: 3	The e will be completely laid waste	824
	24: 4	The e dries up and withers,	824
	24: 4	the exalted of the e languish.	824
	24: 5	The e is defiled by its people;	824
	24: 6	Therefore a curse consumes the e;	824
	24:11	all gaiety is banished from the e.	824
	24:13	be on the e and among the nations,	824
	24:16	From the ends of the e we hear singing:	824
	24:17	O people of the e.	824
	24:18	the foundations of the e shake.	824
	24:19	The e is broken up,	824
	24:19	earth is broken up, the e is split asunder,	824
	24:19	the e is thoroughly shaken.	824
	24:20	The e reels like a drunkard,	824
	24:21	above and the kings on the e below.	141
	25: 8	the disgrace of his people from all the e.	824
	26: 9	When your judgments come upon the e,	824
	26:18	We have not brought salvation to the e;	824
	26:19	the e will give birth to her dead.	824
	26:21	of his dwelling to punish the people of the e	824
	26:21	The e will disclose the blood shed	824
	29: 4	Your voice will come ghostlike from the e;	824
	34: 1	Let the e hear, and all that is in it,	824
	37:16	over all the kingdoms of the e.	824
	37:16	You have made heaven and e,	824
	37:20	so that all kingdoms on e may know	824
	40:12	Who has held the dust of the e in a basket,	824
	40:21	not understood since the e was founded?	824
	40:22	He sits enthroned above the circle of the e,	824
	40:28	the Creator of the ends of the e.	824
	41: 5	the ends of the e tremble.	824
	41: 9	I took you from the ends of the e,	824
	42: 4	till he establishes justice on e.	824
	42: 5	who spread out the e and all that comes out	824
	42:10	his praise from the ends of the e,	824
	43: 6	and my daughters from the ends of the e—	824
	44:23	shout aloud, O e beneath.	824
	44:24	who spread out the e by myself,	824
	45: 8	Let the e open wide, let salvation spring up,	824
	45:12	It is I who made the e and created mankind	824
	45:18	he who fashioned and made the e,	824
	45:22	all you ends of the e;	824
	48:13	My own hand laid the foundations of the e,	824
	48:20	Send it out to the ends of the e;	824
	49: 6	to the ends of the e."	824
	49:13	rejoice, O e; burst into song, O mountains!	824
	51: 6	look at the e beneath;	824
	51: 6	like smoke, the e will wear out like	824
	51:13	and laid the foundations of the e,	824
	51:16	who laid the foundations of the e,	824
	52:10	of the e will see the salvation of our God.	824
	54: 5	he is called the God of all the e.	824
	54: 9	of Noah would never again cover the e.	824
	55: 9	"As the heavens are higher than the e,	824
	55:10	without watering the e and making it bud	824
	60: 2	the e and thick darkness is over the peoples,	824
	62: 7	and makes her the praise of the e.	824
	62:11	to the ends of the e:	824
	65:17	I will create new heavens and a new e.	824
	66: 1	and the e is my footstool.	824
	66:22	and the new e that I make will endure	824
Jer	4:23	I looked at the e,	824
	4:28	Therefore the e will mourn and the heavens	824
	6:19	O e: I am bringing disaster on	824
	6:22	up from the ends of the e.	824
	7:33	the birds of the air and the beasts of the e,	824
	9:24	justice and righteousness on e,	824
	10:10	When he is angry, the e trembles;	824
	10:11	who did not make the heavens and the e,	10077
	10:11	from the e and from under the heavens.' "	10075
	10:12	But God made the e by his power;	824
	10:13	he makes clouds rise from the ends of the e.	824
	15: 3	of the air and the beasts of the e to devour	824
	15: 4	of the e because of what Manasseh son	824
	16: 4	the birds of the air and the beasts of the e."	824
	16:19	the nations will come from the ends of the e	824
	19: 7	the birds of the air and the beasts of the e.	824
	23:24	"Do not I fill heaven and e?"	824
	24: 9	and an offense to all the kingdoms of the e,	824
	25:26	all the kingdoms on the face of the e.	141
	25:29	down a sword upon all who live on the e,	824
	25:30	shout against all who live on the e.	824
	25:31	tumult will resound to the ends of the e,	824
	25:32	from the ends of the e."	824
	25:33	from one end of the e to the other.	824
	26: 6	of cursing among all the nations of the e.' "	824
	27: 5	the e and its people and the animals that are	824
	28:16	about to remove you from the face of the e.	141
	29:18	of the e and an object of cursing and horror,	824
	31: 8	and gather them from the ends of the e—	824
	31:22	The LORD will create a new thing on e—	824
	31:37	the e below be searched out will I reject all	824
	32:17	the heavens and the e by your great power	824
	33: 2	he who made the e,	2023S
	33: 9	and honor before all nations on e that hear	824
	33:25	and the fixed laws of heaven and e,	824
	34:17	to all the kingdoms of the e.	824
	34:20	the birds of the air and the beasts of the e.	824
	44: 8	and reproach among all the nations on e.	824
	46: 8	She says, 'I will rise and cover the e;	824
	46:12	your cries will fill the e.	824
	49:21	At the sound of their fall the e will tremble;	824
	50:23	and shattered is the hammer of the whole e!	824

Jer	50:41	up from the ends of the e.	824
	50:46	of Babylon's capture the e will tremble;	824
	51: 7	she made the whole e drunk.	824
	51:15	"He made the e by his power;	824
	51:16	he makes clouds rise from the ends of the e.	824
	51:25	you who destroy the whole e,"	824
	51:41	the boast of the whole e seized!	824
	51:48	and e and all that is in them will shout	824
	51:49	in all the e have fallen because of Babylon.	824
La	2: 1	the splendor of Israel from heaven to e;	824
	2:15	the joy of the whole e?"	824
	4:12	The kings of the e did not believe,	824
Eze	7:21	and as loot to the wicked of the e,	824
	8: 3	up between e and heaven and in visions	824
	26:20	I will make you dwell in the e below,	824
	27:33	the kings of the e.	824
	28:17	So I threw you to the e;	824
	29: 5	I will give you as food to the beasts of the e	824
	31:12	of the e came out from under its shade	824
	31:14	for the e below, among mortal men,	824
	31:16	were consoled in the e below.	824
	31:18	down with the trees of Eden to the e below;	824
	32: 4	the beasts of the e gorge themselves on you.	824
	32:18	to the e below both her and the daughters	824
	32:24	down uncircumcised to the e below.	824
	34: 6	They were scattered over the whole e,	824
	35:14	whole e rejoices, I will make you desolate.	824
	38:20	the people on the face of the e will tremble	141
	39:18	the e as if they were rams and lambs, goats	824
Da	2:10	a man on e who can do what the king asks!	10309
	2:35	a huge mountain and filled the whole e.	10075
	2:39	one of bronze, will rule over the whole e.	10075
	4:11	it was visible to the ends of the e.	10075
	4:15	with the animals among the plants of the e.	10075
	4:20	visible to the whole e,	10075
	4:22	to distant parts of the e.	10075
	4:35	the peoples of the e are regarded as nothing.	10075
	4:35	of heaven and the peoples of the e.	10075
	6:27	and wonders in the heavens and on the e.	10075
	7:17	that will rise from the e.	10075
	7:23	a fourth kingdom that will appear on e.	10075
	7:23	and will devour the whole e,	10075
	8: 5	the whole e without touching the ground.	824
	8:10	the starry host down to the e and trampled	824
	12: 2	in the dust of the e will awake:	141
Hos	2:21	and they will respond to the e;	824
	2:22	and the e will respond to the grain,	824
	6: 3	like the spring rains that water the e."	824
Joel	2:10	Before them the e shakes, the sky trembles,	824
	2:30	in the heavens and on the e,	824
	3:16	the e and the sky will tremble.	824
Am	3: 2	of all the families of the e;	141
	3: 5	from the e when there is nothing to catch?	141
	4:13	and treads the high places of the e—	824
	8: 9	at noon and darken the e in broad daylight.	824
	9: 5	who touches the e and it melts,	824
	9: 6	on the e, who calls for the waters of the sea	824
	9: 8	I will destroy it from the face of the e—	141
Jnh	2: 6	the e beneath barred me in forever.	824
Mic	1: 2	all of you, listen, O e and all who are in it,	824
	1: 3	down and treads the high places of the e.	824
	4:13	their wealth to the Lord of all the e.	824
	5: 4	his greatness will reach to the ends of the e.	824
	6: 2	listen, you everlasting foundations of the e.	824
	7:13	The e will become desolate because	824
Na	1: 5	The e trembles at his presence,	824
	2:13	I will leave you no prey on the e.	824
Hab	1: 6	across the whole e to seize dwelling places	824
	2:14	For the e will be filled with the knowledge	824
	2:20	let all the e be silent before him."	824
	3: 3	the heavens and his praise filled the e.	824
	3: 6	He stood, and shook the e;	824
	3: 9	Selah You split the e with rivers;	824
	3:12	the e and in anger you threshed the nations.	824
Zep	1: 2	from the face of the e,"	141
	1: 3	when I cut off man from the face of the e,"	141
	1:18	a sudden end of all who live in the e."	824
	3:20	and praise among all the peoples of the e	824
Hag	1:10	and the e its crops.	824
	2: 6	the heavens and the e,	824
	2:21	that I will shake the heavens and the e.	824
Zec	1:10	The LORD has sent to go throughout the e."	824
	1:11	throughout the e and found the whole world	824
	4:10	which range throughout the e.)"	824
	4:14	to serve the Lord of all the e."	824
	5: 9	up the basket between heaven and e.	824
	6: 7	they were straining to go throughout the e,	824
	6: 7	And he said, "Go throughout the e!"	824
	6: 7	So they went throughout the e.	824
	9:10	and from the River to the ends of the e.	824
	12: 1	who lays the foundation of the e,	824
	12: 3	the nations of the e are gathered against her,	824
	14: 9	The LORD will be king over the whole e.	824
	14:17	the e do not go up to Jerusalem to worship	824
Mt	5: 5	for they will inherit the e.	1178
	5:13	"You are the salt of the e.	1178
	5:18	until heaven and e disappear,	1178
	5:35	or by the e, for it is his footstool;	1178
	6:10	your will be done on e as it is in heaven.	1178
	6:19	not store up for yourselves treasures on e,	1178
	9: 6	Son of Man has authority on e to forgive sins...."	1178
	10:34	that I have come to bring peace to the e.	1178
	11:25	"I praise you, Father, Lord of heaven and e,	1178
	12:40	and three nights in the heart of the e.	1178
	12:42	of the e to listen to Solomon's wisdom,	1178
	16:19	whatever you bind on e will be bound	1178

Mt	16:19	in heaven, and whatever you loose on e will	1178
	17:25	the kings of the e collect duty and taxes—	1178
	18:18	whatever you bind on e will be bound	1178
	18:18	and whatever you loose on e will be loosed	1178
	18:19	of you on e agree about anything you ask	1178
	23: 9	And do not call anyone on e 'father,'	1178
	23:35	the righteous blood that has been shed on e,	1178
	24:30	and all the nations of the e will mourn.	1178
	24:35	Heaven and e will pass away,	1178
	27:51	The e shook and the rocks split.	1178
	28:18	in heaven and on e has been given to me.	1178
Mk	2:10	Son of Man has authority on e to forgive sins...."	1178
	13:27	the ends of the e to the ends of the heavens.	1178
	13:31	Heaven and e will pass away,	1178
Lk	2:14	and on e peace to men	1178
	5:24	Son of Man has authority on e to forgive sins...."	1178
	10:21	Father, Lord of heaven and e,	1178
	11:31	of the e to listen to Solomon's wisdom,	1178
	12:49	"I have come to bring fire on the e,	1178
	12:51	Do you think I came to bring peace on e?	1178
	12:56	how to interpret the appearance of the e	1178
	16:17	and e to disappear than for the least stroke	1178
	18: 8	will he find faith on the e?"	1178
	21:25	On the e, nations will be in anguish	1178
	21:33	Heaven and e will pass away,	1178
	21:35	on the face of the whole e.	1178
Jn	3:31	one who is from the e belongs to the earth,	1178
	3:31	one who is from the earth belongs to the e,	1178
	3:31	and speaks as one from the e.	1178
	12:32	But I, when I am lifted up from the e,	1178
	17: 4	on e by completing the work you gave me	1178
Ac	1: 8	and to the ends of the e."	1178
	2:19	the heaven above and signs on the e below,	1178
	3:25	on e will be blessed.'	1178
	4:24	"you made the heaven and the e and	1178
	4:26	The kings of the e take their stand and	1178
	7:49	and the e is my footstool.	1178
	8:33	For his life was taken from the e."	1178
	10:11	like a large sheet being let down to e	1178
	10:12	as well as reptiles of the e and birds of	1178
	11: 6	and saw four-footed animals of the e,	1178
	13:47	to the ends of the e.' "	1178
	14:15	and e and sea and everything in them.	1178
	17:24	the Lord of heaven and e and does not live	1178
	17:26	that they should inhabit the whole e;	1178
	22:22	"Rid the e of him!	1178
Ro	9:17	my name might be proclaimed in all the e."	1178
	9:28	the Lord will carry out his sentence on e	1178
	10:18	"Their voice has gone out into all the e,	1178
1Co	4:13	we have become the scum of the e,	3180
	8: 5	or on e (as indeed there are many "gods"	1178
	10:26	"The e is the Lord's, and everything in it."	1178
	15:47	The first man was of the dust of the e,	1178
	15:48	so are those who are of the e;	5954
Eph	1:10	in heaven and on e together under one head,	1178
	3:15	in heaven and on e derives its name.	1178
	6: 3	and that you may enjoy long life on the e."	1178
Php	2:10	in heaven and on e and under the earth,	2103
	2:10	in heaven and on earth and **under the e,**	2973
Col	1:16	things in heaven and on e,	1178
	1:20	whether things on e or things in heaven,	1178
Heb	1:10	O Lord, you laid the foundations of the e,	1178
	5: 7	During the days of Jesus' **life on e,**	4922
	8: 4	If he were on e, he would not be a priest,	1178
	11:13	that they were aliens and strangers on e,	1178
	12:25	they refused him who warned them on e,	1178
	12:26	At that time his voice shook the e,	1178
	12:26	"Once more I will shake not only the e but	1178
Jas	5: 5	on e in luxury and self-indulgence.	1178
	5:12	not by heaven or by e or by anything else.	1178
	5:18	and the e produced its crops.	1178
2Pe	3: 5	the e was formed out of water and by water.	1178
	3: 7	the present heavens and e are reserved	1178
	3:10	the e and everything in it will be laid bare.	1178
	3:13	to a new heaven and a new e,	1178
Rev	1: 5	and the ruler of the kings of the e.	1178
	1: 7	the peoples of the e will mourn because	1178
	3:10	to test those who live on the e.	1178
	5: 3	on e or under the earth could open the scroll	1178
	5: 3	on earth or under the e could open the scroll	1178
	5: 6	of God sent out into all the e.	1178
	5:10	and they will reign on the e."	1178
	5:13	and on e and under the earth and on the sea,	1178
	5:13	and on earth and under the e and on the sea,	1178
	6: 4	the e and to make men slay each other.	1178
	6: 8	over a fourth of the e to kill by sword,	1178
	6: 8	and by the wild beasts of the e.	1178
	6:10	until you judge the inhabitants of the e	1178
	6:13	and the stars in the sky fell to e,	1178
	6:15	Then the kings of the e, the princes,	1178
	7: 1	at the four corners of the e,	1178
	7: 1	the four winds of the e to prevent any wind	1178
	8: 5	and hurled it on the e;	1178
	8: 7	and it was hurled down upon the e.	1178
	8: 7	A third of the e was burned up,	1178
	8:13	Woe to the inhabitants of the e,	1178
	9: 1	a star that had fallen from the sky to the e.	1178
	9: 3	down upon the e and were given power like	1178
	9: 3	like that of scorpions of the e.	1178
	9: 4	not to harm the grass of the e or any plant	1178
	10: 6	the e and all that is in it,	1178
	11: 4	that stand before the Lord of the e.	1178
	11: 6	and to strike the e with every kind of plague	1178
	11:10	the e will gloat over them and will celebrate	1178
	11:10	had tormented those who live on the e.	1178

Rev	11:18	and for destroying those who destroy the e."	1178
	12: 4	of the sky and flung them to the e.	1178
	12: 9	He was hurled to the e,	1178
	12:12	But woe to the e and the sea,	1178
	12:13	that he had been hurled to the e,	1178
	12:16	But the e helped the woman	1178
	13: 8	All inhabitants of the e will worship	1178
	13:11	I saw another beast, coming out of the e.	1178
	13:12	and made the e and its inhabitants worship	1178
	13:13	to come down from heaven to e in full view	1178
	13:14	he deceived the inhabitants of the e.	1178
	14: 3	who had been redeemed from the e.	1178
	14: 6	to proclaim to those who live on the e—	1178
	14: 7	Worship him who made the heavens, the e,	1178
	14:15	for the harvest of the e is ripe."	1178
	14:16	on the cloud swung his sickle over the e,	1178
	14:16	and the e was harvested.	1178
	14:19	The angel swung his sickle on the e,	1178
	16: 1	the seven bowls of God's wrath on the e."	1178
	16:18	since man has been on e,	1178
	17: 2	the kings of the e committed adultery and	1178
	17: 2	the inhabitants of the e were intoxicated	1178
	17: 5	THE MOTHER OF PROSTITUTES AND OF THE ABOMINATIONS OF THE E.	1178
	17: 8	of the e whose names have not been written	1178
	17:18	that rules over the kings of the e."	1178
	18: 1	and the e was illuminated by his splendor.	1178
	18: 3	The kings of the e committed adultery	1178
	18: 3	and the merchants of the e grew rich	1178
	18: 9	the kings of the e who committed adultery	1178
	18:11	of the e will weep and mourn over her	1178
	18:24	and of all who have been killed on the e."	1178
	19: 2	the great prostitute who corrupted the e	1178
	19:19	Then I saw the beast and the kings of the e—	1178
	20: 8	the nations in the four corners of the e—	1178
	20: 9	across the breadth of the e and surrounded	1178
	20:11	E and sky fled from his presence,	1178
	21: 1	Then I saw a new heaven and a new e,	1178
	21: 1	first heaven and the first e had passed away,	1178
	21:24	the kings of the e will bring their splendor	1178

EARTH'S (6) [EARTH]

Ge	27:28	of heaven's dew and of e richness—	824
	27:39	be away from the e richness,	824
Job	38: 4	were you when I laid the e foundation?	824
Pr	3:19	By wisdom the LORD laid the e foundations,	824
Isa	24: 1	Therefore e inhabitants are burned up,	824
Rev	14:18	the clusters of grapes from the e vine,	1178

EARTHEN (1) [EARTH, EARTHENWARE]

| Hab | 1:10 | they build e ramps and capture them. | 6760 |

EARTHENWARE (1) [EARTHEN]

| Pr | 26:23 | over e are fervent lips with an evil heart. | 3084 |

EARTHLY (15) [EARTH]

Jn	3:12	I have spoken to you of e things and you do	2103
1Co	15:40	also heavenly bodies and there are e bodies;	2103
	15:40	and the splendor of the e bodies is another.	2103
	15:48	As was the e man,	5954
	15:49	as we have borne the likeness of the e man,	5954
2Co	5: 1	that if the e tent we live in is destroyed,	2103
Eph	4: 9	also descended to the lower, e regions?	1178
	6: 5	Slaves, obey your e masters with respect and fear,	2848+4922
Php	3:19	Their mind is on e things.	2103
Col	3: 2	not on e things.	1178
	3: 5	whatever belongs to your e nature;	1178
	3:22	Slaves, obey your e masters in everything;	2848+4922
Heb	9: 1	for worship and also an e sanctuary.	3176
Jas	3:15	not come down from heaven but is e,	2103
1Pe	4: 2	the rest of his e life for evil human desires,	4922

EARTHQUAKE (17) [QUAKE]

1Ki	19:11	After the wind there was an e,	8323
	19:11	but the LORD was not in the e.	8323
	19:12	After the e came a fire,	8323
Isa	29: 6	with thunder and e and great noise,	8323
Eze	38:19	that time there shall be a great e in the land	8323
Am	1: 1	concerning Israel two years before the e,	8323
Zec	14: 5	the e in the days of Uzziah king of Judah.	8323
Mt	27:54	the e and all that had happened,	4939
	28: 2	There was a violent e,	4939
Ac	16:26	Suddenly there was such a violent e that	4939
Rev	6:12	There was a great e.	4939
	8: 5	rumblings, flashes of lightning and an e.	4939
	11:13	a severe e and a tenth of the city collapsed.	4939
	11:13	Seven thousand people were killed in the e,	4939
	11:19	peals of thunder, an e and a great hailstorm.	4939
	16:18	rumblings, peals of thunder and a severe e.	4939
	16:18	No e like it has ever occurred	NIG

EARTHQUAKES (3) [QUAKE]

Mt	24: 7	be famines and e in various places.	4939
Mk	13: 8	There will be e in various places,	4939
Lk	21:11	There will be great e,	4939

EASE (9) [EASIER, EASILY, EASY]

Job	3:18	Captives also enjoy their e;	8631
	7:13	and my couch will e my complaint,	5951
	12: 5	Men at e have contempt for misfortune as	8633
	21:23	completely secure and at e,	8929
Pr	1:33	to me will live in safety and be at e,	8631
Jer	12: 1	Why do all the faithless live at e?	8922
	49:31	"Arise and attack a nation at e,	8929
La	1: 5	her enemies are at e.	8922
Jnh	4: 6	for his head to e his discomfort,	5911

EASIER (7) [EASE]

Mt	9: 5	Which is e: to say, 'Your sins are forgiven,'	2324
	19:24	it is e for a camel to go through the eye of	2324
Mk	2: 9	Which is e: to say to the paralytic,	2324
	10:25	It is e for a camel to go through the eye of	2324
Lk	5:23	Which is e: to say, 'Your sins are forgiven,'	2324
	16:17	It is e for heaven and earth to disappear	2324
	18:25	it is e for a camel to go through the eye of	2324

EASILY (10) [EASE]

Jdg	16: 9	he snapped the thongs as e as a piece	889+3869
	20:43	chased them and e overran them in	4957
Pr	14: 6	but knowledge comes e to the discerning.	7837
	14: 6	do not associate with one e angered,	2779
Hos	7:11	e deceived and senseless—	7331
Ac	24:11	You can e verify that	NIG
1Co	13: 5	it is not self-seeking, it is not e angered,	4236
2Co	11: 4	you put up with it e enough.	2822
2Th	2: 2	not to become e unsettled or alarmed	5441
Heb	12: 1	and the sin that so e entangles,	2342

EAST (188) [EASTERN, EASTWARD, NORTHEASTER, SOUTHEAST]

Ge	2: 8	LORD God had planted a garden in the e,	7710
	2:14	it runs along the e side of Asshur.	7713
	3:24	the e side of the Garden of Eden cherubim	7710
	4:16	and lived in the land of Nod, e of Eden.	7713
	12: 8	there he went on toward the hills e	4946+7710
	12: 8	with Bethel on the west and Ai on the e.	7710
	13:11	of the Jordan and set out toward the e.	7710
	13:14	and look north and south, e and west.	2025+7711
	25: 6	from his son Isaac to the land of the e.	7710
	28:14	you will spread out to the west and to the e,	7711
	41: 6	thin and scorched by the e wind.	7708
	41:23	and thin and scorched by the e wind.	7708
	41:27	of grain scorched by the e wind:	7708
Ex	10:13	an e wind blow across the land all that day	7708
	14:21	a strong e wind and turned it into dry land.	7708
	27:13	On the e end, toward the sunrise,	2025+7711
	38:13	The e end, toward the sunrise,	2025+7711
Lev	1:16	with its contents and throw it to the e side	7711
Nu	2: 3	On the e, toward the sunrise,	7711
	3:38	and his sons were to camp to the e of	7711
	10: 5	the tribes camping on the e are to set out.	7711
	32:19	to us on the e side of the Jordan."	4667
	33: 7	to the e of Baal Zephon,	7156
	34: 3	On the e, your southern boundary will start	7711
	34:11	to Riblah on the e side of Ain and continue	7710
	34:11	the slopes e of the Sea of Kinnereth.	2025+7711
	34:15	on the e side of the Jordan of Jericho,	7711
	35: 5	three thousand feet on the e side,	7711
Dt	1: 1	all Israel in the desert e of the Jordan—	928+6298
	1: 5	E of the Jordan in the territory of Moab,	928+6298
	3: 8	Amorites the territory e of the Jordan,	928+6298
	3:27	look west and north and south and e.	2025+4667
	4:41	Moses set aside three cities e of the Jordan,	928+2025+4667+6298+9087
	4:46	were in the valley near Beth Peor e of	928+6298
	4:47	the two Amorite kings e of the Jordan.	928+4667+6298+9087
	4:49	and included all the Arabah e of the Jordan,	2025+4667+6298
Jos	1:14	that Moses gave you e of the Jordan,	928+6298
	1:15	the servant of the LORD gave you e of	928+6298
	2:10	the two kings of the Amorites e of	928+6298
	7: 2	which is near Beth Aven to the e of Bethel,	7710
	9:10	to the two kings of the Amorites e of	928+6298
	11: 3	to the Canaanites in the e and west;	4667
	11: 8	and to the Valley of Mizpah on the e,	4667
	12: 1	over e of the Jordan,	2021+2025+4667+9087
	13: 3	from the Shihor River on the e of Egypt to	7156
	13: 5	and all Lebanon to the e,	2021+4667+9087
	13: 8	the inheritance that Moses had given them e of the Jordan,	928+2025+4667+6298
	13:27	of Sihon king of Heshbon (the e side of	4667
	13:32	in the plains of Moab across the Jordan e of Jericho,	2025+4667
	14: 3	the two-and-a-half tribes their inheritance e of the Jordan	4946+6298
	16: 1	e of the waters of Jericho,	2025+4667
	16: 5	in the e to Upper Beth Horon.	4667
	16: 6	passing by it to Janoah on the e.	4667
	17: 5	of land besides Gilead and Bashan e of	4946+6298
	17: 7	Asher to Micmethath e of Shechem.	6584+7156
	17:10	on the north and Issachar on the e.	4667
	18: 7	on the e side of the Jordan.	4667
	19:12	It turned e from Sarid toward the sunrise to	2025+7711
	19:27	turned e toward Beth Dagon,	2021+4667+9087
	19:34	and the Jordan on the e.	4667+9087
	20: 8	On the e side of the Jordan	2025+4667
	24: 8	the Amorites who lived e of the Jordan.	928+6298
Jdg	11:18	the route of the nomads e of Nobah	4946+7769
	10: 8	the Israelites on the e side of the Jordan	6298
	20:43	in the vicinity of Gibeah on the e.	4667+9087
	21:19	and e of the road that goes from Bethel	2021+2025+4667+9087
1Sa	13: 5	e of Beth Aven.	7713
	15: 7	to the e of Egypt.	7156
1Ki	4:30	the wisdom of all the men of the E,	7710
	7:25	three facing south and three facing e.	2025+4667
	11: 7	On a hill e of Jerusalem,	6584+7156
	17: 3	e of the Jordan.	6584+7156
	17: 5	e of the Jordan, and stayed there.	6584+7156
2Ki	10:33	e of the Jordan in all the land of Gilead	2021+4667+9087
	13:17	"Open the e window," he said,	2025+7711
	23:13	high places that were e of Jerusalem	6584+7156
1Ch	4:39	the outskirts of Gedor to the e of the valley	4667
	5: 9	the e they occupied the land up to the edge	4667
	5:10	the Hagrites throughout the entire region e	4667
	6:78	the Jordan e of Jericho they received Bezer	4667
	7:28	Naaran to the e,	4667
	9:18	being stationed at the King's Gate on the e,	4667
	9:24	e, west, north and south.	4667
	12:15	to the e and to the west.	4667
	12:37	from e of the Jordan, men of Reuben, Gad	6298
	26:14	The lot for the E Gate fell to Shelemiah.	4667
	26:17	There were six Levites a day on the e,	4667
2Ch	4: 4	three facing south and three facing e.	2025+4667
	5:12	stood on the e side of the altar.	4667
	29: 4	assembled them in the square on the e side	4667
	31:14	keeper of the E Gate,	2025+4667
Ne	3:26	toward the e and the projecting tower.	4667
	3:29	the guard at the E Gate, made repairs.	4667
	12:37	of David to the Water Gate on the e.	4667
Job	1: 3	among all the people of the E.	7710
	15: 2	or fill his belly with the hot e wind?	7708
	18:20	men of the e are seized with horror.	7719
	23: 8	"But if I go to the e, he is not there;	7710
	27:21	The e wind carries him off, and he is gone;	7708
	38:24	or the place where the e winds are scattered	7708
Ps	48: 7	of Tarshish shattered by an e wind.	7708
	75: 6	No one from the e or the west or from	4604
	78:26	the e wind from the heavens and led forth	7708
	103:12	as far as the e is from the west,	4667
	107: 3	from e and west, from north and south.	4667
Isa	2: 6	They are full of superstitions from the E;	7710
	9:12	Arameans from the e and Philistines from	7710
	11:14	the people to the e.	7710
	24:15	Therefore in the e give glory to the LORD;	241
	27: 8	as on a day the e wind blows.	7708
	41: 2	"Who has stirred up one from the e,	4667
	43: 5	from the e and gather you from the west.	4667
	46:11	From the e I summon a bird of prey;	4667
Jer	18:17	Like a wind from the e,	7708
	31:40	the e as far as the corner of the Horse Gate,	4667
	49:28	and destroy the people of the E.	7710
Eze	8:16	of the LORD and their faces toward the e,	7711
	8:16	they were bowing down to the sun in the e.	7711
	10:19	They stopped at the entrance to the e gate	7719
	11: 1	of the house of the LORD that faces e.	2025+7708
	11:23	and stopped above the mountain e	4946+7710
	17:10	when the e wind strikes it—	7708
	19:12	The e wind made it shrivel,	7708
	25: 4	to the people of the E as a possession.	7710
	25:10	with the Ammonites to the people of the E	7710
	27:26	But the e wind will break you to pieces in	7708
	39:11	in the valley of those who travel e toward	7713
	40: 6	Then he went to the gate facing e	2025+7708
	40:10	the e gate were three alcoves on each side;	7708
	40:19	a hundred cubits on the e side as well as on	7708
	40:22	as those of the gate facing e.	7708
	40:23	just as there was on the e.	7708
	40:32	on the e side, and he measured the gateway,	7708
	41:14	The width of the temple courtyard on the e,	7708
	42: 9	on the e side as one enters them from	7708
	42:15	the e gate and measured the area all around;	7708
	42:16	the e side with the measuring rod;	7708
	43: 1	the man brought me to the gate facing e,	7708
	43: 2	of the God of Israel coming from the e.	7708
	43: 4	the temple through the gate facing e.	7708
	43:17	The steps of the altar face e."	7708
	44: 1	the one facing e, and it was shut.	7708
	45: 7	and eastward from the e side,	2025+7711
	46: 1	of the inner court facing e is to be shut on	7708
	46:12	the gate facing e is to be opened for him.	7708
	47: 1	the threshold of the temple toward the e (for	7708
	47: 1	toward the east (for the temple faced e).	7708
	47: 2	the outside to the outer gate facing e,	7708
	47:18	"On the e side the boundary will run	7708
	47:18	This will be the e boundary.	2025+7708
	48: 1	be part of its border from the e side to	7708
	48: 2	it will border the territory of Dan from e	7708
	48: 3	border the territory of Asher from e	2025+7708
	48: 4	territory of Naphtali from e to west.	2025+7708
	48: 5	territory of Manasseh from e to west.	2025+7708
	48: 6	the territory of Ephraim from e to west.	7708
	48: 7	it will border the territory of Reuben from e	7708
	48: 7	the territory of Judah from e to west will be	7708
	48: 8	its length from e to west will equal	2025+7708
	48:10	10,000 cubits wide on the e side and	7708
	48:16	the south side 4,500 cubits, the e side 4,500	7708
	48:17	250 cubits on the e,	7708
	48:18	cubits on the e side and 10,000	7708
	48:23	from the e side to the west side.	2025+7708
	48:24	territory of Benjamin from e to west.	2025+7708
	48:25	border the territory of Simeon from e	2025+7708
	48:26	territory of Issachar from e to west.	2025+7708
	48:27	territory of Zebulun from e to west.	2025+7708
	48:32	"On the e side, which is 4,500 cubits	2025+7708
Da	8: 9	and to the e and toward the Beautiful Land.	4667
	11:44	from the e and the north will alarm him,	4667
Hos	12: 1	he pursues the e wind all day	7708

Hos	13:15	An e wind from the LORD will come, 7708
Am	8:12	from sea to sea and wander from north to e, 4667
Jnh	4: 5	Jonah went out and sat down at a place e of 7710
	4: 8	God provided a scorching e wind, 7708
Zec	8: 7	from the countries of the e and the west. 4667
	14: 4	Mount of Olives, e of Jerusalem 6584+7156+7710
	14: 4	of Olives will be split in two from e 4667
Mt	2: 1	Magi from the e came to Jerusalem 424
	2: 2	in the e and have come to worship him." 424
	2: 9	in the e went ahead of them until it stopped 424
	8:11	I say to you that many will come from the e 424
	24:27	as lightning that comes from the e is visible 424
Lk	13:29	from e and west and north and south, 424
Rev	7: 2	another angel coming up from the e, 424+2463
	16:12	the way for the kings from the E. 424+2463
	21:13	There were three gates on the e, 424

EASTER (KJV) PASSOVER

EASTERN (20) [EAST]

Ge	10:30	in the e hill country. 7710
	29: 1	and came to the land of the e peoples. 7710
Nu	23: 7	the king of Moab from the e mountains. 7710
	34:10	" 'For your e boundary, 2025+7711
Jos	4:19	and camped at Gilgal on the e border 4667
	12: 1	including all the e side of the Arabah; 2025+4667
	12: 3	e Arabah from the Sea of Kinnereth to 2025+4667
	15: 5	The e boundary is the Salt Sea as far 2025+7711
	18:20	the boundary on the e side. 2025+7711
Jdg	6: 3	and other e peoples invaded the country. 7710
	6:33	and other e peoples joined forces 7710
	7:12	the other e peoples had settled in the valley, 7710
	8:10	that were left of the armies of the e peoples; 7710
	11:18	the e side of the country of Moab, 4667+9087
Eze	45: 7	the western to the e border parallel to 2025+7708
	47: 8	toward the e region and goes down into 7716
	47:18	to the e sea and as far as Tamar. 7719
	48:21	cubits of the sacred portion to the e border, NIH
Joel	2:20	with its front columns going into the e sea 7719
Zec	14: 8	half to the e sea and half to the western sea, 7719

EASTWARD (8) [EAST]

Ge	11: 2	As men moved e, 4946+7710
Jos	16: 6	north it curved e to Taanath Shiloh, 2025+4667
	19:13	Then it continued e to Gath Hepher 2025+2025+4667+7711
1Ki	17: 3	turn e and hide in the Kerith Ravine, 2025+7711
Eze	42:12	to the corresponding wall extending e, 7708
	45: 7	the west side and e from the east side, 2025+7708
	47: 3	As the man went e with a measuring line 7708
	48:21	It will extend e from the 25,000 2025+7708

EASY (5) [EASE]

Dt	1:41	thinking it e to go up into the hill country. 2103
2Ki	3:18	an e thing in the eyes of the LORD; 7837
	5:20	"My master was too e on Naaman, 3104
Mt	11:30	For my yoke is e and my burden is light." 5982
Lk	12:19	Take life e; eat, drink and be merry.' ' 399

EAT (514) [ATE, EATEN, EATER, EATING, EATS]

Ge	2:16	"You are free to e from any tree in 430+430
	2:17	not e from the tree of the knowledge 430
	2:17	for when you e of it you will surely die." 430
	3: 1	not e from any tree in the garden'?" 430
	3: 2	"We may e fruit from the trees in the garden, 430
	3: 3	not e fruit from the tree that is in the middle 430
	3: 5	when you e of it your eyes will be opened, 430
	3:11	that I commanded you not to e from?" 430
	3:14	on your belly and you will e dust all 430
	3:17	'You must not e of it,' 430
	3:17	through painful toil you will e of it all 430
	3:18	and you will e the plants of the field. 430
	3:19	of your brow you will e your food 430
	3:22	and take also from the tree of life and e, 430
	9: 4	not eat meat that has its lifeblood still in it. 430
	18: 5	Let me get you something to e, 4312+7326
	24:33	not e until I have told you what I have 430
	27: 4	of tasty food I like and bring it to me to e, 430
	27: 7	and prepare me some tasty food to e, 430
	27:10	Then take it to your father to e, 430
	27:19	Please sit up and e some of my game so 430
	27:25	bring me some of your game to e, 430
	27:31	"My father, sit up and e some of my game, 430
	28:20	and will give me food to e and clothes 430
	32:32	the Israelites do not e the tendon attached to 430
	37:25	As they sat down to e their meal, 430
	40:19	And the birds will e away your flesh." 430
	43:16	they are to e with me at noon." 430
	43:25	they had heard that they were to e there. 430
	43:32	because Egyptians could not e 430
Ex	2:20	Invite him to have something to e." 430
	12: 4	with what each person will e. 430
	12: 7	the doorframes of the houses where they e 430
	12: 8	to e the meat roasted over the fire, 430
	12: 9	Do not e the meat raw or cooked in water, 430
	12:11	This is how you are to e it: 430
	12:11	E it in haste; it is the LORD's Passover. 430
	12:15	For seven days you are to e bread made 430
	12:16	prepare food for everyone to e— 430
	12:18	In the first month you are to e bread made 430
	12:20	E nothing made with yeast. 430

Ex	12:20	you must e unleavened bread." 430
	12:43	"No foreigner is to e of it. 430
	12:44	Any slave you have bought may e of it 430
	12:45	and a hired worker may not e of it. 430
	12:48	No uncircumcised male may e of it. 430
	13: 3	E nothing containing yeast. 430
	13: 6	For seven days e bread made without yeast 430
	13: 7	E unleavened bread during those 430
	16: 8	when he gives you meat to e in the evening 430
	16:12	Tell them, 'At twilight you will e meat, 430
	16:15	the bread the LORD has given you to e. 433
	16:25	"E it today," Moses said, 430
	16:32	so they can see the bread I gave you to e 430
	18:12	to e bread with Moses' father-in-law in 430
	22:31	So do not e the meat of an animal torn 430
	23:11	and the wild animals may e what they leave. 430
	23:15	for seven days e bread made without yeast, 430
	29:32	and his sons are to e the meat of the ram 430
	29:33	They are to e these offerings 430
	29:33	But no one else may e them, 430
	32: 6	down to e and drink and got up to indulge 430
	34:15	and you will e their sacrifices. 430
	34:18	For seven days e bread made without yeast, 430
Lev	3:17	You must not e any fat or any blood.' " 430
	6:16	Aaron and his sons shall e the rest of it, 430
	6:16	they are to e it in the courtyard of the Tent 430
	6:18	Any male descendant of Aaron may e it. 430
	6:26	The priest who offers it shall e it; 430
	6:29	Any male in a priest's family may e it. 430
	7: 6	Any male in a priest's family may e it, 430
	7:19	anyone ceremonially clean may e it. 430
	7:23	'Do not e any of the fat of cattle, 430
	7:24	but you must not e it. 430+430
	7:26	you must not e the blood of any bird 430
	8:31	and e it there with the bread from the basket 430
	8:31	saying, 'Aaron and his sons are to e it.' 430
	10:12	to the LORD by fire and e it prepared 430
	10:13	E it in a holy place, 430
	10:14	and your sons and your daughters may e 430
	10:14	E them in a ceremonially clean place; NIH
	10:17	"Why didn't you e the sin offering in 430
	11: 2	these are the ones you may e: 430
	11: 3	You may e any animal that has 430
	11: 4	but you must not e them. 430
	11: 8	not e their meat or touch their carcasses; 430
	11: 9	you may e any that have fins and scales. 430
	11:11	you must not e their meat 430
	11:13	and not e because they are detestable: 430
	11:21	that walk on all fours that you may e: 430
	11:22	Of these you may e any kind of locust, 430
	11:39	an animal that you are allowed to e dies, 433
	11:42	not to e any creature that moves about on 430
	17:12	"None of you may e blood, 430
	17:12	nor may an alien living among you e blood." 430
	17:14	nor e the blood of any creature, 430
	19:25	But in the fifth year you may e its fruit. 430
	19:26	" 'Do not e any meat with the blood still 430
	21:22	He may e the most holy food of his God, 430
	22: 4	he may not e the sacred offerings 430
	22: 6	He must not e any of the sacred offerings, 430
	22: 7	and after that he may e the sacred offerings, 430
	22: 8	He must not e anything found dead or torn 430
	22:10	a priest's family may e the sacred offering, 430
	22:10	the guest of a priest or his hired worker e it. 430
	22:11	that slave may e his food. 430
	22:12	not e any of the sacred contributions. 430
	22:13	she may e of her father's food. 430
	22:13	however, may e any of it. 430
	22:16	by allowing them to e the sacred offerings 430
	23: 6	for seven days you must e bread made 430
	23:14	You must not e any bread, 430
	24: 9	who are to e it in a holy place, 430
	25:12	only what is taken directly from 430
	25:19	and you will e your fill and live there 430
	25:20	"What will we e in the seventh year 430
	25:22	you will e from the old crop 430
	25:22	from the old crop and will continue to e 430
	26: 5	and you will e all the food you want 430
	26:16	because your enemies will e it. 430
	26:26	You will e, but you will not be satisfied. 430
	26:29	You will e the flesh of your sons and 430
Nu	6: 3	not drink grape juice or e grapes or raisins. 430
	6: 4	he must not e anything that comes from 430
	9:11	They are to e the lamb, 430
	11: 4	"If only we had meat to e! 430
	11:13	'Give us meat to e!' 430
	11:18	when you will e meat. 430
	11:18	"If only we had meat to e!" 430
	11:18	and you will e it. 430
	11:19	You will not e it for just one day, 430
	11:21	'I will give them meat to e for 430
	15:19	and you e the food of the land, 430
	18:10	E it as something most holy; 430
	18:10	every male shall e it. 430
	18:11	who is ceremonially clean may e it. 430
	18:13	who is ceremonially clean may e it. 430
	18:31	You and your households may e the rest 430
	28:17	for seven days e bread made without yeast. 430
Dt	2: 6	to pay them in silver for the food you e and 430
	2:28	to e and water to drink for their price 430
	4:28	which cannot see or hear or e or smell. 430
	6:11	then when you e and are satisfied, 430
	8:12	Otherwise, when you e and are satisfied, 430
	8:16	He gave you manna to e in the desert, 430
	11:15	and you will e and be satisfied. 430
	12: 7	and your families shall e and shall rejoice 430
	12:15	of your towns and e as much of the meat 430

Dt	12:15	ceremonially unclean and the clean may e it. 430
	12:16	But you must not e the blood; 430
	12:17	You must not e in your own towns the tithe 430
	12:18	you are to e them in the presence of 430
	12:20	then you may e as much of it as you want. 430
	12:21	and in your own towns you may e as much 430
	12:22	E them as you would gazelle or deer. 430
	12:22	ceremonially unclean and the clean may e. 430
	12:23	But be sure you do not e the blood, 430
	12:23	and you must not e the life with the meat. 430
	12:24	You must not e the blood; 430
	12:25	Do not e it, so that it may go well with you 430
	12:27	but you may e the meat. 430
	14: 3	Do not e any detestable thing. 430
	14: 4	These are the animals you may e: 430
	14: 6	You may e any animal that has 430
	14: 7	not e the camel, 430
	14: 8	not to e their meat or touch their carcasses. 430
	14: 9	you may e any that has fins and scales. 430
	14:10	not have fins and scales you may not e; 430
	14:11	You may e any clean bird. 430
	14:12	But these you may not e: 430
	14:19	do not e them. 430
	14:20	that is clean you may e. 430
	14:21	Do not e anything you find already dead. 430
	14:21	and he may e it, 430
	14:23	E the tithe of your grain, new wine and oil, 430
	14:26	Then you and your household shall e there 430
	14:29	in your towns may come and e and 430
	15:20	You are to e it in your own towns. 430
	15:22	and your family are to e them in 430
	15:22	and the clean may e it, NIH
	15:23	But you must not e the blood; 430
	16: 3	Do not e it with bread made with yeast, 430
	16: 3	but for seven days e unleavened bread, 430
	16: 7	Roast it and e it at the place 430
	16: 8	For six days e unleavened bread and on 430
	20:19	because you can e their fruit. 430
	23:24	you may e all the grapes you want, 430
	26:12	they may e in your towns and be satisfied. 430
	28:31	but you will e none of it. 430
	28:33	not know will e what your land 430
	28:39	because worms will e them. 430
	28:53	you will e the fruit of the womb, 430
	28:57	For she intends to e them secretly during 430
	31:20	and when they e their fill and thrive, 430
Jos	24:13	and you live in them and e from vineyards 430
Jdg	13: 4	and that you do not e anything unclean, 430
	13: 7	and do not e anything unclean. 430
	13:14	She must not e anything that comes from 430
	13:14	nor e anything unclean. 430
	13:16	I will not e any of your food. 430
	14:14	"Out of the eater, something to e; 4407
	19: 5	Refresh yourself with something to e; 4312+7326
	19: 6	of them sat down to e and drink together. 430
	19:21	they had something to e and drink. 430
1Sa	1: 7	till she wept and would not e. 430
	1: 8	Why don't you e? 430
	2:36	so I can have food to e." ' " 430
	9:13	before he goes up to the high place to e. 430
	9:13	afterward, those who are invited will e 430
	9:19	for today you are to e with me, 430
	9:24	E, because it was set aside for you 430
	14:34	and slaughter them here and e them. 430
	20:24	the king sat down to e. 430
	20:34	that second day of the month he did not e, 430
	28:22	so you may e and have the strength to go 430
	28:23	He refused and said, "I will not e." 430
	30:11	They gave him water to drink and food to e 430
2Sa	3:35	and urged David to e something 1356
	9: 7	and you will always e at my table." 430
	9:10	will always e at my table. 430
	11:11	How could I go to my house to e and drink 430
	12:17	and he would not e any food with them. 1356
	12:21	you get up and e!" 430
	13: 5	give me something to e. 1356
	13: 5	in my sight so I may watch her and then e it 430
	13: 6	so I may e from her hand." 1356
	13: 9	but he refused to e. 430
	13:10	the food here into my bedroom so I may e 1356
	13:11	But when she took it to him to e, 430
	16: 2	the bread and fruit are for the men to e, 430
	17:29	for David and his people to e. 430
1Ki	2: 7	be among those who e at your table. 430
	2: 7	with me and have something to e, 6184
	13: 8	nor would I e bread or drink water here. 430
	13: 9	not e bread or drink water or return by 430
	13:15	"Come home with me and e." 430
	13:16	nor can I e bread or drink water with you 430
	13:17	not e bread or drink water there or return by 430
	13:18	so that he may e bread and drink water.' " 430
	13:22	in the place where he told you not to e or 430
	14:11	Dogs will e those belonging to Jeroboam 430
	16: 4	Dogs will e those belonging to Baasha 430
	17:12	that we may e it—and die." 430
	18:19	who e at Jezebel's table." 430
	18:41	And Elijah said to Ahab, "Go, e and drink, 430
	18:42	So Ahab went off to e and drink, 430
	19: 5	"Get up and e." 430
	19: 7	"Get up and e, 430
	21: 4	He lay on his bed sulking and refused to e. 430
	21: 5	Why won't you e?" 430
	21: 7	Get up and e! 430
	21:24	"Dogs will e those belonging to Ahab 430
2Ki	4: 8	he stopped there to e. 430
	4:40	but as they began to e it, they cried out, 430
	4:40	And they could not e it. 430

2Ki	4:41	"Serve it to the people to e."	430
	4:42	"Give it to the people to e," Elisha said.	430
	4:43	"Give it to the people to e.	430
	4:43	'They will e and have some left over.' "	430
	6:22	that they may e and drink and then go back	430
	6:28	'Give up your son so we may e him today,	430
	6:28	and tomorrow we'll e my son.'	430
	6:29	'Give up your son so we may e him,'	430
	7: 2	"but you will not e any of it!"	430
	7:19	but you will not e any of it!"	430
	18:27	like you, will have to e their own filth	430
	18:31	of you will e from his own vine	430
	19:29	"This year you will e what grows by itself,	430
	19:29	plant vineyards and e their fruit.	430
	25: 3	that there was no food for the people to e.	NIH
2Ch	31:10	we have had enough to e and plenty	430
Ezr	2:63	The governor ordered them not to e any of	430
	9:12	be strong and eat the good things of the land	430
Ne	5: 2	in order for us to e and stay alive,	430
	7:65	not to e any of the most sacred food	430
	8:12	all the people went away to e and drink,	430
	9:36	so they could e its fruit and	430
Est	4:16	Do not e or drink for three days,	430
Job	1: 4	and they would invite their three sisters to e	430
	27:14	his offspring will never have enough to e.	4312
	31: 8	then may others e what I have sown,	430
Ps	14: 4	those who devour my people as men e bread	430
	22:26	The poor will e and be satisfied;	430
	50:13	Do I e the flesh of bulls or drink the blood	430
	53: 4	those who devour my people as men e bread	430
	78:24	he rained down manna for the people to e,	430
	78:25	all the food they could e.	8427
	102: 4	I forget to e my food.	430
	102: 9	For I e ashes as my food	430
	127: 2	toiling for food to e—	430
	128: 2	You will e the fruit of your labor;	430
	141: 4	let me not e of their delicacies.	4310
Pr	1:31	they will e the fruit of their ways and	430
	4:17	They e the bread of wickedness and drink	4310
	9: 5	e my food and drink the wine I have mixed.	4310
	13:25	The righteous e to their hearts' content,	430
	18:21	and those who love it will e its fruit.	430
	23: 6	Do not e the food of a stingy man,	4310
	23: 7	"E and drink," he says to you,	430
	24:13	E honey, my son, for it is good;	430
	25:16	If you find honey, e just enough—	430
	25:21	give him food to e;	430
	25:27	It is not good to e too much honey,	430
	27:18	He who tends a fig tree will e its fruit,	430
	31:27	the affairs of her household and does not e	430
Ecc	2:24	A man can do nothing better than to e	430
	2:25	who can e or find enjoyment?	430
	3:13	That everyone may e and drink,	430
	5:18	and proper for a man to e and drink, and	430
	8:15	a man under the sun than to e and drink and	430
	9: 7	Go, e your food with gladness,	430
	10:17	and whose princes e at a proper time—	430
SS	5: 1	E, O friends, and drink;	430
Isa	1:19	you will e the best from the land;	430
	4: 1	"We will e our own food	430
	7:15	He will e curds and honey	430
	7:22	he will have curds to e.	430
	7:22	All who remain in the land will e curds	430
	9:20	on the left they will e, but not be satisfied.	430
	11: 7	and the lion will e straw like the ox.	430
	21: 5	they spread the rugs, they e, they drink!	430
	22:13	"Let us e and drink," you say,	430
	30:24	that work the soil will e fodder and mash,	430
	36:12	like you, will have to e their own filth	430
	36:16	of you will e from his own vine	430
	37:30	"This year you will e what grows by itself,	430
	37:30	plant vineyards and e their fruit.	430
	49:26	make your oppressors e their own flesh;	430
	50: 9	the moths will e them up.	430
	51: 8	the moth will e them up like a garment;	430
	55: 1	you who have no money, come, buy and e!	430
	55: 2	Listen, listen to me, and e what is good,	430
	62: 9	but those who harvest it will e it and praise	430
	65: 4	who e the flesh of pigs,	430
	65:13	"My servants will e,	430
	65:21	they will plant vineyards and e their fruit.	430
	65:22	or plant and others e.	430
	65:25	and the lion will e straw like the ox,	430
	66:17	the one in the midst of those who e the flesh	430
Jer	2: 7	I brought you into a fertile land to e its fruit	430
	7:21	to your other sacrifices and e	430
	9:15	make this people e bitter food	430
	16: 8	where there is feasting and sit down to e	430
	19: 9	I will make them e the flesh of their sons	430
	19: 9	and they will e one another's flesh during	430
	23:15	make them e bitter food	430
	29: 5	plant gardens and e what they produce.	430
	29:28	plant gardens and e what they produce.' "	430
	52: 6	that there was no food for the people to e.	NIH
La	2:20	Should women e their offspring,	430
Eze	2: 8	open your mouth and e what I give you."	430
	3: 1	e what is before you, eat this scroll;	430
	3: 1	eat what is before you, eat this scroll;	430
	3: 2	gave me the scroll to e.	430
	3: 3	e this scroll I am giving you	430
	4: 9	You are to e it during the 390 days you lie	430
	4:10	of food to e each day and eat it at set times.	430
	4:10	of food to eat each day and e it at set times.	430
	4:12	E the food as you would a barley cake;	430
	4:13	the people of Israel will e defiled food	430
	4:16	The people will e rationed food in anxiety	430
	5:10	in your midst fathers will e their children,	430

Eze	5:10	and children will e their fathers.	430
	12:18	tremble as you e your food,	430
	12:19	They will e their food in anxiety	430
	16:19	olive oil and honey I gave you to e—	430
	18: 2	" 'The fathers e sour grapes,	430
	18: 6	not e at the mountain shrines or look to	430
	18:15	not e at the mountain shrines or look to	430
	22: 9	in you are those who e	430
	24:17	do not cover the lower part of your face or e	430
	24:22	not cover the lower part of your face or e	430
	25: 4	they will e your fruit and drink your milk.	430
	33:25	Since you e meat with the blood still in it	430
	34: 3	You e the curds,	430
	39:17	There you will e flesh and drink blood.	430
	39:18	You will e the flesh of mighty men	430
	39:19	you will e fat till you are glutted	430
	39:20	At my table you will e your fill	8425
	42:13	the LORD will e the most holy offerings.	430
	44: 3	inside the gateway to e in the presence of	430
	44:29	They will e the grain offerings.	430
	44:31	The priests must not e anything,	430
	45:21	during which you shall e bread made	430
Da	1:12	but vegetables for us to e and water to drink.	430
	1:13	that of the young men who e the royal food,	430
	4:25	you will e grass like cattle and	10301
	4:32	you will e grass like cattle.	10301
	7: 5	It was told, 'Get up and e your fill of flesh!'	10030
	11:26	Those who e from	430
Hos	4:10	"They will e but not have enough;	430
	8:13	They offer sacrifices given to me and they e	430
	9: 3	to Egypt and e unclean food in Assyria.	430
	9: 4	all who e them will be unclean.	430
Joel	2:26	You will have plenty to e,	430+430
Am	9:14	they will make gardens and e their fruit.	430
Ob	1: 7	those who e your bread will set a trap	NIH
Jnh	3: 7	do not let them e or drink.	8286
Mic	3: 3	who e my people's flesh, strip off their skin	430
	6:14	You will e but not be satisfied;	430
	7: 1	there is no cluster of grapes to e,	430
Zep	3:13	They will e and lie down	8286
Hag	1: 6	You e, but never have enough.	430
Zec	11: 9	Let those who are left e one another's flesh.	430
	11:16	but will e the meat of the choice sheep,	430
Mt	6:25	what you will e or drink;	2266
	6:31	do not worry, saying, 'What shall we e?'	2266
	9:11	"Why does your teacher e	2266
	12: 1	to pick some heads of grain and e them.	2266
	14:16	You give them something to e."	2266
	15: 2	They don't wash their hands before they e!"	2266
	15:27	"but even the dogs e the crumbs that fall	2266
	15:32	with me three days and have nothing to e.	2266
	24:49	to beat his fellow servants and to e	2266
	25:35	and you gave me something to e,	2266
	25:42	and you gave me nothing to e,	2266
	26:17	to make preparations for you to e	2266
	26:26	saying, "Take and e; this is my body."	2266
Mk	2:16	"Why does he e with tax collectors	2266
	2:26	which is lawful only for priests to e	2266
	3:20	and his disciples were not even able to e.	2266
	5:43	and told them to give her something to e.	2266
	6:31	that they did not even have a chance to e,	2266
	6:36	and buy themselves something to e."	2266
	6:37	"You give them something to e."	2266
	6:37	on bread and give it to them to e?"	2266
	7: 3	(The Pharisees and all the Jews do not e	2266
	7: 4	from the marketplace they do not e	2266
	7:27	"First let the children e all they want,"	5963
	7:28	under the table e the children's crumbs."	2266
	8: 1	Since they had nothing to e,	2266
	8: 2	with me three days and have nothing to e.	2266
	11:14	"May no one ever e fruit from you again."	2266
	14:12	to go and make preparations for you to e	2266
	14:12	I may e the Passover with my disciples?'	2266
	14:14	I may e the Passover with my disciples?'	2266
Lk	5:30	"Why do you e and drink	2266
	6: 1	rub them in their hands and e the kernels	2266
	6: 4	he ate what is lawful only for priests to e	2266
	8:55	Jesus told them to give her something to e.	2266
	9:13	"You give them something to e."	2266
	10: 8	e what is set before you.	2266
	11:37	a Pharisee invited him to e with him;	753
	12:19	Take life easy; e, drink and be merry.'	2266
	12:22	about your life, what you will e;	2266
	12:29	not set your heart on what you will e	2266
	12:45	the menservants and maidservants and to e	2266
	14: 1	to e in the house of a prominent Pharisee,	2266
	14:15	"Blessed is the man who will e at the feast	2266
	16:21	who e what fell from the rich man's table.	5963
	17: 7	'Come along now and sit down to e'?	404
	17: 8	and wait on me while I e and drink;	2266
	17: 8	after that you may e and drink'?	2266
	22: 8	"Go and make preparations for us to e	2266
	22:11	I may e the Passover with my disciples?'	2266
	22:15	to e this Passover with you before I suffer.	2266
	22:16	not e it again until it finds fulfillment	2266
	22:30	so that you may e and drink at my table	2266
	24:41	"Do you have anything here to e?"	1110
Jn	4:31	"Rabbi, e something."	2266
	4:32	to e that you know nothing about."	2266
	6: 5	shall we buy bread for these people to e?"	2266
	6:31	They had all had enough to e,	NIG
	6:31	'He gave them bread from heaven to e.' "	2266
	6:50	which a man may e and not die.	2266
	6:52	"How can this man give us his flesh to e?"	2266
	6:53	unless you e the flesh of the Son of Man	2266
	18:28	they wanted to e the Passover.	2266
Ac	9: 9	and did not e or drink anything.	2266
	10:10	and wanted something to e,	1174

Ac	10:13	"Get up, Peter. Kill and e."	2266
	11: 7	'Get up, Peter. Kill and e.'	2266
	23:12	and bound themselves with an oath not to e	2266
	23:14	not to e anything until we have killed Paul.	1174
	23:21	not to e or drink until they have killed him.	2266
	27:33	before dawn Paul urged them all to e.	3561+5575
	27:35	Then he broke it and began to e.	2266
Ro	14: 2	One man's faith allows him to e everything,	2266
	14: 3	the man who does not e everything must	2266
	14:15	because of what you e,	1109
	14:20	to e anything that causes someone else	2266
	14:21	It is better not to e meat or drink wine or	2266
1Co	5:11	With such a man do not even e.	5303
	8: 7	that when they e such food they think of it	2266
	8: 8	we are no worse if we do not e,	2266
	8:10	to e what has been sacrificed to idols?	2266
	8:13	if what I e causes my brother to fall into sin,	1109
	8:13	I will never e meat again,	2266
	9: 7	a vineyard and does not e of its grapes?	2266
	10: 7	down to e and drink and got up to indulge	2266
	10:18	not those who e the sacrifices participate in	2266
	10:25	E anything sold in the meat market	2266
	10:27	e whatever is put before you	2266
	10:28	then do not e it,	2266
	10:31	whether you e or drink or whatever you do,	2266
	11:20	it is not the Lord's Supper you e,	2266
	11:21	for as you e,	2266
	11:22	Don't you have homes to e and drink in?	2266
	11:26	For whenever you e this bread	2266
	11:33	my brothers, when you come together to e,	2266
	11:34	If anyone is hungry, he should e at home,	2266
	15:32	dead are not raised, "Let us e and drink,	2266
Gal	2:12	he used to e with the Gentiles.	5303
Col	2:16	not let anyone judge you by what you e	1111
2Th	3: 8	nor did we e anyone's food without paying	2266
	3:10	"If a man will not work, he shall not e."	2266
	3:12	to settle down and earn the bread they e.	2266
Heb	13: 7	which are of no value to those who e them.	4344
	13:10	at the tabernacle have no right to e.	2266
Jas	5: 3	against you and e your flesh like fire.	2266
Rev	2: 7	I will give the right to e from the tree	2266
	3:20	I will come in and e with him,	1268
	10: 9	He said to me, "Take it and e it.	2983
	17:16	they will e her flesh and burn her with fire.	2266
	19:18	so that you may e the flesh of kings,	2266

EATEN (66) [EAT]

Ge	3:11	Have you e from the tree	430
	6:21	to take every kind of food that is to be e	430
	14:24	but what my men have e and the share	430
	31:38	nor have I e rams from your flocks.	430
	31:54	After they had e, they spent the night there.	430
	43: 2	So when they had e all	430
Ex	12:46	"It must be e inside one house;	430
	21:28	and its meat must not be e.	430
	29:34	It must not be e, because it is sacred.	430
Lev	6:16	it is to be e without yeast in a holy place;	430
	6:23	it must not be e."	430
	6:26	it is to be e in a holy place,	430
	6:30	in the Holy Place must not be e;	430
	7: 6	but it must be e in a holy place;	430
	7:15	of thanksgiving must be e on	430
	7:16	sacrifice shall be e on the day he offers it,	430
	7:16	but anything left over may be e on	430
	7:18	If any meat of the fellowship offering is e	430+430
	7:19	that touches anything ceremonially unclean must not be e;	430
	10:18	you should have e the goat in	430+430
	10:19	the LORD have been pleased if I had e	430
	11:34	Any food that could be e but has water on it	430
	11:41	it is not to be e.	430
	11:47	between living creatures that may be e	430
	11:47	be eaten and those that may not be e.' "	430
	17:13	that may be e must drain out the blood	430
	19: 6	It shall be e on the day you sacrifice it or	430
	19: 7	If any of it is e on the third day,	430+430
	19:23	it must not be e.	430
	22:30	It must be e that same day;	430
	25: 7	Whatever the land produces may be e.	430
Nu	12:12	with its flesh half e away."	430
Dt	8:10	When you have e and are satisfied,	430
	26:14	not e any of the sacred portion while I was	430
Ru	2:18	over after she had e enough.	8425
1Sa	14:30	if the men had e today some of	430+430
	28:20	for he had e nothing all that day and night.	430
	30:11	for he had not e any food or drunk any water	430
2Sa	19:42	e any of the king's provisions?	430+430
1Ki	13:28	The lion had neither e the body nor mauled	430
Job	6: 6	Is tasteless food e without salt,	430
	13:28	like a garment e by moths.	430
Pr	9:17	food e in secret is delicious!"	NIH
	23: 8	You will vomit up the little you have e	430
	30:17	will be e by the vultures.	430
SS	5: 1	I have e my honeycomb and my honey;	430
Jer	24: 2	so bad they could not be e."	430
	24: 3	the poor ones are so bad they cannot be e."	430
	24: 8	which are so bad they cannot be e,'	430
	29:17	that are so bad they cannot be e.	430
	31:29	'The fathers have e sour grapes,	430
Eze	4:14	now I have never e anything found dead	430
Hos	10:13	you have e the fruit of deception.	430
Joel	1: 4	the great locusts have e;	430
	1: 4	young locusts have e;	430
	1: 4	young locusts have left other locusts have e.	430
	2:25	for the years the locusts have e—	430

Mk	6:44	of the men who *had* e was five thousand.	2266
Jn	6:13	over *by* those who *had* e.	1048
	6:23	the place where the people *had* e the bread	2266
Ac	10:14	*"I have* never e anything impure	2266
	12:23	and he was e by worms and died.	5037
	27:33	*you* haven't e anything.	4689
	27:38	e as much as *they* wanted,	3170
Jas	5: 2	and moths have e your clothes.	1181+4963
Rev	10:10	but when *I had* e it,	2266

EATER (3) [EAT]

Jdg	14:14	He replied, "Out of the e, something to eat;	430
Isa	55:10	for the sower and bread for the e,	430
Na	3:12	the figs fall into the mouth of the e.	430

EATING (56) [EAT]

Ge	40:17	but the birds *were* e them out of the basket	430
Ex	34:28	without e bread or drinking water.	430
Lev	26:10	*be* e last year's harvest when you will have	430
Dt	27: 7	e them and rejoicing in the presence of	430
	28:55	of the flesh of his children that *he is* e.	430
Jdg	9:27	While they were e and drinking,	430
	19: 4	e and drinking, and sleeping there.	430
Ru	3: 3	until he has finished e and drinking.	430
	3: 7	When Boaz *had finished* e and drinking	430
1Sa	1: 9	Once when *they had* finished e and drinking	430
	9:13	The people *will not begin* e	430
	14:33	against the Lᴏʀᴅ by e meat that has blood	430
	14:34	Do not sin against the Lᴏʀᴅ by e meat	430
	30:16	scattered over the countryside, e,	430
1Ki	1:25	Right now they *are* e and drinking with him	430
	13:23	When the man of God had finished e	430
2Ki	6:23	and after *they had finished* e and drinking,	430
1Ch	12:39	with David, e and drinking,	430
Isa	22:13	e *of* meat and drinking of wine!	430
	29: 8	as when a hungry man dreams that *he is* e,	430
Jer	41: 1	While *they were* e together there,	430
Da	5:30	to his palace and spent the night *without* e	10297
Zec	7: 6	And when *you were* e and drinking,	430
Mt	11:18	For John came neither e nor drinking,	2266
	11:19	The Son of Man came e and drinking,	2266
	15:20	but e with unwashed hands does	2266
	24:38	people were e and drinking,	5592
	26:21	And *while* they *were* e, he said,	2266
	26:26	*While* they *were* e, Jesus took bread,	2266
Mk	2:15	and "sinners" *were* e *with* him	5263
	2:16	the law who were Pharisees saw *him* e with	2266
	7: 2	saw some of his disciples e food with hands	2266
	7: 5	of e their food with "unclean" hands?"	2266
	14:18	*While* they were reclining at the table e,	2266
	14:18	one who *is* e with me."	2266
	14:22	*While* they *were* e, Jesus took bread,	2266
	16:14	to the Eleven *as they were* e;	367
Lk	5:29	of tax collectors and others were e	2879
	5:33	but yours *go on* e and drinking."	2266
	7:33	For John the Baptist came neither e bread	2266
	7:34	The Son of Man came e and drinking,	2266
	7:37	that Jesus *was* e at the Pharisee's house,	2879
	10: 7	e and drinking whatever they give you,	2266
	15:16	with the pods that the pigs *were* e,	2266
	17:27	*People were* e, drinking,	2266
	17:28	*People were* e and drinking,	2266
Jn	21:15	When *they had finished* e,	753
Ac	1: 4	On one occasion, *while he was* e with them,	5259
Ro	14:15	Do not *by* your e destroy your brother	1109
	14:17	For the kingdom of God is not a matter of e	1111
	14:23	because his e is not from faith;	NIG
1Co	8: 4	So then, about e food sacrificed to idols:	NIG
	8:10	weak conscience sees you who have this	
		knowledge e in an idol's temple,	2879
Jude	1:12	e *with* you without the slightest qualm—	5307
Rev	2:14	the Israelites to sin by e food sacrificed	2266
	2:20	and the e of food sacrificed to idols.	2266

EATS (41) [EAT]

Ex	12:15	for whoever e anything with yeast in it	430
	12:19	And whoever e anything with yeast	430
Lev	7:18	the person who e any of it will	430
	7:20	But if anyone who is unclean e any meat of	430
	7:21	and then e any of the meat of	430
	7:25	Anyone *who* e the fat of an animal	430
	7:27	If anyone e blood,	430
	11:40	Anyone *who* e some of	430
	14:47	or e in the house must wash his clothes.	430
	17:10	among them who e any blood—	430
	17:10	against that person who e blood	430
	17:14	anyone *who* e it must be cut off."	430
	17:15	who e anything found dead or torn	430
	19: 8	*Whoever* e it will be held responsible	430
	22:14	" 'If anyone e a sacred offering by mistake,	430
1Sa	14:24	"Cursed be any man who e food before	430
	14:28	"Cursed be any man who e food today!' "	430
2Sa	19:35	Can your servant taste what he e	430
Job	18:13	It e away parts of his skin;	430
	39:24	In frenzied excitement he e *up* the ground;	1686
Ps	106:20	for an image of a bull, *which* e grass.	430
Pr	30:20	*She* e and wipes her mouth and says,	430
Ecc	5:12	whether he e little or much,	430
	5:12	All his days he e in darkness,	430
Isa	44:16	he roasts his meat and e *his* fill.	8425
	59: 5	Whoever e their eggs will die,	430
Jer	31:30	whoever e sour grapes—	430
Eze	18:11	*"He* e at the mountain shrines.	430
Lk	15: 2	"This man welcomes sinners and e *with*	5303
Jn	6:51	anyone e of this bread, he will live forever.	2266

Jn	6:54	Whoever e my flesh and drinks my blood	5592
	6:56	Whoever e my flesh and drinks my blood	5592
Ro	14: 2	whose faith is weak, e only vegetables.	2266
	14: 3	The man who e everything must not look	2266
	14: 6	He who e meat, eats to the Lord,	2266
	14: 6	He who eats meat, e to the Lord,	2266
	14:23	man who has doubts is condemned if *he* e,	2266
1Co	11:27	whoever e the bread or drinks the cup of	2266
	11:28	to examine himself before he e of the bread	2266
	11:29	For anyone who e and drinks without	2266
	11:29	the body of the Lord e and drinks judgment	2266

EAVES (1)

| 1Ki | 7: 9 | and from foundation to e, | 3258 |

EBAL (7)

Ge	36:23	Alvan, Manahath, E, Shepho and Onam.	6507
Dt	11:29	and on Mount E the curses.	6507
	27: 4	set up these stones on Mount E,	6506
	27:13	And these tribes shall stand on Mount E	6506
Jos	8:30	Then Joshua built on Mount E an altar to	6506
	8:33	and half of them in front of Mount E.	6506
1Ch	1:40	Alvan, Manahath, E, Shepho and Onam.	6507

EBB (1) [EBBED, EBBING, EBBS]

| La | 2:12 | as their lives e *away* in their mothers' arms. | 9161 |

EBBED (1) [EBB]

| Ps | 107: 5 | and their lives e away. | 6494 |

EBBING (1) [EBB]

| Jnh | 2: 7 | "When my life *was* e away, | 6494 |

EBBS (1) [EBB]

| Job | 30:16 | my life e away; days of suffering grip me. | 9161 |

EBED (6)

Jdg	9:26	of E moved with his brothers	6270
	9:28	Then Gaal son of E said,	6270
	9:30	the city heard what Gaal son of E said,	6270
	9:31	"Gaal son of E and his brothers have come	6270
	9:35	of E had gone out and was standing at	6270
Ezr	8: 6	E son of Jonathan, and with him 50 men;	6270

EBED-MELECH (6)

Jer	38: 7	But E, a Cushite, an official in	6283
	38: 8	E went out of the palace and said to him,	6283
	38:10	Then the king commanded E the Cushite,	6283
	38:11	So E took the men with him and went to	6283
	38:12	E the Cushite said to Jeremiah,	6283
	39:16	"Go and tell E the Cushite, 'This is what	6283

EBENEZER (3)

1Sa	4: 1	The Israelites camped at E,	75
	5: 1	they took it from E to Ashdod.	75
	7:12	He named it E, saying,	75

EBER (16)

Ge	10:21	Shem was the ancestor of all the sons of E.	6299
	10:24	and Shelah the father of E.	6299
	10:25	Two sons were born to E:	6299
	11:14	he became the father of E.	6299
	11:15	And after he became the father of E,	6299
	11:16	When E had lived 34 years,	6299
	11:17	E lived 430 years and had other sons	6299
Nu	24:24	they will subdue Asshur and E,	6299
1Ch	1:18	and Shelah the father of E.	6299
	1:19	Two sons were born to E:	6299
	1:25	E, Peleg, Reu,	6299
	5:13	Sheba, Jorai, Jacan, Zia and E—seven in all.	6299
	8:12	The sons of Elpaal: E, Misham,	6299
	8:22	Ishpan, E, Eliel,	6299
Ne	12:20	of Sallu's, Kallai; of Amok's, E;	6299
Lk	3:35	the son of E, the son of Shelah,	1576

EBEZ (1)

| Jos | 19:20 | Rabbith, Kishion, E, | 82 |

EBIASAPH (3)

1Ch	6:23	Elkanah his son, E his son, Assir his son,	47
	6:37	the son of E, the son of Korah,	47
	9:19	Shallum son of Kore, the son of E,	47

EBONY (1)

| Eze | 27:15 | they paid you with ivory tusks and e. | 2041 |

EBRONAH (KJV) ABRONAH

ECBATANA (1)

| Ezr | 6: 2 | in the citadel of E in the province of Media, | 10020 |

ECHO (2) [ECHOES]

| Hab | 2:11 | and the beams of the woodwork *will* e it. | 6699 |
| Zep | 2:14 | Their calls *will* e through the windows, | 8876 |

ECHOES (1) [ECHO]

| Isa | 15: 8 | Their outcry e *along* the border of Moab; | 5938 |

ED (KJV) WITNESS

EDEN (19) [BETH EDEN]

Ge	2: 8	a garden in the east, in E;	6359
	2:10	the garden flowed from E;	6359
	2:15	in the Garden of E to work it and take care	6359
	3:23	from the Garden of E to work the ground	6359
	3:24	the east side of the Garden of E cherubim	6359
	4:16	and lived in the land of Nod, east of E.	6359
2Ki	19:12	and the people of E who were in Tel Assar?	6361
2Ch	29:12	Joah son of Zimmah and E son of Joah;	6360
	31:15	E, Miniamin, Jeshua, Shemaiah,	6360
Isa	37:12	and the people of E who were in Tel Assar?	6361
	51: 3	he will make her deserts like E,	6359
Eze	27:23	Canneh and E and merchants of Sheba,	6361
	28:13	You were in E, the garden of God;	6359
	31: 9	the envy of all the trees of E in the garden	6359
	31:16	Then all the trees of E,	6359
	31:18	" 'Which of the trees of E can be compared	6359
	31:18	down with the trees of E to the earth below;	6359
	36:35	like the garden of E;	6359
Joel	2: 3	garden of E, behind them, a desert waste—	6359

EDER (4) [MIDGAL EDER]

Jos	15:21	of Edom were: Kabzeel, E,	6375
1Ch	8:15	Zebadiah, Arad, E,	6376
	23:23	Mahli, E and Jerimoth—three in all.	6374
	24:30	the sons of Mushi: Mahli, E and Jerimoth.	6374

EDGE (35) [DOUBLE-EDGED, EDGES]

Ex	13:20	at Etham on the e of the desert.	7895
	26: 4	Make loops of blue material along the e *of*	8557
	26:10	along the e *of* the end curtain in one set and	8557
	26:10	and also along the e *of* the end curtain in	8557
	28:26	of the breastpiece on the inside e next to	8557
	28:32	a woven e like a collar around this opening,	8557
	36:11	along the e *of* the end curtain in one set,	8557
	36:17	along the e *of* the end curtain in one set and	8557
	36:17	and also along the e *of* the end curtain in	8557
	39:19	of the breastpiece on the inside e next to	8557
Nu	20:16	a town on the e *of* your territory.	7895
	22:36	at the e *of* his territory.	7895
	33: 6	on the e *of* the desert.	7895
Jos	3: 8	the e of the Jordan's waters,	7895
	3:15	and their feet touched the water's e,	7895
Jdg	7:17	When I get to the e of the camp,	7895
	7:19	the hundred men with him reached the e *of*	7895
1Sa	9:27	they were going down to the e of the town,	7895
2Ki	7: 5	When they reached the e of the camp,	7895
	7: 8	The men who had leprosy reached the e *of*	7895
1Ch	5: 9	the east they occupied the land up to the e	995
Ps	89:43	You have turned back the e *of* his sword	7644
Ecc	10:10	If the ax is dull and its e unsharpened,	7156
Jer	31:29	and the children's teeth *are* set on e.'	7733
	31:30	his own teeth *will be* set on e.	7733
Eze	18: 2	and the children's teeth *are* set on e'?	7733
	43:13	with a rim of one span around the e.	8557
Am	3:12	be saved, those who sit in Samaria on the e	6991
Mt	9:20	behind him and touched the e of his cloak.	3192
	14:36	to let the sick just touch the e of his cloak,	3192
Mk	4: 1	along the shore at the water's e.	2498
	6:56	to let them touch even the e of his cloak,	3192
Lk	5: 2	he saw at the water's e two boats,	NIG
	8:44	She came up behind him and touched the e	3192
Heb	11:34	and escaped the e *of* the sword;	3479+5125

EDGE (Anglicized) See also LEDGE

EDGES (5) [EDGE]

Lev	19: 9	do not reap to the very e *of* your field	6991
	19:27	of your head or clip off the e *of* your beard.	6991
	21: 5	the e *of* their beards or cut their bodies.	6991
	23:22	do not reap to the very e *of* your field	6991
Job	38:13	the earth by the e and shake the wicked out	4053

EDICT (17) [DICTATE]

Ezr	6:11	I decree that if anyone changes this e,	10601
Est	1:20	Then when the king's e is proclaimed	7330
	2: 8	the king's order and e had been proclaimed,	2017
	3:14	A copy of the text of the e was to be issued	NIH
	3:15	and the e was issued in the citadel of Susa.	2017
	4: 3	In every province to which the e and order	1821
	4: 8	He also gave him a copy of the text of the e	2017
	8:11	The king's e granted the Jews in every city	889S
	8:13	A copy of the text of the e was to be issued	NIH
	8:14	the e was also issued in the citadel of Susa.	2017
	8:17	wherever the e of the king went,	2017
	9: 1	the e commanded by the king was to	2017
	9:13	to carry out this day's e tomorrow also,	2017
	9:14	An e was issued in Susa.	2017
Da	6: 7	that the king should issue an e and enforce	10628
	6:15	the Medes and Persians no decree or e that	10628
Heb	11:23	and they were not afraid of the king's e.	1409

EDIFICATION (1) [EDIFIED, EDIFIES]

| Ro | 14:19 | to do what leads to peace and to mutual e. | 3869 |

EDIFIED (2) [EDIFICATION]

1Co	14: 5	so that the church *may* be e.	3284+3869
	14:17	but the other man *is* not e.	3868

EDIFIES (2) [EDIFICATION]

1Co	14: 4	He who speaks in a tongue e himself,	3868
	14: 4	but he who prophesies e the church.	3868

EDOM (92) [EDOM'S, EDOMITE, EDOMITES, ESAU]

Ge	25:30	(That is why he was also called E.)	121
	32: 3	the country of E.	121
	36: 1	This is the account of Esau (that is, E).	121
	36: 8	(that is, E) settled in the hill country of Seir.	121
	36:16	the chiefs descended from Eliphaz in E;	121+824
	36:17	the chiefs descended from Reuel in E;	121+824
	36:19	These were the sons of Esau (that is, E),	121
	36:21	sons of Seir in E were Horite chiefs.	121+824
	36:31	These were the kings who reigned in E	121+824
	36:32	Bela son of Beor became king of E.	121
	36:43	These were the chiefs of E,	121
Ex	15:15	The chiefs of E will be terrified,	121
Nu	20:14	from Kadesh to the king of E, saying:	121
	20:18	But E answered: "You may	121
	20:20	Then E came out against them with a large	121
	20:21	Since E refused to let them go	121
	20:23	At Mount Hor, near the border of E,	121+824
	21: 4	to go around E,	121+824
	24:18	E will be conquered;	121
	33:37	on the border of E.	121+824
	34: 3	of the Desert of Zin along the border of E.	121
Jos	15: 1	extended down to the territory of E,	121
	15:21	the Negev toward the boundary of E were:	121
Jdg	5: 4	when you marched from the land of E,	121
	11:17	Israel sent messengers to the king of E,	121
	11:17	but the king of E would not listen.	121
	11:18	skirted the lands of E and Moab,	121
1Sa	14:47	Moab, the Ammonites, E,	121
2Sa	8:12	E and Moab, the Ammonites and	121
	8:14	He put garrisons throughout E,	121
1Ki	9:26	which is near Elath in E,	121+824
	11:14	from the royal line of E.	121
	11:15	Earlier when David was fighting with E,	121
	11:15	had struck down all the men in E.	121
	11:16	until they had destroyed all the men in E.	121
	22:47	There was then no king in E;	121
2Ki	3: 8	"Through the Desert of E," he answered.	121
	3: 9	with the king of Judah and the king of E.	121
	3:12	and Jehoshaphat and the king of E went	121
	3:20	water flowing from the direction of E!	121
	3:26	to break through to the king of E,	121
	8:20	E rebelled against Judah and set	121
	8:22	To this day E has been in rebellion	121
	14:10	You have indeed defeated E and	121
1Ch	1:43	These were the kings who reigned in E	121+824
	1:51	The chiefs of E were:	121
	1:54	These were the chiefs of E.	121
	18:11	E and Moab, the Ammonites and	121
	18:13	He put garrisons in E,	121
2Ch	8:17	Ezion Geber and Elath on the coast of E.	121+824
	20: 2	against you from E,	121
	21: 8	E rebelled against Judah and set	121
	21:10	To this day E has been in rebellion	121
	25:19	to yourself that you have defeated E,	121
	25:20	because they sought the gods of E.	121
Ps	60: 8	upon E I toss my sandal;	121
	60: 9	Who will lead me to E?	121
	83: 6	the tents of E and the Ishmaelites,	121
	108: 9	upon E I toss my sandal;	121
	108:10	Who will lead me to E?	121
Isa	11:14	They will lay hands on E and Moab,	121
	34: 5	see, it descends in judgment on E,	121
	34: 6	in Bozrah and a great slaughter in E.	121+824
	34:11	over E the measuring line of chaos and	2023S
	63: 1	Who is this coming from E, from Bozrah,	121
Jer	9:26	E, Ammon, Moab and all who live in	121
	25:21	E, Moab and Ammon;	121
	27: 3	Then send word to the kings of E, Moab,	121
	40:11	E and all the other countries heard that	121
	49: 7	Concerning E: This is what the LORD Almighty says:	121
	49:17	"E will become an object of horror;	121
	49:19	I will chase E from its land in an instant.	5647S
	49:20	the LORD has planned against E,	121
La	4:21	Rejoice and be glad, O Daughter of E,	121
	4:22	But, O Daughter of E,	121
Eze	16:57	by the daughters of E and all her neighbors	121
	25:12	'Because E took revenge on the house	121
	25:13	against E and kill its men and their animals.	121
	25:14	I will take vengeance on E by the hand	121
	25:14	and they will deal with E in accordance	121
	32:29	"E is there, her kings and all her princes;	121
	35:15	O Mount Seir, you and all of E.	121
	36: 5	the rest of the nations, and against all E,	121
Da	11:41	Many countries will fall, but E,	121
Joel	3:19	Egypt will be desolate, E a desert waste,	121
Am	1: 6	and sold them to E,	121
	1: 9	sold whole communities of captives to E,	121
	1:11	"For three sins of E, even for four,	121
	9:12	so that they may possess the remnant of E	121
Ob	1: 1	the Sovereign LORD says about E—	121
	1: 8	"will I not destroy the wise men of E,	121
Mal	1: 4	E may say, "Though we have been crushed,	121

EDOM'S (3) [EDOM]

Isa	34: 9	E streams will be turned into pitch,	2023S
Jer	49:22	that day the hearts of E warriors will be like	121
Am	2: 1	as if to lime, the bones of E king,	121

EDOMITE (8) [EDOM]

Dt	23: 7	Do not abhor an E, for he is your brother.	122
1Sa	21: 7	he was Doeg the E, Saul's head shepherd.	122
	22: 9	But Doeg the E,	122
	22:18	Doeg the E turned and struck them down.	122
	22:22	"That day, when Doeg the E was there,	122
1Ki	11:14	Hadad the E, from the royal line of Edom.	122
	11:17	some E officials who had served his father.	122
Ps	52: T	Doeg the E had gone to Saul and told him:	122

EDOMITES (15) [EDOM]

Ge	36: 9	the account of Esau the father of the E in	121
	36:43	This was Esau the father of the E.	121
2Sa	8:13	from striking down eighteen thousand E in	121
	8:14	and all the E became subject to David.	121
1Ki	11: 1	Moabites, Ammonites, E,	122
2Ki	8:21	The E surrounded him	121
	14: 7	the one who defeated ten thousand E in	121
	16: 6	E then moved into Elath	122
1Ch	18:12	down eighteen thousand E in the Valley	121
	18:13	and all the E became subject to David.	121
2Ch	21: 9	The E surrounded him	121
	25:14	from slaughtering the E,	122
	28:17	The E had again come and attacked Judah	122
Ps	60: T	and struck down twelve thousand E in	121
	137: 7	the E did on the day Jerusalem fell.	121+1201

EDREI (8)

Nu	21:33	to meet them in battle at E.	167
Dt	1: 4	and at E had defeated Og king of Bashan,	167
	3: 1	to meet us in battle at E.	167
	3:10	and all Bashan as far as Salecah and E,	167
Jos	12: 4	who reigned in Ashtaroth and E.	167
	13:12	and E and had survived as one of the last of	167
	13:31	and Ashtaroth and E (the royal cities of Og	167
	19:37	Kedesh, E, En Hazor,	167

EDUCATED (1)

Ac	7:22	Moses was e in all the wisdom of	4084

EFFECT (8) [EFFECTIVE, EFFECTIVELY, EFFECTS]

Job	41:26	The sword that reaches him has no e,	7756
Isa	32:17	The e of righteousness will be quietness	6275
Ac	7:53	that was put into e through angels but have	1408
1Co	15:10	and his grace to me was not without e.	3031
Gal	3:19	The law was put into e through angels by	1411
Eph	1:10	to be put into e when the times	3873
Heb	9:17	it never takes e while the one who made it	2710
	9:18	even the first covenant was not put into e	1590

EFFECTIVE (2) [EFFECT]

1Co	16: 9	a great door for e work has opened to me,	1921
Jas	5:16	of a righteous man is powerful and e.	1919

EFFECTIVELY (1) [EFFECT]

Ac	14: 1	There they spoke so e that a great number	NIG

EFFECTS (1) [EFFECT]

Ac	28: 5	into the fire and suffered no ill e.	2805

EFFEMINATE   (KJV) MALE PROSTITUTES

EFFORT (15) [EFFORTS]

Ecc	2:19	the work into which I have poured my e	6661
Da	6:14	to rescue Daniel and made every e	10700
Lk	13:24	"Make every e to enter through the narrow	76
Jn	5:44	make no e to obtain the praise that	2426
Ro	9:16	therefore, depend on man's desire or e,	5556
	14:19	therefore make every e to do what leads	1503
Gal	3: 3	now trying to attain your goal by human e?	4922
Eph	4: 3	Make every e to keep the unity of the Spirit	5079
1Th	2:16	in their e to keep us from speaking to	NIG
	2:17	intense longing we made every e	5079
Heb	4:11	therefore, make every e to enter that rest,	5079
	12:14	Make every e to live in peace with all men	1503
2Pe	1: 5	make every e to add to your faith goodness;	5082
	1:15	And I will make every e to see that	5079
	3:14	make every e to be found spotless,	5079

EFFORTS (7) [EFFORT]

Job	36:19	or even all your mighty e sustain you	4410
Ecc	2:11	All man's e are for his mouth,	6662
	8:17	Despite all his e to search it out,	6661
Eze	24:12	It has frustrated all e;	9303
	29:20	for his e because he and his army did it	6268
Gal	4:11	that somehow I have wasted my e on you.	3159
1Th	3: 5	and our e might have been useless.	3160

EGG (2) [EGGS]

Job	6: 6	or is there flavor in the white of an e?	2733
Lk	11:12	Or if he asks for an e,	6051

EGGS (7) [EGG]

Dt	22: 6	on the young or on the e,	1070
Job	39:14	She lays her e on the ground	1070
Isa	10:14	as men gather abandoned e,	1070
	34:15	The owl will nest there and lay e,	4880
	59: 5	the e of vipers and spin a spider's web.	1070
	59: 5	Whoever eats their e will die,	1070
Jer	17:11	a partridge that hatches e it did not lay is	1842

EGLAH (2)

2Sa	3: 5	Ithream the son of David's wife E.	6321
1Ch	3: 3	and the sixth, Ithream, by his wife E.	6321

EGLAIM (1) [EN EGLAIM]

Isa	15: 8	their wailing reaches as far as E,	104

EGLATH SHELISHIYAH (2)

Isa	15: 5	as far as E.	6326
Jer	48:34	as far as Horonaim and E,	6326

EGLON (13)

Jos	10: 3	Japhia king of Lachish and Debir king of E.	6324
	10: 5	Jarmuth, Lachish and E—joined forces.	6324
	10:23	Hebron, Jarmuth, Lachish and E.	6324
	10:34	with him moved on from Lachish to E;	6324
	10:36	and all Israel with him went up from E	6324
	10:37	Just as at E, they totally destroyed it	6324
	12:12	the king of E the one the king of Gezer one	6324
	15:39	Lachish, Bozkath, E,	6324
Jdg	3:12	the LORD gave E king of Moab power	6323
	3:13	E came and attacked Israel,	NIH
	3:14	to E king of Moab for eighteen years.	6323
	3:15	with tribute to E king of Moab.	6323
	3:17	He presented the tribute to E king of Moab,	6323

EGYPT (609) [EGYPT'S, EGYPTIAN, EGYPTIAN'S, EGYPTIANS]

Ge	12:10	and Abram went down to E to live there for	5213
	12:11	As he was about to enter E,	5213
	12:14	When Abram came to E,	5213
	13: 1	So Abram went up from E to the Negev,	5213
	13:10	like the land of E, toward Zoar.	5213
	15:18	from the river of E to the great river,	5213
	21:21	his mother got a wife for him from E.	824+5213
	25:18	near the border of E,	5213
	26: 2	"Do not go down to E;	5213
	37:25	on their way to take them down to E.	5213
	37:28	who took him to E.	5213
	37:36	the Midianites sold Joseph in E to Potiphar,	5213
	39: 1	Now Joseph had been taken down to E.	5213
	40: 1	of the king of E offended their master,	5213
	40: 1	their master, the king of E.	5213
	40: 5	cupbearer and the baker of the king of E.	5213
	41: 8	for all the magicians and wise men of E.	5213
	41:19	in all the land of E.	5213
	41:29	throughout the land of E,	5213
	41:30	all the abundance in E will be forgotten,	824+5213
	41:33	and put him in charge of the land of E.	5213
	41:34	E during the seven years of abundance.	824+5213
	41:36	of famine that will come upon E,	824+5213
	41:41	in charge of the whole land of E."	5213
	41:43	in charge of the whole land of E.	5213
	41:44	or foot in all E."	824+5213
	41:45	And Joseph went throughout the land of E.	5213
	41:46	the service of Pharaoh king of E.	5213
	41:46	and traveled throughout E.	824+5213
	41:48	in E and stored it in the cities.	824+5213
	41:53	The seven years of abundance in E	824+5213
	41:54	but in the whole land of E there was food.	5213
	41:55	When all E began to feel the famine,	824+5213
	41:56	for the famine was severe throughout E.	824+5213
	41:57	the countries came to E to buy grain	5213
	42: 1	Jacob learned that there was grain in E,	5213
	42: 2	"I have heard that there is grain in E.	5213
	42: 3	down to buy grain from E.	5213
	43: 2	the grain they had brought from E,	5213
	43:15	to E and presented themselves to Joseph.	5213
	45: 4	the one you sold into E!	5213
	45: 8	his entire household and ruler of all E.	824+5213
	45: 9	God has made me lord of all E.	5213
	45:13	in E and about everything you have seen.	5213
	45:18	of E and you can enjoy the fat of the land.'	5213
	45:19	some carts from E for your children	824+5213
	45:20	because the best of all E will be yours.'	824+5213
	45:23	with the best things of E,	5213
	45:25	up out of E and came to their father Jacob	5213
	45:26	In fact, he is ruler of all E."	824+5213
	46: 3	"Do not be afraid to go down to E,	5213
	46: 4	I will go down to E with you,	5213
	46: 6	and Jacob and all his offspring went to E.	5213
	46: 7	with him to E his sons and grandsons	5213
	46: 8	and his descendants) who went to E:	5213
	46:20	In E, Manasseh and Ephraim were born	824+5213
	46:26	All those who went to E with Jacob—	5213
	46:27	two sons who had been born to Joseph in E,	5213
	46:27	which went to E, were seventy in all.	5213
	47: 6	and the land of E is before you;	5213
	47:11	in E and gave them property in the best	824+5213
	47:13	both E and Canaan wasted away	824+5213
	47:14	found in E and Canaan in payment for	824+5213
	47:15	the people of E and Canaan was gone,	824+5213
	47:15	all E came to Joseph and said,	5213
	47:20	Joseph bought all the land in E for Pharaoh.	5213

Ge	47:21	from one end of E to the other.	5213
	47:26	as a law concerning land in E—	5213
	47:27	Now the Israelites settled in E in the region of Goshen.	824+5213
	47:28	Jacob lived in E seventeen years,	824+5213
	47:29	Do not bury me in E,	5213
	47:30	of E and bury me where they are buried."	5213
	48: 5	in E before I came to you here	824+5213
	50: 7	his court and all the dignitaries of E—	824+5213
	50:14	burying his father, Joseph returned to E,	5213
	50:22	Joseph stayed in E,	5213
	50:26	he was placed in a coffin in E.	5213
Ex	1: 1	of Israel who went to E with Jacob, each	5213
	1: 5	Joseph was already in E.	5213
	1: 8	came to power in E.	5213
	1:15	of E said to the Hebrew midwives,	5213
	1:17	not do what the king of E had told them	5213
	1:18	the king of E summoned the midwives	5213
	2:23	During that long period, the king of E died.	5213
	3: 7	the misery of my people in E.	5213
	3:10	to bring my people the Israelites out of E."	5213
	3:11	and bring the Israelites out of E?"	5213
	3:12	you have brought the people out of E,	5213
	3:16	done to you in E.	5213
	3:17	to bring you up out of your misery in E into	5213
	3:18	the elders are to go to the king of E and say	5213
	3:19	that the king of E will not let you go unless	5213
	4:18	in E to see if any of them are still alive."	5213
	4:19	"Go back to E,	5213
	4:20	on a donkey and started back to E.	824+5213
	4:21	"When you return to E,	5213
	5: 4	But the king of E said, "Moses and Aaron,	5213
	5:12	E to gather stubble to use for straw,	824+5213
	6:11	of E to let the Israelites go out	5213
	6:13	about the Israelites and Pharaoh king of E,	5213
	6:13	to bring the Israelites out of E,	824+5213
	6:26	Israelites out of E by their divisions."	824+5213
	6:27	the ones who spoke to Pharaoh king of E	5213
	6:27	about bringing the Israelites out of E.	5213
	6:28	when the LORD spoke to Moses in E,	824+5213
	6:29	of E everything I tell you."	5213
	7: 3	and wonders in E,	824+5213
	7: 4	Then I will lay my hand on E and	5213
	7: 5	against E and bring the Israelites out of it."	5213
	7:19	over the waters of E—	5213
	7:19	Blood will be everywhere in E,	824+5213
	7:21	Blood was everywhere in E.	824+5213
	8: 5	and make frogs come up on the land of E.' "	5213
	8: 6	over the waters of E,	5213
	8: 7	also made frogs come up on the land of E.	5213
	8:16	the land of E the dust will become gnats."	5213
	8:17	throughout the land of E became gnats.	5213
	8:24	and throughout E the land was ruined	824+5213
	9: 4	the livestock of Israel and that of E,	5213
	9: 9	over the whole land of E,	5213
	9:18	that has ever fallen on E,	5213
	9:22	the sky so that hail will fall all over E	824+5213
	9:22	everything growing in the fields of E."	824+5213
	9:23	So the LORD rained hail on the land of E;	5213
	9:24	the land of E since it had become a nation.	5213
	9:25	Throughout E hail struck everything in	824+5213
	10: 7	Do you not yet realize that E is ruined?"	5213
	10:12	over E so that locusts will swarm over	824+5213
	10:13	So Moses stretched out his staff over E,	824+5213
	10:14	they invaded all E and settled down	824+5213
	10:15	on tree or plant in all the land of E.	5213
	10:19	Not a locust was left anywhere in E.	1473+5213
	10:21	so that darkness will spread over E—	824+5213
	10:22	total darkness covered all E for three days.	824+5213
	11: 1	on Pharaoh and on E.	5213
	11: 3	in E by Pharaoh's officials and by	824+5213
	11: 4	'About midnight I will go throughout E.	5213
	11: 5	Every firstborn son in E will die,	5213
	11: 6	will be loud wailing throughout E—	824+5213
	11: 7	the LORD makes a distinction between E	5213
	11: 9	so that my wonders may be multiplied in E."	824+5213
	12: 1	LORD said to Moses and Aaron in E,	824+5213
	12:12	that same night I will pass through E	824+5213
	12:12	I will bring judgment on all the gods of E.	5213
	12:13	when I strike E.	824+5213
	12:17	that I brought your divisions out of E.	5213
	12:27	of the Israelites in E and spared our homes	5213
	12:29	down all the firstborn in E,	824+5213
	12:30	and there was loud wailing in E,	5213
	12:39	With the dough they had brought from E,	5213
	12:39	of E and did not have time to prepare food	5213
	12:40	Israelite people lived in E was 430 years.	5213
	12:41	all the LORD's divisions left E.	824+5213
	12:42	that night to bring them out of E,	824+5213
	12:51	the LORD brought the Israelites out of E	824+5213
	13: 3	the day you came out of E,	5213
	13: 8	for me when I came out of E.'	5213
	13: 9	For the LORD brought you out of E	5213
	13:14	the LORD brought us out of E,	5213
	13:15	the LORD killed every firstborn in E,	824+5213
	13:16	that the LORD brought us out of E	5213
	13:17	and return to E."	5213
	13:18	The Israelites went up out of E armed	824+5213
	14: 5	king of E was told that the people had fled,	5213
	14: 7	along with all the other chariots in E,	5213
	14: 8	the heart of Pharaoh king of E,	5213
	14:11	"Was it because there were no graves in E	5213
	14:11	to us by bringing us out of E?	5213
	14:12	Didn't we say to you in E, 'Leave us alone;	5213
	14:20	coming between the armies of E and Israel.	5213
Ex	14:25	The LORD is fighting for them against E."	5213
	16: 1	after they had come out of E.	824+5213
	16: 3	by the LORD's hand in E!	824+5213
	16: 6	the LORD who brought you out of E,	824+5213
	16:32	in the desert when I brought you out of E.' "	824+5213
	17: 3	up out of E to make us and our children	5213
	18: 1	the LORD had brought Israel out of E.	5213
	19: 1	In the third month after the Israelites left E—	824+5213
	19: 4	'You yourselves have seen what I did to E,	5213
	20: 2	who brought you out of E,	824+5213
	22:21	for you were aliens in E.	824+5213
	23: 9	because you were aliens in E.	824+5213
	23:15	for in that month you came out of E.	5213
	29:46	of E so that I might dwell among them.	824+5213
	32: 1	Moses who brought us up out of E,	5213
	32: 4	O Israel, who brought you up out of E,	5213
	32: 7	whom you brought up out of E,	5213
	32: 8	O Israel, who brought you up out of E,	5213
	32:11	E with great power and a mighty hand?	824+5213
	32:23	Moses who brought us up out of E,	5213
	33: 1	and the people you brought up out of E,	824+5213
	34:18	for in that month you came out of E.	5213
Lev	11:45	the LORD who brought you out of E	824+5213
	18: 3	You must not do as they do in E,	824+5213
	19:34	for you were aliens in E.	824+5213
	19:36	who brought you out of E.	824+5213
	22:33	brought you out of E to be your God.	824+5213
	23:43	booths when I brought them out of E,	824+5213
	25:38	of E to give you the land of Canaan	5213
	25:42	whom I brought out of E,	824+5213
	25:55	whom I brought out of E,	824+5213
	26:13	E so that you would no longer be slaves	824+5213
	26:45	of E in the sight of the nations to	824+5213
Nu	1: 1	after the Israelites came out of E.	824+5213
	3:13	I struck down all the firstborn in E,	824+5213
	8:17	I struck down all the firstborn in E,	824+5213
	9: 1	second year after they came out of E.	824+5213
	11: 5	We remember the fish we ate in E	5213
	11:18	We were better off in E!"	5213
	11:20	saying, "Why did we ever leave E?" '"	5213
	13:22	before Zoan in E.)	5213
	14: 2	"If only we had died in E!	824+5213
	14: 3	be better for us to go back to E?"	5213
	14: 4	a leader and go back to E."	5213
	14:19	from the time they left E until now."	5213
	14:22	the miraculous signs I performed in E and	5213
	15:41	brought you out of E to be your God.	824+5213
	20: 5	Why did you bring us up out of E	5213
	20:15	Our forefathers went down into E,	5213
	20:16	and sent an angel and brought us out of E.	5213
	21: 5	"Why have you brought us up out of E	5213
	22: 5	Balak said: "A people has come out of E;	5213
	22:11	that has come out of E covers the face of	5213
	23:22	God brought them out of E;	5213
	24: 8	"God brought them out of E;	5213
	26: 4	the Israelites who came out of E:	824+5213
	26:59	who was born to the Levites in E.	5213
	32:11	of E will see the land I promised on oath	5213
	33: 1	the Israelites when they came out of E	824+5213
	33:38	after the Israelites came out of E.	824+5213
	34: 5	join the Wadi of E and end at the Sea.	5213
Dt	1:27	so he brought us out of E to deliver us	824+5213
	1:30	will fight for you, as he did for you in E,	5213
	4:20	of the iron-smelting furnace, out of E,	5213
	4:34	the LORD your God did for you in E	5213
	4:37	of E by his Presence and his great strength,	5213
	4:45	when they came out of E	5213
	4:46	and the Israelites as they came out of E.	5213
	5: 6	who brought you out of E,	824+5213
	5:15	Remember that you were slaves in E	824+5213
	6:12	who brought you out of E,	824+5213
	6:21	tell him: "We were slaves of Pharaoh in E,	5213
	6:22	but the LORD brought us out of E with	5213
	6:22	great and terrible—upon E and Pharaoh	5213
	7: 8	from the power of Pharaoh king of E.	5213
	7:15	on you the horrible diseases you knew in E,	5213
	7:18	to Pharaoh and to all E.	5213
	8:14	who brought you out of E,	824+5213
	9: 7	day you left E until you arrived here,	824+5213
	9:12	of E have become corrupt.	5213
	10:19	for you yourselves were aliens in E.	824+5213
	10:22	down into E were seventy in all,	5213
	11: 3	and the things he did in the heart of E, both	5213
	11: 3	of E and to his whole country;	5213
	11:10	to take over is not like the land of E,	5213
	13: 5	of E and redeemed you from the land	824+5213
	13:10	who brought you out of E,	824+5213
	15:15	Remember that you were slaves in E and	824+5213
	16: 1	the month of Abib he brought you out of E	5213
	16: 3	because you left E in haste—	824+5213
	16: 3	the time of your departure from E,	824+5213
	16: 6	the anniversary of your departure from E.	5213
	16:12	Remember that you were slaves in E,	5213
	17:16	the people return to E to get more of them,	5213
	20: 1	who brought you out of E,	824+5213
	23: 4	on your way when you came out of E,	5213
	24: 9	along the way after you came out of E.	5213
	24:18	Remember that you were slaves in E and	5213
	24:22	Remember that you were slaves in E.	824+5213
	25:17	along the way when you came out of E.	5213
	26: 5	and he went down into E with a few people	5213
	26: 8	So the LORD brought us out of E with	5213
	28:27	with the boils of E and with tumors,	5213
	28:60	He will bring upon you all the diseases of E	5213
Dt	28:68	in ships to E on a journey	5213
	29: 2	that the LORD did in E to Pharaoh,	824+5213
	29:16	yourselves know how we lived in E	824+5213
	29:25	when he brought them out of E.	824+5213
	34:11	the LORD sent him to do in E—	824+5213
Jos	2:10	for you when you came out of E,	5213
	5: 4	All those who came out of E	5213
	5: 4	in the desert on the way after leaving E.	5213
	5: 5	during the journey from E had not.	5213
	5: 6	of military age when they left E had died,	5213
	5: 9	the reproach of E from you."	5213
	9: 9	all that he did in E,	5213
	13: 3	on the east of E to the territory of Ekron on	5213
	15: 4	along to Azmon and joined the Wadi of E,	5213
	15:47	as far as the Wadi of E and the coastline of	5213
	24: 4	but Jacob and his sons went down to E.	5213
	24: 6	When I brought your fathers out of E,	5213
	24:14	beyond the River and in E,	5213
	24:17	and our fathers up out of E,	824+5213
	24:32	which the Israelites had brought up from E,	5213
Jdg	2: 1	"I brought you up out of E and led you into	5213
	2:12	who had brought them out of E.	824+5213
	6: 8	I brought you up out of E,	5213
	6: 9	I snatched you from the power of E and	5213
	6:13	not the LORD bring us up out of E?'	5213
	11:13	"When Israel came up out of E,	5213
	11:16	But when they came up out of E,	5213
	19:30	the day the Israelites came up out of E.	824+5213
1Sa	2:27	to your father's house when they were in E	5213
	8: 8	from the day I brought them up out of E	5213
	10:18	'I brought Israel up out of E,	5213
	10:18	from the power of E and all the kingdoms	5213
	12: 6	brought your forefathers up out of E.	824+5213
	12: 8	"After Jacob entered E,	5213
	12: 8	who brought your forefathers out of E	5213
	15: 2	as they came up from E.	5213
	15: 6	the Israelites when they came up out of E."	5213
	15: 7	to the east of E.	5213
	27: 8	in the land extending to Shur and E.)	824+5213
2Sa	7: 6	the day I brought the Israelites up out of E	5213
	7:23	whom you redeemed from E?	5213
1Ki	3: 1	an alliance with Pharaoh king of E	5213
	4:21	as far as the border of E.	5213
	4:30	and greater than all the wisdom of E.	5213
	6: 1	after the Israelites had come out of E,	824+5213
	8: 9	the Israelites after they came out of E.	824+5213
	8:16	the day I brought my people Israel out of E,	5213
	8:21	when he brought them out of E."	824+5213
	8:51	whom you brought out of E,	5213
	8:53	brought our fathers out of E."	5213
	8:65	from Lebo Hamath to the Wadi of E.	5213
	9: 9	who brought their fathers out of E,	824+5213
	9:16	of E had attacked and captured Gezer.	5213
	10:28	Solomon's horses were imported from E	5213
	10:29	from E for six hundred shekels of silver,	5213
	11:17	But Hadad, still only a boy, fled to E	5213
	11:18	they went to E, to Pharaoh king of Egypt,	5213
	11:18	they went to Egypt, to Pharaoh king of E,	5213
	11:21	While he was in E,	5213
	11:40	but Jeroboam fled to E,	5213
	12: 2	of Nebat heard this (he was still in E,	5213
	12: 2	he returned from E.	5213
	12:28	O Israel, who brought you up out of E."	824+5213
	14:25	Shishak king of E attacked Jerusalem.	5213
2Ki	17: 4	for he had sent envoys to So king of E,	5213
	17: 7	of E from under the power of Pharaoh	824+5213
	17: 7	from under the power of Pharaoh king of E.	5213
	17:36	up out of E with mighty power	5213
	18:21	Look now, you are depending on E,	5213
	18:21	of E to all who depend on him.	5213
	18:24	though you are depending on E for chariots	5213
	19: 9	the Cushite king [of E],	NIH
	19:24	up all the streams of E."	5191
	21:15	from the day their forefathers came out of E	5213
	23:29	he went up to the Euphrates River to help	5213
	23:34	he took Jehoahaz and carried him off to E,	5213
	24: 7	The king of E did not march out	5213
	24: 7	from the Wadi of E to the Euphrates River.	5213
	25:26	fled to E for fear of the Babylonians.	5213
1Ch	13: 5	the Shihor River in E to Lebo Hamath,	5213
	17: 5	from the day I brought Israel up out of E	NIH
	17:21	whom you redeemed from E?	5213
2Ch	1:16	Solomon's horses were imported from E	5213
	1:17	from E for six hundred shekels of silver,	5213
	5:10	with the Israelites after they came out of E.	5213
	6: 5	the day I brought my people out of E,	824+5213
	7: 8	from Lebo Hamath to the Wadi of E.	5213
	7:22	who brought them out of E,	824+5213
	9:26	as far as the border of E.	5213
	9:28	Solomon's horses were imported from E	5213
	10: 2	of Nebat heard this (he was in E,	5213
	10: 2	he returned from E.	5213
	12: 2	Shishak king of E attacked Jerusalem in	5213
	12: 3	and Cushites that came with him from E,	5213
	12: 9	Shishak king of E attacked Jerusalem,	5213
	20:10	to invade when they came from E;	824+5213
	26: 8	his fame spread as far as the border of E	5213
	35:20	of E went up to fight at Carchemish on	5213
	36: 3	The king of E dethroned him in Jerusalem	5213
	36: 4	The king of E made Eliakim,	5213
	36: 4	and carried him off to E.	5213
Ne	9: 9	the suffering of our forefathers in E;	5213
	9:18	who brought you up out of E,'	5213
Ps	68:31	Envoys will come from E;	5213
	78:12	in the sight of their fathers in the land of E,	5213
	78:43	day he displayed his miraculous signs in E,	5213
	78:51	He struck down all the firstborn of E,	5213

Ps	80: 8	You brought a vine out of E;	5213
	81: 5	for Joseph when he went out against E,	824+5213
	81:10	who brought you up out of E.	824+5213
	105:23	Then Israel entered E;	5213
	105:38	E was glad when they left,	5213
	106: 7	When our fathers were in E,	5213
	106:21	who had done great things in E,	5213
	114: 1	When Israel came out of E,	5213
	135: 8	He struck down the firstborn of E,	5213
	135: 9	O E, against Pharaoh and all his servants.	5213
	136:10	who struck down the firstborn of E	5213
Pr	7:16	with colored linens from E.	5213
Isa	7:18	of E and for bees from the land of Assyria.	5213
	10:24	and lift up a club against you, as E did.	5213
	10:26	as he did in E.	5213
	11:11	from **Lower** E, from Upper Egypt,	5213
	11:11	from **Upper** E, from Cush, from Elam,	7356
	11:16	for Israel when they came up from E.	824+5213
	19: 1	An oracle concerning E:	5213
	19: 1	on a swift cloud and is coming to E.	5213
	19: 1	The idols of E tremble before him,	5213
	19: 6	the streams of E will dwindle and dry up.	5191
	19:12	and make known what the LORD Almighty has planned against E.	5213
	19:13	of her peoples have led E astray.	5213
	19:14	they make E stagger in all that she does,	5213
	19:15	There is nothing E can do—	5213
	19:18	in E will speak the language of Canaan	824+5213
	19:19	an altar to the LORD in the heart of E,	824+5213
	19:20	to the LORD Almighty in the land of E;	5213
	19:22	The LORD will strike E with a plague;	5213
	19:23	In that day there will be a highway from E	5213
	19:23	to E and the Egyptians to Assyria.	5213
	19:24	along with E and Assyria,	5213
	19:25	saying, "Blessed be E my people,	5213
	20: 3	as a sign and portent against E and Cush,	5213
	20: 5	in Cush and boasted in E will be afraid	5213
	23: 5	When word comes to E,	5213
	27:12	the flowing Euphrates to the Wadi of E,	5213
	27:13	in E will come and worship the LORD	824+5213
	30: 2	who go down to E without consulting me;	5213
	30: 7	to E, whose help is utterly useless.	5213
	31: 1	Woe to those who go down to E for help,	5213
	36: 6	Look now, you are depending on E,	5213
	36: 6	to all who depend on him.	5213
	36: 9	though you are depending on E for chariots	5213
	37: 9	the Cushite king [of E],	NIH
	37:25	up all the streams of E.'	5191
	43: 3	I give E for your ransom,	5213
	45:14	products of E and the merchandise of Cush,	5213
	52: 4	"At first my people went down to E to live;	5213
Jer	2: 6	who brought us up out of E and led us	824+5213
	2:18	Now why go to E to drink water from	5213
	2:36	You will be disappointed by E as you were	5213
	7:22	I brought your forefathers out of E	824+5213
	7:25	the time your forefathers left E until	824+5213
	9:26	E, Judah, Edom, Ammon, Moab	5213
	11: 4	when I brought them out of E,	824+5213
	11: 7	up from E until today,	824+5213
	16:14	who brought the Israelites up out of E,'	824+5213
	23: 7	who brought the Israelites up out of E,'	824+5213
	24: 8	in this land or live in E.	824+5213
	25:19	Pharaoh king of E,	5213
	26:21	But Uriah heard of it and fled in fear to E.	5213
	26:22	however, sent Elnathan son of Acbor to E,	5213
	26:23	They brought Uriah out of E and took him	5213
	31:32	by the hand to lead them out of E,	824+5213
	32:20	signs and wonders in E and	5213
	32:21	You brought your people Israel out of E	824+5213
	34:13	when I brought them out of E,	824+5213
	37: 5	Pharaoh's army had marched out of E,	5213
	37: 7	will go back to its own land, to E.	5213
	41:17	near Bethlehem on their way to E	5213
	42:14	'No, we will go and live in E,	824+5213
	42:15	to go to E and you do go to settle there,	5213
	42:16	famine you dread will follow you into E,	5213
	42:17	to E to settle there will die by the sword,	5213
	42:18	be poured out on you when you go to E.	5213
	42:19	the LORD has told you, 'Do not go to E.'	5213
	43: 2	'You must not go to E to settle there.'	5213
	43: 7	So they entered E in disobedience to	824+5213
	43:11	He will come and attack E,	824+5213
	43:12	to the temples of the gods of E;	5213
	43:12	so will he wrap E around himself	824+5213
	43:13	temple of the sun in E he will demolish	824+5213
	43:13	down the temples of the gods of E.' "	5213
	44: 1	concerning all the Jews living in **Lower** E—	824+5213
	44: 1	and in **Upper** E:	824+7356
	44: 8	burning incense to other gods in E,	824+5213
	44:12	Judah who were determined to go to E	824+5213
	44:12	They will all perish in E;	824+5213
	44:13	I will punish those who live in E with	824+5213
	44:14	in E will escape or survive to return	824+5213
	44:15	people living in **Lower** and Upper E,	824+5213
	44:24	all you people of Judah in E.	824+5213
	44:26	all Jews living in E:	824+5213
	44:26	in E will ever again invoke my name	824+5213
	44:27	in E will perish by sword and famine	824+5213
	44:28	return to the land of Judah from E will	824+5213
	44:28	in E will know whose word will stand	824+5213
	44:30	of E over to his enemies who seek his life,	5213
	46: 2	Concerning E: This is the message against	5213
	46: 2	of E, which was defeated at Carchemish on	5213
	46: 8	E rises like the Nile,	5213
	46:11	O Virgin Daughter of E.	5213
	46:13	of Babylon to attack E:	824+5213

Jer	46:14	"Announce this in E, and proclaim it	5213
	46:17	'Pharaoh king of E is only a loud noise;	5213
	46:19	you who live in E,	1426+5213
	46:20	"E is a beautiful heifer,	5213
	46:22	E will hiss like a fleeing serpent as	2023S
	46:24	The Daughter of E will be put to shame,	5213
	46:25	on E and her gods and her kings,	5213
	46:26	E will be inhabited as in times past,"	NIH
La	5: 6	to E and Assyria to get enough bread.	5213
Eze	17:15	by sending his envoys to E to get horses	5213
	19: 4	They led him with hooks to the land of E.	5213
	20: 5	and revealed myself to them in E.	824+5213
	20: 6	them that I would bring them out of E	824+5213
	20: 7	do not defile yourselves with the idols of E.	5213
	20: 8	nor did they forsake the idols of E.	5213
	20: 8	and spend my anger against them in E.	824+5213
	20: 9	the Israelites by bringing them out of E.	824+5213
	20:10	of E and brought them into the desert.	824+5213
	20:36	in the desert of the land of E,	5213
	23: 3	They became prostitutes in E,	5213
	23: 8	not give up the prostitution she began in E,	5213
	23:19	when she was a prostitute in E.	5213
	23:21	when in E your bosom was caressed	5213
	23:27	and prostitution you began in E.	824+5213
	23:27	with longing or remember E anymore.	5213
	27: 7	from E was your sail and served	5213
	29: 2	against Pharaoh king of E and prophesy	5213
	29: 2	and prophesy against him and against all E.	5213
	29: 3	" 'I am against you, Pharaoh king of E,	5213
	29: 6	Then all who live in E will know that I am	5213
	29: 9	E will become a desolate wasteland.	824+5213
	29:10	the land of E a ruin and a desolate waste	5213
	29:12	of E desolate among devastated lands,	5213
	29:14	captivity and return them to **Upper** E,	824+7356
	29:16	E will no longer be a source of confidence	NIH
	29:19	to give E to Nebuchadnezzar king	824+5213
	29:20	I have given him E as a reward	824+5213
	30: 4	A sword will come against E,	5213
	30: 4	When the slain fall in E,	5213
	30: 5	by the sword along with E.	4392S
	30: 6	" 'The allies of E will fall	5213
	30: 8	to E and all her helpers are crushed.	5213
	30:10	of E by the hand of Nebuchadnezzar king	5213
	30:11	against E and fill the land with the slain.	5213
	30:13	No longer will there be a prince in E,	824+5213
	30:14	I will lay waste **Upper** E,	7356
	30:15	the stronghold of E;	5213
	30:16	I will set fire to E;	5213
	30:18	At Tahpanhes when I break the yoke of E;	5213
	30:19	So I will inflict punishment on E,	5213
	30:21	the arm of Pharaoh king of E.	5213
	30:22	I am against Pharaoh king of E,	5213
	30:25	and he brandishes it against E.	824+5213
	31: 2	say to Pharaoh king of E and to his hordes:	5213
	32: 2	up a lament concerning Pharaoh king of E	5213
	32:12	They will shatter the pride of E,	5213
	32:15	I make E desolate and strip the land	824+5213
	32:16	for E and all her hordes they will chant it,	5213
	32:18	wail for the hordes of E and consign to	5213
	32:21	the grave the mighty leaders will say of E	2257S
	47:19	along the Wadi [of E] to the Great Sea.	NIH
	48:28	along the Wadi [of E] to the Great Sea.	NIH
Da	9:15	of E with a mighty hand and who made	824+5213
	11: 8	of silver and gold and carry them off to E.	5213
	11:42	E will not escape.	824+5213
	11:43	of gold and silver and all the riches of E,	5213
Hos	2:15	as in the day she came up out of E.	824+5213
	7:11	now calling to E, now turning to Assyria.	5213
	7:16	this they will be ridiculed in the land of E.	5213
	8:13	They will return to E.	5213
	9: 3	to E and eat unclean food in Assyria.	5213
	9: 6	E will gather them,	5213
	11: 1	I loved him, and out of E I called my son.	5213
	11: 5	and will not Assyria rule over them	824+5213
	11:11	like birds from E,	5213
	12: 1	with Assyria and sends olive oil to E.	5213
	12: 9	[who brought you] out of E;	824+5213
	12:13	a prophet to bring Israel up from E,	5213
	13: 4	[who brought you] out of E;	824+5213
Joel	3:19	But E will be desolate,	5213
Am	2:10	"I brought you up out of E,	824+5213
	3: 1	the whole family I brought up out of E:	824+5213
	3: 9	of Ashdod and to the fortresses of E:	824+5213
	4:10	"I sent plagues among you as I did to E.	5213
	8: 8	up and then sink like the river of E.	5213
	9: 5	then sinks like the river of E—	5213
	9: 7	"Did I not bring Israel up from E,	824+5213
Mic	6: 4	of E and redeemed you from the land	824+5213
	7:12	to you from Assyria and the cities of E,	5191
	7:12	from E to the Euphrates and from sea to sea	5191
	7:15	As in the days when you came out of E,	824+5213
Na	3: 9	Cush and E were her boundless strength;	5213
Hag	2: 5	with you when you came out of E.	5213
Zec	10:10	from E and gather them from Assyria.	824+5213
	14:19	be the punishment of E and the punishment	5213
Mt	2:13	the child and his mother and escape to E.	131
	2:14	during the night and left for E,	131
	2:15	"Out of E I called my son."	131
	2:19	in a dream to Joseph in E	131
Ac	2:10	E and the parts of Libya near Cyrene;	131
	7: 9	they sold him as a slave into E.	131
	7:10	to gain the goodwill of Pharaoh king *of* E;	131
	7:10	he made him ruler over E and all his palace.	131
	7:11	"Then a famine struck all E and Canaan,	131
	7:12	that there was grain in E,	131
	7:15	Then Jacob went down to E,	131
	7:17	of our people in E greatly increased.	131

Ac	7:18	became ruler of E.	131
	7:34	the oppression of my people in E.	131
	7:34	Now come, I will send you back to E.'	131
	7:36	of E and did wonders and miraculous signs	NIG
	7:36	did wonders and miraculous signs in E,	131+1178
	7:39	and in their hearts turned back to E.	131
	7:40	this fellow Moses who led us out of E	131+1178
	13:17	people prosper during their stay in E,	131+1178
Heb	3:16	not all those Moses led out of E?	131
	8: 9	by the hand to lead them out of E,	131+1178
	11:22	**exodus** of the Israelites **from** E	2016
	11:26	as of greater value than the treasures *of* E,	131
	11:27	By faith he left E,	131
Jude	1: 5	the Lord delivered his people out of E,	131+1178
Rev	11: 8	which is figuratively called Sodom and E,	131

EGYPT'S (5) [EGYPT]

Isa	20: 4	with buttocks bared—to E shame.	5213
	30: 2	to E shade for refuge.	5213
	30: 3	E shade will bring you disgrace.	5213
Eze	30: 9	of them on the day of E doom,	5213
Zec	10:11	down and E scepter will pass away.	5213

EGYPTIAN (35) [EGYPT]

Ge	16: 1	she had an E maidservant named Hagar;	5212
	16: 3	Sarai his wife took her E maidservant Hagar	5212
	21: 9	the E had borne to Abraham was mocking,	5212
	25:12	whom Sarah's maidservant, Hagar the E,	5212
	39: 1	an E who was one of Pharaoh's officials,	5212
	39: 2	and he lived in the house of his E master.	5212
	39: 5	the LORD blessed the household of the E	5212
Ex	1:19	"Hebrew women are not like E women;	5212
	2:11	He saw an E beating a Hebrew,	5212
	2:12	he killed the E and hid him in the sand.	5212
	2:14	of killing me as you killed the E?"	5212
	2:19	"An E rescued us from the shepherds.	5212
	7:11	the E magicians also did the same things	5213
	7:22	But the E magicians did the same things	5213
	14:24	of fire and cloud at the E army and threw it	5213
Lev	24:10	an Israelite mother and an E father went out	5212
Dt	11: 4	what he did to the E army,	5212
	23: 7	Do not abhor an E,	5212
1Sa	30:11	They found an E in a field and brought him	5212
	30:13	He said, "I am an E,	5212
2Sa	23:21	And he struck down a huge E.	5212
	23:21	Although the E had a spear in his hand,	5212
2Ki	7: 6	of Israel has hired the Hittite and E kings	5213
1Ch	2:34	He had an E servant named Jarha.	5212
	11:23	And he struck down an E who was seven	5212
	11:23	the E had a spear like a weaver's rod	5212
Isa	11:15	up the gulf of the E sea;	5213
	19: 2	"I will stir up E against Egyptian—	5213
	19: 2	"I will stir up Egyptian against E—	5213
	20: 4	the E captives and Cushite exiles, young	5213
Zec	14:18	If the E people do not go up and take part,	5213
Ac	7:24	of them being mistreated by an E,	NIG
	7:24	and avenged him by killing the E.	130
	7:28	to kill me as you killed the E yesterday?'	130
	21:38	"Aren't you the E who started a revolt	130

EGYPTIAN'S (2) [EGYPT]

2Sa	23:21	the spear from the E hand and killed him	5212
1Ch	11:23	the spear from the E hand and killed him	5212

EGYPTIANS (91) [EGYPT]

Ge	12:12	When the E see you, they will say,	5213
	12:14	the E saw that she was	5213
	41:55	Then Pharaoh told all the E,	5213
	41:56	the storehouses and sold grain to the E,	5213
	43:32	and the E who ate with him by themselves,	5213
	43:32	because E could not eat with Hebrews,	5213
	43:32	for that is detestable to E.	5213
	45: 2	he wept so loudly that the E heard him,	5213
	46:34	for all shepherds are detestable to the E."	5213
	47:20	The E, one and all, sold their fields,	5213
	50: 3	And the E mourned for him seventy days.	5213
	50:11	"The E are holding a solemn ceremony	5213
Ex	1:12	so the E came to dread the Israelites	NIH
	1:14	the E used them ruthlessly.	NIH
	3: 8	down to rescue them from the hand of the E	5213
	3: 9	the way the E are oppressing them.	5213
	3:20	and strike the E with all the wonders	5213
	3:21	"And I will make the E favorably disposed	5213
	3:22	And so you will plunder the E."	5213
	6: 5	whom the E are enslaving,	5213
	6: 6	from under the yoke of the E.	5213
	6: 7	from under the yoke of the E.	5213
	7: 5	And the E will know that I am the LORD	5213
	7:18	the E will not be able to drink its water.' "	5213
	7:21	so bad that the E could not drink its water.	5213
	7:24	And all the E dug along the Nile	5213
	8:21	The houses of the E will be full of flies,	5213
	8:26	be detestable to the E,	5213
	9: 6	All the livestock of the E died,	5213
	9:11	that were on them and on all the E.	5213
	10: 2	with the E and how I performed my signs	5213
	10: 6	those of all your officials and all the E—	5213
	11: 3	the E favorably disposed toward the people,	5213
	12:23	through the land to strike down the E,	5213
	12:27	when he struck down the E.' "	5213
	12:30	and all his officials and all the E got up	5213
	12:33	The E urged the people to hurry and leave	5213
	12:35	as Moses instructed and asked **the** E	5213
	12:36	the E favorably disposed toward the people,	5213

Ex	12:36	so they plundered the **E**.	5213
	14: 4	and the **E** will know that I am the LORD."	5213
	14: 9	The **E**—all Pharaoh's horses	5213
	14:10	and there were the **E**, marching after them.	5213
	14:12	let us serve the **E**'?	5213
	14:12	to serve the **E** than to die in the desert!"	5213
	14:13	**E** you see today you will never see again.	5213
	14:17	of the **E** so that they will go in after them.	5213
	14:18	The **E** will know that I am the LORD	5213
	14:23	The **E** pursued them,	5213
	14:25	And the **E** said,	5213
	14:26	so that the waters may flow back over the **E**	5213
	14:27	The **E** were fleeing toward it,	5213
	14:30	from the hands of the **E**,	5213
	14:30	Israel saw the **E** lying dead on the shore.	5213
	14:31	the LORD displayed against the **E**,	5213
	15:26	of the diseases I brought on the **E**,	5213
	18: 8	the LORD had done to Pharaoh and the **E**	5213
	18: 9	in rescuing them from the hand of the **E**,	5213
	18:10	who rescued you from the hand of the **E**	5213
	18:10	the people from the hand of the **E**.	5213
	32:12	Why should the **E** say,	5213
Lev	26:13	be slaves to **the E**;	2157S
Nu	14:13	"Then the **E** will hear about it!	5213
	20:15	The **E** mistreated us and our fathers,	5213
	33: 3	in full view of all the **E**,	5213
Dt	26: 6	But the **E** mistreated us and made us suffer,	5213
Jos	24: 5	and I afflicted the **E** by what I did there,	5213
	24: 6	and the **E** pursued them with chariots	5213
	24: 7	he put darkness between you and the **E**;	5213
	24: 7	with your own eyes what I did to the **E**.	5213
Jdg	10:11	The LORD replied, "When the **E**,	5213
1Sa	4: 8	the **E** with all kinds of plagues in the desert.	5213
	6: 6	Why do you harden your hearts as the **E**	5213
Ezr	9: 1	Ammonites, Moabites, **E** and Amorites.	5212
Ne	9:10	how arrogantly the **E** treated them.	NIH
Isa	19: 1	and the hearts of the **E** melt within them.	5213
	19: 3	The **E** will lose heart,	5213
	19: 4	the **E** over to the power of a cruel master,	5213
	19:16	In that day the **E** will be like women.	5213
	19:17	the land of Judah will bring terror to the **E**;	5213
	19:21	LORD will make himself known to the **E**,	5213
	19:23	The Assyrians will go to Egypt and the **E**	5213
	19:23	The **E** and Assyrians will worship together.	5213
	31: 3	But the **E** are men and not God;	5213
Eze	16:26	engaged in prostitution with the **E**,	1201+5213
	29:12	And I will disperse the **E** among the nations	5213
	29:13	At the end of forty years I will gather the **E**	5213
	30:23	the **E** among the nations and scatter them	5213
	30:26	the **E** among the nations and scatter them	5213
Ac	7:22	the wisdom *of* the **E** and was powerful	130
Heb	11:29	the **E** tried to do so, they were drowned.	130

EHI (1)

Ge	46:21	Bela, Beker, Ashbel, Gera, Naaman,	305

EHUD (12)

Jdg	3:15	**E**, a left-handed man, the son of Gera	179
	3:16	Now **E** had made a double-edged sword	179
	3:18	After **E** had presented the tribute,	NIH
	3:20	**E** then approached him	179
	3:21	**E** reached with his left hand,	179
	3:22	**E** did not pull the sword out.	NIH
	3:23	Then **E** went out to the porch;	179
	3:26	While they waited, **E** got away.	179
	3:31	After **E** came Shamgar son of Anath,	2257S
	4: 1	After **E** died, the Israelites once again did evil in the eyes of the LORD.	179
1Ch	7:10	The sons of Bilhan: Jeush, Benjamin, **E**,	179
	8: 6	These were the descendants of **E**,	287

EIGHT (38) [EIGHTH]

Ge	17:12	among you who is **e** days old must	9046
	21: 4	When his son Isaac was **e** days old,	9046
	22:23	Milcah bore these **e** sons	9046
Ex	26:25	be **e** frames and sixteen silver bases—	9046
	36:30	So there were **e** frames	9046
Nu	7: 8	and he gave four carts and **e** oxen to	9046
	29:29	" 'On the sixth day prepare **e** bulls,	9046
Jdg	3: 8	the Israelites were subject for **e** years.	9046
	12:14	He led Israel **e** years.	9046
1Sa	17:12	Jesse had **e** sons,	9046
2Sa	23: 8	he raised his spear against **e** hundred men,	9046
	24: 9	In Israel there were **e** hundred thousand able-bodied men who could handle	9046
1Ki	7:10	some measuring ten cubits and some **e**.	9046
2Ki	8:17	and he reigned in Jerusalem **e** years.	9046
	22: 1	Josiah was **e** years old	9046
1Ch	24: 4	from Eleazar's descendants and **e** heads	9046
2Ch	13: 3	with **e** hundred thousand able troops.	9046
	21: 5	and he reigned in Jerusalem **e** years.	9046
	21:20	and he reigned in Jerusalem **e** years.	9046
	29:17	For **e** more days they consecrated	9046
	34: 1	Josiah was **e** years old	9046
Ecc	11: 2	Give portions to seven, yes to **e**,	9046
Jer	41:15	and **e** *of* his men escaped from Johanan	9046
Eze	40: 9	it was **e** cubits deep	9046
	40:31	and **e** steps led up to it.	9046
	40:34	and **e** steps led up to it.	9046
	40:37	and **e** steps led up to it.	9046
	40:41	**e** tables in all—	9046
Mic	5: 5	even **e** leaders of men.	9046
Mk	6:37	**e** months of a man's wages!	1324+1357
Lk	9:28	About **e** days after Jesus said this,	3044
	16: 6	" '**E** hundred gallons** of olive oil,'	1004+1669

Lk	16: 7	'Take your bill and make it **e** hundred.'	3837
Jn	6: 7	"**E** months' wages" would not buy	1324+1357
Ac	7: 8	and circumcised him **e** days after his birth.	3838
	9:33	a paralytic who had been bedridden for **e** years.	3893
	25: 6	After spending **e** or ten days with them,	3893
1Pe	3:20	In it only a few people, **e** in all,	3893

EIGHTEEN (15) [EIGHTEENTH, 18]

Jdg	3:14	to Eglon king of Moab for **e** years,	6926+9046
	10: 8	For **e** years they oppressed all the Israelites	6926+9046
	20:25	they cut down another **e** thousand Israelites,	6926+9046
	20:44	**E** thousand Benjamites fell,	6925+9046
2Sa	8:13	striking down **e** thousand Edomites in	6925+9046
1Ki	7:15	each **e** cubits high and twelve cubits	6926+9046
2Ki	24: 8	Jehoiachin was **e** years old	6926+9046
1Ch	18:12	struck down **e** thousand Edomites in	6925+9046
	29: 7	**e** thousand talents of bronze and	547+2256+8052+9046
2Ch	11:21	he had **e** wives and sixty concubines,	6926+9046
	36: 9	Jehoiachin was **e** years old	6926+9046
Jer	52:21	Each of the pillars was **e** cubits high	6926+9046
Lk	13: 4	Or those **e** who died when the tower	1277
	13:11	crippled by a spirit *for* **e** years.	1277
	13:16	kept bound *for* **e** long years,	1274+2779+3893

EIGHTEENTH (11) [EIGHTEEN]

1Ki	15: 1	In the **e** year of the reign of Jeroboam	6926+9046
2Ki	3: 1	in the **e** year of Jehoshaphat king of	6926+9046
	22: 3	In the **e** year of his reign,	6926+9046
	23:23	But in the **e** year of King Josiah,	6926+9046
1Ch	24:15	the **e** to Happizzez,	6925+9046
	24:15	the **e** to Hanani, his sons and relatives,	6925+9046
2Ch	13: 1	In the **e** year of the reign of Jeroboam,	6926+9046
	34: 8	In the **e** year of Josiah's reign,	6926+9046
	35:19	Passover was celebrated in the **e** year	6926+9046
Jer	32: 1	the **e** year of Nebuchadnezzar.	6926+9046
	52:29	Nebuchadnezzar's **e** year, 832 people	6926+9046

EIGHTH (35) [EIGHT]

Ex	22:30	but give them to me on the **e** day.	9029
Lev	9: 1	On the **e** day Moses summoned Aaron	9029
	12: 3	On the **e** day the boy is to be circumcised.	9029
	14:10	On the **e** day he must bring two male lambs	9029
	14:23	"On the **e** day he must bring them	9029
	15:14	On the **e** day he must take two doves	9029
	15:29	On the **e** day she must take two doves	9029
	22:27	From the **e** day on,	9029
	23:36	and on the **e** day hold a sacred assembly	9029
	23:39	and the **e** day also is a day of rest.	9029
	25:22	While you plant during the **e** year,	9029
Nu	6:10	Then on the **e** day he must bring two doves	9029
	7:54	On the **e** day Gamaliel son of Pedahzur,	9029
	29:35	" 'On the **e** day hold an assembly	9029
1Ki	6:38	the **e** month, the temple was finished	9029
	12:32	on the fifteenth day of the **e** month,	9029
	12:33	On the fifteenth day of the **e** month,	9029
2Ki	24:12	In the **e** year of the reign of the king	9046
1Ch	12:12	Johanan the **e**, Elzabad the ninth,	9029
	24:10	the seventh to Hakkoz, the **e** to Abijah,	9029
	25:15	the **e** to Jeshaiah, his sons and relatives, 12	9029
	26: 5	Issachar the seventh and Peullethai the **e**.	9029
	27:11	The **e**, for the eighth month,	9029
	27:11	The eighth, for the **e** month,	9029
2Ch	7: 9	On the **e** day they held an assembly,	9029
	29:17	and by the **e** day of the month they reached	9046
	34: 3	In the **e** year of his reign,	9046
Ne	8:18	and on the **e** day,	9046
Eze	43:27	At the end of these days, from the **e** day on,	9029
Zec	1: 1	In the **e** month of the second year of Darius,	9029
Lk	1:59	the **e** day they came to circumcise the child,	3838
	2:21	the **e** day, when it was time to circumcise	3893
Php	3: 5	circumcised on the **e day**, of the people	3892
Rev	17:11	and now is not, is an **e** king.	3838
	21:20	the seventh chrysolite, the **e** beryl,	3838

EIGHTIETH (1) [EIGHTY]

1Ki	6: 1	and **e** year after the Israelites had come out	9046

EIGHTY (16) [EIGHTIETH, 80]

Ge	35:28	Isaac lived a hundred and **e** years.	9046
Ex	7: 7	Moses was **e** years old	9046
Jdg	3:30	and the land had peace for **e** years.	9046
2Sa	19:32	Barzillai was a very old man, **e** years of age.	9046
	19:35	I am now **e** years old.	9046
1Ki	5:15	and **e** thousand stonecutters in the hills,	9046
	12:21	a hundred and **e** thousand fighting men—	9046
2Ki	6:25	a donkey's head sold for **e** shekels of silver,	9046
	10:24	Now Jehu had posted **e** men outside	9046
2Ch	2: 2	as carriers and **e** thousand as stonecutters in	9046
	11: 1	a hundred and **e** thousand fighting men—	9046
	14: 8	and two hundred and **e** thousand	9046
	26:17	the priest with **e** other courageous priests of	9046
Ps	90:10	or **e**, if we have the strength;	9046
SS	6: 8	**e** concubines, and virgins beyond number;	9046
Jer	41: 5	**e** men who had shaved off their beards,	9046

EIGHTY-FIVE (4)

Jos	14:10	So here I am today, **e** years old!	2256+2822+9046
1Sa	22:18	he killed **e** men who wore	2256+2822+9046
2Ki	19:35	a hundred and **e** thousand men	2256+2822+9046

Isa	37:36	a hundred and **e** thousand men	2256+2822+9046

EIGHTY-FOUR (1)

Lk	2:37	was a widow until she was **e**.	2291+3837+5475

EIGHTY-SIX (1)

Ge	16:16	Abram was **e** years old	2256+9046+9252

EIGHTY-THREE (1)

Ex	7: 7	and Aaron **e** when they spoke to Pharaoh.	2256+8993+9046

EITHER (41)

Ge	31:24	not to say anything to Jacob, **e** good or bad.	4946
	31:29	not to say anything to Jacob, **e** good or bad.	4946
Ex	21:16	"Anyone who kidnaps another **and e**	2256
Lev	1:10	an animal from **e** the herd **or** the flock.	2256
	1:10	from **e** the sheep **or** the goats,	196
	18: 9	**e** your father's daughter **or**	196
	18:17	**e** her son's daughter **or**	2256
	20:17	the daughter of **e** his father **or** his mother,	196
	20:19	the sister of **e** your mother **or** your father,	2256
	22:18	**e** an Israelite **or** an alien living in Israel—	2256
	22:18	**e** to fulfill a vow **or** as a freewill offering,	2256
Nu	22:26	**e** to the right **or** to the left	2256
Dt	1:37	"You shall not enter it, **e**.	1685
	22: 6	in a tree **or** on the ground,	196
1Sa	16: 8	"The LORD has not chosen this one **e**."	1685
	20:27	**e** yesterday or today?"	1685
	26:10	**e** his time will come and he will die,	196
	28:15	**e** by prophets **or** by dreams.	1685
2Sa	13:22	**e** good or bad;	4946
1Ki	10:20	one at **e** end of each step.	2256+2296+2296+4946+4946S
2Ki	9:20	but he isn't coming back **e**.	NIH
	18: 5	**e** before him or after him.	2256
2Ch	9:19	one at **e** end of each step.	2256+2296+2296+4946+4946S
Jer	29:19	And you exiles have not listened **e**,"	NIH
Eze	1:11	the wing of another creature on **e** side,	NIH
	40:34	palm trees decorated the jambs on **e** side,	2256+4946+4946+7024+7024
	40:37	palm trees decorated the jambs on **e** side,	2256+4946+4946+7024+7024
	40:48	they were five cubits wide **on e** side.	2256+4946+4946+7024+7024
	40:48	its projecting walls were three cubits wide **on e** side.	2256+4946+4946+7024+7024
Am	7: 6	"This will not happen **e**,"	1685
Zep	1:12	'The LORD will do nothing, **e** good or bad.'	4202
Mt	5:34	**e** by heaven, for it is God's throne;	3612
	6:24	**E** he will hate the one and love the other,	2445
	12:32	**e** in this age or in the age to come.	4046
Mk	16:13	but they did not believe them **e**.	NIG
Lk	16:13	**E** he will hate the one and love the other,	2445
Jn	19:10	"Don't you realize I have power **e**	NIG
Ro	11:21	he will **not** spare you **e**.	4028
1Co	15:16	then Christ has **not** been raised **e**.	4028
1Jn	3:15	No one who continues to sin has **e** seen him	NIG
Rev	3:15	I wish you were **e** one or the other!	NIG

EJECTED (1)

Ac	18:16	So *he* **had** them **e** from the court.	590

EKED See BETH EKED

EKER (1)

1Ch	2:27	Maaz, Jamin and **E**.	6831

EKRON (24)

Jos	13: 3	on the east of Egypt to the territory of **E** on	6833
	13: 3	Ashdod, Ashkelon, Gath and **E**—	6834
	15:11	It went to the northern slope of **E**,	6833
	15:45	**E**, with its surrounding settlements	6833
	15:46	west of **E**, all that were in the vicinity	6833
	19:43	Elon, Timnah, **E**,	6833
Jdg	1:18	and **E**—each city with its territory.	6833
1Sa	5:10	So they sent the ark of God to **E**.	6833
	5:10	As the ark of God was entering **E**,	6833
	5:10	the **people** of **E** cried out,	6834
	6:16	and then returned that same day to **E**.	6833
	6:17	Gaza, Ashkelon, Gath and **E**.	6833
	17:52	The towns from **E** to Gath that	6833
	17:52	the entrance of Gath and to the gates of **E**.	6833
	17:52	along the Shaaraim road to Gath and **E**.	6833
2Ki	1: 2	"Go and consult Baal-Zebub, the god of **E**,	6833
	1: 3	consult Baal-Zebub, the god of **E**?'	6833
	1: 6	to consult Baal-Zebub, the god of **E**?	6833
	1:16	to consult Baal-Zebub, the god of **E**?	6833
Jer	25:20	Gaza, **E**, and the people left at Ashdod);	6833
Am	1: 8	I will turn my hand against **E**,	6833
Zep	2: 4	be emptied and **E** uprooted.	6833
Zec	9: 5	Gaza will writhe in agony, and **E** too,	6833
	9: 7	and **E** will be like the Jebusites.	6833

EL See IPHTAH EL, MIGDAL EL

EL BETHEL (1) [BETHEL]

Ge	35: 7	and he called the place **E**,	450

EL ELOHE ISRAEL (1) [ISRAEL]
Ge　33:20　up an altar and called it E.　449

EL PARAN (1) [PARAN]
Ge　14: 6　as far as E near the desert.　386

EL-BERITH (1)
Jdg　9:46　into the stronghold of the temple of E.　451

ELA (1)
1Ki　4:18　Shimei son of E—in Benjamin;　452

ELAH (16) [ELAH'S]
Ge	36:41	Oholibamah, E, Pinon,	462
1Sa	17: 2	the Valley of E and drew up their battle line	463
	17:19	and all the men of Israel in the Valley of E,	463
	21: 9	whom you killed in the Valley of E,	463
1Ki	16: 6	And E his son succeeded him as king.	462
	16: 8	E son of Baasha became king of Israel,	462
	16: 9	E was in Tirzah at the time,	2085S
	16:13	and his son E had committed	462
2Ki	15:30	of E conspired against Pekah son	462
	17: 1	Hoshea son of E became king of Israel,	462
	18: 1	In the third year of Hoshea son of E king	462
	18: 9	the seventh year of Hoshea son of E king	462
1Ch	1:52	Oholibamah, E, Pinon,	462
	4:15	Iru, E and Naam.	462
	4:15	The son of E: Kenaz.	462
	9: 8	E son of Uzzi, the son of Micri;	462

ELAH'S (1) [ELAH]
1Ki　16:14　As for the other events of E reign,　462

ELAM (27) [ELAM'S, ELAMITES]
Ge	10:22	E, Asshur, Arphaxad, Lud and Aram.	6520
	14: 1	Kedorlaomer king of E and Tidal king	6520
	14: 9	against Kedorlaomer king of E, Tidal king	6520
1Ch	1:17	E, Asshur, Arphaxad, Lud and Aram.	6521
	8:24	Hananiah, E, Anthothijah,	6521
	26: 3	E the fifth, Jehohanan the sixth	6521
Ezr	2: 7	of E 1,254	6521
	2:31	of the other E 1,254	6521
	8: 7	of the descendants of E, Jeshaiah son	6521
	10: 2	one of the descendants of E, said to Ezra,	6521
	10:26	From the descendants of E:	6521
Ne	7:12	of E 1,254	6521
	7:34	of the other E 1,254	6521
	10:14	Parosh, Pahath-Moab, E, Zattu, Bani,	6521
	12:42	Uzzi, Jehohanan, Malkijah, E and Ezer.	6521
Isa	11:11	from Upper Egypt, from Cush, from E,	6520
	21: 2	the looter takes loot. E,	6520
	22: 6	E takes up the quiver,	6520
Jer	25:25	all the kings of Zimri, E and Media;	6520
	49:34	to Jeremiah the prophet concerning E, early	6520
	49:35	"See, I will break the bow of E,	6520
	49:36	I will bring against E the four winds from	6520
	49:37	I will shatter E before their foes,	6520
	49:38	in E and destroy her king and officials,"	6520
	49:39	"Yet I will restore the fortunes of E in days	6520
Eze	32:24	"E is there, with all her hordes	6520
Da	8: 2	in the citadel of Susa in the province of E;	6520

ELAM'S (1) [ELAM]
Jer　49:36　not be a nation where E exiles do not go.　6520

ELAMITES (2) [ELAM]
Ezr　4: 9　Persia, Erech and Babylon, the E of Susa,　10551
Ac　2: 9　Parthians, Medes and E;　1780

ELAPSED (1)
1Sa　18:26　before the allotted time e,　4202+4848

ELASAH (2)
Ezr　10:22　Ishmael, Nethanel, Jozabad and E.　543
Jer　29: 3　He entrusted the letter to E son of Shaphan　543

ELATED (1) [ELATION]
1Sa　11: 9　to the men of Jabesh, they were e.　8523

ELATH (7)
Dt	2: 8	which comes up from E and Ezion Geber,	397
1Ki	9:26	which is near E in Edom.	393
2Ki	14:22	the one who rebuilt E and restored it	397
	16: 6	Rezin king of Aram recovered E for Aram	397
	16: 6	then moved into E and have lived there	397
2Ch	8:17	Then Solomon went to Ezion Geber and E	393
	26: 2	the one who rebuilt E and restored it	393

ELATION (1) [ELATED]
Pr　28:12　the righteous triumph, there is great e;　9514

ELDAAH (2)
Ge　25: 4　Epher, Hanoch, Abida and E.　456
1Ch　1:33　Ephah, Epher, Hanoch, Abida and E.　456

ELDAD (2)
Nu　11:26　two men, whose names were E and Medad,　455

Nu　11:27　"E and Medad are prophesying in　455

ELDER (6) [ELDERLY, ELDERS]
Isa	3: 2	the soothsayer and e,	2418
1Ti	5:19	Do not entertain an accusation against an e	4565
Tit	1: 6	An e must be blameless,	NIG
1Pe	5: 1	I appeal as a fellow e,	5236
2Jn	1: 1	The e, To the chosen lady and her children,	4565
3Jn	1: 1	The e, To my dear friend Gaius,	4565

ELDER, ELDEST (Anglicized) See also OLDER, OLDEST

ELDERLY (1) [ELDER]
Lev　19:32　show respect for the e and revere your God.　2418

ELDERS (188) [ELDER]
Ex	3:16	assemble the e of Israel and say to them,	2418
	3:18	"The e of Israel will listen to you.	2418
	3:18	the e are to go to the king of Egypt and say	NIH
	4:29	Moses and Aaron brought together all the e	2418
	12:21	Then Moses summoned all the e of Israel	2418
	17: 5	with you some of the e of Israel and take	2418
	17: 6	So Moses did this in the sight of the e	2418
	18:12	and Aaron came with all the e of Israel	2418
	19: 7	and summoned the e of the people and set	2418
	24: 1	and seventy of the e of Israel.	2418
	24: 9	and the seventy e of Israel went up	2418
	24:14	He said to the e,	2418
Lev	4:15	The e of the community are	2418
	9: 1	and his sons and the e of Israel.	2418
Nu	11:16	of Israel's e who are known to you	2418
	11:24	He brought together seventy of their e	2418
	11:25	on him and put the Spirit on the seventy e.	2418
	11:26	They were listed among the e,	NIH
	11:30	Then Moses and the e of Israel returned to	2418
	16:25	and the e of Israel followed him.	2418
	22: 4	The Moabites said to the e of Midian,	2418
	22: 7	The e of Moab and Midian left,	2418
Dt	5:23	of your tribes and your e came to me.	2418
	19:12	the e of his town shall send for him,	2418
	21: 2	your e and judges shall go out and measure	2418
	21: 3	Then the e of the town nearest	2418
	21: 6	Then all the e of the town nearest	2418
	21:19	of him and bring him to the e at the gate	2418
	21:20	They shall say to the e,	2418
	22:15	that she was a virgin to the town e at	2418
	22:16	The girl's father will say to the e,	2418
	22:17	the cloth before the e of the town,	2418
	22:18	the e shall take the man and punish him.	2418
	25: 7	she shall go to the e at the town gate	2418
	25: 8	Then the e of his town shall summon him	2418
	25: 9	up to him in the presence of the e,	2418
	27: 1	and the e of Israel commanded the people:	2418
	29:10	and chief men, your e and officials,	2418
	31: 9	and to all the e of Israel.	2418
	31:28	Assemble before me all the e of your tribes	2418
	32: 7	Ask your father and he will tell you, your e,	2418
Jos	7: 6	The e of Israel did the same,	2418
	8:33	aliens and citizens alike, with their e,	2418
	9:11	And our e and all those living	2418
	20: 4	the city gate and state his case before the e	2418
	23: 2	their e, leaders, judges and officials—	2418
	24: 1	He summoned the e, leaders,	2418
	24:31	of Joshua and of the e who outlived him	2418
Jdg	2: 7	of Joshua and of the e who outlived him	2418
	8:14	the e of the town.	2418
	8:16	He took the e of the town and taught	2418
	11: 5	the e of Gilead went to get Jephthah from	2418
	11: 8	The e of Gilead said to him, "Nevertheless,	2418
	11:10	The e of Gilead replied,	2418
	11:11	So Jephthah went with the e of Gilead,	2418
	21:16	And the e of the assembly said,	2418
Ru	4: 2	Boaz took ten of the e of the town and said,	2418
	4: 4	and in the presence of the e of my people.	2418
	4: 9	Boaz announced to the e and all the people,	2418
	4:11	Then the e and all those at the gate said,	2418
1Sa	4: 3	the e of Israel asked,	2418
	8: 4	the e of Israel gathered together and came	2418
	11: 3	The e of Jabesh said to him,	2418
	15:30	before the e of my people and before Israel;	2418
	16: 4	the e of the town trembled	2418
	30:26	he sent some of the plunder to the e	2418
2Sa	3:17	Abner conferred with the e of Israel	2418
	5: 3	the e of Israel had come to King David	2418
	12:17	The e of his household stood beside him	2418
	17: 4	to Absalom and to all the e of Israel.	2418
	17:15	"Ahithophel has advised Absalom and the e	2418
	19:11	"Ask the e of Judah,	2418
1Ki	8: 1	into his presence at Jerusalem the e	2418
	8: 3	When all the e of Israel had arrived,	2418
	12: 6	the e who had served his father Solomon	2418
	12: 8	the advice the e gave him and consulted	2418
	12:13	Rejecting the advice given him by the e,	2418
	20: 7	The king of Israel summoned all the e of	2418
	20: 8	The e and the people all answered,	2418
	21: 8	and sent them to the e and nobles who lived	2418
	21:11	So the e and nobles who lived	2418
2Ki	6:32	and the e were sitting with him.	2418
	6:32	but before he arrived, Elisha said to the e,	2418
	10: 1	to the officials of Jezreel, to the e and to	2418
	10: 5	the e and the guardians sent this message	2418
	23: 1	the king called together all the e of Judah	2418
1Ch	11: 3	the e of Israel had come to King David	2418

1Ch	15:25	the e of Israel and the commanders of units	2418
	21:16	Then David and the e, clothed in sackcloth,	2418
2Ch	5: 2	to Jerusalem the e of Israel,	2418
	5: 4	When all the e of Israel had arrived,	2418
	10: 6	the e who had served his father Solomon	2418
	10: 8	the advice the e gave him and consulted	2418
	10:13	Rejecting the advice of the e,	2418
	34:29	the king called together all the e of Judah	2418
Ezr	5: 5	of their God was watching over the e of	10675
	5: 9	We questioned the e and asked them,	10675
	6: 7	the Jews and the Jewish e rebuild this house	10675
	6: 8	for these e of the Jews in the construction	10675
	6:14	So the e of the Jews continued to build	10675
	10: 8	with the decision of the officials and the	2418
	10:14	along with the e and judges of each town,	2418
Job	12:20	and takes away the discernment of e.	2418
Ps	105:22	as he pleased and teach his e wisdom.	2418
	107:32	and praise him in the council of the e.	2418
	119:100	I have more understanding than the e,	2418
Pr	31:23	he takes his seat among the e of the land.	2418
Isa	3:14	into judgment against the e and leaders	2418
	9:15	the e and prominent men are the head,	2418
	24:23	and before its e, gloriously.	2418
Jer	19: 1	Take along some of the e of the people and	2418
	26:17	Some of the e of the land stepped forward	2418
	29: 1	to the surviving e among the exiles and to	2418
La	1:19	My priests and my e perished in the city	2418
	2:10	The e of the Daughter of Zion sit on	2418
	4:16	priests are shown no honor, the e no favor.	2418
	5:12	e are shown no respect.	2418
	5:14	The e are gone from the city gate;	2418
Eze	7:26	as will the counsel of the e.	2418
	8: 1	in my house and the e of Judah were sitting	2418
	8:11	of them stood seventy e of the house	2418
	8:12	the e of the house of Israel are doing in	2418
	9: 6	So they began with the e who were in front	2418
	14: 1	Some of the e of Israel came to me and sat	2418
	20: 1	some of the e of Israel came to inquire of	2418
	20: 3	speak to the e of Israel and say to them,	2418
Joel	1: 2	you e; listen, all who live in the land.	2418
	1:14	Summon the e and all who live in the land	2418
	2:16	bring together the e, gather the children,	2418
Mt	15: 2	the tradition of the e?	4565
	16:21	at the hands of the e,	4565
	21:23	and the e of the people came to him.	4565
	26: 3	the e of the people assembled in the palace	4565
	26:47	the chief priests and the e of the people.	4565
	26:57	of the law and the e had assembled.	4565
	27: 1	and the e of the people came to the decision	4565
	27: 3	to the chief priests and the e,	4565
	27:12	by the chief priests and the e,	4565
	27:20	But the chief priests and the e persuaded	4565
	27:41	of the law and the e mocked him.	4565
	28:12	When the chief priests had met with the e	4565
Mk	7: 3	holding to the tradition of the e.	4565
	7: 5	according to the tradition of the e instead	4565
	8:31	and be rejected by the e,	4565
	11:27	the teachers of the law and the e came	4565
	14:43	the teachers of the law, and the e.	4565
	14:53	e and teachers of the law came together.	4565
	15: 1	the chief priests, with the e,	4565
Lk	7: 3	of Jesus and sent some e of the Jews to him,	4565
	9:22	and be rejected by the e,	4565
	20: 1	together with the e, came up to him.	4565
	22:52	the officers of the temple guard, and the e,	4565
	22:66	the council of the e of the people met,	4564
Ac	4: 5	e and teachers of the law met in Jerusalem.	4565
	4: 8	"Rulers and e of the people!	4565
	4:23	that the chief priests and e had said to them.	4565
	5:21	the full assembly of the e of Israel—	1172
	6:12	So they stirred up the people and the e and	4565
	11:30	sending their gift to the e by Barnabas	4565
	14:23	Paul and Barnabas appointed e for them	4565
	15: 2	up to Jerusalem to see the apostles and e	4565
	15: 4	by the church and the apostles and e,	4565
	15: 6	and e met to consider this question.	4565
	15:22	Then the apostles and e,	4565
	15:23	The apostles and e, your brothers,	4565
	16: 4	the decisions reached by the apostles and e	4565
	20:17	Paul sent to Ephesus for the e of the church.	4565
	21:18	and all the e were present.	4565
	23:14	They went to the chief priests and e	4565
	24: 1	down to Caesarea with some of the e and	4565
	25:15	and e of the Jews brought charges	4565
1Ti	4:14	when the body of e laid their hands on you.	4564
	5:17	The e who direct the affairs of the	4565
Tit	1: 5	and appoint e in every town,	4565
Jas	5:14	He should call the e of the church to pray	4565
1Pe	5: 1	To the e among you,	4565
Rev	4: 4	and seated on them were twenty-four e.	4565
	4:10	the twenty-four e fall down	4565
	5: 5	one of the e said to me, "Do not weep!	4565
	5: 6	by the four living creatures and the e.	4565
	5: 8	and the twenty-four e fell down before	4565
	5:11	and the living creatures and the e.	4565
	5:14	and the e fell down and worshiped.	4565
	7:11	around the e and the four living creatures.	4565
	7:13	Then one of the e asked me,	4565
	11:16	And the twenty-four e,	4565
	14: 3	before the four living creatures and the e.	4565
	19: 4	The twenty-four e and the four living	4565

ELEAD (1)
1Ch　7:21　and E were killed by the native-born men　537

ELEADAH (1)

1Ch	7:20	Tahath his son, E his son, Tahath his son,	538

ELEALEH (5)

Nu	32: 3	Dibon, Jazer, Nimrah, Heshbon, E, Sebam,	542
	32:37	And the Reubenites rebuilt Heshbon, E	541
Isa	15: 4	Heshbon and E cry out,	542
	16: 9	O Heshbon, O E, I drench you with tears!	542
Jer	48:34	of their cry rises from Heshbon to E	542

ELEASAH (4)

1Ch	2:39	Helez the father of E,	543
	2:40	E the father of Sismai,	543
	8:37	E his son and Azel his son.	543
	9:43	E his son and Azel his son.	543

ELEAZAR (74) [ELEAZAR'S]

Ex	6:23	and she bore him Nadab and Abihu, E	540
	6:25	E son of Aaron married one of	540
	28: 1	along with his sons Nadab and Abihu, E	540
Lev	10: 6	Then Moses said to Aaron and his sons E	540
	10:12	E and Ithamar, "Take the grain offering left	540
	10:16	he was angry with E and Ithamar,	540
Nu	3: 2	the firstborn and Abihu, E and Ithamar.	540
	3: 4	so only E and Ithamar served as priests.	540
	3:32	The chief leader of the Levites was E son	540
	4:16	"E son of Aaron, the priest,	540
	16:37	"Tell E son of Aaron, the priest, to take	540
	16:39	So E the priest collected	540
	19: 3	Give it to E the priest;	540
	19: 4	Then E the priest is to take some	540
	20:25	and his son E and take them up Mount Hor.	540
	20:26	and put them on his son E, for Aaron will	540
	20:28	and put them on his son E.	540
	20:28	and E came down from the mountain,	540
	25: 7	When Phinehas son of E, the son of Aaron,	540
	25:11	"Phinehas son of E, the son of Aaron,	540
	26: 1	the LORD said to Moses and E son	540
	26: 3	and E the priest spoke with them and said,	540
	26:60	of Nadab and Abihu, E and Ithamar.	540
	26:63	These are the ones counted by Moses and E	540
	27: 2	before Moses, E the priest, the leaders and	540
	27:19	before E the priest and the entire assembly	540
	27:21	He is to stand before E the priest,	540
	27:22	before E the priest and the whole assembly.	540
	31: 6	along with Phinehas son of E, the priest,	540
	31:12	and E the priest and the Israelite assembly	540
	31:13	E the priest and all the leaders of	540
	31:21	Then E the priest said to the soldiers	540
	31:26	"You and E the priest and the family heads	540
	31:29	from their half share and give it to E	540
	31:31	So Moses and E the priest did as	540
	31:41	Moses gave the tribute to E the priest as	540
	31:51	Moses and E the priest accepted from them	540
	31:52	of hundreds that Moses and E presented as	NIH
	31:54	Moses and E the priest accepted the gold	540
	32: 2	So they came to Moses and E the priest and	540
	32:28	to E the priest and Joshua son of Nun and	540
	34:17	E the priest and Joshua son of Nun.	540
Dt	10: 6	and E his son succeeded him as priest.	540
Jos	14: 1	which E the priest,	540
	17: 4	They went to E the priest,	540
	19:51	These are the territories that E the priest,	540
	21: 1	of the Levites approached E the priest,	540
	22:13	So the Israelites sent Phinehas son of E,	540
	22:31	And Phinehas son of E, the priest,	540
	22:32	Then Phinehas son of E, the priest,	540
	24:33	And E son of Aaron died and was buried	540
Jdg	20:28	with Phinehas son of E,	540
1Sa	7: 1	the hill and consecrated E his son to guard	540
2Sa	23: 9	to him was E son of Dodai the Ahohite,	540
	23:10	The troops returned to E,	2257S
1Ch	6: 3	Nadab, Abihu, E and Ithamar.	540
	6: 4	E was the father of Phinehas,	540
	6:50	E his son, Phinehas his son,	540
	9:20	In earlier times Phinehas son of E was	540
	11:12	to him was E son of Dodai the Ahohite,	540
	23:21	The sons of Mahli: E and Kish.	540
	23:22	E died without having sons:	540
	24: 1	Abihu, E and Ithamar.	540
	24: 2	so E and Ithamar served as the priests.	540
	24: 3	of Zadok a descendant of E and Ahimelech	540
	24: 5	of God among the descendants of both E	540
	24: 6	from E and then one from Ithamar.	540
	24:28	From Mahli: E, who had no sons.	540
Ezr	7: 5	the son of Phinehas, the son of E,	540
	8:33	E son of Phinehas was with him,	540
	10:25	Ramiah, Izziah, Malkijah, Mijamin, E,	540
Ne	12:42	Shemaiah, E, Uzzi, Jehohanan, Malkijah,	540
Mt	1:15	Eliud the father of E,	1789
	1:15	E the father of Matthan,	1789

ELEAZAR'S (2) [ELEAZAR]

1Ch	24: 4	among E descendants than	540
	24: 4	from E descendants and eight heads	540

ELECT (11) [ELECTION]

Mt	24:22	sake of the e those days will be shortened.	1723
	24:24	and miracles to deceive even the e—	1723
	24:31	they will gather his e from the four winds,	1723
Mk	13:20	But for the sake of the e,	1723
	13:22	and miracles to deceive the e—	1723
	13:27	And he will send his angels and gather his e	1723

Ro	11: 7	it did not obtain, but the e did.	1724
1Ti	5:21	of God and Christ Jesus and the e angels,	1723
2Ti	2:10	for the sake of the e,	1723
Tit	1: 1	of Jesus Christ for the faith of God's e and	1723
1Pe	1: 1	an apostle of Jesus Christ, To God's e,	1723

ELECTION (3) [ELECT]

Ro	9:11	that God's purpose in e might stand;	1724
	11:28	but as far as e is concerned,	1724
2Pe	1:10	to make your calling and e sure.	1724

ELEGANCE (1) [ELEGANT]

SS	4: 4	like the tower of David, built with e;	9444

ELEGANT (2) [ELEGANCE]

Eze	23:41	You sat on an e couch,	3884
Lk	23:11	Dressing him in an e robe,	3287

ELEMENTARY (2) [ELEMENTS]

Heb	5:12	you need someone to teach you the e truths	794+3836+5122
	6: 1	the e teachings about Christ and go on	794

ELEMENTS (2) [ELEMENTARY]

2Pe	3:10	the e will be destroyed by fire,	5122
	3:12	and the e will melt in the heat.	5122

ELEVATE (1) [ELEVATED, ELEVATING]

2Co	11: 7	in order to e you by preaching the gospel	5738

ELEVATED (1) [ELEVATE]

Est	5:11	how he had e him above the other nobles	5951

ELEVATING (1) [ELEVATE]

Est	3: 1	e him and giving him a seat	5951

ELEVEN (23) [ELEVENTH]

Ge	32:22	and his e sons and crossed the ford of	285+6925
	37: 9	sun and moon and e stars were bowing	285+6925
Ex	26: 7	over the tabernacle—e altogether.	6926+6954
	26: 8	All e curtains are to be the same size	6926+6954
	36:14	over the tabernacle—e altogether.	6926+6954
	36:15	All e curtains were the same size—	6926+6954
Nu	29:20	" 'On the third day prepare e bulls,	6925+6954
Dt	1: 2	(It takes e days to go from Horeb	285+6925
Jos	15:51	e towns and their villages.	285+6926
Jdg	16: 5	will give you e hundred shekels	547+2256+4395
	17: 2	"The e hundred shekels of silver	547+2256+4395
	17: 3	the e hundred shekels of silver to his mother,	547+2256+4395
2Ki	23:36	and he reigned in Jerusalem e years.	285+6926
	24:18	and he reigned in Jerusalem e years.	285+6926
2Ch	36: 5	and he reigned in Jerusalem e years.	285+6926
	36:11	and he reigned in Jerusalem e years.	285+6926
Jer	52: 1	and he reigned in Jerusalem e years.	285+6926
Mt	28:16	Then the e disciples went to Galilee,	1894
Mk	16:14	Later Jesus appeared to the E	1894
Lk	24: 9	they told all these things to the E and to all	1894
	24:33	There they found the E and those	1894
Ac	1:26	so he was added to the e apostles.	1894
	2:14	Then Peter stood up with the E,	1894

ELEVENTH (20) [ELEVEN]

Nu	7:72	On the e day Pagiel son of Ocran,	6925+6954
Dt	1: 3	on the first day of the e month,	6925+6954
1Ki	6:38	In the e year in the month of Bul,	285+6926
2Ki	9:29	(In the e year of Joram son of Ahab,	285+6926
	25: 2	until the e year of King Zedekiah.	6926+6954
1Ch	12:13	and Macbannai the e.	6925+6954
	24:12	the e to Eliashib, the twelfth to Jakim,	6925+6954
	25:18	the e to Azarel, his sons and relatives,	6925+6954
	27:14	The e, for the eleventh month,	6925+6954
	27:14	The eleventh, for the e month,	6925+6954
Jer	1: 3	the e year of Zedekiah son of Josiah	6926+6954
	39: 2	the fourth month of Zedekiah's e year,	6926+6954
	52: 5	until the e year of King Zedekiah.	6926+6954
Eze	26: 1	e year, on the first day of the month,	6926+6954
	30:20	In the e year, in the first month on	285+6926
	31: 1	In the e year, in the third month on	285+6926
Zec	1: 7	the twenty-fourth day of the e month,	6925+6954
Mt	20: 6	About the e hour he went out	1895
	20: 9	about the e hour came and each received	1895
Rev	21:20	the e jacinth, and the twelfth amethyst.	1895

ELHANAN (4)

2Sa	21:19	E son of Jaare-Oregim	481
	23:24	E son of Dodo from Bethlehem,	481
1Ch	11:26	E son of Dodo from Bethlehem,	481
	20: 5	E son of Jair killed Lahmi the brother	481

ELI (33) [ELI'S]

1Sa	1: 3	the two sons of E,	6603
	1: 9	Now E the priest was sitting on a chair by	6603
	1:12	E observed her mouth.	6603
	1:13	E thought she was drunk	6603
	1:17	E answered, "Go in peace,	6603
	1:25	they brought the boy to E,	6603
	2:11	before the LORD under E the priest.	6603
	2:20	E would bless Elkanah and his wife,	6603

1Sa	2:22	Now E, who was very old,	6603
	2:27	a man of God came to E and said to him,	6603
	3: 1	The boy Samuel ministered before the LORD under E.	6603
	3: 2	One night E, whose eyes were becoming	6603
	3: 5	And he ran to E and said, "Here I am;	6603
	3: 5	But E said, "I did not call;	NIH
	3: 6	And Samuel got up and went to E and said,	6603
	3: 6	"My son," E said, "I did not call;	NIH
	3: 8	and Samuel got up and went to E and said,	6603
	3: 8	Then E realized that the LORD was calling	6603
	3: 9	So E told Samuel, "Go and lie down,	6603
	3:12	carry out against E everything I spoke	6603
	3:14	Therefore, I swore to the house of E,	6603
	3:15	He was afraid to tell E the vision,	6603
	3:16	but E called him and said,	6603
	3:17	"What was it he said to you?" E asked.	NIH
	3:18	Then E said, "He is the LORD;	NIH
	4:13	there was E sitting on his chair by the side	6603
	4:14	E heard the outcry and asked,	6603
	4:14	The man hurried over to E,	6603
	4:16	He told E, "I have just come from	6603
	4:16	E asked, "What happened, my son?"	NIH
	4:18	E fell backward off his chair by the side of	NIH
	14: 3	the son of E, the LORD's priest in Shiloh.	6603
1Ki	2:27	at Shiloh about the house of E.	6603

ELI'S (4) [ELI]

1Sa	2:12	E sons were wicked men;	6603
	3:14	'The guilt of E house will never be atoned	6603
	4: 4	And E two sons, Hophni and Phinehas,	6603
	4:11	and E two sons, Hophni and Phinehas,	6603

ELIAB (20)

Nu	1: 9	from Zebulun, E son of Helon;	482
	2: 7	of the people of Zebulun is E son of Helon.	482
	7:24	On the third day, E son of Helon,	482
	7:29	This was the offering of E son of Helon.	482
	10:16	and E son of Helon was over the division of	482
	16: 1	Dathan and Abiram, sons of E,	482
	16:12	the sons of E.	482
	26: 8	The son of Pallu was E,	482
	26: 9	and the sons of E were Nemuel,	482
Dt	11: 6	sons of E the Reubenite.	482
1Sa	16: 6	Samuel saw E and thought,	482
	17:13	The firstborn was E;	482
	17:28	When E, David's oldest brother,	482
1Ch	2:13	Jesse was the father of E his firstborn;	482
	6:27	E his son, Jeroham his son, Elkanah his son	482
	12: 9	the second in command, E the third,	482
	15:18	Unni, E, Benaiah, Maaseiah, Mattithiah,	482
	15:20	Aziel, Shemiramoth, Jehiel, Unni, E,	482
	16: 5	Shemiramoth, Jehiel, Mattithiah, E,	482
2Ch	11:18	the daughter of Jesse's son E.	482

ELIADA (4)

2Sa	5:16	Elishama, E and Eliphelet.	486
1Ki	11:23	Rezon son of E,	486
1Ch	3: 8	Elishama, E and Eliphelet—nine in all.	486
2Ch	17:17	From Benjamin: E, a valiant soldier,	486

ELIAH (KJV) ELIJAH

ELIAHBA (2)

2Sa	23:32	E the Shaalbonite, the sons	494
1Ch	11:33	the Baharumite, E the Shaalbonite,	494

ELIAKIM (15) [ELIAKIM'S, JEHOIAKIM]

2Ki	18:18	E son of Hilkiah the palace administrator,	509
	18:26	Then E son of Hilkiah,	509
	18:37	E son of Hilkiah the palace administrator,	509
	19: 2	He sent E the palace administrator,	509
	23:34	Pharaoh Neco made E son of Josiah king	509
2Ch	36: 4	The king of Egypt made E,	509
Ne	12:41	E, Maaseiah, Miniamin, Micaiah, Elioenai,	509
Isa	22:20	E son of Hilkiah.	509
	36: 3	E son of Hilkiah the palace administrator,	509
	36:11	Then E, Shebna and Joah said to	509
	36:22	E son of Hilkiah the palace administrator,	509
	37: 2	He sent E the palace administrator,	509
Mt	1:13	Abiud the father of E,	1806
	1:13	E the father of Azor,	1806
Lk	3:30	the son of Jonam, the son of E,	1806

ELIAKIM'S (3) [ELIAKIM]

2Ki	23:34	and changed E name to Jehoiakim.	2257S
2Ch	36: 4	and changed E name to Jehoiakim.	2257S
	36: 4	But Neco took E brother Jehoahaz	2257S

ELIAM (2)

2Sa	11: 3	the daughter of E and the wife of Uriah	500
	23:34	E son of Ahithophel the Gilonite,	500

ELIAS (KJV) ELIJAH

ELIASAPH (6)

Nu	1:14	from Gad, E son of Deuel;	498
	2:14	The leader of the people of Gad is E son	498
	3:24	the families of the Gershonites was E son	498
	7:42	On the sixth day E son of Deuel,	498

Nu   7:47   This was the offering of E son of Deuel.   498
   10:20   and E son of Deuel was over the division of   498

ELIASHIB (15) [ELIASHIB'S]

1Ch   3:24   The sons of Elioenai: Hodaviah, E, Pelaiah,   513
   24:12   the eleventh to E, the twelfth to Jakim,   513
Ezr   10: 6   to the room of Jehohanan son of E.   513
   10:24   From the singers: 513
   10:27   From the descendants of Zattu: Elioenai, E,   513
   10:36   Vaniah, Meremoth, E,   513
Ne   3: 1   E the high priest and his fellow priests went   513
   3:20   the angle to the entrance of the house of E   513
   12:10   Joiakim the father of E,   513
   12:10   E the father of Joiada,   513
   12:22   of the Levites in the days of E,   513
   12:23   the time of Johanan son of E were recorded   513
   13: 4   E the priest had been put in charge of   513
   13: 7   about the evil thing E had done   513
   13:28   of E the high priest was son-in-law   513

ELIASHIB'S (1) [ELIASHIB]

Ne   3:21   from the entrance of E house to the end   513

ELIATHAH (2)

1Ch   25: 4   Hanani, E, Giddalti and Romamti-Ezer;   484
   25:27   the twentieth to E, his sons and relatives,   517

ELIDAD (1)

Nu   34:21   E son of Kislon, from the tribe   485

ELIEHOENAI (2)

1Ch   26: 3   Jehohanan the sixth and E the seventh.   492
Ezr   8: 4   E son of Zerahiah, and with him 200 men;   492

ELIEL (10)

1Ch   5:24   Epher, Ishi, E, Azriel, Jeremiah,   483
   6:34   the son of Jeroham, the son of E,   483
   8:20   Elienai, Zillethai, E,   483
   8:22   Ishpan, Eber, E,   483
   11:46   E the Mahavite, Jeribai and Joshaviah   483
   11:47   E, Obed and Jaasiel the Mezobaite.   483
   12:11   Attai the sixth, E the seventh,   483
   15: 9   E the leader and 80 relatives;   483
   15:11   Shemaiah, E and Amminadab the Levites.   483
2Ch   31:13   Asahel, Jerimoth, Jozabad, E, Ismakiah,   483

ELIENAI (1)

1Ch   8:20   E, Zillethai, Eliel,   501

ELIEZER (15)

Ge   15: 2   and the one who will inherit my estate is E   499
Ex   18: 4   and the other was named E,   499
1Ch   7: 8   The sons of Beker: Zemirah, Joash, E,   499
   15:24   and E the priests were to blow trumpets   499
   23:15   The sons of Moses: Gershom and E.   499
   23:17   The descendants of E: 499
   23:17   E had no other sons,   499
   26:25   His relatives through E: 499
   27:16   E son of Zicri;   499
2Ch   20:37   E son of Dodavahu   499
Ezr   8:16   So I summoned E, Ariel, Shemaiah,   499
   10:18   Maaseiah, E, Jarib and Gedaliah.   499
   10:23   Kelita); Pethahiah, Judah and E.   499
   10:31   From the descendants of Harim: E, Ishijah,   499
Lk   3:29   the son of E, the son of Jorim,   1808

ELIHOENAI (KJV) ELIEHOENAI

ELIHOREPH (1)

1Ki   4: 3   E and Ahijah, sons of Shisha—   495

ELIHU (10)

1Sa   1: 1   the son of E, the son of Tohu,   491
1Ch   12:20   Jediael, Michael, Jozabad, E and Zillethai,   491
   26: 7   his relatives E and Semakiah were   490
   27:18   E, a brother of David;   490
Job   32: 2   But E son of Barakel the Buzite,   491
   32: 4   Now E had waited before speaking to Job   490
   32: 6   So E son of Barakel the Buzite said: 491
   34: 1   Then E said: 491
   35: 1   Then E said: 490
   36: 1   E continued: 491

ELIJAH (111) [ELIJAH'S]

1Ki   17: 1   Now E the Tishbite, from Tishbe in Gilead,   489
   17: 2   Then the word of the LORD came to E: 2257S
   17:13   E said to her, "Don't be afraid.   489
   17:15   She went away and did as E had told her.   489
   17:15   So there was food every day for E and for   2085S
   17:16   with the word of the LORD spoken by E.   489
   17:18   She said to E, "What do you have against   489
   17:19   "Give me your son," E replied.   NIH
   17:23   E picked up the child and carried him down   489
   17:24   Then the woman said to E,   489
   18: 1   the word of the LORD came to E: 489
   18: 2   So E went to present himself to Ahab.   489
   18: 7   As Obadiah was walking along, E met him.   489
   18: 7   and said, "Is it really you, my lord E?"   489
   18: 8   "Go tell your master, 'E is here.'"   489

1Ki   18:11   to go to my master and say, 'E is here.'   489
   18:14   to go to my master and say, 'E is here.'   489
   18:15   E said, "As the LORD Almighty lives,   489
   18:16   and Ahab went to meet E.   489
   18:17   When he saw E, he said to him,   489
   18:18   not made trouble for Israel," E replied.   NIH
   18:21   E went before the people and said,   489
   18:22   Then E said to them,   489
   18:25   E said to the prophets of Baal,   489
   18:27   At noon E began to taunt them.   489
   18:30   Then E said to all the people,   489
   18:31   E took twelve stones,   489
   18:36   the prophet E stepped forward and prayed: 489
   18:40   Then E commanded them,   489
   18:40   and E had them brought down to   489
   18:41   And E said to Ahab, "Go, eat and drink,   489
   18:42   but E climbed to the top of Carmel,   489
   18:43   Seven times E said, "Go back."   NIH
   18:44   So E said, "Go and tell Ahab,   NIH
   18:46   The power of the LORD came upon E   489
   19: 1   Ahab told Jezebel everything E had done   489
   19: 2   So Jezebel sent a messenger to E to say,   489
   19: 3   E was afraid and ran for his life.   NIH
   19: 9   "What are you doing here, E?"   489
   19:13   When E heard it,   489
   19:13   "What are you doing here, E?"   489
   19:19   So E went from there and found Elisha son   NIH
   19:19   E went up to him and threw his cloak   489
   19:20   Elisha then left his oxen and ran after E.   489
   19:20   "Go back," E replied.   NIH
   19:21   to follow E and became his attendant.   489
   21:17   word of the LORD came to E the Tishbite: 489
   21:20   Ahab said to E, "So you have found me,   489
   21:28   word of the LORD came to E the Tishbite: 489
2Ki   1: 3   angel of the LORD said to E the Tishbite   488
   1: 4   So E went.   488
   1: 8   The king said, "That was E the Tishbite."   488
   1: 9   to E a captain with his company   2257S
   1: 9   The captain went up to E,   2257S
   1:10   E answered the captain,   489
   1:11   At this the king sent to E another captain   2257S
   1:12   "If I am a man of God," E replied,   488
   1:13   up and fell on his knees before E.   489
   1:15   The angel of the LORD said to E,   489
   1:15   So E got up and went down with him to   NIH
   1:17   the word of the LORD that E had spoken   489
   2: 1   When the LORD was about to take E up   489
   2: 1   E and Elisha were on their way   489
   2: 2   E said to Elisha, "Stay here;   489
   2: 4   Then E said to him, "Stay here, Elisha;   489
   2: 6   Then E said to him, "Stay here;   489
   2: 7   where E and Elisha had stopped   2157+9109S
   2: 8   E took his cloak, rolled it up and struck   489
   2: 9   When they had crossed, E said to Elisha,   489
   2:10   "You have asked a difficult thing," E said,   NIH
   2:11   and E went up to heaven in a whirlwind.   489
   2:13   that had fallen from E and went back   489
   2:14   "Where now is the LORD, the God of E?"   489
   2:15   said, "The spirit of E is resting on Elisha."   489
   3:11   He used to pour water on the hands of E."   489
   9:36   that he spoke through his servant E   489
   10:10   through his servant E."   489
   10:17   to the word of the LORD spoken to E.   489
1Ch   8:27   E and Zicri were the sons of Jeroham.   488
2Ch   21:12   a letter from E the prophet, which said: 489
Ezr   10:21   Maaseiah, E, Shemaiah, Jehiel and Uzziah.   488
   10:26   Zechariah, Jehiel, Abdi, Jeremoth and E.   488
Mal   4: 5   I will send you the prophet E before   488
Mt   11:14   he is the E who was to come.   2460
   16:14   "Some say John the Baptist; others say E;   2460
   17: 3   before them Moses and E,   2460
   17: 4   one for you, one for Moses and one for E."   2460
   17:10   of the law say that E must come first?"   2460
   17:11   E comes and will restore all things.   2460
   17:12   But I tell you, E has already come,   2460
   27:47   they said, "He's calling E."   2460
   27:49   Let's see if E comes to save him."   2460
Mk   6:15   Others said, "He is E."   2460
   8:28   "Some say John the Baptist; others say E;   2460
   9: 4   there appeared before them E and Moses,   2460
   9: 5   one for you, one for Moses and one for E."   2460
   9:11   of the law say that E must come first?"   2460
   9:12   E does come first, and restores all things.   2460
   9:13   But I tell you, E has come,   2460
   15:35   they said, "Listen, he's calling E."   2460
   15:36   Let's see if E comes to take him down,"   2460
Lk   1:17   in the spirit and power of E,   2460
   4:26   Yet E was not sent to any of them,   2460
   9: 8   others that E had appeared,   2460
   9:19   "Some say John the Baptist; others say E;   2460
   9:30   Two men, Moses and E,   2460
   9:33   one for you, one for Moses and one for E."   2460
Jn   1:21   Are you E?"   2460
   1:25   nor E, nor the Prophet?"   2460
Ro   11: 2   the Scripture says in the passage about E—   2460
Jas   5:17   E was a man just like us.   2460

ELIJAH'S (2) [ELIJAH]

1Ki   17:22   The LORD heard E cry,   489
Lk   4:25   in Israel in E time,   2460

ELIKA (1)

2Sa   23:25   Shammah the Harodite, E the Harodite,   508

ELIM (5) [BEER ELIM]

Ex   15:27   Then they came to E,   396
   16: 1   from E and came to the Desert of Sin,   396
   16: 1   which is between E and Sinai,   396
Nu   33: 9   They left Marah and went to E,   396
   33:10   They left E and camped by the Red Sea.   396

ELIMELECH (6)

Ru   1: 2   The man's name was E,   497
   1: 3   Now E, Naomi's husband, died,   497
   2: 1   from the clan of E, a man of standing,   497
   2: 3   who was from the clan of E.   497
   4: 3   of land that belonged to our brother E.   497
   4: 9   from Naomi all the property of E,   497

ELIMINATE (1) [ELIMINATED]

Dt   7:22   You will not be allowed to e them all   3983

ELIMINATED (1) [ELIMINATE]

Dt   2:15   against them until he had completely e them   2169

ELIOENAI (7)

1Ch   3:23   E, Hizkiah and Azrikam—three in all.   493
   3:24   The sons of E: 493
   4:36   also E, Jaakobah, Jeshohaiah,   493
   7: 8   Zemirah, Joash, Eliezer, E, Omri,   493
Ezr   10:22   From the descendants of Pashhur: E,   493
   10:27   From the descendants of Zattu: E, Eliashib,   493
Ne   12:41   Eliakim, Maaseiah, Miniamin, Micaiah, E,   493

ELIPHAL (1)

1Ch   11:35   E son of Ur,   503

ELIPHAZ (14)

Ge   36: 4   Adah bore E to Esau, Basemath bore Reuel,   502
   36:10   E, the son of Esau's wife Adah, and Reuel,   502
   36:11   The sons of E: 502
   36:12   Esau's son E also had   502
   36:15   The sons of E the firstborn of Esau: 502
   36:16   These were the chiefs descended from E   502
1Ch   1:35   E, Reuel, Jeush, Jalam and Korah.   502
   1:36   The sons of E: 502
Job   When Job's three friends, E the Temanite,   502
   4: 1   Then E the Temanite replied: 502
   15: 1   Then E the Temanite replied: 502
   22: 1   Then E the Temanite replied: 502
   42: 7   he said to E the Temanite,   502
   42: 9   So E the Temanite, Bildad the Shuhite   502

ELIPHELEHU (2)

1Ch   15:18   Eliab, Benaiah, Maaseiah, Mattithiah, E,   504
   15:21   E, Mikneiah, Obed-Edom,   504

ELIPHELET (8)

2Sa   5:16   Elishama, Eliada and E.   505
   23:34   E son of Ahasbai the Maacathite,   505
1Ch   3: 6   There were also Ibhar, Elishua, E,   505
   3: 8   Elishama, Eliada and E—nine in all.   505
   8:39   Jeush the second son and E the third.   505
   14: 7   Elishama, Beeliada and E.   505
Ezr   8:13   whose names were E, Jeuel and Shemaiah,   505
   10:33   Mattenai, Mattattah, Zabad, E, Jeremai,   505

ELISABETH (KJV) ELIZABETH

ELISEUS (KJV) ELISHA

ELISHA (90) [ELISHA'S]

1Ki   19:16   and anoint E son of Shaphat   515
   19:17   and E will put to death any who escape   515
   19:19   So Elijah went from there and found E son   515
   19:20   So E left his oxen and ran after Elijah.   NIH
   19:21   So E left and went back.   NIH
2Ki   2: 1   Elijah and E were on their way from Gilgal.   515
   2: 2   Elijah said to E, "Stay here;   515
   2: 2   But E said, "As surely as the LORD lives   515
   2: 3   of the prophets at Bethel came out to E   515
   2: 3   "Yes, I know," E replied.   NIH
   2: 4   Then Elijah said to him, "Stay here, E;   515
   2: 5   at Jericho went up to E and asked him.   515
   2: 7   where Elijah and E had stopped   2157+9109S
   2: 9   When they had crossed, Elijah said to E,   515
   2: 9   a double portion of your spirit," E replied.   515
   2:12   E saw this and cried out, "My father!   515
   2:12   And E saw him no more.   NIH
   2:15   said, "The spirit of Elijah is resting on E."   515
   2:16   "No," E replied, "do not send them."   NIH
   2:18   When they returned to E,   2257S
   2:19   The men of the city said to E, "Look,   515
   2:22   according to the word E had spoken.   515
   2:23   From there E went up to Bethel.   NIH
   3:11   "E son of Shaphat is here.   515
   3:13   E said to the king of Israel,   515
   3:14   E said, "As surely as   515
   3:15   the hand of the LORD came upon E   2257S
   4: 1   the company of the prophets cried out to E,   515
   4: 2   E replied to her, "How can I help you?   515
   4: 3   E said, "Go around   NIH
   4: 8   One day E went to Shunem.   515

2Ki	4:11	One day when E came,	NIH
	4:13	E said to him, "Tell her,	NIH
	4:14	be done for her?" E asked.	NIH
	4:15	Then E said, "Call her."	NIH
	4:16	"About this time next year," E said,	NIH
	4:17	just as E had told her.	515
	4:29	E said to Gehazi,	NIH
	4:31	Gehazi went back to meet E and told him,	2257S
	4:32	When E reached the house,	515
	4:35	E turned away and walked back and forth	NIH
	4:36	E summoned Gehazi and said,	515
	4:38	E returned to Gilgal and there was a famine	515
	4:41	E said, "Get some flour."	NIH
	4:42	"Give it to the people to eat," E said.	NIH
	4:43	E answered, "Give it to the people to eat.	NIH
	5: 8	When E the man of God heard that the king	515
	5:10	E sent a messenger to say to him, "Go,	515
	5:19	"Go in peace," E said.	NIH
	5:20	the servant of E the man of God,	515
	5:25	he went in and stood before his master E.	NIH
	5:25	"Where have you been, Gehazi?" E asked.	515
	5:26	But E said to him,	515
	6: 1	The company of the prophets said to E,	515
	6: 3	"I will," E replied.	NIH
	6: 6	E cut a stick and threw it there,	NIH
	6:10	Time and again E warned the king.	NIH
	6:12	"but E, the prophet who is in Israel,	515
	6:17	And E prayed, "O LORD,	515
	6:17	of horses and chariots of fire all around E.	515
	6:18	E prayed to the LORD,	515
	6:18	as E had asked.	515
	6:19	E told them, "This is not the road	515
	6:20	After they entered the city, E said,	515
	6:21	he asked E, "Shall I kill them, my father?"	515
	6:31	if the head of E son of Shaphat remains	515
	6:32	Now E was sitting in his house,	515
	6:32	but before he arrived, E said to the elders,	2085S
	7: 1	E said, "Hear the word of the LORD.	515
	7: 2	answered E, "but you will not eat any	NIH
	8: 1	Now E had said to the woman	515
	8: 4	about all the great things E has done."	515
	8: 5	the king how E had restored the dead	NIH
	8: 5	the woman whose son E had brought back	515
	8: 5	this is her son whom E restored to life."	515
	8: 7	E went to Damascus,	515
	8: 9	Hazael went to meet E,	2257S
	8:10	E answered, "Go and say to him,	515
	8:13	of Aram," answered E.	515
	8:14	Hazael left E and returned to his master.	515
	8:14	"What did E say to you?"	515
	9: 1	The prophet E summoned a man from	515
	13:14	Now E was suffering from the illness	515
	13:15	E said, "Get a bow and some arrows,"	515
	13:16	E put his hands on the king's hands.	515
	13:17	E said, and he shot.	515
	13:17	arrow of victory over Aram!" E declared.	NIH
	13:18	E told him, "Strike the ground."	NIH
	13:20	E died and was buried.	515
Lk	4:27	with leprosy in the time of E the prophet,	1811

ELISHA'S (4) [ELISHA]

2Ki	5: 9	and stopped at the door of E house.	515
	5:27	from E presence and he was leprous,	2257S
	13:21	so they threw the man's body into E tomb.	515
	13:21	When the body touched E bones,	515

ELISHAH (3)

Ge	10: 4	E, Tarshish, the Kittim and the Rodanim.	511
1Ch	1: 7	E, Tarshish, the Kittim and the Rodanim.	511
Eze	27: 7	of blue and purple from the coasts of E.	511

ELISHAMA (16)

Nu	1:10	from Ephraim, E son of Ammihud;	514
	2:18	of Ephraim is E son of Ammihud.	514
	7:48	On the seventh day E son of Ammihud,	514
	7:53	the offering of E son of Ammihud.	514
	10:22	E son of Ammihud was in command.	514
2Sa	5:16	E, Eliada and Eliphelet.	514
2Ki	25:25	Ishmael son of Nethaniah, the son of E,	514
1Ch	2:41	and Jekamiah the father of E.	514
	3: 8	E, Eliada and Eliphelet—nine in all.	514
	7:26	Ladan his son, Ammihud his son, E his son,	514
	14: 7	E, Beeliada and Eliphelet.	514
2Ch	17: 8	and the priests E and Jehoram.	514
Jer	36:12	E the secretary, Delaiah son of Shemaiah,	514
	36:20	After they put the scroll in the room of E	514
	36:21	from the room of E the secretary and read it	514
	41: 1	the son of E,	514

ELISHAPHAT (1)

2Ch	23: 1	and E son of Zicri.	516

ELISHEBA (1)

Ex	6:23	Aaron married E, daughter of Amminadab	510

ELISHUA (3)

2Sa	5:15	Ibhar, E, Nepheg, Japhia,	512
1Ch	3: 6	There were also Ibhar, E, Eliphelet,	512
	14: 5	Ibhar, E, Elpelet,	512

ELITE (1)

Eze	23: 7	as a prostitute to all the e of the Assyrians	4436

ELIUD (2)

Mt	1:14	Akim the father of E,	1809
	1:15	E the father of Eleazar,	1809

ELIZABETH (10)

Lk	1: 5	his wife E was also a descendant of Aaron.	1810
	1: 7	they had no children, because E was barren;	1810
	1:13	Your wife E will bear you a son,	1810
	1:24	After this his wife E became pregnant and	1810
	1:36	Even E your relative is going to have	1810
	1:40	where she entered Zechariah's home and greeted E.	1810
	1:41	heard Mary's greeting,	1810
	1:41	and E was filled with the Holy Spirit.	1810
	1:56	Mary stayed with E for about three months	899S
	1:57	When it was time for E to have her baby,	1810

ELIZAPHAN (4)

Nu	3:30	of the Kohathite clans was E son of Uzziel.	507
	34:25	of Parnach, the leader from the tribe	507
1Ch	15: 8	the descendants of E, Shemaiah the leader	507
2Ch	29:13	the descendants of E, Shimri and Jeiel;	507

ELIZUR (5)

Nu	1: 5	from Reuben, E son of Shedeur;	506
	2:10	The leader of the people of Reuben is E son	506
	7:30	On the fourth day E son of Shedeur.	506
	7:35	This was the offering of E son of Shedeur.	506
	10:18	E son of Shedeur was in command.	506

ELKANAH (20)

Ex	6:24	of Korah were Assir, E and Abiasaph.	555
1Sa	1: 1	whose name was E son of Jeroham,	555
	1: 4	Whenever the day came for E to sacrifice,	555
	1: 8	E her husband would say to her, "Hannah,	555
	1:19	E lay with Hannah his wife,	555
	1:21	the man E went up with all his family	555
	1:23	E her husband told her.	555
	2:11	Then E went home to Ramah,	555
	2:20	Eli would bless E and his wife, saying,	555
1Ch	6:23	his son, Ebiasaph his son, Assir his son,	555
	6:25	The descendants of E: Amasai, Ahimoth,	555
	6:26	E his son, Zophai his son, Nahath his son,	555
	6:27	E his son and Samuel his son.	555
	6:34	the son of E, the son of Jeroham,	555
	6:35	the son of E, the son of Mahath,	555
	6:36	the son of E, the son of Joel,	555
	9:16	and Berekiah son of Asa, the son of E,	555
	12: 6	E, Isshiah, Azarel, Joezer and Jashobeam	555
	15:23	Berekiah and E were to be doorkeepers for	555
2Ch	28: 7	and E, second to the king.	555

ELKOSHITE (1)

Na	1: 1	The book of the vision of Nahum the E.	556

ELLASAR (2)

Ge	14: 1	Arioch king of E,	536
	14: 9	of Shinar and Arioch king of E—	536

ELMADAM (1)

Lk	3:28	the son of Cosam, the son of E,	1825

ELNAAM (1)

1Ch	11:46	Jeribai and Joshaviah the sons of E,	534

ELNATHAN (7)

2Ki	24: 8	mother's name was Nehushta daughter of E;	535
Ezr	8:16	I summoned Eliezer, Ariel, Shemaiah, E,	535
	8:16	Shemaiah, Elnathan, Jarib, E, Nathan,	535
	8:16	who were leaders, and Joiarib and E,	535
Jer	26:22	however, sent E son of Acbor to Egypt,	535
	36:12	E son of Acbor, Gemariah son of Shaphan,	535
	36:25	though E, Delaiah and Gemariah urged	535

ELOHE   See EL ELOHE ISRAEL

ELOI (4)

Mt	27:46	"E, Eloi, lama sabachthani?"—	1830
	27:46	"Eloi, E, lama sabachthani?"—	1830
Mk	15:34	"E, Eloi, lama sabachthani?"—	1830
	15:34	"Eloi, E, lama sabachthani?"—	1830

ELON (7) [ELONITE]

Ge	26:34	also Basemath daughter of E the Hittite.	390
	36: 2	Adah daughter of E the Hittite,	390
	46:14	The sons of Zebulun: Sered, E and Jahleel.	472
Nu	26:26	through E, the Elonite clan;	472
Jos	19:43	E, Timnah, Ekron,	391
Jdg	12:11	E the Zebulunite led Israel ten years.	390
	12:12	Then E died, and was buried in Aijalon in	390

ELON BETHHANAN (1)

1Ki	4: 9	Beth Shemesh and E;	392

ELONITE (1) [ELON]

Nu	26:26	through Elon, the E clan;	533

ELOQUENCE (1) [ELOQUENT]

1Co	2: 1	with e or superior wisdom as I proclaimed	3364

ELOQUENT (1) [ELOQUENCE]

Ex	4:10	"O Lord, I have never been e,	408+1821

ELOTH   (KJV) ELATH

ELPAAL (3)

1Ch	8:11	By Hushim he had Abitub and E.	551
	8:12	The sons of E:	551
	8:18	Izliah and Jobab were the sons of E.	551

ELPELET (1)

1Ch	14: 5	Ibhar, Elishua, E,	550

ELSE (92) [ELSE'S, ELSEWHERE]

Ge	19:12	"Do you have anyone e here—	6388
	19:12	or anyone e in the city who belongs to you?	NIH
	34:28	and donkeys and everything e of theirs in	889
Ex	4:13	"O Lord, please send someone e to do it."	928+3338S
	10:23	No one could see anyone e	278S
	22:27	What e will he sleep in?	AIT
	29:33	But no one e may eat them,	2424
	33:16	What e will distinguish me and your people	NIH
	36: 6	"No man or woman is to make anything e	6388
Lev	16: 2	or e he will die,	4202
	27:10	or if he has sold it to someone e,	337
Nu	1:51	Anyone e who goes near it shall be put	2424
	3:10	anyone e who approaches	2424
	3:38	Anyone e who approached	2424
	6:21	in addition to whatever e he can afford.	AIT
	12: 3	more humble than anyone e on the face of	132S
	15:14	or anyone e living among you presents	AIT
	18: 4	and no one e may come near where you are.	2424
	18: 7	Anyone e who comes near	2424
	20:19	to pass through on foot—nothing e."	1821
	22:19	and I will find out what e	3578
	31:23	and anything e that can withstand fire must	NIH
Dt	20: 5	in battle and someone e may dedicate it.	337
	20: 6	in battle and someone e enjoy it.	337
	20: 7	in battle and someone e marry her."	337
	20:14	the livestock and everything e in the city,	889S
	23:19	or food or anything e that may earn interest.	NIH
Jdg	18: 7	and had no relationship with anyone e.	NIH
	18:24	What e do I have?	6388
	18:28	and had no relationship with anyone e.	NIH
	20:48	the animals and everything e they found.	NIH
1Sa	17:30	then turned away to someone e and brought	337
	30:19	plunder or anything e they had taken.	AIT
2Sa	3:35	so severely, if I taste bread or anything e	AIT
1Ki	2:36	but do not go anywhere e.	625+625+2025+2025+2256
	2:42	'On the day you leave to go anywhere e,	625+625+2025+2025+2256
	14: 5	pretend to be someone e."	5796
Ezr	7:20	And anything e needed for the temple	10692
Est	1:19	to someone e who is better than she.	8295
Job	17: 3	Who e will put up security for me?	2085
Pr	4:23	Above all e, guard your heart,	5464S
	14:10	and no one e can share its joy.	2424
	27: 2	someone e, and not your own lips.	5799
Ecc	3:16	And I saw something e under the sun:	6388
	8:14	There is something meaningless	NIH
	9:11	I have seen something e under the sun:	8740
Isa	27: 5	Or e let them come to me for refuge;	196
Jer	23:34	and test them, for what e can I do because	375
	23:34	If a prophet or a priest or anyone e claims,	6639S
	26:19	"Did Hezekiah king of Judah or anyone e	AIT
	40: 5	or go anywhere e you please."	AIT
Eze	27:27	and everyone e on board will sink into	3972+7736
Da	5:17	and give your rewards to someone e.	10025
Mal	4: 6	or e I will come and strike the land with	7153
Mt	11: 3	or should we expect someone e?"	2283
Mk	1:38	Jesus replied, "Let us go somewhere e—	250
Lk	7:19	or should we expect someone e?"	257
	7:20	or should we expect someone e?' "	257
	13:31	"Leave this place and go somewhere e.	NIG
	18: 9	and looked down on everybody e,	3370
	22:58	A little later someone e saw him and said,	2283
Jn	5: 7	someone e goes down ahead of me."	257
	5:43	but if someone e comes in his own name,	257
	15:24	not done among them what no one e did,	257
	21:18	and someone e will dress you and lead you	257
Ac	4:12	Salvation is found in no one e,	257
	5:13	No one e dared join them.	3370
	8:34	prophet talking himself or someone e?"	2283
	17:25	and breath and everything e.	NIG
	24:12	in the synagogues or anywhere e in the city.	2848
Ro	2: 1	you who pass judgment on someone e,	NIG
	8:39	nor anything e in all creation,	2283
	14:20	to eat anything that causes someone e	NIG
	14:21	or drink wine or to do anything e	NIG
1Co	1:16	I don't remember if I baptized anyone e.)	257
	3:10	and someone e is building on it.	257
	4: 7	who makes you different from anyone e?	NIG
	7:11	or e be reconciled to her husband.	NIG
	11:21	ahead without waiting for anybody e.	NIG
	15:37	perhaps of wheat or of something e.	3370
2Co	9:13	in sharing with them and with everyone e.	NIG
	11:21	What anyone e dares to boast about—	NIG

2Co 11:28   **Besides everything** e, I face daily the
              pressure of my concern   3836+4211+6006
Gal   6: 4   without comparing himself to **somebody** e,   2283
Php   1:13   *to* everyone that I am in chains for Christ.   3370
     2:20   I have no one e like him,   NIG
     3: 4   If anyone e thinks he has reasons   257
1Th   2: 6   not from you or **anyone** e.   257
     3:12   for each other and for everyone e,   NIG
     5:15   to be kind to each other and to everyone e.   NIG
1Ti   1:10   whatever e is contrary to the sound doctrine   2283
Jas   5:12   not by heaven or by earth or by anything e.   257

ELSE'S (5) [ELSE]
Ge 43:34   as much as anyone e.   4392
Ru   2:22   in **someone** e field you might be harmed."   337
Lk 16:12   with **someone** e property,   259
Ro 14: 4   Who are you to judge **someone** e servant?   259
   15:20   not be building on **someone** e foundation.   259

ELSEWHERE (7) [ELSE, WHERE]
Lev 18: 9   in the same home or e.   2575
2Ch 26: 6   near Ashdod and e among the Philistines.   NIH
Ezr   4:10   and settled in the city of Samaria and e   10692
     4:17   of their associates living in Samaria and e   10692
Ps 84:10   in your courts than a thousand e;   NIH
Jn 12:39   because, as Isaiah says e: 4099
Ac 13:35   So it is stated e: 1877+2283

ELTEKEH
Jos 19:44   **E**, Gibbethon, Baalath,   559
   21:23   Also from the tribe of Dan they received **E**,   558

ELTEKON (1)
Jos 15:59   Beth Anoth and **E**—   560

ELTOLAD (2)
Jos 15:30   **E**, Kesil, Hormah,   557
   19: 4   **E**, Bethul, Hormah,   557

ELUDE (2) [ELUDED]
Job 11:20   and escape *will* e them;   6
Rev   9: 6   but death *will* e them.   608+5771

ELUDED (2) [ELUDE]
1Sa 18:11   But David e him twice.   4946+6015+7156
   19:10   but David e him as Saul drove the spear   7080

ELUL (1)
Ne   6:15   on the twenty-fifth of **E**,   469

ELUZAI (1)
1Ch 12: 5   **E**, Jerimoth, Bealiah, Shemariah   539

ELYMAS (2)
Ac 13: 8   But **E** the sorcerer (for   1829
   13: 9   looked straight at **E** and said,   899S

ELZABAD (2)
1Ch 12:12   Johanan the eighth, **E** the ninth,   479
   26: 7   Othni, Rephael, Obed and **E**;   479

ELZAPHAN (2)
Ex   6:22   of Uzziel were Mishael, **E** and Sithri.   553
Lev 10: 4   Moses summoned Mishael and **E**,   553

EMASCULATE (1) [EMASCULATED]
Gal   5:12   the whole way and e *themselves!*   644

EMASCULATED (1) [EMASCULATE]
Dt 23: 1   No *one* who has **been** e by crushing   7205

EMBALM (1) [EMBALMED, EMBALMING]
Ge 50: 2   in his service to e his father Israel.   2846

EMBALMED (2) [EMBALM]
Ge 50: 2   So the physicians e him,   2846
   50:26   And after *they* e him,   2846

EMBALMING (1) [EMBALM]
Ge 50: 3   for that was the time required for e.   2847

EMBANKMENT (1) [BANK]
Lk 19:43   when your enemies will build an e   5918

EMBARRASS (1) [EMBARRASSED, EMBARRASSMENT]
Ru   2:15   among the sheaves, don't e her.   4007

EMBARRASSED (1) [EMBARRASS]
2Co   7:14   and you *have* not e me.   2875

EMBARRASSMENT (1) [EMBARRASS]
Jdg   3:25   They waited to the point of e,   1017

EMBEDDED (1)
Ecc 12:11   words of the wise are like **firmly** e nails—   5749

EMBERS (2)
Ps 102: 3   my bones burn like **glowing** e.   4611
Pr 26:21   As charcoal to e and as wood to fire,   1624

EMBITTER (1) [BITTER]
Col   3:21   Fathers, *do not* e your children,   2241

EMBITTERED (1) [BITTER]
Ps 73:21   my heart was grieved and my spirit e,   9111

EMBODIMENT (1) [BODY]
Ro   2:20   in the law the e of knowledge and truth—   3673

EMBOLDENED (1) [BOLD]
1Co   8:10   *be* e to eat what has been sacrificed   3868

EMBRACE (5) [EMBRACED, EMBRACES, EMBRACING]
Pr   3:18   She is a tree of life to those *who* e her;   2616
   4: 8   e her, and she will honor you.   2485
   5:20   Why e the bosom of another man's wife?   2485
Ecc   3: 5   a time to e and a time to refrain,   2485
Mic   7: 5   Even with her who lies in your e be careful   2668

EMBRACED (7) [EMBRACE]
Ge 29:13   *He* e him and kissed him and brought him   2485
   33: 4   But Esau ran to meet Jacob and e him;   2485
   45:14   and Benjamin e him, weeping,   6584+7418
   48:10   and his father kissed them and e them.   2485
1Ki   9: 9   and *have* e other gods,   2616
2Ch   7:22   and *have* e other gods,   2616
Ac 20:37   They all wept as *they* e him and kissed him.
              2093+2158+3836+5549

EMBRACES (2) [EMBRACE]
SS   2: 6   and his right arm e me.   2485
   8: 3   under my head and his right arm e me.   2485

EMBRACING (1) [EMBRACE]
Ecc   2: 3   with wine, and e folly—   296

EMBROIDERED (10) [EMBROIDERER, EMBROIDERERS]
Jdg   5:30   as plunder for Sisera, colorful garments e,   8391
   5:30   **highly** e garments for my neck—   8391
Ps 45:14   In e **garments** she is led to the king;   8391
Eze 16:10   an e **dress** and put leather sandals on you.   8391
   16:13   of fine linen and costly fabric and e **cloth.**   8391
   16:18   you took your e clothes to put on them,   8391
   26:16   and take off their e garments.   8391
   27: 7   Fine e linen from Egypt was your sail   8391
   27:16   purple fabric, e **work**, fine linen,   8391
   27:24   e **work** and multicolored rugs   8391

EMBROIDERER (7) [EMBROIDERED]
Ex 26:36   the work of an e.   8387
   27:16   the work of an e—   8387
   28:39   The sash is to be the work of an e.   8387
   36:37   the work of an e;   8387
   38:18   the work of an e;   8387
   38:23   a craftsman and designer, and an e in blue,   8387
   39:29   the work of an e—   8387

EMBROIDERERS (1) [EMBROIDERED]
Ex 35:35   e in blue, purple and scarlet yarn   8387

EMEK   See BETH EMEK, EMEK KEZIZ

EMEK KEZIZ (1)
Jos 18:21   Jericho, Beth Hoglah, **E**,   6681

EMERALD (5)
Ex 28:18   a sapphire and an e;   3402
   39:11   a sapphire and an e;   3402
Eze 28:13   ruby, topaz and e, chrysolite,   3402
Rev   4: 3   A rainbow, resembling an e,   5039
   21:19   the third chalcedony, the fourth e,   5040

EMERODS (KJV) TUMORS

EMERGE (1)
Da   8:22   *that will* e from his nation but will   6641

EMINENT (KJV) MOUND, MOUNDS, LOFTY

EMISSION (6)
Lev 15:16   " 'When a man has an e *of* semen,   8887
   15:18   with a woman and there is an e *of* semen,   8887
   15:32   for anyone made unclean by an e *of* semen,   8887

Lev 22: 4   by a corpse or by anyone who has an e   8887
Dt 23:10   unclean because of a nocturnal e,   7937
Eze 23:20   like those of donkeys and whose e was like   2444

EMITES (3)
Ge 14: 5   the **E** in Shaveh Kiriathaim   400
Dt   2:10   (The **E** used to live there—   400
   2:11   but the Moabites called them **E**.   400

EMMANUEL (KJV) IMMANUEL

EMMOR (KJV) HAMOR

EMMAUS (1)
Lk 24:13   of them were going to a village called **E**,   1843

EMPEROR (1) [EMPIRE]
Ac 25:25   to the **E** I decided to send him to Rome.   4935

EMPEROR'S (1) [EMPIRE]
Ac 25:21   to be held over for the **E** decision,   4935

EMPHATICALLY (1)
Mk 14:31   But Peter insisted e,   1735

EMPIRE (4) [EMPEROR, EMPEROR'S, IMPERIAL]
Est 10: 1   King Xerxes imposed tribute throughout
              the e,   824
Jer 34: 1   and peoples in the e he ruled were fighting   824
Da 11: 4   his e will be broken up and parceled out   4895
   11: 4   his e will be uprooted and given to others.   4895

EMPLOYED (1)
Eze 39:14   " 'Men *will be* regularly e to cleanse   976

EMPTIED (5) [EMPTY]
Ge 24:20   So she quickly e her jar into the trough,   6867
Lev 14:36   to order the house *to be* e before he goes in   7155
Ne   5:13   So may such a man be shaken out and e!"   8199
Zep   2: 4   At midday Ashdod *will be* e   1763
1Co   1:17   lest the cross of Christ *be* e of its power.   3033

EMPTIES (1) [EMPTY]
Eze 47: 8   *When* it e into the Sea,   3655

EMPTY (33) [EMPTY-HANDED, EMPTIED, EMPTIES, EMPTYING]
Ge   1: 2   Now the earth was formless and e,   983
   37:24   the cistern was e; there was no water in it.   8199
Jdg   7:16   he placed trumpets and e jars in the hands   8199
Ru   1:21   but the LORD has brought me back e.   8200
1Sa   6: 3   do not send it away e,   8200
   20:18   because your seat *will be* e.   7212
   20:25   but David's place was e.   7212
   20:27   David's place was e again.   7212
2Ki   4: 3   around and ask all your neighbors for e jars.   8199
   18:20   but you speak only e **words.**   1821+8557
2Ch 24:11   the chief priest would come and e the chest   6867
Job 15: 2   "Would a wise man answer with e notions   8120
   26: 7   the northern *(skies)* over e **space;**   9332
   35:13   God does not listen to their e **plea;**   8736
   35:16   So Job opens his mouth with e **talk;**   2039
Pr 14: 4   Where there are no oxen, the manger is e,   1338
Isa 16: 6   but her boasts are e.   4027+4202
   32: 6   the hungry he **leaves** e and from   8197
   36: 5   but you speak only e **words.**   1821+8557
   45:18   he did not create it to be e,   9332
   55:11   It will not return to me e,   8200
   59: 4   They rely on e arguments and speak lies;   9332
Jer   4:23   and it was formless and e,   983
   48:12   *they will* e her jars and smash her jugs.   8197
   51:34   he has made us an e jar.   8198
Eze   24:11   **E** it piece by piece without casting lots   3655
   24:11   the e pot on the coals till it becomes hot   8199
Am   4: 6   "I gave you e **stomachs** in every city   5931+9094
Mic   6:14   your stomach will still be e.   3803
Lk   1:53   but has sent the rich away e.   3031
Eph   5: 6   Let no one deceive you *with* e words,   3031
1Pe   1:18   from the e way of life handed down to you   3469
2Pe   2:18   For they mouth e, boastful words and,   3470

EMPTY-HANDED (12) [EMPTY, HAND]
Ge 31:42   you would surely have sent me away e.   8200
Ex   3:21   so that when you leave you will not go e.   8200
   23:15   "No one is to appear before me e.   8200
   34:20   "No one is to appear before me e.   8200
Dt 15:13   you release him, do not send him away e.   8200
   16:16   No man should appear before the LORD e: 8200
Ru   3:17   'Don't go back to your mother-in-law e.' "   8200
Job 22: 9   And you sent widows away e and broke   8200
Jer 50: 9   be like skilled warriors who do not return e.   8200
Mk 12: 3   beat him and sent him away e.   3031
Lk 20:10   the tenants beat him and sent him away e.   3031
   20:11   and treated shamefully and sent away e.   3031

EMPTYING (2) [EMPTY]
Ge	42:35	As they were e their sacks,	8197
Hab	1:17	*Is he* to keep on e his net,	8197

EMULATION (KJV) ENVY

EN EGLAIM (1) [EGLAIM]
Eze	47:10	from En Gedi to E there will	6536

EN GANNIM (3)
Jos	15:34	Zanoah, E, Tappuah, Enam,	6528
	19:21	E, En Haddah and Beth Pazzez.	6528
	21:29	Jarmuth and E, together	6528

EN GEDI (6) [HAZAZON TAMAR]
Jos	15:62	the City of Salt and E—	6527
1Sa	23:29	and lived in the strongholds of E.	6527
	24: 1	"David is in the Desert of E."	6527
2Ch	20: 2	in Hazazon Tamar" (that is, E).	6527
SS	1:14	from the vineyards of E.	6527
Eze	47:10	from E to En Eglaim there will	6527

EN HADDAH (1)
Jos	19:21	En Gannim, E and Beth Pazzez.	6532

EN HAKKORE (1)
Jdg	15:19	So the spring was called E,	6530

EN HAZOR (1) [HAZOR]
Jos	19:37	Kedesh, Edrei, E,	6533

EN MISHPAT (1) [KADESH]
Ge	14: 7	and went to E (that is,	6535

EN RIMMON (1) [RIMMON]
Ne	11:29	in E, in Zorah, in Jarmuth,	6538

EN ROGEL (4)
Jos	15: 7	of En Shemesh and came out at E.	6537
	18:16	of the Jebusite city and so to E.	6537
2Sa	17:17	and Ahimaaz were staying at E.	6537
1Ki	1: 9	at the Stone of Zoheleth near E.	6537

EN SHEMESH (1)
Jos	15: 7	It continued along to the waters of E	6539
Jos	18:17	It then curved north, went to E,	6539

EN TAPPUAH (1) [TAPPUAH]
Jos	17: 7	to include the people living at E.	6540

ENABLE (3) [ABLE]
Ecc	6: 2	but God *does* not e him to enjoy them,	8948
Lk	1:74	and to e us to serve him without fear	1443
Ac	4:29	consider their threats and e your servants	1443

ENABLED (6) [ABLE]
Lev	26:13	and e you **to walk** with heads held high.	2143
Ru	4:13	and the LORD e her to conceive,	5989
Jn	6:65	to me unless the Father *has* e him."	1443+1639
Ac	2: 4	in other tongues as the Spirit e them.	1443
	7:10	He gave Joseph wisdom and e him to gain	NIG
Heb	11:11	was e to become a father	1539

ENABLES (5) [ABLE]
2Sa	22:34	he e me **to stand** on the heights.	6641
Ps	18:33	he e me **to stand** on the heights.	6641
Ecc	5:19	and e him to enjoy them,	8948
Hab	3:19	he e me **to go** on the heights.	2005
Php	3:21	by the power that e him to bring everything	1538

ENABLING (1) [ABLE]
Ac	14: 3	the message of his grace *by* e them to do	
		miraculous signs and	1328+1443+3836+5931

ENAIM (2)
Ge	38:14	and then sat down at the entrance to E,	6542
	38:21	beside the road at E?"	6542

ENAM (1)
Jos	15:34	Zanoah, En Gannim, Tappuah, E,	6543

ENAN (5) [HAZAR ENAN]
Nu	1:15	from Naphtali, Ahira son of E."	6544
	2:29	of the people of Naphtali is Ahira son of E.	6544
	7:78	On the twelfth day Ahira son of E,	6544
	7:83	This was the offering of Ahira son of E.	6544
	10:27	and Ahira son of E was over the division of	6544

ENCAMP (9) [CAMP]
Ex	14: 2	"Tell the Israelites to turn back and e	2837
	14: 2	*They are to* e by the sea,	2837
Nu	1:50	they are to take care of it and e around it.	2837
	2: 3	the divisions of the camp of Judah *are to* e	2837
	2:17	in the same order as *they* e,	2837

ENCAMPED (14) [CAMP]
Nu	9:20	at the LORD's command *they would* e,	2837
Job	19:12	they build a siege ramp against me and e	2837
Isa	29: 3	I *will* e against you all around;	2837
Jer	50:29	E all around her; let no one escape.	2837

ENCAMPED (14) [CAMP]
Ge	26:17	So Isaac moved away from there and e in	2837
Nu	2:34	that is the way *they* e under their standards,	2837
	9:17	wherever the cloud settled, the Israelites e.	2837
	9:18	and at his command *they* e.	2837
	9:23	At the LORD's command *they* e,	2837
	12:16	the people left Hazeroth and e in the Desert	2837
	24: 2	and saw Israel e tribe by tribe,	8905
Dt	11:20	He mustered all his men and e at Jahaz	2837
1Sa	26: 5	with the army e around him.	2837
2Sa	23:13	a band of Philistines *was* e in the Valley	2837
1Ki	16:15	The army *was* e near Gibbethon.	2837
2Ki	25: 1	*He* e outside the city	2837
1Ch	11:15	a band of Philistines *was* e in the Valley	2837

ENCAMPS (1) [CAMP]
Ps	34: 7	of the LORD e around those who fear him,	2837

ENCHANTER (4) [ENCHANTERS]
Ps	58: 5	however skillful the e *may be.*	2489+2490
Isa	3: 3	skilled craftsman and clever e.	4318
Da	2:10	a thing of any magician or e or astrologer.	10081
	2:27	Daniel replied, "No wise man, e,	10081

ENCHANTERS (6) [ENCHANTER]
Da	1:20	the magicians and e in his whole kingdom.	879
	2: 2	So the king summoned the magicians, e,	879
	4: 7	When the magicians, e,	10081
	5: 7	The king called out for the e,	10081
	5:11	appointed him chief of the magicians, e,	10081
	5:15	The wise men and e were brought	10081

ENCIRCLE (3) [CIRCLE]
Ps	22:12	strong bulls of Bashan e me.	4193
Isa	29: 3	I *will* e you *with* towers and set	6584+7443
Lk	19:43	and e you and hem you in on every side.	4333

ENCIRCLED (7) [CIRCLE]
1Ki	7:24	Below the rim, gourds e it—	6015+6017
2Ch	4: 3	figures of bulls e it—	6015+6017+6017
Ps	22:16	a band of evil men *has* e me,	5938
SS	7: 2	Your waist is a mound of wheat e by lilies.	6048
Rev	4: 3	resembling an emerald, e the throne.	3239
	5: 6	e by the four living creatures and the elders.	NIG
	5:11	They e the throne and the living creatures	3241

ENCIRCLING (2) [CIRCLE]
1Ki	7:18	in two rows e each network to decorate	6017
2Ch	33:14	as far as the entrance of the Fish Gate and e	6015

ENCLOSE (1) [CLOSE]
SS	8: 9	we will e her *with* panels of cedar.	7443

ENCLOSED (3) [CLOSE]
Est	1: 5	in the e garden of the king's palace,	2958
SS	4:12	you are a spring e, a sealed fountain.	3159
Eze	46:22	of the outer court were e courts,	7788

ENCOUNTER (3)
Ex	23:27	into confusion every nation *you* e.	928+995
2Sa	23: 8	whom he killed in one e.	7193
1Ch	11:11	whom he killed in one e.	7193

ENCOURAGE (24) [ENCOURAGED, ENCOURAGEMENT, ENCOURAGES, ENCOURAGING, ENCOURAGINGLY]
Dt	1:38	E him, because he will lead Israel	2616
	3:28	and e and strengthen him,	2616
2Sa	11:25	Say this to Joab."	2616
	19: 7	Now go out and e your men.	1819+4213+6584
Job	16: 5	But my mouth *would* e you;	599
Ps	10:17	*you* e them, and you listen to their cry,	3922+4213
	64: 5	They e each other in evil plans,	2616
Isa	1:17	Seek justice, e the oppressed.	887
Jer	29: 8	**dreams** you e them to have.	2706+2731
Ac	15:32	said much *to* e and strengthen the brothers.	4151
Ro	12: 8	if it is encouraging, let him e;	4155
Eph	6:22	and that he *may* e you.	4151
Col	4: 8	and that *he may* e your hearts.	4151
1Th	3: 2	to strengthen and e you in your faith,	4151
	4:18	Therefore e each other with these words.	4151
	5:11	e one another and build each other up,	4151
	5:14	warn those who are idle, e the timid,	4170
2Th	2:17	e your hearts and strengthen you	4151
2Ti	4: 2	correct, rebuke and e—	4151
Tit	1: 9	so that he can e others by sound doctrine	4151
	2: 6	the young men to be self-controlled.	4151
	2:15	E and rebuke with all authority.	4151
Heb	3:13	But e one another daily,	4151
	10:25	but let us e one another—	4151

ENCOURAGED (20) [ENCOURAGE]
Jdg	7:11	you *will be* e to attack the camp."	2616+3338

Jdg	20:22	of Israel e one another and again took	2616
2Ch	22: 3	for his mother e him in doing wrong.	3446
	32: 6	and e them with these words:	1819+4222+6584
	35: 2	to their duties and e them in the service of	2616
Eze	13:22	because you e the wicked not to turn	2616+3338
Ac	9:31	and e by the Holy Spirit,	4151
	11:23	he was glad and e them all to remain true to	4151
	16:40	they met with the brothers and e them.	4151
	18:27	The brothers e him and wrote to	4730
	27:36	They were all e and ate some food	2314
	28:15	Paul thanked God and *was* e.	2511+3284
Ro	1:12	*be* **mutually** e by each other's faith.	5220
1Co	14:31	so that everyone *may be* instructed and e.	4151
2Co	7: 4	I *am* **greatly** e;	4155+4444
	7:13	By all this *we are* e.	4151
Php	1:14	most of the brothers in the Lord *have been* e	4275
Col	2: 2	My purpose is that they *may be* e in heart	4151
1Th	3: 7	in all our distress and persecution *we were* e	4151
Heb	6:18	hope offered to us *may be* greatly e.	2400+4155

ENCOURAGEMENT (11) [ENCOURAGE]
Ac	4:36	called Barnabas (which means Son *of* E),	4155
	13:15	if you have a message *of* e for the people,	4155
	20: 2	**speaking** many words *of* e to	4151
Ro	15: 4	the e of the Scriptures we might have hope.	4155
	15: 5	and e give you a spirit of unity	4155
1Co	14: 3	for their strengthening, e and comfort.	4155
2Co	7:13	In addition *to* our own e,	4155
Php	2: 1	If you have any e from being united	4155
2Th	2:16	and by his grace gave us eternal e	4155
Phm	1: 7	Your love has given me great joy and e,	4155
Heb	12: 5	that word *of* e that addresses you as sons:	4155

ENCOURAGES (1) [ENCOURAGE]
Isa	41: 7	The craftsman e the goldsmith,	2616

ENCOURAGING (6) [ENCOURAGE]
Ac	14:22	the disciples and e them to remain true to	4151
	15:31	and were glad for its e **message.**	4155
	20: 1	and, *after* e them, said good-by and set out	4151
Ro	12: 8	if it is e, let him encourage;	4155
1Th	2:12	e, comforting and urging you	4151
1Pe	5:12	e you and testifying that this is	4151

ENCOURAGINGLY (1) [ENCOURAGE]
2Ch	30:22	Hezekiah spoke e to all the Levites,	4213+6584

ENCROACH (2)
Dt	2:37	not e on any of the land of the Ammonites,	7928
Pr	23:10	not move an ancient boundary stone or e on	995

ENCRUSTED (1) [CRUST]
Eze	24: 6	to the pot now e,	2689

END (268) [ENDED, ENDING, ENDS, ENDLESS, ENDLESSLY]
Ge	6:13	"I am going to put an e *to* all people,	7891
	8: 3	At the e *of* the hundred and fifty days	7895
	23: 9	which belongs to him and is at the e	7895
	41:53	of abundance in Egypt *came* to an e,	3983
	47:21	from *one e* of Egypt to the other.	1473+7895
Ex	12:41	At the e of the 430 years, to the very day,	7891
	23:16	the Feast of Ingathering at the e *of* the year,	3655
	25:19	on one e and the second cherub on	7896
	26: 4	along the edge of the e curtain in one set,	7896
	26: 4	the same with the e curtain in the other set.	7812
	26: 5	and fifty loops on the e curtain of	7896
	26:10	the edge of the e curtain in one set and also	7812
	26:10	and also along the edge of the e curtain in	NIH
	26:22	Make six frames for the **far** e, that is,	3752
	26:22	that is, the west e of the tabernacle,	NIH
	26:23	for the corners at the far e.	3752
	26:27	at the **far** e *of* the tabernacle.	3752
	26:28	from e to end at the middle of the frames.	7895
	26:28	from end to e at the middle of the frames.	7895
	27:12	"The west e *of* the courtyard shall	6991
	27:13	On the east e, toward the sunrise,	6991
	32:27	through the camp from *one* e to the other,	9133S
	36:11	along the edge of the e curtain in one set,	7896
	36:11	and the same was done with the e curtain in	7812
	36:12	and fifty loops on the e curtain of	7895
	36:17	the edge of the e curtain in one set and also	7812
	36:17	and also along the edge of the e curtain in	NIH
	36:27	They made six frames for the **far** e, that is,	3752
	36:27	that is, the west e of the tabernacle,	NIH
	36:28	the corners of the tabernacle at the **far** e.	3752
	36:32	at the **far** e *of* the tabernacle.	3752
	36:33	that it extended from e to end at the middle	7895
	36:33	that it extended from end to e at the middle	7895
	37: 8	on one e and the second cherub on	7896
	38:12	The west e was fifty cubits wide	6991
	38:13	The east e, toward the sunrise,	6991
Nu	13:25	At the e of forty days they returned	7891
	14:35	*They will* **meet** their e in this desert;	9462
	16:21	from this assembly so *I can* put an e	3983
	16:45	from this assembly so *I can* put an e	3983
	17:10	*This will* put an e to their grumbling	3983
	23:10	and may my e be like theirs!"	3983
	25:11	that in my zeal I *did* not put an e to them.	3983
	34: 3	from the e of the Salt Sea.	
	34: 5	the Wadi of Egypt and e at the Sea.	2118+9362
	34: 9	to Ziphron and e at Hazar Enan.	2118+9362

Column 1

Nu	34:12	along the Jordan and e *at* the Salt Sea.	2118+9362
Dt	4:32	ask from one e of the heavens to the other.	7895
	8:16	to test you so that in the e it might go well	344
	9:11	At the e of the forty days and forty nights,	7891
	11:12	on it from the beginning of the year to its e.	344
	13: 7	from one e of the land to the other),	7895
	14:28	At the e of every three years,	7895
	15: 1	At the e of every seven years	7891
	28:64	from one e of the earth to the other.	7895
	31:10	"At the e *of* every seven years,	7891
	31:24	the words of this law from beginning to e,	9462
	31:30	the words of this song from beginning to e	9462
	32:20	he said, "and see what their e will be;	344
	32:29	and discern what their e will be!	344
Jos	13:27	up to the e of the Sea of Kinnereth).	7895
	15: 2	the bay at the southern e of the Salt Sea,	7895
	15: 8	at the northern e of the Valley of Rephaim.	7895
	24:20	and bring disaster on you and **make an e**	3983
Ru	3: 7	to lie down at the **far** e of the grain pile.	7895
1Sa	3:12	from beginning to e.	3983
	14:27	so he reached out the e of the staff that was	7895
	14:43	"I merely tasted a little honey with the e	7895
2Sa	2:26	Don't you realize that *this* will e in	
		bitterness?	340+928+2021+2118
	15: 7	At the e of four years,	7891
	24: 8	at the e of nine months and twenty days.	7895
	24:15	on Israel from that morning **until the e** of	6330
1Ki	9:10	At the e *of* twenty years,	7895
	10:20	one **at either** e of each step.	
			2256+2296+2296+4946+4946ˢ
2Ki	8: 3	At the e of the seven years she came back	7895
	10:21	until it was full from one e to the other.	7023
	18:10	the e of three years the Assyrians took it.	7895
	21:16	that he filled Jerusalem from e to end—	7023
	21:16	that he filled Jerusalem from end to e—	7023
	24:20	**in the** e he thrust them from his presence.	6330
1Ch	29:29	from beginning to e,	340
2Ch	8: 1	At the e of twenty years,	7891
	9:19	one **at either** e of each step.	
			2256+2296+2296+4946+4946ˢ
	9:29	of Solomon's reign, from beginning to e,	340
	12:15	of Rehoboam's reign, from beginning to e,	340
	16:11	events of Asa's reign, from beginning to e,	340
	20:16	and you will find them at the e of the gorge	6067
	20:34	Jehoshaphat's reign, from beginning to e,	340
	21:19	at the e of the second year,	7891
	25: 2	of Amaziah's reign, from beginning to e,	340
	26:22	of Uzziah's reign, from beginning to e,	340
	28:26	and all his ways, from beginning to e,	340
	35:27	all the events, from beginning to e,	340
Ezr	9:11	with their impurity from one e to the other.	7023
Ne	3:21	the entrance of Eliashib's house to the e	9417
	4:11	and will kill them and **put an e** *to*	8697
	9:31	in your great mercy you did not put an e	3986
Est	1:18	be **no** e *of* disrespect and discord.	1896+3869
	8: 3	She begged him to **put an e** to the evil plan	6296
Job	4:15	and the hair on my body **stood on e.**	6169
	7: 6	and *they* **come to an e** without hope.	3983
	16: 3	Will your long-winded speeches never e?	7891
	18: 2	"When *will you* e these speeches?	7874+8492
	19:25	that *in the* e he will stand upon the earth.	340
	21:21	when his allotted months **come to an e?**	2951
	28: 3	Man puts an e to the darkness;	7891
Ps	7: 9	**bring to an** e the violence of the wicked	1698
	19: 6	It rises at one e of the heavens	7895
	39: 4	my life's e and the number of my days;	7891
	48:14	he will be our guide even to the e.	4637
	89:44	*You* have **put an** e to his splendor	8697
	102:27	and your years *will* never e.	9462
	107:27	they *were* at their **wits'** e.	1182+2683+3972
	112: 8	**in the** e he will look in triumph on his foes.	
			889+6330
	119:33	then I will keep them **to the e.**	6813
	119:112	My heart is set on keeping your decrees to	
		the very e.	4200+6409+6813
Pr	1:19	the e *of* all who go after ill-gotten gain;	784
	5: 4	but *in the* e she is bitter as gall,	344
	5:11	At the **e of** your **life** you will groan,	344
	14:12	but *in the* e it leads to death.	344
	14:13	and joy may e in grief.	344
	16:25	but *in the* e it leads to death.	344
	19:20	and in the e you will be wise.	344
	20:21	at the beginning will not be blessed at the e.	344
	23:32	the e it bites like a snake and poisons like	344
	25: 8	in the e if your neighbor puts you to shame?	344
	28:23	He who rebukes man will **in the** e gain	
		more favor than	343
	29:21	he will bring grief *in the* e.	344
Ecc	3:11	what God has done from beginning to e.	6067
	4: 8	There was no e to his toil.	7891
	4:16	There was no e to all the people who were	7891
	7: 8	e *of* a matter is better than its beginning,	344
	10:13	at the e they are wicked madness—	344
	12:12	Of making many books there is no e,	7891
Isa	2: 7	there is no e to their treasures.	7897
	2: 7	there is no e to their chariots.	7897
	7: 3	at the e *of* the aqueduct of the Upper Pool,	7895
	9: 7	and peace there will be no e.	7891
	10: 7	to **put an e** to many nations.	4162
	10:25	Very soon my anger against you *will* e	3983
	13:11	I *will* **put an e** to the arrogance of	8697
	14: 4	How the oppressor has **come to an e!**	7891
	16: 4	The oppressor *will* **come to an e,**	699
	16:10	for I have **put an e** to the shouting.	8697
	21: 2	I *will* **bring to an e** all	8697
	21:16	all the pomp of Kedar *will* **come to an e.**	3983
	23:15	But at the e *of* these seventy years,	7891

Column 2

Isa	23:17	At the e *of* seventy years,	7891
	38:12	day and night *you* **made an e** of me.	8966
	38:13	day and night *you* **made an e** of me.	8966
	46:10	I make known the e from the beginning,	344
	60:20	and your days of sorrow *will* e.	8966
	60:20	*they will* **meet** *their* e together,"	6066
Jer	5:31	But what will you do in the e?	344
	7:34	I *will* **bring an e** to the sounds of joy	8697
	12:12	of the LORD will devour from *one* e of	7895
	16: 9	and in your days I *will* **bring an e** to	8697
	17:11	and in the e he will prove to be a fool.	344
	20:18	to see trouble and sorrow and *to* e my days	3983
	25:33	from *one* e of the earth to the other.	7895
	48: 2	'Come, *let us* **put an e** to that nation.'	4162
	48:35	In Moab I *will* **put an e**	8697
	49:37	the sword until I *have* **made an e** *of* them.	3983
	51:13	your e has come,	7891
	51:64	The words of Jeremiah e here.	6330
	52: 3	**in** the e he thrust them from his presence.	6330
La	3:53	*to* e my life in a pit and threw stones at me;	7551
	4:18	Our e was near, our days were numbered,	7891
	4:18	for our e had come.	7891
	4:22	your punishment *will* e;	9462
Eze	3:16	At the e *of* seven days the word of	7895
	5: 2	When the days of your siege **come to an e,**	4848
	7: 2	to the land of Israel: The e!	7891
	7: 2	The e has come upon the four corners of	7891
	7: 3	The e is now upon you	7891
	7: 6	The e has come!	7891
	7: 6	The e has come!	7891
	7:24	I *will* **put an e** *to* the pride of the mighty,	8697
	12:23	I *am going to* **put an e** *to* this proverb,	8697
	20:17	not destroy them or put an e to them in	3986
	22: 4	and the e *of* your years has come.	6961
	22:15	and I *will* **put an e** to your uncleanness.	9462
	23:48	I *will* **put an e** to lewdness in the land,	8697
	26:13	I *will* **put an e** to your noisy songs,	8697
	26:21	I will bring you to a **horrible** e and you will	1166
	27:36	you have come to a **horrible** e and will	1166
	28:19	you have come to a **horrible** e and will	1166
	29:13	At the e *of* forty years I will gather	7891
	30:10	" 'I *will* **put an e** *to* the hordes of Egypt	8697
	30:13	" 'I will destroy the idols and **put an e** *to*	8697
	30:18	there her proud strength *will* **come to an e.**	8697
	33:28	and her proud strength *will* **come to an e.**	8697
	39:14	At the e of the seven months	7895
	40:15	to the **far** e of its portico was fifty cubits.	7164
	41: 4	and its width was twenty cubits across the e	7156
	43:27	*At the* e *of* these days,	3983
	46:19	and showed me a place at the western e.	3752
Da	1:15	the e *of* the ten days they looked healthier	7921
	1:18	At the e *of* the time set by the king	7921
	2:44	**bring** them to an e,	10508
	4:34	At the e *of* that time, I, Nebuchadnezzar,	10636
	5:26	**brought** it to an e.	10719
	6:26	his dominion will **never** e.	10002+10509+10527
	7:28	"This is the e of the matter.	10509
	8:17	that the vision concerns the time of the **e.**"	7891
	8:19	vision concerns the appointed time of the e.	7891
	9:24	to put an e *to* sin, to atone for wickedness,	9462
	9:26	The e will come like a flood:	7891
	9:26	War will continue until the e,	7891
	9:27	of the 'seven' *he will* **put an e** *to* sacrifice	7891
	9:27	the e that is decreed is poured out on him."	3986
	11:18	but a commander *will* **put an e**	8697
	11:27	an e will still come at the appointed time.	7891
	11:35	and made spotless until the time of the e,	7891
	11:40	the e the king of the South will engage him	7891
	11:45	Yet he will come to his e,	7891
	12: 4	of the scroll until the time of the e.	7891
	12: 9	up and sealed until the time of the e.	7891
	12:12	the one who waits for and reaches the e of	NIH
	12:13	"As for you, go your way till the e.	7891
	12:13	and then at the e of the days you will rise	7891
Hos	1: 4	I *will* **put an e** *to* the kingdom of Israel.	8697
	11: 6	of their gates and **put an e** to their plans.	430
Am	6: 7	your feasting and lounging *will* e.	6073
	8:10	an only son and the e *of* it like a bitter day.	344
Na	1: 8	an overwhelming flood he will make an e	3986
	1: 9	against the LORD he will bring to an e;	3986
Hab	2: 3	it speaks of the e and will not prove false.	7891
Zep	1:18	for he will make a sudden e of all who live	3986
Mt	10:22	he who stands firm to the e will be saved.	5465
	13:39	The harvest is the e of the age,	5333
	13:40	so it will be at the e of the age.	5333
	13:49	This is how it will be at the e of the age.	5333
	21:41	**bring** those wretches to a wretched **e,"**	660
	24: 3	be the sign of your coming and of the e	5333
	24: 6	but the e is still to come.	5465
	24:13	he who stands firm to the e will be saved.	5465
	24:14	and then the e will come.	5465
	24:31	from one e of the heavens to the other.	216
	28:20	to the **very** e of the age."	5333
Mk	3:26	his e has come.	5465
	13: 7	but the e is still to come.	5465
	13:13	he who stands firm to the e will be saved.	5465
Lk	1:33	his kingdom will never e."	5465
	4: 2	and *at the* e of them he was hungry.	5334
	17:24	and lights up the sky from one e to	NIG
	21: 9	but the e will not come right away."	NIG
Jn	11: 4	"This sickness *will* not e in death.	1639+4639
Ac	21:26	when the days of purification *would* e and	1741
Ro	10: 4	Christ is the e of the law so that there may	5465
1Co	1: 8	He will keep you strong to the e,	5465
	4: 9	on display at the e of the procession,	2274
	15:24	Then the e will come,	5465
2Co	11:15	Their e will be what their actions deserve.	5465

Column 3

Col	1:29	**To this** I labor,	1650+4005
Heb	1:12	and your years *will* never e."	1722
	3:14	to share in Christ if we hold firmly till the e	5465
	6: 8	In the e it will be burned.	5465
	6:11	to show this same diligence to the very e,	5465
	6:16	the oath confirms what is said and puts an e	4306
	7: 3	without beginning of days or e of life,	2400+5465
	9:26	now he has appeared once for all at the e of	5333
	11:22	By faith Joseph, *when his* e was near,	5462
1Pe	4: 7	The e of all things is near.	5465
2Pe	2:20	they are worse off at the e than they were at	2274
Rev	2:26	does my will to the e, I will give authority	5465
	21: 6	the Beginning and the **E.**	5465
	22:13	the Beginning and the **E.**	5465

ENDANGER (2) [DANGER]

Ru	4: 6	because I might e my own estate.	8845
1Co	15:30	for us, why *do we* e ourselves every hour?	3073

ENDANGERED (1) [DANGER]

Ecc	10: 9	whoever splits logs *may* be e by them.	6124

ENDANGERS (1) [DANGER]

Lev	19:16	**do anything that** e your neighbor's **life.**	
			1947+6584+6641

ENDEAVOUR (KJV) MAKE EVERY EFFORT

ENDED (16) [END]

Jos	15:11	The boundary e at the sea.	2118+9362
	16: 8	to the Kanah Ravine and e at the sea.	2118+9362
	17: 9	the northern side of the ravine and e at	2118+9362
	19:14	and e at the Valley of Iphtah El.	2118+9362
	19:22	and e at the Jordan.	2118+9362
2Ch	31: 1	When all this *had* e,	3983
Job	31:40	The words of Job *are* e.	9462
	39: 3	their labor pains are e.	8938
Ps	78:33	So *he* e their days in futility and their years	3983
Pr	22:10	quarrels and insults *are* e.	8697
Isa	14: 4	How his fury *has* e!	8697
Jer	8:20	"The harvest is past, the summer *has* e,	3983
Am	8: 5	be e that we may market wheat?"—	NIH
Ac	20: 1	When the uproar *had* e,	4264
Rev	20: 3	until the thousand years *were* e.	5464
	20: 5	to life until the thousand years *were* e.)	5464

ENDING (4) [END]

Ge	44:12	with the oldest and e with the youngest.	3983
Jos	15: 4	e at the sea.	2118+9362
	16: 3	e at the sea.	2118+9362
	19:33	to Lakkum and e *at* the Jordan.	2118+9362

ENDLESS (8) [END]

Job	22: 5	Are not your sins e?	401+7891
Ps	9: 6	**E** ruin has overtaken the enemy,	4200+5905
	49:11	dwellings for e **generations,**	1887+1887+2256
	93: 5	holiness adorns your house for e days,	802
	106:31	credited to him as righteousness for e	
		generations to come.	6330+6409
Na	2: 9	The supply is e,	401+7897
	3:19	for who has not felt your e cruelty?	9458
1Ti	1: 4	*to* myths and e genealogies.	596

ENDLESSLY (1) [END]

Heb	10: 1	same sacrifices repeated e year	1457+1650+3836

ENDOR (3)

Jos	17:11	Ibleam and the people of Dor, **E,**	6529
1Sa	28: 7	"There is one in **E,**" they said.	6529
Ps	83:10	at **E** and became like refuse on the ground.	6529

ENDOW (2) [ENDOWED]

Job	39:17	for God *did* not e her *with* wisdom	5960
Ps	72: 1	**E** the king *with* your justice, O God,	5989

ENDOWED (4) [ENDOW]

2Ch	2:12	e *with* intelligence and discernment,	3359
Job	38:36	Who e the heart *with* wisdom	8883
Isa	55: 5	for *he has* e you **with splendor."**	6995
	60: 9	for *he has* e you **with splendor.**	6995

ENDS (66) [END]

Ex	25:18	of hammered gold at the e of the cover.	7896
	25:19	of one piece with the cover, at the two e.	7896
	28:25	the other e of the chains to the two settings,	7896
	37: 7	of hammered gold at the e of the cover.	7896
	37: 8	at the two e he made them of one piece with	7896
	39:18	the other e of the chains to the two settings,	7896
Dt	28:49	from the e of the earth,	7895
	33:17	even those at the e of the earth.	700
1Sa	2:10	The LORD will judge the e of the earth.	700
1Ki	8: 8	These poles were so long that their e could	8031
2Ch	5: 9	These poles were so long that their e,	8031
Job	28:24	the e of the earth and sees everything under	7896
	37: 3	the whole heaven and sends it to the e of	4053
Ps	19: 4	their words to the e of the world.	7895
	22:27	the e of the earth will remember and turn to	700

Ps	46: 9	He makes wars cease to the e *of* the earth;	7895
	48:10	your praise reaches to the e *of* the earth;	7898
	59:13	the e *of* the earth that God rules over Jacob.	700
	61: 2	From the e *of* the earth I call to you,	7895
	65: 5	the e *of* the earth and of the farthest seas,	7898
	67: 7	and all the e *of* the earth will fear him.	700
	72: 8	from sea to sea and from the River to the e	700
	98: 3	all the e *of* the earth have seen the salvation	700
	135: 7	He makes clouds rise from the e *of*	7895
Pr	11:23	The desire of the righteous e only in good,	NIH
	12:24	but laziness e in slave labor.	2118
	16: 4	LORD works out everything for his own e	5102
	17:24	a fool's eyes wander to the e *of* the earth.	7895
	18: 1	An unfriendly man pursues **selfish** e;	9294
	20:17	but he e **up** with a mouth full of gravel.	339
	30: 4	Who has established all the e *of* the earth?	700
Isa	5:26	He whistles for those at the e *of* the earth.	7895
	13: 5	from the e *of* the heavens—	7895
	24:16	From the e *of* the earth we hear singing:	4053
	40:28	the Creator *of* the earth.	7896
	41: 5	the e *of* the earth tremble.	7896
	41: 9	I took you from the e *of* the earth,	7896
	42:10	his praise from the e *of* the earth,	7895
	43: 6	and my daughters from the e *of* the earth—	7895
	45:22	all you e *of* the earth;	700
	48:20	Send it out to the e *of* the earth;	7895
	49: 6	that you may bring my salvation to the e *of*	7895
	52:10	the e *of* the earth will see the salvation	700
	58: 4	Your fasting e in quarreling and strife,	NIH
	62:11	The LORD has made proclamation to the e	7895
Jer	6:22	a great nation is being stirred up from the e	3752
	10:13	he makes clouds rise from the e *of*	7895
	16:19	to you the nations will come from the e *of*	700
	25:31	tumult will resound to the e of the earth,	7895
	25:32	a mighty storm is rising from the e *of*	3752
	31: 8	of the north and gather them from the e *of*	3752
	48:47	Here e the judgment on Moab.	6330
	50:41	up from the e *of* the earth.	3752
	51:16	he makes clouds rise from the e *of*	7895
Eze	15: 4	on the fire as fuel and the fire burns both e	7896
Da	4:11	it was visible to the e *of* the earth.	10509
Mic	5: 4	for then his greatness will reach to the e *of*	700
Zec	9:10	from sea to sea and from the River to the e	700
Mt	12:42	for she came from the e *of* the earth	4306
Mk	13:27	the e *of* the earth to the ends of the heavens.	216
	13:27	the ends of the earth to the e *of* the heavens.	216
Lk	11:31	for she came from the e *of* the earth	4306
Ac	1: 8	and to the e *of* the earth."	2274
	13:47	that you may bring salvation to the e *of*	2274
Ro	10:18	their words to the e *of* the world."	4306

ENDUED (1)

| Ps | 89:13 | Your arm is e **with** power; | 6640 |

ENDURANCE (12) [ENDURE]

Ro	15: 4	so that through e and the encouragement of	5705
	15: 5	May the God who *gives* e	5705
2Co	1: 6	which produces in you **patient** e of	5705
	6: 4	in every way: in great e;	5705
Col	1:11	you may have **great** e and patience,	4246+5705
1Th	1: 3	and your e inspired by hope	5705
1Ti	6:11	godliness, faith, love, e and gentleness.	5705
2Ti	3:10	my purpose, faith, patience, love, e,	5705
Tit	2: 2	and sound in faith, in love and *in* e.	5705
Rev	1: 9	in the suffering and kingdom and **patient** e	5705
	13:10	for **patient** e and faithfulness on the part of	5705
	14:12	This calls for **patient** e on the part of	5705

ENDURE (40) [ENDURANCE, ENDURED, ENDURES, ENDURING]

1Sa	13:14	But now your kingdom *will* not e;	7756
2Sa	7:16	and your kingdom *will* e forever	586
Job	14: 2	like a fleeting shadow, *he does* not e.	6641
	15:29	be rich and his wealth *will* not e,	7756
	20:21	his prosperity *will* not e.	2656
Ps	37:18	and their inheritance *will* e forever.	2118
	49:12	But man, despite his riches, *does* not e;	4328
	55:12	*I could* e it;	5951
	69: 7	For *I* scorn for your sake,	5951
	69:10	When I weep and fast, I *must* e scorn;	2118+4200
	72: 5	*He will* e as long as the sun,	799
	72:17	*May* his name e forever;	2118
	89:29	**as long as** the heavens e,	3427+3869
	89:36	and his throne e before me like the sun;	NIH
	101: 5	him *will* I not e.	3523
	104:31	*May* the glory of the LORD e forever;	2118
	119:91	Your laws e to this day,	6641
Pr	12:19	Truthful lips e forever,	3922
	27:24	for riches do not e forever,	NIH
Ecc	3:14	that everything God does *will* e forever;	2118
Isa	66:22	and the new earth that I make *will* e	6641
	66:22	"so *will* your name and descendants e.	6641
Jer	10:10	the nations cannot e his wrath.	3920
	10:19	"This is my sickness, and *I must* e it."	5951
	44:22	LORD could no longer e your wicked actions	5951
Eze	22:14	*Will* your courage e or your hands	NIH
Da	2:44	but *it will* itself e forever.	10624
Joel	2:11	Who can e it?	3920
Na	1: 6	Who *can* e his fierce anger?	7756
Mal	3: 2	But who *can* e the day of his coming?	3920
1Co	4:12	when we are persecuted, *we* e it;	462
2Co	1: 8	far beyond our ability to e,	NIG
2Ti	2: 3	E hardship **with** us like a good soldier	5155
	2:10	Therefore *I* e everything for the sake of	5702

2Ti	2:12	if *we* e, we will also reign	5702
Heb	12: 7	E hardship as discipline;	5702
1Pe	2:20	a beating for doing wrong and e it?	5702
	2:20	if you suffer for doing good and *you* e it,	5702
Rev	3:10	you have kept my command **to** e **patiently**,	5705

ENDURED (8) [ENDURE]

Ps	123: 3	for *we have* e much contempt.	8425
	123: 4	We *have* e much ridicule from the proud,	8425
	132: 1	remember David and all *the* hardships he e.	6700
Ac	13:18	he e their conduct for about forty years in	5574
2Ti	3:11	Iconium and Lystra, the persecutions *I* e.	5722
Heb	12: 2	who for the joy set before him e the cross,	5702
	12: 3	Consider him who e such opposition	5702
Rev	2: 3	You have persevered and *have* e hardships	1002

ENDURES (60) [ENDURE]

Ge	8:22	"As long as the earth e,	3427
1Ch	16:34	his love e forever.	NIH
	16:41	"for his love e forever."	NIH
2Ch	5:13	his love e forever."	NIH
	7: 3	his love e forever."	NIH
	7: 6	saying, "His love e forever."	NIH
	20:21	for his love e forever."	NIH
Ezr	3:11	his love to Israel e forever."	NIH
Ps	100: 5	the LORD is good and his love e forever;	NIH
	102:12	your renown e through all generations.	NIH
	106: 1	his love e forever.	NIH
	107: 1	his love e forever.	NIH
	111: 3	and his righteousness e forever.	6641
	112: 3	and his righteousness e forever.	6641
	112: 9	his righteousness e forever;	6641
	117: 2	the faithfulness of the LORD e forever.	NIH
	118: 1	his love e forever.	NIH
	118: 2	Let Israel say: "His love e forever."	NIH
	118: 3	"His love e forever."	NIH
	118: 4	"His love e forever."	NIH
	118:29	his love e forever.	NIH
	119:90	you established the earth, and *it* e.	6641
	125: 1	which cannot be shaken but e forever.	3782
	135:13	Your name, O LORD, e forever,	NIH
	136: 1	His love e forever.	NIH
	136: 2	His love e forever.	NIH
	136: 3	His love e forever.	NIH
	136: 4	His love e forever.	NIH
	136: 5	His love e forever.	NIH
	136: 6	His love e forever.	NIH
	136: 7	His love e forever.	NIH
	136: 8	His love e forever.	NIH
	136: 9	His love e forever.	NIH
	136:10	the firstborn of Egypt His love e forever.	NIH
	136:11	from among them His love e forever.	NIH
	136:12	His love e forever.	NIH
	136:13	the Red Sea asunder His love e forever.	NIH
	136:14	His love e forever.	NIH
	136:15	His love e forever.	NIH
	136:16	His love e forever.	NIH
	136:17	His love e forever.	NIH
	136:18	killed mighty kings—His love e forever.	NIH
	136:19	of the Amorites His love e forever.	NIH
	136:20	Og king of Bashan—His love e forever.	NIH
	136:21	His love e forever.	NIH
	136:22	His love e forever.	NIH
	136:23	in our low estate His love e forever.	NIH
	136:24	His love e forever.	NIH
	136:25	His love e forever.	NIH
	136:26	His love e forever.	NIH
	138: 8	your love, O LORD, e forever—	NIH
	145:13	your dominion e through all generations.	NIH
Jer	33:11	his love e forever."	NIH
La	5:19	your throne e from generation	NIH
Da	4: 3	his dominion e from generation	NIH
	4:34	his kingdom e from generation	NIH
	6:26	"For he is the living God and he e forever;	10629
	9:15	and who made for yourself a name that e	NIH
Jn	6:27	but for food that e to eternal life,	3531
2Co	9: 9	his righteousness e forever."	3531

ENDURING (7) [ENDURE]

1Ki	11:38	a dynasty as e as the one I built for David	586
Ps	19: 9	The fear of the LORD is pure, e forever.	6641
Pr	8:18	e wealth and prosperity.	6982
Jer	5:15	an ancient and e nation,	419
2Th	1: 4	in all the persecutions and trials you are e.	462
Heb	13:14	For here we do not have an e city,	3531
1Pe	1:23	through the living and e word of God.	3531

ENEMIES (275) [ENEMY]

Ge	14:20	who delivered your e into your hand."	7640
	22:17	take possession of the cities of their e,	8533
	24:60	offspring possess the gates of their e."	8533
	49: 8	your hand will be on the neck of your e;	367
Ex	1:10	if war breaks out, will join our e,	8533
	23:22	I will be an enemy to your e	367
	23:27	I will make all your e turn their backs	367
	32:25	and so become a laughingstock to their e.	7756
Lev	26: 7	You will pursue your e,	367
	26: 8	your e will fall by the sword before you.	367
	26:16	because your e will eat it.	367
	26:17	so that you will be defeated by your e;	367
	26:32	that your e who live there will be appalled.	367
	26:34	and you are in the country of your e;	367
	26:36	in the lands of their e that the sound of	367

Lev	26:37	you will not be able to stand before your e.	367
	26:38	the land of your e will devour you.	367
	26:39	in the lands of their e because of their sins;	367
	26:41	so that I sent them into the land of their e—	367
	26:44	when they are in the land of their e,	367
Nu	10: 9	and rescued from your e.	367
	14:42	You will be defeated by your e,	367
	23:11	I brought you to curse my e,	367
	24:10	"I summoned you to curse my e,	367
	25:17	"**Treat** the Midianites **as** e and kill them,	7675
	25:18	because they **treated** you **as** e	7675
	32:21	until he has driven his e out before him—	367
Dt	1:42	You will be defeated by your e.' "	367
	6:19	thrusting out all your e before you,	367
	12:10	and he will give you rest from all your e	367
	20: 1	against your e and see horses and chariots	367
	20: 3	into battle against your e.	367
	20: 4	for you against your e to give you victory."	367
	20:14	And you may use the plunder from your e	
		your God gives you from your e.	367
	21:10	When you go to war against your e and	367
	23: 9	When you are encamped against your e,	367
	23:14	to protect you and to deliver your e to you.	367
	25:19	from all the e around you in	367
	28: 7	The LORD will grant that the e who rise	367
	28:25	to be defeated before your e.	367
	28:31	Your sheep will be given to your e,	367
	28:48	you will serve the e the LORD sends	367
	28:68	for sale to your e as male and female slaves,	367
	30: 7	on your e who hate and persecute you.	367
	32:31	as even our e concede.	367
	32:43	on his e and make atonement for his land	7640
	33:29	Your e will cower before you,	367
Jos	5:13	"Are you for us or for our e?"	7640
	7: 8	now that Israel has been routed by its e?	367
	7:12	the Israelites cannot stand against their e;	367
	7:13	against your e until you remove it.	367
	10:13	till the nation avenged itself on its e,	367
	10:19	Pursue your e, attack them from the rear	367
	10:25	to all the e you are going to fight."	367
	21:44	Not one of their e withstood them;	367
	21:44	the LORD handed all their e over to them.	367
	22: 8	divide with your brothers the plunder from	
		your e."	367
	23: 1	from all their e around them,	367
Jdg	2:14	He sold them to their e all around,	367
	2:18	and saved them out of the hands of their e	367
	5:31	"So may all your e perish, O LORD!	367
	8:34	from the hands of all their e on every side.	367
	11:36	that the LORD has avenged you of your e,	367
1Sa	2: 1	My mouth boasts over my e,	367
	4: 3	with us and save us from the hand of our e."	367
	12:10	But now deliver us from the hands of our e,	367
	12:11	from the hands of your e on every side,	367
	14:24	before I have avenged myself on my e!"	367
	14:30	of the plunder they took from their e.	367
	14:47	he fought against their e on every side:	367
	18:25	to take revenge on his e.' "	367
	20:15	of David's e from the face of the earth."	367
	20:16	the LORD call David's e to account."	367
	25:26	may your e and all who intend	367
	25:29	But the lives of your e he will hurl away as	367
	29: 8	Why can't I go and fight against the e	367
	30:26	for you from the plunder of the LORD's e."	367
2Sa	3:18	and from the hand of all their e.' "	367
	5: 8	and blind! *who are* David's e."	5883+8533
	5:20	the LORD has broken out against my e	367
	7: 1	from all his e around him,	367
	7: 9	I have cut off all your e from before you.	367
	7:11	I will also give you rest from all your e.	367
	12:14	because by doing this you have made the e	367
	18:19	from the hand of his e."	367
	18:32	the e *of* my lord the king and all who rise	367
	19: 9	king delivered us from the hand of our e;	367
	22: 1	from the hand of all his e and from the hand	367
	22: 4	and I am saved from my e.	367
	22:15	He shot arrows and scattered [**the** e],	4392S
	22:38	"I pursued my e and crushed them;	367
	22:41	You made my e turn their backs in flight,	367
	22:49	who sets me free from my e.	367
	24:13	Or three months of fleeing from your e	7640
1Ki	3:11	for the death of your e but for discernment	367
	5: 3	until the LORD put **his** e under his feet.	4392S
	8:44	your people go to war against their e,	367
	8:48	of their e who took them captive, and pray	367
2Ki	17:39	from the hand of all your e."	367
	21:14	and hand them over to their e.	367
1Ch	12:17	But if you have come to betray me to my e	7640
	14:11	God has broken out against my e	367
	17: 8	I have cut off all your e from before you.	367
	17:10	I will also subdue all your e.	367
	21:12	of being swept away before your e,	7640
	22: 9	and I will give him rest from all his e	367
2Ch	1:11	riches or honor, nor for the death of your e,	8533
	6:28	when e besiege them in any of their cities,	367
	6:34	your people go to war against their e,	367
	20:27	to rejoice over their e.	367
	20:29	how the LORD had fought against the e	367
	26:13	to support the king against his e.	367
Ezr	4: 1	When the e *of* Judah and Benjamin heard	7640
	8:22	and horsemen to protect us from e on	367
	8:31	and he protected us from e and bandits	367
Ne	4: 1	Also our e said,	7640
	4:15	When our e heard that we were aware	367
	5: 9	to avoid the reproach of our Gentile e?	367
	6: 1	of our e that I had rebuilt the wall and not	367

Ne	6:16	When all our e heard about this,	367
	9:27	So you handed them over to their e,	7640
	9:27	who rescued them from the hand of their e.	7640
	9:28	to the hand of their e so that they ruled	367
Est	8:11	and to plunder the property of their e.	4392S
	8:13	on that day to avenge themselves on their e.	367
	9:1	On this day the e of the Jews had hoped	367
	9:5	The Jews struck down all their e with	367
	9:16	and get relief from their e.	367
	9:22	time when the Jews got relief from their e,	367
Job	8:22	Your e will be clothed in shame,	8533
	19:11	he counts me among his e.	7640
	27:7	"May my e be like the wicked,	367
Ps	3:7	Strike all my e on the jaw;	367
	5:8	in your righteousness because of my e—	8806
	6:10	All my e will be ashamed and dismayed;	367
	7:6	rise up against the rage of my e.	7675
	8:2	because of your e,	7675
	9:3	My e turn back;	367
	9:13	O LORD, see how my e persecute me!	8533
	10:5	he sneers at all his e.	7675
	17:9	from my mortal e who surround me.	367
	18:T	from the hand of all his e and from the hand	367
	18:3	and I am saved from my e.	367
	18:14	He shot his arrows and scattered [the e],	4392
	18:37	I pursued my e and overtook them;	367
	18:40	You made my e turn their backs in flight,	367
	18:48	who saves me from my e.	367
	21:8	Your hand will lay hold on all your e;	367
	23:5	a table before me in the presence of my e.	7675
	25:2	nor let my e triumph over me.	367
	25:19	See how my e have increased and	367
	27:2	when my e and my foes attack me,	7640
	27:6	be exalted above the e who surround me;	367
	30:1	of the depths and did not let my e gloat	367
	31:11	Because of all my e,	7675
	31:15	from my e and from those who pursue me.	367
	35:19	Let not those gloat over me who are my e	367
	37:20	The LORD's e will be like the beauty of	367
	38:19	Many are those who are my vigorous e;	367
	41:5	My e say of me in malice,	367
	41:7	All my e whisper together against me;	8533
	44:5	Through you we push back our e;	7640
	44:7	but you give us victory over our e,	7640
	45:5	the hearts of the king's e;	367
	55:15	Let death take my e by surprise;	4564S
	56:9	my e will turn back when I call for help.	367
	59:1	Deliver me from my e, O God;	367
	60:12	and he will trample down our e.	7640
	66:3	So great is your power that your e cringe	367
	68:1	May God arise, may his e be scattered;	367
	68:21	Surely God will crush the heads of his e,	367
	69:4	many are my e without cause,	367
	69:19	all my e are before you.	7675
	71:10	For my e speak against me;	367
	72:9	before him and his e will lick the dust.	367
	74:23	the uproar of your e,	7756
	78:53	but the sea engulfed their e.	367
	78:66	He beat back his e;	7640
	80:6	and our e mock us.	367
	81:14	how quickly would I subdue their e	367
	83:2	See how your e are astir,	367
	86:17	that my e may see it and be put to shame,	8533
	89:10	with your strong arm you scattered your e.	367
	89:42	you have made all his e rejoice.	367
	89:51	the taunts with which your e have mocked,	367
	92:9	For surely your e, O LORD,	367
	92:9	O LORD, surely your e will perish;	367
	102:8	All day long my e taunt me;	367
	106:42	Their e oppressed them and subjected them	367
	108:13	and he will trample down our e.	7640
	110:1	"Sit at my right hand until I make your e	367
	110:2	you will rule in the midst of your e.	367
	118:7	I will look in triumph on my e.	8533
	119:98	Your commands make me wiser than my e,	367
	119:139	for my e ignore your words.	7640
	127:5	to shame when they contend with their e in	367
	132:18	I will clothe his e with shame,	367
	136:24	and freed us from our e,	7640
	139:22	I count them my e.	367
	143:9	Rescue me from my e, O LORD,	367
	143:12	In your unfailing love, silence my e;	367
	144:6	Send forth lightning and scatter [the e],	4392S
Pr	16:7	he makes even his e live at peace with him.	367
Isa	1:24	from my foes and avenge myself on my e.	367
	9:11	against them and has spurred their e on.	367
	11:13	and Judah's e will be cut off;	7675
	26:11	the fire reserved for your e consume them.	7640
	29:5	But your many e will become like fine dust,	2424
	41:12	Though you search for your e,	408+5194
	42:13	the battle cry and will triumph over his e.	367
	59:18	to his e and retribution to his foes;	7640
	62:8	as food for your e,	367
	63:18	our e have trampled down your sanctuary.	7640
	64:2	down to make your name known to your e	7640
	66:6	the LORD repaying his e all they deserve.	367
Jer	12:7	the one I love into the hands of her e.	367
	15:9	the survivors to the sword before their e,"	367
	15:11	surely I will make your e plead with you	367
	15:14	I will enslave you to your e in a land you do	367
	17:4	I will enslave you to your e in a land you do	367
	18:17	I will scatter them before their e;	367
	19:7	by the sword before their e,	367
	19:9	on them by the e who seek their lives.'	367
	20:4	by the sword of their e.	367
	20:5	over to their e all the wealth of this city—	367
	21:7	and to their e who seek their lives.	367

Jer	30:16	all your e will go into exile.	367
	34:20	over to their e who seek their lives.	367
	34:21	over to their e who seek their lives,	367
	44:30	of Egypt over to his e who seek his life,	367
	50:7	their e said, 'We are not guilty,	7640
	51:55	Waves [of e] will rage like great waters;	2157S
La	1:2	they have become her e.	367
	1:5	her e are at ease.	367
	1:7	Her e looked at her and laughed	7640
	1:21	All your e have heard of my distress;	367
	2:16	All your e open their mouths wide	367
	3:46	"All our e have opened their mouths wide	367
	3:52	Those who were my e	367
	3:62	what my e whisper and mutter	7756
	4:12	that e and foes could enter the gates	367
Eze	16:27	I gave you over to the greed of your e,	8533
	39:23	from them and handed them over to their e,	7640
	39:27	from the countries of their e,	367
Da	4:19	the dream applied to your e and its meaning	10686
Am	9:4	into exile by their e,	367
Mic	4:10	of the hand of your e.	367
	5:9	be lifted up in triumph over your e,	7640
	7:6	a man's e are the members	367
Na	1:2	and maintains his wrath against his e.	367
	3:13	gates of your land are wide open to your e;	367
Mt	5:44	Love your e and pray	2398
	10:36	a man's e will be the members	2398
	22:44	"Sit at my right hand until I put your e	2398
Mk	12:36	"Sit at my right hand until I put your e	2398
Lk	1:71	salvation from our e and from the hand	2398
	1:74	to rescue us from the hand of our e,	2398
	6:27	"But I tell you who hear me: Love your e,	2398
	6:35	But love your e, do good to them,	2398
	19:27	But those e of mine who did not want me to	2398
	19:43	when your e will build an embankment	2398
	20:43	until I make your e a footstool	2398
	23:12	before this they had been e.	1877+2397
Ac	2:35	until I make your e a footstool	2398
Ro	5:10	For if, when we were God's e,	2398
	11:28	they are e on your account;	2398
1Co	15:25	For he must reign until he has put all his e	2398
Php	3:18	many live as e of the cross of Christ.	2398
Col	1:21	from God and were e in your minds	2398
Heb	1:13	"Sit at my right hand until I make your e	2398
	10:13	Since that time he waits for his e to	2398
	10:27	and of raging fire that will consume the e	5641
Rev	11:5	from their mouths and devours their e.	2398
	11:12	while their e looked on.	2398

ENEMY (107) [ENEMIES, ENEMY'S, ENMITY]

Ex	15:6	Your right hand, O LORD, shattered the e.	367
	15:9	"The e boasted, 'I will pursue,	367
	23:22	I will be an e to your enemies	366
Lev	26:25	and you will be given into e hands.	367
Nu	10:9	against an e who is oppressing you,	7640
	24:18	Edom will be conquered; Seir, his e,	367
	35:23	not his e and he did not intend to harm him,	367
Dt	28:53	the suffering that your e will inflict on you	367
	28:55	because of the suffering your e will inflict	367
	28:57	in the distress that your e will inflict on you	367
	32:27	of the e, lest the adversary misunderstand	367
	32:42	the heads of the e leaders."	367
	33:27	He will drive out your e before you, saying,	367
Jdg	3:28	"for the LORD has given Moab, your e,	367
	16:23	"Our god has delivered Samson, our e,	367
	16:24	"Our god has delivered our e	367
1Sa	18:29	and he remained his e the rest of his days.	367
	19:17	and send my e away so that he escaped?"	367
	24:4	'I will give your e into your hands for you	367
	24:19	When a man finds his e,	367
	26:8	"Today God has delivered your e	367
	28:16	from you and become your e?	6839
2Sa	4:8	your e, who tried to take your life.	367
	22:18	He rescued me from my powerful e,	367
1Ki	8:33	an e because they have sinned against you,	367
	8:37	an e besieges them in any of their cities,	367
	8:46	with them and give them over to the e,	367
	21:20	"So you have found me, my e!"	367
2Ki	6:18	As the e came down toward him,	NIH
2Ch	6:24	an e because they have sinned against you	367
	6:36	over to the e, who takes them captive to	367
	25:8	God will overthrow you before the e,	367
Est	3:10	the Agagite, the e of the Jews.	7675
	7:6	"The adversary and e is this vile Haman."	367
	8:1	Haman, the e of the Jews.	7675
	9:10	Haman son of Hammedatha, the e of the Jews.	7675
	9:24	the Agagite, the e of all the Jews,	7675
Job	6:23	deliver me from the hand of the e,	7640
	13:24	and consider me your e?	367
	33:10	he considers me his e.	367
Ps	7:5	then let my e pursue and overtake me;	367
	9:6	Endless ruin has overtaken the e,	367
	13:2	How long will my e triumph over me?	367
	13:4	my e will say,	367
	18:17	He rescued me from my powerful e,	367
	31:8	You have not handed me over to the e	367
	41:11	for my e does not triumph over me.	367
	42:9	oppressed by the e?"	367
	43:2	oppressed by the e?"	367
	44:10	You made us retreat before the e,	7640
	44:16	because of the e, who is bent on revenge.	367
	55:3	of the e, at the stares of the wicked;	367
	55:12	If an e were insulting me, I could endure it;	367
	60:11	Give us aid against the e,	7640

Ps	64:1	protect my life from the threat of the e.	367
	74:3	all this destruction the e has brought on	367
	74:10	How long will the e mock you, O God?	7640
	74:18	Remember how the e has mocked you,	367
	78:61	his splendor into the hands of the e.	7640
	89:22	No e will subject him to tribute;	367
	106:10	from the hand of the e he redeemed them.	367
	108:12	Give us aid against the e,	7640
	143:3	The e pursues me, he crushes me to	367
Pr	24:17	Do not gloat when your e falls;	367
	25:21	If your e is hungry, give him food to eat;	8533
	27:6	but an e multiplies kisses.	8533
	29:24	The accomplice of a thief is his own e;	8533
Isa	22:3	having fled while the e was still far away.	NIH
	63:10	and became their e and he himself fought	367
Jer	6:25	for the e has a sword,	367
	30:14	as an e would and punished you as would	367
	31:16	"They will return from the land of the e.	367
	44:30	the e who was seeking his life.'"	NIH
	46:22	a fleeing serpent as the e advances in force;	NIH
	47:3	of e chariots and the rumble of their wheels.	2257S
La	1:7	When her people fell into e hands,	7640
	1:9	on my affliction, for the e has triumphed."	367
	1:10	The e laid hands on all her treasures;	7640
	1:16	because the e has prevailed."	367
	2:3	at the approach of the e.	367
	2:4	Like an e he has strung his bow;	367
	2:5	The Lord is like an e;	367
	2:7	He has handed over to the e the walls	367
	2:17	he has let the e gloat over you,	367
	2:22	for and reared, my e has destroyed."	367
Eze	36:2	The e said of you, "Aha!	367
Hos	8:3	an e will pursue him.	367
Am	3:11	"An e will overrun the land;	7640
Mic	2:8	Lately my people have risen up like an e.	367
	7:8	Do not gloat over me, my e!	367
	7:10	Then my e will see it and will be covered	367
Na	3:11	into hiding and seek refuge from the e.	367
Zep	3:15	he has turned back your e.	367
Zec	8:10	about his business safely because of his e,	7640
Mt	5:43	'Love your neighbor and hate your e.'	2398
	13:25	his e came and sowed weeds among	2398
	13:28	"'An e did this,' he replied.	476+2398
	13:39	and the e who sows them is the devil.	2398
Lk	10:19	and to overcome all the power of the e;	2398
Ac	13:10	a child of the devil and an e of everything	2398
Ro	12:20	"If your e is hungry, feed him;	2398
1Co	15:26	The last e to be destroyed is death.	2398
Gal	4:16	Have I now become your e by telling you	2398
2Th	3:15	Yet do not regard him as an e,	2398
1Ti	5:14	and to give the e no opportunity for slander.	512
Jas	4:4	a friend of the world becomes an e of God.	2398
1Pe	5:8	Your e the devil prowls around like	508

ENEMY'S (3) [ENEMY]

Ex	23:4	across your e ox or donkey wandering off,	367
Job	31:29	"If I have rejoiced at my e misfortune	8533
Jer	8:16	snorting of the e horses is heard from Dan;	2257S

ENERGY (1)

Col	1:29	struggling with all his e,	1918

ENFOLDS (1) [FOLD]

Isa	25:7	the shroud that e all peoples, the sheet	4286

ENFORCE (1) [FORCE]

Da	6:7	that the king should issue an edict and e	10772

ENGAGE (9) [ENGAGED, ENGAGES, ENGAGING]

Ex	31:5	and to e in all kinds of craftsmanship.	6913
	35:33	to e in all kinds of artistic craftsmanship.	6913
Dt	2:24	to take possession of it and e him in battle.	1741
	20:12	If they refuse to make peace and they e you	6913
1Sa	7:10	the Philistines drew near to e Israel	NIH
2Ch	35:22	but disguised himself to e him in battle.	4309
Jer	11:15	When you e in your wickedness,	NIH
Da	11:40	of the South will e him in battle,	5590
Hos	4:10	they will e in prostitution but	2388

ENGAGED (7) [ENGAGE]

Jdg	12:2	"I and my people were e in a great struggle	2118
1Ki	16:17	the people e in all the detestable practices	6913
Eze	16:17	and e in prostitution with them.	2388
	16:26	You e in prostitution with the Egyptians,	2388
	16:28	You e in prostitution with the Assyrians	2388
	23:5	"Oholah e in prostitution	2388
1Co	7:36	improperly toward the virgin he is e to,	NIG

ENGAGES (1) [ENGAGE]

Dt	18:10	interprets omens, e in witchcraft,	4175

ENGAGING (1) [ENGAGE]

Eze	23:3	e in prostitution from their youth.	2388

ENGRAFTED (KJV) PLANTED

ENGRAVE (4) [ENGRAVED, ENGRAVES, ENGRAVING]

Ex	28:9	"Take two onyx stones and e on them	7338

Ex	28:11	E the names of the sons of Israel *on*
	28:36	"Make a plate of pure gold and e on it
Zec	3: 9	and I *will* e an inscription on it,'

7338
7334+7338
7338

ENGRAVED (10) [ENGRAVE]

Ex	28:21	each *like* a seal with the name of one of	7334
	32:16	the writing was the writing of God, e on	3100
	39: 6	and e them *like* a seal with the names	7334+7338
	39:14	each *like* a seal with the name of one of	7334
	39:30	out of pure gold and e on it,	4180
1Ki	7:36	*He* e cherubim, lions and palm trees on	7338
Job	19:24	or e in rock forever!	2933
Isa	49:16	I *have* e you on the palms of my hands;	2980
Jer	17: 1	"Judah's sin *is* e with an iron tool,	4180
2Co	3: 7	*which was* e in letters on stone,	*1963*

ENGRAVES (1) [ENGRAVE]

Ex	28:11	on the two stones the way a gem cutter e	7334

ENGRAVING (3) [ENGRAVE]

1Ki	7:31	Around its opening there was e.	5237
2Ch	2: 7	and experienced in the **art of** e,	7334+7338
	2:14	**experienced in** all kinds of e	7334+7338

ENGROSSED (1)

1Co	7:31	as if not e in them.	2974

ENGULF (3) [ENGULFED, ENGULFING]

Ps	69: 2	the floods e me.	8851
	69:15	*Do not let* the floodwaters e me or	8851
Hos	7: 2	Their sins e them;	6015

ENGULFED (3) [ENGULF]

Ps	78:53	but the sea e their enemies.	4059
	88:17	*they have* completely e me.	5938
	124: 4	the flood *would have* e us,	8851

ENGULFING (1) [ENGULF]

Jnh	2: 5	The e waters threatened me,	705

ENHANCES (1)

Ro	3: 7	"If my falsehood e God's truthfulness and	*4355*

ENJOIN, ENJOINED (KJV) ORDER, ORDERED

ENJOY (39) [JOY]

Ge	45:18	of Egypt and *you can* e the fat of the land.'	430
Ex	30:38	like it to e its **fragrance** must be cut off	8193
Lev	26:34	Then the land *will* e its sabbath years all	8354
	26:34	then the land will rest and e its sabbaths	8354
	26:43	be deserted by them and *will* e its sabbaths	8354
Nu	14:31	in *to* e the land you have rejected.	3359
Dt	6: 2	and so that you *may* e **long life.**	799+3427
	20: 6	a vineyard and *not begun to* e it?	2725
	20: 6	in battle and someone else e it.	2725
	28:30	but *you will* not *even begin to* e its fruit.	2725
Jdg	19: 6	"Please stay tonight and e yourself."	3512
	19: 9	Stay and e yourself.	3512
Ne	8:10	"Go and e choice food and sweet drinks,	430
Job	3:18	Captives also e *their* **ease;**	8631
	20:17	*He will* not e the streams,	8011
	20:18	*he will* not e the profit from his trading.	6632
	33:28	and I will live *to* e the light.'	8011
Ps	37: 3	dwell in the land and e **safe pasture.**	8286
	37:11	the land and e great peace.	6695
	37:19	in days of famine they *will* e **plenty.**	8425
	106: 5	I *may* e the prosperity of your chosen ones,	8011
Pr	7:18	*let's* e **ourselves** with love!	6632
	28:16	he who hates ill-gotten gain *will* e **a long life.**	799+3427
Ecc	3:22	for a man than *to* e his work,	8523
	5:19	and enables him to e them,	430
	6: 2	but God does not enable him to e them,	430
	6: 3	if he cannot e his prosperity and does	8425
	6: 6	over but fails to e his prosperity.	8011
	9: 9	E life with your wife, whom you love,	8011
	11: 8	*let him* e them all.	8523
Isa	3:10	for *they will* e the fruit of their deeds.	430
	65:22	my chosen ones *will* **long** e the works	1162
Jer	31: 5	the farmers will plant them and e their fruit.	2725
	33: 6	and *will* **let them** e abundant peace.	1655
Jn	5:35	and you chose for a time *to* e his light.	*22*
Ro	15: 2	and the whole church here e,	*NIG*
Eph	6: 3	and that *you may* e **long life** on	*1639+3432*
Heb	11:25	of God rather than *to* e the pleasures of sin	*2400*
3Jn	1: 2	I pray that you *may* e **good health** and	*5617*

ENJOYED (9) [JOY]

Jdg	3:30	the land e **peace** forty years.	9200
1Ch	29:28	having a **long** life, wealth and honor.	3427+8428
2Ch	36:21	The land e its sabbath rests;	8354
Job	21:25	never *having* e anything good.	430
Ps	55:14	with whom *I* once e **sweet** fellowship	5517
Ac	7:46	who e God's favor and asked	*2351*
	9:31	Galilee and Samaria e a time of peace.	*2400*
	24: 2	"We have e a long period of peace under you,	*5593*
Ro	15:24	after *I* have e your **company** for a while.	*1855*

ENJOYING (3) [JOY]

Jdg	19:22	*While* they were e themselves,	3512
Ne	9:35	e your great goodness to them in	NIH
Ac	2:47	praising God and e the **favor** of all	*2400+5921*

ENJOYMENT (4) [JOY]

Ecc	2:25	for without him, who can eat or **find** e?	2591
	4: 8	"and why am I depriving myself of e?"	3208
	8:15	So I commend the e of life,	8525
1Ti	6:17	with everything for our e.	*656*

ENJOYS (3) [JOY]

Pr	13: 2	the fruit of his lips a man e good things,	430
Ecc	6: 2	and a stranger e them instead.	430
Hab	1:16	for by his net he lives in luxury and e	NIH

ENLARGE (4) [LARGE]

Ex	34:24	before you and e your territory,	8143
1Ch	4:10	that you would bless me and e my territory!	8049
Isa	54: 2	"E the place of your tent,	8143
2Co	9:10	and increase your store of seed and *will* e	*889*

ENLARGED (5) [LARGE]

Dt	12:20	the LORD your God *has* e your territory	8143
Isa	9: 3	*You have* e the nation	8049
	26:15	*You have* e the nation, O LORD;	3578
	26:15	*you have* e the nation.	3578
Jer	20:17	her womb e forever.	2226

ENLARGES (4) [LARGE]

Dt	19: 8	If the LORD your God e your territory,	8143
	33:20	"Blessed is *he who* e Gad's domain!	8143
Job	12:23	*he* e nations, and disperses them.	8848
Isa	5:14	the grave e its appetite and opens its mouth	8143

ENLIGHTEN (1) [LIGHT]

Isa	40:14	Whom did the LORD consult *to* e him,	1067

ENLIGHTENED (2) [LIGHT]

Eph	1:18	*be* e in order that you may know the hope	*5894*
Heb	6: 4	for those who *have* once *been* e,	*5894*

ENMITY (1) [ENEMY]

Ge	3:15	I will put e between you and the woman,	368

ENOCH (13)

Ge	4:17	she became pregnant and gave birth to E.	2840
	4:17	and he named it after his son E.	2840
	4:18	To E was born Irad,	2840
	5:18	he became the father of E.	2840
	5:19	And after he became the father of E,	2840
	5:21	When E had lived 65 years,	2840
	5:22	E walked with God 300 years	2840
	5:23	Altogether, E lived 365 years.	2840
	5:24	E walked with God;	2840
1Ch	1: 3	E, Methuselah, Lamech, Noah.	2840
Lk	3:37	the son of E, the son of Jared,	1970
Heb	11: 5	By faith E was taken from this life,	*1970*
Jude	1:14	E, the seventh from Adam,	*1970*

ENORMOUS (3)

Da	2:31	e, dazzling statue, awesome in appearance.	10647
	4:10	Its height was e.	10678
Rev	12: 3	an e red dragon with seven heads	*3489*

ENOS (KJV) ENOSH

ENOSH (8)

Ge	4:26	Seth also had a son, and he named him E.	633
	5: 6	he became the father of E.	633
	5: 7	And after he became the father of E,	633
	5: 9	When E had lived 90 years,	633
	5:10	E lived 815 years and had other sons	633
	5:11	Altogether, E lived 905 years,	633
1Ch	1: 1	Adam, Seth, E,	633
Lk	3:38	the son *of* E,	*1968*

ENOUGH (98)

Ge	19:20	Look, here is a town *near* e to run to,	AIT
	22: 3	he had cut e **wood** *for* the burnt offering,	AIT
	24:20	and drew e **for** all his camels.	AIT
	30:15	But she said to her, "**Wasn't** it e	5071
	47:15	from Pharaoh and **had food** e *from*	430
Ex	9:28	for we have had e thunder and hail.	8041
	16: 4	to go out each day and gather e for that day.	1821
	23:30	until *you have* **increased** e	AIT
	36: 5	"The people are bringing more than e	1896
	36: 7	what they already had was more than e	1896
Lev	25:21	in the sixth year that the land will yield e	9311
Nu	11:22	*Would* they **have** e if flocks	5162
	11:22	*Would* they **have** e if all the fish in	5162
	16: 9	**Isn't** it e for you that the God	5071
	16:13	**Isn't** it e that you have brought us up out of	5071
	20:12	in me e to honor me as holy in the sight of	NIH
Dt	1: 6	"You have stayed **long** e at this mountain.	8041
	2: 3	around this hill country **long** e;	8041
	2: 5	not **even** e to put your foot on.	6330
	3:26	"That is e," the LORD said.	8041

ENRAGED (8) [RAGE]

2Ki	6:11	This e the king of Aram.	4213+6192
2Ch	16:10	he was so e that he put him in prison.	2408
Est	3: 5	or pay him honor, he was e.	2779+4848
Isa	8:21	*they will become* e and, looking upward,	7911
	57:17	*I was* e by his sinful greed;	7911
Eze	16:43	the days of your youth but e me	8074
Mt	22: 7	The king was e.	*3974*
Rev	12:17	the dragon *was* e at the woman and went off	*3974*

ENRICH (2) [RICH]

Ps	65: 9	*you* e it abundantly.	6947
Pr	5:10	and your toil e another man's house.	NIH

ENRICHED (3) [RICH]

Isa	23: 2	whom the seafarers *have* e.	4848

Dt	9: 8	the LORD's wrath so that he *was* **angry** e	AIT
	9:19	for *he was* **angry** e with you to destroy you.	AIT
	9:20	And the LORD was **angry** e with Aaron	4394
	19:15	One witness is not e to **convict**	AIT
Jos	17:16	"The hill country *is* not e for us,	5162
	22:17	Was **not** the sin of Peor e for us?	5071
Jdg	21:14	But there were not e for all of them.	4027
Ru	2:18	over after she *had* **eaten** e.	8425
2Sa	18:18	And as if this *were* not e in your sight,	6388+1791
	24:16	the angel who was afflicting the people, "**E!**	8041
1Ki	18:32	around it **large** e to hold two seahs of seed.	3869
	19: 4	"I have had e, LORD," he said.	8041
	20:10	if e dust *remains* in Samaria to give each	8563
1Ch	17:17	And as if this *were* not e in your sight,	7781
	21:15	to the angel who was destroying the people, "**E!**	8041
2Ch	13: 7	and indecisive and not **strong** e	AIT
	22: 9	the house of Ahaziah **powerful** e to retain	AIT
	30: 3	not e priests had consecrated themselves	1896+4200+4537
	31:10	we *have* **had** e to eat and plenty to spare,	8425
Ezr	9:14	not be angry e with us to destroy us,	6330
Ne	2:14	not e room for my mount to get through;	NIH
Job	15:11	Are God's consolations **not** e for you,	5071
	19:22	*Will you* never **get** e of my flesh?	8425
	27:14	his offspring *will* never **have** e to eat.	8425
	41:10	No one is **fierce** e to rouse him.	AIT
Ps	49: 8	**no** payment *is* ever e—	2532
	78:29	They ate till *they* **had** more than e,	8425
Pr	25:16	If you find honey, eat **just** e—	1896
	30:15	four that never say, '**E!**':	2104
	30:16	and fire, which never says, '**E!**'	2104
Ecc	1: 8	The eye never **has** e of seeing,	8425
	5:10	Whoever loves money never **has** money e;	8425
Isa	1:11	"*I have more than* e of burnt offerings,	8425
	7:13	Is it **not** e to try the patience of men?	5071
	7:15	and honey when he **knows** e to reject	AIT
	7:15	before the boy **knows** e to reject the wrong	AIT
	40:16	nor its animals e *for* burnt offerings.	1896
	56:11	they never have e.	8429
Jer	9:12	What man is **wise** e to understand this?	AIT
La	5: 6	to Egypt and Assyria to **get** e bread.	8425
Eze	16: 5	with pity or **had compassion** e to do any	AIT
	16: 8	and saw that you were **old** e for love,	AIT
	16:20	Was your prostitution **not** e?	5071
	30:21	in a splint so as to **become strong** e to hold	AIT
	34:18	Is it **not** e for you to feed on	5071
	34:18	Is it not e for you to drink clear water?	NIH
	44: 6	E of your detestable practices,	8041
	45: 9	You have **gone far** e, O princes of Israel!	8041
	47: 5	**deep** e to swim in—	8467
Hos	4:10	"They will eat but not **have** e;	8425
Joel	2:19	e to **satisfy** you **fully;**	AIT
Am	4: 8	to town for water but *did not* **get** e to drink,	8425
Jnh	4: 9	"I am angry e to die."	6330
Na	2:12	The lion killed e *for* his cubs and strangled	1896
Hag	1: 6	You eat, but never **have** e.	8425
Zec	10:10	and *there will* not **be room** e for them.	5162
Mal	3:10	that you will not have **room** e for it.	1896
Mt	6:34	Each day has e trouble of its own.	*757*
	10:25	It is e for the student to be like his teacher,	*757*
	15:33	"Where could we get e bread	*5537*
	25: 9	'*there may* not be e for both us and you.	*758*
Mk	5: 4	No one was strong e to subdue him.	*NIG*
	8: 4	in this remote place can anyone get e bread	*NIG*
	14:41	"Are you still sleeping and resting? **E!**	*600*
Lk	14:28	to see if *he* **has** e money to complete it?	*1650+2400*
	16: 3	I'm not strong e to dig,	*NIG*
	22:38	"That is e," he replied.	*2653*
Jn	6: 7	not buy e bread for each one to have	*758*
	6:12	When *they* **had** all **had** e to eat,	*1855*
	14: 8	show us the Father and *that will* be e."	*758*
Ac	24: 4	that you be kind e to hear us briefly.	*NIG*
	24:25	"That's e for now!"	*NIG*
1Co	1: 5	that there is nobody among you wise e	*NIG*
	14:17	You may be giving thanks well e,	*NIG*
2Co	11: 4	you put up with it easily.	*NIG*
1Th	3: 9	How can we thank God e for you in return	*NIG*
1Pe	4: 3	For you have spent e time in the	*757*
Rev	12: 8	But he was not strong e,	*NIG*

ENQUIRE, ENQUIRED, ENQUIREST, ENQUIRY (Anglicized, KJV) ASK, ASKS, ASKING, BRING UP, FIND OUT, GREET, INQUIRE, INQUIRED, INQUIRING, QUESTION, SEEKING

Eze	27:33	and your wares *you* e the kings of	6947
1Co	1: 5	For in him *you have been* e in every way—	4457

ENROLL (2) [ENROLLED, ENROLLMENT]

2Sa	24: 2	of Israel from Dan to Beersheba and e	7212
	24: 4	of the king to e the fighting men of Israel.	7212

ENROLLED (1) [ENROLL]

2Ch	31:17	e by their families **in the genealogical records**	3509

ENROLLMENT (1) [ENROLL]

2Ch	17:14	Their e by families was as follows:	7213

ENSAMPLE (KJV) EXAMPLE, MODEL, PATTERN

ENSLAVE (3) [SLAVE]

Jer	15:14	*I will* e you *to* your enemies in	6268
	17: 4	*I will* e you *to* your enemies in	6268
	30: 8	no longer *will* foreigners e them.	6268

ENSLAVED (9) [SLAVE]

Ge	15:13	be e and mistreated four hundred years.	6268
Ne	5: 5	Some of our daughters *have already* **been e,**	3899
Jer	25:14	be e by many nations and great kings;	6268
	34:11	the slaves they had freed and e them again.	
		2256+3899+4200+4200+6269+9148	
Eze	34:27	from the hands of those *who* e them.	6268
Na	3: 4	who e nations by her prostitution	4835
Ac	7: 6	a country not their own, and *they will* be e	1530
Gal	4: 9	Do you wish *to* be e by them all	1526
Tit	3: 3	deceived and e by all kinds of passions	1526

ENSLAVES (1) [SLAVE]

2Co	11:20	up with anyone who e you or exploits you	2871

ENSLAVING (1) [SLAVE]

Ex	6: 5	whom the Egyptians *are* e,	6268

ENSNARE (7) [SNARE]

Pr	5:22	The evil deeds of a wicked man e him;	4334
Ecc	7:26	but the sinner *will* e.	4334
Isa	29:21	*who* e the defender in court and	7772
Eze	13:18	for their heads in order to e people.	7421
	13:18	*Will you* e the lives of my people	7421
	13:20	with which you e people like birds	7421
	13:20	I will set free the people that you e	7421

ENSNARED (5) [SNARE]

Dt	7:25	or *you will* be e by it,	3704
	12:30	not *to* be e by inquiring about their gods,	5943
Ps	9:16	the wicked *are* e by the work of their hands.	3704
Pr	6: 2	e by the words of your mouth,	4334
	22:25	you may learn his ways and get yourself e.	4613

ENSUE (KJV) PURSUE

ENSURE (1)

Ps	119:122	E your servant's well-being;	6842

ENTANGLE (1) [ENTANGLED, ENTANGLES]

Ps	35: 8	*may* the net they hid e them,	4334

ENTANGLED (4) [ENTANGLE]

Ps	18: 4	The cords of death e me;	705
	116: 3	The cords of death e me,	705
Na	1:10	*They will be* e among thorns and drunk	6018
2Pe	2:20	and Savior Jesus Christ and *are* again e **in** it	1861

ENTANGLES (1) [ENTANGLE]

Heb	12: 1	that hinders and the sin that so **easily,** e	2342

ENTER (168) [ENTERED, ENTERING, ENTERS, ENTRANCE, ENTRANCES, ENTRYWAY, REENTERED]

Ge	6:18	and *you will* e the ark—	448+995
	12:11	As he was about to e Egypt,	995
	49: 6	*Let* me not e their council,	928+995
Ex	12:23	not permit the destroyer to e your houses	448+995
	12:25	When *you* e the land that	995
	28:43	his sons must wear them whenever they e	448+995
	30:20	Whenever they e the Tent of Meeting,	448+995
	40:35	Moses could not e the Tent of Meeting	448+995
Lev	14:34	"When *you* e the land of Canaan,	448+995
	16: 3	how Aaron *is to* e the sanctuary area:	995
	19:23	'When *you* e the land and plant any kind	448+995
	21:11	not e a place where there is a dead body	995+6584
	23:10	'When *you* e the land I am going	448+995
	25: 2	*you* e the land I am going to give you,	448+995
Nu	5:22	that brings a curse e your body so	928+995
	5:24	and this water *will* e her	928+995
	14:30	Not one of you *will* e the land I swore	448+995
	15: 2	*you* e the land I am giving you as a home	448+995

Nu	15:18	you e the land to which I am taking you	448+995
	20:24	*He will* not e the land I give the Israelites,	448+995
	34: 2	'When you e Canaan, the land that will	448+995
Dt	1:37	"You *shall* not e, either.	995
	1:38	your assistant, Joshua son of Nun, *will* e it.	995
	1:39	they *will* e the land.	995
	4:21	not cross the Jordan and e the good land	448+995
	8: 1	and increase and *may* e and possess the land	995
	10:11	so that *they may* e and possess the land	995
	11:31	to cross the Jordan to e and take possession	448+995
	17:14	When *you* e the land	448+995
	18: 9	When *you* e the land	448+995
	23: 1	crushing or cutting *may* e the assembly	928+995
	23: 2	of his descendants *may* e the assembly of	928+995
	23: 3	Moabite or any of his descendants *may* e	928+995
	23: 8	born to them *may* e the assembly of	928+995
	23:24	If *you* e your neighbor's vineyard,	928+995
	23:25	If *you* e your neighbor's grainfield,	928+995
	27: 3	when you have crossed over to e	448+995
	29:12	You are standing here in order to e into	6296
	30:18	in the land you are crossing the Jordan to e	995
	32:52	not e the land I am giving to the people	448+995
Jos	2:18	*when* we e the land,	928+995
Jdg	11:18	*They did* not e the territory of Moab,	928+995
1Sa	5: 5	nor any *others* who e Dagon's temple	995
	9:13	As soon as you e the town,	995
2Sa	5: 8	'blind and lame' *will* not e the palace."	448+995
1Ki	22:30	"*I will* e the battle in disguise,	928+995
2Ki	11:16	as she reached the place where the horses e	4427
	19:32	not e this city or shoot an arrow here.	448+995
	19:33	he will not e this city, declares the LORD.	448+995
2Ch	23: 6	not e the temple of the LORD because	448+995
	18:29	"*I will* e the battle in disguise,	928+995
	23: 6	*to* e the temple of the LORD except	995
	23: 6	they *may* e because they are consecrated,	995
	23:19	in any way unclean *might* e.	995
	27: 2	but unlike him *he did* not e the temple of	448+995
	31:16	all who *would* e the temple of the LORD	995+4200
Ne	9:23	into the land that you told their fathers to e	995
Est	1:19	that Vashti *is* never again *to* e the presence	995
	4: 2	in sackcloth was allowed to e it.	448+995
Ps	45:15	*they* e the palace of the king.	928+995
	95:11	"*They will* never e my rest."	448+995
	100: 4	E his gates with thanksgiving and his courts	995
	118:19	*I will* e and give thanks to the LORD.	928+995
	118:20	through which the righteous *may* e.	995
	132: 3	"*I will* not e my house or go to my bed	928+995
Pr	2:10	For wisdom *will* e your heart,	995
Isa	10:28	*They* e Aiath; they pass	995+6584
	13: 2	beckon to them *to* e the gates of the nobles.	995
	26: 2	the gates that the righteous nation *may* e,	995
	26:20	e your rooms and shut the doors	928+995
	35:10	*They will* e Zion with singing;	995
	37:33	not e this city or shoot an arrow here.	448+995
	37:34	*he will* not e this city,"	448+995
	51:11	*They will* e Zion with singing;	995
	52: 1	and defiled *will* not e you again.	928+995
	57: 2	Those who walk uprightly e *into* peace;	995
	59:14	in the streets, honesty cannot e.	995
Jer	3:16	*It will* never e their minds or	6584+6590
	7:31	nor *did it* e my mind.	6584+6590
	16: 5	not e a house where there is a funeral meal;	995
	16: 8	not e a house where there is feasting and sit	995
	19: 5	nor *did it* e my mind.	6584+6590
	21:13	Who *can* e our refuge?"	928+995
	32:35	nor *did it* e my mind,	6584+6590
La	1:10	she saw pagan nations e her sanctuary—	995
	1:10	*to* e your assembly.	928+995
	4:12	and foes *could* e the gates of Jerusalem.	928+995
Eze	7:22	robbers *will* e it and desecrate it.	928+995
	13: 9	nor *will they* e the land of Israel.	448+995
	20:38	yet *they will* not e the land of Israel.	448+995
	26:10	when he enters your gates as *men* e	4427
	37: 5	I *will* **make** breath e you,	995
	42:14	Once the priests e the holy precincts,	995
	44: 2	no one *may* e through it.	995
	44: 3	*to* e by way of the portico of the gateway	995
	44: 9	in heart and flesh *is to* e my sanctuary,	448+995
	44:16	They alone *are to* e my sanctuary;	448+995
	44:17	when *they* e the gates of the inner court,	448+995
	46: 2	*to* e from the outside through the portico of	995
Da	1: 5	after that *they* were *to* e the king's **service.**	
		4200+6641+7156	
	11: 7	the king of the North and e his fortress;	928+995
Joel	2: 9	like thieves *they* e through the windows.	995
	3: 2	There *I will* e **into judgment** against them	9149
Zec	5: 4	and it *will* e the house of the thief and	448+995
Mt	5:20	*you will* certainly not e the kingdom	1656
	7:13	"E through the narrow gate.	1656
	7:13	and many e through it.	1639+1656
	7:21	Lord,' *will* e the kingdom of heaven,	1656
	10: 5	not go among the Gentiles or e any town of	1656
	10:11	"Whatever town or village *you* e,	1656
	10:12	*As you* e the home, give it your greeting.	1656
	12:29	how can anyone e a strong man's house	1656
	18: 3	*you will* never e the kingdom of heaven.	1656
	18: 8	for you *to* e life maimed or crippled than	1656
	18: 9	*to* e life with one eye than to have two eyes	1656
	19:17	If you want *to* e life,	1656
	19:23	for a rich man *to* e the kingdom of heaven.	1656
	19:24	the eye of a needle than for a rich man *to* e	1656
	23:13	You yourselves *do* not e,	1656
	23:13	nor will you let those who are trying to	1656
Mk	1:45	Jesus could no longer e a town openly	1656
	3:27	no one can e a strong man's house	1656
	6:10	Whenever *you* e a house,	1656

Mk	9:25	come out of him and never e him again."	1656
	9:43	*to* e life maimed than with two hands to go	1656
	9:45	*to* e life crippled than to have two feet and	1656
	9:47	It is better for you *to* e the kingdom of God	1656
	10:15	of God like a little child *will* never e it."	1656
	10:23	for the rich *to* e the kingdom of God!"	1656
	10:24	how hard it is *to* e the kingdom of God	1656
	10:25	the eye of a needle than for a rich man *to* e	1656
	11: 2	and just as *you* e it,	1660
	13:15	down or e the house to take anything out.	1656
Lk	9: 4	Whatever house *you* e,	1656
	10: 5	"When *you* e a house, first say,	1656
	10: 8	"When *you* e a town and are welcomed,	1656
	10:10	when *you* e a town and are not welcomed,	1656
	13:24	"Make every effort *to* e	1656
	13:24	will try *to* e and will not be able to.	1656
	18:17	of God like a little child *will* never e it."	1656
	18:24	for the rich *to* e the kingdom of God!	1660
	18:25	the eye of a needle than for a rich man *to* e	1656
	19:30	and *as you* e it,	1660
	21:21	*and let* those in the country not e the city.	1656
	22:10	He replied, "As you e the city,	1656
	24:26	to suffer these things and then e his glory?"	1656
Jn	3: 4	e a second time **into** his mother's womb	1656
	3: 5	no one can e the kingdom of God	1656
	10: 1	the man who *does* not e the sheep pen by	1656
	18:28	the Jews *did* not e the palace;	1656
Ac	3: 3	When he saw Peter and John about to e,	1655
	14:22	"We must go through many hardships *to* e	1656
	16: 7	they tried *to* e Bithynia,	1650+4513
Heb	3:11	'*They shall* never e my rest.' "	1656
	3:18	that they would never e his rest if not	1656
	3:19	So we see that they were not able *to* e,	1656
	4: 3	Now *we* who have believed e that rest,	1656
	4: 3	'*They shall* never e my rest.' "	1656
	4: 5	"*They shall* never e my rest."	1656
	4: 6	It still remains that some *will* e that rest,	1656
	4:11	therefore, make every effort *to* e that rest,	1656
	9:12	He did not e by means of the blood of goats	1656
	9:24	For Christ *did* not e a man-made sanctuary	1656
	9:25	Nor did he e heaven to offer himself again	NIG
	10:19	*to* e the Most Holy Place by the blood	1658
Rev	15: 8	and no one could e the temple until	1656
	21:27	Nothing impure will ever e it,	1656

ENTERED (107) [ENTER]

Ge	7: 7	his wife and his sons' wives e the ark	448+995
	7: 9	came to Noah and e the ark,	NIH
	7:13	and the wives of his three sons, e the ark.	448+995
	7:15	of life in them came to Noah and e the ark.	NIH
	19: 3	they did go with him and e his house.	448+995
	31:33	he e Rachel's tent.	928+995
	41:46	when he e **the service** *of* Pharaoh king of Egypt.	4200+6641+7156
Ex	19: 2	*they* e the Desert of Sinai,	995
	24:18	Then Moses e the cloud as he went on up	928+995+9348
	33: 8	watching Moses until he e the tent.	995+2025
	34:34	But whenever he e the LORD's presence	995
	40:32	They washed whenever they e the Tent	448+995
Lev	16:23	the linen garments he put on before he e	448+995
Nu	7:89	When Moses e the Tent of Meeting	448+995
	17: 8	The next day Moses e the Tent of	448+995
Dt	26: 1	When *you have* e the land	448+995
Jos	2: 1	So they went and e the house of	995
	2: 3	men who came to you and e your house,	995+4200
	8:19	*They* e the city and captured it	995
Jdg	4:18	So *he* e her tent,	448+6073
	18: 2	The men e the hill country of Ephraim	995
1Sa	4:13	When the man e the town	928+995
	12: 8	"After Jacob e Egypt,	995
	14:25	The entire army e the woods,	928+995
	16:21	David came to Saul and e his **service.**	4200+6641+7156
	19:16	But when the men e,	995
1Ki	2:30	So Benaiah e the tent of the LORD	448+995
2Ki	6:20	After they e the city, Elisha said, "LORD,	995
	7: 8	edge of the camp and e one of the tents.	448+995
	7: 8	and e another tent and took some things	448+995
	9:31	As Jehu e the gate, she asked,	928+995
	10:25	and then e the inner shrine of	2143+6330
1Ch	5:17	were e in the **genealogical records**	3509
	24:19	ministering when they e the temple of	995+4200
	27:24	and the number *was* not e in the book of	6590
2Ch	8:11	the ark of the LORD *has* e are holy."	448+995
	15:12	*They* e into a covenant to seek the LORD,	995
	20:28	*They* e Jerusalem **and went** to the temple of	995
	26:16	and e the temple of the LORD	448+995
Est	6: 4	Now Haman *had just* e the outer court	995+4200
	6: 6	When Haman e, the king asked him,	995
Job	3: 6	among the days of the year nor *be* e in any	995
	38:22	"*Have you* e the storehouses of the snow	448+995
Ps	73:17	till *I* e the sanctuary of God;	448+995
	105:23	Then Israel e Egypt;	995
	109:18	*it* e into his body like water,	995
Isa	28:15	"We have e *into* a covenant with death,	4162
Jer	9:21	and *has* e our fortresses;	928+995
	34:10	and people who e into this covenant agreed	995
	43: 7	So *they* e Egypt in disobedience to	995
	51:51	foreigners *have* e the holy places of	995+6584
Eze	4:14	No unclean meat *has ever* e my mouth."	928+995
	16: 8	I gave you my solemn oath and e into	995
	23:39	*they* e my sanctuary and desecrated it.	448+995
	37:10	and breath e them;	928+995
	43: 4	The glory of the LORD e the temple	448+995
	44: 2	the God of Israel, *has* e through it.	995

Eze	46: 9	to return through the gate by which *he* e,	928+995
Da	1:19	so *they* e the king's **service.**	4200+6641+7156
Am	5:19	as though he e his house and rested his hand	995
Ob	1:11	and foreigners e his gates and cast lots	995
Mt	8: 5	When Jesus had e Capernaum,	1656
	9:23	When Jesus e the ruler's house and saw	1650+2262
	12: 4	He e the house of God,	1656
	21:10	When Jesus e Jerusalem,	1656
	21:12	Jesus e the temple area	1656
	21:23	Jesus e the temple courts, and,	1650+2262
	24:38	up to the day Noah e the ark;	1656
	26:58	He e and sat down with the guards to see	1656
Mk	2: 1	when Jesus again e Capernaum,	1656
	2:26	he e the house of God and ate	1656
	3:20	Then Jesus e a house,	1650+2262
	7:17	After *he* had left the crowd and e the house,	1656
	7:24	He e a house and did not want anyone	1656
	11:11	Jesus e Jerusalem and went to the temple.	1656
	11:15	Jesus e the temple area	1656
	16: 5	As they e the tomb,	1656
Lk	1:40	where *she* e Zechariah's home	1656
	6: 4	*He* e the house of God,	1656
	7: 1	the hearing of the people, he e Capernaum.	1656
	7:45	but this woman, from the time *I* e,	1656
	9:34	and they were afraid as they e the cloud.	1656
	11:52	*You* yourselves have not e,	1656
	17:27	in marriage up to the day Noah e the ark.	1656
	19: 1	Jesus e Jericho and was passing through.	1656
	19:45	Then *he* e the temple area	1656
	22: 3	Then Satan e Judas, called Iscariot,	1656
	24: 3	but *when they* e,	1656
Jn	6:22	and that Jesus had not e it with his disciples,	5291
	11:30	Now Jesus *had* not yet e the village,	2262
	13:27	Satan e *into* him.	1656
	16:28	I came from the Father and e the world	1650+2262
Ac	5:21	At daybreak *they* e the temple courts,	1656
	9:17	Then Ananias went to the house and e it.	1656
	10:25	As Peter e the house,	1181+1656
	11: 8	or unclean *has* ever e my mouth.'	1656
	11:12	and *we* e the man's house.	1656
	13:14	On the Sabbath they e the synagogue	1656
	19: 8	Paul e the synagogue	1656
	25:23	with great pomp and e the audience room	1656
Ro	5:12	just as sin e the world through one man,	1656
Heb	6:20	who went before us, *has* e on our behalf.	1656
	9: 6	the priests e regularly *into* the outer room	1655
	9: 7	But only the high priest e the inner room,	NIG
	9:12	but he e the Most Holy Place once for all	NIG
	9:24	he e heaven itself,	NIG
Rev	11:11	a breath of life from God e them,	1656

ENTERING (24) [ENTER]

Nu	32: 9	e the land the LORD had given them.	448+995
Dt	4: 5	the land you *are* e to take possession of it.	995
	7: 1	the land you *are* e to possess and drives out	995
	11:10	The land you *are* e to take over is not like	995
	11:29	into the land you *are* e to possess,	995
	23:20	to in the land you *are* e to possess.	995
	28:21	from the land you *are* e to possess.	995
	28:63	be uprooted from the land you *are* e	995
	30:16	in the land you *are* e to possess.	995
	31:16	to the foreign gods of the land they *are* e.	928+995+7931
1Sa	5:10	As the ark of God *was* e Ekron,	995
	9:14	and *as* they *were* e it, there was Samuel,	928+995+9348
	23: 7	for David has imprisoned himself by e	928+995
2Sa	6:16	As the ark of David *was* e the City	995
	15:37	at Jerusalem as Absalom *was* e the city.	995
	17:17	they could not risk being seen e the city.	995+2025
1Ki	15:17	leaving or e the territory of Asa king	995+4200
2Ki	11:19	e by way of the gate of the guards.	NIH
1Ch	15:29	the ark of the covenant of the LORD was e	995+6330
		the City of David,	
2Ch	16: 1	leaving or e the territory of Asa king	995+4200
Ezr	9:11	'The land you *are* e to possess is	995
Mt	21:31	e the kingdom of God **ahead of**	4575
Lk	11:52	and you have hindered those who *were* e."	1656
Heb	4: 1	since the promise *of* e his rest still stands,	1656

ENTERS (25) [ENTER]

Ex	28:29	"Whenever Aaron e the Holy Place,	448+995
	28:30	be over Aaron's heart whenever he e	995
	28:35	be heard when he e the Holy Place	448+995
Nu	19:14	Anyone who e the tent and anyone who	448+995
2Ki	5:18	When my master e the temple of Rimmon	995
	12: 9	on the right side as one e the temple of	995
2Ch	23: 7	Anyone *who* e the temple must be put	448+995
Isa	3:14	The LORD into judgment against	995
Eze	26:10	and chariots when he e your gates	928+995
	42: 9	entrance on the east side as one e them	995+4200
	42:12	by which *one* e the rooms.	995
	44:21	to drink wine when he e the inner court.	448+995
	46: 8	When the prince e,	995
	46: 9	whoever e by the north gate to worship is	995
	46: 9	and whoever e by the south gate is to go out	995
	47: 8	where it e the Sea.	995+2025
Mt	15:17	that whatever e the mouth goes into	1660
Mk	7:18	"Don't you see that nothing that e a man	1660
	14:14	Say to the owner of the house he e,	1656
Lk	22:10	Follow him to the house that he e,	1660
Jn	10: 2	The man who e by the gate is the shepherd	1656
	10: 9	whoever e through me will be saved.	1656
Heb	4:10	for anyone who e God's rest also rests	1656
	6:19	It e the inner sanctuary behind the curtain,	1656

ENTERTAIN (4) [ENTERTAINED, ENTERTAINMENT]

Jdg	16:25	they shouted, "Bring out Samson to e us."	8471
Mt	9: 4	Why *do you* e evil **thoughts** in your hearts?	1926
1Ti	5:19	*Do* not e an accusation against an elder	4138
Heb	13: 2	Do not forget to e **strangers,**	5810

ENTERTAINED (2) [ENTERTAIN]

Ac	28: 7	and for three days e us hospitably.	3826
Heb	13: 2	for by so doing some people *have* e angels	3826

ENTERTAINMENT (1) [ENTERTAIN]

Da	6:18	and without any e being brought to him.	10166

ENTHRALLED (1)

Ps	45:11	The king *is* e *by* your beauty;	203

ENTHRONED (20) [THRONE]

1Sa	4: 4	who is e *between* the cherubim.	3782
2Sa	6: 2	who is e *between* the cherubim that are on	3782
2Ki	19:15	God of Israel, e *between* the cherubim,	3782
1Ch	13: 6	who is e *between* the cherubim—	3782
Ps	2: 4	The *One* e in heaven laughs;	3782
	9:11	Sing praises to the LORD, e *in* Zion;	3782
	22: 3	Yet you *are* e as the Holy One;	3782
	29:10	The LORD sits e over the flood;	3782
	29:10	the LORD *is* e as King forever.	3782
	55:19	God, who *is* e forever,	3782
	61: 7	May he be e in God's presence forever;	3782
	80: 1	you *who* sit *between* the cherubim,	3782
	99: 1	he *sits* e *between* the cherubim;	3782
	102:12	But you, O LORD, **sit** e forever;	3782
	113: 5	the *One* who *sits* e on high,	3782
	132:14	here *I* will sit e, for I have desired it—	3782
Isa	14:13	*I* will **sit** e on the mount of assembly,	3782
	37:16	God of Israel, e *between* the cherubim,	3782
	40:22	He sits e above the circle of the earth,	3782
	52: 2	rise up, **sit** e, O Jerusalem.	3782

ENTHRONES (1) [THRONE]

Job	36: 7	he e them with kings	2021+3782+4058+4200

ENTHUSIASM (2)

2Co	8:17	but he is coming to you with *much* e and	5080
	9: 2	your e has stirred most of them to action.	2419

ENTICE (7) [ENTICED, ENTICES, ENTICING]

1Ki	22:20	'Who *will* e Ahab into attacking	7331
	22:21	'I *will* e him.'	7331
2Ch	18:19	'Who *will* e Ahab king of Israel	7331
	18:20	'I *will* e him.'	7331
Pr	1:10	My son, if sinners e you,	7331
2Pe	2:18	*they* e people who are just escaping	1284
Rev	2:14	who taught Balak *to* e the Israelites to sin	965+1967+4998

ENTICED (8) [ENTICE]

Dt	4:19	*do* not *be* e into bowing down to them	5615
	11:16	*be* e to turn away and worship other gods	4222+7331
2Ki	17:21	Jeroboam e Israel away from following	5615
Job	31: 9	"If my heart *has* *been* e by a woman,	7331
	31:27	so that my heart was secretly e	7331
Eze	14: 9	if the prophet *is* e to utter a prophecy,	7331
	14: 9	I the LORD *have* e that prophet,	7331
Jas	1:14	*he is* dragged away and e.	1284

ENTICES (3) [ENTICE]

Dt	13: 6	or your closest friend secretly e you,	6077
Job	36:18	Be careful that no *one* e you by riches;	6077
Pr	16:29	A violent man e his neighbor and leads him	7331

ENTICING (2) [ENTICE]

1Ki	22:22	" 'You will succeed *in* e him,'	7331
2Ch	18:21	" 'You will succeed *in* e him,'	7331

ENTIRE (89) [ENTIRELY]

Ge	2:11	it winds through the e land of Havilah,	3972
	2:13	it winds through the e land of Cush.	3972
	7:19	under all the heavens were covered.	3972
	19:25	and the e plain, including all those living in	3972
	45: 8	of his e household and ruler of all Egypt.	3972
Ex	14:28	the e army of Pharaoh that had followed	3972
	16: 3	into this desert to starve this e assembly	3972
	16: 9	"Say to the e Israelite community,	3972
	29:18	Then burn the e ram on the altar.	3972
Lev	3: 9	the e fat tail cut off close to the backbone,	9459
	8: 3	and gather the e assembly at the entrance to	3972
	9: 5	the e assembly came near and stood before	3972
	19: 2	to the e assembly of Israel and say to them:	3972
	24:14	and the e assembly is to stone him.	3972
	24:16	The e assembly must stone him.	3972
	27:32	The e tithe of the herd and flock—	3972
Nu	4:16	in charge of the e tabernacle and everything	3972
	5:30	the LORD and is to apply this e law to her.	3972
	6: 5	" 'During the e period of his vow	3972

ENTIRELY (5) [ENTIRE]

Ex	28:31	the robe of the ephod e *of* blue cloth,	4003
	39:22	the robe of the ephod e *of* blue cloth—	4003
Jer	30:11	**let you go** e **unpunished.'**	5927+5927
	46:28	**let you go** e **unpunished."**	5927+5927
2Co	8: 3	e on their own,	882

ENTRAILS (1)

Zep	1:17	be poured out like dust and their e like filth.	4302

ENTRANCE (144) [ENTER]

Ge	18: 1	while he was sitting at the e to his tent in	7339
	18: 2	from the e of his tent to meet them	7339
	18:10	Sarah was listening at the e to the tent,	7339
	38:14	and then sat down at the e to Enaim,	7339
	43:19	and spoke to him at the e to the house.	7339
Ex	26:36	the e to the tent make a curtain of blue,	7339
	27:14	to be on one side of the e,	NIH
	27:16	"For the e to the courtyard	9133
	29: 4	e to the Tent of Meeting and wash them	7339
	29:11	the LORD's presence at the e to the Tent	7339
	29:32	At the e to the Tent of Meeting,	7339
	29:42	to be made regularly at the e to the Tent	7339
	32:26	So he stood at the e to the camp and said,	9133
	33: 9	down and stay at the e,	7339
	33:10	the pillar of cloud standing at the e *to*	7339
	33:10	each at the e to his tent.	7339
	35:15	for the doorway at the e to the tabernacle;	7339
	35:17	and the curtain for the e to the courtyard;	9133
	36:37	For the e *to* the tent they made a curtain	7339
	38: 8	the women who served at the e to the Tent	7339
	38:14	on one side of the e,	NIH
	38:15	on the other side of the e to the courtyard,	9133
	38:18	The curtain for the e *to* the courtyard was	9133

Nu	14: 7	and said to the e Israelite assembly,	3972
	16:19	of the LORD appeared to the e assembly.	3972
	16:22	the e assembly when only one man sins?"	3972
	20:29	the e house of Israel mourned	3972
	21:23	He mustered his e army and marched out	3972
	27:19	before Eleazar the priest and the e assembly	3972
	27:21	At his command the e army and the e community of	3972
Dt	2:14	By then, that e generation	3972
Jos	6:23	They brought out her e family and put them	3972
	8:11	The e force that was with him marched up	3972
	9: 1	and along the e coast of the Great Sea as far	3972
	9:24	and water carriers for the e community."	3972
	10: 7	up from Gilgal with his e army,	3972
	11:16	So Joshua took this e land:	3972
	11:23	So Joshua took the e land,	3972
	13:21	the plateau and the e realm of Sihon king of	3972
	13:30	the e realm of Og king of Bashan—	3972
	24:17	on our e journey and among all the nations	3972
Jdg	8:12	routing their e army.	3972
1Sa	14:25	The e army entered the woods,	3972
2Sa	6:11	LORD blessed him and his e household.	3972
	6:15	and the e house of Israel brought up the ark	3972
	7:17	to David all the words of this e revelation.	3972
	8: 9	that David had defeated the e army	3972
	10: 7	David sent Joab out with the e army	3972
	12:29	So David mustered his e army and went	3972
	12:31	David and his e army returned to Jerusalem.	3972
	15:16	with his e household following him;	3972
	20:14	and through the e *region* of the Berites,	3972
	20:23	Joab was over Israel's e army;	3972
	24: 8	After they had gone through the e land,	3972
1Ki	8: 5	the e assembly of Israel that had gathered	3972
	20: 1	of Aram mustered his e army.	3972
2Ki	6:24	of Aram mobilized his e army and marched	3972
	15:18	During his e reign he did not turn away	3972
	17: 5	The king of Assyria invaded the e land,	3972
	17:13	the e Law that I commanded your fathers	3972
	24:16	also deported to Babylon the e army	3972
1Ch	4:27	so their e clan did not become as numerous	3972
	5:10	of the Hagrites throughout the e region east	3972
	17:15	to David all the words of this e revelation.	3972
	18: 9	the e army of Hadadezer king of Zobah,	3972
	19: 8	David sent Joab out with the e army	3972
	20: 3	David and his e army returned to Jerusalem.	3972
2Ch	5: 6	the e assembly of Israel that had gathered	3972
	26:14	bows and slingstones for the e army.	3972
	29:18	"We have purified the e temple of	3972
	30:25	The e assembly of Judah rejoiced,	3972
	34: 9	Ephraim and the e remnant of Israel and	3972
	35:16	the e service of the LORD was carried out	3972
Ezr	4: 5	and frustrate their plans during the e reign	3972
	8:34	and the e weight was recorded at that time.	3972
Job	16: 7	you have devastated my e household.	3972
Isa	39: 2	the spices, the fine oil, his e armory	3972
Jer	26:17	and said to the e assembly of people,	3972
	36:23	until the e scroll was burned in the fire.	3972
	37:10	if you were to defeat the e Babylonian army	3972
	42: 2	to the LORD your God for this e remnant.	3972
	51:31	of Babylon that his e city is captured,	4946+7895
Eze	9: 8	the e remnant of Israel in this outpouring	3972
	10:12	Their e bodies, including their backs,	3972
	20:40	the land the e house of Israel will serve me,	3972
	45: 1	the e area will be holy.	3972
	48:20	The e portion will be a square, 25,000	3972
Da	2:48	the e province of Babylon and placed him	10353
	11:17	of his e kingdom and will make an alliance	3972
Lk	2: 1	be taken of the e Roman world.	4246
Ac	11:28	over the e Roman world.	3910
	18: 8	and his e household believed in the Lord;	3910
Gal	5:14	The e law is summed up in	4246

Ex	38:30	They used it to make the bases for the e *to*	7339
	38:31	and those for its e and all the tent pegs for	9133
	39:38	and the curtain for the e to the tent;	7339
	39:40	and the curtain for the e to the courtyard;	9133
	40: 5	the Testimony and put the curtain at the e *to*	7339
	40: 6	in front of the e *to* the tabernacle, the Tent	7339
	40: 8	around it and put the curtain at the e *to*	9133
	40:12	the e *to* the Tent of Meeting and wash them	7339
	40:28	up the curtain at the e to the tabernacle.	7339
	40:29	He set the altar of burnt offering near the e	7339
	40:33	and altar and put up the curtain at the e *to*	9133
Lev	1: 3	the e *to* the Tent of Meeting so that it will	7339
	1: 5	on all sides at the e *to* the Tent of Meeting.	7339
	3: 2	of his offering and slaughter it at the e *to*	7339
	4: 4	He is to present the bull at the e *to* the Tent	7339
	4: 7	of the altar of burnt offering at the e *to*	7339
	4:18	of the altar of burnt offering at the e *to*	7339
	8: 3	and gather the entire assembly at the e *to*	7339
	8: 4	the assembly gathered at the e *to* the Tent	7339
	8:31	the e *to* the Tent of Meeting and eat it there	7339
	8:33	Do not leave the e *to* the Tent of Meeting	7339
	8:35	the e *to* the Tent of Meeting day and night	7339
	10: 7	Do not leave the e *to* the Tent of Meeting	7339
	12: 6	to the priest at the e *to* the Tent of Meeting	7339
	14:11	and his offerings before the LORD at the e	7339
	14:23	to the priest at the e *to* the Tent of Meeting,	7339
	15:14	the e *to* the Tent of Meeting and give them	7339
	15:29	to the priest at the e *to* the Tent of Meeting.	7339
	16: 7	and present them before the LORD at the e	7339
	17: 4	to the e *to* the Tent of Meeting to present it as	7339
	17: 5	at the e *to* the Tent of Meeting	7339
	17: 6	the LORD at the e *to* the Tent of Meeting	7339
	17: 9	not bring it to the e *to* the Tent of Meeting	7339
	19:21	a ram to the e *to* the Tent of Meeting for	7339
Nu	3:25	the curtain at the e *to* the Tent of Meeting,	7339
	3:26	at the e *to* the courtyard surrounding	7339
	4:25	for the e *to* the Tent of Meeting,	7339
	4:26	the curtain for the e,	7339+9133
	6:10	to the priest at the e *to* the Tent of Meeting.	7339
	6:13	be brought to the e *to* the Tent of Meeting.	7339
	6:18	" "Then at the e *to* the Tent of Meeting	7339
	10: 3	to assemble before you at the e *to* the Tent	7339
	11:10	each at the e *to* his tent.	7339
	12: 5	at the e *to* the Tent and summoned Aaron	7339
	16:18	and stood with Moses and Aaron at the e *to*	7339
	16:19	in opposition to them at the e *to* the Tent	7339
	16:50	Then Aaron returned to Moses at the e *to*	7339
	20: 6	and Aaron went from the assembly to the e	7339
	25: 6	of Israel while they were weeping at the e	7339
	27: 2	the Tent of Meeting and stood	7339
Dt	31:15	and the cloud stood over the e *to* the Tent.	7339
Jos	8:29	from the tree and throw it down at the e *of*	7339
	19:51	the LORD at the e *to* the Tent of Meeting.	7339
	20: 4	in the e *of* the city gate and state his case	7339
Jdg	9:35	at the e *to* the city gate just as Abimelech	7339
	9:40	all the way to the e *to* the gate.	7339
	9:44	to a position at the e *to* the city gate.	7339
	9:52	as he approached the e *to* the tower to set it	7339
	18:16	armed for battle, stood at the e	7339
	18:17	the six hundred armed men stood at the e	7339
1Sa	2:22	the women who served at the e *to* the Tent	7339
	17:52	and pursued the Philistines to the e *of* Gath	995
2Sa	10: 8	and drew up in battle formation at the e *to*	7339
	11: 9	But Uriah slept at the e *to* the palace	7339
	11:23	but we drove them back to the e *to*	7339
1Ki	6: 8	The e *to* the lowest floor was on	7339
	6:31	the e *of* the inner sanctuary he made doors	7339
	6:33	of olive wood for the e *to* the main hall.	7339
	14:27	on duty at the e *to* the royal palace.	7339
	22:10	at the threshing floor by the e *of* the gate	7339
2Ki	7: 3	with leprosy at the e *of* the city gate	7339
	10: 8	at the e *of* the city gate until morning."	7339
	12: 9	The priests who guarded the e put into	6197
	23: 8	at the e *to* the Gate of Joshua,	7339
	23:11	He removed from the e *to* the temple of	995
1Ch	9:19	for guarding the e *to* the dwelling of	4427
	9:21	of Meshelemiah was the gatekeeper at the e	7339
	19: 9	up in battle formation at the e *to* their city,	7339
2Ch	12:10	on duty at the e *to* the royal palace.	7339
	18: 9	at the threshing floor by the e *to* the gate	7339
	23:13	standing by his pillar at the e.	4427
	23:15	So they seized her as she reached the e *of*	4427
	33:14	the e *of* the Fish Gate and encircling the hill	995
Ne	3:20	the angle to the e *of* the house of Eliashib	7339
	3:21	from the e *of* Eliashib's house to the end	7339
Est	5: 1	on his royal throne in the hall, facing the e.	7339
Isa	24:10	the e *to* every house is barred.	995
Jer	1:15	and set up their thrones in the e *of* the gates	7339
	19: 2	near the e *of* the Potsherd Gate,	7339
	26:10	the LORD and took their places at the e *of*	7339
	36:10	which was in the upper courtyard at the e	7339
	38:14	to the third in the temple of the LORD.	4427
	43: 9	at the e *to* Pharaoh's palace in Tahpanhes.	7339
Eze	8: 3	to the e *to* the north gate of the inner court,	7339
	8: 5	and in the e north of the gate of	929
	8: 7	Then he brought me to the court.	7339
	8:14	to the e *to* the north gate of the house of	7339
	8:16	and there at the e *to* the temple,	7339
	10:19	They stopped at the e *to* the east gate of	7339
	11: 1	at the e *to* the gate were twenty-five men,	7339
	40:11	Then he measured the width of the e	7339
	40:15	The distance from the e *of* the gateway to	415
	40:40	the e *to* the north gateway were two tables,	7339
	40:48	The width of the e was fourteen cubits	9133
	41: 2	The e was ten cubits wide,	7339
	41: 3	and measured the jambs of the e;	7339
	41: 3	The e was six cubits wide,	7339

Eze	41:17	the e *to* the inner sanctuary and on the walls	7339
	41:20	From the floor to the area above the e,	7339
	42: 9	The lower rooms had an e on the east side	4427
	44: 5	Give attention to the e *of* the temple and all	4427
	46: 3	in the presence of the LORD at the e *to*	7339
	46:19	Then the man brought me through the e at	4427
	47: 1	The man brought me back to the e *of*	7339
Mt	27:60	in front of the e *to* the tomb and went away.	2598
Mk	15:46	he rolled a stone against the e of the tomb.	2598
	16: 3	"Who will roll the stone away from the e *of*	2598
Jn	11:38	It was a cave with a stone laid across the e.	NIG
	20: 1	that the stone had been removed from the e.	NIG
Ac	12: 6	and sentries stood guard at the e.	2598
	12:13	Peter knocked at the **outer** e,	2598+4784

ENTRANCE (Anglicized) See also ENTRYWAY

ENTRANCES (5) [ENTER]
Ex	33: 8	all the people rose and stood at the e	7339
Nu	16:27	and little ones at the e *to* their tents.	7339
Pr	8: 3	at the e, she cries aloud:	4427+7339
Eze	41:11	There were e *to* the side rooms from	7339
	43:11	its arrangement, its exits and e—	4569

ENTREAT (3) [ENTREATY]
Zec	7: 2	to e the LORD	906+2704+7156
	8:21	'Let us go at once to e the LORD and seek	906+2704+7156
	8:22	to seek the LORD Almighty and to e him."	906+2704+7156

ENTREATY (2) [ENTREAT]
2Ch	33:13	the LORD **was moved by** his e	6983
	33:19	God **was moved by** his e,	6983

ENTRIES, ENTRY (KJV) DOORS, ENTRANCE, ENTRANCES, ENTRYWAY, GATEWAY

ENTRUST (4) [TRUST]
Ge	42:37	E him to my care,	5989
2Ki	22: 5	*Have them* e it to the men appointed	5989
Jn	2:24	But Jesus *would* not e himself to them,	4409
2Ti	2: 2	in the presence of many witnesses e	4192

ENTRUSTED (35) [TRUST]
Ge	39: 4	and *he* e to his care everything he owned.	5989
	39: 8	everything he owns *he has* e to my care.	5989
Lev	6: 2	deceiving his neighbor about **something** e	5989
	6: 4	or what **was** e to him,	7212+7214
1Ki	15:18	He e it to his officials and sent them	5989
2Ki	22: 7	But they need not account for the money e	5989
	22: 9	and **have** e it to the workers and supervisors	5989
1Ch	9:26	e with the responsibility for the rooms	575+928
	9:31	was e with the responsibility for baking	575+928
2Ch	34:10	Then *they* e it to the men appointed	5989
	34:17	in the temple of the LORD have e it to	5989
Ezr	7:19	to the God of Jerusalem all the articles e	10314
Est	2: 8	was taken to the king's palace and e to	448+3338
	6: 9	Then *let* the robe and horse *be* e to one of	5989
Jer	13:20	Where is the flock *that was* e to you,	5989
	29: 3	He e the letter to Elasah son of Shaphan	928+3338
Mt	25:14	who called his servants and e his property	4140
	25:20	he said, 'you e me with five talents.	4140
	25:22	he said, 'you e me with two talents;	4140
Lk	12:48	from the one who *has been* e with much,	4192
Jn	5:22	but *has* e all judgment to the Son,	1443
Ro	3: 2	*they have been* e with the very words	4409
	6:17	the form of teaching to which *you were* e.	4140
1Co	4: 1	as *those* e with the secret things of God.	3874
Gal	2: 7	that *I had been* e with the task of preaching	4409
1Th	2: 4	as men approved by God *to be* e with	4409
1Ti	1:11	which he e to me.	4409
	6:20	**what has been** e to *your* **care.**	4146
2Ti	1:12	that he is able to guard what I have e to him	4146
	1:14	Guard the good **deposit** that was e to you—	4146
Tit	1: 3	to light through the preaching e to me by	4409
	1: 7	Since an overseer is e with God's **work,**	3874
1Pe	2:23	he *himself* to him who judges justly.	4140
	5: 3	not lording it over those e to you,	NIG
Jude	1: 3	the faith that was once for all e to the saints.	4140

ENTRYWAY (2) [ENTER]
2Ki	16:18	and removed the royal e outside the temple	4427
Mk	14:68	he said, and went out into the e.	4580

ENTWINES (1)
Job	8:17	it e its roots around a pile of rocks	6018

ENVELOPED (4)
Isa	42:25	It e them in flames,	4946+6017
Mt	17: 5	he was still speaking, a bright cloud e them,	2173
Mk	9: 7	Then a cloud appeared and e them,	2173
Lk	9:34	a cloud appeared and e them,	2173

ENVIED (2) [ENVY]
Ge	26:14	and servants that the Philistines e him.	7861
Ps	73: 3	For *I* e the arrogant when I saw	7861

ENVIES (1) [ENVY]
Jas	4: 5	the spirit he caused to live in us e intensely?	5784

ENVIOUS (7) [ENVY]
Dt	32:21	I *will* **make** them e by those who are not	7861
Ps	37: 1	of evil men or *be* e of those who do wrong;	7861
	106:16	In the camp *they* grew e of Moses and	7861
Pr	24:19	because of evil men or *be* e of the wicked,	7861
Mt	20:15	Or are you e because I am generous?'	1639+3836+4057+4505
Ro	10:19	"I *will* **make** you e by those who are not	4143
	11:11	to the Gentiles to **make** Israel e.	4143

ENVOY (3) [ENVOYS]
Pr	13:17	but a trustworthy e brings healing.	7495
Jer	49:14	An e was sent to the nations to say,	7495
Ob	1: 1	An e was sent to the nations to say, "Rise,	7495

ENVOYS (12) [ENVOY]
1Ki	5: 1	he sent his e to Solomon,	6269
2Ki	17: 4	for he had sent e to So king of Egypt,	4855
2Ch	32:31	when e were sent *by* the rulers of Babylon	4885
Ps	68:31	E will come from Egypt;	3134
Isa	14:32	What answer shall be given to the e of	4855
	18: 2	which sends e by sea in papyrus boats over	7495
	30: 4	in Zoan and their e have arrived in Hanes,	4855
	30: 6	the e carry their riches on donkeys' backs,	NIH
	33: 7	the e *of* peace weep bitterly.	4855
	39: 2	Hezekiah received **the** e gladly	2157S
Jer	27: 3	through the e who have come to Jerusalem	4855
Eze	17:15	by sending his e to Egypt to get horses and	4855

ENVY (21) [ENVIED, ENVIES, ENVIOUS, ENVYING]
Job	5: 2	and e slays the simple.	7863
Ps	68:16	Why **gaze in** e, O rugged mountains,	8353
Pr	3:31	*Do* not e a violent man or choose any	7861
	14:30	but e rots the bones.	7863
	23:17	*Do* not *let* your heart e sinners,	7861
	24: 1	*Do* not e wicked men,	7861
Ecc	4: 4	and all achievement spring from man's e	7863
Eze	31: 9	*the* e of all the trees of Eden in the garden	7861
Mt	27:18	of e that they had handed Jesus over to him.	5784
Mk	7:22	e, slander, arrogance and folly.	4057+4505
	15:10	of e that the chief priests had handed Jesus	5784
Ro	1:29	They are full of e, murder, strife,	5784
	11:14	**arouse** my own people to e	4143
1Co	13: 4	*It does* not e, it does not boast,	2420
Gal	5:21	and e; drunkenness, orgies,	5784
Php	1:15	that some preach Christ out of e and rivalry,	5784
1Ti	6: 4	and quarrels about words that result in e,	5784
Tit	3: 3	We lived in malice and e,	5784
Jas	3:14	if you harbor bitter e and selfish ambition	2419
	3:16	For where you have e and selfish ambition,	2419
1Pe	2: 1	hypocrisy, e, and slander of every kind.	5784

ENVYING (1) [ENVY]
Gal	5:26	provoking and e each other.	5783

EPAENETUS (KJV) EPENETUS

EPAPHRAS (3)
Col	1: 7	You learned it from E,	2071
	4:12	E, who is one of you and a servant	2071
Phm	1:23	E, my fellow prisoner in Christ Jesus,	2071

EPAPHRODITUS (2)
Php	2:25	to send back to you E,	2073
	4:18	I have received from E the gifts you sent.	2073

EPENETUS (1)
Ro	16: 5	Greet my dear friend E,	2045

EPHAH (52)
Ge	25: 4	The sons of Midian were E, Epher,	6549
Ex	16:36	(An omer is one tenth of an e.)	406
	29:40	of an e of fine flour mixed with a quarter of	NIH
Lev	5:11	for his sin a tenth of an e of fine flour for	406
	6:20	a tenth of an e of fine flour as	406
	14:10	with three-tenths of an e of fine flour mixed	NIH
	14:21	a tenth of an e of fine flour mixed with oil	406
	19:36	An honest e and an honest hin.	406
	23:13	with its grain offering of two-tenths of an e	NIH
	23:17	bring two loaves made of three-tenths of an e	NIH
	24: 5	using two-tenths of an e for each loaf.	NIH
Nu	5:15	a tenth of an e of barley flour on her behalf.	406
	15: 4	of an e of fine flour mixed with a quarter of	NIH
	15: 6	an e of fine flour mixed with a third of a hin	NIH
	15: 9	of an e of fine flour mixed with half a hin	NIH
	28: 5	of an e of fine flour mixed with a quarter of	406
	28: 9	and a grain offering of two-tenths of an e	NIH
	28:12	to be a grain offering of three-tenths of an e	NIH
	28:12	of two-tenths of an e of fine flour mixed	NIH
	28:13	a tenth of an e of fine flour mixed with oil.	NIH
	28:20	of three-tenths of an e of fine flour mixed	NIH
	28:28	to be a grain offering of three-tenths of an e	NIH
	29: 3	of three-tenths of an e of fine flour mixed	NIH
	29: 9	of three-tenths of an e of fine flour mixed	NIH
	29:14	of three-tenths of an e of fine flour mixed	NIH
Jdg	6:19	an e of flour he made bread without yeast.	406

Ru	2:17	and it amounted to about an e.	406
1Sa	1:24	an e of flour and a skin of wine,	406
	17:17	"Take this e of roasted grain	406
1Ch	1:33	E, Epher, Hanoch, Abida and Eldaah.	6549
	2:46	Caleb's concubine E was the mother	6549
	2:47	Jotham, Geshan, Pelet, E and Shaaph.	6549
Isa	5:10	a homer of seed only an e of grain."	406
	60: 6	young camels of Midian and E.	6548
Eze	45:10	an accurate e and an accurate bath.	406
	45:11	The e and the bath are to be the same size,	406
	45:11	of a homer and the e a tenth of a homer;	406
	45:13	an e from each homer of wheat and a sixth	406
	45:13	a sixth of an e from each homer of barley	406
	45:24	as a grain offering an e for each bull and	406
	45:24	for each bull and an e for each ram,	406
	45:24	along with a hin of oil for each e.	406
	46: 5	with the ram is to be an e,	406
	46: 5	along with a hin of oil for each e.	406
	46: 7	He is to provide as a grain offering one e	406
	46: 7	one e with the ram,	406
	46: 7	along with a hin of oil with each e.	406
	46:11	the grain offering is to be an e with a bull,	406
	46:11	an e with a ram,	406
	46:11	along with a hin of oil for each e.	406
	46:14	of a sixth of an e with a third of a hin of oil	406
Mic	6:10	your ill-gotten treasures and the short e,	406

EPHAI (1)

Jer	40: 8	the sons of E the Netophathite,	6550

EPHER (4)

Ge	25: 4	The sons of Midian were Ephah, E,	6761
1Ch	1:33	Ephah, E, Hanoch, Abida and Eldaah.	6761
	4:17	Jether, Mered, E and Jalon.	6761
	5:24	These were the heads of their families: E,	6761

EPHES DAMMIM (1)

1Sa	17: 1	They pitched camp at E,	702

EPHESIAN (1) [EPHESUS]

Ac	21:29	(They had previously seen Trophimus the E	2386

EPHESIANS (2) [EPHESUS]

Ac	19:28	"Great is Artemis of the E!"	2386
	19:34	"Great is Artemis of the E!"	2386

EPHESUS (18) [EPHESIAN, EPHESIANS]

Ac	18:19	They arrived at E,	2387
	18:21	Then he set sail from E.	2387
	18:24	a native of Alexandria, came to E.	1650
	19: 1	through the interior and arrived at E.	2387
	19:17	to the Jews and Greeks living in E,	2387
	19:26	in E and in practically the whole province	2387
	19:35	"Men of E, doesn't all the world know that	2386
	19:35	the city of E is the guardian of the temple	2386
	20:16	to sail past E to avoid spending time in	2387
	20:17	Paul sent to E for the elders of the church.	2387
1Co	15:32	in E for merely human reasons,	2387
	16: 8	But I will stay on at E until Pentecost,	2387
Eph	1: 1	To the saints in E,	2387
1Ti	1: 3	in E so that you may command certain men	2387
2Ti	1:18	in how many ways he helped me in E.	2387
	4:12	I sent Tychicus to E.	2387
Rev	1:11	to E, Smyrna, Pergamum, Thyatira, Sardis,	2387
	2: 1	"To the angel of the church in E write:	2387

EPHLAL (2)

1Ch	2:37	Zabad the father of E,	697
	2:37	E the father of Obed,	697

EPHOD (50)

Ex	25: 7	to be mounted on the e and breastpiece.	680
	28: 4	a breastpiece, an e, a robe, a woven tunic,	680
	28: 6	"Make the e of gold, and of blue,	680
	28: 8	of one piece with the e and made with gold,	5647S
	28:12	of the e as memorial stones for the sons	680
	28:15	Make it like the e:	680
	28:25	to the shoulder pieces of the e at the front.	680
	28:26	on the inside edge next to the e.	680
	28:27	of the shoulder pieces on the front of the e,	680
	28:27	the seam just above the waistband of the e.	680
	28:28	be tied to the rings of the e with blue cord,	680
	28:28	not swing out from the e.	680
	28:31	the robe of the e entirely of blue cloth,	680
	29: 5	the robe of the e,	680
	29: 5	the e itself and the breastpiece.	680
	29: 5	Fasten the e on him	680
	35: 9	to be mounted on the e and breastpiece.	680
	35:27	to be mounted on the e and breastpiece.	680
	39: 2	They made the e of gold, and of blue,	680
	39: 4	They made shoulder pieces for the e,	2257S
	39: 5	of one piece with the e and made with gold,	5647S
	39: 7	of the e as memorial stones for the sons	680
	39: 8	They made it like the e:	680
	39:18	to the shoulder pieces of the e at the front.	680
	39:19	on the inside edge next to the e.	680
	39:20	of the shoulder pieces on the front of the e,	680
	39:20	the seam just above the waistband of the e.	680
	39:21	of the e with blue cord, connecting it to	680
	39:21	not swing out from the e—	680
	39:22	the robe of the e entirely of blue cloth—	680
Lev	8: 7	clothed him with the robe and put the e	680

Lev	8: 7	He also tied the e to him	680
Nu	34:23	Hanniel son of E, the leader from the tribe	681
Jdg	8:27	Gideon made the gold into an e,	680
	17: 5	an e and some idols and installed one	680
	18:14	that one of these houses has an e.	680
	18:17	inside and took the carved image, the e,	680
	18:18	the e, the other household gods and	680
	18:20	He took the e, the other household gods	680
1Sa	2:18	a boy wearing a linen e.	680
	2:28	and to wear an e in my presence.	680
	14: 3	who was wearing an e.	680
	21: 9	it is wrapped in a cloth behind the e.	680
	22:18	That day he killed eighty-five men who	
		wore the linen e.	680
	23: 6	the e down with him when he fled to David	680
	23: 9	he said to Abiathar the priest, "Bring the e."	680
	30: 7	the son of Ahimelech, "Bring me the e."	680
2Sa	6:14	David, wearing a linen e.	680
1Ch	15:27	David also wore a linen e.	680
Hos	3: 4	without e or idol.	680

EPHPHATHA (1)

Mk	7:34	and with a deep sigh said to him, "E!"	2395

EPHRAIM (157) [EPHRAIM'S, EPHRAIMITE, EPHRAIMITES]

Ge	41:52	The second son he named E and said,	713
	46:20	Manasseh and E were born to Joseph	713
	48: 1	So he took his two sons Manasseh and E	713
	48: 5	E and Manasseh will be mine,	713
	48:13	E on his right toward Israel's left hand	713
	48:20	'May God make you like E	713
	48:20	So he put E ahead of Manasseh.	713
Nu	1:10	from E, Elishama son of Ammihud;	713
	1:32	From the descendants of E:	713
	1:33	number from the tribe of E was 40,500.	713
	2:18	of the camp of E under their standard.	713
	2:18	of E is Elishama son of Ammihud.	713
	2:24	All the men assigned to the camp of E,	713
	7:48	the leader of the people of E,	713
	10:22	divisions of the camp of E went next,	713+1201
	13: 8	from the tribe of E, Hoshea son of Nun;	713
	26:28	through Manasseh and E were:	713
	26:35	the descendants of E by their clans:	713
	26:37	These were the clans of E;	713+1201
	34:24	leader from the tribe of E son of Joseph;	713+1201
Dt	33:17	Such are the ten thousands of E;	713
	34: 2	the territory of E and Manasseh,	713
Jos	14: 4	sons of Joseph had become two tribes—	
		Manasseh and E.	713
	16: 4	So Manasseh and E,	713
	16: 5	This was the territory of E, clan by clan:	713+1201
	16:10	the Canaanites live among the people of E	713
	17: 9	to E lying among the towns of Manasseh,	713
	17:10	On the south the land belonged to E,	713
	17:15	if the hill country of E is too small for you,	713
	17:17	to E and Manasseh—	713
	19:50	Timnath Serah in the hill country of E.	713
	20: 7	Shechem in the hill country of E,	713
	21: 5	from the clans of the tribes of E,	713
	21:20	from the tribe of E:	713
	21:21	of E they were given Shechem (a city	713
	24:30	at Timnath Serah in the hill country of E,	713
	24:33	to his son Phinehas in the hill country of E.	713
Jdg	1:29	Nor did E drive out the Canaanites living	713
	2: 9	at Timnath Heres in the hill country of E,	713
	3:27	he blew a trumpet in the hill country of E,	713
	4: 5	and Bethel in the hill country of E,	713
	5:14	Some came from E, whose roots were	713
	7:24	throughout the hill country of E,	713
	7:24	the men of E were called out and they took	713
	10: 1	He lived in Shamir, in the hill country of E.	713
	10: 9	Benjamin and the house of E;	713
	12: 1	The men of E called out their forces,	713
	12: 4	the men of Gilead and fought against E.	713
	12: 4	"You Gileadites are renegades from E	713
	12: 5	the fords of the Jordan leading to E,	713
	12: 5	and whenever a survivor of E said,	713
	12:15	and was buried at Pirathon in E,	713+824
	17: 1	from the hill country of E	713
	17: 8	to Micah's house in the hill country of E.	713
	18: 2	the hill country of E and came to the house	713
	18:13	on to the hill country of E and came	713
	19: 1	a remote area in the hill country of E took	713
	19:16	an old man from the hill country of E,	713
	19:18	to a remote area in the hill country of E	713
1Sa	1: 1	a Zuphite from the hill country of E,	713
	9: 4	of E and through the area around Shalisha,	713
	14:22	of E heard that the Philistines were on	713
2Sa	2: 9	and also over E, Benjamin and all Israel.	713
	13:23	at Baal Hazor near the border of E,	713
	18: 6	and the battle took place in the forest of E.	713
	20:21	from the hill country of E,	713
1Ki	4: 8	in the hill country of E;	713
	12:25	in the hill country of E and lived there.	713
2Ki	5:22	to me from the hill country of E.	713
	14:13	the wall of Jerusalem from the E Gate to	713
1Ch	6:66	as their territory towns from the tribe of E.	713
	6:67	of E they were given Shechem (a city	713
	7:20	The descendants of E:	713
	7:22	Their father E mourned	713
	9: 3	and from E and Manasseh who lived	713+1201
	12:30	men of E, brave warriors, famous	713
2Ch	13: 4	in the hill country of E, and said,	713
	15: 8	the towns he had captured in the hills of E	713

2Ch	15: 9	and Benjamin and the people from E,	713
	17: 2	of E that his father Asa had captured.	713
	19: 4	the hill country of E and turned them back	713
	25: 7	not with any of the people of E.	713
	25:10	the troops who had come to him from E	713
	25:23	the wall of Jerusalem from the E Gate to	713
	28:12	Then some of the leaders in E—	713+1201
	30: 1	and also wrote letters to E and Manasseh,	713
	30:10	couriers went from town to town in E	713+824
	30:18	of the many people who came from E,	713
	31: 1	throughout Judah and Benjamin and in E	713
	34: 6	In the towns of Manasseh, E and Simeon,	713
	34: 9	E and the entire remnant of Israel and	713
Ne	8:16	and the one by the Gate of E.	713
	12:39	over the Gate of E.	713
Ps	60: 7	E is my helmet, Judah my scepter.	713
	78: 9	The men of E, though armed with bows,	713
	78:67	he did not choose the tribe of E;	713
	80: 2	before E, Benjamin	713
	108: 8	E is my helmet, Judah my scepter.	713
Isa	7: 2	"Aram has allied itself with E";	713
	7: 5	Aram, E and Remaliah's son have plotted	
		your ruin,	713
	7: 8	Within sixty-five years E will	713
	7: 9	The head of E is Samaria,	713
	7:17	a time unlike any since E broke away	713
	9: 9	E and the inhabitants of Samaria—	713
	9:21	Manasseh will feed on E, and Ephraim	713
	9:21	and E on Manasseh;	713
	11:13	E will not be jealous of Judah,	713
	11:13	nor Judah hostile toward E.	713
	17: 3	The fortified city will disappear from E,	713
Jer	4:15	proclaiming disaster from the hills of E.	713
	7:15	the people of E.'	713
	31: 6	when watchmen cry out on the hills of E,	713
	31: 9	and E is my firstborn son.	713
	31:20	Is not E my dear son,	713
	50:19	be satisfied on the hills of E and Gilead.	713
Eze	48: 5	"E will have one portion;	713
	48: 6	it will border the territory of E from east	713
Hos	4:17	E is joined to idols; leave him alone!	713
	5: 3	I know all about E;	713
	5: 3	E, you have now turned to prostitution;	713
	5: 5	the Israelites, even E, stumble in their sin;	713
	5: 9	E will be laid waste on the day	713
	5:11	E is oppressed, trampled in judgment,	713
	5:12	I am like a moth to E,	713
	5:13	"When E saw his sickness,	713
	5:13	then E turned to Assyria,	713
	5:14	For I will be like a lion to E,	713
	6: 4	"What can I do with you, E?	713
	6:10	There E is given to prostitution	713
	7: 1	the sins of E are exposed and the crimes	713
	7: 8	"E mixes with the nations;	713
	7: 8	E is a flat cake not turned over.	713
	7:11	"E is like a dove,	713
	8: 9	E has sold herself to lovers.	713
	8:11	E built many altars for sin offerings,	713
	9: 3	E will return to Egypt and eat unclean food	713
	9: 8	is the watchman over E,	713
	9:13	I have seen E, like Tyre,	713
	9:13	But E will bring out their children to	713
	9:16	E is blighted, their root is withered,	713
	10: 6	E will be disgraced;	713
	10:11	E is a trained heifer that loves to thresh;	713
	10:11	I will drive E, Judah must plow,	713
	11: 3	It was I who taught E to walk,	713
	11: 8	"How can I give you up, E?	713
	11: 9	nor will I turn and devastate E.	713
	11:12	E has surrounded me with lies,	713
	12: 1	E feeds on the wind;	713
	12: 8	E boasts, "I am very rich;	713
	12:14	But E has bitterly provoked him to anger;	713
	13: 1	When E spoke, men trembled;	713
	13:12	The guilt of E is stored up,	713
	14: 8	O E, what more have I to do with idols?	713
Ob	1:19	They will occupy the fields of E	713
Zec	9:10	from E and the war-horses from Jerusalem,	713
	9:13	as I bend my bow and fill it with E.	713
Jn	11:54	to a village called E,	2394

EPHRAIM'S (12) [EPHRAIM]

Ge	48:14	and put it on E head,	713
	48:17	on E head he was displeased;	713
	48:17	of his father's hand to move it from E head	713
	50:23	and saw the third generation of E children.	713
Jdg	8: 2	Aren't the gleanings of E grapes better than	713
Isa	11:13	E jealousy will vanish,	713
	28: 1	the pride of E drunkards,	713
	28: 3	That wreath, the pride of E drunkards,	713
Jer	31:18	"I have surely heard E moaning:	713
Eze	37:16	and write on it, 'E stick,	713
	37:19	which is in E hand,	713
Hos	9:11	E glory will fly away like a bird—	713

EPHRAIMITE (6) [EPHRAIM]

Jdg	12: 5	"Are you an E?"	718
1Sa	1: 1	the son of Tohu, the son of Zuph, an E.	718
1Ki	11:26	an E from Zeredah,	718
1Ch	27:10	was Helez the Pelonite, an E.	713+1201
	27:14	was Benaiah the Pirathonite, an E.	713+1201
2Ch	28: 7	an E warrior, killed Maaseiah	713

EPHRAIMITES (8) [EPHRAIM]

Jos	16: 8	the inheritance of the tribe of the E,	713+1201

Jos	16: 9	that were set aside for the E within	713+1201
	17: 8	belonged to the E.)	713+1201
Jdg	8: 1	Now the E asked Gideon,	408+713
	12: 4	down because the E had said,	713
	12: 6	Forty-two thousand E were killed at	713+4946
1Ch	27:20	over the E: Hoshea son of Azaziah;	713+1201
Zec	10: 7	The E will become like mighty men,	713

EPHRAIN (KJV) EPHRON

EPHRATH (5) [EPHRATHITE, EPHRATHITES]

Ge	35:16	from E, Rachel began to give birth	714
	35:19	and was buried on the way to E (that is,	714
	48: 7	a little distance from E.	714
	48: 7	So I buried her there beside the road to E"	714
1Ch	2:19	When Azubah died, Caleb married E,	715

EPHRATHAH (5) [BETHLEHEM, CALEB EPHRATHAH]

Ru	4:11	May you have standing in E and be famous	716
1Ch	2:50	The sons of Hur the firstborn of E:	717
	4: 4	the firstborn of E and father of Bethlehem.	717
Ps	132: 6	We heard it in E,	716
Mic	5: 2	"But you, Bethlehem E,	716

EPHRATHITE (1) [EPHRATH]

1Sa	17:12	David was the son of an E named Jesse,	718

EPHRATHITES (1) [EPHRATH]

Ru	1: 2	They were E from Bethlehem, Judah.	718

EPHRON (10) [EPHRON'S]

Ge	23: 8	then listen to me and intercede with E son	6766
	23:10	E the Hittite was sitting among his people	6766
	23:13	and he said to E in their hearing,	6766
	23:14	E answered Abraham,	6766
	25: 9	in the field of E son of Zohar the Hittite,	6766
	49:29	with my fathers in the cave in the field of E	6766
	49:30	as a burial place from E the Hittite,	6766
	50:13	as a burial place from E the Hittite,	6766
Jos	15: 9	came out at the towns of Mount E and went	6767
2Ch	13:19	the towns of Bethel, Jeshanah and E,	6767

EPHRON'S (2) [EPHRON]

Ge	23:16	to E terms and weighed out for him	6766
	23:17	So E field in Machpelah near Mamre—	6766

EPICUREAN (1)

Ac	17:18	A group of E and Stoic philosophers began	2134

EPISTLE (KJV) LETTER

EQUAL (18) [EQUALED, EQUALITY, EQUALLY, EQUITY, EQUIVALENT]

Ge	44:18	though you are e to Pharaoh himself.	4017
	47: 9	not e the years of the pilgrimage	5952
Ex	30:34	frankincense, all in e amounts,	928+963+963
Dt	33:25	and your strength will e your days.	3869
1Sa	9: 2	an impressive young man without e among the Israelites—	401+3202+4946
1Ki	3:13	so that in your lifetime you will have no e	4017
Job	41:33	Nothing on earth is his e—	5444
Isa	40:25	Or who is my e?"	8750
	46: 5	or count me e?	8750
Eze	31: 8	nor could the pine trees e its boughs,	1948
	45:12	Twenty shekels plus twenty-five shekels plus fifteen shekels e one mina.	NIH
	48: 8	and its length from east to west will e one	3869
Da	1:19	and he found none e to Daniel, Hananiah,	3869
Mt	20:12	'and you have made them e	2698
Jn	5:18	making himself e with God.	2698
1Co	12:25	but that its parts should have e concern	899+3836
2Co	2:16	And who is e to such a task?	2653
	11:12	an opportunity to be considered e with us in the things they boast about.	1609+2777+2779

EQUALED (2) [EQUAL]

Mt	24:21	and never to be e again.	NIG
Mk	13:19	and never to be e again.	NIG

EQUALITY (3) [EQUAL]

2Co	8:13	but that there might be e.	2699
	8:14	Then there will be e,	2699
Php	2: 6	did not consider e with God something to be grasped,	1639+2698+3836

EQUALLY (5) [EQUAL]

Ex	21:35	divide both the money and the dead animal e.	2936
Lev	7:10	belongs e to all the sons of Aaron.	278+408+2257+3869
Dt	18: 8	He is to share e in their benefits,	3869
Ecc	11: 6	or whether both will do e well.	285+3869
Eze	47:14	You are to divide it e among them.	278+408+2257+3869

EQUIP (1) [EQUIPMENT, EQUIPPED]

Heb	13:21	e you with everything good	2936

EQUIPMENT (10) [EQUIP]

Nu	3:36	all its e, and everything related to their use,	3998
	4:26	the ropes and all the e used in its service.	3998
	4:32	all their e and everything related	3998
Dt	23:13	As part of your e have something to dig	266
1Sa	8:12	to make weapons of war and e	3998
1Ki	19:21	the plowing e to cook the meat and gave it	3998
2Ki	7:15	and e the Arameans had thrown away	3998
2Ch	20:25	a great amount of e and clothing and	8214
Ne	13: 9	then I put back into them the e of the house	3998
Zec	11:15	"Take again the e of a foolish shepherd.	3998

EQUIPPED (4) [EQUIP]

2Ch	14: 8	e with large shields and with spears,	5951
Ne	4:16	while the other half were e with spears,	2616
Da	11:13	he will advance with a huge army fully e.	8214
2Ti	3:17	so that the man of God may be thoroughly e	1992

EQUITY (3) [EQUAL]

Ps	96:10	he will judge the peoples with e.	4797
	98: 9	in righteousness and the peoples with e.	4797
	99: 4	you have established e;	4797

EQUIVALENT (2) [EQUAL]

Lev	27: 2	to the LORD by giving e values,	6886
Eze	45:14	for ten baths are e to a homer).	NIH

ER (10)

Ge	38: 3	who was named E.	6841
	38: 6	Judah got a wife for E, his firstborn,	6841
	38: 7	But E, Judah's firstborn,	6841
	46:12	The sons of Judah: E, Onan, Shelah.	6841
	46:12	Perez and Zerah (but E and Onan had died	6841
Nu	26:19	E and Onan were sons of Judah,	6841
1Ch	2: 3	The sons of Judah: E, Onan and Shelah.	6841
	2: 3	E, Judah's firstborn, was wicked in	6841
	4:21	E the father of Lecah,	6841
Lk	3:28	the son of Elmadam, the son of E,	2474

ERAN (1) [ERANITE]

Nu	26:36	through E, the Eranite clan.	6896

ERANITE (1) [ERAN]

Nu	26:36	through Eran, the E clan.	6897

ERASTUS (3)

Ac	19:22	He sent two of his helpers, Timothy and E,	2235
Ro	16:23	E, who is the city's director	2235
2Ti	4:20	E stayed in Corinth,	2235

ERECH (2)

Ge	10:10	E, Akkad and Calneh, in Shinar.	804
Ezr	4: 9	E and Babylon, the Elamites of Susa,	10074

ERECT (3) [ERECTED]

Dt	16:22	and do not e a sacred stone,	7756
Eze	4: 2	E siege works against it,	1215
	21:22	to build a ramp and to e siege works.	1215

ERECTED (9) [ERECT]

Ex	40:18	he put the bases in place, e the frames,	8492
2Sa	18:18	e it in the King's Valley as a monument	5893
1Ki	7:21	He e the pillars at the portico of the temple.	7756
2Ki	21: 3	he also e altars to Baal and made	7756
	23:12	down the altars the kings of Judah had e on	6913
2Ch	3:17	He e the pillars in the front of the temple,	7756
	33: 3	he also e altars to the Baals	7756
Est	6: 4	on the gallows he had e for him.	3922
Eze	17:17	and siege works e to destroy many lives.	1215

ERI (2) [ERITE]

Ge	46:16	Zephon, Haggi, Shuni, Ezbon, E,	6878
Nu	26:16	through E, the Erite clan;	6878

ERITE (1) [ERI]

Nu	26:16	through Eri, the E clan;	6879

ERODES (1)

Job	14:18	"But as a mountain e and crumbles and as	5877

ERRAND (KJV) HAVE TO SAY, MESSAGE

ERRED (2) [ERROR]

Nu	15:28	the one who e by sinning unintentionally,	8704
1Sa	26:21	I have acted like a fool and have e greatly."	8706

ERROR (12) [ERRED, ERRORS]

Job	4:18	if he charges his angels with e,	9334
	19: 4	my e remains my concern alone.	5413
Ecc	10: 5	the sort of e that arises from a ruler:	8705
Isa	32: 6	He practices ungodliness and spreads e	9360
	47:15	Each of them goes on in his e;	9494
Mt	22:29	"You are in e because you do not know	4414

Mk	12:24	"Are you not in e because you do not know	4414
1Th	2: 3	the appeal we make does not spring from e	4415
Jas	5:20	a sinner from the e of his way will save him	4415
2Pe	2:18	from those who live in e.	4415
	3:17	not be carried away by the e of lawless men	4415
Jude	1:11	for profit into Balaam's e;	4415

ERRORS (2) [ERROR]

Ps	19:12	Who can discern his e?	8709
Ecc	10: 4	calmness can lay great e to rest.	2628

ESARHADDON (3)

2Ki	19:37	And E his son succeeded him as king.	675
Ezr	4: 2	to him since the time of E king of Assyria,	675
Isa	37:38	And E his son succeeded him as king.	675

ESAU (87) [EDOM, ESAU'S]

Ge	25:25	so they named him E.	6916
	25:27	and E became a skillful hunter,	6916
	25:28	who had a taste for wild game, loved E,	6916
	25:29	E came in from the open country, famished.	6916
	25:32	"Look, I am about to die," E said.	6916
	25:34	Then Jacob gave E some bread	6916
	25:34	So E despised his birthright.	6916
	26:34	When E was forty years old,	6916
	27: 1	he called for E his older son and said	6916
	27: 5	as Isaac spoke to his son E.	6916
	27: 5	When E left for the open country	6916
	27: 6	to your brother E,	6916
	27:11	"But my brother E is a hairy man,	6916
	27:15	the best clothes of E her older son,	6916
	27:19	"I am E your firstborn.	6916
	27:21	to know whether you really are my son E	6916
	27:22	but the hands are the hands of E."	6916
	27:23	like those of his brother E;	6916
	27:24	"Are you really my son E?"	6916
	27:30	his brother E came in from hunting.	6916
	27:32	he answered, "your firstborn, E."	6916
	27:34	When E heard his father's words,	6916
	27:36	E said, "Isn't he rightly named Jacob?	NIH
	27:37	Isaac answered E, "I have made him lord	6916
	27:38	E said to his father,	6916
	27:38	Then E wept aloud.	6916
	27:41	E held a grudge against Jacob because of	6916
	27:42	Rebekah was told what her older son E had said,	6916
	27:42	"Your brother E is consoling himself with	6916
	28: 5	who was the mother of Jacob and E.	6916
	28: 6	Now E learned that Isaac had blessed Jacob	6916
	28: 8	E then realized how displeasing	6916
	32: 3	of him to his brother E in the land of Seir,	6916
	32: 4	to say to my master E:	6916
	32: 6	they said, "We went to your brother E,	6916
	32: 8	"If E comes and attacks one group,	6916
	32:11	I pray, from the hand of my brother E,	6916
	32:13	a gift for his brother E:	6916
	32:17	"When my brother E meets you and asks,	6916
	32:18	They are a gift sent to my lord E.	6916
	32:19	the same thing to E when you meet him.	6916
	33: 1	Jacob looked up and there was E,	6916
	33: 4	But E ran to meet Jacob and embraced him;	6916
	33: 5	Then E looked up and saw the women	NIH
	33: 8	E asked, "What do you mean	NIH
	33: 9	E said, "I already have plenty, my brother.	6916
	33:11	And because Jacob insisted, E accepted it.	NIH
	33:12	Then E said, "Let us be on our way;	NIH
	33:15	E said, "Then let me leave some of my men	6916
	33:16	that day E started on his way back to Seir.	6916
	35: 1	from your brother E."	6916
	35:29	And his sons E and Jacob buried him.	6916
	36: 1	This is the account of E (that is, Edom).	6916
	36: 2	E took his wives from the women	6916
	36: 4	Adah bore Eliphaz to E,	6916
	36: 5	These were the sons of E,	6916
	36: 6	E took his wives and sons and daughters	6916
	36: 8	So E (that is, Edom) settled in the hill	6916
	36: 9	the account of E the father of the Edomites	6916
	36:14	whom she bore to E:	6916
	36:15	The sons of Eliphaz the firstborn of E:	6916
	36:19	These were the sons of E (that is, Edom),	6916
	36:40	These were the chiefs descended from E,	6916
	36:43	This was E the father of the Edomites.	6916
Dt	2: 4	of your brothers the descendants of E,	6916
	2: 5	I have given E the hill country of Seir	6916
	2: 8	on past our brothers the descendants of E,	6916
	2:12	but the descendants of E drove them out.	6916
	2:22	the same for the descendants of E,	6916
	2:29	the descendants of E, who live in Seir, and	6916
Jos	24: 4	and to Isaac I gave Jacob and E.	6916
	24: 4	I assigned the hill country of Seir to E,	6916
1Ch	1:34	The sons of Isaac: E and Israel.	6916
	1:35	The sons of E:	6916
Jer	49: 8	for I will bring disaster on E at	6916
	49:10	But I will strip E bare;	6916
Ob	1: 6	But how E will be ransacked,	6916
	1: 8	of understanding in the mountains of E?	6916
	1:18	the house of E will be stubble,	6916
	1:18	be no survivors from the house of E."	6916
	1:19	the Negev will occupy the mountains of E,	6916
	1:21	to govern the mountains of E.	6916
Mal	1: 2	"Was not E Jacob's brother?	6916
	1: 3	but E I have hated,	6916
Ro	9:13	"Jacob I loved, but E I hated."	2481
Heb	11:20	By faith Isaac blessed Jacob and E	2481
	12:16	or is godless like E,	2481

ESAU'S (14) [ESAU]

Ge	25:26	with his hand grasping **E** heel;	6916
	36:10	These are the names of **E** sons:	6916
	36:10	Eliphaz, the son of **E** wife Adah, and Reuel,	6916
	36:10	and Reuel, the son of **E** wife Basemath.	6916
	36:12	**E** son Eliphaz also had a concubine	6916
	36:12	These were grandsons of **E** wife Adah.	6916
	36:13	These were grandsons of **E** wife Basemath.	6916
	36:14	The sons of **E** wife Oholibamah daughter	6916
	36:15	the chiefs among **E** descendants:	6916
	36:17	The sons of **E** son Reuel:	6916
	36:17	they were grandsons of **E** wife Basemath.	6916
	36:18	The sons of **E** wife Oholibamah	6916
	36:18	from **E** wife Oholibamah daughter of Anah.	6916
Ob	1: 9	and everyone in **E** mountains will be cut	6916

ESCAPE (66) [ESCAPED, ESCAPES, ESCAPING]

Ge	7: 7	entered the ark *to* **e** the waters of the flood.	4946+7156
	32: 8	the group that is left may **e**."	7129
Jos	8:20	they had no chance to **e** in any direction,	5674
Jdg	20:42	but they **could not e** the battle.	1815
1Sa	19:10	That night David **made good** *his* **e**.	2256+4880+5674
	19:18	When David had fled and **made** *his* **e**,	4880
	27: 1	The best thing I can do *is to* **e** to the land of	
		the Philistines.	4880+4880
2Sa	15:14	or none of us will **e** from Absalom.	7129
	20: 6	he will find fortified cities and **e** *from* us."	5911
1Ki	12:18	to get into his chariot and **e** to Jerusalem.	5674
	19:17	Jehu will put to death any *who* **e** the sword	4880
	19:17	and Elisha will put to death any *who* **e**	4880
2Ki	10:24	of the men I am placing in your hands **e**,	4880
	10:25	*let* no one **e**."	3655
2Ch	10:18	to get into his chariot and **e** to Jerusalem.	5674
Est	4:13	you alone of all the Jews *will* **e**.	4880
Job	11:20	and **e** will elude them;	4960
	15:30	*He* will not **e** the darkness;	6073
Ps	56: 7	On no account **let** them **e**;	7117
	68:20	comes **e** from death.	9362
	88: 8	*I* am confined and cannot **e**;	3655
Pr	11: 9	but through knowledge the righteous **e**.	2740
Ecc	7:26	The man who pleases God *will* **e** her,	4880
Isa	20: 6	How then *can* we **e**?'"	4880
Jer	11:11	on them a disaster they cannot **e**.	3655
	21: 9	he will **e** with his life.	4200+8965
	25:35	the leaders of the flock no **place to e**.	7129
	32: 4	Zedekiah king of Judah *will* not **e** out of	4880
	34: 3	You *will* not **e** from his grasp but will	4880
	35:11	**e** the Babylonian and Aramean armies	4946+7156
	38: 2	He will **e** with his life; he will live.'	4200+8965
	38:18	not **e** from their hands.'"	4880
	38:23	not **e** from their hands but will be captured	4880
	39:18	by the sword but will **e** with your life,	4200+8965
	41:18	to **e** the Babylonians.	4946+7156
	42:17	or the disaster I will bring on them.'	7127
	44:14	to live in Egypt will **e** or survive to return	7127
	44:28	*Those who* **e** the sword and return to	7127
	45: 5	wherever you go I will let you **e** with	4200+8965
	46: 6	"The swift cannot flee nor the strong **e**.	4880
	48: 8	and not a town *will* **e**.	4880
	50:29	Encamp all around her; let no *one* **e**.	7129
La	3: 7	He has walled me in so *I* cannot **e**;	3655
Eze	6: 8	for some of you will **e** the sword	7127
	6: 9	*those who* **e** will remember me—	7127
	7:16	All who survive and **e** will be in	7127
	17:15	*Will he* who does such things **e**?	4880
	17:15	Will he break the treaty and yet **e**?	4880
	17:18	*he shall* not **e**.	4880
Da	11:42	Egypt will not **e**.	7129
Hos	9: 6	Even if *they* **e** from destruction,	2143
Am	2:14	The swift *will* **not e**,	6+4960
	9: 1	Not one will get away, none *will* **e**.	4880+7127
Hab	2: 9	to **e** the clutches of ruin!	5911
Zec	2: 7	**E**, you who live in the Daughter	4880
Mal	3:15	and even those who challenge God **e**.'"	4880
Mt	2:13	the child and his mother and **e** to Egypt.	5771
	23:33	How *will you* **e** being condemned to hell?	5771
Lk	21:36	that you may be able *to* **e** all that is about	1767
Ac	27:30	In an attempt *to* **e** from the ship,	5771
Ro	2: 3	do you think you *will* **e** God's judgment?	1767
1Th	5: 3	and *they will* not **e**.	1767
2Ti	2:26	that they will come to their senses and **e**	NIG
Heb	2: 3	how *shall* we **e** if we ignore such	1767
	12:25	If they *did* not **e** when they refused him	1767
2Pe	1: 4	and **e** the corruption in the world	709

ESCAPED (38) [ESCAPE]

Ge	14:13	One who *had* **e** came and reported this	7127
Jdg	3:26	He passed by the idols and **e** to Seirah.	4880
	3:29	not a man **e**.	4880
	9: 5	the youngest son of Jerub-Baal, **e** by hiding.	3855
1Sa	19:12	and he fled and **e**.	4880
	19:17	and send my enemy away so that he **e**?"	4880
	22: 1	David left Gath and **e** to the cave	4880
	22:20	**e** and fled to join David.	4880
	23:13	When Saul was told that David had **e**	4880
2Sa	1: 3	"I have **e** from the Israelite camp."	4880
1Ki	20:20	of Aram **e** on horseback with some	4880
	20:30	The rest of them **e** to the city of Aphek.	5674
2Ki	9:27	but he **e** to Megiddo and died there.	5674
	13: 5	and *they* **e** from the power of Aram.	3655
	19:37	and they **e** *to* the land of Ararat.	4880
1Ch	4:43	the remaining Amalekites who had **e**,	7129
2Ch	16: 7	of the king of Aram *has* **e** from your hand.	4880
	20:24	no one had **e**.	7129
	30: 6	who have **e** from the hand of the kings	7129
	36:20	who **e** *from* the sword,	4946
Job	1:15	I am the only one *who has* **e** to tell you!"	4880
	1:16	I am the only one *who has* **e** to tell you!"	4880
	1:17	I am the only one *who has* **e** to tell you!"	4880
	1:19	I am the only one *who has* **e** to tell you!"	4880
	19:20	*I have* **e** with only the skin of my teeth.	4880
Ps	124: 7	We have **e** like a bird out of	4880
	124: 7	the snare has been broken, and we have **e**.	4880
Isa	37:38	and they **e** *to* the land of Ararat.	4880
Jer	41:15	of his men **e** from Johanan and fled to	4880
	51:50	You *who* have **e** the sword,	7128
La	2:22	of the LORD's anger no one **e** or survived;	7127
Eze	33:21	**man who** *had* **e** from Jerusalem came to me	7127
Jn	10:39	but *he* **e** their grasp.	2002
Ac	16:27	because he thought the prisoners *had* **e**.	1767
	26:26	that none of this *has* **e** his **notice**.	3291
	28: 4	for *though* he **e** from the sea,	1407
Heb	11:34	and **e** the edge of the sword;	5771
2Pe	2:20	If *they* have **e** the corruption of the world	709

ESCAPES (3) [ESCAPE]

Ps	33:16	no warrior **e** by his great strength.	5911
Pr	12:13	but a righteous man **e** trouble.	3655
Joel	2: 3	a desert waste—nothing **e** them.	2118+7129

ESCAPING (7) [ESCAPE]

Jdg	9:21	Then Jotham fled, **e** to Beer,	1368
Job	15:22	He despairs of **e** the darkness;	8740
Jer	48:19	Ask the man fleeing and the *woman* **e**,	4880
Hos	13: 3	like smoke **e** through a window.	NIH
Ac	27:42	of them from swimming away and **e**.	1423
1Co	3:15	but only as one **e** through the flames.	NIG
2Pe	2:18	they entice people who *are* just **e from**	709

ESCORT (2) [ESCORTED]

Da	11: 6	together with her royal **e** and her father and	995
Ac	16:37	*Let them* come themselves and **e** us **out**."	1974

ESCORTED (4) [ESCORT]

1Ki	1:38	on King David's mule and **e** him to Gihon.	2143
SS	3: 7	**e** by sixty warriors, the noblest of Israel,	6017
Ac	16:39	They came to appease them and **e** them	1974
	17:15	The men who **e** Paul brought him to Athens	2770

ESAIAS (KJV) ISAIAH

ESCHEW (KJV) TURN FROM

ESEK (1)

Ge	26:20	So he named the well **E**,	6922

ESH-BAAL (2) [BAAL, ISH-BOSHETH]

1Ch	8:33	Malki-Shua, Abinadab and **E**.	843
	9:39	Malki-Shua, Abinadab and **E**.	843

ESHAN (1)

Jos	15:52	Arab, Dumah, **E**,	878

ESHBAN (2)

Ge	36:26	Hemdan, **E**, Ithran and Keran.	841
1Ch	1:41	Hemdan, **E**, Ithran and Keran.	841

ESHCOL (6)

Ge	14:13	a brother of **E** and Aner.	866
	14:24	to Aner, **E** and Mamre.	866
Nu	13:23	When they reached the Valley of **E**,	865
	13:24	the Valley of **E** because of the cluster	865
	32: 9	up to the Valley of **E** and viewed the land,	865
Dt	1:24	came to the Valley of **E** and explored it.	865

ESHEAN (KJV) ESHAN

ESHEK (1)

1Ch	8:39	The sons of his brother **E**:	6944

ESHKALONITES (KJV) ASHKELON

ESHTAOL (7) [ESHTAOLITES]

Jos	15:33	In the western foothills: **E**, Zorah, Ashnah,	900
	19:41	Zorah, **E**, Ir Shemesh,	900
Jdg	13:25	between Zorah and **E**.	900
	16:31	and **E** in the tomb of Manoah his father.	900
	18: 2	and **E** to spy out the land and explore it.	900
	18: 8	When they returned to Zorah and **E**,	900
	18:11	armed for battle, set out from Zorah and **E**.	900

ESHTAOLITES (1) [ESHTAOL]

1Ch	2:53	From these descended the Zorathites and **E**.	901

ESHTARAH See BE ESHTARAH

ESHTEMOA (5)

Jos	21:14	Jattir, **E**,	904
1Sa	30:28	to those in Aroer, Siphmoth, **E**	904
1Ch	4:17	Shammai and Ishbah the father of **E**.	904
	4:19	the father of Keilah the Garmite, and **E**	904
	6:57	(a city of refuge), and Libnah, Jattir, **E**,	904

ESHTEMOH (1)

Jos	15:50	Anab, **E**, Anim,	903

ESHTON (2)

1Ch	4:11	who was the father of **E**.	902
	4:12	**E** was the father of Beth Rapha.	902

ESLI (1)

Lk	3:25	the son of Nahum, the son *of* **E**,	2268

ESPECIALLY (15) [SPECIAL]

Jos	2: 1	look over the land," he said, "**e** Jericho."	2256
Est	8:10	who rode fast horses **e** **bred** for the king.	1201+2021+8247
Ac	25:26	and **e** before you, King Agrippa,	3436
	26: 3	and **e** so because you are well acquainted	3436
1Co	14: 1	**e** the gift of prophecy.	3437
2Co	1:12	and **e** in our relations with you,	4359
	7:13	we were **e** delighted to see	3437
Gal	6:10	**e** to those who belong to the family	3436
Php	4:22	**e** those who belong to Caesar's household.	3436
1Ti	4:10	and **e** of those who believe.	3436
	5: 8	and **e** for his immediate family,	3436
	5:17	**e** those whose work is preaching	3436
2Ti	4:13	and my scrolls, **e** the parchments.	3436
Tit	1:10	**e** those of the circumcision group.	3436
2Pe	2:10	This is **e** true of those who follow	3436

ESPIED, ESPY (KJV) EXPLORE, SAW, SEARCHED OUT, WATCHED

ESPOUSALS, ESPOUSED (KJV) BETROTHED, PLEDGED TO BE MARRIED, PROMISED

ESROM (KJV) HEZRON

ESTABLISH (37) [ESTABLISHED, ESTABLISHES, ESTABLISHING, REESTABLISHED]

Ge	6:18	But *I* will **e** my covenant with you,	7756
	9: 9	"I now **e** my covenant with you and	7756
	9:11	*I* **e** my covenant with you:	7756
	17: 7	I will **e** my covenant as	7756
	17:19	I will **e** my covenant with him as	7756
	17:21	my covenant *I will* **e** with Isaac,	7756
Ex	23:31	"I will **e** your borders from the Red Sea to	8883
Dt	28: 9	The LORD *will* **e** you as his holy people,	7756
1Sa	2:35	I will firmly **e** his house,	1215
2Sa	3:10	and **e** David's throne over Israel and Judah	7756
	7:11	that the LORD *himself will* **e** a house	6913
	7:12	and I will **e** his kingdom.	3922
	7:13	I will **e** the throne of his kingdom forever.	3922
1Ki	8:32	and so **e** his innocence.	5989
	9: 5	I will **e** your royal throne	7756
1Ch	17:11	and I will **e** his kingdom.	3922
	17:12	and I will **e** his throne forever.	3922
	18: 3	to **e** his control along the Euphrates River.	5893
	22:10	And *I will* **e** the throne of his kingdom	3922
	28: 7	I will **e** his kingdom forever	3922
2Ch	6:23	not guilty and so **e** his innocence.	5989
	7:18	I will **e** your royal throne,	7756
Est	9:27	upon themselves *to* **e the custom** that they	7756
	9:31	*to* **e** these days of Purim	7756
Ps	87: 5	and the Most High himself *will* **e** her."	3922
	89: 4	'I will **e** your line forever	3922
	89:29	I will **e** his line forever,	8492
	90:17	**e** the work of our hands for us—	3922
	90:17	yes, **e** the work of our hands.	3922
Isa	26:12	LORD, *you* **e** peace for us;	9189
Eze	16:60	I will **e** an everlasting covenant with you.	7756
	16:62	So I will **e** my covenant with you,	7756
	37:26	I will **e** them and increase their numbers,	5989
Da	11:16	He will **e** *himself* in the Beautiful Land	6641
Ro	10: 3	from God and sought *to* **e** their own,	2705
	16:25	*to* him who is able *to* **e** you by my gospel	5114
Heb	10: 9	He sets aside the first to **e** the second.	2705

ESTABLISHED (75) [ESTABLISH]

Ge	9:17	"This is the sign of the covenant *I have* **e**	7756
	47:26	So Joseph **e** it as a law concerning land	8492
Ex	6: 4	also **e** my covenant with them to give them	7756
	15:17	the sanctuary, O Lord, your hands **e**.	3922
Lev	26:46	and the regulations that the LORD **e**	5989
Dt	19:15	A matter *must be* **e** by the testimony	7756
1Sa	13:13	if you had, he *would have* **e** your kingdom	3922
	20:31	neither you nor your kingdom *will be* **e**.	3922
	24:20	and that the kingdom of Israel *will be* **e**	7756
2Sa	5:12	And David knew that the LORD *had* **e** him	3922
	7:16	your throne will be **e** forever.'"	3922
	7:24	*You have* **e** your people Israel	3922
	7:26	of your servant David will be **e** before you.	3922

1Ki	2:12	and his rule was firmly e.	3922
	2:24	*he who has e* me securely on the throne	3922
	2:46	The kingdom was now **firmly e**	3922
1Ch	14: 2	And David knew that the LORD *had e* him	3922
	16:30	The world is firmly e; it cannot be moved.	3922
	17:14	his throne will be e forever.' "	3922
	17:23	and his house be e forever.	586
	17:24	so that *it will be e* and that your name will	586
	17:24	of your servant David *will be e* before you.	3922
2Ch	1: 1	Solomon son of David e himself firmly	2616
	12: 1	After Rehoboam's position as king *was e*	3922
	12:13	King Rehoboam e himself firmly	2616
	17: 5	The LORD e the kingdom	3922
	21: 4	When Jehoram e himself firmly	7756
Ezr	8:20	and the officials *had e* to assist the Levites.	5989
Est	9:31	and as *they had e* for themselves	7756
Job	12:19	and overthrows *men* long e.	419
	21: 8	They see their children e around them,	3922
	24:22	though *they become* e,	7756
	28:25	When he e the force of the wind	6913
Ps	9: 7	he has e his throne for judgment.	3922
	24: 2	for he founded it upon the seas and e it	3922
	74:16	you e the sun and moon.	3922
	78: 5	He decreed statutes for Jacob and e the law	8492
	78:69	like the earth that *he e* forever.	3569
	81: 5	*He* e it as a statute for Joseph	8492
	89: 2	*you* e your faithfulness in heaven itself.	3922
	89:37	*it will be e* forever like the moon,	3922
	93: 1	The world is **firmly e**; it cannot be moved.	3922
	93: 2	Your throne **was e** long ago;	3922
	96:10	The world is firmly e, it cannot be moved;	3922
	99: 4	you *have* e equity;	3922
	102:28	their descendants *will be e* before you."	3922
	103:19	The LORD *has* e his throne in heaven,	3922
	119:90	*you* e the earth, and it endures.	3922
	119:152	from your statutes that *you* e them	3569
	140:11	*Let* slanderers *not be e* in the land;	3922
Pr	8:28	when he e the clouds above	599
	12: 3	A man cannot be e through wickedness,	3922
	16:12	for a throne is e through righteousness.	3922
	24: 3	and through understanding *it is* e;	3922
	25: 5	his throne *will be e* through righteousness.	3922
	30: 4	Who *has* e all the ends of the earth?	7756
Isa	2: 2	of the LORD's temple will be e as chief	3922
	14:32	"The LORD *has* e Zion,	3569
	16: 5	In love a throne *will be* e;	3922
	44: 7	since I *e* my ancient people, and what is yet	8492
	54:14	In righteousness *you will be* e:	3922
Jer	12:16	then *they will be* e among my people.	1215
	30:20	and their community *will be e* before me;	3922
	33: 2	the LORD who formed it and e it—	3922
	33:25	not e my covenant *with* day and night and	8492
Mic	4: 1	of the LORD's temple will be e as chief	3922
Mt	18:16	that 'every matter *may be* e by the testimony	2705
Ro	13: 1	that which God *has* e.	5679
	13: 1	The authorities that exist *have been* e	5435
2Co	13: 1	"Every matter *must be* e by the testimony	2705
Gal	3:15	to a human covenant *that has been* **duly e,**	3263
	3:17	not set aside the covenant **previously e**	4623
Eph	3:17	I pray that you, *being* rooted and e in love,	2530
Col	1:23	in your faith, e and firm, not moved from	2530
2Pe	1:12	and *are* **firmly** e in the truth you now have.	5114

ESTABLISHES (5) [ESTABLISH]

Job	25: 2	he e order in the heights of heaven.	6913
Isa	42: 4	not falter or be discouraged till *he e* justice	8492
	62: 7	till *he e* Jerusalem and makes her the praise	3922
Mic	7: 9	until he pleads my case and e my right.	6913
Hab	2:12	with bloodshed and e a town by crime!	3922

ESTABLISHING (1) [ESTABLISH]

Isa	9: 7	e and upholding it with justice	3922

ESTATE (10)

Ge	15: 2	and the one who will inherit my e is Eliezer	1074
	31:14	in the inheritance of our father's e?	1074
Ru	4: 6	because I might endanger my own e.	5709
Est	8: 1	the e *of* Haman.	1074
	8: 2	And Esther appointed him over Haman's e.	1074
	8: 7	I have given his e to Esther,	1074
Ps	136:23	in our **low** e His love endures forever.	9165
Lk	15:12	'Father, give me my share *of* the e.'	4045
Ac	28: 7	an e nearby that belonged to Publius,	6005
Gal	4: 1	although he owns **the whole** e.	AIT

ESTEEM (3) [ESTEEMED]

Est	10: 3	and **held in high** e by his many fellow Jews,	8354
Pr	4: 8	E her, and she will exalt you;	6147
Isa	66: 2	"This is the one *I* e:	5564

ESTEEMED (5) [ESTEEM]

Pr	22: 1	to be e is better than silver or gold.	2834
Isa	53: 3	and *we* e him not.	3108
Da	9:23	for you are **highly** e.	2776
	10:11	He said, "Daniel, you who are **highly** e,	2776
	10:19	"Do not be afraid, O man **highly e,**" he said.	2776

ESTHER (42) [ESTHER'S]

Est	2: 7	This girl, who was also known as **E,**	676
	2: 8	E also was taken to the king's palace	676
	2:10	E had not revealed her nationality	676
	2:11	how E was and what was happening to her.	676
	2:15	for E (the girl Mordecai had adopted,	676

Est	2:15	And E won the favor of everyone	676
	2:17	Now the king was attracted to E more than	676
	2:20	E had kept secret her family background	676
	2:22	about the plot and told Queen E,	676
	4: 5	Then E summoned Hathach,	676
	4: 8	to show to E and explain it to her,	676
	4: 9	and reported to E what Mordecai had said.	676
	4:15	Then E sent this reply to Mordecai:	676
	5: 1	On the third day E put on her royal robes	676
	5: 2	When he saw Queen E standing in	676
	5: 2	So E approached and touched the tip of	676
	5: 3	the king asked, "What is it, Queen E?	676
	5: 4	"If it pleases the king," replied E,	676
	5: 5	"so that we may do what E asks."	676
	5: 5	to the banquet E had prepared.	676
	5: 6	the king again asked E,	676
	5:12	"I'm the only person Queen E invited	676
	6:14	to the banquet E had prepared.	676
	7: 1	and Haman went to dine with Queen E,	676
	7: 2	"Queen E, what is your petition?	676
	7: 3	Then Queen E answered,	676
	7: 5	King Xerxes asked Queen E, "Who is he?	676
	7: 6	E said, "The adversary and enemy	676
	7: 7	stayed behind to beg Queen E for his life.	676
	7: 8	on the couch where E was reclining.	676
	8: 1	That same day King Xerxes gave Queen E	676
	8: 1	for E had told how he was related to her.	676
	8: 2	And E appointed him over Haman's estate.	676
	8: 3	E again pleaded with the king,	676
	8: 4	to E and she arose and stood before him.	676
	8: 7	to Queen E and to Mordecai the Jew,	676
	8: 7	I have given his estate to E,	676
	9:12	The king said to Queen E,	676
	9:13	"If it pleases the king," E answered,	676
	9:29	So Queen E, daughter of Abihail,	676
	9:31	the Jew and Queen E had decreed for them,	676

ESTHER'S (5) [ESTHER]

Est	2:18	the king gave a great banquet, E banquet,	676
	4: 4	When E maids and eunuchs came	676
	4:12	When E words were reported to Mordecai,	676
	4:17	and carried out all of E instructions.	676
	9:32	E decree confirmed these regulations	676

ESTIMATE (1)

Lk	14:28	*Will he* not first sit down and e the cost	6028

ESTRANGED (2) [STRANGE]

2Sa	14:14	so that a banished person *may not remain* e	5615
Job	19:13	my acquaintances *are* completely e	2319

ETAM (5)

Jdg	15: 8	down and stayed in a cave in the rock of E.	6515
	15:11	down to the cave in the rock of E and said	6515
1Ch	4: 3	These were the sons of E:	6515
	4:32	Their surrounding villages were E, Ain,	6515
2Ch	11: 6	Bethlehem, E, Tekoa,	6515

ETERNAL (81) [ETERNALLY, ETERNITY]

Ge	21:33	upon the name of the LORD, the E God.	6409
Dt	33:27	The e God is your refuge,	7710
1Ki	10: 9	the LORD's e love for Israel,	4200+6409
Ps	16:11	with e pleasures at your right hand.	5905
	21: 6	you have granted him e blessings	4200+6329
	111:10	To him belongs e praise.	4200+6329
	119:89	Your word, O LORD, is e;	4200+6409
	119:160	all your righteous laws are e.	4200+6409
Ecc	12: 5	to his e home and mourners go about	6409
Isa	26: 4	for the LORD, the LORD, is the Rock e.	6409
	47: 7	'I will continue forever—the e queen!'	6329
Jer	10:10	he is the living God, the e King.	6409
Da	4: 3	His kingdom is an e kingdom;	10550
	4:34	His dominion is an e dominion;	10550
Hab	3: 6	His ways are e.	6409
Mt	18: 8	or two feet and be thrown into e fire.	173
	19:16	what good thing must I do to get e life?"	173
	19:29	as much and will inherit e life.	173
	25:41	into the e fire prepared for the devil	173
	25:46	"Then they will go away to e punishment,	173
	25:46	but the righteous to e life."	173
Mk	3:29	he is guilty of an e sin."	173
	10:17	he asked, "what must I do to inherit e life?"	173
	10:30	persecutions) and in the age to come, e life.	173
Lk	10:25	he asked, "what must I do to inherit e life?"	173
	16: 9	you will be welcomed into e dwellings.	173
	18:18	what must I do to inherit e life?"	173
	18:30	in the age to come, e life.	173
Jn	3:15	in him may have e life.	173
	3:16	in him shall not perish but have e life.	173
	3:36	Whoever believes in the Son has e life,	173
	4:14	a spring of water welling up to e life."	173
	4:36	even now he harvests the crop for e life,	173
	5:24	and believes him who sent me has e life	173
	5:39	that by them you possess e life.	173
	6:27	but for food that endures to e life,	173
	6:40	and believes in him shall have e life,	173
	6:54	and drinks my blood has e life,	173
	6:68	You have the words *of* e life.	173
	10:28	I give them e life, and they shall never perish	173
	12:25	in this world will keep it for e life.	173
	12:50	I know that his command leads to e life.	173
	17: 2	over all people that he might give e life	173
	17: 3	Now this is e life: that they may know you,	173

Ac	13:46	not consider yourselves worthy *of* e life,	173
	13:48	all who were appointed for e life believed.	173
Ro	1:20	his e power and divine nature—	132
	2: 7	honor and immortality, he will give e life.	173
	5:21	through righteousness to bring e life	173
	6:22	and the result is e life.	173
	6:23	of God is e life in Christ Jesus our Lord.	173
	16:26	the e God, so that all nations might believe	173
2Co	4:17	an e glory that far outweighs them all.	173
	4:18	but what is unseen is e.	173
	5: 1	an e house in heaven,	173
Gal	6: 8	from the Spirit will reap e life.	173
Eph	3:11	to his e purpose which he accomplished	172
2Th	2:16	and by his grace gave us e encouragement	173
1Ti	1:16	on him and receive e life.	173
	1:17	Now to the King e, immortal, invisible,	172
	6:12	*of* the e life to which you were called	173
2Ti	2:10	that is in Christ Jesus, with e glory.	173
Tit	1: 2	on the hope *of* e life,	173
	3: 7	the hope *of* e life.	173
Heb	5: 9	he became the source of e salvation	173
	6: 2	of the dead, and e judgment.	173
	9:12	having obtained e redemption.	173
	9:14	the e Spirit offered himself unblemished	173
	9:15	the promised e inheritance—	173
	13:20	the blood *of* the e covenant brought back	173
1Pe	5:10	who called you to his e glory in Christ,	173
2Pe	1:11	a rich welcome into the e kingdom	173
1Jn	1: 2	and we proclaim to you the e life,	173
	2:25	this is what he promised us—even e life.	173
	3:15	and you know that no murderer has e life	173
	5:11	God has given us e life,	173
	5:13	so that you may know that you have e life,	173
	5:20	He is the true God and e life.	173
Jude	1: 7	the punishment *of* e fire.	173
	1:21	to bring you to e life.	173
Rev	14: 6	the e gospel to proclaim to those who live	173

ETERNALLY (2) [ETERNAL]

Gal	1: 8	let him be e **condemned!**	353
	1: 9	let him be e **condemned!**	353

ETERNITY (3) [ETERNAL]

Ps	93: 2	you are from **all** e.	6409
Pr	8:23	I was appointed from e,	6409
Ecc	3:11	He has also set e in the hearts of men;	6409

ETH KAZIN (1)

Jos	19:13	to Gath Hepher and E;	6962

ETHAM (4)

Ex	13:20	After leaving Succoth they camped at E on	918
Nu	33: 6	They left Succoth and camped at E,	918
	33: 7	They left E, turned back to Pi Hahiroth,	918
	33: 8	for three days in the Desert of E,	918

ETHAN (8)

1Ki	4:31	including E the Ezrahite—	420
1Ch	2: 6	Zimri, E, Heman, Calcol and Darda—	420
	2: 8	The son of E: Azariah.	420
	6:42	the son of E, the son of Zimmah,	420
	6:44	E son of Kishi, the son of Abdi,	420
	15:17	and from their brothers the Merarites, E son	420
	15:19	and E were to sound the bronze cymbals;	420
Ps	89: T	A maskil of E the Ezrahite.	420

ETHANIM (1)

1Ki	8: 2	at the time of the festival in the month of E,	923

ETHBAAL (1)

1Ki	16:31	also married Jezebel daughter of E king of	909

ETHER (2)

Jos	15:42	Libnah, E, Ashan,	6987
	19: 7	Rimmon, E and Ashan—	6987

ETHIOPIA (KJV) CUSH

ETHIOPIAN (2) [ETHIOPIANS]

Jer	13:23	Can the E change his skin or	3934
Ac	8:27	and on his way he met an E eunuch,	134+467

ETHIOPIANS (1) [ETHIOPIAN]

Ac	8:27	treasury of Candace, queen *of* the E.	134

ETHNAN (1)

1Ch	4: 7	The sons of Helah: Zereth, Zohar, E,	925

ETHNI (1)

1Ch	6:41	the son of E, the son of Zerah,	922

EUBULUS (1)

2Ti	4:21	E greets you, and so do Pudens, Linus,	2300

EUNICE (1)

2Ti	1: 5	grandmother Lois and in your mother E	2332

EUNUCH (10) [EUNUCHS]

Est	2: 3	king's **e**, who is in charge of the women;	6247
	2:14	the king's **e** who was in charge of	6247
	2:15	king's **e** who was in charge of the harem,	6247
Isa	56: 3	And let not any **e** complain,	6247
Ac	8:27	and on his way he met an Ethiopian **e**,	2336
	8:32	The **e** was reading this passage of Scripture:	NIG
	8:34	The **e** asked Philip, "Tell me, please,	2336
	8:36	they came to some water and the **e** said,	2336
	8:38	Then both Philip and the **e** went down into	2336
	8:39	and the **e** did not see him again,	2336

EUNUCHS (11) [EUNUCH]

2Ki	9:32	Two or three **e** looked down at him.	6247
	20:18	and they will become **e** in the palace of	6247
Est	1:10	the seven **e** who served him—	6247
	1:15	of King Xerxes that the **e** have taken	6247
	4: 4	and **e** came and told her about Mordecai,	6247
	4: 5	one of the king's **e** assigned to attend her,	6247
	6:14	the king's **e** arrived	6247
	7: 9	Harbona, one of the **e** attending the king,	6247
Isa	39: 7	and they will become **e** in the palace of	6247
	56: 4	"To the **e** who keep my Sabbaths,	6247
Mt	19:12	For some are **e** because they were born	2336

EUODIA (1)

Php	4: 2	with **E** and I plead with Syntyche to agree	2337

EUPHRATES (20) [TRANS-EUPHRATES]

Ge	2:14	And the fourth river is the **E**.	7310
	15:18	the river of Egypt to the great river, the **E**—	7310
Dt	1: 7	as far as the great river, the **E**.	7310
	11:24	and from the **E** River to the western sea.	7310
Jos	1: 4	and from the great river, the **E**—	7310
2Sa	8: 3	to restore his control along the **E** River.	7310
2Ki	23:29	to the **E** River to help the king of Assyria.	7310
	24: 7	from the Wadi of Egypt to the **E** River.	7310
1Ch	5: 9	of the desert that extends to the **E** River,	7310
	18: 3	to establish his control along the **E** River.	7310
2Ch	35:20	up to fight at Carchemish on the **E**,	7310
Isa	11:15	over the **E** River.	NIH
	27:12	the LORD will thresh from the flowing **E**	5643S
Jer	46: 2	on the **E** River by Nebuchadnezzar king	7310
	46: 6	In the north by the **E** they stumble	7310
	46:10	in the land of the north by the River **E**.	7310
	51:63	tie a stone to it and throw it into the **E**.	7310
Mic	7:12	from Egypt to the **E** and from sea to sea	5643S
Rev	9:14	at the great river **E**."	2371
	16:12	on the great river **E**,	2371

EUROCLYDON (KJV) NORTHEASTER

EUTYCHUS (1)

Ac	20: 9	in a window was a young man named **E**,	2366

EVANGELIST (2) [EVANGELISTS]

Ac	21: 8	and stayed at the house *of* Philip the **e**,	2296
2Ti	4: 5	endure hardship, do the work *of* an **e**,	2296

EVANGELISTS (1) [EVANGELIST]

Eph	4:11	some to be prophets, some to be **e**,	2296

EVE (4)

Ge	3:20	Adam named his wife **E**,	2558
	4: 1	Adam lay with his wife **E**,	2558
2Co	11: 3	But I am afraid that just as **E** was deceived	2293
1Ti	2:13	For Adam was formed first, then **E**.	2293

EVEN (565) [EVENLY]

Ge	8:21	because of man, **e** though every inclination	3954
	14:23	not **e** a thread or the thong of a sandal,	561
	24:41	be released from my oath **e** if they refuse	2256
	31:28	You didn't **e** let me kiss my grandchildren	2256
	31:50	**e** though no one is with us,	NIH
	39:10	he refused to go to bed with her or **e** be	NIH
	40:15	and **e** here I have done nothing	1685
	41:21	But **e** after they ate them,	2256
	44: 8	We **e** brought back to you from the land	2176
	48:14	**e** though Manasseh was the firstborn.	3954
Ex	1:10	or *they will become* **e** more **numerous** and,	AIT
	1:20	and became **e more** numerous.	4394
	2:19	He **e** drew water for us and watered	1685
	7:19	**e** in the wooden buckets and stone jars."	2256
	7:23	and did not take **e** this to heart.	1685
	8:21	and **e** the ground where they are.	1685
	9: 7	and found that not **e** one of the animals of	6330
	10:24	**E** your women and children may go	1685
	19:22	**E** the priests, who approach the LORD,	1685+2256
	33: 5	If I were to go with you **e** for a moment,	NIH
	34: 3	not **e** the flocks and herds may graze	1685
	34:21	**e** during the plowing season	NIH
Lev	4:13	**e though** the community is unaware of	2256
	5: 2	**e though** he is unaware of it,	2256
	5: 3	**e though** he is unaware of it,	2256
	5: 4	**e though** he is unaware of it,	2256
	5:17	**e though** he does not know it,	2256
	13:55	**e though** it has not spread, it is unclean.	2256
	18:25	**E** the land was defiled;	2256
	21:11	**e** for his father or mother,	NIH
	25:54	" '**E** if he is not redeemed in any	2256
	26:17	you will flee **e when** no one is pursuing you	2256

Lev	26:36	**e though** no one is pursuing them.	2256
	26:37	**e though** no one is pursuing them.	2256
Nu	4:20	**e for** a moment, or they will die."	3869
	5:14	or if he is jealous and suspects her **e though**	2256
	6: 4	not **e** the seeds or skins.	6330
	6: 7	**E** if his own father or mother or brother	2256
	13:28	We **e** saw descendants of Anak there.	1685+2256
	17:13	Anyone who **e comes near** the tabernacle of the LORD will die.	7929+7929
	22:18	"**E if** Balak gave me his palace filled	561
	24:13	'**E if** Balak gave me his palace filled	561
	32:14	making the LORD **e** more angry with Israel.	6388
Dt	1:28	We **e** saw the Anakites there.' "	1685
	2: 5	not **e enough** to put your foot on.	6330
	2:36	**e** as far as Gilead,	2256
	5:24	a man can live **e** if God speaks with him.	NIH
	7:20	among them until **e** the survivors who hide	2256
	10:14	**e** the highest heavens,	2256
	12:31	They **e** burn their sons and daughters	1685+3954
	18: 8	**e though** he has received money from	963+4200
	19: 6	and kill him **e though** he is not deserving	2256
	23: 2	**e** down to the tenth generation.	1685
	23: 3	**e** down to the tenth generation.	1685
	24: 6	not **e** the upper one—	2256
	28:30	but *you will not* **e** *begin to* **enjoy** its fruit.	AIT
	28:54	**E** the most gentle and sensitive man	NIH
	29:19	**e though** I persist in going my own way."	3954
	30: 4	**E if** you have been banished to	561
	31:21	**e** before I bring them into	NIH
	32:31	as **e** our enemies concede.	2256
	33:17	**e** those at the ends of the earth.	3481
Jos	22:17	**e though** a plague fell on the community of	2256
Jdg	2:19	to ways **e** more corrupt **than** those	4946
	3:22	**E** the handle sank in after the blade,	1685
	3:16	"**E though** you detain me,	561
	14:16	"I haven't **e** explained it to my father	2180
	15: 3	**have a right to get e**	5927
Ru	1:12	**E if** I thought there was still hope for me—	3954
	1:12	**e** if I had a husband tonight and	1685
	2:15	"**E if** she gathers among the sheaves,	1685
	2:21	Ruth the Moabitess said, "He **e** said to me,	3954
1Sa	2:15	But **e** before the fat was burned,	NIH
	12:12	**e though** the LORD your God was your king	2256
	13: 7	Some Hebrews **e** crossed the Jordan to	2256
	14:30	the slaughter of the Philistines have been **e**	3954
	14:39	**e** if it lies with my son Jonathan,	3954
	17:29	"Can't I **e** speak?"	NIH
	18: 4	and **e** his sword, his bow and his belt.	6330
	19:23	But the Spirit of God came **e** upon him,	1685
	20:15	from my family—not **e** when	2256
	21: 5	The men's things are holy **e** on missions	2256
	23:17	**E** my father Saul knows this."	1685+2256
	25:29	**E though** someone is pursuing you	2256
2Sa	5: 6	**e** the blind and the lame can ward you	561+3954
	6:22	I will become **e** more undignified than this,	6388
	12: 3	drank from his cup **and e** slept in his arms.	2256
	12: 8	*I would have* **given** *you* **e more.**	2179+2179+2256+3578+3869+3869
	17: 9	**E** now, he is hidden in a cave	2180
	17:10	Then **e** the bravest soldier,	1685
	17:13	to the valley until not **e** a piece of it can	1685
	18: 3	"**E** if half of us die, they won't care;	2256
	18:12	"**E** if a thousand shekels were weighed out	2256
	19:43	of Judah responded **e** more harshly **than**	4946
	23:19	**e though** he was not included among them.	2256
1Ki	1: 1	not keep warm **e when** they put covers	2256
	1:37	**make** his throne **e greater**	AIT
	1:42	**E** as he was speaking,	6388
	8:27	The heavens, **e** the highest heaven,	2256
	10: 7	Indeed, **not e** half was told me;	AIT
	12:11	I *will* **make** it **e heavier.**	3578
	12:14	I *will* **make** it **e heavier.**	3578
	12:30	the people went **e as far as** Dan to worship	6330
	12:31	**e though** they were not Levites.	889
	13: 8	"**E if** you were to give me half	561
	13:33	**E** after this, Jeroboam did not change	NIH
	14:14	Yes, **e** now.	1685
	14:24	There were **e** male shrine prostitutes in	1685+2256
	15:13	He **e** deposed his grandmother Maacah	1685+2256
	18:35	The water ran down around the altar and **e**	1685
	22:46	male shrine prostitutes who remained there **e after** the reign	928
2Ki	3:14	I would not look at you or **e** notice you.	2256
	5:16	And **e though** Naaman urged him,	2256
	7: 2	*e if* the LORD *should* **open**	AIT
	7:19	*e if* the LORD *should* **open**	AIT
	16: 3	of Israel and **e** sacrificed his son in the fire,	1685
	17:19	and **e** Judah did not keep the commands of	1685
	17:41	**E while** these people were worshiping	2256
	18:24	**e though** you are depending on Egypt	2256
	23:15	**E** the altar at Bethel,	1685+2256
	23:15	**e** that altar and high place he demolished.	1685
1Ch	10:13	of the LORD and consulted a medium	1685
	11: 2	In the past, **e while** Saul was king,	1685
	11:21	**e though** he was not included among them.	2256
2Ch	2: 6	**e** the highest heavens, cannot contain him?	2256
	6:18	The heavens, **e** the highest heavens,	2256
	9: 6	**not e** half the greatness	AIT
	10:11	I *will* **make** it **e heavier.**	3578
	10:14	I *will* **make** it **e heavier.**	3578
	11:14	The Levites **e** abandoned their pasturelands	3954
	16:12	**e** in his illness he did not seek help from the LORD,	1685+2256
	24: 7	of God and had used **e** its sacred objects for	1685
	25: 8	**E** if you go and fight courageously	3954
	28:22	King Ahaz became **e** more unfaithful	2256
	30:19	**e if** he is not clean according to the rules of	2256

Ezr	5:14	He **e** removed from the temple of Babylon	10059+10221
Ne	1: 9	then **e if** your exiled people are at	561
	4: 3	if **e** a fox climbed up on it,	561
	4:23	**e** when he went for water.	NIH
	6: 7	and have **e** appointed prophets	1685
	9: 6	**e** the highest heavens,	NIH
	9:18	**e** when they cast for themselves an image	677
	9:22	allotting to them **e** the remotest frontiers.	NIH
	9:35	**E while** they were in their kingdom,	2256
	13:26	**but e** he was led into sin	1685
Est	4:16	**e though** it is against the law.	889
	5: 3	**E** up to half the kingdom,	NIH
	5: 6	**E** up to half the kingdom,	NIH
	7: 2	**E** up to half the kingdom,	NIH
	7: 8	"Will he **e** molest the queen while she is	1685
Job	5: 5	taking it **e** from among thorns,	2256
	6:14	**e though** he forsakes the fear of	2256
	6:27	You would **e** cast lots for the fatherless	677
	7:14	**e then** you frighten me with dreams	2256
	7:19	or let me alone **e** for an instant?	NIH
	8: 6	**e** now he will rouse himself on your behalf	3954
	9:13	**e** the cohorts of Rahab cowered at his feet.	NIH
	9:16	**E if** I summoned him and he responded,	561
	9:20	**E if** I were innocent,	561
	9:30	**E if** I washed myself with soap	561
	9:31	so that **e** my clothes would detest me.	NIH
	10:15	**E if** I am innocent, I cannot lift my head,	2256
	10:22	where **e** the light is like darkness."	2256
	11: 6	God has **e** forgotten some of your sin.	3954
	15: 4	**But** you **e** undermine piety	677
	15:10	men **e older** than your father.	AIT
	15:15	if **e** the heavens are not pure in his eyes,	2256
	16:19	**E** now my witness is in heaven;	1685
	19:18	**E** the little boys scorn me;	1685
	21:22	since he judges **e** the highest?	NIH
	22: 2	Can a **e** wise man benefit him?	3954
	22:30	He will deliver **e** one who is not innocent,	NIH
	23: 2	"**E** today my complaint is bitter;	1685
	25: 5	If **e** the moon is not bright and the stars are	6330
	28:21	concealed **e** from the birds of the air.	2256
	33:29	twice, **e** three times—	NIH
	36:13	**e** when he fetters them,	3954
	36:19	Would your wealth **or e**	AIT
	36:33	**e** the cattle make known its approach.	677
Ps	9: 6	**e** the memory of them has perished.	NIH
	14: 3	there is no one who does good, not **e** one.	1685
	15: 4	who keeps his oath **e** when it hurts,	NIH
	16: 7	**e** at night my heart instructs me.	677
	22: 9	in you **e** at my mother's breast.	NIH
	23: 4	**E though** I walk through the valley of	1685
	27: 3	**e then** will I be confident.	NIH
	33:22	O LORD, **e as** we put our hope in you.	889+3869
	36: 4	**E** on his bed he plots evil;	NIH
	38:10	**e** the light has gone from my eyes.	2256
	39: 2	**not e** saying anything good,	AIT
	41: 9	**E** my close friend, whom I trusted,	1685
	48:14	he will be our guide **e** to the end.	NIH
	53: 3	there is no one who does good, not **e** one.	1685
	55:18	**e though** many oppose me.	3954
	58: 3	**E** from birth the wicked go astray;	NIH
	68:13	**E** while you sleep among the campfires,	2256
	68:18	**e** from the rebellious—	677+2256
	71:18	**E** when I am old and gray,	1685+2256
	78: 6	the children yet to be born,	NIH
	78:30	**e** while it was still in their mouths,	NIH
	83: 8	**E** Assyria has joined them to lend strength	1685
	84: 2	My soul yearns, **e** faints,	1685+2256
	84: 3	**E** the sparrow has found a home,	1685
	91: 9	**e** the LORD, who is my refuge—	NIH
	106: 6	We have sinned, **e as** our fathers did;	6640
	112: 4	**E** in darkness light dawns for the upright,	NIH
	133: 3	the LORD bestows his blessing, **e**	NIH
	139:10	**e** there your hand will guide me,	1685
	139:12	**e** the darkness will not be dark to you;	1685
Pr	11:24	One man gives freely, yet gains **e more;**	6388
	14:13	**E** in laughter the heart may ache,	1685
	14:20	The poor are shunned by their neighbors,	1685
	14:32	**but e** in death the righteous have a refuge.	2256
	14:33	in the heart of the discerning **and e**	2256
	16: 4	**e** the wicked for a day of disaster.	1685+2256
	16: 7	he makes **e** his enemies live at peace	1685
	17:28	**E** a fool is thought wise if he keeps silent,	1685
	19:24	he will not **e** bring it back to his mouth!	1685
	20:11	**E** a child is known by his actions,	1685
	22:19	I teach you today, **e** you.	677
	27: 7	to the hungry **e** what is bitter tastes sweet.	3972
	28: 9	**e** his prayers are detestable.	1685
Ecc	1:11	and **e** those who are yet to come will not	1685
	2:23	**e** at night his mind does not rest.	1685
	6: 6	**e** if he lives a thousand years twice over	2256
	8:17	**E** if a wise man claims he knows,	1685+2256
	9: 4	**e** a live dog is better off than a dead lion!	3954
	9: 5	**e** the memory of them is forgotten.	3954
	10: 3	**E** as he walks along the road,	1685+2256
	10:20	Do not revile the king **e** in your thoughts,	1685
Isa	1:15	**e** if you offer many prayers,	1685
	5:30	**e** the light will be darkened by the clouds.	2256
	14: 8	**E** the pine trees and the cedars	1685
	23:12	**e** there you will find no rest."	1685
	26:10	**e** in a land of uprightness they go	NIH
	32: 7	**e** when the plea of the needy is just.	2256
	33:23	and **e** the lame will carry off plunder.	NIH
	36: 9	**e though** you are depending on Egypt	2256
	40:30	**E** youths grow tired and weary,	2256
	43:11	I, **e** I, am the LORD.	NIH
	43:25	**e** I, am he who blots out your transgressions	NIH

Isa	44:19	I e baked bread over its coals,	677
	46: 4	E to your old age and gray hairs I am he,	2256
	47: 6	E on the aged you laid a very heavy yoke,	NIH
	47:14	They cannot e save themselves from	NIH
	48:15	I, e I, have spoken; yes, I have called him.	NIH
	51:12	"I, e I, am he who comforts you.	NIH
	56:12	or e far better."	3856+4394
	64:10	e Zion is a desert, Jerusalem a desolation.	NIH
Jer	2:33	E the worst of women can learn	1685
	4: 6	e terrible destruction."	2256
	5:18	"Yet e in those days," declares the LORD,	1685
	6: 1	For disaster looms out of the north,	2256
	6:15	they do not e know how to blush.	1685
	8: 7	E the stork in the sky knows	1685
	8:12	they do not e know how to blush.	2256
	9:26	and e the whole house	2256
	11:23	Not a remnant will be left to them,	2256
	12: 6	e they have betrayed you;	1685
	12:16	e as they once taught my people to swear by Baal—	889+3869
	14: 5	E the doe in the fields deserts her	1685+3954
	15: 1	"E if Moses and Samuel were to stand	561
	16: 7	not e for a father or a mother—	2256
	17: 2	E their children remember their altars	3869
	22:24	as I live," declares the LORD, "e if you,	3954
	23:11	e in my temple I find their wickedness,"	1685
	23:38	e though I told you that you must not claim,	2256
	27: 6	I will make e the wild animals subject	1685
	28:14	I will e give him control over	1685
	29:31	e though I did not send him,	2256
	34:15	You e made a covenant before me in	2256
	36:25	E though Elnathan, Delaiah	1685
	37:10	E if you were to defeat	3954
	38:15	E if I did give you counsel,	2256
	48:34	for e the waters of Nimrim are dried up.	1685
	49:37	e my fierce anger," declares the LORD.	NIH
	51:53	E if Babylon reaches the sky	3954
La	3: 8	E when I call out or cry for help,	1685
	4: 3	E jackals offer their breasts	1685
Eze	5: 7	You have not e conformed to the standards	2256
	8: 6	that are e more detestable."	1524
	8:13	that are e more detestable."	1524
	8:15	that are e more detestable than this."	1524
	14:14	e if these three men—	2256
	14:16	e if these three men were in it,	NIH
	14:18	e if these three men were in it,	2256
	14:20	declares the Sovereign LORD, e if Noah,	2256
	16:28	and e after that,	2256
	16:29	but e with this you were not satisfied.	1685+2256
	16:56	not e mention your sister Sodom in the day	2256
	16:57	E so, you are now scorned by the daughters	4017
	17:10	E if it is transplanted, will it thrive?	2256
	21:14	Let the sword strike twice, e three times.	NIH
	23:37	they e sacrificed their children,	1685+2256
	23:40	"They e sent messengers for	677+2256+3954
	24:12	not been removed, not e by fire.	NIH
	35:10	e though the LORD was there,	2256
	36:10	e the whole house of Israel.	NIH
	44: 9	and flesh is to enter my sanctuary, not e	3972
Da	2:41	e as you saw iron mixed with clay.	10168+10353+10619
	3:18	But e if he does not, we want you to know,	10213
	4:36	and became e greater than before.	NIH
	5: 9	King Belshazzar became e more terrified	10678
	9: 9	e though we have rebelled against him;	3954
	11: 5	one of his commanders will become e stronger than he	AIT
	11:15	e their best troops will not have the strength	2256
Hos	4:18	E when their drinks are gone,	NIH
	5: 5	the Israelites, e Ephraim,	2256
	9: 6	E if they escape from destruction,	2180
	9:12	E if they rear children,	3954
	9:16	E if they bear children,	1685
	10: 3	But e if we had a king,	NIH
	11: 7	E if they call to the Most High,	2256
	11:12	e against the faithful Holy One.	2256
	13:15	e though he thrives among his brothers.	3954
Joel	1:18	E the flocks of sheep are suffering.	1685
	1:20	E the wild animals pant for you;	1685
	2:12	"E now," declares the LORD,	1685+2256
	2:29	E on my servants, both men and women, I will pour out my Spirit	1685+2256
Am	1: 3	"For three sins of Damascus, e for four,	2256
	1: 6	"For three sins of Gaza, e for four,	2256
	1: 9	"For three sins of Tyre, e for four,	2256
	1:11	"For three sins of Edom, e for four,	2256
	1:13	"For three sins of Ammon, e for four,	2256
	2: 1	"For three sins of Moab, e for four,	2256
	2: 4	"For three sins of Judah, e for four,	2256
	2: 6	"For three sins of Israel, e for four,	2256
	2:16	E the bravest warriors will flee naked on	2256
	5:22	E though you bring me burnt offerings	3954
	8: 6	selling e the sweepings with the wheat.	2256
Jnh	1:13	for the sea grew e wilder than before.	2143+2256+6192
Mic	1: 9	e to Jerusalem itself.	NIH
	1:12	e to the gate of Jerusalem.	NIH
	5: 5	e eight leaders of men.	2256
	5: 5	E with her who lies in your embrace	NIH
	7:10	e now she will be trampled underfoot	NIH
	7:12	e from Egypt to the Euphrates and from sea	2256
Hab	1: 5	e if you were told.	3954
Zec	9:12	e now I announce that I will restore twice	1685
Mal	1: 5	e beyond the borders of Israel!"	4946+6584
	2:12	e though he brings offerings to	2256
	3:15	and e those who challenge God escape.' "	1685

Mt	5:36	you cannot make e one hair white or black.	NIG
	5:46	Are not e the tax collectors doing that?	2779
	5:47	Do not e pagans do that?	2779
	6:29	Yet I tell you that not e Solomon	4028
	8:27	E the winds and the waves obey him!"	2779
	10:30	And e the very hairs of your head are all numbered.	2779
	10:42	if anyone gives e a cup of cold water to one	3668
	13:12	e what he has will be taken from him.	2779
	15:27	"but e the dogs eat the crumbs that fall	2779
	18:17	and if he refuses to listen e to the church,	2779
	21:32	And e after you saw this,	NIG
	24:24	and miracles to deceive e the elect—	2779
	24:27	that comes from the east is visible e in	2401
	24:33	E so, when you see all these things,	2779
	24:36	not e the angels in heaven, nor the Son,	4028
	25:29	e what he has will be taken from him.	2779
	26:33	"E if all fall away on account of you,	NIG
	26:35	Peter declared, "E if I have to die with you,	2779
	27:14	not e to a single charge."	4028
Mk	1:27	He e gives orders to evil spirits	2779
	2: 2	not e outside the door,	3593
	2:28	the Son of Man is Lord e of the Sabbath."	2779
	3:20	he and his disciples were not e able to eat.	3593
	4: 8	sixty, or e a hundred times."	2779
	4:20	sixty or e a hundred times what was sown."	2779
	4:24	measured to you—and e more.	2779+4707+5148
	4:25	e what he has will be taken from him.	2779
	4:41	E the wind and the waves obey him!"	2779
	5: 3	not e with a chain.	4028
	6: 2	that he e does miracles!	2779
	6:31	and going that they did not e have a chance	2779
	6:56	let them touch e the edge of his cloak,	1569+2779
	7:28	"but e the dogs under the table eat	2779
	7:37	"He e makes the deaf hear and	2779
	10:26	The disciples were e more amazed,	4360
	10:45	For e the Son of Man did not come to	2779
	13:29	E so, you see when these things happening,	2779
	13:32	not e the angels in heaven, nor the Son,	4028
	14:29	Peter declared, "E if all fall away,	2779
	14:31	"E if I have to die with you,	NIG
	14:59	Yet e then their testimony did not agree.	2779
Lk	1:15	and he will be filled with the Holy Spirit e	2285
	1:36	E Elizabeth your relative is going to have	2779
	1:55	e as he said to our fathers."	2777
	6:32	E 'sinners' love those who love them.	2779
	6:33	E 'sinners' do that.	2779
	6:34	E 'sinners' lend to 'sinners,'	2779
	7: 7	not e consider myself worthy to come	NIG
	7: 9	not found such great faith e in Israel."	NIG
	7:29	(All the people, e the tax collectors,	2779
	7:49	"Who is this who e forgives sins?"	2779
	8:18	not have, e what he thinks he has will	2779
	8:25	He commands e the winds and the water,	2779
	9:42	E while the boy was coming,	2285
	10:11	'E the dust of your town that sticks	2779
	10:17	e the demons submit to us in your name."	2779
	12:27	Yet I tell you, not e Solomon	4028
	12:38	e if he comes in the second or third watch	2779
	14:26	yes, e his own life—	2779
	15:29	Yet you never gave me e	2779
	16:21	E the dogs came and licked his sores.	2779
	16:31	they will not be convinced e	4028
	18: 4	'E though I don't fear God or care	2779
	18:11	or e like this tax collector.	2779
	18:13	He would not e look up to heaven,	4024+4028
	19:26	e what he has will be taken away.	2779
	19:42	e you, had only known	2779
	20:37	e Moses showed that the dead rise,	2779
	21:16	You will be betrayed by parents, brothers,	2779
	21:31	E so, when you see these things happening,	2779
	23:35	and the rulers e sneered at him.	2779
Jn	4:36	E now the reaper draws his wages,	2453
	4:36	e now he harvests the crop for eternal life,	2779
	5:18	but he was e calling God his own Father,	2779
	5:20	to your amazement he will show him e	2779
	5:21	e so the Son gives life to whom	2779
	7: 5	e his own brothers did not believe in him.	4028
	8:14	"E if I testify on my own behalf,	2779
	8:30	E as he spoke, many put their faith in him.	AIT
	9:29	we don't e know where he comes from."	NIG
	10:38	if I do it, e though you do not believe me,	2779
	11:22	But I know that e now God will give you	2779
	11:25	believes in me will live, e though he dies;	2779
	12:37	E after Jesus had done all these miraculous signs in their presence,	1254
	12:42	Yet at the same time many e among	2779
	14: 9	e after I have been among you such	2779
	14:12	He will do e greater things than these,	2779
	15: 2	so that it will be e more fruitful.	NIG
	16:30	and that you do not e need	NIG
	17:16	not of the world, e as I am not of it.	2777
	17:23	that you sent me and have loved them e as	2777
	19: 8	he was e more afraid,	NIG
	21:11	but e with so many the net was not torn.	2779
	21:25	e the whole world would not	4028
Ac	2:18	E on my servants, both men and women,	2779
	3:20	who has been appointed for you—e Jesus.	NIG
	5:13	e though they were highly regarded,	247
	7: 5	not e a foot of ground.	4028
	7: 5	e though at that time Abraham had no child.	NIG
	7:52	They e killed those who predicted	2779
	10:45	of the Holy Spirit had been poured out e on	2779
	11:18	God has granted e the Gentiles repentance	2779
	13:41	e if someone told you.' "	NIG
	14:18	E with these words,	2779
	16:37	e though we are Roman citizens,	AIT

Ac	17:23	I e found an altar with this inscription:	2779
	19: 2	we have not e heard that there is	4028
	19:12	so that e handkerchiefs and aprons	2779
	19:31	E some of the officials of the province,	2779
	19:32	not e know why they were there.	NIG
	20:30	E from your own number men will arise	2779
	22: 5	I e obtained letters from them	2779
	22:25	to flog a Roman citizen who hasn't e	2779
	24: 6	and e tried to desecrate the temple;	2779
	26:11	I e went to foreign cities to persecute them.	2779
	28:23	and came in e larger numbers to the place	NIG
Ro	1:26	E their women exchanged natural relations	5445
	2:14	e though they do not have	AIT
	2:15	now e defending them.)	2779
	2:27	e though you have the written code	NIG
	3:10	"There is no one righteous, not e one;	4028
	3:12	there is no one who does good, not e one."	2401
	5:14	e over those who did not sin by breaking	2779
	7: 3	e though she marries another man.	AIT
	9:24	e us, whom he also called, not only from	2779
	15: 3	For e Christ did not please himself but,	2779
1Co	2:10	e the deep things of God.	2779
	4: 3	indeed, I do not e judge myself.	4028
	4:15	E though you have ten thousand guardians	1142+1569
	5: 1	a kind that does not occur e among pagans:	4028
	5: 3	E though I am not physically present,	1142+3525
	5:11	With such a man do not e eat.	3593
	6: 4	appoint as judges e men of little account in	NIG
	7:38	he who does not marry her does e better.	NIG
	8: 5	For e if there are so-called gods,	2779
	9: 2	E though I may not be an apostle to others,	1623
	10:33	e as I try to please everybody in every way.	2777
	13:12	I shall know fully, e as I am fully known.	2779
	14: 7	E in the case of lifeless things	3940
	14:21	but e then they will not listen to me,"	2779
	15: 9	and do not e deserve to be called an apostle,	NIG
	15:13	then not e Christ has been raised.	4028
	16: 6	or e spend the winter,	2779
2Co	1: 8	so that we despaired of life.	2779
	1: 8	will not the ministry of the Spirit be e	4802
	3:15	E to this day when Moses is read,	247
	4: 3	And e if our gospel is veiled,	2779
	7: 8	E if I caused you sorrow by my letter,	2779
	7:12	So e though I wrote to you,	2779
	8: 3	and e beyond their ability.	2779
	8:22	and now e more so because	4498+5080S
	10: 8	For e if I boast somewhat freely about	5445
	10:13	a field that reaches e to you.	2779
	11:20	you e put up with anyone who enslaves you	NIG
	12: 6	E if I should choose to boast,	1569
	12:11	e though I am nothing.	2779
	13: 7	the test but that you will do what is right e	1254
Gal	1: 8	But e if we or an angel from heaven	2779
	2: 3	Yet not e Titus, who was with me,	4028
	2: 3	e though he was a Greek.	AIT
	2:13	so that by their hypocrisy e	2779
	4:14	E though my illness was a trial to you,	2779
	6:13	Not e those who are circumcised obey	4028
	6:16	e to the Israel of God.	2779
Eph	1:10	on earth together under one head, e Christ.	NIG
	2: 5	with Christ e when we were dead	2779
	5: 3	But among you there must not be e a hint	3593
	5:12	For it is shameful e to mention what	2779
Php	2: 8	e death on a cross!	1254
	2:17	But e if I am being poured out like	2779
	3:18	before and now say again with tears,	2779
	4:16	for e when I was in Thessalonica,	2779
	4:18	I have received full payment and e more;	NIG
2Th	2: 9	For e when we were with you,	2779
1Ti	1:13	E though I was once a blasphemer and	AIT
	5: 6	for pleasure is dead e while she lives.	AIT
	5:25	and e those that are not cannot be hidden.	2779
	6: 2	Instead, they are to serve them e better,	NIG
2Ti	2: 9	e to the point of being chained	3588
Tit	1:12	E one of their own prophets has said,	NIG
Phm	1:16	He is very dear to me but e dearer to you,	NIG
	1:16	knowing that you will do e more than I ask.	2779
Heb	4:12	it penetrates e to dividing soul and spirit,	948
	6: 9	E though we speak like this, dear friends,	2779
	7: 4	E the patriarch Abraham gave him a tenth	NIG
	7: 5	e though their brothers are descended	2788
	7: 9	One might e say that Levi,	2229+3306+6055
	7:15	And what we have said is e more clear	2285
	9:18	This is why e the first covenant was not put	NIG
	11: 4	e though he is dead.	AIT
	11: 8	e though he did not know	AIT
	11:11	e though he was past age—	2779
	11:18	e though God had said to him,	NIG
	12:20	"If e an animal touches the mountain,	2779
Jas	1:11	the rich man will fade away e while he goes	NIG
	2:19	E the demons believe that—and shudder.	2779
	2:25	was not e Rahab the prostitute	2779
	4:14	not e know what will happen tomorrow.	NIG
1Pe	1: 7	which perishes e though refined by fire—	1254
	1: 8	e though you do not see	AIT
	1:12	E angels long to look into these things.	NIG
	3:14	But e if you should suffer for what is right,	2779
	4: 6	the gospel was preached e to those who are	2779
	4:15	or e as a meddler.	NIG
2Pe	1: 2	e though you know them	2788
	2: 1	They will secretly introduce destructive heresies, e denying the sovereign Lord	2779
	2:11	yet e angels, although they are stronger	3963
1Jn	2:18	e now many antichrists have come.	2779
	2:25	this is what he promised us—e eternal life.	NIG
	4: 3	which you have heard is coming and e	2779

1Jn	5: 4	the victory that has overcome the world, **e**	NIG
	5:20	**e** in his Son Jesus Christ.	NIG
3Jn	1: 2	**e as** your soul is getting along well.	2777
	1: 5	**e though** they are strangers to you.	2779
	1:12	**and e** by the truth itself.	2779
Jude	1: 9	But **e** the archangel Michael,	NIG
	1:23	hating **e** the clothing stained by corrupted	2779
Rev	1: 7	**e** those who pierced him;	2779
	2:10	**e to the point of** death,	948
	2:13	**e** in the days of Antipas,	2779
	4: 8	eyes all around, **e** under his wings.	2779
	5: 3	could open the scroll **or e** look inside it.	4046
	13:13	**e** causing fire to come down from heaven	2779

EVEN-TEMPERED (1) [TEMPER]

Pr	17:27	and a man of understanding is **e**.	7922+8120

EVENING (142) [EVENINGS]

Ge	1: 5	And there was **e**, and there was morning—	6847
	1: 8	And there was **e**, and there was morning—	6847
	1:13	And there was **e**, and there was morning—	6847
	1:19	And there was **e**, and there was morning—	6847
	1:23	And there was **e**, and there was morning—	6847
	1:31	And there was **e**, and there was morning—	6847
	8:11	When the dove returned to him in the **e**,	6847
	19: 1	The two angels arrived at Sodom in the **e**,	6847
	24:11	it was toward **e**,	6847
	24:63	He went out to the field one **e** to meditate,	6847
	29:23	But when **e** came,	6847
	30:16	when Jacob came in from the fields that **e**,	6847
	49:27	in the **e** he divides the plunder."	6847
Ex	12:18	the **e** of the fourteenth day until the evening	6847
	12:18	the evening of the fourteenth day until the **e**	6847
	16: 6	"*In the* **e** you will know that it was	6847
	16: 8	to eat in the **e** and all the bread you want in	6847
	16:13	That **e** quail came and covered the camp,	6847
	18:13	they stood around him from morning till **e**.	6847
	18:14	around you from morning till **e**?"	6847
	27:21	before the LORD from **e** till morning.	6847
Lev	6:20	half of it in the morning and half in the **e**.	6847
	11:24	be unclean till **e**.	6847
	11:25	and he will be unclean till **e**.	6847
	11:27	be unclean till **e**.	6847
	11:28	and he will be unclean till **e**.	6847
	11:31	will be unclean till **e**.	6847
	11:32	Put it in water; it will be unclean till **e**,	6847
	11:39	the carcass will be unclean till **e**.	6847
	11:40	and he will be unclean till **e**.	6847
	11:40	and he will be unclean till **e**.	6847
	14:46	while it is closed up will be unclean till **e**.	6847
	15: 5	and he will be unclean till **e**.	6847
	15: 6	and he will be unclean till **e**.	6847
	15: 7	and he will be unclean till **e**.	6847
	15: 8	and he will be unclean till **e**.	6847
	15:10	that were under him will be unclean till **e**;	6847
	15:10	and he will be unclean till **e**.	6847
	15:11	and he will be unclean till **e**.	6847
	15:16	and he will be unclean till **e**.	6847
	15:17	and it will be unclean till **e**.	6847
	15:18	and they will be unclean till **e**.	6847
	15:19	be unclean till **e**.	6847
	15:21	and he will be unclean till **e**.	6847
	15:22	and he will be unclean till **e**.	6847
	15:23	he will be unclean till **e**.	6847
	15:27	and he will be unclean till **e**.	6847
	17:15	and he will be ceremonially unclean till **e**;	6847
	22: 6	be unclean till **e**.	6847
	23:32	From the **e** of the ninth day of the month	6847
	23:32	of the month until the following **e** you are	6847
	24: 3	to tend the lamps before the LORD from **e**	6847
Nu	9:15	From **e** till morning the cloud above	6847
	9:21	the cloud stayed only from **e** till morning,	6847
	19: 7	but he will be ceremonially unclean till **e**.	6847
	19: 8	and he too will be unclean till **e**.	6847
	19:10	and he will be unclean till **e**.	6847
	19:19	and that **e** he will be clean.	6847
	19:21	the water of cleansing will be unclean till **e**.	6847
	19:22	who touches it becomes unclean till **e**."	6847
Dt	16: 4	the **e** of the first day remain until morning.	6847
	16: 6	the Passover in the **e**,	6847
	23:11	But as **e** approaches he is to wash himself,	6847
	28:67	"If only it were **e**!"	6847
	28:67	and in the **e**, "If only it were morning!"—	6847
Jos	5:10	On the **e** of the fourteenth day of the month,	6847
	7: 6	remaining there till **e**.	6847
	8:29	a tree and left him there until **e**.	2021+6847+6961
	10:26	they were left hanging on the trees until **e**.	6847
Jdg	19: 9	said, "Now look, it's almost **e**.	6845
	19:16	That **e** an old man from the hill country	6847
	20:23	up and wept before the LORD until **e**,	6847
	20:26	until **e** and presented burnt offerings	6847
	21: 2	where they sat before God until **e**,	6847
Ru	2:17	So Ruth gleaned in the field until **e**.	6847
1Sa	14:24	be any man who eats food before **e** comes,	6847
	17:16	and **e** and took his stand.	6845
	20: 5	and hide in the field until the **e** of the day	6847
	20:19	The day after tomorrow, **toward e**,	3718+4394
	30:17	David fought them from dusk until the **e** of	6847
2Sa	1:12	They mourned and wept and fasted till **e**	6847
	11: 2	One **e** David got up from his bed	6847
	11:13	in the **e** Uriah went out to sleep on his mat	6847
1Ki	17: 6	in the morning and bread and meat in the **e**,	6847
	18:29	until the time for the **e sacrifice**.	4966+6590
	22:35	and that **e** he died.	6847
2Ki	16:15	and the **e** grain offering.	6847

1Ch	16:40	of burnt offering regularly, morning and **e**,	6847
	23:30	They were to do the same in the **e**	6847
2Ch	2: 4	and **e** and on Sabbaths and New Moons and	6847
	13:11	and **e** they present burnt offerings	928+928+2021+2021+6847+6847
	13:11	the lamps on the gold lampstand **every e**.	928+928+2021+2021+6847+6847
	18:34	in his chariot facing the Arameans until **e**.	6847
Ezr	3: 3	burnt offerings and for both the morning and **e** sacrifices.	6847
	9: 4	I sat there appalled until the **e** sacrifice.	6847
	9: 5	Then, at the **e** sacrifice,	6847
Ne	13:19	When **e shadows** fell *on* the gates	7511
Est	2:14	In the **e** she would go there and in	6847
Job	7: 2	Like a slave longing for the **e shadows**,	7498
Ps	55:17	**E**, morning and noon I cry out in distress,	6847
	59: 6	They return at **e**,	6847
	59:14	They return at **e**,	6847
	65: 8	and **e** fades you call forth songs of joy.	6847
	90: 6	by **e** it is dry and withered.	6847
	102:11	My days are like the **e** shadow;	5742
	104:23	to his labor until **e**.	6847
	109:23	I fade away like an **e** shadow;	5742
	141: 2	up of my hands be like the **e** sacrifice.	6847
Ecc	11: 6	and at **e** let not your hands be idle,	6847
Isa	17:14	In the **e**, sudden terror!	6847
Jer	6: 4	and the shadows of **e** grow long.	6847
Eze	12: 4	Then in the **e**, while they are watching,	6847
	12: 7	the **e** I dug through the wall with my hands.	6847
	24:18	and in the **e** my wife died.	6847
	33:22	Now the **e** before the man arrived,	6847
	46: 2	but the gate will not be shut until **e**.	6847
Da	9:21	about the time of the **e** sacrifice.	6847
Zep	2: 7	In the **e** they will lie down in the houses	6847
	3: 3	her rulers are **e** wolves,	6847
Zec	14: 7	When **e** comes, there will be light.	6847
Mt	8:16	When **e** came, many who were demon-possessed were brought to him,	4070
	14:15	As **e** approached, the disciples came to him	4070
	14:23	When **e** came, he was there alone,	4070
	16: 2	He replied, "When **e** comes, you say,	4070
	20: 8	"When **e** came, the owner of	4070
	26:20	When **e** came, Jesus was reclining at	4070
	27:57	As **e** approached, there came a rich man	4070
Mk	1:32	That **e** after sunset the people brought	1181+4070
	4:35	That day when **e** came,	4070
	6:47	When **e** came, the boat was in the middle of	4070
	11:19	When **e** came, they went out of the city.	4067
	13:35	whether **in the e**, or at midnight,	4067
	14:17	When **e** came, Jesus arrived with	4070
	15:42	So as **e** approached,	4070
Lk	21:37	and **each e** he went out to spend the night on the hill	3816+3836
	24:29	for it is nearly **e**; the day is almost over."	2270
Jn	6:16	When **e** came, his disciples went down to	4070
	13: 2	The **e meal** was being served,	4070
	20:19	On the **e** of that first day of the week,	1639+4070
Ac	4: 3	and because it was **e**,	2270
	28:23	till **e** he explained and declared to them	2270

EVENINGS (2) [EVENING]

Da	8:14	"It will take 2,300 **e** and mornings;	6847
	8:26	"The vision of the **e** and mornings	6847

EVENLY (1) [EVEN]

1Ki	6:35	and overlaid them with gold **hammered e** over the carvings.	3837

EVENT (KJV) DESTINY, FATE

EVENTS (56)

1Ki	11:41	As for the other **e** *of* Solomon's reign—	1821
	12:15	for this **turn of e** was from the LORD,	6016
	14:19	The other **e** *of* Jeroboam's reign,	1821
	14:29	As for the other **e** *of* Rehoboam's reign,	1821
	15: 7	As for the other **e** *of* Abijah's reign,	1821
	15:23	As for all the other **e** *of* Asa's reign,	1821
	15:31	As for the other **e** *of* Nadab's reign,	1821
	16: 5	As for the other **e** *of* Baasha's reign,	1821
	16:14	As for the other **e** *of* Elah's reign,	1821
	16:20	As for the other **e** *of* Zimri's reign,	1821
	16:27	As for the other **e** *of* Omri's reign,	1821
	22:39	As for the other **e** *of* Ahab's reign,	1821
	22:45	As for the other **e** *of* Jehoshaphat's reign,	1821
2Ki	1:18	As for all the other **e** *of* Ahaziah's reign,	1821
	8:23	As for the other **e** *of* Jehoram's reign,	1821
	10:34	As for the other **e** *of* Jehu's reign,	1821
	12:19	As for the other **e** *of* the reign of Joash,	1821
	13: 8	As for the other **e** *of* the reign of Jehoahaz,	1821
	13:12	As for the other **e** *of* the reign of Jehoash,	1821
	14:15	As for the other **e** *of* the reign of Jehoash,	1821
	14:18	As for the other **e** *of* Amaziah's reign,	1821
	14:28	As for the other **e** *of* Jeroboam's reign,	1821
	15: 6	As for the other **e** *of* Azariah's reign,	1821
	15:11	The other **e** *of* Zechariah's reign are written	1821
	15:15	The other **e** *of* Shallum's reign,	1821
	15:21	As for the other **e** *of* Menahem's reign,	1821
	15:26	The other **e** *of* Pekahiah's reign,	1821
	15:31	As for the other **e** *of* Pekah's reign,	1821
	15:36	As for the other **e** *of* Jotham's reign,	1821
	16:19	As for the other **e** *of* the reign of Ahaz,	1821
	20:20	As for the other **e** *of* Hezekiah's reign,	1821
	21:17	As for the other **e** *of* Manasseh's reign,	1821
	21:25	As for the other **e** *of* Amon's reign,	1821

2Ki	23:28	As for the other **e** *of* Josiah's reign,	1821
	24: 5	As for the other **e** *of* Jehoiakim's reign,	1821
1Ch	29:29	As for the **e** *of* King David's reign,	1821
2Ch	9:29	As for the other **e** *of* Solomon's reign,	1821
	10:15	for this **turn of e** was from God,	5813
	12:15	As for the other **e** *of* Rehoboam's reign,	1821
	13:22	The other **e** *of* Abijah's reign,	1821
	16:11	The **e** *of* Asa's reign,	1821
	20:34	The other **e** *of* Jehoshaphat's reign,	1821
	25:26	As for the other **e** *of* Amaziah's reign,	1821
	26:22	The other **e** *of* Uzziah's reign,	1821
	27: 7	The other **e** *in* Jotham's reign,	1821
	28:26	The other **e** *of* his reign and all his ways,	1821
	32:32	The other **e** *of* Hezekiah's reign	1821
	33:18	The other **e** *of* Manasseh's reign,	1821
	35:26	The other **e** *of* Josiah's reign and his acts	1821
	35:27	all the **e**, from beginning to end, are written	1821
	36: 8	The other **e** *of* Jehoiakim's reign,	1821
Est	3: 1	After these **e**, King Xerxes honored Haman	1821
	9:20	Mordecai recorded these **e**,	1821
Lk	21:11	**fearful e** and great signs from heaven.	5831
Ac	5:11	and all who heard about these **e**.	AIT
	19:40	with rioting because of today's **e**.	NIG

EVENTUALLY (1)

Lk	18: 5	so that she won't **e** wear me out	1650+5465

EVER (248) [EVERLASTING, FOREVER, FOREVERMORE]

Ge	24:16	no man had **e lain** with her.	AIT
Ex	5:23	**E since** I went to Pharaoh to speak	255+4946
	9:18	the worst hailstorm that has **e** fallen	4202
	10: 6	nor your forefathers have **e** seen from	AIT
	10:14	nor *will* there **e** be again.	AIT
	11: 6	worse than *there has* **e** been or ever will	AIT
	11: 6	or **e** will be **again**.	AIT
	15:18	The LORD will reign for **e** and ever."	6409
	15:18	The LORD will reign for **e** and ever."	6329
Nu	11:20	saying, "Why *did we* **e** leave Egypt?" '"	AIT
	14:23	of them *will* **e** see the land I promised	AIT
	14:23	with contempt *will* **e** see it.	AIT
	35:26	if the accused **e** goes outside the limits	3655+3655
Dt	4:32	*Has* anything so great as this **e** happened,	AIT
	4:32	or *has* anything like it **e** been heard of?	AIT
	4:34	*Has* any god **e** tried to take for himself	AIT
	5:26	For what mortal man has **e** heard the voice	3972
	8:19	If *you* **e** forget the LORD your God	8894+8894
	9:24	the LORD **e since** I have known you.	3427+4946
	34:12	For no one has **e** shown the mighty power	NIH
Jos	7: 7	**e bring** this people **across**	AIT
	7:26	called the Valley of Achor **e since**.	2021+2021+2296+3427+6330
	14:14	belonged to Caleb son of Jephunneh the Kenizzite **e since**,	2021+2021+2296+3427+6330
	22:28	"And we said, 'If they **e** say this to us,	4737
Jdg	11:25	*Did he* **e quarrel** with Israel or fight	AIT
	16:17	"No razor *has e been* **used** on my head,"	AIT
Ru	1:17	LORD deal with me, be it **e** so severely,	3907
1Sa	1:11	and no razor *will e be* **used** on his head."	3907
	3:17	May God deal with you, be it **e** so severely,	3907
	14:44	"May God deal with me, be it **e** so severely,	3907
	20:13	LORD deal with me, be it **e** so severely,	3907
	20:15	and do not **e** cut off your kindness	6330+6409
	25:22	God deal with David, be it **e** so severely,	3907
	27: 6	belonged to the kings of Judah **e since**.	2021+2021+2296+3427+6330
2Sa	3: 9	God deal with Abner, be it **e** so severely,	3907
	3:35	"May God deal with me, be it **e** so severely,	3907
	6: 9	*can* the ark of the LORD **e** come to me?"	AIT
	7: 7	*did I* **e** say of their rulers	1819+1821
	7:11	and have done **e since**	4946
	13:32	This has been Absalom's expressed intention **e since**	4946
	19:13	May God deal with me, be it **e** so severely,	3907
1Ki	2:23	"May God deal with me, be it **e** so severely,	3907
	3:12	nor will there **e** be.	339
	10:20	Nothing like it *had* **e been made**	AIT
	12: 9	the gods deal with me, be it **e** so severely,	3907
	20:10	the gods deal with me, be it **e** so severely,	3907
	22:28	Micaiah declared, "If *you* **e** return safely,	8740+8740
2Ki	6:31	"May God deal with me, be it **e** so severely,	3907
1Ch	13:12	god of any nation **e** delivered his land	5911+5911
	13:12	"How can *I* **e bring** the ark of God to me?"	AIT
	17: 6	*did I* **e** say to any of their leaders	AIT
	17:10	and have done **e since**	4946
	29:25	as no king over Israel **e** had before.	3972
2Ch	1:12	such as no king who was before you **e had**	AIT
	9:11	like them had **e been** seen in Judah.)	4200+7156
	9:19	Nothing like it *had* **e been made**	AIT
	18:27	Micaiah declared, "If *you* **e** return safely,	8740+8740
	32:13	the gods of those nations **e able** to deliver their land	3523+3523
	35:18	of the kings of Israel *had* **e celebrated** such	AIT
Ne	13:1	that no Ammonite or Moabite should **e**	6330+6409
Job	4: 7	Who, being innocent, *has* **e perished**?	AIT
	4: 7	were the upright **e destroyed**?	AIT
	6:22	Have I said, 'Give something	3954
	15: 7	"Are you the **first** man **e** born?	AIT
	20: 4	**e since** man was placed on the earth,	4974
	29:20	the bow **e** new in my hand.'	AIT
	38:12	"Have you **e** given orders to the morning,	3427+4946
Ps	5:11	let them **e** sing for joy.	4200+6409

Ps
9: 5 you have blotted out their name for e 6409
9: 5 blotted out their name for ever and e. 6329
9:18 nor the hope of the afflicted e perish. 4200+6329
10:16 The LORD is King for e and ever; 6409
10:16 The LORD is King for ever and e; 6329
21: 4 length of days, for e and ever. 6409
21: 4 length of days, for ever and e. 6329
25: 3 No one whose hope is in you will e be put 1685
25:15 My eyes are e on the LORD, 9458
26: 3 for your love is e before me, NIH
38:17 and my pain is e with me. 9458
45: 6 O God, will last for e and ever; 6409
45: 6 O God, will last for ever and e; 6329
45:17 the nations will praise you for e and ever. 6409
45:17 the nations will praise you for ever and e. 6329
48:14 For this God is our God for e and ever; 6409
48:14 For this God is our God for ever and e; 6329
49: 8 no payment is e enough— 4200+6409
50: 8 which are e before me. 9458
52: 8 in God's unfailing love for e and ever. 6409
52: 8 in God's unfailing love for ever and e. 6329
61: 8 Then will I e sing praise to your name 4200+6329
71: 6 I will e praise you. 9458
72:15 May people e pray for him 9458
74:15 you dried up the e flowing rivers. 419
83:17 May they e be ashamed and dismayed; 6329+6330
84: 4 they are e praising you. 6388
89:33 nor will I e betray my faithfulness. AIT
111: 8 They are steadfast for e and ever, 6329
111: 8 They are steadfast for ever and e, 4200+6409
119:44 I will always obey your law, for e and ever. 6409
119:44 I will always obey your law, for ever and e. 6329
119:98 for they are e with me. 4200+6409
132:12 on your throne for e and ever." 6329
132:12 on your throne for ever and e." 6329
132:14 "This is my resting place for e and ever; 6329
132:14 "This is my resting place for ever and e; 6329
132:16 and her saints will e sing for joy. 8264+8264
141: 5 Yet my prayer is e against the deeds 6388
145: 1 I will praise your name for e and ever. 6409
145: 1 I will praise your name for ever and e. 6329
145: 2 and extol your name for e and ever. 6409
145: 2 and extol your name for ever and e. 6329
145:21 praise his holy name for e and ever. 6409
145:21 praise his holy name for ever and e. 6329
148: 6 He set them in place for e and ever; 6329
148: 6 He set them in place for ever and e; 4200+6409

Pr
4:18 shining e brighter till the full light of day.
239+2143+2256
5:19 may you e be captivated by her love. 9458
30:13 those whose eyes are e so haughty, 4537

Ecc
1: 6 e returning on its course. AIT

Isa
6: 9 Be e hearing, but never understanding 9048+9048
6: 9 be e seeing, but never perceiving." 8011+8011
34:10 e pass through it again. 4200+5905+5905
36:18 the god of any nation e delivered his land AIT
49:16 your walls are e before me. 9458
59:12 Our offenses are e with us, NIH
66: 8 Who has e heard of such a thing? AIT
66: 8 Who has e seen such things? AIT

Jer
2:10 see if there has e been anything like this: AIT
2:11 Has a nation e changed its gods? AIT
6: 7 her sickness and wounds are e before me. 9458
7: 7 in the land I gave your forefathers for e 4946+6409
7: 7 for ever and e. 6330+6409
18:13 Who has e heard anything like this? AIT
18:14 of Lebanon e vanish from its rocky slopes? AIT
18:14 from distant sources e cease to flow? AIT
19: 4 nor the kings of Judah e knew, AIT
20:18 Why did I e come out of the womb AIT
25: 5 to you and your fathers for e and ever. 4946+6409
25: 5 to you and your fathers for ever and e. 6330+6409
31:36 "will the descendants of Israel e cease to be
a nation before me." 2021+3427+3972
33:18 e fail to have a man to stand AIT
35: 6 your descendants must e drink wine. 6330+6409
35: 8 and daughters have e drunk wine 3427+3972
44: 3 nor you nor your fathers e knew, AIT
44:18 But e since we stopped burning incense 255+4946
44:18 in Egypt will e again invoke my name 6388

La
2:20 Whom have you e treated like this? AIT

Eze
4:14 No unclean meat has e entered my mouth." AIT
15: 3 Is wood e taken from it AIT
16:16 nor should they e occur. AIT
27:32 "Who was e silenced like Tyre, NIH
31:14 the waters are e to tower proudly on high, AIT
31:14 so well-watered are e to reach such AIT

Da
2:10 has e asked such a thing of any magician AIT
2:20 to the name of God for e and ever; 10002+10550
2:20 name of God for ever and e; 10002+10527+10550
6:22 Nor have I e done any wrong before you, AIT
7:18 yes, for e and ever.' 10550
7:18 yes, for ever and e.' 10002+10550
9:12 the whole heaven nothing has e been done AIT
12: 3 like the stars for e and ever. 6409
12: 3 like the stars for ever and e. 6329

Joel
1: 2 like this e happened in your days or in AIT
2: 2 as never was of old nor e will be in ages 3578

Mic
4: 5 in the name of the LORD our God for e 6409
4: 5 of the LORD our God for ever and e. 6329

Mal
3: 7 E since the time of your forefathers 4200+4946

Mt
9:33 "Nothing like this has e 4030
13:14 be e hearing but never understanding; 198+201
13:14 you will be e seeing but never perceiving.
1063+1063

Mk
4:12 "'they may be e seeing but never
perceiving, 1063+1063

Mk
4:12 and e hearing but never understanding; 201+201
11: 2 which no one has e ridden. 4037
11:14 "May no one e eat fruit from you again."
172+1650+3836

Lk
9:39 It scarcely e leaves him 3653
19:30 which no one has e ridden. 4799

Jn
1:18 No one has e seen God, 4799
3:13 No one has e gone into heaven except NIG
4:29 see a man who told me everything I e did. 4012
4:39 "He told me everything I e did." NIG
7:46 "No one e spoke the way this man does," 4030
9:32 Nobody has e heard of opening the eyes of
a man born blind. 172+1666+3836
10: 8 All who e came before me were thieves 4012
19:41 in which no one had e been laid. 4031

Ac
7:52 Was there e a prophet your fathers did 5515
11: 8 Nothing impure or unclean has e 4030
20:25 the kingdom will e see me again. 4033
26: 4 "The Jews all know the way I have lived e NIG
28:26 be e hearing but never understanding; 198+201
28:26 you will be e seeing but never perceiving."
1063+1063

Ro
11:35 "Who has e given to God, NIG
2Co
7: 7 so that my joy was greater than e. 3437
Gal
1: 5 to whom be glory for e and ever. Amen. 172
1: 5 to whom be glory for ever and e. Amen. 172
Eph
1:15 e since I heard about AIT
3:21 throughout all generations, for e and ever! 172
3:21 throughout all generations, for ever and e! 172
5:29 After all, no one e hated his own body, 4537
Php
4:20 To our God and Father be glory for e 172
4:20 and Father be glory for ever and e. 172
1Ti
1:17 be honor and glory for e and ever. 172
1:17 be honor and glory for ever and e. 172
2Ti
4:18 To him be glory for e and ever. 172
4:18 To him be glory for ever and e. 172
Heb
1: 5 For to which of the angels did God e say, 4537
1: 8 O God, will last for e and ever; 172
1: 8 O God, will last for ever and e; 172
1:13 To which of the angels did God e say, 4537
7:13 and no one from that tribe has e served at AIT
13:21 to whom be glory for e and ever. 172
13:21 to whom be glory for ever and e. 172
1Pe
4:11 be the glory and the power for e and ever. 172
4:11 be the glory and the power for ever and e. 172
5:11 To him be the power for e and ever. Amen. 172
5:11 To him be the power for ever and e. Amen. 172
2Pe
3: 4 E since our fathers died, 608+4005
1Jn
3: 2 No one has e seen God; 4799
Rev
1: 6 to him be glory and power for e and ever! 172
1: 6 to him be glory and power for ever and e! 172
1:18 and behold I am alive for e and ever! 172
1:18 and behold I am alive for ever and e! 172
4: 9 on the throne and who lives for e and ever, 172
4: 9 on the throne and who lives for ever and e, 172
4:10 and worship him who lives for e and ever 172
4:10 and worship him who lives for ever and e 172
5:13 and glory and power, for e and ever!" 172
5:13 and glory and power, for ever and e!" 172
7:12 and power and strength be to our God for e 172
7:12 and strength be to our God for ever and e. 172
10: 6 he swore by him who lives for e and ever, 172
10: 6 he swore by him who lives for ever and e, 172
11:15 and he will reign for e and ever." 172
11:15 and he will reign for ever and e." 172
14:11 smoke of their torment rises for e and ever. 172
14:11 smoke of their torment rises for ever and e. 172
15: 7 who lives for e and ever. 172
15: 7 who lives for ever and e. 172
16:18 No earthquake like it has e occurred since
man has been 608+4005
18:18 'Was there e a city like this great city?' 5515
18:22 No workman of any trade will e be found 3590
19: 3 smoke from her goes up for e and ever." 172
19: 3 smoke from her goes up for ever and e." 172
20:10 They will be tormented day and night for e 172
20:10 be tormented day and night for ever and e. 172
21:25 e be shut, for there will be no 3590+4024
21:27 Nothing impure will e enter it, 3590
22: 5 And they will reign for e and ever. 172
22: 5 And they will reign for ever and e. 172

EVER-INCREASING (2) [INCREASE]
Ro
6:19 in slavery to impurity and to e wickedness,
490+490+1650+3836
2Co
3:18 being transformed into his likeness with e
glory, 608+1518+1518+1650

EVER-PRESENT (1) [PRESENT]
Ps
46: 1 an e help in trouble. 4394+5162

EVERLASTING (71) [EVER]
Ge
9:16 and remember the e covenant between God 6409
17: 7 as an e covenant between me and you 6409
17: 8 I will give as an e possession to you 6409
17:13 in your flesh is to be an e covenant. 6409
17:19 an e covenant for his descendants after him. 6409
48: 4 and I will give this land as an e possession 6409
Nu
18:19 It is an e covenant of salt before the LORD 6409
Dt
33:15 and the fruitfulness of the e hills, 6409
33:27 and underneath are the e arms. 6409
2Sa
23: 5 Has he not made with me an e covenant, 6409
1Ch
16:17 to Israel as an e covenant; 6409
16:36 the God of Israel, from e to everlasting. 6409
16:36 the God of Israel, from everlasting to e. 6409

1Ch
29:10 from e to everlasting. 6409
29:10 from everlasting to e. 6409
Ezr
9:12 to your children as an e inheritance.' 6330+6409
Ne
9: 5 who is from e to everlasting." 6409
9: 5 who is from everlasting to e." 6409
Ps
41:13 the God of Israel, from e to everlasting. 6409
41:13 the God of Israel, from everlasting to e. 6409
52: 5 God will bring you down to e ruin: 4200+5905
74: 3 Turn your steps toward these e ruins, 5905
78:66 he put them to e shame. 6409
90: 2 from e to everlasting you are God. 6409
90: 2 from everlasting to e you are God. 6409
103:17 from e to everlasting the LORD's love is 6409
103:17 from everlasting to e the LORD's love is 6409
105:10 to Israel as an e covenant: 6409
106:48 the God of Israel, from e to everlasting. 6409
106:48 the God of Israel, from everlasting to e. 6409
119:142 Your righteousness is e 4200+6409
139:24 and lead me in the way e. 6409
145:13 Your kingdom is an e kingdom, 3972+6409
Isa
9: 6 Mighty God, E Father, Prince of Peace. 6329
24: 5 the statutes and broken the e covenant. 6409
30: 8 days to come it may be an e witness. 6330+6409
33:14 Who of us can dwell with e burning?" 6409
35:10 e joy will crown their heads. 6409
40:28 The LORD is the e God, 6409
45:17 be saved by the LORD with an e salvation; 6409
45:17 be put to shame or disgraced, to ages e. 6329
51:11 e joy will crown their heads. 6409
54: 8 but with e kindness I will have compassion 6409
55: 3 I will make an e covenant with you, 6409
55:13 for an e sign, which will not be destroyed." 6409
56: 5 I will give them an e name that will not 6409
60:15 the e pride and the joy of all generations. 6409
60:19 for the LORD will be your e light, 6409
60:20 the LORD will be your e light, 6409
61: 7 and e joy will be theirs. 6409
61: 8 and make an e covenant with them. 6409
63:12 to gain for himself e renown, 6409
Jer
5:22 an e barrier it cannot cross. 6409
23:40 I will bring upon you e disgrace— 6409
23:40 e shame that will not be forgotten." 6409
25: 9 object of horror and scorn, and an e ruin. 6409
31: 3 "I have loved you with an e love; 6409
32:40 I will make an e covenant with them: 6409
50: 5 to the LORD in an e covenant that will not 6409
Eze
16:60 and I will establish an e covenant with you. 6409
37:26 it will be an e covenant. 6409
Da
7:14 His dominion is an e dominion that will 10550
7:27 His kingdom will be an e kingdom, 10550
9:24 to bring in e righteousness, 6409
12: 2 some to e life, 6409
12: 2 others to shame and e contempt. 6409
Mic
5: 2 listen, you e foundations of the earth. 419
Hab
1:12 O LORD, are you not from e? 7710
Jn
6:47 he who believes has e life. 173
2Th
1: 9 be punished with e destruction and shut out 173
Jude
1: 6 bound with e chains for judgment on 132

EVERY (628) [EVERYBODY, EVERYBODY'S, EVERYDAY, EVERYONE, EVERYONE'S, EVERYTHING, EVERYWHERE]
Ge
1:21 and e living and moving thing with which 3972
1:21 and e winged bird according to its kind. 3972
1:28 the air and over e living creature that moves 3972
1:29 "I give you e seed-bearing plant on the face 3972
1:29 of the whole earth and e tree that has fruit 3972
1:30 I give e green plant for food." 3972
6: 5 and that e inclination of the thoughts 3972
6:17 e creature that has the breath of life in it. NIH
6:20 Two of e kind of bird, NIH
6:20 of e kind of animal and of every kind NIH
6:20 and of e kind of creature that moves along 3972
6:21 to take e kind of food that is to be eaten 3972
7: 2 with you seven of e kind of clean animal, 3972
7: 2 and two of e kind of unclean animal, NIH
7: 3 and also seven of e kind of bird, NIH
7: 4 of the earth e living creature I have made." 3972
7:14 with them e wild animal according 3972
7:14 e creature that moves along the ground 3972
7:14 the ground according to its kind and e bird 3972
7:16 in were male and female of e living thing, 3972
7:21 E living thing that moved on 3972
7:23 E living thing on the face of 3972
8:17 Bring out e kind of living creature that is 3972
8:21 even though e inclination of his heart is evil NIH
9: 2 upon e creature that moves along 3972
9: 5 I will demand an accounting from e animal. 3972
9:10 with e living creature that was with you— 3972
9:10 e living creature on earth. 3972
9:12 and e living creature with you, a covenant 3972
9:15 and you and all living creatures of e kind. 3972
9:16 and all living creatures of e kind on 3972
17:10 E male among you shall be circumcised. 3972
17:12 For the generations to come e male 3972
17:23 e male in his household, 3972
17:27 And e male in Abraham's household, 3972
19: 4 from e part of the city of Sodom— 7895
20:18 up e womb in Abimelech's household 3972
24: 1 and the LORD had blessed him in e way. 3972
30:32 from them e speckled or spotted sheep, 3972
30:32 e dark-colored lamb and every spotted 3972
30:32 every dark-colored lamb and e spotted 928
34:24 and e male in the city was circumcised. 3972

Ge	34:25	the unsuspecting city, killing e male.	3972
Ex	1:22	"E boy that is born you must throw into	3972
	1:22	but let e girl live."	3972
	3:22	E woman is to ask her neighbor	AIT
	9:19	the hail will fall on e man and animal	3972
	9:25	in the fields and stripped e tree.	3972
	10: 5	including e tree that is growing	3972
	10:14	in e area of the country in great numbers.	3972
	11: 5	E firstborn son in Egypt will die,	3972
	12:12	and strike down e firstborn—	3972
	13: 2	"Consecrate to me e firstborn male.	3972
	13: 2	of e womb among the Israelites belongs	3972
	13:12	to the LORD the first offspring of e womb.	3972
	13:13	Redeem with a lamb e firstborn donkey,	3972
	13:13	Redeem e firstborn among your sons.	3972
	13:15	the LORD killed e firstborn in Egypt,	3972
	13:15	the first male offspring of e womb	3972
	18:22	but have them bring e difficult case to you;	3972
	23:27	into confusion e nation you encounter.	3972
	30: 7	burn fragrant incense on the altar e morning	
		928+928+1332+2021+2021	
	34:19	first offspring of e womb belongs to me,	3972
	35:25	E skilled woman spun with her hands	3972
	36: 1	Oholiab and e skilled person to whom	3972
	36: 2	and Oholiab and e skilled person to whom	3972
Lev	2:11	"E grain offering you bring to	3972
	6:12	E morning the priest is to add firewood	
		928+928+1332+1332+2021+2021	
	6:23	E grain offering of a priest shall	3972
	7: 9	E grain offering baked in an oven	3972
	7:10	and e grain offering,	3972
	11:26	"E animal that has a split hoof	3972
	11:41	"E creature that moves about on	3972
	11:46	e living thing that moves in the water	3972
	11:46	in the water and e creature that moves about	3972
	17:14	because the life of e creature is its blood.	3972
	17:14	because the life of e creature is its blood;	3972
	27:25	E value is to be set according to	3972
	27:32	e tenth animal that passes under	3972
Nu	1: 2	listing them by name, one by one.	3972
	3:12	first male offspring of e Israelite woman.	3972
	3:13	I set apart for myself e firstborn in Israel,	3972
	3:15	Count e male a month old or more."	3972
	3:39	including e male a month old or more,	3972
	7: 3	ox from each leader and a cart from e two.	NIH
	8:16	first male offspring from e Israelite woman.	3972
	8:17	E firstborn male in Israel,	3972
	11:10	Moses heard the people of e family wailing,	2257S
	14:29	e one of you twenty years old	3972
	16: 3	e one of them,	3972
	18:10	e male shall eat it.	3972
	18:15	The first offspring of e womb,	3972
	18:15	But you must redeem e firstborn son	NIH
	18:15	and e firstborn male of unclean animals.	NIH
	19:15	and e open container without a lid fastened	3972
	28:10	the burnt offering for e Sabbath,	928+8701+8701
	28:11	"'On the first of e month,	4013S
	28:24	the food for the offering made by fire e day	4200
	30: 4	then all her vows and e pledge	3972
	31: 7	and killed e man.	3972
	31:17	And kill e woman who has slept with	3972
	31:18	for yourselves e girl who has never slept	3972
	31:20	Purify e garment as well	3972
	31:28	for the LORD one out of e five hundred,	2021
	31:30	select one out of e fifty, whether persons,	2021
	31:47	Moses selected one out of e fifty persons	2021
	32:18	until e Israelite has received his inheritance.	408
	32:27	But your servants, e man armed for battle,	3972
	32:29	e man armed for battle,	3972
	34:12	with its boundaries on e side.'"	6017
	36: 7	for e Israelite shall keep	408
	36: 8	E daughter who inherits land	3972
	36: 8	that e Israelite will possess the inheritance	408
Dt	1:41	So e one of you put on his weapons,	408
	3: 6	of Heshbon, destroying e city—	3972
	7:15	The LORD will keep you free from e disease.	3972
	8: 1	to follow e command I am giving you today,	3972
	8: 3	but on e word that comes from the mouth of	3972
	11: 6	their tents and e living thing that belonged	3972
	11:24	E place where you set your foot will	3972
	12: 2	and on the hills and under e spreading tree	3972
	14:28	At the end of e three years,	NIH
	15: 1	of e seven years you must cancel debts.	NIH
	15: 2	E creditor shall cancel the loan he has made	3972
	15:19	for the LORD your God e firstborn male	3972
	16:18	for each of your tribes in e town	3972
	28:61	The LORD will also bring on you e kind	3972
	31:10	"At the end of e seven years,	NIH
Jos	1: 3	I will give you e place	3972
	6: 5	the people will go up, e man straight in."	2257
	6:20	so e man charged straight in,	408
	6:21	and destroyed with the sword e living thing	3972
	8:24	and when e one of them had been put to	3972
	21:44	The LORD gave them rest on e side,	6017
	21:45	e one was fulfilled.	3972
	23:14	E promise has been fulfilled.	3972
	23:15	But just as e good promise of the LORD	3972
Jdg	8:34	hands of all their enemies on e side.	4946+6017
	15: 4	He then fastened a torch to e pair of tails,	NIH
	20:10	of e hundred from all the tribes of Israel,	2021
	21:11	"Kill e male and every woman who is not	3972
	21:11	"Kill every male and e woman who is not	3972
1Sa	2:29	of e offering made by my people Israel?'	3972
	2:33	E one of you that I do not cut off	408
	4:10	the Israelites were defeated and e man fled	AIT
	11: 2	that I gouge out the right eye of e man	6017
	12:11	from the hands of your enemies on e side,	6017

1Sa	14:47	he fought against their enemies on e side:	6017
	17:16	the Philistine came forward e morning	AIT
	20:15	not even when the LORD has cut off e one	408
	25:12	When they arrived, they reported e word.	3972
	25:30	for my master e good thing he promised	3972
	26:23	The LORD rewards e man for his	2021
2Sa	2:23	And e man stopped when he came to	3972
	8: 2	E two lengths of them were put to death,	NIH
	13:37	But King David mourned for his son e day.	3972
	20: 1	E man to his tent, O Israel!"	AIT
	23: 5	arranged and secured in e part?	3972
	23: 5	and grant me my e desire?	3972
1Ki	1:29	who has delivered me out of e trouble,	3972
	5: 4	on e side, and there is no adversary	6017
	7:36	in e available space,	408
	10:22	Once e three years it returned,	4200
	12:24	Go home, e one of you,	408
	14:10	I will cut off from Jeroboam e last male	928+7815+8874
	14:23	and Asherah poles on e high hill and	3972
	14:23	and under e spreading tree.	3972
	17:15	So there was food e day for Elijah and for	3427
	21:21	cut off from Ahab e last male	928+7815+8874
	22:36	"E man to his town; everyone to his land!"	AIT
2Ki	3:19	You will overthrow e fortified city	3972
	3:19	and e major town.	3972
	3:19	You will cut down e good tree,	3972
	3:19	and ruin e good field with stones."	3972
	3:21	so e man, young and old,	3972
	3:25	a stone on e good field until it was covered.	3972
	3:25	up all the springs and cut down e good tree.	3972
	10:11	cut off from Ahab e last male	928+7815+8874
	12: 5	Let e priest receive the money from one of	408
	13:20	to enter the country e spring.	995+9102
	14:12	and e man fled to his home.	AIT
	15:20	E wealthy man had to contribute fifty	3972
	16: 4	on the hilltops and under e spreading tree.	3972
	17:10	and Asherah poles on e high hill and	3972
	17:10	and under e spreading tree.	3972
	17:11	At e high place they burned incense,	3972
	18:31	Then e one of you will eat	408
	25: 9	E important building he burned down.	3972
1Ch	9:32	preparing for e Sabbath the bread set out	
		on the table.	8701+8701
	12:33	with e type of weapon, to help David	3972
	12:37	armed with e type of weapon—120,000.	3972
	14:17	So David's fame spread throughout e land,	3972
	21:12	of the LORD ravaging e part of Israel.'	3972
	22: 9	from all his enemies on e side.	4946+6017
	22:15	as well as men skilled in e kind of work	3972
	22:18	has he not granted you rest on e side?	4946+6017
	23:30	They were also to stand e morning to thank	
		928+928+1332+1332+2021+2021	
	26:32	of Manasseh for e matter pertaining to God	3972
	28: 9	for the LORD searches e heart	3972
	28: 9	and understands e motive behind	3972
	28:21	and e willing man skilled	3972
	28:21	the people will obey your e command."	3972
2Ch	2: 4	and for making burnt offerings e morning	4200
	9:21	Once e three years it returned,	4200
	11: 4	Go home, e one of you,	408
	11:16	from e tribe of Israel who set their hearts	3972
	13:11	E morning and evening they present burnt	
		offerings 928+928+1332+1332+2021+2021	
	13:11	light the lamps on the gold lampstand e	
		evening. 928+928+2021+2021+6847+6847	
	14: 5	the high places and incense altars in e town	3972
	14: 7	and he has given us rest on e side."	4946+6017
	15: 6	with e kind of distress.	3972
	15:15	So the LORD gave them rest on e side.	4946+6017
	19:10	In e case that comes before you	3972
	20: 4	indeed, they came from e town in Judah	3972
	20:30	his God had given him rest on e side.	4946+6017
	25:22	and e man fled to his home.	AIT
	28: 4	on the hilltops and under e spreading tree.	3972
	28:24	up altars at e street corner in Jerusalem.	3972
	28:25	In e town in Judah he built high places	3972
	30:21	priests sang to the LORD e day,	928+3427+3427
	31:19	to distribute portions to e male among them	3972
	32:22	He took care of them on e side.	4946+6017
Ne	4:22	"Have e man and his helper stay	AIT
	5:13	and possessions e man who does	3972
	5:18	and e ten days an abundant supply of wine	1068
	10:31	E seventh year we will forgo working	2021
	10:35	of our crops and e fruit tree.	3972
	11: 1	the people cast lots to bring one out of e ten	2021
Est	1:22	in each people's tongue that e man should	3972
	2: 3	in e province of his realm	3972
	2:11	E day he walked back and forth near the	
		courtyard 2256+3427+3427+3972	
	3:14	as law in e province and made known to	3972
	3:14	to the people of e nationality so they would	3972
	4: 3	In e province to which the edict and order	3972
	8:11	The king's edict granted the Jews in e city	3972
	8:13	as law in e province and made known to	3972
	8:13	of e nationality so that the Jews would	3972
	8:17	In e province and in every city,	3972
	8:17	In every province and in e city,	3972
	9:27	without fail observe these two days e year,	3972
	9:28	in e generation by every family,	3972
	9:28	in every generation by e family,	2256+5476+5476
	9:28	in e province and in every city.	2256+4519+4519
	9:28	in every province and in e city.	2256+6551+6551
Job	7:18	that you examine him e morning	4200
	7:18	and test him e moment?	4200
	12:10	of e creature and the breath of all mankind.	3972
	18:11	Terrors startle him on e side	6017

Job	18:11	on every side and dog his e step.	AIT
	19:10	He tears me down on e side till I am gone;	6017
	28:21	It is hidden from the eyes of e living thing,	3972
	31: 4	not see my ways and count my e step?	3972
	31:37	I would give him an account of my e step;	AIT
	34:21	he sees their e step.	3972
	37: 7	he stops e man from his labor.	3972
	40:11	look at e proud man and bring him low,	3972
	40:12	look at e proud man and humble him,	3972
Ps	3: 6	of thousands drawn up against me on e side.	6017
	7:11	a God who expresses his wrath e day.	3972
	12: 3	all flattering lips and e boastful tongue	NIH
	13: 2	with my thoughts and e day have sorrow	3429
	31:13	there is terror on e side;	4946+6017
	50:10	for e animal of the forest is mine,	3972
	50:11	I know e bird in the mountains,	3972
	52: 4	You love e harmful word,	3972
	73:14	I have been punished e morning.	4200
	74: 8	They burned e place	3972
	82: 7	you will fall like e other ruler."	AIT
	88: 9	I call to you, O LORD, e day;	3972
	89:51	with which they have mocked e step	AIT
	97: 3	before him and consumes his foes on e side.	6017
	101: 8	E morning I will put to silence all	4200
	101: 8	I will cut off e evildoer from the city of	3972
	105:35	they ate up e green thing in their land,	3972
	118:11	They surrounded me on e side,	6015
	119:101	I have kept my feet from e evil path so	3972
	119:104	therefore I hate e wrong path.	3972
	119:128	I hate e wrong path.	3972
	136:25	and who gives food to e creature.	3972
	140: 2	in their hearts and stir up war e day.	3972
	144:13	Our barns will be filled with e kind of	
		provision. 448+2385+2385+4946	
	145: 2	E day I will praise you and extol your name	3972
	145:16	and satisfy the desires of e living thing.	3972
	145:21	Let e creature praise his holy name for ever	3972
Pr	2: 9	right and just and fair—e good path.	3972
	7:12	now in the squares, at e corner she lurks.)	3972
	13:16	E prudent man acts out of knowledge,	3972
	16:33	but its e decision is from the LORD.	3972
	20: 3	but e fool is quick to quarrel.	3972
	30: 5	"E word of God is flawless;	3972
Ecc	3: 1	and a season for e activity under heaven:	3972
	3:17	for there will be a time for e activity,	3972
	3:17	a time for e deed."	3972
	7: 2	for death is the destiny of e man;	3972
	7:21	Do not pay attention to e word people say,	3972
	8: 6	a proper time and procedure for e matter,	3972
	12:14	For God will bring e deed into judgment,	3972
	12:14	including e hidden thing,	3972
SS	4:14	with e kind of incense tree,	3972
	7:13	and at our door is e delicacy,	3972
Isa	2:15	for e lofty tower and every fortified wall,	3972
	2:15	for every lofty tower and e fortified wall,	3972
	2:16	for e trading ship and every stately vessel.	3972
	2:16	for every trading ship and e stately vessel.	3972
	7:23	in e place where there were	3972
	9: 5	E warrior's boot used in battle	3972
	9: 5	in battle and e garment rolled in blood will	NIH
	9:17	e mouth speaks vileness.	3972
	13: 7	e man's heart will melt.	3972
	15: 2	E head is shaved and every beard cut off.	3972
	15: 2	Every head is shaved and e beard cut off.	3972
	19: 7	E sown field along	3972
	21: 8	e night I stay at my post.	3972
	24:10	the entrance to e house is barred.	3972
	30:25	on e high mountain and every lofty hill.	3972
	30:25	on every high mountain and e lofty hill.	3972
	30:32	E stroke the LORD lays on them	3972
	31: 7	in that day e one of you will reject the idols	408
	32:20	sowing your seed by e stream,	3972
	33: 2	Be our strength e morning,	4200
	36:16	Then e one of you will eat	408
	40: 4	E valley shall be raised up,	3972
	40: 4	e mountain and hill made low;	3972
	45:23	Before me e knee will bow;	3972
	45:23	by me e tongue will swear.	3972
	49: 9	the roads and find pasture on e barren hill.	3972
	51:13	that you live in constant terror e day	3972
	51:20	they lie at the head of e street,	3972
	54:17	you will refute e tongue that accuses you.	3972
	57: 5	among the oaks and under e spreading tree;	3972
	58: 6	to set the oppressed free and break e yoke?	3972
Jer	2:20	Indeed, on e high hill and	3972
	2:20	and under e spreading tree you lay down as	3972
	3: 6	She has gone up on e high hill and	3972
	3: 6	and under e spreading tree	3972
	3:13	to foreign gods under e spreading tree,	3972
	4:25	e bird in the sky had flown away.	3972
	4:29	of horsemen and archers e town takes	3972
	6:25	and there is terror on e side.	4946+6017
	9: 4	For e brother is a deceiver,	3972
	9: 4	and e friend a slanderer.	3972
	10:14	e goldsmith is shamed by his idols.	3972
	12: 4	the land lie parched and the grass in e field	3972
	13:12	E wineskin should be filled with wine.'	3972
	13:12	that e wineskin should be filled with wine?'	3972
	16:16	down on e mountain and hill and from	3972
	19:15	around it e disaster I pronounced	3972
	20:10	many whispering, "Terror on e side!	4946+6017
	21:12	"'Administer justice e morning;	4200
	23:36	e man's own word becomes his oracle	AIT
	30: 6	Then why do I see e strong man	3972
	30: 6	e face turned deathly pale?	3972
	34:14	'E seventh year each of you must	4946+7891
	35:17	in Jerusalem e disaster I pronounced	3972

Jer	36: 3	about e disaster I plan to inflict on them,	3972
	36:31	the people of Judah e disaster I pronounced	3972
	46: 5	and there is terror **on e side,"**	4946+6017
	48: 8	The destroyer will come against e town,	3972
	48:37	**E** head is shaved and every beard cut off;	3972
	48:37	Every head is shaved and e beard cut off;	3972
	48:37	e hand is slashed and every waist is covered	3972
	48:37	every hand is slashed and e waist is covered	NIH
	49: 5	"**E** one of you will be driven away,	408
	49:29	will shout to them, 'Terror **on e side!'**	4946+6017
	49:32	on them from e side,"	3972
	50:15	Shout against her **on e side!**	6017
	51: 2	will oppose her **on e side** in the day	4946+6017
	51:17	"**E** man is senseless and without knowledge	3972
	51:17	e goldsmith is shamed by his idols.	3972
	52:13	**E** important building he burned down.	3972
La	2: 3	In fierce anger he has cut off e horn	3972
	2:19	faint from hunger at the head of e street.	3972
	2:22	you summoned against me terrors **on e side.**	
			4946+6017
	3:23	They are new e morning;	4200
	4: 1	scattered at the head of e street.	3972
	4:18	Men stalked us at e step,	AIT
Eze	6:13	on e high hill and all the mountaintops,	3972
	6:13	under e spreading tree	3972
	6:13	and e leafy oak—	3972
	7:17	**E** hand will go limp,	3972
	7:17	and e knee will become as weak as water.	3972
	12:22	'The days go by and e vision comes	3972
	12:23	'The days are near when e vision will	3972
	14:22	e disaster I have brought upon it.	3972
	16:24	and made a lofty shrine in e public square.	3972
	16:25	of e street you built your lofty shrines	3972
	16:31	of e street and made your lofty shrines	3972
	16:31	made your lofty shrines in e public square,	3972
	16:33	**E** prostitute receives a fee,	3972
	17:23	Birds of e kind will nest in it;	3972
	18: 4	For e living soul belongs to me,	3972
	20:26	the sacrifice of e firstborn—	3972
	20:39	Go and serve your idols, **e one** of you!	408
	20:47	and e face from south to north will	3972
	21: 7	**E** heart will melt and every hand go limp;	3972
	21: 7	Every heart will melt and e hand go limp;	3972
	21: 7	e spirit will become faint	3972
	21: 7	and e knee become as weak as water.'	3972
	21:10	The sword despises e such stick.	3972
	21:14	**closing in** on them **from e side.**	2539
	23:22	against you from e side—	6017
	23:24	take up positions against you **on e side** with	6017
	26:16	trembling e moment, appalled at you.	4200
	27:11	and Helech manned your walls **on e side;**	6017
	28:13	e precious stone adorned you:	3972
	28:23	with the sword against her **on e side.**	4946+6017
	29:18	e head was rubbed bare	3972
	29:18	and e shoulder made raw.	3972
	32:10	of them will tremble e moment for his life.	4200
	34: 6	over all the mountains and on e high hill.	3972
	36: 3	and hounded you **from e side** so	4946+6017
	38:20	e creature that moves along the ground,	3972
	38:20	the cliffs will crumble and e wall will fall to	3972
	38:21	**E man's** sword will be against his brother.	AIT
	39:17	to e kind of bird and all the wild animals:	3972
	39:20	mighty men and soldiers of e kind,'	3972
	45:15	be taken from e flock of two hundred from	2021
	45:23	**E** day during the seven days of	4200
	46:13	" 'E day you are to provide a year-old lamb	
			2021+3427+4200
	47:12	**E** month they will bear,	4200
Da	1: 4	showing aptitude for e kind of learning,	3972
	1:20	In e matter of wisdom and understanding	3972
	3: 4	O peoples, nations and **men of e language:**	10392
	3: 7	nations and **men of e language** fell down	10392
	4: 1	nations and **men of e language,**	10392
	4:12	from it e creature was fed.	10353
	5:19	nations and **men of e language** dreaded	10392
	6: 4	to rescue Daniel and **made e effort**	10700
	6:25	nations and **men of e language** throughout	10392
	6:26	in e part of my kingdom people must fear	10353
	7:14	and **men of e language** worshiped him.	10392
	11:36	above e god and will say unheard-of things	3972
Hos	9: 1	of a prostitute at e threshing floor.	3972
	9:12	I will bereave them of e one.	132
Joel	2: 6	e face turns pale.	3972
	3:11	all you nations **from e side,**	4946+6017
	3:12	to judge all the nations **on e side.**	4946+6017
Am	2: 8	beside e altar on garments taken in pledge.	3972
	4: 4	Bring your sacrifices e morning,	4200
	4: 4	your tithes e three years.	4200
	4: 6	in e city and lack of bread in every town,	3972
	4: 6	in every city and lack of bread in e town."	3972
	5:16	and cries of anguish in e public square.	3972
Mic	4: 4	**E man** will sit under his own vine and	AIT
Na	2:10	bodies tremble, e face grows pale.	3972
	3:10	to pieces at the head of e street.	3972
Zep	1: 4	I will cut off from this place **e remnant**	AIT
	2:11	The nations on e shore will worship him,	3972
	2:11	e one in its own land.	408
	2:14	creatures of e kind.	3972
	3: 5	and e new day he does not fail,	4200
	3:19	I will give them praise and honor in e land	3972
Zec	5: 3	e thief will be banished,	3972
	8:10	for I had turned e man against his neighbor.	3972
	10: 4	from him the battle bow, from him e ruler.	3972
	12: 4	On that day I will strike e horse with panic	3972
	13: 4	"On that day e prophet will be ashamed	408
	14:21	**E** pot in Jerusalem and Judah will be holy	3972
Mal	1:11	In e place incense and pure offerings will	3972

Mal	4: 1	the arrogant and e evildoer will be stubble,	3972
Mt	3:10	and e tree that does not produce good fruit	4246
	4: 4	but on e word that comes from the mouth	4246
	4:23	and healing e disease and sickness among	4246
	7:17	Likewise e good tree bears good fruit.	4246
	7:19	**E** tree that does not bear good fruit is cut	4246
	9:35	of the kingdom and healing e disease	4246
	10: 1	to drive out evil spirits and to heal e disease	4246
	12:25	"**E** kingdom divided against itself will	4246
	12:25	and e city or household divided	4246
	12:31	e sin and blasphemy will be forgiven men,	4246
	12:36	for e careless word they have spoken.	4246
	13:52	"Therefore e teacher of the law	4246
	15:13	"**E** plant that my heavenly Father has	4246
	18:16	so that 'e matter may be established by	4246
	19: 3	to divorce his wife for **any and** e reason?"	4246
	24: 2	e one will be thrown down."	NIG
	26:55	**E day** I sat in the temple courts	2465+2848
Mk	13: 2	e one will be thrown down."	NIG
	14:49	**E day** I was with you,	2465+2848
Lk	2:23	"**E** firstborn male is to be consecrated to	4246
	2:41	E year his parents went to Jerusalem for	2848
	3: 5	**E** valley shall be filled in,	4246
	3: 5	e mountain and hill made low.	4246
	3: 9	and e tree that does not produce good fruit	4246
	5:17	who had come from e village of Galilee and	4246
	10: 1	of him to e town and place where he was	4246
	13:24	"**Make e effort** to enter through	76
	16:19	and fine linen and lived in luxury e day.	2848
	19:43	and encircle you and hem you in **on e side.**	4119
	19:47	**E** day he was teaching at the temple.	2848
	21: 6	e one of them will be thrown down."	NIG
	22:53	**E** day I was with you in the temple courts,	2848
Jn	1: 9	that gives light to e man was coming into	4246
	13:10	you are clean, though not e one of you."	4246
	13:11	that was why he said not e one was clean.	4246
	15: 2	He cuts off e branch in me that bears no	4246
	15: 2	in me that bears no fruit, while e branch	4246
	21:25	If e one of them were written down,	2848
Ac	2: 5	from e nation under heaven.	4246
	2:38	"Repent and be baptized, **e one** of you,	1667
	2:46	**E** day they continued to meet together in	2848
	3: 2	where he was put e day to beg	2848
	10:35	but accepts men from e nation who fear him	4246
	13:27	of the prophets that are read e Sabbath.	2848+4246
	15:21	For Moses has been preached **in** e city from	2848
	15:21	in the synagogues on e Sabbath."	4246
	17:11	and examined the Scriptures e day to see	2848
	17:22	I see that in e way you are very religious.	4246
	17:26	From one man he made e nation of men,	4246
	18: 4	**E** Sabbath he reasoned in the synagogue,	
			2848+4246
	20:23	that **in** e city the Holy Spirit warns me	2848
	24: 3	Everywhere and **in** e way,	4118
Ro	1:29	They have become filled **with** e kind	4246
	2: 9	for e human being who does evil:	4246
	3: 2	Much in e way!	4246
	3: 4	Let God be true, and e man a liar.	4246
	3:19	so that e mouth may be silenced and	4246
	7: 8	produced in me e kind of covetous desire.	4246
	12: 3	the grace given me I say to e one of you:	4246
	14: 5	another man considers e day alike.	4246
	14:11	says the Lord, 'e knee will bow before me;	4246
	14:11	e tongue will confess to God.' "	4246
	14:19	therefore **make e effort** to do what leads	1503
1Co	1: 5	For in him you have been enriched in e way	4246
	4:17	with what I teach everywhere in e church.	4246
	10:33	even as I try to please everybody **in** e way.	4246
	11: 3	to realize that the head of e man is Christ,	4246
	11: 4	**E** man who prays or prophesies	4246
	11: 5	And e woman who prays or prophesies	4246
	12:18	e one of them, just as he wanted them to be.	1667
	12:26	If one part suffers, e part suffers with it;	4246
	12:26	one part is honored, **e** part rejoices with it.	4246
	14: 5	like **e one** of you to speak in tongues,	4246
	15:30	us, why do we endanger ourselves e hour?	4246
	15:31	I die e day—	2848
	16: 2	On the first day of e week,	NIG
2Co	4: 2	to e man's conscience in the sight of God.	4246
	4: 8	We are hard pressed on e **side,**	4246
	6: 4	of God we commend ourselves in e **way:**	4246
	7: 5	but we were harassed at e turn—	4246
	7:11	At e **point** you have proved yourselves to	4246
	9: 8	you will abound in e good work.	4246
	9:11	be made rich in e way so that you can	4246
	9:11	so that you can be generous on e **occasion,**	4246
	10: 5	and e pretension that sets itself up against	4246
	10: 5	and we take captive e thought	4246
	10: 6	be ready to punish e act of disobedience,	4246
	11: 6	perfectly clear to you in e way.	4246
	13: 1	"**E** matter must be established by	4246
Gal	5: 3	Again I declare **to** e man who lets himself	4246
Eph	1: 3	with e spiritual blessing in Christ.	4246
	1:21	and e title that can be given,	4246
	1:23	of him who fills everything in e way.	4246
	4: 3	**Make e effort** to keep the unity of the Spirit	5079
	4:14	**by** e wind of teaching and by the cunning	4246
	4:16	and held together by e supporting ligament,	4246
	4:19	over to sensuality so as to indulge in e kind	4246
	4:31	along with e **form** of malice.	4246
Php	1: 3	making the most of e opportunity,	NIG
	1: 3	I thank my God e time I remember you.	4246
	1:18	The important thing is that **in** e way,	4246
	2: 9	the name that is above e name,	4246
	2:10	at the name of Jesus e knee should bow,	4246
	2:11	e tongue confess that Jesus Christ is Lord,	4246
	4:12	of being content in any and e **situation,**	4246

Col	1:10	of the Lord and may please him in e **way:**	4246
	1:10	bearing fruit in e good work,	4246
	1:23	and that has been proclaimed to e creature	4246
	2:10	who is the head **over** e power and authority.	4246
	4: 5	make the most of e opportunity.	NIG
1Th	2:17	out of our intense longing we made e effort	4359
	5:22	Avoid e kind of evil.	1667
2Th	1: 3	and the love e one of you has	1667
	1:11	by his power may fulfill e good purpose	4246
	1:11	of yours and e act prompted by your faith.	NIG
	2:10	and in e **sort** of evil that deceives	4246
	2:17	and strengthen you in e good deed	4246
	3: 6	from e brother who is idle and does not live	4246
	3:16	at all times and in e way.	4246
2Ti	3:17	be thoroughly equipped for e good work.	4246
	4:18	The Lord will rescue me from e evil attack	4246
Tit	1: 5	and appoint elders in e town,	2848
	2:10	so that in e **way** they will make the teaching	4246
Phm	1: 6	**of** e good thing we have in Christ.	4246
Heb	2: 2	by angels was binding, and e violation	4246
	2:17	to be made like his brothers in e **way,**	4246
	3: 4	For e house is built by someone,	4246
	4:11	therefore, **make e effort** to enter that rest,	5079
	4:15	in e way, just as we are—	4246
	5: 1	**E** high priest is selected from among men	4246
	8: 3	**E** high priest is appointed to offer both gifts	4246
	9:19	Moses had proclaimed e commandment	4246
	9:25	the Most Holy Place e year with blood	2848
	10:11	Day after day e priest stands	4246
	12:14	**Make e effort** to live in peace with all men	1503
	13:18	and desire to live honorably in e **way.**	4246
Jas	1:17	**E** good and perfect gift is from above,	4246
	3:16	there you find disorder and e evil practice.	4246
1Pe	2: 1	hypocrisy, envy, and slander of e **kind.**	4246
	2:13	for the Lord's sake to e authority instituted	4246
2Pe	1: 5	make e effort to add to your faith goodness;	4246
	1:15	And **I will make e effort** to see that	5079
	3:14	**make e effort** to be found spotless,	5079
1Jn	4: 1	Dear friends, do not believe e spirit,	4246
	4: 2	**E** spirit that acknowledges that Jesus Christ	4246
	4: 3	but e spirit that does not acknowledge	4246
Rev	1: 7	and e eye will see him,	4246
	5: 9	from e tribe and language and people	4246
	5:13	Then I heard e creature in heaven and	4246
	6:14	and e mountain and island was removed	4246
	6:15	and e slave and every free man hid in caves	4246
	6:15	and every slave and e free man hid in caves	NIG
	7: 9	from e nation, tribe, people and language,	4246
	7:17	God will wipe away e tear from their eyes."	4246
	11: 6	to strike the earth with e **kind** of plague	4246
	11: 9	and a half days men from e people,	NIG
	13: 7	And he was given authority over e tribe,	4246
	14: 6	to e nation, tribe, language and people.	4246
	16: 3	and e living thing in the sea died.	4246
	16:20	**E** island fled away and the mountains could	4246
	18: 2	for demons and a haunt **for** e evil spirit,	4246
	18: 2	a haunt **for** e unclean and detestable bird.	4246
	18:12	e **sort** of citron wood,	4246
	18:12	and articles of e kind made of ivory,	4246
	18:17	"**E** sea captain, and all who travel by ship,	4246
	21: 4	He will wipe e tear from their eyes.	4246
	21:19	the city walls were decorated **with** e kind	4246
	22: 2	yielding its fruit e month.	1667

EVERYBODY (8) [BODY, EVERY]

Lk	9:15	The disciples did so, and e sat down.	570
	18: 9	and looked down on e **else,**	3370
Ac	4:16	"**E** living in Jerusalem knows they have	
		done an outstanding miracle,	4246
	21:24	Then e will know there is no truth	4246
Ro	1: 8	to do what is right in the eyes of e.	476+4246
1Co	10:33	even as I try to please e in every way.	4246
	14:24	in while e is prophesying,	4246
2Co	3: 2	written on our hearts, known and read by e.	
			476+4246

EVERYBODY'S (1) [BODY, EVERY]

Ac	16:26	and e chains came loose.	4246

EVERYDAY (1) [DAY, EVERY]

Gal	3:15	let me take an example **from** e life.	476+2848

EVERYONE (216) [EVERY, ONE]

Ge	16:12	against e and everyone's hand against him,	3972
	21: 6	e who hears about this will laugh with me."	3972
	45: 1	"Have e leave my presence!"	408+3972
Ex	12:16	except to prepare food for e to eat—	3972+5883
	16:21	Each morning e gathered as much	408
	16:29	**E** is to stay where he is on the seventh day;	408
	19:16	**E** in the camp trembled.	2021+3972+6639
	35: 5	**E** who is willing is to bring to the LORD	3972
	35:21	and e who was willing	408+3972
	35:23	**E** who had blue, purple or scarlet yarn	408+3972
	35:24	and e who had acacia wood for any part of	3972
	38:26	from e who had crossed over	3972
Lev	18:29	" '**E** who does any of these detestable	3972
	25:13	of Jubilee e is to return to his own property.	408
Nu	15:13	'**E** who is native-born must do these things	3972
	15:29	to e who sins unintentionally,	2021[S]
	18:11	**E** in your household who is ceremonially	
		clean may eat it.	3972
	18:13	**E** in your household who is ceremonially	
		clean may eat it.	3972
Dt	4: 3	e who followed the Baal of Peor,	408+2021+3972

Dt	12: 8	e as he sees fit,	408
Jos	10:28	and totally destroyed e in it.	2021+3972+5883
	10:30	The city and e in it Joshua put to the sword.	
			2021+3972+5883
	10:32	The city and e in it he put to the sword,	
			2021+3972+5883
	10:35	to the sword and totally destroyed e in it,	
			2021+3972+5883
	10:37	its villages and e in it.	2021+3972+5883
	10:37	totally destroyed it and e in it.	2021+3972+5883
	10:39	E in it they totally destroyed.	3972+5883
	11:11	E in it they put to the sword.	2021+3972+5883
Jdg	9:25	to ambush and rob e who passed by,	3972
	17: 6	e did as he saw fit,	408
	19:30	E who saw it said,	3972
	21:25	e did as he saw fit.	408
1Sa	2:36	Then e left in your family line will come	3972
	3:11	that will make the ears of e who hears	3972
	8:22	"E go back to his town."	408
	14:34	So e brought his ox that night	2021+3972+6639
2Sa	13: 9	"Send e out of here," Amnon said.	408+3972
	13: 9	So e left him.	408+3972
	15: 4	Then e who has a complaint	408+3972
	16:21	hands of e with you will be strengthened."	3972
	20:12	that e who came up to Amasa stopped,	3972
1Ki	10:25	e who came brought a gift—	408
	22:36	e to his land!"	408
2Ki	10:11	So Jehu killed e in Jezreel who remained of	3972
	14:26	how bitterly e in Israel, whether slave	NIH
	15:16	attacked Tiphsah and e in the city	3972
	21:12	that the ears of e who hears of it will tingle.	3972
1Ch	12:15	and they put to flight e living in	3972
2Ch	9:24	e who came brought a gift—	408
	29:29	the king and e present with him knelt down	3972
	30:18	the LORD, who is good, pardon e	3972
	34:32	Then he had e in Jerusalem	3972
Ezr	1: 5	e whose heart God had moved—	3972
	8:22	of our God is on e who looks to him,	3972
	9: 4	Then e who trembled at the words of	3972
	10:14	Then let e in our towns who has married	3972
Est	2:15	And Esther won the favor of e who saw her.	3972
Job	17: 6	"God has made me a byword to e,	6639
	34:26	for their wickedness where e can see them,	AIT
	42:11	and e who had known him before came	3972
Ps	12: 2	E lies to his neighbor;	408
	32: 6	Therefore let e who is godly pray to you	3972
	53: 3	E has turned away,	3972
Pr	19: 6	and e is the friend of a man who gives gifts.	3972
Ecc	3:13	That e may eat and drink,	132+2021+3972
	10: 3	the fool lacks sense and shows e	3972
Isa	6:12	until the LORD has sent e far away and	132
	9:17	for e is ungodly and wicked,	3972
	19:17	e to whom Judah is mentioned will	3972
	30: 5	e will be put to shame because of	3972
	43: 7	e who is called by my name,	3972
Jer	1: 7	You must go to e I send you to	3972
	10:14	E is senseless and without knowledge;	132+3972
	15:10	yet e curses me.	3972
	17:20	and e living in Jerusalem who come	3972
	19: 3	that will make the ears of e who hears	3972
	20: 7	I am ridiculed all day long; e mocks me.	3972
	31:30	Instead, e will die for his own sin;	408
	32:19	you reward e according to his conduct and	408
	34: 9	E was to free his Hebrew slaves,	408
	35:17	to bring on Judah and on e living	3972
	50:16	the oppressor let e return to his own people,	408
	50:16	let e flee to his own land.	408
Eze	16:44	" 'E who quotes proverbs will quote this	
		proverb	3972
	20:48	E will see that I the LORD have kindled it;	
			1414+3972
	21: 4	my sword will be unsheathed against e	1414+3972
	23: 7	with all the idols of e she lusted after.	3972
	27:27	and e else on board will sink into	3972+7736
Da	3:10	e who hears the sound of the horn,	10050+10353
	11: 2	he will stir up e against the kingdom	3972
	12: 1	e whose name is found written in	3972
Joel	2:32	And e who calls on the name of	3972
Ob	9	and e in Esau's mountains will be cut down	408
Jnh	3: 8	Let e call urgently on God.	AIT
Na	3:19	E who hears the news	3972
Hab	2:17	have destroyed lands and cities and e	3782+3972
	2:17	have destroyed lands and cities and e	3782+3972
Zec	5: 3	e who swears falsely will be banished.	3972
	10: 1	and plants of the field to e.	408
	11: 6	"I will hand e over to his neighbor	132
Mt	5:15	and it gives light to e in the house.	4246
	7: 8	For e who asks receives;	4246
	7:21	"Not e who says to me, 'Lord, Lord,'	4246
	7:24	"Therefore e who hears these words	4246
	7:26	But e who hears these words of mine	476
	13:25	But while e was sleeping,	476
	19:11	Jesus replied, "Not e can accept this word,	4246
	19:29	And e who has left houses or brothers	4246
	25:29	For e who has will be given more,	4246
Mk	1:37	"E is looking for you!"	4246
	2:12	This amazed e and they praised God,	4246
	3: 3	"Stand up in front of e."	3545+3836
	7:14	"Listen to me, e, and understand this.	4246
	9:49	E will be salted with fire.	4246
	11:32	for e held that John really was a prophet.)	570
	13:37	What I say to you, I say to e: 'Watch!' "	4246
	14:50	Then e deserted him and fled.	4246
Lk	1:66	E who heard this wondered about it, asking,	4246
	2: 3	e went to his own town to register.	1667+4246
	2:47	E who heard him was amazed	4246
	4:15	and e praised him.	4246

Lk	4:20	of e in the synagogue were fastened	4246
	5:26	E was amazed and gave praise to God.	570
	6: 8	"Get up and stand in front of e."	3545+3836
	6:30	Give to e who asks you,	4246
	6:40	but e who is fully trained will be	4246
	9:43	While e was marveling at all that Jesus did,	4246
	11: 4	for we also forgive e who sins against us.	4246
	11:10	For e who asks receives;	4246
	12:10	And e who speaks a word against the Son	4246
	12:41	are you telling this parable to us, or to e?"	4246
	12:48	From e who has been given much,	4246
	14:11	For e who exalts himself will be humbled,	4246
	14:29	e who sees it will ridicule him	4246
	16:16	and e is forcing his way into it.	4246
	18:14	For e who exalts himself will be humbled,	4246
	19:26	"He replied, 'I tell you that to e who has,	4246
	20:18	E who falls on that stone will be broken	4246
Jn	2:10	"E brings out the choice wine first and	476+4246
	3: 8	So it is with e born of the Spirit."	3836+4246
	3:15	that e who believes in him may have eternal	
		life.	4246
	3:20	E who does evil hates the light,	4246
	3:26	he is baptizing, and e is going to him."	4246
	4:13	"E who drinks this water will	4246
	6:40	For my Father's will is that e who looks to	4246
	6:45	E who listens to the Father and learns	4246
	8:34	e who sins is a slave to sin.	4246
	11:48	e will believe in him,	4246
	18:37	E on the side of truth listens to me."	4246
Ac	1:19	E in Jerusalem heard about this,	4246
	2:21	And e who calls on the name of	323+4246
	2:43	E was filled with awe,	4246+6034
	8:19	that e on whom I lay my hands may receive	1569
	10:43	about him that e who believes	4246
	13:39	Through him e who believes is justified	4246
	27:44	In this way e reached land in safety.	4246
Ro	1:16	of God for the salvation of e who believes;	4246
	2:10	honor and peace for e who does good:	4246
	10: 4	be righteousness for e who believes.	4246
	10:13	"E who calls on the name of the Lord will	4246
	12:18	live at peace with e.	476+4246
	13: 1	E must submit himself to	4246+6034
	13: 7	Give e what you owe him:	4246
	16:19	E has heard about your obedience,	4246
1Co	8: 7	But not e knows this.	4246
	9:19	I make myself a slave to e,	4246
	9:25	E who competes in the games goes	3836
	14: 3	But e who prophesies speaks to men	3836
	14:23	and e speaks in tongues,	4246
	14:26	When you come together, e has a hymn,	1667
	14:31	so that e may be instructed and encouraged.	4246
	16:16	as these and to e who joins in the work,	4246
2Co	9:13	in sharing with them and with e else.	4246
Gal	3:10	"Cursed is e who does not continue	4246
	3:13	"Cursed is e who is hung on a tree."	4246
Eph	3: 9	and to make plain to e the administration	4246
	6: 8	that the Lord will reward e	1667
Php	1:13	and to e else that I am in chains for Christ,	4246
	2:21	For e looks out for his own interests,	4246
Col	1:28	and teaching with all wisdom,	476+4246
	1:28	that we may present e perfect in Christ.	476+4246
	4: 6	that you may know how to answer e.	1651+1667
1Th	3:12	and overflow for each other and for e else,	4246
	5:14	help the weak, be patient with e.	4246
	5:15	to be kind to each other and to e else.	4246
2Th	3: 2	for not e has faith.	4246
1Ti	2: 1	and thanksgiving be made for e—	476+4246
	4:15	so that e may see your progress.	4246
2Ti	1:15	You know that e in the province	4246
	2:19	and, "E who confesses the name of	4246
	2:24	instead, he must be kind to e, able to teach,	4246
	3: 9	their folly will be clear to e.	4246
	3:12	e who wants to live a godly life	4246
	4:16	but e deserted me.	4246
Tit	3: 8	and profitable for e.	476
	3:15	E with me sends you greetings.	4246
Heb	2: 9	the grace of God he might taste death for e.	4246
	12: 6	and he punishes e he accepts as a son."	4246
	12: 8	(and e undergoes discipline),	4246
Jas	1:19	E should be quick to listen,	476+4246
1Pe	2:17	Show proper respect to e:	4246
	3:15	to e who asks you to give the reason for	4246
2Pe	3: 9	to perish, but e to come to repentance.	4246
1Jn	2:29	that e who does what is right has been born	4246
	3: 3	E who has this hope	4246
	3: 4	E who sins breaks the law;	4246
	4: 7	E who loves has been born of God	4246
	5: 1	E who believes that Jesus is	4246
	5: 1	and e who loves the father loves his child	4246
	5: 4	for e born of God overcomes the world.	4246
3Jn	1:12	Demetrius is well spoken of by e—	4246
Jude	1:15	judge e, and to convict all the ungodly	2848+4246
Rev	13:16	He also forced e, small and great,	4246
	22:12	to e according to what he has done.	1667
	22:15	and e who loves and practices falsehood.	4246
	22:18	I warn e who hears the words of	4246

EVERYONE'S (4) [EVERY, ONE]

Ge	16:12	against everyone and e hand against him,	3972
Jos	2:11	our hearts melted and e courage failed	408+928
Lk	1:63	and to e astonishment he wrote,	3972
Ac	1:24	Then they prayed, "Lord, you know e heart.	4246

EVERYTHING (386) [EVERY, THING]

| Ge | 1:30 | e that has the breath of life in it— | NIH |

Ge	6:17	E on earth will perish.	3972
	6:22	Noah did e just as God commanded him.	3972
	7:14	and every bird according to its kind, e	3972
	7:22	E on dry land that had the breath of life	3972
	8:19	e that moves on the earth—	3972
	9: 3	E that lives and moves will be food for you.	3972
	9: 3	I now give you e.	3972
	12:20	with his wife and e he had.	3972
	13: 1	with his wife and e he had,	3972
	14:20	Then Abram gave him a tenth of e.	3972
	21:22	"God is with you in e you do.	3972
	24:36	and he has given him e he owns.	3972
	25: 5	Abraham left e he owned to Isaac.	3972
	31: 1	"Jacob has taken e our father owned	3972
	31:34	through e in the tent but found nothing.	3972
	34:28	and donkeys and e else of theirs in the city	889
	34:29	taking as plunder e in the houses.	3972
	39: 3	the LORD gave him success in e he did,	3972
	39: 4	and he entrusted to his care e he owned.	3972
	39: 5	of the LORD was on e Potiphar had,	3972
	39: 6	So he left in Joseph's care e he had;	3972
	39: 8	e he owns he has entrusted to my care.	3972
	42:36	E is against me!"	3972+5626
	45:13	in Egypt and about e you have seen.	3972
	45:27	told him e Joseph had said to them,	1821+3972
	46:32	and herds and e they own.'	3972
	47: 1	with their flocks and herds and e they own,	3972
Ex	4:28	Then Moses told Aaron e the LORD	3972
	4:30	Aaron told them e the LORD had said	1821+3972
	6:29	Tell Pharaoh king of Egypt e I tell you."	3972
	7: 2	You are to say e I command you,	3972
	9:19	now to bring your livestock and e you have	3972
	9:22	and animals and on e growing in the fields	3972
	9:25	Throughout Egypt hail struck e in	3972
	9:25	it beat down e growing in the fields	3972
	10:12	the land and devour e growing in the fields,	3972
	10:12	e left by the hail."	3972
	10:15	e growing in the fields and the fruit on	3972
	18: 1	heard of e God had done for Moses and	3972
	18: 8	about e the LORD had done to Pharaoh	3972
	18:24	to his father-in-law and did e he said.	3972
	19: 8	"We will do e the LORD has said."	3972
	23:13	"Be careful to do e I have said to you.	3972
	24: 3	"E the LORD has said we will do.	
			1821+2021+3972
	24: 4	then wrote down e the LORD had said.	3972
	24: 7	"We will do e the LORD has said;	3972
	29:35	and his sons e I have commanded you,	3972
	31: 6	to make e I have commanded you:	3972
	35:10	and make e the LORD has commanded:	3972
	38:22	made e the LORD commanded Moses;	3972
	39:32	The Israelites did e just as the LORD	3972
	40: 9	and anoint the tabernacle and e in it;	3972
	40:16	Moses did e just as the LORD	3972
Lev	8:10	and anointed the tabernacle and e in it,	3972
	8:36	and his sons did e the LORD commanded	
			1821+2021+3972
	11:33	e in it will be unclean,	3972
	15: 9	" 'E the man sits on when riding will	3972
	27:28	e so devoted is most holy to the LORD.	3972
	27:30	" 'A tithe of e from the land,	3972
Nu	1:50	over all its furnishings and e belonging	3972
	2:34	So the Israelites did e the LORD	3972
	3:26	and e related to their use.	3972
	3:31	the curtain, and e related to their use.	3972
	3:36	and e related to their use,	3972
	4:16	in charge of the entire tabernacle and e in it,	3972
	4:32	all their equipment and e related	3972
	9: 5	The Israelites did e just as the LORD	3972
	16:30	with e that belongs to them,	3972
	16:33	with e they owned;	3972
	18: 7	in connection with e at the altar	1821+3972
	18:14	"E in Israel that is devoted to	3972
	18:29	the best and holiest part of e given to you.'	3972
	22: 4	"This horde is going to lick up e around us,	3972
	30: 2	not break his word but must do e he said.	3972
	31:20	Purify every garment as well as e	3972+3998
Dt	1:18	at that time I told you e you were to do.	
			1821+2021+3972
	5:28	E they said was good.	3972
	10:14	the earth and e in it.	3972
	12: 7	in e you have put your hand to,	3972
	12:11	there you are to bring e I command you:	3972
	12:14	and there observe e I command you.	3972
	12:18	in e you put your hand to.	3972
	15:10	and in e you put your hand to.	3972
	15:18	your God will bless you in e you do.	3972
	17:10	Be careful to do e they direct you to do.	3972
	18:18	and he will tell them e I command him.	3972
	20:14	the livestock and e else in the city,	3972
	23: 9	keep away from e impure.	1821+3972
	23:20	in e you put your hand to in	3972
	26:14	I have done e you commanded me.	3972
	28: 8	and on e you put your hand to,	3972
	28:20	and rebuke in e you put your hand to,	3972
	28:29	You will be unsuccessful in e you do;	2006
	29: 9	so that you may prosper in e you do.	3972
	30: 2	according to e I command you today,	3972
Jos	1: 8	that you may be careful to do e written in it.	3972
	2:23	and told him e that had happened to them.	3972
	4:10	in the middle of the Jordan until e the LORD	
			1821+2021+3972
	6:24	Then they burned the whole city and e in it,	3972
	22: 2	and you have obeyed me in e I commanded.	3972
	23: 3	You yourselves have seen e	3972
	24:31	and who had experienced e	3972+5126
Jdg	13:14	She must do e I have commanded her."	3972

Jdg	16:17	So he told her e.	3972+4213
	16:18	Delilah saw that he had told her e,	3972+4213
	16:18	he has told me e."	3972+4213
	20:48	including the animals and e else they found.	3972
Ru	3: 6	and did e her mother-in-law told her to do.	3972
	3:16	Then she told her e Boaz had done for her	3972
1Sa	2:22	about e his sons were doing to all Israel and	3972
	3:12	against Eli I spoke against his family—	3972
	3:18	So Samuel told him e,	1821+2021+3972
	9: 6	and e he says comes true.	3972
	12: 1	to e you said to me and have set a king	3972
	15: 3	attack the Amalekites and totally destroy e	3972
	15: 9	e that was good.	3972
	15: 9	but e that was despised	2021+3972+4856
	18:14	In e he did he had great success,	3972
	30:18	David recovered e the Amalekites had taken	3972
	30:19	David brought e back.	2021+3972
2Sa	3:19	to Hebron to tell David e that Israel and	3972
	3:25	and find out e you are doing."	3972
	3:36	indeed, the king did please them.	3972
	6:12	the household of Obed-Edom and e he has,	3972
	9: 9	"I have given your master's grandson e	3972
	11:22	he arrived he told David e Joab had sent him	3972
	14:20	he knows e that happens in the land."	3972
	19:30	"Let him take e,	3972
	21:14	and did e the king commanded.	3972
1Ki	6:18	E was cedar; no stone was to be seen.	3972
	14:26	He took e, including all	3972
	19: 1	Now Ahab told Jezebel e Elijah had done	3972
	20: 6	They will seize e you value	3972
	22:43	In e he walked in the ways of his father Asa	3972
2Ki	4:26	"E is all right," she said.	NIH
	5:21	"Is all right?"	NIH
	5:22	"E is all right," Gehazi answered.	NIH
	8: 6	"Give back e that belonged to her,	3972
	9:11	one of them asked him, "Is e all right?	NIH
	14: 3	In e he followed the example	3972
	20:13	and e found among his treasures.	3972
	20:15	"They saw e in my palace," Hezekiah said.	3972
	20:17	surely come when e in your palace,	3972
	21: 8	to do e I commanded them and will keep	3972
	22:16	according to e written in the book the king	3972
1Ch	10:11	the inhabitants of Jabesh Gilead heard of e	3972
	13:14	LORD blessed his household and e he had.	3972
	16:32	let the fields be jubilant, and e in them!	3972
	16:40	in accordance with e written in the Law of	3972
	26:28	And e dedicated by Samuel the seer and	3972
	29: 3	over and above e I have provided	3972
	29:11	for e in heaven and earth is yours.	3972
	29:14	E comes from you,	3972
	29:19	and to do e to build the palatial structure	3972
2Ch	12: 9	took e, including the gold shields Solomon had made.	3972
	21:14	sons, your wives and e that is yours,	3972+8214
	29:16	of the LORD's temple is unclean	3972
	31: 5	They brought a great amount, a tithe of e.	3972
	31:21	In e that he undertook in the service	3972+5126
	32:30	He succeeded in e he undertook.	3972
	32:31	God left him to test him and to know e	3972
	33: 8	to do e I commanded them concerning all	3972
	34:16	"Your officials are doing e	3972
	36:19	they burned all the palaces and destroyed e of value there.	3972+3998
Ezr	7: 6	The king had granted him e he asked,	3972
	8:34	E was accounted for by number	3972
Ne	9: 6	You give life to e,	3972
	13:30	the priests and the Levites of e foreign,	3972
Est	4: 7	Mordecai told him e that had happened	3972
	6:13	and all his friends e that had happened	3972
	9:26	Because of e written in this letter and	3972
Job	1:10	and his household and e he has?	3972
	1:11	and strike e he has,	3972
	1:12	"Very well, then, e he has is in your hands,	3972
	28:24	for he views the ends of the earth and sees e	3972
	33: 1	pay attention to e I say.	3972
	41:11	E under heaven belongs to me.	3972
Ps	8: 6	you put e under his feet;	3972
	24: 1	The earth is the LORD's, and e in it,	4850
	33:15	who considers e they do.	3972
	96:12	and e in them.	3972
	98: 7	Let the sea resound, and e in it, the world,	4850
	146: 6	the sea, and e in them—	3972
	150: 6	Let e that has breath praise the LORD.	3972
Pr	16: 4	LORD works out e for his own ends—	3972
Ecc	1: 2	E is meaningless."	3972
	2:11	e was meaningless, a chasing after the wind;	3972
	3: 1	There is a time for e,	3972
	3:11	He has made e beautiful in its time.	3972
	3:14	I know that e God does will endure forever;	3972
	3:19	E is meaningless.	3972
	8: 9	as I applied my mind to e done under	3972+5126
	9: 3	The evil in e that happens under the sun:	3972
	10:19	but money is the answer for e.	3972
	11: 8	E to come is meaningless.	3972
	12: 8	"E is meaningless!"	3972
Isa	8:12	"Do not call conspiracy e that these people	3972
	39: 2	the fine oil, his entire armory and e found	3972
	39: 4	"They saw e in my palace," Hezekiah said.	3972
	39: 6	surely come when e in your palace,	3972
Jer	8:16	They have come to devour the land and e in	4850
	11: 4	I said, 'Obey me and do e I command you,	3972
	21:14	a fire in your forests that will consume e	3972
	26: 2	Tell them e I command you;	1821+2021+3972
	26: 8	as Jeremiah finished telling all the people e	3972
	35: 8	We have obeyed e our forefather Jonadab	3972
	35:10	have fully obeyed e our forefather Jonadab commanded us.	3972

Jer	35:18	and have done e he ordered.'	3972
	36: 8	Baruch son of Neriah did e Jeremiah	3972
	36:13	Micaiah told them e he had heard Baruch read	1821+2021+3972
	36:20	to the king in the courtyard and reported e to him.	1821+2021+3972
	38:27	and he told them e the king had ordered	3972
	42: 4	I will tell you e the LORD says	1821+2021+3972
	42: 5	with e the LORD your God sends you to tell us.	1821+2021+3972
	42:20	tell us e he says and we will do it.'	3972
	43: 1	e the LORD had sent him to tell them—	465+1821+2021+2021+3972
	44:17	We will certainly do e we said we would:	1821+2021+3972
	47: 2	They will overflow the land and e in it,	4850
	50:21	"Do e I have commanded you.	3972
La	2: 3	like a flaming fire that consumes e around	6017
Eze	7:14	they blow the trumpet and get e ready,	3972
	11:25	the exiles e the LORD had shown me.	1821+3972
	12:19	be stripped of e in it because of the violence	4850
	23:29	and take away e you have worked for.	3972
	30:12	the land and e in it.	4850
	32:15	and strip the land of e in it,	4850
	40: 4	and pay attention to e I am going	3972
	40: 4	Tell the house of Israel e you see."	3972
	41:16	e beyond and including	NIH
	44: 5	and give attention to e I tell you	3972
	44:29	and e in Israel devoted to	3972
	47: 9	so where the river flows e will live.	3972
Da	2:40	for iron breaks and smashes e—	10353
	4:37	e he does is right and all his ways are just.	10353
	8:12	It prospered in e it did,	NIH
	9:14	for the LORD our God is righteous in e he does;	3972+5126
Am	6: 8	I will deliver up the city and e in it."	4850
Zep	1: 2	"I will sweep away e from the face of	3972
Mt	5:18	from the Law until e is accomplished.	4246
	7:12	So in e, do to others	3972
	13:41	and they will weed out of his kingdom e	4246
	13:46	and sold e he had and bought it.	4012+4246
	17:12	but have done to him e they wished.	4012
	18:26	he begged, 'and I will pay back e.'	4246
	18:31	and told their master e that had happened.	4246
	19:27	"We have left e to follow you!	4246
	22: 4	and e is ready.	4246
	23: 3	you must obey them and do e they tell you.	1569+4012+4246
	23: 5	"E they do is done for men to see:	4246
	23:20	by the altar swears by it and by e on it.	4246
	23:27	of dead men's bones and e unclean.	4246
	28:11	the city and reported to the chief priests e	570
	28:20	to obey e I have commanded you.	4012+4246
Mk	4:11	to those on the outside e is said in parables	3836+4246
	4:34	with his own disciples, he explained e.	4246
	7:37	"He has done e well," they said.	4246
	8:25	his sight was restored, and he saw e clearly.	570
	9:13	and they have done to him e they wished,	4012
	9:23	"E is possible for him who believes."	4246
	10:21	"Go, sell e you have and give to the poor,	4012
	10:28	"We have left e to follow you!"	4246
	11:11	He looked around at e,	4246
	12:44	but she, out of her poverty, put in e—	4246
	13:23	I have told you e ahead of time.	4246
	14:36	Father," he said, "e is possible for you.	4246
Lk	1: 3	since I myself have carefully investigated e	4246
	2:39	When Joseph and Mary had done e required	4246
	5:11	left e and followed him.	4246
	5:28	and Levi got up, left e and followed him.	4246
	11:41	and e will be clean for you.	4246
	14:17	'Come, for e is now ready.'	NIG
	14:33	not give up e he has cannot be my disciple.	4246
	15:14	After he had spent e,	4246
	15:31	and e I have is yours.	4246
	17:10	when you have done e you were told to do,	4246
	18:22	Sell e you have and give to the poor,	4012+4246
	18:31	and e that is written by the prophets about	4246
	24:14	with each other about e that had happened.	4246
	24:44	E must be fulfilled that is written about me	4246
Jn	3:35	The Father loves the Son and has placed e	4246
	4:25	When he comes, he will explain e to us."	570
	4:29	see a man who told me e I ever did.	4246
	4:39	"He told me e I ever did."	4246
	14:26	and will remind you of e I have said to you.	4246
	15:15	for e that I learned from my Father	4246
	17: 7	e you have given me comes from you.	4012+4246
Ac	2:44	All the believers were together and had e in common.	570
	3:21	until the time comes for God to restore e,	4246
	3:22	you must listen to e he tells you.	323+4012+4246
	4:24	the earth and the sea, and e in them.	4246
	4:32	but they shared e they had.	570
	10: 8	He told them e that had happened	570
	10:33	to listen to e the Lord has commanded you	4246
	10:39	of e he did in the country of the Jews and	4246
	11: 4	and explained e to them precisely	NIG
	12:11	from Herod's clutches and from e	4246
	13:10	of the devil and an enemy of e that is right!	4246
	13:22	he will do e I want him to do.'	4246
	13:39	from e you could not be justified from by	4246
	14:15	who made heaven and earth and sea and e	4246
	15: 4	to whom they reported e God had done	4012
	17:24	"The God who made the world and e in it is	4246
	17:25	he gives all men life and breath and e else.	4246
	20:35	In e I did, I showed you that by this kind	4246
	24:14	I believe e that agrees with the Law and	4246

Ro	14: 2	One man's faith allows him to eat e,	4246
	14: 3	The man who eats e must not look down	NIG
	14: 3	and the man who does not eat e must	NIG
	14:23	and e that does not come from faith is sin.	4246
	15: 4	For e that was written in the	4012
1Co	6:12	"E is permissible for me"—	4246
	6:12	but not e is beneficial.	4246
	6:12	"E is permissible for me"—	4246
	10:23	"E is permissible"—	4246
	10:23	but not e is beneficial.	4246
	10:23	"E is permissible"—	4246
	10:23	but not e is constructive.	4246
	10:26	for, "The earth is the Lord's, and e in it."	4445
	11: 2	for remembering me in e and for holding to	4246
	11:12	But e comes from God.	3836+4246
	14:40	But e should be done in a fitting	4246
	15:27	For he "has put e under his feet."	4246
	15:27	it says that "e" has been put under him,	4246
	15:27	who put e under Christ.	3836+4246
	15:28	be made subject to him who put e	3836+4246
	16:14	Do e in love.	4246
2Co	2: 9	the test and be obedient in e.	4246
	6:10	having nothing, and yet possessing e.	4246
	7: 1	from e that contaminates body and spirit,	4246
	7:14	But just as e we said to you was true,	4246
	8: 7	But just as you excel in e—	4246
	11:28	Besides e else, I face daily the pressure of my concern	3836+4211+6006
	12:15	spend for you e I have and expend	1682
	12:19	and e we do, dear friends,	4246
Gal	3:10	not continue to do e written in the Book of	4246
Eph	1:11	of him who works out e in conformity with	4246
	1:22	and appointed him to be head over e for	4246
	1:23	of him who fills e in every way.	3836+4246
	5:13	But e exposed by the light becomes visible,	4246
	5:14	for it is light that makes e visible.	4246
	5:20	to God the Father for e,	4246
	5:24	wives should submit to their husbands in e.	4246
	6:13	and after you have done e, to stand.	570
	6:21	will tell you e, so that you also may know	4246
Php	2:14	Do e without complaining or arguing,	4246
	3: 8	I consider e a loss compared to	4246
	3:21	by the power that enables him to bring e under his control,	3836+4246
	4: 6	Do not be anxious about anything, but in e,	4246
	4:13	I can do e through him who gives me strength.	4246
Col	1:18	so that in e he might have the supremacy.	4246
	3:20	Children, obey your parents in e,	4246
	3:22	Slaves, obey your earthly masters in e;	4246
	4: 9	They will tell you e that is happening here.	4246
1Th	5:21	Test e. Hold on to the good.	4246
2Th	2: 4	over e that is called God or is worshiped,	4246
1Ti	3:11	but temperate and trustworthy in e.	4246
	4: 4	For e God created is good,	4246
	6:13	In the sight of God, who gives life to e,	4246
	6:17	who richly provides us with e	4246
2Ti	2:10	Therefore I endure e for the sake of	4246
Tit	2: 7	In e set them an example	4246
	2: 9	to be subject to their masters in e,	4246
	3:13	Do e you can to help Zenas the lawyer	5081
	3:13	and see that they have e they need.	3309+3594
Heb	2: 8	and put e under his feet."	4246
	2: 8	In putting e under him,	3836+4246
	2: 8	at present we do not see e subject to him.	4246
	2:10	for whom and through whom e exists,	3836+4246
	3: 4	but God is the builder of e.	4246
	4:13	E is uncovered and laid bare before the eyes	4246
	7: 2	and Abraham gave him a tenth of e.	4246
	8: 5	"See to it that you make e according to	4246
	9: 6	When e had been arranged like this,	4047
	9:21	the tabernacle and e used in its ceremonies.	4246
	9:22	the law requires that nearly e be cleansed	4246
	12: 1	let us throw off e that hinders and the sin	4246
	13:21	equip you with e good for doing his will,	4246
2Pe	1: 3	His divine power has given us e we need	4246
	3: 4	e goes on as it has since the beginning	4246
	3:10	and the earth and e in it will be laid bare.	NIG
	3:11	Since e will be destroyed in this way,	4246
1Jn	2:16	For e in the world—	4246
	3:20	and he knows e.	4246
Rev	1: 2	who testifies to e he saw—	4012
	21: 5	"I am making e new!"	4246

EVERYWHERE (25) [EVERY, WHERE]

Ge	20:13	E we go, say of me, "He is my brother." '	2021+3972+5226
Ex	7:19	Blood will be e in Egypt,	3972
	7:21	Blood was e in Egypt.	3972
Lev	25: 9	the trumpet sounded e on the tenth day of	NIH
1Ch	18: 6	LORD gave David victory e he went.	928+3972
	18:13	LORD gave David victory e he went.	928+3972
Ps	103:22	all his works e in his dominion.	3972+5226
Pr	15: 3	The eyes of the LORD are e,	928+3972+5226
	24:31	thorns had come up e,	3972
Jer	8: 3	by the LORD will be e—	NIH
Eze	16:33	to you from e for your illicit favors.	6017
Am	8: 3	Many, many bodies—flung e!	3972+5226
Mk	1:45	Yet the people still came to him from e.	4119
	16:20	Then the disciples went out and preached e,	4116
Lk	9: 6	preaching the gospel and healing people e.	4116
Ac	8:13	And he followed Philip e,	4674
	17:30	now he commands all people e to repent.	4116
	21:28	This is the man who teaches all men e	4116
	24: 3	E and in every way, most excellent Felix,	4116
	28:22	that people e are talking against this sect."	4116

1Co	1: 2	all those e who call on the name	1877+4246+5536
	4:17	with what I teach e in every church.	4116
2Co	2:14	through us spreads e the fragrance of the knowledge of him.	1877+4246+5536
1Th	1: 8	your faith in God has become known e.	1877+4246+5536
1Ti	2: 8	I want men e to lift up holy hands in prayer,	4246+5536

EVI (2)

Nu	31: 8	Among their victims were E, Rekem, Zur,	209
Jos	13:21	E, Rekem, Zur, Hur and Reba—	209

EVIDENCE (8) [EVIDENT]

Ex	22:13	the remains as e and he will not be required	6332
1Sa	12: 7	because I am going to confront you with e	9149
Mt	26:59	for false e against Jesus so	6019
Mk	14:55	and the whole Sanhedrin were looking for e	3456
Jn	14:11	at least believe on the e of the miracles	1328
Ac	11:23	When he arrived and saw the e of the grace	NIG
2Th	1: 5	All this is e that God's judgment is right,	1891
Jas	2:20	do you want e that faith without works is useless?	1182

EVIDENT (3) [EVIDENCE, EVIDENTLY]

1Ch	4:41	as is e to this day.	NIH
Gal	2:17	it becomes e that we ourselves are sinners,	2351
Php	4: 5	Let your gentleness be e to all.	1182

EVIDENTLY (1) [EVIDENT]

Gal	1: 7	E some people are throwing you	1623+3590

EVIL (454) [EVILDOER, EVILDOERS, EVILS]

Ge	2: 9	the tree of the knowledge of good and e.	8273
	2:17	the tree of the knowledge of good and e,	8273
	3: 5	knowing good and e."	8273
	3:22	knowing good and e."	8273
	6: 5	of the thoughts of his heart was only e all	8273
	8:21	though every inclination of his heart is e	8273
	44: 4	'Why have you repaid good with e?	8288
Ex	10:10	Clearly you are bent on e.	8288
	32:12	with intent that he brought them out,	8288
	32:22	how prone these people are to e.	8273
Lev	5: 4	whether good or e	8317
Nu	32:13	of those who had done e	8273
Dt	1:35	"Not a man of this e generation shall see	8273
	4:25	doing e in the eyes of the LORD your God	8273
	9:18	doing what was e in the LORD's sight and	8273
	13: 5	You must purge the e from among you.	8273
	13:11	among you will do such an e thing again.	8273
	17: 2	the LORD gives you is found doing e in	8273
	17: 5	or woman who has done this e deed	8273
	17: 7	You must purge the e from among you.	8273
	17:12	You must purge the e from Israel.	8273
	19:19	You must purge the e from among you.	8273
	19:20	and never again will such an e thing	8273
	21:21	You must purge the e from among you.	8273
	22:21	You must purge the e from among you.	8273
	22:22	You must purge the e from Israel.	8273
	22:24	You must purge the e from among you.	8273
	24: 7	You must purge the e from among you.	8273
	28:20	of the e you have done in forsaking him.	8278
	31:29	upon you because you will do e in the sight	8273
Jos	23:15	on you all the e he has threatened,	8273
Jdg	2:11	Then the Israelites did e in the eyes of	8273
	2:19	They refused to give up their e practices	5095
	3: 7	The Israelites did e in the eyes of	8273
	3:12	Once again the Israelites did e in the	8273
	3:12	and because they did this e	8273
	4: 1	the Israelites once again did e in the eyes of	8273
	6: 1	Again the Israelites did e in the eyes of	8273
	9:23	God sent an e spirit between Abimelech	8273
	10: 6	Again the Israelites did e in the eyes of	8273
	13: 1	Again the Israelites did e in the eyes of	8273
	20:13	to death and purge the e from Israel."	8288
1Sa	12:17	an e thing you did in the eyes of the LORD	8288
	12:19	for we have added to all our other sins the e	8288
	12:20	"You have done all this e;	8288
	12:25	Yet if you persist in doing e,	8317+8317
	15:19	on the plunder and do e in the eyes of	8273
	15:23	and arrogance like the e of idolatry.	224
	16:14	an e spirit from the LORD tormented him.	8273
	16:15	an e spirit from God is tormenting you.	8273
	16:16	the e spirit from God comes upon you,	8273
	16:23	and the e spirit would leave him.	8273
	18:10	an e spirit from God came forcefully	8273
	19: 9	an e spirit from the LORD came upon Saul	8273
	24:13	'From evildoers come e deeds,'	8400
	25:21	He has paid me back for good.	8288
	30:22	But all the e men and troublemakers	8273
2Sa	3:39	the evildoer according to his e deeds!"	8288
	12: 9	the LORD by doing what is e in his eyes?	8273
	14:17	an angel of God in discerning good and e.	8273
	22:22	I have not done e by turning from my God.	8399
	23: 6	e men are all to be cast aside like thorns,	1175
1Ki	1:52	but if e is found in him, he will die."	8288
	11: 6	Solomon did e in the eyes of the LORD;	8273
	13:33	this, Jeroboam did not change his e ways,	8273
	14: 9	You have done more e than all who lived	8317
	14:22	Judah did e in the eyes of the LORD.	8273
	15:26	He did e in the eyes of the LORD,	8273
	15:34	He did e in the eyes of the LORD,	8273

1Ki	16: 7	because of all the e he had done in the eyes	8288
	16:19	doing e in the eyes of the LORD	8273
	16:25	But Omri did e in the eyes of the LORD	8273
	16:30	Ahab son of Omri did more e in the eyes of	8273
	21:20	"because you have sold yourself to do e in	8273
	21:25	who sold himself to do e in the eyes of	8273
	22:52	He did e in the eyes of the LORD,	8273
2Ki	3: 2	He did e in the eyes of the LORD,	8273
	8:18	He did e in the eyes of the LORD and did	8273
	8:27	the ways of the house of Ahab and did e in	8273
	13: 2	He did e in the eyes of the LORD	8273
	13:11	He did e in the eyes of the LORD and did	8273
	14:24	He did e in the eyes of the LORD and did	8273
	15: 9	He did e in the eyes of the LORD.	8273
	15:18	He did e in the eyes of the LORD.	8273
	15:24	Pekahiah did e in the eyes of the LORD.	8273
	15:28	He did e in the eyes of the LORD,	8273
	17: 2	He did e in the eyes of the LORD,	8273
	17:13	"Turn from your e ways.	8273
	17:17	and sorcery and sold themselves to do e in	8273
	21: 2	He did much e in the eyes of the LORD,	8273
	21: 6	He did much e in the eyes of the LORD,	8273
	21: 9	so that they did more e than the nations	8273
	21:11	He has done more e than	8317
	21:15	because they have done e in my eyes	8273
	21:16	so that they did e in the eyes of the LORD.	8273
	21:20	He did e in the eyes of the LORD,	8273
	23:32	He did e in the eyes of the LORD,	8273
	23:37	And he did e in the eyes of the LORD,	8273
	24: 9	He did e in the eyes of the LORD,	8273
	24:19	He did e in the eyes of the LORD,	8273
1Ch	21: 7	This command was also e in the sight	8317
2Ch	12:14	He did e because he had not set his heart	8273
	21: 6	He did e in the eyes of the LORD,	8273
	22: 4	He did e in the eyes of the LORD,	8273
	29: 6	they did e in the eyes of	8273
	33: 2	He did e in the eyes of the LORD,	8273
	33: 6	He did much e in the eyes of the LORD,	8273
	33: 9	so that they did more e than the nations	8273
	33:22	He did e in the eyes of the LORD,	8273
	36: 5	He did e in the eyes of the LORD his God.	8273
	36: 9	He did e in the eyes of the LORD,	8273
	36:12	He did e in the eyes of the LORD his God	8273
Ezr	9:13	a result of our e deeds and our great guilt,	8273
Ne	9:28	they again did what was e in your sight.	8273
	9:35	not serve you or turn from their e ways.	8273
	13: 7	about the e thing Eliashib had done	8288
Est	8: 3	an end to the e plan of Haman the Agagite,	8288
	8: 5	the e scheme Haman had devised against	8288
Job	1: 1	he feared God and shunned e.	8273
	1: 8	a man who fears God and shuns e."	8273
	2: 3	a man who fears God and shuns e.	8273
	4: 8	those who plow e and those who sow	224
	11:11	and when he sees e, does he not take note?	224
	11:14	that is in your hand and allow no e to dwell	6406
	15:16	who drinks up e like water!	6406
	15:35	They conceive trouble and give birth to e;	224
	16:11	to e men and thrown me into the clutches of	6397
	18:21	Surely such is the dwelling of an e man;	6405
	20:12	"Though e is sweet in his mouth	8288
	21:30	e man is spared from the day of calamity,	8273
	22:15	to the old path that e men have trod?	224
	24:20	e men are no longer remembered	6406
	28:28	and to shun e is understanding.' "	8273
	30:26	Yet when I hoped for good, e came;	8273
	34:10	Far be it from God to do e,	8400
	36:10	and commands them to repent of their e.	224
	36:21	Beware of turning to e,	224
Ps	5: 4	You are not a God who takes pleasure in e;	8400
	6: 8	Away from me, all you who do e,	224
	7: 4	if I have done e to him who is at peace	8273
	7:14	with e and conceives trouble gives birth	224
	10: 7	trouble and e are under his tongue.	224
	10:15	Break the arm of the wicked and e man;	8273
	18:21	I have not done e by turning from my God.	8399
	21:11	Though they plot e against you	8288
	22:16	a band of e men has encircled me,	8317
	23: 4	I will fear no e, for you are with me;	8273
	27: 2	When e men advance against me	8317
	28: 3	with those who do e,	224
	28: 4	for their deeds and for their e work;	8278
	34:13	from e and your lips from speaking lies.	8273
	34:14	Turn from e and do good;	8273
	34:16	of the LORD is against those who do e,	8273
	34:21	E will slay the wicked;	8288
	35:12	They repay me e for good	8288
	36: 4	Even on his bed he plots e;	224
	37: 1	Do not fret because of e men or be envious	8317
	37: 8	it leads only to e.	8317
	37: 9	For e men will be cut off,	8317
	37:27	Turn from e and do good;	8273
	38:20	who repay my good with e slander me	8288
	49: 5	Why should I fear when e days come,	8273
	50:19	for e and harness your tongue to deceit.	8288
	51: 4	have I sinned and done what is e	8273
	52: 1	Why do you boast of e, you mighty man?	8288
	52: 3	You love e rather than good,	8273
	54: 5	Let e recoil on those who slander me;	8273
	55:15	for e finds lodging among them.	8273
	64: 5	They encourage each other in e plans,	8273
	71: 4	from the grasp of e and cruel men.	6401
	73: 7	the e conceits of their minds know no limits.	5381
	97:10	Let those who love the LORD hate e,	8273
	101: 4	I will have nothing to do with e.	8288
	109: 5	They repay me e for good,	8288
	109: 6	Appoint an e man to oppose him;	8401
	109:20	to those who speak e of me.	8273

Ps	119:101	I have kept my feet from every e path so	8273
	125: 3	the righteous might use their hands to do e.	6406
	139:20	They speak of you with e intent;	4659
	140: 1	Rescue me, O LORD, from e men;	8273
	140: 2	who devise e plans in their hearts and stir	8273
	141: 4	Let not my heart be drawn to what is e,	8273
Pr	2:14	and rejoice in the perverseness of e,	8273
	3: 7	fear the LORD and shun e.	8273
	4:14	of the wicked or walk in the way of e men.	8273
	4:16	For they cannot sleep till they do e;	8317
	4:27	keep your foot from e.	8273
	5:22	The e deeds of a wicked man ensnare him;	6411
	6:14	who plots e with deceit in his heart—	8273
	6:18	feet that are quick to rush into e,	8288
	8:13	To fear the LORD is to hate e;	8273
	8:13	e behavior and perverse speech.	8273
	10:23	A fool finds pleasure in e conduct,	2365
	10:29	but it is the ruin of those who do e.	224
	11: 6	but the unfaithful are trapped by e desires.	2094
	11:19	but he who pursues e goes to his death.	8288
	11:27	but e comes to him who searches for it.	8288
	12:12	The wicked desire the plunder of e men,	8273
	12:13	An e man is trapped by his sinful talk,	8273
	12:20	in the hearts of those who plot e,	8273
	13:19	but fools detest turning from e.	8273
	14:16	A wise man fears the LORD and shuns e,	8273
	14:19	E men will bow down in the presence of	8273
	14:22	Do not those who plot e go astray?	8273
	15:28	but the mouth of the wicked gushes e.	8288
	16: 6	the fear of the LORD a man avoids e.	8273
	16:17	The highway of the upright avoids e;	8273
	16:27	A scoundrel plots e,	8288
	16:30	he who purses his lips is bent on e.	8288
	17: 4	A wicked man listens to e lips;	224
	17:11	An e man is bent only on rebellion;	8273
	17:13	If a man pays back e for good,	8288
	17:13	e will never leave his house.	8288
	19:28	and the mouth of the wicked gulps down e.	224
	20: 8	he winnows out all e with his eyes.	8273
	20:30	Blows and wounds cleanse away e,	8273
	21:10	The wicked man craves e;	8273
	21:27	much more so when brought with e intent!	2365
	24: 8	He who plots e will be known as a schemer.	8317
	24:19	Do not fret because of e men or be envious	8317
	24:20	for the e man has no future hope,	8273
	26:23	are fervent lips with an e heart.	8273
	28: 5	E men do not understand justice,	8273
	28:10	along an e path will fall into his own trap,	8273
	29: 6	An e man is snared by his own sin,	8273
	30:32	or if you have planned e,	2372
Ecc	4: 3	who has not seen the e that is done under	8273
	5:13	I have seen a grievous e under the sun:	8288
	5:16	This too is a grievous e:	8288
	6: 1	I have seen another e under the sun,	8288
	6: 2	This is meaningless, a grievous e.	2716
	9: 3	This is the e in everything that happens	8273
	9: 3	of e and there is madness in their hearts	8273
	9:12	in a snare, so men are trapped by e times	8288
	10: 5	There is an e I have seen under the sun,	8288
	12:14	whether it is good or e.	8273
Isa	1:13	I cannot bear your e assemblies.	224
	1:16	Take your e deeds out of my sight!	8278
	5:20	to those who call e good and good evil,	8273
	5:20	to those who call evil good and good e,	8273
	13:11	I will punish the world for its e,	8288
	26:10	land of uprightness they go on doing e	6401
	29:20	and all who have an eye for e will	224
	32: 6	fool speaks folly, his mind is busy with e:	224
	32: 7	he makes up e schemes to destroy the poor	2365
	33:15	shuts his eyes against contemplating e—	8273
	55: 7	and the e man his thoughts.	224
	56: 2	and keeps his hand from doing any e."	8273
	57: 1	to be spared from e.	8288
	59: 4	they conceive trouble and give birth to e.	224
	59: 6	Their deeds are e deeds,	224
	59: 7	Their thoughts are e thoughts;	224
	59:15	and whoever shuns e becomes a prey.	8273
	65:12	You did e in my sight	8273
	66: 4	They did e in my sight	8273
Jer	2:19	and realize how e and bitter it is for you	8273
	3: 5	but you do all the e you can."	8273
	3:17	the stubbornness of their e hearts.	8273
	4: 4	like fire because of the e you have done—	8278
	4:14	wash the e from your heart and be saved.	8288
	4:22	They are skilled in doing e;	8317
	5:28	Their e deeds have no limit;	8273
	7:24	the stubborn inclinations of their e hearts.	8273
	7:26	and did more e than their forefathers.'	8317
	7:30	" 'The people of Judah have done e	8273
	8: 3	of this e nation will prefer death to life,	8273
	11: 8	the stubbornness of their e hearts.	8273
	11:15	doing in my temple as she works out her e schemes	4659
	11:17	of Judah have done e and provoked me	8273
	13:23	Neither can you do good who are accustomed to doing e.	8317
	16:12	the stubbornness of his e heart instead	8273
	18: 8	and if that nation I warned repents of its e,	8288
	18:10	it does e in my sight and does not obey me,	8273
	18:11	So turn from your e ways, each one of you,	8273
	18:12	the stubborn inclinations of their e heart.' "	8273
	18:20	Should good be repaid with e?	8288
	21:12	like fire because of the e you have done—	8278
	23: 2	on you for the e you have done,"	8278
	23:10	an e course and use their power unjustly.	8288
	23:22	from their e ways and from their evil deeds.	8273
	23:22	from their evil ways and from their e deeds.	8278

Jer	25: 5	from your e ways and your evil practices,	8273
	25: 5	from your evil ways and your e practices,	8278
	26: 3	and each will turn from his e way.	8273
	26: 3	because of the e they have done.	8278
	32:30	of Israel and Judah have done nothing but e	8273
	32:32	by all the e they have done—	8288
	44: 3	because of the e they have done.	8288
	52: 2	He did e in the eyes of the LORD,	8273
Eze	3:18	to dissuade him from his e ways in order	8401
	3:19	or from his e ways, he will die for his sin;	8401
	3:20	from his righteousness and does e,	6404
	6: 9	for the e they have done and	8288
	11: 2	these are the men who are plotting e	224
	13:22	from their e ways and so save their lives,	8273
	20:43	for all the e you have done.	8288
	20:44	to your e ways and your corrupt practices,	8288
	30:12	of the Nile and sell the land to e men;	8273
	33:11	Turn from your e ways!	8273
	33:13	in his righteousness and does e, none of	6404
	33:13	he will die for the e he has done.	6404
	33:15	and does no e, he will surely live;	6404
	33:18	from his righteousness and does e,	6404
	36:31	Then you will remember your e ways	8273
	38:10	and you will devise an e scheme.	8273
Da	11:27	The two kings, with their hearts bent on e,	5334
Hos	7: 2	not realize that I remember all their e deeds.	8288
	7:15	but they plot e against me.	8273
	10:13	planted wickedness, you have reaped e,	6406
Am	5:13	quiet in such times, for the times are e.	8273
	5:14	Seek good, not e, that you may live.	8273
	5:15	Hate e, love good;	8273
	6: 3	You put off the e day and bring near a reign	8273
	9: 4	I will fix my eyes upon them for e and not	8288
Jnh	3: 8	up their e ways and their violence.	8273
	3:10	and how they turned from their e ways,	8273
Mic	2: 1	to those who plot e on their beds!	8273
	3: 2	you who hate good and love e;	8273
	3: 4	from because of the e they have done.	8317
	7: 3	Both hands are skilled in doing e;	8273
Na	1:11	has one come forth who plots e against	8288
Hab	1:13	Your eyes are too pure to look on e;	8273
Zec	1: 4	from your e ways and your evil practices.'	8273
	1: 4	from your evil ways and your e practices,	8273
	7:10	In your hearts do not think e of each other.'	8288
	8:17	do not plot e against your neighbor,	8288
Mal	2:17	"All who do e are good in the eyes of	8273
Mt	5:11	persecute you and falsely say all kinds of e	4505
	5:37	beyond this comes from the e one.	4505
	5:39	But I tell you, Do not resist an e person.	4505
	5:45	He causes his sun to rise on the e and	4505
	6:13	but deliver us from the e one.'	4505
	7:11	If you, then, though you are e,	4505
	9: 4	"Why do you entertain e thoughts	4505
	10: 1	to drive out e spirits and	176
	12:34	how can you who are e say anything good?	4505
	12:35	and the good man brings good things out of	4505
	12:35	and the evil man brings e things out of	4505
	12:35	of the e stored up in him.	4505
	12:43	"When an e spirit comes out of a man,	176
	13:19	the e one comes and snatches away	4505
	13:38	The weeds are the sons of the e one,	4505
	13:41	that causes sin and all who do e.	490
	15:19	For out of the heart come e thoughts,	4505
	22:18	But Jesus, knowing their e intent, said,	4504
Mk	1:23	by an e spirit cried out,	176
	1:26	The e spirit shook the man violently	176
	1:27	He even gives orders to e spirits	176
	3: 4	to do good or to do e,	2803
	3:11	Whenever the e spirits saw him,	176
	3:30	"He has an e spirit."	176
	5: 2	a man with an e spirit came from the tombs	176
	5: 8	"Come out of this man, you e spirit!"	176
	5:13	e spirits came out and went into the pigs.	176
	6: 7	and gave them authority over e spirits.	176
	7:21	come e thoughts, sexual immorality, theft,	2805
	7:25	by an e spirit came and fell at his feet.	176
	9:25	he rebuked the e spirit.	176
Lk	3:19	and all the other e things he had done,	4505
	4:33	a man possessed by a demon, an e spirit.	176
	4:36	and power he gives orders to e spirits	176
	6: 9	to do good or to do e,	2803
	6:18	Those troubled by e spirits were cured,	176
	6:22	and insult you and reject your name as e,	4505
	6:45	and the e man brings evil things out of	4505
	6:45	and the evil man brings e things out of	4505
	6:45	of the e stored up in his heart.	4505
	7:21	sicknesses and e spirits,	4505
	8: 2	of e spirits and diseases:	4505
	8:29	For Jesus had commanded the e spirit	176
	9:42	but Jesus rebuked the e spirit,	176
	11:13	If you then, though you are e,	4505
	11:24	"When an e spirit comes out of a man,	176
	11:34	of light because their eyes were e.	4505
Jn	3:19	Everyone who does e hates the light,	5765
	5:29	to live, and those who have done e will rise	5765
	7: 7	because I testify that what it does is e.	4505
	17:15	but that you protect them from the e one.	4505
Ac	5:16	and those tormented by e spirits,	176
	8: 7	With shrieks, e spirits came out of many,	176
	19:12	and the e spirits left them.	4505
	19:13	around driving out e spirits tried to invoke	2020
	19:15	[One day] the e spirit answered them,	4505
	19:16	Then the man who had the e spirit jumped	4505
	19:18	and openly confessed their e deeds.	NIG
	23: 5	'Do not speak e about the ruler	2809
Ro	1:29	e, greed and depravity.	4504
	1:30	they invent ways of doing e;	2805

Ro	2: 8	and who reject the truth and follow e,	94
	2: 9	for every human being who does e:	2805
	3: 8	"Let us do e that good may result"?	2805
	6:12	so that you obey its e desires.	2123
	7:19	no, the e I do not want to do—	2805
	7:21	I want to do good, e is right there with me.	2805
	12: 9	Hate what is e; cling to what is good.	4505
	12:17	Do not repay anyone e for evil.	2805
	12:17	Do not repay anyone evil for e.	2805
	12:21	Do not be overcome by e,	2805
	12:21	but overcome e with good.	2805
	14:16	to be spoken of as e.	1059
	16:19	and innocent about what is e.	2805
1Co	10: 6	from setting our hearts on e things	2805
	13: 6	Love does not delight in e but rejoices with	94
	14:20	In regard to e be infants,	2798
Gal	1: 4	to rescue us from the present e age,	4505
Eph	5:16	because the days are e.	4505
	6:12	and against the spiritual forces of e in	4504
	6:13	so that when the day of e comes,	4505
	6:16	the flaming arrows of the e one.	4505
Php	3: 2	those men who do e,	2805
Col	1:21	in your minds because of your e behavior.	4505
	3: 5	lust, e desires and greed, which is idolatry.	2805
1Th	5:22	Avoid every kind of e.	4505
2Th	2:10	of e that deceives those who are perishing.	94
	3: 2	be delivered from wicked and e men,	4505
	3: 3	and protect you from the e one.	4505
1Ti	6: 4	in envy, strife, malicious talk, e suspicions	4505
	6:10	love of money is a root of all kinds of e.	2805
2Ti	2:22	Flee the e desires of youth,	2123
	3: 6	and are swayed by all kinds of e desires,	2123
	3:13	while e men and impostors will go	4505
	4:18	from every e attack	4505
Tit	1:12	"Cretans are always liars, e brutes,	2805
Heb	5:14	to distinguish good from e.	2805
Jas	1:13	For God cannot be tempted by e,	2805
	1:14	is tempted when, by his own e desire,	2123
	1:21	the e that is so prevalent and humbly accept	2798
	2: 4	and become judges with e thoughts?	4505
	3: 6	a world of e among the parts of the body.	94
	3: 8	It is a restless e, full of deadly poison.	2805
	3:16	there you find disorder and every e practice.	5765
	4:16	All such boasting is e.	4505
1Pe	1:14	do not conform to the e desires you had	2123
	2:16	not use your freedom as a cover-up for e;	2798
	3: 9	not repay e with evil or insult with insult,	2805
	3: 9	not repay evil with e or insult with insult,	2805
	3:10	from e and his lips from deceitful speech.	2805
	3:11	He must turn from e and do good;	2805
	3:12	face of the Lord is against those who do e."	2805
	3:17	to suffer for doing good than for doing e.	2803
	4: 2	of his earthly life for e human desires,	2123
2Pe	1: 4	in the world caused by e desires.	2123
	2: 3	scoffing and following their own e desires.	2123
1Jn	2:13	because you have overcome the e one.	4505
	2:14	and you have overcome the e one.	4505
	3:12	to the e one and murdered his brother.	4505
	3:12	Because his own actions were e	4505
	5:18	and the e one cannot harm him.	4505
	5:19	under the control of the e one.	4505
3Jn	1:11	do not imitate what is e but what is good.	2805
	1:11	Anyone who does what is e has	2803
Jude	1:16	they follow their own e desires;	2123
Rev	16:13	I saw three e spirits that looked like frogs;	176
	18: 2	for demons and a haunt for every e spirit,	176

EVIL-MERODACH (2)

| 2Ki | 25:27 | in the year E became king of Babylon, | 213 |
| Jer | 52:31 | in the year E became king of Babylon, | 213 |

EVILDOER (3) [EVIL]

2Sa	3:39	May the LORD repay the e according	6913+8288
Ps	101: 8	I will cut off every e from the city of	224+7188
Mal	4: 1	arrogant and every e will be stubble,	6913+8402

EVILDOERS (29) [EVIL]

1Sa	24:13	'From e come evil deeds,'	8401
Job	8:20	or strengthen the hands of e.	8317
	34: 8	He keeps company with e;	224+7188
	34:22	no deep shadow, where e can hide.	224+7188
Ps	14: 4	Will e never learn—	224+7188
	14: 6	You e frustrate the plans of the poor,	NIH
	26: 5	I abhor the assembly of e and refuse to sit	8317
	36:12	See how the e lie fallen—	224+7188
	53: 4	Will the e never learn—	224+7188
	59: 2	Deliver me from e and save me from	224+7188
	64: 2	from that noisy crowd of e.	224+7188
	92: 7	up like grass and all e flourish,	224+7188
	92: 9	all e will be scattered.	224+7188
	94: 4	all the e are full of boasting.	224+7188
	94:16	Who will take a stand for me against e?	224+7188
	119:115	Away from me, you e,	8317
	125: 5	the LORD will banish with the e.	224+7188
	141: 4	in wicked deeds with men who are e;	224+7188
	141: 5	my prayer is ever against the deeds of e;	8288
	141: 9	from the traps set by e.	224+7188
Pr	21:15	joy to the righteous but terror to e.	224+7188
Isa	1: 4	a brood of e, children given to corruption!	8317
	31: 2	against those who help e.	224+7188
Jer	23:14	They strengthen the hands of e,	8317
Hos	10: 9	Did not war overtake the e in Gibeah?	1201+6594
Mal	3:15	Certainly the e prosper,	6913+8402
Mt	7:23	Away from me, you e!'	490+2237+3836
Lk	13:27	Away from me, all you e!'	94+2239

| Lk | 18:11 | robbers, e, adulterers— | 96 |

EVILS (1) [EVIL]

| Mk | 7:23 | All these e come from inside and make | 4505 |

EWE (6) [EWES]

Ge	21:28	Abraham set apart seven e lambs from	3898
	21:29	of these seven e lambs you have set apart	3898
Lev	14:10	and one e lamb a year old,	3898
Nu	6:14	for a burnt offering, a year-old e lamb	3898
2Sa	12: 3	poor man had nothing except one little e	
		lamb he had bought.	3898
	12: 4	the e lamb that belonged to the poor man	3898

EWES (2) [EWE]

| Ge | 32:14 | two hundred e and twenty rams, | 8161 |
| | 33:13 | the e and cows that are nursing their young. | 7366 |

EXACT (6) [EXACTED, EXACTING, EXACTLY]

Ge	43:21	the e weight—in the mouth of his sack.	5486
Est	4: 7	including the e amount	7308
Mt	2: 7	found out from them the e	208
Jn	4:53	the father realized that this was the e time	NIG
Ac	3: 9	and the e places where they should live.	3999
Heb	1: 3	of God's glory and the e representation	5917

EXACTED (3) [EXACT]

2Ki	15:20	Menahem e this money from Israel.	3655
	18:14	The king of Assyria e from Hezekiah king	8492
	23:35	and e the silver and gold from the people of	5601

EXACTING (2) [EXACT]

| Ne | 5: 7 | You are e usury from your own countrymen | 5957 |
| | 5:10 | But let the e of usury stop! | 5391 |

EXACTLY (9) [EXACT]

Ge	41:13	And things turned out e	4027
Ex	25: 9	all its furnishings e like	889+3869+3972+4027
Nu	8: 4	lampstand was made e like the pattern	3869+4027
		he must do e as you do.	889+3869+4027
Dt	24: 8	careful to do e as the priests,	889+3869+3972
Jdg	7:17	do e as I do.	889+3869+4027
2Ki	7:17	And that is e what happened to him,	4027
Jn	14:31	I do e what my Father has commanded me.	4048
Ac	22:30	to find out e why Paul was being accused	855

EXALT (28) [EXALTED, EXALTS]

Ex	15: 2	my father's God, and I will e him.	8123
Jos	3: 7	"Today I will begin to e you in the eyes	1540
1Sa	2:10	to his king and e the horn of his anointed."	8123
1Ch	25: 5	through the promises of God to e him.	1540
Job	19: 5	If indeed you would e yourselves	1540
Ps	30: 1	I will e you, O LORD,	8123
	34: 3	let us e his name together.	8123
	35:26	may all who e themselves over me	1540
	37:34	He will e you to inherit the land;	1540
	38:16	not let them gloat or e themselves over me	1540
	75: 6	the east or the west or from the desert can e	8123
	89:17	and by your favor you e our horn.	8123
	99: 5	E the LORD our God and worship	8123
	99: 9	E the LORD our God and worship	8123
	107:32	Let them e him in the assembly of	8123
	118:28	you are my God, and I will e you.	8123
	145: 1	I will e you, my God the King;	8123
Pr	4: 8	Esteem her, and she will e you;	8123
	25: 6	Do not e yourself in the king's presence,	2075
Isa	24:15	e the name of the LORD,	NIH
	25: 1	I will e you and praise your name,	8123
Eze	21:26	of kingdoms and will never again e itself	5951
Da	4:37	praise and e and glorify the King of heaven,	10659
	11:36	e and magnify himself above every god	8123
	11:37	but will e himself above them all.	1540
Hos	11: 7	he will by no means e them.	8123
2Th	2: 4	and will e himself over everything	5643

EXALTED (67) [EXALT]

Ex	15: 1	for he is highly e.	1448+1448
	15:21	"Sing to the LORD, for he is highly e.	1448+1448
Nu	24: 7	their kingdom will be e.	5951
Jos	4:14	That day the LORD e Joshua in the sight	1540
2Sa	5:12	as king over Israel and had e his kingdom	5951
	22:47	E be God, the Rock, my Savior!	8123
	22:49	You e me above my foes;	8123
	23: 1	the oracle of the man e by the Most High,	7756
1Ch	14: 2	and that his kingdom had been highly e for	5951
	17:17	as though I were the most of men,	5092+9366
	29:11	you are e as head over all.	5951
	29:25	The LORD highly e Solomon in the sight	1540
Ne	9: 5	may it be e above all blessing and praise.	8123
Job	24:24	For a little while they are e,	8250
	36:22	"God is e in his power.	8435
	37:23	The Almighty is beyond our reach and e	8438
Ps	18:46	E be God my Savior!	8123
	18:48	You e me above my foes;	8123
	21:13	Be e, O LORD, in your strength;	8123
	27: 6	be e above the enemies who surround me;	8123
	35:27	may they always say, "The LORD be e,	1540
	40:16	"The LORD be e!"	8123
	46:10	I will be e among the nations,	8123

Ps	46:10	*I will be* e in the earth."	8123
	47: 9	*he is* greatly e.	6590
	57: 5	Be e, O God, above the heavens;	8123
	57:11	Be e, O God, above the heavens;	8123
	70: 4	"*Let God be* e!"	1540
	89:13	your hand is strong, your right hand e.	8123
	89:19	*I have* e a young man from among	8123
	89:24	and through my name his horn *will be* e.	8123
	89:27	the **most** e of the kings of the earth.	6609
	89:42	*You have* e the right hand of his foes;	8123
	92: 8	But you, O LORD, are e forever.	5294
	92:10	*You have* e my horn like that of a wild ox;	8123
	97: 9	you **are** e far above all gods.	6590
	99: 2	he **is** e over all the nations.	8123
	108: 5	Be e, O God, above the heavens,	8123
	113: 4	The LORD *is* e over all the nations,	8123
	138: 2	for *you have* e above all things your name	1540
	148:13	for his name alone **is** e;	8435
Pr	11:11	the blessing of the upright a city *is* e,	8123
	30:32	you have played the fool and e **yourself,**	5951
Isa	2:11	the LORD alone *will be* e in that day.	8435
	2:12	for all *that* **is** e (and they will be humbled),	5951
	2:17	the LORD alone *will be* e in that day,	8435
	5:16	LORD Almighty *will be* e by his justice,	1467
	6: 1	the Lord seated on a throne, high and e, and	5951
	12: 4	and proclaim that his name *is* e.	8435
	24: 4	the e *of* the earth languish.	5294+6639
	33: 5	The LORD **is** e, for he dwells on high;	8435
	33:10	"Now *will I* be e; now will I be lifted up.	8123
	52:13	he will be raised and lifted up and highly e.	1467
Jer	17:12	A glorious throne, e from the beginning,	5294
La	2:17	*he has* e the horn of your foes.	8123
Eze	21:26	The lowly *will be* e and the exalted will	1467
	21:26	be exalted and the e will be brought low.	1469
Hos	13: 1	he *was* e in Israel.	5951
Mic	6: 6	and bow down before the e God?	5294
Mt	23:12	and whoever humbles himself *will be* e.	5738
Lk	14:11	and he who humbles himself *will be* e."	5738
	18:14	and he who humbles himself *will be* e."	5738
Ac	2:33	E to the right hand of God,	5738
	5:31	God e him to his own right hand as Prince	5738
Php	1:20	as always Christ *will be* e in my body,	3486
	2: 9	Therefore God e him **to the highest place**	5671
Heb	7:26	set apart from sinners, e **above** the heavens.	5734

EXALTS (7) [EXALT]

1Sa	2: 7	he humbles and he e.	8123
Job	36: 7	with kings and e *them* forever.	1467
Ps	75: 7	He brings one down, *he* e another.	8123
Pr	14:34	Righteousness e a nation,	8123
Mt	23:12	For whoever e himself will be humbled,	5738
Lk	14:11	everyone who e himself will be humbled,	5738
	18:14	everyone who e himself will be humbled,	5738

EXAMINE (36) [CROSS-EXAMINED, EXAMINED, EXAMINES, EXAMINING]

Ge	37:32	E it *to see* whether it is your son's robe."	5795
Lev	13: 3	The priest *is to* e the sore on his skin,	8011
	13: 5	On the seventh day the priest *is to* e him,	8011
	13: 6	*to* e him again, and if the sore has faded	8011
	13: 8	The priest *is to* e him,	8011
	13:10	The priest *is to* e him,	8011
	13:13	the priest *is to* e him,	8011
	13:17	The priest *is to* e him,	8011
	13:20	the priest *is to* e it,	8011
	13:25	the priest *is to* e the spot,	8011
	13:27	On the seventh day the priest *is to* e him,	8011
	13:30	the priest *is to* e the sore, and if it appears	8011
	13:32	the seventh day the priest *is to* e the sore,	8011
	13:34	the seventh day the priest *is to* e the itch,	8011
	13:36	*to* e him, and if the itch has spread in	8011
	13:39	the priest *is to* e them, and if	8011
	13:43	The priest *is to* e him,	8011
	13:50	The priest *is to* e the mildew and isolate	8011
	13:51	On the seventh day *he is to* e it,	8011
	13:55	the priest *is to* e it,	8011
	14: 3	to go outside the camp and e him.	8011
	14:36	to be emptied before he goes in to e	8011
	14:37	*He is to* e the mildew on the walls,	8011
	14:44	to go and e it and, if the mildew has spread	8011
	14:48	the priest comes *to* e it and the mildew has	8011
Job	7:18	that *you* e him every morning	7212
	34:23	God *has* no *need to* e men further,	8492
Ps	11: 4	his eyes e them.	1043
	17: 3	you probe my heart and e me at night,	7212
	26: 2	and try me, e my heart and my mind,	7671
Jer	17:10	the LORD search the heart and e the mind,	1043
	20:12	you *who* e the righteous and probe the heart	1043
La	3:40	*Let us* e our ways and test them,	2924
Eze	21:21	he will consult his idols, *he will* e the liver.	8011
1Co	11:28	A man *ought to* e himself before he eats of	1507
2Co	13: 5	E yourselves *to see* whether you are in the faith;	4279

EXAMINED (5) [EXAMINE]

Job	5:27	"*We have* e this, and it is true.	2983
	13: 9	Would it turn out well if *he* e you?	2983
Lk	23:14	*I have* e him in your presence	373
Ac	17:11	the message with great eagerness and e	373
	28:18	They e me and wanted to release me,	373

EXAMINES (8) [EXAMINE]

Lev	13: 3	When the priest e him,	8011
	13:21	But if, when the priest e it,	8011

Lev	13:26	if the priest e it and there is no white hair in	8011
	13:31	But if, when the priest e this kind of sore,	8011
	13:53	"But if, when the priest e it,	8011
	13:56	If, when the priest e it,	8011
Ps	11: 5	The LORD e the righteous,	1043
Pr	5:21	and *he* e all his paths.	7143

EXAMINING (3) [EXAMINE]

Ne	2:13	e the walls of Jerusalem,	8431
	2:15	so I went up the valley by night, e the wall.	8431
Ac	24: 8	*By* e him yourself you will be able to learn	373

EXAMPLE (19) [EXAMPLES]

2Ki	14: 3	In everything *he* **followed the** e	3869+6913+6913
Ecc	9:13	I also saw under the sun **this** e *of* wisdom	AIT
Eze	14: 8	that man and make him an e and a byword.	253
Jn	13:15	an e that you should do as I have done	5682
Ro	7: 2	**For** e, by law a married woman is bound	1142
1Co	10: 1	**Follow** my e, as I follow the example	1181+3629
	11: 1	as I follow the e of Christ.	NIG
Gal	3:15	*let me* **take an** e from everyday life.	3306
Php	3:17	**Join with others** in following my e,	1181+5213
2Th	3: 7	how you ought *to* follow our e.	3628
1Ti	1:16	as an e for those who would believe on him	5721
	4:12	but set an e for the believers in speech,	5596
Tit	2: 7	an e by doing what is good.	5596
Heb	4:11	so that no one will fall by following their e	5682
Jas	3: 4	Or take ships as an e.	NIG
	5:10	as an e of patience in the face of suffering,	5682
1Pe	2:21	leaving you an e, that you should follow	5681
2Pe	2: 6	and made them an e of what is going	5682
Jude	1: 7	as an e of those who suffer the punishment	1257

EXAMPLES (3) [EXAMPLE]

1Co	10: 6	Now these things occurred as e to keep us	5596
	10:11	as e and were written down as warnings	5595
1Pe	5: 3	but being e to the flock.	5596

EXASPERATE (1)

Eph	6: 4	Fathers, *do* not e your children;	4239

EXCEED (2) [EXCEEDED, EXCEEDINGLY, EXCESSIVE]

Nu	3:46	273 firstborn Israelites who e **the number**	6369
Job	14: 5	and have set limits *he* cannot e.	6296

EXCEEDED (3) [EXCEED]

Nu	3:49	from those *who* e **the number** redeemed by	6369
1Ki	10: 7	in wisdom and wealth *you have* **far** e	3578
2Ch	9: 6	*you have* **far** e the report I heard.	3578

EXCEEDINGLY (6) [EXCEED]

Ge	30:43	In this way the man grew e prosperous	4394+4394
Ex	1: 7	and became e numerous,	928+4394+4394
Nu	11:10	The LORD became e angry,	4394
	14: 7	through and explored is e good.	4394+4394
2Ch	1: 1	with him and made him e great.	2025+4200+5087
Eze	9: 9	of Israel and Judah is e great;	928+4394+4394

EXCEL (4) [EXCELLED, EXCELLENCY, EXCELLENT, EXCELLING]

Ge	49: 4	*you* will no longer e,	3855
1Co	14:12	try to e in gifts that build up the church.	4355
2Co	8: 7	But just as *you* e in everything—	4355
	8: 7	*see that* you also e in this grace of giving.	4355

EXCELLED (1) [EXCEL]

Isa	10:10	kingdoms whose images e those	4946

EXCELLENCY (1) [EXCEL]

Ac	23:26	*To His* **E**, Governor Felix: Greetings.	3196

EXCELLENT (8) [EXCEL]

Ps	45: 2	*You are the* **most** e of men	3636
Lk	1: 3	for you, **most** e Theophilus,	3196
Ac	24: 3	Everywhere and in every way, **most** e Felix,	3196
	26:25	"I am not insane, **most** e Festus,"	3196
1Co	12:31	now I will show you the **most** e way.	2848+5651
Php	4: 8	if anything is e or praiseworthy—	746
1Ti	3:13	an e standing and great assurance	2819
Tit	3: 8	These things are e and profitable	2819

EXCELLING (2) [EXCEL]

Ge	49: 3	the first sign of my strength, e *in* honor,	3856
	49: 3	excelling in honor, e *in* power.	3856

EXCEPT (94) [EXCEPTION, EXCEPTIONAL]

Ge	39: 6	did not concern himself with anything e	561+3954
	39: 9	withheld nothing from me e you,	561+3954
	47:18	for our lord e our bodies and our land.	561+1194
Ex	8: 9	e *for* those that remain in the Nile.	8370
	12:16	e to prepare food for everyone to eat—	421
Lev	13:33	be shaved e *for* the diseased area,	2256+4202
	21: 2	e *for* a close relative,	561+3954
Nu	14:30	e Caleb son of Jephunneh and Joshua son of Nun.	561+3954
	16:40	that no one e a descendant of Aaron	889+4202

Nu	26:65	was left e Caleb son of Jephunneh	561+3954
	32:12	not one e Caleb son of Jephunneh	1194
	35:33	e by the blood of the one who shed it.	561+3954
Dt	1:36	e Caleb son of Jephunneh.	2314
	16: 6	e in the place he will choose as a dwelling for his Name.	561+3954
Jos	6:15	e that on that day they circled	8370
	8: 2	e that you may carry off their plunder	8370
	11:13	e Hazor, which Joshua burned.	2314
	11:19	E for the Hivites living in Gibeon,	1194
Jdg	11:34	E for her he had neither son nor daughter.	4946
Ru	2: 7	e for a short rest in the shelter."	2296
	4: 4	For no one has the right to do it e you,	2314
1Sa	21: 6	there was no bread there e the bread	561+3954
	30:17	e four hundred young men who rode off	561+3954
2Sa	12: 3	poor man had nothing e one little ewe lamb he had bought.	561+3954
	22:32	And who is the Rock e our God?	1187+4946
1Ki	3: 3	e that he offered sacrifices	8370
	8: 9	in the ark e the two stone tablets	8370
	15: 5	e in the case of Uriah the Hittite.	8370
	17: 1	in the next few years e at my word."	561+3954
	22:31	small or great, e the king of Israel."	561+3954
2Ki	4: 2	she said, "e a little oil."	561+3954
	5:15	that there is no God in all the world e	561+3954
	9:35	they found nothing e her skull,	561+3954
	13: 7	the army of Jehoahaz e fifty horsemen,	561+3954
2Ch	2: 6	e as a place to burn sacrifices before him?	561+3954
	5:10	There was nothing in the ark e	8370
	18:30	small or great, e the king of Israel."	561+3954
	21:17	Not a son was left to him e Ahaziah,	561+3954
	23: 6	of the LORD e the priests and Levites	561+3954
Ne	2:12	with me e the one I was riding on.	561+3954
Ps	18:31	And who is the Rock e our God?	2314
Ecc	5:11	what benefit are they to the owner e	561+3954
Jer	44:14	none will return e a few fugitives."	561+3954
Da	2:11	No one can reveal it to the king e the gods,	10386
	3:28	or worship any god e their own God.	10386
	6: 7	e to you, O king,	10386
	6:12	who prays to any god or man e to you,	10386
	10:21	supports me against them e Michael,	561+3954
Hos	13: 4	no God but me, no Savior e me.	1194
Mt	5:13	e to be thrown out and trampled by men.	1623+3590
	5:32	e for marital unfaithfulness,	4211
	11:27	No one knows the Son e the Father,	1623+3590
	11:27	no one knows the Father e the Son and	1623+3590
	12:39	e the sign of the prophet Jonah.	1623+3590
	16: 4	will be given it e the sign of Jonah."	1623+3590
	17: 8	they saw no one e Jesus.	1623+3590
	19: 9	e for marital unfaithfulness,	3590
	21:19	but found nothing on it e leaves.	1623+3590
Mk	5:37	follow him e Peter, James and John	1623+3590
	6: 5	e lay his hands on a few sick people	1623+3590
	6: 8	"Take nothing for the journey e a staff	1623+3590
	8:14	e for one loaf they had with them in	1623+3590
	9: 8	no longer saw anyone with them e Jesus.	247
	10:18	"No one is good—e God alone.	1623+3590
Lk	8:51	not let anyone go in with him e Peter,	1623+3590
	10:22	No one knows who the Son is e the Father,	1623+3590
	10:22	knows who the Father is e the Son and	1623+3590
	11:29	will be given it e the sign of Jonah.	1623+3590
	17:18	give praise to God e this foreigner?"	1623+3590
	18:19	"No one is good—e God alone.	1623+3590
Jn	1:33	e that the one who sent me to baptize	247
	3:13	No one has ever gone into heaven e	1623+3590
	6:46	No one has seen the Father e the one	1623+3590
	14: 6	No one comes to the Father e through me.	1623+3590
	17:12	None has been lost e the one doomed	1623+3590
Ac	8: 1	and all e the apostles were scattered	4440
	26:29	to me today may become what I am, e **for**	4211
Ro	7: 7	not have known what sin was e through the law.	1623+3590
	13: 1	for there is no authority e that which	1623+3590
	13: 8	e the continuing debt to love one another,	1623+3590
	15:18	of anything e what Christ has accomplished	NIG
1Co	1:14	I did not baptize any of you e Crispus and Gaius,	1623+3590
	2: 2	e Jesus Christ and him crucified.	1623+3590
	2:11	knows the thoughts of a man e the man's spirit	1623+3590
	2:11	no one knows the thoughts of God e the Spirit of God.	1623+3590
	7: 5	not deprive each other e by mutual consent	323+1623+3614
	10:13	No temptation has seized you e what is common to man.	1623+3590
	12: 3	"Jesus is Lord," e by the Holy Spirit.	1623+3590
2Co	12:13	e that I was never a burden to you?	1623+3590
Gal	6:14	May I never boast e in the cross	1623+3590
Eph	4: 9	(What does "he ascended" mean e that	1623+3590
Php	4:15	of giving and receiving, e you only;	1623+3590
Rev	14: 3	No one could learn the song e the 144,000 who had been redeemed	1623+3590

EXCEPTION (1) [EXCEPT]

Est	4:11	The **only** e to this is for the king to	963+4200

EXCEPTIONAL (1) [EXCEPT]

Da	6: 3	by his e qualities that the king planned	10339

EXCESSIVE (6) [EXCEED]

Eze	18: 8	He does not lend at usury or take e interest.	9552
	18:13	He lends at usury and takes e interest.	9552
	18:17	from sin and takes no usury or e interest.	9552
	22:12	and e interest and make unjust gain	9552
2Co	2: 7	he will not be overwhelmed by e sorrow.	4358
Rev	18: 3	of the earth grew rich from her e luxuries."	1539

EXCHANGE (13) [EXCHANGED, EXCHANGING]

Ge	47:16	"I will sell you food in e for your livestock,	928
	47:17	and he gave them food in e for their horses,	928
	47:17	with food in e for all their livestock.	928
	47:19	Buy us and our land in e for food,	928
Lev	27:10	He must not e it or substitute a good one for	2736
Dt	14:25	then e your tithe for silver,	5989
1Ki	21: 2	In e I will give you a better vineyard or,	9393
Isa	43: 4	I will give men in e for you,	9393
	43: 4	and people in e for your life.	9393
Eze	48:14	They must not sell or e any of it.	4614
Mt	16:26	Or what can a man give in e for his soul?	498
Mk	8:37	Or what can a man give in e for his soul?	498
2Co	6:13	As a fair e—I speak as to my children—	521

EXCHANGED (13) [EXCHANGE]

Ps	106:20	They e their Glory for an image of a bull,	4614
Jer	2:11	But my people have e their Glory	4614
Eze	27:12	they e silver, iron, tin and lead	5989
	27:13	they e slaves and articles of bronze	5989
	27:14	" 'Men of Beth Togarmah e work horses,	5989
	27:16	they e turquoise, purple fabric,	5989
	27:18	they e wheat from Minnith and confections,	5989
	27:19	they e wrought iron,	5989
	27:22	for your merchandise they e the finest	5989
Hos	4: 7	they e their Glory for something disgraceful	4614
Ro	1:23	and e the glory of the immortal God	248
	1:25	They e the truth of God for a lie,	3563
	1:26	Even their women e natural relations	3563

EXCHANGING (1) [EXCHANGE]

Jn	2:14	and others sitting at tables e money.	3048

EXCITEMENT (1)

Job	39:24	In frenzied e he eats up the ground;	8075

EXCLAIM (3) [EXCLAIMED, EXCLAIMING]

Ps	35:10	My whole being will e, "Who is like you,	606
Jer	46:17	There they will e, 'Pharaoh king	7924
Rev	18:18	the smoke of her burning, they will e,	3189

EXCLAIMED (12) [EXCLAIM]

Jdg	6:22	he e, "Ah, Sovereign LORD!	606
Ru	1:19	and the women e, "Can this be Naomi?"	606
	2:10	She e, "Why have I found such favor	606
2Ki	3:10	"What!" e the king of Israel.	606
Est	7: 8	The king e, "Will he even molest the queen	606
Mt	27:54	and e, "Surely he was the Son of God!"	3306
Mk	1:37	they e, "Everyone is looking for you!"	3306
	9:24	Immediately the boy's father e,	3189
Lk	1:42	In a loud voice she e: "Blessed are you	430
Jn	8:52	At this the Jews e, "Now we know	3306
Ac	8:10	gave him their attention and e,	3306
	12:14	without opening it and e,	550

EXCLAIMING (1) [EXCLAIM]

1Co	14:25	So he will fall down and worship God, e,	550

EXCLUDE (4) [EXCLUDED, EXCLUSIVELY]

Isa	56: 3	"The LORD will surely e me	976+976
	66: 5	and e you because of my name, have said,	5612
Lk	6:22	when they e you and insult you	928
Rev	11: 2	But the outer court;	1675

EXCLUDED (6) [EXCLUDE]

2Ch	26:21	and e from the temple of the LORD.	1615
Ezr	2:62	so were e from the priesthood as unclean.	4946
Ne	7:64	so were e from the priesthood as unclean.	4946
	13: 3	they e from Israel all who were	976
Ro	3:27	It is e.	1710
Eph	2:12	e from citizenship in Israel and foreigners	558

EXCLUSIVELY (1) [EXCLUDE]

Ac	18: 5	Paul devoted himself e to preaching,	AIT

EXCREMENT (3)

Dt	23:13	dig a hole and cover up your e.	7362
Eze	4:12	using human e for fuel."	1645+7362
	4:15	over cow manure instead of human e."	1645

EXCUSE (6) [EXCUSES]

Ps	25: 3	to shame who are treacherous without e.	8200
Lk	14:18	Please e me.'	2400+4148
	14:19	Please e me.'	2400+4148
Jn	15:22	Now, however, they have no e for their sin.	4733
Ro	1:20	so that men are without e.	406
	2: 1	You, therefore, have no e,	406

EXCUSES (1) [EXCUSE]

Lk	14:18	"But they all alike began to make e.	4148

EXECRATION (KJV) OBJECT OF CURSING

EXECUTE (11) [EXECUTED, EXECUTING, EXECUTION, EXECUTIONER]

2Ch	2:14	of engraving and can e any design given	3108
Isa	66:16	the LORD will e judgment upon all men,	9149
Eze	11:10	and I will e judgment on you at	9149
	11:11	I will e judgment on you at the borders	9149
	17:20	I will bring him to Babylon and e judgment	9149
	20:35	face to face, I will e judgment upon you.	9149
	38:22	I will e judgment upon him with plague	9149
Da	2:24	the king had appointed to e the wise men	10005
	2:24	"Do not e the wise men of Babylon."	10005
Hab	1:12	you have appointed them to e judgment;	NIH
Jn	18:31	"But we have no right to e anyone,"	650

EXECUTED (10) [EXECUTE]

2Ki	14: 5	the kingdom was firmly in his grasp, he e	5782
	25:21	the king had them e.	2256+4637+5782
2Ch	24:24	judgment was e on Joash.	6913
	25: 3	the kingdom was firmly in his control, he e	2222
Jer	52:27	the king had them e.	2256+4637+5782
Da	2:18	and his friends might not be e with the rest	10005
Mt	27:20	to ask for Barabbas and to have Jesus e.	660
Lk	23:32	were also led out with him to be e.	359
Ac	12:19	the guards and ordered that they be e.	552
	13:28	they asked Pilate to have him e.	359

EXECUTING (1) [EXECUTE]

2Ch	22: 8	While Jehu was e judgment on the house	9149

EXECUTION (1) [EXECUTE]

Da	2:12	so angry and furious that he ordered the e	10005

EXECUTIONER (1) [EXECUTE]

Mk	6:27	So he immediately sent an e with orders	5063

EXEMPT (4)

1Sa	17:25	e his father's family from taxes	2930+6913
1Ki	15:22	an order to all Judah—no one was e—	5929
1Ch	9:33	were e from other duties	7080
Mt	17:26	"Then the sons are e," Jesus said to him.	1801

EXERCISE (5) [EXERCISED, EXERCISES, EXERTED]

Mt	20:25	their high officials e authority over them.	2980
Mk	10:42	their high officials e authority over them.	2980
Lk	22:25	and those who e authority over	2027
1Co	8: 9	that the e of your freedom does not become	2026
Rev	13: 5	and to e his authority for forty-two months.	4472

EXERCISED (2) [EXERCISE]

Da	11: 4	nor will it have the power he e,	5440
Rev	13:12	He e all the authority of the first beast	4472

EXERCISES (1) [EXERCISE]

Jer	9:24	that I am the LORD, who e kindness,	6913

EXERTED (1) [EXERCISE]

Eph	1:20	which he e in Christ when he raised him	1919

EXHAUST (2) [EXHAUSTED]

Jer	51:58	the peoples e themselves for nothing,	3333
Hab	2:13	that the nations e themselves for nothing?	3615

EXHAUSTED (13) [EXHAUST]

Jdg	4:21	to him while he lay fast asleep, e.	6545
	8: 4	e yet keeping up the pursuit,	6546
	8:15	give bread to your e men?' "	6546
1Sa	14:31	from Micmash to Aijalon, they were e.	4394+6545
	30:10	for two hundred men were too e to cross	7006
	30:21	to the two hundred men who had been too e	7006
2Sa	16: 2	the wine is to refresh those who become e	3617
	16:14	with him arrived at their destination e.	6546
	21:15	and he became e;	6545
Jer	51:30	Their strength is e,	5980
Da	8:27	I, Daniel, was e and lay ill for several days.	2118
Lk	12:33	a treasure in heaven that will not be e,	444
	22:45	he found them asleep, e from sorrow.	NIG

EXHORT (1) [EXHORTATION, EXHORTED]

1Ti	5: 1	but e him as if he were your father.	4151

EXHORTATION (1) [EXHORT]

Heb	13:22	I urge you to bear with my word of e,	4155

EXHORTED (1) [EXHORT]

Lk	3:18	with many other words John e the people	4151

EXILE (78) [EXILED, EXILES]

2Sa	15:19	an e from your homeland.	1655

2Ki	17:23	taken from their homeland into e	1655
	24:14	He carried into e all Jerusalem:	1655+1655
	25:11	the commander of the guard carried into e	1655
	25:27	of the e of Jehoiachin king of Judah,	1661
1Ch	5: 6	of Assyria took into e.	1655
	5:22	And they occupied the land until the e.	1583
	5:26	took the Reubenites, the Gadites and the half-tribe of Manasseh into e.	1655
	6:15	sent Judah and Jerusalem into e	1655
2Ch	36:20	He carried into e to Babylon the remnant,	1655
Ezr	6:21	Israelites who had returned from the e ate it,	1583
Ne	1: 2	the Jewish remnant that survived the e,	8660
	1: 3	"Those who survived the e and are back in	8660
	8:17	from e built booths and lived in them.	8660
Est	2: 6	who had been carried into e from Jerusalem	1655
Isa	5:13	Therefore my people will go into e	1655
	27: 8	By warfare and e you contend with her—	8938
Jer	1: 3	when the people of Jerusalem went into e.	1655
	13:19	All Judah will be carried into e,	1655
	20: 6	in your house will go into e to Babylon.	8660
	22:22	and your allies will go into e.	8660
	24: 1	the artisans of Judah were carried into e	1655
	27:20	carried Jehoiachin son of Jehoiakim king of Judah into e	1655
	29: 1	other people Nebuchadnezzar had carried into e	1655
	29: 2	and the artisans had gone into e	NIH
	29: 4	to all those I carried into e from Jerusalem	1655
	29: 7	the city to which I have carried you into e.	1655
	29:14	the place from which I carried you into e."	1655
	29:16	not go with you into e—	1583
	30:10	your descendants from the land of their e.	8660
	30:16	all your enemies will go into e.	8660
	39: 9	of the imperial guard carried into e	1655
	40: 1	and Judah who were being carried into e	1655
	40: 7	and who had not been carried into e	1655
	43: 3	so they may kill us or carry us into e	1655
	46:19	Pack your belongings for e,	1583
	46:27	your descendants from the land of their e.	8660
	48: 7	and Chemosh will go into e,	1583
	48:11	she has not gone into e.	1583
	48:46	into e and your daughters into captivity.	8660
	49: 3	for Molech will go into e,	1583
	52:15	of the guard carried into e some of	1655
	52:28	the people Nebuchadnezzar carried into e:	1655
	52:30	745 Jews taken into e by Nebuzaradan	1655
	52:31	of the e of Jehoiachin king of Judah,	1661
La	1: 3	Judah has gone into e.	1655
	1: 5	Her children have gone into e,	8660
	1:18	and maidens have gone into e.	8660
	4:22	he will not prolong your e.	1655
Eze	1: 2	the fifth year of the e of King Jehoiachin—	1661
	3:11	to your countrymen in e and speak to them.	1583
	12: 3	pack your belongings for e and in	1583
	12: 4	bring out your belongings packed for e.	1583
	12: 4	go out like those who go into e.	1583
	12: 7	During the day I brought out my things packed for e,	1583
	12:11	They will go into e as captives.	1583
	25: 3	the people of Judah when they went into e,	1583
	33:21	In the twelfth year of our e,	1655
	39:23	the people of Israel went into e for their sin,	1655
	39:28	I sent them into e among the nations,	1655
	40: 1	In the twenty-fifth year of our e,	1661
Hos	10: 5	taken from them into e.	1655
Am	1: 5	The people of Aram will go into e to Kir,"	1655
	1:15	Her king will go into e,	1583
	5: 5	For Gilgal will surely go into e,	1655+1655
	5:27	I will send you into e beyond Damascus,"	1655
	6: 7	be among the first to go into e;	1655+1655
	7:11	and Israel will surely go into e,	1655+1655
	7:17	And Israel will certainly go into e,	1655+1655
	9: 4	Though they are driven into e	8660
Mic	1:16	go from you into e.	1655
Na	3:10	Yet she was taken captive and went into e.	8660
Zec	14: 2	Half of the city will go into e,	1583
Mt	1:11	and his brothers at the time of the e	3578
	1:12	After the e to Babylon.	3578
	1:17	fourteen from David to the e to Babylon,	3578
	1:17	and fourteen from the e to the Christ.	3578
Ac	7:43	Therefore I will send you into e'	3579

EXILED (8) [EXILE]

2Ki	17:28	So one of the priests who had been e	1655
Ne	1: 9	if your e people are at the farthest horizon,	5615
Isa	27:13	and those who were e in Egypt will come	5615
	49:21	I was e and rejected.	1655
Jer	22:10	rather, weep bitterly for him who is e,	2143
La	2: 9	and her princes are e among the nations,	NIH
Am	9:14	I will bring back my e people Israel,	8654
Na	2: 7	that [the city] be e and carried away.	1655

EXILES (38) [EXILE]

Ezr	1:11	the e came up from Babylon to Jerusalem.	1583
	2: 1	up from the captivity of the e,	1583
	4: 1	that the e were building a temple for	1201+1583
	6:16	the priests, the Levites and the rest of the e—	10120+10145
	6:19	the e celebrated the Passover.	1201+1583
	6:20	the Passover lamb for all the e,	1201+1583
	8:35	Then the e who had returned	1201+1583
	9: 4	because of this unfaithfulness of the e.	1583
	10: 6	to mourn over the unfaithfulness of the e.	1583
	10: 7	and Jerusalem for all the e to assemble	1201+1583

Ezr 10: 8 be expelled from the assembly of the e. 1583
10:16 So the e did as was proposed. 1201+1583
Ne 7: 6 of the e whom Nebuchadnezzar king 1583
Ps 147: 2 he gathers the e of Israel. 5615
Isa 11:12 for the nations and gather the e of Israel; 5615
20: 4 the Egyptian captives and Cushite e, young 1661
45:13 He will rebuild my city and set my e free, 1661
56: 8 he who gathers the e of Israel. 5615
Jer 24: 5 I regard as good the e from Judah, 1661
28: 4 and all the other e from Judah who went 1661
28: 6 of the LORD's house and all the e back 1583
29: 1 to the surviving elders among the e and to 1583
29:19 And you e have not listened either," NIH
29:20 all you e whom I have sent away 1583
29:22 all the e from Judah who are 1661
29:31 "Send this message to all the e: 1583
49:36 not be a nation where Elam's e do not go. 5615
Eze 1: 1 I was among the e by the Kebar River, 1583
3:15 I came to the e who lived at Tel Abib near 1583
11:24 to the e in Babylonia in the vision given by 1583
11:25 the e everything the LORD had shown me. 1583
Da 2:25 a man among the e from Judah who can tell
the king what his dream means." 10120+10145
5:13 Daniel, one of the e my father the king
brought from Judah? 10120+10145
6:13 "Daniel, who is one of the e from Judah,
10120+10145
Ob 1:20 This company of Israelite e who are 1661
1:20 the e from Jerusalem who are 1661
Mic 4: 6 the e and those I have brought to grief. 5615
Zec 6:10 "Take [silver and gold] from the e Heldai, 1583

EXIST (1) [EXISTED, EXISTS]
Ro 13: 1 The authorities that e have been established 1639

EXISTED (1) [EXIST]
2Pe 3: 5 the heavens e and the earth was formed out 1639

EXISTS (3) [EXIST]
Ecc 6:10 Whatever e has already been named, 2118
Heb 2:10 for whom and through whom everything e, NIG
11: 6 to him must believe that he e and 1639

EXITS (4)
Eze 42:11 with similar e and dimensions. 4604
43:11 its arrangement, its e and entrances— 4604
44: 5 of the temple and all the e of the sanctuary. 4604
48:30 "These will be the e of the city: 9362

EXODUS (1)
Heb 11:22 e of the Israelites from Egypt 2016

EXORBITANT (1)
Pr 28: 8 by e interest amasses it for 2256+5968+9552

EXORCISTS (KJV) DRIVING OUT EVIL
SPIRITS

EXPAND (1) [EXPANSE]
2Co 10:15 of activity among you will greatly e, 3486

EXPANSE (13) [EXPAND, EXPANSES]
Ge 1: 6 an e between the waters to separate water 8385
1: 7 So God made the e and separated the water 8385
1: 7 and separated the water under the e from 8385
1: 8 God called the e "sky." 8385
1:14 in the e of the sky to separate the day from 8385
1:15 be lights in the e of the sky to give light on 8385
1:17 in the e of the sky to give light on the earth, 8385
1:20 and let birds fly above the earth across the e 8385
Eze 1:22 like an e, sparkling like ice, 8385
1:23 the e their wings were stretched out one 8385
1:25 Then there came a voice from above the e 8385
1:26 the e over their heads was what looked like 8385
10: 1 of a throne of sapphire above the e that was 8385

EXPANSES (1) [EXPANSE]
Job 38:18 Have you comprehended the vast e of 8144

EXPECT (13) [EXPECTANT,
EXPECTANTLY, EXPECTATION,
EXPECTED, EXPECTING]
Isa 58: 4 e your voice to be heard 9048
64: 3 you did awesome things that we did not e, 7747
Eze 13: 6 yet they e their words to be fulfilled. 3498
Mt 11: 3 or should we e someone else?" 4659
24:44 at an hour when you do not e him. 1506
24:50 when he does not e him and at an hour he is 4659
Lk 6:34 to those from whom you e repayment, 1827
7:19 or should we e someone else?" 4659
7:20 or should we e someone else?' " 4659
12:40 at an hour when you do not e him." 1506
12:46 when he does not e him and at an hour he is 4659
2Co 10: 2 as I e to be toward some people who think 3357
Php 1:20 I eagerly e and hope that I will in no way 638

EXPECTANT (1) [EXPECT]
Jer 31: 8 e mothers and women in labor; 2226

EXPECTANTLY (2) [EXPECT]
Job 29:21 "Men listened to me e, 3498
Lk 3:15 The people were waiting e 4659

EXPECTATION (4) [EXPECT]
Ps 5: 3 before you and wait in e. 7595
Eze 19: 5 she saw her hope unfulfilled, her e gone, 9536
Ro 8:19 The creation waits in eager e for the sons 638
Heb 10:27 a fearful e of judgment and of raging fire 1693

EXPECTED (8) [EXPECT]
Ge 48:11 "I never e to see your face again, 7136
Pr 11: 7 all he e from his power comes to nothing. 9347
Hag 1: 9 "You e much, but see, 7155
Mt 20:10 they e to receive more. 3787
Ac 16:13 where we e to find a place of prayer. 3787
25:18 with any of the crimes I had e. 5706
28: 6 The people e him to swell up 4659
2Co 8: 5 And they did not do as we e, 1827

EXPECTING (7) [EXPECT]
Lk 2: 5 to be married to him and was e a child. 1607
6:34 e to be repaid in full. 2671
6:35 without e to get anything back. 594
8:40 for they were all e him. 4659
Ac 3: 5 e to get something from them. 4659
10:24 Cornelius was e them 4659
1Co 16:11 I am e him along with the brothers. 1683

EXPEDIENT (KJV) BENEFICIAL, BEST,
BETTER, GAINED, GOOD

EXPEL (1) [EXPELLED]
1Co 5:13 "E the wicked man from among you." 1976

EXPELLED (5) [EXPEL]
1Sa 28: 3 Saul had e the mediums and spiritists from 6073
1Ki 15:12 He e the male shrine prostitutes from 6296
Ezr 10: 8 and would himself be e from the assembly 976
Eze 28:16 and I e you, O guardian cherub, 6
Ac 13:50 and e them from their region. 1675

EXPEND (1) [EXPENSE]
2Co 12:15 spend for you everything I have and e 1682

EXPEND (Anglicized) See also SPEND

EXPENSE (2) [EXPEND, EXPENSES,
EXPENSIVE]
Lk 10:35 for any extra e you may have.' 4655
1Co 9: 7 Who serves as a soldier at his own e? 4072

EXPENSES (3) [EXPENSE]
2Ki 12:12 met all the other e 3655
Ezr 6: 8 The e of these men are to be fully paid out 10486
Ac 21:24 in their purification rites and pay their e, 1251

EXPENSIVE (5) [EXPENSE]
Mt 26: 7 with an alabaster jar of very e perfume, 988
Mk 14: 3 with an alabaster jar of very e perfume, 4500
Lk 7:25 those who wear e clothes and indulge 1902
Jn 12: 3 about a pint of pure nard, an e perfume; 4501
1Ti 2: 9 or gold or pearls or e clothes, 4500

EXPERIENCE (3) [EXPERIENCED]
Nu 16:29 and e only what usually happens to men, 7212
Jdg 3: 2 not had previous battle e); 3359
Heb 11: 5 so that he did not e death; 3972

EXPERIENCED (13) [EXPERIENCE]
Dt 11: 2 not the ones who saw and e the discipline 3359
Jos 24:31 and who had e everything 3359
Jdg 3: 1 to test all those Israelites who had not e any 3359
2Sa 17: 8 Besides, your father is an e fighter; 408+4878
1Ki 7:14 Huram was highly skilled and e 1981+2256+9312
1Ch 12:33 e soldiers prepared for battle 3655+7372
12:36 e soldiers prepared for battle— 3655+7372
2Ch 2: 7 in the art of engraving, 3359
2:14 e in all kinds of engraving 7334+7338
17:13 He also kept e fighting men in Jerusalem.
408+1475+2657+4878
Ecc 1:16 I have e much of wisdom and knowledge." 8011
SS 3: 8 all of them wearing the sword, all e in battle 4340
Ro 11:25 Israel has e a hardening in part until 1181

EXPERT (4) [EXPERTS]
Mt 22:35 One of them, an e in the law, 3788
Lk 10:25 On one occasion an e in the law stood up 3788
10:37 The e in the law replied, 1254+3836S
1Co 3:10 I laid a foundation as an e builder, 5055

EXPERTS (7) [EXPERT]
Est 1:13 for the king to consult e in matters of law 3359
Lk 7:30 and e in the law rejected God's purpose 3788
11:45 One of the e in the law answered him, 3788
11:46 Jesus replied, "And you e in the law, 3788

EXPERTS (continued)
Lk 11:52 "Woe to you e in the law, 3788
14: 3 Jesus asked the Pharisees and e in the law, 3788
2Pe 2:14 are e in greed—an accursed brood! 1214+2840

EXPIRED (KJV) ELAPSED, END, OVER,
PASSED, SPRING

EXPLAIN (20) [EXPLAINED, EXPLAINING,
EXPLAINS, EXPLANATION]
Ge 41:24 but none could e it to me." 5583
Dt 32: 7 your elders, and they will e to you. 606
Jdg 14:16 he replied, "so why should I e it to you?" 5583
1Ki 10: 3 nothing was too hard for the king to e 5583
2Ch 9: 2 nothing was too hard for him to e to her. 5583
Est 4: 8 to show to Esther and e it to her, 5583
Job 15:17 "Listen to me and I will e to you; 2555
Jer 9:12 by the LORD and can e it? 5583
Da 2: 6 But if you tell me the dream and e 10600
2:27 magician or diviner can e to the king 10252
5:12 e riddles and solve difficult problems. 10252
5:15 but they could not e it. 10252+10600
10:14 to e to you what will happen to your people 1067
Mt 13:36 "E to us the parable of the weeds in 1397
15:15 Peter said, "E the parable to us." 5851
16:21 to e to his disciples that he must go 1259
Jn 4:25 he comes, will e everything to us." 334
Ac 2:14 let me e this to you; 1196+1639
Heb 5:11 but it is hard to e because you are slow 1549
Rev 17: 7 I will e to you the mystery of the woman 3306

EXPLAINED (12) [EXPLAIN]
Jdg 14:16 "I haven't even e it to my father or mother," 5583
14:17 She in turn e the riddle to her people. 5583
14:19 and gave their clothes to those who had e 5583
1Sa 10:25 Samuel e to the people the regulations of 1819
Da 2:15 Arioch then e the matter to Daniel. 10313
2:17 and e the matter to his friends Hananiah, 10313
Zec 1:10 the man standing among the myrtle trees e, 6699
Mk 4:34 with his own disciples, he e everything. 2147
Lk 24:27 e to them what was said 1450
Ac 11: 4 and e everything to them precisely 1758
18:26 they invited him to their home and e to him 1758
28:23 From morning till evening he e and declared 1758

EXPLAINING (3) [EXPLAIN]
Jdg 14:15 "Coax your husband into e the riddle for us, 5583
Isa 28: 9 To whom is he e his message? 1067
Ac 17: 3 e and proving that the Christ had to suffer 1380

EXPLAINS (1) [EXPLAIN]
Ac 8:31 he said, "unless someone e it to me?" 3842

EXPLANATION (2) [EXPLAIN]
Ecc 8: 1 Who knows the e of things? 7323
Da 7:23 "He gave me this e: 10042

EXPLOIT (5) [EXPLOITED, EXPLOITING,
EXPLOITS]
Pr 22:22 Do not e the poor because they are poor 1608
Isa 58: 3 you as you please and e all your workers. 5601
2Co 12:17 Did I e you through any of the men I sent 4430
12:18 Titus did not e you, did he? 4430
2Pe 2: 3 In their greed these teachers will e you 1864

EXPLOITED (1) [EXPLOIT]
2Co 7: 2 we have e no one. 4430

EXPLOITING (1) [EXPLOIT]
Jas 2: 6 Is it not the rich who are e you? 2872

EXPLOITS (8) [EXPLOIT]
2Sa 23:17 Such were the e of the three mighty men. 6913
23:20 who performed great e. 7189
23:22 the e of Benaiah son of Jehoiada; 6913
1Ki 22:45 the things he achieved and his military e, 4309
1Ch 11:19 Such were the e of the three mighty men. 6913
11:22 who performed great e. 7189
11:24 the e of Benaiah son of Jehoiada; 6913
2Co 11:20 up with anyone who enslaves you or e you 2983

EXPLORE (11) [EXPLORED, EXPLORING]
Nu 13: 2 "Send some men to e the land of Canaan, 9365
13:16 the names of the men Moses sent to e 9365
13:17 When Moses sent them to e Canaan, 9365
14:36 So the men Moses had sent to e the land, 9365
14:38 Of the men who went to e the land, 9365
Jos 14: 7 from Kadesh Barnea to e the land. 8078
Jdg 18: 2 and Eshtaol to spy out the land and e it. 2983
18: 2 They told them, "Go, e the land." 2983
2Sa 10: 3 Hasn't David sent them to you to e the city 2983
1Ch 19: 3 to you to e and spy out the country 2983
Ecc 1:13 to study and to e by wisdom all that is done 9365

EXPLORED (7) [EXPLORE]
Nu 13:21 and e the land from the Desert of Zin as far 9365
13:32 a bad report about the land they had e. 9365
13:32 "The land we e devours those living in it. 6296+9365

Nu 14: 6 who were among those *who had* e the land, 9365
14: 7 through and e is exceedingly good. 9365
14:34 for each of the forty days *you* e the land— 9365
Dt 1:24 and came to the Valley of Eshcol and e it. 8078

EXPLORING (1) [EXPLORE]

Nu 13:25 of forty days they returned from the land. 9365

EXPORTED (2)

1Ki 10:29 also e *them* to all the kings of the Hittites 3655
2Ch 1:17 also e *them* to all the kings of the Hittites 3655

EXPOSE (10) [EXPOSED, EXPOSES, EXPOSING]

Nu 25: 4 **kill** them **and** e them in broad daylight 3697
Job 20:27 The heavens *will* e his guilt; 1655
Isa 57:12 I will e your righteousness 5583
La 2:14 not e your sin to ward off your captivity. 1655
4:22 and e your wickedness. 1655
Eze 25: 9 therefore I *will* e the flank of Moab, 7337
Hos 2:10 now I *will* e her lewdness before the eyes 1655
Mt 1:19 did not want to e her **to public disgrace**, 1258
1Co 4: 5 and *will* e the motives of men's hearts. 5746
Eph 5:11 but rather e them. 1794

EXPOSED (24) [EXPOSE]

Ex 20:26 lest your nakedness **be** e on it.' 1655
Lev 20:18 *he has* e the source of her flow, 6867
2Sa 21: 6 to us *to be* **killed and** e before the LORD 3697
21: 9 *who* **killed and** e them on a hill before 3697
21:13 *who had* **been killed and** e were gathered up 3697
22:16 of the sea *were* e and the foundations of 8011
Ne 4:13 of the wall at the e **places**, 7460
Est 6: 2 that Mordecai *had* e Bigthana and Teresh, 5583
Ps 18:15 of the sea *were* e and the foundations of 8011
Pr 26:26 his wickedness *will* **be** e in the assembly. 1655
Isa 47: 3 Your nakedness *will* **be** e 1655
Jer 8: 2 They *will be* e to the sun and the moon 8848
36:30 be thrown out and e to the heat by day and NIH
Eze 16:36 your nakedness in your promiscuity 1655
23:18 and e her nakedness, 1655
23:29 the shame of your prostitution *will* **be** e. 1655
Hos 5: 1 the sins of Ephraim *are* e and the crimes 1655
Hab 2:16 Drink and be e! 6887
Zep 2:14 the beams of cedar *will be* e. 6867
Jn 3:20 the light for fear their deeds *will be* e. 1794
2Co 11:23 and been e **to death** again and again. 2505
Eph 5:13 everything e by the light becomes visible, 1794
Heb 10:33 Sometimes *you* were **publicly** e to insult 2518
Rev 16:15 he may not go naked and *be* shamefully e." 1063

EXPOSES (1) [EXPOSE]

Pr 13:16 but a fool e his folly. 7298

EXPOSING (1) [EXPOSE]

Ge 30:37 and e the white inner wood of the branches. 4741

EXPOUND (2)

Dt 1: 5 Moses began *to* e this law, saying: 930
Ps 49: 4 with the harp I *will* e my riddle: 7337

EXPRESS (8) [EXPRESSED, EXPRESSES, EXPRESSING, EXPRESSION, EXPRESSIONS]

2Sa 10: 2 David sent a delegation to e his **sympathy** 5714
10: 3 by sending men to you *to* e sympathy? 5714
1Ch 19: 2 David sent a delegation to e his **sympathy** 5714
19: 2 in the land of the Ammonites to e **sympathy** 5714
19: 3 by sending men to you *to* e sympathy? 5714
Eze 33:31 With their mouths they e devotion, 6913
Ro 8:26 for us with groans *that* **words cannot** e. 227
Col 4: 8 I am sending him to you **for the** e **purpose** that you may know 899+1650+4047

EXPRESSED (2) [EXPRESS]

2Sa 13:32 This has been Absalom's e intention 6584+7023
Eph 2: 7 grace, e in his kindness to us in Christ Jesus. NIG

EXPRESSES (1) [EXPRESS]

Ps 7:11 a God *who* e his **wrath** every day. 2404

EXPRESSING (2) [EXPRESS]

1Co 2:13 e spiritual truths in spiritual words. 5173
Gal 5: 6 The only thing that counts is faith e *itself* 1919

EXPRESSION (2) [EXPRESS]

Lev 7:12 " 'If he offers it as an e **of thankfulness**, 9343
Job 9:27 I will change my e, and smile,' 7156

EXPRESSIONS (1) [EXPRESS]

2Co 9:12 but is also overflowing in many e **of thanks** 2374

EXTEND (20) [EXTENDED, EXTENDING, EXTENDS, EXTENSIVE, EXTENT]

Ge 9:27 May God e **the territory** of Japheth; 7332
49:13 his border will e **toward** Sidon. 6584
Ex 25:32 Six branches *are* to e from the sides of 3655

Ex 26:28 The center crossbar is *to* e from end to end 1368
will e **out** fifteen hundred feet 2025+2575
Dt 11:24 Your territory *will* e from the desert 2118
Jos 1: 4 Your territory *will* e from the desert 2118
1Ch 11:10 gave his kingship strong support to e it over 4887
Est 4:11 to this is for the king *to* e the gold scepter 3804
Ps 109:12 May no *one* e kindness to him or take pity 5432
110: 2 The LORD *will* e your mighty scepter 8938
Isa 66:12 "I *will* e peace to her like a river, 5742
Eze 45: 7 It will e **westward** from the west side 2025+3542
47:17 The boundary *will* e from the sea 2118
48:21 It will e **eastward** from the 25,000 2025+7708
48:23 it will e **from** the east side to the west side. 4946
Da 11:42 He *will* e his power over many countries; 8938
Am 1:13 of Gilead in order to e his borders, 8143
Zec 9:10 His rule will e **from** sea to sea and from 4946
14: 5 for it *will* e to Azel. 5595

EXTENDED (16) [EXTEND]

Ex 36:33 They made the center crossbar so that *it* e 1368
37:18 Six branches e from the sides of 3655
Dt 4:48 This land e **from** Aroer on the rim of 4946
Jos 13: 9 It e **from** Aroer on the rim of 4946
15: 1 e down to the territory of Edom, 2118
17: 7 The territory of Manasseh e from Asher 2118
19:11 and e to the ravine near Jokneam. 7003
1Ki 6: 3 main hall of the temple e the width of 6584+7156
6:21 and *he* e gold chains across the front of 6296
1Ch 5:16 the pasturelands of Sharon as far as they e. 9362
21:16 with a drawn sword in his hand e 5742
2Ch 3:13 wings of these cherubim e twenty cubits. 7298
Ezr 7:28 and *who* has e his good favor to me before 5742
Est 8: 4 Then the king e the gold scepter to Esther 3804
Isa 26:15 *you have* e all the borders of the land. 8178
Eze 42: 7 it e in front of the rooms for fifty cubits. 802

EXTENDING (11) [EXTEND]

Ex 25:33 for all six branches e from the lampstand. 3655
25:35 be under the first pair of branches e from 3655
37:19 for all six branches e from the lampstand. 3655
37:21 under the first pair of branches e from 3655
Nu 21:13 in the desert e into Amorite territory. 3655
Dt 3:16 and the Gadites I gave the territory e **from** 4946
Jos 13:30 The territory e from Mahanaim 2118
1Sa 27: 8 in the land e to Shur and Egypt.) 995
2Ch 5: 9 e **from** the ark, could be seen from front 4946
Eze 42:12 to the corresponding wall e eastward, 2006
Mic 7:11 the day *for* e your boundaries. 8178

EXTENDS (5) [EXTEND]

Nu 21:30 which e to Medeba." 6330
1Ch 5: 9 desert that e to the Euphrates River, 4200+4946
Pr 31:20 to the poor and e her hands to the needy. 8938
Da 4:22 and your dominion e **to** distant parts of 10378
Lk 1:50 His mercy e to those who fear him, NIG

EXTENSIVE (3) [EXTEND]

1Ch 22: 5 David made e preparations before his death. 4200+8044
2Ch 27: 3 and did e work on the wall at 4200+8044
Ne 4:19 "The work is e and spread out, 2221

EXTENT (3) [EXTEND]

Jn 13: 1 showed them **the full** e of his love. 1650+5465
1Co 11:18 and to some e I believe. 3538
2Co 2: 5 grieved all of you, **to some** e— 247+608+3538

EXTERMINATE (2) [EXTERMINATING]

1Ki 9:21 whom the Israelites could not e— 3049
Eze 25: 7 the nations and e you from the countries. 6

EXTERMINATING (1) [EXTERMINATE]

Jos 11:20 e them without mercy, 9012

EXTERNAL (2)

Gal 2: 6 not **judge** by e **appearance** 476+3284+4725
Heb 9:10 e regulations applying until the time of 4922

EXTINCT (KJV) CUT SHORT, EXTINGUISHED

EXTINGUISH (1) [EXTINGUISHED]

Eph 6:16 with which you can e all the flaming arrows 4931

EXTINGUISHED (2) [EXTINGUISH]

2Sa 21:17 so that the lamp of Israel *will* not *be* e." 3882
Isa 43:17 and they lay there, never to rise again, e, 1980

EXTOL (11)

Job 36:24 Remember *to* e his work, 8434
Ps 34: 1 I *will* e the LORD at all times; 1385
68: 4 e him who rides on the clouds— 6148
95: 2 with thanksgiving and e him with music 8131
109:30 With my mouth I *will* greatly e 3344
111: 1 I *will* e the LORD with all my heart in 3344
115:18 it is we *who* e the LORD, 1385
117: 1 e him, all *you* peoples. 8655
145: 2 and e your name for ever and ever. 2146
145:10 your saints *will* e you, 1385

Ps 147:12 E the LORD, O Jerusalem; 8655

EXTORT (1) [EXTORTION]

Lk 3:14 He replied, "Don't e **money** 1398

EXTORTION (9) [EXTORT]

Lev 6: 4 stolen or **taken by** e, 6943+6945
Ps 62:10 not trust in e or take pride in stolen goods; 6945
Ecc 7: 7 E turns a wise man into a fool, 6945
Isa 33:15 who rejects gain from e and keeps his hand 5131
Jer 22:17 and on oppression and e." 5298
Eze 18:18 because *he* **practiced** e, 6943+6945
22:12 from your neighbors by e, 6945
22:29 The people of the land **practice** e and 6943+6945
Hab 2: 6 and makes himself wealthy *by* e! 6294

EXTRA (4)

Mt 10:10 or e tunic, or sandals or a staff; 1545
Mk 6: 9 Wear sandals but not an e tunic. 1545
Lk 9: 3 no bag, no bread, no money, no e tunic. 324+1545
10:35 for any e **expense** you may have.' 4655

EXTRAORDINARY (1)

Ac 19:11 God did e miracles through Paul 3836+4024+5593

EXTREME (2) [EXTREMES, EXTREMELY]

Jos 15: 1 to the Desert of Zin in the e south. 7895
2Co 8: 2 and their e poverty welled up 958+2848

EXTREMELY (2) [EXTREME]

Pr 30:24 yet they *are* e wise: 2681+2682
Gal 1:14 of my own age and was e zealous for 4359

EXTREMES (1) [EXTREME]

Ecc 7:18 The man who fears God will avoid all [e]. 4392S

EXULT (3)

Ps 89:16 *they* e in your righteousness. 8123
Isa 14: 8 the cedars of Lebanon e over you and say, 8523
45:25 be found righteous and *will* e. 2146

EYE (72) [EYEBROWS, EYED, EYELIDS, EYES, EYESIGHT]

Ge 2: 9 trees that were pleasing to the e and good 5260
3: 6 good for food and pleasing to the e, 6524
Ex 21:24 e for eye, tooth for tooth, hand 6524
21:24 eye for e, tooth for tooth, hand for hand, 6524
21:26 or maidservant in the e and destroys it, 6524
21:26 the servant go free to compensate for the e. 6524
Lev 21:20 or who has any e defect, 6524
24:20 e for eye, tooth for tooth. 6524
24:20 eye for e, tooth for tooth. 6524
Nu 24: 3 the oracle of one whose e sees clearly, 6524
24: 3 the oracle of one whose e sees clearly, 6524
Dt 19:21 life for life, e for eye, tooth for tooth, 6524
19:21 life for life, eye for e, tooth for tooth, 6524
32:10 he guarded him as the apple of his e, 6524
1Sa 11: 2 on the condition that I gouge out the right e 6524
18: 9 Saul **kept** a **jealous** e **on** David. 6523
Ezr 5: 5 But the e *of* their God was watching over 10540
Job 7: 8 e that now sees me will see me no longer; 6524
10:18 I wish I had died before any e saw me. 6524
14: 3 Do you fix your e on such a one? 6524
20: 9 The e that saw him will not see him again; 6524
24:15 The e of the adulterer watches for dusk; 6524
24:15 he thinks, 'No e will see me,' 6524
28: 7 no falcon's e has seen it. 6524
Ps 17: 8 Keep me as the apple of your e; 6524
35:19 without reason maliciously wink the e. 6524
94: 9 Does he who formed the e not see? 6524
Pr 6:13 who winks with his e, 6524
7: 2 guard my teachings as the apple of your e. 6524
16:30 with his e is plotting perversity; 6524
30:17 "The e that mocks a father, 6524
Ecc 1: 8 The e never has enough of seeing, 6524
6: 9 the e sees than the roving of the appetite. 6524
Isa 29:20 and all *who* **have an** e for evil will 9193
64: 4 no e has seen any God besides you, 6524
La 2: 4 Like a foe he has slain all who were pleasing to the e; 6524
Zec 2: 8 touches you touches the apple of his e— 6524
11:17 the sword strike his arm and his right e! 6524
11:17 his right e be **totally blinded**! 6524
12: 4 "I will keep a watchful e over the house 6524
Mt 5:29 If your right e causes you to sin, 4057
5:38 'E for eye, and tooth for tooth.' 4057
5:38 'Eye for e, and tooth for tooth.' 4057
6:22 "The e is the lamp of the body. 4057
7: 3 at the speck of sawdust in your brother's e 4057
7: 3 to the plank in your own e? 4057
7: 4 'Let me take the speck out of your e,' 4057
7: 4 the time there is a plank in your own e? 4057
7: 5 first take the plank out *of* your own e, 4057
7: 5 to remove the speck from your brother's e. 4057
18: 9 And if your e causes you to sin, 4057
18: 9 to have two eyes and 3669
19:24 a camel to go through the e of a needle than 5585
Mk 9:47 if your e causes you to sin, pluck it out. 4057
9:47 to enter the kingdom of God with **one** e than 3669
10:25 a camel to go through the e of a needle than 5584
Lk 6:41 at the speck of sawdust in your brother's e 4057

Lk	6:41	to the plank in your own e?	4057
	6:42	let me take the speck out of your e,'	4057
	6:42	to see the plank in your own e?	4057
	6:42	first take the plank out of your e,	4057
	6:42	to remove the speck from your brother's e.	4057
	11:34	Your e is the lamp of your body.	4057
	18:25	a camel to go through the e of a needle than	5557
1Co	2: 9	However, as it is written: "No e has seen,	4057
	12:16	the ear should say, "Because I am not an e,	4057
	12:17	If the whole body were an e,	4057
	12:21	The e cannot say to the hand,	4057
	15:52	in the twinkling of an e, at the last trumpet.	4057
Eph	6: 6	win their favor when their e is on you,	4056
Col	3:22	and do it, not only when their e is on you	4056
Rev	1: 7	and every e will see him,	4057

EYEBROWS (1) [EYE]

Lev 14: 9 his beard, his e and the rest of his hair. 1461+6524

EYED (1) [EYE]

Ecc 5: 8 for one official is e by a higher one, 9068

EYELIDS (3) [EYE]

Ps 132: 4 no slumber to my e, 6757
Pr   6: 4 no slumber to your e. 6757
Jer 9:18 with tears and water streams from our e. 6757

EYES (522) [EYE]

Ge	3: 5	when you eat of it your e will be opened,	6524
	3: 7	Then the e of both of them were opened,	6524
	6: 8	Noah found favor in the e of the LORD.	6524
	13:14	"Lift up your e from where you are	6524
	18: 3	He said, "If I have found favor in your e,	6524
	19:19	Your servant has found favor in your e,	6524
	21:19	Then God opened her e and she saw a well	6524
	27: 1	When Isaac was old and his e were so weak	6524
	29:17	Leah had weak e,	6524
	30:27	"If I have found favor in your e,	6524
	31:40	and sleep fled from my e.	6524
	32: 5	that I may find favor in your e.' "	6524
	33: 8	"To find favor in your e, my lord," he said.	6524
	33:10	"If I have found favor in your e,	6524
	33:15	"Just let me find favor in the e of my lord."	6524
	34:11	"Let me find favor in your e,	6524
	39: 4	in his e and became his attendant.	6524
	39:21	and granted him favor in the e of	6524
	42:24	from them and bound before their e.	6524
	46: 4	And Joseph's own hand will close your e."	6524
	47:15	Why should we die before your e?	NIH
	47:19	Why should we perish before your e—	6524
	47:25	"May we find favor in the e of our lord;	6524
	47:29	"If I have found favor in your e,	6524
	48:10	Israel's e were failing because of old age,	6524
	49:12	His e will be darker than wine,	6524
	50: 4	"If I have found favor in your e,	6524
Ex	8:26	that are detestable in their e,	6524
	15:26	and do what is right in his e,	6524
	34: 9	"O Lord, if I have found favor in your e,"	6524
Lev	20: 4	If the people of the community close their e	6524
	20:17	be cut off before the e of their people.	6524
Nu	10:31	and you can be our e.	6524
	11:15	if I have found favor in your e—	6524
	13:33	We seemed like grasshoppers in our own e,	6524
	15:39	after the lusts of your own hearts and e.	6524
	16:14	Will you gouge out the e of these men?	6524
	20: 8	before their e and it will pour out its water.	6524
	22:31	Then the LORD opened Balaam's e,	6524
	24: 4	and whose e are opened;	6524
	24:16	and whose e are opened:	6524
	25: 6	the e of Moses and the whole assembly	6524
	27:14	to honor me as holy before their e."	6524
	32: 5	If we have found favor in your e," they said,	6524
	33:55	to remain will become barbs in your e	6524
Dt	1:30	before your very e,	6524
	3:21	"You have seen with your own e all that	6524
	3:27	Look at the land with your own e,	6524
	4: 3	with your own e what the LORD did	6524
	4: 9	the things your e have seen or let them slip	6524
	4:25	doing evil in the e of the LORD your God	6524
	4:34	for you in Egypt before your very e?	6524
	6:22	Before our e the LORD sent miraculous signs	6524
	7:19	You saw with your own e the great trials,	6524
	9:17	breaking them to pieces before your e.	6524
	10:21	with your own e.	6524
	11: 7	But it was your own	6524
	11:12	the e of the LORD your God are continually	6524
	12:25	be doing what is right in the e of the LORD	6524
	12:28	and right in the e of the LORD your God.	6524
	13:18	and doing what is right in his e.	6524
	16:19	a bribe blinds the e of the wise and twists	6524
	17: 2	the e of the LORD your God in violation	6524
	21: 7	nor did our e see it done.	6524
	21: 9	since you have done what is right in the e	6524
	24: 4	be detestable in the e of the LORD.	4200+6524
	25: 3	your brother will be degraded in your e.	6524
	28:31	Your ox will be slaughtered before your e,	6524
	28:32	and you will wear out your e watching	6524
	28:65	e weary with longing,	6524
	28:67	and the sights that your e will see.	6524
	29: 2	Your e have seen all that the LORD did	6524
	29: 3	With your own e you saw those great trials,	6524
	29: 4	a mind that understands or e that see or ears	6524
	34: 4	I have let you see it with your e,	6524
	34: 7	his e were not weak nor his strength gone.	6524

Jos	3: 7	"Today I will begin to exalt you in the e	6524
	23:13	whips on your backs and thorns in your e,	6524
	24: 7	You saw with your own e what I did to	6524
	24:17	performed those great signs before our e.	6524
Jdg	2:11	the Israelites did evil in the e of the LORD	6524
	3: 7	The Israelites did evil in the e of the LORD;	6524
	3:12	Once again the Israelites did evil in the e of	6524
	4: 1	the Israelites once again did evil in the e of	6524
	6: 1	Again the Israelites did evil in the e of	6524
	6:17	"If now I have found favor in your e,	6524
	10: 6	Again the Israelites did evil in the e of	6524
	13: 1	Again the Israelites did evil in the e of	6524
	16:21	gouged out his e and took him down	6524
	16:28	on the Philistines for my two e."	6524
Ru	2: 2	behind anyone in whose e I find favor."	6524
	2:10	"Why have I found such favor in your e	6524
	2:13	"May I continue to find favor in your e,	6524
1Sa	1:18	"May your servant find favor in your e."	6524
	2:33	be spared only to blind your e with tears	6524
	3: 2	whose e were becoming so weak	6524
	3:18	let him do what is good in his e."	6524
	4:15	and whose e were set so that he could	6524
	12: 3	a bribe to make me shut my e?	6524
	12:16	the LORD is about to do before your e!	6524
	12:17	an evil thing you did in the e of the LORD	6524
	14:27	and his e brightened.	6524
	14:29	how my e brightened when I tasted a little	6524
	15:17	you were once small in your own e,	6524
	15:19	on the plunder and do evil in the e of	6524
	20: 3	that I have found favor in your e,	6524
	20:29	If I have found favor in your e,	6524
	24:10	This day you have seen with your own e	6524
	27: 5	"If I have found favor in your e,	6524
	29: 9	that you have been as pleasing in my e as	6524
2Sa	6:22	and I will be humiliated in my own e.	6524
	12: 9	the LORD by doing what is evil in his e?	6524
	12:11	Before your very e I will take your wives	6524
	14:22	that he found favor in your e,	6524
	15:25	If I find favor in the LORD's e,	6524
	16: 4	"May I find favor in your e,	6524
	22:28	but your e are on the haughty	6524
	24: 3	and may the e of my lord the king see it.	6524
1Ki	1:20	the e of all Israel are on you,	6524
	1:48	who has allowed my e to see a successor	6524
	8:29	May your e be open toward this temple	6524
	8:52	"May your e be open to your servant's plea	6524
	9: 3	My e and my heart will always be there.	6524
	10: 7	until I came and saw with my own e.	6524
	11: 6	Solomon did evil in the e of the LORD;	6524
	11:33	nor done what is right in my e,	6524
	11:38	in my ways and do what is right in my e	6524
	14: 8	doing only what was right in my e.	6524
	14:22	Judah did evil in the e of the LORD.	6524
	15: 5	For David had done what was right in the e	6524
	15:11	Asa did what was right in the e of the LORD	6524
	15:26	He did evil in the e of the LORD,	6524
	15:34	He did evil in the e of the LORD,	6524
	16: 7	the evil he had done in the e of the LORD,	6524
	16:19	in the e of the LORD and walking in	6524
	16:25	But Omri did evil in the e of the LORD	6524
	16:30	Ahab son of Omri did more evil in the e of	6524
	20:38	with his headband down over his e.	6524
	20:41	the headband from his e,	6524
	21:20	to do evil in the e of the LORD.	6524
	21:25	who sold himself to do evil in the e of	6524
	22:43	he did what was right in the e of the LORD	6524
	22:52	He did evil in the e of the LORD,	6524
2Ki	3: 2	He did evil in the e of the LORD,	6524
	3:18	an easy thing in the e of the LORD;	6524
	4:34	mouth to mouth, e to eyes, hands to hands.	6524
	4:34	mouth to mouth, eyes to eyes, hands to hands.	6524
	4:35	and opened his e.	6524
	6:17	"O LORD, open his e so he may see."	6524
	6:17	Then the LORD opened the servant's e,	6524
	6:20	open the e of these men so they can see."	6524
	6:20	the LORD opened their e and they looked,	6524
	7: 2	"You will see it with your own e,"	6524
	7:19	"You will see it with your own e,	6524
	8:18	He did evil in the e of the LORD.	6524
	8:27	the house of Ahab and did evil in the e of	6524
	9:30	Jezebel heard about it, she painted her e,	6524
	10:30	in accomplishing what is right in my e	6524
	12: 2	the e of the LORD all the years Jehoiada	6524
	13: 2	the e of the LORD by following the sins	6524
	13:11	the e of the LORD and did not turn away	6524
	14: 3	He did what was right in the e of the LORD	6524
	14:24	the e of the LORD and did not turn away	6524
	15: 3	He did what was right in the e of the LORD,	6524
	15: 9	He did evil in the e of the LORD,	6524
	15:18	He did evil in the e of the LORD.	6524
	15:24	Pekahiah did evil in the e of the LORD.	6524
	15:28	He did evil in the e of the LORD.	6524
	15:34	He did what was right in the e of the LORD	6524
	16: 2	he did not do what was right in the e of	6524
	17: 2	He did evil in the e of the LORD,	6524
	17:17	and sold themselves to do evil in the e of	6524
	18: 3	He did what was right in the e of the LORD,	6524
	19:16	open your e, O LORD, and see;	6524
	19:22	and lifted your e in pride?	6524
	20: 3	and have done what is good in your e."	6524
	21: 2	He did evil in the e of the LORD,	6524
	21: 6	He did much evil in the e of the LORD,	6524
	21:15	in my e and have provoked me to anger	6524
	21:16	so that they did evil in the e of the LORD.	6524
	21:20	He did evil in the e of the LORD,	6524
	22: 2	in the e of the LORD and walked in all	6524
	22:20	Your e will not see all	6524

2Ki	23:32	He did evil in the e of the LORD,	6524
	23:37	And he did evil in the e of the LORD,	6524
	24: 9	He did evil in the e of the LORD,	6524
	24:19	He did evil in the e of the LORD,	6524
	25: 7	the sons of Zedekiah before his e.	6524
	25: 7	Then they put out his e,	6524
2Ch	6:20	May your e be open toward this temple day	6524
	6:40	may your e be open and your ears attentive	6524
	7:15	Now my e will be open	6524
	7:16	My e and my heart will always be there.	6524
	9: 6	until I came and saw with my own e.	6524
	14: 2	Asa did what was good and right in the e of	6524
	16: 9	For the e of the LORD range throughout	6524
	20:12	but our e are upon you."	6524
	20:32	he did what was right in the e of the LORD	6524
	21: 6	He did evil in the e of the LORD.	6524
	22: 4	He did evil in the e of the LORD,	6524
	24: 2	Joash did what was right in the e of	6524
	25: 2	He did what was right in the e of the LORD	6524
	26: 4	He did what was right in the e of the LORD	6524
	27: 2	He did what was right in the e of the LORD	6524
	28: 1	he did not do what was right in the e of	6524
	29: 2	He did what was right in the e of the LORD	6524
	29: 6	in the e of the LORD our God	6524
	29: 8	as you can see with your own e.	6524
	33: 2	He did evil in the e of the LORD,	6524
	33: 6	He did much evil in the e of the LORD,	6524
	33:22	He did evil in the e of the LORD,	6524
	34: 2	the e of the LORD and walked in the ways	6524
	34:28	Your e will not see all	6524
	36: 5	He did evil in the e of the LORD his God.	6524
	36: 9	He did evil in the e of the LORD.	6524
	36:12	He did evil in the e of the LORD his God	6524
Ezr	9: 8	to our e and a little relief in our bondage.	6524
Ne	1: 6	let your ear be attentive and your e open	6524
	9:32	do not let all this hardship seem trifling in your e—	4200+7156
Job	3:10	the womb for to hide trouble from my e.	6524
	4:16	A form stood before my e,	6524
	7: 7	my e will never see happiness again.	6524
	10: 4	Do you have e of flesh?	6524
	11:20	But the e of the wicked will fail,	6524
	13: 1	"My e have seen all this,	6524
	15:12	and why do your e flash,	6524
	15:15	if even the heavens are not pure in his e,	6524
	16: 9	my opponent fastens on me his piercing e.	6524
	16:16	deep shadows ring my e;	6757
	16:20	as my e pour out tears to God;	6524
	17: 2	my e must dwell on their hostility.	6524
	17: 5	the e of his children will fail.	6524
	17: 7	My e have grown dim with grief;	6524
	19:27	I myself will see him with my own e—	6524
	21: 8	their offspring before their e.	6524
	21:20	Let his own e see his destruction;	6524
	24:23	but his e are on their ways.	6524
	25: 5	and the stars are not pure in his e,	6524
	27:19	when he opens his e, all is gone.	6524
	28:10	his e see all its treasures.	6524
	28:21	from the e of every living thing,	6524
	29:15	I was e to the blind and feet to the lame.	6524
	31: 1	a covenant with my e not to look lustfully	6524
	31: 7	if my heart has been led by my e,	6524
	31:16	or let the e of the widow grow weary,	6524
	32: 1	because he was righteous in his own e.	6524
	34:21	"His e are on the ways of men;	6524
	36: 7	He does not take his e off the righteous;	6524
	39:29	his e detect it from afar.	6524
	40:24	Can anyone capture him by the e,	6524
	41:18	his e are like the rays of dawn.	6524
	42: 5	of you but now my e have seen you.	6524
Ps	6: 7	My e grow weak with sorrow;	6524
	11: 4	his e examine them.	6757
	13: 3	Give light to my e, or I will sleep in death;	6524
	17: 2	may your e see what is right.	6524
	17:11	with e alert, to throw me to the ground.	6524
	18:27	but bring low those whose e are haughty.	6524
	19: 8	giving light to the e.	6524
	25:15	My e are ever on the LORD,	6524
	31: 9	my e grow weak with sorrow,	6524
	33:18	e of the LORD are on those who fear him,	6524
	34:15	The e of the LORD are on the righteous	6524
	35:21	With our own e we have seen it."	6524
	36: 1	There is no fear of God before his e.	6524
	36: 2	in his own e he flatters himself too much	6524
	38:10	even the light has gone from my e.	6524
	52: 1	you who are a disgrace in the e of God?	AIT
	54: 7	my e have looked in triumph on my foes.	6524
	66: 7	his e watch the nations—	6524
	69: 3	My e fail, looking for my God.	6524
	69:23	May their e be darkened so they cannot see,	6524
	77: 4	You kept my e from closing;	6524
	79:10	Before our e, make known among	6524
	88: 9	my e are dim with grief.	6524
	91: 8	You will only observe with your e and see	6524
	92:11	My e have seen the defeat	6524
	101: 3	I will set before my e no vile thing.	6524
	101: 5	whoever has haughty e and a proud heart,	6524
	101: 6	My e will be on the faithful in the land,	6524
	115: 5	They have mouths, but cannot speak, e,	6524
	116: 8	my e from tears, my feet from stumbling,	6524
	118:23	and it is marvelous in our e.	6524
	119:18	Open my e that I may see wonderful things	6524
	119:37	Turn my e away from worthless things;	6524
	119:82	My e fail, looking for your promise;	6524
	119:123	My e fail, looking for your salvation,	6524
	119:136	Streams of tears flow from my e,	6524
	119:148	My e stay open through the watches of	6524

Ps	121: 1	I lift up my e to the hills—	6524
	123: 1	I lift up my e to you,	6524
	123: 2	As the e of slaves look to the hand	6524
	123: 2	as the e of a maid look to the hand	6524
	123: 2	so our e look to the LORD our God,	6524
	131: 1	O LORD, my e are not haughty;	6524
	132: 4	I will allow no sleep to my e,	6524
	135:16	They have mouths, but cannot speak, e,	6524
	139:16	your e saw my unformed body.	6524
	141: 8	But my e are fixed on you,	6524
	145:15	The e of all look to you,	6524
Pr	3: 7	Do not be wise in your own e;	6524
	4:25	Let your e look straight ahead,	6524
	6: 4	Allow no sleep to your e,	6524
	6:17	haughty e, a lying tongue, hands	6524
	6:25	or let her captivate you with her e,	6757
	10:26	As vinegar to the teeth and smoke to the e,	6524
	15: 3	The e of the LORD are everywhere,	6524
	17:24	a fool's e wander to the ends of the earth.	6524
	20: 8	he winnows out all evil with his e.	6524
	20:12	Ears that hear and e that see—	6524
	21: 4	Haughty e and a proud heart,	6524
	22:12	The e of the LORD keep watch	6524
	23:26	give me your heart and let your e keep	6524
	23:29	Who has bloodshot e?	6524
	23:33	Your e will see strange sights	6524
	25: 7	What you have seen with your e	6524
	26: 5	or he will be wise in his own e.	6524
	26:12	Do you see a man wise in his own e?	6524
	26:16	The sluggard is wiser in his own e than	
		seven men who answer discreetly.	6524
	27:20	and neither are the e of man.	6524
	28:11	A rich man may be wise in his own e,	6524
	28:27	but he who closes his e	6524
	29:13	The LORD gives sight to the e of both.	6524
	30:12	in their own e and yet are not cleansed	6524
	30:13	those whose e are ever so haughty,	6524
Ecc	2:10	I denied myself nothing my e desired;	6524
	2:14	The wise man has e in his head,	6524
	4: 8	yet his e were not content with his wealth.	6524
	5:11	to the owner except to feast his e on them?	6524
	8:16	his e not seeing sleep day or night—	6524
	11: 7	and it pleases the e to see the sun.	6524
	11: 9	of your heart and whatever your e see,	6524
SS	1:15	Your e are doves.	6524
	4: 1	Your e behind your veil are doves.	6524
	4: 9	with one glance of your e,	6524
	5:12	His e are like doves by the water streams,	6524
	6: 5	Turn your e from me; they overwhelm me.	6524
	7: 4	Your e are the pools of Heshbon by the gate	6524
	8:10	in his e like one bringing contentment.	6524
Isa	1:15	I will hide my e from you;	6524
	2:11	The e of the arrogant man will be humbled	6524
	3:16	flirting with their e,	6524
	5:15	the e of the arrogant humbled.	6524
	5:21	in their own e and clever in their own sight.	6524
	6: 5	and my e have seen the King,	6524
	6:10	make their ears dull and close their e.	6524
	6:10	Otherwise they might see with their e,	6524
	10:12	of his heart and the haughty look in his e.	6524
	11: 3	with his e, or decide by what he hears	6524
	13:16	be dashed to pieces before their e;	6524
	17: 7	and turn their e to the Holy One of Israel.	6524
	29:10	He has sealed your e (the prophets);	6524
	29:18	and darkness the e of the blind will see.	6524
	30:20	with your own e you will see them.	6524
	32: 3	Then the e of those who see will no longer	6524
	33:15	against plots of murder and shuts his e	6524
	33:17	Your e will see the king in his beauty	6524
	33:20	your e will see Jerusalem, a peaceful abode,	6524
	35: 5	the e of the blind be opened and the ears of	6524
	37:17	open your e, O LORD, and see;	6524
	37:23	and lifted your e in pride?	6524
	38: 3	and have done what is good in your e."	6524
	38:14	My e grew weak as I looked to the heavens.	6524
	40:26	Lift your e and look to the heavens:	6524
	42: 7	to open e that are blind,	6524
	43: 8	Lead out those who have e but are blind,	6524
	44:18	their e are plastered over	6524
	49: 5	for I am honored in the e of the LORD	6524
	49:18	Lift up your e and look around;	6524
	51: 6	Lift up your e to the heavens,	6524
	52: 8	they will see it with their own e.	6524
	59:10	feeling our way like men without e.	6524
	60: 4	"Lift up your e and look about you:	6524
	65:16	be forgotten and hidden from my e.	6524
Jer	4:30	Why shade your e with paint?	6524
	5: 3	O LORD, do not your e look for truth?	6524
	5:21	who have e but do not see,	6524
	7:30	of Judah have done evil in my e,	6524
	9: 1	of water and my e a fountain of tears!	6524
	9:18	over us till our e overflow with tears	6524
	13:17	my e will weep bitterly,	6524
	13:20	up your e and see those who are coming	6524
	14:17	" 'Let my e overflow with tears night	6524
	16: 9	Before your eyes and in your days I will bring	6524
	16:17	My e are on all their ways;	6524
	16:17	nor is their sin concealed from my e.	6524
	20: 4	with your own e you will see them fall by	6524
	22:17	"But your e and your heart are set only	6524
	24: 6	My e will watch over them for their good,	6524
	29:21	to death before your very e.	6524
	31:16	from weeping and your e from tears,	6524
	32: 4	to face and see him with his own e.	6524
	32:19	Your e are open to all the ways of men;	6524
	34: 3	the king of Babylon with your own e,	6524
	39: 6	of Zedekiah before his e and also killed all	6524

Jer	39: 7	Then he put out Zedekiah's e	6524
	39:16	be fulfilled before your e.	4200+7156
	51:24	"Before your e I will repay Babylon	6524
	52: 2	He did evil in the e of the LORD,	6524
	52:10	the sons of Zedekiah before his e;	6524
	52:11	Then he put out Zedekiah's e,	6524
La	1:16	"This is why I weep and my e overflow	6524
	2:11	My e fail from weeping,	6524
	2:18	give yourself no relief, your e no rest.	1426+6524
	3:48	Streams of tears flow from my e	6524
	3:49	My e will flow unceasingly, without relief,	6524
	4:17	our e failed, looking in vain for help;	6524
	5:17	because of these things our e grow dim	6524
Eze	1:18	and all four rims were full of e all around.	6524
	6: 9	from me, and by their e,	6524
	10:12	were completely full of e,	6524
	12: 2	They have e to see but do not see and ears	6524
	20: 7	of the vile images you have set your e on,	6524
	20: 8	of the vile images they had set their e on,	6524
	20: 9	the e of the nations they lived among and	6524
	20:14	from being profaned in the e of the nations	6524
	20:22	from being profaned in the e of the nations	6524
	20:24	and their e [lusted] after their fathers' idols.	6524
	22:16	When you have been defiled in the e of	6524
	22:26	and they shut their e to the holy	6524
	23:40	painted your e and put on your jewelry.	6524
	24:16	to take away from you the delight of your e.	6524
	24:21	the delight of your e, the object of your	6524
	24:25	the delight of their e, their heart's desire,	6524
	36:23	through you before their e.	6524
	37:20	before their e the sticks you have written on	6524
	38:16	through you before their e.	6524
	40: 4	look with your e and hear with your ears	6524
Da	4:34	raised my e toward heaven,	10540
	7: 8	This horn had e like the eyes of a man and	10540
	7: 8	This horn had eyes like the e of a man and	10540
	7:20	the others and that had e and a mouth	10540
	8: 5	a prominent horn between his e came from	6524
	8:21	large horn between his e is the first king.	6524
	9:18	open your e and see the desolation of	6524
	10: 6	his e like flaming torches.	6524
Hos	2:10	now I will expose her lewdness before the e	6524
Joel	1:16	not the food been cut off before our very e	6524
Am	9: 4	I will fix my e upon them for evil and not	6524
	9: 8	"Surely the e of the Sovereign LORD are	6524
Mic	4:11	let our e gloat over Zion!"	6524
	7:10	My e will see her downfall;	6524
Hab	1:13	Your e are too pure to look on evil;	6524
Zep	3:20	before your very e,"	6524
Zec	3: 9	There are seven e on that one stone,	6524
	4:10	"(These seven are the e of the LORD,	6524
	9: 1	the e of men and all the tribes of Israel are	6524
	14:12	their e will rot in their sockets.	6524
Mal	1: 5	You will see it with your own e and say,	6524
	2:17	"All who do evil are good in the e of	6524
Mt	6:22	If your e are good,	4057
	6:23	But if your e are bad,	4057
	9:29	Then he touched their e and said,	4057
	13:15	and they have closed their e.	4057
	13:15	Otherwise they might see with their e,	4057
	13:16	But blessed are your e because they see,	4057
	18: 9	to enter life with one eye than to have two e	4057
	20:34	on them and touched their e.	3921
	21:42	and it is marvelous in our e'?	4057
	26:43	because their e were heavy.	4057
Mk	8:18	Do you have e but fail to see,	4057
	8:23	spit on the man's e and put his hands on him	3921
	8:25	put his hands on the man's e.	4057
	8:25	Then his e were opened,	1332
	9:47	of God with one eye than to have two e and	4057
	12:11	and it is marvelous in our e'?"	4057
	14:40	because their e were heavy.	4057
Lk	2:30	For my e have seen your salvation,	4057
	4:20	The e of everyone in the synagogue	4057
	10:23	"Blessed are the e that see what you see.	4057
	11:34	When your e are good,	4057
	16:15	the ones who justify yourselves in the e of	1967
	19:42	but now it is hidden from your e.	4057
	24:31	Then their e were opened	4057
Jn	4:35	open your e and look at the fields!	2048+4057
	9: 6	and put it on the man's e.	4057
	9:10	"How then were your e opened?"	4057
	9:11	and put it on my e.	4057
	9:14	and opened the man's e was a Sabbath.	4057
	9:15	"He put mud on my e," the man replied,	4057
	9:17	It was your e he opened."	4057
	9:21	how he can see now, or who opened his e,	4057
	9:26	How did he open your e?"	4057
	9:30	yet he opened my e.	4057
	9:32	Nobody has ever heard of opening the e of	4057
	10:21	Can a demon open the e of the blind?"	4057
	11:37	the e of the blind man have kept this man	4057
	12:40	"He has blinded their e	4057
	12:40	so they can neither see with their e,	4057
Ac	1: 9	he was taken up before their very e,	899+1063
	9: 8	when he opened his e he could see nothing.	4057
	9:18	something like scales fell from Saul's e,	4057
	9:40	She opened her e,	4057
	26:18	to open their e and turn them from darkness	4057
	28:27	and they have closed their e.	4057
	28:27	Otherwise they might see with their e,	4057
Ro	3:18	"There is no fear of God before their e."	4057
	11: 8	e so that they could not see and ears so	4057
	11:10	May their e be darkened so they cannot see,	4057
	12:17	to do what is right in the e of everybody.	1967
2Co	4:18	fix our e not on what is seen, but on	5023
	8:21	not only in the e of the Lord but also in	1967

2Co	8:21	in the eyes of the Lord but also in the e	1967
Gal	3: 1	Before your very e Jesus Christ was clearly	
		portrayed as crucified.	4057
	4:15	you would have torn out your e	4057
Eph	1:18	that the e of your heart may be enlightened	4057
Heb	4:13	and laid bare before the e of him	4057
	12: 2	Let us fix our e on Jesus,	927
Jas	2: 5	not God chosen those who are poor in the e	NIG
1Pe	3:12	For the e of the Lord are on the righteous	4057
2Pe	2:14	With e full of adultery,	4057
1Jn	1: 1	which we have seen with our e,	4057
	2:16	the cravings of sinful man, the lust of his e	4057
Rev	1:14	and his e were like blazing fire.	4057
	2:18	the Son of God, whose e are like blazing	
		fire	2400+4057
	3:18	and salve to put on your e, so you can see.	4057
	4: 6	and they were covered with e,	4057
	4: 8	and was covered with e all around,	4057
	5: 6	He had seven horns and seven e,	4057
	7:17	God will wipe away every tear from their e.	4057
	19:12	His e are like blazing fire,	4057
	21: 4	He will wipe every tear from their e.	4057

EYESIGHT (1) [EYE]

| Jer | 14: 6 | their e fails for lack of pasture." | 6524 |

EYEWITNESSES (2) [WITNESS]

| Lk | 1: 2 | the first were e and servants of the word. | 898 |
| 2Pe | 1:16 | but we were e of his majesty. | 2228 |

EZBAI (1)

| 1Ch | 11:37 | Hezro the Carmelite, Naarai son of E, | 256 |

EZBON (2)

| Ge | 46:16 | The sons of Gad: Zephon, Haggi, Shuni, E, | 719 |
| 1Ch | 7: 7 | The sons of Bela: E, Uzzi, Uzziel, | 719 |

EZEKIEL (2)

| Eze | 1: 3 | word of the LORD came to E the priest, | 3489 |
| | 24:24 | E will be a sign to you; | 3489 |

EZEKIAS (KJV) HEZEKIAH

EZEL (1) [BETH EZEL]

| 1Sa | 20:19 | and wait by the stone E. | 262 |

EZEM (3)

Jos	15:29	Baalah, Iim, E,	6796
	19: 3	Hazar Shual, Balah, E,	6796
1Ch	4:29	Bilhah, E, Tolad,	6796

EZER (10)

Ge	36:21	Dishon, E and Dishan.	733
	36:27	The sons of E: Bilhan, Zaavan and Akan.	733
	36:30	Dishon, E and Dishan.	733
1Ch	1:38	Zibeon, Anah, Dishon, E and Dishan.	733
	1:42	The sons of E: Bilhan, Zaavan and Akan.	733
	4: 4	and E the father of Hushah.	6470
	7:21	E and Elead were killed by	6470
	12: 9	E was the chief,	6470
Ne	3:19	Next to him, E son of Jeshua,	6470
	12:42	Uzzi, Jehohanan, Malkijah, Elam and E.	6472

EZION GEBER (7) [GEBER]

Nu	33:35	They left Abronah and camped at E.	6787
	33:36	They left E and camped at Kadesh,	6787
Dt	2: 8	which comes up from Elath and E,	6787
1Ki	9:26	King Solomon also built ships at E,	6787
	22:48	they were wrecked at E.	6787
2Ch	8:17	to E and Elath on the coast of Edom.	6787
	20:36	After these were built at E,	6787

EZRA (26) [EZRA'S]

Ezr	7: 1	E son of Seraiah, the son of Azariah,	6474
	7: 6	this E came up from Babylon.	6474
	7: 8	E arrived in Jerusalem in the fifth month of	NIH
	7:10	For E had devoted himself to the study	6474
	7:11	the letter King Artaxerxes had given to E	6474
	7:12	king of kings, To E the priest,	10537
	7:21	to provide with diligence whatever E	10537
	7:25	E, in accordance with the wisdom	10537
	10: 1	While E was praying and confessing,	6474
	10: 2	one of the descendants of Elam, said to E,	6474
	10: 5	So E rose up and put the leading priests	6474
	10: 6	Then E withdrew from before the house	6474
	10:10	E the priest stood up and said to them,	6474
	10:16	E the priest selected men who were family	
		heads,	6474
Ne	8: 1	They told E the scribe to bring out	6474
	8: 2	So on the first day of the seventh month E	6474
	8: 4	E the scribe stood on	6474
	8: 5	E opened the book.	6474
	8: 6	E praised the LORD, the great God;	6474
	8: 9	E the priest and scribe,	6474
	8:13	around E the scribe to give attention to	6474
	8:18	E read from the Book of the Law of God.	NIH
	12: 1	with Jeshua: Seraiah, Jeremiah, E,	6474
	12:26	the governor and of E the priest and scribe.	6474
	12:33	along with Azariah, E, Meshullam,	6474
	12:36	E the scribe led the procession.	6474

EZRA'S (1) [EZRA]

Ne	12:13	of E, Meshullam; of Amariah's,	6474

EZRAH (1) [EZRAHITE]

1Ch	4:17	The sons of E:	6477

EZRAHITE (3) [EZRAH]

1Ki	4:31	including Ethan the E—	276
Ps	88: T	A maskil of Heman the E.	276
	89: T	A maskil of Ethan the E.	276

EZRI (1)

1Ch	27:26	E son of Kelub was in charge of	6479

F

FABLES (KJV) See MYTHS, STORIES

FABRIC (6)

Jdg	16:13	into the f [on the loom] and tighten it with	5018
	16:13	wove them into the f	5018
	16:14	up the pin and the loom, with the f.	5018
Eze	16:13	and costly f and embroidered cloth.	5429
	27:16	they exchanged turquoise, purple f,	NIH
	27:24	with you beautiful garments, blue f,	1659

FACE (313) [FACED, FACEDOWN, FACES, FACING, STERN-FACED]

Ge	1:29	on the f of the whole earth and every tree	7156
	4: 5	and his f was downcast.	7156
	4: 6	Why is your f downcast?	7156
	6: 7	from the f of the earth—	7156
	7: 4	and I will wipe from the f of	7156
	7:23	on the f of the earth was wiped out;	7156
	11: 4	be scattered over the f of the whole earth."	7156
	11: 9	the LORD scattered them over the f of	7156
	19: 1	to meet them and bowed down with his f to	678
	30:40	but made the rest f the streaked	5989+7156
	32:30	saying, "It is because I saw God f to face,	7156
	32:30	saying, "It is because I saw God face to f,	7156
	33:10	to see your f is like seeing the face of God,	7156
	33:10	to see your face is like seeing the f of God,	7156
	38:15	for she had covered her f.	7156
	43: 3	not see my f again unless your brother is	7156
	43: 5	not see my f again unless your brother is	7156
	43:31	After he had washed his f,	7156
	44:23	you will not see my f again.'	7156
	44:26	the man's f unless our youngest brother is	7156
	48:11	"I never expected to see your f again,	7156
	48:12	and bowed down with his f to the ground.	678
Ex	3: 6	At this, Moses hid his f,	7156
	10: 5	They will cover the f of the ground so	6524
	10:28	The day you see my f you will die."	7156
	13:17	For God said, "If they f war,	8011
	25:20	The cherubim are to f each other,	7156
	32:12	in the mountains and to wipe them off the f	7156
	33:11	The LORD would speak to Moses f	7156
	33:11	to Moses face to f,	7156
	33:16	the other people on the f of the earth?"	7156
	33:20	But," he said, "you cannot see my f,	7156
	33:23	but my f must not be seen."	7156
	34:29	he was not aware that his f was radiant	6425+7156
	34:30	his f was radiant,	6425+7156
	34:33	he put a veil over his f.	7156
	34:35	they saw that his f was radiant.	6425+7156
	34:35	over his f until he went in to speak with	7156
Lev	13:45	lower part of his f	8559
	17:10	I will set my f against	7156
	20: 3	I will set my f against that man	7156
	20: 5	I will set my f against that man	7156
	20: 6	" 'I will set my f against	7156
	26:17	I will set my f against you so that you will	7156
Nu	6:25	the LORD make his f shine upon you and	7156
	6:26	the LORD turn his f toward you	7156
	11:15	and do not let me f my own ruin."	8011
	12: 3	more humble than anyone else on the f of	7156
	12: 8	With him I speak f to face,	7023
	12: 8	With him I speak face to f,	7023
	12:14	"If her father had spit in her f,	7156
	14:14	O LORD, have been seen f to face,	6524
	14:14	and your face is like seeing face to f,	6524
	14:43	and Canaanites will f you there.	4200+7156
	22: 5	the f of the land and have settled next	6524
	22:11	that has come out of Egypt covers the f of	6524
	24: 1	but turned his f toward the desert.	7156
Dt	5: 4	The LORD spoke to you face to f out of	7156
	5: 4	The LORD spoke to you f to face out of	6524
	6:15	he will destroy you from the f of the land.	7156
	7: 6	of all the peoples on the f of the earth to	6524
	7:10	he will repay to their f by destruction;	7156
	7:10	to repay to their f those who hate him.	7156
	14: 2	Out of all the peoples on the f of the earth,	7156
	25: 9	spit in his f and say,	7156

Dt	31:17	I will hide my f from them,	7156
	31:18	And I will certainly hide my f on that day	7156
	32:20	"I will hide my f from them," he said,	7156
	34:10	Moses, whom the LORD knew f to face,	7156
	34:10	Moses, whom the LORD knew face to f,	7156
Jos	5: 1	they no longer had the courage to f	4946+7156
	7:10	What are you doing down on your f?	7156
Jdg	6:22	I have seen the angel of the LORD f	7156
	6:22	the angel of the LORD face to f!"	7156
Ru	2:10	she bowed down with her f to the ground.	7156
1Sa	1:18	and her f was no longer downcast.	7156
	5: 3	fallen on his f on the ground before the ark	7156
	5: 4	fallen on his f on the ground before the ark	7156
	20:15	of David's enemies from the f of	7156
	20:41	with his f to the ground.	678
	24: 8	down and prostrated himself with his f to	678
	25:23	and bowed down before David with her f	678
	25:41	She bowed down with her f to the ground	678
	28:14	down and prostrated himself with his f to	678
2Sa	2:22	look your brother Joab in the f?"	448+5951+7156
	14: 4	with her f to the ground to pay him honor,	678
	14: 7	nor descendant on the f of the earth."	678
	14:22	with his f to the ground to pay him honor,	678
	14:24	he must not see my f."	7156
	14:24	to his own house and did not see the f of	7156
	14:28	in Jerusalem without seeing the king's f.	7156
	14:32	Now then, I want to see the king's f,	7156
	14:33	and he came in and bowed down with his f	678
	18:28	He bowed down before the king with his f	678
	19: 4	The king covered his f and cried aloud,	7156
	21: 1	so David sought the f of the LORD.	7156
	24:20	and bowed down before the king with his f	678
1Ki	1:23	before the king and bowed with his f to	678
	1:31	Then Bathsheba bowed low with her f to	678
	13:34	to its destruction from the f of the earth.	7156
	18:42	the ground and put his f between his knees.	7156
	19:13	he pulled his cloak over his f and went out	7156
	22:24	up and slapped Micaiah in the f.	4305
2Ki	4:29	Lay my staff on the boy's f."	7156
	4:31	on ahead and laid the staff on the boy's f,	7156
	8:15	in water and spread it over the king's f,	7156
	14: 8	"Come, meet me f to face."	7156
	14: 8	"Come, meet me face to f."	7156
	20: 2	Hezekiah turned his f to the wall	7156
1Ch	16:11	seek his f always.	7156
	21:21	and bowed down before David with his f	678
2Ch	7:14	and pray and seek my f and turn	7156
	18:23	up and slapped Micaiah in the f.	4305
	20:12	we have no power to f this vast army	4200+7156
	20:17	Go out to f them tomorrow,	4200+7156
	20:18	Jehoshaphat bowed with his f to	678
	25:17	"Come, meet me f to face."	7156
	25:17	"Come, meet me face to f."	7156
	30: 9	not turn his f from you if you return	7156
Ezr	9: 6	and disgraced to lift up my f to you,	7156
Ne	2: 2	"Why does your f look so sad	7156
	2: 3	Why should my f not look sad when	7156
	4: 5	they have thrown insults in the f of	4200+5584
Est	7: 8	they covered Haman's f.	7156
Job	1:11	and he will surely curse you to your f."	7156
	2: 5	and he will surely curse you to your f."	7156
	4:15	A spirit glided past my f,	7156
	6:28	Would I lie to your f?	7156
	11:15	then you will lift up your f without shame;	7156
	13:15	I will surely defend my ways to his f.	7156
	13:24	Why do you hide your f	7156
	15:27	"Though his f is covered with fat	7156
	16:16	My f is red with weeping,	7156
	17: 6	a man in whose f people spit.	7156
	17:12	in the f of darkness they say,	7156
	21:31	Who denounces his conduct to his f?	7156
	22:26	in the Almighty and will lift up your f	7156
	23:17	by the thick darkness that covers my f.	7156
	24:15	and he keeps his f concealed.	7156
	26: 9	He covers the f of the full moon,	7156
	26:10	the horizon on the f of the waters for	7156
	29:24	the light of my f was precious to them.	7156
	30:10	they do not hesitate to spit in my f.	7156
	33:26	he sees God's f and shouts for joy;	7156
	34:29	If he hides his f, who can see him?	7156
	37:12	around over the f of the whole earth	7156
Ps	4: 6	Let the light of your f shine upon us,	7156
	10:11	he covers his f and never sees."	7156
	11: 7	upright men will see his f.	7156
	13: 1	How long will you hide your f from me?	7156
	17:15	And I—in righteousness I will see your f;	7156
	22:24	not hidden his f from him but has listened	7156
	24: 6	who seek your f, O God of Jacob.	7156
	27: 8	My heart says of you, "Seek his f!"	7156
	27: 8	Your f, LORD, I will seek.	7156
	27: 9	Do not hide your f from me,	7156
	30: 7	but when you hid your f, I was dismayed.	7156
	31:16	Let your f shine on your servant;	7156
	34:16	the f of the LORD is	7156
	44: 3	and the light of your f, for you loved them.	7156
	44:15	and my f is covered with shame	7156
	44:22	Yet for your sake we f death all day long;	2222
	44:24	Why do you hide your f	7156
	50:21	I will rebuke you and accuse you to your f.	6524
	51: 9	Hide your f from my sins	7156
	67: 1	and bless us and make his f shine upon us,	7156
	69: 7	and shame covers my f.	7156
	69:17	Do not hide your f from your servant;	7156
	80: 3	make your f shine upon us,	7156
	80: 7	make your f shine upon us,	7156
	80:19	make your f shine upon us,	7156
	88:14	do you reject me and hide your f from me?	7156

Ps	102: 2	Do not hide your f from me when I am	7156
	104:15	oil to make his f shine,	7156
	104:29	When you hide your f, they are terrified;	7156
	104:30	and you renew the f of the earth.	7156
	105: 4	seek his f always.	7156
	119:58	I have sought your f with all my heart;	7156
	119:135	Make your f shine upon your servant	7156
	143: 7	Do not hide your f from me or I will be	7156
Pr	7:13	and with a brazen f she said:	7156
	8:27	when he marked out the horizon on the f	7156
	15:13	A happy heart makes the f cheerful,	7156
	16:15	When a king's f brightens, it means life;	7156
	27:19	water reflects a f,	2021+2021+4200+7156+7156
Ecc	7: 3	because a sad f is good for the heart.	7156
	8: 1	a man's f and changes its hard appearance.	7156
SS	2:14	show me your f, let me hear your voice;	5260
	2:14	your voice is sweet, and your f is lovely.	5260
Isa	8:17	who is hiding his f from the house	7156
	23:17	with all the kingdoms on the f of the earth.	7156
	24: 1	he will ruin its f and scatter its inhabitants—	7156
	38: 2	Hezekiah turned his f to the wall	7156
	50: 6	not hide my f from mocking and spitting.	7156
	50: 7	Therefore have I set my f like flint,	7156
	50: 8	Let us f each other!	6641
	54: 8	of anger I hid my f from you for a moment,	7156
	57:17	I punished him, and hid my f in anger,	NIH
	59: 2	your sins have hidden his f from you,	7156
	64: 7	for you have hidden your f from us	7156
	65: 3	to my very f, offering sacrifices in gardens	7156
Jer	13:26	over your f that your shame may be seen—	7156
	18:17	I will show them my back and not my f in	7156
	25:26	all the kingdoms on the f of the earth.	7156
	28:16	'I am about to remove you from the f of	7156
	30: 6	every f turned deathly pale?	7156
	32: 4	and will speak with him f to face	7023
	32: 4	to f and see him with his own eyes.	7023
	33: 5	I will hide my f from this city because	7156
	34: 3	and he will speak with you f to face.	7023
	34: 3	and he will speak with you face to f.	7023
La	3:29	Let him bury his f in the dust—	7023
Eze	1:10	Each of the four had the f of a man,	7156
	1:10	on the right side each had the f of a lion,	7156
	1:10	and on the left the f of an ox;	7156
	1:10	each also had the f of an eagle.	7156
	4: 3	between you and the city and turn your f	7156
	4: 7	Turn your f toward the siege of Jerusalem	7156
	6: 2	set your f against the mountains of Israel;	7156
	7:22	I will turn my f away from them,	7156
	10:14	One f was that of a cherub,	7156
	10:14	the second the f of a man,	7156
	10:14	the third the f of a lion,	7156
	10:14	and the fourth the f of an eagle.	7156
	12: 6	Cover your f so that you cannot see	7156
	12:12	He will cover his f so that he cannot see	7156
	13:17	set your f against the daughters	7156
	14: 4	a wicked stumbling block before his f and	7156
	14: 7	a wicked stumbling block before his f and	7156
	14: 8	I will set my f against that man	7156
	15: 7	I will set my f against them.	7156
	15: 7	And when I set my f against them,	7156
	20:35	into the desert of the nations and there, f	7156
	20:35	of the nations and there, face to f,	7156
	20:46	set your f toward the south;	7156
	20:47	and every f from south to north will	7156
	21: 2	set your f against Jerusalem and preach	7156
	24:17	lower part of your f	8559
	24:22	lower part of your f	8559
	25: 2	set your f against the Ammonites	7156
	28:21	set your f against Sidon;	7156
	29: 2	set your f against Pharaoh king of Egypt	7156
	35: 2	set your f against Mount Seir;	7156
	38: 2	set your f against Gog,	7156
	38:20	on the f of the earth will tremble	7156
	39:23	So I hid my f from them and handed them	7156
	39:24	and I hid my f from them.	7156
	39:29	I will no longer hide my f from them,	7156
	41:19	the f of a man toward the palm tree	7156
	41:19	and the f of a lion toward the palm tree on	7156
	43:17	The steps of the altar f east."	7155
Da	5: 6	His f turned pale and he was so frightened	10228
	5: 9	and his f grew more pale.	10228
	7:28	and my f turned pale,	10228
	8:18	with my f to the ground.	7156
	10: 6	his f like lightning,	7156
	10: 8	my f turned deathly pale	2086
	10: 9	I fell into a deep sleep, my f to the ground.	7156
	10:15	I bowed with my f toward the ground	7156
Hos	2: 2	from her f and the unfaithfulness from	7156
	5:15	And they will seek my f;	7156
Joel	2: 6	every f turns pale.	7156
Am	5: 8	of the sea and pours them out over the f of	7156
	9: 6	of the sea and pours them out over the f of	7156
	9: 8	I will destroy it from the f of the earth—	7156
Mic	3: 4	At that time he will hide his f from them	7156
Na	2:10	bodies tremble, every f grows pale.	7156
	3: 5	"I will lift your skirts over your f.	7156
Zep	1: 2	"I will sweep away everything from the f	7156
	1: 3	and rubble when I cut off man from the f	7156
Mt	6:17	put oil on your head and wash your f,	4725
	17: 2	His f shone like the sun,	4725
	18:10	that their angels in heaven always see the f	4725
	26:39	he fell with his f to the ground and prayed,	4725
	26:67	in his f and struck him with their fists.	4725
Mk	10:22	At this the man's f fell.	5145
Lk	5:12	with his f to the ground and begged him,	4725
	9:29	the appearance of his f changed,	4725
	21:35	upon all those who live on the f of	4725

Jn	11:44	and a cloth around his **f**.	4071
	18:22	**struck** him **in the f**.	1443+4825
	19: 3	**struck** him **in the f**.	1443+4825
Ac	6:15	and they saw that his **f** was like the face of	4725
	6:15	and they saw that his face was like the **f** of	4725
	16:19	into the marketplace **to f** the authorities.	2093
	20:38	that they would never see his **f** again.	4725
Ro	8:36	"For your sake we **f death** all day long;	2506
1Co	7:28	But those who marry will **f** many troubles	2400
	13:12	then we shall see **f** to face.	4725
	13:12	then we shall see face to **f**.	4725
2Co	3: 7	not look steadily at the **f** of Moses because	4725
	3:13	over his **f** to keep the Israelites from gazing	4725
	4: 6	the knowledge of the glory of God in the **f**	4725
	10: 1	am "timid" **when f to face** with you,	2848+4725
	10: 1	am "timid" **when face to f** with you,	2848+4725
	11:20	or slaps you in the **f**.	4725
	11:28	I **f** daily the pressure of my concern for all	NIG
Gal	2:11	I opposed him to his **f**,	4725
Heb	9:27	and after that to **f** judgment,	NIG
	10:32	in a great contest in the **f** of suffering,	NIG
Jas	1: 2	whenever you **f** trials of many kinds,	4346
	1:23	like a man who looks at his **f** in a mirror	4725
	5:10	example of patience in the **f** of suffering,	NIG
1Pe	3:12	**f** of the Lord is against those who do evil."	4725
2Jn	1:12	to visit you and talk with you **f** to face,	5125
	1:12	to visit you and talk with you face to **f**,	5125
3Jn	1:14	and we will talk **f** to face.	5125
	1:14	and we will talk face to **f**.	5125
Rev	1:16	His **f** was like the sun shining	4071
	4: 7	the third had a **f** like a man,	4725
	6:16	and hide us from the **f** of him who sits on	4725
	10: 1	his **f** was like the sun,	4725
	22: 4	They will see his **f**,	4725

FACED (20) [FACE]

Ex	37: 9	The cherubim **f** each other,	7156
Nu	8: 3	the lamps so that they **f forward**	448+4578+7156
2Ki	14:11	He and Amaziah king of Judah **f each other**	7156+8011
	23:29	but Neco **f** him and killed him at Megiddo.	8011
2Ch	25:21	He and Amaziah king of Judah **f each other**	7156+8011
Ne	8: 3	he **f** the square before the Water Gate	4200+7156
Eze	1:17	of the four directions the creatures **f**;	NIH
	10:11	of the four directions the cherubim **f**;	NIH
	10:11	in whatever direction the head **f**;	7155
	40: 9	The portico of the gateway **f** the temple.	4946
	40:16	the openings all around **f** inward.	4200
	40:31	Its portico **f** the outer court;	448
	40:34	Its portico **f** the outer court;	4200
	40:37	Its portico **f** the outer court;	4200
	42: 2	The building whose door **f** north was	448+7156
	42: 3	gallery **f** gallery at the three levels.	448+7156
	47: 1	toward the east (for the temple **f** east).	7156
Ac	25:16	any man before he has **f** his accusers	2848+4725
Ro	4:19	he **f the fact** that his body was as good	2917
Heb	11:36	Some **f** jeers and flogging,	3284+4278

FACEDOWN (20) [FACE]

Ge	17: 3	Abram fell **f**, and God said to him,	6584+7156
	17:17	Abraham fell **f**; he laughed	6584+7156
Lev	9:24	they shouted for joy and fell **f**.	6584+7156
Nu	14: 5	Moses and Aaron fell **f** in front of	6584+7156
	16: 4	When Moses heard this, he fell **f**.	6584+7156
	16:22	Moses and Aaron fell **f** and cried out,	6584+7156
	16:45	And they fell **f**.	6584+7156
	20: 6	to the Tent of Meeting and fell **f**,	6584+7156
	22:31	So he bowed low and **fell f**.	678+2556+4200
Jos	5:14	Joshua fell **f** to the ground in reverence,	448+7156
	7: 6	Joshua tore his clothes and fell **f** to	6584+7156
1Sa	17:49	and he fell **f** on the ground.	6584+7156
1Ch	21:16	clothed in sackcloth, fell **f**.	6584+7156
Eze	1:28	When I saw it, I fell **f**,	6584+7156
	3:23	and I fell **f**.	6584+7156
	9: 8	I fell **f**, crying out, "Ah,	6584+7156
	11:13	I fell **f** and cried out in a loud voice,	6584+7156
	43: 3	and I fell **f**.	448+7156
	44: 4	and I fell **f**.	448+7156
Mt	17: 6	they fell **f** to the ground, terrified.	2093+4725

FACES (61) [FACE]

Ge	9:23	Their **f** were turned the other way so	7156
	40: 7	"Why are your **f** so sad today?"	7156
	42: 6	they bowed down to him with their **f** to	678
Nu	21:11	desert that **f** Moab toward the sunrise.	6584+7156
Jos	15: 7	which **f** the Pass of Adummim south of	5790
	18:17	which **f** the Pass of Adummim,	5790
Jdg	13:20	and his wife fell with their **f** to the ground.	7156
	16: 3	to the top of the hill that **f** Hebron.	6584+7156
1Sa	26: 1	the hill of Hakilah, which **f** Jeshimon?	6584+7156
1Ki	7: 9	with a saw on their inner and **outer f**.	AIT
1Ch	12: 8	Their **f** were the faces of lions,	7156
	12: 8	Their faces were the **f** of lions,	7156
2Ch	7: 3	on the pavement with their **f** to the ground,	678
	29: 6	They turned their **f** away from	7156
Ne	8: 6	and worshiped the LORD with their **f** to	678
Job	40:13	shroud their **f** in the grave.	7156
Ps	34: 5	their **f** are never covered with shame.	7156
	83:16	Cover their **f** with shame so	7156
Isa	3: 9	The look on their **f** testifies against them;	7156
	3:15	by crushing my people and grinding the **f**	7156
	6: 2	With two wings they covered their **f**,	7156
	13: 8	at each other, their **f** aflame.	7156
	25: 8	LORD will wipe away the tears from all **f**;	7156

Isa	29:22	no longer will their **f** grow pale.	7156
	49:23	down before you with their **f** to the ground;	678
	53: 3	Like one from whom men hide their **f**	7156
Jer	2:27	to me and not their **f**;	7156
	5: 3	They made their **f** harder than stone	7156
	32:33	to me and not their **f**;	7156
	50: 5	the way to Zion and turn their **f** toward it.	7156
	51:51	and shame covers our **f**,	7156
Eze	1: 6	each of them had four **f** and four wings.	7156
	1: 8	All four of them had **f** and wings,	7156
	1:10	Their **f** looked like this:	7156
	1:11	Such were their **f**.	7156
	1:15	beside each creature with its four **f**.	7156
	7:18	Their **f** will be covered with shame	7156
	8:16	of the LORD and their **f** toward the east,	7156
	9: 2	of the upper gate, which **f** north, each with	7155
	10:14	Each of the cherubim had four **f**:	7156
	10:21	Each had four **f** and four wings,	7156
	10:22	Their **f** had the same appearance	7156
	11: 1	of the house of the LORD that **f** east.	7155
	14: 3	put wicked stumbling blocks before their **f**.	7156
	27:35	with horror and their **f** are distorted	7156
	40:10	the same measurements, and the **f** of	NIH
	40:14	the **f** of the projecting walls all around the	NIH
	40:16	The **f** of the projecting walls were decorated with palm trees.	NIH
	40:26	it had palm tree decorations **on the f** of	448
	41:18	Each cherub had two **f**:	7156
Mic	3: 7	They will all cover their **f**	8559
Mal	2: 3	I will spread on your **f** the offal	7156
Mt	6:16	for they disfigure their **f**	4725
	23:13	the kingdom of heaven in men's **f**.	1869
Lk	24: 5	the women bowed down with their **f** to	4725
	24:17	They stood still, their **f** downcast.	NIG
2Co	3:18	with unveiled **f** all reflect the Lord's glory,	4725
Rev	7:11	They fell down on their **f** before the throne	4725
	9: 7	and their **f** resembled human faces.	4725
	9: 7	and their faces resembled human **f**.	4725
	11:16	fell on their **f** and worshiped God,	4725

FACING (48) [FACE]

Jos	8:33	**f** those who carried it—	5584
	18:14	the hill **f** Beth Horon on the south	6584+7156
	18:16	to the foot of the hill **f** the Valley	6584+7156
	19:46	with the area **f** Joppa.	4578
1Sa	13:18	the Valley of Zeboim **f** the desert.	2025
	17:21	up their lines **f each other**.	5120+7925
	26: 3	on the hill of Hakilah **f** Jeshimon,	6584+7156
1Ki	7: 4	in sets of three, **f each other**.	448+4691+4691
	7: 5	in sets of three, **f each other**.	448+4691+4691
	7:25	Sea stood on twelve bulls, three **f** north,	7155
	7:25	three facing north, three **f** west,	7155
	7:25	three **f** south and three facing east.	7155
	7:25	three facing south and three **f** east.	7155
	22:35	the king was propped up in his chariot **f**	5584
2Ki	2: 7	**f** the place where Elijah	4946+5584
2Ch	3:13	They stood on their feet, **f** the main hall.	7156
	4: 4	Sea stood on twelve bulls, three **f** north,	7156
	4: 4	three facing north, three **f** west,	7155
	4: 4	three **f** south and three facing east.	7155
	4: 4	three facing south and three **f** east.	7155
	18:34	in his chariot **f** the Arameans until evening.	5790
Ne	3:19	a point **f** the ascent to the armory as far as	5584
Est	5: 1	on his royal throne in the hall, **f**	5790
Eze	40: 6	Then he went to the gate **f** east.	7156
	40: 7	the portico **f** the temple was one rod deep.	4946
	40:14	The measurement was up to the **portico f**	AIT
	40:20	the length and width of the gate **f** north,	7156
	40:22	as those of the gate **f** east.	7156
	40:23	a gate to the inner court **f** the north gate,	5584
	40:24	to the south side and I saw a gate **f** south.	2006
	40:27	The inner court also had a gate **f** south,	2006
	40:44	at the side of the north gate and **f** south,	7156
	40:44	at the side of the south gate and **f** north,	7156
	40:45	"The room **f** south is for	7156
	40:46	and the room **f** north is for	7156
	41:12	The building **f** the temple courtyard on	448+7156
	41:15	the building **f** the courtyard at the rear	448+7156
	41:15	inner sanctuary and the **portico f** the court,	AIT
	42:13	south rooms **f** the temple courtyard are	448+7156
	43: 1	the man brought me to the gate **f** east,	7155
	44: 1	the man through the gate **f** east.	7156
	44: 1	the one **f** east, and it was shut.	7155
	46: 1	of the inner court **f** east is to be shut on	7155
	46:12	the gate **f** east is to be opened for him.	7156
	46:19	of the gate to the sacred rooms **f** north,	7155
	47: 2	around the outside to the outer gate **f** east,	7155
Ac	20:23	that prison and hardships are **f** me.	3531
	27:12	**f** both southwest and northwest.	1063

FACT (33) [FACTS]

Ge	45:26	**In f**, he is ruler of all Egypt."	3954
	47:18	"We cannot hide from our lord the **f that**	AIT
2Sa	13:15	with intense hatred. **In f**	3954
2Ki	8:10	to me that he will **in f die**."	4637+4637
Ezr	5:17	to see if King Cyrus did in **f** issue a decree	10029
Mk	3:27	**In f**, no one can enter a strong man's house	247
	7:25	**In f**, as soon as she heard about him,	247
	12:22	**In f**, none of the seven left any children.	2779
Jn	4: 2	although in **f** it was not Jesus who baptized,	2793
	4:18	The **f is**, you have had five husbands,	1142
	9:37	**in f**, he is the one speaking with you."	2779
	10: 5	But they will never follow a stranger; **in f**,	247
	16: 2	**in f**, a time is coming	247
	18:37	**In f**, for this reason I was born,	NIG

Ac	2:32	and we are all witnesses **of the f**.	4005S
	13:34	**The f that** God raised him from the dead,	4022
Ro	4: 2	If, **in f**, Abraham was justified by works,	1142
	4:19	he **faced the f** that his body was as good	2917
1Co	6: 7	The very **f** that you have lawsuits among you	NIG
	10: 1	I do not want you to be ignorant of the **f**,	NIG
	12:18	**in f** God has arranged the parts in the body,	3815
	15:15	But he did not raise him **if in f** the dead	726+1642
2Co	11:20	**In f**, you even put up anyone who enslaves	247
1Th	3: 4	**In f**, when we were with you,	1142+2779
	4: 1	to please God, as **in f** you are living.	2779
	4:10	And **in f**, you do love all the brothers	1142
	5:11	just as **in f** you are doing.	2779
1Ti	5:13	Some have **in f** already turned away	1142
2Ti	3:12	**In f**, everyone who wants to live	1254+2779
Tit	1:15	**In f**, both their minds and consciences	247
Heb	5:12	**In f**, though by this time you ought to	1142+2779
	9:22	**In f**, the law requires that nearly everything	2779
1Jn	3: 4	**in f**, sin is lawlessness.	2779

FACTIONS (3)

1Ki	16:21	the people of Israel were split into **two f**;	AIT
2Co	12:20	**f**, slander, gossip, arrogance and disorder.	2249
Gal	5:20	of rage, selfish ambition, dissensions, **f**	146

FACTS (1) [FACT]

Ac	19:36	Therefore, since these **f** are undeniable,	AIT

FADE (6) [FADED, FADES, FADING]

Ps	109:23	I **f** away like an evening shadow;	2143
Isa	17: 4	"In that day the glory of Jacob will **f**;	1937
Na	1: 4	and the blossoms of Lebanon **f**.	581
Jas	1:11	the rich man will **f** away even	3447
1Pe	1: 4	that can never perish, spoil or **f**—	278
	5: 4	the crown of glory that will **never f** away.	277

FADED (5) [FADE]

Lev	13: 6	sore has **f** and has not spread in the skin,	3908
	13:21	and it is not more than skin deep and has **f**,	3908
	13:26	if it is not more than skin deep and has **f**,	3908
	13:28	in the skin but has **f**, it is a swelling from	3908
	13:56	the mildew has **f** after	3908

FADES (2) [FADE]

Ps	65: 8	and evening **f** you call forth songs of joy.	NIH
Ecc	12: 4	and the sound of grinding **f**;	9164

FADING (8) [FADE]

Pr	7: 9	as the day was **f**, as the dark of night set in.	6847
Isa	1:30	You will be like an oak with **f** leaves,	5570
	28: 1	to the **f** flower, his glorious beauty,	5570
	28: 4	That **f** flower, his glorious beauty,	5570
Jer	6: 4	But, alas, the daylight is **f**,	7155
2Co	3: 7	because of its glory, **f** though it was,	2934
	3:11	And if what was **f away** came with glory,	2934
	3:13	at it while the radiance was **f** away.	2934

FAIL (55) [FAILED, FAILING, FAILINGS, FAILS, FAILURE]

Lev	20: 4	to Molech and they **f** to put him to death,	1194
	26:15	and **f** to carry out all my commands and	1194
Nu	15:22	" 'Now if you unintentionally **f** to keep any	4202
	32:23	"But if you **f** to do this,	4202
2Sa	7:16	**cross over without f**,	6296+6296
1Ki	2: 4	you will never **f to have** a man on the	4162+4200
	8:25	'You shall never **f to have** a man to sit	4162+4200
	9: 5	'You shall never **f to have** a man on	4162+4200
2Ki	10:10	against the house of Ahab will **f**.	824+2025+5877
1Ch	28:20	not **f** you or forsake you until all the work	8332
2Ch	6:16	'You shall never **f to have** a man to	4162+4200
	7:18	'You shall never **f to have** a man to	4162+4200
	34:33	they did not **f** to follow the LORD,	4946+6073
Ezr	6: 9	must be given them daily without **f**,	10712
Est	9:27	without **f** observe these two days every year,	6296
Job	11:20	But the eyes of the wicked will **f**,	3983
	14: 7	and its new shoots will not **f**.	2532
	17: 5	the eyes of his children will **f**.	3983
	21:10	Their bulls never **f** to breed;	1718
	41:12	"I will not **f to speak** of his limbs,	3087
Ps	6: 7	they **f** because of all my foes.	6980
	69: 3	My eyes **f**, looking for my God.	3983
	73:26	My flesh and my heart may **f**,	3983
	89:28	and my covenant with him will **never f**.	586
	89:31	if they violate my decrees and **f**	4202
	119:82	My eyes **f**, looking for your promise;	3983
	119:123	My eyes **f**, looking for your salvation,	3983
Pr	15:22	Plans **f** for lack of counsel,	7296
Isa	32:10	the grape harvest will **f**,	3983
	33:16	and water will not **f** him.	586
	51: 6	my righteousness will never **f**.	3169
	58:11	like a spring whose waters never **f**.	3941
Jer	20:11	They will **f** and be thoroughly disgraced;	4202+8505
	33:17	David will never **f to have** a man to sit	4162+4200
	33:18	Levites, ever **f to have** a man to stand	4162+4200
	35:19	Recab will never **f to have** a man to	4162+4200
La	2:11	My eyes **f** from weeping,	3983
	3:22	for his compassions never **f**.	3983
Eze	2: 5	And whether they listen or **f** to listen—	2532
	2: 7	whether they listen or **f** to listen.	2532
	3:11	whether they listen or **f** to listen."	2532
	30: 6	and her proud strength will **f**.	3718

Eze	47:12	nor *will* their fruit **f**.	9462
Hos	9: 2	the new wine *will* **f** them.	3950
	13:15	his spring *will* **f** and his well dry up.	3312
Zep	3: 5	and every new day he does not **f**,	6372
Mk	8:18	Do you have eyes but **f** to see,	4024
	8:18	and ears but **f** to hear?	4024
	10:30	**f** to receive a hundred times as much	1569+3590
Lk	6:42	when you yourself **f** to see the plank	4024
	18:30	will **f** to receive many times as much	3590+4049
	22:32	Simon, that your faith *may* not **f**.	1722
Jn	1:20	He did not **f** to confess,	766
Ac	5:38	or activity is of human origin, *it will* **f**.	2907
2Co	13: 5	unless, of course, *you* **f the test**?	99+1639

FAILED (24) [FAIL]

Lev	5:16	for what he *has* **f** to do in regard to	2627
Jos	2:11	our hearts melted and everyone's courage **f**	4202+6388+7756
	21:45	good promises to the house of Israel **f**;	5877
	23:14	the LORD your God gave you *has* **f**.	5877
	23:14	has been fulfilled; not one *has* **f**.	5877
Jdg	1:21	however, **f** to dislodge the Jebusites,	4202
	8:35	They also **f** to show kindness to the family	4202
	21: 5	the tribes of Israel has **f** to assemble before	4202
	21: 5	that anyone who **f** to assemble before	4202
	21: 8	of the tribes of Israel **f** to assemble before	4202
1Sa	3:13	and he **f** to restrain them.	4202
	25:37	his heart **f** him and he became like a stone.	4637
1Ki	8:56	Not one word *has* **f** of all	5877
	15: 5	*had* not **f to keep** any of the LORD's	
		commands all the days of his life—	4946+6073
2Ki	3:26	to the king of Edom, but *they* **f**.	3523+4202
Ezr	10: 8	Anyone who **f** to appear within three days	4202
Ne	9:17	They refused to listen and **f** to remember	4202
Job	32:15	words *have* **f** them.	4946+6980
Ps	77: 8	*Has* his promise **f** for all time?	1698
La	4:17	our eyes **f**, looking in vain for help;	3983
Ro	9: 6	It is not as though God's word *had* **f**.	1738
2Co	13: 6	that we *have* not **f the test**.	99+1639
	13: 7	even though we *may* seem **to have f**.	99+1639
Jas	5: 4	The wages *you* **f to pay** the workmen	691

FAILING (3) [FAIL]

Ge	48:10	Israel's eyes *were* **f** because of old age,	3877
Dt	8:11	**f** to observe his commands,	1194
1Sa	12:23	that I should sin against the LORD by **f**	2532

FAILINGS (1) [FAIL]

| Ro | 15: 1 | We who are strong ought to bear with the **f** | 821 |

FAILS (17) [FAIL]

Ex	21:33	a pit or digs one and **f** to cover it and an ox	4202
Nu	9:13	on a journey **f** to celebrate the Passover,	2532
	19:13	of anyone who **f** to purify himself defiles	4202
2Ki	10:19	Anyone who **f to come** will no longer live."	7212
Ps	31:10	my strength **f** because of my affliction,	4173
	38:10	My heart pounds, my strength **f** me;	6440
	40:12	and my heart **f** within me.	6440
	143: 7	O LORD; my spirit **f**.	3983
Pr	8:36	But *whoever* **f to find** me harms himself;	2627
Ecc	6: 6	over but **f** to enjoy his prosperity.	4202
Isa	65:20	he who **f to reach** a hundred will	2627
Jer	14: 6	their eyesight **f** for lack of pasture."	3983
	15:18	like a spring *that* **f**?	586+4202
	17: 8	a year of drought and never **f** to bear fruit."	4631
Joel	1:10	the new wine is dried up, the oil **f**.	581
Hab	3:17	olive crop **f** and the fields produce no food,	3950
1Co	13: 8	Love never **f**.	4406

FAILURE (1) [FAIL]

| 1Th | 2: 1 | brothers, that our visit to you was not a **f**. | 3031 |

FAIN (KJV) See LONGED

FAINT (31) [FAINTED, FAINTHEARTED, FAINTING, FAINTS]

1Sa	14:28	That is why the men *are* **f**."	6545
Job	23:16	God *has* **made** my heart **f**;	8216
	26:14	how **f** the whisper we hear of him!	9066
Ps	6: 2	Be merciful to me, LORD, for I am **f**;	583
	61: 2	I call as my heart *grows* **f**;	6494
	77: 3	I mused, and my spirit *grew* **f**.	6494
	102: T	When *he is* **f** and pours out his lament	6494
	142: 3	When my spirit *grows* **f** within me,	6494
	143: 4	So my spirit *grows* **f** within me;	6494
Ecc	12: 4	but all their songs *grow* **f**;	8820
SS	2: 5	refresh me with apples, for I *am* **f with** love.	2703
	5: 8	Tell him I *am* **f** with love.	2703
Isa	15: 4	and their hearts *are* **f**.	3760
	29: 8	that he is drinking, but he awakens **f**,	6546
	40:31	they will walk and not be **f**.	3615
	44:12	he drinks no water and *grows* **f**.	3615
	57:10	and so *you* did not **f**.	2703
	57:16	the spirit of man *would* **grow** **f** before me—	6494
Jer	8:18	my heart is **f** within me.	1868
	15: 9	of seven *will* **grow** **f** and breathe her last.	581
	31:25	I will refresh the weary and satisfy the **f**."	1790+5883
La	1:13	He made me desolate, **f** all the day long.	1865
	1:22	My groans are many and my heart is **f**."	1868
	2:11	because children and infants **f** in the streets	6494
	2:12	as they **f** like wounded men in the streets	6494

La	2:19	who **f** from hunger at the head	6488
	5:17	Because of this our hearts are **f**,	1865
Eze	21: 7	every spirit *will become* **f**	3908
Am	8:13	and strong young men *will* **f** because	6634
Jnh	4: 8	on Jonah's head so that *he grew* **f**.	6634
Lk	21:26	Men *will* **f** from terror,	715

FAINTED (1) [FAINT]

| Isa | 51:20 | Your sons *have* **f**; | 6634 |

FAINTHEARTED (2) [FAINT, HEART]

| Dt | 20: 3 | *Do* not *be* **f** or afraid; | 4222+8216 |
| | 20: 8 | shall add, "Is any man afraid or **f**? | 4222+8205 |

FAINTING (1) [FAINT]

| Jer | 4:31 | I *am* **f**; my life is given over to murderers." | 6545 |

FAINTS (2) [FAINT]

| Ps | 84: 2 | My soul yearns, even **f**, for the courts of | 3983 |
| | 119:81 | My soul **f with longing** for your salvation, | 3983 |

FAIR (9) [FAIR HAVENS, FAIRLY, FAIRNESS]

Jdg	9:16	and if you have been **f** to Jerub-Baal	3208
Job	26:13	By his breath the skies became **f**;	9185
Pr	1: 3	doing what is right and just and **f**;	4797
	2: 9	understand what is right and just and **f**—	4797
SS	6:10	**f** as the moon, bright as the sun,	3637
Hos	10:11	so I will put a yoke on her **f** neck.	3206
Mt	16: 2	'It will be **f** weather, for the sky is red,'	2304
2Co	6:13	As a **f** exchange—	NIG
Col	4: 1	with what is right and **f**,	2699

FAIR HAVENS (1)

| Ac | 27: 8 | and came to a place called **F**, | 2816 |

FAIRLY (5) [FAIR]

Lev	19:15	but judge your neighbor **f**.	928+7406
Dt	1:16	between your brothers and judge **f**,	7406
	16:18	and they shall judge the people **f**.	7406
Pr	31: 9	Speak up and judge **f**;	7406
Eze	18: 8	and judges **f** between man and man.	622

FAIRNESS (1) [FAIR]

| Pr | 29:14 | If a king judges the poor with **f**, | 622 |

FAIRS (KJV) See MERCHANDISE, WARES

FAITH (270) [FAITHFUL, FAITHFULLY, FAITHFULNESS, FAITHLESS]

Ex	21: 8	because he *has* **broken f** with her.	953
Dt	32:51	*of you* **broke f** with me in the presence of	5085
Jos	22:16	'How *could you* **break f** with the God	5085+5086
Jdg	9:16	in **good f** when you made Abimelech king,	9459
	9:19	and in **good f** toward Jerub-Baal	9459
1Sa	14:33	"You have **broken f**," he said.	953
2Ch	20:20	**Have f** in the LORD your God	586
	20:20	**have f** in his prophets and you will	586
Isa	7: 9	**stand firm in** your **f**,	586
	26: 2	the nation that keeps **f**.	574
Hab	2: 4	but the righteous will live by his **f**—	575
Mal	2:10	the covenant of our fathers *by* **breaking f**	953
	2:11	Judah *has* **broken f**.	953
	2:14	because you *have* **broken f** with her,	953
	2:15	*do* not **break f** with the wife of your youth.	953
	2:16	and *do* not **break f**.	953
Mt	6:30	*O* you **of little f**?	3899
	8:10	found anyone in Israel with such great **f**.	4411
	8:26	He replied, "You **of little f**,	3899
	9: 2	When Jesus saw their **f**, he said	4411
	9:22	he said, "your **f** has healed you."	4411
	9:29	"According to your **f** it will be done	4411
	13:58	miracles there because of their **lack of f**.	602
	14:31	"You **of little f**," he said,	3899
	15:28	"Woman, you have great **f**!	4411
	16: 8	Jesus asked, "You **of little f**,	3899
	17:20	"Because you have so **little f**.	3898
	17:20	if you have **f** as small as a mustard seed,	4411
	21:21	if you have **f** and do not doubt,	4411
	24:10	the **f** and will betray and hate each other,	NIG
Mk	2: 5	When Jesus saw their **f**,	4411
	4:40	Do you still have no **f**?"	4411
	5:34	"Daughter, your **f** has healed you.	4411
	6: 6	And he was amazed at their **lack of f**.	602
	10:52	"Go," said Jesus, "your **f** has healed you."	4411
	11:22	"Have **f** in God," Jesus answered.	4411
	16:14	he rebuked them for their **lack of f**	602
Lk	5:20	When Jesus saw their **f**, he said, "Friend,	4411
	7: 9	not found such great **f** even in Israel."	4411
	7:50	"Your **f** has saved you; go in peace."	4411
	8:25	"Where is your **f**?"	4411
	8:48	"Daughter, your **f** has healed you.	4411
	12:28	*O* you **of little f**!	3899
	17: 5	to the Lord, "Increase our **f**!"	4411
	17: 6	"If you have **f** as small as a mustard seed,	4411
	17:19	your **f** has made you well."	4411
	18: 8	will he find **f** on the earth?"	4411
	18:42	your **f** has healed you."	4411
	22:32	Simon, that your **f** may not fail.	4411
Jn	2:11	and his disciples **put** *their* **f** in him.	4409

Jn	7:31	Still, many in the crowd **put** *their* **f** in him.	4409
	8:30	Even as he spoke, many **put** *their* **f** in him.	4409
	11:45	**put** *their* **f** in him.	4409
	12:11	over to Jesus and **putting** *their* **f** in him.	4409
	12:42	not confess their **f** for fear they would	NIG
	14:12	anyone who *has* **f** in me will do what I	4409
Ac	3:16	By **f** in the name of Jesus,	4411
	3:16	It is Jesus' name and the **f** that comes	4411
	6: 5	a man full *of* **f** and of the Holy Spirit;	4411
	6: 7	of priests became obedient *to* the **f**.	4411
	11:24	full of the Holy Spirit and **f**,	4411
	13: 8	and tried to turn the proconsul from the **f**.	4411
	14: 9	saw that he had **f** to be healed	4411
	14:22	to remain true to the **f**.	4411
	14:27	and how he had opened the door *of* **f** to	4411
	15: 9	for he purified their hearts *by* **f**.	4411
	16: 5	So the churches were strengthened *in the* **f**	4411
	20:21	in repentance and have **f** in our Lord Jesus.	4411
	24:24	to him as he spoke about **f** in Christ Jesus.	4411
	26:18	among those who are sanctified *by* **f**.	4411
	27:25	for *I have* **f** in God that it will happen just	4409
Ro	1: 5	to the obedience that comes *from* **f**.	4411
	1: 8	your **f** is being reported all over the world.	4411
	1:12	be mutually encouraged by each other's **f**.	4411
	1:17	**f from first to last**,	1650+4411+4411
	1:17	"The righteous will live by **f**."	4411
	3: 3	What if some *did* **not have f**?	601
	3: 3	Will their **lack of f** nullify God's	
		faithfulness?	602
	3:22	from God comes through **f** in Jesus Christ	4411
	3:25	atonement, through **f** in his blood.	4411
	3:26	one who justifies those who **have f**	1666+4411
	3:27	No, but on that *of* **f**.	4411
	3:28	is justified *by* **f** apart from observing the law.	4411
	3:30	who will justify the circumcised *by* **f** and	4411
	3:30	and the uncircumcised through that same **f**.	4411
	3:31	Do we, then, nullify the law by this **f**?	4411
	4: 5	his **f** is credited as righteousness.	4411
	4: 9	that Abraham's **f** was credited to him	4411
	4:11	a seal of the righteousness that he had *by* **f**	4411
	4:12	but who also walk in the footsteps of the **f**	4411
	4:13	through the righteousness that comes *by* **f**.	4411
	4:14	**f** has no value and the promise is worthless,	4411
	4:16	Therefore, the promise comes by **f**,	4411
	4:16	of the law but also to those who are of the **f**	4411
	4:19	Without weakening *in his* **f**,	4411
	4:20	strengthened *in his* **f** and gave glory to God,	4411
	5: 1	since we have been justified through **f**,	4411
	5: 2	*by* **f** into this grace in which we now stand.	4411
	9:30	a righteousness that is by **f**;	4411
	9:32	Because they pursued it not by **f** but as	4411
	10: 6	But the righteousness that is by **f** says:	4411
	10: 8	that is, the word *of* **f** we are proclaiming:	4411
	10:17	**f** comes from hearing the message,	4411
	11:20	and you stand *by* **f**.	4411
	12: 3	with the measure *of* God has given you.	4411
	12: 6	let him use it in proportion to his **f**.	4411
	14: 1	Accept him whose **f** is weak,	4411
	14: 2	One man's **f** allows him to eat everything,	4409
	14: 2	whose **f** is weak, eats only vegetables.	NIG
	14:23	because his eating is not from **f**;	4411
	14:23	that does not come from **f** is sin.	4411
1Co	2: 5	your **f** might not rest on men's wisdom,	4411
	12: 9	to another **f** by the same Spirit,	4411
	13: 2	and if I have a **f** that can move mountains,	4411
	13:13	now these three remain: **f**, hope and love.	4411
	15:14	our preaching is useless and so is your **f**.	4411
	15:17	if Christ has not been raised, your **f** is futile;	4411
	16:13	Be on your guard; stand firm in the **f**;	4411
2Co	1:24	Not that we lord it over your **f**,	4411
	1:24	because it is *by* **f** you stand firm.	4411
	4:13	With that same spirit *of* **f** we also believe	4411
	5: 7	We live by **f**, not by sight.	4411
	8: 7	But just as you excel in everything—in **f**,	4411
	10:15	as your **f** continues to grow,	4411
	13: 5	to see whether you are in the **f**;	4411
Gal	1:23	now preaching the **f** he once tried	4411
	2:16	but *by* **f** in Jesus Christ.	4411
	2:16	*have* **put** our **f** in Christ Jesus that we may	4409
	2:16	that we may be justified *by* **f** in Christ and	4411
	2:20	I live by **f** in the Son of God,	4411
	3: 8	by **f**, and announced the gospel in advance	4411
	3: 9	So those who **have f** are blessed along	1666+4411
	3: 9	Abraham, the man *of* **f**.	4412
	3:11	because, "The righteous will live by **f**."	4411
	3:12	The law is not based on **f**;	4411
	3:14	so that by **f** we might receive the promise	4411
	3:22	being given through **f** in Jesus Christ.	4411
	3:23	Before this **f** came, we were held prisoners	4411
	3:23	locked up until **f** should be revealed.	4411
	3:24	to Christ that we might be justified by **f**.	4411
	3:25	Now that **f** has come,	4411
	3:26	You are all sons of God through **f**	4411
	5: 5	*by* **f** we eagerly await through the Spirit	4411
	5: 6	that counts is **f** expressing itself	4411
Eph	1:15	since I heard about your **f** in the Lord Jesus	4411
	2: 8	by grace you have been saved, through **f**—	4411
	3:12	through **f** in him we may approach God	4411
	3:17	Christ may dwell in your hearts through **f**.	4411
	4: 5	one Lord, one **f**, one baptism;	4411
	4:13	*in the* **f** and in the knowledge of the Son	4411
	6:16	take up the shield *of* **f**,	4411
	6:23	and love with **f** from God the Father and	4411
Php	1:25	of you for your progress and joy *in the* **f**,	4411
	1:27	contending as one man *for* the **f** of	4411
	2:17	and service *coming from* your **f**,	4411
	3: 9	but that which is through **f** in Christ—	4411

Php	3: 9	that comes from God and is by f.	4411
Col	1: 4	because we have heard of your f	4411
	1: 5	the f and love that spring from the hope	NIG
	1:23	if you continue in your f,	4411
	2: 5	how orderly you are and how firm your f	4411
	2: 7	strengthened in the f as you were taught,	4411
	2:12	and raised with him through your f in	4411
1Th	1: 3	and Father your work produced by f,	4411
	1: 8	f in God has become known everywhere.	4411
	3: 2	to strengthen and encourage you in your f,	4411
	3: 5	I sent to find out about your f.	4411
	3: 6	and has brought good news about your f	4411
	3: 7	about you because of your f.	4411
	3:10	and supply what is lacking in your f.	4411
	5: 8	putting on f and love as a breastplate,	4411
2Th	1: 3	because your f is growing more and more,	4411
	1: 4	about your perseverance and f in all	4411
	1:11	of yours and every act prompted by your f.	4411
	3: 2	for not everyone has f.	4411
1Ti	1: 2	To Timothy my true son in the f:	4411
	1: 4	God's work—which is by f.	4411
	1: 5	and a good conscience, and a sincere f.	4411
	1:14	with the f and love that are in Christ Jesus.	4411
	1:19	holding on to f and a good conscience.	4411
	1:19	and so have shipwrecked their f.	4411
	2: 7	and a teacher of the true f to the Gentiles.	4411
	2:15	if they continue in f,	4411
	3: 9	of the f with a clear conscience.	4411
	3:13	and great assurance in their f	4411
	4: 1	that in later times some will abandon the f	4411
	4: 6	the truths of the f and of the good teaching	4411
	4:12	in life, in love, in f and in purity.	4411
	5: 8	the f and is worse than an unbeliever.	4411
	6:10	from the f and pierced themselves	4411
	6:11	and pursue righteousness, godliness, f,	4411
	6:12	Fight the good fight of the f.	4411
	6:21	and in so doing have wandered from the f.	4411
2Ti	1: 5	I have been reminded of your sincere f,	4411
	1:13	with f and love in Christ Jesus.	4411
	2:18	and they destroy the f of some.	4411
	2:22	and pursue righteousness, f,	4411
	3: 8	as far as the f is concerned, are rejected.	4411
	3:10	my purpose, f, patience, love, endurance,	4411
	3:15	to make you wise for salvation through f	4411
	4: 7	I have finished the race, I have kept the f.	4411
Tit	1: 1	of Jesus Christ for the f of God's elect and	4411
	1: 2	a f and knowledge resting on the hope	NIG
	1: 4	my true son in our common f:	4411
	1:13	so that they will be sound in the f	4411
	2: 2	and sound in f, in love and in endurance.	4411
	3:15	Greet those who love us in the f.	4411
Phm	1: 5	I hear about your f in the Lord Jesus	4411
	1: 6	that you may be active in sharing your f,	4411
Heb	4: 2	those who heard did not combine it with f.	4411
	4:14	let us hold firmly to the f we profess.	NIG
	6: 1	and of f in God,	4411
	6:12	but to imitate those who through f	4411
	10:22	with a sincere heart in full assurance of f,	4411
	10:38	But my righteous one will live by f.	4411
	11: 1	Now f is being sure of what we hope for	4411
	11: 3	By f we understand that the universe	4411
	11: 4	By f Abel offered God a better sacrifice	4411
	11: 4	By f he was commended as	4005S
	11: 4	by f he still speaks, even though he is dead.	899S
	11: 5	By f Enoch was taken from this life,	4411
	11: 6	without f it is impossible to please God,	4411
	11: 7	By f Noah, when warned about things not	4411
	11: 7	By his f he condemned the world	4005S
	11: 7	of the righteousness that comes by f.	4411
	11: 8	By f Abraham, when called to go to	4411
	11: 9	By f he made his home in the promised land	4411
	11:11	By f Abraham, even though he was past age	4411
	11:13	All these people were still living by f	4411
	11:17	By f Abraham, when God tested him,	4411
	11:20	By f Isaac blessed Jacob and Esau	4411
	11:21	By f Jacob, when he was dying,	4411
	11:22	By f Joseph, when his end was near,	4411
	11:23	By f Moses' parents hid him	4411
	11:24	By f Moses, when he had grown up,	4411
	11:27	By f he left Egypt,	4411
	11:28	By f he kept the Passover and	4411
	11:29	By f the people passed through the Red Sea	4411
	11:30	By f the walls of Jericho fell,	4411
	11:31	By f the prostitute Rahab,	4411
	11:33	who through f conquered kingdoms,	4411
	11:39	These were all commended for their f,	4411
	12: 2	the author and perfecter of our f,	4411
	13: 7	of their way of life and imitate their f.	4411
Jas	1: 3	of your f develops perseverance.	4411
	2: 5	in the eyes of the world to be rich in f and	4411
	2:14	if a man claims to have f but has no deeds?	4411
	2:14	Can such f save him?	4411
	2:17	In the same way, f by itself,	4411
	2:18	But someone will say, "You have f;	4411
	2:18	Show me your f without deeds,	4411
	2:18	and I will show you my f by what I do.	4411
	2:20	that f without deeds is useless?	4411
	2:22	You see that his f and his actions were	4411
	2:22	his f was made complete by what he did.	4411
	2:24	by what he does and not by f alone.	4411
	2:26	so f without deeds is dead.	4411
	5:15	And the prayer offered in f will make	4411
1Pe	1: 5	through f are shielded by God's power	4411
	1: 7	These have come so that your f—	4411
	1: 9	for you are receiving the goal of your f,	4411
	1:21	and so your f and hope are in God.	4411
	5: 9	Resist him, standing firm in the f,	4411

2Pe	1: 1	have received a f as precious as ours:	4411
	1: 5	to add to your f goodness;	4411
1Jn	5: 4	that has overcome the world, even our f.	4411
Jude	1: 3	for the f that was once for all entrusted to	4411
	1:20	build yourselves up in your most holy f	4411
Rev	2:13	You did not renounce your f in me,	4411
	2:19	I know your deeds, your love and f,	4411

FAITHFUL (83) [FAITH]

Nu	12: 7	he is f in all my house.	586
Dt	7: 9	he is the f God,	586
	32: 4	A f God who does no wrong,	575
1Sa	2:35	I will raise up for myself a f priest,	586
2Sa	20:19	We are the peaceful and f in Israel.	573
	22:26	"To the f you show yourself faithful,	2883
	22:26	"To the faithful you show yourself f,	2874
1Ki	3: 6	he was f to you and righteous	622+928+2143
2Ch	31:18	they were f in consecrating themselves.	575
	31:20	and right and f before the LORD his God.	622
Ne	9: 8	You found his heart f to you,	586
Ps	12: 1	the f have vanished from among men.	574
	18:25	To the f you show yourself faithful,	2883
	18:25	To the faithful you show yourself f,	2874
	25:10	the ways of the LORD are loving and f	622
	31:23	The LORD preserves the f,	573
	33: 4	he is f in all he does.	575
	37:28	the just and will not forsake his f ones.	2883
	78: 8	whose spirits were not f to him.	586
	78:37	they were not f to his covenant.	586
	89:19	to your f people you said:	2883
	89:24	My f love will be with him,	575
	89:37	the f witness in the sky."	586
	97:10	the lives of his f ones and delivers them	2883
	101: 6	My eyes will be on the f in the land,	586
	111: 7	The works of his hands are f and just;	622
	145:13	The LORD is f to all his promises	586
	146: 6	the LORD, who remains f forever.	622
Pr	2: 8	the just and protects the way of his f ones.	2883
	20: 6	but a f man who can find?	574
	28:20	A f man will be richly blessed,	575
	31:26	and f instruction is on her tongue.	2876
Isa	1:21	See how the f city has become a harlot!	586
	1:26	the City of Righteousness, the F City."	586
	49: 7	because of the LORD, who is f,	586
	55: 3	my f love promised to David.	586
Jer	42: 5	be a true and f witness against us if we do	586
Eze	43:11	down before them so that they may be f	9068
	48:11	who were f in serving me and did	9068
Hos	11:12	even against the f Holy One.	586
Zec	8: 8	be my people, and I will be f and righteous	622
Mt	24:45	"Who then is the f and wise servant,	4412
	25:21	'Well done, good and f servant!	4412
	25:21	You have been f with a few things;	4412
	25:23	'Well done, good and f servant!	4412
	25:23	You have been f with a few things;	4412
Lk	12:42	"Who then is the f and wise manager,	4412
Ro	12:12	patient in affliction, f in prayer.	4674
1Co	1: 9	with his Son Jesus Christ our Lord, is f.	4412
	4: 2	a trust must prove f.	4412
	4:17	my son whom I love, who is f in the Lord.	4412
	10:13	God is f; he will not let you be tempted beyond what you can bear.	4412
2Co	1:18	But as surely as God is f,	4412
Eph	1: 1	the f in Christ Jesus:	4412
	6:21	the dear brother and f servant in the Lord,	4412
Col	1: 2	To the holy and f brothers in Christ	4412
	1: 7	who is a f minister of Christ on our behalf,	4412
	4: 7	a f minister and fellow servant in the Lord.	4412
	4: 9	our f and dear brother, who is one of you.	4412
1Th	5:24	one who calls you is f and he will do it.	4412
2Th	3: 3	But the Lord is f, and he will strengthen	4412
1Ti	1:12	that he considered me f,	4412
	5: 9	has been f to her husband,	467+1222+1651
2Ti	2:13	if we are faithless, he will remain f,	4412
Heb	2:17	a merciful and f high priest in service	4412
	3: 2	He was f to the one who appointed him,	4412
	3: 2	just as Moses was f in all God's house.	NIG
	3: 5	Moses was f as a servant in all God's house,	4412
	3: 6	But Christ is f as a son over God's house.	NIG
	8: 9	they did not remain f to my covenant,	1844
	10:23	for he who promised is f.	4412
	11:11	he considered him f who had made	4412
1Pe	4:19	to their f Creator and continue to do good.	4412
	5:12	whom I regard as a f brother,	4412
1Jn	1: 9	he is f and just and will forgive us our sins	4412
3Jn	1: 5	you are f in what you are doing for	4412
Rev	1: 5	who is the f witness,	4412
	2:10	Be f, even to the point of death,	4412
	2:13	even in the days of Antipas, my f witness,	4412
	3:14	the f and true witness,	4411
	14:12	and remain f to Jesus.	4411
	17:14	chosen and f followers."	4412
	19:11	whose rider is called F and True.	4412

FAITHFULLY (18) [FAITH]

Dt	11:13	So if you f obey the commands	9048+9048
Jos	24: 2	and f when the LORD gives us the land."	622
1Sa	12:24	be sure to fear the LORD and serve him f	622+928
1Ki	2: 4	they live, and if they walk f before me	622+928
2Ki	20: 3	how I have walked before you f and	622+928
	22: 7	because they are acting f."	575+928
2Ch	19: 9	"You must serve f and wholeheartedly in	575+928
	31:12	Then they f brought in the contributions,	575+928
	31:15	Shecaniah assisted him f in the towns	575+928
	32: 1	After all that Hezekiah had so f done,	622

2Ch	34:12	The men did the work f.	575+928
Ne	9:33	you have acted f, while we did wrong.	622
	13:14	and do not blot out what I have so f done	2876
Isa	38: 3	how I have walked before you f and	622+928
Jer	23:28	but let the one who has my word speak it f.	622
Eze	18: 9	and f keeps my laws.	622+6913
	44:15	of Zadok and who f carried out the duties	9068
1Pe	4:10	f administering God's grace	2819+6055

FAITHFULNESS (59) [FAITH]

Ge	24:27	who has not abandoned his kindness and f	622
	24:49	Now if you will show kindness and f	622
	32:10	and f you have shown your servant.	622
	47:29	that you will show me kindness and f.	622
Ex	34: 6	slow to anger, abounding in love and f,	622
Jos	24:14	the LORD and serve him with all f.	622
1Sa	26:23	for his righteousness and f.	575
2Sa	2: 6	the LORD now show you kindness and f,	622
	15:20	May kindness and f be with you."	622
Ps	30: 9	Will it proclaim your f?	622
	36: 5	reaches to the heavens, your f to the skies.	575
	40:10	I speak of your f and salvation.	622
	54: 5	in your f destroy them.	622
	57: 3	God sends his love and his f.	622
	57:10	your f reaches to the skies.	622
	61: 7	appoint your love and f to protect him.	622
	71:22	I will praise you with the harp for your f,	622
	85:10	Love and f meet together;	622
	85:11	F springs forth from the earth,	575
	86:15	slow to anger, abounding in love and f.	622
	88:11	your f in Destruction?	575
	89: 1	with my mouth I will make your f known	575
	89: 2	that you established your f in heaven itself.	575
	89: 5	O LORD, your f too,	575
	89: 8	O LORD, and your f surrounds you.	575
	89:14	love and f go before you.	622
	89:33	nor will I ever betray my f.	575
	89:49	which in your f you swore to David?	622
	91: 4	his f will be your shield and rampart.	622
	92: 2	in the morning and your f at night,	575
	98: 3	He has remembered his love and his f to	575
	100: 5	his f continues through all generations.	575
	108: 4	your f reaches to the skies.	622
	111: 8	done in f and uprightness.	622
	115: 1	because of your love and f.	622
	117: 2	and the f of the LORD endures forever.	622
	119:75	and in f you have afflicted me.	575
	119:90	Your f continues through all generations;	575
	138: 2	for your love and your f,	622
	143: 1	in your f and righteousness come	575
Pr	3: 3	Let love and f never leave you;	622
	14:22	those who plan what is good find love and f.	622
	16: 6	Through love and f sin is atoned for;	622
	20:28	Love and f keep a king safe;	622
Isa	11: 5	be his belt and f the sash around his waist.	575
	16: 5	in f a man will sit on it—	622
	25: 1	in perfect f you have done marvelous things,	575
	38:18	down to the pit cannot hope for your f.	622
	38:19	fathers tell their children about your f.	622
	42: 3	In f he will bring forth justice;	622
	61: 8	In my f I will reward them and make	622
La	3:23	They are new every morning; great is your f.	575
Hos	2:20	I will betroth you in f,	575
	4: 1	"There is no f, no love,	622
Mt	23:23	more important matters of the law—justice, mercy and f.	4411
Ro	3: 3	Will their lack of faith nullify God's f?	4411
Gal	5:22	joy, peace, patience, kindness, goodness, f,	4411
3Jn	1: 3	and tell about your f to the truth and	NIG
Rev	13:10	for patient endurance and f on the part of	4411

FAITHLESS (13) [FAITH]

Ps	78:57	Like their fathers they were disloyal and f,	953
	101: 3	The deeds of f men I hate;	6091
	119:158	I look on the f with loathing,	953
Pr	14:14	f will be fully repaid for their ways,	4213+6047
Jer	3: 6	"Have you seen what f Israel has done?	5412
	3: 8	I gave f Israel her certificate of divorce	5412
	3:11	"F Israel is more righteous than unfaithful Judah.	5412
	3:12	" 'Return, f Israel,' declares the LORD,	5412
	3:14	"Return, f people," declares the LORD,	8743
	3:22	f people; I will cure you of backsliding."	8743
	12: 1	Why do all the f live at ease?	953+954
Ro	1:31	they are senseless, f, heartless, ruthless.	853
2Ti	2:13	if we are f, he will remain faithful,	601

FALCON (1) [FALCON'S, FALCONS]

Dt	14:13	the red kite, the black kite, any kind of f,	1901

FALCON'S (1) [FALCON]

Job	28: 7	no f eye has seen it.	370

FALCONS (1) [FALCON]

Isa	34:15	there also the f will gather,	1901

FALL (228) [FALLEN, FALLING, FALLS, FELL, FELLED, FELLING]

Ge	2:21	caused the man to f into a deep sleep;	5877
	9: 2	and dread of you will f upon all the beasts	2118
	27:13	"My son, let the curse f on me.	NIH
Ex	9:19	the hail will f on every man and animal	3718
	9:22	the sky so that hail will f all over Egypt—	2118

Ex	15:16	terror and dread *will* f upon them.	5877
Lev	26: 7	and *they will* f by the sword before you.	5877
	26: 8	and your enemies *will* f by the sword	5877
	26:36	and *they will* f,	5877
Nu	1:53	the Testimony so that wrath *will* not f on	2118
	14: 3	to this land only to *let us* f by the sword?	5877
	14:29	In this desert your bodies *will* f—	5877
	14:32	you—your bodies *will* f in this desert.	5877
	14:43	be with you and *you will* f by the sword."	5877
	18: 5	wrath *will* not f on the Israelites again.	2118
Dt	28:52	in which you trust f **down.**	3718
	29:20	All the curses written in this book *will* f	8069
	31:29	disaster *will* f **upon** you	7925
	32: 2	*Let* my teaching f like rain	6903
Jos	9:20	so that wrath *will* not f on us for breaking	2118
Jdg	15:18	now die of thirst and f into the hands of	5877
1Sa	3:19	*let* none of his words f	5877
	14:45	not a hair of his head *will* f to the ground,	5877
	18:25	Saul's plan was to have David f by	5877
	26:20	not *let* my blood f to the ground far from	5877
2Sa	3:29	*May* his blood f upon the head of Joab and	2565
	14:11	"not one hair of your son's head *will* f to	5877
	17:12	and we will f on him as dew settles on	NIH
	24:14	*Let us* f into the hands of the LORD,	5877
	24:14	but *do not let me* f into the hands of men."	5877
	24:17	*Let* your hand f upon me and my family."	2118
1Ki	1:52	not a hair of his head *will* f to the ground,	5877
2Ki	6: 6	The man of God asked, "Where *did it* f?"	5877
	9:18	**"F** in behind me."	448+6015
	9:19	**F** in behind me."	448+6015
1Ch	21:13	*Let me* f into the hands of the LORD,	5877
	21:13	but *do not let me* f into the hands of men."	5877
	21:17	*let* your hand f upon me and my family,	2118
2Ch	34:11	kings of Judah *had* **allowed to** f into ruin.	8845
Est	8: 6	can I bear to see disaster f **on** my people?	5162
Job	13:11	*Would* not the dread of him f on you?	5877
	31:22	then *let* my arm f from the shoulder,	5877
	36:28	and abundant **showers** f on mankind.	8319
	37: 6	He says to the snow, 'F on the earth,'	2092
Ps	10:10	*they* f under his strength.	5877
	13: 4	and my foes will rejoice when *I* f.	4572
	20: 8	They are brought to their knees and f,	5877
	27: 2	*they will* stumble and f,	5877
	35: 8	*may they* f into the pit, to their ruin.	5877
	37:24	*he will* not f,	3214
	38:17	For I am about to f,	7520
	45: 5	*let* the nations f beneath your feet.	5877
	46: 2	the earth give way and the mountains f into	4572
	46: 5	God is within her, *she will* not f;	4572
	46: 6	Nations are in uproar, kingdoms f;	4572
	55:22	he will never let the righteous f.	4572
	69: 9	the insults of those who insult you f on me.	5877
	82: 7	*you will* f like every other ruler."	5877
	91: 7	A thousand *may* f at your side,	5877
	106:26	that he *would* **make** them f in the desert,	5877
	106:27	**make** their descendants f	5877
	118:13	I was pushed back and *about to* f,	5877
	140:10	**Let** burning coals f upon them;	4572
	141:10	*Let* the wicked f into their own nets,	5877
	145:14	The LORD upholds all those *who* f	5877
Pr	4:16	of slumber till *they* **make** someone f.	4173
	11:28	Whoever trusts in his riches *will* f,	5877
	16:18	a haughty spirit before a f.	4174
	22:14	under the LORD's wrath *will* f *into* it.	5877
	26:27	If a man digs a pit, *he will* f into it;	5877
	28:10	along an evil path *will* f into his own trap,	5877
	28:18	he whose ways are perverse *will* suddenly f.	5877
Ecc	9:12	by evil times that f unexpectedly	5877
	10: 8	Whoever digs a pit *may* f into it;	5877
Isa	3:25	Your men *will* f by the sword,	5877
	8:14	to stumble and a rock that **makes** them f.	4842
	8:15	*they will* f and be broken,	5877
	9: 8	*it will* f on Israel.	5877
	10: 4	among the captives or f among the slain.	5877
	10:34	Lebanon *will* f before the Mighty One.	5877
	13:15	all who are caught *will* f by the sword.	5877
	22:25	it will be sheared off and *will* f,	5877
	24:18	Whoever flees at the sound of terror *will* f	5877
	28:13	so that they will go and f backward,	4173
	30:25	when the towers f,	5877
	31: 3	he who is helped *will* f;	5877
	31: 8	"Assyria *will* f by a sword that is not	5877
	31: 9	Their stronghold *will* f because of terror;	6296
	34: 4	the starry host *will* f like withered leaves	5570
	34: 7	And the wild oxen *will* f with them,	3718
	40: 7	The grass withers and the flowers f,	5570
	40: 8	The grass withers and the flowers f,	5570
	40:30	and young men **stumble and** f;	4173+4173
	47:11	A calamity *will* f upon you	5877
	51:23	'F prostrate that we may walk over you.'	8817
Jer	6:15	So *they will* f among the fallen;	5877
	8: 4	" 'When *men* f **down,** do they not get up?	5877
	8:12	So *they will* f among the fallen;	5877
	13:18	for your glorious crowns *will* f	3718
	19: 7	*I will* **make** them f by the sword	5877
	20: 4	with your own eyes will see *them* f by	5877
	23:12	to darkness and there *they will* f.	5877
	25:27	and vomit, and f to rise no more because of	5877
	25:34	you *will* f and be shattered	5877
	34:17	'freedom' to f by the sword,	NIH
	39:18	not f by the sword but will escape	5877
	44:12	*they will* f by the sword or die	5877
	46: 6	by the River Euphrates they stumble and f.	5877
	46:12	both *will* f **down** together."	5877
	46:16	*they will* f over each other.	5877
	48:16	"The f of Moab is at hand;	369
	48:44	"Whoever flees from the terror *will* f into	5877

Jer	49:21	the sound of their f the earth will tremble;	5877
	49:26	her young men *will* f in the streets;	5877
	50:15	She surrenders, her towers f,	5877
	50:30	her young men *will* f in the streets;	5877
	50:32	The arrogant one will stumble and f	5877
	51: 4	*They will* f **down** slain in Babylon,	5877
	51: 8	Babylon *will* suddenly f and be broken.	5877
	51:44	And the wall of Babylon *will* f.	5877
	51:49	"Babylon *must* f because of Israel's slain,	5877
	51:64	And her people *will* f.' "	3615
La	1: 9	Her f was astounding;	3718
Eze	5:12	a third will f by the sword	5877
	6: 7	Your *people will* f slain among you,	5877
	6:11	for *they will* f by the sword,	5877
	6:12	and he that is near *will* f by the sword,	5877
	11:10	*You will* f by the sword,	5877
	13:11	with whitewash that *it is going to* f.	2118
	13:13	of rain *will* f with destructive fury.	2118
	13:21	*they will* no longer f prey to your power.	2118
	17:21	All his fleeing troops *will* f by the sword,	5877
	23:25	of you who are left *will* f by the sword.	5877
	24:21	and daughters you left behind *will* f by	5877
	25:13	and from Teman to Dedan *they will* f by	5877
	26:11	your strong pillars *will* f to the ground.	3718
	26:15	at the sound of your f,	5147
	26:18	coastlands tremble on the day of your f;	5147
	28:23	The slain *will* f within her,	5877
	29: 5	*You will* f on the open field and not	5877
	30: 4	When the slain f in Egypt,	5877
	30: 5	and the people of the covenant land *will* f	5877
	30: 6	" 'The allies of Egypt *will* f	5877
	30: 6	From Migdol to Aswan *they will* f by	5877
	30:17	of Heliopolis and Bubastis *will* f by	5877
	30:22	and **make** the sword f from his hand.	5877
	30:25	but the arms of Pharaoh *will* f **limp.**	5877
	31:16	at the sound of its f when I brought it down	5147
	32:12	**cause** your hordes **to** f	5877
	32:20	*They will* f among those killed by	5877
	33:12	not **cause** him *to* f when he turns from it.	4173
	33:27	those who are left in the ruins *will* f by	5877
	35: 8	by the sword *will* f on your hills and	5877
	36:15	**cause** your nation **to** f,	4173
	38:20	and every wall *will* f to the ground.	5877
	39: 4	On the mountains of Israel *you will* f,	5877
	39: 5	*You will* f in the open field,	5877
	40: 1	the fourteenth year after the f *of the city*—	5782
	44:12	**made** the house of Israel f	2118+4200+4842
Da	3: 5	*you must* f **down** and worship the image	10484
	3: 6	not f **down** and worship will immediately	10484
	3:10	pipes and all kinds of music *must* f **down**	10484
	3:11	not f **down** and worship will be thrown into	10484
	3:15	*to* f **down** and worship the image I made,	10484
	11:19	of his own country but will stumble and f,	5877
	11:26	and many *will* f **in battle.**	2728+5877
	11:33	though for a time *they will* f by the sword	4173
	11:34	When they f, they will receive a little help,	4173
	11:41	Many countries *will* f, but Edom,	4173
Hos	7: 7	All their kings f, and none of them calls on	5877
	7:16	Their leaders *will* f by the sword because	5877
	10: 8	and to the hills, "F on us!"	5877
	13:16	*They will* f by the sword;	5877
Am	3: 5	*Does* a bird f into a trap on the ground	5877
	3:14	the altar will be cut off and f to the ground.	5877
	7:17	and your sons and daughters *will* f by	5877
	8:14	*they will* f, never to rise again."	5877
Na	3:12	the figs f into the mouth of the eater.	5877
	3:19	about you claps his hands at your f,	NIH
Hag	2:22	horses and their riders *will* f,	3718
Mt	7:25	beat against that house; yet *it did* not f,	4406
	10:29	not one of them *will* f to the ground apart	4406
	11: 6	the man who *does* not f **away** on account	4997
	15:14	both *will* f **into** a pit."	4406
	15:27	"but even the dogs eat the crumbs that f	4406
	24:29	the stars *will* f from the sky,	4406
	26:31	"This very night *you will all* f **away**	4997
	26:33	"Even if all f **away** on account of you,	4997
	26:41	so that *you will* not f **into** temptation.	1656
Mk	4:17	*they* quickly f **away.**	4997
	13:25	the stars *will* f from the sky,	1639+4406
	14:27	"You will all f **away**," Jesus told them,	4997
	14:29	Peter declared, "Even if all f **away**,	4997
	14:38	so that *you will* not f into temptation.	2262
Lk	6:39	*Will they* not both f into a pit?	1860
	7:23	the man who *does* not f **away** on account	4997
	8:13	but in the time of testing *they* f **away.**	923
	10:18	"I saw Satan f like lightning from heaven.	4406
	11:17	and a house divided against itself *will* f.	4406
	21:24	*They will* f by the sword and will be taken	4406
	22:40	that *you will* not f **into** temptation."	1656
	22:46	so that *you will* not f **into** temptation."	1656
	23:30	Then " 'they will say to the mountains, "F	4406
Ac	5:15	so that at least Peter's shadow *might* f **on**	2173
	27:32	that held the lifeboat and let it f **away.**	1738
	28: 6	to swell up or suddenly f dead,	2928
Ro	3:23	for all have sinned and f **short** of the glory	5728
	9:33	to stumble and a rock that **makes** them f,	4998
	11:11	so as to f beyond recovery?	4406
	14:21	that *will* **cause** your brother *to* f.	4684
1Co	8:13	**causes** my brother *to* f **into sin,**	4997
	8:13	so that *I will* not **cause** him *to* f.	4997
	10:12	be careful that *you* don't f!	4098
	14:25	So he will f **down** and worship God,	4406
1Th	4:13	to be ignorant about those who f **asleep,**	3121
1Ti	3: 6	or he may become conceited and f	1860
	3: 7	not f into disgrace and into the devil's trap.	1860
	6: 9	want to get rich f into temptation and a trap	1860
Heb	4:11	so that no one *will* f by following their	4406

Heb	6: 6	if they f **away,** to be brought back	4178
	10:31	It is a dreadful thing *to* f into the hands of the living God.	1860
1Pe	1:24	the grass withers and the flowers f,	1738
	2: 8	to stumble and a rock that **makes** them."	4998
2Pe	1:10	if you do these things, *you will* never f,	4760
	3:17	by the error of lawless men and f **from**	1738
Rev	3: 9	and f **down** at your feet and acknowledge	4686
	4:10	the twenty-four elders f **down**	4406
	6:16	"F on us and hide us from the face	4406

FALLEN (77) [FALL]

Ge	15:17	When the sun had set and darkness *had* f,	2118
Ex	9:18	the worst hailstorm that *has* ever f	2118
	23: 5	of someone who hates you f **down**	8069
Lev	19:10	or pick up the **grapes that have** f.	7261
Dt	22: 4	or his ox f on the road,	5877
	29:22	the calamities that *have* f on the land and	NIH
Jos	2: 9	to you and that a great fear of you *has* f	5877
Jdg	3:25	There they saw their lord f to the floor,	5877
	8:10	and twenty thousand swordsmen *had* f.	5877
	19:27	concubine, f *in* the doorway of the house,	5877
1Sa	5: 3	f on his face on the ground before the ark	5877
	5: 4	f on his face on the ground before the ark	5877
	20:37	to the place where Jonathan's arrow *had* f,	3721
	31: 8	and his three sons f on Mount Gilboa.	5877
2Sa	1:10	because I knew that after he *had* f he could	5877
	1:12	because *they had* f by the sword.	5877
	1:19	How the mighty *have* f!	5877
	1:25	"How the mighty *have* f in battle!	5877
	1:27	"How the mighty *have* f!	5877
	2:23	to the place where Asahel *had* f and died.	5877
	3:38	and a great man *has* f in Israel this day?	5877
2Ki	1: 2	Now Ahaziah *had* f through the lattice	5877
	1:14	fire *has* f from heaven and consumed	3718
	2:13	that *had* f from Elijah and went back	5877
	2:14	Then he took the cloak that *had* f from him	5877
1Ch	10: 8	and his sons f on Mount Gilboa.	5877
2Ch	14:14	the terror of the LORD *had* f upon them,	2118
	29: 8	the LORD *has* f on Judah and Jerusalem;	2118
	29: 9	This is why our fathers *have* f by the sword	5877
Ps	9:15	nations *have* f into the pit they have dug;	3190
	16: 6	The boundary lines *have* f for me	5877
	36:12	See how the evildoers lie f—	5877
	57: 6	but *they have* f into it *themselves.*	5877
	68:14	it was like **snow** f on Zalmon.	8919
	105:38	because dread of Israel *had* f on them.	5877
Pr	6: 3	*you have* f into your neighbor's hands;	995
Isa	9:10	"The bricks *have* f **down,**	5877
	14:12	How *you have* f from heaven,	5877
	21: 9	'Babylon *has* f, has fallen!	5877
	21: 9	'Babylon has fallen, *has* f!	5877
Jer	3: 3	and no spring rains *have* f.	2118
	6:15	So they will fall among the f;	5877
	8:12	So they will fall among the f;	5877
	48:32	The destroyer *has* f on your ripened fruit	5877
	51:47	be disgraced and her slain *will* all lie f	5877
	51:49	in all the earth *have* f because of Babylon.	5877
La	2:21	my young men and maidens *have* f by	5877
	5:16	The crown *has* f from our head.	5877
Eze	21:15	So that hearts may melt and the f be many,	4842
	31:13	All the birds of the air settled on the f tree,	5147
	32:22	all *who have* f by the sword.	5877
	32:23	f by the sword.	5877
	32:24	All of them are slain, f by the sword.	5877
	32:27	other uncircumcised warriors *who have* f,	5877
	33:21	"The city *has* f!"	5782
Am	5: 2	"F is Virgin Israel,	5877
	9:11	"In that day I will restore David's f tent.	5877
Mic	7: 8	Though *I have* f, I will rise.	5877
Zec	11: 1	Wail, O pine tree, for the cedar *has* f;	5877
Jn	11:11	"Our friend Lazarus *has* f **asleep;**	3121
Ac	15:16	this I will return and rebuild David's f tent.	4406
Ro	15: 3	of those who insult you *have* f **on** me."	2158
1Co	11:30	and a number of you *have* f **asleep.**	3121
	15: 6	though some *have* f asleep.	3121
	15:18	also who *have* f asleep in Christ are lost.	3121
	15:20	the firstfruits *of* those who *have* f **asleep.**	3121
Gal	5: 4	*you have* f **away** from grace.	1738
1Th	4:14	with Jesus those who *have* f **asleep** in him.	3121
	4:15	not precede those who *have* f **asleep.**	3121
Heb	4: 1	that none of you be found *to have* f **short**	5728
Rev	2: 5	the height from which *you have* f!	4406
	9: 1	and I saw a star *that had* f from the sky to	4406
	14: 8	A second angel followed and said, "F!	4406
	14: 8	F is Babylon the Great,	4406
	17:10	Five *have* f, one is, the other has not yet come;	4406
	18: 2	With a mighty voice he shouted: "F!	4406
	18: 2	F is Babylon the Great!	4406

FALLING (11) [FALL]

Ge	8: 2	and the rain *had* **stopped** f from the sky.	3973
Est	7: 8	Haman *was* f on the couch	5877
	8: 3	f at his feet and weeping.	5877
Ps	72: 6	He will be like rain f on a mown field,	3718
	133: 3	the dew of Hermon *were* f on Mount Zion.	3718
Isa	3: 8	Jerusalem staggers, Judah *is* f;	5877
Mk	15:19	F on their knees, they paid homage to him.	5502
Lk	2:34	to cause the f and rising of many in Israel,	4774
	22:44	and his sweat was like drops of blood f to	2849
Heb	6: 7	in the rain often f on it and that produces	2262
Jude	1:24	To him who is able to keep you from f and	720

FALLOW (KJV) See UNPLOWED

FALLOWDEER (KJV) See ROE DEER

FALLS (42) [FALL]

Ex	21:33	to cover it and an ox or a donkey f into it,	5877
Lev	11:32	of them dies and f on something,	5877
	11:33	If one of them f into a clay pot,	5877
	11:35	of their carcasses f on becomes unclean;	5877
	11:37	If a carcass f on any seeds that are to	5877
	11:38	on the seed and a carcass f on it,	5877
	16: 9	Aaron shall bring the goat whose lot f to	6590
Nu	24: 4	from the Almighty, *who* f prostrate,	5877
	24:16	from the Almighty, *who* f prostrate,	5877
	33:54	Whatever f to them by lot will be theirs.	3655
Dt	20:20	until the city at war with you f.	3718
	22: 8	on your house if someone f from the roof.	5877
2Sa	3:29	or leprosy or who leans on a crutch or who f	5877
	3:34	You fell as *one* f before wicked men."	5877
Job	4:13	when deep sleep f on men,	5877
	9:24	a land f into the hands of the wicked,	5989
	18:12	disaster is ready for him when he f.	7520
	33:15	when deep sleep f on men as they slumber	5877
Ps	7:15	and scoops it out f into the pit he has made.	5877
Pr	11:14	For lack of guidance a nation f,	5877
	13:17	A wicked messenger f into trouble,	5877
	17:20	he whose tongue is deceitful f into trouble.	5877
	24:16	for though a righteous man f seven times,	5877
	24:17	Do not gloat when your enemy f;	5877
	28:14	but he who hardens his heart f into trouble.	5877
Ecc	4:10	If one f down, his friend can help him up.	5877
	4:10	But pity the man who f and has no one	5877
	11: 3	a tree f to the south or to the north,	5877
	11: 3	in the place where it f, there it will lie.	5877
Isa	24:20	upon it is the guilt of its rebellion that *it* f—	5877
Eze	13:14	When *it* f, you will be destroyed in it;	5877
Mt	12:11	"If any of you has a sheep and it f into a pit	1860
	13:21	he quickly f away.	4997
	17:15	*He* often f into the fire or into the water.	4406
	21:44	He who f on this stone will be broken	4406
	21:44	but he on whom *it* f will be crushed."	4406
Lk	14: 5	"If one of you has a son or an ox that f into	4406
	20:18	Everyone who f on that stone will	4406
	20:18	but he on whom *it* f will be crushed."	4406
Jn	12:24	a kernel of wheat f to the ground and dies,	4406
Ro	14: 4	To his own master he stands or f.	4406
Jas	1:11	its blossom f and its beauty is destroyed.	1738

FALSE (85) [FALSEHOOD, FALSELY]

Ex	20:16	not give f testimony against your neighbor.	9214
	23: 1	"Do not spread f reports.	8736
	23: 7	Have nothing to do with a f charge and do	9214
Dt	5:20	not give f testimony against your neighbor.	8736
	19:18	giving f testimony against his brother,	9214
Job	24:25	who *can* prove me f and reduce my words	3941
	36: 4	Be assured that my words are not f;	9214
	41: 9	Any hope of subduing him *is* f;	3941
Ps	4: 2	and seek f gods?	3942
	24: 4	up his soul to an idol or swear by *what* is f.	5327
	27:12	for f witnesses rise up against me,	9214
	35:20	but devise f accusations	5327
	40: 4	to those who turn aside to f gods.	3942
	44:17	though we had not forgotten you or *been* f	9213
Pr	6:19	a f witness who pours out lies and	9214
	12:17	but a f witness tells lies.	9214
	13: 5	The righteous hate what is f,	9214
	14: 5	but a f witness pours out lies.	9214
	14:25	but a f witness is deceitful.	3942
	19: 5	A f witness will not go unpunished,	9214
	19: 9	A f witness will not go unpunished,	9214
	21:28	A f witness will perish,	3942
	25:18	the man who gives f testimony	9214
Isa	29:21	and with f testimony deprive the innocent	9332
	41:29	See, they are all f!	224
	44:25	of f prophets and makes fools of diviners,	967
	57:11	so dreaded and feared that *you have been* f	3941
	63: 8	sons *who will* not *be* f to me";	9213
Jer	13:25	and trusted in f gods.	9214
	14:14	They are prophesying to you f visions,	9214
	16:19	"Our fathers possessed nothing but f gods,	9214
	23:16	fill you with f hopes.	2038
	23:32	against those who prophesy f dreams,"	9214
	50:36	A sword against her f prophets!	967
La	2:14	of your prophets were f and worthless;	8736
	2:14	The oracles they gave you were f	8736
Eze	12:24	For there will be no more f visions	8736
	13: 6	Their visions are f and their divinations	8736
	13: 7	Have you not seen f visions	8736
	13: 8	Because of your f words and lying visions,	8736
	13: 9	be against the prophets who see f visions	8736
	13:23	therefore you will no longer see f visions	8736
	21:23	It will seem like a f omen	8736
	21:29	Despite f visions concerning you	8736
	22:28	for them by f visions and lying divinations."	8736
Hos	10: 4	take f oaths and make agreements;	8736
Am	2: 4	they have been led astray by f gods,	3942
Mic	6:11	with a bag of f weights?	5327
Hab	2: 3	it speaks of the end and *will* not prove f.	3941
Zec	10: 2	they tell dreams that are f,	8736
Mal	2: 6	in his mouth and nothing f was found	6406
Mt	7:15	"Watch out for f prophets.	6021
	15:19	sexual immorality, theft, f testimony,	6019
	19:18	do not steal, *do* not give f testimony,	6018
	24:11	and many f prophets will appear	6021
	24:24	For f Christs and f prophets will appear	6023
	24:24	For false Christs and f prophets will appear	6021
	26:59	looking for f evidence against Jesus so	6019

Mt	26:60	though many f witnesses came forward.	6019
Mk	10:19	*do* not give f testimony, do not defraud,	6018
	13:22	For f Christs and false prophets will appear	6023
	13:22	For false Christs and f prophets will appear	6021
	14:57	up and gave this f testimony against him:	6018
Lk	6:26	how their fathers treated the f prophets.	6021
	18:20	do not steal, *do* not give f testimony,	6018
Jn	1:47	in whom there is nothing f."	1515
	7:18	there is nothing f about him.	94+4024
Ac	6:13	They produced f witnesses, who testified,	6014
	13: 6	and f prophet named Bar-Jesus,	6021
1Co	15:15	then found to be f witnesses about God,	6020
2Co	11:13	For such men are f apostles,	6013
	11:26	and in danger from f brothers.	6012
Gal	2: 4	some f brothers had infiltrated our ranks	6012
Php	1:18	whether *from* f motives or true,	4733
Col	2:18	not let anyone who delights in f humility	NIG
	2:23	their f humility and their harsh treatment of	NIG
1Ti	1: 3	not to teach f doctrines any longer	2281
	6: 3	If anyone teaches f doctrines and does	2281
2Pe	2: 1	But there were also f prophets among	6021
	2: 1	just as there will be f teachers among you.	6015
1Jn	4: 1	because many f prophets have gone out	6021
Rev	2: 2	and have found them f.	6014
	16:13	and out of the mouth *of* the f prophet.	6021
	19:20	with him the f prophet who had performed	6021
	20:10	and the f prophet had been thrown.	6021

FALSEHOOD (10) [FALSE]

Job	21:34	Nothing is left of your answers but f!"	5086
	31: 5	in f or my foot has hurried after deceit—	8736
Ps	52: 3	f rather than speaking the truth.	9214
	119:163	I hate and abhor f but I love your law.	9214
Pr	30: 8	Keep f and lies far from me;	8736
Isa	28:15	a lie our refuge and f our hiding place."	9214
Ro	3: 7	"If my f enhances God's truthfulness and	6025
Eph	4:25	of you must put off f and speak truthfully	6022
1Jn	4: 6	the Spirit of truth and the spirit *of* f.	4415
Rev	22:15	and everyone who loves and practices f.	6022

FALSELY (16) [FALSE]

Ge	21:23	before God that *you* will not deal f	9213
Lev	6: 3	or if he swears f,	6584+9214
	6: 5	he swore f about.	2021+4200+9214
	19:12	" 'Do not swear f by my name	2021+4200+9214
Ps	41: 6	to see me, he speaks f,	8736
	101: 7	no one who speaks f will stand	9214
Jer	5: 2	still they are swearing f."	2021+4200+9214
	8: 8	of the scribes has handled it f?	2021+4200+9214
Da	6:24	the men who *had* accused Daniel were brought	10030+10642
Zec	5: 3	everyone who swears f will be banished.	8678
	5: 4	and the house of him who swears f	9214
	8:17	and do not love to swear f.	9214
Mt	5:11	persecute you and f say all kinds of evil	6017
Mk	14:56	Many testified f against him,	6018
Lk	3:14	and don't accuse people f—	5193
1Ti	6:20	*of* what *is* f called knowledge,	6024

FALTER (2) [FALTERED, FALTERING, FALTERS]

Pr	24:10	If you f in times of trouble,	8332
Isa	42: 4	*he* will not f or be discouraged	3908

FALTERED (1) [FALTER]

Ps	105:37	and from among their tribes no *one* f.	4173

FALTERING (3) [FALTER]

Ex	6:12	since I speak with f lips?"	6888
	6:30	"Since I speak with f lips,	6888
Job	4: 4	you have strengthened f knees.	4156

FALTERS (1) [FALTER]

Isa	21: 4	My heart f, fear makes me tremble;	9494

FAME (16) [FAMOUS]

Dt	26:19	in praise, f and honor high above all	9005
Jos	6:27	and his f spread throughout the land.	9053
	9: 9	because of the f *of* the LORD your God.	9005
1Ki	4:31	his f spread to all the surrounding nations.	9005
	10: 1	When the queen of Sheba heard about the f	9051
1Ch	14:17	So David's f spread throughout every land,	9005
	22: 5	of great magnificence and f	9005
2Ch	9: 1	the queen of Sheba heard of Solomon's f,	9051
	26: 8	his f spread as far as the border of Egypt,	9005
	26:15	His f spread far and wide,	9005
Isa	66:19	not heard of my f or seen my glory.	9051
Jer	48:17	all who know her f;	9005
Eze	16:14	And your f spread among the nations	9005
	16:15	in your beauty and used your f to become	9005
Hos	14: 7	his f will be like the wine from Lebanon.	2352
Hab	3: 2	LORD, I have heard of your f;	9051

FAMILIAR (3)

Ps	139: 3	*you are* f with all my ways.	6122
Isa	53: 3	a man of sorrows, and f with suffering.	3359
Ac	26:26	The king *is* f with these things,	2179

FAMILIES (109) [FAMILY]

Ge	45:18	bring your father and your f back to me.	1074
Ex	1:21	he gave them f of their own.	1074

Ex	6:14	These were the heads of their f:	3+1074
	6:25	These were the heads of the Levite f,	3
	12:21	for your f and slaughter the Passover lamb.	5476
Nu	1: 2	by their clans and f,	3+1074
	1:18	by their clans and f,	3+1074
	1:20	to the records of their clans and f,	3+1074
	1:22	to the records of their clans and f,	3+1074
	1:24	to the records of their clans and f,	3+1074
	1:26	to the records of their clans and f,	3+1074
	1:28	to the records of their clans and f,	3+1074
	1:30	to the records of their clans and f,	3+1074
	1:32	to the records of their clans and f,	3+1074
	1:34	to the records of their clans and f,	3+1074
	1:36	to the records of their clans and f,	3+1074
	1:38	to the records of their clans and f,	3+1074
	1:40	to the records of their clans and f,	3+1074
	1:42	to the records of their clans and f,	3+1074
	1:45	according to their f.	3+1074
	1:47	The f of the tribe of Levi, however,	3
	2:32	counted according to their f.	3+1074
	3:15	"Count the Levites by their f and clans.	3+1074
	3:20	according to their f.	3+1074
	3:24	the f of the Gershonites was Eliasaph son	3+1074
	3:30	The leader of the f of the Kohathite clans	3+1074
	3:35	the f of the Merarite clans was Zuriel son	3+1074
	4: 2	of the Levites by their clans and f.	3+1074
	4:22	of the Gershonites by their clans and f.	3+1074
	4:29	"Count the Merarites by their clans and f.	3+1074
	4:34	the Kohathites by their clans and f.	3+1074
	4:38	by their clans and f.	3
	4:40	counted by their clans and f, were 2,630.	3+1074
	4:42	by their clans and f.	3
	4:46	the Levites by their clans and f.	3+1074
	7: 2	the heads of f who were the tribal leaders	3+1074
	26: 2	of the whole Israelite community by f—	3+1074
	34:14	because the f of the tribe of Reuben,	3+1074
	36: 1	the heads of the Israelite f.	3
Dt	12: 7	you and your f shall eat and shall rejoice	1074
Jos	7:17	of the Zerahites come forward by f,	1505
	21: 1	and the heads of the other tribal f of Israel	3
2Sa	15:22	on with all his men and the f that were	3251
1Ki	8: 1	the tribes and the chiefs of the Israelite f,	3
2Ki	10:13	f of the king and the queen mother."	1201
1Ch	4:38	Their f increased greatly,	3+1074
	5:13	Their relatives, by f, were:	3
	5:24	These were the heads of their f:	3+1074
	5:24	famous men, and heads of their f.	3+1074
	7: 2	heads of their f.	3
	7: 7	Uzzi, Uzziel, Jerimoth and Iri, heads of f—	3+1074
	7: 9	the heads of f and 20,200	3+1074
	7:11	All these sons of Jediael were heads of f,	3
	7:40	heads of f, choice men,	3+1074
	8: 6	who were heads of f of those living	3
	8:10	These were his sons, heads of f.	3
	8:13	who were heads of f of those living	3
	8:28	All these were heads of f,	3
	9: 9	All these men were heads of their f.	3+1074
	9:13	The priests, who were heads of f,	3+1074
	9:33	heads of Levite f,	3
	9:34	All these were heads of Levite f,	3
	12:39	their f had supplied provisions for them.	278
	15:12	"You are the heads of the Levitical f;	3
	16:28	Ascribe to the LORD, O f of nations,	5476
	23: 9	These were the heads of the f of Ladan.	3
	23:24	the descendants of Levi by their f,	3+1074
	23:24	the heads of f as they were registered	3
	24: 4	of f from Eleazar's descendants	3+1074
	24: 4	of f from Ithamar's descendants.	3+1074
	24: 6	of Abiathar and the heads of f of the priests	3+1074
	24:30	according to their f.	3
	24:31	heads of f of the priests and of the Levites.	3
	24:31	The f of the oldest brother were treated	3
	26:13	according to their f, young and old alike.	3+1074
	26:21	of f belonging to Ladan the Gershonite,	3
	26:26	the heads of f who were the commanders	3
	26:31	to the genealogical records of their f.	3
	26:32	who were able men and heads of f,	3
	27: 1	heads of f, commanders of thousands	3
	29: 6	Then the leaders of f,	3
2Ch	1: 2	to all the leaders in Israel, the heads of f—	3
	5: 2	the tribes and the chiefs of the Israelite f,	3
	17:14	Their enrollment by f was as follows:	3+1074
	19: 8	of Israelite f to administer the law of	3
	23: 2	the heads of Israelite f from all the towns.	3
	25: 5	and assigned them according to their f	3+1074
	31:17	by their f in the genealogical records	3509
	35: 4	Prepare yourselves by f in your divisions,	3+1074
	35: 5	of Levites for each subdivision of the f	3+1074
	35:12	to give them to the subdivisions of the f	3
Ezr	2:59	that their f were descended from Israel:	3+1074
	2:68	of the heads of the f gave freewill offerings	3
	4: 2	to Zerubbabel and to the heads of the f	3
	4: 3	the heads of the f of Israel answered,	3
Ne	4:13	posting them by f, with their swords,	5476
	7: 5	the common people for registration by f.	3509
	7:61	that their f were descended from Israel:	3+1074
	7:70	the heads of the f contributed to the work.	3
	7:71	the heads of the f gave to the treasury for	3
	8:13	the heads of all the f,	3
	10:34	to determine when each of our f is to bring	3+1074
	11:13	who were heads of f—	3
	12:12	these were the heads of the priestly f:	3
Ps	22:27	and all the f of the nations will bow down	5476
	68: 6	God sets the lonely in f,	1074
	96: 7	Ascribe to the LORD, O f of nations,	5476
	107:41	of their affliction and increased their f	5476
Am	3: 2	"You only have I chosen of all the f *of*	5476

FAMILY (177) [FAMILIES]

Ref	Text	#
Ge 7: 1	"Go into the ark, you and your whole f,	1074
16: 2	perhaps *I can* **build a f** through her."	1215
19:32	then lie with him and preserve our f line	2446
19:34	with him so we can preserve our f line	2446
24:38	but go to my father's f and to my own clan,	1074
24:40	from my own clan and from my father's f.	1074
30: 3	and that through her I too *can* **build a f**."	1215
43: 7	about ourselves and our f.	4580
46:27	the members of Jacob's f,	1074
50:22	along with all his father's f.	1074
Ex 1: 1	each with his f:	1074
12: 3	to take a lamb for his f,	3+1074
Lev 6:29	Any male in a priest's f may eat it;	NIH
7: 6	Any male in a priest's f may eat it,	NIH
20: 5	and his f and all who follow him from their people	5476
22:10	" 'No one **outside a priest's** f may eat	2424
25:10	to his f **property** and each to his own clan.	299
27:16	the LORD part of his f **land,** its value is	299+8441
27:22	which is not part of his f **land,**	299+8441
27:28	whether man or animal or f **land—**	299+8441
Nu 1: 4	each the head of his f, is to help you.	3+1074
1:44	each one representing his f.	3+1074
2: 2	with the banners of his f."	3+1074
2:34	each with his clan and f.	3+1074
3: 1	the **account of the** f of Aaron and Moses	9352
11:10	Moses heard the people of every f wailing,	5476
18: 1	your sons and your father's f are to bear	1074
25: 6	to his f a Midianite woman right before	278
25:14	the leader of a Simeonite	3+1074
25:15	a tribal chief of a Midianite f.	3+1074
31:26	"You and Eleazar the priest and the f heads	3
32:28	and Joshua son of Nun and to the f heads	3
36: 1	The f heads of the clan of Gilead son	3
Dt 5:16	and your f and is well off with you,	1074
15:20	Each year you and your f are to eat them in	1074
18: 8	from the sale of f **possessions.**	3
25: 5	his widow must not marry **outside the f.**	2021+2025+2424+2575
25: 9	not build up his brother's f **line.**"	1074
25:10	in Israel as The F of the Unsandaled.	1074
Jos 2:12	that you will show kindness to my f,	3+1074
2:18	and all your f into your house.	3+1074
6:23	They brought out her entire f and put them	5476
6:25	with her f and all who belonged to her,	3+1074
7:14	that the LORD takes shall come forward f	NIH
7:14	that the LORD takes shall come forward family by f;	1074
7:14	the f that the LORD takes shall come forward	1074
7:18	Joshua had his f come forward man	1074
13:29	the f of the descendants of Manasseh, clan	4751
21: 1	Now the f heads of the Levites	3
22:14	of a f division among the Israelite clans.	3
Jdg 1:25	but spared the man and his whole f.	5476
6:15	and I am the least in my f."	1074
6:27	because he was afraid of his f and the men	3+1074
8:27	and it became a snare to Gideon and his f.	1074
8:35	They also failed to show kindness to the f	1074
9:16	and his f, and if you have treated him	1074
9:18	revolted against my father's f,	1074
9:19	toward Jerub-Baal and his f today,	1074
11: 2	not going to get any inheritance in our f,"	3+1074
16:31	and his father's whole f went down	1074
18:25	and you and your f will lose your lives."	1074
Ru 4:10	from among his f or from the town records.	278
4:12	may your f be like that of Perez,	1074
4:18	This, then, is the f line *of* Perez:	9352
1Sa 1:21	with all his f to offer the annual sacrifice to	1074
2:31	there will not be an old man in your f **line**	1074
2:32	in your f **line** there will never be	1074
2:36	in your f **line** will come and bow down	1074
3:12	against Eli everything I spoke against his f	1074
3:13	that I would judge his f forever because of	1074
9:20	if not to you and all your father's f?"	1074
17:25	in marriage and will exempt his father's f	1074
18:18	what is my f or my father's clan in Israel,	2646
20:15	not ever cut off your kindness from my f—	5476
20:29	because our f is observing a sacrifice in	5476
22:11	of Ahitub and his father's whole f,	1074
22:15	or any of his father's f,	1074
22:16	Ahimelech, you and your father's whole **f.**"	1074
22:22	for the death of your father's whole f.	1074
24:21	or wipe out my name from my father's **f.**"	1074
27: 3	Each man had his f with him,	1074
2Sa 2: 3	men who were with him, each with his f,	1074
3: 8	to the house of your father Saul and to his f	278
7:18	O Sovereign LORD, and what is my f,	1074
9: 9	that belonged to Saul and his f,	1074
14: 9	the blame rest on me and on my father's f,	1074
16: 5	from the same clan as Saul's f came out	1074
21: 4	or gold from Saul or his f,	1074
24:17	Let your hand fall upon me and my f."	3+1074
1Ki 14:14	a king over Israel who will cut off the f	1074
15:29	he killed Jeroboam's whole f.	1074
16:11	he killed off Baasha's whole f,	1074
16:12	So Zimri destroyed the whole f *of* Baasha,	1074
17:15	for Elijah and for the woman and her f.	1074
18:18	"But you and your father's f have.	1074
2Ki 8: 1	"Go away with your f and stay for a	1074
8: 2	and her f went away and stayed in the land	1074
8:27	for he was related by marriage to Ahab's f.	1074
10:17	he killed all who were left there of Ahab's f;	NIH
11: 1	she proceeded to destroy the whole royal f	2446
1Ch 5:15	the son of Guni, was head of their f.	3+1074
7: 4	According to their f genealogy,	3+1074
7:23	because there had been misfortune in his f.	1074
1Ch 9:19	his f (the Korahites) were responsible for	3+1074
12:27	leader of the f of Aaron, with 3,700 men,	195
12:28	with 22 officers from his f;	3+1074
13:14	of God remained with the f of Obed-Edom	1074
16:43	and David returned home to bless his f.	1074
17:16	O LORD God, and what is my f,	1074
21:17	let your hand fall upon me and my f,	3+1074
23:11	as one f with one assignment.	3+1074
24: 6	one f being taken from Eleazar and	3+1074
26: 6	who were leaders in their father's f	1074
27:15	from the f of Othniel.	NIH
28: 4	chose me from my whole f to be king	3+1074
28: 4	from the house of Judah he chose my f,	3+1074
2Ch 22:10	she proceeded to destroy the whole royal f	2446
26:12	The total number of f leaders over	3
31:10	from the f of Zadok, answered,	1074
Ezr 1: 5	Then the f heads of Judah and Benjamin,	3
2:36	the descendants of Jedaiah (through the f	1074
2:62	These searched for their f records,	3509
3:12	the older priests and Levites and f heads,	3
8: 1	These are the f heads and those registered	3
8:29	and the Levites and the f heads of Israel."	3
10:16	the priest selected men who were f heads,	3
10:16	one from each f division.	3
Ne 7:39	the descendants of Jedaiah (through the f	1074
7:64	These searched for their f records,	3509
12:12	of Seraiah's f, Meraiah;	NIH
12:22	The f heads of the Levites in the days	3
12:23	The f heads among the descendants of Levi	3
Est 2:10	Esther had not revealed her nationality and f **background,**	4580
2:20	Esther had kept secret her f **background**	4580
4:14	but you and your father's f will perish.	1074
8: 6	to see the destruction of my f?"	4580
9:28	in every generation by **every** f,	2256+5476+5476
Job 21:21	For what does he care about the f he leaves	1074
32: 2	the Buzite, of the f of Ram,	5476
Pr 11:29	on his f will inherit only wind,	1074
15:27	A greedy man brings trouble to his f,	1074
27:27	of goats' milk to feed you and your f and	1074
31:15	for her f and portions for her servant girls.	1074
Isa 22:24	All the glory of his f will hang on him:	3+1074
Jer 12: 6	Your brothers, your own f—	3+1074
35: 2	to the Recabite f and invite them to come	1074
35: 3	the whole f *of* the Recabites.	1074
35: 5	the men of the Recabite f and said to them,	1074
35:18	Jeremiah said to the f *of* the Recabites,	1074
38:17	you and your f will live.	1074
Eze 17:13	a member of the royal f and made a treaty	2446
43:19	who are Levites, of the f of Zadok,	2446
Da 1: 3	in some of the Israelites from the royal f	2446
11: 7	her f **line** will arise to take her place.	5916+9247
Am 3: 1	the whole f I brought up out of Egypt:	5476
Mk 3:21	When his f heard about this,	3836+4123
5:19	to **your** f and tell them how much	3836+5050
Lk 9:61	and say good-by to my f."	3875
12:52	be five in one f divided against each other,	3875
Jn 7:42	that the Christ will come from David's f	5065
8:35	a slave has no permanent place in the f,	3864
Ac 4: 6	and the other men of the high priest's f.	1169
7:13	and Pharaoh learned about Joseph's f.	1169
7:14	for his father Jacob and his whole f,	5149
10: 2	and all his f were devout and God-fearing;	3875
16:33	immediately he and all his f were baptized.	3836
16:34	believe in God—he and his **whole f.**	4109
Gal 6:10	to those who **belong to** the f of believers.	3858
Eph 3:15	from whom his whole f in heaven and	4255
1Ti 3: 4	He must manage his own f well and see	3875
3: 5	not know how to manage his own f,	3875
5: 4	into practice by caring for their own f and	3875
5: 8	and especially for his **immediate f,**	3858
5:16	a believer has widows in her f,	NIG
Heb 2:11	those who are made holy are of the same f.	NIG
11: 7	in holy fear built an ark to save his f.	3836+3875
1Pe 4:17	for judgment to begin with the f of God;	3875

FAMINE (102) [FAMINES]

Ref	Text	#
Ge 12:10	Now there was a f in the land,	8280
12:10	for a while because the f was severe.	8280
26: 1	Now there was a f in the land—	8280
26: 1	besides the earlier f of Abraham's time—	8280
41:27	They are seven years of f.	8280
41:30	but seven years of f will follow them.	8280
41:30	and the f will ravage the land.	8280
41:31	the f that follows it will be so severe.	8280
41:36	during the seven years of f that will come	8280
41:36	that the country may not be ruined by the f."	8280
41:50	Before the years of f came,	8280
41:54	and the seven years of f began,	8280
41:54	There was f in all the other lands,	8280
41:55	When all Egypt *began to* **feel the f,**	8279
41:56	the f had spread over the whole country,	8280
41:56	for the f was severe throughout Egypt.	8280
41:57	because the f was severe in all the world.	8280
42: 5	for the f was in the land of Canaan also.	8280
43: 1	Now the f was still severe in the land.	8280
45: 6	two years now there has been f in the land,	8280
45:11	because five years of f are still to come.	8280
47: 4	because the f is severe in Canaan	8280
47:13	the whole region because the f was severe;	8280
47:13	and Canaan wasted away because of the f.	8280
47:20	because the f was too severe for them.	8280
Dt	I will send wasting f against them,	8280
Ru 1: 1	there was a f in the land,	8280
2Sa 21: 1	there was a f for three successive years;	8280
24:13	upon you three years of f in your land?	8280
1Ki 8:37	"When f or plague comes to the land,	8280
18: 2	Now the f was severe in Samaria,	8280
2Ki 4:38	Elisha returned to Gilgal and there was a f	8280
6:25	There was a great f in the city;	8280
7: 4	the f is there, and we will die.	8280
8: 1	a f in the land that will last seven years."	8280
25: 3	the ninth day of the [fourth] month the f in	8280
1Ch 21:12	three years of f, three months of being	8280
2Ch 6:28	"When f or plague comes to the land,	8280
20: 9	sword of judgment, or plague or f,	8280
Ne 5: 3	and our homes to get grain during the f."	8280
Job 5:20	In f he will ransom you from death,	8280
5:22	You will laugh at destruction and f,	4103
Ps 33:19	from death and keep them alive in f.	8280
37:19	in days of f they will enjoy plenty.	8282
105:16	He called down f on the land	8280
Isa 14:30	But your root I will destroy by f;	8280
51:19	ruin and destruction, f and sword—	8280
Jer 5:12	we will never see sword or f.	8280
11:22	their sons and daughters by f.	8280
14:12	with the sword, f and plague."	8280
14:13	'You will not see the sword or suffer f.	8280
14:15	'No sword or f will touch this land.'	8280
14:15	same prophets will perish by sword and f.	8280
14:16	of Jerusalem because of the f and sword.	8280
14:18	if I go into the city, I see the ravages of f.	8280
16: 4	They will perish by sword and f,	8280
18:21	So give their children over to f;	8280
21: 7	and f, to Nebuchadnezzar king of Babylon	8280
21: 9	in this city will die by the sword, f	8280
24:10	sword, f and plague against them	8280
27: 8	sword, f and plague, declares the LORD,	8280
27:13	sword, f and plague with which	8280
29:17	the sword, f and plague against them	8280
29:18	sword, f and plague and will make them	8280
32:24	Because of the sword, f and plague,	8280
32:36	sword, f and plague it will be handed over	8280
34:17	to fall by the sword, plague and f.	8280
38: 2	in this city will die by the sword, f	8280
42:16	the f you dread will follow you into Egypt,	8280
42:17	to settle there will die by the sword, f	8280
42:22	You will die by the sword, f and plague in	8280
44:12	they will fall by the sword or die from f.	8280
44:12	they will die by sword or f.	8280
44:13	f and plague, as I punished Jerusalem.	8280
44:18	and have been perishing by sword and f."	8280
44:27	by sword and f until they are all destroyed.	8280
52: 6	By the ninth day of the fourth month the f	8280
La 2:19	sword are better off than those who die of f;	8280
Eze 5:12	of the plague or perish by f inside you;	8280
5:16	and destructive arrows of f,	8280
5:16	I will bring more and more f upon you	8280
5:17	I will send f and wild beasts against you,	8280
6:11	of Israel, for they will fall by the sword, f	8280
6:12	he that survives and is spared will die of f.	8280
7:15	inside are plague and f;	8280
7:15	and those in the city will be devoured by f	8280
12:16	of them from the sword, f and plague, so	8280
14:13	to cut off its food supply and send f upon it	8280
14:21	sword and f and wild beasts and plague—	8280
34:29	be victims of f in the land or bear the scorn	8280
36:29	and make it plentiful and will not bring f	8280
36:30	among the nations because of f.	8280
Am 8:11	"when I will send a f through the land—	8280
8:11	not a f of food or a thirst for water,	8280
8:11	but a f of hearing the words of the LORD.	NIH
Lk 4:25	and a half years and then there was a severe f	3350
15:14	there was a severe f in that whole country,	3350
Ac 7:11	"Then a f struck all Egypt and Canaan,	3350
11:28	that a severe f would spread over	3350
Ro 8:35	or persecution or f or nakedness or danger	3350
Rev 6: 8	over a fourth of the earth to kill by sword, f	3350
18: 8	death, mourning and f.	3350

FAMINES (3) [FAMINE]

Ref	Text	#
Mt 24: 7	be f and earthquakes in various places.	3350
Mk 13: 8	be earthquakes in various places, and f.	3350
Lk 21:11	f and pestilences in various places,	3350

FAMISHED (3) [FAMISH]

Ref	Text	#
Ge 25:29	Esau came in from the open country, f.	6546
25:30	let me have some of that red stew! I'm f!"	6546
Isa 8:21	when *they are* f, they will become enraged	8279

FAMOUS (11) [FAME]

Ref	Text	#
Ru 4:11	in Ephrathah and *be* f in Bethlehem.	7924+9005
4:14	*May he become* f throughout Israel!	7924+9005
2Sa 8:13	And David **became** f after he returned	6913+9005
23:18	and as f as the Three.	9005
23:22	he too was as f as the three mighty men.	9005
1Ki 1:47	**make** Solomon's name more f	3512
1Ch 5:24	They were brave warriors, f men,	9005
11:20	and so he became as f as the Three.	9005
11:24	he too was as f as the three mighty men.	9005
12:30	brave warriors, f in their own clans—	408+9005
Isa 66:19	to the Libyans and Lydians (f as archers),	NIH

FAN (1) [FANS]

Ref	Text	#
2Ti 1: 6	*to* f **into flame** the gift of God,	351

FANGS (5) [FANG]

Ref	Text	#
Dt 32:24	against them the f *of* wild beasts,	9094
Job 20:16	the f of an adder will kill him.	4383
29:17	I broke the f of the wicked and snatched	5506

Ps	58: 6	tear out, O LORD, the *f* of the lions!	4922
Joel	1: 6	it has the teeth of a lion, the *f* of a lioness.	5506

FANNERS (KJV) See FOREIGNERS

FANS (1) [FAN]

Isa	54:16	the blacksmith *who* f the coals *into* flame	5870

FANTASIES (3)

Ps	73:20	O Lord, you will despise them as f.	7513
Pr	12:11	but he who chases f lacks judgment.	8199
	28:19	but the one who chases f will have his fill	8199

FAR (244) [AFAR, FAR-OFF, FARAWAY, FARTHER, FARTHEST]

Ge	10:19	from Sidon toward Gerar as f as Gaza,	6330
	10:19	Admah and Zeboiim, as f as Lasha.	6330
	12: 6	Abram traveled through the land as f as	6330
	14: 6	as f as El Paran near the desert.	6330
	14:14	in his household and went in pursuit as f as	6330
	14:15	pursuing them as f as Hobah,	6330
	18:25	F be it from you to do such a thing—	2721
	18:25	F be it from you!	2721
	44: 4	not gone from the city when Joseph said	8178
	44: 7	F be it from your servants to do anything	2721
	44:17	"F be it from me to do such a thing!"	2721
Ex	3: 1	the f side of the desert and came to Horeb,	339
	8:28	must not go very f.	8178+8178
	26:22	Make six frames for the f end, that is,	3752
	26:23	for the corners at the f end.	3752
	26:27	at the f end of the tabernacle.	3752
	36:27	They made six frames for the f end, that is,	3752
	36:28	the corners of the tabernacle at the f end.	3752
	36:32	at the f end of the tabernacle.	3752
Lev	13:12	so f as the priest can see,	3972+4200
Nu	11:31	as f as a day's walk in any direction.	3869
	13:21	the land from the Desert of Zin as f as	6330
	16: 3	"You have gone too f!	8041
	16: 7	You Levites have gone too f!"	8041
	21:24	but only as f as the Ammonites,	6330
	21:26	and had taken from him all his land as f as	6330
	21:30	We have demolished them as f as Nophah,	6330
Dt	1: 7	as f as the great river, the Euphrates.	6330
	2:23	Avvites who lived in villages as f as Gaza,	6330
	2:36	even as f as Gilead,	6330
	3: 8	the Arnon Gorge as f as Mount Hermon.	6330
	3:10	and all Bashan as f as Salecah and Edrei,	6330
	3:14	took the whole region of Argob as f as	6330
	4:49	as f as the Sea of the Arabah,	6330
	12:21	to put his Name is too f away from you,	8178
	13: 7	whether near or f,	8158
	14:24	to put his Name is so f away),	8178
	28:49	a nation against you from f away,	7368
	34: 2	all the land of Judah as f as the western sea,	6330
	34: 3	the City of Palms, as f as Zoar.	6330
Jos	7: 5	from the city gate as f as the stone quarries	6330
	8: 4	Don't go very f from it.	8178
	9: 1	the Great Sea as f as Lebanon	448+4578
	13: 4	from Arah of the Sidonians as f as Aphek,	6330
	13: 9	the whole plateau of Medeba as f as Dibon,	6330
	13:11	all of Mount Hermon and all Bashan as f as	6330
	13:25	and half the Ammonite country as f as	6330
	15: 5	the Salt Sea as f as the mouth of the Jordan,	6330
	15:47	and villages, as f as the Wadi of Egypt and	6330
	16: 3	to the territory of the Japhletites as f as	6330
	19: 8	the villages around these towns as f as	6330
	19:10	of their inheritance went as f as Sarid.	6330
	19:28	Hammon and Kanah, as f as Greater Sidon.	6330
	22:29	"F be it from us to rebel against	2721
	24: 6	with chariots and horsemen as f as	NIH
	24:16	"F be it from us to forsake the LORD	2721
Jdg	4:16	and army as f as Harosheth Haggoyim.	6330
	7:22	to Beth Shittah toward Zererah as f as	6330
	7:24	of the Jordan ahead of them as f as	6330
	7:24	the waters of the Jordan as f as Beth Barah.	6330
	11:33	as f as Abel Keramim.	6330
	20:45	the Benjamites as f as Gidom and struck	6330
Ru	3: 7	to lie down at the f end of the grain pile.	7895
1Sa	2:30	the LORD declares: 'F be it from me!	2721
	6:12	of the Philistines followed them as f as	6330
	7:12	"Thus f has the LORD helped us."	2178+6330
	12:23	f be it from me that I should sin against	2721
	24: 3	David and his men were f back in the cave.	928+3752
	26:20	not let my blood fall to the ground f from the presence of the LORD.	4946+5584
2Sa	7:18	that you have brought me this f?	2151+6330
	19:15	king returned and went as f as the Jordan.	6330
	20:20	"F be it from me!"	2721
	20:20	"F be it from me to swallow up or destroy!	2721
	23:17	"F be it from me, O LORD, to do this!"	2721
1Ki	4:21	as f as the border of Egypt.	6330
	8:46	to his own land, f away or near;	8158
	10: 7	in wisdom and wealth you have f exceeded	3578
	12:30	the people went even as f as Dan	6330
2Ki	7:15	They followed them as f as the Jordan,	6330
	18: 8	as f as Gaza and its territory.	6330
1Ch	4:33	the villages around these towns as f as	6330
	5:11	as f as Salecah:	6330
	5:16	on all the pasturelands of Sharon as f as	6584
	12:40	their neighbors from as f away as Issachar,	6330
	13: 2	let us send word f and wide to the rest	7287
	17:16	that you have brought me this f?	2151+6330
	18: 3	as f as Hamath,	2025

2Ch	6:36	who takes them captive to a land f away	8158
	9: 6	you have f exceeded the report I heard.	3578
	9:26	as f as the border of Egypt.	6330
	12: 4	of Judah and came as f as Jerusalem.	6330
	14: 9	and came as f as Mareshah.	6330
	14:13	and Asa and his army pursued them as f as	6330
	26: 8	his fame spread as f as the border of Egypt,	6330
	26:15	fame spread f and wide,	4200+4946+6330+8158
	30:10	as f as Zebulun,	6330
	33:14	as f as the entrance of the Fish Gate	2256
	34: 6	Ephraim and Simeon, as f as Naphtali,	6330
Ezr	3:13	And the sound was heard f away.	4200+4946+6330+8158
Ne	3: 1	building as f as the Tower of the Hundred,	6330
	3: 1	and as f as the Tower of Hananel.	6330
	3: 8	They restored Jerusalem as f as	6330
	3:13	of the wall as f as the Dung Gate.	6330
	3:15	as f as the steps going down from the City	6330
	3:16	as f as the artificial pool and the House of	6330
	3:19	point facing the ascent to the armory as f as	NIH
	3:31	made repairs as f as the house of	6330
	3:31	and as f as the room above the corner;	6330
	5: 8	"As f as possible,	1896+3869
	12:39	as f as the Sheep Gate.	6330
	12:43	in Jerusalem could be heard f away.	4946+8158
Est	4: 2	But he went only as f as the king's gate,	6330
	9:20	the provinces of King Xerxes, near and f,	8158
Job	5: 4	His children are f from safety,	8178
	13:21	Withdraw your hand f from me,	8178
	22:23	If you remove wickedness f from your tent	8178
	28:22	F from where people dwell he cuts a shaft,	4946
	28: 4	f from men he dangles and sways.	4946
	34:10	F be it from God to do evil,	2721
	38:11	'This f you may come and no farther;	6330+7024
Ps	10: 1	O LORD, do you stand f off?	928+8158
	10: 5	haughty and your laws are f from him;	4946+5584
	22: 1	Why are you so f from saving me,	8158
	22: 1	so f from the words of my groaning?	NIH
	22:11	Do not be f from me,	8178
	22:19	But you, O LORD, be not f off;	8178
	35:22	Do not be f from me, O Lord.	8178
	38:11	my neighbors stay f away.	4946+8158
	38:21	be not f from me, O my God.	8178
	49:14	f from their princely mansions.	4946
	55: 7	I would flee f away and stay in the desert;	8178
	55: 8	f from the tempest and storm."	4946
	65: 8	Those living f away fear your wonders;	7921
	71:12	Be not f from me, O God;	8178
	73:27	Those who are f from you will perish;	8179
	80:11	its shoots as f as the River.	448
	97: 9	you are exalted f above all gods.	4394
	101: 4	Men of perverse heart shall be f from me;	6073
	103:12	as f as the east is from the west,	8178
	103:12	so f has he removed our transgressions	8178
	109:17	may it be f from him.	8178
	119:150	but they are f from your law.	8178
	119:155	Salvation is f from the wicked,	8158
	139: 9	if I settle on the f side of the sea,	344
Pr	4:24	keep corrupt talk f from your lips.	8178
	5: 8	Keep to a path f from her,	8178
	5:29	The LORD is f from the wicked	8158
	22: 5	he who guards his soul stays f from them.	8178
	22:15	rod of discipline will drive it f from him.	8178
	27:10	a neighbor nearby than a brother f away.	8158
	30: 8	Keep falsehood and lies f from me;	8178
	31:10	She is worth f more than rubies.	8158
Ecc	2: 9	I became greater by f than anyone	3578
	7:24	it is f off and most profound—	8158
Isa	6:12	until the LORD has sent everyone f away	8178
	15: 5	her fugitives flee as f as Zoar,	6330
	15: 5	as f as Eglath Shelishiyah.	NIH
	15: 8	their wailing reaches as f as Eglaim,	6330
	15: 8	their lamentation as f as Beer Elim.	NIH
	16: 8	Their shoots spread out and went as f as	6296
	17:13	he rebukes them they flee f away,	4946+5305
	18: 2	people feared f and wide,	2085+2134+2256+4946
	18: 7	people feared f and wide,	2085+2134+2256+4946
	22: 3	while the enemy was still f away.	4946+8158
	29:13	but their hearts are f from me.	8178
	33:13	You who are f away, hear what I have done;	8178
	46:12	you who are f from righteousness.	8158
	46:13	it is not f away;	8178
	49:19	those who devoured you will be f away.	8178
	54:14	Tyranny will be f from you;	8178
	54:14	Terror will be f removed;	NIH
	56:12	or even f better."	3856+4394
	57: 9	You sent your ambassadors f away;	4946+8158
	57:19	Peace, peace, to those f and near,"	8158
	59: 9	So justice is f from us,	8178
	59:11	for deliverance, but it is f away.	8178
Jer	2: 5	that they strayed so f from me?	8178
	8:19	to the cry of my people from a land f away:	5305
	12: 2	on their lips but f from their hearts.	8158
	23:23	"and not a God f away?	4946+8158
	25:26	near and f, one after the other—	8158
	27:10	that will only serve to remove you f	8178
	31:40	to the Kidron Valley on the east as f as	6330
	43: 7	to the LORD and went as f as Tahpanhes.	6330
	48:24	to all the towns of Moab, f and near.	8158
	48:32	Your branches spread as f as the sea;	NIH
	48:32	they reached as f as the sea of Jazer.	6330
	48:34	from Zoar as f as Horonaim	6330
Eze	6:12	He that is f away will die of the plague,	6330
	8: 6	that will drive me f from my sanctuary?	8178
	10: 5	the cherubim could be heard as f away as	6330
	11:15	'They are f from the LORD;	8178
	11:16	Although I sent them f away among	8178

Eze	22: 5	and those *who* are f away will mock you,	8158
	23:40	for men who came from f away,	5305
	29:10	as f as the border of Cush.	6330
	38: 6	from the f north with all its troops—	3752
	38:15	from your place in the f north,	3752
	39: 2	from the f north and send you against	3752
	40:15	to the f end of its portico was fifty cubits,	7164
	44:10	"'The Levites who went f from me	8178
	45: 9	You have gone f enough,	8041
	47:16	as f as Hazer Hatticon,	NIH
	47:18	to the eastern sea and as f as Tamar.	NIH
	47:19	from Tamar as f as the waters	6330
Da	9: 7	of Jerusalem and all Israel, both near and f,	8158
	11: 2	who will be f richer than all the others.	1524
	11:10	and carry the battle as f as his fortress.	6330
Joel	2:20	drive the northern army f	8178
	3: 6	*you might* send them f from their homeland.	8178
	3: 8	a nation f away."	8158
Ob	1:20	in Canaan will possess [the land] as f as	6330
Mic	4: 3	for strong nations f and wide.	6330+8158
Zec	13: 5	*Those who* are f away will come and help	8158
Mt	15: 8	but their hearts are f from me.	4522
Mk	7: 6	but their hearts are f from me.	4522
	12:34	"You are not f from the kingdom of God."	3426
Lk	7: 6	He was not f from the house when	3426
	16:23	he looked up and saw Abraham f away,	608+3427
Jn	6: 1	to the f shore of the Sea of Galilee (that is,	4305
	6: 9	but how f will they go among	1639+4047+5515
	21: 8	for they were not f from shore,	3426
Ac	2:39	children and for all who are f off—	1650+3426
	11:19	in connection with Stephen traveled as f as	2401
	17:27	though he is not f from each one of us.	3426
	22:21	I will send you f away to the Gentiles.' "	3426
	23:31	during the night and brought him as f as	1650
	28:15	and they traveled as f as the Forum	948
Ro	11:28	As f as the gospel is concerned,	3525
	11:28	but as f as election is concerned,	1254
	12:18	f as it depends on you,	AIT
2Co	1: 8	f beyond our ability to endure,	NIG
	4:17	that f outweighs them all.	983+1650+2848+5651+5651
	10:14	*We are* not *going too* f in our boasting,	5657
	10:14	for we did get as f as you with the gospel	948
Eph	1:21	f above all rule and authority,	5645
	2:13	in Christ Jesus you who once were f away have been brought near	3426
	2:17	peace to you who were f away and peace	3426
Php	1:23	which is better by f;	4498
2Ti	3: 9	as f as the faith is concerned, are rejected.	NIG
	3: 9	But *they will* not *get very* f	2093+4498+4621
Rev	18:10	they will stand f off and cry: " 'Woe!	608+3427
	18:15	will stand f off, terrified at her torment.	608+3427
	18:17	from the sea, will stand f off.	608+3427

FAR-OFF (2) [FAR]

Isa	23: 7	to settle in f lands?	8158
	46:11	from a f land, a man to fulfill my purpose.	5305

FARAWAY (1) [FAR]

Isa	13: 5	They come from f lands,	5305

FARE (2) [FARED]

Isa	55: 2	your soul will delight in the richest of f.	2016
Jnh	1: 3	After paying the f, he went aboard	8510

FARED (2) [FARE]

Ge	30:29	how your livestock has f under my care.	2118
Isa	10: 9	'Has not Calno f like Carchemish?	3869

FAREWELL (1)

Ac	15:29	do well to avoid these things. F.	4874

FARM (3) [FARMED, FARMER, FARMERS]

2Sa	9:10	and your servants are to f the land for him	6268
2Ch	31:19	on the f lands around their towns or	4494
Eze	48:19	from the city who f it will come from all	6268

FARMED (2) [FARM]

1Ch	27:26	in charge of the field workers who f	6275
Heb	6: 7	for whom it is f receives the blessing	1175

FARMER (9) [FARM]

Isa	28:24	When a f plows for planting,	3086
Jer	51:23	with you I shatter f and oxen,	438
Zec	13: 5	I am not a prophet. I am a f;	141+408+6268
Mt	13: 3	"A f went out to sow his seed.	5062
Mk	4: 3	"Listen! A f went out to sow his seed.	5062
	4:14	The f sows the word.	5062
Lk	8: 5	"A f went out to sow his seed.	5062
2Ti	2: 6	The hardworking f should be the first	1177
Jas	5: 7	See how the f waits for the land	1177

FARMERS (8) [FARM]

Jer	14: 4	the f are dismayed and cover their heads.	438
	31: 5	will plant vines and enjoy their fruit.	5749
	31:24	f and those who move about	438
Joel	1:11	Despair, you f, wail, you vine growers;	438
Am	5:16	the f will be summoned to weep and	438
Mt	21:33	the vineyard to some f and went away on	1177
Mk	12: 1	the vineyard to some f and went away on	1177
Lk	20: 9	*to* some f and went away for a long time.	1177

FARTHER (6) [FAR]

1Ki	7: 8	palace in which he was to live, set f back,	337+2021+2958
Job	38:11	'This far you may come and no f;	
Mt	26:39	Going a little f,	4601
Mk	1:19	When he had gone a little f,	4581
	14:35	Going a little f,	4601
Lk	24:28	Jesus acted as if he were going f.	4522

FARTHEST (5) [FAR]

Jos	17:18	Clear it, and its f limits will be yours;	9362
Ne	1: 9	if your exiled people are at the f horizon,	7895
Job	28: 3	he searches the f recesses for ore in	3972+9417
Ps	65: 5	the ends of the earth and of the f seas,	8158
Isa	41: 9	from its f corners I called you.	721

FARTHING (KJV) See PENNY

FASHION (1) [FASHIONED, FASHIONING, FASHIONS]

Ex	28:15	"F a breastpiece for making decisions—	6913

FASHIONED (5) [FASHION]

Ex	39: 8	They f the breastpiece—	6913
2Ki	19:18	f by men's hands.	5126
Isa	37:19	f by human hands.	5126
	45:18	he who f and made the earth, he founded it;	3670
Hos	13: 2	from their silver, cleverly f images,	9312

FASHIONING (1) [FASHION]

Ex	32: 4	cast in the shape of a calf, f it with a tool.	7445

FASHIONS (3) [FASHION]

Job	15:35	their womb f deceit."	3922
Isa	40:19	with gold and f silver chains for it.	7671
	44:15	But he also f a god and worships it;	7188

FAST (50) [FASTED, FASTING, FASTS]

Dt	4: 4	but all of you who held f to	1816
	10:20	Hold f to him and take your oaths	1815
	11:22	in all his ways and to hold f to him—	1815
	13: 4	serve him and hold f to him.	1815
	30:20	listen to his voice, and hold f to him.	1815
Jos	22: 5	to obey his commands, to hold f to him	1815
	23: 8	to hold f to the LORD your God,	1815
Jdg	4:21	to him while he lay f asleep,	8101
2Sa	12:23	But now that he is dead, why should I f?	7426
1Ki	11: 2	Solomon held f to them in love.	1815
	21:12	a f and seated Naboth in a prominent place	7427
2Ki	18: 6	He held f to the LORD and did not cease	1815
2Ch	20: 3	and he proclaimed a f for all Judah.	7427
Ezr	8:21	by the Ahava Canal, I proclaimed a f,	7427
Est	4:16	all the Jews who are in Susa, and f for me.	7426
	4:16	I and my maids will f as you do.	7426
	8:10	who rode f horses especially bred for	8224
Job	18: 9	a snare holds him f.	2616
	36: 8	held f by cords of affliction,	4334
	41:17	They are joined f to one another;	1815
Ps	69:10	When I weep and f, I must endure scorn;	7427
	119:31	I hold f to your statutes, O LORD;	1815
	139:10	your right hand will hold me f.	296
Pr	5:22	the cords of his sin hold him f.	9461
Isa	56: 2	the man who holds it f,	2616
	56: 4	who choose what pleases me and hold f	2616
	56: 6	without desecrating it and who hold f	2616
	58: 4	You cannot f as you do today	7426
	58: 5	Is this the kind of f I have chosen,	7427
	58: 5	Is that what you call a f,	7427
Jer	14:12	they f, I will not listen to their cry;	7426
	50:33	All their captors hold them f,	2616
Joel	1:14	Declare a holy f; call a sacred assembly.	7427
	2:15	Blow the trumpet in Zion, declare a holy f,	7427
Jnh	3: 5	They declared a f, and all of them,	7427
Zec	7: 3	"Should I mourn and f in the fifth month,	5692
Mt	6:16	"When you f, do not look somber as	3764
	6:17	But when you f, put oil on your head	3764
	9:14	"How is it that we and the Pharisees f,	3764
	9:14	but your disciples do not f?"	3764
	9:15	then they will f.	3764
Mk	2:19	of the bridegroom f while he is with them?	3764
	2:20	and on that day they will f.	3764
Lk	5:33	"John's disciples often f and pray,	3764
	5:34	of the bridegroom f while he is with them?	3764
	5:35	in those days they will f."	3764
	18:12	I f twice a week and give a tenth	3764
Ac	27: 9	because by now it was after the F.	3763
	27:41	The bow stuck f and would not move,	2242
1Pe	5:12	Stand f in it.	2705

FASTED (15) [FAST]

Jdg	20:26	They f that day until evening	7426
1Sa	7: 6	that day they f and there they confessed,	7426
	31:13	and they f seven days.	7426
2Sa	1:12	They mourned and wept and f till evening	7426
	12:16	He f and went into his house and spent	7426+7427
	12:21	While the child was alive, you f and wept,	7426
	12:22	I f and wept.	7426
1Ki	21:27	he tore his clothes, put on sackcloth and f.	7426
1Ch	10:12	and they f seven days.	7426
Ezr	8:23	So we f and petitioned our God about this,	7426
Ne	1: 4	and f and prayed before the God of heaven.	7426

Isa	58: 3	'Why have we f,' they say,	7426
Zec	7: 5	'When you f and mourned in the fifth	7426
	7: 5	was it really for me that you f?	7426+7426
Ac	13: 3	So after they had f and prayed,	3764

FASTEN (15) [FASTENED, FASTENS]

Ex	25:12	Cast four gold rings for it and f them	5989
	25:26	for the table and f them to the four corners,	5989
	26: 6	and use them to f the curtains together so	2489
	26:11	in the loops to f the tent together as a unit.	2489
	28:12	and f them on the shoulder pieces of	8492
	28:23	Make two gold rings for it and f them	5989
	28:24	F the two gold chains to the rings at	5989
	28:37	F a blue cord to it to attach it to the turban;	8492
	29: 5	F the ephod on him	679
	36:13	to f the two sets of curtains together so	2489
	36:18	to f the tent together as a unit.	2489
Job	13:27	You f my feet in shackles;	8492
Pr	6:21	f them around your neck.	6698
Isa	22:21	with your robe and f your sash around him	2616
Jer	10: 4	they f it with hammer and nails so it will	2616

FASTENED (19) [FASTEN]

Ex	28: 7	so it can be f.	2489
	37: 3	He cast four gold rings for it and f them	NIH
	37:13	for the table and f them to the four corners,	5989
	39: 4	so it could be f.	2489
	39: 7	Then they f them on the shoulder pieces of	8492
	39:16	and f them to the tops of the corners of	5989
	39:17	They f the two gold chains to the rings at	5989
	39:31	Then they f a blue cord to it to attach it to	5989
Lev	8: 7	so it was f on him.	679
Nu	19:15	and every open container without a lid f	7348
Jdg	16: 7	to each to every pair of tails,	8492
1Sa	17:39	David f on his sword over the tunic	2520
	31:10	of the Ashtoreths and f his body to the wall	9546
Est	1: 6	f with cords of white linen	296
Eze	24:17	Keep your turban f and your sandals	2502
Lk	4:20	of everyone in the synagogue were f	867
Jn	19:1	Pilate had a notice prepared and f to	5502
Ac	16:24	he put them in the inner cell and f their feet	856
	28: 3	f itself on his hand.	2750

FASTENS (2) [FASTEN]

Job	16: 9	my opponent f on me his piercing eyes.	4323
	33:11	He f my feet in shackles;	8492

FASTING (21) [FAST]

1Ki	21: 9	"Proclaim a day of f and seat Naboth in	7427
Ne	9: 1	f and wearing sackcloth and having dust	7427
Est	4: 3	with f, weeping and wailing.	7427
	9:31	to their times of f and lamentation.	7427
Ps	35:13	on sackcloth and humbled myself with f.	7427
	109:24	My knees give way from f;	7427
Isa	58: 3	'Yet on the day of your f,	7427
	58: 4	Your f ends in quarreling and strife,	7426
	58: 6	"Is not this the kind of f I have chosen:	7427
Jer	36: 6	of f and read to the people from the scroll	7427
	36: 9	a time of f before the LORD	7427
Da	9: 3	in f, and in sackcloth and ashes.	7427
Joel	2:12	with f and weeping and mourning."	7427
Mt	4: 2	After f forty days and forty nights,	3764
	6:16	to show men they are f.	3764
	6:18	be obvious to men that you are f, but only	3764
Mk	2:18	John's disciples and the Pharisees were f.	3764
	2:18	and the disciples of the Pharisees are f,	3764
Lk	2:37	the temple but worshiped night and day, f	3763
Ac	13: 2	they were worshiping the Lord and f,	3764
	14:23	with prayer and f, committed them	3763

FASTS (1) [FAST]

Zec	8:19	"The f of the fourth, fifth, seventh and tenth	7427

FAT (93) [FATTENED, FATTENING]

Ge	4: 4	But Abel brought f portions from some of	2693
	41: 2	sleek and f, and they grazed among	1374+1414
	41: 4	and gaunt ate up the seven sleek, f cows.	1374
	41:18	the river there came up seven cows, f	1374+1414
	41:20	up the seven f cows that came up first.	1374
	45:18	the land of Egypt and you can enjoy the f	2693
Ex	23:18	"The f of my festival offerings must not	2693
	29:13	Then take all the f around the inner parts,	2693
	29:13	and both kidneys with the f on them,	2693
	29:22	"Take from this ram the f, the fat tail,	2693
	29:22	"Take from this ram the fat, the f tail,	487
	29:22	the fat tail, the f around the inner parts,	2693
	29:22	both kidneys with the f on them,	2693
Lev	1: 8	including the head and the f,	7022
	1:12	including the head and the f,	7022
	3: 3	all the f that covers the inner parts	2693
	3: 4	both kidneys with the f on them near	2693
	3: 9	its f, the entire fat tail cut off close to	2693
	3: 9	entire f tail cut off close to the backbone,	487
	3: 9	to the backbone, all the f that covers	2693
	3:10	both kidneys with the f on them near	2693
	3:14	all the f that covers the inner parts	2693
	3:15	both kidneys with the f on them near	2693
	3:16	All the f is the LORD's.	2693
	3:17	You must not eat any f or any blood.' "	2693
	4: 8	He shall remove all the f from the bull of	2693
	4: 8	the f that covers the inner parts	2693
	4: 9	with the f on them near the loins, and	2693
	4:10	the f is removed from the ox sacrificed as	NIH

Lev	4:19	the f from it and burn it on the altar,	2693
	4:26	the f on the altar as he burned the fat of	2693
	4:26	the fat on the altar as he burned the f of	2693
	4:31	He shall remove all the f,	2693
	4:31	just as the f is removed from	2693
	4:35	He shall remove all the f,	2693
	4:35	just as the f is removed from the lamb of	2693
	6:12	the burnt offering on the fire and burn the f	2693
	7: 3	All its f shall be offered:	2693
	7: 3	the f tail and the fat that covers	487
	7: 3	and the f that covers the inner parts,	2693
	7: 4	both kidneys with the f on them near	2693
	7:23	'Do not eat any of the f of cattle,	2693
	7:24	The f of an animal found dead or torn	2693
	7:25	the f of an animal from which an offering	2693
	7:30	he is to bring the f,	2693
	7:31	The priest shall burn the f on the altar,	2693
	7:33	of Aaron who offers the blood and the f of	2693
	8:16	also took all the f around the inner parts,	2693
	8:16	and both kidneys and their f,	2693
	8:20	the pieces and the f.	7022
	8:25	He took the f, the fat tail,	2693
	8:25	He took the fat, the f tail,	487
	8:25	the fat tail, all the f around the inner parts,	2693
	8:25	both kidneys and their f and the right thigh.	2693
	8:26	on the f portions and on the right thigh.	2693
	9:10	On the altar he burned the f,	2693
	9:19	But the f portions of the ox and the ram—	2693
	9:19	the f tail, the layer of fat,	487
	9:19	the fat tail, the layer of f,	4833
	9:20	and then Aaron burned the f on the altar.	2693
	9:24	the burnt offering and the f portions on	2693
	10:15	with the f portions of the offerings made	2693
	16:25	He shall also burn the f of the sin offering	2693
	17: 6	the f as an aroma pleasing to the LORD.	2693
Nu	18:17	and burn their f as an offering made	2693
Dt	32:15	Jeshurun grew f and kicked;	9042
	32:38	the f of their sacrifices and drank the wine	2693
Jdg	3:17	Eglon king of Moab, who was a very f man.	1374
	3:22	and the f closed in over it.	2693
1Sa	2:15	But even before the f was burned,	2693
	2:16	"Let the f be burned up first,	2693
	15: 9	the f calves and lambs—	5458
	15:22	and to heed is better than the f of rams.	2693
1Ki	8:64	and the f of the fellowship offerings,	2693
	8:64	and the f of the fellowship offerings,	2693
2Ch	7: 7	and the f of the fellowship offerings,	2693
	7: 7	the grain offerings and the f portions.	2693
	29:35	with the f of the fellowship offerings and	2693
	35:14	the burnt offerings and the f portions	2693
Job	15:27	with f and his waist bulges with flesh,	2693
Ps	66:15	I will sacrifice f animals to you and	4671
Isa	1:11	of rams and the f of fattened animals;	2693
	10:27	be broken because you have grown so f.	9043
	17: 4	the f of his body will waste away.	5458
	34: 6	it is covered with f—	2693
	34: 6	f from the kidneys of rams.	2693
	34: 7	and the dust will be soaked with f.	2693
	43:24	or lavished on me the f of your sacrifices.	2693
Jer	5:28	and have grown f and sleek.	9042
Eze	34:20	between the f sheep and the lean sheep.	1374
	39:19	you will eat f till you are glutted	2693
	44: 7	f and blood, and you broke my covenant.	2693
	44:15	to stand before me to offer sacrifices of f	2693

FATAL (5)

Jer	42:20	that you made a f mistake when you sent	
		me to the LORD your God	928+5883+9494
Na	3:19	your injury is f.	2703
Rev	13: 3	of the beast seemed to have had a f wound,	2505
	13: 3	but the f wound had been healed.	2505
	13:12	whose f wound had been healed.	2505

FATALLY (1)

Jer	51: 4	f wounded in her streets.	1991

FATE (13)

Est	7: 7	that the king had already decided his f,	8288
Job	12: 5	as the f of those whose feet are slipping.	5787
	18:20	Men of the west are appalled at his f;	3427
	20:29	Such is the f God allots the wicked,	2750
	21:17	the f God allots in his anger?	2475
	27:13	"Here is the f God allots to the wicked,	2750
	27:14	their f is the sword;	NIH
Ps	49:13	the f of those who trust in themselves,	2006
Ecc	2:14	that the same f overtakes them both.	5247
	2:15	"The f of the fool will overtake me also.	5247
	3:19	Man's f is like that of the animals;	5247
	3:19	the same f awaits them both:	5247
Isa	14:16	they ponder your f:	NIH

FATFLESHED (KJV) See FAT

FATHER (1082) [FATHER-IN-LAW, FATHER'S, FATHERED, FATHERLESS, FATHERS, FATHERS', FOREFATHER, FOREFATHER'S, FOREFATHERS, GRANDFATHER, GRANDFATHER'S]

Ge	2:24	a man will leave his f and mother and	3
	4:18	and Irad was the f of Mehujael,	3528
	4:18	and Mehujael was the f of Methushael,	3528
	4:18	and Methushael was the f of Lamech.	3528

Ge	4:20	he was the f of those who live in tents	3
	4:21	the f of all who play the harp and flute.	3
	5: 6	he became the f of Enosh.	3528
	5: 7	And after he became the f of Enosh,	3528
	5: 9	he became the f of Kenan.	3528
	5:10	And after he became the f of Kenan,	3528
	5:12	he became the f of Mahalalel.	3528
	5:13	And after he became the f of Mahalalel,	3528
	5:15	he became the f of Jared.	3528
	5:16	And after he became the f of Jared,	3528
	5:18	he became the f of Enoch.	3528
	5:19	And after he became the f of Enoch,	3528
	5:21	he became the f of Methuselah.	3528
	5:22	And after he became the f of Methuselah,	3528
	5:25	he became the f of Lamech.	3528
	5:26	And after he became the f of Lamech,	3528
	5:32	he became the f of Shem,	3528
	9:18	(Ham was the f of Canaan.)	3
	9:22	Ham, the f of Canaan,	3
	10: 8	Cush was the f of Nimrod,	3528
	10:13	Mizraim was the f of the Ludites,	3528
	10:15	Canaan was the f of Sidon his firstborn,	3528
	10:24	Arphaxad was the f of Shelah,	3528
	10:24	and Shelah the f of Eber.	3528
	10:26	Joktan was the f of Almodad, Sheleph,	3528
	11:10	he became the f of Arphaxad.	3528
	11:11	And after he became the f of Arphaxad,	3528
	11:12	he became the f of Shelah.	3528
	11:13	And after he became the f of Shelah,	3528
	11:14	he became the f of Eber.	3528
	11:15	And after he became the f of Eber,	3528
	11:16	he became the f of Peleg.	3528
	11:17	And after he became the f of Peleg,	3528
	11:18	he became the f of Reu.	3528
	11:19	And after he became the f of Reu,	3528
	11:20	he became the f of Serug.	3528
	11:21	And after he became the f of Serug,	3528
	11:22	he became the f of Nahor.	3528
	11:23	And after he became the f of Nahor,	3528
	11:24	he became the f of Terah.	3528
	11:25	And after he became the f of Terah,	3528
	11:26	he became the f of Abram,	3528
	11:27	Terah became the f of Abram,	3528
	11:27	And Haran became the f of Lot.	3528
	11:28	While his f Terah was still alive,	3
	11:29	the f of both Milcah and Iscah.	3
	17: 4	You will be the f of many nations.	3
	17: 5	for I have made you a f of many nations.	3
	17:20	He will be the f of twelve rulers,	3528
	19:31	"Our f is old, and there is no man around	3
	19:32	Let's get our f to drink wine and then lie	3
	19:32	and preserve our family line through our f."	3
	19:33	That night they got their f to drink wine,	3
	19:34	"Last night I lay with my f.	3
	19:34	can preserve our family line through our f."	3
	19:35	So they got their f to drink wine that night	3
	19:36	both of Lot's daughters became pregnant	
		by their f.	3
	19:37	he is the f of the Moabites of today.	3
	19:38	he is the f of the Ammonites of today.	3
	20:12	daughter of my f though not of my mother;	3
	22: 7	Isaac spoke up and said to his f Abraham,	3
	22: 7	up and said to his father Abraham, "F?"	3
	22:21	Buz his brother, Kemuel (the f of Aram),	3
	22:23	Bethuel became the f of Rebekah.	3528
	25: 3	Jokshan was the f of Sheba and Dedan;	3528
	25:19	Abraham became the f of Isaac.	3528
	26: 3	the oath I swore to your f Abraham.	3
	26:15	in the time of his f Abraham,	3
	26:18	in the time of his f Abraham,	3
	26:18	the same names his f had given them.	3
	26:24	"I am the God of your f Abraham.	3
	27: 6	I overheard your f say	3
	27: 9	so I can prepare some tasty food for your f,	3
	27:10	Then take it to your f to eat,	3
	27:12	What if my f touches me?	3
	27:14	just the way his f liked it.	3
	27:18	He went to his f and said, "My father."	3
	27:18	He went to his father and said, "My f."	3
	27:19	Jacob said to his f,	3
	27:22	Jacob went close to his f Isaac,	3
	27:26	Then his f Isaac said to him, "Come here,	3
	27:31	and brought it to his f.	3
	27:31	Then he said to him, "My f,	3
	27:32	His f Isaac asked him, "Who are you?"	3
	27:34	with a loud and bitter cry and said to his f,	3
	27:34	"Bless me—me too, my f!"	3
	27:38	Esau said to his f,	3
	27:38	"Do you have only one blessing, my f?	3
	27:38	Bless me too, my f!"	3
	27:39	His f Isaac answered him,	3
	27:41	of the blessing his f had given him.	3
	27:41	"The days of mourning for my f are near;	3
	28: 2	to the house of your mother's f Bethuel.	3
	28: 7	and that Jacob had obeyed his f and mother	3
	28: 8	the Canaanite women were to his f Isaac;	3
	28:13	of your f Abraham and the God of Isaac.	3
	29:12	a relative of her f and a son of Rebekah.	3
	29:12	So she ran and told her f.	3
	31: 1	"Jacob has taken everything our f owned	3
	31: 1	from what belonged to our f."	3
	31: 5	but the God of my f has been with me.	3
	31: 6	You know that I've worked for your f	3
	31: 7	yet your f has cheated me	3
	31:16	from our f belongs to us and our children.	3
	31:18	to go to his f Isaac in the land of Canaan.	3
	31:29	but last night the God of your f said to me,	3

Ge	31:35	Rachel said to her f, "Don't be angry,	3
	31:42	If the God of my f,	3
	31:53	the God of their f, judge between us."	3
	31:53	in the name of the Fear of his f Isaac.	3
	32: 9	Jacob prayed, "O God of my f Abraham,	3
	32: 9	God of my f Isaac, O LORD,	3
	33:19	Hamor, the f of Shechem,	3
	34: 4	And Shechem said to his f Hamor,	3
	34: 6	Then Shechem's f Hamor went out to talk	3
	34:11	Shechem said to Dinah's f and brothers,	3
	34:13	as they spoke to Shechem and his f Hamor.	3
	35:18	But his f named him Benjamin.	3
	35:27	Jacob came home to his f Isaac in Mamre,	3
	36: 9	the account of Esau the f of the Edomites	3
	36:24	the donkeys of his f Zibeon.	3
	36:43	This was Esau the f of the Edomites.	3
	37: 1	in the land where his f had stayed,	3
	37: 2	he brought their f a bad report about them.	3
	37: 4	that their f loved him more than any	3
	37:10	When he told his f as well as his brothers,	3
	37:10	his f rebuked him and said,	3
	37:11	but his f kept the matter in mind.	3
	37:22	from them and take him back to his f.	3
	37:32	the ornamented robe back to their f	3
	37:35	So his f wept for him.	3
	42:13	The youngest is now with our f,	3
	42:29	to their f Jacob in the land of Canaan,	3
	42:32	We were twelve brothers, sons of one f.	3
	42:32	The youngest is now with our f in Canaan.'	3
	42:35	they and their f saw the money pouches,	3
	42:36	Their f Jacob said to them,	3
	42:37	Then Reuben said to his f,	3
	43: 2	their f said to them,	3
	43: 7	'Is your f still living?'	3
	43: 8	Then Judah said to Israel his f,	3
	43:11	Then their f Israel said to them,	3
	43:23	Your God, the God of your f,	3
	43:27	"How is your aged f you told me about?	3
	43:28	"Your servant our f is still alive and well."	3
	44:17	go back to your f in peace."	3
	44:19	'Do you have a f or a brother?'	3
	44:20	And we answered, 'We have an aged f,	3
	44:20	and his f loves him.'	3
	44:22	'The boy cannot leave his f;	3
	44:22	if he leaves him, his f will die.'	3
	44:24	When we went back to your servant my f,	3
	44:25	"Then our f said,	3
	44:27	"Your servant my f said to us,	3
	44:30	when I go back to your servant my f and	3
	44:30	to your servant my father and if my f,	NIH
	44:31	the gray head of our f down to the grave	3
	44:32	the boy's safety to my f.	3
	44:32	I will bear the blame before you, my f,	3
	44:34	How can I go back to my f if the boy is not	3
	44:34	the misery that would come upon my f."	3
	45: 3	Is my f still living?"	3
	45: 8	He made me f to Pharaoh,	3
	45: 9	Now hurry back to my f and say to him,	3
	45:13	Tell my f about all the honor accorded me	3
	45:13	And bring my f down here quickly."	3
	45:18	bring your f and your families back to me.	3
	45:19	and get your f and come.	3
	45:23	And this is what he sent to his f:	3
	45:25	up out of Egypt and came to their f Jacob	3
	45:27	the spirit of their f Jacob revived.	3
	46: 1	to the God of his f Isaac.	3
	46: 3	"I am God, the God of your f," he said.	3
	46: 5	and Israel's sons took their f Jacob	3
	46:29	and went to Goshen to meet his f Israel.	3
	46:29	he threw his arms around his f and wept for	2257S
	47: 1	"My f and brothers,	3
	47: 5	"Your f and your brothers have come	3
	47: 6	settle your f and your brothers in	3
	47: 7	Then Joseph brought his f Jacob in	3
	47:11	So Joseph settled his f and his brothers	3
	47:12	Joseph also provided his f and his brothers	3
	48: 1	"Your f is ill."	3
	48: 9	Joseph said to his f.	3
	48:10	and his f kissed them and embraced them.	NIH
	48:17	Joseph saw his f placing his right hand	3
	48:18	Joseph said to him, "No, my f,	3
	48:19	But his f refused and said, "I know,	3
	49: 2	listen to your f Israel.	3
	49:28	and this is what their f said to them	3
	50: 1	Joseph threw himself upon his f and wept	3
	50: 2	in his service to embalm his f Israel.	3
	50: 5	'My f made me swear an oath and said,	3
	50: 5	Now let me go up and bury my f;	3
	50: 6	Pharaoh said, "Go up and bury your f,	3
	50: 7	So Joseph went up to bury his f.	3
	50:10	a seven-day period of mourning for his f.	3
	50:14	After burying his f,	3
	50:14	with him to bury his f.	3
	50:15	Joseph's brothers saw that their f was dead,	3
	50:16	"Your f left these instructions	3
	50:17	of the servants of the God of your f."	3
Ex	2:18	When the girls returned to Reuel their f,	3
	3: 6	Then he said, "I am the God of your f,	3
	20:12	"Honor your f and your mother,	3
	21:15	"Anyone who attacks his f or mother must	3
	21:17	"Anyone who curses his f or mother must	3
	22:17	her f absolutely refuses to give her to him,	3
	40:15	Anoint them just as you anointed their f,	3
Lev	16:32	to succeed his f as high priest is	3
	18: 7	" 'Do not dishonor your f	3
	18: 8	that would dishonor your f.	3
	18:11	born to your f; she is your sister.	3

Lev	19: 3	of you must respect his mother and f,	3
	20: 9	" 'If anyone curses his f or mother,	3
	20: 9	He has cursed his f or his mother,	3
	20:11	he has dishonored his f.	3
	20:17	the daughter of either his f or his mother,	3
	20:19	the sister of either your mother or your f,	3
	21: 2	such as his mother or f,	3
	21: 9	she disgraces her f	3
	21:11	even for his f or mother,	3
	24:10	and an Egyptian f went out among	408
Nu	3: 4	during the lifetime of their f Aaron.	3
	6: 7	Even if his own f or mother or brother	3
	12:14	"If her f had spit in her face,	3
	26:29	Makirite clan (Makir was the f of Gilead);	3528
	26:60	Aaron was the f of Nadab and Abihu,	3528
	27: 3	"Our f died in the desert.	3
	27:11	If his f had no brothers,	3
	30: 4	and her f hears about her vow or pledge	3
	30: 5	if her f forbids her when he hears about it,	3
	30: 5	because her f has forbidden her.	3
	30:16	a f and his young daughter still living	3
	36: 6	within the tribal clan of their f.	3
Dt	1:31	as a f carries his son,	408
	5:16	"Honor your f and your mother,	3
	21:13	and mourned her f and mother for	3
	21:18	and rebellious son who does not obey his f	3
	21:19	his f and mother shall take hold of him	3
	22:15	the girl's f and mother shall bring proof	3
	22:16	The girl's f will say to the elders,	3
	22:19	of silver and give them to the girl's f,	3
	22:29	he shall pay the girl's f fifty shekels	3
	26: 5	"My f was a wandering Aramean,	3
	27:16	"Cursed is the man who dishonors his f	3
	27:22	of his f or the daughter of his mother."	3
	32: 6	Is he not your F, your Creator,	3
	32: 7	Ask your f and he will tell you,	3
	33: 9	He said of his f and mother,	3
Jos	2:13	that you will spare the lives of my f	3
	2:18	you have brought your f and mother,	3
	6:23	her f and mother and brothers	3
	15:18	she urged him to ask her f for a field.	3
	17: 4	along with the brothers of their f,	3
	24: 2	including Terah the f of Abraham	3
	24: 3	But I took your f Abraham from the land	3
	24:32	Hamor, the f of Shechem.	3
Jdg	1:14	she urged him to ask her f for a field.	3
	8:32	of his f Joash in Ophrah of the Abiezrites.	3
	9:17	and to think that my f fought for you,	3
	9:28	Serve the men of Hamor, Shechem's f!	3
	9:56	to his f by murdering his seventy brothers.	3
	11: 1	His f was Gilead;	3528
	11:36	"My f," she replied, "you have given your	
		word to the LORD.	3
	11:39	to her f and he did to her as he had vowed.	3
	14: 2	he returned, he said to his f and mother,	3
	14: 3	His f and mother replied,	3
	14: 3	But Samson said to his f, "Get her for me.	3
	14: 5	to Timnah together with his f and mother.	3
	14: 6	But he told neither his f	3
	14:10	Now his f went down to see the woman.	3
	14:16	even explained it to my f or mother,"	3
	15: 1	But her f would not let him go in.	3
	15: 6	up and burned her and her f to death.	3
	16:31	and Eshtaol in the tomb of Manoah his f.	3
	17:10	"Live with me and be my f and priest,	3
	18:19	Come with us, and be our f and priest.	3
	19: 3	and when her f saw him,	3
	19: 4	His father-in-law, the girl's f,	3
	19: 5	but the girl's f said to his son-in-law,	3
	19: 6	Afterward the girl's f said,	3
	19: 8	when he rose to go, the girl's f said,	3
	19: 9	his father-in-law, the girl's f, said,	3
Ru	2:11	how you left your f and mother	3
	4:17	He was the f of Jesse, the father of David.	3
	4:17	He was the father of Jesse, the f of David.	3
	4:18	Perez was the f of Hezron,	3528
	4:19	Hezron the f of Ram,	3528
	4:19	Ram the f of Amminadab,	3528
	4:20	Amminadab the f of Nahshon,	3528
	4:20	Nahshon the f of Salmon,	3528
	4:21	Salmon the f of Boaz,	3528
	4:21	Boaz the f of Obed,	3528
	4:22	Obed the f of Jesse,	3528
	4:22	and Jesse the f of David.	3528
1Sa	2: 8	I chose your f out of all the tribes of Israel	2257S
	9: 3	to Saul's f Kish were lost,	3
	9: 5	or my f will stop thinking about	3
	10: 2	And now your f has stopped thinking	3
	10:12	"And who is their f?"	3
	14: 1	But he did not tell his f.	3
	14:27	not heard that his f had bound the people	3
	14:28	"Your f bound the army under a strict oath,	3
	14:29	"My f has made trouble for the country.	3
	14:51	Saul's f Kish and Abner's father Ner were	
		sons of Abiel.	
	14:51	and Abner's f Ner were sons of Abiel.	3
	19: 2	"My f Saul is looking for a chance	3
	19: 3	with my f in the field where you are.	3
	19: 4	of David to Saul his f and said to him, "Let	3
	20: 1	How have I wronged your f,	3
	20: 2	Look, my f doesn't do anything,	3
	20: 3	"Your f knows very well	3
	20: 8	If your f misses me at all, tell him,	3
	20: 8	Why hand me over to your f?"	3
	20: 9	the least inkling that my f was determined	3
	20:10	if your f answers you harshly?"	3
	20:12	surely sound out my f by this time the day	3

Ref	Text	Num
1Sa 20:13	But if my **f** is inclined to harm you,	3
20:13	be with you as he has been with my **f**.	3
20:32	Jonathan asked his **f**.	3
20:33	Then Jonathan knew that his **f** intended	3
22: 3	"Would you let my **f** and mother come	3
23:17	"My **f** Saul will not lay a hand on you.	3
23:17	Even my **f** Saul knows this."	3
24:11	my **f**, look at this piece of your robe	3
2Sa 3: 8	the house of your **f** Saul and to his family	3
6:21	who chose me rather than your **f** or anyone	3
7:14	I will be his **f**, and he will be my son.	3
9: 7	for the sake of your **f** Jonathan.	3
10: 2	just as his **f** showed kindness to me."	3
10: 2	to Hanun concerning his **f**.	3
10: 3	"Do you think David is honoring your **f**	3
13: 5	"When your **f** comes to see you,	3
16:19	Just as I served your **f**,	3
17: 8	You know your **f** and his men;	3
17: 8	Besides, your **f** is an experienced fighter,	3
17:10	for all Israel knows that your **f** is a fighter	3
19:37	in my own town near the tomb of my **f**	3
21:14	in the tomb of Saul's **f** Kish,	3
1Ki 1: 6	(His **f** had never interfered with him	3
2:12	Solomon sat on the throne of his **f** David,	3
2:24	the throne of my **f** David and has founded	3
2:26	the Sovereign LORD before my **f** David	3
2:32	of my **f** David he attacked two men	3
2:44	the wrong you did to my **f** David.	3
3: 3	according to the statutes of his **f** David,	3
3: 6	my **f** David, because he was faithful to you	3
3: 7	in place of my **f** David.	3
3:14	and commands as David your **f** did,	3
5: 1	to succeed his **f** David,	3
5: 3	of the wars waged against my **f** David	3
5: 5	as the LORD told my **f** David,	3
6:12	the promise I gave to David your **f**.	3
7:14	of Naphtali and whose **f** was a man of Tyre	3
7:51	in the things his **f** David had dedicated—	3
8:15	with his own mouth to my **f** David.	3
8:17	"My **f** David had it in his heart to build	3
8:18	But the LORD said to my **f** David,	3
8:20	I have succeeded David my **f** and now I sit	3
8:24	to your servant David my **f**;	3
8:25	keep for your servant David my **f**	3
8:26	let your word that you promised your	
	servant David my **f** come true.	3
9: 4	as David your **f** did,	3
9: 5	as I promised David your **f** when I said,	3
11: 4	as the heart of David his **f** had been.	3
11: 6	as David his **f** had done.	3
11:12	Nevertheless, for the sake of David your **f**,	3
11:17	Edomite officials who had served his **f**	3
11:27	in the wall of the city of David his **f**.	3
11:33	and laws of David, Solomon's **f**,	3
11:43	and was buried in the city of David his **f**.	3
12: 4	"Your **f** put a heavy yoke on us,	3
12: 6	the elders who had served his **f** Solomon	3
12: 9	'Lighten the yoke your **f** put on us'?"	3
12:10	'Your **f** put a heavy yoke on us,	3
12:11	My **f** laid on you a heavy yoke;	3
12:11	My **f** scourged you with whips;	3
12:14	"My **f** made your yoke heavy;	3
12:14	My **f** scourged you with whips;	3
13:11	They also told their **f** what he had said to	3
13:12	Their **f** asked them,	3
15: 3	He committed all the sins his **f** had done	3
15:11	as his **f** David had done.	3
15:15	the articles that he and his **f** had dedicated.	3
15:19	there was between my **f** and your father.	3
15:19	there was between my father and your **f**.	3
15:24	with them in the city of his **f** David.	3
15:26	walking in the ways of his **f** and in his sin,	3
19:20	"Let me kiss my **f** and mother good-by,"	3
20:34	the cities my **f** took from your father,"	3
20:34	the cities my father took from your **f**,"	3
20:34	as my **f** did in Samaria."	3
22:43	in the ways of his **f** Asa and did not stray	3
22:46	even after the reign of his **f** Asa.	3
22:50	with them in the city of David his **f**.	3
22:52	because he walked in the ways of his **f**	3
22:53	to anger, just as his **f** had done.	3
2Ki 2:12	Elisha saw this and cried out, "My **f**!	3
2:12	and cried out, "My father! My **f**!	3
3: 2	but not as his **f** and mother had done.	3
3: 2	of Baal that his **f** had made.	3
3:13	of your **f** and the prophets of your mother."	3
4:18	and one day he went out to his **f**,	3
4:19	he said to his **f**.	3
4:19	His **f** told a servant,	NIH
5:13	"My **f**, if the prophet had told you	3
6:21	he asked Elisha, "Shall I kill them, my **f**?	3
9:25	in chariots behind Ahab his **f** when	3
13:14	and wept over him. "My **f**!	3
13:14	over him. "My father! My **f**!"	3
13:25	in battle from his **f** Jehoahaz.	3
14: 3	but not as his **f** David had done.	3
14: 3	the example of his **f** Joash.	3
14: 5	the officials who had murdered his **f**	3
14:21	in place of his **f** Amaziah.	3
15: 3	just as his **f** Amaziah had done.	3
15:34	just as his **f** Uzziah had done.	3
15:38	the city of his **f**.	3
16: 2	Unlike David his **f**,	3
18: 3	just as his **f** David had done.	3
20: 5	the God of your **f** David, says:	3
21: 3	high places his **f** Hezekiah had destroyed;	3
21:20	as his **f** Manasseh had done.	3

Ref	Text	Num
2Ki 21:21	He walked in all the ways of his **f**;	3
21:21	the idols his **f** had worshiped,	3
22: 2	and walked in all the ways of his **f** David,	3
23:30	and made him king in place of his **f**.	3
23:34	of Josiah king in place of his **f** Josiah	3
24: 9	just as his **f** had done.	3
1Ch 1:10	Cush was the **f** of Nimrod,	3528
1:11	Mizraim was the **f** of the Ludites,	3528
1:13	Canaan was the **f** of Sidon his firstborn,	3528
1:18	Arphaxad was the **f** of Shelah,	3528
1:18	and Shelah the **f** of Eber.	3528
1:20	Joktan was the **f** of Almodad, Sheleph,	3528
1:34	Abraham was the **f** of Isaac.	3528
2:10	Ram was the **f** of Amminadab,	3528
2:10	and Amminadab the **f** of Nahshon,	3528
2:11	Nahshon was the **f** of Salmon,	3528
2:11	Salmon the **f** of Boaz,	3528
2:12	the **f** of Obed and Obed the father of Jesse.	3528
2:12	the father of Obed and Obed the **f** of Jesse.	3528
2:13	Jesse was the **f** of Eliab his firstborn,	3528
2:17	whose **f** was Jether the Ishmaelite.	3
2:20	Hur was the **f** of Uri,	3528
2:20	and Uri the **f** of Bezalel.	3528
2:21	Makir the **f** of Gilead.	3
2:22	Segub was the **f** of Jair,	3
2:23	All these were descendants of Makir the **f**	3
2:24	of Hezron bore him Ashhur the **f** of Tekoa.	3
2:31	Ishi, who was the **f** of Sheshan.	1201S
2:31	Sheshan was the **f** of Ahlai.	1201S
2:36	Attai was the **f** of Nathan,	3528
2:36	Nathan the **f** of Zabad,	3528
2:37	Zabad the **f** of Ephlal,	3528
2:37	Ephlal the **f** of Obed,	3528
2:38	Obed the **f** of Jehu,	3528
2:38	Jehu the **f** of Azariah,	3528
2:39	Azariah the **f** of Helez,	3528
2:39	Helez the **f** of Eleasah,	3528
2:40	Eleasah the **f** of Sismai,	3528
2:40	Sismai the **f** of Shallum,	3528
2:41	Shallum the **f** of Jekamiah,	3528
2:41	and Jekamiah the **f** of Elishama.	3528
2:42	who was the **f** of Ziph,	3
2:42	who was the **f** of Hebron.	3
2:44	Shema was the **f** of Raham,	3528
2:44	and Raham the **f** of Jorkeam.	3
2:44	Rekem was the **f** of Shammai.	3528
2:45	and Maon was the **f** of Beth Zur.	3
2:46	Haran was the **f** of Gazez.	3528
2:49	to Shaaph the **f** of Madmannah and	3
2:49	to Sheva the **f** of Macbenah and Gibea.	3
2:50	Shobal the **f** of Kiriath Jearim,	3
2:51	Salma the **f** of Bethlehem,	3
2:51	and Hareph the **f** of Beth Gader.	3
2:52	of Shobal the **f** of Kiriath Jearim were:	3
2:55	the **f** of the house of Recab.	3
4: 2	Reaiah son of Shobal was the **f** of Jahath,	3528
4: 2	and Jahath the **f** of Ahumai and Lahad.	3528
4: 4	Penuel was the **f** of Gedor,	3
4: 4	and Ezer the **f** of Hushah.	3
4: 4	firstborn of Ephrathah and **f** of Bethlehem.	3
4: 5	Ashhur the **f** of Tekoa had two wives,	3
4: 8	who was the **f** of Anub and Hazzobebah	3528
4:11	Shuhah's brother, was the **f** of Mehir,	3528
4:11	who was the **f** of Eshton.	3
4:12	Eshton was the **f** of Beth Rapha,	3528
4:12	Paseah and Tehinnah the **f** of Ir Nahash.	3
4:14	Meonothai was the **f** of Ophrah.	3528
4:14	Seraiah was the **f** of Joab,	3528
4:14	the **f** of Ge Harashim.	3
4:17	Shammai and Ishbah the **f** of Eshtemoa.	3
4:18	(His Judean wife gave birth to Jered the **f**	3
4:18	Heber the **f** of Soco,	3
4:18	and Jekuthiel the **f** of Zanoah.)	3
4:19	the **f** of Keilah the Garmite,	3
4:21	Er the **f** of Lecah,	3
4:21	Laadah the **f** of Mareshah and the clans of	3
6: 4	Eleazar was the **f** of Phinehas,	3528
6: 4	Phinehas the **f** of Abishua,	3528
6: 5	Abishua the **f** of Bukki,	3528
6: 5	Bukki the **f** of Uzzi,	3528
6: 6	Uzzi the **f** of Zerahiah,	3528
6: 6	Zerahiah the **f** of Meraioth,	3528
6: 7	Meraioth the **f** of Amariah,	3528
6: 7	Amariah the **f** of Ahitub,	3528
6: 8	Ahitub the **f** of Zadok,	3528
6: 8	Zadok the **f** of Ahimaaz,	3528
6: 9	Ahimaaz the **f** of Azariah,	3528
6: 9	Azariah the **f** of Johanan,	3528
6:10	Johanan the **f** of Azariah (it was he who	3528
6:11	Azariah the **f** of Amariah,	3528
6:11	Amariah the **f** of Ahitub,	3528
6:12	Ahitub the **f** of Zadok,	3528
6:12	Zadok the **f** of Shallum,	3528
6:13	Shallum the **f** of Hilkiah,	3528
6:13	Hilkiah the **f** of Azariah,	3528
6:14	Azariah the **f** of Seraiah,	3528
6:14	and Seraiah the **f** of Jehozadak.	3528
7:14	She gave birth to Makir the **f** of Gilead.	3
7:22	Their **f** Ephraim mourned	3
7:31	who was the **f** of Birzaith.	3
7:32	Heber the **f** of Japhlet,	3528
8: 1	Benjamin was the **f** of Bela his firstborn,	3528
8: 7	and who was the **f** of Uzza and Ahihud.	3528
8:29	Jeiel the **f** of Gibeon lived in Gibeon.	3
8:32	who was the **f** of Shimeah.	3528
8:33	Ner was the **f** of Kish,	3528
8:33	Kish the **f** of Saul,	3528

Ref	Text	Num
1Ch 8:33	and Saul the **f** of Jonathan, Malki-Shua,	3528
8:34	Merib-Baal, who was the **f** of Micah.	3528
8:36	Ahaz was the **f** of Jehoaddah,	3528
8:36	Jehoaddah was the **f** of Alemeth,	3528
8:36	and Zimri the **f** of Moza.	3528
8:37	Moza was the **f** of Binea;	3528
9:35	Jeiel the **f** of Gibeon lived in Gibeon.	3
9:38	Mikloth was the **f** of Shimeam.	3528
9:39	Ner was the **f** of Kish,	3528
9:39	Kish the **f** of Saul,	3528
9:39	and Saul the **f** of Jonathan, Malki-Shua,	3528
9:40	Merib-Baal, who was the **f** of Micah.	3528
9:42	Ahaz was the **f** of Jadah,	3528
9:42	Jadah the **f** of Alemeth,	3528
9:42	and Zimri the **f** of Moza.	3528
9:43	Moza was the **f** of Binea;	3528
14: 3	the **f** of more sons and daughters.	3528
17:13	I will be his **f**, and he will be my son.	3
19: 2	because his **f** showed kindness to me."	3
19: 2	to Hanun concerning his **f**.	3
19: 3	"Do you think David is honoring your **f**	3
22:10	He will be my son, and I will be his **f**.	3
24: 2	Nadab and Abihu died before their **f** did,	3
25: 3	under the supervision of their **f** Jeduthun,	3
26:10	his **f** had appointed him the first),	3
28: 6	and I will be his **f**.	3
28: 9	acknowledge the God of your **f**,	3
29:10	O LORD, God of our **f** Israel,	3
29:23	the LORD as king in place of his **f** David.	3
2Ch 1: 8	to David my **f** and have made me king	3
1: 9	let your promise to my **f** David	3
2: 3	for my **f** David when you sent him cedar	3
2: 7	whom my **f** David provided.	3
2:14	from Dan and whose **f** was from Tyre.	3
2:14	and with those of my lord, David your **f**.	3
2:17	after the census his **f** David had taken,	3
3: 1	the LORD had appeared to his **f** David.	3
5: 1	in the things his **f** David had dedicated—	3
6: 4	with his mouth to my **f** David.	3
6: 7	"My **f** David had it in his heart to build	3
6: 8	But the LORD said to my **f** David,	3
6:10	I have succeeded David my **f** and now I sit	3
6:15	to your servant David my **f**;	3
6:16	keep for your servant David my **f**	3
7:17	if you walk before me as David your **f** did,	3
7:18	as I covenanted with David your **f**	3
8:14	with the ordinance of his **f** David,	3
9:31	and was buried in the city of David his **f**.	3
10: 4	"Your **f** put a heavy yoke on us,	3
10: 6	the elders who had served his **f** Solomon	3
10: 9	'Lighten the yoke your **f** put on us'?"	3
10:10	'Your **f** put a heavy yoke on us,	3
10:11	My **f** laid on you a heavy yoke;	3
10:11	My **f** scourged you with whips;	3
10:14	"My **f** made your yoke heavy;	NIH
10:14	My **f** scourged you with whips;	3
15:18	the articles that he and his **f** had dedicated.	3
16: 3	there was between my **f** and your father.	3
16: 3	there was between my father and your **f**.	3
17: 2	of Ephraim that his **f** Asa had captured.	3
17: 3	in the ways his **f** David had followed.	3
17: 4	but sought the God of his **f**	3
20:32	He walked in the ways of his **f** Asa and did	3
21: 3	Their **f** had given them many gifts of silver	3
21:12	the God of your **f** David, says:	3
21:12	of your **f** Jehoshaphat or of Asa king	3
24:22	kindness Zechariah's **f** Jehoiada had shown	3
25: 3	the officials who had murdered his **f**	3
26: 1	made him king in place of his **f** Amaziah	3
26: 4	just as his **f** Amaziah had done.	3
27: 2	just as his **f** Uzziah had done,	3
28: 1	Unlike David his **f**,	3
29: 2	just as his **f** David had done.	3
33: 3	high places his **f** Hezekiah had demolished;	3
33:22	as his **f** Manasseh had done.	3
33:23	But unlike his **f** Manasseh,	3
34: 2	and walked in the ways of his **f** David,	3
34: 3	he began to seek the God of his **f** David.	3
36: 1	in Jerusalem in place of his **f**.	3
Ne 12:10	Jeshua was the **f** of Joiakim,	3528
12:10	Joiakim the **f** of Eliashib,	3528
12:10	Eliashib the **f** of Joiada,	NIH
12:11	Joiada the **f** of Jonathan,	3528
12:11	and Jonathan the **f** of Jaddua.	3528
Est 2: 7	up because she had neither **f** nor mother.	3
2: 7	as his own daughter when her **f**	3
Job 15:10	men even older than your **f**.	3
17:14	'You are my **f**,' and to the worm,	3
29:16	I was a **f** to the needy;	3
31:18	from my youth I reared him as would a **f**,	3
38:28	Does the rain have a **f**?	3
42:15	and their **f** granted them an inheritance	3
Ps 2: 7	today I have become your **F**.	3528
27:10	Though my **f** and mother forsake me,	3
68: 5	A **f** to the fatherless,	3
89:26	He will call out to me, 'You are my **F**,	3
103:13	As a **f** has compassion on his children,	3
Pr 3:12	as a **f** the son he delights in.	3
10: 1	A wise son brings joy to his **f**,	3
15:20	A wise son brings joy to his **f**,	3
17:21	there is no joy for the **f** of a fool.	3
17:25	A foolish son brings grief to his **f**,	3
19:26	He who robs his **f**	3
20:20	If a man curses his **f** or mother,	3
23:22	Listen to your **f**, who gave you life,	3
23:24	The **f** of a righteous man has great joy;	3
23:25	May your **f** and mother be glad;	3

Pr	27:10	and the friend of your **f**, and do not go	3
	28: 7	a companion of gluttons disgraces his **f**.	3
	28:24	He who robs his **f** or mother and says,	3
	29: 3	man who loves wisdom brings joy to his **f**,	3
	30:17	"The eye that mocks a **f**,	3
Isa	7:17	on your people and on the house of your **f**	3
	8: 4	Before the boy knows how to say 'My **f**'	3
	9: 6	Everlasting **F**, Prince of Peace.	3
	22:21	be a **f** to those who live in Jerusalem and to	3
	22:23	be a seat of honor for the house of his **f**.	3
	38: 5	the God of your **f** David, says:	3
	43:27	Your first **f** sinned;	3
	45:10	Woe to him who says to his **f**,	3
	51: 2	your **f**, and to Sarah, who gave you birth.	3
	58:14	to feast on the inheritance of your **f** Jacob."	3
	63:16	But you are our **F**,	3
	63:16	you, O L ORD, are our **F**,	3
	64: 8	Yet, O L ORD, you are our **F**.	3
Jer	2:27	They say to wood, 'You are my **f**,'	3
	3: 4	Have you not just called to me: 'My **F**,	3
	3:19	I thought you would call me '**F**' and	3
	16: 7	not even for a **f** or a mother—	3
	20:15	be the man who brought my **f** the news,	3
	22:11	who succeeded his **f** as king of Judah	3
	22:15	Did not your **f** have food and drink?	3
	31: 9	because I am Israel's **f**,	3
Eze	16: 3	your **f** was an Amorite and your mother	3
	16:45	Your mother was a Hittite and your **f**	3
	18: 4	the **f** as well as the son—	3
	18:11	(though the **f** has done none of them):	2085 S
	18:14	a son who sees all the sins his **f** commits,	3
	18:18	But his **f** will die for his own sin,	3
	18:19	the son not share the guilt of his **f**?'	3
	18:20	The son will not share the guilt of the **f**,	3
	18:20	nor will the **f** share the guilt of the son.	3
	22: 7	In you they have treated **f** and mother	3
	44:25	if the dead person was his **f** or mother,	3
Da	5: 2	that Nebuchadnezzar his **f** had taken from	10003
	5:11	of your **f** he was found to have insight	10003
	5:11	King Nebuchadnezzar your **f**—	10003
	5:11	your **f** the king, I say—	10003
	5:13	one of the exiles my **f** the king brought	10003
	5:18	the Most High God gave your **f**	
		Nebuchadnezzar sovereignty	10003
	11: 6	together with her royal escort and her **f** and	3528
Am	2: 7	**F** and son use the same girl and	3
Mic	7: 6	For a son dishonors his **f**,	3
Zec	13: 3	if anyone still prophesies, his **f** and mother,	3
Mal	1: 6	son honors his **f**, and a servant his master.	3
	1: 6	If I am a **f**, where is the honor due me?	3
	2:10	Have we not all one **F**?	3
Mt	1: 2	Abraham was the **f** of Isaac,	1164
	1: 2	Isaac the **f** of Jacob,	1164
	1: 2	Jacob the **f** of Judah and his brothers,	1164
	1: 3	Judah the **f** of Perez and Zerah,	1164
	1: 3	Perez the **f** of Hezron,	1164
	1: 3	Hezron the **f** of Ram,	1164
	1: 4	Ram the **f** of Amminadab,	1164
	1: 4	Amminadab the **f** of Nahshon,	1164
	1: 4	Nahshon the **f** of Salmon,	1164
	1: 5	Salmon the **f** of Boaz,	1164
	1: 5	Boaz the **f** of Obed,	1164
	1: 5	Obed the **f** of Jesse,	1164
	1: 6	and Jesse the **f** of King David.	1164
	1: 6	David was the **f** of Solomon,	1164
	1: 7	Solomon the **f** of Rehoboam,	1164
	1: 7	Rehoboam the **f** of Abijah,	1164
	1: 7	Abijah the **f** of Asa,	1164
	1: 8	Asa the **f** of Jehoshaphat,	1164
	1: 8	Jehoshaphat the **f** of Jehoram,	1164
	1: 8	Jehoram the **f** of Uzziah,	1164
	1: 9	Uzziah the **f** of Jotham,	1164
	1: 9	Jotham the **f** of Ahaz,	1164
	1: 9	Ahaz the **f** of Hezekiah,	1164
	1:10	Hezekiah the **f** of Manasseh,	1164
	1:10	Manasseh the **f** of Amon,	1164
	1:10	Amon the **f** of Josiah,	1164
	1:11	Josiah the **f** of Jeconiah and his brothers at	1164
	1:12	Jeconiah was the **f** of Shealtiel,	1164
	1:12	Shealtiel the **f** of Zerubbabel,	1164
	1:13	Zerubbabel the **f** of Abiud,	1164
	1:13	Abiud the **f** of Eliakim,	1164
	1:13	Eliakim the **f** of Azor,	1164
	1:14	Azor the **f** of Zadok,	1164
	1:14	Zadok the **f** of Akim,	1164
	1:14	Akim the **f** of Eliud,	1164
	1:15	Eliud the **f** of Eleazar,	1164
	1:15	Eleazar the **f** of Matthan,	1164
	1:15	Matthan the **f** of Jacob,	1164
	1:16	and Jacob the **f** of Joseph,	1164
	2:22	in Judea in place of his **f** Herod,	4252
	3: 9	'We have Abraham as our **f**.'	4252
	4:21	They were in a boat with their **f** Zebedee,	4252
	4:22	the boat and their **f** and followed him.	4252
	5:16	and praise your **F** in heaven.	4252
	5:45	that you may be sons of your **F** in heaven.	4252
	5:48	therefore, as your heavenly **F** is perfect.	4252
	6: 1	you will have no reward from your **F**	4252
	6: 4	Then your **F**, who sees what is done	4252
	6: 6	close the door and pray to your **F**,	4252
	6: 6	Then your **F**, who sees what is done	4252
	6: 8	for your **F** knows what you need	4252
	6: 9	" 'Our **F** in heaven,	4252
	6:14	your heavenly **F** will also forgive you.	4252
	6:15	your **F** will not forgive your sins.	4252
	6:18	but only to your **F**, who is unseen;	4252
	6:18	and your **F**, who sees what is done	4252

Mt	6:26	and yet your heavenly **F** feeds them.	4252
	6:32	your heavenly **F** knows that you need	4252
	7:11	how much more will your **F** in heaven give	4252
	7:21	the will of my **F** who is in heaven.	4252
	8:21	"Lord, first let me go and bury my **f**."	4252
	10:20	the Spirit of your **F** speaking through you.	4252
	10:21	and a **f** his child;	4252
	10:29	the ground apart from the will of your **F**.	4252
	10:32	I will also acknowledge him before my **F**	4252
	10:33	I will disown him before my **F** in heaven.	4252
	10:35	I have come to turn " 'a man against his **f**,	4252
	10:37	"Anyone who loves his **f** or mother more	4252
	11:25	At that time Jesus said, "I praise you, **F**,	4252
	11:26	Yes, **F**, for this was your good pleasure.	4252
	11:27	committed to me by my **F**.	4252
	11:27	No one knows the Son except the **F**,	4252
	11:27	no one knows the **F** except the Son	4252
	12:50	does the will of my **F** in heaven is my	4252
		brother and sister	
	13:43	like the sun in the kingdom of their **F**.	4252
	15: 4	'Honor your **f** and mother'	4252
	15: 4	and 'Anyone who curses his **f** or mother	4252
	15: 5	But you say that if a man says to his **f**	4252
	15: 6	he is not to 'honor his **f**' with it.	4252
	15:13	that my heavenly **F** has not planted will	4252
	16:17	but by my **F** in heaven.	4252
	18:10	in heaven always see the face of my **F**	4252
	18:14	In the same way your **F** in heaven is	4252
	18:19	it will be done for you by my **F** in heaven.	4252
	18:35	"This is how my heavenly **F** will treat each	4252
	19: 5	'For this reason a man will leave his **f**	4252
	19:19	honor your **f** and mother,'	4252
	19:29	or sisters or **f** or mother or children	4252
	20:23	for whom they have been prepared by my **F**.	4252
	21:30	"Then the **f** went to the other son and said	NIG
	21:31	"Which of the two did what his **f** wanted?"	4252
	23: 9	And do not call anyone on earth '**f**,'	4252
	23: 9	for you have one **F**, and he is in heaven.	4252
	24:36	nor the Son, but only the **F**.	4252
	25:34	'Come, you who are blessed by my **F**;	4252
	26:39	"My **F**, if it is possible, may this cup be	4252
	26:42	"My **F**, if it is not possible for this cup to	4252
	26:53	Do you think I cannot call on my **F**,	4252
	28:19	the **F** and of the Son and of the Holy Spirit,	4252
Mk	1:20	and they left their **f** Zebedee in the boat	4252
	5:40	he took the child's **f** and mother and	4252
	7:10	'Honor your **f** and your mother,' and,	4252
	7:10	'Anyone who curses his **f** or mother must	4252
	7:11	But you say that if a man says to his **f**	4252
	7:12	let him do anything for his **f** or mother.	4252
	9:21	Jesus asked the boy's **f**,	4252
	9:24	Immediately the boy's **f** exclaimed,	4252
	10: 7	'For this reason a man will leave his **f**	4252
	10:19	honor your **f** and mother.'	4252
	10:29	or mother or **f** or children or fields for me	4252
	11:10	the coming kingdom of our **f** David!"	4252
	11:25	so that your **F** in heaven may forgive you	4252
	13:12	and a **f** his child.	4252
	13:32	nor the Son, but only the **F**.	4252
	14:36	**F**," he said, "everything is possible for you.	4252
	15:21	Simon, the **f** of Alexander and Rufus,	4252
Lk	1:32	the throne of his **f** David,	4252
	1:59	to name him after his **f** Zechariah,	4252
	1:62	Then they made signs to his **f**,	4252
	1:67	His **f** Zechariah was filled with	4252
	1:73	the oath he swore to our **f** Abraham:	4252
	2:33	The child's **f** and mother marveled	4252
	2:48	Your **f** and I have been anxiously searching	4252
	3: 8	'We have Abraham as our **f**.'	4252
	6:36	Be merciful, just as your **F** is merciful.	4252
	8:51	and the child's **f** and mother.	4252
	9:26	the glory of the **F** and of the holy angels.	4252
	9:42	healed the boy and gave him back to his **f**.	4252
	9:59	"Lord, first let me go and bury my **f**."	4252
	10:21	"I praise you, **F**, Lord of heaven and earth,	4252
	10:21	Yes, **F**, for this was your good pleasure.	4252
	10:22	committed to me by my **F**.	4252
	10:22	No one knows who the Son is except the **F**,	4252
	10:22	no one knows who the **F** is except the Son	4252
	11: 2	" '**F**, hallowed be your name,	4252
	11:13	how much more will your **F** in heaven give	4252
	12:30	and your **F** knows that you need them.	4252
	12:32	for your **F** has been pleased to give you	4252
	12:53	**f** against son and son against father,	4252
	12:53	father against son and son against **f**,	4252
	14:26	to me and does not hate his **f** and mother,	4252
	15:12	The younger one said to his **f**, 'Father,	4252
	15:12	The younger one said to his father, '**F**,	4252
	15:18	I will set out and go back to my **f** and say	4252
	15:18	**F**, I have sinned against heaven and	4252
	15:20	So he got up and went to his **f**.	4252
	15:20	his **f** saw him and was filled	4252
	15:21	"The son said to him, '**F**,	4252
	15:22	"But the **f** said to his servants, 'Quick!	4252
	15:27	'and your **f** has killed the fattened calf	4252
	15:28	So his **f** went out and pleaded with him.	4252
	15:29	But he answered his **f**, 'Look!	4252
	15:31	" 'My son,' the **f** said,	1254+3836 S
	16:24	So he called to him, '**F** Abraham,	4252
	16:27	"He answered, 'Then I beg you, **f**,	4252
	16:30	" 'No, **f** Abraham,' he said,	4252
	18:20	honor your **f** and mother.' "	4252
	22:29	just as my **F** conferred one on me,	4252
	22:42	"**F**, if you are willing, take this cup	4252
	23:34	Jesus said, "**F**, forgive them,	4252
	23:46	Jesus called out with a loud voice, "**F**,	4252
	24:49	to send you what my **F** has promised;	4252

Jn	1:14	the One and Only, who came from the **F**,	4252
	3:35	The **F** loves the Son and has placed	4252
	4:12	Are you greater than our **f** Jacob,	4252
	4:21	when you will worship the **F** neither	4252
	4:23	the true worshipers will worship the **F**	4252
	4:23	the kind of worshipers the **F** seeks.	4252
	4:53	the **f** realized that this was the exact time	4252
	5:17	"My **F** is always at his work	4252
	5:18	but he was even calling God his own **F**,	4252
	5:19	he can do only what he sees his **F** doing,	4252
	5:19	whatever **the F** does the Son also does.	1697 S
	5:20	**F** loves the Son and shows him all he does.	4252
	5:21	as the **F** raises the dead and gives them life,	4252
	5:22	Moreover, the **F** judges no one,	4252
	5:23	the Son just as they honor the **F**.	4252
	5:23	not honor the Son does not honor the **F**,	4252
	5:26	For as the **F** has life in himself,	4252
	5:36	For the very work that the **F** has given me	4252
	5:36	testifies that the **F** has sent me.	4252
	5:37	the **F** who sent me has himself testified	4252
	5:45	do not think I will accuse you before the **F**.	4252
	6:27	the **F** has placed his seal of approval."	4252
	6:32	but it is my **F** who gives you the true bread	4252
	6:37	All that the **F** gives me will come to me,	4252
	6:42	whose **f** and mother we know?	4252
	6:44	to me unless the **F** who sent me draws him,	4252
	6:45	to the **F** and learns from him comes to me.	4252
	6:46	the **F** except the one who is from God;	4252
	6:46	only he has seen the **F**.	4252
	6:57	the living **F** sent me and I live because of	4252
	6:57	and I live because of the **F**,	4252
	6:65	to me unless the **F** has enabled him."	4252
	8:16	I stand with the **F**, **who** sent me.	4252
	8:18	my other witness is the **F**, **who** sent me."	4252
	8:19	Then they asked him, "Where is your **f**?"	4252
	8:19	"You do not know me or my **F**,"	4252
	8:19	you would know my **F** also."	4252
	8:27	that he was telling them about his **F**.	4252
	8:28	but speak just what the **F** has taught me.	4252
	8:38	you do what you have heard from your **f**."	4252
	8:39	"Abraham is our **f**," they answered.	4252
	8:41	You are doing the things your own **f** does."	4252
	8:41	"The only **F** we have is God himself."	4252
	8:42	Jesus said to them, "If God were your **F**,	4252
	8:44	You belong to your **f**, the devil,	4252
	8:44	for he is a liar and the **f** of lies.	4252
	8:49	"but I honor my **F** and you dishonor me.	4252
	8:53	Are you greater than our **f** Abraham?	4252
	8:54	My **F**, whom you claim as your God,	4252
	8:56	Your **f** Abraham rejoiced at the thought	4252
	10:15	the **F** knows me and I know the Father—	4252
	10:15	as the Father knows me and I know the **F**—	4252
	10:17	The reason my **F** loves me is that I lay	4252
	10:18	This command I received from my **F**."	4252
	10:29	My **F**, who has given them to me,	4252
	10:30	I and the **F** are one."	4252
	10:32	"I have shown you many great miracles	
		from the **F**.	4252
	10:36	what about the one whom the **F** set apart	4252
	10:37	not believe me unless I do what my **F** does.	4252
	10:38	and understand that the **F** is in me,	4252
	10:38	the Father is in me, and I in the **F**."	4252
	11:41	Then Jesus looked up and said, "**F**,	4252
	12:26	My **F** will honor the one who serves me.	4252
	12:27	'**F**, save me from this hour'?	4252
	12:28	**F**, glorify your name!"	4252
	12:49	the **F** who sent me commanded me what	4252
	12:50	the **F** has told me to say."	4252
	13: 1	for him to leave this world and go to the **F**.	4252
	13: 3	the **F** had put all things under his power,	4252
	14: 6	No one comes to the **F** except through me.	4252
	14: 7	you would know my **F** as well.	4252
	14: 8	show us the **F** and that will be enough	4252
	14: 9	Anyone who has seen me has seen the **F**.	4252
	14: 9	How can you say, 'Show us the **F**'?	4252
	14:10	Don't you believe that I am in the **F**,	4252
	14:10	and that the **F** is in me?	4252
	14:10	Rather, it is the **F**, living in me,	4252
	14:11	that I am in the **F** and the Father is in me;	4252
	14:11	that I am in the Father and the **F** is in me;	4252
	14:12	because I am going to the **F**.	4252
	14:13	so that the Son may bring glory to the **F**.	4252
	14:16	And I will ask the **F**, and he will give you	4252
	14:20	that day you will realize that I am in my **F**,	4252
	14:21	He who loves me will be loved by my **F**,	4252
	14:23	My **F** will love him,	4252
	14:24	they belong to the **F** who sent me.	4252
	14:26	whom the **F** will send in my name,	4252
	14:28	be glad that I am going to the **F**,	4252
	14:28	for the **F** is greater than I.	4252
	14:31	the world must learn that I love the **F** and	4252
	14:31	I do exactly what my **F** has commanded me.	4252
	15: 1	and my **F** is the gardener.	4252
	15: 9	the **F** has loved me, so have I loved you.	4252
	15:15	from my **F** I have made known to you.	4252
	15:16	Then the **F** will give you whatever you ask	4252
	15:23	He who hates me hates my **F** as well.	4252
	15:24	and yet they have hated both me and my **F**.	4252
	15:26	whom I will send to you from the **F**,	4252
	15:26	the Spirit of truth who goes out from the **F**,	4252
	16: 3	because they have not known the **F** or me.	4252
	16:10	because I am going to the **F**,	4252
	16:15	All that belongs to the **F** is mine.	4252
	16:17	and 'Because I am going to the **F**'?	4252
	16:23	my **F** will give you whatever you ask	4252
	16:25	but will tell you plainly about my **F**,	4252
	16:26	I am not saying that I will ask the **F**	4252

Jn	16:27	the F himself loves you	4252
	16:28	I came from the F and entered the world;	4252
	16:28	the world and going back to the F."	4252
	16:32	Yet I am not alone, for my F is with me.	4252
	17: 1	"F, the time has come.	4252
	17: 5	now, F, glorify me in your presence with	4252
	17:11	Holy F, protect them by the power	4252
	17:21	F, just as you are in me and I am in you.	4252
	17:24	"F, I want those you have given me to be	4252
	17:25	"Righteous F, though the world does	4252
	18:11	not drink the cup the F has given me?"	4252
	20:17	for I have not yet returned to the F.	4252
	20:17	'I am returning to my F and your Father,	4252
	20:17	'I am returning to my Father and your F.	4252
	20:21	As the F has sent me, I am sending you."	4252
Ac	1: 4	but wait for the gift my F promised,	4252
	1: 7	or dates the F has set by his own authority.	4252
	2:33	from the F the promised Holy Spirit	4252
	4:25	the death of his F,	4252
	7: 2	of glory appeared to our f Abraham	4252
	7: 4	After the death of his f,	4252
	7: 8	And Abraham became the f of Isaac,	1164
	7: 8	Later Isaac became the f of Jacob,	NIG
	7: 8	the f of the twelve patriarchs.	NIG
	7:14	for his f Jacob and his whole family,	4252
	13:33	today I have become your F.'	1164
	16: 1	but whose f was a Greek.	4252
	16: 3	for they all knew that his f was a Greek.	4252
	28: 8	His f was sick in bed,	4252
Ro	1: 7	and peace to you from God our F and from	4252
	4:11	he is the f of all who believe but have	4252
	4:12	And he is also the f of the circumcised who	4252
	4:12	of the faith that our f Abraham had	4252
	4:16	He is the f of us all.	4252
	4:17	"I have made you a f of many nations."	4252
	4:17	He is our f in the sight of God,	NIG
	4:18	and so became the f of many nations,	4252
	6: 4	from the dead through the glory of the F,	4252
	8:15	And by him we cry, "Abba, F."	4252
	9:10	Rebekah's children had one and the same f,	NIG
	9:10	and the same father, our f Isaac.	4252
	15: 6	and mouth you may glorify the God and F	4252
1Co	1: 3	from God our F and the Lord Jesus Christ.	4252
	4:15	for in Christ Jesus I became your f through	1164
	8: 6	the F, from whom all things came and	4252
	15:24	the F after he has destroyed all dominion,	4252
2Co	1: 2	from God our F and the Lord Jesus Christ.	4252
	1: 3	to the God and F of our Lord Jesus Christ,	4252
	1: 3	the F of compassion and the God	4252
	6:18	"I will be a F to you,	4252
	11:31	The God and F of the Lord Jesus,	4252
Gal	1: 1	but by Jesus Christ and God the F,	4252
	1: 3	from God our F and the Lord Jesus Christ.	4252
	1: 4	according to the will of our God and F,	4252
	4: 2	and trustees until the time set by his f.	4252
	4: 6	the Spirit who calls out, "Abba, F."	4252
Eph	1: 2	from God our F and the Lord Jesus Christ.	4252
	1: 3	to the God and F of our Lord Jesus Christ.	4252
	1:17	of our Lord Jesus Christ, the glorious F,	4252
	2:18	through him we both have access to the F	4252
	3:14	For this reason I kneel before the F,	4252
	4: 6	one God and F of all,	4252
	5:20	always giving thanks to God the F	4252
	5:31	"For this reason a man will leave his f	4252
	6: 2	"Honor your f and mother"—	4252
	6:23	from God the F and the Lord Jesus Christ.	4252
Php	1: 2	from God our F and the Lord Jesus Christ.	4252
	2:11	to the glory of God the F.	4252
	2:22	as a son with his f he has served with me in	4252
	4:20	To our God and F be glory for ever	4252
Col	1: 2	Grace and peace to you from God our F.	4252
	1: 3	the F of our Lord Jesus Christ,	4252
	1:12	giving thanks to the F,	4252
	3:17	giving thanks to God the F through him.	4252
1Th	1: 1	in God the F and the Lord Jesus Christ:	4252
	1: 3	before our God and F your work produced	4252
	2:11	that we dealt with each of you as a f deals	4252
	3:11	our God and F himself and our Lord Jesus	4252
	3:13	and holy in the presence of our God and F	4252
2Th	1: 1	in God the F and the Lord Jesus Christ:	4252
	1: 2	from God the F and the Lord Jesus Christ.	4252
	2:16	and God our F, who loved us	4252
1Ti	1: 2	from God the F and Christ Jesus our Lord.	4252
	5: 1	but exhort him as if he were your f.	4252
2Ti	1: 2	from God the F and Christ Jesus our Lord.	4252
Tit	1: 4	the F and Christ Jesus our Savior.	4252
Phm	1: 3	from God our F and the Lord Jesus Christ.	4252
Heb	1: 5	today I have become your F"?	1164
	1: 5	Or again, "I will be his F,	4252
	1: 5	today I have become your F."	1164
	7: 3	Without f or mother, without genealogy,	574
	11:11	was enabled to become a f	2856+3284+5065
	12: 7	For what son is not disciplined by his f?	4252
	12: 9	to the F of our spirits and live!	4252
Jas	1:17	down from the F of the heavenly lights,	4252
	1:27	Religion that God our F accepts as pure	4252
	3: 9	With the tongue we praise our Lord and F,	4252
1Pe	1: 2	the foreknowledge of God the F, through	4252
	1: 3	to the God and F of our Lord Jesus Christ!	4252
	1:17	F who judges each man's work impartially,	4252
2Pe	1:17	when the voice came to him from	4252
1Jn	1: 2	which was with the F and has appeared	4252
	1: 3	And our fellowship is with the F and	4252
	2: 1	we have one who speaks to the F	4252
	2:13	because you have known the F.	4252
	2:15	the love of the F is not in him.	4252
	2:16	comes not from the F but from the world.	4252

1Jn	2:22	he denies the F and the Son.	4252
	2:23	No one who denies the Son has the F;	4252
	2:23	the Son has the F also.	4252
	2:24	also will remain in the Son and in the F.	4252
	3: 1	How great is the love the F has lavished	4252
	4:14	and testify that the F has sent his Son to be	4252
	5: 1	the f loves his child as well.	1164
2Jn	1: 3	from God the F and from Jesus Christ,	4252
	1: 4	just as the F commanded us.	4252
	1: 9	in the teaching has both the F and the Son.	4252
Jude	1: 1	by God the F and kept by Jesus Christ:	4252
Rev	1: 6	and priests to serve his God and F—	4252
	2:27	as I have received authority from my F.	4252
	3: 5	before my F and his angels.	4252
	3:21	just as I overcame and sat down with my F	4252

FATHER'S (149) [FATHER]

Ge	9:22	the father of Canaan, saw his f nakedness	3
	9:23	in backward and covered their f nakedness.	3
	9:23	that they would not see their f nakedness.	3
	12: 1	your people and your f household and go	3
	20:13	from my f household, I said to her, 'This is	3
	24: 7	who brought me out of my f household	3
	24:23	in your f house for us to spend the night?"	3
	24:38	but go to my f family and to my own clan,	3
	24:40	from my own clan and from my f family.	3
	26:15	So all the wells that his f servants had dug	3
	27:30	and Jacob had scarcely left his f presence,	3
	27:34	When Esau heard his f words,	3
	28:21	so that I return safely to my f house,	3
	29: 9	Rachel came with her f sheep,	3+4200
	31: 5	"I see that your f attitude toward me is	3
	31: 9	So God has taken away your f livestock	3
	31:14	in the inheritance of our f estate?	3
	31:19	Rachel stole her f household gods.	3+4200
	31:30	to return to your f house.	3
	34:19	the most honored of all his f household,	3
	35:22	in and slept with his f concubine Bilhah,	3
	37: 2	his f wives, and he brought their father	3
	37:12	to graze their f flocks near Shechem,	3
	38:11	"Live as a widow in your f house	3
	38:11	So Tamar went to live in her f house.	3
	41:51	and all my f household."	3
	46:31	to his brothers and his f household,	3
	46:31	'My brothers and my f household,	3
	47:12	and his brothers and all his f household	3
	48:17	so he took hold of his f hand to move it	3
	49: 4	for you went up onto your f bed,	3
	49: 8	your f sons will bow down to you.	3
	49:25	because of your f God,	3
	49:26	Your f blessings are greater than	3
	50: 8	and those belonging to his f household.	3
	50:22	along with all his f family.	3
Ex	2:16	and fill the troughs to water their f flock.	3
	6:20	Amram married his f sister Jochebed,	1860
	15: 2	and I will praise him, my f God,	3
	18: 4	for he said, "My f God was my helper;	3
Lev	18: 8	not have sexual relations with your f wife;	3
	18: 9	your f daughter or your mother's daughter,	3
	18:11	with the daughter of your f wife, born	3
	18:12	not have sexual relations with your f sister;	3
	18:12	she is your f close relative.	3
	18:14	" 'Do not dishonor your f brother	3
	20:11	" 'If a man sleeps with his f wife,	3
	22:13	and she returns to live in her f house as	3
	22:13	she may eat of her f food.	3
Nu	18: 1	your sons and your f family are to bear	3
	27: 4	Why should our f name disappear	3
	27: 4	Give us property among our f relatives."	3
	27: 7	as an inheritance among their f relatives	3
	27: 7	and turn their f inheritance over to them.	3
	27:10	give his inheritance to his f brothers.	3
	30: 3	in her f house makes a vow to the LORD	3
	36: 8	in her f tribal clan,	3
	36:11	married their cousins on their f side.	1201+1856
	36:12	in their f clan and tribe.	3
Dt	21:17	That son is the first sign of his f strength.	2257S
	22:21	the door of her f house and there the men	3
	22:21	while still in her f house.	3
	22:30	A man is not to marry his f wife;	3
	22:30	he must not dishonor his f bed.	3
	27:20	the man who sleeps with his f wife,	3
	27:20	for he dishonors his f bed."	3
Jdg	6:25	"Take the second bull from your f herd,	3
	6:25	down your f altar to Baal and cut down	3+4200
	9: 5	He went to his f home in Ophrah and	3
	9:18	revolted against my f family,	3
	11: 7	and drive me from my f house?	3
	14:15	or we will burn you and your f household	3
	14:19	he went up to his f house.	3
	16:31	and his f whole family went down	3
	19: 2	and went back to her f house in Bethlehem.	3
	19: 3	She took him into her f house,	3
1Sa	2:25	however, did not listen to their f rebuke,	3
	2:27	to your f house when they were in Egypt	3
	2:28	I also gave your f house all	3
	2:30	and your f house would minister	3
	2:31	and the strength of your f house,	3
	9:20	if not to you and all your f family?"	3
	17:15	from Saul to tend his f sheep at Bethlehem.	3
	17:25	in marriage and will exempt his f family	3
	17:34	Your servant has been keeping his f sheep	3+4200
	18: 2	and did not let him return to his f house.	3
	18:18	what is my family or my f clan in Israel,	3
	20:34	at his f shameful treatment of David.	3
	22: 1	and his f household heard about it,	3

1Sa	22:11	of Ahitub and his f whole family,	3
	22:15	or any of his f family,	3
	22:16	Ahimelech, you and your f whole family."	3
	22:22	for the death of your f whole family.	3
	24:21	or wipe out my name from my f family."	3
2Sa	2:32	and buried him in his f tomb at Bethlehem.	3
	3: 7	"Why did you sleep with my f concubine?"	3
	3:29	the head of Joab and upon all his f house!	3
	14: 9	the blame rest on me and on my f family,	3
	15:34	I was your f servant in the past,	3
	16:21	"Lie with your f concubines whom he left	3
	16:21	a stench in your f nostrils,	3
	16:22	and he lay with his f concubines in	3
	17:23	So he died and was buried in his f tomb.	3
1Ki	2:26	and shared all my f hardships."	3
	2:31	and so clear me and my f house of the guilt	3
	12:10	'My little finger is thicker than my f waist.	3
	18:18	"But you and your f family have.	3
2Ki	10: 3	and set him on his f throne.	3
1Ch	5: 1	but when he defiled his f marriage bed,	3
	26: 6	who were leaders in their f family	3
	28: 4	and from my f sons he was pleased	3
2Ch	10:10	'My little finger is thicker than my f waist.	3
	21: 4	over his f kingdom,	3
	21:13	members of your f house,	3
	22: 4	after his f death they became his advisers,	3
Ne	1: 6	including myself and my f house,	3
Est	4:14	but you and your f family will perish.	3
Ps	45:10	Forget your people and your f house.	3
Pr	1: 8	to your f instruction and do	3
	4: 1	Listen, my sons, to a f instruction;	3
	4: 3	When I was a boy in my f house,	3
	6:20	keep your f commands and do	3
	13: 1	A wise son heeds his f instruction,	3
	15: 5	A fool spurns his f discipline,	3
	19:13	A foolish son is his f ruin,	3
Isa	3: 6	at his f home, and say, "You have	3
Eze	18:17	He will not die for his f sin;	3
	22:11	his own f daughter.	3
Mt	16:27	of Man is going to come in his F glory	4252
	26:29	with you in my F kingdom."	4252
Mk	8:38	of him when he comes in his F glory with	4252
Lk	2:49	"Didn't you know I had to be in my F house?"	4252
	15:17	'How many of my f hired men have food	4252
	16:27	father, send Lazarus to my f house,	4252
Jn	1:18	who is at the F side, has made him known.	4252
	2:16	How dare you turn my F house into	4252
	5:43	I have come in my F name,	4252
	6:40	For my F will is that everyone who looks	4252
	8:38	what I have seen in the F presence,	4252
	8:44	and you want to carry out your f desire.	4252
	10:25	miracles I do in my F name speak for me,	4252
	10:29	no one can snatch them out of my F hand.	4252
	14: 2	In my F house are many rooms;	4252
	15: 8	This is to my F glory,	4252
	15:10	just as I have obeyed my F commands	4252
Ac	7:20	he was cared for in his f house.	4252
1Co	5: 1	A man has his f wife.	4252
2Jn	1: 3	the F Son, will be with us in truth and love.	4252
Rev	14: 1	and his F name written on their foreheads.	4252

FATHER-IN-LAW (24) [FATHER]

Ge	38:13	"Your f is on his way to Timnah	2767
	38:25	she sent a message to her f.	2767
Ex	3: 1	the flock of Jethro his f,	3162
	4:18	Then Moses went back to Jethro his f	3162
	18: 1	the priest of Midian and f of Moses,	3162
	18: 2	his f Jethro received her	3162
	18: 5	Moses' f, together with Moses' sons	3162
	18: 6	to him, "I, your f Jethro, am coming to you	3162
	18: 7	So Moses went out to meet his f	3162
	18: 8	Moses told his f about everything	3162
	18:12	Then Jethro, Moses' f,	3162
	18:12	to eat bread with Moses' f in the presence	3162
	18:14	When his f saw all that Moses was doing	3162
	18:17	Moses' f replied, "What you are doing is	3162
	18:24	to his f and did everything he said.	3162
	18:27	Then Moses sent his f on his way,	3162
Nu	10:29	Moses' f, "We are setting out for the place	3162
Jdg	1:16	The descendants of Moses' f, the Kenite,	3162
	19: 4	His f, the girl's father,	3162
	19: 7	the man got up to go, his f persuaded him,	3162
1Sa	4:19	up to leave, his f, the girl's father, said,	3162
	4:19	and that her f and her husband were dead,	2767
	4:21	of the ark of God and the deaths of her f	2767
Jn	18:13	Annas, who was the f of Caiaphas,	4290

FATHERED (1) [FATHER]

Dt	32:18	You deserted the Rock, who f you;	3528

FATHERLESS (39) [FATHER]

Ex	22:24	will become widows and your children f.	3846
Dt	10:18	He defends the cause of the f and	3846
	14:29	the aliens, the f and the widows who live	3846
	16:11	the f and the widows living among you.	3846
	16:14	the aliens, the f and the widows who live	3846
	24:17	Do not deprive the alien or the f of justice,	3846
	24:19	Leave it for the alien, the f and the widow,	3846
	24:20	the alien, the f and the widow.	3846
	24:21	the alien, the f and the widow.	3846
	26:12	the alien, the f and the widow,	3846
	26:13	the alien, the f and the widow,	3846
	27:19	the alien, the f or the widow."	3846
Job	6:27	for the f and barter away your friend.	3846

Job	22:9	and broke the strength of the **f**.	3846
	24:9	The **f** child is snatched from the breast;	3846
	29:12	and the **f** who had none to assist him.	3846
	31:17	not sharing it with the **f**—	3846
	31:21	if I have raised my hand against the **f**,	3846
Ps	10:14	you are the helper of the **f**.	3846
	10:18	defending the **f** and the oppressed,	3846
	68:5	A father to the **f**, a defender of widows,	3846
	82:3	Defend the cause of the weak and **f**;	3846
	94:6	they murder the **f**.	3846
	109:9	May his children be **f** and his wife	3846
	109:12	or take pity on his **f children**.	3846
	146:9	the alien and sustains the **f** and the widow,	3846
Pr	23:10	or encroach on the fields of the **f**,	3846
Isa	1:17	Defend the cause of the **f**,	3846
	1:23	They do not defend the cause of the **f**;	3846
	9:17	nor will he pity the **f** and widows,	3846
	10:2	and robbing the **f**.	3846
Jer	5:28	do not plead the case of the **f** to win it,	3846
	7:6	not oppress the alien, the **f** or the widow	3846
	22:3	violence to the alien, the **f** or the widow,	3846
La	5:3	We have become orphans and **f**,	3+401
Eze	22:7	and mistreated the **f** and the widow.	3846
Hos	14:3	for in you the **f** find compassion."	3846
Zec	7:10	Do not oppress the widow or the **f**,	3846
Mal	3:5	who oppress the widows and the **f**,	3846

FATHERS (312) [FATHER]

Ge	15:15	will go to your **f** in peace and be buried at	3
	31:3	to the land of your **f** and to your relatives,	3
	46:34	just as our **f** did.'	3
	47:3	"just as our **f** were."	3
	47:9	the years of the pilgrimage of my **f**."	3
	47:30	but when I rest with my **f**,	3
	48:15	"May the God before whom my **f** Abraham	3
	48:16	and the names of my **f** Abraham and Isaac,	3
	48:21	and take you back to the land of your **f**	3
	49:29	with my **f** in the cave in the field of Ephron	3
Ex	3:13	'The God of your **f** has sent me to you,'	3
	3:15	'The LORD, the God of your **f**—	3
	3:16	'The LORD, the God of your **f**—	3
	4:5	the LORD, the God of your **f**—	3
	10:6	something neither your **f**	3
	20:5	the children for the sin of the **f** to the third	3
	34:7	of the **f** to the third and fourth generation."	3
Lev	26:40	and the sins of their **f**—	3
Nu	14:18	he punishes the children for the sin of the **f**	3
	20:15	The Egyptians mistreated us and our **f**,	3
	32:8	This is what your **f** did when I sent them	3
	32:14	the place of your **f** and making the LORD	3
	36:8	the inheritance of his **f**.	3
Dt	1:8	the LORD swore he would give to your **f**—	3
	1:11	May the LORD, the God of your **f**,	3
	1:21	the LORD, the God of your **f**, told you.	3
	4:1	the LORD, the God of your **f**, is giving you.	3
	5:3	It was not with our **f** that	3
	5:9	the children for the sin of the **f** to the third	3
	6:3	just as the LORD, the God of your **f**,	3
	6:10	to your **f**, to Abraham, Isaac and Jacob,	3
	8:3	which neither you nor your **f** had known,	3
	8:16	something your **f** had never known,	3
	9:5	to accomplish what he swore to your **f**,	3
	10:11	and possess the land that I swore to their **f**	3
	12:1	the LORD, the God of your **f**,	3
	13:6	that neither you nor your **f** have known,	3
	24:16	**F** shall not be put to death	3
	24:16	nor children put to death for their **f**;	3
	26:7	the LORD, the God of your **f**,	3
	27:3	just as the LORD, the God of your **f**,	3
	28:36	to a nation unknown to you or your **f**.	3
	28:64	which neither you nor your **f** have known.	3
	29:13	and as he swore to your **f**,	3
	29:25	the LORD, the God of their **f**,	3
	30:5	to the land that belonged to your **f**,	3
	30:5	and numerous than your **f**.	3
	30:9	just as he delighted in your **f**,	3
	30:20	in the land he swore to give to your **f**,	3
	31:16	"You are going to rest with your **f**,	3
	32:...	gods your **f** did not fear.	3
Jos	4:21	when your descendants ask their **f**,	3
	5:6	that he had solemnly promised their **f**	3
	18:3	the LORD, the God of your **f**, has given you?	3
	22:28	of the LORD's altar, which our **f** built,	3
	24:6	When I brought your **f** out of Egypt,	3
	24:17	and our **f** up out of Egypt,	3
Jdg	2:10	to their **f**, another generation grew	3
	2:12	the LORD, the God of their **f**,	3
	2:17	Unlike their **f**, they quickly turned from	NIH
	2:17	from the way in which their **f** had walked,	3
	2:19	even more corrupt than those of their **f**,	3
	6:13	Where are all his wonders that our **f** told us	3
	21:22	When their **f** or brothers complain to us,	3
1Sa	12:7	by the LORD for you and your **f**.	3
	12:15	as it was against your **f**.	3
2Sa	7:12	over and you rest with your **f**,	3
1Ki	1:21	the king is laid to rest with his **f**,	3
	2:10	David rested with his **f** and was buried in	3
	8:21	of the LORD that he made with our **f**	3
	8:34	to the land you gave to their **f**.	3
	8:40	in the land you gave our **f**.	3
	8:48	toward the land you gave their **f**, toward	3
	8:53	brought our **f** out of Egypt."	3
	8:57	be with us as he was with our **f**;	3
	8:58	decrees and regulations he gave our **f**.	3
	9:9	who brought their **f** out of Egypt,	3
	11:21	with his **f** and that Joab the commander of	3

1Ki	11:43	Then he rested with his **f** and was buried in	3
	13:22	not be buried in the tomb of your **f**.'"	3
	14:20	and then rested with his **f**.	3
	14:22	stirred up his jealous anger more than their **f** had done.	3
	14:31	Rehoboam rested with his **f** and was buried	3
	15:8	Abijah rested with his **f** and was buried	3
	15:12	and got rid of all the idols his **f** had made.	3
	15:24	Then Asa rested with his **f** and was buried	3
	16:6	Baasha rested with his **f** and was buried	3
	16:28	Omri rested with his **f** and was buried	3
	21:3	the inheritance of my **f**."	3
	21:4	not give you the inheritance of my **f**."	3
	22:40	Ahab rested with his **f**.	3
	22:50	with his **f** and was buried with them in	3
2Ki	8:24	Jehoram rested with his **f** and was buried	3
	9:28	with his **f** in his tomb in the City of David.	3
	10:35	with his **f** and was buried in Samaria.	3
	12:18	the sacred objects dedicated by his **f**—	3
	12:21	and was buried with his **f** in the City	3
	13:9	Jehoahaz rested with his **f** and was buried	3
	13:13	Jehoash rested with his **f**,	3
	14:6	"**F** shall not be put to death	3
	14:6	nor children put to death for their **f**;	3
	14:16	with his **f** and was buried in Samaria with	3
	14:20	and was buried in Jerusalem with his **f**,	3
	14:22	to Judah after Amaziah rested with his **f**.	3
	14:29	Jeroboam rested with his **f**,	3
	15:7	Azariah rested with his **f** and was buried	3
	15:9	as his **f** had done.	3
	15:22	Menahem rested with his **f**.	3
	15:38	Jotham rested with his **f** and was buried	3
	16:20	with his **f** and was buried with them in	3
	17:13	the entire Law that I commanded your **f**	3
	17:14	and were as stiff-necked as their **f**,	3
	17:15	the covenant he had made with their **f** and	3
	17:41	to do as their **f** did.	3
	20:17	all that your **f** have stored up until this day,	3
	20:21	Hezekiah rested with his **f**.	3
	21:18	Manasseh rested with his **f** and was buried	3
	21:22	He forsook the LORD, the God of his **f**,	3
	22:13	against us because our **f** have not obeyed	3
	22:20	Therefore I will gather you to your **f**,	3
	23:32	just as his **f** had done.	3
	23:37	just as his **f** had done.	3
	24:6	Jehoiakim rested with his **f**.	3
1Ch	5:25	of their **f** and prostituted themselves to	3
	6:19	of the Levites listed according to their **f**:	3
	9:19	as their **f** had been responsible for guarding	3
	12:17	may the God of our **f** see it and judge you."	3
	17:11	over and you go to be with your **f**,	3
	25:6	the supervision of their **f** for the music of	3
	29:18	O LORD, God of our **f** Abraham,	3
	29:20	the LORD, the God of their **f**;	3
2Ch	6:25	to the land you gave to them and their **f**.	3
	6:31	in the land you gave our **f**.	3
	6:38	and pray toward the land you gave their **f**,	3
	7:22	the LORD, the God of their **f**,	3
	9:31	Then he rested with his **f** and was buried in	3
	11:16	the LORD, the God of their **f**,	3
	12:16	Rehoboam rested with his **f** and was buried	3
	13:12	the LORD, the God of your **f**,	3
	13:18	the LORD, the God of their **f**.	3
	14:1	Abijah rested with his **f** and was buried in	3
	14:4	the LORD, the God of their **f**,	3
	15:12	the LORD, the God of their **f**,	3
	16:13	of his reign Asa died and rested with his **f**.	3
	19:4	the LORD, the God of their **f**.	3
	20:6	"O LORD, God of our **f**,	3
	20:33	not set their hearts on the God of their **f**.	3
	21:1	Jehoshaphat rested with his **f** and was	3
	21:10	the LORD, the God of their **f**.	3
	21:19	as they had for his **f**.	3
	24:18	the LORD, the God of their **f**,	3
	24:24	the LORD, the God of their **f**,	3
	25:4	"**F** shall not be put to death	3
	25:4	nor children put to death for their **f**;	3
	25:28	by horse and was buried with his **f** in	3
	26:2	to Judah after Amaziah rested with his **f**.	3
	26:23	Uzziah rested with his **f** and was buried	3
	27:9	Jotham rested with his **f** and was buried	3
	28:6	the LORD, the God of their **f**.	3
	28:9	the LORD, the God of your **f**, was angry with Judah,	3
	28:25	provoked the LORD, the God of his **f**, to anger.	3
	28:27	Ahaz rested with his **f** and was buried in	3
	29:5	the LORD, the God of their **f**.	3
	29:6	Our **f** were unfaithful;	3
	29:9	This is why our **f** have fallen by the sword	3
	30:7	Do not be like your **f** and brothers,	3
	30:7	the LORD, the God of their **f**,	3
	30:8	Do not be stiff-necked, as your **f** were;	3
	30:19	the LORD, the God of his **f**—	3
	30:22	praised the LORD, the God of their **f**.	3
	32:13	not know what I and my **f** have done to all	3
	32:14	that my **f** destroyed has been able	3
	32:15	from my hand or the hand of my **f**.	3
	32:33	with his **f** and was buried on the hill where	3
	33:12	before the God of his **f**.	3
	33:20	Manasseh rested with his **f** and was buried	3
	34:21	on us because our **f** have not kept the word	3
	34:28	Now I will gather you to your **f**.	3
	34:32	covenant of God, the God of their **f**.	3
	34:33	follow the LORD, the God of their **f**.	3
	35:24	He was buried in the tombs of his **f**,	3
	36:15	the LORD, the God of their **f**,	3

Ezr	5:12	because our **f** angered the God of heaven,	10003
	7:27	Praise be to the LORD, the God of our **f**,	3
	8:28	offering to the LORD, the God of your **f**.	3
	10:11	the LORD, the God of your **f**, and do his will.	3
Ne	2:3	the city where my **f** are buried lies in ruins,	3
	2:5	the city in Judah where my **f** are buried so	3
	9:2	and the wickedness of their **f**.	3
	9:23	into the land that you told their **f** to enter	3
	9:32	upon our **f** and all your people,	3
	9:34	and our **f** did not follow your law;	3
Job	8:8	and find out what their **f** learned,	3
	15:18	hiding nothing received from their **f**	3
	30:1	whose **f** I would have disdained to put	3
	38:28	Who **f** the drops of dew?	3528
Ps	22:4	In you our **f** put their trust;	3
	39:12	a stranger, as all my **f** were.	3
	44:1	our **f** have told us what you did	3
	44:2	the nations and planted **our f**;	4392S
	44:2	the peoples and made **our f** flourish.	4392S
	45:16	Your sons will take the place of your **f**;	3
	49:19	he will join the generation of his **f**,	3
	78:3	what our **f** have told us.	3
	78:12	in the sight of their **f** in the land of Egypt,	3
	78:57	Like their **f** they were disloyal	3
	79:8	Do not hold against us the sins of the **f**;	8037
	95:9	where your **f** tested and tried me,	3
	106:6	We have sinned, even as our **f** did;	3
	106:7	When our **f** were in Egypt,	3
	109:14	of his **f** be remembered before the LORD;	3
Pr	30:11	"There are those who curse their **f** and do	3
Isa	38:19	**f** tell their children about your faithfulness.	3
	39:6	all that your **f** have stored up until this day,	3
	49:23	Kings will be your **foster f**,	587
	64:11	where our **f** praised you,	3
	65:7	both your sins and the sins of your **f**,"	3
Jer	2:5	"What fault did your **f** find in me,	3
	3:25	both we and our **f**;	3
	6:21	**F** and sons alike will stumble over them;	3
	7:14	the place I gave to you and your **f**.	3
	7:18	children gather wood, the **f** light the fire,	3
	9:14	as their **f** taught them."	3
	9:16	that neither they nor their **f** have known,	3
	13:14	**f** and sons alike, declares the LORD.	3
	14:20	and the guilt of our **f**;	3
	16:3	and the men who are their **f**,	3
	16:11	'It is because your **f** forsook me,'	3
	16:12	you have behaved more wickedly than your **f**	3
	16:13	a land neither you nor your **f** have known,	3
	16:19	"Our **f** possessed nothing but false gods,	3
	19:4	in it to gods that neither they nor their **f** nor	3
	23:27	just as their **f** forgot my name	3
	23:39	with the city I gave to you and your **f**.	3
	24:10	from the land I gave to them and your **f**.'"	3
	25:5	the land the LORD gave to you and your **f**	3
	31:29	'The **f** have eaten sour grapes,	3
	34:5	a funeral fire in honor of your **f**,	3
	34:14	Your **f**, however, did not listen to me	3
	35:15	in the land I have given to you and your **f**."	3
	44:3	nor you nor your **f** ever knew.	3
	44:9	the wickedness committed by your **f** and	3
	44:10	and the decrees I set before you and your **f**.	3
	44:17	to her just as we and our **f**,	3
	44:21	the streets of Jerusalem by you and your **f**,	3
	47:3	**F** will not turn to help their children;	3
	50:7	the LORD, the hope of their **f**.'	3
La	5:7	Our **f** sinned and are no more,	3
Eze	2:3	and their **f** have been in revolt against me	3
	5:10	in your midst **f** will eat their children,	3
	5:10	and children will eat their **f**.	3
	18:2	" 'The **f** eat sour grapes,	3
	20:4	with the detestable practices of their **f**	3
	20:18	the statutes of your **f** or keep their laws	3
	20:27	In this also your **f** blasphemed me	3
	20:30	the way your **f** did and lust	3
	20:36	As I judged your **f** in the desert of the land	3
	20:42	with uplifted hand to give to your **f**,	3
	37:25	the land where your **f** lived.	3
Da	2:23	I thank and praise you, O God of my **f**:	10003
	9:6	our princes and our **f**,	3
	9:8	and our **f** are covered with shame	3
	9:16	the iniquities of our **f** have made Jerusalem	3
	11:24	and will achieve what neither his **f**	3
	11:37	for the gods of his **f** or the one desired	3
	11:38	to his **f** he will honor with gold and silver,	3
Hos	9:10	when I saw your **f**,	3
Mic	7:20	on oath to our **f** in days long ago.	3
Zec	8:14	when your **f** angered me,"	3
Mal	2:10	Why do we profane the covenant of our **f**	3
	4:6	of the **f** to their children, and the hearts of	3
	4:6	and the hearts of the children to their **f**;	3
Lk	1:17	to turn the hearts of the **f** to their children	4252
	1:55	even as he said to our **f**."	4252
	1:72	to show mercy to our **f** and	4252
	6:23	For that is how their **f** treated the prophets.	4252
	6:26	how their **f** treated the false prophets.	4252
	11:11	"Which of you **f**, if your son asks for	4252
Jn	4:20	Our **f** worshiped on this mountain,	4252
Ac	3:13	Isaac and Jacob, the God of our **f**,	4252
	3:25	and of the covenant God made with your **f**.	4252
	5:30	God of our **f** raised Jesus from the dead—	4252
	7:2	"Brothers and **f**, listen to me!	4252
	7:11	and our **f** could not find food.	4252
	7:12	he sent our **f** on their first visit.	4252
	7:15	where he and our **f** died.	4252
	7:32	'I am the God of your **f**,	4252
	7:38	on Mount Sinai, and with our **f**;	4252
	7:39	"But our **f** refused to obey him.	4252

Ac	7:45	our f under Joshua brought it with them	4252
	7:51	You are just like your f:	4252
	7:52	Was there ever a prophet your f did	4252
	13:17	God of the people of Israel chose our f;	4252
	13:32	What God promised our f	4252
	13:36	with his f and his body decayed.	4252
	15:10	that neither we nor our f have been able	4252
	22: 1	"Brothers and f, listen now	4262
	22: 3	in the law of our f and was just as zealous	4262
	22:14	of our f has chosen you to know his will	4262
	24:14	the God of our f as a follower of the Way,	4262
	26: 6	of my hope in what God has promised our f	4252
1Co	4:15	you do not have many f,	4252
Gal	1:14	for the traditions of my f.	4257
Eph	6: 4	F, do not exasperate your children;	4252
Col	3:21	F, do not embitter your children,	4252
1Ti	1: 9	for those who kill their f or mothers,	4260
Heb	3: 9	where your f tested and tried me and	4252
	12: 9	we have all had human f who disciplined us	4252
	12:10	Our f disciplined us for a little while	3525+3836ˢ
2Pe	3: 4	Ever since our f died,	4252
1Jn	2:13	I write to you, f,	4252
	2:14	I write to you, f,	4252

FATHERS' (5) [FATHER]

Lev	26:39	of their f' sins they will waste away.	3
Jer	3:24	the fruits of our f' labor—	3
	32:18	for the f' sins into the laps of their children	3
Eze	20:24	and their eyes [lusted] after their f' idols.	3
	22:10	In you are those who dishonor their f' bed;	3

FATHOM (5) [FATHOMED]

Job	11: 7	"Can you f the mysteries of God?	5162
Ps	145: 3	his greatness no one can f.	2984
Ecc	3:11	yet they cannot f what God has done	5162
Isa	40:28	and his understanding no one can f.	2984
1Co	13: 2	the gift of prophecy and can f all mysteries	3857

FATHOMED (2) [FATHOM]

Job	5: 9	He performs wonders that cannot be f,	2984
	9:10	He performs wonders that cannot be f,	2984

FATLING (KJV) See YEARLING

FATTED (KJV) See FATTENED

FATTENED (16) [FAT]

Dt	32:14	and flock and with f lambs and goats,	2693
1Sa	28:24	The woman had a f calf at the house,	5272
2Sa	6:13	he sacrificed a bull and a f calf.	5309
1Ki	1: 9	and f calves at the Stone of Zoheleth	5309
	1:19	f calves, and sheep, and has invited all	5309
	1:25	sacrificed great numbers of cattle, f calves,	5309
Pr	15:17	where there is love than a f calf	80
Isa	1:11	of rams and the fat of f animals;	5309
Jer	46:21	in her ranks are like f calves.	5272
Eze	39:18	all of them f animals from Bashan.	5309
Am	5:22	You dine on choice lambs and f calves.	5272
Mt	22: 4	and f cattle have been butchered,	4990
Lk	15:23	Bring the f calf and kill it.	4988
	15:27	the f calf because he has him back safe	4988
	15:30	you kill the f calf for him!'	4988
Jas	5: 5	You have f yourselves in the day	5555

FATTENING (1) [FAT]

1Sa	2:29	by f yourselves on the choice parts	1344

FAULT (13) [FAULTFINDERS, FAULTLESS, FAULTS, FAULTY]

Ex	5:16	but the f is with your own people."	2627
1Sa	29: 3	I have found no f in him."	4399
	29: 6	I have found no f in you,	8288
Job	33:10	Yet God has found f with me;	9481
Jer	2: 5	"What f did your fathers find in me,	6404
	17: 4	Through your own f you will lose	928
Jnh	1:12	I know that it is my f	928+4200+8611
Mt	18:15	go and show him his f,	1794
Php	2:15	children of God without f in a crooked	320
Heb	8: 8	But God found f with the people and said:	3522
Jas	1: 5	to all without finding f,	3943
	3: 2	If anyone is never at f in what he says,	4760
Jude	1:24	before his glorious presence without f and	320

FAULTFINDERS (1) [FAULT, FIND]

Jude	1:16	These men are grumblers and f;	3523

FAULTLESS (3) [FAULT]

Pr	8: 9	they are f to those who have knowledge.	3838
Php	3: 6	as for legalistic righteousness, f.	289+1181
Jas	1:27	as pure and f is this:	299

FAULTS (2) [FAULT]

Job	10: 6	that you must search out my f and probe	6411
Ps	19:12	Forgive my hidden f.	AIT

FAULTY (2) [FAULT]

Ps	78:57	as unreliable as a f bow.	8244
Hos	7:16	they are like a f bow.	8244

FAVOR (117) [FAVORABLE, FAVORABLY, FAVORED, FAVORITE, FAVORITISM, FAVORS]

Ge	4: 4	The LORD looked with f on Abel	9120
	4: 5	and his offering he did not look with f.	9120
	6: 8	Noah found f in the eyes of the LORD.	2834
	18: 3	He said, "If I have found f in your eyes,	2834
	19:19	Your servant has found f in your eyes,	2834
	30:27	"If I have found f in your eyes, please stay.	2834
	32: 5	that I may find f in your eyes.' "	2834
	33: 8	"To find f in your eyes, my lord," he said.	2834
	33:10	"If I have found f in your eyes,	2834
	33:15	"Just let me find f in the eyes of my lord."	2834
	34:11	"Let me find f in your eyes,	2834
	39: 4	Joseph found f in his eyes	2834
	39:21	he showed him kindness and granted him f	2834
	47:25	"May we find f in the eyes of our lord;	2834
	47:29	"If I have found f in your eyes,	2834
	50: 4	"If I have found f in your eyes,	2834
Ex	32:11	Moses sought the f of the LORD his God.	906+2704+7156
	33:12	'I know you by name and you have found f	2834
	33:13	so I may know you and continue to find f	2834
	34: 9	"O Lord, if I have found f in your eyes,"	2834
Lev	26: 9	I will look on you with f	7155
Nu	11:15	if I have found f in your eyes—	2834
	32: 5	If we have found f in your eyes," they said,	2834
Dt	33:16	and its fullness and the f of him who dwelt	8356
	33:23	"Naphtali is abounding with the f of	8356
Jos	15:19	She replied, "Do me a special f.	1388
Jdg	1:15	She replied, "Do me a special f.	1388
	6:17	"If now I have found f in your eyes,	2834
Ru	2: 2	behind anyone in whose eyes I find f."	2834
	2:10	"Why have I found such f in your eyes	2834
	2:13	"May I continue to find f in your eyes,	2834
1Sa	1:18	"May your servant find f in your eyes."	2834
	2:26	and in f with the LORD and with men.	3202
	13:12	not sought the LORD's f.'	2704+7156
	20: 3	that I have found f in your eyes,	2834
	20:29	If I have found f in your eyes,	2834
	27: 5	"If I have found f in your eyes,	2834
	29: 4	How better could he regain his master's f	8354
		than by taking the heads	
2Sa	2: 6	the same f because you have done this.	3208
	14:22	that he has found f in your eyes,	2834
	15:25	If I find f in the LORD's eyes,	2834
	16: 4	"May I find f in your eyes,	2834
2Ki	13: 4	Jehoahaz sought the LORD's f,	906+2704+7156
2Ch	33:12	In his distress he sought the f of	906+2704+7156
Ezr	7:28	and who has extended his good f to me	2876
Ne	1:11	by granting him f in the presence	8171
	2: 5	and if your servant has found f in his sight,	3512
	5:19	Remember me with f, O my God,	3208
	13:31	Remember me with f, O my God.	3208
Est	2: 9	The girl pleased him and won his f.	2876
	2:15	the f of everyone who saw her.	2834
	2:17	and she won his f and approval	2834
	5: 8	the king regards me with f and if it pleases	2834
	7: 3	"If I have found f with you, O king,	2834
	8: 5	and if he regards me with f and thinks it	2834
Job	11:19	and many will court your f.	2704+7156
	33:26	He prays to God and finds f with him,	8354
	34:19	to princes and does not f the rich over	5795
Ps	5:12	you surround them with your f as with	8356
	30: 5	but his f lasts a lifetime;	8356
	45:12	men of wealth will seek your f.	2704+7156
	69:13	O LORD, in the time of your f;	8356
	77: 7	Will he never show his f again?	8354
	84: 9	look with f on your anointed one.	5564+7156
	84:11	the LORD bestows f and honor;	2834
	85: 1	You showed f to your land, O LORD;	8354
	89:17	and by your f you exalt our horn.	8356
	90:17	the f of the Lord our God rest upon us;	5840
	102:13	for it is time to show f to her;	2858
	106: 4	when you show f to your people,	8356
Pr	3: 4	Then you will win f and a good name in	2834
	8:35	and receives f from the LORD.	8356
	12: 2	A good man obtains f from the LORD,	8356
	13:15	Good understanding wins f,	2834
	16:15	his f is like a rain cloud in spring.	8356
	18:22	a wife finds what is good and receives f	8356
	19: 6	Many curry f with a ruler,	2704+7156
	19:12	but his f is like dew on the grass.	8356
	28:23	in the end gain more f than he who has	2834
Ecc	9:11	or wealth to the brilliant or f to the learned;	2834
Isa	27:11	and their Creator shows them no f.	2858
	49: 8	"In the time of my f I will answer you,	8356
	60:10	in f I will show you compassion.	8356
	61: 2	to proclaim the year of the LORD's f and	8356
Jer	16:13	for I will show you no f.'	2850
	26:19	the LORD and seek his f?	906+2704+7156
	31: 2	the sword will find f in the desert;	2834
La	4:16	priests are shown no honor, the elders no f.	2858
Eze	1:13	I myself will withdraw my f;	1757
	36: 9	and will look on you with f;	7155
Da	1: 9	Now God had caused the official to show f	2876
	7:22	and pronounced judgment in f of the saints	10378
	9:13	not sought the f of the LORD our God	906+2704+7156
	9:17	look with f on your desolate sanctuary.	239+7156
	11:30	and show f to those who forsake	1067
Hos	12: 4	he wept and begged for his f.	2858
Zec	11: 7	Then I took two staffs and called one F and	5840
	11:10	Then I took my staff called F and broke it,	5840
Mt	20:20	kneeling down, asked a f of him.	160

Lk	1:25	"In these days he has shown his f	2078
	1:30	Mary, you have found f with God.	5921
	2:14	peace to men on whom his f rests."	2306
	2:52	and in f with God and men.	5921
	4:19	to proclaim the year of the Lord's f."	1283
Jn	5:32	There is another who testifies in my f,	4309
Ac	2:47	praising God and enjoying the f of all	2400+5921
	7:46	who enjoyed God's f and asked	5921
	24:27	Felix wanted to grant a f to the Jews,	5921
	25: 3	as a f to them,	5921
	25: 9	Festus, wishing to do the Jews a f,	5921
2Co	1:11	on our behalf for the gracious f granted us	5922
	6: 2	he says, "In the time of my f I heard you,	1283
	6: 2	I tell you, now is the time of God's f,	2347
Eph	6: 6	not only to win their f when their eye is	473
Col	3:22	when their eye is on you and to win their f,	473
Phm	1:14	that any f you do will be spontaneous and	19
Rev	2: 6	But you have this in your f:	NIG

FAVORABLE (5) [FAVOR]

Ge	40:16	that Joseph had given a f interpretation,	3202
1Sa	25: 8	Therefore be f toward my young men,	928+2834+5162+6524
1Ki	12: 7	and serve them and give them a f answer,	3202
2Ch	10: 7	and please them and give them a f answer,	3202
Jer	42: 6	Whether it is f or unfavorable,	3202

FAVORABLY (7) [FAVOR]

Ge	33:10	now that you have received me f.	8354
Ex	3:21	I will make the Egyptians f disposed toward this people,	928+2834+6524
	11: 3	The LORD made the Egyptians f disposed toward the people,	928+2834+6524
	12:36	The LORD had made the Egyptians f disposed toward the people,	928+2834+6524
1Sa	20:12	If he is f disposed toward you,	3201
1Ki	22:13	with theirs, and speak f."	3202
2Ch	18:12	with theirs, and speak f."	3202

FAVORED (6) [FAVOR]

Dt	33: 8	and Urim belong to the man you f.	2883
	33:24	let him be f by his brothers,	8354
Ps	30: 7	O LORD, when you f me,	8356
Eze	32:19	Say to them, 'Are you more f than others?	5838
Lk	1:28	"Greetings, you who are highly f!	5923
	1:43	But why am I so f,	NIG

FAVORITE (1) [FAVOR]

SS	6: 9	the f of the one who bore her.	1338

FAVORITISM (9) [FAVOR]

Ex	23: 3	do not show f to a poor man in his lawsuit.	2075
Lev	19:15	do not show partiality to the poor or f	2075+7156
Ac	10:34	how true it is that God does not show f	1639+4720
Ro	2:11	For God does not show f.	1639+4721
Eph	6: 9	and there is no f with him.	4721
Col	3:25	and there is no f.	4721
1Ti	5:21	and to do nothing out of f.	2848+4680
Jas	2: 1	as believers in our glorious Lord Jesus Christ, don't show f.	1877+4721
	2: 9	But if you show f, you sin	4719

FAVORS (6) [FAVOR]

2Sa	20:11	and said, "Whoever f Joab, and whoever is	2911
Ecc	9: 7	for it is now that God f what you do.	8354
Jer	3:13	you have scattered your f to foreign gods	2006
Eze	16:15	You lavished your f on anyone who passed	9373
	16:33	from everywhere for your illicit f.	9373
	16:34	runs after you for your f.	339+2388

FAWN (2) [FAWNS]

Job	39: 1	Do you watch when the doe bears her f?	NIH
Jer	14: 5	the doe in the field deserts her newborn f	AIT

FAWNS (4) [FAWN]

Ge	49:21	a doe set free that bears beautiful f.	611
SS	4: 5	Your two breasts are like two f,	6762
	4: 5	like twin f of a gazelle that browse among	NIH
	7: 3	Your breasts are like two f,	6762

FEAR (260) [AFRAID, FEARED, FEARFUL, FEARFULLY, FEARING, FEARLESSLY, FEARS, FEARSOME, FRIGHT, FRIGHTEN, FRIGHTENED, FRIGHTENING, GOD-FEARING]

Ge	9: 2	The f and dread of you will fall upon all	4616
	20:11	'There is surely no f of God in this place,	3711
	22:12	Now I know that you f God,	3710
	31:42	the God of Abraham and the F of Isaac,	7065
	31:53	So Jacob took an oath in the name of the F	7065
	32: 7	In great f and distress Jacob divided	3707
	42:18	"Do this and you will live, for I f God:	3710
Ex	9:30	that you and your officials still do not f	3707
	18:21	men who f God,	3710
	20:18	they trembled with f.	3707
	20:20	the f of God will be with you to keep you	3711
Lev	19:14	but f your God.	3707
	25:17	but f your God.	3707
	25:36	but f your God,	3707
	25:43	but f your God.	3707

Dt	2:25	the terror and f of you on all the nations	3711
	5:29	to f me and keep all my commands always,	3707
	6: 2	after them *may* f the LORD your God	3707
	6:13	F the LORD your God,	3707
	6:24	to obey all these decrees and to f	3707
	7:19	the same to all the peoples you now f.	3707
	10:12	the LORD your God ask of you but to f	3707
	10:20	F the LORD your God and serve him.	3707
	11:25	the terror and f of you on the whole land,	4616
	25:18	*they* had no f of God.	3707
	28:10	and *they* will f you.	3707
	31:12	and learn *to* f the LORD your God	3707
	31:13	and learn to f the LORD your God as long	3707
	32:17	gods your fathers *did not* f.	8549
Jos	2: 9	to you and that a **great** f of you has fallen	399
	2: 9	in this country are **melting in** f because	4570
	2:24	the people *are* **melting in** f because of us."	4570
	4:24	and so that *you might* always f	3707
	14: 8	**made** the hearts of the people **melt with** f.	4998
	22:24	We did it for f that some day	1796
	24:14	"Now f the LORD and serve him	3707
Jdg	7: 3	*with* f may turn back	3710
1Sa	12:14	If *you* f the LORD and serve him	3707
	12:24	*to* f the LORD and serve him faithfully	3707
	13: 7	the troops with him *were* **quaking with** f.	3006
	17:24	they all ran from him *in great* f.	3707
	28:20	**filled with** f because of Samuel's words.	
			3707+4394
2Sa	17:10	*will* **melt with** f, for all Israel knows	5022+5022
	23: 3	when he rules in the f *of God*,	3711
1Ki	1:50	But Adonijah, *in* f of Solomon,	3707
	8:40	that *they will* f you all the time they live	3707
	8:43	the earth may know your name and f you,	3707
2Ki	25:26	fled to Egypt for f of the Babylonians.	3707
1Ch	14:17	and the LORD made all the nations f him.	7065
2Ch	6:31	so that *they will* f you and walk	3707
	6:33	the earth may know your name and f you,	3707
	12: 5	in Jerusalem **for** f of Shishak,	4946+7156
	17:10	The f *of the* LORD fell on all	7065
	19: 7	Now let the f *of the* LORD be upon you.	7065
	19: 9	and wholeheartedly in the f *of the* LORD.	3711
	20:29	The f *of God* came upon all the kingdoms	7065
	26: 5	who instructed him in the f *of God*.	3711
Ezr	3: 3	Despite their f of the peoples around them,	399
	10: 3	of those *who* f the commands of our God.	3007
Ne	5: 9	in the f of our God to avoid the reproach	3711
Est	5: 9	that he neither rose nor **showed** f	2316
	8:17	because f of the Jews had seized them.	7065
	9: 3	because f of Mordecai had seized them.	7065
Job	1: 9	"*Does* Job f God for nothing?"	3707
	4:14	f and trembling seized me	7065
	5:21	and *need not* f when destruction comes.	3707
	5:22	and *need not* f the beasts of the earth.	3707
	6:14	though he forsakes the f of the Almighty.	3711
	9:35	Then I would speak up without f of him,	3707
	11:15	you will stand firm and without f.	3707
	19:29	*you should* f the sword yourselves;	1593
	21: 9	Their homes are safe and free from f;	7065
	23:15	when I think of all this, *I* f him.	7064
	28:28	And he said to man, 'The f of the Lord—	3711
	31:23	and **for** f of his splendor I could	4946
	33: 7	No f *of me* should alarm you,	399
	39:22	He laughs at f, afraid of nothing;	7065
	41:33	a creature without f.	3145
Ps	2:11	Serve the LORD with f and rejoice	3711
	3: 6	*I will* not f the tens of thousands drawn	3707
	15: 4	but honors *those who* f the LORD,	3710
	19: 9	f *of the* LORD is pure, enduring forever.	3711
	22:23	You *who* f the LORD, praise him!	3710
	22:25	*those who* f you will I fulfill my vows.	3710
	23: 4	*I will* f no evil, for you are with me;	3707
	25:14	The LORD confides in *those who* f him;	3707
	27: 1	my salvation—whom *shall* I f?	3707
	27: 3	an army besiege me, my heart *will* not f;	3707
	31:19	up for *those who* f you,	3710
	33: 8	*Let* all the earth f the LORD;	3372
	33:18	eyes of the LORD are on *those who* f him,	3710
	34: 7	around *those who* f him,	3710
	34: 9	F the LORD, *you* his saints,	3707
	34: 9	for *those who* f him lack nothing.	3707
	34:11	I will teach you the f of the LORD.	3711
	36: 1	There is no f *of God* before his eyes.	7065
	40: 3	Many will see and f and put their trust	3707
	46: 2	Therefore *we will* not f,	3707
	49: 5	Why *should* I f when evil days come,	3707
	52: 6	The righteous will see and f;	3707
	55: 5	F and trembling have beset me;	3711
	55:19	and *have* no f *of God*.	3707
	60: 4	But for *those who* f you,	3710
	61: 5	the heritage of *those who* f your name.	3710
	64: 4	they shoot at him suddenly, without f.	3707
	64: 9	All mankind *will* f;	3707
	65: 8	*Those* living far away f your wonders;	3707
	66:16	all you *who* f God;	3710
	67: 7	and all the ends of the earth *will* f him.	3707
	85: 9	his salvation is near *those who* f him,	3710
	86:11	that I *may* f your name.	3707
	90:11	For your wrath is as great as the f	3711
	91: 5	*You will* not f the terror of night,	3707
	102:15	The nations *will* f the name of	3707
	103:11	so great is his love for *those who* f him;	3710
	103:13	on *those who* f him;	3710
	103:17	with *those who* f him, and his righteousness	3710
	111: 5	He provides food for *those who* f him;	3710
	111:10	The f *of the* LORD is the beginning	3711
	112: 7	*He will* **have** no f of bad news;	3707
	112: 8	His heart is secure, *he will* **have** no f;	3707

Ps	115:11	You *who* f him, trust in the LORD—	3710
	115:13	he will bless *those who* f the LORD—	3710
	118: 4	Let *those who* f the LORD say:	3710
	119:63	I am a friend to all who f you,	3707
	119:74	May *those who* f you rejoice	3710
	119:79	May *those who* f you turn to me,	3710
	119:120	My flesh trembles in f *of you*;	7065
	128: 1	Blessed are all *who* f the LORD,	3710
	135:20	you *who* f him, praise the LORD.	3710
	145:19	He fulfills the desires of *those who* f him;	3710
	147:11	the LORD delights in *those who* f him,	3710
Pr	1: 7	The f *of the* LORD is the beginning	3711
	1:29	and did not choose to f the LORD,	3711
	1:33	be at ease, without f *of harm*."	7065
	2: 5	you will understand the f *of the* LORD	3711
	3: 7	f the LORD and shun evil.	3707
	3:25	*Have* no f of sudden disaster or of the ruin	3707
	8:13	To f the LORD is to hate evil;	3711
	9:10	"The f *of the* LORD is the beginning	3711
	10:27	The f *of the* LORD adds length to life,	3711
	14:27	The f *of the* LORD is a fountain of life,	3711
	15:16	with the f *of the* LORD than great wealth	3711
	15:33	f *of the* LORD teaches a man wisdom,	3711
	16: 6	the f *of the* LORD a man avoids evil.	3711
	19:23	The f *of the* LORD leads to life:	3711
	22: 4	and the f *of the* LORD bring wealth	3711
	23:17	always be zealous for the f *of the* LORD.	3711
	24:21	F the LORD and the king, my son,	3707
	29:25	F *of man* will prove to be a snare,	3010
	31:21	it snows, *she has* no f for her household;	3707
Ecc	8:13	Yet because the wicked do not f God,	3710
	12:13	F God and keep his commandments,	3707
Isa	7:25	you will no longer go there *for* f	3711
	8:12	*do not* f what they fear, and do not dread it.	3707
	8:12	do not fear *what they* f, and do not dread it.	4616
	8:13	he is the one you are to f,	4616
	11: 2	of knowledge and of the f *of the* LORD—	3711
	11: 3	and he will delight in the f *of the* LORD.	3711
	19:16	*with* f at the uplifted hand that	7064
	21: 4	My heart falters, f makes me tremble;	7146
	33: 6	f *of the* LORD is the key to this treasure.	3711
	35: 4	"Be strong, *do not* f;	3707
	41: 5	The islands have seen it and f;	3707
	41:10	So *do not* f, for I am with you;	3707
	41:13	*Do not* f; I will help you.	3707
	41:23	we will be dismayed and **filled with** f.	3707
	43: 1	"F not, for I have redeemed you;	3707
	51: 7	*Do not* f the reproach of men or be terrified	3707
	51:12	Who are you that *you* f mortal men,	3707
	54: 4	*Do not* f **disgrace**;	4007
	54:14	*you will* have nothing *to* f.	3707
	57:11	that *you do* not f me?	3372
	59:19	*men will* f the name of the LORD,	3707
Jer	3: 8	that her unfaithful sister Judah *had* no f;	3707
	5:22	*Should you* not f me?"	3707
	5:24	'*Let us* f the LORD our God,	3707
	10: 5	*Do not* f them;	3707
	17: 8	*It does* not f when heat comes;	3707
	22:25	to those who seek your life, those you f—	3328
	26:19	*Did* not Hezekiah f the LORD	3707
	26:21	Uriah heard of it and fled in f to Egypt.	3707
	30: 5	'Cries of f are heard—terror, not peace.	3010
	30:10	"'So *do not* f, O Jacob my servant,	3707
	32:39	so that they *will* always f me	3707
	32:40	and I will inspire them to f me,	3711
	36:16	**looked** at each other in f	7064
	36:24	all his attendants who heard all these words	
		showed no f,	7064
	39:17	you will not be handed over to those you f.	3328
	42:11	king of Babylon, whom you now f.	3710
	42:16	the sword you f will overtake you there,	3710
	46:27	*Do not* f, O Jacob my servant;	3707
	46:28	*Do not* f, O Jacob my servant,	3707
La	3:57	and you said, "*Do not* f."	3707
Eze	11: 8	You f the sword, and the sword	2719
	12:18	and shudder in f as you drink your water.	1796
	27:35	and their faces *are* **distorted with** f.	8307
	30:13	and I will spread f throughout the land.	3711
Da	6:26	in every part of my kingdom people must f	10227
Hos	10: 5	in Samaria f for the calf-idol of Beth Aven.	1593
Am	3: 8	The lion has roared—who *will* not f?	3707
Mic	6: 9	and *to* f your name is wisdom—	
	7:17	*they will* **turn in** f to the LORD our God	7064
Na	2:11	*you will* f me and accept correction!'	3707
Zep	3: 7	never again *will you* f any harm.	3707
	3:15	"*Do not* f, O Zion;	3707
	3:16		
Hag	2: 5	my Spirit remains among you. *Do not* f.'	3707
Zec	9: 5	Ashkelon will see it and f;	3372
Mal	3: 5	but *do not* f me," says the LORD	3707
Mt	14:26	"It's a ghost," they said, and cried out in f.	5832
Mk	5:33	trembling with f, told him the whole truth.	5828
Lk	1:12	was startled and **was gripped with** f.	2158+5832
	1:50	His mercy extends *to* those who f him,	5828
	1:74	and to enable us to serve him **without** f	925
	8:25	In f and amazement they asked one	5828
	8:37	because they were overcome *with* f.	3489+5832
	12: 5	But I will show you whom *you should* f:	5828
	12: 5	f him who, after the killing of the body,	5828
	12: 5	Yes, I tell you, f him.	5828
	18: 4	though *I don't* f God or care about men,	5828
	23:40	"*Don't* you f God," he said,	5828
Jn	3:20	will not come into the light **for** f that	2671+3590
	7:13	about him for f of the Jews.	5832
	12:42	not confess their faith for f they would	NIG
	20:19	with the doors locked for f of the Jews,	5832
Ac	5: 5	And great f seized all who heard	5832

Ac	5:11	Great f seized the whole church	5832
	7:32	Moses **trembled with** f and did not	1181+1958
	9:31	living *in the* f of the LORD.	5832
	10: 4	Cornelius stared at him in f.	1181+1873
	10:35	from every nation who f him	5828
	19:17	they *were* all **seized with** f,	2158+5832
Ro	3:18	"There is no f of God before their eyes."	5832
	8:15	a spirit that makes you a slave again to f,	5832
	13: 3	Do you want *to be* **free from** f of the one in	
		authority?	3590+5828
1Co	2: 3	I came to you in weakness and f,	5832
	16:10	see to it that he has **nothing to** f while he is	925
2Co	5:11	then, we know what it is to f the Lord,	5832
	7:15	receiving him with f and trembling.	5832
	12:20	I f that there may be quarreling, jealousy,	NIG
Gal	2: 2	**for** f that I was running or had run	3590+4803
	4:11	I f for you, that somehow I have wasted my	5828
Eph	6: 5	Slaves, obey your earthly masters with	
		respect and f,	5571
Php	2:12	continue to work out your salvation with f	5832
Heb	2:15	in slavery *by* their f of death.	5832
	11: 7	in holy f built an ark to save his family.	2326
	12:21	"I am trembling **with** f."	1769
1Pe	1:17	as strangers here in **reverent** f.	5832
	2:17	Love the brotherhood of believers, f God,	5828
	3: 6	and *do* not give way to f.	5828
	3:14	"*Do* not f what they fear;	5828
	3:14	"Do not fear what they f;	5832
1Jn	4:18	There is no f in love.	5832
	4:18	But perfect love drives out f,	5832
	4:18	because f has to do with punishment.	5832
Jude	1:23	to others show mercy, mixed with f—	5832
Rev	14: 7	"F God and give him glory,	5828
	15: 4	Who *will* not f you, O Lord,	5828
	19: 5	you who f him, both small and great!"	5828

FEARED (37) [FEAR]

Ex	1:17	f God and did not do what the king	3707
	1:21	And because the midwives f God,	3707
	9:20	Those officials of Pharaoh who f the word	3707
	14:31	the people f the LORD and put their trust	3707
Dt	9:19	*I* f the anger and wrath of the LORD,	3336
Jos	9:24	So *we* f for our lives because of you,	3707
1Sa	4:13	because his heart f for the ark of God.	2118+3007
	14:26	because they f the oath.	3707
1Ch	16:25	he *is to be* f above all gods.	3707
Ne	7: 2	and f God more than most men do.	3710
Job	1: 1	*he* f God and shunned evil.	3710
	3:25	What *I* f has come upon me;	7064
	31:34	because *I* so f the crowd and so dreaded	6907
Ps	76: 7	You alone *are* *to be* f.	3707
	76: 8	and the land f and was quiet—	3372
	76:11	to the One *to be* f.	4616
	76:12	*he* **is** f by the kings of the earth.	3707
	89: 7	of the holy ones God is greatly f;	6907
	96: 4	he *is to be* f above all gods.	3707
	119:38	so that you *may be* f.	3711
	130: 4	therefore *you* are f.	3372
Isa	18: 2	to a people f far and wide,	3707
	18: 7	from a people f far and wide,	3707
	57:11	so dreaded and f that you have been false	3707
Da	5:19	of every language dreaded and f him.	10167
Jnh	1:16	At this the men greatly f the LORD,	3707+3711
Hab	1: 7	They are a f and dreaded people;	398
Hag	1:12	And the people f the LORD.	3707
Mal	1:14	my name *is to be* f among the nations.	3707
	3:16	Then *those who* f the LORD talked	3710
	3:16	in his presence concerning *those who* f	3710
Mk	6:20	because Herod f John and protected him,	5828
	11:18	for a way to kill him, for *they* f him,	5828
	11:32	(They f the people,	5828
Lk	18: 2	a judge *who* neither f God nor cared	5828
Jn	19:38	but secretly because he f the Jews.	5832
Ac	5:26	*they* f that the people would stone them.	5832

FEARFUL (7) [FEAR]

Lev	26:36	I will make their hearts *so* f in the lands	5322
Dt	28:59	the LORD *will* send f plagues on you	7098
Job	32: 6	that is why I *was* f,	2324
Isa	8:22	and darkness and f gloom,	7442
	35: 4	say to *those with* f hearts, "Be strong, do	4554
Lk	21:11	and f **events** and great signs from heaven.	5831
Heb	10:27	but only a f expectation of judgment and	5829

FEARFULLY (1) [FEAR]

| Ps | 139:14 | because I am f and wonderfully made; | 3707 |

FEARING (4) [FEAR]

Jos	22:25	might cause ours to stop f the LORD.	3707
Ac	27:17	F that they would run aground on	3590+5828
	27:29	F that we would be dashed against	3590+5828
Heb	11:27	not f the king's anger;	5828

FEARLESSLY (4) [FEAR]

Ac	9:27	in Damascus he *had* **preached** f in the name	4245
Eph	6:19	so that I will **make** known the mystery of	4244
	6:20	Pray that I may declare it f, as I should.	4245
Php	1:14	the word of God more courageously and f.	925

FEARS (15) [FEAR]

Job	1: 8	a man *who* f God and shuns evil."	3710
	2: 3	a man *who* f God and shuns evil.	3710
Ps	25:12	Who, then, is the man *that* f the LORD?	3710

Ps	34: 4	he delivered me from all my **f**,	4475
	112: 1	Blessed is the man *who* **f** the LORD,	3707
	128: 4	Thus is the man blessed *who* **f** the LORD.	3710
Pr	14: 2	He whose walk is upright **f** the LORD,	3707
	14:16	A wise man **f** the LORD and shuns evil,	3707
	14:26	*He who* **f** the LORD has a secure fortress,	3711
	28:14	the man *who* always **f** the LORD,	7064
	31:30	a woman *who* **f** the LORD is to be praised.	3710
Ecc	7:18	*man who* **f** God will avoid all [extremes].	3710
Isa	50:10	Who among you **f** the LORD and obeys	3710
2Co	7: 5	conflicts on the outside, **f** within.	5832
1Jn	4:18	The one who **f** is not made perfect in love.	5828

FEARSOME (1) [FEAR]

Job	41:14	ringed about with his **f** teeth?	399

FEAST (97) [FEASTED, FEASTING, FEASTS]

Ge	21: 8	on the day Isaac was weaned Abraham held a great **f**.	5492
	26:30	Isaac then made a **f** for them,	5492
	29:22	the people of the place and gave a **f**.	5492
	40:20	and he gave a **f** for all his officials.	5492
Ex	12:17	**F** of Unleavened Bread,	5174
	23:15	"Celebrate the **F** of Unleavened Bread;	2504
	23:16	the **F** of Harvest with the firstfruits of	2504
	23:16	the **F** of Ingathering at the end of the year,	2504
	34:18	"Celebrate the **F** *of* Unleavened Bread.	2504
	34:22	the **F** *of* Weeks with the firstfruits of	2504
	34:22	the **F** *of* Ingathering at the turn of the year.	2504
	34:25	of the sacrifice from the Passover **F** remain	2504
Lev	23: 6	the LORD's **F** of Unleavened Bread	2504
	23:34	the LORD's **F** of Tabernacles begins,	2504
Nu	28:26	of new grain during the **F** of Weeks,	8651
Dt	16:10	**F** of Weeks to the LORD your God	2504
	16:13	the **F** of Tabernacles for seven days	2504
	16:14	Be joyful at your **F**—	2504
	16:15	For seven days **celebrate the F** to	2510
	16:16	at the **F** of Unleavened Bread,	2504
	16:16	of Unleavened Bread, the **F** of Weeks and	2504
	16:16	of Weeks and the **F** *of* Tabernacles.	2504
	31:10	during the **F** *of* Tabernacles,	2504
	33:19	they will **f** on the abundance of the seas,	3567
Jdg	14:10	And Samson made a **f** there,	5492
	14:12	the answer within the seven days of the **f**,	5492
	14:17	She cried the whole seven days of the **f**.	5492
2Sa	3:20	David prepared a **f** for him and his men.	5492
1Ki	1:41	as they were finishing their **f**.	430
	3:15	Then he gave a **f** for all his court.	5492
2Ki	6:23	So *he* **prepared** a great **f** for them,	4127+4130
2Ch	8:13	the **F** of Unleavened Bread,	2504
	8:13	of Unleavened Bread, the **F** *of* Weeks and	2504
	8:13	of Weeks and the **F** *of* Tabernacles.	2504
	30:13	to celebrate the **F** *of* Unleavened Bread in	2504
	30:21	the **F** of Unleavened Bread for seven days	2504
	35:17	the **F** *of* Unleavened Bread for seven days.	2504
Ezr	3: 4	they celebrated the **F** *of* Tabernacles with	2504
	6:22	with joy the **F** *of* Unleavened Bread.	2504
Ne	8:14	in booths during the **f** of the seventh month	2504
	8:18	They celebrated the **F** for seven days,	2504
Job	39:30	His young ones **f** on blood,	6633
Ps	22:29	the rich of the earth *will* **f** and worship;	430
	36: 8	*They* **f** on the abundance of your house;	8115
	81: 3	on the day of our **F**;	2504
Pr	5:10	lest strangers **f** on your wealth	8425
	15:15	but the cheerful heart has a continual **f**.	5492
Ecc	5:11	to the owner except to **f** his eyes on them?	8021
	10:16	and whose princes **f** in the morning.	430
	10:19	A **f** is made for laughter,	4312
Isa	25: 6	a **f** of rich food for all peoples, a banquet	5492
	58:14	of the land and *to* **f** on the inheritance	430
Jer	51:39	a **f** *for* them and make them drunk, so	5492
La	2: 7	as on the day of an **appointed f**.	4595
	2:22	"As you summon to a **f** day,	4595
Eze	45:21	a **f** *lasting* seven days,	2504
	45:23	of the **F** he is to provide seven bulls	2504
	45:25	" 'During the seven days of the **F**,	2504
Zec	14:16	and to celebrate the **F** *of* Tabernacles.	2504
	14:18	up to celebrate the **F** *of* Tabernacles,	2504
	14:19	up to celebrate the **F** *of* Tabernacles.	2504
Mt	8:11	take *their* **places at the f** with Abraham,	369
	26: 5	"But not during the **f**," they said,	2038
	26:17	**F** of Unleavened Bread,	109
	27:15	Now it was the governor's custom at the **F**	2038
Mk	14: 1	**F** of Unleavened Bread	109
	14: 2	"But not during the **F**," they said,	2038
	14:12	**F** of Unleavened Bread,	109
	15: 6	Now it was the custom at the **F** to release	2038
Lk	2:41	to Jerusalem *for* the **F** of the Passover.	2038
	2:42	they went up to the **F**,	2038
	2:43	After the **F** was over,	NIG
	13:29	take *their* **places at the f** in the kingdom	369
	14: 8	"When someone invites you to a **wedding f**,	1141
	14:15	"Blessed is the man who will eat at the **f** in	756
	15:23	Let's **have a f** and celebrate.	2266
	22: 1	Now the **F** of Unleavened Bread,	2038
Jn	2:23	he was in Jerusalem at the Passover **F**,	2038
	4:45	in Jerusalem at the **Passover F**,	2038
	5: 1	Jesus went up to Jerusalem for a **f** of	2038
	6: 4	The Jewish Passover **F** was near.	2038
	7: 2	the Jewish **F** of Tabernacles was near,	2038
	7: 8	You go to the **F**.	2038
	7: 8	I am not yet going up to this **F**,	2038
	7:10	after his brothers had left for the **F**,	2038
	7:11	at the **F** the Jews were watching for him	2038

Jn	7:14	until halfway through the **F** did Jesus go up	2038
	7:37	On the last and greatest day of the **F**,	2038
	10:22	came the **F** of Dedication at Jerusalem.	1589
	11:56	Isn't he coming to the **F** at all?"	2038
	12:12	the great crowd that had come for the **F**	2038
	12:20	up to worship at the **F**.	2038
	13: 1	It was just before the Passover **F**.	2038
	13:29	to buy what was needed for the **F**,	2038
Ac	12: 3	**F** of Unleavened Bread.	109
	20: 6	**F** of Unleavened Bread,	109+2465
2Pe	2:13	reveling in their pleasures *while they* **f** with	5307

FEASTED (1) [FEAST]

Ge	43:34	So *they* **f** and drank freely with him.	9272

FEASTING (13) [FEAST]

Est	8:17	with **f** and celebrating.	5492
	9:17	and made it a day of **f** and joy.	5492
	9:18	and made it a day of **f** and joy.	5492
	9:19	of the month of Adar as a day of joy and **f**,	5492
	9:22	of **f** and joy and giving presents of food	5492
Job	1: 5	When a period of **f** had run its course,	5492
	1:13	and daughters *were* **f** and drinking wine at	430
	1:18	and daughters *were* **f** and drinking wine at	430
Pr	17: 1	with peace and quiet than a house full of **f**,	2285
Ecc	7: 2	of **f**, for death is the destiny of every man;	5492
Jer	16: 8	a house where there is **f** and sit down to eat	5492
Am	6: 7	your **f** and lounging will end.	5301
Zec	7: 6	*were* you not just **f** *for* yourselves?	430+2256+9272

FEASTS (30) [FEAST]

Lev	23: 2	'These are my **appointed f**,	4595
	23: 2	the **appointed f**—'These are	4595
	23: 4	" 'These are the LORD's **appointed f**,	4595
	23:37	(" 'These are the LORD's **appointed f**,	4595
	23:44	to the Israelites the **appointed f** of	4595
Nu	10:10	your **appointed f** and New Moon	4595
	29:39	for the LORD at your **appointed f:**	4595
1Ch	23:31	at New Moon festivals and at **appointed f**.	4595
2Ch	2: 4	at the **appointed f** *of* the LORD our God.	4595
	8:13	New Moons and the three annual **f**—	4595
	31: 3	New Moons and **appointed f** as written in	4595
Ezr	3: 5	the sacrifices for all the **appointed** sacred **f**	4595
Ne	10:33	New Moon festivals and **appointed f;**	4595
Job	1: 4	to take turns holding **f** in their homes,	5492
	24:20	womb forgets them, the worm **f** on them;	5517
Isa	1:14	and your **appointed f** my soul hates.	4595
La	1: 4	for no one comes to her **appointed f**.	4595
	2: 6	LORD has made Zion forget her **appointed f**	4595
Eze	36:38	at Jerusalem during her **appointed f**.	4595
	44:24	and my decrees for all my **appointed f**,	4595
	45:17	the **appointed f** *of* the house of Israel.	4595
	46: 9	before the LORD at the **appointed f**,	4595
	46:11	" 'At the festivals and the **appointed f**,	4595
Hos	2:11	all her **appointed f**.	4595
	9: 5	on the day of your **appointed f**,	4595
	9: 5	as in the days of your **appointed f**.	4595
Am	5:21	"I hate, I despise your **religious f;**	2504
	8:10	I will turn your **religious f** into mourning	2504
Zep	3:18	the **appointed f** I will remove from you;	4595
Jude	1:12	These men are blemishes at your **love f**,	27

FEAT (1)

2Ki	8:13	a mere dog, accomplish such a **f?**"	1524+1821

FEATHERS (6)

Job	39:13	with the pinions and **f** of the stork.	5681
	39:18	**spreads** *her* **f to run**,	928+2021+5257+5294
Ps	68:13	its **f** with shining gold."	89
	91: 4	He will cover you with his **f**,	89
Eze	17: 3	A great eagle with powerful wings, long **f**	88
Da	4:33	until his hair grew like the **f** of an eagle	NIH

FEATURES (3)

1Sa	16:12	with a fine appearance and handsome **f**.	8024
Est	2: 7	Esther, was lovely in form and **f**,	5260
Job	38:14	its **f** stand out like those of a garment.	NIH

FED (10) [FEED]

Dt	32:13	on the heights of the land and **f** him *with*	430
Jdg	19:21	into his house and **f** his donkeys.	1176
Ps	80: 5	*You have* **f** them *with* the bread of tears;	430
	81:16	you *would be* **f** with the finest of wheat;	430
Da	4:12	from it every creature *was* **f**.	10226
Hos	13: 6	When I **f** them, they were satisfied;	5338
Na	2:11	the **place where** they **f** their young,	5337
Lk	6:25	Woe to you who *are* **well f** now,	1855
Php	4:12	whether **well f** or hungry,	5963
Jas	2:16	**keep** warm and **well f**,"	5963

FEE (2)

Nu	22: 7	taking with them the **f for divination**,	7877
Eze	16:33	Every prostitute receives a **f**,	5613

FEEBLE (8) [FEEBLEST]

Ne	4: 2	he said, "What are those **f** Jews doing?	584
Job	4: 3	how you have strengthened **f** hands.	8333
	26: 2	How you have saved the arm that is **f!**	4202+6437
Ps	38: 8	I *am* **f** and utterly crushed;	7028
Isa	16:14	her survivors will be very few and **f**."	3888+4202

Isa	35: 3	Strengthen the **f** hands,	8333
Jer	49:24	Damascus *has become* **f**,	8332
Heb	12:12	strengthen your **f** arms and weak knees.	4223

FEEBLEMINDED (KJV) See TIMID

FEEBLEST (1) [FEEBLE]

Zec	12: 8	that the **f** among them will be like David,	4173

FEED (33) [FED, FEEDING, FEEDS, OVERFED, PASTURE-FED, STALL-FED, WELL-FED]

Ge	42:27	of them opened his sack to get **f**	5028
1Ki	14:11	the birds of the air *will* **f** on those who die	430
	16: 4	the birds of the air *will* **f** on those who die	430
	17: 4	I have ordered the ravens to **f** you there."	3920
	21:24	the birds of the air *will* **f** on those who die	430
Ps	49:14	and death *will* **f** on them.	8286
	80:13	and the creatures of the field **f** on it.	8286
Pr	27:27	of goats' milk to **f** you and your family and	4312
Isa	5:17	lambs *will* **f** *among* the ruins of the rich.	430
	9:20	Each *will* **f** on the flesh	430
	9:21	Manasseh will **f** on Ephraim, and Ephraim	NIH
	11: 7	The cow *will* **f** with the bear,	8286
	18: 6	the birds will **f** on them all summer,	6584
	49: 9	"They will **f** beside the roads	8286
	61: 6	*You will* **f** on the wealth of nations,	430
	65:25	The wolf and the lamb *will* **f** together,	8286
Eze	34:10	the shepherds *can* no longer **f** themselves.	8286
	34:14	and there *they will* **f** *in* a rich pasture on	8286
	34:18	for you *to* **f** on the good pasture?	8286
	34:19	*Must* my flock **f** on	8286
Hos	4: 8	*They* **f** on the sins of my people	430
	9: 2	and winepresses *will* not **f** the people;	8286
	11: 4	from their neck and bent down *to* **f** them.	430
Mic	7:14	Let them **f** in Bashan and Gilead as	8286
Zec	11:16	or heal the injured, or **f** the healthy,	3920
Mt	15:33	in this remote place to **f** such a crowd?"	5963
	25:37	when did we see you hungry and **f** you,	5555
Mk	8: 4	in this remote place can anyone get enough bread to **f** them?"	5963
Lk	15:15	who sent him to his fields *to* **f** pigs.	1081
Jn	21:15	Jesus said, "**F** my lambs."	1081
	21:17	Jesus said, "**F** my sheep.	1081
Ro	12:20	"If your enemy is hungry, **f** him;	6039
Jude	1:12	shepherds who **f** only themselves.	NIG

FEEDING (4) [FEED]

Dt	8: 3	to hunger and then **f** you *with* manna,	430
Mt	8:30	from them a large herd of pigs was **f**.	1081
Mk	5:11	of pigs was **f** on the nearby hillside.	1081
Lk	8:32	A large herd of pigs was **f** there on	1081

FEEDS (10) [FEED]

Job	40:15	with you and *which* **f** on grass like an ox.	430
Pr	15:14	but the mouth of a fool **f** on folly.	8286
Isa	44:20	*He* **f** on ashes,	8286
Hos	12: 1	Ephraim **f** on the wind;	8286
Mic	3: 5	if one **f** them, they proclaim 'peace';	928+5966+9094
Mt	6:26	and yet your heavenly Father **f** them.	5555
Lk	12:24	no storeroom or barn; yet God **f** them.	5555
Jn	6:57	one who **f** on me will live because of me.	5592
	6:58	he who **f** on this bread will live forever."	5592
Eph	5:29	but *he* **f** and cares for it,	1763

FEEL (19) [FEELING, FEELINGS, FEELS, FELT]

Ge	41:55	When all Egypt *began to* **f the famine**,	8279
Jdg	16:26	where I *can* **f** the pillars that support	4630
1Sa	16:16	and you *will* **f better**."	3201
	16:23	he *would* **f** better,	3201
2Ki	9:15	Jehu said, "If this is the way you **f**,	5883
Ps	58: 9	Before your pots *can* **f** [the heat of]	1067
	115: 7	but cannot **f**, feet, but they cannot walk;	4630
Pr	23:35	They beat me, but *I don't* **f** it!	3359
Isa	32: 9	you daughters *who* **f secure**,	1053
	32:10	a year you *who* **f secure** will tremble;	1053
	32:11	shudder, you daughters *who* **f secure!**	1053
Da	8:25	When *they* **f secure**,	8932
	11:21	the kingdom when its people **f secure**,	8932
	11:24	When the richest provinces **f secure**,	8932
Am	6: 1	and *to* you *who* **f secure** on Mount Samaria	1053
Zec	1:15	with the nations that I **f secure**,	8633
2Co	11:29	Who is weak, and *I do* not **f weak?**	820
Php	1: 7	It is right for me *to* **f** this way about all	5858
2Th	3:14	in order that *he may* **f** ashamed.	1956

FEELING (2) [FEEL]

Job	24:23	He may let them rest in a **f** of security,	1055
Isa	59:10	**f** our **way** like men without eyes.	1779

FEELINGS (2) [FEEL]

Nu	5:14	and if **f** of jealousy come over her husband	8120
	5:30	or when **f** of jealousy come over a man	8120

FEELS (3) [FEEL]

Ex	23: 9	you yourselves know **how it f** to be aliens,	5883
Job	14:22	*He* **f** but *the* **pain** of his own body	3872
1Co	7:36	along in years and he **f** he ought to marry,	NIG

FEET (281) [FOOT]

Ge	6:15	The ark is to be **450 f** long,	564+4395+8993
	6:15	**75 f** wide and 45 feet high.	564+2822
	6:15	75 feet wide and **45 f** high.	564+8993
	7:20	to a depth of more than **twenty f.**	564+2822+6926
	8: 9	dove could find no place to set its **f**	4090+8079
	18: 4	and then you may all wash your **f** and rest	8079
	19: 2	You can wash your **f** and spend the night	8079
	24:32	water for him and his men to wash their **f.**	8079
	43:24	to wash their **f** and provided fodder	8079
	49:10	nor the ruler's staff from between his **f,**	8079
	49:33	he drew his **f** up into the bed,	8079
Ex	4:25	and touched [Moses'] **f** with it.	8079
	12:11	on your **f** and your staff in your hand.	8079
	24:10	Under his **f** was something like	8079
	25:12	for it and fasten them to its four **f,**	7193
	29:20	and on the big toes of their right **f,**	8079
	30:19	and his sons are to wash their hands and **f**	8079
	30:21	they shall wash their hands and **f** so	8079
	37: 3	for it and fastened them to its four **f,**	7193
	40:31	to wash their hands and **f.**	8079
Lev	8:24	and on the big toes of their right **f,**	8079
	11:42	or walks on all fours or on many **f;**	8079
Nu	11:31	the camp to about **three f** above the ground,	564
	35: 4	will extend out **fifteen hundred f**	547+564
	35: 5	**three thousand f** on the east side,	547+564
Dt	1:36	and his descendants the land he set his **f**	2005
	3:11	and was **more than thirteen f** long	564+9596
	3:11	and **six f** wide.	564+752
	8: 4	not wear out and your **f** did not swell	8079
	22: 4	**get it to its f.**	7756+7756
	28:35	the soles of your **f** to the top of your head.	8079
	29: 5	nor did the sandals on your **f.**	8079
	33: 3	At your **f** they all bow down,	8079
	33:24	and let him bathe his **f** in oil.	8079
Jos	3:15	and their **f** touched the water's edge,	8079
	4:18	No sooner had they set their **f** on	4090+8079
	9: 5	on their **f** and wore old clothes.	8079
	10:24	"Come here and put your **f** on the necks	8079
	10:24	So they came forward and placed their **f**	8079
	14: 9	on which your **f** have walked will	8079
Jdg	5:27	At her **f** he sank, he fell; there he lay.	8079
	5:27	At her **f** he sank, he fell;	8079
	19:21	After they had washed their **f,**	8079
Ru	3: 4	Then go and uncover his **f** and lie down.	5274
	3: 7	uncovered his **f** and lay down.	5274
	3: 8	and discovered a woman lying at his **f.**	5274
	3:14	So she lay at his **f** until morning,	5274
1Sa	2: 9	He will guard the **f** of his saints,	8079
	14:13	using his hands and **f,**	8079
	17: 4	He was **over nine f** tall.	564+2256+2455+9252
	25:24	She fell at his **f** and said:	8079
	25:41	and wash the **f** of my master's servants."	8079
2Sa	2: 9	your **f** were not fettered.	8079
	4: 4	of Saul had a son who was lame in **both f.**	8079
	4:12	They cut off their hands and **f** and hung	8079
	9: 3	he is crippled in **both f."**	8079
	9:13	and he was crippled in **both f.**	8079
	11: 8	"Go down to your house and wash your **f."**	8079
	19:24	of his **f** or trimmed his mustache	8079
	22:10	dark clouds were under his **f.**	8079
	22:34	He makes my **f** like the **f** of a deer;	8079
	22:34	He makes my feet like the **f** of a deer;	NIH
	22:39	they fell beneath my **f.**	8079
	22:40	you made my adversaries bow **at** my **f.**	9393
1Ki	2: 5	around his waist and the sandals on his **f**	8079
	5: 3	the LORD put his enemies under his **f.**	4090+8079
	15:23	however, his **f** became diseased.	8079
2Ki	4:27	she took hold of his **f.**	8079
	4:37	fell at his **f** and bowed to the ground.	8079
	9:35	her **f** and her hands.	8079
	13:21	the man came to life and stood up on his **f.**	8079
	14:13	section **about six hundred f** long.	564+752+4395
	19:24	With the soles of my **f** I have dried up all	7193
	21: 8	the **f** of the Israelites wander from	8079
	25:17	Each pillar was **twenty-seven f** high.	564+6926+9046
	25:17	**four and a half f** high	564+8993
1Ch	11:23	**seven and a half f** tall.	564+928+2021+2822
	28: 2	King David rose to his **f** and said:	8079
2Ch	3:13	They stood on their **f,** facing the main hall.	8079
	16:12	with a disease in his **f.**	8079
	25:23	section **about six hundred f** long.	564+752+4395
	33: 8	not again make the **f** of the Israelites leave	8079
Ezr	6: 3	**ninety f** high and ninety feet wide,	10039+10749
	6: 3	ninety feet high and **ninety f** wide,	10039+10749
Ne	9:21	nor did their **f** become swollen.	8079
Est	5:14	"Have a gallows built, **seventy-five f** high,	564+2822
	7: 9	"A gallows **seventy-five f** high stands	564+2822
	8: 3	falling at his **f** and weeping.	8079
Job	2: 7	with painful sores from the soles of his **f** to	8079
	9:13	the cohorts of Rahab cowered **at** his **f.**	9393
	12: 5	as the fate of those whose **f** are slipping.	8079
	13:27	You fasten my **f** in shackles;	8079
	13:27	by putting marks on the soles of my **f,**	8079
	18: 8	His **f** thrust him into a net and he wanders	8079
	23:11	My **f** have closely followed his steps;	8079
	29: 8	and the old men rose to **their f,**	6641
	29:15	I was eyes to the blind and **f** to the lame.	8079
	30:12	they lay snares for my **f,**	8079
	33:11	He fastens my **f** in shackles;	8079
Ps	8: 6	you put everything under his **f:**	8079
	9:15	**f** are caught in the net they have hidden.	8079
	17: 5	my **f** have not slipped.	7193
	18: 9	dark clouds were under his **f.**	8079

Ps	18:33	He makes my **f** like the feet of a deer;	8079
	18:33	He makes my feet like the **f** of a deer;	NIH
	18:38	they fell beneath my **f.**	8079
	18:39	you made my adversaries bow **at** my **f.**	9393
	22:16	they have pierced my hands and my **f.**	8079
	25:15	only he will release my **f** from the snare.	8079
	26:12	My **f** stand on level ground;	8079
	31: 8	over to the enemy but have set my **f** in	8079
	37:31	his **f** do not slip.	892
	40: 2	he set my **f** on a rock and gave me	892
	44:18	our **f** had not strayed from your path.	892
	45: 5	let the nations fall beneath your **f.**	NIH
	47: 3	peoples under our **f.**	8079
	56:13	from death and my **f** from stumbling,	8079
	57: 6	They spread a net for my **f—**	7193
	58:10	when they bathe their **f** in the blood of	7193
	66: 9	he has preserved our lives and kept our **f**	8079
	68:23	that you may plunge your **f** in the blood	7272
	73: 2	But as for me, my **f** had almost slipped;	7272
	105:18	They bruised his **f** with shackles,	8079
	110: 1	a footstool for your **f."**	8079
	115: 7	but cannot feel, **f,** but they cannot walk;	8079
	116: 8	my eyes from tears, my **f** from stumbling,	8079
	119:101	I have kept my **f** from every evil path so	8079
	119:105	Your word is a lamp to my **f** and a light	8079
	122: 2	Our **f** are standing in your gates,	8079
	140: 4	of violence who plan to trip my **f.**	7193
Pr	1:16	for their **f** rush into sin,	8079
	4:26	for your **f** and take only ways that are firm.	8079
	5: 5	Her **f** go down to death;	8079
	6:13	with his **f** and motions with his fingers,	8079
	6:18	**f** that are quick to rush into evil,	8079
	6:28	on hot coals without his **f** being scorched?	8079
	7:11	her **f** never stay at home;	8079
	26: 6	Like cutting off one's **f**	7272
	29: 5	a net for his **f.**	7193
SS	5: 3	I have washed my **f—**	8079
	7: 1	How beautiful your sandaled **f,**	7193
Isa	20: 2	and the sandals from your **f."**	8079
	23: 7	whose **f** have taken her to settle	8079
	26: 6	F trample it down—	8079
	26: 6	the **f** of the oppressed,	8079
	37:25	With the soles of my **f** I have dried up all	7193
	41: 2	by a path his **f** have not traveled before.	8079
	49:23	they will lick the dust at your **f.**	8079
	52: 7	How beautiful on the mountains are the **f**	8079
	58:13	"If you keep your **f** from breaking	8079
	59: 7	Their **f** rush into sin;	8079
	60:13	and I will glorify the place of my **f.**	8079
	60:14	will bow down at your **f** and	4090+8079
Jer	2:25	until your **f** are bare and your throat is dry.	8079
	13:16	before your **f** stumble on	7272
	14:10	they do not restrain their **f.**	8079
	18:22	and have hidden snares for my **f.**	8079
	38:22	Your **f** are sunk in the mud;	8079
La	1:13	a net for my **f** and turned me back.	8079
Eze	1: 7	their **f** were like those of a calf	4090+8079
	2: 1	stand up on your **f** and I will speak to you."	8079
	2: 2	into me and raised me to my **f,**	8079
	3:24	Spirit came into me and raised me to my **f.**	8079
	6:11	and stamp your **f** and cry out "Alas!"	8079
	24:17	and your sandals on your **f;**	8079
	24:23	on your heads and your sandals on your **f.**	8079
	25: 6	and stamped your **f,**	7272
	32: 2	with your **f** and muddying the streams,	7272
	34:18	the rest of your pasture with your **f?**	7272
	34:18	also muddy the rest with your **f?**	7272
	34:19	and drink what you have muddied with your **f?**	8079
	37:10	they came to life and stood up on their **f—**	8079
	43: 7	and the place for the soles of my **f.**	8079
Da	2:33	its **f** partly of iron and partly of baked clay.	10655
	2:34	on its **f** of iron and clay and smashed them.	10655
	2:41	as you saw that the **f** and toes were partly	10655
	3: 1	**ninety f** high and nine feet wide,	10039+10747
	3: 1	ninety feet high and **nine f** wide,	10039+10747
	3:24	King Nebuchadnezzar **leaped to** his **f**	10624
	7: 4	from the ground so that it stood on **two f**	10655
	8:18	Then he touched me and raised me to my **f.**	6642
Na	1: 3	and clouds are the dust of his **f.**	8079
	1:15	the **f** of one who brings good news,	8079
Hab	3:19	he makes my **f** like the feet of a deer,	8079
	3:19	he makes my feet like the **f** of a deer,	NIH
Zec	5: 2	**thirty f** long and fifteen feet wide."	564+928+2021+6929
	5: 2	thirty feet long and **fifteen f** wide."	564+928+2021+6924
	14: 4	On that day his **f** will stand on the Mount	8079
	14:12	while they are still standing on their **f,**	8079
Mal	4: 3	they will be ashes under the soles of your **f**	8079
Mt	7: 6	they may trample them under their **f,**	4546
	10:14	shake the dust off your **f** when you leave	4546
	15:30	and laid them at his **f;** and he healed them.	4546
	18: 8	or crippled than to have two hands or two **f**	4546
	22:44	until I put your enemies under your **f."** '	4546
	28: 9	clasped his **f** and worshiped him.	4546
Mk	5: 4	and broke the **irons on** his **f.**	4267
	5:22	he fell at his **f.**	4546
	5:33	came and **fell at** his **f** and,	4700
	6:11	shake the dust off your **f** when you leave,	4546
	7:25	by an evil spirit came and fell at his **f.**	4546
	9:27	by the hand and lifted him to his **f,**	NIG
	9:45	to enter life crippled than to have two **f** and	4546
	10:49	**On your f!** He's calling you."	1586
	10:50	he **jumped to his f** and came to Jesus.	403
	12:36	until I put your enemies under your **f."** '	4546

Lk	1:79	to guide our **f** into the path of peace."	4546
	7:38	as she stood behind him at his **f** weeping,	4546
	7:38	she began to wet his **f** with her tears.	4546
	7:44	You did not give me any water for my **f,**	4546
	7:44	but she wet my **f** with her tears	4546
	7:45	has not stopped kissing my **f.**	4546
	7:46	but she has poured perfume on my **f.**	4546
	8:28	he cried out and **fell at** his **f,**	4700
	8:35	at Jesus' **f,** dressed and in his right mind;	4546
	8:41	came and fell at Jesus' **f,**	4700
	8:47	came trembling and **fell at** his **f.**	4700
	9: 5	shake the dust off your **f**	4546
	10:11	that sticks to our **f** we wipe off against you.	4546
	10:39	at the Lord's **f** listening to what he said.	4546
	15:22	a ring on his finger and sandals on his **f.**	4546
	17:16	at Jesus' **f** and thanked him—	4546
	20:43	a footstool **for your f.** '	4546
	24:39	Look at my hands and my **f.**	4546
	24:40	he showed them his hands and **f.**	4546
Jn	11: 2	on the Lord and wiped his **f** with her hair.	4546
	11:32	she fell at his **f** and said, "Lord,	4546
	11:44	his hands and **f** wrapped with strips	4546
	12: 3	she poured it on Jesus' **f** and wiped his feet	4546
	12: 3	she poured it on Jesus' **feet** and wiped his **f**	4546
	13: 5	a basin and began to wash his disciples' **f,**	4546
	13: 6	"Lord, are you going to wash my **f?"**	4546
	13: 8	said Peter, "you shall never wash my **f."**	4546
	13: 9	"not just my **f** but my hands and my head	4546
	13:10	who has had a bath needs only to wash his **f**	4546
	13:12	When he had finished washing their **f,**	4546
	13:14	have washed your **f,**	4546
	13:14	you also should wash one another's **f.**	4546
Ac	2:35	a footstool **for your f.** '	4546
	3: 7	the man's **f** and ankles became strong.	1000
	3: 8	**He** jumped **to his f** and began to walk.	2705
	4:35	and put it at the apostles' **f,**	4546
	4:37	the money and put it at the apostles' **f.**	4546
	5: 2	the rest and put it at the apostles' **f.**	4546
	5: 9	**f** of the men who buried your husband are at the door,	4546
	5:10	At that moment she fell down at his **f**	4546
	7:58	the witnesses laid their clothes at the **f** of	4546
	9:41	**helped** her **to her f.**	482
	10:25	Cornelius met him and fell at his **f**	4546
	13:51	the dust from their **f** in protest against them	4546
	14: 8	In Lystra there sat a man crippled in his **f,**	4546
	14:10	"Stand up on your **f!"**	4546
	16:24	in the inner cell and fastened their **f** in	4546
	21:11	tied his own hands and **f** with it and said,	4546
	26:16	'Now get up and stand on your **f.**	4546
	27:28	**a hundred and twenty f** deep.	1633+3976
	27:28	and found it was **ninety f** deep.	1278+3976
Ro	3:15	"Their **f** are swift to shed blood;	4546
	10:15	the **f** of those who bring good news!"	4546
	16:20	of peace will soon crush Satan under your **f.**	4546
1Co	12:21	And the head cannot say to the **f,**	4546
	15:25	until he has put all his enemies under his **f.**	4546
	15:27	For he "has put everything under his **f."**	4546
Eph	1:22	under his **f** and appointed him to be head	4546
	6:15	and with your **f** fitted with the readiness	4546
1Ti	5:10	washing the **f** of the saints,	4546
Heb	1:13	a footstool **for your f"?**	4546
	2: 8	and put everything under his **f."**	4546
	12:13	"Make level paths **for your f,"**	4546
Jas	2: 3	or "Sit on the floor by my **f,"**	5711
Rev	1:13	**a robe reaching down to** his **f**	4468
	1:15	His **f** were like bronze glowing in	4546
	1:17	I fell at his **f** as though dead.	4546
	2:18	and whose **f** are like burnished bronze.	4546
	3: 9	and fall down at your **f** and acknowledge	4546
	11:11	and they stood on their **f,**	4546
	12: 1	with the sun, with the moon under her **f**	4546
	13: 2	but had **f** like those of a bear and a mouth	4546
	19:10	At this I fell at his **f** to worship him.	4546
	22: 8	I fell down to worship at the **f** of	4546

FEIGN, FEIGNED (Anglicized, KJV) See PRETEND, PRETENDED

FELIX (10)

Ac	23:24	that he may be taken safely to Governor **F."**	5772
	23:26	**To** His Excellency, Governor **F:** Greetings.	5772
	24: 2	Tertullus presented his case before **F:**	NIG
	24: 3	most excellent **F,** we acknowledge this	5772
	24:22	Then **F,** who was well acquainted with	5772
	24:24	Several days later **F** came	5772
	24:25	**F** was afraid and said,	5772
	24:27	**F** was succeeded by Porcius Festus,	5772
	24:27	**F** wanted to grant a favor to the Jews,	5772
	25:14	a man here whom **F** left as a prisoner.	5772

FELL (186) [FALL]

Ge	7:12	And rain **f** on the earth forty days	2118
	14:10	of the men **f** into them and the rest fled to	5877
	15:12	Abram **f** into a deep sleep,	5877
	17: 3	Abram **f** facedown, and God said to him,	5877
	17:17	Abraham **f** facedown;	5877
	35: 5	and the terror of God **f** upon the towns all	2118
	41: 5	He **f asleep** again and had a second dream:	3822
Ex	9:24	hail **f** and lightning flashed back and forth.	2118
Lev	9:24	they shouted for joy and **f** facedown.	5877
Nu	11: 9	**f dead** before the LORD when they made	4637
	14: 5	Then Moses and Aaron **f** facedown in front	5877
	16: 4	When Moses heard this, he **f** facedown.	5877

Nu 16:22 and Aaron **f** facedown and cried out, 5877
16:45 And *they* **f** facedown. 5877
20: 3 when our brothers **f dead** before 1588
20: 6 to the Tent of Meeting and **f** facedown, 5877
22:31 he bowed low and **f facedown.** 678+2556+4200
Dt 9:18 Then once again *I* **f** prostrate before 5877
19: 5 and as he swings his ax to **f** a tree, 4162
Jos 5:14 Then Joshua **f** facedown to the ground 5877
7: 6 and **f** facedown to the ground before 5877
8:25 Twelve thousand men and women **f**, 5877
21:10 because the first lot **f** to them): 2118
22:17 plague **f** on the community of the LORD! 2118
Jdg 4:16 All the troops of Sisera **f** by the sword; 5877
5:27 At her feet he sank, *he* **f**; there he lay. 5877
5:27 At her feet he sank, *he* **f**; 5877
5:27 where he sank, there *he* **f**—dead. 5877
8:11 of Nobah and Jogbehah and **f upon** 5782
9:40 and many **f** wounded in the flight— 5877
13:20 Manoah and his wife **f** with their faces to 5877
16: 4 *he* **f in love with** a woman in the Valley 170
19:26 **f down** *at* the door and lay there 5877
20:31 about thirty men **f** in the open field and on NIH
20:44 Eighteen thousand Benjamites **f**, 5877
20:46 On that day twenty-five thousand
Benjamite swordsmen **f**, 5877
1Sa 4:18 Eli **f** backward off his chair by the side of 5877
11: 7 the terror of the LORD **f** on the people, 5877
14:13 The Philistines **f** before Jonathan, 5877
17:49 and *he* **f** facedown on the ground. 5877
25:24 *She* **f** at his feet and said: 5877
28:20 Immediately Saul **f** full length on 5877
31: 1 and *many* **f** slain on Mount Gilboa. 5877
31: 4 so Saul took his own sword and **f** on it. 5877
31: 5 he too **f** on his sword and died with him. 5877
2Sa 1: 2 *he* **f** to the ground to pay him honor. 5877
1: 4 Many of them **f** and died. 5877
2:16 and *they* **f down** together. 5877
2:23 *He* **f** there and died on the spot. 5877
3:34 *You* **f** as one falls before wicked men." 5877
4: 4 *he* **f** and became crippled. 5877
11:17 some of the men in David's army **f**, 5877
13: 1 Amnon son of David **f in love with** 170
14: 4 **f** with her face to the ground 5877
14:22 Joab **f** with his face to the ground 5877
19:18 *he* **f** prostrate before the king 5877
21: 9 All seven of them **f** together; 5877
21:22 *they* **f** at the hands of David and his men. 5877
22:39 *they* **f** beneath my feet. 5877
1Ki 18:38 the LORD **f** and burned up the sacrifice, 5877
18:39 *they* **f** prostrate and cried, "The LORD— 5877
19: 5 he lay down under the tree and **f asleep.** 3822
2Ki 1:10 Then fire **f** from heaven and consumed 3718
1:12 of God **f** from heaven and consumed him 3718
1:13 up and **f** on his knees before Elijah. 4156
4:37 **f** at his feet and bowed to the ground. 5877
6: 5 the iron axhead **f** into the water. 5877
1Ch 5:22 and many others **f** slain, 5877
10: 1 and *many* **f** slain on Mount Gilboa. 5877
10: 4 so Saul took his own sword and **f** on it. 5877
10: 5 he too **f** on his sword and died. 5877
20: 8 *they* **f** at the hands of David and his men. 5877
21:14 and seventy thousand men of Israel **f dead.** 5877
21:16 clothed in sackcloth, **f** facedown. 5877
24: 7 The first lot **f** to Jehoiarib, 3655
25: 9 **f** to Joseph, his sons and relatives, 3655
26:14 The lot for the East Gate **f** to Shelemiah. 5877
26:14 and the lot for the North Gate **f** to his 3655
26:15 lot for the South Gate **f** to Obed-Edom, NIH
26:15 and the lot for the storehouse **f** to his sons. NIH
26:16 on the upper road **f** to Shuppim and Hosah. NIH
29:20 they bowed low and **f prostrate** before 2556
2Ch 14:13 of Cushites **f** that they could not recover; 5877
17:10 of the LORD **f** on all the kingdoms of 2118
20:18 of Judah and Jerusalem **f down** in worship 5877
Ezr 9: 5 and **f** on my knees 4156
Ne 13:19 When **evening shadows f** on the gates 7511
Est 3: 7 And the lot **f** on the twelfth month, NIH
Job 1:16 "The fire of God **f** from the sky and burned 5877
1:20 Then *he* **f** to the ground in worship 5877
29:22 my words **f gently** on their ears. 5752
Ps 18:38 *they* **f** beneath my feet. 5877
105:44 *they* **f heir** *to* what others had toiled for— 3769
137: 7 the Edomites did on the day Jerusalem **f**. NIH
La 1: 7 When her people **f** into enemy hands, 5877
Eze 1:28 When I saw it, *I* **f** facedown. 5877
3:23 and *I* **f** facedown. 5877
9: 8 *I* **f** facedown, crying out, "Ah, 5877
11:13 *I* **f** facedown and cried out in a loud voice, 5877
31:12 Its boughs **f** on the mountains and in all 5877
39:23 and they all **f** by the sword. 5877
43: 3 and *I* **f** facedown. 5877
44: 4 and *I* **f** facedown. 5877
Da 2:46 Then King Nebuchadnezzar **f** prostrate 10484
3: 7 nations and men of every language **f down** 10484
3:23 firmly tied, **f** into the blazing furnace. 10484
7:20 before which three of *them* **f**— 10484
8:17 I was terrified and **f** prostrate. 5877
10: 9 *I* **f** into a deep sleep, 8101
Jnh 1: 5 he lay down and **f** into a deep sleep. 8101
1: 7 They cast lots and the lot **f** on Jonah. 5877
Mt 7:27 and *it* **f** with a great crash." 4406
13: 4 some **f** along the path, 4406
13: 5 Some **f** on rocky places, 4406
13: 7 Other seed **f** among thorns, 4406
13: 8 Still other seed **f** on good soil, 4406
13:20 The one who **received** the **seed** that **f** 5062
13:22 The one who **received** the **seed** that **f** 5062

Mt 13:23 the one who **received** the **seed** that **f** 5062
17: 6 *they* **f** facedown to the ground, terrified. 4406
18:26 "The servant **f** on his knees before him. 4406
18:29 "His fellow servant **f** to his knees 4406
25: 5 and they all became drowsy and **f asleep.** 2761
26:39 **f** with his face **to the ground** 4406
Mk 3:11 *they* **f down** before him and cried out, 4700
4: 4 some **f** along the path, 4406
4: 5 Some **f** on rocky places, 4406
4: 7 Other seed **f** among thorns, 4406
4: 8 Still other seed **f** on good soil. 4406
5: 6 he **f** on his **knees in front of** 4686
5:22 *he* **f** at his feet 4406
5:33 came and **f** at his **feet** and, 4700
7:25 by an evil spirit came and **f** at his feet. 4700
9:20 He **f** to the ground and rolled around, 4406
10:17 **f** on his **knees before** 1206
10:22 At this man's **face f**. 5145
14:35 *he* **f** to the ground and prayed that 4406
Lk 5: 8 *he* **f** at Jesus' knees and said, 4700
5:12 he **f** with his face to the ground 4406
8: 5 some **f** along the path; 4406
8: 6 Some **f** on rock, and when it came up, 2928
8: 7 Other seed **f** among thorns, 4406
8: 8 Still other seed **f** on good soil. 4406
8:14 The seed that **f** among thorns stands 4406
8:23 As they sailed, *he* **f asleep.** 934
8:28 he cried out and **f** at his **feet,** 4700
8:41 came and **f** at Jesus' feet, 4700
8:47 came trembling and **f** at his **feet.** 4700
10:30 **f** into the **hands** of robbers. 4346
10:36 a neighbor to the man who **f** into the hands 1860
13: 4 when the tower in Siloam **f** on them— 4406
16:21 to eat what **f** from the rich man's table. 4406
Jn 11:32 *she* **f** at his feet and said, "Lord, 4406
18: 6 they drew back and **f** to the ground. 4406
Ac 1:18 there *he* **f headlong,** 1181+4568
1:26 they cast lots, and the lot **f** to Matthias; 4406
5: 5 he **f down** and died. 4406
5:10 At that moment *she* **f down** at his feet 4406
7:60 Then he **f** on his knees and cried out, 5502
7:60 When he had said this, *he* **f asleep.** 3121
9: 4 He **f** to the ground and heard a voice say 4406
9:18 something like scales **f** from Saul's eyes, 674
10:10 he **f** into a **trance.** 1181+1749+2093
10:25 Cornelius met him and **f** at his feet 4406
12: 7 he said, and the chains **f off** Peter's wrists. 1738
13:36 in his own generation, *he* **f asleep;** 3121
16:29 in and **f** trembling **before** Paul and Silas. 4700
19:35 **image, which f from heaven?** 1479
20: 9 *he* **f** to the ground from the third story 4406
22: 7 *I* **f** to the ground and heard a voice say 4406
22:17 I **f** into a trance 1181
26:14 We all **f** to the ground, 2928
Ro 11:22 sternness to those who **f,** 4406
Heb 3:17 whose bodies **f** in the desert? 4406
11:30 By faith the walls of Jericho **f,** 4406
Rev 1:17 *I* **f** at his feet as though dead. 4406
5: 8 and the twenty-four elders **f down** before 4406
5:14 and the elders **f down** and worshiped. 4406
6:13 and the stars in the sky **f** to earth, 4406
7:11 *They* **f down** on their faces before 4406
8:10 **f** from the sky on a third of the rivers and 4406
11:16 **f** on their faces and worshiped God, 4406
16:21 about a hundred pounds each **f** upon men. 2849
19: 4 and the four living creatures **f down** 4406
19:10 At this *I* **f** at his feet to worship him. 4406
22: 8 *I* **f down** to worship at the feet of 4406

FELLED (2) [FALL]

Isa 9:10 the fig trees *have* **been f,** 1548
10:33 The lofty trees *will* **be f,** 1548

FELLER (KJV) See WOODSMAN

FELLING (1) [FALL]

1Ki 5: 6 that we have no one so skilled in **f** timber 4162

FELLOW (91) [FELLOW'S, FELLOWMAN, FELLOWS, FELLOWSHIP]

Ge 9: 5 an accounting for the life of his **f man.** AIT
19: 9 they said, "This **f** came here as an alien, 285ˢ
34:20 their city to speak to their **f townsmen.** 408+6551
Ex 2:13 "Why are you hitting your **f** Hebrew?". 8276
32: 1 As for this **f** Moses who brought us up out 408
32:23 As for this **f** Moses who brought us up out 408
Lev 25:46 not rule over your **f** Israelites ruthlessly. 278
Nu 16:10 He has brought you and all your **f** Levites 278
18: 2 Bring your **f** Levites 278
18: 6 I myself have selected your **f** Levites from 278
Dt 15: 2 the loan he has made to his **f Israelite.** 8276
15: 2 not require payment from his **f Israelite.** 8276
15:12 If a **f** Hebrew, a man or a woman, 278
18: 7 like all his **f** Levites who serve there in 278
Jdg 20:13 not listen to their **f** Israelites. 278
Ru 1:19 All my **f townsmen** know that you 6639+9133
1Sa 10:27 "How can this **f** save us?" AIT
21:15 that you have to bring **this f** here to carry AIT
2Sa 6:20 of his servants as any **vulgar f** would!" AIT
1Ki 22:27 Put **this f** in prison and give him nothing AIT
2Ki 9:11 Why does this **f** send someone to me to AIT
9:11 When Jehu went out to his **f officers,** 123+6269
23: 9 with their **f** priests. 278
1Ch 6:48 Their **f** Levites were assigned to all 278

1Ch 9:19 and his **f** gatekeepers from his family 278
15:12 you and your **f** Levites are 278
16:39 David left Zadok the priest and his **f** priests 278
26:20 Their **f** Levites were in charge of 278
2Ch 18:26 Put **this f** in prison and give him nothing AIT
19:10 from your **f countrymen** who live in 278
28:11 Send back your **f countrymen** you have 278
28:15 to their **f countrymen** at Jericho, 278
31:15 distributing to their **f** priests according 278
35: 5 of the families of your **f countrymen,** 278
35: 6 [the lambs] for your **f countrymen,** 278
35:15 because their **f** Levites made 278
Ezr 3: 2 and his **f** priests and Zerubbabel son 278
6: 6 their **f** officials of that province, 10360
Ne 6: 1 **f** priests went to work and rebuilt 278
Est 10: 3 held in high esteem by his many **f Jews,** 278
Job 30: 5 They were banished from their **f** men, 1569
Jer 34: 9 no one was to hold a **f** Jew in bondage. 278
34:14 of you must free any **f** Hebrew who has
sold himself 278
34:17 for your **f** countrymen. 278
Mt 9: 3 **"This f** is blaspheming!" AIT
12:24 that **this f** drives out demons." AIT
18:28 *of* his **f servants** who owed him 5281
18:29 "His **f servant** fell to his knees 5281
18:33 on your **f servant** just as I had on you?' 5281
24:49 to beat his **f servants** and to eat and drink 5281
26:61 and declared, **"This f** said, 'I am able AIT
26:71 **"This f** was with Jesus of Nazareth." AIT
Mk 2: 7 "Why does **this f** talk like that? AIT
14:69 **"This f** is one of them. AIT
Lk 5:21 "Who is **this f** who speaks blasphemy? AIT
14:10 in the presence of all your **f guests.** 5263
14:30 'This **f** began to build and was not able 476
22:59 "Certainly **this f** was with him, AIT
Jn 9:29 "Who is **this f** who told you to pick it up 476
9:29 but as for **this f,** AIT
Ac 2:14 **"F** Jews and all of you who live NIG
6:13 **"This f** never stops speaking 476
7:23 he decided to visit his **f** Israelites. 81
7:40 for **this f** Moses who led us out of Egypt— AIT
19:26 and hear how **this f** Paul has convinced AIT
19:38 Demetrius and his **f** craftsmen have a
grievance 899+3836+5250
Ro 16: 3 my **f workers** in Christ Jesus. 5301
16: 9 Greet Urbanus, our **f worker** in Christ, 5301
16:21 Timothy, my **f worker,** 5301
1Co 3: 9 For we are God's **f workers;** 5301
2Co 6: 1 As God's **f workers** we urge you not 5300
8:23 he is my partner and **f worker** among you; 5301
12:16 Yet, **crafty** that I am, AIT
Eph 2:19 but **f citizens with** God's people 5232
Php 2:25 my brother, **f worker** and fellow soldier, 5301
2:25 my brother, fellow worker and **f soldier,** 5369
4: 3 with Clement and the rest of my **f workers,** 5301
Col 1: 7 Epaphras, our dear **f servant,** 5281
4: 7 a faithful minister and **f servant** in 5281
4:10 My **f prisoner** Aristarchus sends you his
greetings, 5257
4:11 the only Jews among my **f workers** for 5301
1Th 3: 2 and God's **f worker** in spreading the gospel 5301
Phm 1: 1 *To* Philemon our dear friend and **f worker,** 5301
1: 2 *to* Archippus our **f soldier** and to 5369
1:23 Epaphras, my **f prisoner** in Christ Jesus, 5257
1:24 Demas and Luke, my **f workers.** 5301
Heb 13: 3 in prison as if you were their **f prisoners,** 5279
1Pe 5: 1 I appeal as a **f elder,** 5236
Rev 6:11 of their **f servants** and brothers who were 5281
19:10 I am a **f servant with** you and with 5281
22: 9 I am a **f servant with** you and with 5281

FELLOW'S (2) [FELLOW]

1Sa 25:21 all my watching over **this f** property 2296+4200ˢ
Jn 9:28 "You are **this f** disciple! AIT

FELLOWCITIZENS (KJV) See FELLOW CITIZEN

FELLOWLABOURER (KJV) See FELLOW WORKERS

FELLOWMAN (3) [FELLOW, MAN]

Ps 15: 3 and casts no slur on his **f,** 7940
Mic 2: 2 a **f** of his inheritance. 408
Ro 13: 8 for he who loves **his f** has fulfilled the law. 2283+3836ˢ

FELLOWPRISONER (KJV) See FELLOW PRISONER

FELLOWS (3) [FELLOW]

1Sa 14: 6 to the outpost of those **uncircumcised f.** AIT
31: 4 or these **uncircumcised f** will come AIT
1Ch 10: 4 or these **uncircumcised f** will come AIT

FELLOWSERVANT (KJV) See FELLOW SERVANT

FELLOWSHIP (99) [FELLOW]

Ex 20:24 on it your burnt offerings and **f offerings,** 8968

Ex	24: 5	and sacrificed young bulls as **f** offerings to	8968
	29:28	to the LORD from their **f** offerings.	8968
	32: 6	and presented **f offerings.**	8968
Lev	3: 1	" 'If someone's offering is a **f** offering,	8968
	3: 3	From the **f** offering he is to bring	8968
	3: 6	an animal from the flock as a **f** offering to	8968
	3: 9	From the **f** offering he is to bring	8968
	4:10	from the ox sacrificed as a **f** offering.	8968
	4:26	as he burned the fat of the **f** offering.	8968
	4:31	as the fat is removed from the **f** offering,	8968
	4:35	from the lamb of the **f** offering,	8968
	6:12	the fire and burn the fat of the **f offerings**	8968
	7:11	for the **f** offering a person may present to	8968
	7:13	with his **f** offering of thanksgiving he is	8968
	7:14	the blood of the **f offerings.**	8968
	7:15	of his **f** offering of thanksgiving must	8968
	7:18	of the **f** offering is eaten on the third day,	8968
	7:20	of the **f** offering belonging to the LORD,	8968
	7:21	of the **f** offering belonging to the LORD,	8968
	7:29	a **f** offering to the LORD is to bring part	8968
	7:32	to give the right thigh of your **f** offerings to	8968
	7:33	of the **f offering** shall have the right thigh	8968
	7:34	From the **f** offerings of the Israelites,	8968
	7:37	the ordination offering and the **f** offering,	8968
	9: 4	a **f offering** to sacrifice before the LORD,	8968
	9:18	and the ram as the **f** offering for the people.	8968
	9:22	the burnt offering and the **f offering,**	8968
	10:14	as your share of the Israelites' **f** offerings.	8968
	17: 5	and sacrifice them as **f** offerings.	8968
	19: 5	" 'When you sacrifice a **f** offering to	8968
	22:21	or flock a **f** offering to the LORD to fulfill	8968
	23:19	each a year old, for a **f** offering.	8968
Nu	6:14	a ram without defect for a **f offering,**	8968
	6:17	and is to sacrifice the ram as a **f** offering to	8968
	6:18	that is under the sacrifice of the **f** offering.	8968
	7:17	to be sacrificed as a **f offering.**	8968
	7:23	to be sacrificed as a **f offering.**	8968
	7:29	to be sacrificed as a **f offering.**	8968
	7:35	to be sacrificed as a **f offering.**	8968
	7:41	to be sacrificed as a **f offering.**	8968
	7:47	to be sacrificed as a **f offering.**	8968
	7:53	to be sacrificed as a **f offering.**	8968
	7:59	to be sacrificed as a **f offering.**	8968
	7:65	to be sacrificed as a **f offering.**	8968
	7:71	to be sacrificed as a **f offering.**	8968
	7:77	to be sacrificed as a **f offering.**	8968
	7:83	to be sacrificed as a **f offering.**	8968
	7:88	the **f offering** came to twenty-four oxen,	8968
	10:10	over your burnt offerings and **f** offerings,	8968
	15: 8	special vow or a **f offering** to the LORD,	8968
	29:39	drink offerings and **f offerings.' "**	8968
Dt	27: 7	Sacrifice **f** offerings there,	8968
Jos	8:31	and sacrificed **f offerings.**	8968
	22:23	or to sacrifice **f** offerings on it,	8968
	22:27	sacrifices and **f offerings.**	8968
Jdg	20:26	and **f offerings** to the LORD.	8968
	21: 4	presented burnt offerings and **f offerings.**	8968
1Sa	10: 8	to sacrifice burnt offerings and **f** offerings,	8968
	11:15	There they sacrificed **f** offerings before	8968
	13: 9	the burnt offering and the **f offerings.**"	8968
2Sa	6:17	and **f offerings** before the LORD.	8968
	6:18	the burnt offerings and **f offerings,**	8968
	24:25	sacrificed burnt offerings and **f** offerings.	8968
1Ki	3:15	sacrificed burnt offerings and **f offerings.**	8968
	8:63	Solomon offered a sacrifice of **f** offerings	8968
	8:64	and the fat of the **f offerings,**	8968
	8:64	and the fat of the **f offerings.**	8968
	9:25	and **f offerings** on the altar he had built for	8968
2Ki	16:13	and sprinkled the blood of his **f offerings**	8968
1Ch	16: 1	and **f offerings** before God.	8968
	16: 2	the burnt offerings and **f offerings,**	8968
	21:26	sacrificed burnt offerings and **f offerings.**	8968
2Ch	7: 7	and the fat of the **f offerings,**	8968
	29:35	together with the fat of the **f offerings** and	8968
	30:22	and offered **f** offerings and praised	8968
	31: 2	to offer burnt offerings and **f offerings,**	8968
	33:16	of the LORD and sacrificed **f** offerings	8968
Ps	55:14	with whom I once enjoyed sweet **f**	6051
Pr	7:14	"I have **f** offerings at home;	8968
Eze	43:27	and **f offerings** on the altar.	8968
	45:15	and **f offerings** to make atonement for	8968
	45:17	and **f offerings** to make atonement for	8968
	46: 2	and his **f offerings.**	8968
	46:12	whether a burnt offering or **f offerings—**	8968
	46:12	or his **f offerings** as he does on	8968
Am	5:22	Though you bring choice **f offerings,**	8968
Ac	2:42	to the apostles' teaching and to the **f,**	3126
1Co	1: 9	into **f** with his Son Jesus Christ our Lord,	3126
	5: 2	with grief and have put out of your **f**	3545
2Co	6:14	Or what **f** can light have with darkness?	3126
	13:14	and the **f** of the Holy Spirit be with you all.	3126
Gal	2: 9	of **f** when they recognized the grace given	3126
Php	2: 1	if any **f** with the Spirit,	3126
	3:10	of his resurrection and the **f of sharing**	3126
1Jn	1: 3	so that you also may have **f** with us.	3126
	1: 3	And our **f** is with the Father and	3126
	1: 6	If we claim to have **f** with him yet walk in	3126
	1: 7	we have **f** with one another,	3126

FELLOWSOLDIER (KJV) See FELLOW SOLDIER

FELLOWWORKERS (KJV) See FELLOW WORKERS

FELT (13) [FEEL]

Ge	2:25	both naked, and they **f** no **shame.**	1017
Ex	2: 6	He was crying, and she **f sorry** for him.	2798
	10:21	darkness that can be **f.**"	5491
1Sa	13:12	So I **f compelled** to offer	706
2Ki	8:11	with a fixed gaze until Hazael **f ashamed.**	1017
Ps	30: 6	I **f secure,** I said, "I will never be shaken."	8930
Jer	5: 3	You struck them, but they **f** no **pain;**	2655
	22:21	I warned you when you **f secure,**	8932
Na	3:19	for who has not **f** your endless cruelty?	6296
Mk	5:29	and she **f** in her body that she was freed	1182
2Co	1: 9	in our hearts we **f** the sentence of death.	2400
Heb	10: 2	and would no longer have **f guilty**	5287
Jude	1: 3	If I had to write and urge you to contend	2400

FEMALE (37) [FEMALES]

Ge	1:27	male and **f** he created them.	5922
	5: 2	He created them male and **f**	5922
	6:19	male and **f,** to keep them alive with you.	5922
	7: 3	and **f,** to keep their various kinds alive	5922
	7: 9	and **f,** came to Noah and entered the ark,	5922
	7:16	were male and **f** of every living thing,	5922
	12:16	male and **f** donkeys,	912
	20:14	and **f** slaves and gave them to Abraham,	9148
	30:35	and all the speckled or **spotted** **f** goats	AIT
	32:14	two hundred **f** goats	NIH
	32:15	thirty **f** camels with their young,	3567
	32:15	twenty **f donkeys** and ten male donkeys.	912
	45:23	and ten **donkeys** loaded with grain	912
Ex	21:20	a man beats his male or **f** slave with a rod	563
	21:32	If the bull gores a male or **f** slave,	563
Lev	3: 1	whether male or **f,**	5922
	3: 6	he is to offer a male or **f** without defect.	5922
	4:28	offering for the sin he committed a **f** goat	5922
	4:32	he is to bring a **f** without defect.	5922
	5: 6	the LORD a **f** lamb or goat from the flock	5922
	25:44	" 'Your male and **f** slaves are to come from	563
	27: 4	and if it is a **f,**	5922
	27: 5	at twenty shekels and of a **f** at ten shekels.	5922
	27: 6	and that of a **f** at three shekels of silver.	5922
	27: 7	at fifteen shekels and of a **f** at ten shekels.	5922
Nu	5: 3	Send away male and **f** alike;	5922
	15:27	a **year-old** **f** goat for a sin offering.	AIT
Dt	23:18	not bring the earnings of a **f prostitute** or	AIT
	28:68	to your enemies as male and **f** slaves,	9148
Est	2: 7	as male and **f** slaves,	9148
Ecc	2: 7	I bought male and **f** slaves	9148
Jer	34: 9	both male and **f;**	9148
	34:10	that they would free their male and **f** slaves	9148
	34:16	the male and **f** slaves you had set free to go	9148
Mt	19: 4	the Creator 'made them male and **f,'**	2559
Mk	10: 6	of creation God 'made them male and **f.'**	2559
Gal	3:28	Jew nor Greek, slave nor free, male nor **f,**	2559

FEMALES (1) [FEMALE]

Ge	30:41	Whenever the **stronger** **f** were in heat,	AIT

FENCE (1)

Ps	62: 3	this leaning wall, this tottering **f?**	1555

FENCED (KJV) See BLOCKED, DUG UP, FORTIFIED, KNIT TOGETHER, WALLS

FERMENTED (10)

Lev	10: 9	or other **f drink** whenever you go into	8911
Nu	6: 3	he must abstain from wine and other **f drink**	8911
	6: 3	from wine or from other **f drink.**	8911
	28: 7	a quarter of a hin of **f drink** with each lamb.	8911
Dt	14:26	cattle, sheep, wine or other **f drink,**	8911
	29: 6	and drank no wine or other **f drink.**	8911
Jdg	13: 4	to it that you drink no wine or other **f drink**	8911
	13: 7	drink no wine or other **f drink** and do	8911
	13:14	or other **f drink** nor eat anything unclean.	8911
Lk	1:15	He is never to take wine or other **f drink,**	4975

FEROCIOUS (4)

Ge	37:20	and say that a **f** animal devoured him.	8273
	37:33	Some **f** animal has devoured him.	8273
Isa	35: 9	nor will any **f** beast get up on it;	7264
Mt	7:15	but inwardly they are **f** wolves.	774

FERTILE (16) [FERTILIZE]

Nu	13:20	Is it **f** or poor?	9045
2Ch	26:10	in the hills and in the **f lands.**	4149
Ne	9:25	They captured fortified cities and **f** land;	9045
	9:35	in the spacious and **f** land you gave them,	9045
Isa	5: 1	a vineyard on a **f** hillside.	1201+9043
	10:18	and **f fields** it will completely destroy,	4149
	28: 1	set on the head of a **f** valley—	9043
	28: 4	set on the head of a **f** valley,	9043
	29:17	into a **f field** and the fertile field seem like	4149
	29:17	into a fertile field and the **f field** seem like	4149
	32:15	and the desert becomes a **f field,**	4149
	32:15	and the **f field** seems like a forest.	4149
	32:16	and righteousness live in the **f field.**	4149
Jer	2: 7	I brought you into a **f** land to eat its fruit	4149
Eze	17: 5	of the seed of your land and put it in **f** soil.	2446
Mic	7:14	by itself in a forest, in **f pasturelands.**	4149

FERTILIZE (1) [FERTILE]

Lk	13: 8	and I'll dig around it and **f** it.	965+3162

FERVENT (1) [FERVOR]

Pr	26:23	of glaze over earthenware are **f** lips with	1944

FERVOR (2) [FERVENT]

Ac	18:25	and he spoke **with great f** and	2417+3836+4460
Ro	12:11	but keep your spiritual **f,** serving the Lord.	2417

FESTAL (1) [FESTIVAL]

Ps	118:27	the **f procession** up to the horns of the altar.	2504

FESTER (1) [FESTERING]

Ps	38: 5	My wounds **f** and are loathsome because	5245

FESTERING (6) [FESTER]

Ex	9: 9	and **f** boils will break out on men	81
	9:10	and **f** boils broke out on men and animals.	81
Lev	21:20	or who has **f** or running sores.	1734
	22:22	anything with warts or **f** or running sores.	1734
Dt	28:27	**f sores** and the itch,	1734
Job	7: 5	my skin is broken and **f.**	4416

FESTIVAL (32) [FESTAL, FESTIVALS, FESTIVE]

Ex	5: 1	so that they may **hold a f** to me in	2510
	10: 9	because we are to celebrate a **f to**	2504
	12:14	to come you shall celebrate it as a **f to**	2504
	13: 6	on the seventh day hold a **f** to the LORD.	2504
	23:14	a year you are to **celebrate a f** to me.	2510
	23:18	"The fat of my **f offerings** must not	2504
	32: 5	"Tomorrow there will be a **f** to	2504
Lev	23:39	the **f** to the LORD for seven days;	2504
	23:41	a **f** to the LORD for seven days each year.	2504
Nu	15: 3	or freewill offerings or **f offerings—**	4595
	28:17	of this month there is to be a **f;**	2504
	29:12	Celebrate a **f** to the LORD for seven days.	2504
Jdg	9:27	they held a **f** in the temple of their god.	2136
	21:19	the annual **f** of the LORD in Shiloh,	2504
1Sa	20: 5	"Look, tomorrow is the **New Moon f,**	2544
	20:18	"Tomorrow is the **New Moon f.**	2544
	20:24	and when the **New Moon f** came,	2544
1Ki	8: 2	the time of the **f** in the month of Ethanim,	2504
	8:65	So Solomon observed the **f** at that time,	2504
	12:32	He instituted a **f** on the fifteenth day of	2504
	12:32	like the **f** held in Judah,	2504
	12:33	So he instituted the **f** for the Israelites,	2504
2Ch	5: 3	at the time of the **f** in the seventh month.	2504
	7: 8	So Solomon observed the **f** at that time	2504
	7: 9	of the altar for seven days and the **f**	2504
	30:23	to celebrate the **f** seven more days;	NIH
Isa	30:29	as on the night you celebrate a holy **f;**	2504
Hos	7: 5	On the day of the **f** of our king	NIH
	9: 5	on the **f** days of the LORD?	2504
Mal	2: 3	the offal from your **f sacrifices,**	2504
1Co	5: 8	Therefore let us **keep the F,**	2037
Col	2:16	or with regard to a **religious f,**	2038

FESTIVALS (12) [FESTIVAL]

Nu	10:10	appointed feasts and **New Moon f—**	2544+8031
1Ch	23:31	the LORD on Sabbaths and at **New Moon f**	2544
Ne	10:33	**New Moon f** and appointed feasts;	2544
Isa	1:14	Your **New Moon f**	2544
	29: 1	to year and let your cycle of **f** go on.	2504
	33:20	Look upon Zion, the city of our **f;**	4595
Eze	45:17	grain offerings and drink offerings at the **f,**	2504
	46:11	" 'At the **f** and the appointed feasts,	2504
Hos	2:11	her **yearly f,** her New Moons,	2504
	5: 7	Now their **New Moon f** will devour them	2544
Na	1:15	Celebrate your **f,** O Judah,	2504
Zec	8:19	and glad occasions and happy **f** for Judah.	4595

FESTIVE (2) [FESTIVAL]

1Sa	25: 8	since we come at a **f** time.	3202
Ps	42: 4	and thanksgiving among the **f** throng.	2510

FESTOONED (1)

1Ki	7:17	of interwoven chains **f** the capitals on top	1544

FESTUS (14) [PORCIUS]

Ac	24:27	Felix was succeeded by Porcius **F,**	5776
	25: 1	**F** went up from Caesarea to Jerusalem,	5776
	25: 3	They urgently requested **F,**	899S
	25: 4	**F** answered, "Paul is being held	5776
	25: 9	**F,** wishing to do the Jews a favor,	5776
	25:12	After **F** had conferred with his council,	5776
	25:13	at Caesarea to pay their respects to **F.**	5776
	25:14	**F** discussed Paul's case with the king.	5776
	25:22	Then Agrippa said to **F,**	5776
	25:23	At the command of **F,**	5776
	25:24	**F** said: "King Agrippa,	5776
	26:24	At this point **F** interrupted Paul's defense.	5776
	26:25	"I am not insane, most excellent **F,"**	5776
	26:32	Agrippa said to **F,**	5776

FETCH, FETCHED (KJV) See BRING, BROUGHT, CAPTURE, COME BACK, GET, ESCORT, TAKE

FETTERED (1) [FETTERS]
2Sa	3:34	your feet were not f.	4200+5602+5733

FETTERS (3) [FETTERED]
Job	36:13	when *he* f them, they do not cry for help.	673
Ps	2: 3	they say, "and throw off their f."	6310
	149: 8	to bind their kings with f,	2414

FEVER (11) [FEVERISH]
Lev	26:16	and f that will destroy your sight	7707
Dt	28:22	with f and inflammation,	7707
Job	30:30	my body burns with f.	2996
Mt	8:14	Peter's mother-in-law lying in bed **with a f.**	4789
	8:15	He touched her hand and the f left her,	4790
Mk	1:30	Simon's mother-in-law was in bed **with a f,**	4789
	1:31	The f left her and she began to wait	4790
Lk	4:38	suffering *from* a high f,	4790
	4:39	So he bent over her and rebuked the f,	4790
Jn	4:52	"The f left him yesterday at	4790
Ac	28: 8	suffering from f and dysentery.	4790

FEVERISH (1) [FEVER]
La	5:10	Our skin is hot as an oven, f from hunger.	2363

FEW (76) [FEWEST]
Ge	29:20	but they seemed like **only a f** days to him	285
	34:30	We are f in number,	5493
	47: 9	My years have been f and difficult,	5071
Lev	25:16	and when the years *are* f,	5070
	25:52	If **only a f** years remain until the Year	5071
	26:22	**make** you *so* **f in number**	5070
Nu	9:20	over the tabernacle **only a f** days;	5031
	13:18	or weak, f or many.	5071
	35: 8	but f from one that has few."	5070
	35: 8	but few from one that has f."	5070
Dt	4:27	and **only a f** of you will survive	5031+5493
	26: 5	with a f people and lived there and became	5071
	28:62	in the sky will be left but **f in number,**	5071+5493
	33: 6	nor his men be f."	5031
Jos	7: 3	for **only a f** men are there."	5071
	10:20	f who were left reached their fortified cities.	8586
1Sa	14: 6	whether by many or by f."	5071
	17:28	with whom did you leave those f sheep in	5071
1Ki	17: 1	in the **next** *f* years except at my word."	AIT
	17:12	a f sticks to take home and make a meal	9109
2Ki	4: 3	Don't ask for **just a f.**	5070
1Ch	16:19	When they were but f *in* number,	5493
	16:19	they were but few in number, f indeed,	5071
2Ch	24:24	with **only a f** men,	5203
	29:34	were **too f** to skin all the burnt offerings;	5071
Ne	2:12	I set out during the night with a f men.	5071
	7: 4	but there were f people in it.	5071
Job	10:20	Are not my f days almost over?	5071
	14: 1	"Man born of woman is of f days and full	7920
	16:22	"Only a f years will pass before I go on	5031
Ps	105:12	When they were but f *in* number,	5493
	105:12	they were but few in number, f indeed,	3869+5071
	109: 8	May his days be f;	5071
Ecc	2: 3	to do under heaven during the f days	5031
	5: 2	so let your words be f.	5071
	5:18	the days of life God has given him—	5031
	6:12	the f and meaningless days he passes	5031
	9:14	a small city with **only a f** people in it.	5071
	12: 3	the grinders cease because *they are* f,	5070
Isa	10:19	be *so* f that a child could write them down.	5031
	16:14	survivors will be **very f** and feeble."	4663+5071
	21:17	the warriors of Kedar, *will be* f."	5071
	24: 6	and **very f** are left.	632+4663
	65:20	be in it an infant who lives but a *f* **days,**	AIT
Jer	42: 2	now **only a f** are left.	5071
	44:14	none will return except a *f* **fugitives."**	AIT
	44:28	of Judah from Egypt will be f."	5031+5493
	49: 9	would they not leave a **f grapes?**	6622
Eze	5: 3	a f strands of hair and tuck them away in	
		the folds of your garment.	928+5031+5071
	5: 4	f of these and throw them into the fire	4946
	12:16	I will spare a f of them from the sword,	5031
	13:19	a *f* **handfuls** *of* barley and scraps of bread.	AIT
Da	11:20	In a f years, however, he will be destroyed,	285
	11:23	with **only a f** people he will rise to power.	5071
Ob	1: 5	would they not leave a **f grapes?**	6622
Mt	7:14	and only a f find it.	3900
	9:37	but the workers are f.	3900
	15:34	"Seven," they replied, "and a f small fish."	3900
	22:14	"For many are invited, but f are chosen."	3900
	25:21	You have been faithful with a f *things;*	3900
	25:23	You have been faithful with a f *things;*	3900
Mk	2: 1	A f days later,	NIG
	6: 5	except lay his hands on a f sick people	3900
	8: 7	They had a f small fish as well;	3900
Lk	10: 2	but the workers are f.	3900
	12:48	be beaten with f blows.	3900
	13:23	are only a f people going to be saved?"	3900
Jn	2:12	There they stayed *for* a f days.	4024+4498
Ac	1: 5	in a f days you will be baptized with	4024+4498
	10:48	to stay with them *for* a f days.	5516
	17: 4	and not a f prominent women.	3900
	17:34	A *f* men became followers of Paul	AIT
	25:13	A *f* days later King Agrippa	AIT
1Pe	3:20	In it only a f people, eight in all,	3900
Rev	2:14	Nevertheless, I have a f *things* against you:	3900
	3: 4	a f people in Sardis who have	3900

FEWEST (1) [FEW]
Dt	7: 7	for you were the f of all peoples.	5071

FIDELITY (KJV) See TRUSTED

FIELD (216) [BATTLEFIELD, FIELDS, FIELDSTONES, GRAINFIELD, GRAINFIELDS]
Ge	2: 5	and no shrub of the f had yet appeared on	8441
	2: 5	and no plant of the f had yet sprung up,	8441
	2:19	of the ground all the beasts of the f and all	8441
	2:20	of the air and all the beasts of the f.	8441
	3:18	and you will eat the plants of the f.	8441
	4: 8	"Let's go out to the f."	8441
	4: 8	And while they were in the f,	8441
	23: 9	to him and is at the end of his f.	8441
	23:11	"Listen to me; I give you the f,	8441
	23:13	I will pay the price of the f.	8441
	23:17	Ephron's f in Machpelah near Mamre—	8441
	23:17	both the f and the cave in it,	8441
	23:17	all the trees within the borders of the f—	8441
	23:19	the f *of* Machpelah near Mamre (which is	8441
	23:20	So the f and the cave in it were deeded	8441
	24:63	He went out to the f one evening	8441
	24:65	that man in the f coming to meet us?"	8441
	25: 9	in the f *of* Ephron son of Zohar the Hittite,	8441
	25:10	f Abraham had bought from the Hittites.	8441
	27:27	The smell of my son is like the smell of a f	8441
	29: 2	There he saw a well in the f,	8441
	37: 7	in the f when suddenly my sheaf rose	8441
	39: 5	both in the house and in the f.	8441
	49:29	in the cave in the f *of* Ephron the Hittite,	8441
	49:30	the cave in the f *of* Machpelah,	8441
	49:30	along with the f.	NIH
	49:32	The f and the cave in it were bought from	8441
	50:13	and buried him in the cave in the f	8441
	50:13	along with the f.	8441
Ex	9: 3	a terrible plague on your livestock in the f—	8441
	9:19	and everything you have in the f to a place	8441
	9:19	not been brought in and is still out in the f,	8441
	9:21	and livestock in the f.	8441
	22: 5	in a f or vineyard and lets them stray	8441
	22: 5	and they graze in another man's f,	8441
	22: 5	from the best of his own f or vineyard.	8441
	22: 6	of grain or standing grain or the *whole* f,	8441
	23:16	of the crops you sow in your f."	8441
	23:16	when you gather in your crops from the f.	8441
Lev	19: 9	do not reap to the very edges of your f	8441
	19:19	not plant your f with two kinds of seed.	8441
	23:22	do not reap to the very edges of your f	8441
	26: 4	and the trees of their f their fruit.	8441
	27:17	If he dedicates his f during the Year	8441
	27:18	But if he dedicates his f after the Jubilee,	8441
	27:19	If the man who dedicates the f wishes	8441
	27:19	and the f will again become his.	NIH
	27:20	If, however, he does not redeem the f,	8441
	27:21	When the f is released in the Jubilee,	8441
	27:21	like a f devoted to the LORD;	8441
	27:22	to the LORD a f he has bought,	8441
	27:24	In the Year of Jubilee the f will revert to	8441
Nu	20:17	We will not go through any f or vineyard,	8441
	21:22	not turn aside into any f or vineyard.	8441
	22: 4	as an ox licks up the grass of the f."	8441
	22:23	she turned off the road into a f.	8441
	23:14	to the f *of* Zophim on the top of Pisgah,	8441
Dt	20:19	Are the trees of the f people,	8441
	21: 1	lying in a f in the land	8441
	24:19	in your f and you overlook a sheaf,	8441
	28:38	in the f but you will harvest little,	5070
Jos	15:18	she urged him to ask her father for a f.	8441
Jdg	1:14	she urged him to ask her father for a f.	8441
	5:18	so did Naphtali on the heights of the f.	8441
	13: 9	to the woman while she was out in the f;	8441
	20:31	that about thirty men fell in the **open f** and	8441
Ru	2: 3	she found herself working in a f belonging	
		to Boaz,	2754+8441
	2: 7	into the f and has worked steadily	NIH
	2: 8	in another f and don't go away from here.	8441
	2: 9	Watch the f where the men are harvesting,	8441
	2:17	So Ruth gleaned in the f until evening.	8441
	2:22	in someone else's f you might be harmed."	8441
1Sa	6:14	to the f *of* Joshua of Beth Shemesh,	8441
	6:18	is a witness to this day in the f *of* Joshua	8441
	14:15	those in the camp and f,	8441
	17:44	the birds of the air and the beasts of the f!"	8441
	19: 3	with my father in the f where you are.	8441
	20: 5	and hide in the f until the evening of	8441
	20:11	Jonathan said, "let's go out into the f."	8441
	20:24	So David hid in the f,	8441
	20:35	In the morning Jonathan went out to the f	8441
	30:11	an Egyptian in a f and brought him	8441
2Sa	14: 6	into a fight with each other in the f,	8441
	14:30	"Look, Joab's f is next to mine,	2754
	14:30	So Absalom's servants set the f on fire.	2754
	14:31	"Why have your servants set my f on fire?"	2754
	18: 6	The army marched into the f to fight Israel,	8441
	20:12	from the road into a f and threw a garment	8441
	23:11	where there was a f full of lentils,	2754+8441
	23:12	in the middle of the f.	2754
2Ki	3:19	and ruin every good f with stones."	2754
	3:25	on every good f until it was covered.	2754
	9:25	and throw him on the f *that belonged*	2754+8441
	18:17	his chief officer and his f **commander** with	8072
	18:17	on the road to the Washerman's F.	8441

2Ki	18:19	The f **commander** said to them,	8072
	18:26	Shebna and Joah said to the f **commander,**	8072
	18:37	told him what the f **commander** had said.	8072
	19: 4	the words of the f **commander,**	8072
	19: 8	When the f **commander** heard that the king	8072
	19:26	They are like plants in the f,	8441
1Ch	11:13	where there was a f full of barley,	2754+8441
	11:14	they took their stand in the middle of the f.	2754
	27:26	in charge of the f workers who farmed	8441
2Ch	26:23	near them in a f *for* burial that belonged to	8441
Job	5:23	a covenant with the stones of the f,	8441
Ps	8: 7	and the beasts of the f,	8442
	50:11	and the creatures of the f are mine.	8442
	72: 6	He will be like rain falling on a **mown** f,	1600
	72:16	let it thrive like the grass of the f.	824
	80:13	and the creatures of the f feed on it.	8442
	103:15	he flourishes like a flower of the f;	8441
	104:11	They give water to all the beasts of the f;	8442
Pr	13:23	poor man's f may produce abundant food,	5776
	24:30	I went past the f of the sluggard,	8441
	27:26	and the goats with the price of a f.	8441
	31:16	She considers a f and buys it;	8441
SS	2: 7	by the gazelles and by the does of the f:	8441
	3: 5	by the gazelles and by the does of the f:	8441
Isa	1: 8	like a hut in a f **of melons,**	5252
	5: 8	to you who add house to house and join f	8441
	5: 8	to f till no space is left and you live alone	8441
	7: 3	on the road to the Washerman's F.	8441
	19: 7	Every **sown** f *along*	4669
	28:25	barley in its plot, and spelt in its f?	1474
	29:17	will not Lebanon be turned into a **fertile** f	4149
	29:17	into a fertile field and the **fertile** f seem	4149
	32:15	and the desert becomes a **fertile** f,	4149
	32:15	and the **fertile** f seems like a forest.	4149
	32:16	and righteousness live in the **fertile** f.	4149
	36: 2	the king of Assyria sent his f **commander**	8072
	36: 2	on the road to the Washerman's F,	8441
	36: 4	The f **commander** said to them,	8072
	36:11	Shebna and Joah said to the f **commander,**	8072
	36:22	told him what the f **commander** had said.	8072
	37: 4	the words of the f **commander,**	8072
	37: 8	When the f **commander** heard that the king	8072
	37:27	They are like plants in the f,	8441
	40: 6	all their glory is like the flowers of the f.	8441
	55:12	all the trees of the f will clap their hands.	8441
Jer	4:17	They surround her like men guarding a f,	8442
	7:20	on man and beast, on the trees of the f and	8441
	9:22	of men will lie like refuse on the open f,	8441
	12: 4	and the grass in every f be withered?	8441
	12:10	and trample down my f;	2754
	12:10	they will turn my pleasant f into	2754
	14: 5	the doe in the f deserts her newborn fawn	8441
	26:18	" 'Zion will be plowed like a f,	8441
	32: 7	'Buy my f at Anathoth,	8441
	32: 8	'Buy my f at Anathoth in the territory	8441
	32: 9	the f at Anathoth from my cousin Hanamel	8441
	32:25	'Buy the f with silver and have	8441
	41: 8	oil and honey, hidden in a f."	8441
La	4: 9	for lack of food from the f.	8442
Eze	16: 5	you were thrown out into the open f,	8441
	16: 7	I made you grow like a plant of the f.	8441
	17:24	of the f will know that I the LORD bring	8441
	29: 5	You will fall on the open f and not	8441
	31: 4	to all the trees of the f.	8441
	31: 5	the trees of the f;	8441
	31: 6	of the f gave birth under its branches;	8441
	31:13	of the f were among its branches.	8441
	31:15	and all the trees of the f withered away.	8441
	32: 4	on the land and hurl you on the open f,	8441
	34:27	The trees of the f will yield their fruit and	8441
	36:30	the fruit of the trees and the crops of the f,	8441
	38:20	the birds of the air, the beasts of the f	8441
	39: 5	You will fall in the open f,	7156
Da	2:38	the beasts of the f and the birds of the air.	10119
	4:12	Under it the beasts of the f found shelter,	10119
	4:15	remain in the ground, in the grass of the f.	10119
	4:21	giving shelter to the beasts of the f,	10119
	4:23	in the grass of the f,	10119
Hos	2:18	a covenant for them with the beasts of the f	8441
	4: 3	the f and the birds of the air and the fish of	8441
	10: 4	up like poisonous weeds in a plowed f.	8442
	12:11	be like piles of stones on a plowed f.	8442
Joel	1:11	because the harvest of the f is destroyed.	8441
	1:12	all the trees of the f—are dried up.	8441
	1:19	up all the trees of the f.	8441
Am	4: 7	One f had rain;	2754
Mic	3:12	Zion will be plowed like a f,	8441
	4:10	the city to camp in the **open f.**	8441
Zec	10: 1	and plants of the f to everyone.	8441
Mt	6:28	See how the lilies of the f grow.	69
	6:30	that is how God clothes the grass *of* the f,	69
	9:38	to send out workers into his **harvest."**	2546
	13:24	like a man who sowed good seed in his f.	69
	13:27	'Sir, didn't you sow good seed in your f?	69
	13:31	which a man took and planted in his f.	69
	13:36	to us the parable of the weeds *in* the f."	69
	13:38	The f is the world,	69
	13:44	of heaven is like treasure hidden in a f.	69
	13:44	and sold all he had and bought that f.	69
	22: 5	one to his f, another to his business.	69
	24:18	Let no one in the f go back to get his cloak.	69
	24:40	Two men will be in the f;	69
	27: 7	to use the money to buy the potter's f as	69
	27: 8	That is why it has been called the F	69
	27:10	and they used them to buy the potter's f,	69
Mk	13:16	Let no one in the f go back to get his cloak.	69

Lk	10: 2	to send out workers into his **harvest** f.	2546
	12:28	that is how God clothes the grass of the f,	69
	14:18	The first said, 'I have just bought a f,	69
	15:25	"Meanwhile, the older son was in the f.	69
	17: 7	the servant when he comes in from the f,	69
	17:31	in the f should go back for anything.	69
Ac	1:18	Judas bought a f;	6005
	1:19	that f in their language Akeldama,	6005
	1:19	that is, F of Blood.)	6005
	4:37	sold a f he owned and brought the money	69
1Co	3: 9	you are God's f, God's building.	1176
2Co	10:13	to us,	2834+3586+3836
	10:13	a f that reaches even to you.	3586
1Pe	1:24	all their glory is like the flowers *of* the f;	5965

FIELDS (107) [FIELD]

Ge	30:14	into the f and found some mandrake plants,	8441
	30:16	Jacob came in from the f that evening,	8441
	31: 4	to come out to the f where his flocks were.	8441
	34: 5	his sons were in the f with his livestock;	8441
	34: 7	Now Jacob's sons had come in from the f	8441
	34:28	of theirs in the city and out in the f.	8441
	37:15	around in the f and asked him,	8441
	41:48	the food grown in the f surrounding it.	8441
	47:20	The Egyptians, one and all, sold their f,	8441
	47:24	as seed for the f and as food for yourselves	8441
Ex	1:14	and with all kinds of work in the f,	8441
	8:13	in the courtyards and in the f.	8441
	9:22	on everything growing in the f *of* Egypt."	8441
	9:25	Throughout Egypt hail struck everything in the f—	8441
	9:25	it beat down everything growing in the f	8441
	10: 5	that is growing in your f.	8441
	10:12	and devour everything growing in the f,	824
	10:15	everything growing in the f and the fruit on	824
	23:10	"For six years you are to sow your f	824
Lev	14: 7	he is to release the live bird in the open f.	8441
	14:53	to release the live bird in the open f outside	8441
	17: 5	now making in the open f.	8441
	25: 3	For six years sow your f,	8441
	25: 4	Do not sow your f or prune your vineyards.	8441
	25:12	eat only what is taken directly from the f.	8441
Nu	16:14	and honey or given us an inheritance of f	8441
Dt	11:15	I will provide grass in the f for your cattle,	8441
	14:22	a tenth of all that your f produce each year.	8441
	32:13	the land and fed him with the fruit of the f,	8442
	32:32	of Sodom and from the f *of* Gomorrah.	8727
Jos	8:24	the men of Ai in the f and in the desert	8441
	21:12	But the f and villages around	8441
Jdg	9:27	After they had gone out into the f	8441
	9:32	and lie in wait in the f.	8441
	9:42	the people of Shechem went out to the f,	8441
	9:43	and set an ambush in the f.	8441
	9:44	upon those in the f and struck them down.	8441
	19:16	came in from his work in the f.	8441
Ru	2: 2	to the f and pick up the leftover grain	8441
	2: 3	So she went out and began to glean in the f	8441
1Sa	8:14	of your f and vineyards and olive groves	8441
	11: 5	Just then Saul was returning from the f,	8441
	22: 7	of Jesse give all of you f and vineyards?	8441
	25:15	and the whole time we were out in the f	8441
2Sa	1:21	nor f *that yield* offerings [of grain].	8441
	11:11	are camped in the open f.	8441
	19:29	I order you and Ziba to divide the f."	8441
1Ki	2:26	"Go back to your f in Anathoth.	8441
2Ki	4:39	the f to gather herbs and found a wild vine.	8441
	23: 4	He burned them outside Jerusalem in the f	8727
	25:12	of the land to work the vineyards and f	3320
1Ch	6:56	But the f and villages around	8441
	16:32	let the f be jubilant,	8441
2Ch	26:10	**working** his f **and vineyards**	4144
	31: 5	oil and honey and all that the f produced.	8441
Ne	5: 3	"We are mortgaging our f,	8441
	5: 4	the king's tax on our f and vineyards.	8441
	5: 5	because our f and our vineyards belong	8441
	5:11	Give back to them immediately their f,	8441
	11:25	As for the villages with their f,	8441
	11:30	in Lachish and its f,	8441
	12:44	the f *around* the towns they were to bring	8441
	13:10	the service had gone back to their own f.	8441
Job	24: 6	They gather fodder in the f and glean in	8441
Ps	37:20	like the beauty of the f, they will vanish—	4120
	96:12	let the f be jubilant,	8442
	107:37	They sowed f and planted vineyards	8441
	132: 6	we came upon it in the f *of* Jaar:	8441
	144:13	by tens of thousands in our f;	2575
Pr	8:26	before he made the earth or its f or any of	2575
	23:10	or encroach on the f *of* the fatherless,	8441
	24:27	and get your f ready;	8441
Ecc	5: 9	the king himself profits from the f.	8441
Isa	1: 7	your f are being stripped	141
	6:11	the houses are left deserted and the f ruined	141
	10:18	and **fertile** f it will completely destroy,	4149
	16: 8	The f *of* Heshbon wither,	8727
	32:12	Beat your breasts for the pleasant f,	8441
	61: 5	foreigners will **work** your f and vineyards.	438
Jer	6:12	together with their f and their wives,	8441
	6:25	Do not go out to the f or walk on the roads,	8441
	8:10	to other men and their f to new owners.	8441
	13:27	on the hills and in the f.	8441
	32:15	f and vineyards will again be bought	8441
	32:43	Once more f will be bought in this land	8441
	32:44	F will be bought for silver,	8441
	35: 9	to live in or had vineyards, f or crops.	8441
	39:10	at that time he gave vineyards and f.	3321
	48:33	from the orchards and f *of* Moab.	824

Jer	52:16	of the land to work the vineyards and f.	3320
Eze	39:10	not need to gather wood from the f or cut it	8441
Hos	5: 7	Now their New Moon festivals will devour them and their f.	2750
Joel	1:10	The f are ruined, the ground is dried up;	8441
Ob	1:19	They will occupy the f *of* Ephraim	8441
Mic	2: 2	They covet f and seize them, and houses,	8441
	2: 4	He assigns our f to traitors.' "	8441
Hab	3:17	olive crop fails and the f produce no food,	8727
Hag	1:11	for a drought on the f and the mountains,	824
Mal	3:11	the vines in your f will not cast their fruit,"	8441
Mt	19:29	or children or f for my sake will receive	69
Mk	10:29	or mother or father or children or f for me	69
	10:30	brothers, sisters, mothers, children and f—	69
	11: 8	spread branches they had cut in the f.	69
Lk	2: 8	shepherds living out in the f nearby,	6001
	15:15	who sent him to his f to feed pigs.	69
Jn	4:35	I tell you, open your eyes and look at the f!	6001
Jas	5: 4	workmen who mowed your f are crying out	6001

FIELDSTONES (1) [FIELD, STONE]

| Dt | 27: 6 | the altar of the LORD your God with f | 74+8969 |

FIERCE (49) [FIERCE-LOOKING, FIERCELY, FIERCER, FIERCEST]

Ge	49: 7	Cursed be their anger, so f, and their fury,	6434
Ex	32:12	Turn from your f anger;	3019
Nu	25: 4	that the LORD's f anger may turn away	3019
Dt	13:17	that the LORD will turn from his f anger;	3019
	29:23	which the LORD overthrew in f anger.	2779
	29:24	Why this f, burning anger?"	1524
Jos	7:26	Then the LORD turned from his f anger	3019
1Sa	20:34	Jonathan got up from the table in f anger;	3034
	28:18	the LORD or carry out his f wrath against	3019
	31: 3	The fighting **grew** f around Saul,	3877
2Sa	2:17	The battle that day was very f,	7997
	17: 8	as f as a wild bear robbed of her cubs.	5253+5883
2Ki	23:26	not turn away from the heat of his f anger,	1524
1Ch	10: 3	The fighting **grew** f around Saul,	3877
2Ch	28:11	for the LORD's f anger rests on you."	3019
	28:13	and his f anger rests on Israel."	3019
	29:10	so that his f anger will turn away from us.	3019
	30: 8	so that his f anger will turn away from you.	3019
Ezr	10:14	until the f anger of our God	3019
Job	41:10	No *one* is f *enough* to rouse him.	425
Ps	7	F men conspire against me for no offense	6434
	69:24	let your f anger overtake them.	3019
	85: 3	and turned from your f anger.	3019
Pr	26:13	a f **lion** roaming the streets!"	787
Isa	7: 4	because of the f anger of Rezin and Aram	3034
	13: 9	a cruel day, with wrath and f anger—	3019
	19: 4	and a f king will rule over them,"	6434
	27: 1	his f, great and powerful sword,	7997
	27: 8	with his f blast he drives her out,	7997
	49:24	or captives rescued from the f?	6883
	49:25	and plunder retrieved from the f;	6883
Jer	4: 8	for the f anger of the LORD has	3019
	4:26	before the LORD, before his f anger.	3019
	12:13	because of the LORD's f anger."	3019
	25:37	be laid waste because of the f anger of	3019
	25:38	and because of the LORD's f anger.	3019
	30:24	The f anger of the LORD will	3019
	44: 6	Therefore, my f anger was poured out;	2779
	49:37	even my f anger," declares the LORD.	3019
	51:45	Run from the f anger of the LORD.	3019
La	1:12	on me in the day of his f anger?	3019
	2: 3	In f anger he has cut off every horn	3034
	2: 6	in his f anger he has spurned both king	2405
	4:11	he has poured out his f anger.	3019
Hos	11: 9	I will not carry out my f anger,	3019
Jnh	3: 9	and with compassion turn from his f anger	3019
Na	1: 6	Who can endure his f anger?	3019
Zep	2: 2	the f anger of the LORD comes upon you,	3019
	3: 8	all my f anger.	3019

FIERCE-LOOKING (1) [FIERCE]

| Dt | 28:50 | a f nation without respect for the old | 6434+7156 |

FIERCELY (4) [FIERCE]

Job	39:21	He paws f, rejoicing in his strength,	928+2021+6677
Ps	25:19	and how f they hate me!	2805
Jer	6:29	The bellows **blow** f to burn away the lead	5723
Lk	11:53	of the law began to oppose him f and	1267

FIERCER (1) [FIERCE]

| Hab | 1: 8 | f than wolves at dusk. | 2523 |

FIERCEST (1) [FIERCE]

| 2Sa | 11:15 | in the front line where the fighting is f. | 2617 |

FIERY (16) [FIRE]

Ps	11: 6	On the wicked he will rain f coals	836
	21: 9	like a f furnace.	836
Eze	21:31	and breathe out my f anger against you;	836
	22:20	into a furnace to melt it with a f blast,	836
	22:21	and I will blow on you with my f wrath,	836
	22:31	and consume them with my f anger,	836
	28:14	you walked among the f stones.	836
	28:16	from among the f stones.	836
	38:19	In my zeal and f wrath I declare that at	836
Mt	13:42	They will throw them into the f furnace,	4786

Mt	13:50	and throw them into the f furnace,	4786
Rev	6: 4	Then another horse came out, a f **red** *one*.	4794
	9:17	Their breastplates were f **red**, dark blue,	4791
	10: 1	and his legs were like f pillars,	4786
	19:20	of them were thrown alive into the f lake	4786
	21: 8	be in the f lake of burning sulfur.	4786

FIFTEEN (18) [FIFTEENTH]

Ex	27:14	Curtains f cubits long are to be on	2822+6926
	27:15	and curtains f cubits long are to be on	2822+6926
	38:14	Curtains f cubits long were on one	2822+6926
	38:15	and curtains f cubits long were on the	2822+6926
Lev	27: 7	set the value of a male at f shekels	2822+6925
Nu	35: 4	will extend out f **hundred feet**	547+564
Jdg	8:10	about f thousand men, all that were	2822+6925
2Sa	9:10	Ziba had f sons and twenty servants.)	2822+6925
	19:17	and his f sons and twenty servants.	2822+6925
1Ki	7: 3	forty-five beams, f to a row.	2822+6925
2Ki	14:17	for f years after the death of Jehoash	2822+6926
	20: 6	I will add f years to your life.	2822+6926
2Ch	25:25	for f years after the death of Jehoash	2822+6926
Isa	38: 5	I will add f years to your life.	2822+6926
Eze	45:12	Twenty shekels plus twenty-five shekels plus f shekels equal one mina.	2256+2822+6927
Hos	3: 2	So I bought her for f shekels of silver	2822+6925
Zec	5: 2	thirty feet long and f **feet** wide."	2822+6925
			564+928+2021+6924
Gal	1:18	with Peter and stayed with him f days.	1278

FIFTEENTH (18) [FIFTEEN]

Ex	16: 1	on the f day of the second month	2822+6925
Lev	23: 6	On the f day of that month the LORD's Feast of Unleavened Bread	2822+6925
	23:34	'On the f day of the seventh month	2822+6925
	23:39	with the f day of the seventh month,	2822+6925
Nu	28:17	On the f day of this month there is	2822+6925
	29:12	" 'On the f day of the seventh month,	2822+6925
	33: 3	on the f day of the first month,	2822+6925
1Ki	12:32	on the f day of the eighth month,	2822+6925
	12:33	On the f day of the eighth month,	2822+6925
2Ki	14:23	In the f year of Amaziah son of Joash	2822+6926
1Ch	24:14	the f to Bilgah, the sixteenth to Immer,	2822+6925
	25:22	the f to Jerimoth, his sons and	2822+6926
2Ch	15:10	in the third month of the f year	2822+6926
Est	9:18	on the f they rested and made it a day	2822+6925
	9:21	the fourteenth and f days of the month	2822+6925
Eze	32:17	on the f day of the month,	2822+6925
	45:25	in the seventh month on the f day,	2822+6925
Lk	3: 1	the f year of the reign of Tiberius Caesar—	4298

FIFTH (55) [FIVE]

Ge	1:23	and there was morning—the f day.	2797
	30:17	and bore Jacob a f son.	2797
	41:34	the land *to* **take a f** *of* the harvest of Egypt.	2821
	47:24	give a f of it to Pharaoh.	2797
	47:26	that a f of the produce belongs to Pharaoh.	2823
Lev	5:16	add a f of the value to that and give it all	2797
	6: 5	add a f of the value to it and give it all to	2797
	19:25	But in the f year you may eat its fruit.	2797
	22:14	to the priest for the offering and add a f *of*	2797
	27:13	he must add a f to its value.	2797
	27:15	he must add a f to its value,	2797
	27:19	he must add a f to its value,	2797
	27:27	adding a f *of* the value to it.	2797
	27:31	he must add a f *of* the value to it.	2797
Nu	5: 7	add **one** f to it and give it all to	2797
	7:36	On the f day Shelumiel son of Zurishaddai,	2797
	29:26	" 'On the f day prepare nine bulls,	2797
	33:38	of the f month of the fortieth year after	2797
Jos	19:24	The f lot came out for the tribe of Asher,	2797
Jdg	19: 8	On the morning of the f day,	2797
2Sa	3: 4	the f, Shephatiah the son of Abital;	2797
1Ki	14:25	In the f year of King Rehoboam,	2797
2Ki	8:16	In the f year of Joram son of Ahab king	2822
	25: 8	On the seventh day of the f month,	2797
1Ch	2:14	the fourth Nethanel, the f Raddai,	2797
	3: 3	the f, Shephatiah the son of Abital;	2797
	8: 2	Nohah the fourth and Rapha the f.	2797
	12:10	Mishmannah the fourth, Jeremiah the f,	2797
	24: 9	the f to Malkijah, the sixth to Mijamin,	2797
	25:12	the f to Nethaniah,	2797
	26: 3	the f, Jehohanan the sixth and Eliehoenai	2797
	26: 4	Sacar the fourth, Nethanel the f,	2797
	27: 8	The f, for the fifth month,	2797
	27: 8	The fifth, for the f month,	2797
2Ch	12: 2	of Egypt attacked Jerusalem in the f year	2797
Ezr	7: 8	the f month of the seventh year of the king.	2797
	7: 9	on the first day of the f month,	2797
Ne	6: 5	Then, the f time, Sanballat sent his aide	2797
Jer	1: 3	down to the f month of the eleventh year	2797
	28: 1	In the f month of that same year,	2797
	36: 9	the f year of Jehoiakim son of Josiah king	2797
	52:12	On the tenth day of the f month,	2797
Eze	1: 1	in the fourth month on the f day,	2822
	1: 2	On the f of the month—	2822
	1: 2	it was the f year of the exile	2797
	8: 1	in the sixth month on the f day,	2822
	20: 1	in the f month on the tenth day,	2797
	33:21	in the tenth month on the f day,	2822
Zec	7: 3	"Should I mourn and fast in the f month,	2797
	7: 5	and mourned in the f and seventh months	2797
	8:19	"The fasts of the fourth, f,	2797
Rev	6: 9	When he opened the f seal,	4286
	9: 1	The f angel sounded his trumpet,	4286
	16:10	The f angel poured out his bowl on	4286

Rev	21:20	the **f** sardonyx, the sixth carnelian,	4286

FIFTIES (5) [FIFTY]

Ex	18:21	as officials over thousands, hundreds, **f**	2822
	18:25	over thousands, hundreds, **f** and tens.	2822
Dt	1:15	of **f** and of tens and as tribal officials.	2822
1Sa	8:12	of thousands and commanders of **f**,	2822
Mk	6:40	they sat down in groups of hundreds and **f**.	4299

FIFTIETH (3) [FIFTY]

Lev	25:10	Consecrate the **f** year and proclaim liberty	2822
	25:11	The **f** year shall be a jubilee for you;	2822
2Ki	15:23	In the **f** year of Azariah king of Judah,	2822

FIFTY (81) [FIFTIES, FIFTIETH, 50]

Ge	7:24	the earth for a hundred and **f** days.	2822
	8: 3	the hundred and **f** days the water had gone	2822
	18:24	if there are **f** righteous people in the city?	2822
	18:24	for the sake of the **f** righteous people in it?	2822
	18:26	"If I find **f** righteous people in the city	2822
	18:28	of the righteous is five less than **f**?	2822
Ex	26: 5	Make **f** loops on one curtain and fifty loops	2822
	26: 5	Make fifty loops on one curtain and **f** loops	2822
	26: 6	Then make **f** gold clasps and use them	2822
	26:10	Make **f** loops along the edge of	2822
	26:11	Then make **f** bronze clasps and put them in	2822
	27:12	of the courtyard shall be **f** cubits wide	2822
	27:13	the courtyard shall also be **f** cubits wide.	2822
	27:18	be a hundred cubits long and **f** cubits wide,	2822
	36:12	They also made **f** loops on one curtain	2822
	36:12	and **f** loops on the end curtain of	2822
	36:13	Then they made **f** gold clasps	2822
	36:17	They then made **f** loops along the edge of	2822
	36:18	They made **f** bronze clasps to fasten	2822
	38:12	The west end was **f** cubits wide	2822
	38:13	toward the sunrise, was also **f** cubits wide.	2822
Lev	23:16	Count off **f** days up to the day after	2822
	27: 3	and sixty at **f** shekels of silver, according	2822
	27:16	**f** shekels of silver to a homer	2822
Nu	4: 3	Count all the men from thirty to **f** years	2822
	4:23	Count all the men from thirty to **f** years	2822
	4:30	Count all the men from thirty to **f** years	2822
	4:35	from thirty to **f** years of age who came	2822
	4:39	from thirty to **f** years of age who came	2822
	4:43	from thirty to **f** years of age who came	2822
	4:47	to **f** years of age who came to do the work	2822
	8:25	but at the age of **f**,	2822
	31:30	select one out of every **f**, whether persons,	2822
	31:47	Moses selected one out of every **f** persons	2822
Dt	22:29	he shall pay the girl's father **f** shekels	2822
Jos	7:21	and a wedge of gold weighing **f** shekels,	2822
2Sa	15: 1	a chariot and horses and with **f** men to run	2822
	24:24	and the oxen and paid **f** shekels of silver	2822
1Ki	1: 5	with **f** men to run ahead of him.	2822
	7: 2	**f** wide and thirty high,	2822
	7: 6	a colonnade **f** cubits long and thirty wide.	2822
	10:29	and a horse for a hundred and **f**.	2822
	18: 4	**f** in each, and had supplied them with food	2822
	18:13	in two caves, **f** in each, and supplied them	2822
	18:19	And bring the four hundred and **f** prophets	2822
	18:22	but Baal has four hundred and **f** prophets.	2822
2Ki	1: 9	a captain with his *company of* **f** men.	2822
	1:10	and consume you and your **f** men!"	2822
	1:11	to Elijah another captain with his **f** men.	2822
	1:12	and consume you and your **f** men!"	2822
	1:12	and consumed him and his **f** men.	2822
	1:13	the king sent a third captain with his **f** men.	2822
	1:13	for my life and the lives of these **f** men,	2822
	2: 7	**F** men of the company of the prophets	2822
	2:16	"we your servants have **f** able men.	2822
	2:17	And they sent **f** men,	2822
	13: 7	the army of Jehoahaz except **f** horsemen,	2822
	15:20	to contribute **f** shekels of silver to be given	2822
	15:25	Taking **f** men of Gilead with him,	2822
1Ch	5:21	of the Hagrites—**f** thousand camels,	2822
	5:21	two hundred **f** thousand sheep	2822
2Ch	1:17	and a horse for a hundred and **f**.	2822
	3: 9	The gold nails weighed **f** shekels.	2822
	8:10	two hundred and **f** officials supervising	2822
	8:18	and **f** talents of gold,	2822
Ne	5:17	and **f** Jews and officials ate at my table,	2822
Isa	3: 3	the captain of **f** and man of rank,	2822
Eze	40:15	to the far end of its portico was **f** cubits.	2822
	40:21	It was **f** cubits long	2822
	40:25	It was **f** cubits long	2822
	40:29	It was **f** cubits long	2822
	40:33	It was **f** cubits long	2822
	40:36	It was **f** cubits long	2822
	42: 2	a hundred cubits long and **f** cubits wide.	2822
	42: 7	in front of the rooms for **f** cubits.	2822
	42: 8	to the outer court was **f** cubits long,	2822
Hag	2:16	to a wine vat to draw **f** measures	2822
Lk	7:41	five hundred denarii, and the other **f**.	4299
	9:14	down in groups of about **f** each."	4299
Jn	8:57	"You are not yet **f** years old,"	4299
Ac	19:19	total came to **f** thousand drachmas.	3689+4297

FIFTY-FIVE (2)

2Ki	21: 1	he reigned in Jerusalem **f** years.	2256+2822+2822
2Ch	33: 1	he reigned in Jerusalem **f** years.	2256+2822+2822

FIFTY-SECOND (1) [FIFTY-TWO]

2Ki	15:27	In the **f** year of Azariah king of Judah,	2256+2822+9109

FIFTY-TWO (3) [FIFTY-SECOND, 52]

2Ki	15: 2	he reigned in Jerusalem **f** years.	2256+2822+9109
2Ch	26: 3	he reigned in Jerusalem **f** years.	2256+2822+9109
Ne	6:15	twenty-fifth of Elul, in **f** days.	2256+2822+9109

FIG (41) [FIGS, SYCAMORE-FIG, SYCAMORE-FIGS]

Ge	3: 7	so they sewed **f** leaves together	9300
Dt	8: 8	vines and **f** trees, pomegranates,	9300
Jdg	9:10	"Next, the trees said to the **f** tree,	9300
	9:11	"But the **f** tree replied,	9300
1Ki	4:25	each man under his own vine and **f** tree.	9300
2Ki	18:31	from his own vine and **f** tree	9300
1Ch	12:40	**f** cakes, raisin cakes, wine, oil,	1811
Ps	105:33	down their vines and **f** trees and shattered	9300
Pr	27:18	He who tends a **f** tree will eat its fruit,	9300
SS	2:13	The **f** tree forms its early fruit;	9300
Isa	9:10	the **f** trees have been felled,	9204
	28: 4	will be like a **f** ripe before harvest—	1136
	34: 4	like shriveled figs from the **f** tree.	9300
	36:16	from his own vine and **f** tree	9300
Jer	5:17	devour your vines and **f** trees.	9300
Hos	2:12	I will ruin her vines and her **f** trees,	9300
	9:10	like seeing the early fruit on the **f** tree.	9300
Joel	1: 7	and ruined my **f** trees.	9300
	1:12	vine is dried up and the **f** tree is withered;	9300
	2:22	the **f** tree and the vine yield their riches.	9300
Am	4: 9	Locusts devoured your **f** and olive trees,	9300
Mic	4: 4	and under his own **f** tree,	9300
Na	3:12	like **f** trees with their first ripe fruit;	9300
Hab	3:17	Though the **f** tree does not bud	9300
Hag	2:19	Until now, the vine and the **f** tree,	9300
Zec	3:10	to sit under his vine and **f** tree,'	9300
Mt	21:19	Seeing a **f** tree by the road,	5190
	21:20	"How did the **f** tree wither so quickly?"	5190
	21:21	do what was done to the **f** tree,	5190
	24:32	"Now learn this lesson from the **f** tree:	5190
Mk	11:13	Seeing in the distance a **f** tree in leaf,	5190
	11:20	they saw the **f** tree withered from the roots.	5190
	11:21	The **f** tree you cursed has withered!"	5190
	11:28	"Now learn this lesson from the **f** tree:	5190
Lk	13: 6	"A man had a **f** tree,	5190
	13: 7	on this **f** tree and haven't found any.	5190
	21:29	"Look at the **f** tree and all the trees.	5190
Jn	1:48	under the **f** tree before Philip called you."	5190
	1:50	I saw you under the **f** tree.	5190
Jas	3:12	My brothers, can a **f** tree bear olives,	5190
Rev	6:13	as late figs drop *from* a **f** tree when shaken	899S

FIGHT (111) [FIGHTER, FIGHTERS, FIGHTING, FIGHTS, FOUGHT]

Ex	1:10	**f** against us and leave the country."	4309
	14:14	The LORD *will* **f** for you;	4309
	17: 9	of our men and go out to **f** the Amalekites.	4309
Lev	24:10	and a **f** broke out in the camp between him	5897
Nu	22:11	be able to **f** them and drive them away.' "	4309
	32:27	will cross over to **f** before the LORD,	4878
Dt	1:30	*will* **f** for you, as he did for you in Egypt,	4309
	1:41	We will go up and **f**,	4309
	1:42	"Tell them, 'Do not go up and **f**,	4309
	3:22	the LORD your God himself *will* **f**	4309
	20: 4	with you to **f** for you against your enemies	4309
	29: 7	and Og king of Bashan came out to **f**	4878
Jos	10:25	to all the enemies you *are going to* **f**."	4309
	11: 5	to **f** against Israel.	4309
	24: 9	prepared *to* **f** against Israel,	4309
Jdg	1: 1	"Who will be the first to go up and **f** for us	4309
	1: 3	*to* **f** against the Canaanites.	4309
	1: 9	down to **f** against the Canaanites living in	4309
	2:15	Whenever Israel went out to **f**,	NIH
	8: 1	when you went to **f** Midian?"	4309
	9:38	Go out and **f** them!"	4309
	10: 9	to **f** against Judah, Benjamin and the house	4309
	11: 6	so *we can* **f** the Ammonites."	4309
	11: 8	come with us *to* **f** the Ammonites,	4309
	11: 9	"Suppose you take me back to **f**	4309
	11:25	Did he ever quarrel with Israel or **f**	4309+4309
	11:32	Jephthah went over to **f** the Ammonites,	4309
	12: 1	to **f** the Ammonites without calling us	4309
	12: 3	and crossed over to **f** the Ammonites,	NIH
	12: 3	why have you come up today to **f** me?"	4309
	15:10	"Why have you come to **f** us?"	6584
	18:23	**called out** your men to **f**?"	2410
	20:14	to **f** against the Israelites.	2021+3655+4200+4878
	20:18	"Who of us shall go first to **f** against	4878
	20:20	of Israel went out to **f** the Benjamites	4878
1Sa	4: 1	Now the Israelites went out to **f** against	4878
	4: 9	Be men, and **f**!"	4309
	8:20	and to go out before us and **f** our battles."	4309
	13: 5	The Philistines assembled to **f** Israel,	4309
	17: 9	If he is able to **f** and kill me,	4309
	17:10	Give me a man and *let us* **f** each other."	4309
	17:32	your servant will go and **f** him."	4309
	17:33	to go out against this Philistine and **f** him;	4309
	18:17	only serve me bravely and **f** the battles of	4309
	28: 1	the Philistines gathered their forces to **f**	4309
	29: 8	Why can't I go and **f** against the enemies	4309
2Sa	2:14	the young men get up and **f** hand to hand	8471
	2:28	nor did they **f** anymore.	4309
	10:12	and *let us* **f** bravely for our people and	2616
	10:13	with him advanced to **f** the Arameans,	4878
	11:20	'Why did you get so close to the city to **f**?	4309
	14: 6	*They* **got into** a **f** with each other in	5897
	18: 6	The army marched into the field to **f** Israel,	7925
	21:15	with his men *to* **f** against the Philistines,	4309
1Ki	12:24	Do not go up *to* **f** against your brothers,	4309
	20:23	But if *we* **f** them on the plains,	4309
	20:25	so *we can* **f** Israel on the plains.	4309
	20:26	and went up to **f** against Israel.	4878
	22: 4	with me to **f** against Ramoth Gilead?"	4878
	22:31	"Do not **f** with anyone, small or great,	4309
2Ki	3: 7	Will you go with me to **f** against Moab?"	4878
	3:21	that the kings had come to **f** against them;	4309
	10: 3	Then **f** for your master's house."	4309
	16: 5	of Israel marched up to **f** against Jerusalem	4878
	19: 9	was marching out to **f** against him.	4309
1Ch	12:19	when he went with the Philistines to **f**	4878
	19:13	and *let us* **f** bravely for our people and	2616
	19:14	with him advanced to **f** the Arameans,	4878
2Ch	11: 4	Do not go up to **f** against your brothers.	4309
	13:12	Men of Israel, *do not* **f** against the LORD,	4309
	18:30	"Do not **f** with anyone, small or great,	4309
	20:17	You *will* not *have* to **f** this **battle.**	4309
	25: 8	if you go and **f** courageously in battle,	6913
	32: 8	to help us and to **f** our battles."	4309
	35:20	up to **f** at Carchemish on the Euphrates,	4309
	35:22	but went to **f** him on the plain of Megiddo.	4309
Ne	4: 8	and **f** against Jerusalem and stir up trouble	4309
	4:14	**f** for your brothers,	4309
	4:20	Our God *will* **f** for us!"	4309
Ps	35: 1	**f** against those who fight against me.	4309
	35: 1	fight against *those who* **f** *against* me.	4309
Isa	7: 1	of Remaliah king of Israel marched up to **f**	4878
	19: 2	brother *will* **f** against brother,	4309
	29: 7	Then the hordes of all the nations that **f**	7371
	29: 8	be with the hordes of all the nations that **f**	7371
	37: 9	was marching out to **f** against him.	4309
Jer	1:19	*They will* **f** against you but will	4309
	15:20	*they will* **f** against you but will	4309
	21: 4	in your hands, which you are using to **f**	4309
	21: 5	*I myself will* **f** against you with	4309
	32: 5	If *you* **f** against the Babylonians,	4309
	33: 5	*in the* **f** with the Babylonians,	4309
	34:22	*They will* **f** against it,	4309
	41:12	and went to **f** Ishmael son of Nethaniah.	4309
Da	10:20	Soon I will return to **f** against the prince	4309
	11: 7	*he will* **f** against them and be victorious.	6913
	11:11	of the South will march out in a rage and **f**	4309
Zec	10: 5	*they will* **f** and overthrow the horsemen.	4309
	14: 2	the nations to Jerusalem to **f** against it;	4878
	14: 3	Then the LORD will go out and **f**	4309
	14:14	Judah too *will* **f** at Jerusalem.	4309
Jn	18:36	my servants would **f** to prevent my arrest	76
1Co	9:26	*I do not* **f** like a man beating the air.	4782
2Co	10: 4	The **weapons** we **f** with are not the	
		weapons of the world.	3836+3960+5127
1Ti	1:18	so that by following them *you may* **f**	5129
	1:18	by following them you may fight the good **f**,	5127
	6:12	**F** the good fight of the faith.	76
	6:12	Fight the good **f** of the faith.	74
2Ti	4: 7	I have fought the good **f**,	74
Jas	4: 2	You quarrel and **f**.	4482
Rev	2:16	and *will* **f** against them with the sword	4482

FIGHTER (4) [FIGHT]

2Sa	17: 8	your father is an **experienced f**;	408+4878
	17:10	for all Israel knows that your father is a **f**	1475
	23:20	Benaiah son of Jehoiada was a **valiant f**	408+1201+2657
1Ch	11:22	Benaiah son of Jehoiada was a **valiant f**	408+1201+2657

FIGHTERS (4) [FIGHT]

Jos	10: 2	and all its men were **good f**.	1475
Jdg	20:44	all of them **valiant f**.	408+2657
	20:46	all of them **valiant f**.	408+2657
2Sa	17: 8	they are **f**, and as fierce as a wild bear	1475

FIGHTING (66) [FIGHT]

Ex	2:13	and saw two Hebrews **f**.	5897
	14:25	The LORD *is* **f** for them against Egypt."	4309
	21:22	"If men *who are* **f** hit a pregnant woman	5897
Nu	31:42	from that of the **f** men—	7371
Dt	2:14	of **f** men had perished from the camp,	4878
	2:16	of these **f** men among the people had died,	4878
	20:19	**f** against it to capture it,	4309
	25:11	If two men *are* **f** and the wife of one	5897
Jos	1:14	but all your **f** men, fully armed,	1475+2657
	6: 2	along with its king and its **f** men.	1475+2657
	8: 3	of his **best f men** and sent them out	1475+2657
	10: 7	including all the **best f men**.	1475+2657
	10:14	Surely the LORD *was* **f** for Israel!	4309
Jdg	20:17	all of them **f** men.	4878
	20:34	The **f** was so heavy that the Benjamites did	
	21:10	assembly sent twelve thousand **f** men	1201+2657
1Sa	17:19	**f** against the Philistines."	4309
	17:33	and he has been a **f** man from his youth."	4878
	23: 1	the Philistines *are* **f** against Keilah	4309
	28:15	"The Philistines are **f** against me,	4309
	29: 4	or he will turn against us during the **f**.	4878
	31: 3	The **f** grew fierce around Saul,	4878
2Sa	10: 7	with the entire army of **f** men.	1475
	10:14	So Joab returned from **f** the Ammonites	6584
	11:15	in the front line where the **f** is fiercest.	4878
	24: 2	to Beersheba and enroll the **f** men,	6639
	24: 4	the presence of the king to enroll the **f** men	6639
	24: 9	Joab reported the number of the **f** men to	6639
	24:10	after he had counted the **f** men,	6639
1Ki	9:22	they were his **f** men,	4878

1Ki	11:15	Earlier when David *was* **f** with Edom,	907+2118
	12:21	a hundred and eighty thousand **f** men	4878+6913
	22:34	"Wheel around and get me out of the **f**.	4722
2Ki	19: 8	and found the king **f** against Libnah.	4309
	24:14	all the officers and **f** men,	1475+2657
	24:16	the entire force of seven thousand **f** men,	2657
	25:19	he took the officer in charge of the **f** men	4878
1Ch	5:20	They were helped in **f** them,	6584
	7: 2	descendants of Tola listed as **f** men	1475+2657
	7: 5	The relatives who were **f** men	1475+2657
	7: 7	record listed 22,034 **f** men.	1475+2657
	7: 9	heads of families and 20,200 **f** men.	1475+2657
	7:11	**f** men ready to go out to war.	1475+2657
	10: 3	The **f** grew fierce around Saul,	4878
	12:38	All these were **f** men who volunteered	4878
	19: 8	with the entire army of **f** men.	1475
	21: 5	Joab reported the number of the **f** men	6639
	21:17	not I who ordered the **f** men to be counted?	6639
2Ch	8: 9	they were his **f** men,	4878
	11: 1	a hundred and eighty thousand **f** men,	4878+6913
	13: 3	of four hundred thousand able **f** men,	4878
	14: 8	All these were **brave f** men.	1475+2657
	17:13	He also kept **experienced f** men in Jerusalem	408+1475+2657+4878
	17:14	the commander, with 300,000 **f** men;	1475+2657
	18:33	"Wheel around and get me out of the **f**.	4722
	25: 6	a hundred thousand **f** men from Israel	1475+2657
	26:12	leaders over the **f** men was 2,600.	1475+2657
	32:21	the **f** men and the leaders and officers	1475+2657
Isa	37: 8	and found the king **f** against Libnah.	4309
Jer	34: 1	and peoples in the empire he ruled *were* **f**	4309
	34: 7	of Babylon *was* **f** against Jerusalem and	4309
	51:30	Babylon's warriors have stopped **f**;	4309
	52:25	he took the officer in charge of the **f** men,	4878
Joel	3: 9	Let all the **f** men draw near and attack.	4878
Ac	5:39	you will only find yourselves **f against** God	2534
	7:26	upon two Israelites *who were* **f**.	3481

FIGHTS (6) [FIGHT]

Jos	23:10	because the LORD your God **f** for you,	4309
Jdg	6:31	Whoever **f** for him shall be put to death	8189
1Sa	25:28	because he **f** the LORD's battles.	4309
Isa	30:32	*as* he **f** them in battle *with* the blows	4309
Zec	14: 3	as he **f** in the day of battle.	4309
Jas	4: 1	What causes **f** and quarrels among you?	4483

FIGS (24) [FIG]

Nu	13:23	along with some pomegranates and **f**.	9300
	20: 5	It has no grain or **f**,	9300
1Sa	25:18	and two hundred **cakes of pressed f**,	1811
	30:12	a **cake of pressed f** and two cakes of raisins.	1811
2Sa	16: 1	a hundred **cakes of f** and a skin of wine.	7811
2Ki	20: 7	Then Isaiah said, "Prepare a poultice of **f**."	9300
Ne	13:15	grapes, **f** and all other kinds of loads.	9300
Isa	34: 4	like shriveled **f** from the fig tree.	NIH
	38:21	"Prepare a poultice of **f** and apply it to	9300
Jer	8:13	There will be no **f** on the tree,	9300
	24: 1	of **f** placed in front of the temple of	9300
	24: 2	One basket had very good **f**,	9300
	24: 2	the other basket had very poor **f**,	9300
	24: 3	"F," I answered.	9300
	24: 5	'Like these good **f**,	9300
	24: 8	"'But like the poor **f**,	9300
	29:17	and I will make them like poor **f** that are	9300
Mic	7: 1	none of the **early f** that I crave.	1136
Na	3:12	the **f** fall into the mouth of the eater.	NIH
Mt	7:16	or **f** from thistles?	5192
Mk	11:13	because it was not the season *for* **f**.	5192
Lk	6:44	People do not pick **f** from thornbushes,	5192
Jas	3:12	or a grapevine bear **f**?	5192
Rev	6:13	as late **f** drop from a fig tree when shaken	5190

FIGURATIVELY (4) [FIGURE]

Jn	16:25	"Though I have been speaking **f**,	1877+4231
Gal	4:24	These things may be taken **f**,	251
Heb	11: 9	**f** speaking, he did receive Isaac back	1877+4130
Rev	11: 8	which is **f** called Sodom and Egypt,	4462

FIGURE (4) [FIGURATIVELY, FIGURES]

Eze	1:26	and high above on the throne was a **f** like	1952
	8: 2	I looked, and I saw a **f** like that of a man.	1952
Jn	7: 4	to become a **public f** acts in secret.	1877+4244
	10: 6	Jesus used this **f** of speech,	4231

FIGUREHEAD (1) [HEAD]

Ac	28:11	the **f** of the twin gods Castor and Pollux.	4185

FIGURES (3) [FIGURE]

2Ch	4: 3	Below the rim, **f** of bulls encircled it—	1952
Eze	23:14	**f** of Chaldeans portrayed in red,	7512
Jn	16:29	and without **f** of speech.	4231

FILIGREE (6)

Ex	28:11	Then mount the stones in gold **f** settings	5401
	28:13	Make gold **f** settings	5401
	28:20	Mount them in gold **f** settings.	8687
	39: 6	in gold **f** settings and engraved them like	5401
	39:13	They were mounted in gold **f** settings.	5401
	39:16	They made two gold **f** settings	5401

FILL (68) [FILLED, FILLING, FILLS, FULL,

FULLNESS, FULLY]

Ge	1:22	and increase in number and **f** the water in	4848
	1:28	**f** the earth and subdue it.	4848
	9: 1	"Be fruitful and increase in number and **f**	4848
	42:25	Joseph gave orders *to* **f** their bags	4848
	44: 1	"F the men's sacks *with* as much food	4848
Ex	2:16	and they came to draw water and **f**	4848
	10: 6	*They will* **f** your houses and those	4848
Lev	25:19	you will eat your **f** and live there in safety.	8427
Dt	28:67	of the terror that *will* **f** your hearts and	7064
	31:20	and when they eat *their* **f** and thrive,	8425
1Sa	16: 1	**F** your horn *with* oil and be on your way;	4848
1Ki	18:33	"F four large jars *with* water and pour it on	4848
Job	8:21	*He will* yet **f** your mouth *with* laughter	8427
	15: 2	with empty notions or **f** his belly *with*	4848
	15:21	Terrifying sounds **f** his ears;	928
	15:24	Distress and anguish **f** him *with* terror;	1286
	23: 4	and **f** my mouth *with* arguments.	4848
	31:31	'Who *has* not *had his* **f** of Job's meat?'—	8425
	41: 7	*Can you* **f** his hide with harpoons	4848
Ps	16:11	you will **f** me *with* joy in your presence,	8427
	74:20	of violence **f** the dark places of the land.	4848
	81:10	Open wide your mouth and I *will* **f** it.	4848
	129: 7	*with* it the reaper cannot **f** his hands,	4848
	129: 7	nor the one who gathers **f** his arms.	NIH
Pr	1:13	of valuable things and **f** our houses	4848
	12:21	but the wicked *have* *their* **f** of trouble.	4848
	26:25	for seven abominations **f** his heart.	928
	28:19	one who chases fantasies *will* *have his* **f**	8425
Ecc	1: 8	nor the ear *its* **f** of hearing.	4848
SS	5: 1	**drink** your **f**, O lovers.	8910
Isa	13:21	jackals *will* **f** her houses;	4848
	27: 6	and blossom and **f** all the world *with* fruit.	4848
	33: 5	he *will* **f** Zion *with* justice	4848
	34: 5	My sword *has* **drunk** *its* **f** in the heavens;	8115
	44:16	he roasts his meat and **eats** *his* **f**.	4848
	56:12	*Let us* **drink** our **f** of beer!	6010
	65:11	who spread a table for Fortune and **f** bowls	4848
Jer	13:13	*to* **f** with drunkenness all who live	4848
	23:16	**f** you *with* false hopes.	2038
	23:24	"Do not I **f** heaven and earth?"	4848
	46:12	your cries *will* **f** the earth.	4848
	50:10	all who plunder her *will have their* **f**,"	8425
	51:14	I *will* surely **f** you *with* men,	4848
Eze	3: 3	and **f** your stomach *with* it."	4848
	7:19	not satisfy their hunger or **f** their stomachs	4848
	8:17	*Must they* also **f** the land *with* violence	4848
	9: 7	the temple and **f** the courts *with* the slain.	4848
	10: 2	**F** your hands with burning coals from	4848
	20:26	that *I might* **f** them *with* horror	9037
	24: 4	**F** it *with* the best of these bones;	4848
	30:11	against Egypt and **f** the land *with* the slain.	4848
	32: 5	and **f** the valleys *with* your remains.	4848
	35: 8	I *will* **f** your mountains *with* the slain;	4848
	39:20	At my table *you will* **eat** *your* **f** of horses	8425
Da	7: 5	'Get up and eat your **f** of flesh!'	10678
Zep	1: 9	who **f** the temple of their gods	4848
Hag	1: 6	You drink, but never *have* *your* **f**.	8910
	2: 7	and *I will* **f** this house *with* glory,'	4848
Zec	9:13	I will bend Judah as I bend my bow and **f** it	4848
Mt	23:32	**F** up, then, the measure of the sin	4444
Lk	15:16	He longed *to* **f** his stomach with the pods	1153
Jn	2: 7	"F the jars *with* water."	1153
	6:26	because you ate the loaves and *had* your **f**.	5963
Ac	2:28	*you will* **f** me *with* joy in your presence.'	4444
Ro	15:13	May the God of hope **f** you *with* all joy	4444
Eph	4:10	in order to **f** the whole universe.)	4444
Col	1: 9	*to* **f** you *with* the knowledge of his will	4444
	1:24	and I **f up** in my flesh what is still lacking	499

FILLED (184) [FILL]

Ge	6: 6	and his heart *was* **f with** pain.	6772
	6:13	earth *is* **f** with violence because of them.	4848
	21:19	and **f** the skin *with* water and gave the boy	4848
	24:16	**f** her jar and came up again.	4848
	34: 7	They *were* **f with** grief and fury,	6772
Ex	1: 7	so that the land *was* **f** with them.	4848
	16:12	in the morning *you will be* **f** with bread.	8425
	31: 3	and *I have* **f** him *with* the Spirit of God,	4848
	35:31	and he *has* **f** him *with* the Spirit of God,	4848
	35:35	He *has* **f** them *with* skill to do all kinds	4848
	40:34	the glory of the LORD **f** the tabernacle.	4848
	40:35	the glory of the LORD **f** the tabernacle.	4848
Lev	19:29	or the land will turn to prostitution and *be* **f**	4848
Nu	7:13	each **f** *with* fine flour mixed with oil as	4849
	7:14	one gold dish weighing ten shekels, **f** *with* incense;	4849
	7:19	each **f** *with* fine flour mixed with oil as	4849
	7:20	one gold dish weighing ten shekels, **f** *with* incense;	4849
	7:25	each **f** *with* fine flour mixed with oil as	4849
	7:26	one gold dish weighing ten shekels, **f** *with* incense;	4849
	7:31	each **f** *with* fine flour mixed with oil as	4849
	7:32	one gold dish weighing ten shekels, **f** *with* incense;	4849
	7:37	each **f** *with* fine flour mixed with oil as	4849
	7:38	one gold dish weighing ten shekels, **f** *with* incense;	4849
	7:43	each **f** *with* fine flour mixed with oil as	4849
	7:44	one gold dish weighing ten shekels, **f** *with* incense;	4849
	7:49	each **f** *with* fine flour mixed with oil as	4849
	7:50	one gold dish weighing ten shekels, **f** *with* incense;	4849
	7:55	each **f** *with* fine flour mixed with oil as	4849

Nu	7:56	one gold dish weighing ten shekels, **f** *with* incense;	4849
	7:61	each **f** *with* fine flour mixed with oil as	4849
	7:62	one gold dish weighing ten shekels, **f** *with* incense;	4849
	7:67	each **f** *with* fine flour mixed with oil as	4849
	7:68	one gold dish weighing ten shekels, **f** *with* incense;	4849
	7:73	each **f** *with* fine flour mixed with oil as	4849
	7:74	one gold dish weighing ten shekels, **f** *with* incense;	4849
	7:79	each **f** *with* fine flour mixed with oil as	4849
	7:80	one gold dish weighing ten shekels, **f** *with* incense;	4849
	7:86	The twelve gold dishes **f** with incense	4849
	22: 3	Moab *was* **f with** dread because of	7762
	22:18	if Balak gave me his palace **f** *with* silver	4850
	24:13	if Balak gave me his palace **f** *with* silver	4850
Dt	6:11	houses **f** with all kinds	4849
	28:66	**f with** dread both night and day,	7064
	32:15	**f with** food, he became heavy and sleek.	9042
	32:32	Their **grapes** *are* **f** with poison,	AIT
	34: 9	of Nun *was* **f** with the spirit of wisdom	4848
Jos	9:13	And these wineskins that *we* **f** were new,	4848
Ru	1:21	a drink from the water jars the men *have* **f**."	8612
1Sa	5:11	death *had* **f** the city *with* panic;	928+2118+3972
	28: 5	**terror f** his heart.	3006+4394
	28:20	**f with** fear because of Samuel's words.	3707+4394
1Ki	3:26	The woman whose son was alive *was* **f with**	4023
	8:10	the cloud **f** the temple of the LORD.	4848
	8:11	for the glory of the LORD **f** his temple.	4848
	11:27	the supporting terraces and *had* **f in** the gap	6037
	18:35	around the altar and even **f** the trench.	4848
2Ki	3:17	yet this valley *will be* **f** *with* water,	4848
	3:20	And the land *was* **f** *with* water.	4848
	4: 4	Pour oil into all the jars, and as each is **f**,	4849
	4:39	of its gourds and the fold of his cloak.	4850
	21:16	so much innocent blood that *he* **f** Jerusalem	4848
	24: 4	For *he had* **f** Jerusalem with innocent blood,	4848
2Ch	5:13	temple of the LORD *was* **f** with a cloud,	4848
	5:14	glory of the LORD **f** the temple of God.	4848
	7: 1	and the glory of the LORD **f** the temple.	4848
	7: 2	because the glory of the LORD **f** it.	4848
Ezr	6:22	the LORD *had* **f** them **with joy** by changing	8523
	9:11	By their detestable practices *they have* **f** it	4848
Ne	9:25	of houses **f** with all kinds of good things,	4849
Est	5: 9	he *was* **f** *with* rage against Mordecai.	4848
Job	3:15	who **f** their houses with silver.	4848
	3:22	who are **f with gladness** and	448+1637+8524
	20:23	When he has **f** his belly,	4848
	22:18	Yet it was he *who* **f** their houses	4848
Ps	4: 7	*You have* **f** my heart *with* greater joy than	5989
	5: 9	their heart is **f** with destruction.	NIH
	38: 7	My back is **f** with searing pain;	4848
	48:10	your right hand is **f** with righteousness.	4848
	65: 4	*We are* **f** with the good things	8425
	65: 9	The streams of God *are* **f** with water	4848
	71: 8	My mouth is **f** with your praise,	4848
	72:19	*may* the whole earth *be* **f** *with* his glory.	4848
	80: 9	and it took root and **f** the land.	4848
	119:64	The earth *is* **f** with your love, O LORD;	4848
	126: 2	Our mouths *were* **f** with laughter,	4848
	126: 3	and we are **f** with joy.	8524
	144:13	Our barns will be **f** *with* every kind	4849
Pr	1:31	and *be* **f** with the fruit of their schemes.	8425
	3:10	then your barns *will be* **f** to overflowing,	4848
	7:20	He took his **purse f** *with* money	AIT
	8:30	I was **f with delight** day after day,	9141
	12:14	of his lips a man *is* **f** *with* good things as	8425
	18:20	of his mouth a man's stomach *is* **f**;	8425
	24: 4	through knowledge its rooms are **f**	4848
Ecc	8:11	the people *are* **f** with schemes to do wrong.	4848
Isa	6: 1	and the train of his robe **f** the temple.	4848
	6: 4	and thresholds shook and the temple was **f**	4848
	41:23	that we will be dismayed and **f** with **fear**.	AIT
	51:20	They are **f** *with* the wrath of the LORD	4848
	6:11	it is **f with** oppression.	928+7931
Jer	13:12	Every wineskin *should be* **f** *with* wine.'	4848
	13:12	that every wineskin *should be* **f**	4848
	15:17	on me and *you had* **f** me *with* indignation.	4848
	16:18	and *have* **f** my inheritance	4848
	19: 4	and *they have* **f** this place *with* the blood of	4848
	25:15	from my hand this **cup f** *with* the wine	AIT
	31:14	and my people *will be* **f** *with* my bounty,"	8425
	33: 5	'They *will be* **f** with the dead bodies of	4848
	41: 9	Ishmael son of Nethaniah **f** it *with*	4848
	50: 2	be put to shame, Marduk *will be* **f with terror**.	3169
	50: 2	to shame and her idols **f with terror**.'	3169
	50:36	*They will be* **f with terror**.	3169
	51:34	and **f** his stomach with our delicacies,	4848
La	3:15	*He has* **f** me with bitter herbs and sated me	8425
	3:30	and *let him be* **f** with disgrace.	8425
Eze	10: 3	and a cloud **f** the inner court.	4848
	10: 4	The cloud **f** the temple,	4848
	11: 6	in this city and **f** its streets *with* the dead.	4848
	23:33	*You will be* **f** *with* drunkenness	4848
	27:25	*You are* **f** with heavy cargo in the heart of	4848
	28:16	Through your widespread trade you *were* **f**	4848
	32: 6	and the ravines *will be* **f** with your flesh.	4848
	36:38	the ruined cities be **f** with flocks of people.	4849
	43: 5	and the glory of the LORD **f** the temple.	4848
Da	2:35	the statue became a huge mountain and **f**	10416
	11:12	king of the South *will be* **f with pride**	4222+8123
Joel	2:24	The threshing floors *will be* **f** with grain;	4848
Am	4:10	*I* **f** your nostrils *with* the stench	6590
Mic	3: 8	But as for me, *I am* **f** with power,	4848

Na	1: 2	the LORD takes vengeance and is f **with**	1251
Hab	2:14	For the earth *will be* f with the knowledge	4848
	2:16	*You will be* f with shame instead of glory.	8425
	3: 3	the heavens and his praise f the earth.	4848
Zec	8: 5	The city streets *will be* f *with* boys	4848
Mt	5: 6	for they *will be* f.	5963
	9: 8	they were f **with awe;**	5828
	17:23	And the disciples *were* f with grief.	3382+5379
	22:10	and the wedding hall *was* f with guests.	4398
	27:48	*He* f it with wine vinegar, put it on a stick,	4398
	28: 8	afraid yet f **with joy,**	3489+5915
Mk	1:41	F **with compassion,** Jesus reached out his hand	5072
	15:36	f a sponge with wine vinegar,	1153
Lk	1:15	and *he will be* f with the Holy Spirit even	4398
	1:41	and Elizabeth *was* f with the Holy Spirit.	4398
	1:53	*He has* f the hungry with good things	1855
	1:65	The neighbors were all f with awe,	NIG
	1:67	His father Zechariah *was* f with the Holy Spirit and prophesied.	4398
	2:40	he *was* f with wisdom,	4444
	3: 5	Every valley *shall be* f **in,**	4444
	5: 7	and f both boats so full that they began	4398
	5:26	*They were* f with awe and said,	4398
	7:16	They were all f **with awe** and praised God.	3284+5832
	15:20	and *was* f **with compassion** for him;	5072
Jn	2: 7	so *they* f them to the brim.	1153
	6:13	So they gathered them and f twelve baskets	1153
	12: 3	And the house *was* f with the fragrance of	4444
	16: 6	you *are* f **with** grief.	4444
Ac	2: 2	of a violent wind came from heaven and f	4444
	2: 4	All of them *were* f with the Holy Spirit	4398
	2:43	Everyone *was* f with awe,	1181
	3:10	and *they were* f with wonder	4398
	4: 8	Peter, f with the Holy Spirit, said to them:	4398
	4:31	And *they were* all f with the Holy Spirit	4398
	5: 3	how is it that Satan *has* so f your heart	4444
	5:17	*were* f with jealousy.	4398
	5:28	"Yet *you have* f Jerusalem	4444
	9:17	so that you may see again and be f with	4398
	13: 9	f with the Holy Spirit,	4398
	13:45	*they were* f with jealousy	4398
	13:52	And the disciples *were* f with joy and with	4444
	16:34	*he was* f **with joy** because he had come	22
Ro	1:29	*They have* become f with every kind	4444
1Co	5: 2	Shouldn't *you* rather *have* been f **with grief**	4291
Eph	3:19	that *you may be* f to the measure of all	4444
	5:18	Instead, *be* f **with the Spirit.**	4444
Php	1:11	f **with the fruit** of righteousness that comes	4444
2Ti	1: 4	so that *I may be* f with joy.	4444
1Pe	1: 8	f **with** an inexpressible and glorious **joy,**	22+5915
Rev	8: 5	f it with fire from the altar,	1153
	12:12	*He is* f **with** fury,	2400
	15: 7	the seven angels seven golden bowls f with	1154
	15: 8	And the temple *was* f with smoke from	1153
	16:19	and gave her the cup f with the wine of	NIG
	17: 4	with abominable things and the filth	1154

FILLET, FILLETED   (KJV) See BANDS

FILLING   (3) [FILL]

Ge	26:15	Philistines stopped up, f them *with* earth.	4848
Eze	44: 4	I looked and saw the glory of the LORD f	4848
Na	2:12	f his lairs *with* the kill and his dens *with*	4848

FILLS   (6) [FILL]

Nu	14:21	the glory of the LORD f the whole earth,	4848
Job	20:11	The youthful vigor *that* f his bones will lie	4848
	36:32	He f his hands *with* lightning	4059
Ps	107: 9	for he satisfies the thirsty and f the hungry	4848
Ac	14:17	f your hearts **with joy."**	2372
Eph	1:23	of him who f everything in every way.	4444

FILTH   (9) [FILTHINESS, FILTHY]

2Ki	18:27	who, like you, will have to eat their own f	2989
Pr	30:12	and yet are not cleansed of their f;	7363
Isa	4: 4	The Lord will wash away the f	7363
	28: 8	and there is not a spot without f.	7363
	36:12	who, like you, will have to eat their own f	2989
Na	3: 6	I will pelt you with f,	9199
Zep	1:17	like dust and their entrails like f.	1672
Jas	1:21	get rid of all **moral** f and the evil that is	4864
Rev	17: 4	filled with abominable things and the f	176

FILTHINESS   (1) [FILTH]

La	1: 9	Her f clung to her skirts;	3240

FILTHY   (5) [FILTH]

Isa	64: 6	and all our righteous acts are like f rags;	6340
Zec	3: 3	in f clothes as he stood before the angel.	7364
	3: 4	"Take off his f clothes."	7364
Col	3: 8	slander, and f **language** from your lips.	155
2Pe	2: 7	who was distressed by the f lives	816

FINAL   (6) [FINALITY, FINALLY]

Ru	4: 7	and transfer of property to *become* f,	7756
Ps	73:17	then I understood their f **destiny.**	344
Isa	41:22	and know their f **outcome.**	344
Mt	12:45	the f *condition* of that man is worse than	2274
Lk	11:26	the f *condition* of that man is worse than	2274
Ac	28:25	after Paul had made this f statement:	NIG

FINALITY   (1) [FINAL]

Ro	9:28	on earth *with* speed and f."	5334

FINALLY   (36) [FINAL]

Nu	10:25	F, as the rear guard for all the units,	2256
Jdg	9:14	"F all the trees said to the thornbush,	2256
	14:17	So on the seventh day she f told him,	NIH
1Sa	10:21	F Saul son of Kish was chosen.	2256
	19:22	F, he himself left for Ramah and went	1685+2256
2Sa	24: 7	F, they went on to Beersheba in the Negev	2256
1Ki	17:17	and f stopped breathing.	889+6330
	22:21	F, a spirit came forward,	2256
2Ch	18:20	F, a spirit came forward,	2256
Ne	2:15	F, I turned back and reentered through	2256
Da	2:40	F, there will be a fourth kingdom,	10221
	4: 8	F, Daniel came into my presence	10024+10221+10527
	6: 5	F these men said,	10008
	12: 7	power of the holy people has been f broken,	3983
Mt	22:27	F, the woman died.	4246+5731
	26:60	F two came forward,	5731
Mk	6:21	F the opportune time came.	NIG
Lk	18: 4	But f he said to himself,	3552+4047
	20:32	F, the woman died too.	5731
Jn	1:22	F they said, "Who are you?	4036
	7:45	F the temple guards went back to	4036
	9:17	F they turned again to the blind man,	4036
	19:16	F Pilate handed him over to them to	5538
	20: 8	F the other disciple,	4036+5538
Ac	16:18	F Paul became so troubled that he turned	1254
	20: 2	and f arrived in Greece,	NIG
	27:20	we f gave up all hope of being saved.	3370
2Co	13:11	F, brothers, good-by.	3370
Gal	6:17	F, let no one cause me trouble,	3370+3836
Eph	6:10	F, be strong in the Lord and	3370+3836
Php	3: 1	F, my brothers, rejoice in the Lord!	3370+3836
	4: 8	F, brothers, whatever is true,	3370+3836
1Th	4: 1	F, brothers, we instructed you how to live	3370
2Th	3: 1	F, brothers, pray for us that	3370+3836
Jas	5:11	have seen what the Lord f brought about.	5465
1Pe	3: 8	F, all of you, live in harmony	3836+5465

FINANCIAL   (1)

1Ti	6: 5	think that godliness is a **means to** f **gain.**	4516

FIND   (230) [FINDING, FINDS, FOUND]

Ge	8: 9	the dove *could* f no place to set its feet	5162
	18:26	"If *I* f fifty righteous people in the city	5162
	18:28	"If *I* f forty-five there," he said,	5162
	18:30	"I will not do it if *I* f thirty there."	5162
	19:11	with blindness so that they could not f	5162
	27:20	"How *did you* f it so quickly, my son?"	5162
	31:32	But if *you* f anyone who has your gods,	5162
	31:35	but *could* not f the household gods.	5162
	32: 5	that *I may* f favor in your eyes.' "	5162
	33: 8	"To f favor in your eyes, my lord," he said.	5162
	33:15	"Just *let me* f favor in the eyes	5162
	34:11	"Let me f favor in your eyes,	5162
	38:20	but *he did* not f her.	5162
	38:22	"I didn't f her.	5162
	38:23	but you didn't f her."	5162
	41:38	"Can *we* f anyone like this man,	5162
	44:15	f things out by divination?"	5727+5727
	47:25	"May *we* f favor in the eyes of our lord;	5162
Ex	5:11	get your own straw wherever *you can* f it,	5162
	16:25	not f any of it on the ground today.	5162
	33:13	and *continue to* f favor with you.	5162
Nu	9: 8	until *I* f out what the LORD commands	9048
	10:33	during those three days to f them a place	9365
	22:19	and *I will* f out what else	3359
	32:23	be sure that your sin *will* f you **out.**	5162
Dt	4:29	*you will* f him if you look for him	5162
	13: 3	to f out whether you love him	3359
	14:21	Do not eat anything you f already dead.	NIH
	22: 3	Do the same if you f your brother's donkey	NIH
	22:14	*I did* not f proof of her virginity,"	5162
	22:17	'*I did* not f your daughter to be a virgin.'	5162
	28:65	Among those nations *you will* f no **repose,**	8089
Jos	2:16	to the hills so the pursuers *will* not f you.	7003
	20: 3	and f protection from the avenger of blood.	2118
Jdg	18: 8	"How did you f **things?"**	4537
	18:10	*you will* f an unsuspecting people and	448+995
Ru	1: 9	that each of you *will* f rest in the home	5162
	2: 2	behind anyone in whose eyes *I* f favor."	5162
	2:13	"May *I continue to* f favor in your eyes,	5162
	3: 1	*should I* not **try to** f a home for you,	1335
	3:18	until *you* f out what happens.	3359
1Sa	1:18	"May your servant f favor in your eyes."	5162
	9: 4	but *they did* not f **them.**	5162
	9: 4	but *they* did not f them.	5162
	9:13	*you will* f him before he goes up to	5162
	9:13	*you should* f him about this time."	5162
	14:38	*let us* f **out** what sin has been committed today.	2256+3359+8011
	16:17	"F someone who plays well and bring him	8011
	17:56	"F **out** whose son this young man is."	8626
	19: 3	about you and will tell you what *I* f **out."**	8011
	20:21	Then I will send a boy and say, 'Go, f	5162
	20:36	"Run and f the arrows I shoot."	5162
	21: 3	or whatever *you can* f."	5162
	23:16	and **helped** him f **strength**	906+2616+3338
	23:22	F **out** where David usually goes	2256+3359+8011
	23:23	F **out** about all the hiding places he uses	2256+3359+8011

1Sa	25: 8	and your son David whatever you can f	5162
	28: 7	"F me a woman who is a medium,	1335
2Sa	3:25	and f **out** everything you are doing."	3359
	11: 3	David sent someone to f **out** about her.	2011
	15:25	If *I* f favor in the LORD's eyes,	5162
	16: 4	"May *I* f favor in your eyes,"	5162
	20: 6	or *he will* f fortified cities and escape	5162
1Ki	18: 5	Maybe *we can* f some grass to keep	5162
	18:10	he made them swear *they could* not f you.	5162
	18:12	If I go and tell Ahab and *he* doesn't f you,	5162
	22:25	"You *will* f **out** on the day you go to hide	8011
2Ki	2:17	for three days but *did* not f him.	5162
	6:13	"Go, f **out** where he is," the king ordered,	8011
	7:13	let us send men to f **out** what happened."	8011
	7:14	"Go and f **out** what has happened."	8011
2Ch	18:24	"You *will* f **out** on the day you go to hide	8011
	20:16	and *you will* f them at the end of	5162
	32: 4	of Assyria come and f **plenty** of water?"	5162
Ezr	2:62	not f them and so were excluded from	5162
	4:15	In these records *you will* f that this city is	10708
Ne	5: 8	because *they could* f nothing to say.	5162
	7:64	not f them and so were excluded from	5162
Est	2:11	near the courtyard of the harem to f **out**	3359
	4: 5	to f **out** what was troubling Mordecai	3359
Job	5:24	of your property and f nothing **missing.**	2627
	8: 8	and f **out** what their fathers learned,	3922
	9:14	*How can I* f words to argue with him?	1047
	17:10	*I will* not f a wise man among you.	5162
	22:26	then *you will* f **delight** in the Almighty	6695
	23: 3	If only I knew where to f him;	5162
	23: 5	*I would* f **out** what he would answer me,	3359
	23: 8	if I go to the west, *I do* not f him.	1067
	27:10	*Will he* f **delight** in the Almighty?	6695
	32:20	I must speak and f **relief;**	8118
Ps	17: 3	though you test me, *you will* f nothing;	5162
	36: 7	and low among men f **refuge** in the shadow	2879
	62: 5	F **rest,** O my soul, in God alone;	1957
	91: 4	and under his wings *you will* f **refuge;**	2879
	119:35	for there *I* f **delight.**	2911
	119:52	O LORD, and *I* f **comfort** in them.	5714
	132: 5	till *I* f a place for the LORD,	5162
Pr	2: 5	they will look for me but will not f me.	5162
	2: 5	of the LORD and f the knowledge of God.	5162
	4:22	for they are life to those who f them	5162
	8:17	and those who seek me f me.	5162
	8:36	But *whoever* **fails to** f me harms himself;	2627
	14: 7	for *you will* not f knowledge on his lips.	3359
	14:22	But those who plan what is good f love	NIH
	20: 6	but a faithful man who can f?	5162
	23:35	will I wake up so *I can* f another drink?"	1335
	24:14	if *you* f it, there is a future hope for you,	5162
	25:16	If *you* f honey, eat just enough—	5162
	31:10	A wife of noble character who *can* f?	5162
Ecc	2: 1	with pleasure *to* f **out** what is good."	8011
	2:24	and drink and f satisfaction in his work.	8011
	2:25	who can eat or f **enjoyment?**	2591
	3:13	and f satisfaction in all his toil—	8011
	5:18	to f satisfaction in his toilsome labor under	8011
	7:26	I f more bitter than death	5162
	11: 1	for after many days *you will* f it *again.*	5162
	12: 1	"I f no pleasure in them"—	4200
	12:10	Teacher searched to f just the right words,	5162
SS	3: 1	I looked for him but *did* not f him.	5162
	3: 2	So I looked for him but *did* not f him.	5162
	5: 6	I looked for him but *did* not f him.	5162
	5: 8	if *you* f my lover, what will you tell him?	5162
Isa	14:30	The poorest of the poor *will* f pasture,	8286
	14:32	in her his afflicted people *will* f **refuge.**	2879
	23:12	even there you *will* f **no rest."**	5663
	34:14	the night creatures will also repose and f	5162
	41:12	*you will* not f **them.**	5162
	49: 9	and f pasture on every barren hill.	NIH
	57: 2	*they* f **rest** as they lie in death.	5663
	58:14	then *you will* f your **joy** in the LORD,	6695
	59:11	We look for justice, but f none;	NIH
Jer	2: 5	"What fault *did* your fathers f in me,	5162
	2:24	at mating time *they will* f her.	5162
	2:34	On your clothes **men** f the lifeblood of	5162
	5: 1	*If you can* f but one person	5162
	6:10	*they* f **no pleasure** in it.	2911
	6:16	and *you will* f **rest** for your souls.	5162
	14: 3	they go to the cisterns but f no water.	5162
	23:11	even in my temple *I* f their wickedness,"	5162
	29: 6	f **wives** for your sons	4374
	29:13	and f me when you seek me	5162
	31: 2	the sword *will* f favor in the desert;	5162
	45: 3	with groaning and f **no rest.'** "	5162
La	1: 6	Her princes are like deer *that* f no pasture;	5162
	2: 9	and her prophets no longer f visions from	5162
	5: 5	we are weary and f **no rest.**	5663
Eze	17:23	*they will* f **shelter** in the shade	8905
Da	6: 4	the satraps tried to f grounds for charges	10708
	6: 4	*They could* f no corruption in him,	10708
	6: 5	"We will never f any basis for charges	10708
Hos	2: 6	in so that *she* cannot f her way.	5162
	2: 7	she will look for them but not f them.	5162
	5: 6	*they will* not f **him.**	5162
	12: 8	With all my wealth *they will* not f	5162
	14: 3	for in you the fatherless f **compassion."**	8163
Am	8:12	but *they will* not f it.	5162
Jnh	1: 7	let us cast lots to f **out** who is responsible	3359
Na	3: 7	Where *can I* f anyone to comfort you?"	1335
Zep	2: 3	there *they will* f **pasture.**	8286
Zec	2: 2	to f **out** how wide and how long it is."	8011
Mt	2: 8	As soon as *you* f him, report to me,	2351
	7: 7	seek and *you will* f;	2351
	7:14	that leads to life, and only a few f it.	1639+2351

Mt	10:39	whoever loses his life for my sake will f it.	2351
	11:29	and you will f rest for your souls.	2351
	12:43	seeking rest and does not f it.	2351
	16:25	but whoever loses his life for me will f it.	2351
	17:27	and you will f a four-drachma coin.	2351
	21: 2	at once you will f a donkey tied there,	2351
	22: 9	and invite to the banquet anyone you f.'	2351
	22:10	and gathered all the people they could f,	2351
	26:60	But they did not f any,	2351
Mk	11: 2	you will f a colt tied there,	2351
	11:13	he went to f out if it had any fruit.	2351
	13:36	do not let him f you sleeping.	2351
	14:55	but they did not f any.	2351
Lk	1:62	to f out what he would like to name	NIG
	2:12	You will f a baby wrapped in cloths	2351
	2:45	When they did not f him,	2351
	5:19	When they could not f a way to do this	2351
	9:12	and countryside and f food and lodging,	2351
	11: 9	seek and you will f;	2351
	11:24	seeking rest and does not f it.	2351
	13: 6	to look for fruit on it, but did not f any.	2351
	18: 8	will he f faith on the earth?"	2351
	19:15	in order to f out what they had gained	1182
	19:30	you will f a colt tied there,	2351
	19:48	Yet they could not f any way to do it,	2351
	23: 4	"I f no basis for a charge against this man."	2351
	24: 3	they did not f the body of the Lord Jesus.	2351
	24:23	but didn't f his body.	2351
Jn	1:41	to f his brother Simon and tell him,	2351
	4:27	and were surprised to f him talking with	NIG
	7:17	he will f out whether my teaching comes	1182
	7:34	but you will not f me;	2351
	7:35	to go that we cannot f him?	2351
	7:36	but you will not f me,' and 'Where I am,	2351
	7:51	to f out what he is doing?"	1182
	7:52	and you f that a prophet does	3972
	10: 9	He will come in and go out, and f pasture.	2351
	18:38	"I f no basis for a charge against him.	2351
	19: 4	to you to let you know that I f no basis for	2351
	19: 6	I f no basis for a charge against him."	2351
	21: 6	of the boat and you will f some."	2351
Ac	5:22	the officers did not f them there.	2351
	5:39	you will only f yourselves fighting	2351
	7:11	and our fathers could not f food.	2351
	12:19	for him and did not f him,	2351
	16:13	where we expected to f a place of prayer.	1639
	17: 6	But when they did not f them,	2351
	17:27	and perhaps reach out for him and f him,	2351
	22:24	to f out why the people were shouting	2105
	22:30	to f out exactly why Paul was being accused	1182
	23: 9	"We f nothing wrong with this man,"	2351
	24:12	My accusers did not f me arguing	2351
	24:25	When I f it convenient,	2789+3561
Ro	7:21	So I f this law at work:	2351
1Co	4:19	and then I will f out not only	1182
2Co	2:13	because I did not f my brother Titus there.	2351
	9: 4	with me and f you unprepared, we—	2351
	12:20	when I come I may not f you as I want you	2351
	12:20	and you may not f me as you want me	2351
Eph	5:10	and f out what pleases the Lord.	1507
1Th	3: 5	I sent to f out about your faith.	1182
2Ti	1:18	the Lord grant that he will f mercy from	2351
Heb	4:16	and f grace to help us in our time of need.	2351
Jas	3:16	there you f disorder and every evil practice.	NIG
1Pe	1:11	trying to f out the time and circumstances	2236
2Jn	1: 4	to f some of your children walking in the truth,	2351
Rev	9: 6	men will seek death, but will not f it;	2351

FINDING (12) [FIND]

Ex	15:22	in the desert without f water.	5162
Jos	2:22	the road and returned without f them.	5162
Jdg	5:30	'Are they not f and dividing the spoils:	5162
	15:15	F a fresh jawbone of a donkey,	5162
Job	36:26	The number of his years is past f out.	2984
Ps	107: 4	f no way to a city where they could settle.	5162
Ecc	7:28	while I was still searching but not f—	5162
Hos	9:10	it was like f grapes in the desert;	NIH
Jn	1:43	F Philip, he said to him, "Follow me."	2351
Ac	5:10	the young men came in and, f her dead,	2351
	21: 4	F the disciples there,	461
Jas	1: 5	to all without f fault,	3943

FINDS (45) [FIND]

Ge	4:14	and whoever f me will kill me."	5162
Lev	6: 3	or if he f lost property and lies about it, or	5162
Nu	35:27	the avenger of blood f him outside the city,	5162
Dt	24: 1	because he f something indecent about her,	5162
Jdg	9:33	do whatever your hand f to do."	5162
1Sa	10: 7	do whatever your hand f to do,	5162
	24:19	When a man f his enemy,	5162
Job	33:20	so that his very being f food repulsive	2299
	33:26	He prays to God and f favor with him,	8354
Ps	55:15	for evil f lodging among them.	NIH
	62: 1	My soul f rest in God alone;	NIH
	112: 1	who f great delight in his commands.	2911
	119:162	in your promise like one who f great spoil.	5162
Pr	3:13	Blessed is the man who f wisdom,	5162
	8:35	For whoever f me finds life	5162
	8:35	For whoever finds me f life	5162
	10:23	A fool f pleasure in evil conduct,	4200
	11:27	He who seeks good f goodwill,	1335
	14: 6	The mocker seeks wisdom and f none,	AIT
	15:23	A man f joy in giving an apt reply—	NIH
	18: 2	A fool f no pleasure in understanding	2911

Pr	18:22	He who f a wife finds what is good	5162
	18:22	a wife f what is good and receives favor	5162
	20: 4	so at harvest time he looks but f nothing.	NIH
	21:21	who pursues righteousness and love f life,	5162
	28:13	and renounces them f mercy.	8163
Ecc	9:10	Whatever your hand f to do,	5162
Isa	38:16	and my spirit f life in them too.	NIH
La	1: 3	she f no resting place.	5162
Mt	7: 8	he who seeks f;	2351
	10:39	Whoever f his life will lose it,	2351
	12:44	it f the house unoccupied,	2351
	18:13	And if he f it, I tell you the truth,	1181+2351
	24:46	for that servant whose master f him doing	2351
Lk	11:10	he who seeks f;	2351
	11:25	it f the house swept clean and put	2351
	12:37	good for those servants whose master f them watching	2351
	12:38	those servants whose master f them ready,	2351
	12:43	for that servant whom the master f doing	2351
	15: 4	and go after the lost sheep until he f it?	2351
	15: 5	And when he f it,	2351
	15: 8	and search carefully until she f it?	2351
	15: 9	And when she f it,	2351
	22:16	not eat it again until it f fulfillment in the kingdom of God."	4444
1Co	14:16	how can one who f himself among those	405

FINE (123) [FINE-LOOKING, FINE-SOUNDING, FINED, FINELY, FINERY, FINES, FINEST]

Ge	18: 6	"get three seahs of f flour and knead it	6159
	41:42	He dressed him in robes of f linen and put	9254
Ex	2: 2	When she saw that he was a f child,	3202
	9: 9	It will become f dust over the whole land	85
	25: 4	purple and scarlet yarn and f linen;	9254
	28: 5	purple and scarlet yarn, and f linen.	9254
	28:39	the tunic of f linen and make the turban	9254
	28:39	and make the turban of f linen.	9254
	29: 2	And from f wheat flour, without yeast,	6159
	29:40	a tenth of an ephah of f flour mixed with	6159
	30:23	"Take the following f spices:	8031
	35: 6	purple and scarlet yarn and f linen;	9254
	35:23	purple and scarlet yarn or f linen,	9254
	35:25	blue, purple or scarlet yarn or f linen.	9254
	35:35	purple and scarlet yarn and f linen—	9254
	38:23	purple and scarlet yarn and f linen.)	9254
	39: 3	purple and scarlet yarn and f linen—	9254
	39:27	they made tunics of f linen—	9254
	39:28	and the turban of f linen,	9254
Lev	2: 1	his offering is to be of f flour.	6159
	2: 2	a handful of the f flour and oil,	6159
	2: 4	it is to consist of f flour:	6159
	2: 5	it is to be made of f flour mixed with oil,	6159
	2: 7	it is to be made of f flour and oil.	6159
	5:11	of an ephah of f flour for a sin offering.	6159
	6:15	The priest is to take a handful of f flour	6159
	6:20	of f flour as a regular grain offering,	6159
	7:12	of f flour well-kneaded and mixed	6159
	14:10	of an ephah of f flour mixed with oil for	6159
	14:21	with a tenth of an ephah of f flour mixed	6159
	23:13	of an ephah of f flour mixed with oil—	6159
	23:17	of two-tenths of an ephah of f flour,	6159
	24: 5	"Take f flour and bake twelve loaves	6159
Nu	6:15	cakes made of f flour mixed with oil,	6159
	7:13	each filled with f flour mixed with oil as	6159
	7:19	each filled with f flour mixed with oil as	6159
	7:25	each filled with f flour mixed with oil as	6159
	7:31	each filled with f flour mixed with oil as	6159
	7:37	each filled with f flour mixed with oil as	6159
	7:43	each filled with f flour mixed with oil as	6159
	7:49	each filled with f flour mixed with oil as	6159
	7:55	each filled with f flour mixed with oil as	6159
	7:61	each filled with f flour mixed with oil as	6159
	7:67	each filled with f flour mixed with oil as	6159
	7:73	each filled with f flour mixed with oil as	6159
	7:79	each filled with f flour mixed with oil as	6159
	8: 8	with its grain offering of f flour mixed	6159
	15: 4	a tenth of an ephah of f flour mixed with	6159
	15: 6	an ephah of f flour mixed with a third of	6159
	15: 9	an ephah of f flour mixed with half a hin	6159
	28: 5	a tenth of an ephah of f flour mixed with	6159
	28: 9	of an ephah of f flour mixed with oil.	6159
	28:12	of an ephah of f flour mixed with oil;	6159
	28:12	of an ephah of f flour mixed with oil;	6159
	28:13	of a tenth of an ephah of f flour mixed	6159
	28:20	of an ephah of f flour mixed with oil;	6159
	28:28	of an ephah of f flour mixed with oil;	6159
	29: 3	of an ephah of f flour mixed with oil;	6159
	29: 9	of an ephah of f flour mixed with oil;	6159
	29:14	of an ephah of f flour mixed with oil.	6159
Dt	3:25	that f hill country and Lebanon."	3202
	8:12	when you build f houses and settle down,	3202
	9:21	to powder as f as dust and threw the dust	1990
	22:19	They shall f him a hundred shekels	6740
1Sa	16:12	f appearance and handsome features.	3637
2Sa	22:43	I beat them as f as the dust of the earth;	8835
1Ki	4:22	of f flour and sixty cors of meal,	6159
	10:18	with ivory and overlaid with f gold.	7059
2Ki	20:13	silver, the gold, the spices and the f oil—	3202
1Ch	15:27	David was clothed in a robe of f linen,	1009
	29: 2	and all kinds of f stone and marble—	3701
2Ch	2:14	and blue and crimson yarn and f linen.	1009
	3: 5	with f gold and decorated it with palm tree	3202
	3: 8	inside with six hundred talents of f gold.	3202
	3:14	purple and crimson yarn and f linen,	1009

2Ch	5:12	dressed in f linen and playing cymbals,	1009
	8:27	and two f articles of polished bronze,	3202
Est	8:15	of gold and a purple robe of f linen.	1009
Job	16: 4	I could make f speeches against you	928+2488+4863
Ps	18:42	I beat them as f as dust borne on the wind;	8835
	92:10	f oils have been poured upon me.	8316
Pr	8:19	My fruit is better than f gold;	7058
	25:12	of f gold is a wise man's rebuke to	4188
	31:22	she is clothed in f linen and purple.	9254
Ecc	7: 1	A good name is better than f perfume,	9043
Isa	3:22	the f robes and the capes and cloaks,	4711
	3:24	instead of f clothing, sackcloth;	7345
	5: 9	the f mansions left without occupants.	1524+2256+3202
	19: 9	the weavers of f linen will lose hope.	2583
	23:18	for abundant food and f clothes,	6971
	29: 5	your many enemies will become like f dust,	1987
	39: 2	the silver, the gold, the spices, the f oil,	3202
	40:15	the islands as though they were f dust.	1987
Jer	22: 7	up your f cedar beams and throw them into	4436
	25:34	you will fall and be shattered like f pottery.	2775
La	4: 1	the f gold become dull!	3202
Eze	16:10	I dressed you in f linen and covered you	9254
	16:13	your clothes were of f linen	9254
	16:13	Your food was f flour,	6159
	16:17	You also took the f jewelry I gave you,	9514
	16:19	the f flour, olive oil	6159
	16:39	of your clothes and take your f jewelry	9514
	23:26	of your clothes and take your f jewelry.	9514
	26:12	and demolish your f houses	2775
	27: 7	F embroidered linen from Egypt	9254
	27:16	purple fabric, embroidered work, f linen,	1009
Mt	11: 8	A man dressed in f clothes?	3434
	11: 8	who wear f clothes are in kings' palaces.	3434
	13:45	like a merchant looking for f pearls.	2819
Mk	7: 9	a f way of setting aside the commands	2822
Lk	7:25	A man dressed in f clothes?	3434
	13: 9	If it bears fruit next year, f!	NIG
	16:19	and f linen and lived in luxury every day.	1116
Gal	4:18	It is f to be zealous,	2819
Jas	2: 2	a gold ring and f clothes,	3287
	2: 3	to the man wearing f clothes and say,	3287
1Pe	3: 3	the wearing of gold jewelry and f clothes.	NIG
Rev	18:12	f linen, purple, silk and scarlet cloth;	1115
	18:13	of f flour and wheat;	4947
	18:16	Woe, O great city, dressed in f linen,	1115
	19: 8	F linen, bright and clean,	1115
	19: 8	F linen stands for the righteous acts of	1115
	19:14	on white horses and dressed in f linen,	1115

FINE-LOOKING (1) [FINE, LOOK]

1Sa	16:18	He speaks well and is a f man.	9307

FINE-SOUNDING (1) [FINE, SOUND]

Col	2: 4	no one may deceive you by f arguments.	4391

FINED (1) [FINE]

Ex	21:22	the offender must be f whatever	6740+6740

FINELY (22) [FINE]

Ex	26: 1	with ten curtains of f twisted linen	8813
	26:31	purple and scarlet yarn and f twisted linen,	8813
	26:36	and scarlet yarn and f twisted linen—	8813
	27: 9	and is to have curtains of f twisted linen,	8813
	27:16	and scarlet yarn and f twisted linen—	8813
	27:18	of f twisted linen five cubits high,	8813
	28: 6	and of f twisted linen—	8813
	28: 8	and with f twisted linen.	8813
	28:15	and of f twisted linen.	8813
	36: 8	with ten curtains of f twisted linen	8813
	36:35	purple and scarlet yarn and f twisted linen,	8813
	36:37	and scarlet yarn and f twisted linen—	8813
	38: 9	and had curtains of f twisted linen,	8813
	38:16	the courtyard were of f twisted linen.	8813
	38:18	and scarlet yarn and f twisted linen—	8813
	39: 2	and of f twisted linen.	8813
	39: 5	and with f twisted linen,	8813
	39: 8	and of f twisted linen.	8813
	39:24	and scarlet yarn and f twisted linen around	8813
	39:28	and the undergarments of f twisted linen.	8813
	39:29	The sash was of f twisted linen and blue,	8813
Lev	16:12	of f ground fragrant incense and take them	1987

FINER (KJV) See SILVERSMITH

FINERY (2) [FINE]

2Sa	1:24	who clothed you in scarlet and f,	6358
Isa	3:18	that day the Lord will snatch away their f:	9514

FINES (1) [FINE]

Am	2: 8	of their god they drink wine taken as f.	6711

FINEST (19) [FINE]

Nu	18:12	the f olive oil and all the finest new wine	2693
	18:12	and all the f new wine and grain they give	2693
Dt	32:14	of Bashan and the f kernels of wheat.	2693
	33:14	with the best the sun brings forth and the f	4458
Jdg	20:34	Then ten thousand of Israel's f men made	1047
2Ki	9:23	as a gift forty camel-loads of all the f wares	3206
	19:23	the f of its forests.	3623+4149
Job	28:15	It cannot be bought with the f gold,	6034

Ps	81:16	But you would be fed with the **f** of wheat;	2693
	147:14	to your borders and satisfies you with the **f**	2693
SS	4:14	with myrrh and aloes and all the **f** spices.	8031
Isa	17:10	the **f** plants and plant imported vines,	5846
	25: 6	the best of meats and the **f** of wines.	2423
	37:24	the **f** of its forests.	3623+4149
Jer	48:15	her **f** young men will go down in	4436
Eze	27:22	for your merchandise they exchanged the **f**	8031
Da	10: 5	a belt of the **f** gold around his waist.	233+4188
Joel	3: 5	and my gold and carried off my **f** treasures	3202
Am	6: 6	by the bowlful and use the **f** lotions,	8040

FINGER (31) [FINGERS]

Ge	41:42	from his **f** and put it on Joseph's finger.	3338
	41:42	from his finger and put it on Joseph's **f**.	3338
Ex	8:19	"This is the **f** of God."	720
	29:12	on the horns of the altar with your **f**,	720
	31:18	tablets of stone inscribed by the **f** of God.	720
Lev	4: 6	He is to dip his **f** into the blood	720
	4:17	He shall dip his **f** into the blood	720
	4:25	of the sin offering with his **f** and put it on	720
	4:30	the blood with his **f** and put it on the horns	720
	4:34	of the sin offering with his **f** and put it on	720
	8:15	and with his **f** he put it on all the horns of	720
	9: 9	and he dipped his **f** into the blood	720
	14:16	and his **f** sprinkle some of it before	720
	16:14	of the bull's blood and with his **f** sprinkle it	720
	16:14	of it with his **f** seven times before	720
	16:19	of the blood on it with his **f** seven times	720
Nu	19: 4	on his **f** and sprinkle it seven times toward	720
Dt	9:10	inscribed by the **f** of God.	720
1Ki	12:10	'My little **f** is thicker than my father's waist.	7782
2Ch	10:10	'My little **f** is thicker than my father's waist.	7782
Est	3:12	So the king took his signet ring from his **f**	3338
Job	1:12	but on the man himself do not lay a **f**."	3338
Isa	58: 9	with the pointing **f** and malicious talk,	720
Mt	23: 4	not willing to **lift a f** to move them.	1235
Lk	11:20	But if I drive out demons by the **f** of God,	1235
	11:46	and you yourselves will not lift one **f**	1235
	15:22	Put a ring on his **f** and sandals on his feet.	5931
	16:24	and send Lazarus to dip the tip of his **f**	1235
Jn	8: 6	to write on the ground with his **f**.	1235
	20:25	the nail marks in his hands and put my **f**	1235
	20:27	Then he said to Thomas, "Put your **f** here;	1235

FINGERS (14) [FINGER]

2Sa	21:20	with six **f** on each hand and six toes	720
1Ch	20: 6	with six **f** on each hand and six toes	720
Ps	8: 3	the work of your **f**, the moon and the stars,	720
	144: 1	trains my hands for war, my **f** for battle.	720
Pr	6:13	with his feet and motions with his **f**,	720
	7: 3	Bind them on your **f**;	720
	31:19	and grasps the spindle with her **f**.	4090
SS	5: 5	my **f** with flowing myrrh,	720
Isa	2: 8	to what their **f** have made.	720
	17: 8	and the incense altars their **f** have made.	720
	59: 3	stained with blood, your **f** with guilt.	720
Jer	52:21	each was four **f** thick, and hollow.	720
Da	5: 5	the **f** of a human hand appeared and wrote	10064
Mk	7:33	Jesus put his **f** into the man's ears.	1235

FINING POT (KJV) See CRUCIBLE

FINISH (18) [FINISHED, FINISHING]

Ge	6:16	and **f** the ark to within 18 inches of the top.	3983
	29:27	**F** this daughter's bridal week;	4848
Ru	2:21	until they **f** harvesting all my grain.' "	3983
1Ch	27:24	to count the men but did not **f**.	3983
Ne	4: 2	Will they **f** in a day?	3983
Ps	90: 9	we **f** our years with a moan.	3983
Pr	24:27	**F** your outdoor work	3922
Jer	51:63	When you **f** reading this scroll,	3983
Da	9:24	and your holy city to **f** transgression,	3974
Mt	10:23	you will not **f** going through the cities	5464
Lk	14:29	the foundation and is not able to **f** it,	1754
	14:30	to build and was not able to **f**.'	1754
Jn	4:34	of him who sent me and to **f** his work.	5457
	5:36	that the Father has given me to **f**,	5457
Ac	20:24	if only I may **f** the race and complete	5457
2Co	8:11	Now **f** the work,	2200
	9: 5	**f the arrangements for** the generous gift	4616
Jas	1: 4	Perseverance must **f** its work so	2400+5455

FINISHED (90) [FINISH]

Ge	2: 2	By the seventh day God had **f** the work	3983
	17:22	When he had **f** speaking with Abraham,	3983
	18:33	the LORD had **f** speaking with Abraham,	3983
	24:15	Before he had **f** praying,	3983
	24:19	until they have **f** drinking."	3983
	24:22	When the camels had **f** drinking,	3983
	24:45	"Before I **f** praying in my heart,	3983
	27:30	After Isaac **f** blessing him	3983
	29:28	He **f** the week with Leah,	4848
	49:33	Jacob had **f** giving instructions to his sons,	3983
Ex	31:18	When the LORD **f** speaking to Moses	3983
	34:33	When Moses **f** speaking to them,	3983
	40:33	And so Moses **f** the work.	3983
Lev	16:20	"When Aaron has **f** making atonement for	3983
Nu	4:15	"After Aaron and his sons have **f** covering	3983
	7: 1	When Moses **f** setting up the tabernacle,	3983
	16:31	As soon as he **f** saying all this,	3983
Dt	20: 9	the officers have **f** speaking to the army,	3983
	26:12	When you have **f** setting aside a tenth	3983
	31:24	After Moses **f** writing in a book the words	3983

Dt	32:45	When Moses **f** reciting all these words	3983
Jos	4: 1	the whole nation had **f** crossing the Jordan,	9462
	8:24	When Israel had **f** killing all the men of Ai	3983
	19:49	When they had **f** dividing the land	3983
	19:51	And so they **f** dividing the land.	3983
Jdg	15:17	When he **f** speaking, he threw away	3983
Ru	2:23	until the barley and wheat harvests were **f**.	3983
	3: 3	until he has **f** eating and drinking.	3983
	3: 7	When Boaz had **f** eating and drinking	AIT
1Sa	1: 9	Once when they had **f** eating and drinking	339
	13:10	Just as he **f** making the offering,	3983
	18: 1	After David had **f** talking with Saul,	3983
	24:16	When David **f** saying this, Saul asked,	3983
2Sa	6:18	After he had **f** sacrificing the burnt offerings	3983
	11:19	"When you have **f** giving the king this	3983
	13:36	As he **f** speaking, the king's sons came in,	3983
	15:24	and all the people had **f** leaving the city.	9462
1Ki	3: 1	of David until he **f** building his palace and	3983
	6:38	the temple was **f** in all its details according	3983
	7:40	So Huram **f** all the work he had undertaken	3983
	7:51	the temple of the LORD was **f**, he brought	8966
	8:54	When Solomon had **f** all these prayers	3983
	9: 1	When Solomon had **f** building the temple of	3983
	13:23	the man of God had **f** eating and drinking,	339
2Ki	6:23	and after they had **f** eating and drinking,	AIT
	10:25	as Jehu had **f** making the burnt offering,	3983
	16:11	and it before King Ahaz returned.	6913
1Ch	16: 2	After David **f** sacrificing	3983
	28:20	of the temple of the LORD is **f**.	3983
2Ch	4:11	So Huram **f** the work he had undertaken	3983
	5: 1	the temple of the LORD was **f**, he brought	8966
	7: 1	When Solomon **f** praying,	3983
	7:11	When Solomon had **f** the temple of	3983
	8:16	So the temple of the LORD was **f**.	8966
	20:23	After they **f** slaughtering the men	3983
	24:14	When they had **f**, they brought the rest of	3983
	29:29	When the offerings were **f**,	3983
	29:34	the Levites helped them until the task was **f**	3983
	31: 7	the third month and **f** in the seventh month.	3983
Ezr	5:11	one that a great king of Israel built and **f**.	10354
	5:16	under construction but is not yet **f**."	10719
	6:14	They **f** building the temple according to	10354
	6:15	of the first month they **f** dealing with all	3983
Isa	10:12	When the Lord has **f** all his work	1298
Jer	26: 8	But as soon as Jeremiah **f** telling all	3983
	43: 1	When Jeremiah **f** telling the people all	3983
Eze	4: 6	"After you have **f** this, lie down again,	3983
	4: 8	from one side to the other until you have **f**	3983
	42:15	When he had **f** measuring what was inside	3983
	43:23	When you have **f** purifying it,	3983
Mt	7:28	When Jesus had **f** saying these things,	5464
	11: 1	After Jesus had **f** instructing his twelve disciples,	5464
	13:53	When Jesus had **f** these parables,	5464
	19: 1	When Jesus had **f** saying these things,	5464
	26: 1	When Jesus had **f** saying all these things,	5464
Lk	4:13	When the devil had **f** all this tempting,	5334
	5: 4	When he had **f** speaking, he said to Simon,	4264
	7: 1	When Jesus had **f** saying all this in	4444
	11: 1	When he **f**, one of his disciples said to him,	4264
	11:37	When Jesus had **f** speaking,	NIG
Jn	12:36	When he had **f speaking**,	AIT
	13:12	When he had **f washing** their feet,	AIT
	18: 1	When he had **f praying**,	AIT
	19:30	Jesus said, "It is **f**."	5464
	21:15	When they had **f eating**,	AIT
Ac	12:25	Barnabas and Saul had **f** their mission,	4444
	15:13	When they **f**, James spoke up:	4967
2Ti	4: 7	I have **f** the race, I have kept the faith.	5464
Heb	4: 3	yet his work has been **f** since the creation	1181
Rev	11: 7	Now when they have **f** their testimony,	5464

FINISHING (2) [FINISH]

1Ki	1:41	with him heard it as they were **f** their feast.	3983
2Ch	29:17	**f** on the sixteenth day of the first month.	3983

FINS (5)

Lev	11: 9	you may eat any that have **f** and scales	6181
	11:10	or streams that do not have **f** and scales—	6181
	11:12	the water that does not have **f** and scales is	6181
Dt	14: 9	you may eat any that has **f** and scales you may	6181
	14:10	that does not have **f** and scales you may	6181

FIR (2) [FIRS]

Isa	41:19	the **f** and the cypress together,	9329
	60:13	the pine, the **f** and the cypress together,	9329

FIRE (459) [AFIRE, CAMPFIRES, FIERY, FIREBRANDS, FIRELIGHT, FIREPANS, FIREPOT, FIRES, FIREWOOD]

Ge	22: 6	and he himself carried the **f** and the knife.	836
	22: 7	"The **f** and wood are here," Isaac said.	836
Ex	3: 2	the LORD appeared to him in flames of **f**	836
	3: 2	though the bush was on **f** it did not burn up.	836+928+1277+2021
	12: 8	to eat the meat roasted over the **f**,	836
	12: 9	but roast it over the **f**—	836
	13:21	by night in a pillar of **f** to give them light,	836
	13:22	the pillar of **f** by night left its place in front	836
	14:24	down from the pillar of **f** and cloud at	836
	19:18	because the LORD descended on it in **f**.	836
	22: 6	a **f** breaks out and spreads into thornbushes	836
	22: 6	who started the **f** must make restitution.	1282

Ex	24:17	like a consuming **f** on top of the mountain.	836
	29:18	**offering made** to the LORD by **f**.	852
	29:25	**offering made** to the LORD by **f**.	852
	29:41	**offering made** to the LORD by **f**.	852
	30:20	**offering made** to the LORD by **f**,	852
	32:20	and burned it in the **f**;	836
	32:24	and I threw it into the **f**,	836
	35: 3	Do not light a **f** in any of your dwellings	836
	40:38	and **f** was in the cloud by night,	836
Lev	1: 7	The sons of Aaron the priest are to put **f** on	836
	1: 7	on the altar and arrange wood on the **f**.	836
	1: 9	It is a burnt offering, an **offering made by f**,	852
	1:13	It is a burnt offering, an **offering made by f**,	852
	1:17	on the wood that is on the **f** on the altar.	836
	1:17	It is a burnt offering, an **offering made by f**,	852
	2: 2	an **offering made by f**,	852
	2: 3	**offerings made** to the LORD by **f**.	852
	2: 9	on the altar as an **offering made by f**,	852
	2:10	**offerings made** to the LORD by **f**.	852
	2:11	**offering made** to the LORD by **f**.	852
	2:14	of new grain roasted in the **f**.	836
	2:16	**offering made** to the LORD by **f**.	852
	3: 3	**sacrifice** made to the LORD by **f**:	852
	3: 5	as an **offering made by f**,	852
	3: 9	**sacrifice** made to the LORD by **f**:	852
	3:11	**offering made** to the LORD by **f**.	852
	3:14	**offering** to the LORD by **f**:	852
	3:16	an **offering made by f**, a pleasing aroma.	852
	4:12	and burn it in a wood **f** on the ash heap.	836
	4:35	**offerings made** to the LORD by **f**.	852
	5:12	**offerings made** to the LORD by **f**.	852
	6: 9	and the **f** must be kept burning on the altar.	836
	6:10	the burnt offering that the **f** has consumed	836
	6:12	The **f** on the altar must be kept burning;	836
	6:12	the burnt offering on the **f** and burn the fat	1277
	6:13	The **f** must be kept burning on	836
	6:17	**offerings made** to me by **f**.	852
	6:18	**offerings made** to the LORD by **f**.	852
	7: 5	**offering made** to the LORD by **f**.	852
	7:25	from which an **offering made** by **f** may be made	852
	7:30	**offering made** to the LORD by **f**,	852
	7:35	**offerings made** to the LORD by **f**.	852
	8:21	**offering made** to the LORD by **f**,	852
	8:28	**offerings made** to the LORD by **f**.	852
	9:24	**F** came out from the presence of the LORD	836
	10: 1	put **f** in them and added incense;	836
	10: 1	and they offered unauthorized **f** before	836
	10: 2	**f** came out from the presence of the LORD	836
	10: 6	for those the LORD has **destroyed by f**.	8596
	10:12	**offerings made** to the LORD by **f**;	852
	10:13	**offerings made** to the LORD by **f**.	852
	10:15	the fat portions of the **offerings made by f**,	852
	13:55	Burn it with **f**,	836
	13:57	the mildew must be burned with **f**.	836
	16:13	the incense on the **f** before the LORD,	836
	20:14	Both he and they must be burned in the **f**,	836
	21: 6	**offerings made** to the LORD by **f**,	852
	21: 9	she must be burned in the **f**.	836
	21:21	**offerings made** to the LORD by **f**.	852
	22:22	**offering made** to the LORD by **f**.	852
	22:27	**offering made** to the LORD by **f**.	852+7933
	23: 8	**offering made** to the LORD by **f**.	852
	23:13	**offering made** to the LORD by **f**.	852
	23:18	an **offering made by f**,	852
	23:25	**offering made** to the LORD by **f**.' "	852
	23:27	**offering made** to the LORD by **f**.	852
	23:36	**offering made** to the LORD by **f**,	852
	23:36	**offering made** to the LORD by **f**,	852
	23:37	**offerings made** to the LORD by **f**—	852
	24: 7	**offering made** to the LORD by **f**.	852
	24: 9	**offerings made** to the LORD by **f**."	852
Nu	3: 4	an offering with unauthorized **f** before him	836
	6:18	and put it in the **f** that is under the sacrifice	836
	9:15	above the tabernacle looked like **f**.	836
	9:16	and at night it looked like **f**.	836
	11: 1	Then **f** from the LORD burned	836
	11: 2	to the LORD and the **f** died down.	836
	11: 3	**f** from the LORD had burned among them.	836
	14:14	in a pillar of cloud by day and a pillar of **f**	836
	15: 3	to the LORD **offerings made by f**, from	852
	15:10	It will be an **offering made by f**,	852
	15:13	an **offering made by f** as an aroma pleasing	852
	15:14	an **offering made by f** as an aroma pleasing	852
	15:25	for their wrong an offering **made by f** and	852
	16: 7	and tomorrow put **f** and incense in them	836
	16:18	put **f** and incense in it,	836
	16:35	And **f** came out from the LORD	836
	16:46	along with **f** from the altar,	836
	18: 9	that is kept from the **f**.	836
	18:17	and burn their fat as an **offering made by f**,	852
	21:28	"**F** went out from Heshbon,	836
	26:10	whose followers died when the **f** devoured	836
	26:61	before the LORD with unauthorized **f**.)	836
	28: 2	the food for my offerings made by **f**,	852
	28: 3	'This is the **offering made by f** that you are	852
	28: 6	**offering made** to the LORD by **f**.	852
	28: 8	This is an **offering made by f**,	852
	28:13	**offering made** to the LORD by **f**.	852
	28:19	to the LORD an **offering made by f**,	852
	28:24	for the **offering made by f** every day	852
	29: 6	**offerings made** to the LORD by **f**—	852
	29:13	an **offering made by f** as an aroma pleasing	852
	29:36	an **offering made by f** as an aroma pleasing	852
	31:23	and anything else that can withstand **f** must	836
	31:23	be put through the **f**,	836
	31:23	And whatever cannot withstand **f** must	836
Dt	1:33	in **f** by night and in a cloud by day,	836

Dt	4:11	while it blazed with f to the very heavens,	836
	4:12	Then the LORD spoke to you out of the f.	836
	4:15	to you at Horeb out of the f.	836
	4:24	the LORD your God is a consuming f,	836
	4:33	the voice of God speaking out of f,	836
	4:36	On earth he showed you his great f,	836
	4:36	and you heard his words from out of the f.	836
	5: 4	to face out of the f on the mountain.	836
	5: 5	of the f and did not go up the mountain.)	836
	5:22	of the f, the cloud and the deep darkness;	836
	5:23	while the mountain was ablaze with f,	836
	5:24	and we have heard his voice from the f.	836
	5:25	This great f will consume us,	836
	5:26	of the living God speaking out of f,	836
	7: 5	and burn their idols in the f.	836
	7:25	of their gods you are to burn in the f.	836
	9: 3	across ahead of you like a devouring f.	836
	9:10	to you on the mountain out of the f,	836
	9:15	the mountain while it was ablaze with f.	836
	9:21	and burned it in the f.	836
	10: 4	out of the f, on the day of the assembly.	836
	12: 3	and burn their Asherah poles in the f;	836
	12:31	even burn their sons and daughters in the f	836
	18: 1	**offerings made** to the LORD **by** f,	852
	18:10	or daughter in the f,	836
	18:16	nor see this great f anymore,	836
	32:22	For a f has been kindled by my wrath,	836
Jos	7:15	the devoted things shall be destroyed by f,	836
	8: 8	When you have taken the city, **set it on** f.	
			836+928+2021+3675
	8:19	and captured it and quickly **set it on** f.	
			836+928+2021+3675
	13:14	the **offerings made by** f to the LORD,	852
Jdg	1: 8	the city to the sword and set it on f.	836
	6:21	F flared from the rock,	836
	9:15	if not, then let f come out of the thornbush	836
	9:20	let f come out from Abimelech	836
	9:20	and let f come out from you,	836
	9:49	and **set it on** f over the people inside.	
			836+928+2021+3675
	9:52	the entrance to the tower to **set it on** f,	
			836+928+2021+8596
	20:48	the towns they came across they set on f.	836
1Sa	2: 28	the **offerings made with** f **by** the Israelites.	852
	30: 3	by f and their wives and sons	836
2Sa	14:30	Go and **set it on** f."	836+928+2021+3675
	14:30	**set the field on** f.	836+928+2021+3675
	14:31	**set my field on** f?"	836+928+2021+3675
	22: 9	consuming f came from his mouth,	836
1Ki	9:16	He **had set** the palace **on** f	836+928+2021+8596
	16:18	**set the palace on** f	836+928+2021+8596
	18:23	and put it on the wood but not set f to it.	836
	18:23	and put it on the wood but not set f to it.	836
	18:24	The god who answers by f—he is God."	836
	18:25	but do not light the f."	836
	18:38	Then the f of the LORD fell and burned	836
	19:12	After the earthquake came a f,	836
	19:12	but the LORD was not in the f.	836
	19:12	And after the f came a gentle whisper.	836
2Ki	1:10	may f come down from heaven	836
	1:10	Then f fell from heaven and consumed	836
	1:12	"may f come down from heaven	836
	1:12	Then the f of God fell from heaven	836
	1:14	f has fallen from heaven and consumed	836
	2:11	a chariot of f and horses of fire appeared	836
	2:11	a chariot of fire and horses of f appeared	836
	6:17	the hills full of horses and chariots of f all	836
	8:12	"You will **set** f to their fortified places,	
			836+928+2021+8938
	16: 3	and even sacrificed his son in the f,	836
	17:17	and daughters in the f,	836
	17:31	in the f as sacrifices to Adrammelech	836
	19:18	They have thrown their gods into the f	836
	21: 6	He sacrificed his own son in the f,	836
	23:10	to sacrifice his son or daughter in the f	836
	25: 9	He **set** f to the temple of the LORD,	8596
1Ch	14:12	David gave orders to burn them in the f.	836
	21:26	and the LORD answered him with f	836
2Ch	7: 1	f came down from heaven and consumed	836
	7: 3	the Israelites saw the f coming down and	836
	16:14	and they made a huge f in his honor.	8599
	21:19	His people made no f in his honor,	8599
	28: 3	and sacrificed his sons in the f,	836
	33: 6	He sacrificed his sons in the f in the Valley	836
	35:13	the Passover animals over the f	836
	36:19	They **set** God's temple and broke	8596
Ne	1: 3	and its gates have been burned with f."	836
	2: 3	and its gates have been destroyed by f?"	836
	2:13	which had been destroyed by f,	836
	2:17	and its gates have been burned with f.	836
	9:12	with a pillar of f to give them light on	836
	9:19	of f by night to shine on the way they were	836
Job	1:16	"The f of God fell from the sky	836
	15:34	and f will consume the tents	836
	18: 5	the flame of his f stops burning.	836
	18:15	F resides in his tent;	4442
	20:26	A f unfanned will consume him	836
	22:20	and f devours their wealth.'	836
	28: 5	is transformed below as by f;	836
	31:12	It is a f that burns to Destruction,	836
	41:19	sparks of f shoot out.	836
	41:20	as from a boiling pot over a f of reeds.	NIH
Ps	18: 8	consuming f came from his mouth,	836
	21: 9	and his f will consume them.	836
	39: 3	and as I meditated, the f burned;	836
	46: 9	he burns the shields with f.	836
	50: 3	a f devours before him,	836

Ps	66:12	we went through f and water,	836
	68: 2	as wax melts before the f,	836
	78:14	by day and with light from the f all night.	836
	78:21	his f broke out against Jacob,	836
	78:63	F consumed their young men,	836
	79: 5	How long will your jealousy burn like f?	836
	80:16	Your vine is cut down, it is burned with f;	836
	83:14	As f consumes the forest or a flame sets	836
	89:46	How long will your wrath burn like f?	836
	97: 3	F goes before him and consumes his foes	836
	104: 4	flames of f his servants.	836
	105:39	and f to give light at night.	836
	106:18	F blazed among their followers;	836
	140:10	may they be thrown into the f,	836
Pr	6:27	Can a man scoop f into his lap	836
	16:27	and his speech is like a scorching f.	836
	26:20	Without wood a f goes out;	836
	26:21	As charcoal to embers and as wood to f,	836
	30:16	which is never satisfied with water, and f,	836
SS	8: 6	It burns like blazing f, like a mighty flame.	836
Isa	1: 7	your cities burned with f;	836
	1:31	with no one to **quench** the f."	3882
	4: 4	by a spirit of judgment and a spirit of f.	1277
	4: 5	of smoke by day and a glow of flaming f	836
	5:24	of f lick up straw and as dry grass sinks	836
	9: 5	will be fuel for the f.	836
	9:18	Surely wickedness burns like a f;	836
	9:19	and the people will be fuel for the f;	836
	10:16	a f will be kindled like a blazing flame.	3679
	10:17	The Light of Israel will become a f,	836
	26:11	let the f reserved for your enemies	836
	27: 4	**set** them all **on** f.	7455
	29: 6	and tempest and flames of a devouring f.	836
	30:27	and his tongue is a consuming f.	836
	30:30	with raging anger and consuming f,	836+4258
	30:33	Its f **pit** has been made deep and wide,	4509
	30:33	with an abundance of f and wood;	836
	31: 9	declares the LORD, whose f is in Zion,	241
	33:11	your breath is a f that consumes you.	836
	33:14	of us can dwell with the consuming f?	836
	37:19	They have thrown their gods into the f	836
	43: 2	When you walk through the f,	836
	44:15	he **kindles** a f and bakes bread.	5956
	44:16	Half of the wood he burns in the f;	836
	44:16	I am warm; I see the f."	241
	47:14	the f will burn them up.	836
	47:14	here is no f to sit by.	241
	64: 2	when f sets twigs ablaze and causes water	836
	64:11	has been burned with f,	836
	65: 5	a f that keeps burning all day.	836
	66:15	See, the LORD is coming with f,	836
	66:15	and his rebuke with flames of f.	836
	66:16	For with f and with his sword	836
	66:24	nor will their f be quenched,	836
Jer	4: 4	like f because of the evil you have done—	836
	5:14	a f and these people the wood it consumes.	836
	6:29	the lead with f, but the refining goes on	836
	7:18	the fathers light the f,	836
	7:31	to burn their sons and daughters in the f—	836
	11:16	of a mighty storm he will **set it on** f,	836+3675
	15:14	for my anger will kindle a f that will burn	836
	17:27	then I will kindle an unquenchable f in	836
	19: 5	to burn their sons in the f as offerings	836
	20: 9	his word is in my heart like a f,	836
	20: 9	a f shut up in my bones.	1277
	21:10	and he will destroy it with f.'	836
	21:12	like f because of the evil you have done—	836
	21:14	I will kindle a f in your forests	836
	22: 7	and throw them into the f.	836
	23:29	"Is not my word like f,"	836
	29:22	the king of Babylon burned in the f.'	836
	32:29	come in and **set it on** f;	836+928+2021+3675
	34: 5	As people made a **funeral** f in honor	5386
	34: 5	so they will **make** a f in your honor	8596
	36:22	a f burning in the firepot in front of him.	836
	36:23	until the entire scroll was burned in the f.	836
	36:32	of Judah had burned in the f.	836
	39: 8	The Babylonians **set** f to the royal palace	
			836+928+2021+8596
	43:12	He will **set** f to the temples of the gods	836+3675
	48:45	for a f has gone out from Heshbon,	836
	49: 2	its surrounding villages will be **set on** f.	
			836+928+2021+3675
	49:27	"I will **set** f to the walls of Damascus;	836+3675
	50:32	I will kindle a f in her towns	836
	51:30	Her dwellings are **set on** f;	836
	51:32	the marshes **set on** f,	836+928+2021+8596
	51:58	be leveled and her high gates **set on** f;	
			836+928+2021+3675
	52:13	He **set** f to the temple of the LORD,	8596
La	1:13	"From on high he sent f,	836
	2: 3	like a flaming f that consumes everything	836
	2: 4	like f on the tent of the Daughter of Zion.	836
	4:11	a f in Zion that consumed her foundations.	836
Eze	1: 4	of the f looked like glowing metal,	836
	1: 5	and in the f was what looked	2023S
	1:13	like burning coals of f or like torches.	836
	1:13	F moved back and forth among	2085S
	1:27	like glowing metal, as if full of f,	836
	1:27	and that from there down he looked like f;	836
	5: 2	a third of the hair with f inside the city.	241
	5: 4	a few of these and throw them into the f	836
	5: 4	A f will spread from there to	836
	5: 4	to be his waist down he was like f,	836
	10: 6	"Take f from among the wheels,	836
	10: 7	the cherubim reached out his hand to the f	836
	15: 4	on the f as fuel and the fire burns both ends	836

Eze	15: 4	on the fire as fuel and the f burns both ends	836
	15: 5	when the f has burned it and it is charred?	836
	15: 6	the trees of the forest as fuel for the f,	836
	15: 7	Although they have come out of the f,	836
	15: 7	the f will yet consume them.	836
	19:12	and f consumed them.	836
	19:14	F spread from one of its main branches	836
	20:31	the sacrifice of your sons in the f—	836
	20:47	I am about to **set** f to you,	836+3675
	21:32	You will be fuel for the f,	836
	23:25	of you who are left will be consumed by f.	836
	24:10	So heap on the wood and kindle the f.	836
	24:12	not been removed, not even by f.	836
	28:18	So I made a f come out from you,	836
	30: 8	when I set f to Egypt	836
	30:14	set f to Zoan and inflict punishment	836
	30:16	I will set f to Egypt;	836
	39: 6	I will send f on Magog and	836
	46:23	with **places for** f built all around under	4453
Da	3:22	flames of the f killed the soldiers who took	10471
	3:24	that we tied up and threw into the f?"	10471
	3:25	I see four men walking around in the f,	10471
	3:26	Meshach and Abednego came out of the f,	10471
	3:27	the f had not harmed their bodies, nor was	10471
	3:27	and there was no smell of f on them.	10471
	7: 9	His throne was flaming with f,	10471
	7:10	A river of f was flowing,	10471
	7:11	and thrown into the blazing f.	10080
Hos	7: 4	an oven whose f the baker need not stir	NIH
	7: 6	in the morning it blazes like a flaming f.	836
	8:14	But I will send f upon their cities	836
Joel	1:19	for f has devoured the open pastures	836
	1:20	of water have dried up and f has devoured	836
	2: 3	Before them f devours,	836
	2: 5	like a crackling f consuming stubble,	836+4258
	2:30	blood and f and billows of smoke.	836
Am	1: 4	I will send f upon the house of Hazael	836
	1: 7	I will send f upon the walls of Gaza	836
	1:10	I will send f upon the walls of Tyre	836
	1:12	I will send f upon Teman	836
	1:14	I will **set** f to the walls of Rabbah	836+3675
	2: 2	I will send f upon Moab that will consume	836
	2: 5	I will send f upon Judah that will consume	836
	4:11	like a burning stick snatched from the f,	8599
	5: 6	through the house of Joseph like a f;	836
	7: 4	for judgment by f;	836
Ob	1:18	be a f and the house of Joseph a flame;	836
	1:18	and they will **set it on** f and consume it.	1944
Mic	1: 4	like wax before the f,	836
	1: 7	all her temple gifts will be burned with f;	836
Na	1: 6	His wrath is poured out like f;	836
	3:13	f has consumed their bars.	836
	3:15	There the f will devour you;	836
Hab	2:13	the people's labor is only **fuel for** the f,	
			836+928+1896
Zep	1:18	the f of his jealousy the whole world will	836
	3: 8	be consumed by the f of my jealous anger.	836
Zec	2: 5	And I myself will be a wall of f around it,'	836
	3: 2	a burning stick snatched from the f?"	836
	9: 4	and she will be consumed by f.	836
	11: 1	so that f may devour your cedars!	836
	13: 9	This third I will bring into the f;	836
Mal	3: 2	be like a refiner's f or a launderer's soap.	836
	4: 1	that day that is coming will **set** them **on** f,"	4265
Mt	3:10	be cut down and thrown into the f.	4786
	3:11	with the Holy Spirit and with f.	4786
	3:12	up the chaff with unquenchable f."	4786
	5:22	will be in danger of the f of hell.	4786
	6:30	and tomorrow is thrown into the f,	3106
	7:19	down and thrown into the f.	4786
	13:40	up and burned in the f,	4786
	17:15	He often falls into the f or into the water.	4786
	18: 8	or two feet and be thrown into eternal f.	4786
	18: 9	to have two eyes and be thrown into the f	4786
	25:41	into the eternal f prepared for the devil	4786
Mk	9:22	"It has often thrown him into f or water	4786
	9:43	where the f never goes out.	4786
	9:48	and the f is not quenched.'	4786
	9:49	Everyone will be salted with f.	4786
	14:54	the guards and warmed himself at the f.	5890
Lk	3: 9	be cut down and thrown into the f."	4786
	3:16	with the Holy Spirit and with f."	4786
	3:17	up the chaff with unquenchable f."	4786
	9:54	do you want us to call f down from heaven	4786
	12:28	and tomorrow is thrown into the f,	3106
	12:49	"I have come to bring f on the earth,	4786
	16:24	because I am in agony in this f.'	5825
	17:29	f and sulfur rained down from heaven	4786
	22:55	when they had kindled a f in the middle of	4786
Jn	15: 6	thrown into the f and burned.	4786
	18:18	around a f they had made to keep warm.	471
	21: 9	a f **of burning coals** there with fish on it,	471
Ac	2: 3	to be tongues of f that separated and came	4786
	2:19	blood and f and billows of smoke.	4786
	28: 2	They built a f and welcomed us all	4787
	28: 3	as he put it on the f, a viper,	4787
	28: 5	But Paul shook the snake off into the f	4786
1Co	3:13	It will be revealed with f,	4786
	3:13	will test the quality of each man's work.	4786
1Th	5:19	Do not put out the Spirit's f;	NIG
2Th	1: 7	in blazing f with his powerful angels.	4786
Heb	1: 7	his servants flames of f."	4786
	10:27	of raging f that will consume the enemies	4786
	12:18	be touched and that is burning with f;	4786
	12:29	for our "God is a consuming f."	4786
Jas	3: 5	Consider what a great forest is **set on** f by	409
	3: 6	The tongue also is a f,	4786

Jas	3: 6	sets the whole course of his life on f,	5824
	3: 6	and is itself set on f by hell.	5824
	5: 3	against you and eat your flesh like f.	4786
1Pe	1: 7	which perishes even though refined by f—	4786
2Pe	3: 7	and earth are reserved for f,	4786
	3:10	the elements will be destroyed by f,	3012
	3:12	about the destruction of the heavens by f,	4792
Jude	1: 7	the punishment of eternal f.	4786
	1:23	snatch others from the f and save them;	4786
Rev	1:14	and his eyes were like blazing f.	4786
	2:18	of God, whose eyes are like blazing f.	4786
	3:18	to buy from me gold refined in the f,	4786
	8: 5	filled it with f from the altar,	4786
	8: 7	there came hail and f mixed with blood,	4786
	9:17	and out of their mouths came f,	4786
	9:18	by the three plagues of f,	4786
	11: 5	f comes from their mouths	4786
	13:13	even causing f to come down from heaven	4786
	14:18	who had charge of the f,	4786
	15: 2	like a sea of glass mixed with f and,	4786
	16: 8	to scorch people with f	4786
	17:16	they will eat her flesh and burn her with f.	4786
	18: 8	She will be consumed by f,	4786
	19:12	His eyes are like blazing f,	4786
	20: 9	But f came down from heaven	4786
	20:14	and Hades were thrown into the lake of f.	4786
	20:14	The lake of f is the second death.	4786
	20:15	he was thrown into the lake of f.	4786

FIREBRANDS (2) [FIRE]

Job	41:19	F stream from his mouth;	4365
Pr	26:18	a madman shooting f or deadly arrows	2415

FIRELIGHT (1) [FIRE]

Lk	22:56	A servant girl saw him seated there in the f.	5890

FIREPANS (3) [FIRE]

Ex	27: 3	sprinkling bowls, meat forks and f.	4746
	38: 3	sprinkling bowls, meat forks and f.	4746
Nu	4:14	including the f, meat forks,	4746

FIREPOT (4) [FIRE]

Ge	15:17	a smoking f with a blazing torch appeared	9486
Jer	36:22	with a fire burning in the f in front of him.	279
	36:23	a scribe's knife and threw them into the f,	279
Zec	12: 6	leaders of Judah like a f in a woodpile.	836+3963

FIRES (5) [FIRE]

Isa	27:11	and women come and make f with them.	239
	40:16	Lebanon is not sufficient for altar f,	1277
	50:11	all you who light f and provide yourselves	836
	50:11	walk in the light of your f and of	836
Mal	1:10	so that you would not light useless f	239

FIREWOOD (2) [FIRE]

Lev	6:12	to add f and arrange the burnt offering on	6770
Isa	7: 4	because of these two smoldering stubs of f	202

FIRKINS (KJV) See GALLONS

FIRM (54) [FIRMLY]

Ex	14:13	Stand f and you will see the deliverance	3656
	15: 8	The surging waters stood f like a wall;	5893
Jos	3:17	of the LORD stood f on dry ground in	3922
2Ch	20:17	stand f and see the deliverance	6641
Ezr	9: 8	and giving us a f place in his sanctuary,	3845
Job	11:15	you will stand f and without fear.	3668
	36: 5	he is mighty, and f in his purpose.	3946
	41:23	they are f and immovable.	3668
Ps	20: 8	but we rise up and stand f.	6386
	30: 7	you made my mountain stand f;	6437
	33: 9	he commanded, and it stood f.	6641
	33:11	the plans of the LORD stand f forever,	6641
	37:23	he makes his steps f;	3922
	40: 2	on a rock and gave me a f place to stand.	3922
	75: 3	it is I who hold its pillars f.	9419
	78:13	made the water stand f	5893
	89: 2	that your love stands f forever,	1215
	89: 4	and make your throne f	1215
	93: 5	Your statutes stand f;	586+4394
	119:89	it stands f in the heavens.	5893
Pr	4:26	for your feet and take only ways that are f.	3922
	10:25	but the righteous stand f forever.	3572
	12: 7	but the house of the righteous stands f.	6641
Isa	7: 9	stand f in your faith,	586
	22:17	to take f hold of you and hurl you away,	6487+6487
	22:23	I will drive him like a peg into a f place;	586
	22:25	peg driven into the f place will give way;	586
Eze	13: 5	the house of Israel so that it will stand f	6641
Zec	8:23	and nations will take f hold of one Jew	2616
Mt	10:22	he who stands f to the end will be saved.	5702
	24:13	he who stands f to the end will be saved.	5702
Mk	13:13	he who stands f to the end will be saved.	5702
Lk	21:19	By standing f you will gain life.	5705
1Co	10:12	So, if you think you are standing f,	2705
	15:58	Therefore, my dear brothers, stand f.	1181+1612
	16:13	Be on your guard; stand f in the faith;	2705
2Co	1: 7	And our hope for you is f,	1010
	1:21	makes both us and you stand f	1011
	1:24	because it is by faith you stand f.	2705
Gal	5: 1	Stand f, then, and do not let yourselves	2705

Eph	6:14	Stand f then, with the belt of truth buckled	2705
Php	1:27	I will know that you stand f in one spirit,	2705
	4: 1	is how you should stand f in the Lord,	2705
Col	1:23	and f, not moved from the hope held out in	1612
	2: 5	how orderly you are and how f your faith	5106
	4:12	that you may stand f in all the will of God,	2705
1Th	3: 8	since you are standing f in the Lord.	2705
2Th	2:15	stand f and hold to the teachings	2705
1Ti	6:19	as a f foundation for the coming age,	2819
2Ti	2:19	God's solid foundation stands f,	2705
Heb	6:19	as an anchor for the soul, f and secure.	855
Jas	5: 8	You too, be patient and stand f,	2840+3836+5114
1Pe	5: 9	Resist him, standing f in the faith,	5104
	5:10	and make you strong, f and steadfast.	4964

FIRMAMENT (KJV) See EXPANSE

FIRMLY (22) [FIRM]

Ge	41:32	that the matter has been f decided by God,	3922
1Sa	2:35	I will f establish his house,	586
1Ki	2:12	and his rule was f established.	4394
	2:46	The kingdom was now f established	3922
2Ki	14: 5	After the kingdom was f in his grasp,	2616
1Ch	16:30	The world is f established;	3922
2Ch	1: 1	of David established himself f	2616
	12:13	King Rehoboam established himself f	2616
	21: 4	When Jehoram established himself f	2616
	25: 3	After the kingdom was f in his control,	2616
Ps	93: 1	The world is f established;	3922
	96:10	The world is f established;	3922
Ecc	12:11	like f embedded nails—	5749
Da	2: 5	"This is what I have f decided:	10014
	2: 8	that this is what I have f decided:	10014
	3:23	f tied, fell into the blazing furnace.	10366
	11:32	who know their God will f resist him.	2616
1Co	15: 2	you hold f to the word I preached to you.	2988
Tit	1: 9	He must hold f to the trustworthy message	504
Heb	3:14	to share in Christ if we hold f till the end	1010
	4:14	let us hold f to the faith we profess.	3195
2Pe	1:12	and are f established in the truth you	5114

FIRS (1) [FIR]

SS	1:17	our rafters are f.	1361

FIRST (377) [FIRSTBORN, FIRSTFRUITS]

Ge	1: 5	and there was morning—the f day.	285
	2:11	The name of the f is the Pishon;	285
	8: 5	on the f day of the tenth month the tops of	285
	8:13	By the f day of the first month	285
	8:13	of the f month of Noah's six hundred	8037
	8:13	of Noah's six hundred and f year,	285
	10:10	The f centers of his kingdom	8040
	13: 4	and where he had f built an altar.	8037
	25:25	The f to come out was red,	8037
	25:31	Jacob replied, "F sell me your birthright."	2021+3427+3869
	25:33	But Jacob said, "Swear to me f."	3427+3869
	38:28	"This one came out f."	8037
	41:20	up the seven fat cows that came up f.	8037
	43:18	that was put back into our sacks the f time.	9378
	43:20	down here the f time to buy food.	9378
	49: 3	my might, the f sign of my strength,	8040
Ex	4: 8	or pay attention to the f miraculous sign,	8037
	12: 2	"This month is to be for you the f month,	8031
	12: 2	the f month of your year.	8037
	12:15	On the f day remove the yeast	8037
	12:15	from the f day through the seventh must	8037
	12:16	On the f day hold a sacred assembly,	8037
	12:18	In the f month on the fourteenth day eat bread made	8037
	13: 2	The f offspring of every womb among	7081
	13:12	to give over to the LORD the f offspring	7081
	13:15	the f male offspring of every womb	7081
	21:10	he must not deprive the f one of her food,	NIH
	25:35	be under the f pair of branches extending	NIH
	28:17	In the f row there shall be a ruby,	285
	29:40	With the f lamb offer a tenth of an ephah	285
	34: 1	two stone tablets like the f ones,	8037
	34: 1	the words that were on the f tablets,	8037
	34: 4	the f ones and went up Mount Sinai early	8037
	34:19	f offspring of every womb belongs to me,	7081
	37:21	under the f pair of branches extending	NIH
	39:10	In the f row there was a ruby,	285
	40: 2	on the f day of the first month.	285
	40: 2	on the first day of the f month.	8037
	40:17	So the tabernacle was set up on the f day	285
	40:17	up on the first day of the f month in	8037
Lev	4:21	and burn it as he burned the f bull.	8037
	5: 8	who shall f offer the one for	8037
	9:15	for a sin offering as he did with the f one.	8037
	23: 5	on the fourteenth day of the f month.	8037
	23: 7	On the f day hold a sacred assembly;	8037
	23:10	the priest a sheaf of the f grain you harvest.	8040
	23:24	'On the f day of the seventh month you are	285
	23:35	The f day is a sacred assembly;	8037
	23:39	the f day is a day of rest,	8037
	23:40	the f day you are to take choice fruit from	8037
Nu	1: 1	of Sinai on the f day of the second month	285
	1:18	the whole community together on the f day	285
	2: 9	They will set out f.	8037
	3:12	in place of the f male offspring	1147+7081+8167
	7:12	the f day was Nahshon son of Amminadab	8037
	8:16	the f male offspring from every Israelite	1147
	9: 1	of Sinai in the f month of the second year	8037
	9: 5	on the fourteenth day of the f month.	8037

Nu	10:13	They set out, this f time,	8037
	10:14	The divisions of the camp of Judah went f,	8037
	13:20	(It was the season for the f ripe grapes.)	1137
	15:20	the f of your ground meal and present it as	8040
	15:21	from the f of your ground meal.	8040
	18:15	The f offspring of every womb,	7081
	20: 1	In the f month the whole Israelite	8037
	22:15	and more distinguished than the f.	465S
	24:20	"Amalek was f among the nations,	8040
	28:11	"'On the f of every month,	8031
	28:16	day of the f month the LORD's Passover	8037
	28:18	On the f day hold a sacred assembly	8037
	29: 1	"'On the f day of the seventh month hold	285
	33: 3	on the fifteenth day of the f month,	8037
	33:38	on the f day of the fifth month of	285
Dt	1: 3	on the f day of the eleventh month,	285
	10: 1	like the f ones and come up to me on	8037
	10: 2	the words that were on the f tablets,	8037
	10: 3	two stone tablets like the f ones,	8037
	10:10	as I did the f time,	8037
	13: 9	Your hand must be the f in putting him	8037
	16: 4	on the evening of the f day remain	8037
	17: 7	the witnesses must be the f in putting him	8037
	18: 4	the f wool from the shearing of your sheep,	8040
	21:17	the f sign of his father's strength.	8040
	24: 4	then her f husband, who divorced her	8037
	25: 6	The f son she bears shall carry on	1147
Jos	4:19	of the f month the people went up from	8037
	21: 4	The f lot came out for the Kohathites,	NIH
	21:10	because the f lot held to them):	8037
Jdg	1: 1	"Who will be the f to go up and fight for us	9378
	20:18	"Who of us shall go f to fight against the Benjamites?"	928+2021+9378
	20:18	LORD replied, "Judah shall go f."	928+2021+9378
	20:22	they had stationed themselves the f day.	8037
	20:39	"We are defeating them as in the f battle."	8037
1Sa	2:16	"Let the fat be burned up f,	2021+3427+3869
	14:14	In that f attack Jonathan	8037
	14:35	it was the f time he had done this.	2725
	22:15	Was that day the f time I inquired of God	2725
2Sa	17: 9	If he should attack your troops f,	928+2021+9378
	18:27	the f one runs like Ahimaaz son of Zadok."	8037
	19:20	the f of the whole house of Joseph to come	8037
	19:43	the f to speak of bringing back our king?"	8037
	21: 9	they were put to death during the f days of	8037
1Ki	3:22	But the f one insisted, "No!	2296S
	3:27	"Give the living baby to the f woman.	2023S
	6:24	of the f cherub was five cubits long, and	285
	17:13	But f make a small cake of bread for me	928+2021+8037
	18:25	"Choose one of the bulls and prepare it f,	8037
	20: 9	'Your servant will do all you demanded the f time,	8037
	20:17	of the provincial commanders went out f.	8037
	22: 5	F seek the counsel of the LORD.	2021+3427+3869
2Ki	1:14	the f two captains and all their men.	8037
	4:42	from the f ripe grain,	1137
	17:25	When they f lived there,	9378
	6:54	because the f lot was for them):	NIH
1Ch	9: 2	Now the f to resettle on their own property	8037
	11: 6	Joab son of Zeruiah went up f,	8037
	12:15	the Jordan in the f month	8037
	15:13	did not bring it up the f time that	8037
	16: 7	That day David f committed to Asaph,	8031
	23: 8	Jehiel the f, Zetham and Joel—three in all.	8031
	23:11	Jahath was the f and Ziza the second,	8031
	23:16	Shubael was the f.	8031
	23:17	Rehabiah was the f.	8031
	23:18	The sons of Izhar: Shelomith was the f.	8031
	23:19	Jeriah the f, Amariah the second,	8031
	23:20	Micah the f and Isshiah the second.	8031
	24: 7	The f lot fell to Jehoiarib,	8037
	24:21	Rehabiah, from his sons: Isshiah was the f.	8031
	24:23	Jeriah the f, Amariah the second,	8031
	25: 9	The f lot, which was for Asaph,	8031
	26:10	the f (although he was not the firstborn,	8031
	26:10	his father had appointed him the f),	8031
	27: 2	In charge of the f division,	8037
	27: 2	for the f month, was Jashobeam	8037
	27: 2	of all the army officers for the f month.	8037
2Ch	3:11	of the f cherub was five cubits long	NIH
	3:12	touched the wing of the f cherub.	285
	18: 4	F seek the counsel of the LORD.	2021+3427+3869
	29: 3	In the f month of the first year of his reign,	8037
	29: 3	In the first month of the f year of his reign,	8037
	29:17	They began the consecration on the f day	285
	29:17	on the first day of the f month,	8037
	29:17	on the sixteenth day of the f month.	8037
	35: 1	on the fourteenth day of the f month.	8037
	36:22	In the f year of Cyrus king of Persia,	285
Ezr	1: 1	In the f year of Cyrus king of Persia,	285
	3: 6	the f day of the seventh month they began	285
	5:13	In the f year of Cyrus king of Babylon,	10248
	6: 3	In the f year of King Cyrus, the king issued	10248
	6:19	On the fourteenth day of the f month,	8037
	7: 9	on the f day of the first month,	8037
	7: 9	on the first day of the f month,	8037
	7: 9	and he arrived in Jerusalem on the f day of	285
	8:31	the twelfth day of the f month we set out	8037
	10:16	the f day of the tenth month they sat down	8037
	10:17	and by the f day of the first month	8037
	10:17	from the f month they finished dealing with all	8037
Ne	4:21	from the f light of dawn till the stars came out.	6590+8840
	7: 5	of those who had been the f to return.	8037
	8: 2	So on the f day of the seventh month Ezra	285
	8:18	Day after day, from the f day to the last,	8037

Ne	10:37	to the priests, the f of our ground meal,	8040
Est	3: 7	in the f month, the month of Nisan,	8037
	3:12	Then on the thirteenth day of the f month	8037
Job	3: 9	for daylight in vain and not see the f rays	6757
	15: 7	"Are you the f man *ever* born?	8037
	40:19	He ranks f among the works of God,	8040
	42:12	the latter part of Job's life more than the f.	8040
	42:14	The f daughter he named Jemimah,	285
Pr	4:18	the righteous is like the f *gleam of* dawn.	AIT
	8:22	the f of his works, before his deeds of old;	8040
	18:17	The f to present his case seems right,	8037
Isa	41: 4	with the f of them and with the last—	8037
	41:27	I was the f to tell Zion, 'Look,	8037
	43:27	Your f father sinned;	8037
	44: 6	I am the f and I am the last;	8037
	48:12	I am the f and I am the last.	8037
	48:16	the announcement I have not spoken	8031
	52: 4	"At f my people went down to Egypt	8037
Jer	4:31	a groan as of *one* **bearing** *her* f child—	1144
	7:12	now to the place in Shiloh where I f made a dwelling	928+2021+8037
	25: 1	the f year of Nebuchadnezzar king	8038
	36:28	on it all the words that were on the f scroll,	8037
	50:17	f to devour him was the king of Assyria;	8037
Eze	26: 1	in the f month of the month,	285
	29:17	in the f month on the first day,	8037
	29:17	in the first month on the f day,	285
	30:20	in the f month on the seventh day,	8037
	31: 1	in the third month on the f day,	285
	32: 1	in the twelfth month on the f day,	285
	40:21	as those of f gateway.	8037
	44:30	the f *portion of* your ground meal so that	8040
	45:18	the f month on the first day you are to take	8037
	45:18	the first month on the f day you are to take	285
	45:21	the f month on the fourteenth day you are	8037
Da	1:21	And Daniel remained there until the f year	285
	6:19	At the f *light* of dawn,	10459
	7: 1	the f year of Belshazzar king of Babylon,	10248
	7: 4	"The f was like a lion,	10623
	7: 8	and three of the f horns were uprooted	10623
	8:21	large horn between his eyes is the f king.	8037
	9: 1	the f year of Darius son of Xerxes (a Mede	285
	9: 2	in the f year of his reign,	285
	10: 4	On the twenty-fourth day of the f month,	8037
	10:12	Since the f day that you set your mind	8037
	10:21	but f I will tell you what is written in	NIH
	11: 1	And in the f year of Darius the Mede,	285
	11:13	larger than the f;	8037
Hos	2: 7	'I will go back to my husband as at f,	8037
Am	6: 7	Therefore you will be among the f to go	8031
Jnh	3: 4	On the f day, Jonah started into the city.	285
Na	3:12	like fig trees with their f **ripe fruit;**	1137
Hag	1: 1	on the f day of the sixth month,	285
Zec	6: 2	The f chariot had red horses,	8037
	12: 7	the dwellings of Judah f,	8037
	14:10	the Benjamin Gate to the site of the F Gate,	8037
Mt	5:24	F go and be reconciled to your brother;	4754
	6:33	seek f his kingdom and his righteousness,	4754
	7: 5	f take the plank out of your own eye,	4754
	8:21	"Lord, f let me go and bury my father."	4754
	10: 2	f, Simon (who is called Peter)	4755
	12:29	unless he f ties up the strong man?	4754
	12:45	of that man is worse than the f.	4755
	13:30	F collect the weeds and tie them in bundles	4754
	17:10	of the law say that Elijah must come f?"	4754
	17:25	Jesus *was the* f to speak.	4740
	17:27	Take the f fish you catch;	4755
	19:30	But many who are f will be last,	4755
	19:30	and many who are last will be f.	4755
	20: 8	the last ones hired and going on to the f.'	4755
	20:10	So when those came who were hired f,	4755
	20:16	the last will be f, and the first will be last."	4755
	20:16	the last will be first, and the f will be last."	4755
	20:27	and whoever wants to be f must	4755
	21:28	He went to the f and said, 'Son,	4755
	21:31	"The f," they answered.	4755
	21:36	more than the f time,	4755
	22:25	The f one married and died,	4755
	22:38	This is the f and greatest commandment.	4755
	23:26	F clean the inside of the cup and dish,	4754
	26:17	On the f day of the Feast of Unleavened	4755
	27:64	be worse than the f."	4755
	28: 1	at dawn on the f day of the week,	1651
Mk	3:27	unless he f ties up the strong man.	4754
	4:28	f the stalk, then the head,	4754
	7:27	"F let the children eat all they want,"	4754
	9:11	of the law say that Elijah must come f?"	4754
	9:12	Elijah does come f, and restores all things.	4754
	9:35	"If anyone wants to be f,	4754
	10:31	But many who are f will be last,	4755
	10:31	and the last f."	4755
	10:44	whoever wants to be f must be slave of all.	4755
	12:20	The f one married and died	4754
	13:10	gospel must f be preached to all nations.	4754
	14:12	*On* the f day of the Feast of Unleavened	4755
	16: 2	Very early *on* the f day of the week,	1651
	16: 9	When Jesus rose early *on* the f day of	4755
	16: 9	he appeared f to Mary Magdalene,	4754
Lk	1: 2	by those who from the f were eyewitnesses	794
	2: 2	(This was the f census that took place	4755
	6:42	f take the plank out of your eye,	4754
	9:59	"Lord, f let me go and bury my father."	4754
	9:61	but f let me go back and say good-by	4754
	10: 5	"When you enter a house, f say,	4754
	11:26	of that man is worse than the f."	4755
	11:38	that Jesus did not f wash before the meal,	4754
	12: 1	Jesus began to speak f to his disciples,	4754

Lk	13:30	be f, and first who will	4755
	13:30	and f who will be last."	4755
	14:18	The f said, 'I have just bought a field,	4755
	14:28	Will he not f sit down and estimate the cost	4754
	14:31	Will he not f sit down	4754
	16: 5	He asked the f,	4755
	17:25	But f he must suffer many things and	4754
	19:16	"The f one came and said, 'Sir,	4755
	20:29	The f one married a woman	4755
	21: 9	These things must happen f,	4754
	24: 1	*On* the f day of the week,	1651
Jn	1:41	The f thing Andrew did was	4754
	2:10	"Everyone brings out the choice wine f and	4754
	2:11	This, the f of his miraculous signs,	794
	7:51	without f hearing him	4754
	8: 7	let him be the f to throw a stone at her."	4755
	8: 9	the older ones f, until only Jesus was left,	806
	12:16	At f his disciples did	4754
	15:18	keep in mind that it hated me f.	4754
	16: 4	I did not tell you this at f because I was	794
	18:13	and brought him f to Annas,	4754
	19:32	of the f man who had been crucified	4755
	20: 1	Early *on* the f day of the week,	1651
	20: 4	and reached the tomb f.	4755
	20: 8	who had reached the tomb f,	4755
	20:19	On the evening *of* that f day of the week,	1651
Ac	3:26	he sent him f to you to bless you	4754
	7:12	he sent our fathers on their f visit.	4755
	11:26	The disciples were called Christians f	4759
	12:10	They passed the f and second guards	4755
	13:46	to speak the word of God to you f.	4755
	15:14	at f showed his concern by taking from	4754
	20: 7	On the f day of the week we came together	1651
	20:18	the f day I came into the province of Asia.	4755
	26:20	To those in Damascus,	4754
	26:23	as the f to rise from the dead,	4755
	27:43	to jump overboard f and get to land.	4755
Ro	1: 8	I thank my God through Jesus Christ	4754
	1:16	f for the Jew, then for the Gentile.	4754
	1:17	by **faith** from f to last,	1650+4411+4411
	2: 9	f for the Jew, then for the Gentile;	4754
	2:10	f for the Jew, then for the Gentile;	4754
	3: 2	F of all, they have been entrusted with	4754
	10:19	F, Moses says, "I will make you envious	4755
	13:11	now than when we f believed.	NIG
	16: 5	the f convert to Christ in the province	569
1Co	11:18	In the f place, I hear that when you come	4754
	12:28	church God has appointed f of all apostles,	4754
	14:30	the f speaker should stop.	4755
	15: 3	on to you as of f importance:	1877+4755
	15:45	"The f man Adam became a living being";	4755
	15:46	The spiritual did not come f,	4754
	15:47	The f man was of the dust of the earth,	4755
	16: 2	On the f day of every week,	1651
	16:15	of Stephanas were the f converts in Achaia,	569
2Co	1:15	I planned to visit you f so	4728
	8: 5	but they gave themselves f to the Lord and	4754
	8:10	Last year you *were* **the** f not only to give	4599
Gal	4:13	of an illness that I f preached the gospel	4728
Eph	1:12	who were the f to hope in Christ,	4598
	6: 2	the f commandment with a promise—	4755
Php	1: 5	in the gospel from the f day until now,	4755
1Th	4:16	and the dead in Christ will rise f.	4754
1Ti	2: 1	I urge, then, f of all, that requests, prayers,	4754
	2:13	For Adam was formed f, then Eve.	4755
	3:10	They must f be tested;	4754
	5: 4	these should learn f of all	4755
	5:12	because they have broken their f pledge.	4755
2Ti	1: 5	which f lived in your grandmother Lois	4754
	2: 6	The hardworking farmer should be the f	4755
	4:16	At my f defense,	4755
Heb	2: 3	which was f announced by the Lord,	794
	3:14	till the end the confidence we had at f.	794
	7: 2	F, his name means "king of righteousness"	4754
	7:27	f for his own sins,	4728
	8: 7	with that f covenant,	4755
	8:13	he has made the f one obsolete;	4755
	9: 1	f covenant had regulations for worship	4755
	9: 2	In its f room were the lampstand,	4755
	9: 8	as the f tabernacle was still standing.	4755
	9:15	the sins committed under the f covenant.	4755
	9:18	even the f covenant was not put into effect	4755
	10: 8	F he said, "Sacrifices and offerings,	542
	10: 9	He sets aside the f to establish the second.	4755
	10:15	about this. He says:	3552+3836
Jas	3:17	that comes from heaven is f of all pure;	4754
2Pe	3: 3	F of all, you must understand that in	4047+4754
1Jn	4:19	We love because he f loved us.	4755
3Jn	1: 9	but Diotrephes, who **loves to be** f,	5812
Rev	1:17	I am the F and the Last.	4755
	2: 4	You have forsaken your f love.	4755
	2: 5	Repent and do the things you did at f.	4755
	2: 8	the words of him who is the F and the Last,	4755
	2:19	now doing more than you did at f.	4755
	4: 1	And the voice I had f heard speaking to me	4755
	4: 7	The f living creature was like a lion,	4755
	6: 1	the Lamb opened the f of the seven seals,	1651
	8: 7	The f angel sounded his trumpet,	4755
	9:12	The f woe is past;	1651
	13:12	He exercised all the authority *of* the f beast	4755
	13:12	and its inhabitants worship the f beast,	4755
	13:14	to do on behalf of the f beast,	NIG
	13:15	to give breath to the image of the f beast,	NIG
	16: 2	The f angel went and poured out his bowl	4755
	20: 5	This is the f resurrection.	4755
	20: 6	who have part in the f resurrection.	4755
	21: 1	for the f heaven and the first earth	4755

Rev	21: 1	heaven and the f earth had passed away,	4755
	21:19	The f foundation was jasper,	4755
	22:13	the F and the Last,	4755

FIRSTBEGOTTEN (KJV) See
FIRSTBORN

FIRSTBORN (132) [FIRST, BEAR]

Ge	4: 4	from some of the f of his flock.	1147
	10:15	Canaan was the father of Sidon his f,	1147
	22:21	the f, Buz his brother, Kemuel (the father	1147
	25:13	Nebaioth the f of Ishmael, Kedar, Adbeel,	1147
	27:19	Jacob said to his father, "I am Esau your f.	1147
	27:32	"I am your son," he answered, "your f,	1147
	35:23	Reuben the f of Jacob, Simeon, Levi,	1147
	36:15	The sons of Eliphaz the f of Esau:	1147
	38: 6	Judah got a wife for Er, his f,	1147
	38: 7	Judah's f, was wicked in	1147
	41:51	Joseph named his f Manasseh and said,	1147
	43:33	from the f to the youngest;	1147
	46: 8	Reuben the f of Jacob.	1147
	48:14	even though Manasseh was the f.	1147
	48:18	"No, my father, this one is the f;	1147
	49: 3	"Reuben, you are my f, my might,	1147
Ex	4:22	Israel is my f son,	1147
	4:23	so I will kill your f son.' "	1147
	6:14	of Reuben the f son of Israel were Hanoch	1147
	11: 5	Every f son in Egypt will die,	1147
	11: 5	from the f son of Pharaoh,	1147
	11: 5	to the f son of the slave girl,	1147
	11: 5	and all the f of the cattle as well.	1147
	12:12	through Egypt and strike down every f—	1147
	12:29	the LORD struck down all the f in Egypt,	1147
	12:29	from the f of Pharaoh,	1147
	12:29	to the f of the prisoner,	1147
	12:29	and f of all the livestock as well.	1147
	13: 2	"Consecrate to me every f *male.*	1147
	13:12	All the f males *of* your livestock belong to the LORD.	7081+8715
	13:13	Redeem with a lamb every f donkey,	7081
	13:13	Redeem every f among your sons.	7081
	13:15	the LORD killed every f in Egypt,	1147
	13:15	and redeem each of my f sons.'	1147
	22:29	"You must give me the f of your sons.	1147
	34:19	including all the f males *of* your livestock,	7081
	34:20	Redeem the f donkey with a lamb,	7081
	34:20	Redeem all your f sons.	1147
Lev	27:26	however, may dedicate the f of an animal,	1147
	27:26	the f already **belongs to the** LORD;	1144+4200
Nu	1:20	From the descendants of Reuben the f *son*	1147
	3: 2	of Aaron were Nadab the f and Abihu,	1147
	3:13	for all the f are mine.	1147
	3:13	When I struck down all the f in Egypt,	1147
	3:13	I set apart for myself every f in Israel,	1147
	3:40	the Israelite males who are a month old	1147
	3:41	Take the Levites for me in place of all the f	1147
	3:41	of all the f of the livestock of the Israelites.	1147
	3:42	So Moses counted all the f of the Israelites.	1147
	3:43	The total number of f males a month old	1147
	3:45	the Levites in place of all the f of Israel,	1147
	3:46	the 273 f Israelites who exceed the number	1147
	3:50	From the f of the Israelites	1147
	8:16	as my own in place of the f,	7082
	8:17	Every f **male** in Israel,	1147
	8:17	When I struck down all the f in Egypt,	1147
	8:18	the Levites in place of all the f *sons*	1147
	18:15	But you must redeem every f son	1147
	18:15	and every f **male** of unclean animals.	1147
	18:17	"But you must not redeem the f of an ox,	1147
	26: 5	Reuben, the f *son* of Israel, were:	1147
	33: 4	who were burying all their f, whom	1147
Dt	12: 6	and the f of your herds and flocks.	1147
	12:17	or the f of your herds and flocks,	1147
	14:23	and the f of your herds and flocks in	1147
	15:19	for the LORD your God every f male	1147
	15:19	Do not put the f of your oxen to work,	1147
	15:19	and do not shear the f of your sheep.	1147
	21:15	and both bear him sons but the f is the son	1147
	21:16	not **give the rights of the** f to the son	1144
	21:16	in preference to his actual f,	1147
	21:17	of his unloved wife as the f by giving him	1147
	21:17	The right of the f belongs to him.	1148
	33:17	In majesty he is like a f bull;	1147
Jos	6:26	of his f *son* will he lay its foundations;	1147
	17: 1	for the tribe of Manasseh as Joseph's f,	1147
	17: 1	that is, for Makir, Manasseh's f.	1147
1Sa	8: 2	The name of his f was Joel and the name	1147
	17:13	The f was Eliab;	1147
2Sa	3: 2	His f was Amnon the son of Ahinoam	1147
1Ki	16:34	at the cost of his f *son* Abiram,	1147
2Ki	3:27	Then he took his f son,	1147
1Ch	1:13	Canaan was the father of Sidon his f,	1147
	1:29	Nebaioth the f of Ishmael, Kedar, Adbeel,	1147
	2: 3	Judah's f, was wicked in the LORD's sight	1147
	2:13	Jesse was the father of Eliab his f;	1147
	2:25	The sons of Jerahmeel the f of Hezron:	1147
	2:25	Ram his f, Bunah, Oren,	1147
	2:27	The sons of Ram the f of Jerahmeel:	1147
	2:42	Mesha his f, who was the father of Ziph,	1147
	2:50	The sons of Hur the f of Ephrathah:	1147
	3: 1	The f was Amnon the son of Ahinoam	1147
	3:15	Johanan the f, Jehoiakim the second son,	1147
	4: 4	of Ephrathah and father of Bethlehem.	1147
	5: 1	The sons of Reuben the f of Israel (he was	1147
	5: 1	the firstborn of Israel (he was the f, but	1147

1Ch	5: 1	his **rights as** f were given to the sons	1148
	5: 2	the **rights of the** f belonged to Joseph)—	1148
	5: 3	the sons of Reuben the f *of* Israel:	1147
	6:28	Joel the f and Abijah the second son.	1147
	8: 1	Benjamin was the father of Bela his f,	1147
	8:30	and his f son was Abdon,	1147
	8:39	The sons of his brother Eshek: Ulam his f,	1147
	9: 5	Asaiah the f and his sons.	1147
	9:31	the f son of Shallum the Korahite,	1147
	9:36	and his f son was Abdon,	1147
	26: 2	Meshelemiah had sons: Zechariah the f,	1147
	26: 4	Obed-Edom also had sons: Shemaiah the f,	1147
	26:10	Shimri the first (although he was not the f,	1147
2Ch	21: 3	to Jehoram because he was his f son.	1147
Ne	10:36	we will bring the f of our sons and	1147
Job	18:13	death's f devours his limbs.	1147
Ps	78:51	He struck down all the f of Egypt,	1147
	89:27	I will also appoint him my f,	1147
	105:36	Then he struck down all the f in their land,	1147
	135: 8	He struck down the f of Egypt,	1147
	135: 8	of men and animals.	NIH
	136:10	the f *of* Egypt His love endures forever.	1147
Jer	31: 9	and Ephraim is my f son.	1147
Eze	20:26	the sacrifice of every f—	7081+8167
Mic	6: 7	Shall I offer my f for my transgression,	1147
Zec	12:10	for him as one grieves for a f son.	1147
Lk	2: 7	and she gave birth to her f,	4758
	2:23	"Every f male is to be consecrated to	1380+3616
Ro	8:29	be the f among many brothers.	4758
Col	1:15	the f over all creation.	4758
	1:18	he is the beginning and the f from among	4758
Heb	1: 6	when God brings his f into the world,	4758
	11:28	that the destroyer of the f would not touch	4758
	11:28	of the firstborn would not touch **the** f	899S
	12:23	to the church of the f,	4758
Rev	1: 5	the f from the dead,	4758

FIRSTFRUITS (29) [FIRST]

Ex	23:16	of Harvest with the f *of* the crops you sow	1137
	23:19	the best of the f *of* your soil to the house	1137
	34:22	of Weeks with the f *of* the wheat harvest,	1137
	34:26	the best of the f *of* your soil to the house	1137
Lev	2:12	to the LORD as an offering of the f,	8040
	2:14	" 'If you bring a grain offering of f to	1137
	23:17	as a wave offering of f to the LORD.	1137
	23:20	together with the bread of the f.	1137
Nu	18:12	the LORD as the f of their **harvest.**	8040
	18:13	All the land's f that they bring to	1137
	28:26	" 'On the day of f,	1137
Dt	18: 4	You are to give them the f *of* your grain,	8040
	26: 2	f of all that you produce from the soil	7262+8040
	26:10	now I bring the f *of* the soil that you,	7262+8040
2Ch	31: 5	the Israelites generously gave the f	8040
Ne	10:35	of the LORD each year the f *of* our crops	1137
	12:44	of the storerooms for the contributions, f	8040
	13:31	and for the f.	1137
Ps	78:51	the f *of* manhood in the tents of Ham.	8040
	105:36	the f of all their manhood.	8040
Pr	3: 9	with the f *of* all your crops;	8040
Jer	2: 3	the f *of* his harvest;	8040
Eze	44:30	The best of all the f and	1137
Ro	8:23	who have the f of the Spirit,	569
	11:16	If the part of the dough offered as f is holy,	569
1Co	15:20	the f of those who have fallen asleep.	569
	15:23	But each in his own turn: Christ, the f;	569
Jas	1:18	be a kind of f of all he created.	569
Rev	14: 4	from among men and offered as f to God	569

FIRSTLING (KJV) See FIRSTBORN

FISH (64) [FISHERMEN, FISHERS, FISHHOOK, FISHHOOKS, FISHING]

Ge	1:26	and let them rule over the f of the sea and	1836
	1:28	over the f of the sea and the birds of the air	1836
	9: 2	and upon all the f of the sea;	1834
Ex	7:18	The f in the Nile will die,	1836
	7:21	The f in the Nile died,	1836
Nu	11: 5	We remember the f we ate in Egypt	1836
	11:22	the f *in* the sea were caught for them?"	1834
Dt	4:18	the ground or any f in the waters below.	1836
1Ki	4:33	about animals and birds, reptiles and f.	1834
2Ch	33:14	as the entrance of the F Gate and encircling	1834
Ne	3: 3	The F Gate was rebuilt by the sons	1834
	12:39	the Jeshanah Gate, the F Gate,	1834
	13:16	in f and all kinds of merchandise	1794
Job	12: 8	or let the f of the sea inform you.	1834
Ps	8: 8	and the f of the sea,	1834
	105:29	causing their f to die.	1836
Ecc	9:12	As f are caught in a cruel net,	1834
Isa	50: 2	their f rot for lack of water and die	1836
Eze	29: 4	the f *of* your streams stick to your scales.	1836
	29: 4	with all the f sticking to your scales.	1836
	29: 5	you and all the f *of* your streams.	1836
	38:20	The f of the sea, the birds of the air,	1834
	47: 9	There will be large numbers of f,	1836
	47:10	The f will be of many kinds—	1836
	47:10	like the f of the Great Sea.	1836
Hos	4: 3	the field and the birds of the air and the f	1834
Jnh	1:17	But the LORD provided a great f	1834
	1:17	inside the three days and three nights.	1834
	2: 1	the f Jonah prayed to the LORD his God.	1836
	2:10	And the LORD commanded the f,	1834
Hab	1:14	You have made men like f *in* the sea,	1834
Zep	1: 3	the birds of the air and the f *of* the sea.	1834

Zep	1:10	"a cry will go up from the F Gate,	1834
Mt	7:10	Or if he asks for a f, will give him a snake?	2716
	12:40	and three nights in the belly of a **huge** f,	3063
	13:47	into the lake and caught all kinds of f.	NIG
	13:48	down and collected the good f in baskets,	NIG
	14:17	of bread and two f,"	2716
	14:19	the five loaves and the two f and looking	2716
	15:34	"Seven," they replied, "and a few **small** f."	2715
	15:36	Then he took the seven loaves and the f,	2716
	17:27	Take the first f you catch;	2716
Mk	6:38	they said, "Five—and two f."	2716
	6:41	the five loaves and the two f and looking	2716
	6:41	He also divided the two f among them all.	2716
	6:43	of broken pieces of bread and f.	2716
	8: 7	They had a few **small** f as well;	2715
Lk	5: 6	a large number of f that their nets began	2716
	5: 9	at the catch of f they had taken,	2716
	9:13	of bread and two f—	2716
	9:16	the five loaves and the two f and looking	2716
	11:11	if your son asks for a f,	2716
	24:42	They gave him a piece *of* broiled f,	2716
Jn	6: 9	and two **small** f,	4066
	6:11	He did the same with the f.	4066
	21: 3	"I'm going out to f,"	244
	21: 5	"Friends, haven't any any f?"	4709
	21: 6	the net in because of the large number of f.	2716
	21: 8	towing the net full of f,	2716
	21: 9	a fire of burning coals there with f on it,	4066
	21:10	"Bring some *of* the f you have just caught."	4066
	21:11	It was full of large f, 153,	2716
	21:13	and did the same with the f.	4066
1Co	15:39	birds another and f another.	2716

FISHERMEN (7) [FISH]

Isa	19: 8	The f will groan and lament,	1900
Jer	16:16	"But now I will send for many f,"	1900
Eze	47:10	F will stand along the shore;	1854
Mt	4:18	for they were f.	243
	13:48	it was full, the f pulled it up on the shore.	NIG
Mk	1:16	for they were f.	243
Lk	5: 2	left there by the f,	243

FISHERS (2) [FISH]

Mt	4:19	Jesus said, "and I will make you f of men."	243
Mk	1:17	Jesus said, "and I will make you f of men."	243

FISHHOOK (1) [FISH, HOOK]

Job	41: 1	a f or tie down his tongue with a rope?	2676

FISHHOOKS (1) [FISH, HOOK]

Am	4: 2	the last of you with f.	1855+6106

FISHING (1) [FISH]

Job	41: 7	with harpoons or his head with f spears?	1834

FISHING NETS (Anglicized) See FISHNETS

FISHNETS (2) [NET]

Eze	26: 5	the sea she will become a place to spread f,	3052
	26:14	and you will become a place to spread f.	3052

FISHPOOL (KJV) See POOL

FIST (4) [FISTS, TIGHTFISTED]

Ex	21:18	a stone or with his f and he does not die	114
Nu	35:21	with his f so that he dies, that person shall	3338
Job	15:25	because he shakes his f at God	3338
Isa	10:32	they will shake their f at the mount of	3338

FISTS (4) [FIST]

Isa	58: 4	and in striking each other with wicked f.	114
Zep	2:15	by her scoff and shake their f.	3338
Mt	26:67	**struck** him **with** *their* f.	3139
Mk	14:65	**struck** him **with** *their* f,	3139

FIT (13) [FITS, FITTED, FITTING, FITTINGS]

Ge	49:20	he will provide **delicacies** f *for* a king.	AIT
Dt	12: 8	everyone as he sees f,	3838
Jdg	5:25	in a **bowl** f for nobles	AIT
	17: 6	everyone did as he saw f.	3838
	21:25	everyone did as he saw f.	3838
2Ki	24:16	strong and f for war,	6913
Isa	54:16	into flame and forges a weapon f **for**	4200
Eze	19:11	f for a ruler's scepter.	448
	19:14	No strong branch is left on it for	NIH
Mt	3:11	whose sandals I am not f to carry.	2653
Lk	9:62	the plow and looks back is f **for service** in	2310
	14:35	It is f neither for the soil nor for	2310
Ac	22:22	He's not f to live!"	2763

FITCHES (KJV) See CARAWAY

FITS (1) [FIT]

Gal	5:20	hatred, discord, jealousy, f of rage,	2596

FITTED (3) [FIT]

Ex	26:24	and f into a single ring;	3481+9447
	36:29	the top and f into a single ring;	3481+9447
Eph	6:15	and with your feet f with the readiness	5686

FITTING (8) [FIT]

Ps	33: 1	it is f for the upright to praise him.	5534
	147: 1	how pleasant and f to praise him!	5534
Pr	10:32	The lips of the righteous know *what* is f,	8356
	19:10	It is not f for a fool to live in luxury—	5534
	26: 1	honor is not f for a fool.	5534
1Co	14:40	But everything should be done in a f	2361
Col	3:18	as *is* f in the Lord.	465
Heb	2:10	*it was* f that God,	4560

FITTINGS (1) [FIT]

1Ch	22: 3	for the doors of the gateways and for the f,	4677

FIVE (209) [FIFTH, FIVE-SIDED, FOUR-FIFTHS]

Ge	14: 9	four kings against f.	2822
	18:28	of the righteous is f less than fifty?	2822
	18:28	the whole city because of f **people?"**	2822
	43:34	Benjamin's portion was f times as much	2822
	45: 6	the next f years there will not be plowing	2822
	45:11	because f years of famine are still to come.	2822
	45:22	of silver and f sets of clothes.	2822
	47: 2	He chose f of his brothers	2822
Ex	22: 1	he must pay back f head of cattle for the ox	2822
	26: 3	Join f of the curtains together,	2822
	26: 3	and do the same with the other f.	2822
	26: 9	Join f of the curtains into one set	2822
	26:26	f for the frames on one side of	2822
	26:27	f for those on the other side,	2822
	26:27	and f for the frames on the west,	2822
	26:37	and f posts of acacia wood overlaid	2822
	26:37	And cast f bronze bases for them.	2822
	27: 1	f cubits long and five cubits wide.	2822
	27: 1	five cubits long and f cubits wide.	2822
	27:18	of finely twisted linen f cubits high,	2822
	36:10	They joined f of the curtains together	2822
	36:10	and did the same with the other f.	2822
	36:16	They joined f of the curtains into one set	2822
	36:31	f for the frames on one side of	2822
	36:32	f for those on the other side,	2822
	36:32	and f for the frames on the west,	2822
	36:38	and they made f posts with hooks for them.	2822
	36:38	with gold and made their f bases of bronze.	2822
	38: 1	f cubits long and five cubits wide.	2822
	38: 1	five cubits long and f cubits wide.	2822
	38:18	the curtains of the courtyard, f cubits high,	2822
Lev	26: 8	F of you will chase a hundred,	2822
	27: 5	a person between the ages of f and twenty,	2822
	27: 6	a person between one month and f years,	2822
	27: 6	set the value of a male at f shekels of silver	2822
Nu	3:47	collect f shekels for each one,	2822
	7:17	and two oxen, f rams, five male goats	2822
	7:17	f male goats and five male lambs	2822
	7:17	five male goats and f male lambs	2822
	7:23	and two oxen, f rams, five male goats	2822
	7:23	f male goats and five male lambs	2822
	7:23	five male goats and f male lambs	2822
	7:29	and two oxen, f rams, five male goats	2822
	7:29	f male goats and five male lambs	2822
	7:29	five male goats and f male lambs	2822
	7:35	and two oxen, f rams, five male goats	2822
	7:35	f male goats and five male lambs	2822
	7:35	five male goats and f male lambs	2822
	7:41	and two oxen, f rams, five male goats	2822
	7:41	f male goats and five male lambs	2822
	7:41	five male goats and f male lambs	2822
	7:47	and two oxen, f rams, five male goats	2822
	7:47	f male goats and five male lambs	2822
	7:47	five male goats and f male lambs	2822
	7:53	and two oxen, f rams, five male goats	2822
	7:53	f male goats and five male lambs	2822
	7:53	five male goats and f male lambs	2822
	7:59	and two oxen, f rams, five male goats	2822
	7:59	f male goats and five male lambs	2822
	7:59	five male goats and f male lambs	2822
	7:65	and two oxen, f rams, five male goats	2822
	7:65	f male goats and five male lambs	2822
	7:65	five male goats and f male lambs	2822
	7:71	and two oxen, f rams, five male goats	2822
	7:71	f male goats and five male lambs	2822
	7:71	five male goats and f male lambs	2822
	7:77	and two oxen, f rams, five male goats	2822
	7:77	f male goats and five male lambs	2822
	7:77	five male goats and f male lambs	2822
	7:83	and two oxen, f rams, five male goats	2822
	7:83	f male goats and five male lambs	2822
	7:83	five male goats and f male lambs	2822
	11:19	or two days, or f, ten or twenty days,	2822
	18:16	at the redemption price set at f shekels	2822
	31: 8	the f kings of Midian.	2822
	31:28	for the LORD one out of every f hundred,	2822
Jos	8:12	Joshua had taken about f thousand men	2822
	10: 5	Then the f kings of the Amorites—	2822
	10:16	the f kings had fled and hidden in the cave	2822
	10:17	that the f kings had been found hiding in	2822
	10:22	of the cave and bring those f kings out	2822
	10:23	they brought the f kings out of the cave—	2822
	10:26	the kings and hung them on f trees,	2822
	13: 3	(the territory of the f Philistine rulers	2822
Jdg	3: 3	the f rulers of the Philistines,	2822
	18: 2	So the Danites sent f warriors from Zorah	2822

Jdg	18: 7	So the f men left and came to Laish,	2822
	18:14	Then the f men who had spied out the land	2822
	18:17	The f men who had spied out the land went	2822
	20:45	the Israelites cut down f thousand men	2822
1Sa	6: 4	"F gold tumors and five gold rats,	2822
	6: 4	"Five gold tumors and f gold rats,	2822
	6:16	The f rulers of the Philistines saw all this	2822
	6:18	to the f rulers—	2822
	17: 5	of bronze weighing f thousand shekels;	2822
	17:40	chose f smooth stones from the stream,	2822
	21: 3	Give me f loaves of bread,	2822
	25:18	f dressed sheep, five seahs of roasted grain,	2822
	25:18	five dressed sheep, f seahs of roasted grain,	2822
	25:42	attended by her f maids,	2822
2Sa	4: 4	He was f years old when the news	2822
	21: 8	with the f sons of Saul's daughter Merab,	2822
	24: 9	and in Judah f hundred thousand.	2822
1Ki	4:32	and his songs numbered a thousand and f.	2822
	6: 6	The lowest floor was f cubits wide,	2822
	6:10	The height of each was f cubits,	2822
	6:24	of the first cherub was f cubits long, and	2822
	6:24	and the other wing f cubits—	2822
	7:16	each capital was f cubits high.	2822
	7:23	from rim to rim and f cubits high.	2822
	7:39	He placed f of the stands on the south side	2822
	7:39	on the south side of the temple and f on	2822
	7:49	the lampstands of pure gold f on the right	2822
	7:49	on the right and f on the left, in front of	2822
2Ki	6:25	quarter of a cab of seed pods for f shekels.	2822
	7:13	"Have some men take f of the horses	2822
	13:19	"You should have struck the ground f	2822
	25:19	of the fighting men and f royal advisers.	2822
1Ch	2: 4	Judah had f sons in all.	2822
	2: 6	and Darda—f in all.	2822
	3:20	There were also f others:	2822
	4:32	and Ashan—f towns—	2822
	4:42	And f hundred of these Simeonites,	2822
	7: 3	All f of them were chiefs.	2822
	7: 7	of families—f in all.	2822
	29: 7	on the temple of God f thousand talents	2822
2Ch	3:11	of the first cherub was f cubits long	2822
	3:11	while its other wing, also f cubits long,	2822
	3:12	of the second cherub was f cubits long	2822
	3:12	and its other wing, also f cubits long,	2822
	3:15	with a capital on top measuring f cubits.	2822
	4: 2	from rim to rim and f cubits high.	2822
	4: 6	for washing and placed f on the south side	2822
	4: 6	and placed five on the south side and f on	2822
	4: 7	f on the south side and five on the north.	2822
	4: 7	five on the south side and f on the north.	2822
	4: 8	f on the south side and five on the north.	2822
	4: 8	five on the south side and f on the north.	2822
	6:13	a bronze platform, f cubits long,	2822
	6:13	f cubits wide and three cubits high,	2822
	13:17	there were f hundred thousand casualties	2822
	35: 9	provided f thousand Passover offerings	2822
	35: 9	and f hundred head of cattle for	2822
Ne	3:13	repaired f hundred yards of the wall	547+564
Est	9: 6	Jews killed and destroyed f hundred men.	2822
	9:12	and destroyed f hundred men and	2822
Job	1: 3	f hundred yoke of oxen	2822
	1: 3	of oxen and f hundred donkeys,	2822
Isa	17: 6	four or f on the fruitful boughs,"	2822
	19:18	In that day f cities in Egypt will speak	2822
	30:17	at the threat of f you will all flee away,	2822
Jer	52:22	on top of the one pillar was f cubits high	2822
Eze	40: 7	between the alcoves were f cubits thick.	2822
	40:30	and f cubits deep.)	2822
	40:48	they were f cubits wide on either side.	2822
	41: 2	on each side of it were f cubits wide.	2822
	41: 9	of the side rooms was f cubits thick.	2822
	41:11	the open area was f cubits wide all around.	2822
	41:12	the building was f cubits thick all around,	2822
	42:16	it was f hundred cubits.	2822
	42:17	it was f hundred cubits by	2822
	42:18	it was f hundred cubits by	2822
	42:19	it was f hundred cubits by	2822
	42:20	f hundred cubits long	2822
	42:20	and f hundred cubits wide,	2822
Mt	14:17	"We have here only f loaves of bread	4297
	14:19	the f loaves and the two fish and looking	4297
	14:21	who ate was about f thousand men,	4295
	16: 9	Don't you remember the f loaves for	4297
	16: 9	the five loaves for the f thousand,	4295
	25: 2	F of them were foolish and five were wise.	4297
	25: 2	Five of them were foolish and f were wise.	4297
	25:15	To one he gave f talents of money,	4297
	25:16	the f talents went at once	4297
	25:16	to work and gained f more.	4297
	25:20	the f talents brought the other five.	4297
	25:20	the five talents brought the other f.	4297
	25:20	he said, 'you entrusted me with f talents.	4297
	25:20	See, I have gained f more.'	4297
Mk	6:38	When they found out, they said, "F—	4297
	6:41	the f loaves and the two fish and looking	4297
	6:44	of the men who had eaten was f thousand.	4295
	8:19	I broke the f loaves for the five thousand,	4297
	8:19	the five loaves for the f thousand,	4295
Lk	1:24	and for f months remained in seclusion.	4297
	7:41	One owed him f hundred denarii,	4296
	9:13	"We have only f loaves of bread	4297
	9:14	(About f thousand men were there.)	4295
	9:16	the f loaves and the two fish and looking	4297
	12: 6	Are not f sparrows sold for two pennies?	4297
	12:52	on there will be f in one family divided	4297
	14:19	'I have just bought f yoke of oxen,	4297
	16:28	for I have f brothers.	4297

Lk	19:18	'Sir, your mina has earned f more.'	4297
	19:19	'You take charge of f cities.'	4297
Jn	4:18	The fact is, you have had f husbands,	4297
	5: 2	by f covered colonnades.	4297
	6: 9	"Here is a boy with f small barley loaves	4297
	6:10	men sat down, about f thousand of them.	4295
	6:13	with the pieces of the f barley loaves left	4297
Ac	4: 4	number of men grew to about f thousand.	4297
	20: 6	f days later joined the others at Troas,	4297
	24: 1	F days later the high priest Ananias went	4297
1Co	14:19	in the church I would rather speak f	
		intelligible words to instruct others	4297
	15: 6	to more than f hundred of the brothers at	4296
2Co	11:24	F times I received from the Jews	4294
Rev	9: 5	but only to torture them for f months.	4297
	9:10	to torment people for f months.	4297
	17:10	F have fallen, one is,	4297

FIVE-SIDED (1) [FIVE, SIDE]

| 1Ki | 6:31 | of olive wood with f jambs. | 2797 |

FIX (8) [AFFIXING, FIXED]

Dt	11:18	F these words of mine in your hearts	8492
Job	14: 3	Do you f your eye on such a one?	7219
Pr	4:25	f your gaze directly before you.	3837
Isa	46: 8	"Remember this, f it in mind,	899
Am	9: 4	I will f my eyes upon them for evil and	8492
2Co	4:18	f our eyes not on what is seen, but on	5023
Heb	3: 1	f your thoughts on Jesus,	2917
	12: 2	Let us f our eyes on Jesus,	927

FIXED (6) [FIX]

2Ki	8:11	He stared at him with a f gaze until Hazael	
			906+2256+6641+7156+8492
Job	38:10	when I f limits for it and set its doors	8689
Ps	141: 8	But my eyes are f on you,	448
Pr	8:28	and f securely the fountains of the deep,	6451
Jer	33:25	and the f laws of heaven and earth,	2978
Lk	16:26	and you a great chasm has been f,	5114

FLAG (KJV) See REED

FLAGSTAFF (1) [STAFF]

| Isa | 30:17 | till you are left like a f on a mountaintop, | 9568 |

FLAKES (1)

| Ex | 16:14 | thin f like frost on the ground appeared on | 2892 |

FLAME (16) [AFLAME, FLAMED, FLAMES, FLAMING]

Jdg	13:20	As the f blazed up from the altar	4258
	13:20	the angel of the LORD ascended in the f.	4258
	16: 9	of string snaps when it comes close to a f.	836
Job	15:30	a f will wither his shoots,	8927
	18: 5	the f of his fire stops burning.	8663
Ps	83:14	the forest or a f sets the mountains ablaze,	4259
	106:18	a f consumed the wicked.	4259
SS	8: 6	It burns like blazing fire, like a mighty f.	8928
Isa	10:16	a fire will be kindled like a blazing f.	836
	10:17	their Holy One a f;	4259
	47:14	from the power of the f.	4259
	54:16	into f and forges a weapon fit for its work.	836
Eze	20:47	The blazing f will not be quenched,	8927
Joel	2: 3	behind them a f blazes.	4259
Ob	1:18	be a fire and the house of Joseph a f;	4259
2Ti	1: 6	For this reason I remind you to fan into f	351

FLAMED (1) [FLAME]

| Am | 1:11 | and his fury f unchecked, | 5905+9068 |

FLAMES (16) [FLAME]

Ex	3: 2	of the LORD appeared to him in f of fire	4225
Job	41:21	and f dart from his mouth.	4258
Ps	104: 4	f of fire his servants.	4265
Isa	5:24	down in the f, so their roots will decay	4259
	29: 6	and tempest and f of a devouring fire.	4258
	42:25	It enveloped them in f,	4265
	43: 2	the f will not set you ablaze.	4259
	66:15	and his rebuke with f of fire.	4258
Jer	51:58	the nations' labor is only fuel for the f."	
			836+928+1896
Da	3:22	the f of the fire killed the soldiers who took	10695
Joel	1:19	the open pastures and f have burned up all	4259
Ac	7:30	an angel appeared to Moses in the f of	5825
1Co	3:15	but only as one escaping through the f,	4786
	13: 3	to the poor and surrender my body to the f,	2794
Heb	1: 7	his servants f of fire."	5825
	11:34	the fury of the f, and escaped the edge of	4786

FLAMING (11) [FLAME]

Ge	3:24	a f sword flashing back and forth to guard	4267
Ps	7:13	he makes ready his f arrows.	1944
Isa	4: 5	of smoke by day and a glow of f fire	4259
	50:11	and provide yourselves with f torches,	2338
La	2: 3	a f fire that consumes everything around it.	4259
Da	7: 9	His throne was f with fire,	10695
	10: 6	his eyes like f torches,	836
Hos	7: 6	in the morning it blazes like a f fire.	4259
Na	2: 4	They look like f torches;	4365
Zec	12: 6	like a f torch among sheaves.	836

| Eph | 6:16 | the f arrows of the evil one. | 4792 |

FLANK (2)

| Eze | 25: 9 | therefore I will expose the f of Moab, | 4190 |
| | 34:21 | Because you shove with f and shoulder, | 7396 |

FLAP (1) [FLAPPED]

| Job | 39:13 | "The wings of the ostrich f joyfully, | 6632 |

FLAPPED (1) [FLAP]

| Isa | 10:14 | not one f a wing, | 5610 |

FLARE (2) [FLARED]

| 2Sa | 11:20 | the king's anger may f up, | 6590 |
| Ps | 2:12 | for his wrath can f up in a moment. | 1277 |

FLARED (3) [FLARE]

Jdg	6:21	Fire f from the rock,	6590
1Sa	20:30	Saul's anger f up at Jonathan and he said	3013
Ps	124: 3	when their anger f against us,	3013

FLASH (9) [FLASHED, FLASHES, FLASHING]

Job	15:12	and why do your eyes f,	8141
	37:15	makes his lightning f?	3649
Eze	21:10	polished to f like lightning!	1398
	21:15	It is made to f like lightning,	1398
	21:28	to consume and to f like lightning!	1398
Hos	11: 6	Swords will f in their cities,	2565
Zec	9:14	his arrow will f like lightning.	3655
Lk	9:29	as bright as a f of lightning.	1993
1Co	15:52	in a f, in the twinkling of an eye, at	875

FLASHED (8) [FLASH]

Ex	9:23	and lightning f down to the ground.	2143
	9:24	and lightning f back and forth.	928+4374+9348
Ps	77:17	your arrows f back and forth.	2143
Eze	1:13	it was bright, and lightning f out of it.	3655
Hos	6: 5	my judgments f like lightning upon you.	3655
Hab	3: 4	rays f from his hand,	NIH
Ac	9: 3	suddenly a light from heaven f around	4313
	22: 6	a bright light from heaven f around me.	4313

FLASHES (10) [FLASH]

Job	41:18	His snorting throws out f of light;	2145
Ps	29: 7	of the LORD strikes with f of lightning.	4259
Eze	1:14	and forth like f of lightning.	1027
Am	5: 9	he f destruction on the stronghold	1158
Na	2: 3	The metal on the chariots f on	836+928
Lk	17:24	which f and lights up the sky from one end	848
Rev	4: 5	From the throne came f of lightning,	847
	8: 5	f of lightning and an earthquake,	847
	11:19	And there came f of lightning,	847
	16:18	Then there came f of lightning,	847

FLASHING (7) [FLASH]

Ge	3:24	a flaming sword f back and forth to guard	2200
Dt	32:41	when I sharpen my f sword	1398
Job	39:23	along with the f spear and lance.	4258
Ps	76: 3	There he broke the f arrows,	8404
Eze	1: 4	an immense cloud with lightning	4374
Na	3: 3	f swords and glittering spears!	4258
Hab	3:11	at the lightning of your f spear.	5586

FLASK (3)

1Sa	10: 1	Then Samuel took a f of oil and poured it	7095
2Ki	9: 1	take this f of oil with you and go	7095
	9: 3	the f and pour the oil on his head	7095

FLAT (1) [FLATS, FLATTENS]

| Hos | 7: 8 | Ephraim is a f cake not turned over. | 6314 |

FLATS (1) [FLAT]

| Job | 39: 6 | the salt f as his habitat. | 4877 |

FLATTENS (1) [FLAT]

| Isa | 32:19 | Though hail f the forest and | 3718 |

FLATTER (3) [FLATTERING, FLATTERS, FLATTERY]

Job	32:21	nor will I f any man;	4033
Ps	78:36	then they would f him with their mouths,	7331
Jude	1:16	they boast about themselves and f others	2513+4725

FLATTERING (5) [FLATTER]

Ps	12: 2	their f lips speak with deception.	2747
	12: 3	May the LORD cut off all f lips	2747
Pr	26:28	and a f mouth works ruin.	2747
	28:23	He who rebukes a man will in the end gain more favor than he who has a f tongue.	2744
Eze	12:24	or f divinations among the people of Israel.	2728

FLATTERS (2) [FLATTER]

| Ps | 36: 2 | For in his own eyes he f himself too much | 2744 |
| Pr | 29: 5 | Whoever f his neighbor is spreading a net | 2744 |

FLATTERY (4) [FLATTER]

Job	32:22	for if I were skilled in f,	4033
Da	11:32	With f he will corrupt those who have violated the covenant,	2747
Ro	16:18	By smooth talk and f they deceive	2330
1Th	2: 5	You know we never used f,	3135

FLAVOR (1)

Job	6: 6	or is there f in the white of an egg?	3248

FLAW (3) [FLAWLESS]

Dt	15:21	is lame or blind, or has any serious f,	4583
	17: 1	ox or a sheep that has any defect or f	1821+8273
SS	4: 7	there is no f in you.	4583

FLAWLESS (6) [FLAW]

2Sa	22:31	the word of the LORD is f.	7671
Job	11: 4	'My beliefs are f and I am pure	2341
Ps	12: 6	And the words of the LORD are f,	3196
	18:30	the word of the LORD is f.	7671
Pr	30: 5	"Every word of God is f;	7671
SS	5: 2	my sister, my darling, my dove, my f one.	9447

FLAX (6)

Ex	9:31	(The f and barley were destroyed,	7325
	9:31	barley had headed and the f was in bloom.	7325
Jos	2: 6	the stalks of f she had laid out on the roof.)	7324
Jdg	15:14	on his arms became like charred f,	7324
Pr	31:13	and f and works with eager hands.	7324
Isa	19: 9	with combed f will despair,	7324

FLAY (KJV) See SKIN, STRIP OFF

FLEA (2)

1Sa	24:14	A dead dog? A f?	7282
	26:20	of Israel has come out to look for a f—	7282

FLED (118) [FLEE]

Ge	14:10	when the kings of Sodom and Gomorrah f,	5674
	14:10	of the men fell into them and the rest f to	5674
	16: 6	Sarai mistreated Hagar; so she f from her.	1368
	31:21	So he f with all he had,	1368
	31:22	that Jacob had f.	1368
	31:40	and sleep f from my eyes.	5610
Ex	2:15	but Moses f from Pharaoh and went to live	1368
	14: 5	of Egypt was told that the people had f,	1368
Nu	16:34	all the Israelites around them f, shouting,	5674
	35:25	to the city of refuge to which he f.	5674
	35:26	of the city of refuge to which he has f	5674
	35:32	not accept a ransom for anyone who has f to	5674
Jos	8:15	and they f toward the desert.	5674
	10:11	As they f before Israel on the road down	5674
	10:16	the five kings had f and hidden in the cave	5674
	20: 6	in the town from which he f."	5674
Jdg	1: 6	Adoni-Bezek f, but they chased him	5674
	4:15	Sisera abandoned his chariot and f on foot.	5674
	4:17	however, f on foot to the tent of Jael,	5674
	7:21	all the Midianites ran, crying out as they f.	5674
	7:22	The army f to Beth Shittah toward Zererah	5674
	8:12	f, but he pursued them and captured them,	5674
	9:21	Then Jotham f, escaping to Beer,	5674
	9:51	all the people of the city—f.	5674
	11: 3	So Jephthah f from his brothers and settled	1368
	20:42	f before the Israelites in	7155
	20:45	As they turned and f toward the desert to	5674
	20:47	But six hundred men turned and f into	5674
1Sa	4:10	and every man f to his tent.	5674
	4:16	I f from it this very day."	5674
	4:17	"Israel f before the Philistines,	5674
	19: 8	He struck them with such force that they f	5674
	19:12	and he f and escaped.	1368
	19:18	When David had f and made his escape,	1368
	20: 1	Then David f from Naioth at Ramah	1368
	21:10	That day David f from Saul and went	1368
	22:20	escaped and f to join David.	1368
	23: 6	with him when he f to David at Keilah.)	1368
	27: 4	Saul was told that David had f to Gath,	1368
	30:17	on camels and f.	5674
	31: 1	the Israelites f before them,	5674
	31: 7	the Jordan saw that the Israelite army had f	5674
	31: 7	they abandoned their towns and f.	5674
2Sa	1: 4	He said, "The men f from the battle.	5674
	4: 3	because the people of Beeroth f to Gittaim	1368
	4: 4	His nurse picked him up and f,	5674
	10:13	and they f before him.	5674
	10:14	they f before Abishai and went inside	5674
	10:18	But they f before Israel,	5674
	13:29	mounted their mules and f.	5674
	13:34	Meanwhile, Absalom had f.	1368
	13:37	Absalom f and went to Talmai son	1368
	13:38	After Absalom f and went to Geshur,	1368
	18:17	all the Israelites f to their homes.	5674
	19: 8	the Israelites had f to their homes.	5674
	19: 9	he has f the country because of Absalom;	1368
	23:11	Israel's troops f from them.	5674
1Ki	2: 7	when I f from your brother Absalom.	1368
	2:28	he f to the tent of the LORD	5674
	2:29	King Solomon was told that Joab had f to	5674
	11:17	But Hadad, still only a boy, f to Egypt	1368
	11:23	who had f from his master,	1368
	11:40	but Jeroboam f to Egypt,	1368
	12: 2	where he had f from King Solomon),	1368

1Ki	20:20	At that, the Arameans f,	5674
	20:30	And Ben-Hadad f to the city and hid in	5674
2Ki	3:24	up and fought them until they f.	5674
	7: 7	and f in the dusk and abandoned their tents	5674
	8:21	his army, however, f back home.	5674
	9:23	Joram turned about and f,	5674
	9:27	he f up the road to Beth Haggan.	5674
	14:12	and every man f to his home.	5674
	14:19	and he f to Lachish,	5674
	25: 4	the whole army f at night through the gate	NIH
	25: 4	They f toward the Arabah,	2143
	25:26	f to Egypt for fear of the Babylonians.	995
1Ch	10: 1	the Israelites f before them,	5674
	10: 7	in the valley saw that the army had f and	5674
	10: 7	they abandoned their towns and f.	5674
	11:13	the troops f from the Philistines.	5674
	19:14	and they f before him.	5674
	19:15	they too f before his brother Abishai	5674
	19:18	But they f before Israel,	5674
2Ch	10: 2	where he had f from King Solomon),	1368
	13:16	The Israelites f before Judah,	5674
	14:12	and Judah. The Cushites f,	5674
	25:22	and every man f to his home.	5674
	25:27	against him in Jerusalem and he f	5674
Ps	3: T	When he f from his son Absalom.	1368
	48: 5	they f in terror.	2905
	57: T	When he had f from Saul into the cave.	1368
	104: 7	But at your rebuke the waters f,	5674
	114: 3	sea looked and f, the Jordan turned back;	5674
	114: 5	Why was it, O sea, that you f, O Jordan,	5674
Isa	20: 6	those we f to for help and deliverance from	5674
	22: 3	All your leaders have f together;	5610
	22: 3	All you who were caught were taken prisoner together, having f while	1368
Jer	9:10	the birds of the air have f and the animals are gone.	5610
	26:21	Uriah heard of it and f in fear to Egypt.	1368
	39: 4	and all the soldiers saw them, they f;	1368
	41:15	of his men escaped from Johanan and f to	2143
	52: 7	and the whole army f.	1368
	52: 7	They f toward the Arabah,	2143
La	1: 6	in weakness they have f before the pursuer.	2143
Da	10: 7	that they f and hid themselves.	1368
Hos	12:12	Jacob f to the country of Aram;	1368
Am	5:19	as though a man f from a lion only to meet	5674
Zec	14: 5	You will flee as you f from the earthquake	5674
Mt	26:56	Then all the disciples deserted him and f.	5771
Mk	14:50	Then everyone deserted him and f.	5771
	14:52	he f naked, leaving his garment behind.	5771
	16: 8	the women went out and f from the tomb.	5771
Ac	7:29	When Moses heard this, he f to Midian,	5771
	14: 6	to the Lycaonian cities of Lystra	2966
Heb	6:18	we who have f to take hold of the hope	2966
Rev	12: 6	The woman f into the desert to a place	5771
	16:20	Every island f away and	5771
	20:11	Earth and sky f from his presence,	5771

FLEE (89) [FLED, FLEEING, FLEES]

Ge	19:17	one of them said, "F for your lives!	4880
	19:17	F to the mountains or you will	4880
	19:19	But I can't f to the mountains;	4880
	19:20	Let me f to it—it is very small, isn't it?	4880
	19:22	But f there quickly,	4880
	27:43	F at once to my brother Laban in Haran.	1368
Ex	21:13	he is to f to a place I will designate.	5674
Lev	26:17	over you, and you will f even	5674
Nu	10:35	may your foes f before you."	5674
	35: 6	a person who has killed someone may f.	5674
	35:11	person who has killed someone accidentally may f.	5674
	35:15	anyone who has killed another accidentally can f there.	5674
Dt	4:42	a person could f if he had unintentionally	5674
	4:42	He could f into one of these cities	5674
	19: 3	so that anyone who kills a man may f there.	5674
	19: 5	That man may f to one of these cities	5674
	28: 7	from one direction but f from you in seven.	5674
	28:25	at them from one direction but f from them	5674
Jos	8: 5	as they did before, we will f from them.	5674
	8: 6	So when we f from them,	5674
	20: 3	and unintentionally may f there	5674
	20: 9	who killed someone accidentally could f	5674
2Sa	15:14	We must f, or none of us will escape	1368
	17: 2	and then all the people with him will f.	5674
	18: 3	if we are forced to f,	5674+5674
	19: 3	in who are ashamed when they f	5674
2Ki	19:21	of Jerusalem tosses her head as you f.	339
Job	41:28	Arrows do not make him f;	1368
Ps	11: 1	"F like a bird to your mountain.	5653
	31:11	those who see me on the street f from me.	5610
	55: 7	I would f far away and stay in the desert;	5610
	68: 1	may his foes f before him.	5674
	68:12	"Kings and armies f in haste;	5610+5610
	139: 7	Where can I f from your presence?	1368
SS	2:17	Until the day breaks and the shadows f,	5674
	4: 6	Until the day breaks and the shadows f,	5674
Isa	2:19	Men will f to caves in the rocks and	995
	2:21	They will f to caverns in the rocks and to	995
	13:14	each will f to his native land.	5674
	15: 5	her fugitives f as far as Zoar,	NIH
	17:13	when he rebukes them they f far away,	5674
	21:15	They f from the sword,	5610
	30:16	You said, 'No, we will f on horses.'	5674
	30:16	Therefore you will f!	5674
	30:17	A thousand will f at the threat of one;	NIH
	30:17	at the threat of five you will all f away,	5674
	31: 8	They will f before the sword	5674

Isa	33: 3	the thunder of your voice, the peoples f;	5610
	35:10	and sorrow and sighing will f away.	5674
	37:22	of Jerusalem tosses her head as you f.	339
	48:20	Leave Babylon, f from the Babylonians!	1368
	51:11	and sorrow and sighing will f away.	5674
Jer	4: 5	Let us f to the fortified cities!'	995
	4: 6	F for safety without delay!	6395
	6: 1	"F for safety, people of Benjamin!	6395
	6: 1	F from Jerusalem!	NIH
	8:14	Let us f to the fortified cities	995
	25:35	The shepherds will have nowhere to f,	4960
	46: 5	They f in haste without looking back,	4960+5674
	46: 6	"The swift cannot f nor the strong escape.	5674
	46: 6	They too will turn and f together,	5674
	48: 6	F! Run for your lives;	5674
	49: 8	Turn and f, hide in deep caves,	5674
	49:24	to f and panic has gripped her;	5674
	49:30	"F quickly away!	5674
	50: 3	both men and animals will f away.	5653
	50: 8	"F out of Babylon;	5653
	50:16	let everyone f to his own land.	5674
	51: 6	"F from Babylon!	5674
La	4:15	When they f and wander about,	5680
Da	4:14	the animals f from under it and the birds	10469
Am	2:16	bravest warriors will f naked on that day,"	5674
Jnh	1: 3	he went aboard and sailed for Tarshish to f	NIH
	4: 2	That is why I was so quick to f to Tarshish.	1368
Na	3: 7	All who see you will f from you and say,	5610
Zec	2: 6	F from the land of the north,"	5674
	14: 5	You will f by my mountain valley,	5674
	14: 5	You will f as you fled from the earthquake	5674
Mt	3: 7	warned you to f from the coming wrath?	5771
	10:23	When you are persecuted in one place, f	5771
	24:16	then let those who are in Judea f to	5771
Mk	13:14	then let those who are in Judea f to	5771
Lk	3: 7	warned you to f from the coming wrath?	5771
	21:21	Then let those who are in Judea f to	5771
1Co	6:18	F from sexual immorality.	5771
	10:14	Therefore, my dear friends, f from idolatry.	5771
1Ti	6:11	But you, man of God, f from all this,	5771
2Ti	2:22	Flee the evil desires of youth,	5771
Jas	4: 7	Resist the devil, and he will f from you.	5771

FLEE, FLEETH (KJV) See FLED, FLEE, FLEES, FLEETING, FLY, RUNS AWAY

FLEECE (7)

Jdg	6:37	I will place a wool f on the threshing floor.	1603
	6:37	If there is dew only on the f and all	1603
	6:38	he squeezed the f and wrung out the dew—	1603
	6:39	Allow me one more test with the f.	1603
	6:39	the f dry and the ground covered	1603
	6:40	Only the f was dry;	1603
Job	31:20	for warming him with the f from my sheep,	1600

FLEEING (13) [FLEE]

Ge	35: 1	when you were f from your brother Esau."	1368
	35: 7	to him when he was f from his brother.	1368
Ex	14:27	The Egyptians were f toward it,	5674
Lev	26:36	They will run as though f from the sword,	4961
	26:37	over one another as though f from	NIH
Jos	8:20	for the Israelites who had been f toward	5674
1Sa	22:17	They knew he was f,	1368
2Sa	10:14	Ammonites saw that the Arameans were f,	5674
	24:13	Or three months of f from your enemies	5674
1Ch	19:15	Ammonites saw that the Arameans were f,	5674
Jer	46:22	a f serpent as the enemy advances in force;	2143
	48:19	Ask the man f and the woman escaping,	5674
Eze	17:21	All his f troops will fall by the sword,	4451

FLEES (9) [FLEE]

Dt	19: 4	the man who kills another and f there	5674
	19:11	and then f to one of these cities,	5674
Jos	20: 4	"When he f to one of these cities,	5674
Job	20:24	Though he f from an iron weapon,	1368
	27:22	as he f headlong from its power.	1368+1368
Pr	28: 1	The wicked man f though no one pursues,	5674
Isa	10:29	Ramah trembles; Gibeah of Saul f.	5674
	24:18	Whoever f at the sound of terror will fall	5674
Jer	48:44	"Whoever f from the terror will fall into	5674

FLEET (6) [FLEETING]

1Ki	9:27	to serve in the f with Solomon's men.	639
	10:22	The king had a f of trading ships at sea	639+9576
	22:48	a f of trading ships to go to Ophir for gold,	641+9576
2Ch	9:21	king had a f of trading ships	641+2143+9576
	20:36	a f of trading ships.	641+2143+4200+9576
Da	11:40	and cavalry and a great f of ships.	641

FLEET-FOOTED (2) [FOOT]

2Sa	2:18	Now Asahel was as f as a wild gazelle.	928+7824+8079
Am	2:15	the f soldier will not get away,	928+7824+8079

FLEETING (6) [FLEET]

Job	14: 2	like a f shadow, he does not endure.	1368
Ps	39: 4	let me know how f is my life.	2534
	89:47	Remember how f my life.	2698
	144: 4	his days are like a f shadow.	6296
Pr	21: 6	by a lying tongue is a f vapor and	5622
	31:30	Charm is deceptive, and beauty is f;	2039

FLESH (130)

Ge	2:21	and closed up the place with f.	1414
	2:23	now bone of my bones and f of my flesh;	1414
	2:23	now bone of my bones and flesh of my f;	1414
	2:24	and they will become one f.	1414
	17:13	in your f is to be an everlasting covenant.	1414
	17:14	who has not been circumcised in the f,	1414
	29:14	"You are my own f and blood."	1414
	37:27	all, he is our brother, our own f and blood."	1414
	40:19	And the birds will eat away your f."	1414
Ex	4:7	it was restored, like the rest of his f.	1414
	29:14	the bull's f and its hide and its offal outside	1414
Lev	4:11	But the hide of the bull and all its f,	1414
	6:27	of the f will become holy,	1414
	8:17	and its f and its offal he burned up outside	1414
	9:11	the f and the hide he burned up outside	1414
	13:10	the hair white and if there is raw f in	1414
	13:14	But whenever raw f appears on him,	1414
	13:15	When the priest sees the raw f,	1414
	13:15	The raw f is unclean;	1414
	13:16	Should the raw f change and turn white,	1414
	13:24	or white spot appears in the raw f of	4695
	16:27	their hides, f and offal are to be burned up.	1414
	26:29	You will eat the f of your sons and	1414
	26:29	of your sons and the f of your daughters.	1414
Nu	12:12	with its f half eaten away."	1414
	19:5	its hide, f, blood and offal.	1414
Dt	28:53	the f of the sons and daughters	1414
	28:55	to one of them any of the f of his children	1414
	32:42	while my sword devours f:	1414
Jdg	8:7	I will tear your f with desert thorns	1414
	9:2	Remember, I am your f and blood."	1414
1Sa	17:44	"and I'll give your f to the birds of the air	1414
2Sa	1:22	from the f of the mighty,	2693
	5:1	"We are your own f and blood.	1414
	16:11	"My son, who is of my own f,	5055
	19:12	You are my brothers, my own f and blood.	1414
	19:13	'Are you not my own f and blood?	1414
1Ki	8:19	who is your own f and blood—	2743+3655+4946
2Ki	5:10	and your f will be restored and you will	1414
	5:14	and his f was restored and became clean	1414
	9:36	at Jezreel dogs will devour Jezebel's f.	1414
	20:18	your own f and blood,	3655+3870+4946
1Ch	11:1	"We are your own f and blood.	1414
2Ch	6:9	who is your own f and blood—	2743+3655+4946
	32:8	With him is only the arm of f,	1414
Ne	5:5	Although we are of the same f and blood	1414
Job	2:5	But stretch out your hand and strike his f	1414
	6:12	Is my f bronze?	1414
	10:4	Do you have eyes of f?	1414
	10:11	and f and knit me together with bones	1414
	15:27	with fat and his waist bulges with f,	6913+7089
	19:22	Will you never get enough of my f?	1414
	19:26	yet in my f I will see God;	1414
	33:21	His f wastes away to nothing,	1414
	33:25	then his f is renewed like a child's;	1414
	41:23	The folds of his f are tightly joined;	1414
Ps	27:2	against me to devour my f,	1414
	50:13	the f of bulls or drink the blood of goats?	1414
	73:26	My f and my heart may fail,	8638
	78:39	He remembered that they were but f,	1414
	79:2	f of your saints to the beasts of the earth.	1414
	84:2	and my f cry out for the living God.	1414
	119:120	My f trembles in fear of you;	1414
Pr	5:11	when your f and body are spent.	1414
Isa	9:20	on the f of his own offspring:	1414
	31:3	their horses are f and not spirit.	1414
	39:7	your own f and blood	3655+3870+4946
	49:26	I will make your oppressors eat their own f;	1414
	58:7	to turn away from your own f and blood?	1414
	65:4	who eat the f of pigs,	1414
	66:17	in the midst of those who eat the f of pigs	1414
Jer	9:25	"when I will punish all who are circumcised only in the f—	6889
	17:5	in man, who depends on f for his strength	1414
	19:9	I will make them eat the f of their sons	1414
	19:9	and they will eat one another's f during	1414
	51:35	May the violence done to our f be	8638
La	3:4	He has made my skin and my f grow old	6425
Eze	11:19	of stone and give them a heart of f.	1414
	32:5	I will spread your f on the mountains	1414
	32:6	and the ravines will be filled with your f.	NIH
	36:26	of stone and give you a heart of f.	1414
	37:6	and make f come upon you and cover you	1414
	37:8	and tendons and f appeared on them	1414
	39:17	There you will eat f and drink blood.	1414
	39:18	You will eat the f of mighty men and drink	1414
	40:43	The tables were for the f of the offerings.	1414
	44:7	in heart and f into my sanctuary,	1414
	44:9	in heart and f is to enter my sanctuary,	1414
Da	7:5	It was told, 'Get up and eat your fill of f!'	10125
Mic	3:2	from my people and the f from their bones;	8638
	3:3	who eat my people's f, strip off their skin	8638
	3:3	like f for the pot?"	1414
Zec	11:9	Let those who are left eat one another's f."	1414
	14:12	Their f will rot while they are still standing	8638
Mal	2:15	In f and spirit they are his.	8638
Mt	19:5	and the two will become one f'?	4922
Mk	10:8	and the two will become one f.'	4922
Lk	24:39	a ghost does not have f and bones,	4922
Jn	1:14	The Word became f and made his dwelling	4922
	3:6	F gives birth to flesh,	4922
	3:6	Flesh gives birth to f,	4922
	6:51	This bread is my f,	4922
	6:52	"How can this man give us his f to eat?"	4922
	6:53	unless you eat the f of the Son of Man	4922

Jn	6:54	Whoever eats my f and drinks my blood	4922
	6:55	For my f is real food	4922
	6:56	Whoever eats my f and drinks my blood	4922
	6:63	Spirit gives life; the f counts for nothing.	4922
1Co	6:16	For it is said, "The two will become one f."	4922
	15:39	All f is not the same:	4922
	15:39	Men have one kind of f,	4922
	15:50	that f and blood cannot inherit the kingdom	4922
2Co	12:7	there was given me a thorn in my f,	4922
Gal	6:13	that they may boast about your f.	4922
Eph	2:15	in his f the law with its commandments	4922
	5:31	and the two will become one f."	4922
	6:12	For our struggle is not against f and blood,	4922
Php	3:2	those mutilators of the f.	NIG
	3:3	and who put no confidence in the f—	4922
	3:4	to put confidence in the f, I have more:	4922
Col	1:24	up in my f what is still lacking in regard	4922
Heb	2:14	Since the children have f and blood,	4922
Jas	5:3	against you and eat your f like fire.	4922
1Jn	4:2	acknowledges that Jesus Christ has come in the f is from God,	4922
		Jesus Christ is coming in the f,	4922
2Jn	1:7	Jesus Christ as coming in the f,	4922
Jude	1:23	even the clothing stained by corrupted f.	4922
Rev	17:16	they will eat her f and burn her with fire.	4922
	19:18	so that you may eat the f of kings,	4922
	19:18	and the f of all people, free and slave,	4922
	19:21	all the birds gorged themselves on their f.	4922

FLESH (KJV) See also BIRTH, BODY, CREATURES, EARTHLY, HUMAN ANCESTRY, HUMAN EFFORT, HUMAN NATURE, HUMAN STANDARDS, KIND, LIFE, MAN, MANKIND, MEAT, MORTAL, ONE, ORDINARY, OUTWARDLY, NATURAL, PEOPLE, PHYSICAL, SINFUL NATURE, SENSUAL, WORLD, WORLDLY

FLESHHOOK (KJV) See HOOK

FLEW (4) [FLY]

2Sa	22:11	He mounted the cherubim and f;	6414
Ps	18:10	He mounted the cherubim and f;	6414
Isa	6:6	of the seraphs f to me with a live coal	6414
Ac	16:26	At once all the prison doors f open,	487

FLIES (15) [FLY]

Ex	8:21	I will send swarms of f on you	6856
	8:21	of the Egyptians will be full of f,	6856
	8:22	no swarms of f will be there,	6856
	8:24	Dense swarms of f poured	6856
	8:24	the land was ruined by the f.	6856
	8:29	the f will leave Pharaoh and his officials	6856
	8:31	the f left Pharaoh and his officials	6856
Dt	4:17	like any animal on earth or any bird that f	6414
Job	20:8	Like a dream he f away,	6414
Ps	78:45	He sent swarms of f that devoured them,	6856
	91:5	nor the arrow that f by day,	6414
	105:31	He spoke, and there came swarms of f,	6856
Ecc	10:1	As dead f give perfume a bad smell,	2279
Isa	7:18	that day the LORD will whistle for f from	2279
	51:6	like a garment and its inhabitants die like f.	4031

FLIGHT (15) [FLY]

Lev	26:36	of a windblown leaf will put them to f.	8103
Dt	32:30	put ten thousand to f,	5674
Jdg	9:40	and many fell wounded in the f—	5674
2Sa	22:41	You made my enemies turn their backs in f,	NIH
2Ki	7:15	in their headlong f.	2905
1Ch	12:15	and they put to f everyone living in	1368
Job	39:26	"Does the hawk take f by your wisdom	87
Ps	18:40	You made my enemies turn their backs in f,	NIH
	104:7	the sound of your thunder they took to f;	2905
Isa	10:31	Madmenah is in f,	5610
	52:12	But you will not leave in haste or go in f;	4961
Jer	48:9	and archers every town takes to f.	1368
Eze	40:49	It was reached by a f of stairs,	5092
Da	9:21	came to me in swift f about the time	3616+3618
Mt	24:20	that your f will not take place in winter or	5870

FLIMSY (1)

Eze	13:10	and because, when a f wall is built,	2666

FLINGING (1) [FLUNG]

Ac	22:23	and throwing off their cloaks and f dust	965

FLINT (8) [FLINTY]

Ex	4:25	But Zipporah took a f knife,	7644
Jos	5:2	"Make f knives and circumcise	7644
	5:3	So Joshua made f knives and circumcised	7644
Isa	5:28	their horses' hoofs seem like f,	7641
	50:7	Therefore have I set my face like f,	2734
Jer	17:1	inscribed with a f point,	9032
Eze	3:9	like the hardest stone, harder than f.	7644
Zec	7:12	They made their hearts as hard as f	9032

FLINTY (2) [FLINT]

Dt	32:13	and with oil from the f crag,	2734
Job	28:9	the f rock and lays bare the roots of	2734

FLIRTING (1)

Isa	3:16	f with their eyes,	8568

FLOAT (4) [FLOATED]

1Ki	5:9	and I will f them in rafts by sea to	8492
2Ki	6:6	and made the iron f.	7429
2Ch	2:16	that you need and will f them in rafts	995
Hos	10:7	and its king will f away like a twig on	1950

FLOATED (1) [FLOAT]

Ge	7:18	and the ark f on the surface of the water.	2143

FLOCK (99) [FLOCKING, FLOCKS]

Ge	4:4	from some of the firstborn of his f.	7366
	21:28	set apart seven ewe lambs from the f,	7366
	27:9	the f and bring me two choice young goats,	7366
	30:40	the young of the f by themselves,	4166
	31:10	with the f were streaked,	7366
	31:12	with the f are streaked,	7366
	38:17	"I'll send you a young goat from my f,"	7366
Ex	2:16	and fill the troughs to water their father's f.	7366
	2:17	to their rescue and watered their f.	7366
	2:19	even drew water for us and watered the f."	7366
	3:1	the f of Jethro his father-in-law,	7366
	3:1	and he led the f to the far side of the desert	7366
	34:19	whether from herd or f.	8445
Lev	1:2	an animal from either the herd or the f,	7366
	1:10	the offering is a burnt offering from the f,	7366
	3:6	" 'If he offers an animal from the f as	7366
	5:6	a female lamb or goat from the f as	7366
	5:15	the LORD as a penalty a ram from the f,	7366
	5:18	as a guilt offering a ram from the f,	7366
	6:6	his guilt offering, a ram from the f,	7366
	22:21	from the herd or f a fellowship offering to	7366
	27:32	The entire tithe of the herd and f—	7366
Nu	15:3	from the herd or the f,	7366
Dt	15:14	Supply him liberally from your f,	7366
	16:2	an animal from your f or herd at the place	7366
	32:14	with curds and milk from herd and f and	7366
1Sa	17:20	Early in the morning David left the f with	7366
	17:34	and carried off a sheep from the f,	6373
2Sa	7:8	from the pasture and from following the f	7366
1Ch	17:7	from the pasture and from following the f,	7366
Ezr	10:19	a ram from the f as a guilt offering.)	7366
Job	21:11	They send forth their children as a f;	7366
Ps	77:20	like a f by the hand of Moses and Aaron.	7366
	78:52	But he brought his people out like a f;	7366
	80:1	you who lead Joseph like a f;	7366
	95:7	the f under his care.	7366
SS	1:7	where you graze your f and	8286
	4:1	Your hair is like a f of goats descending	6373
	4:2	Your teeth are like a f of sheep just shorn,	6373
	6:5	like a f of goats descending from Gilead.	6373
	6:6	Your teeth are like a f of sheep coming up	6373
Isa	40:11	He tends his f like a shepherd:	6373
	63:11	with the shepherd of his f?	7366
Jer	13:17	not prosper and all their f is scattered.	5338
	13:17	the LORD's f will be taken captive.	6373
	13:20	Where is the f that was entrusted to you,	6373
	23:2	"Because you have scattered my f	7366
	23:3	the remnant of my f out of all the countries	7366
	25:34	roll in the dust, you leaders of the f.	7366
	25:35	the leaders of the f no place to escape.	7366
	25:36	the wailing of the leaders of the f,	7366
	31:10	and will watch over his f like a shepherd.'	6373
	49:20	The young of the f will be dragged away;	7366
	50:8	and be like the goats that lead the f.	7366
	50:17	a scattered f that lions have chased away.	8445
	50:45	The young of the f will be dragged away;	7366
	51:23	with you I shatter shepherd and f,	6373
Eze	24:5	take the pick of the f.	7366
	34:2	Should not shepherds take care of the f?	7366
	34:3	but you do not take care of the f.	7366
	34:8	because my f lacks a shepherd and	7366
	34:8	not search for my f but cared	7366
	34:8	for themselves rather than for my f,	7366
	34:10	and will hold them accountable for my f.	7366
	34:10	I will remove them from tending the f so	7366
	34:10	I will rescue my f from their mouths,	6373
	34:12	after his scattered f when he is with them,	6373
	34:16	I will shepherd the f with justice.	5626S
	34:17	" 'As for you, my f,	7366
	34:19	Must my f feed on what you have trampled	7366
	34:22	I will save my f,	7366
	43:23	to offer a young bull and a ram from the f,	7366
	43:25	a young bull and a ram from the f,	7366
	45:15	be taken from every f of two hundred from	7366
Am	7:15	But the LORD took me from tending the f	7366
Jnh	3:7	Do not let any man or beast, herd or f,	6373
Mic	2:12	like a f in its pasture;	6373
	4:8	As for you, O watchtower of the f,	6373
	5:4	shepherd his f in the strength of the LORD.	8286
	7:14	the f of your inheritance,	7366
Zec	9:16	on that day as the f of his people.	7366
	10:3	the LORD Almighty will care for his f,	6373
	11:4	"Pasture the f marked for slaughter.	7366
	11:7	So I pastured the f marked for slaughter,	7366
	11:7	particularly the oppressed of the f.	7366
	11:7	and I pastured the f.	7366
	11:8	The f detested me,	4392+5883S
	11:11	the f who were watching me knew it was	7366
	11:17	who deserts the f!	7366
Mal	1:14	an acceptable male in his f and vows	6373
Mt	26:31	and the sheep of the f will be scattered.'	4479

Lk 12:32 "Do not be afraid, little **f,** 4480
Jn 10:12 Then the wolf attacks **the f** and scatters it. 899S
10:16 and there shall be one **f** and one shepherd. 4479
Ac 20:28 Keep watch over yourselves and all the **f** 4480
20:29 in among you and will not spare the **f.** 4480
1Co 9: 7 Who tends a **f** and does not drink of 4479
1Pe 5: 2 of God's **f** that is under your care, serving 4480
5: 3 but being examples *to* the **f.** 4480

FLOCKING (1) [FLOCK]

Hos 7:12 I hear them **f together,** I will catch them. 6337

FLOCKS (100) [FLOCK]

Ge 4: 2 Abel kept **f,** and Cain worked the soil. 7366
13: 5 also had **f** and herds and tents. 7366
26:14 He had so many **f** and herds and 5238+7366
29: 2 with three **f** of sheep lying near it because 6373
29: 2 because the **f** were watered from that well. 6373
29: 3 When all the **f** were gathered there, 6373
29: 7 it is not time for the **f** to be gathered. 5238
29: 8 "until all the **f** are gathered and 6373
30:31 on tending your **f** and watching over them: 7366
30:32 through all your **f** today and remove 7366
30:36 to tend the rest of Laban's **f.** 7366
30:38 be directly in front of the **f** when they came 7366
30:38 When the **f** were in heat and came to drink, 7366
30:40 Thus he made separate **f** for himself 6373
30:43 and came to own large **f,** 7366
31: 4 to come out to the fields where his **f** were. 7366
31: 8 then all the **f** gave birth to speckled young; 7366
31: 8 then all the **f** bore streaked young. 7366
31:38 nor have I eaten rams from your **f.** 7366
31:41 and six years for your **f,** 7366
31:43 and the **f** are my flocks. 7366
31:43 and the flocks are my **f.** 7366
32: 7 and the **f** and herds and camels as well. 7366
34:28 They seized their **f** and herds and donkeys 7366
37: 2 was tending the **f** with his brothers, 7366
37:12 to graze their father's **f** near Shechem, 7366
37:13 your brothers *are* **grazing the f** 8286
37:14 with your brothers and with the **f,** 7366
37:16 where they *are* **grazing their f?"** 8286
45:10 your **f** and herds, and all you have. 7366
46:32 and they have brought along their **f** 7366
47: 1 with their **f** and herds 7366
47: 4 and your servants' **f** have no pasture. 7366
50: 8 and their **f** and herds were left in Goshen. 7366
Ex 10: 9 and with our **f** and herds, 7366
10:24 only leave your **f** and herds behind." 7366
12:32 Take your **f** and herds, as you have said, 7366
12:38 both **f** and herds. 7366
34: 3 not even the **f** and herds may graze in front 7366
Nu 11:22 if **f** and herds were slaughtered for them? 7366
31: 9 **f** and goods as plunder. 5238
32: 1 who had very large **herds and f,** 5238
32:24 and pens for your **f,** 7366
32:26 our **f** and herds will remain here in 5238
32:36 and built pens for their **f.** 7366
35: 3 **f** and all their other livestock. 8214
Dt 7:13 of your herds and the lambs of your **f** in 7366
8:13 and when your herds and **f** grow large 7366
12: 6 and the firstborn of your herds and **f,** 7366
12:17 or the firstborn of your herds and **f,** 7366
12:21 the herds and the LORD has given you, 7366
14:23 and the firstborn of your herds and **f** in 7366
15:19 of your herds and **f.** 7366
28: 4 of your herds and the lambs of your **f.** 7366
28:18 of your herds and the lambs of your **f.** 7366
28:51 or lambs of your **f** until you are ruined. 7366
Jos 14: 4 with pastureland for their **f** and herds. 5238
Jdg 5:16 to hear the whistling for the **f?** 6373
1Sa 8:17 He will take a tenth of your **f,** 7366
30:20 He took all the **f** and herds, 7366
1Ki 20:27 like two **small f** of goats, 3105
2Ki 5:26 **f,** herds, or menservants and maidservants? 7366
1Ch 4:39 the valley in search of pasture for their **f.** 7366
4:41 because there was pasture for their **f.** 7366
27:31 Jaziz the Hagrite was in charge of the **f.** 7366
2Ch 17:11 and the Arabs brought him **f:** 7366
31: 6 also brought a tithe of their herds and **f** and 7366
32:28 and pens for the **f.** 6373
32:29 and acquired great numbers of **f** and herds, 7366
Ne 10:36 of our herds and of our **f** to the house 7366
Job 1:10 that his **f and herds** are spread throughout 5238
24: 2 they pasture **f** they have stolen. 6373
Ps 8: 7 all **f** and herds, and the beasts of the field, 7556
65:13 The meadows are covered with **f** and 7366
107:41 and increased their families like **f.** 7366
Pr 27:23 Be sure you know the condition of your **f,** 7366
Ecc 2: 7 I also owned more herds and **f** than anyone 7366
SS 1: 7 be like a veiled woman beside the **f** 6373
Isa 13:20 no shepherd *will* **rest his f** there. 8069
17: 2 of Aroer will be deserted and left to **f,** 6373
32:14 the delight of donkeys, a pasture for **f,** 6373
60: 7 All Kedar's **f** will be gathered to you, 7366
61: 5 Aliens will shepherd your **f;** 7366
65:10 Sharon will become a pasture for **f,** 7366
Jer 3:24 their **f** and herds, their sons and daughters. 7366
5:17 they will devour your **f** and herds, 7366
6: 3 with their **f** will come against her; 6373
31:12 the young of the **f** and herds. 7366
31:24 and those who move about with their **f.** 6373
33:12 be pastures for shepherds to rest their **f.** 7366
33:13 **f** will again pass under the hand of 7366
49:29 Their tents and their **f** will be taken. 7366

Eze 36:38 as numerous as the **f** for offerings 7366
36:38 the ruined cities will be filled with **f** of people. 7366
Hos 5: 6 with their **f** and herds to seek the LORD, 7366
Joel 1:18 even the **f** of sheep are suffering. 6373
Mic 5: 8 like a young lion among **f** of sheep, 6373
Zep 2:14 **F and herds** will lie down there, 6373
Lk 2: 8 keeping watch over their **f** at night. 4479
Jn 4:12 as did also his sons and his **f and herds?"** 2576

FLOG (8) [FLOGGED, FLOGGING, FLOGGINGS]

Pr 17:26 or to **f** officials for their integrity. 5782
19:25 A mocker, and the simple will learn 5782
Mt 10:17 over to the local councils and **f** you 3463
23:34 others *you will* **f** in your synagogues 3463
Mk 10:34 spit on him, **f** him and kill him. 3463
Lk 18:32 insult him, spit on him, **f** him and kill him. 3463
Ac 22:25 As they stretched him out *to* **f** him, 2666
22:25 for you *to* **f** a Roman citizen who hasn't 3464

FLOGGED (11) [FLOG]

Dt 25: 2 down and **have** him **f** in his presence with 5782
25: 3 If he *is* **f** more than that, 4804+5782
Mt 20:19 over to the Gentiles to *be* mocked and **f** 3463
27:26 But he **had** Jesus **f,** 5849
Mk 13: 9 the local councils and **f** in the synagogues. 1296
15:15 He **had** Jesus **f,** 5849
Jn 19: 1 Then Pilate took Jesus and had him **f.** 3463
Ac 5:40 They called the apostles in and *had them* **f.** 1296
16:23 *After* they had been severely **f,** 2202+4435
22:24 He directed that he be **f** and questioned 3465
2Co 11:23 been **f** more severely, 4435

FLOGGING (2) [FLOG]

Ps 89:32 their iniquity with **f;** 5596
Heb 11:36 Some faced jeers and **f,** 3465

FLOGGINGS (1) [FLOG]

2Sa 7:14 with **f** inflicted *by* men. 5596

FLOOD (33) [FLOODED, FLOODGATES, FLOODING, FLOODS, FLOODWATERS]

Ge 7: 7 the ark to escape the waters of the **f.** 4429
7:17 For forty days the **f** kept coming on 4429
9:11 be cut off by the waters of a **f;** 4429
9:11 never again will there be a **f** to destroy 4429
9:15 the waters become a **f** to destroy all life. 4429
9:28 After the **f** Noah lived 350 years. 4429
10: 1 who themselves had sons after the **f.** 4429
10:32 over the earth after the **f.** 4429
11:10 Two years after the **f,** 4429
Jos 3:15 the Jordan *is* **at f stage** all during harvest. 1536+3972+4848+6584
4:18 an **at f stage** as before. 1536+3972+6584
Job 20:28 A **f** will carry off his house, 4429
22:11 and why a **f** of water covers you. 9180
22:16 their foundations washed away by a **f.** 5643
27:20 Terrors overtake him like a **f;** 4784
38:34 to the clouds and cover yourself with a **f** 9180
Ps 6: 6 all night long *I* **f** my bed with weeping 8466
29:10 The LORD sits enthroned over the **f;** 4429
88:17 All day long they surround me like a **f;** 4784
124: 4 the **f** would have engulfed us, 4784
Isa 59:19 For he will come like a pent-up **f** that 5643
Da 9:26 The end will come like a **f:** 8852
11:10 on like an irresistible **f** and carry the battle 8851
11:40 and sweep through them like a **f.** 8851
Hos 5:10 I will pour out my wrath on them like a **f** NIH
Na 1: 8 but with an overwhelming **f** he will make 8852
Mal 2:13 *You* **f** the LORD's altar *with* tears. 4059
Mt 24:38 For in the days before the **f,** 2886
24:39 about what would happen until the **f** came 2886
Lk 6:48 When a **f** came, the torrent struck that house 4439
17:27 Then the **f** came and destroyed them all. 2886
1Pe 4: 4 with them into the same **f** of dissipation, 431
2Pe 2: 5 the ancient world when he brought the **f** 2886

FLOODED (1) [FLOOD]

Ge 7:24 The waters **f** the earth for a hundred 1504

FLOODGATES (6) [FLOOD]

Ge 7:11 and the **f** of the heavens were opened. 748
8: 2 and the **f** of the heavens had been closed, 748
2Ki 7: 2 LORD should open the **f** of the heavens, 748
7:19 LORD should open the **f** of the heavens, 748
Isa 24:18 The **f** of the heavens are opened, 748
Mal 3:10 if I will not throw open the **f** of heaven 748

FLOODING (2) [FLOOD]

Isa 28: 2 like a driving rain and a **downpour,** 3888+8851
66:12 and the wealth of nations like a **f** stream; 8851

FLOODS (1) [FLOOD]

Ps 69: 2 the **f** engulf me. 8673

FLOODWATERS (5) [FLOOD]

Ge 6:17 bring **f** on the earth to destroy all life 4429+4784
7: 6 when the **f** came on the earth. 4429+4784
7:10 And after the seven days the **f** came on 4429+4784
Ps 69:15 the **f** engulf me or the depths swallow 4784+8673

Isa 8: 7 to bring against them the mighty **f** of 4784+8041

FLOOR (58) [FLOORS]

Ge 50:10 When they reached the **threshing f** of Atad, 1755
50:11 the mourning at the **threshing f** of Atad, 1755
Ex 16:14 on the ground appeared on the desert **f.** 7156
Nu 5:17 and put some dust from the tabernacle **f** 7977
15:20 as an offering from the **threshing f,** 1755
18:27 to you as grain from the **threshing f** or juice 1755
18:30 to you as the product of the **threshing f** or 1755
Dt 15:14 your **threshing f** and your winepress. 1755
16:13 of your **threshing f** and your winepress. 1755
Jdg 3:25 There they saw their lord fallen to the **f,** 824
6:37 I will place a wool fleece on the **threshing f** 1755
Ru 3: 2 be winnowing barley on the **threshing f.** 1755
3: 3 Then go down to the **threshing f,** 1755
3: 6 So she went down to the **threshing f** 1755
3:14 that a woman came to the **threshing f."** 1755
2Sa 6: 6 they came to the **threshing f** of Nacon, 1755
24:16 at the **threshing f** of Araunah the Jebusite. 1755
24:18 on the **threshing f** of Araunah the Jebusite." 1755
24:21 "To buy your **threshing f,"** David answered 1755
24:24 So David bought the **threshing f** and 1755
1Ki 6: 6 The lowest **f** was five cubits wide, 3666
6: 6 the middle **f** six cubits and NIH
6: 6 and the third **f** seven. NIH
6: 8 to the lowest **f** was on the south side of 7521
6:15 paneling them from the **f** of the temple to 7977
6:15 the **f** of the temple with planks of pine. 7977
6:16 with cedar boards from **f** to ceiling to form 7977
7: 7 he covered it with cedar from **f** to ceiling. 7977
22:10 at the **threshing f** *by* the entrance of the gate 1755
22:35 The blood from his wound ran onto the **f** 2668
2Ki 6:27 From the **threshing f?** 1755
1Ch 13: 9 they came to the **threshing f** of Kidon, 1755
21:15 then standing at the **threshing f** of Araunah 1755
21:18 on the **threshing f** of Araunah the Jebusite. 1755
21:21 he left the **threshing f** and bowed down 1755
21:22 of your **threshing f** so I can build an altar to 1755
21:28 on the **threshing f** of Araunah the Jebusite, 1755
2Ch 3: 1 at the **threshing f** *by* the entrance of the gate 1755
18: 9 at the **threshing f** *by* the entrance of the gate 1755
Job 39:12 and gather it to your **threshing f?** 1755
Isa 21:10 O my people, crushed on the **threshing f,** 1755
Jer 51:33 like a **threshing f** at the time it is trampled; 1755
Eze 37: 2 a great many bones on the **f** of the valley, 7156
41: 7 from the **lowest f** to the top floor through AIT
41: 7 from the lowest floor to the **top f** through AIT
41: 7 to the top floor through the **middle f.** AIT
41:16 The **f,** the wall up to the windows, 824
41:20 From the **f** to the area above the entrance, 824
42: 6 The rooms *on the third f* had no pillars, AIT
42: 6 so they were smaller in **f** space than those 824
Da 2:35 like chaff on a **threshing f** *in* the summer. 10010
6:24 And before they reached the **f** of the den, 10076
Hos 9: 1 of a prostitute at every **threshing f.** 1755+1841
13: 3 like chaff swirling from a **threshing f,** 1755
Mic 4:12 like sheaves to the **threshing f.** 1755
Mt 3:12 and he will clear his **threshing f,** 272
Lk 3:17 in his hand to clear his **threshing f** and 272
Jas 2: 3 "You stand there" or "Sit on the **f** NIG

FLOORS (6) [FLOOR]

1Sa 23: 1 and are looting the **threshing f,"** 1755
1Ki 6:30 the **f** of both the inner and outer rooms of 7977
Eze 42: 5 on the lower and **middle f** of the building. AIT
42: 6 on the lower and **middle f.** AIT
Hos 9: 2 **Threshing f** and winepresses will not feed 1755
Joel 2:24 The **threshing f** will be filled with grain; 1755

FLORAL (2) [FLOWER]

1Ki 7:49 the gold **f** work and lamps and tongs; 7258
2Ch 4:21 the gold **f** work and lamps and tongs 7258

FLOUR (68)

Ge 18: 6 "get three seahs of fine **f** and knead it 7854
Ex 29: 2 And from **fine f,** without yeast, 6159
29:40 an ephah of **fine f** mixed with a quarter of 6159
Lev 2: 1 his offering is to be of **fine f.** 6159
2: 2 The priest shall take a handful of the **fine f** 6159
2: 4 it is to consist of **fine f:** 6159
2: 5 it is to be made of **fine f** mixed with oil, 6159
2: 7 it is to be made of **fine f** and oil. 6159
5:11 for his sin a tenth of an ephah of **fine f** for 6159
6:15 The priest is to take a handful of **fine f** 6159
6:20 of **fine f** as a regular grain offering, 6159
7:12 of **fine f** well-kneaded and mixed with oil. 6159
14:10 of an ephah of **fine f** mixed with oil *for* 6159
14:21 a tenth of an ephah of **fine f** mixed with oil 6159
23:13 of two-tenths of an ephah of **fine f** mixed 6159
23:17 of two-tenths of an ephah of **fine f,** 6159
24: 5 "Take **fine f** and bake twelve loaves 6159
Nu 5:15 of an ephah of barley **f** on her behalf. 7854
6:15 cakes made of **fine f** mixed with oil, 6159
7:13 each filled with **fine f** mixed with oil as 6159
7:19 each filled with **fine f** mixed with oil as 6159
7:25 each filled with **fine f** mixed with oil as 6159
7:31 each filled with **fine f** mixed with oil as 6159
7:37 each filled with **fine f** mixed with oil as 6159
7:43 each filled with **fine f** mixed with oil as 6159
7:49 each filled with **fine f** mixed with oil as 6159
7:55 each filled with **fine f** mixed with oil as 6159
7:61 each filled with **fine f** mixed with oil as 6159
7:67 each filled with **fine f** mixed with oil as 6159

Nu	7:73	each filled with **fine f** mixed with oil as — 6159
	7:79	each filled with **fine f** mixed with oil as — 6159
	8: 8	with its grain offering of **fine f** mixed — 6159
	15: 4	of a tenth of an ephah of **fine f** mixed with — 6159
	15: 6	of an ephah of **fine f** mixed with a third of — 6159
	15: 9	of an ephah of **fine f** mixed with half a hin — 6159
	28: 5	of a tenth of an ephah of **fine f** mixed with — 6159
	28: 9	of two-tenths of an ephah of **fine f** mixed — 6159
	28:12	of three-tenths of an ephah of **fine f** mixed — 6159
	28:12	of two-tenths of an ephah of **fine f** mixed — 6159
	28:13	of a tenth of an ephah of **fine f** mixed — 6159
	28:20	of three-tenths of an ephah of **fine f** mixed — 6159
	28:28	of three-tenths of an ephah of **fine f** mixed — 6159
	29: 3	of three-tenths of an ephah of **fine f** mixed — 6159
	29: 9	of three-tenths of an ephah of **fine f** mixed — 6159
	29:14	of three-tenths of an ephah of **fine f** mixed — 6159
Jdg	6:19	an ephah of f he made bread without yeast. — 7854
1Sa	1:24	an ephah of f and a skin of wine, — 7854
	28:24	She took *some* f, kneaded it — 7854
2Sa	17:28	f and roasted grain, beans and lentils, — 7854
1Ki	4:22	of **fine f** and sixty cors of meal, — 6159
	17:12	only a handful of f in a jar and a little oil in — 7854
	17:14	'The jar of f will not be used up and — 7854
	17:16	For the jar of f was not used up and the jug — 7854
2Ki	4:41	Elisha said, "Get *some* f." — 7854
	7: 1	of f will sell for a shekel and two seahs — 6159
	7:16	So a seah of f sold for a shekel, — 6159
	7:18	of f will sell for a shekel and two seahs — 6159
1Ch	9:29	as well as the f and wine, and the oil, — 6159
	12:40	There were plentiful supplies of f, — 7854
	23:29	the f for the grain offerings, — 6159
Isa	47: 2	Take millstones and grind f; — 7854
Eze	16:13	Your food was **fine f**, honey and olive oil. — 6159
	16:19	the **fine f**, olive oil and honey I gave you — 6159
	46:14	with a third of a hin of oil to moisten the f. — 6159
Hos	8: 7	The stalk has no head; it will produce no f. — 7854
Mt	13:33	of f until it worked all through the dough." — 236
Lk	13:21	mixed into a **large amount of f** — 236+4929+5552
Rev	18:13	of wine and olive oil, of **fine f** and wheat; — 4947

FLOURISH (13) [FLOURISHES, FLOURISHING]

Ge	26:22	and *we will* f in the land." — 7238
Job	15:32	and his branches *will not* f. — 8315
Ps	44: 2	the peoples and **made** our fathers f. — 8938
	72: 7	In his days the righteous *will* f; — 7255
	72:16	*Let* its fruit f like Lebanon; — 7437
	92: 7	up like grass and all evildoers f, — 7437
	92:12	The righteous *will* f like a palm tree, — 7255
	92:13	*they will* f in the courts of our God. — 7255
Pr	14:11	but the tent of the upright *will* f. — 7255
Isa	55:10	the earth and making it bud and f, — 7541
	66:14	your heart will rejoice and you *will* f — 7255
Eze	17:24	**make** the dry tree f. — 7255
Hos	14: 7	*He will* f like the grain. — 2649

FLOURISHES (2) [FLOURISH]

Ps	103:15	he f like a flower of the field; — 7437
Pr	12:12	but the root of the righteous f. — 5989

FLOURISHING (4) [FLOURISH]

Dt	6:10	a land with large, f cities you did not build, — 3202
Ps	37:35	I have seen a wicked and ruthless man f — 6590
	52: 8	But I am like an olive tree f in the house — 8316
Ecc	2: 6	to water groves of f trees. — 7541

FLOW (31) [FLOWED, FLOWING, FLOWS]

Ex	14:26	the sea so that the waters *may* f **back** over — 8740
Lev	12: 7	be ceremonially clean from her f *of* blood. — 5227
	15:19	When a woman has her **regular** f of blood, — 928+1414+2307
	15:24	with her and her **monthly** f touches him, — 5614
	20:18	he has exposed the source of her f, — 1947
Nu	13:27	and it *does* f with milk and honey! — 2307
	24: 7	Water *will* f from their buckets. — 5688
Jos	4: 7	that the f *of* the Jordan was cut off before — 4784
Job	6:17	but that **cease to** f in the dry season, — 7551
Ps	78:16	of a rocky crag and **made** water f **down** — 3718
	119:136	Streams of tears f *from* my eyes, — 3718
	147:18	he stirs up his breezes, and the waters f. — 5688
Ecc	1: 7	All streams f into the sea, — 2143
Isa	30:25	of water will f on every high mountain — 3298
	41:18	*I will* **make** rivers f on barren heights, — 7337
	48:21	*he* **made** water f for them from the rock; — 5688
Jer	18:14	from distant sources ever cease *to* f? — 5688
	48:33	I have stopped the f of wine from — NIH
La	2:18	**let** your tears f like a river day and night; — 3718
	3:48	Streams of tears f *from* my eyes — 3718
	3:49	My eyes *will* f unceasingly, — 5599
Eze	28:23	upon her and make blood f in her streets. — NIH
	32:14	and **make** her streams f like oil, — 2143
Joel	3:18	and the hills *will* f with milk; — 2143
	3:18	A fountain *will* f **out** of the LORD's house — 3655
Am	9:13	from the mountains and f *from* all the hills. — 4570
Zec	14: 8	On that day living water *will* f **out** from — 3655
Jn	7:38	of living water *will* f **from** within him." — 4835
	19:34	bringing a sudden f of blood and water. — NIG
2Co	1: 5	For just as the sufferings of Christ f *over* — 4355
Jas	3:11	*Can* both fresh water and salt water f from — 1108

FLOWED (10) [FLOW]

Ge	2:10	A river watering the garden f from Eden; — 3655
Ex	14:28	The water f **back** and covered the chariots — 8740

Dt	9:21	and threw the dust into a stream that f **down** — 3718
1Ki	18:28	as was their custom, until their blood f. — 9161
2Ch	32: 4	the springs and the stream that f through — 8851
Ps	78:20	and streams f **abundantly.** — 8851
	104: 8	*they* f **over** the mountains, — 6590
	105:41	like a river *it* f in the desert. — 2143
Eze	31: 4	their streams f all around its base — 2143
Rev	14:20	and blood f **out** of the press, — 2002

FLOWER (6) [FLORAL, FLOWERLIKE, FLOWERS]

Job	14: 2	He springs up like a f and withers away; — 7488
Ps	103:15	he flourishes like a f *of* the field; — 7488
Isa	18: 5	the blossom is gone and the f becomes — 5900
	28: 1	to the fading f, his glorious beauty, — 7488
	28: 4	That fading f, his glorious beauty, — 7491
Jas	1:10	because he will pass away like a wild f. — 470

FLOWERLIKE (2) [FLOWER]

Ex	25:31	its f cups, buds and blossoms shall be — NIH
	37:17	its f cups, buds and blossoms were — NIH

FLOWERS (15) [FLOWER]

Ex	25:33	Three cups **shaped like almond** f with buds — 5481
	25:34	to be four cups **shaped like almond** f — 5481
	37:19	Three cups **shaped like almond** f with buds — 5481
	37:20	were four cups **shaped like almond** f — 5481
1Ki	6:18	carved with gourds and open f. — 7488
	6:29	he carved cherubim, palm trees and open f. — 7488
	6:32	palm trees and open f, — 7488
	6:35	and open f on them and overlaid them — 7488
SS	2:12	F appear on the earth; — 5890
Isa	5:24	and their f blow away like dust; — 7258
	40: 6	and all their glory is like the f *of* the field. — 7488
	40: 7	The grass withers and the f fall, — 7488
	40: 8	The grass withers and the f fall, — 7488
1Pe	1:24	and all their glory is like the f *of* the field; — 470
	1:24	the grass withers and the f fall, — 470

FLOWING (45) [FLOW]

Ex	3: 8	a land f *with* milk and honey— — 2307
	3:17	a land f *with* milk and honey.' — 2307
	13: 5	a land f *with* milk and honey— — 2307
	33: 3	Go up to the land f *with* milk and honey. — 2307
Lev	15: 3	Whether it *continues* f *from* his body — 8201
	20:24	a land f *with* milk and honey, — 2307
Nu	14: 8	a land f *with* milk and honey, — 2307
	16:13	of a land f *with* milk and honey to kill us in — 2307
	16:14	a land f *with* milk and honey or given us — 2307
Dt	6: 3	that you may increase greatly in a land f — 2307
	8: 7	with springs in the valleys and hills; — 3655
	11: 9	a land f *with* milk and honey. — 2307
	21: 4	or planted and where there is a f **stream.** — 419
	26: 9	a land f *with* milk and honey, — 2307
	26:15	a land f *with* milk and honey." — 2307
	27: 3	a land f *with* milk and honey. — 2307
	31:20	When I have brought them into the land f — 2307
Jos	3:13	in the Jordan, its waters f downstream will — 3718
	3:16	the water from upstream stopped f. — 3718
	3:16	the water f **down** to the Sea of the Arabah — 3718
	5: 6	a land f *with* milk and honey. — 2307
2Ki	3:20	water f from the direction of Edom! — 995
	4: 6	Then the oil stopped f. — NIH
Job	20:17	the **rivers** f *with* honey and cream. — AIT
	39:19	or clothe his neck with a f **mane?** — 8310
Ps	74:15	you dried up the **ever** f rivers. — 419
	107:33	f **springs** into thirsty ground, — 4604+4784
	107:35	and the parched ground into f **springs;** — 4604+4784
SS	4:15	of f water streaming down from Lebanon. — 2645
	5: 5	my fingers with f **myrrh,** — 6296
	7: 9	f **gently** *over* lips and teeth. — 1803
Isa	8: 6	the gently f waters of Shiloah and rejoices — 2143
	27:12	from the f Euphrates to the Wadi of Egypt, — 8673
	44: 4	like poplar trees by f **streams.** — 3298+4784
Jer	11: 5	a land f *with* milk and honey'— — 2307
	32:22	a land f *with* milk and honey. — 2307
Eze	20: 6	a land f *with* milk and honey, — 2307
	20:15	a land f *with* milk and honey, — 2307
	23:15	with belts around their waists and f turbans — 6242
	32: 6	I will drench the land with your f blood and — 7597
	47: 2	and the water *was* f from the south side. — 7096
Da	7:10	A river of fire *was* f, — 10457
Mk	12:38	to walk around in f **robes** and be greeted in — 5124
Lk	20:46	around in f **robes** and love to be greeted in — 5124
Rev	22: 1	f **from** the throne of God and of the Lamb — 1744

FLOWN (1) [FLY]

Jer	4:25	every bird in the sky *had* f **away.** — 5610

FLOWS (8) [FLOW]

Ezr	8:15	I assembled them at the canal that f — 995
Ps	58: 7	Let them vanish like water *that* f **away;** — 2143
	104:10	*it* f between the mountains. — 2143
Eze	47: 8	"This water f toward the eastern region — 3655
	47: 9	creatures will live wherever the river f — 995
	47: 9	because this water f there and makes — 995
	47: 9	so where the river f everything will live. — 995
	47:12	the water from the sanctuary f *to* them. — 3655

FLUENT (1)

Isa	32: 4	stammering tongue *will be* f and clear. — 1819+4200+4554

FLUNG (2) [FLINGING]

Am	8: 3	Many, many bodies—f everywhere! — 8959
Rev	12: 4	of the stars out of the sky and f them to — *965*

FLUTE (15) [FLUTES]

Ge	4:21	the father of all who play the harp and f. — 6385
Job	21:12	they make merry to the sound of the f. — 6385
	30:31	and my f to the sound of wailing. — 6385
Ps	150: 4	praise him with the strings and f, — 6385
Jer	48:36	"So my heart laments for Moab like a f; — 2720
	48:36	like a f for the men of Kir Hareseth. — 2720
Da	3: 5	f, zither, lyre, harp, pipes and all kinds — 10446
	3: 7	f, zither, lyre, harp and all kinds of music, — 10446
	3:10	f, zither, lyre, harp, pipes and all kinds — 10446
	3:15	when you hear the sound of the horn, f, — 10446
Mt	9:23	and saw the f **players** and the noisy crowd, — 886
	11:17	'We played the f for you, and you did not — 884
Lk	7:32	'We played the f for you, and you did not — 884
1Co	14: 7	such as the f or harp, — 888
Rev	18:22	f **players** and trumpeters, — 886

FLUTES (5) [FLUTE]

1Sa	10: 5	f and harps being played before them, — 2720
1Ki	1:40	playing f and rejoicing greatly, — 2720
Ps	5: T	For the director of music. For f. — 5704
Isa	5:12	tambourines and f and wine, — 2720
	30:29	when people go up with f to the mountain — 2720

FLUTTERING (2)

Pr	26: 2	Like a f sparrow or a darting swallow, — 5653
Isa	16: 2	Like f birds pushed from the nest, — 5610

FLUX (KJV) See DYSENTERY

FLY (14) [FLEW, FLIES, FLIGHT, FLOWN, FLYING]

Ge	1:20	and *let* birds f above the earth across — 6414
Ex	8:31	not a f remained. — NIH
Dt	19: 5	the head *may* f **off** and hit his neighbor — 5970
Job	5: 7	to trouble as surely as sparks f upward. — 6414
	9:25	*they* f **away** without a glimpse of joy. — 1368
Ps	55: 6	*I would* f **away** and be at rest— — 6414
	90:10	for they quickly pass, and *we* f **away.** — 6414
Pr	23: 5	for they will surely sprout wings and f **off** — 6414
Isa	60: 8	"Who are these *that* f **along** like clouds, — 6414
Hos	9:11	Ephraim's glory *will* f **away** like a bird— — 6414
Na	3:16	the land and then f **away.** — 6414
	3:17	but when the sun appears *they* f **away,** — 5610
Hab	1: 8	*They* f like a vulture swooping to devour; — 6414
Rev	12:14	so that *she might* f to the place prepared — 4375

FLYING (13) [FLY]

Ge	8: 7	and *it kept* f back and forth until — 3655
Lev	11:20	" 'All f insects that walk on all fours are to — 6416
Dt	14:19	All f insects that swarm are unclean — 6416
Ps	78:27	f birds like sand on the seashore. — 4053
	148:10	small creatures and f birds, — 4053
Isa	6: 2	and with two *they were* f. — 6414
Hab	1: 8	in the heavens at the glint of your f arrows, — 2143
Zec	5: 1	and there before me was a f scroll! — 6414
	5: 2	I answered, "I see a f scroll, — 6414
Rev	4: 7	the fourth was like a f eagle. — 4375
	8:13	an eagle *that was* f in midair call out in — 4375
	14: 6	Then I saw another angel f in midair, — 4375
	19:17	who cried in a loud voice *to* all the birds f — 4375

FOAL (2)

Zec	9: 9	on a colt, the f of a donkey. — 1201
Mt	21: 5	on a colt, the f of a donkey.' " — *5626*

FOAM (2) [FOAMING, FOAMS]

Job	24:18	"Yet they are f on the surface of the water; — 7824
Ps	46: 3	though its waters roar and f and — 2812

FOAMING (4) [FOAM]

Dt	32:14	You drank the f blood of the grape. — 2815
Ps	75: 8	of the LORD is a cup full of f wine mixed — 2812
Mk	9:20	f **at the mouth.** — *930*
Jude	1:13	wild waves of the sea, f **up** their shame; — *2072*

FOAMS (2) [FOAM]

Mk	9:18	*He* f **at the mouth,** — *930*
Lk	9:39	into convulsions so that he f **at the mouth.** — *931*

FODDER (7)

Ge	24:25	she added, "We have plenty of straw and f, — 5028
	24:32	Straw and f were brought for the camels, — 5028
	43:24	and provided f for their donkeys. — 5028
Jdg	19:19	both straw and f for our donkeys and bread — 5028
Job	6: 5	or an ox bellow when it has f? — 1173
	24: 6	They gather in the fields and glean in — 1173
Isa	30:24	and donkeys that work the soil will eat — 1173

FOE (10) [FOES]

Ps	7: 4	or without cause have robbed my f— — 7675
	8: 2	to silence the f and the avenger. — 367
	55:12	if a f were raising himself against me, — 8533
	61: 3	a strong tower against the f. — 367

Ps	74:10	Will the f revile your name forever?	367
	106:10	He saved them from the hand of the f;	8533
	107: 2	those he redeemed from the hand of the f,	7640
La	1: 5	captive before the f.	7640
	2: 4	Like a f he has slain all who were pleasing	7640
Hab	1:15	wicked f pulls all of them up with hooks,	NIH

FOES (52) [FOE]

Nu	10:35	may your f flee before you."	8533
Dt	33: 7	Oh, be his help against his f!"	7640
	33:11	strike his f till they rise no more."	8533
2Sa	22:18	from my f, who were too strong for me.	8533
	22:41	and I destroyed my f.	8533
	22:49	You exalted me above my f;	7756
2Ki	21:14	be looted and plundered by all their f.	367
Job	22:20	'Surely our f are destroyed,	7799
Ps	3: 1	O LORD, how many are my f!	7640
	6: 7	they fail because of all my f.	7675
	13: 4	and my f will rejoice when I fall.	7640
	17: 7	in you from their f.	7756
	18:17	from my f, who were too strong for me.	8533
	18:40	and I destroyed my f.	8533
	18:48	You exalted me above my f;	7756
	21: 8	your right hand will seize your f.	8533
	27: 2	when my enemies and my f attack me,	367
	27:12	Do not turn me over to the desire of my f,	7640
	34:21	f of the righteous will be condemned.	8533
	41: 2	and not surrender him to the desire of his f.	367
	42:10	as my f taunt me,	7675
	44: 5	through your name we trample our f.	7756
	54: 7	my eyes have looked in triumph on my f.	367
	68: 1	may his f flee before him.	8533
	68:23	in the blood of your f,	367
	69:18	redeem me because of my f.	367
	74: 4	Your f roared in the place where you met	7675
	81:14	and turn my hand against their f!	7640
	83: 2	how your f rear their heads.	8533
	89:23	I will crush his f before him and strike	7640
	89:42	You have exalted the right hand of his f;	7640
	92:11	the rout of my wicked f.	7756
	97: 3	Fire goes before him and consumes his f	7640
	105:24	he made them too numerous for their f,	7640
	106:41	and their f ruled over them.	8533
	112: 8	in the end he will look in triumph on his f.	7640
	119:157	Many are the f who persecute me,	7640
	138: 7	against the anger of my f,	367
	143:12	destroy all my f, for I am your servant.	7675
Isa	1:24	"Ah, I will get relief from my f	7640
	9:11	But the LORD has strengthened Rezin's f	7640
	59:18	to his enemies and retribution to his f;	367
	66:14	but his fury will be shown to his f.	367
Jer	46:10	a day of vengeance, for vengeance on his f	7640
	49:37	I will shatter Elam before their f,	367
La	1: 5	Her f have become her masters;	7640
	1:17	for Jacob that his neighbors become his f;	7640
	2:17	he has exalted the horn of your f,	7640
	4:12	and f could enter the gates of Jerusalem.	7640
Mic	5: 9	and all your f will be destroyed.	367
Na	1: 2	The LORD takes vengeance on his f	7640
	1: 8	he will pursue his f into darkness.	367

FOILS (2)

Ps	33:10	The LORD f the plans of the nations;	7296
Isa	44:25	who f the signs of false prophets	7296

FOLD (4) [ENFOLDS, FOLDED, FOLDING, FOLDS]

Ex	26: 9	F the sixth curtain double	4100
2Ki	4:39	of its gourds and filled the f of his cloak.	955
Hag	2:12	a person carries consecrated meat in the f	4053
	2:12	and that f touches some bread or stew,	4053

FOLDED (3) [FOLD]

Ex	28:16	and a span wide—and f double.	4100
	39: 9	and a span wide—and f double.	4100
Jn	20: 7	The cloth was f up by itself,	1962

FOLDING (2) [FOLD]

Pr	6:10	a little f of the hands to rest—	2486
	24:33	a little f of the hands to rest—	2486

FOLDS (5) [FOLD]

Ne	5:13	I also shook out the f of my robe and said,	2950
Job	41:23	The f of his flesh are tightly joined;	5139
Ps	74:11	the f of your garment and destroy them!	7931
Ecc	4: 5	The fool f his hands and ruins himself.	2485
Eze	5: 3	in the f of your garment.	4053

FOLIAGE (4)

Eze	19:11	It towered high above the thick f,	6291
	31: 3	it towered on high, its top above the thick f.	6291
	31:10	lifting its top above the thick f,	6291
	31:14	lifting their tops above the thick f.	6291

FOLK (KJV) See MEN, CREATURES, PEOPLE

FOLLOW (189) [FOLLOWED, FOLLOWER, FOLLOWERS, FOLLOWING, FOLLOWS]

Ge	41:30	but seven years of famine will f them.	339+7756

Ex	11: 8	'Go, you and all the people who f you!'	928+8079
	16: 4	see whether they will f my instructions.	928+2143
	23: 2	"Do not f the crowd in doing wrong.	339+2118
	23:24	or worship them or f their practices.	3869+6913
Lev	18: 3	Do not f their practices.	2143
	18: 4	and be careful to f my decrees.	2143
	18:30	Keep my requirements and do not f any of	6913
	19:37	and all my laws and f them,	6913
	20: 5	both him and all who f him	339
	20: 8	Keep my decrees and f them,	6913
	20:22	Keep all my decrees and laws and f them,	6913
	22:31	"Keep my commands and f them.	6913
	25:18	" 'F my decrees and be careful	6913
	26: 3	" 'If you f my decrees and are careful	2143
Nu	9:12	they must f all the regulations.	3869
Dt	4: 1	F them so that you may live and may go in	6913
	4: 5	so that you may f them in	4027+6913
	4:13	which he commanded you to f and	6913
	4:14	to f in the land that you are crossing	6913
	5: 1	Learn them and be sure to f them.	6913
	5:31	and laws you are to teach them to f in	6913
	6:14	Do not f other gods,	339+2143
	7:11	Therefore, take care to f the commands,	6913
	7:12	to these laws and are careful to f them,	6913
	8: 1	to f every command I am giving you today,	6913
	8:19	the LORD your God and f other gods	339+2143
	11:22	If you carefully observe all these commands I am giving you to f—	6913
	12: 1	be careful to f in the land that the LORD,	6913
	13: 2	"Let us f other gods" (gods you have	339+2143
	13: 4	It is the LORD your God you must f,	339+2143
	13: 5	turn you from the way the LORD your God commanded you to f.	928+2143
	15: 5	f all these commands I am giving you today.	6913
	16:12	and f carefully these decrees.	6913
	16:20	F justice and justice alone,	8103
	17:19	and f carefully all the words of this law	6913
	19: 9	carefully f all these laws I command you today—	6913
	20:18	to f all the detestable things they do	3869+6913
	24: 8	You must f carefully what I have commanded them.	6913
	26:16	to f these decrees and laws;	6913
	27:10	the LORD your God and f his commands	6913
	28: 1	carefully f all his commands I give you today,	6913
	28:13	and carefully f them,	6913
	28:15	and do not carefully f all his commands	6913
	28:58	not carefully f all the words of this law,	6913
	29: 9	Carefully f the terms of this covenant,	6913
	29:22	Your children who f you	339+4946+7756
	29:29	that we may f all the words of this law.	6913
	30: 8	f all his commands I am giving you today.	6913
	31:12	and f carefully all the words of this law.	6913
Jos	3: 3	move out from your positions and f it.	339+2143
	22:27	and you and the generations that f,	339
Jdg	3:28	"F me," he ordered, "for the LORD	8103
	6:34	summoning the Abiezrites to f him.	339
	7:17	"F my lead.	4027+6913
	9: 3	they were inclined to f Abimelech,	339
Ru	2: 9	and f along after the girls.	2143
1Sa	11: 7	of anyone who does not f Saul	339+3655
	12:14	over you f the LORD your God—	339+2118
	25:19	on ahead; I'll f you."	339+995
	25:27	be given to the men who f you.	928+2143+8079
	30:21	to f him and who were left behind at	339+2143
2Sa	17: 9	among the troops who f Absalom.'	339
	20: 2	of Israel deserted David to f Sheba son	339
	20:11	and whoever is for David, let him f Joab!"	339
1Ki	6:12	if you f my decrees,	928+2143
	6: 6	he did not f the LORD completely,	339
	11:10	had forbidden Solomon to f other gods,	339+2143
	18:21	If the LORD is God, f him;	339+2143
	18:21	but if Baal is God, f him."	339+2143
	19:21	to f Elijah and became his attendant.	339+2143
2Ki	6:19	F me, and I will lead you to	339+2143
	18: 6	to the LORD and did not cease to f him;	339
	23: 3	to f the LORD and keep his commands,	339+2143
1Ch	28: 8	Be careful to f all the commands of	2011
2Ch	34:31	to f the LORD and keep his commands,	339+2143
	34:33	they did not fail to f the LORD,	339
Ne	9:34	and our fathers did not f your law;	6913
	10:29	f the Law of God given through Moses	928+2143
Est	2:20	to f Mordecai's instructions	6913
Job	21:33	all men f after him,	5432
Ps	23: 6	and love will f me all the days of my life,	8103
	45:14	her virgin companions f her	339
	81:12	to f their own devices.	928+2143
	81:13	if Israel would f my ways,	928+2143
	89:30	and do not f my statutes,	928+2143
	94:15	and all the upright in heart will f it.	339
	111:10	all who f his precepts have good understanding.	6913
	119:33	Teach me, O LORD, to f your decrees;	2006
	119:63	to all who f your precepts.	9068
	119:106	that I will f your righteous laws.	9068
	119:166	O LORD, and I f your commands.	6913
Ecc	1:11	not be remembered by those who f.	340
	11: 9	F the ways of your heart	928+2143
SS	1: 8	f the tracks of the sheep	3655
Isa	8:11	not to f the way of this people.	928+2143
	42:24	For they would not f his ways;	928+2143
Jer	3:17	No longer will they f the stubbornness	339+2143
	7: 6	do not f other gods to your own harm,	339+2143
	7: 9	and after other gods you have not known,	339+2143
	11: 6	to the terms of this covenant and f them.	6913
	11: 8	the covenant I had commanded them to f	6913

Jer	13:10	who f the stubbornness of their hearts	928+2143
	18:12	each of us will f the stubbornness	6913
	23:10	The [prophets] f an evil course	2118
	23:17	And to all who f the stubbornness	928+2143
	25: 6	Do not f other gods to serve	339+2143
	26: 4	If you do not listen to me and f my law,	928+2143
	32:23	but they did not obey you or f your law;	928+2143
	35:15	do not f other gods to serve them.	339+2143
	42:16	and the famine you dread will f you	339+1815
Eze	9: 5	"F him through the city and kill,	339+6296
	11:20	Then they will f my decrees and	928+2143
	13: 3	foolish prophets who f their own spirit	339+2143
	20:13	not f my decrees but rejected my laws	928+2143
	20:16	and did not f my decrees	928+2143
	20:18	"Do not f the statutes of your fathers	928+2143
	20:19	f my decrees and be careful	928+2143
	20:21	They did not f my decrees,	928+2143
	36:27	I will put my Spirit in you and move you to f my decrees	928+2143
	37:24	They will f my laws and be careful	928+2143
	43:11	to its design and f all its regulations.	6913
	48: 1	f the Hethlon road to Lebo Hamath;	448+3338
Hos	11:10	They will f the LORD;	339+2143
Mt	4:19	"Come, f me," Jesus said,	3958
	8:19	"Teacher, I will f you wherever you go."	199
	8:22	But Jesus told him, "F me,	199
	9: 9	"F me," he told him,	199
	10:38	anyone who does not take his cross and f me is not worthy of me.	199+3958
	16:24	and take up his cross and f me.	199
	19:21	Then come, f me."	199
	19:27	"We have left everything to f you!	199
Mk	1:17	"Come, f me," Jesus said,	3958
	2:14	"F me," Jesus told him,	199
	5:37	He did not let anyone f him except Peter,	5258
	8:34	and take up his cross and f me.	199
	10:21	Then come, f me."	199
	10:28	"We have left everything to f you!"	199
	14:13	of water will meet you. F him.	199
Lk	5:27	"F me," Jesus said to him,	199
	9:23	and take up his cross daily and f me.	199
	9:57	"I will f you wherever you go."	199
	9:59	He said to another man, "F me."	199
	9:61	Still another said, "I will f you, Lord;	199
	14:27	not carry his cross and f me cannot	2262+3958
	18:22	Then come, f me."	199
	18:28	"We have left all we had to f you!"	199
	21: 8	Do not f them.	3958+4513
	22:10	F him to the house that he enters,	199
Jn	1:43	Finding Philip, he said to him, "F me."	199
	10: 4	and his sheep f him	199
	10: 5	But they will never f a stranger;	199
	10:27	I know them, and they f me.	199
	12:26	Whoever serves me must f me;	199
	13:36	"Where I am going, you cannot f now,	199
	13:36	but you will f later."	199
	13:37	"Lord, why can't I f you now?	199
	21:19	Then he said to him, "F me!"	199
	21:22	You must f me."	199
Ac	12: 8	"Wrap your cloak around you and f me,"	199
Ro	12: 9	and reject the truth and f evil,	4275
	15: 5	among yourselves as you f Christ Jesus,	NIG
1Co	1:12	One of you says, "I f Paul";	1639
	1:12	another, "I f Apollos";	NIG
	1:12	another, "I f Cephas";	NIG
	1:12	still another, "I f Christ."	NIG
	3: 4	For when one says, "I f Paul," and another,	1639
	3: 4	"I follow Paul," and another, "I f Apollos,"	NIG
	11: 1	F my example, as I follow the	1181+3629
	11: 1	as I f the example of Christ.	NIG
	14: 1	The way of love	1503
2Co	12:18	in the same spirit and f the same course?	2717
Gal	2:14	you force Gentiles to f Jewish customs?	2678
	6:16	Peace and mercy to all who f this rule,	5123
2Th	3: 7	how you ought to f our example.	3628
	3: 9	to make ourselves a model for you to f.	3628
1Ti	4: 1	and f deceiving spirits and things taught	4668
	5:15	in fact already turned away to f Satan.	3958
1Pe	1:11	of Christ and the glories that would f.	3552+4047
	2:21	that you should f in his steps.	2051
2Pe	1:16	We did not f cleverly invented stories	1979
	2: 2	Many will f their shameful ways	1979
	2:10	This is especially true of those who f	3958+4513
	2:15	the straight way and wandered off to f	1979
Jude	1:16	they f their own evil desires;	4513
	1:18	scoffers who will f their own ungodly desires."	4513
	1:19	who f mere natural instincts	6035
Rev	14: 4	They f the Lamb wherever he goes.	199
	14:13	for their deeds will f them."	199

FOLLOWED (134) [FOLLOW]

Ge	32:19	and all the others who f the herds:	339+2143
Ex	14:23	and chariots and horsemen f them into	339+995
	14:28	of Pharaoh that had f the Israelites into	339+995
	15:20	and all the women f her,	339+3655
Nu	16:25	and the elders of Israel f him.	339+2143
	25: 8	and f the Israelite into the tent.	339+995
	31:16	the ones who f Balaam's advice and were	928
	32:11	not me wholeheartedly, f me or	339
	32:12	for they f the LORD wholeheartedly.'	339
Dt	1:36	because he f the LORD wholeheartedly."	339
	4: 3	among you everyone who f the Baal	339+2143
Jos	6: 8	the ark of the LORD's covenant f them.	339+2143
	6: 9	and the rear guard f the ark.	339+2143
	6:13	and the rear guard f the ark of the LORD,	339+2143

Jos	14: 8	f the LORD my God wholeheartedly.	339
	14: 9	because you have f	339
	14:14	because he f the LORD, the God of Israel,	339
Jdg	2:12	*They* f and worshiped various gods of	339+2143
	3:28	So they f him down and,	339
	4:10	Ten thousand men f him,	928+6590+8079
	4:14	f *by* ten thousand men.	339
	5:14	Benjamin was with the people who f you.	339
	9:49	the men cut branches and f Abimelech.	339+2143
	10: 3	He *was* f by Jair of Gilead,	339+7756
	11: 3	around him and f him.	3655+6640
	13:11	Manoah got up and f his wife.	339+2143
1Sa	6:12	Philistines f them as far as the border	339+2143
	14:13	his armor-bearer f and killed behind him.	NIH
	17:13	Jesse's three oldest sons *had* f Saul to	339+2143
	17:14	The three oldest f Saul,	339+2143
	26: 3	When he saw that Saul *had* f him there,	339+995
2Sa	2:10	The house of Judah, however, f David.	339+2118
	17:23	that his advice *had* not been f,	6913
	20:14	who gathered together and f him.	339+995
1Ki	11: 5	He f Ashtoreth the goddess of	339+2143
	12:14	he f the advice of the young men and said,	3869
	14: 8	who kept my commands and f me	339+2143
	18:18	the LORD's commands and have f	339+2143
2Ki	4:30	So he got up and f her.	339+2143
	7:15	*They* f them as far as the Jordan,	339+2143
	14: 3	In everything he f *the example*	3869+6913+6913
	17: 8	and f the practices of the nations	928+2143
	17:15	*They* f worthless idols	339+2143
	17:19	f the practices Israel had introduced.	928+2143
1Ch	8:30	f by Zur, Kish, Baal, Ner, Nadab,	2256
	9:36	f by Zur, Kish, Baal, Ner, Nadab,	2256
2Ch	10:14	he f the advice of the young men and said,	3869
	11:16	f the Levites *to* Jerusalem	339+995
	17: 3	in the ways his father David had f.	NIH
	17: 4	and f his commands rather than	928+2143
	22: 5	He also f their counsel when he went	928+2143
	26:17	of the LORD f him in.	339+995
Ne	12:32	and half the leaders of Judah f them,	339+2143
	12:38	I f them on top of the wall,	339
Est	2: 4	appealed to the king, and *he* f it.	4027+6913
Job	23:11	My feet *have* closely f his steps;	296
Pr	7:22	All at once he f her like an ox going to	339+2143
Ecc	4:15	and walked under the sun f the youth,	6640
Jer	2: 2	as a bride you loved me and f me	339+2143
	2: 5	*They* f worthless idols	339+2143
	7:24	instead, *they* f the stubborn inclinations	928+2143
	8: 2	and which *they have* f and consulted	339+2143
	9:13	they have not obeyed me or f my law.	928+2143
	9:14	*they have* f the stubbornness of their hearts;	339+2143
	9:14	they have f the Baals,	339
	11: 8	f the stubbornness of their evil hearts.	928+2143
	11:10	They *have* f other gods to serve them.	339+2143
	16:11	'and f other gods and served	339+2143
	35:18	and *have* f all his instructions	9068
	44:10	nor *have they* f my law and	928+2143
	44:23	not obeyed him or f his law or his decrees	928+2143
Eze	5: 6	and *has* not f my decrees.	2143
	5: 7	*have* not f my decrees or kept my laws.	2143
	11:12	not f my decrees or kept my laws	2143
Am	2: 4	the gods their ancestors f,	339+2143
Mic	6:16	and *you have* f their traditions.	928+2143
Hab	3: 5	pestilence f his steps.	3655
Mal	2: 9	not f my ways but have shown partiality	9068
Mt	4:20	At once they left their nets and f him.	199
	4:22	the boat and their father and f him.	199
	4:25	and the region across the Jordan f him.	199
	8: 1	large crowds f him.	199
	8:23	he got into the boat and his disciples f him.	199
	9: 9	and Matthew got up and f him.	199
	9:27	two blind men f him, calling out,	199
	12:15	Many f him, and he healed all their sick,	199
	14:13	the crowds f him on foot from the towns.	199
	19: 2	Large crowds f him,	199
	19:28	you who *have* f me will also sit	199
	20:29	a large crowd f him.	199
	20:34	they received their sight and f him.	199
	21: 9	ahead of him and those that f shouted,	199
	26:58	But Peter f him at a distance,	199
	27:55	They *had* f Jesus from Galilee to care	199
Mk	1:18	At once *they* left their nets and f him.	199
	1:20	the boat with the hired men and f him.	599+3958
	2:14	Jesus told him, and Levi got up and f him.	199
	2:15	for there were many who f him.	199
	3: 7	and a large crowd from Galilee f.	199
	5:24	A large crowd f and pressed around him.	199
	10:32	while those who f were afraid.	199
	10:52	and f Jesus along the road.	199
	11: 9	ahead and those who f shouted,	199
	14:54	Peter f him at a distance,	199
	15:41	In Galilee these women had f him	199
Lk	5:11	left everything and f him.	199
	5:28	and Levi got up, left everything and f him.	199
	9:11	but the crowds learned about it and f him.	199
	18:43	he received his sight and f Jesus,	199
	22:39	and his disciples f him.	199
	22:54	Peter f at a distance.	199
	23:27	A large number of people f him,	199
	23:49	the women who *had* f him from Galilee,	5258
	23:55	with Jesus from Galilee f Joseph and saw	2887
Jn	1:37	When the two disciples heard him say this,	
		they f Jesus.	199
	1:40	and who *had* f Jesus.	199
	6: 2	and a great crowd of people f him	199
	6:66	turned back and no longer f him.	3552+4344

Jn	11:31	*they* f her, supposing she was going to	199
	21: 8	The other disciples f in the boat,	2262
Ac	8:11	*They* f him because he had amazed them	4668
	8:13	And he f Philip everywhere,	4674
	12: 9	Peter f him out of the prison,	199+2002
	13:43	and devout converts to Judaism f Paul	199
	16:17	This girl f Paul and the rest of us, shouting,	2887
	21:36	The crowd that f kept shouting,	199
	27:11	f the advice of the pilot and of the owner	NIG
Ro	5:16	The judgment f one sin	NIG
	5:16	but the gift f many trespasses	1666
Eph	2: 2	to live when you f the ways of this world	2848
1Ti	4: 6	and of the good teaching that *you have* f.	4158
Rev	13: 3	The whole world was astonished and f	3958
	14: 8	A second angel f and said, "Fallen!	199
	14: 9	A third angel f them and said in	199

FOLLOWER (1) [FOLLOW]

Ac	24:14	the God of our fathers as a f of the Way,	2848

FOLLOWERS (24) [FOLLOW]

Nu	16: 5	Then he said to Korah and all his f:	6337
	16: 6	You, Korah, and all your f are to do this:	6337
	16:11	and all your f have banded together.	6337
	16:16	"You and all your f are to appear before	6337
	16:19	When Korah had gathered all his f	6337
	16:40	or he would become like Korah and his f.	6337
	26: 9	and Aaron and were among Korah's f	6337
	26:10	whose f died when the fire devoured	6337
	27: 3	He was not among Korah's f,	6337
Jdg	9: 4	who became his f.	339+2143
1Sa	30:22	and troublemakers among David's f said,	408+889+2143+6640
1Ki	16:22	But Omri's f proved stronger than those of Tibni	339+889+2021+6639
Ne	11: 8	and his f, Gabbai and Sallai—928 men.	339
Ps	49:13	and of their f, who approve their sayings.	339
	106:18	Fire blazed among their f;	6337
Da	11:24	loot and wealth among his f.	2157S
Lk	11:19	by whom do your f drive them out?	5626
	22:49	When Jesus' f saw what was going to happen,	1254+3836S
Ac	5:36	He was killed, all his f were dispersed.	4275
	5:37	and all his f were scattered.	4275
	9:25	But his f took him by night	3412
	17:34	A few men became f of Paul and believed.	3140
	22: 4	the f of this Way to their death,	NIG
Rev	17:14	chosen and faithful f."	AIT

FOLLOWING (64) [FOLLOW]

Ge	47:18	they came to him the f year and said,	9108
Ex	30:23	"Take the f fine spices:	NIH
Lev	20: 6	to prostitute himself by f them,	339
	23:32	of the month until the f evening you are	NIH
Nu	32:15	If you turn away from f him,	339
Dt	7: 4	from f me to serve other gods,	339
	11:28	I command you today by f other gods,	339+2143
	28:14	f other gods and serving them.	339+2143
Jos	18:21	clan by clan, had the f cities:	NIH
	21: 3	the Israelites gave the Levites the f towns	465S
	21: 9	and Simeon they allotted the f towns	465S
Jdg	2:19	f other gods and serving	339+2143
1Sa	5: 4	But the f morning when they rose,	4740
2Sa	7: 8	the pasture and from f the flock to be ruler	339
	15:12	and Absalom's f kept on increasing.	907+6639
	15:16	with his entire household f him;	928+8079
	15:17	king set out, with all the people f him,	928+8079
1Ki	8:66	On the f day he sent the people away.	9029S
2Ki	13: 2	He did evil in the eyes of the LORD *by* f	339+2143
	16: 3	the detestable ways of the nations	3869
	17:21	Jeroboam enticed Israel away from f	339
	21: 2	f the detestable practices of the nations	3869
1Ch	6:71	The Gershonites received the f:	NIH
	6:77	(the rest of the Levites) received the f:	NIH
	17: 7	I took you from the pasture and from f	339
2Ch	25:27	the time that Amaziah turned away from f	339
	28: 3	f the detestable ways of the nations	3869
	29:15	f the word of the LORD.	928
	30:12	f the word of the LORD.	928
	33: 2	f the detestable practices of the nations	3869
	36:14	f all the detestable practices of the nations	3869
Ezr	2:59	The f came up from the towns	465S
	10:18	the f had married foreign women:	5162
Ne	7:61	The f came up from the towns	465S
Job	34:27	from f him and had no regard for any	339
Ps	119:14	I rejoice in f your statutes as one rejoices	2006
Isa	66:17	f the one in the midst of those who eat	339
Jer	2: 8	by Baal, f worthless idols.	339+2143
	3:19	and not turn away from f me.	339
	16:12	each of you *is* f the stubbornness	339+2143
Zep	1: 6	those who turn back from f the LORD	339
Mt	8:10	he was astonished and said *to* those f him,	199
	10: 5	with the f instructions:	NIG
Mk	13:24	"But in those days, f that distress,	3552
	14:51	but a linen garment, *was* f Jesus.	5258
Lk	7: 9	and turning *to* the crowd f him, he said,	199
Jn	1:38	Jesus saw them f and asked,	199
	18:15	and another disciple *were* f Jesus.	199
	21:20	the disciple whom Jesus loved *was* f them.	199
Ac	10: 9	the f day as they were on their journey	2069
	10:24	The f day he arrived in Caesarea.	2069
	15:23	With them they sent the f letter:	NIG
	15:28	with anything beyond the f requirements:	4047
	20:15	and *on* the f day arrived at Miletus.	2400
	23:11	The f night the Lord stood near Paul	2079

Ac	28:13	and on the f day we reached Puteoli,	1308
1Co	11:17	In the f directives I have no praise for you,	4047
Eph	2: 3	of our sinful nature and f its desires	4472
Php	3:17	Join with others in f my example,	1181+5213
1Ti	1:18	by f them you may fight the good fight,	NIG
Heb	4:11	so that no one will fall by f their example	NIG
2Pe	3: 3	scoffing and f their own evil desires.	4513
Rev	6: 8	and Hades *was* f close behind him.	199
	19:14	The armies of heaven *were* f him,	199

FOLLOWS (16) [FOLLOW]

Ge	41:31	the famine that f it will be so severe.	339+4027
Nu	14:24	a different spirit and f me wholeheartedly,	339
2Ki	11:15	and put to the sword anyone *who* f her."	339+995
2Ch	23:14	Their enrollment by families was as f:	465
	23:14	and put to the sword anyone *who* f her."	339+995
Ezr	4:11	to Artaxerxes the king as f:	10358
	5: 7	The report they sent him read as f:	10180+10341
Jer	4:20	Disaster f disaster; the whole land lies in ruins.	6584+7925
	51:31	One courier f another	7925
	51:31	and messenger f messenger to announce to	7925
Eze	18: 9	*He* f my decrees and faithfully keeps	928+2143
	18:17	He keeps my laws and f my decrees.	928+2143
	33:15	the decrees that give life,	928+2143
Hos	4: 2	and bloodshed f bloodshed.	5595
Jn	8:12	Whoever f me will never walk in darkness,	199
Ac	23:25	He wrote a letter as f:	2400+3836+4047+5596

FOLLY (37) [FOOL]

1Sa	25:25	his name is Fool, and f goes with him.	5576
Job	42: 8	and not deal with you according to your f.	5576
Ps	38: 5	and are loathsome because of my sinful f.	222
	69: 5	You know my f, O God;	222
	85: 8	but let them not return to f.	4074
Pr	5:23	led astray by his own great f.	222
	9:13	The woman F is loud;	4070
	12:23	but the heart of fools blurts out f.	222
	13:16	but a fool exposes his f.	222
	14: 8	but the f of fools is deception.	222
	14:18	The simple inherit f,	222
	14:24	but the f of fools yields folly.	222
	14:24	but the folly of fools yields f.	222
	14:29	but a quick-tempered man displays f.	222
	15: 2	but the mouth of the fool gushes f.	222
	15:14	but the mouth of a fool feeds on f.	222
	15:21	F delights a man who lacks judgment,	222
	16:22	but f brings punishment to fools.	222
	17:12	of her cubs than a fool in his f.	222
	18:13	that is his f and his shame.	222
	19: 3	A man's own f ruins his life,	222
	22:15	F is bound up in the heart of a child,	222
	24: 9	The schemes of f are sin,	222
	26: 4	Do not answer a fool according to his f,	222
	26: 5	Answer a fool according to his f,	222
	26:11	so a fool repeats his f.	222
	27:22	you will not remove his f from him.	222
Ecc	1:17	and also of madness and f,	8508
	2: 3	with wine, and embracing f—	6121
	2:12	and also madness and f.	6121
	2:13	I saw that wisdom is better than f,	6121
	7:25	of wickedness and the madness of f.	6121
	10: 1	so a little f outweighs wisdom and honor.	6121
	10:13	At the beginning his words are f;	6121
Isa	32: 6	fool speaks f, his mind is busy with evil:	5576
Mk	7:22	lewdness, envy, slander, arrogance and f.	932
2Ti	3: 9	their f will be clear to everyone.	486

FOMENTING (1)

Isa	59:13	f oppression and revolt,	1819

FOND (1)

1Sa	19: 1	But Jonathan *was* very f of David	2911

FONDLED (2)

Eze	23: 3	In that land their breasts were f	5080
	23:21	and your young breasts f.	5080

FOOD (317) [FOODS]

Ge	1:29	They will be yours for f.	433
	1:30	I give every green plant for f."	433
	2: 9	pleasing to the eye and good for f.	4407
	3: 6	of the tree was good for f and pleasing to	4407
	3:19	the sweat of your brow you will eat your f	4312
	6:21	to take every kind of f that is to be eaten	4407
	6:21	be eaten and store it away as f for you and	433
	9: 3	Everything that lives and moves will be f	433
	14:11	of Sodom and Gomorrah and all their f;	431
	21:14	the next morning Abraham took *some* f and	4312
	24:33	Then f was set before him, but he said,	430
	27: 4	the kind of tasty f I like and bring it to me	4761
	27: 7	and prepare me *some* tasty f to eat,	4761
	27: 9	I can prepare *some* tasty f for your father,	4761
	27:14	and she prepared *some* tasty f,	4761
	27:17	the tasty f and the bread she had made.	4761
	27:31	He too prepared *some* tasty f	4761
	28:20	and will give me f to eat and clothes	4312
	39: 6	with anything except the f he ate.	4312
	41:35	the f of these good years that are coming	431
	41:35	to be kept in the cities for f.	431
	41:36	This f should be held in reserve for	431
	41:48	the f produced *in* those seven years	431
	41:48	the f grown *in* the fields surrounding it.	431

Ge	41:54	but in the whole land of Egypt there was f.	4312
	41:55	the people cried to Pharaoh for f.	4312
	42: 7	they replied, "to buy f."	431
	42:10	"Your servants have come to buy f.	431
	42:33	take f for your starving households and go.	NIH
	43: 2	"Go back and buy us a little more f."	431
	43: 4	we will go down and buy f for you.	431
	43:20	down here the first time to buy f.	431
	43:22	additional silver with us to buy f.	431
	43:31	controlling himself, said, "Serve the f."	4312
	44: 1	"Fill the men's sacks with as much f	431
	44:25	'Go back and buy a little more f.'	431
	47:12	and all his father's household with f,	4312
	47:13	There was no f, however,	4312
	47:15	to Joseph and said, "Give us f.	4312
	47:16	"I will sell you f in exchange	NIH
	47:17	and he gave them f in exchange	4312
	47:17	with f in exchange for all their livestock.	4312
	47:19	Buy us and our land in exchange for f,	4312
	47:22	from Pharaoh and had f enough *from*	430
	47:24	as f *for* yourselves and your households	431
	49:20	"Asher's f will be rich;	4312
Ex	12:16	**prepare f** for everyone **to eat**—	430
	12:39	of Egypt and did not have time to prepare f	7476
	16: 3	of meat and ate all the f we wanted,	4312
	21:10	he must not deprive the first one of her f,	8638
	23:11	the poor among your people *may* **get** f	430
	23:25	his blessing will be on your f and water.	4312
Lev	3:11	The priest shall burn them on the altar as f,	4312
	3:16	The priest shall burn them on the altar as f,	4312
	11:34	Any f that could be eaten but has water	431
	21: 6	the f *of* their God, they are to be holy.	4312
	21: 8	because they offer up the f *of* your God.	4312
	21:17	a defect may come near to offer the f	4312
	21:21	not come near to offer the f *of* his God.	4312
	21:22	He may eat the most holy f *of* his God,	4312
	21:22	as well as the holy f;	NIH
	22: 7	for they are his f.	4312
	22:11	that slave may eat his f.	4312
	22:13	she may eat of her father's f.	4312
	22:25	of a foreigner and offer them as the f	4312
	25: 6	during the sabbath year will be f for you—	433
	25:37	not lend him money at interest or sell him f	431
	26: 5	and you will eat all the f you want and live	4312
Nu	11: 4	with them *began to* **crave** other f,	203+9294
	11:34	the people who *had* **craved** other f.	203
	15:19	and you eat the f *of* the land,	4312
	21: 5	And we detest this miserable f!"	4312
	28: 2	the f for my offerings made by fire,	4312
	28:24	In this way prepare the f *for*	4312
Dt	2: 6	to pay them in silver for the f you eat and	431
	2:28	Sell us f to eat and water to drink	431
	10:18	giving him f and clothing.	4312
	23:19	or f or anything else that may earn interest.	431
	28:26	Your carcasses will be f for all the birds of	4407
	32:15	**filled with** f, he became heavy and sleek.	9042
Jos	5:12	the day after they ate this f *from* the land;	6289
	9: 5	All the bread of their f **supply** was dry	7474
Jdg	13:16	I will not eat any of your f.	4312
	17:10	your clothes and your f."	4695
Ru	1: 6	to the aid of his people by providing f	4312
1Sa	2: 5	Those who were full hire themselves out for f,	4312
	2:36	to some priestly office so I can have f	4312+7326
	9: 7	The f in our sacks is gone.	4312
	14:24	"Cursed be any man who eats f	4312
	14:24	So none of the troops tasted f.	4312
	14:28	'Cursed be any man who eats f today!'	4312
	28:22	and let me give you some f so you may eat	4312
	30:11	They gave him water to drink and f	4312
	30:12	not eaten *any* f or drunk any water	4312
2Sa	3:35	or who falls by the sword or who lacks f."	4312
	12: 3	It shared his f,	7326
	12:17	and he would not eat any f with them.	4312
	12:20	and at his request they served him f,	4312
	13: 5	the f in my sight so I may watch her and	1376
	13: 7	of your brother Amnon and prepare some f	1376
	13:10	the f here into my bedroom so I may eat	1376
1Ki	5: 9	by providing f for my royal household."	4312
	5:11	of wheat as f for his household,	4818
	10: 5	the f on his table,	4407
	11:18	a house and land and provided him with f.	4312
	17: 9	a widow in that place to **supply** you **with** f.	3920
	17:15	So *there was* f every day for Elijah and for	430
	18: 4	and had supplied them with f and water.)	4312
	18:13	and supplied them with f and water.	4312
	19: 8	Strengthened by that f,	428
2Ki	6:22	Set f and water before them so	4312
	25: 3	so severe that there was no f for the people	4312
1Ch	12:40	and Naphtali came bringing f on donkeys,	4312
2Ch	9: 4	the f on his table,	4407
	11:11	with supplies of f, olive oil and wine.	4407
Ezr	2:63	of the **most sacred** f until there was	AIT
	3: 7	and gave f and drink and oil to the people	4407
	10: 6	he ate no f and drank no water,	4312
Ne	5:14	nor my brothers ate the f *allotted to*	4312
	5:15	from them in addition to f and wine.	4312
	5:18	I never demanded the f *allotted to*	4312
	7:65	the **most sacred** f until there should be	7731+7731
	8:10	"Go and enjoy **choice** f and sweet drinks,	5460
	8:12	to send **portions of** f and to celebrate	4950
	13: 2	with f and water but had hired Balaam	4312
	13:15	I warned them against selling f on that day.	7474
Est	2: 9	with her beauty treatments and **special** f.	4950
	9:22	of feasting and joy and giving **presents** of f	4950
Job	3:24	For sighing comes to me instead of f;	4312

Job	6: 6	Is **tasteless** *f* eaten without salt,	AIT
	6: 7	I refuse to touch it; such f makes me ill.	4312
	12:11	the ear test words as the tongue tastes f?	431
	15:23	He wanders about—for vultures;	4312
	20:14	yet his f will turn sour in his stomach;	4312
	22: 7	to the weary and you withheld f from	4312
	24: 5	the poor go about their labor of foraging f;	3272
	24: 5	the wasteland provides f for their children.	4312
	28: 5	The earth, from which f comes,	4312
	30: 4	and their f was the root of the broom tree.	4312
	33:20	so that his very being finds f repulsive	4312
	34: 3	the ear tests words as the tongue tastes f.	430
	36:16	of your table laden with **choice** f.	2016
	36:31	the nations and provides f in abundance.	431
	38:41	Who provides f for the raven	7474
	38:41	to God and wander about for lack of f?	431
	39:29	From there he seeks out his f;	431
Ps	42: 3	My tears have been my f day and night,	4312
	59:15	They wander about for f and howl if	430
	63:10	be given over to the sword and become f	4987
	69:21	They put gall in my f and gave me vinegar	1362
	74:14	the heads of Leviathan and gave him as f	4407
	78:18	to the test by demanding the f they craved.	431
	78:20	But can he also give us f?	4312
	78:25	he sent them all the f they could eat.	7476
	78:30	before they turned from the f they craved,	431
	79: 2	of your servants as f to the birds of the air,	4407
	102: 4	I forget to eat my f.	4312
	102: 9	as my f and mingle my drink with tears	4312
	104:14	bringing forth f from the earth:	4312
	104:21	for their prey and seek their f from God.	431
	104:27	These all look to you to give them their f at	431
	105:16	and destroyed all their supplies of f;	4312
	107:18	They loathed all f and drew near the gates	431
	111: 5	He provides f for those who fear him;	3272
	127: 2	toiling for f to eat—	4312
	132:15	her poor will I satisfy with f.	4312
	136:25	and who gives f to every creature.	4312
	145:15	you give them their f at the proper time.	431
	146: 7	of the oppressed and gives f to the hungry.	4312
	147: 9	He provides f for the cattle and for	4312
Pr	6: 8	in summer and gathers its f at harvest.	4407
	9: 5	eat my f and drink the wine I have mixed.	4312
	9:17	f eaten in secret is delicious!"	4312
	12: 9	to be somebody and have no f.	4312
	12:11	He who works his land will have abundant f	4312
	13:23	poor man's field may produce abundant f,	431
	20:13	stay awake and you will have f to spare.	4312
	20:17	F gained by fraud tastes sweet to a man,	4312
	21:20	the house of the wise are stores of **choice** *f*	AIT
	22: 9	for he shares his f with the poor.	4312
	23: 3	for that f is deceptive.	4312
	23: 6	Do not eat the f *of* a stingy man,	4312
	25:21	If your enemy is hungry, give him f to eat;	4312
	28:19	He who works his land will have abundant f	4312
	30:22	a fool who is full of f,	4312
	30:25	yet they store up their f in the summer;	4312
	31:14	bringing her f from afar.	4312
	31:15	she provides f for her family and portions	3272
Ecc	9: 7	Go, eat your f with gladness,	4312
	9:11	or the battle to the strong, nor does f come	4312
Isa	3: 1	all supplies of f and all supplies of water,	4312
	3: 7	I have no f or clothing in my house;	4312
	4: 1	"We will eat our own f	4312
	21:14	bring f *for* the fugitives.	4312
	23:18	for abundant f and fine clothes.	430
	25: 6	a feast of **rich** f for all peoples, a banquet	9043
	30:23	the f that comes from the land will be rich	4312
	58: 7	Is it not to share your f with the hungry	4312
	62: 8	"Never again will I give your grain as f	4407
	65:25	but dust will be the serpent's f.	4312
Jer	5:17	They will devour your harvests and f,	4312
	7:33	the carcasses of this people will become f	4407
	9:15	**make** this people **eat** bitter f	430
	16: 4	and their dead bodies will become f for	4407
	16: 7	No *one will* **offer** f to comfort	7271
	19: 7	as f to the birds of the air and the beasts of	4407
	22:15	*Did* not your father **have** f and drink?	430
	23:15	*I will* **make** them **eat** bitter f	430
	34:20	Their dead bodies will become f for	4407
	44:17	At that time we had plenty of f	4312
	52: 6	so severe that there was no f for the people	4312
La	1:11	they barter their treasures for f	431
	1:19	in the city while they searched for f	4312
	4: 9	with hunger, they waste away for lack of f	9482
	4:10	who became their f	1356
Eze	4:10	of f to eat each day and eat it at set times.	4407
	4:12	Eat **the** f as you would a barley cake;	5626S
	4:13	the people of Israel will eat defiled f—	4312
	4:16	I will cut off the supply of f in Jerusalem.	4312
	4:16	The people will eat rationed f in anxiety	4312
	4:17	for f and water will be scarce.	4312
	5:16	upon you and cut off your supply of f.	4312
	12:18	tremble as you eat your f,	4312
	12:19	They will eat their f in anxiety	4312
	14:13	to cut off its f supply and send famine	4312
	16:13	*Your* f was fine flour, honey and olive oil.	430
	16:19	Also the f I provided for you—	4312
	16:20	to me and sacrificed them as f to the idols.	430
	18: 7	He does not commit robbery but gives his f	4312
	18:16	He does not commit robbery but gives his f	4312
	23:37	whom they bore to me, as f for them.	433
	24:17	or eat the customary f [of mourners]."	4312
	24:22	or eat the customary f [of mourners].	4312
	29: 5	as f to the beasts of the earth and the birds	433
	34: 5	when they were scattered they became f,	433
	34: 8	and has become f for all the wild animals,	433

Eze	34:10	and it will no longer be f for them.	433
	39: 4	as f to all kinds of carrion birds and to	433
	44: 7	while you offered me f,	4312
	47:12	Their fruit will serve for f and their leaves	4407
	48:18	Its produce will supply f for the workers of	4312
Da	1: 5	of f and wine *from* the king's table.	7329
	1: 8	to defile himself with the royal f and wine,	7329
	1:10	who has assigned your f and drink.	4407
	1:13	that of the young men who eat the royal f,	7329
	1:15	of the young men who ate the royal f.	7329
	1:16	So the guard took away their **choice** f and	7329
	4:12	its fruit abundant, and on it was f for all.	10410
	4:21	providing f for all, giving shelter to	10410
	10: 3	I ate no choice f;	4312
Hos	2: 5	who give me my f and my water,	4312
	9: 3	to Egypt and eat unclean f in Assyria.	NIH
	9: 4	This f will be for themselves;	4312
Joel	1:16	the f been cut off before our very eyes—	431
Am	8:11	not a famine of f or a thirst for water,	4312
Hab	1:16	in luxury and enjoys the choicest f.	4407
	3:17	olive crop fails and the fields produce no f,	431
Hag	2:12	some wine, oil or other f,	4407
Zec	9: 7	the **forbidden** f from between their teeth.	9199
Mal	1: 7	"You place defiled f on my altar.	4312
	1:12	and of its f, 'It is contemptible.'	431
	3:10	that there may be f in my house.	3272
Mt	3: 4	His f was locusts and wild honey.	5575
	6:25	Is not life more important than f,	5575
	14:15	to the villages and buy themselves some f."	1109
	24:45	in his household to give them their f at	5575
Mk	7: 2	of his disciples eating f with hands	788
	7: 5	of eating their f with 'unclean' hands?"	788
Lk	3:11	the one who has f should do the same.	1109
	9:12	and countryside and find f and lodging,	2169
	9:13	unless we go and buy f for all this crowd."	1109
	12:23	Life is more than f,	5575
	12:42	to give them their f **allowance** at	4991
	15:17	of my father's hired men have f to spare,	788
Jn	4: 8	into the town to buy f.)	5575
	4:32	"I have f to eat that you know nothing about	1111
	4:33	"Could someone have brought him f?"	2266
	4:34	"My f," said Jesus, "is to do the will	1109
	6:27	Do not work for f that spoils,	1111
	6:27	but for f that endures to eternal life,	1111
	6:55	For my flesh is real f	1111
Ac	6: 1	in the daily distribution of f.	NIG
	7:11	and our fathers could not find f.	5964
	9:19	and after taking some f,	5575
	12:20	on the king's country for their f **supply.**	5555
	14:17	with plenty *of* f and fills your hearts	5575
	15:20	telling them to abstain from f polluted	NIG
	15:29	abstain from f **sacrificed to idols,**	1628
	21:25	abstain from f **sacrificed to idols,**	1628
	27:21	the men had gone a long time **without** f,	826
	27:33	and have gone **without** f—	827
	27:34	Now I urge you to take some f.	5575
	27:36	and ate some f themselves.	5575
Ro	14:14	I am fully convinced that no f is unclean	NIG
	14:20	the work of God for the sake of f.	1109
	14:20	All f is clean, but it is wrong for a man to	NIG
1Co	3: 2	I gave you milk, not **solid** f,	1109
	6:13	"F for the stomach and the stomach	1109
	6:13	for the stomach and the stomach *for* f"—	1109
	8: 1	Now about f **sacrificed to idols:**	1628
	8: 4	So then, about eating f sacrificed to idols:	1111
	8: 7	to idols that when they eat **such** f they think	1628
	8: 8	But f does not bring us near to God;	1109
	9: 4	Don't we have the right *to* f and drink?	2266
	9:13	in the temple **get** *their* f from the temple,	2266
	10: 3	They all ate the same spiritual f	1109
2Co	9:10	the sower and bread for f will also supply	1111
	9:11	and thirst and have often **gone without** f,	3763
2Th	3: 8	did we eat anyone's f without paying for it.	788
1Ti	6: 8	But if we have f and clothing,	1418
Heb	5:12	You need milk, not **solid** f!	5575
	5:14	But solid f is for the mature,	5575
	9:10	They are only a matter of f and drink	1109
Jas	2:15	or sister is without clothes and daily f.	5575
Rev	2:14	to sin by eating f **sacrificed to idols** and	1628
	2:20	the eating of f **sacrificed to idols.**	1628

FOODS (4) [FOOD]

Ps	63: 5	be satisfied as with the **richest of** f;	
			2016+2256+2693
Mk	7:19	Jesus declared all f "clean.")	1109
1Ti	4: 3	and order them to abstain from certain f,	1109
Heb	13: 9	not *by* ceremonial f,	1109

FOOL (82) [FOLLY, FOOL'S, FOOLISH, FOOLISHLY, FOOLISHNESS, FOOLS]

Nu	22:29	"You have **made a** f of me!	6618
Jdg	16:10	"You have **made a** f of me; you lied to me.	9438
	16:13	*you have been* **making a** f of me and lying	9438
	16:15	This is the third time *you have* **made a** f of	9438
1Sa	25:25	his name is F, and folly goes with him.	5572
	26:21	Surely *I have* **acted like a** f	6118
Job	5: 2	Resentment kills a f,	211
	5: 3	I myself have seen a f taking root,	211
Ps	14: 1	The f says in his heart, "There is no God."	5572
	53: 1	The f says in his heart, "There is no God."	5572
Pr	10: 8	but a chattering f comes to ruin.	211
	10:10	and a chattering f comes to ruin.	211
	10:14	but the mouth of a f invites ruin.	211
	10:18	and whoever spreads slander is a f.	4067
	10:23	A f finds pleasure in evil conduct,	4067

Pr	11:29	and the f will be servant to the wise.	211
	12:15	The way of a f seems right to him,	211
	12:16	A f shows his annoyance at once,	211
	13:16	but a f exposes his folly.	4067
	14:16	but a f is hotheaded and reckless.	4067
	15: 2	but the mouth of the f gushes folly.	4067
	15: 5	A f spurns his father's discipline,	211
	15:14	but the mouth of a f feeds on folly.	4067
	17: 7	Arrogant lips are unsuited to a f,	5572
	17:10	a hundred lashes a f.	4067
	17:12	to meet a bear robbed of her cubs than a f	4067
	17:16	Of what use is money in the hand of a f,	4067
	17:21	To have a f for a son brings grief;	4067
	17:21	there is no joy for the father of a f.	5572
	17:28	Even a f is thought wise if he keeps silent,	211
	18: 2	A f finds no pleasure in understanding	4067
	19: 1	a f whose lips are perverse.	4067
	19:10	It is not fitting for a f to live in luxury—	4067
	20: 3	but every f is quick to quarrel.	211
	23: 9	Do not speak to a f,	4067
	24: 7	Wisdom is too high for a f;	211
	26: 1	honor is not fitting for a f.	4067
	26: 4	Do not answer a f according to his folly,	4067
	26: 5	Answer a f according to his folly,	4067
	26: 6	of a message by the hand of a f.	4067
	26: 7	a proverb in the mouth of a f.	4067
	26: 8	in a sling is the giving of honor to a f.	4067
	26: 9	a proverb in the mouth of a f.	4067
	26:10	at random is he who hires a f	4067
	26:11	so a f repeats his folly.	4067
	26:12	There is more hope for a f than for him.	4067
	27: 3	but provocation by a f is heavier than both.	211
	27:22	Though you grind a f in a mortar,	211
	28:26	He who trusts in himself is a f,	4067
	29: 9	If a wise man goes to court with a f,	211
	29: 9	the f rages and scoffs,	NIH
	29:11	A f gives full vent to his anger,	4067
	29:20	There is more hope for a f than for him.	4067
	30:22	a f who is full of food,	5572
	30:32	"If you have played the f	5571
Ecc	2:14	while the f walks in the darkness.	4067
	2:15	"The fate of the f will overtake me also.	4067
	2:16	For the wise man, like the f,	4067
	2:16	Like the f, the wise man too must die!	4067
	2:19	whether he will be a wise man or a f?	6119
	4: 5	The f folds his hands and ruins himself.	4067
	5: 3	speech of a f when there are many words.	4067
	6: 8	What advantage has a wise man over a f?	4067
	7: 7	Extortion turns a wise man into a f,	2147
	7:17	Do not be overwicked, and do not be a f—	6119
	10: 2	but the heart of the f to the left.	4067
	10: 3	the f lacks sense and shows everyone	6119
	10:12	but a f is consumed by his own lips.	4067
	10:14	and the f multiplies words.	6119
Isa	32: 5	No longer will the f be called noble nor	5572
	32: 6	f speaks folly, his mind is busy with evil:	5572
Jer	17:11	and in the end he will prove to be a f.	5572
Hos	9: 7	the prophet is considered a f,	211
Mt	5:22	But anyone who says, 'You f!'	3704
Lk	12:20	"But God said to him, 'You f!	933
1Co	3:18	a "f" so that he may become wise.	3704
2Co	11:16	I repeat: Let no one take me for a f.	933
	11:16	then receive me just as you would a f,	933
	11:17	not talking as the Lord would, but as a f.	932
	11:21	I am speaking as a f—	932+1877
	12: 6	I would not be a f,	933
	12:11	I have made a f of myself.	933

FOOL'S (5) [FOOL]

Pr	14: 3	A f talk brings a rod to his back,	211
	17:24	a f eyes wander to the ends of the earth.	4067
	18: 6	A f lips bring him strife,	4067
	18: 7	A f mouth is his undoing,	4067
Ecc	10:15	A f work wearies him;	4067

FOOLISH (46) [FOOL]

Ge	31:28	You have done a f thing.	6118
Dt	32: 6	O f and unwise people?	5572
2Sa	24:10	I have done a very f thing."	6118
1Ch	21: 8	I have done a very f thing."	6118
2Ch	16: 9	You have done a f thing.	6118
Job	2:10	"You are talking like a f woman.	5572
Ps	49:10	the f and the senseless alike perish	4067
	74:18	how f people have reviled your name.	5572
Pr	8: 5	you who are f, gain understanding.	4067
	10: 1	but a f son grief to his mother.	4067
	14: 1	the f one tears hers down.	222
	14: 7	Stay away from a f man,	4067
	14:17	A quick-tempered man does f things,	222
	15:20	but a f man despises his mother.	4067
	17:25	A f son brings grief to his father	4067
	19:13	A f son is his father's ruin,	4067
	21:20	but a f man devours all he has.	4067
Ecc	2: 2	"Laughter," I said, "is	2147
	4:13	an old but f king who no longer knows	4067
Jer	5: 4	they are f, for they do not know the way of	3282
	5:21	you f and senseless people,	5572
	10: 8	They are all senseless and f;	4071
Eze	13: 3	the f prophets who follow their own spirit	5572
Zec	11:15	"Take again the equipment of a f shepherd.	216
Mt	7:26	like a f man who built his house on sand.	3704
	25: 2	Five of them were f and five were wise.	3704
	25: 3	The f ones took their lamps but did	3704
	25: 8	The f ones said to the wise,	3704
Lk	11:40	You f people!	933

Lk	24:25	He said to them, "How f you are,	485+6043
Ro	1:14	both to the wise and the f.	485
	1:21	and their f hearts were darkened.	852
	2:20	an instructor of the f, a teacher of infants,	933
1Co	1:20	not God made f the wisdom of the world?	3701
	1:27	But God chose the f things of the world	3704
	15:36	How f! What you sow does	933
Gal	3: 1	You f Galatians!	485
	3: 3	Are you so f?	485
Eph	5: 4	f talk or coarse joking,	3703
	5:17	Therefore do not be f,	933
1Ti	6: 9	a trap and into many f and harmful desires	485
2Ti	2:23	to do with f and stupid arguments,	3704
Tit	3: 3	At one time we too were f, disobedient,	485
	3: 9	But avoid f controversies and genealogies	3704
Jas	2:20	You f man, do you want evidence that faith	3031
1Pe	2:15	the ignorant talk of f men.	933

FOOLISHLY (2) [FOOL]

Nu	12:11	against us the sin we have so f committed.	3282
1Sa	13:13	"You acted f," Samuel said.	6118

FOOLISHNESS (8) [FOOL]

2Sa	15:31	turn Ahithophel's counsel into f."	6118
1Co	1:18	of the cross is f to those who are perishing,	3702
	1:21	through the f of what was preached	3702
	1:23	a stumbling block to Jews and f	3702
	1:25	the f of God is wiser than man's wisdom,	3704
	2:14	Spirit of God, for they are f to him,	3702
	3:19	wisdom of this world is f in God's sight.	3702
2Co	11: 1	up with a little of my f;	932

FOOLS (41) [FOOL]

2Sa	13:13	You would be like one of the wicked f	5572
Job	12:17	and makes f of judges.	2147
Ps	39: 8	do not make me the scorn of f.	5572
	74:22	remember how f mock you all day long.	5572
	92: 6	f do not understand,	4067
	94: 8	you f, when will you become wise?	4067
	107:17	Some became f through their rebellious	211
Pr	1: 7	but f despise wisdom and discipline.	211
	1:22	in mockery and hate knowledge?	4067
	1:32	the complacency of f will destroy them;	4067
	3:35	but f he holds up to shame.	4067
	10:21	but f die for lack of judgment.	211
	12:23	but the heart of f blurts out folly.	4067
	13:19	but f detest turning from evil.	4067
	13:20	but a companion of f suffers harm.	4067
	14: 8	but the folly of f is deception.	4067
	14: 9	F mock at making amends for sin,	211
	14:24	but the folly of f yields folly.	4067
	14:33	even among f she lets herself be known.	4067
	15: 7	not so the hearts of f.	4067
	16:22	but folly brings punishment to f.	211
	19:29	and beatings for the backs of f.	4067
	26: 3	and a rod for the backs of f!	4067
Ecc	5: 1	to offer the sacrifice of f,	4067
	5: 4	He has no pleasure in f; fulfill your vow.	4067
	7: 4	the heart of f is in the house of pleasure.	4067
	7: 5	to listen to the song of f.	4067
	7: 6	so is the laughter of f.	4067
	7: 9	for anger resides in the lap of f.	4067
	9:17	to be heeded than the shouts of a ruler of f.	4067
	10: 6	F are put in many high positions,	6120
Isa	19:11	The officials of Zoan are nothing but f;	211
	19:13	The officials of Zoan have become f,	3282
	35: 8	wicked f will not go about on it.	211
	44:25	false prophets and makes f of diviners,	2147
Jer	4:22	"My people are f; they do not know me.	211
	50:36	They will become f.	3282
Mt	23:17	You blind f!	3704
Ro	1:22	to be wise, they became f	3701
1Co	4:10	We are f for Christ,	3704
2Co	11:19	You gladly put up with f since you are	933

FOOT (86) [BAREFOOT, AFOOT, FEET, FLEET-FOOTED, FOOTHOLD, FOOTINGS, FOOTPRINTS, FOUR-FOOTED, UNDERFOOT]

Ge	41:44	will lift hand or f in all Egypt."	8079
Ex	12:37	about six hundred thousand men on f,	8081
	19:12	not go up the mountain or touch the f of it.	7895
	19:17	and they stood at the f of the mountain.	9397
	21:24	tooth for tooth, hand for hand, foot for	8079
	21:24	tooth for tooth, hand for hand, foot for f,	8079
	24: 4	and built an altar at the f of the mountain	9393
	32:19	breaking them to pieces at the f of	9393
Lev	8:23	and on the big toe of his right f.	8079
	13:12	of the infected person from head to f,	8079
	14:14	and on the big toe of his right f,	8079
	14:17	and on the big toe of his right f,	8079
	14:25	and on the big toe of his right f.	8079
	14:28	and on the big toe of his right f.	8079
	21:19	no man with a crippled f or hand,	8079
Nu		among six hundred thousand men on f,	8081
	20:19	We only want to pass through on f—	8079
	22:25	crushing Balaam's f against it.	8079
Dt	2: 5	not even enough to put your f on.	4090+8079
	2:28	Only let us pass through on f—	8079
	4:11	near and stood at the f of the mountain	9393
	11:10	by f as in a vegetable garden.	8079
	11:24	Every place where you set your f will	4090+8079
	19:21	tooth for tooth, hand for hand, for foot.	8079

Dt	19:21	tooth for tooth, hand for hand, foot for f.	8079
	28:56	to touch the ground with the sole of her f—	8079
	28:65	no resting place for the sole of your f.	8079
	32:35	In due time their f will slip;	8079
Jos	1: 3	where you set your f,	4090+8079
	3:13	set f in the Jordan,	4090+8079
	18:16	down to the f of the hill facing the Valley	7895
Jdg	3:16	sword about a f and a half long,	1688
	4:15	Sisera abandoned his chariot and fled on f,	8079
	4:17	however, fled on f to the tent of Jael,	8079
1Sa	4:10	Israel lost thirty thousand f soldiers.	8081
	15: 4	two hundred thousand f soldiers.	8081
2Sa	8: 4	and twenty thousand f soldiers.	408+8081
	10: 6	hired twenty thousand Aramean f soldiers	8081
	10:18	and forty thousand of their f soldiers.	8081
	14:25	to the sole of his f there was no blemish	8079
	21:20	on each hand and six toes on each f—	8079
1Ki	14:12	When you set f in your city,	8079
	20:29	on the Aramean f soldiers in one day.	8081
2Ki	13: 7	ten chariots and ten thousand f soldiers.	8081
1Ch	18: 4	and twenty thousand f soldiers.	408+8081
	19:18	and forty thousand of their f soldiers.	408+8081
	20: 6	on each hand and six toes on each f—	NIH
Job	18: 4	in places forgotten by the f of man;	8079
	28: 8	Proud beasts do not set f on it,	2005
	31: 5	or my f has hurried after deceit—	8079
	39:15	unmindful that a f may crush them,	8079
Ps	36:11	the f of the proud not come against me,	8079
	38:16	over me when my f slips."	8079
	66: 6	they passed through the waters on f—	8079
	91:12	you will not strike your f against a stone.	8079
	94:18	When I said, "My f is slipping," your love,	8079
	121: 3	He will not let your f slip—	8079
Pr	1:15	do not set f on their paths;	8079
	3:23	and your f will not stumble;	8079
	3:26	be your confidence and will keep your f	8079
	4:14	not set f on the path of the wicked or walk	995
	4:27	keep your f from evil.	8079
	25:17	Seldom set f in your neighbor's house—	8079
	25:19	Like a bad tooth or a lame f is reliance on	8079
Ecc	10: 7	while princes go on f like slaves.	824+2021+6584
Isa	1: 6	From the sole of your f to the top	8079
Jer	12: 5	with men on f and they have worn you out,	8079
Eze	29:11	No f of man or animal will pass through it;	8079
	32:13	be stirred by the f of man or muddied by	8079
Hab	3:13	you stripped him from head to f.	3572
Mt	4: 6	so that you will not strike your f against	4546
	14:13	crowds followed him on f from the towns.	4270
	18: 8	If your hand or your f causes you to sin,	4546
	22:13	'Tie him hand and f,	4546
Mk	5: 4	For he had often been chained hand and f,	4267
	6:33	and ran on f from all the towns	4270
	9:45	And if your f causes you to sin, cut it off.	4546
Lk	8:29	though he was chained hand and f and kept	4267
Jn	20:12	one at the head and the other at the f.	4546
Ac	7: 5	not even a f of ground.	1037+4546
	20:13	because he was going there on f.	4269
1Co	12:15	If the f should say, "Because I am not	4546
Heb	10:29	trampled the Son of God under f,	2922
Rev	10: 2	He planted his right f on the sea	4546
	10: 2	on the sea and his left f on the land,	NIG

FOOTHILLS (20) [HILL]

Dt	1: 7	in the mountains, in the western f,	9169
Jos	9: 1	those in the hill country, in the western f,	9169
	10:40	the western f and the mountain slopes,	9169
	11: 2	in the western f and in Naphoth Dor on	9169
	11:16	the whole region of Goshen, the western f,	9169
	11:16	and the mountains of Israel with their f,	9169
	12: 8	the western f, the Arabah,	9169
	15:33	In the western f: Eshtaol, Zorah, Ashnah,	9169
Jdg	1: 9	the Negev and the western f.	9169
1Ki	10:27	as plentiful as sycamore-fig trees in the f.	9169
1Ch	27:28	and sycamore-fig trees in the western f.	9169
2Ch	1:15	as plentiful as sycamore-fig trees in the f.	9169
	9:27	as plentiful as sycamore-fig trees in the f.	9169
	26:10	because he had much livestock in the f and	9169
	28:18	the Philistines had raided towns in the f	9169
Jer	17:26	the territory of Benjamin and the western f,	9169
	32:44	of the western f and of the Negev,	9169
	33:13	of the western f and of the Negev,	9169
Ob	1:19	and people from the f will possess the land	9169
Zec	7: 7	Negev and the western f were settled?'"	9169

FOOTHOLD (3) [FOOT]

Ps	69: 2	where there is no f.	5097
	73: 2	I had nearly lost my f.	892
Eph	4:27	and do not give the devil a f.	5536

FOOTINGS (1) [FOOT]

Job	38: 6	On what were its f set,	149

FOOTMEN (KJV) See MEN ON FOOT

FOOTPRINTS (2) [FOOT]

Ps	77:19	though your f were not seen.	6811
Hos	6: 8	stained with f of blood.	6814

FOOTSTEPS (5) [STEP]

1Ki	14: 6	So when Ahijah heard the sound of her f at	8079
2Ki	6:32	the sound of his master's f behind him?"	8079
Ps	119:133	Direct my f according to your word;	7193

Isa	26: 6	the feet of the oppressed, the **f** of the poor.	7193
Ro	4:12	but who also walk *in* the **f** of the faith	2717

FOOTSTOOL (13) [STOOL]

1Ch	28: 2	for the **f** of our God,	2071+8079
2Ch	9:18	and a **f** of gold was attached to it.	3900
Ps	99: 5	LORD our God and worship at his **f**;	2071+8079
	110: 1	until I make your enemies a **f**	2071
	132: 7	let us worship at his **f**—	2071+8079
Isa	66: 1	and the earth is my **f**.	2071+8079
La	2: 1	he has not remembered his **f** in the day of his anger.	2071+8079
Mt	5:35	or by the earth, for it is his **f**;	5711
Lk	20:43	until I make your enemies a **f**	5711
Ac	2:35	until I make your enemies a **f**	5711
	7:49	and the earth is my **f**.	3836+4546+5711
Heb	1:13	until I make your enemies a **f**	5711
	10:13	for his enemies to be made his **f**,	5711

FOR (7282) See Index of Articles Etc.

FORAGING (1)

Job	24: 5	the poor go about their labor of **f** food;	8838

FORBAD (KJV) See DETER, STOP

FORBEARANCE (1)

Ro	3:25	because in his **f** he had left the sins committed beforehand unpunished—	496

FORBID (7) [FORBIDDEN, FORBIDS]

Nu	30:11	but says nothing to her and *does* not **f** her,	5648
1Sa	24: 6	"The LORD **f** that I should do such	2721
	26:11	But the LORD **f** that I should lay a hand	2721
1Ki	21: 3	"The LORD **f** that I should give you	2721
1Ch	11:19	"God **f** that I should do this!"	2721
1Co	14:39	and *do* not **f** speaking in tongues.	3266
1Ti	4: 3	*They* **f** people to marry and order them	3266

FORBIDDEN (15) [FORBID]

Lev	4: 2	and does what *is* **f** in any of	4202+6913
	4:13	and does what *is* **f** in any of	4202+6913
	4:22	and does what *is* **f** in any of	4202+6913
	4:27	and does what *is* **f** in any of	4202+6913
	5:17	a person sins and does what *is* **f** in any	4202+6913
	19:23	*regard* its fruit as **f**.	6887+6889
	19:23	For three years you are to consider it **f**;	6888
Nu	30: 5	because her father *has* **f** her,	5648
Dt	4:23	of anything the LORD your God *has* **f**.	7422
	23: 2	one born of a **f** marriage	4927
1Ki	11:10	*he had* **f** Solomon to follow other gods	1194+7422
2Ki	17:15	the things the LORD had **f** them to do.	NIH
Est	2:10	because Mordecai *had* **f** her to do so.	4202+7422
La	1:10	*you had* **f** to enter your assembly.	4202+7422
Zec	9: 7	the **f** food from between their teeth.	9199

FORBIDS (3) [FORBID]

Nu	30: 5	if her father **f** her when he hears about it,	5648
	30: 8	if her husband **f** her when he hears about it,	5648
Jn	5:10	the law **f** you to carry your mat."	2003+4024

FORECAST (KJV) See PLOT

FORCE (37) [ENFORCE, FORCED, FORCEFUL, FORCEFULLY, FORCES, FORCIBLY, FORCING]

Ge	31:31	**take** your daughters away from me by **f**.	1608
	47:26	**still** in **f** today—	6330
Ex	9:14	the **full** *of* my plagues against you and	3972
	19:21	not **f** *their* **way through** to see the LORD	2238
	19:24	the people *must* not **f** *their* **way through**	2238
Jos	8:11	The entire **f** that was with him marched up	4878+6639
Jdg	7:13	the tent with such **f** that the tent overturned	5877S
	8:10	with a **f** of about fifteen thousand men, all	4722
1Sa	2:16	if you don't, I'll take it by **f**."	2622
	19: 8	He struck them with such **f** that they fled	4804
2Sa	5:17	they went up **in full f** to search for him,	3972
	13:12	"Don't **f** me. Such a thing should not be	6700
1Ki	9:21	for his slave **labor f**,	4989
	11:28	the whole **f** *of* the house of Joseph.	6023
2Ki	6:14	and chariots and a strong **f** there.	2657
	24:16	also deported to Babylon the **entire f**	AIT
1Ch	14: 8	they went up **in full f** to search for him,	3972
2Ch	8: 8	for his slave **labor f**,	4989
	13: 3	Abijah went into battle with a **f**	2657
	26:13	a powerful **f** to support the king	2657
	32: 4	A large **f** *of men* assembled,	6639
Ezr	4:23	in Jerusalem and compelled them by **f**	10013
Est	8:11	to destroy, kill and annihilate any **armed f**	2657
Job	19:12	His troops advance in **f**;	3480
	20:22	the full **f** *of* misery will come upon him.	3338
	24: 4	**f** all the poor of the land **into hiding.**	2461
	28:25	When he established the **f** of the wind	5486
Jer	46:22	as the enemy advances in **f**;	2657
Am	5:11	on the poor and **f** him **to give** you grain.	4374
Ob		All your allies *will* **f** you to the border;	8938
Jn	6:15	to come and make him king by **f**,	773
Ac	5:26	They did not **use f**,	1040+3552
	23:10	**take** him away from them **by f**	773

Ac	26:11	and *I tried to* **f** them to blaspheme.	337
	27:14	Before very long, a wind **of hurricane f**,	5607
Gal	2:14	*you* **f** Gentiles to follow Jewish customs?	337
Heb	9:17	will is **in f** only when somebody has died;	1010

FORCED (24) [FORCE]

Ge	49:15	to the burden and submit to **f labor**.	4989
Ex	1:11	over them to oppress them with **f labor**,	6026
Dt	20:11	the people in it shall be subject to **f labor**	4989
Jos	16:10	of Ephraim but are required to do **f labor**.	4989
	17:13	they subjected the Canaanites to **f labor**	4989
Jdg	1:28	they pressed the Canaanites into **f labor**,	4989
	1:30	but they did subject them to **f labor**,	4989
	1:33	and Beth Anath became **f laborers**	4989
	1:35	they too were pressed into **f labor**.	4989
2Sa	18: 3	if *we are* **f to flee**,	5674+5674
	20:24	Adoniram was in charge of **f labor**;	4989
1Ki	4: 6	in charge of **f labor**.	4989
	5:14	Adoniram was in charge of the **f labor**.	4989
	9:15	of the **f labor** King Solomon conscripted	4989
	12:18	who was in charge of **f labor**,	4989
2Ch	10:18	who was in charge of **f labor**,	4989
Job	30: 6	They were **f** to live in the dry stream beds,	4200
Ps	69: 4	*I am* **f to restore** what I did not steal.	8740
Isa	31: 8	be put to **f labor**.	4989
Jer	34:16	you **f** them	3899
Mt	27:32	and *they* **f** him to carry the cross.	30
Mk	15:21	and *they* **f** him to carry the cross.	30
Phm	1:14	will be spontaneous and not **f**.	340+2848
Rev	13:16	He also **f** everyone, small and great,	4472

FORCEFUL (2) [FORCE]

Mt	11:12	and **f** men lay hold of it.	1043
2Co	10:10	some say, "His letters are weighty and **f**,	2708

FORCEFULLY (3) [FORCE]

1Sa	18:10	an evil spirit from God **came f** upon Saul.	7502
Isa	28: 2	he will throw it **f** to the ground.	928+3338
Mt	11:12	kingdom of heaven *has been* **f advancing**,	1041

FORCES (36) [FORCE]

Ge	14: 3	All these latter kings **joined f** in the Valley	2489
	21:22	the commander of his **f** said to Abraham,	7372
	21:32	and Phicol the commander of his **f** returned	7372
	26:26	and Phicol the commander of his **f**.	7372
	34:30	*if they* **join f** against me and attack me,	665
Jos	10: 5	Jarmuth, Lachish and Eglon—**joined f**.	665
	10: 6	the hill country *have* **joined f** against us."	7695
	11: 5	All these kings **joined f**	3585
Jdg	6:33	and other eastern peoples **joined f**	665+3481
	12: 1	The men of Ephraim called out their **f**,	NIH
1Sa	4: 2	The Philistines **deployed** *their* **f**	6885
	14:17	"**Muster** *the* **f** and see who has left us."	7212
	17: 1	Now the Philistines gathered their **f** for war	4722
	23: 3	if we go to Keilah against the Philistine **f**!"	5120
	23: 8	And Saul called up all his **f** for battle,	6639
	23:26	As Saul and his **f** were closing in on David	408
	28: 1	the Philistines gathered their **f** to fight	4722
	29: 1	The Philistines gathered all their **f**	4722
	30:23	and handed over to us the **f** that came	1522
1Ki	11:24	when David destroyed the **f** [of Zobah],	4392S
	15:20	the commanders of his **f** against the towns	2657
1Ch	20: 1	Joab led out the **armed f**	2657+7372
2Ch	14:13	before the LORD and his **f**.	4722
	16: 4	the commanders of his **f** against the towns	2657
	32: 9	and all his **f** were laying siege to Lachish,	4939
Job	10:17	your **f** come against me wave upon wave.	7372
	25: 3	Can his **f** be numbered?	1522
Ps	48: 4	When the kings **joined f**,	3585
	55:11	**Destructive f** are at work in the city;	2095
Da	11: 7	He will attack the **f** of the king of	2657
	11:15	The **f** of the South will be powerless	2432
	11:31	"His **armed f** will rise up to desecrate	2432
Joel	2:11	his **f** are beyond number,	4722
Zec	9: 8	I will defend my house against marauding **f**.	7372
Mt	5:41	If someone **f** you to go one mile,	30
Eph	6:12	and against the spiritual **f** of evil in	NIG

FORCIBLY (2) [FORCE]

Ge	40:15	For *I was* **f carried off** from the land	1704+1704
Dt	28:31	Your donkey *will* **be f taken** from you	1608

FORCING (2) [FORCE]

Lk	16:16	and everyone *is* **f** his **way** into it.	1041
Ac	7:19	and oppressed our forefathers **by f** them	4472

FORD (2) [FORDED, FORDS]

Ge	32:22	and his eleven sons and crossed the **f** *of*	5044
2Sa	19:18	the **f** to take the king's household over and	6302

FORDED (1) [FORD]

Jos	2:23	**f** the river and came to Joshua son of Nun	6296

FORDS (7) [FORD]

Jos	2: 7	on the road that leads to the **f** of the Jordan.	5045
Jdg	3:28	taking possession of the **f** of the Jordan	5045
	12: 5	the **f** of the Jordan leading to Ephraim;	5045
	12: 6	they seized him and killed him at the **f** *of*	5045
2Sa	15:28	at the **f** *in* the desert until word comes	6302
	17:16	not spend the night at the **f** *in* the desert;	6302
Isa	16: 2	the women of Moab at the **f** of the Arnon.	5045

FOREFATHER (13) [FATHER]

Nu	26:58	(Kohath *was the* **f** of Amram;	3528
Jos	15:13	(Arba *was the* **f** *of* Anak.	3
	19:47	in Leshem and named it Dan after their **f**.)	3
	21:11	(Arba *was the* **f** *of* Anak.	3
Jdg	18:29	They named it Dan after their **f** Dan,	3
1Ki	15: 3	as the heart of David his **f** had been.	3
1Ch	24: 1	for them by their **f** Aaron,	3
Jer	35: 6	because our **f** Jonadab son	3
	35: 8	We have obeyed everything our **f** Jonadab	3
	35:10	have fully obeyed everything our **f** Jonadab commanded us.	3
	35:16	the command their **f** gave them,	3
	35:18	the command of your **f** Jonadab	3
Ro	4: 1	Abraham, our **f**, discovered in this matter?	4635

FOREFATHER'S (1) [FATHER]

Jer	35:14	because they obey their **f** command.	3

FOREFATHERS (98) [FATHER]

Ex	10: 6	nor your **f** have ever seen from	3+3
	13: 5	the land he swore to your **f** to give you,	3
	13:11	as he promised on oath to you and your **f**,	3
Lev	25:41	to his own clan and to the property of his **f**?	3
Nu	11:12	the land you promised on oath to their **f**?	3
	14:23	the land I promised on oath to their **f**.	3
	20:15	Our **f** went down into Egypt,	3
	36: 4	from the tribal inheritance of our **f**."	3
	36: 7	the tribal land inherited from his **f**.	3
Dt	1:35	the good land I swore to give your **f**,	3
	4:31	or forget the covenant with your **f**,	3
	4:37	Because he loved your **f**	3
	6:18	the LORD promised on oath to your **f**,	3
	6:23	the land that he promised on oath to our **f**.	3
	7: 8	to your **f** that he brought you out with	3
	7:12	as he swore to your **f**.	3
	7:13	that he swore to your **f** to give you.	3
	8: 1	the LORD promised on oath to your **f**.	3
	8:18	which he swore to your **f**, as it is today.	3
	10:15	Yet the LORD set his affection on your **f**	3
	10:22	Your **f** who went down into Egypt	3
	11: 9	the LORD swore to your **f** to give to them	3
	11:21	that the LORD swore to give your **f**,	3
	13:17	as he promised on oath to your **f**,	3
	19: 8	as he promised on oath to your **f**,	3
	26: 3	the LORD swore to our **f** to give us."	3
	26:15	as you promised on oath to our **f**,	3
	28:11	in the land he swore to your **f** to give you.	3
	31: 7	the land he swore to their **f** to give them,	3
	31:20	the land I promised on oath to their **f**,	3
Jos	1: 6	the land I swore to their **f** to give them.	3
	21:43	the land he had sworn to give their **f**,	3
	21:44	just as he had sworn to their **f**.	3
	24: 2	'Long ago your **f**,	3
	24:14	Throw away the gods your **f** worshiped	3
	24:15	the gods your **f** served beyond the River,	3
Jdg	2: 1	into the land that I swore to give to your **f**.	3
	2:20	down for their **f** and has not listened to me,	3
	2:22	of the LORD and walk in it as their **f** did."	3
	3: 4	which he had given their **f** through Moses.	3
1Sa	12: 6	and Aaron and brought your **f** up out	3
	12: 8	who brought your **f** out of Egypt	3
1Ki	14:15	from this good land that he gave to their **f**	3
2Ki	19:12	that were destroyed by my **f** deliver them:	3
	21: 8	from the land I gave their **f**,	3
	21:15	from the day their **f** came out of Egypt	3
1Ch	29:15	as were all our **f**.	3
2Ch	33: 8	the land I assigned to your **f**,	3
Ezr	9: 7	From the days of our **f** until now,	3
Ne	9: 9	"You saw the suffering of our **f** in Egypt;	3
	9:16	our **f**, became arrogant and stiff-necked,	3
	9:36	slaves in the land you gave our **f**	3
	13:18	Didn't your **f** do the same things,	3
Ps	78: 3	which he commanded our **f**	3
	78: 8	They would not be like their **f**—	3
Pr	22:28	an ancient boundary stone set up by your **f**.	3
Isa	14:21	to slaughter his sons for the sins of their **f**;	3
	37:12	by my **f** deliver them—	3
Jer	3:18	a northern land to the land I gave your **f** as	3
	7: 7	in the land I gave your **f** for ever and ever.	3
	7:22	For when I brought your **f** out of Egypt	3
	7:25	From the time your **f** left Egypt until now,	3
	7:26	and did more evil than their **f**.'	3
	11: 4	the terms I commanded your **f**	3
	11: 5	I will fulfill the oath I swore to your **f**,	3
	11: 7	the time I brought your **f** up from Egypt	3
	11:10	They have returned to the sins of their **f**,	3+8037
	11:10	the covenant I made with their **f**.	3
	16:15	to the land I gave their **f**.	3
	17:22	as I commanded your **f**.	3
	30: 3	and restore them to the land I gave their **f**	3
	31:32	not be like the covenant I made with their **f**	3
	32:22	to give their **f**,	3
	33:15	with your **f** when I brought them out	3
Eze	36:28	You will live in the land I gave your **f**;	3
	47:14	with uplifted hand to give it to your **f**,	3
Da	11:24	nor his **f** did.	3+3
Joel	1: 2	in your days or in the days of your **f**?	3
Zec	1: 2	"The LORD was very angry with your **f**.	3
	1: 4	Do not be like your **f**,	3
	1: 5	Where are your **f** now?	3
	1: 5	the prophets, overtake your **f**?	3
Mal	3: 7	the time of your **f** you have turned away	3
Mt	23:30	'If we had lived in the days of our **f**,	4252
	23:32	then, the measure of the sin *of* your **f**!	4252

Lk	11:47	and it was your f who killed them.	4252
	11:48	that you approve of what your f did;	4252
Jn	6:31	Our f ate the manna in the desert;	4252
	6:49	Your f ate the manna in the desert,	4252
	6:58	Your f ate manna and died,	4252
Ac	7:19	and oppressed our f by forcing them	4252
	7:44	"Our f had the tabernacle of the Testimony	4252
	28:25	"The Holy Spirit spoke the truth to your f	4252
1Co	10: 1	that our f were all under the cloud and	4252
2Ti	1: 3	I thank God, whom I serve, as my f did,	4591
Heb	1: 1	In the past God spoke to our f through	4252
	8: 9	not be like the covenant I made *with* their f	4252
1Pe	1:18	**handed down** to you from your f,	4261

FOREFINGER (2)

Lev	14:16	dip his right f into the oil in his palm,	720
	14:27	and with his right f sprinkle some of the oil	720

FOREFRONT (KJV) See FRONT, INSIDE, OUTSIDE

FOREHEAD (17) [FOREHEADS]

Ex	13: 9	hand and a reminder **on** your f that	1068+6524
	13:16	hand and a symbol **on** your f that	1068+6524
	28:38	It will be on Aaron's f,	5195
	28:38	on Aaron's f continually so that they will	5195
Lev	13:41	the front of his scalp and has a **bald** f,	1477
	13:42	a reddish-white sore on his bald head or f,	1478
	13:42	on his head or f.	1478
	13:43	on his head or f is reddish-white like	1478
1Sa	17:49	and struck the Philistine on the f.	5195
	17:49	The stone sank into his f,	5195
2Ch	26:19	leprosy broke out on his f.	5195
	26:20	they saw that he had leprosy on his f,	5195
Isa	48: 4	of your neck were iron, your f was bronze.	5195
Eze	3: 9	I will make your f like the hardest stone,	5195
Rev	13:16	a mark on his right hand or on his f,	3587
	14: 9	and receives his mark on the f or on	3587
	17: 5	This title was written on her f:	3587

FOREHEADS (10) [FOREHEAD]

Nu	24:17	He will crush the f *of* Moab,	6991
Dt	6: 8	your hands and bind them **on** your f.	1068+6524
	11:18	your hands and bind them **on** your f.	1068+6524
Jer	48:45	it burns the f *of* Moab,	6991
Eze	9: 4	on the f *of* those who grieve and lament	5195
Rev	7: 3	a seal on the f *of* the servants of our God."	3587
	9: 4	not have the seal of God on their f.	3587
	14: 1	and his Father's name written on their f.	3587
	20: 4	and had not received his mark on their f	3587
	22: 4	and his name will be on their f.	3587

FOREIGN (51) [FOREIGNER, FOREIGNERS, FOREIGNERS']

Ge	35: 2	"Get rid of the f gods you have with you,	5797
	35: 4	So they gave Jacob all the f gods they had	5797
Ex	2:22	"I have become an alien in a f land."	5799
	18: 3	"I have become an alien in a f land,"	5799
Dt	31:16	to the f gods of the land they are entering.	5797
	32:12	no f god was with him.	5797
	32:16	They made him jealous with their f gods	2424
Jos	24:20	you forsake the LORD and serve f gods,	5797
	24:23	"throw away the f gods that are among you	5797
Jdg	10:16	of the f gods among them and served	5797
1Sa	7: 3	then rid yourselves of the f gods and	5797
1Ki	11: 1	Solomon, however, loved many f women besides Pharaoh's daughter—	5799
	11: 8	He did the same for all his f wives,	5799
2Ki	19:24	I have dug wells in f *lands* and drunk	2424
2Ch	14: 3	the f altars and the high places,	5797
	33:15	of the f gods and removed the image from	5797
Ezr	9: 7	and humiliation at the hand of f kings,	824
	10: 2	by marrying f women from the peoples	5799
	10:10	you have married f women.	5799
	10:11	around you and from your f wives."	5799
	10:14	a f woman come at a set time,	5799
	10:17	the men who had married f women.	5799
	10:18	the following had married f women:	5799
	10:44	All these had married f women,	5799
Ne	13: 3	from Israel all who were of f descent.	6850
	13:26	but even he was led into sin by f women.	5799
	13:27	to our God by marrying f women?"	5799
	13:30	the priests and the Levites of everything f,	5797
Ps	44:20	or spread out our hands to a f god,	2424
	81: 9	You shall have no f god among you;	2424
	114: 1	house of Jacob from a people of f **tongue**,	4357
	137: 4	the songs of the LORD while in a f land?	5797
Isa	28:11	Very well then, with f lips	4353
	37:25	I have dug wells in f lands and drunk	NIH
	43:12	I, and not *some* f god among you.	2424
Jer	2:25	I love f gods, and I must go after them.'	2424
	3:13	you have scattered your favors to f gods	2424
	5:19	and served f gods in your own land,	5797
	8:19	with their worthless f idols?"	5797
	19: 4	**made** this a place of f gods;	5796
	25:20	and all the f **people** there;	6850
	25:24	and all the kings of the f **people** who live	6850
Eze	31:12	the most ruthless of f nations cut it down	2424
Da	11:39	with the help of a f god	5797
Zep	1: 8	and all those clad in f clothes.	5799
Hag	2:22	and shatter the power of the f kingdoms.	1580
Mal	2:11	by marrying the daughter of a f god.	5797
Ac	17:18	"He seems to be advocating f gods."	3828

Ac	26:11	I even went to f cities to persecute them.	2032
Heb	11: 9	like a stranger in a f country;	NIG
	11:34	in battle and routed f armies.	259

FOREIGNER (20) [FOREIGN]

Ge	17:12	or bought with money from a f—	1201+5797
	17:27	in his household or bought from a f,	1201+5797
Ex	12:43	"No f is to eat of it.	1201+5797
Lev	22:25	such animals from the hand of a f	1201+5797
Dt	14:21	and he may eat it, or you may sell it to a f.	5799
	15: 3	You may require payment from a f,	5799
	17:15	Do not place a f over you,	5799
	23:20	You may charge a f interest.	5799
Ru	2:10	that you notice me—a f?"	5799
2Sa	15:19	You are a f, an exile from your homeland.	5799
1Ki	8:41	"As for the f who does not belong	5799
	8:43	and do whatever the f asks of you,	5799
2Ch	6:32	"As for the f who does not belong	5799
	6:33	and do whatever the f asks of you,	5799
Isa	56: 3	Let no f who has bound himself	1201+2021+5797
Eze	44: 9	No f uncircumcised in heart and flesh	1201+5797
Lk	17:18	and give praise to God except this f?"	254
Ac	7:29	where he **settled** as a f and had two sons.	4230
1Co	14:11	I am a f to the speaker,	975
	14:11	and he is a f to me.	975

FOREIGNERS (37) [FOREIGN]

Ge	31:15	Does he not regard us as f?	5799
Ex	21: 8	He has no right to sell her to f,	5799+6639
Dt	29:22	and f who come from distant lands will see	5799
2Sa	22:45	and f come cringing to me;	1201+5797
Ne	9: 2	Those of Israelite descent had separated themselves from all f.	1201+5797
Ps	18:44	f cringe before me.	1201+5797
	144: 7	the mighty waters, from the hands of f	1201+5797
	144:11	rescue me from the hands of f	1201+5797
Isa	1: 7	your fields are being stripped by f right	2424
	25: 5	You silence the uproar of f,	2424
	56: 6	f who bind themselves to the LORD to serve him,	1201+2021+5797
	60:10	"F will rebuild your walls,	1201+5797
	61: 5	f will work your fields and vineyards.	1201+5797
	62: 8	never again will f drink the new wine	1201+5797
Jer	5:19	you will serve f in a land not your own.'	2424
	30: 8	no longer will f enslave them.	2424
	50:37	against her horses and chariots and all the f	6850
	51: 2	I will send f to Babylon to winnow her and	2424
	51:51	because f have entered the holy places of	2424
La	5: 2	our homes to f.	5799
Eze	7:21	as plunder to f and as loot to the wicked of	2424
	11: 9	over to f and inflict punishment on you.	2424
	28: 7	to bring f against you, the most ruthless	2424
	28:10	of the uncircumcised at the hands of f.	2424
	30:12	by the hand of f I will lay waste the land	2424
	44: 7	you brought f uncircumcised in heart	1201+5797
	44: 9	the f who live among the Israelites.	1201+5797
Hos	7: 9	F sap his strength,	2424
	8: 7	f would swallow it up.	2424
Joel	3:17	never again will f invade her.	2424
Ob	1:11	and f entered his gates and cast lots	5799
Zec	9: 6	F will occupy Ashdod,	4927
Mt	27: 7	the potter's field as a burial place *for* f.	3828
Ac	17:21	f who lived there spent their time doing nothing	3828
1Co	14:21	the lips *of* f I will speak to this people,	2283
Eph	2:12	excluded from citizenship in Israel and f to	3828
	2:19	you are no longer f and aliens,	3828

FOREIGNERS' (1) [FOREIGN]

Isa	25: 2	the f' stronghold a city no more;	2424

FOREKNEW (2) [KNOW]

Ro	8:29	For those God f he also predestined to	4589
	11: 2	God did not reject his people, whom *he* f.	4589

FOREKNOW (KJV) See FOREKNEW

FOREKNOWLEDGE (2) [KNOW]

Ac	2:23	over to you *by* God's set purpose and f;	4590
1Pe	1: 2	who have been chosen according to the f	4590

FOREMAN (3) [FOREMEN]

Ru	2: 5	Boaz asked the f of his harvesters,	5853+5893
	2: 6	The f replied, "She is the Moabitess	5853+5893
Mt	20: 8	the owner of the vineyard said *to* his f,	2208

FOREMEN (8) [FOREMAN]

Ex	5: 6	to the slave drivers and f in charge of	8853
	5:10	and the f went out and said to the people,	8853
	5:14	The Israelite f appointed by Pharaoh's	8853
	5:15	Israelite f went and appealed to Pharaoh:	8853
	5:19	The Israelite f realized they were in trouble	8853
1Ki	5:16	thirty-three hundred f who supervised	5893+8569
2Ch	2: 2	and thirty-six hundred as f over them.	5904
	2:18	f over them to keep the people working.	5904

FOREMOST (2) [MOST]

Jer	31: 7	shout for the f *of* the nations.	8031
Am	6: 1	you notable men of the f nation,	8040

FOREORDAINED (KJV) See CHOSEN

FOREPART (KJV) See BOW, FRONT, INNER

FORERUNNER (KJV) See WENT BEFORE

FORESAIL (1) [SAIL]

Ac	27:40	the f to the wind and made for the beach.	784

FORESAW (1) [FORESEE]

Gal	3: 8	The Scripture f that God would justify	4632

FORESEE (1) [FORESAW, FORESIGHT]

Isa	47:11	catastrophe *you* cannot f will suddenly come	3359

FORESEETH (KJV) See SEES

FORESHIP (KJV) See BOW

FORESIGHT (1) [FORESEE]

Ac	24: 2	of peace under you, and your f has brought	4630

FORESKIN (1) [FORESKINS]

Ex	4:25	Zipporah took a flint knife, cut off her son's f	6889

FORESKINS (3) [FORESKIN]

1Sa	18:25	for the bride than a hundred Philistine f,	6889
	18:27	He brought their f and presented	6889
2Sa	3:14	for the price of a hundred Philistine f."	6889

FOREST (41) [FORESTED, FORESTS]

Dt	19: 5	a man may go into the f with his neighbor	3623
Jos	17:15	the f and clear land for yourselves there in	3623
1Sa	22: 5	So David left and went to the f of Hereth.	3623
2Sa	18: 6	the battle took place in the f of Ephraim.	3623
	18: 8	and the f claimed more lives that day than	3623
	18:17	a big pit in the f and piled up a large heap	3623
1Ki	7: 2	Palace of the F of Lebanon a hundred cubits	3623
	10:17	The king put them in the Palace of the F	3623
	10:21	Palace of the F of Lebanon were pure gold.	3623
1Ch	16:33	Then the trees of the f will sing,	3623
2Ch	9:16	The king put them in the Palace of the F	3623
	9:20	Palace of the F of Lebanon were pure gold.	3623
Ne	2: 8	keeper of the king's f,	7236
Ps	50:10	for every animal of the f is mine,	3623
	80:13	Boars from the f ravage it and the creatures	3623
	83:14	the f or a flame sets the mountains ablaze,	3623
	96:12	Then all the trees of the f will sing for joy;	3623
	104:20	and all the beasts of the f prowl.	3623
SS	2: 3	among the trees of the f is my lover among	3623
Isa	7: 2	as the trees of the f are shaken by the wind.	3623
	9:18	it sets the f thickets ablaze,	3623
	10:34	He will cut down the f thickets with an ax;	3623
	22: 8	to the weapons in the Palace of the F;	3623
	29:17	and the fertile field seem like a f?	3623
	32:15	and the fertile field seems like a f.	3623
	32:19	the f and the city is leveled completely,	3623
	44:14	He let it grow among the trees of the f,	3623
	56: 9	come and devour, all you beasts of the f!	3623
Jer	5: 6	a lion from the f will attack them,	3623
	10: 3	they cut a tree out of the f,	3623
	12: 8	to me like a lion in the f.	3623
	46:23	They will chop down her f,"	3623
Eze	15: 2	of a branch on any of the trees in the f?	3623
	15: 6	the vine among the trees of the f as fuel for	3623
	20:46	the south and prophesy against the f of	3623
	20:47	Say to the southern f:	3623
	31: 3	beautiful branches overshadowing the f;	3091
Mic	5: 8	like a lion among the beasts of the f,	3623
	7:14	which lives by itself in a f,	3623
Zec	11: 2	the dense f has been cut down!	3623
Jas	3: 5	Consider what a great f is set on fire by	5627

FORESTED (1) [FOREST]

Jos	17:18	but the f hill country as well.	3623

FORESTS (9) [FOREST]

2Ki	19:23	the **finest** of its f.	3623+4149
Ps	29: 9	the oaks and strips the f bare.	3623
Isa	10:18	The splendor of his f,	3623
	10:19	the remaining trees of his f will be so few	3623
	37:24	the **finest** of its f.	3623+4149
	44:23	you mountains, you f and all your trees,	3623
Jer	21:14	in your f that will consume everything	3623
Eze	34:25	in the desert and sleep in the f in safety.	3623
	39:10	from the fields or cut it from the f,	3623

FORETELL (2) [FORETELLS, FORETOLD]

Isa	44: 7	yes, *let him* f what will come.	5583
	44: 8	Did I not proclaim this and f it long ago?	5583

FORETELLS (1) [FORETELL]

Dt	13: 1	If a prophet, or *one who* f **by dreams**,	2706+2731

FORETOLD (12) [FORETELL]

2Ki	7:17	the man of God *had* f when the king came	1819
	23:16	by the man of God who f these things.	7924
Ps	105:19	till **what** he f came to pass,	1821
Isa	41:26	No one told of this, no *one* f it,	9048
	43: 9	Which of them f this and proclaimed to us	5583
	45:21	Who f this long ago,	9048
	48: 3	*I* f the former things long ago,	5583
	48:14	Which of [the idols] *has* f these things?	5583
	52: 6	that day they will know that it is I who f it.	1819
Ac	3:18	how God fulfilled what *he had* f through all	4615
	3:24	as many as have spoken, *have* f these days.	2859
Jude	1:17	the apostles of our Lord Jesus Christ f.	4625

FOREVER (290) [EVER]

Ge	3:22	the tree of life and eat, and live f."	4200+6409
	6: 3	My Spirit will not contend with man f,	4200+6409
	13:15	to you and to your offspring	6330+6409
Ex	3:15	This is my name f,	4200+6409
	31:17	a sign between me and the Israelites f,	4200+6409
	32:13	and it will be their inheritance f.'"	4200+6409
Dt	5:29	with them and their children f!	4200+6409
	13:16	It is to remain a ruin f, never to be rebuilt.	6409
	28:46	wonder to you and your descendants f.	6330+6409
	29:29	to us and to our children f,	6330+6409
	32:40	As surely as I live f,	4200+6409
Jos	4: 7	a memorial to the people of Israel f."	6330+6409
	14: 9	and that of your children f,	6330+6409
1Sa	2:30	and your father's house would minister before me f.'	6330+6409
	3:13	that I would judge his family f because	6330+6409
	20:23	the LORD is witness between you and me f."	6330+6409
	20:42	descendants and my descendants f.'"	6330+6409
	27:12	the Israelites, that he will be my servant f."	6409
2Sa	2:26	"Must the sword devour f?	4200+5905
	3:28	"I and my kingdom are f innocent	6330+6409
	7:13	I will establish the throne of his kingdom f.	4200+6409
	7:16	your kingdom will endure f before me;	6330+6409
	7:16	your throne will be established f.'"	6330+6409
	7:24	as your very own f,	6330+6409
	7:25	keep f the promise you have made	4200+6409
	7:26	so that your name will be great f.	4200+6409
	7:29	that it may continue f in your sight;	4200+6409
	7:29	house of your servant will be blessed f	4200+6409
	22:51	to David and his descendants f."	6330+6409
1Ki	1:31	"May my lord King David live f!"	4200+6409
	2:33	blood rest on the head of Joab and his descendants f.	4200+6409
	2:33	may there be the LORD's peace f."	6330+6409
	2:45	before the LORD f."	6330+6409
	8:13	a place for you to dwell f."	6409
	9: 3	by putting my Name there f.	4200+6409
	9: 5	I will establish your royal throne over Israel f,	4200+6409
	11:39	because of this, but not f.'"	2021+3427+3972
2Ki	5:27	to you and to your descendants f."	4200+6409
	8:19	a lamp for David and his descendants f.	2021+3427+3972
	21: 7	I will put my Name f.	4200+6409
1Ch	15: 2	and to minister before him f."	6330+6409
	16:15	He remembers his covenant f,	4200+6409
	16:34	his love endures f.	4200+6409
	16:41	"for his love endures f."	4200+6409
	17:12	and I will establish his throne f.	6330+6409
	17:14	my house and my kingdom f;	2021+6330+6409
	17:14	his throne will be established f.'"	6330+6409
	17:22	You made your people Israel your very own f,	6330+6409
	17:23	and his house be established f.	6330+6409
	17:24	and that your name will be great f.	6330+6409
	17:27	that it may continue f in your sight;	4200+6409
	17:27	blessed it, and it will be blessed f."	4200+6409
	22:10	throne of his kingdom over Israel f.'	6330+6409
	23:13	he and his descendants f,	6330+6409
	23:13	to pronounce blessings in his name f.	6330+6409
	23:25	come to dwell in Jerusalem f,	4200+6330+6409
	28: 4	to be king over Israel f.	6330+6409
	28: 7	I will establish his kingdom f	4200+6330+6409
	28: 8	an inheritance to your descendants f.	6330+6409
	28: 9	if you forsake him, he will reject you f	4200+6329
	29:18	in the hearts of your people f,	4200+6409
2Ch	5:13	his love endures f."	4200+6409
	6: 2	a place for you to dwell f."	6409
	7: 3	his love endures f."	4200+6409
	7: 6	saying, "His love endures f."	4200+6409
	7:16	so that my Name may be there f.	6330+6409
	9: 8	Israel and his desire to uphold them f,	4200+6409
	13: 5	Israel to David and his descendants f	4200+6409
	20: 7	give it to the descendants of Abraham your friend?	4200+6409
	20:21	for his love endures f."	4200+6409
	21: 7	a lamp for him and his descendants f.	2021+3427+3972
	30: 8	which he has consecrated f.	4200+6409
	33: 4	My Name will remain in Jerusalem f.	4200+6409
	33: 7	I will put my Name f. .	4200+6409
Ezr	3:11	his love to Israel endures f."	4200+6409
Ne	2: 3	"May the king live f!"	4200+6409
Job	4:20	unnoticed, they perish f.	4200+5905
	7:16	I despise my life; I would not live f.	4200+6409
	19:24	or engraved in rock f!	4200+6329
	20: 7	he will perish f, like his own dung;	4200+5905
	23: 7	I would be delivered f from my judge.	4200+5905

Job	36: 7	with kings and exalts them f.	4200+5905
Ps	9: 7	The LORD reigns f;	4200+6409
	12: 7	and protect us from such people f.	4200+6409
	13: 1	Will you forget me f?	5905
	18:50	to David and his descendants f.	6330+6409
	19: 9	The fear of the LORD is pure, enduring f.	4200+6329
	22:26	may your hearts live f!	4200+6329
	23: 6	I will dwell in the house of the LORD.	802+3427+4200
	28: 9	their shepherd and carry them f.	2021+6330+6409
	29:10	the LORD is enthroned as King f.	4200+6409
	30:12	I will give you thanks f.	4200+6409
	33:11	But the plans of the LORD stand firm f,	4200+6409
	37:18	and their inheritance will endure f.	4200+6409
	37:27	then you will dwell in the land f.	4200+6409
	37:28	They will be protected f,	4200+6409
	37:29	the land and dwell in it f.	4200+6329
	41:12	and set me in your presence f.	4200+6409
	44: 8	and we will praise your name f.	4200+6409
	44:23	Do not reject us f.	4200+5905
	45: 2	since God has blessed you f.	4200+6409
	48: 8	God makes her secure f.	6330+6409
	49: 9	he should live on f and not see decay.	4200+5905
	49:11	Their tombs will remain their houses f,	4200+6409
	52: 9	I will praise you f for what you have done;	4200+6409
	55:19	God, who is enthroned f,	7710
	61: 4	in your tent f and take refuge in the shelter	6409
	61: 7	May he be enthroned in God's presence f;	6409
	66: 7	He rules f by his power,	6409
	68:16	where the LORD himself will dwell f?	4200+5905
	69:23	and their backs be bent f.	9458
	72:17	May his name endure f;	4200+6409
	72:19	Praise be to his glorious name f;	4200+6409
	73:26	strength of my heart and my portion f.	4200+6409
	74: 1	Why have you rejected us f, O God?	4200+5905
	74:10	Will the foe revile your name f?	4200+5905
	74:19	the lives of your afflicted people f.	4200+5905
	75: 9	As for me, I will declare this f;	4200+6409
	77: 7	"Will the Lord reject f?	4200+6409
	77: 8	Has his unfailing love vanished f?	4200+5905
	78:69	like the earth that he established f.	4200+6409
	79: 5	Will you be angry f?	4200+5905
	79:13	will praise you f;	4200+6409
	81:15	and their punishment would last f.	4200+6409
	85: 5	Will you be angry with us f?	4200+6409
	86:12	I will glorify your name f.	4200+6409
	89: 1	I will sing of the LORD's great love f;	6409
	89: 2	I will declare that your love stands firm f,	6409
	89: 4	'I will establish your line f	6330+6409
	89:28	I will maintain my love to him f,	4200+6409
	89:29	I will establish his line f,	4200+6329
	89:36	that his line will continue f	4200+6409
	89:37	it will be established f like the moon,	6409
	89:46	Will you hide yourself f?	4200+5905
	89:52	Praise be to the LORD f!	4200+6409
	92: 7	they will be f destroyed.	6329+6330
	92: 8	But you, O LORD, are exalted f.	4200+6409
	100: 5	LORD is good and his love endures f;	4200+6409
	102:12	But you, O LORD, sit enthroned f;	4200+6409
	103: 9	nor will he harbor his anger f;	4200+6409
	104:31	May the glory of the LORD endure f;	4200+6409
	105: 8	He remembers his covenant f,	4200+6409
	106: 1	his love endures f.	4200+6409
	107: 1	his love endures f.	4200+6409
	109:19	like a belt tied f around him.	9458
	110: 4	"You are a priest f,	4200+6409
	111: 3	and his righteousness endures f.	4200+6329
	111: 5	he remembers his covenant f.	4200+6409
	111: 9	he ordained his covenant f—	4200+6409
	112: 3	and his righteousness endures f.	4200+6329
	112: 6	a righteous man will be remembered f.	6409
	112: 9	his righteousness endures f;	4200+6329
	117: 2	the faithfulness of the LORD endures f.	4200+6409
	118: 1	his love endures f.	4200+6409
	118: 2	Let Israel say: "His love endures f."	4200+6409
	118: 3	"His love endures f."	4200+6409
	118: 4	"His love endures f."	4200+6409
	118:29	his love endures f.	4200+6409
	119:111	Your statutes are my heritage f;	4200+6409
	119:144	Your statutes are f right;	4200+6409
	119:152	that you established them to last f.	4200+6409
	125: 1	which cannot be shaken but endures f.	4200+6409
	135:13	Your name, O LORD, endures f,	4200+6409
	136: 1	His love endures f.	4200+6409
	136: 2	His love endures f.	4200+6409
	136: 2	His love endures f.	4200+6409
	136: 3	His love endures f.	4200+6409
	136: 4	His love endures f.	4200+6409
	136: 5	His love endures f.	4200+6409
	136: 6	His love endures f.	4200+6409
	136: 7	His love endures f.	4200+6409
	136: 8	His love endures f.	4200+6409
	136: 9	His love endures f.	4200+6409
	136:10	His love endures f.	4200+6409
	136:11	His love endures f.	4200+6409
	136:12	His love endures f.	4200+6409
	136:13	His love endures f.	4200+6409
	136:14	His love endures f.	4200+6409
	136:15	His love endures f.	4200+6409
	136:16	His love endures f.	4200+6409
	136:17	His love endures f.	4200+6409
	136:18	His love endures f.	4200+6409
	136:19	His love endures f.	4200+6409
	136:20	His love endures f.	4200+6409
	136:21	His love endures f.	4200+6409
	136:22	His love endures f.	4200+6409

Ps	136:23	His love endures f.	4200+6409
	136:24	His love endures f.	4200+6409
	136:25	His love endures f.	4200+6409
	136:26	His love endures f.	4200+6409
	138: 8	your love, O LORD, endures f—	4200+6409
	146: 6	the LORD, who remains faithful f.	4200+6409
	146:10	The LORD reigns f, your God, O Zion,	4200+6409
Pr	6:21	Bind them upon your heart f;	9458
	10:25	but the righteous stand firm f.	6409
	12:19	Truthful lips endure f,	4200+6329
	21:28	listens to him will be destroyed f.	4200+5905
	27:24	for riches do not endure f,	4200+6409
Ecc	1: 4	but the earth remains f.	4200+6409
	3:14	everything God does will endure f;	4200+6409
Isa	9: 7	and righteousness from that time on and f.	6330+6409
	25: 8	he will swallow up death f.	4200+5905
	26: 4	Trust in the LORD f, for the LORD,	6329+6330
	28:28	so one does not go on threshing it f.	4200+5905
	32:14	watchtower will become a wasteland f,	6330+6409
	32:17	be quietness and confidence f.	6330+6409
	34:10	its smoke will rise f.	4200+6409
	34:17	They will possess it f and dwell there	6330+6409
	40: 8	but the word of our God stands f."	4200+6409
	47: 7	You said, 'I will continue f—	4200+6409
	51: 6	But my salvation will last f,	4200+6409
	51: 8	But my righteousness will last f,	4200+6409
	57:15	he who lives f, whose name is holy:	6329
	57:16	I will not accuse f,	6330+6409
	59:21	from this time on and f,"	6330+6409
	60:21	and they will possess the land f.	4200+6409
	64: 9	do not remember our sins f.	4200+6329
	65:18	and rejoice f in what I will create,	6329+6330
Jer	3: 5	Will your wrath continue f?'	4200+5905
	3:12	the LORD, 'I will not be angry f.	4200+6409
	17: 4	and it will burn f."	6330+6409
	17:25	and this city will be inhabited f.	4200+6409
	20:17	her womb enlarged f.	6409
	25:12	"and will make it desolate f.	6409
	33:11	his love endures f."	4200+6409
	49:13	and all its towns will be in ruins."	6409
	49:33	a desolate place f.	6330+6409
	51:26	for you will be desolate f,"	6409
	51:39	then sleep f and not awake,"	6409
	51:57	they will sleep f and not awake,"	6409
	51:62	it will be desolate f.'	6409
La	3:31	For men are not cast off by the Lord f.	4200+6409
	5:19	You, O LORD, reign f;	4200+6409
Eze	35: 9	I will make you desolate f;	6409
	37:25	children's children will live there f,	6330+6409
	37:25	David my servant will be their prince f	4200+6409
	37:26	I will put my sanctuary among them f.	4200+6409
	37:28	when my sanctuary is among them f.'	4200+6409
	43: 7	I will live among the Israelites f.	4200+6409
	43: 9	and I will live among them f.	4200+6409
Da	2: 4	the king in Aramaic, "O king, live f!	10378+10550
	2:44	but it will itself endure	10002+10378+10550
	3: 9	Nebuchadnezzar, "O king, live f!	10378+10550
	4:34	I honored and glorified him who lives f.	10002+10550
	5:10	"O king, live f!"	10378+10550
	6: 6	"O King Darius, live f!	10378+10550
	6:21	Daniel answered, "O king, live f!	10378+10550
	6:26	"For he is the living God and he endures f;	10378+10550
	7:18	the kingdom and will possess it f—	10002+10527+10550
	7:26	be taken away and completely destroyed f.	10002+10509+10527
	12: 7	and I heard him swear by him who lives f,	6409
Hos	2:19	I will betroth you to me f;	4200+6409
Joel	3:20	Judah will be inhabited f and	4200+6409
Ob	1:10	you will be destroyed f.	4200+6409
Jnh	2: 6	the earth beneath barred me in f.	4200+6409
Mic	2: 9	from their children f.	4200+6409
	4: 7	in Mount Zion from that day and f.	6330+6409
	7:18	You do not stay angry f but delight to show mercy.	4200+6329
Zep	2: 9	weeds and salt pits, a wasteland f.	6330+6409
Zec	1: 5	And the prophets, do they live f?	6330+6409
Lk	1:33	he will reign over the house of Jacob f;	172+1650+3836
	1:55	Abraham and his descendants f,	172+1650+3836
Jn	6:51	If anyone eats of this bread, he will live f.	172+1650+3836
	6:58	but he who feeds on this bread will live f."	172+1650+3836
	8:35	but a son belongs to it f.	172+1650+3836
	12:34	that the Christ will remain f,	172+1650+3836
	14:16	to be with you f—	172+1650+3836
Ro	1:25	who is f praised.	172+1650+3836
	9: 5	who is God over all, f praised!	172+1650+3836
	11:10	and their backs be bent f."	1328+4246
	11:36	To him be the glory f!	172+1650+3836
	16:27	be glory f through Jesus Christ!	172+1650+3836
1Co	9:25	we do it to get a crown that will last f.	915
2Co	9: 9	his righteousness endures f."	172+1650+3836
	11:31	who is to be praised f,	172+1650+3836
1Th	4:17	And so we will be with the Lord f.	4121
1Ti	6:16	To him be honor and might f.	173
Heb	5: 6	"You are a priest f,	172+1650+3836
	6:20	He has become a high priest f,	172+1650+3836
	7: 3	like the Son of God he remains a priest f.	1457+1650+3836
	7:17	it is declared: "You are a priest f,	172+1650+3836
	7:21	'You are a priest f.'"	172+1650+3836
	7:24	but because Jesus lives f,	172+1650+3836

Heb 7:28 who has been made perfect f. 172+1650+3836
     10:14 by one sacrifice he has made perfect f those
           who are being made holy. 1457+1650+3836
     13: 8 Jesus Christ is the same yesterday and
           today and f. 172+1650+3836
1Pe 1:25 but the word of the Lord stands f. 172+1650+3836
2Pe 3:18 To him be glory both now and f! 172+1650+2465
1Jn 2:17 the man who does the will of God lives f.
            172+1650+3836
2Jn 1: 2 the truth, which lives in us and will be with
         us f: 172+1650+3836
Jude 1:13 for whom blackest darkness has been
           reserved f. 172+1650

FOREVERMORE (7) [EVER]

Ps 113: 2 the LORD be praised, both now and f. 6330+6409
  115:18 extol the LORD, both now and f. 6330+6409
  121: 8 coming and going both now and f. 6330+6409
  125: 2 surrounds his people both now and f. 6330+6409
  131: 3 in the LORD both now and f. 6330+6409
  133: 3 For there the LORD bestows his blessing,
          even life f. 2021+6330+6409
Jude 1:25 before all ages, now and f! 172+1650+3836+4246

FOREWARN (KJV) See SHOW

FORFEIT (4) [FORFEITING, FORFEITS]

Ezr 10: 8 within three days would f all his property, 3049
Jnh 2: 8 to worthless idols f the grace that could 6440
Mk 8:36 gain the whole world, yet f his soul? 2423
Lk 9:25 and yet lose or f his very self? 2423

FORFEITING (1) [FORFEIT]

Hab 2:10 shaming your own house and f your life. 2627

FORFEITS (2) [FORFEIT]

Pr 20: 2 he who angers him f his life. 2627
Mt 16:26 gains the whole world, yet f his soul? 2423

FORGAT (KJV) See FORGOT

FORGAVE (7) [FORGIVE]

Ps 32: 5 and you f the guilt of my sin. 5951
   65: 3 you f our transgressions. 4105
  78:38 he f their iniquities and did 4105
  85: 2 You f the iniquity of your people 5951
Eph 4:32 just as in Christ God f you. 5919
Col 2:13 He f us all our sins, 5919
    3:13 Forgive as the Lord f you. 5919

FORGED (2) [FORGES]

Ge 4:22 who f all kinds of tools out of bronze 4323
Isa 54:17 no weapon f against you will prevail, 3670

FORGES (2) [FORGED]

Isa 44:12 he f it with the might of his arm. 7188
  54:16 into flame and f a weapon fit for its work. 3655

FORGET (58) [FORGETS, FORGETTING, FORGOT, FORGOTTEN]

Ge 41:51 because God has made me f all my trouble 5960
Dt 4: 9 not f the things your eyes have seen 8894
   4:23 to f the covenant of the LORD your God 8894
   4:31 or f the covenant with your forefathers, 8894
   6:12 be careful that you do not f the LORD, 8894
   8:11 that you do not f the LORD your God, 8894
   8:14 and you will f the LORD your God, 8894
   8:19 If you ever f the LORD your God 8894+8894
   9: 7 and never f how you provoked 8894
  25:19 Do not f! 8894
1Sa 1:11 and not f your servant but give her a son, 8894
2Ki 17:38 not f the covenant I have made with you, 8894
Job 8:13 Such is the destiny of all who f God; 8894
   9:27 If I say, 'I will f my complaint, 8894
  11:16 You will surely f your trouble, 8894
Ps 9:17 all the nations that f God. 8895
  10:12 Do not f the helpless. 8894
  13: 1 Will you f me forever? 8894
  44:24 and f our misery and oppression? 8894
  45:10 F your people and your father's house. 8894
  50:22 "Consider this, you who f God, 8894
  59:11 O Lord our shield, or my people will f. 8894
  74:19 do not f the lives 8894
  78: 7 in God and would not f his deeds 8894
  102: 4 I f to eat my food. 8894
  103: 2 O my soul, and f not all his benefits— 8894
  119:61 I will not f your law. 8894
  119:83 I do not f your decrees. 8894
  119:93 I will never f your precepts, 8894
 119:109 I will not f your law. 8894
 119:141 I do not f your precepts. 8894
  137: 5 If I f you, O Jerusalem, 8894
  137: 5 may my right hand f [its skill]. 8894
Pr 3: 1 My son, do not f my teaching, 8894
  4: 5 do not f my words or swerve from them, 8894
  31: 5 lest they drink and f what the law decrees, 8894
  31: 7 let them drink and f their poverty 8894
Isa 43:18 "F the former things; 440+2349
  44:21 O Israel, I will not f you. 5960
  49:15 "Can a mother f the baby at her breast 8894

Isa 49:15 Though she may f, I will not forget you! 8894
  49:15 Though she may forget, I will not f you! 8894
  51:13 that you f the LORD your Maker, 8894
  54: 4 You will f the shame of your youth 8894
  65:11 the LORD and f my holy mountain, 8895
Jer 2:32 Does a maiden f her jewelry, 8894
  23:27 dreams they tell one another will make my
          people f my name, 8894
  23:39 I will surely f you and cast you out 5960+5960
La 2: 6 LORD has made Zion f her appointed feasts 8894
  5:20 Why do you always f us? 8894
Eze 39:26 They will f their shame and all 5960
Am 8: 7 "I will never f anything they have done. 8894
Mic 6:10 Am I still to f, O wicked house, 5960
Heb 6:10 he will not f your work and 2140
  13: 2 Do not f to entertain strangers, 2140
  13:16 not f to do good and to share with others, 2140
2Pe 3: 5 But they deliberately f that long ago 3291
  3: 8 But do not f this one thing, dear friends: 3291

FORGETS (4) [FORGET]

Ge 27:45 with you and f what you did to him, 8894
Job 24:20 womb f them, the worm feasts on them; 8894
Jn 16:21 her baby is born she f the anguish 3648+4033
Jas 1:24 and immediately f what he looks like. 2140

FORGETTING (2) [FORGET]

Php 3:13 F what is behind and straining 2140
Jas 1:25 not f what he has heard, but doing it— 2144

FORGIVE (74) [FORGAVE, FORGIVEN, FORGIVENESS, FORGIVES, FORGIVING]

Ge 50:17 I ask you to f your brothers the sins and 5951
  50:17 Now please f the sins of the servants of 5951
Ex 10:17 Now f my sin once more and pray to 5951
  23:21 he will not f your rebellion, 5951
  32:32 But now, please f their sin— 5951
  34: 9 f our wickedness and our sin, 6142
Nu 14:19 f the sin of these people, 6142
Dt 29:20 The LORD will never be willing to f him; 6142
Jos 24:19 He will not f your rebellion and your sins. 5951
1Sa 15:25 f my sin and come back with me, 5951
  25:28 Please f your servant's offense. 5951
1Ki 8:30 your dwelling place, and when you hear, f. 6142
  8:34 then hear from heaven and f the sin 6142
  8:36 from heaven and f the sin of your servants, 6142
  8:39 your dwelling place. F and act; 6142
  8:50 And f your people, who have sinned 6142
  8:50 f all the offenses they have committed NIH
2Ki 5:18 But may the LORD f your servant 6142
  5:18 may the LORD f your servant for this." 6142
  24: 4 and the LORD was not willing to f. 6142
2Ch 6:21 and when you hear, f. 6142
  6:25 then hear from heaven and f the sin 6142
  6:27 from heaven and f the sin of your servants, 6142
  6:30 F, and deal with each man according 6142
  6:39 And f your people, 6142
  7:14 from heaven and will f their sin 6142
Job 7:21 not pardon my offenses and f my sins? 6296
Ps 19:12 F my hidden faults. 5927
  25:11 O Lord, f my iniquity, though it is great. 6142
  79: 9 and f our sins for your name's sake. 4105
Isa 2: 9 do not f them. 5951
Jer 5: 1 I will f this city. 6142
  5: 7 "Why should I f you? 6142
  18:23 Do not f their crimes or blot out their sins 4105
  31:34 "For I will f their wickedness 6142
  33: 8 and will f all their sins of rebellion 6142
  36: 3 I will f their wickedness and their sin." 6142
  50:20 for I will f the remnant I spare. 6142
Da 9:19 O Lord, listen! O Lord, f! 6142
Hos 1: 6 that I should at all them. 5951+5951
  14: 2 "F all our sins and receive us graciously, 5951
Am 7: 2 I cried out, "Sovereign LORD, f! 6142
Mt 6:12 F us our debts, as we also have forgiven 918
  6:14 if you f men when they sin against you, 918
  6:14 your heavenly Father will also f you. 918
  6:15 But if you do not f men their sins, 918
  6:15 your Father will not f your sins. 918
  9: 6 Son of Man has authority on earth to f sins 918
  18:21 how many times shall I f my brother 918
  18:35 of you unless you f your brother 918
Mk 2: 7 Who can f sins but God alone?" 918
  2:10 Son of Man has authority on earth to f sins 918
  11:25 if you hold anything against anyone, f him, 918
  11:25 your Father in heaven may f you your sins." 918
Lk 5:21 Who can f sins but God alone?" 918
  5:24 Son of Man has authority on earth to f sins 918
  6:37 F, and you will be forgiven. 668
  11: 4 F us our sins, for we also forgive 918
  11: 4 for we also f everyone who sins against us. 918
  17: 3 rebuke him, and if he repents, f him. 918
  17: 4 to you and says, 'I repent,' f him." 918
  23:34 Jesus said, "Father, f them, 918
Jn 20:23 If you f anyone his sins, they are forgiven; 918
  20:23 if you do not f them, 3195
Ac 8:22 Perhaps he will f you for having such 918
2Co 2: 7 instead, you ought to f and comfort him, 5919
  2:10 If you f anyone, I also forgive him. 5919
  2:10 If you forgive anyone, I also f him. NIG
  2:10 if there was anything to f— 5919
  12:13 F me this wrong! 5919
Col 3:13 and f whatever grievances you may have 5919
  3:13 F as the Lord forgave you. NIG

Heb 8:12 For I will f their wickedness 1639+2664
1Jn 1: 9 and will f us our sins and purify us 918

FORGIVEN (45) [FORGIVE]

Lev 4:20 and they will be f. 6142
  4:26 and he will be f. 6142
  4:31 and he will be f. 6142
  4:35 and he will be f. 6142
  5:10 and he will be f. 6142
  5:13 and he will be f. 6142
  5:16 and he will be f. 6142
  5:18 and he will be f. 6142
  6: 7 and he will be f for any 6142
  19:22 and his sin will be f. 6142
Nu 14:20 The LORD replied, "I have f them, 6142
  15:25 and they will be f. 6142
  15:26 the aliens living among them will be f, 6142
  15:28 he will be f. 6142
Ps 32: 1 Blessed is he whose transgressions are f, 5951
Isa 33:24 the sins of those who dwell there will be f. 5951
La 3:42 and rebelled and you have not f. 6142
Mt 6:12 as we also have f our debtors. 918
  9: 2 "Take heart, son; your sins are f." 918
  9: 5 Which is easier: to say, 'Your sins are f,' 918
  12:31 every sin and blasphemy will be f men, 918
  12:31 blasphemy against the Spirit will not be f. 918
  12:32 a word against the Son of Man will be f, 918
  12:32 against the Holy Spirit will not be f. 918
Mk 2: 5 "Son, your sins are f." 918
  2: 9 to say to the paralytic, 'Your sins are f,' 918
  3:28 and blasphemies of men will be f them. 918
  3:29 against the Holy Spirit will never be f; 912+2400
  4:12 otherwise they might turn and be f!' " 918
Lk 5:20 he said, "Friend, your sins are f." 918
  5:23 Which is easier: to say, 'Your sins are f,' 918
  7:47 I tell you, her many sins have been f— 918
  7:47 But he who has been f little loves little." 918
  7:48 Then Jesus said to her, "Your sins are f." 918
  12:10 a word against the Son of Man will be f, 918
  12:10 against the Holy Spirit will not be f. 918
Jn 20:23 If you forgive anyone his sins, they are f; 918
  20:23 if you do not forgive them, they are not f." 3195
Ro 4: 7 Blessed are they whose transgressions are f, 5919
2Co 2:10 And what I have f— 5919
  2:10 I have f in the sight of Christ for your sake, NIG
Heb 10:18 And where these have been f, 912
Jas 5:15 If he has sinned, he will be f. 918
1Jn 2:12 because your sins have been f on account 918

FORGIVENESS (14) [FORGIVE]

Ps 130: 4 But with you there is f; 6145
Mt 26:28 which is poured out for many for the f 912
Mk 1: 4 a baptism of repentance for the f of sins. 912
Lk 1:77 the knowledge of salvation through the f 912
  3: 3 preaching a baptism of repentance for the f 912
  24:47 and f of sins will be preached in his name 912
Ac 2:38 of Jesus Christ for the f of your sins. 912
  5:31 that he might give repentance and f of sins 912
  10:43 in him receives f of sins 912
  13:38 I want you to know that through Jesus the f 912
  26:18 that they may receive f of sins and a place 912
Eph 1: 7 redemption through his blood, the f of sins, 912
Col 1:14 in whom we have redemption, the f of sins. 912
Heb 9:22 without the shedding of blood there is no f. 912

FORGIVES (3) [FORGIVE]

Ps 103: 3 who f all your sins 6142
Mic 7:18 who pardons sin and f the transgression of 6296
Lk 7:49 "Who is this who even f sins?" 918

FORGIVING (7) [FORGIVE]

Ex 34: 7 and f wickedness, rebellion and sin. 5951
Nu 14:18 abounding in love and f sin and rebellion. 5951
Ne 9:17 But you are a f God, 6145
Ps 86: 5 You are f and good, O Lord, 6143
  99: 8 you were to Israel a f God, 5951
Da 9: 9 The Lord our God is merciful and f, 6145
Eph 4:32 to one another, f each other, just as 5919

FORGO (1)

Ne 10:31 Every seventh year we will f working 5759

FORGOT (12) [FORGET]

Ge 40:23 not remember Joseph; he f him. 8894
Dt 32:18 you f the God who gave you birth. 8894
Jdg 3: 7 they f the LORD their God and served 8894
1Sa 12: 9 "But they f the LORD their God; 8894
Ps 78:11 They f what he had done, 8894
 106:13 But they soon f what he had done and did 8894
 106:21 They f the God who saved them, 8894
Jer 23:27 just as their fathers f my name 8894
  50: 6 and f their own resting place. 8894
Hos 2:13 and went after her lovers, but me she f," 8894
  13: 6 then they f me. 8894
Mt 16: 5 the disciples f to take bread. 2140

FORGOTTEN (39) [FORGET]

Ge 41:30 Then all the abundance in Egypt will be f, 8894
Dt 26:13 from your commands nor have I any 8894
  31:21 it will not be f by their descendants. 8894
Job 11: 6 God has even f some of your sin. 5960

Job	19:14	my friends *have* f me.	8894
	28: 4	in places f by the foot of man;	8894
Ps	9:18	But the needy *will* not always *be* f,	8894
	10:11	He says to himself, "God *has* f;	8894
	31:12	*I am* f by them as though I were dead;	4213+4946+8894
	42: 9	"Why *have you* f me?	8894
	44:17	not f you or been false to your covenant.	8894
	44:20	If *we had* f the name of our God	8894
	77: 9	*Has* God f to be merciful?	8894
	119:153	for *I have* not f your law.	8894
	119:176	for *I have* not f your commands.	8894
Ecc	2:16	in days to come both *will be* f.	8894
	9: 5	and even the memory of them *is* f.	8894
Isa	17:10	*You have* f God your Savior,	8894
	23:15	that time Tyre *will be* f for seventy years,	8894
	23:16	walk through the city, O prostitute f;	8894
	49:14	the Lord *has* f me."	8894
	65:16	For the past troubles *will be* f and hidden	8894
Jer	2:32	Yet my people *have* f me,	8894
	3:21	and *have* f the LORD their God.	8894
	13:25	*you have* f me and trusted in false gods.	8894
	18:15	Yet my people *have* f me;	8894
	20:11	their dishonor *will* never *be* f.	8894
	23:40	everlasting shame that *will* not *be* f."	8894
	30:14	All your allies *have* f you;	8894
	44: 9	*Have you* f the wickedness committed	8894
	50: 5	an everlasting covenant *that will* not *be* f.	8894
La	3:17	*I have* f what prosperity is.	5960
Eze	22:12	And *you have* f me,	8894
	23:35	Since *you have* f me and thrust me	8894
Hos	8:14	Israel *has* f his Maker and built palaces;	8894
Mk	8: 6	The disciples *had* f to bring bread,	2140
Lk	12: 6	Yet not one of them *is* f by God.	2140
Heb	12: 5	And *you have* f that word	1720
2Pe	1: 9	and *has* f that he has been cleansed	3284+3330

FORK (7) [FORKS]

1Sa	2:13	with a three-pronged f in his hand.	4657
	2:14	for himself whatever the f brought up.	4657
Isa	30:24	spread out with f and shovel.	8181
Jer	15: 7	a **winnowing** f at the city gates of the land.	4665
Eze	21:21	of Babylon will stop at the f *in* the road, at	562
Mt	3:12	His **winnowing** f is in his hand,	4768
Lk	3:17	His **winnowing** f is in his hand	4768

FORKS (6) [FORK]

Ex	27: 3	sprinkling bowls, **meat** f and firepans.	4657
	38: 3	sprinkling bowls, **meat** f and firepans.	4657
Nu	4:14	**meat** f, shovels and sprinkling bowls.	4657
1Sa	13:21	of a shekel for sharpening f and axes and	7849
1Ch	28:17	for the f, sprinkling bowls and pitchers;	4657
2Ch	4:16	shovels, **meat** f and all related articles.	4657

FORLORN (1)

| Ps | 35:12 | for good and leave my soul f. | 8890 |

FORM (30) [DEFORMED, FORMATION, FORMED, FORMING, FORMS]

Ge	29:17	but Rachel was lovely in f, and beautiful.	9307
Ex	20: 4	in the f of anything in heaven above or on	9454
Nu	12: 8	he sees the f of the LORD.	9454
Dt	4:12	the sound of words but saw no f;	9454
	4:15	You saw no f of any kind the day	9454
	4:23	do not make for yourselves an idol in the f	9454
	5: 8	in the f of anything in heaven above or on	9454
1Ki	6:16	with cedar boards from floor to ceiling *to* f	1215
Est	2: 7	was lovely in f and features,	9307
Job	4:16	A f stood before my eyes,	9454
	31:15	the same one f us both within our mothers?	3922
	41:12	his strength and his graceful f.	6886
Ps	83: 5	*they* f an alliance against you—	4162
Isa	44:13	He shapes it in the f *of* man,	9322
	45: 7	I f the light and create darkness,	3670
	52:14	and his f marred beyond human likeness—	9307
Jer	11:16	with fruit beautiful in f.	9307
Eze	1: 5	In appearance their f was that of a man,	1952
Mk	16:12	Afterward Jesus appeared in a different f	3671
Lk	3:22	on him in bodily f like a dove.	1626
Jn	5:37	have never heard his voice nor seen his f,	1626
Ac	7:41	**made** an idol in the f **of a calf.**	3674
	14:11	down to us in human f!"	3929
Ro	6:17	you wholeheartedly obeyed the f	5596
	12: 5	so in Christ *we* who are many f one body,	1639
1Co	7:31	this world in its present f is passing away.	5386
	12:12	all its parts are many, *they* f one body.	1639
Eph	4:31	along with **every** f of malice.	AIT
Col	2: 9	the fullness of the Deity lives **in bodily** f,	5395
2Ti	3: 5	a f of godliness but denying its power.	3673

FORMATION (4) [FORM]

2Sa	10: 8	and drew up in **battle** f at the entrance	4878
1Ch	19: 9	up in **battle** f at the entrance to their city,	4878
Jer	6:23	like men in **battle** f to attack you,	6885
	50:42	like men in battle f to attack you,	6885

FORMED (43) [FORM]

Ge	2: 7	the LORD God f the man *from* the dust of	3670
	2: 8	and there he put the man *he had* f.	3670
	2:19	the LORD God *had* f out of the ground all	3670
Dt	4:16	whether f *like* a man or a woman,	9322
	32: 6	your Creator, who made and f you?	3922
Jos	18:20	The Jordan f **the boundary** on	1487

2Sa	2:25	*They* f themselves into a group	2118
	10:17	The Arameans f *their* **battle lines**	6885
1Ch	19:17	and f *his* **battle lines** opposite them.	6885
	19:17	David f his **lines** to meet the Arameans	6885
Job	1:17	"The Chaldeans f three raiding parties	8492
Ps	65: 6	*who* f the mountains by your power,	3922
	94: 9	Does he *who* f the eye not see?	3670
	95: 5	and his hands f the dry land.	3670
	103:14	for he knows how we are f,	3671
	104:26	which *you* f to frolic there.	3670
	119:73	Your hands made me and f me;	3922
Ecc	11: 5	or how the body is f in a mother's womb,	NIH
Isa	29:16	Shall *what* is f say to him who formed it,	5126
	29:16	Shall *what is* formed say to *him who* f it,	6913
	43: 1	he who created you, O Jacob, *he who* f you,	3670
	43: 7	whom *I* f and made."	3670
	43:10	Before me no god *was* f,	3670
	43:21	the people *I* f for myself	3670
	44: 2	he who made you, *who* f you in the womb,	3670
	44:24	your Redeemer, *who* f you in the womb:	3670
	45:18	but f it to be inhabited—	3670
	49: 5	*he who* f me in the womb to be his servant	3670
Jer	1: 5	"Before *I* f you in the womb I knew you,	3670
	18: 4	so the potter f it *into* another pot,	6913
	33: 2	the LORD *who* f it and established it—	3670
Eze	16: 7	Your breasts *were* f and your hair grew,	3922
	45: 7	the land bordering each side of the area f	NIH
	48:21	"What remains on both sides of the area f	NIH
Mt	13:26	When the wheat sprouted and f heads,	4472
Ac	17: 5	f **a mob** and started a riot in the city.	4062
	23:12	The next morning the Jews f a conspiracy	4472
Ro	9:20	"Shall what **is** f say to him who formed it,	4420
	9:20	"Shall what is formed say to *him who* f it,	4421
Gal	4:19	in the pains of childbirth until Christ *is* f	3672
1Ti	2:13	For Adam *was* f first, then Eve.	4421
Heb	11: 3	that the universe *was* f at God's command,	2936
2Pe	3: 5	the heavens existed and the earth *was* f out	5319

FORMER (32) [FORMERLY]

Nu	21:26	who had fought against the f king of Moab	8037
Dt	4:32	Ask now about the f days,	8037
1Ki	16:24	the name of the f owner of the hill.	NIH
2Ki	17:34	To this day they persist in their f practices.	8037
	17:40	however, but persisted in their f practices.	8037
Ezr	3:12	who had seen the f temple,	8037
Job	8: 8	"Ask the f generations	8037
Ps	77: 5	I thought about the f days,	4946+7710
	89:49	where is your f great love,	8037
Isa	33:18	In your thoughts you will ponder the f terror	NIH
	41:22	Tell us what the f *things* were,	8037
	42: 9	See, the f *things* have taken place,	8037
	43: 9	and proclaimed to us the f *things?*	8037
	43:18	"Forget the f *things,*	8037
	46: 9	Remember the f *things,* those of long ago;	8037
	48: 3	I foretold the f *things* long ago,	8037
	65: 7	the full payment for their f deeds."	8037
	65:17	The f *things* will not be remembered,	8037
Jer	34: 5	the f kings who preceded you,	8037
Eze	33:12	to live because of **his** f righteousness.'	2023S
	38:17	the one I spoke of in f days by my servants	7719
Da	7: 7	It was different from all the f beasts,	10621
Mic	4: 8	the f dominion will be restored to you;	8037
Hag	2: 3	who saw this house in its f glory?	8037
	2: 9	be greater than the glory of the f house,'	8037
Mal	3: 4	as in days gone by, as in f years.	7719
Mt	23:23	without neglecting the f.	1697S
Lk	11:42	the latter without leaving **the** f undone.	1697S
Ac	1: 1	In *my* f book, Theophilus,	4755
Eph	4:22	with regard to your f way of life,	4728
Php	1:17	The f preach Christ out of selfish ambition,	1254
Heb	7:18	The f regulation is set aside	4575

FORMERLY (15) [FORMER]

Jos	8:33	of the LORD had f commanded	928+2021+8037
	15:15	in Debir (f called Kiriath Sepher).	4200+7156
Jdg	1:10	in Hebron (f called Kiriath Arba)	4200+7156
	1:11	in Debir (f called Kiriath Sepher).	4200+7156
	1:23	to spy out Bethel (f called Luz),	4200+7156
1Sa	9: 9	(F in Israel, if a man went to inquire	4200+7156
	10:11	When all those who had f known him saw	
		him prophesying	919+4946+8997
1Ch	4:40	Some Hamites had lived there. f	4200+7156
Ne	13: 5	with a large room f used to store	4200+7156
Jn	9: 8	those who had f seen him begging asked,	4728
Gal	1:23	"The man who f persecuted us is	4537
	4: 8	F, when you did not know God,	5538
Eph	2:11	remember that f you who are Gentiles	4537
Phm	1:11	F he was useless to you,	4537
Heb	6: 4	and those who f had the gospel preached	4728

FORMING (3) [FORM]

Isa	30: 1	f **an alliance**, but not by my Spirit,	5011+5818
Eze	41: 8	f the foundation of the side rooms.	NIH
Zec	14: 4	f a great valley,	NIH

FORMLESS (2)

| Ge | 1: 2 | Now the earth was f and empty, | 9332 |
| Jer | 4:23 | and it was f and empty; | 9332 |

FORMS (9) [FORM]

Ge	41:32	the dream was given to Pharaoh in two f is	7193
Lev	26:30	on the **lifeless** f of your idols,	7007
Ps	33:15	he *who* f the hearts of all,	3670
	49:14	their f will decay in the grave,	7451

SS	2:13	The fig tree f its early fruit;	2845
Jer	16:18	with the **lifeless** f of their vile images.	5577
Am	4:13	*He who* f the mountains, creates the wind,	3670
Zec	12: 1	and *who* f the spirit of man within him,	3670
1Pe	4:10	God's grace in its various f.	NIG

FORMULA (2)

| Ex | 30:32 | and do not make any oil with the same f. | 5504 |
| | 30:37 | Do not make any incense with this f | 5504 |

FORNICATION (KJV) See MARITAL UNFAITHFULNESS, PROSTITUTE, SEXUAL IMMORALITY

FORSAKE (44) [FORSAKEN, FORSAKES, FORSAKING, FORSOOK]

Dt	31: 6	he will never leave you nor f you."	6440
	31: 8	he will never leave you nor f you.	6440
	31:16	*They will* f me and break	6440
	31:17	with them and f them;	6440
Jos	1: 5	I will never leave you nor f you.	6440
	24:16	*to* f the LORD to serve other gods!	6440
	24:20	you f the LORD and serve foreign gods,	6440
1Ki	8:57	may he never leave us nor f us.	5759
2Ki	21:14	*I will* f the remnant of my inheritance	5759
1Ch	28: 9	but if *you* f him, he will reject you forever.	6440
	28:20	or f you until all the work for the service of	6440
2Ch	7:19	"But if you turn away and f the decrees	6440
	15: 2	he will be found by you, but if *you* f him,	6440
	15: 2	but if you forsake him, *he will* f you.	6440
Ezr	8:22	but his great anger is against all *who* f him."	6440
Ps	27: 9	Do not reject me or f me,	6440
	27:10	Though my father and mother f me,	6440
	37:28	the just and *will* not f his faithful ones.	6440
	38:21	O LORD, *do* not f me;	6440
	71: 9	*do* not f me when my strength is gone.	6440
	71:18	Even when I am old and gray, *do* not f me,	6440
	89:30	"If his sons f my law and do	6440
	94:14	*he will* never f his inheritance.	6440
	119: 8	*do* not utterly f me.	6440
Pr	1: 8	and *do* not f your mother's teaching.	5759
	4: 2	so *do* not f my teaching.	6440
	4: 6	*Do* not f wisdom, and she will protect you;	6440
	6:20	and *do* not f your mother's teaching.	5759
	27:10	*Do* not f your friend and the friend	6440
	28: 4	*Those who* f the law praise the wicked,	6440
Isa	1:28	and *those who* f the LORD will perish.	6440
	41:17	I, the God of Israel, *will* not f them.	6440
	42:16	*I will* not f them.	6440
	55: 7	*Let* the wicked f his way and	6440
	65:11	"But as for *you who* f the LORD	6440
Jer	2:19	how evil and bitter it is for you *when* you f	6440
	12: 7	"I *will* f my house,	6440
	14: 9	we bear your name; *do* not f us!	5663
	17:13	all *who* f you will be put to shame.	6440
	23:33	*I will* f you, declares the LORD.'	5759
La	5:20	Why *do you* f us so long?	6440
Eze	20: 8	nor *did they* f the idols of Egypt.	6440
Da	11:30	to *those who* f the holy covenant.	6440
Heb	13: 5	"Never will I leave you; never *will I* f you."	1593

FORSAKEN (39) [FORSAKE]

Jdg	10:13	But you *have* f me and served other gods,	6440
1Sa	8: 8	we *have* f the LORD and served the Baals	6440
1Ki	9: 9	'Because *they have* f the LORD their God,	6440
	11:33	I will do this because *they have* f me	6440
2Ki	22:17	Because *they have* f me and burned incense	6440
2Ch	7:22	'Because *they have* f the LORD,	6440
	13:10	and *we have* not f him.	6440
	13:11	But you *have* f him.	6440
	21:10	because Jehoram *had* f the LORD,	6440
	24:20	Because *you have* f the LORD,	6440
	24:20	*he has* f you.' "	6440
	24:24	Because Judah *had* f the LORD,	6440
	28: 6	because Judah *had* f the LORD,	6440
	34:25	Because *they have* f me and burned incense	6440
Ps	9:10	LORD, have never f those who seek you.	6440
	22: 1	My God, my God, why *have you* f me?	6440
	37:25	yet I have never seen the righteous f	6440
	71:11	They say, "God *has* f him;	6440
	119:53	*who have* f your law.	6440
	119:87	but I *have* not f your precepts.	6440
Isa	1: 4	*They have* f the LORD;	6440
	6:12	and the land **is** utterly f.	6440
	27:10	an abandoned settlement, f like the desert;	6440
	49:14	But Zion said, "The LORD *has* f me,	6440
	58: 2	and *has* not f the commands of its God.	6440
	60:15	"Although you have been f and hated,	6440
Jer	2:13	*They have* f me, the spring of living water,	6440
	5: 7	Your children *have* f me and sworn	6440
	5:19	'As *you have* f me and served foreign gods	6440
	9:13	"It is because they *have* f my law,	6440
	17:13	in the dust because *they have* f the LORD,	6440
	19: 4	For *they have* f me and made this a place	6440
	22: 9	'Because *they have* f the covenant of the	6440
	51: 5	and Judah have not been f by their God,	527
Eze	8:12	the LORD *has* f the land.' "	6440
	9: 9	They say, 'The LORD *has* f the land;	6440
Mt	27:46	"My God, my God, why *have you* f me?"	1593
Mk	15:34	"My God, my God, why *have you* f me?"	1593
Rev	2: 4	*You have* f your first love.	918

FORSAKES (1) [FORSAKE]
Job 6:14 even though *he* f the fear of the Almighty. 6440

FORSAKING (7) [FORSAKE]
Dt 28:20 of the evil you have done *in* f him. 6440
Jdg 10:10 f our God and serving the Baals." 6440
1Sa 8: 8 f me and serving other gods, 6440
Isa 57: 8 F me, you uncovered your bed, 907+4946
Jer 1:16 because of their wickedness *in* f me, 6440
2:17 *by* f the LORD your God when he led you 6440
Eze 20:27 your fathers blasphemed me by f me: 5085+5086

FORSOMUCH (KJV) See BECAUSE

FORSOOK (8) [FORSAKE]
Jdg 2:12 *They* f the LORD, 6440
2:13 because *they* f him and served Baal and 6440
10: 6 And because the Israelites f the LORD 6440
2Ki 17:16 *They* f all the commands of 6440
21:22 *He* f the LORD, the God of his fathers, 6440
2Ch 29: 6 the eyes of the LORD our God and f him. 6440
Jer 16:11 'It is because your fathers f me,' 6440
16:11 *They* f me and did not keep my law. 6440

FORSWEAR (KJV) See BREAK OATH

FORT (KJV) See FORTRESS

FORTH (64)
Ge 3:24 and a flaming sword **flashing back and** f 2200
4: 1 the help of the LORD *I* have **brought** f 7865
7:11 the springs of the great deep **burst** f, 1324
8: 7 and f until the water had dried up from 3655
Ex 9:24 lightning **flashed back and** f. 928+4374+9348
32:27 and f through the camp from one end to 6296
Dt 33: 2 he **shone** f from Mount Paran. 3649
33:14 with the best the sun **brings** f and the finest 9311
1Sa 17:15 but David **went** back and f from Saul 2143
2Sa 22:13 of his presence bolts of lightning **blazed** f. 1277
2Ki 4:35 Elisha turned away and walked back and f 285+285+2178+2178+2256
Est 2143 Every day he **walked** back and f near 2143
Job 1: 7 through the earth and **going** back and f 2143
2: 2 through the earth and **going** back and f 2143
8:10 *Will they* not **bring** f words 3655
14: 9 of water it will bud and **put** f shoots like 6913
15: 7 *Were* you **brought** f before the hills? 2655
21:11 *They* **send** their children as a flock; 8938
23:10 *I will* **come** f as gold. 3655
24:14 in the night *he* **steals** f like a thief. 2118
38: 8 the sea behind doors when it burst f from 3655
38:32 *Can you* **bring** f the constellations 3655
39: 3 They crouch down and **bring** f their young; 7114
Ps 19: 2 Day after day *they* **pour** f speech; 5580
19: 5 a bridegroom **coming** f from his pavilion, 3655
43: 3 **Send** f your light and your truth, 8938
45: 4 In your majesty **ride** f victoriously in behalf 8206
50: 2 From Zion, perfect in beauty, God **shines** f. 3649
60: 1 O God, and **burst** f upon us; 7287
65: 8 *you* **call** f songs of joy. 8264
68: 6 he **leads** the prisoners with singing; 3655
71: 6 you **brought** me f from my mother's womb, 1602
77:17 your arrows **flashed** back and f. 2143
78:26 from the heavens and **led** f the south wind 5627
80: 1 enthroned between the cherubim, **shine** f 3649
85:11 Faithfulness **springs** f from the earth, 7541
90: 2 the mountains were born or *you* **brought** f 2655
94: 1 O God who avenges, **shine** f. 3649
104:14 **bringing** f food from the earth; 3655
107:20 *He* **sent** f his word and healed them; 8938
144: 6 **Send** f lightning and scatter 1397+1398
Pr 8:22 "The LORD **brought** me f as the first 7865
10:31 mouth of the righteous **brings** f wisdom, 5649
27: 1 you do not know what a day *may* **bring** f. 3528
Isa 35: 6 Water *will* **gush** f in the wilderness 1324
41: 4 **calling** f the generations from 7924
41:21 "**Set** f your arguments," 5602
42: 3 In faithfulness *he will* **bring** f justice; 3655
55:12 You will go out in joy and *be* **led** f 3297
58: 8 Then your light *will* **break** f like the dawn, 1324
65: 9 *I will* **bring** f descendants from Jacob, 3655
66: 8 or a nation *be* **brought** f in a moment? 3528
Eze 1:13 Fire **moved** back and f among the creatures; 2143
1:14 The creatures **sped** back and f like flashes 8351
7:10 Doom *has* **burst** f, the rod has budded, 3655
13:11 and violent winds *will* **burst** f. 1324
17: 2 **set** f an allegory and tell the house of Israel 2554
37: 2 He led me **back and** f among them, 6017+6017
Hos 10: 1 *he* **brought** f fruit for himself. 8751
Na 1:11 *has one* **come** f who plots evil against 3655
2: 4 **rushing** back and f through the squares. 9212
2Co 4: 2 **setting** f the truth plainly 5748
Gal 4:27 **break** f and cry aloud, 4838
Eph 4:14 **tossed** back and f by the waves, 3115

FORTHWITH (KJV) See AS SOON AS, AT ONCE, IMMEDIATELY, SUDDEN, SUDDENLY, QUICKLY

FORTIETH (3) [FORTY]
Nu 33:38 the first day of the fifth month of the f year 752
Dt 1: 3 In the f year, on the first day of the eleventh 752
1Ch 26:31 In the f year of David's reign 752

FORTIFICATIONS (1) [FORTRESS]
2Sa 20:15 and it stood against the **outer** f. 2658

FORTIFIED (63) [FORTRESS]
Nu 13:19 Are they unwalled or f? 4448
13:28 and the cities are f and very large. 1290
21:24 because their border was f. 6434
32:17 and children will live in f cities, 4448
32:36 Beth Nimrah and Beth Haran as f cities, 4448
Dt 3: 5 All these cities were f with high walls and 1290
28:52 throughout your land until the high f walls 1290
Jos 10:20 the few who were left reached their f cities. 4448
14:12 and their cities were large and f, 1290
19:29 toward Ramah and went to the f city 4448
19:35 The f cities were Ziddim, Zer, Hammath, 4448
1Sa 6:18 the f towns with their country villages. 4448
2Sa 20: 6 or he will find f cities and escape from us." 4448
1Ki 12:25 Then Jeroboam f Shechem in 1215
15:17 and f Ramah to prevent anyone 1215
22:39 and the cities *he* f, 1215
2Ki 3:19 You will overthrow every f city 4448
8:12 "You will set fire to their f places, 4448
10: 2 a f city and weapons, 4448
17: 9 From watchtower to f city they built 4448
18: 8 From watchtower to f city, 4448
18:13 of Assyria attacked all the f cities of Judah 1290
19:25 you have turned f cities into piles of stone. 1290
2Ch 8: 5 and Lower Beth Horon as f cities, 5190
11:10 These were f cities in Judah and Benjamin. 5193
11:23 and to all the f cities. 5193
12: 4 he captured the f cities of Judah and came 5193
14: 6 He built up the f cities of Judah, 5193
16: 1 and f Ramah to prevent anyone 1215
17: 2 in all the f cities of Judah and put garrisons 1290
17:19 besides those he stationed in the f cities 4448
19: 5 in each of the f cities of Judah. 1290
21: 3 as well as f cities in Judah, 5193
26: 9 and *he* f them. 2616
32: 1 He laid siege to the f cities, 1290
33:14 in all the f cities in Judah. 1290
Ne 9:25 They captured f cities and fertile land; 1290
Ps 60: 9 Who will bring me to the f city? 5190
108:10 Who will bring me to the f city? 4448
Pr 10:15 The wealth of the rich is their f city. 6437
18:11 The wealth of the rich is their f city; 6437
18:19 a f city, and disputes are like 6437
Isa 2:15 for every lofty tower and every f wall, 1290
17: 3 The f city will disappear from Ephraim, 4448
25: 2 The f town a ruin, 1290
25:12 down your high f walls and lay them low; 4448
27:10 The f city stands desolate, 1290
36: 1 of Assyria attacked all the f cities of Judah 1290
37:26 you have turned f cities into piles of stone. 1290
Jer 1:18 Today I have made you a f city, 4448
4: 5 Let us flee to the f cities!' 4448
5:17 the sword they will destroy the f cities 4448
8:14 Let us flee to the f cities and perish there! 4448
15:20 a f wall of bronze; 1290
34: 7 These were the only f cities left in Judah. 4448
48:18 up against you and ruin your f **cities.** 4448
Eze 21:20 and another against Judah and f Jerusalem. 1290
36:35 are now f and inhabited." 1290
Da 11:15 up siege ramps and will capture a city. 4448
Hos 8:14 Judah has f many towns. 1290
Am 5: 9 on the stronghold and brings f **city** 4448
Hab 1:10 They laugh at all f **cities;** 4448
Zep 1:16 the f cities and against the corner towers. 1290

FORTIFIES (1) [FORTRESS]
Jer 51:53 the sky and f her lofty stronghold, 1307

FORTRESS (35) [FORTIFICATIONS, FORTIFIED, FORTIFIES, FORTRESSES, FORTS]
2Sa 5: 7 David captured the f *of* Zion, 5181
5: 9 then took up residence in the f and called it 5181
22: 2 LORD is my rock, my f and my deliverer; 5181
24: 2 toward the f *of* Tyre and all the towns of 4448
1Ch 11: 5 David captured the f *of* Zion, 5181
11: 7 David then took up residence in the f, 5171
Ps 18: 2 LORD is my rock, my f and my deliverer; 5181
28: 8 a f of salvation for his anointed one. 5057
31: 2 a **strong** f to save me. 1074+5181
31: 3 Since you are my rock and my f, 5181
46: 7 the God of Jacob is our f. 5369
46:11 the God of Jacob is our f. 5369
48: 3 he has shown himself to be her f. 5369
59: 9 you, O God, are my f, 5369
59:16 for you are my f, 5369
59:17 you, O God, are my f, my loving God. 5369
62: 2 he is my f, I will never be shaken. 5369
62: 6 he is my f, I will never be shaken. 5369
71: 3 for you are my rock and my f. 5181
91: 2 "He is my refuge and my f, my God, 5181
94:22 But the LORD has become my f, 5369
144: 2 He is my loving God and my f, 5181
Pr 14:26 He who fears the LORD has a secure f, 6437
Isa 17:10 not remembered the Rock, your f. 5057
23: 4 O f *of* the sea, for she has spoken: 5057
23:14 your f is destroyed! 5057
29: 7 that attack her and her f and besiege her, 5183
32:14 The f will be abandoned, 810
33:16 whose refuge will be the mountain f. 5171
Jer 16:19 O LORD, my strength and my f, 5057
Da 11: 7 of the king of the North and enter his f; 5057
11:10 and carry the battle as far as his f. 5057
11:31 to desecrate the temple f and will abolish 5057
Na 2: 1 Guard the f, watch the road, 5193
Zec 9:12 Return to your f, O prisoners of hope; 1315

FORTRESSES (26) [FORTRESS]
Isa 23:11 an order concerning Phoenicia that her f 5058
23:13 they stripped its f bare and turned it into 810
Jer 6: 5 let us attack at night and destroy her f!" 810
9:21 and has entered our f; 810
17:27 of Jerusalem that will consume her f.' " 810
49:27 it will consume the f of Ben-Hadad." 810
Da 11:19 the f *of* his own country but will stumble 5057
11:24 He will plot the overthrow of f— 4448
11:38 Instead of them, he will honor a god of f; 5057
11:39 He will attack the **mightiest** f with 4448+5057
Hos 8:14 upon their cities that will consume their f." 810
10:14 so that all your f will be devastated— 4448
Am 1: 4 the house of Hazael that will consume the f 810
1: 7 the walls of Gaza that will consume her f. 810
1:10 the walls of Tyre that will consume her f." 810
1:12 upon Teman that will consume the f 810
1:14 that will consume her f amid war cries on 810
2: 2 upon Moab that will consume the f 810
2: 5 that will consume the f *of* Jerusalem." 810
3: 9 to the f *of* Ashdod and to the fortresses 810
3: 9 to the fortresses *of* Ashdod and to the f 810
3:10 "who hoard plunder and loot in their f." 810
3:11 down your strongholds and plunder your f." 810
6: 8 the pride of Jacob and detest his f; 810
Mic 5: 5 and marches through our f, 810
Na 3:12 All your f are like fig trees 4448

FORTS (2) [FORTRESS]
2Ch 17:12 he built f and store cities in Judah 1072
27: 4 He built towns in the Judean hills and f 1072

FORTUNATE (1) [FORTUNE]
Ac 26: 2 I consider myself f to stand before you 3421

FORTUNATUS (1)
1Co 16:17 F and Achaicus arrived, 5847

FORTUNE (4) [FORTUNATE, FORTUNE-TELLING, FORTUNES]
Ge 30:11 Then Leah said, "What **good** f!" 1513
Job 31:25 the f my hands had gained, 3888
Pr 21: 6 A f made by a lying tongue is 238
Isa 65:11 a table for F and fill bowls of mixed wine 1513

FORTUNE-TELLING (1) [FORTUNE]
Ac 16:16 a great deal of money for her owners *by* f. 3446

FORTUNES (19) [FORTUNE]
Dt 30: 3 the LORD your God will restore your f 8654
Ps 14: 7 the LORD restores the f of his people, 8654
53: 6 When God restores the f *of* his people, 8654
85: 1 you restored the f of Jacob. 8669
126: 4 Restore our f, O LORD. 8669
Jer 30:18 the f *of* Jacob's tents and have compassion 8654
32:44 because I will restore their f," 8654
33:11 the f *of* the land as they were before,' 8654
33:26 For I will restore their f 8654
48:47 "Yet I will restore the f *of* Moab in days 8654
49: 6 I will restore the f *of* the Ammonites," 8654
49:39 "Yet I will restore the f *of* Elam in days 8654
Eze 16:53 the f *of* Sodom and her daughters and 8669
16:53 and your f along with them, 8669
Hos 6:11 "Whenever I would restore the f 8654
Joel 3: 1 I restore the f *of* Judah and Jerusalem, 8654
Mic 3:11 and her prophets **tell** f for money. 7876
Zep 2: 7 he will restore their f. 8654
3:20 of the earth when I restore your f 8654

FORTY (95) [FORTIETH, 40]
Ge 7: 4 now I will send rain on the earth for f days 752
7: 4 on the earth for forty days and f nights, 752
7:12 on the earth f days and forty nights. 752
7:12 on the earth forty days and f nights. 752
7:17 For f days the flood kept coming on 752
8: 6 After f days Noah opened 752
18:29 "What if only f are found there?" 752
18:29 He said, "For the sake of f, 752
25:20 and Isaac was f years old 752
26:34 When Esau was f years old, 752
32:15 f cows and ten bulls, 752
50: 3 taking a full f days, 752
Ex 16:35 The Israelites ate manna f years, 752
24:18 on the mountain f days and f nights. 752
24:18 on the mountain forty days and f nights. 752
26:19 make f silver bases to go underneath 752
26:21 and f silver bases—two under each frame. 752
34:28 Moses was there with the LORD f days 752
34:28 with the LORD forty days and f nights 752

Ex	36:24	made *f* silver bases to go under them—	752
	36:26	and *f* silver bases—two under each frame.	752
Nu	13:25	of *f* days they returned from exploring	752
	14:33	be shepherds here for *f* years,	752
	14:34	For *f* years—one year	752
	14:34	of the *f* days you explored the land—	752
	32:13	in the desert *f* years,	752
Dt	2: 7	These *f* years the LORD your God has been with you,	752
	8: 2	the way in the desert these *f* years,	752
	8: 4	not swell during these *f* years.	752
	9: 9	on the mountain *f* days and forty nights;	752
	9: 9	on the mountain forty days and *f* nights;	752
	9:11	At the end of the *f* days and forty nights,	752
	9:11	At the end of the forty days and *f* nights,	752
	9:18	the LORD for *f* days and forty nights;	752
	9:18	the LORD for forty days and *f* nights;	752
	9:25	the LORD those *f* days and forty nights	752
	9:25	the LORD those forty days and *f* nights	752
	10:10	Now I had stayed on the mountain *f* days	752
	25: 3	he must not give him more than *f* lashes.	752
	29: 5	During the *f* years that I led you through	752
Jos	4:13	About *f* thousand armed for battle crossed	752
	5: 6	about in the desert *f* years until all	752
	14: 7	I was *f* years old when Moses the servant	752
Jdg	3:11	So the land had peace for *f* years,	752
	5: 8	or spear was seen among *f* thousand	752
	5:31	Then the land had peace *f* years.	752
	8:28	the land enjoyed peace *f* years.	752
	12:14	He had *f* sons and thirty grandsons,	752
	13: 1	into the hands of the Philistines for *f* years.	752
1Sa	4:18	He had led Israel *f* years.	752
	17:16	For *f* days the Philistine came forward every morning	752
2Sa	2:10	Ish-Bosheth son of Saul was *f* years old	752
	5: 4	and he reigned *f* years.	752
	10:18	and *f* thousand of their foot soldiers.	752
1Ki	2:11	he had reigned *f* years over Israel—	752
	6:17	in front of this room was *f* cubits long.	752
	7:38	each holding *f* baths	752
	11:42	in Jerusalem over all Israel *f* years.	752
	19: 8	he traveled *f* days and forty nights	752
	19: 8	and *f* nights until he reached Horeb,	752
2Ki	8: 9	a gift *f* camel-loads of all the finest wares	752
	12: 1	and he reigned in Jerusalem *f* years.	752
1Ch	19:18	and *f* thousand of their foot soldiers.	752
	29:27	He ruled over Israel *f* years.	752
2Ch	9:30	in Jerusalem over all Israel *f* years.	752
	24: 1	and he reigned in Jerusalem *f* years.	752
Ne	5:15	on the people and took *f* shekels of silver	752
	9:21	For *f* years you sustained them in	752
Job	42:16	After this, Job lived a hundred and *f* years;	752
Ps	95:10	*f* years I was angry with that generation;	752
Eze	29:11	no one will live there for *f* years.	752
	29:12	and her cities will lie desolate *f* years	752
	29:13	of *f* years I will gather the Egyptians from	752
	41: 2	it was *f* cubits long and twenty cubits wide.	752
	46:22	*f* cubits long and thirty cubits wide;	752
Am	2:10	and I led you *f* years in the desert	752
	5:25	and offerings *f* years in the desert,	752
Jnh	3: 4	"F more days and Nineveh will	752
Mt	4: 2	After fasting *f* days and forty nights,	5477
	4: 2	After fasting forty days and *f* nights,	5477
Mk	1:13	and he was in the desert *f* days,	5477
Lk	4: 2	for *f* days he was tempted by the devil.	5477
Ac	1: 3	to them over a period *of f* days and spoke	5477
	4:22	miraculously healed was over *f* years old.	5477
	7:23	"When Moses *was* **f years** old,	5478
	7:30	"After *f* years had passed,	5477
	7:36	at the Red Sea and *for* **f** years in the desert.	5478
	7:42	and offerings *f* years in the desert,	5477
	13:18	he endured their conduct *for* about **f years**	5478
	13:21	of the tribe of Benjamin, who ruled *f* years.	5477
	23:13	More than *f* men were involved in this plot,	5477
	23:21	because more than *f* of them are waiting	5477
2Co	11:24	from the Jews the *f* lashes minus one.	5477
Heb	3: 9	and *for f* years saw what I did.	5477
	3:17	And with whom was he angry *for f* years?	5477

FORTY-EIGHT (2)

Nu	35: 7	In all you must give the Levites *f* towns,	752+2256+9046
Jos	21:41	held by the Israelites were *f*	752+2256+9046

FORTY-FIRST (1)

2Ch	16:13	in the *f* year of his reign Asa died	285+752+2256

FORTY-FIVE (3) [45]

Ge	18:28	"If I find *f* there," he said,	752+2256+2822
Jos	14:10	he has kept me alive for *f* years	752+2256+2822
1Ki	7: 3	*f* beams, fifteen to a row.	752+2256+2822

FORTY-NINE (1)

Lev	25: 8	amount to a period of *f* years.	752+2256+9596

FORTY-ONE (4)

1Ki	14:21	*f* years old when he became king,	285+752+2256
	15:10	he reigned in Jerusalem *f* years.	285+752+2256
2Ki	14:23	and he reigned *f* years.	285+752+2256
2Ch	12:13	*f* years old when he became king,	285+752+2256

FORTY-SEVEN (1)

Ge	47:28	of his life were a hundred and **f.**	752+2256+8679

FORTY-SIX (1)

Jn	2:20	"It has taken *f* years to build this temple,	1971+2779+5477

FORTY-TWO (6) [42]

Nu	35: 6	give them *f* other towns.	752+2256+9109
Jdg	12: 6	F thousand Ephraimites were killed at that time.	752+2256+9109
1Sa	13: 1	he reigned over Israel [*f*] years.	752+2256+9109
2Ki	2:24	and mauled *f* of the youths.	752+2256+9109
	10:14	of Beth Eked—*f* men.	752+2256+9109
Rev	13: 5	to exercise his authority *for* **f** months.	1545+5477

FORUM (1)

Ac	28:15	and they traveled as far as the F of Appius	5842

FORWARD (55)

Ge	19: 9	and moved *f* to break down the door.	5602
Lev	8: 6	**brought** Aaron and his sons *f*	7928
	8:13	**brought** Aaron's sons *f*,	7928
	8:24	**brought** Aaron's sons *f*	7928
	16:20	he shall **bring** *f* the live goat.	7928
Nu	8: 3	the lamps so that they **faced** *f on*	448+4578+7156
	12: 5	When both of them **stepped** *f*,	3655
Dt	20: 2	the priest *shall* **come** *f* and address	5602
	21: 5	The priests, the sons of Levi, *shall* **step** *f*,	5602
Jos	6: 8	before the LORD **went** *f*,	6296
	6:13	the seven trumpets **went** *f*,	2143
	7:14	the LORD takes *shall* **come** *f* clan by clan;	7928
	7:14	that the LORD takes *shall* **come** *f* family	7928
	7:14	that the LORD takes *shall* **come** *f* man	7928
	7:16	the next morning Joshua had Israel **come** *f*	7928
	7:17	The clans of Judah **came** *f*,	7928
	7:17	had the clan of the Zerahites **come** *f*	7928
	7:18	had his family **come** *f*	7928
	8:19	from their position and **rushed** *f*.	8132
	10:24	So they **came** *f* and placed their feet	7928
Jdg	8:21	So Gideon **stepped** *f* and killed them,	7756
	9:44	and the companies with him **rushed** *f* to	7320
1Sa	10:21	Then he **brought** *f* the tribe of Benjamin,	7928
	17:16	the Philistine **came** *f* every morning	5602
	17:52	Then the men of Israel and Judah **surged** *f*	7756
2Sa	20: 8	he **stepped** *f*, it dropped out of its sheath.	3655
1Ki	1: 5	**put himself** *f* and said, "I will be king."	5951
	18:36	the prophet Elijah **stepped** *f* and prayed:	5602
	22:21	Finally, a spirit **came** *f*,	3655
2Ki	20: 9	*Shall* the shadow **go** *f* ten steps,	2143
	20:10	for the shadow to **go** *f* ten steps,"	5742
2Ch	18:20	Finally, a spirit **came** *f*,	3655
Ps	35:11	Ruthless witnesses **come** *f*;	7756
Pr	18:17	till another **comes** *f* and questions him.	AIT
Isa	41: 1	*Let them* **come** *f* and speak;	5602
	41: 5	They approach and **come** *f*;	910
	47:13	*Let* your astrologers **come** *f*,	6641
	63: 1	**striding** *f* in the greatness of his strength?	7579
Jer	7:24	They went backward and not *f*.	4200+7156
	26:17	of the elders of the land **stepped** *f* and said	7756
Eze	39:22	that day the house of Israel will know	2134
Da	3: 8	At this time some astrologers **came** *f*	10638
Zec	5: 5	the angel who was speaking to me **came** *f*	3655
Mt	26:50	Then the **men stepped** *f*,	4665
	26:60	*though* many false witnesses **came** *f*.	4665
	26:60	Finally two **came** *f*	4665
Mk	3:10	with diseases *were* **pushing** *f* to touch him.	2158
Lk	2:38	the child *to* all who *were* **looking** *f* to	4657
	13:12	he **called** her *f* and said to her, "Woman,	4715
Ac	5: 6	Then the young men **came** *f*,	482
2Co	11:20	or **pushes** *himself f* or slaps you in the face.	2048
Heb	11:10	For he was **looking** *f* to the city	1683
2Pe	3:12	*as you* **look** *f* to the day of God	4659
	3:13	with his promise *we are* **looking** *f* to	4659
	3:14	*since* you *are* **looking** *f* to this,	4659

FORWARDNESS (KJV) See
EAGERNESS, EARNESTNESS

FOSTER (1)

Isa	49:23	Kings will be your *f* fathers,	587

FOUGHT (46) [FIGHT]

Ex	17:10	So Joshua *f* the Amalekites	4309
Nu	21:23	When he reached Jahaz, he *f* with Israel.	4309
	21:26	who *had f* against the former king of Moab	4309
	31: 7	*They f* against Midian,	7371
	31:28	From the soldiers who *f* in the battle,	3655+4200
	31:36	of those who *f* in the battle was:	928+3655
Jos	10:42	the God of Israel, *f* for Israel.	4309
	23: 3	it was the LORD your God who *f* for you.	4309
	24: 8	*They f* against you,	4309
	24:11	The citizens of Jericho *f* against you,	4309
Jdg	1: 5	that they found Adoni-Bezek and *f*	4309
	5:19	"Kings came, *they f*; the kings of Canaan	4309
	5:19	of Canaan *f* at Taanach by the waters	4309
	5:20	From the heavens they *f*,	4309
	5:20	from their courses *they f* against Sisera.	4309
	9:17	and to think that my father *f* for you,	4309
	9:39	the citizens of Shechem and *f* Abimelech.	4309
	11:20	and encamped at Jahaz and *f* with Israel.	4309
	12: 4	the men of Gilead and *f* Ephraim.	4309
1Sa	4:10	So the Philistines *f*,	4309
	12: 9	the Philistines and the king of Moab, *who f*	4309
	14:47	he *f* against their enemies on every side:	4309

1Sa	14:48	He *f* valiantly and defeated the Amalekites,	6913
	19: 8	and David went out and *f* the Philistines.	4309
	23: 5	So David and his men went to Keilah, *f*	4309
	30:17	David *f* them from dusk until the evening	5782
	31: 9	Now the Philistines *f* against Israel;	4309
2Sa	8: 3	David *f* Hadadezer son of Rehob,	5782
	10:17	to meet David and *f* against him.	4309
	11:17	the city came out and *f* against Joab, some	4309
	12:26	Meanwhile Joab *f* against Rabbah of	4309
	12:27	"*I have f* against Rabbah	4309
2Ki	3:23	"Those kings **must have f**	2991+2991
	3:24	the Israelites rose up and *f* them	5782
1Ch	10: 1	Now the Philistines *f* against Israel;	4309
	18: 3	David *f* Hadadezer king of Zobah,	5782
	19:17	and *they f* against him.	4309
	22: 8	and have *f* many wars.	6913
2Ch	20:29	how the LORD *had f* against the enemies	4309
Ps	60: T	he *f* Aram Naharaim and Aram Zobah,	5897
Isa	63:10	and became their enemy and *he* himself *f*	4309
Zec	14:12	the LORD will strike all the nations that *f*	7371
1Co	15:32	If *I f* wild beasts in Ephesus	2562
2Ti	4: 7	*I have* **f** the good fight,	76
Rev	12: 7	and his angels *f* against the dragon,	4482
	12: 7	and the dragon and his angels *f* back.	4482

FOUL (KJV) See EVIL, MUDDY, RED, STORMY

FOUND (336) [FIND]

Ge	2:20	But for Adam no suitable helper *was* **f.**	5162
	4:15	so that no one *who* **f** him would kill him.	5162
	6: 8	Noah *f* favor in the eyes of the LORD.	5162
	7: 1	I *have f* you righteous in this generation.	4200+7156+8011
	9:24	and *f out* what his youngest son had done	3359
	11: 2	*they f* a plain in Shinar and settled there.	5162
	16: 7	of the LORD *f* Hagar near a spring in	5162
	18: 3	He said, "If I *have f* favor in your eyes,	5162
	18:29	"What if only forty *are f* there?"	5162
	18:30	What if only thirty *can be f* there?"	5162
	18:31	what if only twenty *can be f* there?"	5162
	18:32	What if only ten *can be f* there?"	5162
	19:19	Your servant *has f* favor in your eyes,	5162
	24:30	he went out to the man and *f* him standing	2180
	26:32	They said, "*We've f* water!"	5162
	30:14	into the fields and *f* some mandrake plants,	5162
	30:27	"If I *have f* favor in your eyes, please stay.	5162
	31:33	but *he f* nothing.	5162
	31:34	in the tent but *f* nothing.	5162
	31:37	what *have you f* that belongs	5162
	33:10	"If I *have f* favor in your eyes,	5162
	37:15	a man *f* him wandering around in the fields	5162
	37:17	after his brothers and *f* them near Dothan.	5162
	37:32	to their father and said, "We *f* this.	5162
	39: 4	Joseph *f* favor in his eyes	5162
	43:21	and each of us *f* his silver—	2180
	44: 8	of Canaan the silver we *f* inside the mouths	5162
	44: 9	If any of your servants is *f* to have *it*,	5162
	44:10	is *f* to have *it* will become my slave;	5162
	44:12	And the cup was *f* in Benjamin's sack.	5162
	44:16	we ourselves and the one who was *f* to have	5162
	44:17	Only the man who was *f* to have	5162
	47:14	*to be f* in Egypt and Canaan in payment for	5162
	47:29	"If I *have f* favor in your eyes,	5162
	50: 4	"If I *have f* favor in your eyes,	5162
Ex	5:20	*they f* Moses and Aaron waiting	7003
	9: 7	Pharaoh sent men to investigate and *f that*	2180
	16:27	For seven days no yeast *is to be f*	5162
	16:27	but *they f* none.	5162
	22: 4	"If the stolen animal is *f* alive in his possession—	5162+5162
	22: 8	But if the thief is not *f*,	5162
	33:12	'I know you by name and *you have f* favor	5162
	34: 9	"O Lord, if I *have f* favor in your eyes,"	5162
Lev	6: 4	or the lost property he *f*,	5162
	7:24	The fat of an **animal f dead** or torn	5577
	10:16	about the goat of the sin offering and *f*	2180
	17:15	who eats **anything f dead** or torn	5577
	22: 8	He must not eat **anything f dead** or torn	5577
Nu	11:15	if I *have f* favor in your eyes—	5162
	15:32	a man *was f* gathering wood on	5162
	15:33	Those *who f* him gathering wood brought him to Moses and Aaron	5162
	23: 6	So he went back to him and *f* him standing	2180
	23:17	and *f* him standing beside his offering,	2180
	32: 5	If *we have f* favor in your eyes," they said,	5162
Dt	13:17	of those condemned things *shall be f*	1815
	15: 9	and you will be *f* guilty of sin.	NIH
	16: 4	*Let* no yeast be *f* in your possession	8011
	17: 2	the LORD gives you is *f* doing evil in	5162
	18:10	*Let* no one be *f* among you who	5162
	21: 1	If a *man* is *f* slain,	5162
	22:20	and no proof of the girl's virginity *can be f*,	5162
	22:22	man is *f* sleeping with another man's wife,	5162
	22:27	for the man the girl out in the country,	5162
	32:10	In a desert land he *f* him,	5162
Jos	10:17	the five kings *had been f* hiding in the cave	5162
Jdg	1: 5	It was there that *they f* Adoni-Bezek	5162
	3:24	and the doors of the upper room locked.	8011
	6:17	"If now I *have f* favor in your eyes,	5162
	20:48	the animals and everything else they *f*.	5162
	21: 9	they *f* that none of the people	2180
	21:12	*They f* among the people living	5162
Ru	2: 3	she *f* herself working in a field belonging	NIH
	2:10	"Why *have I f* such favor in your eyes	5162

1Sa	9:20	they have **been f.** 5162
	10: 2	donkeys you set out to look for *have* **been f.** 5162
	10:14	"But when we saw they were not to be f, NIH
	10:16	He assured us that the donkeys *had* **been f.** 5162
	10:21	they looked for him, *he was* not to be f. 5162
	12: 5	that *you have* not f anything in my hand." 5162
	13:19	a blacksmith *could be* f in the whole land 5162
	14:20	They f the Philistines in total confusion, 2180
	20: 3	that *I have* f favor in your eyes, 5162
	20:29	If *I have* f favor in your eyes, 5162
	25:28	*Let* no wrongdoing be f in you as long 5162
	27: 5	"If *I have* f favor in your eyes, 5162
	29: 3	*I have* f no fault in him." 5162
	29: 6	*I have* f no fault in him. 5162
	29: 8	"What *have you* f against your servant 5162
	30: 3	they f it destroyed by fire and their wives 2180
	30: 6	But David f **strength** in 2616
	30:11	*They* f an Egyptian in a field 5162
	31: 8	it *they* f Saul and his three sons fallen 5162
2Sa	2:30	nineteen of David's men were f **missing.** 7212
	7:27	So your servant *has* f courage 5162
	14:22	that he *has* f favor in your eyes, 5162
	17:12	we will attack him wherever he *may* be f, 5162
	17:13	until not even a piece of it *can* be f." 5162
	17:20	The men searched but f no one, 5162
1Ki	1: 3	for a beautiful girl and f Abishag, 5162
	1:52	but if evil is f in him, he will die." 5162
	13:14	*He* f him sitting under an oak tree 5162
	13:28	and f the body thrown down on the road, 5162
	14:13	the God of Israel, *has* f anything good. 5162
	19:19	So Elijah went from there and f Elisha son 5162
	20:36	a lion f him and killed him. 5162
	20:37	The prophet f another man and said, 5162
	21:20	Ahab said to Elijah, "So *you have* f me, 5162
	21:20	"*I have* f you," he answered, 5162
2Ki	4:39	the fields to gather herbs and f a wild vine. 5162
	7:15	and they f the whole road strewn with 2180
	9: 5	he f the army officers sitting together. 2180
	9:35	they f nothing except her skull, 5162
	12: 5	be used to repair whatever damage is f in 5162
	12:18	the gold f in the treasuries of the temple of 5162
	14:14	the gold and silver and all the articles f *in* 5162
	16: 8	and gold f in the temple of the LORD and 5162
	18:15	that was f in the temple of the LORD and 5162
	19: 8	and f the king fighting against Libnah. 5162
	20:13	and everything f among his treasures. 5162
	22: 8	"*I have* f the Book of the Law in the temple 5162
	22:13	in this book that *has* **been f.** 5162
	23: 2	which *had* **been f** in the temple of 5162
	25:19	of the land and sixty of his men who **were f** 5162
1Ch	4:40	*They* f rich, good pasture, 5162
	10: 8	they f Saul and his sons fallen 5162
	17:25	So your servant *has* f **courage** to pray 5162
	20: 2	its weight had f to be a talent of gold, 5162
	24: 4	A larger number of leaders were f 5162
	26:31	the Hebronites were f at Jazer in Gilead. 5162
	28: 9	If you seek him, *he will* be f by you; 5162
2Ch	2:17	and *they* were f to be 153,600. 5162
	15: 2	If you seek him, *he will* be f by you, 5162
	15: 4	and sought him, and he was f by them. 5162
	15:15	and he was f by them. 5162
	20:25	and *they* f among them a great amount 5162
	21:17	invaded it and carried off all the goods f in 5162
	22: 8	he f the princes of Judah and the sons 5162
	25: 5	those twenty years old or more and f 5162
	25:24	the gold and silver and all the articles f in 5162
	29:16	that *they* f in the temple of the LORD. 5162
	34:14	Hilkiah the priest f the Book of the Law of 5162
	34:15	"*I have* f the Book of the Law in the temple 5162
	34:21	in this book that *has* **been f.** 5162
	34:30	which *had* **been f** in the temple of 5162
	36: 8	and all that was f against him, 5162
Ezr	4:19	and it was f that this city has 10708
	6: 2	A scroll was f in the citadel of Ecbatana in 10708
	8:15	I f no Levites there. 5162
Ne	2: 5	and if your servant *has* f **favor** in his sight. 3512
	7: 5	*I* f the genealogical record 5162
	7: 5	This is what *I* f written there: 5162
	8:14	*They* f written in the Law, 5162
	9: 8	*You* f his heart faithful to you, 5162
	13: 1	of the people and there *it* was f written 5162
Est	2:22	But Mordecai f **out** about the plot 3359
	2:23	report was investigated and f to be true, 5162
	6: 2	*It* was f recorded there 5162
	7: 3	"If *I have* f favor with you, O king, 5162
Job	9:29	Since *I am already* f **guilty,** AIT
	12:12	Is not wisdom f among the aged? NIH
	20: 8	no more to be f, 5162
	28:12	"But where *can* wisdom **be f?** 5162
	28:13	it cannot **be f** in the land of the living. 5162
	32: 3	because *they had* f no way to refute Job, 5162
	32:13	Do not say, '*We have* f wisdom; 5162
	33:10	Yet God *has* f fault with me; 5162
	33:24	*I have* f a ransom for him'— 5162
	42:15	Nowhere in all the land **were** *there* f women 5162
Ps	10:15	*that* would not be f **out.** 5162
	32: 6	to you while you *may* be f; 5162
	37:10	you look for them, they will not be f. NIH
	37:36	though I looked for him, he *could* not be f. 5162
	69:20	for comforters, but *I* f none. 5162
	84: 3	Even the sparrow *has* f a home, 5162
	89:20	*I have* f David my servant; 5162
	109: 7	When he is tried, *let him be* f guilty, 3655
	109:17	he f no **pleasure** in blessing— 2911
Pr	7:15	I looked for you and *have* f you! 5162
	10: 9	he who takes crooked paths *will* be f **out.** 3359
	10:13	Wisdom **is** f on the lips of the discerning, 5162

Pr	13:10	but wisdom is f in those who take advice. NIH
	14: 9	but goodwill is f among the upright. NIH
	19: 7	they are nowhere to be **f.** NIH
	30:28	yet it is f in kings' palaces. NIH
Ecc	7:28	*I* f one [upright] man among a thousand, 5162
	7:29	This only have *I* f: 5162
SS	3: 3	The watchmen f me as they made their 5162
	3: 4	Scarcely had I passed them when *I* f 5162
	5: 7	The watchmen f me as they made their 5162
	8: 1	Then, if *I* f you outside, I would kiss you, 5162
Isa	30:14	a fragment *will be* f for taking coals from 5162
	35: 9	*they will* not **be f** there. 5162
	37: 8	and f the king fighting against Libnah 5162
	39: 2	and everything f among his treasures. 5162
	45:25	of Israel *will be* f **righteous** and will exult. AIT
	51: 3	Joy and gladness *will be* f in her, 5162
	55: 6	Seek the LORD while he *may* be f; 5162
	57:10	*You* f renewal of your strength, 5162
	59:15	Truth is **nowhere to be f,** 6372
	65: 1	*I was* f by those who did not seek me. 5162
	65: 8	when juice is *still* f in a cluster of grapes 5162
Jer	29:14	*I will* be f by you," declares the LORD, 5162
	40: 1	He had f Jeremiah bound in chains 4374
	40: 2	the commander of the guard f Jeremiah, 4374
	50: 7	Whoever f them devoured them; 5162
	50:20	but none *will* be f, 5162
	50:24	*you* were f and captured 5162
	52:25	of the land and sixty of his men who **were f** 5162
Eze	4:14	now I have never eaten **anything** f **dead** 5577
	16:37	with whom *you* f **pleasure,** 6844
	22:30	but *I* f none. 5162
	26:21	but *you will* never again **be f,** 5162
	28:15	till wickedness **was f** in you. 5162
	44:31	f **dead** or torn by wild animals. 5577
Da	1:19	and he f none equal to Daniel, Hananiah, 5162
	1:20	he f them ten times better than all 5162
	2:25	"*I have* f a man among the exiles 10708
	4:12	Under it the beasts of the field f **shelter,** 10300
	5:11	of your father he *was* f to have insight 10708
	5:12	*was* f to have a keen mind and knowledge 10708
	5:27	on the scales and f wanting. 10708
	6:11	and f Daniel praying and asking God 10708
	6:22	because I *was* f innocent in his sight. 10708
	6:23	no wound *was* f on him, 10708
	12: 1	everyone whose name **is** f written in 5162
Hos	9:10	"When *I* f Israel, it was like finding grapes 5162
	12: 4	*He* f him at Bethel and talked 5162
Jnh	1: 3	where he f a ship bound for that port. 5162
Mic	1:13	the transgressions of Israel **were f** in you. 5162
Zep	3:13	nor *will* deceit **be f** in their mouths. 5162
Zec	1:11	and the whole world at rest and in peace." 2180
Mal	2: 6	in his mouth and nothing false **was f** 5162
Mt	1:18	but before they came together, *she was* f to 2351
	2: 7	f **out** from them the **exact** time 208
	8:10	not f anyone in Israel with such great faith. 2351
	13:44	**When** a man f it, he hid it again, 2351
	13:46	*When* he f one of great value, 2351
	18:28	"But when that servant went out, *he* f one 2351
	20: 6	and f still others standing around. 2351
	21:19	up to it but f nothing on it except leaves. 2351
	26:40	to his disciples and f them sleeping. 2351
	26:43	he again f them sleeping, 2351
Mk	1:37	and when *they* f him, they exclaimed: 2351
	6:38	*When they* f **out,** they said, "Five— 1182
	7:30	*She* went home and f her child lying on 2351
	11: 4	They went and f a colt outside in the street, 2351
	11:13	he f nothing but leaves, 2351
	14:16	and f things just as Jesus had told them. 2351
	14:37	to his disciples and f them sleeping. 2351
	14:40	he again f them sleeping, 2351
Lk	1:30	Mary, *you have* f favor with God. 2351
	2:16	So they hurried off and f Mary and Joseph, 461
	2:46	After three days *they* f him in 2351
	4:17	he f the place where it is written: 2351
	7: 9	not f such great faith even in Israel." 2351
	7:10	to the house and f the servant well. 2351
	8:35	they f the man from whom 2351
	9:36	*they* f that Jesus was alone. 2351
	13: 7	for fruit on this fig tree and haven't f any. 2351
	15: 6	*I have* f my lost sheep.' 2351
	15: 9	*I have* f my lost coin.' 2351
	15:24	he was lost and is **f.'** 2351
	15:32	he was lost and is **f.'** " 2351
	17:18	*Was* no one f to return and give praise 2351
	19:32	and f it just as he had told them. 2351
	22:13	and f things just as Jesus had told them. 2351
	22:45	he f them asleep, exhausted from sorrow. 2351
	23: 2	"We have f this man subverting our nation. 2351
	23:14	in your presence and *have* f no basis 2351
	23:22	*I have* f in him no grounds for 2351
	24: 2	*They* f the stone rolled away from 2351
	24:24	and f it just as the women had said, 2351
	24:33	There *they* f the Eleven and those 2351
Jn	1:41	"We have f the Messiah" (that is, the Christ) 2351
	1:45	Philip f Nathanael and told him, 2351
	1:45	"We have f the one Moses wrote about in 2351
	2:14	In the temple courts he f men selling cattle, 2351
	5:14	Later Jesus f him at the temple and said 2351
	6:25	*When they* f him on the other side of 2351
	9:35	and when he f him, he said, 2351
	11:17	Jesus f that Lazarus had already been in 2351
	11:57	that if anyone f **out** where Jesus was, 1182
	12: 9	Meanwhile a large crowd of Jews f **out** 1182
	12:14	Jesus f a young donkey and sat upon it, 2351
	19:33	to Jesus and f that he was already dead, 3972
Ac	4:12	Salvation is f in no one else, NIG
	5:23	"We f the jail securely locked, with 2351

Ac	5:23	when we opened them, *we* f no one inside." 2351
	9: 2	if he f any there who belonged to the Way, 2351
	9:33	There he f a man named Aeneas, 2351
	10:17	the men sent by Cornelius f **out** 1452
	10:27	Peter went inside and f a large gathering 2351
	11:26	and *when he* f him, 2351
	13:22	'*I have* f David son of Jesse a man 2351
	13:28	Though *they* f no proper ground for 2351
	14: 6	But *they* f **out** about it and fled to 5328
	17:23	*I* even f an altar with this inscription: 2351
	19: 1	There he f some disciples 2351
	21: 2	We f a ship crossing over to Phoenicia, 2351
	22:25	hasn't even **been f guilty?"** 185
	23:29	*I* f that the accusation had to do 2351
	24: 5	"We have f this man to be a troublemaker, 2351
	24:18	I was ceremonially clean when *they* f me 2351
	24:20	who are here should state what crime *they* f 2351
	25:25	I f he had done nothing deserving of death, 2898
	27: 6	the centurion f an Alexandrian ship sailing 2351
	27:28	and f that the water was a hundred 2351
	27:28	and f it was ninety feet deep. 2351
	28: 1	*we* f **out** that the island was called Malta. 2105
	28:14	There *we* f some brothers who invited us 2351
Ro	7:10	*I* f that the very commandment 2351
	10:20	"*I was* f by those who did not seek me; 2351
1Co	15:15	then f to be false witnesses about God, 2351
2Co	2:12	of Christ and f that the Lord had opened NIG
	5: 3	we will not be f naked. 2351
Php	2: 8	And *being* f in appearance as a man, 2351
	3: 9	and *be* f in him, not having a righteousness 2351
Col	2:17	the reality, however, is f in Christ. NIG
2Ti	1:17	he searched hard for me until he f me. 2351
Heb	3: 1	Jesus *has been* f **worthy** of greater honor 546
	4: 1	that none of you be f to have fallen short 1506
	8: 8	But God f **fault with** the people and said: 3522
	11: 5	he *could* not be f, 2351
Jas	2: 8	If you really keep the royal law f **in** 2848
1Pe	2:22	and no deceit *was* f in his mouth." 2351
2Pe	3:14	make every effort *to be* f spotless, 2351
Rev	2: 2	and *have* f them false. 2351
	3: 2	for *I have* not f your deeds complete in 2351
	3: 4	because no one f who was worthy 2351
	14: 5	No lie *was* f in their mouths; 2351
	16:20	and the mountains *could* not be **f.** 2351
	18:21	never *to be* f again. 2351
	18:22	No workman of any trade *will ever be* f 2351
	18:24	In her *was* f the blood of prophets and of 2351
	20:15	If anyone's name *was* not f written in 2351
	21:16	He measured the city with the rod and f it NIG

FOUNDATION (39) [FOUNDATIONS, FOUNDED]

1Ki	5:17	to **provide** a f of dressed stone for 3569
	6:37	**The** f of the temple of the LORD **was laid** 3569
	7: 9	to the great courtyard and from f to eaves, 4996
2Ch	3: 3	**The** f Solomon **laid** for building 3569
	8:16	of the temple of the LORD was **laid** 4586
	23: 5	the royal palace and a third at the **F** Gate, 3572
Ezr	3: 3	on its f and sacrificed burnt offerings on it 4807
	3: 6	the f of the LORD's temple *had not yet been* **laid.** 3569
	3:10	When the builders **laid the f** of the temple 3569
	3:11	**the f** of the house of the LORD **was laid.** 3569
	3:12	**the f** of this temple being **laid,** 3569
Job	38: 4	were you when I **laid** the earth's f? 3569
Ps	87: 1	He has set his f on the holy mountain; 3573
	89:14	and justice are the f of your throne; 4806
	97: 2	and justice are the f of his throne. 4806
Isa	28:16	a precious cornerstone for a sure f; 4586
		He will be the **sure f** for your times, 575
Jer	51:26	nor any stone for a f, 4589
Eze	13:14	to the ground so that its f will be laid bare. 3572
	41: 8	forming the f of the side rooms. 4588
Am	9: 6	in the heavens and sets its f on the earth, 99
Hag	2:18	**the f** of the LORD's temple **was laid.** 3569
Zec	4: 9	"The hands of Zerubbabel *have* **laid the f** 3569
	8: 9	when the **f was laid** *for* the house of 3569
	12: 1	who **lays the f** of the earth, 3569
Mt	7:25	because *it had its* f on the rock. 2530
Lk	6:48	who dug down deep and laid the f on rock. 2529
	6:49	a house on the ground without a f. 2529
	14:29	if he lays the f and is not able to finish it, 2529
Ro	15:20	not be building on someone else's f. 2529
1Co	3:10	I laid a f as an expert builder, 2529
	3:11	For no one can lay any f other than 2529
	3:12	If any man builds on this f using gold, 2529
Eph	2:20	built on the f of the apostles and prophets, 2529
1Ti	3:15	the pillar and f of the truth. 1613
	6:19	up treasure for themselves as a firm f for 2529
2Ti	2:19	Nevertheless, God's solid f stands firm, 2529
Heb	6: 1	the f of repentance from acts that lead 2529
Rev	21:19	The first f was jasper, the second sapphire, 2529

FOUNDATIONS (38) [FOUNDATION]

Dt	32:22	the earth and its harvests and set afire the f 4587
Jos	6:26	of his firstborn son *will* he **lay** its f; 3569
1Sa	2: 8	"For the f of the earth are the LORD's; 5187
2Sa	22: 8	the f of the heavens shook; 4589
	22:16	the f of the earth laid bare at the rebuke of 4589
1Ki	5:17	**The f were laid** *with* large stones 3569
	16:34	He **laid** its f at the cost 3569
Ezr	4:12	the walls and repairing the f. 10079
	5:16	So this Sheshbazzar came and **laid the f** of 10079
	6: 3	and let its f be **laid.** 10079
Job	4:19	whose f are in the dust, 3572

Job	22:16	their f washed away by a flood.	3572
Ps	11: 3	When the f are being destroyed,	9268
	18: 7	and the f of the mountains shook;	4587
	18:15	the f of the earth laid bare at your rebuke,	4589
	82: 5	all the f of the earth are shaken.	4587
	102:25	the beginning *you* **laid the** f of the earth,	3569
	104: 5	He set the earth on its f;	4806
	137: 7	they cried, "tear it down to its f!"	3572
Pr	3:19	By wisdom the LORD **laid** the earth's f,	3569
	8:29	and when he marked out the f of the earth.	4587
Isa	24:18	the f of the earth shake.	4587
	44:28	and of the temple, "*Let its* f *be laid.*" '	3569
	48:13	My own hand **laid the** f of the earth,	3569
	51:13	the heavens and **laid the** f of the earth,	3569
	51:16	*who* **laid the** f of the earth,	3569
	54:11	your f with sapphires,	3569
	58:12	and will raise up the age-old f;	4587
Jer	31:37	be measured and the f of the earth below	4587
La	4:11	a fire in Zion that consumed her f.	3572
Eze	30: 4	be carried away and her f torn down.	3572
Mic	1: 6	into the valley and lay bare her f.	3572
	6: 2	listen, you everlasting f of the earth.	4587
Ac	16:26	that the f of the prison were shaken.	2528
Heb	1:10	O Lord, you **laid the** f of the earth,	2530
	11:10	he was looking forward to the city with f,	2529
Rev	21:14	The wall of the city had twelve f,	2529
	21:19	The f of the city walls were decorated	2529

FOUNDED (11) [FOUNDATION]

Ex	9:18	from the day it **was** f till now.	3569
1Ki	2:24	on the throne of my father David and **has** f	6913
Ps	24: 2	for he f it upon the seas and established it	3569
	89:11	you f the world and all that is in it.	3569
	94:15	Judgment will again be f on righteousness,	6330
	107:36	and *they* f a city where they could settle.	3922
Isa	40:21	not understood since the earth was f?	4589
	45:18	and made the earth, he f it;	3922
Jer	10:12	he f the world by his wisdom	3922
	51:15	he f the world by his wisdom	3922
Heb	8: 6	and it *is* f on better promises.	3793

FOUNTAIN (15) [FOUNTAINS]

Ne	2:14	on toward the F Gate and the King's Pool,	6524
	3:15	The F Gate was repaired by Shallun son	6524
	12:37	At the F Gate they continued directly up	6524
Ps	36: 9	For with you is the f of life;	5227
Pr	5:18	May your f be blessed,	5227
	10:11	The mouth of the righteous is a f *of* life,	5227
	13:14	The teaching of the wise is a f *of* life,	5227
	14:27	The fear of the LORD is a f *of* life,	5227
	16:22	a f *of* life to those who have it,	5227
	18: 4	but the f *of* wisdom is a bubbling brook.	5227
SS	4:12	you are a spring enclosed, a sealed f.	1644
	4:15	You are a garden f,	5078
Jer	9: 1	a spring of water and my eyes a f *of* tears!	5227
Joel	3:18	A f will flow out of the LORD's house	5078
Zec	13: 1	a f will be opened to the house of David	5227

FOUNTAINS (2) [FOUNTAIN]

Ps	87: 7	"All my f are in you."	5078
Pr	8:28	and fixed securely the f of the deep,	6524

FOUR (225) [FOUR-DRACHMA, FOUR-FIFTHS, FOUR-FOOTED, FOUR-SIDED, FOURS, FOURTH]

Ge	2:10	from there it was separated into f headwaters.	752
	14: 9	f kings against five.	752
	14:11	The f kings seized all the goods of Sodom	NIH
	15:13	and mistreated f hundred years.	752
	23:15	land is worth f hundred shekels of silver,	752
	23:16	f hundred shekels of silver,	752
	32: 6	and f hundred men are with him."	752
	33: 1	coming with his f hundred men;	752
Ex	22: 1	for the ox and f sheep for the ox.	752
	25:12	Cast f gold rings for it and fasten them	752
	25:12	for it and fasten them to its f feet,	752
	25:26	Make f gold rings for the table	752
	25:26	the table and fasten them to the f corners,	752
	25:26	where the f legs are.	752
	25:34	the lampstand there are to be f cups shaped	752
	26: 2	twenty-eight cubits long and f cubits wide.	752
	26: 8	thirty cubits long and f cubits wide.	752
	26:32	Hang it with gold hooks on f posts	752
	26:32	with gold and standing on f silver bases.	752
	27: 2	Make a horn at each of the f corners,	752
	27: 4	a bronze ring at each of the f corners of	752
	27:16	with f posts and four bases.	752
	27:16	with four posts and f bases.	752
	28:17	mount f rows of precious stones on it.	752
	36: 9	twenty-eight cubits long and f cubits wide.	752
	36:15	thirty cubits long and f cubits wide.	752
	36:36	They made f posts of acacia wood for it	752
	36:36	for them and cast their f silver bases.	752
	37: 3	He cast f gold rings for it	752
	37: 3	for it and fastened them to its f feet,	752
	37:13	They cast f gold rings for the table	752
	37:13	and fastened them to the f corners,	752
	37:13	where the f legs were.	752
	37:20	And on the lampstand were f cups shaped	752
	38: 2	Make a horn at each of the f corners,	752
	38: 5	for the f corners of the bronze grating,	752
	38:19	with f posts and four bronze bases.	752
	38:19	with four posts and f bronze bases.	752

Ex	39:10	Then they mounted f rows	752
Lev	11:23	that have f legs you are to detest.	752
Nu	7: 7	He gave two carts and f oxen to	752
	7: 8	and he gave f carts and eight oxen to	752
	7:85	silver dishes weighed two thousand f hundred shekels,	752
Dt	22:12	on the f corners of the cloak you wear.	752
Jos	19: 7	f towns and their villages—	752
	21:18	with their pasturelands—f towns.	752
	21:22	with their pasturelands—f towns.	752
	21:24	with their pasturelands—f towns.	752
	21:29	with their pasturelands—f towns.	752
	21:31	with their pasturelands—f towns.	752
	21:35	with their pasturelands—f towns.	752
	21:37	with their pasturelands—f towns.	752
	21:39	f towns in all.	752
Jdg	9:34	near Shechem in f companies.	752
	11:40	of Israel go out for f days to commemorate	752
	19: 2	After she had been there f months,	752
	20: 2	f hundred thousand soldiers armed	752
	20:17	mustered f hundred thousand swordsmen,	752
	20:47	where they stayed f months.	752
	21:12	in Jabesh Gilead f hundred young women who had never slept with a man,	752
1Sa	4: 2	about f thousand of them on the battlefield.	752
	22: 2	About f hundred men were with him.	752
	25:13	About f hundred men went up with David,	752
	27: 1	in Philistine territory a year and f months.	752
	30:10	and f hundred men continued the pursuit.	752
	30:17	except f hundred young men who rode off	752
2Sa	12: 6	He must pay for that lamb f *times over,*	752
	15: 7	At the end of f years,	752
	21:22	These f were descendants of Rapha	752
1Ki	4:26	Solomon had f thousand stalls	752
	6: 1	In the f hundred and eightieth year after	752
	7: 2	and thirty high, with f rows	752
	7:19	in the shape of lilies, f cubits high.	752
	7:27	each was f cubits long,	752
	7:27	f wide and three high.	752
	7:30	Each stand had f bronze wheels,	752
	7:30	and each had a basin resting on f supports,	752
	7:32	The f wheels were under the panels,	752
	7:34	Each stand had f handles,	752
	7:38	and measuring f cubits across,	752
	7:42	the f hundred pomegranates for	752
	18:19	And bring the f hundred and fifty prophets	752
	18:19	and the f hundred prophets of Asherah,	752
	18:22	but Baal has f hundred and fifty prophets.	752
	18:33	"Fill f large jars with water and pour it on	752
	22: 6	about f hundred men—	752
2Ki	7: 3	Now there were f men with leprosy at	752
	25:17	pillar was f **and a half feet** high	564+8993
1Ch	3: 5	These f were by Bathsheba daughter	752
	7: 1	and Shimron—f in all.	752
	9:24	The gatekeepers were on the f sides:	752
	9:26	But the f principal gatekeepers,	752
	21: 5	including f hundred and seventy thousand	752
	21:20	his f sons who were	752
	23: 5	f thousand are to be gatekeepers	752
	23: 5	be gatekeepers and f thousand are to praise	752
	23:10	These were the sons of Shimei—f in all.	752
	23:12	and Uzziel—f in all.	752
	26:17	f a day on the north,	752
	26:17	f a day on the south and two at a time at	752
	26:18	there were f at the road and two at	752
2Ch	4:13	the f hundred pomegranates for	752
	8:18	sailed to Ophir and brought back f hundred	752
	9:25	Solomon had f thousand stalls for horses	752
	13: 3	of f hundred thousand able fighting men,	752
	18:15	the prophets—f hundred men—	752
Ezr	6:17	f hundred male lambs and,	10065
Ne	6: 4	F times they sent me the same message,	752
Job	1:19	from the desert and struck the f corners of	752
Pr	30:15	f that never say, 'Enough!':	752
	30:18	f that I do not understand:	752
	30:21	under f it cannot bear up:	752
	30:24	"F things on earth are small,	752
	30:29	f that move with stately bearing:	752
Isa	11:12	of Judah from the f quarters of the earth.	752
	17: 6	f or five on the fruitful boughs,"	752
Jer	15: 3	"I will send f kinds of destroyers	752
	36:23	or f columns of the scroll,	752
	49:36	I will bring against Elam the f winds from	752
	49:36	the four winds from the f quarters of	752
	49:36	I will scatter them to the f winds,	3972S
	52:21	each was f fingers thick, and hollow.	752
Eze	1: 5	like f living creatures.	752
	1: 6	each of them had f faces and four wings.	752
	1: 6	each of them had four faces and f wings.	752
	1: 8	Under their wings on their f sides they had	752
	1: 8	*All* f of them had faces and wings,	752
	1:10	Each of the f had the face of a man,	752
	1:15	beside each creature with its f faces.	752
	1:16	and all f looked alike.	752
	1:17	of the f directions the creatures faced;	752
	1:18	and all f rims were full of eyes all around.	752
	7: 2	The end has come upon the f corners of	752
	10: 9	and I saw beside the cherubim f wheels,	752
	10:10	the f of them looked alike;	752
	10:11	of the f directions the cherubim faced;	752
	10:12	as were their f wheels.	752
	10:14	Each of the cherubim had f faces:	752
	10:21	Each had f faces and four wings,	752
	10:21	Each had four faces and f wings,	752
	14:21	against Jerusalem my f dreadful judgments—	752
	37: 9	Come from the f winds, O breath,	752
	40:41	So there were f tables on one side of	752

Eze	40:41	on one side of the gateway and f on	752
	40:42	There were also f tables of dressed stone	752
	41: 5	around the temple was f cubits wide.	752
	42:20	So he measured the area on *all* f sides.	752
	43:14	up to the larger ledge it is f cubits high and	752
	43:15	The altar hearth is f cubits high,	752
	43:15	f horns project upward from the hearth.	752
	43:20	and put it on the f horns of the altar and on	752
	43:20	on the f corners of the upper ledge and all	752
	45:19	the f corners of the upper ledge of the altar	752
	46:21	and led me around to its f corners,	752
	46:21	In f corners of the outer court	752
	46:22	each of the courts in the f corners was	752
	46:23	of each of the f courts was a ledge of stone,	752
Da	1:17	To these f young men God gave knowledge	752
	3:25	I see f men walking around in the fire,	10065
	7: 2	and there before me were the f winds	10065
	7: 3	F great beasts, each different from	10065
	7: 6	And on its back it had f wings like those of	10065
	7: 6	This beast had f heads,	10065
	7:17	'The f great beasts are four kingdoms	10065
	7:17	The four great beasts are f kingdoms	10065
	8: 8	and in its place f prominent horns grew up	752
	8: 8	up toward the f winds of heaven.	752
	8:22	The f horns that replaced the one	752
	8:22	that was broken off represent f kingdoms	752
	11: 4	up and parceled out toward the f winds	752
Am	1: 3	"For three sins of Damascus, even for f,	752
	1: 6	"For three sins of Gaza, even for f,	752
	1: 9	"For three sins of Tyre, even for f,	752
	1:11	"For three sins of Edom, even for f,	752
	1:13	"For three sins of Ammon, even for f,	752
	2: 1	"For three sins of Moab, even for f,	752
	2: 4	"For three sins of Judah, even for f,	752
	2: 6	"For three sins of Israel, even for f,	752
Zec	1:18	and there before me were f horns!	752
	1:20	Then the LORD showed me f craftsmen.	752
	2: 6	"for I have scattered you to the f winds	752
	6: 1	before me were f chariots coming out from	752
	6: 5	"These are the f spirits of heaven,	752
Mt	15:38	of those who ate was f **thousand,**	5483
	16:10	Or the seven loaves *for* the f **thousand,**	5483
	24:31	they will gather his elect from the f winds,	5475
Mk	8: 9	About f **thousand** *men* were present.	5483
	8:20	I broke the seven loaves for the f **thousand,**	5483
	13:27	and gather his elect from the f winds,	5475
Lk	16: 6	sit down quickly, and make it f **hundred.**'	4299
	19: 8	I will pay back f **times** the amount."	5486
Jn	4:35	'F months more and then the harvest'?	5485
	11:17	in the tomb *for* f days.	5475
	11:39	for he has been there f days."	5479
	19:23	dividing them into f shares,	5475
Ac	5:36	and about f **hundred** men rallied to him.	5484
	7: 6	enslaved and mistreated f **hundred** years.	5484
	10:11	down to earth *by* its f corners.	5475
	10:30	"F days ago I was in my house praying	5480
	11: 5	down from heaven *by* its f corners,	5475
	12: 4	handing him over to be guarded *by* f **squads**	5482
	12: 4	by four squads *of* f soldiers each.	5475
	21: 9	He had f unmarried daughters who prophesied.	5475
	21:23	There are f men with us who have made	5475
	21:38	a revolt and led f **thousand** terrorists out	5483
	27:29	they dropped f anchors from the stern	5475
Rev	4: 6	around the throne, were f living creatures,	5475
	4: 8	Each of the f living creatures had six wings	5475
	5: 6	*by* the f living creatures and the elders.	5475
	5: 8	the f living creatures and the twenty-four	5475
	5:14	The f living creatures said, "Amen,"	5475
	6: 1	of the f living creatures say in a voice	5475
	6: 6	like a voice among the f living creatures,	5475
	7: 1	After this I saw f angels standing at	5475
	7: 1	at the f corners of the earth,	5475
	7: 1	holding back the f winds of the earth	5475
	7: 2	*to* the f angels who had been given power	5475
	7:11	around the elders and the f living creatures.	5475
	9:14	"Release the f angels who are bound at	5475
	9:15	And the f angels who had been kept ready	5475
	14: 3	before the f living creatures and the elders.	5475
	15: 7	Then one of the f living creatures gave to	5475
	19: 4	and the f living creatures fell down	5475
	20: 8	the nations in the f corners of the earth—	5475

FOUR-DRACHMA (1) [DRACHMAS, FOUR]

Mt	17:27	open its mouth and you will find a f **coin.**	5088

FOUR-FIFTHS (1) [FIVE, FOUR]

Ge	47:24	The *other* f you may keep as seed for	752+3338

FOUR-FOOTED (2) [FOUR, FOOT]

Ac	10:12	It contained all kinds of f **animals,**	5488
	11: 6	into it and saw f **animals** of the earth,	5488

FOUR-SIDED (1) [FOUR, SIDE]

1Ki	6:33	In the same way he made f jambs	8055

FOURFOLD (KJV) See FOUR TIMES

FOURS (4) [FOUR]

Lev	11:20	that walk on **all** f are to be detestable	752
	11:21	some winged creatures that walk on **all** f	752

Lev 11:27 Of all the animals that walk on **all f**, 752
11:42 or walks on **all f** or on many feet; 752

FOURSCORE (KJV) See EIGHTY, EIGHT HUNDRED

FOURSQUARE (KJV) See SQUARE

FOURTEEN (27) [FOURTEENTH]
Ge 31:41 for you **f** years for your two daughters 752+6926
46:22 to Jacob—**f** in all. 752+6925
Nu 29:13 two rams and **f** male lambs a year old, 752+6925
29:15 and with each of the **f** lambs, one-tenth. 752+6925
29:17 two rams and **f** male lambs a year old, 752+6925
29:20 two rams and **f** male lambs a year old, 752+6925
29:23 two rams and **f** male lambs a year old, 752+6925
29:26 two rams and **f** male lambs a year old, 752+6925
29:29 two rams and **f** male lambs a year old, 752+6925
29:32 two rams and **f** male lambs a year old, 752+6925
Jos 15:36 **f** towns and their villages. 752+6926
18:28 **f** towns and their villages. 752+6926
1Ki 8:65 **f** days in all. 752+6926
10:26 he had **f hundred** chariots 547+752+2256+4395
1Ch 25: 5 God gave Heman **f** sons 752+6926
2Ch 1:14 he had **f hundred** chariots 547+752+2256+4395
13:21 He married **f** wives 752+6926
Job 42:12 He had **f** thousand sheep, 752+6926
Eze 40:48 The width of the entrance was **f** cubits 752+6926
43:17 **f** cubits long and fourteen cubits wide, 752+6926
43:17 fourteen cubits long and **f** cubits wide, 752+6926
Mt 1:17 Thus there were **f** generations in all 1280
1:17 **f** from David to the exile to Babylon, 1280
1:17 and **f** from the exile to the Christ. 1280
Ac 27:33 "For the last **f** days," he said, 5476
2Co 12: 2 in Christ who **f** years ago was caught up to 1280
Gal 2: 1 **F** years later I went up again to Jerusalem, 1280

FOURTEENTH (24) [FOURTEEN]
Ge 14: 5 In the **f** year, Kedorlaomer and 752+6926
Ex 12: 6 of them until the **f** day of the month, 752+6925
12:18 evening of the **f** day until the evening 752+6925
Lev 23: 5 twilight on the **f** day of the first month. 752+6925
Nu 9: 3 at twilight on the **f** day of this month, 752+6925
9: 5 Desert of Sinai at twilight on the **f** day 752+6925
9:11 **f** day of the second month at twilight. 752+6925
28:16 " 'On the **f** day of the first month 752+6925
Jos 5:10 the evening of the **f** day of the month, 752+6925
2Ki 18:13 In the **f** year of King Hezekiah's reign, 752+6926
1Ch 24:13 the **f** to Jeshebeab, 752+6925
25:21 the **f** to Mattithiah, 752+6925
2Ch 30:15 on the **f** day of the second month. 752+6925
35: 1 on the **f** day of the first month. 752+6925
Ezr 6:19 On the **f** day of the first month, 752+6925
Est 9:15 in Susa came together on the **f** day of 752+6925
9:17 on the **f** they rested and made it a day 752+6925
9:18 had assembled on the thirteenth and **f**, 752+6925
9:19 observe the **f** of the month of Adar as 752+6925
9:21 to have them celebrate annually the **f** 752+6925
Isa 36: 1 In the **f** year of King Hezekiah's reign, 752+6926
Eze 40: 1 in the **f** year after the fall of the city— 752+6926
45:21 **f** day you are to observe the Passover, 752+6925
Ac 27:27 On the **f** night we were still being driven 5476

FOURTH (72) [FOUR]
Ge 1:19 and there was morning—the **f** day. 8055
2:14 And the **f** river is the Euphrates. 8055
15:16 In the **f** generation your descendants will come back here, 8055
Ex 20: 5 of the fathers to the third and **f generation** 8067
28:20 in the **f** row a chrysolite, 8055
34: 7 of the fathers to the third and **f generation**." 8067
39:13 in the **f** row a chrysolite, 8055
Lev 19:24 In the **f** year all its fruit will be holy, 8055
Nu 7:30 On the **f** day Elizur son of Shedeur, 8055
14:18 the fathers to the third and **f generation**.' 8067
23:10 of Jacob or number the **f part** of Israel? 8065
29:23 " 'On the **f** day prepare ten bulls, 8055
Dt 5: 9 of the fathers to the third and **f generation** 8067
Jos 19:17 **f** lot came out for Issachar, clan by clan. 8055
Jdg 14:15 On the **f** day, they said to Samson's wife, 8055
19: 5 the **f** day they got up early and he prepared 8055
2Sa 3: 4 the **f**, Adonijah the son of Haggith; 8055
1Ki 6: 1 the **f** year of Solomon's reign over Israel, 8055
6:37 of the LORD was laid in the **f** year, 8055
22:41 of Asa became king of Judah in the **f** year 752
2Ki 10:30 on the throne of Israel to the **f generation**." 8055
15:12 on the throne of Israel to the **f generation**." 8055
18: 9 In King Hezekiah's **f** year, 8055
25: 3 the ninth day of the **[f]** month the famine NIH
1Ch 2:14 the Nethanel, the fifth Raddai, 8055
3: 2 the **f**, Adonijah the son of Haggith; 8055
3:15 Zedekiah the third, Shallum the **f**. 8055
8: 2 Nohah the **f** and Rapha the fifth. 8055
12:10 Mishmannah the **f**, Jeremiah the fifth, 8055
23:19 Jahaziel the third and Jekameam the **f**. 8055
24: 8 the third to Harim, the **f** to Seorim, 8055
24:23 Jahaziel the third and Jekameam the **f**. 8055
25:11 the **f** to Izri, his sons and relatives, 12 8055
26: 2 Zebadiah the third, Jathniel the **f**, 8055
26: 4 Sacar the third, Nethanel the fifth, 8055
26:11 Tabaliah the **f** and Zechariah the fifth. 8055
27: 7 The **f**, for the fourth month, 8055
27: 7 The fourth, for the **f** month, 8055

2Ch 3: 2 the second month in the **f** year of his reign. 752
20:26 On the **f** day they assembled in the Valley 8055
Ezr 8:33 On the **f** day, in the house of our God, 8055
Job 42:16 and their children to the **f** generation. 752
Jer 25: 1 the **f** year of Jehoiakim son of Josiah king 8055
28: 1 the **f** year, early in the reign 8055
36: 1 the **f** year of Jehoiakim son of Josiah king 8055
39: 2 of the **f** month of Zedekiah's eleventh year, 8055
45: 1 the **f** year of Jehoiakim son of Josiah king 8055
46: 2 the **f** year of Jehoiakim son of Josiah king 8055
51:59 with Zedekiah king of Judah in the **f** year 8055
52: 6 By the ninth day of the **f** month the famine 8055
Eze 1: 1 in the **f** month on the fifth day, 8055
10:14 and the **f** the face of an eagle. 8055
Da 2:40 Finally, there will be a **f** kingdom, 10651
3:25 and the **f** looks like a son of the gods." 10651
7: 7 and there before me was a **f** beast— 10651
7:19 of the **f** beast, which was different from all 10651
7:23 'The **f** beast is a fourth kingdom 10651
7:23 a **f** kingdom that will appear on earth. 10651
11: 2 and then a **f**, who will be far richer 8055
Zec 6: 3 and the **f** dappled—all of them powerful. 8055
7: 1 In the **f** year of King Darius, 752
7: 1 the LORD came to Zechariah on the **f** day 752
8:19 "The fasts of the **f**, fifth, 8055
Mt 14:25 the **f** watch of the night Jesus went out 5480
Mk 6:48 About the **f** watch of the night he went out 5480
Rev 4: 7 the **f** was like a flying eagle. 5480
6: 7 When the Lamb opened the **f** seal, 5480
6: 7 the voice of the **f** living creature say, 5480
6: 8 over a **f** of the earth to kill by sword, 5480
8:12 The **f** angel sounded his trumpet, 5480
16: 8 The **f** angel poured out his bowl on 5480
21:19 the third chalcedony, the **f** emerald, 5480

FOURTH (Anglicized) See also QUARTER

FOWL (1) [FOWLER, FOWLER'S]
1Ki 4:23 gazelles, roebucks and choice **f**. 1350

FOWLER (1) [FOWL]
Pr 6: 5 like a bird from the snare of the **f**. 3687

FOWLER'S (2) [FOWL]
Ps 91: 3 the **f** snare and from the deadly pestilence. 3687
124: 7 like a bird out of the **f** snare; 3704

FOWLS (KJV) See BIRDS

FOX (2) [FOXES]
Ne 4: 3 if even a **f** climbed up on it, 8785
Lk 13:32 He replied, "Go tell that **f**, 273

FOXES (6) [FOX]
Jdg 15: 4 So he went out and caught three hundred **f** 8785
15: 5 and let the **f** loose in the standing grain of NIH
SS 2:15 Catch for us the **f**, 8785
2:15 the little **f** that ruin the vineyards, 8785
Mt 8:20 "**F** have holes and birds of the air have nests 273
Lk 9:58 "**F** have holes and birds of the air have nests 273

FRACTION (1)
Mk 12:42 copper coins, worth only **a f of a penny**. 3119

FRACTURE (2) [FRACTURES]
Lev 24:20 **f** for fracture, eye for eye, tooth 8691
24:20 fracture for **f**, eye for eye, tooth 8691

FRACTURES (1) [FRACTURE]
Ps 60: 2 mend its **f**, for it is quaking. 8691

FRAGILE (1)
Job 8:14 What he trusts in is **f**; 3684

FRAGMENT (1)
Isa 30:14 that among its pieces not a **f** will be found 3084

FRAGRANCE (14) [FRAGRANT]
Ex 30:38 like it to **enjoy** its **f** must be cut off 8193
SS 1: 3 Pleasing is the **f** of your perfumes; 8194
1:12 my perfume spread its **f**. 8194
2:13 the blossoming vines spread their **f**. 8194
4:10 and the **f** of your perfume than any spice! 8194
4:11 The **f** of your garments is like that 8194
4:16 that its **f** may spread abroad. 1411
7: 8 the **f** of your breath like apples, 8194
7:13 The mandrakes send out their **f**, 8194
Isa 3:24 Instead of **f** there will be a stench; 1411
Hos 14: 6 his **f** like a cedar of Lebanon. 8194
Jn 12: 3 house was filled with the **f** of the perfume. 4011
2Co 2:14 and through us spreads everywhere the **f** of 4011
2:16 to the other, the **f** of life. 4011

FRAGRANT (28) [FRAGRANCE]
Ex 25: 6 for the anointing oil and for the **f** incense; 6160
30: 7 "Aaron must burn **f** incense on 6160
30:23 250 shekels) of **f** cinnamon, 1411
30:23 250 shekels of **f** cane, 1411

Ex 30:25 a **f** blend, the work of a perfumer. 5351
30:34 the LORD said to Moses, "Take **f spices**— 6160
30:35 and make a **f blend** of incense, 8381
31:11 and the anointing oil and incense for 6160
35: 8 for the anointing oil and for the **f** incense; 6160
35:15 the anointing oil and the **f** incense; 6160
35:28 for the anointing oil and for the **f** incense. 6160
37:29 **f** incense—the work of a perfumer. 6160
39:38 the anointing oil, the **f** incense, 6160
40:27 and burned **f** incense on it, 6160
Lev 4: 7 on the horns of the altar of **f** incense that is 6160
16:12 of finely ground **f** incense and take them 6160
Nu 4:16 the **f** incense, the regular grain offering and 6160
2Ch 2: 4 to dedicate it to him for burning **f** incense 6160
13:11 and **f** incense to the LORD. 6160
Ps 45: 8 All your robes are **f** with myrrh and aloes NIH
Isa 43:24 You have not bought any **f calamus** 7866
Eze 6:13 places where they offered **f incense** 5767+8194
8:11 and a **f** cloud of incense was rising. 6986
16:19 you offered as **f incense** before them. 5767+8194
20:28 presented their **f incense** 5767+8194
20:41 as **f incense** when I bring you out from 5767+8194
Eph 5: 2 as a **f** offering and sacrifice to God. 2380+4011
Php 4:18 They are a **f** offering, 2380+4011

FRAIL (KJV) See FLEETING

FRAME (14) [FRAMES]
Ex 26:16 Each **f** is to be ten cubits long and a cubit 7983
26:19 two bases for each **f**, 7983
26:21 and forty silver bases—two under each **f**. 7983
26:25 two under each **f**. 7983
36:21 Each **f** was ten cubits long and a cubit and 7983
36:24 two bases for each **f**, 7983
36:26 and forty silver bases—two under each **f**. 7983
36:30 two under each **f**. 7983
Nu 4:10 of sea cows and put it on a **carrying f**. 4573
4:12 of sea cows and put them on a **carrying f**. 4573
1Ki 7:31 that had a **circular f** one cubit deep. 4196
Job 17: 7 my whole **f** is but a shadow. 3674
Ps 139:15 My **f** was not hidden from you 6798
Isa 58:11 and will strengthen your **f**. 6795

FRAMES (29) [FRAME]
Ex 26:15 "Make upright **f** of acacia wood for 7983
26:17 the **f** of the tabernacle in this way. 7983
26:18 Make twenty **f** for the south side of 7983
26:20 of the tabernacle, make twenty **f** 7983
26:22 Make six **f** for the far end, that is, 7983
26:23 make two **f** for the corners at the far end. 7983
26:25 be eight **f** and sixteen silver bases— 7983
26:26 five for the **f** on one side of the tabernacle, 7983
26:27 and five for the **f** on the west, 7983
26:28 from end to end at the middle of the **f**. 7983
35:11 clasps, **f**, crossbars, posts and bases; 7983
36:20 They made upright **f** of acacia wood for 7983
36:22 They made all the **f** of the tabernacle 7983
36:23 They made twenty **f** for the south side of 7983
36:25 they made twenty **f** 7983
36:27 They made six **f** for the far end, that is, 7983
36:28 and two **f** were made for the corners of 7983
36:29 At these two corners the **f** were double NIH
36:30 So there were eight **f** 7983
36:31 five for the **f** on one side of the tabernacle, 7983
36:32 and five for the **f** on the west, 7983
36:33 from end to end at the middle of the **f**. 7983
36:34 the **f** with gold and make gold rings to hold 7983
39:33 the tent and all its furnishings, its clasps, **f**, 7983
40:18 he put the bases in place, erected the **f**, 7983
Nu 3:36 to take care of the **f** of the tabernacle, 7983
4:31 to carry the **f** of the tabernacle. 7983
1Ki 7: 5 All the doorways had rectangular **f**; 9208

FRANKINCENSE (2) [INCENSE]
Ex 30:34 and pure **f**, all in equal amounts, 4247
Rev 18:13 myrrh and **f**, of wine and olive oil, 3337

FRANKLY (1)
Lev 19:17 **Rebuke** your neighbor **f** 3519+3519

FRANTIC (1)
1Ki 18:29 and they continued their **f** prophesying 5547

FRAUD (3) [DEFRAUD]
Pr 20:17 Food gained by **f** tastes sweet to a man, 9214
Jer 10:14 His images are a **f**; 9214
51:17 His images are a **f**; 9214

FRAY (1)
Job 39:21 and charges into the **f**. 5977

FRECKLED (KJV) See RASH

FREE (111) [FREED, FREEDMAN, FREEDMEN, FREEDOM, FREEING, FREELY]
Ge 2:16 "You are **f to eat** from any tree in 430+430
44:10 the rest of you will be **f from blame**." 5929
49:21 a doe **set f** that bears beautiful fawns. 8938

Ex	6: 6	I will *f* you from being slaves to them,	5911
	21: 2	But in the seventh year, he shall go *f*,	2930
	21: 3	If he comes alone, *he is to* go *f* alone;	3655
	21: 4	and only the man *shall* go *f*.	3655
	21: 5	and children and do not want to go *f*,'	2930
	21: 7	*she is* not *to* go *f* as menservants do.	3655
	21:11	*she is to* go *f*,	3655
	21:26	the servant go *f* to compensate for the eye.	2930
	21:27	he must let the servant go *f* to compensate	2930
Nu	5:28	not defiled herself and is *f* **from impurity**,	3196
	32:22	*f* from your **obligation** to the LORD and	5929
Dt	7:15	The LORD *will* **keep** you *f*	6073
	15:12	in the seventh year you must let him go *f*.	2930
	15:18	a hardship *to* **set** your **servant** *f*,	2930+8938
	24: 5	be *f* to stay at home and bring happiness to	5929
	32:36	and no one is left, slave or *f*.	6440
Jdg	16:20	"I'll go out as before and **shake myself** *f*."	5850
2Sa	22:49	*who* **sets** me *f* from my enemies.	3655
1Ki	14:10	every last male in Israel—slave or *f*,	6440
	20:34	"On the basis of a treaty I *will* **set** you *f*."	8938
	20:42	'You have **set** *f* a man	3338+4946+8938
	21:21	every last male in Israel—slave or *f*.	6440
2Ki	9: 8	every last male in Israel—slave or *f*.	6440
	14:26	whether slave or *f*, was suffering;	6440
1Ch	4:10	from harm so that I will be *f* **from** pain."	1194
	12:17	when my hands are *f* **from** violence	928+4202
Job	10: 1	therefore I *will* **give** *f* **rein**	6440
	16:17	yet my hands have been *f* of violence	4202
	21: 9	Their homes are safe and *f* **from** fear;	4946
	33: 9	I am clean and *f* **from** guilt.	4202
	36:16	to a spacious place *f* **from** restriction,	4202
	39: 5	"Who let the wild donkey go *f*?	2930
Ps	25:17	*f* me from my anguish.	3655
	31: 4	*F* me from the trap that is set for me,	3655
	73: 5	They are *f* **from** the burdens common	401
	81: 6	their hands *were* **set** *f* from the basket.	6296
	105:20	the ruler of peoples **set** him *f*.	7337
	118: 5	and he answered by **setting** me *f*.	5303
	119:32	for *you have* **set** my heart *f*.	8143
	129: 4	he has **cut** me *f* *from* the cords of	7915
	142: 7	**Set** me *f* from my prison,	3655
	146: 7	The LORD **sets** prisoners *f*,	6002
Pr	6: 3	my son, *to* *f* **yourself**,	5911
	6: 5	*F* **yourself**, like a gazelle from the hand of	5911
	11:21	but those who are righteous *will* **go** *f*.	4880
	19: 5	and he who pours out lies will not go *f*.	4880
Isa	32:20	and **letting** your cattle and donkeys **range** *f*.	8079+8938
	42: 7	to *f* captives from prison and to release	3655
	45:13	and **set** my exiles *f*,	8938
	49: 9	and to those in darkness, '*Be* *f*!'	1655
	51:14	The cowering prisoners *will* soon be **set** *f*;	7337
	52: 2	*F* **yourself** *from* the chains on your neck,	7337
	58: 6	the cords of the yoke, to set the oppressed *f*	2930
Jer	2:31	'*We are f* to **roam**;	AIT
	34: 9	Everyone was to *f* his Hebrew slaves,	2930+8938
	34:10	that they *would* *f* their male	2930+8938
	34:10	They agreed, and **set** them *f*.	8938
	34:14	each of *you must* *f* any fellow Hebrew who	8938
	34:14	you must let him go *f*.'	2930
	34:16	the male and female slaves you had set *f*	2930
	37: 4	Now Jeremiah *was f to* **come** and go among	AIT
La	5: 8	and there is none *to* *f* us from their hands.	7293
Eze	13:20	I *will* **set** *f* the people that you ensnare	8938
Zec	9:11	I *will* *f* your prisoners from	8938
Lk	13:12	*you are* **set** *f* from your infirmity."	668
	13:16	be **set** *f* on the Sabbath day	3395
Jn	8:32	and the truth *will* **set** you *f*."	1802
	8:33	How can you say that we shall be **set** *f*?"	1801
	8:36	the Son **sets** you *f*, you will be free indeed.	1802
	8:36	the Son sets you free, you will be *f* indeed.	1801
	19:10	power either *to* *f* you or to crucify you?"	668
	19:12	From then on, Pilate tried *to* **set** Jesus *f*,	668
Ac	7:34	and have come down *to* **set** them *f*.	1975
	26:32	"This man could *have been* **set** *f* if he had	668
Ro	6:18	*You have been* **set** *f* from sin	1802
	6:20	you were *f* from the control	1801
	6:22	But now *that you have been* **set** *f* from sin	1802
	8: 2	of the Spirit of life **set** me *f* from the law	1802
	13: 3	Do you want *to be f* **from** fear of the	3590+5828
1Co	7:22	similarly, he who was a *f* *man*	1801
	7:32	I would like you to be *f* **from** concern.	291
	7:39	she is *f* to marry anyone she wishes,	1801
	9: 1	Am I not *f*?	1801
	9:18	the gospel I may offer it *f* of **charge**,	78
	9:19	I am *f* and **belong to no man**,	1666+1801+4246
	9:21	the law (though I am not *f* from God's **law**	491
	12:13	whether Jews or Greeks, slave or *f*—	1801
2Co	11: 7	the gospel of God to you *f* of **charge**?	1562
Gal	3:28	slave nor *f*, male nor female,	1801
	4:22	and the other by the *f* **woman**.	1801
	4:23	by the *f* *woman* was born as the result of	1801
	4:26	But the Jerusalem that is above is *f*,	1801
	4:30	in the inheritance with the *f* **woman's** son."	1801
	4:31	but of the *f* **woman**.	1801
	5: 1	It is for freedom that Christ *has* **set** us *f*.	1802
	5:13	You, my brothers, were called to be *f*.	1800
Eph	6: 8	whether he is slave or *f*.	1801
Col	1:22	without blemish and *f* **from** accusation—	441
	3:11	slave or *f*, but Christ is all, and is in all.	1801
Heb	2:15	and those who all their lives were held	557
	9:15	that he has died as a ransom to set them *f*	NIG
	13: 5	*f* **from** the love of money	921
1Pe	2:16	Live as *f* **men**, but do not use your freedom	1801
Rev	6:15	and every *f* **man** hid in caves and among	1801
	13:16	small and great, rich and poor, *f* and slave,	1801
	19:18	and the flesh *of* all people, *f* and slave,	1801

Rev	20: 3	After that, he must *be* **set** *f* for a short time.	3395
	22:17	let him take the *f* **gift** of the water of life.	1562

FREED (10) [FREE]

Lev	19:20	because *she* had not **been** *f*.	2926
Job	3:19	and the slave is *f* from his master.	2930
Ps	116:16	*you have* *f* me from my chains.	7337
	136:24	and *f* us from our enemies,	7293
Jer	34:11	and took back the slaves *they had* *f*	2930+8938
	52:31	of Judah and *f* him from prison on	3655
Mk	5:29	and she felt in her body that *she was* *f*	2615
	5:34	Go in peace and be *f* **from** your suffering."	5618
Ro	6: 7	anyone who has died *has* **been** *f* from sin.	1467
Rev	1: 5	and *has* *f* us from our sins by his blood,	3395

FREEDMAN (1) [FREE]

1Co	7:22	by the Lord is the Lord's *f*;	592

FREEDMEN (1) [FREE]

Ac	6: 9	from members of the Synagogue *of the* F	3339

FREEDOM (24) [FREE]

Lev	19:20	not been ransomed or given her *f*,	2928
Ps	119:45	I will walk about in *f*,	8146
Isa	61: 1	to proclaim *f* for the captives and release	2002
Jer	34: 8	in Jerusalem to proclaim *f* for *the* slaves.	2002
	34:15	of you proclaimed *f* to his countrymen.	2002
	34:17	you have not proclaimed *f*	2002
	34:17	So I now proclaim '*f*' for you,	2002
	34:17	'*f*' to fall by the sword, plague and famine.	NIH
Eze	46:17	the servant may keep it until the year of *f*;	2002
Lk	4:18	He has sent me to proclaim *f* for	912
Ac	24:23	to give him some *f* and permit his friends	457
Ro	8:21	to decay and brought into the glorious *f* of	1800
1Co	7:21	although if you can **gain** *your* *f*, do so.	1181+1801
	8: 9	that the **exercise of** your *f* does not become	2026
	10:29	For why should my *f* be judged	1800
2Co	3:17	where the Spirit of the Lord is, there is *f*.	1800
Gal	2: 4	to spy on the *f* we have in Christ Jesus and	1800
	5: 1	It is *for* *f* that Christ has set us free.	1800
	5:13	not use your *f* to indulge the sinful nature;	1800
Eph	3:12	in him we may approach God with *f*	4244
Jas	1:25	the perfect law that *gives* *f*, and continues	1800
	2:12	to be judged by the law that **gives** *f*,	1800
1Pe	2:16	but do not use your *f* as a cover-up for evil;	1800
2Pe	2:19	They promise them *f*,	1800

FREEING (2) [FREE]

Jer	40: 4	But today I *am* *f* you from the chains	7337
Ac	2:24	*f* him from the agony of death,	3395

FREELY (22) [FREE]

Ge	43:34	So they feasted and **drank** *f* with him.	8910
Dt	15: 8	and **lend** him whatever he needs.	6292+6292
	23:23	because you made your vow *f* to	5607
1Ch	29: 9	for *they had* **given** *f* and wholeheartedly to	5605
Ezr	7:15	that the king and his advisers *have* *f* **given**	10461
Ps	12: 8	The wicked *f* **strut** about	2143
	37:26	They are always generous and **lend** *f*;	4278
	112: 5	to him who is generous and **lends** *f*,	4278
Pr	11:24	*One man* **gives** *f*, yet gains even more;	7061
Isa	55: 7	and to our God, for *he will f* **pardon**.	8049
Hos	14: 4	heal their waywardness and love them *f*,	5607
Mt	10: 8	*F* you have received, freely give.	1562
	10: 8	Freely you have received, *f* give.	1562
Mk	1:45	Instead he went out and began to talk *f*,	4498
Jn	1:20	He did not fail to confess, but confessed *f*,	NIG
Ac	9:28	**moved about** *f* in Jerusalem,	1660+1744+2779
	26:26	and I can speak *f* to him.	4245
Ro	3:24	and are justified *f* by his grace through	1562
1Co	2:12	we may understand what God *has* *f* **given** us	5919
2Co	6:11	We *have* **spoken** *f* to you, Corinthians,	487+3836+5125
	10: 8	if I boast somewhat *f* about the authority	4358
Eph	1: 6	which *he has* **given** us in the One he loves.	5923

FREEMAN (KJV) See FREE MAN

FREEWILL (22) [WILL]

Ex	35:29	to the LORD *f* **offerings** for all the work	5607
	36: 3	to bring *f* **offerings** morning after morning.	5607
Lev	7:16	the result of a vow or is a *f* **offering**,	5607
	22:18	either to fulfill a vow or as a *f* **offering**,	5607
	22:21	to fulfill a special vow or as a *f* **offering**,	5607
	22:23	present as a *f* **offering** an ox or a sheep	5607
	23:38	the *f* **offerings** you give to the LORD.)	5607
Nu	15: 3	or *f* **offerings** or festival offerings—	5607
	29:39	and your *f* **offerings**, prepare these for	5607
Dt	12: 6	to give and your *f* **offerings**,	5607
	12:17	or your *f* **offerings** or special gifts.	5607
	16:10	a *f* **offering** in proportion to the blessings	5607
2Ch	31:14	in charge of the *f* **offerings** *given* to God,	5607
Ezr	1: 4	and with *f* **offerings** for the temple of God	5607
	1: 6	in addition to all the *f* **offerings**.	5605
	2:68	the heads of the families **gave** *f* **offerings**	5605
	3: 5	**brought as** *f* **offerings**	5605+5607
	7:16	as the offerings *of* the people and priests	10461
	8:28	and gold are a *f* **offering** to the LORD.	5607
Ps	54: 6	I will sacrifice a *f* **offering** to you;	5607
Eze	46:12	When the prince provides a *f* **offering** to	5607
Am	4: 5	and brag about your *f* **offerings**—	5607

FREEWOMAN (KJV) See FREE WOMAN

FRENZIED (1)

Job	39:24	In *f* excitement he eats up the ground;	8323

FREQUENT (1) [FREQUENTLY]

1Ti	5:23	of your stomach and your *f* illnesses.	4781

FREQUENTLY (2) [FREQUENT]

Ac	24:26	so he sent for him *f* and talked with him.	4781
2Co	11:23	been in prison **more** *f*,	4359

FRESH (18) [FRESH-CUT, FRESHLY]

Ge	26:19	and discovered a well of *f* water there.	2645
Lev	14: 5	that one of the birds be killed over *f* water	2645
	14: 6	of the bird that was killed over the *f* water.	2645
	14:50	He shall kill one of the birds over *f* water	2645
	14:51	the blood of the dead bird and the *f* water,	2645
	14:52	the *f* water, the live bird, the cedar wood,	2645
	15:13	and bathe himself with *f* water,	2645
Nu	19:17	into a jar and pour *f* water over them.	2645
Jdg	15:15	Finding a *f* jawbone of a donkey,	3269
	16: 7	"If anyone ties me with seven *f* thongs	4300
	16: 8	the Philistines brought her seven *f* thongs	4300
Job	29:20	My glory will remain *f* in me,	2543
Ps	92:14	they will stay *f* and green,	2015
Eze	47: 8	the water there becomes *f*.	8324
	47: 9	**makes** the salt water *f*;	8324
	47:11	swamps and marshes *will* not *become* *f*;	8324
Jas	3:11	Can both *f* water and salt water flow from	1184
	3:12	Neither can a salt spring produce *f* water.	1184

FRESH-CUT (1) [CUT, FRESH]

Ge	30:37	however, took *f* branches from poplar,	4300

FRESHLY (1) [FRESH]

Ge	8:11	there in its beak was a *f* **plucked** olive leaf!	3273

FRET (4)

Ps	37: 1	*Do* not *f* because of evil men or be envious	3013
	37: 7	*do* not *f* when men succeed in their ways,	3013
	37: 8	*do* not *f*—it leads only to evil.	3013
Pr	24:19	*Do* not *f* because of evil men or be envious	3013

FRICTION (1)

1Ti	6: 5	**constant** *f* between men of corrupt mind,	1384

FRIEND (70) [FRIENDLY, FRIENDS, FRIENDSHIP]

Ge	38:12	his *f* Hirah the Adullamite went with him.	8276
	38:20	the young goat by his *f* the Adullamite	8276
Ex	32:27	each killing his brother and *f*	8276
	33:11	as a man speaks with his *f*.	8276
Dt	13: 6	or your **closest** *f* secretly entices you,	889+3869+3870+5883+8276
Jdg	7:13	as a man was telling a *f* his dream.	8276
	7:14	His *f* responded, "This can	8276
	14:20	the *f* who had attended him at his wedding.	5335
	15: 2	he said, "that I gave her to your *f*.	5335
	15: 6	because his wife was given to his *f*."	5335
Ru	4: 1	"Come over here, my *f*, and sit down."	532+7141
2Sa	13: 3	Now Amnon had a *f* named Jonadab son	8276
	15:37	So David's *f* Hushai arrived at Jerusalem	8291
	16:16	Then Hushai the Arkite, David's *f*,	8291
	16:17	"Is this the love you show your *f*?	8276
	16:17	Why didn't you go with your *f*?"	8276
1Ki	16:11	whether relative or *f*.	8276
1Ch	27:33	Hushai the Arkite was the king's *f*.	8276
2Ch	20: 7	to the descendants of Abraham your *f*?	170
Job	6:27	for the fatherless and barter away your *f*.	8276
	16:20	My intercessor is my *f*	8276
	16:21	with God as a man pleads for his *f*.	8276
Ps	35:14	I went about mourning as though for my *f*	8276
	41: 9	Even my **close** *f*, whom I trusted,	408+8934
	55:13	my companion, my **close** *f*,	3359
	88:18	the darkness *is* my **closest** *f*."	3359
	119:63	I am a *f* to all who fear you,	2492
Pr	17:17	A *f* loves at all times,	8276
	18:24	there is a *f* who sticks closer than a brother.	170
	19: 4	but a poor man's *f* deserts him.	8276
	19: 6	everyone is the *f* of a man who gives gifts.	8276
	22:11	will have the king for his *f*.	8276
	27: 6	Wounds from a *f* can be trusted,	170
	27: 9	of one's *f* springs from his earnest counsel.	8276
	27:10	Do not forsake your *f* and the friend	8276
	27:10	and the *f* of your father, and do not go	8276
Ecc	4:10	his *f* can help him up.	2492
SS	5:16	This is my lover, this my *f*,	8276
Isa	41: 8	you descendants of Abraham my *f*,	170
Jer	3: 4	'My Father, my *f* from my youth,	476
	9: 4	and every *f* a slanderer.	8276
	9: 4	*F* deceives friend, and no one speaks	408S
	9: 5	Friend deceives *f*, and no one speaks	8276
	23:35	of you keeps on saying to his *f* or relative:	8276
Mic	7: 5	put no confidence in a *f*.	476
Mt	11:19	a *f* of tax collectors and "sinners." '	5813
	20:13	"But he answered one of them, '*F*,	2279
	22:12	'*F*,' he asked, 'how did you get in here	2279
	26:50	Jesus replied, "*F*, do what you came for."	2279
Lk	7:15	When Jesus saw their faith, he said, "*F*,	476

Lk	7:34	a f of tax collectors and "sinners." '	5813
	11: 5	"Suppose one of you has a f,	5813
	11: 5	'F, lend me three loaves of bread,	5813
	11: 6	a f of mine on a journey has come to me,	5813
	11: 8	and give him the bread because he is his f,	5813
	14:10	'F, move up to a better place.'	5813
Jn	3:29	The f who attends the bridegroom waits	5813
	11:11	"Our f Lazarus has fallen asleep;	5813
	19:12	you are no f of Caesar.	5813
Ro	16: 5	Greet my dear f Epenetus,	28
	16: 9	and my dear f Stachys,	28
	16:12	Greet my dear f Persis,	28
Col	4:14	Our dear f Luke, the doctor,	28
Phm	1: 1	To Philemon our dear f and fellow worker,	28
Jas	2:23	and he was called God's f.	5813
	4: 4	a f of the world becomes an enemy of God.	5813
3Jn	1: 1	The elder, To my dear f Gaius,	28
	1: 2	Dear f, I pray	28
	1: 5	Dear f, you are faithful	28
	1:11	Dear f, do not imitate what is evil	28

FRIENDLY (3) [FRIEND]

Ge	34:21	"These men are f toward us," they said.	8969
Jdg	4:17	because there were f relations	8934
1Ki	5: 1	he had always been on f terms with David.	170

FRIENDS (91) [FRIEND]

Ge	19: 7	and said, "No, my f. Don't do this wicked	278
Jdg	11:37	to roam the hills and weep with my f,	8292
	19:23	"No, my f, don't be so vile.	278
1Sa	30:26	who were his f, saying,	8276
2Sa	3: 8	of your father Saul and to his family and f.	5335
2Ki	10:11	his close f and his priests,	3359
Est	5:10	Calling together his f and Zeresh, his wife,	170
	5:14	His wife Zeresh and all his f said to him,	170
	6:13	and all his f everything that had happened	170
Job	2:11	When Job's three f, Eliphaz the Temanite,	8276
	6:14	should have the devotion of his f,	5335
	12: 4	"I have become a laughingstock to my f,	8276
	17: 5	If a man denounces his f for reward,	8276
	19:14	my f have forgotten me.	3359
	19:19	All my intimate f detest me;	5493
	19:21	"Have pity on me, my f, have pity,	8276
	24:17	they make f with the terrors of darkness.	5795
	32: 3	He was also angry with the three f,	8276
	35: 4	like to reply to you and to your f with you.	8276
	42: 7	"I am angry with you and your two f,	8276
	42:10	After Job had prayed for his f,	8276
Ps	31:11	I am a dread to my f—	3359
	38:11	My f and companions avoid me because	170
	55:20	My companion attacks his f;	8934
	88: 8	You have taken from me my closest f	3359
	122: 8	For the sake of my brothers and f,	8276
Pr	14:20	but the rich have many f.	170
	16:28	and a gossip separates close f.	476
	17: 9	whoever repeats the matter separates close f.	476
	19: 4	Wealth brings many f,	8276
	19: 7	how much more do his f avoid him!	5335
	22:24	Do not make f with a hot-tempered man,	8287
SS	1: 7	beside the flocks of your f?	2492
	5: 1	Eat, O f, and drink;	8276
	8:13	You who dwell in the gardens with f	2492
Jer	6:21	neighbors and f will perish."	8276
	9: 4	"Beware of your f;	8276
	20: 4	a terror to yourself and to all your f;	170
	20: 6	and all your f to whom you prophesied lies.'	170
	20:10	All my f are waiting for me to slip,	632+8934
	38:22	those trusted f of yours.	408+8934
	38:22	your f have deserted you.'	NIH
La	1: 2	All her f have betrayed her;	8276
Da	2:13	for Daniel and his f to put them to death.	10245
	2:17	and explained the matter to his f Hananiah,	10245
	2:18	so that he and his f might not be executed	10245
Ob	1: 7	your f will deceive and overpower you;	408+8934
Zec	13: 6	wounds I was given at the house of my f.'	170
Lk	2:44	for him among their relatives and f.	1196
	7: 6	the house when the centurion sent f to say	5813
	12: 4	"I tell you, my f,	5813
	14:12	do not invite your f,	5813
	15: 6	Then he calls his f and neighbors together	5813
	15: 9	she calls her f and neighbors together	5813
	15:29	so I could celebrate with my f.	5813
	16: 9	use worldly wealth to gain f	5813
	21:16	brothers, relatives and f,	5813
	23:12	That day Herod and Pilate became f—	5813
Jn	15:13	that he lay down his life for his f.	5813
	15:14	You are my f if you do what I command.	5813
	15:15	Instead, I have called you f,	5813
	21: 5	He called out to them, "F,	4086
Ac	10:24	called together his relatives and close f.	5813
	19:31	to you with our dear f Barnabas and Paul—	5813
	19:31	f of Paul, sent him a message begging him	5813
	24:23	to give him some freedom and permit his f	2625
	27: 3	to go to his f so they might provide	5813
Ro	12:19	Do not take revenge, my f,	28
1Co	10: 1	Therefore, my dear f, flee from idolatry.	28
2Co	7: 1	Since we have these promises, dear f,	28
	12:19	and everything we do, dear f,	28
Php	2:12	my dear f, as you have always obeyed—	28
	4: 1	stand firm in the Lord, dear f!	28
Heb	6: 9	Even though we speak like this, dear f,	28
1Pe	2:11	Dear f, I urge you, as aliens and strangers	28
	4:12	Dear f, do not be surprised at	28
2Pe	3: 1	Dear f, this is now my second letter to you.	28
	3: 8	But do not forget this one thing, dear f:	28

2Pe	3:14	then, dear f, since you are looking forward	28
	3:17	dear f, since you already know this,	28
1Jn	2: 7	Dear f, I am not writing you a new command	28
	3: 2	Dear f, now we are children of God,	28
	3:21	Dear f, if our hearts do not condemn us,	28
	4: 1	Dear f, do not believe every spirit,	28
	4: 7	Dear f, let us love one another,	28
	4:11	Dear f, since God so loved us,	28
3Jn	1:14	The f here send their greetings.	5813
	1:14	Greet the f there by name.	5813
Jude	1: 3	Dear f, although I was very eager to write	28
	1:17	But, dear f, remember what the apostles	28
	1:20	But you, dear f, build yourselves up	28

FRIENDSHIP (8) [FRIEND]

Dt	23: 6	not seek a treaty of f with them	2256+3208+8934
1Sa	20:42	for we have sworn f with each other in	NIH
Ezr	9:12	not seek a treaty of f with them	2256+3208+8934
Job	29: 4	when God's intimate f blessed my house,	6051
Ps	109: 4	In return for my f they accuse me,	173
	109: 5	and hatred for my f.	173
Pr	12:26	A righteous man is cautious in f,	8276
Jas	4: 4	that f with the world is hatred toward God?	5802

FRIGHT (1) [FEAR]

Lk	24: 5	In their f the women bowed down	1181+1873

FRIGHTEN (7) [FEAR]

Dt	28:26	and there will be no one to f them away.	3006
Ne	6: 9	They were all trying to f us, thinking,	3707
Job	7:14	then you f me with dreams and terrify me	3169
	9:34	so that his terror would f me no more.	1286
Jer	7:33	and there will be no one to f them away.	3006
Eze	30: 9	to f Cush out of her complacency.	3006
2Co	10: 9	I do not want to seem to be trying to f you	1768

FRIGHTENED (9) [FEAR]

Ge	42:35	the money pouches, they were f.	3707
	43:18	Now the men were f when they were taken	3707
Isa	31: 4	against him, he is not f by their shouts	3169
Da	5: 6	so that his knees knocked together	10097
Mk	5: 6	not knowing what to say, they were so f.)	1769
Lk	21: 9	wars and revolutions, do not be f.	4765
	24:37	They were startled and f,	1873
Php	1:28	without being f in any way	4769
1Pe	3:14	"Do not fear what they fear; do not be f."	5429

FRIGHTENING (2) [FEAR]

Job	13:21	and stop f me with your terrors.	1286
Da	7: 7	terrifying and f and very powerful.	10028

FRINGE (1)

Job	26:14	And these are but the outer f of his works;	7896

FRO (2)

Ps	39: 6	Man is a mere phantom as he goes to and f;	2143
	104:26	There the ships go to and f,	2143

FROGS (14)

Ex	8: 2	I will plague your whole country with f.	7630
	8: 3	The Nile will teem with f.	7630
	8: 4	The f will go up on you and your people	7630
	8: 5	make f come up on the land of Egypt.' "	7630
	8: 6	and the f came up and covered the land.	7630
	8: 7	also made f come up on the land of Egypt.	7630
	8: 8	to take the f away from me and my people,	7630
	8: 9	and your houses may be rid of the f,	7630
	8:11	The f will leave you and your houses,	7630
	8:12	to the LORD about the f he had brought	7630
	8:13	The f died in the houses,	7630
Ps	78:45	and f that devastated them.	7630
	105:30	Their land teemed with f,	7630
Rev	16:13	I saw three evil spirits that looked like f;	1005

FROLIC (2)

Ps	104:26	which you formed to f there.	8471
Jer	50:11	because you f like a heifer threshing grain	7055

FROM (5013) See Index of Articles Etc.

FRONDS (1)

Lev	23:40	and palm f, leafy branches and poplars,	4093

FRONT (159) [FRONTAL]

Ge	30:38	so that they would be directly in f of	4200+5790
	30:39	they mated in f of the branches.	448
	30:41	the branches in the troughs in f of	4200+6524
	31:37	Put it here in f of your relatives and mine,	5584
	32:17	owns all these animals in f of you?'	7156
	33: 2	the maidservants and their children in f,	8037
	40: 9	"In my dream I saw a vine in f of me,	4200+7156
Ex	7:10	Aaron threw his staff down in f of Pharaoh	4200+7156
	13:22	night left its place in f of the people.	4200+7156
	14:19	who had been traveling in f of	4200+7156
	14:19	The pillar of cloud also moved from in f	7156
	16:34	the manna in f of the Testimony,	4200+7156
	19: 2	in the desert in f of the mountain.	5584
	25:37	up on it so that they light the space in f of	7156

Ex	26: 9	the sixth curtain double at the f of the tent.	7156
	27:21	the curtain that is in f of the Testimony,	6584
	28:25	to the shoulder pieces of the ephod at the f.	7156
	28:27	the shoulder pieces on the f of the ephod,	7156
	28:37	it is to be on the f of the turban.	7156
	29:10	the bull to the f of the Tent of Meeting.	7156
	30: 6	altar in f of the curtain that is before	4200+7156
	30:36	and place it in f of the Testimony in	4200+7156
	32: 5	an altar in f of the calf and announced,	4200+7156
	32:15	on both sides, f and back.	2296S
	33:19	to pass in f of you,	6584+7156
	34: 3	herds may graze in f of the mountain."	448+4578
	34: 6	he passed in f of Moses, proclaiming,	6584+7156
	39:18	to the shoulder pieces of the ephod at the f.	7156
	39:20	the shoulder pieces on the f of the ephod,	7156
	40: 5	altar of incense in f of the ark of the Testimony	4200+7156
	40: 6	Place the altar of burnt offering in f of	4200+7156
	40:26	the Tent of Meeting in f of the curtain	4200+7156
Lev	3: 8	of his offering and slaughter it in f of	4200+7156
	3:13	and slaughter it in f of the Tent	4200+7156
	4: 6	in f of the curtain of the sanctuary.	907+7156
	4:17	sprinkle it before the LORD seven times in f of the curtain.	907+7156
	6:14	in f of the altar.	448+7156
	8: 9	the sacred diadem, on the f of it,	7156
	9: 5	the things Moses commanded to the f of	7156
	10: 4	away from the f of the sanctuary."	7156
	13:41	the f of his scalp and has a bald forehead,	6991
	16: 2	the curtain in f of the atonement cover	448+7156
	16:14	and with his finger sprinkle it on the f of	7156
	16:15	on the atonement cover and in f of it.	4200+7156
	17: 4	to the LORD in f of the tabernacle of	4200+7156
	19:14	put a stumbling block in f of the blind,	4200+7156
Nu	3:38	in f of the Tent of Meeting.	4200+7156
	8: 2	to light the area in f of the lampstand.' "	448+4578+7156
	8: 9	the Levites to the f of the Tent of Meeting	7156
	8:13	Have the Levites stand in f of Aaron	4200+7156
	14: 5	and Aaron fell facedown in f of	4200+7156
	16:43	Then Moses and Aaron went to the f of	7156
	17: 4	Tent of Meeting in f of the Testimony,	4200+7156
	17:10	"Put back Aaron's staff in f of	4200+7156
	19: 4	and sprinkle it seven times toward the f of	7156
	20:10	the assembly together in f of the rock	448+7156
Dt	14: 1	shave the f of your heads for the dead,	1068+6524
	26: 4	and set it down in f of the altar	4200+7156
Jos	4:12	armed, in f of the Israelites,	4200+7156
	5:13	saw a man standing in f of him with	4200+5584
	6: 4	of rams' horns in f of the ark.	4200+7156
	6: 6	seven priests carry trumpets in f of	4200+7156
	8:11	and approached the city and arrived in f of	5584
	8:33	the people stood in f of Mount Gerizim	448+4578
	8:33	and half of them in f of Mount Ebal,	448+4578
Jdg	18:21	livestock and their possessions in f of	4200+7156
1Sa	8:11	and they will run in f of his chariots.	4200+7156
	9:24	what was on it and set it in f of Saul.	4200+7156
	16: 8	and had him pass in f of Samuel.	4200+7156
	17:41	with his shield bearer in f of him,	4200+7156
	21:15	to carry on like this in f of me?	6584
2Sa	2:14	up and fight hand to hand in f of us."	4200+7156
	3:31	and walk in mourning in f of	4200+7156
	5:23	attack them in f of the balsam trees.	4578+4946
	5:24	the LORD has gone out in f of you	4200+7156
	6: 4	and Ahio was walking in f of it.	4200+7156
	10: 9	Joab saw that there were battle lines in f of him and behind him;	4946+7156
	11:15	"Put Uriah in the f line where	448+4578+7156
1Ki	6: 3	The portico at the f of the main hall of	7156
	6: 3	and projected ten cubits from the f of	7156
	6:17	The main hall in f of this room	4200+7156
	6:21	and he extended gold chains across the f	7156
	7: 5	they were in f part in sets of three,	4578
	7: 6	In f of it was a portico,	6584+7156
	7: 6	and in f of that were pillars and	6584+7156
	7:49	in f of the inner sanctuary);	4200+7156
	8: 8	Holy Place in f of the inner sanctuary,	6584+7156
	8:22	of the LORD in f of the whole assembly	5584
	8:64	middle part of the courtyard in f of	4200+7156
2Ki	11:18	killed Mattan the priest of Baal in f of	4200+7156
	15:10	He attacked him in f of the people,	7692
	16:14	before the LORD he brought from the f	7156
1Ch	14:14	attack them in f of the balsam trees.	4578+4946
	14:15	will mean God has gone out in f of	4200+7156
	19:10	Joab saw that there were battle lines in f of	7156
2Ch	1: 5	in Gibeon in f of the tabernacle of	4200+7156
	3: 4	The f of the temple was twenty cubits long	7156
	3:15	In the f of the temple he made two pillars,	4200+7156
	3:17	the pillars in the f of the temple,	7156
	4:20	to burn in f of the inner sanctuary	4200+7156
	5: 9	seen from in f of the inner sanctuary,	6584+7156
	6:12	of the LORD in f of the whole assembly	5584
	7: 7	middle part of the courtyard in f of	4200+7156
	8:12	of the LORD that he had built in f of	4200+7156
	13:13	while he was in f of Judah the ambush	7156
	13:14	that they were being attacked at both f	7156
	15: 8	the LORD that was in f of the portico	4200+7156
	20: 5	the LORD in f of the new courtyard	4200+7156
	23:17	killed Mattan the priest of Baal in f of	4200+7156
	29:17	They are now in f of the LORD's altar.	4200+7156
Ne	3:23	and Hasshub made repairs in f of	5584
	3:28	each in f of his own house.	4200+5584
Est	4: 6	in the open square of the city in f of	5790
	5: 1	in f of the king's hall.	5790
Ps	68:25	In f are the singers,	7709
Pr	21:29	A wicked man puts up a bold f,	928+6451+7156

Jer	24: 1	of figs placed **in f** of the temple of	4200+7156
	36:22	fire burning in the firepot **in f** of him.	4200+7156
Eze	4: 1	put it **in f** of you and draw the city	4200+7156
	6: 4	slay your people **in f** of your idols.	4200+7156
	6: 5	the dead bodies of the Israelites **in f** of	4200+7156
	8:11	**In f** of them stood seventy elders of	4200+7156
	9: 6	the elders who were **in f** of the temple.	4200+7156
	14: 1	Israel came to me and sat down **in f** of	4200+7156
	16:37	from all around and will strip you **in f** of	448
	20: 1	and they sat down **in f** of me.	4200+7156
	40:12	**In f** of each alcove was	4200+7156
	40:47	And the altar was **in f** of the temple.	4200+7156
	40:49	and twelve cubits **from f to back.**	8145
	41:14	including the **f** of the temple,	7156
	41:21	the **f** of the Most Holy Place was similar.	7156
	41:25	a wooden overhang on the **f** of the portico.	7156
	42: 4	**In f** of the rooms was	4200+7156
	42: 7	it extended **in f** of the rooms	448+7156
	42:11	with a passageway **in f** of them.	4200+7156
	44: 4	of the north gate to the **f** of the temple.	7156
Joel	2:20	with its **f columns** going into	7156
Zec	3: 9	See, the stone I have set **in f** of Joshua!	4200+7156
	14:20	like the sacred bowls **in f** of the altar.	4200+7156
Mt	5:24	leave your gift there **in f** of the altar.	1869
	27:24	he took water and washed his hands **in f** of	595
	27:29	a staff in his right hand and knelt **in f** of	1869
	27:60	**rolled** a big stone **in f** of the entrance	4685
Mk	3: 3	"Stand up **in f** of everyone."	3545+3836
	5: 6	**fell** on his **knees in f** of him.	4686
	15:39	who stood there **in f** of Jesus,	1666+1885
Lk	5:19	right **in f** of Jesus.	1869
	5:25	Immediately he stood up **in f** of them,	1967
	6: 8	"Get up and stand **in f** of everyone."	3545+3836
	14: 2	There **in f** of him was a man suffering	1869
	19:27	bring them here and kill them **in f** of	1869
Ac	18:17	the synagogue ruler and beat him **in f** of	1869
	19:33	**pushed** Alexander **to the f,**	4582
	27:35	and gave thanks to God **in f** of them all.	1967
1Co	6: 6	and this **in f** of unbelievers!	2093
Gal	2:14	I said to Peter **in f** of them all,	1869
Rev	4: 6	covered with eyes, **in f** and in back.	1869
	7: 9	before the throne and **in f** of the Lamb.	1967
	12: 4	The dragon stood **in f** of the woman	1967

FRONTAL (1) [FRONT]
Jdg 20:34 of Israel's finest men made a **f** attack   4946+5584

FRONTIER (2) [FRONTIERS]
| Eze | 25: 9 | beginning at its **f** towns— | 7895 |
| | 48: 1 | the northern **f,** Dan will have one portion; | 7895 |

FRONTIERS (1) [FRONTIER]
Ne 9:22 allotting to them even the **remotest f.**   6992

FROST (5)
Ex	16:14	thin flakes like **f** on the ground appeared	4095
Job	38:29	Who gives birth to the **f** from the heavens	4095
Ps	147:16	like wool and scatters the **f** like ashes.	4095
Jer	36:30	and exposed to the heat by day and the **f**	7943
Zec	14: 6	there will be no light, no cold or **f.**	7885

FROWARD (KJV) See CORRUPT, CROOKED, DEVIOUS, HARSH, PERVERSE, WICKED, WILY

FROWN (1)
Jer 3:12 'I will **f** on you no longer,   5877+7156

FROZE (1) [FROZEN]
2Sa 23:10 the Philistines till his hand grew tired and **f**   1815

FROZEN (2) [FROZE]
| Job | 37:10 | and the broad waters become **f.** | 3668 |
| | 38:30 | when the surface of the deep **is f?** | 4334 |

FRUIT (172) [FIRSTFRUITS, FRUITAGE, FRUITFUL, FRUITFULNESS, FRUITION, FRUITLESS, FRUITS]
Ge	1:11	and trees on the land that bear **f** with seed	7262
	1:12	according to their kinds and trees bearing **f**	7262
	1:29	of the whole earth and every tree that has **f**	7262
	3: 2	"We may eat **f** from the trees in the garden,	7262
	3: 3	'You must not eat **f** from the tree that is in	7262
	3: 6	that the **f** of the tree was good for food	7262
	3:12	she gave me some **f** from the tree,	NIH
Ex	10:15	everything growing in the fields and the **f**	7262
Lev	19:23	the land and plant any kind of **f** tree,	4407
	19:23	regard its **f** as forbidden.	7262
	19:24	In the fourth year all its **f** will be holy,	7262
	19:25	But in the fifth year you may eat its **f.**	7262
	23:40	the first day you are to take choice **f** from	7262
	25:19	Then the land will yield its **f,**	7262
	26: 4	and the trees of the field their **f.**	7262
	26:20	nor will the trees of the land yield their **f.**	7262
	27:30	from the soil or **f** from the trees, belongs to	7262
Nu	13:20	Do your best to bring back some of the **f**	7262
	13:26	the whole assembly and showed them the **f**	7262
	13:27	Here is its **f.**	7262
Dt	1:25	with them some of the **f** of the land,	7262
	7:13	He will bless the **f** of your womb,	7262

Dt	20:19	because you can eat their **f.**	NIH
	20:20	that you know are not **f** trees and use them	NIH
	22: 9	not only the crops you plant but also the **f**	9311
	28: 4	The **f** of your womb will be blessed,	7262
	28:11	in the **f** of your womb,	7262
	28:18	The **f** of your womb will be cursed,	7262
	28:30	but you will not even begin to enjoy its **f.**	NIH
	28:53	you will eat the **f** of the womb,	7262
	30: 9	of your hands and in the **f** of your womb,	7262
	32:13	of the land and fed him with the **f** of	9482
Jdg	9:11	the fig tree replied, 'Should I give up my **f,**	9482
2Sa	16: 2	the bread and **f** are for the men to eat,	7811
2Ki	19:29	plant vineyards and eat their **f.**	7262
	19:30	and bear **f** above.	7262
Ne	9:25	olive groves and **f** trees in abundance.	4407
	9:36	so they could eat its **f** and	7262
	10:35	of our crops and of every **f** tree.	7262
	10:37	the **f** of all our trees and of our new wine	7262
Ps	1: 3	which yields its **f** in season	7262
	72: 3	the hills the **f** of righteousness.	NIH
	72:16	Let its **f** flourish like Lebanon;	7262
	92:14	*They will still* **bear f** in old age,	5649
	104:13	the earth is satisfied by the **f** of his work.	7262
	128: 2	You will eat the **f** of your labor;	3330+4090
	148: 9	**f** trees and all cedars,	7262
Pr	1:31	they will eat the **f** of their ways and	7262
	1:31	and be filled with the **f** of their schemes.	NIH
	8:19	My **f** is better than fine gold;	7262
	11:30	The **f** of the righteous is a tree of life,	7262
	12:14	From the **f** of his lips a man is filled	7262
	13: 2	the **f** of his lips a man enjoys good things,	7262
	18:20	From the **f** of his mouth	7262
	18:21	and those who love it will eat its **f.**	7262
	27:18	He who tends a fig tree will eat its **f,**	7262
Ecc	2: 5	and parks and planted all kinds of **f** trees	7262
SS	2: 3	and his **f** is sweet to my taste.	7262
	2:13	The fig tree forms its **early f;**	7001
	7: 7	and your breasts like **clusters of f.**	864
	7: 8	I will take hold of its **f."**	6180
	8:11	for its **f** a thousand shekels of silver.	7262
	8:12	two hundred are for those who tend its **f.**	7262
Isa	3:10	for they will enjoy the **f** of their deeds.	7262
	4: 2	the **f** of the land will be the pride and glory	7262
	5: 2	but it yielded only **bad f.**	946
	11: 1	from his roots a Branch *will* **bear f.**	7238
	14:29	its **f** will be a darting, venomous serpent.	7262
	16: 9	The shouts of joy over your **ripened f** and	7811
	27: 6	and blossom and fill all the world with **f.**	9482
	32:10	and the **harvest of f** will not come.	668
	32:17	The **f** of righteousness will be peace;	5126
	37:30	plant vineyards and eat their **f.**	7262
	37:31	and bear **f** above.	7262
	65:21	they will plant vineyards and eat their **f.**	7262
Jer	2: 7	I brought you into a fertile land to eat its **f**	7262
	6:19	the **f** of their schemes.	7262
	7:20	on the trees of the field and on the **f** of	7262
	11:16	a thriving olive tree with **f** beautiful	7262
	11:19	saying, "Let us destroy the tree and its **f;**	4312
	12: 2	they grow and bear **f.**	7262
	17: 8	a year of drought and never fails to bear **f."**	7262
	31: 5	farmers will plant them and enjoy their **f.**	NIH
	40:10	harvest the wine, **summer f** and oil,	7811
	40:12	an abundance of wine and **summer f.**	7811
	48:32	The destroyer has fallen on your **ripened f**	7811
Eze	17: 8	bear **f** and become a splendid vine.	7262
	17: 9	Will it not be uprooted and stripped of its **f**	7262
	17:23	and bear **f** and become a splendid cedar.	7262
	19:12	it was stripped of its **f;**	7262
	19:14	of its main branches and consumed its **f.**	7262
	25: 4	they will eat your **f** and drink your milk.	7262
	34:27	The trees of the field will yield their **f** and	7262
	36: 8	will produce branches and **f**	7262
	36:30	the **f** of the trees and the crops of the field,	7262
	47:12	**F** trees of all kinds will grow on	4407
	47:12	nor will their **f** fail.	7262
	47:12	Their **f** will serve for food and their leaves	7262
Da	4:12	Its leaves were beautiful, its **f** abundant,	10004
	4:14	strip off its leaves and scatter its **f.**	10004
	4:21	with beautiful leaves and abundant **f,**	10004
Hos	9:10	like seeing the **early f** on the fig tree.	1136
	9:16	their root is withered, they yield no **f.**	7262
	10: 1	he brought forth **f** for himself.	7262
	10: 1	As his **f** increased, he built more altars;	7262
	10:12	reap the **f** of unfailing love,	7023
	10:13	you have eaten the **f** of deception.	7262
	14: 2	that we may offer the **f** of our lips.	7262
Joel	2:22	The trees are bearing their **f;**	7262
Am	2: 9	I destroyed his **f** above	7262
	6:12	and the **f** of righteousness into bitterness—	7262
	8: 1	a basket of **ripe f.**	7811
	8: 2	"A basket of **ripe f,**" I answered.	7811
	9:14	they will make gardens and eat their **f.**	7262
Mic	6: 7	the **f** of my body for the sin of my soul?	7262
	7: 1	I am like one who gathers **summer f** at	7811
Na	3:12	like fig trees with their **first ripe f;**	1137
Hag	1:10	and the olive tree **have** not **borne f.**	5951
Zec	8:12	the vine will yield its **f,**	7262
Mal	3:11	in your fields *will* not **cast** *their* **f,"**	8897
Mt	3: 8	**Produce f** in keeping with repentance.	2843
	3:10	that does not produce good **f** will be cut	2843
	7:16	By their **f** you will recognize them.	2843
	7:17	Likewise every good tree bears good **f,**	2843
	7:17	but a bad tree bears bad **f.**	2843
	7:18	A good tree cannot bear bad **f,**	2843
	7:18	and a bad tree cannot bear good **f.**	2843
	7:19	Every tree that does not bear good **f** is cut	2843
	7:20	Thus, by their **f** you will recognize them.	2843

Mt	12:33	"Make a tree good and its **f** will be good,	2843
	12:33	or make a tree bad and its **f** will be bad,	2843
	12:33	for a tree is recognized by its **f.**	2843
	21:19	"May you never bear **f** again!"	2843
	21:34	to the tenants to collect his **f.**	2843
	21:43	to a people who will produce its **f.**	2843
	26:29	not drink of this **f** of the vine from now on	1163
Mk	11:13	he went to find out if it had any **f.**	NIG
	11:14	"May no one ever eat **f** from you again."	2843
	12: 2	from them some of the **f** of the vineyard.	2843
	14:25	I will not drink again of the **f** of the vine	1163
Lk	3: 8	**Produce f** in keeping with repentance.	2843
	3: 9	that does not produce good **f** will be cut	2843
	6:43	"No good tree bears bad **f,**	2843
	6:43	nor does a bad tree bear good **f.**	2843
	6:44	Each tree is recognized by its own **f.**	2843
	13: 6	and he went to look for **f** on it,	2843
	13: 7	for **f** on this fig tree and haven't found any.	2843
	13: 9	If it bears **f** next year, fine!	2843
	20:10	so they would give him some of the **f** of	2843
	22:18	For I tell you I will not drink again of the **f**	1163
Jn	15: 2	cuts off every branch in me that bears no **f,**	2843
	15: 2	that does bear **f** he prunes so that it will be	2843
	15: 4	No branch can bear **f** by itself;	2843
	15: 4	Neither can you bear **f** unless you remain	NIG
	15: 5	he will bear much **f;**	2843
	15: 8	that you bear much **f,**	2843
	15:16	and appointed you to go and bear **f—**	2843
	15:16	**f** that will last.	2843
Ro	7: 4	in order that *we might* **bear f** to God.	2844
	7: 5	so that *we* **bore f** for death.	2844
	15:28	that they have received this **f,**	2843
Gal	5:22	But the **f** of the Spirit is love, joy, peace,	2843
Eph	5: 9	the **f** of the light consists in all goodness,	2843
Php	1:11	with the **f** of righteousness that comes	2843
Col	1: 6	All over the world this gospel is **bearing f**	2844
	1:10	**bearing f** in every good work,	2844
Heb	13:15	the **f** of lips that confess his name.	2843
Jas	3:17	submissive, full of mercy and good **f,**	2843
Jude	1:12	autumn trees, **without f** and uprooted—	182
Rev	18:14	'The **f** you longed for is gone from you.	3967
	22: 2	the tree of life, bearing twelve crops of **f,**	2843
	22: 2	yielding its **f** every month.	2843

FRUITAGE (1) [FRUIT]
Isa 27: 9 and this will be the full **f** of the removal   7262

FRUITFUL (30) [FRUIT]
Ge	1:22	"**Be f** and increase in number and fill	7238
	1:28	"*Be* **f** and increase in number;	7238
	8:17	so they can multiply on the earth and be **f**	7238
	9: 1	"*Be* **f** and increase in number and fill	7238
	9: 7	As for you, *be* **f** and increase in number;	7238
	17: 6	*I will* **make** you very **f;**	7238
	17:20	*I will* **make** him **f**	7238
	28: 3	and **make** you **f** and increase your numbers	7238
	35:11	*be* **f** and increase in number.	7238
	41:52	because God *has* **made** me **f** in the land	7238
	47:27	They acquired property there and *were* **f**	7238
	48: 4	'I *am going to* **make** you **f**	7238
	49:22	"Joseph is a **f vine,**	1201+7238
	49:22	a **f vine** near a spring,	1201+7238
Ex	1: 7	the Israelites *were* **f** and multiplied greatly	7238
Lev	26: 9	and **make** you **f** and increase your numbers,	7238
Ps	105:24	**made** his people very **f;**	7238
	107:34	and **f** land into a salt waste,	7262
	107:37	that yielded a **f** harvest;	7262
	128: 3	*be* like a **f vine** within your house;	7238
Isa	5: 1	four or five on the **f boughs!**	7238
	5: 1	In that day—"Sing about a **f vineyard:**	2774
	32:12	for the **f vines**	7238
Jer	4:26	I looked, and the **f land** was a desert,	4149
	23: 3	*they will be* **f** and increase in number.	7238
	49: 4	boast of your valleys *so* **f?**	2307
Eze	19:10	it was **f** and full of branches because	7238
	36:11	and *they will be* **f** and become numerous.	7238
Jn	15: 2	so that *it will be* even more **f.**	2843+5770
Php	1:22	this will mean **f labor** for me.	2843

FRUITFULNESS (2) [FRUITFUL]
| Dt | 33:15 | and the **f** of the everlasting hills; | 4458 |
| Hos | 14: 8 | your **f** comes from me." | 7262 |

FRUITION (1) [FRUIT]
2Sa 23: 5 *Will he* not **bring to f** my salvation   7541

FRUITLESS (1) [FRUIT]
Eph 5:11 Have nothing to do with the **f** deeds   182

FRUITS (5) [FRUIT]
Ge	4: 3	Cain brought some of the **f** of the soil as	7262
Ps	109:11	may strangers plunder the **f** of his labor.	3330
SS	4:13	an orchard of pomegranates with choice **f,**	7262
	4:16	into his garden and taste its choice **f.**	7262
Jer	3:24	consumed **f** of our fathers' **labor—**	3330

FRUSTRATE (4) [FRUSTRATED, FRUSTRATES, FRUSTRATING, FRUSTRATION]
2Sa	17:14	to **f** the good advice of Ahithophel in order	7296
Ezr	4: 5	and **f** their plans during the entire reign	7296
Ps	14: 6	*You* evildoers **f** the plans of the poor,	1017

1Co 1:19 the intelligence of the intelligent *I* will *f.*" 119

FRUSTRATED (3) [FRUSTRATE]
2Sa 13: 2 Amnon *became* f to the point of illness 7674
Ne 4:15 of their plot and that God had f it, 7296
Eze 24:12 It has f all efforts; 4206

FRUSTRATES (2) [FRUSTRATE]
Ps 146: 9 but *he* f the ways of the wicked. 6430
Pr 22:12 but *he* f the words of the unfaithful. 6156

FRUSTRATING (1) [FRUSTRATE]
2Sa 15:34 you can help me by f Ahithophel's advice. 7296

FRUSTRATION (2) [FRUSTRATE]
Ecc 5:17 with great f, affliction and anger. 4088
Ro 8:20 For the creation was subjected to f, 3470

FRYINGPAN (KJV) See PAN

FUEL (13)
Isa 9: 5 will be f *for the fire. 4409
9:19 be scorched and the people will be f *for 4409
44:15 It is man's f for burning; NIH
44:19 "Half of it *I* used for f; 836+1198+8596
Jer 51:58 the nations' labor is only f for the flames." 836+928+1896
Eze 4:12 using human excrement for f." NIH
15: 4 on the fire as f and the fire burns both ends 433
15: 6 the vine among the trees of the forest as f 433
21:32 You will be f for the fire, 433
39: 9 use the weapons for f 1277
39: 9 seven years *they* will use them for f. 836+1277
39:10 use the weapons for f 836+1277
Hab 2:13 the people's labor is only f for the fire, 836+928+1896

FUGITIVE (2) [FUGITIVES]
Pr 28:17 the guilt of murder *will be a* f till death; 5674
Eze 24:26 that day a f will come to tell you the news. 7127

FUGITIVES (14) [FUGITIVE]
Nu 21:29 up his sons as f and his daughters 7129
Jos 8:22 leaving them neither survivors nor f. 7127
Isa 15: 5 her f flee as far as Zoar, 1371
15: 9 the f of Moab and upon those who remain 7129
16: 3 Hide the f, do not betray the refugees. 5615
16: 4 Let the Moabite f stay with you; 5615
21:14 you who live in Tema, bring food for the f. 5610
43:14 and bring down as f all the Babylonians, 1371
45:20 assemble, you f *from the nations. 7127
Jer 44:14 none will return except a few f." 7128
48:45 the f stand helpless, for a fire has gone out 5674
49: 5 and no one will gather the f. 5610
50:28 the f and refugees from Babylon declaring 5674
Ob 1:14 at the crossroads to cut down their f, 7129

FULFILL (50) [FULFILLED, FULFILLING, FULFILLMENT, FULFILLS]
Ge 38: 8 f *your* duty to her **as a brother-in-law** 3302
Lev 22:18 either to f a vow or as a freewill offering, 4200
22:21 to the LORD to f a special vow or as 5624+7098
Nu 6:21 He must f the vow he has made, 3869+4027+6913+7023
23:19 Does he promise and not f? 7756
Dt 25: 5 f the duty of a brother-in-law to her. 3302
25: 7 He will not f the duty of a brother-in-law 3302
1Sa 1:21 to the LORD and to f his vow, NIH
2Sa 5: 7 "Let me go to Hebron and f a vow I made 8966
1Ki 6:12 I will f through you the promise I gave 7756
12:15 to f the word the LORD had spoken 7756
2Ki 23:24 to f the requirements of the law written in 7756
2Ch 10:15 to f the word the LORD had spoken 7756
36:22 to f the word of the LORD spoken 3983
Ezr 1: 1 to f the word of the LORD spoken 3983
Est 5: 8 to grant my petition and f my request, 6913
Job 22:27 and *you will* f your vows. 8966
Ps 22:25 those who fear you *will* f my vows. 8966
50:14 f your vows to the Most High, 8966
61: 8 to your name and f my vows day after day. 8966
66:13 with burnt offerings and f my vows 8966
76:11 to the LORD your God and f them; 8966
116:14 I will f my vows to the LORD in 8966
116:18 I will f my vows to the LORD in 8966
119:38 F your promise to your servant, 7756
138: 8 The LORD *will* f [his purpose] for me; 1698
Ecc 5: 4 He has no pleasure in fools; f your vow. 8966
5: 5 not to vow than to make a vow and not f it. 8966
Isa 46:11 from a far-off land, a **man** to f my purpose. AIT
Jer 11: 5 Then I will f the oath I swore 7756
28: 6 May the LORD f the words 7756
29:10 to you and f my gracious promise 7756
33:14 'when I will f the gracious promise 7756
39:16 I am about to f my words against this city 995
Eze 12:25 I will f whatever I say, 6913
Na 1:15 O Judah, and f your vows. 8966
Mt 1:22 to f what the Lord had said through 4444
3:15 for us to do this to f all righteousness." 4444
4:14 to f what was said through 4444
5:17 not come to abolish them but to f them. 4444
8:17 This was to f what was spoken through 4444

Mt 12:17 This was to f what was spoken through 4444
21: 4 to f what was spoken through the prophet: 4444
Jn 12:38 to f the word of Isaiah the prophet: 4444
13:18 But this is to f the scripture: 4444
15:25 But this is to f what is written in their Law: 4444
Ac 7:17 the time drew near for God to f his promise NIG
1Co 7: 3 The husband *should* f his marital duty 625
Gal 6: 2 in this way *you will* f the law of Christ. 405
2Th 1:11 by his power he *may* f every good purpose 4444

FULFILLED (60) [FULFILL]
Jos 21:45 every one *was* f. 995
23:14 Every promise *has been* f; 995
Jdg 13:12 "When your words *are* f, 995
1Sa 10: 7 Once these signs *are* f, 995
10: 9 and all these signs *were* f that day. 995
1Ki 8:15 with his own hand *has* f what he promised 4848
8:24 and with your hand *you have* f it— 4848
9:25 f the temple **obligations.** 8966
2Ki 15:12 of the LORD spoken to Jehu *was* f: 2118+4027
2Ch 6: 4 *who* with his hands *has* f what he promised 4848
6:15 and with your hand *you have* f it— 4848
Ps 65: 1 to you our vows *will* be f. 8966
Pr 7:14 today *I* f my vows. 8966
13:12 but a longing f is a tree of life. 995
13:19 A longing f is sweet to the soul, 2118
Jer 1:12 to *see that* my word *is* f." 6913
17:15 *Let* it now *be* f!" 995
25:12 "But when the seventy years *are* f, 4848
34:18 not f the terms of the covenant they made 7756
39:16 that time *they* will be f before your eyes. 2118
La 2:17 he has f his word, 1298
Eze 12:23 days are near when every vision will be f. 1821
12:25 and *it shall* be f without delay. 6913
12:28 whatever I say *will* be f, 6913
13: 6 yet they expect their words to *be* f. 7756
Da 4:33 about Nebuchadnezzar *was* f. 10508
8:13 "How long will it take for the vision to be f NIH
9:12 *You have* f the words spoken against us and 7756
12: 6 be before these astonishing things are f?" 7891
Mt 2:15 so *was* f what the Lord had said through 4444
2:17 through the prophet Jeremiah *was* f: 4444
2:23 *was* f what was said through the prophets: 4444
13:14 In them *is* f the prophecy of Isaiah: 405
13:35 So *was* f what was spoken through 4444
26:54 the Scriptures *be* f that say it must happen 4444
26:56 that the writings of the prophets *might be* f." 4444
27: 9 by Jeremiah the prophet *was* f: 4444
Mk 13: 4 be the sign that they are all about to *be* f?" 5334
14:49 But the Scriptures *must be* f." 4444
Lk 1: 1 an account of the things that *have been* f 4442
4:21 "Today this scripture *is* f in your hearing." 4444
18:31 about the Son of Man *will be* f. 5464
21:24 until the times of the Gentiles *are* f. 4444
22:37 and I tell you that this must *be* f in me. 5464
24:44 *be* f that is written about me in the Law 4444
Jn 17:12 to destruction so that Scripture *would be* f. 4444
18: 9 that the words he had spoken *would be* f: 4444
18:32 of death he was going to die *would be* f. 4444
19:24 that the scripture *might be* f which said, 4444
19:28 and so that the Scripture *would be* f, 5464
19:36 so that the scripture *would be* f: 4444
Ac 1:16 *be* f which the Holy Spirit spoke long ago 4444
3:18 But this is how God f what he had foretold 4444
13:27 yet in condemning him *they* f the words of 4444
13:33 he has f for us, their children, 1740
23: 1 I have f my duty to God 4488
26: 7 to *see* f as they earnestly serve God day 2918
Ro 13: 8 he who loves his fellowman has f the law. 4444
Jas 2:23 And the scripture *was* f that says, 4444
Rev 17:17 until God's words *are* f. 5464

FULFILLING (3) [FULFILL]
Nu 3: 8 f the obligations of the Israelites **by doing** 6268
1Ki 2:27 f the word the LORD had spoken 4848
Ecc 5: 4 do not delay in f it. 8966

FULFILLMENT (10) [FULFILL]
Lev 22:23 but it will not be accepted in f of a vow. 4200
2Ch 36:21 the seventy years were completed in f of 4848
Da 11:14 among your own people will rebel in f of 6641
Lk 9:31 which he was about to bring to f 4444
21:22 For this is the time of punishment in f 4398
22:16 until it **finds** f in the kingdom of God." 4444
22:37 what is written about me is reaching its f." 5465
Ro 13:10 Therefore love is the f of the law. 4445
1Co 10:11 on whom the f of the ages has come. 5465
Eph 1:10 when the times will have reached their f— 4445

FULFILLS (3) [FULFILL]
Ps 57: 2 to God, *who* f [his purpose] for me. 1698
145:19 *He* f the desires of those who fear him; 6913
Isa 44:26 and f the predictions of his messengers, 8966

FULL (200) [FILL]
Ge 6:11 in God's sight and *was* f of violence. 4848
14:10 the Valley of Siddim was f of tar **pits,** 931+931
15:16 not yet reached its f **measure."** 8969
23: 9 for the f price as a burial site among you." 4849
25: 8 an old man and f of years; 8428
35:29 old and f of years, 8428
41: 1 When *two* f **years** had passed, 3427+9102
41: 7 up the seven healthy, f heads. 4849
41:22 f and good, growing on a single stalk. 4849

Ge 50: 3 **taking** a f forty days, 4848
Ex 5:18 you must produce your **quota** of bricks." 9420
8:21 The houses of the Egyptians *will be* f 4848
9:14 the f **force** of my plagues against you and 3972
16:20 *it was* f of maggots and began to smell. 8249
23:26 I will **give** you a f life span. 4848
Lev 6: 5 He must make restitution in f, 8031
16:12 a censer f of burning coals from the altar 4850
23:15 count off seven f weeks. 9459
25:29 he retains the right of redemption a f year 9448
25:30 not redeemed before a f year has passed, 9459
Nu 5: 7 He must **make** f restitution *for* his wrong, 928+8031+8740
33: 3 They marched out boldly in **view** of all 6524
Dt 21:13 and mother for a f month, 3427
33:23 of the LORD and *is* f of his blessing, 4848
Jos 10:13 and delayed going down about a f day. 9459
Jdg 8: 2 the f **grape harvest** of Abiezer? 1292
Ru 1:21 I went away f, but the LORD has brought me 4849
1Sa 2: 5 *Those who were* f hire themselves out 8428
18:27 and **presented the** f **number** to the king so 4848
28:20 Immediately Saul fell f length on 4850
2Sa 5:17 they went up in f force to search for him, 3972
11:18 Joab sent David a f account of the battle. 3972
23:11 a place where there was a field f of lentils, 4848
2Ki 3:16 Make this valley f of ditches. 1463+1463
4: 6 When all the jars were f, 4848
6:17 and he looked and saw the hills f of horses 4848
10:21 until it *was* f from one end to the other. 4848
1Ch 11:13 a place where there was a field f of barley, 4849
14: 8 they went up in f force to search for him, 3972
21:22 Sell it to me at the f price." 4849
21:24 "No, I insist on paying the f price. 4849
23: 1 When David was old and f of years, 8425
2Ch 24:10 dropping them into the chest until it *was* f. 3983
24:10 Now Jehoiada and f of years, 8425
Ne 9:25 They ate to the f and were well-nourished; 8425
Est 1: 4 a f 180 days he displayed the vast wealth 8041
9:29 wrote with f authority to confirm this 3972
10: 2 together with a f **account** of the greatness 7308
Job 5:26 You will come to the grave in f **vigor**, 3995
10:15 for I am f of shame and drowned 8428
14: 1 "Man born of woman is of few days and f 8428
15:32 Before his time *he will* **be paid** in f, 4848
20:22 the f **force** of misery will come upon him. 3972
21:23 One man dies in f vigor, 9448
21:27 "I know f **well** what you are thinking, 2176
26: 9 He covers the face of the f **moon,** 4057
32:12 **gave** you *my* f **attention.** 1067
32:18 For *I am* f of words, 4848
42:17 And so he died, old and f of years. 8428
Ps 10: 7 His mouth *is* f of curses and lies 4848
26:10 whose right hands *are* f of bribes. 4848
31:23 but the proud he pays back in f. 3856
33: 5 the earth *is* f of his unfailing love. 4848
75: 8 In the hand of the LORD is a cup f 4848
78:38 and did not stir up his f wrath. 3972
81: 3 and when the **moon** is f, 4057
88: 3 For my soul *is* f of trouble 8425
94: 4 all the evildoers *are* f of **boasting.** 607
104:24 the earth *is* f of your creatures. 4848
116: 5 our God is f of **compassion.** 8163
127: 5 Blessed is the man whose quiver *is* f 4848
130: 7 and with him is f redemption. 2221
139:14 I know that f **well.** 4394
144: 8 whose mouths *are* f of lies, 1819
144:11 of foreigners whose mouths *are* f of lies, 1819
Pr 1:17 How useless to spread a net in **view** of all 6524
4:18 shining ever brighter till the f **light** of day. 3922
5:21 man's ways are in f **view** of the LORD, 5790+6524
7:20 and will not be home till f **moon.**" 3427+4057
8:21 **making** their treasuries f. 4848
17: 1 and quiet than a house f of feasting, 4849
20:17 but he ends up with a mouth f of gravel. 4848
27: 7 He who is f loathes honey, 8428
29:11 A fool gives f vent to his anger, 3972
30:22 a fool *who is* f of food, 8425
31:11 Her husband **has** f confidence in her 1053+4213
Ecc 1: 7 yet the sea is never f. 4849
9: 3 *are* f of evil and there is madness 4848
11: 3 If clouds are f of water, 4848
Isa 1:15 Your hands *are* f of blood; 4849
1:21 She once was f of justice! 4849
2: 6 *They are* f of superstitions from the East; 4848
2: 7 Their land *is* f of silver and gold; 4848
2: 7 Their land *is* f of horses; 4848
2: 8 Their land *is* f of idols; 4848
6: 3 the whole earth is f of his glory." 4850
11: 9 for the earth *will be* f of the knowledge 4848
15: 9 Dimon's waters *are* f of blood, 4848
22: 2 O town f of commotion, 4849
22: 7 Your choicest valleys *are* f of chariots, 4848
27: 9 be the f fruitage of the removal of his sin: 3972
30:26 like the light of seven f **days,** AIT
30:27 his lips *are* f of wrath, 4848
47: 9 They will come upon you in f **measure,** 9448
65: 6 not keep silent but will **pay back** in f; 8966
65: 7 **measure** into their laps **the** f payment 4499
Jer 5:27 Like cages f of birds, 4849
5:27 their houses are f of deceit; 4849
6:11 But *I am* f of the wrath of the LORD. 4848
23:10 The land *is* f of adulterers; 4849
35: 5 Then I set bowls f of wine and some cups 4849
51: 5 though their land *is* f of guilt before 4848
51:56 he will **repay** in f. 8966+8966
La 1: 1 deserted lies the city, once *so* f of people! 8041
4:11 The LORD *has* **given** f vent to his wrath; 3983

Eze	1:18	and all four rims were **f** of eyes all around.	4849
	1:27	like glowing metal, as if **f** of fire,	1074+6017
	7:23	because the land *is* **f** of bloodshed and	4848
	7:23	of bloodshed and the city *is* **f** of violence.	4848
	9: 9	the land *is* **f** of bloodshed and	4848
	9: 9	of bloodshed and the city *is* **f** of injustice.	4848
	10: 4	the court *was* **f** of the radiance of the glory	4848
	10:12	were completely **f** of eyes,	4849
	17: 3	and **f** plumage of varied colors came	4849
	17: 7	with powerful wings and **f** plumage.	8041
	19:10	it was fruitful and **f** of branches because	6734
	22: 5	O infamous city, **f** of turmoil.	8041
	23:12	warriors in **f** dress, mounted horsemen,	4814
	28:12	**f** of wisdom and perfect in beauty.	4849
	37: 1	it was **f** of bones.	4849
Joel	2:26	until *you are* **f**, and you will praise	8425
	3:13	the winepress *is* **f** and the vats overflow—	4848
Na	3: 1	Woe to the city of blood, **f** *of* lies,	3972
	3: 1	**f** *of* plunder, never without victims!	4849
Zec	9:15	be **f** like a bowl used for sprinkling	4848
Mt	6: 2	**received** their reward **in f.**	600
	6: 5	**received** their reward **in f.**	600
	6:16	**received** their reward **in f.**	600
	6:22	your whole body will be **f of light.**	5893
	6:23	your whole body will be **f of darkness.**	5027
	13:48	When it was **f**, the fishermen pulled it up	4444
	23:25	but inside *they are* **f** of greed	1154
	23:27	but on the inside *are* **f** of dead men's bones	1154
	23:28	but on the inside you are **f** of hypocrisy	3550
Mk	2:12	took his mat and walked out **in f view of**	1869
	4:28	then the head, then the **f** kernel in the head.	4441
Lk	4: 1	Jesus, **f** of the Holy Spirit,	4441
	5: 7	and filled both boats so **f** that they began	NIG
	6:34	expecting to be repaid **in f.**	2698+3836
	10:21	Jesus, **f of joy** through the Holy Spirit, said,	22
	11:34	your whole body also is **f of light.**	5893
	11:34	your body also is **f of darkness.**	5027
	11:36	if your whole body is **f of light,**	5893
	11:39	inside you are **f** of greed and wickedness.	1154
	14:23	so that my house will be **f.**	1153
Jn	1:14	came from the Father, **f** of grace and truth.	4445
	3:29	and is **f of joy** when he hears	5897+5915
	10:10	that they may have life, and have it **to the f.**	4356
	13: 1	showed them the **f extent** of his love.	1650+5465
	17:13	that they may have the **f** measure of my joy	4444
	21: 8	towing the net **f** of fish,	NIG
	21:11	It was **f** of large fish, 153,	3550
Ac	5: 2	*With* his wife's **f knowledge** he kept back part of the money	5323
	5:20	the people the **f** message of this new life."	4246
	5:21	the **f** assembly of the elders of Israel—	4246
	6: 3	from among you who are known to be **f**	4441
	6: 5	a man of faith and of the Holy Spirit;	4441
	6: 8	a man **f** of God's grace and power,	4441
	7:55	But Stephen, **f** of the Holy Spirit,	4441
	8:23	that you are **f** of bitterness and captive	1650
	11:24	**f** of the Holy Spirit and faith,	4441
	13:10	You are **f** of all kinds of deceit	4441
	17:16	to see that the city was **f of idols.**	2977
Ro	1:29	They are **f** of envy, murder, strife,	3550
	3:14	"Their mouths *are* **f** of cursing	1154
	11:25	the **f** number of the Gentiles has come in.	4445
	13: 6	who give *their* **f** time to governing.	4674
	15:14	that you yourselves are **f** of goodness,	3550
	15:29	I will come in the **f measure** of the blessing	4445
	16:19	so I am **f of joy** over you;	5897
Gal	4: 5	that we might receive the **f rights of sons.**	5625
Eph	6:11	Put on the **f armor** of God so	4110
	6:13	Therefore put on the **f armor** of God,	4110
Php	4:18	I have received **f** payment and even more;	4246
Col	2: 2	the **f** riches of complete understanding,	4246
	4: 6	Let your conversation be always **f** of grace,	NIG
1Ti	1:15	that deserves **f** acceptance:	4246
	2:11	in quietness and **f** submission.	4246
	4: 9	that deserves **f** acceptance	4246
	6: 1	*of* **f** respect, so that God's name	4246
Phm	1: 6	so that you will have a **f understanding**	2106
Heb	10:22	with a sincere heart in **f** assurance of faith,	4443
Jas	3: 8	It is a restless evil, **f** of deadly poison.	3550
	3:17	submissive, **f** of mercy and good fruit,	3550
	5:11	The Lord is **f of compassion** and mercy.	4499
2Pe	2:14	With eyes **f** of adultery,	3550
Rev	5: 8	they were holding golden bowls **f** of incense	1154
	13:13	down from heaven to earth in **f view of**	1967
	14:10	which has been poured **f strength** into	204
	21: 9	the seven bowls **f** of the seven last plagues	1154

FULL-GROWN (1) [GROW]

Jas	1:15	and sin, *when* it is **f**, gives birth to death.	699

FULLER (KJV) See SOAP

FULLER'S (KJV) See WASHERMAN'S

FULLNESS (10) [FILL]

Dt	33:16	and its **f** and the favor of him who dwelt in	4850
Jn	1:16	From the **f** of his grace we have all received	4445
Ro	11:12	how much greater riches will their **f** bring!	4445
Eph	3:19	of him who fills everything in every way.	4445
	3:19	be filled to the measure of all the **f** of God.	4445
	4:13	to the whole measure of the **f** of Christ.	4445
Col	1:19	For God was pleased to have all his **f** dwell	4445
	1:25	**present** to you the word of God **in its f**—	4444
	2: 9	For in Christ all the **f** of the Deity lives	4445

Col	2:10	and *you* have been **given f** in Christ,	1639+4444

FULLY (45) [FILL]

Ex	19: 5	if *you* **obey** me **f** and keep my covenant,	928+7754+9048+9048
Dt	15: 5	if only *you* **f obey** the LORD your God	928+7754+9048+9048
	28: 1	If *you* **f obey** the LORD your God	928+7754+9048+9048
Jos	1:14	but all your fighting men, **f armed,**	2821
	1:17	Just as we **f obeyed** Moses,	3972
1Ki	8:61	be **f committed** to the LORD our God,	8969
	11: 4	not **f devoted** to the LORD his God,	8969
	15: 3	not **f devoted** to the LORD his God,	8969
	15:14	Asa's heart was **f committed** to	8969
1Ch	12:38	came to Hebron **f determined** to make David king	928+4222+8969
2Ch	15:17	Asa's heart was **f committed**	8969
	16: 9	to strengthen those whose hearts are **f committed** to him.	8969
Ezr	6: 8	to be **f** paid out of the royal treasury,	10056
Ps	62: 4	They **f** intend to topple him	421
	106: 2	of the LORD or **f** declare his praise?	3972
	119: 4	down precepts that are to be **f** obeyed.	4394
	119:138	they are **f** trustworthy.	4394
Pr	13: 4	the desires of the diligent **are f satisfied.**	2014
	14:14	faithless *will be* **f repaid** for their ways.	8425
	28: 5	those who seek the LORD understand it **f.**	3972
Isa	21: 7	let him be alert, **f alert."**	8041
Jer	23:20	not turn back until he **f accomplishes** the purposes of his heart.	2256+6913+7756
	30:24	not turn back until he **f accomplishes** the purposes of his heart.	2256+6913+7756
	35:10	have **f obeyed** everything our forefather Jonadab commanded us.	2256+6913+9048
Eze	38: 4	your horses, your horsemen **f armed,**	4814
Da	11:13	with a huge army **f equipped.**	8041
Joel	2:19	new wine and oil, *enough to* **satisfy** you **f;**	8425
Lk	6:40	but everyone *who is* **f trained** will be	2936
	9:32	but *when* they became **f awake,**	1340
	11:21	"When a strong man, **f armed,**	2774
Ro	4:21	*being* **f persuaded** that God had power	4442
	8: 4	of the law *might be* **f met** in us,	4444
	14: 5	Each one *should be* **f convinced**	4442
	14:14	*I am* **f convinced** that no food is unclean	2779+3857+4275
	15:19	I *have* **f** proclaimed the gospel of Christ.	4444
1Co	13:12	I *shall* **know f**, even as I am fully **known.**	2105
	13:12	I shall know fully, even as *I am* **f known.**	2105
	15:58	Always **give** *yourselves* **f** to the work of	4355
2Co	1:14	to understand **f** that you can boast	2401+5465
Gal	4: 4	But when the time had **f** come,	4445
Col	4:12	mature and **f assured.**	4442
2Ti	4:17	the message *might be* **f** proclaimed and all	4442
Tit	2:10	but to show that they can be **f** trusted,	4246
1Pe	1:13	set your hope **f** on the grace to be given you	5458
2Jn	1: 8	but that you may be rewarded **f.**	4441

FUN (1)

Ac	2:13	Some, however, **made f** of them and said,	1430

FUNCTION (2)

Ex	27:19	whatever their **f**, including all the tent pegs	NIH
Ro	12: 4	these members do not all have the same **f,**	4552

FUNERAL (2)

Jer	16: 5	not enter a house where there is a **f meal;**	5301
	34: 5	As people made a **f fire** *in* honor	5386

FURBISHED (KJV) See POLISHED

FURIOUS (16) [FURY]

Dt	29:28	In **f** anger and in great wrath	2779
2Sa	13:21	King David heard all this, he *was* **f.**	3013+4394
2Ch	25:10	They were **f** with Judah and left	678+3013+4394
Est	1:12	king *became* **f** and burned with anger.	4394+7911
Jer	32:37	where I banish them in my **f** anger	2779
Da	2:12	and **f** that he ordered the execution of all	10633
	3:13	**F** with rage, Nebuchadnezzar summoned	10270
	3:19	Then Nebuchadnezzar *was* **f**	10270+10416
Mt	2:16	outwitted by the Magi, *he was* **f**, and	2597+3336
	8:24	A **furious** storm came up on the lake,	3489
Mk	4:37	A **f** squall came up,	3489
Lk	4:28	the synagogue *were* **f** when they heard	2596+4398
	6:11	But they *were* **f** and began to discuss	486+4398
Ac	5:33	*they were* **f** and wanted to put them	1391
	7:54	*they were* **f** and gnashed their teeth at him,	1391
	19:28	they *were* **f** and began shouting:	2596+4441

FURIOUSLY (2) [FURY]

Jer	46: 9	**Drive f**, O charioteers!	2147
Da	8: 7	I saw him attack the ram **f,**	5352

FURLONGS (KJV) See MILES, STADIA

FURNACE (31)

Ge	19:28	like smoke from a **f.**	3901
Ex	9: 8	of soot from a **f** and have Moses toss it into	3901
	9:10	So they took soot from a **f** and stood	3901
	19:18	up from it like smoke from a **f,**	3901
Dt	4:20	and brought you out of the iron-smelting **f,**	3929

1Ki	8:51	out of that iron-smelting **f.**	3929
Ps	12: 6	like silver refined in a **f** of clay,	6612
	21: 9	like a fiery **f.**	9486
Pr	17: 3	The crucible for silver and the **f** for gold,	3929
	27:21	The crucible for silver and the **f** for gold,	3929
Isa	31: 9	whose **f** is in Jerusalem.	9486
	48:10	I have tested you in the **f** of affliction.	3929
Jer	11: 4	out of the iron-smelting **f.'**	3929
Eze	22:18	tin, iron and lead left inside a **f.**	3929
	22:20	and tin into a **f** to melt it with a fiery blast,	3929
	22:22	As silver is melted in a **f,**	3929
Da	3: 6	be thrown into a blazing **f."**	10086
	3:11	be thrown into a blazing **f.**	10086
	3:15	be thrown immediately into a blazing **f.**	10086
	3:17	If we are thrown into the blazing **f,**	10086
	3:19	the **f** heated seven times hotter than usual	10086
	3:20	and throw them into the blazing **f.**	10086
	3:21	were bound and thrown into the blazing **f.**	10086
	3:22	so urgent and the **f** so hot that the flames of	10086
	3:23	firmly tied, fell into the blazing **f.**	10086
	3:26	the opening of the blazing **f** and shouted,	10086
Mal	4: 1	the day is coming; it will burn like a **f.**	9486
Mt	13:42	They will throw them into the fiery **f,**	2825
	13:50	and throw them into the fiery **f,**	2825
Rev	1:15	His feet were like bronze glowing in a **f,**	2825
	9: 2	from it like the smoke *from* a gigantic **f.**	2825

FURNISHED (4) [FURNISHINGS]

Eze	16:52	for *you have* **f** *some* **justification**	7136
Mk	14:15	a large upper room, **f** and ready.	5143
Lk	22:12	He will show you a large upper room, all **f.**	5143
Ac	28:10	*they* **f** us **with** the supplies we needed.	2202

FURNISHINGS (23) [FURNISHED]

Ex	25: 9	Make this tabernacle and all its **f** exactly	3998
	31: 7	and all the other **f** of the tent—	3998
	39:33	the tent and all its **f**, its clasps, frames,	3998
	39:40	all the **f** for the tabernacle,	3998
	40: 9	consecrate it and all its **f,**	3998
Nu	1:50	over all its **f** and everything belonging to it.	3998
	1:50	to carry the tabernacle and all its **f;**	3998
	3: 8	They are to take care of all the **f** of	3998
	4:15	the **holy f** and all the holy articles,	7731
	4:16	including its **holy f** and articles.	7731
	7: 1	and consecrated it and all its **f.**	3998
	18: 3	near the **f** of the sanctuary or the altar,	3998
	19:18	the water and sprinkle the tent and all the **f**	3998
1Ki	7:48	Solomon also made all the **f** that were in	3998
	7:51	the silver and gold and the **f**—	3998
	8: 4	the Tent of Meeting and all the sacred **f**	3998
1Ch	9:29	Others were assigned to take care of the **f**	3998
2Ch	4:19	Solomon also made all the **f** that were	3998
	5: 1	the silver and gold and all the **f**—	3998
	5: 5	the Tent of Meeting and all the sacred **f**	3998
	28:24	Ahaz gathered together the **f** *from*	3998
Jer	27:18	the **f** remaining in the house of the LORD	3998
	27:19	and the other **f** that are left in this city,	3998

FURNITURE (KJV) See ACCESSORIES, ARTICLES, FURNISHINGS, SADDLES, TREASURES, UTENSILS

FURROW (1) [FURROWS]

Job	39:10	Can you hold him to the **f** with a harness?	9439

FURROWS (3) [FURROW]

Job	31:38	against me and all its **f** are wet with tears,	9439
Ps	65:10	You drench its **f** and level its ridges;	9439
	129: 3	and made their **f** long.	5103

FURTHER (17) [FURTHERMORE]

1Sa	10:22	So they inquired **f** of the LORD,	6388
	3:22	Go and make **f** preparation.	6388
2Ch	32:16	Sennacherib's officers spoke **f** against	6388
Job	34:23	God has no need to examine men **f,**	6388
	35:15	and **f**, that his anger never punishes	6964
Ecc	9: 5	they have no **f** reward,	6388
Eze	23:14	**carried** her prostitution **still f.**	3578
Hos	11: 2	the **f** they went from me.	4027
Zec	1:17	"Proclaim **f:** This is what the LORD Almighty says:	6388
Ac	4:17	stop this thing from spreading **any f**	2093+4498
	4:21	*After* **f threats** they let them go.	4653
	11:18	they had no **f** objections and praised God,	NIG
	13:42	the people invited them to speak **f**	NIG
	19:39	If there is anything **f** you want to bring up,	4304
	24: 4	But in order not to weary you **f,**	4498
1Co	11:34	And when I come I will give **f** directions.	3370
Heb	12:19	that no **f word** be **spoken** to them,	3364+4707

FURTHER (Anglicized) See also FARTHER

FURTHERMORE (12) [FURTHER]

2Sa	16:19	**F,** whom should I serve?	2021+2256+9108
2Ki	18:25	**F,** have I come to attack	6964
	23:24	**F,** Josiah got rid of the mediums	1685+2256
2Ch	17: 6	**f,** he removed the high places and	2256+6388
	36:14	all the leaders of the priests and	1685
Ezr	4:13	**F,** the king should know that	10363
	6:11	**F,** I decree that if anyone changes this	10221
Ne	5:17	**F,** a hundred and fifty Jews	2256

Isa 36:10	F, have I come to attack	2256+6964
Jer 21: 8	"F, tell the people, 'This is what	2256
26:24	F, Ahikam son of Shaphan	421
Ro 1:28	F, since they did not think it worthwhile	2779

FURY (24) [FURIOUS, FURIOUSLY]

Ge 27:44	for a while until your brother's f subsides.	2779
34: 7	They were filled with grief and f,	3013+4394
49: 7	so fierce, and their, f, so cruel!	6301
2Ki 3:27	The f against Israel was great;	7912
Est 7:10	Then the king's f subsided.	2779
Job 40:11	Unleash the f of your wrath,	6301
Pr 6:34	for jealousy arouses a husband's f,	2779
22: 8	and the rod of his f will be destroyed.	6301
27: 4	Anger is cruel and f overwhelming,	678
Isa 14: 4	How his f has ended!	4502
14: 6	and in f subdued nations	678
66:14	but his f will be shown to his foes.	2404
66:15	he will bring down his anger with f,	2779
Jer 21: 5	and a mighty arm in anger and f	2779
Eze 13:13	of rain will fall with destructive f.	2779
19:12	But it was uprooted in f and thrown to	2779
23:25	and they will deal with you in f.	2779
Da 11:30	and vent his f against the holy covenant.	2404
Am 1:11	and his f flamed unchecked,	6301
Heb 11:34	the f of the flames, and escaped the edge of	1539
Rev 6:12	He is filled with f,	2596+3489
14:10	too, will drink of the wine of God's f,	2596
16:19	the cup filled with the wine of the f	2596
19:15	of the f of the wrath of God Almighty.	2596

FUTILE (6) [FUTILITY]

Ps 94:11	he knows that they are f,	2039
Jer 48:30	I know her insolence but it is f,"	4027+4202
Mal 3:14	"You have said, 'It is f to serve God.	8736
Ro 1:21	but their thinking became f	3471
1Co 3:20	that the thoughts of the wise are f."	3469
15:17	Christ has not been raised, your faith is f;	3469

FUTILITY (4) [FUTILE]

Job 7: 3	so I have been allotted months of f,	8736
Ps 78:33	So he ended their days in f and their years	2039
89:47	For what f you have created all men!	8736
Eph 4:17	in the f of their thinking.	3470

FUTURE (33)

Ge 30:33	my honesty will testify for me in the f,	3427+4737
Dt 6:20	In the f, when your son asks you,	4737
Jos 4: 6	In the f, when your children ask you,	4737
4:21	to the Israelites, "In the f	4737
22:27	Then in the f your descendants will not	4737
2Sa 7:19	the f of the house of your servant.	4946+8158
1Ch 17:17	you have spoken about the f of the house of	
	your servant.	4946+8158
Job 8: 7	so prosperous will your f be.	344
Ps 22:30	f generations will be told about the Lord.	995
37:37	there is a f for the man of peace.	344
37:38	the f of the wicked will be cut off.	344
102:18	Let this be written for a f generation,	340
Pr 23:18	There is surely a f hope for you,	344
24:14	if you find it, there is a f hope for you,	344
24:20	for the evil man has no f hope,	344
Ecc 7:14	a man cannot discover anything about his f.	339
8: 7	Since no man knows the f,	2118+4537+8611
Isa 9: 1	the f he will honor Galilee of the Gentiles,	340
41:23	tell us what the f holds,	294
Jer 29:11	plans to give you hope and a f.	344
31:17	So there is hope for your f,"	344
La 1: 9	she did not consider her f.	344
Eze 12:27	and he prophesies about the distant f.'	6961
38: 8	In f years you will invade a land	344
Da 2:45	God has shown the king what will take	
	place in the f.	10021+10180
8:26	for it concerns the distant f."	3427+8041
10:14	to your people in the f,	344+3427
Mt 26:64	In the f you will see the Son of Man	608+785
Ac 16:16	spirit by which she predicted the f.	4460+4780
Ro 8:38	neither the present nor the f,	3516
1Co 3:22	or life or death or the present or the f—	3516
Heb 3: 5	testifying to what would be said in the f.	AIT
11:20	and Esau in regard to their f.	3516

G

GAAL (10)

Jdg 9:26	Now G son of Ebed moved	1720
9:28	Then G son of Ebed said,	1720
9:30	of the city heard what G son of Ebed said,	1720
9:31	"G son of Ebed and his brothers have come	1720
9:33	When G and his men come out against you,	2085ˢ
9:35	Now G son of Ebed had gone out	1720
9:36	When G saw them, he said to Zebul,	1720
9:37	But G spoke up again:	1720
9:39	So G led out the citizens of Shechem	1720
9:41	and Zebul drove G and his brothers out	1720

GAASH (4)

Jos 24:30	north of Mount G.	1724
Jdg 2: 9	north of Mount G.	1724
2Sa 23:30	Hiddai from the ravines of G,	1724
1Ch 11:32	Hurai from the ravines of G,	1724

GABA (KJV) See GEBA

GABBAI (1)

Ne 11: 8	and his followers, G and Sallai—928 men.	1480

GABBATHA (1)

Jn 19:13	Stone Pavement (which in Aramaic is G).	1119

GABRIEL (4)

Da 8:16	a man's voice from the Ulai calling, "G,	1508
9:21	G, the man I had seen in the earlier vision,	1508
Lk 1:19	The angel answered, "I am G.	1120
1:26	God sent the angel G to Nazareth,	1120

GAD (55) [BAAL GAD, DIBON GAD, GAD'S, GADITES, MIGDAL GAD]

Ge 30:11	So she named him G.	1514
35:26	of Leah's maidservant Zilpah: G and Asher.	1514
46:16	The sons of G:	1514
49:19	"G will be attacked by a band of raiders,	1514
Ex 1: 4	Dan and Naphtali; G and Asher.	1514
Nu 1:14	from G, Eliasaph son of Deuel;	1514
1:24	From the descendants of G:	1514
1:25	number from the tribe of G was 45,650.	1514
2:14	The tribe of G will be next.	1514
2:14	of the people of G is Eliasaph son of Deuel.	1514
7:42	the leader of the people of G,	1514
10:20	over the division of the tribe of G.	1201+1514
13:15	from the tribe of G, Geuel son of Maki.	1514
26:15	The descendants of G by their clans were:	1514
26:18	These were the clans of G;	1201+1514
34:14	the tribe of G and the half-tribe	1201+1532
Dt 27:13	Reuben, G, Asher, Zebulun,	1514
33:20	About G he said:	1514
33:20	G lives there like a lion,	NIH
Jos 4:12	G and the half-tribe of Manasseh crossed	1514
13:24	to the tribe of G, clan by clan:	1514
18: 7	And G, Reuben and the half-tribe	1514
20: 8	Ramoth in Gilead in the tribe of G,	1514
21: 7	from the tribes of Reuben, G and Zebulun.	1514
21:38	from the tribe of G,	1514
22:13	G and the half-tribe of Manasseh	1201+1514
22:15	G and the half-tribe of Manasseh—	1201+1514
22:21	G and the half-tribe of Manasseh	1201+1514
22:30	G and Manasseh had to say,	1201+1514
22:31	said to Reuben, G and Manasseh,	1201+1514
1Sa 13: 7	even crossed the Jordan to the land of G	1514
22: 5	But the prophet G said to David,	1514
2Sa 24: 5	and then went through G and on to Jazer.	1514
24:11	of the LORD had come to the G the prophet,	1514
24:13	So G went to David and said to him,	1514
24:14	David said to G, "I am in deep distress.	1514
24:18	that day G went to David and said to him,	1514
24:19	as the LORD had commanded through G.	1514
2Ki 10:33	in all the land of Gilead (the region of G,	1532
1Ch 2: 2	Joseph, Benjamin, Naphtali, G and Asher.	1514
6:63	from the tribes of Reuben, G and Zebulun.	1514
6:80	from the tribe of G they received Ramoth	1514
12:37	G and the half-tribe of Manasseh,	1532
21: 9	The LORD said to G, David's seer,	1514
21:11	So G went to David and said to him,	1514
21:13	David said to G, "I am in deep distress.	1514
21:18	of the LORD ordered G to tell David to go	1514
21:19	in obedience to the word that G had spoken	1514
29:29	of Nathan the prophet and the records of G	1514
2Ch 29:25	by David and G the king's seer and Nathan	1514
Jer 49: 1	then has Molech taken possession of G?	1514
Eze 48:27	"G will have one portion;	1514
48:28	of G will run south from Tamar to	1514
48:34	the gate of G,	1514
Rev 7: 5	from the tribe of G 12,000,	1122

GAD'S (1) [GAD]

Dt 33:20	"Blessed is he who enlarges G domain!	1514

GADARENES (1)

Mt 8:28	at the other side in the region of the G,	1123

GADDAH See HAZAR GADDAH

GADDEST (KJV) See GO ABOUT

GADDI (1)

Nu 13:11	G son of Susi;	1534

GADDIEL (1)

Nu 13:10	from the tribe of Zebulun, G son of Sodi;	1535

GADER See BETH GADER

GADFLY (1)

Jer 46:20	a g is coming against her from the north.	7976

GADI (2)

2Ki 15:14	Then Menahem son of G went from Tirzah	1533
15:17	Menahem son of G became king of Israel,	1533

GADITES (29) [GAD]

Nu 32: 1	The Reubenites and G,	1201+1514
32: 6	Moses said to the G and Reubenites,	1201+1514
32:25	The G and Reubenites said to Moses,	1201+1514
32:29	to them, "If the G and Reubenites,	1201+1514
32:31	The G and Reubenites answered,	1201+1514
32:33	Then Moses gave to the G,	1201+1514
32:34	The G built up Dibon, Ataroth, Aroer,	1201+1514
Dt 3:12	the Reubenites and the G the territory north	1532
3:16	and the G I gave the territory extending	1532
4:43	Ramoth in Gilead, for the G;	1532
29: 8	the G and the half-tribe of Manasseh.	1532
Jos 1:12	the G and the half-tribe of Manasseh,	1532
12: 6	the G and the half-tribe of Manasseh to	1532
13: 8	the Reubenites and the G had received	1532
13:28	the inheritance of the G,	1201+1514
22: 1	the G and the half-tribe of Manasseh	1532
22: 9	the G and the half-tribe of Manasseh	1201+1514
22:10	the G and the half-tribe of Manasseh	1201+1514
22:25	you Reubenites and G!	1201+1514
22:32	with the Reubenites and G in Gilead	1201+1514
22:33	where the Reubenites and the G lived.	1201+1514
22:34	And the Reubenites and the G gave	1201+1514
1Ch 5: 1	The G lived next to them in Bashan,	1201+1514
5:16	The G lived in Gilead,	NIH
5:18	the G and the Reubenites	1532
5:26	the G and the half-tribe of Manasseh	1532
12: 8	Some G defected to David at his stronghold	1532
12:14	These G were army commanders;	1201+1514
26:32	the G and the half-tribe of Manasseh	1532

GAHAM (1)

Ge 22:24	Tebah, G, Tahash and Maacah.	1626

GAHAR (2)

Ezr 2:47	Giddel, G, Reaiah,	1627
Ne 7:49	Hanan, Giddel, G,	1627

GAIETY (2)

Isa 24: 8	The g of the tambourines is stilled,	5375
24:11	all g is banished from the earth.	5375

GAIN (68) [GAINED, GAINING, GAINS, REGAIN, REGAINED]

Ge 15: 8	how can I know that I will g possession	3769
37:26	"What will we g if we kill our brother	1299
Ex 14: 4	But I will g glory for myself	3877
14:17	And I will g glory through Pharaoh	3877
14:18	that I am the LORD when I g glory	3877
18:21	trustworthy men who hate dishonest g—	1299
1Sa 8: 3	after dishonest g and accepted bribes	1299
2Ki 15:19	a thousand talents of silver to g his support	
		907+2118+3338
Job 21:15	What would we g by praying to him?'	3603
22: 3	would he g if your ways were blameless?	1299
35: 3	and what do I g by not sinning?'	3603
Ps 30: 9	"What g is there in my destruction,	1299
60:12	With God we will g the victory,	6913
90:12	that we may g a heart of wisdom.	995
108:13	With God we will g the victory,	6913
119:36	and not toward selfish g.	1299
119:104	I g understanding from your precepts;	1067
Pr 1:19	all who go after ill-gotten g;	1298+1299
4: 1	pay attention and g understanding.	3359
8: 5	You who are simple, g prudence;	1067
8: 5	you who are foolish, g understanding.	1067
11:16	but ruthless men g only wealth.	9461
16: 8	a little with righteousness than much g	9311
19:25	and he will g knowledge.	1067
21:11	a mocker is punished, the simple g wisdom;	AIT
28:16	but he who hates ill-gotten g will enjoy	1299
28:23	He who rebukes a man will in the end g	
	more favor than	5162
Ecc 1: 3	What does man g from all his labor	3862
2:15	What then do I g by being wise?"	3463
3: 9	What does the worker g from his toil?	3862
5:16	so he departs, and what does he g,	3862
6: 8	What does a poor man g by knowing how	4200
Isa 29:24	wayward in spirit will g understanding;	3359
33:15	who rejects g from extortion	1299
56:11	each seeks his own g.	1299
63:12	to g for himself everlasting renown,	6913
Jer 6:13	all are greedy for g;	1299
8:10	all are greedy for g;	1299
12:13	they will wear themselves out but g nothing.	3603
22:17	and your heart are set only on dishonest g,	1299
Eze 22:12	and excessive interest and make unjust g	1298
22:13	at the unjust g you have made and at	1299
22:27	and kill people to make unjust g.	1298+1299
28:22	O Sidon, and I will g glory within you.	3877
33:31	but their hearts are greedy for unjust g.	1299
Da 2: 8	"I am certain that you are trying to g time,	10223
10:12	to g understanding and to humble yourself	1067
11:43	He will g control of the treasures of gold	5440
Hab 2: 9	to him who builds his realm by unjust g	1299
Mal 3:14	What did we g by carrying out his	1299
Mk 8:36	to g the whole world, yet forfeit is soul?	3045
Lk 9:25	to g the whole world, and yet lose or forfeit	
	his very self?	3045

Lk 16: 9 use worldly wealth *to g* friends 4472
    21:19 By standing firm *you will g* life. 3227
Jn 7:18 on his own does so *to g* honor for himself, 2426
Ac 7:10 to g the goodwill of Pharaoh king of Egypt; NIG
1Co 7:21 if you can g *your freedom,* do so. 1181+1801
    13: 3 but have not love, *I* g nothing. 6067
Php 1:21 For to me, to live is Christ and to die is g. 3046
    3: 8 I consider them rubbish, that *I may* g Christ 3045
1Ti 3: 8 and not **pursuing dishonest** g. 153
    3:13 Those who have served well g 4347
    6: 5 that godliness is a **means to financial** g. 4516
    6: 6 But godliness with contentment is great g. 4516
2Ti 3: 6 and g **control over** weak-willed women, 170
Tit 1: 7 not violent, not **pursuing dishonest** g. 153
    1:11 and that for the sake of dishonest g. 3046
Heb 11:35 so that *they might* g a better resurrection. 5593

GAINED (23) [GAIN]

Ge 31: 1 and *has* g all this wealth 6913
2Sa 15:12 And so the conspiracy g strength, 2118
2Ch 32: 8 And the people g **confidence** 6164
Job 31:25 the fortune my hands *had* g, 5162
Ps 129: 2 but *they have* not g **the victory** over me. 3523
Pr 20:17 **Food** g by fraud tastes sweet to a man, AIT
    20:21 An inheritance **quickly** g at 987
Ecc 2:11 nothing was g under the sun. 3862
Isa 26:15 g **glory for yourself;** 3877
Jer 32:20 and *have* g the renown that is still yours. 6913
Eze 28: 4 and understanding *you have* g wealth 6913
Da 11: 2 When he has g **power** by his wealth, 2621
Mt 25:16 and put his money to work and g five more. 3045
    25:17 the one with the two talents g two more. 3045
    25:20 See, *I have* g five more.' 3045
    25:22 see, *I have* g two more.' 3045
Lk 19:15 in order to find out what *they had* g with it. 1390
Ro 5: 2 through whom *we* **have** g access by faith AIT
1Co 15:32 what have I g? 4055
2Co 12: 1 *Although* there is nothing *to be* g, 5237
Gal 2:21 if righteousness could be g through the law, NIG
Heb 11:33 and g what was promised; 2209
Rev 18:15 and g their **wealth** 4456

GAINING (3) [GAIN]

Ge 3: 6 and also desirable for g **wisdom,** 8505
Ps 44:12 g nothing from their sale. 8049
Jn 4: 1 The Pharisees heard that Jesus *was* g 4472

GAINS (8) [GAIN]

Pr 3:13 the man *who* g understanding, 7049
    11:16 A kindhearted woman g respect, 9461
    11:24 One man gives freely, yet g even more; 3578
    15:32 whoever heeds correction g understanding. 7864
    29:23 but a man of lowly spirit g honor. 9461
Jer 17:11 the *man who* g riches by unjust means. 6913
Mic 4:13 You will devote their **ill-gotten** g to 1299
Mt 16:26 What good will it be for a man if *he* g 3045

GAINSAY, GAINSAYERS (KJV) See OPPOSE, RESIST

GAINSAYING (KJV) See OBSTINATE, RAISING OBJECTION, REBELLION

GAIUS (5)

Ac 19:29 The people seized G and Aristarchus, 1127
    20: 4 G from Derbe, Timothy also, 1127
Ro 16:23 G, whose hospitality I and 1127
1Co 1:14 of you except Crispus and G, 1127
3Jn 1: 1 The elder, *To* my dear friend G, 1127

GALAL (3)

1Ch 9:15 Heresh, G and Mattaniah son of Mica, 1674
    9:16 the son of G, the son of Jeduthun; 1674
Ne 11:17 and Abda son of Shammua, the son of G, 1674

GALATIA (5) [GALATIAN, GALATIANS]

Ac 16: 6 throughout the region of Phrygia and G, 1131
    18:23 throughout the region of G and Phrygia, 1131
Gal 1: 2 To the churches *in* G: 1130
2Ti 4:10 Crescens has gone to G, 1130
1Pe 1: 1 G, Cappadocia, Asia and Bithynia, 1130

GALATIAN (1) [GALATIA]

1Co 16: 1 Do what I told the G churches to do. 1130

GALATIANS (1) [GALATIA]

Gal 3: 1 You foolish G! 1129

GALBANUM (1)

Ex 30:34 gum resin, onycha and g— 2697

GALE (3)

Job 21:18 like chaff swept away by a g? 6070
Isa 17:13 like tumbleweed before a g. 6070
    41:16 and a g will blow them away. 6194

GALEED (2)

Ge 31:47 and Jacob called it G. 1681

Ge 31:48 That is why it was called G. 1681

GALILEAN (4) [GALILEE]

Mk 14:70 you are one of them, for you are a G." 1134
Lk 22:59 this fellow was with him, for he is a G. 1134
    23: 6 Pilate asked if the man was a G. 1134
Ac 5:37 Judas the G appeared in the days of the census 1134

GALILEANS (5) [GALILEE]

Lk 13: 1 about the G whose blood Pilate had mixed 1134
    13: 2 that these G were worse sinners than all 1134
    13: 2 the other G because they suffered this way? 1134
Jn 4:45 the G welcomed him. 1134
Ac 2: 7 not all these men who are speaking G? 1134

GALILEE (70) [GALILEAN, GALILEANS, TIBERIAS]

Jos 20: 7 in G in the hill country of Naphtali, 1665
    21:32 in G (a city of refuge for one accused 1665
1Ki 9:11 King Solomon gave twenty towns in G 824+1665
2Ki 15:29 He took Gilead and G, 1665
1Ch 6:76 of Naphtali they received Kedesh in G, 1665
Isa 9: 1 the future he will honor G *of* the Gentiles, 1665
Mt 2:22 he withdrew to the district *of* G, 1133
    3:13 Then Jesus came from G to the Jordan to 1133
    4:12 he returned to G. 1133
    4:15 along the Jordan, G of the Gentiles— 1133
    4:18 As Jesus was walking beside the Sea of G, 1133
    4:23 Jesus went throughout G, 1133
    4:25 Large crowds from G, the Decapolis, 1133
    11: 1 to teach and preach in the towns of G. NIG
    15:29 and went along the Sea *of* G. 1133
    17:22 When they came together in G, 1133
    19: 1 he left G and went into the region of Judea 1133
    21:11 the prophet from Nazareth in G." 1133
    26:32 I have risen, I will go ahead of you into G." 1133
    26:69 "You also were with Jesus *of* G," she said. 1133
    27:55 They had followed Jesus from G to care 1133
    28: 7 the dead and is going ahead of you into G. 1133
    28:10 Go and tell my brothers to go to G; 1133
    28:16 the eleven disciples went to G, 1133
Mk 1: 9 that time Jesus came from Nazareth *in* G 1133
    1:14 Jesus went into G, 1133
    1:16 As Jesus walked beside the Sea *of* G, 1133
    1:28 over the whole region *of* G. 1133
    1:39 So he traveled throughout G, 1133
    3: 7 and a large crowd from G followed. 1133
    6:21 and the leading men *of* G. 1133
    7:31 down to the Sea *of* G and into the region of 1133
    9:30 They left that place and passed through G. 1133
    14:28 I have risen, I will go ahead of you into G." 1133
    15:41 In G these women *had* followed him 1133
    16: 7 'He is going ahead of you into G. 1133
Lk 1:26 Nazareth, a town *in* G, 1133
    2: 4 from the town of Nazareth *in* G to Judea, 1133
    2:39 they returned to G to their own town 1133
    3: 1 *of* G, his brother Philip tetrarch of Iturea 1133
    4:14 Jesus returned to G in the power of 1133
    4:31 he went down to Capernaum, a town *in* G, 1133
    5:17 who had come from every village *of* G and 1133
    8:26 which is across the lake *from* G. 1133
    17:11 along the border between Samaria and G. 1133
    23: 5 in G and has come all the way here." 1133
    23:49 the women who had followed him from G, 1133
    23:55 from G followed Joseph and saw the tomb 1133
    24: 6 while he was still with you in G: 1133
Jn 1:43 The next day Jesus decided to leave for G. 1133
    2: 1 a wedding took place at Cana in G. 1133
    2:11 Jesus performed at Cana *in* G. 1133
    4: 3 and went back once more to G. 1133
    4:43 After the two days he left for G. 1133
    4:45 When he arrived in G, 1133
    4:46 Once more he visited Cana *in* G, 1133
    4:47 that Jesus had arrived in G from Judea, 1133
    4:54 having come from Judea to G. 1133
    6: 1 to the far shore of the Sea of G (that is, 1133
    7: 1 After this, Jesus went around in G, 1133
    7: 9 Having said this, he stayed in G. 1133
    7:41 "How can the Christ come from G? 1133
    7:52 They replied, "Are you from G, too? 1133
    7:52 that a prophet does not come out of G." 1133
    12:21 who was from Bethsaida *in* G, 1133
    21: 2 Nathanael from Cana *in* G, 1133
Ac 1:11 "Men *of* G," they said, 1134
    9:31 G and Samaria enjoyed a time of peace. 1133
    10:37 in G after the baptism that John preached— 1133
    13:31 by those who had traveled with him from G 1133

GALL (6) [GALLED]

Job 16:13 he pierces my kidneys and spills my g on 5354
Ps 69:21 They put g in my food and gave me vinegar 8032
Pr 5: 4 but in the end she is bitter as g, 4360
La 3:15 with bitter herbs and sated me with g. 4360
    3:19 the bitterness and the g. 4360
Mt 27:34 to drink, mixed with g; 5958

GALLED (1) [GALL]

1Sa 18: 8 Saul was very angry; this refrain g him. 928+6524+8317

GALLERIES (3) [GALLERY]

Eze 41:15 including its g on each side; 916

Eze 41:16 the narrow windows and g around the three 916
    42: 5 the g took more space from them than from 916

GALLERY (2) [GALLERIES]

Eze 42: 3 g faced gallery at the three levels. 916
    42: 3 gallery faced g at the three levels. 916

GALLEY (1)

Isa 33:21 No g *with* oars will ride them, 639

GALLIM (2)

1Sa 25:44 to Paltiel son of Laish, who was from G. 1668
Isa 10:30 Cry out, O Daughter of G! 1668

GALLIO (3)

Ac 18:12 While G was proconsul of Achaia, 1136
    18:14 G said to the Jews, 1136
    18:17 But G showed no concern whatever. 1136

GALLONS (2)

Lk 16: 6 " 'Eight hundred g of olive oil,' 1004+1669
Jn 2: 6 each holding from **twenty to thirty** g. 1545+2445+3583+5552

GALLOP (1) [GALLOPING, GALLOPS]

Joel 2: 4 *they* g along like cavalry. 8132

GALLOPING (4) [GALLOP]

Jdg 5:22 g, galloping go his mighty steeds. 1852
    5:22 galloping, g go his mighty steeds. 1852
Jer 47: 3 at the sound of the hoofs of g steeds. 9121
Na 3: 2 g horses and jolting chariots! 1851

GALLOPS (1) [GALLOP]

Hab 1: 8 Their cavalry g **headlong;** 7055

GALLOWS (9)

Est 2:23 the two officials were hanged on a g. 6770
    5:14 "Have a g built, seventy-five feet high, 6770
    5:14 and he had the g built. 6770
    6: 4 on the g he had erected for him. 6770
    7: 9 "A g seventy-five feet high stands 6770
    7:10 on the g he had prepared for Mordecai. 6770
    8: 7 and they have hanged him on the g. 6770
    9:13 and let Haman's ten sons be hanged on g." 6770
    9:25 he and his sons should be hanged on the g. 6770

GAMALIEL (7)

Nu 1:10 from Manasseh, G son of Pedahzur; 1697
    2:20 of the people of Manasseh is G son 1697
    7:54 On the eighth day G son of Pedahzur, 1697
    7:59 This was the offering of G son of Pedahzur. 1697
    10:23 G son of Pedahzur was over the division of 1697
Ac 5:34 But a Pharisee named G, 1137
    22: 3 Under G I was thoroughly trained in 1137

GAME (10) [GAMES]

Ge 25:28 Isaac, who had a taste for **wild** g, 7473
    27: 3 to the open country to hunt *some* **wild** g 7473
    27: 5 for the open country to hunt g 7473
    27: 7 'Bring me *some* g 7473
    27:19 Please sit up and eat some of my g so 7473
    27:25 "My son, bring me some of your g to eat, 7473
    27:31 "My father, sit up and eat some of my g, 7473
    27:33 that, who hunted g and brought it to me? 7473
Ps 76: 4 more majestic than mountains rich with g. 3272
Pr 12:27 The lazy man does not roast his g, 7473

GAMES (1) [GAME]

1Co 9:25 Everyone who **competes in the** g goes 76

GAMMAD (1)

Eze 27:11 **men of** G were in your towers. 1689

GAMUL (1) [BETH GAMUL]

1Ch 24:17 the twenty-second to G, 1690

GANGRENE (1)

2Ti 2:17 Their teaching will spread like g. 1121

GANNIM See EN GANNIM

GAP (4) [GAPS]

Jdg 21:15 LORD had made a g in the tribes of Israel. 7288
1Ki 11:27 and had filled in the g **in the wall** of 7288
Ne 6: 1 the wall and not a g was left in it— 7288
Eze 22:30 and stand before me in the g on behalf of 7288

GAPE (1) [GAPING]

Ps 35:21 *They* g at me and say, "Aha! 7023+8143

GAPING (1) [GAPE]

Job 30:14 They advance as through a g breach; 8146

GAPS (1) [GAP]

Ne	4: 7	ahead and that the **g** were being closed,	7287

GARDEN (53) [GARDENER, GARDENS]

Ge	2: 8	the LORD God had planted a **g** in the east,	1703
	2: 9	the middle of the **g** were the tree of life and	1703
	2:10	A river watering the **g** flowed from Eden;	1703
	2:15	the G of Eden to work it and take care of it.	1703
	2:16	"You are free to eat from any tree in the **g**,	1703
	3: 1	'You must not eat from any tree in the **g**'?"	1703
	3: 2	"We may eat fruit from the trees in the **g**,	1703
	3: 3	from the tree that is in the middle of the **g**,	1703
	3: 8	the LORD God as he was walking in the **g**	1703
	3: 8	the LORD God among the trees of the **g**.	1703
	3:10	He answered, "I heard you in the **g**,	1703
	3:23	the LORD God banished him from the G	1703
	3:24	on the east side of the G of Eden cherubim	1703
	13:10	like the **g** of the LORD,	1703
Dt	11:10	and irrigated it by foot as in a vegetable **g**.	1703
1Ki	21: 2	to use for a vegetable **g**,	1703
2Ki	21:18	and was buried in his palace **g**,	1703
	21:18	in his palace garden, the **g** of Uzza.	1703
	21:26	He was buried in his grave in the **g**	1703
	25: 4	between the two walls near the king's **g**,	1703
Ne	3:15	by the King's G,	1703
Est	1: 5	in the enclosed **g** of the king's palace,	1708
	1: 6	**g** had hangings of white and blue linen,	NIH
	7: 7	left his wine and went out into the palace **g**.	1708
	7: 8	Just as the king returned from the palace **g**	1708
Job	8:16	spreading its shoots over the **g**;	1708
SS	4:12	You are a **g** locked up, my sister, my bride;	1703
	4:15	You are a **g** fountain,	1703
	4:16	Blow on my **g**,	1703
	4:16	into his **g** and taste its choice fruits.	1703
	5: 1	I have come into my **g**, my sister,	1703
	6: 2	My lover has gone down to his **g**,	1703
Isa	1:30	like a **g** without water.	1708
	5: 7	the men of Judah are the **g** of his delight.	5750
	51: 3	her wastelands like the **g** of the LORD.	1703
	58:11	You will be like a well-watered **g**,	1703
	61:11	the sprout come up and a **g** causes seeds	1708
Jer	31:12	They will be like a well-watered **g**,	1703
	39: 4	the city at night by way of the king's **g**,	1703
	52: 7	between the two walls near the king's **g**,	1703
La	2: 6	He has laid waste his dwelling like a **g**;	1703
Eze	28:13	You were in Eden, the **g** of God;	1703
	31: 8	cedars in the **g** of God could not rival it,	1703
	31: 8	in the **g** of God could match its beauty.	1703
	31: 9	the envy of all the trees of Eden in the **g**	1703
	36:35	that was laid waste has become like the **g**	1703
Joel	2: 3	Before them the land is like the **g** of Eden,	1703
Mt	13:32	it is the largest of **g plants** and becomes	3303
Mk	4:32	and becomes the largest of all **g plants,**	3303
Lk	11:42	rue and all other kinds of **g herbs,**	3303
	13:19	which a man took and planted in his **g**.	3057
Jn	19:41	where Jesus was crucified, there was a **g**,	3057
	19:41	and in the **g** a new tomb,	3057

GARDENER (2) [GARDEN]

Jn	15: 1	"I am the true vine, and my Father is the **g**.	1177
	20:15	Thinking he was the **g**, she said, "Sir,	3058

GARDENS (11) [GARDEN]

Nu	24: 6	like **g** beside a river,	1708
Ecc	2: 5	I made **g** and parks and planted all kinds	1708
SS	6: 2	to browse in the **g** and to gather lilies.	1703
	8:13	You who dwell in the **g** with friends	1703
Isa	1:29	because of the **g** that you have chosen.	1708
	65: 3	offering sacrifices in **g** and burning incense	1708
	66:17	into the **g**, following the one in the midst	1708
Jer	29: 5	plant **g** and eat what they produce.	1708
	29:28	plant **g** and eat what they produce.' "	1708
Am	4: 9	"Many times I struck your **g** and vineyards,	1708
	9:14	they will make **g** and eat their fruit.	1708

GAREB (3)

2Sa	23:38	Ira the Ithrite, G the Ithrite	1735
1Ch	11:40	Ira the Ithrite, G the Ithrite,	1735
Jer	31:39	from there straight to the hill of G and	1736

GARLAND (2)

Pr	1: 9	They will be a **g** to grace your head and	4292
	4: 9	a **g** of grace on your head and present you	4292

GARLIC (1)

Nu	11: 5	melons, leeks, onions and **g**.	8770

GARMENT (47) [GARMENTS, UNDERGARMENT, UNDERGARMENTS]

Ge	9:23	But Shem and Japheth took a **g** and laid it	8529
	25:25	and his whole body was like a hairy **g**;	168
Ex	22: 9	a donkey, a sheep, a **g**,	8515
Lev	6:27	and if any of the blood is spattered on a **g**,	955
Nu	31:20	Purify every **g** as well as everything made	955
Jdg	8:25	So they spread out a **g**,	8529
Ru	3: 9	"Spread the **corner of** your **g** over me,	4053
1Sa	19:13	with a **g** and putting some goats' hair at	955
2Sa	13:18	of the virgin daughters of the king wore.	5077
	20:12	from the road into a field and threw a **g**	955
2Ki	1: 8	"He was a man with a **g of hair** and with	8552
Job	13:28	like a **g** eaten by moths.	955

Job	30:18	he binds me like the neck of my **g**.	4189
	31:19	or a needy man without a **g**,	4064
	38: 9	the clouds its **g** and wrapped it	4230
	38:14	its features stand out like those of a **g**.	4230
Ps	74:11	from the folds of your **g** and destroy them!	2668
	102:26	they will all wear out like a **g**.	955
	104: 2	He wraps himself in light as with a **g**;	8515
	104: 6	You covered it with the deep as with a **g**;	4230
	109:18	He wore cursing as his **g**;	4496
Pr	20:16	Take the **g** of one who puts up security for	955
	25:20	Like one who takes away a **g** on a cold day,	955
	27:13	Take the **g** of one who puts up security for	955
Isa	9: 5	and every **g** rolled in blood will be destined	8529
	50: 9	They will all wear out like a **g**;	955
	51: 6	like smoke, the earth will wear out like a **g**	955
	51: 8	For the moth will eat them up like a **g**;	955
	61: 3	a **g** of praise instead of a spirit of despair.	5073
Jer	43:12	As a shepherd wraps his **g** around him,	955
Eze	5: 3	in the **folds of** your **g**.	4053
	16: 8	I spread the **corner of** my **g** over you	4053
	44:17	not wear any **woolen g** while ministering at	7547
Hag	2:12	in the fold of his **g**,	955
Zec	13: 4	on a **prophet's g** of hair in order to deceive.	168
Mal	2:16	with violence as well as with his **g**,"	4230
Mt	9:16	a patch of unshrunk cloth on an old **g**,	2668
	9:16	for the patch will pull away from the **g**,	2668
Mk	2:21	a patch of unshrunk cloth on an old **g**.	2668
	14:51	wearing nothing but a **linen g**,	4984
	14:52	he fled naked, leaving his **g** behind.	4984
Lk	5:36	from a new **g** and sews it on an old one.	2668
	5:36	If he does, he will have torn the new **g**	NIG
Jn	19:23	This **g** was seamless,	5945
	21: 7	he wrapped his **outer g** around him	2087
Heb	1:11	they will all wear out like a **g**.	2668
	1:12	like a **g** they will be changed.	2668

GARMENTS (73) [GARMENT]

Ge	3:21	The LORD God made **g** of skin for Adam	4189
	49:11	he will wash his **g** in wine,	4230
Ex	28: 2	Make sacred **g** for your brother Aaron,	955
	28: 3	in such matters that they are to make **g**	955
	28: 4	These are the **g** they are to make:	955
	28: 4	They are to make these sacred **g**	955
	29: 5	Take the **g** and dress Aaron with the tunic,	955
	29:21	and sprinkle it on Aaron and his **g** and	955
	29:21	and on his sons and their **g**.	955
	29:21	Then he and his sons and their **g** will	955
	29:29	"Aaron's sacred **g** will belong	955
	31:10	and also the woven **g**,	955
	31:10	both the sacred **g** for Aaron the priest and	955
	31:10	for Aaron the priest and the **g** for his sons	955
	35:19	the woven **g** worn for ministering in	955
	35:19	both the sacred **g** for Aaron the priest and	955
	35:19	for Aaron the priest and the **g** for his sons	955
	35:21	for all its service, and for the sacred **g**.	955
	39: 1	purple and scarlet yarn they made woven **g**	955
	39: 1	They also made sacred **g** for Aaron,	955
	39:41	and the woven **g** worn for ministering in	955
	39:41	both the sacred **g** for Aaron the priest and	955
	39:41	the **g** for his sons when serving as priests.	955
	40:13	Then dress Aaron in the sacred **g**,	955
Lev	8: 2	their **g**, the anointing oil,	955
	8:30	and sprinkled them on Aaron and his **g** and	955
	8:30	and on his sons and their **g**.	955
	8:30	and his **g** and his sons and their garments.	955
	8:30	and his garments and his sons and their **g**.	955
	16: 4	These are sacred **g**;	955
	16:23	of Meeting and take off the linen **g** he put	955
	16:24	in a holy place and put on his regular **g**.	955
	16:32	He is to put on the sacred linen **g**	955
	21:10	to wear the priestly **g**,	955
Nu	15:38	to make tassels on the corners of your **g**,	955
	20:26	Remove Aaron's **g** and put them	955
	20:28	Moses removed Aaron's **g** and put them	955
Jdg	5:30	colorful **g** as plunder for Sisera,	7389
	5:30	colorful **g** embroidered,	7389
	5:30	highly embroidered **g** for my neck—	7389
	8:26	the purple **g** worn by the kings of Midian or	955
	14:12	I will give you thirty **linen g** and thirty sets	6041
	14:13	you must give me thirty **linen g**	6041
2Sa	1:24	who adorned your **g** with ornaments	4230
	10: 4	cut off their **g** in the middle at the buttocks,	4503
1Ch	19: 4	cut off their **g** in the middle at the buttocks,	4503
Ezr	2:69	5,000 minas of silver and 100 priestly **g**.	4189
Ne	7:70	50 bowls and 530 **g** for priests.	4189
	7:72	2,000 minas of silver and 67 **g** for priests.	4189
Est	8:15	the king's presence wearing royal **g** of blue	4230
Ps	22:18	They divide my **g** among them and cast lots	955
	45:14	In **embroidered g** she is led to the king;	8391
Pr	31:24	She makes **linen g** and sells them,	6041
SS	4:11	The fragrance of your **g** is like that	8515
Isa	3:23	and the **linen g** and tiaras and shawls.	6041
	52: 1	Put on your **g** of splendor, O Jerusalem;	955
	59:17	the **g** of vengeance and wrapped himself	955
	61:10	For he has clothed me with **g** of salvation	955
	63: 1	from Bozrah, with his **g** stained crimson?	955
	63: 2	Why are your **g** red,	4230
	63: 3	their blood spattered my **g**,	955
La	4:14	that no one dares to touch their **g**.	4230
Eze	16:10	and covered you with **costly g**.	5429
	16:16	of your **g** to make gaudy high places,	955
	26:16	and take off their embroidered **g**.	955
	27:24	with you **beautiful g**,	4815
	42:14	the outer court until they leave behind the **g**	955
	44:19	the people by means of their **g**.	955
Joel	2:13	Rend your heart and not your **g**.	955

Am	2: 8	They lie down beside every altar on **g** taken	955
Zec	3: 4	and I will put **rich g** on you."	4711
Mt	23: 5	and the tassels *on* their **g** long;	2668
Jn	19:24	"They divided my **g** among them,	2668

GARMITE (1)

1Ch	4:19	the father of Keilah the G,	1753

GARNER, GARNERS (KJV) See BARN, BARNS, STOREHOUSES

GARRISON (2) [GARRISONS]

2Sa	23:14	and the Philistine **g** was at Bethlehem.	5163
1Ch	11:16	and the Philistine **g** was at Bethlehem.	5907

GARRISONS (5) [GARRISON]

2Sa	8: 6	He put **g** in the Aramean kingdom	5907
	8:14	He put **g** throughout Edom,	5907
1Ch	18: 6	He put **g** in the Aramean kingdom	NIH
	18:13	He put **g** in Edom,	5907
2Ch	17: 2	in all the fortified cities of Judah and put **g**	5907

GASP (2) [GASPING]

Job	11:20	their hope will become a dying **g**."	5134
Isa	42:14	I cry out, I **g** and pant.	5971

GASPING (1) [GASP]

Jer	4:31	cry of the Daughter of Zion **g for breath,**	3640

GAT (KJV) See ACQUIRED, CAME, CLIMBED, GET, LEFT, MOUNTED, MOVED, SET OUT, TRAVELED, WENT

GATAM (3)

Ge	36:11	Teman, Omar, Zepho, G and Kenaz.	1725
	36:16	Korah, G and Amalek.	1725
1Ch	1:36	Teman, Omar, Zepho, G and Kenaz;	1725

GATE (222) [GATEKEEPERS, GATEPOST, GATEPOSTS, GATES, GATEWAY, GATEWAYS]

Ge	23:10	of all the Hittites who had come to the **g** of	9133
	23:18	of all the Hittites who had come to the **g** of	9133
	28:17	this is the **g** of heaven."	9133
	34:20	and his son Shechem went to the **g**	9133
	34:24	the men who went out of the city **g** agreed	9133
Dt	17: 5	to your **city g** and stone that person	9133
	21:19	of him and bring him to the elders at the **g**	9133
	22:15	a virgin to the town elders at the **g**.	9133
	22:24	you shall take both of them to the **g** of	9133
	25: 7	she shall go to the elders at the **town g**	9133
Jos	2: 5	when it was time to close the **city g**,	9133
	2: 7	the **g** was shut.	9133
	7: 5	from the **city g** as far as the stone quarries	9133
	8:29	down at the entrance of the **g**.	9133
	20: 4	the entrance of the city **g** and state his case	9133
Jdg	9:35	the entrance to the **city g** just as Abimelech	9133
	9:40	all the way to the entrance to the **g**.	9133
	9:44	to a position at the entrance to the **city g**.	9133
	16: 2	in wait for him all night at the **city g**.	9133
	16: 3	up and took hold of the doors of the **city g**,	9133
	18:16	stood at the entrance of the **g**.	9133
	18:17	at the entrance to the **g**.	9133
Ru	4: 1	Meanwhile Boaz went up to the **town g**	9133
	4:11	Then the elders and all those at the **g** said,	9133
1Sa	4:18	by the side of the **g**.	9133
	21:13	the **g** and letting saliva run down his beard.	9133
2Sa	10: 8	at the entrance to their **city g**,	9133
	11:23	to the entrance to the **city g**.	9133
	15: 2	the side of the road leading to the **city g**.	9133
	18: 4	beside the **g** while all the men marched out	9133
	23:15	a drink of water from the well near the **g**	9133
	23:16	near the **g** of Bethlehem and carried it back	9133
1Ki	4:13	with bronze **g bars**);	1378
	17:10	When he came to the town **g**,	7339
	22:10	the threshing floor by the entrance of the **g**	9133
2Ki	7: 1	and two seahs of barley for a shekel at the **g**	9133
	7: 3	with leprosy at the entrance of the **city g**.	9133
	7:17	on whose arm he leaned in charge of the **g**,	9133
	7:18	and two seahs of barley for a shekel at the **g**	9133
	9:31	As Jehu entered the **g**, she asked,	9133
	10: 8	at the entrance of the **city g** until morning."	9133
	11: 6	at the Sur **G**, and a third at the gate behind	9133
	11: 6	and a third at the **g** behind the guard,	9133
	11:19	entering by way of the **g** of the guards.	9133
	14:13	the wall of Jerusalem from the Ephraim **G**	9133
	14:13	from the Ephraim Gate to the Corner **G**—	9133
	15:35	the Upper **G** of the temple of the LORD.	9133
	23: 8	at the entrance to the **G** of Joshua,	9133
	23: 8	which is on the left of the city **g**.	9133
	25: 4	the whole army fled at night through the **g**	9133
1Ch	9:18	being stationed at the King's **G** on the east,	9133
	11:17	a drink of water from the well near the **g**	9133
	11:18	near the **g** of Bethlehem and carried it back	9133
	16:42	of Jeduthun were stationed at the **g**.	9133
	26:13	Lots were cast for **each g**,	2256+9133+9133
	26:14	The lot for the East **G** fell to Shelemiah.	NIH
	26:14	and the lot for the North **G** fell to him.	NIH
	26:15	The lot for the South **G** fell to Obed-Edom,	NIH

1Ch	26:16	for the West G and the Shalleketh Gate on	NIH
	26:16	and the Shalleketh G on the upper road fell	9133
2Ch	23: 5	and a third at the Foundation G,	9133
	23:15	as she reached the entrance of the Horse G	9133
	23:20	through the Upper G and seated the king on	9133
	24: 8	at the g of the temple of the LORD.	9133
	25:23	the wall of Jerusalem from the Ephraim G	9133
	25:23	from the Ephraim Gate to the Corner G—	9133
	26: 9	in Jerusalem at the Corner G,	9133
	26: 9	at the Valley G and at the angle of the wall,	9133
	27: 3	Jotham rebuilt the Upper G of the temple	9133
	31:14	**keeper of** the East G,	8788
	32: 6	before him in the square at the city g	9133
	33:14	as the entrance of the Fish G and encircling	9133
	35:15	The gatekeepers at **each g**	2256+9133+9133
Ne	2:13	By night I went out through the Valley G	9133
	2:13	toward the Jackal Well and the Dung G,	9133
	2:14	toward the Fountain G and the King's Pool,	9133
	2:15	and reentered through the Valley G.	9133
	3: 1	to work and rebuild the Sheep G.	9133
	3: 3	The Fish G was rebuilt by the sons	9133
	3: 6	The Jeshanah G was repaired by Joiada son	9133
	3:13	The Valley G was repaired by Hanun and	9133
	3:13	of the wall as far as the Dung G.	9133
	3:14	The Dung G was repaired by Malkijah son	9133
	3:15	The Fountain G was repaired	9133
	3:26	up to a point opposite the Water G toward	9133
	3:28	Above the Horse G,	9133
	3:29	the guard at the East G, made repairs.	9133
	3:31	opposite the Inspection G,	9133
	3:32	the room above the corner and the Sheep G	9133
	8: 1	in the square before the Water G.	9133
	8: 3	as he faced the square before the Water G	9133
	8:16	the square by the Water G and the one by	9133
	8:16	by the Water Gate and the one by the G	9133
	12:31	toward the Dung G.	9133
	12:37	the Fountain G they continued directly up	9133
	12:37	above the house of David to the Water G	9133
	12:39	over the G of Ephraim,	9133
	12:39	the Jeshanah G, the Fish Gate,	9133
	12:39	the Jeshanah Gate, the Fish G,	9133
	12:39	as far as the Sheep G.	9133
	12:39	At the G of the Guard they stopped.	9133
Est	2:19	Mordecai was sitting at the king's g.	9133
	2:21	Mordecai was sitting at the king's g,	9133
	3: 2	All the royal officials at the king's g knelt	9133
	3: 3	at the king's g asked Mordecai,	9133
	4: 2	But he went only as far as the king's g,	9133
	4: 6	of the city in front of the king's g.	9133
	5: 9	But when he saw Mordecai at the king's g	9133
	5:13	that Jew Mordecai sitting at the king's g."	9133
	6:10	Mordecai the Jew, who sits at the king's g.	9133
	6:12	Mordecai returned to the king's g.	9133
Job	29: 7	to the g of the city and took my seat in	9133
Ps	69:12	Those who sit at the g mock me,	9133
	118:20	This is the g of the LORD through which	9133
	127: 5	with their enemies in the g.	9133
Pr	17:19	he who builds a high g invites destruction.	7339
	24: 7	the **assembly at the** g he has nothing to say.	9133
	31:23	Her husband is respected at the **city g,**	9133
	31:31	her works bring her praise at the **city g.**	9133
SS	7: 4	of Heshbon by the g of Bath Rabbim.	9133
Isa	14:31	Wail, O g!	9133
	24:12	its g is battered to pieces.	9133
	28: 6	to those who turn back the battle at the g.	9133
Jer	7: 2	"Stand at the g of the LORD's house	9133
	17:19	"Go and stand at the g of the people,	9133
	19: 2	near the entrance of the Potsherd G.	9133
	20: 2	in the stocks at the Upper G of Benjamin at	9133
	26:10	of the New G of the LORD's house.	9133
	31:38	the Tower of Hananel to the Corner G,	9133
	31:40	the east as far as the corner of the Horse G,	9133
	36:10	at the entrance of the New G of the temple,	9133
	37:13	But when he reached the Benjamin G,	9133
	38: 7	the king was sitting in the Benjamin G,	9133
	39: 3	and took seats in the Middle G:	9133
	39: 4	through the g between the two walls,	9133
	52: 7	through the g between the two walls near	9133
La	5:14	The elders are gone from the **city g;**	9133
Eze	8: 3	to the north g of the inner court,	9133
	8: 5	the g of the altar I saw this idol of jealousy.	9133
	8:14	the entrance to the north g of the house of	9133
	9: 2	from the direction of the upper g,	9133
	10:19	They stopped at the entrance to the east g	9133
	11: 1	up and brought me to the g of the house of	9133
	11: 1	the entrance to the g were twenty-five men,	9133
	26: 2	The g to the nations is broken,	1946
	40: 6	Then he went to the g facing east.	9133
	40: 6	and measured the threshold of the g;	9133
	40: 7	And the threshold of the g next to	9133
	40:10	the east g were three alcoves on each side;	9133
	40:10	the length and width of the g facing north,	9133
	40:22	as those of the g facing east.	9133
	40:23	a g to the inner court facing the north gate,	9133
	40:23	a gate to the inner court facing the north g,	9133
	40:23	from one g to the opposite one;	9133
	40:24	to the south side and I saw a g facing south.	9133
	40:27	The inner court also had a g facing south,	9133
	40:27	and he measured from this g to	9133
	40:27	to the outer g on the south side;	9133
	40:28	into the inner court through the south g,	9133
	40:28	and he measured the south g;	9133
	40:35	Then he brought me to the north g	9133
	40:44	Outside the inner g, within the inner court,	9133
	40:44	at the side of the north g and facing south,	9133
	40:44	at the side of the south g and facing north.	9133

Eze	42:15	the east g and measured the area all around;	9133
	43: 1	the man brought me to the g facing east,	9133
	43: 4	the temple through the g facing east.	9133
	44: 1	the man brought me back to the outer g of	9133
	44: 2	"This g is to remain shut.	9133
	44: 2	the g will not be shut until evening.	9133
	44: 4	the man brought me by way of the north g	9133
	46: 1	The g of the inner court facing east is to	9133
	46: 2	but the g will be shut until evening.	9133
	46: 9	whoever enters by the north g to worship is	9133
	46: 9	to worship is to go out the south g;	9133
	46: 9	by the south g is to go out the north gate.	9133
	46: 9	by the south gate is to go out the north g.	9133
	46: 9	through the g by which he entered,	9133
	46: 9	but each is to go out the opposite g.	NIH
	46:12	the g facing east is to be opened for him.	9133
	46:12	the g will be shut.	9133
	46:19	through the entrance at the side of the g to	9133
	47: 2	He then brought me out through the north g	9133
	47: 2	the outside to the outer g facing east,	9133
	48:31	on the north side will be the g of Reuben,	9133
	48:31	the g of Judah and the gate of Levi.	9133
	48:31	the gate of Judah and the g of Levi.	9133
	48:32	the g of Joseph,	9133
	48:32	the g of Benjamin and the gate of Dan.	9133
	48:32	the gate of Benjamin and the g of Dan.	9133
	48:33	the g of Simeon,	9133
	48:33	the g of Issachar and the gate of Zebulun.	9133
	48:33	the gate of Issachar and the g of Zebulun.	9133
	48:34	the g of Gad,	9133
	48:34	the g of Asher and the gate of Naphtali.	9133
	48:34	the gate of Asher and the g of Naphtali.	9133
Am	1: 5	I will break down the g of Damascus;	1378
Mic	1: 9	It has reached the very g of my people,	9133
	1:12	even to the g of Jerusalem.	9133
	2:13	they will break through the g and go out.	9133
Zep	1:10	"a cry will go up from the Fish G,	9133
Zec	14:10	the Benjamin G to the site of the First Gate,	9133
	14:10	to the site of the First G,	9133
	14:10	to the Corner G, and from the Tower	9133
Mt	7:13	"Enter through the narrow g,	4783
	7:13	For wide is the g and broad is the road	4783
	7:14	the g and narrow the road that leads to life,	4783
Lk	7:12	As he approached the town g,	4783
	16:20	At his g was laid a beggar named Lazarus,	4784
Jn	5: 2	Now there is in Jerusalem near the **Sheep G**	4583
	10: 1	who does not enter the sheep pen by the g,	2598
	10: 2	enters by the g is the shepherd of his sheep.	2598
	10: 3	The watchman opens the g for him,	NIG
	10: 7	I am the g for the sheep.	2598
	10: 9	I am the g; whoever enters through me will	2598
		be saved.	
Ac	3: 2	to the temple g called Beautiful,	2598
	3:10	at the temple g called Beautiful,	4783
	10:17	and stopped at the g.	4784
	12:10	and came to the iron g leading to the city.	4784
	16:13	On the Sabbath we went outside the **city g**	4783
Heb	13:12	so Jesus also suffered outside the **city g**	4783
Rev	21:21	each g made of a single pearl.	4784

GATEKEEPER (2) [GATE, KEEP]

2Sa	18:26	and he called down to the g, "Look,	8788
1Ch	9:21	of Meshelemiah was the g at the entrance	8788

GATEKEEPERS (34) [GATE, KEEP]

2Ki	7:10	to the city and told them, "We went into	8788
	7:11	The g shouted the news,	8788
1Ch	9:17	The g: Shallum, Akkub,	8788
	9:18	the g belonging to the camp of the Levites.	8788
	9:19	and his fellow g from his family	NIH
	9:20	of Eleazar was in charge of **the g,**	2157S
	9:22	to be g at the thresholds numbered 212.	8788
	9:22	**The g** had been assigned to their positions	2156S
	9:24	The g were on the four sides:	8788
	9:26	But the four principal g, who were Levites,	8788
	15:18	Mikneiah, Obed-Edom and Jeiel, the g.	8788
	16:38	and also Hosah, were g.	8788
	23: 5	to be g and four thousand are to praise	8788
	26: 1	The divisions of the g:	8788
	26:12	These divisions of the g,	8788
	26:19	of the g who were descendants of Korah	8788
2Ch	8:14	He also appointed the g by divisions for	8788
	35:15	The g at each gate did not need to leave	8788
Ezr	2:42	The g of the temple:	8788
	2:70	the g and the temple servants settled	8788
	7: 7	Levites, singers, g and temple servants,	8788
	7:24	on any of the priests, Levites, singers, g,	10777
	10:24	From the g: Shallum, Telem and Uri.	8788
Ne	7: 1	the g and the singers and	8788
	7: 3	While the g are still on duty,	2156S
	7:45	The g: the descendants of Shallum,	8788
	7:73	The priests, the Levites, the g,	8788
	10:28	priests, Levites, g, singers,	8788
	10:39	the g and the singers stay.	8788
	11:19	The g: Akkub, Talmon	8788
	12:25	Talmon and Akkub were g who guarded	8788
	12:45	as did also the singers and g,	8788
	12:47	the daily portions for the singers and g,	8788
	13: 5	singers and g, as well as the contributions	8788

GATEPOST (1) [GATE, POST]

Eze	46: 2	of the gateway and stand by the g.	4647+9133

GATEPOSTS (1) [GATE, POST]

Eze	45:19	and on the g of the inner court.	4647+9133

GATES (111) [GATE]

Ge	24:60	your offspring possess the g of their enemies	9133
Ex	20:10	nor the alien within your g.	9133
Dt	3: 5	with high walls and with g and bars,	1946
	5:14	nor the alien within your g,	9133
	6: 9	of your houses and on your g.	9133
	11:20	of your houses and on your g,	9133
	20:11	If they accept and open their g,	NIH
	33:25	**bolts of** your g will be iron and bronze,	NIH
Jos	6:26	the cost of his youngest he will set up its g."	1946
Jdg	5: 8	war came to the **city g,**	9133
	5:11	of the LORD went down to the **city g.**	9133
1Sa	17:52	the entrance of Gath and to the g of Ekron.	9133
	23: 7	by entering a town with g and bars."	1946
2Sa	18:24	between the inner and outer g,	9133
1Ki	16:34	and he set up its g at the cost	1946
2Ki	15:16	because they refused to open their g.	NIH
	23: 8	He broke down the shrines at the g—	9133
1Ch	9:23	in charge of guarding the g of the house of	9133
2Ch	8: 5	with walls and with g and bars,	1946
	8:14	by divisions for the **various g,**	2256+9133+9133
	14: 7	with towers, g and bars.	1946
	23:19	He also stationed doorkeepers at the g of	9133
	31: 2	to give thanks and to sing praises at the g	9133
Ne	1: 3	and its g have been burned with fire."	9133
	2: 3	and its g have been destroyed by fire?"	9133
	2: 8	to make beams for the g of the citadel by	9133
	2:13	and its g, which had been destroyed by fire.	9133
	2:17	and its g have been burned with fire.	9133
	6: 1	to that time I had not set the doors in the g	9133
	7: 3	"The g of Jerusalem are not to be opened	9133
	11:19	who kept watch at the g—172 men.	9133
	12:25	the storerooms at the g.	9133
	12:30	they purified the people, the g and the wall.	9133
	13:19	on the g of Jerusalem before the Sabbath,	9133
	13:19	I stationed some of my own men at the g so	9133
	13:22	the g in order to keep the Sabbath day holy.	9133
Job	17:16	Will it go down to the g of death?	964
	38:17	Have the g of death been shown to you?	9133
	38:17	Have you seen the g of the shadow	9133
Ps	9:13	Have mercy and lift me up from the g	9133
	9:14	that I may declare your praises in the g of	9133
	24: 7	up your heads, O g;	9133
	24: 9	Lift up your heads, O you g;	9133
	87: 2	the g of Zion more than all the dwellings	9133
	100: 4	Enter his g with thanksgiving	9133
	107:16	for he breaks down g of bronze and cuts	1946
	107:18	They loathed all food and drew near the g	9133
	118:19	Open for me the g of righteousness;	9133
	122: 2	Our feet are standing in your g,	9133
	147:13	the bars of your g and blesses your people	9133
Pr	8: 3	beside the g leading into the city, at	9133
	14:19	and the wicked at the g of the righteous.	9133
	18:19	disputes are like the barred g of a citadel.	1378
Isa	3:26	The g of Zion will lament and mourn;	7339
	13: 2	beckon to them to enter the g of the nobles.	7339
	22: 7	and horsemen are posted at the **city g;**	9133
	26: 2	the g that the righteous nation may enter,	9133
	38:10	of my life must I go through the g of death	9133
	45: 1	to open doors before him so that g will not	9133
	45: 2	down g of bronze and cut through bars	1946
	54:12	your g of sparkling jewels,	9133
	60:11	Your g will always stand open,	9133
	60:18	and your g Praise.	9133
	62:10	Pass through, pass through the g!	9133
Jer	1:15	up their thrones in the entrance of the g	9133
	7: 2	through these g to worship the LORD.	9133
	15: 7	a winnowing fork at the **city g** of the land.	9133
	17:19	stand also at all the other g of Jerusalem.	9133
	17:20	in Jerusalem who come through these g.	9133
	17:21	on the Sabbath day or bring it through the g	9133
	17:24	and bring no load through the g of this city	9133
	17:25	on David's throne will come through the g	9133
	17:27	as you come through the g of Jerusalem on	9133
	17:27	an unquenchable fire in the g of Jerusalem	9133
	22: 2	and your people who come through these g	9133
	22: 4	on David's throne will come through the g	9133
	22:19	and thrown outside the g of Jerusalem."	9133
	49:31	"a nation that has neither g nor bars;	1946
	51:30	the **bars of** her g are broken.	1378
	51:58	be leveled and her high g set on fire;	9133
La	2: 9	Her g have sunk into the ground;	9133
	4:12	and foes could enter the g of Jerusalem.	9133
Eze	21:15	the sword for slaughter at all their g,	9133
	21:22	to set battering rams against the g,	9133
	26:10	wagons and chariots when he enters your g	9133
	38:11	of them living without walls and without g	1946
	44:11	of the g of the temple and serving in it;	9133
	44:17	" 'When they enter the g of the inner court,	9133
	44:17	at the g of the inner court or inside	9133
	48:31	the g of the city will be named after	9133
	48:31	The three g on the north side will be	9133
	48:32	which is 4,500 cubits long, will be three g:	9133
	48:33	cubits, will be three g:	9133
	48:34	which is 4,500 cubits long, will be three g:	9133
Hos	11: 6	will destroy the **bars of** their g and put	964
Ob	1:11	and foreigners entered his g and cast lots	9133
	1:13	not march through the g of my people in	9133
Na	2: 6	The river g are thrown open and	9133
	3:13	The g of your land are wide open	9133
Mt	16:18	and the g of Hades will not overcome it.	4783
Ac	9:24	on the **city g** in order to kill him.	4783
	14:13	the **city g** because he and the crowd wanted	4784
	21:30	and immediately the g were shut.	2598
Rev	21:12	It had a great, high wall with twelve g,	4784
	21:12	and with twelve angels at the g.	4784

Rev	21:12	On the g were written the names of the	
		twelve tribes of Israel.	NIG
	21:13	There were three g on the east,	4784
	21:15	its g and its walls.	4784
	21:21	The twelve g were twelve pearls,	4784
	21:25	On no day will its g ever be shut,	4784
	22:14	to the tree of life and may go through the g	4784

GATEWAY (35) [GATE, WAY]

Ge	19: 1	and Lot was sitting in the g of the city.	9133
1Sa	9:18	Saul approached Samuel in the g	9133
2Sa	3:27	Joab took him aside into the g,	9133
	18:24	the watchman went up to the roof of the g	9133
	18:33	up to the room over the g and wept.	9133
	19: 8	the king got up and took his seat in the g.	9133
	19: 8	"The king is sitting in the g,"	9133
2Ki	7:17	and the people trampled him in the g,	9133
	7:20	for the people trampled him in the g,	9133
Eze	27: 3	Say to Tyre, situated at the g to the sea,	4427
	40: 3	the g with a linen cord and a measuring rod	9133
	40: 8	Then he measured the portico of the g;	9133
	40: 9	The portico of the g faced the temple.	9133
	40:11	the width of the entrance to the g;	9133
	40:13	Then he measured the g from the top of	9133
	40:14	around the inside of the g—	9133
	40:15	The distance from the entrance of the g to	9133
	40:16	inside the g were surmounted	9133
	40:16	from the inside of the lower g to the outside	9133
	40:21	as those of the first g.	9133
	40:25	The g and its portico had narrow openings	
		all around,	2257S
	40:29	its g and its portico had openings all	2257S
	40:32	and he measured the g;	9133
	40:33	The g and its portico had openings all	2257S
	40:39	In the portico of the g were two tables	9133
	40:40	By the outside wall of the portico of the g,	9133
	40:40	the entrance to the north g were two tables,	9133
	40:41	on one side of the g and four on the other—	9133
	44: 3	the only one who may sit inside the g to eat	2257S
	44: 3	He is to enter by way of the portico of the g	9133
	46: 2	through the portico of the g and stand by	9133
	46: 2	He is to worship at the threshold of the g	9133
	46: 3	of the LORD at the entrance to that g.	9133
	46: 8	he is to go in through the portico of the g,	9133
Mt	26:71	Then he went out to the g,	4784

GATEWAYS (6) [GATE, WAY]

1Ch	22: 3	to make nails for the doors of the g and for	9133
Pr	1:21	in the g of the city she makes her speech:	7339+9133
La	1: 4	All her g are desolate, her priests groan,	9133
Eze	40:18	of the g and was as wide as they were long;	9133
	40:30	(The porticoes of the g around	NIH
	40:38	by the portico in each of the inner g,	9133

GATH (36) [GATH HEPHER, GATH RIMMON, MORESHETH GATH]

Jos	11:22	G and Ashdod did any survive.	1781
	13: 3	Ashdod, Ashkelon, G and Ekron—	1785
1Sa	5: 8	the ark of the god of Israel moved to G."	1781
	6:17	Gaza, Ashkelon, G and Ekron.	1781
	7:14	to G that the Philistines had captured	1781
	17: 4	Goliath, who was from G,	1781
	17:23	Goliath, the Philistine champion from G,	1781
	17:52	the entrance of G and to the gates of Ekron.	1781
	17:52	along the Shaaraim road to G and Ekron.	1781
	21:10	from Saul and went to Achish king of G.	1781
	21:12	of Achish king of G.	1781
	22: 1	David left G and escaped to the cave	9004S
	27: 2	over to Achish son of Maoch king of G.	1781
	27: 3	and his men settled in G with Achish.	1781
	27: 4	Saul was told that David had fled to G,	1781
	27:11	a man or woman alive to be brought to G,	1781
2Sa	1:20	"Tell it not in G, proclaim it not	1781
	15:18	from G marched before the king.	1781
	21:20	which took place at G,	1781
	21:22	These four were descendants of Rapha in G,	1781
1Ki	2:39	king of G, and Shimei was told,	1781
	2:39	"Your slaves are in G."	1781
	2:40	to Achish at G in search of his slaves.	1781
	2:40	and brought the slaves back from G.	1781
	2:41	that Shimei had gone from Jerusalem to G	1781
2Ki	12:17	went up and attacked G and captured it.	1781
1Ch	7:21	by the native-born men of G,	1781
	8:13	and who drove out the inhabitants of G.	1781
	18: 1	and he took G and its surrounding villages	1781
	20: 6	which took place at G,	1781
	20: 8	These were descendants of Rapha in G,	1781
2Ch	11: 8	G, Mareshah, Ziph,	1781
	26: 6	and broke down the walls of G,	1781
Ps	56: T	When the Philistines had seized him in G.	1781
Am	6: 2	and then go down to G in Philistia.	1781
Mic	1:10	Tell it not in G; weep not at all.	1781

GATH HEPHER (2) [GATH, HEPHER]

| Jos | 19:13 | Then it continued eastward to G | 1783 |
| 2Ki | 14:25 | Jonah son of Amittai, the prophet from G. | 1783 |

GATH RIMMON (4) [GATH, RIMMON]

Jos	19:45	Jehud, Bene Berak, G,	1784
	21:24	Aijalon and G, together with their	1784
	21:25	Taanach and G, together with their	1784
1Ch	6:69	Aijalon and G, together with their	1784

GATHER (118) [GATHERED, GATHERING, GATHERS, INGATHERING]

Ge	31:46	He said to his relatives, "G some stones."	4377
	49: 1	G around so I can tell you what will happen	665
Ex	5: 7	let them go and g their own straw.	8006
	5:12	over Egypt to g stubble to use for straw.	8006
	16: 4	to go out each day and g enough for	4377
	16: 5	and that is to be twice as much as they g on	4377
	16:16	'Each one is to g as much as he needs.	4377
	16:26	Six days you are to g it,	4377
	16:27	on the seventh day to g it,	4377
	23:16	when you g in your crops from the field.	4377
Lev	8: 3	and g the entire assembly at the entrance to	7735
	19: 9	not reap to the very edges of your field or g	4377
	23:22	not reap to the very edges of your field or g	4377
	25: 3	prune your vineyards and g their crops.	665
Nu	10: 7	To g the assembly, blow the trumpets,	7735
	19: 9	"A man who is clean shall g up the ashes	665
	20: 8	g the assembly together.	7735
	21:16	"G the people together	665
Dt	11:14	so that you may g in your grain,	665
	13:16	G all the plunder of the town into	7695
	28:39	not drink the wine or g the grapes,	112
	30: 3	on you and g you again from all the nations	7695
	30: 4	the LORD your God will g you	7695
Ru	2: 7	'Please let me glean and g among	665
2Ki	4:39	the fields to g herbs and found a wild vine.	4377
	22:20	Therefore I will g you to your fathers,	665
1Ch	16:35	g us and deliver us from the nations,	7695
2Ch	34:28	Now I will g you to your fathers,	665
Ne	1: 9	I will g them from there and bring them	7695
Est	4:16	g together all the Jews who are in Susa,	4043
Job	24: 6	They g fodder in the fields and glean in	7917
	39:12	and g it to your threshing floor?	665
Ps	2: 2	the rulers g together against the LORD	3570
	7: 7	Let the assembled peoples g around you.	6015
	50: 5	"G to me my consecrated ones,	665
	104:28	When you give it to them, they g it up;	4377
	106:47	and g us from the nations,	7695
	142: 7	the righteous will g about me because	4193
Ecc	3: 5	time to scatter stones and a time to g them,	4043
SS	6: 2	to browse in the gardens and to g lilies.	4377
Isa	10:14	as men g abandoned eggs,	665
	11:12	He will raise a banner for the nations and g	665
	34:15	there also the falcons will g,	7695
	34:16	and his Spirit will g them together.	7695
	43: 5	from the east and g you from the west.	7695
	43: 9	All the nations g together and	7695
	45:20	"G together and come;	7695
	49: 5	and g Israel to himself, for I am honored in	665
	49:18	all your sons g and come to you.	7695
	56: 8	"I will g still others to them	7695
	62: 9	and those who g the grapes will drink it in	7695
	66:18	to come and g all nations and tongues,	7695
Jer	3:17	and all nations will g in Jerusalem	7748
	4: 5	Cry aloud and say: 'G together!	665
	7:18	The children g wood,	4377
	8:14	"Why are we sitting here? G together!	665
	9:22	with no one to g them.'"	665
	10:17	G up your belongings to leave the land,	665
	12: 9	Go and g all the wild beasts;	665
	21: 4	And I will g them inside this city.	665
	23: 3	"I myself will g the remnant	7695
	29:14	I will g you from all the nations	7695
	31: 8	from the land of the north and g them from	7695
	31:10	'He who scattered Israel will g them	7695
	32:37	I will surely g them from all the lands	7695
	49: 5	and no one will g the fugitives.	7695
Eze	11:17	I will g you from the nations	7695
	16:37	therefore I am going to g all your lovers,	7695
	16:37	I will g them against you from all around	7695
	20:34	I will bring you from the nations and g you	7695
	20:41	the nations and g you from the countries	7695
	22:19	I will g you into Jerusalem.	7695
	22:20	As men g silver, copper, iron,	7697
	22:20	so will I g you in my anger and my wrath	7695
	22:21	I will g you and I will blow on you	4043
	28:25	When I g the people of Israel from	7695
	29:13	of forty years I will g the Egyptians from	7695
	34:13	the nations and g them from the countries,	7695
	36:24	I will g you from all the countries	7695
	37:21	I will g them from all around	7695
	39:10	not need to g wood from the fields or cut it	5951
	39:28	I will g them to their own land,	4043
Hos	7:14	They g together for grain and new wine	1591
	8:10	I will now g them together.	7695
	9: 6	Egypt will g them,	7695
Joel	2:16	G the people, consecrate the assembly;	665
	2:16	bring together the elders, g the children,	665
	3: 2	I will g all nations and bring them down	7695
Mic	2:12	"I will surely g all of you, O Jacob;	665+665
	4: 6	declares the LORD, "I will g the lame;	665
Na	3:18	on the mountains with no one to g them.	7695
Hab	1: 9	like a desert wind and g prisoners like sand.	665
Zep	2: 1	G together, gather together,	8006
	2: 1	Gather together, g together,	8006
	3: 8	to g the kingdoms and	7695
	3:19	and g those who have been scattered.	7695
	3:20	At that time I will g you;	7695
Zec	10: 8	I will signal for them and g them in.	7695
	10:10	from Egypt and g them from Assyria.	7695
	14: 2	I will g all the nations to Jerusalem	665
Mt	12:30	and he who does not g with me scatters.	5251
	13:30	then g the wheat and bring it	5251
	23:37	I have longed to g your children together,	2190
	24:28	there the vultures will g.	5251

Mt	24:31	they will g his elect from the four winds,	2190
	25:26	that I harvest where I have not sown and g	5251
Mk	13:27	And he will send his angels and g his elect	2190
Lk	3:17	to clear his threshing floor and to g	5251
	11:23	and he who does not g with me, scatters.	5251
	13:34	I have longed to g your children together,	2190
	17:37	there the vultures will g."	2190
Jn	6:12	"G the pieces that are left over.	5251
Ac	4:26	the rulers g together against the Lord and	5251
2Ti	4: 3	they will g around them a great number	2197
Rev	14:18	"Take your sharp sickle and g the clusters	5582
	16:14	to g them for the battle on the great day	5251
	19:17	g together for the great supper of God,	5251
	20: 8	Gog and Magog—to g them for battle.	5251

GATHERED (136) [GATHER]

Ge	1: 9	the water under the sky be g to one place,	7748
	1:10	and the g waters he called "seas."	5224
	25: 8	and he was g to his people.	665
	25:17	and he was g to his people.	665
	29: 3	When all the flocks were g there,	665
	29: 7	it is not time for the flocks to be g.	665
	29: 8	"until all the flocks are g and	665
	35:29	and died and was g to his people,	665
	37: 7	while your sheaves g around mine	6015
	49:29	"I am about to be g to my people.	665
	49:33	breathed his last and was g to his people.	665
Ex	16:17	some g much, some little.	4377
	16:18	he who g much did not have too much,	8049
	16:18	and he who g little did not have too little.	5070
	16:18	Each one g as much as he needed.	4377
	16:21	Each morning everyone g as much	4377
	16:22	On the sixth day, they g twice as much—	4377
	32: 1	they g around Aaron and said, "Come,	7735
Lev	8: 4	the assembly g at the entrance to the Tent	7735
	23:39	after you have g the crops of the land,	665
Nu	11:32	the people went out and g quail.	665
	11:32	No one g less than ten homers.	665
	14: 5	of the whole Israelite assembly g there.	7736
	16:19	When Korah had g all his followers	7735
	16:42	But when the assembly g in opposition	7735
	20: 2	people g in opposition to Moses and Aaron.	7735
	20:10	g the assembly together	7735
	20:24	"Aaron will be g to his people.	665
	20:26	for Aaron will be g to his people;	665
	27:13	you too will be g to your people,	665
	31: 2	After that, you will be g to your people."	665
Dt	16:13	for seven days after you have g the produce	665
	32:50	you will die and be g to your people,	665
	32:50	on Mount Hor and was g to his people.	665
Jos	18: 1	The whole assembly of the Israelites g	7735
	22:12	the whole assembly of Israel g at Shiloh	7735
Jdg	2:10	After that whole generation had been g	665
	4:13	Sisera g together his nine hundred iron	
		chariots	2410
	9: 6	the citizens of Shechem and Beth Millo g	665
	9:27	and g the grapes and trodden them,	1305
	11: 3	where a group of adventurers g around him	4377
Ru	2:17	Then she threshed the barley she had g,	4377
	2:18	her mother-in-law saw how much she had g.	4377
1Sa	8: 4	of Israel g together and came to Samuel	7695
	17: 1	Now the Philistines g their forces for war	665
	17:47	All those g here will know that it is not	7736
	22: 2	or in debt or discontented g around him,	7695
	28: 1	In those days the Philistines g their forces	7695
	28: 4	while Saul g all the Israelites and set	7695
	29: 1	The Philistines g all their forces at Aphek,	7695
2Sa	10:17	When David was told of this, he g all Israel,	665
	17:11	be g to you, with you yourself leading	665+665
	20:14	who g together and followed him.	7735
	21:13	and exposed were g up.	665
	23: 6	which are not g with the hand.	4374
	23: 9	when they taunted the Philistines g	665
1Ki	8: 5	and the entire assembly of Israel that had g	3585
	11:24	He g men around him and became	7695
2Ki	4:39	He g some of its gourds and filled the fold	4377
1Ch	11:13	when the Philistines g there for battle.	665
	19:17	he g all Israel and crossed the Jordan;	665
	23: 2	He also g together all the leaders of Israel,	665
2Ch	5: 6	and the entire assembly of Israel that had g	3585
	13: 7	Some worthless scoundrels g around him	7695
	23: 2	throughout Judah and the Levites and	7695
	28:24	Ahaz g together the furnishings from	665
	29:20	g the city officials together	665
Ezr	7:28	and g leading men from Israel to go up	7695
	9: 4	the words of the God of Israel g around me	665
	10: 1	and children—g around him.	665
	10: 9	of Judah and Benjamin had g in Jerusalem	7695
Ne	8:13	g around Ezra the scribe to give attention to	665
	9: 1	the Israelites g together,	665
Job	5:26	like sheaves g in season.	6590
	24:24	they are brought low and g up	7890
	30: 4	In the brush they g salt herbs,	7786
Ps	35:15	But when I stumbled, they g in glee;	665
	35:15	attackers g against me when I was unaware.	665
	107: 3	those he g from the lands,	7695
Pr	27:25	and the grass from the hills is g in,	665
	30: 4	Who has g up the wind in the hollow	665
SS	5: 1	I have g my myrrh with my spice.	768
Isa	24:13	so I g all the countries;	665
	27:12	O Israelites, will be g up one by one.	4377
	56: 8	to them besides those already g."	7695
	60: 7	All Kedar's flocks will be g to you,	7695
Jer	6:11	the street and on the young men g together;	6051
	8: 2	They will not be g up or buried,	665
	25:33	not be mourned or g up or buried,	665

Jer	40:15	cause all the Jews who *are* g around you to	7695
Eze	29: 5	on the open field and not **be** g picked up.	665
	38: 7	you and all the hordes g about you,	7735
	38: 8	whose *people* were g from many nations to	7695
	38:12	against the resettled ruins and the people g	665
	38:13	*Have you* g your hordes to loot,	7735
	39:27	from the nations and *have* g them from	7695
Hos	10:10	nations *will* be g against them to put them	665
Mic	1: 7	Since she g her gifts from the wages	7695
	4:11	But now many nations *are* g against you.	665
Zec	12: 3	all the nations of the earth *are* g against her,	665
Mt	13: 2	Such large crowds g around him that he got	5251
	16: 9	and how many basketfuls *you* g?	3284
	16:10	and how many basketfuls *you* g?	3284
	22:10	and g all the people they could find,	5251
	22:41	While the Pharisees were g **together,**	5251
	25:32	All nations *will be* g before him,	5251
	27:17	So when the crowd *had* g, Pilate asked	5251
	27:27	the Praetorium and g the whole company	5251
Mk	1:33	The whole town g at the door,	1639+2190
	2: 2	So many g that there was no room left,	5251
	3:20	Jesus entered a house, and again a crowd g,	5302
	4: 1	The crowd that g around him was so large	5251
	5:21	a large crowd g around him while he was	5251
	6:30	The apostles g around Jesus and reported	5251
	7: 1	of the law who had come from Jerusalem g	5251
	8: 1	During those days another large crowd g.	1639
Lk	12: 1	when a crowd of many thousands *had* g,	2190
	23:48	When all the people who *had* g	5219
Jn	6:13	So *they* g them and filled twelve baskets	5251
	8: 2	where all the people g around him,	2262
	10:24	The Jews g **around** him, saying,	3240
Ac	5:16	Crowds g also from the towns	5302
	6: 2	g all the disciples **together**	4673
	12:12	many people had g and were praying.	5255
	13:44	the next Sabbath almost the whole city g	5251
	14:20	But after the disciples *had* g **around** him,	3240
	14:27	they g the church **together** and reported all	5251
	15:30	where *they* g the church **together**	5251
	16:13	to speak to the women *who had* g there.	5302
	28: 3	Paul g a pile of brushwood and,	5370
2Co	8:15	"He who g much did not have too much,"	NIG
	8:15	and he who g little did not have too little."	NIG
2Th	2: 1	of our Lord Jesus Christ and our *being* **g to**	2191
Rev	14:19	g its grapes and threw them into	5582
	16:16	Then *they* g the kings **together** to the place	5251
	19:19	and their armies **together** to make war	5251

GATHERING (12) [GATHER]

Nu	11: 8	The people went around g it,	4377
	15:32	a man was found g wood on the Sabbath	8006
	15:33	Those who found him g wood brought him	8006
1Ki	17:10	a widow was there g sticks.	8006
	17:12	I am g a few sticks to take home and make	8006
Ecc	2:26	the sinner he gives the task of g and storing	665
Jer	6: 9	over the branches again, like one g grapes."	1305
Mt	3:12	g his wheat into the barn and burning up	5251
	25:24	harvesting where you have not sown and g	5251
Lk	8: 4	While a large crowd *was* g	5290
	15: 1	and "sinners" were all g **around** to hear him	1581
Ac	10:27	Peter went inside and found a large g	5302

GATHERS (18) [GATHER]

Nu	19:10	The *man who* g up the ashes of	665
Ru	2:15	"Even if *she* g among the sheaves,	4377
Ps	33: 7	He g the waters of the sea into jars;	4043
	41: 6	he speaks falsely, *while* his heart g slander;	7695
	129: 7	nor the *one who* g fill his arms.	6682
	147: 2	he g the exiles of Israel.	4043
Pr	6: 8	in summer and g its food at harvest.	112
	10: 5	He who g **crops** in summer is a wise son,	112
	13:11	but he who g money little by little	7695
Isa	17: 5	a reaper g the standing grain and harvests	665
	40:11	He g the lambs in his arms	7695
	56: 8	he who g the exiles of Israel:"	7695
Mic	4:12	not understand his plan, he who g them	7695
	7: 1	like one who g summer fruit at the gleaning	668
Hab	1:15	he g them **up** in his dragnet;	665
	2: 5	he g to himself all the nations	665
Mt	23:37	as a hen g her chicks under her wings,	2190
Lk	13:34	as a hen g her chicks under her wings,	NIG

GAUDY (1)

Eze	16:16	of your garments to make g high places,	3229

GAUNT (3) [GAUNTNESS]

Ge	41: 3	seven other cows, ugly and g,	1414+1987
	41: 4	ugly and g ate up the seven sleek, fat	1414+1987
Ps	109:24	my body is thin and g.	4946+9043

GAUNTNESS (1) [GAUNT]

Job	16: 8	my g rises up and testifies against me.	3951

GAVE (659) [GIVE]

Ge	2:20	So the man g names to all the livestock,	7924
	3: 6	*She* also g some to her husband,	5989
	3:12	she g me some fruit from the tree,	5989
	4: 1	she became pregnant and g **birth** *to* Cain.	3528
	4: 2	Later *she* g **birth** *to* his brother Abel.	3528
	4:17	she became pregnant and g **birth** *to* Enoch.	3528
	4:20	Adah g **birth** *to* Jabal;	3528
	4:25	*she* g **birth** *to* a son and named him Seth,	3528
	9: 3	Just as *I* g you the green plants,	5989

Ge	12:20	Pharaoh g **orders** about Abram *to* his men,	7422
	14:20	Then Abram g him a tenth of everything.	5989
	16: 3	and g her to her husband to be his wife.	5989
	16:13	*She* g this name to the LORD who spoke	7924
	16:15	and Abram g the name Ishmael to	7924
	18: 7	tender calf and g it to a servant,	5989
	20:14	and female slaves and g them to Abraham,	5989
	21: 3	Abraham g the name Isaac to	7924
	21:14	and a skin of water and g them to Hagar.	5989
	21:19	and g the boy **a drink.**	9197
	21:27	and cattle and g them to Abimelech,	5989
	24:18	the jar to her hands and g him **a drink.**	9197
	24:53	of clothing and g them to Rebekah;	5989
	24:53	he also g costly gifts to her brother and	5989
	25: 6	he g gifts to the sons of his concubines	5989
	25:26	when Rebekah g birth *to* them.	3528
	25:34	Then Jacob g Esau some bread	5989
	26:11	So Abimelech g **orders** to all the people:	7422
	26:18	he g them the same names his father had	7924
	27:20	"The LORD your God g me **success,"**	7936
	28: 4	the land God g to Abraham."	5989
	29:22	the people of the place and g a feast.	6913
	29:23	he took his daughter Leah and g her	995
	29:24	And Laban g his servant girl Zilpah	5989
	29:28	and then Laban g him his daughter Rachel	5989
	29:29	Laban g his servant girl Bilhah	5989
	29:32	Leah became pregnant and g **birth** *to* a son.	3528
	29:33	and when *she* g **birth** *to* a son she said,	3528
	29:33	*he* g me this one too."	5989
	29:34	and when *she* g **birth** *to* a son she said,	3528
	29:35	and when *she* g **birth** *to* a son she said,	3528
	30: 4	So *she* g him her servant Bilhah as a wife.	5989
	30: 9	she took her maidservant Zilpah and g her	5989
	30:21	Some time later *she* g **birth** *to* a daughter	3528
	30:23	She became pregnant and g **birth** *to* a son	3528
	30:25	After Rachel g **birth** *to* Joseph,	3528
	31: 8	all the flocks g **birth** to speckled young;	3528
	35: 4	So *they* g Jacob all the foreign gods	5989
	35:12	The land *I* g to Abraham and Isaac I	5989
	38: 3	she became pregnant and g **birth** *to* a son,	3528
	38: 4	and g **birth** *to* a son and named him Onan.	3528
	38: 5	*She* g **birth** *to* still another son	3528
	38: 5	It was at Kezib that she g **birth** *to* him.	3528
	38:18	So *he* g them to her and slept with her,	5989
	39: 3	with him and that the LORD g him **success**	7503
	39:23	and g him **success** in whatever he did.	7503
	40:20	and *he* g a feast for all his officials.	6913
	41:45	g Joseph the name Zaphenath-Paneah	7924
	41:45	and g him Asenath daughter of Potiphera,	5989
	42:25	Joseph g **orders** to fill their bags with grain,	7422
	43:24	g them water to wash their feet	5989
	44: 1	Now Joseph g *these* **instructions** *to*	7422
	45:21	Joseph g them carts,	5989
	45:21	he also g them provisions for their journey.	5989
	45:22	To each of them he g new clothing,	5989
	45:22	but to Benjamin he g three hundred shekels	5989
	47:11	and g them property in the best part of	5989
	47:17	and he g them food in exchange	5989
	47:22	from the allotment Pharaoh g them.	5989
	49:29	g them *these* **instructions:**	7422
Ex	1:21	*he* g them families of their own.	6913
	1:22	Pharaoh g *this* **order** to all his people:	7422
	2: 2	she became pregnant and g **birth** *to* a son.	3528
	2:21	who g his daughter Zipporah to Moses **in marriage.**	5989
	2:22	Zipporah g **birth** *to* a son,	3528
	4:11	"Who g man his mouth?	8492
	5: 6	That same day Pharaoh g *this* **order** *to*	7422
	12:36	*they* g them **what** they **asked for;**	8626
	16:32	so they can see the bread *I* g you **to eat** in	430
	31:18	*he* g him the two tablets of the Testimony,	5989
	32:24	Then *they* g me the gold,	5989
	34:32	g them all *the* **commands** the LORD	**7422**
	36: 6	Then Moses g **an order**	7422
Lev	7:38	which the LORD g Moses on Mount Sinai	7422
	27:34	the LORD g Moses on Mount Sinai for	7422
Nu	3:51	Moses g the redemption money to Aaron	5989
	7: 6	and oxen and g them to the Levites.	5989
	7: 7	*He* g two carts and four oxen to	5989
	7: 8	and *he* g four carts and eight oxen to	5989
	13:16	g Hoshea son of Nun *the* **name**	7924
	13:27	g Moses *this* **account:**	6218
	15:22	of these commands the LORD g Moses—	1819
	15:23	the LORD g them and continuing through	7422
	17: 6	and their leaders g him twelve staffs,	5989
	21: 3	and g the Canaanites **over**	5989
	22:18	if Balak g me his palace filled with silver	5989
	22:40	and g some to Balaam and	8938
	24:13	if Balak g me his palace filled with silver	5989
	30:16	the regulations the LORD g Moses	7422
	31:21	of the law that the LORD g Moses:	5989
	31:41	Moses g the tribute to Eleazar the priest as	5989
	31:47	and g them to the Levites,	5989
	32:28	Then Moses g **orders** about them *to* Eleazar	7422
	32:33	Then Moses g to the Gadites	5989
	32:38	*They* g names to the cities they rebuilt.	7924
	32:40	So Moses g Gilead to the Makirites,	5989
	36: 5	LORD's command Moses g *this* **order**	7422
	36:13	the LORD g through Moses to the Israelites	7422
Dt	2:12	as Israel did in the land the LORD g them	5989
	2:36	The LORD our God g us all of them.	5989
	3: 3	also g into our hands Og king of Bashan	5989
	3:12	*I* g the Reubenites and the Gadites	5989
	3:13	*I* g to the half tribe of Manasseh.	5989
	3:15	And *I* g Gilead to Makir.	5989
	3:16	and the Gadites *I* g the territory extending	5989
	4:45	decrees and laws Moses g them	1819

Dt	5:22	on two stone tablets and g them to me.	5989
	8:16	g you manna **to eat**	430
	9:10	The LORD g me two stone tablets inscribed	5989
	9:11	the LORD g me the two stone tablets,	5989
	10: 4	And the LORD g them to me.	5989
	22:16	g my daughter **in marriage**	851+4200+5989
	26: 9	and g us this land, a land flowing with milk	5989
	28:45	the commands and decrees *he* g you.	7422
	29: 8	and g it as an inheritance to the Reubenites,	5989
	31: 9	So Moses wrote down this law and g it to	5989
	31:23	The LORD g *this* **command** to Joshua son	7422
	31:25	he g *this* **command** *to* the Levites	7422
	32: 8	g the nations their **inheritance,**	5706
	32:18	you forgot the God *who* g you **birth.**	2655
	33: 4	the law that Moses g us,	7422
Jos	1: 7	the law my servant Moses g you;	7422
	1:13	the servant of the LORD g you:	7422
	1:14	that Moses g you east of the Jordan,	5989
	1:15	the LORD g you east of the Jordan toward	5989
	6:20	when the people g a loud **shout,**	8131+9558
	8:33	when he g instructions to bless the people	NIH
	10:12	the LORD g the Amorites **over** to Israel,	5989
	10:27	At sunset Joshua g *the* **order**	7422
	10:30	The LORD also g that city and its king	5989
	11: 8	the LORD g them into the hand of Israel.	5989
	11:23	and he g it as an inheritance to Israel	5989
	12: 6	the LORD g their land to the Reubenites,	5989
	12: 7	toward Seir (their lands Joshua g as	5989
	13:14	But to the tribe of Levi he g no inheritance,	5989
	14:13	and g him Hebron as his inheritance.	5989
	15:13	Joshua g to Caleb son of Jephunneh	5989
	15:17	Caleb g his daughter Acsah to him **in marriage.**	851+4200+5989
	15:19	So Caleb g her the upper and lower springs.	5989
	17: 4	So Joshua g them an inheritance along with	5989
	18: 7	the servant of the LORD g it to them."	5989
	19:49	the Israelites g Joshua son of Nun	5989
	19:50	*They* g him the town he asked for—	5989
	21: 3	the Israelites g the Levites	5989
	21:11	*They* g them Kiriath Arba (that is,	5989
	21:13	the priest *they* g Hebron (a city of refuge	5989
	21:17	the tribe of Benjamin they g them Gibeon,	NIH
	21:43	So the LORD g Israel all	5989
	21:44	The LORD g them **rest** on every side,	5663
	22: 3	the mission the LORD your God g you.	5184
	22: 4	that Moses the servant of the LORD g you	5989
	22: 5	the servant of the LORD g you:	7422
	22: 7	the other half of the tribe Joshua g land on	5989
	22:34	the altar *this* **name:** A Witness Between	7924
	23:14	not one of all the good promises the LORD your God g you has failed.	1819
	24: 3	and g him **many** descendants.	8049
	24: 3	*I* g him Isaac,	5989
	24: 4	and to Isaac *I* g Jacob and Esau.	5989
	24: 8	but *I* g them into your hands.	5989
	24:11	but *I* g them into your hands.	5989
	24:13	So *I* g you a land on which you did not toil	5989
Jdg	1: 4	the LORD g the Canaanites and Perizzites	5989
	1:13	Caleb g his daughter Acsah to him **in marriage.**	851+4200+5989
	1:15	Caleb g her the upper and lower springs.	5989
	3: 6	and g their own daughters to their sons,	5989
	3:10	The LORD g Cushan-Rishathaim king	5989
	3:12	the LORD g Eglon king of Moab **power**	2616
	3:15	and he g them a deliverer—	7756
	4:19	She opened a skin of milk, g him **a drink,**	9197
	5:25	He asked for water, and *she* g him milk;	5989
	6: 1	for seven years he g them into the hands of	5989
	6: 9	from before you and g you their land.	5989
	8: 3	God g Oreb and Zeeb,	5989
	9: 4	*They* g him seventy shekels of silver from	5989
	11:21	Sihon and all his men into Israel's hands,	5989
	11:32	and the LORD g them into his hands.	5989
	12: 3	the LORD g me the **victory** over them.	5989
	12: 9	g his daughters **away in marriage**	928+3338+5989
	13:24	The woman g **birth** *to* a boy	3528
	14: 9	he g them some, and they too ate it.	5989
	14:19	of their belongings and g their clothes	5989
	15: 2	he said, "that *I* g her to your friend.	5989
	17: 4	of silver and g them to a silversmith,	5989
Ru	1:12	if I had a husband tonight and then g **birth**	3528
	2:15	Boaz g **orders** to his men,	7422
	2:18	also brought out and g her what she had left	5989
	3:17	"He g me these six measures of barley,	5989
	4: 7	one party took off his sandal and g it to	5989
	4:13	and *she* g **birth** *to* a son.	3528
1Sa	1: 5	But to Hannah he g a double portion	5989
	1:20	of time Hannah conceived and g **birth** *to*	3528
	2:20	the place of the one she prayed for and g to	8626
	2:21	she conceived and g **birth** *to* three sons	3528
	2:28	*I* also g your father's house all	5989
	4:19	she went into labor and g **birth,**	3528
	9:23	"Bring the piece of meat *I* g you,	5989
	13:13	the command the LORD your God g you;	7422
	15:24	I was afraid of the people and so *I* g in	928+7754+9048
	18: 4	the robe he was wearing and g it to David,	5989
	18: 5	g him a **high rank** in the army.	6584+8492
	18:13	and g him command over a thousand men,	8492
	18:27	Saul g him his daughter Michal **in marriage.**	851+4200+5989
	20:40	Jonathan g his weapons to the boy and said,	5989
	21: 6	So the priest g him the consecrated bread,	5989
	22:10	he also g him provisions and the sword	5989
	24:22	So David g **his oath** to Saul.	8678
	25: 9	*they* g Nabal this message	1819

1Sa	27: 6	So on that day Achish g him Ziklag,	5989
	30:11	*They* g him water to drink and food	5989
2Sa	3:15	So Ish-Bosheth g orders	8938
	4:10	That was the reward I g him for his news!	5989
	4:12	So David g *an order* to his men,	7422
	6:19	Then *he* g a loaf of bread,	2745
	8: 6	The LORD g David victory wherever he went.	3828
	8:14	The LORD g David victory wherever he went.	3828
	12: 8	I g your master's house to you,	5989
	12: 8	I g the house of Israel and Judah.	5989
	12:24	She g birth *to* a son,	3528
	13:25	but g him *his* blessing,	1385
	14:16	and my son from the inheritance God g us.'	NIH
	16:23	the advice Ahithophel g was like	3619+6783
	19:28	g your servant a place among those	8883
	19:39	and g him *his* blessing,	1385
1Ki	1: 7	and they g him *their* support.	339+6468
	2: 1	*he* g a charge to Solomon his son.	7422
	2:25	So King Solomon g orders to Benaiah son	8938
	2:43	and obey the command *I* g you?"	7422
	2:46	Then the king g the order to Benaiah son	7422
	3:15	Then *he* g a feast for all his court.	6913
	3:25	He then g an order:	606
	3:27	Then the king g *his* ruling:	6699
	4:29	God g Solomon wisdom	5989
	5:11	Solomon g Hiram twenty thousand cors	5989
	5:12	The LORD g Solomon wisdom,	5989
	6:12	I will fulfill through you the promise *I* g	1819
	8:34	and bring them back to the land *you* g	5989
	8:36	on the land *you* g your people for	5989
	8:40	in the land *you* g our fathers.	5989
	8:48	toward the land *you* g their fathers, toward	5989
	8:56	of all the good promises he g	1819
	8:58	decrees and regulations he g our fathers.	7422
	9:11	King Solomon g twenty towns in Galilee	5989
	9:16	then g it as a wedding gift to his daughter,	5989
	10:10	And *she* g the king 120 talents of gold,	5989
	10:10	the queen of Sheba g to King Solomon.	5989
	10:13	King Solomon g the queen all she desired	5989
	11:18	who g Hadad a house and land	5989
	11:19	g him a sister of his own wife, Queen Tahpenes, in marriage,	851+5989
	12: 8	rejected the advice the elders g him	3619+6783
	13: 3	That same day the man of God g a sign:	5989
	13:21	the command the LORD your God g you.	7422
	14: 8	from the house of David and g it to you,	5989
	14:15	from this good land that *he* g	5989
	15: 4	for David's sake the LORD his God g him	5989
	17:23	He g him to his mother and said, "Look,	5989
	19:21	to cook the meat and g it to the people,	5989
2Ki	4:17	about that same time *she* g birth *to* a son,	3528
	5:23	He g them to two of his servants,	5989
	11:10	Then he g the commanders the spears	5989
	12:11	*they* g the money to the men appointed	5989
	12:15	an accounting from those to whom *they* g	5989
	15:19	and Menahem g him a thousand talents	5989
	16:15	King Ahaz then g *these orders* to Uriah	7422
	17:20	he afflicted them and g them into the hands	5989
	17:27	Then the king of Assyria g *this order:*	7422
	17:34	that the LORD g the descendants of Jacob,	7422
	18:15	So Hezekiah g him all the silver	5989
	18:16	and g it to the king of Assyria.	5989
	21: 8	from the land *I* g their forefathers	5989
	21: 8	that my servant Moses g them."	7422
	22: 8	He g it to Shaphan, who read it.	5989
	22:12	He g *these orders* to Hilkiah the priest,	7422
	23:21	The king g *this order* *to* all the people:	7422
	25:28	and g him a seat of honor higher than those	5989
	25:30	the king g Jehoiachin a regular allowance	5989
1Ch	2:35	g his daughter in marriage	851+4200+5989
	2:49	*She* also g birth *to* Shaaph the father	3528
	4: 9	saying, "*I* g birth to him in pain."	3528
	4:17	One of Mered's wives g birth *to* Miriam,	2225
	4:18	(His Judean wife g birth *to* Jered the father	3528
	6:64	So the Israelites g the Levites these towns	5989
	6:70	the tribe of Manasseh the Israelites g Aner	NIH
	7:14	*She* g birth *to* Makir the father of Gilead.	3528
	7:16	Makir's wife Maacah g birth *to* Ishhod	3528
	7:18	His sister Hammoleketh g birth *to* Ishhod	3528
	7:23	she became pregnant and g birth *to* a son.	3528
	11:10	g his kingship strong support	2616+6640
	14:12	and David g orders to burn them in the fire.	606
	16: 3	Then *he* g a loaf of bread,	2745
	18: 6	The LORD g David victory everywhere he went.	3828
	18:13	The LORD g David victory everywhere he went.	3828
	22: 2	So David g orders to assemble	606
	22:13	that the LORD g Moses for Israel.	7422
	25: 5	God g Heman fourteen sons	5989
	28:11	Then David g his son Solomon the plans	5989
	28:12	He g him the plans of all that	NIH
	28:13	He g him instructions for the divisions of	NIH
	28:18	He also g him the plan for the chariot,	NIH
	28:19	*he* g me understanding *in* all the details	8505
	29: 6	in charge of the king's work g willingly.	5605
	29: 7	*They* g toward the work on the temple	5989
	29: 8	Any who had precious stones g them to	5989
2Ch	2: 1	Solomon g orders to build a temple for	606
	6:25	to the land *you* g to them and their fathers.	5989
	6:27	on the land *you* g your people for	5989
	6:31	in the land *you* g our fathers.	5989
	6:38	toward the land *you* g their fathers, toward	5989
	7: 3	they worshiped and g thanks to the LORD.	3344
	7: 6	and which were used when he g thanks,	2146
2Ch	9: 9	Then *she* g the king 120 talents of gold,	5989
	9: 9	the queen of Sheba g to King Solomon.	5989
	9:12	Solomon g the queen of Sheba all she	5989
	9:12	he g her more than she had brought to him.	NIH
	10: 8	rejected the advice the elders g him	3619+6783
	11:23	He g them abundant provisions	5989
	14: 6	for the LORD g him rest.	5663
	15:15	So the LORD g them rest on every side.	5663
	19: 9	He g them these orders:	7422
	20:11	the possession *you* g us as an inheritance.	3769
	23: 9	Then he g the commanders of units of	5989
	24:12	The king and Jehoiada g it to	5989
	26: 5	God g him success.	7503
	28: 9	he g them into your hand.	5989
	28:14	the soldiers g up the prisoners and plunder	6440
	28:20	but *he* g him trouble instead of help.	7674
	29:27	Hezekiah g the order to sacrifice	606
	31: 5	the Israelites generously g the firstfruits	8049
	31:11	Hezekiah g orders to prepare storerooms in	606
	32:24	who answered him and g him	5989
	34: 9	and g him the money that had been brought	5989
	34:11	also g money to the carpenters and builders	5989
	34:15	He g it to Shaphan.	5989
	34:20	He g these orders to Hilkiah,	7422
	35: 8	the administrators of God's temple, g	5989
Ezr	2:68	the families g freewill offerings toward	5605
	2:69	to their ability they g to the treasury	5989
	3: 7	they g money to the masons and carpenters,	5989
	3: 7	and g food and drink and oil to the people	NIH
	3:11	all the people g a great shout of praise	8131+9558
	5:11	This is the answer they g us:	10754
	5:14	"Then King Cyrus g them to them	10314
	8:36	who then g assistance to the people and to	5951
	9:11	you g through your servants the prophets	7422
	10:19	g their hands in pledge to put away	5989
Ne	1: 7	and laws *you* g your servant Moses.	7422
	1: 8	the instruction *you* g your servant Moses,	7422
	2: 1	I took the wine and g it to the king.	5989
	2: 9	of Trans-Euphrates and g them	5989
	6: 4	and each time *I* g them the same answer.	8740
	7:70	The governor g to the treasury 1,000	5989
	7:71	the heads of the families g to the treasury	5989
	9:13	*You* g them regulations and laws	5989
	9:14	and g them commands,	7422
	9:15	In their hunger *you* g them bread	5989
	9:20	*You* g your good Spirit to instruct them.	5989
	9:20	and *you* g them water for their thirst.	5989
	9:22	"*You* g them kingdoms and nations,	5989
	9:27	in your great compassion *you* g them deliverers,	5989
	9:34	or the warnings *you* g them.	6343+6386
	9:35	in the spacious and fertile land *you* g them,	5989
	9:36	slaves in the land *you* g our forefathers	5989
	12:40	The two choirs that g thanks	9343
	13: 9	*I* g orders to purify the rooms,	606
Est	1: 3	of his reign he g a banquet for all his nobles	6913
	1: 5	the king g a banquet, lasting seven days,	6913
	1: 9	Queen Vashti also g a banquet for	6913
	2:18	And the king g a great banquet,	6913
	3:10	and g it to Haman son of Hammedatha,	5989
	4: 8	*He* also g him a copy of the text of the edict	5989
	5:12	the king to the banquet *she* g.	6913
	8: 1	That same day King Xerxes g Queen Esther	5989
Job	1:21	The LORD g and and the LORD has taken	5989
	8: 4	*he* g them *over* to the penalty of their sin.	8938
	10:12	You g me life and showed me kindness,	NIH
	22: 7	*You* g no water to the weary	9197
	32:12	g you my full attention.	1067
	38:36	the heart with wisdom or g understanding	5989
	39: 6	*I* g him the wasteland as his home,	8492
	42:10	and g him twice as much as he had before.	3578
	42:11	and each one g him a piece of silver and	5989
	42:11	and *you* g it to him—	5989
Ps	21: 4	the victories you g, his glory is great;	NIH
	21: 5	on a rock and g me a firm place to stand.	3922
	40: 2	You g us up to be devoured like sheep	5989
	44:11	You g abundant showers, O God;	5678
	68: 9	They put gall in my food and g me vinegar	9197
	69:21	The heads of Leviathan and g him as food to	5989
	74:14	the desert and g them water as abundant as	9197
	78:15	Yet he g a command to the skies above	7422
	78:23	he g them the grain of heaven.	5989
	78:24	*He* g their crops to the grasshopper,	5989
	78:46	*He* g over their cattle to the hail,	6037
	78:48	not spare them from death but g them over	6037
	78:50	*He* g his people over to the sword;	6037
	78:62	So *I* g them over to their stubborn hearts	8938
	81:12	and the decrees he g them.	5989
	99: 7	he g them the lands of the nations,	5989
	105:44	*they* g no thought to your miracles;	8505
	106: 7	g in to their craving;	203+9294
	106:14	So he g them what they asked for,	5989
	106:15	and he g their land as an inheritance,	5989
	135:12	and g their land as an inheritance,	5989
	136:21	he g a decree that will never pass away.	5989
	148: 6	when I called and no one g heed	7992
Pr	1:24	when he g the sea its boundary so	8492
	8:29	Listen to your father, who g you life,	3528
	23:22	may she who g you birth rejoice!	3528
	23:25	and the spirit returns to God who g it.	5989
Ecc	12: 7	there she who was in labor g you birth.	3528
SS	8: 5	and she conceived and g birth *to* a son.	3528
Isa	8: 3	who g you permission to cut out a grave	4200
	22:16	we writhed in pain, but g birth *to* wind.	3528
	26:18	*I* g to Jerusalem a messenger	5989
	41:27	*I* g them into your hand.	5989
	47: 6	your father, and to Sarah, *who* g you birth.	2655
	51: 2		
Isa	63: 5	I was appalled that no *one* g support;	6164
Jer	2:27	and to stone, 'You g me birth.'	3528
	3: 8	*I* g faithless Israel her certificate of divorce	5989
	3:18	g your forefathers *as an inheritance.*	5706
	7: 7	in the land *I* g your forefathers for ever	5989
	7:14	the place *I* g to you and your fathers.	5989
	7:23	but *I* g them this command:	7422
	12:14	the inheritance *I* g my people Israel,	5706
	15:10	Alas, my mother, that you g me birth,	3528
	16:15	to the land *I* g their forefathers.	5989
	17: 4	the inheritance *I* g you.	5989
	22:26	and the mother who g you birth	3528
	23:39	with the city *I* g to you and your fathers.	5989
	24:10	until they are destroyed from the land *I* g	5989
	25: 5	and you can stay in the land the LORD g	5989
	27:12	*I* g the same message to Zedekiah king of Judah.	465+1819+1821+2021+3972
	30: 3	to the land *I* g their forefathers to possess,'	5989
	32:12	and *I* g this deed to Baruch son of Neriah,	5989
	32:13	g Baruch *these instructions:*	7422
	32:22	*You* g them this land you had sworn	5989
	35: 6	son of Recab g us *this command:*	7422
	35:16	the command their forefather g them,	7422
	36:32	and g it to the scribe Baruch son of Neriah,	5989
	37:21	King Zedekiah then g orders for Jeremiah	7422
	39:10	at that time *he* g them vineyards and fields.	5989
	40: 5	Then the commander g him provisions and	5989
	50:12	*she* who g you birth will be disgraced.	3528
	51:59	This is the message Jeremiah g *to*	7422
	52:32	and g him a seat of honor higher than those	5989
	52:34	by day the king of Babylon of Jehoiachin	5989
La	2:14	The oracles they g you were false	2600
Eze	3: 2	g me the scroll *to eat.*	430
	16: 8	g you *my* solemn oath	8678
	16:17	You also took the fine jewelry *I* g you,	5989
	16:19	olive oil and honey *I* g you to eat—	430
	16:27	*I* g you *over* to the greed of your enemies,	5989
	16:36	because *you* g them your children's blood,	5989
	20:11	*I* g them my decrees and made known	5989
	20:12	Also *I* g them my Sabbaths as a sign	5989
	20:25	I also g them *over* to statutes that were	5989
	23: 4	They were mine and g birth *to* sons	3528
	23: 7	*She* g herself as a prostitute to all the elite	5989
	28:25	which *I* g to my servant Jacob.	5989
	31: 6	of the field g birth under its branches;	3528
	36:28	in the land *I* g your forefathers;	5989
	37:25	in the land *I* g to my servant Jacob,	5989
Da	1: 7	The chief official g them new names:	8492
	1:16	to drink and g them vegetables instead.	5989
	1:17	To these four young men God g knowledge	5989
	5: 1	King Belshazzar g a great banquet for	10522
	5: 2	he g orders to bring in the gold	10042
	5: 6	and his legs g way.	10742
	5:18	the Most High God g your father Nebuchadnezzar sovereignty	10314
	5:19	Because of the high position he g him,	10314
	6:16	So the king g the order,	10042
	6:23	and g orders to lift Daniel out of the den.	10042
	7:16	and g me the interpretation of these things:	10313
	7:23	"*He* g me this explanation:	10042
	9:10	the laws he g us through his servants	5989
	10:18	like a man touched me and g me strength.	2616
Hos	1: 6	Gomer conceived again and g birth *to*	3528
	2: 8	the *one* who g her the grain, the new wine	5989
	2:12	g them many visions and told parables	8049
	13:11	So in my anger *I* g you a king,	5989
Am	4: 6	"I g you empty stomachs in every city	5989
Hag	1:13	g this message of the LORD to the people:	606
Zec	3: 6	of the LORD g this charge to Joshua:	6386
Mal	2: 5	covenant of life and peace, and *I* g them to	5989
	4: 4	and laws *I* g him at Horeb for all Israel.	7422
Mt	1:25	with her until she g birth *to* a son.	5503
	1:25	And he g him the name Jesus.	2813
	2:16	and he g orders to kill all the boys	690
	8:18	he g orders to cross to the other side of	3027
	10: 1	to him and g them authority	1443
	14:19	he g thanks and broke the loaves.	2328
	14:19	Then he g them to the disciples,	1443
	14:19	and the disciples g them to the people.	NIG
	15:36	he broke them and g them to the disciples,	1443
	20:14	the same as I g you.	NIG
	21:23	"And who g you this authority?"	1443
	25:15	To one he g five talents of money,	1443
	25:35	For I was hungry and *you* g me something	1443
	25:35	g me something to drink,	4540
	25:42	I was hungry and *you* g me nothing to eat,	1443
	25:42	g me nothing to drink,	4540
	26:26	Jesus took bread, g thanks and broke it,	2328
	26:26	and g it to his disciples, saying,	1443
	26:27	g thanks and offered it to them, saying,	2373
	27:12	he g no answer.	646
	27:50	he g up his spirit.	918
	28:12	*they* g the soldiers a large sum of money,	1443
Mk	2:26	And *he* also g some to his companions."	1443
	3:12	But *he* g them strict orders not	2203
	3:16	Simon (to whom *he* g the name Peter);	2202
	3:17	(to them *he* g the name Boanerges,	2202
	5:13	*He* g them permission,	2205
	5:43	*He* g strict orders not to let anyone know	1403
	6: 7	and g them authority over evil spirits.	1443
	6:21	On his birthday Herod g a banquet	4472
	6:28	and she g it to her mother.	1443
	6:41	he g thanks and broke the loaves.	2328
	6:41	Then he g them to his disciples to set before	1443
	8: 6	he broke them and g them to his disciples	1443
	8: 7	*he* g thanks for them also and told	2328
	9: 9	Jesus g them orders not to tell	1403

Mk	11:28	"And who g you authority to do this?"	1443
	12:44	*They* all g out of their wealth;	965
	14:22	Jesus took bread, g **thanks** and broke it,	2328
	14:22	and g it to his disciples, saying, "Take it;	1443
	14:23	the cup, g **thanks** and offered it to them,	2373
	14:57	g this **false testimony**	6018
	14:61	But Jesus remained silent and g no **answer.**	646
	15:45	*he* g the body to Joseph.	1563
Lk	1:57	*she* g **birth** to a son.	1164
	2: 7	and *she* g **birth** to her firstborn,	5503
	2:38	*she* g **thanks** to God and spoke about	469
	4:20	g it **back** to the attendant and sat down.	625
	5:26	Everyone was amazed and g **praise** to God.	1519
	6: 4	And *he* also g some to his companions."	1443
	7:15	and Jesus g him **back** to his mother.	1443
	7:21	and g sight to many who were blind.	5919
	8:32	and *he* g them **permission.**	2205
	9: 1	*he* g them power and authority	1443
	9:16	*he* g **thanks** and broke them.	2328
	9:16	Then *he* g them to the disciples to set before	1443
	9:42	healed the boy and g him **back** to his father.	625
	10:35	and g them to the innkeeper.	1443
	11:27	"Blessed is the mother who g you **birth**	1002
	15:16	but no one g him anything.	1443
	15:29	Yet *you* never g me even a young goat	1443
	19:13	of his servants and g them ten minas.	1443
	20: 2	"Who g you this authority?"	1443
	21: 4	All these people g their gifts out	965+1650
	22:17	After taking the cup, *he* g **thanks** and said,	2373
	22:19	And he took bread, g **thanks** and broke it,	2373
	22:19	gave thanks and broke it, and g it to them,	1443
	23: 9	but Jesus g him no **answer.**	646
	24:30	*he* took bread, g **thanks,**	2328
	24:42	They g him a piece of broiled fish,	2113
Jn	1:12	*he* g the right to become children of God—	1443
	1:32	Then John g this **testimony.**	3455
	3:16	the world that *he* g his one and only Son,	1443
	4:12	who g us the well and drank	1443
	5:19	Jesus g them this **answer:**	646
	5:35	John was a lamp that burned and g **light,**	5743
	6:11	Jesus then took the loaves, g **thanks,**	2373
	6:31	'*He* g them bread from heaven to eat.' "	1443
	7:22	because Moses g you circumcision	1443
	13:26	*he* g it to Judas Iscariot, son of Simon.	1443
	17: 4	on earth by completing the work *you* g me	1443
	17: 6	to those whom *you* g me out of the world.	1443
	17: 6	*you* g them to me and they have obeyed	1443
	17: 8	For *I* g them the words you gave me	1443
	17: 8	For I gave them the words *you* g me	1443
	17:11	power of your name—the name *you* g me—	1443
	17:12	and kept them safe by that name *you* g me.	1443
	17:22	I have given them the glory that *you* g me,	1443
	18: 9	"I have not lost one of those *you* g me."	1443
	19: 9	he asked Jesus, but Jesus g him no answer.	1443
	19:30	he bowed his head and g **up** his spirit.	4140
	21:13	Jesus came, took the bread and g it to them,	1443
Ac	1: 3	to these men and g many convincing proofs	NIG
	1: 4	*he* g them this **command:**	4133
	2:45	*they* g to anyone as he had need.	1374
	3: 5	So the man g him his **attention,**	AIT
	5:28	"We g you **strict orders** not to teach	4132+4133
	7: 5	*He* g him no inheritance here,	1443
	7: 8	Then *he* g Abraham the covenant	1443
	7:10	*He* g Joseph wisdom and enabled him	1443
	7:42	But God turned away and g them **over** to	4140
	8:10	g him *their* **attention** and exclaimed,	AIT
	8:38	And *he* g **orders** to stop the chariot.	3027
	10: 2	g generously to those in **need**	1797+4472
	11:17	if God g them the same gift as he gave us,	1443
	11:17	if God gave them the same gift as he g us,	NIG
	13:19	and g their land **to** his people **as** their **inheritance.**	2883
	13:20	God g them judges until the time of Samuel	1443
	13:21	and *he* g them Saul son of Kish,	1443
	19:16	g them such a **beating** that they ran out	2710
	21:14	*we* g up and said, "The Lord's will be done	2483
	27:15	so *we* g **way** to it and were driven along.	2113
	27:20	*we* finally g **up** all hope of being saved.	4311
	27:20	and g **thanks** to God in front of them all.	2373
Ro	1:21	glorified him as God nor g **thanks** to him,	2373
	1:24	Therefore God g them **over** in	4140
	1:26	of this, God g them **over** to shameful lusts.	4140
	1:28	he g them **over** to a depraved mind,	4140
	4:20	in his faith and g glory to God,	1443
	8:32	but g him **up** for us all—	4140
	11: 8	"God g them a spirit of stupor,	1443
	15:15	because of the grace God g me	1443
1Co	3: 2	*I* g you milk, not solid food,	4540
2Co	5:18	and g us the ministry of reconciliation;	1443
	8: 3	that they g as much as they were able,	NIG
	8: 5	but *they* g themselves first to the Lord and	1443
	10: 8	the authority the Lord g us for building you	1443
	13: 2	**already** g you a **warning**	4625
	13: 2	the Lord g me for building you up,	1443
Gal	1: 4	who g himself for our sins to rescue us	1443
	2: 9	g me and Barnabas the right hand	1443
	2:20	who loved me and g himself for me.	4140
	3:18	but God **in** his **grace** g it to Abraham	5919
Eph	4: 8	he led captives in his train and g gifts	1443
	4:11	It was he who g some to be apostles,	1443
	5: 2	as Christ loved us and g himself up for us	4140
	5:25	as Christ loved the church and g himself **up**	4140
Php	2: 9	the highest place and g him the name that is	5919
	3:17	according to the pattern we g *you.*	2400
Col	1:25	the commission God g me to present to you	1443
1Th	1: 9	what kind of reception you g us.	2400+4639
	4: 2	For you know what instructions *we* g you	1443

2Th	2:16	by his grace g us eternal encouragement	1443
	3:10	we were with you, *we* g you this **rule:**	4133
1Ti	2: 6	who g himself as a ransom for all men—	1443
2Ti	4:17	Lord stood at my side and g me **strength,**	1904
Tit	2:14	who g himself for us to redeem us	1443
Heb	7: 2	and Abraham g him a tenth of everything.	3532
	7: 4	Even the patriarch Abraham g him a tenth	1443
	11:22	and g **instructions** about his bones.	1948
Jas	2:25	for what she did *when she* g **lodging** to	5685
	5:18	Again he prayed, and the heavens g rain,	1443
2Pe	3:15	with the wisdom that God g him.	1443
1Jn	3:24	We know it by the Spirit *he* g us.	1443
3Jn	1: 3	*It* g me great **joy** to have some of the	AIT
Jude	1: 7	g themselves **up to sexual immorality**	1745
Rev	1: 1	which God g him	1443
	10: 3	and *he* g a loud **shout** like the roar of	3189+5889
	11:13	and the survivors were terrified and g glory	1443
	12: 5	*She* g **birth** to a son, a male child,	5503
	13: 2	The dragon g the beast his power	1443
	15: 7	Then one of the four living creatures g to	1443
	16:19	and g her the cup filled with the wine of	1443
	18: 7	**glory** and luxury *she* g herself.	1519
	20:13	The sea g **up** the dead that were in it,	1443
	20:13	and Hades g **up** the dead that were in them,	1443

GAVE (Anglicized) See also DELIVERED

GAY (KJV) See FINE

GAZA (23)

Ge	10:19	from Sidon toward Gerar as far as G,	6445
Dt	2:23	Avvites who lived in villages as far as G,	6445
Jos	10:41	to G and from the whole region of Goshen	6445
	11:22	in G, Gath and Ashdod did any survive.	6445
	13: 3	of the five Philistine rulers in G,	6484
	15:47	and G, its settlements and villages,	6445
Jdg	1:18	The men of Judah also took G,	6445
	6: 4	the crops all the way to G and did not spare	6445
	16: 1	One day Samson went to G,	6445
	16: 2	**people of** G were told, "Samson is here!"	6484
	16:21	and took him down to G.	6445
1Sa	6:17	one each for Ashdod, G, Ashkelon,	6445
1Ki	4:24	from Tiphsah to G,	6445
2Ki	18: 8	as far as G and its territory.	6445
Jer	25:20	G, Ekron, and the people left at Ashdod);	6445
	47: 1	the Philistines before Pharaoh attacked G:	6445
	47: 5	G will shave her head in mourning;	6445
Am	1: 6	"For three sins of G, even for four,	6445
	1: 7	of G that will consume her fortresses.	6445
Zep	2: 4	G will be abandoned and Ashkelon left	6445
Zec	9: 5	G will writhe in agony, and Ekron too,	6445
	9: 5	G will lose her king and Ashkelon will	6445
Ac	8:26	that goes down from Jerusalem to G."	1124

GAZATHITES (KJV) See GAZA

GAZE (11) [GAZING]

2Ki	8:11	*He* stared *at* him **with a fixed g**	906+2256+6641+7156+8492
Job	35: 5	g *at* the clouds so high above you.	8800
	36:25	men g *on* it from afar.	5564
Ps	27: 4	to g upon the beauty of the LORD	2600
	68:16	Why g in envy, O rugged mountains,	8353
Pr	4:25	fix your g directly before you.	6757
	23:31	*Do not* g *at* wine when it is red,	8011
SS	6:13	come back, that *we may* g on you!	2600
	6:13	Why *would you* g on the Shulammite as	2600
Hab	2:15	so that *he can* g on their naked bodies.	5564
Rev	11: 9	language and nation *will* g on their bodies	1063

GAZELLE (12) [GAZELLES]

Dt	12:15	as if it were g or deer.	7383
	12:22	Eat them as you would g or deer.	7383
	14: 5	the g, the roe deer, the wild goat, the ibex,	7383
	15:22	as if it were g or deer.	7383
2Sa	2:18	Asahel was as fleet-footed as a wild g.	7383
Pr	6: 5	like a g from the hand of the hunter,	7383
SS	2: 9	My lover is like a g or a young stag.	7383
	2:17	a g or like a young stag on the rugged hills.	7383
	4: 5	like twin fawns of a g that browse among	7386
	7: 3	like two fawns, twins of a g.	7386
	8:14	and be like a g or like a young stag on	7383
Isa	13:14	Like a hunted g,	7383

GAZELLES (4) [GAZELLE]

1Ki	4:23	g, roebucks and choice fowl.	7383
1Ch	12: 8	they were as swift as g in the mountains.	7373
SS	2: 7	I charge you by the g and by the does of	7374
	3: 5	I charge you by the g and by the does of	7374

GAZER (KJV) See GEZER

GAZEZ (2)

1Ch	2:46	the mother of Haran, Moza and G.	1606
	2:46	Haran was the father of G.	1606

GAZING (3) [GAZE]

SS	2: 9	g through the windows,	8708
Da	10: 8	So I was left alone, I g *at* this great vision;	8011
2Co	3:13	over his face to keep the Israelites from g	867

GAZINGSTOCK (KJV) See PUBLICLY EXPOSED, SPECTACLE

GAZITES (KJV) See GAZA

GAZZAM (2)

Ezr	2:48	Rezin, Nekoda, G,	1613
Ne	7:51	G, Uzza, Paseah,	1613

GE HARASHIM (1)

1Ch	4:14	father of Joab, the father of G.	1629

GEBA (15)

Jos	18:24	Kephar Ammoni, Ophni and G—	1494
	21:17	of Benjamin they gave Gibeon, G,	1494
1Sa	13: 3	the Philistine outpost at G,	1494
	14: 5	the other to the south toward G.	1494
1Ki	15:22	With them King Asa built up G	1494
2Ki	23: 8	from G to Beersheba,	1494
1Ch	6:60	G, Alemeth and Anathoth,	1494
	8: 6	of those living in G and were deported	1494
2Ch	16: 6	With them he built up G and Mizpah.	1494
Ezr	2:26	of Ramah and G 621	1494
Ne	7:30	of Ramah and G 621	1494
	11:31	the Benjamites from G lived in Micmash,	1494
	12:29	and from the area of G and Azmaveth,	1494
Isa	10:29	and say, "We will camp overnight at G."	1494
Zec	14:10	The whole land, from G to Rimmon,	1494

GEBAL (3) [GEBALITES]

1Ki	5:18	the **men of** G cut and prepared the timber	1490
Ps	83: 7	G, Ammon and Amalek, Philistia, with	1489
Eze	27: 9	Veteran craftsmen of G were on board	1488

GEBALITES (1) [GEBAL]

Jos	13: 5	the area of the G;	1490

GEBER (1) [BEN-GEBER, EZION GEBER]

1Ki	4:19	G son of Uri—in Gilead	1506

GEBIM (1)

Isa	10:31	the people of G take cover.	1481

GECKO (1)

Lev	11:30	the g, the monitor lizard, the wall lizard,	652

GEDALIAH (31) [GEDALIAH'S]

2Ki	25:22	of Babylon appointed G son of Ahikam,	1546
	25:23	that the king of Babylon had appointed G	1546
	25:23	they came to G at Mizpah—	1546
	25:24	G took an oath to reassure them	1546
	25:25	came with ten men and assassinated G and	1546
1Ch	25: 3	As for Jeduthun, from his sons: G, Zeri,	1546
	25: 9	the second to G, he and his relatives and	1546
Ezr	10:18	Maaseiah, Eliezer, Jarib and G.	1545
Jer	38: 1	G son of Pashhur,	1546
	39:14	They turned him over to G son of Ahikam,	1546
	40: 5	"Go back to G son of Ahikam,	1545
	40: 6	to G son of Ahikam at Mizpah and stayed	1545
	40: 7	of Babylon had appointed G son of Ahikam	1546
	40: 8	they came to G at Mizpah—	1546
	40: 9	G son of Ahikam, the son of Shaphan,	1546
	40:11	and had appointed G son of Ahikam,	1546
	40:12	to G at Mizpah,	1546
	40:13	in the open country came to G at Mizpah	1546
	40:14	But G son of Ahikam did not believe them.	1546
	40:15	of Kareah said privately to G at Mizpah,	1546
	40:16	But G son of Ahikam said to Johanan son	1546
	41: 1	came with ten men to G son of Ahikam	1546
	41: 2	with him got up and struck down G son	1546
	41: 3	also killed all the Jews who were with G	1546
	41: 6	he said, "Come to G son of Ahikam."	1546
	41: 9	of the men he had killed along with G was	1546
	41:10	of the imperial guard had appointed G son	1546
	41:16	after he had assassinated G son of Ahikam:	1545
	41:18	of Nethaniah had killed G son of Ahikam,	1546
	43: 6	of the imperial guard had left with G son	1546
Zep	1: 1	the son of G, the son of Amariah,	1545

GEDALIAH'S (1) [GEDALIAH]

Jer	41: 4	The day after G assassination.	1546

GEDEON (KJV) See GIDEON

GEDER (1) [GEDERITE]

Jos	12:13	the king of Debir one the king of G one	1554

GEDERAH (2) [GEDERATHITE]

Jos	15:36	Adithaim and G (or Gederothaim)—	1557
1Ch	4:23	the potters who lived at Netaim and G;	1557

GEDERATHITE (1) [GEDERAH]

1Ch	12: 4	Jahaziel, Johanan, Jozabad the G,	1561

GEDERITE (1) [GEDER]

1Ch	27:28	Baal-Hanan the G was in charge of	1559

GEDEROTH (2)

Jos	15:41	G, Beth Dagon, Naamah and Makkedah—	1558
2Ch	28:18	Aijalon and G, as well as Soco,	1558

GEDEROTHAIM (1)

Jos	15:36	Adithaim and Gederah (or G)—	1562

GEDI See EN GEDI

GEDOR (7)

Jos	15:58	Halhul, Beth Zur, G,	1530
1Ch	4: 4	Penuel was the father of G,	1529
	4:18	to Jered the father of G,	1529
	4:39	the outskirts of G to the east of the valley	1530
	8:31	G, Ahio, Zeker	1529
	9:37	G, Ahio, Zechariah and Mikloth.	1529
	12: 7	and Zebadiah the sons of Jeroham from G.	1530

GEHAZI (20)

2Ki	4:12	He said to his servant, G,	1634
	4:14	G said, "Well, she has no son	1634
	4:25	the man of God said to his servant G,	1634
	4:27	G came over to push her away,	1634
	4:29	Elisha said to G,	1634
	4:31	G went on ahead and laid the staff on	1634
	4:31	G went back to meet Elisha and told him,	NIH
	4:36	Elisha summoned G and said,	1634
	5:20	G, the servant of Elisha the man	1634
	5:21	So G hurried after Naaman.	1634
	5:22	"Everything is all right," G answered.	NIH
	5:23	He urged G to accept them,	2257S
	5:23	and they carried them ahead of G.	2257S
	5:24	When G came to the hill,	NIH
	5:25	"Where have you been, G?"	1634
	5:25	"Your servant didn't go anywhere," G answered.	NIH
	5:27	Then G went from Elisha's presence	NIH
	8: 4	The king was talking to G,	1634
	8: 5	Just as G was telling the king	2085S
	8: 5	G said, "This is the woman,	1634

GELILOTH (3)

Jos	18:17	went to En Shemesh, continued to G,	1667
	22:10	to G near the Jordan in the land of Canaan,	1667
	22:11	the altar on the border of Canaan at G near	1667

GEM (1) [GEMS]

Ex	28:11	the two stones the way a g cutter engraves	74

GEMALLI (1)

Nu	13:12	from the tribe of Dan, Ammiel son of G;	1696

GEMARIAH (5)

Jer	29: 3	to Elasah son of Shaphan and to G son	1701
	36:10	From the room of G son of Shaphan	1702
	36:11	When Micaiah son of G,	1702
	36:12	Elnathan son of Acbor, G son of Shaphan,	1702
	36:25	and G urged the king not to burn the scroll,	1702

GEMS (4) [GEM]

Ex	25: 7	and onyx stones and other g to be mounted	74
	35: 9	and onyx stones and other g to be mounted	74
	35:27	and other g to be mounted on the ephod	74
La	4: 1	The sacred g are scattered at the head	74

GENDER (KJV) See MATE, PRODUCE

GENEALOGICAL (11) [GENEALOGY]

1Ch	4:33	And they kept a g record.	3509
	5: 1	not be listed in the g record	3509
	5: 7	listed according to their g records:	9352
	5:17	were entered in the g records	3509
	7: 7	Their g record listed 22,034 fighting men.	3509
	7: 9	Their g record listed the heads of families	9352
	26:31	according to the g records of their families.	9352
2Ch	31:16	whose names were in the g records—	3509
	31:17	enrolled by their families in the g records	3509
	31:18	whole community listed in these g records.	3509
Ne	7: 5	the g record of those who had been the first	3510

GENEALOGIES (5) [GENEALOGY]

1Ch	9: 1	All Israel was listed in the g	3509
2Ch	12:15	and of Iddo the seer that deal with g?	3509
	31:19	were recorded in the g of the Levites.	3509
1Ti	1: 4	devote themselves to myths and endless g.	1157
Tit	3: 9	avoid foolish controversies and g and	1157

GENEALOGY (10) [GENEALOGICAL, GENEALOGIES]

1Ch	7: 2	in their g numbered 22,600.	9352
	7: 4	According to their family g,	9352
	7: 5	as listed in their g, were 87,000 in all.	3509
	7:40	as listed in their g, was 26,000.	3509
	8:28	chiefs as listed in their g,	9352
	9: 9	as listed in their g, numbered 956.	9352
	9:22	They were registered by g in their villages.	3509
	9:34	chiefs as listed in their g,	9352
Mt	1: 1	of the g of Jesus Christ the son of David,	1161

GENERAL (KJV) See COMMANDER

GENERALS (2)

Rev	6:15	the kings of the earth, the princes, the g,	5941
	19:18	so that you may eat the flesh of kings, g,	5941

GENERATION (84) [GENERATIONS]

Ge	7: 1	I have found you righteous in this g.	1887
	15:16	In the fourth g your descendants will come back here,	1887
	50:23	and saw the third g of Ephraim's children.	9000
Ex	1: 6	and all his brothers and all that g died,	1887
	3:15	by which I am to be remembered from g	1887
	3:15	to be remembered from generation to g.	1887
	17:16	be at war against the Amalekites from g	1887
	17:16	the Amalekites from generation to g."	1887
	20: 5	of the fathers to the third and fourth g,	8067
	34: 7	of the fathers to the third and fourth g."	8067
Nu	14:18	of the fathers to the third and fourth g,	8067
	32:13	the whole g of those who had done evil	1887
Dt	1:35	"Not a man of this evil g shall see	1887
	2:14	that entire g of fighting men had perished	1887
	5: 9	of the fathers to the third and fourth g,	8067
	23: 2	even down to the tenth g.	1887
	23: 3	even down to the tenth g.	1887
	23: 8	The third g of children born	1887
	32: 5	but a warped and crooked g.	1887
	32:20	for they are a perverse g,	1887
Jdg	2:10	After that whole g had been gathered	1887
	2:10	another g grew up, who knew neither	1887
2Ki	10:30	on the throne of Israel to the fourth g."	8055
	15:12	on the throne of Israel to the fourth g."	8055
Est	9:28	and observed in every g by every family,	1887
Job	42:16	and their children to the fourth g.	1887
Ps	24: 6	Such is the g of those who seek him,	1887
	48:13	that you may tell of them to the next g.	1887
	49:19	he will join the g of his fathers,	1887
	71:18	till I declare your power to the next g,	1887
	78: 4	the next g the praiseworthy deeds of	1887
	78: 6	so the next g would know them,	1887
	78: 8	a stubborn and rebellious g,	1887
	79:13	g to generation we will recount your praise.	1887
	79:13	generation to g we will recount your praise.	1887
	95:10	For forty years I was angry with that g;	1887
	102:18	Let this be written for a future g,	1887
	109:13	their names blotted out from the next g.	1887
	112: 2	the g of the upright will be blessed.	1887
	145: 4	One g will commend your works	1887
Isa	34:10	From g to generation it will lie desolate;	1887
	34:10	From generation to g it will lie desolate;	1887
	34:17	and dwell there from g to generation.	1887
	34:17	and dwell there from generation to g.	1887
Jer	2:31	of this g, consider the word of the LORD:	1887
	7:29	and abandoned this g that is	1887
	50:39	or lived in from g to generation.	1887
	50:39	or lived in from generation to g.	1887
La	5:19	your throne endures from g to generation.	1887
	5:19	your throne endures from generation to g.	1887
Da	4: 3	his dominion endures from g to generation.	10183
	4: 3	his dominion endures from generation to g.	10183
	4:34	his kingdom endures from g to generation.	10183
	4:34	his kingdom endures from generation to g.	10183
Joel	1: 3	and their children to the next g.	1887
Mt	11:16	"To what can I compare this g?	1155
	12:39	"A wicked and adulterous g asks for	1155
	12:41	at the judgment with this g and condemn it;	1155
	12:42	at the judgment with this g and condemn it;	1155
	12:45	That is how it will be with this wicked g."	1155
	16: 4	A wicked and adulterous g looks for	1155
	17:17	"O unbelieving and perverse g,"	1155
	23:36	all this will come upon this g.	1155
	24:34	this g will certainly not pass away	1155
Mk	8:12	"Why does this g ask for a miraculous sign?	1155
	8:38	in this adulterous and sinful g,	1155
	9:19	"O unbelieving g," Jesus replied,	1155
	13:30	this g will certainly not pass away	1155
Lk	1:50	who fear him, from g to generation.	1155
	1:50	who fear him, from generation to g.	1155
	7:31	then, can I compare the people of this g?	1155
	9:41	"O unbelieving and perverse g,"	1155
	11:29	Jesus said, "This is a wicked g.	1155
	11:30	so also will the Son of Man be to this g.	1155
	11:31	with the men of this g and condemn them;	1155
	11:32	at the judgment with this g and condemn it;	1155
	11:50	Therefore this g will be held responsible	1155
	11:51	this g will be held responsible for it all.	1155
	17:25	and be rejected by this g.	1155
	21:32	this g will certainly not pass away	1155
Ac	2:40	"Save yourselves from this corrupt g."	1155
	13:36	in his own g, he fell asleep;	1155
Php	2:15	without fault in a crooked and depraved g,	1155
Heb	3:10	That is why I was angry with that g,	1155

GENERATIONS (80) [GENERATION]

Ge	9:12	a covenant for all g to come:	1887
	17: 7	after you for the g to come.	1887
	17: 9	after you for the g to come.	1887
	17:12	For the g to come every male	1887
Ex	12:14	for the g to come you shall celebrate it as	1887
	12:17	as a lasting ordinance for the g to come.	1887
	12:42	to honor the LORD for the g to come.	1887
	16:32	of manna and keep it for the g to come,	1887

GENERATIONS (continued)

Ex	16:33	the LORD to be kept for the g to come."	1887
	20: 6	to a thousand [g] of those who love me	NIH
	27:21	among the Israelites for the g to come.	1887
	29:42	"For the g to come this burnt offering is to	1887
	30: 8	before the LORD for the g to come.	1887
	30:10	the atoning sin offering for the g to come.	1887
	30:21	and his descendants for the g to come."	1887
	30:31	for the g to come.	1887
	31:13	between me and you for the g to come,	1887
	31:16	for the g to come as a lasting covenant.	1887
	40:15	that will continue for all g to come."	1887
Lev	3:17	a lasting ordinance for the g to come,	1887
	6:18	to the LORD by fire for the g to come.	1887
	7:36	as their regular share for the g to come.	1887
	10: 9	a lasting ordinance for the g to come,	1887
	17: 7	for them and for the g to come.'	1887
	21:17	'For the g to come none	1887
	22: 3	"Say to them: 'For the g to come,	1887
	23:14	to be a lasting ordinance for the g to come,	1887
	23:21	to be a lasting ordinance for the g to come,	1887
	23:31	to be a lasting ordinance for the g to come,	1887
	23:41	to be a lasting ordinance for the g to come;	1887
	24: 3	to be a lasting ordinance for the g to come.	1887
Nu	10: 8	for you and the g to come.	1887
	15:14	For the g to come,	1887
	15:15	this is a lasting ordinance for the g to come.	1887
	15:21	the g to come you are to give this offering	1887
	15:23	and continuing through the g to come—	1887
	15:38	the g to come you are to make tassels on	1887
	18:23	a lasting ordinance for the g to come.	1887
	35:29	for you throughout the g to come,	1887
Dt	5:10	to a thousand [g] of those who love me	NIH
	7: 9	to a thousand g of those who love him	1887
	29:22	Your children who follow you in later g	1887
	32: 7	consider the g long past.	1887+1887+2256+9102
Jos	22:27	be a witness between us and you and the g	1887
1Ch	16:15	the word he commanded, for a thousand g,	1887
Job	8: 8	"Ask the former g and find out	1887
Ps	22:30	future g will be told about the Lord.	1887
	33:11	the purposes of his heart through all g.	1887+1887+2256
	45:17	I will perpetuate your memory through all g;	1887+1887+2256
	49:11	their dwellings for endless g,	1887+1887+2256
	61: 6	his years for many g.	1887+1887+2256
	72: 5	as long as the moon, through all g.	1887+1887
	85: 5	Will you prolong your anger through all g?	1887+1887+2256
	89: 1	my mouth I will make your faithfulness known through all g.	1887+1887+2256
	89: 4	and make your throne firm through all g.' "	1887+1887+2256
	90: 1	you have been our dwelling place throughout all g.	1887+1887+2256
	100: 5	his faithfulness continues through all g.	1887+1887+2256
	102:12	your renown endures through all g.	1887+1887+2256
	102:24	your years go on through all g.	1887+1887
	105: 8	the word he commanded, for a thousand g,	1887
	106:31	as righteousness for endless g to come.	1887+1887+2256
	119:90	Your faithfulness continues through all g;	1887+1887+2256
	135:13	your renown, O LORD, through all g.	1887+1887+2256
	145:13	and your dominion endures through all g.	1887+1887+2256
	146:10	your God, O Zion, for all g.	1887+1887+2256
Pr	27:24	a crown is not secure for all g.	1887+1887+2256
Ecc	1: 4	G come and generations go,	1887
	1: 4	Generations come and go,	1887
Isa	13:20	be inhabited or lived in through all g;	1887+1887+2256
	41: 4	calling forth the g from the beginning?	1887
	51: 8	my salvation through all g."	1887+1887
	51: 9	awake, as in days gone by, as in g of old.	1887
	60:15	the everlasting pride and the joy of all g.	1887+1887+2256
	61: 4	that have been devastated for g.	1887+1887+2256
Joel	3:20	and Jerusalem through all g.	1887+1887+2256
Mt	1:17	Thus there were fourteen g in all	1155
Lk	1:48	From now on all g will call me blessed,	1155
Eph	3: 5	not made known to men in other g as it has	1155
	3:21	and in Christ Jesus throughout all g,	1155
Col	1:26	that has been kept hidden for ages and g,	1155

GENEROSITY (3) [GENEROUS]

2Co	8: 2	their extreme poverty welled up in rich g.	605
	9:11	and through us your g will result in thanksgiving to God.	4015S
	9:13	and for your g in sharing with them and	605

GENEROUS (9) [GENEROSITY, GENEROUSLY]

Ps	37:26	They are always g and lend freely;	2858
	112: 5	to him who is g and lends freely,	2858
Pr	11:25	A g man will prosper;	1388
	22: 9	A g man will himself be blessed,	3202+6524
Mt	20:15	Or are you envious because I am g?'	19
2Co	9: 5	for the g gift you had promised.	2330
	9: 5	Then it will be ready as a g gift,	2330
	9:11	so that you can be g on every occasion,	605
1Ti	6:18	and to be g and willing to share.	2331

GENEROUSLY (10) [GENEROUS]

Dt	15:10	**Give g** to him and do so without	5989+5989
1Ch	29:14	that we should be able to **give** as **g** as this?	5605
2Ch	31: 5	the Israelites **g** gave the firstfruits	8049
Ps	37:21	but the righteous give **g**;	2858
Ac	10: 2	he gave **g** to those in need and prayed	4498
Ro	12: 8	to the needs of others, let him give **g**;	605+1877
2Co	9: 6	sows **g** will also reap generously.	2093+2330
	9: 6	sows generously will also reap **g**.	2093+2330
Tit	3: 6	he poured out on us **g** through Jesus Christ	4455
Jas	1: 5	who gives **g** to all without finding fault,	607

GENITALS (1)

Eze	23:20	whose **g** were like those of donkeys	1414

GENNESARET (3)

Mt	14:34	they landed at **G**.	1166
Mk	6:53	they landed at **G** and anchored there.	1166
Lk	5: 1	as Jesus was standing by the Lake *of* **G**,	1166

GENTILE (11) [GENTILES]

Ezr	6:21	the unclean practices of their **G** neighbors	1580
Ne	5: 9	to avoid the reproach of our **G** enemies?	1580
Ac	10:28	for a Jew to associate with a **G** or visit him.	260
	15:23	To the **G** believers in Antioch,	1620+1666
	21:25	As for the **G** believers,	1620
Ro	1:16	first for the Jew, then *for* the **G**.	1818
	2: 9	first for the Jew, then for the **G**;	1818
	2:10	first for the Jew, then for the **G**.	1818
	10:12	there is no difference between Jew and **G**—	1818
Gal	2:14	yet you live **like a G** and not like a Jew.	1619
	2:15	Jews by birth and not "**G** sinners"	1620

GENTILES (93) [GENTILE]

Ne	5: 8	we have bought back our Jewish brothers	
		who were sold to the **G**.	1580
Isa	9: 1	in the future he will honor Galilee of the **G**,	1580
	42: 6	for the people and a light for the **G**,	1580
	49: 6	I will also make you a light for the **G**,	1580
	49:22	"See, I will beckon to the **G**,	1580
Mt	4:15	along the Jordan, Galilee of the **G**—	1620
	10: 5	"Do not go among the **G** or enter any town	1620
	10:18	as witnesses to them and *to* the **G**.	1620
	20:19	over *to* the **G** to be mocked and flogged	1620
	20:25	"You know that the rulers of the **G** lord it	1620
Mk	10:33	to death and will hand him over *to* the **G**,	1620
	10:42	as rulers *of* the **G** lord it over them,	1620
Lk	2:32	a light for revelation *to* the **G** and for glory	1620
	18:32	He will be handed over *to* the **G**.	1620
	21:24	be trampled on by the **G** until the times of	1620
	21:24	until the times *of* the **G** are fulfilled.	1620
	22:25	"The kings of the **G** lord it over them;	1620
Ac	4:27	and Pontius Pilate met together with the **G**	1620
	9:15	the **G** and their kings and before the people	1620
	10:45	Spirit had been poured out even on the **G**.	1620
	11: 1	the **G** also had received the word of God.	1620
	11:18	even the **G** repentance unto life."	1620
	13:16	of Israel and you **G** who worship God,	NIV
	13:26	and **you God-fearing G**,	2536+3836+5828
	13:46	we now turn to the **G**.	1620
	13:47	" 'I have made you a light *for* the **G**,	1620
	13:48	When the **G** heard this,	1620
	14: 1	a great number *of* Jews and **G** believed.	1818
	14: 2	up the **G** and poisoned their minds against	1620
	14: 5	There was a plot afoot *among* the **G**	1620
	14:27	opened the door of faith *to* the **G**.	1620
	15: 3	they told how the **G** had been converted.	1620
	15: 5	"**The G** must be circumcised and required	899S
	15: 7	the **G** might hear from my lips the message	1620
	15:12	and wonders God had done among the **G**	1620
	15:14	by taking from the **G** a people for himself.	1620
	15:17	and all the **G** who bear my name,	1620
	15:19	for the **G** who are turning to God.	1620
	18: 6	From now on I will go to the **G**."	1620
	21:11	and will hand him over to the **G**.' "	1620
	21:19	in detail what God had done among the **G**	1620
	21:21	among the **G** to turn away from Moses,	1620
	22:21	I will send you far away to the **G**.' "	1620
	26:17	from your own people and from the **G**.	1620
	26:20	and *to* the **G** also,	1620
	26:23	to his own people and *to* the **G**."	1620
	28:28	that God's salvation has been sent *to* the **G**,	1620
Ro	1: 5	from among all the **G** to the obedience	1620
	1:13	just as I have had among the other **G**.	1620
	2:14	(Indeed, when **G**, who do not have the law,	1620
	2:24	"God's name is blasphemed among the **G**	1620
	3: 9	the charge that Jews and **G** alike are all	1818
	3:29	Is he not the God *of* **G** too?	1620
	3:29	of Gentiles too? Yes, *of* **G** too,	1620
	9:24	only from the Jews but also from the **G**?	1620
	9:30	the **G**, who did not pursue righteousness	1620
	11:11	*to* the **G** to make Israel envious.	1620
	11:12	and their loss means riches *for* the **G**,	1620
	11:13	I am talking to you **G**.	1620
	11:13	Inasmuch as I am the apostle *to* the **G**,	1620
	11:25	until the full number *of* the **G** has come in.	1620
	15: 9	that the **G** may glorify God for his mercy,	1620
	15: 9	"Therefore I will praise you among the **G**;	1620
	15:10	it says, "Rejoice, *O* **G**, with his people."	1620
	15:11	And again, "Praise the Lord, all you **G**,	1620
	15:12	the **G** will hope in him."	1620
	15:16	the **G** with the priestly duty of proclaiming	1620
	15:16	the **G** might become an offering acceptable	1620
	15:18	through me in leading the **G** to obey God	1620

Ro	15:27	For if the **G** have shared in the Jews'	1620
	16: 4	the churches of the **G** are grateful to them.	1620
1Co	1: 23	to Jews and foolishness *to* **G**,	1620
2Co	11:26	my own countrymen, in danger from **G**;	1620
Gal	1:16	so that I might preach him among the **G**,	1620
	2: 2	the gospel that I preach among the **G**.	1620
	2: 7	the task of preaching the gospel *to* the **G**,	213
	2: 8	in my ministry as an apostle to the **G**.	1620
	2: 9	They agreed that we should go to the **G**,	1620
	2:12	he used to eat with the **G**.	1620
	2:12	from the **G** because he was afraid	NIG
	2:14	that you force **G** to follow Jewish customs?	1620
	3: 8	the **G** by faith, and announced the gospel	1620
	3:14	blessing given to Abraham might come to	
		the **G** through Christ Jesus,	1620
Eph	2:11	remember that formerly you who are **G**	1620
	3: 1	of Christ Jesus for the sake of you **G**—	1620
	3: 6	through the gospel the **G** are heirs together	1620
	3: 8	*to* the **G** the unsearchable riches of Christ,	1620
	4:17	that you must no longer live as the **G** do,	1620
Col	1:27	the **G** the glorious riches of this mystery,	1620
1Th	2:16	from speaking *to* the **G** so that they may	1620
1Ti	2: 7	and a teacher of the true faith *to* the **G**.	1620
2Ti	4:17	and all the **G** might hear it.	1620
Rev	11: 2	because it has been given *to* the **G**.	1620

GENTLE (18) [GENTLENESS, GENTLY]

Dt	28:54	Even the most **g** and sensitive man	8205
	28:56	most **g** and sensitive woman among you—	8205
	28:56	and **g** that she would not venture to touch	8204
2Sa	18: 5	"Be **g** with the young man Absalom	351
1Ki	19:12	And after the fire came a **g** whisper.	1987
Job	41: 3	Will he speak to you with **g** words?	8205
Pr	15: 1	A **g** answer turns away wrath,	8205
	25:15	and a **g** tongue can break a bone.	8205
Jer	11:19	like a **g** lamb led to the slaughter;	476
Zec	9: 9	**g** and riding on a donkey, on a colt,	6714
Mt	11:29	for I am **g** and humble in heart,	4558
	21: 5	**g** and riding on a donkey, on a colt,	4558
Ac	27:13	**g** south wind *began* to **blow**,	5710
1Co	4:21	or in love and with a **g** spirit?	4559
Eph	4: 2	Be completely humble and **g**;	4559
1Th	2: 7	but we were **g** among you,	2473
1Ti	3: 3	not violent but **g**, not quarrelsome,	2117
1Pe	3: 4	the unfading beauty *of* a **g** and quiet spirit,	4558

GENTLENESS (6) [GENTLE]

2Co	10: 1	By the meekness and **g** of Christ,	2117
Gal	5:23	**g** and self-control. Against such things	4559
Php	4: 5	Let your **g** be evident to all.	2117
Col	3:12	kindness, humility, **g** and patience.	4559
1Ti	6:11	godliness, faith, love, endurance and **g**.	4557
1Pe	3:15	But do this with **g** and respect,	4559

GENTLY (8) [GENTLE]

Job	15:11	words spoken **g** to you?	351+4200
	29:22	my words **fell g** on their ears.	5752
SS	7: 9	**flowing g** *over* lips and teeth.	1803
Isa	8: 6	the **g** flowing waters of Shiloah	351+4200
	40:11	*he* **g** leads those that have young.	5633
Gal	6: 1	you who are spiritual should restore him **g**.	1877+4460+4559
2Ti	2:25	who oppose him he must **g** instruct,	1877+4559
Heb	5: 2	*to* **deal g** with those who are ignorant	3584

GENUBATH (2)

1Ki	11:20	of Tahpenes bore him a son named **G**,	1707
	11:20	There **G** lived with Pharaoh's own children.	1707

GENUINE (3)

2Co	6: 8	**g**, yet regarded as impostors;	239
Php	2:20	who takes a **g** interest in your welfare.	1189
1Pe	1: 7	may be **proved g** and may result in praise,	1510

GERA (9)

Ge	46:21	Bela, Beker, Ashbel, **G**, Naaman, Ehi,	1733
Jdg	3:15	the son of **G** the Benjamite.	1733
2Sa	16: 5	His name was Shimei son of **G**,	1733
	19:16	Shimei son of **G**,	1733
	19:18	When Shimei son of **G** crossed the Jordan,	1733
1Ki	2: 8	you have with you Shimei son of **G**,	1733
1Ch	8: 3	The sons of Bela were: Addar, **G**, Abihud,	1733
	8: 5	**G**, Shephuphan and Huram.	1733
	8: 7	and **G**, who deported them and who was	1733

GERAHS (5)

Ex	30:13	sanctuary shekel, which weighs twenty **g**.	1743
Lev	27:25	sanctuary shekel, twenty **g** to the shekel.	1743
Nu	3:47	sanctuary shekel, which weighs twenty **g**.	1743
	18:16	sanctuary shekel, which weighs twenty **g**.	1743
Eze	45:12	The shekel is to consist of twenty **g**.	1743

GERAR (10)

Ge	10:19	of Canaan reached from Sidon toward **G**	1761
	20: 1	For a while he stayed in **G**,	1761
	20: 2	Then Abimelech king of **G** sent for Sarah	1761
	26: 1	to Abimelech king of the Philistines in **G**.	1761
	26: 6	So Isaac stayed in **G**.	1761
	26:17	in the Valley of **G** and settled there.	1761
	26:20	of **G** quarreled with Isaac's herdsmen	1761
	26:26	Abimelech had come to him from **G**,	1761
2Ch	14:13	Asa and his army pursued them as far as **G**.	1761

2Ch	14:14	They destroyed all the villages around **G**,	1761

GERASENES (3)

Mk	5: 1	across the lake to the region *of* the **G**.	*1170*
Lk	8:26	They sailed to the region *of* the **G**,	*1170*
	8:37	*of* the **G** asked Jesus to leave them,	*1170*

GERIZIM (4)

Dt	11:29	to proclaim on Mount **G** the blessings,	1748
	27:12	these tribes shall stand on Mount **G** to bless	1748
Jos	8:33	of the people stood in front of Mount **G**	1748
Jdg	9: 7	the top of Mount **G** and shouted to them,	1748

GERSHOM (7)

Ex	2:22	and Moses named him **G**, saying,	1768
	18: 3	One son was named **G**, for Moses said,	1768
Jdg	18:30	and Jonathan son of **G**, the son of Moses,	1768
1Ch	23:15	The sons of Moses: **G** and Eliezer.	1768
	23:16	descendants of **G**: Shubael was the first.	1768
	26:24	a descendant of **G** son of Moses,	1768
Ezr	8: 2	of the descendants of Phinehas, **G**;	1768

GERSHON (15) [GERSHONITE, GERSHONITES]

Ge	46:11	The sons of Levi: **G**, Kohath and Merari.	1767
Ex	6:16	**G**, Kohath and Merari.	1767
	6:17	The sons of **G**, by clans,	1767
Nu	3:17	**G**, Kohath and Merari.	1767
	3:21	To **G** belonged the clans of the Libnites	1767
	26:57	through **G**, the Gershonite clan;	1767
Jos	21: 6	of **G** were allotted thirteen towns from	1767
1Ch	6: 1	The sons of Levi: **G**, Kohath and Merari.	1767
	6:16	The sons of Levi: **G**, Kohath and Merari.	1768
	6:17	These are the names of the sons of **G**:	1768
	6:20	Of **G**: Libni his son,	1768
	6:43	the son of **G**, the son of Levi;	1768
	6:62	The descendants of **G**, clan by clan,	1768
	15: 7	from the descendants of **G**, Joel the leader	1768
	23: 6	**G**, Kohath and Merari.	1767

GERSHONITE (10) [GERSHON]

Nu	3:18	These were the names of the **G** clans:	1201+1767
	3:21	these were the **G** clans.	1769
	3:23	The **G** clans were to camp on the west,	1769
	4:24	the **g** clans as they work and carry burdens:	1769
	4:28	of the **G** clans at the Tent of Meeting.	1201+1769
	4:41	the total of those in the **G** clans	1201+1767
	26:57	through Gershon, the **G** clan;	1769
Jos	21:33	All the towns of the **G** clans were thirteen,	1769
1Ch	26:21	of families belonging to Ladan the **G**,	1769
	29: 8	the LORD in the custody of Jehiel the **G**.	1769

GERSHONITES (12) [GERSHON]

Nu	3:24	of the families of the **G** was Eliasaph son	1769
	3:25	the **G** were responsible for the care of	1201+1767
	4:22	of the **G** by their families and clans.	1201+1767
	4:26	The **G** are to do all that needs to be done	NIH
	4:38	The **G** were counted by their clans	1201+1767
	7: 7	gave two carts and four oxen to the **G**,	1201+1767
	10:17	the **G** and Merarites, who carried it,	1201+1767
Jos	21:27	The Levite clans of the **G** were given:	1201+1767
1Ch	6:71	The **G** received the following:	1201+1768
	23: 7	Belonging to the **G**: Ladan and Shimei.	1769
	26:21	who were **G** through Ladan.	1201+1769
2Ch	29:12	the **G**, Joah son of Zimmah and Eden son	1769

GERUTH KIMHAM (1) [KIMHAM]

Jer	41:17	at **G** near Bethlehem on their way	1745

GESHAN (1)

1Ch	2:47	The sons of Jahdai: Regem, Jotham, **G**,	1642

GESHEM (4)

Ne	2:19	Tobiah the Ammonite official and **G**	1774
	6: 1	**G** the Arab and the rest of our enemies	1774
	6: 2	Sanballat and **G** sent me this message:	1774
	6: 6	and **G** says it is true—	1776

GESHUR (11) [GESHURITES]

Jos	12: 5	the border of the **people of G** and Maacah,	1771
	13:11	of the **people of G** and Maacah, all	1771
	13:13	not drive out the **people of G** and Maacah,	1771
2Sa	3: 3	of Maacah daughter of Talmai king of **G**;	1770
	13:37	the king of **G**.	1770
	13:38	After Absalom fled and went to **G**,	1770
	14:23	to **G** and brought Absalom back	1770
	14:32	"Why have I come from **G**?	1770
	15: 8	While your servant was living at **G**	1770
1Ch	2:23	(But **G** and Aram captured Havvoth Jair,	1770
	3: 2	of Maacah daughter of Talmai king of **G**;	1770

GESHURITES (3) [GESHUR]

Dt	3:14	as the border of the **G** and the Maacathites;	1771
Jos	13: 2	all the regions of the Philistines and **G**;	1771
1Sa	27: 8	and his men went up and raided the **G**,	1771

GET (312) [GETS, GETTING, GOT, ILL-GOTTEN]

Ge	18: 5	*Let me* **g** you something to eat,	4374

Ge	18: 6	"g three seahs of fine flour and knead it	NIH
	19: 9	"G out of our way," they replied.	5602
	19:12	G them out of here,	3655
	19:14	He said, "Hurry and g out of this place,	3655
	19:32	Let's g our father to drink wine	9197
	19:34	Let's g him to drink wine again tonight,	9197
	21:10	"G rid of that slave woman and her son,	1763
	24: 3	that you will not g a wife for my son from	4374
	24: 4	to my country and my own relatives and g	4374
	24: 7	so that you can g a wife for my son	4374
	24:37	not a wife for my son from the daughters	4374
	24:38	and g a wife for my son.'	4374
	24:40	so that you can g a wife for my son	4374
	24:48	on the right road to g the granddaughter	4374
	27: 3	Now then, g your weapons—	5951
	27:13	Just do what I say; go and g them for me."	4374
	29:20	So Jacob served seven years to g Rachel,	928
	34: 4	"G me this girl as my wife."	4374
	35: 2	"G rid of the foreign gods you have	6073
	38:20	the Adullamite in order to g his pledge back	4374
	40:14	to Pharaoh and g me out of this prison.	3655
	42:16	of your number to g your brother;	4374
	42: 7	of them opened his sack to g feed	5989
	45:19	and g your father and come.	5951
	46:28	of him to Joseph to g directions to Goshen.	3723
Ex	2: 5	the reeds and sent her slave girl to g it.	4374
	2: 7	and g one of the Hebrew women to nurse	7924
	5: 4	G back to your work!"	2143
	5:11	g your own straw wherever you can find it,	4374
	5:18	Now g to work.	2143
	7:24	along the Nile to g drinking water,	AIT
	8:20	"G up early in the morning	8899
	9:13	"G up early in the morning	8899
	10:26	and until we g there we will	995
	10:28	Pharaoh said to Moses, "G out of my sight!	2143
	14:25	"Let's g away from the Israelites!	5674
	16:24	and it did not stink or g maggots in it.	2118
	23:11	the poor among your people may g food	430
	32:25	that Aaron had let them g out of control	7277
Nu	11:13	Where can I g meat for all these people?	5989
	16:10	but now you are trying to g the priesthood	1335
	16:45	"G away from this assembly so I can put	8250
	17: 2	the Israelites and twelve staffs from them,	4374
	20:25	G Aaron and his son Eleazar and take them	4374
	22:23	Balaam beat her to g her back on the road.	5742
Dt	2:13	"Now g up and cross the Zered Valley."	7756
	6: 7	when you lie down and when you g up.	7756
	11:19	when you lie down and when you g up.	7756
	17:16	make the people return to Egypt to g more	8049
	22: 4	Help him g it to its feet.	7756+7756
	24:10	into his house to g what he is offering as	6292
	24:19	do not go back to g it.	4374
	30:12	into heaven to g it and proclaim it to us	4374
	30:13	the sea to g it and proclaim it to us	4374
Jos	1: 2	g ready to cross the Jordan River into	7756
	1:11	'G your supplies ready.	3922
	18: 7	however, do not g a portion among you,	4200
	22:26	'Let us g ready and build an altar—	6913
Jdg	1:24	"Show us how to g into the city	4427
	7: 9	"G up, go down against the camp,	7756
	7:15	to the camp of Israel and called out, "G up!	7756
	7:17	When I g to the edge of the camp,	995
	9:29	Then I would g rid of him.	6073
	11: 2	"You are not going to g any inheritance	5706
	11: 5	of Gilead went to g Jephthah from the land	4374
	14: 2	now g her for me as my wife."	4374
	14: 3	the uncircumcised Philistines to g a wife?"	4374
	14: 3	Samson said to his father, "G her for me.	4374
	15: 3	have a right to g even	5927
	15: 7	I won't stop until I g my revenge on you."	5933
	16:28	let me with one blow g revenge on the Philistines for my two eyes."	5933+5934
	16:31	family went down to g him.	5951
	18:10	When you g there,	995
	19: 9	Early tomorrow morning you can g up	8899
	19:28	He said to her, "G up; let's go."	7756
	20:10	to g provisions for the army.	4374
	21:22	we did not g wives for them during the war,	4374
Ru	2: 9	go and g a drink from the water jars	9272
1Sa	1:14	G rid of your wine.	6073
	6: 7	"Now then, g a new cart ready,	4374
	9:26	on the roof, "G ready, and I will send you	7756
	18: 8	What more can he g but the kingdom?"	4200
	19:17	"He said to me, 'Let me g away.	8938
	20:29	let me g away to see my brothers.'	4880
	23:26	hurrying to get away from Saul.	2143
	24:19	does he let him g away unharmed?	928+2006+8938
	26:11	Now g the spear and water jug that are	4374
	26:22	of your young men come over and g it.	4374
	29:10	Now g up early,	8899
2Sa	2:14	the young men g up and fight hand to hand	7756
	4: 6	of the house as if to g some wheat,	4374
	5: 6	"You will not g in here;	995
	5: 6	They thought, "David cannot g in here."	995
	11: 4	Then David sent messengers to g her.	4374
	11:20	'Why did you g so close to the city	5602
	11:21	Why did you g so close to the wall?'	5602
	12:17	beside him to g him up from the ground,	7756
	12:21	you g up and eat!"	7756
	13:13	Where could I g rid of my disgrace?	2143
	13:15	Amnon said to her, "Get up and get out!"	7756
	13:15	Amnon said to her, "Get up and g out!"	2143
	13:17	"G this woman out of here and	2021+2025+2575+8938
	14: 7	then we will g rid of the heir as well.'	9012
	15: 2	He would g up early and stand by the side	8899

2Sa	16: 7	As he cursed, Shimei said, "G out, get out,	3655
	16: 7	As he cursed, Shimei said, "Get out, g out,	3655
	20:18	'G your answer at Abel,' and that settled it.	8626+8626
	23:15	that someone would g me a drink of water	9197
1Ki	12:18	managed to g into his chariot and escape	6590
	17:11	As she was going to g it, he called,	4374
	18:23	G two bulls for us.	5989
	18:40	Don't let anyone g away!"	4880
	19: 5	"G up and eat."	7756
	19: 7	"G up and eat,	7756
	19:15	you g there, anoint Hazael king over Aram.	995
	20:33	"Go and g him," the king said.	4374
	21: 7	G up and eat!	7756
	21: 7	I'll g you the vineyard of Naboth	5989
	21:15	"G up and take possession of the vineyard	7756
	22:34	around and g me out of the fighting.	3655
2Ki	4:41	Elisha said, "G some flour."	4374
	5:20	after him and g something from him."	4374
	6: 2	where each of us can g a pole;	4374
	6:27	where can I g help for you?	3828
	7:12	and then we will take them alive and g into	995
	9: 2	When you g there,	995
	9: 2	g him away from his companions	7756
	9:17	"G a horseman," Joram ordered.	4374
	13:15	Elisha said, "G a bow and some arrows,"	4374
	22: 4	the high priest and have him g ready	9462
1Ch	11: 5	"You will not g in here."	995
	11:17	that someone would g me a drink of water	9197
2Ch	10:18	managed to g into his chariot and escape	6590
	18:33	around and g me out of the fighting.	3655
Ne	2: 6	and when will you g back?"	8740
	2:14	for my mount to g through;	6296
	5: 2	to eat and stay alive, we must g grain."	4374
	5: 3	our vineyards and our homes to g grain	4374
	6: 7	Now this report will g back to the king;	9048
	6: 9	"Their hands will g too weak for the work,	AIT
Est	6:10	"G the robe and the horse and do just	4374
	9:16	to protect themselves and g relief	5663
Job	7: 4	'How long before I g up?'	7756
	15:31	for he will g nothing in return.	2118
	19: 7	I g no response;	6699
	19:22	Will you never g enough of my flesh?	8425
	33:27	but I did not g what I deserved."	8750
	36: 3	I g my knowledge from afar;	5951
Ps	39: 6	not knowing which will g it.	665
	41: 8	he will never g up from the place	7756
Pr	1: 5	and let the discerning g guidance—	7864
	1:13	we will g all sorts of valuable things	5162
	1:19	it takes away the lives of those who g it.	1251
	4: 5	G wisdom, get understanding;	7864
	4: 5	Get wisdom, g understanding;	7864
	4: 7	Wisdom is supreme; therefore g wisdom.	7864
	4: 7	it cost all you have, g understanding.	7864
	6: 9	When will you g up from your sleep?	7756
	16:16	How much better to g wisdom than gold,	7864
	16:16	since he has no desire to g wisdom?	7864
	22:25	and g yourself ensnared.	4374
	23: 4	Do not wear yourself out to g rich;	AIT
	23:23	g wisdom, discipline and understanding.	NIH
	24:27	and g your fields ready;	6963
	28:20	one eager to g rich will not go unpunished.	6947
	28:22	A stingy man is eager to g rich	NIH
Ecc	2:22	a man g for all the toil and anxious striving	2093
	8:14	righteous men who g what	5595
	8:14	and wicked men who g what	5595
SS	3: 2	I will g up now and go about the city,	7756
Isa	1:24	"Ah, I will g relief from my foes	5714
	21: 5	G up, you officers, oil the shields!	7756
	30:11	Leave this way, g off this path,	5742
	35: 9	nor will any ferocious beast g up on it;	6590
	56:12	"Come," each one cries, "let me g wine!	4374
Jer	1:17	"G yourself ready!	273+5516
	8: 4	" 'When men fall down, do they not g up?	7756
	13: 6	"Go now to Perath and g the belt I told you	4374
	25:27	Drink, g drunk and vomit,	8910
	28:13	but in its place you will g a yoke of iron.	6913
	35: 3	So I went to g Jaazaniah son of Jeremiah,	4374
	36:21	The king sent Jehudi to g the scroll,	4374
	37:12	g his share of the property	2745
	46:11	"Go up to Gilead and g balm,	4374
	46:14	'Take your positions and g ready,	3922
	46:16	They will say, 'G up,	7756
	51: 8	G balm for her pain;	4374
	51:61	"When you g to Babylon,	995
La	3:44	a cloud so that no prayer can g through.	6296
	5: 6	to Egypt and Assyria to g enough bread.	8425
	5: 9	We g our bread at the risk of our lives	995
Eze	3:22	"G up and go out to the plain,	7756
	7:14	the trumpet and g everything ready,	3922
	7:26	They will try to g a vision from	1335
	17:15	by sending him envoys to Egypt to g horses	5989
	18:31	and g a new heart and a new spirit.	6913
	20: 7	And I said to them, "Each of you, g rid of	8959
	20: 8	they did not g rid of the vile images	8959
	38: 7	" 'G ready; be prepared,	3922
Da	7: 5	'G up and eat your fill of flesh!'	10624
Hos	12:12	Israel served to g a wife,	928
Am	2:15	the fleet-footed soldier will not g away,	4880
	4: 8	for water but did not g enough to drink,	8425
	7:12	Amaziah said to Amos, "G out, you seer!	2143
	9: 1	Not one will g away, none will escape.	5674+5674
Jnh	1: 6	G up and call on your god!	7756
Mic	2:10	G up, go away!	7756
Zep	2:10	This is what they will g in return	4200
Mt	2:13	"G up," he said, "take the child	1586
	2:20	"G up, take the child and his mother and go	1586

Mt	5:26	you will not g out until you have paid	2002
	5:46	what reward will you g?	2400
	9: 5	or to say, 'G up and walk'?	1586
	9: 6	Then he said to the paralytic, "G up,	1586
	13:54	"Where did this man g this wisdom	NIG
	13:56	then did this man g all these things?"	NIG
	14:22	Immediately Jesus made the disciples g	1832
	15:33	"Where could we g enough bread	NIG
	16:23	and said to Peter, "G behind me, Satan!	5632
	17: 7	"G up," he said.	1586
	19:16	what good thing must I do to g eternal life?"	2400
	22:12	'how did you g in here	1656
	24:18	in the field go back to g his cloak.	149
	24:32	As soon as its twigs g tender	1181
Mk	2: 4	not g him to Jesus because of the crowd,	1586
	2: 9	or to say, 'G up, take your mat and walk'?	1586
	2:11	g up, take your mat and go home."	1586
	5:41	"Little girl, I say to you, g up!").	1586
	6: 2	"Where did this man g these things?"	NIG
	6:31	to a quiet place and g some rest."	399
	6:45	Immediately Jesus made his disciples g	1832
	8: 4	this remote place can anyone g enough bread	NIG
	8:33	"G behind me, Satan!"	5632
	13:16	in the field go back to g his cloak.	149
	13:28	As soon as its twigs g tender	1181
	15:24	they cast lots to see what each would g.	149
	16:18	and they will g well."	2400
Lk	5:23	or to say, 'G up and walk'?	1586
	5:24	g up, take your mat and go home."	1586
	6: 8	"G up and stand in front of everyone."	1586
	6:35	without expecting to g anything back.	594
	7:14	He said, "Young man, I say to you, g up!"	1586
	8:19	but they were not able to g near him	5344
	8:54	by the hand and said, "My child, g up!"	1586
	9:52	into a Samaritan village to g things ready	2286
	11: 7	I can't g up and give you anything.'	482
	11: 8	though he will not g up and give him	482
	11: 8	because of the man's boldness he will g up	1586
	12:20	Then who will g what you have prepared	1639
	12:45	and to eat and drink and g drunk.	3499
	12:47	and does not g ready or does	2286
	12:59	you will not g out until you have paid	2002
	14:24	of those men who were invited will g a taste	1174
	17: 8	g yourself ready and wait on me	4322
	17:31	should go down to g them.	149
	18: 8	I tell you, he will see that they g justice,	4472
	18:12	a week and give a tenth of all I g.'	3227
	21:21	let those in the city g out,	1774
	22: 2	for some way to g rid of Jesus,	359
	22:46	"G up and pray so that you will not fall	482
Jn	2:16	"G these out of here!	149
	4:11	Where can you g this living water?	2400
	4:15	give me this water so that I won't g thirsty	1498
	5: 6	he asked him, "Do you want to g well?"	1181
	5: 8	While I am trying to g in,	2262
	5: 8	Then Jesus said to him, "G up!	1586
	6:25	"Rabbi, when did you g here?"	1181
	7:15	"How did this man g such learning	1207+3857
	11:12	"Lord, if he sleeps, he will g better."	5392
	19:24	"Let's decide by lot who will g it."	NIG
	20:15	and I will g him."	149
Ac	3: 5	expecting to g something from them.	3284
	9: 6	"Now g up and go into the city,	482
	9:34	G up and take care of your mat."	482
	9:40	he said, "Tabitha, g up."	482
	10:13	Then a voice told him, "G up, Peter.	482
	10:20	So g up and go downstairs.	482
	10:26	But Peter made him g up.	1586
	11: 7	I heard a voice telling me, 'G up, Peter.	482
	12: 7	"Quick, g up!"	482
	16:37	now do they want to g rid of us quietly?	1675
	21:34	not g at the truth because of the uproar,	855+1182
	22:10	" 'G up,' the Lord said,	482
	22:16	G up, be baptized and wash your sins away,	482
	23:23	"G ready a detachment	2286
	23:35	when your accusers g here."	4134
	26:16	'Now g up and stand on your feet.	482
	27:43	to jump overboard first and g to land.	1996
	27:44	The rest were to g there on planks or	NIG
1Co	5: 7	G rid of the old yeast that you may be	1705
	7:36	They should g married.	1138
	9:13	in the temple g their food from the temple,	2266
	9:24	Run in such a way as to g the prize.	2898
	9:25	They do it to g a crown that will not last;	3284
	9:25	we do it to g a crown that will last forever.	NIG
	14: 8	who will g ready for battle?	4186
2Co	10:14	for we did g as far as you with the gospel	5777
Gal	1:18	I went up to Jerusalem to g acquainted with Peter	2707
	4:30	"G rid of the slave woman and her son,	1675
Eph	4:31	G rid of all bitterness, rage and anger,	149
	5:18	Do not g drunk on wine,	3499
1Th	5: 7	and those who g drunk, get drunk at night.	3499
	5: 7	and those who get drunk, g drunk at night.	3501
1Ti	5:13	g into the habit of being idle	3443
	6: 9	to g rich fall into temptation and a trap and	4456
2Ti	3: 9	But they will not g very far	2093+4498+4621
	4:11	G Mark and bring him with you,	377
	4:21	Do your best to g here before winter.	2262
Jas	1:21	g rid of all moral filth and the evil that is	700
	4: 2	You want something but don't g it.	2400
	4: 3	that you may spend what you g	NIG

GETHER (2)

Ge	10:23	Uz, Hul, G and Meshech.	1788
1Ch	1:17	Uz, Hul, G and Meshech.	1788

GETHSEMANE (2)

Mt	26:36	with his disciples to a place called **G**,	*1149*
Mk	14:32	They went to a place called **G**,	*1149*

GETS (18) [GET]

Ex	21:19	if the other **g** up and walks around outside	7756
	21:21	to be punished if the slave **g** up after a day	6641
2Sa	15: 4	see that he **g** justice."	7405
Pr	13: 4	The sluggard craves and **g** nothing,	AIT
	19: 8	*He who* **g** wisdom loves his own soul;	7864
	21:10	his neighbor **g** no mercy from him.	2858
	21:11	a wise man is instructed, *he* **g** knowledge.	4374
	29:26	it is from the LORD that man **g** justice.	NIH
	31:15	*She* **g** up while it is still dark;	7756
Isa	44:12	*He* **g** hungry and loses his strength;	AIT
Mt	28:14	If this report **g** to the governor,	*NIG*
Mk	4:27	Night and day, whether he sleeps or **g** up,	*1586*
Lk	13:25	the owner of the house **g** up and closes	*1586*
	18: 5	see that she **g** justice,	*1688*
Ac	23:15	We are ready to kill him before he **g** here."	*1581*
1Co	9:24	but only one **g** the prize?	3284
	11:21	One remains hungry, another **g** drunk.	3501
2Ti	2: 4	No one serving as a soldier **g** involved in	AIT

GETTING (13) [GET]

Jdg	3:13	**G** the Ammonites and Amalekites *to* join	AIT
1Sa	1:14	"How long *will you* keep on **g** drunk?	8910
1Ki	16: 9	**g** drunk in the home of Arza,	8893+9272
	20:16	with him were in their tents **g** drunk.	8893+9272
Jnh	1:11	The sea *was* **g** rougher and rougher.	AIT
Mt	14:15	and *it's* already **g** late.	4216
	27:24	Pilate saw that *he* was **g** nowhere,	4029+6067
Mk	5:18	As Jesus *was* **g** into the boat,	1832
	5:26	yet instead of **g** better she grew worse.	6067
Lk	23:41	for *we are* **g** what our deeds deserve.	655
Jn	12:19	"See, *this is* **g** us nowhere.	4024+4029+6067
1Co	7:36	and if she is **g** along in years	5644
3Jn	1: 2	even as your soul is **g** along well.	2338

GEUEL (1)

Nu	13:15	from the tribe of Gad, **G** son of Maki.	1451

GEZER (14)

Jos	10:33	of **G** had come up to help Lachish,	1618
	12:12	the king of Eglon one the king of **G** one	1618
	16: 3	of Lower Beth Horon and on to **G**,	1618
	16:10	not dislodge the Canaanites living in **G**;	1618
	21:21	for one accused of murder) and **G**,	1618
Jdg	1:29	the Canaanites living in **G**,	1618
2Sa	5:25	the way from Gibeon to **G**.	1618
1Ki	9:15	and Hazor, Megiddo and **G**.	1618
	9:16	of Egypt had attacked and captured **G**.	1618
	9:17	And Solomon rebuilt **G**.)	1618
1Ch	6:67	(a city of refuge), and **G**,	1618
	7:28	**G** and its villages to the west,	1618
	14:16	all the way from Gibeon to **G**.	1618
	20: 4	war broke out with the Philistines, at **G**.	1618

GEZRITES (KJV) See GIRZITES

GHOST (4) [GHOSTLIKE]

Mt	14:26	"It's a **g**," they said, and cried out in fear.	5753
Mk	6:49	they thought he was a **g**.	5753
Lk	24:37	thinking they saw a **g**.	4460
	24:39	a **g** does not have flesh and bones,	4460

[GIVE UP THE] GHOST (KJV) See
BREATHED HIS LAST, DIE, DIED, DYING
GASP, GAVE UP HIS SPIRIT, PERISHED

[HOLY] GHOST (KJV) See [HOLY] SPIRIT

GHOSTLIKE (1) [GHOST]

Isa	29: 4	Your voice will come **g** from the earth;	200+3869

GIAH (1)

2Sa	2:24	near **G** on the way to the wasteland	1632

GIANT (KJV) See RAPHA, REPHAITES,
WARRIOR

GIBBAR (1)

Ezr	2:20	of **G** 95	1507

GIBBETHON (5)

Jos	19:44	Eltekeh, **G**, Baalath,	1510
	21:23	the tribe of Dan they received Eltekeh, **G**,	1510
1Ki	15:27	and he struck him down at **G**,	1510
	16:15	The army was encamped near **G**,	1510
	16:17	with him withdrew from **G** and laid siege	1510

GIBEA (1) [GIBEATHITE]

1Ch	2:49	to Sheva the father of Macbenah and **G**.	1495

GIBEAH (48)

Jos	15:57	Kain, **G** and Timnah—	1497
Jos	18:28	(that is, Jerusalem), **G** and Kiriath—	1497
	24:33	of Aaron died and was buried at **G**,	1497
Jdg	19:12	We will go on to **G**."	1497
	19:13	to reach **G** or Ramah and spend the night	1497
	19:14	the sun set as they neared **G** in Benjamin.	1497
	19:16	who was living in **G** (the men of	1497
	20: 4	and my concubine came to **G** in Benjamin	1497
	20: 5	the night the men of **G** came after me	1497
	20: 9	But now this is what we'll do to **G**:	1497
	20:10	when the army arrives at **G** in Benjamin,	1497
	20:13	Now surrender those wicked men of **G** so	1497
	20:14	From their towns they came together at **G**	1497
	20:15	from those living in **G**.	1497
	20:19	up and pitched camp near **G**.	1497
	20:20	up battle positions against them at **G**.	1497
	20:21	The Benjamites came out of **G** and cut	1497
	20:25	when the Benjamites came out from **G**	1497
	20:29	Then Israel set an ambush around **G**.	1497
	20:30	against **G** as they had done before.	1497
	20:31	to Bethel and the other to **G**,	1497
	20:33	of its place on the west of **G**.	1497
	20:34	a frontal attack on **G**.	1497
	20:36	on the ambush they had set near **G**.	1497
	20:37	in ambush made a sudden dash into **G**,	1497
	20:43	and easily overran them in the vicinity of **G**	1497
1Sa	10: 5	"After that you will go to **G** *of* God,	1497
	10:10	When they arrived at **G**,	1497
	10:26	Saul also went to his home in **G**,	1497
	11: 4	When the messengers came to **G** *of* Saul	1497
	13: 2	and a thousand were with Jonathan at **G**	1497
	13:15	Then Samuel left Gilgal and went up to **G**	1497
	13:16	with them were staying in **G** *in* Benjamin,	1497
	14: 2	the outskirts of **G** under a pomegranate tree	1497
	14:16	Saul's lookouts at **G** *in* Benjamin saw	1497
	15:34	but Saul went up to his home in **G** *of* Saul.	1497
	22: 6	under the tamarisk tree on the hill at **G**,	1497
	23:19	The Ziphites went up to Saul at **G** and said,	1497
	26: 1	The Ziphites went to Saul at **G** and said,	1497
2Sa	21: 6	and exposed before the LORD at **G**	1497
	23:29	Ithai son of Ribai from **G** *in* Benjamin,	1497
1Ch	11:31	Ithai son of Ribai from **G** *in* Benjamin,	1497
2Ch	13: 2	a daughter of Uriel of **G**.	1497
Isa	10:29	Ramah trembles; **G** *of* Saul flees.	1497
Hos	5: 8	"Sound the trumpet in **G**,	1497
	9: 9	as in the days of **G**.	1497
	10: 9	"Since the days of **G**, you have sinned,	1497
	10: 9	Did not war overtake the evildoers in **G**?	1497

GIBEATH HAARALOTH (1)

Jos	5: 3	the Israelites at **G**.	1502

GIBEATHITE (1) [GIBEA]

1Ch	12: 3	and Joash the sons of Shemaah the **G**;	1503

GIBEON (40) [GIBEONITE, GIBEONITES]

Jos	9: 3	of **G** heard what Joshua had done to Jericho	1500
	9:17	**G**, Kephirah, Beeroth and Kiriath Jearim.	1500
	10: 1	of **G** had made a treaty of peace with Israel	1500
	10: 2	because **G** was an important city,	1500
	10: 4	"Come up and help me attack **G**," he said,	1500
	10: 5	up positions against **G** and attacked it.	1500
	10:10	who defeated them in a great victory at **G**.	1500
	10:12	"O sun, stand still over **G**, O moon,	1500
	10:41	and from the whole region of Goshen to **G**.	1500
	11:19	Except for the Hivites living in **G**,	1500
	18:25	**G**, Ramah, Beeroth,	1500
	21:17	the tribe of Benjamin they gave them **G**,	1500
2Sa	2:12	left Mahanaim and went to **G**.	1500
	2:13	and met them at the pool of **G**.	1500
	2:16	in **G** was called Helkath Hazzurim.	1500
	2:24	on the way to the wasteland of **G**.	1500
	3:30	killed their brother Asahel in the battle at **G**.	1500
	5:25	the Philistines all the way from **G** to Gezer.	1500
	20: 8	While they were at the great rock in **G**,	1500
1Ki	3: 4	The king went to **G** to offer sacrifices,	1500
	3: 5	At **G** the LORD appeared to Solomon	1500
	9: 2	as he had appeared to him at **G**.	1500
1Ch	6:60	the tribe of Benjamin they were given **G**,	1500
	8:29	Jeiel the father of **G** lived in Gibeon.	1500
	8:29	Jeiel the father of Gibeon lived in **G**.	1500
	9:35	Jeiel the father of **G** lived in Gibeon.	1500
	9:35	Jeiel the father of Gibeon lived in **G**.	1500
	14:16	all the way from **G** to Gezer.	1500
	16:39	of the LORD at the high place in **G**	1500
	21:29	at that time on the high place at **G**.	1500
2Ch	1: 3	to the high place at **G**,	1500
	1: 5	in **G** in front of the tabernacle of	NIH
	1:13	to Jerusalem from the high place at **G**,	1500
Ne	3: 7	repairs were made by men from **G**	1500
	3: 7	Melatiah of **G** and Jadon of Meronoth—	1498
	7:25	of **G** 95	1500
Isa	28:21	he will rouse himself as in the Valley of **G**	1500
Jer	28: 1	who was from **G**, said to me in the house	1500
	41:12	up with him near the great pool in **G**.	1500
	41:16	and court officials he had brought from **G**.	1500

GIBEONITE (1) [GIBEON]

1Ch	12: 4	and Ishmaiah the **G**, a mighty man among	1498

GIBEONITES (10) [GIBEON]

Jos	9:16	after they made the treaty with **the G**,	2157S
	9:22	Then Joshua summoned the **G** and said,	2157S
	9:27	That day he made the **G** woodcutters	4392S
	10: 6	The **G** then sent word to Joshua in	408+1500

2Sa	21: 1	it is because he put the **G** to death."	1498
	21: 2	The king summoned the **G** and spoke	1498
	21: 2	(Now the **G** were not a part of Israel	1498
	21: 3	David asked the **G**,	1498
	21: 4	The **G** answered him,	1498
	21: 9	He handed them over to the **G**,	1498

GIBLITES (KJV) See GEBALITES

GIDDALTI (2)

1Ch	25: 4	Hanani, Eliathah, **G** and Romamti-Ezer;	1547
	25:29	the twenty-second to **G**,	1547

GIDDEL (4)

Ezr	2:47	**G**, Gahar, Reaiah,	1543
	2:56	Jaala, Darkon, **G**,	1543
Ne	7:49	Hanan, **G**, Gahar,	1543
	7:58	Jaala, Darkon, **G**,	1543

GIDEON (47) [GIDEON'S, JERUB-BAAL]

Jdg	6:11	where his son **G** was threshing wheat in	1549
	6:12	the angel of the LORD appeared to **G**,	2257S
	6:13	**G** replied, "if the LORD is with us,	1549
	6:15	**G** asked, "how can I save Israel?	NIH
	6:17	**G** replied, "If now I have found favor	NIH
	6:19	**G** went in, prepared a young goat,	1549
	6:20	And **G** did so.	NIH
	6:22	**G** realized that it was the angel of the LORD,	1549
	6:24	So **G** built an altar to the LORD there	1549
	6:27	So **G** took ten of his servants and did as	1549
	6:29	they were told, "**G** son of Joash did it."	1549
	6:32	So that day they called **G** "Jerub-Baal,"	2257S
	6:34	the Spirit of the LORD came upon **G**,	1549
	6:36	**G** said to God, "If you will save Israel	1549
	6:38	**G** rose early the next day;	NIH
	6:39	**G** said to God, "Do not be angry with me.	1549
	7: 1	**G**) and all his men camped at the spring	1549
	7: 2	The LORD said to **G**,	1549
	7: 4	But the LORD said to **G**,	1549
	7: 5	So **G** took the men down to the water.	1549
	7: 7	The LORD said to **G**,	1549
	7: 8	So **G** sent the rest of the Israelites	NIH
	7: 9	During that night the LORD said to **G**,	2257S
	7:13	**G** arrived just as a man was telling	1549
	7:14	be nothing other than the sword of **G** son	1549
	7:15	When **G** heard the dream	1549
	7:18	'For the LORD and for **G**.' "	1549
	7:19	**G** and the hundred men with him reached	1549
	7:20	"A sword for the LORD and for **G**!"	1549
	7:24	**G** sent messengers throughout	1549
	7:25	the heads of Oreb and Zeeb to **G**,	1549
	8: 1	Now the Ephraimites asked **G**,	2257S
	8: 4	**G** and his three hundred men,	1549
	8: 7	Then **G** replied, "Just for that,	1549
	8:11	**G** went up by the route of the nomads east	1549
	8:13	**G** son of Joash then returned from	1549
	8:15	**G** came and said to the men of Succoth,	NIH
	8:19	**G** replied, "Those were my brothers,	NIH
	8:21	So **G** stepped forward and killed them,	1549
	8:22	The Israelites said to **G**, "Rule over us—	1549
	8:23	But **G** told them, "I will not rule over you,	1549
	8:27	**G** made the gold into an ephod,	1549
	8:27	and it became a snare to **G** and his family.	1549
	8:32	**G** son of Joash died at a good old age	1549
	8:33	No sooner had **G** died than	1549
	8:35	**G**) for all the good things he had done	1549
Heb	11:32	I do not have time to tell about **G**, Barak,	*1146*

GIDEON'S (1) [GIDEON]

Jdg	8:28	not raise its head again. During **G** lifetime,	1549

GIDEONI (5)

Nu	1:11	from Benjamin, Abidan son of **G**;	1551
	2:22	the people of Benjamin is Abidan son of **G**.	1551
	7:60	On the ninth day Abidan son of **G**,	1551
	7:65	This was the offering of Abidan son of **G**.	1551
	10:24	and Abidan son of **G** was over the division	1551

GIDOM (1)

Jdg	20:45	after the Benjamites as far as **G** and struck	1550

GIER (KJV) See OSPREY

GIFT (83) [GIFTED, GIFTS]

Ge	30:20	"God has presented me with a precious **g**.	2273
	32:13	from what he had with him he selected a **g**	4966
	32:18	They are a **g** sent to my lord Esau.	4966
	33:10	accept this **g** from me.	4966
	34:12	and the **g** I am to bring as great as you like,	5508
	43:11	and take them down to the man as a **g**—	4966
Lev	2: 1	a **g** for a burnt offering to the LORD,	7933
Nu	18: 6	from among the Israelites as a **g** to you,	5510
	18: 7	the service of the priesthood as a **g**.	5510
	31:52	that Moses and Eleazar presented as a **g** to	9556
Dt	16:17	Each of you must bring a **g** in proportion to	5510
1Sa	9: 7	We have no **g** to take to the man of God.	9593
	25:27	And let this **g**, which you servant has	1388
2Sa	11: 8	and a **g** *from* the king was sent after him.	5368
1Ki	9:16	then gave it as a wedding **g** to his daughter,	8933
	10:25	everyone who came brought a **g**—	4966
	13: 7	and I will give you a **g**."	5522

1Ki	15:19	I am sending you a g of silver and gold.	8816
2Ki	5:15	Please accept now a g from your servant."	1388
	8: 8	"Take a g with you and go to meet the man	4966
	8: 9	a g forty camel-loads of all the finest wares	4966
	16: 8	and sent it as a g to the king of Assyria.	8816
	20:12	of Babylon sent Hezekiah letters and a g,	4966
2Ch	9:24	everyone who came brought a g—	4966
Ps	45:12	The Daughter of Tyre will come with a g,	4966
Pr	18:16	A g opens the way for the giver	5508
	21:14	A g given in secret soothes anger,	5508
Ecc	3:13	in all his toil—this is the g of God.	5522
	5:19	be happy in his work—this is a g of God.	5522
Isa	39: 1	of Babylon sent Hezekiah letters and a g,	4966
Eze	45:13	" 'This is the special g you are to offer:	9556
	45:16	of the land will participate in this special g	9556
	46:16	If the prince makes a g from his inheritance	5510
	46:17	he makes a g from his inheritance to one	5510
	48: 8	portion you are to present as a special	9556
	48:12	a special g to them from the sacred portion	9557
	48:20	As a special g you will set aside	8123
Mt	5:23	if you are offering your g at the altar	1565
	5:24	leave your g there in front of the altar.	1565
	5:24	then come and offer your g.	1565
	8: 4	and offer the g Moses commanded,	1565
	15: 5	from me is a g devoted to God,'	NIV
	23:18	but if anyone swears by the g on it,	1565
	23:19	g, or the altar that makes the gift sacred?	1565
	23:19	gift, or the altar that makes the g sacred?	1565
Mk	7:11	Corban' (that is, a g devoted to God),	1565
Jn	4:10	the g of God and who it is that asks you for	1561
Ac	1: 4	but wait for the g my Father promised,	NIV
	2:38	you will receive the g of the Holy Spirit.	1561
	8:20	because you thought you could buy the g	1561
	10:45	with Peter were astonished that the g of	1561
	11:17	if God gave them the same g as he gave us,	1561
	11:30	sending their g to the elders by Barnabas	NIV
Ro	1:11	so that I may impart to you some spiritual g	5922
	4: 4	his wages are not credited to him as a g,	5921
	5:15	But the g is not like the trespass.	5922
	5:15	how much more did God's grace and the g	1561
	5:16	the g of God is not like the result of	1564
	5:16	but the g followed many trespasses	5922
	5:17	of grace and of the g of righteousness reign	1561
	6:23	but the g of God is eternal life	5922
	12: 6	If a man's g is prophesying,	NIV
1Co	1: 7	Therefore you do not lack any spiritual g	5922
	7: 7	But each man has his own g from God;	5922
	7: 7	one has this g, another has that.	NIV
	13: 2	If I have the g of prophecy	4735
	14: 1	especially the g of prophecy.	NIV
	16: 3	and send them with your g to Jerusalem.	5921
2Co	8:12	g is acceptable according to what one has,	NIV
	8:20	of the way we administer this liberal g	NIV
	9: 5	for the generous g you had promised.	2330
	9: 5	Then it will be ready as a generous g,	2330
	9:15	Thanks be to God for his indescribable g!	1561
Eph	2: 8	not from yourselves, it is the g of God—	1565
	3: 7	by the g of God's grace given me through	1561
Php	4:17	Not that I am looking for a g,	1517
1Ti	4:14	Do not neglect your g,	5922
2Ti	1: 6	to fan into flame the g of God,	5922
Heb	6: 4	who have tasted the heavenly g,	1561
Jas	1:17	Every good and perfect g is from above,	1564
1Pe	3: 7	as heirs with you of the gracious g of life,	5921
	4:10	Each one should use whatever g he has received	5922
Rev	22:17	let him take the free g of the water of life.	1562

GIFTED (1) [GIFT]

1Co	14:37	a prophet or spiritually g,	NIV

GIFTS (87) [GIFT]

Ge	24:53	he also gave costly g to her brother and	4458
	25: 6	he gave g to the sons of his concubines	5510
	32:20	with these g I am sending on ahead;	4966
	32:21	So Jacob's g went on ahead of him,	4966
	43:15	the men took the g and double the amount	4966
	43:25	They prepared their g for Joseph's arrival	4966
	43:26	the g they had brought into the house,	4966
Ex	28:38	in the sacred g the Israelites consecrate,	7731
	28:38	whatever their g may be.	5510
Lev	23:38	to your g and whatever you have vowed	5510
Nu	5:10	Each man's sacred g are his own,	7731
	7: 3	They brought as their g before	7933
	8:19	as g to Aaron and his sons to do the work at	5989
	18: 9	the g they bring me as most holy offerings,	7933
	18:11	from the g of all the wave offerings of	8641
Dt	12: 6	your tithes and special g,	3338+9556
	12:11	your tithes and special g,	3338+9556
	12:17	or your freewill offerings or special g.	3338+9556
	33:15	the choicest g of the ancient mountains and	8031
	33:16	with the best g of the earth and its fullness	NIH
1Sa	10:27	They despised him and brought him no g.	4966
2Ki	12:18	g he himself had dedicated	7731
2Ch	5: 1	and all Judah brought g to Jehoshaphat,	4966
	17:11	Some Philistines brought Jehoshaphat g	4966
	21: 3	Their father had given them many g	5510
	31:12	tithes and dedicated g.	7731
	31:14	the LORD and also the consecrated g.	7731+7731
	32:23	and valuable g for Hezekiah king	4458
Ezr	1: 6	and with valuable g,	4458
Est	2:18	throughout the provinces and distributed g	5368
	9:22	of food to one another and g to the poor.	5510
Ps	68:18	you received g from men,	5510
	68:29	at Jerusalem kings will bring you g.	8856

Ps	72:10	of Sheba and Seba will present him g.	868
	76:11	the neighboring lands bring g to the One to	8856
	112: 9	He has scattered abroad his g to the poor,	5989
Pr	19: 6	the friend of a man who gives g,	5508
	22:16	to increase his wealth and he who gives g to	5989
	25:14	who boasts of g he does not give.	5522+9214
Isa	1:23	they all love bribes and chase after g.	8988
	18: 7	At that time g will be brought to	8856
	18: 7	the g will be brought to Mount Zion,	NIH
Eze	16:33	but you give g to all your lovers,	5621
	20:26	I let them become defiled through their g—	5510
	20:31	When you offer your g—	5510
	20:39	with your g and idols.	5510
	20:40	and your choice g,	5368
	44:30	and of all your special g will belong to	9556
Da	2: 6	from me g and rewards and great honor.	10448
	2:48	in a high position and lavished many g	10448
	5:17	"You may keep your g for yourself	10448
	11:38	with precious stones and costly g.	2776
Mic	1: 7	all her temple g will be burned with fire;	924
	1: 7	Since she gathered her g from the wages	NIH
	1:14	Therefore you will give parting g	8933
	7: 3	the ruler demands g,	NIH
Mt	2:11	with g of gold and of incense and of myrrh.	1565
	7:11	know how to give good g to your children,	1517
	7:11	your Father in heaven give good g	NIG
Lk	11:13	know how to give good g to your children,	1517
	21: 1	Jesus saw the rich putting their g into	1565
	21: 4	All these people gave their g out	1565
	21: 5	and with g dedicated to God.	356
Ac	10: 4	"Your prayers and g to the poor have come	1797
	10:31	and remembered your g to the poor.	1797
	24:17	to bring my people g for the poor and	1797
Ro	11:29	for God's g and his call are irrevocable.	5922
	12: 6	We have different g, according to the grace	5922
1Co	12: 1	Now about spiritual g, brothers,	NIG
	12: 4	There are different kinds of g,	5922
	12: 9	to another a g of healing by that one Spirit,	5922
	12:28	also those having g of healing,	5922
	12:28	those with g of administration,	3236
	12:30	Do all have g of healing?	5922
	12:31	But eagerly desire the greater g.	5922
	14: 1	way of love and eagerly desire spiritual g,	NIG
	14:12	Since you are eager to have spiritual g,	NIG
	14:12	try to excel in g that build up the church.	NIG
2Co	9: 9	"He has scattered abroad his g to the poor;	1443
Eph	4: 8	he led captives in his train and gave g	1517
Php	4:18	received from Epaphroditus the g you sent.	NIG
Heb	2: 4	and g of the Holy Spirit distributed	3536
	5: 1	to offer g and sacrifices for sins,	1565
	8: 3	to offer both g and sacrifices,	1565
	8: 4	the g prescribed by the law.	1565
	9: 9	that the g and sacrifices being offered were	1565
Rev	11:10	and will celebrate by sending each other g,	1565

GIGANTIC (1)

Rev	9: 2	from it like the smoke from a g furnace.	3489

GIHON (6)

Ge	2:13	The name of the second river is the G;	1633
1Ki	1:33	on my own mule and take him down to G.	1633
	1:38	and escorted him to G.	1633
	1:45	the prophet have anointed him king at G.	1633
2Ch	32:30	the G spring and channeled the water down	1633
	33:14	west of the G spring in the valley,	1633

GILALAI (1)

Ne	12:36	Shemaiah, Azarel, Milalai, G, Maai,	1675

GILBOA (8)

1Sa	28: 4	the Israelites and set up camp at G.	1648
	31: 1	and many fell slain on Mount G.	1648
	31: 8	and his three sons fallen on Mount G.	1648
2Sa	1: 6	"I happened to be on Mount G,"	1648
	1:21	"O mountains of G,	1648
	21:12	after they struck Saul down on G.)	1648
1Ch	10: 1	and many fell slain on Mount G.	1648
	10: 8	and his sons fallen on Mount G.	1648

GILEAD (97) [GILEAD'S, GILEADITE, GILEADITES, JABESH GILEAD, RAMOTH GILEAD]

Ge	31:21	he headed for the hill country of G.	1680
	31:23	up with him in the hill country of G.	1680
	31:25	of G when Laban overtook him,	1680
	37:25	a caravan of Ishmaelites coming from G.	1680
Nu	26:29	Makirite clan (Makir was the father of G);	1680
	26:29	through G, the Gileadite clan.	1680
	26:30	These were the descendants of G:	1680
	27: 1	the son of G, the son of Makir,	1680
	32: 1	that the lands of Jazer and G were suitable	1680
	32:26	in the cities of G.	1680
	32:29	give them the land of G as their possession.	1680
	32:39	of Makir son of Manasseh went to G,	1680
	32:40	So Moses gave G to the Makirites,	1680
	36: 1	The family heads of the clan of G son	1201+1680
Dt	2:36	even as far as G,	1680
	3:10	the plateau, and all G, and all Bashan as far	1680
	3:12	including half the hill country of G,	1680
	3:13	The rest of G and also all of Bashan,	1680
	3:15	And I gave G to Makir.	1680
	3:16	the territory extending from G down to	1680
	4:43	Ramoth in G, for the Gadites;	1680

Dt	34: 1	from G to Dan,	1680
Jos	12: 2	This included half of G.	1680
	12: 5	and half of G to the border of Sihon king	1680
	13:11	also included G, the territory of the people	1680
	13:25	of G and half the Ammonite country as far	1680
	13:31	half of G, and Ashtaroth and Edrei	1680
	17: 1	who had received G and Bashan because	1680
	17: 3	Zelophehad son of Hepher, the son of G,	1680
	17: 5	of land besides G and Bashan east of	1680
	17: 6	The land of G belonged to the rest of	1680
	20: 8	Ramoth in G in the tribe of Gad,	1680
	21:38	in G (a city of refuge for one accused	1680
	22: 9	at Shiloh in Canaan to return to G,	824+1680
	22:13	the priest, to the land of G—	1680
	22:15	When they went to G—	824+1680
	22:32	with the Reubenites and Gadites in G	824+1680
Jdg	5:17	G stayed beyond the Jordan.	1680
	7: 3	and leave Mount G.' "	1680
	10: 3	He was followed by Jair of G,	1682
	10: 4	They controlled thirty towns in G,	824+1680
	10: 8	on the east side of the Jordan in G,	1680
	10:17	to arms and camped in G,	1680
	10:18	of the people of G said to each other,	1680
	10:18	be the head of all those living in G."	1680
	11: 1	His father was G;	1680
	11: 5	the elders of G went to get Jephthah from	1680
	11: 8	The elders of G said to him, "Nevertheless,	1680
	11: 8	you will be our head over all who live in G.	1680
	11:10	The elders of G replied,	1680
	11:11	So Jephthah went with the elders of G,	1680
	11:29	He crossed G and Manasseh,	1680
	11:29	passed through Mizpah of G,	1680
	12: 4	Jephthah then called together the men of G	1680
	12: 4	the men of G asked him,	1680
	12: 7	and was buried in a town in G.	1680
	20: 1	of G came out as one man and assembled	1680
1Sa	13: 7	the Jordan to the land of Gad and G.	1680
2Sa	2: 9	He made him king over G,	1680
	17:26	and Absalom camped in the land of G.	1680
	24: 6	to G and the region of Tahtim Hodshi,	1680
1Ki	2: 7	the sons of Barzillai of G and let them be	1682
	4:13	of Jair son of Manasseh in G were his,	1680
	4:19	in G (the country of Sihon king of	824+1680
	17: 1	Now Elijah the Tishbite, from Tishbe in G,	1680
2Ki	10:33	the Jordan in all the land of G (the region	1680
	10:33	from Aroer by the Arnon Gorge through G	1680
	15:25	Taking fifty men of G with him,	1201+1682
	15:29	He took G and Galilee.	1680
1Ch	2:21	Makir the father of G (he had married her	1680
	2:22	controlled twenty-three towns in G.	824+1680
	2:23	of Makir the father of G.	1680
	5: 9	their livestock had increased in G.	824+1680
	5:10	throughout the entire region east of G.	1680
	5:14	the son of G, the son of Michael,	1680
	5:16	The Gadites lived in G,	1680
	6:80	of Gad they received Ramoth in G,	1680
	7:14	She gave birth to Makir the father of G.	1680
	7:17	These were the sons of G son of Makir.	1680
	26:31	the Hebronites were found at Jazer in G.	1680
	27:21	over the half-tribe of Manasseh in G:	1680
Ps	60: 7	G is mine, and Manasseh is mine;	1680
	108: 8	G is mine, Manasseh is mine;	1680
SS	4: 1	a flock of goats descending from Mount G.	1680
	6: 5	like a flock of goats descending from G.	1680
Jer	8:22	Is there no balm in G?	1680
	22: 6	"Though you are like G to me,	1680
	46:11	"Go up to G and get balm,	1680
	50:19	be satisfied on the hills of Ephraim and G.	1680
Eze	47:18	along the Jordan between G and the land	1680
Hos	6: 8	G is a city of wicked men,	1680
	12:11	Is G wicked?	1680
Am	1: 3	Because she threshed G	1680
	1:13	of G in order to extend his borders,	1680
Ob	1:19	and Benjamin will possess G.	1680
Mic	7:14	in Bashan and G as in days long ago.	1680
Zec	10:10	I will bring them to G and Lebanon,	824+1680

GILEAD'S (1) [GILEAD]

Jdg	11: 2	G wife also bore him sons,	1680

GILEADITE (8) [GILEAD]

Nu	26:29	through Gilead, the G clan.	1682
Jdg	11: 1	Jephthah the G was a mighty warrior.	1682
	11:40	the daughter of Jephthah the G.	1682
	12: 7	Then Jephthah the G died,	1682
2Sa	17:27	and Barzillai the G from Rogelim	1682
	19:31	Barzillai the G also came down from Rogelim	1682
Ezr	2:61	a daughter of Barzillai the G and was called	1682
Ne	7:63	a daughter of Barzillai the G and was called	1682

GILEADITES (4) [GILEAD]

Jos	17: 1	Makir was the ancestor of the G,	1680
Jdg	12: 4	The G struck them down because	408+1680
	12: 4	"You G are renegades from Ephraim	1680
	12: 5	The G captured the fords of	1680

GILGAL (39) [BETH GILGAL]

Dt	11:30	in the Arabah in the vicinity of G.	1652
Jos	4:19	up from the Jordan and camped at G on	1652
	4:20	at G the twelve stones they had taken out of	1652
	5: 9	So the place has been called G to this day.	1652
	5:10	while camped at G on the plains of Jericho,	1652
	9: 6	the camp at G and said to him and the men	1652
	10: 6	then sent word to Joshua in the camp at G:	1652

Jos	10: 7	marched up from G with his entire army,	1652
	10: 9	After an all-night march from G,	1652
	10:15	with all Israel to the camp at G.	1652
	10:43	with all Israel to the camp at G.	1652
	12:23	the king of Goyim in G one	1652
	14: 6	the men of Judah approached Joshua at G,	1652
	15: 7	the Valley of Achor and turned north to G,	1652
Jdg	2: 1	The angel of the Lord went up from G	1652
	3:19	At the idols near G he himself turned back	1652
1Sa	7:16	on a circuit from Bethel to G to Mizpah,	1652
	10: 8	"Go down ahead of me to G.	1652
	11:14	to G and there reaffirm the kingship."	1652
	11:15	the people went to G and confirmed Saul	1652
	13: 4	people were summoned to join Saul at G.	1652
	13: 7	Saul remained at G,	1652
	13: 8	but Samuel did not come to G,	1652
	13:12	down against me at G,	1652
	13:15	Then Samuel left G and went up to Gibeah	1652
	15:12	and has turned and gone on down to G."	1652
	15:21	to the Lord your God at G."	1652
	15:33	to death before the Lord at G.	1652
2Sa	19:15	of Judah had come to G to go out and meet	1652
	19:40	When the king crossed over to G,	1652
2Ki	2: 1	and Elisha were on their way from G.	1652
	4:38	Elisha returned to G and there was a famine	1652
Hos	4:15	"Do not go to G;	1652
	9:15	"Because of all their wickedness in G,	1652
	12:11	Do they sacrifice bulls in G?	1652
Am	4: 4	go to G and sin yet more.	1652
	5: 5	do not go to G,	1652
	5: 5	For G will surely go into exile,	1652
Mic	6: 5	from Shittim to G,	1652

GILOH (2)

Jos	15:51	Goshen, Holon and G—eleven towns	1656
2Sa	15:12	David's counselor, to come from G,	1656

GILONITE (2)

2Sa	15:12	he also sent for Ahithophel the G,	1639
	23:34	Eliam son of Ahithophel the G,	1639

GIMZO (1)

2Ch	28:18	as well as Soco, Timnah and G,	1693

GIN (KJV) See TRAP

GINATH (2)

1Ki	16:21	half supported Tibni son of G for king,	1640
	16:22	of Tibni son of G.	1640

GINNETHON (2) [GINNETHON'S]

Ne	10: 6	Daniel, G, Baruch,	1715
	12: 4	Iddo, G, Abijah,	1715

GINNETHON'S (1) [GINNETHON]

Ne	12:16	of Iddo's, Zechariah; of G, Meshullam;	1715

GIRD (1)

Ps	45: 3	G your sword upon your side,	2520

GIRDED (KJV) See ARMED, CLOAK TUCKED INTO BELT, CLOTHED, DRESSED, FASTENED, PUT ON, STRENGTHENED, TIED, WEARING, WRAPPED

GIRGASHITES (7)

Ge	10:16	Jebusites, Amorites, G,	1739
	15:21	Amorites, Canaanites, G and Jebusites."	1739
Dt	7: 1	the Hittites, G, Amorites, Canaanites,	1739
Jos	3:10	Perizzites, G, Amorites and Jebusites.	1739
	24:11	Perizzites, Canaanites, Hittites, G,	1739
1Ch	1:14	Jebusites, Amorites, G,	1739
Ne	9: 8	Amorites, Perizzites, Jebusites and G.	1739

GIRGASITE (KJV) See GIRGASHITES

GIRL (57) [GIRL'S, GIRLS]

Ge	24:14	May it be that when I say to a g,	5855
	24:16	The g was very beautiful, a virgin;	5855
	24:28	The g ran and told her mother's household	5855
	24:55	"Let the g remain with us ten days or so;	5855
	24:57	"Let's call the g and ask her about it."	5855
	29:24	And Laban gave his servant g Zilpah	9148
	29:29	Laban gave his servant g Bilhah	9148
	34: 3	he loved the g and spoke tenderly to her.	5855
	34: 4	"Get me this g as my wife."	3530
	34:12	Only give me the g as my wife."	5855
Ex	1:16	but if it is a g, let her live."	1426
	1:22	but let every g live."	1426
	2: 5	the reeds and sent her slave g to get it.	563
	2: 8	And the g went and got the baby's mother.	6625
	11: 5	to the firstborn son of the slave g,	9148
Lev	12: 7	the woman who gives birth to a boy or a g.	5922
	19:20	with a woman who is a slave g promised	563
Nu	31:18	every g who has never slept with a man	851+3251
Dt	22:24	the g because she was in a town and did	5855
	22:25	a g pledged to be married and rapes her,	5855

Dt	22:26	Do nothing to the g;	5855
	22:27	for the man found the g out in the country,	2023S
	22:27	and though the betrothed g screamed,	5855
	22:29	He must marry the g,	NIH
Jdg	5:30	a g or two for each man,	8167
	9:18	the son of his slave g,	563
1Sa	30:19	young or old, boy or g,	1426
2Sa	17:17	A servant g was to go and inform them,	9148
1Ki	1: 3	for a beautiful g and found Abishag,	5855
	1: 4	The g was very beautiful;	5855
2Ki	5: 2	and had taken captive a young g	5855
	5: 4	to his master and told him what the g	5855
Est	2: 4	the g who pleases the king be queen instead	5855
	2: 7	This g, who was also known as Esther,	5855
	2: 9	The g pleased the king and won his favor.	5855
	2:15	for Esther (the g Mordecai had adopted,	889S
Job	31: 1	with my eyes not to look lustfully at a g.	1435
Am	2: 7	the same g and so profane my holy name.	5855
Mt	9:24	The g is not dead but asleep."	3166
	9:25	he went in and took the g by the hand,	3166
	14:11	in on a platter and given to the g,	3166
	26:69	and a servant g came to him.	4087
	26:71	where another g saw him and said to	AIT
Mk	5:41	(which means, "Little g, I say to you,	3166
	5:42	Immediately the g stood up and walked	3166
	6:22	The king said to the g,	3166
	6:25	At once the g hurried in to the king with	NIG
	6:28	He presented it to the g,	3166
	14:69	When the servant g saw him there,	4087
Lk	8:42	a g of about twelve, was dying.	NIG
	22:56	A servant g saw him seated there in	4087
Jn	18:16	to the g on duty there and brought Peter in.	2601
	18:17	the g at the door asked Peter.	4087
Ac	12:13	a servant g named Rhoda came to answer	4087
	16:16	we were met by a slave g who had a spirit	4087
	16:17	This g followed Paul and the rest of us,	AIT
	16:19	When the owners of the slave g realized	899S

GIRL'S (11) [GIRL]

Dt	22:15	the g father and mother shall bring proof	5855
	22:16	The g father will say to the elders,	5855
	22:19	of silver and give them to the g father.	5855
	22:20	and no proof of the g virginity can	4200+5855
	22:29	he shall pay the g father fifty shekels	5855
Jdg	19: 4	His father-in-law, the g father,	5855
	19: 5	but the g father said to his son-in-law,	5855
	19: 6	Afterward the g father said,	5855
	19: 8	when he rose to go, the g father said,	5855
	19: 9	his father-in-law, the g father, said,	5855
Est	2:12	a g turn came to go in to King Xerxes,	5855

GIRLS (24) [GIRL]

Ge	20:17	his wife and his slave g	563
Ex	2:18	When the g returned to Reuel their father,	AIT
Jdg	11:38	She and the g went into the hills and wept	8292
	21:21	When the g of Shiloh come out to join in	1426
	21:21	of you seize a wife from the g of Shiloh	1426
	21:23	While the g were dancing,	AIT
Ru	2: 8	Stay here with my servant g.	5855
	2: 9	and follow along after the g.	2177S
	2:13	the standing of one of your servant g."	9148
	2:22	my daughter, to go with his g,	5855
	2:23	to the servant g of Boaz to glean until	5855
	3: 2	with whose servant g you have been,	5855
1Sa	9:11	they met some g coming out to draw water,	5855
2Sa	6:20	in the sight of the slave g of his servants	563
	6:22	But by these slave g you spoke of,	563
Est	2: 3	all these beautiful g into the harem	1435+5855
	2: 8	many g were brought to the citadel of Susa	5855
Job	41: 5	a bird or put him on a leash for your g?	5855
Pr	27:27	and to nourish your servant g.	5855
	31:15	and portions for her servant g.	5855
Joel	3: 3	they sold g for wine that they might drink.	3530
Na	2: 7	Its slave g moan like doves and beat	563
Zec	8: 5	be filled with boys and g playing there."	3530
Mk	14:66	the servant g of the high priest came by.	4087

GIRZITES (1)

1Sa	27: 8	the G and the Amalekites.	1747

GISHPA (1)

Ne	11:21	and Ziha and G were in charge of them.	1778

GITTAH-HEPHER (KJV) See GATH HEPHER

GITTAIM (2)

2Sa	4: 3	of Beeroth fled to G and have lived there	1786
Ne	11:33	in Hazor, Ramah and G,	1786

GITTITE (8) [GITTITES]

2Sa	6:10	to the house of Obed-Edom the G.	1785
	6:11	of Obed-Edom the G for three months,	1785
	15:19	The king said to Ittai the G,	1785
	15:22	So Ittai the G marched on with all his men	1785
	18: 2	and a third under Ittai the G.	1785
	21:19	the Bethlehemite killed Goliath the G,	1785
1Ch	13:13	to the house of Obed-Edom the G.	1785
	20: 5	the brother of Goliath the G,	1785

GITTITES (1) [GITTITE]

2Sa	15:18	six hundred G who had accompanied him	1785

GITTITH (3)

Ps	8: T	According to g. A Psalm of David.	1787
	81: T	According to g. Of Asaph.	1787
	84: T	According to g. Of the sons of Korah.	1787

GIVE (908) [GAVE, GIVEN, GIVER, GIVES, GIVING, LIFE-GIVING]

Ge	1:15	in the expanse of the sky to g light on	239
	1:17	in the expanse of the sky to g light on	239
	1:29	"I g you every seed-bearing plant on	5989
	1:30	I g every green plant for food."	NIH
	3:16	with pain you will g birth to children.	3528
	9: 3	I now g you everything.	NIH
	12: 7	"To your offspring I will g this land."	5989
	13:15	All the land that you see I will g to you	5989
	14:21	"G me the people and keep the goods	5989
	15: 2	what can you g me since I remain childless	5989
	15: 7	to g you this land to take possession of it."	5989
	15:18	"To your descendants I g this land,	5989
	17: 8	I will g as an everlasting possession	5989
	17:16	I will bless her and will surely g you a son	5989
	23:11	"Listen to me; I g you the field,	5989
	23:11	and I g you the cave that is in it.	5989
	23:11	I g it to you in the presence of my people.	5989
	24: 7	'To your offspring I will g this land'—	5989
	24:12	g me success today,	7936
	24:17	"Please g me a little water from your jar."	1686
	24:41	from my oath even if they refuse to g her	5989
	24:45	and I said to her, 'Please g me a drink.'	9197
	25:24	When the time came for her to g birth,	3528
	26: 3	your descendants I will g all these lands	5989
	26: 4	in the sky and will g them all these lands,	5989
	27: 4	that I may g you my blessing before I die."	1385
	27: 7	so that I may g you my blessing in	1385
	27:10	so that he may g you his blessing	1385
	27:19	so that you may g me your blessing."	1385
	27:25	so that I may g you my blessing."	1385
	27:28	May God g you of heaven's dew and	5989
	27:31	so that you may g me your blessing."	1385
	28: 4	May he g you and your descendants	5989
	28:13	I will g you and your descendants	5989
	28:20	and will g me food to eat and clothes	5989
	28:22	and of all that you g me I will give you	5989
	28:22	that you give me I will g you a tenth."	6923+6923
	29:19	that I g her to you than to some other man.	5989
	29:21	Then Jacob said to Laban, "G me my wife.	2035
	29:26	g the younger daughter in marriage	5989
	29:27	then we will g you the younger one also,	5989
	30: 1	So she said to Jacob, "G me children,	2035
	30:14	Please g me some of your son's mandrakes.	5989
	30:26	G me my wives and children,	5989
	30:31	"What shall I g you?"	5989
	30:31	"Don't g me anything," Jacob replied.	5989
	34: 8	Please g her to him as his wife.	5989
	34: 9	g us your daughters and take our daughters	5989
	34:11	and I will g you whatever you ask.	5989
	34:12	Only g me the girl as my wife."	5989
	34:14	we can't g our sister to a man who is	5989
	34:15	We will g our consent to you	252
	34:16	Then we will g you our daughters	5989
	34:23	So let us g our consent to them,	252
	35:12	to Abraham and Isaac I also g to you,	5989
	35:12	and I will g this land to your descendants	5989
	35:16	to g birth and had great difficulty.	3528
	38:16	what will you g me to sleep with you?"	5989
	38:17	"Will you g me something as a pledge	5989
	38:18	He said, "What pledge should I g you?"	5989
	38:26	since I wouldn't g her to my son Shelah."	5989
	38:27	When the time came for her to g birth,	3528
	41:16	God will g Pharaoh the answer he desires."	6699
	42:22	Now we must g an accounting	2011
	42:25	and to g them provisions for their journey.	5989
	42:34	Then I will g your brother back to you,	5989
	45:18	I will g you the best of the land of Egypt	5989
	47:15	to Joseph and said, "G us food.	2035
	47:19	G us seed so that we may live and not die,	5989
	47:24	g a fifth of it to Pharaoh.	5989
	48: 4	and I will g this land as	5989
	48:22	I g the ridge of land I took from	5989
Ex	1:19	and g birth before the midwives arrive."	3528
	5: 7	'I will not g you any more straw,	5989
	6: 4	with them to g them the land of Canaan,	5989
	6: 8	to the land I swore with uplifted hand to g	5989
	6: 8	I will g it to you as a possession.	5989
	9:19	G an order now to bring your livestock	8938
	12:25	the Lord will g you as he promised,	5989
	13: 5	land he swore to your forefathers to g you,	5989
	13:12	to g over to the Lord the first offspring	6296
	13:21	by night in a pillar of fire to g them light,	239
	17: 2	"G us water to drink."	5989
	18:19	now to me and I will g you some advice,	3619
	20:16	"You shall not g false testimony	6699
	22:17	If her father absolutely refuses to g her	5989
	22:29	"You must g me the firstborn of your sons.	5989
	22:30	but g them to me on the eighth day.	5989
	23: 2	When you g testimony in a lawsuit,	6699
	23:26	I will g you a full life span.	4848
	24:12	and I will g you the tablets of stone,	5989
	25: 2	each man whose heart prompts him to g.	5605
	25:16	which I will g you.	5989
	25:21	which I will g you.	5989

Ex	25:22	with you and g you all my commands for	1819
	28: 2	to g him dignity and honor.	NIH
	28:40	to g them dignity and honor.	NIH
	30:13	over to those already counted *is to g*	5989
	30:14	*are to* g an offering to the LORD.	5989
	30:15	not *to* g **more** than a half shekel and	8049
	30:15	a half shekel and the poor *are* not *to* g **less**	5070
	32:13	*I will* g your descendants all this land I promised them,	5989
	33: 1	saying, '*I will* g it to your descendants.'	5989
	33:14	and *I will* g you **rest.**"	5663
Lev	5:16	add a fifth of the value to that and g it all to	5989
	6: 5	the value to it and g it all to the owner on	5989
	6: 9	"G Aaron and his sons *this* **command:**	7422
	7:32	*You are to* g the right thigh	5989
	7:36	that the Israelites g this to them	5989
	15:14	to the Tent of Meeting and g them to	5989
	18:21	not g any of your children to be sacrificed	5989
	20:24	I *will* g it to you as an inheritance,	5989
	23:10	*to* g you and you reap its harvest,	5989
	23:38	and all the freewill offerings *you* g to	5989
	25: 2	you enter the land I *am going to* g you,	5989
	25:38	of Egypt to g you the land of Canaan and to	5989
Nu	3: 9	G the Levites to Aaron and his sons;	5989
	3:48	G the money for the redemption of	5989
	5: 7	and g it to the person he has wronged.	5989
	6:26	toward you and g you peace." '	8492
	7: 5	G them to the Levites	5989
	7: 9	But Moses *did* not g any to the Kohathites;	5989
	10:29	'*I will* g it to you.'	5989
	11:12	*Did* I g them **birth?**	3528
	11:13	'G us meat to eat!'	5989
	11:18	Now the LORD *will* g you meat,	5989
	11:21	'*I will* g them meat to eat for	5989
	14: 8	and *will* g it to us.	5989
	15:21	*to* g this offering to the LORD from	5989
	18: 8	the holy offerings the Israelites g me I give	NIH
	18: 8	the Israelites give me I g to you	5989
	18:11	*I* g this to you and your sons	5989
	18:12	"I g you all the finest olive oil and all	5989
	18:12	and all the finest new wine and grain *they* g	5989
	18:19	to the LORD *I* g to you and your sons	5989
	18:21	"I g to the Levites all the tithes in Israel	5989
	18:24	*I* g to the Levites as their inheritance	5989
	18:26	the tithe *I* g you as your inheritance,	5989
	18:28	From these tithes *you must* g	5989
	19: 3	G it to Eleazar the priest;	5989
	20:12	into the land *I* g them."	5989
	20:24	He will not enter the land *I* g the Israelites,	5989
	21:16	and *I will* g them water."	5989
	23: 5	"Go back to Balak and g him this **message.**"	1819
	23:16	"Go back to Balak and g him this **message.**"	1819
	26:54	To a larger group g a **larger** inheritance,	8049
	27: 4	G us property among our father's relatives."	5989
	27: 7	*You* **must certainly** g them property	5989+5989
	27: 9	g his inheritance to his brothers.	5989
	27:10	g his inheritance to his father's brothers.	5989
	27:11	g his inheritance to the nearest relative	5989
	27:20	G him some of your authority so	5989
	28: 2	"G *this* **command** *to* the Israelites and say	7422
	31:29	from their half share and g it to Eleazar	5989
	31:30	G them to the Levites,	5989
	32:29	g them the land of Gilead	5989
	33:54	To a larger group g a **larger** inheritance,	8049
	33:55	*They will* g you **trouble** in the land	7675
	35: 2	the Israelites *to* g the Levites towns to live	5989
	35: 2	And g them pasturelands around the towns.	5989
	35: 4	around the towns that *you* g	5989
	35: 6	the towns *you* g the Levites will be cities	5989
	35: 6	In addition, g them forty-two other towns.	5989
	35: 7	In all *you must* g	5989
	35: 8	The towns *you* g the Levites from the land	5989
	35:13	These six towns *you* g will be your cities	5989
	35:14	G three on this side of the Jordan and three	5989
	36: 2	the LORD commanded my lord to g	5989
	36: 2	he ordered you to g the inheritance	5989
Dt	1: 8	the land that the LORD swore *he would* g	5989
	1:35	the **good** land I swore to g your forefathers,	5989
	1:36	and *I will* g him and his descendants	5989
	1:39	*I will* g it to them and they will take	5989
	2: 4	G the people *these* **orders:**	7422
	2: 5	for *I will* not g you any of their land,	5989
	2: 9	for *I will* not g you any part of their land.	5989
	2:19	not g you possession of any land belonging	5989
	2:30	and his heart obstinate in order to g him	5989
	4: 2	of the LORD your God that I g you.	7422
	4:38	to bring you into their land to g it to you	5989
	5:20	"You shall not g false testimony	6699
	5:31	so that I *may* g you all the commands,	1819
	6: 2	and commands that I g you,	7422
	6: 6	that I g you today are to be	7422
	6:10	to Abraham, Isaac and Jacob, to g you—	5989
	6:23	and g us the land that he promised on oath	5989
	7: 3	*Do* not g your daughters to their sons	5989
	7:11	decrees and laws I g you today.	7422
	7:13	that he swore to your forefathers to g you.	5989
	7:24	*He will* g their kings into your hand,	5989
	10:11	that I swore to their fathers to g them."	5989
	11: 9	the LORD swore to your forefathers to g	5989
	11:21	the LORD swore to g your forefathers.	5989
	12: 6	to g and your freewill offerings,	NIH
	12:10	and *he will* g you **rest**	5663
	12:17	or whatever you have vowed to g,	NIH
	12:26	and whatever you have vowed to g,	NIH
	14:21	*You may* g it to an alien living in any	5989
	15: 9	and g him nothing.	5989
	15:10	G **generously** to him and do so	5989+5989

Dt	15:14	G to him as the LORD your God has blessed	5989
	15:15	That is why I g you this command today.	7422
	17: 9	of them and *they will* g you the verdict.	5583
	17:10	according to the decisions *they* g you at	5583
	17:11	and the decisions *they* g you.	606
	18: 4	*to* g them the firstfruits of your grain,	5989
	20: 3	be terrified or g **way to panic** before them.	6907
	20: 4	against your enemies to g you **victory.**"	3828
	21:16	g **the rights of the firstborn**	1144
	22: 2	Then g it **back** to him.	8740
	22:19	a hundred shekels of silver and g them to	5989
	22:19	g him more than forty **lashes.**	5782
	26: 3	to our forefathers to g us."	5989
	26:12	*you shall* g it to the Levite, the alien,	5989
	27: 1	all these commands that I g you today.	7422
	27:10	and decrees that I g you today."	7422
	28: 1	follow all his commands I g you today,	7422
	28:11	to your forefathers to g you.	5989
	28:13	the LORD your God that I g you this day	7422
	28:14	from any of the commands I g you today,	7422
	28:55	and he *will* not g to one of them any of	5989
	28:65	the LORD *will* g you an anxious mind,	5989
	30:20	and he *will* g you many years in	3782
	30:20	in the land he swore to g to your fathers,	5989
	31: 7	to their forefathers to g them,	5989
	32:38	*Let them* g you **shelter!**	2118+6261
	34: 4	'*I will* g it to your descendants.'	5989
Jos	1: 2	into the land I *am about to* g to them—	5989
	1: 3	*I will* g you every place	5989
	1: 6	to their forefathers to g them.	5989
	2:12	G me a sure sign	5989
	5: 6	to g us, a land flowing with milk	5989
	6: 5	*have* all the people g a loud **shout;**	8131+9558
	6:10	"*Do* not g **a war cry,**	8131
	7:19	g glory to the LORD, the God of Israel,	8492
	7:19	the God of Israel, and g him the praise.	5989
	8: 7	The LORD your God *will* g it	5989
	9:24	to g you the whole land and	5989
	14:12	Now g me this hill country that	5989
	15:16	"*I will* g my daughter Acsah **in marriage**	851+4200+5989
	15:19	g me also springs of water."	5989
	17: 4	to g us an inheritance among our brothers."	5989
	20: 4	into their city and g him a place to live	5989
	21: 2	through Moses that you g us towns to live	5989
	21:43	the land he had sworn to g their forefathers,	5989
Jdg	1:12	"*I will* g my daughter Acsah **in marriage**	851+4200+5989
	1:15	g me also springs of water."	5989
	2: 1	and led you into the land that I swore to g	NIH
	2:19	*They* refused *to* g **up** their evil practices	5877
	4: 7	to the Kishon River and g him	5989
	4:19	"Please g me some **water.**"	9197
	6:17	g me a sign that it is really you talking	6913
	7: 7	and g the Midianites into your hands.	5989
	7: 9	because I *am going to* g it into your hands.	5989
	8: 5	"G my troops some bread;	5989
	8: 6	Why *should we* g bread to your troops?"	5989
	8:15	Why *should we* g bread to your exhausted	5989
	8:24	of you g me an earring from your share of	5989
	8:25	"*We'll be* **glad to** g them."	5989+5989
	9: 9	'*Should I* g up my oil,	2532
	9:11	fig tree replied, '*Should I* g up my fruit,	2532
	9:13	vine answered, '*Should I* g up my wine,	2532
	11:13	Now g it **back** peaceably."	8740
	11:17	'G us permission to go	AIT
	11:30	If *you* g the Ammonites into my hands	5989+5989
	11:37	"G me two months to roam the hills	8332
	13: 5	you will conceive and g **birth** *to* a son.	3528
	13: 7	'You will conceive and g **birth** to a son.	3528
	14:12	"*If you can* g me *the* **answer** within	5583+5583
	14:12	*I will* g you thirty linen garments	5989
	14:13	you *must* g me thirty linen garments	5989
	14:14	For three days they could not g the answer.	5583
	16: 5	of us *will* g you eleven hundred shekels	5989
	17: 3	*I will* g it **back** to you."	8740
	17:10	and I'll g you ten shekels of silver a year,	5989
	20: 7	speak up and g your verdict."	2035
	20:10	it *can* g them what they deserve	6913
	20:28	tomorrow I *will* g them into your hands."	5989
	21: 1	g his daughter **in marriage**	851+4200+5989
	21: 7	oath by the LORD not *to* g them any of our daughters **in marriage?**"	851+4200+5989
	21:18	We can't g our daughters as wives,	5989
	21:22	you *did* not g your daughters to them.' "	5989
1Sa	1: 4	*he would* g portions of the meat	5989
	1:11	and not forget your servant but g her a son,	5989
	1:11	then *I will* g him to the LORD for all	5989
	1:28	So now I g him to the LORD.	8626
	2:10	"He will g strength to his king and exalt	5989
	2:15	"G the priest some meat to roast;	5989
	2:20	the LORD g you children by this woman	8492
	8: 6	when they said, "G us a king to lead us,"	5989
	8:14	and vineyards and olive groves and g them	5989
	8:15	and of your vintage and g it to his officials	5989
	8:22	"Listen to them and g them a **king.**"	4887+4889
	9: 7	"If we go, what *can we* g the man?	995
	9: 8	*I will* g it to the man of God so	5989
	9:27	so that I *may* g you a message from God."	9048
	11: 3	"G us seven days	8332
	14:37	*Will you* g them into Israel's hand?"	5989
	14:41	the God of Israel, "G me the right answer."	2035
	17:10	G me a man and let us fight each other."	5989
	17:25	The king *will* g **great wealth** to	6947+6648
	17:25	g him his daughter **in marriage**	5989
	17:44	"and I'll g your flesh to the birds of	5989
	17:46	Today I *will* g the carcasses of	5989

1Sa	17:47	and *he will* g all of you into our hands."	5989
	18:17	g her to you **in marriage;**	851+4200+5989
	18:21	"*I will* g her to him," he thought,	5989
	21: 3	G me five loaves of bread,	928+3338+5989
	21: 9	"There is none like it; g it to me."	5989
	22: 7	of Jesse g all of you fields and vineyards?	5989
	23: 4	*to* g the Philistines into your hand."	5989
	23:14	but God *did* not g David into his hands.	5989
	24: 4	'I *will* g your enemy into your hands	5989
	25: 8	Please g your servants	5989
	25:11	and g it to men coming	5989
	25:14	our master his **greetings,**	1385
	27: 1	Then Saul *will* g **up** searching	3286
	28:22	and *let me* g you some food	8492
2Sa	2:23	But Asahel refused to g **up** *the* **pursuit;**	6073
	3:14	demanding, "G me my wife Michal,	5989
	7:11	also g you **rest** from all your enemies.	5663
	12:11	and g them to one who is close to you,	5989
	13: 5	g me something **to eat.**	1356
	16: 3	*will* g me **back** my grandfather's kingdom.'	8740
	16:20	"G us your advice.	2035
	17: 6	If not, g us your **opinion.**"	1819
	18: 3	now for you to g us **support** from the city.	6468
	18:11	Then I would have had to g you ten shekels	5989
	21: 6	So the king said, "I *will* g them to you."	5989
	22:36	*You* g me your shield of victory;	5989
1Ki	2:17	*to* g me Abishag the Shunammite	5989
	3: 5	"Ask for whatever you want *me to* g you."	5989
	3: 9	So g your servant a discerning heart	5989
	3:12	*I will* g you a wise and discerning mind,	5989
	3:13	*I will* g you what you have	5989
	3:14	*I will* g you a **long life.**"	799
	3:25	the living child in two and g half to one	5989
	3:26	"Please, my lord, g her the living baby!	5989
	3:27	"G the living baby to the first woman.	5989
	5: 6	"So g **orders** that cedars of Lebanon be cut	7422
	8:28	Yet **attention** to your servant's prayer	7155
	8:46	with them and g them **over** to the enemy,	5989
	11:11	the kingdom away from you and g it to one	5989
	11:13	but *will* g him one tribe for the sake	5989
	11:31	of Solomon's hand and g you ten tribes.	5989
	11:35	from his son's hands and g you ten tribes.	5989
	11:36	*I will* g one tribe to his son so	5989
	11:38	the one I built for David and *will* g Israel	5989
	12: 7	g them a favorable **answer,**	1819+1821
	12:27	**again** g their **allegiance**	4213+8740
	13: 7	and *I will* g you a gift."	5989
	13: 8	if *you were to* g me half your possessions,	5989
	14: 5	g her such and such **an answer.**	1819
	14:16	And *he will* g Israel **up** because of	5989
	17:19	"G me your son," Elijah replied.	5989
	20:10	in Samaria to g each of my men a handful."	NIH
	20:13	*I will* g it into your hand today,	5989
	21: 2	In exchange *I will* g you a better vineyard	5989
	21: 3	"The LORD forbid that I *should* g you	5989
	21: 4	not g you the inheritance of my fathers."	5989
	21: 6	*I will* g you another vineyard	5989
	21: 6	he said, '*I will* not g you my vineyard.' '	5989
	22: 6	the Lord *will* g it into the king's hand."	5989
	22:12	the LORD *will* g it into the king's hand."	5989
	22:15	the LORD *will* g it into the king's hand."	5989
	22:27	Put this fellow in prison and g him nothing	430S
2Ki	4:42	"G it to the people to eat," Elisha said.	5989
	4:43	Elisha answered, "G it to the people to eat.	5989
	5:22	Please g them a talent of silver and two sets	5989
	6:28	'G up your son so we may eat him today,	5989
	6:29	'G up your son so we may eat him,'	5989
	8: 6	"G **back** everything that belonged to her,	8740
	10:15	"If so," said Jehu, "g me your hand."	5989
	14: 9	'G your daughter to my son **in marriage.**'	851+4200+5989
	18:23	*I will* g you two thousand horses—	5989
	19:16	G **ear,** O LORD, and hear;	265+5742
1Ch	16: 4	to g **thanks,** and to praise the LORD,	3344
	16: 8	G **thanks** to the LORD, call on his name;	3344
	16:18	"To you *I will* g the land of Canaan as	5989
	16:34	G **thanks** to the LORD, for he is good;	3344
	16:35	that we *may* g **thanks** to your holy name,	3344
	16:41	and designated by name to g **thanks** to	3344
	21:23	*I will* g the oxen for the burnt offerings,	5989
	21:23	*I will* g all this."	5989
	22: 9	and *I will* g him **rest** from all his enemies	5663
	22:12	*May* the LORD g you discretion	5989
	29: 3	of my God I *now* g my personal treasures	5989
	29:12	and power to exalt and g **strength** to all.	2616
	29:13	Now, our God, we g you **thanks,**	3344
	29:14	that we should be able to g as **generously**	5605
	29:19	And g my son Solomon the wholehearted	5989
2Ch	1: 7	"Ask for whatever you want *me to* g you."	5989
	1:10	G me wisdom and knowledge,	5989
	1:12	And *I will* also g you wealth,	5989
	2:10	*I will* g your servants,	5989
	5:13	to g **praise** and thanks to the LORD.	2146
	6:19	Yet **attention** to your servant's prayer	7155
	6:36	with them and g them **over** to the enemy,	5989
	10: 7	g them a favorable **answer,**	1819+1821
	12: 7	but *will* soon g them deliverance.	5989
	15: 7	as for you, be strong and *do* not g **up,**	3338+8332
	18: 5	"for God *will* g it into the king's hand."	5989
	18:11	the LORD *will* g it into the king's hand."	5989
	18:26	Put this fellow in prison and g him nothing	430S
	19: 6	who is with you whenever you g a verdict.	NIH
	20: 7	before your people Israel and g it forever to	5989
	20:17	the deliverance the LORD *will* g you,	6640
	20:21	"G **thanks** to the LORD,	3344
	25: 9	"The LORD *can* g you much more than that."	5989

2Ch	25:18	'G your daughter to my son **in marriage.**'	851+4200+5989
	30:12	of God was on the people to g them unity	5989
	31: 2	to minister, to g **thanks** and to sing praises	3344
	31: 4	in Jerusalem to g the portion due the priests	5989
	35:12	They set aside the burnt offerings to g them	5989
Ezr	9:12	g your daughters **in marriage**	5989
Ne	1:11	G your servant **success**	7503
	2: 8	so *he will* g me timber to make beams for	5989
	2:20	"The God of heaven *will* g us **success.**	7503
	4: 4	G them **over** as plunder in a land	5989
	5:11	G **back** to them immediately their fields,	8740
	5:12	"We will g it **back**," they said.	8740
	6:13	and then they *would* g me a bad name	2118+4200
	8:13	the scribe to g **attention** to the words of	8505
	9: 6	You g **life** to everything,	2649
	9: 8	a covenant with him to g to his descendants	5989
	9:12	with a pillar of fire to g them **light on**	239
	9:15	with uplifted hand to g them.	5989
	10:30	g our daughters **in marriage**	5989
	10:32	for carrying out the commands to g a third	5989
	12:24	who stood opposite them to g **praise**	2146
	12:31	I also assigned two large **choirs to g thanks**	9343
	13:25	g your daughters **in marriage**	5989
Est	1:19	Also *let* the king g her royal position	5989
	4:14	"g the Jews in Susa **permission**	5989
Job	2: 4	"A man *will* g all he has for his own life.	5989
	6:22	'G something on my behalf,	2035
	7:17	that *you* g him so much attention,	8883
	9:16	I do not believe *he would* g me **a hearing.**	263+7754
	10: 1	therefore *I will* g **free rein** to my complaint	6440
	15:35	They conceive trouble and g **birth** *to* evil;	3528
	17: 3	"G me, O God, the pledge you demand.	8492
	20:10	his own hands *must* g **back** his wealth.	8740
	20:18	What he toiled for he *must* g **back** uneaten;	8740
	21: 2	let this be the consolation you g me.	NIH
	22: 3	What pleasure would it g the Almighty	4200
	31:37	*I would* g him an account of my every step;	5583
	35: 7	If you are righteous, what *do you* g to him,	5989
	39: 1	when the mountain goats g **birth?**	3528
	39: 2	Do you know the time they g **birth?**	3528
	39:17	wisdom or g her **a share** of good sense.	2745
	39:19	"*Do you* g the horse his strength	5989
Ps	4: 1	G me **relief** from my distress;	8143
	5: 1	G **ear** to my words, O LORD,	263
	7:17	*I will* g **thanks** to the LORD because	3344
	13: 3	G **light** to my eyes,	239
	17: 1	G **ear** to my prayer—	263
	17: 6	g **ear** to me and hear my prayer.	265+5742
	18:35	*You* g me your shield of victory,	5989
	20: 4	*May he* g you the desire of your heart	5989
	21: 1	How great is his joy in the victories you g!	NIH
	28: 7	for joy and *I will* g **thanks** *to* him in song.	3344
	30:12	*I will* g you **thanks** forever.	3344
	35:18	*I will* g you **thanks** in the great assembly;	3344
	36: 8	*you* g them **drink** *from* your river	9197
	37: 4	and *he will* g you the desires of your heart.	5989
	37:21	but the righteous g generously;	5989
	44: 7	but *you* g us **victory** over our enemies,	3828
	45:10	Listen, O daughter, consider and g **ear:**	265+5742
	46: 2	the earth g **way** and the mountains fall into	4614
	49: 3	from my heart will g **understanding.**	NIH
	49: 7	No man can redeem the life of another or g	5989
	60:11	G us aid against the enemy,	2035
	71: 3	g *the* **command** to save me,	7422
	75: 1	*We* g **thanks** to you, O God, we give thanks	3344
	75: 1	We give thanks to you, O God, *we* g **thanks**	3344
	78:20	But can he also g us food?	5989
	85:12	The LORD *will* indeed g what is good,	5989
	86:11	g me an **undivided** heart,	3479
	86:17	G me a sign of your goodness,	6913
	100: 4	g **thanks** to him and praise his name.	3344
	104:11	*They* g **water** *to* all the beasts of the field;	9197
	104:27	These all look to you to g them their food	5989
	104:28	*When you* g it to them, they gather it up;	5989
	105: 1	G **thanks** to the LORD, call on his name;	3344
	105:11	"To you *I will* g the land of Canaan as	5989
	105:39	and a fire to g **light** at night.	239
	106: 1	G **thanks** to the LORD, for he is good;	3344
	106:47	that we *may* g **thanks** to your holy name	3344
	107: 1	G **thanks** to the LORD, for he is good;	3344
	107: 8	*Let them* g **thanks** to the LORD	3344
	107:15	*Let them* g **thanks** to the LORD	3344
	107:21	*Let them* g **thanks** to the LORD	3344
	107:31	*Let them* g **thanks** to the LORD	3344
	108:12	G us aid against the enemy,	2035
	109:24	My knees g **way** from fasting,	4173
	118: 1	G **thanks** to the LORD, for he is good;	3344
	118:19	I will enter and g **thanks** *to* the LORD.	3344
	118:21	*I will* g you **thanks**, for you answered me;	3344
	118:28	You are my God, and *I will* g you **thanks;**	3344
	118:29	G **thanks** to the LORD, for he is good;	3344
	119:34	G me **understanding,**	1067
	119:62	to g you **thanks** for your righteous laws.	3344
	119:73	g me **understanding** to learn your commands.	1067
	119:125	g me **discernment** that I may understand your statutes.	1067
	119:144	g me **understanding** that I may live.	1067
	119:169	g me **understanding** according	1067
	136: 1	G **thanks** to the LORD, for he is good.	3344
	136: 2	G **thanks** to the God of gods.	3344
	136: 3	G **thanks** to the Lord of lords:	3344
	136:26	G **thanks** to the God of heaven.	3344
	141: 8	*do not* g me **over to death.**	6867
	145:15	you g them their food at the proper time.	5989

Pr	1:10	if sinners entice you, *do not* g **in** to them.	995
	3:28	*I'll* g it tomorrow"—	5989
	4: 2	I g you sound learning,	5989
	5: 9	lest *you* g your best strength to others	5989
	14: 8	The wisdom of the prudent is *to* g **thought**	1067
	21:26	but the righteous g without sparing.	5989
	22:21	so that *you can* g sound answers	8740
	23:26	g me your heart and let your eyes keep	8740
	25:14	who boasts of **gifts he does not g.**	5522+9214
	25:21	g him food to eat;	430
	25:21	g him water **to drink,**	9197
	27:23	g careful attention to your herds;	8883
	29:17	and he will g you **peace;**	5663
	30: 8	g me neither poverty nor riches,	5989
	30: 8	but g me only my daily bread.	3271
	30:15	"The leech has two daughters. **'G! Give!**	2035
	30:15	"The leech has two daughters. **'Give! G!"**	2035
	31: 6	G beer to those who are perishing,	5989
	31:31	G her the reward she has earned,	5989
Ecc	3: 6	a time to search and a time to g **up,**	6
	10: 1	As dead flies g perfume **a bad smell,**	944+5580
	11: 2	G portions to seven, yes to eight,	5989
	11: 9	and *let* your heart g you **joy** in the days	3512
SS	7:12	there *I will* g you my love.	5989
	8: 2	g you spiced wine **to drink,**	9197
	8: 7	If one *were to* g all the wealth of his house	5989
	8:12	But my own vineyard is mine to g;	4200+7156
Isa	7:14	Therefore the Lord himself *will* g you	5989
	7:14	be with child and *will* g **birth** *to* a son,	3528
	7:22	of the abundance of the milk *they* g,	6913
	11: 4	with justice *he will* g **decisions** for the poor	5989
	12: 4	"G **thanks** to the LORD, call on his name;	3344
	13:10	and the moon *will* not g its light.	5585
	16: 3	"G us counsel, render a decision.	995
	19:11	of Pharaoh g senseless advice.	1279
	22:25	peg driven into the firm place *will* g **way;**	4631
	24:15	in the east g **glory** *to* the LORD;	3877
	26:17	to g **birth** writhes and cries out in her pain,	3528
	26:19	the earth *will* g **birth** *to* her dead.	5877
	29:11	And if *you* g the scroll to someone who can	5989
	29:12	if *you* g the scroll to someone who cannot	5989
	30:10	"G us **no more visions**	2600
	33:11	You conceive chaff, *you* g **birth** *to* straw;	3528
	34: 2	he will g them **over** to slaughter.	5989
	35: 3	steady the knees *that* g **way;**	4173
	36: 8	*I will* g you two thousand horses—	5989
	37:17	G **ear,** O LORD, and hear;	265+5742
	41:28	one among them **to g counsel,**	3446
	41:28	no *one* to g answer when I ask them.	8740
	42: 8	not g my glory to another or my praise	5989
	42:12	*Let them* g glory to the LORD	8492
	43: 3	*I* g Egypt for your ransom,	5989
	43: 4	*I will* g men in exchange for you,	5989
	43: 6	I will say to the north, '**G** them **up!'**	5989
	43:20	to g **drink** to my people, my chosen,	9197
	45: 3	*I will* g you the treasures of darkness,	5989
	45:11	g me **orders** about the work of my hands?	7422
	49:20	g me **more space** to live in."	5602
	53:12	Therefore *I will* g him **a portion** among	2745
	55: 3	G **ear** and come to me;	265+5742
	56: 5	to them *I will* g within my temple	5989
	56: 5	*I will* g them an everlasting name	5989
	56: 7	and g them **joy** in my house of prayer.	8523
	59: 4	they conceive trouble and g **birth** *to* evil.	3528
	62: 6	g yourselves no rest,	4200
	62: 7	and g him no rest	5989
	62: 8	"Never again *will I* g your grain as food	5989
	65:15	but to his servants *he will* g another name.	7924
	66: 9	the moment of birth and not g **delivery?"**	3528
Jer	3:15	Then *I will* g you shepherds	5989
	3:19	like sons and g you a desirable land,	5989
	6:10	To whom can I speak and g **warning?**	6386
	7:22	I *did* not *just* g them **commands**	7422
	8:10	Therefore *I will* g their wives	5989
	11: 5	to g them a land flowing with milk	5989
	12: 7	*I will* g the one I love into the hands	5989
	13:16	G glory to the LORD your God	5989
	14:13	*I will* g you lasting peace in this place.' "	5989
	15:13	Your wealth and your treasures *I will* g	5989
	16: 7	nor *will anyone* g them **a drink**	3926+9197
	17: 3	and all your treasures *I will* g **away**	5989
	18: 2	and there *I will* g you my message."	9048
	18:21	So g their children **over** to famine;	5989
	19: 7	and *I will* g their carcasses as food to	5989
	20:13	G **praise** *to* the LORD!	2146
	24: 7	*I will* g them a heart to know me,	5989
	27: 4	G them **a message** for their masters and say,	7422
	27: 5	and *I* g it to anyone I please.	5989
	28:14	I will even g him iron control over	5989
	29: 6	g your daughters **in marriage,**	408+4200+5989
	29:11	plans to g you hope and a future.	5989
	31: 2	I will come to g **rest** to Israel."	8089
	31:13	*I will* g them **comfort** and joy instead	5714
	32:22	to g their forefathers,	5989
	32:39	*I will* g them singleness of heart	5989
	32:42	on this people, so I *will* g them all	995
	33:11	saying, "G **thanks** to the LORD Almighty,	3344
	34:22	I am going to g **the order,**	7422
	35: 2	g them wine **to drink."**	9197
	38:15	"If *I* g you **an answer,** will you not kill me?	5583
	38:15	Even if *I did* g you **counsel,**	3619
La	2: 6	g yourself no relief, your eyes no rest.	5989
Eze	2: 8	open your mouth and eat what I g you."	5989
	3:17	the word I speak and g them **warning**	2302
	11:17	and *I will* g you **back** the land	5989
	11:19	*I will* g them an undivided heart and put	5989
	11:19	from them their heart of stone and g them	5989

Eze	16:33	but you g gifts to all your lovers,	5989
	16:34	for you g payment and none is given	5989
	16:61	*I will* g them to you as daughters,	5989
	20:28	to g them and they saw any high hill	5989
	20:42	the land I had sworn with uplifted hand to g	5989
	21:22	to g *the* **command** to slaughter,	7023+7337
	21:27	to him *I will* g it.'	5989
	23: 8	She did *not* g **up** the prostitution she began	6440
	23:46	Bring a mob against them and g them **over**	5989
	25: 4	therefore *I am going to* g you to the people	5989
	25: 7	and g you as plunder to the nations.	5989
	25:10	*I will* g Moab along with the Ammonites	5989
	29: 5	*I will* g you as food to the beasts of	5989
	29:19	to g Egypt to Nebuchadnezzar king	5989
	32: 7	and the moon *will* not g its **light.**	239+240
	33: 7	the word I speak and g them **warning**	2302
	33:15	follows the **decrees** *that* g **life,**	AIT
	33:27	the country *I will* g to the wild animals to	5989
	35: 6	*I will* g you **over** to bloodshed	6913
	36:26	*I will* g you a new heart and put	5989
	36:26	from you your heart of stone and g you	5989
	39: 4	*I will* g you as food to all kinds	5989
	39:11	" 'On that day *I am to* g Gog a burial place	5989
	43:19	*You are to* g a young bull as a sin offering	5989
	44: 5	and g attention *to* everything I tell you	8492
	44: 5	G attention to the entrance of the temple	8492
	44:28	*You are to* g them no possession in Israel;	5989
	44:30	*You are to* g them the first portion	5989
	45: 6	*to* g the city as its property an area 5,000	5989
	45: 9	G **up** your violence and oppression	6073
	46: 7	the lambs as much as he **wants to g,**	3338+5952
	46:18	g his sons their **inheritance**	5706
	47:14	Because I swore with uplifted hand to g it	5989
	47:23	there *you are to* g him his inheritance,"	5989
Da	1:12	G us nothing but vegetables to eat	5989
	3:28	*to* g **up** their lives rather than serve	10314
	5:16	you are able to g **interpretations**	10599+10600
	5:17	and g your rewards to someone else.	10314
	9:18	G **ear,** O God, and hear;	265+5742
	9:22	to g you **insight** and understanding.	8505
	11:17	g him a daughter **in marriage**	851+2021+5989
Hos	2: 5	who g me my food and my water,	5989
	2:15	There *I will* g her **back** her vineyards,	5989
	4:10	the LORD to g **themselves**	9068
	5: 7	*they* g **birth** to illegitimate children.	3528
	9:14	G them, O LORD—	5989
	9:14	what *will you* g them?	5989
	9:14	G them wombs that miscarry and breasts	5989
	11: 8	"How *can I* g you **up,** Ephraim?	5989
	13:10	"G me a king and princes"?	5989
Am	2:10	to g you the land of the Amorites.	3769
	5:11	on the poor and **force** him to g you grain.	4374
	9: 9	"For *I will* g *the* **command,**	7422
Jnh	3: 2	and proclaim to it the message I g you."	1819
	3: 8	*Let* them g **up** their evil ways	4946+8740
	4: 6	and made it grow up over Jonah to g shade	2118
Mic	1:14	Therefore *you will* g parting gifts	5989
	4:13	for *I will* g you horns of iron;	8492
	4:13	*I will* g you hoofs of bronze	8492
	6:14	what you save *I will* g to the sword.	5989
	6:16	Therefore *I will* g you **over** to ruin	5989
Na	2:10	Hearts melt, knees g **way,** bodies tremble,	7211
Hab	2: 1	what **answer** *I am to* g to this complaint.	8740
	2:19	*Can* it g **guidance?**	3723
Zep	3:19	*I will* g them praise and honor	8492
	3:20	*I will* g you honor and praise among all	5989
Hag	1: 5	"G **careful thought** to your ways.	4222+8492
	1: 7	"G **careful thought** to your ways.	4222+8492
	2:15	" 'Now g **careful thought** to this	4222+8492
	2:18	g **careful thought** to the day when	4222+8492
	2:18	G **careful thought:**	4222+8492
Zec	3: 7	of my courts, and *I will* g you a place	5989
	8:12	all these things **as an inheritance**	5706
	10: 2	*they* g **comfort** in vain.	5714
	11:12	"If you think it best, g me my pay;	2035
Mal	1:14	in his flock and **vows to** g it,	5623
Mt	1:21	*She will* g **birth** to a son,	5503
	1:21	and *you are to* g him the name Jesus,	2813
	1:23	be with child and *will* g **birth** to a son,	5503
	4: 9	"All this *I will* g you," he said,	1443
	5:31	'Anyone who divorces his wife *must* g her	1443
	5:42	G to the one who asks you,	1443
	6: 2	"So when *you* g **to the needy,**	1797+4472
	6: 3	But *when you* g **to the needy,**	1797+4472
	6:11	G us today our daily bread.	1443
	7: 6	"*Do not* g dogs what is sacred;	1443
	7: 9	if his son asks for bread, *will* g him a stone?	2113
	7:10	if he asks for a fish, *will* g him a snake?	2113
	7:11	know how to g good gifts to your children,	1443
	7:11	will your Father in heaven g good gifts	1443
	10: 8	Freely you have received, freely g.	1443
	10:12	As you enter the home, g your **greeting.**	832
	11:28	weary and burdened, and *I will* g you **rest.**	399
	12:36	g **account** on the day of judgment **for**	625
	14: 7	with an oath to g her whatever she asked.	1443
	14: 8	"G me here on a platter the head of John	1443
	14:16	You g them something to eat."	1443
	16:19	*I will* g you the keys of the kingdom	1443
	16:26	what *can* a man g in exchange for his soul?	1443
	17:27	and g it to them for my tax and yours."	1443
	19: 7	"did Moses command that a man g his wife	1443
	19:18	do not steal, *do not* g **false testimony,**	6018
	19:21	go, sell your possessions and g to the poor,	1443
	20:14	*to* g the man who was hired last the same	1443
	20:28	g his life as a ransom for many."	1443
	21:41	g him *his* **share of** the crop	625
	22:21	"G to Caesar what is Caesar's,	625

Mt	23:23	*You* **g a tenth of** your spices—	620
	24:29	and the moon *will* not **g** its light;	1443
	24:45	in his household *to* **g** them their food at	1443
	25: 8	'**G** us some of your oil;	1443
	25:28	and **g** it to the one who has the ten talents.	1443
	25:37	**g** you something **to drink?**	4540
	26:15	*to* **g** me if I hand him over to you?"	1443
	27:64	So **g** the **order** for the tomb to	3027
Mk	5:43	and told them *to* **g** her something to eat.	1443
	6:22	and *I'll* **g** it to you."	1443
	6:23	"Whatever you ask I *will* **g** you,	1443
	6:25	"I want you *to* **g** me right now the head	1443
	6:37	"You **g** them something to eat."	1443
	6:37	to go and spend that much on bread and **g** it	1443
	7: 3	**g** their hands a ceremonial **washing,**	AIT
	8:37	what can a man **g** in exchange for his soul?	1443
	10:19	*do* not **g** false testimony, do not defraud,	6018
	10:21	sell everything you have and **g** to the poor,	1443
	10:45	and *to* **g** his life as a ransom for many."	1443
	12: 9	He will come and kill those tenants and **g**	1443
	12:17	"**G** to Caesar what is Caesar's and	625
	13:24	and the moon *will* not **g** its light;	1443
	14:11	to hear this and promised *to* **g** him money.	1443
Lk	1:13	and *you are to* **g** him the name John.	2813
	1:31	You will be with child and **g birth to** a son,	5503
	1:31	and *you are to* **g** him the name Jesus.	2813
	1:32	The Lord God *will* **g** him the throne	1443
	1:77	*to* **g** his people the knowledge of salvation	1443
	4: 6	"I *will* **g** you all their authority	1443
	4: 6	and I *can* **g** it to anyone I want to.	1443
	6:30	**G** to everyone who asks you,	1443
	6:38	**G,** and it will be given to you.	1443
	7:44	*You* did not **g** me any water for my feet,	1443
	7:45	*You* did not **g** me a kiss, but this woman,	1443
	8:55	Jesus told them *to* **g** her something to eat.	1443
	9:13	He replied, "You **g** them something to eat."	1443
	10: 7	eating and drinking *whatever* they **g** you,	3836
	11: 3	**G** us each day our daily bread.	1443
	11: 7	I can't get up and **g** you anything.'	1443
	11: 8	though *he will* not get up and **g** him	1443
	11: 8	up and **g** him as much as he needs.	1443
	11:11	asks for a fish, *will* **g** him a snake instead?	2113
	11:12	if he asks for an egg, *will* **g** him a scorpion?	2113
	11:13	know how *to* **g** good gifts to your children,	1443
	11:13	will your Father in heaven **g** the Holy Spirit	1443
	11:41	**g** what is inside [the dish] **to the poor,**	1443+1797
	11:42	**g God a tenth of** you mint, rue and	620
	12:32	for your Father has been pleased *to* **g** you	1443
	12:33	Sell your possessions and **g to the poor.**	1443+1797
	12:42	*to* **g** them their food allowance at	1443+3836
	13:15	from the stall and lead it out *to* **g** it **water?**	4540
	14: 9	'**G** this man your seat.'	1443
	14:12	"When *you* **g** a luncheon or dinner,	4472
	14:13	But when *you* **g** a banquet, invite the poor,	4472
	14:33	not **g up** everything he has cannot	698
	15:12	'Father, **g** me my share of the estate.'	1443
	16: 2	**G** an account of your management,	625
	16:12	who *will* **g** you property of your own?	1443
	17:18	and **g** praise to God except this foreigner?"	1443
	18: 1	that they should always pray and not **g up.**	1591
	18:12	I fast twice a week and **g a tenth of**	620
	18:20	do not steal, *do* not **g** false testimony,	6018
	18:22	Sell everything you have and **g** to the poor,	1344
	19: 8	Here and *now* I **g** half of my possessions to	1443
	19:24	'Take his mina away from him and **g** it	1443
	20:10	to the tenants *so they would* **g** him some of	1443
	20:16	He will come and kill those tenants and **g**	1443
	20:25	"Then **g** to Caesar what is Caesar's,	625
	21:15	For I *will* **g** you words and wisdom	1443
	22: 5	and agreed *to* **g** him money.	1443
	24:30	broke it and *began to* **g** it to them.	2113
Jn	1:22	**G** us an answer to take back	NIG
	4: 7	Jesus said to her, "*Will you* **g** me a drink?"	1443
	4:14	the water I **g** him will never thirst.	1443
	4:14	the water I **g** him will become in him	1443
	4:15	**g** me this water so that I won't get thirsty	1443
	5:21	Son gives life to whom he is pleased to **g** it.	NIG
	6:27	which the Son of Man *will* **g** you.	1443
	6:30	"What miraculous sign then *will* you **g**	4472
	6:34	they said, "from now on **g** us this bread."	1443
	6:51	which I *will* **g** for the life of the world."	1443
	6:52	"How can this man **g** us his flesh to eat?"	1443
	9:24	"**G** glory to God," they said.	1443
	10:28	I **g** them eternal life, and they shall never perish;	1443
	11:22	now God *will* **g** you whatever you ask."	1443
	13:26	"It is the one to whom I *will* **g** this piece	1443
	13:29	or to **g** something to the poor.	1443
	13:34	new command I **g** you: Love one another.	1443
	14:16	and *he will* **g** you another Counselor to be	1443
	14:27	Peace I leave with you; my peace I **g** you.	1443
	14:27	I *do* not **g** to you as the world gives.	1443
	15:16	the Father *will* **g** you whatever you ask	1443
	16:23	my Father *will* **g** you whatever you ask	1443
	17: 2	over all people that *he might* **g** eternal life	1443
	18:40	**G** us Barabbas!"	NIG
Ac	3: 6	but what I *have* I **g** you.	1443
	5:31	*that he might* **g** repentance and forgiveness	1443
	6: 4	and *will* **g** our **attention** to prayer and	4674
	8:19	"**G** me also this ability so that everyone	1443
	12:23	because Herod *did* not **g** praise to God,	1443
	13:34	" 'I *will* **g** you the holy and sure blessings	1443
	20:32	which can build you up and **g** you	1443
	20:35	'It is more blessed *to* **g** than to receive.' "	1443
	21:26	to the temple *to* **g notice of** the date when	1334
	23:21	Don't **g in** to them,	4275

Ac	24:23	under guard but *to* **g** him some freedom	2400
Ro	2: 6	God "*will* **g** to each person according	625
	2: 7	he will **g** eternal life.	NIG
	8:11	also **g** life to your mortal bodies	2443
	8:32	along with him, **graciously g** us all things?	5919
	12: 8	to the needs of others, let him **g** generously;	NIG
	12:20	**g** him something **to drink.**	4540
	13: 6	*who g their* **full time** to this,	4674
	13: 7	**G** everyone what you owe him:	625
	14:12	of us *will* **g** an account of himself to God.	1443
	15: 5	and encouragement **g** you a spirit of unity	1443
	16: 2	*to* **g** her any help she may need from you,	4225
1Co	7:10	To the married I **g this command** (not I,	4133
	7:25	I have no command from the Lord, but I **g**	1443
	10:16	cup of thanksgiving for which *we* **g thanks**	2328
	11:34	when I come I *will* **g** further **directions.**	1411
	13: 3	**g** all I possess **to the poor**	6039
	15:58	**g** yourselves **fully** to the work of the Lord,	4355
	16: 3	I will **g** letters of introduction to the men	NIG
2Co	1:11	many *will* **g thanks** on our behalf **for**	2373
	4: 6	made his light shine in our hearts to **g** us	NIG
	8:10	Last year you were the first not only to **g**	4472
	9: 2	in Achaia were ready to **g**;	NIG
	9: 7	Each man should **g** what he has decided	NIG
	9: 7	in his heart to **g**,	NIG
Gal	2: 5	*We* did not **g in** to them for a moment,	1634+3836+5717
	3: 5	*Does* God **g** you his Spirit and work	2220
	6: 9	a harvest *if we do* not **g up.**	1725
Eph	1:17	*may* **g** you the Spirit of wisdom	1443
	4:27	and *do* not **g** the devil a foothold.	1443
Php	2:30	up for the help you *could not* **g** me.	5729
Col	4:15	**G** my **greetings** to the brothers at Laodicea	832
1Th	5:18	**g thanks** in all circumstances,	2373
2Th	1: 7	and relief to you who are troubled,	NIG
	3:16	of peace himself **g** you peace at all times	1443
1Ti	1:18	I **g** you this instruction in keeping with	4192
	4:15	**g** yourself **wholly** to them,	3509
	5: 3	**G** proper **recognition** to those widows	5506
	5: 7	**G** the people these **instructions,**	4133
	5:14	*to* **g** the enemy no opportunity for slander.	1443
2Ti	1: 7	For God *did* not **g** us a spirit of timidity,	1443
	2: 7	the Lord *will* **g** you insight into all this.	1443
	4: 1	I **g** you this **charge:**	1371
Heb	4:13	of him to whom we must **g** account.	NIG
	6:14	**g** you **many descendants.**"	4437+4437
	10:25	*Let* us not **g up** meeting together,	1593
	13:17	over you as men *who must* **g** an account.	625
Jas	1:18	*He* chose *to* **g** us **birth** through the word	652
1Pe	3: 6	if you do what is right and do not **g way**	4766
	3:15	to **g** an answer to everyone who asks you	NIG
	3:15	to **g** the reason for the hope that you have.	NIG
	4: 5	to **g** account to him who is ready to judge	625
1Jn	5:16	he should pray and God *will* **g** him life.	1443
Rev	2: 7	I *will* **g** the right to eat from the tree	1443
	2:10	and I *will* **g** you the crown of life.	1443
	2:17	I *will* **g** some of the hidden manna.	1443
	2:17	I *will* also **g** him a white stone with	1443
	2:26	I *will* **g** authority over the nations—	1443
	2:28	I *will* also **g** him the morning star.	1443
	3:21	I *will* **g** the right to sit with me	1443
	4: 9	Whenever the living creatures **g** glory,	1443
	10: 9	and asked him *to* **g** me the little scroll.	1443
	11: 3	And I *will* **g** power to my two witnesses,	1443
	11:17	"*We* **g thanks** to you, Lord God Almighty,	2373
	12: 2	in pain *as she was about to* **g birth.**	5503+6048
	12: 4	of the woman who was about to **g birth,**	5503
	13:15	*to* **g** breath to the image of the first beast,	1443
	14: 7	"Fear God and **g** him glory,	1443
	17:13	and *will* **g** their power and authority to	1443
	17:17	to accomplish his purpose by agreeing *to* **g**	1443
	18: 6	**G back** to her as she has given;	625
	18: 7	**G** her as much torture and grief as the glory	1443
	19: 7	and be glad and **g** him glory!	1443
	21: 6	To him who is thirsty I *will* **g** to drink	1443
	22: 5	for the Lord God *will* **g** them **light.**	5894
	22:12	and I *will* **g** to everyone according	625
	22:16	have sent my angel *to* **g** you this **testimony**	3455

GIVE, GIVEN (Anglicized) See also DELIVERED, TURN

GIVEN (472) [GIVE]

Ge	9: 2	they **are g** into your hands.	5989
	15: 3	Abram said, "*You* have **g** me no children;	5989
	24:19	After *she had* **g** him a **drink,** she said,	9197
	24:35	*He has* **g** him sheep and cattle,	5989
	24:36	and *he has* **g** him everything he owns.	5989
	26:18	the same names his father *had* **g** them.	7924
	26:22	"Now the LORD *has* **g** us **room**	8143
	27:41	because of the blessing his father *had* **g** him.	1385
	28: 4	and your descendants the **blessing g**	AIT
	30: 6	he has listened to my plea and **g** me a son."	5989
	31: 9	and *has* **g** them to me.	5989
	33: 5	children God *has* **graciously g** your servant.	2858
	38:14	she *had* not **been g** to him as his wife.	5989
	38:30	came out and he *was* **g** the name Zerah.	7924
	40:16	**g** a favorable **interpretation,**	7354
	41:32	the dream *was* **g** to Pharaoh in two forms is	9101
	43:23	*has* **g** you treasure in your sacks;	5989
	46:18	whom Laban *had* **g** to his daughter Leah—	5989
	46:25	whom Laban *had* **g** to his daughter Rachel—	5989
	48: 9	"They are the sons God *has* **g** me here,"	5989
Ex	4:21	the wonders I *have* **g** you the power to do.	8492
	5:16	Your servants **are g** no straw,	5989

Ex	5:18	You *will* not be **g** any straw,	5989
	16:15	"It is the bread the LORD *has* **g** you to eat.	5989
	16:29	Bear in mind that the LORD *has* **g** you	5989
	28: 3	the skilled men *to* whom I *have* **g** wisdom	4848
	31: 6	Also I *have* **g** skill to all the craftsmen	5989
	34:32	the LORD *had* **g** him on Mount Sinai.	1819
	35:34	And *he has* **g** both him and Oholiab son	5989
	36: 1	to whom the LORD *has* **g** skill and ability	5989
	36: 2	*to* whom the LORD *had* **g** ability	5989
Lev	6:17	I *have* **g** it as their share of the offerings	5989
	7:34	the thigh that is presented and *have* **g** them	5989
	10:11	the LORD *has* **g** them through Moses."	1819
	10:14	they *have* **been g** to you and your children	5989
	10:17	it *was* **g** to you to take away the guilt of	5989
	17:11	and I *have* **g** it to you to make atonement	5989
	19:20	not been ransomed *or* **g** her freedom,	5989
	26:25	and *you will* be **g** into enemy hands.	5989
	27: 9	an animal **g** to the LORD becomes holy.	5989
Nu	1: 7	Aaron took these men whose names *had* been **g,**	5918
	3: 9	Israelites *who are to* be **g** wholly to him.	5989+5989
	5: 8	to the LORD and must be **g** to the priest,	NIH
	8:16	Israelites *who are to* be **g** wholly to me.	5989+5989
	8:19	I *have* **g** the Levites as gifts to Aaron	5989
	16:14	a land flowing with milk and honey or **g** us	5989
	18:29	and holiest part of everything **g** *to* you.'	5510
	21:29	*He has* **g up** his sons as fugitives	5989
	27:12	the Abarim range and see the land I *have* **g**	5989
	32: 5	"*let* this land *be* **g** to your servants	5989
	32: 7	over into the land the LORD *has* **g** them?	5989
	32: 9	the land the LORD *had* **g** them.	5989
	33:53	for I *have* **g** you the land to possess.	5989
	34:13	that it *be* **g** to the nine and a half tribes,	5989
	35: 8	the land the Israelites possess *are to* be **g**	5989
Dt	1: 8	See, I *have* **g** you this land.	5989
	1:21	the LORD your God *has* **g** you the land.	5989
	2: 5	I *have* **g** Esau the hill country of Seir	5989
	2: 9	I *have* **g** Ar to the descendants of Lot as	5989
	2:19	I *have* **g** it as a possession to	5989
	2:24	I *have* **g** into your hand Sihon the Amorite,	5989
	3:18	"The LORD your God *has* **g** you this land	5989
	3:19	in the towns I *have* **g** you,	5989
	3:20	to the possession I *have* **g** you."	5989
	6:17	the stipulations and decrees he *has* **g** you.	7422
	8:10	for the good land he *has* **g** you.	5989
	9:23	of the land I *have* **g** you."	5989
	12: 1	*has* **g** you to possess—	5989
	12:21	the herds and flocks the LORD *has* **g** you,	5989
	16:10	**blessings** the LORD your God *has* **g**	1385
	22:19	because this man *has* **g** an Israelite virgin	3655
	26:10	O LORD, *have* **g** me."	5989
	26:11	the good things the LORD your God *has* **g** you	5989
	26:13	the sacred portion and *have* **g** it to	5989
	26:15	and the land you *have* **g** us as you promised	5989
	28:31	Your sheep *will* be **g** to your enemies,	5989
	28:32	and daughters *will* be **g** to another nation,	5989
	28:53	the LORD your God *has* **g** you.	5989
	29: 4	to this day the LORD *has* not **g** you a mind	5989
	29:26	gods *he had* not **g** them.	2745
	32:30	unless the LORD *had* **g** them **up?**	6037
Jos	2: 9	the LORD *has* **g** this land to you and that	5989
	2:24	"The LORD *has* surely **g** the whole land	5989
	6:16	For the LORD *has* **g** you the city!	5989
	9:19	"We *have* **g** our **oath** by the LORD,	8678
	10: 8	I *have* **g** them into your hand.	5989
	10:19	for the LORD your God *has* **g** them	5989
	13: 8	the inheritance that Moses *had* **g** them east	5989
	13:15	This is what Moses *had* **g** to the tribe	5989
	13:24	This is what Moses *had* **g** to the tribe	5989
	13:29	This is what Moses *had* **g** to the half-tribe	5989
	13:32	This is the **inheritance** Moses *had* **g**	5706
	13:33	Moses *had* **g** no inheritance.	5989
	15:19	Since *you* have **g** me land in the Negev,	5989
	17:14	"Why *have you* **g** us only one allotment	5989
	18: 3	the God of your fathers, *has* **g** you?	5989
	21:12	around the city *they* had **g** to Caleb son	5989
	21:21	of Ephraim they *were* **g** Shechem (a city	5989
	21:26	and their pasturelands were **g** to the rest of	NIH
	21:27	The Levite clans of the Gershonites were **g:**	4200
	21:34	(the rest of the Levites) were **g:**	4200
	22: 4	LORD your God *has* **g** your brothers **rest**	5663
	22: 7	the half-tribe of Manasseh Moses *had* **g** land	5989
	23: 1	and the LORD *had* **g** Israel **rest**	5663
	23:13	which the LORD your God *has* **g** you.	5989
	23:15	from this good land he *has* **g** you.	5989
	23:16	from the good land he *has* **g** you."	5989
Jdg	1: 2	I *have* **g** the land into their hands."	5989
	1:15	Since *you* have **g** me land *in* the Negev,	5989
	1:20	Hebron *was* **g** to Caleb,	5989
	3: 4	which he *had* **g** their forefathers	7422
	3:28	"for the LORD *has* **g** Moab, your enemy,	5989
	4:14	the LORD *has* **g** Sisera into your hands.	5989
	7:14	God *has* **g** the Midianites and	5989
	7:15	The LORD *has* **g** the Midianite camp	5989
	8: 7	the LORD *has* **g** Zebah and Zalmunna	5989
	11:24	whatever the LORD our God *has* **g** us,	3769
	11:36	"you *have* **g** your **word** to the LORD.	906+7023+7198
	14:11	he *was* **g** thirty companions,	4374
	14:16	*You've* **g** my people a riddle,	2554
	14:20	And Samson's wife *was* **g** to	2118
	15: 6	because his wife *was* **g** to his friend."	5989
	15:18	"You *have* **g** your servant this great victory.	5989
	20:36	men of Israel *had* **g** way before Benjamin,	5989
	21:14	at that time and *were* **g** the women	5989

Ru	2:13	*"You have* g me **comfort**	5714
	4:15	*has* g him **birth."**	3528
1Sa	1:28	For his whole life he *will* **be** g over to	8626
	4:20	*you have* g **birth** *to* a son."	3528
	14:10	that the LORD *has* g them into our hands."	5989
	14:12	the LORD *has* g them into the hand	5989
	15:28	of Israel from you today and *has* g it to one	5989
	18:19	Saul's daughter, *to be* g to David,	5989
	18:19	she *was* g **in marriage** to Adriel of Meholah.	851+4200+5989
	25:27	**be** g to the men who follow you.	5989
	25:44	But Saul *had* g his daughter Michal,	5989
	28:17	the kingdom out of your hands and g it	5989
	30:23	not do that with what the LORD *has* g us.	5989
2Sa	7:1	in his palace and the LORD *had* g him **rest**	5663
	9:9	*I have* g your master's grandson everything	5989
	12:8	*I would have* g you **even more.** 2179+2179+2256+3578+3869+3869	
	13:28	*Have* not I g you *this* **order?**	7422
	17:6	*Ahithophel has* g this advice.	1819
	17:7	**advice** Ahithophel *has* g	3619+6783
	21:6	*let* seven of his male descendants *be* g	5989
1Ki	2:21	Shunammite *be* g **in marriage**	851+4200+5989
	3:6	to him and *have* g him a son to sit	5989
	3:28	all Israel heard the verdict the king *had* g,	9149S
	5:4	But now the LORD my God *has* g me **rest**	5663
	5:7	for *he has* g David a wise son to rule	5989
	8:56	who *has* g rest to his people Israel just	5663
	9:6	the commands and decrees *I have* g you	5989
	9:7	from the land *I have* g them	5989
	9:12	to see the towns that Solomon *had* g him,	5989
	9:13	of towns are these *you have* g me,	5989
	10:13	besides what *he had* g her out	5989
	12:13	Rejecting the **advice** g him by the elders,	3619+6783
	13:5	according to the sign g *by* the man of God	5989
	13:26	The LORD *has* g him **over** to the lion,	5989
	15:29	of the LORD g through his servant Ahijah	1819
	18:26	they took the bull g them and prepared it.	5989
	20:27	also mustered and g **provisions,**	3920
2Ki	5:1	through him the LORD *had* g victory	5989
	5:17	**be** g as much earth as a pair	5989
	15:20	to contribute fifty shekels of silver to *be* g	5989
	17:15	and the **warnings** *he had* g	6343+6030
	18:6	the commands the LORD *had* g Moses.	7422
	18:30	this city *will* not *be* g into the hand of	5989
	22:10	"Hilkiah the priest *has* g me a book."	5989
1Ch	5:1	as firstborn *were* g to the sons of Joseph son	5989
	6:55	They *were* g Hebron in Judah	5989
	6:56	the city *were* g to Caleb son of Jephunneh.	5989
	6:57	So the descendants of Aaron *were* g Hebron	5989
	6:60	the tribe of Benjamin they *were* g Gibeon,	NIH
	6:66	Some of the Kohathite clans *were* g	2118
	6:67	of Ephraim they *were* g Shechem (a city	5989
	6:40	which *he had* g Israel.	7422
	25:5	They *were* g him through the promises	NIH
	28:5	and the LORD *has* g me **many—**	5989
	29:9	for *they had* g **freely** and wholeheartedly to	5605
	29:14	and *we have* g you only what comes	5989
	29:17	All these things *have* I g **willingly** and	5605
	29:17	**willingly** your people who are here *have* g	5605
2Ch	1:12	wisdom and knowledge *will* **be** g you.	5989
	2:12	*He has* g King David a wise son,	5989
	2:14	of engraving and can execute any design g	5989
	7:19	the decrees and commands *I have* g you	5989
	7:20	which *I have* g them,	5989
	8:2	the villages that Hiram *had* g him,	5989
	13:5	*has* g the kingship of Israel to David	5989
	14:7	and *he has* g us **rest** on every side."	5663
	18:14	"for *they will* **be** g into your hand."	5989
	20:27	g them **cause to rejoice**	8523
	20:30	for his God *had* g him **rest** on every side.	5663
	21:3	Their father *had* g them many gifts of silver	5989
	21:3	but *he had* g the kingdom to Jehoram	5989
	28:5	*He was* also g into the hands of the king	5989
	31:14	was in charge of the **freewill offerings** g	AIT
	32:29	for God *had* g him very great riches.	5989
	33:8	decrees and ordinances g through Moses."	NIH
	34:14	the LORD that had been g through Moses.	NIH
	34:18	"Hilkiah the priest *has* g me a book."	5989
	36:23	of heaven, *has* g me all the kingdoms of	5989
Ezr	1:2	of heaven, *has* g me all the kingdoms of	5989
	6:9	must be g them daily without fail,	10314
	7:6	which the LORD, the God of Israel, *had* g.	5989
	7:11	of the letter King Artaxerxes *had* g to Ezra	5989
	7:15	that the king and his advisers have **freely** g	10461
	9:9	and repair its ruins, and he *has* g us a wall	5989
	9:13	and *have* g us a remnant like this.	5989
Ne	7:72	The total g by the rest of the people	5989
	10:29	of God g through Moses the servant of God	5989
	12:43	because God *had* g them great **joy.**	8523+8525
	13:10	to the Levites *had* not been g to them,	5989
Est	2:3	and *let* beauty treatments *be* g to them.	5989
	2:13	Anything she wanted *was* g her to take	5989
	5:3	up to half the kingdom, *it will* **be** g you."	5989
	5:6	*It will* **be** g you.	5989
	7:2	*It will* **be** g you.	5989
	8:7	*I have* g his estate to Esther,	5989
	9:12	*It will* **be** g you.	5989
Job	3:20	"Why is light g to those in misery,	5989
	3:23	Why is life g to a man whose way is hidden	NIH
	15:19	the land *was* g whom no alien passed	5989
	38:12	*"Have you* ever g **orders** *to* the morning,	7422
Ps	60:3	*you have* g us wine that makes us stagger.	9197
	61:5	*you have* g me the heritage	3498
	63:10	*be* g **over** *to* the sword and	3338+5599+6584
	72:15	*May* gold from Sheba *be* g him.	5989

Ps	74:9	*We are* g no miraculous signs;	8011
	78:29	for *he had* g them what they craved.	995
	79:2	*They have* g the dead bodies	5989
	94:17	Unless the LORD *had* g me help,	NIH
	105:42	For he remembered his holy promise g to	907
	115:16	but the earth he *has* g to man.	5989
	118:18	but *he has* not g me **over** to death.	5989
	119:49	for *you have* g me **hope.**	3498
	122:4	of the LORD according to the statute g to	4200
Pr	8:24	When there were no oceans, *I was* g **birth,**	2655
	8:25	before the hills, *I was* g **birth,**	2655
	21:14	A gift g in secret soothes anger,	NIH
	23:2	to your throat if you are g to **gluttony.**	1251+5883
Ecc	5:18	the few days of life God *has* g him—	5989
	8:15	the days of the life God *has* g him under	5989
	9:9	of this meaningless life that God *has* g you	5989
	12:11	firmly embedded nails—g by one Shepherd.	5989
Isa	1:4	children g to **corruption!**	8845
	8:18	and the children the LORD *has* g me.	5989
	9:6	For to us a child is born, to us a son is g,	5989
	14:32	What **answer** *shall be* g to the envoys of	6699
	23:4	"I have neither been in labor nor g **birth;**	3528
	23:11	He *has* g **an order** concerning Phoenicia	7422
	26:18	*we have* not g **birth** to people of the world.	5877
	34:16	For it is his mouth that *has* g the **order,**	7422
	35:2	The glory of Lebanon *will be* g to it,	5989
	36:15	this city *will* not *be* g into the hand of	5989
	50:4	The Sovereign LORD *has* g me	5989
	63:10	they *were* g **rest** by the Spirit of	5663
Jer	4:31	my life is g **over** to murderers."	4200
	8:13	What *I have* g them will be taken	5989
	8:14	g us poisoned water **to drink,**	9197
	21:10	*It will be* g into the hands of the king	5989
	32:16	"After *I had* g the deed of purchase	5989
	35:15	the land *I have* g to you and your fathers."	5989
	37:21	the courtyard of the guard and g bread from	5989
	38:16	who *has* g us breath,	6913
	39:11	of Babylon *had* g *these* **orders**	7422
La	3:58	LORD *has* g **full vent** *to* his wrath;	3983
Eze	11:15	this land *was* g to us as our possession.'	5989
	11:24	to the exiles in Babylonia in the vision g **by**	928
	15:6	As *I have* g the wood of the vine among	5989
	16:14	splendor *I had* g you made your beauty perfect,	8492
	16:34	for you give payment and none *is* g to you.	5989
	17:18	g his hand **in pledge**	5989
	20:15	not bring them into the land *I had* g them—	5989
	29:20	*I have* g him Egypt as a reward	5989
	33:24	the land *has been* g to us as our possession.'	5989
	35:12	and *have been* g **over** to us to devour."	5989
	46:5	The grain offering g with the ram is to be	NIH
Da	2:23	*You have* g me wisdom and power,	10314
	2:37	of heaven *has* g you dominion and power	10314
	4:16	that of a man and *let* him *be* g the mind of	10314
	5:21	from people and g the mind of an animal;	10702
	5:28	and g to the Medes and Persians."	10314
	7:4	and the heart of a man *was* g to it.	10314
	7:6	and it *was* g authority to rule.	10314
	7:14	He *was* g authority, glory	10314
	8:12	and the daily sacrifice *were* g **over** to it.	5989
	8:26	and mornings that *has been* g you is true,	606
	9:2	of the LORD g to Jeremiah the prophet,	2118
	9:23	as you began to pray, an answer *was* g,	3655
	10:1	a revelation *was* g to Daniel	1655
	10:19	my lord, since *you have* g me **strength."**	2616
	11:4	be uprooted and g to others.	4200
	11:21	a contemptible person who *has* not *been* g	5989
Hos	6:10	There Ephraim is g to prostitution	4200
	8:13	They offer sacrifices g *to* me and they eat	2037
Joel	2:23	for *he has* g you the autumn rains	5989
Am	6:11	For the LORD *has* g **the command,**	7422
	9:15	be uprooted from the land *I have* g them,"	5989
Na	1:14	The LORD *has* g a **command**	7422
Zec	6:8	the north country *have* g my Spirit **rest** in	5663
	6:14	The crown will be g to Heldai, Tobijah,	4200
Mt	6:33	all these things *will be* g to you as well.	4707
	7:7	"Ask and *it will* **be** g to you;	1443
	9:8	who *had* g such authority to men.	1443
	10:19	At that time you *will* **be** g what to say,	1443
	12:39	*be* g it except the sign of the prophet Jonah.	1443
	13:11	the kingdom of heaven *has been* g to you,	1443
	13:12	Whoever has *will* **be** g **more,**	1443
	14:11	His head was brought in on a platter and g	1443
	15:36	and *when he had* g **thanks,**	2373
	16:4	but none *will* **be** g it except the sign	1443
	19:11	but only those to whom *it has been* g.	1443
	21:43	and g to a people who will produce its fruit.	1443
	22:30	nor *be* g **in marriage;**	1139
	25:29	For everyone who has *will be* g **more,**	1443
	26:9	a high price and the money g to the poor."	1443
	27:58	Pilate ordered that *it be* g to him.	625
	28:18	in heaven and on earth *has been* g to me.	1443
Mk	4:11	of the kingdom of God *has been* g to you.	1443
	4:25	Whoever has *will* **be** g **more;**	1443
	6:2	"What's this wisdom that *has been* g him,	1443
	6:17	For Herod himself *had* g **orders**	690
	8:6	the seven loaves and g **thanks,**	2373
	8:12	I tell you the truth, no sign *will* **be** g to it."	1443
	12:25	nor *be* g **in marriage;**	1139
	12:28	g them a good **answer,**	646
	13:11	Just say whatever *is* g you at the time,	1443
	14:5	a year's wages and the money g to	1443
Lk	2:21	Jesus, the name the angel *had* g him	2813
	4:6	*be* g to me,	4140
	6:38	Give, and *it will* **be** g to you.	1443
	8:10	the kingdom of God *has been* g to you,	1443

Lk	8:18	Whoever has *will be* g **more;**	1443
	10:19	*I have* g you authority to trample	1443
	11:9	Ask and *it will be* g to you;	1443
	11:29	none *will be* g it except the sign of Jonah.	1443
	12:48	From everyone who *has been* g much,	1443
	17:27	marrying and *being* g **in marriage** up to	1139
	19:15	the servants to whom *he had* g the money,	1443
	19:26	to everyone who has, more *will be* g,	1443
	20:34	of this age marry and *are* g **in marriage.**	1140
	20:35	nor *be* g **in marriage,**	1139
	22:19	saying, "This is my body g for you;	1443
Jn	1:17	For the law *was* g through Moses;	1443
	3:27	"A man can receive only what *is* g him	1443
	4:5	of ground Jacob *had* g to his son Joseph.	1443
	4:10	and he would *have* g you living water."	1443
	5:27	And he *has* g him authority to judge	1443
	5:36	For the very work that the Father *has* g me	1443
	6:23	the bread *after* the Lord *had* g **thanks.**	2373
	6:32	it is not Moses who *has* g you the bread	1443
	6:39	that I shall lose none of all that *he has* g me,	1443
	7:19	*Has* not Moses g you the law?	1443
	7:39	Up to that time the Spirit had not been g,	NIG
	10:29	My Father, who *has* g them to me,	1443
	11:57	the chief priests and Pharisees *had* g **orders**	1443
	12:2	Here a dinner *was* g in Jesus' honor.	4472
	12:5	and the money g to the poor?	1443
	12:18	that he *had* g this miraculous sign,	4472
	15:7	ask whatever you wish, and *it will be* g you.	1181
	17:2	to all those *you have* g him.	1443
	17:7	that everything *you have* g me comes	1443
	17:9	but for those *you have* g me,	1443
	17:14	*I have* g them your word and	1443
	17:22	*I have* g them the glory that you gave me,	1443
	17:24	I want those *you have* g me to be with me	1443
	17:24	the glory *you have* g me	1443
	18:11	not drink the cup the Father *has* g me?"	1443
	19:11	over me if it were not g to you from above.	1443
	19:35	The man who saw it *has* g **testimony,**	3455
Ac	3:16	that *has* g this complete healing to him,	1443
	4:12	under heaven g to men by which we must	1443
	5:32	whom God *has* g to those who obey him."	1443
	8:18	When Simon saw that the Spirit *was* g at	1443
	17:31	*He has* g **proof** of this to all men	4218+4411
	20:24	the task the Lord Jesus *has* g me—	3284
	27:24	and God *has* **graciously** g you the lives	5919
Ro	5:5	the Holy Spirit, whom *he has* g us.	1443
	5:13	for before the law was g,	NIG
	11:35	"Who *has* ever g to God,	4594
	12:3	the grace g me I say to every one of you:	1443
	12:3	with the measure of faith God *has* g you.	3532
	12:6	according to the grace g us.	1443
1Co	1:4	because of his grace g you in Christ Jesus.	1443
	2:12	may understand what God *has* **freely** g us.	5919
	3:10	By the grace God *has* g me,	1443
	4:2	*have been* g a trust must prove faithful.	3874
	11:15	For long hair *is* g to her as a covering.	1443
	11:24	and *when he had* g **thanks,** he broke it	2373
	12:7	of the Spirit *is* g for the common good.	1443
	12:8	To one *there is* g through the Spirit	1443
	12:13	g the one Spirit **to drink.**	4540
	12:24	of the body and *has* g greater honor to	1443
2Co	4:11	we who are alive *are* always *being* g **over**	4140
	5:5	for this very purpose and *has* g us the Spirit	1443
	7:7	but also by the comfort you *had* g him,	4151
	8:1	that God *has* g the Macedonian churches,	1443
	9:5	not as **one** grudgingly g.	4432
	9:14	of the surpassing grace God *has* g you.	NIG
	12:7	*there was* g me a thorn in my flesh,	1443
Gal	2:9	when they recognized the grace g to me.	1443
	3:18	He redeemed us in order that the blessing g	NIG
	3:21	if a law *had been* g that could impart life,	1443
	3:22	being g through faith in Jesus Christ,	NIG
	3:22	*might be* g to those who believe.	NIG
	4:15	and g them to me.	1443
Eph	1:6	which *he has* **freely** g us in	5923
	1:21	and every **title** *that can be* g,	3950+3951
	3:2	of God's grace that *was* g to me for you,	1443
	3:7	of God's grace g me through the working	1443
	3:8	this grace *was* g me:	1443
	4:7	But to each one of us grace *has been* g	1443
	4:19	they *have* g themselves **over** to sensuality	4140
	6:19	words *may be* g me so	1443
Php	1:19	that through your prayers and the **help** g by	2221
Col	1:6	*you have been* g **fullness** in Christ,	1639+4444
1Th	1:6	the joy g by the **Holy Spirit.**	AIT
1Ti	1:12	Jesus my Lord, who *has* g me strength,	1904
	2:6	the testimony g in its proper time.	NIG
	3:3	not g **to drunkenness,** not violent	4232
	4:14	which *was* g you through	1443
2Ti	1:9	This grace *was* g us in Christ Jesus before	1443
Tit	1:7	not quick-tempered, not g **to drunkenness,**	1443
Phm	1:7	Your love *has* g me great joy.	2400
Heb	2:13	and the children God *has* g me."	1443
	4:8	For if Joshua *had* g them **rest,**	2924
	7:11	the basis of it the **law** *was* g to the people),	3793
Jas	1:5	and *it will be* g to him.	1443
1Pe	1:3	In his great mercy he *has* g us **new birth**	335
	1:13	set your hope fully on the grace to *be* g you	5770
2Pe	1:3	His divine power *has* g us everything we need for life and godliness	1563
	1:4	Through these he *has* g us his very great	1563
	3:2	and the command g by our Lord and Savior	NIG
1Jn	4:13	because he *has* g us of his Spirit.	1443
	4:21	And he *has* g us this command:	608+2400
	5:9	which *he has* g about his Son.	3455S
	5:10	the testimony God *has* g about his Son.	3455S

1Jn	5:11	God *has* g us eternal life,	1443
	5:20	and *has* g us understanding,	1443
2Jn	1: 4	*It has* g me great **joy** to find some	AIT
Rev	2:21	*I have* g her time to repent	1443
	6: 2	Its rider held a bow, and he *was* g a crown,	1443
	6: 4	Its rider *was* g power to take peace from	1443
	6: 4	To him *was* g a large sword.	1443
	6: 8	They *were* g power over a fourth of	1443
	6:11	Then each of them *was* g a white robe,	1443
	7: 2	to the four angels who *had been* g power	1443
	8: 2	and to them *were* g seven trumpets.	1443
	8: 3	He *was* g much incense to offer,	1443
	9: 1	star *was* g the key to the shaft of the Abyss.	1443
	9: 3	down upon the earth and *were* g power like	1443
	9: 5	They *were* not g power to kill them,	1443
	11: 1	I *was* g a reed like a measuring rod	1443
	11: 2	because *it has been* g to the Gentiles.	1443
	12:13	he pursued the woman who *had* g **birth to**	5503
	12:14	The woman *was* g the two wings of	1443
	13: 4	the dragon because he *had* g authority to	1443
	13: 5	The beast *was* g a mouth to utter proud	1443
	13: 7	He *was* g power to make war against	1443
	13: 7	And he *was* g authority over every tribe,	1443
	13:14	the signs he *was* g power to do on behalf of	1443
	13:15	He *was* g power to give breath to the image	1443
	15: 2	They held harps g them by God	NIG
	16: 6	and *you have* g them blood to drink	1443
	16: 8	sun *was* g power to scorch people with fire.	1443
	18: 6	Give back to her as she *has* g;	625
	19: 8	bright and clean, *was* g her to wear."	1443
	20: 4	on which were seated *those* who *had been* g authority to judge.	1443

GIVER (2) [GIVE]

Pr	18:16	for the g and ushers him into the presence	132ˢ
2Co	9: 7	for God loves a cheerful g.	1522

GIVES (139) [GIVE]

Ex	4:11	Who g him sight or makes him blind?	NIH
	13:11	the land of the Canaanites and g it to you,	5989
	16: 8	that it was the LORD when *he* g you meat	5989
	16:29	that is why on the sixth day he g you bread	5989
	21: 4	If his master g him a wife	5989
	21:22	and she g **birth** prematurely	3529+3655
	22: 7	"If a man g his neighbor silver or goods	5989
	22:10	"If a man g a donkey, an ox,	5989
Lev	12: 2	and g **birth** *to* a son will be ceremonially	3528
	12: 5	If *she* g **birth** *to* a daughter, for two weeks	3528
	12: 7	regulations for the *woman who* g **birth** to	3528
	20: 2	or any alien living in Israel who g any	5989
	20: 4	that man g one of his children to Molech	5989
Nu	5:10	but what he g to the priest will belong to	5989
	10:32	whatever good things the LORD g us."	3512
	22: 8	the answer the LORD g me."	1819
Dt	3:20	until the LORD g **rest** to your brothers	5663
	4:40	the LORD your God g you for all time.	5989
	7:16	the peoples the LORD your God g **over**	5989
	8:18	for it is he who g you the ability	5989
	12:15	to the blessing the LORD your God g you.	5989
	16: 5	in any town the LORD your God g you	5989
	17: 2	the LORD g you is found doing evil in	5989
	19: 8	g you the whole land he promised them,	5989
	20:14	the plunder the LORD your God g you	5989
	22:14	and slanders her and g her a bad name,	3655
	24: 1	g it to her and sends her from his house,	5989
	24: 3	g it to her and sends her from his house,	5989
	25:19	the LORD your God g you **rest** from all	5663
Jos	1:15	until the LORD g them **rest,**	5663
	2:14	and faithfully when the LORD g us	5989
Jdg	11: 9	the Ammonites and the LORD g them	5989
	11:24	not take what your god Chemosh g you?	3769
	21:18	be *anyone who* g a wife to a Benjamite.'	5989
Ru	4:12	the LORD g you by this young woman,	5989
2Sa	22:51	*He* g his king **great** victories;	1540
	24:23	O king, Araunah g all this to the king."	5989
1Ki	17:14	not run dry until the day the LORD g rain	5989
Ezr	9: 8	and so our God g **light** to our eyes and	239
Est	5:13	But all this g me no **satisfaction** as long	8750
Job	8:15	He leans on his web, but *it* g **way;**	4202+6641
	32: 8	*that* g him **understanding.**	1067
	33: 4	the breath of the Almighty g me **life.**	2649
	35:10	*who* g songs in the night,	5989
	36: 6	He does not keep the wicked alive but g	5989
	38:29	Who g **birth** *to* the frost from the heavens	3528
Ps	7:14	with evil and conceives trouble g **birth**	3528
	18:50	*He* g his king **great** victories;	1540
	29:11	The LORD g strength to his people;	5989
	68:35	the God of Israel g power and strength	5989
	82: 1	*he* g **judgment** among the "gods":	9149
	119:130	The unfolding of your words g **light;**	239
	119:130	*it* g **understanding** *to* the simple.	1067
	136:25	and *who* g food to every creature.	5989
	144:10	to the One who g **victory** to kings,	5989
	146: 7	of the oppressed and g food to the hungry.	5989
	146: 8	the LORD g **sight** *to* the blind,	7219
Pr	2: 6	For the LORD g **wisdom,**	5989
	3:34	He mocks proud mockers but g **grace** to	5989
	5: 6	*She* g no **thought** *to* the way of life;	7143
	11:24	*One man* g **freely,** yet gains even more;	7061
	12:17	A truthful witness g **honest** testimony,	7032
	14:15	but a prudent man g **thought** to his steps.	1067
	14:30	A heart at peace g life to the body,	NIH
	15:30	and good news g **health** to the bones.	2014
	16:20	*Whoever* g **heed** to instruction prospers,	8505
	17: 8	A bribe is a charm to the **one who** g it;	1251

Pr	19: 6	everyone is the friend of a **man** *who* g gifts.	AIT
	19:11	A man's wisdom g him **patience;**	678+799
	21:29	but an upright man g **thought** *to* his ways.	1067
	22:16	to increase his wealth and *he who* g **gifts** to	5989
	25:18	the man *who* g false **testimony**	6699
	25:26	a polluted well is a righteous man *who* g **way** to the wicked.	4572
	28:27	*he who* g to the poor will lack nothing,	5989
	29: 4	By justice a king g a country **stability,**	6641
	29:11	A fool g full **vent** to his anger.	3655
	29:13	The LORD g **sight** *to* the eyes of both.	239
Ecc	2:26	God g wisdom, knowledge and happiness,	5989
	2:26	but to the sinner *he* g the task of gathering	5989
	5:19	God g any man wealth and possessions,	5989
	5:19	God g a man wealth,	5989
Isa	14: 3	the LORD g you **relief** from suffering	5663
	21: 9	And he g back *the* **answer:**	6699
	30:20	the Lord g you the bread of adversity and	5989
	40:29	*He* g strength to the weary and increases	5989
	42: 5	*who* g breath to its people,	5989
	66: 7	"Before she goes into labor, *she* g **birth;**	3528
	66: 8	in labor than *she* g **birth** *to* her children.	3528
Jer	5:24	who g autumn and spring rains in season,	5989
La	4: 4	but no *one* g it to them.	7298
Eze	18: 7	He does not commit robbery but g his food	5989
	18:16	He does not commit robbery but g his food	5989
	33:15	if he g **back** what he took in pledge for	8740
Da	2:21	g wisdom to the wise and knowledge to	10314
	4:17	and g them to anyone he wishes and sets	10498
	4:25	of men and g them to anyone he wishes.	10498
	4:32	of men and g them to anyone he wishes."	10498
Mic	5: 3	the time when she who is in labor g **birth**	3528
Hab	2:15	"Woe to *him who* g **drink** *to* his neighbors,	9197
Zec	10: 1	*He* g showers of rain to men,	5989
Mt	5:15	and *it* g **light** to everyone in the house.	3290
	10:42	g even a cup of cold **water to**	4540
	26:73	for your accent g you **away."**	1316+4472
Mk	1:27	*He* even g **orders** to evil spirits	2199
	9:41	anyone who g you **a cup** of water	4539+4540
Lk	4:36	With authority and power *he* g **orders**	2199
Jn	1: 9	that g **light** *to* every man was coming into	5894
	3: 6	Flesh g **birth** to flesh,	1164
	3: 6	but the Spirit g **birth** to spirit.	1164
	3:34	for God g the Spirit without limit.	1443
	5:21	the Father raises the dead and g them **life,**	2443
	5:21	so the Son g **life** to whom he is pleased	2443
	6:32	but it is my Father who g you	1443
	6:33	down from heaven and g life to the world."	1443
	6:37	All that the Father g me will come to me,	1443
	6:63	Spirit g **life;** the flesh counts for	1639+2443
	14:27	I do not give to you as the world g.	1443
Ac	17:25	*because* he himself g all men life	1443
Ro	4:17	the God who g **life** to the dead	2443
	14: 6	eats to the Lord, for *he* g **thanks** to God;	2373
	14: 6	does so to the Lord and g **thanks** to God.	2373
	15: 5	g **endurance** and **encouragement**	AIT
1Co	12:11	and *he* g them to each one,	1349
	15:38	But God g it a body as he has determined,	1443
	15:38	and to each kind of seed he g its own body.	NIG
	15:57	He g us the **victory** through our Lord	1443
2Co	3: 6	for the letter kills, but the Spirit g **life.**	2443
Php	4:13	through him who g me **strength.**	1904
1Th	4: 8	God, who g you his Holy Spirit.	1443
1Ti	6:13	God, who g **life to** everything,	2441
Jas	1: 5	God, who g generously to all	1443
	1:15	desire has conceived, *it* g **birth to** sin;	5503
	1:15	when *it is* full-grown, g **birth** to death.	652
	1:25	that g **freedom,** and continues to do this,	AIT
	2:12	to be judged by the law that g **freedom,**	AIT
	4: 6	But *he* g us more grace.	1443
	4: 6	opposes the proud but g grace to the humble.	1443
1Pe	5: 5	opposes the proud but g grace to the humble.	1443
Rev	21:23	for the glory of God g it **light,**	5894

GIVING (117) [GIVE]

Ge	13:17	for *I am* g it to you."	5989
	20:16	"*I am* g your brother a thousand shekels	5989
	30:18	for g my maidservant to my husband."	5989
	38:28	As she *was* g **birth,**	3528
	41:12	g each man *the* **interpretation**	7354
	49:28	g each the **blessing** appropriate to him.	1385+1388
	49:33	When Jacob had finished g **instructions**	7422
Ex	20:12	in the land the LORD your God g you.	5989
Lev	14:34	which *I am* g you as your possession,	5989
	20: 3	for *by* g his children to Molech,	5989
	27: 2	to the LORD by g equivalent **values,**	NIH
Nu	13: 2	which *I am* g to the Israelites.	5989
	15: 2	you enter the land *I am* g you as a home	5989
	18: 7	*I am* g you the service of the priesthood as	5989
Dt	1:20	which the LORD our God *is* g us.	5989
	1:25	that the LORD our God *is* g us."	5989
	2:29	into the land the LORD our God *is* g us."	5989
	3:20	that the LORD your God *is* g them,	5989
	4: 1	the God of your fathers, *is* g you.	5989
	4:21	the LORD your God *is* g you	5989
	4:40	which *I am* g you today,	7422
	5:16	in the land the LORD your God *is* g you	5989
	5:31	in the land *I am* g them to possess."	5989
	8: 1	to follow every command *I am* g you today,	7422
	8:11	and his decrees that *I am* g you this day.	7422
	9: 6	LORD your God *is* g you this good land	5989
	10:13	of the LORD that *I am* g you for your own good?	7422
	10:18	g him food and clothing.	5989
	11: 8	the commands *I am* g you today,	7422
	11:13	the commands *I am* g you today—	7422
	11:17	from the good land the LORD *is* g you.	5989

Dt	11:22	observe all these commands I *am* g you	7422
	11:27	the LORD your God that I *am* g you today;	7422
	11:31	of the land the LORD your God *is* g us.	5989
	12: 9	the LORD your God *is* g you.	5989
	12:10	g you **as an inheritance,**	5706
	12:28	to obey all these regulations I *am* g you,	7422
	13:12	the towns the LORD your God *is* g you	5989
	13:18	commands that I *am* g you today	7422
	15: 4	in the land the LORD your God *is* g you	5989
	15: 5	follow all these commands I *am* g you today	7422
	15: 7	that the LORD your God *is* g you,	5989
	16:10	*by* g a freewill offering in proportion to	5989
	16:18	the LORD your God *is* g you,	5989
	16:20	the land the LORD your God *is* g you.	5989
	17:14	the land the LORD your God *is* g you	5989
	18: 9	the land the LORD your God *is* g you.	5989
	19: 1	the nations whose land he *is* g you,	5989
	19: 2	the LORD your God *is* g you to possess.	5989
	19: 3	g you **as an inheritance,**	5706
	19:10	which the LORD your God *is* g you	5989
	19:14	the LORD your God *is* g you to possess.	5989
	19:18	g false **testimony** against his brother,	6699
	20:16	the nations the LORD your God *is* g you	5989
	21: 1	the LORD your God *is* g you to possess,	5989
	21:17	as the firstborn by g him a double share	5989
	21:23	the land the LORD your God *is* g you as	5989
	24: 4	the land the LORD your God *is* g you as	5989
	25:15	in the land the LORD your God *is* g you.	5989
	25:19	in the land he *is* g you to possess as	5989
	26: 1	the land the LORD your God *is* g you as	5989
	26: 2	of the land the LORD your God *is* g you,	5989
	27: 2	the land the LORD your God *is* g you,	5989
	27: 3	the land the LORD your God *is* g you,	5989
	28: 8	in the land he *is* g you.	5989
	28:15	and decrees I *am* g you today,	7422
	28:52	the land the LORD your God *is* g you.	5989
	30: 8	follow all his commands I *am* g you today.	7422
	32:49	the land I *am* g the Israelites	5989
	32:52	the land I *am* g to the people of Israel."	5989
Jos	1:11	of the land the LORD your God *is* g you	5989
	1:13	'The LORD your God *is* g you **rest**	5663
	1:15	that the LORD your God *is* g them.	5989
	3: 3	g **orders** to the people:	7422
Jdg	2:23	he did not drive them out at once by g them	5989
1Sa	22:13	g him bread and a sword and inquiring	5989
2Sa	11:19	"When you have finished g	1819
	18: 5	And all the troops heard the king g **orders**	7422
	24:12	I am g you three options.	5747
1Ch	21:10	I *am* g you three options.	5742
Ezr	9: 9	and g us a firm place in his sanctuary,	5989
Ne	4:10	"The strength of the laborers *is* g **out,**	4173
	8: 8	making it clear and g the meaning so that	8492
Est	2:22	g **credit** to Mordecai.	928+9005
	3: 1	and g him a seat of honor higher than that	8492
	9:19	a day for g presents to each other.	5447
	9:22	of feasting and joy and g presents of food	5447
Ps	19: 8	g **joy** *to* the heart.	8523
	19: 8	g **light** *to* the eyes.	239
	100: T	A psalm. For g **thanks.**	9343
	106: 5	and join your inheritance in g **praise.**	2146
	111: 6	g them the lands of other nations.	5989
Pr	1: 4	for g **prudence** to the simple, knowledge	5989
	15:23	A man finds joy in g **an apt reply**—	5101+7023
	26: 8	a stone in a sling is the g of honor to a fool.	5989
Eze	3: 3	eat this scroll I *am* g you	5989
	11: 2	and g wicked **advice** in this city.	3619+6783
	16:54	of all you have done in g them **comfort.**	5714
Da	4:21	g **shelter** to the beasts of the field,	AIT
	6:10	g **thanks** to his God,	10312
	9:13	by turning from our sins and g **attention**	8505
Mt	24:38	marrying and g **in marriage,**	1139
Jn	16:21	A woman g **birth to a child** has pain	5503
Ac	1: 2	*after* g **instructions** through the Holy Spirit	1948
	8: 1	Saul was there, g **approval** to his death.	5306
	14:17	He has shown kindness *by* g rain	1443
	15: 8	that he accepted them *by* g the Holy Spirit	1443
	22:20	I stood there g my **approval** and guarding	5306
1Co	14:17	You *may be* g **thanks** well enough,	2373
2Co	5:12	*are* g you an opportunity to take pride in us,	1443
	8: 7	see that you also excel in this grace of g.	NIG
Eph	1:16	I have not stopped g **thanks** for you,	2373
	5:20	always g **thanks** to God the Father	2373
Php	4:15	with me in the matter of g and receiving,	1521
Col	1:12	g **thanks** to the Father,	2373
	3:17	g **thanks** to God the Father through him.	2373

GIZONITE (1)

1Ch	11:34	the sons of Hashem the G,	1604

GLAD (77) [GLADDENS, GLADLY, GLADNESS]

Ex	4:14	and his heart *will be* g when he sees you.	8523
Jos	22:33	They *were* g to hear the report	928+3512+6524
Jdg	8:25	answered, "We'll be g to give them."	5989+5989
	18:20	Then the priest was g.	3512+4213
1Sa	19: 5	and you saw it and *were* g.	8523
2Sa	1:20	lest the daughters of the Philistines *be* g,	8523
1Ki	8:66	joyful and g in heart for all the good things	3202
1Ch	16:31	Let the heavens rejoice, *let* the earth *be* g;	1635
2Ch	7:10	joyful and g in heart for the good things	3202
Ps	5:11	But *let* all who take refuge in you *be* g;	8523
	9: 2	I *will be* g and rejoice in you;	8523
	14: 7	let Jacob rejoice and Israel *be* g!	8523
	16: 9	Therefore my heart *is* g	8523

Ps	21: 6	and **made** him g with the joy	2525
	31: 7	*I will be* g and rejoice in your love,	1635
	32:11	Rejoice in the LORD and *be* g,	8523
	40:16	But may all who seek you rejoice and *be* g	8523
	45: 8	the music of the strings **makes** you g.	8523
	46: 4	There is a river whose streams **make** g	8523
	48:11	of Judah *are* g because of your judgments.	1635
	53: 6	let Jacob rejoice and Israel *be* g!	8523
	58:10	*be* g when they are avenged,	8523
	67: 4	May the nations *be* g and sing for joy,	8523
	68: 3	the righteous *be* g and rejoice before God;	8523
	69:32	The poor will see and *be* g—	8523
	70: 4	But may all who seek you rejoice and *be* g	8523
	90:14	we may sing for joy and *be* g all our days.	8523
	90:15	**Make** us g for as many days	8523
	92: 4	*you* **make** me g by your deeds, O LORD;	8523
	96:11	Let the heavens rejoice, *let* the earth *be* g;	1635
	97: 1	The LORD reigns, *let* the earth *be* g;	8523
	97: 8	and rejoices and the villages of Judah *are* g	1635
	105:38	Egypt *was* g when they left,	8523
	107:30	*They were* g when it grew calm,	8523
	118:24	let us rejoice and *be* g in it.	8523
	149: 2	let the people of Zion *be* g in their King.	1635
Pr	23:15	then my heart *will be* g;	8523
	23:25	*May* your father and mother *be* g;	8523
	29: 6	but a righteous one can sing and *be* g.	8523
Ecc	8:15	the sun than to eat and drink and *be* g.	8523
Isa	25: 9	let us rejoice and *be* g in his salvation."	8523
	35: 1	desert and the parched land *will be* g;	8464
	65:18	But *be* g and rejoice forever	8464
	66:10	"Rejoice with Jerusalem and *be* g for her,	1635
Jer	20:15	*who* **made** him **very** g, saying,	8523+8523
	31:13	Then maidens *will* dance and *be* g,	8523
	41:13	with him, *they were* g.	8523
	50:11	"Because you rejoice and *are* g,	6600
La	4:21	Rejoice and *be* g, O Daughter of Edom,	8523
Joel	2:21	Be not afraid, O land; *be* g and rejoice.	1635
	2:23	Be g, O people of Zion,	1635
Hab	1:15	and so he rejoices and *is* g.	1635
Zep	3:14	*Be* g and rejoice with all your heart,	8523
Zec	2:10	"Shout and *be* g, O Daughter of Zion.	8523
	8:19	and g **occasions** and happy festivals	8525
	10: 7	and their hearts *will be* g as with wine.	8523
Mt	5:12	Rejoice and *be* g, because great is your	22
Lk	15:32	But we had to celebrate and *be* g,	5897
Jn	4:36	the sower and the reaper *may* **be** g together.	5897
	8:56	he saw it and *was* g."	5897
	11:15	and for your sake *I am* g I was not there,	5897
	14:28	*you* would *be* g that I am going to	5897
Ac	2:26	my heart *is* g and my tongue rejoices;	2370
	2:46	and ate together with g and sincere hearts,	21
	11:23	he was g and encouraged them all	5897
	13:48	*they were* g and honored the word of	5897
	15: 3	This news made all the brothers very g.	5915
	15:31	and *were* g for its encouraging message.	5897
1Co	16:17	*I was* g when Stephanas,	5897
2Co	2: 2	who is left to **make** me g but you	2370
	7:16	*I am* g I can have complete confidence	5897
	13: 9	*We are* g whenever we are weak	5897
Gal	4:27	For it is written: "*Be* g, O barren woman,	2370
Php	2:17	*I am* g and rejoice with all of you.	5897
	2:18	you too *should be* g and rejoice with me.	5897
	2:28	that when you see him again *you may be* g	5897
Rev	19: 7	and **be** g and give him glory!	22

GLADDENS (1) [GLAD]
Ps	104:15	wine *that* g the heart of man,	8523

GLADLY (11) [GLAD]
Dt	28:47	and g in the time of prosperity,	928+3206+4222
Jdg	19: 3	he g welcomed him.	8523
2Ch	24:10	the people brought their contributions g,	8523
Isa	39: 2	Hezekiah **received** the envoys g	6584+8523
	64: 5	to the help of *those who* g do right,	8464
Jer	3:19	" 'How g would I treat you like sons	375
Lk	19: 6	he came down at once and welcomed him g.	5897
Ac	24:10	so I g make my defense.	2315
2Co	11:19	You g put up with fools since you are	2452
	12: 9	Therefore I will boast all the more g	2452
	12:15	So I will **very** g spend for you everything	2452

GLADNESS (23) [GLAD]
2Ch	29:30	sang praises with g and bowed their heads	8525
Est	8:16	a time of happiness and joy, g and honor.	8607
	8:17	there was joy and g among the Jews,	8525
Job	3:22	who are **filled with** g and rejoice	448+1637+8524
Ps	35:27	in my vindication shout for joy and g;	8523
	45:15	They are led in with joy and g;	1637
	51: 8	Let me hear joy and g;	8525
	65:12	the hills are clothed with g.	1637
	100: 2	Worship the LORD with g;	8525
Ecc	5:20	God keeps him occupied with g *of* heart.	8525
	9: 7	Go, eat your food with g,	8525
Isa	16:10	and g are taken away from the orchards;	1637
	35:10	G and joy will overtake them,	8607
	51: 3	Joy and g will be found in her,	8525
	51:11	G and joy will overtake them,	8525
	61: 3	the oil of g instead of mourning,	8607
Jer	7:34	to the sounds of joy and g and to the voices	8525
	16: 9	to the sounds of joy and g and to the voices	8525
	25:10	from them the sounds of joy and g,	8525
	31:13	I will turn their mourning into g;	8607
	33:11	the sounds of joy and g, the voices of bride	8607
	48:33	and g are gone from the orchards and fields	1637
Joel	1:16	joy and g from the house of our God?	1637

GLANCE (2) [GLANCES, GLANCING]
Pr	23: 5	Cast but a g at riches, and they are gone,	6524
SS	4: 9	you have stolen my heart with one g	NIH

GLANCES (1) [GLANCE]
Pr	30:13	whose g are so disdainful;	6757

GLANCING (1) [GLANCE]
Ex	2:12	G this way and that and seeing no one,	7155

GLASS (4)
Rev	4: 6	was what looked like a sea **of** g,	5612
	15: 2	like a sea **of** g mixed with fire and,	5612
	21:18	and the city of pure gold, as pure as g.	5613
	21:21	of pure gold, like transparent g.	5613

GLASSES (KJV) See MIRROR

GLAZE (1)
Pr	26:23	of g over earthenware are fervent lips with	6213

GLEAM (2) [GLEAMED, GLEAMING]
Pr	4:18	The path of the righteous is like the *first* g	240
Da	10: 6	and legs like the g of burnished bronze,	6524

GLEAMED (2) [GLEAM]
Eze	1: 7	their feet were like those of a calf and g	5913
Lk	24: 4	two men in clothes **that** g like lightning	848

GLEAMING (1) [GLEAM]
Job	20:25	the g point out of his liver.	1398

GLEAN (8) [GLEANED, GLEANING, GLEANINGS, GLEANS]
Ru	2: 3	So she went out and *began to* g in the fields	4377
	2: 7	'Please *let me* g and gather among	4377
	2: 8	in another field and don't go away	4377
	2:15	As she got up to g,	4377
	2:19	"Where *did you* g today?	4377
	2:23	to the servant girls of Boaz to g until	4377
Job	24: 6	They gather fodder in the fields and g *in*	4380
Jer	6: 9	g the remnant of Israel as **thoroughly**	6618+6618

GLEANED (1) [GLEAN]
Ru	2:17	So Ruth g in the field until evening.	4377

GLEANING (1) [GLEAN]
Mic	7: 1	like one who gathers summer fruit at the g	6622

GLEANINGS (5) [GLEAN]
Lev	19: 9	the very edges of your field or gather the g	4378
	23:22	the very edges of your field or gather the g	4378
Jdg	8: 2	g of Ephraim's **grapes** are better than	6622
Isa	17: 6	Yet *some* g will remain,	6622
	24:13	or as when g are left after the grape harvest.	6622

GLEANS (1) [GLEAN]
Isa	17: 5	as *when a man* g heads of grain in the	4377

GLEE (2)
Ps	35:15	But when I stumbled, they gathered *in* g;	8523
Eze	36: 5	and against all Edom, for with g and	8525

GLIDE (1) [GLIDED, GLIDING]
Dt	32:24	the venom of vipers *that* g in the dust.	2323

GLIDED (1) [GLIDE]
Job	4:15	A spirit g **past** my face,	2736

GLIDING (2) [GLIDE]
Job	26:13	his hand pierced the g serpent.	1371
Isa	27: 1	Leviathan the g serpent,	1371

GLIMPSE (2)
Job	9:25	they fly away without a g *of* joy.	8011
	23: 9	he turns to the south, I **catch** no g of him.	8011

GLINT (1)
Hab	3:11	and moon stood still in the heavens at the g	240

GLISTENING (1)
Job	41:32	Behind him *he* **leaves** a g wake;	239

GLITTERING (3)
Na	3: 3	flashing swords and g spears!	1398
Rev	17: 4	and *was* g with gold,	5998
	18:16	purple and scarlet, and g with gold,	5998

GLOAT (12) [GLOATED, GLOATING, GLOATS]
Ps	22:17	people stare and g over me.	8011
	30: 1	of the depths and *did* not **let** my enemies g	8523
	35:19	not *those* g over me who are my enemies	8523
	35:24	*do not let* them g over me.	8523
	35:26	May all *who* g over my distress be put	8524
	38:16	not *let* them g or exalt themselves over me	8523
	59:10	God will go before me and *will* **let** me g	8011
Pr	24:17	*Do* not g when your enemy falls;	8523
La	2:17	he has **let** the enemy g over you,	8523
Mic	4: 1	*let* our eyes g over Zion!"	2600
	7: 8	*Do* not g over me, my enemy!	8523
Rev	11:10	The inhabitants of the earth *will* g	5897

GLOATED (1) [GLOAT]
Job	31:29	or g *over* the trouble that came to him—	6424

GLOATING (1) [GLOAT]
Hab	3:14	g as though about to devour	6617

GLOATS (1) [GLOAT]
Pr	17: 5	*whoever* g over disaster will	8523

GLOOM (13) [GLOOMY]
Job	10:21	to the land of g and deep shadow,	3125
Ps	107:10	Some sat in darkness and the **deepest** g,	7516
	107:14	the **deepest** g and broke away their chains.	7516
Isa	8:22	and darkness and fearful g,	5066
	9: 1	there will be no more g for those who were	4599
	24:11	all joy **turns to** g,	6845
	29:18	and out of g and darkness the eyes of	694
Jer	13:16	to thick darkness and change it to **deep** g.	6906
Eze	31:15	clothed Lebanon **with** g,	7722
Joel	2: 2	a day of darkness and g,	696
Zep	1:15	a day of darkness and g,	696
Heb	12:18	to darkness, g and storm;	2432
Jas	4: 9	to mourning and your joy to g.	2993

GLOOMY (1) [GLOOM]
2Pe	2: 4	into g dungeons to be held for judgment;	2432

GLORIES (1) [GLORY]
1Pe	1:11	of Christ and the g that would follow.	1518

GLORIFIED (17) [GLORY]
Isa	66: 5	have said, 'Let the LORD *be* g,	3877
Eze	39:13	and the day I **am** g will be a memorable day	3877
Da	4:34	I honored and g him who lives forever.	10198
Jn	7:39	since Jesus *had* not yet *been* g.	1519
	11: 4	for God's glory so that God's Son *may be* g	1519
	12:16	Only after Jesus *was* g did they realize	1519
	12:23	for the Son of Man *to be* g.	1519
	12:28	a voice came from heaven, "I have g it,	1519
	13:31	the Son of Man g and God is glorified	1519
	13:31	the Son of Man glorified and God *is* g	1519
	13:32	If God *is* g in him,	1519
Ac	3:13	*has* g his servant Jesus.	1519
Ro	1:21	*they* neither g him as God nor gave thanks	1519
	8:30	those he justified, *he* also g.	1519
2Th	1:10	*be* g in his holy people and to be marveled	1901
	1:12	so that the name of our Lord Jesus *may be* g	1901
1Pe	1:21	raised him from the dead and g him,	1443+1518

GLORIFIES (2) [GLORY]
Lk	1:46	And Mary said: "My soul g the Lord	3486
Jn	8:54	your God, is the one who g me.	1519

GLORIFY (19) [GLORY]
Ps	34: 3	G the LORD with me;	1540
	63: 3	my lips *will* g you.	8655
	69:30	I will praise God's name in song and g him	1540
	86:12	*I will* g your name forever.	3877
Isa	60:13	and *I will* g the place of my feet.	3877
Da	4:37	praise and exalt and g the King of heaven,	10198
Jn	8:54	Jesus replied, "If I g myself, my glory	1519
	12:28	Father, g your name!"	1519
	12:28	"I have glorified it, and *will* g it again."	1519
	13:32	God *will* g the Son in himself,	1519
	13:32	and *will* g him at once.	1519
	17: 1	G your Son, that your Son may glorify you.	1519
	17: 1	Glorify your Son, that your Son *may* g you.	1519
	17: 5	g me in your presence with the glory I had	1519
	21:19	of death by which Peter *would* g God.	1519
Ro	15: 6	so that with one heart and mouth *you may* g	1519
	15: 9	that the Gentiles *may* g God for his mercy,	1519
1Pe	2:12	*they may* see your good deeds and g God on	1519
Rev	16: 9	but they refused to repent and g him.	1443+1518

GLORIFYING (1) [GLORY]
Lk	2:20	g and praising God for all the things	1519

GLORIOUS (50) [GLORY]
Dt	28:58	do not revere this g and awesome name—	3877
	33:29	and helper and your g sword.	1452
1Ch	29:13	and praise your g name.	9514
Ne	9: 5	"Blessed be your g name,	3883
Ps	16: 3	the g *ones* in whom is all my delight.	129
	45:13	All g is the princess within [her chamber];	3884
	66: 2	make his praise g!	3883
	72:19	Praise be to his g name forever;	3883
	87: 3	G *things* are said of you, O city of God;	3877
	111: 3	G and majestic are his deeds,	2086
	145: 5	of the g splendor of your majesty,	3883

Ps	145:12	of your mighty acts and the g splendor	3883
Isa	3: 8	defying his g presence.	3883
	4: 2	of the LORD will be beautiful and g,	3883
	11:10	and his place of rest will be g.	3883
	12: 5	for he has done g things;	1455
	28: 1	to the fading flower, his g beauty,	9514
	28: 4	That fading flower, his g beauty,	9514
	28: 5	the LORD Almighty will be a g crown,	9514
	42:21	to make his law great and g.	158
	60: 7	and I will adorn my g temple.	9514
	63:12	who sent his g arm of power to be	9514
	63:14	to make for yourself a g name.	9514
	63:15	and see from your lofty throne, holy and g.	9514
	64:11	Our holy and g temple,	9514
Jer	13:18	your g crowns will fall from your heads."	9514
	14:21	do not dishonor your g throne.	3883
	17:12	A g throne, exalted from the beginning,	3883
	48:17	how broken the g staff!'	9514
Mt	19:28	when the Son of Man sits on his g throne,	1518
Lk	9:31	appeared in g splendor,	1518
Ac	2:20	before the coming of the great and g day of	2212
Ro	8:21	to decay and brought into the g freedom of	1518
2Co	3: 8	ministry of the Spirit be even more g?	1518+1877
	3: 9	If the ministry that condemns men is g,	1518
	3: 9	how much more g is the ministry that	1518
	3:10	For what was g has no glory now	1519
Eph	1: 6	to the praise of his g grace,	1518
	1:17	of our Lord Jesus Christ, the g Father,	1518
	1:18	the riches of his g inheritance in the saints,	1518
	3:16	of his g riches he may strengthen you	1518
Php	3:21	so that they will be like his g body.	1518
	4:19	according to his g riches in Christ Jesus.	1518
Col	1:11	with all power according to his g might so	1518
	1:27	the Gentiles the g riches of this mystery,	1518
1Ti	1:11	to the gospel of the blessed God,	1518
Tit	2:13	the g appearing of our great God	1518
Jas	2: 1	as believers in our g Lord Jesus Christ,	1518
1Pe	1: 8	with an inexpressible and g joy,	1519
Jude	1:24	and to present you before his g presence	1518

GLORIOUSLY (1) [GLORY]

Isa	24:23	and before its elders, g.	3883

GLORY (295) [GLORIES, GLORIFIED, GLORIFIES, GLORIFY, GLORIFYING, GLORIOUS, GLORIOUSLY]

Ex	14: 4	I will gain g for myself through Pharaoh	3877
	14:17	And I will gain g through Pharaoh	3877
	14:18	the LORD when I gain g through Pharaoh,	3877
	15:11	majestic in holiness, awesome in g,	9335
	16: 7	the morning you will see the g of the LORD	3883
	16:10	the g of the LORD appearing in the cloud.	3883
	24:16	g of the LORD settled on Mount Sinai.	3883
	24:17	the Israelites the g of the LORD looked	3883
	29:43	and the place will be consecrated by my g.	3883
	33:18	Then Moses said, "Now show me your g."	3883
	33:22	When my g passes by,	3883
	40:34	the g of the LORD filled the tabernacle.	3883
	40:35	the g of the LORD filled the tabernacle.	3883
Lev	9: 6	the g of the LORD may appear to you."	3883
	9:23	g of the LORD appeared to all the people.	3883
Nu	14:10	the g of the LORD appeared at the Tent	3883
	14:21	as I live and as surely as the g of the LORD	3883
	14:22	not one of the men who saw my g and	3883
	16:19	the g of the LORD appeared to	3883
	16:42	the cloud covered it and the g of the LORD	3883
	20: 6	and the g of the LORD appeared to them.	3883
Dt	5:24	"The LORD our God has shown us his g	3883
Jos	7:19	give to the LORD, the God of Israel,	3883
1Sa	4:21	saying, "The g has departed from Israel"—	3883
	4:22	She said, "The g has departed from Israel,	3883
	15:29	He who is the g of Israel does not lie	5905
2Sa	1:19	"Your g, O Israel, lies slain	7382
1Ki	8:11	for the g of the LORD filled his temple.	3883
2Ki	14:10	G in your victory, but stay at home!	3877
1Ch	16:10	G in his holy name;	2146
	16:24	Declare his g among the nations,	3883
	16:28	ascribe to the LORD g and strength,	3883
	16:29	ascribe to the LORD the g due his name.	3883
	16:35	that we may g in your praise."	8655
	29:11	and the g and the majesty and the splendor	9514
2Ch	5:14	g of the LORD filled the temple of God.	3883
	7: 1	and the g of the LORD filled the temple.	3883
	7: 2	of the LORD because the g of the LORD	3883
	7: 3	and the g of the LORD above the temple,	3883
Est	1: 4	of his kingdom and the splendor and g	9514
Job	29:20	My g will remain fresh in me,	3883
	40:10	Then adorn yourself with g and splendor,	1454
Ps	3: 3	you bestow g on me and lift up my head.	3883
	4: 2	O men, will you turn my g into shame?	3883
	8: 1	You have set your g above the heavens.	2086
	8: 5	and crowned him with g and honor.	3883
	19: 1	The heavens declare the g of God;	3883
	21: 5	the victories you gave, his g is great;	3883
	24: 7	that the King of g may come in.	3883
	24: 8	Who is this King of g?	3883
	24: 9	that the King of g may come in.	3883
	24:10	Who is he, this King of g?	3883
	24:10	LORD Almighty—he is the King of g.	3883
	26: 8	O LORD, the place where your g dwells.	3883
	29: 1	ascribe to the LORD g and strength.	3883
	29: 2	Ascribe to the LORD the g due his name;	3883
	29: 3	the God of g thunders,	3883
	29: 9	And in his temple all cry, "G!"	3883
	57: 5	let your g be over all the earth.	3883

Ps	57:11	let your g be over all the earth.	3883
	63: 2	and beheld your power and your g.	3883
	66: 2	Sing the g of his name;	3883
	72:19	may the whole earth be filled with his g.	3883
	73:24	and afterward you will take me into g.	3883
	79: 9	O God our Savior, for the g of your name;	3883
	85: 9	that his g may dwell in our land.	3883
	86: 9	they will bring g to your name.	3877
	89:17	For you are their g and strength,	9514
	96: 3	Declare his g among the nations,	3883
	96: 6	strength and g are in his sanctuary.	9514
	96: 7	ascribe to the LORD g and strength.	3883
	96: 8	Ascribe to the LORD the g due his name;	3883
	97: 6	and all the peoples see his g.	3883
	102:15	all the kings of the earth will revere your g.	3883
	102:16	and appear in his g.	3883
	104:31	May the g of the LORD endure forever;	3883
	105: 3	G in his holy name;	2146
	106:20	They exchanged their G for an image of	3883
	106:47	to your holy name and g in your praise.	8655
	108: 5	and let your g be over all the earth.	3883
	113: 4	his g above the heavens.	3883
	115: 1	not to us but to your name be the g,	3883
	138: 5	for the g of the LORD is great.	3883
	145:11	They will tell of the g of your kingdom	3883
	149: 9	This is the g of all his saints.	2077
Pr	14:28	A large population is a king's g,	2079
	19:11	it is to his g to overlook an offense.	9514
	20:29	The g of young men is their strength,	9514
	25: 2	It is the g of God to conceal a matter;	3883
	25: 2	to search out a matter is the g of kings.	3883
Isa	4: 2	be the pride and g of the survivors in Israel.	9514
	4: 5	over all the g will be a canopy.	3883
	6: 3	the whole earth is full of his g."	3883
	13:19	the g of the Babylonians' pride,	9514
	17: 3	the remnant of Aram will be like the g of	3883
	17: 4	"In that day the g of Jacob will fade;	3883
	22:24	All the g of his family will hang on him:	3883
	23: 9	to bring low the pride of all g and	7382
	24:15	Therefore in the east give g to the LORD;	3877
	24:16	"G to the Righteous One."	7382
	26:15	gained g for yourself;	3877
	35: 2	The g of Lebanon will be given to it,	3883
	35: 2	they will see the g of the LORD,	3883
	40: 5	And the g of the LORD will be revealed,	3883
	40: 6	all their g is like the flowers of the field.	2876
	41:16	the LORD and g in the Holy One of Israel.	2146
	42: 8	I will not yield my g to another.	3883
	42:12	Let them give g to the LORD	3883
	43: 7	whom I created for my g,	3883
	44:13	of man in all his g,	9514
	44:23	he displays his g in Israel.	6995
	48:11	I will not yield my g to another.	3883
	58: 8	g of the LORD will be your rear guard.	3883
	59:19	they will revere his g.	3883
	60: 1	and the g of the LORD rises upon you.	3883
	60: 2	upon you and his g appears over you.	3883
	60:13	"The g of Lebanon will come to you,	3883
	60:19	and your God will be your g.	9514
	62: 2	and all kings your g;	3883
	66:18	and they will come and see my g.	3883
	66:19	not heard of my fame or seen my g.	3883
	66:19	They will proclaim my g among	3883
Jer	2:11	But my people have exchanged their G	3883
	4: 2	be blessed by him and in him they will g."	2146
	13:16	Give g to the LORD your God	3883
	48:18	from your g and sit on the parched ground,	3883
Eze	1:28	the appearance of the likeness of the g of	3883
		the LORD.	
	3:12	May the g of the LORD be praised	3883
	3:23	the g of the LORD was standing there,	3883
	3:23	like the g I had seen by the Kebar River,	3883
	8: 4	And there before me was the g of the God	3883
	9: 3	Now the g of the God of Israel went up	3883
	10: 4	Then the g of the LORD rose from above	3883
	10: 4	the court was full of the radiance of the g	3883
	10:18	Then the g of the LORD departed from	3883
	10:19	the g of the God of Israel was above them.	3883
	11:22	the g of the God of Israel was above them.	3883
	11:23	The g of the LORD went up from within	3883
	24:25	their joy and g, the delight of their eyes,	9514
	25: 9	of that land.	7382
	28:22	O Sidon, and I will gain g within you.	3877
	39:21	"I will display my g among the nations,	3883
	43: 2	the g of the God of Israel coming from	3883
	43: 2	and the land was radiant with his g.	3883
	43: 4	The g of the LORD entered the temple	3883
	43: 5	and the g of the LORD filled the temple.	3883
	44: 4	the g of the LORD filling the temple of	3883
Da	2:37	and power and might and g;	10331
	4:30	by my mighty power and for the g	10331
	4:36	and splendor were returned to me for the g	10331
	5:18	and greatness and g and splendor.	10331
	5:20	from his royal throne and stripped of his g.	10331
	7:14	and sovereign power;	10331
Hos	4: 7	they exchanged their G for something	3883
	9:11	Ephraim's g will fly away like a bird—	3883
Mic	1:15	the g of Israel will come to Adullam.	3883
Hab	2:14	with the knowledge of the g of the LORD,	3883
	2:16	You will be filled with shame instead of g.	3883
	2:16	and disgrace will cover your g.	3883
	3: 3	His g covered the heavens	2086
Hag	2: 3	saw this house in its former g?	3883
	2: 7	and I will fill this house with g,'	3883
	2: 9	'The g of this present house will	3883
	2: 9	be greater than the g of the former house,'	NIH
Zec	2: 5	'and I will be its g within.'	3883

Mt	16:27	of Man is going to come in his Father's g	1518
	24:30	clouds of the sky, with power and great g.	1518
	25:31	"When the Son of Man comes in his g,	1518
	25:31	he will sit on his throne in heavenly g.	1518
Mk	8:38	of him when he comes in his Father's g	1518
	10:37	and the other at your left in your g."	1518
	13:26	in clouds with great power and g.	1518
Lk	2: 9	and the g of the Lord shone around them,	1518
	2:14	"G to God in the highest,	1518
	2:32	for revelation to the Gentiles and for g	1518
	9:26	be ashamed of him when he comes in his g	1518
	9:26	when he comes in his glory and in the g of	NIG
	9:32	they saw his g and the two men standing	1518
	19:38	"Peace in heaven and g in the highest!"	1518
	21:27	in a cloud with power and great g.	1518
	24:26	to suffer these things and then enter his g?"	1518
Jn	1:14	We have seen his g,	1518
	1:14	the g of the One and Only,	1518
	2:11	He thus revealed his g,	1518
	8:50	I am not seeking g for myself;	1518
	8:54	"If I glorify myself, my g means nothing.	1518
	9:24	"Give g to God," they said.	1518
	11: 4	it is for God's g so that God's Son may	1518
	11:40	you would see the g of God?"	1518
	12:41	Isaiah said this because he saw Jesus' g	1518
	14:13	so that the Son may bring g to the Father.	1519
	15: 8	This is to my Father's g,	1519
	16:14	He will bring g to me by taking	1519
	17: 4	I have brought you g on earth	1519
	17: 5	in your presence with the g I had with you	1519
	17:10	And g has come to me through them.	1519
	17:22	I have given them the g that you gave me,	1518
	17:24	to see my g, the glory you have given me	1518
	17:24	the g you have given me	4005S
Ac	7: 2	God of g appeared to our father Abraham	1518
	7:55	looked up to heaven and saw the g of God,	1518
Ro	1:23	the g of the immortal God for images made	1518
	2: 7	by persistence in doing good seek g,	1518
	2:10	but g, honor and peace	1518
	3: 7	and so increases his g,	1518
	3:23	for all have sinned and fall short of the g	1518
	4:20	in his faith and gave g to God,	1518
	5: 2	we rejoice in the hope of the g of God.	1518
	6: 4	from the dead through the g of the Father,	1518
	8:17	in order that we may also share in his g.	5280
	8:18	not worth comparing with the g that will	1518
	9: 4	theirs the divine g, the covenants,	1518
	9:23	of his g known to the objects of his mercy,	1518
	9:23	whom he prepared in advance for g—	1518
	11:36	To him be the g forever!	1518
	15:17	I g in Christ Jesus in my service to	2400+3018
	16:27	be g forever through Jesus Christ!	1518
1Co	2: 7	and that God destined for our g	1518
	2: 8	not have crucified the Lord of g.	1518
	10:31	do it all for the g of God.	1518
	11: 7	since he is the image and g of God;	1518
	11: 7	but the woman is the g of man.	1518
	11:15	if a woman has long hair, it is her g?	1518
	15:31	I g over you in Christ Jesus our Lord.	2400+3018
	15:43	it is sown in dishonor, it is raised in g;	1518
2Co	1:20	the "Amen" is spoken by us to the g	1518
	3: 7	came with g, so that the Israelites could	1518
	3: 7	at the face of Moses because of its g,	1518
	3:10	For what was glorious has no g now	1519
	3:10	now in comparison with the surpassing g.	1518
	3:11	And if what was fading away came with g,	1518
	3:11	much greater is the g of that which lasts!	1518
	3:18	with unveiled faces all reflect the Lord's g,	1518
	3:18	with ever-increasing g,	608+1518+1518+1650
	4: 4	the light of the gospel of the g of Christ,	1518
	4: 6	the light of the knowledge of the g of God	1518
	4:15	to overflow to the g of God.	1518
	4:17	an eternal g that far outweighs them all.	1518
	6: 8	g and dishonor, bad report and good report;	1518
Gal	1: 5	to whom be g for ever and ever. Amen.	1518
Eph	1:12	might be for the praise of his g.	1518
	1:14	to the praise of his g.	1518
	3:13	my sufferings for you, which are your g.	1518
	3:21	be g in the church and in Christ Jesus	1518
Php	1:11	to the g and praise of God.	1518
	2:11	to the g of God the Father.	1518
	3: 3	who g in Christ Jesus,	3016
	3:19	and their g is in their shame.	1518
	4:20	To our God and Father be g for ever	1518
Col	1:27	which is Christ in you, the hope of g.	1518
	3: 4	then you also will appear with him in g.	1518
1Th	2:12	who calls you into his kingdom and g.	1518
	2:19	or the crown in which we will g in	3018
	2:20	Indeed, you are our g and joy.	1518
2Th	2:14	in the g of our Lord Jesus Christ.	1518
1Ti	1:17	be honor and g for ever and ever.	1518
	3:16	believed on in the world, was taken up in g.	1518
2Ti	2:10	that is in Christ Jesus, with eternal g.	1518
	4:18	To him be g for ever and ever.	1518
Heb	1: 3	of God's g and the exact representation	1518
	2: 7	you crowned him with g and honor	1518
	2: 9	now crowned with g and honor	1518
	2:10	In bringing many sons to g,	1518
	5: 5	Christ also did not take upon himself the g	1519
	9: 5	Above the ark were the cherubim of the G,	1518
	13:21	to whom be g for ever and ever.	1518
1Pe	1: 7	g and honor when Jesus Christ is revealed.	1518
	1:24	all their g is like the flowers of the field;	1518
	4:11	be the g and the power for ever and ever.	1518
	4:13	be overjoyed when his g is revealed.	1518
	4:14	for the Spirit of g and of God rests on you.	1518
	5: 1	and one who also will share in the g to	1518

1Pe	5: 4	the crown of g that will never fade away.	1518
	5:10	who called you to his eternal g in Christ,	1518
2Pe	1: 3	of him who called us by his own g	1518
	1:17	For he received honor and g from God	1518
	1:17	the voice came to him from the Majestic G,	1518
	3:18	To him be g both now and forever!	1518
Jude	1:25	to the only God our Savior be g,	1518
Rev	1: 6	to him be g and power for ever and ever!	1518
	4: 9	Whenever the living creatures give g,	1518
	4:11	to receive g and honor and power,	1518
	5:12	and wisdom and strength and honor and g	1518
	5:13	and to the Lamb be praise and honor and g	1518
	7:12	and g and wisdom and thanks and honor	1518
	11:13	and the survivors were terrified and gave g	1518
	14: 7	"Fear God and give him g,	1518
	15: 4	O Lord, and **bring g** to your name?	1519
	15: 8	from the g of God and from his power,	1519
	18: 7	g and luxury she **gave** herself.	1519
	19: 1	and g and power belong to our God,	1518
	19: 7	Let us rejoice and be glad and give him g!	1518
	21:11	It **shone with** the g of God,	1518+2400
	21:23	for the g of God gives it light,	1518
	21:26	The g and honor of the nations will	1518

GLOW (1) [GLOWING, GLOWS]
Isa	4: 5	of smoke by day and a g of flaming fire	5586

GLOWING (5) [GLOW]
Ps	102: 3	my bones burn like g embers.	4611
Eze	1: 4	The center of the fire looked like g **metal**,	3133
	1:27	up he looked like g **metal**, as if full of fire,	3133
	8: 2	as bright as g metal.	3133
Rev	1:15	His feet were like bronze g in a furnace,	4792

GLOWS (1) [GLOW]
Eze	24:11	and its copper g so its impurities may	3081

GLUTTED (1) [GLUTTON]
Eze	39:19	till you are g and drink blood	8429

GLUTTON (2) [GLUTTED, GLUTTONS, GLUTTONY]
Mt	11:19	and they say, 'Here is a g and a drunkard,	5741
Lk	7:34	and you say, 'Here is a g and a drunkard,	5741

GLUTTONS (3) [GLUTTON]
Pr	23:21	for drunkards and g become poor,	2361
	28: 7	but a companion of g disgraces his father.	2361
Tit	1:12	Cretans are always liars, evil brutes, lazy g.	1143

GLUTTONY (1) [GLUTTON]
Pr	23: 2	put a knife to your throat if you are **given to g.**	1251+5883

GNASH (3) [GNASHED, GNASHES, GNASHING]
Ps	37:12	the righteous and g their teeth at them;	3080
	112:10	he will g his teeth and waste away;	3080
La	2:16	they scoff and g their teeth and say,	3080

GNASHED (2) [GNASH]
Ps	35:16	they g their teeth at me.	3080
Ac	7:54	they were furious and g their teeth at him.	1107

GNASHES (2) [GNASH]
Job	16: 9	and tears me in his anger and g his teeth	3080
Mk	9:18	g his teeth and becomes rigid.	5563

GNASHING (7) [GNASH]
Mt	8:12	there will be weeping and g of teeth."	1106
	13:42	where there will be weeping and g of teeth.	1106
	13:50	where there will be weeping and g of teeth.	1106
	22:13	where there will be weeping and g of teeth.	1106
	24:51	where there will be weeping and g of teeth.	1106
	25:30	there will be weeping and g of teeth.'	1106
Lk	13:28	will be weeping there, and g of teeth,	1106

GNAT (1) [GNATS]
Mt	23:24	You strain out a g but swallow a camel.	3270

GNATS (6) [GNAT]
Ex	8:16	the land of Egypt the dust will become g."	4031
	8:17	g came upon men and animals.	4038
	8:17	throughout the land of Egypt became g.	4031
	8:18	But when the magicians tried to produce g	4031
	8:18	And the g were on men and animals.	4038
Ps	105:31	and g throughout their country.	4031

GNAWED (1) [GNAWING]
Rev	16:10	Men g their tongues in agony	3460

GNAWING (1) [GNAWED]
Job	30:17	my g **pains** never rest.	6908

GO (1413) [GOES, GOING, GONE, WENT]
Ge	4: 8	"Let's g out to the field."	2143
Ge	7: 1	LORD then said to Noah, "G into the ark,	995
	11: 7	let us g down and confuse their language	3718
	11:31	from Ur of the Chaldeans to g to Canaan.	2143
	12: 1	and your father's household and g to	NIH
	12:19	Take her and g!"	2143
	13: 9	If you g to the left, I'll go to the right;	NIH
	13: 9	If you go to the left, I'll **g to the right**;	3554
	13: 9	if you g to the right, I'll go to the left."	NIH
	13: 9	if you go to the right, I'll **g to the left**."	8521
	13:17	G, walk through the length and breadth of	7756
	15:15	will g to your fathers in peace and	995
	16: 2	G, sleep with my maidservant;	448+995
	16: 9	"G back to your mistress and submit	8740
	18: 5	be refreshed and then g on your way—	6296
	18:21	that I will g down and see	3718
	19: 2	then g on your way early in the morning."	2143
	19: 3	But he insisted so strongly that they did g	6073
	19:34	and you g in and lie with him	995
	20:13	Everywhere we g, say of me,	995
	22: 2	and g to the region of Moriah.	2143
	22: 5	with the donkey while I and the boy g	2143
	24: 4	but will g to my country	2143
	24:11	the time the women g out to draw water.	3655
	24:38	but g to my father's family and	2143
	24:41	Then, when you g to my clan,	995
	24:51	Here is Rebekah; take her and g,	2143
	24:55	then you may g."	2143
	24:56	on my way so I may g to my master."	2143
	24:58	"Will you g with this man?"	2143
	24:58	"I will g," she said.	2143
	25:18	as you g toward Asshur.	995
	26: 2	"Do not g down to Egypt;	3718
	27: 3	and g out to the open country	3655
	27: 9	G out to the flock	2143
	27:13	Just do what I say; g and get them for me."	2143
	28: 2	G at once to Paddan Aram,	2143
	28:15	and will watch over you wherever you g,	2143
	30:25	so I can g back to my own homeland.	2143
	30:31	I will g on tending your flocks	8740
	30:32	Let me g through all your flocks today	6296
	31: 3	"G back to the land of your fathers and	8740
	31:13	at once and g back to your native land.'"	8740
	31:18	to g to his father Isaac in the land	995
	31:52	that I will not g past this heap to your side	6296
	31:52	to harm you and that you will not g past	6296
	32: 9	'G back to your country and your relatives,	8740
	32:16	and said to his servants, "G ahead of me,	6296
	32:26	man said, "Let me g, for it is daybreak."	8938
	32:26	not let you g unless you bless me."	8938
	33:14	So let my lord g on ahead of his servant,	6296
	34:17	we'll take our sister and g."	2143
	35: 1	"G up to Bethel and settle there,	7756
	35: 3	Then come, let us g up to Bethel.	6590
	37:14	"G and see if all is well with your brothers	2143
	37:17	"I heard them say, 'Let's g to Dothan.'"	2143
	37:35	"in mourning will I g down to the grave	3718
	39:10	he refused to g to bed with her or	725+8886
	41:55	"G to Joseph and do what he tells you."	2143
	42: 2	G down there and buy some for us,	3718
	42:19	while the rest of you g and take grain back	2143
	42:33	for your starving households and g.	2143
	42:38	"My son will not g down there with you;	3718
	43: 2	"G back and buy us a little more food."	8740
	43: 4	we will g down and buy food for you.	3718
	43: 5	you will not send him, we will not g down,	3718
	43: 8	along with me and we will g at once,	2143
	43:13	Take your brother also and g back to	8740
	44: 4	"G after those men at once,	8103
	44:17	g back to your father in peace."	6590
	44:25	'G back and buy a little more food.'	8740
	44:26	But we said, 'We cannot g down.	3718
	44:26	youngest brother is with us will we g.	3718
	44:30	when I g back to your servant my father and	995
	44:34	How can I g back to my father if the boy is	6590
	45:28	I will g and see him before I die."	2143
	46: 3	"Do not be afraid to g down to Egypt,	3718
	46: 4	I will g down to Egypt with you,	3718
	46:31	"I will g up and speak to Pharaoh	6590
	50: 5	Now let me g up and bury my father;	6590
	50: 6	Pharaoh said, "G up and bury your father,	6590
Ex	2: 7	"Shall I g and get one of the Hebrew	2143
	2: 8	"Yes, g," she answered.	2143
	3: 3	"I will g over and see this strange sight—	6073
	3:10	So now, g. I am sending you to Pharaoh	2143
	3:11	that I should g to Pharaoh and bring	2143
	3:13	"Suppose I g to the Israelites and say	995
	3:16	"G, assemble the elders of Israel and say	2143
	3:18	and the elders are to g to the king of Egypt	995
	3:19	the king of Egypt will not let you g unless	2143
	3:20	After that, he will let you g.	8938
	3:21	you leave you will not g empty-handed.	2143
	4:12	Now g; I will help you speak	2143
	4:18	"Let me g back to my own people in Egypt	2143
	4:18	Jethro said, "G, and I wish you well."	2143
	4:19	"G back to Egypt,	2143
	4:21	so that he will not let the people g.	8938
	4:23	"Let my son g, so he may worship me."	8938
	4:23	But you refused to let him g;	8938
	4:27	"G into the desert to meet Moses."	2143
	5: 1	'Let my people g,	8938
	5: 2	that I should obey him and let Israel g?	8938
	5: 2	and I will not let Israel g."	8938
	5: 7	let them g and gather their own straw.	2143
	5: 8	'Let us g and sacrifice to our God.'	2143
	5:11	G and get your own straw wherever you can find it,	2143
	5:17	'Let us g and sacrifice to the LORD.'	2143
Ex	6: 1	of my mighty hand he will let them g;	8938
	6:11	"G, tell Pharaoh king of Egypt to let	995
	6:11	to let the Israelites g out of his country."	8938
	7: 2	to tell Pharaoh to let the Israelites g out	8938
	7:14	he refuses to let the people g.	8938
	7:15	G to Pharaoh in the morning as he goes out	2143
	7:16	Let my people g,	8938
	8: 1	"G to Pharaoh and say to him,	995
	8: 1	Let my people g,	8938
	8: 2	If you refuse to let them g,	8938
	8: 4	The frogs will g up on you	6590
	8: 8	and I will let your people g	8938
	8:20	Let my people g,	8938
	8:21	If you do not let my people g,	8938
	8:25	"G, sacrifice to your God here in the land."	2143
	8:28	"I will let you g to offer sacrifices to	8938
	8:28	but you must not g very far.	2143
	8:29	not letting the people g to offer sacrifices	8938
	8:32	and would not let the people g.	8938
	9: 1	"G to Pharaoh and say to him,	995
	9: 1	Let my people g,	8938
	9: 2	If you refuse to let them g and continue	8938
	9: 7	and he would not let the people g.	8938
	9:13	Let my people g,	8938
	9:17	and will not let them g.	8938
	9:28	I will let you g;	8938
	9:35	and he would not let the Israelites g,	8938
	10: 1	the LORD said to Moses, "G to Pharaoh,	995
	10: 3	Let my people g,	8938
	10: 4	If you refuse to let them g,	8938
	10: 7	Let the people g,	8938
	10: 8	"G, worship the LORD your God,"	2143
	10: 9	"We will g with our young and old,	2143
	10:10	if I let you g,	8938
	10:11	Have only the men g;	2143
	10:20	and he would not let the Israelites g.	8938
	10:24	Pharaoh summoned Moses and said, "G,	2143
	10:24	your women and children may g with you;	2143
	10:26	Our livestock too must g with us;	2143
	10:27	and he was not willing to let them g.	8938
	11: 1	After that, he will let you g from here,	8938
	11: 4	'About midnight I will g	3655
	11: 8	bowing down before me and saying, 'G,	3655
	11:10	not let the Israelites g out of his country.	8938
	12:21	"G at once and select the animals	5432
	12:22	of you shall g out the door of his house	3655
	12:31	G, worship the LORD	2143
	12:32	as you have said, and g.	2143
	13:15	Pharaoh stubbornly refused to **let us g,**	8938
	13:17	When Pharaoh let the people g,	8938
	14: 5	We have let the Israelites g	8938
	14:16	so that the Israelites can g through the sea	995
	14:17	of the Egyptians so that they will g in	995
	16: 4	to g out each day and gather enough for	3655
	16:29	no one is to g out."	3655
	17: 5	with which you struck the Nile, and g.	2143
	17: 9	"Choose some of our men and g out	3655
	18:23	and all these people will g home satisfied."	995
	19:10	"G to the people and consecrate them today	2143
	19:12	that you do not g up the mountain or touch	6590
	19:13	a long blast may they g up to the mountain."	6590
	19:21	"G down and warn the people so they do	3718
	19:24	"G down and bring Aaron up with you.	2143
	20:26	And do not g up to my altar on steps,	6590
	21: 2	But in the seventh year, he shall g free,	3655
	21: 3	If he comes alone, he is to g free alone;	3655
	21: 3	she is to g with him.	3655
	21: 4	and only the man shall g free.	3655
	21: 5	and children and do not want to g free,'	3655
	21: 7	she is not to g free as menservants do.	3655
	21:11	she is to g free,	3655
	21:26	he must let the servant g free	8938
	21:27	he must let the servant g free	8938
	23:23	My angel will g ahead of you	2143
	24:14	and anyone involved in a dispute can g	5602
	26:19	make forty silver bases to g under them—	NIH
	32: 1	make us gods who will g before us.	2143
	32: 7	Then the LORD said to Moses, "G down,	2143
	32:23	'Make us gods who will g before us.	2143
	32:27	G back and forth through the camp	8740
	32:30	But now I will g up to the LORD.	6590
	32:34	Now g, lead the people to the place I spoke	2143
	32:34	and my angel will g before you.	2143
	33: 1	and g up to the land I promised on oath	6590
	33: 3	G up to the land flowing with milk	NIH
	33: 3	But I will not g with you,	6590
	33: 5	I were to g with you even for a moment,	6590
	33: 7	Anyone inquiring of the LORD would g	3655
	33:14	"My Presence will g with you,	2143
	33:15	"If your Presence does not g with us,	2143
	33:16	and with your people unless you g with us?	2143
	34: 9	he said, "then let the Lord g with us.	2143
	34:24	when you g up three times each year	6590
	36:24	made forty silver bases to g under them—	NIH
Lev	6: 6	must be kept burning; it must not g out.	3882
	6:13	continuously; it must not g out.	3882
	10: 9	or other fermented drink whenever you g,	995
	12: 4	She must not touch anything sacred or g to	995
	13:16	he must g to the priest.	995
	14: 3	to outside the camp and examine him.	3655
	14:35	the owner of the house must g and tell	995
	14:36	the priest is to g in and inspect the house.	995
	14:38	the priest shall g out the doorway of	3655
	14:44	the priest is to g and examine it and, if	995
	16:23	g into the Tent of Meeting and take off	995
	19:10	g over your vineyard a **second time**	6618
	19:16	"'Do not g **about** spreading slander	2143

Lev	21:23	not g near the curtain or approach the altar, 995
	25:27	he can then g back to his own property. 8740
	25:28	and he can then g back to his property. 8740
	25:41	and he will g back to his own clan and to 8740
Nu	4: 5	to g in and take down the shielding curtain 995
	4:19	and his sons are to g into the sanctuary 995
	4:20	But the Kohathites must not g in to look at 995
	5:27	water that brings a curse, it will g into her 995
	6: 6	to the LORD he must not g near 995
	8:19	when they g near the sanctuary." 5602
	10: 9	When you g into battle in your own land 995
	10:30	He answered, "No, I will not g; 2143
	11:26	but did not g out to the Tent. 3655
	13:17	"G up through the Negev and on into 6590
	13:30	"We should g up and take possession 6590+6590
	14: 3	Wouldn't it be better for us to g back 8740
	14: 4	"We should choose a leader and g back 8740
	14:14	that you g before them in a pillar of cloud 2143
	14:40	"We will g up to the place 6590
	14:42	Do not g up, because the LORD is not with 6590
	16:30	and they g down alive into the grave, 3718
	18: 3	but they must not g near the furnishings of 7928
	18:22	From now on the Israelites must not g near 7928
	20:17	not g through any field or vineyard, 6296
	20:19	"We will g along the main road, 6590
	20:21	to let them g through their territory, 6296
	21: 4	to g around Edom. 6015
	22:12	God said to Balaam, "Do not g with them. 2143
	22:13	"G back to your own country, 2143
	22:13	LORD has refused to let me g with you." 2143
	22:18	not do anything great or small to g beyond 6296
	22:20	g with them, but do only what I tell you." 2143
	22:34	Now if you are displeased, I will g back." 8740
	22:35	"G with the men, 2143
	23: 3	beside your offering while I g aside. 2143
	23: 5	"G back to Balak 8740
	23:16	"G back to Balak 8740
	24:11	Now leave at once and g home! NIH
	24:13	to g beyond the command of the LORD— 6296
	27:12	"G up this mountain in the Abarim range 6590
	27:17	to g out and come in before them, 3655
	27:21	of the Israelites will g out, 3655
	31: 3	to g to war against the Midianites and 2118
	32: 6	"Shall your countrymen g to war 995
	32:17	But we are ready to arm ourselves and g NIH
	32:21	if all of you will g armed over the Jordan 6296
	34: 4	on to Zin and south of Kadesh Barnea. 2118
	34: 4	Then it will g to Hazar Addar and over 3655
	34: 8	Then the boundary will g to Zedad, 2118
	34:11	The boundary will g down from Shepham 3718
	34:12	the boundary will g down along the Jordan 3718
	35:32	a city of refuge and so allow him to g back 8740
Dt	1: 2	to g from Horeb to Kadesh Barnea by NIH
	1: 7	g to all the neighboring peoples in 995
	1: 8	G in and take possession of the land that 995
	1:21	G up and take possession of it as 6590
	1:26	But you were unwilling to g up; 6590
	1:28	Where can we g? 6590
	1:33	and to show you the way you should g. 2143
	1:41	We will g up and fight, 6590
	1:41	to g up into the hill country. 6590
	1:42	"Tell them, 'Do not g up and fight, 6590
	3:20	each of you may g back to 8740
	3:25	Let me g over and see the good land 6296
	3:27	G up to the top of Pisgah and look west 6590
	4: 1	and may g in and take possession of 995
	4:40	so that it may g well with you 3512
	5: 5	of the fire and did not g up the mountain.) 6590
	5:16	that it may g well with you in the land 3512
	5:27	G near and listen to all that 7928
	5:29	so that it might g well with them 3512
	5:30	"G, tell them to return to their tents. 2143
	6: 3	be careful to obey so that it may g well 3512
	6:18	so that it may g well with you 3512
	6:18	with you and you may g in and take over 995
	8:16	that in the end it might g well with you. 3512
	9: 1	to g in and dispossess nations greater 995
	9:12	"G down from here at once, 3718
	9:23	"G up and take possession of the land 6590
	10:11	"G," the LORD said to me, 7756
	11: 8	the strength to g in and take over the land 995
	11:25	of you on the whole land, wherever you g. 2005
	12: 5	To that place you must g; 995
	12:25	so that it may g well with you 3512
	12:26	and g to the place the LORD will choose. 995
	12:28	so that it may always g well with you 3512
	13: 6	"Let us g and worship other gods" (gods 2143
	13:13	of their town astray, saying, "Let us g 2143
	14:25	the silver with you and g to the place 2143
	15:12	the seventh year you must let him g free. 8938
	17: 9	G to the priests, who are Levites, 995
	17:16	"You are not to g back that way again." 8740
	19: 5	a man may g into the forest 995
	19:13	so that it may g well with you. 3201
	20: 1	When you g to war against your enemies 3655
	20: 2	When you are about to g into battle, 7928
	20: 5	Let him g home, or he may die 2143+2256+8740
	20: 6	Let him g home, or he may die 2143+2256+8740
	20: 7	Let him g home, or he may die 2143+2256+8740
	20: 8	Let him g home so that his brothers will not become disheartened too." 2143+2256+8740
	21: 2	and judges shall g out and measure 3655
	21:10	When you g to war against your enemies 3655
	21:13	then you may g to her and be her husband 995
	21:14	let her g wherever she wishes. 8938
	22: 6	be sure to let the mother g, 8938+8938
	22: 7	so that it may g well with you 3512

Dt	23:10	he is to g outside the camp and stay there. 3655
	23:12	a place outside the camp where you can g 3655
	24:10	do not g into his house 995
	24:12	do not g to sleep with his pledge 8886
	24:19	do not g back to get it. 8740
	24:20	not g over the branches a second time 339+6994
	24:21	do not g over the vines again. 339+6618
	25: 7	she shall g to the elders at the town gate 6590
	25: 9	his brother's widow shall g up to him in 5602
	26: 2	Then g to the place the LORD your God 2143
	28: 6	in and blessed when you g out. 3655
	28:19	in and cursed when you g out. 3655
	28:41	because they will g into captivity. 2143
	29:18	from the LORD our God to g and worship 2143
	31: 7	for you must g with this people into 995
	32:49	"G up into the Abarim Range 6590
Jos	1: 7	you may be successful wherever you g. 2143
	1: 9	be with you wherever you g." 2143
	1:11	"G through the camp and tell the people, 6296
	1:11	the Jordan here to g in and take possession 995
	1:15	you may g back and occupy your own land, 8740
	1:16	and wherever you send us we will g. 2143
	2: 1	"G, look over the land," he said, 2143
	2: 5	G after them quickly. 8103
	2:16	"G to the hills so the pursuers will 2143
	2:16	and then g on your way." 2143
	3: 4	Then you will know which way to g, 2143
	3: 4	and the ark; do not g near it." 7928
	3: 8	g and stand in the river.' " NIH
	3:11	of the Lord of all the earth will g into 6296
	4: 5	"G over before the ark of the LORD 6296
	6: 5	and the people will g up, 6590
	6:19	the LORD and must g into his treasury." 995
	6:22	"G into the prostitute's house 995
	7: 2	"G up and spy out the region." 6590
	7: 3	the people will have to g up against Ai. 6590
	7:13	"G, consecrate the people. 7756
	8: 1	and g up and attack Ai. 7756
	8: 4	Don't g very far from it. 8178
	8:17	in Ai or Bethel who did not g after Israel. 3655
	9:11	g and meet them and say to them, 2143
	14:11	I'm just as vigorous to g out to battle now 3655
	17:15	g up into the forest and clear land 6590
	18: 8	"G and make a survey of the land and write 2143
	20: 6	Then he may g back to his own home in 995
	22:12	of Israel gathered at Shiloh to g to war 6590
	23:14	"Now I am about to g the way of all 2143
	23:16	and g and serve other gods and bow down 2143
Jdg	1: 1	be the first to g up and fight for us against 6590
	1: 2	The LORD answered, "Judah is to g; 6590
	1: 3	We in turn will g with you into yours." 2143
	4: 6	'G, take with you ten thousand men 2143
	4: 8	Barak said to her, "If you g with me, 2143
	4: 8	"If you go with me, I will g; 2143
	4: 8	but if you don't g with me, I won't go." 2143
	4: 8	but if you don't go with me, I won't g." 2143
	4: 9	"Very well," Deborah said, "I will g 2143+2143
	4:14	Then Deborah said to Barak, "G! 7756
	5:22	galloping, galloping g his mighty steeds. NIH
	6:14	"G in the strength you have 2143
	6:18	Please do not g away until I come back 4631
	7: 4	If I say, 'This one shall g with you,' 2143
	7: 4	'This one shall g with you,' he shall g; 2143
	7: 4	'This one shall not g with you,' 2143
	7: 4	not go with you,' he shall not g." 2143
	7: 7	Let all the other men g, 2143
	7: 9	"Get up, g down against the camp, 3718
	7:10	go down to the camp with your servant Purah 3718
	9:38	G out and fight them!" 3655
	10:14	G and cry out to the gods you have chosen. 2143
	11:17	to g through your country,' 6296
	11:38	"You may g," he said. 2143
	11:38	And he let her g for two months. 8938
	11:40	the young women of Israel g out 2143
	12: 1	"Why did you g to fight the Ammonites 6296
	12: 1	the Ammonites without calling us to g 2143
	14: 3	Must you g to the uncircumcised 2143
	15: 1	But her father would not let him g in. 995
	16:20	"I'll g out as before 3655
	18: 2	They told them, "G, explore the land." 2143
	18: 6	The priest answered them, "G in peace. 2143
	18: 9	Don't hesitate to g there and take it over. 2143
	19: 5	then you can g." 2143
	19: 7	And when the man got up to g, 2143
	19: 8	when he rose to g, the girl's father said, 2143
	19:12	We won't g into an alien city, 6073
	19:12	We will g on to Gibeah." 6296
	19:25	and at dawn they let her g. 8938
	19:28	He said to her, "Get up; let's g." 2143
	20: 8	saying, "None of us will g home. 2143
	20: 9	We'll g up against it as the lot directs. NIH
	20:18	"Who of us shall g first to fight against 2143
	20:18	The LORD replied, "Judah shall g first." NIH
	20:23	"Shall we g up again to battle against 5602
	20:23	"G up against them." 6590
	20:28	"Shall we g up again to battle 3655
	20:28	The LORD responded, "G up," 6590
	21:10	with instructions to g to Jabesh Gilead 2143
	21:20	"G and hide in the vineyards 2143
	21:21	from the girls of Shiloh and g to the land 2143
Ru	1: 8	"G back, each of you, 2143
	1:10	"We will g back with you to your people." 8740
	1:12	G back with her." 8740
	1:15	"G back with her." 8740
	1:16	Where you g I will go, 2143
	1:16	Where you go I will g, 2143
	1:18	that Ruth was determined to g with her, 2143
	2: 2	"Let me g to the fields and pick up 2143

Ru	2: 2	Naomi said to her, "G ahead, my daughter. 2143
	2: 8	Don't g and glean in another field 2143
	2: 8	in another field and don't g away from here. 6296
	2: 9	g and get a drink from the water jars 2143
	2:22	my daughter, to g with his girls, 3655
	3: 3	Then g down to the threshing floor, 3718
	3: 4	Then g and uncover his feet and lie down. 995
	3:16	Naomi asked, "How did it g, my daughter?" 905+4769
	3:17	of barley, saying, 'Don't g back 995
1Sa	1:17	Eli answered, "G in peace, 2143
	1:22	Hannah did not g. 6590
	2:20	Then they would g home. 2143
	2:28	to g up to my altar, to burn incense, 6590
	3: 5	g back and lie down." 8740
	3: 6	g back and lie down." 8740
	3: 9	So Eli told Samuel, "G and lie down, 2143
	4: 3	so that it may g with us and save us from 995
	5:11	let it g back to its own place, 8740
	6: 6	so they could g on their way? 2143
	6:20	To whom will the ark g up from here?" 6590
	8:20	to g out before us and fight our battles." 3655
	8:22	"Everyone g back to his town." 2143
	9: 3	of the servants with you and g and look for 2143
	9: 5	with him, "Come, let's g back, 8740
	9: 6	Let's g there now. 2143
	9: 7	Saul said to his servant, "If we g, 2143
	9: 9	"Come, let us g to the seer," 2143
	9:10	"Come, let's g." 2143
	9:13	those who are invited will eat. G up now; 6590
	9:19	"G up ahead of me to the high place, 6590
	9:19	and in the morning I will let you g 8938
	9:27	"Tell the servant to g on ahead of us"— 6296
	10: 3	"Then you will g from there 2736
	10: 5	"After that you will g to Gibeah of God, 995
	10: 8	"G down ahead of me to Gilgal. 3718
	11:14	let us g to Gilgal and there reaffirm 2143
	14: 1	let's g over to the Philistine outpost on 6296
	14: 6	let's g over to the outpost 6296
	14: 7	"G ahead; I am with you heart and soul." 5742
	14: 9	we will stay where we are and not g up 6590
	14:34	"G out among the men and tell them, 7046
	14:36	"Let us g down after the Philistines 3718
	14:37	"Shall I g down after the Philistines?" 3718
	15: 3	Now g, attack the Amalekites 2143
	15: 6	Then he said to the Kenites, "G away, 2143
	15:18	And he sent you on a mission, saying, 'G 2143
	15:26	"I will not g back with you. 8740
	15:35	he did not g to see Saul again, NIH
	16: 2	But Samuel said, "How can I g? 2143
	17:32	your servant will g and fight him." 2143
	17:33	not able to g out against this Philistine 2143
	17:37	Saul said to David, "G, 2143
	17:39	"I cannot g in these," he said to Saul, 2143
	18:30	continued to g out to battle, 3655
	19: 2	g into hiding and stay there. 3782
	19: 3	I will g out and stand with my father in 3655
	20: 5	but let me g and hide in the field until 8938
	20:11	Jonathan said, "let's g out into the field." 3655
	20:19	g to the place where you hid 995
	20:21	Then I will send a boy and say, 'G, 2143
	20:22	then you must g, 2143
	20:28	for permission to g to Bethlehem. NIH
	20:29	He said, 'Let me g, 8938
	20:38	Then he shouted, "Hurry! G quickly! 2590
	20:40	G, carry them back to town." 2143
	20:42	Jonathan said to David, "G in peace, 2143
	22: 5	G into the land of Judah." 2143
	23: 2	"Shall I g and attack these Philistines?" 2143
	23: 2	The LORD answered him, "G, 2143
	23: 3	if we g to Keilah against the Philistine 2143
	23: 4	"G down to Keilah 3718
	23: 8	to g down to Keilah to besiege David 3718
	23:13	he did not g there. 3655
	23:22	G and make further preparation. 2143
	23:23	Then I will g with you; 2143
	25: 5	"G up to Nabal at Carmel and greet him 995
	25:19	Then she told her servants, "G on ahead; 6296
	25:35	g home in peace. 2143
	26: 6	"Who will g down into the camp with me 3718
	26: 6	"I'll g with you," said Abishai. 3718
	26:10	or he will g into battle and perish. 3718
	26:11	that are near his head, and let's g." 2143
	26:19	'G, serve other gods.' 2143
	27:10	"Where did you g raiding today?" 7320
	28: 7	so I may g and inquire of her." 2143
	28:22	so you may eat and have the strength to g 2143
	29: 4	He must not g with us into battle, 3718
	29: 7	Turn back and g in peace; 2143
	29: 8	Why can't I g and fight against 995
	29: 9	'He must not g up with us into battle.' 6590
	29:11	to g back to the land of the Philistines, 2143
	30:22	"Because they did not g out with us, 2143
	30:22	and children and g." 2143
2Sa	1:15	David called one of his men and said, "G, 5602
	2: 1	"Shall I g up to one of the towns 6590
	2: 1	The LORD said, "G up." 6590
	2: 1	David asked, "Where shall I g?" 6590
	3:16	Then Abner said to him, "G back home!" 2143
	3:21	"Let me g at once and assemble all Israel 2143
	3:24	Why did you let him g? 8938
	5:19	"Shall I g and attack the Philistines? 6590
	5:19	The LORD answered him, "G, 6590
	5:23	and he answered, "Do not g straight up, 6590
	7: 3	you have in mind, for g and do it, 2143
	7: 5	"G and tell my servant David, 'This is what 2143
	11: 1	at the time when kings g off to war, 3655

2Sa	11: 8	"**G down** to your house	3718
	11: 9	and *did* not **g down** to his house.	3718
	11:10	David was told, "Uriah *did* not **g home**,"	3718
	11:10	Why didn't *you* **g home**?"	3718
	11:11	*How could* I **g** to my house to eat and drink	995
	11:13	he *did* not **g** home.	3718
	12:23	I *will* **g** to him, but he will not return to me.	8886
	13: 5	"**G** to bed and pretend to be ill,"	2143
	13: 7	"**G** to the house of your brother Amnon	2143
	13:25	"All of us *should* not **g**;	2143
	13:25	Absalom urged him, he still refused to **g**,	2143
	13:26	"Why *should* he **g** with you?"	8132
	13:39	spirit of the king longed to **g** to Absalom,	3655
	14: 3	Then **g** to the king and speak these words	995
	14: 8	The king said to the woman, "**G home**,	2143
	14:21	**G,** bring back the young man Absalom."	2143
	14:24	the king said, "He *must* **g** to his own house;	6015
	14:30	**G** and set it on fire."	2143
	14:31	Then Joab **g** to Absalom's house	995
	15: 7	"*Let me* **g** to Hebron and fulfill	2143
	15: 9	The king said to him, "**G in peace**."	2143
	15:19	"**G back** and stay with King Absalom.	8740
	15:20	**G back,** and take your countrymen.	8740
	15:22	David said to Ittai, "**G ahead,** march on."	2143
	15:27	**G back** to the city in peace,	8740
	15:33	David said to him, "If you **g** with me,	6296
	16: 9	*Let me* **g over** and cut off his head."	6296
	16:17	Why didn't *you* **g** with your friend?"	2143
	17:17	A servant girl *was* to **g** and inform them,	2143
	17:17	and they *were* to **g** and tell King David,	2143
	18: 3	But the men said, "*You* must not **g** out;	3655
	18:21	Then Joab said to a Cushite, "**G,**	2143
	18:22	"My son, why *do* you *want* to **g?**	8132
	19: 7	Now **g** out and encourage your men.	7756
	19: 7	by the LORD that if you don't **g out,**	3655
	19:15	to **g out** and meet the king and bring him	2143
	19:25	"Why didn't *you* **g** with me,	2143
	19:26	so *I can* **g** with the king."	2143
	19:34	I *should* **g up** to Jerusalem with the king?	6590
	21:17	"Never again *will you* **g out** with us	3655
	24: 1	"**G** and take a census of Israel and Judah."	2143
	24: 2	"**G** throughout the tribes of Israel from Dan	8763
	24:12	"**G** and tell David, 'This is what	2143
	24:18	"**G up** and build an altar to the LORD on	6590
1Ki	1:13	**G in** to King David and say to 995+2143+2256	
	1:35	Then *you are* to **g up** with him,	6590
	1:53	and Solomon said, "**G** to your home."	2143
	2: 2	"I *am* about to **g** the way of all the earth,"	2143
	2: 3	in all you do and wherever you **g,**	7155
	2: 6	*do* not **let** his gray head **g down**	3718
	2:26	"**G back** to your fields in Anathoth.	2143
	2:29	"**G,** strike him down!"	2143
	2:36	but *do* not **g** anywhere else.	3655
	2:42	'On the day you leave to **g** anywhere else,	2143
	7:38	one basin to **g** on each of the ten stands.	NIH
	8:44	your people to **g** to war against their enemies,	3655
	9: 6	and decrees I have given you and **g off**	2143
	11:21	Then Hadad said to Pharaoh, "*Let me* **g,**	8938
	11:22	"to **g back** to your own country?"	2143
	11:22	Hadad replied, "but *do let* me **g!**" 8938+8938	
	12: 5	"**G away** for three days and then come back	2143
	12:24	*Do* not **g up** to fight against your brothers,	6590
	12:24	**G home,** every one of you,	8740
	12:27	If these people **g up** to offer sacrifices at	6590
	12:28	"It is too much for you *to* **g up**	6590
	13: 8	I *would* not **g** with you,	995
	13:12	"Which way *did he* **g?**"	2143
	13:16	"I cannot turn back and **g** with you,	995
	14: 2	"**G,** disguise yourself,	7756
	14: 2	Then **g** to Shiloh.	2143
	14: 3	cakes and a jar of honey, and **g** to him.	995
	14: 7	**G,** tell Jeroboam that this is what	2143
	14:12	"As for you, **g back** home.	8740
	17: 9	"**G at once** to Zarephath of Sidon	2143
	17:13	**G home** and do as you have said.	995
	18: 1	"**G** and present yourself to Ahab,	2143
	18: 5	"**G** through the land to all the springs	2143
	18: 8	"**G** tell your master, 'Elijah is here.' "	2143
	18:11	now you tell me *to* **g** to my master and say,	2143
	18:12	*I* **g** and tell Ahab and he doesn't find you,	995
	18:14	now you tell me *to* **g** to my master and say,	2143
	18:41	And Elijah said to Ahab, "**G,** eat and drink,	6590
	18:43	and look toward the sea,"	6590
	18:43	Seven times Elijah said, "**G back.**"	8740
	18:44	So Elijah said, "**G** and tell Ahab,	6590
	18:44	'Hitch up your chariot and **g down** before	3718
	19:11	"**G out** and stand on the mountain in	3655
	19:15	"**G back** the way you came,	2143
	19:15	and **g** to the Desert of Damascus.	NIH
	19:20	"**G back,**" Elijah replied,	2143
	20:31	*Let us* **g** to the king of Israel	3655
	20:33	"**G** and get him," the king said.	995
	20:34	he made a treaty with him, and **let** him **g.**	8938
	21:18	"**G down** to meet Ahab king of Israel,	7756
	22: 4	"*Will you* **g** with me to fight	2143
	22: 6	"*Shall* I **g** to war against Ramoth Gilead,	2143
	22: 6	"**G,**" they answered, "for	6590
	22:15	*shall we* **g** to war against Ramoth Gilead,	2143
	22:17	*Let each* one **g** home in peace.' "	8740
	22:22	" ' *I will* **g out** and be a lying spirit in	3655
	22:22	'**G** and do it.'	3655
	22:24	the spirit from the LORD **g** when he went	6296
	22:25	"You will find out on the day *you* **g** to hide	995
	22:48	of trading ships to **g** to Ophir for gold,	2143
2Ki	1: 2	"**G** and consult Baal-Zebub,	2143
	1: 3	"**G up** and meet the messengers of the king	6590
	1: 6	'**G back** to the king who sent you	2143

2Ki	1:15	"**G down** with him;	3718
	2:16	*Let them* **g** and look for your master.	2143
	2:18	"Didn't I tell you not to **g?**"	2143
	2:23	"**G on up,** you baldhead!"	6590
	2:23	"**G on up,** you baldhead!"	6590
	3: 7	*Will* you **g** with me to fight	2143
	3: 7	"*I will* **g** with you," he replied.	6590
	3:13	**G** to the prophets of your father and	2143
	4: 3	"**G** around and ask all your neighbors	2143
	4: 4	Then **g** *inside* and shut the door	995
	4: 7	"**G,** sell the oil and pay your debts.	2143
	4:22	**g** to the man of God **quickly**	8132
	4:23	"Why **g** to him today?"	2143
	5: 5	"**By all means, g,**" 995+2143	
	5:10	Elisha sent a messenger to say to him, "**G,**	2143
	5:19	"**G in peace,**" Elisha said.	2143
	5:25	"Your servant didn't **g** anywhere,"	2143
	6: 2	*Let us* **g** to the Jordan,	2143
	6: 2	And he said, "**G.**"	2143
	6:13	"**G,** find out where he is," the king ordered,	2143
	6:22	that they may eat and drink and then **g back**	2143
	7: 4	If we say, '*We'll* **g into** the city'—	995
	7: 4	So *let's* **g over** to the camp of the Arameans	2143
	7: 9	*Let's* **g at once** and report this to 995+2143+2256	
	7:14	"**G** and find out what has happened."	2143
	8: 1	"**G away** with your family and stay for a	2143
	8: 8	with you and **g** to meet the man of God.	2143
	8:10	Elisha answered, "**G** and say to him,	2143
	9: 1	of oil with you and **g** *to* Ramoth Gilead.	2143
	9: 2	**G** to him, get him away	995
	9:15	the city to **g** and tell the news in Jezreel."	2143
	10:25	"**G in** and kill them; let no one escape."	995
	11: 7	*that* normally **g off** Sabbath duty are all	3655
	17:27	"Have one of the priests you took captive	
		from Samaria **g** back to live there	2143
	19:27	where you stay and when you come and **g**	3655
	20: 5	"**G back** and tell Hezekiah, the leader	8740
	20: 5	On the third day from now you *will* **g up**	6590
	20: 8	and that *I will* **g up** to the temple of	6590
	20: 9	*Shall* the shadow **g forward** ten steps,	2143
	20: 9	or *shall* it **g back** ten steps?"	8740
	20:10	for the shadow to **g forward** ten steps,"	5742
	20:10	"Rather, *have* it **g back** ten steps."	345+8740
	20:11	made the shadow **g back** the ten steps	8740
	22: 4	"**G up** to Hilkiah the high priest	6590
	22:13	"**G** and inquire of the LORD for me and	2143
	25:24	and *it will* **g well** with you."	3512
1Ch	7:11	fighting men **ready to g out** to war. 3655+7372	
	14:10	"*Shall* I **g** and attack the Philistines?	6590
	14:10	The LORD answered him, "**G,**	6590
	14:14	"*Do* not **g straight up,**	6590
	17: 4	"**G** and tell my servant David, 'This is what	2143
	17:11	When your days are over and you **g** to be	2143
	20: 1	at the time when kings **g off** to war,	3655
	21: 2	"**G** and count the Israelites from Beersheba	2143
	21:10	"**G** and tell David, 'This is what	2143
	21:18	*to* **g up** and build an altar to the LORD on	6590
	21:30	But David could not **g** before it to inquire	2143
2Ch	6:34	your people **g** to war against their enemies,	3655
	7:19	and commands I have given you and **g off**	2143
	11: 4	*Do* not **g up** to fight against your brothers.	6590
	11: 4	**G home,** every one of you,	8740
	18: 3	"*Will* you **g** with me against Ramoth Gilead	2143
	18: 5	"*Shall we* **g** to war against Ramoth Gilead,	2143
	18: 5	"**G,**" they answered, "for God will give it	6590
	18:14	*shall we* **g** to war against Ramoth Gilead,	2143
	18:16	*Let each* one **g** home in peace.' "	8740
	18:21	" '*I will* **g** and be a lying spirit in	3655
	18:21	'**G** and do it.'	3655
	18:23	the spirit from the LORD **g** when he went	6296
	18:24	"You will find out on the day *you* **g** to hide	995
	20:17	**G out** to face them tomorrow,	3655
	24: 5	"**G** to the towns of Judah and collect	3655
	25: 8	if you **g** and fight courageously in battle,	995
	26:11	**ready to g out** by divisions according	3655+7372
	34:21	"**G** and inquire of the LORD for me and	2143
	36:23	and *let him* **g up.**'"	6590
Ezr	1: 3	may his God be with him, and *let him* **g up**	6590
	1: 5	to **g up** and build the house of the LORD	6590
	4: 4	and made them afraid to **g** on **building.**	AIT
	5: 5	not stopped until a report *could* **g** to Darius	10207
	5:15	'Take these articles and **g** and deposit them	10016
	7:13	who wish to **g** to Jerusalem with you,	10207
	7:13	to go to Jerusalem with you, *may* **g.**	10207
	7:28	from Israel to **g up** with me.	6590
	8:31	from the Ahava Canal to **g** *to* Jerusalem.	2143
Ne	6: 2	on a great project and cannot **g down.**	3718
	6: 3	the work stop while I leave it and **g down**	3718
	6:11	like me **g** into the temple to save his life?	995
	6:11	I *will* not **g!**"	995
	8:10	"**G** and enjoy choice food and sweet drinks,	2143
	8:15	"**G out** into the hill country	3655
	9:15	you told them to **g in** and take possession	995
	12:31	had the leaders of Judah **g up**	6590
	13:22	and **g** and guard the gates in order to keep	995
Est	2:12	a girl's turn came to **g in** to King Xerxes,	995
	2:13	And this is how she *would* **g** to the king:	995
	2:14	In the evening she *would* **g** there and in	995
	2:15	the daughter of his uncle Abihail) to **g** to	995
	4: 8	to urge her to **g** into the king's presence	995
	4:11	since I was called to **g** to the king."	995
	4:16	"**G,** gather together all the Jews who are	2143
	4:16	When this is done, *I will* **g** to the king,	995
	5:14	**g** with the king to the dinner and	995
	6:10	"**G at once,**" the king commanded Haman.	4554
Job	2:11	by agreement to **g** and sympathize with him	995
	6:18	*they* **g up** into the wasteland and perish.	6590

Job	10:14	**let** my offense **g unpunished.**	5927
	10:21	before *I* **g** to the place of no return,	2143
	11: 2	*Are* all these words to **g unanswered?** 4202+6699	
	16: 6	and if I refrain, *it does* not **g** away.	2143
	16:22	"Only a few years will pass before *I* **g** on	2143
	17:16	*Will* it **g down** to the gates of death?	3718
	20:13	*to let* it **g** and keeps it in his mouth,	6440
	21:13	in prosperity and **g down** *to* the grave	5737
	23: 3	if only *I could* **g** to his dwelling!	995
	23: 8	"But if I **g** to the east, he is not there;	2143
	23: 8	if I **g** to the west, I do not find him;	NIH
	24: 5	poor **g** about their labor of foraging food;	3655
	24:10	Lacking clothes, *they* **g about** naked;	2143
	24:10	they carry the sheaves, but still **g hungry.**	NIH
	27: 6	and never let **g** of it;	8332
	30:28	*I* **g about** blackened, but not by the sun;	2143
	31:34	that I kept silent and *would* not **g** outside	3655
	39: 5	"Who **let** the wild donkey **g** free?	8938
	42: 8	now take seven bulls and seven rams and **g**	2143
Ps	22:29	all *who* **g down** to the dust will kneel	3718
	26: 6	and **g about** your altar, O LORD,	6015
	32: 8	and teach you in the way you *should* **g**;	2143
	38: 6	all day long *I* **g about** mourning.	2143
	42: 2	When *can I* **g** and meet with God?	995
	42: 4	how *I used* to **g** with the multitude,	6296
	42: 9	Why *must I* **g about** mourning,	2143
	43: 2	Why *must I* **g about** mourning,	2143
	43: 4	Then *will I* **g** to the altar of God, to God,	995
	44: 9	you no *longer* **g out** with our armies.	3655
	48:12	Walk about Zion, **g around** her,	5938
	55:15	let them **g down** alive to the grave,	3718
	58: 3	Even from birth the wicked **g astray**;	2319
	59:10	God *will* **g before** me and will let me gloat	7709
	60:10	and no longer **g out** with our armies?	3655
	63: 9	*they* will **g down** to the depths of the earth.	995
	68:21	hairy crowns of *those who* **g on** in their sins.	2143
	71: 3	to which I *can* always **g**;	995
	84: 7	*They* **g** from strength to strength,	2143
	88: 4	I am counted among *those who* **g down** to	3718
	89:14	love and faithfulness **g before** you.	7709
	95:10	"They are a people whose hearts **g astray**,	9494
	102:24	your years **g** on through all generations.	NIH
	104:19	and the sun knows when to **g down.**	4427
	104:26	There the ships **g** to and fro,	2143
	108:11	and no longer **g out** with our armies?	3655
	115:17	those *who* **g down** to silence;	3718
	122: 1	"*Let us* **g** to the house of the LORD."	2143
	122: 4	That is where the tribes **g up,**	6590
	132: 3	not enter my house or **g** to my bed—	6590
	132: 7	"*Let us* **g** to his dwelling place;	995
	139: 7	Where *can I* **g** from your Spirit?	2143
	139: 8	If *I* **g up** to the heavens, you are there;	6158
	143: 7	or I will be like *those who* **g down** to the pit.	3718
	143: 8	Show me the way *I should* **g,**	2143
Pr	1:12	and whole, like *those who* **g down** to the pit;	3718
	1:15	*do* not **g** along with them,	928+2006+2143
	1:19	all *who* **g after ill-gotten gain**;	1298+1299
	2:19	None *who* **g** to her return or attain the paths	995
	3:23	Then *you will* **g** on your way in safety,	2143
	4:13	Hold on to instruction, *do* not let it **g**;	8332
	4:15	turn from it and **g on** *your* way.	6296
	5: 5	Her feet **g down** to death;	3718
	5: 8	*do* not **g near** the door of her house,	7928
	6: 3	**G** and humble yourself;	2143
	6: 6	**G** to the ant, you sluggard;	2143
	6:29	no one who touches her *will* **g unpunished.**	5927
	9:15	*who* **g straight on** their way.	3837
	10: 3	**let** the righteous **g hungry**	8279
	11:21	The wicked *will* not **g unpunished,**	5927
	11:21	but those who are righteous *will* **g** free.	4880
	14:22	*Do* not those who plot evil **g astray?**	9494
	16: 5	Be sure of this: They *will* not **g unpunished.**	5927
	17: 5	over disaster *will* not **g unpunished.**	5927
	18: 8	they **g down** *to* a man's inmost parts.	3718
	19: 5	A false witness *will* not **g unpunished,**	5927
	19: 5	and he who pours out lies *will* not **g** free.	4880
	19: 9	A false witness *will* not **g unpunished,**	5927
	22: 6	a child *in the way* he *should* **g,** 2006+6584+7023	
	23:30	*who* **g** to sample bowls of mixed wine.	995
	24:25	But *it will* **g well** with those who convict	5838
	26:22	they **g down** *to* a man's inmost parts.	3718
	27:10	and *do* not **g** *to* your brother's house	995
	28:12	wicked rise to power, men **g into hiding.**	2924
	28:20	one eager to get rich *will* not **g unpunished.**	5927
	28:28	wicked rise to power, people **g into hiding**;	6259
	31:18	and her lamp *will* not **g** out at night.	3882
Ecc	1: 4	Generations come and generations **g,**	995
	3:20	All **g** to the same place;	2143
	5: 1	Guard your steps when *you* **g** to the house	2143
	5: 1	**G near** to listen rather than to offer	7928
	6: 6	*Do* not all **g** to the same place?	2143
	7: 2	It is better to **g** to a house of mourning than	2143
	7: 2	to go to a house of mourning than *to* **g** to	2143
	7:18	It is good to grasp the one and not let **g** of	
		the other.	906+3338+5663
	8:10	those who used to come and **g** from	2143
	8:12	I know that *it will* **g** better	2118
	8:13	*it will* not **g** well with them,	2118
	9: 7	**G,** eat your food with gladness,	2143
	10: 7	while princes **g** on foot like slaves.	2143
	12: 5	to his eternal home and mourners **g about**	6015
SS	3: 2	I will get up now and **g about** the city,	6015
	3: 4	I held him and *would* not **let** him **g**	8332
	4: 6	I *will* **g** to the mountain of myrrh and	2143
	7: 9	*May* the wine **g** straight to my lover,	2143
	7:11	my lover, *let us* **g** to the countryside,	3655
	7:12	*Let us* **g** early to the vineyards to see if	8899

Isa	2: 3	*let us* **g up** to the mountain of the LORD	6590
	2: 3	The law *will* **g out** from Zion,	3655
	2:10	**G** into the rocks, hide in the ground	995
	5:13	Therefore my people *will* **g into exile**	1655
	6: 8	And who *will* **g** for us?"	2143
	6: 9	He said, "**G** and tell this people:	2143
	7: 3	Then the LORD said to Isaiah, "**G out,**	3655
	7:24	*Men will* **g** there with bow and arrow,	995
	7:25	*you will* no longer **g** there for fear of	995
	10:29	*They* **g over** the pass, and say,	6296
	13: 7	Because of this, all hands *will* **g limp,**	8332
	14:17	and *would* not **let** his captives **g** home?"	7337
	15: 5	*They* **g up** the way to Luhith,	6590
	15: 5	weeping as they **g;**	NIH
	18: 2	**G,** swift messengers, to a people tall	2143
	19:23	The Assyrians *will* **g** to Egypt and	995
	21: 6	This is what the Lord says to me: "**G,**	2143
	22:15	"**G,** say to this steward, to Shebna,	995+2143
	23:18	Her profits *will* **g** to those who live before	2118
	26:10	a land of uprightness *they* **g** on **doing evil**	AIT
	26:20	**G,** my people, enter your rooms and shut	2143
	28:13	so that *they will* **g** and fall backward,	2143
	28:28	so *one does* not **g** on **threshing** it forever.	1889+1889
	29: 1	*let* your **cycle** of festivals **g on.**	5938
	29:15	Woe to those *who* **g** to great depths	6676
	30: 2	who **g** down to Egypt	2143
	30: 8	**g** now, write it on a tablet for them,	995
	30:29	your hearts will rejoice as *when* people **g up**	2143
	31: 1	Woe to those *who* **g down** to Egypt for help,	3718
	35: 8	wicked fools *will* not **g about** on it.	9494
	37:28	where you stay and when you come and **g**	3655
	38: 5	"**G** and tell Hezekiah, 'This is what	2143
	38: 8	**make** the shadow cast by the sun **g**	8740
	38:10	"In the prime of my life *must I* **g** through	2143
	38:18	*those who* **g down** to the pit cannot hope	3718
	38:22	"What will be the sign that *I will* **g up** to	6590
	40: 9	**g up** on a high mountain.	6590
	42:10	you *who* **g down** to the sea,	3718
	45: 2	I *will* **g** before you and will level	2143
	45:16	*they will* **g off** into disgrace together.	2143
	46: 2	*they* themselves **g off** into captivity.	2143
	47: 1	"**G down,** sit in the dust,	3718
	47: 5	"Sit in silence, **g** into darkness,	995
	48:17	who directs you in the way *you should* **g.**	2143
	50:11	**g,** walk in the light of your fires and of	AIT
	51: 4	The law *will* **g out** from me;	3655
	52:11	Depart, depart, **g out** from there!	3655
	52:12	you will not leave in haste or **g** in flight;	2143
	52:12	for the LORD *will* **g** before you,	2143
	55:12	*You will* **g out** in joy and be led forth	3655
	58: 8	then your righteousness *will* **g** before you,	2143
	63:14	like cattle *that* **g down** to the plain,	3718
	65:13	but you *will* **g hungry;**	AIT
	65:13	but you *will* **g thirsty;**	AIT
	66:17	and purify themselves to **g** into the gardens,	NIH
	66:24	"And *they will* **g out** and look upon	3655
Jer	1: 7	*You must* **g** to everyone I send you to	2143
	2: 2	"**G** and proclaim in the hearing	2143
	2:18	Now why **g** to Egypt to drink water from	2006
	2:18	And why **g** to Assyria to drink water from	2006
	2:25	and *I must* **g** after them.'	2143
	2:36	Why *do you* **g about** so much,	261
	3:12	**G,** proclaim this message toward the north:	2143
	4: 1	of my sight and no longer **g astray,**	5653
	4: 6	Raise the signal to **g** to Zion!	NIH
	4:29	*Some* **g** into the thickets;	995
	5: 1	"**G up and down** the streets of Jerusalem	8763
	5: 5	*I will* **g** to the leaders and speak to them;	2143
	5:10	"**G** through her vineyards and ravage them,	6590
	6:25	*Do* not **g out** to the fields or walk on	3655
	7:12	" "**G** now to the place in Shiloh	2143
	7:21	**G** ahead, **add** your burnt offerings	AIT
	7:23	that *it may* **g well** with you.	3512
	9: 2	so that I might leave my people and **g away**	2143
	9: 3	*They* **g** from one sin to another;	3655
	11:12	of Jerusalem *will* **g** and cry out to the gods	2143
	12: 9	**G** and gather all the wild beasts;	2143
	13: 1	"**G** and buy a linen belt and put it	2143
	13: 4	and **g** now to Perath and hide it there in	2143
	13: 6	"**G** now to Perath and get the belt I told you	2143
	13:10	the stubbornness of their hearts and **g**	2143
	14: 3	*they* **g** to the cisterns but find no water.	995
	14:18	If *I* **g** into the country,	3655
	14:18	if *I* **g** into the city,	995
	15: 1	my heart would not **g** out to this people.	NIH
	15: 1	them away from my presence! Let them **g!**	3655
	15: 2	And if they ask you, 'Where *shall* we **g?'**	3655
	16: 5	*do* not **g** to mourn or show sympathy,	2143
	17:19	"**G** and stand at the gate of the people,	2143
	17:19	through which the kings of Judah **g in**	995
	18: 2	"**G down** to the potter's house,	3718
	19: 1	"**G** and buy a clay jar from a potter.	2143
	19: 2	and **g** out to the Valley of Ben Hinnom,	3655
	19:10	while those who **g** with you are watching,	2143
	20: 6	in your house *will* **g** into exile to Babylon.	2143
	22: 1	"**G down** to the palace of the king of Judah	3718
	22:20	"**G up** to Lebanon and cry out,	6590
	22:22	and your allies *will* **g** into exile.	2143
	25:16	and **g mad** because of the sword I will send	2147
	25:29	and *will* you **indeed g** **unpunished?**	5927+5927
	25:29	you will not **g** **unpunished,**	5927
	28:13	"**G** and tell Hananiah, 'This is what	2143
	29:16	your countrymen who *did* not **g** with you	2143
	30:11	**let** you **g entirely unpunished.'**	5927+5927
	30:16	all your enemies *will* **g** into exile.	2143
	31: 4	up your tambourines and **g out** to dance	3655

Jer	31: 6	'Come, *let us* **g up** to Zion,	6590
	34: 2	**G** to Zedekiah king of Judah and tell him,	2143
	34: 3	And *you will* **g** to Babylon.	995
	34:14	*you must* **let** him **g** free.'	8938
	34:16	and female slaves you had set free to **g**	NIH
	35: 2	"**G** to the Recabite family and invite them	2143
	35:11	*we must* **g** to Jerusalem to escape	995
	35:13	**G** and tell the men of Judah and the people	2143
	36: 5	I cannot **g** to the LORD's temple.	995
	36: 6	So *you* **g** to the house of the LORD on	995
	36:19	"You and Jeremiah, **g** and hide.	2143
	37: 4	Now Jeremiah was free to come and **g**	3655
	37: 7	*will* **g back** to its own land, to Egypt.	8740
	37:12	the city to **g** to the territory of Benjamin	2143
	38:20	Then *it will* **g well** with you,	3512
	39:16	"**G** and tell Ebed-Melech the Cushite,	2143
	40: 4	**g** wherever you please."	2143
	40: 5	However, before Jeremiah **turned to g,**	8740
	40: 5	"**G back** to Gedaliah son of Ahikam,	8740
	40: 5	or **g** anywhere else you please."	2143
	40: 5	and a present and **let** him **g.**	8938
	40: 9	and *it will* **g well** with you.	3512
	42: 3	your God will tell us where *we should* **g**	2143
	42: 6	so that *it will* **g well** with us,	3512
	42:14	'No, *we will* **g** and live in Egypt,	995
	42:15	to **g** to Egypt and you do go to settle there,	995
	42:15	to go to Egypt and *you do* **g** to settle there,	995
	42:17	to **g** to Egypt to settle there will die by	995
	42:18	be poured out on you when you **g**	995
	42:19	'*Do* not **g** to Egypt.'	995
	42:22	in the place where you want to **g** to settle."	995
	43: 2	'*You must* not **g** to Egypt to settle there.'	995
	44:12	of Judah who were determined to **g**	995
	44:25	"*G ahead* then, do what you promised!"	AIT
	45: 5	but wherever *you* **g** I will let you escape	2143
	46:11	"**G up** to Gilead and get balm,	6590
	46:16	*let us* **g back** to our own people	8740
	46:28	not **let** you **g entirely unpunished."**	5927+5927
	48: 5	*They* **g up** the way to Luhith,	6590
	48: 5	weeping bitterly as they **g;**	NIH
	48: 7	and Chemosh *will* **g** into exile,	3655
	48:15	her finest young men *will* **g down** in	3718
	49: 3	for Molech *will* **g** into exile,	2143
	49:12	why *should* you **g unpunished?**	5927+5927
	49:12	*You will* not **g unpunished,**	5927
	49:36	be a nation where Elam's exiles *do* not **g.**	995
	50: 4	the people of Judah together *will* **g** in tears	995
	50:27	*let them* **g down** to the slaughter!	3718
	50:33	refusing to **let** them **g.**	8938
	50:38	idols *that will* **g mad** with terror.	2147
	51: 9	let us leave her and each **g** to his own land,	2143
La	4:15	"**G away!** You are unclean!"	6073
Eze	1:12	Wherever the spirit *would* **g,**	2143
	1:12	the spirit would go, *they would* **g,**	2143
	1:17	*they would* **g** in any one of	2143
	1:20	Wherever the spirit *would* **g,**	2143
	1:20	*they would* **g,** and the wheels would rise	2143
	3: 1	then **g** and speak to the house of Israel."	2143
	3: 4	of man, **g** now to the house of Israel	995+2143
	3:11	**G** now to your countrymen in exile	995+2143
	3:22	"Get up and **g out** to the plain,	3655
	3:24	"**G,** shut yourself inside your house.	995
	3:25	you will be bound so that *you* cannot **g out**	3655
	7:14	no one *will* **g** into battle,	2143
	7:17	Every hand *will* **g limp,**	8332
	8: 9	"**G** in and see the wicked	995
	9: 4	"**G** throughout the city of Jerusalem	6296
	9: 7	and fill the courts with the slain. **G!"**	3655
	10: 2	"**G** in among the wheels beneath	995
	10:11	*they would* **g** in any one of the four	2143
	12: 3	and **g** from where you are to another place.	1655
	12: 4	**g** out like those who go into exile.	3655
	12: 4	go out like *those who* **g** into exile.	4604
	12:11	*They will* **g** into exile as captives.	2143
	12:12	be dug in the wall for him to **g** through.	3655
	12:16	where *they* **g** they may acknowledge all	995
		their detestable practices.	
	12:22	'The days **g** by and every vision comes	799
	20:29	What is this high place you **g** to?' "	995
	20:39	And serve your idols, every one of you!	2143
	21: 7	and every hand **g limp;**	8332
	24: 6	whose deposit *will* not **g** away!	3655
	26:20	down with *those who* **g down** to the pit,	3718
	26:20	with *those who* **g down** to the pit,	3718
	30: 9	that day messengers *will* **g out** from me	3655
	30:17	the cities themselves *will* **g** into captivity,	2143
	30:18	and her villages *will* **g** into captivity.	2143
	31:14	with *those who* **g down** to the pit.	3718
	31:16	down to the grave with *those who* **g down** to	3718
	32:18	with *those who* **g down** to the pit.	3718
	32:19	**G down** and be laid among	3718
	32:24	with *those who* **g down** to the pit.	3718
	32:25	with *those who* **g down** to the pit;	3718
	32:29	with *those who* **g down** to the pit.	3718
	32:30	bear their shame with *those who* **g down**	3718
	35: 7	and cut off from it all who come and **g,**	8740
	38: 9	and the many nations with you *will* **g up,**	6590
	39: 9	of Israel *will* **g out** and use the weapons	3655
	39:14	*Some will* **g** throughout the land and,	6296
	39:15	As they **g** through the land and one	6296
	42:14	to **g** into the outer court until they leave	3655
	42:14	to put on other clothes before *they* **g near**	7928
	44: 3	of the gateway and **g** out the same way."	3655
	44:19	When they **g out** into the outer court where	3655
	46: 2	of the gateway and then **g out,**	3655
	46: 8	to **g** in through the portico of the gateway,	995

Eze	46: 9	by the north gate to worship *is to* **g out**	3655
	46: 9	the south gate *is to* **g out** the north gate.	3655
	46: 9	but *each is to* **g** out the opposite gate.	3655
	46:10	going in when they **g in** and going out	995
	46:10	in and going out when they **g out.**	3655
	46:12	Then *he shall* **g out,**	3655
	48:11	and *did* not **g astray** as the Levites did	9494
Da	10:20	when I **g,** the prince of Greece will come;	3655
	11: 4	It will not **g** to his descendants.	NIH
	11: 6	the king of the South *will* **g** to the king of	995
	12: 4	Many *will* **g here and there**	8763
	12: 9	He replied, "**G** *your way,* Daniel,	2143
	12:13	"As for you, **g** *your way* till the end.	2143
Hos	1: 2	the LORD said to him, "**G,** take to yourself	2143
	2: 5	She said, '*I will* **g** after my lovers,	2143
	2: 7	'*I will* **g back** to my husband as at first,	2143
	3: 1	The LORD said to me, "**G,** show your love	2143
	4:15	"*Do* not **g** to Gilgal;	995
	4:15	*do* not **g up** to Beth Aven.	6590
	5: 6	*When they* **g** with their flocks and herds	2143
	5:14	I will tear them to pieces and **g away;**	2143
	5:15	Then *I will* **g** back to my place	2143
	7:12	*they,* I will throw my net over them;	2143
Joel	2:20	its stench *will* **g up;** its smell will rise."	6590
Am	1: 5	The people of Aram *will* **g** into exile	1655
	1:15	Her king *will* **g** into exile,	2143
	2: 2	Moab *will* **g down** in great tumult	4637
	4: 3	*You will* **g** each straight **out**	3655
	4: 4	"**G** to Bethel and sin;	995
	4: 4	**g** to Gilgal and sin yet more.	NIH
	5: 5	*do* not **g** to Gilgal,	995
	5: 5	For Gilgal *will* **surely** **g** into exile,	1655+1655
	6: 2	**G** to Calneh and look at it;	6296
	6: 2	**g** from there *to* great Hamath,	2143
	6: 2	and then **g down** to Gath in Philistia.	3718
	6: 7	be among the first to **g** into exile;	1655+1655
	7:11	and Israel *will* **surely g** into exile,	1655+1655
	7:12	**G back** to the land of Judah.	1368
	7:15	'**G,** prophesy to my people Israel.'	2143
	7:17	Israel *will* **certainly g** into exile,	1655+1655
	8: 9	"*I will* **make** the sun **g down**	995
Ob	1: 1	and *let us* **g** against her for battle"—	7756
	1:21	Deliverers *will* **g up** on Mount Zion	6590
Jnh	1: 2	"**G** to the great city of Nineveh and preach	2143
	3: 2	"**G** to the great city of Nineveh	2143
Mic	1: 8	*I will* **g about** barefoot and naked.	2143
	1:16	**g** from you **into exile.**	1655
	2:10	Get up, **g away!**	2143
	2:13	One who breaks open the way *will* **g up**	6590
	2:13	they will break through the gate and **g out.**	3655
	3: 6	and the day *will* **g dark** for them.	7722
	4: 2	*let us* **g up** to the mountain of the LORD,	6590
	4: 2	The law *will* **g out** from Zion,	3655
	4:10	*You will* **g** to Babylon;	995
Na	3:11	*you will* **g** into hiding and seek refuge	2118
Hab	1:11	they sweep past like the wind and **g on—**	6296
	2: 6	How long must this **g** on?'	NIH
	3:19	he **enables** me to **g** on the heights.	2005
Zep	1:10	"a cry will **g** up from the Fish Gate,	NIH
Hag	1: 8	**G up** *into* the mountains and bring	6590
Zec	1:10	the LORD has sent to **g** throughout	2143
	6: 7	they were straining to **g** throughout	2143+2143
	6: 7	he said, "**G** throughout the earth!"	2143+2143
	6:10	**G** the same day *to* the house of Josiah son	995
	6:14	behind them that no one could come or **g.**	6296
	8:10	No one *could* **g about** *his* **business** safely	995+2256+3655
	8:21	and the inhabitants of one city *will* **g**	2143
	8:21	'*Let us* **g at once** to entreat the LORD	2143+2143
	8:23	'*Let us* **g** with you,	2143
	11: 5	buyers slaughter them and **g unpunished.**	AIT
	14: 2	Half of the city *will* **g** into exile,	3655
	14: 3	Then the LORD *will* **g out** and fight	3655
	14:16	that have attacked Jerusalem *will* **g up**	6590
	14:17	not **g up** to Jerusalem to worship the King,	6590
	14:18	If the Egyptian people *do* not **g up**	6590
	14:18	on the nations that *do* not **g up** to celebrate	6590
	14:19	the nations that *do* not **g up** to celebrate	6590
Mal	4: 2	And *you will* **g out** and leap	3655
Mt	2: 8	"**G** and make a careful search for the child.	4513
	2: 8	so that I too may **g** and worship him."	2262
	2:12	in a dream not to **g back** to Herod,	366
	2:20	and his mother and **g** to the land of Israel,	4513
	2:22	he was afraid to **g** there.	599
	5:24	First **g** and be reconciled to your brother;	5632
	5:30	of your body than for your whole body to **g**	599
	5:41	If someone forces you to **g** one mile,	NIG
	5:41	**g** with him two miles.	5632
	6: 6	But when you pray, **g** into your room,	1656
	8: 4	But **g,** show yourself to the priest and offer	5632
	8: 7	Jesus said to him, "I will **g** and heal him."	2262
	8: 9	I tell this one, '**G,**' and he goes;	4513
	8:13	Then Jesus said to the centurion, "**G!**	5632
	8:19	I will follow you wherever you **g.**	599
	8:21	"Lord, first let me **g** and bury my father."	599
	8:32	He said to them, "**G!"**	5632
	9: 6	"Get up, take your mat and **g home.**	5632
	9:13	But **g** and learn what this means:	4513
	9:24	he said, "**G away.** The girl is not dead	432
	10: 5	not among the Gentiles or enter any town	599
	10: 6	**G** rather to the lost sheep of Israel.	4513
	10: 7	*As you* **g,** preach this message:	4513
	11: 4	"**G back** and report to John what you hear	4513
	11: 7	"What *did you* **g out** into the desert to see?	2002
	11: 8	If not, what *did you* **g out** to see?	2002
	11: 9	Then what *did you* **g out** to see?	2002
	11:23	No, *you will* **g down** to the depths.	2849

Mt 12:45 and they **g** in and live there. 1656
13:28 'Do you want us *to* **g** and pull them up?' 599
14:15 so they can **g** to the villages 599
14:16 Jesus replied, "They do not need *to* **g away.** 599
14:22 and **g on ahead of** him to the other side, 4575
16:21 to his disciples that he must **g** to Jerusalem 599
17:27 **g** to the lake and throw out your line. 4513
18:12 not leave the ninety-nine on the hills and **g** 4513
18:15 **g** and show him his fault, 5632
18:27 canceled the debt and **let** him **g.** 668
19:21 "If you want to be perfect, **g,** 5632
19:24 it is easier for a camel *to* **g through** the eye 1451
20: 4 'You also **g** and work in my vineyard.' 5632
20: 7 'You also **g** and work in my vineyard.' 5632
20:14 Take your pay and **g.** 5632
21: 2 "**G** to the village ahead of you, 4513
21:21 but also you can say to this mountain, '**G,** 149
21:28 'Son, **g** and work today in the vineyard.' 5632
21:30 He answered, 'I will, sir,' but *he* did not **g.** 599
22: 9 **G** to the street corners and invite to 4513
24:17 *Let* no one on the roof of his house **g down** 2849
24:18 in the field **g** back to get his cloak. 2188
24:26 out in the desert,' *do* not **g out;** 2002
25: 9 to those who sell oil and buy some 4513
25:39 or in prison and **g** to visit you?' 2262
25:46 they **will g away** to eternal punishment, 599
26:18 "**G** into the city to a certain man 5632
26:24 The Son of Man **will g** just as it is written 5632
26:32 *I* will **g ahead of** you into Galilee. 4575
26:36 "Sit here while I **g over** there and pray." 599
26:46 Rise, *let us* **g!** Here comes my betrayer!" 72
27:65 "**G,** make the tomb as secure 5632
28: 7 Then **g** quickly and tell his disciples. 4513
28:10 **g** and tell my brothers to go to Galilee; 5632
28:10 Go and tell my brothers to **g** to Galilee; 599
28:16 where Jesus had told them to **g.** NIG
28:19 **g** and make disciples of all nations, 4513

Mk 1:38 Jesus replied, "*Let us* **g** somewhere else— 72
1:44 But **g,** show yourself to the priest and offer 5632
2:11 get up, take your mat and **g** home." 5632
4:35 "*Let us* **g over** to the other side." 1451
5:12 allow *us to* **g into** them." 1656
5:18 begged to **g** with him. 1639
5:19 "**G** home to your family and tell them 5632
5:34 **G** in peace and be freed 5632
6:36 Send the people away so they can **g** to 599
6:37 Are we to **g** and spend that much on bread 599
6:38 he asked. "**G** and see." 5632
6:45 and **g on ahead of** him to Bethsaida, 4575
7: 8 *You have* **let g of** the commands of God 918
7:19 For *it* doesn't **g into** his heart but 1660
7:29 he told her, "For such a reply, *you may* **g;** 5632
8:26 saying, "Don't **g into** the village." 1656
9:43 with two hands to **g into** hell, 599
10:21 "**G,** sell everything you have and give to 5632
10:25 It is easier for a camel *to* **g through** the eye 1451
10:52 "**G,**" said Jesus, "your faith has healed you. 5632
11: 2 "**G** to the village ahead of you, 5632
11: 6 and the *people* **let** them **g.** 918
11:23 if anyone says to this mountain, '**G,** 149
13:15 *Let* no one on the roof of his house **g down** 2849
13:16 in the field **g** back to get his cloak. 2188
14:12 *to* **g** and make preparations for you to eat 599
14:13 telling them, "**G into** the city, 5632
14:21 The Son of Man *will* **g** just as it is written 5632
14:28 *I will* **g ahead of** you into Galilee." 4575
14:42 Rise! *Let us* **g!** Here comes my betrayer!" 72
16: 1 so that they might **g** to anoint Jesus' body. 2262
16: 7 But **g,** tell his disciples and Peter, 5632
16:15 "**G** into all the world and preach 4513

Lk 1: 9 to **g into** the temple of the Lord 1656
1:17 And he *will* **g on** before the Lord 4601
1:76 for *you will* **g on** before the Lord 4638
2:15 "*Let's* **g** to Bethlehem and see this thing 1451
5: 8 "**G away** from me, Lord; 2002
5:14 "Don't tell anyone, but **g,** 599
5:24 get up, take your mat and **g** home." 4513
5:33 **g on eating** and **drinking.**" AIT
6:25 for *you will* **g hungry.** 4277
7: 8 I tell this one, '**G,**' and he goes; 4513
7:22 "**G back** and report to John 4513
7:24 "What *did you* **g out** into the desert to see? 2002
7:25 If not, what *did you* **g out** to see? 2002
7:26 But what *did you* **g out** to see? 2002
7:50 "Your faith has saved you; **g** in peace." 4513
8:14 but *as they* **g on** their **way** they are choked 4513
8:22 "*Let's* **g over** to the other side of the lake." 1451
8:31 not to order them *to* **g** into the Abyss. 599
8:32 to let them **g into** them, 1656
8:38 the demons had gone out begged *to* **g** 1639
8:47 seeing that *she could* not **g unnoticed,** 3291
8:48 your faith has healed you. **G** in peace." 4513
8:51 not let anyone **g** in with him except Peter, 1656
9:12 so *they can* **g** to the surrounding villages 4513
9:13 we **g** and buy food for all this crowd." 4513
9:57 "I will follow you wherever *you* **g.**" 599
9:59 "Lord, first let me **g** and bury my father." 599
9:60 you **g** and proclaim the kingdom of God." 599
9:61 but first let me **g** back and say good-by NIG
10: 1 and place where he was about to **g.** 2262
10: 3 **G!** I am sending you out like lambs 5632
10:10 **g** into its streets and say, 2002
10:15 No, *you will* **g down** to the depths. 2849
10:37 Jesus told him, "**G** and do likewise." 4513
11:26 and they **g** in and live there. 1656
13:31 "Leave this place and **g** somewhere else. 4513
13:32 He replied, "**G** tell that fox, 4513

Lk 14:18 and *I* must **g** and see it. 2002
14:21 '**G out** quickly into the streets and alleys 2002
14:23 '**G out** to the roads and country lanes 2002
14:31 Or suppose a king is about *to* **g** to **war** 4483+5202
15: 4 the open country and **g** after the lost sheep 4513
15:18 and **g back** to my father and say to him: 4513
15:28 and refused *to* **g in.** 1656
16:26 so that those who want to **g** from here 1329
17:14 When he saw them, he said, "**G,** 4513
17:19 Then he said to him, "Rise and **g;** 4513
17:23 *Do* not **g running off after** them. 599+1503+3593
17:31 *should* **g down** to get them. 2849
17:31 in the field *should* **g** back for anything. 2188
18:25 it is easier for a camel *to* **g through** the eye 1656
19:30 "**G** to the village ahead of you, 5632
22: 8 "**G** and make preparations for us to eat 4513
22:22 of Man *will* **g** as it has been decreed, 4513
22:33 I am ready to **g** with you to prison and 4513

Jn 4: 4 Now he had *to* **g through** Samaria. 1451
4:16 "**G,** call your husband and come back." 5632
4:50 Jesus replied, "*You may* **g.** 4513
6: 9 how far will they **g** among 1639+4047+5515
6:35 He who comes to me will never **g hungry,** 4277
6:68 "Lord, to whom *shall we* **g?** 599
7: 3 "You ought to leave here and **g** to Judea, 5632
7: 8 You **g** to the Feast. 326
7:14 the Feast *did* Jesus **g up** to the temple courts 326
7:33 and then *I* **g** to the one who sent me. 5632
7:35 "Where does this man intend *to* **g** 4513
7:35 Will *he* **g** where our people live scattered 4513
8: 9 those who heard *began to* **g away** one at 2002
8:11 "**G** now and leave your life of sin." 4513
8:21 Where I **g,** you cannot come." 5632
8:22 Is that why he says, 'Where I **g,** 5632
9: 7 "**G,**" he told him, "wash in the Pool 5632
9:11 He told me *to* **g** to Siloam and wash. 5632
10: 9 He will come in and **g out,** 2002
11: 7 "*Let us* **g** back to Judea." 72
11:15 But *let us* **g** to him." 72
11:16 "*Let* us also **g,** that we may die with him." 72
11:44 "Take off the grave clothes and let him **g.**" 5632
13: 1 to leave this world and **g** to the Father. NIG
14: 3 And if *I* **g** and prepare a place for you, 4513
15:16 and appointed you to **g** and bear fruit— 5632
16: 1 so that *you will* not **g astray.** 4997
16: 7 Unless *I* **g away,** the Counselor will 599
16: 7 but if *I* **g,** I will send him to you. 4513
18: 8 then let these men **g.**" 5632
19:12 "If you let this man **g,** 668
20: 5 of linen lying there but *did* not **g in.** 1656
20:17 **G** instead to my brothers and tell them, 4513
21: 3 and they said, "We'll **g** with you." 2262
21:18 and lead you where you do not want to **g.**" NIG

Ac 1:11 in the same way you have seen him **g** 4513
1:25 which Judas left *to* **g** where he belongs." 4198
3:13 though he had decided *to* **let** him **g.** 668
4:21 After further threats they **let** them **g.** 668
5:20 "**G,** stand in the temple courts," he said, 4513
5:38 **Let** them **g!** 918
5:40 and **let** them **g.** 668
7: 3 'and **g** to the land I will show you.' 1306
7:40 'Make us gods who *will* **g before** us. 4638
8:26 "**G** south to the road— 4513
8:29 "**G** to that chariot and stay near it." 4665
9: 6 "Now get up and **g into** the city, 1656
9:11 "**G** to the house of Judas on Straight Street 4513
9:15 But the Lord said to Ananias, "**G!** 4198
10:20 So get up and **g downstairs.** 2849
10:20 Do not hesitate *to* **g** with them, 4513
14:16 he let all nations **g** their own way. 4198
14:22 "We must **g through** many hardships 1328
15: 2 *to* **g up** to Jerusalem to see the apostles 326
15:36 "*Let us* **g back** and visit the brothers in all 2188
16:36 Now you can leave. **G** in peace." 4513
17: 9 and the others posted bond and **let** them **g.** 668
18: 6 From now on *I will* **g** to the Gentiles." 4513
18:27 When Apollos wanted *to* **g** to Achaia, 1451
19:21 Paul decided *to* **g** to Jerusalem, 4513
20: 3 he decided to **g back** through Macedonia. 5715
21: 4 the Spirit they urged Paul not *to* **g on** 2094
21:12 with Paul not *to* **g up** to Jerusalem. 326
22:10 the Lord said, 'and **g** into Damascus. 4513
22:21 "Then the Lord said to me, '**G;** 4513
23:10 to **g down** and take him away from them 2849
23:23 and two hundred spearmen to **g** to Caesarea 4513
23:32 The next day they let the cavalry **g on** 599
25: 9 "Are you willing to **g up** to Jerusalem 326
25:12 To Caesar *you will* **g!**" 4513
25:20 if he would be willing to **g** to Jerusalem 4513
27: 3 *to* **g** to his friends so they might provide 4513
28:26 "'**G** to this people and say, "You will 4513

Ro 6: 1 *Shall we* **g on** sinning so that grace can 2152
15:24 I plan to do so when *I* **g** to Spain. 4513
15:28 *I will* **g** to Spain and visit you on 599

1Co 4: 6 "Do not **g** beyond what is written." NIG
4:11 To this very hour we **g hungry** and thirsty, 4277
10:27 to a meal and you want to **g,** 4513
16: 4 If it seems advisable for me *to* **g** also, 4513
16: 5 After *I* **g through** Macedonia, 1451
16: 6 on my journey, wherever *I* **g.** 4513
16:12 strongly urged him to **g** to you with 2262
16:12 He was quite unwilling to **g** now, 2262
16:12 but *he will* **g** when he has the opportunity. 2262

2Co 9:14 their **hearts g** out to you. 2160
10:15 Neither do we **g** beyond our limits NIG
12: 1 I must **g on boasting.** AIT

2Co 12: 1 *I will* **g on** to visions and revelations 2262
12:18 to **g** to you and I sent our brother with him. NIG
Gal 1:17 nor *did I* **g up** to Jerusalem 456
2: 9 that we should **g** to the Gentiles, NIG
5:12 I wish they would **g** the whole way NIG
Eph 4:26 the sun **g down** while you are still angry, 2115
6: 3 "that *it may* **g** well with you and 1181
Php 1:22 If I am *to* **g** on living in the body, AIT
2:23 as soon as I see how things **g with** me. 4309
2Ti 3:13 and impostors *will* **g** from bad to worse, 4621
Heb 4: 6 the gospel preached to them did not **g in,** 1656
6: 1 about Christ and **g on** to maturity, 5770
11: 8 *to* a place he would later receive 2002
13:13 *Let us,* then, **g** to him outside the camp, 2002
Jas 2:16 "**G,** I wish you well; 1645+1877+5632
3: 4 the pilot wants *to* **g.** 2316
4:13 or tomorrow *we will* **g** to this or that city, 4513
1Jn 3: 9 he cannot **g on sinning,** AIT
3Jn 1: 2 and that all *may* **g** well with you, 2338
Rev 10: 8 "**G,** take the scroll that lies open in 5632
11: 1 **g** and measure the temple of God and 1586
13:10 If anyone is *to* **g** into captivity, NIG
13:10 into captivity he *will* **g.** 5632
16: 1 the temple saying to the seven angels, "**G,** 5632
16:14 they **g out** to the kings of the whole world, 1744
16:15 not **g** naked and be shamefully exposed." 4344
17: 8 and will come up out of the Abyss and **g** 2002
20: 8 and *will* **g out** to deceive the nations in 2002
22:14 *may* **g** through the gates **into** the city. 1656

GO (Anglicized) See also GET AWAY

GOAD (KJV) See OXGOAD

GOADS (3)
1Sa 13:21 and axes and for repointing **g.** 1995
Ecc 12:11 The words of the wise are like **g,** 1996
Ac 26:14 It is hard for you to kick against the **g.**' 3034

GOAH (1)
Jer 31:39 to the hill of Gareb and then turn to **G.** 1717

GOAL (6)
Lk 13:32 and on the third day *I will* **reach** *my* **g.**' 5457
2Co 5: 9 So we **make it** *our* **g** to please him, 5818
Gal 3: 3 *are you* now *trying to* **attain** *your* **g** 2200
Php 3:14 I press on toward the **g** to win the prize 5024
1Ti 1: 5 The **g** of this command is love, 5056
1Pe 1: 9 for you are receiving the **g** of your faith, 5465

GOAT (86) [GOAT'S, GOATS, GOATS', GOATSKINS, HE-GOAT, SCAPEGOAT]
Ge 15: 9 a **g** and a ram, each three years old, 6436
30:32 and every spotted or speckled **g.** 6436
30:33 Any **g** in my possession that is not speckled 6436
37:31 slaughtered a **g** and dipped the robe in 6436+8538
38:17 "I'll send you a **young g** from my flock," 1531+6436
38:20 Judah sent the **young g** by his friend 1531+6436
38:23 After all, I did send her this **young g,** 1531
Ex 23:19 not cook a **young g** in its mother's milk. 1531
25: 4 and fine linen; **g hair;** 6436
26: 7 of **g hair** for the tent over the tabernacle— 6436
34:26 not cook a **young g** in its mother's milk." 1531
35: 6 and fine linen; **g hair;** 6436
35:23 or fine linen, or **g hair,** ram skins dyed red 6436
35:26 and had the skill spun the **g hair.** 6436
36:14 of **g hair** for the tent over the tabernacle— 6436
Lev 3:12 " 'If his offering is a **g,** 6436
4:23 as his offering a male **g** without defect. 6436+8538
4:28 for the sin he committed a female **g** 6436+8544
5: 6 to the LORD a female lamb or **g** from 6436+8544
9: 3 'Take a **male g** for a sin offering, 6436+8538
9:15 He took the **g** for the people's sin offering 8538
10:16 about the **g** of the sin offering and found 8538
10:18 you should have eaten the **g in** 2023S
16: 9 Aaron shall bring the **g** whose lot falls to 8538
16:10 the **g** chosen by lot as the scapegoat shall 8538
16:15 then slaughter the **g** for the sin offering for 8538
16:20 he shall bring forward the live **g.** 8538
16:21 the head of the live **g** and confess over it all 8538
16:21 He shall send the **g** away into the desert in NIH
16:22 The **g** will carry on itself all their sins to 8538
16:26 the man who releases the **g** as a scapegoat 8538
16:27 The bull and the **g** for the sin offerings, 8538
17: 3 a lamb or a **g** in the camp or outside of it 6436
17: 7 of their sacrifices to the **g idols** 8539
22:27 a lamb or a **g** is born, 6436
23:19 sacrifice one **male g** for a sin offering 6436+8538
Nu 7:16 one **male g** for a sin offering; 6436+8538
7:22 one **male g** for a sin offering; 6436+8538
7:28 one **male g** for a sin offering; 6436+8538
7:34 one **male g** for a sin offering; 6436+8538
7:40 one **male g** for a sin offering; 6436+8538
7:46 one **male g** for a sin offering; 6436+8538
7:52 one **male g** for a sin offering; 6436+8538
7:58 one **male g** for a sin offering; 6436+8538
7:64 one **male g** for a sin offering; 6436+8538
7:70 one **male g** for a sin offering; 6436+8538
7:76 one **male g** for a sin offering; 6436+8538
15:11 Each bull or ram, each lamb or **young g,** 6436
15:24 and a **male g** for a sin offering. 6436+8538

Nu	15:27	a year-old female **g** for a sin offering.	6436
	18:17	a sheep or a **g**; they are holy.	6436
	28:15	one **male g** is to be presented to	6436+8538
	28:22	Include one **male g** as a sin offering	8538
	28:30	Include one **male g** to make atonement	6436+8538
	29: 5	Include one **male g** as a sin offering,	6436+8538
	29:11	Include one **male g** as a sin offering,	6436+8538
	29:16	Include one **male g** as a sin offering,	6436+8538
	29:19	Include one **male g** as a sin offering,	6436+8538
	29:22	Include one **male g** as a sin offering,	8538
	29:25	Include one **male g** as a sin offering,	6436+8538
	29:28	Include one **male g** as a sin offering,	8538
	29:31	Include one **male g** as a sin offering,	8538
	29:34	Include one **male g** as a sin offering,	8538
	29:38	Include one **male g** as a sin offering,	8538
	31:20	**g** hair or wood."	6436
Dt	14: 4	the ox, the sheep, the **g**,	6436+8445
	14: 5	the gazelle, the roe deer, the **wild g**,	735
	14:21	Do not cook a **young g** in its mother's milk.	1531
Jdg	6:19	Gideon went in, prepared a **young g**,	1531+6436
	13:15	until we prepare a **young g** for you."	1531+6436
	13:19	Then Manoah took a **young g**,	1531+6436
	14: 6	as he might have torn a **young g**.	1531
	15: 1	a **young g** and went to visit his wife.	1531+6436
1Sa	16:20	a **young g** and sent them with his son	1531+6436
2Ch	11:15	and for the **g** and calf **idols** he had made.	8539
Isa	11: 6	the leopard will lie down with the **g**,	1531
Eze	43:22	a **male g** without defect for a sin offering,	6436+8538
	43:25	to provide a **male g** daily for a sin offering;	8538
	45:23	and a **male g** for a sin offering.	6436+8538
Da	8: 5	suddenly a **g** with a prominent horn	6436+8538
	8: 7	the **g** knocked him to the ground	NIH
	8: 8	The **g** became very great,	6436+7618
	8:21	The shaggy **g** is the king of Greece.	7618
Lk	15:29	Yet you never gave me even a **young g**	2253
Rev	6:12	like sackcloth made of **g** hair,	NIG

GOAT'S (3) [GOAT]

Lev	4:24	on the **g** head and slaughter it at the place	8538
	16:18	of the bull's blood and some of the **g** blood	8538
	16:21	and put them on the **g** head.	8538

GOATH (KJV) See GOAH

GOATS (79) [GOAT]

Ge	27: 9	and bring me two choice **young g**,	1531+6436
	30:35	That same day he removed all the **male g**	9411
	30:35	and all the speckled or spotted female **g**	6436
	31:10	up and saw that the **male g** mating with	6966
	31:12	'Look up and see that all the **male g** mating	6966
	31:38	Your sheep and **g** have not miscarried,	6436
	32: 5	I have cattle and donkeys, **sheep and g**,	7366
	32:14	two hundred female **g**	6436
	32:14	and twenty **male g**,	9411
	47:17	their **sheep and g**, their cattle and	5238+7366
Ex	9: 3	and on your cattle and **sheep and g**,	7366
	12: 5	you may take them from the sheep or the **g**.	6436
	20:24	your **sheep and g** and your cattle.	7366
Lev	1:10	from either the sheep or the **g**,	6436
	7:23	not eat any of the fat of cattle, sheep or **g**.	6436
	16: 5	to take two **male g** for a sin offering	6436+8538
	16: 7	to take the two **g** and present them before	8538
	16: 8	He is to cast lots for the two **g**—	8538
	22:19	sheep or **g** in order that it may be accepted	6436
Nu	7:17	five **male g** and five male lambs a year old,	6966
	7:23	five **male g** and five male lambs a year old,	6966
	7:29	five **male g** and five male lambs a year old,	6966
	7:35	five **male g** and five male lambs a year old,	6966
	7:41	five **male g** and five male lambs a year old,	6966
	7:47	five **male g** and five male lambs a year old,	6966
	7:53	five **male g** and five male lambs a year old,	6966
	7:59	five **male g** and five male lambs a year old,	6966
	7:65	five **male g** and five male lambs a year old,	6966
	7:71	five **male g** and five male lambs a year old,	6966
	7:77	five **male g** and five male lambs a year old,	6966
	7:83	five **male g** and five male lambs a year old,	6966
	7:87	Twelve **male g** were used for	6436+8538
	7:88	sixty **male g** and sixty male lambs	6966
	31:28	persons, cattle, donkeys, **sheep or g**.	7366
	31:30	cattle, donkeys, **sheep, g** or other animals.	7366
Dt	32:14	and flock and with fattened lambs and **g**,	6966
1Sa	10: 3	One will be carrying three **young g**,	1531
	24: 2	and his men near the Crags of the **Wild G**.	3604
	25: 2	a thousand **g** and three thousand sheep.	6436
1Ki	4:23	and a hundred **sheep and g**,	7366
	8:63	hundred and twenty thousand **sheep and g**.	7366
	20:27	like two small flocks of **g**,	6436
2Ch	7: 5	hundred and twenty thousand **sheep and g**.	7366
	14:15	and carried off droves of **sheep and g**	7366
	15:11	of cattle and seven thousand **sheep and g**	7366
	17:11	and seven thousand seven hundred **g**.	9411
	29:21	seven male lambs and seven **male g**	6436+7618
	29:23	The **g** for the sin offering were brought	8538
	29:24	The priests then slaughtered the **g**	4392S
	29:33	and three thousand **sheep and g**,	7366
	30:24	and seven thousand **sheep and g** for	7366
	30:24	and ten thousand **sheep and g**.	7366
	35: 7	total of thirty thousand sheep and **g**	1201+6436
Ezr	6:17	a sin offering for all Israel, twelve **male g**,	10535+10615
	8:35	as a sin offering, twelve **male g**.	7618
Job	39: 1	when the mountain **g** give birth?	3604
Ps	50: 9	from your stall or of **g** from your pens,	6966
	50:13	the flesh of bulls or drink the blood of **g**?	

Ps	66:15	I will offer bulls and **g**.	6966
	104:18	The high mountains belong to the **wild g**;	3604
Pr	27:26	and the **g** with the price of a field.	6966
SS	1: 8	of the sheep and graze your **young g** by	1537
	4: 1	Your hair is like a flock of **g** descending	6436
	6: 5	like a flock of **g** descending from Gilead.—	6436
Isa	1:11	in the blood of bulls and lambs and **g**.	6966
	7:21	a young cow and two **g**,	7360
	13:21	and there the **wild g** will leap about.	8538
	34: 6	the blood of lambs and **g**,	6966
	34:14	and **wild g** will bleat to each other;	8538
Jer	50: 8	and be like the **g** that lead the flock.	6966
	51:40	like rams also.	6966
Eze	27:21	with you in lambs, rams and **g**.	6966
	34:17	and between rams and **g**.	6966
	39:18	if they were rams and lambs, **g** and bulls—	6966
Mt	25:32	a shepherd separates the sheep from the **g**.	2253
	25:33	He will put the sheep on his right and the **g**	2252
Heb	9:12	by means of the blood **of g** and calves;	5543
	9:13	The blood **of g** and bulls and the ashes of	5543
	10: 4	the blood of bulls and **g** to take away sins.	5543

GOATS' (3) [GOAT]

1Sa	19:13	a garment and putting some **g' hair** at	3889+6436
	19:16	and at the head was some **g' hair**.	3889+6436
Pr	27:27	You will have plenty of **g'** milk to feed you	6436

GOATSKINS (2) [GOAT, SKIN]

Ge	27:16	the smooth part of his neck with the **g**.	1531+6425+6436
Heb	11:37	They went about in sheepskins and **g**,	128+1293

GOB (2)

2Sa	21:18	with the Philistines, at **G**.	1570
	21:19	In another battle with the Philistines at **G**,	1570

GOBLET (3) [GOBLETS]

SS	7: 2	a rounded **g** that never lacks blended wine.	110
Isa	51:17	its dregs the **g** that makes men stagger.	3926+7694
	51:22	from that cup, the **g** **of** my wrath,	3926+7694

GOBLETS (6) [GOBLET]

1Ki	10:21	All King Solomon's **g** were gold,	3998+5482
2Ch	9:20	All King Solomon's **g** were gold,	3998+5482
Est	1: 7	Wine was served in **g** of gold,	3998
Da	5: 2	to bring in the gold and silver **g**	10398
	5: 3	in the gold **g** that had been taken from	10398
	5:23	You had the **g** from his temple brought	10398

GOD (3969) [GOD'S, GOD-BREATHED, GOD-FEARING, GOD-HATERS, GODDESS, GODLESS, GODLESSNESS, GODLINESS, GODLY, GODS]

Ge	1: 1	In the beginning **G** created the heavens and	466
	1: 2	Spirit of **G** was hovering over the waters.	466
	1: 3	And **G** said, "Let there be light,"	466
	1: 4	**G** saw that the light was good,	466
	1: 5	**G** called the light "day,"	466
	1: 6	And **G** said, "Let there be an expanse	466
	1: 7	So **G** made the expanse and separated	466
	1: 8	**G** called the expanse "sky."	466
	1: 9	And **G** said, "Let the water under the sky	466
	1:10	**G** called the dry ground "land,"	466
	1:10	And **G** saw that it was good.	466
	1:11	**G** said, "Let the land produce vegetation:	466
	1:12	And **G** saw that it was good.	466
	1:14	And **G** said, "Let there be lights in	466
	1:16	**G** made two great lights—	466
	1:17	**G** set them in the expanse of the sky	466
	1:18	And **G** saw that it was good.	466
	1:20	And **G** said, "Let the water teem	466
	1:21	So **G** created the great creatures of the sea	466
	1:21	And **G** saw that it was good.	466
	1:22	**G** blessed them and said,	466
	1:24	And **G** said, "Let the land produce	466
	1:25	**G** made the wild animals according	466
	1:25	And **G** saw that it was good.	466
	1:26	Then **G** said, "Let us make man	466
	1:27	So **G** created man in his own image,	466
	1:27	in the image of **G** he created him;	466
	1:28	**G** blessed them and said to them,	466
	1:29	**G** said, "I give you every seed-bearing plant	466
	1:31	**G** saw all that he had made,	466
	2: 2	By the seventh day **G** had finished	466
	2: 3	And **G** blessed the seventh day	466
	2: 4	When the LORD **G** made the earth and	466
	2: 5	the LORD **G** had not sent rain on the earth	466
	2: 7	the LORD **G** formed the man from	466
	2: 8	LORD **G** had planted a garden in the east,	466
	2: 9	And the LORD **G** made all kinds	466
	2:15	The LORD **G** took the man and put him in	466
	2:16	And the LORD **G** commanded the man,	466
	2:18	The LORD **G** said, "It is not good for the man	466
	2:19	Now the LORD **G** had formed out of	466
	2:21	the LORD **G** caused the man to fall into	466
	2:22	Then the LORD **G** made a woman from	466
	3: 1	the wild animals the LORD **G** had made.	466
	3: 1	He said to the woman, "Did **G** really say,	466
	3: 3	but **G** did say, 'You must not eat	466
	3: 5	"For **G** knows that when you eat	466
	3: 5	and you will be like **G**,	466
	3: 8	of the LORD **G** as he was walking in	466

Ge	3: 8	and they hid from the LORD **G** among	466
	3: 9	But the LORD **G** called to the man,	466
	3:13	Then the LORD **G** said to the woman,	466
	3:14	So the LORD **G** said to the serpent,	466
	3:21	The LORD **G** made garments of skin	466
	3:22	And the LORD **G** said,	466
	3:23	So the LORD **G** banished him from	466
	4:25	"**G** has granted me another child in place	466
	5: 1	When **G** created man,	466
	5: 1	he made him in the likeness of **G**.	466
	5:22	with **G** 300 years and had other sons	466
	5:24	Enoch walked with **G**; then he was no more,	466
	5:24	he was no more, because **G** took him away.	466
	6: 2	the sons of **G** saw that the daughters	466
	6: 4	the sons of **G** went to the daughters of men	466
	6: 9	and he walked with **G**.	466
	6:12	**G** saw how corrupt the earth had become,	466
	6:13	So **G** said to Noah,	466
	6:22	as **G** commanded him.	466
	7: 9	as **G** had commanded Noah.	466
	7:16	as **G** had commanded Noah.	466
	8: 1	But **G** remembered Noah and all	466
	8:15	Then **G** said to Noah,	466
	9: 1	Then **G** blessed Noah and his sons,	466
	9: 6	for in the image of **G** has God made man.	466
	9: 6	in the image of God has **G** made man.	NIH
	9: 8	**G** said to Noah and to his sons with him:	466
	9:12	And **G** said, "This is the sign of	466
	9:16	the everlasting covenant between **G**	466
	9:17	So **G** said to Noah,	466
	9:26	"Blessed be the LORD, the **G** of Shem!	466
	9:27	May **G** extend the territory of Japheth;	466
	14:18	He was priest of **G** Most High,	446
	14:19	"Blessed be Abram by **G** Most High,	446
	14:20	And blessed be **G** Most High,	446
	14:22	**G** Most High, Creator of heaven and earth,	446
	16:13	"You are the **G** who sees me," for she said,	446
	17: 1	"I am **G** Almighty; walk before me	446
	17: 3	Abram fell facedown, and **G** said to him,	466
	17: 7	be your **G** and the God of your descendants	466
	17: 7	be your God and the **G** of your descendants	NIH
	17: 8	and I will be their **G**."	466
	17: 9	Then **G** said to Abraham, "As for you,	466
	17:15	**G** also said to Abraham,	466
	17:18	And Abraham said to **G**,	466
	17:19	Then **G** said, "Yes,	466
	17:22	**G** went up from him.	466
	17:23	and circumcised them, as **G** told him.	466
	19:29	So when **G** destroyed the cities of the plain,	466
	20: 3	But **G** came to Abimelech in a dream	466
	20: 6	Then **G** said to him in the dream, "Yes,	466
	20:11	'There is surely no fear of **G** in this place,	466
	20:13	And when **G** had me wander	466
	20:17	Then Abraham prayed to **G**,	466
	20:17	and **G** healed Abimelech,	466
	21: 2	at the very time **G** had promised him.	466
	21: 4	as **G** commanded him.	466
	21: 6	Sarah said, "**G** has brought me laughter,	466
	21:12	But **G** said to him,	466
	21:17	**G** heard the boy crying,	466
	21:17	the angel of **G** called to Hagar from heaven	466
	21:17	**G** has heard the boy crying as he lies there.	466
	21:19	Then **G** opened her eyes and she saw a well	466
	21:20	**G** was with the boy as he grew up.	466
	21:22	"**G** is with you in everything you do.	466
	21:23	before **G** that you will not deal falsely	466
	21:33	the name of the LORD, the Eternal **G**.	446
	22: 1	Some time later **G** tested Abraham.	466
	22: 2	Then **G** said, "Take your son,	NIH
	22: 3	for the place **G** had told him about.	466
	22: 8	"**G** himself will provide the lamb for	466
	22: 9	the place **G** had told him about,	466
	22:12	Now I know that you fear **G**,	466
	24: 3	the **G** of heaven and the God of earth,	466
	24: 3	the God of heaven and the **G** of earth,	466
	24: 7	"The LORD, the **G** of heaven,	466
	24:12	"O LORD, **G** of my master Abraham,	466
	24:27	the **G** of my master Abraham,	466
	24:42	'O LORD, **G** of my master Abraham,	466
	24:48	the **G** of my master Abraham,	466
	25:11	**G** blessed his son Isaac,	466
	26:24	"I am the **G** of your father Abraham.	466
	27:20	"The LORD your **G** gave me success,"	466
	27:28	May **G** give you of heaven's dew and	466
	28: 3	May **G** Almighty bless you	446
	28: 4	the land **G** gave to Abraham."	466
	28:12	of **G** were ascending and descending on it.	466
	28:13	the **G** of your father Abraham and the God	466
	28:13	of your father Abraham and the **G** of Isaac.	466
	28:17	This is none other than the house of **G**;	466
	28:20	"If **G** will be with me and will watch	466
	28:21	then the LORD will be my **G**	466
	30: 2	"Am I in the place of **G**,	466
	30: 6	Then Rachel said, "**G** has vindicated me;	466
	30:17	**G** listened to Leah, and she became pregnant	466
	30:18	"**G** has rewarded me	466
	30:20	"**G** has presented me with a precious gift.	466
	30:22	**G** remembered Rachel;	466
	30:23	"**G** has taken away my disgrace."	466
	31: 5	but the **G** of my father has been with me.	466
	31: 7	**G** has not allowed him to harm me.	466
	31: 9	**G** has taken away your father's livestock	466
	31:11	The angel of **G** said to me in the dream,	466
	31:13	I am the **G** of Bethel,	446
	31:16	that **G** took away from our father belongs	466
	31:16	So do whatever **G** has told you."	466
	31:24	Then **G** came to Laban the Aramean in	466

Ge
31:29 last night the G of your father said to me, 466
31:42 If the G of my father, the God of Abraham 466
31:42 the G of Abraham and the Fear of Isaac, 466
31:42 But G has seen my hardship and the toil 466
31:50 remember that G is a witness between you 466
31:53 the G of Abraham and the God of Nahor, 466
31:53 the God of Abraham and the G of Nahor, 466
31:53 the G of their father, judge between us." 466
32: 1 and the angels of G met him. 466
32: 2 he said, "This is the camp of G!" 466
32: 9 Jacob prayed, "O G of my father Abraham, 466
32: 9 G of my father Isaac, O Lord, 466
32:28 with G and with men and have overcome." 466
32:30 saying, "It is because I saw G face to face, 466
33: 5 the children G has graciously given your servant. 466
33:10 to see your face is like seeing the face of G, 466
33:11 for G has been gracious to me 466
35: 1 Then G said to Jacob, 466
35: 1 and build an altar there to G, 446
35: 3 where I will build an altar to G, 466
35: 5 of G fell upon the towns all around them so 466
35: 7 that G revealed himself to him 466
35: 9 G appeared to him again and blessed him. 466
35:10 G said to him, "Your name is Jacob, 466
35:11 And G said to him, "I am God Almighty; 466
35:11 And God said to him, "I am G Almighty; 446
35:13 Then G went up from him at the place 466
35:14 at the place where G had talked with him, NIH
35:15 Jacob called the place where G had talked 466
39: 9 a wicked thing and sin against G?" 466
40: 8 "Do not interpretations belong to G? 466
41:16 "but G will give Pharaoh the answer 466
41:25 G has revealed to Pharaoh what he is about 466
41:28 G has shown Pharaoh what he is about 466
41:32 the matter has been firmly decided by G, 466
41:32 and G will do it soon. 466
41:38 one in whom is the spirit of G?" 466
41:39 "Since G has made all this known to you, 466
41:51 G has made me forget all my trouble 466
41:52 because G has made me fruitful in the land 466
42:18 "Do this and you will live, for I fear G: 466
42:28 "What is this that G has done to us?" 466
43:14 And may G Almighty grant you mercy 446
43:23 Your G, the God of your father, 466
43:23 Your God, the G of your father, 466
43:29 he said, "G be gracious to you, my son." 466
44:16 G has uncovered your servants' guilt. 466
45: 5 because it was to save lives that G sent me 466
45: 7 But G sent me ahead of you to preserve 466
45: 8 it was not you who sent me here, but G. 466
45: 9 G has made me lord of all Egypt. 466
46: 1 he offered sacrifices to the G of his father 466
46: 2 And G spoke to Israel in a vision at night 466
46: 3 "I am G, the God of your father," he said. 446
46: 3 "I am God, the G of your father," he said. 466
48: 3 "G Almighty appeared to me at Luz in 446
48: 9 "They are the sons G has given me here," 466
48:11 and now G has allowed me to see your 466
48:15 the G before whom my fathers Abraham 466
48:15 G who has been my shepherd all my life 466
48:20 'May G make you like Ephraim 466
48:21 but G will be with you and take you back 466
49:25 because of your father's G, 466
50:17 of the servants of the G of your father." 466
50:19 Am I in the place of G? 466
50:20 to harm me, but G intended it for good 466
50:24 But G will surely come to your aid 466
50:25 "G will surely come to your aid, 466

Ex
1:17 feared G and did not do what the king 466
1:20 So G was kind to the midwives and 466
1:21 And because the midwives feared G, 466
2:23 because of their slavery went up to G. 466
2:24 G heard their groaning 466
2:25 So G looked on the Israelites 466
3: 1 came to Horeb, the mountain of G. 466
3: 4 G called to him from within the bush, 466
3: 5 "Do not come any closer," G said. NIH
3: 6 Then he said, "I am the G of your father, 466
3: 6 the G of Abraham, 466
3: 6 the G of Isaac and the God of Jacob." 466
3: 6 the God of Isaac and the G of Jacob." 466
3: 6 because he was afraid to look at G. 466
3:11 But Moses said to G, "Who am I, 466
3:12 And G said, "I will be with you. NIH
3:12 you will worship G on this mountain." 466
3:13 Moses said to G, "Suppose I go 466
3:13 'The G of your fathers has sent me to you,' 466
3:14 G said to Moses, "Say to the Israelites, 466
3:15 G also said to Moses, "Say to the Israelites, 466
3:15 'The Lord, the G of your fathers 466
3:15 the G of Abraham, the God of Isaac and 466
3:15 the G of Isaac and the God of Jacob— 466
3:15 the God of Isaac and the G of Jacob— 466
3:16 'The Lord, the G of your fathers— 466
3:16 the G of Abraham, Isaac and Jacob— 466
3:18 the G of the Hebrews, has met with us. 466
3:18 to offer sacrifices to the Lord our G.' 466
4: 5 the G of their fathers— 466
4: 5 the G of Abraham, the God of Isaac and 466
4: 5 the G of Isaac and the God of Jacob— 466
4: 5 the God of Isaac and the G of Jacob— 466
4:16 if he were your mouth and as if you were G 466
4:20 And he took the staff of G in his hand. 466
4:27 So he met Moses at the mountain of G 466
5: 1 "This is what the Lord, the G of Israel, 466
5: 3 "The G of the Hebrews has met with us. 466

Ex
5: 3 to offer sacrifices to the Lord our G, 466
5: 8 'Let us go and sacrifice to our G.' 466
6: 2 G also said to Moses, "I am the Lord. 466
6: 3 to Isaac and to Jacob as G Almighty, 446
6: 7 and I will be your G. 466
6: 7 that I am the Lord your G, 466
7: 1 "See, I have made you like G to Pharaoh, 466
7:16 'The Lord, the G of the Hebrews, 466
8:10 like the Lord our G. 466
8:19 "This is the finger of G." 466
8:25 "Go, sacrifice to your G here in the land." 466
8:26 the Lord our G would be detestable to 466
8:27 to offer sacrifices to the Lord our G, 466
8:28 to offer sacrifices to the Lord your G in 466
9: 1 the G of the Hebrews, says: 466
9:13 the G of the Hebrews, says: 466
9:30 not fear the Lord G." 466
10: 3 the G of the Hebrews, says: 466
10: 7 that they may worship the Lord their G. 466
10: 8 "Go, worship the Lord your G," he said. 466
10:16 against the Lord your G and against you. 466
10:17 and pray to the Lord your G 466
10:25 to present to the Lord our G. 466
10:26 of them in worshiping the Lord our G, 466
13:17 G did not lead them on the road through 466
13:17 For G said, "If they face war, 466
13:18 So G led the people around by 466
13:19 "G will surely come to your aid, 466
14:19 Then the angel of G, 466
15: 2 He is my G, and I will praise him, 466
15: 2 and I will praise him, my father's G, 466
15:26 of the Lord your G and do what is right 466
16:12 that I am the Lord your G.' " 466
17: 9 of the hill with the staff of G in my hands." 466
18: 1 heard of everything G had done for Moses 466
18: 4 for he said, "My father's G was my helper, 466
18: 5 near the mountain of G. 466
18:12 a burnt offering and other sacrifices to G, 466
18:12 in the presence of G. 466
18:19 and may G be with you 466
18:19 before G and bring their disputes to him. 466
18:21 men who fear G, trustworthy 466
18:23 If you do this and G so commands, 466
19: 3 Then Moses went up to G, 466
19:17 the people out of the camp to meet with G, 466
19:19 and the voice of G answered him. 466
20: 1 And G spoke all these words: 466
20: 2 "I am the Lord your G, who brought you 466
20: 5 for I, the Lord your G, am a jealous God, 466
20: 5 I, the Lord your God, am a jealous G, 446
20: 7 not misuse the name of the Lord your G, 466
20:10 a Sabbath to the Lord your G. 466
20:12 the land the Lord your G is giving you. 466
20:19 do not have G speak to us or we will die." 466
20:20 G has come to test you, 466
20:20 the fear of G will be with you to keep you 2257S
20:21 the thick darkness where G was. 466
21:13 but G lets it happen, 466
22:20 "Whoever sacrifices to any g other than 466
22:28 "Do not blaspheme G or curse the ruler 466
23:19 to the house of the Lord your G. 466
23:25 Worship the Lord your G, 466
24:10 and saw the G of Israel. 466
24:11 But G did not raise his hand NIH
24:11 they saw G, and they ate and drank. 466
24:13 and Moses went up on the mountain of G. 466
29:45 among the Israelites and be their G. 466
29:46 that I am the Lord their G, 466
29:46 I am the Lord their G. 466
31: 3 and I have filled him with the Spirit of G, 466
31:18 of stone inscribed by the finger of G. 466
32:11 the favor of the Lord his G. 466
32:16 The tablets were the work of G; 466
32:16 the writing was the writing of G, 466
32:27 "This is what the Lord, the G of Israel, 466
34: 6 the compassionate and gracious G, 446
34:14 Do not worship any other g, 446
34:14 whose name is Jealous, is a jealous G. 466
34:23 the Sovereign Lord, the G of Israel. 466
34:24 to appear before the Lord your G. 466
34:26 to the house of the Lord your G. 466
35:31 and he has filled him with the Spirit of G, 466

Lev
2:13 of your G out of your grain offerings; 466
4:22 of the commands of the Lord his G, 466
11:44 I am the Lord your G; 466
11:45 brought you up out of Egypt to be your G; 466
18: 2 'I am the Lord your G. 466
18: 4 I am the Lord your G. 466
18:21 you must not profane the name of your G; 466
18:30 I am the Lord your G.' " 466
19: 2 'Be holy because I, the Lord your G, 466
19: 3 I am the Lord your G. 466
19: 4 I am the Lord your G. 466
19:10 I am the Lord your G. 466
19:12 and so profane the name of your G. 466
19:14 but fear your G. 466
19:25 I am the Lord your G. 466
19:31 I am the Lord your G. 466
19:32 for the elderly and revere your G. 466
19:34 I am the Lord your G. 466
19:36 I am the Lord your G. 466
20: 7 because I am the Lord your G. 466
20:24 I am the Lord your G. 466
21: 6 to their G and must not profane the name 466
21: 6 and must not profane the name of their G. 466
21: 6 the food of their G, they are to be holy. 466
21: 7 because priests are holy to their G. 466

Lev
21: 8 because they offer up the food of your G. 466
21:12 the sanctuary of his G or desecrate it, 466
21:12 by the anointing oil of his G. 466
21:17 near to offer the food of his G. 466
21:21 not come near to offer the food of his G. 466
21:22 He may eat the most holy food of his G, 466
22:25 and offer them as the food of your G. 466
22:33 of Egypt to be your G. 466
23:14 very day you bring this offering to your G. 466
23:22 I am the Lord your G.' " 466
23:28 for you before the Lord your G. 466
23:40 before the Lord your G for seven days. 466
23:43 I am the Lord your G.' " 466
24:15 'If anyone curses his G, 466
24:22 I am the Lord your G.' " 466
25:17 but fear your G. 466
25:17 I am the Lord your G. 466
25:36 but fear your G, 466
25:38 I am the Lord your G, 466
25:38 to give you the land of Canaan and to be your G. 466
25:43 but fear your G. 466
25:55 I am the Lord your G. 466
26: 1 I am the Lord your G. 466
26:12 I will walk among you and be your G, 466
26:13 I am the Lord your G, 466
26:44 I am the Lord their G. 466
26:45 in the sight of the nations to be their G. 466

Nu
6: 7 of his separation to G is on his head. 466
10: 9 be remembered by the Lord your G 466
10:10 be a memorial for you before your G. 466
10:10 I am the Lord your G." 466
12:13 So Moses cried out to the Lord, "O G, 446
15:40 and will be consecrated to your G. 466
15:41 I am the Lord your G, 466
15:41 of Egypt to be your G. 466
15:41 I am the Lord your G.' " 466
16: 9 that the G of Israel has separated you from 466
16:22 "O G, God of the spirits of all mankind, 446
16:22 "O God, G of the spirits of all mankind, 466
21: 5 they spoke against G and against Moses, 466
22: 9 G came to Balaam and asked, 466
22:10 Balaam said to G, "Balak son of Zippor, 466
22:12 G said to Balaam, "Do not go with them. 466
22:18 beyond the command of the Lord my G. 466
22:20 That night G came to Balaam and said, 466
22:22 But G was very angry when he went, 466
22:38 I must speak only what G puts 466
23: 4 G met with him, and Balaam said, 466
23: 8 can I curse those whom G has not cursed? 446
23:19 G is not a man, that he should lie, 466
23:21 The Lord their G is with them; 466
23:22 G brought them out of Egypt; 446
23:23 'See what G has done!' 466
23:27 Perhaps it will please G 466
24: 2 the Spirit of G came upon him 466
24: 4 of one who hears the words of G, who sees 446
24: 8 "G brought them out of Egypt; 446
24:16 the words of G, who has knowledge from 446
24:23 "Ah, who can live when G does this? 446
25:13 the honor of his G and made atonement for 466
27:16 the G of the spirits of all mankind, 466

Dt
1: 6 The Lord our G said to us at Horeb, 466
1:10 Lord your G has increased your numbers 466
1:11 May the Lord, the G of your fathers, 466
1:17 for judgment belongs to G. 466
1:19 Then, as the Lord our G commanded us, 466
1:20 which the Lord our G is giving us. 466
1:21 the Lord your G has given you the land. 466
1:21 the G of your fathers, told you. 466
1:25 that the Lord our G is giving us." 466
1:26 the command of the Lord your G. 466
1:30 The Lord your G, who is going before you, 466
1:31 how the Lord your G carried you, 466
1:32 you did not trust in the Lord your G, 466
1:41 as the Lord our G commanded us." 466
2: 7 The Lord your G has blessed you in all 466
2: 7 the Lord your G has been with you, 466
2:29 the land the Lord our G is giving us." 466
2:30 Lord your G had made his spirit stubborn 466
2:33 the Lord our G delivered him over to us 466
2:36 The Lord our G gave us all of them. 466
2:37 with the command of the Lord our G, 466
3: 3 So the Lord our G also gave 466
3:18 "The Lord your G has given you this land 466
3:20 that the Lord your G is giving them, 466
3:21 that the Lord your G has done 466
3:22 the Lord your G himself will fight 466
3:24 For what g is there in heaven or 446
4: 1 the G of your fathers, is giving you. 466
4: 2 of the Lord your G that I give you. 466
4: 3 The Lord your G destroyed from 466
4: 4 to the Lord your G are still alive today. 466
4: 5 as the Lord my G commanded me, 466
4: 7 near them the way the Lord our G is 466
4:10 before the Lord your G at Horeb, 466
4:19 the Lord your G has apportioned to all 466
4:21 the Lord your G is giving you 466
4:23 the Lord your G that he made with you; 466
4:23 the Lord your G has forbidden. 466
4:24 For the Lord your G is a consuming fire, 466
4:24 a consuming fire, a jealous G. 446
4:25 doing evil in the eyes of the Lord your G 466
4:29 if from there you seek the Lord your G, 466
4:30 to the Lord your G and obey him. 466
4:31 For the Lord your G is a merciful God; 466
4:31 For the Lord your God is a merciful G; 446

Dt	4:32	from the day G created man on the earth;	466
	4:33	the voice of G speaking out of fire,	466
	4:34	Has any g ever tried to take	466
	4:34	the things the LORD your G did for you	466
	4:35	that you might know that the LORD is G;	466
	4:39	that the LORD is G in heaven above and	466
	4:40	the LORD your G gives you for all time.	466
	5: 2	The LORD our G made a covenant	466
	5: 6	"I am the LORD your G, who brought you	466
	5: 9	for I, the LORD your G, am a jealous God,	466
	5: 9	I, the LORD your God, am a jealous G,	446
	5:11	not misuse the name of the LORD your G,	466
	5:12	as the LORD your G has commanded you.	466
	5:14	a Sabbath to the LORD your G.	466
	5:15	that the LORD your G brought you out	466
	5:15	the LORD your G has commanded you	466
	5:16	as the LORD your G has commanded you	466
	5:16	the land the LORD your G is giving you.	466
	5:24	"The LORD our G has shown us his glory	466
	5:24	a man can live even if G speaks with him.	466
	5:25	the voice of the LORD our G any longer.	466
	5:26	the voice of the living G speaking out	466
	5:27	and listen to all that the LORD our G says.	466
	5:27	the LORD our G tells you.	466
	5:32	the LORD your G has commanded you;	466
	5:33	the LORD your G has commanded you,	466
	6: 1	and laws the LORD your G directed me	466
	6: 2	after them may fear the LORD your G	466
	6: 3	just as the LORD, the G of your fathers,	466
	6: 4	The LORD our G, the LORD is one.	466
	6: 5	Love the LORD your G with all your heart	466
	6:10	When the LORD your G brings you into	466
	6:13	Fear the LORD your G,	466
	6:15	for the LORD your G, who is among you,	466
	6:15	is a jealous G and his anger will	446
	6:16	Do not test the LORD your G as you did	466
	6:17	of the LORD your G and the stipulations	466
	6:20	the LORD our G has commanded you?"	466
	6:24	and to fear the LORD our G,	466
	6:25	before the LORD our G,	466
	7: 1	When the LORD your G brings you into	466
	7: 2	the LORD your G has delivered them over	466
	7: 6	a people holy to the LORD your G.	466
	7: 6	The LORD your G has chosen you out	466
	7: 9	Know therefore that the LORD your G is God;	466
	7: 9	therefore that the LORD your God is G;	466
	7: 9	he is the faithful G, keeping his covenant	446
	7:12	the LORD your G will keep his covenant	466
	7:16	the peoples the LORD your G gives over	466
	7:18	the LORD your G did to Pharaoh and	466
	7:19	the LORD your G brought you out.	466
	7:19	The LORD your G will do the same to all	466
	7:20	the LORD your G will send the hornet	466
	7:21	for the LORD your G, who is among you,	466
	7:21	is a great and awesome G.	446
	7:22	The LORD your G will drive out those nations	466
	7:23	the LORD your G will deliver them over	466
	7:25	for it is detestable to the LORD your G.	466
	8: 2	how the LORD your G led you all the way	466
	8: 5	so the LORD your G disciplines you.	466
	8: 6	the commands of the LORD your G,	466
	8: 7	For the LORD your G is bringing you into	466
	8:10	praise the LORD your G for	466
	8:11	that you do not forget the LORD your G,	466
	8:14	and you will forget the LORD your G,	466
	8:18	But remember the LORD your G,	466
	8:19	the LORD your G and follow other gods	466
	8:20	for not obeying the LORD your G.	466
	9: 3	that the LORD your G is the one who goes	466
	9: 4	the LORD your G has driven them out	466
	9: 5	the LORD your G will drive them out	466
	9: 6	LORD your G is giving you this good land	466
	9: 7	the LORD your G to anger in the desert.	466
	9:10	stone tablets inscribed by the finger of G.	466
	9:16	against the LORD your G;	466
	9:23	the command of the LORD your G.	466
	10: 9	as the LORD your G told them.)	466
	10:12	the LORD your G ask of you but to fear	466
	10:12	of you but to fear the LORD your G,	466
	10:12	the LORD your G with all your heart and	466
	10:14	To the LORD your G belong the heavens,	466
	10:17	For the LORD your G is God of gods	466
	10:17	For the LORD your God is G of gods	466
	10:17	the great G, mighty and awesome,	446
	10:20	Fear the LORD your G and serve him.	466
	10:21	He is your praise; he is your G,	466
	10:22	and now the LORD your G has made you	466
	11: 1	Love the LORD your G and keep his	466
	11: 2	the discipline of the LORD your G:	466
	11:12	It is a land the LORD your G cares for;	466
	11:12	of the LORD your G are continually on it	466
	11:13	to love the LORD your G and to serve him	466
	11:22	to love the LORD your G, to walk in all	466
	11:25	The LORD your G, as he promised you,	466
	11:27	the commands of the LORD your G	466
	11:28	the LORD your G and turn from the way	466
	11:29	When the LORD your G has brought you	466
	11:31	the land the LORD your G is giving you.	466
	12: 1	the LORD, the G of your fathers,	466
	12: 4	You must not worship the LORD your G	466
	12: 5	the place the LORD your G will choose	466
	12: 7	in the presence of the LORD your G,	466
	12: 7	the LORD your G has blessed you.	466
	12: 9	the LORD your G is giving you.	466
	12:10	the land the LORD your G is giving you	466

Dt	12:11	the place the LORD your G will choose as	466
	12:12	there rejoice before the LORD your G,	466
	12:15	the blessing the LORD your G gives you.	466
	12:18	in the presence of the LORD your G at	466
	12:18	the place the LORD your G will choose—	466
	12:18	to rejoice before the LORD your G	466
	12:20	LORD your G has enlarged your territory	466
	12:21	where the LORD your G chooses	466
	12:27	on the altar of the LORD your G,	466
	12:27	beside the altar of the LORD your G,	466
	12:28	and right in the eyes of the LORD your G.	466
	12:29	the LORD your G will cut off before you	466
	12:31	You must not worship the LORD your G	466
	13: 3	The LORD your G is testing you	466
	13: 4	It is the LORD your G you must follow,	466
	13: 5	the LORD your G, who brought you out	466
	13: 5	the LORD your G commanded you	466
	13:10	to turn you away from the LORD your G,	466
	13:12	the towns the LORD your G is giving you	466
	13:16	whole burnt offering to the LORD your G.	466
	13:18	because you obey the LORD your G,	466
	14: 1	You are the children of the LORD your G.	466
	14: 2	a people holy to the LORD your G.	466
	14:21	a people holy to the LORD your G.	466
	14:23	in the presence of the LORD your G at	466
	14:23	to revere the LORD your G always.	466
	14:24	blessed by the LORD your G	466
	14:25	the place the LORD your G will choose.	466
	14:26	in the presence of the LORD your G	466
	14:29	so that the LORD your G may bless you	466
	15: 4	the LORD your G is giving you to possess	466
	15: 5	if only you fully obey the LORD your G	466
	15: 6	For the LORD your G will bless you	466
	15: 7	that the LORD your G is giving you,	466
	15:10	of this the LORD your G will bless you	466
	15:14	as the LORD your G has blessed you.	466
	15:15	and the LORD your G redeemed you.	466
	15:18	And the LORD your G will bless you	466
	15:19	for the LORD your G every firstborn male	466
	15:20	in the presence of the LORD your G at	466
	15:21	not sacrifice it to the LORD your G.	466
	16: 1	the Passover of the LORD your G,	466
	16: 2	as the Passover to the LORD your G	466
	16: 5	in any town the LORD your G gives you	466
	16: 7	at the place the LORD your G will choose.	466
	16: 8	to the LORD your G and do no work.	466
	16:10	of Weeks to the LORD your G by giving	466
	16:10	the LORD your G has given you.	466
	16:11	And rejoice before the LORD your G at	466
	16:15	the Feast to the LORD your G at the place	466
	16:15	For the LORD your G will bless you	466
	16:16	must appear before the LORD your G at	466
	16:17	the LORD your G has blessed you.	466
	16:18	the LORD your G is giving you,	466
	16:20	the land the LORD your G is giving you.	466
	16:21	the altar you build to the LORD your G,	466
	16:22	for these the LORD your G hates.	466
	17: 1	not sacrifice to the LORD your G an ox or	466
	17: 2	the eyes of the LORD your G in violation	466
	17: 8	the place the LORD your G will choose.	466
	17:12	to the LORD your G must be put to death.	466
	17:14	the land the LORD your G is giving you	466
	17:15	the king the LORD your G chooses.	466
	17:19	the LORD his G and follow carefully all	466
	18: 5	for the LORD your G has chosen them	466
	18: 7	minister in the name of the LORD his G	466
	18: 9	the land the LORD your G is giving you,	466
	18:12	LORD your G will drive out those nations	466
	18:13	be blameless before the LORD your G.	466
	18:14	the LORD your G has not permitted you	466
	18:15	The LORD your G will raise up for you	466
	18:16	the LORD your G at Horeb on the day of	466
	18:16	not hear the voice of the LORD our G	466
	19: 1	When the LORD your G has destroyed	466
	19: 2	the land the LORD your G is giving you	466
	19: 3	the land the LORD your G is giving you	466
	19: 8	the LORD your G enlarges your territory,	466
	19: 9	the LORD your G and to walk always	466
	19:10	which the LORD your G is giving you	466
	19:14	the land the LORD your G is giving you	466
	20: 1	because the LORD your G,	466
	20: 4	For the LORD your G is the one who goes	466
	20:13	LORD your G delivers it into your hand,	466
	20:14	the plunder the LORD your G gives you	466
	20:16	the LORD your G is giving you as	466
	20:17	as the LORD your G has commanded you.	466
	20:18	you will sin against the LORD your G.	466
	21: 1	the land the LORD your G is giving you	466
	21: 5	for the LORD your G has chosen them	466
	21:10	and the LORD your G delivers them	466
	21:23	the land the LORD your G is giving you	466
	22: 5	LORD your G detests anyone who does this.	466
	23: 5	the LORD your G would not listen	466
	23: 5	because the LORD your G loves you.	466
	23:14	For the LORD your G moves about	466
	23:18	of the LORD your G to pay any vow,	466
	23:18	the LORD your G detests them both.	466
	23:20	so that the LORD your G may bless you	466
	23:21	If you make a vow to the LORD your G,	466
	23:21	the LORD your G will certainly demand it	466
	23:23	the LORD your G with your own mouth.	466
	24: 4	the land the LORD your G is giving you	466
	24: 9	Remember what the LORD your G did	466
	24:13	in the sight of the LORD your G.	466
	24:18	and the LORD your G redeemed you	466
	24:19	so that the LORD your G may bless you	466
	25:15	the land the LORD your G is giving you.	466

Dt	25:16	LORD your G detests anyone who does these things,	466
	25:18	they had no fear of G.	466
	25:19	the LORD your G gives you rest from all	466
	26: 1	the land the LORD your G is giving you	466
	26: 2	the land the LORD your G is giving you	466
	26: 2	the place the LORD your G will choose as	466
	26: 3	to the LORD your G that I have come to	466
	26: 4	in front of the altar of the LORD your G.	466
	26: 5	before the LORD your G:	466
	26: 7	the LORD, the G of our fathers,	466
	26:10	Place the basket before the LORD your G	466
	26:11	the LORD your G has given to you	466
	26:13	Then say to the LORD your G:	466
	26:14	I have obeyed the LORD my G;	466
	26:16	LORD your G commands you this day	466
	26:17	that the LORD is your G and	466
	26:19	be a people holy to the LORD your G,	466
	27: 2	the land the LORD your G is giving you,	466
	27: 3	the land the LORD your G is giving you,	466
	27: 3	just as the LORD, the G of your fathers,	466
	27: 5	Build there an altar to the LORD your G,	466
	27: 6	of the LORD your G with fieldstones	466
	27: 6	on it to the LORD your G.	466
	27: 7	in the presence of the LORD your G.	466
	27: 9	the people of the LORD your G.	466
	27:10	Obey the LORD your G and follow his	466
	28: 1	If you fully obey the LORD your G	466
	28: 1	the LORD your G will set you high	466
	28: 2	if you obey the LORD your G:	466
	28: 8	The LORD your G will bless you in	466
	28: 9	the LORD your G and walk in his ways.	466
	28:13	the LORD your G that I give you this day	466
	28:15	if you do not obey the LORD your G	466
	28:45	not obey the LORD your G and observe	466
	28:47	the LORD your G joyfully and gladly in	466
	28:52	the land the LORD your G is giving you.	466
	28:53	the LORD your G has given you.	466
	28:58	the LORD your G—	466
	28:62	not obey the LORD your G.	466
	29: 6	that I am the LORD your G.	466
	29:10	in the presence of the LORD your G—	466
	29:12	into a covenant with the LORD your G,	466
	29:13	that he may be your G as he promised you	466
	29:15	the presence of the LORD our G but also	466
	29:18	from the LORD our G to go and worship	466
	29:25	the G of their fathers,	466
	29:29	secret things belong to the LORD our G,	466
	30: 1	the LORD your G disperses you among	466
	30: 2	to the LORD your G and obey him	466
	30: 3	LORD your G will restore your fortunes	466
	30: 4	the LORD your G will gather you	466
	30: 6	The LORD your G will circumcise your hearts	466
	30: 7	The LORD your G will put all these curses	466
	30: 9	LORD your G will make you most prosperous	466
	30:10	the LORD your G and keep his commands	466
	30:10	the LORD your G with all your heart and	466
	30:16	the LORD your G, to walk in his ways,	466
	30:16	and the LORD your G will bless you in	466
	30:20	and that you may love the LORD your G,	466
	31: 3	The LORD your G himself will cross over	466
	31: 6	for the LORD your G goes with you;	466
	31:11	to appear before the LORD your G at	466
	31:12	the LORD your G and follow carefully all	466
	31:13	and learn to fear the LORD your G as long	466
	31:17	upon us because our G is not with us?'	466
	31:26	of the covenant of the LORD your G.	466
	32: 3	Oh, praise the greatness of our G!	466
	32: 4	A faithful G who does no wrong,	446
	32:12	no foreign g was with him.	446
	32:15	He abandoned the G who made him	468
	32:17	They sacrificed to demons, which are not G	468
	32:18	you forgot the G who gave you birth.	446
	32:21	They made me jealous by what is no g	446
	32:39	There is no g besides me.	446
	33: 1	the man of G pronounced on the Israelites	466
	33:26	"There is no one like the G of Jeshurun,	446
	33:27	The eternal G is your refuge,	466
Jos	1: 9	be discouraged, for the LORD your G will	466
	1:11	the land the LORD your G is giving you	466
	1:13	'The LORD your G is giving you rest	466
	1:15	that the LORD your G is giving them.	466
	1:17	Only may the LORD your G be with you	466
	2:11	the LORD your G is God in heaven above	466
	2:11	the LORD your God is G in heaven above	466
	3: 3	of the covenant of the LORD your G,	466
	3: 9	to the words of the LORD your G.	466
	3:10	how you will know that the living G is	446
	4: 5	over before the ark of the LORD your G	466
	4:23	For the LORD your G dried up the Jordan	466
	4:23	the LORD your G did to the Jordan	466
	4:24	the LORD your G."	466
	7:13	for this is what the LORD, the G of Israel,	466
	7:19	give glory to the LORD, the G of Israel,	466
	7:20	the LORD, the G of Israel,	466
	8: 7	The LORD your G will give it	466
	8:30	the LORD, the G of Israel,	466
	9: 9	because of the fame of the LORD your G.	466
	9:18	the LORD, the G of Israel.	466
	9:19	the LORD, the G of Israel.	466
	9:23	and water carriers for the house of my G."	466
	9:24	the LORD your G had commanded his servant Moses	466
	10:19	for the LORD your G has given them	466
	10:40	just as the LORD, the G of Israel,	466
	10:42	because the LORD, the G of Israel,	466

Jos 13:14	made by fire to the LORD, the G of Israel,	466
13:33	the LORD, the G of Israel, is their inheritance	466
14: 6	the man of G at Kadesh Barnea about you	466
14: 8	followed the LORD my G wholeheartedly.	466
14: 9	the LORD my G wholeheartedly.'	466
14:14	the LORD, the G of Israel, wholeheartedly.	466
18: 3	the G of your fathers, has given you?	466
18: 6	in the presence of the LORD our G.	466
22: 3	the mission the LORD your G gave you.	466
22: 4	LORD your G has given your brothers rest	466
22: 5	to love the LORD your G,	466
22:16	'How could you break faith with the G	466
22:19	other than the altar of the LORD our G.	466
22:22	"The Mighty One, G, the LORD!	466
22:22	The Mighty One, G, the LORD!	466
22:24	the LORD, the G of Israel?	466
22:29	the altar of the LORD our G that stands	466
22:33	to hear the report and praised G.	466
22:34	A Witness Between Us that the LORD is G.	466
23: 3	the LORD your G has done	466
23: 3	the LORD your G who fought for you.	466
23: 5	The LORD your G himself will drive them out of your way.	466
23: 5	as the LORD your G promised you.	466
23: 8	you are to hold fast to the LORD your G,	466
23:10	because the LORD your G fights for you,	466
23:11	be very careful to love the LORD your G.	466
23:13	the LORD your G will no longer drive out these nations	466
23:13	which the LORD your G has given you.	466
23:14	the LORD your G gave you has failed.	466
23:15	of the LORD your G has come true,	466
23:16	the covenant of the LORD your G,	466
24: 1	and they presented themselves before G.	466
24: 2	"This is what the LORD, the G of Israel,	466
24:17	the LORD our G himself who brought us	466
24:18	because he is our G."	466
24:19	He is a holy G; he is a jealous God.	466
24:19	He is a holy God; he is a jealous G.	446
24:23	the LORD, the G of Israel."	466
24:24	the LORD our G and obey him."	466
24:26	in the Book of the Law of G.	466
24:27	against you if you are untrue to your G."	466
Jdg 1: 7	Now G has paid me back for what I did	466
2:12	the G of their fathers,	466
3: 7	they forgot the LORD their G and served	466
3:20	"I have a message from G for you."	466
4: 6	the G of Israel, commands you:	466
4:23	On that day G subdued Jabin,	466
5: 3	I will make music to the LORD, the G	466
5: 5	before the LORD, the G of Israel.	466
6: 8	"This is what the LORD, the G of Israel,	466
6:10	I said to you, 'I am the LORD your G;	466
6:20	The angel of G said to him,	466
6:26	a proper kind of altar to the LORD your G	466
6:31	If Baal really is a g,	466
6:36	Gideon said to G, "If you will save Israel	466
6:39	Then Gideon said to G,	466
6:40	That night G did so.	466
7:14	G has given the Midianites and	466
7:15	and its interpretation, he worshiped G.	NIH
8: 3	G gave Oreb and Zeeb,	466
8:33	They set up Baal-Berith as their g	466
8:34	and did not remember the LORD their G,	466
9: 7	so that G may listen to you.	466
9:23	G sent an evil spirit between Abimelech	466
9:24	G did this in order that the crime	NIH
9:27	they held a festival in the temple of their g.	466
9:56	Thus G repaid the wickedness	466
9:57	G also made the men of Shechem pay	466
10:10	forsaking our G and serving the Baals.	466
11:21	"Then the LORD, the G of Israel,	466
11:23	"Now since the LORD, the G of Israel,	466
11:24	not take what your g Chemosh gives you?	466
11:24	whatever the LORD our G has given us,	466
13: 5	set apart to G from birth,	466
13: 6	"A man of G came to me.	466
13: 6	He looked like an angel of G,	466
13: 7	be a Nazirite of G from birth until the day	466
13: 8	let the man of G you sent to us come again	466
13: 9	G heard Manoah, and the angel	466
13: 9	the angel of G came again to the woman	466
13:22	"We have seen G!"	466
15:19	G opened up the hollow place in Lehi,	466
16:17	a Nazirite set apart to G since birth.	466
16:23	to offer a great sacrifice to Dagon their g	466
16:23	"Our g has delivered Samson, our enemy,	466
16:24	the people saw him, they praised their g,	466
16:24	"Our g has delivered our enemy	466
16:28	O G, please strengthen me just once more,	466
18: 5	of G to learn whether our journey will	466
18:10	a spacious land that G has put	466
18:31	all the time the house of G was in Shiloh,	466
20: 2	in the assembly of the people of G,	466
20:18	up to Bethel and inquired of G.	466
20:27	the ark of the covenant of G was there,	466
21: 2	where they sat before G until evening,	466
21: 3	"O LORD, the G of Israel," they cried,	466
Ru 1:16	be my people and your G my God.	466
1:16	be my people and your God my G.	466
2:12	rewarded by the LORD, the G of Israel,	466
1Sa 1:17	and may the G of Israel grant you	466
2: 2	there is no Rock like our G.	466
2: 3	for the LORD is a G who knows,	446
2:25	G may mediate for him;	466
2:27	a man of G came to Eli and said to him,	466
2:30	"Therefore the LORD, the G of Israel,	466
1Sa 3: 3	The lamp of G had not yet gone out,	466
3: 3	where the ark of G was.	466
3:17	May G deal with you,	466
4: 4	with the ark of the covenant of G.	466
4: 7	"A g has come into the camp," they said.	466
4:11	The ark of G was captured.	466
4:13	because his heart feared for the ark of G.	466
4:17	and the ark of G has been captured."	466
4:18	When he mentioned the ark of G,	466
4:19	that the ark of G had been captured and	466
4:21	because of the capture of the ark of G and	466
4:22	for the ark of G has been captured."	466
5: 1	the Philistines had captured the ark of G,	466
5: 7	the g of Israel must not stay here with us,	466
5: 7	upon us and upon Dagon our g."	466
5: 8	"What shall we do with the ark of the g	466
5: 8	the ark of the g of Israel moved to Gath."	466
5: 8	So they moved the ark of the G of Israel.	466
5:10	So they sent the ark of G to Ekron.	466
5:10	As the ark of G was entering Ekron,	466
5:10	of the g of Israel around to us to kill us	466
5:11	"Send the ark of the g of Israel away;	466
6: 3	"If you return the ark of the g of Israel,	466
6: 5	and pay honor to Israel's g.	466
6:19	But G struck down some of the men	NIH
6:20	the presence of the LORD, this holy G?	466
7: 8	not stop crying out to the LORD our G	466
9: 6	"Look, in this town there is a man of G;	466
9: 7	We have no gift to take to the man of G.	466
9: 8	of G so that he will tell us what way	466
9: 9	if a man went to inquire of G,	466
9:10	for the town where the man of G was.	466
9:27	so that I may give you a message from G."	466
10: 3	up to G at Bethel will meet you there.	466
10: 5	"After that you will go to Gibeah of G,	466
10: 7	your hand finds to do, for G is with you.	466
10: 9	G changed Saul's heart,	466
10:10	the Spirit of G came upon him in power,	466
10:18	"This is what the LORD, the G of Israel,	466
10:19	But you have now rejected your G,	466
10:26	by valiant men whose hearts G had touched.	466
11: 6	the Spirit of G came upon him in power,	466
12: 9	"But they forgot the LORD their G;	466
12:12	though the LORD your G was your king.	466
12:14	over you follow the LORD your G—	466
12:19	to the LORD your G for your servants so	466
13:13	the command the LORD your G gave you;	466
14:15	It was a panic sent by G.	466
14:18	Saul said to Ahijah, "Bring the ark of G."	466
14:36	the priest said, "Let us inquire of G here."	466
14:37	So Saul asked G,	466
14:37	But G did not answer him that day.	NIH
14:41	Saul prayed to the LORD, the G of Israel,	466
14:44	Saul said, "May G deal with me,	466
15:15	to sacrifice to the LORD your G,	466
15:21	the best of what was devoted to G,	3051
15:21	to sacrifice them to the LORD your G	466
15:30	so that I may worship the LORD your G."	466
16:15	an evil spirit from G is tormenting you.	466
16:16	the evil spirit from G comes upon you,	466
16:23	the spirit from G came upon Saul,	466
17:26	the armies of the living G?"	466
17:36	he has defied the armies of the living G.	466
17:45	the G of the armies of Israel,	466
17:46	the whole world will know that there is a G	466
18:10	an evil spirit from G came forcefully	466
19:20	the Spirit of G came upon Saul's men	466
19:23	But the Spirit of G came even upon him,	466
20:12	"By the LORD, the G of Israel,	466
22: 3	with you until I learn what G will do	466
22:13	and a sword and inquiring of G for him,	466
22:15	Was that day the first time I inquired of G	466
23: 7	and he said, "G has handed him over to me,	466
23:10	David said, "O LORD, G of Israel,	466
23:11	O LORD, G of Israel, tell your servant."	466
23:14	but G did not give David into his hands.	466
23:16	and helped him find strength in G.	466
25:22	May G deal with David,	466
25:29	of the living by the LORD your G.	466
25:32	"Praise be to the LORD, the G of Israel,	466
25:34	as surely as the LORD, the G of Israel,	466
26: 8	"Today G has delivered your enemy	466
28:15	and G has turned away from me.	466
29: 9	as pleasing in my eyes as an angel of G;	466
30: 6	David found strength in the LORD his G.	466
30:15	to me before G that you will not kill me	466
2Sa 2:27	Joab answered, "As surely as G lives,	466
3: 9	May G deal with Abner,	466
3:35	saying, "May G deal with me,	466
5:10	The LORD G Almighty was with him.	466
6: 2	to bring up from there the ark of G,	466
6: 3	the ark of G on a new cart and brought it	466
6: 4	with the ark of G on it,	466
6: 6	and took hold of the ark of G,	466
6: 6	therefore G struck him down	466
6: 7	down and he died there beside the ark of G.	466
6:12	because of the ark of G."	466
6:12	and brought up the ark of G from the house	466
7: 2	while the ark of G remains in a tent."	466
7:22	and there is no G but you,	466
7:23	the one nation on earth that G went out	466
7:24	and you, O LORD, have become their G.	466
7:25	And now, LORD G, keep forever the promise	466
7:26	'The LORD Almighty is G over Israel!'	466
7:27	"O LORD Almighty, G of Israel,	466
7:28	O Sovereign LORD, you are G!	466
10:12	for our people and the cities of our G.	466
2Sa 12: 7	This is what the LORD, the G of Israel,	466
12:16	David pleaded with G for the child.	466
14:11	"Then let the king invoke the LORD his G	466
14:13	a thing like this against the people of G?	466
14:14	But G does not take away life;	466
14:16	from the inheritance G gave us.'	466
14:17	an angel of G in discerning good and evil.	466
14:17	May the LORD your G be with you.' "	466
14:20	like that of an angel of G—	466
15:24	the ark of the covenant of G,	466
15:24	They set down the ark of G,	466
15:25	"Take the ark of G back into the city.	466
15:29	of G back to Jerusalem and stayed there.	466
15:32	where people used to worship G,	466
16:23	like that of one who inquires of G.	466
18:28	"Praise be to the LORD your G!	466
19:13	May G deal with me, and ever so severely,	466
19:27	My lord the king is like an angel of G;	466
21:14	G answered prayer in behalf of the land.	466
22: 3	my G is my rock, in whom I take refuge,	466
22: 7	I called out to my G.	466
22:22	I have not done evil by turning from my G.	466
22:30	with my G I can scale a wall.	466
22:31	"As for G, his way is perfect;	446
22:32	For who is G besides the LORD?	446
22:32	And who is the Rock except our G?	446
22:33	It is G who arms me with strength	446
22:47	Exalted be G, the Rock, my Savior!	446
22:48	He is the G who avenges me,	446
23: 1	the man anointed by the G of Jacob,	466
23: 3	The G of Israel spoke,	466
23: 3	when he rules in the fear of G,	466
23: 5	"Is not my house right with G?	446
24: 3	the LORD your G multiply the troops	466
24:23	"May the LORD G accept you."	466
24:24	to the LORD my G burnt offerings	466
1Ki 1:17	to me your servant by the LORD your G:	466
1:30	the LORD, the G of Israel,	466
1:36	the G of my lord the king, so declare it.	466
1:47	'May your G make Solomon's name more famous than yours	466
1:48	'Praise be to the LORD, the G of Israel,	466
2: 3	observe what the LORD your G requires:	466
2:23	"May G deal with me,	466
3: 5	during the night in a dream, and G said,	466
3: 7	"Now, O LORD my G,	466
3:11	So G said to him,	466
3:28	he had wisdom from G to administer justice	466
4:29	G gave Solomon wisdom	466
5: 3	a temple for the Name of the LORD his G	466
5: 4	now the LORD my G has given me rest	466
5: 5	a temple for the Name of the LORD my G,	466
8:15	"Praise be to the LORD, the G of Israel,	466
8:17	the LORD, the G of Israel.	466
8:20	the Name of the LORD, the G of Israel.	466
8:23	"O LORD, G of Israel,	466
8:23	of Israel, there is no G like you in heaven	466
8:25	"Now LORD, G of Israel,	466
8:26	And now, O G of Israel,	466
8:27	"But will G really dwell on earth?	466
8:28	O LORD my G.	466
8:57	the LORD our G be with us as he was	466
8:59	be near to the LORD our G day and night,	466
8:60	the earth may know that the LORD is G	466
8:61	be fully committed to the LORD our G,	466
8:65	They celebrated it before the LORD our G	466
9: 9	they have forsaken the LORD their G,	466
10: 9	Praise be to the LORD your G,	466
10:24	to hear the wisdom G had put in his heart.	466
11: 4	not fully devoted to the LORD his G,	466
11: 5	the detestable g of the Ammonites	9199
11: 7	a high place for Chemosh the detestable g	9199
11: 7	the detestable g of the Ammonites.	9199
11: 9	the LORD, the G of Israel,	466
11:23	And G raised up against Solomon	466
11:31	for this is what the LORD, the G of Israel,	466
11:33	Chemosh the g of the Moabites,	466
11:33	and Molech the g of the Ammonites,	466
12:22	of G came to Shemaiah the man of God:	466
12:22	of God came to Shemaiah the man of G:	466
13: 1	of the LORD a man of G came from Judah	466
13: 3	That same day the man of G gave a sign:	NIH
13: 4	of G cried out against the altar at Bethel,	466
13: 5	the sign given by the man of G by the word	466
13: 6	Then the king said to the man of G,	466
13: 6	with the LORD your G and pray for me	466
13: 6	the man of G interceded with the LORD,	466
13: 7	The king said to the man of G,	466
13: 8	But the man of G answered the king,	466
13:11	that the man of G had done that day.	466
13:12	the man of G from Judah had taken.	466
13:14	and rode after the man of G.	466
13:14	the man of G who came from Judah?"	466
13:16	The man of G said,	NIH
13:19	So the man of G returned with him and ate	NIH
13:21	to the man of G who had come from Judah,	NIH
13:21	the command the LORD your G gave you.	466
13:23	When the man of G had finished eating	NIH
13:26	"It is the man of G who defied the word of	466
13:29	up the body of the man of G,	466
13:31	in the grave where the man of G is buried;	466
14: 7	the LORD, the G of Israel, says:	466
14:13	the G of Israel, has found anything good.	466
15: 3	not fully devoted to the LORD his G,	466
15: 4	the LORD his G gave him a lamp	466
15:30	provoked the LORD, the G of Israel, to anger	466
16:13	provoked the LORD, the G of Israel, to anger	466

1Ki 16:26	the LORD, the G of Israel, to anger	466
16:33	the LORD, the G of Israel, to anger	466
17: 1	"As the LORD, the G of Israel, lives,	466
17:12	"As surely as the LORD your G lives,"	466
17:14	this is what the LORD, the G of Israel,	466
17:18	"What do you have against me, man of G?	466
17:20	"O LORD my G,	466
17:21	"O LORD my G,	466
17:24	"Now I know that you are a man of G and	466
18:10	As surely as the LORD your G lives,	466
18:21	If the LORD is G, follow him;	466
18:21	but if Baal is G, follow him."	NIH
18:24	Then you call on the name of your g,	466
18:24	The g who answers by fire—he is God."	466
18:24	The god who answers by fire—he is G."	466
18:25	Call on the name of your g,	466
18:27	"Surely he is a g!	466
18:36	"O LORD, G of Abraham,	466
18:36	be known today that you are G in Israel and	466
18:37	that you, O LORD, are G, and	466
18:39	"The LORD—he is G!	466
18:39	The LORD—he is G!"	466
19: 8	he reached Horeb, the mountain of G.	466
19:10	for the LORD G Almighty.	466
19:14	for the LORD G Almighty.	466
20:28	of G came up and told the king of Israel,	466
20:28	a g of the hills and not a god of the valleys,	466
20:28	a god of the hills and not a g of the valleys,	466
21:10	that he has cursed both G and the king.	466
21:13	"Naboth has cursed both G and the king.	466
22:53	the G of Israel, to anger,	466
2Ki 1: 2	consult Baal-Zebub, the g of Ekron,	466
1: 3	'Is it because there is no G in Israel	466
1: 3	to consult Baal-Zebub, the g of Ekron?'	466
1: 6	Is it because there is no G in Israel	466
1: 6	to consult Baal-Zebub, the g of Ekron?	466
1: 9	"Man of G, the king says, 'Come down!'"	466
1:10	"If I am a man of G,	466
1:11	The captain said to him, "Man of G,	466
1:12	"If I am a man of G," Elijah replied,	466
1:12	of G fell from heaven and consumed him	466
1:13	"Man of G," he begged,	466
1:16	Is it because there is no G in Israel for you	466
1:16	to consult Baal-Zebub, the g of Ekron?	466
2:14	Where now the LORD, the G of Elijah?"	466
4: 7	She went and told the man of G,	466
4: 9	comes our way a holy man of G.	466
4:16	"Don't mislead your servant, O man of G!"	466
4:21	and laid him on the bed of the man of G,	466
4:22	to the man of G quickly and return."	466
4:25	So she set out and came to the man of G	466
4:25	the man of G said to his servant Gehazi,	466
4:27	she reached the man of G at the mountain,	466
4:27	but the man of G said, "Leave her alone!	466
4:40	"O man of G, there is death in the pot!"	466
4:42	of G twenty loaves of barley bread baked	466
5: 7	he tore his robes and said, "Am I G?	466
5: 8	When Elisha the man of G heard that	466
5:11	and call on the name of the LORD his G,	466
5:14	as the man of G had told him,	466
5:15	went back to the man of G.	466
5:15	that there is no G in all the world except	466
5:17	and sacrifices to any other g but	466
5:20	the servant of Elisha the man of G,	466
6: 6	The man of G asked, "Where did it fall?"	466
6: 9	of G sent word to the king of Israel:	466
6:10	on the place indicated by the man of G,	466
6:15	of the man of G got up and went out early	466
6:31	He said, "May G deal with me,	466
7: 2	the king was leaning said to the man of G,	466
7:17	just as the man of G had foretold when	466
7:18	It happened as the man of G had said to	466
7:19	The officer had said to the man of G,	466
7:19	The man of G had replied,	NIH
8: 2	to do as the man of G said.	466
8: 4	the servant of the man of G, and had said,	466
8: 7	"The man of G has come all the way	466
8: 8	with you and go to meet the man of G.	466
8:11	Then the man of G began to weep.	466
9: 6	"This is what the LORD, the G of Israel,	466
10:31	the LORD, the G of Israel, with all his heart.	466
13:19	of G was angry with him and said,	466
14:25	the LORD, the G of Israel,	466
16: 2	in the eyes of the LORD his G.	466
17: 7	against the LORD their G,	466
17: 9	the LORD their G that were not right.	466
17:14	who did not trust in the LORD their G.	466
17:16	the commands of the LORD their G	466
17:19	the commands of the LORD their G.	466
17:26	of Samaria do not know what the g of	466
17:27	the people what the g of the land requires."	466
17:39	Rather, worship the LORD your G;	466
18: 5	trusted in the LORD, the G of Israel.	466
18:12	not obeyed the LORD their G,	466
18:22	"We are depending on the LORD our G"—	466
18:33	the g of any nation ever delivered his land	466
19: 4	the LORD your G will hear all the words	466
19: 4	has sent to ridicule the living G,	466
19: 4	for the words the LORD your G has heard.	466
19:10	Do not let the g you depend on deceive you	466
19:15	"O LORD, G of Israel,	466
19:15	you alone are G over all the kingdoms of	466
19:16	to insult the living G.	466
19:19	Now, O LORD our G,	466
19:19	that you alone, O LORD, are G."	466
19:20	"This is what the LORD, the G of Israel,	466
19:37	in the temple of his g Nisroch,	466

2Ki 20: 5	the LORD, the G of your father David, says:	466
21:12	the LORD, the G of Israel, says:	466
21:22	the LORD, the G of his fathers,	466
22:15	"This is what the LORD, the G of Israel,	466
22:18	'This is what the LORD, the G of Israel,	466
23:13	for Chemosh the vile g of Moab,	9199
23:13	the detestable g of the people of Ammon.	9359
23:16	by the man of G who foretold these things.	466
23:17	of the man of G who came from Judah	466
23:21	the Passover to the LORD your G,	466
1Ch 4:10	Jabez cried out to the G of Israel, "Oh,	466
4:10	And G granted his request.	466
5:20	and G handed the Hagrites	466
5:25	But they were unfaithful to the G	466
5:25	whom G had destroyed before them.	466
5:26	So the G of Israel stirred up the spirit	466
6:48	the tabernacle, the house of G.	466
6:49	the servant of G had commanded.	466
9:11	the official in charge of the house of G;	466
9:13	for ministering in the house of G.	466
9:26	the rooms and treasuries in the house of G.	466
9:27	the night stationed around the house of G,	466
11: 2	And the LORD your G said to you,	466
11:19	"G forbid that I should do this!"	466
12:17	the G of our fathers see it and judge you."	466
12:18	for your G will help you."	466
12:22	like the army of G.	466
13: 2	and if it is the will of the LORD our G,	466
13: 3	Let us bring the ark of our G back to us,	466
13: 5	to bring the ark of G from Kiriath Jearim.	466
13: 6	the ark of G the LORD, who is enthroned	466
13: 7	of G from Abinadab's house on a new cart,	466
13: 8	with all their might before G,	466
13:10	So he died there before G.	466
13:12	David was afraid of G that day and asked,	466
13:12	"How can I ever bring the ark of G to me?"	466
13:14	The ark of G remained with the family	466
14:10	so David inquired of G:	466
14:11	G has broken out against my enemies	466
14:14	so David inquired of G again,	466
14:14	and G answered him,	466
14:15	because that will mean G has gone out	466
14:16	So David did as G commanded him,	466
15: 1	a place for the ark of G and pitched a tent	466
15: 2	but the Levites may carry the ark of G,	466
15:12	and bring up the ark of the LORD, the G	466
15:13	that the LORD our G broke out in anger	466
15:14	the ark of the LORD, the G of Israel.	466
15:15	And the Levites carried the ark of G with	466
15:24	to blow trumpets before the ark of G.	466
15:26	Because G had helped the Levites	466
16: 1	They brought the ark of G and set it inside	466
16: 1	and fellowship offerings before G.	466
16: 4	and to praise the LORD, the G of Israel:	466
16: 6	before the ark of the covenant of G.	466
16:14	He is the LORD our G;	466
16:35	Cry out, "Save us, O G our Savior;	466
16:36	Praise be to the LORD, the G of Israel,	466
17: 2	do it, for G is with you."	466
17: 3	That night the word of G came to Nathan,	466
17:16	"Who am I, O LORD G,	466
17:17	if this were not enough in your sight, O G,	466
17:17	the most exalted of men, O LORD G.	466
17:20	O LORD, and there is no G but you.	466
17:21	the one nation on earth whose G went out	466
17:22	and you, O LORD, have become their G.	466
17:24	'The LORD Almighty, the G over Israel,	466
17:24	the God over Israel, is Israel's G!'	466
17:25	my G, have revealed to your servant	466
17:26	O LORD, you are G!	466
19:13	for our people and the cities of our G.	466
21: 7	also evil in the sight of G,	466
21: 8	Then David said to G, "I have sinned	466
21:15	And G sent an angel to destroy Jerusalem.	466
21:17	David said to G, "Was it not I who ordered	466
21:17	O LORD my G, let your hand fall upon me	466
21:30	not go before it to inquire of G,	466
22: 1	"The house of the LORD G is to be here,	466
22: 2	for building the house of G.	466
22: 6	a house for the LORD, the G of Israel.	466
22: 7	a house for the Name of the LORD my G.	466
22:11	and build the house of the LORD your G,	466
22:12	the law of the LORD your G.	466
22:18	"Is not the LORD your G with you?	466
22:19	and soul to seeking the LORD your G.	466
22:19	to build the sanctuary of the LORD G,	466
22:19	and the sacred articles belonging to G into	466
23:14	of G were counted as part of the tribe	466
23:25	"Since the LORD, the G of Israel,	466
23:28	of other duties at the house of G.	466
24: 5	of the sanctuary and officials of G among	466
24:19	the G of Israel, had commanded him.	466
25: 5	through the promises of G to exalt him.	466
25: 5	G gave Heman fourteen sons	466
25: 6	for the ministry at the house of G.	466
26: 5	(For G had blessed Obed-Edom.)	466
26:20	in charge of the treasuries of the house of G	466
26:32	for every matter pertaining to G and for	466
28: 2	for the footstool of our G,	466
28: 3	But G said to me,	466
28: 4	"Yet the LORD, the G of Israel,	466
28: 8	and in the hearing of our G:	466
28: 8	the commands of the LORD your G,	466
28: 9	acknowledge the G of your father,	466
28:12	for the treasuries of the temple of G and for	466
28:20	for the LORD G, my God, is with you.	466
28:20	for the LORD God, my G, is with you.	466

1Ch 28:21	for all the work on the temple of G,	466
29: 1	the one whom G has chosen,	466
29: 1	not for man but for the LORD G.	466
29: 2	for the temple of my G—	466
29: 3	of my G I now give my personal treasures	466
29: 3	and silver for the temple of my G, over and	466
29: 7	on the temple of G five thousand talents	466
29:10	O LORD, G of our father Israel,	466
29:13	Now, our G, we give you thanks,	466
29:16	O LORD our G, as for all this abundance	466
29:17	I know, my G, that you test the heart	466
29:18	O LORD, G of our fathers Abraham,	466
29:20	"Praise the LORD your G."	466
29:20	praised the LORD your G of their fathers;	466
2Ch 1: 1	for the LORD his G was with him	466
1: 4	Now David had brought up the ark of G	466
1: 7	That night G appeared to Solomon and said	466
1: 8	Solomon answered G,	466
1: 9	Now, LORD G, let your promise	466
1:11	G said to Solomon,	466
2: 4	a temple for the Name of the LORD my G	466
2: 4	the appointed feasts of the LORD our G.	466
2: 5	our G is greater than all other gods.	466
2:12	"Praise be to the LORD, the G of Israel,	466
3: 3	the temple of G was sixty cubits long	466
4:11	for King Solomon in the temple of G:	466
5:14	glory of the LORD filled the temple of G.	466
6: 4	"Praise be to the LORD, the G of Israel,	466
6: 7	for the Name of the LORD, the G of Israel.	466
6:10	for the Name of the LORD, the G of Israel.	466
6:14	He said: "O LORD, G of Israel,	466
6:14	of Israel, there is no G like you in heaven	466
6:16	"Now LORD, G of Israel,	466
6:17	And now, O LORD, G of Israel,	466
6:18	will G really dwell on earth with men?	466
6:19	O LORD my G.	466
6:40	"Now, my G, may your eyes be open	466
6:41	"Now arise, O LORD G,	466
6:41	May your priests, O LORD G,	466
6:42	O LORD G, do not reject your anointed one.	466
7: 5	the people dedicated the temple of G.	466
7:22	forsaken the LORD, the G of their fathers,	466
8:14	the man of G had ordered.	466
9: 8	Praise be to the LORD your G,	466
9: 8	as king to rule for the LORD your G.	466
9: 8	the love of your G for Israel and his desire	466
9:23	to hear the wisdom G had put in his heart.	466
10:15	for this turn of events was from G,	466
11: 2	to Shemaiah the man of G:	466
11:16	the LORD, the G of Israel,	466
11:16	the LORD, the G of their fathers.	466
13: 5	the LORD, the G of Israel,	466
13:10	"As for us, the LORD is our G,	466
13:11	the requirements of the LORD our G.	466
13:12	G is with us; he is our leader.	466
13:12	the LORD, the G of your fathers,	466
13:15	G routed Jeroboam and all Israel	466
13:16	and G delivered them into their hands.	466
13:18	relied on the LORD, the G of their fathers.	466
14: 2	and right in the eyes of the LORD his G.	466
14: 4	to seek the LORD, the G of their fathers,	466
14: 7	we have sought the LORD our G;	466
14:11	Asa called to the LORD his G and said,	466
14:11	Help us, O LORD our G,	466
14:11	O LORD, you are our G;	466
15: 1	The Spirit of G came upon Azariah son	466
15: 3	a long time Israel was without the true G,	466
15: 4	the LORD, the G of Israel, and sought him,	466
15: 6	because G was troubling them	466
15: 9	when they saw that the LORD his G was	466
15:12	seek the LORD, the G of their fathers,	466
15:13	the G of Israel, were to be put to death,	466
15:15	They sought G eagerly,	2084s
15:18	into the temple of G the silver and gold and	466
16: 7	of Aram and not on the LORD your G,	466
17: 4	but sought the G of his father	466
18: 5	"for G will give it into the king's hand."	466
18:13	I can tell him only what my G says."	466
18:31	G drew them away from him,	466
19: 3	and have set your heart on seeking G."	466
19: 4	the G of their fathers.	466
19: 7	with the LORD our G there is no injustice	466
20: 6	"O LORD, G of our fathers,	466
20: 6	are you not the G who is in heaven?	466
20: 7	O our G, did you not drive out	466
20:12	O our G, will you not judge them?	466
20:19	the G of Israel, with very loud voice.	466
20:20	the LORD your G and you will be upheld;	466
20:29	The fear of G came upon all the kingdoms	466
20:30	for his G had given him rest on every side.	466
20:33	not set their hearts on the G	466
21:10	forsaken the LORD, the G of his fathers.	466
21:12	the LORD, the G of your father David, says:	466
22: 7	G brought about Ahaziah's downfall.	466
22:12	with them at the temple of G for six years	466
23: 3	with the king at the temple of G.	466
23: 9	and that were in the temple of G.	466
24: 5	to repair the temple of your G.	466
24: 7	of G and had used even its sacred objects	466
24: 9	that Moses the servant of G had required	466
24:13	They rebuilt the temple of G according	466
24:16	of the good he had done in Israel for G	466
24:18	the LORD, the G of their fathers,	466
24:20	of G came upon Zechariah son of Jehoiada	466
24:20	"This is what G says:	466
24:24	forsaken the LORD, the G of their fathers,	466
24:27	of G are written in the annotations on	466

2Ch	25: 7	But a man of G came to him and said,	466
	25: 8	G will overthrow you before the enemy,	466
	25: 8	G has the power to help or to overthrow."	466
	25: 9	Amaziah asked the man of G,	466
	25: 9	The man of G replied,	466
	25:16	that G has determined to destroy you,	466
	25:20	for G so worked that he might hand them	466
	25:24	and all the articles found in the temple of G	466
	26: 5	He sought G during the days of Zechariah,	466
	26: 5	who instructed him in the fear of G.	466
	26: 5	G gave him success.	466
	26: 7	G helped him against the Philistines and	466
	26:16	He was unfaithful to the LORD his G,	466
	26:18	you will not be honored by the LORD G."	466
	27: 6	before the LORD his G.	466
	28: 5	Therefore the LORD his G handed him	466
	28: 6	the LORD, the G of their fathers,	466
	28: 9	the LORD, the G of your fathers,	466
	28:10	of sins against the LORD your G?	466
	28:24	from the temple of G and took them away.	466
	28:25	the LORD, the G of his fathers, to anger.	466
	29: 5	the LORD, the G of your fathers.	466
	29: 6	of the LORD our G and forsook him.	466
	29: 7	at the sanctuary to the G of Israel.	466
	29:10	the LORD, the G of Israel,	466
	29:36	at what G had brought about for his people,	466
	30: 1	Passover to the LORD, the G of Israel.	466
	30: 5	Passover to the LORD, the G of Israel.	466
	30: 6	return to the LORD, the G of Abraham,	466
	30: 7	the LORD, the G of their fathers,	466
	30: 8	Serve the LORD your G,	466
	30: 9	for the LORD your G is gracious	466
	30:12	of G was on the people to give them unity	466
	30:16	in the Law of Moses the man of G.	466
	30:19	who sets his heart on seeking G—	466
	30:19	the LORD, the G of his fathers—	466
	30:22	praised the LORD, the G of their fathers.	466
	30:27	and G heard them,	NIH
	31: 6	to the LORD their G,	466
	31:13	the official in charge of the temple of G.	466
	31:14	of the freewill offerings given to G,	466
	31:20	and faithful before the LORD his G.	466
	31:21	he sought his G	466
	32: 8	with us is the LORD our G to help us and	466
	32:11	'The LORD our G will save us from	466
	32:14	then can your G deliver you from my hand?	466
	32:15	for no g of any nation	468
	32:15	How much less will your g deliver you	466
	32:16	against the LORD G and	466
	32:17	G of Israel, and saying this against him:	466
	32:17	from my hand, so the g of Hezekiah will	466
	32:19	about the G of Jerusalem as they did about	466
	32:21	And when he went into the temple of his g,	466
	32:29	for G had given him very great riches.	466
	32:31	G left him to test him and	466
	33: 7	of which G had said to David and	466
	33:12	the favor of the LORD his G	466
	33:12	and humbled himself greatly before the G	466
	33:13	Then Manasseh knew that the LORD is G.	466
	33:16	to serve the LORD, the G of Israel.	466
	33:17	but only to the LORD their G.	466
	33:18	including his prayer to his G and the words	466
	33:18	the LORD, the G of Israel,	466
	33:19	how G was moved by his entreaty, as well	NIH
	34: 3	he began to seek the G of his father David.	466
	34: 8	to repair the temple of the LORD his G.	466
	34: 9	that had been brought into the temple of G,	466
	34:23	"This is what the LORD, the G of Israel,	466
	34:26	'This is what the LORD, the G of Israel,	466
	34:27	before G when you heard what he spoke	466
	34:32	in accordance with the covenant of their	466
	34:32	covenant of God, the G of their fathers.	466
	34:33	in Israel serve the LORD their G.	466
	34:33	the LORD, the G of their fathers.	466
	35: 3	the LORD your G and his people Israel.	466
	35:21	G has told me to hurry;	466
	35:21	so stop opposing G, who is with me,	466
	36: 5	He did evil in the eyes of the LORD his G.	466
	36:12	He did evil in the eyes of the LORD his G	466
	36:13	not turn to the LORD, the G of Israel.	466
	36:15	The LORD, the G of their fathers,	466
	36:17	G handed all of them over	NIH
	36:18	the articles from the temple of G,	466
	36:23	" 'The LORD, the G of heaven,	466
	36:23	may the LORD his G be with him,	466
Ezr	1: 2	" 'The LORD, the G of heaven,	466
	1: 3	may his G be with him,	466
	1: 3	and build the temple of the LORD, the G	466
	1: 3	the G who is in Jerusalem.	466
	1: 4	with freewill offerings for the temple of G	466
	1: 5	everyone whose heart G had moved—	466
	1: 7	and had placed in the temple of his g.	466
	2:68	the rebuilding of the house of G on its site.	466
	3: 2	the G of Israel to sacrifice burnt offerings	466
	3: 2	in the Law of Moses the man of G.	466
	3: 8	after their arrival at the house of G	466
	3: 9	on the house of G.	466
	4: 1	temple for the LORD, the G of Israel,	466
	4: 2	we seek your G and have been sacrificing	466
	4: 3	with us in building a temple to our G.	466
	4: 3	the G of Israel, as King Cyrus,	466
	4:24	of G in Jerusalem came to a standstill until	10033
	5: 1	and Jerusalem in the name of the G	10033
	5: 2	to rebuild the house of G in Jerusalem.	10033
	5: 2	And the prophets of G were with them,	10033
	5: 5	of their G was watching over the elders of	10033
	5: 8	to the temple of the great G.	10033

Ezr	5:11	the servants of the G of heaven and earth,	10033
	5:12	our fathers angered the G of heaven,	10033
	5:13	a decree to rebuild this house of G.	10033
	5:14	and silver articles of the house of G,	10033
	5:15	And rebuild the house of G on its site.	10033
	5:16	and laid the foundations of the house of G	10033
	5:17	to rebuild this house of G in Jerusalem.	10033
	6: 3	concerning the temple of G in Jerusalem:	10033
	6: 5	gold and silver articles of the house of G,	10033
	6: 5	they are to be deposited in the house of G.	10033
	6: 7	with the work on this temple of G.	10033
	6: 7	the Jewish elders rebuild this house of G	10033
	6: 8	in the construction of this house of G:	10033
	6: 9	to the G of heaven, and wheat, salt, wine	10033
	6:10	to the G of heaven and pray for	10033
	6:12	May G, who has caused his Name	10033
	6:14	of the G of Israel and the decrees of Cyrus,	10033
	6:16	celebrated the dedication of the house of G	10033
	6:17	of G they offered a hundred bulls,	10033
	6:18	in their groups for the service of G	10033
	6:21	seek the LORD, the G of Israel.	466
	6:22	in the work on the house of G,	466
	6:22	house of God, the G of Israel.	466
	7: 6	which the LORD, the G of Israel,	466
	7: 6	the hand of the LORD his G was on him.	466
	7: 9	for the gracious hand of his G was on him.	466
	7:12	a teacher of the Law of the G of heaven:	10033
	7:14	with regard to the Law of your G,	10033
	7:15	and his advisers have freely given to the G	10033
	7:16	for the temple of their G in Jerusalem.	10033
	7:17	of the temple of your G in Jerusalem.	10033
	7:18	in accordance with the will of your G.	10033
	7:19	the G of Jerusalem all the articles entrusted	10033
	7:19	to you for worship in the temple of your G.	10033
	7:20	of your G that you may have occasion	10033
	7:21	a teacher of the Law of the G of heaven,	10033
	7:23	Whatever the G of heaven has prescribed,	10033
	7:23	with diligence for the temple of the G	10033
	7:24	or other workers at this house of G.	10033
	7:25	in accordance with the wisdom of your G,	10033
	7:25	all who know the laws of your G.	10033
	7:26	Whoever does not obey the law of your G	10033
	7:27	Praise be to the LORD, the G of our fathers,	466
	7:28	the hand of the LORD my G was on me,	466
	8:17	to us for the house of our G.	466
	8:18	the gracious hand of our G was on us,	466
	8:21	before our G and ask him for a safe journey	466
	8:22	of our G is on everyone who looks to him,	466
	8:23	we fasted and petitioned our G about this,	466
	8:25	for the house of our G.	466
	8:28	offering to the LORD, the G of your fathers.	466
	8:30	to the house of our G in Jerusalem.	466
	8:31	The hand of our G was on us,	466
	8:33	On the fourth day, in the house of our G,	466
	8:35	burnt offerings to the G of Israel:	466
	8:36	to the people and to the house of G.	466
	9: 4	the G of Israel gathered around me because	466
	9: 5	my hands spread out to the LORD my G	466
	9: 6	"O my G, I am too ashamed and disgraced	466
	9: 6	to lift up my face to you, my G,	466
	9: 8	the LORD our G has been gracious	466
	9: 8	and so our G gives light to our eyes and	466
	9: 9	our G has not deserted us in our bondage.	466
	9: 9	the house of our G and repair its ruins,	466
	9:10	now, O our G, what can we say after this?	466
	9:13	and our great guilt, and yet, our G,	466
	9:15	O LORD, G of Israel, you are righteous!	466
	10: 1	down before the house of G, a large crowd	466
	10: 2	to our G by marrying foreign women from	466
	10: 3	before our G to send away all these women	466
	10: 3	of those who fear the commands of our G.	466
	10: 6	before the house of G and went to the room	466
	10: 9	in the square before the house of G,	466
	10:11	the G of your fathers, and do his will.	466
	10:14	of our G in this matter is turned away	466
Ne	1: 4	and prayed before the G of heaven.	466
	1: 5	Then I said: "O LORD, G of heaven,	466
	1: 5	God of heaven, the great and awesome G,	446
	2: 4	Then I prayed to the G of heaven,	466
	2: 8	the gracious hand of my G was upon me,	466
	2:12	I had not told anyone what my G had put	466
	2:18	about the gracious hand of my G upon me	466
	2:20	"The G of heaven will give us success.	466
	4: 4	Hear us, O our G, for we are despised.	466
	4: 9	to our G and posted a guard day and night	466
	4:15	of their plot and that G had frustrated it,	466
	4:20	Our G will fight for us!"	466
	5: 9	in the fear of our G to avoid the reproach	466
	5:13	"In this way may G shake out of his house	466
	5:15	of reverence for G I did not act like that.	466
	5:19	Remember me with favor, O my G,	466
	6:10	He said, "Let us meet in the house of G,	466
	6:12	I realized that G had not sent him,	466
	6:14	Remember Tobiah and Sanballat, O my G,	466
	6:14	with the help of our G.	466
	7: 2	and feared G more than most men do.	466
	7: 5	So my G put it into my heart to assemble	466
	8: 6	Ezra praised the LORD, the great G;	466
	8: 8	They read from the Book of the Law of G,	466
	8: 9	"This day is sacred to the LORD your G.	466
	8:16	of G and in the square before the Water Gate	466
	8:18	Ezra read from the Book of the Law of G.	466
	9: 3	the Law of the LORD their G for a quarter	466
	9: 3	and in worshiping the LORD their G.	466
	9: 4	with loud voices to the LORD their G.	466
	9: 5	"Stand up and praise the LORD your G,	466
	9: 7	"You are the LORD G,	466

Ne	9:17	But you are a forgiving G,	468
	9:18	'This is your g, who brought you up out of	466
	9:31	for you are a gracious and merciful G.	446
	9:32	"Now therefore, O our G, the great,	466
	9:32	the great, mighty and awesome G,	446
	10:28	of the Law of G, together with their wives	466
	10:29	and an oath to follow the Law of G given	466
	10:29	the servant of G and to obey carefully all	466
	10:32	for the service of the house of our G:	466
	10:33	and for all the duties of the house of our G.	466
	10:34	to the house of our G at set times each year	466
	10:34	to burn on the altar of the LORD our G,	466
	10:36	and of our flocks to the house of our G,	466
	10:37	to the storerooms of the house of our G,	466
	10:38	of the tithes up to the house of our G,	466
	10:39	"We will not neglect the house of our G."	466
	11:11	supervisor in the house of G,	466
	11:16	of the outside work of the house of G;	466
	11:22	for the service of the house of G.	466
	12:24	as prescribed by David the man of G.	466
	12:36	by] David the man of G.	466
	12:40	then took their places in the house of G;	466
	12:43	because G had given them great joy.	466
	12:45	They performed the service of their G and	466
	12:46	the songs of praise and thanksgiving to G.	466
	13: 1	be admitted into the assembly of G,	466
	13: 2	(Our G, however, turned the curse into	466
	13: 4	of the storerooms of the house of our G.	466
	13: 7	a room in the courts of the house of G,	466
	13: 9	into them the equipment of the house of G,	466
	13:11	"Why is the house of G neglected?"	466
	13:14	Remember me for this, O my G,	466
	13:14	so faithfully done for the house of my G	466
	13:18	that our G brought all this calamity upon us	466
	13:22	Remember me for this also, O my G,	466
	13:26	He was loved by his G,	466
	13:26	and G made him king over all Israel,	466
	13:27	to our G by marrying foreign women?"	466
	13:29	Remember them, O my G,	466
	13:31	Remember me with favor, O my G.	466
Job	1: 1	he feared G and shunned evil.	466
	1: 5	and cursed G in their hearts.	466
	1: 8	a man who fears G and shuns evil."	466
	1: 9	"Does Job fear G for nothing?"	466
	1:16	"The fire of G fell from the sky and burned	466
	1:22	not sin by charging G with wrongdoing.	466
	2: 3	a man who fears G and shuns evil.	466
	2: 9	Curse G and die!"	466
	2:10	Shall we accept good from G,	466
	3: 4	may G above not care about it;	468
	3:23	whom G has hedged in?	468
	4: 9	At the breath of G they are destroyed;	468
	4:17	'Can a mortal be more righteous than G?	468
	4:18	If G places no trust in his servants,	NIH
	5: 8	"But if it were I, I would appeal to G;	446
	5:17	"Blessed is the man whom G corrects;	468
	6: 8	that G would grant what I hope for,	468
	6: 9	that G would be willing to crush me,	468
	7: 7	O G, that my life is but a breath;	NIH
	8: 3	Does G pervert justice?	446
	8: 5	But if you will look to G and plead with	446
	8:13	Such is the destiny of all who forget G;	468
	8:20	"Surely G does not reject a blameless man	446
	9: 2	how can a mortal be righteous before G?	446
	9:13	G does not restrain his anger;	468
	10: 2	I will say to G: Do not condemn me,	468
	11: 4	You say to G, 'My beliefs are flawless	NIH
	11: 5	Oh, how I wish that G would speak,	468
	11: 6	G has even forgotten some of your sin.	468
	11: 7	"Can you fathom the mysteries of G?	468
	12: 4	though I called upon G and he answered—	468
	12: 6	and those who provoke G are secure—	446
	12: 6	those who carry their g in their hands.	468
	12:13	"To G belong wisdom and power;	2257S
	13: 3	the Almighty and to argue my case with G.	446
	13: 8	Will you argue the case for G?	446
	13:20	"Only grant me these two things, O G,	446
	15: 4	and hinder devotion to G.	446
	15:13	so that you vent your rage against G	446
	15:15	If G places no trust in his holy ones,	NIH
	15:25	at G and vaunts himself against	446
	16: 7	Surely, O G, you have worn me out;	NIH
	16: 9	G assails me and tears me in his anger	NIH
	16:11	G has turned me over to evil men	446
	16:20	as my eyes pour out tears to G;	468
	16:21	of a man he pleads with G as a man pleads	468
	17: 3	"Give me, O G, the pledge you demand.	NIH
	17: 6	"G has made me a byword to everyone,	NIH
	18:21	such is the place of one who knows not G."	446
	19: 6	that G has wronged me and drawn his net	468
	19:21	have pity, for the hand of G has struck me.	468
	19:22	Why do you pursue me as G does?	446
	19:26	yet in my flesh I will see G;	468
	20:15	G will make his stomach vomit them up.	446
	20:23	G will vent his burning anger against him	NIH
	20:29	Such is the fate G allots the wicked,	466
	20:29	the heritage appointed for them by G."	446
	21: 9	the rod of G is not upon them.	468
	21: 9	Yet they say to G, 'Leave us alone!	468
	21:17	the fate G allots in his anger?	446
	21:19	'G stores up a man's punishment	NIH
	21:22	"Can anyone teach knowledge to G,	468
	22: 2	"Can a man be of benefit to G?	446
	22:12	"Is not G in the heights of heaven?	468
	22:13	Yet you say, 'What does G know?	446
	22:17	They said to G, 'Leave us alone!	446
	22:21	"Submit to G and be at peace with him;	2257S

Ps	71:12	Be not far from me, O G;	466
	71:12	come quickly, O my G, to help me.	466
	71:17	Since my youth, O G, you have taught me,	466
	71:18	do not forsake me, O G,	466
	71:19	O G, you who have done great things.	466
	71:19	Who, O G, is like you?	466
	71:22	the harp for your faithfulness, O my G;	466
	72: 1	Endow the king with your justice, O G,	466
	72:18	Praise be to the LORD G,	466
	72:18	the G of Israel,	466
	73: 1	Surely G is good to Israel,	466
	73:11	They say, "How can G know?	446
	73:17	till I entered the sanctuary of G;	446
	73:26	but G is the strength of my heart	466
	73:28	But as for me, it is good to be near G.	466
	74: 1	Why have you rejected us forever, O G?	466
	74: 8	where G was worshiped in the land.	466
	74:10	How long will the enemy mock you, O G?	466
	74:12	But you, O G, are my king from of old;	466
	74:22	Rise up, O G, and defend your cause;	466
	75: 1	We give thanks to you, O G,	466
	75: 7	But it is G who judges:	466
	75: 9	I will sing praise to the G of Jacob.	466
	76: 1	In Judah G is known;	466
	76: 6	At your rebuke, O G of Jacob,	466
	76: 9	O G, rose up to judge,	466
	76:11	to the LORD your G and fulfill them;	466
	77: 1	I cried out to G for help;	466
	77: 1	I cried out to G to hear me.	466
	77: 3	I remembered you, O G, and I groaned;	466
	77: 9	Has G forgotten to be merciful?	446
	77:13	Your ways, O G, are holy.	466
	77:13	What g is so great as our God?	446
	77:13	What god is so great as our G?	466
	77:14	You are the G who performs miracles;	446
	77:16	O G, the waters saw you and writhed;	466
	78: 7	Then they would put their trust in G	466
	78: 8	whose hearts were not loyal to G,	466
	78:18	They willfully put G to the test	466
	78:19	They spoke against G, saying,	466
	78:19	saying, "Can G spread a table in the desert?	446
	78:22	not believe in G or trust in his deliverance.	466
	78:34	Whenever G slew them,	446
	78:35	They remembered that G was their Rock,	466
	78:35	that G Most High was their Redeemer.	466
	78:41	Again and again they put G to the test;	446
	78:56	But they put G to the test and rebelled	466
	78:59	When G heard them, he was very angry;	466
	79: 1	O G, the nations have invaded your inheritance;	466
	79: 9	Help us, O G our Savior,	466
	79:10	"Where is their G?"	466
	80: 3	Restore us, O G; make your face shine upon us,	466
	80: 4	O LORD G Almighty,	466
	80: 7	Restore us, O G Almighty;	466
	80:14	Return to us, O G Almighty!	466
	80:19	Restore us, O LORD G Almighty;	466
	81: 1	Sing for joy to G our strength;	466
	81: 1	shout aloud to the G of Jacob!	466
	81: 4	an ordinance of the G of Jacob.	466
	81: 9	You shall have no foreign g among you;	446
	81: 9	you shall not bow down to an alien g.	446
	81:10	I am the LORD your G,	466
	82: 1	G presides in the great assembly;	466
	82: 8	Rise up, O G, judge the earth,	466
	83: 1	O G, do not keep silent;	466
	83: 1	be not quiet, O G, be not still.	446
	83:12	of the pasturelands of G."	466
	83:13	Make them like tumbleweed, O my G,	466
	84: 2	and my flesh cry out for the living G.	446
	84: 3	O LORD Almighty, my King and my G.	466
	84: 7	till each appears before G in Zion.	466
	84: 8	Hear my prayer, O LORD G Almighty;	466
	84: 8	listen to me, O G of Jacob.	466
	84: 9	upon our shield, O G;	466
	84:10	in the house of my G than dwell in the tents	466
	84:11	For the LORD G is a sun and shield;	466
	85: 4	Restore us again, O G our Savior,	466
	85: 8	I will listen to what G the LORD will say;	446
	86: 2	You are my G;	466
	86:10	you alone are G.	466
	86:12	I will praise you, O Lord my G,	466
	86:14	The arrogant are attacking me, O G;	466
	86:15	are a compassionate and gracious G,	446
	87: 3	O city of G:	466
	88: 1	O LORD, the G who saves me,	466
	89: 7	of the holy ones G is greatly feared;	446
	89: 8	O LORD G Almighty, who is like you?	466
	89:26	my G, the Rock my Savior.'	446
	90: T	A prayer of Moses the man of G.	466
	90: 2	from everlasting to everlasting you are G.	446
	90:17	the favor of the Lord our G rest upon us;	466
	91: 2	"He is my refuge and my fortress, my G,	446
	92:13	they will flourish in the courts of our G.	466
	94: 1	O LORD, the G who avenges,	446
	94: 1	the God who avenges, O G who avenges,	466
	94: 7	the G of Jacob pays no heed."	466
	94:22	and my G the rock in whom I take refuge.	466
	94:23	the LORD our G will destroy them.	466
	95: 3	For the LORD is the great G,	446
	95: 7	for he is our G and we are the people	466
	98: 3	of the earth have seen the salvation of our G.	466
	99: 5	Exalt the LORD our G and worship	466
	99: 8	O LORD our G, you answered them;	466
	99: 8	you were to Israel a forgiving G,	446
	99: 9	Exalt the LORD our G and worship	466

Ps	99: 9	for the LORD our G is holy.	466
	100: 3	Know that the LORD is G.	466
	102:24	So I said: "Do not take me away, O my G,	446
	104: 1	O LORD my G, you are very great;	466
	104:21	for their prey and seek their food from G.	466
	104:33	I will sing praise to my G as long as I live.	466
	105: 7	He is the LORD our G;	466
	106:14	in the wasteland they put G to the test.	446
	106:21	They forgot the G who saved them,	466
	106:33	for they rebelled against the Spirit of G,	2257S
	106:47	Save us, O LORD our G,	466
	106:48	Praise be to the LORD, the G of Israel,	466
	107:11	the words of G and despised the counsel of	466
	108: 1	My heart is steadfast, O G;	466
	108: 5	Be exalted, O G, above the heavens,	466
	108: 7	G has spoken from his sanctuary:	466
	108:11	Is it not you, O G,	466
	108:13	With G we will gain the victory,	466
	109: 1	O G, whom I praise, do not remain silent,	466
	109:26	Help me, O LORD my G;	466
	113: 5	Who is like the LORD our G,	466
	114: 7	at the presence of the G of Jacob,	468
	115: 2	"Where is their G?"	466
	115: 3	Our G is in heaven;	466
	116: 5	our G is full of compassion.	466
	118:27	The LORD is G,	446
	118:28	You are my G, and I will give you thanks;	466
	118:28	you are my G, and I will exalt you.	466
	119:115	that I may keep the commands of my G!	466
	122: 9	the sake of the house of the LORD our G,	466
	123: 2	so our eyes look to the LORD our G,	466
	135: 2	in the courts of the house of our G.	466
	136: 2	Give thanks to the G of gods.	466
	136:26	Give thanks to the G of heaven.	466
	139:17	to me are your thoughts, O G!	466
	139:19	If only you would slay the wicked, O G!	468
	139:23	Search me, O G, and know my heart;	446
	140: 6	I say to you, "You are my G."	466
	143:10	for you are my G;	466
	144: 2	He is my loving G and my fortress,	NIH
	144: 9	I will sing a new song to you, O G;	466
	144:15	the people whose G is the LORD.	466
	145: 1	I will exalt you, my G the King,	466
	146: 2	I will sing praise to my G as long as I live.	466
	146: 5	Blessed is he whose help is the G of Jacob,	446
	146: 5	whose hope is in the LORD his G,	466
	146:10	The LORD reigns forever, your G,	466
	147: 1	How good it is to sing praises to our G,	466
	147: 7	make music to our G on the harp.	466
	147:12	praise your G, O Zion;	466
	149: 6	May the praise of G be in their mouths and	446
	150: 1	Praise G in his sanctuary;	466
Pr	2: 5	the LORD and find the knowledge of G.	466
	2:17	the covenant she made before G.	466
	3: 4	and a good name in the sight of G and man.	466
	14:31	but whoever is kind to the needy honors G.	2257S
	25: 2	It is the glory of G to conceal a matter;	466
	30: 5	"Every word of G is flawless;	468
	30: 9	and so dishonor the name of my G.	466
Ecc	1:13	What a heavy burden G has laid on men!	466
	2:24	This too, I see, is from the hand of G,	466
	2:26	G gives wisdom, knowledge and happiness,	NIH
	2:26	to hand it over to the one who pleases G.	466
	3:10	I have seen the burden G has laid on men.	466
	3:11	yet they cannot fathom what G has done	466
	3:13	this is the gift of G.	466
	3:14	that everything G does will endure forever;	466
	3:14	G does it so that men will revere him.	466
	3:15	and G will call the past to account.	466
	3:17	"G will bring to judgment both	466
	3:18	G tests them so that they may see	466
	5: 1	when you go to the house of G.	466
	5: 2	in your heart to utter anything before G,	466
	5: 2	G is in heaven and you are on earth,	466
	5: 4	When you make a vow to G,	466
	5: 6	Why should G be angry at what you say	466
	5: 7	Therefore stand in awe of G.	466
	5:18	the few days of life G has given him—	466
	5:19	G gives any man wealth and possessions,	466
	5:19	this is a gift of G.	466
	5:20	because G keeps him occupied	466
	6: 2	G gives a man wealth,	466
	6: 2	but G does not enable him to enjoy them,	466
	7:13	Consider what G has done:	466
	7:14	G has made the one as well as the other.	466
	7:18	man who fears G will avoid all [extremes].	466
	7:26	The man who pleases G will escape her,	466
	7:29	G made mankind upright,	466
	8: 2	I say, because you took an oath before G.	466
	8:12	who are reverent before G.	2257S
	8:13	Yet because the wicked do not fear G,	466
	8:15	the days of the life G has given him under	466
	8:17	then I saw all that G has done.	466
	9: 7	for it is now that G favors what you do.	466
	9: 9	that G has given you under the sun—	NIH
	11: 5	so you cannot understand the work of G,	466
	11: 9	that for all these things G will bring you	466
	12: 7	and the spirit returns to G who gave it.	466
	12:13	Fear G and keep his commandments,	466
	12:14	For G will bring every deed into judgment,	466
Isa	1:10	listen to the law of our G,	466
	2: 3	to the house of the G of Jacob.	466
	5:16	and the holy G will show himself holy	446
	5:19	"Let G hurry, let him hasten his work	NIH
	7:11	"Ask the LORD your G for a sign,	466
	7:13	Will you try the patience of my G also?	466
	8:10	but it will not stand, for G is with us.	446

Isa	8:19	should not a people inquire of their G?	466
	8:21	will curse their king and their G.	466
	9: 6	Mighty G, Everlasting Father,	446
	10:21	of Jacob will return to the Mighty G.	466
	12: 2	Surely G is my salvation;	446
	13:19	will be overthrown by G like Sodom	466
	14:13	I will raise my throne above the stars of G;	446
	17: 6	declares the LORD, the G of Israel.	466
	17:10	You have forgotten G your Savior;	466
	21:10	from the G of Israel.	466
	21:17	The LORD, the G of Israel, has spoken.	466
	24:15	the G of Israel, in the islands of the sea.	466
	25: 1	O LORD, you are my G;	466
	25: 9	"Surely this is our G;	466
	25:11	G will bring down their pride despite	NIH
	26: 1	G makes salvation its walls and ramparts.	NIH
	26:13	our G, other lords besides you have ruled	466
	28:11	and strange tongues G will speak	NIH
	28:26	His G instructs him and teaches him	466
	29:23	and will stand in awe of the G of Israel.	466
	30:18	For the LORD is a G of justice.	466
	31: 3	But the Egyptians are men and not G;	446
	34:11	G will stretch out over Edom	NIH
	35: 2	the splendor of our G.	466
	35: 4	your G will come, he will come	466
	36: 7	"We are depending on the LORD our G"—	466
	36:18	the g of any nation ever delivered his land	466
	37: 4	that the LORD your G will hear the words	466
	37: 4	has sent to ridicule the living G,	466
	37: 4	for the words the LORD your G has heard.	466
	37:10	Do not let the g you depend on deceive you	466
	37:16	G of Israel, enthroned between	466
	37:16	you alone are G over all the kingdoms of	466
	37:17	to insult the living G.	466
	37:20	Now, O LORD our G,	466
	37:20	that you alone, O LORD, are G."	NIH
	37:21	"This is what the LORD, the G of Israel,	466
	37:38	in the temple of his g Nisroch,	466
	38: 5	the G of your father David, says:	466
	40: 1	Comfort, comfort my people, says your G.	466
	40: 3	in the wilderness a highway for our G.	466
	40: 8	but the word of our G stands forever."	466
	40: 9	say to the towns of Judah, "Here is your G!"	466
	40:18	To whom, then, will you compare G?	446
	40:27	my cause is disregarded by my G"?	466
	40:28	The LORD is the everlasting G,	466
	41:10	do not be dismayed, for I am your G.	466
	41:13	For I am the LORD, your G,	466
	41:17	I, the G of Israel, will not forsake them.	466
	42: 5	This is what G the LORD says—	446
	43: 3	For I am the LORD, your G,	466
	43:10	Before me no g was formed,	466
	43:12	I, and not some foreign g among you.	NIH
	43:12	declares the LORD, "that I am G.	446
	44: 6	apart from me there is no G.	466
	44: 8	Is there any G besides me?	468
	44:10	Who shapes a g and casts an idol,	446
	44:15	But he also fashions a g and worships it;	446
	44:17	From the rest he makes a g, his idol;	446
	44:17	"Save me; you are my g."	446
	45: 3	I am the LORD, the G of Israel,	466
	45: 5	apart from me there is no G.	466
	45:14	saying, 'Surely G is with you,	446
	45:14	there is no other g.' "	466
	45:15	Truly you are a G who hides himself,	446
	45:15	O G and Savior of Israel.	466
	45:18	he who created the heavens, he is G;	466
	45:21	And there is no G apart from me,	466
	45:21	a righteous G and a Savior;	446
	45:22	for I am G, and there is no other.	466
	46: 6	they hire a goldsmith to make it into a g,	446
	46: 9	I am G, and there is no other;	446
	46: 9	I am G, and there is none like me.	466
	48: 1	of the LORD and invoke the G of Israel—	466
	48: 2	the holy city and rely on the G of Israel—	466
	48: 5	and metal g ordained them.'	5822
	48:17	"I am the LORD your G,	466
	49: 4	and my reward is with my G."	466
	49: 5	and my G has been my strength—	466
	50:10	the name of the LORD and rely on his G.	466
	51:15	For I am the LORD your G,	466
	51:20	of the LORD and the rebuke of your G.	466
	51:22	your G, who defends his people:	466
	52: 7	who say to Zion, "Your G reigns!"	466
	52:10	of the earth will see the salvation of our G.	466
	52:12	the G of Israel will be your rear guard.	466
	53: 4	yet we considered him stricken by G,	466
	54: 5	he is called the G of all the earth.	466
	54: 6	only to be rejected," says your G.	466
	55: 5	because of the LORD your G,	466
	55: 7	and to our G, for he will freely pardon.	466
	57:21	"There is no peace," says my G,	466
	58: 2	not forsaken the commands of its G.	466
	58: 2	and seem eager for G to come near them.	466
	59: 2	But your iniquities have separated you from your G;	466
	59:13	turning our backs on our G,	466
	60: 9	to the honor of the LORD your G,	466
	60:19	your G will be your glory.	466
	61: 2	and the day of vengeance of our G,	466
	61: 6	you will be named ministers of our G.	466
	61:10	my soul rejoices in my G.	466
	62: 3	a royal diadem in the hand of your G.	466
	62: 5	so will your G rejoice over you.	466
	64: 4	no eye has seen any G besides you,	466
	65:16	a blessing in the land will do so by the G	466
	65:16	in the land will swear by the G of truth.	466

Isa	66: 9	says your **G**.	466
Jer	2:17	the LORD your **G** when he led you in	466
	2:19	when you forsake the LORD your **G**	466
	3:13	against the LORD your **G**,	466
	3:21	and have forgotten the LORD their **G**.	466
	3:22	for you are the LORD our **G**.	466
	3:23	the LORD our **G** is the salvation of Israel.	466
	3:25	We have sinned against the LORD our **G**,	466
	3:25	not obeyed the LORD our **G**."	466
	5: 4	the requirements of their **G**.	466
	5: 5	the requirements of their **G**."	466
	5:14	the LORD Almighty says:	466
	5:19	'Why has the LORD our **G** done all this	466
	5:24	'Let us fear the LORD our **G**,	466
	7: 3	the LORD Almighty, the **G** of Israel, says:	466
	7:21	the LORD Almighty, the **G** of Israel, says:	466
	7:23	I will be your **G** and you will be my people.	466
	7:28	not obeyed the LORD its **G** or responded	466
	8:14	the LORD our **G** has doomed us to perish	466
	9:15	the LORD Almighty, the **G** of Israel, says:	466
	10:10	But the LORD is the true **G**;	466
	10:10	he is the living **G**, the eternal King.	466
	10:12	But **G** made the earth by his power;	NIH
	11: 3	the LORD, the **G** of Israel, says:	466
	11: 4	and I will be your **G**.	466
	11:13	to burn incense to that **shameful g** Baal are	1425
	13:12	'This is what the LORD, the **G** of Israel,	466
	13:16	to the LORD your **G** before he brings	466
	14:22	No, it is you, O LORD our **G**.	466
	15:16	O LORD **G** Almighty.	466
	16: 9	the LORD Almighty, the **G** of Israel, says:	466
	16:10	against the LORD our **G**?'	466
	19: 3	the **G** of Israel, says: Listen!	466
	19:15	the **G** of Israel, says: 'Listen!	466
	21: 4	the LORD, the **G** of Israel, says:	466
	22: 9	of the LORD their **G** and have worshiped	466
	23: 2	the LORD, the **G** of Israel, says to	466
	23:23	"Am I only a **G** nearby,"	466
	23:23	"and not a **G** far away?	466
	23:36	so you distort the words of the living **G**,	466
	23:36	the LORD Almighty, our **G**.	466
	24: 5	the LORD, the **G** of Israel, says:	466
	24: 7	and I will be their **G**,	466
	25:15	This is what the LORD, the **G** of Israel,	466
	25:27	the LORD Almighty, the **G** of Israel, says:	466
	26:13	and obey the LORD your **G**.	466
	26:16	to us in the name of the LORD our **G**."	466
	27: 4	the LORD Almighty, the **G** of Israel, says:	466
	27:21	the **G** of Israel, says about the things	466
	28: 2	the LORD Almighty, the **G** of Israel, says:	466
	28:14	the LORD Almighty, the **G** of Israel, says:	466
	29: 4	the **G** of Israel, says to all those I carried	466
	29: 8	the LORD Almighty, the **G** of Israel, says:	466
	29:21	the **G** of Israel, says about Ahab son	466
	29:25	the LORD Almighty, the **G** of Israel, says:	466
	30: 2	the LORD, the **G** of Israel, says:	466
	30: 9	the LORD their **G** and David their king,	466
	30:22	and I will be your **G**.' "	466
	31: 1	"I will be the **G** of all the clans of Israel,	466
	31: 6	let us go up to Zion, to the LORD our **G**.' "	466
	31:18	because you are the LORD my **G**.	466
	31:23	the LORD Almighty, the **G** of Israel, says:	466
	31:33	I will be their **G**,	466
	32:14	the LORD Almighty, the **G** of Israel, says:	466
	32:15	the LORD Almighty, the **G** of Israel, says:	466
	32:18	O great and powerful **G**,	446
	32:27	the **G** of all mankind.	466
	32:36	the LORD, the **G** of Israel, says:	466
	32:38	and I will be their **G**.	466
	33: 4	this is what the LORD, the **G** of Israel,	466
	34: 2	the LORD, the **G** of Israel, says:	466
	34:13	the LORD, the **G** of Israel, says:	466
	35: 4	of Hanan son of Igdaliah the man of **G**.	466
	35:13	the LORD, the **G** of Israel, says:	466
	35:17	this is what the LORD **G** Almighty,	466
	35:17	the **G** of Israel, says: 'Listen!	466
	35:18	the LORD Almighty, the **G** of Israel, says:	466
	35:19	the LORD Almighty, the **G** of Israel, says:	466
	37: 3	"Please pray to the LORD our **G** for us."	466
	37: 7	the LORD, the **G** of Israel, says:	466
	38:17	"This is what the LORD **G** Almighty,	466
	38:17	the LORD Almighty, the **G** of Israel, says:	466
	39:16	the LORD Almighty, the **G** of Israel, says:	466
	40: 2	"The LORD your **G** decreed this disaster	466
	42: 2	the LORD your **G** for this entire remnant.	466
	42: 3	Pray that the LORD your **G** will tell us	466
	42: 4	"I will certainly pray to the LORD your **G**	466
	42: 5	the LORD your **G** sends you to tell us.	466
	42: 6	we will obey the LORD our **G**,	466
	42: 6	for we will obey the LORD our **G**."	466
	42: 9	"This is what the LORD, the **G** of Israel,	466
	42:13	and so disobey the LORD your **G**,	466
	42:15	the LORD Almighty, the **G** of Israel, says:	466
	42:18	the LORD Almighty, the **G** of Israel, says:	466
	42:20	when you sent me to the LORD your **G**	466
	42:20	'Pray to the LORD our **G** for us;	466
	42:21	the LORD your **G** in all he sent me	466
	43: 1	the words of the LORD their **G**—	466
	43: 2	The LORD our **G** has not sent you to say,	466
	43:10	the LORD Almighty, the **G** of Israel, says:	466
	44: 2	the LORD Almighty, the **G** of Israel, says:	466
	44: 7	"Now this is what the LORD **G** Almighty,	466
	44: 7	the LORD Almighty, the **G** of Israel, says:	466
	44:11	the LORD Almighty, the **G** of Israel, says:	466
	44:25	the LORD Almighty, the **G** of Israel, says:	466
	45: 2	the **G** of Israel, says to you, Baruch:	466
	46:25	the LORD Almighty, the **G** of Israel, says:	466

Jer	46:25	to bring punishment on Amon **g** of Thebes,	NIH
	48: 1	the LORD Almighty, the **G** of Israel, says:	466
	50: 4	in tears to seek the LORD their **G**.	466
	50:18	the LORD Almighty, the **G** of Israel, says:	466
	50:28	the LORD our **G** has taken vengeance,	466
	50:40	As **G** overthrew Sodom and Gomorrah	466
	51: 5	not been forsaken by their **G**,	466
	51:10	in Zion what the LORD our **G** has done.'	466
	51:33	the LORD Almighty, the **G** of Israel, says:	466
	51:56	For the LORD is a **G** of retribution;	446
La	3:41	up our hearts and our hands to **G** in heaven,	446
Eze	1: 1	and I saw visions of **G**.	466
	8: 3	and heaven and in visions of **G** he took me	466
	8: 4	And there before me was the glory of the **G**	466
	9: 3	Now the glory of the **G** of Israel went up	466
	10: 5	the voice of **G** Almighty when he speaks.	446
	10:19	glory of the **G** of Israel was above them.	466
	10:20	the **G** of Israel by the Kebar River,	466
	11:20	and I will be their **G**.	466
	11:22	glory of the **G** of Israel was above them.	466
	11:24	in the vision given by the Spirit of **G**.	466
	14:11	and I will be their **G**,	466
	20: 5	"I am the LORD your **G**."	466
	20: 7	I am the LORD your **G**."	466
	20:19	I am the LORD your **G**;	466
	20:20	that I am the LORD your **G**."	466
	28: 2	the pride of your heart you say, "I am a **g**;	446
	28: 2	the throne of a **g** in the heart of the seas."	466
	28: 2	But you are a man and not a **g**,	446
	28: 2	though you think you are as wise as a **g**.	446
	28: 6	you think you are wise, as wise as a **g**,	466
	28: 9	Will you then say, "I am a **g**,"	446
	28: 9	You will be but a man, not a **g**,	446
	28:13	You were in Eden, the garden of **G**;	466
	28:14	You were on the holy mount of **G**;	466
	28:16	in disgrace from the mount of **G**,	466
	28:26	that I am the LORD their **G**.' "	466
	31: 8	cedars in the garden of **G** could not rival it,	466
	31: 8	in the garden of **G** could match its beauty.	466
	31: 9	of all the trees of Eden in the garden of **G**.	466
	34:24	I the LORD will be their **G**,	466
	34:30	they will know that I, the LORD their **G**,	466
	34:31	are people, and I am your **G**,	466
	36:28	and I will be your **G**.	466
	37:23	and I will be their **G**.	466
	37:27	I will be their **G**,	466
	39:22	that I am the LORD their **G**.	466
	39:28	that I am the LORD their **G**.	466
	40: 2	In visions of **G** he took me to the land	466
	43: 2	the glory of the **G** of Israel coming from	466
	44: 2	the **G** of Israel, has entered through it.	466
Da	1: 2	of the articles from the temple of **G**.	466
	1: 2	the temple of his **g** in Babylonia and put in	466
	1: 2	and put in the treasure house of his **g**.	466
	1: 9	Now **G** had caused the official	466
	1:17	To these four young men **G** gave knowledge	466
	2:18	the **G** of heaven concerning this mystery,	10033
	2:19	Then Daniel praised the **G** of heaven	10033
	2:20	be to the name of **G** for ever and ever;	10033
	2:23	I thank and praise you, O **G** of my fathers:	10033
	2:28	a **G** in heaven who reveals mysteries.	10033
	2:37	The **G** of heaven has given you dominion	10033
	2:44	the **G** of heaven will set up a kingdom	10033
	2:45	"The great **G** has shown	10033
	2:47	"Surely your **G** is the God of gods and	10033
	2:47	the **G** of gods and the Lord of kings and	10033
	3:15	Then what **g** will be able to rescue you	10033
	3:17	the **G** we serve is able to save us from it,	10033
	3:26	servants of the Most High **G**, come out!	10033
	3:28	"Praise be to the **G** of Shadrach,	10033
	3:28	or worship any **g** except their own God.	10033
	3:28	or worship any **g** except their own **G**.	10033
	3:29	or language who say anything against the **G**	10033
	3:29	for no other **g** can save in this way."	10033
	4: 2	the Most High **G** has performed for me.	10033
	4: 8	after the name of my **g**,	10033
	5: 3	that had been taken from the temple of **G**	10033
	5:18	the Most High **G** gave your father	
		Nebuchadnezzar sovereignty	10033
	5:21	that the Most High **G** is sovereign over	10033
	5:23	But you did not honor the **G** who holds	10033
	5:26	**G** has numbered the days of your reign	10033
	6: 5	to do with the law of his **G**."	10033
	6: 7	to any **g** or man during the next thirty days,	10033
	6:10	giving thanks to his **G**.	10033
	6:11	and found Daniel praying and asking **G**	10033
	6:12	to any **g** or man except to you,	10033
	6:16	The king said to Daniel, "May your **G**,	10033
	6:20	servant of the living **G**, has your God,	10033
	6:20	has your **G**, whom you serve continually,	10033
	6:22	My **G** sent his angel,	10033
	6:23	because he had trusted in his **G**.	10033
	6:26	and reverence the **G** of Daniel.	10033
	6:26	he is the living **G** and he endures forever;	10033
	9: 3	the Lord **G** and pleaded with him in prayer	466
	9: 4	to the LORD my **G** and confessed:	466
	9: 4	"O Lord, the great and awesome **G**,	446
	9: 9	The Lord our **G** is merciful and forgiving,	466
	9:10	we have not obeyed the LORD our **G**	466
	9:11	the law of Moses, the servant of **G**,	466
	9:13	the LORD our **G** by turning from our sins	466
	9:14	for the LORD our **G** is righteous	466
	9:15	"Now, O Lord our **G**,	466
	9:17	"Now, our **G**, hear the prayers and petitions	466
	9:18	Give ear, O **G**, and hear;	466
	9:19	For your sake, O my **G**, do not delay,	466
	9:20	to the LORD my **G** for his holy hill—	466

Da	10:12	and to humble yourself before your **G**,	466
	11:32	who know their **G** will firmly resist him.	466
	11:36	and magnify himself above every **g**	446
	11:36	against the **G** of gods.	446
	11:37	nor will he regard any **g**,	468
	11:38	he will honor a **g** of fortresses;	468
	11:38	a **g** unknown to his fathers he will honor	468
	11:39	with the help of a foreign **g**	468
Hos	1: 7	but by the LORD their **G**."	466
	1: 9	and I am not your **G**.	NIH
	1:10	they will be called 'sons of the living **G**.'	446
	2:23	and they will say, 'You are my **G**.' "	466
	3: 5	the LORD their **G** and David their king.	466
	4: 1	no acknowledgment of **G** in the land.	466
	4: 6	you have ignored the law of your **G**,	466
	4:12	they are unfaithful to their **G**.	466
	5: 4	not permit them to return to their **G**.	466
	6: 6	of **G** rather than burnt offerings.	466
	7:10	not return to the LORD his **G** or search	466
	8: 2	Israel cries out to me, 'O our **G**,	466
	8: 6	a craftsman has made it; it is not **G**.	466
	9: 1	For you have been unfaithful to your **G**;	466
	9: 8	The prophet, along with my **G**,	466
	9: 8	and hostility in the house of his **G**.	466
	9: 9	**G** will remember their wickedness	NIH
	9:17	My **G** will reject them because they have	466
	11: 9	For I am **G**, and not man—	446
	11:12	And Judah is unruly against **G**,	446
	12: 3	as a man he struggled with **G**.	466
	12: 5	the LORD **G** Almighty,	466
	12: 6	But you must return to your **G**;	466
	12: 6	and wait for your **G** always.	466
	12: 9	"I am the LORD your **G**,	466
	13: 4	"But I am the LORD your **G**,	466
	13: 4	You shall acknowledge no **G** but me,	466
	13:16	because they have rebelled against their **G**.	466
	14: 1	Return, O Israel, to the LORD your **G**.	466
Joel	1:13	you who minister before my **G**;	466
	1:13	from the house of your **G**.	466
	1:14	to the house of the LORD your **G**,	466
	1:16	joy and gladness from the house of our **G**?	466
	2:13	Return to the LORD your **G**,	466
	2:14	and drink offerings for the LORD your **G**.	466
	2:17	'Where is their **G**?' "	466
	2:23	rejoice in the LORD your **G**,	466
	2:26	the name of the LORD your **G**,	466
	2:27	that I am the LORD your **G**,	466
	3:17	you will know that I, the LORD your **G**,	466
Am	2: 8	the house of their **g** they drink wine taken	466
	3:13	declares the Lord, the LORD **G** Almighty.	466
	4:12	prepare to meet your **G**, O Israel."	466
	4:13	the LORD **G** Almighty is his name.	466
	5:14	the LORD **G** Almighty will be with you,	466
	5:15	the LORD **G** Almighty will have mercy	466
	5:16	the LORD **G** Almighty, says:	466
	5:26	the pedestal of your idols, the star of your **g**	466
	5:27	whose name is **G** Almighty.	466
	6: 8	the LORD **G** Almighty declares:	466
	6:14	For the LORD **G** Almighty declares,	466
	8:14	or say, 'As surely as your **g** lives, O Dan,'	466
	8:14	'As surely as the **g** of Beersheba lives'—	2006
	9:15	says the LORD your **G**.	466
Jnh	1: 5	and each cried out to his own **g**.	466
	1: 6	Get up and call on your **g**!	466
	1: 9	I worship the LORD, the **G** of heaven,	466
	2: 1	the fish Jonah prayed to the LORD his **G**.	466
	2: 6	O LORD my **G**.	466
	3: 5	The Ninevites believed **G**.	466
	3: 8	Let everyone call urgently on **G**.	466
	3: 9	**G** may yet relent and with compassion turn	466
	3:10	When **G** saw what they did and	466
	4: 2	a gracious and compassionate **G**,	446
	4: 2	a **g** who relents from sending calamity.	NIH
	4: 6	Then the LORD **G** provided a vine	466
	4: 7	at dawn the next day provided a worm,	466
	4: 8	**G** provided a scorching east wind,	466
	4: 9	But **G** said to Jonah,	466
Mic	3: 7	because there is no answer from **G**."	466
	4: 2	to the house of the **G** of Jacob,	466
	4: 5	in the name of the LORD our **G** for ever	466
	5: 4	of the name of the LORD his **G**.	466
	6: 6	and bow down before the exalted **G**?	466
	6: 8	and to walk humbly with your **G**.	466
	7: 4	the day **G** visits you.	NIH
	7: 7	I wait for **G** my Savior;	466
	7: 7	my **G** will hear me.	466
	7:10	"Where is the LORD your **G**?"	466
	7:17	the LORD our **G** and will be afraid of you.	466
	7:18	Who is a **G** like you,	446
Na	1: 2	The LORD is a jealous and avenging **G**;	466
Hab	1:11	guilty men, whose own strength is their **g**."	468
	1:12	My **G**, my Holy One, we will not die.	466
	3: 3	**G** came from Teman,	468
	3:18	I will be joyful in **G** my Savior.	466
Zep	2: 7	The LORD their **G** will care for them;	466
	2: 9	the **G** of Israel, "surely Moab will become	466
	3: 2	she does not draw near to her **G**.	466
	3:17	The LORD your **G** is with you,	466
Hag	1:12	of the LORD their **G** and the message of	466
	1:12	because the LORD their **G** had sent him.	466
	1:14	the house of the LORD Almighty, their **G**,	466
Zec	4: 7	the capstone to shouts of '**G** bless it!	NIH
	4: 7	'**G** bless it!' "	NIH
	6:15	if you diligently obey the LORD your **G**."	466
	8: 8	be faithful and righteous to them as their **G**.	466
	8:23	we have heard that **G** is with you.' "	466
	9: 7	Those who are left will belong to our **G**	466

Zec 9:16 The LORD their G will save them on — 466
10: 6 the LORD their G and I will answer them. — 466
11: 4 This is what the LORD my G says: — 466
12: 5 because the LORD Almighty is their G.' — 466
12: 8 and the house of David will be like G, — 466
13: 9 and they will say, 'The LORD is our G.' " — 466
14: 5 Then the LORD my G will come, — 466
Mal 1: 9 "Now implore G to be gracious to us. — 446
2:10 Did not one G create us? — 446
2:11 by marrying the daughter of a foreign g. — 446
2:16 says the LORD G of Israel, — 466
2:17 with them" or "Where is the G of justice?" — 466
3: 8 "Will a man rob G? — 466
3:14 "You have said, 'It is futile to serve G. — 466
3:15 and even those who challenge G escape.' " — 466
3:18 between those who serve G — 466
Mt 1:23 Immanuel"—which means, "G with us." — 2536
3: 9 of these stones G can raise up children — 2536
3:16 and he saw the Spirit of G descending like — 2536
4: 3 "If you are the Son of G, — 2536
4: 4 that comes from the mouth of G.' " — 2536
4: 6 "If you are the Son of G," he said, — 2536
4: 7 'Do not put the Lord your G to the test.' " — 2536
4:10 'Worship the Lord your G, — 2536
5: 8 for they will see G. — 2536
5: 9 for they will be called sons of G — 2536
6:24 You cannot serve both G and Money. — 2536
6:30 that is how G clothes the grass of the field, — 2536
8:29 "What do you want with us, Son of G?" — 2536
9: 8 and they praised G, — 2536
12: 4 He entered the house of G, — 2536
12:28 if I drive out demons by the Spirit of G, — 2536
12:28 then the kingdom of G has come upon you. — 2536
14:33 saying, "Truly you are the Son of G." — 2536
15: 3 "And why do you break the command of G — 2536
15: 4 For G said, 'Honor your father and mother' — 2536
15: 5 from me is a gift devoted to G,' — NIG
15: 6 Thus you nullify the word of G for — 2536
15:31 And they praised the G of Israel. — 2536
16:16 the Son of the living G." — 2536
16:23 you do not have in mind the things of G, — 2536
19: 6 Therefore what G has joined together, — 2536
19:24 for a rich man to enter the kingdom of G." — 2536
19:26 but with G all things are possible." — 2536
21:31 the kingdom of G ahead of you. — 2536
21:43 that the kingdom of G will be taken away — 2536
22:16 the way of G in accordance with the truth. — 2536
22:21 and to G what is God's." — 2536
22:29 not know the Scriptures or the power of G. — 2536
22:31 have you not read what G said to you, — 2536
22:32 'I am the G of Abraham, — 2536
22:32 the G of Isaac, and the God of Jacob'? — 2536
22:32 the God of Isaac, and the God of Jacob'? — 2536
22:32 not the G of the dead but of the living." — 2536
22:37 " 'Love the Lord your G with all your heart — 2536
26:61 to destroy the temple of G and rebuild it — 2536
26:63 "I charge you under oath by the living G: — 2536
26:63 Tell us if you are the Christ, the Son of G." — 2536
27:40 if you are the Son of G!" — 2536
27:43 He trusts in G. — 2536
27:43 Let G rescue him now if he wants him, — NIG
27:43 for he said, 'I am the Son of G.' " — 2536
27:46 which means, "My G, my God, why — 2536
27:46 which means, "My God, my G, why — 2536
27:54 "Surely he was the Son of G!" — 2536
Mk 1: 1 Jesus Christ, the Son of G. — 2536
1:14 proclaiming the good news of G. — 2536
1:15 "The kingdom of G is near. — 2536
1:24 I know who you are—the Holy One of G!" — 2536
2: 7 Who can forgive sins but G alone?" — 2536
2:12 This amazed everyone and they praised G, — 2536
2:26 of G and ate the consecrated bread, — 2536
3:11 "You are the Son of G," — 2536
4:11 the kingdom of G has been given to you. — 2536
4:26 "This is what the kingdom of G is like. — 2536
4:30 "What shall we say the kingdom of G is — 2536
5: 7 Jesus, Son of the Most High G? — 2536
5: 7 Swear to G that you won't torture me!" — 2536
7: 8 of the commands of G and are holding on — 2536
7: 9 of setting aside the commands of G — 2536
7:11 Corban' (that is, a gift devoted to G), — 1565
7:13 the word of G by your tradition — 2536
8:33 "You do not have in mind the things of G, — 2536
9: 1 before they see the kingdom of G come — 2536
9:47 of G with one eye than to have two eyes — 2536
10: 6 of creation G 'made them male — NIG
10: 9 Therefore what G has joined together, — 2536
10:14 the kingdom of G belongs to such as these. — 2536
10:15 of G like a little child will never enter it." — 2536
10:18 "No one is good—except G alone. — 2536
10:23 for the rich to enter the kingdom of G!" — 2536
10:24 how hard it is to enter the kingdom of G! — 2536
10:25 for a rich man to enter the kingdom of G." — 2536
10:27 man this is impossible, but not with G; — 2536
10:27 all things are possible with G." — 2536
11:22 "Have faith in G," Jesus answered. — 2536
12:14 the way of G in accordance with the truth. — 2536
12:17 and to G what is God's." — 2536
12:24 the Scriptures or the power of G? — 2536
12:26 how G said to him, — 2536
12:26 'I am the G of Abraham, the God of Isaac, — 2536
12:26 'I am the God of Abraham, the G of Isaac, — 2536
12:26 the God of Isaac, and the G of Jacob'? — 2536
12:27 He is not the G of the dead, — 2536
12:29 'Hear, O Israel, the Lord our G, — 2536
12:30 Love the Lord your G with all your heart — 2536
12:32 in saying that G is one and there is no other — NIG

Mk 12:34 "You are not far from the kingdom of G." — 2536
13:19 when G created the world, until now— — 2536
14:25 when I drink it anew in the kingdom of G." — 2536
15:34 which means, "My G, my God, why — 2536
15:34 which means, "My God, my G, why — 2536
15:39 "Surely this man was the Son of G!" — 2536
15:43 waiting for the kingdom of G, — 2536
16:19 and he sat at the right hand of G. — 2536
Lk 1: 6 of them were upright in the sight of G, — 2536
1: 8 and he was serving as priest before G, — 2536
1:16 bring back to the Lord their G. — 2536
1:19 I stand in the presence of G, — 2536
1:26 G sent the angel Gabriel to Nazareth, — 2536
1:30 Mary, you have found favor with G. — 2536
1:32 The Lord G will give him the throne — 2536
1:35 to be born will be called the Son of G. — 2536
1:37 For nothing is impossible with G." — 2536
1:47 and my spirit rejoices in G my Savior, — 2536
1:64 and he began to speak, praising G. — 2536
1:68 "Praise be to the Lord, the G of Israel, — 2536
1:78 because of the tender mercy of our G, — 2536
2:13 praising G and saying, — 2536
2:14 "Glory to G in the highest, — 2536
2:20 glorifying and praising G for all — 2536
2:28 in his arms and praised G, saying: — 2536
2:38 she gave thanks to G and spoke about — 2536
2:40 and the grace of G was upon him. — 2536
2:52 and in favor with G and men. — 2536
3: 2 word of G came to John son of Zechariah in — 2536
3: 8 of these stones G can raise up children — 2536
3:38 the son of Adam, the son of G. — 2536
4: 3 "If you are the Son of G, — 2536
4: 8 the Lord your G and serve him only.' " — 2536
4: 9 "If you are the Son of G," he said, — 2536
4:12 'Do not put the Lord your G to the test.' " — 2536
4:34 I know who you are—the Holy One of G!" — 2536
4:41 shouting, "You are the Son of G!" — 2536
4:43 the kingdom of G to the other towns also, — 2536
5: 1 around him and listening to the word of G, — 2536
5:21 Who can forgive sins but G alone?" — 2536
5:25 on and went home praising G. — 2536
5:26 and gave praise to G. — 2536
6: 4 He entered the house of G, — 2536
6:12 and spent the night praying to G. — 2536
6:20 for yours is the kingdom of G. — 2536
7:16 with awe and praised G. — 2536
7:16 "G has come to help his people." — 2536
7:28 in the kingdom of G is greater than he." — 2536
8: 1 the good news of the kingdom of G. — 2536
8:10 the kingdom of G has been given to you, — 2536
8:11 The seed is the word of G. — 2536
8:28 Jesus, Son of the Most High G? — 2536
8:39 and tell how much G has done for you." — 2536
9: 2 to preach the kingdom of G and to heal — 2536
9:11 to them about the kingdom of G, — 2536
9:20 Peter answered, "The Christ of G." — 2536
9:27 before they see the kingdom of G. — 2536
9:43 they were all amazed at the greatness of G. — 2536
9:60 you go and proclaim the kingdom of G." — 2536
9:62 for service in the kingdom of G." — 2536
10: 9 'The kingdom of G is near you.' — 2536
10:11 be sure of this: The kingdom of G is near.' — 2536
10:27 " 'Love the Lord your G with all your heart — 2536
11:20 if I drive out demons by the finger of G, — 2536
11:20 then the kingdom of G has come to you. — 2536
11:28 the word of G and obey it." — 2536
11:42 you give a tenth of your mint, rue and — 620
11:42 but you neglect justice and the love of G. — 2536
11:49 Because of this, G in his wisdom said, — 2536
12: 6 Yet not one of them is forgotten by G. — 2536
12: 8 before the angels of G. — 2536
12: 9 be disowned before the angels of G. — 2536
12:20 "But G said to him, 'You fool! — 2536
12:21 for himself but is not rich toward G." — 2536
12:24 yet G feeds them. And how much more — 2536
12:28 that is how G clothes the grass of the field, — 2536
13:13 she straightened up and praised G. — 2536
13:18 "What is the kingdom of G like? — 2536
13:20 compare the kingdom of G to? — 2536
13:28 and all the prophets in the kingdom of G, — 2536
13:29 at the feast in the kingdom of G. — 2536
14:15 at the feast in the kingdom of G." — 2536
15:10 of G over one sinner who repents. — 2536
16:13 You cannot serve both G and Money." — 2536
16:15 but G knows your hearts. — 2536
16:16 of the kingdom of G is being preached, — 2536
17:15 came back, praising G in a loud voice. — 2536
17:18 to G except this foreigner?" — 2536
17:20 when the kingdom of G would come, — 2536
17:20 "The kingdom of G does not come — 2536
17:21 because the kingdom of G is within you." — 2536
18: 2 a judge who neither feared G nor cared — 2536
18: 4 though I don't fear G or care about men, — 2536
18: 7 And will not G bring about justice — 2536
18:11 'G, I thank you that I am not like other men — 2536
18:13 'G, have mercy on me, a sinner.' — 2536
18:14 went home justified before G. — 1467
18:16 the kingdom of G belongs to such as these. — 2536
18:17 of G like a little child will never enter it." — 2536
18:19 "No one is good—except G alone. — 2536
18:24 for the rich to enter the kingdom of G! — 2536
18:25 for a rich man to enter the kingdom of G." — 2536
18:27 with men is possible with G." — 2536
18:29 for the sake of the kingdom of G — 2536
18:43 and followed Jesus, praising G. — 2536
18:43 all the people saw it, they also praised G. — 2536
19:11 that the kingdom of G was going to appear — 2536

Lk 19:37 of disciples began joyfully to praise G — 2536
20:21 but teach the way of G in accordance with — 2536
20:25 and to G what is God's." — 2536
20:37 for he calls the Lord 'the G of Abraham, — 2536
20:37 and the G of Isaac, and the God of — 2536
20:37 and the God of Isaac, and the G of Jacob.' — 2536
20:38 He is not the G of the dead, — 2536
21: 5 and with gifts dedicated to G. — 356
21:31 you know that the kingdom of G is near. — 2536
22:16 in the kingdom of G." — 2536
22:18 of the vine until the kingdom of G comes." — 2536
22:69 be seated at the right hand of the mighty G." — 2536
22:70 "Are you then the Son of G?" — 2536
23:35 if he is the Christ of G, — 2536
23:40 "Don't you fear G," he said, — 2536
23:47 seeing what had happened, praised G — 2536
23:51 and he was waiting for the kingdom of G — 2536
24:19 powerful in word and deed before G and all — 2536
24:53 continually at the temple, praising G. — 2536
Jn 1: 1 and the Word was with G, — 2536
1: 1 and the Word was G. — 2536
1: 2 He was with G in the beginning. — 2536
1: 6 There came a man who was sent from G; — 2536
1:12 he gave the right to become children of G— — 2536
1:13 or a husband's will, but born of G. — 2536
1:18 No one has ever seen G, — 2536
1:18 but the One and Only, — 2536
1:29 "Look, the Lamb of G, — 2536
1:34 and I testify that this is the Son of G." — 2536
1:36 he said, "Look, the Lamb of G!" — 2536
1:49 "Rabbi, you are the Son of G; — 2536
1:51 of G ascending and descending on the Son — 2536
3: 2 a teacher who has come from G. — 2536
3: 2 if G were not with him." — 2536
3: 3 the kingdom of G unless he is born again." — 2536
3: 5 the kingdom of G unless he is born — 2536
3:16 "For G so loved the world — 2536
3:17 For G did not send his Son into the world — 2536
3:21 that what he has done has been done — 2536
through G." — 2536
3:33 has certified that G is truthful. — 2536
3:34 the one whom G has sent speaks the words — 2536
3:34 speaks the words of G, — 2536
3:34 for G gives the Spirit without limit. — NIG
4:10 the gift of G and who it is that asks you for — 2536
4:24 G is spirit, and his worshipers must
worship in spirit and in truth." — 2536
5:18 but he was even calling G his own Father, — 2536
5:18 making himself equal with G. — 2536
5:25 the Son of G and those who hear will live. — 2536
5:42 I know that you do not have the love of G — 2536
5:44 the praise that comes from the only G? — 2536
6:27 On him G the Father has placed his seal — 2536
6:28 to do the works G requires?" — 2536
6:29 Jesus answered, "The work of G is this: — 2536
6:33 For the bread of G is he who comes down — 2536
6:45 'They will all be taught by G.' — 2536
6:46 the Father except the one who is from G; — 2536
6:69 and know that you are the Holy One of G." — 2536
7:17 from G or whether I speak on my own. — 2536
8:40 the truth that I heard from G. — 2536
8:41 "The only Father we have is G himself." — 2536
8:42 Jesus said to them, "If G were your Father, — 2536
8:42 for I came from G and now am here. — 2536
8:47 He who belongs to G hears what G says. — 2536
8:47 He who belongs to God hears what G says. — 2536
8:47 not hear is that you do not belong to G." — 2536
8:54 My Father, whom you claim as your G, — 2536
9: 3 so that the work of G might be displayed — 2536
9:16 "This man is not from G, — 2536
9:24 "Give glory to G," they said. — 2536
9:29 We know that G spoke to Moses, — 2536
9:31 We know that G does not listen to sinners. — 2536
9:33 If this man were not from G, — 2536
10:33 because you, a mere man, claim to be G." — 2536
10:35 to whom the word of G came— — 2536
11:22 now G will give you whatever you ask." — 2536
11:27 you are the Christ, the Son of G, — 2536
11:40 you would see the glory of G?" — 2536
11:52 but also for the scattered children of G, — 2536
12:43 from men more than praise from G. — 2536
13: 3 that he had come from G and was returning — 2536
13: 3 from God and was returning to G; — 2536
13:31 the Son of Man glorified and G is glorified — 2536
13:32 If G is glorified in him, — 2536
13:32 will glorify the Son in himself, — 2536
14: 1 Trust in G; trust also in me. — 2536
16: 2 will think he is offering a service to G. — 2536
16:27 and have believed that I came from G. — 2536
16:30 that you came from G." — 2536
17: 3 that they may know you, the only true G, — 2536
19: 7 because he claimed to be the Son of G." — 2536
20:17 to my G and your God.' — 2536
20:17 to my God and your G.' " — 2536
20:28 Thomas said to him, "My Lord and my G!" — 2536
20:31 that Jesus is the Christ, the Son of G, — 2536
21:19 of death by which Peter would glorify G. — 2536
Ac 1: 3 and spoke about the kingdom of G. — 2536
2:11 we hear them declaring the wonders of G — 2536
2:17 G says, I will pour out my Spirit — 2536
2:22 a man accredited by G to you by miracles, — 2536
2:22 which G did among you through him, — 2536
2:24 But G raised him from the dead, — 2536
2:30 and knew that G had promised him on oath — 2536
2:32 G has raised this Jesus to life, — 2536
2:33 Exalted to the right hand of G, — 2536
2:36 G has made this Jesus, — 2536

Ac	2:39	for all whom the Lord our **G** will call."	2536
	2:47	praising **G** and enjoying the favor of all	2536
	3: 8	walking and jumping, and praising **G**.	2536
	3: 9	When all the people saw him walking and	
		praising **G**,	2536
	3:13	The **G** of Abraham, Isaac and Jacob,	2536
	3:13	Isaac and Jacob, the **G** of our fathers,	2536
	3:15	but **G** raised him from the dead.	2536
	3:18	how **G** fulfilled what he had foretold	2536
	3:19	Repent, then, and turn to **G**,	NIG
	3:21	the time comes for **G** to restore everything,	2536
	3:22	'The Lord your **G** will raise up for you	2536
	3:25	of the prophets and of the covenant **G** made	2536
	3:26	When **G** raised up his servant,	2536
	4:10	whom you crucified but whom **G** raised	2536
	4:19	in God's sight to obey you rather than **G**.	2536
	4:21	because all the people were praising **G**	2536
	4:24	raised their voices together in prayer to **G**.	2536
	4:31	and spoke the word of **G** boldly.	2536
	5: 4	You have not lied to men but to **G**."	2536
	5:29	"We must obey **G** rather than men!	2536
	5:30	The **G** of our fathers raised Jesus from	2536
	5:31	**G** exalted him to his own right hand	2536
	5:32	the Holy Spirit, whom **G** has given	2536
	5:39	But if it is from **G**, you will not be able to	2536
	5:39	you will only find yourselves **fighting against G**."	2534
	6: 2	of the word of **G** in order to wait on tables.	2536
	6: 7	So the word of **G** spread.	2536
	6:11	blasphemy against Moses and against **G**."	2536
	7: 2	The **G** of glory appeared	2536
	7: 3	and your people,' **G** said, 'and go to	NIG
	7: 4	**G** sent him to this land where you are	NIG
	7: 5	But **G** promised him that he	NIG
	7: 6	**G** spoke to him in this way:	2536
	7: 7	**G** said, 'and afterward they will come out	2536
	7: 9	But **G** was with him	2536
	7:17	for **G** to fulfill his promise to Abraham,	2536
	7:25	that **G** was using him to rescue them,	2536
	7:32	'I am the **G** of your fathers,	2536
	7:32	the **G** of Abraham, Isaac and Jacob.'	2536
	7:35	to be their ruler and deliverer by **G** himself,	2536
	7:37	'**G** will send you a prophet like me	2536
	7:42	But **G** turned away and gave them over to	2536
	7:43	of Molech and the star of your **g** Rephan,	2536
	7:44	It had been made as **G** directed Moses,	NIG
	7:45	from the nations **G** drove out before them.	2536
	7:46	a dwelling place for the **G** of Jacob.	2536
	7:55	up to heaven and saw the glory of **G**,	2536
	7:55	and Jesus standing at the right hand of **G**.	2536
	7:56	Son of Man standing at the right hand of **G**.	2536
	8:12	the good news of the kingdom of **G** and	2536
	8:14	that Samaria had accepted the word of **G**,	2536
	8:20	could buy the gift of **G** with money!	2536
	8:21	because your heart is not right before **G**.	2536
	9:20	the synagogues that Jesus is the Son of **G**.	2536
	10: 2	to those in need and prayed to **G** regularly.	2536
	10: 3	He distinctly saw an angel of **G**,	2536
	10: 4	up as a memorial offering before **G**.	2536
	10:15	that **G** has made clean."	2536
	10:28	But **G** has shown me that I should	2536
	10:31	**G** has heard your prayer	2536
	10:33	in the presence of **G** to listen to everything	2536
	10:34	"I now realize how true it is that **G** does	2536
	10:36	the message **G** sent to the people of Israel,	NIG
	10:38	how **G** anointed Jesus of Nazareth with	2536
	10:38	because **G** was with him.	2536
	10:40	but **G** raised him from the dead on	2536
	10:41	by witnesses whom **G** had already chosen—	2536
	10:42	the one whom **G** appointed as judge of	2536
	10:46	in tongues and praising **G**.	2536
	11: 1	also had received the word of **G**.	2536
	11: 9	that **G** has made clean.'	2536
	11:17	if **G** gave them the same gift as he gave us,	2536
	11:17	who was I to think that I could oppose **G**?"	2536
	11:18	and praised **G**, saying, "So	2536
	11:18	**G** has granted even the Gentiles	2536
	11:23	and saw the evidence of the grace of **G**,	2536
	12: 5	but the church was earnestly praying to **G**	2536
	12:22	They shouted, "This is the voice of a **g**,	2536
	12:23	because Herod did not give praise to **G**,	2536
	12:24	But the word of **G** continued to increase	2536
	13: 5	the word of **G** in the Jewish synagogues.	2536
	13: 7	because he wanted to hear the word of **G**.	2536
	13:16	of Israel and you Gentiles who worship **G**,	2536
	13:17	**G** of the people of Israel chose our fathers;	2536
	13:20	**G** gave them judges until the time	NIG
	13:23	"From this man's descendants **G** has brought to Israel the Savior Jesus,	2536
	13:30	But **G** raised him from the dead,	2536
	13:32	What **G** promised our fathers	NIG
	13:34	The fact that **G** raised him from the dead,	NIG
	13:37	the one whom **G** raised from the dead did	2536
	13:43	to continue in the grace of **G**.	2536
	13:46	to speak the word of **G** to you first.	2536
	14:15	from these worthless things to the living **G**,	2536
	14:22	to enter the kingdom of **G**,"	2536
	14:26	of **G** for the work they had now completed.	2536
	14:27	that **G** had done through them and	2536
	15: 4	they reported everything **G** had done	2536
	15: 7	you know that some time ago **G** made	2536
	15: 8	**G**, who knows the heart,	2536
	15:10	why do you try to test **G** by putting on	2536
	15:12	and wonders **G** had done among	2536
	15:14	to us how **G** at first showed his concern	2536
	15:19	for the Gentiles who are turning to **G**.	2536
	16:10	concluding that **G** had called us to preach	2536

Ac	16:14	who was a worshiper of **G**.	2536
	16:17	servants of the Most High **G**,	2536
	16:25	and singing hymns to **G**,	2536
	16:34	because he had come to believe in **G**—	2536
	17:13	that Paul was preaching the word of **G**	2536
	17:23	this inscription: TO AN UNKNOWN **G**.	2536
	17:24	"The **G** who made the world	2536
	17:27	**G** did this so that men would seek him	NIG
	17:30	In the past **G** overlooked such ignorance,	2536
	18: 7	Titius Justus, a worshiper of **G**.	2536
	18:11	teaching them the word of **G**.	2536
	18:13	to worship **G** in ways contrary to the law."	2536
	18:26	to him the way of **G** more adequately.	2536
	19: 8	about the kingdom of **G**.	2536
	19:11	**G** did extraordinary miracles through Paul,	2536
	20:21	that they must turn to **G** in repentance	2536
	20:27	to proclaim to you the whole will of **G**.	2536
	20:28	Be shepherds of the church of **G**,	2536
	20:32	"Now I commit you to **G** and to the word	2536
	21:19	and reported in detail what **G** had done	2536
	21:20	When they heard this, they praised **G**.	2536
	22: 3	of our fathers and was just as zealous for **G**	2536
	22:14	'The **G** of our fathers has chosen you	2536
	23: 1	to **G** in all good conscience to this day."	2536
	23: 3	Then Paul said to him, "**G** will strike you,	2536
	24:14	I admit that I worship the **G** of our fathers	2536
	24:15	I have the same hope in **G** as these men,	2536
	24:16	to keep my conscience clear before **G**	2536
	26: 6	in what **G** has promised our fathers	2536
	26: 7	as they earnestly serve **G** day and night.	NIG
	26: 8	of you consider it incredible that **G** raises	2536
	26:18	and from the power of Satan to **G**,	2536
	26:20	and turn to **G** and prove their repentance	2536
	26:29	I pray that not only you	2536
	27:23	the **G** whose I am and whom I serve stood	2536
	27:24	and **G** has graciously given you the lives	2536
	27:25	for I have faith in **G** that it will happen just	2536
	27:35	and gave thanks to **G** in front of them all.	2536
	28: 6	and said he was a **g**.	2536
	28:15	At the sight of these men Paul thanked **G**	2536
	28:23	and declared to them the kingdom of **G**	2536
	28:31	the kingdom of **G** and taught about	2536
Ro	1: 1	an apostle and set apart for the gospel of **G**	2536
	1: 4	to be the Son of **G** by his resurrection from	2536
	1: 7	in Rome who are loved by **G** and called to	2536
	1: 7	Grace and peace to you from **G** our Father	2536
	1: 8	I thank my **G** through Jesus Christ for all	2536
	1: 9	**G**, whom I serve with my whole heart	2536
	1:16	the power of **G** for the salvation	2536
	1:17	from **G** is revealed, a righteousness that is	2536
	1:18	wrath of **G** is being revealed from heaven	2536
	1:19	since what may be known about **G** is plain	2536
	1:19	because **G** has made it plain to them.	2536
	1:21	For although they knew **G**,	2536
	1:21	they neither glorified him as **G**	2536
	1:23	and exchanged the glory of the immortal **G**	2536
	1:24	Therefore **G** gave them over in	2536
	1:25	They exchanged the truth of **G** for a lie,	2536
	1:26	of this, **G** gave them over to shameful lusts.	2536
	1:28	to retain the knowledge of **G**,	2536
	2: 6	**G** "will give to each person according	4005S
	2:11	For **G** does not show favoritism.	2536
	2:16	on the day when **G** will judge men's secrets	2536
	2:17	and brag about your relationship to **G**;	2536
	2:23	do you dishonor **G** by breaking the law?	2536
	2:29	not from men, but from **G**.	2536
	3: 2	with the very words of **G**.	2536
	3: 4	Let **G** be true, and every man a liar.	2536
	3: 5	**G** is unjust in bringing his wrath on us?	2536
	3: 6	how could **G** judge the world?	2536
	3:11	no one who seeks **G**.	2536
	3:18	"There is no fear of **G** before their eyes."	2536
	3:19	the whole world held accountable to **G**.	2536
	3:21	But now a righteousness from **G**,	2536
	3:22	from **G** comes through faith in Jesus Christ	2536
	3:23	sinned and fall short of the glory of **G**,	2536
	3:25	**G** presented him as a sacrifice	2536
	3:29	Is **G** the God of Jews only?	NIG
	3:29	Is **G**od the God of Jews only?	2536
	3:29	Is he not the **G** of Gentiles too?	NIG
	3:30	since there is only one **G**,	2536
	4: 2	but not before **G**.	2536
	4: 3	"Abraham believed **G**, and it was credited	2536
	4: 5	but trusts **G** who justifies the wicked,	NIG
	4: 6	to whom **G** credits righteousness apart	2536
	4:17	He is our father in the sight of **G**,	NIG
	4:17	the **G** who gives life to the dead	2536
	4:20	regarding the promise of **G**,	2536
	4:20	in his faith and gave glory to **G**,	2536
	4:21	being fully persuaded that **G** had power	NIG
	4:24	to whom **G** will credit righteousness—	NIG
	5: 1	with **G** through our Lord Jesus Christ,	2536
	5: 2	we rejoice in the hope of the glory of **G**.	2536
	5: 5	because **G** has poured out his love	2536
	5: 8	**G** demonstrates his own love for us in this:	2536
	5:11	in **G** through our Lord Jesus Christ,	2536
	5:16	the gift of **G** is not like the result of	NIG
	6:10	but the life he lives, he lives to **G**.	2536
	6:11	count yourselves dead to sin but alive to **G**	2536
	6:13	but rather offer yourselves to **G**,	2536
	6:17	But thanks be to **G** that,	2536
	6:22	from sin and have become slaves to **G**,	2536
	7: 4	in order that we might bear fruit to **G**.	2536
	7:25	Thanks be to **G**—	2536
	8: 3	**G** did by sending his own Son in	2536
	8: 7	the sinful mind is hostile to **G**.	2536

Ro	8: 8	by the sinful nature cannot please **G**.	2536
	8: 9	if the Spirit of **G** lives in you.	2536
	8:14	by the Spirit of **G** are sons of God.	2536
	8:14	by the Spirit of God are sons of **G**.	2536
	8:17	heirs of **G** and co-heirs with Christ,	2536
	8:19	in eager expectation for the sons of **G** to	2536
	8:21	the glorious freedom of the children of **G**.	2536
	8:28	And we know that in all things **G** works for	NIG
	8:29	For those **G** foreknew he also predestined	NIG
	8:31	If **G** is for us, who can be against us?	2536
	8:33	against those whom **G** has chosen?	2536
	8:33	It is **G** who justifies.	2536
	8:34	the right hand of **G** and is also interceding	2536
	8:39	be able to separate us from the love of **G**	2536
	9: 5	who is **G** over all, forever praised!	2536
	9:14	Is **G** unjust? Not at all!	2536
	9:18	Therefore **G** has mercy on whom he wants	NIG
	9:19	"Then why does **G** still blame us?	NIG
	9:20	who are you, O man, to talk back to **G**?	2536
	9:22	What if **G**, choosing to show his wrath	2536
	9:26	they will be called 'sons of the living **G**.' "	2536
	10: 1	to **G** for the Israelites is that they may	2536
	10: 2	about them that they are zealous for **G**,	2536
	10: 3	from **G** and sought to establish their own,	2536
	10: 9	and believe in your heart that **G** raised him	2536
	11: 1	I ask then: Did **G** reject his people?	2536
	11: 2	**G** did not reject his people,	2536
	11: 2	how he appealed to **G** against Israel:	2536
	11: 8	"**G** gave them a spirit of stupor,	2536
	11:21	For if **G** did not spare the natural branches,	2536
	11:22	therefore the kindness and sternness of **G**:	2536
	11:23	for **G** is able to graft them in again.	2536
	11:30	to **G** have now received mercy as a result	2536
	11:32	For **G** has bound all men over	2536
	11:33	of the wisdom and knowledge of **G**!	2536
	11:35	"Who has ever given to **G**,	899S
	11:35	that **G** should repay him?"	NIG
	12: 1	holy and pleasing to **G**—	2536
	12: 3	with the measure of faith **G** has given you.	2536
	13: 1	that which **G** has established.	2536
	13: 1	that exist have been established by **G**.	2536
	13: 2	against what **G** has instituted,	2536
	14: 3	for **G** has accepted him.	2536
	14: 6	eats to the Lord, for he gives thanks to **G**;	2536
	14: 6	does so to the Lord and gives thanks to **G**.	2536
	14:11	every tongue will confess to **G**.' "	2536
	14:12	of us will give an account of himself to **G**.	2536
	14:17	of **G** is not a matter of eating and drinking,	2536
	14:18	in this way is pleasing to **G** and approved	2536
	14:20	Do not destroy the work of **G** for the sake	2536
	14:22	between yourself and **G**.	2536
	15: 5	May the **G** who gives endurance	2536
	15: 6	the **G** and Father of our Lord Jesus Christ.	2536
	15: 7	in order to bring praise to **G**.	2536
	15: 9	the Gentiles may glorify **G** for his mercy,	2536
	15:13	May the **G** of hope fill you with all joy	2536
	15:15	because of the grace **G** gave me	2536
	15:16	of proclaiming the gospel of **G**,	2536
	15:16	an offering acceptable to **G**,	NIG
	15:17	I glory in Christ Jesus in my service to **G**.	2536
	15:18	the Gentiles to obey **G** by what I have said	NIG
	15:30	to join me in my struggle by praying to **G**	2536
	15:33	The **G** of peace be with you all. Amen.	2536
	16:20	The **G** of peace will soon crush Satan	2536
	16:26	by the command of the eternal **G**,	2536
	16:27	to the only wise **G** be glory forever	2536
1Co	1: 1	an apostle of Christ Jesus by the will of **G**,	2536
	1: 2	church of **G** in Corinth, to those sanctified	2536
	1: 3	Grace and peace to you from **G** our Father	2536
	1: 4	I always thank **G** for you because	2536
	1: 9	**G**, who has called you into fellowship	2536
	1:18	who are being saved it is the power of **G**.	2536
	1:20	Has not **G** made foolish the wisdom of	2536
	1:21	For since in the wisdom of **G** the world	2536
	1:21	**G** was pleased through the foolishness	2536
	1:24	but to those whom **G** has called,	NIG
	1:24	the power of **G** and the wisdom of God.	2536
	1:24	the power of God and the wisdom of **G**.	2536
	1:25	the foolishness of **G** is wiser than man's wisdom,	2536
	1:25	the weakness of **G** is stronger than man's strength.	2536
	1:27	But **G** chose the foolish things of the world	2536
	1:27	**G** chose the weak things of the world	2536
	1:30	who has become for us wisdom from **G**—	2536
	2: 1	to you the testimony about **G**.	2536
	2: 7	that has been hidden and that **G** destined	2536
	2: 9	no mind has conceived what **G** has prepared	2536
	2:10	but **G** has revealed it to us by his Spirit.	2536
	2:10	even the deep things of **G**.	2536
	2:11	the thoughts of **G** except the Spirit of God.	2536
	2:11	the thoughts of God except the Spirit of **G**.	2536
	2:12	of the world but the Spirit who is from **G**,	2536
	2:12	we may understand what **G** has freely given us.	2536
	2:14	the things that come from the Spirit of **G**,	2536
	3: 6	Apollos watered it, but **G** made it grow.	2536
	3: 7	but only **G**, who makes things grow.	2536
	3:10	By the grace **G** has given me,	2536
	3:17	destroys God's temple, **G** will destroy him;	2536
	3:23	and you are of Christ, and Christ is of **G**.	2536
	4: 1	with the secret things of **G**.	2536
	4: 5	time each will receive his praise from **G**.	2536
	4: 9	to me that **G** has put us apostles on display	2536
	4:20	of **G** is not a matter of talk but of power.	2536
	5:13	**G** will judge those outside.	2536
	6: 9	not inherit the kingdom of **G**?	2536

1Co	6:10	will inherit the kingdom of G.	2536
	6:11	and by the Spirit of our G.	2536
	6:13	but G will destroy them both.	2536
	6:14	By his power G raised the Lord from	2536
	6:19	whom you have received from G?	2536
	6:20	Therefore honor G with your body.	2536
	7: 7	But each man has his own gift from G;	2536
	7:15	G has called us to live in peace.	2536
	7:17	to him and to which G has called him.	2536
	7:20	in when G called him.	NIG
	7:24	Brothers, each man, as responsible to G,	2536
	7:24	in the situation G called him to.	NIG
	7:40	and I think that I too have the Spirit of G.	2536
	8: 3	the man who loves G is known by God.	2536
	8: 3	the man who loves God is known by G.	899S
	8: 4	in the world and that there is no G but one.	2536
	8: 6	yet for us there is but one G, the Father,	2536
	8: 8	But food does not bring us near to G;	2536
	9: 9	Is it about oxen that G is concerned?	2536
	10: 5	G was not pleased with most of them;	2536
	10:13	And G is faithful;	2536
	10:20	to demons, not to G, and I do not want you	2536
	10:30	because of something I thank G for?	NIG
	10:31	do it all for the glory of G.	2536
	10:32	whether Jews, Greeks or the church of G—	2536
	11: 3	and the head of Christ is G.	2536
	11: 7	since he is the image and glory of G;	2536
	11:12	But everything comes from G.	2536
	11:13	to pray to G with her head uncovered?	2536
	11:16	nor do the churches of G.	2536
	11:22	Or do you despise the church of G	2536
	12: 3	by the Spirit of G says,	2536
	12: 6	the same G works all of them in all men.	2536
	12:18	in fact G has arranged the parts in the body,	2536
	12:24	But G has combined the members of	2536
	12:28	And in the church G has appointed first	2536
	14: 2	a tongue does not speak to men but to G.	2536
	14:16	If you are praising G with your spirit,	NIG
	14:18	I thank G that I speak in tongues more than	2536
	14:25	So he will fall down and worship G,	2536
	14:25	exclaiming, "G is really among you!"	2536
	14:28	in the church and speak to himself and G.	2536
	14:33	For G is not a God of disorder but of peace.	2536
	14:33	For God is not a G of disorder but of peace.	NIG
	14:36	Did the word of G originate with you?	2536
	15: 9	because I persecuted the church of G.	2536
	15:10	But by the grace of G I am what I am,	2536
	15:10	not I, but the grace of G that was with me.	2536
	15:15	then found to be false witnesses about G,	2536
	15:15	about G that he raised Christ from the dead.	2536
	15:24	when he hands over the kingdom to G	2536
	15:27	that this does not include G himself.	NIG
	15:28	so that G may be all in all.	2536
	15:34	for there are some who are ignorant of G—	2536
	15:38	But G gives it a body as he has determined,	2536
	15:50	cannot inherit the kingdom of G,	2536
	15:57	But thanks be to G!	2536
2Co	1: 1	an apostle of Christ Jesus by the will of G,	2536
	1: 1	To the church of G in Corinth,	2536
	1: 2	Grace and peace to you from G our Father	2536
	1: 3	the G and Father of our Lord Jesus Christ,	2536
	1: 3	of compassion and the G of all comfort,	2536
	1: 4	with the comfort we ourselves have received from G.	2536
	1: 9	not rely on ourselves but on G,	2536
	1:12	the holiness and sincerity that are from G.	2536
	1:18	But as surely as G is faithful,	2536
	1:19	For the Son of G, Jesus Christ,	2536
	1:20	no matter how many promises G has made,	2536
	1:20	by us to the glory of G.	2536
	1:21	Now it is G who makes both us and you	2536
	1:23	I call G as my witness that it was in order	2536
	2:14	But thanks be to G,	2536
	2:15	For we are to G the aroma of Christ	2536
	2:17	we do not peddle the word of G for profit.	2536
	2:17	in Christ we speak before G with sincerity,	2536
	2:17	like men sent from G.	2536
	3: 3	with ink but with the Spirit of the living G,	2536
	3: 4	as this is ours through Christ before G.	2536
	3: 5	but our competence comes from G.	2536
	4: 2	nor do we distort the word of G.	2536
	4: 2	every man's conscience in the sight of G.	2536
	4: 4	The g of this age has blinded the minds	2536
	4: 4	Christ, who is the image of G.	2536
	4: 6	For G, who said, "Let light shine out	2536
	4: 6	the knowledge of the glory of G in the face	2536
	4: 7	that this all-surpassing power is from G and	2536
	4:15	to overflow to the glory of G.	2536
	5: 1	we have a building from G,	2536
	5: 5	Now it is G who has made us	2536
	5:11	What we are is plain to G,	2536
	5:13	out of our mind, it is for the sake of G;	2536
	5:18	All this is from G, who reconciled us	2536
	5:19	that G was reconciling the world to himself	2536
	5:20	G were making his appeal through us.	2536
	5:20	Be reconciled to G.	2536
	5:21	G made him who had no sin to be sin	NIG
	5:21	we might become the righteousness of G.	2536
	6: 4	of G we commend ourselves in every way:	2536
	6: 7	in truthful speech and in the power of G;	2536
	6:16	between the temple of G and idols?	2536
	6:16	For we are the temple of the living G.	2536
	6:16	As G has said: "I will live with them	2536
	6:16	and I will be their G,	2536
	7: 1	perfecting holiness out of reverence for G.	2536
	7: 6	But G, who comforts the downcast,	2536
	7: 9	For you became sorrowful as G intended	2536

2Co	7:12	that before G you could see for yourselves	2536
	8: 1	that G has given the Macedonian churches.	2536
	8:16	I thank G, who put into the heart of Titus	2536
	9: 7	for G loves a cheerful giver.	2536
	9: 8	G is able to make all grace abound to you,	2536
	9:11	generosity will result in thanksgiving to G.	2536
	9:12	in many expressions of thanks to G.	2536
	9:13	men will praise G for the obedience	2536
	9:14	of the surpassing grace G has given you.	2536
	9:15	Thanks be to G for his indescribable gift!	2536
	10: 5	sets itself up against the knowledge of G,	2536
	10:13	to the field G has assigned to us,	2536
	11: 7	by preaching the gospel of G to you free	2536
	11:11	G knows I do!	2536
	11:31	The G and Father of the Lord Jesus,	2536
	12: 2	I do not know—G knows.	2536
	12: 3	the body I do not know, but G knows—	2536
	12:19	We have been speaking in the sight of G	2536
	12:21	when I come again my G will humble me	2536
	13: 7	to G that you will not do anything wrong.	2536
	13:11	the G of love and peace will be with you.	2536
	13:14	and the love of G,	2536
Gal	1: 1	but by Jesus Christ and G the Father,	2536
	1: 3	Grace and peace to you from G our Father	2536
	1: 4	according to the will of our G and Father,	2536
	1:10	to win the approval of men, or of G?	2536
	1:13	how intensely I persecuted the church of G	2536
	1:15	But when G, who set me apart from birth	2536
	1:20	I assure you before G that what I	2536
	1:24	And they praised G because of me.	2536
	2: 6	G does not judge by external appearance—	2536
	2: 8	For G, who was at work in the ministry	3836S
	2:19	to the law so that I might live for G.	2536
	2:20	I live by faith in the Son of G,	2536
	2:21	I do not set aside the grace of G,	2536
	3: 5	Does G give you his Spirit and work	3836S
	3: 6	Consider Abraham: "He believed G,	2536
	3: 8	The Scripture foresaw that G would justify	2536
	3:11	Clearly no one is justified before G by	2536
	3:17	the covenant previously established by G	2536
	3:18	but in his grace gave it to Abraham	2536
	3:20	but G is one.	2536
	3:21	therefore, opposed to the promises of G?	2536
	3:26	You are all sons of G through faith	2536
	4: 4	the time had fully come, G sent his Son,	2536
	4: 6	G sent the Spirit of his Son into our hearts,	2536
	4: 7	you are a son, G has made you also an heir.	2536
	4: 8	Formerly, when you did not know G,	2536
	4: 9	But now that you know G—	2536
	4: 9	or rather are known by G—	2536
	4:14	as if I were an angel of G,	2536
	5:21	like this will not inherit the kingdom of G.	2536
	6: 7	Do not be deceived: G cannot be mocked.	2536
	6:16	even to the Israel of G.	2536
Eph	1: 1	an apostle of Christ Jesus by the will of G,	2536
	1: 2	Grace and peace to you from G our Father	2536
	1: 3	the G and Father of our Lord Jesus Christ,	2536
	1:17	that the G of our Lord Jesus Christ,	2536
	1:22	And G placed all things under his feet	NIG
	2: 4	But because of his great love for us, G,	2536
	2: 6	And G raised us up with Christ	NIG
	2: 8	this not from yourselves, it is the gift of G—	2536
	2:10	which G prepared in advance for us to do.	2536
	2:12	without hope and without G in the world.	117
	2:16	to reconcile both of them to G through	2536
	2:22	a dwelling in which G lives by his Spirit.	2536
	3: 9	which for ages past was kept hidden in G,	2536
	3:10	of G should be made known to the rulers	2536
	3:12	in him we may approach G with freedom	NIG
	3:19	to the measure of all the fullness of G.	2536
	4: 6	one G and Father of all,	2536
	4:13	and in the knowledge of the Son of G	2536
	4:18	and separated from the life of G because of	2536
	4:24	like G in true righteousness and holiness.	2536
	4:30	And do not grieve the Holy Spirit of G,	2536
	4:32	just as in Christ G forgave you.	2536
	5: 1	Be imitators of G, therefore,	2536
	5: 2	as a fragrant offering and sacrifice to G.	2536
	5: 5	in the kingdom of Christ and of G.	2536
	5:20	always giving thanks to G the Father	2536
	6: 6	doing the will of G from your heart.	2536
	6:11	of G so that you can take your stand	2536
	6:13	Therefore put on the full armor of G,	2536
	6:17	which is the word of G.	2536
	6:23	and love with faith from G the Father and	2536
Php	1: 2	Grace and peace to you from G our Father	2536
	1: 3	I thank my G every time I remember you.	2536
	1: 8	G can testify how I long for all of you with	2536
	1:11	to the glory and praise of G.	2536
	1:14	to speak the word of G more courageously	2536
	1:28	that you will be saved—and that by G.	2536
	2: 6	Who, being in very nature G,	2536
	2: 6	did not consider equality with G something	2536
	2: 9	Therefore G exalted him to the highest	2536
	2:11	to the glory of G the Father.	2536
	2:13	for it is G who works in you to will and	2536
	2:15	children of G without fault in a crooked	2536
	2:27	But G had mercy on him,	2536
	3: 3	we who worship by the Spirit of G,	2536
	3: 9	the righteousness that comes from G and is	2536
	3:14	for which G has called me heavenward	2536
	3:15	that too G will make clear to you.	2536
	3:19	their g is their stomach,	2536
	4: 6	present your requests to G.	2536
	4: 7	And the peace of G,	2536
	4: 9	And the G of peace will be with you.	2536
	4:18	an acceptable sacrifice, pleasing to G.	2536

Php	4:19	And my G will meet all your needs	2536
	4:20	To our G and Father be glory for ever	2536
Col	1: 1	an apostle of Christ Jesus by the will of G,	2536
	1: 2	Grace and peace to you from G our Father.	2536
	1: 3	We always thank G, the Father of our Lord	2536
	1: 9	not stopped praying for you and asking G	NIG
	1:10	growing in the knowledge of G,	2536
	1:15	He is the image of the invisible G,	2536
	1:19	For G was pleased to have all his fullness	NIG
	1:21	from G and were enemies in your minds	NIG
	1:25	by the commission G gave me to present	2536
	1:25	to you the word of G in its fullness—	2536
	1:27	To them G has chosen to make known	2536
	2: 2	that they may know the mystery of G,	2536
	2:12	through your faith in the power of G,	2536
	2:13	G made you alive with Christ.	NIG
	2:19	grows as G causes it to grow.	2536
	3: 1	Christ is seated at the right hand of G.	2536
	3: 3	your life is now hidden with Christ in G.	2536
	3: 6	of these, the wrath of G is coming.	2536
	3:16	with gratitude in your hearts to G.	2536
	3:17	giving thanks to G the Father through him.	2536
	4: 3	that G may open a door for our message,	2536
	4:11	fellow workers for the kingdom of G,	2536
	4:12	you may stand firm in all the will of G.	2536
1Th	1: 1	in G the Father and the Lord Jesus Christ:	2536
	1: 2	We always thank G for all of you,	2536
	1: 3	We continually remember before our G	2536
	1: 4	For we know, brothers loved by G,	2536
	1: 8	in G has become known everywhere.	2536
	1: 9	They tell how you turned to G from idols	2536
	1: 9	from idols to serve the living and true G,	2536
	2: 2	of our G we dared to tell you his gospel	2536
	2: 4	as men approved by G to be entrusted with	2536
	2: 4	We are not trying to please men but G,	2536
	2: 5	G is our witness.	2536
	2: 8	to share with you not only the gospel of G	2536
	2: 9	while we preached the gospel of G to you.	2536
	2:10	You are witnesses, and so is G,	2536
	2:12	and urging you to live lives worthy of G,	2536
	2:13	And we also thank G continually because,	2536
	2:13	when you received the word of G,	2536
	2:13	but as it actually is, the word of G,	2536
	2:15	They displease G and are hostile to all men	2536
	2:16	The wrath of G has come upon them	2536
	3: 9	How can we thank G enough for you	2536
	3: 9	in the presence of our G because of you?	2536
	3:11	Now may our G and Father himself	2536
	3:13	in the presence of our G and Father	2536
	4: 1	how to live in order to please G,	2536
	4: 5	who do not know G;	2536
	4: 7	For G did not call us to be impure,	2536
	4: 8	not reject man but G,	2536
	4: 9	for you yourselves have been taught by G	2531
	4:14	and so we believe that G will bring	2536
	4:16	and with the trumpet call of G,	2536
	5: 9	For G did not appoint us to suffer wrath but	2536
	5:23	May G himself, the God of peace,	NIG
	5:23	May God himself, the G of peace,	2536
2Th	1: 1	in G our Father and the Lord Jesus Christ:	2536
	1: 2	Grace and peace to you from G the Father	2536
	1: 3	We ought always to thank G for you,	2536
	1: 5	be counted worthy of the kingdom of G,	2536
	1: 6	G is just: He will pay back trouble to those	2536
	1: 8	He will punish those who do not know G	2536
	1:11	our G may count you worthy of his calling,	2536
	1:12	according to the grace of our G and	2536
	2: 4	that is called G or is worshiped,	2536
	2: 4	proclaiming himself to be G.	2536
	2:11	For this reason G sends them	2536
	2:13	But we ought always to thank G for you,	2536
	2:13	because from the beginning G chose you to	2536
	2:16	and G our Father, who loved us	2536
1Ti	1: 1	by the command of G our Savior and	2536
	1: 2	Grace, mercy and peace from G the Father	2536
	1:11	to the glorious gospel of the blessed G,	2536
	1:17	immortal, invisible, the only G,	2536
	2: 3	This is good, and pleases G our Savior,	2536
	2: 5	For there is one G and one mediator	2536
	2: 5	and one mediator between G and men,	2536
	2:10	for women who profess to worship G.	2537
	3:15	which is the church of the living G,	2536
	4: 3	which G created to be received	2536
	4: 4	For everything G created is good,	2536
	4: 5	because it is consecrated by the word of G	2536
	4:10	that we have put our hope in the living G,	2536
	5: 4	for this is pleasing to G.	2536
	5: 5	in need and left all alone puts her hope in G	2536
	5: 5	to pray and to ask G for help.	4666
	5:21	of G and Christ Jesus and the elect angels,	2536
	6:11	But you, man of G, flee from all this,	2536
	6:13	In the sight of G, who gives life	2536
	6:15	which G will bring about in his own time—	NIG
	6:15	G, the blessed and only Ruler,	NIG
	6:17	but to put their hope in G,	2536
2Ti	1: 1	an apostle of Christ Jesus by the will of G,	2536
	1: 2	Grace, mercy and peace from G the Father	2536
	1: 3	I thank G, whom I serve,	2536
	1: 6	to fan into flame the gift of G,	2536
	1: 7	For G did not give us a spirit of timidity,	2536
	1: 8	by the power of G,	2536
	2:14	before G against quarreling about words;	2536
	2:15	to present yourself to G as one approved,	2536
	2:25	will grant them repentance leading to	2536
	3: 4	lovers of pleasure rather than lovers of G—	5806
	3:17	the man of G may be thoroughly equipped	2536
	4: 1	In the presence of G and of Christ Jesus,	2536

Ref	Text	Num
Tit 1:1	servant of G and an apostle of Jesus Christ	2536
1:2	which G, who does not lie,	2536
1:3	to me by the command of G our Savior,	2536
1:4	Grace and peace from G the Father	2536
1:16	They claim to know G,	2536
2:5	so that no one will malign the word of G.	2536
2:10	the teaching about G our Savior attractive.	2536
2:11	of G that brings salvation has appeared	2536
2:13	the glorious appearing of our great G	2536
2:13	and love of G our Savior appeared,	2536
3:8	in G may be careful to devote themselves	2536
Phm 1:3	Grace to you and peace from G our Father	2536
1:4	I always thank my G as I remember you	2536
Heb 1:1	the past G spoke to our forefathers through	2536
1:5	For to which of the angels did G ever say,	NIG
1:6	when G brings his firstborn into the world,	NIG
1:8	about the Son he says, "Your throne, O G,	2536
1:9	therefore G, your God, has set you above	2536
1:9	therefore God, your G, has set you above	2536
1:13	To which of the angels did G ever say,	NIG
2:4	G also testified to it by signs,	2536
2:8	G left nothing that is not subject to him.	NIG
2:9	that by the grace of G he might taste death	2536
2:10	it was fitting that G,	899S
2:13	and the children G has given me."	2536
2:17	and faithful high priest in service to G,	2536
3:4	but G is the builder of everything.	2536
3:12	that turns away from the living G.	2536
3:18	And to whom did G swear	NIG
4:3	enter that rest, just as G has said,	NIG
4:4	"And on the seventh day G rested	2536
4:7	Therefore G again set a certain day,	NIG
4:8	G would not have spoken later	NIG
4:9	then, a Sabbath-rest for the people of G;	2536
4:10	just as G did from his.	2536
4:12	For the word of G is living and active.	2536
4:14	Jesus the Son of G,	2536
5:1	to represent men in matters related to G,	2536
5:4	he must be called by G, just as Aaron was.	2536
5:5	But G said to him, "You are my Son;	3836S
5:10	and was designated by G to be high priest	2536
6:1	and of faith in G,	2536
6:3	And G permitting, we will do so.	2536
6:5	of G and the powers of the coming age,	2536
6:6	of G all over again and subjecting him	2536
6:7	receives the blessing of G.	2536
6:10	G is not unjust; he will not forget	2536
6:13	When G made his promise to Abraham,	2536
6:17	Because G wanted to make	2536
6:18	G did this so that,	NIG
6:18	in which it is impossible for G to lie,	2536
7:1	king of Salem and priest of G Most High.	2536
7:3	the Son of G he remains a priest forever.	2536
7:19	by which we draw near to G.	2536
7:21	a priest with an oath when G said to him:	NIG
7:25	to save completely those who come to G	2536
8:8	But G found fault with the people and said:	NIG
8:10	I will be their G, and they will be my	2536
9:14	to G, cleanse our consciences from acts	2536
9:14	so that we may serve the living G!	2536
9:20	which G has commanded you to keep."	2536
10:7	I have come to do your will, O G.'"	2536
10:12	he sat down at the right hand of G,	2536
10:21	we have a great priest over the house of G,	2536
10:22	to G with a sincere heart in full assurance	NIG
10:27	that will consume the enemies of G.	NIG
10:29	trampled the Son of G under foot,	2536
10:31	to fall into the hands of the living G.	2536
10:36	so that when you have done the will of G,	2536
11:3	By faith Abel offered G a better sacrifice	2536
11:4	when G spoke well of his offerings.	2536
11:5	because G had taken him away.	2536
11:5	he was commended as one who pleased G.	2536
11:6	without faith it is impossible to please G,	NIG
11:10	whose architect and builder is G.	2536
11:16	G is not ashamed to be called their God,	2536
11:16	God is not ashamed to be called their G,	2536
11:17	By faith Abraham, when G tested him,	NIG
11:18	even though G had said to him,	NIG
11:19	Abraham reasoned that G could raise	2536
11:25	with the people of G rather than to enjoy	2536
11:40	G had planned something better for us so	2536
12:2	down at the right hand of the throne of G.	2536
12:7	G is treating you as sons.	2536
12:10	but G disciplines us for our good,	3836S
12:15	the grace of G and that no bitter root grows	2536
12:22	heavenly Jerusalem, the city of the living G.	2536
12:23	You have come to G, the judge of all men,	2536
12:28	so worship G acceptably with reverence	2536
12:29	for our "G is a consuming fire."	2536
13:4	for G will judge the adulterer and all	2536
13:5	G has said, "Never will I leave you;	899S
13:7	who spoke the word of G to you.	2536
13:15	let us continually offer to G a sacrifice	2536
13:16	for with such sacrifices G is pleased.	2536
13:20	May the G of peace,	2536
Jas 1:1	servant of G and of the Lord Jesus Christ,	2536
1:5	he should ask G,	2536
1:12	that G has promised to those who love him.	NIG
1:13	no one should say, "G is tempting me."	2536
1:13	For G cannot be tempted by evil,	2536
1:20	about the righteous life that G desires.	2536
1:27	Religion that G our Father accepts as pure	2536
2:5	Has not G chosen those who are poor in	2536
2:19	You believe that there is one G.	2536
2:23	"Abraham believed G, and it was credited	2536
4:2	You do not have, because you do not ask G.	NIG
Jas 4:4	with the world is hatred toward G?	2536
4:4	of the world becomes an enemy of G.	2536
4:6	"G opposes the proud but gives grace to	2536
4:7	Submit yourselves, then, to G.	2536
4:8	near to G and he will come near to you.	2536
1Pe 1:2	to the foreknowledge of G the Father,	2536
1:3	the G and Father of our Lord Jesus Christ!	2536
1:21	Through him you believe in G,	2536
1:21	and so your faith and hope are in G.	2536
1:23	through the living and enduring word of G.	2536
2:4	but chosen by G and precious to him—	2536
2:5	offering spiritual sacrifices acceptable to G	2536
2:9	a holy nation, a people belonging to G,	NIG
2:10	but now you are the people of G;	2536
2:12	and glorify G on the day he visits us.	2536
2:16	live as servants of G.	2536
2:17	Love the brotherhood of believers, fear G,	2536
2:19	because he is conscious of G.	2536
2:20	this is commendable before G.	2536
3:5	of the past who put their hope in G used	2536
3:18	to bring you to G.	2536
3:20	when G waited patiently in the days	2536
3:21	the pledge of a good conscience toward G.	2536
4:2	but rather for the will of G.	2536
4:6	live according to G in regard to the spirit.	2536
4:11	as one speaking the very words of G.	2536
4:11	with the strength G provides,	2536
4:11	so that in all things G may be praised	2536
4:14	the Spirit of glory and of G rests on you.	2536
4:16	but praise G that you bear that name.	2536
4:17	to begin with the family of G;	2536
4:17	not obey the gospel of G?	2536
5:2	you are willing, as G wants you to be;	2536
5:5	"G opposes the proud but gives grace to	2536
5:10	And the G of all grace,	2536
5:12	that this is the true grace of G.	2536
2Pe 1:1	through the righteousness of our G	2536
1:2	the knowledge of G and of Jesus our Lord.	2536
1:17	For he received honor and glory from G	2536
1:21	but men spoke from G as they were carried	2536
2:4	if G did not spare angels when they sinned,	2536
3:12	to the day of G and speed its coming.	2536
3:15	with the wisdom that G gave him.	NIG
1Jn 1:5	G is light; in him there is no darkness at all.	2536
2:14	and the word of G lives in you,	2536
2:17	man who does the will of G lives forever.	2536
3:1	that we should be called children of G!	2536
3:2	Dear friends, now we are children of G,	2536
3:8	The reason the Son of G appeared was	2536
3:9	No one who is born of G will continue	2536
3:9	because he has been born of G.	2536
3:10	the children of G are and who the children	2536
3:10	not do what is right is not a child of G;	2536
3:17	how can the love of G be in him?	2536
3:20	For G is greater than our hearts,	2536
3:21	we have confidence before G	2536
4:1	the spirits to see whether they are from G,	2536
4:2	how you can recognize the Spirit of G:	2536
4:2	Jesus Christ has come in the flesh is from G	2536
4:3	not acknowledge Jesus is not from G.	2536
4:4	are from G and have overcome them,	2536
4:6	We are from G, and whoever knows God	2536
4:6	and whoever knows G listens to us;	2536
4:6	whoever is not from G does not listen to us.	2536
4:7	for love comes from G.	2536
4:7	Everyone who loves has been born of G	2536
4:7	has been born of God and knows G.	2536
4:8	Whoever does not love does not know G,	2536
4:8	because G is love.	2536
4:9	This is how G showed his love among us:	2536
4:10	This is love: not that we loved G,	2536
4:11	Dear friends, since G so loved us,	2536
4:12	No one has ever seen G;	2536
4:12	G lives in us and his love is made complete	2536
4:15	that Jesus is the Son of G,	2536
4:15	G lives in him and he in God.	2536
4:15	God lives in him and he in G.	2536
4:16	we know and rely on the love G has for us.	2536
4:16	G is love.	2536
4:16	Whoever lives in love lives in G,	2536
4:16	and G in him.	2536
4:20	If anyone says, "I love G,"	2536
4:20	cannot love G, whom he has not seen.	2536
4:21	Whoever loves G must also love	2536
5:1	that Jesus is the Christ is born of G,	2536
5:2	that we love the children of G,	2536
5:2	by loving G and carrying out his	2536
5:3	This is love for G: to obey his commands.	2536
5:4	everyone born of G overcomes the world.	2536
5:5	that Jesus is the Son of G.	2536
5:9	because it is the testimony of G,	2536
5:10	of G has this testimony in his heart.	2536
5:10	not believe G has made him out to be a liar,	2536
5:10	the testimony G has given about his Son.	2536
5:11	G has given us eternal life,	2536
5:12	not have the Son of G does not have life.	2536
5:13	of the Son of G so that you may know	2536
5:14	the confidence we have in approaching G:	899S
5:16	he should pray and G will give him life.	NIG
5:18	anyone born of G does not continue to sin;	2536
5:18	the one who was born of G keeps him safe,	2536
5:19	We know that we are children of G,	2536
5:20	We know also that the Son of G has come	2536
5:20	He is the true G and eternal life.	2536
2Jn 1:3	from G the Father and from Jesus Christ,	2536
1:9	in the teaching of Christ does not have G;	2536
3Jn 1:6	on their way in a manner worthy of G.	2536
3Jn 1:11	Anyone who does what is good is from G.	2536
1:11	Anyone who does what is evil has not seen G.	2536
Jude 1:1	by G the Father and kept by Jesus Christ:	2536
1:4	of our G into a license for immorality	2536
1:25	to the only G our Savior be glory,	2536
Rev 1:1	revelation of Jesus Christ, which G gave	2536
1:2	that is, the word of G and the testimony	2536
1:6	to be a kingdom and priests to serve his G	2536
1:8	says the Lord G, "who is, and who was,	2536
1:9	the word of G and the testimony of Jesus.	2536
2:7	which is in the paradise of G.	2536
2:18	These are the words of the Son of G,	2536
3:1	the seven spirits of G and the seven stars.	2536
3:2	your deeds complete in the sight of my G.	2536
3:12	a pillar in the temple of my G.	2536
3:12	the name of my G and the name of the city	2536
3:12	and the name of the city of my G,	2536
3:12	down out of heaven from my G;	2536
4:5	These are the seven spirits of G.	2536
4:8	"Holy, holy, holy is the Lord G Almighty,	2536
4:11	"You are worthy, our Lord and G,	2536
5:6	which are the seven spirits of G sent out	2536
5:9	with your blood you purchased men for G	2536
5:10	to be a kingdom and priests to serve our G,	2536
6:9	because of the word of G and	2536
7:2	having the seal of the living G.	2536
7:3	on the foreheads of the servants of our G."	2536
7:10	"Salvation belongs to our G,	2536
7:11	before the throne and worshiped G,	2536
7:12	and strength be to our G for ever and ever.	2536
7:15	before the throne of G and serve him day	2536
7:17	And G will wipe away every tear	2536
8:2	I saw the seven angels who stand before G,	2536
8:4	went up before G from the angel's hand.	2536
9:4	not have the seal of G on their foreheads.	2536
9:13	of the golden altar that is before G.	2536
10:7	the mystery of G will be accomplished,	2536
11:1	and measure the temple of G and the altar,	2536
11:11	a breath of life from G entered them,	2536
11:13	and gave glory to the G of heaven.	2536
11:16	who were seated on their thrones before G,	2536
11:16	fell on their faces and worshiped G,	2536
11:17	"We give thanks to you, Lord G Almighty,	2536
12:5	And her child was snatched up to G and	2536
12:6	the desert to a place prepared for her by G,	2536
12:10	and the power and the kingdom of our G,	2536
12:10	who accuses them before our G day	2536
13:6	He opened his mouth to blaspheme G,	2536
14:4	among men and offered as firstfruits to G	2536
14:7	"Fear G and give him glory,	2536
15:2	They held harps given them by G	2536
15:3	the servant of G and the song of the Lamb:	2536
15:3	and marvelous are your deeds, Lord G Almighty.	2536
15:7	golden bowls filled with the wrath of G,	2536
15:8	from the glory of G and from his power,	2536
16:7	"Yes, Lord G Almighty,	2536
16:9	and they cursed the name of G,	2536
16:11	the G of heaven because of their pains	2536
16:14	the battle on the great day of G Almighty.	2536
16:19	G remembered Babylon the Great	2536
16:21	And they cursed G on account of	2536
17:17	For G has put it into their hearts	2536
18:5	and G has remembered her crimes.	2536
18:8	for mighty is the Lord G who judges her.	2536
18:20	G has judged her for the way she treated	2536
19:1	and glory and power belong to our G,	2536
19:4	fell down and worshiped G,	2536
19:5	"Praise our G, all you his servants,	2536
19:6	For our Lord G Almighty reigns.	2536
19:9	he added, "These are the true words of G."	2536
19:10	to the testimony of Jesus. Worship G!	2536
19:13	and his name is the Word of G.	2536
19:15	of the fury of the wrath of G Almighty.	2536
19:17	gather together for the great supper of G,	2536
20:4	for Jesus and because of the word of G.	2536
20:6	be priests of G and of Christ and will reign	2536
21:2	coming down out of heaven from G,	2536
21:3	"Now the dwelling of G is with men,	2536
21:3	and G himself will be with them and	2536
21:3	be with them and be their G.	2536
21:7	and I will be his G and he will be my son.	2536
21:10	coming down out of heaven from G.	2536
21:11	It shone with the glory of G,	2536
21:22	because the Lord G Almighty and	2536
21:23	for the glory of G gives it light,	2536
22:1	from the throne of G and of the Lamb	2536
22:3	The throne of G and of the Lamb will be in	2536
22:5	for the Lord G will give them light.	2536
22:6	the G of the spirits of the prophets,	2536
22:9	keeps the words of this book. Worship G!"	2536
22:18	G will add to him the plagues described	2536
22:19	G will take away from him his share in	2536

GOD'S (207) [GOD]

Ref	Text	Num
Ge 6:11	Now the earth was corrupt in G sight	466
28:22	up as a pillar will be G house,	466
Ex 18:15	the people come to me to seek G will.	466
18:16	and inform them of G decrees and laws."	466
Dt 21:23	on a tree is under G curse.	466
1Sa 5:11	G hand was very heavy upon it.	466
14:45	for he did this today with G help."	466
2Sa 9:3	of Saul to whom I can show G kindness?"	466
1Ch 5:22	because the battle was G.	466+4946
2Ch 1:3	for G Tent of Meeting was there,	466

2Ch	4:19	the furnishings that were in G temple:	466
	5: 1	in the treasuries of G temple.	466
	20:15	For the battle is not yours, but G.	466+4200
	24:18	G anger came upon Judah and Jerusalem.	NIH
	31:21	the service of G temple and in obedience to	466
	32:12	Hezekiah himself remove this g high places	2257S
	33: 7	and put it in G temple,	466
	35: 8	the administrators of G temple,	466
	35:22	at G command but went to fight him on	466
	36:13	who had made him take an oath in G name.	466
	36:16	But they mocked G messengers,	466
	36:19	They set fire to G temple and broke down	466
Ne	13:25	I made them take an oath in G name	466
Job	6: 4	G terrors are marshaled against me.	468
	9:34	someone to remove G rod from me,	2257S
	13: 7	Will you speak wickedly on G behalf?	446
	15: 8	Do you listen in on G council?	468
	15:11	Are G consolations not enough for you,	468
	15:30	the breath of G mouth will carry him away.	2257S
	20:28	rushing waters on the day of G wrath.	2257S
	29: 4	intimate friendship blessed my house,	468
	33:26	he sees G face and shouts for joy;	2257S
	36: 2	that there is more to be said in G behalf.	468
	37: 5	G voice thunders in marvelous ways;	446
	37:14	stop and consider G wonders.	446
	38:33	Can you set up [G] dominion over	2257S
	40: 9	Do you have an arm like G,	446
Ps	52: 8	I trust in G unfailing love for ever and ever.	466
	61: 7	be enthroned in G presence forever;	466
	63:11	all who swear by G name will praise him,	2257S
	69:30	I will praise G name in song	466
	78:10	they did not keep G covenant and refused	466
	78:31	G anger rose against them;	466
	114: 2	Judah became G sanctuary,	2257S
Ecc	9: 1	the wise and what they do are in G hands,	466
Mt	5:34	either by heaven, for it is G throne;	2536
	22:21	and to God what is G."	2536
	23:22	by G throne and by the one who sits on it.	2536
Mk	3:35	Whoever does G will is my brother	2536
	12:17	and to God what is G."	2536
Lk	3: 6	And all mankind will see G salvation.' "	2536
	7:29	acknowledged that G way was right,	2536
	7:30	the law rejected G purpose for themselves,	2536
	8:21	and brothers are those who hear G word	2536
	16:15	among men is detestable in G sight.	2536
	19:44	not recognize the time of G coming	NIG
	20:25	and to God what is G."	2536
	20:36	They are G children,	2536
Jn	3:18	in the name of G one and only Son.	2536
	3:36	for G wrath remains on him."	2536
	7:17	If anyone chooses to do G will,	899S
	10:36	blasphemy because I said, 'I am G Son'?	2536
	11: 4	it is for G glory so that God's Son may	2536
	11: 4	so that G Son may be glorified through it."	2536
Ac	2:23	by G set purpose and foreknowledge;	2536
	4:19	for yourselves whether it is right in G sight	2536
	6: 8	Stephen, a man full of G grace and power,	NIG
	7:46	who enjoyed G favor and asked	2536
	13:36	"For when David had served G purpose	2536
	17:29	"Therefore since we are G offspring,	2536
	18:21	"I will come back if it is G will."	2536
	20:24	task of testifying to the gospel of G grace.	2536
	23: 4	"You dare to insult G high priest?"	2536
	26:22	But I have had G help to this very day,	2536
	28:28	to know that G salvation has been sent to	2536
Ro	1:10	by G will the way may be opened for me	2536
	1:20	of the world G invisible qualities—	899S
	1:32	Although they know G righteous decree	2536
	2: 2	Now we know that G judgment	2536
	2: 3	do you think you will escape G judgment?	2536
	2: 4	not realizing that G kindness leads you	2536
	2: 5	against yourself for the day of G wrath,	2536
	2:13	it is not those who hear the law who are righteous in G sight,	2536+3836+4123
	2:24	"G name is blasphemed among	2536
	3: 3	of faith nullify G faithfulness?	2536
	3: 5	But if our unrighteousness brings out G righteousness more clearly,	2536
	3: 7	"If my falsehood enhances G truthfulness	2536
	5: 9	be saved from G wrath through him!	NIG
	5:10	For if, when we were G enemies,	NIG
	5:15	how much more did G grace and the gift	2536
	5:17	much more will those who receive G abundant provision of grace	NIG
	7:22	For in my inner being I delight in G law;	2536
	7:25	I myself in my mind am a slave to G law,	2536
	8: 7	It does not submit to G law,	2536
	8:16	with our spirit that we are G children.	2536
	8:27	for the saints in accordance with G will.	2536
	9: 6	It is not as though G word had failed.	2536
	9: 8	not the natural children who are G children,	2536
	9:11	G purpose in election might stand;	2536
	9:16	man's desire or effort, but on G mercy.	2536
	10: 3	they did not submit to G righteousness.	2536
	11: 4	And what was G answer to him?	5977
	11:29	for G gifts and his call are irrevocable.	2536
	11:31	now receive mercy as a result of G mercy	NIG
	12: 1	I urge you, brothers, in view of G mercy,	2536
	12: 2	to test and approve what G will is—	2536
	12:13	Share with G people who are in need.	41
	12:19	my friends, but leave room for G wrath,	3836S
	13: 4	For he is G servant to do you good.	2536
	13: 4	He is G servant, an agent of wrath	2536
	13: 6	for the authorities are G servants,	2536
	14:10	we will all stand before G judgment seat.	2536
	15: 8	a servant of the Jews on behalf of G truth,	2536
	15:32	that by G will I may come to you with joy	2536

1Co	2: 5	not rest on man's wisdom, but on G power.	2536
	2: 7	No, we speak of G secret wisdom,	2536
	3: 9	For we are G fellow workers;	2536
	3: 9	you are G field, God's building.	2536
	3: 9	you are God's field, G building.	2536
	3:16	that you yourselves are G temple and	2536
	3:16	and that G Spirit lives in you?	2536
	3:17	If anyone destroys G temple,	2536
	3:17	G temple is sacred, and you are that temple.	2536
	3:19	the wisdom of this world is foolishness in G sight.	2536+4123
	7:19	Keeping G commands is what counts.	2536
	9:21	(though I am not free from G law	2536
	11:19	to show which of you have G approval.	NIG
	16: 1	Now about the collection for G people:	41
2Co	1:12	but according to G grace.	2536
	4: 1	through G mercy we have this ministry,	NIG
	6: 1	As G fellow workers we urge you not	NIG
	6: 1	not to receive G grace in vain.	2536
	6: 2	I tell you, now is the time of G favor,	NIG
	8: 5	and then to us in keeping with G will.	2536
	9:12	not only supplying the needs of G people	41
	13: 4	yet he lives by G power.	2536
	13: 4	yet by G power we will live with him	2536
Eph	1: 7	in accordance with the riches of G grace	899S
	1:14	of those who are G possession—	NIG
	2:10	For we are G workmanship,	899S
	2:19	but fellow citizens with G people	41
	2:19	and members of G household,	2536
	3: 2	of G grace that was given to me for you,	2536
	3: 7	the Spirit to G holy apostles and prophets.	899S
	3: 7	of G grace given me through the working	2536
	3: 8	I am less than the least of all G people,	41
	4:12	to prepare G people for works of service,	41
	5: 3	these are improper for G holy people.	41
	5: 6	for because of such things G wrath comes	2536
Php	1: 7	all of you share in G grace with me.	NIG
Col	1: 6	and understood G grace in all its truth.	2536
	3:12	Therefore, as G chosen people,	2536
1Th	2:14	became imitators of G churches in Judea,	2536
	3: 2	who is our brother and G fellow worker	2536
	4: 3	It is G will that you should be sanctified:	2536
	5:18	for this is G will for you in Christ Jesus.	2536
2Th	1: 4	among G churches we boast	2536
	1: 5	that G judgment is right,	2536
	2: 4	so that he sets himself up in G temple,	2536
	2:16	May the Lord direct your hearts into G love	2536
1Ti	1: 4	These promote controversies rather than G work—	2536
	3: 5	how can he take care of G church?)	2536
	3:15	to conduct themselves in G household,	2536
	6: 1	so that G name and our teaching may not	2536
2Ti	2: 9	But G word is not chained.	2536
	2:19	G solid foundation stands firm,	2536
Tit	1: 1	of Jesus Christ for the faith of G elect and	2536
	1: 7	Since an overseer is entrusted with G work,	NIG
Heb	1: 3	of G glory and the exact representation	NIG
	1: 6	he says, "Let all G angels worship him."	2536
	3: 2	just as Moses was faithful in all G house.	899S
	3: 5	as a servant in all G house,	899S
	3: 6	But Christ is faithful as a son over G house.	899S
	4:10	for anyone who enters G rest also rests	899S
	4:13	from G sight Everything is uncovered	899S
	5:12	the elementary truths of G word all	2536
	9:24	now to appear for us in G presence.	2536
	11: 3	the universe was formed at G command,	2536
	13:24	Greet all your leaders and all G people.	41
Jas	2:23	and he was called G friend.	2536
	3: 9	who have been made in G likeness.	2536
1Pe	1: 1	an apostle of Jesus Christ, To G elect,	NIG
	1: 5	who through faith are shielded by G power until	2536
	2:15	For it is G will that by doing good	2536
	3: 4	which is of great worth in G sight.	2536
	3:17	It is better, if it is G will, to suffer for	2536
	3:22	into heaven and is at G right hand—	2536
	4:10	faithfully administering G grace	2536
	4:19	to G will should commit themselves	2536
	5: 2	of G flock that is under your care, serving	2536
	5: 6	therefore, under G mighty hand,	2536
2Pe	3: 5	by G word the heavens existed and	2536
1Jn	2: 5	G love is truly made complete in him.	2536
	3: 9	because G seed remains in him;	899S
	5: 9	but G testimony is greater because it is	2536
Jude	1:21	Keep yourselves in G love as you wait for	2536
Rev	3:14	faithful witness, the ruler of G creation.	2536
	11:19	Then G temple in heaven was opened,	2536
	12:17	those who obey G commandments	2536
	14:10	too, will drink of the wine of G fury,	2536
	14:12	of the saints who obey G commandments	2536
	14:19	into the great winepress of G wrath.	2536
	15: 1	because with them G wrath is completed.	2536
	16: 1	the seven bowls of G wrath on the earth."	2536
	17:17	until G words are fulfilled.	2536
	20: 9	and surrounded the camp of G people,	41
	22:21	The grace of the Lord Jesus be with G people.	41

GOD-BREATHED (1) [GOD, BREATH]

2Ti	3:16	All Scripture is G and is useful	2535

GOD-FEARING (8) [GOD, FEAR]

Ecc	8:12	I know that it will go better with G men,	466+2021+3710
Ac	2: 5	in Jerusalem G Jews from every nation	2327
	10: 2	his family were devout and G;	2536+3836+5828

Ac	10:22	He is a righteous and G man,	2536+3836+5828
	13:26	"Brothers, children of Abraham, and you G Gentiles,	2536+3836+5828
	13:50	the G women of high standing and	4936
	17: 4	as did a large number of G Greeks and not	4936
	17:17	with the Jews and the G Greeks,	4936

GOD-HATERS (1) [GOD, HATE]

Ro	1:30	G, insolent, arrogant and boastful;	2539

GOD-WARD (KJV) See BEFORE GOD, IN GOD

GODDESS (6) [GOD]

1Ki	11: 5	followed Ashtoreth the g of the Sidonians,	466
	11:33	worshiped Ashtoreth the g of the Sidonians,	466
2Ki	23:13	of Israel had built for Ashtoreth the vile g	9199
Ac	19:27	that the temple of the great g Artemis will	2516
	19:27	and the g herself, who is worshiped	NIG
	19:37	nor blasphemed our g.	2536

GODHEAD (KJV) See DEITY, DIVINE BEING, DIVINE NATURE

GODLESS (16) [GOD]

Job	8:13	so perishes the hope of the g.	2868
	13:16	for no g man would dare come before him!	2868
	15:34	For the company of the g will be barren,	2868
	20: 5	the joy of the g lasts but a moment.	2868
	27: 8	For what hope has the g when he is cut off,	2868
	34:30	to keep a g man from ruling,	2868
	36:13	"The g in heart harbor resentment;	2868
Pr	11: 9	With his mouth the g destroys his neighbor,	2868
Isa	10: 6	I send him against a g nation,	2868
	33:14	trembling grips the g;	2868
Jer	23:11	"Both prophet and priest are g;	2866
1Ti	4: 7	to do with g myths and old wives' tales;	1013
	6:20	from g chatter and the opposing ideas	1013
2Ti	2:16	Avoid g chatter, because those who indulge	1013
Heb	12:16	or is g like Esau, who for a single meal	1013
Jude	1: 4	They are g men, who change the grace of	815

GODLESSNESS (2) [GOD]

Ro	1:18	the g and wickedness of men who suppress	813
	11:26	he will turn g away from Jacob.	813

GODLINESS (12) [GOD]

Ac	3:12	or g we had made this man walk?	2354
1Ti	2: 2	and quiet lives in all g and holiness.	2354
	3:16	the mystery of g is great:	2354
	4: 8	but g has value for all things,	2354
	6: 5	of the truth and who think that g is a means	2354
	6: 6	But g with contentment is great gain.	2354
	6:11	g, faith, love, endurance and gentleness.	2354
2Ti	3: 5	having a form of g but denying its power.	2354
Tit	1: 1	the knowledge of the truth that leads to g—	2354
2Pe	1: 3	for life and g through our knowledge	2354
	1: 6	and to perseverance, g;	2354
	1: 7	and to g, brotherly kindness;	2354

GODLY (16) [GOD]

Ps	4: 3	the LORD has set apart the g for himself;	2883
	12: 1	Help, LORD, for the g are no more;	2883
	32: 6	Therefore let everyone who is g pray to you	2883
Mic	7: 2	The g have been swept from the land;	2883
Mal	2:15	Because he was seeking g offspring.	2883
Jn	9:31	He listens to the g man who does his will.	2538
Ac	8: 2	G men buried Stephen and mourned deeply	2327
2Co	7:10	G sorrow brings repentance that leads	2536+2848
	7:11	See what this g sorrow has produced	2536+2848
	11: 2	I am jealous for you with a g jealousy.	2536
1Ti	4: 7	rather, train yourself to be g.	2354
	6: 3	of our Lord Jesus Christ and to g teaching,	2354
2Ti	3:12	a life in Christ Jesus will be persecuted,	2357
Tit	2:12	upright and g lives in this present age,	2357
2Pe	2: 9	how to rescue g men from trials and to hold	2356
	3:11	You ought to live holy and g lives	2354

GODS (271) [GOD]

Ge	31:19	Rachel stole her father's household g.	9572
	31:30	But why did you steal my g?"	466
	31:32	But if you find anyone who has your g,	466
	31:32	not know that Rachel had stolen the g	4392S
	31:34	Now Rachel had taken the household g	9572
	31:35	but could not find the household g	9572
	35: 2	of the foreign g you have with you,	466
	35: 4	the foreign g they had and the rings	466
Ex	12:12	I will bring judgment on all the g of Egypt.	466
	15:11	"Who among the g is like you, O LORD?	446
	18:11	that the LORD is greater than all other g,	446
	20: 3	"You shall have no other g before me.	466
	20:23	Do not make any g to be alongside me;	NIH
	20:23	not make for yourselves g of silver or gods	466
	20:23	not make for yourselves gods of silver or g	466
	23:13	Do not invoke the names of other g;	466
	23:24	down before their g or worship them	466
	23:32	a covenant with them or with their g.	466
	23:33	of their g will certainly be a snare to you."	466
	32: 1	"Come, make us g who will go before us.	466
	32: 4	Then they said, "These are your g, O Israel,	466

Ex	32: 8	'These are your **g**, O Israel,	466
	32:23	'Make us **g** who will go before us.	466
	32:31	They have made themselves **g** of gold.	466
	34:15	when they prostitute themselves to their **g**	466
	34:16	to their **g**, they will lead your sons to do	466
Lev	19: 4	not turn to idols or make **g** of cast metal	466
Nu	25: 2	to the sacrifices to their **g**.	466
	25: 2	and bowed down before these **g**.	466
	33: 4	LORD had brought judgment on their **g**.	466
Dt	4: 7	as to have their **g** near them the way	466
	4:28	There you will worship man-made **g**	466
	5: 7	"You shall have no other **g** before me.	466
	6:14	Do not follow their **g**,	466
	6:14	the **g** of the peoples around you;	466
	7: 4	from following me to serve other **g**,	466
	7:16	on them with pity and do not serve their **g**,	466
	7:25	images of their **g** you are to burn in the fire.	466
	8:19	the LORD your God and follow other **g**	466
	10:17	the LORD your God is God of **g** and Lord	466
	11:16	to turn away and worship other **g** and bow	466
	11:28	by following other **g**,	466
	12: 2	you are dispossessing worship their **g**.	466
	12: 3	of their **g** and wipe out their names	466
	12:30	to be ensnared by inquiring about their **g**,	466
	12:30	"How do these nations serve their **g**?	466
	12:31	because in worshiping their **g**,	466
	12:31	in the fire as sacrifices to their **g**.	466
	13: 2	"Let us follow other **g**" (gods you have	466
	13: 2	"Let us follow other gods" ("g you have	4392S
	13: 6	and worship other **g**" (gods that neither you	466
	13: 6	and worship other gods" (**g** that neither you	NIH
	13: 7	**g** of the peoples around you,	466
	13:13	and worship other **g**" (gods you have	466
	13:13	and worship other gods" ("g you have	889S
	17: 3	to my command has worshiped other **g**,	466
	18:20	prophet who speaks in the name of other **g**,	466
	20:18	in worshiping their **g**,	466
	28:14	following other **g** and serving them.	466
	28:36	There you will worship other **g**,	466
	28:36	**g** of wood and stone.	NIH
	28:64	There you will worship other **g**—	466
	28:64	**g** of wood and stone,	NIH
	29:18	to go and worship the **g** of those nations;	466
	29:26	and worshiped other **g** and bowed down	466
	29:26	**g** they did not know,	466
	29:26	**g** he had not given them.	NIH
	30:17	to bow down to other **g** and worship them,	466
	31:16	the foreign **g** of the land they are entering.	466
	31:18	in turning to other **g**.	466
	31:20	they will turn to other **g** and worship them,	466
	32:16	They made him jealous with their foreign **g**	NIH
	32:17	**g** they had not known,	466
	32:17	**g** that recently appeared,	NIH
	32:17	**g** your fathers did not fear.	4392S
	32:37	He will say: "Now where are their **g**,	466
	32:38	the **g** who ate the fat of their sacrifices	NIH
Jos	23: 7	do not invoke the names of their **g** or swear	466
	23:16	and serve other **g** and bow down to them,	466
	24: 2	beyond the River and worshiped other **g**.	466
	24:14	the **g** your forefathers worshiped beyond	466
	24:15	whether the **g** your forefathers served	466
	24:15	or the **g** of the Amorites,	466
	24:16	to forsake the LORD to serve other **g**!	466
	24:20	the LORD and serve foreign **g**,	466
	24:23	"throw away the foreign **g** that are	466
Jdg	2: 3	be [thorns] in your sides and their **g** will be	466
	2:12	They followed and worshiped various **g** of	466
	2:17	but prostituted themselves to other **g**	466
	2:19	following other **g** and serving	466
	3: 6	and served their **g**.	466
	5: 8	When they chose new **g**,	466
	6:10	do not worship the **g** of the Amorites,	466
	9: 9	by which both **g** and men are honored,	466
	9:13	which cheers both **g** and men,	466
	10: 6	and the **g** of Aram, the gods of Sidon,	466
	10: 6	and the gods of Aram, the **g** of Sidon,	466
	10: 6	the gods of Sidon, the **g** of Moab,	466
	10: 6	the **g** of the Ammonites and the gods of	466
	10: 6	the Ammonites and the **g** of the Philistines.	466
	10:13	you have forsaken me and served other **g**,	466
	10:14	Go and cry out to the **g** you have chosen.	466
	10:16	of the foreign **g** among them and served	466
	18:14	other **household g**, a carved image and	9572
	18:17	the other **household g** and the cast idol	9572
	18:18	the other **household g** and the cast idol,	9572
	18:20	the other **household g** and the carved image	9572
	18:24	He replied, "You took the **g** I made,	466
Ru	1:15	to her people and her **g**.	466
1Sa	4: 8	from the hand of these mighty **g**?	466
	4: 8	They are the **g** who struck the Egyptians	466
	6: 5	from you and your **g** and your land.	466
	7: 3	then rid yourselves of the foreign **g** and	466
	8: 8	forsaking me and serving other **g**,	466
	17:43	And the Philistine cursed David by his **g**.	466
	26:19	and have said, 'Go, serve other **g**.'	466
2Sa	7:23	by driving out nations and their **g** from	466
1Ki	9: 6	to serve other **g** and worship them,	466
	9: 9	and have embraced other **g**,	466
	11: 2	surely turn your hearts after their **g**."	466
	11: 4	his wives turned his heart after other **g**,	466
	11: 8	and offered sacrifices to their **g**.	466
	11:10	to follow other **g**,	466
	12:28	Here are your **g**, O Israel,	466
	14: 9	You have made for yourself other **g**,	466
	19: 2	"May the **g** deal with me,	466
	20:10	"May the **g** deal with me,	466
	20:23	"Their **g** are gods of the hills.	466

1Ki	20:23	"Their gods are **g** of the hills.	466
2Ki	17: 7	They worshiped other **g**	466
	17:29	each national group made its own **g** in	466
	17:31	and Anammelech, the **g** of Sepharvaim.	466
	17:33	also served their own **g** in accordance with	466
	17:35	"Do not worship any other **g** or bow down	466
	17:37	Do not worship other **g**.	466
	17:38	and do not worship other **g**.	466
	18:34	Where are the **g** of Hamath and Arpad?	466
	18:34	are the **g** of Sepharvaim, Hena and Ivvah?	466
	18:35	of all the **g** of these countries has been able	466
	19:12	the **g** of the nations that were destroyed	466
	19:12	the **g** of Gozan, Haran,	NIH
	19:18	They have thrown their **g** into the fire	466
	19:18	they were not **g** but only wood and stone,	466
	22:17	to other **g** and provoked me to anger by all	466
	23:24	the mediums and spiritists, the **household g**,	9572
1Ch	5:25	prostituted themselves to the **g** of	466
	10:10	They put his armor in the temple of their **g**	466
	14:12	The Philistines had abandoned their **g** there,	466
	16:25	he is to be feared above all **g**.	466
	16:26	For all the **g** of the nations are idols,	466
2Ch	2: 5	because our God is greater than all other **g**.	466
	7:19	to serve other **g** and worship them,	466
	7:22	and have embraced other **g**,	466
	13: 8	that Jeroboam made to be your **g**.	466
	13: 9	a priest of what are not **g**.	466
	25:14	he brought back the **g** of the people of Seir.	466
	25:14	He set them up as his own **g**,	466
	25:15	"Why do you consult this people's **g**,	466
	25:20	because they sought the **g** of Edom.	466
	28:23	He offered sacrifices to the **g** of Damascus,	466
	28:23	**g** of the kings of Aram have helped them,	466
	28:25	to burn sacrifices to other **g** and provoked	466
	32:13	Were the **g** of those nations ever able	466
	32:14	Who of all the **g** of these nations	466
	32:17	the **g** of the peoples of the other lands did	466
	32:19	as they did about the **g** of the other peoples	466
	33:15	the foreign **g** and removed the image from	466
	34:25	to other **g** and provoked me to anger by all	466
Ps	4: 2	and seek **false g**?	3942
	16: 4	of those will increase who run after **other g**.	337
	40: 4	to those who turn aside to **false g**.	3942
	82: 1	he gives judgment among the "g":	466
	82: 6	"I said, 'You are "g";	466
	86: 8	Among the **g** there is none like you,	466
	95: 3	the great King above all **g**.	466
	96: 4	he is to be feared above all **g**.	466
	96: 5	For all the **g** of the nations are idols,	466
	97: 7	worship him, all you **g**!	466
	97: 9	you are exalted far above all **g**.	466
	106:28	and ate sacrifices offered to lifeless **g**;	NIH
	135: 5	that our Lord is greater than all **g**.	466
	136: 2	Give thanks to the God of **g**.	466
	138: 1	before the "g" I will sing your praise.	466
Isa	21: 9	All the images of its **g** lie shattered on	466
	36:19	Where are the **g** of Hamath and Arpad?	466
	36:19	Where are the **g** of Sepharvaim?	466
	36:20	of all these countries has been able	466
	37:12	the **g** of the nations that were destroyed	466
	37:12	the **g** of Gozan, Haran,	NIH
	37:19	They have thrown their **g** into the fire	466
	37:19	they were not **g** but only wood and stone,	466
	41:23	so we may know that you are **g**.	466
	42:17	who say to images, 'You are our **g**,'	466
	45:20	who pray to **g** that cannot save.	446
Jer	1:16	in burning incense to other **g** and	466
	2:11	Has a nation ever changed its **g**?	466
	2:11	(Yet they are not **g** at all.)	466
	2:25	I love foreign **g**, and I must go after them.'	NIH
	2:28	then are the **g** you made for yourselves?	466
	2:28	For you have as many **g** as you have towns,	466
	3:13	you have scattered your favors to foreign **g**	NIH
	3:24	From our youth **shameful g** have consumed	1425
	5: 7	and sworn by **g** that are not gods.	NIH
	5: 7	and sworn by gods that are not **g**.	466
	5:19	and served foreign **g** in your own land,	466
	7: 6	not follow other **g** to your own harm,	466
	7: 9	and follow other **g** you have not known,	466
	7:18	They pour out drink offerings to other **g**	466
	10:11	"Tell them this: 'These **g**, who did not	10033
	11:10	They have followed other **g** to serve them.	466
	11:12	of Jerusalem will go and cry out to the **g**	466
	11:13	You have as many **g** as you have towns,	466
	13:10	of their hearts and go after other **g** to serve	466
	13:25	and trusted in **false g**.	9214
	16:11	'and followed other **g** and served	466
	16:13	there you will serve other **g** day and night,	466
	16:19	but **false g**, worthless idols	9214
	16:20	Do men make their own **g**?	466
	16:20	Yes, but they are not **g**!"	466
	19: 4	and made this a place of foreign **g**;	NIH
	19: 4	in it to **g** that neither they nor their fathers	466
	19:13	and poured out drink offerings to other **g**.' "	466
	22: 9	and have worshiped and served other **g**.' "	466
	25: 6	Do not follow other **g** to serve	466
	32:29	by pouring out drink offerings to other **g**.	466
	35:15	do not follow other **g** to serve them.	466
	43:12	He will set fire to the temples of the **g**	466
	43:12	and take **their g** captive.	4392S
	43:13	and will burn down the temples of the **g**	466
	44: 3	and by worshiping other **g** that neither they	466
	44: 5	or stop burning incense to other **g**.	466
	44: 8	burning incense to other **g** in Egypt,	466
	44:15	to other **g**, along with all	466
	46:25	on Egypt and her **g** and her kings,	466
	48:35	the high places and burn incense to their **g**,"	466

Da	2:11	can reveal it to the king except the **g**,	10033
	2:47	of **g** and the Lord of kings and a revealer	10033
	3:12	They neither serve your **g** nor worship	10033
	3:14	that you do not serve my **g** or worship	10033
	3:18	that we will not serve your **g** or worship	10033
	3:25	and the fourth looks like a son of the **g**."	10033
	4: 8	and the spirit of the holy **g** is in him.)	10033
	4: 9	I know that the spirit of the holy **g** is	10033
	4:18	because the spirit of the holy **g** is in you."	10033
	5: 4	they praised the **g** of gold and silver,	10033
	5:11	the spirit of the holy **g** in him.	10033
	5:11	and wisdom like that of the **g**.	10033
	5:14	I have heard that the spirit of the **g** is in you	10033
	5:23	You praised the **g** of silver and gold,	10033
	11: 8	He will also seize their **g**,	466
	11:36	against the God of **g**.	446
	11:37	the **g** of his fathers or for the one desired	466
Hos	3: 1	to other **g** and love the sacred raisin cakes."	466
	14: 3	We will never again say 'Our **g**'	466
Am	2: 4	they have been led astray by **false g**,	3942
	2: 4	the **g** their ancestors followed,	889S
Mic	4: 5	in the name of their **g**;	466
Na	1:14	that are in the temple of your **g**.	466
Zep	1: 9	who fill the temple of their **g** with violence	123
	2:11	when he destroys all the **g** of the land.	466
Jn	10:34	'I have said you are "g"?	2536
	10:35	If he called them 'g,'	2536
Ac	7:40	'Make us **g** who will go before us.	2536
	14:11	"The **g** have come down to us	2536
	17:18	"He seems to be advocating foreign **g**."	1228
	19:26	He says that man-made **g** are no gods at all.	3836S
	19:26	He says that man-made gods are no **g** at all.	2536
	28:11	the **twin g Castor and Pollux.**	1483
1Co	8: 5	For even if there are so-called **g**,	2536
	8: 5	or on earth (as indeed there are many "g"	2536
Gal	4: 8	to those who by nature are not **g**.	2536

GOES (96) [GO]

Ge	40:14	But when **all g** well with you,	3512
Ex	7:15	Go to Pharaoh in the morning *as he* **g** out	3655
	8:20	the morning and confront Pharaoh as he **g**	3655
	12:23	the LORD **g** through the land to strike	6296
Lev	14:36	to be emptied before he **g** in to examine	995
	14:46	"Anyone *who* **g** into the house	995
	16:17	the time Aaron **g** in to make atonement in	995
	22: 7	When the sun **g** down, he will be clean,	995
Nu	1:51	Anyone else who **g** near it shall be put	7929
	5:12	'If a man's wife **g** astray and is unfaithful	8474
	5:29	the law of jealousy when a woman **g** astray	8474
	35:26	if the accused **ever g outside** the limits of	
		the city of refuge	3655+3655
Dt	9: 3	the *one who* **g across** ahead of you like	6296
	16: 6	when the sun **g** down,	995
	20: 4	For the LORD your God is the *one who* **g**	2143
	31: 6	for the LORD your God **g** with you;	2143
	31: 8	The LORD himself **g** before you and will	2143
Jos	2:19	If anyone **g** outside your house into	3655
Jdg	21:19	of the road that **g** from Bethel to Shechem,	6590
1Sa		If *it* **g** up to its own territory,	6590
	9:13	before *he* **g** up to the high place to eat.	6590
	23:22	Find out where David *usually* **g**	2118+8079
	24:13	As the old saying **g**,	606
	25:25	his name is Fool, and folly **g** with him.	NIH
2Ki	11: 8	Stay close to the king **wherever he g**."	
			928+928+995+2256+3655
2Ch	23: 7	Stay close to the king **wherever he g**."	
			928+928+995+2256+3655
Ne	9:37	its abundant harvest **g** to the kings	NIH
Job	7: 9	he who **g down** *to* the grave does not return.	3718
	9:11	when *he* **g** by, I cannot perceive him.	2736
	18: 6	the lamp beside him **g** out.	1980
	21:33	and a countless throng **g** before him.	NIH
	22:14	as *he* **g about** in the vaulted heavens.'	2143
	24:18	so that no *one* **g** to the vineyards.	7155
	41:22	dismay **g** before him.	1881
Ps	19: 4	Their voice **g** out into all the earth,	3655
	39: 6	Man is a mere phantom *as he* **g to and fro**:	2143
	41: 6	then *he* **g** out and spreads it abroad.	3655
	85:13	Righteousness **g** before him and prepares	2143
	97: 3	Fire **g** before him and consumes his foes	2143
	104:23	Then man **g** out to his work,	3655
	126: 6	He who **g** out weeping,	2143+2143
Pr	6:12	*who* **g about** with a corrupt mouth,	2143
	11:19	but he who pursues evil **g** to his death.	NIH
	13:25	but the stomach of the wicked **g hungry**.	2893
	16:18	Pride **g** before destruction,	NIH
	19:15	and the shiftless man **g hungry**.	8279
	20:14	**off** *he* **g** and boasts about his purchase.	261
	22:10	Drive out the mocker, and **out g** strife;	3655
	23:31	when *it* **g down** smoothly!	2143
	26:20	Without wood a fire **g** out;	3882
	29: 9	If a wise man **g** to court with a fool,	9149
Ecc	1: 6	round and round *it* **g**,	2143
	3:21	and if the spirit of the animal **g down** into	
		the earth?"	3718+4200+4752
	8:17	No one can comprehend what **g** on under	6913
	12: 5	Then man **g** to his eternal home	2143
Isa	15: 2	Dibon **g** up to its temple,	6590
	16:12	*she* **g** to her shrine to pray, it is to no avail.	995
	47:15	Each of them **g** on in his error;	6298
	55:11	so is my word that **g** out from my mouth:	3655
	66: 7	"Before *she* **g into labor**, she gives birth;	2655
Jer	6:29	but *the* **refining g** on in vain;	7671+7671
	14: 2	and a cry **g up** from Jerusalem.	6590
	21: 9	But whoever **g out** and surrenders to	3655
	38: 2	or plague, but whoever **g over** to	3655

Eze	14: 4	before his face and then **g** to a prophet,	995
	14: 7	and then **g** to a prophet to inquire of me,	995
	44:27	On the day he **g** into the inner court of	995
	47: 8	toward the eastern region and **g down** into	3718
Mic	5: 8	which mauls and mangles as it **g**,	6296
Mt	8: 9	I tell this one, 'Go,' and he **g**;	4513
	12:43	it **g through** arid places seeking rest	1451
	12:45	Then it **g** and takes with it	4513
	15:11	What **g into** a man's mouth does	1656
	15:17	the mouth into the stomach and then out	6003
Mk	9:43	where the fire **never g out**.	812
Lk	7: 8	I tell this one, 'Go,' and he **g**;	4513
	11: 5	and he **g** to him at midnight and says,	4513
	11:24	it **g through** arid places seeking rest	1451
	11:26	Then it **g** and takes seven other spirits more	4513
	15: 6	and home. Then he calls his friends	2262
	16:30	'but if someone from the dead **g** to them,	4513
	19:37	near the **place where the road g down**	2853
Jn	5: 7	someone else **g down** ahead of me."	2849
	10: 4	he **g** on ahead of them,	4513
	5: 5	Spirit of truth who **g out** from the Father,	1744
Ac	8:26	that **g down** from Jerusalem to Gaza."	2849
1Co	6: 6	one brother **g** to law against another—	3212
	9:25	in the games **g into** strict **training.**	1603
	11:21	each of you **g** ahead without waiting	4624
Col	2:18	**g into** great detail about what he has	1836
Jas	1:11	even while he **g about his business.**	4512
	1:24	and, after looking at himself, **g away**	599
2Pe	2: 2	that is washed **g** back to her wallowing in	NIG
	3: 4	everything **g** on as it has since	1373
Rev	14: 4	They follow the Lamb wherever he **g.**	5632
	19: 3	The smoke from her **g up** for ever	326

GOG (12)

1Ch	5: 4	Shemaiah his son, **G** his son,	1573
Eze	38: 2	set your face against **G,**	1573
	38: 3	I am against you, O **G,**	1573
	38:14	son of man, prophesy and say to **G:**	1573
	38:16	In days to come, O **G,**	1573
	38:18	When **G** attacks the land of Israel,	1573
	38:21	a sword against **G** on all my mountains,	2257S
	39: 1	"Son of man, prophesy against **G** and say:	1573
	39: 1	I am against you, O **G,**	1573
	39:11	" 'On that day I will give **G** a burial place	1573
	39:11	**G** and all his hordes will be buried there.	1573
Rev	20: 8	**G** and Magog—to gather them for battle.	1223

GOIIM (2)

Ge	14: 1	of Elam and Tidal king of **G**	1582
	14: 9	Tidal king of **G,** Amraphel king of Shinar	1582

GOING (309) [GO]

Ge	6:13	"I am **g** to put an end to all people,	AIT
	6:13	surely **g** to **destroy** both them and the earth.	AIT
	6:17	I am **g** to **bring** floodwaters on the earth	AIT
	7:16	The animals **g in** were male and female	995
	16: 8	and where are you **g?**"	2143
	19:13	because we are **g** to **destroy** this place.	AIT
	32:17	and where are you **g**,	2143
	37:13	Come, I am **g** to **send** you to them."	AIT
	48: 4	**g** to make you **fruitful.**	AIT
Ex	10: 8	"But just who will be **g?**"	2143
	19: 9	"I am **g** to **come** to you in a dense cloud,	AIT
	34:12	in the land where you are **g.**	995
Lev	18:24	how the nations that I am **g** to **drive out**	AIT
	20:23	the nations I am **g** to **drive out** before you.	AIT
	23:10	the land I am **g** to **give** you	AIT
	25: 2	you enter the land I am **g** to **give** you,	AIT
Nu	10:30	I am **g** back to my own land	2143
	11:15	If this is how you are **g** to **treat** me,	AIT
	15:39	not prostitute yourselves by **g** after the lusts	9365
	16:34	The earth is **g** to **swallow** us too!"	AIT
	17:13	Are we all **g** to **die?**"	AIT
	22: 4	"This horde is **g** to lick up everything	6964
	24:14	Now I am **g** back to my people, but come,	2143
	32: 7	the Israelites from **g over** into the land	6296
Dt	1:30	LORD your God, who is **g** before you,	2143
	3:21	**over** there where you are **g.**	6296
	3:27	since you are not **g** to **cross** this Jordan.	AIT
	9: 4	**g** to **drive** them **out**	AIT
	9: 5	that you are **g in** to take possession	995
	20: 3	"Hear, O Israel, today you are **g** into battle	7929
	29:19	even though I persist in **g** my own way."	2143
	31:16	"You are **g** to **rest** with your fathers,	AIT
	33:18	"Rejoice, Zebulun, in your **g out**, and you,	3655
Jos	6: 9	with the armed guard **g** ahead of the ark of	6296
	8:21	and that smoke was **g up** from the city,	6590
	10:10	the road **g up** to Beth Horon and cut them	5090
	10:13	in the middle of the sky and delayed **g down**	995
	10:25	to all the enemies you are **g** to **fight.**"	AIT
	19:11	**G** west it ran to Maralah,	4200
	22:33	about **g** to war against them to devastate	6590
Jdg	4: 9	because of the way you are **g** about this,	2143
	6:23	You are not **g** to **die.**"	AIT
	6:31	**g** to **plead** Baal's **cause?**	AIT
	7: 9	because I am **g** to **give** it into your hands.	AIT
	11: 2	not **g** to **get** any **inheritance**	AIT
	12: 1	We're **g** to **burn down** your house	AIT
	13: 3	but you are **g** to **conceive** and have a son.	AIT
	15: 1	He said, "I'm **g** to my wife's room."	995
	18: 9	**Aren't** you **g** to **do something?**	AIT
	19:17	the old man asked, "Where are you **g?**	2143
	19:18	and now I am **g** to the house of the LORD.	2143
	20:40	and saw the smoke of the whole city **g up**	6590
Ru	1:11	Am I **g** to have any more sons,	NIH

Ru	1:15	"your sister-in-law is **g** back to her people	8740
1Sa	9:11	As they were **g up** the hill to the town,	6590
	9:27	they were **g down** to the edge of the town,	3718
	10: 3	Three men **g up** to God at Bethel	6590
	12: 7	**g** to **confront** you **with evidence**	AIT
	17:20	He reached the camp as the army was **g out**	3655
	17:55	As Saul watched David **g out** to meet	3655
	20: 2	"You are not **g** to **die!**	AIT
	23: 4	for I am **g** to **give** the Philistines	AIT
	23:26	Saul was **g** along one side of the mountain,	2143
	26:14	"Aren't you **g** to **answer** me, Abner?"	AIT
2Sa	11: 7	how the war was **g.**	4200+8934
	12:11	" 'Out of your own household I am **g** to **bring** calamity	AIT
	12:13	You are not **g** to **die.**	AIT
	14:18	the answer to what I am **g** to **ask** you."	AIT
	15:20	I do not know where I am **g?**	889+2143+2143+6584
	16:13	along the road while Shimei was **g** along	2143
	18: 9	while the mule he was riding kept on **g.**	6296
	18:14	"I'm not **g** to **wait** like this for you."	AIT
1Ki	11:29	that time Jeroboam was **g out** of Jerusalem,	3655
	11:31	'See, I am **g** to **tear** the kingdom out	AIT
	14:10	I am **g** to **bring** disaster on the house	AIT
	17:11	As she was **g** to get it, he called,	2143
	18: 6	Ahab **g** in one direction and Obadiah	2143
	20: 6	tomorrow I am **g** to **send** my officials	AIT
	21:21	'I am **g** to **bring** disaster on you.	AIT
	21:26	He behaved in the vilest manner by **g**	2143
	22:20	and **g** to his **death** there?'	5877
2Ki	1: 3	that you are **g off** to consult Baal-Zebub,	2143
	2: 3	that the LORD is **g** to **take** your master	AIT
	2: 5	that the LORD is **g** to **take** your master	AIT
	6: 9	because the Arameans are **g down** there."	5741
	10:19	I am **g** to hold a great sacrifice for Baal.	NIH
	11: 5	the three companies that are **g on** duty on	995
	11: 9	those who were **g on** duty on the Sabbath	995
	11: 9	the Sabbath and those who were **g off** duty	3655
	19: 7	I am **g** to **put** such a spirit in him that	AIT
	20: 1	because you are **g** to **die**;	AIT
	21:12	I am **g** to **bring** such disaster on Jerusalem	AIT
	22:16	I am **g** to **bring** disaster on this place	AIT
	22:20	the disaster I am **g** to **bring** on this place.' "	AIT
2Ch	2: 5	"The temple I am **g** to **build** will be great,	AIT
	18:19	and **g** to his **death** there?'	5877
	23: 4	you priests and Levites who are **g on** duty	995
	23: 8	those who were **g on** duty on the Sabbath	995
	23: 8	the Sabbath and those who were **g off** duty	3655
	34:24	I am **g** to **bring** disaster on this place	AIT
	34:28	the disaster I am **g** to **bring** on this place	AIT
Ne	3:15	as the steps **g down** from the City of David.	3718
	13: 6	But while all this was **g** on,	NIH
Job	1: 7	through the earth and **g back and forth**	2143
	2: 2	through the earth and **g back and forth**	2143
	33:24	'Spare him from **g down** to the pit;	3718
	33:28	He redeemed my soul from **g down** to	6296
Ps	30: 3	you spared me from **g down** into the pit.	3718
	30: 9	in my **g down** into the pit?	3718
	121: 8	over your coming and **g** both now	3655
	139: 3	You discern my **g out** and my lying down;	782
	144:14	no **g into** captivity,	3448
Pr	7: 8	He was **g down** the street near her corner,	6296
	7:22	All at once he followed her like an ox as **g**	995
	15:24	for the wise to keep him from **g down** to	4752
	22: 3	but the simple keep **g** and suffer for it.	6296
	27:12	but the simple keep **g** and suffer for it.	6296
Ecc	9:10	for in the grave, where you are **g**,	2143
Isa	5: 5	Now I will tell you what I am **g** to **do**	AIT
	20: 2	he did so, **g** around stripped and barefoot.	2143
	24: 1	the LORD is **g** to **lay waste** the earth	AIT
	37: 7	I am **g** to **put** a spirit in him so that	AIT
	38: 1	because you are **g** to **die**;	AIT
	41:22	to tell us what is **g** to **happen.**	AIT
	58:13	and if you honor it by not **g** your own way	6913
Jer	6:28	hardened rebels, **g about** to slander.	2143
	13:13	I am **g** to **fill** with drunkenness all who	AIT
	19: 3	I am **g** to **bring** a disaster on this place	AIT
	19:15	I am **g** to **bring** on this city and the villages	AIT
	28:16	This very year you are **g** to **die**;	AIT
	32: 7	of Shallum your uncle is **g** to **come** to you	AIT
	34:22	**g** to **give** the order,	AIT
	35:17	I am **g** to **bring** on Judah and	AIT
	38:14	"I am **g** to **ask** you something,"	AIT
	44:30	'I am **g** to **hand** Pharaoh Hophra king of Egypt **over**	AIT
Eze	9: 8	Are you **g** to **destroy** the entire remnant	AIT
	11: 5	but I know what is **g through** your mind.	5091
	12:23	I am **g** to **put an end** to this proverb	AIT
	13:11	with whitewash that it is **g** to **fall.**	AIT
	16:37	therefore I am **g** to **gather** all your lovers,	AIT
	21: 3	Because I am **g** to **cut off** the righteous	AIT
	25: 4	therefore I am **g** to **give** you to the people of	AIT
	26: 7	From the north I am **g** to **bring**	AIT
	28: 7	I am **g** to **bring** foreigners against you,	AIT
	29:19	I am **g** to **give** Egypt to Nebuchadnezzar	AIT
	36:22	that I am **g** to **do** these things,	AIT
	37: 1	I am **g** to **open** your graves and bring you up from them;	AIT
	37:19	I am **g** to **take** the stick of Joseph—	AIT
	40: 4	to everything I am **g** to **show** you,	AIT
	44:25	not defile himself by **g** near a dead person;	995
	46:10	**g in** when they go in and going out	995
	46:10	going in when they go in and **g out**	3655
Da	2:29	revealer of mysteries showed you what is **g** to **happen.**	AIT
	8:19	"I am **g** to **tell** you what will happen later	AIT
Hos	2:14	"Therefore I am now **g** to **allure** her;	AIT

Joel	2:20	with its front columns **g** into the eastern sea	NIH
	3: 7	I am **g** to **rouse** them out of the places	AIT
Hab	1: 5	For I am **g** to **do** something in your days	AIT
Zec	2: 2	I asked, "Where are you **g?**"	2143
	3: 8	I am **g** to **bring** my servant, the Branch.	AIT
	5: 3	the curse will **g** out over the whole land;	3655
	6: 5	**g out** from standing in the presence of	3655
	6: 6	The one with the black horses is **g** toward	3655
	6: 8	Then he called to me, "Look, those **g**	3655
	8:21	I myself am **g.**'	2143
	11:16	For I am **g** to **raise up** a shepherd over	AIT
	12: 2	"I am **g** to **make** Jerusalem a cup	AIT
	12: 8	the Angel of the LORD **g** before them.	NIH
Mal	3:14	and **g** about like mourners before	2143
Mt	2:13	for Herod is **g** to **search** for the child	3516
	4:21	**G** on from there, he saw two other brothers,	4581
	8:25	We're **g** to **drown!**"	AIT
	9:32	While they were **g out**,	2002
	10:23	you will not finish **g** through the cities	NIG
	12: 9	**G** on from that place,	3553
	16:27	of Man is **g** to **come** in his Father's glory	3516
	17:12	In the same way the Son of Man is **g** to	3516
	17:22	of Man is **g** to be betrayed into the hands	3516
	20: 8	the last ones hired and **g** on to the first.'	2401
	20:17	Now as Jesus was **g up** to Jerusalem,	326
	20:18	"We are **g up** to Jerusalem,	326
	20:22	"Can you drink the cup I am **g** to **drink?**"	3516
	20:30	and when they heard that Jesus was **g** by,	4135
	25: 8	our lamps are **g out.**'	4931
	25:14	it will be like a man **g** on a journey,	623
	26:18	I am **g** to **celebrate** the Passover	AIT
	26:39	**G** a little **farther,**	4601
	26:49	**G** at once to Jesus, Judas said, "Greetings,	4665
	26:62	"Are you not **g** to **answer?**	AIT
	27:32	As they were **g out**,	2002
	27:40	"You who are **g** to **destroy** the temple	AIT
	27:58	**G** to Pilate, he asked for Jesus' body,	4665
	28: 2	**g** to the tomb, rolled back the stone	4665
	28: 7	from the dead and is **g** ahead of you	4575
Mk	2:23	One Sabbath Jesus was **g** through	4182
	6:31	and **g** that they did not even have a chance	5632
	7:15	a man can make him 'unclean' by **g into**	1660
	9:31	of Man is **g** to be **betrayed** into the hands	AIT
	10:32	and told them what was **g** to happen	3516
	10:33	"We are **g up** to Jerusalem," he said,	326
	13:34	It's like a man **g away.**	624
	14:35	**G** a little **farther,**	4601
	14:45	**G** at once to Jesus, Judas said, "Rabbi!"	2262
	14:60	"Are you not **g** to **answer?**	646
	15: 4	"Aren't you **g** to **answer?**	646
	15:29	You who are **g** to **destroy** the temple	AIT
	16: 7	'He is **g** ahead of you into Galilee.	4575
Lk	1:36	Even Elizabeth your relative is **g** to **have**	AIT
	1:59	and they were **g** to **name** him	AIT
	1:66	asking, "What then is this child **g** to **be?**"	AIT
	6: 1	One Sabbath Jesus was **g** through	1388
	8:24	"Master, Master, we're **g** to **drown!**"	AIT
	9: 7	the tetrarch heard about all that was **g** on.	1181
	9:44	of Man is **g** to be betrayed into the hands	3516
	10:30	man was **g down** from Jerusalem to Jericho,	2849
	10:31	A priest happened to be **g down**	2849
	12:54	immediately you say, 'It's **g** to **rain**,'	2262+3915
	12:55	you say, 'It's **g** to be **hot**,' and it is.	AIT
	12:58	As you are **g** with your adversary to	5632
	13:23	are only a few people **g** to be **saved?**"	AIT
	13:33	I must keep **g** today and tomorrow and	4513
	15:26	and asked him what was **g** on.	323+4047+5515
	17:12	As he was **g into** a village,	1656
	18:31	"We are **g up** to Jerusalem,	326
	18:36	When he heard the crowd **g** by,	1388
	19:11	that the kingdom of God was **g** to **appear**	3516
	19:28	he went on ahead, **g up** to Jerusalem.	326
	22:21	of him who is **g** to **betray** me is with mine	AIT
	22:49	Jesus' followers saw what was **g** to **happen**,	AIT
	23:52	**G** to Pilate, he asked for Jesus' body.	4665
	24:13	of them were **g** to a village called Emmaus,	4513
	24:21	the one who was **g** to **redeem** Israel.	3516
	24:28	the village to which they were **g**,	4513
	24:28	Jesus acted as if he were **g** farther.	4513
	24:49	I am **g** to **send** you what my Father has promised;	AIT
Jn	2:20	and you are **g** to **raise** it in three days?"	AIT
	3: 8	where it comes from or where it is **g.**	5632
	3:26	he is baptizing, and everyone is **g** to him."	2262
	5:47	how are you **g** to **believe** what I say?"	AIT
	6: 6	for he already had in mind what he was **g** to	3516
	7: 8	I am not yet **g up** to this Feast,	326
	8:14	where I came from and where I am **g.**	5632
	8:14	where I come from or where I am **g.**	5632
	8:21	"I am **g** away, and you will look for me,	5632
	11: 8	and yet you are **g** back there?"	5632
	11:11	but I am **g** there to wake him up."	4513
	11:31	supposing she was **g** to the tomb	5632
	12:11	of him many of the Jews were **g over**	5632
	12:33	to show the kind of death he was **g** to die.	3516
	12:35	"You are **g** to **have** the light just a little	AIT
	12:35	in the dark does not know where he is **g.**	5632
	13: 6	"Lord, are you **g** to **wash** my feet?"	AIT
	13:11	For he knew who was **g** to **betray** him,	AIT
	13:21	one of you is **g** to **betray** me."	AIT
	13:33	Where I am **g**, you cannot come.	5632
	13:36	"Lord, where are you **g?**"	5632
	13:36	Jesus replied, "Where I am **g**,	5632
	14: 2	I am **g** there to prepare a place for you.	4513
	14: 4	the way to the place where I am **g.**"	5632
	14: 5	"Lord, we don't know where you are **g**,	5632
	14:12	because I am **g** to the Father.	4513

Jn	14:28	'I am g away and I am coming back	5632
	14:28	be glad that I am g to the Father,	4513
	16: 5	"Now I am g to him who sent me,	5632
	16: 5	'Where are you g?'	5632
	16: 7	It is for your good that I am g away.	599
	16:10	because I am g to the Father,	5632
	16:17	and 'Because I am g to the Father'?"	5632
	16:28	now I am leaving the world and g back to	4513
	18: 4	knowing all that was g to happen to him,	2262
	18:32	of death he was g to die would be fulfilled.	3516
	21: 3	"I'm g out to fish," Simon Peter told them,	5632
	21:20	"Lord, who is g to betray you?")	AIT
Ac	1: 6	at this time g to restore the kingdom	AIT
	1:10	up into the sky as he was g,	4513
	3: 1	One day Peter and John were g up to	326
	3: 2	to beg from those g into the temple courts.	1660
	4:16	"What are we g to do with these men?"	AIT
	8: 3	G from house to house,	1660
	11:12	to have no hesitation about g with them.	5302
	13:11	You are g to be blind,	AIT
	13:41	for I am g to do something in your days	AIT
	14:24	After g through Pisidia,	1451
	16:16	Once when we were g to the place of prayer,	4513
	17:23	as something unknown I am g to proclaim	AIT
	18:10	and no one is g to attack and harm you,	AIT
	20:13	where we were g to take Paul aboard.	3516
	20:13	because he was g there on foot.	3516
	20:22	I am g to Jerusalem,	4513
	22:26	"What are you g to do?"	3516
	25: 4	and I myself am g there soon.	1744
	26:12	of these journeys I was g to Damascus	4513
	27:10	that our voyage is g to be disastrous	3516
	27:30	pretending they were g to	3516
1Co	16: 5	for I will be g through Macedonia.	1451
2Co	10:14	We are not g too far in our boasting,	5657
Php	1:30	since you are g through	2400
1Ti	5:13	into the habit of being idle and g about	4320
Heb	3:10	'Their hearts are always g astray,	4414
	5: 2	and are g astray,	4414
	11: 8	though he did not know where he was g.	2262
Jas	2:12	as those who are g to be judged by the law	3516
1Pe	2:25	For you were like sheep g astray,	4414
	3:13	Who is g to harm you if you are eager	AIT
2Pe	2: 6	of what is g to happen to the ungodly;	3516
1Jn	2:11	he does not know where he is g,	5632
	2:19	but their g showed that none	NIG
Rev	3:10	that is g to come upon the whole world	3516
	17:11	to the seven and is g to his destruction.	5632

GOLAN (4)

Dt	4:43	and G in Bashan, for the Manassites.	1584
Jos	20: 8	and G in Bashan in the tribe of Manasseh.	1584
	21:27	of Manasseh, G in Bashan (a city of refuge	1584
1Ch	6:71	the half-tribe of Manasseh they received G	1584

GOLD (455) [GOLD-COVERED, GOLDEN, GOLDSMITH, GOLDSMITHS]

Ge	2:11	the entire land of Havilah, where there is g.	2298
	2:12	(The g of that land is good;	2298
	13: 2	in livestock and in silver and g.	2298
	24:22	the man took out a g nose ring weighing	2298
	24:22	and two g bracelets weighing ten shekels.	2298
	24:35	and g, menservants and maidservants,	2298
	24:53	the servant brought out g and silver jewelry	2298
	41:42	in robes of fine linen and put a g chain	2298
	44: 8	So why would we steal silver or g	2298
Ex	3:22	for articles of silver and g and for clothing.	2298
	11: 2	for articles of silver and g."	2298
	12:35	for articles of silver and g and for clothing.	2298
	20:23	for yourselves gods of silver or gods of g.	2298
	25: 3	g, silver and bronze;	2298
	25:11	Overlay it with pure g, both inside and out,	2298
	25:11	and make a g molding around it.	2298
	25:12	Cast four g rings for it and fasten them	2298
	25:13	of acacia wood and overlay them with g.	2298
	25:17	"Make an atonement cover of pure g—	2298
	25:18	of hammered g at the ends of the cover.	2298
	25:24	with pure g and make a gold molding	2298
	25:24	with pure gold and make a g molding	2298
	25:25	a handbreadth wide and put a g molding on	2298
	25:26	Make four g rings for the table	2298
	25:28	overlay them with g and carry the table	2298
	25:29	And make its plates and dishes of pure g,	2298
	25:31	a lampstand of pure g and hammer it out,	2298
	25:36	hammered out of pure g.	2298
	25:38	and trays are to be of pure g.	2298
	25:39	of pure g is to be used for the lampstand	2298
	26: 6	Then make fifty g clasps and use them	2298
	26:29	the frames with g and make gold rings	2298
	26:29	and make g rings to hold the crossbars.	2298
	26:29	Also overlay the crossbars with g.	2298
	26:32	Hang it with g hooks on four posts	2298
	26:32	with g and standing on four silver bases.	2298
	26:37	Make g hooks for this curtain	2298
	26:37	of acacia wood overlaid with g.	2298
	28: 5	Have them use g, and blue,	2298
	28: 6	"Make the ephod of g, and of blue,	2298
	28: 8	with the ephod and made with g,	2298
	28:11	Then mount the stones in g filigree settings	2298
	28:13	Make g filigree settings	2298
	28:14	and two braided chains of pure g,	2298
	28:15	of g, and of blue, purple and scarlet yarn,	2298
	28:20	Mount them in g filigree settings.	2298
	28:22	breastpiece make braided chains of pure g,	2298
	28:23	Make two g rings for it and fasten them	2298

Ex	28:24	the two g chains to the rings at the corners	2298
	28:26	Make two g rings and attach them to	2298
	28:27	Make two more g rings and attach them to	2298
	28:33	with g bells between them.	2298
	28:34	The g bells and the pomegranates are	2298
	28:36	"Make a plate of pure g and engrave on it	2298
	30: 3	and all the sides and the horns with pure g,	2298
	30: 3	and make a g molding around it.	2298
	30: 4	Make two g rings for the altar below	2298
	30: 5	of acacia wood and overlay them with g.	2298
	31: 4	to make artistic designs for work in g,	2298
	31: 8	the pure g lampstand and all its accessories,	NIH
	32: 2	"Take off the g earrings that your wives,	2298
	32:24	I told them, 'Whoever has any g jewelry,	2298
	32:24	Then they gave me the g,	NIH
	32:31	They have made themselves gods of g.	2298
	35: 5	to bring to the LORD an offering of g,	2298
	35:22	came and brought g jewelry of all kinds:	2298
	35:22	They all presented their g as	2298
	35:32	to make artistic designs for work in g,	2298
	36:13	Then they made fifty g clasps	2298
	36:34	the frames with g and made gold rings	2298
	36:34	and made g rings to hold the crossbars.	2298
	36:34	They also overlaid the crossbars with g.	2298
	36:36	for it and overlaid them with g.	2298
	36:36	They made g hooks for them	2298
	36:38	with g and made their five bases of bronze.	2298
	37: 2	He overlaid it with pure g,	2298
	37: 2	and made a g molding around it.	2298
	37: 3	He cast four g rings for it	2298
	37: 4	of acacia wood and overlaid them with g.	2298
	37: 6	He made the atonement cover of pure g—	2298
	37: 7	of hammered g at the ends of the cover.	2298
	37:11	Then they overlaid it with pure g and made	2298
	37:11	with pure gold and made a g molding	2298
	37:12	a handbreadth wide and put a g molding on	2298
	37:13	They cast four g rings for the table	2298
	37:15	of acacia wood and were overlaid with g.	2298
	37:16	And they made from pure g the articles for	2298
	37:17	of pure g and hammered it out, base	2298
	37:22	hammered out of pure g.	2298
	37:23	its wick trimmers and trays, of pure g.	2298
	37:24	from one talent of pure g.	2298
	37:26	and all the sides and the horns with pure g,	2298
	37:26	and made a g molding around it.	2298
	37:27	They made two g rings below	2298
	37:28	of acacia wood and overlaid them with g.	2298
	38:24	of the g from the wave offering used for all	2298
	39: 2	They made the ephod of g, and of blue,	2298
	39: 3	of g and cut strands to be worked into	2298
	39: 5	with the ephod and made with g,	2298
	39: 6	in g filigree settings and engraved them	2298
	39: 8	of g, and of blue, purple and scarlet yarn,	2298
	39:13	They were mounted in g filigree settings.	2298
	39:15	For the breastpiece they made braided chains of pure g,	2298
	39:16	They made two g filigree settings	2298
	39:16	and two g rings,	2298
	39:17	They fastened the two g chains to the rings	2298
	39:19	They made two g rings and attached them	2298
	39:20	Then they made two more g rings	2298
	39:25	of pure g and attached them around	2298
	39:30	out of pure g and engraved on it,	2298
	39:37	the pure g lampstand with its row of lamps	NIH
	39:38	the g altar, the anointing oil,	2298
	40: 5	the g altar of incense in front of the ark of	2298
	40:26	the g altar in the Tent of Meeting in front	2298
Lev	8: 9	on Aaron's head and set the g plate,	2298
	24: 4	The lamps on the pure g lampstand before	NIH
	24: 6	on the table of pure g before the LORD.	NIH
Nu	4:11	the g altar they are to spread a blue cloth	2298
	7:14	one g dish weighing ten shekels, filled	2298
	7:20	one g dish weighing ten shekels, filled	2298
	7:26	one g dish weighing ten shekels, filled	2298
	7:32	one g dish weighing ten shekels, filled	2298
	7:38	one g dish weighing ten shekels, filled	2298
	7:44	one g dish weighing ten shekels, filled	2298
	7:50	one g dish weighing ten shekels, filled	2298
	7:56	one g dish weighing ten shekels, filled	2298
	7:62	one g dish weighing ten shekels, filled	2298
	7:68	one g dish weighing ten shekels, filled	2298
	7:74	one g dish weighing ten shekels, filled	2298
	7:80	one g dish weighing ten shekels, filled	2298
	7:84	and twelve g dishes.	2298
	7:86	The twelve g dishes filled	2298
	7:86	the g dishes weighed a hundred	2298
	8: 4	It was made of hammered g—	2298
	22:18	gave me his palace filled with silver and g,	2298
	24:13	gave me his palace filled with silver and g,	2298
	31:22	G, silver, bronze, iron, tin, lead	2298
	31:50	the g articles each of us acquired—	2298
	31:51	the priest accepted from them the g—	2298
	31:52	the g from the commanders of thousands	2298
	31:54	Moses and Eleazar the priest accepted the g	2298
Dt	7:25	Do not covet the silver and g on them,	2298
	8:13	and your silver and g increase	2298
	17:17	large amounts of silver and g.	2298
	29:17	idols of wood and stone, of silver and g.	2298
Jos	6:19	the silver and g and the articles of bronze	2298
	6:24	but they put the silver and g and the articles	2298
	7:21	and a wedge of g weighing fifty shekels,	2298
	7:24	the g wedge, his sons and daughters,	2298
	22: 8	with large herds of livestock, with silver, g,	2298
Jdg	8:24	of the Ishmaelites to wear g earrings.)	2298
	8:26	The weight of the g earrings he asked	2298
	8:27	Gideon made the g into an ephod,	2257S
1Sa	6: 4	"Five g tumors and five gold rats,	2298

1Sa	6: 4	"Five gold tumors and five g rats,	2298
	6: 8	the g objects you are sending back to him	2298
	6:11	along with it the chest containing the g rats	2298
	6:15	with the chest containing the g objects,	2298
	6:17	These are the g tumors the Philistines sent	2298
	6:18	And the number of the g rats was according	2298
2Sa	1:24	garments with ornaments of g.	2298
	8: 7	the g shields that belonged to the officers	2298
	8:10	with him articles of silver and g	2298
	8:11	and g from all the nations he had subdued:	2298
	12:30	its weight was a talent of g,	2298
	21: 4	"We have no right to demand silver or g	2298
1Ki	6:20	He overlaid the inside with pure g,	2298
	6:21	the inside of the temple with pure g,	2298
	6:21	and he extended g chains across the front of	2298
	6:21	which was overlaid with g.	2298
	6:22	So he overlaid the whole interior with g.	2298
	6:22	also overlaid with g the altar that belonged	2298
	6:28	He overlaid the cherubim with g.	2298
	6:30	and outer rooms of the temple with g.	2298
	6:32	the cherubim and palm trees with beaten g.	2298
	6:35	and overlaid them with g hammered evenly	2298
	7:49	the lampstands of pure g (five on the right	2298
	7:49	the g floral work and lamps and tongs;	2298
	7:50	the pure g basins, wick trimmers,	2298
	7:50	and the g sockets for the doors of	2298
	7:51	the silver and g and the furnishings—	2298
	9:11	the cedar and pine and g he wanted.	2298
	9:14	Hiram had sent to the king 120 talents of g.	2298
	9:28	to Ophir and brought back 420 talents of g,	2298
	10: 2	large quantities of g, and precious stones—	2298
	10:10	And she gave the king 120 talents of g.	2298
	10:11	(Hiram's ships brought g from Ophir;	2298
	10:14	The weight of the g that Solomon	2298
	10:16	King Solomon made two hundred large shields of hammered g;	2298
	10:16	six hundred bekas of g went	2298
	10:17	of hammered g, with three minas of gold	2298
	10:17	with three minas of g in each shield.	2298
	10:18	with ivory and overlaid with fine g.	2298
	10:21	All King Solomon's goblets were g,	2298
	10:21	of the Forest of Lebanon were pure g.	2298
	10:22	carrying g, silver and ivory,	2298
	10:25	articles of silver and g, robes,	2298
	14:26	the g shields Solomon had made.	2298
	15:15	the LORD the silver and g and the articles	2298
	15:18	then took all the silver and g that was left	2298
	15:19	See, I am sending you a gift of silver and g.	2298
	20: 3	'Your silver and g are mine,	2298
	20: 5	'I sent to demand your silver and g,	2298
	20: 7	my silver and my g, I did not refuse him."	2298
	22:48	a fleet of trading ships to go to Ophir for g,	2298
2Ki	5: 5	six thousand shekels of g and ten sets	2298
	7: 8	g and clothes, and went off and hid them.	2298
	12:13	or silver for the temple of the LORD;	2298
	12:18	the g found in the treasuries of the temple	2298
	14:14	the g and silver and all the articles found in	2298
	16: 8	and g found in the temple of the LORD	2298
	18:14	of silver and thirty talents of g.	2298
	18:16	the g with which he had covered the doors	NIH
	20:13	silver, the g, the spices and the fine oil—	2298
	23:33	a hundred talents of silver and a talent of g.	2298
	23:35	the silver and g he demanded.	2298
	23:35	and g from the people of the land according	2298
	24:13	the g articles that Solomon king of Israel	2298
	25:15	all that were made of pure g or silver.	2298+2298
1Ch	18: 7	the g shields carried by the officers	2298
	18:10	Hadoram brought all kinds of articles of g	2298
	18:11	and g he had taken from all these nations:	2298
	20: 2	its weight was found to be a talent of g,	2298
	21:25	six hundred shekels of g for the site.	2298
	22:14	a hundred thousand talents of g,	2298
	22:16	in g and silver, bronze and iron—	2298
	28:14	the weight of g for all the gold articles to	2298
	28:14	the weight of gold for all the g articles to	2298
	28:15	the weight of g for the gold lampstands	2298
	28:15	for the g lampstands and their lamps, with	2298
	28:16	of g for each table for consecrated bread;	2298
	28:17	of pure g for the forks, sprinkling bowls	2298
	28:17	the weight of g for each gold dish;	2298
	28:17	the weight of gold for each g dish;	NIH
	28:18	and the weight of the refined g for the altar	2298
	28:18	the cherubim of g that spread their wings	2298
	29: 2	g for the gold work, silver for the silver,	2298
	29: 2	gold for the g work, silver for the silver,	2298
	29: 3	of g and silver for the temple of my God,	2298
	29: 4	three thousand talents of g (gold of Ophir)	2298
	29: 4	three thousand talents of gold (g of Ophir)	2298
	29: 5	for the g work and the silver work,	2298
	29: 7	and ten thousand darics of g,	2298
2Ch	1:15	and g as common in Jerusalem as stones,	2298
	2: 7	a man skilled to work in g and silver,	2298
	2:14	He is trained to work in g and silver,	2298
	3: 4	He overlaid the inside with pure g.	2298
	3: 5	with fine g and decorated it with palm tree	2298
	3: 6	And the g he used was gold of Parvaim.	2298
	3: 6	And the gold he used was g of Parvaim.	2298
	3: 7	walls and doors of the temple with g,	2298
	3: 8	inside with six hundred talents of fine g.	2298
	3: 9	The g nails weighed fifty shekels.	2298
	3: 9	He also overlaid the upper parts with g.	2298
	3:10	and overlaid them with g.	2298
	4: 7	He made ten g lampstands according to	2298
	4: 8	also made a hundred g sprinkling bowls	2298
	4:20	of pure g with their lamps, to burn in front	2298
	4:21	the g floral work and lamps	2298
	4:21	and lamps and tongs (they were solid g);	2298

2Ch	4:22	the pure g wick trimmers,	2298
	4:22	and the g doors of the temple:	2298
	5: 1	the silver and g and all the furnishings—	2298
	8:18	and fifty talents of g,	2298
	9: 1	large quantities of g, and precious stones—	2298
	9: 9	Then she gave the king 120 talents of g,	2298
	9:10	the men of Solomon brought g from Ophir;	2298
	9:13	The weight of the g	2298
	9:14	the land brought g and silver to Solomon.	2298
	9:15	King Solomon made two hundred large	
		shields of hammered g;	2298
	9:15	six hundred bekas of hammered g went	2298
	9:16	of hammered g, with three hundred bekas	2298
	9:16	with three hundred bekas of g	2298
	9:17	with ivory and overlaid with pure g.	2298
	9:18	and a footstool of g was attached to it.	2298
	9:20	All King Solomon's goblets were g,	2298
	9:20	of the Forest of Lebanon were pure g.	2298
	9:21	carrying g, silver and ivory,	2298
	9:24	articles of silver and g, and robes,	2298
	12: 9	including the g shields Solomon had made.	2298
	13:11	on the g lampstand every evening.	2298
	15:18	into the temple of God the silver and g and	2298
	16: 2	the silver and g out of the treasuries of	2298
	16: 3	See, I am sending you silver and g.	2298
	21: 3	of silver and g and articles of value,	2298
	24:14	and also dishes and other objects of g	2298
	25:24	the g and silver and all the articles found in	2298
	32:27	and he made treasuries for his silver and g	2298
	36: 3	a hundred talents of silver and a talent of g.	2298
Ezr	1: 4	to provide him with silver and g,	2298
	1: 6	with articles of silver and g,	2298
	1: 9	dishes 30 silver dishes 1,000	2298
	1:10	g bowls 30 matching silver bowls 410	2298
	1:11	there were 5,400 articles of g and of silver.	2298
	2:69	drachmas of g, 5,000 minas of silver	2298
	5:14	of Babylon the g and silver articles of	10160
	6: 5	g and silver articles of the house of God,	10160
	7:15	you are to take with you the silver and g	10160
	7:16	and g you may obtain from the province	10160
	7:18	with the rest of the silver and g,	10160
	8:25	the offering of silver and g and the articles	2298
	8:26	100 talents of g,	2298
	8:27	20 bowls of g valued at 1,000	2298
	8:27	as precious as g.	2298
	8:28	and g are a freewill offering to the LORD,	2298
	8:30	and Levites received the silver and g	2298
	8:33	and g and the sacred articles into the hands	2298
Ne	7:70	the treasury 1,000 drachmas of g, 50 bowls	2298
	7:71	drachmas of g and 2,200 minas of silver.	2298
	7:72	of g, 2,000 minas of silver and 67 garments	2298
Est	1: 6	There were couches of g and silver on	2298
	1: 7	Wine was served in goblets of g,	2298
	4:11	for the king to extend the g scepter to him	2298
	5: 2	and held out to her the g scepter that was	2298
	8: 4	the king extended the g scepter to Esther	2298
	8:15	a large crown of g and a purple robe	2298
Job	3:15	with rulers who had g	2298
	22:24	your g of Ophir to the rocks in the ravines,	234
	22:25	then the Almighty will be your g,	1309
	23:10	I will come forth as g.	2298
	28: 1	for silver and a place where g is refined.	2298
	28: 6	and its dust contains nuggets of g.	2298
	28:15	It cannot be bought with the finest g,	6034
	28:16	It cannot be bought with the g of Ophir,	4188
	28:17	Neither g nor crystal can compare with it,	2298
	28:17	nor can it be had for jewels of g.	7058
	28:19	it cannot be bought with pure g.	4188
	31:24	"If I have put my trust in g or said	2298
	31:24	or said to pure g,	4188
	42:11	a piece of silver and a g ring.	2298
Ps	19:10	They are more precious than g,	2298
	19:10	than much pure g;	7058
	21: 3	and placed a crown of pure g on his head.	7058
	45: 9	at your right hand is the royal bride in g	4188
	45:13	her gown is interwoven with g.	2298
	68:13	its feathers with shining g."	3021
	72:15	May g from Sheba be given him.	2298
	105:37	laden with silver and g,	2298
	115: 4	But their idols are silver and g,	2298
	119:72	of pieces of silver and g.	2298
	119:127	Because I love your commands more than g,	2298
	119:127	more than pure g,	7058
	135:15	The idols of the nations are silver and g,	2298
Pr	3:14	and yields better returns than g.	3021
	8:10	knowledge rather than choice g,	3021
	8:19	My fruit is better than fine g;	7058
	11:22	Like a g ring in a pig's snout is	2298
	16:16	How much better to get wisdom than g,	3021
	17: 3	crucible for silver and the furnace for g,	2298
	20:15	G there is, and rubies in abundance,	2298
	22: 1	to be esteemed is better than silver or g.	2298
	25:11	A word aptly spoken is like apples of g	2298
	25:12	Like an earring of g or an ornament	2298
	25:12	of fine g is a wise man's rebuke to	4188
	27:21	crucible for silver and the furnace for g,	2298
Ecc	2: 8	I amassed silver and g for myself,	2298
SS	1:11	We will make you earrings of g,	2298
	3:10	Its posts he made of silver, its base of g.	2298
	5:11	His head is purest g;	4188+7058
	5:14	His arms are rods of g set with chrysolite.	2298
	5:15	of marble set on bases of pure g.	7058
Isa	2: 7	Their land is full of silver and g;	2298
	2:20	and bats their idols of silver and idols of g,	2298
	13:12	I will make man scarcer than pure g,	7058
	13:12	more rare than the g of Ophir.	4188
	13:17	not care for silver and have no delight in g.	2298

Isa	30:22	and your images covered with g;	2298
	31: 7	and g your sinful hands have made.	2298
	39: 2	the silver, the g, the spices, the fine oil,	2298
	40:19	with g and fashions silver chains for it.	2298
	46: 6	Some pour out g from their bags	2298
	60: 6	bearing g and incense and proclaiming	2298
	60: 9	with their silver and g,	2298
	60:17	Instead of bronze I will bring you g,	2298
Jer	4:30	in scarlet and put on jewels of g?	2298
	10: 4	They adorn it with silver and g;	2298
	10: 9	from Tarshish and g from Uphaz.	2298
	51: 7	Babylon was a g cup in the LORD's hand;	2298
	52:19	all that were made of pure g or silver.	2298+2298
La	4: 1	How the g has lost its luster,	2298
	4: 1	the fine g become dull!	4188
	4: 2	once worth their weight in g,	7058
Eze	7:19	and their g will be an unclean thing.	2298
	7:19	and g will not be able to save them in	2298
	16:13	So you were adorned with g and silver;	2298
	16:17	the jewelry made of my g and silver,	2298
	27:22	of spices and precious stones,	2298
	28: 4	and amassed g and silver in your treasuries.	2298
	28:13	and mountings were made of g;	2298
	38:13	to carry off silver and g,	2298
Da	2:32	The head of the statue was made of pure g,	10160
	2:35	the silver and the g were broken to pieces	10160
	2:38	You are that head of g.	10160
	2:45	the clay, the silver and the g to pieces.	10160
	3: 1	King Nebuchadnezzar made an image of g,	10160
	3: 5	of g that King Nebuchadnezzar has set up.	10160
	3: 7	of g that King Nebuchadnezzar had set up.	10160
	3:10	down and worship the image of g,	10160
	3:12	the image of g you have set up."	10160
	3:14	or worship the image of g I have set up?	10160
	3:18	or worship the image of g you have set up."	10160
	5: 2	to bring in the g and silver goblets	10160
	5: 3	in the g goblets that had been taken from	10160
	5: 4	they praised the gods of g and silver,	10160
	5: 7	and have a g chain placed around his neck,	10160
	5:16	in purple and have a g chain placed	10160
	5:23	You praised the gods of silver and g,	10160
	5:29	a g chain was placed around his neck,	10160
	10: 5	a belt of the finest g around his waist.	233+4188
	11: 8	of silver and g and carry them off to Egypt.	2298
	11:38	to his fathers he will honor with g	2298
	11:43	of g and silver and all the riches of Egypt,	2298
Hos	2: 8	who lavished on her the silver and g—	2298
	8: 4	With their silver and g they make idols	2298
Joel	3: 5	For you took my silver and my g	2298
Na	2: 9	Plunder the g!	2298
Hab	2:19	It is covered with g and silver;	2298
Zep	1:18	Neither their silver nor their g will be able	2298
Hag	2: 8	'The silver is mine and the g is mine,'	2298
Zec	4: 2	a solid g lampstand with a bowl at the top	2298
	4:12	the two g pipes that pour out golden oil?"	2298
	6:10	"Take [silver and g] from the exiles Heldai,	NIH
	6:11	Take the silver and g and make a crown,	2298
	9: 3	and g like the dirt of the streets.	3021
	13: 9	like silver and test them like g.	2298
	14:14	great quantities of g and silver	2298
Mal	3: 3	the Levites and refine them like g	2298
Mt	2:11	with gifts of g and of incense and of myrrh.	5996
	10: 9	Do not take along any g or silver or copper	5996
	23:16	but if anyone swears by the g of the temple,	5996
	23:17	Which is greater:	5996
	23:17	or the temple that makes the g sacred?	5996
Ac	3: 6	Then Peter said, "Silver or g I do not have,	5992
	17:29	not think that the divine being is like g	5996
	20:33	I have not coveted anyone's silver or g	5992
1Co	3:12	on this foundation using g,	5996
1Ti	2: 9	or g or pearls or expensive clothes,	5992
2Ti	2:20	not only of g and silver, but also of wood	5991
Heb	9: 4	This ark contained the g jar of manna,	5991
Jas	2: 2	into your meeting wearing a g ring	5993
	5: 3	Your g and silver are corroded.	5996
1Pe	1: 7	your faith—of greater worth than g,	5992
	1:18	as silver or g that you were redeemed from	5992
	3: 3	the wearing of g jewelry and fine clothes.	5992
Rev	3:18	I counsel you to buy from me g refined in	5992
	4: 4	and had crowns of g on their heads.	5991
	9: 7	wore something like crowns of g,	5996
	9:20	and idols of g, silver, bronze,	5991
	14:14	a crown of g on his head and a sharp sickle	5991
	17: 4	and was glittering with g,	5992
	18:12	of g, silver, precious stones and pearls;	5996
	18:16	purple and scarlet, and glittering with g,	5992
	21:15	a measuring rod of g to measure the city,	5991
	21:18	and the city of pure g, as pure as glass.	5992
	21:21	The great street of the city was of pure g,	5992

GOLD-COVERED (1) [GOLD, COVER]

Heb	9: 4	and the g ark of the covenant.	4119+4328+5992

GOLDEN (21) [GOLD]

1Ki	7:48	in the LORD's temple: the g altar;	2298
	7:48	the g table on which was the bread of	2298
	12:28	the king made two g calves.	2298
2Ki	10:29	the worship of the g calves at Bethel	2298
2Ch	4:19	In God's temple: the g altar;	2298
	13: 8	a vast army and have with you the g calves	2298
Job	37:22	Out of the north he comes in g splendor;	2298
Ecc	12: 6	or the g bowl is broken;	2298
Zec	4:12	the two gold pipes that pour out g oil?"	2298
Heb	9: 4	which had the g altar of incense and	5991
Rev	1:12	when I turned I saw seven g lampstands,	5991

Rev	1:13	and with a g sash around his chest.	5991
	1:20	and of the seven g lampstands is this:	5991
	2: 1	and walks among the seven g lampstands;	5991
	5: 8	a harp and they were holding g bowls full	5991
	8: 3	Another angel, who had a g censer,	5991
	8: 3	on the g altar before the throne.	5991
	9:13	the horns of the g altar that is before God.	5991
	15: 6	and wore g sashes around their chests.	5991
	15: 7	the seven angels seven g bowls filled with	5991
	17: 4	She held a g cup in her hand,	5991

GOLDSMITH (6) [GOLD]

Isa	40:19	and a g overlays it with gold	7671
	41: 7	The craftsman encourages the g,	7671
	46: 7	they hire a g to make it into a god,	7671
Jer	10: 9	and g have made is then dressed in blue	7671
	10:14	every g is shamed by his idols.	7671
	51:17	every g is shamed by his idols.	7671

GOLDSMITHS (3) [GOLD]

Ne	3: 8	Uzziel son of Harhaiah, one of the g,	7671
	3:31	Next to him, Malkijah, one of the g,	7672
	3:32	above the corner and the Sheep Gate the g	7671

GOLGOTHA (3)

Mt	27:33	G (which means The Place of the Skull).	1201
Mk	15:22	G (which means The Place of the Skull).	1201
Jn	19:17	the Skull (which in Aramaic is called G).	1201

GOLIATH (7)

1Sa	17: 4	A champion named G, who was from Gath,	1669
	17: 8	G stood and shouted to the ranks of Israel,	NIH
	17:23	As he was talking with them, G,	1669
	21: 9	"The sword of G the Philistine,	1669
	22:10	and the sword of G the Philistine."	1669
2Sa	21:19	of Jaare-Oregim the Bethlehemite killed G	1669
1Ch	20: 5	of Jair killed Lahmi the brother of G	1669

GOMER (8)

Ge	10: 2	The sons of Japheth: G, Magog, Madai,	1699
	10: 3	The sons of G:	1699
1Ch	1: 5	The sons of Japheth: G, Magog, Madai,	1699
	1: 6	The sons of G:	1699
Eze	38: 6	also G with all its troops,	1699
Hos	1: 3	So he married G daughter of Diblaim,	1700
	1: 6	G conceived again and gave birth to	NIH
	1: 8	G had another son.	NIH

GOMORRAH (23)

Ge	10:19	G, Admah and Zeboiim, as far as Lasha.	6686
	13:10	the LORD destroyed Sodom and G.)	6686
	14: 2	Birsha king of G, Shinab king of Admah,	6686
	14: 8	Then the king of Sodom, the king of G,	6686
	14:10	and when the kings of Sodom and G fled,	6686
	14:11	of Sodom and G and all their food;	6686
	18:20	and G is so great and their sin so grievous	6686
	19:24	down burning sulfur on Sodom and G—	6686
	19:28	He looked down toward Sodom and G,	6686
Dt	29:23	be like the destruction of Sodom and G,	6686
	32:32	the vine of Sodom and from the fields of G.	6686
Isa	1: 9	we would have been like G.	6686
	1:10	to the law of our God, you people of G!	6686
	13:19	be overthrown by God like Sodom and G,	6686
Jer	23:14	the people of Jerusalem are like G."	6686
	49:18	As Sodom and G were overthrown,	6686
	50:40	and G along with their neighboring towns,"	6686
Am	4:11	of you as I overthrew Sodom and G.	6686
Zep	2: 9	the Ammonites like G—	6686
Mt	10:15	it will be more bearable for Sodom and G	1202
Ro	9:29	we would have been like G."	1202
2Pe	2: 6	if he condemned the cities of Sodom and G	1202
Jude	1: 7	Sodom and G and the surrounding towns	1202

GONE (207) [GO]

Ge	8: 3	and fifty days the water had g down,	2893
	19: 4	Before they had g to bed,	8886
	20: 4	Now Abimelech had not g near her,	7928
	21:15	When the water in the skin was g,	3983
	28: 7	and mother and had g to Paddan Aram.	2143
	31:19	When Laban had g to shear his sheep,	2143
	31:30	you have g off because you longed	2143+2143
	35: 3	with me wherever I have g."	2143
	37:12	Now his brothers had g	2143
	43:10	we could have g and returned twice."	NIH
	44: 4	not g far from the city when Joseph said	3655
	47:15	of the people of Egypt and Canaan was g,	9462
	47:16	since your money is g."	699
	47:18	the fact that since our money is g	9462
	50:14	his brothers and all the others who had g	6590
Ex	3: 4	the LORD saw that he had g over to look,	6073
	9:29	"When I have g out of the city,	3655
	16:14	When the dew was g,	6590
	19:14	After Moses had g down the mountain to	3718
Lev	14:48	because the mildew is g.	8324
Nu	5:19	with you and you have not g astray	8474
	5:20	But if you have g astray while married	8474
	13:31	But the men who had g up with him said,	6590
	14: 9	their protection is g,	6073
	16: 3	"You have g too far!	8041
	16: 7	You Levites have g too far!"	8041
	16:33	and they perished and were g from	4946+9348
	31:21	the soldiers who had g into battle,	995

Nu	32:13	who had done evil in his sight *was* g.	9462
Dt	32:36	when he sees their strength *is* g	261
	34: 7	his eyes were not weak nor his strength g.	5674
Jos	2: 7	and as soon as the pursuers *had* g out,	3655
Jdg	3:24	After he *had* g,	3655
	4:12	of Abinoam *had* g up to Mount Tabor,	6590
	4:14	*Has* not the LORD g ahead of you?"	3655
	9:27	After *they had* g out into the fields	3655
	9:35	of Ebed *had* g out and was standing at	3655
	18:22	When *they had* some distance	8178
	19:11	near Jebus and the day *was* almost g,	3718
	20: 3	that the Israelites *had* g up to Mizpah.)	6590
Ru	1:13	the LORD's hand *has* g out against me!"	3655
1Sa	3: 3	The lamp of God *had* not yet g out,	3882
	9: 7	The food in our sacks *is* g.	261
	13:23	Now a detachment of Philistines *had* g out	3655
	14:21	with the Philistines and *had* g up with them	6590
	15:12	but he was told, "Saul has g to Carmel.	995
	15:12	in his own honor and has turned and g on	6296
	20:41	After the boy *had* g,	995
	23: 7	Saul was told that David *had* g to Keilah,	995
	28:20	His strength *was* g,	928+2118+4202
2Sa	3:22	and *he had* g.	2143
	3:23	king had sent him away and that *he had* g	2143
	3:24	Now *he is* g!	2143+2143
	4: 7	*They had* g into the house	995
	5:24	the LORD *has* g out in front of you	3655
	7: 9	I have been with you wherever *you have* g,	2143
	12:15	After Nathan *had* g home,	6296
	16: 1	When David *had* g a short distance beyond	6296
	17:21	After the men *had* g,	2143
	24: 8	After *they had* g through the entire land,	8763
1Ki	1:25	Today *he has* g down	3718
	1:45	From there *they have* g up cheering,	6590
	2:15	and the kingdom *has* g to my brother;	2118
	2:41	When Solomon was told that Shimei *had* g	2143
	11:15	*who had* g up to bury the dead,	6590
	12: 1	the Israelites *had* g there to make him king.	995
	14: 4	his sight *was* g because of his age.	7756
	14:10	as one burns dung, until it *is* all g.	9462
	21:18	where *he has* g to take possession of it.	3718
	22:13	The messenger who *had* g	2143
2Ki	3:26	the king of Moab saw that the battle *had* g	2616S
	4:13	g to all this trouble	3006+3010
	5: 2	from Aram *had* g out and had taken captive	3655
	9:16	and Ahaziah king of Judah *had* g down	3718
	20:11	ten steps *it had* g down on the stairway	345+3718
	25:11	of the populace and those who *had* g over to	5877
1Ch	14:15	because that will mean God *has* g out	3655
	17: 8	I have been with you wherever *you have* g,	2143
2Ch	10: 1	the Israelites *had* g there to make him king.	995
	18:2	The messenger who *had* g	2143
Ezr	4:12	up to us from you *have* g to Jerusalem	10085
Ne	2:16	The officials did not know where *I had* g	2143
	4: 7	the repairs to Jerusalem's walls *had* g ahead	6590
	13:10	the service *had* g back to their own fields.	1368
Job	7: 9	As a cloud vanishes and *is* g,	2143
	11:16	recalling it only as waters g by.	6296
	14:20	You overpower him once for all, and *he is* g	2143
	19: 4	If it is true that *I have* g astray,	8706
	19:10	down on every side till *I am* g;	2143
	19:14	My kinsmen *have* g away;	2532
	24:14	When daylight is g, the murderer rises up	NIH
	24:24	and then they are g;	401
	27:19	when he opens his eyes, all is g.	401
	27:21	The east wind carries him off, and *he is* g;	2143
	29: 2	"How I long for the months g by,	7710
	30: 2	since their vigor *had* g from them?	6
Ps	28: 1	be like *those who have* g down to the pit.	3718
	38:10	even the light has g from my eyes.	401+907
	52: T	the Edomite *had* g to Saul and told him:	995
	52: T	"David *has* g to the house of Ahimelech."	995
	54: T	When the Ziphites *had* g to Saul and said,	995
	71: 9	do not forsake me when my strength *is* g.	3983
	90: 4	like a day that *has* just g by,	6296
	103:16	the wind blows over it and it is g,	401
Pr	7:19	he has g on a long journey.	2143
	10:25	the storm has swept by, the wicked are g,	401
	23: 5	Cast but a glance at riches, and they are g,	401
	30: 4	Who *has* g up to heaven and come down?	6590
Ecc	6:12	will happen under the sun after he is g?	NIH
	7:29	men *have* g in search of many schemes."	1335
SS	2:11	The winter is past; the rains are over and g.	2143
	5: 6	but my lover had left; he was g.	6296
	6: 1	*has* your lover g, most beautiful of women?	2143
	6: 2	My lover *has* g down to his garden,	3718
Isa	15: 6	vegetation *is* g and nothing green is left.	3983
	17:14	Before the morning, they are g!	401
	18: 5	the blossom *is* g and the flower becomes	9462
	20: 3	"Just as my servant Isaiah *has* g stripped	2143
	22: 1	that you have all g up on the roofs,	6590
	38: 8	the sun go back the ten steps *it has* g down	3718
	38: 8	the ten steps *it had* g down.	3718
	51: 9	awake, as in days g by,	7710
	53: 6	We all, like sheep, *have* g astray,	9494
Jer	3: 6	She *has* g up on every high hill and	2143
	4:23	and at the heavens, and their light was g.	401
	5:23	they have turned aside and g away.	2143
	9:10	of the air have fled and the animals *are* g.	2143
	10:20	My sons *are* g from me and are no more;	2143
	14:18	Both prophet and priest *have* g to	6086
	17:11	When his life is half g,	AIT
	22:11	as king of Judah but *has* g from this place:	3655
	29: 2	the craftsmen and the artisans *had* g	3655
	37:21	until all the bread in the city *was* g.	9462
	38:19	"I am afraid of the Jews who *have* g over to	5877
	39: 9	along with those who *had* g over to him,	5877

Jer	44:14	of the remnant of Judah who *have* g to live	995
	48:11	*she has* not g into exile.	2143
	48:33	Joy and gladness *are* g from the orchards	665
	48:36	The wealth they acquired *is* g.	6
	48:45	for a fire *has* g out from Heshbon,	3655
	51: 7	therefore they *have* now g mad.	2147
	52:15	of the craftsmen and those who *had* g over	5877
La	1: 3	Judah *has* g into exile.	1655
	1: 5	Her children *have* g into exile,	2143
	1:18	My young men and maidens *have* g into	2143
	3:18	"My splendor *is* g and all that I had hoped	6
	5:14	The elders *are* g from the city gate;	8697
	5:15	is g *from* our hearts;	8697
Eze	11:16	in the countries where *they have* g.'	995
	13: 5	not g up to the breaks in the wall to repair it	6590
	13:15	"The wall is g and so are those who	401
	19: 5	her expectation g, she took another	6
	23:31	have g the way of your sister;	2143
	27:34	and all your company *have* g down	5877
	31:17	*had* also g down to the grave with it,	3718
	36:21	among the nations where *they had* g.	995
	36:22	among the nations where *you have* g.	995
	37:11	'Our bones are dried up and our hope *is* g;	6
	37:21	of the nations where *they have* g.	2143
	45: 9	You have g far enough, O princes of Israel!	8041
	46:12	he shall go out, and after he has g out,	3655
Da	2:14	*had* g out to put to death the wise men	10485
	10:17	My strength *is* g and I can hardly breathe."	928+4202+6641
Hos	4:18	Even when their drinks *are* g,	6073
	8: 9	For they *have* g up to Assyria like	6590
Jnh	1: 5	But Jonah *had* g below deck,	3718
Zec	1:11	"We have g throughout the earth and found	2143
Mal	3: 4	as in days g by, as in former years.	6409
Mt	2:13	*When they had* g, an angel of the Lord	432
	9:28	When *he had* g indoors,	2262
Mk	1:19	When *he had* g a little **farther**,	4581
	5:30	At once Jesus realized that power *had* g out	2002
	7:30	and the demon g.	2002
	9:28	After Jesus *had* g indoors,	1656
Lk	2:15	the angels had left them and g into heaven,	NIG
	8:30	because many demons *had* g into him.	1656
	8:35	the man from whom the demons *had* g out,	2002
	8:38	from whom the demons *had* g begged	2002
	8:46	I know that power *has* g out from me."	2002
	16: 9	so that when *it is* g,	1722
	19: 7	"He *has* g to be the guest of a 'sinner.'"	1656
Jn	2: 3	When the wine *was* g,	5728
	3:13	No one *has* ever g into heaven except	326
	4: 8	(His disciples *had* g into the town	599
	6:22	but that they *had* g away alone.	599
	7:50	who *had* g to Jesus earlier and was one	2262
	12:19	how the whole world *has* g after him!"	599
	13:31	When *he was* g, Jesus said,	2002
Ac	8:27	This man *had* g to Jerusalem to worship,	2262
	9:23	After many days *had* g by,	4444
	10: 7	When the angel who spoke to him *had* g,	599
	16:19	that their hope of making money *was* g,	2002
	20:25	among whom *I have* g about preaching	1451
	27:21	the men *had* g a long time without food,	5639
	27:33	in constant suspense and have g	NIG
Ro	10:18	"Their voice has g out into all the earth,	2002
2Co	5:17	the old *has* g, the new has come!	4216
	11:27	I have often g without sleep;	71+1877
	11:27	and thirst and have often g without food;	3763
2Ti	4:10	has deserted me and *has* g to Thessalonica.	4513
	4:10	Crescens has g to Galatia,	NIG
Heb	4:14	a great high priest *who has* g **through**	1451
1Pe	3:22	who has g into heaven and is	4513
1Jn	4: 1	because many false prophets *have* g out	2002
2Jn	1: 7	*have* g out into the world.	2002
Rev	12:12	because the devil *has* g down to you!	2849
	18:14	'The fruit you longed for is g from you.	599

GONG (1)

1Co	13: 1	a resounding g or a clanging cymbal.	5910

GOOD (601) [BETTER, BEST, GOODNESS]

Ge	1: 4	God saw that the light was g,	3202
	1:10	And God saw that it was g.	3202
	1:12	And God saw that it was g.	3202
	1:18	And God saw that it was g.	3202
	1:21	And God saw that it was g.	3202
	1:25	And God saw that it was g.	3202
	1:31	and it was very g.	3202
	2: 9	trees that were pleasing to the eye and g	3202
	2: 9	and the tree of the knowledge of g and evil.	3202
	2:12	(The gold of that land is g;	3202
	2:17	not eat from the tree of the knowledge of g	3202
	2:18	"It is not g for the man to be alone.	3202
	3: 5	like God, knowing g and evil."	3202
	3: 6	fruit of the tree was g for food and pleasing	3202
	3:22	like one of us, knowing g and evil.	3202
	15:15	in peace and be buried at a g old age.	3202
	20: 3	"You *are* as g as dead because of	4637
	24:10	taking with him all kinds of g **things**	3206
	25: 8	at a g old age, an old man and full of years;	3202
	25:32	"What g is the birthright to me?"	AIT
	30:11	Then Leah said, "What g fortune!"	1513
	31:24	to say anything to Jacob, either g or bad."	3202
	31:29	to say anything to Jacob, either g or bad.'	3202
	34:18	Their proposal seemed g to Hamor	3512
	41: 5	Seven heads of grain, healthy and g,	3202
	41:22	full and g, growing on a single stalk.	3202
	41:24	of grain swallowed up the seven g heads.	3202

Ge	41:26	The seven g cows are seven years,	3202
	41:26	the seven g heads of grain are seven years;	3202
	41:35	of these g years that are coming and store	3202
	41:37	The plan seemed g to Pharaoh and	3512
	44: 4	'Why have you repaid g with evil?'	3208
	49:15	When he sees how g is his resting place	3202
	50:20	God intended it for g to accomplish what is	3208
Ex	3: 8	into a g and spacious land, a land flowing	3202
	18: 9	the g things the LORD had done for Israel	3208
	18:17	"What you are doing is not g.	3202
Lev	5: 4	takes an oath to **do** anything, whether g	3512
	27:10	not exchange it or substitute a g one for	3202
	27:10	or a bad one for a g one;	3202
	27:12	who will judge its quality as g or bad.	3202
	27:14	the priest will judge its quality as g or bad.	3202
	27:33	He must not pick out the g from the bad	3202
Nu	10:29	for the LORD has promised g *things*	3202
	10:32	we will share with you whatever g things	3202
	13:19	Is it g or bad?	3202
	14: 7	through and explored is exceedingly g.	3202
	24:13	g or bad, to go beyond the command of	3208
Dt	1:14	"What you propose to do is g."	3202
	1:23	The idea seemed g to me,	3512
	1:25	"It is a g land that the LORD our God	3202
	1:35	the g land I swore to give your forefathers,	3202
	1:39	your children who do not yet know g	3202
	3:25	Let me go over and see the g land beyond	3202
	4:21	not cross the Jordan and enter the g land	3202
	4:22	over and take possession of that g land.	3202
	5:28	Everything they said was g.	3512
	6:11	with all kinds of g *things* you did	3206
	6:18	and g in the LORD's sight,	3202
	6:18	and you may go in and take over the g land	3202
	8: 7	God is bringing you into a g land—	3202
	8:10	for the g land he has given you.	3202
	9: 6	LORD your God is giving you this g land	3202
	10:13	I am giving you today for your own g?	3202
	11:17	from the g land the LORD is giving you.	3202
	12:28	be doing what is g and right in the eyes of	3202
	18:17	"What they say *is* g.	3512
	26:11	among you shall rejoice in all the g *things*	3202
Jos	9:25	to us whatever seems g and right to you."	3202
	10: 2	and all its men were g fighters.	1475
	21:45	of all the LORD's g promises to the house	3202
	23:13	until you perish from this g land,	3202
	23:14	and soul that not one of all the g promises	3202
	23:15	But just as every g promise of	3202
	23:15	from this g land he has given you.	3202
	23:16	from the g land he has given you."	3202
	24:20	after *he has* been g to you."	3512
Jdg	8:32	of Joash died at a g old age and was buried	3202
	8:35	for all the g **things** he had done for them.	3208
	9:11	'Should I give up my fruit, so g and sweet,	3202
	9:16	in g **faith** when you made Abimelech king,	9459
	9:19	and in g **faith** toward Jerub-Baal	9459
	17:13	I know that the LORD *will be* g to me,	3512
	18: 9	We have seen that the land is very g.	3202
Ru	2:22	"It will be g for you, my daughter,	3202
	3: 7	and drinking and *was* in g spirits,	3512+4213
	3:13	in the morning if he wants to redeem, g;	3202
1Sa	1:23	only *may* the LORD **make** g his word."	7756
	2:24	not a g report that I hear spreading among	3202
	2:32	Although *will be* **done** *to* Israel,	3512
	3:18	let him do what is g in his eyes."	3202
	9:10	"G," Saul said to his servant.	3202
	11:10	you can do to us whatever seems g to you."	3202
	12:14	follow the LORD your God—g!	NIH
	12:21	*They can* do you no g,	3603
	12:23	I will teach you the way that is g and right.	3208
	15: 9	everything that was g.	3202
	19:10	night David **made** g *his* escape.	2256+4880+5674
	24:18	You have just now told me of the g you did	3208
	25: 6	G health to you and your household!	8934
	25: 6	And g **health** to all that is yours!	8934
	25:15	Yet these men were very g to us.	3202
	25:21	He has paid me back evil for g.	3202
	25:30	for my master every g thing he promised	3208
	25:33	May you be blessed for your g **judgment**	3248
	26:16	What you have done is not g.	3202
2Sa	3:13	"G," said David.	3202
	4:10	and thought he was **bringing** g **news**,	1413
	7:28	and you have promised these g **things**	3208
	10:12	The LORD will do what is g in his sight."	3202
	13:22	either g or bad; he hated Amnon	3202
	14:17	an angel of God in discerning g and evil.	3202
	15:26	let him do to me whatever seems g to him."	3202
	16:12	and repay me with g for the cursing	3208
	17: 4	This plan seemed g to Absalom and to all	3837
	17: 7	Ahithophel has given is not g this time.	3202
	17:14	to frustrate the g advice of Ahithophel	3202
	18:25	"If he is alone, he must have g **news.**"	1415
	18:26	"He *must be* **bringing** g **news**, too."	1413
	18:27	"He's a g man," the king said.	3202
	18:27	"He comes with g news."	3202
	18:31	"My lord the king, **hear** the g **news!**	1413
	19:35	Can I tell the difference between what is g	3202
1Ki	1:42	like you must be bringing g news."	3202
	2:38	"What you say is g.	3202
	2:42	'What you say is g.	3202
	7:10	with large stones of g **quality**,	3701
	8:56	of all the g promises he gave	3202
	8:66	joyful and glad in heart for all the g **things**	3208
	14:13	the God of Israel, has found anything g.	3202
	14:15	He will uproot Israel from this g land	3202
	18:24	and the people said, "What you say is g."	3202
	20:33	**took** this as a g sign	5727
	22: 8	because he never prophesies *anything* g	3202

1Ki	22:18	that he never prophesies *anything* g	3202
2Ki	3:19	You will cut down every g tree,	3202
	3:19	and ruin every g field with stones."	3202
	3:25	on every g field until it was covered.	3202
	3:25	the springs and cut down every g tree.	3202
	7: 9	a day of g news and we are keeping it	1415
	20: 3	and have done what is g in your eyes."	3202
	20:19	of the LORD you have spoken is g,"	3202
1Ch	4:40	They found rich, g pasture,	3202
	13: 2	"If it seems g to you and if it is the will of	3202
	16:34	Give thanks to the LORD, for he is g;	3202
	17:26	You have promised these g **things**	3208
	19:13	The LORD will do what is g in his sight.	3202
	28: 8	that you may possess this g land and pass it	3202
	29:28	He died at a g old age,	3202
2Ch	5:13	"He is g; his love endures forever."	3202
	7: 3	saying, "He is g; his love endures forever."	3202
	7:10	the g things the LORD had done for David	3208
	12:12	Indeed, there was some g in Judah.	3202
	14: 2	Asa did what was g and right in the eyes of	3202
	18: 7	because he never prophesies *anything* g	3208
	18:17	that he never prophesies *anything* g	3202
	19: 3	There is, however, some g in you,	3202
	24:16	because of the g he had done in Israel	3208
	30:18	saying, "May the LORD, who is g,	3202
	30:22	who showed g understanding of the service	3202
	31:20	doing what was g and right and faithful	3202
Ezr	3:11	they sang to the LORD: "He is g;	3202
	7:28	and who has extended his g **favor** to me	2876
	9:12	and eat the g **things** *of* the land and leave it	3206
Ne	2:18	So they began this g **work.**	3208
	5: 5	and though our sons are as g as theirs,	3869
	6:19	they kept reporting to me his g **deeds** and	3208
	9:13	and decrees and commands that are g.	3202
	9:20	You gave your g Spirit to instruct them.	3202
	9:25	of houses filled with all kinds of g things,	3206
	9:36	and the other g **things** it *produces.*	3206
Est	10: 3	because he worked for the g of his people	3202
Job	2:10	Shall we accept g from God,	3202
	21:25	never having enjoyed anything g.	3208
	22:18	with g **things,** so I stand aloof from	3202
	30:26	Yet when I hoped for g, evil came;	3202
	34: 4	let us learn together what is g.	3202
	39:17	with wisdom or give her a share of g **sense.**	1069
Ps	4: 6	"Who can show us any g?"	3202
	13: 6	for *he has* **been** g to me.	1694
	14: 1	there is no one who does g.	3202
	14: 3	there is no one who does g, not even one.	3202
	16: 2	apart from you I have no g **thing."**	3208
	25: 7	for you are g, O LORD.	3206
	25: 8	G and upright is the LORD;	3202
	34: 8	Taste and see that the LORD is g;	3202
	34:10	those who seek the LORD lack no g *thing.*	3202
	34:12	and desires to see many g days,	3202
	34:14	Turn from evil and do g,	3202
	35:12	for g and leave my soul forlorn.	3208
	36: 3	he has ceased to be wise and to **do** g.	3512
	37: 3	Trust in the LORD and do g;	3202
	37:27	Turn from evil and do g;	3202
	38:20	Those who repay my g with evil	3208
	38:20	when I pursue *what is* g.	3202
	39: 2	not even saying *anything* g,	3202
	51:18	In your g **pleasure** make Zion prosper;	8356
	52: 3	You love evil rather than g,	3202
	52: 9	for your name is g.	3202
	53: 1	there is no one who does g.	3202
	53: 3	there is no one who does g, not even one.	3202
	54: 6	O LORD, for it is g.	3202
	65: 4	with the g **things** *of* your house,	3206
	73: 1	Surely God is g to Israel,	3202
	73:28	But as for me, it is g to be near God.	3202
	84:11	no g *thing* does he withhold	3202
	85:12	The LORD will indeed give what is g,	3202
	86: 5	You are forgiving and g, O Lord,	3202
	92: 1	It is g to praise the LORD and make music	3202
	100: 5	LORD is g and his love endures forever;	3202
	103: 5	with g **things** so that your youth is renewed	3202
	104:28	they are satisfied with g *things.*	3202
	106: 1	Give thanks to the LORD, for he is g;	3202
	107: 1	Give thanks to the LORD, for he is g;	3202
	107: 9	and fills the hungry with g *things.*	3202
	109: 5	They repay me evil for g,	3208
	111:10	all who follow his precepts have g understanding.	3202
	112: 5	G will come to him who is generous	3202
	116: 7	for the LORD *has been* g to you.	1694
	118: 1	Give thanks to the LORD, for he is g;	3202
	118:29	Give thanks to the LORD, for he is g;	3202
	119:17	**Do** g to your servant, and I will live;	1694
	119:39	for your laws are g.	3202
	119:65	Do g to your servant according	3202
	119:66	Teach me knowledge and g judgment,	3206
	119:68	You are g, and what you do is g;	3512
	119:68	You are good, and *what you* **do** *is* g;	3512
	119:71	It was g for me to be afflicted so	3202
	125: 4	**Do** g, O LORD, to those who are good,	3512
	125: 4	Do good, O LORD, to those *who* are g,	3202
	133: 1	How g and pleasant it is	3202
	135: 3	Praise the LORD, for the LORD is g;	3202
	136: 1	Give thanks to the LORD, for he is g.	3202
	143:10	may your g Spirit lead me on level ground.	3202
	145: 9	The LORD is g to all;	3202
	147: 1	How g it is to sing praises to our God,	3202
Pr	2: 9	and fair—every g path.	3202
	2:20	the ways of g **men** and keep to the paths of	3202
	3: 4	and a g name in the sight of God and man.	3202
	3:27	not withhold g from those who deserve it,	3202
Pr	11:23	The desire of the righteous ends only in g,	3202
	11:27	He who seeks g finds goodwill,	3202
	12: 2	A g **man** obtains favor from the LORD,	3202
	12:14	of his lips a man is filled with g *things* as	3202
	13: 2	the fruit of his lips a man enjoys g *things,*	3202
	13:15	G understanding wins favor,	3202
	13:22	A g *man* leaves an inheritance	3202
	14:14	and the g man rewarded for his.	3202
	14:19	down in the presence of the g,	3202
	14:22	But those who plan *what* is g find love	3202
	15: 3	keeping watch on the wicked and the g.	3202
	15:23	and how g is a timely word!	3202
	15:30	and g news gives health to the bones.	3202
	16:29	and leads him down a path that is not g.	3202
	17:13	If a man pays back evil for g,	3208
	17:22	A cheerful heart is g medicine,	3512
	17:26	It is not g to punish an innocent man,	3202
	18: 5	It is not g to be partial to the wicked or	3202
	18:22	a wife finds *what* is g and receives favor	3202
	19: 2	It is not g to have zeal without knowledge,	3202
	20:14	"It's no g, it's no good!"	8273
	20:14	"It's no good, it's no g!"	8273
	22: 1	g name is more desirable than great riches;	NIH
	24:13	Eat honey, my son, for it is g;	3202
	24:23	To show partiality in judging is not g:	3202
	25:25	is g news from a distant land.	3202
	25:27	It is not g to eat too much honey,	3202
	28:10	the blameless will receive a g inheritance.	3202
	28:21	To show partiality is not g—	3202
	31:12	She brings him g, not harm,	3202
Ecc	2: 1	with pleasure to find out *what* is g."	3202
	3:12	to be happy and do g while they live.	3202
	4: 9	because they have a g return for their work:	3202
	5:18	Then I realized that it is g and proper for	3202
	6:12	For who knows what is g for a man in life,	3202
	7: 1	A g name is better than fine perfume,	3202
	7: 3	because a sad face *is* g *for* the heart.	3512
	7:11	is a g *thing* and benefits those who see	3202
	7:14	When times are g, be happy;	3202
	7:18	It is g to grasp the one and not let go of	3202
	9: 2	the g and the bad,	3202
	9: 2	As it is with the g *man,* so with the sinner;	3202
	9:18	but one sinner destroys much g.	3208
	12:14	whether it is g or evil.	3202
Isa	5: 2	Then he looked for a crop of g **grapes,**	6694
	5: 4	When I looked for g **grapes,**	6694
	5:20	Woe to those who call evil g and good evil,	3202
	5:20	Woe to those who call good evil and g evil,	3202
	38: 3	and have done what is g in your eyes."	3202
	39: 8	of the LORD you have spoken is g,"	3202
	40: 9	You *who* **bring** g **tidings** *to* Zion,	1413
	40: 9	You *who* **bring** g **tidings** *to* Jerusalem,	1413
	41: 7	He says of the welding, "It is g."	3202
	41:23	**Do** *something,* whether g	3512
	41:27	I gave to Jerusalem a **messenger of** g **tidings.**	1413
	52: 7	the feet of *those who* **bring** g **news,**	1413
	52: 7	who proclaim peace, who bring g tidings,	3202
	55: 2	Listen, listen to me, and eat *what* is g,	3202
	61: 1	to **preach** g **news** *to* the poor.	1413
	63: 7	the many g **things** he has done for the house	3206
	65: 2	who walk in ways not g,	3202
	65: 8	'Don't destroy it, there is yet *some* g in it,'	1388
Jer	4: 2	they know not how to **do** g."	3512
	5:25	your sins have deprived you of g.	3202
	6:16	ask where the g way is, and walk in it,	3202
	8:15	We hoped for peace but no g has come,	3202
	10: 5	they can do no harm nor *can* they **do** *any* g.	3512
	13:23	Neither can you **do** g who are accustomed	3512
	14:19	We hoped for peace but no g has come,	3202
	15:11	"Surely I will deliver you for a g *purpose;*	3202
	16:19	worthless idols *that* **did** them no g.	3603
	18:10	reconsider the g I had intended to **do**	3208+3512
	18:20	Should g be repaid with evil?	3208
	21:10	to do this city harm and not g,	3208
	24: 2	One basket had very g figs,	3202
	24: 3	"The g ones are very good,	3202
	24: 3	"The good ones are very g,	3202
	24: 5	'Like these g figs,	3202
	24: 5	I regard as g the exiles from Judah,	3208
	24: 6	My eyes will watch over them for their g,	3208
	26:14	with me whatever you think is g and right.	3202
	29:32	the g **things** I will do for my people,	3202
	32:39	for their own g and the good	3202
	32:39	and the g of their children after them.	NIH
	32:40	I will never stop **doing** g *to* them,	3512
	32:41	I will rejoice in **doing** them g	3201
	33: 9	on earth that hear of all the g **things** I do	3208
	33:11	for the LORD is g;	3202
	38: 4	the g of these people but their ruin."	8934
	44:27	over them for harm, not for g;	3208
La	3:25	LORD is g to those whose hope is in him,	3202
	3:26	it is g to wait quietly for the salvation of	3202
	3:27	It is g for a man to bear the yoke	3202
	3:38	that both calamities and g things come?	3202
Eze	17: 8	in g soil by abundant water so	3202
	20:25	not g and laws they could not live by;	3202
	30:22	the g arm as well as the broken one,	2617
	34:14	I will tend them in a g pasture,	3202
	34:14	There they will lie down in g grazing land,	3202
	34:18	for you to feed on the g pasture?	3202
Da	3:15	and worship the image I made, very g.	NIH
Hos	8: 3	But Israel has rejected what is g;	3202
Am	5:14	Seek g, not evil, that you may live.	3202
	5:15	love g; maintain justice in the courts.	3202
	9: 4	upon them for evil and not for g."	3208
Jnh	2: 9	What I have vowed *I* **will** **make** g.	8966
Mic	2: 7	"*Do not my words* **do** g	3512
	3: 2	you who hate g and love evil;	3202
	6: 8	He has showed you, O man, what is g.	3202
Na	1: 7	LORD is g, a refuge in times of trouble.	3202
	1:15	the feet of *one who* **brings** g **news,**	1413
Zep	1:12	'The LORD will do nothing, either g or bad.'	3512
Zec	8:15	"so now I have determined to **do** g again	3512
Mal	2:17	"All who do evil are g in the eyes of	3202
Mt	3:10	that does not produce g fruit will be cut	2819
	4:23	preaching the g news of the kingdom,	2295
	5:13	*It is* no longer g for anything,	2710
	5:16	that they may see your g deeds	2819
	5:45	to rise on the evil and the g,	19
	6:22	If your eyes are g,	604
	7:11	know how to give g gifts to your children,	19
	7:11	will your Father in heaven give g gifts	19
	7:17	Likewise every g tree bears good fruit,	19
	7:17	Likewise every good tree bears g fruit,	2819
	7:18	A g tree cannot bear bad fruit,	19
	7:18	and a bad tree cannot bear g fruit.	2819
	7:19	not bear g fruit is cut down and thrown into	2819
	9:35	preaching the g news of the kingdom	2295
	11: 5	**the g news is preached** to the poor.	2294
	11:26	Yes, Father, for this was your g **pleasure.**	2306
	12:12	it is lawful to do g on the Sabbath."	2822
	12:33	"Make a tree g and its fruit will be good,	2819
	12:33	"Make a tree good and its fruit will be g,	2819
	12:34	how can you who are evil say anything g?	19
	12:35	The g man brings good things out of	19
	12:35	The good man brings g *things* out of	19
	12:35	of the g stored up in him,	19
	13: 8	Still other seed fell on g soil,	2819
	13:23	on g soil is the man who hears the word	2819
	13:24	of heaven is like a man who sowed g seed	2819
	13:27	'Sir, didn't you sow g seed in your field?	2819
	13:37	"The one who sowed the g seed is the Son	2819
	13:38	g seed stands for the sons of the kingdom.	2819
	13:48	Then they sat down and collected the g fish	2819
	16:26	What g *will it be* **for** a man if he gains the	6067
	17: 4	"Lord, it is g for us to be here.	2819
	19:16	what g *thing* must I do to get eternal life?"	19
	19:17	"Why do you ask me about what is g?"	19
	19:17	"There is only One who is g.	19
	22:10	people they could find, both g and bad,	19
	24:46	It will be g for that servant whose master	3421
	25:21	'Well done, g and faithful servant!	19
	25:23	'Well done, g and faithful servant!	19
Mk	1:14	proclaiming the g **news of God.**	2295
	1:15	Repent and believe the g **news!"**	2295
	3: 4	to do g or to do evil, to save life or to kill?"	19
	4: 8	Still other seed fell on g soil.	2819
	4:20	Others, like seed sown on g soil,	2819
	8:36	What g *is it* for a man to gain	6067
	9: 5	"Rabbi, it is g for us to be here.	2819
	9:50	"Salt is g, but if it loses its saltiness,	2819
	10:17	"G teacher," he asked,	19
	10:18	"Why do you call me g?"	19
	10:18	No one is g—except God alone.	19
	12:28	that Jesus had given them a g answer,	2822
	16:15	Go into all the world and preach the g **news**	2295
Lk	1: 3	*it seemed* g also to me to write	1506
	1:19	**tell** you this g **news.**	2294
	1:53	He has filled the hungry **with** g *things*	19
	2:10	*I* **bring** you g **news** of great joy that will be	2294
	3: 9	that does not produce g fruit will be cut	2819
	3:18	people and **preached** the g **news** to them.	2294
	4:18	to **preach** g **news** to the poor.	2294
	4:43	"I must **preach the** g **news** of the kingdom	2294
	6: 9	to **do** g or to do evil,	16
	6:27	do g to those who hate you,	2822
	6:33	if *you* **do** g to those who **are** g to you,	16
	6:33	if you do good *to* those who **are** g to you,	16
	6:35	But love your enemies, **do** g to them,	16
	6:38	A measure, pressed down,	2819
	6:43	"No g tree bears bad fruit,	2819
	6:43	nor does a bad tree bear g fruit.	2819
	6:45	The g man brings good things out of	19
	6:45	The good man brings g things out of	19
	6:45	of the g stored up in his heart,	19
	7:22	**the** g **news** *is* **preached** to the poor.	2294
	8: 1	**proclaiming the** g **news** of the kingdom	2294
	8: 8	Still other seed fell on g soil.	2819
	8:15	But the seed on g soil stands for those with	2819
	8:15	for those with a noble and g heart,	2819
	9:25	What g *is it* for a man to gain	6067
	9:33	"Master, it is g for us to be here.	2819
	10:21	Yes, Father, for this was your g **pleasure.**	2306
	11:13	know how to give g gifts to your children,	19
	11:34	When your eyes are g,	604
	12:16	of a certain rich man **produced a** g **crop.**	2369
	12:19	"You have plenty of g *things* laid up	19
	12:37	It will be g for those servants who master	3421
	12:38	It will be g for those servants who master	3421
	12:43	It will be g for that servant whom	3421
	14:34	"Salt is g, but if it loses its saltiness,	2819
	16:16	**the** g **news** of the kingdom of God *is being* **preached,**	2294
	16:25	in your lifetime you received your g *things,*	19
	18:18	A certain ruler asked him, "G teacher,	19
	18:19	"Why do you call me g?"	19
	18:19	"No one is g—except God alone.	19
	19:17	"'Well done, my g servant!'	19
	23:50	a g and upright man,	19
Jn	1:46	Can anything g come from there?"	19
	5:29	those who have done g will rise to live,	19
	7:12	Some said, "He is a g **man."**	19
	10:11	"I am the g shepherd.	2819

Jn	10:11	g shepherd lays down his life for the sheep.	2819
	10:14	"I am the g shepherd;	2819
	16: 7	It is for your g that I am going away.	5237
	18:14	that it would be g if one man died for	5237
Ac	5:42	proclaiming the g news that Jesus is	2294
	8:12	as he preached the g news of the kingdom	2294
	8:35	told him the g news about Jesus.	2294
	9:36	who was always doing g and helping	19
	10:33	and it was g of you to come.	2822
	10:36	telling the g news of peace	2294
	10:38	around doing g and healing all who were	2308
	11:20	telling them the g news about the Lord	2294
	11:24	He was a g man,	19
	13:32	tell you the g news:	2294
	14: 7	where they continued to preach the g news.	2294
	14:15	We are bringing you g news,	2294
	14:21	They preached the g news in that city	2294
	15:28	It seemed g to the Holy Spirit and to us not	1506
	17:18	because Paul was preaching the g news	2294
	19:25	"Men, you know we receive a g income	2345
	19:27	our trade will lose its g name,	591+1650+2262
	23: 1	to God in all g conscience to this day."	19
Ro	2: 7	by persistence in doing g seek glory,	19
	2:10	honor and peace for everyone who does g:	19
	3: 8	"Let us do evil that g may result"?	19
	3:12	there is no one who does g, not even one."	5983
	4:19	the fact that his body was as g as dead	2453+3739
	5: 7	g man someone might possibly dare to die.	19
	7:12	the commandment is holy, righteous and g.	19
	7:13	Did that which is g, then, become death to	2819
	7:13	produced death in me through what was g,	19
	7:16	I agree that the law is g.	2819
	7:18	I know that nothing g lives in me, that is,	19
	7:18	For I have the desire to do what is g,	NIG
	7:19	For what I do is not the g I want to do;	19
	7:21	I want to do g, evil is right there with me.	2819
	8:28	that in all things God works for the g	19
	9:11	the twins were born or had done anything g	19
	10:15	the feet of those who bring g news!"	19
	10:16	not all the Israelites accepted the g news.	2295
	12: 2	his g, pleasing and perfect will.	19
	12: 9	Hate what is evil; cling to what is g.	19
	12:21	but overcome evil with g.	19
	13: 4	For he is God's servant to do you g.	19
	14:16	not allow what you consider g to be spoken	19
	15: 2	of us should please his neighbor for his g,	19
	16:19	but I want you to be wise about what is g,	19
1Co	5: 6	Your boasting is not g.	2819
	7: 1	It is g for a man not to marry.	2819
	7: 8	It is g for them to stay unmarried, as I am.	2819
	7:26	that it is g for you to remain as you are.	2819
	7:35	I am saying this for your own g,	5239
	10:24	Nobody should seek his own g,	NIG
	10:24	but the g of others.	NIG
	10:33	not seeking my own g but the good	5239
	10:33	not seeking my own good but the g	NIG
	11:17	for your meetings do more harm than g.	3202
	12: 7	of the Spirit is given for the common g.	5237
	14: 6	what g will I be to you,	6067
	15:33	"Bad company corrupts g character."	5982
2Co	5:10	done while in the body, whether g or bad.	19
	6: 8	bad report and g report;	2367
	9: 8	you will abound in every g work.	19
Gal	4:17	zealous to win you over, but for no g.	2822
	4:18	provided the purpose is g,	2819
	5: 7	You were running a g race.	2822
	6: 6	in the word must share all g things	19
	6: 9	Let us not become weary in doing g,	2819
	6:10	let us do g to all people,	19
	6:12	to make a g impression outwardly	2349
Eph	1: 9	of his will according to his g pleasure,	2306
	2:10	created in Christ Jesus to do g works,	19
	6: 8	for whatever g he does,	19
Php	1: 6	a g work in you will carry it on	19
	2:13	and to act according to his g purpose.	2306
	4:14	Yet it was g of you to share in my troubles.	2822
Col	1:10	bearing fruit in every g work,	19
1Th	3: 6	and has brought g news about your faith	2294
	5:21	Test everything. Hold on to the g.	2819
2Th	1:11	by his power he may fulfill every g purpose	20
	2:16	by his grace gave us eternal encouragement	
		and g hope,	19
	2:17	and strengthen you in every g deed	19
1Ti	1: 5	from a pure heart and a g conscience and	19
	1: 8	that the law is g if one uses it properly.	2819
	1:18	by following them you may fight the g fight,	2819
	1:19	holding on to faith and a g conscience.	19
	2: 3	This is g, and pleases God our Savior,	2819
	2:10	but with g deeds, appropriate for women	19
	3: 7	also have a g reputation with outsiders,	2819
	4: 4	For everything God created is g,	2819
	4: 6	you will be a g minister of Christ Jesus,	2819
	4: 6	the truths of the faith and of the g teaching	2819
	5:10	and is well known for her g deeds,	2819
	5:10	to all kinds of g deeds.	19
	5:25	In the same way, g deeds are obvious,	2819
	6:12	Fight the g fight of the faith.	2819
	6:12	when you made your g confession in	2819
	6:13	before Pontius Pilate made the g confession,	2819
	6:18	Command them to do g,	14
	6:18	to be rich in g deeds, and to be generous	2819
2Ti	1:14	the g deposit that was entrusted to you—	2819
	2: 3	Endure hardship with us like a g soldier	2819
	2:21	the Master and prepared to do any g work.	19
	3: 3	brutal, not lovers of g.	920
	3:17	be thoroughly equipped for every g work.	19
	4: 7	I have fought the g fight,	2819

Tit	1: 8	one who loves what is g,	5787
	1:16	disobedient and unfit for doing anything g.	19
	2: 3	but to teach what is g.	2815
	2: 7	an example by doing what is g.	2819
	2:14	eager to do what is g.	2819
	3: 1	to be ready to do whatever is g,	19
	3: 8	to devote themselves to doing what is g.	2819
	3: 8	to devote themselves to doing what is g,	2819
Phm	1: 6	of every g thing we have in Christ.	19
	1:15	that you might have him back for g—	NIG
Heb	5:14	to distinguish g from evil.	2819
	9:11	of the g things that are already here,	19
	10: 1	a shadow of the g things that are coming—	19
	10:24	one another on toward love and g deeds.	2819
	11:12	so from this one man, and he as g as dead,	NIG
	12:10	but God disciplines us for our g,	5237
	13: 9	It is g for our hearts to be strengthened	2819
	13:16	not forget to do g and to share with others,	2343
	13:21	with everything g for doing his will,	19
Jas	1:17	Every g and perfect gift is from above,	19
	2: 3	"Here's a g seat for you,"	2822
	2:14	What g is it, my brothers,	4055
	2:16	about his physical needs, what g is it?	4055
	2:19	that there is one God. G!	2822+4472
	3:13	Let him show it by his g life,	2819
	3:17	submissive, full of mercy and g fruit,	19
	4:17	the g he ought to do and doesn't do it,	2819
1Pe	2: 3	now that you have tasted that the Lord is g.	5982
	2:12	Live such g lives among the pagans that,	2819
	2:12	they may see your g deeds and glorify God	2819
	2:15	that by doing g you should silence	16
	2:18	only to those who are g and considerate,	19
	2:20	if you suffer for doing g and you endure it,	16
	3:10	and see g days must keep his tongue	19
	3:11	He must turn from evil and do g;	19
	3:13	to harm you if you are eager to do g?	19
	3:16	against your g behavior in Christ may	19
	3:17	to suffer for doing g than for doing evil.	16
	3:21	the body but the pledge of a g conscience	19
	4:19	and continue to do g.	17
3Jn	1: 2	I pray that you may enjoy g health and	5617
	1:11	do not imitate what is evil but what is g.	19
	1:11	Anyone who does what is g is from God.	16

GOOD-BY (8)

Ge	31:28	kiss my grandchildren and my daughters g.	5975
Ru	1:14	Orpah kissed her mother-in-law g,	5975
1Ki	19:20	kiss my father and mother g,"	5975
Lk	9:61	but first let me go back and say g	698
Ac	20: 1	said g and set out for Macedonia.	832
	21: 6	After saying g to each other,	571
2Co	2:13	I said g to them and went on to Macedonia.	698
	13:11	Finally, brothers, g.	5897

GOODLIER, GOODLIEST, GOODLY
(KJV) See ADORNED, BEAUTIFUL, BEST,
DELIGHTFUL, FINE, FINEST,
FLOURISHING, HANDSOME, HUGE,
MIGHTY, PROUD, SPLENDID,
WELL-BUILT, WITHOUT EQUAL

GOODMAN (KJV) See HUSBAND,
LANDOWNER, OWNER

GOODNESS (20) [GOOD]

Ex	33:19	"I will cause all my g to pass in front	3206
2Ch	6:41	may your saints rejoice in your g.	3202
Ne	9:25	they reveled in your great g.	3206
	9:35	enjoying your great g to them in	3206
Ps	23: 6	Surely g and love will follow me all	3202
	27:13	I will see the g of the LORD in the land of	3206
	31:19	How great is your g,	3206
	69:16	O LORD, out of the g of your love;	3202
	86:17	Give me a sign of your g,	3208
	109:21	out of the g of your love, deliver me.	3202
	116:12	can I repay the LORD for all his g to me?	9326
	142: 7	about me because of your g to me.	1694
	145: 7	They will celebrate your abundant g	3206
Ro	15:14	that you yourselves are full of g,	20
Gal	5:22	peace, patience, kindness, g, faithfulness,	20
Eph	5: 9	(for the fruit of the light consists in all g,	20
Heb	6: 5	the g of the word of God and the powers of	2819
2Pe	1: 3	by his own glory and g.	746
	1: 5	make every effort to add to your faith g;	746
	1: 5	and to g, knowledge;	746

GOODS (26)

Ge	14:11	The four kings seized all the g of Sodom	8214
	14:16	the g and brought back his relative Lot	8214
	14:21	the people and keep the g for yourself."	8214
	31:18	the g he had accumulated in Paddan Aram,	8214
	31:37	that you have searched through all my g,	3998
	36: 6	and all the g he had acquired in Canaan,	7871
	40:17	In the top basket were all kinds of baked g	685+4407+5126
Ex	22: 7	or g for safekeeping and they are stolen	3998
Nu	31: 9	flocks and g as plunder.	2657
2Ch	21:17	invaded it and carried off all the g found in	8214
Ezr	1: 4	with g and livestock,	8214
	1: 6	with g and livestock.	8214
Ne	13: 8	and threw all Tobiah's household g out of	3998

Ne	13:20	of g spent the night outside Jerusalem.	4928
Est	3:13	the month of Adar, and to plunder their g.	8965
Ps	62:10	in extortion or take pride in stolen g;	1610
Ecc	5:11	g increase, so do those who consume them.	3208
Jer	49:29	be carried off with all their g and camels.	3998
Eze	27:12	because of your great wealth of g;	2104
	27:18	and great wealth of g,	2104
	38:12	rich in livestock and g,	7871
	38:13	and g to seize much plunder?" '	7871
Hab	2: 6	to him who piles up stolen g	2257+4200+4202
Lk	12:18	there I will store all my grain and my g.	19
	17:31	roof of his house, with his g inside,	5007
Ac	2:45	Selling their possessions and g,	5638

GOODWILL (5)

Est	9:30	words of g and assurance—	8934
Pr	11:27	He who seeks good finds g,	8356
	14: 9	but g is found among the upright.	8356
Ac	7:10	to gain the g of Pharaoh king of Egypt;	5921
Php	1:15	out of envy and rivalry, but others out of g.	2306

GOPHER [WOOD] (KJV) See CYPRESS

GORE (3) [GORES, GORING]

Dt	33:17	With them he will g the nations,	5590
1Ki	22:11	'With these you will g the Arameans	5590
2Ch	18:10	'With these you will g the Arameans	5590

GORES (3) [GORE]

Ex	21:28	"If a bull g a man or a woman to death,	5590
	21:31	also applies if the bull g a son or daughter.	5590
	21:32	If the bull g a male or female slave,	5590

GORGE (22) [GORGED]

Ex	15: 9	I will g myself on them.	4848
Dt	2:24	"Set out now and cross the Arnon G.	5707
	2:36	From Aroer on the rim of the Arnon G,	5707
	2:36	and from the town in the g,	5707
	3: 8	from the Arnon G as far as Mount Hermon.	5707
	3:12	of Aroer by the Arnon G,	5707
	3:16	the Arnon G (the middle of the gorge being	5707
	3:16	the Arnon Gorge (the middle of the g being	5707
	4:48	on the rim of the Arnon G to Mount Siyon	5707
Jos	12: 1	from the Arnon G to Mount Hermon,	5707
	12: 2	from Aroer on the rim of the Arnon G—	5707
	12: 2	from the middle of the g—	5707
	13: 9	from Aroer on the rim of the Arnon G,	5707
	13: 9	and from the town in the middle of the g,	5707
	13:16	from Aroer on the rim of the Arnon G,	5707
	13:16	and from the town in the middle of the g,	5707
	15: 7	the Pass of Adummim south of the g.	5707
2Sa	24: 5	south of the town in the g,	5707
2Ki	10:33	from Aroer by the Arnon G through Gilead	5707
2Ch	20:16	and you will find them at the end of the g	5707
Pr	23:20	or g themselves on meat,	2361
Eze	32: 4	and all the beasts of the earth g themselves	8425

GORGED (1) [GORGE]

Rev	19:21	all the birds g themselves on their flesh.	5963

GORGEOUS (KJV) See ELEGANT

GORING (2) [GORE]

Ex	21:29	of g and the owner has been warned but has	5591
	21:36	that the bull had the habit of g,	5591

GOSHEN (15)

Ge	45:10	You shall live in the region of G and be	1777
	46:28	of him to Joseph to get directions to G.	1777
	46:28	When they arrived in the region of G,	1777
	46:29	and went to G to meet his father Israel.	1777
	46:34	be allowed to settle in the region of G,	1777
	47: 1	the land of Canaan and are now in G."	824+1777
	47: 4	please let your servants settle in G."	824+1777
	47: 6	Let them live in G.	824+1777
	47:27	in Egypt in the region of G.	1777
	50: 8	their flocks and herds were left in G.	824+1777
Ex	8:22	with the land of G, where my people live;	1777
	9:26	only place it did not hail was the land of G,	1777
Jos	10:41	and from the whole region of G to Gibeon.	1777
	11:16	all the Negev, the whole region of G,	1777
	15:51	G, Holon and Giloh—	1777

GOSPEL (96)

Mt	24:14	And this g of the kingdom will be preached	2295
	26:13	wherever this g is preached throughout	2295
Mk	1: 1	The beginning of the g about Jesus Christ,	2295
	8:35	for me and for the g will save it.	2295
	10:29	or children or fields for me and the g	2295
	13:10	the g must first be preached to all nations.	2295
	14: 9	the g is preached throughout the world,	2295
Lk	9: 6	from village to village, preaching the g	2294
	20: 1	in the temple courts and preaching the g,	2294
Ac	8:25	preaching the g in many Samaritan villages.	2294
	8:40	preaching the g in all the towns	2294
	15: 7	from my lips the message of the g	2295
	16:10	that God had called us to preach the g	2294
	20:24	task of testifying to the g of God's grace.	2295
Ro	1: 1	an apostle and set apart for the g of God—	2295

Ro	1: 2	**the** g he promised beforehand	4005ˢ
	1: 9	with my whole heart in **preaching** the g	2295
	1:15	so eager *to* **preach the** g also to you who	2294
	1:16	I am not ashamed of the g,	2295
	1:17	For in **the** g a righteousness from God	899ˢ
	2:16	through Jesus Christ, as my g declares.	2295
	11:28	As far as the g is concerned,	2295
	15:16	with the priestly duty of **proclaiming** the g	2295
	15:19	I have fully proclaimed the g of Christ.	2295
	15:20	*to* **preach the** g where Christ was	2294
	16:25	to him who is able to establish you by my g	2295
1Co	1: 17	but *to* **preach the** g—	2294
	4:15	in Christ Jesus I became your father	
		through the g	2295
	9:12	up with anything rather than hinder the g	2295
	9:14	the g should receive their living from	2295
	9:14	should receive their living from the g,	2295
	9:16	Yet when *I* **preach the** g, I cannot boast,	2294
	9:16	Woe to me if *I do* not **preach the** g!	2294
	9:18	that *in* **preaching the** g I may offer it free	2294
	9:23	I do all this for the sake of the g,	2295
	15: 1	to remind you of the g I preached to you,	2295
	15: 2	By **this** g you are saved,	4005ˢ
2Co	2:12	to Troas to **preach** the g of Christ and found	2295
	4: 3	And even if our g is veiled,	2295
	4: 4	so that they cannot see the light *of* the g of	2295
	8:18	by all the churches for his service *to* the g.	2295
	9:13	that accompanies your confession of the g	2295
	10:14	for we did get as far as you with the g	2295
	10:16	*so that we* can **preach** the g in the regions	2294
	11: 4	or a different g from the one you accepted,	2295
	11: 7	to elevate you by **preaching** the g	2294+2295
Gal	1: 6	of Christ and are turning to a different g—	
	1: 7	which is really no g at all.	257ˢ
	1: 7	and are trying to pervert the g of Christ.	2295
	1: 8	from heaven *should* **preach a** g other than	2294
	1: 9	**preaching** to you a g other than what	2294
	1:11	that the g I **preached** is not something	2294+2295
	2: 2	to a revelation and set before them the g	2295
	2: 5	the truth *of* the g might remain with you.	2295
	2: 7	the task *of* **preaching** the g to the Gentiles,	2295
	2:14	not acting in line with the truth *of* the g,	2295
	3: 8	**announced** the g in advance	4603
	4:13	an illness that *I* first **preached** the g to you.	2294
Eph	1:13	the g of your salvation.	2295
	3: 6	the g the Gentiles are heirs together	2295
	3: 7	I became a servant of **this** g by the gift	4005ˢ
	6:15	with the readiness that comes *from* the g	2295
	6:19	the mystery of the g,	2295
Php	1: 5	because of your partnership in the g from	2295
	1: 7	or defending and confirming the g,	2295
	1:12	to me has really served to advance the g.	2295
	1:16	that I am put here for the defense *of* the g.	2295
	1:27	in a manner worthy *of* the g of Christ.	2295
	1:27	as one man for the faith *of* the g	2295
	2:22	with me in the work *of* the g.	2295
	4: 3	at my side in the cause of the g,	2295
	4:15	*with* the g, when I set out from Macedonia,	2295
Col	1: 5	about in the word *of* truth, the g	2295
	1: 6	All over the world **this** g is bearing fruit	NIG
	1:23	not moved from the hope held out in the g.	2295
	1:23	This is the g that you heard and	NIG
1Th	1: 5	our g came to you not simply with words,	2295
	2: 2	of our God we dared to tell you his g	2295
	2: 4	by God to be entrusted with the g.	2295
	2: 8	not only the g of God but our lives as well,	2295
	2: 9	to anyone while we preached the g of God	2295
	3: 2	and God's fellow worker in **spreading** the g	2295
2Th	1: 8	and do not obey the g of our Lord Jesus.	2295
	2:14	He called you to this through our g,	2295
1Ti	1:11	to the glorious g of the blessed God,	2295
2Ti	1: 8	But join with me in suffering *for* the g,	2295
	1:10	and immortality to light through the g.	2295
	1:11	And of **this** g I was appointed a herald and	4005ˢ
	2: 8	descended from David. This is my g,	2295
Phm	1:13	while I am in chains *for* the g.	2295
Heb	4: 2	For we also have had the g **preached** *to* us,	2294
	4: 6	those who formerly **had the g preached**	2294
1Pe	1:12	by those who **have preached the** g to you	2294
	4: 6	For this is the reason the g **was preached**	2294
	4:17	be for those who do not obey the g of God?	2295
Rev	14: 6	the eternal g **to proclaim** to those	2294+2295

GOSSIP (7) [GOSSIPING, GOSSIPS]

Pr	11:13	A g betrays a confidence,	2143+8215
	16:28	and a g separates close friends.	8087
	18: 8	The words of a g are like choice morsels,	8087
	20:19	A g betrays a confidence,	2143+8215
	26:20	without a g a quarrel dies down.	8087
	26:22	The words of a g are like choice morsels,	8087
2Co	12:20	factions, slander, g, arrogance and disorder.	6030

GOSSIPING (1) [GOSSIP]

| 3Jn | 1:10 | g maliciously **about** us. | 5826 |

GOSSIPS (2) [GOSSIP]

| Ro | 1:29 | and malice. They are g, | 6031 |
| 1Ti | 5:13 | but also g and busybodies, | 5827 |

GOT (159) [GET]

Ge	18:16	When the men g up to leave,	7756
	19: 1	*he* g up to meet them and bowed down	7756
	19:27	**Early** the next morning Abraham g up	8899
	19:33	*they* g their father **to drink** wine	9197

Ge	19:33	of it when she lay down or when she g up.	7756
	19:35	*they* g their father **to drink** wine	9197
	19:35	of it when she lay down or when she g up.	7756
	21:21	his mother g a wife for him from Egypt.	4374
	22: 3	**Early** the next morning Abraham g up	8899
	24:54	When *they* g up the next morning, he said,	7756
	24:61	Then Rebekah and her maids g **ready**	7756
	24:64	She g down from her camel	5877
	25:34	He ate and drank, and then g up and left.	7756
	27:14	and g them and brought them to his mother.	4374
	32:22	That night Jacob g up and took his two	7756
	37:31	Then *they* g Joseph's robe,	4374
	38: 6	Judah g a wife for Er, his firstborn,	4374
Ex	2: 3	*she* g a papyrus basket for him and coated it	4374
	2: 8	And the girl went and g the baby's mother.	7924
	2:17	but Moses g up and came to their rescue	7756
	12:30	and all the Egyptians g up during the night,	7756
	24: 4	*He* g up early the next morning and built	8899
	32: 6	down to eat and drink and g up to indulge	7756
Nu	16:25	Moses g up and went to Dathan	7756
	22:13	The next morning Balaam g up and said	7756
	22:21	Balaam g up in the morning,	7756
	24:25	Then Balaam g up and returned home	7756
Jos	6:12	Joshua g up early the next morning and	8899
	6:15	*they* g up at daybreak and marched around	8899
	15:18	When *she* g off her donkey,	4946+6584+7563
Jdg	1:14	When *she* g off her donkey,	4946+6584+7563
	3:26	While they waited, Ehud g away.	4880
	6:28	when the men of the town g up,	8899
	7: 6	All the rest g down on their knees to drink.	4156
	10:16	Then *they* g rid of the foreign gods	6073
	13:11	Manoah g up and followed his wife.	7756
	16: 3	Then *he* g up and took hold of the doors of	7756
	19: 5	On the fourth day *they* g up early	8899
	19: 7	And when the man g up to go,	7756
	19: 9	g up to leave, his father-in-law,	7756
	19:27	When her master g up in the morning	7756
	20:11	of Israel g **together** and united as one man	665
	20:19	The next morning the Israelites g up	7756
Ru	2:15	As *she* g up to glean,	7756
	3:14	g up before anyone could be recognized;	7756
1Sa	3: 6	And Samuel g up and went to Eli and said,	7756
	3: 8	and Samuel g up and went to Eli and said,	7756
	9:26	When Saul g **ready**,	7756
	15:12	**Early** in the morning Samuel g up	8899
	20:34	Jonathan g up from the table	7756
	20:41	David g up from the south side	7756
	25:23	she quickly g off her donkey	3718+4946+6584
	25:42	Abigail quickly g on a donkey and,	8206
	28:23	*He* g up from the ground and sat on	7756
	28:25	That same night *they* g up and left.	7756
	29:11	and his men g up early in the morning	8899
	30:17	and none of them g away,	4880
2Sa	11: 2	One evening David g up from his bed	7756
	12:20	Then David g up from the ground.	7756
	13:29	Then all the king's sons g up,	7756
	14: 6	*They* g **into a fight** with each other in	5897
	18: 9	Absalom's head g **caught** in the tree.	AIT
	19: 8	king g up and took his seat in the gateway.	7756
	24:11	Before David g up the next morning,	7756
1Ki	1: 5	g chariots and horses **ready**,	6913
	3:20	So *she* g up in the middle of the night	7756
	3:21	*I* g up to nurse my son—and he was dead!	7756
	14:17	Then Jeroboam's wife g up and left	7756
	15:12	from the land and g rid of all	6073
	19: 8	So *he* g up and ate and drank.	7756
	21:16	he g up and went down to take possession	7756
2Ki	1:15	So Elijah g up and went down with him to	7756
	3: 2	*He* g rid of the sacred stone of Baal	6073
	3:22	When *they* g up early in the morning,	8899
	4:30	So *he* g up and followed her.	7756
	4:34	Then *he* g on the bed and lay upon the boy,	6590
	4:35	and forth in the room and then g on the bed	6590
	5:21	*he* g down from the chariot to meet him.	5877
	5:26	when the man g down from his chariot	2200
	6:15	of the man of God g up and went out early	7756
	7: 5	At dusk *they* g up and went to the camp of	7756
	7: 7	So *they* g up and fled in the dusk	7756
	7:12	The king g up in the night and said	7756
	9: 6	Jehu g up and went into the house.	7756
	9:16	he g **into** *his* chariot and rode to Jezreel.	8206
	19:35	When *the people* g up the next morning—	8899
	23:24	Josiah g rid of the mediums and spiritists,	1278
2Ch	33:15	*He* g rid of the foreign gods and removed	6073
Est	6:11	So Haman g the robe and the horse.	4374
	7: 7	The king g up in a rage,	7756
	9: 1	and the Jews g **the upper hand**	8948
	9:22	when the Jews g **relief** from their enemies,	5663
Job	1:20	Job g up and tore his robe	7756
Isa	37:36	When *the people* g up the next morning—	8899
Jer	41: 2	and the ten men who were with him g up	7756
Eze	3:23	So *I* g up and went out to the plain.	7756
	29:18	Yet his army g no reward from	2118+4200
Da	6:10	Three times a day he g **down** on his knees	10121
	6:19	the king g up and hurried to the lions' den.	10624
	6:19	*I* g up and went about the king's business.	7756
Zec	11: 8	In one month *I* g rid of	3948
Mt	2:14	So he g up, took the child and his mother	1586
	2:21	So he g up, took the child and his mother	1586
	8:15	and *she* g up and began to wait on him.	1586
	8:23	Then he g **into** the boat	1832
	8:26	Then he g up and rebuked the winds and	1586
	9: 7	And the man g up and went home.	1586
	9: 9	and Matthew g up and followed him.	482
	9:19	Jesus g up and went with him,	1586
	9:25	and *she* g up.	1586
	13: 2	around him that he g into a boat and sat	1832

Mt	14:29	Then Peter g **down** out of the boat,	2849
	15:39	*he* g **into** the boat and went to the vicinity	1832
	22:34	the Pharisees g **together.**	5251
	27:48	one of them ran and g a sponge.	3284
Mk	1:35	while it was still dark, Jesus g up,	482
	2:12	He g up, took his mat and walked out	1586
	2:14	and Levi g up and followed him.	482
	4: 1	that he g into a boat and sat in it out on	1832
	4:39	He g up, rebuked the wind and said to	1444
	5: 2	*When* Jesus g **out** of the boat,	2002
	6:33	from all the towns and g there ahead of	4601
	6:54	As soon as they g **out** of the boat,	2002
	8:10	he g into the boat with his disciples	1832
	8:13	g back into the boat and crossed to	1832
Lk	1:39	At that time Mary g **ready** and hurried to	482
	4:29	They g up, drove him out of the town,	482
	4:39	She g at once and began to wait	482
	5: 3	He g into one of the boats,	1832
	5:28	and Levi g up, left everything and followed	482
	6: 8	So *he* g up and stood there.	2705
	8:22	So they g into a boat and set out.	1832
	8:24	He g up and rebuked the wind and	1444
	8:37	So he g into the boat and left.	1832
	14:20	"Still another said, '*I* just g **married,**	1138+1222
	15:13	the younger son g **together** all he had,	5251
	15:20	So he g up and went to his father.	482
	24:12	Peter, however, g up and ran to the tomb.	482
	24:33	They g up and returned at once	482
Jn	4:52	as to the time when his son g better,	2400
	6:17	where *they* g into a boat and set off across	1832
	6:24	they g into the boats and went	1832
	11:29	she g up quickly and went to him.	1586
	11:31	noticed how quickly she g up and went out,	482
	13: 4	so *he* g up from the meal,	1586
	21: 3	So they went out and g **into** the boat,	1832
Ac	1:18	(With the reward he g for his wickedness,	NIG
	5: 8	the price *you* and Ananias g for the land?"	625
	9: 8	Saul g up from the ground,	1586
	9:18	He g up and was baptized,	482
	9:34	Immediately Aeneas g up.	482
	9:40	then *he* g **down** on his knees and prayed,	5502
	14:20	he g up and went back into the city.	482
	15: 7	Peter g up and addressed them:	482
	16:10	we g **ready** at once to leave for Macedonia,	2426
	21:15	we g **ready** and went up to Jerusalem.	2171
	25:18	*When* his accusers g up to speak,	2705
	28:16	When *we* g to Rome,	1656
1Co	10: 7	down to eat and drink and g up to indulge	482

GOUGE (4) [GOUGED]

Nu	16:14	*Will you* g **out** the eyes of these men?	5941
1Sa	11: 2	with you only on the condition that I g **out**	5941
Mt	5:29	g it **out** and throw it away.	1975
	18: 9	g it **out** and throw it away.	1975

GOUGED (1) [GOUGE]

| Jdg | 16:21 | g **out** his eyes and took him down to Gaza. | 5941 |

GOURD (KJV) See VINE

GOURDS (4)

1Ki	6:18	carved with g and open flowers.	7225
	7:24	Below the rim, g encircled it—	7225
	7:24	The g were cast in two rows in one piece	7225
2Ki	4:39	of its g and filled the fold of his cloak.	7226

GOVERN (17) [GOVERNED, GOVERNING, GOVERNMENT, GOVERNOR, GOVERNOR'S, GOVERNORS, GOVERNS]

Ge	1:16	the greater light to g the day and the lesser	4939
	1:16	to govern the day and the lesser light to g	4939
	1:18	to g the day and the night,	5440
1Sa	9:17	he *will* g my people."	6806
1Ki	3: 9	a discerning heart to g your people and	9149
	3: 9	For who is able to g this great people	9149
2Ch	1:10	for who *is able* to g this great people	9149
	1:11	for wisdom and knowledge *to* g my people	9149
Job	34:17	Can he who hates justice g?	2502
Ps	9: 8	*he will* g the peoples with justice.	1906
	136: 8	the sun to g the day,	4939
	136: 9	the moon and stars to g the night;	4939
Pr	8:16	by me princes g,	8606
Isa	3: 4	mere children *will* g them.	5440
Ob	1:21	on Mount Zion to g the mountains of Esau.	9149
Zec	3: 7	then you *will* g my house and have charge	1906
Ro	12: 8	if it is leadership, let him g diligently;	NIG

GOVERNED (3) [GOVERN]

Jdg	9:22	After Abimelech *had* g Israel three years,	8606
2Ki	15: 5	of the palace and g the people of the land.	9149
2Ch	26:21	of the palace and g the people of the land.	9149

GOVERNING (2) [GOVERN]

| Ro | 13: 1 | to the g authorities, | 5660 |
| | 13: 6 | who give their full time to g. | 899+4047ˢ |

GOVERNMENT (4) [GOVERN]

1Ki	9:22	his g **officials,** his officers, his captains,	6269
Isa	9: 6	and the g will be on his shoulders.	5385
	9: 7	the increase of his g and peace there will	5385
Da	6: 4	against Daniel in his conduct of g **affairs,**	10424

GOVERNMENTS (KJV) See ADMINISTRATION

GOVERNOR (50) [GOVERN]

Ge	42: 6	Now Joseph was the g of the land,	8954
Jdg	9:30	the g of the city heard that Gaal son	8569
1Ki	4:19	He was the only g over the district.	5907
2Ki	10: 5	So the palace administrator, the city g,	889+6584S
	23: 8	to the Gate of Joshua, the city g,	8569
	25:23	king of Babylon **appointed** Gedaliah **as g,**	7212
Ezr	2:63	The g ordered them not to eat any of	9579
	5: 3	Tattenai, g of Trans-Euphrates,	10580
	5: 6	Tattenai, g of Trans-Euphrates,	10580
	5:14	whom he had appointed g,	10580
	6: 6	Now then, Tattenai, g of Trans-Euphrates,	10580
	6: 7	Let the g of the Jews and	10580
	6:13	Tattenai, g of Trans-Euphrates,	10580
Ne	3: 7	the authority of the g of Trans-Euphrates,	7068
	5:14	when I was appointed to be their g in	7068
	5:14	the food allotted to the g,	7068
	5:18	the food allotted to the g,	7068
	7:65	The g, therefore, ordered them not	9579
	7:70	The g gave to the treasury 1,000	9579
	8: 9	Then Nehemiah the g,	9579
	10: 1	Nehemiah the g, the son of Hacaliah.	9579
	12:26	in the days of Nehemiah the g and of Ezra	7068
Isa	60:17	I will make peace your g	7213
Jer	40: 7	**appointed** Gedaliah son of Ahikam **as g**	7212
	40:11	**appointed** Gedaliah son of Ahikam, the son of Shaphan, **as g**	7212
	41: 2	the king of Babylon had **appointed as g**	**7212**
	41:18	the king of Babylon had **appointed as g**	7212
Hag	1: 1	g of Judah, and to Joshua son	7068
	1:14	of Zerubbabel son of Shealtiel, g of Judah,	7068
	2: 2	g of Judah, to Joshua son of Jehozadak,	7068
	2:21	"Tell Zerubbabel g of Judah that	7068
Mal	1: 8	Try offering them to your g!	7068
Mt	27: 2	and handed him over to Pilate, the g.	2450
	27:11	Meanwhile Jesus stood before the g,	2450
	27:11	and the g asked him, "Are you the king	2450
	27:14	to the great amazement of the g.	2450
	27:21	want me to release to you?" asked the g.	2450
	28:14	If this report gets to the g,	2450
Lk	2: 2	that took place while Quirinius was g	2448
	3: 1	when Pontius Pilate was g of Judea,	2448
	20:20	over to the power and authority of the g.	2450
Jn	18:28	to the **palace of the** Roman g.	4550
Ac	23:24	so that he may be taken safely to G Felix."	2450
	23:26	To His Excellency, G Felix: Greetings.	2450
	23:33	the letter to the g and handed Paul over	2450
	23:34	The g read the letter and asked	NIG
	24: 1	against Paul before the g.	2450
	24:10	When the g motioned for him to speak,	2450
	26:30	the g and Bernice and those sitting	2450
2Co	11:32	In Damascus the g under King Aretas had	1617

GOVERNOR'S (2) [GOVERN]

Mt	27:15	Now it was the g custom at the Feast	2450
	27:27	Then the g soldiers took Jesus into	2450

GOVERNORS (24) [GOVERN]

1Ki	4: 7	also had twelve **district** g over all Israel,	5893
	10:15	and from all the Arabian kings and the g of	7068
2Ch	9:14	Also all the kings of Arabia and the g of	7068
Ezr	8:36	and to the g of Trans-Euphrates,	7068
Ne	2: 7	to the g of Trans-Euphrates,	7068
	2: 9	to the g of Trans-Euphrates and gave them	7068
	5:15	But the earlier g—those preceding me—	7068
Est	3:12	satraps, the g of the various provinces and	7068
	8: 9	the satraps, g and nobles of	7068
	9: 3	the g and the king's administrators helped	7068
Jer	51:23	with you I shatter g and officials.	7068
	51:28	their g and all their officials,	7068
	51:57	her g, officers and warriors as well;	7068
Eze	23: 6	in blue, and commanders, all	7068
	23:12	g and commanders, warriors in full dress,	7068
	23:23	all of them g and commanders,	7068
Da	3: 2	He then summoned the satraps, prefects, g,	10580
	3: 3	So the satraps, prefects, g, advisers,	10580
	3:27	g and royal advisers crowded around them.	10580
	6: 7	advisers and g have all agreed that	10580
Mt	10:18	be brought before g and kings as witnesses	2450
Mk	13: 9	On account of me you will stand before g	2450
Lk	21:12	you will be brought before kings and g,	2450
1Pe	2:14	or to g, who are sent by him	2450

GOVERNS (1) [GOVERN]

Job	36:31	the way he g the nations and provides food	1906

GOWN (1)

Ps	45:13	her g is interwoven with gold.	4230

GOYIM (1)

Jos	12:23	of Dor (in Naphoth Dor) one the king of G	1582

GOZAN (5)

2Ki	17: 6	in G on the Habor River and in the towns	1579
	18:11	in G on the Habor River and in towns of	1579
	19:12	the gods of G, Haran,	1579
1Ch	5:26	Habor, Hara and the river of G,	1579
Isa	37:12	the gods of G, Haran,	1579

GRABBED (4)

Jdg	15:15	he g it and struck down a thousand men.	4374
2Sa	2:16	Then each man g his opponent by the head	2616
	13:11	she took it to him to eat, he g her and said,	2616
Mt	18:28	He g him and began to choke him.	3195

GRACE (131) [GRACIOUS, GRACIOUSLY]

Ps	45: 2	and your lips have been anointed with g,	2834
Pr	1: 9	They will be a garland to g your head and	2834
	3:22	an **ornament to** g your neck.	2834
	3:34	He mocks proud mockers but gives g to	2834
	4: 9	She will set a garland of g on your head	2834
Isa	26:10	Though g is **shown** to the wicked,	2858
Jnh	2: 8	to worthless idols forfeit the g that could	2876
Zec	12:10	of Jerusalem a spirit of g and supplication.	2834
Lk	2:40	and the g of God was upon him.	5921
Jn	1:14	came from the Father, full of g and truth.	5921
	1:16	of his g we have all received one blessing	NIG
	1:17	g and truth came through Jesus Christ.	5921
Ac	4:33	and much g was upon them all.	5921
	6: 8	Stephen, a man full of God's g and power,	5921
	11:23	and saw the evidence of the g of God,	5921
	13:43	and urged them to continue in the g of God.	5921
	14: 3	the message of his g by enabling them	5921
	14:26	where they had been committed to the g	5921
	15:11	the g of our Lord Jesus that we are saved,	5921
	15:40	commended by the brothers to the g of	5921
	18:27	to those who by g had believed.	5921
	20:24	task of testifying to the gospel of God's g.	5921
	20:32	to God and to the word of his g,	5921
Ro	1: 5	we received g and apostleship	5921
	1: 7	G and peace to you from God our Father	5921
	3:24	by his g through the redemption that came	5921
	4:16	that it may be by g and may be guaranteed	5921
	5: 2	by faith into this g in which we now stand.	5921
	5:15	how much more did God's g and the gift	5921
	5:15	the gift that came by the g of the one man,	5921
	5:17	of g and of the gift of righteousness reign	5921
	5:20	sin increased, g increased all the more,	5921
	5:21	so also g might reign through righteousness	5921
	6: 1	on sinning so that g may increase?	5921
	6:14	because you are not under law, but under g.	5921
	6:15	we are not under law but under g?	5921
	11: 5	a remnant chosen by g.	5921
	11: 6	And if by g, then it is no longer by works;	5921
	11: 6	if it were, g would no longer be grace.	5921
	11: 6	if it were, grace would no longer be g.	5921
	12: 3	the g given me I say to every one of you:	5921
	12: 6	according to the g given us.	5921
	15:15	because of the g God gave me	5921
	16:20	The g of our Lord Jesus be with you.	5921
1Co	1: 3	G and peace to you from God our Father	5921
	1: 4	because of his g given you in Christ Jesus.	5921
	3:10	By the g God has given me,	5921
	15:10	But by the g of God I am what I am,	5921
	15:10	and his g to me was not without effect.	5921
	15:10	not I, but the g of God that was with me.	5921
	16:23	The g of the Lord Jesus be with you.	5921
2Co	1: 2	G and peace to you from God our Father	5921
	1:12	but according to God's g.	5921
	4:15	so that the g that is reaching more	5921
	6: 1	not to receive God's g in vain.	5921
	8: 1	to know about the g that God has given	5921
	8: 6	to completion this **act of** g on your part.	5921
	8: 7	see that you also excel in this g of giving.	5921
	8: 9	you know the g of our Lord Jesus Christ,	5921
	9: 8	God is able to make all g abound to you,	5921
	9:14	of the surpassing g God has given you.	5921
	12: 9	he said to me, "My g is sufficient for you,	5921
	13:14	May the g of the Lord Jesus Christ,	5921
Gal	1: 3	G and peace to you from God our Father	5921
	1: 6	the one who called you by the g of Christ	5921
	1:15	from birth and called me by his g,	5921
	2: 9	when they recognized the g given to me.	5921
	2:21	I do not set aside the g of God,	5921
	3:18	but God in his g gave it to Abraham	5919
	5: 4	you have fallen away from g.	5921
	6:18	The g of our Lord Jesus Christ be	5921
Eph	1: 2	G and peace to you from God our Father	5921
	1: 6	to the praise of his glorious g,	5921
	1: 7	in accordance with the riches of God's g	5921
	2: 5	it is by g you have been saved.	5921
	2: 7	the incomparable riches of his g,	5921
	2: 8	For it is by g you have been saved,	5921
	3: 2	of God's g that was given to me for you,	5921
	3: 7	of God's g given me through the working	5921
	3: 8	this g was given me:	5921
	4: 7	But to each one of us g has been given	5921
	6:24	G to all who love our Lord Jesus Christ	5921
Php	1: 2	G and peace to you from God our Father	5921
	1: 7	all of you share in God's g with me.	5921
	4:23	The g of the Lord Jesus Christ be	5921
Col	1: 2	G and peace to you from God our Father.	5921
	1: 6	and understood God's g in all its truth.	5921
	4: 6	Let your conversation be always full of g,	5921
	4:18	G be with you.	5921
1Th	1: 1	G and peace to you.	5921
	5:28	The g of our Lord Jesus Christ be with you.	5921
2Th	1: 2	G and peace to you from God our Father	5921
	1:12	the g of our God and the Lord Jesus Christ.	5921
	2:16	and by his g gave us eternal encouragement	5921
	3:18	The g of our Lord Jesus Christ be with you all.	5921
1Ti	1: 2	G, mercy and peace from God the Father	5921
	1:14	The g of our Lord was poured out	5921
	6:21	G be with you.	5921
2Ti	1: 2	G, mercy and peace from God the Father	5921
	1: 9	but because of his own purpose and g.	5921
	1: 9	This g was given us in Christ Jesus before	NIG
	2: 1	be strong in the g that is in Christ Jesus.	5921
	4:22	G be with you.	5921
Tit	1: 4	G and peace from God the Father	5921
	2:11	For the g of God	5921
	3: 7	having been justified by his g,	5921
	3:15	G be with you all.	5921
Phm	1: 3	G to you and peace from God our Father	5921
	1:25	The g of the Lord Jesus Christ be	5921
Heb	2: 9	so that by the g of God he might taste death	5921
	4:16	Let us then approach the throne of g	5921
	4:16	and find g to help us in our time of need.	5921
	10:29	and who has insulted the Spirit of g?	5921
	12:15	the g of God and that no bitter root grows	5921
	13: 9	for our hearts to be strengthened by g,	5921
	13:25	G be with you all.	5921
Jas	4: 6	But he gives us more g.	5921
	4: 6	"God opposes the proud but gives g to the humble."	5921
1Pe	1: 2	G and peace be yours in abundance.	5921
	1:10	who spoke of the g that was to come	5921
	1:13	set your hope fully on the g to be given you	5921
	4:10	faithfully administering God's g	5921
	5: 5	"God opposes the proud but gives g to the humble."	5921
	5:10	And the God of all g, who called you	5921
	5:12	and testifying that this is the true g of God.	5921
2Pe	1: 2	G and peace be yours in abundance through	5921
	3:18	in the g and knowledge of our Lord	5921
2Jn	1: 3	G, mercy and peace from God the Father	5921
Jude	1: 4	who change the g of our God into a license	5921
Rev	1: 4	G and peace to you from him who is,	5921
	22:21	g of the Lord Jesus be with God's people.	5921

GRACEFUL (3)

Job	41:12	his strength and his g form,	2665
Pr	5:19	A loving doe, a g deer—	2834
SS	7: 1	Your g legs are like jewels,	2788

GRACIOUS (42) [GRACE]

Ge	21: 1	the LORD was g to Sarah as he had said,	7212
	33:11	for God has been g to me	2858
	43:29	And he said, "God be g to you, my son."	2858
Ex	34: 6	the LORD, the compassionate and g God,	2843
Nu	6:25	upon you and be g to you;	2858
1Sa	2:21	And the LORD was g to Hannah;	7212
2Sa	1:23	in life they were loved and g,	5833
	12:22	The LORD may be g to me and let	2858
2Ki	13:23	But the LORD was g to them	2858
2Ch	30: 9	LORD your God is g and compassionate.	2843
Ezr	7: 9	for the g hand of his God was on him.	3202
	8:18	Because the g hand of our God was on us,	3202
	8:22	"The g hand of our God is on everyone	3208
	9: 8	the LORD our God has been g	9382
Ne	2: 8	And because the g hand of my God was	3202
	2:18	also told them about the g hand of my God	3202
	9:17	a forgiving God, g and compassionate,	2843
	9:31	for you are a g and merciful God.	2843
Job	33:24	to be g to him and say, 'Spare him	2858
Ps	25:16	Turn to me and be g to me,	2858
	67: 1	May God be g to us and bless us	2858
	86:15	O Lord, are a compassionate and g God,	2843
	103: 8	The LORD is compassionate and g,	2843
	111: 4	the LORD is g and compassionate.	2843
	112: 4	g and compassionate and righteous man.	2843
	116: 5	The LORD is g and righteous;	2843
	119:29	be g to me through your law.	2858
	119:58	be g to me according to your promise.	2858
	145: 8	The LORD is g and compassionate,	2843
Pr	22:11	and whose speech is g will have the king	2834
Ecc	10:12	Words from a wise man's mouth are g,	2834
Isa	30:18	Yet the LORD longs to be g to you;	2858
	30:19	How g he will be when you cry for help!	2858+2858
	33: 2	O LORD, be g to us; we long for you.	2858
Jer	29:10	I will come to you and fulfill my g promise	3202
	33:14	'when I will fulfill the g promise I made to	3202
Joel	2:13	for he is g and compassionate,	2843
Jnh	4: 2	that you are a g and compassionate God,	2843
Mal	1: 9	"Now implore God to be g to us.	2858
Lk	4:22	and were amazed at the g words that came	5921
2Co	1:11	on our behalf for the g **favor granted** us	5922
1Pe	3: 7	and as heirs with you of the g **gift** of life,	5921

GRACIOUSLY (4) [GRACE]

Ge	33: 5	the children God has g **given** your servant."	2858
Hos	14: 2	"Forgive all our sins and receive us g,	3202
Ac	27:24	and God has g **given** you the lives	5919
Ro	8:32	along with him, g give us all things?	5919

GRAFF, GRAFFED (KJV) See GRAFTED

GRAFT (1) [GRAFTED]

Ro	11:23	for God is able to g them **in** again.	1596

GRAFTED (5) [GRAFT]

Ro	11:17	have been g **in among** the others and	1596
	11:19	were broken off so that I could be g **in.**"	1596
	11:23	they will be g **in,** for God is able to graft	1596
	11:24	to nature were g into a cultivated olive tree,	1596
	11:24	be g **into** their own olive tree!	1596

GRAIN (265) [GRAINS, GRANARIES]

Ge	27:28	an abundance of g and new wine.	1841
	27:37	I have sustained him with g and new wine.	1841
	37: 7	We were binding **sheaves of** g out in	524
	41: 5	Seven **heads of** g, healthy and good,	8672
	41: 6	seven other **heads of** g sprouted—	8672
	41: 7	The thin **heads of** g swallowed up	8672
	41:22	"In my dreams I also saw seven **heads of** g,	8672
	41:24	The thin **heads of** g swallowed up	8672
	41:26	the seven good **heads of** g are seven years;	8672
	41:27	the seven worthless **heads of** g scorched by	8672
	41:35	that are coming and store up the g under	1339
	41:49	Joseph stored up huge quantities of g,	1339
	41:56	Joseph opened the storehouses and **sold** g	8690
	41:57	the countries came to Egypt to **buy** g	8690
	42: 1	Jacob learned that there was g in Egypt,	8692
	42: 2	"I have heard that there is g in Egypt.	8692
	42: 3	of Joseph's brothers went down to buy g	1339
	42: 5	among those who went to **buy** g,	8690
	42: 6	the *one who* **sold** g to all its people.	8690
	42:19	while the rest of you go and take g back	8692
	42:25	Joseph gave orders to fill their bags with g,	1339
	42:26	they loaded their g on their donkeys	8692
	43: 2	the g they had brought from Egypt,	8692
	44: 2	along with the silver for his g."	8692
	45:23	and ten female donkeys loaded with g	1339
	47:14	in payment for the g they were buying,	8692
Ex	22: 6	so that it burns **shocks of** g or standing grain	1538
	22: 6	that it burns shocks of grain or **standing** g	7850
	29:41	the same g **offering** and its drink offering	4966
	30: 9	or any burnt offering or g **offering,**	4966
	40:29	on it burnt offerings and g **offerings,**	4966
Lev	2: 1	" 'When someone brings a g **offering** to	4966
	2: 3	The rest of the g **offering** belongs to Aaron	4966
	2: 4	" 'If you bring a g **offering** baked in	4966
	2: 5	If your g **offering** is prepared on a griddle,	4966
	2: 6	it is a g **offering.**	4966
	2: 7	If your g **offering** is cooked in a pan,	4966
	2: 8	Bring the g **offering** made of these things	4966
	2: 9	from the g **offering** and burn it on the altar	4966
	2:10	The rest of the g **offering** belongs to Aaron	4966
	2:11	" 'Every g **offering** you bring to	4966
	2:13	Season all your g **offerings** with salt.	4966
	2:13	of your God out of your g **offerings;**	4966
	2:14	" 'If you bring a g **offering** *of* firstfruits to	4966
	2:14	offer crushed heads of **new** g roasted in	4152
	2:15	Put oil and incense on it; it is a g **offering.**	4966
	2:16	the memorial portion of the **crushed** g and	1762
	5:13	as in the case of the g **offering.'** "	4966
	6:14	the regulations for the g **offering:**	4966
	6:15	with all the incense on the g **offering,**	4966
	6:20	of fine flour as a regular g **offering,**	4966
	6:21	and present the g **offering** broken in pieces	4966
	6:23	Every g **offering** of a priest shall	4966
	7: 9	Every g **offering** baked in an oven	4966
	7:10	and every g **offering,**	4966
	7:37	the g **offering,** the sin offering,	4966
	9: 4	together with a g **offering** mixed with oil.	4966
	9:17	He also brought the g **offering,**	4966
	10:12	"Take the g **offering** left over from	4966
	14:10	with oil for a g **offering,**	4966
	14:20	together with the g **offering,**	4966
	14:21	with oil for a g **offering,**	4966
	14:31	together with the g **offering,**	4966
	23:10	**sheaf of** the first g you harvest.	6684
	23:13	together with its g **offering** *of* two-tenths	4966
	23:14	or roasted or **new** g,	4152
	23:16	and then present an **offering of** new g to	4966
	23:18	together with their g **offerings**	4966
	23:37	the burnt offerings and g **offerings,**	4966
	27:30	whether g *from* the soil or fruit from	2446
Nu	4:16	the regular g **offering** and	4966
	5:15	because it is a g **offering** for jealousy,	4966
	5:18	the g **offering** for jealousy,	4966
	5:25	from her hands the g **offering** for jealousy,	4966
	5:26	then to take a handful of the g **offering** as	4966
	6:15	with their g **offerings** and drink offerings,	4966
	6:17	with its g **offering** and drink offering.	4966
	7:13	fine flour mixed with oil as a g **offering;**	4966
	7:19	fine flour mixed with oil as a g **offering;**	4966
	7:25	fine flour mixed with oil as a g **offering;**	4966
	7:31	fine flour mixed with oil as a g **offering;**	4966
	7:37	fine flour mixed with oil as a g **offering;**	4966
	7:43	fine flour mixed with oil as a g **offering;**	4966
	7:49	fine flour mixed with oil as a g **offering;**	4966
	7:55	fine flour mixed with oil as a g **offering;**	4966
	7:61	fine flour mixed with oil as a g **offering;**	4966
	7:67	fine flour mixed with oil as a g **offering;**	4966
	7:73	fine flour mixed with oil as a g **offering;**	4966
	7:79	fine flour mixed with oil as a g **offering;**	4966
	7:87	together with their g **offering.**	4966
	8: 8	with its g **offering** *of* fine flour mixed	4966
	15: 4	to the LORD a g **offering** *of* a tenth of	4966
	15: 6	a ram prepare a g **offering** *of* two-tenths of	4966
	15: 9	with the bull a g **offering** *of* three-tenths	4966
	15:24	along with its prescribed g **offering**	4966
	18: 9	whether g or sin or guilt offerings,	4966
	18:12	and g they give the LORD as the firstfruits	1841
	18:27	to you as from the threshing floor or juice	1841
	20: 5	It has no g or figs,	2446
	28: 5	with a g **offering** of a tenth of an ephah	4966
	28: 8	along with the same kind of g **offering**	4966
	28: 9	and a g **offering** of two-tenths of an ephah	4966
	28:12	a g **offering** of three-tenths of an ephah	4966
	28:12	with the ram, a g **offering** of two-tenths of	4966
	28:13	a g **offering** of a tenth of	4966

Nu	28:20	a g **offering** of three-tenths of an ephah	4966
	28:26	to the LORD an **offering of** new g during	4966
	28:28	be a g **offering** of three-tenths of an ephah	4966
	28:31	and its g **offering.**	4966
	29: 3	the bull prepare a g **offering** of three-tenths	4966
	29: 6	with their g **offerings** and drink offerings	4966
	29: 9	the bull prepare a g **offering** of three-tenths	4966
	29:11	with its g **offering,** and their drink offerings	4966
	29:14	of the thirteen bulls prepare a g **offering**	4966
	29:16	with its g **offering** and drink offering.	4966
	29:18	prepare their g **offerings** and drink offerings	4966
	29:19	with its g **offering,** and their drink offerings	4966
	29:21	prepare their g **offerings** and drink offering.	4966
	29:22	with its g **offering** and drink offering.	4966
	29:24	prepare their g **offerings** and drink offerings	4966
	29:25	with its g **offering** and drink offering.	4966
	29:27	prepare their g **offerings** and drink offerings	4966
	29:28	with its g **offering** and drink offering.	4966
	29:30	prepare their g **offerings** and drink offering.	4966
	29:31	with its g **offering** and drink offering.	4966
	29:33	prepare their g **offerings** and drink offerings	4966
	29:34	with its g **offering** and drink offering.	4966
	29:37	prepare their g **offerings** and drink offerings	4966
	29:38	with its g **offering** and drink offering.	4966
	29:39	your burnt offerings, g **offerings,**	4966
Dt	7:13	your g, new wine and oil—	1841
	11:14	so that you may gather in your g,	1841
	12:17	the tithe of your g and new wine and oil,	1841
	14:23	Eat the tithe of your g, new wine and oil,	1841
	16: 9	to put the sickle to the **standing** g.	7850
	18: 4	to give them the firstfruits of your g,	1841
	23:25	you must not put a sickle to his **standing** g.	7850
	25: 4	an ox while it *is* **treading out** *the* g.	1889
	28:51	They will leave you no g, new wine or oil,	1841
	33:28	Jacob's spring is secure in a land of g	1841
Jos	5:11	unleavened bread and **roasted** g.	7828
	22:23	to offer burnt offerings and g **offerings,**	4966
	22:29	g **offerings** and sacrifices,	4966
Jdg	13:19	together with the g **offering,**	4966
	13:23	and g **offering** from our hands,	4966
	15: 5	and let the foxes loose in the **standing g** of	7850
	15: 5	He burned up the shocks and **standing** g,	7850
Ru	2: 2	and pick up the **leftover** g behind anyone	8672
	2:14	he offered her *some* **roasted** g.	7039
	2:21	until they finish **harvesting** all my g.' "	7907
	3: 7	to lie down at the far end of the g pile.	6894
1Sa	8:15	of your g and of your vintage and give it	2446
	17:17	of **roasted** g and these ten loaves of bread	7833
	25:18	five dressed sheep, five seahs of **roasted** g,	7833
2Sa	1:21	nor fields that yield offerings [of g].	NIH
	17:19	over the opening of the well and scattered g	8195
	17:28	flour and **roasted** g, beans and lentils,	7833
1Ki	8:64	g **offerings** and the fat of	4966
	8:64	the g **offerings** and the fat of	4966
2Ki	4:42	of barley bread baked from the **first ripe** g,	1137
	4:42	along with *some* **heads of** new g.	4152
	16:13	up his burnt offering and g **offering,**	4966
	16:15	and the evening g **offering,**	4966
	16:15	and his g **offering,**	4966
	16:15	their g **offering** and their drink offering.	4966
	18:32	a land of g and new wine,	1841
1Ch	21:23	and the wheat for the g **offering.**	4966
	23:29	the flour for the g **offerings,**	4966
2Ch	7: 7	the g **offerings** and the fat portions.	4966
	31: 5	the firstfruits of their g,	1841
	32:28	to store the harvest of g, new wine and oil;	1841
Ezr	7:17	with their g **offerings** and drink offerings,	10432
Ne	5: 2	for us to eat and stay alive, we must get g."	1841
	5: 3	and our homes to get g during the famine."	1841
	5:10	also lending the people money and g.	1841
	5:11	the hundredth part of the money, g,	1841
	10:31	or g to sell on the Sabbath,	8692
	10:33	the regular g **offerings** and burnt offerings;	4966
	10:37	of our [g] offerings,	NIH
	10:39	are to bring their contributions of g,	1841
	13: 5	to store the g **offerings** and incense	4966
	13: 5	and also the tithes of g,	1841
	13: 9	with the g **offerings** and the incense.	4966
	13:12	All Judah brought the tithes of g,	1841
	13:15	on the Sabbath and bringing in g	6894
Job	24:24	they are cut off like heads of g.	8672
	31:10	*may* my wife **grind** another man's g,	3221
	39:12	Can you trust him to bring in your g	2446
Ps	4: 7	when their g and new wine abound.	1841
	65: 9	with water to provide the people with g,	1841
	65:13	and the valleys are mantled with g;	1339
	72:16	Let g abound throughout the land;	1339
	78:24	he gave them the g of heaven.	1841
Pr	11:26	People curse the man who holds g,	1339
	27:22	grinding him like g with a pestle,	8195
Isa	5:10	a homer of seed only an ephah of g."	NIH
	17: 5	a reaper gathers the **standing** g and harvests	7850
	17: 5	the standing grain and harvests the g	8672
	17: 5	when a man gleans **heads of** g in the Valley	8672
	19:21	with sacrifices and g **offerings;**	4966
	23: 3	the great waters came the g of the Shihor;	2446
	28:28	G must be ground to make bread;	NIH
	36:17	a land of g and new wine,	1841
	43:23	I have not burdened you with g **offerings**	4966
	57: 6	and offered g **offerings.**	4966
	62: 8	"Never again will I give your g as food	1841
	66: 3	whoever makes a g **offering** is	4966
	66:20	as the Israelites bring their g **offerings,**	4966
Jer	5:17	like **cut** g behind the reaper,	6658
	14:12	and g **offerings,** I will not accept them.	4966
	17:26	g **offerings,** incense and thank offerings to	4966
	23:28	For what has straw to do with g?"	1339

Jer	31:12	the g, the new wine and the oil,	1841
	33:18	to burn g **offerings** and to present	4966
	41: 5	bringing g **offerings** and incense with them	4966
	50:11	a heifer **threshing** g and neigh like stallions,	1889
	50:26	pile her up like **heaps of** g.	6894
Eze	36:29	I will call for the g and make it plentiful	1841
	42:13	the g **offerings,** the sin offerings and	4966
	44:29	They will eat the g **offerings,**	4966
	45:15	These will be used for the g **offerings,**	4966
	45:17	g **offerings** and drink offerings at	4966
	45:17	the sin offerings, g **offerings,**	4966
	45:24	as a g **offering** an ephah for each bull and	4966
	45:25	burnt offerings, g **offerings** and oil.	4966
	46: 5	The g **offering** given with the ram is to be	4966
	46: 5	and the g **offering** with the lambs is to be	4966
	46: 7	He is to provide as a g **offering** one ephah	4966
	46:11	the g **offering** is to be an ephah with a bull,	4966
	46:14	with it morning by morning a g **offering,**	4966
	46:14	The presenting of this g **offering** to	4966
	46:15	So the lamb and the g **offering** and	4966
	46:20	the sin offering and bake the g **offering,**	4966
Hos	2: 8	the g, the new wine and oil, who lavished	1841
	2: 9	"Therefore I will take away my g	1841
	2:22	and the earth will respond to the g,	1841
	7:14	for g and new wine but turn away from me.	1841
	8: 7	Were it to yield g, foreigners would	NIH
	14: 7	He will flourish like the g.	1841
Joel	1: 9	G **offerings** and drink offerings are cut off	4966
	1:10	the g is destroyed, the new wine is dried up	1841
	1:13	for the g **offerings** and drink offerings	4966
	1:17	for the g has dried up.	1841
	2:14	g **offerings** and drink offerings for	4966
	2:19	"I am sending you g, new wine and oil,	1841
	2:24	The threshing floors will be filled with g;	1339
Am	2:13	as a cart crushes when loaded with g.	6658
	5:11	on the poor and force him to give you g.	1339
	5:22	and g **offerings,** I will not accept them.	4966
	8: 5	be over that we may sell g, and the Sabbath	8692
	8: 5	among all the nations as g is shaken in	NIH
Hag	1:11	on the g, the new wine,	1841
Zec	9:17	G will make the young men thrive,	1841
Mt	12: 1	to pick some **heads of** g and eat them.	5092
Mk	2:23	they began to pick some **heads of** g.	5092
	4: 7	so that they did not bear g.	2843
	4:28	All by itself the soil **produces** g—	2844
	4:29	As soon as the g is ripe,	2843
Lk	6: 1	his disciples began to pick some **heads of** g,	5092
	12:18	there I will store all my g and my goods.	4992
	17:35	Two women will be **grinding** g together;	241
Ac	7:12	When Jacob heard that there was g	4989
	27:38	they lightened the ship by throwing the g	4992
1Co	9: 9	an ox *while it is* **treading out the** g."	262
1Ti	5:18	the ox *while it is* **treading out the** g,"	262

GRAINFIELD (1) [FIELD]

Dt	23:25	If you enter your neighbor's g,	7850

GRAINFIELDS (3) [FIELD]

Mt	12: 1	At that time Jesus went through the g on	5077
Mk	2:23	through the g, and as his disciples walked	5077
Lk	6: 1	through the g, and his disciples began	5077

GRAIN, GRAINS (Anglicized) See also KERNEL, KERNELS

GRAINS (3) [GRAIN]

Job	29:18	my days as numerous as the g of sand.	2567
Ps	139:18	they would outnumber the g of sand.	2567
Isa	48:19	your children like its **numberless** g;	5054

GRANARIES (3) [GRAIN]

Ex	22:29	"Do not hold back offerings from your g	4852
Jer	50:26	Break open her g; pile her up like heaps	4393
Joel	1:17	the g have been broken down,	4923

GRANDCHILDREN (7) [CHILD]

Ge	31:28	You didn't even let me kiss my g	1201
	31:55	Early the next morning Laban kissed his g	1201
	45:10	you, your children and g,	1201+1201
Ex	10: 2	that you may tell your children and g	1201+1201
Dt	4:25	After you have had children and g	1201+1201
2Ki	17:41	To this day their children and g	1201+1201
1Ti	5: 4	But if a widow has children or g,	1681

GRANDDAUGHTER (5) [DAUGHTER]

Ge	24:48	get the g *of* my master's brother for his son.	1426
	36: 2	and Oholibamah daughter of Anah and	1426
	36:14	and of Zibeon, whom she bore to Esau:	1426
2Ki	8:26	Athaliah, a g *of* Omri king of Israel.	1426
2Ch	22: 2	Athaliah, a g *of* Omri.	1426

GRANDDAUGHTERS (1) [DAUGHTER]

Ge	46: 7	grandsons and his daughters and g—	1201+1426

GRANDFATHER (1) [FATHER]

2Sa	9: 7	the land that belonged to your g Saul,	3

GRANDFATHER'S (2) [FATHER]

2Sa	16: 3	of Israel will give me back my g kingdom.'	3
	19:28	All my g descendants deserved nothing	3

GRANDMOTHER (3) [MOTHER]

1Ki	15:13	He even deposed his g Maacah	562
2Ch	15:16	King Asa also deposed his g Maacah	562
2Ti	1: 5	in your g Lois and in your mother Eunice	3439

GRANDMOTHER'S (1) [MOTHER]

1Ki	15:10	His g name was Maacah daughter	562

GRANDPARENTS (1) [PARENTS]

1Ti	5: 4	and so repaying their **parents and g,**	4591

GRANDSON (9) [SON]

Ge	11:31	his g Lot son of Haran,	1201+1201
	29: 5	"Do you know Laban, Nahor's g?"	1201
Jdg	8:22	you, your son and your g—	1201+1201
2Sa	9: 9	"I have given your master's g everything	1201
	9:10	that your master's g may be provided for.	1201
	9:10	And Mephibosheth, g of your master,	1201
	16: 3	"Where is your master's g?"	1201
	19:24	Mephibosheth, Saul's g,	1201
Jer	27: 7	his g until the time for his land comes;	1201+1201

GRANDSONS (7) [SON]

Ge	36:12	These were g of Esau's wife Adah.	1201
	36:13	These were g of Esau's wife Basemath.	1201
	36:16	they were g of Adah.	1201
	36:17	they were g of Esau's wife Basemath.	1201
	46: 7	took with him to Egypt his sons and g	1201+1201
Jdg	12:14	He had forty sons and thirty g,	1201+1201
1Ch	8:40	had many sons and g—150 in all.	1201+1201

GRANT (35) [GRANTED, GRANTING, GRANTS]

Ge	19:21	"Very well, *I will* g this request too;	5951+7156
	24:42	please g success *to* the journey	7503
	43:14	And *may* God Almighty g you mercy before	5989
Ex	21: 9	he must g her the rights of a daughter.	6913
Lev	26: 6	" *'I will* g peace in the land,	5989
Dt	28: 7	The LORD *will* g that the enemies	5989
	28:11	The LORD *will* g you **abundant** prosperity	3855
Jdg	11:37	But g me this one request," she said.	6913
Ru	1: 9	the LORD g that each of you will find rest	5989
1Sa	1:17	of Israel g you what you have asked	5989
2Sa	23: 5	and g me my every desire?	NIH
1Ki	5: 9	*to* g my wish by providing food	6913
1Ch	22: 9	and *I will* g Israel peace and quiet	5989
Est	5: 8	and if it pleases the king to g my petition	5989
	7: 3	g me my life—this is my petition.	5989
Job	6: 8	that God *would* g what I hope for,	5989
	13:20	"Only g me these two things, O God,	6913
Ps	20: 2	the sanctuary and g you **support** from Zion.	6184
	20: 5	*May* the LORD g all your requests.	4848
	51:12	of your salvation and g me a willing spirit,	NIH
	85: 7	O LORD, and g us your salvation.	5989
	86:16	g your strength to your servant and save	5989
	94:13	you g him **relief** from days of trouble,	9200
	118:25	O LORD, save us; O LORD, g us **success.**	7503
	140: 8	not g the wicked their desires, O LORD;	5989
Isa	46:13	*I will* g salvation to Zion,	5989
Hag	2: 9	'And in this place *I will* g peace,'	5989
Mt	20:21	"G that one of these two sons	3306
	20:23	to sit at my right or left is not for me *to* g.	1443
Mk	10:40	to sit at my right or left is not for me *to* g.	1443
Lk	18: 3	'G me **justice** against my adversary.'	AIT
	23:24	So Pilate g to their demand.	1181
Ac	24:27	Felix wanted *to* g a favor to the Jews,	2960
2Ti	1:18	the Lord g that he will find mercy from	1443
	2:25	God *will* g them repentance leading them	1443

GRANTED (31) [GRANT]

Ge	4:25	"God has g me another child in place	8883
	24:56	the LORD *has* g **success** *to* my journey.	7503
	39:21	he showed him kindness and g him favor in	5989
Jos	1:13	and *has* g you this land,'	5989
	14: 3	Moses *had* g the two-and-a-half tribes their inheritance east of the Jordan	5989
	14: 3	not g the Levites an inheritance among	5989
1Sa	1:27	the LORD *has* g me what I asked of him.	5989
	25:35	I have heard your words and g your **request."**	5951+7156
2Sa	14:22	the king *has* g his servant's request."	6913
1Ch	4:10	And God g his request.	995
	22:18	And *has* he not g you **rest** on every side?	5663
	23:25	*has* g rest to his people and has come	5663
Ezr	7: 6	The king *had* g everything he asked,	5989
	9: 9	He *has* g us new life to rebuild the house	5989
Ne	2: 8	the king g my **requests.**	5989
Est	5: 6	Even up to half the kingdom, *it will* be g."	6913
	7: 2	Even up to half the kingdom, *it will* be g."	6913
	8:11	The king's edict g the Jews in every city	5989
	9:12	*It will* also be g."	6913
Job	42:15	and their father g them an inheritance along	5989
Ps	21: 2	*You have* g him the desire of his heart	5989
	21: 6	Surely *you have* g him eternal blessings	8883
Pr	10:24	what the righteous desire *will be* g.	5989
Mt	14: 9	he ordered that her request *be* g	1443
	15:28	Your request *is* g."	1181
Jn	5:26	so *he has* g the Son to have life in himself.	1443
	17: 2	For *you* g him authority over all people	1443
Ac	11:18	God *has* g even the Gentiles repentance	1443
Ro	11:20	G. But they were broken off	2822
2Co	1:11	on our behalf for the **gracious favor** g us	5922

GRANTING (1) [GRANT]

Ne	1:11	*by* g him favor in the presence	5989

GRANTS (2) [GRANT]

Ps	127: 2	for *he* g sleep to those he loves.	5989
	147:14	He g peace *to* your borders	8492

GRAPE (10) [GRAPES, GRAPEVINE, GRAPEVINES]

Lev	26: 5	Your threshing will continue until g harvest	1292
	26: 5	the g harvest will continue until planting,	1292
Nu	6: 3	not drink g juice or eat grapes or raisins.	6694
Dt	32:14	You drank the foaming blood of the g.	6694
Jdg	8: 2	the **full** g harvest *of* Abiezer?	1292
Isa	18: 5	and the flower becomes a ripening g,	1235
	24:13	when gleanings are left after the g harvest.	1292
	32:10	the g harvest will fail,	1292
Jer	49: 9	If g pickers came to you,	1305
Ob	1: 5	If g pickers came to you,	1305

GRAPES (43) [GRAPE]

Ge	40:10	and its clusters ripened into g.	6694
	40:11	and I took the g,	6694
	49:11	his robes in the blood of g.	6694
Lev	19:10	or pick up the g **that have fallen.**	7261
	25: 5	or harvest the g of your untended vines.	6694
Nu	6: 3	He must not drink grape juice or eat g **or raisins.**	2256+3313+4300+6694
	13:20	(It was the season for the first ripe g.)	6694
	13:23	a branch bearing a single cluster of g.	6694
	13:24	the **cluster of** g the Israelites cut off there.	864
Dt	23:24	you may eat all the g you want,	6694
	24:21	When *you* **harvest** *the* g in your vineyard,	1305
	28:39	not drink the wine or **gather** *the* g,	112
	32:32	Their g are *filled with* poison,	6694
Jdg	8: 2	**gleanings** of Ephraim's g	6622
	9:27	and gathered the g and trodden them,	4142
Ne	13:15	g, figs and all other kinds of loads.	6694
Job	15:33	be like a vine stripped of its **unripe** g,	1235
Ps	80:12	so that all who pass by pick its g?	NIH
Isa	5: 2	Then he looked for a crop of **good** g,	6694
	5: 4	When I looked for **good** g,	6694
	62: 9	and those who gather **the** g will drink it in	2257S
	65: 8	when juice is still found in a **cluster of** g	864
Jer	6: 9	the branches again, like *one* **gathering** g."	1305
	8:13	There will be no g on the vine.	6694
	25:30	He will shout like those who tread the g,	NIH
	31:29	'The fathers have eaten **sour** g,	1235
	31:30	whoever eats **sour** g—his own teeth will be	1235
	48:32	on your ripened fruit and g.	1292
	49: 9	would they not leave a **few** g?	6622
Eze	18: 2	" 'The fathers eat **sour** g,	1235
Hos	9:10	it was like finding g in the desert;	6694
Joel	3:13	Come, **trample the** g,	8097
Am	9:13	and the planter by the one treading g.	6694
Ob	1: 5	would they not leave a **few** g?	6622
Mic	6:15	you will crush g but not drink the wine.	9408
	7: 1	there is no **cluster of** g to eat,	864
Hab	3:17	the fig tree does not bud and there are no g	3292
Mt	7:16	Do people pick g from thornbushes,	5091
Lk	6:44	or g from briers.	5091
1Co	9: 7	a vineyard and does not eat of its g?	2843
Rev	14:18	the **clusters of** g from the earth's vine,	1084
	14:18	because its g are ripe."	5091
	14:19	gathered its g and threw them into	306

GRAPEVINE (3) [GRAPE, VINE]

Nu	6: 4	Nazirite, he must not eat anything that comes from the g,	1728+3516
Jdg	13:14	She must not eat anything that comes from the g,	1728+3516
Jas	3:12	can a fig tree bear olives, or a g bear figs?	306

GRAPEVINES (1) [GRAPE, VINE]

Nu	20: 5	It has no grain or figs, g or pomegranates.	1728

GRASP (9) [GRASPED, GRASPING, GRASPS]

2Ki	14: 5	After the kingdom was firmly in his g,	3338
Ps	71: 4	from the g of evil and cruel men.	4090
Ecc	7:18	It is good *to* g the one and not let go of	296
Jer	15:21	the wicked and redeem you from the g of	4090
	34: 3	You will not escape from his g but will	3338
Lk	9:45	so that *they did* not g it,	150
Jn	10:39	but he escaped their g.	5931
1Co	14:11	If then *I do* not **g the meaning**	1539+3836+3857
Eph	3:18	*to* g how wide and long and high	2898

GRASPED (6) [GRASP]

Ge	19:16	the men g his hand and the hands	2616
Eze	21:11	to *be* g with the hand;	9530
	21:15	*it is* g for slaughter.	6487
	29: 7	When they g you with their hands,	9530
Hos	12: 3	In the womb *he* g his brother's **heel;**	6810
Php	2: 6	with God **something to be** g,	772

GRASPING (3) [GRASP]

Ge	25:26	with his hand g Esau's heel;	296

GRASPS (2) [GRASP]

Dt	32:41	and my hand g it in judgment,	296
Pr	31:19	In her hand she holds the distaff and g	9461

GRASS (53)

Nu	22: 4	as an ox licks up the g *of* the field."	3764
Dt	11:15	I will provide g in the fields for your cattle,	6912
	32: 2	like showers on **new** g,	2013
2Sa	23: 4	after rain that brings the g from the earth.'	2013
1Ki	18: 5	Maybe we can find *some* g to keep	2945
2Ki	19:26	like g *sprouting* on the roof,	2945
Job	5:25	your descendants like the g *of* the earth.	6912
	6: 5	Does a wild donkey bray when it has g,	2013
	8:12	they wither more quickly than g.	2945
	38:27	and make it sprout with g?	2013+4604
	40:15	with you and which feeds on g like an ox.	2945
Ps	37: 2	for like the g they will soon wither,	2945
	72:16	let it thrive like the g of the field.	6912
	90: 5	they are like the new g of the morning—	2945
	92: 7	that though the wicked spring up like g	6912
	102: 4	My heart is blighted and withered like g;	6912
	102:11	I wither away like g.	6912
	103:15	As for man, his days are like g,	2945
	104:14	He makes g grow for the cattle,	6912
	106:20	for an image of a bull, which eats g,	6912
	129: 6	May they be like g *on* the roof,	2945
	147: 8	the earth with rain and makes g grow on	6912
Pr	19:12	but his favor is like dew on the g.	6912
	27:25	and new growth appears and the g *from*	6912
Isa	5:24	and as **dry** g sinks down in the flames,	3143
	15: 6	up and the g is withered;	2945
	35: 7	g and reeds and papyrus will grow.	2945
	37:27	like g *sprouting* on the roof,	2945
	40: 6	"All men are like g,	2945
	40: 7	The g withers and the flowers fall,	2945
	40: 7	Surely the people are g.	2945
	40: 8	The g withers and the flowers fall,	2945
	44: 4	They will spring up like g in a meadow,	2945
	51:12	the sons of men, who are but g,	2945
	66:14	and you will flourish like g;	2013
Jer	12: 4	and the g *in* every field be withered?	6912
	14: 5	because there is no g.	2013
Da	4:15	remain in the ground, in the g of the field.	10187
	4:23	in the g of the field,	10187
	4:25	you will eat g like cattle and be drenched	10572
	4:32	you will eat g like cattle.	10572
	4:33	He was driven away from people and ate g	10572
	5:21	with the wild donkeys and ate g like cattle;	10572
Mic	5: 7	like showers on the g,	6912
Mt	6:30	If that is how God clothes the g of the field,	5965
	14:19	he directed the people to sit down on the g.	5965
Mk	6:39	down in groups on the green g.	5965
Lk	12:28	If that is how God clothes the g of the field,	5965
Jn	6:10	There was plenty *of* g in that place,	5965
1Pe	1:24	For, "All men are like g,	5965
	1:24	the g withers and the flowers fall,	5965
Rev	8: 7	and all the green g was burned up.	5965
	9: 4	not to harm the g of the earth or any plant	5965

GRASSHOPPER (3) [GRASSHOPPERS]

Lev	11:22	of locust, katydid, cricket or g.	2506
Ps	78:46	He gave their crops to the g,	2885
Ecc	12: 5	and the g drags himself along	2506

GRASSHOPPERS (7) [GRASSHOPPER]

Nu	13:33	We seemed like g in our own eyes,	2506
1Ki	8:37	or blight or mildew, locusts or g,	2885
2Ch	6:28	or blight or mildew, locusts or g,	2885
Ps	105:34	and the locusts came, g without number;	3540
Isa	40:22	and its people are like g.	2506
Na	3:15	the sword will cut you down and, like g,	3540
	3:15	Multiply like g, multiply like locusts!	3540

GRASSLANDS (1) [LAND]

Ps	65:12	The g *of* the desert overflow;	5661

GRATEFUL (1) [GRATIFY, GRATIFYING, GRATITUDE]

Ro	16: 4	the churches of the Gentiles *are* g to them.	2373

GRATIFY (2) [GRATEFUL]

Ro	13:14	and do not think about how to g the desires	NIG
Gal	5:16	not g the desires of the sinful nature.	5464

GRATIFYING (1) [GRATEFUL]

Eph	2: 3	g the cravings of our sinful nature	NIG

GRATING (6)

Ex	27: 4	Make a g for it, a bronze network,	4803
	35:16	altar of burnt offering with its bronze g,	4803
	38: 4	They made a g for the altar,	4803
	38: 5	for the four corners of the bronze g.	4803
	38:30	with its bronze g and all its utensils,	4803
	39:39	the bronze altar with its bronze g, its poles	4803

GRATITUDE (2) [GRATEFUL]

Ac	24: 3	we acknowledge this with profound g.	2374

Other entries at top of columns:

Php	1:29	For *it has been* g to you on behalf	5919
Jdg	7:20	G the torches in their left hands	2616
Pr	27:16	or g oil *with* the hand.	7924

Col 3:16 and spiritual songs with **g** in your hearts   5921

GRAVE (84) [GRAVES]

Ge	37:35	"in mourning will I go down to the **g**	8619
	42:38	you will bring my gray head down to the **g**	8619
	44:29	you will bring my gray head down to the **g**	8619
	44:31	the gray head of our father down to the **g**	8619
Nu	16:30	and they go down alive into the **g**,	8619
	16:33	They went down alive into the **g**,	8619
	19:16	anyone who touches a human bone or a **g**,	7700
	19:18	or a **g** or someone who has been killed	7700
Dt	34:6	but to this day no one knows where his **g** is.	7690
1Sa	2:6	he brings down to the **g** and raises up.	8619
2Sa	22:6	The cords of the **g** coiled around me;	8619
1Ki	2:6	not let his gray head go down to the **g**	8619
	2:9	Bring his gray head down to the **g**	8619
	2:9	in the **g** where the man of God is buried;	7700
2Ki	21:26	He was buried in his **g** in the garden	7690
Job	3:22	and rejoice when they reach the **g**?	7700
	5:26	You will come to the **g** in full vigor,	7700
	7:9	he who goes down to the **g** does not return.	8619
	10:19	from the womb to the **g**!	7700
	11:8	They are deeper than the **depths of the g—**	8619
	14:13	"If only you would hide me in the **g**	8619
	17:1	my days are cut short, the **g** awaits me.	7700
	17:13	If the only home I hope for is the **g**,	8619
	21:13	in prosperity and go down to the **g**,	8619
	21:32	He is carried to the **g**,	8619
	24:19	**g** snatches away those who have sinned.	8619
	40:13	shroud their faces in the **g**.	3243
Ps	5:9	Their throat is an open **g**;	7700
	6:5	Who praises you from the **g**?	8619
	9:17	The wicked return to the **g**,	7700
	16:10	because you will not abandon me to the **g**,	8619
	18:5	The cords of the **g** coiled around me;	8619
	30:3	O LORD, you brought me up from the **g**;	8619
	31:17	be put to shame and lie silent in the **g**.	8619
	49:14	Like sheep they are destined for the **g**,	8619
	49:14	their forms will decay in the **g**,	8619
	49:15	But God will redeem my life from the **g**;	8619
	55:15	let them go down alive to the **g**,	8619
	86:13	from the depths of the **g**.	8619
	88:3	of trouble and my life draws near the **g**.	8619
	88:5	like the slain who lie in the **g**,	7700
	88:11	Is your love declared in the **g**,	7700
	89:48	or save himself from the power of the **g**?	7700
	107:20	he rescued them from the **g**.	8827
	116:3	the anguish of the **g** came upon me;	8619
	141:7	at the mouth of the **g**."	8619
Pr	1:12	let's swallow them alive, like the **g**,	8619
	5:5	her steps lead straight to the **g**.	8619
	7:27	Her house is a highway to the **g**,	8619
	9:18	that her guests are in the depths of the **g**.	8619
	15:24	to keep him from going down to the **g**.	8619
	30:16	the **g**, the barren womb,	8619
Ecc	9:10	do it with all your might, for in the **g**,	8619
SS	8:6	its jealousy unyielding as the **g**.	8619
Isa	5:14	Therefore the **g** enlarges its appetite	8619
	14:9	The **g** below is all astir to meet you	8619
	14:11	to the **g**, along with the noise of your harps;	8619
	14:15	But you are brought down to the **g**,	8619
	22:16	and who gave you permission to cut out a **g**	7700
	22:16	hewing your **g** on the height	7700
	28:15	with the **g** we have made an agreement.	8619
	28:18	your agreement with the **g** will not stand.	8619
	38:18	For the **g** cannot praise you,	8619
	53:9	He was assigned a **g** with the wicked,	7700
	57:9	you descended to the **g** itself!	8619
Jer	5:16	Their quivers are like an open **g**;	7700
	20:17	with my mother as my **g**,	7700
Eze	31:15	down to the **g** I covered the deep springs	8619
	31:16	to the **g** with those who go down to the pit.	8619
	31:17	had also gone down to the **g** with it,	8619
	32:21	the **g** the mighty leaders will say of Egypt	8619
	32:23	of the pit and her army lies around her **g**.	7690
	32:24	with all her hordes around her **g**,	7690
	32:25	with all her hordes around her **g**.	7700
	32:27	who went down to the **g** with their weapons	8619
Hos	13:14	from the power of the **g**;	8619
	13:14	Where, O **g**, is your destruction?	8619
Am	9:2	they dig down to the **depths of the g**,	8619
Jnh	2:2	From the depths of the **g** I called for help,	8619
Na	1:14	I will prepare your **g**, for you are vile."	7700
Hab	2:5	as the **g** and like death is never satisfied,	8619
Jn	11:44	"Take off the **g** clothes and let him go."	NIG
Ac	2:27	because you will not abandon me to the **g**,	87
	2:31	that he was not abandoned to the **g**,	87

GRAVECLOTHES (KJV) See STRIPS OF LINEN

GRAVED, GRAVEN (KJV) See CARVED, ENGRAVED, IDOL, INSCRIBED

GRAVEDIGGERS (1) [DIG]

Eze 39:15 a marker beside it until the **g** have buried it   7699

GRAVEL (2)

Pr 20:17 but he ends up with a mouth full of **g**.   2953
La 3:16 He has broken my teeth with **g**;   2953

GRAVES (14) [GRAVE]

Ex	14:11	"Was it because there were no **g** in Egypt	7700
2Ki	23:6	to powder and scattered the dust over the **g**	7700
2Ch	34:4	the **g** of those who had sacrificed to them.	7700
Isa	65:4	who sit among the **g** and spend their nights	7700
Jer	8:1	of Jerusalem will be removed from their **g**.	7700
Eze	32:22	she is surrounded by the **g** of all her slain,	7700
	32:23	Their **g** are in the depths of the pit	7700
	32:26	with all their hordes around their **g**.	7700
	37:12	I am going to open your **g** and bring you up	7700
	37:13	I open your **g** and bring you up from them.	7700
Mt	23:29	for the prophets and decorate the **g** of	3646
Lk	11:44	because you are like unmarked **g**,	3646
Jn	5:28	all who are in their **g** will hear his voice	3646
Ro	3:13	"Their throats are open **g**;	5439

GRAVITY (KJV) See PROPER RESPECT, SERIOUSNESS

GRAY (11)

Ge	42:38	you will bring my **g head** down to the grave	8484
	44:29	you will bring my **g head** down to the grave	8484
	44:31	the **g head** of our father down to the grave	8484
1Sa	12:2	As for me, I am old and **g**,	8482
1Ki	2:6	not let his **g head** go down to the grave	8484
	2:9	Bring his **g head** down to the grave	8484
Ps	71:18	Even when I am old and **g**,	8484
Pr	16:31	**G** hair is a crown of splendor;	8484
	20:29	**g hair** the splendor of the old.	8484
Isa	46:4	Even to your old age and **g hairs** I am he,	8484
Hos	7:9	His **hair** is sprinkled with **g**,	8484

GRAY-HAIRED (2) [HAIR]

Dt 32:25 women will perish, infants and **g** men.   8484
Job 15:10 The **g** and the aged are on our side,   8482

GRAYHEADED (KJV) See GRAY, GRAY-HAIRED

GRAZE (9) [GRAZED, GRAZES, GRAZING]

Ge	37:12	to **g** their father's flocks near Shechem.	8286
Ex	22:5	or vineyard and lets them stray and they **g**	1278
	34:3	not even the flocks and herds may **g** in front	8286
SS	1:7	where you **g** your **flock** and	8286
	1:8	of the sheep and **g** your young goats by	8286
Isa	5:17	Then sheep will **g** as in their own pasture;	8286
	27:10	there the calves **g**, there they lie down;	8286
	30:23	In that day your cattle will **g**	8286
Jer	50:19	to his own pasture and he will **g** on Carmel	8286

GRAZED (2) [GRAZE]

Ge 41:2 sleek and fat, and they **g** among the reeds.   8286
   41:18 fat and sleek, and they **g** among the reeds.   8286

GRAZES (1) [GRAZE]

Ex 22:5 a man **g** his livestock in a field or vineyard   1278

GRAZING (7) [GRAZE]

Ge	36:24	the hot springs in the desert while he was **g**	8286
	37:13	your brothers are **g the flocks**	8286
	37:16	where they are **g** their **flocks**?"	8286
1Ch	27:29	the Sharonite was in charge of the herds **g**	8286
Job	1:14	and the donkeys were **g** nearby,	8286
Eze	34:14	of Israel will be their **g land.**	5659
	34:14	There they will lie down in good **g land**,	5659

GREASE (KJV) See CALLOUS

GREAT (702) [GREATER, GREATEST, GREATLY, GREATNESS]

Ge	1:16	God made two **g** lights—	1524
	1:21	the **g** creatures of the sea and every living	1524
	6:5	The LORD saw how **g** man's wickedness	8041
	7:11	the springs of the **g** deep burst forth,	8041
	10:12	Nineveh and Calah; that is the **g** city.	1524
	12:2	into a **g** nation and I will bless you;	1524
	12:2	I will **make** your name **g**,	1540
	12:6	the site of the **g tree** of Moreh at Shechem.	471
	13:6	for their possessions were **g**	8041
	13:18	and went to live near the **g trees** of Mamre	471
	14:13	near the **g trees** of Mamre the Amorite,	471
	15:1	I am your shield, your very **g** reward."	2221
	15:14	and afterward they will come out with **g** possessions.	1524
	15:18	from the river of Egypt to the **g** river,	1524
	17:20	and I will make him into a **g** nation.	1524
	18:1	the **g trees** of Mamre while he was sitting	471
	18:18	surely become a **g** and powerful nation,	1524
	18:20	against Sodom and Gomorrah is so **g**	8045
	19:13	to the LORD against its people is so **g**	1540
	19:19	and you have shown such **g** kindness to me	1540
	20:9	you have brought such **g** guilt upon me	1524
	21:8	on the day Isaac was weaned Abraham held a **g** feast.	1524
	21:18	for I will make him into a **g** nation."	1524
	30:8	"I have had a **g** struggle with my sister,	466
	32:7	In **g** fear and distress Jacob divided	4394
	34:12	**Make** the price for the bride and the gift I am to bring as **g** as **you like**,	4394+8049

Ge	35:16	to give birth and had **g difficulty.**	7996
	35:17	And as she was **having g difficulty**	7996
	36:7	Their possessions were too **g** for them	8041
	41:29	Seven years of **g** abundance are coming	1524
	45:7	and to save your lives by a **g** deliverance.	1524
	46:3	for I will make you into a **g** nation there.	1524
	48:19	and he too will become **g**.	1540
Ex	10:14	area of the country in **g numbers.**	3878+4394
	14:31	the **g** power the LORD displayed against	1524
	32:10	Then I will make you into a **g** nation."	1524
	32:11	of Egypt with **g** power and a mighty hand?	1524
	32:21	that you led them into such a **g** sin?"	1524
	32:30	"You have committed a **g** sin.	1524
	32:31	what a **g** sin these people have committed!	1524
Lev	11:18	the little owl, the cormorant, the **g** owl,	3568
	11:29	the weasel, the rat, any kind of **g lizard**,	7370
	19:15	to the poor or favoritism to the **g**,	1524
Nu	13:32	All the people we saw there are of **g size.**	4500
	14:19	In accordance with your **g** love,	1542
	22:18	not do anything **g** or small to go beyond	1524
	34:6	be the coast of the **G** Sea.	1524
	34:7	run a line from the **G** Sea to Mount Hor	1524
Dt	1:7	as far as the **g** river, the Euphrates.	1524
	1:17	hear both small and **g** alike.	1524
	3:5	there were also a **g** many unwalled villages.	4394
	4:6	"Surely this **g** nation is a wise	1524
	4:7	so **g** as to have their gods near them	1524
	4:8	so **g** as to have such righteous decrees	1524
	4:32	Has anything so **g** as this ever happened,	1524
	4:34	or by **g** and awesome deeds,	1524
	4:36	On earth he showed you his **g** fire,	1524
	4:37	of Egypt by his Presence and his **g** strength,	1524
	5:25	This **g** fire will consume us,	1524
	6:22	and wonders—**g** and terrible—	1524
	7:19	You saw with your own eyes the **g** trials,	1524
	7:21	is a **g** and awesome God.	1524
	7:23	into **g** confusion until they are destroyed.	1524
	9:26	by your **g power** and brought out of Egypt	1542
	9:29	that you brought out by your **g** power	1524
	10:17	the **g** God, mighty and awesome,	1524
	10:21	who performed for you those **g**	1524
	11:7	that saw all these **g** things	1524
	11:30	near the **g trees** of Moreh,	471
	14:16	the little owl, the **g** owl, the white owl,	3568
	17:16	must not **acquire g numbers** of horses for	8049
	18:16	nor see this **g** fire anymore,	1524
	19:6	overtake him if the distance is too **g**,	8049
	26:5	and lived there and became a **g** nation,	1524
	26:8	with **g** terror and with miraculous signs	1524
	29:3	With your own eyes you saw those **g** trials,	1524
	29:3	those miraculous signs and **g** wonders.	1524
	29:28	and in **g** wrath the LORD uprooted them	1524
Jos	1:4	and from the **g** river, the Euphrates—	1524
	1:4	to the **G** Sea on the west.	1524
	2:9	to you and that a **g fear** of you has fallen	399
	3:16	It piled up in a heap a **g** distance away,	4394
	7:9	then will you do for your own **g** name?"	1524
	9:1	of the **G** Sea as far as Lebanon (the kings of	1524
	10:10	who defeated them in a **g** victory	1524
	15:12	the coastline of the **G** Sea.	1524
	15:47	of Egypt and the coastline of the **G** Sea.	1524
	17:1	because the Makirites were **g soldiers**.	408+4878
	22:8	to your homes with your **g** wealth—	8041
	22:8	and a **g quantity** of clothing—	2221+4394
	23:4	the Jordan and the **G** Sea in the west.	1524
	23:9	"The LORD has driven out before you **g**	1524
	24:17	performed those **g** signs before our eyes.	1524
Jdg	2:7	the **g** things the LORD had done for Israel.	1524
	2:15	They were in **g** distress.	4394
	4:11	by the **g tree** in Zaanannim near Kedesh.	471
	9:6	and Beth Millo gathered beside the **g tree**	471
	10:9	and Israel was in **g** distress.	4394
	12:2	in a **g** struggle with the Ammonites,	4394
	15:18	"You have given your servant this **g** victory.	1524
	16:5	the secret of his **g** strength and	1524
	16:6	of your **g** strength and how you can be tied	1524
	16:15	the secret of your **g** strength."	1524
	16:23	to offer a **g** sacrifice to Dagon their god and	1524
	20:38	up a **g** cloud of smoke from the city,	8049
1Sa	1:16	of my **g** anguish and grief."	8044
	2:17	This sin of the young men was very **g** in	1524
	4:5	all Israel raised such a **g** shout that	1524
	4:10	The slaughter was very **g**;	1524
	5:9	throwing it into a **g** panic.	1524+4394
	6:9	then the LORD has brought this **g** disaster	1524
	10:3	on from there until you reach the **g tree**	471
	11:15	and all the Israelites held a **g** celebration.	4394
	12:16	and see this **g** thing the LORD is about	1524
	12:22	For the sake of his **g** name the LORD will	1540
	14:45	about this **g** deliverance in Israel?	1524
	17:24	they all ran from him in **g** fear.	4394
	17:25	The king will give **g** wealth to	1524
	18:14	In everything he did he had **g success**,	8505
	19:5	The LORD won a **g** victory for all Israel,	1524
	19:22	for Ramah and went to the **g** cistern	1524
	20:2	my father doesn't do anything, **g** or small,	1524
	26:25	you will do **g** things and surely triumph."	6913+6913
	28:15	"I am in **g** distress," Saul said.	4394
	30:16	of the **g amount** of plunder they had taken	1524
2Sa	3:22	from a raid and brought with them a **g deal**	8041
	3:38	and a **g man** has fallen in Israel this day?	1524
	7:9	Now I will make your name **g**,	1524
	7:21	you have done this **g thing**	1525
	7:22	"How **g you** are, O Sovereign LORD!	1540
	7:23	and to perform **g** and awesome wonders	1525

2Sa
7:26 so that your name *will be* g forever. 1540
8: 8 David took a g **quantity** of bronze. 2221+4394
12:30 He took a g **quantity** of plunder from 2221+4394
18: 7 and the casualties that day were g— 1524
18:29 "I saw g confusion just as Joab was about 1524
20: 8 While they were at the g rock in Gibeon, 1524
22:36 you stoop down *to* **make** me g. 8049
22:51 *He* **gives** his king g victories; 1540
23:10 The LORD brought about a g victory 1524
23:12 and the LORD brought about a g victory. 1524
23:20 who performed g exploits. 8041
24:14 for his mercy is g; 8041

1Ki
1:19 He has sacrificed g **numbers** of cattle, 8044
1:25 down and sacrificed g **numbers** of cattle, 8044
3: 6 "You have shown g kindness 1524
3: 6 You have continued this g kindness to him 1524
3: 8 the people you have chosen, a g people, 8041
3: 9 For who is able to govern this g nation. 3878
4:29 gave Solomon wisdom and very g insight, 2221
5: 7 a wise son to rule over this g nation. 8041
7: 9 from the outside to the g courtyard and 1524
7:12 The g courtyard was surrounded by a wall 1524
8:42 of your g name and your mighty hand 1524
10: 2 at Jerusalem with a very g caravan— 3878
10:11 and from there they brought g **cargoes** 2221+4394
10:18 the king made a g throne inlaid with ivory 1524
19:11 Then a g and powerful wind tore 1524
22:13 "Do not fight with anyone, small or g, 1524

2Ki
3:27 The fury against Israel was g; 1524
5: 1 He was a g man in the sight of his master 1524
5:13 prophet had told you to do some g thing, 1524
6:23 So he prepared a g feast for them, 1524
6:25 There was a g famine in the city; 1524
7: 6 of chariots and horses and a g army, 1524
8: 4 about all the g **things** Elisha has done." 1524
10:19 I am going to hold a g sacrifice for Baal. 1524
17:21 and caused them to commit a g sin. 1524
18:19 " 'This is what the g king, 1524
18:28 "Hear the word of the g king, 1524
22:13 G is the LORD's anger that burns 1524

1Ch
11: 6 under the g **tree** in Jabesh. 461
11:14 and the LORD brought about a g victory. 1524
11:22 who performed g exploits. 8041
12:22 until he had a g army, 1524
16:25 g is the LORD and most worthy of praise; 1524
17:19 you have done this g **thing** 1525
17:19 and made known all these *promises*. 1525
17:21 and to perform g and awesome wonders 1525
17:24 and that your name *will be* g forever. 1540
18: 8 David took a g quantity of bronze, 4394
20: 2 He took a g **quantity** of plunder from 2221+4394
21:13 for his mercy is very g; 8041
22: 5 of g magnificence and fame and splendor 1540
22:14 "I have **taken** g **pains** to provide for 928+6715
22:14 bronze and iron too g to be weighed, 4200+8044
29: 1 The task is g, because this palatial 1524
29:22 with g joy in the presence of the LORD 1524

2Ch
1: 1 and **made** him exceedingly g. 1540
1: 8 "You have shown g kindness 1524
1:10 for who is able to govern this g people 1524
2: 5 "The temple I am going to build will be g, 1524
2:13 Huram-Abi, a man of g **skill**, 1069+2682+3359
6:32 from a distant land because of your g name 1524
6:42 Remember the g **love** *promised* 2876
9: 1 Arriving with a g caravan— 3878
9:17 the king made a g throne inlaid with ivory 1524
14:13 a g number of Cushites fell that they could NIH
15: 5 of the lands were in g turmoil. 8041
15:13 were to be put to death, whether small or g, 1524
16: 8 a mighty army with g **numbers** 2221+4394
17: 5 so that he had g wealth and honor, 4200+8044
18: 1 Jehoshaphat had g wealth and honor, 4200+8044
18:30 "Do not fight with anyone, small or g, 1524
20:25 a g **amount** of equipment and clothing 4200+8044
21:19 and he died in g pain. 8273
24:11 and collected a g **amount** of money. 4200+8044
25:10 Judah and left for home in a g **rage**. 678+3034
25:13 and carried off g **quantities** of plunder. 8041
28: 8 They also took a g **deal** of plunder. 8041
28:13 For our guilt is already g, 8041
30:21 for seven days with g rejoicing. 1524
30:24 A g **number** of priests consecrated
    themselves. 4200+8044
30:26 There was g joy in Jerusalem. 1524
31: 5 They brought a g **amount**, 4200+8044
31:10 and this g **amount** is left over." 2162
32:27 Hezekiah had very g riches and honor, 2221
32:29 and acquired g **numbers** of flocks and
    herds, 4200+8044
32:29 for God had given him very g riches. 8041
34:21 G is the LORD's anger that is poured out 1524

Ezr
3:11 And all the people gave a g shout of praise 1524
4:10 the g and honorable Ashurbanipal deported 10647
5: 8 to the temple of the g God. 10647
5:11 that a g king of Israel built and finished. 10647
8:22 his g anger is against all who forsake him." 6437
9: 7 until now, our guilt has been g. 1524
9:13 a result of our evil deeds and our g guilt, 1524

Ne
1: 3 the province are in g trouble and disgrace. 1524
1: 5 God of heaven, the g and awesome God, 1524
1:10 by your g strength and your mighty hand. 1524
3:27 the g projecting tower to the wall of Ophel. 1524
4:14 Remember the Lord, who is g and awesome, 1524
5: 1 the men and their wives raised a g outcry 1524
6: 3 on a g project and cannot go down. 1524
8: 6 Ezra praised the LORD, the g God; 1524
8:12 of food and to celebrate with g joy, 1524

Ne
8:17 And their joy was very g. 1524
9:19 "Because of your g compassion you did 8041
9:25 they reveled in your g goodness. 1524
9:27 in your g compassion you gave them
    deliverers, 8041
9:31 But in your g mercy you did not put an end 8041
9:32 "Now therefore, O our God, the g 1524
9:35 enjoying your g goodness to them in 8041
9:37 We are in g distress. 1524
12:43 And on that day they offered g sacrifices, 1524
12:43 because God had given them g joy. 1524
13:22 to me according to your g love. 8044

Est
2:18 And the king gave a g banquet. 1524
4: 3 there was g mourning among the Jews, 4394
4: 4 she was in g distress. 1524

Job
2:13 they saw how g his suffering *was*. 1540+4394
3:19 The small and the g are there, 1524
4:10 yet the teeth of the g lions are broken. 4097
12:23 *He* **makes** nations g, and destroys them; 8434
21:28 You say, 'Where now is the g **man's** house, 5618
22: 5 Is not your wickedness g? 8041
23: 6 Would he oppose me with g power? 8041
26: 3 what g insight you have displayed! 4200+8044
30:18 In his g power [God] becomes like clothing 8044
31:25 if I have rejoiced over my g wealth, 8041
36:26 *How* g is God—beyond our understanding! 8438
37: 5 he does g **things** beyond our understanding. 1524
37:23 in his justice and g righteousness, 8044
39:11 Will you rely on him for his g strength? 8041

Ps
2: 1 But I, by your g love, 8044
17: 7 Show the wonder of your g **love**, 2876
17:12 like a g **lion** crouching in cover. 4097
18:14 g bolts of lightning and routed them. 8041
18:35 you stoop down *to* **make** me g. 8049
18:50 *He* **gives** his king g victories; 1540
19:11 in keeping them there is g reward. 8041
19:13 innocent of g transgression. 8041
21: 1 How g is his joy in the victories you give! 4394
21: 5 the victories you gave, his glory is g; 1524
22:25 the theme of my praise in the g assembly; 8041
25: 6 O LORD, your g **mercy** and love, 8171
25:11 forgive my iniquity, though it is g. 8041
26:12 in the g **assembly** I will praise the LORD. 5220
31:19 How g is your goodness, 8041
33:16 no warrior escapes by his g strength. 8044
33:17 despite *all* its g strength it cannot save. 8044
35:18 I will give you thanks in the g assembly; 8041
36: 6 your justice like the g deep. 8041
37:11 the land and enjoy g peace. 8044
40: 9 I proclaim righteousness in the g assembly; 8041
40:10 and your truth from the g assembly. 8041
47: 2 the g King over all the earth! 1524
48: 1 G is the LORD, and most worthy of praise, 1524
48: 2 the city of the G King. 8041
49: 6 in their wealth and boast of their g riches? 8044
51: 1 g compassion blot out my transgressions. 8044
52: 7 but trusted in his g wealth and grew strong 8044
57:10 For g is your love, reaching to the heavens; 1524
66: 3 *So* g is your power 8044
68:11 and g was the company 8041
68:26 Praise God in the g congregation; 5220
68:27 there the g **throng** of Judah's princes, 8086
69:13 in your g love, O God, 8041
69:16 in your g mercy turn to me. 8044
71:19 O God, you who have done g *things*. 1524
76: 1 his name is g in Israel. 1524
77:13 What god is *so* g as our God? 1524
82: 1 God presides in the g assembly; 446
86:10 For you are g and do marvelous deeds; 1524
86:13 For g is your love toward me; 1524
89: 1 I will sing of the LORD's g **love** forever; 2876
89:49 where is your former g **love**, 2876
90:11 For your wrath is as g as the fear NIH
91:13 you will trample the g **lion** and 4097
92: 5 How g *are* your works, O LORD, 1540
93: 4 Mightier than the thunder of the g waters, 8041
94:19 When anxiety was g within me, 8044
95: 3 For the LORD is the g God, 1524
95: 3 the g King above all gods. 1524
96: 4 g is the LORD and most worthy of praise; 1524
99: 2 G is the LORD in Zion; 1524
99: 3 Let them praise your g 1524
102:10 because of your g **wrath**, 2256+2405+7912
103:11 *so* g *is* his love for those who fear him; 1504
104: 1 O LORD my God, *you are* very g; 1540
106:21 who had done g *things* in Egypt, 1524
106:45 and out of his g love he relented. 8044
107:43 and consider the g **love** *of* the LORD. 2876
108: 4 For g is your love, higher than the heavens; 1524
109:30 in the g **throng** I will praise him. 8041
111: 2 G are the works of the LORD; 1524
112: 1 who finds g delight in his commands. 4394
115:13 who fear the LORD—small and g alike. 1524
116: 6 *when I was* in g **need**, he saved me. 1937
117: 2 For g *is* his love toward us, 1504
119:14 as one rejoices in g riches. 3972
119:156 Your compassion is g, O LORD; 8041
119:162 in your promise like one who finds g spoil. 8041
119:165 G **peace** have they who love your law, 8041
126: 2 "The LORD has done g *things* for them." 1540
126: 3 The LORD has done g *things* for us, 1540
131: 1 I do not concern myself with g *matters* 1524
135: 5 I know that the LORD is g, 1524
136: 4 to him who alone does g wonders, 1524
136: 7 who made the g **lights**— 1524
136:17 who struck down g kings, 1524
138: 5 for the glory of the LORD is g. 1524

Ps
145: 3 G is the LORD and most worthy of praise; 1524
145: 6 and I will proclaim your g **deeds**. 1525
147: 5 G is our Lord and mighty in power; 1524
148: 7 you g **sea creatures** and all ocean depths, 9490

Pr
5:23 led astray by his own g folly. 8044
6:35 he will refuse the bribe, however g it is. 8049
13: 7 to be poor, yet has g wealth. 8041
14:29 A patient man has g understanding, 8041
15: 6 house of the righteous contains g treasure, 8041
15:16 of the LORD than g wealth with turmoil. 8041
18:16 and ushers him into the presence of the g. 1524
21:14 in the cloak pacifies g wrath. 6434
22: 1 good name is more desirable than g riches; 8041
23:24 father of a righteous man *has* g joy; 1635+1635
24: 5 A wise man has g power, 6437
25: 6 and do not claim a place among g *men*; 1524
28:12 the righteous triumph, there is g elation; 8041

Ecc
2: 4 *I* **undertook** g projects: 1540
2:21 This too is meaningless and a g misfortune. 8041
5:17 with g frustration, affliction and anger. 2221
10: 4 calmness can lay g errors to rest. 1524

Isa
5: 9 "Surely the g houses will become desolate, 8041
9: 2 in darkness have seen a g light; 1524
10:33 will lop off the boughs with g **power**. 5124
12: 6 for g is the Holy One of Israel among you." 1524
13: 4 like that of a g multitude! 8041
17:12 they roar like the roaring of g waters! 3888
23: 3 the g waters came the grain of the Shihor, 8041
27: 1 his fierce, g and powerful sword, 1524
27:13 And in that day a g trumpet will sound. 1524
29: 6 with thunder and earthquake and g noise, 1524
29:15 Woe to those *who* go to g depths 6676
30:25 In the day of g slaughter, 8041
31: 1 and in the g strength of their horsemen, 4394
31: 4 "As a lion growls, a g **lion** over his prey— 4097
32: 2 and the shadow of a g rock in a thirsty land. 3878
34: 6 a sacrifice in Bozrah and a g slaughter 1524
34: 7 the bull calves and the g bulls. 52
34:11 the g **owl** and the raven will nest there. 3568
36: 4 "Tell Hezekiah, " 'This is what the g king, 1524
36:13 "Hear the word of the g king, 1524
40:26 of his g power and mighty strength, 8044
42:21 of his righteousness *to* **make** *his* law g 1540
51:10 the waters of the g deep, 8041
53:12 a portion among the g, 8041
54:13 and g will be your children's peace. 8041

Jer
2:12 O heavens, and shudder with g horror," 4394
2:31 a desert to Israel or a land of g **darkness?** 4420
5: 6 for their rebellion is g 8045
6:22 a g nation is being stirred up from the ends 1524
9:19 How g is our shame! 4394
10: 6 No one is like you, O LORD; you are g, 1524
10:22 a g commotion from the land of the north! 1524
13: 9 of Judah and the g pride of Jerusalem. 8041
14: 7 For our backsliding *is* g; 8045
16:10 the LORD decreed such a g disaster 1524
21: 5 in anger and fury and g wrath. 1524
22: 8 done such a thing to this g city?' 1524
22:14 a g palace with spacious upper rooms.' 4500
25:14 be enslaved by many nations and g kings; 1524
27: 5 With my g power and outstretched arm 1524
27: 7 and g kings will subjugate him. 1524
28: 8 against many countries and g kingdoms. 1524
30:14 your guilt is *so* g and your sins so many. 8044
30:15 Because of your g guilt I have done 8044
31: 8 a g throng will return. 1524
31:15 mourning and g weeping, 9476
31:20 *I have* g compassion *for* him," 8163+8163
32:17 the heavens and the earth by your g power 1524
32:18 O g and powerful God, 1524
32:19 g are your purposes. 1524
32:21 and an outstretched arm and with g terror. 1524
32:37 in my furious anger and g wrath; 1524
32:42 As I have brought all this g calamity 1524
33: 3 to me and I will answer you and tell you g 1524
36: 7 against this people by the LORD are g." 1524
41:12 They caught up with him near the g pool 8041
44: 2 the g disaster I brought on Jerusalem and 3972
44: 7 Why bring *such* g disaster on yourselves 1524
44:26 'I swear by my g name,' says the LORD, 1524
45: 5 Should you then seek g *things* for yourself? 1524
48: 3 cries of g havoc and destruction. 1524
50: 9 against Babylon an alliance of g nations 1524
50:22 the noise of g destruction! 1524
50:41 a g nation and many kings are being stirred 1524
51:54 the sound of g destruction from the land of 1524
51:55 Waves [of enemies] will rage like g waters; 8041

La
1: 1 who once was g among the nations! 8041
3:22 Because of the LORD's g **love** we are 2876
3:23 new every morning; g is your faithfulness. 8041
3:32 so g is his unfailing love. 8044

Eze
1: 4 of Israel and Judah is exceedingly g; 1524
14: 4 in keeping with his g idolatry. 8044
17: 3 A g eagle with powerful wings, 1524
17: 7 " 'But there was another g eagle 1524
17:17 with his mighty army and g horde will be 8041
21:14 a sword for g slaughter, 1524
25:17 I will carry out g vengeance on them 1524
26: 7 with horsemen and a g army. 1524
27:12 because of your g wealth of goods; 3972+8044
27:18 of your many products and g wealth 3972+8044
27:33 with your g wealth and your wares 8044
28: 5 By your g skill in trading 8044
31: 6 all the g nations lived in its shade. 8041
32: 3 a g throng of people I will cast my net 8041
36:23 I will show the holiness of my g name, 1524

Eze 37: 2 a g many bones on the floor of the valley, 4394
38: 4 and a g horde with large and small shields, 8041
38:15 all of them riding on horses, a g horde, 1524
38:19 at that time there shall be a g earthquake in 1524
39:17 the g sacrifice on the mountains of Israel. 1524
47: 7 I saw a g number of trees on each side of 4394
47:10 like the fish of the G Sea. 1524
47:15 the north side it will run from the G Sea by 1524
47:19 along the Wadi [of Egypt] to the G Sea. 1524
47:20 the G Sea will be the boundary to 1524
48:28 along the Wadi [of Egypt] to the G Sea. 1524
Da 2: 6 from me gifts and rewards and g honor. 10678
2:10 No king, however g and mighty, 10647
2:45 "The g God has shown the king 10647
4: 3 How g are his signs, 10647
4:22 You have become g and strong; 10648
4:30 "Is not this the g Babylon I have built as 10647
5: 1 a g banquet for a thousand of his nobles 10647
7: 2 winds of heaven churning up the g sea. 10647
7: 3 Four g beasts, each different from 10647
7:17 'The four g beasts are four kingdoms 10647
8: 4 He did as he pleased and became g. 1540
8: 6 the canal and charged at him in g rage. 3946
8: 8 The goat became very g, 1540
8:11 It set itself up to be as g as the Prince 1540
9: 4 "O Lord, the g and awesome God, 1524
9:12 by bringing upon us g disaster. 1524
9:18 but because of your g mercy. 8041
10: 1 and it concerned a g war. 1524
10: 4 as I was standing on the bank of the g river, 1524
10: 8 So I was left alone, gazing at this g vision; 1524
11: 3 with g power and do as he pleases. 8041
11: 5 will rule his own kingdom with g power. 8041
11:10 for war and assemble a g army, 8041
11:28 to his own country with g wealth. 1524
11:40 with chariots and cavalry and a g fleet 8041
11:44 in a g rage to destroy and annihilate many. 4774
12: 1 the g prince who protects your people, 1524
Hos 1:11 for g will be the day of Jezreel. 1524
5:13 and sent to the g king for help. 3714
5:14 like a g lion to Judah. 4097
9: 7 so many and your hostility so g, 8041
10: 6 to Assyria as tribute for the g king. 3714
10:15 Bethel, because your wickedness is g. 8288+8288
Joel 1: 4 the g locusts have eaten; 746
1: 4 what the g locusts have left 746
2:11 The day of the LORD is g; it is dreadful. 1524
2:20 Surely he has done g things. 1540
2:21 Surely the LORD has done g things. 1540
2:25 the g locust and the young locust, 746
2:25 my g army that I sent among you. 1524
2:31 before the coming of the g and dreadful day 3489
3:13 so g is their wickedness!" 8041
Am 2: 2 in g tumult amid war cries and the blast 8623
3: 9 the g unrest within her and the oppression 8041
5:12 and how g your sins. 6786
6: 2 go from there to g Hamath, 8041
6:11 the g house into pieces and the small house 1524
7: 4 up the g deep and devoured the land. 8041
Jnh 1: 2 the g city of Nineveh and preach against it, 1524
1: 4 Then the LORD sent a g wind on the sea, 1524
1:12 that this g storm has come upon you." 1524
1:17 LORD provided a g fish to swallow Jonah, 1524
3: 2 "Go to the g city of Nineveh and proclaim 1524
4:11 not be concerned about that g city?" 1524
Na 1: 3 LORD is slow to anger and g in power; 1524
3:10 and all her g men were put in chains. 1524
Hab 3:15 churning the g waters. 8041
Zep 1:14 "The g day of the LORD is near— 1524
3:17 He will take g delight in you, 928+8464+8525
Zec 2: 4 a city without walls because of the g
number of men and livestock 8044
12:11 the weeping in Jerusalem will be g, 1540
14: 4 forming a g valley, 1524+4394
14:13 be stricken by the LORD with g panic. 8041
14:14 g quantities of gold and silver 4200+4394+8044
Mal 1: 5 'G is the LORD 1540
1:11 My name will be g among the nations, 1524
1:11 my name will be g among the nations," 1524
1:14 For I am a g king," 1524
4: 5 before that g and dreadful day of 1524
Mt 2:18 weeping and g mourning, 4498
4:16 in darkness have seen a g light; 3489
5:12 because g is your reward in heaven. 4498
5:19 be called g in the kingdom of heaven. 3489
5:35 for it is the city of the G King. 3489
6:23 how g is that darkness! 4531
7:27 beat against that house, and it fell with a g
crash." 899+1639+3489+3836+4774
8:10 not found anyone in Israel with such g faith. 5537
13:46 When he found one of g value, 4501
15:28 Jesus answered, "Woman, you have g faith! 4501
15:30 G crowds came to him, bringing the lame, 4498
19:22 he went away sad, because he had g wealth. 4498
20:26 to become g among you must 3489
24:21 For then there will be g distress, 3489
24:24 and perform g signs and miracles 3489
24:30 with power and g glory. 4498
27:14 to the g amazement of the governor. 3336
27:19 a g deal today in a dream because of him." 4498
Mk 5:26 She had suffered a g deal under the care 4498
10:22 because he had g wealth. 4498
10:43 to become g among you must 3489
13: 2 "Do you see all these g buildings?" 3489
13:26 of Man coming in clouds with g power 4498
Lk 1:15 for he will be g in the sight of the Lord. 3489
1:32 He will be g and will be called the Son of 3489

Lk 1:49 Mighty One has done g things for me— 3489
1:58 that the Lord had shown her g mercy, 3486
2:10 I bring you good news of g joy that will be 3489
2:13 a g company of the heavenly host appeared 4436
5:29 Then Levi held a g banquet for Jesus 3489
6:17 a g number of people from all over Judea, 4498
6:23 because g is your reward in heaven. 4498
6:35 Then your reward will be g, 4498
7: 9 not found such g faith even in Israel." 5537
7:16 "A g prophet has appeared among us," 3489
8:23 and they were in g danger. NIG
14:16 "A certain man was preparing a g banquet 3489
16:26 and you a g chasm has been fixed, 3489
18:23 because he was a man of g wealth. 5379
21:11 There will be g earthquakes, 3489
21:11 and fearful events and g signs from heaven. 3489
21:23 There will be g distress in the land 3489
21:27 in a cloud with power and g glory. 4498
24:52 and returned to Jerusalem with g joy. 3489
Jn 5: 3 a g number of disabled people used to lie— 4436
6: 2 and a g crowd of people followed him 4498
6: 5 up and saw a g crowd coming toward him, 4498
10:32 "I have shown you many g miracles from 2819
12:12 The next day the g crowd that had come for 4498
Ac 2:20 before the coming of the g and glorious day 3489
4:29 to speak your word with g boldness. 4246
4:33 With g power the apostles continued 3489
5: 5 g fear seized all who heard what had 3489
5:11 G fear seized the whole church 3489
6: 8 did g wonders and miraculous signs among 3489
7:11 bringing g suffering, and our fathers could 3489
8: 1 that day a g persecution broke out against 3489
8: 8 So there was g joy in that city. 4498
8: 9 He boasted that he was someone g, 3489
8:10 the divine power known as the G Power." 3489
8:13 by the g signs and miracles he saw. 3489
11:21 a g number of people believed and turned 4498
11:24 and a g number of people were brought to 2653
11:26 the church and taught g numbers of people. 2653
14: 1 a g number of Jews and Gentiles believed. 4498
16:16 She earned a g deal of money 4498
17:11 with g eagerness and examined 4246
18:25 and he spoke with g fervor and 2417+3836+4460
18:27 he was a g help to those who 4498
19:23 there arose a g disturbance 3900+4024+5431
19:27 the g goddess Artemis will be discredited, 3489
19:28 "G is Artemis of the Ephesians!" 3489
19:34 "G is Artemis of the Ephesians!" 3489
19:35 the guardian of the temple of the g Artemis 3489
20:19 Lord with g humility and with tears, 4246+5425
21:35 of the mob was so g he had to be carried by NIG
23: 9 There was a g uproar, 3489
25:23 Agrippa and Bernice came with g pomp 4498
26:22 and testify to small and g alike. 3489
26:24 "Your g learning is driving you insane." 4498
27:10 to be disastrous and bring g loss to ship 4498
Ro 9: 2 I have g sorrow and unceasing anguish 3489
9:22 with g patience the objects of his wrath— 4498
16: 2 for she has been a g help to many people, NIG
1Co 1: 8 We were under g pressure, 2848+5651
2: 4 of distress and anguish of heart and 4498
6: 4 in every way: in g endurance; 4498
7: 4 I have g confidence in you; 4498
7: 4 I take g pride in you. 4498
8:22 even more so because of his g confidence 4498
12: 7 of these surpassingly g revelations, 5651
12:12 were done among you with g perseverance. 4246
Eph 1:19 and his incomparably g power 3490
2: 4 But because of his g love for us, God, 4498
Php 2:29 Welcome him in the Lord with g joy, 4246
Col 1:11 so that you may have g endurance 4246+5705
2:18 goes into g detail about what he has seen, 1836
1Ti 3:13 an excellent standing and g assurance 4498
3:16 the mystery of godliness is g: 3489
6: 6 But godliness with contentment is g gain. 4246
2Ti 4: 2 g patience and careful instruction. 3429+4246
4: 3 they will gather around them a g number NIG
4:14 the metalworker did me a g deal of harm. 4498
Tit 2:13 the glorious appearing of our g God 3489
Phm 1: 7 Your love has given me g joy 4498
Heb 2: 3 if we ignore such a g salvation? 5496
4:14 since we have a g high priest who has gone 3489
7: 4 Just think how g he was: 4383
10:21 we have a g priest over the house of God, 3489
10:32 when you stood your ground in a g contest 4498
12: 1 since we are surrounded by such a g cloud 5537
13:20 that g Shepherd of the sheep, 3489
Jas 3: 5 but it makes g boasts. 3489
3: 5 Consider what a g forest is set on fire by 2462
1Pe 1: 3 In his g mercy he has given us new birth 4498
1: 4 which is of g worth in God's sight. 4500
2Pe 1: 4 Through these he has given us his very g 3492
1Jn 3: 1 How g is the love the Father has lavished 4534
2Jn 1: 4 It has given me g joy to find some 3336
3Jn 1: 3 It gave me g joy to have some of 3336
Jude 1: 6 for judgment on the g Day, 3489
1:24 without fault and with g joy— 21
Rev 6:12 There was a g earthquake. 3489
6:17 For the g day of their wrath has come, 3489
7: 9 and there before me was a g multitude 4498
7:14 who have come of the g tribulation; 3489
8:10 and a g star, blazing like a torch, fell 3489
9:14 who are bound at the g river Euphrates." 3489
11: 8 the g city, which figuratively is called 3489
11:17 because you have taken your g power 3489
11:18 reverence your name, both small and g— 3489

Rev 11:19 an earthquake and a g hailstorm. 3489
12: 1 A g and wondrous sign appeared in heaven: 3489
12: 9 The g dragon was hurled down— 3489
12:14 the two wings of a g eagle, 3489
13: 2 and his throne and g authority. 3489
13:13 And he performed g and miraculous signs, 3489
13:16 He also forced everyone, small and g, 3489
14: 8 Fallen is Babylon the G, 3489
14:19 into the g winepress of God's wrath. 3489
15: 1 in heaven another g and marvelous sign: 3489
15: 3 "G and marvelous are your deeds, 3489
16:12 on the g river Euphrates. 3489
16:14 to gather them for the battle on the g day 3489
16:19 The g city split into three parts, 3489
16:19 the G and gave her the cup filled with 3489
17: 1 the punishment of the g prostitute, 3489
17:18 MYSTERY BABYLON THE G 3489
17:18 The woman you saw is the g city that rules 3489
18: 1 He had g authority, 3489
18: 2 Fallen is Babylon the G! 3489
18:10 Woe, O g city, O Babylon, city of power! 3489
18:16 Woe, O g city, dressed in fine linen, 3489
18:17 In one hour such g wealth has been brought 5537
18:18 'Was there ever a city like this g city?' 3489
18:19 O g city, where all who had ships on 3489
18:21 the g city of Babylon will be thrown down, 3489
18:23 Your merchants were the world's g men. 3491
19: 1 of a g multitude in heaven shouting: 4498
19: 2 the g prostitute who corrupted the earth 3489
19: 5 you who fear him, both small and g!" 3489
19: 6 I heard what sounded like a g multitude, 4498
19:17 gather together for the g supper of God, 3489
19:18 free and slave, small and g." 3489
20: 1 and holding in his hand a g chain. 3489
20:11 a g white throne and him who was seated 3489
20:12 And I saw the dead, g and small, 3489
21:10 in the Spirit to a mountain g and high, 3489
21:12 It had a g, high wall with twelve gates, 3489
21:21 The g street of the city was of pure gold, 4423
22: 2 down the middle of the g street of the city. 4423

GREATER (80) [GREAT]

Ge 1:16 the g light to govern the day and 1524
39: 9 No one is g in this house than I am. 1524
41:40 to the throne will I be g than you." 1540
48:19 his younger brother will be g than he, 1540
49:26 Your father's blessings are g than 1504
Ex 18:11 that the LORD is g than all other gods, 1524
Nu 14:12 into a nation g and stronger than they." 1524
24: 7 "Their king will be g than Agag; 8123
Dt 4:38 before you nations g and stronger than you 1524
9: 1 the Jordan to go in and dispossess nations g 1524
20: 1 and chariots and an army g than yours, 8041
Ru 3:12 "This kindness is g than 3512
1Sa 14:30 of the Philistines have been even g?" 8049
2Sa 13:16 a g wrong than what you have already done 1524
19:43 g claim on David than you have. 4946
23:19 Was he not held in g honor than the Three? 3954
23:23 He was held in g honor than any of 4946
1Ki 1:37 make his throne even g than 1540
1:47 and his throne g than yours!' 1540
4:30 Solomon's wisdom was g than the wisdom 8049
4:30 and g than all the wisdom of Egypt. NIH
10:23 King Solomon was g in riches 1540
1Ch 11:25 He was held in g honor than any of 4946
2Ch 2: 5 because our God is g than all other gods. 1524
9:22 King Solomon was g in riches 1540
32: 7 there is a g power with us than with him. 8041
Job 33:12 for God is g than man. 8049
Ps 4: 7 You have filled my heart with g joy than 4946
135: 5 that our Lord is g than all gods. 4946
Ecc 2: 9 I became g by far than anyone 1540
La 4: 6 The punishment of my people is g than 1540
Da 2:30 I have g wisdom than other living men, 10427
4:36 became even g than before. 10323+10339+10650
Hag 2: 9 be g than the glory of the former house,' 1524
Zec 12: 7 not be g than that of Judah. 1540
Mt 11:11 not risen anyone g than John the Baptist; 3505
11:11 in the kingdom of heaven is g than he. 3505
12: 6 I tell you that one g than the temple is here. 3505
12:41 and now one g than Jonah is here. 4498
12:42 and now one g than Solomon is here. 4498
23:17 You blind fools! Which is g: 3505
23:19 You blind men! Which is g: 3505
Mk 12:31 There is no commandment g than these." 3505
Lk 7:28 of women there is no one g than John; 3505
7:28 in the kingdom of God is g than he." 3505
11:31 and now one g than Solomon is here. 4498
11:32 and now one g than Jonah is here. 4498
22:27 For who is g, the one who is at the table or 3505
Jn 1:50 You shall see g things than that." 3505
3:30 He must become g; I must become less. 889
4:12 Are you g than our father Jacob, 3505
5:20 he will show him even g things than these. 3505
8:53 Are you g than our father Abraham? 3505
10:29 who has given them to me, is g than all; 3505
13:16 no servant is g than his master, 3505
13:16 a messenger g than the one who sent him. 3505
14:12 He will do even g things than these, 3505
14:28 for the Father is g than I. 3505
15:13 G love has no one than this, that he lay 3505
15:20 'No servant is g than his master.' 3505
19:11 over to you is guilty of a g sin." 3505
Ro 9:12 how much g riches will their fullness bring! 3437
1Co 12:24 the body and has given g honor to the parts 4358
12:31 But eagerly desire the g gifts. 3505

1Co	14: 5	He who prophesies is g than one who	3505
		speaks in tongues,	
2Co	3:11	how much g is the glory of that which lasts!	3437
	7: 7	so that my joy was g than ever.	3437
	7:15	for you is all the g when he remembers	4359
Heb	3: 3	found worthy of g honor than Moses,	4498
	3: 3	as the builder of a house has g honor *than*	4498
	6:13	there was no one g for him to swear by,	3505
	6:16	Men swear by *someone* g than themselves,	3505+3836
	7: 7	the lesser person is blessed by the g.	3202
	9:11	through the g and more perfect tabernacle	3505
	11:26	as *of* g value than the treasures of Egypt,	3505
1Pe	1: 7	your faith—of g worth than gold,	4501
1Jn	3:20	For God is g than our hearts,	3505
	4: 4	because the one who is in you is g than	3505
	5: 9	but God's testimony is g because it is	3505
3Jn	1: 4	I have no g joy than to hear	3504

GREATER SIDON (2) [SIDON]

Jos	11: 8	and pursued them all the way to S,	7478
	19:28	Hammon and Kanah, as far as S.	7478

GREATEST (31) [GREAT]

Jos	14:15	who was the g man among the Anakites.)	1524
2Sa	7: 9	like the names of the g *men* of the earth.	1524
2Ki	23: 2	all the people from the least to the g.	1524
	25:26	all the people from the least to the g,	1524
1Ch	12:14	and the g for a thousand.	1524
	17: 8	like the names of the g *men* of the earth.	1524
2Ch	34:30	all the people from the least to the g.	1524
Est	1: 5	for all the people from the least to the g,	1524
	1:20	from the least to the g."	1524
Job	1: 3	the g man among all the people of the East.	1524
Jer	6:13	"From the least to the g,	1524
	8:10	From the least to the g,	1524
	31:34	from the least of them to the g,"	1524
	42: 1	from the least to the g approached	1524
	42: 8	and all the people from the least to the g,	1524
	44:12	From the least to the g,	1524
Jnh	3: 5	from the g to the least, put on sackcloth.	1524
Mt	18: 1	"Who is the g in the kingdom of heaven?"	3505
	18: 4	like this child is the g in the kingdom	3505
	22:36	which is the g commandment in the Law?"	3489
	22:38	This is the first and g commandment.	3489
	23:11	The g among you will be your servant.	3505
Mk	9:34	they had argued about who was the g.	3505
Lk	9:46	as to which of them would be the g.	3505
	9:48	he who is least among you all—he is the g."	3489
	22:24	as to which of them was considered to be g.	3505
	22:26	g among you should be like the youngest,	3505
Jn	7:37	On the last and g day of the Feast,	3489
1Co	13:13	But the g of these is love.	3505
Heb	8:11	from the least of them to the g.	3489
1Pe	1:10	**searched intently and with the g care,**	1699+2001+2779

GREATLY (73) [GREAT]

Ge	3:16	"I will g increase your pains	8049+8049
	7:18	The waters rose and increased g on	4394
	7:19	They rose g on the earth,	4394+4394
	13:13	of Sodom were wicked and were sinning g	4394
	17: 2	will g increase your numbers."	928+4394+4394
	17:20	and will g increase his numbers.	928+4394+4394
	21:11	The matter distressed Abraham g	4394
	30:30	before I came has increased g,	4200+8044
	47:27	and were fruitful and increased g	4394
	48:16	may they increase g upon the earth."	4200+8044
Ex	1: 7	the Israelites were fruitful and multiplied g	8049
Dt	6: 3	that you may increase g in a land flowing	4394
1Sa	19: 4	and what he has done has benefited you g.	4394
	26:21	I have acted like a fool and have erred g."	2221+4394
	28:21	to Saul and saw that he was g shaken,	4394
	30: 6	David was g distressed because	4394
2Sa	24:10	"I have sinned g in what I have done.	4394
1Ki	1:40	playing flutes and rejoicing g,	1524
	5: 7	he was g pleased and said,	4394
1Ch	4:38	Their families increased g,	4200+8044
	19: 5	for they were g humiliated.	4394
	21: 8	"I have sinned g by doing this.	4394
	29: 9	David the king also rejoiced g.	1524
2Ch	26:15	he was g helped until he became powerful.	7098
	33:12	the LORD his God and humbled himself g	4394
Ezr	10: 9	g distressed by the occasion and because of	8283
	10:13	because *we have* sinned g in this thing.	8049
Ne	4: 1	he became angry and was g incensed.	2221
	13: 8	I was g displeased and threw all Tobiah's	4394
Job	20: 2	to answer because I am g disturbed.	2591
Ps	47: 9	he is g exalted.	4394
	89: 7	of the holy ones God is g feared;	8041
	107:38	and their numbers g increased,	4394
	109:30	With my mouth I will g extol the LORD;	4394
	116:10	therefore I said, "I am g afflicted."	4394
	119:167	I obey your statutes, for I love them g.	4394
	129: 1	They have g oppressed me from my youth,	8041
	129: 2	they have g oppressed me from my youth,	8041
Ecc	9:13	example of wisdom that g impressed me:	1524
Isa	31: 6	to him you *have so* g revolted against,	6676
	35: 2	*it will* **rejoice** g and shout for joy	677+1635+1638
	61:10	I **delight** g in the LORD;	8464+8464
	66:10	**rejoice** g with her.	5375+8464
Jer	3:16	**numbers** *have* increased g in	2256+7238+8049
	14:10	"They g love to wander;	4027

Jer	50:12	your mother will be g ashamed;	4394
La	1: 8	Jerusalem *has* **sinned** g and	2627+2628
Da	4: 1	*May* you prosper g!	10677
	4:19	(also called Belteshazzar) *was* g perplexed	10724
	6:14	he was g distressed;	10678
	6:25	"*May* you prosper g!"	10677
	11:39	*will* g honor those who acknowledge him.	8049
Jnh	1:16	At this the men g feared the LORD,	1524
	4: 1	Jonah was g displeased and became angry.	1524
Zec	9: 9	Rejoice g, O Daughter of Zion!	4394
Mt	17:15	"He has seizures and is suffering g.	2809
	18:31	they were g distressed and went	5379
	19:25	they were g astonished and asked,	5379
Mk	6:20	When Herod heard John, he was g puzzled;	4498
	6:26	The king was g distressed,	4337
Lk	1:29	Mary was g troubled at his words	1410
	23: 8	When Herod saw Jesus, he was g pleased,	3336
Ac	4: 2	*They were* g disturbed because	1387
	7:17	number of our people in Egypt g increased.	889+2779+4437
	17:16	he *was* g distressed to see that	4236
	20:12	and were g comforted.	3585+4024
2Co	7: 4	I am g encouraged;	4155+4444
	10:15	of activity among you will g expand,	1650+4353
Php	4:10	I rejoice g in the Lord that at all you	3487
Heb	6:18	the hope offered to us may be g encouraged.	2708
1Pe	1: 6	In this *you* g rejoice, though now	22
Rev	17: 6	When I saw her, I was g astonished.	3489

GREATNESS (16) [GREAT]

Ex	15: 7	In the g of your majesty you threw	8044
Dt	3:24	to show to your servant your g	1542
	32: 3	Oh, praise the g of our God!	1542
1Ch	29:11	is the g and the power and the glory and	1525
2Ch	9: 6	half the g of your wisdom was told me;	5270
Est	10: 2	with a full account of the g *of* Mordecai	1525
Ps	145: 3	his g no one can fathom.	1525
	150: 2	praise him for his surpassing g.	1542
Isa	63: 1	striding forward in the g of his strength?	8044
Eze	38:23	And so *I will* **show** *my* g and my holiness,	1540
Da	4:22	your g has grown until it reaches the sky,	10650
	5:18	and g and glory and splendor.	10650
	7:27	power and g of the kingdoms under	10650
Mic	5: 4	*his* g will reach to the ends of the earth.	1540
Lk	9:43	And they were all amazed at the g of God.	3484
Php	3: 8	a loss compared to the **surpassing** g	5660

GREAVES (1)

1Sa	17: 6	on his legs he wore bronze g,	5196

GRECIA, GRECIANS (KJV) See GREEK

GRECIAN (2) [GREECE]

Ac	6: 1	the G Jews among them complained against	1821
	9:29	He talked and debated with the G Jews,	1821

GREECE (7) [GRECIAN, GREEK, GREEKS]

Isa	66:19	to Tubal and G, and to the distant islands	3430
Eze	27:13	"'G, Tubal and Meshech traded with you;	3430
Da	8:21	The shaggy goat is the king of G,	3430
	10:20	and when I go, the prince of G will come;	3430
	11: 2	up everyone against the kingdom of G.	3430
Zec	9:13	O G, and make you like a warrior's sword.	3430
Ac	20: 2	and finally arrived in G,	1817

GREED (12) [GREEDY]

Isa	57:17	I was enraged by his sinful g;	1299
Eze	16:27	I gave you over to the g of your enemies.	5883
Mt	23:25	but inside they are full of g	771
Mk	7:22	g, malice, deceit, lewdness,	4432
Lk	11:39	but inside you are full of g and wickedness.	771
	12:15	Be on your guard against all kinds of *g*;	4432
Ro	1:29	with every kind of wickedness, evil,	4432
Eph	5: 3	or of any kind of impurity, or of g,	4432
Col	3: 5	lust, evil desires and g, which is idolatry.	4432
1Th	2: 5	nor did we put on a mask to cover up g—	4432
2Pe	2: 3	In their g these teachers will exploit you	4432
	2:14	they are experts in g—an accursed brood!	4432

GREEDY (13) [GREED]

Ps	10: 3	he blesses the g and reviles the LORD.	1298
Pr	15:27	A g *man* brings trouble to his family,	1298+1299
	28:25	A g *man* stirs up dissension,	5883+8146
	29: 4	but *one who is* g for bribes tears it down.	AIT
Jer	6:13	all *are* g for gain;	1298
	8:10	all *are* g for gain;	1298
Eze	33:31	but their hearts *are* g for unjust gain.	339+2143
Hab	2: 5	Because he *is* as g as the grave and	8143
1Co	5:10	or the g and swindlers, or idolaters.	4431
	5:11	a brother but is sexually immoral or g,	4431
	6:10	nor the g nor drunkards nor slanderers	4431
Eph	5: 5	No immoral, impure or g **person**—	4431
1Pe	5: 2	not g **for money**, but eager to serve;	154

GREEK (11) [GREECE]

Mk	7:26	The woman was a G,	1820
Jn	19:20	in Aramaic, Latin and G.	1822
Ac	16: 1	but whose father was a G.	1818
	16: 3	for they all knew that his father was a G.	1818
	17:12	also a number of prominent G women	1820
	17:12	prominent Greek women and many G men.	NIG
	21:37	"Do you speak G?"	1822

Gal	2: 3	even though he was a G.	1818
	3:28	There is neither Jew nor G, slave nor free,	1818
Col	3:11	Here there is no G or Jew,	1818
Rev	9:11	in Hebrew is Abaddon, and in G, Apollyon.	1819

GREEKS (18) [GREECE]

Eze	27:19	and G from Uzal bought your merchandise;	3430
Joel	3: 6	of Judah and Jerusalem to the G,	1201+3436
Jn	7:35	scattered among the G, and teach	1818
	7:35	and teach the G?	1818
	12:20	Now there were some G among those	1818
Ac	11:20	went to Antioch and began to speak to G	1821
	17: 4	a large number *of* God-fearing G and not	1818
	17:17	*with* the Jews and the **God-fearing** G,	4936
	18: 4	trying to persuade Jews and G.	1818
	19:10	the Jews and G who lived in the province	1818
	19:17	*to* the Jews and G living in Ephesus,	1818
	20:21	both Jews and G that they must turn to God	1818
	21:28	he has brought G into the temple area	1818
Ro	1:14	I am obligated both *to* G and non-Greeks,	1818
1Co	1:22	Jews demand miraculous signs and G look	1818
	1:24	whom God has called, both Jews and G,	1818
	10:32	whether Jews, G or the church of God—	1818
	12:13	whether Jews or G, slave or free—	1818

GREEN (22) [GREENISH]

Ge	1:30	I give every g plant for food."	3764
	9: 3	Just as I gave you the g plants,	3764
Ex	10:15	Nothing g remained on tree or plant in all	3764
2Ki	19:26	like tender g shoots,	2013
Job	39: 8	for his pasture and searches for any g thing.	3728
Ps	23: 2	He makes me lie down in g pastures,	2013
	37: 2	like g plants they will soon die away.	2013
	37:35	and ruthless man flourishing like a g tree	8316
	58: 9	whether they be g or dry—	2645
	92:14	they will stay fresh and g,	8316
	105:35	they ate up every g thing in their land,	6912
Pr	11:28	but the righteous will thrive like a g **leaf.**	6591
Isa	15: 6	the vegetation is gone and nothing g is left.	3764
	37:27	like tender g shoots,	2013
Jer	17: 8	its leaves are always g.	8316
Eze	17:24	up the g tree and make the dry tree flourish.	4300
	20:47	and it will consume all your trees, both g	4300
Hos	14: 8	I am like a g pine tree;	8316
Joel	2:22	for the open pastures *are becoming* g.	2012
Mk	6:39	down in groups on the g grass.	5952
Lk	23:31	if men do these things when the tree is g,	5619
Rev	8: 7	and all the g grass was burned up.	5952

GREENISH (2) [GREEN]

Lev	13:49	or any leather article, is g or reddish,	3768
	14:37	and if it has g or reddish depressions	3768

GREET (39) [GREETED, GREETING, GREETINGS, GREETS]

1Sa	10: 4	*They will* g you and offer you two loaves	4200+8626+8934
	13:10	and Saul went out to g him.	1385+7925
	25: 5	to Nabal at Carmel and g him	4200+8626+8934
2Sa	8:10	to g him and congratulate him	4200+8626+8934
2Ki	4:29	If you meet anyone, *do* not g him,	1385
	10:13	and we have come down to g the families	8934
1Ch	18:10	to g him and congratulate him	4200+8626+8934
Isa	14: 9	the spirits of the departed to g you—	NIH
Mt	5:47	And if *you* g only your brothers,	832
Mk	9:15	with wonder and ran to g him.	832
Lk	10: 4	and *do* not g anyone on the road.	832
Ro	16: 3	G Priscilla and Aquila,	832
	16: 5	G also the church that meets at their house.	NIG
	16: 5	G my dear friend Epenetus,	832
	16: 6	G Mary, who worked very hard for you.	832
	16: 7	G Andronicus and Junias,	832
	16: 8	G Ampliatus, whom I love in the Lord.	832
	16: 9	G Urbanus, our fellow worker in Christ,	832
	16:10	G Apelles, tested and approved in Christ.	832
	16:10	G those who belong to the household	832
	16:11	G Herodion, my relative.	832
	16:11	G those in the household of Narcissus	832
	16:12	G Tryphena and Tryphosa,	832
	16:12	G my dear friend Persis,	832
	16:13	G Rufus, chosen in the Lord,	832
	16:14	G Asyncritus, Phlegon, Hermes, Patrobas,	832
	16:15	G Philologus, Julia, Nereus and his sister,	832
	16:16	G one another with a holy kiss.	832
	16:16	g you in the Lord.	832
1Co	16:19	Aquila and Priscilla g you warmly in the Lord,	832
	16:20	G one another with a holy kiss.	832
2Co	13:12	G one another with a holy kiss.	832
Php	4:21	G all the saints in Christ Jesus.	832
1Th	5:26	G all the brothers with a holy kiss.	832
2Ti	4:19	G Priscilla and Aquila and the household	832
Tit	3:15	G those who love us in the faith.	832
Heb	13:24	G all your leaders and all God's people.	832
1Pe	5:14	G one another with a kiss of love.	832
3Jn	1:14	G the friends there by name.	832

GREETED (13) [GREET]

Ex	18: 7	*They* g each other and then	4200+8626+8934
Jdg	18:15	at Micah's place and g him.	4200+8626+8934
Ru	2: 4	then Boaz arrived from Bethlehem and g	606
1Sa	17:22	battle lines and g his brothers.	4200+8626+8934
	30:21	his men approached, *he* g them.	4200+8626+8934

2Ki	10:15	Jehu **g** him and said,	1385
Mt	23: 7	they love to be **g** in the marketplaces and	833
Mk	12:38	to walk around in flowing robes and be **g** in	833
Lk	1:40	where she entered Zechariah's home and **g** Elizabeth.	832
	20:46	and love to be **g** in the marketplaces	833
Ac	18:22	at Caesarea, he went up and **g** the church	832
	21: 7	where *we* **g** the brothers and stayed	832
	21:19	Paul **g** them and reported in detail	832

GREETING (7) [GREET]

Mt	10:12	As you enter the home, **give** it *your* **g**.	832
Lk	1:29	and wondered what kind of **g** this might be.	833
	1:41	When Elizabeth heard Mary's **g**,	833
	1:44	as the sound *of* your **g** reached my ears,	833
1Co	16:21	I, Paul, write this **g** in my own hand.	833
Col	4:18	I, Paul, write this **g** in my own hand.	833
2Th	3:17	I, Paul, write this **g** in my own hand,	833

GREETINGS (31) [GREET]

1Sa	25:14	*to* **give** our master his **g**,	1385
Ezr	4:17	and elsewhere in Trans-Euphrates: **G**.	10720
	5: 7	To King Darius: **Cordial g**.	
			10002+10002+10353+10720
	7:12	of the Law of the God of heaven: **G**.	10147
Mt	26:49	Going at once to Jesus, Judas said, "**G**,	5897
	28: 9	Suddenly Jesus met them. "**G**," he said.	5897
Lk	1:28	The angel went to her and said, "**G**,	5897
	11:43	the synagogues and **g** in the marketplaces.	833
Ac	15:23	in Antioch, Syria and Cilicia: **G**.	5897
	23:26	To His Excellency, Governor Felix: **G**.	5897
Ro	16:16	All the churches of Christ **send g**.	832
	16:21	Timothy, my fellow worker, **sends** *his* **g** to	832
	16:23	**sends** you *his* **g**.	832
	16:23	and our brother Quartus **send** you *their* **g**.	832
1Co	16:19	churches in the province of Asia **send** you **g**.	832
	16:20	All the brothers here **send** you **g**.	832
2Co	13:13	All the saints **send** *their* **g**.	832
Php	4:21	The brothers who are with me **send g**.	832
	4:22	All the saints **send** you **g**,	832
Col	4:10	My fellow prisoner Aristarchus **sends** you *his* **g**,	832
	4:11	Jesus, who is called Justus, also sends **g**.	NIG
	4:12	and a servant of Christ Jesus, **sends g**.	832
	4:14	the doctor, and Demas **send g**.	832
	4:15	**Give** my **g** to the brothers at Laodicea, and	832
Tit	3:15	Everyone with me **sends** you **g**.	832
Phm	1:23	in Christ Jesus, **sends** you **g**.	832
Heb	13:24	Those from Italy **send** you *their* **g**.	832
Jas	1: 1	among the nations: **G**.	5897
1Pe	5:13	**sends** you her **g**, and so does my son Mark.	832
2Jn	1:13	children of your chosen sister **send** *their* **g**.	832
3Jn	1:14	The friends here **send** *their* **g**.	832

GREETS (2) [GREET]

2Ki	4:29	do not greet him, and if anyone **g** you,	1385
2Ti	4:21	Eubulus **g** you, and so do Pudens, Linus,	832

GREW (72) [GROW]

Ge	10: 8	who **g** to be a mighty warrior on the earth.	2725
	21: 8	The child **g** and was weaned,	1540
	21:20	God was with the boy as he **g up**.	1540
	25:27	The boys **g up**, and Esau became	1540
	30:43	the man **g** exceedingly **prosperous**	AIT
Ex	2:10	When the child **g** older,	1540
	16:21	and when the sun **g** hot, it melted away.	AIT
	17:12	When Moses' hands **g** tired,	NIH
	19:19	**g louder and louder.**	2143+2256+2618+4394
Nu	21: 4	But the people **g impatient** on the way;	AIT
Dt	32:15	Jeshurun **g** fat and kicked;	9042
Jos	17:13	However, when the Israelites **g stronger,**	AIT
Jdg	2:10	another generation **g up**, who knew neither	7756
	4:24	**g stronger and stronger**	2143+2256+7997
	13:24	He **g** and the LORD blessed him,	1540
Ru	1:13	would you wait until *they* **g up?**	1540
1Sa	2:21	the boy Samuel **g up** in the presence of	1540
	3:19	The LORD was with Samuel as he **g up**,	1540
	8: 1	When Samuel **g** old, he appointed his sons	2416
	31: 3	The fighting **g fierce** around Saul,	AIT
2Sa	3: 1	David **g stronger and stronger**	2143+2256+2618
	3: 1	while the house of Saul **g weaker and weaker.**	1924+2143+2256
	12: 3	and *it* **g up** with him and his children.	1540
	23:10	the Philistines till his hand **g** tired and froze	AIT
1Ki	11: 4	As Solomon **g** old, his wives turned his	2420
	17:17	He **g worse and worse,**	2118+2617+2716+4394
	18:45	Meanwhile, the sky **g black** with clouds,	AIT
2Ki	4:18	The child **g**, and one day he went out	1540
	4:34	the boy's body **g warm.**	AIT
1Ch	1:10	who **g** to be a mighty warrior on earth.	2725
	10: 3	The fighting **g fierce** around Saul,	3877
2Ch	13:21	But Abijah **g in strength.**	2616
	27: 6	Jotham **g powerful** because he walked	AIT
Ps	39: 3	My heart **g** hot within me,	AIT
	52: 7	but trusted in his great wealth and **g strong**	AIT
	77: 3	I mused, and my spirit **g faint.**	AIT
	106:16	In the camp *they* **g envious** of Moses and	AIT
	107:30	They were glad when *it* **g calm,**	AIT
Isa	38:14	My eyes **g weak** as I looked to the heavens.	AIT
	53: 2	*He* **g up** before him like a tender shoot,	6590
Eze	16: 7	You **g up** and developed and became	8049
	16: 7	Your breasts were formed and your hair **g,**	7541
	17:10	wither away in the plot where it **g?' "**	7542
	31: 5	and its branches **g long,**	AIT

Da	4:11	The tree **g large** and strong	10648
	4:20	tree you saw, which **g large** and strong,	10648
	4:33	until his hair **g** like the feathers of an eagle	10648
	5: 9	and his face **g** more pale.	10731
	8: 3	the other but **g up** later.	6590
	8: 8	and in its place four prominent horns **g up**	6590
	8: 9	but **g** in power to the south and to the east	1540
	8:10	It **g** until it reached the host of	1540
Jnh	1:13	for the sea **g even wilder** than before.	2143+2256+6192
	1:15	and the raging sea **g calm.**	AIT
	4: 8	on Jonah's head so that *he* **g faint.**	AIT
Zec	11: 8	and I **g weary** of them	7918
Mt	13: 7	which **g up** and choked the plants.	326
Mk	4: 7	which **g up** and choked the plants,	326
	4: 8	It came up, **g** and produced a crop,	889
	5:26	yet instead of getting better *she* **g** worse.	1650+2262+3836
Lk	1:80	the child **g** and became strong in spirit;	889
	2:40	And the child **g** and became strong;	889
	2:52	And Jesus **g** in wisdom and stature,	4621
	8: 7	which **g up** with it and choked the plants.	5243
	13:19	It **g** and became a tree,	889
Jn	6:18	and the waters **g rough.**	1444
Ac	4: 4	number of men **g** to about five thousand.	1181
	9:22	Saul **g** more and more **powerful**	AIT
	9:31	by the Holy Spirit, *it* **g in numbers,**	4437
	16: 5	in the faith and daily in numbers.	4355
	19:20	of the Lord spread widely and **g** in power.	2710
Rev	18: 3	and the merchants of the earth **g rich**	4456

GREY, GREYHEADED (KJV, Anglicized)
See GRAY

GREYHOUND (KJV) See ROOSTER

GRIDDLE (3)

Lev	2: 5	If your grain offering is prepared on a **g**,	4679
	6:21	Prepare it with oil on a **g**;	4679
	7: 9	or on a **g** belongs to the priest who offers it,	4679

GRIEF (33) [GRIEFS, GRIEVANCE, GRIEVANCES, GRIEVE, GRIEVED, GRIEVES, GRIEVING, GRIEVOUS]

Ge	26:35	a **source of g** to Isaac and Rebekah.	5289+8120
	34: 7	They **were filled with g** and fury,	6772
	38:12	When Judah **had recovered from** his **g**,	5714
1Sa	1:16	of my great anguish and **g."**	4088
Est	6:12	with his head covered in **g,**	63
Job	17: 7	My eyes have grown dim with **g**;	4089
Ps	10:14	But you, O God, do see trouble and **g**;	4088
	31: 9	my soul and my body with **g.**	NIH
	35:14	I bowed my head *in* **g** as though weeping	7722
	88: 9	my eyes are dim with **g.**	6715
Pr	10: 1	but a foolish son **g** to his mother.	9342
	10:10	He who winks maliciously causes **g,**	6780
	14:13	and joy may end in **g.**	9342
	17:21	To have a fool for a son brings **g**;	9342
	17:25	A foolish son brings **g** to his father	4088
	29:21	he will bring **g** in the end.	4959
Ecc	1:18	the more knowledge, the more **g.**	4799
	2:23	All his days his work is pain and **g**;	4088
La	1: 5	The LORD **has brought** her **g** because	3324
	3:32	Though **he brings g,**	3324
	3:33	not willingly bring affliction or **g** to	3324
	3:51	What I see **brings g** to my soul because	6618
Eze	13:22	when I **had brought** them no **g,**	3872
	21: 6	before them with broken heart and **bitter g.**	5320
Mic	4: 6	the exiles and those *I* **have brought to g.**	8317
Mt	17:23	And the disciples **were filled with g.**	3382+5379
Jn	16: 6	you are filled with **g.**	3383
	16:20	You will grieve, but your **g** will turn to joy.	3383
	16:21	is *your* **time of g,**	2400+3383
1Co	5: 2	Shouldn't *you* rather **have been filled with g**	4291
2Co	2: 5	If anyone **has caused g,**	3382
1Pe	1: 6	a little while you may have had *to* **suffer g**	3382
Rev	18: 7	Give her as much torture and **g** as the glory	4292

GRIEFS (1) [GRIEF]

1Ti	6:10	and pierced themselves *with* many **g**.	3850

GRIEVANCE (2) [GRIEF]

Job	31:13	and maidservants when they had a **g**	8190
Ac	19:38	and his fellow craftsmen have a **g**	3364

GRIEVANCES (1) [GRIEF]

Col	3:13	and forgive whatever **g** you may have	3664

GRIEVE (18) [GRIEF]

1Sa	2:33	with tears and **g** to your heart,	117
2Sa	1:26	I **g** for you, Jonathan my brother;	7639
Ne	8:10	*Do* not **g**, for the joy of the LORD	6772
	8:11	for this is a sacred day. Do not **g."**	6772
Isa	16: 7	Lament and **g** for the men of Kir Hareseth.	5778
	61: 3	and provide for *those who* **g** in Zion—	63
La	1: 4	her maidens **g**, and she is in bitter anguish.	3324
Eze	7:12	Let not the buyer rejoice nor the seller **g,**	61
	9: 4	on the foreheads of those who **g** and lament	634
Joel	1:11	**g** for the wheat and the barley,	NIH
Am	6: 6	but *you* do not **g** over the ruin of Joseph.	2703
Zec	12:10	and **g bitterly** for him as one grieves for	5352

Jn	16:20	You **will g**, but your grief will turn to joy.	3382
2Co	2: 2	For if I **g** you, who is left to make me glad	3382
	2: 4	not to **g** *you* but to let you know the depth	3382
Eph	4:30	And *do* not **g** the Holy Spirit of God,	3382
1Th	4:13	or to **g** like the rest of men,	3382
Jas	4: 9	**G**, mourn and wail.	5415

GRIEVED (22) [GRIEF]

Ge	6: 6	The LORD **was g** that he had made man on	5714
	6: 7	for *I* **am g** that I have made them."	5714
Dt	34: 8	The Israelites **g** *for* Moses in the plains	1134
Jdg	21: 6	Now the Israelites **g** for their brothers,	5714
	21:15	The people **g** for Benjamin,	5714
1Sa	15:11	"*I* **am g** that I have made Saul king,	5714
	15:35	the LORD **was g** that he had made Saul king	5714
	20: 3	must not know this or *he* **will be g.'**	6772
	20:34	the month he did not eat, because *he* **was g**	6772
2Sa	24:16	The LORD **was g** because of the calamity	5714
1Ch	21:15	and **was g** because of the calamity and said	5714
Job	30:25	*Has* not my soul **g** for the poor?	6327
Ps	73:21	my heart **was g** and my spirit embittered,	2806
	78:40	in the desert and **g** him in the wasteland!	6772
Isa	63:10	Yet they rebelled and **g** his Holy Spirit.	6772
Jer	42:10	for *I* **am g** over the disaster I have inflicted	5714
Eze	6: 9	*I* **have been g** *by* their adulterous hearts,	8689
Ac	20:38	What **g** them most was his statement	3849
2Co	2: 2	to make me glad but you whom I **have g**?	3382
	2: 5	so much **g** me as he has grieved all of you,	3382
	2: 5	so much grieved me as he has **g** all of you,	NIG
	12:21	be **g over** many who have sinned earlier	4291

GRIEVES (1) [GRIEF]

Zec	12:10	and grieve bitterly for him as *one* **g** for	5352

GRIEVING (3) [GRIEF]

2Sa	14: 2	like a woman *who has spent* many days **g**	61
	19: 2	"The king *is* **g** for his son."	6772
Joel	1: 8	in sackcloth **g** for the husband of her youth.	NIH

GRIEVOUS (7) [GRIEF]

Ge	18:20	and Gomorrah is so great and their sin so **g**	3877
Ecc	2:17	the work that is done under the sun was **g**	8273
	5:16	I have seen a **g** evil under the sun:	2703
	6: 2	This too *is* a **g** evil.	8273
Jer	14:17	has suffered a **g** wound, a crushing blow.	1524
	15:18	Why is my pain unending and my wound **g**	631

GRIND (5) [GRINDERS, GRINDING]

Ex	30:36	**G** some of it to powder and place it in front	8835
Job	31:10	*may* my wife **g** another man's **grain**,	3221
Pr	27:22	Though *you* **g** a fool in a mortar,	4197
Isa	28:28	his horses *do* not **g** it.	1990
	47: 2	Take millstones and **g** flour;	3221

GRINDERS (1) [GRIND]

Ecc	12: 3	when the **g** cease because they are few,	3223

GRINDING (6) [GRIND]

Jdg	16:21	they set him to **g** in the prison.	3221
Pr	27:22	**g** him like grain with a pestle,	NIH
Ecc	12: 4	and the sound of **g** fades;	3222
Isa	3:15	by crushing my people and **g** the faces of	3221
Mt	24:41	Two *women will be* **g** with a hand mill;	241
Lk	17:35	Two women will be **g grain** together;	241

GRIP (4) [GRIPPED, GRIPS]

Ex	15:14	anguish *will* **g** the people of Philistia.	296
Job	30:16	my life ebbs away; days of suffering **g** me.	296
Isa	13: 8	pain and anguish *will* **g** them;	296
Jer	13:21	*Will* not pain **g** you like that of a woman	296

GRIPPED (4) [GRIP]

Jer	6:24	Anguish *has* **g** us,	2616
	49:24	she has turned to flee and panic *has* **g** her;	2616
	50:43	Anguish *has* **g** him,	2616
Lk	1:12	he was startled and *was* **g with fear.**	2158+5832

GRIPS (3) [GRIP]

Ps	119:53	Indignation **g** me because of the wicked,	296
Isa	33:14	trembling **g** the godless;	296
Jer	8:21	I mourn, and horror **g** me.	2616

GRISLED (KJV) See SPOTTED, DAPPLED

GROAN (19) [GROANED, GROANING, GROANS]

Ps	38: 8	*I* **g** in anguish of heart.	8613
Pr	5:11	At the end of your life *you* will **g**,	5637
	29: 2	when the wicked rule, the people **g**.	634
Isa	19: 8	The fishermen *will* **g** and lament,	627
	24: 7	all the merrymakers *will* **g**.	634
Jer	4:31	a **g** as of one bearing her first child—	7650
	22:23	*you will* **g** when pangs come upon you,	634
	51:52	throughout her land the wounded *will* **g**.	650
La	1: 4	All her gateways are desolate, her priests **g**,	634
	1:11	All her people **g** as they search for bread;	634
Eze	21: 6	"Therefore **g**, son of man!	634
	21: 6	**G** before them with broken heart	634

Eze	24:17	G quietly; do not mourn for the dead.	650
	24:23	of your sins and g among yourselves.	5637
	26:15	the sound of your fall, when the wounded g	650
	30:24	and he will g before him like	5543+5544
Ro	8:23	g inwardly as we wait eagerly for	5100
2Co	5:2	Meanwhile we g, longing to be clothed	5100
	5:4	we g and are burdened,	5100

GROANED (3) [GROAN]

Ex	2:23	The Israelites g in their slavery	634
Jdg	2:18	as they g under those who oppressed	5544
Ps	77:3	I remembered you, O God, and I g;	2159

GROANING (15) [GROAN]

Ex	2:24	God heard their g	5544
	6:5	I have heard the g of the Israelites,	5544
Job	23:2	his hand is heavy in spite of my g.	635
Ps	6:6	I am worn out from g;	635
	12:5	of the oppression of the weak and the g of	651
	22:1	so far from the words of my g?	8614
	31:10	by anguish and my years by g;	635
	32:3	through my g all day long.	8614
	102:5	Because of my loud g I am reduced to skin	635
Isa	21:2	I will bring to an end all the g she caused.	635
Jer	45:3	I am worn out with g and find no rest.' '	635
La	1:21	"People have heard my g,	634
Eze	21:7	And when they ask you, 'Why are you g?'	634
Ac	7:34	I have heard their g and have come down	5099
Ro	8:22	that the whole creation has been g as in	5367

GROANS (7) [GROAN]

Job	3:24	my g pour out like water.	8614
	24:12	The g of the dying rise from the city,	5543
Ps	79:11	the g of the prisoners come before you;	651
	102:20	to hear the g of the prisoners	651
La	1:8	she herself g and turns away.	634
	1:22	My g are many and my heart is faint."	635
Ro	8:26	the Spirit himself intercedes for us with g	5099

GROPE (5) [GROPED]

Dt	28:29	At midday you will g about like	5491
Job	5:14	at noon they g as in the night.	5491
	12:25	They g in darkness with no light;	5491
Isa	59:10	Like the blind we g along the wall,	1779
La	4:14	Now they g through the streets	5675

GROPED (1) [GROPE]

Ac	13:11	and he g about,	4310

GROSS (KJV) See THICK, CALLOUSED

GROUND (308) [AGROUND, GROUNDS]

Ge	1:9	and let dry g appear.	3317
	1:10	God called the dry g "land,"	3317
	1:24	livestock, creatures that move along the g,	NIH
	1:25	and all the creatures that move along the g	141
	1:26	over all the creatures that move along the g.	824
	1:28	that moves on the g."	824
	1:30	and all the creatures that move on the g—	824
	2:5	and there was no man to work the g,	141
	2:6	and watered the whole surface of the g—	141
	2:7	the man from the dust of the g and breathed	141
	2:9	of trees grow out of the g—	141
	2:19	the LORD God had formed out of the g all	141
	3:17	"Cursed is the g because of you;	141
	3:19	to the g, since from it you were taken;	141
	3:23	from the Garden of Eden to work the g	141
	4:10	brother's blood cries out to me from the g.	141
	4:11	under a curse and driven from the g,	141
	4:12	When you work the g,	141
	5:29	by the g the LORD has cursed."	141
	6:7	creatures that move along the g,	8254
	6:20	that moves along the g will come to you to	141
	7:8	and of all creatures that move along the g,	141
	7:14	that moves along the g according to its kind	824
	7:23	and the creatures that move along the g and	NIH
	8:8	from the surface of the g.	141
	8:13	and saw that the surface of the g was dry.	141
	8:17	all the creatures that move along the g—	824
	8:19	the creatures that move along the g and all	NIH
	8:21	"Never again will I curse the g because	141
	9:2	the g, and upon all the fish of the sea;	141
	18:2	to meet them and bowed low to the g.	824
	19:1	and bowed down with his face to the g.	824
	24:52	he bowed down to the g before the LORD.	824
	33:3	and bowed down to the g seven times	824
	33:19	the plot of g where he pitched his tent.	8441
	37:10	and bow down to the g before you?"	824
	38:9	his semen on the g to keep from producing	824
	42:6	down to him with their faces to the g.	824
	43:26	and they bowed down before him to the g.	824
	44:11	of them quickly lowered his sack to the g	824
	44:14	they threw themselves to the g before him.	824
	47:23	here is seed for you so you can plant the g.	141
	48:12	and bowed down with his face to the g.	824
Ex	3:5	the place where you are standing is holy g."	141
	4:3	The LORD said, "Throw it on the g."	824
	4:3	Moses threw it on the g and it became	824
	4:9	from the Nile and pour it on the dry g.	3317
	4:9	from the river will become blood on the g."	3318
	8:16	and strike the dust of the g,'	824
	8:17	with the staff and struck the dust of the g,	824

Ex	8:21	and even the g where they are.	141
	9:23	and lightning flashed down to the g.	824
	10:5	the face of the g so that it cannot be seen.	824
	10:15	They covered all the g until it was black.	824
	14:16	Israelites went through the sea on dry g	3317
	14:22	the Israelites went through the sea on dry g,	3317
	14:29	the Israelites went through the sea on dry g	3317
	15:19	Israelites walked through the sea on dry g.	3317
	16:14	thin flakes frost on the g appeared on	824
	16:25	You will not find any of it on the g today.	8441
	32:20	then he g it to powder,	3221
	34:8	to the g at once and worshiped.	824
Lev	5:2	creatures that move along the g—	9238
	11:21	that have jointed legs for hopping on the g.	824
	11:29	" 'Of the animals that move about on the g,	824
	11:31	Of all those that move along the g,	NIH
	11:41	that moves about on the g is detestable;	824
	11:42	on the g, whether it moves on its belly	824
	11:44	by any creature that moves about on the g.	824
	11:46	that moves about on the g.	824
	16:12	of finely g fragrant incense and take them	1987
	20:25	or bird or anything that moves along the g—	141
	26:4	and the g will yield its crops and the trees	824
	26:19	like iron and the g beneath you like bronze.	824
Nu	11:8	g it in a handmill or crushed it in a mortar.	3221
	11:31	the camp to about three feet above the g,	824
	15:20	Present a cake from the first of your g meal	6881
	15:21	the LORD from the first of your g meal.	6881
	16:31	the g under them split apart	141
Dt	4:18	along the g or any fish in the waters below.	141
	9:21	and g it to powder as fine as dust	3221+3512
	11:17	not rain and the g will yield no produce,	141
	12:16	pour it out on the g like water.	824
	12:24	pour it out on the g like water.	824
	15:23	pour it out on the g like water.	824
	22:6	either in a tree or on the g,	824
	28:11	of your livestock and the crops of your g—	141
	28:23	the g beneath you iron.	824
	28:56	that she would not venture to touch the g	824
Jos	3:17	of the LORD stood firm on dry g in	3000
	3:17	completed the crossing on dry g.	3000
	4:18	on the dry g than the waters of	3000
	4:22	'Israel crossed the Jordan on dry g.'	3317
	5:14	Joshua fell facedown to the g in reverence,	824
	7:6	and fell facedown to the g before the ark of	824
	7:21	They are hidden in the g inside my tent,	824
Jdg	4:21	the peg through his temple into the g,	824
	6:37	on the fleece and all the g is dry,	824
	6:39	the fleece dry and the g covered with dew."	824
	6:40	all the g was covered with dew.	824
	13:20	and his wife fell with their faces to the g.	824
Ru	2:10	she bowed down with her face to the g.	824
1Sa	3:19	and he let none of his words fall to the g.	824
	4:5	a great shout that the g shook.	824
	5:3	fallen on his face on the g before the ark of	824
	5:4	fallen on his face on the g before the ark of	824
	8:12	others to plow his g and reap his harvest,	3045
	14:15	and the g shook.	824
	14:25	and there was honey on the g,	8441
	14:32	they butchered them on the g and ate them,	824
	14:45	not a hair of his head will fall to the g.	824
	17:49	and he fell facedown on the g.	824
	20:41	three times, with his face to the g.	824
	24:8	prostrated himself with his face to the g.	824
	25:23	down before David with her face to the g.	824
	25:41	She bowed down with her face to the g	824
	26:7	with his spear stuck in the g near his head.	824
	26:8	Now let me pin him to the g with one thrust	824
	26:20	the g far from the presence of the LORD.	824
	28:13	"I see a spirit coming up out of the g."	824
	28:14	prostrated himself with his face to the g,	824
	28:20	Immediately Saul fell full length on the g,	824
	28:23	He got up from the g and sat on the couch.	824
2Sa	1:2	he fell to the g to pay him honor.	824
	8:2	down on the g and measured them off with	824
	12:16	and spent the nights lying on the g.	824
	12:17	beside him to get him up from the g,	824
	12:20	Then David got up from the g.	824
	13:31	tore his clothes and lay down on the g;	824
	14:4	with her face to the g to pay him honor,	824
	14:11	of your son's head will fall to the g."	824
	14:14	Like water spilled on the g,	824
	14:22	with his face to the g to pay him honor,	824
	14:33	down with his face to the g before the king.	824
	17:12	on him as dew settles on the g.	141
	18:11	strike him to the g right there?	824
	18:28	down before the king with his face to the g	824
	20:10	and his intestines spilled out on the g.	824
	23:10	but he stood his g and struck down	7756
	24:20	down before the king with his face to the g.	824
1Ki	1:23	the king and bowed with his face to the g.	824
	1:31	bowed low with her face to the g and,	824
	1:40	so that the g shook with the sound.	824
	1:52	not a hair of his head will fall to the g;	824
	18:7	bowed down to the g,	5877+6584+7156
	18:42	to the g and put his face between his knees.	824
2Ki	2:8	and the two of them crossed over on dry g.	3000
	2:15	to meet him and bowed to the g before him.	824
	4:37	fell at his feet and bowed to the g.	824
	8:12	dash their little children to the g,	8187
	9:10	dogs will devour her on the plot of g	2750
	9:21	the plot of g that had belonged to Naboth	2754
	9:26	make you pay for it on this plot of g,	2754
	9:36	On the plot of g at Jezreel dogs will devour	2750
	9:37	be like refuse on the g in the plot at Jezreel	8441
	13:18	Elisha told him, "Strike the g."	824
	13:19	"You should have struck the g five	NIH

2Ki	23:6	He g it to powder and scattered the dust	1990
	23:15	the high place and g it to powder,	1990
1Ch	21:21	down before David with his face to the g.	824
2Ch	2:10	twenty thousand cors of g wheat,	4804
	7:3	the g, and they worshiped and gave thanks	824
	20:18	Jehoshaphat bowed with his face to the g,	824
	20:24	they saw only dead bodies lying on the g;	824
Ne	8:6	the LORD with their faces to the g.	824
	9:11	so that they passed through it on dry g,	3317
	10:37	to the priests, the first of our g meal,	6881
Job	1:20	Then he fell to the g in worship	824
	2:13	on the g with him for seven days	824
	3:16	not hidden in the g like a stillborn child,	NIH
	5:6	nor does trouble sprout from the g,	141
	14:8	in the g and its stump die in the soil,	824
	16:13	and spills my gall on the g.	824
	18:10	A noose is hidden for him on the g;	824
	30:6	among the rocks and in holes in the g.	6760
	39:14	on the g and lets them warm in the sand,	824
	39:24	In frenzied excitement he eats up the g;	824
Ps	7:5	to the g and make me sleep in the dust.	824
	17:11	with eyes alert, to throw me to the g.	824
	26:12	My feet stand on level g;	4793
	44:25	our bodies cling to the g.	824
	73:18	Surely you place them on slippery g;	AIT
	74:7	They burned your sanctuary to the g;	824
	80:9	You cleared the g for it,	7155
	83:10	at Endor and became like refuse on the g.	141
	89:44	to his splendor and cast his throne to the g.	824
	107:33	flowing springs into thirsty g,	7536
	107:35	and the parched g into flowing springs;	824
	143:3	he crushes me to the g;	824
	143:10	may your good Spirit lead me on level g.	824
	146:4	their spirit departs, they return to the g;	141
	147:6	the humble but casts the wicked to the g.	824
Pr	24:31	the g was covered with weeds,	7156
Ecc	12:7	and the dust returns to the g it came from,	824
Isa	2:10	hide in the g from dread of the LORD	6760
	2:19	to holes in the g from dread of the LORD	6760
	3:26	destitute, she will sit on the g.	824
	21:9	of its gods lie shattered on the g!' "	824
	25:12	he will bring them down to the g,	824
	26:5	he levels it to the g and casts it down to	824
	28:2	he will throw it forcefully to the g.	824
	28:28	Grain must be g to make bread;	1990
	29:4	Brought low, you will speak from the g;	824
	30:23	for the seed you sow in the g,	141
	35:7	the thirsty g bubbling springs.	7536
	40:4	the rough g shall become level,	6815
	40:24	no sooner do they take root in the g,	824
	41:18	and the parched g into springs.	824
	44:3	and streams on the dry g;	3317
	45:9	a potsherd among the potsherds on the g.	141
	47:1	sit on the g without a throne,	824
	49:23	down before you with their faces to the g;	824
	51:23	And you made your back like the g,	824
	53:2	and like a root out of dry g.	824
	63:6	and poured their blood on the g."	824
Jer	4:3	up your unplowed g and do not sow	5776
	7:20	of the field and on the fruit of the g,	141
	8:2	but will be like refuse lying on the g.	141
	14:4	The g is cracked because there is no rain in	141
	16:4	but will be like refuse lying on the g.	141
	25:33	but will be like refuse lying on the g.	141
	46:21	they will not stand their g,	6641
	48:18	from your glory and sit on the parched g,	7533
La	2:2	and its princes down to the g in dishonor.	824
	2:9	Her gates have sunk into the g;	824
	2:10	the Daughter of Zion sit on the g in silence;	824
	2:10	Jerusalem have bowed their heads to the g.	824
	2:11	on the g because my people are destroyed,	824
Eze	1:15	I saw a wheel on the g beside each creature	824
	1:19	when the living creatures rose from the g,	824
	1:21	and when the creatures rose from the g,	824
	10:16	spread their wings to rise from the g,	824
	10:19	and rose from the g,	824
	13:14	with whitewash and will level it to the g so	824
	19:12	it was uprooted in fury and thrown to the g.	824
	24:7	she did not pour it on the g,	824
	26:11	and your strong pillars will fall to the g.	824
	26:16	Clothed with terror, they will sit on the g,	824
	28:18	the g in the sight of all who were watching.	824
	34:27	and the g will yield its crops;	824
	38:20	every creature that moves along the g,	141
	38:20	and every wall will fall to the g.	824
	39:14	others will bury those that remain on the g	824
	43:14	From the gutter on the g up to	824
	44:30	of your g meal so that a blessing may rest	6881
Da	4:15	remain in the g, in the grass of the field.	10075
	4:23	while its roots remain in the g.	10075
	7:4	the g so that it stood on two feet like a man,	10075
	8:5	the whole earth without touching the g.	824
	8:7	the goat knocked him to the g and trampled	824
	8:12	and truth was thrown to the g.	824
	8:18	I was in a deep sleep, with my face to the g.	824
	10:9	I fell into a deep sleep, my face to the g.	824
	10:15	I bowed with my face toward the g	824
Hos	2:18	and the creatures that move along the g.	141
	10:11	and Jacob must break up the g.	8440
	10:12	and break up your unplowed g;	5776
	10:14	when mothers were dashed to the g	8187
	13:16	little ones will be dashed to the g,	8187
Joel	1:10	The fields are ruined, the g is dried up;	141
Am	2:7	of the oppressed.	
	2:15	The archer will not stand his g,	6641
	3:5	a trap on the g where no snare has been set?	824
	3:14	of the altar will be cut off and fall to the g.	824

Am	5: 7	and cast righteousness to the g	824
	9: 9	and not a pebble will reach the g.	824
Ob	1: 3	'Who can bring me down to the g?'	824
Mic	7:17	like creatures that crawl on the g.	824
Hag	1:11	the oil and whatever the g produces,	141
Zec	4: 7	Zerubbabel you will become level g.	4793
	8:12	the g will produce its crops,	824
Mt	10:29	to the g apart from the will of your Father.	1178
	15:35	He told the crowd to sit down on the g.	NIG
	17: 6	they fell facedown to the g, terrified.	1178
	25:18	a hole in the g and hid his master's money.	1178
	25:25	and went out and hid your talent in the g.	1178
	26:39	fell with his face to the g	4406
Mk	4:26	A man scatters seed on the g.	1178
	4:31	the smallest seed you plant in the g.	1178
	8: 6	He told the crowd to sit down on the g.	1178
	9:18	it throws him to the g.	4838
	9:20	He fell to the g and rolled around,	1178
	14:35	he fell to the g and prayed that if possible	1178
Lk	5:12	with his face to the g and begged him,	NIG
	6:49	a man who built a house on the g without	1178
	9:42	the demon threw him to the g	4838
	12:16	"The g of a certain rich man produced	6001
	19:44	They will dash you to the g,	1610
	22:44	like drops of blood falling to the g.	1178
	23: 5	down with their faces to the g,	1178
Jn	4: 5	near the plot of g Jacob had given	6005
	8: 6	and started to write on the g with his finger.	1178
	8: 8	Again he stooped down and wrote on the g.	1178
	9: 6	Having said this, he spit on the g,	5912
	12:24	a kernel of wheat falls to the g and dies,	1178
	18: 6	"I am he," they drew back and fell to the g.	5912
Ac	7: 5	not even a foot of g.	1037+4546
	7:33	the place where you are standing is holy g.	1178
	9: 4	to the g and heard a voice say to him,	1178
	9: 8	Saul got up from the g,	1178
	13:28	Though they found no proper g for	162
	20: 9	he fell to the g from the third story	3004
	22: 7	I fell to the g and heard a voice say to me,	1611
	26:14	We all fell to the g, and I heard a voice	1178
2Co	11:12	to cut the g from under those who want	929
Eph	6:13	you may be able to stand your g,	468
Heb	10:32	when you stood your g in a great contest	5702
	11:38	and in caves and holes in the g.	1178

GROUNDS (5) [GROUND]

2Ki	11:16	where the horses enter the palace g,	1074+4889
2Ch	23:15	of the Horse Gate on the palace g,	1074+4889
Da	6: 4	and the satraps tried to find g for charges	10544
Lk	23:22	in him no g for the death penalty.	165+2505
Jn	8:59	slipping away from the temple g.	2639

GROUP (25) [GROUPS, REGROUPED]

Ge	32: 8	"If Esau comes and attacks one g,	4722
	32: 8	the g that is left may escape."	4722
	48:19	and his descendants will become a g	4850
Nu	16: 3	They came as a g to oppose Moses	7735
	26:54	To a larger g give a larger inheritance,	AIT
	26:54	and to a smaller g a smaller one;	AIT
	26:55	What each g inherits will be according to	NIH
	33:54	To a larger g give a larger inheritance,	AIT
	33:54	and to a smaller g a smaller one.	AIT
Jdg	11: 3	a g of adventurers gathered around him	408
1Sa	19:20	they saw a g of prophets prophesying,	4272
2Sa	2:13	One g sat down on one side of the pool	465S
	2:13	down on one side of the pool and one g on	465S
	2:25	a g took their stand on top of a hill.	99
2Ki	17:29	each national g made its own gods	1580+1580
2Ch	35: 5	"Stand in the holy place with a g of Levites	3+1074+2755
Da	6: 6	the satraps went as a g to the king and said:	10656
	6:11	Then these men went as a g	10656
	6:15	the men went as a g to the king and said	10656
Jn	8: 3	They made her stand before the g	1877+3545
Ac	1:15	among the believers (a g numbering about	4063
	6: 5	This proposal pleased the whole g.	4436
	17:18	A g of Epicurean and Stoic philosophers	AIT
Gal	2:12	who belonged to the circumcision g.	AIT
Tit	1:10	especially those of the circumcision g.	AIT

GROUPS (8) [GROUP]

Ge	32: 7	the people who were with him into two g,	4722
	32:10	but now I have become two g.	4722
Nu	26:56	by lot among the larger and smaller g."	NIH
1Ch	23: 6	the Levites into g corresponding to the sons	4713
Ezr	6:18	the Levites in their g for the service of God	10412
Mk	6:39	sit down in g on the green grass.	5235+5235
	6:40	sat down in g of hundreds and fifties.	4555+4555
Lk	9:14	sit down in g of about fifty each."	3112

GROVE (5) [GROVES]

Ex	23:11	with your vineyard and your olive g.	2339
SS	6:11	the g of nut trees to look at the new growth	1708
Jn	18: 1	On the other side there was an olive g,	3057
	18: 3	So Judas came to the g,	1695S
	18:26	"Didn't I see you with him in the olive g?"	3057

GROVES (8) [GROVE]

Dt	6:11	vineyards and olive g you did not plant—	2339
Jos	24:13	from vineyards and olive g that you did	2339
Jdg	15: 5	together with the vineyards and olive g.	2339
1Sa	8:14	and vineyards and olive g and give them	2339
2Ki	5:26	or to accept clothes, olive g, vineyards,	2339
Ne	5:11	vineyards, olive g and houses,	2339

Ne	9:25	olive g and fruit trees in abundance.	2339
Ecc	2: 6	to water g of flourishing trees.	3623

GROW (72) [FULL-GROWN, GREW, GROWERS, GROWING, GROWN, GROWS, GROWTH, OVERGROWN]

Ge	2: 9	the LORD God made all kinds of trees g	7541
	26:13	to g until he became very wealthy.	2143
	27:40	But when you g restless,	AIT
Nu	6: 5	he must let the hair of his head g long.	1540
	24:18	will be conquered, but Israel will g strong.	6913
Dt	8:13	and when your herds and flocks g large	8049
Jdg	16:22	But the hair on his head began to g again	7541
1Sa	2:26	the boy Samuel continued to g in stature	2143
Ezr	4:22	Why let this threat g,	10677
Job	8:11	Can papyrus g tall where there is no marsh?	1448
	8:19	and from the soil other plants g.	7541
	14: 8	Its roots may g old in the ground	2416
	17: 9	those with clean hands will g stronger.	601+3578
	31:16	or let the eyes of the widow g weary,	3983
	39: 4	Their young thrive and g strong in	2730
Ps	6: 7	My eyes g weak with sorrow;	AIT
	31: 9	my eyes g weak with sorrow,	AIT
	31:10	and my bones g weak.	AIT
	34:10	The lions may g weak and hungry,	AIT
	92:12	they will g like a cedar of Lebanon;	8436
	104:14	He makes grass g for the cattle,	7541
	129: 6	which withers before it can g;	8990
	132:17	"Here I will make a horn g for David	7541
	147: 8	the earth with rain and makes grass g on	7541
Pr	13:11	gathers money little by little makes it g.	8049
	20:13	Do not love sleep or you will g poor;	3769
Ecc	12: 2	the light and the moon and the stars g dark,	AIT
	12: 3	those looking through the windows g dim;	AIT
	12: 4	but all their songs g faint;	AIT
Isa	5: 6	and briers and thorns will g there.	6590
	17:11	you make them g,	8451
	29:22	no longer will their faces g pale.	2578
	35: 7	grass and reeds and papyrus will g.	NIH
	40:28	He will not g tired or weary,	AIT
	40:30	Even youths g tired and weary,	AIT
	40:31	they will run and not g weary,	AIT
	44:14	He let it g among the trees of the forest,	599
	44:14	or planted a pine, and the rain made it g.	1540
	45: 8	let righteousness g with it;	7541
	55:13	of the thornbush will g the pine tree,	6590
	55:13	and instead of briers the myrtle will g.	6590
	57:16	spirit of man would g faint before me—	AIT
	61:11	up and a garden causes seeds to g,	7541
Jer	4:28	and the heavens above g dark,	AIT
	6: 4	and the shadows of evening g long.	5742
	12: 2	they g and bear fruit.	2143
	15: 9	of seven will g faint and breathe her last.	AIT
La	3: 4	made my skin and my flesh g old	1162
	5:17	because of these things our eyes g dim	AIT
Eze	16: 7	I made you g like a plant of the field.	8047
	17:24	make the low tree g tall.	1467
	29:21	that day I will make a horn g for the house	7541
	31: 4	deep springs made it g tall;	8123
	44:20	or let their hair g long,	8938
	47:12	of all kinds will g on both banks of	6590
Hos	10: 8	Thorns and thistles will g up	6590
	14: 6	his young shoots will g.	2143
Jnh	4: 6	and made it g up over Jonah to give shade	6590
	4:10	though you did not tend it or make it g.	1540
Zec	8:12	"The seed will g well,	8934
Mt	6:28	See how the lilies of the field g.	889
	13:30	Let both g together until the harvest.	5277
	24:12	the love of most will g cold,	6038
Lk	12:27	"Consider how the lilies g.	889
1Co	3: 6	Apollos watered it, but God made it g.	889
	3: 7	but only God, who makes things g.	889
2Co	10:15	as your faith continues to g,	889
Eph	4:15	in all things g up into him who is the Head,	889
Col	2:19	grows as God causes it to g.	890
Heb	12: 3	that you will not g weary and lose heart.	2827
1Pe	2: 2	so that by it you may g up in your salvation,	889
2Pe	3:18	But g in the grace and knowledge	889

GROWERS (1) [GROW]

Joel	1:11	Despair, you farmers, wail, you vine g;	4144

GROWING (13) [GROW]

Ge	41: 5	healthy and good, were g on a single stalk.	6590
	41:22	full and good, g on a single stalk.	6590
Ex	9:22	and on everything g in the fields of Egypt."	6912
	9:25	it beat down everything g in the fields	6912
	10: 5	including every tree that is g	7541
	10:12	over the land and devour everything g in	6912
	10:15	everything g in the fields and the fruit on	6912
Dt	29:23	nothing sprouting, no vegetation g on it.	6590
Job	8:12	While still g and uncut,	4
	21: 7	g old and increasing in power?	6980
Col	1: 6	the world this gospel is bearing fruit and g,	889
	1:10	g in the knowledge of God,	889
2Th	1: 3	because your faith is g more and more,	5647

GROWL (5) [GROWLED, GROWLS]

Job	4:10	The lions may roar and g,	7754
Isa	5:29	they g as they seize their prey	5637
	59:11	We all g like bears;	2159
Jer	51:38	they g like lion cubs.	5849
Am	3: 4	Does he g in his den when	5989+7754

GROWLED (1) [GROWL]

Jer	2:15	Lions have roared; they have g at him.	5989+7754

GROWLS (1) [GROWL]

Isa	31: 4	"As a lion g, a great lion over his prey—	2047

GROWN (21) [GROW]

Ge	38:14	she saw that, though Shelah had now g up,	1540
	41:48	the food g in the fields surrounding it.	AIT
Ex	2:11	One day, after Moses had g up,	1540
Lev	13:37	and black hair has g in it,	7541
Jdg	11: 2	and when they were g up,	1540
2Sa	10: 5	"Stay at Jericho till your beards have g,	7541
1Ki	12: 8	and consulted the young men who had g up	1540
	12:10	The young men who had g up	1540
1Ch	19: 5	"Stay at Jericho till your beards have g,	7541
2Ch	10: 8	and consulted the young men who had g up	1540
	10:10	The young men who had g up	1540
Job	17: 7	My eyes have g dim with grief;	3908
Ecc	1:16	I have g and increased in wisdom more	1540
SS	8: 8	and her breasts are not yet g.	NIH
Isa	10:27	the yoke will be broken because you have g	NIH
Jer	5:28	and have g fat and sleek.	AIT
Eze	7:11	Violence has g into a rod	7756
	28: 5	of your wealth your heart has g proud.	AIT
Da	4:22	your greatness has g until it reaches the sky,	10648
Heb	11:24	By faith Moses, when he had g up,	1181+3489
Rev	2: 3	and have not g weary.	3159

GROWS (23) [GROW]

Ge	38:11	until my son Shelah g up."	1540
Lev	25: 5	Do not reap what g of itself or harvest	6206
	25:11	and do not reap what g of itself or harvest	6206
1Ki	4:33	of Lebanon to the hyssop that g out	3655
2Ki	19:26	scorched before it g up.	7756
	19:29	"This year you will eat what g by itself,	6206
Job	30:30	My skin g black and peels;	8837
Ps	49:16	not be overawed when a man g rich, when	AIT
	61: 2	I call as my heart g faint;	AIT
	142: 3	When my spirit g faint within me,	AIT
	143: 4	So my spirit g faint within me;	AIT
Pr	13:20	He who walks with the wise g wise,	AIT
Isa	5:27	Not one of them g tired or stumbles,	NIH
	37:27	scorched before it g up.	7756
	37:30	"This year you will eat what g by itself,	6206
	44:12	he drinks no water and g faint.	AIT
Na	2:10	bodies tremble, every face g pale.	6999+7695
Mt	13:32	when it g, it is the largest of garden plants	889
Mk	4:27	the seed sprouts and g,	3602
	4:32	it g and becomes the largest of all	326
Eph	4:16	g and builds itself up in love,	890+4472
Col	2:19	g as God causes it to grow.	889
Heb	12:15	and that no bitter root g up to cause trouble	5886

GROWTH (3) [GROW, UNDERGROWTH]

Pr	27:25	the hay is removed and new g appears and	2013
SS	6:11	to the grove of nut trees to look at the new g	4
Eze	17: 9	All its new g will wither.	7542

GRUDGE (4) [GRUDGING, GRUDGINGLY]

Ge	27:41	Esau held a g against Jacob because of	8475
	50:15	What if Joseph holds a g against us	8475
Lev	19:18	" 'Do not seek revenge or bear a g against	5757
Mk	6:19	So Herodias nursed a g against John	1923

GRUDGING (1) [GRUDGE]

Dt	15:10	to him and do so without a g heart;	8317

GRUDGINGLY (1) [GRUDGE]

2Co	9: 5	not as one g given.	4432

GRUMBLE (8) [GRUMBLED, GRUMBLERS, GRUMBLING]

Ex	16: 7	that you should g against us?"	4296
Nu	14:27	"How long will this wicked community g	4296
	14:36	made the whole community g	4296
	16:11	Who is Aaron that you should g	4296
Mt	20:11	they began to g against the landowner.	1197
Jn	6:41	At this the Jews began to g about him	1197
1Co	10:10	And do not g, as some of them did—	1197
Jas	5: 9	Don't g against each other, brothers,	5100

GRUMBLED (9) [GRUMBLE]

Ex	15:24	So the people g against Moses, saying,	4296
	16: 2	the whole community g against Moses	4296
	17: 3	and they g against Moses.	4296
Nu	14: 2	the Israelites g against Moses and Aaron,	4296
	14:29	in the census who has g against me.	4296
	16:41	the whole Israelite community g	4296
Dt	1:27	You g in your tents and said,	8087
Jos	9:18	The whole assembly g against the leaders,	4296
Ps	106:25	They g in their tents and did not obey	8087

GRUMBLERS (1) [GRUMBLE]

Jude	1:16	These men are g and faultfinders;	1199

GRUMBLING (11) [GRUMBLE]

Ex	16: 7	because he has heard your g against him.	9442
	16: 8	he has heard your g against him.	4296+9442

Ex	16: 8	You are not g against us,"	9442
	16: 9	for he has heard your g.' "	9442
	16:12	"I have heard the g of the Israelites.	9442
Nu	14:27	the complaints of these g Israelites.	4296
	17: 5	I will rid myself of this constant g	4296+9442
	17:10	This will put an end to their g against me,	9442
Jn	6:43	"Stop g among yourselves,"	1197
	6:61	Aware that his disciples were g about this,	1197
1Pe	4: 9	Offer hospitality to one another without g.	1198

GUARANTEE (2) [GUARANTEED, GUARANTEEING]

Ge	43: 9	I myself will g his safety;	6842
Heb	7:22	Jesus has become the g of a better covenant.	1583

GUARANTEED (2) [GUARANTEE]

Ge	44:32	Your servant g the boy's safety	6842
Ro	4:16	and may be g to all Abraham's offspring—	1010

GUARANTEEING (3) [GUARANTEE]

2Co	1:22	as a deposit, g what is to come.	NIG
	5: 5	the Spirit as a deposit, g what is to come.	775
Eph	1:14	who is a deposit g our inheritance	775

GUARD (126) [BODYGUARD, GUARDED, GUARDIAN, GUARDIANS, GUARDING, GUARDROOM, GUARDS, SAFEGUARD]

Ge	3:24	and forth to g the way to the tree of life.	9068
	37:36	of Pharaoh's officials, the captain of the g.	3184
	39: 1	of Pharaoh's officials, the captain of the g,	3184
	40: 3	in the house of the captain of the g,	3184
	40: 4	The captain of the g assigned them	3184
	41:10	in the house of the captain of the g.	3184
	41:12	a servant of the captain of the g.	3184
Ex	22:20	to g you along the way and to bring you to	9068
Nu	10:25	Finally, as the rear g for all the units,	665
Jos	6: 7	with the armed g going ahead of the ark of	2741
	6: 9	The armed g marched ahead of the	2741
	6: 9	and the rear g followed the ark.	665
	6:13	the rear g followed the ark of the LORD,	665
	10:18	and post some men there to g it.	9068
Jdg	7:19	just after they had changed the g.	9068
1Sa	2:31	He will g the feet of his saints,	9068
	7: 1	and consecrated Eleazar his son to g the ark	9068
	19: 2	Be on your g tomorrow morning;	9068
	26:15	Why didn't you g your lord the king?	9068
	26:16	because you did not g your master.	9068
2Sa	16: 6	and the special g were on David's right	1475
	20: 3	the palace and put them in a house under g.	5466
	20:10	Amasa was not on his g against the dagger	9068
1Ki	1: 8	Shimei and Rei and David's special g did	1475
	1:10	or the special g or his brother Solomon.	1475
	14:27	to the commanders of the g on duty at	8132
	20:39	to me with a captive and said, 'G this man.	9068
2Ki	6:10	so that he was on his g in such places.	9068
	11: 6	and a third at the gate behind the g,	9068
	11: 7	to g the temple for the king.	5466+9068
	25: 8	commander of the imperial g,	3184
	25:10	under the commander of the imperial g,	3184
	25:11	the commander of the g carried into exile	3184
	25:15	of the imperial g took away the censers	3184
	25:18	commander of the g took as prisoners	3184
1Ch	9:27	because they had to g it;	5466
	26:16	G was alongside of guard:	5464
	26:16	Guard was alongside of g:	5464
2Ch	12:10	to the commanders of the g on duty at	8132
	12:10	to g what the LORD has assigned	9068
Ezr	8:29	G them carefully until you weigh them out	9193
Ne	3:25	the upper palace near the court of the g.	4766
	3:29	the g at the East Gate, made repairs.	9068
	4: 9	to our God and posted a g day and night	5464
	12:39	At the Gate of the G they stopped.	4766
	13:22	to purify themselves and go and g the gates	9068
Job	7:12	that you put me under g?	5464+6584
Ps	25:20	My life and rescue me;	9068
	86: 2	G my life, for I am devoted to you.	9068
	91:11	concerning you to g you in all your ways;	9068
	127: 1	the watchmen stand g in vain.	9193
	141: 3	Set a g over my mouth, O LORD;	9072
Pr	2:11	and understanding will g you.	5915
	4:13	g it well, for it is your life.	5915
	4:23	Above all else, g your heart,	5915
	7: 2	g my teachings as the apple of your eye.	NIH
Ecc	5: 1	G your steps when you go to the house	9068
Isa	27: 3	I g it day and night so that no one may harm	5915
	52:12	the God of Israel will be your rear g.	665
	58: 8	glory of the LORD will be your rear g.	665
Jer	32: 2	in the courtyard of the g in the royal palace	4766
	32: 8	to me in the courtyard of the g and said,	4766
	32:12	the Jews sitting in the courtyard of the g.	4766
	33: 1	confined in the courtyard of the g,	4766
	37:13	the captain of the g	7215
	37:21	the courtyard of the g and given bread from	4766
	37:21	in the courtyard of the g.	4766
	38: 6	which was in the courtyard of the g.	4766
	38:13	in the courtyard of the g.	4766
	38:28	the g until the day Jerusalem was captured.	4766
	39: 9	the imperial g carried into exile to Babylon	3184
	39:10	the g left behind in the land of Judah some	3184
	39:11	commander of the imperial g:	3184
	39:13	So Nebuzaradan the commander of the g,	3184
	39:14	taken out of the courtyard of the g.	4766
	39:15	the g, the word of the LORD came to him:	4766

Jer	40: 1	the imperial g had released him at Ramah.	3184
	40: 2	the commander of the g found Jeremiah.	3184
	41:10	the imperial g had appointed Gedaliah son	3184
	43: 6	the imperial g had left with Gedaliah son	3184
	51:12	Reinforce the g, station the watchmen,	5464
	52:12	commander of the imperial g,	3184
	52:14	of the imperial g broke down all the walls	3184
	52:15	of the g carried into exile some of	3184
	52:19	of the imperial g took away the basins,	3184
	52:24	of the g took as prisoners Seraiah	3184
	52:30	the commander of the imperial g.	3184
Da	1:11	the g whom the chief official had appointed	4915
	1:16	So the g took away their choice food and	4915
	2:14	Arioch, the commander of the king's g,	10295
Na	2: 1	G the fortress, watch the road,	5915
Mal	2:15	So g yourself in your spirit,	9068
	2:16	So g yourself in your spirit,	9068
Mt	10:17	"Be on your g against men;	4668
	16: 6	"Be on your g against the yeast of	4668
	16:11	But be on your g against the yeast of	4668
	16:12	not telling them to g against the yeast used	4668
	27:65	"Take a g," Pilate answered.	3184
	27:66	a seal on the stone and posting the g.	3184
Mk	13: 9	"You must be on your g.	1063
	13:23	So be on your g;	1063
	13:33	Be on g! Be alert!	70
	14:44	arrest him and lead him away under g."	857
Lk	4:10	concerning you to g you carefully;	1428+3836
	8:29	and foot and kept under g,	5875
	12: 1	"Be on your g against the yeast of	4668
	12:15	Be on your g against all kinds of greed;	5875
	22: 4	and the officers of the temple g	5130
	22:52	and the officers of the temple g,	5130
Ac	4: 1	of the temple g and the Sadducees came up	NIG
	5:24	the captain of the temple g and	2639
	12: 6	and sentries stood g at the entrance.	5871
	16:23	jailer was commanded to g them carefully;	5498
	20:31	So be on your g!	1213
	23:35	Paul be kept under g in Herod's palace.	5875
	24:23	the centurion to keep Paul under g but	5498
	28:16	with a soldier to g him.	5875
1Co	16:13	Be on your g; stand firm in the faith;	1213
Php	1:13	the whole palace g and to everyone else	4550
	4: 7	will g your hearts and your minds	5864
1Ti	6:20	g what has been entrusted to your care.	5875
2Ti	1:12	that he is able to g what I have entrusted	5875
	1:14	G the good deposit that was entrusted	5875
	1:14	g it with the help of the Holy Spirit	NIG
	4:15	You too should be on your g against him,	5875
2Pe	3:17	be on your g so that you may not	5875

GUARDED (8) [GUARD]

Dt	32:10	he g him as the apple of his eye,	5915
	33: 9	over your word and g your covenant.	5915
2Ki	12: 9	The priests who g the entrance put into	9068
Ne	12:25	and Akkub were gatekeepers who g	5464+9068
Est	2:21	of the king's officers who g the doorway,	9068
	6: 2	of the king's officers who g the doorway,	9068
Ac	12: 6	be g by four squads of four soldiers each.	5875
2Co	11:32	of the Damascenes g in order to arrest me.	5864

GUARDIAN (3) [GUARD]

Eze	28:14	You were anointed as a g cherub,	6114
	28:16	O g cherub, from among the fiery stones.	6114
Ac	19:35	the city of Ephesus is the g of the temple	3753

GUARDIANS (4) [GUARD]

2Ki	10: 1	and to the g of Ahab's children.	587
	10: 5	the elders and the g sent this message	587
1Co	4:15	though you have ten thousand g in Christ,	4080
Gal	4: 2	He is subject to g and trustees until	2208

GUARDING (9) [GUARD]

2Ki	11: 5	a third of you g the royal palace,	5466+9068
	11: 6	who take turns g the temple—	5466+9068
1Ch	9:19	(the Korahites) were responsible for g	9068
	9:19	as their fathers had been responsible for g	9068
	9:23	of g the gates of the house of the LORD—	5466
Jer	4:17	They surround her like men g a field,	9068
Mt	27:54	and those with him who were g Jesus saw	5498
Lk	22:63	The men who were g Jesus began mocking	5309
Ac	22:20	I stood there giving my approval and g	5875

GUARDROOM (2) [GUARD]

1Ki	14:28	afterward they returned them to the g.	8132+9288
2Ch	12:11	afterward they returned them to the g.	8132+9288

GUARDS (40) [GUARD]

1Sa	22:17	Then the king ordered the g at his side:	8132
1Ki	14:28	the g bore the shields,	8132
2Ki	10:25	he ordered the g and officers:	8132
	10:25	The g and officers threw the bodies out and	8132
	11: 4	the Carites and the g and had them brought	8132
	11:11	The g, each with his weapon in his hand,	8132
	11:13	the noise made by the g and the people,	8132
	11:18	Then Jehoiada the priest posted g at	7213
	11:19	the g and all the people of the land,	8132
	11:19	entering by way of the gate of the g.	8132
2Ch	12:11	the g went with him, bearing the shields,	8132
Ne	4:22	as g by night and workmen by day."	5464
	4:23	nor the g with me took off our clothes;	408+5464
	7: 3	Also appoint residents of Jerusalem as g,	5466
Ps	97:10	for he g the lives of his faithful ones	9068

Pr	2: 8	for he g the course of the just and protects	5915
	13: 3	He who g his lips guards his life,	5915
	13: 3	He who guards his lips g his life,	9068
	13: 6	Righteousness g the man of integrity,	5915
	16:17	he who g his way guards his life.	5915
	16:17	he who guards his way g his life.	9068
	19:16	He who obeys instructions g his life,	9068
	21:23	He who g his mouth and his tongue	9068
	22: 5	but he who g his soul stays far from them.	9068
	24:12	Does not he who g your life know it?	5915
Eze	9: 1	"Bring the g of the city here,"	7213
	40: 7	The alcoves for the g were one rod long	9288
Na	3:17	Your g are like locusts,	4964
Mt	26:58	and sat down with the g to see the outcome.	5677
	28: 4	The g were so afraid of him that they shook	5498
	28:11	of the g went into the city and reported to	3184
Mk	14:54	There he sat with the g and warmed himself	5677
	14:65	And the g took him and beat him.	5677
Lk	11:21	a strong man, fully armed, g his own house,	5875
Jn	7:32	the Pharisees sent temple g to arrest him.	5677
	7:45	the temple g went back to the chief priests	5677
	7:46	the way this man does," the g declared.	5677
Ac	5:23	with the g standing at the doors;	5874
	12:10	They passed the first and second g	5871
	12:19	the g and ordered that they be executed.	5874

GUDGODAH (1)

Dt	10: 7	From there they traveled to G and on	1516

GUEST (8) [GUESTS]

Lev	22:10	the g of a priest or his hired worker eat it.	9369
Jdg	19:23	Since this man is my g,	448+995+1074
Est	5: 8	the king's command each g was allowed	NIH
Mk	14:14	Where is my g room,	2906
Lk	19: 7	"He has gone to be the g of a 'sinner.' "	2907
	22:11	Where is the g room,	2906
Ac	10:32	He is a g in the home of Simon the tanner,	3826
Phm	1:22	Prepare a g room for me,	3825

GUESTCHAMBER (KJV) See GUEST ROOM

GUESTS (20) [GUEST]

1Sa	9:24	from the time I said, 'I have invited g.' "	6639
2Sa	15:11	They had been invited as g	7924
1Ki	1:41	and all the g who were with him heard it	7924
	1:49	all Adonijah's g rose in alarm	7924
Job	19:15	My g and my maidservants count me	1074+1591
Pr	9:18	that her g are in the depths of the grave.	7924
Mt	9:15	the g of the bridegroom mourn while he is	5626
	14: 9	but because of his oaths and his dinner g,	5263
	22:10	and the wedding hall was filled with g.	367
	22:11	"But when the king came in to see the g,	367
Mk	2:19	the g of the bridegroom fast while he is	5626
	6:22	she pleased Herod and his dinner g.	5263
	6:26	but because of his oaths and his dinner g,	367
Lk	5:34	the g of the bridegroom fast while he is	5626
	7:49	The other g began to say	5263
	14: 7	how the g picked the places of honor at	2813
	14:10	in the presence of all your fellow g,	5263
	14:16	a great banquet and invited many g.	NIG
Jn	2:10	after the g have had too much to drink;	NIG
Ac	10:23	the men into the house to be his g.	3826

GUIDANCE (7) [GUIDE]

2Ki	3:11	I will use the bronze altar for seeking g."	1329
1Ch	10:13	and even consulted a medium for g,	2011
Pr	1: 5	and let the discerning get g—	9374
	11:14	For lack of g a nation falls,	9374
	20:18	if you wage war, obtain g.	9374
	24: 6	for waging war you need g,	9374
Hab	2:19	Can it give g? It is covered with gold	3723

GUIDE (22) [GUIDANCE, GUIDED, GUIDEPOSTS, GUIDES, GUIDING]

Ex	13:21	a pillar of cloud to g them on their way and	5697
	15:13	In your strength you will g them	5633
Ne	9:19	the pillar of cloud did not cease to g them	5697
Ps	25: 5	g me in your truth and teach me,	2005
	31: 3	for the sake of your name lead and g me.	5633
	43: 3	your light and your truth, let them g me;	5697
	48:14	he will be our g even to the end.	5627
	67: 4	the peoples justly and g the nations of	5697
	73:24	You g me with your counsel,	5697
	139:10	even there your hand will g me,	5697
Pr	4:11	I g you in the way of wisdom and lead you	3723
	6:22	When you walk, they will g you;	5697
Isa	9:16	Those who g this people mislead them,	886
	42:16	along unfamiliar paths I will g them;	2005
	49:10	on them will g them and lead them	5627
	51:18	the sons she bore there was none to g her;	5633
	57:18	I will g him and restore comfort to him,	5697
	58:11	The LORD will g you always;	5697
Lk	1:79	to g our feet into the path of peace."	2985
Jn	16:13	comes, he will g you into all truth.	3842
Ac	1:16	as g for those who arrested Jesus—	3843
Ro	2:19	if you are convinced that you are a g for	3843

GUIDED (6) [GUIDE]

Job	31:18	and from my birth I g the widow;	5697
Ps	78:14	He g them with the cloud by day and	5697
	78:53	He g them safely, so they were unafraid;	5697

Ps	107:30	and *he* g them to their desired haven.	5697
Isa	9:16	and *those who* **are** g are led astray.	886
	63:14	This is how *you* g your people to make	5627

GUIDEPOSTS (1) [GUIDE]

Jer	31:21	"Set up road signs; put up g.	9477

GUIDES (8) [GUIDE]

Ps	23: 3	*He* g me in paths of righteousness	5697
	25: 9	*He* g the humble in what is right	2005
Pr	11: 3	The integrity of the upright g them,	5697
	16:23	A wise man's heart g his mouth,	8505
Isa	3:12	O my people, your g lead you astray.	886
Mt	15:14	Leave them; they are blind g.	3843
	23:16	"Woe to you, blind g!	3843
	23:24	*You* blind g! You strain out a gnat	3843

GUIDING (4) [GUIDE]

2Sa	6: 3	sons of Abinadab, *were* g the new cart	5627
1Ch	13: 7	with Uzzah and Ahio g it.	5627
Ecc	2: 3	my mind *still* g me with wisdom.	5627
Jn	18: 3	g a detachment of soldiers	3284

GUILE (KJV) See FALSE, TRICKERY, DECEIT

GUILT (105) [BLOODGUILT, GUILTLESS, GUILTY]

Ge	20: 9	that you have brought such great g	2631
	26:10	and you would have brought g upon us."	871
	44:16	God has uncovered your servants' g.	6411
Ex	28:38	and he will bear the g *involved in*	6411
	28:43	so that they will not incur g and die.	6411
Lev	4: 3	bringing g *on* the people,	873
	5:15	It is a g offering.	871
	5:16	for him with the ram as a g **offering**	871
	5:18	to bring to the priest as a g **offering** a ram	871
	5:19	It is a g offering.	871
	6: 5	on the day he presents his g **offering.**	873
	6: 6	that is, to the LORD, his g **offering,**	871
	6:17	Like the sin offering and the g **offering,**	871
	7: 1	for the g **offering,** which is most holy:	871
	7: 2	The g **offering** is to be slaughtered in	871
	7: 5	It is a g **offering.**	871
	7: 7	to both the sin offering and the g **offering:**	871
	7:37	the sin offering, the g **offering,**	871
	10:17	it was given to you to take away the g *of*	6411
	14:12	the male lambs and offer it as a g **offering,**	871
	14:13	the g **offering** belongs to the priest;	871
	14:14	to take some of the blood of the g **offering**	871
	14:17	on top of the blood of the g **offering**	871
	14:21	he must take one male lamb as a g **offering**	871
	14:24	take the lamb for the g **offering,**	871
	14:25	the lamb for the g **offering** and take some	871
	14:28	the blood of the g **offering**—	871
	19:17	so you will not share in his g.	2628
	19:21	of Meeting for a g **offering** to the LORD.	871
	19:22	With the ram of the g **offering** the priest is	871
	22:16	so bring upon them g requiring payment.	6411
Nu	5:15	a reminder offering to draw attention to g.	6411
	5:28	she *will* **be cleared** of g and will be able	5927
	6:12	a year-old male lamb as a g **offering.**	871
	15:31	his g remains on him.' "	6411
	18: 9	whether grain or sin or g **offerings,**	871
	30:15	then he is responsible for her g."	6411
Dt	19:13	g **of shedding** innocent **blood,**	1947
	21: 9	g **of shedding** innocent **blood,**	1947
	22: 8	not bring the g **of bloodshed** on your house	1947
1Sa	3:14	'The g *of* Eli's house will never be atoned	6411
	6: 3	but by all means send a g **offering** to him.	871
	6: 4	"What g **offering** should we send to him?"	871
	6: 8	sending back to him as a g **offering.**	871
	6:17	the Philistines sent as a g **offering** to	871
2Sa	14: 9	let the king and his throne be **without** g."	5929
	24:10	I beg you, take away the g *of* your servant.	6411
1Ki	2:31	g *of* the innocent **blood** that Joab	1947
	2:33	May the g *of* their **blood** rest on the head	1947
2Ki	12:16	from the g **offerings** and sin offerings was	871
1Ch	21: 3	Why should he bring g on Israel?"	873
	21: 8	I beg you, take away the g *of* your servant.	6411
2Ch	24:18	Because of their g, God's anger came upon	873
	28:13	Do you intend to add to our sin and g?	873
	28:13	For our g is already great,	873
	33:23	Amon increased his g.	873
Ezr	9: 6	and our g has reached to the heavens.	873
	9: 7	until now, our g has been great.	873
	9:13	a result of our evil deeds and our great g,	873
	9:15	Here we are before you in our g,	873
	10:10	married foreign women, adding to Israel's g.	873
	10:19	for their g they each presented a ram from	873
	10:19	a ram from the flock as a g **offering.**)	871
Ne	4: 5	not cover up their g or blot out their sins	6411
Job	20:27	The heavens will expose his g;	6411
	31:33	by hiding my g in my heart	6411
	33: 9	I am clean and free from g.	6411
Ps	7: 3	if I have done this and there is g	6404
	32: 5	and you forgave the g *of* my sin.	6411
	38: 4	My g has overwhelmed me like	6411
	69: 5	my g is not hidden from you.	873
Pr	28:17	A man tormented by the g **of murder** will be a fugitive till death;	1947+5883
Isa	1: 4	Ah, sinful nation, a people loaded with g,	6411
	6: 7	your g is taken away	6411

Isa	24: 6	its people *must* bear *their* g.	870
	24:20	so heavy upon it is the g *of* its **rebellion**	7322
	27: 9	By this, then, will Jacob's g be atoned for,	6411
	53:10	the LORD makes his life a g **offering,**	871
	59: 3	stained with blood, your fingers with g.	6411
Jer	2:22	the stain of your g is still before me,"	6411
	3:13	Only acknowledge your g—	6411
	14:20	we acknowledge our wickedness and the g	6411
	25:12	the land of the Babylonians, for their g,"	6411
	26:15	the g *of* innocent **blood** on yourselves and	1947
	30:14	your g is so great and your sins so many.	6411
	30:15	Because of your great g and many sins	6411
	50:20	"search will be made for Israel's g,	6411
	51: 5	though their land is full of g before	871
Eze	14:10	They will bear their g—	6411
	18:19	the son not share the g *of* his father?'	6411
	18:20	The son will not share the g *of* the father,	6411
	18:20	nor will the father share the g *of* the son.	6411
	21:23	but he will remind them of their g	6411
	21:24	to mind your g by your open rebellion,	6411
	40:39	and g offerings were slaughtered.	871
	42:13	the sin offerings and the g **offerings**—	871
	44:29	the sin offerings and the g **offerings,**	871
	46:20	where the priests will cook the g **offering**	871
Hos	5:15	to my place until they **admit** *their* g.	870
	10: 2	and now *they* must bear *their* g.	870
	12:14	the g *of* his **bloodshed** and will repay him	1947
	13:12	The g *of* Ephraim is stored up,	6411
	13:16	The people of Samaria *must* bear *their* g,	870
Jn	9:41	that you claim you can see, your g remains.	281
	16: 8	he will **convict** the world **of** g	1794

GUILTLESS (4) [GUILT]

Ex	20: 7	not **hold** anyone g who misuses his name.	5927
Dt	5:11	not **hold** anyone g who misuses his name.	5927
1Sa	26: 9	on the LORD's anointed and *be* g?	5927
Job	34: 6	considered a liar; although I am g,	1172+7322

GUILTY (83) [GUILT]

Ge	38:24	"Your daughter-in-law Tamar *is* g *of* prostitution,	2388
Ex	22: 2	the defender is not g *of* bloodshed;	1947
	22: 3	he is g *of* bloodshed.	1947
	22: 9	the judges **declare** g must pay back double	8399
	23: 7	for I will not acquit the g.	8399
	34: 7	not **leave** the g unpunished;	5927+5927
Lev	4:13	unaware of the matter, *they are* g,	870
	4:22	commands of the LORD his God, *he is* g,	870
	4:27	in any of the LORD's commands, *he is* g.	870
	5: 2	he has become unclean and is g.	870
	5: 3	when he learns of it *he will be* g.	870
	5: 4	when he learns of it *he will be* g.	870
	5: 5	" 'When *anyone is* g in any of these ways,	870
	5:17	*he is* g and will be held responsible.	870
	5:19	*he has been* g *of* **wrongdoing** against	870+870
	6: 4	when he thus sins and *becomes* g,	870
	6: 7	of these things he did that made him g."	873
	17: 4	be considered g *of* bloodshed;	1947
	22: 9	not **become** g and die for treating them with contempt.	2628+5951+6584
Nu	5: 6	to the LORD, that person *is* g	870
	14:18	not **leave** the g unpunished;	5927+5927
	18:32	of it *you will* not *be* g in this matter;	2628+1945
	35:27	the accused without being g *of* **murder.**	1947
Dt	15: 9	and you will be found g *of* sin.	2628
	19:10	and so that you will not be g *of* **bloodshed.**	1947
	21: 8	not hold your people g *of* the **blood** of	1947
	21:22	a man g *of* a capital offense is put to death	2628
	23:21	demand it of you and you will be g *of* sin.	2628
	23:22	from making a vow, you will not be g.	2628
	24:15	and you will be g *of* sin.	2628
	25: 1	the innocent and condemning the g.	8401
	25: 2	If the g *man* deserves to be beaten,	8401
1Sa	20: 8	If I am g, then kill me yourself!	6411
	24:11	I am not g *of* wrongdoing or rebellion,	928+3338
	26:18	and what wrong am I g *of*?	928+3338
2Sa	14:32	and if I am g of anything,	6411
	19:19	"May my lord not hold me g.	6411
1Ki	8:32	condemning the g and bringing down	8401
	8:32	**Declare** the innocent **not** g,	7405
2Ch	6:23	repaying the g by bringing down	8401
	6:23	**Declare** the innocent **not** g	7405
	20:35	who *was* g *of* wickedness.	8399
	28:10	aren't you also g *of* sins against the LORD	873
	28:13	"or we will be g *before* the LORD.	873
Job	9:20	it would **pronounce** me g.	6835
	9:29	Since I am *already found* g,	8399
	10: 7	though you know that I *am* not g and	8399
	10:15	If *I am* g—woe to me!	8399
	34:31	'I *am* g but will offend no more.	5951
Ps	5:10	**Declare** them g, O God!	870
	109: 7	When he is tried, let him be found g,	8401
Pr	17:15	Acquitting the g and condemning the innocent—	8401
	21: 8	The way of the g is devious,	2261
	24:24	to the g, "You are innocent"—	8401
	24:25	with those who convict the g,	NIH
Isa	5:23	who acquit the g for a bribe,	8401
	29:21	who with a word **make** a man **out to be** g,	2627
Jer	2: 3	all who devoured her *were* **held** g,	870
	50: 7	their enemies said, 'We *are* not g,	870
Eze	14:10	be as g as the one who consults him.	870
	18:24	the **unfaithfulness** *he is* g *of*	5085+5086
	22: 4	*you* **have become** g because of	870
	25:12	and **became very** g by doing so,	870+870

Hos	1: 2	the land *is* g **of the vilest adultery**	2388+2388
	4:15	O Israel, *let* not Judah **become** g.	870
	13: 1	But he became g **of** Baal worship and died.	870
Na	1: 3	not **leave** the g unpunished.	5927+5927
Hab	1:11	g *men,* whose own strength is their god."	870
Mk	3:29	he is g of an eternal sin."	1944
Lk	13: 4	do you think they were more g than all	4050
Jn	8:46	**Can** any of you **prove** me g of sin?	1794
	9:41	*you* would not **be** g **of** sin;	281+2400
	15:22	*they* would not **be** g **of** sin.	281+2400
	15:24	*they* would not **be** g **of** sin.	281+2400
	19:11	g *of* a greater **sin.**"	281+2400
Ac	5:28	and are determined *to* **make** us g **of**	2042+2093
	22:25	hasn't even **been** found g?"	185
	23:11	*I am* g *of* doing anything deserving death,	92
	28:18	not g *of* any **crime** deserving death.	162
1Co	11:27	be g **of sinning against** the body and blood	1944
Heb	10: 2	would no longer have **felt** g for their sins.	5287
	10:22	to cleanse us from a g **conscience**	4505+5287
Jas	2:10	at just one point is g of breaking all of it.	1944

GULF (1)

Isa	11:15	The LORD will dry up the g *of* the Egyptian	4383

GULL (2)

Lev	11:16	the screech owl, the g, any kind of hawk,	8830
Dt	14:15	the screech owl, the g, any kind of hawk,	8830

GULPS (1)

Pr	19:28	and the mouth of the wicked g **down** evil.	1180

GUM (1)

Ex	30:34	g resin, onycha and galbanum—	5753

GUNI (4) [GUNITE]

Ge	46:24	Jahziel, G, Jezer and Shillem.	1586
Nu	26:48	through G, the Gunite clan;	1586
1Ch	5:15	Ahi son of Abdiel, the son of G,	1586
	7:13	Jahziel, G, Jezer and Shillem—	1586

GUNITE (1) [GUNI]

Nu	26:48	through Guni, the G clan;	1587

GUR (1) [GUR BAAL]

2Ki	9:27	in his chariot on the way up to G	1595

GUR BAAL (1) [BAAL, GUR]

2Ch	26: 7	the Arabs who lived in G and against	1597

GUSH (1) [GUSHED, GUSHES]

Isa	35: 6	Water *will* g **forth** in the wilderness	1324

GUSHED (4) [GUSH]

Nu	20:11	Water g **out,** and the community	3655+8041
Ps	78:20	When he struck the rock, water g **out,**	2307
	105:41	He opened the rock, and water g **out;**	2307
Isa	48:21	he split the rock and water g **out.**	2307

GUSHES (2) [GUSH]

Pr	15: 2	but the mouth of the fool g folly.	5580
	15:28	but the mouth of the wicked g evil.	5580

GUTTER (3)

Eze	43:13	Its g is a cubit deep and a cubit wide,	2668
	43:14	From the g *on* the ground up to	2668
	43:17	of half a cubit and a g of a cubit all around.	2668

H

HA (1) [AHA]

Lk	4:34	"H! What do you want with us,	1568

HAAHASHTARI (1)

1Ch	4: 6	Hepher, Temeni and H.	2028

HAARALOTH See GIBEATH HAARALOTH

HABAIAH (KJV) See HOBAIAH

HABAKKUK (2)

Hab	1: 1	The oracle that H the prophet received.	2487
	3: 1	A prayer of H the prophet. On shigionoth.	2487

HABAZZINIAH (1)

Jer	35: 3	son of H, and his brothers and all his sons—	2484

HABERGEONS (KJV) See COAT OF ARMOR, ARMOR

HABIT (5)

Ex	21:29	bull has **had the** h of goring	4946+8997+9453
	21:36	if it was known that the bull **had the** h	
			4946+8997+9453
Nu	22:30	*Have I* been in the h of this to you?	6122+6122
1Ti	5:13	*they* **get into the** h of being idle	3443
Heb	10:25	as some are **in the** h of doing,	1621

HABITAT (1) [INHABIT]

Job	39: 6	the salt flats as his h.	5438

HABITATION (KJV) See ABODE, ANCESTRY, DWELLING, FOUNDATION, HAUNT, HEAVENS, HOME, HOMELAND, HOUSE, LIVE, NEST, PASTURES, PLACE, PROPERTY, REFUGE, SETTLE, SETTLEMENT, THRONE

HABOR (3)

2Ki	17: 6	in Gozan on the **H** River and in the towns of	2466
	18:11	on the **H** River and in towns of the Medes.	2466
1Ch	5:26	He took them to Halah, **H**,	2466

HACALIAH (2)

Ne	1: 1	The words of Nehemiah son of **H**:	2678
	10: 1	Nehemiah the governor, the son of **H**.	2678

HACHALIAH (KJV) See HACALIAH

HACHILAH (KJV) See HAKILAH

HACHMONI (KJV) See HACMONI

HACHMONITE (KJV) See HACMONITE

HACK (1)

Eze	16:40	who will stone you and h you **to pieces**	1438

HACMONI (1) [HACMONITE]

1Ch	27:32	Jehiel son of **H** took care of the king's sons.	2685

HACMONITE (1) [HACMONI]

1Ch	11:11	a **H**, was chief of the officers;	1201+2685

HAD (530 of 2791) [HAVE] See Index of Articles Etc. for an Exhaustive Listing (See Introduction, page x)

Ge	4:22	Zillah also h **a son**, Tubal-Cain,	3528
	4:26	Seth also h a son, and he named him Enosh.	3528
	5: 3	*he* h **a son** in his own likeness,	3528
	5: 4	Adam lived 800 years and h other sons	3528
	5: 7	Seth lived 807 years and h other sons	3528
	5:10	Enosh lived 815 years and h other sons	3528
	5:13	Kenan lived 840 years and h other sons	3528
	5:16	Mahalalel lived 830 years and h other sons	3528
	5:19	Jared lived 800 years and h other sons	3528
	5:22	with God 300 years and h other sons	3528
	5:26	and h other sons and daughters.	3528
	5:28	Lamech had lived 182 years, *he* h a son.	3528
	5:30	Lamech lived 595 years and h other sons	3528
	6: 4	to the daughters of men and h **children**	3528
	6:10	Noah h three sons: Shem, Ham and Japheth.	3528
	10: 1	who themselves h sons after the flood.	3528
	11: 1	Now the whole world h one language and	2118
	11:11	Shem lived 500 years and h other sons	3528
	11:13	Arphaxad lived 403 years and h other sons	3528
	11:15	Shelah lived 403 years and h other sons	3528
	11:17	Eber lived 430 years and h other sons	3528
	11:19	Peleg lived 209 years and h other sons	3528
	11:21	Reu lived 207 years and h other sons	3528
	11:23	Serug lived 200 years and h other sons	3528
	11:25	Nahor lived 119 years and h other sons	3528
	11:30	Now Sarai was barren; she h no children.	4200
	12:20	with his wife and everything he h.	4200
	13: 1	with his wife and everything he h,	4200
	13: 5	also h flocks and herds and tents.	2118+4200
	16: 1	But she h an Egyptian maidservant	4200
	19:37	The older daughter h a son,	3528
	19:38	The younger daughter also h a son,	3528
	20:13	And when God h me **wander**	9494
	22:24	whose name was Reumah, also h **sons:**	3528
	24: 2	in charge of all that he h,	4200
	24:11	h the camels **kneel down**	1384
	24:29	Now Rebekah h a brother named Laban,	4200
	25:28	Isaac, who h a taste for wild game,	928
	26:14	He h so many flocks and herds and servants	4200
	27:15	which she h in the house,	907
	28:12	*He* h **a dream** in which he saw	2731
	29:16	Now Laban h two daughters;	4200
	30: 8	h a great **struggle** with my sister,	5887+7349
	30:30	The little you h before I came	2118+4200
	31: 2	toward him was not what *it* h been.	8997+9453
Ge	31:10	"In breeding season *I once* h a dream	8011ˢ
	31:21	So he fled with all he h,	4200
	32:10	I h only my staff	928
	32:13	what he h *with* him he selected a gift	928+3338
	35: 4	the foreign gods they h and the rings	928+3338
	35:22	Jacob h twelve sons:	2118
	36:12	also h a concubine named Timna.	2118+4200
	37: 5	Joseph h a dream,	2706+2731
	37: 6	to them, "Listen to this **dream** *I* h:	2706+2731
	37: 9	Then *he* h another **dream,**	2706+2731
	37: 9	"Listen," he said, "*I* h another **dream,**	2706+2731
	37:10	"What is this **dream** you h?	2706+2731
	39: 5	The blessing of the LORD was on everything Potiphar h,	3780+4200
	39: 6	So he left in Joseph's care everything he h;	4200
	40: 5	h a dream the same night,	2706+2731
	40: 5	and each dream h a meaning of its own.	3869
	40: 8	"We both h **dreams,**" they answered,	2706+2731
	40:16	he said to Joseph, "I too h a dream:	NIH
	41: 1	Pharaoh h **a dream:**	2731
	41: 5	He fell asleep again and h a second **dream:**	2731
	41:11	Each of us h **a dream** the same night,	2706+2731
	41:11	and each dream h a meaning of its own.	3869
	41:15	Pharaoh said to Joseph, "*I* h a dream,	2706+2731
	41:43	He h him **ride** in a chariot	8206
	43: 6	by telling the man you h another brother?"	4200
	47:22	from Pharaoh and h **food enough** *from*	430
Ex	2:16	Now a priest of Midian h seven daughters,	4200
	5:13	just as when you h straw."	2118
	9:28	for we *have* h enough thunder and hail.	2118
	10:23	all the Israelites h light in the places	2118+4200
	14: 6	So he h his chariot **made ready**	673
	14:25	so that they h difficulty driving.	2118
	21:29	bull has **h the habit** of goring	4946+8997+9453
	21:36	if it was known that the bull h **the habit**	
			4946+8997+9453
	35:23	Everyone who h blue, purple or	907+5162
	35:24	and everyone who h acacia wood	907+5162
	35:26	And all the women who were willing and h	928
	36: 7	what *they already* h was more than enough	2118
	37: 9	The cherubim h their wings spread upward,	2118
	38: 9	and h curtains of finely twisted linen,	4200
	38:11	a hundred cubits long and h twenty posts	4200
	38:12	and h curtains, with ten posts and ten bases,	4200
Lev	23:43	that *I* h the Israelites **live** in booths	3782
Nu	3: 4	They h no sons;	2118+4200
	5:18	the priest *has* h the woman **stand** before	6641
	11: 4	"If only we h meat **to eat!**	430
	11:18	"If only we h meat **to eat!**	430
	11:24	of their elders and h them **stand** around	6641
	12:10	toward her and saw that *she* h leprosy;	7665
	22:29	If I h a sword in my hand,"	3780
	26:33	(Zelophehad son of Hepher h no sons;	2118+4200
	26:33	he h only daughters,	NIH
	27: 4	from his clan because he h no son?	4200
	27:11	If his father h no brothers,	4200
	27:22	and h him **stand** before Eleazar the priest	6641
	32: 1	who h very large herds and flocks,	2118+4200
Dt	4:25	After *you have* h children	3528
Jos	5: 1	they no longer h the courage to face	928+2118
	5: 5	during the journey from Egypt h not.	4576ˢ
	7:16	next morning Joshua h Israel **come forward**	7928
	7:17	h the clan of the Zerahites **come forward**	7928
	7:18	h his family **come forward**	7928
	7:24	his tent and all that he h,	4200
	8:13	h the soldiers **take up** *their* **positions**—	8492
	8:20	they h no **chance** to escape	928+2118+3338
	11:10	(Hazor h **been** the head	4200+7156
	11:23	Then the land h rest from war.	9200
	14:15	Then the land h rest from war.	9200
	17: 3	h no sons but only daughters.	2118+4200
	17: 8	(Manasseh h the land of Tappuah,	2118+4200
	17:11	Manasseh also h Beth Shan,	2118+4200
	18:21	clan by clan, h the following cities:	2118+4200
	19:47	h **difficulty taking possession of**	3655+4946
	21:42	these towns h pasturelands surrounding it;	2118
Jdg	1:19	because they h iron chariots.	4200
	2:18	for the LORD h **compassion** *on* them	5714
	3: 2	h previous **battle experience**)	3359
	3:11	So the land h **peace** for forty years,	9200
	3:30	and the land h **peace** for eighty years.	9200
	4: 3	Because he h nine hundred iron chariots	4200
	5:31	Then the land h **peace** forty years.	9200
	7:13	"*I* h **a dream,**" he was saying.	2706+2731
	8: 8	but they answered as the men of Succoth h.	6699ˢ
	8:30	He h seventy sons of his own,	2118+4200
	8:30	for he h many wives.	2118+4200
	10: 4	He h thirty sons, who rode thirty donkeys.	
			2118+4200
	11:34	for her he h neither son nor daughter.	4200
	12: 9	He h thirty sons and thirty daughters.	2118+4200
	12:14	He h forty sons and thirty grandsons,	2118+4200
	13: 2	h a wife who was sterile	2118
	17: 5	Now this man Micah h a shrine,	4200
	17: 6	In those days Israel h no king;	928
	18: 1	In those days Israel h no king.	928
	18: 7	from the Sidonians and h no relationship	4200
	18:28	and h no relationship with anyone else.	4200
	19: 1	In those days Israel h no king,	928
	21:25	In those days Israel h no king;	928
Ru	1:12	if *I* h a husband tonight and then	2118+4200
	2: 1	Naomi h a relative on her husband's side,	4200
	2:14	and h some **left over.**	3855
	2:18	and gave her what *she* h **left over.**	3855
1Sa	1: 2	He h two wives;	4200
	1: 2	Peninnah h children, but Hannah had none.	
			2118+4200
1Sa	1: 2	Peninnah had children, but Hannah h none.	4200
	2:12	*they* h no **regard** for the LORD.	3359
	9: 2	He h a son named Saul,	2118+4200
	13: 3	Then Saul h the trumpet **blown** throughout	9546
	13:22	and Jonathan h a sword or spear in his hand;	5162
	13:22	Saul and his son Jonathan h them.	4200+5162
	16: 8	Then Jesse called Abinadab and h him **pass**	6296
	16: 9	Jesse then h Shammah **pass by,**	6296
	16:10	h seven of his sons **pass**	6296
	16:12	So he sent and h him **brought in.**	995
	17:12	Jesse h eight sons,	4200
	18:14	In everything he did he h **great success,**	8505
	20: 9	"If *I* h **the least inkling**	3359+3359
	20:17	And Jonathan h David **reaffirm** his oath out	3578
	25: 2	He h a thousand goats	4200
	28:24	The woman h a fattened calf at the house,	4200
	30: 4	until they h no strength left to weep.	928
2Sa	3: 7	Now Saul had h a concubine named Rizpah	4200
	3:37	that the king h no **part** in the murder	2118+4946
	4: 2	Saul's son h two men who were leaders	2118
	4: 4	(Jonathan son of Saul h a son who was lame	2118+4200
	6:23	Michal daughter of Saul h no children	2118+4200
	9: 5	King David h him **brought** from Lo Debar,	
			2256+4374+8938
	9:10	Ziba h fifteen sons and twenty servants.)	4200
	9:12	Mephibosheth h a young son named Mica,	4200
	10:16	Hadadezer h Arameans **brought** from	3655
	11:27	David h her **brought** to his house,	665
	12: 2	The rich man h a very large number	2118+4200
	12: 3	poor man h nothing except one little ewe lamb he had bought.	4200
	12: 6	because he did such a thing and h no **pity.**"	2798
	13: 3	Now Amnon h a friend named Jonadab son	4200
	14: 2	h a wise woman **brought** from there.	4374
	14: 6	I your servant h two sons.	4200
	17:18	He h a well in his courtyard,	4200
	18:11	Then I would have h to give you	6584
1Ki	1: 4	the king h no **intimate relations with**	3359
	2:19	*He* h a throne **brought** for the king's mother,	8492
	3:17	*I* h **a baby** while she was there with me.	3528
	3:18	this woman also h a baby.	3528
	3:28	because they saw that he h wisdom	928+7931
	4: 7	Solomon also h twelve district governors	4200
	4: 7	Each one h to provide supplies	2118+6584
	4:24	and h peace on all sides.	2118+4200
	4:26	Solomon h four thousand stalls	2118+4200
	5:15	Solomon h seventy thousand carriers	2118+4200
	7:28	They h side panels attached to uprights.	4200
	7:30	Each stand h four bronze wheels	4200
	7:30	and each h a basin resting on four supports,	4200
	8:17	"My father David h *it* in his heart to build	2118
	9: 1	and h achieved all he had desired to do,	NIH
	10: 2	with him about all that *she* h on her mind.	2118
	10:19	The throne h six steps,	4200
	10:19	and its back h a rounded top.	NIH
	10:22	The king h a fleet of trading ships at sea	4200
	10:26	he h fourteen hundred chariots	2118+4200
	11: 3	h seven hundred wives of royal birth	2118+4200
	20:33	Ahab h him **come up** into his chariot.	6590
2Ki	1:17	Because Ahaziah h no son,	2118+4200
	3: 9	army h no more water for themselves	2118+4200
	4:44	and they ate and h *some* **left over,**	3855
	5: 1	He was a valiant soldier, but he h leprosy.	7665
	7: 8	The **men** who h leprosy reached the edge of	7665
	10:16	Then *he* h him **ride** along in his chariot.	8206
	11: 4	and the guards and h them **brought** to him	995
	13:23	and h **compassion** and showed concern	8163
	15: 5	the king's son h **charge** of the palace	6584
	23:16	*he* h the bones **removed** from	2256+4374+8938
1Ch	2: 9	of Hezron h **children** by his wife Azubah	3528
	2:26	Jerahmeel h another wife,	2118+4200
	2:34	Sheshan h no sons—only daughters.	2118+4200
	2:34	He h an Egyptian servant named Jarha.	4200
	4: 5	the father of Tekoa h two wives,	2118+4200
	4:27	Shimei h sixteen sons and six daughters,	4200
	7: 4	they h 36,000 men ready for battle,	6584
	7: 4	for *they* h **many** wives and children.	8049
	7:15	who h only daughters.	2118+4200
	8: 9	By his wife Hodesh *he* h Jobab, Zibia,	3528
	8:11	By Hushim *he* h Abitub and Elpaal.	3528
	8:38	Azel h six sons, and these were their names:	4200
	8:40	*They* h **many** sons and grandsons—	8049
	9:27	because they h to guard it;	6584
	9:27	and they h **charge** of the key	6584
	9:44	Azel h six sons, and these were their names:	4200
	13:14	and everything he h.	4200
	19:16	and h Arameans **brought** from beyond	3655
	22: 7	"My son, I h *it* in my heart to build a house	2118
	23:17	Eliezer h no other sons,	2118+4200
	23:22	he h only daughters.	NIH
	23:22	and they h no sons;	2118+4200
	24:28	From Mahli: Eleazar, who h no sons,	2118+4200
	26: 2	Meshelemiah h these sons: Zechariah	4200
	26: 4	Obed-Edom also h sons:	4200
	26: 6	His son Shemaiah also h sons,	3528
	26: 9	Meshelemiah h sons and relatives,	4200
	26:10	Hosah the Merarite h sons:	4200
	26:12	h duties for ministering in the temple of	4200
	29: 8	Any who h precious stones gave them	907+5162
	29:25	as no king over Israel ever h before.	2118+6584
		such as no king who was before you ever h	2118
2Ch	1:14	he h fourteen hundred chariots	2118+4200
	6: 7	"My father David h *it* in his heart to build	2118
	7:11	and had succeeded in carrying out all he h	995
	9: 1	with him about all *she* h on her mind.	2118
	9:18	The throne h six steps,	4200

2Ch	9:21	The king **h** a fleet of trading ships manned	4200
	9:25	Solomon **h** four thousand stalls for horses	2118+4200
	11:21	he **h** eighteen wives and sixty concubines,	5951
	13:21	fourteen wives and **h** twenty-two sons	3528
	14: 8	Asa **h** an army	2118+4200
	17: 5	so that he **h** great wealth and honor.	2118+4200
	17:13	**h** large supplies in the towns of Judah.	2118+4200
	18: 1	Jehoshaphat **h** great wealth and honor,	2118+4200
	24: 3	and *he* **h** sons and daughters.	3528
	26:10	he **h** much livestock in the foothills	2118+4200
	26:11	Uzziah **h** a well-trained army,	2118+4200
	26:20	they saw that he **h leprosy** on his forehead,	7665
	26:21	King Uzziah **h leprosy** until	7665
	26:21	Jotham **h** in **charge of** the palace	6584
	26:23	for people said, "He **h leprosy.**"	7665
	30:17	the Levites **h** to kill the Passover lambs	6584
	31:10	we *have* **h enough** to eat and plenty to spare	8425
	32:27	Hezekiah **h** very great riches and honor,	
	34:13	**h charge of** the laborers and supervised all	6584
	34:32	**h** everyone in Jerusalem and Benjamin **pledge**	6641
	34:33	**h** all who were present in Israel **serve**	6641
	35:24	in the other chariot he **h** and brought him	4200
	36:15	because he **h pity** on his people and	2798
Ezr	1: 8	of Persia **h** them **brought** by Mithredath	3655
	2:65	also **h** 200 men and women singers.	4200
	2:66	They **h** 736 horses, 245 mules,	NIH
	4:20	Jerusalem *has* **h** powerful kings ruling over	10201+10542
	10:44	some of them **h** children by these wives.	8492
Ne	7:67	also **h** 245 men and women singers.	4200
	7:73	and the Israelites **h** settled in their towns,	NIH
	11:16	who **h charge of** the outside work of	6584
	12:31	**h** the leaders of Judah **go up**	6590
Est	1:14	who **h special access to** the king	7156+8011
	2: 7	up because she **h** neither father nor mother.	4200
	2: 8	who **h charge of** the harem.	9068
Job	1: 2	He **h** seven sons and three daughters,	3528
	3:15	with rulers who **h** gold,	4200
	28:17	nor can it be **h** for jewels of gold.	9455
	31:31	'Who *has* not **h** *his* **fill of** Job's meat?'—	8425
	31:35	that I **h** someone to hear me!	4200
	32: 5	the three men **h** nothing more to say,	928+7023
	34:27	and **h** no **regard for** any of his ways.	8505
	42:10	and gave him twice as much as he **h** before.	4200
	42:12	He **h** fourteen thousand sheep,	2118+4200
	42:13	also **h** seven sons and three daughters.	2118+4200
Ps	55: 6	I said, "Oh, that I **h** the wings of a dove!"	4200
	78:29	They ate till *they* **h** more than **enough,**	8425
	78:63	and their maidens **h** no **wedding songs;**	2146
Ecc	2: 7	and **h** other slaves who were born	2118+4200
	4: 8	he **h** neither son nor brother.	4200
SS	8:11	Solomon **h** a vineyard in Baal Hamon;	2118+4200
Isa	5: 1	My loved one **h** a vineyard on	2118+4200
	53: 2	He **h** no beauty or majesty to attract us	4200
Jer	20: 2	**h** Jeremiah the prophet **beaten**	5782
	23:25	They say, '*I* **h** a dream!	2731
	23:25	'*I* **h** a dream!'	2731
	26:23	who **h** him **struck down** with a sword	5782
	32:10	and sealed the deed, **h** it **witnessed,**	6332+6386
	35: 9	built houses to live in or **h** vineyards,	2118+4200
	37:15	and **h** him **beaten** and imprisoned in	5782
	44:17	At that time we **h** plenty *of* food	8425
	44:18	we *have* **h nothing** and have been	2893+3972
	52:27	the king **h** them **executed.**	2256+4637+5782
La	5: 4	our wood *can be* **h** at a price.	995S
Eze	1: 6	each of them **h** four faces and four wings.	4200
	1: 8	Under their wings on their four sides they **h**	NIH
	1: 8	All four of them **h** faces and wings,	4200
	1:10	Each of the four **h** the face of a man,	4200
	1:10	on the right side each **h** the face of a lion,	4200
	1:10	each also **h** the face of an eagle.	4200
	1:11	each **h** two wings,	4200
	1:23	and each **h** two wings covering its body.	4200
	10:14	Each of the cherubim **h** four faces:	4200
	10:21	Each **h** four faces and four wings,	4200
	10:22	Their faces **h** the same appearance	NIH
	16: 5	with pity or **h compassion** *enough* to do any	2798
	22:24	that *has* **h** no **rain** or showers in the day	4763
	36:21	*I* **h** concern for my holy name,	2798
	40:10	the three **h** the same measurements,	4200
	40:10	on each side **h** the same measurements.	4200
	40:21	and its portico **h** the same measurements	2118
	40:24	and they **h** the same measurements as	NIH
	40:25	and its portico **h** narrow openings all	4200
	40:26	it **h** palm tree decorations on the faces of	4200
	40:27	The inner court also **h** a gate facing south,	4200
	40:28	it **h** the same measurements as the others.	NIH
	40:29	and its portico **h** the same measurements as	NIH
	40:29	and its portico **h** openings all around.	4200
	40:32	it **h** the same measurements as the others.	NIH
	40:33	and its portico **h** the same measurements	NIH
	40:33	and its portico **h** openings all around.	4200
	40:35	It **h** the same measurements as the others,	NIH
	40:36	and it **h** openings all around.	4200
	41: 8	that the temple **h** a raised base all around it,	4200
	41:18	Each cherub **h** two faces:	
	41:21	outer sanctuary **h** a rectangular doorframe,	NIH
	41:23	and the Most Holy Place **h** double doors.	4200
	41:24	Each door **h** two leaves—	4200
	41:26	of the temple also **h** overhangs.	NIH
	42: 6	The rooms on the third floor **h** no pillars,	4200
	42: 6	as the courts **h;**	NIH
	42:11	they **h** the same length and width,	NIH
	42:20	It **h** a wall around it,	4200

Da	2: 1	Nebuchadnezzar **h** dreams;	2706+2731
	2: 3	"*I have* **h** a **dream** that troubles me	2706+2731
	4: 5	*I* **h** a dream that made me afraid.	10255S
	4:18	King Nebuchadnezzar, **h.**	10255S
	7: 1	Daniel **h** a dream,	10255S
	7: 4	and it **h** the wings of an eagle.	10378
	7: 6	And on its back it **h** four wings like those	10378
	7: 6	This beast **h** four heads,	10378
	7: 7	It **h** large iron teeth;	10378
	7: 7	and it **h** ten horns.	10378
	7: 8	This horn **h** eyes like the eyes of a man	10089
	7:20	the others and that **h** eyes and a mouth	10378
	8: 1	I, Daniel, **h** a vision,	8011S
	10: 8	I **h** no strength left,	928
Hos	1: 3	Gomer **h** another son.	3528
	10: 3	if we **h** a king, what could he do for us?"	NIH
Am	4: 7	One field **h** rain;	4763
	4: 7	another **h** none and dried up.	4763S
Zec	1: 8	During the night *I* **h** a vision—	8011
	5: 9	They **h** wings like those of a stork,	4200
	6: 2	The first chariot **h** red horses,	928
Mt	1:19	he **h** in **mind** to divorce her quietly.	1089
	7:29	because he taught as one who **h** authority,	2400
	8:33	including **what h happened to**	3836
	9:33	**man who h been mute** spoke.	3273
	9:36	he **h compassion** on them,	5072
	13: 6	and they withered because they **h** no root.	2400
	13:44	in his joy went and sold all he **h** and bought	2400
	13:46	and sold everything he **h** and bought it.	2400
	14:14	he **h compassion** on them	5072
	18:25	and all that he **h** to be sold to repay the debt.	2400
	18:33	Shouldn't you *have* **h mercy on**	1796
	18:33	on your fellow servant just as I **h** on you?'	1796S
	19:22	because he **h** great wealth.	1639+2400
	20:34	Jesus **h compassion** on them	5072
	22:25	There was a man who **h** two sons.	2400
	22:25	and *since* he **h** no children,	2400
	27:16	At that time *they* **h** a notorious prisoner,	2400
	27:26	But he **h** Jesus **flogged,**	5849
Mk	1:22	he taught them as *one who* **h** authority,	2400
	1:34	Jesus healed many *who* **h** various diseases.	2400
	4: 6	and they withered because they **h** no root.	2400
	5:19	and how he *has* **h mercy on** you."	1796
	5:26	many doctors and had spent all she **h,**	3836+4123S
	6:34	he **h compassion** on them,	5072
	8: 1	Since *they* **h** nothing to eat,	2400
	8: 7	They **h** a few small fish as well;	2400
	8:14	for one loaf *they* **h** with them in the boat.	2400
	10:22	because he **h** great wealth.	1639+2400
	12: 6	"He **h** one left to send, a son,	2400
	12:44	out of her poverty, put in everything—all she **h** to live on."	2400
	15:15	He **h** Jesus **flogged,**	5849
Lk	1: 7	But they **h** no children,	1639
	2:49	"Didn't you know I **h** to be in my Father's house?"	1256
	4:32	his message **h authority.**	1639+1877+2026
	4:40	to Jesus all who **h** various kinds of sickness,	2400
	5:17	who **h** come from every village of Galilee	1639
	7:42	of them **h** the money to pay him back,	2400
	8: 6	plants withered because they **h** no moisture.	2400
	10:37	"The one who **h** mercy on him."	4472
	10:39	She **h** a sister called Mary,	1639
	11:14	**man who h been mute** spoke,	3273
	13: 6	"A man **h** a fig tree, planted in his vineyard,	2400
	14: 6	And *they* **h** nothing to say.	2710
	15:11	"There was a man who **h** two sons.	2400
	15:32	But *we* **h** to celebrate and be glad,	1256
	17: 7	of you **h** a servant plowing or looking after	2400
	17:12	ten men who **h leprosy** met him.	3320
	18:28	"We have left **all** *we* **h** to follow you!"	2625+3836
	21: 4	of her poverty put in all *she* **h** to live on."	2400
	22: 7	the Passover lamb **h** to be sacrificed.	1256
	23:51	who **h** not consented to their decision	1639
	23:55	The women who **h** come with Jesus	1639
Jn	2:10	after the guests *have* **h too much to drink;**	3499
	4: 4	Now he **h** to go through Samaria.	1256
	4:18	The fact is, *you have* **h** five husbands,	2400
	5: 5	One who was there **h** been an invalid	2400
	5: 6	and learned that *he* **h** been in this condition	2400
	6:12	When *they had* **h** enough to eat,	1855
	9:13	to the Pharisees the man who **h** been blind.	4537
	12:29	and heard said *it* **h** thundered;	1181
	13:10	"A person who *has* **h a bath** needs only	3374
	13:29	Since Judas **h charge of** the money,	2400
	17: 5	in your presence with the glory *I* **h**	2400
	18:10	Then Simon Peter, who **h** a sword,	2400
	18:16	but Peter **h** to **wait** outside at the door.	2705
	18:40	**h taken part in a rebellion.**	1639+3334
	19:19	Pilate **h a notice prepared** and	1211+5518
	20: 9	not understand from Scripture that Jesus **h** to rise from the dead."	1256
	21: 7	(for he **h** taken it off) and jumped into	1639
Ac	1:16	the Scripture **h** to be fulfilled which	1256
	2:13	"*They have* **h too much** wine."	1639+3551
	2:44	the believers were together and **h** everything	2400
	2:45	they gave to anyone as he **h** need.	2400
	4:32	but they shared everything **they h.**	899+1639
	4:35	was distributed to anyone as he **h** need.	323+2400
	7: 5	*though* at that time Abraham **h** no child.	1639
	7:29	he settled as a foreigner and **h** two sons.	1164
	7:30	"**After** forty years **h passed,**	4444
	7:44	"Our forefathers **h** the tabernacle of	1639
	11: 4	to them precisely **as it h happened:**	2759
	12: 9	but **h** no **idea** that what	3857
	12:12	many people **h** gathered and were praying.	1639
	13:46	"We **h** to speak the word of God	338+1639

Ac	14: 9	saw that he **h** faith to be healed	2400
	15: 3	how the Gentiles **h been converted.**	2189+3836
	15:39	They **h** such a sharp disagreement that they parted company.	1181
	16: 9	the night Paul **h a vision** of a man	3969+3972
	16:16	we were met by a slave girl who **h** a spirit	2400
	17: 3	the Christ **h** to suffer and rise from the dead.	1256
	18:16	So he **h** them **ejected from** the court.	590
	19:12	and aprons **that h touched** him	608+3836+5999
	19:16	the man who **h** the evil spirit jumped	1639+1877
	21: 9	He **h** four unmarried daughters who prophesied.	1639
	21:35	the mob was so great he **h to** be carried by	5201
	25:16	and has **h** an opportunity to defend himself	3284
	25:19	*they* **h** some points of dispute with him	2400
	26:22	But I *have* **h** God's help to this very day,	5593
	28:19	not that I **h** any charge to bring	2400
Ro	1:13	just as I have **h** among the other Gentiles.	NIG
	4: 2	he **h** something to boast about—	2400
	4:21	fully persuaded that God **h** power	1543+1639
	9:10	but Rebekah's children **h** one and the same father,	2400
1Co	7:29	as if *they* **h** none;	2400
2Co	2:13	*I* still **h** no peace of mind,	2400
	5:21	God made him who **h** no sin to be sin	1182
	7: 5	this body of ours **h** no rest,	2400
Gal	4:22	For it is written that Abraham **h** two sons,	2400
Php	2:27	But God **h mercy on** him,	1796
	4:10	but *you* **h** no **opportunity** to show it.	177
Heb	2:17	For this reason *he* **h** to be made	4053
	4: 2	*we* also *have* **h** the gospel preached to us,	1639
	4: 6	those who formerly **h the gospel preached**	2294
	7: 6	from Abraham and blessed him who **h**	2400
	9: 1	the first covenant **h** regulations for worship	2400
	9: 4	which **h** the golden altar of incense and	2400
	9:26	Then Christ *would have* **h**	1256
	10:34	that you yourselves **h** better	2400
	11:15	*they* would *have* **h** opportunity to return.	2400
	11:39	none of them received **what h been promised.**	2039+3836
	12: 9	*we have* all **h** human fathers who disciplined us	2400
1Pe	1: 6	while you may *have* **h** to suffer grief	1256+1639
1Jn	2: 7	which *you have* **h** since the beginning.	2400
2Jn	1: 5	a new command but one *we have* **h** from	2400
Jude	1: 3	I felt I **h** to write and urge you to contend	340
Rev	4: 7	the third **h** a face like a man,	2400
	4: 8	Each of the four living creatures **h** six wings	2400
	5: 6	He **h** seven horns and seven eyes,	2400
	5: 8	Each one **h** a harp	2400
	8: 3	Another angel, who **h** a golden censer,	2400
	8: 6	Then the seven angels who **h**	2400
	9: 9	*They* **h** breastplates like breastplates of iron,	2400
	9:10	*They* **h** tails and stings like scorpions,	2400
	9:11	*They* **h** as king over them the angel of	2400
	9:14	It said to the sixth angel who **h** the trumpet,	2400
	13: 1	He **h** ten horns and seven heads,	2400
	13: 2	but **h** feet like those of a bear and a mouth	899
	13: 3	the beast seemed *to have* **h** a fatal **wound,**	5377
	13:11	He **h** two horns like a lamb,	2400
	13:17	so that no one could buy or sell unless he **h**	2400
	14: 1	144,000 who **h** his name and his Father's	2400
	14: 6	and *he* **h** the eternal gospel to proclaim	2400
	14:17	and he too **h** a sharp sickle.	2400
	14:18	Still another angel, *who* **h** charge of the fire,	2400
	14:18	a loud voice *to* him who **h** the sharp sickle,	2400
	16: 2	on the people who **h** the mark of the beast	2400
	16: 9	who **h** control over these plagues,	2400
	16:11	they refused to repent of what they **h** done.	2240
	17: 1	One of the seven angels who **h** the seven	2400
	17: 3	with blasphemous names and **h** seven heads	2400
	18: 1	He **h** great authority,	2400
	18:19	where all who **h** ships on the sea	2400
	21: 9	the seven angels who **h** the seven bowls full	2400
	21:12	It **h** a great, high wall with twelve gates,	2400
	21:14	The wall of the city **h** twelve foundations,	2400
	21:15	with me **h** a measuring rod of gold	2400

HADAD (17) [BEN-HADAD, HADAD RIMMON]

Ge	25:15	**H,** Tema, Jetur, Naphish and Kedemah.	2524
	36:35	When Husham died, **H** son of Bedad,	2060
	36:36	When **H** died, Samlah from Masrekah	2060
	36:39	**H** succeeded him as king.	2060
1Ki	11:14	**H** the Edomite, from the royal line of Edom.	2060
	11:17	But **H,** still only a boy,	119
	11:18	who gave **H** a house and land	2257S
	11:19	so pleased with **H** that he gave him a sister	2060
	11:21	**H** heard that David rested with his fathers	2060
	11:21	Then **H** said to Pharaoh, "Let me go,	2060
	11:22	"Nothing," **H** replied, "but do let me go!"	NIH
	11:25	adding to the trouble caused by **H.**	2060
1Ch	1:30	Mishma, Dumah, Massa, **H,** Tema,	2524
	1:46	When Husham died, **H** son of Bedad,	2060
	1:47	When **H** died, Samlah from Masrekah	2060
	1:50	Baal-Hanan died, **H** succeeded him as king.	2060
	1:51	**H** also died.	2060

HADAD RIMMON (1) [HADAD, RIMMON]

Zec	12:11	like the weeping of **H** in the plain	2062

HADADEZER (17) [HADADEZER'S]

2Sa	8: 3	Moreover, David fought **H** son of Rehob,	2061
	8: 5	of Damascus came to help **H** king of Zobah,	2061

2Sa	8: 7	to the officers of H and brought them	2061
	8: 8	towns that belonged to H,	2061
	8: 9	the entire army of H,	2061
	8:10	on his victory in battle over H,	2061
	8:12	also dedicated the plunder taken from H son	2061
	10:16	H had Arameans brought from beyond	2061
	10:19	of H saw that they had been defeated	2061
1Ki	11:23	H king of Zobah.	2061
1Ch	18: 3	Moreover, David fought H king of Zobah,	2061
	18: 5	of Damascus came to help H king of Zobah,	2061
	18: 7	the gold shields carried by the officers of H	2061
	18: 8	towns that belonged to H	2061
	18: 9	the entire army of H king of Zobah,	2061
	18:10	on his victory in battle over H,	2061
	19:19	of H saw that they had been defeated	2061

HADADEZER'S (2) [HADADEZER]

2Sa	10:16	the commander of H army leading them.	2061
1Ch	19:16	the commander of H army leading them.	2061

HADASHAH (1)

Jos	15:37	Zenan, H, Migdal Gad,	2546

HADASSAH (1)

Est	2: 7	Mordecai had a cousin named H,	2073

HADATTAH See HAZOR HADATTAH

HADDAH See EN HADDAH

HADES (5)

Mt	16:18	and the gates of H will not overcome it.	87
Rev	1:18	And I hold the keys of death and H.	87
	6: 8	and H was following close behind him.	87
	20:13	and death and H gave up the dead that were	87
	20:14	Then death and H were thrown into the lake	87

HADID (3)

Ezr	2:33	of Lod, H and Ono 725	2531
Ne	7:37	of Lod, H and Ono 721	2531
	11:34	in H, Zeboim and Neballat,	2531

HADLAI (1)

2Ch	28:12	and Amasa son of H—	2536

HADORAM (4)

Ge	10:27	H, Uzal, Diklah,	2066
1Ch	1:21	H, Uzal, Diklah,	2066
	18:10	sent his son H to King David to greet him	2067
	18:10	H brought all kinds of articles of gold	NIH

HADRACH (1)

Zec	9: 1	of the LORD is against the land of H	2541

HAELEPH (1)

Jos	18:28	H, the Jebusite city (that is, Jerusalem),	2030

HAFT (KJV) See HANDLE

HAGAB (1)

Ezr	2:46	H, Shalmai, Hanan,	2507

HAGABA (1)

Ne	7:48	Lebana, H, Shalmai,	2509

HAGABAH (1)

Ezr	2:45	Lebanah, H, Akkub,	2509

HAGAR (15)

Ge	16: 1	she had an Egyptian maidservant named H;	2057
	16: 3	Sarai his wife took her Egyptian maidservant H	2057
	16: 4	He slept with H, and she conceived.	2057
	16: 6	Sarai mistreated H; so she fled from her.	2023S
	16: 7	of the LORD found H near a spring in	2023S
	16: 8	And he said, "H, servant of Sarai,	2057
	16:15	So H bore Abram a son,	2057
	16:16	when H bore him Ishmael.	2057
	21: 9	the son whom H the Egyptian had borne	2057
	21:14	and a skin of water and gave them to H.	2057
	21:17	the angel of God called to H from heaven	2057
	21:17	"What is the matter, H?	2057
	25:12	whom Sarah's maidservant, H the Egyptian,	2057
Gal	4:24	children who are to be slaves: This is H.	29
	4:25	Now H stands for Mount Sinai in Arabia	29

HAGARENES (KJV) See HAGAR

HAGARITES, HAGERITE (KJV) See HAGRITE

HAGGAI (11)

Ezr	5: 1	H the prophet and Zechariah the prophet,	10247
	6:14	and prosper under the preaching of H	10247
Hag	1: 1	of the LORD came through the prophet H	2516

Hag	1: 3	of the LORD came through the prophet H:	2516
	1:12	and the message of the prophet H,	2516
	1:13	Then H, the LORD's messenger,	2516
	2: 1	of the LORD came through the prophet H:	2516
	2:10	word of the LORD came to the prophet H:	2516
	2:13	Then H said, "If a person defiled by contact	2516
	2:14	Then H said, " 'So it is with this people	2516
	2:20	to H a second time on the twenty-fourth day	2516

HAGGAN See BETH HAGGAN

HAGGARD (2)

2Sa	13: 4	look so h morning after morning?	1924
Job	30: 3	H from want and hunger,	1678

HAGGEDOLIM (1)

Ne	11:14	Their chief officer was Zabdiel son of H.	2045

HAGGERI (KJV) See HAGRI

HAGGI (2) [HAGGITE]

Ge	46:16	The sons of Gad: Zephon, H, Shuni, Ezbon,	2515
Nu	26:15	through H, the Haggite clan;	2515

HAGGIAH (1)

1Ch	6:30	H his son and Asaiah his son.	2517

HAGGIDGAD See HOR HAGGIDGAD

HAGGITE (1) [HAGGI]

Nu	26:15	through Haggi, the H clan;	2515

HAGGITES (KJV) See HAGGI

HAGGITH (5)

2Sa	3: 4	Adonijah the son of H;	2518
1Ki	1: 5	Now Adonijah, whose mother was H,	2518
	1:11	Adonijah, the son of H, has become king	2518
	2:13	Now Adonijah, the son of H;	2518
1Ch	3: 2	the fourth, Adonijah the son of H;	2518

HAGGOYIM See HAROSHETH HAGGOYIM

HAGRI (2) [HAGRITE, HAGRITES]

2Sa	23:36	son of Nathan from Zobah, the son of H,	2058
1Ch	11:38	the brother of Nathan, Mibhar son of H,	2058

HAGRITE (1) [HAGRI]

1Ch	27:31	Jaziz the H was in charge of the flocks.	2058

HAGRITES (6) [HAGRI]

1Ch	5:10	the H, who were defeated at their hands;	2058
	5:10	of the H throughout the entire region east	2157S
	5:19	They waged war against the H, Jetur,	2058
	5:20	and God handed the H and all their allies	2058
	5:21	They seized the livestock of the H—	2157S
Ps	83: 6	and the Ishmaelites, of Moab and the H,	2058

HAHIROTH See PI HAHIROTH

HAI (KJV) See AI

HAIL (29) [HAILSTONES, HAILSTORM]

Ex	9:19	the h will fall on every man and animal	1352
	9:22	the sky so that h will fall all over Egypt—	1352
	9:23	the LORD sent thunder and h,	1352
	9:23	the LORD rained h on the land of Egypt;	1352
	9:24	h fell and lightning flashed back and forth.	1352
	9:25	Throughout Egypt h struck everything in	1352
	9:26	The only place it did not h was the land	1352
	9:28	for we have had enough thunder and h.	1352
	9:29	and there will be no more h,	1352
	9:33	the thunder and h stopped,	1352
	9:34	that the rain and h and thunder had stopped,	1352
	10: 5	the h, including every tree that is growing	1352
	10:12	everything left by the h."	1352
	10:15	They devoured all that was left after the h—	1352
Job	38:22	the snow or seen the storehouses of the h,	1352
Ps	78:47	with h and their sycamore-figs with sleet.	1352
	78:48	He gave over their cattle to the h,	1352
	105:32	He turned their rain into h,	1352
	147:17	He hurls down his h like pebbles.	7943
	148: 8	and h, snow and clouds, stormy winds	1352
Isa	28:17	h will sweep away your refuge, the lie,	1352
	30:30	with cloudburst, thunderstorm and h.	74+1352
	32:19	Though h flattens the forest and	1351
Hag	2:17	mildew and h, yet you did not turn to me,'	1352
Mt	27:29	"H, king of the Jews!"	5897
Mk	15:18	And they began to call out to him, "H,	5897
Jn	19: 3	saying, "H, king of the Jews!"	5897
Rev	8: 7	and there came h and fire mixed with blood,	5898
	16:21	on account of the plague of h,	5898

HAILSTONES (7) [HAIL]

Jos	10:11	the LORD hurled large h down on them	74
	10:11	more of them died from the h than were	74+1352
Ps	18:12	with h and bolts of lightning.	1352
Eze	13:11	and I will send h hurtling down,	74+453
	13:13	in my anger h and torrents of rain will fall	74+453
	38:22	down torrents of rain, h and burning sulfur	74+453
Rev	16:21	From the sky huge h of about	5898

HAILSTORM (3) [HAIL]

Ex	9:18	the worst h that has ever fallen on Egypt,	1352
Isa	28: 2	Like a h and a destructive wind,	1352+2443
Rev	11:19	an earthquake and a great h.	5898

HAIR (95) [GRAY-HAIRED, HAIRS, HAIRY]

Ex	25: 4	and fine linen; goat h;	6436
	26: 7	of goat h for the tent over the tabernacle—	6436
	35: 6	and fine linen; goat h;	6436
	35:23	or fine linen, or goat h, ram skins dyed red	6436
	35:26	and had the skill spun the goat h.	6436
	36:14	of goat h for the tent over the tabernacle—	6436
Lev	10: 6	"Do not let your h become unkempt,	8031
	13: 3	and if the h in the sore has turned white and	8552
	13: 4	be more than skin deep and the h in it has	8552
	13:10	in the skin that has turned the h white and	8552
	13:20	to be more than skin deep and the h	8552
	13:21	there is no white h in it and it is	8552
	13:25	and if the h in it has turned white,	8552
	13:26	and there is no white h in the spot and	8552
	13:30	to be more than skin deep and the h	8552
	13:31	and there is no black h in it,	8552
	13:32	and there is no yellow h in it and it does	8552
	13:36	priest does not need to look for yellow h;	8552
	13:37	and black h has grown in it,	8552
	13:40	When a man has lost his h and is bald,	5307+8031
	13:41	If he has lost his h from the front	5307+8031
	13:45	let his h be unkempt,	8031
	14: 8	shave off all his h and bathe with water;	8552
	14: 9	the seventh day he must shave off all his h;	8552
	14: 9	his eyebrows and the rest of his h.	8552
	19:27	" 'Do not cut the h at the sides of your head	5938
	21:10	must not let his h become unkempt	8031
Nu	5:18	he shall loosen her h and place in her hands	8031
	6: 5	must let the h of his head grow long.	7279+8552
	6: 9	thus defiling the h he has dedicated,	8031
	6:18	the Nazirite must shave off the h	8552
	6:18	to take the h and put it in the fire that is	8552
	6:18	" 'After the Nazirite has shaved off the h	NIH
	31:20	made of leather, goat h or wood."	6436
Jdg	16:19	a man to shave off the seven braids of his h,	8031
	16:22	But the h on his head began to grow again	8552
	20:16	each of whom could sling a stone at a h and	8553
1Sa	14:45	not a h of his head will fall to the ground,	8552
	17:35	When it turned on me, I seized it by its h,	2417
	19:13	putting some goats' h at the head.	3889+6436
	19:16	and at the head was some goats' h.	3889+6436
2Sa	14:11	"not one h of your son's head	8553
	14:26	Whenever he cut the h of his head—	1662
	14:26	he used to cut his h from time to time	1662
1Ki	1:52	not a h of his head will fall to the ground;	8553
2Ki	1: 8	with a garment of h and with a leather belt	8552
	9:30	arranged her h and looked out of a window.	8031
Ezr	9: 3	pulled h from my head and beard and sat	8552
Ne	13:25	of the men and pulled out their h.	5307
Job	4:15	and the h on my body stood on end.	8553
	41:32	one would think the deep had white h.	8484
Pr	16:31	Gray h is a crown of splendor,	8484
	20:29	gray h the splendor of the old.	8484
SS	4: 1	Your h is like a flock of goats descending	8552
	5: 2	my h with the dampness of the night."	7767
	5:11	his h is wavy and black as a raven.	7767
	6: 5	Your h is like a flock of goats descending	8552
	7: 5	Your h is like royal tapestry;	1929+8031
Isa	3:24	instead of well-dressed h, baldness;	5126+5250
	7:20	to shave your head and the h of your legs,	8552
	22:12	to tear out your h and put on sackcloth.	7947
Jer	7:29	Cut off your h and throw it away;	5694
Eze	5: 1	take a set of scales and divide up the h.	4392S
	5: 2	burn a third of the h with fire inside the city.	NIH
	5: 3	a few strands of h and tuck them away in	NIH
	8: 3	a hand and took me by the h of my head.	7492
	16: 7	Your breasts were formed and your h grew,	8552
	44:20	or let their h grow long,	7279
	44:20	keep the h of their heads trimmed.	4080+4080
Da	3:27	nor was a h of their heads singed;	8177
	4:33	with the dew of heaven until his h grew like	10687
	7: 9	the h of his head was white like wool.	10687
Hos	7: 9	h is sprinkled with gray,	8484
Zec	13: 4	not put on a prophet's garment of h in order	8552
Mt	5:36	you cannot make even one h white or black.	2582
Mk	1: 6	John wore clothing made of camel's h,	2582
Lk	7:38	Then she wiped them with her h,	2582
	7:44	with her tears and wiped them with her h.	2582
	21:18	But not a h of your head will perish.	2582
Jn	11: 2	on the Lord and wiped his feet with her h.	2582
	12: 3	on Jesus' feet and wiped his feet with her h.	2582
Ac	18:18	he had his h cut off at Cenchrea because of	3051
	27:34	of you will lose a single h from his head."	2582
1Co	11: 6	she should have her h cut off;	NIG
	11: 6	a woman to have her h cut or shaved off,	3025
	11:14	that if a man has long h, it is a disgrace to	3150
	11:15	that if a woman has long h, it is her glory?	3151
	11:15	For long h is given to her as a covering.	3151
1Ti	2: 9	not with braided h or gold or pearls	4427

1Pe	3: 3	such as braided **h** and the wearing	2582
Rev	1:14	His head and **h** were white like wool,	2582
	6:12	like sackcloth **made of** goat **h,**	5570
	9: 8	**Their h** was like women's hair,	2400+2582
	9: 8	Their hair was like women's **h,**	NIG

HAIRS (5) [HAIR]

Ps	40:12	They are more than the **h** *of* my head,	8553
	69: 4	outnumber the **h** of my head;	8553
Isa	46: 4	Even to your old age and **gray h** I am he,	8484
Mt	10:30	the very **h** of your head are all numbered.	2582
Lk	12: 7	the very **h** of your head are all numbered.	2582

HAIRY (4) [HAIR]

Ge	25:25	and his whole body was like a **h** garment;	8552
	27:11	"But my brother Esau is a **h** man,	8537
	27:23	for his hands were **h** like those of his	8537
Ps	68:21	**h** crowns of those who go on in their sins.	8552

HAKILAH (3)

1Sa	23:19	on the hill of **H,** south of Jeshimon?	2677
	26: 1	"Is not David hiding on the hill of **H,**	2677
	26: 3	the road on the hill of **H** facing Jeshimon,	2677

HAKKATAN (1)

Ezr	8:12	Johanan son of **H,** and with him 110 men;	2214

HAKKEREM   See BETH HAKKEREM

HAKKORE   See EN HAKKORE

HAKKOZ (5)

1Ch	24:10	the seventh to **H,** the eighth to Abijah,	2212
Ezr	2:61	**H** and Barzillai (a man who had married	2212
Ne	3: 4	Meremoth son of Uriah, the son of **H,**	2212
	3:21	the son of **H,** repaired another section,	2212
	7:63	the descendants of Hobaiah, **H** and Barzillai	2212

HAKUPHA (2)

Ezr	2:51	Bakbuk, **H,** Harhur,	2979
Ne	7:53	Bakbuk, **H,** Harhur,	2979

HALAH (3)

2Ki	17: 6	He settled them in **H,**	2712
	18:11	to Assyria and settled them in **H,**	2712
1Ch	5:26	He took them to **H,** Habor,	2712

HALAK (2)

Jos	11:17	from Mount **H,** which rises toward Seir,	2748
	12: 7	in the Valley of Lebanon to Mount **H,**	2748

HALE   (KJV) See DRAG OFF

HALF (114) [HALF-DISTRICT, HALF-TRIBE, HALFWAY, HALVES, TWO-AND-A-HALF]

Ge	15:10	the birds, however, he did not **cut in h.**	1439
Ex	24: 6	Moses took **h** of the blood and put it	2942
	24: 6	and the other **h** he sprinkled on the altar.	2942
	25:10	two and a **h** cubits long,	2942
	25:10	a cubit and a **h** wide,	2942
	25:10	and a cubit and a **h** high.	2942
	25:17	a **h** cubits long and a cubit and a half wide.	2942
	25:17	a half cubits long and a cubit and a **h** wide.	2942
	25:23	a cubit wide and a cubit and a **h** high.	2942
	26:12	the **h** curtain that is left over is to hang	2942
	26:16	be ten cubits long and a cubit and a **h** wide,	2942
	30:13	to give a **h** shekel, according to	4734
	30:13	This **h** shekel is an offering to the LORD.	4734
	30:15	a **h** shekel and the poor are not to give less	4734
	30:23	**H** as much (that is, 250 shekels)	4734
	36:21	and a cubit and a **h** wide,	2942
	37: 1	two and a **h** cubits long,	2942
	37: 1	a cubit and a **h** wide,	2942
	37: 1	and a cubit and a **h** high.	2942
	37: 6	a **h** cubits long and a cubit and a half wide.	2942
	37: 6	a half cubits long and a cubit and a **h** wide.	2942
	37:10	a cubit wide, and a cubit and a **h** high.	2942
	38:26	one beka per person, that is, **h** a shekel,	4734
Lev	6:20	of fine flour as a regular grain offering, **h**	4734
	6:20	of it in the morning and **h** in the evening.	4734
Nu	12:12	with its flesh **h** eaten away."	2942
	15: 9	of an ephah of fine flour mixed with **h** a hin	2942
	15:10	bring a hin of wine as a drink offering.	2942
	28:14	to be a drink offering of **h** a hin of wine;	2942
	31:29	from their **h** share and give it to Eleazar	4734
	31:30	From the Israelites' **h,**	2942
	31:36	The **h** share of those who fought in	4733
	31:42	The **h** belonging to the Israelites,	4734
	31:43	the community's **h**—was 337,500 sheep,	4733
	31:47	From the Israelites' **h,** Moses selected	4734
	34:13	that it be given to the nine and a **h** tribes,	2942
	34:15	a **h** tribes have received their inheritance on	2942
Dt	3:12	including the hill country of Gilead,	2942
	3:13	I gave to the **h** tribe of Manasseh.	2942
Jos	8:33	**H** of the people stood in front	2942
	8:33	of Mount Gerizim and **h** of them in front	2942
	12: 2	This included **h** of Gilead.	2942
	12: 5	of Gilead to the border of Sihon king	2942
	13: 7	an inheritance among the nine tribes and **h**	2942

Jos	13: 8	**The other h of Manasseh,**	2257S
	13:25	of Gilead and **h** the Ammonite country	2942
	13:29	to **h** the family of the descendants	2942
	13:31	**h** of Gilead, and Ashtaroth and Edrei	2942
	13:31	for **h** of the sons of Makir, clan by clan.	2942
	21: 5	Dan and **h** of Manasseh.	2942
	21:25	From **h** the tribe of Manasseh	4734
	22: 7	the other **h** of the tribe Joshua gave land on	2942
Jdg	3:16	sword **about a foot and a h** long,	1688
1Sa	14:14	in an area of about **h** an acre.	2942
2Sa	10: 4	shaved off **h** of each man's beard,	2942
	18: 3	Even if **h** of us die, they won't care;	2942
	19:40	of Judah and **h** the troops of Israel had taken	2942
1Ki	3:25	the living child in two and give **h** to one	2942
	3:25	and give half to one and **h** to the other."	2942
	7:31	it measured a cubit and a **h.**	2942
	7:32	of each wheel was a cubit and a **h.**	2942
	7:35	of the stand there was a circular band **h**	2942
	10: 7	Indeed, not even **h** was told me;	2942
	13: 8	if you were to give me **h** your possessions,	2942
	16: 9	who had command of **h** his chariots,	4734
	16:21	**h** supported Tibni son of Ginath for king,	2942
	16:21	and the other **h** supported Omri.	2942
2Ki	25:17	pillar was **four and a h feet** high	564+8993
1Ch	2:52	Haroeh, **h** the Manahathites,	2942
	2:54	Atroth Beth Joab, **h** the Manahathites,	2942
	6:61	from the clans of **h** the tribe of Manasseh.	4734
	6:70	And from **h** the tribe of Manasseh	4734
	11:23	**seven and a h feet** tall.	564+928+2021+2822
	12:31	men of **h** the tribe of Manasseh, designated	2942
	27:20	over **h** the tribe of Manasseh:	2942
2Ch	9: 6	not even **h** the greatness of your wisdom	2942
Ne	3:17	Hashabiah, ruler of **h** the district of Keilah.	2942
	4: 6	the wall till all of it reached **h** its height,	2942
	4:16	**h** of my men did the work,	2942
	4:16	the other **h** were equipped with spears,	2942
	4:21	the work with **h** the men holding spears,	2942
	12:32	and **h** the leaders of Judah followed them,	2942
	12:38	together with **h** the people—	2942
	12:40	so did I, together with **h** the officials,	2942
	13:24	**H** of their children spoke the language	2942
Est	5: 3	up to **h** the kingdom, it will be given you."	2942
	5: 6	up to **h** the kingdom, it will be granted."	2942
	7: 2	up to **h** the kingdom, it will be granted."	2942
Ps	55:23	not **live out h** their days.	2936
Isa	44:16	**H** of the wood he burns in the fire;	2942
	44:19	"**H** of it I used for fuel;	2942
Jer	17:11	When his life is **h** *gone,*	2942
Eze	16:51	Samaria did not commit **h** the sins you did.	2942
	40:42	each a cubit and a **h** long,	2942
	40:42	a cubit and a **h** wide and a cubit high.	2942
	43:17	with a rim of **h** a cubit and a gutter of	2942
Da	7:25	for a time, times and **h** a time.	10584
	12: 7	"It will be for a time, times and **h** a time.	2942
Zec	14: 2	**H** of the city will go into exile,	2942
	14: 4	with **h** of the mountain moving north	2942
	14: 4	and **h** moving south.	2942
	14: 8	**h** to the eastern sea and half to	2942
	14: 8	to the eastern sea and **h** to the western sea,	2942
Mk	6:23	up to **h** my kingdom."	2468
Lk	4:25	sky was shut for three and a **h** years	1971+3604
	10:30	leaving him **h** dead.	2467
	19: 8	Here and now I give **h** of my possessions to	2468
Jn	6:19	they rowed **three or three and a h miles,**	1633+2445+4297+5084+5558
Ac	18:11	So Paul stayed for a year and a **h,**	1971+3604
Jas	5:17	on the land *for* three and a **h** years.	1971+3604
Rev	8: 1	silence in heaven for about **h an hour.**	2469
	11: 9	and a **h** days men from every people,	2468
	11:11	after the three and a **h** days a breath of life	2468
	12:14	for a time, times and **h** a time,	2468

HALF-DISTRICT (4) [HALF, DISTRICT]

Ne	3: 9	ruler of a **h** of Jerusalem,	2942+7135
	3:12	ruler of a **h** of Jerusalem,	2942+7135
	3:16	ruler of a **h** of Beth Zur,	2942+7135
	3:18	ruler of the other **h** of Keilah.	2942+7135

HALF-TRIBE (24) [HALF, TRIBE]

Nu	32:33	the Reubenites and the **h** of Manasseh	2942+8657
	34:14	tribe of Gad and the **h** of Manasseh	2942+4751
Dt	29: 8	the Gadites and the **h** of Manasseh.	2942+8657
Jos	1:12	the Gadites and the **h** of Manasseh,	2942+8657
	4:12	and the **h** of Manasseh crossed over,	2942+8657
	12: 6	**h** of Manasseh to be their possession.	2942+8657
	13:29	This is what Moses had given to the **h**	2942+8657
	18: 7	Reuben and the **h** of Manasseh	2942+8657
	21: 6	and the **h** of Manasseh in Bashan.	2942+4751
	21:27	from the **h** of Manasseh,	2942+4751
	22: 1	the Gadites and the **h** of Manasseh	2942+8657
	22: 7	**h** of Manasseh Moses had given land	2942+8657
	22: 9	the **h** of Manasseh left the Israelites	2942+8657
	22:10	Gadites and the **h** of Manasseh built	2942+8657
	22:13	Reuben, Gad and the **h** of Manasseh	2942+8657
	22:15	Reuben, Gad and the **h** of Manasseh—	2942+8657
	22:21	and the **h** of Manasseh replied to	2942+8657
1Ch	5:18	the **h** of Manasseh had 44,760 men	2942+8657
	5:23	of the **h** of Manasseh were numerous;	2942+8657
	5:26	Gad and the **h** of Manasseh	2942+8657
	6:71	**h** of Manasseh they received Golan	2942+4751
	12:37	Gad and the **h** of Manasseh,	2942+8657
	26:32	Gad and the **h** of Manasseh	2942+8657
	27:21	over the **h** of Manasseh in Gilead:	2942

HALFWAY (3) [HALF]

Ex	27: 5	under the ledge of the altar so that it is **h** up	2942
	38: 4	to be under its ledge, **h** up the altar.	2942
Jn	7:14	Not until **h** through the Feast did Jesus go	3548

HALHUL (1)

Jos	15:58	**H,** Beth Zur, Gedor,	2713

HALI (1)

Jos	19:25	Their territory included: Helkath, **H,** Beten,	2718

HALL (19)

1Sa	9:22	and his servant into the **h** and seated them at	4384
1Ki	6: 3	the **main h** of the temple extended the width	2121
	6: 5	of the **main h** and inner sanctuary he built	2121
	6:17	The **main h** in front of this room	2121
	6:33	olive wood for the entrance to the **main h.**	2121
	7: 7	He built the throne **h,** the Hall of Justice,	395
	7: 7	He built the throne hall, the **H** of Justice,	395
	7: 8	a palace like this **h** for Pharaoh's daughter,	395
	7:50	for the doors of the **main h** of the temple.	2121
2Ch	3: 5	the **main h** with pine and covered it	1074
	3:13	They stood on their feet, facing the **main h.**	1074
	4:22	and the doors of the **main h.**	2121
Est	5: 1	in front of the king's **h.**	1074
	5: 1	on his royal throne in the **h,**	1074
	7: 8	from the palace garden to the banquet **h,**	1074
SS	2: 4	He has taken me to the **banquet h,**	1074+3516
Da	5:10	came into the banquet **h.**	10103
Mt	22:10	and the **wedding h** was filled with guests.	1141
Ac	19: 9	and had discussions daily in the **lecture h**	5391

HALLELUJAH (4)

Rev	19: 1	in heaven shouting: "**H!**	252
	19: 3	And again they shouted: "**H!**	252
	19: 4	And they cried: "Amen, **H!**"	252
	19: 6	of thunder, shouting: "**H!**	252

HALLOHESH (2)

Ne	3:12	Shallum son of **H,**	2135
	10:24	**H,** Pilha, Shobek,	2135

HALLOW, HALLOWED   (KJV) See CONSECRATE, CONSECRATED, HOLY, SACRED, SET APART

HALLOWED (2) [HOLY]

Mt	6: 9	" 'Our Father in heaven, **h** *be* your name,	39
Lk	11: 2	" 'Father, **h** *be* your name,	39

HALOHESH   (KJV) See HALLOHESH

HALT (4) [HALTED]

2Sa	2:28	and all the men **came to a h;**	6641
	20:12	that all the troops **came to a h** there.	6641
Job	38:11	here is where your proud waves **h**'?	8883
Isa	10:32	This day they *will* **h** at Nob;	6641

HALTED (2) [HALT]

2Sa	15:17	and *they* **h** at a place some distance away.	6641
	18:16	stopped pursuing Israel, for Joab **h** them.	3104

HALTER (1)

Pr	26: 3	A whip for the horse, a **h** for the donkey,	5496

HALVES (3) [HALF]

Ge	15:10	and arranged the **h** opposite each other;	1440
SS	4: 3	Your temples behind your veil are like the **h**	7115
	6: 7	Your temples behind your veil are like the **h**	7115

HAM (16) [HAMITES]

Ge	5:32	the father of Shem, **H** and Japheth.	2769
	6:10	Noah had three sons: Shem, **H** and Japheth.	2769
	7:13	and his sons, Shem, **H** and Japheth, together	2769
	9:18	of the ark were Shem, **H** and Japheth.	2769
	9:18	(**H** was the father of Canaan.)	2769
	9:22	**H,** the father of Canaan,	2769
	10: 1	This is the account of Shem, **H** and Japheth,	2769
	10: 6	sons of **H:** Cush, Mizraim, Put and Canaan.	2769
	10:20	the sons of **H** by their clans and languages,	2769
	14: 5	the Zuzites in **H,** the Emites in Shaveh	2154
1Ch	1: 4	The sons of Noah: Shem, **H** and Japheth.	2769
	1: 8	sons of **H:** Cush, Mizraim, Put and Canaan.	2769
Ps	78:51	the firstfruits of manhood in the tents of **H.**	2769
	105:23	Jacob lived as an alien in the land of **H.**	2769
	105:27	his wonders in the land of **H.**	2769
	106:22	of **H** and awesome deeds by the Red Sea.	2769

HAMAN (44) [HAMAN'S]

Est	3: 1	King Xerxes honored **H** son	2172
	3: 2	knelt down and paid honor to **H,**	2172
	3: 4	Therefore they told **H** about it	2172
	3: 5	When **H** saw that Mordecai would not kneel	2172
	3: 6	Instead **H** looked for a way to destroy	2172
	3: 7	the presence of **H** to select a day and month.	2172
	3: 8	Then **H** said to King Xerxes,	2172
	3:10	and gave it to **H** son of Hammedatha,	2172

Est 3:11 "Keep the money," the king said to **H**, 2172
3:15 The king and **H** sat down to drink, 2172
4: 7 the exact amount of money **H** had promised 2172
5: 4 "let the king, together with **H**, 2172
5: 5 "Bring **H** at once," the king said, 2172
5: 5 So the king and **H** went to the banquet 2172
5: 8 let the king and **H** come tomorrow to 2172
5: 9 **H** went out that day happy and 2172
5:10 **H** restrained himself and went home. 2172
5:11 **H** boasted to them about his vast wealth, 2172
5:12 "And that's not all," **H** added. 2172
5:14 This suggestion delighted **H**, 2172
6: 4 Now **H** had just entered the outer court of 2172
6: 5 "**H** is standing in the court." 2172
6: 6 When **H** entered, the king asked him, 2172
6: 6 Now **H** thought to himself, 2172
6:10 "Go at once," the king commanded **H**. 2172
6:11 So **H** got the robe and the horse. 2172
6:12 But **H** rushed home, 2172
6:14 and hurried **H** away to the banquet 2172
7: 1 king and **H** went to dine with Queen Esther, 2172
7: 6 "The adversary and enemy is this vile **H**." 2172
7: 6 **H** was terrified before the king and queen. 2172
7: 7 But **H**, realizing that the king had already 2172
7: 8 **H** was falling on the couch where Esther 2172
7:10 So they hanged **H** on the gallows he had 2172
8: 1 gave Queen Esther the estate of **H**, 2172
8: 2 which he had reclaimed from **H**, 2172
8: 3 an end to the evil plan of **H** the Agagite, 2172
8: 5 the dispatches that **H** son of Hammedatha, 2172
8: 7 "Because **H** attacked the Jews, 2172
9:10 the ten sons of **H** son of Hammedatha, 2172
9:12 and the ten sons of **H** in the citadel of Susa. 2172
9:14 and they hanged the ten sons of **H**. 2172
9:24 For **H** son of Hammedatha, the Agagite, 2172
9:25 that the evil scheme **H** had devised against 2257[S]

HAMAN'S (5) [HAMAN]

Est 3:12 the language of each people all **H** orders to 2172
7: 8 they covered **H** face. 2172
7: 9 "A gallows seventy-five feet high stands by **H** house. 2172
8: 2 And Esther appointed him over **H** estate. 2172
9:13 and let **H** ten sons be hanged on gallows." 2172

HAMATH (24) [HAMATH ZOBAH, HAMATHITES, LEBO HAMATH]

2Sa 8: 9 king of **H** heard that David had defeated 2828
2Ki 14:28 for Israel both Damascus and **H**, 2828
17:24 **H** and Sepharvaim and settled them in 2828
17:30 and the men from **H** made Ashima; 2828
18:34 Where are the gods of **H** and Arpad? 2828
19:13 Where is the king of **H**, the king of Arpad 2828
23:33 land of **H** so that he might not reign in Jerusalem, 2828
25:21 There at Riblah, in the land of **H**, 2828
1Ch 18: 3 king of Zobah, as far as **H**, 2828
18: 9 king of **H** heard that David had defeated 2828
2Ch 8: 4 and all the store cities he had built in **H**. 2828
Isa 10: 9 Is not **H** like Arpad, 2828
11:11 from **H** and from the islands of the sea. 2828
36:19 Where are the gods of **H** and Arpad? 2828
37:13 Where is the king of **H**, the king of Arpad, 2828
Jer 39: 5 of Babylon at Riblah in the land of **H**, 2828
49:23 "**H** and Arpad are dismayed, 2828
52: 9 of Babylon at Riblah in the land of **H**, 2828
52:27 There at Riblah, in the land of **H**, 2828
Eze 47:16 on the border between Damascus and **H**), 2828
47:17 with the border of **H** to the north. 2828
48: 1 of Damascus next to **H** will be part 2828
Am 6: 2 go from there to great **H**, 2828
Zec 9: 2 and upon **H** too, which borders on it, 2828

HAMATH ZOBAH (1) [HAMATH, ZOBAH]

2Ch 8: 3 then went to **H** and captured it. 2832

HAMATHITES (2) [HAMATH]

Ge 10:18 Arvadites, Zemarites and **H**. 2833
1Ch 1:16 Arvadites, Zemarites and **H**. 2833

HAMITES (2) [HAM]

1Ch 4:40 Some **H** had lived there formerly. 2769
4:41 They attacked the **H** in their dwellings and NIH

HAMMAHLEKOTH   See SELA HAMMAHLEKOTH

HAMMATH (2)

Jos 19:35 The fortified cities were Ziddim, Zer, **H**, 2829
1Ch 2:55 These are the Kenites who came from **H**, 2830

HAMMEDATHA (5)

Est 3: 1 King Xerxes honored Haman son of **H**, 2158
3:10 and gave it to Haman son of **H**, 2158
8: 5 the dispatches that Haman son of **H**, 2158
9:10 the ten sons of Haman son of **H**, 2158
9:24 For Haman son of **H**, the Agagite, 2158

HAMMELECH (KJV) See THE KING

HAMMER (9) [HAMMERED, HAMMERS]

Ex 25:31 a lampstand of pure gold and **h** it **out**, 5251+6913
Nu 16:38 the censers *into* sheets to overlay 6913+8393
Jdg 4:21 a tent peg and a **h** and went quietly to him 5216
5:26 her right hand for the workman's **h**. 2153
1Ki 6: 7 at the quarry were used, and no **h**, chisel 5216
Isa 41: 7 the **h** spurs on him who strikes the anvil. 7079
Jer 10: 4 they fasten it with **h** and nails so it 5216
23:29 "and like a **h** that breaks a rock in pieces? 7079
50:23 and shattered is the **h** *of* the whole earth! 7079

HAMMERED (17) [HAMMER]

Ex 25:18 And make two cherubim out of **h** gold at 5251
25:36 of pure gold. 5251
37: 7 Then he made two cherubim out of **h** gold 5251
37:17 of pure gold and **h** it **out**, base and shaft; 5251
37:22 **h** out *of* pure gold. 5251
39: 3 *They* **h** out thin sheets of gold 8392
Nu 8: 4 It was made of **h** gold— 5251
10: 2 "Make two trumpets of **h** silver, 5251
16:39 and he had them **h** out to overlay the altar, 8392
1Ki 6:35 and overlaid them with gold **h** evenly over 3837
7:29 the lions and bulls were wreaths of **h** work. 4618
10:16 King Solomon made two hundred large shields of **h** gold; 8822
10:17 of **h** gold, with three minas of gold 8822
2Ch 9:15 King Solomon made two hundred large shields of **h** gold; 8822
9:15 six hundred bekas of **h** gold went 8822
9:16 of **h** gold, with three hundred bekas of gold 8822
Jer 10: 9 **H** silver is brought from Tarshish and gold 8392

HAMMERS (1) [HAMMER]

Isa 44:12 he shapes an idol with **h**, 5216

HAMMOLEKETH (1)

1Ch 7:18 His sister **H** gave birth to Ishhod, 2168

HAMMON (2)

Jos 19:28 It went to Abdon, Rehob, **H** and Kanah, 2785
1Ch 6:76 in Galilee, **H** and Kiriathaim, together 2785

HAMMOTH DOR (1) [DOR]

Jos 21:32 **H** and Kartan, together 2831

HAMMUEL (1)

1Ch 4:26 The descendants of Mishma: **H** his son, 2781

HAMON See BAAL HAMON, HAMON GOG

HAMON GOG (2) [BAAL HAMON]

Eze 39:11 So it will be called the Valley of **H**. 2163
39:15 in the Valley of **H**. 2163

HAMONAH (1)

Eze 39:16 (Also a town called **H** will be there.) 2164

HAMOR (13)

Ge 33:19 he bought from the sons of **H**, 2791
34: 2 When Shechem son of **H** the Hivite, 2791
34: 4 And Shechem said to his father **H**, 2791
34: 6 Then Shechem's father **H** went out to talk 2791
34: 8 But **H** said to them, 2791
34:13 as they spoke to Shechem and his father **H**. 2791
34:18 Their proposal seemed good to **H** 2791
34:20 So **H** and his son Shechem went to the gate 2791
34:24 of the city gate agreed with **H** 2791
34:26 put **H** and his son Shechem to the sword 2791
Jos 24:32 of silver from the sons of **H**, 2791
Jdg 9:28 Serve the men of **H**, Shechem's father! 2791
Ac 7:16 the sons *of* **H** at Shechem for a certain sum *1846*

HAMPERED (1)

Pr 4:12 When you walk, your steps *will* not *be* **h**; 7674

HAMSTRING (1) [HAMSTRUNG]

Jos 11: 6 *to* **h** their horses and burn their chariots." 6828

HAMSTRUNG (4) [HAMSTRING]

Ge 49: 6 in their anger and **h** oxen as they pleased. 6828
Jos 11: 9 *He* **h** their horses and burned their chariots. 6828
2Sa 8: 4 He **h** all but a hundred of the chariot horses. 6828
1Ch 18: 4 He **h** all but a hundred of the chariot horses. 6828

HAMUEL (KJV) See HAMMUEL

HAMUL (3) [HAMULITE]

Ge 46:12 The sons of Perez: Hezron and **H**. 2783
Nu 26:21 through **H**, the Hamulite clan. 2783
1Ch 2: 5 The sons of Perez: Hezron and **H**. 2783

HAMULITE (1) [HAMUL]

Nu 26:21 through Hamul, the **H** clan. 2784

HAMUTAL (3)

2Ki 23:31 His mother's name was **H** daughter 2782
24:18 His mother's name was **H** daughter 2782
Jer 52: 1 His mother's name was **H** daughter 2782

HANAMEL (4)

Jer 32: 7 **H** son of Shallum your uncle is going 2856
32: 8 my cousin **H** came to me in the courtyard of 2856
32: 9 the field at Anathoth from my cousin **H** 2856
32:12 in the presence of my cousin **H** and of 2856

HANAN (12) [BAAL-HANAN, BEN-HANAN]

1Ch 8:23 Abdon, Zicri, **H**, 2860
8:38 Bokeru, Ishmael, Sheariah, Obadiah and **H**. 2860
9:44 Bokeru, Ishmael, Sheariah, Obadiah and **H**. 2860
11:43 **H** son of Maacah, Joshaphat the Mithnite, 2860
Ezr 2:46 Hagab, Shalmai, **H**, 2860
Ne 7:49 **H**, Giddel, Gahar, 2860
8: 7 Kelita, Azariah, Jozabad, **H** and Pelaiah— 2860
10:10 Shebaniah, Hodiah, Kelita, Pelaiah, **H**, 2860
10:22 Pelatiah, **H**, Anaiah, 2860
10:26 Ahiah, **H**, Anan, 2860
13:13 in charge of the storerooms and made **H** son 2860
Jer 35: 4 the room of the sons of **H** son of Igdaliah 2860

HANANEL (4)

Ne 3: 1 and as far as the Tower of **H**. 2861
12:39 of **H** and the Tower of the Hundred, 2861
Jer 31:38 be rebuilt for me from the Tower of **H** to 2861
Zec 14:10 the Tower of **H** to the royal winepresses. 2861

HANANI (11)

1Ki 16: 1 word of the LORD came to Jehu son of **H** 2862
16: 7 the prophet Jehu son of **H** to Baasha 2862
1Ch 25: 4 Hananiah, **H**, Eliathah, Giddalti 2862
25:25 the eighteenth to **H**, 2862
2Ch 16: 7 At that time **H** the seer came to Asa king 2862
19: 2 Jehu the seer, the son of **H**, went out 2862
20:34 are written in the annals of Jehu son of **H**, 2862
Ezr 10:20 of Immer: **H** and Zebadiah. 2862
Ne 1: 2 **H**, one of my brothers, came from Judah 2862
7: 2 I put in charge of Jerusalem my brother **H**, 2862
12:36 Gilalai, Maai, Nethanel, Judah and **H**— 2862

HANANIAH (28)

1Ch 3:19 The sons of Zerubbabel: Meshullam and **H**. 2863
3:21 The descendants of **H**: 2863
8:24 **H**, Elam, Anthothijah, 2863
25: 4 **H**, Hanani, Eliathah, Giddalti 2863
25:23 the sixteenth to **H**, his sons and relatives, 2864
2Ch 26:11 the officer under the direction of **H**, 2864
Ezr 10:28 Jehohanan, **H**, Zabbai and Athlai. 2863
Ne 3: 8 and **H**, one of the perfume-makers, 2863
3:30 Next to him, **H** son of Shelemiah, 2863
7: 2 along with **H** the commander of the citadel, 2863
10:23 Hoshea, **H**, Hasshub, 2863
12:12 Meraiah; of Jeremiah's, **H**; 2863
12:41 Zechariah and **H** with their trumpets— 2863
Jer 28: 1 the prophet **H** son of Azzur, 2863
28: 5 replied to the prophet **H** before the priests 2863
28:10 the prophet **H** took the yoke off the neck of 2863
28:12 after the prophet **H** had broken the yoke off 2863
28:13 and tell **H**, 'This is what the LORD says: 2863
28:15 the prophet Jeremiah said to **H** the prophet, 2863
28:15 to Hananiah the prophet, "Listen, **H**! 2863
28:17 **H** the prophet died. 2863
36:12 of Shaphan, Zedekiah son of **H**, 2864
37:13 the son of **H**, arrested him and said, 2863
Da 1: 6 Daniel, **H**, Mishael and Azariah. 2863
1: 7 the name Belteshazzar; to **H**, Shadrach; 2863
1:11 **H**, Mishael and Azariah, 2863
1:19 and he found none equal to Daniel, **H**, 2863
2:17 and explained the matter to his friends **H**, 10275

HAND (847) [HANDBREADTH, HANDED, HANDFUL, HANDFULS, HANDING, HANDS, LEFT-HANDED, OPENHANDED, RIGHT-HANDED]

Ge 3:22 to reach out his **h** and take also from the tree 3338
4:11 to receive your brother's blood from your **h**. 3338
8: 9 He reached out his **h** and took the dove 3338
14:20 who delivered your enemies into your **h**." 3338
14:22 "I have raised my **h** to the LORD, 3338
16:12 his **h** will be against everyone 3338
16:12 be against everyone and everyone's **h** 3338
19:16 the men grasped his **h** and the hands 3338
21:18 Lift the boy up and take him by the **h**, 3338
21:30 from my **h** as a witness that I dug this well." 3338
22:10 Then he reached out his **h** and took 3338
22:12 "Do not lay a **h** on the boy," he said. 3338
24: 2 "Put your **h** under my thigh. 3338
24: 9 So the servant put his **h** under the thigh 3338
25:26 with his **h** grasping Esau's heel; 3338
32:11 I pray, from the **h** *of* my brother Esau, 3338
37:22 but don't lay a **h** on him." 3338
38:18 and the staff in your **h**," she answered. 3338
38:28 one of them put out his **h**, 3338
38:29 But when he drew back his **h**, 3338
39:12 He left his cloak in her **h** and ran out of 3338
39:13 in her **h** and had run out of the house, 3338
40:11 Pharaoh's cup was in my **h**, 3338

Ge	40:11	into Pharaoh's cup and put the cup in his **h.**	4090
	40:13	and you will put Pharaoh's cup in his **h,**	3338
	40:21	he once again put the cup into Pharaoh's **h,**	4090
	41:44	without your word no one will lift **h** or foot	3338
	46:4	And Joseph's own **h** will close your eyes."	3338
	47:29	put your **h** under my thigh and promise	3338
	48:13	Ephraim on his right toward Israel's left **h**	NIH
	48:13	on his left toward Israel's right **h,**	NIH
	48:14	But Israel reached out his right **h** and put it	NIH
	48:14	he put his left **h** on Manasseh's head,	NIH
	48:17	Joseph saw his father placing his right **h**	3338
	48:17	so he took hold of his father's **h** to move it	NIH
	48:18	put your right **h** on his head."	NIH
	49:8	your **h** will be on the neck of your enemies;	3338
	49:24	of the **h** of the Mighty One of Jacob,	3338
Ex	3:8	to rescue them from the **h** of the Egyptians	3338
	3:19	unless a mighty **h** compels him.	3338
	3:20	So I will stretch out my **h** and strike	3338
	4:2	"What is that in your **h?**"	3338
	4:4	"Reach out your **h** and take it by the tail."	3338
	4:4	and it turned back into a staff in his **h.**	4090
	4:6	"Put your **h** inside your cloak."	3338
	4:6	So Moses put his **h** into his cloak,	3338
	4:7	So Moses put his **h** back into his cloak,	3338
	4:17	But take this staff in your **h**	3338
	4:20	And he took the staff of God in his **h.**"	3338
	5:21	and have put a sword in their **h** to kill us."	3338
	6:1	Because of my mighty **h** he will let them go;	3338
	6:1	of my mighty **h** he will drive them out	3338
	6:8	to the land I swore with uplifted **h** to give	3338
	7:4	Then I will lay my **h** on Egypt and	3338
	7:5	when I stretch out my **h** against Egypt	3338
	7:15	in your **h** the staff that was changed into	3338
	7:17	in my **h** I will strike the water of the Nile,	3338
	7:19	'Take your staff and stretch out your **h** over	3338
	8:5	'Stretch out your **h** with your staff over	3338
	8:6	So Aaron stretched out his **h** over the waters	3338
	8:17	and when Aaron stretched out his **h** with	3338
	9:3	the **h** of the LORD will bring	3338
	9:15	For by now I could have stretched out my **h**	3338
	9:22	"Stretch out your **h** toward the sky so	3338
	10:12	"Stretch out your **h** over Egypt so	3338
	10:21	"Stretch out your **h** toward the sky so	3338
	10:22	Moses stretched out his **h** toward the sky,	3338
	11:5	who is at her **h** mill,	8160
	12:11	on your feet and your staff in your **h.**	3338
	13:3	out of it with a mighty **h.**	3338
	13:9	for you like a sign on your **h** and a reminder	3338
	13:9	brought you out of Egypt with his mighty **h.**	3338
	13:14	'With a mighty **h** the LORD brought us out	3338
	13:16	like a sign on your **h** and a symbol on your	3338
	13:16	out of Egypt with his mighty **h.**"	3338
	14:16	and stretch out your **h** over the sea to divide	3338
	14:21	Then Moses stretched out his **h** over the sea,	3338
	14:26	"Stretch out your **h** over the sea so that	3338
	14:27	Moses stretched out his **h** over the sea,	3338
	15:6	"Your right **h,** O LORD,	NIH
	15:6	Your right **h,** O LORD,	NIH
	15:6	and my **h** will destroy them.'	3338
	15:12	You stretched out your right **h** and	NIH
	15:20	Aaron's sister, took a tambourine in her **h,**	3338
	16:3	"If only we had died by the LORD's **h**	3338
	17:5	in your **h** the staff with which you struck	3338
	18:9	for Israel in rescuing them from the **h** of	3338
	18:10	from the **h** of the Egyptians and of Pharaoh,	3338
	18:10	and who rescued the people from the **h** of	3338
	19:13	not a **h** is to be laid on him.	3338
	21:24	tooth for tooth, **h** for hand, foot for foot,	3338
	21:24	tooth for tooth, hand for **h,** foot for foot,	3338
	23:31	*I will* **h** *over to* you the people	928+3338+5989
	24:11	not raise his **h** against these leaders of	3338
	32:11	of Egypt with great power and a mighty **h?**	3338
	33:22	a cleft in the rock and cover you with my **h**	4090
	33:23	Then I will remove my **h** and you will see	4090
Lev	1:4	He is to lay his **h** on the head of the burnt	3338
	3:2	He is to lay his **h** on the head of his offering	3338
	3:8	He is to lay his **h** on the head of his offering	3338
	3:13	He is to lay his **h** on its head and slaughter it	3338
	4:4	He is to lay his **h** on its head and slaughter it	3338
	4:24	He is to lay his **h** on the goat's head,	3338
	4:29	to lay his **h** on the head of the sin offering	3338
	4:33	He is to lay his **h** on its head and slaughter it	3338
	8:23	the thumb of his right **h** and on the big toe	3338
	14:14	the thumb of his right **h** and on the big toe	3338
	14:15	**palm** of his own left **h,**	4090
	14:17	the thumb of his right **h** and on the big toe	3338
	14:25	the thumb of his right **h** and on the big toe	3338
	14:26	**palm** of his own left **h,**	4090
	14:28	be cleansed, on the thumb of his right **h** and	3338
	21:19	no man with a crippled foot or **h,**	3338
	22:25	from the **h** of a foreigner and offer them as	3338
Nu	14:30	with uplifted **h** to make your home,	3338
	22:23	in the road with a drawn sword in his **h,**	3338
	22:29	If I had a sword in my **h,**	3338
	25:7	took a spear in his **h**	3338
	27:18	and lay your **h** on him.	3338
	35:17	if anyone has a stone in his **h** that could kill,	3338
	35:18	in his **h** that could kill, and he hits someone	3338
Dt	2:15	The LORD's **h** was against them	3338
	2:24	I have given into your **h** Sihon the Amorite,	3338
	3:24	your greatness and your strong **h,**	3338
	4:34	by a mighty **h** and an outstretched arm,	3338
	5:15	with a mighty **h** and an outstretched arm,	3338
	6:21	out of Egypt with a mighty **h.**	3338
	7:8	a mighty **h** and redeemed you from the land	3338
	7:19	the mighty **h** and outstretched arm,	3338
	7:24	He will give their kings into your **h,**	3338

Dt	9:26	and brought out of Egypt with a mighty **h.**	3338
	11:2	his majesty, his mighty **h,**	3338
	12:7	in everything you have put your **h** to,	3338
	12:18	in everything you put your **h** to	3338
	13:9	Your **h** must be the first in putting him	3338
	15:10	and in everything you put your **h** to.	3338
	15:18	as much as that of a **hired h.**	8502
	19:12	**h** him **over** *to* the avenger of blood to die.	3338
			928+3338+5989
	19:21	tooth for tooth, **h** for hand, foot for foot.	3338
	19:21	tooth for tooth, hand for **h,** foot for foot.	3338
	20:13	LORD your God delivers it into your **h,**	3338
	23:15	*do* not **h** him **over** to his master.	6037
	23:20	in everything you put your **h** to	3338
	25:12	you shall cut off her **h.** Show her no pity.	4090
	26:8	with a mighty **h** and an outstretched arm,	3338
	28:8	and on everything you put your **h** to.	3338
	28:20	and rebuke in everything you put your **h** to,	3338
	28:32	powerless to lift a **h.**	3338
	32:27	'Our **h** has triumphed;	3338
	32:39	and no one can deliver out of my **h.**	3338
	32:40	I lift my **h** to heaven and declare:	3338
	32:41	and my **h** grasps it in judgment,	3338
	33:3	all the holy ones are in your **h.**	3338
Jos	2:19	his blood will be on our head if a **h** is laid	3338
	4:24	that the **h** of the LORD is powerful and so	3338
	5:13	in front of him with a drawn sword in his **h.**	3338
	8:7	The LORD your God will give it into your **h.**	3338
	8:18	toward Ai the javelin that is in your **h,**	3338
	8:18	for into your **h** I will deliver the city."	3338
	8:26	not draw back the **h** that held out his javelin	3338
	10:8	I have given them into your **h.**	3338
	10:19	for the LORD your God has given them into your **h.**"	3338
	10:30	that city and its king into Israel's **h.**	3338
	11:6	**h** all of them **over** to Israel, slain.	5989
	11:8	the LORD gave them into the **h** of Israel.	3338
	22:31	the Israelites from the LORD's **h.**"	3338
	24:10	and I delivered you out of his **h.**	3338
Jdg	2:15	the **h** of the LORD was against them	3338
	3:21	Ehud reached with his left **h,**	3338
	4:9	for the LORD will **h** Sisera **over** *to a*	928+3338+4835
		woman."	
	4:24	And the **h** of the Israelites grew stronger	3338
	5:26	Her **h** reached for the tent peg,	3338
	5:26	her right **h** for the workman's hammer.	NIH
	6:9	from the power of Egypt and from the **h**	3338
	6:13	and put us into the **h** of Midian."	4090
	6:14	and save Israel out of Midian's **h.**	4090
	6:21	With the tip of the staff that was in his **h,**	3338
	6:36	by my **h** as you have promised—	3338
	6:37	that you will save Israel by my **h,**	3338
	8:7	and Zalmunna into my **h,**	3338
	8:22	you have saved us out of the **h** of Midian."	3338
	9:17	risked his life to rescue you from the **h**	3338
	9:33	do whatever your **h** finds to do.	3338
	15:12	to tie you up and **h** you **over**	928+3338+5989
	15:13	only tie you up and **h** you **over**	928+3338+5989
	16:26	Samson said to the servant who held his **h,**	3338
	16:29	his right **h** on the one and his left hand on	NIH
	16:29	his right hand on the one and his left **h** on	NIH
Ru	1:13	the LORD's **h** has gone out against me!"	3338
1Sa	2:13	with a three-pronged fork in his **h.**	3338
	2:16	"No, **h** it over now;	5989
	4:3	and save us from the **h** of our enemies."	4090
	4:8	from the **h** of these mighty gods?	3338
	5:6	The LORD's **h** was heavy upon the people	3338
	5:7	because his **h** is heavy upon us and	3338
	5:9	the LORD's **h** was against that city,	3338
	5:11	God's **h** was very heavy upon it.	3338
	6:3	and you will know why his **h** has	3338
	6:5	Perhaps his **h** will lift his **h** from you	3338
	6:9	not his **h** that struck us and that it happened	3338
	7:3	and he will deliver you out of the **h** of	3338
	7:8	that he may rescue us from the **h** of	3338
	7:13	**h** of the LORD was against the Philistines.	3338
	9:16	he will deliver my people from the **h** of	3338
	10:7	do whatever your **h** finds to do,	3338
	12:3	From whose **h** have I accepted a bribe	3338
	12:4	not taken anything from anyone's **h.**"	3338
	12:5	that you have not found anything in my **h.**"	3338
	12:9	so he sold them into the **h** of Sisera,	3338
	12:15	his **h** will be against you,	3338
	13:22	and Jonathan had a sword or spear in his **h;**	3338
	14:12	the LORD has given them into the **h**	3338
	14:19	to the priest, "Withdraw your **h.**"	3338
	14:26	yet no one put his **h** to his mouth,	3338
	14:27	the staff that was in his **h** and dipped it into	3338
	14:27	He raised his **h** to his mouth,	3338
	14:37	Will you give them into Israel's **h?**"	3338
	17:37	of the bear will deliver me from the **h**	3338
	17:40	Then he took his staff in his **h,**	3338
	17:40	with his sling in his **h,**	3338
	17:46	This day the LORD *will* **h** you **over** to me,	928+3338+6037
	17:50	without a sword in his **h** he struck down	3338
	18:10	Saul had a spear in his **h**	3338
	18:17	"I will not raise a **h** against him.	3338
	18:21	and so that the **h** of the Philistines may be	3338
	19:9	in his house with his spear in his **h.**	3338
	20:8	Why **h** me **over** to your father?"	995
	21:3	then, what *do* you **have on h?**	3338+3780+9393
	21:4	**have** any ordinary bread on **h,**	448+3338+9393
	22:6	And Saul, spear in **h,**	3338
	22:17	not willing to raise a **h** to strike the priests	3338
	23:4	to give the Philistines into your **h.**"	3338
	23:17	"My father Saul will not lay a **h** on you.	3338

1Sa	24:6	or lift my **h** against him;	3338
	24:10	'I will not lift my **h** against my master,	3338
	24:11	look at this piece of your robe in my **h!**	3338
	24:12	but my **h** will not touch you.	3338
	24:13	so my **h** will not touch you.	3338
	24:15	by delivering me from your **h.**"	3338
	25:35	from her **h** what she had brought him	3338
	26:9	Who can lay a **h** on the LORD's anointed	3338
	26:11	But the LORD forbid that I should lay a **h**	3338
	26:23	not lay a **h** on the LORD's anointed.	3338
	27:1	of these days I will be destroyed by the **h**	3338
	27:1	and I will slip out of his **h.**"	3338
	28:19	The LORD *will* **h** **over** both Israel	928+3338+5989
	28:19	The LORD *will* also **h** **over** the army of	928+3338+5989
		Israel	
	30:15	or **h** me **over** to my master,	928+3338+6037
2Sa	1:14	"Why were you not afraid to lift your **h**	3338
	2:14	the young men get up and **fight h to** hand	8471
	2:14	the young men get up and **fight hand to h**	8471
	3:18	the **h** of the Philistines and from the hand	3338
	3:18	the hand of the Philistines and from the **h**	3338
	4:11	now demand his blood from your **h** and rid	3338
	5:19	*Will* you **h** them **over** *to* me?"	928+3338+5989
	5:19	**surely h** the Philistines **over** to you	928+3338+5989+5989
	12:7	and I delivered you from the **h** of Saul.	3338
	13:5	and then eat it from her **h.**'"	3338
	13:6	so I may eat from her **h.**"	3338
	13:10	into my bedroom so I may eat from your **h.**"	3338
	13:19	She put her **h** on her head and went away,	3338
	14:7	'**H over** the one who struck his brother	5989
	14:16	the **h** of the man who is trying to cut off	4090
	14:19	"Isn't the **h** of Joab with you in all this?"	3338
	15:5	Absalom would reach out his **h,**	3338
	18:12	I would not lift my **h** against the king's son.	3338
	18:14	So he took three javelins in his **h**	4090
	18:19	the LORD has delivered him from the **h**	3338
	19:9	"The king delivered us from the **h**	4090
	19:9	he is the one who rescued us from the **h** of	4090
	20:9	by the beard with his right **h** to kiss him.	3338
	20:10	on his guard against the dagger in Joab's **h,**	3338
	20:21	has lifted up his **h** against the king,	3338
	20:21	**H over** this one man,	5989
	21:20	with six fingers on each **h** and six toes	3338
	22:1	when the LORD delivered him from the **h**	4090
	22:1	the hand of all his enemies and from the **h**	4090
	23:6	which are not gathered with the **h.**	3338
	23:10	the Philistines till his **h** grew tired and froze	3338
	23:21	Although the Egyptian had a spear in his **h,**	3338
	23:21	He snatched the spear from the Egyptian's **h**	3338
	24:16	When the angel stretched out his **h**	3338
	24:16	Withdraw your **h.**"	3338
	24:17	Let your **h** fall upon me and my family."	3338
1Ki	2:19	and she sat down at his right **h.**	NIH
	8:15	with his own **h** has fulfilled what he	
		promised	3338
	8:24	and with your **h** you have fulfilled it—	—
	8:42	of your great name and your mighty **h**	3338
	11:12	I will tear it out of the **h** of your son.	3338
	11:31	of Solomon's **h** and give you ten tribes.	3338
	11:34	the whole kingdom out of Solomon's **h;**	3338
	13:4	he stretched out his **h** from the altar	3338
	13:4	But the **h** he stretched out toward	3338
	13:6	and pray for me that my **h** may be restored."	3338
	13:6	and the king's **h** was restored and became	3338
	18:44	"A cloud as small as a man's **h** is rising	4090
	20:13	I will give it into your **h** today,	3338
	22:6	"for the Lord will give it into the king's **h.**"	3338
	22:12	the LORD will give it into the king's **h.**"	3338
	22:15	the LORD will give it into the king's **h.**"	3338
2Ki	3:10	to **h** us **over** *to* Moab?"	928+3338+5989
	3:13	to **h** us **over** to Moab.	928+3338+5989
	3:15	the **h** of the LORD came upon Elisha	3338
	3:18	*he will* also **h** Moab **over** *to* you.	928+3338+5989
	4:29	take my staff in your **h** and run.	3338
	5:11	wave his **h** over the spot and cure me	3338
	6:7	Then the man reached out his **h** and took it.	3338
	10:15	"If so," said Jehu, "give me your **h.**"	3338
	11:8	each man with his weapon in his **h.**	3338
	11:11	The guards, each with his weapon in his **h,**	3338
	12:7	but **h** it **over** for repairing the temple."	5989
	14:27	he saved them by the **h** of Jeroboam son	3338
	16:7	of the **h** of the king of Aram and of the king	4090
	17:39	it is he who will deliver you from the **h**	3338
	18:21	a man's **h** and wounds him if he leans on it!	4090
	18:29	He cannot deliver you from my **h.**	3338
	18:30	be given into the **h** of the king of Assyria.'	3338
	18:33	from the **h** of the king of Assyria?	3338
	18:34	Have they rescued Samaria from my **h?**	3338
	18:35	the LORD deliver Jerusalem from my **h?**"	3338
	19:19	O LORD our God, deliver us from his **h,**	3338
	20:6	and this city from the **h** of the king	4090
	21:14	my inheritance and **h** them **over**	928+3338+5989
1Ch	4:10	Let your **h** be with me,	3338
	6:15	into exile by the **h** of Nebuchadnezzar.	3338
	6:39	who served at his right **h,**	NIH
	6:44	the Merarites, at his left **h:**	NIH
	11:23	a spear like a weaver's rod in his **h,**	3338
	11:23	He snatched the spear from the Egyptian's **h**	3338
	13:9	Uzzah reached out his **h** to steady the ark,	3338
	13:10	down because he had put his **h** on the ark.	3338
	14:10	*Will* you **h** them **over** *to* me?"	928+3338+5989
	14:10	"Go, *I will* **h** them **over** *to* you,	928+3338+5989
	14:11	against my enemies by my **h.**"	3338
	20:6	with six fingers on each **h** and six toes	NIH
	21:15	Withdraw your **h.**"	3338
	21:16	with a drawn sword in his **h** extended	3338

1Ch	21:17	let your **h** fall upon me and my family,	3338
	28:19	"I have in writing from the **h** of the LORD	3338
	29:14	and we have given you only what comes from your **h**.	
	29:16	it comes from your **h**,	3338
2Ch	6:15	and with your **h** you have fulfilled it—	3338
	6:32	of your great name and your mighty **h**.	3338
	16: 7	the king of Aram has escaped from your **h**.	3338
	16: 8	he delivered them into your **h**.	3338
	18: 5	"for God will give it into the king's **h**."	3338
	18:11	the LORD will give it into the king's **h**."	3338
	18:14	"for they will be given into your **h**."	3338
	20: 6	Power and might are in your **h**,	3338
	23: 7	each man with his weapons in his **h**.	3338
	23:10	each with his weapon in his **h**,	3338
	25:15	not save their own people from your **h**?"	3338
	25:20	that he *might* **h** them *over* to	928+3338+5989
	26:19	a censer in his **h** ready to burn incense,	3338
	26:19	he gave them into your **h**.	3338
	30: 6	who have escaped from the **h** of the kings	4090
	30:12	in Judah the **h** of God was on the people	3338
	32:11	from the **h** of the king of Assyria,	4090
	32:13	to deliver their land from my **h**?	3338
	32:14	then can your god deliver you from my **h**?	3338
	32:15	to deliver his people from my **h** or the hand	3338
	32:15	to deliver his people from my hand or the **h**	3338
	32:15	will your god deliver you from my **h**!"	3338
	32:17	not rescue their people from my **h**,	3338
	32:17	not rescue his people from my **h**."	3338
	32:22	from the **h** of Sennacherib king of Assyria	3338
	32:22	of Assyria and from the **h** of all others.	3338
Ezr	6:12	or people who lifts a **h** to change this decree	10311
	7: 6	the **h** of the LORD his God was on him.	3338
	7: 9	for the gracious **h** of his God was on him.	3338
	7:14	the Law of your God, which is in your **h**.	10311
	7:28	the **h** of the LORD my God was on me,	3338
	8:18	the gracious **h** of our God was on us,	3338
	8:22	"The gracious **h** of our God is	3338
	8:31	The **h** of our God was on us,	3338
Ne	9: 7	and humiliation at the **h** of foreign kings.	3338
	1:10	by your great strength and your mighty **h**.	3338
	2: 8	And because the gracious **h** of my God was	3338
	2:18	about the gracious **h** of my God upon me	3338
	4:17	with one **h** and held a weapon in the other,	3338
	6: 5	and in his **h** was an unsealed letter	3338
	9:15	of the land you had sworn with uplifted **h**	3338
	9:27	who rescued them from the **h**	3338
	9:28	to the **h** of their enemies so that they ruled	3338
Est	5: 2	to her the gold scepter that was in his **h**.	3338
	9: 1	and the Jews **got the upper h**.	8948
Job	1:11	But stretch out your **h** and strike everything	
	2: 5	But stretch out your **h** and strike his flesh	3338
	6: 9	to let loose his **h** and cut me off!	3338
	6:23	deliver me from the **h** of the enemy,	3338
	9:33	to lay his **h** upon us both,	3338
	10: 7	that no one can rescue me from your **h**?	3338
	11:14	if you put away the sin that is in your **h**	
	12: 9	Which of all these does not know that the **h**	3338
	12:10	In his **h** is the life of every creature and	3338
	13:21	Withdraw your **h** far from me,	4090
	15:23	he knows the day of darkness is at **h**.	3338
	19:21	have pity, for the **h** of God has struck me.	3338
	21: 5	clap your **h** over your mouth.	3338
	23: 2	his **h** is heavy in spite of my groaning.	3338
	26:13	his **h** pierced the gliding serpent.	3338
	28: 9	Man's **h** assaults the flinty rock	3338
	29:20	the bow ever new in my **h**.'	3338
	30:21	with the might of your **h** you attack me.	3338
	30:24	a **h** on a broken man when he cries for help	3338
	31:21	if I have raised my **h** against the fatherless,	3338
	31:27	and my **h** offered them a kiss of homage,	3338
	33: 7	nor should my **h** be heavy upon you.	437
	34:20	the mighty are removed without human **h**.	3338
	35: 7	or what does he receive from your **h**?	3338
	40: 4	I put my **h** over my mouth.	3338
	40:14	to you that your own right **h** can save you.	NIH
	41: 8	If you lay a **h** on him,	4090
Ps	10:12	Lift up your **h**, O God.	3338
	10:14	you consider it to take it in **h**.	3338
	16: 8	he is at my right **h**, I will not be shaken.	NIH
	16:11	with eternal pleasures at your right **h**.	NIH
	17: 7	by your right **h** those who take refuge	NIH
	17:14	by your **h** save me from such men,	3338
	18: T	when the LORD delivered him from the **h**	4090
	18: T	the hand of all his enemies and from the **h**	3338
	18:35	and your right **h** sustains me;	NIH
	20: 6	with the saving power of his right **h**.	NIH
	21: 8	Your **h** will lay hold on all your enemies;	3338
	21: 8	your right **h** will seize your foes.	NIH
	32: 4	day and night your **h** was heavy upon me;	3338
	36:11	nor the **h** of the wicked drive me away.	3338
	37:24	for the LORD upholds him with his **h**.	3338
	38: 2	and your **h** has come down upon me.	3338
	39:10	I am overcome by the blow of your **h**.	3338
	44: 2	With your **h** you drove out the nations	3338
	44: 3	it was your right **h**, your arm,	NIH
	45: 4	let your right **h** display awesome deeds.	NIH
	45: 9	at your right **h** is the royal bride in gold	NIH
	48:10	your right **h** is filled with righteousness.	NIH
	60: 5	Save us and help us with your right **h**,	NIH
	63: 8	your right **h** upholds me.	NIH
	71: 4	O my God, from the **h** of the wicked,	3338
	73:23	you hold me by my right **h**.	3338
	74:11	Why do you hold back your **h**,	3338
	74:11	Why do you hold back your hand, your right **h**?	NIH
	74:19	*Do* not **h** *over* the life of your dove	5989

Ps	75: 8	In the **h** of the LORD is a cup full	3338
	77:10	the years of the right **h** of the Most High."	NIH
	77:20	like a flock by the **h** of Moses and Aaron.	NIH
	78:54	to the hill country his right **h** had taken.	NIH
	80:15	the root your right **h** has planted,	NIH
	80:17	Let your **h** rest on the man	3338
	80:17	on the man at your right **h**,	NIH
	81:14	and turn my **h** against their foes!	3338
	82: 4	deliver them from the **h** of the wicked.	3338
	89:13	your **h** is strong, your right hand exalted.	3338
	89:13	your hand is strong, your right **h** exalted.	NIH
	89:21	My **h** will sustain him;	3338
	89:25	I will set his **h** over the sea,	3338
	89:25	his right **h** over the rivers.	NIH
	89:42	You have exalted the right **h** of his foes;	NIH
	91: 7	ten thousand at your right **h**,	NIH
	95: 4	In his **h** are the depths of the earth,	3338
	97:10	and delivers them from the **h** of the wicked.	3338
	98: 1	right **h** and his holy arm have worked salvation for him.	NIH
	104:28	when you open your **h**,	3338
	106:10	He saved them from the **h** of the foe;	3338
	106:10	from the **h** of the enemy he redeemed them.	3338
	106:26	So he swore to them with uplifted **h**	3338
	107: 2	those he redeemed from the **h** of the foe,	3338
	108: 6	Save us and help us with your right **h**,	NIH
	109: 6	let an accuser stand at his right **h**.	3338
	109:27	Let them know that it is your **h**, that you,	3338
	109:31	he stands at the right **h** of the needy one,	NIH
	110: 1	"Sit at my right **h** until I make your enemies	NIH
	110: 5	The Lord is at your right **h**;	NIH
	118:15	LORD's right **h** has done mighty things!	NIH
	118:16	The LORD's right **h** is lifted high;	NIH
	118:16	the LORD's right **h** has done mighty things!"	NIH
	118:27	**With** boughs in **h**,	928
	119:173	May your **h** be ready to help me,	3338
	121: 5	the LORD is your shade at your right **h**;	NIH
	123: 2	of slaves look to the **h** of their master,	3338
	123: 2	eyes of a maid look to the **h** of her mistress,	3338
	136:12	with a mighty **h** and outstretched arm;	3338
	137: 5	may my right **h** forget [its skill].	NIH
	138: 7	you stretch out your **h** against the anger	3338
	138: 7	with your right **h** you save me.	NIH
	139: 5	you have laid your **h** upon me.	4090
	139:10	even there your **h** will guide me,	3338
	139:10	your right **h** will hold me fast.	NIH
	144: 7	Reach down your **h** from on high;	3338
	145:16	You open your **h** and satisfy the desires	3338
Pr	1:24	when I stretched out my **h**,	3338
	3:16	Long life is in her right **h**;	NIH
	3:16	in her left **h** are riches and honor.	NIH
	6: 5	like a gazelle from the **h** of the hunter,	3338
	17:16	Of what use is money in the **h** of a fool,	3338
	19:24	The sluggard buries his **h** in the dish;	3338
	21: 1	The king's heart is in the **h** of the LORD;	3338
	26: 6	the sending of a message by the **h** of a fool.	3338
	26: 9	a thornbush in a drunkard's **h** is a proverb in	3338
	26:15	The sluggard buries his **h** in the dish;	3338
	27:16	the wind or grasping oil with the **h**.	3545
	30:28	a lizard can be caught with the **h**,	3338
	30:32	clap your **h** over your mouth!	3338
	31:19	In her **h** she holds the distaff and grasps	3338
Ecc	2:24	This too, I see, is from the **h** of God,	3338
	2:26	to **h** it *over* to the one who pleases God.	5989
	5:15	from his labor that he can carry in his **h**.	3338
	9:10	Whatever your **h** finds to do,	3338
SS	5: 4	My lover thrust his **h** through the	3338
Isa	1:25	I will turn my **h** against you;	3338
	5:25	his is raised and he strikes them down.	3338
	5:25	his **h** is still upraised.	3338
	6: 6	to me with a live coal in his **h**,	3338
	8:11	The LORD spoke to me with his strong **h**	3338
	9:12	his **h** is still upraised.	3338
	9:17	his **h** is still upraised.	3338
	9:21	his **h** is still upraised.	3338
	10: 4	his **h** is still upraised.	3338
	10: 5	in whose **h** is the club of my wrath!	3338
	10:10	As my **h** seized the kingdoms of the idols,	3338
	10:13	" 'By the strength of my **h** I have done this,	3338
	10:14	my **h** reached for the wealth of the nations;	3338
	11: 8	young child put his **h** into the viper's nest.	3338
	11:11	the Lord will reach out his **h** a second time	3338
	11:15	with a scorching wind he will sweep his **h**	3338
	13:22	Her time *is* at **h**,	995+4200+7940
	14:26	this is the **h** stretched out over all nations.	3338
	14:27	His **h** is stretched out,	3338
	19: 4	*I will* **h** the Egyptians *over* to the power	6127
	19:16	They will shudder with fear at the uplifted **h**	3338
	22:21	and **h** your authority *over*	928+3338+5989
	23:11	The LORD has stretched out his **h** over	3338
	25:10	The **h** of the LORD will rest	3338
	26:11	O LORD, your **h** is lifted high,	3338
	28: 4	as someone sees it and takes it in his **h**,	4090
	31: 3	When the LORD stretches out his **h**,	3338
	33:15	and keeps his **h** from accepting bribes,	4090
	34:17	his **h** distributes them by measure.	3338
	36: 6	a man's **h** and wounds him if he leans on it!	4090
	36:15	be given into the **h** of the king of Assyria.'	3338
	36:18	from the **h** of the king of Assyria?	3338
	36:19	Have they rescued Samaria from my **h**?	3338
	36:20	the LORD deliver Jerusalem from my **h**?	3338
	37:20	O LORD our God, deliver us from his **h**,	3338
	38: 6	and this city from the **h** of the king	4090
	40: 2	from the LORD's **h** double for all her sins.	3338
	40:12	the waters in the **hollow of** his **h**,	9123
	40:12	or with the **breadth** of his **h** marked off	2455
	41:10	I will uphold you with my righteous right **h**.	NIH

Isa	41:13	of your right **h** and says to you, Do not fear;	NIH
	41:20	that the **h** of the LORD has done this,	3338
	42: 6	I will take hold of your **h**.	3338
	43:13	No one can deliver out of my **h**.	3338
	44: 5	still another will write on his **h**,	3338
	44:20	"Is not this thing in my right **h** a lie?"	NIH
	45: 1	whose right **h** I take hold of	3338
	47: 6	I gave them into your **h**,	3338
	48:13	My own **h** laid the foundations of the earth,	3338
	48:13	and my right **h** spread out the heavens;	NIH
	49: 2	in the shadow of his **h** he hid me;	3338
	49: 4	Yet what is due me is in the LORD's **h**,	907
	50:11	This is what you shall receive from my **h**:	3338
	51:16	and covered you with the shadow of my **h**—	3338
	51:17	the **h** of the LORD the cup of his wrath,	3338
	51:18	to take her by the **h**.	3338
	51:22	of your **h** the cup that made you stagger;	3338
	53:10	the will of the LORD will prosper in his **h**.	3338
	56: 1	for my salvation is close at **h**,	995
	56: 2	and keeps his **h** from doing any evil."	3338
	62: 3	be a crown of splendor in the LORD's **h**,	3338
	62: 3	a royal diadem in the **h** of your God.	4090
	62: 8	The LORD has sworn by his right **h** and	NIH
	63:12	of power to be at Moses' right **h**,	NIH
	64: 8	we are all the work of your **h**.	3338
	66: 2	Has not my **h** made all these things,	3338
	66:14	the **h** of the LORD will be made known	3338
Jer	1: 9	Then the LORD reached out his **h**	3338
	6: 9	pass your **h** over the branches again,	3338
	6:12	when I stretch out my **h**	3338
	15:17	I sat alone because your **h** was on me	3338
	18: 6	"Like clay in the **h** of the potter,	3338
	18: 6	so are you in my **h**, O house of Israel.	3338
	18:21	**h** them *over* to the power of the sword.	5599
	20: 4	*I will* **h** all Judah *over* to the king	928+3338+5989
	20: 5	*I will* **h** *over* to their enemies all	928+3338+5989
	21: 5	an outstretched **h** and a mighty arm in anger	3338
	21: 7	*I will* **h** *over* Zedekiah king of Judah,	928+3338+5989
	21:12	rescue from the **h** of his oppressor	3338
	22: 3	Rescue from the **h** of his oppressor	3338
	22:24	were a signet ring on my right **h**,	3338
	22:25	*I will* **h** you *over*	928+3338+5989
	25:15	from my **h** this cup filled with the wine	3338
	25:17	the cup from the LORD's **h** and made all	3338
	25:28	if they refuse to take the cup from your **h**	3338
	27: 6	**h** all your countries *over*	928+3338+5989
	27: 8	until I destroy it by his **h**.	3338
	29:21	"I *will* **h** them *over*	928+3338+5989
	31:11	from the **h** of those stronger than they.	3338
	31:32	when I took them by the **h** to lead them out	3338
	32: 3	*to* **h** this city *over* to the king of Babylon,	928+3338+5989
	32:21	by a mighty **h** and an outstretched arm and	3338
	32:28	*to* **h** this city *over* to the Babylonians	928+3338+5989
	33:13	under the **h** of the one who counts them,'	3338
	34: 2	*to* **h** this city *over* to the king of Babylon,	928+3338+5989
	34:20	*I will* **h** *over*	928+3338+5989
	34:21	**h** Zedekiah king of Judah and his officials *over*	928+3338+5989
	36:14	to them with the scroll in his **h**.	3338
	38:16	I will neither kill you nor **h** you *over*	928+3338+5989
	38:19	for the Babylonians *may* **h** me *over* *to* them	928+3338+5989
	38:20	*"They will* not **h** you *over*,"	5989
	43: 3	against us to **h** us *over* *to* the Babylonians,	928+3338+5989
	44:30	**h** Pharaoh Hophra king of Egypt *over*	928+3338+5989
	46:26	*I will* **h** them *over* to those	928+3338+5989
	48:16	"The fall of Moab *is* at **h**;	995+7940
	48:37	every **h** is slashed	3338
	51: 7	Babylon was a gold cup in the LORD's **h**;	3338
	51:25	"I will stretch out my **h** against you,	3338
La	2: 3	He has withdrawn his right **h** at	NIH
	2: 4	his right **h** is ready.	NIH
	2: 8	and did not withhold his **h** from destroying.	3338
	3: 3	he has turned his **h** against me again	3338
	4: 6	in a moment without a **h** turned to help her.	3338
Eze	1: 3	There the **h** of the LORD was upon him.	3338
	2: 9	I looked, and I saw a **h** stretched out to me.	3338
	3:14	with the strong **h** of the LORD upon me.	3338
	3:22	The **h** of the LORD was upon me there,	3338
	6:14	And I will stretch out my **h** against them	3338
	7:17	Every **h** will go limp,	3338
	7:21	*I will* **h** it all *over* as plunder	928+3338+5989
	8: 1	the **h** of the Sovereign LORD came	3338
	8: 3	like a **h** and took me by the hair of my head.	3338
	8:11	Each had a censer in his **h**,	3338
	9: 1	each with a weapon in his **h**."	3338
	9: 2	each with a deadly weapon in his **h**.	3338
	10: 7	of the cherubim reached out his **h** to the fire	3338
	11: 9	and **h** you *over* to foreigners	928+3338+5989
	13: 9	My **h** will be against	3338
	14: 9	and I will stretch out my **h** against him	3338
	14:13	by being unfaithful and I stretch out my **h**	3338
	16:27	So I stretched out my **h** against you	3338
	16:39	*I will* **h** you *over* to your lovers,	928+3338+5989
	17:18	Because he had given his **h** in pledge and	3338
	18: 8	He withholds his **h** from doing wrong	3338
	18:17	He withholds his **h** from sin	3338
	20: 5	I swore with uplifted **h** to the descendants	3338
	20: 5	With uplifted **h** I said to them,	3338
	20:15	with uplifted **h** I swore to them in the desert	3338

Eze	20:22	But I withheld my **h**,	3338

Eze 20:22 But I withheld my **h**, — 3338
20:23 with uplifted **h** I swore to them in the desert — 3338
20:33 with a mighty **h** and an outstretched arm — 3338
20:34 with a mighty **h** and an outstretched arm — 3338
20:42 the land I had sworn with uplifted **h** to give — 3338
21: 7 Every heart will melt and every **h** go limp; — 3338
21:11 to be grasped with the **h**; — 4090
21:11 made ready for the **h** of the slayer. — 3338
21:22 Into his right **h** will come the lot — NIH
21:31 *I will* **h** *you* over *to brutal men,* — 928+3338+5989
23:28 *about to* **h** *you* over *to those you hate,* — 928+3338+5989
23:31 so I will put her cup into your **h**. — 3338
25: 7 therefore I will stretch out my **h** against you — 3338
25:13 I will stretch out my **h** against Edom — 3338
25:14 I will take vengeance on Edom by the **h** — 3338
25:16 to stretch out my **h** against the Philistines, — 3338
30:10 of Egypt by the **h** *of* Nebuchadnezzar king — 3338
30:12 the **h** of foreigners I will lay waste the land — 3338
30:22 and make the sword fall from his **h**. — 3338
30:24 of Babylon and put my sword in his **h**, — 3338
30:25 when I put my sword into the **h** *of* the king — 3338
33:22 the **h** of the LORD was upon me, — 3338
35: 3 and I will stretch out my **h** against you — 3338
36: 7 I swear with uplifted **h** that the nations — 3338
37: 1 The **h** *of* the LORD was upon me, — 3338
37:17 so that they will become one in your **h**. — 3338
37:19 which is in Ephraim's **h**— — 3338
37:19 and they will become one in my **h**.' — 3338
38:12 and turn my **h** against the resettled ruins and — 3338
39: 3 strike the bow from your left **h** — 3338
39: 3 make your arrows drop from your right **h**. — 3338
39:21 the punishment I inflict and the **h** I lay — 3338
40: 1 on that very day the **h** *of* the LORD was — 3338
40: 3 a linen cord and a measuring rod in his **h**. — 3338
40: 5 in the man's **h** was six long cubits, — 3338
44:12 therefore I have sworn with uplifted **h** — 3338
47: 3 with a measuring line in his **h**, — 3338
47:14 with uplifted **h** to give it to your forefathers, — 3338
Da 1: 2 Jehoiakim king of Judah into his **h**, — 3338
3:15 be able to rescue you from my **h**?" — 10311
3:17 and he will rescue us from your **h**, O king. — 10311
4:35 No one can hold back his **h** or say to him: — 10311
5: 5 the fingers of a human **h** appeared — 10311
5: 5 The king watched the **h** as it wrote. — 10311+10589
5:23 the God who holds in his **h** your life — 10311
5:24 Therefore he sent the **h** that wrote — 10311+10589
9:15 with a mighty **h** and who made for yourself — 3338
10:10 A **h** touched me and set me trembling — 3338
11:41 of Ammon will be delivered from his **h**. — 3338
12: 7 lifted his right hand and his left hand — NIH
12: 7 lifted his right hand and his left **h** — NIH
Hos 9: 7 the days of reckoning *are* at **h**. — 995
11: 8 How can I **h** you over, Israel? — 4481
Joel 2: 1 It is **close at h**— — 7940
Am 1: 8 I will turn my **h** against Ekron, — 3338
5:19 though he entered his house and rested his **h** — 3338
7: 7 with a plumb line in his **h**. — 3338
9: 2 from there my **h** will take them. — 3338
Ob 1:14 nor **h** over their survivors in the day — 6037
Jnh 4:11 people who cannot tell their right **h** from their left, — NIH
Mic 4:10 the LORD will redeem you out of the **h** — 4090
5: 9 Your **h** will be lifted up in triumph — 3338
Hab 2:16 from the LORD's right **h** is coming around — NIH
3: 4 rays flashed from his **h**, — 3338
Zep 1: 4 "I will stretch out my **h** against Judah and — 3338
2:13 He will stretch out his **h** against the north — 3338
Zec 2: 1 a man with a measuring line in his **h**! — 3338
2: 9 I will surely raise my **h** against them so — 3338
4:10 the plumb line in the **h** *of* Zerubbabel. — 3338
8: 4 each with cane in **h** because of his age. — 3338
11: 6 "I will **h** everyone over to his neighbor — 928+3338+5162
13: 7 and I will turn my **h** against the little ones. — 3338
14:13 Each man will seize the **h** of another, — 3338
Mt 3:12 His winnowing fork is in his **h**, — 5931
5:25 or he *may* **h** *you* over to the judge, — 4140
5:25 and the judge may **h** you over to the officer, — NIG
5:30 And if your right **h** causes you to sin, — 5931
6: 3 do not let your **left h** know what your right hand is doing, — 754
6: 3 do not let your left hand know what your right **h** is doing, — 1288
8: 3 Jesus reached out his **h** and touched — 5931
8:15 He touched her **h** and the fever left her, — 5931
9:18 But come and put your **h** on her, — 5931
9:25 he went in and took the girl *by* the **h**, — 5931
10:17 they will **h** you over to the local councils — 4140
12:10 and a man with a shriveled **h** was there. — 5931
12:13 he said to the man, "Stretch out your **h**." — 5931
14:31 Immediately Jesus reached out his **h** — 5931
18: 8 If your **h** or your foot causes you to sin, — 5931
22:13 'Tie him **h** and foot, and throw him outside, — 5931
22:44 "Sit at my **right h** until I put your enemies — 1288
24:41 be grinding with a **h** mill; — 3685
26:15 to give me if I **h** him over to you?" — 4140
26:16 for an opportunity to **h** him over. — 4140
26:23 "The one who has dipped his **h** into — 5931
26:64 sitting at the **right h** of the Mighty One — 1288
27:29 They put a staff in his right **h** and knelt — 1288
Mk 1:31 took her **h** and helped her up. — 5931
1:41 Jesus reached out his **h** and touched — 5931
3: 1 and a man with a shriveled **h** was there. — 5931
3: 3 Jesus said to the man with the shriveled **h**, — 5931
3: 5 said to the man, "Stretch out your **h**." — 5931
3: 5 and his **h** was completely restored. — 5931

Mk 5: 4 he had often *been* **chained h** and foot, — 268+1313
5:41 He took her *by* the **h** and said to her, — 5931
7:32 they begged him to place his **h** on the man. — 5931
8:23 the blind man by the **h** and led him outside — 5931
9:27 But Jesus took him by the **h** and lifted him — 5931
9:43 If your **h** causes you to sin, cut it off. — 5931
10:33 and *will* **h** him over to the Gentiles, — 4140
12:36 "Sit at my **right h** until I put your enemies — 1288
14:11 for an opportunity to **h** him over. — 4140
14:62 sitting at the **right h** of the Mighty One — 1288
16:19 into heaven and he sat at the **right** h of God. — 1288
Lk 1:66 For the Lord's **h** was with him. — 5931
1:71 salvation from our enemies and from the **h** — 5931
1:74 to rescue us from the **h** of our enemies, — 5931
3:17 in his **h** to clear his threshing floor and — 5931
5:13 Jesus reached out his **h** and touched — 5931
6: 6 man was there whose right **h** was shriveled. — 5931
6: 8 and said to the man with the shriveled **h**, — 5931
6:10 "Stretch out your **h**." — 5931
6:10 and his **h** was completely restored. — 5931
8:29 though *he was* **chained h** and foot and — 268+1297
8:54 But he took her *by* the **h** and said, — 5931
9:62 "No one who puts his **h** to the plow — 5931
20:20 so that *they might* **h** him **over** to the power — 4140
20:42 "Sit at my **right h** — 1288
22: 6 for an opportunity to **h** Jesus **over** to them — 4140
22:21 the **h** of him who is going to betray me is — 5931
22:53 and you did not lay a **h** on me. — 5931
22:69 be seated at the **right h** of the mighty God." — 1288
Jn 7:30 but no one laid a **h** on him, — 5931
7:44 but no one laid a **h** on him. — 5931
10:12 The **hired h** is not the shepherd who owns — 3638
10:13 because he is a **hired h** and cares nothing — 3638
10:28 no one can snatch them out of my **h**. — 5931
10:29 no one can snatch them out of my Father's **h** — 5931
20:25 and put my **h** into his side, — 5931
20:27 Reach out your **h** and put it into my side. — 5931
Ac 2:25 he is at my **right h**, I will not be shaken. — 1288
2:33 Exalted *to* the **right h** of God, — 1288
2:34 "Sit at my **right h** — 1288
3: 7 Taking him by the right **h**, — 5931
4:30 Stretch out your **h** to heal — 5931
5:31 *to* his own **right h** as Prince and Savior — 1288
7:50 Has not my **h** made all these things?' — 5931
7:55 and Jesus standing at the **right h** of God. — 1288
7:56 and the Son of Man standing at the **right h** — 1288
9: 8 So they led him *by* the **h** into Damascus. — 5932
9:41 He took her *by* the **h** and helped her — 5931
11:21 The Lord's **h** was with them, — 5931
12:17 Peter motioned *with* his **h** for them to — 5931
13:11 Now the **h** of the Lord is against you. — 5931
13:11 someone to lead him *by* the **h**. — 5933
13:16 Paul motioned *with* his **h** and said: — 5931
21:11 *will* **h** him **over** to the Gentiles.' — 1650+4140+5931
22:11 My companions **led** me *by* the **h** — 5932
23:19 took the young man *by* the **h**, — 5931
25:11 no one has the right *to* **h** me **over** to them. — 5919
25:16 not the Roman custom *to* **h over** any man — 5919
26: 1 with his **h** and began his defense: — 5931
28: 3 fastened itself on his **h**. — 5931
28: 4 the snake hanging from his **h**, they said — 5931
Ro 8:34 at the **right h** of God and is also interceding — 1288
1Co 5: 5 **h** this man **over** to Satan, — 4140
12:15 the foot should say, "Because I am not a **h**, — 5931
12:21 The eye cannot say *to* the **h**, — 5931
16:21 I, Paul, write this greeting *in* my own **h**. — 5931
2Co 6: 7 weapons of righteousness *in* the **right h** and — 1288
Gal 2: 9 and Barnabas the **right h** of fellowship — 1288
6:11 as I write to you *with* my own **h**! — 5931
Eph 1:20 from the dead and seated him at his **right h** — 1288
Col 3: 1 where Christ is seated at the **right h** of God. — 1288
4:18 I, Paul, write this greeting *in* my own **h**. — 5931
2Th 3:17 I, Paul, write this greeting *in* my own **h**, — 5931
Phm 1:19 I, Paul, am writing this *with* my own **h**. — 5931
Heb 1: 3 he sat down at the **right h** of the Majesty — 1288
1:13 "Sit at my **right h** until I make your enemies a footstool — 1288
8: 1 a high priest, who sat down at the **right h** of — 1288
8: 9 when I took them *by* the **h** to lead them out — 5931
10:12 he sat down at the **right h** of God. — 1288
12: 2 sat down at the **right h** of the throne of God. — 1288
1Pe 3:22 into heaven and is at God's **right h**— — 1288
5: 6 therefore, under God's mighty **h**, — 5931
Rev 1:16 In his **right h** he held seven stars, — 5931
1:17 Then he placed his **right h** on me and said: — 1288
1:20 the seven stars that you saw in my **right h** — 1288
2: 1 the seven stars in his **right h** and walks — 1288
5: 1 Then I saw in the **right h** of him who sat on — 1288
5: 7 the scroll from the **right h** of him who sat — 1288
6: 5 a pair of scales in his **h**. — 5931
8: 4 went up before God from the angel's **h**. — 5931
10: 2 which lay open in his **h**. — 5931
10: 8 and on the land raised his right **h** to heaven. — 5931
10: 8 the **h** of the angel who is standing on the sea — 5931
10:10 the little scroll from the angel's **h** and ate it. — 5931
13:16 a mark on his right **h** or on his forehead, — 5931
14: 9 his mark on the forehead or on the **h**, — 5931
14:14 on his head and a sharp sickle in his **h**. — 5931
17: 4 She held a golden cup in her **h**, — 5931
20: 1 the key to the Abyss and holding in his **h** — 5931

HANDBREADTH (8) [HAND]

Ex 25:25 a **h** *wide* and put a gold molding on the rim. — 3256
37:12 a **h** wide and put a gold molding on the rim. — 3256
1Ki 7:26 It was a **h** in thickness, — 3255
2Ch 4: 5 It was a **h** in thickness, — 3255

Ps 39: 5 You have made my days a mere **h**; — 3257
Eze 40: 5 each of which was a cubit and a **h**. — 3256
40:43 And double-pronged hooks, each a **h** long, — 3256
43:13 that cubit being a cubit and a **h**: — 3256

HAND, HANDED (Anglicized) See also TURN, TURNED

HANDCRAFTED (Anglicized) See CRAFTED

HANDED (77) [HAND]

Ge 27:17 Then *she* **h** *to* her son Jacob the tasty food
Ex 32: 4 He took what they **h** him and made it into — 3338
Lev 9:12 His sons **h** him the blood, — 5162
9:13 *They* **h** him the burnt offering piece — 5162
9:18 His sons **h** him the blood, — 5162
Nu 21:34 for *I have* **h** him **over** to you, — 928+3338+5989
Dt 3: 2 for *I have* **h** him **over** to you — 928+3338+5989
Jos 10:32 LORD **h** Lachish **over** to Israel, — 928+3338+5989
21:44 **h** all their enemies **over** — 928+3338+5989
Jdg 2:14 the LORD **h** them **over** to raiders — 928+3338+5989
1Sa 23: 7 said, "God has **h** him **over** to me, — 928+3338+5796
30:23 and **h over** to us the forces that — 928+3338+5989
2Sa 3: 8 *I haven't* **h** *you* **over** to David. — 928+3338+5162
16: 8 LORD has **h** the kingdom **over** — 928+3338+5989
21: 9 **h** them **over** to the Gibeonites, — 928+3338+5989
2Ki 19:10 'Jerusalem *will not* be **h over** to the king of Assyria. — 928+3338+5989
1Ch 5:20 God **h** the Hagrites and all their allies **over** — 928+3338+5989
22:18 **h** the inhabitants of the land **over** — 928+3338+5989
2Ch 28: 5 the LORD his God **h** him **over** to the king of Aram. — 928+3338+5989
30:16 The priests sprinkled the blood **h** to them by — 3338
35:11 priests sprinkled the blood **h** *to them,* — 3338+4946
36:17 God **h** all of them **over** — 928+3338+5989
Ezr 5:12 he **h** them **over** to Nebuchadnezzar — 10089+10311+10314
Ne 9:24 **h** the Canaanites **over** to them, — 928+3338+5989
9:27 *you* **h** them **over** to their enemies — 928+3338+5989
9:30 so *you* **h** them **over** — 928+3338+5989
Ps 31: 8 *You have not* **h** me **over** to the enemy — 928+3338+6037
106:41 *He* **h** them **over** to the nations, — 928+3338+5989
Isa 37:10 'Jerusalem *will not* be **h over** to the king of Assyria. — 928+3338+5989
42:24 Who **h** Jacob **over** to become loot, — 5989
Jer 26:24 he *was not* **h over** to the people — 928+3338+5989
32: 4 but *will* **certainly** be **h over** to the king of Babylon, — 928+3338+5989+5989
32:24 the city *will* be **h over** to the Babylonians, — 928+3338+5989
32:25 the city *will* be **h over** to the Babylonians, — 928+3338+5989
32:36 *it will* be **h over** to the king — 928+3338+5989
32:43 for *it has been* **h over** to the Babylonians.' — 928+3338+5989
34: 3 surely be captured and **h over** — 928+3338+5989
37:17 "*you will* be **h over** to the king — 928+3338+5989
38: 3 'This city *will* **certainly** be **h over** *to the* army — 928+3338+5989+5989
38:18 this city *will* be **h over** to the Babylonians — 928+3338+5989
39:17 *you will not* be **h over** to those you fear. — 928+3338+5989
44:30 **h** Zedekiah king of Judah **over** — 928+3338+5989
46:24 **h over** to the people of the north."928+3338+5989
La 1:14 *He has* **h** me **over** to those — 928+3338+5989
2: 7 *He has* **h over** to the enemy the — 928+3338+6037
Eze 23: 9 *I* **h** her **over** to her lovers, — 928+3338+5989
31:11 *I* **h** it **over** to the ruler of the nations, — 5989
39:23 **h** them **over** to their enemies, — 928+3338+5989
Da 7:25 The saints *will* be **h over** to him for a time, — 10089+10311+10314
7:27 under the whole heaven *will* be **h over** to — 10314
11: 6 In those days she *will* be **h over**, — 5989
Mt 24: 9 be **h over** to be persecuted and put to death, — 4140
26: 2 of Man *will* be **h over** to be crucified." — 4140
27: 2 led him away and **h** him **over** to Pilate. — 4140
27:18 of envy that *they had* **h** Jesus **over** to him. — 4140
27:26 and **h** him **over** to be crucified. — 4140
Mk 7:13 by your tradition that *you have* **h down**. — 4140
13: 9 be **h over** to the local councils and flogged — 4140
15: 1 led him away and **h** him **over** to Pilate. — 4140
15:10 the chief priests *had* **h** Jesus **over** to him. — 4140
15:15 and **h** him **over** to be crucified. — 4140
Lk 1: 2 as *they were* **h down** to us by those who — 4140
4:17 The scroll of the prophet Isaiah *was* **h** — 2113
18:32 *He will* be **h over** to the Gentiles. — 4140
24:20 The chief priests and our rulers **h** him **over** — 4140
Jn 18:30 "*we would not have* **h** him **over** to you." — 4140
19:11 the one who **h** me **over** to you is guilty of — 4140
19:16 Finally Pilate **h** him **over** to them to — 4140
Ac 2:23 This man *was* **h over** to you — 1692
3:13 You **h** him **over** to be killed, — 4140
6:14 and change the customs Moses **h down** — 4140
22:33 the letter to the governor and Paul **over** — 4225
27: 1 Paul and some other prisoners *were* **h over** — 4140
28:17 *I was* arrested in Jerusalem and **h over** to — 4140
1Ti 1:20 whom *I have* **h over** to Satan to be taught — 4140
1Pe 1:18 **h down** to you *from* your forefathers, — 4261

HANDFUL (8) [HAND]

Lev	2: 2	The priest *shall* **take a h** of the fine flour	4850+7858+7859
	5:12	who *shall* **take a h** of it as	4850+7858+7859
	6:15	The priest is to take a **h** of fine flour and oil,	7859
	9:17	**took a h** of it and burned it on the altar	4090+4848
Nu	5:26	then *to* **take a h** of the grain offering as	7858
1Ki	17:12	a **h** *of* flour in a jar and a little oil in	4090+4850
	20:10	in Samaria to give each of my men a **h.**	9123
Ecc	4: 6	Better *one* **h** with tranquillity	4090+4850

HANDFULS (4) [HAND]

Ex	9: 8	"Take **h** of soot from a furnace	2908+4850
Lev	16:12	and **two h** of finely ground fragrant incense	2908+4850
Ecc	4: 6	with tranquillity than *two* **h** with toil	2908+4850
Eze	13:19	for a *few* **h** of barley and scraps of bread.	9123

HANDING (3) [HAND]

1Sa	23:20	for **h** him **over** *to* the king."	928+3338+6037
1Ki	18: 9	*are* **h** your servant **over** *to* Ahab	928+3338+5989
Ac	12: 4	**h** him **over** to be guarded by four squads	4140

HANDIWORK (1)

Isa	19:25	Assyria my **h,** and Israel my inheritance."	3338+5126

HANDKERCHIEFS (1)

Ac	19:12	so that even **h** and aprons	5051

HANDLE (10) [HANDLED, HANDLES, HANDLING]

Ex	18:18	you cannot **h** it alone.	6913
Jdg	3:22	Even the **h** sank in after the blade,	5896
2Sa	24: 9	able-bodied men *who could* **h** a sword,	8990
1Ch	5:18	able-bodied men *who could* **h** shield	5951
	8:40	of Ulam were brave warriors *who could* **h**	2005
	12: 8	ready for battle and *able to* **h** the shield	6885
	21: 5	men *who could* **h** a sword,	8990
2Ch	25: 5	*able to* **h** the spear and shield.	296
Eze	27:29	All *who* **h** the oars will abandon their ships;	9530
Col	2:21	"*Do* not **h**! Do not taste! Do not touch!"?	721

HANDLED (1) [HANDLE]

Jer	8: 8	the lying pen of the scribes *has* **h** it falsely?	6913

HANDLES (3) [HANDLE]

1Ki	7:34	Each stand had four **h,** one on each corner,	4190
SS	5: 5	on the **h** of the lock.	4090
2Ti	2:15	be ashamed and *who* **correctly h** the word	3982

HANDLING (1) [HANDLE]

Lk	16:11	not been trustworthy in **h** worldly wealth,	NIG

HANDMAID (KJV) See MAIDSERVANT, SERVANT

HANDMILL (1) [MILL]

Nu	11: 8	ground it in a **h** or crushed it in a mortar.	8160

HANDS (527) [HAND]

Ge	5:29	the labor and painful toil of our **h** caused by	3338
	9: 2	they are given into your **h.**	3338
	16: 6	"Your servant is in your **h,**" Abram said.	3338
	19:16	the **h** of his wife and of his two daughters	3338
	20: 5	with a clear conscience and clean **h.**"	4090
	24:18	the jar to her **h** and gave him a drink.	3338
	27:16	She also covered his **h** and the smooth part	3338
	27:22	but the **h** are the hands of Esau."	3338
	27:22	but the hands are the **h** of Esau."	3338
	27:23	for his **h** were hairy like those	3338
	31:42	and the toil of my **h,**	4090
	37:21	he tried to rescue him from their **h.**	3338
	37:27	to the Ishmaelites and not lay our **h** on him;	3338
Ex	9:29	I will spread out my **h** in prayer to	4090
	9:33	He spread out his **h** toward the LORD;	4090
	14:30	That day the LORD saved Israel from the **h**	3338
	15:17	the sanctuary, O Lord, your **h** established.	3338
	17: 9	of the hill with the staff of God in my **h.**"	3338
	17:11	As long as Moses held up his **h,**	3338
	17:11	but whenever he lowered his **h,**	3338
	17:12	When Moses' **h** grew tired,	3338
	17:12	Aaron and Hur held his **h** up—	3338
	17:12	so that his **h** remained steady till sunset.	3338
	17:16	**h** were lifted up to the throne of the LORD,	3338
	22: 8	to determine whether he has laid his **h** on	3338
	22:11	the LORD that the neighbor did not lay **h**	3338
	29:10	and his sons shall lay their **h** on its head.	3338
	29:15	and his sons shall lay their **h** on its head.	3338
	29:19	and his sons shall lay their **h** on its head.	3338
	29:20	on the thumbs of their right **h,**	3338
	29:24	the **h** of Aaron and his sons and wave them	4090
	29:25	Then take them from their **h** and burn them	3338
	30:19	to wash their **h** and feet with water from it.	3338
	30:21	they shall wash their **h** and feet so	3338
	32:15	the two tablets of the Testimony in his **h.**	3338
	32:19	and he threw the tablets out of his **h,**	3338
	34: 4	and he carried the two stone tablets in his **h.**	3338
	34:29	the two tablets of the Testimony in his **h,**	3338

Ex	35:25	with her **h** and brought what she had spun—	3338
	40:31	and his sons used it to wash their **h** and feet.	3338
Lev	4:15	to lay their **h** on the bull's head before	3338
	7:30	With his own **h** he is to bring	3338
	8:14	Aaron and his sons laid their **h** on its head.	3338
	8:18	Aaron and his sons laid their **h** on its head.	3338
	8:22	Aaron and his sons laid their **h** on its head.	3338
	8:24	on the thumbs of their right **h** and on	3338
	8:27	He put all these in the **h** of Aaron	4090
	8:28	from their **h** and burned them on the altar	4090
	9:22	Then Aaron lifted his **h** toward the people	3338
	15:11	a discharge touches without rinsing his **h**	3338
	16:21	to lay both **h** on the head of the live goat	3338
	24:14	who heard him are to lay their **h**	3338
	26:25	and you will be given into enemy **h.**	3338
Nu	5:18	he shall loosen her hair and place in her **h**	4090
	5:25	from her **h** the grain offering for jealousy,	3338
	6:19	in his **h** a boiled shoulder of the ram,	4090
	8:10	and the Israelites are to lay their **h** on them.	3338
	8:12	Levites lay their **h** on the heads of the bulls,	3338
	21: 2	"If you will deliver these people into our **h,**	3338
	24:10	He struck his **h** together and said to him,	4090
	27:23	he laid his **h** on him and commissioned him,	3338
Dt	1:27	into the **h** *of* the Amorites to destroy us.	3338
	2: 7	blessed you in all the work of your **h.**	3338
	2:30	in order to give him into your **h,**	3338
	3: 3	also gave into our **h** Og king of Bashan	3338
	6: 8	on your **h** and bind them on your foreheads.	3338
	8:17	of my **h** have produced this wealth for me."	3338
	9:15	two tablets of the covenant were in my **h.**	3338
	9:17	the two tablets and threw them out of my **h,**	3338
	10: 3	the mountain with the two tablets in my **h.**	3338
	11:18	on your **h** and bind them on your foreheads.	3338
	13: 9	and then the **h** of all the people.	3338
	13:17	in your **h,** so that the LORD will turn	3338
	14:29	in all the work of your **h.**	3338
	16:15	and in all the work of your **h,**	3338
	17: 7	The **h** of the witnesses must be the first	3338
	17: 7	and then the **h** of all the people.	3338
	21: 6	the town nearest the body shall wash their **h**	3338
	21: 7	"Our **h** did not shed this blood,	3338
	21:10	into your **h** and you take captives,	3338
	23:25	you may pick kernels with your **h,**	3338
	24:19	bless you in all the work of your **h.**	3338
	26: 4	The priest shall take the basket from your **h**	3338
	27:15	the work of the craftsman's **h—**	3338
	28:12	and to bless all the work of your **h,**	3338
	30: 9	of your **h** and in the fruit of your womb,	3338
	31:29	to anger by what your **h** have made."	3338
	33: 7	With his own **h** he defends his cause.	3338
	33:11	and be pleased with the work of his **h.**	3338
	34: 9	because Moses had laid his **h** of him.	3338
Jos	2:24	surely given the whole land into our **h;**	3338
	6: 2	"See, I have delivered Jericho into your **h,**	3338
	7: 7	across the Jordan to deliver us into the **h** of	3338
	8: 1	I have delivered into your **h** the king of Ai,	3338
	9:25	We are now in your **h.**	3338
	24: 8	but I gave them into your **h.**	3338
	24:11	but I gave them into your **h.**	3338
Jdg	1: 2	I have given the land into their **h.**"	3338
	1: 4	and Perizzites into their **h** and they struck	3338
	2:16	who saved them out of the **h**	3338
	2:18	with the judge and saved them out of the **h**	3338
	2:23	at once by giving them into the **h** of Joshua.	3338
	3: 8	against Israel so that he sold them into the **h**	3338
	3:10	king of Aram into the **h** of Othniel,	3338
	3:28	given Moab, your enemy, into your **h.**"	3338
	4: 2	the LORD sold them into the **h** of Jabin,	3338
	4: 7	and give him into your **h.**' "	3338
	4:14	the LORD has given Sisera into your **h.**	3338
	6: 1	and for seven years he gave them into the **h**	3338
	7: 2	for me to deliver Midian into their **h,**	3338
	7: 6	Three hundred men lapped with their **h.**	3338
	7: 7	and give the Midianites into your **h.**	3338
	7: 9	because I am going to give it into your **h.**	3338
	7:14	and the whole camp into his **h.**"	3338
	7:15	the Midianite camp into your **h.**"	3338
	7:16	he placed trumpets and empty jars in the **h**	3338
	7:19	and broke the jars that were in their **h.**	3338
	7:20	The torches in their left **h** and holding	3338
	7:20	in their right **h** the trumpets they were	3338
	8: 3	the Midianite leaders, into your **h.**	3338
	8: 6	"Do you already have the **h** of Zebah	4090
	8:15	'Do you already have the **h** of Zebah	4090
	8:34	the **h** *of* all their enemies on every side.	3338
	10: 7	the **h** of the Philistines and the Ammonites,	3338
	10:12	did I not save you from their **h?**	3338
	11:21	gave Sihon and all his men into Israel's **h,**	3338
	11:30	"If you give the Ammonites into my **h,**	3338
	11:32	and the LORD gave them into his **h.**	3338
	12: 2	you didn't save me out of their **h.**	3338
	12: 3	I took my life in my **h** and crossed over	4090
	13: 1	so the LORD delivered them into the **h** of	3338
	13: 5	of Israel from the **h** of the Philistines."	3338
	13:23	and grain offering from our **h,**	3338
	14: 6	so that he tore the lion apart with his bare **h**	3338
	14: 9	which he scooped out with his **h** and ate	4090
	15:14	and the bindings dropped from his **h.**	3338
	15:18	Must I now die of thirst and fall into the **h**	3338
	16:18	with the silver in their **h.**	3338
	16:23	delivered Samson, our enemy, into our **h.**"	4090
	16:24	into our **h,** the one who laid waste our land	4090
	18:10	that God has put into your **h,**	3338
	19:27	with her **h** on the threshold.	3338
	20:28	for tomorrow I will give them into your **h.**"	3338
1Sa	5: 4	His head and **h** had been broken off	3338+4090
	12: 9	and into the **h** of the Philistines	3338

1Sa	12:10	now deliver us from the **h** of our enemies,	3338
	12:11	from the **h** of your enemies on every side,	3338
	14:10	that the LORD has given them into our **h.**"	3338
	14:13	Jonathan climbed up, using his **h** and feet,	3338
	14:48	the **h** of those who had plundered them.	3338
	17:47	and he will give all of you into our **h.**"	3338
	18:25	Saul's plan was to have David fall by the **h**	3338
	19: 5	He took his life in his **h** when he killed	4090
	21:13	he was in their **h,** he acted like a madman,	3338
	23:14	but God did not give David into his **h.**	3338
	24: 4	'I will give your enemy into your **h** for you	3338
	24:10	how the LORD delivered you into my **h** in	3338
	24:18	the LORD delivered me into your **h,**	3338
	24:20	of Israel will be established in your **h.**	3338
	25:26	from avenging yourself with your own **h,**	3338
	25:33	and from avenging myself with my own **h.**	3338
	26: 8	God has delivered your enemy into your **h.**	3338
	26:23	The LORD delivered you into my **h** today,	3338
	28:17	the kingdom out of your **h** and given it	3338
	28:21	in my **h** and did what you told me to do.	4090
2Sa	3:34	Your **h** were not bound,	3338
	4:12	They cut off their **h** and feet and hung	3338
	16:21	and the **h** of everyone with you will	3338
	18:12	into my **h,** I would not lift my hand against	4090
	18:28	the men who lifted their **h** against my lord	3338
	21:22	and they fell at the **h** of David and his men.	3338
	22:21	the cleanness of my **h** he has rewarded me.	3338
	22:35	He trains my **h** for battle;	3338
	24:14	Let us fall into the **h** of the LORD,	3338
	24:14	but do not let me fall into the **h** of men."	3338
1Ki	2:46	now firmly established in Solomon's **h.**	3338
	8:22	spread out his **h** toward heaven	4090
	8:38	spreading out his **h** toward this temple—	4090
	8:54	with his **h** spread out toward heaven.	4090
	11:35	from his son's **h** and give you ten tribes.	3338
	20:28	I will deliver this vast army into your **h,**	3338
2Ki	3:11	He used to pour water on the **h** of Elijah."	3338
	4:34	mouth to mouth, eyes to eyes, **h** to hands.	4090
	4:34	mouth to mouth, eyes to eyes, hands to **h.**	4090
	9:35	her skull, her feet and her **h.**	3338+4090
	10:24	of the men I am placing in your **h** escape,	3338
	11:12	and the people clapped their **h** and shouted,	4090
	13:16	"Take the bow in your **h,**"	3338
	13:16	Elisha put his **h** on the king's hands.	3338
	13:16	Elisha put his hands on the king's **h.**	3338
	17:20	he afflicted them and gave them into the **h**	3338
	19:18	wood and stone, fashioned by men's **h.**	3338
	22:17	to anger by all the idols their **h** have made,	3338
1Ch	5:10	who were defeated at their **h;**	3338
	12:17	to my enemies when my **h** are free	4090
	20: 8	and they fell at the **h** of David and his men.	3338
	21:13	Let me fall into the **h** of the LORD,	3338
	21:13	but do not let me fall into the **h** of men."	3338
	29:12	In your **h** are strength and power to exalt	3338
2Ch	6: 4	with his **h** has fulfilled what he promised	3338
	6:12	of Israel and spread out his **h.**	4090
	6:13	and spread out his **h** toward heaven.	4090
	6:29	and pains, and spreading out his **h**	4090
	13: 8	which is in the **h** of David's descendants.	3338
	13:16	and God delivered them into their **h.**	3338
	23:18	of the temple of the LORD in the **h** of	3338
	24:24	the LORD delivered into their **h**	3338
	28: 5	also given into the **h** of the king of Israel,	3338
	29:23	and they laid their **h** on them.	3338
	32:19	the work of men's **h.**	3338
	34:25	to anger by all that their **h** have made,	3338
Ezr	8:33	and gold and the sacred articles into the **h**	3338
	9: 5	and fell on my knees with my **h** spread out	4090
	10: 4	Rise up; this matter is in your **h.**	6584
	10:19	(They all gave their **h** in pledge	3338
Ne	6: 9	"Their **h** will get too weak for the work,	3338
	6: 9	[But I prayed,] "Now strengthen my **h.**"	3338
	8: 6	all the people lifted their **h** and responded,	3338
	13:21	If you do this again, I will lay **h** on you."	3338
Est	9:10	But they did not lay their **h** on the plunder.	3338
	9:15	but they did not lay their **h** on the plunder.	3338
	9:16	but did not lay their **h** on the plunder.	3338
Job	1:10	You have blessed the work of his **h,**	3338
	1:12	then, everything he has is in your **h,**	3338
	2: 6	"Very well, then, he is in your **h;**	3338
	4: 3	how you have strengthened feeble **h.**	3338
	5:12	so that their **h** achieve no success.	3338
	5:18	he injures, but his **h** also heal.	3338
	8:20	a blameless man or strengthen the **h**	3338
	9:24	When a land falls into the **h** of the wicked,	3338
	9:30	with soap and my **h** with washing soda,	4090
	10: 3	to spurn the work of your **h,**	4090
	10: 8	"Your **h** shaped me and made me.	3338
	11:13	to him and stretch out your **h** to him,	4090
	12: 6	those who carry their god in their **h.**	3338
	13:14	in jeopardy and take my life in my **h?**	4090
	14:15	for the creature your **h** have made.	3338
	16:17	yet my **h** have been free of violence	4090
	17: 9	and those with clean **h** will grow stronger.	3338
	20:10	his own **h** must give back his wealth.	3338
	21:16	But their prosperity is not in their own **h,**	4090
	22:30	through the cleanness of your **h.**"	4090
	27:23	It claps its **h** in derision and hisses him out	4090
	29: 9	and covered their mouths with their **h.**	4090
	30: 2	Of what use was the strength of their **h**	3338
	31: 7	or if my **h** have been defiled,	4090
	34:19	the fortune my **h** had gained,	3338
	34:19	for they are all the work of his **h?**	3338
	34:37	**scornfully** he **claps** his **h** among us	6215
	36:32	He fills his **h** with lightning	4090
Ps	7: 3	if I have done this and there is guilt on my **h**	4090
	8: 6	made him ruler over the works of your **h;**	3338

Ps	9:16	wicked are ensnared by the work of their **h**.	4090
	18:20	the cleanness of my **h** he has rewarded me.	3338
	18:24	to the cleanness of my **h** in his sight.	3338
	18:34	He trains my **h** for battle;	3338
	19: 1	the skies proclaim the work of his **h**.	3338
	22:16	they have pierced my **h** and my feet.	3338
	24: 4	He who has clean **h** and a pure heart,	4090
	26: 6	I wash my **h** in innocence,	4090
	26:10	in whose **h** are wicked schemes,	3338
	26:10	whose right **h** are full of bribes.	NIH
	28: 2	I lift up my **h** toward your Most Holy Place.	3338
	28: 4	for what their **h** have done and bring back	3338
	28: 5	of the LORD and what his **h** have done,	3338
	31: 5	Into your **h** I commit my spirit;	3338
	31:15	My times are in your **h**;	3338
	44:20	the name of our God or spread out our **h** to	4090
	47: 1	Clap your **h**, all you nations;	4090
	58: 2	and your **h** mete out violence on the earth.	3338
	63: 4	and in your name I will lift up my **h**.	4090
	73:13	in vain have I washed my **h** in innocence.	4090
	76: 5	not one of the warriors can lift his **h**.	3338
	77: 2	at night I stretched out untiring **h**	3338
	78:61	his splendor into the **h** of the enemy.	3338
	78:72	with skillful **h** he led them.	4090
	81: 6	their **h** were set free from the basket.	4090
	88: 9	I spread out my **h** to you.	4090
	90:17	establish the work of our **h** for us—	3338
	90:17	yes, establish the work of our **h**.	3338
	91:12	they will lift you up in their **h**,	4090
	92: 4	I sing for joy at the works of your **h**.	3338
	95: 5	and his **h** formed the dry land.	3338
	98: 8	Let the rivers clap their **h**,	4090
	102:25	and the heavens are the work of your **h**.	3338
	111: 7	The works of his **h** are faithful and just;	3338
	115: 4	made by the **h** of men.	3338
	115: 7	they have **h**, but cannot feel, feet,	3338
	119:48	I lift up my **h** to your commands,	4090
	119:73	Your **h** made me and formed me;	3338
	119:109	Though I constantly take my life in my **h**,	4090
	125: 3	the righteous might use their **h** to do evil.	3338
	127: 4	in the **h** of a warrior are sons born	3338
	129: 7	with it the reaper cannot fill his **h**,	4090
	134: 2	Lift up your **h** in the sanctuary and praise	3338
	135:15	made by the **h** of men.	3338
	138: 8	do not abandon the works of your **h**.	3338
	140: 4	O LORD, from the **h** of the wicked;	3338
	141: 2	up of my **h** be like the evening sacrifice.	4090
	143: 5	and consider what your **h** have done.	3338
	143: 6	I spread out my **h** to you;	3338
	144: 1	who trains my **h** for war,	3338
	144: 7	the mighty waters, from the **h** of foreigners	3338
	144: 8	whose right **h** are deceitful.	NIH
	144:11	the **h** of foreigners whose mouths are full	3338
	144:11	whose right **h** are deceitful.	NIH
	149: 6	and a double-edged sword in their **h**,	3338
Pr	6: 1	if you have struck **h** in pledge for another,	4090
	6: 3	you have fallen into your neighbor's **h**:	4090
	6:10	a little folding of the **h** to rest—	3338
	6:17	a lying tongue, **h** that shed innocent blood,	3338
	10: 4	Lazy **h** make a man poor,	4090
	10: 4	but diligent **h** bring wealth.	3338
	11:15	to **strike h in pledge** is safe.	9364
	12:14	as surely as the work of his **h** rewards him.	3338
	12:24	Diligent **h** will rule,	3338
	14: 1	but with her own **h** the foolish one tears	3338
	17:18	in judgment strikes **h** in pledge and puts	4090
	21:25	because his **h** refuse to work.	3338
	22:26	not be a man who strikes **h** in pledge or puts	4090
	24:33	a little folding of the **h** to rest—	3338
	30: 4	up the wind in the **hollow of** his **h**?	2908
	31:13	and flax and works with eager **h**.	4090
	31:20	to the poor and extends her **h** to the needy.	3338
Ecc	2:11	Yet when I surveyed all that my **h** had done	3338
	4: 5	The fool folds his **h** and ruins himself.	3338
	5: 6	and destroy the work of your **h**?	3338
	7:26	a trap and whose **h** are chains.	3338
	9: 1	the wise and what they do are in God's **h**,	3338
	10:18	if his **h** are idle, the house leaks.	3338
	11: 6	and at evening let not your **h** be idle,	3338
SS	5: 5	and my **h** dripped with myrrh,	3338
	7: 1	the work of a craftsman's **h**.	3338
Isa	1:15	When you spread out your **h** in prayer,	4090
	1:15	Your **h** are full of blood;	3338
	2: 6	the Philistines and **clasp h** with pagans.	8562
	2: 8	they bow down to the work of their **h**,	3338
	3:11	be paid back for what their **h** have done.	3338
	5:12	no respect for the work of his **h**.	3338
	11:14	They will lay **h** on Edom and Moab,	3338
	13: 7	Because of this, all **h** will go limp,	3338
	17: 8	the altars, the work of their **h**,	3338
	25:11	They will spread out their **h** in it,	3338
	25:11	as a swimmer spreads out his **h** to swim.	NIH
	25:11	despite the cleverness of their **h**.	3338
	29:23	their children, the work of my **h**,	3338
	31: 7	of silver and gold your sinful **h** have made.	3338
	35: 3	Strengthen the feeble **h**,	3338
	37:19	wood and stone, fashioned by human **h**.	3338
	41: 2	He **h** nations **over** to him and subdues kings	5989
	45: 9	Does your work say, 'He has no **h**'?	3338
	45:11	or give me orders about the work of my **h**?	3338
	45:12	My own **h** stretched out the heavens;	3338
	49:16	I have engraved you on the **palms of** my **h**;	4090
	51:23	I will put it into the **h** of your tormentors,	3338
	55:12	and all the trees of the field will clap their **h**.	4090
	59: 3	For your **h** are stained with blood,	4090
	59: 6	and acts of violence are in their **h**.	4090
	60:21	shoot I have planted, the work of my **h**,	3338

Isa	65: 2	All day long I have held out my **h** to	3338
	65:22	will long enjoy the works of their **h**.	3338
Jer	1:16	and in worshiping what their **h** have made.	3338
	2:37	You will also leave that place with your **h**	3338
	4:31	stretching out her **h** and saying, "Alas!	4090
	6:24	and our **h** hang limp.	3338
	11:21	of the LORD or you will die by our **h**'—	3338
	12: 7	the one I love into the **h** of her enemies.	4090
	15: 6	So I will lay **h** on you and destroy you;	3338
	15:21	the **h** of the wicked and redeem you from	3338
	18: 4	from the clay was marred in his **h**;	3338
	19: 7	at the **h** of those who seek their lives,	3338
	20:13	He rescues the life of the needy from the **h**	3338
	21: 4	the weapons of war that are in your **h**,	3338
	21:10	be given into the **h** of the king of Babylon,	3338
	23:14	They strengthen the **h** of evildoers,	3338
	25: 6	to anger with what your **h** have made.	3338
	25: 7	with what your **h** have made,	3338
	25:14	to their deeds and the work of their **h**."	3338
	26:14	As for me, I am in your **h**;	3338
	30: 6	with his **h** on his stomach like a woman	3338
	32: 4	the **h** of the Babylonians but will certainly	3338
	32:30	with what their **h** have made,	3338
	38: 5	"He is in your **h**," King Zedekiah answered.	3338
	38:18	you yourself will not escape from their **h**.'"	3338
	38:23	from their **h** but will be captured by the king	3338
	42:11	and deliver you from his **h**.	3338
	44: 8	to anger with what your **h** have made,	3338
	47: 3	their **h** will hang limp.	3338
	50:43	and his **h** hang limp.	3338
La	1: 7	When her people fell into enemy **h**,	3338
	1:10	The enemy laid **h** on all her treasures;	3338
	1:14	by his **h** they were woven together.	3338
	1:17	Zion stretches out her **h**,	3338
	2:15	All who pass your way clap their **h** at you;	4090
	2:19	Lift up your **h** to him for the lives	4090
	3:41	up our hearts and our **h** to God in heaven,	4090
	3:64	O LORD, for what their **h** have done.	3338
	4: 2	the work of a potter's **h**!	3338
	4:10	With their own **h** compassionate women	
		have cooked their own children,	3338
	5: 8	and there is none to free us from their **h**.	3338
	5: 8	Princes have been hung up by their **h**;	3338
Eze	1: 8	on their four sides they had the **h** of a man.	3338
	6:11	Strike your **h** together and stamp your feet	4090
	7:27	the **h** of the people of the land will tremble.	3338
	10: 2	Fill your **h** with burning coals from among	2908
	10: 7	He took up some of it and put it into the **h**	2908
	10: 8	be seen what looked like the **h** of a man.)	3338
	10:12	their backs, their **h** and their wings,	3338
	10:21	what looked like the **h** of a man.	3338
	12: 7	through the wall with my **h**.	3338
	13:21	and save my people from your **h**,	3338
	13:23	I will save my people from your **h**.	3338
	21:14	and strike your **h together**.	448+4090+4090
	21:17	I too will strike my **h together**,	448+4090+4090
	22:13	" 'I will surely strike my **h** together at	4090
	22:14	or your **h** be strong in the day I deal	3338
	23:37	and blood is on their **h**.	3338
	23:45	they are adulterous and blood is on their **h**.	3338
	25: 6	Because you have clapped your **h**	3338
	28: 9	not a god, in the **h** of those who slay you.	3338
	28:10	of the uncircumcised at the **h** of foreigners.	3338
	29: 7	When they grasped you with their **h**,	4090
	34:27	of their yoke and rescue them from the **h**	3338
	48:14	of the land and **must** not **pass into other h**,	6296
Da	2:34	a rock was cut out, but not by human **h**.	10311
	2:38	in your **h** he has placed mankind and	10311
	2:45	but not by human **h**—	10311
	10:10	set me trembling on my **h** and knees.	3338+4090
Hos	2:10	no one will take her out of my **h**.	3338
	7: 5	and he joins **h** with the mockers.	3338
	14: 3	to what our own **h** have made,	3338
Mic	5:13	down to the work of your **h**.	3338
	7: 3	Both **h** are skilled in doing evil;	4090
	7:16	They will lay their **h** on their mouths	3338
Na	3:19	the news about you claps his **h** at your fall,	4090
Zep	3:16	do not let your **h** hang limp.	3338
Hag	1:11	and on the labor of your **h**."	4090
	2:17	I struck all the work of your **h** with blight,	3338
Zec	4: 9	"The **h** of Zerubbabel have laid the	3338
	4: 9	his **h** will also complete it.	3338
	8: 9	let your **h** be strong so that the temple may	3338
	8:13	Do not be afraid, but let your **h** be strong."	3338
	11: 6	and I will not rescue them from their **h**."	3338
Mal	1: 9	With such offerings from your **h**,	3338
	1:10	"and I will accept no offering from your **h**.	3338
	1:13	should I accept them from your **h**?"	3338
	2:13	or accepts them with pleasure from your **h**.	3338
Mt	4: 6	and they will lift you up in their **h**,	5931
	15: 2	They don't wash their **h** before they eat!"	5931
	15:20	but eating with unwashed **h** does	5931
	16:21	and suffer many things at the **h** of	608
	17:12	the Son of Man is going to suffer **at their h**."	899+5679
	17:22	"The Son of Man is going to be betrayed into the **h**	5931
	18: 8	or crippled than to have two **h** or two feet	5931
	19:13	to place his **h** on them and pray for them.	5931
	19:15	When he had placed his **h** on them,	5931
	26:45	and the Son of Man is betrayed into the **h**	5931
	27:24	he took water and washed his **h** in front of	5931
Mk	5:23	Please come and put your **h** on her so	5931
	6: 5	except lay his **h** on a few sick people	5931
	7: 2	saw some of his disciples eating food **with h**	5931
	7: 3	the Jews do not eat unless they give their **h**	5931
	7: 5	of eating their food **with** 'unclean' **h**?"	5931

Mk	8:23	on the man's eyes and put his **h** on him,	5931
	8:25	Jesus put his **h** on the man's eyes.	5931
	9:31	is going to be betrayed into the **h** of men.	5931
	9:43	for you to enter life maimed than with two **h**	5931
	10:16	put his **h** on them and blessed them.	5931
	14:41	the Son of Man is betrayed into the **h** of sinners.	5931
	16:18	they will pick up snakes with their **h**;	5931
	16:18	they will place their **h** on sick people,	5931
Lk	4:11	they will lift you up in their **h**,	5931
	4:40	and laying his **h** on each one,	5931
	6: 1	rub them **in** their **h** and eat the kernels.	5931
	9:44	of Man is going to be betrayed into the **h**	5931
	10:30	when **he fell into the h** of robbers.	4346
	10:36	to the man who fell into the **h** of robbers?"	NIG
	13:13	Then he put his **h** on her,	5931
	21:12	they will lay **h** on you and persecute you.	5931
	23:46	"Father, into your **h** I commit my spirit."	5931
	24: 7	be delivered into the **h** of sinful men,	5931
	24:39	Look at my **h** and my feet.	5931
	24:40	he showed them his **h** and feet.	5931
	24:50	he lifted up his **h** and blessed them.	5931
Jn	3:35	the Son and has placed everything in his **h**.	5931
	11:44	his **h** and feet wrapped with strips of linen,	5931
	13: 9	"not just my feet but my **h** and my head	5931
	20:20	he showed them his **h** and side.	5931
	20:25	the nail marks in his **h** and put my finger	5931
	20:27	"Put your finger here; see my **h**.	5931
	21:18	you are old you will stretch out your **h**,	5931
Ac	6: 6	who prayed and laid their **h** on them.	5931
	7:41	in honor of what their **h** had made.	5931
	8:17	Then Peter and John placed their **h** on them,	5931
	8:18	at the laying on of the apostles' **h**,	5931
	8:19	on whom I lay my **h** may receive	5931
	9:12	a man named Ananias come and place his **h**	5931
	9:17	Placing his **h** on Saul, he said,	5931
	13: 3	they placed their **h** on them	5931
	17:24	and does not live in temples **built by h**.	5935
	17:25	And he is not served by human **h**,	5931
	19: 6	When Paul placed his **h** on them,	5931
	20:34	You yourselves know that these **h**	5931
	21:11	tied his own **h** and feet with it and said,	5931
	27:19	ship's tackle overboard **with** their own **h**.	901
	28: 8	placed his **h** on him and healed him.	5931
Ro	10:21	"All day long I have held out my **h** to	5931
1Co	4:12	We work hard **with** our own **h**.	5931
	15:24	when he **h over** the kingdom to God	4140
2Co	5: 1	house in heaven, not **built by human h**.	942
	11:33	in the wall and slipped through his **h**.	5931
Eph	2:11	**done** in the body by the **h** of men)—	5935
	4:28	doing something useful **with** his own **h**,	5931
Col	2:11	**not** with a circumcision **done by the h of men**	942
1Th	4:11	and to work **with** your **h**,	5931
1Ti	2: 8	I want men everywhere to lift up holy **h**	5931
	4:14	when the body of elders laid their **h** on you.	5931
	5:22	Do not be hasty in the laying on of **h**,	5931
2Ti	1: 6	in you through the laying on of my **h**,	5931
Heb	1:10	and the heavens are the work of your **h**.	5931
	6: 2	about baptisms, the laying on of **h**,	5931
	10:31	It is a dreadful thing to fall into the **h** of	5931
Jas	4: 8	Wash your **h**, you sinners,	5931
1Jn	1: 1	at and our **h** have touched—	5931
Rev	7: 9	and were holding palm branches in their **h**.	5931
	9:20	not repent of the work of their **h**;	5931
	20: 4	on their foreheads or their **h**.	5931

HANDSOME (11) [HANDSOMELY]

Ge	39: 6	Now Joseph was well-built and **h**,	3637+5260
1Sa	16:12	with a fine appearance and **h** features.	3202
	17:42	ruddy and **h**, and he despised him.	3637+5260
2Sa	14:25	so highly praised for his **h appearance**	3637
1Ki	1: 6	He was also very **h** and was born next	3202+9307
SS	1:16	How **h** you are, my lover!	3637
Eze	23: 6	all of them **h** young men,	2774
	23:12	mounted horsemen, all **h** young men.	2774
	23:23	the Assyrians with them, **h** young men, all	2774
Da	1: 4	**h**, showing aptitude for every kind	3202+5260
Zec	11:13	the **h** price at which they priced me!	159

HANDSOMELY (2) [HANDSOME]

Nu	22:17	because I **will reward** you **h**	3877+3877+4394
	24:11	I said I **would reward** you **h**,	3877+3877

HANDSTAVES (KJV) See WAR CLUB

HANDWRITTEN (KJV) See WRITTEN

HANDYWORK (KJV) See WORK OF HIS HANDS

HANES (1)

Isa	30: 4	in Zoan and their envoys have arrived in **H**,	2865

HANG (16) [HANGED, HANGING, HANGINGS, HANGS, HUNG, OVERHANG, OVERHANGING, OVERHANGS]

Ge	40:19	will lift off your head and **h** you on a tree.	9434
Ex	26:12	that is left over **is to h down** at the rear of	6243
	26:13	what is left **will h** over the sides of	6243

Ex	26:32	H it *with* gold hooks on four posts	5989
	26:33	H the curtain from the clasps and place	5989
Est	7: 9	The king said, "H him on it!"	9434
Job	37:16	Do you know how the clouds **h** poised,	5146
Pr	26: 7	a lame man's legs *that* **h** limp is a proverb	1927
SS	4: 4	on it **h** a thousand shields,	9434
Isa	22:24	All the glory of his family *will* **h** on him:	9434
Jer	6:24	and our hands **h** limp.	8332
	47: 3	their hands will **h** limp.	8342
	50:43	and his hands **h** limp.	8332
Eze	15: 3	Do they make pegs from it to **h** things on?	9434
Zep	3:16	*do not let* your hands **h** limp.	8332
Mt	22:40	All the Law and the Prophets **h**	*3203*

HANGED (11) [HANG]

Ge	40:22	but he **h** the chief baker,	9434
	41:13	and the other man *was* **h**."	9434
2Sa	17:23	in order and then **h** himself.	2871
Est	2:23	the two officials were **h** on a gallows.	9434
	5:14	in the morning *to have* Mordecai **h**	9434
	7:10	So they **h** Haman on the gallows he had	9434
	8: 7	and they have **h** him on the gallows.	9434
	9:13	*let* Haman's ten sons be **h** on gallows."	9434
	9:14	and they **h** the ten sons of Haman.	9434
	9:25	he and his sons *should be* **h** on the gallows.	9434
Mt	27: 5	Then *he* went away and **h** himself.	*551*

HANGING (10) [HANG]

Jos	10:26	they were *left* **h** on the trees until evening.	9434
1Sa	25:17	because disaster is **h** over our master	3983
2Sa	18: 9	He was left **h** in midair,	5989
	18:10	"I just saw Absalom **h** in an oak tree."	9434
Est	6: 4	to speak to the king about **h** Mordecai on	9434
Isa	22:25	and the load **h** on it will be cut down."	6584
Ac	5:30	whom you killed *by* **h** him on a tree.	*3203*
	10:39	They killed him *by* **h** him on a tree,	*3203*
	28: 4	the islanders saw the snake **h** from his hand,	*3203*
2Pe	2: 3	Their condemnation has long been **h**	*NIG*

HANGINGS (1) [HANG]

Est	1: 6	**h** of white and blue **linen,**	4158

HANGS (1) [HANG]

Isa	33:23	Your rigging **h** loose:	5759

HANIEL (KJV) See HANNIEL

HANNAH (14)

1Sa	1: 2	one was called **H** and the other Peninnah.	2839
	1: 2	Peninnah had children, but **H** had none.	2839
	1: 5	But to **H** he gave a double portion	2839
	1: 7	Whenever **H** went up to the house of	2023S
	1: 8	Elkanah her husband would say to her, "**H**,	2839
	1: 9	eating and drinking in Shiloh, **H** stood up.	2839
	1:10	bitterness of soul **H** wept much and prayed	2085S
	1:13	**H** was praying in her heart,	2839
	1:15	"Not so, my lord," **H** replied,	2839
	1:19	Elkanah lay with **H** his wife,	2839
	1:20	**H** conceived and gave birth to a son.	2839
	1:22	**H** did not go.	2839
	2: 1	Then **H** prayed and said:	2839
	2:21	And the LORD was gracious to **H**;	2839

HANNATHON (1)

Jos	19:14	the boundary went around on the north to **H**	2872

HANNIEL (2)

Nu	34:23	**H** son of Ephod, the leader from the tribe	2848
1Ch	7:39	The sons of Ulla: Arah, **H** and Rizia.	2848

HANOCH (6) [HANOCHITE]

Ge	25: 4	The sons of Midian were Ephah, Epher, **H**,	2840
	46: 9	**H**, Pallu, Hezron and Carmi.	2840
Ex	6:14	of Reuben the firstborn son of Israel were **H**	2840
Nu	26: 5	through **H**, the Hanochite clan;	2840
1Ch	1:33	Ephah, Epher, **H**, Abida and Eldaah.	2840
	5: 3	**H**, Pallu, Hezron and Carmi.	2840

HANOCHITE (1) [HANOCH]

Nu	26: 5	through Hanoch, the **H** clan;	2854

HANUN (13)

2Sa	10: 1	and his son **H** succeeded him as king.	2842
	10: 2	"I will show kindness to **H** son of Nahash,	2842
	10: 2	a delegation to express his sympathy to **H**	NIH
	10: 3	the Ammonite nobles said to **H** their lord,	2842
	10: 4	So **H** seized David's men,	2842
1Ch	19: 2	"I will show kindness to **H** son of Nahash,	2842
	19: 2	a delegation to express his sympathy to **H**	2257S
	19: 2	When David's men came to **H** in the land of	2842
	19: 3	the Ammonite nobles said to **H**,	3842
	19: 4	So **H** seized David's men, shaved them,	2842
	19: 6	**H** and the Ammonites sent	2842
Ne	3:13	The Valley Gate was repaired by **H** and	2842
	3:30	Hananiah son of Shelemiah, and, **H**,	2842

HAP (KJV) See AS IT TURNED OUT

HAPHARAIM (1)

Jos	19:19	**H**, Shion, Anaharath,	2921

HAPLY (KJV) See BETTER, FIND, PERHAPS

HAPPEN (57) [HAPPENED, HAPPENING, HAPPENS]

Ge	49: 1	so I can tell you what *will* **h** to you in days	7925
Ex	2: 4	at a distance to see what *would* **h** to him.	6913
	21:13	but God lets *it* **h**,	628+3338+4200
1Ki	14: 3	He will tell you what *will* **h** to the boy.	2118
2Ki	7: 2	floodgates of the heavens, *could* this **h**?"	2118
	7:19	floodgates of the heavens, *could* this **h**?"	2118
Ecc	3:22	For who can bring him to see what *will* **h**	2118
	6:12	Who can tell him what *will* **h** under the sun	2118
	9:11	but time and chance **h** to them all.	7936
	10:14	who can tell him what *will* **h** after him?	2118
Isa	7: 7	" 'It will not take place, *it* will not **h**,	2118
	23:15	*it will* **h** to Tyre as in the song of	2118
	41:22	in [your idols] to tell us what *is going to* **h**.	7936
	47: 7	or reflect on **what** might **h**.	344
Jer	6:18	observe, O witnesses, what will **h** to them.	NIH
La	3:37	and have it **h** if the Lord has not decreed it?	2118
Eze	16:16	*Such things* should not **h**,	995
	20:32	But what you have in mind *will* never **h**.	2118
	38:18	*This is what will* **h** in that day:	2118
Da	2:28	He has shown King Nebuchadnezzar what	
		will **h** in days to come.	10201
	2:29	mysteries showed you what *is going to* **h**.	10201
	8:19	"I am going to tell you what *will* **h** later in	2118
	10:14	to you what *will* **h** to your people in	7936
Hos	10:15	Thus *will it* **h** to you, O Bethel,	6913
Am	7: 3	"*This will* not **h**," the LORD said.	2118
	7: 6	"This *will* not **h** either,"	2118
Jnh	4: 5	in its shade and waited to see what *would* **h**	2118
Zec	6:15	*This will* **h** if you diligently obey	2118
Mt	16:22	"This *shall* never **h** to you!"	*1639*
	24: 3	"Tell us," they said, "when *will* this **h**,	*1639*
	24: 6	Such things must **h**,	*1181*
	24:39	and they knew nothing about what would **h**	*NIG*
	26:54	the Scriptures be fulfilled that say it must **h**	*1181*
Mk	10:32	and told them what was going to **h** to him.	*5201*
	11:23	but believes that what he says *will* **h**,	*1181*
	13: 4	when *will* these things **h**?	*1639*
	13: 7	Such things must **h**, but the end is still	*1181*
Lk	21: 7	they asked, "when *will* these things **h**?	*1639*
	21: 9	These things must **h** first,	*1181*
	21:36	be able to escape all that is about to **h**,	*1181*
	22:49	Jesus' followers saw what *was going to* **h**,	*1639*
	23:31	what *will* **h** when it is dry?"	*1181*
Jn	5:14	Stop sinning or something worse *may* **h**	*1181*
	13:19	*it does* **h** you will believe that I am He.	*1181*
	14:29	so that when *it does* **h** you will believe.	*1181*
	18: 4	knowing all that *was* **going** to **h** to him,	*2262*
Ac	4:28	and will had decided beforehand *should* **h**.	*1181*
	8:24	so that nothing you have said *may* **h** to me."	*2088*
	13:40	what the prophets have said *does* not **h** to	*2088*
	20:22	not knowing what *will* **h** to me there.	*5267*
	26:22	the prophets and Moses said would **h**—	*1181*
	27:25	for I have faith in God that *it will* **h** just	*1639*
	28: 6	a long time and seeing nothing unusual **h**	*1181*
Ro	9:26	"It will **h** that in the very place	*1639*
2Th	1: 7	This will **h** when the Lord Jesus is revealed	*NIG*
Jas	4:14	not even know **what** will **h** tomorrow.	*3836+4481*
2Pe	2: 6	of what is *going to* **h** to the ungodly;	*3516*

HAPPENED (109) [HAPPEN]

Ge	20: 8	and when he told them all that had **h**,	
			465+1821+2021+2021
	34: 7	the fields as soon as they heard what had **h**.	NIH
	42:29	they told him all that had **h** to them.	7936
Ex	32: 1	we don't know what *has* **h** to him."	2118
	32:23	we don't know what *has* **h** to him.'	2118
Lev	10:19	but such things as this *have* **h** to me.	7925
Nu	31:16	from the LORD in what **h** at Peor,	1821
Dt	4:30	in distress and all these things *have* **h**	5162
	4:32	*Has* anything so great as this *ever* **h**,	2118
Jos	2:23	and told him everything that *had* **h** to them.	5162
Jdg	6:13	why *has* all this **h** to us?	5162
	6:38	And that *is what* **h**.	2118
	20: 3	"Tell us how this awful thing **h**."	2118
	21: 3	they cried, "why *has* this **h** to Israel?	2118
1Sa	4: 7	Nothing like this *has* **h** before.	2118
	4:13	man entered the town and told what had **h**,	NIH
	4:16	Eli asked, "What **h**, my son?"	2118
	6: 9	not his hand that struck us but that *it* **h** to us	2118
	10:11	"What is this *that has* **h** to the son of Kish?	2118
	20:26	"**Something** must have **h** to David	5247
2Sa	1: 4	"What **h**?" David asked.	2118
	1: 6	"*I* **h** to be on Mount Gilboa,"	7925+7936
	13:35	*it has* **h** just as your servant said."	2118
	18: 9	Now Absalom **h** to meet David's men.	7925
	20: 1	a Benjamite, **h** to be there.	7925
2Ki	7:14	So let us send them to find out what **h**."	NIH
	7:17	"Go and find out what has **h**."	NIH
	7:18	*It* **h** as the man of God had said to	2118
	7:20	that is exactly *what* **h** to him.	2118
	9:27	Ahaziah king of Judah saw what had **h**,	NIH
	18:12	This **h** because they had not obeyed	NIH
	24: 3	Surely *these things* **h** to Judah according to	2118

HAPPENING (10) [HAPPEN]

Ge	25:22	and she said, "Why is this **h** to me?"	NIH
1Sa	5: 7	When the men of Ashdod saw what was **h**,	4027S
Ne	6: 8	"Nothing like what you are saying *is* **h**;	2118
Est	2:11	to find out how Esther was and what *was* **h**	6913
Mk	14:29	Even so, when you see these things **h**,	*1181*
Lk	18:36	he asked what was **h**.	*4047S*
	21:31	Even so, when you see these things **h**,	*1181*
Ac	12: 9	that what the angel was doing was really **h**;	*1181*
Col	4: 9	They will tell you everything that is **h** here.	*NIG*
1Pe	4:12	as though something strange *were* **h** to you.	*5201*

HAPPENS (17) [HAPPEN]

Ex	22: 3	but if it **h** after sunrise,	NIH
Nu	16:29	experience only **what** usually **h**	7213
Dt	22:23	a man **h** *to meet* in a town a virgin pledged	AIT
	22:25	a man **h** *to meet* a girl pledged to be married	AIT
	22:28	a man **h** *to meet* a virgin who is not pledged	AIT
Ru	3:18	my daughter, until you find out what **h**.	5877
1Sa	2:34	" 'And what **h** to your two sons,	995
2Sa	14:20	he knows everything that **h** in the land."	2118
Ecc	9: 3	the evil in everything that **h** under the sun:	6913
	9: 6	a part in anything that **h** under the sun.	6913
Isa	48:16	at the time it **h**, I am there."	2118
Jer	12: 4	"He will not see **what** **h** to us."	344
Eze	24:24	When this **h**, you will know that I am	995

2Ki	24:20	anger that *all this* **h** to Jerusalem and Judah,	2118
Ezr	9:13	"What *has* **h** to us is a result	995
Ne	9:33	In all that *has* **h** to us, you have been just;	995
Est	1: 1	*This is what* **h** during the time of Xerxes,	2118
	4: 7	Mordecai told him everything that *had* **h**	7936
	6:13	and all his friends everything that *had* **h**	7936
	9:17	This **h** on the thirteenth day of the month	NIH
	9:26	of what they had seen and what *had* **h**	5595
Job	3:25	what I dreaded *has* **h** to me.	995
Ps	44:17	All this **h** *to* us,	995
Isa	20: 6	'See **what** *has* **h** *to* those we relied on,	3907
	44: 7	and lay out before me **what** *has* **h**	2023S
	48: 5	before *they* **h** I announced them to you so	995
Jer	5:30	"A horrible and shocking thing *has* **h** in	2118
	13:22	"Why *has* this **h** to me?"—	7925
	32:24	What you said *has* **h**, as you now see.	2118
	40: 3	All this **h** because you people sinned against	2118
	48:19	ask them, 'What *has* **h**?'	2118
	52: 3	that *all this* **h** to Jerusalem and Judah,	2118
La	4:13	But it **h** because of the sins of her prophets	NIH
	5: 1	Remember, O LORD, what *has* **h** to us;	2118
Eze	16:19	*That is what* **h**, declares the Sovereign	2118
Da	4:28	All this **h** to King Nebuchadnezzar.	10413
	12: 1	be a time of distress such as *has* not **h** from	2118
Joel	1: 2	*Has* anything like this *ever* **h** in your days or	2118
Mt	8:33	including **what** had **h** to the	*3836*
	14:13	When Jesus heard what had **h**,	*NIG*
	18:31	When the other servants saw what had **h**,	*1181*
	18:31	and told their master everything that had **h**.	*1181*
	22:26	The same thing **h** to the second and third	*NIG*
	24:34	not pass away until all these things have **h**.	*1181*
	27:54	the earthquake and all that had **h**,	*1181*
	28:11	to the chief priests everything that had **h**.	*1181*
Mk	5:14	the people went out to see what had **h**.	*1181+1639*
	5:16	told the people what had **h** to	*1181*
	5:33	the woman, knowing what had **h** to her,	*1181*
	13:30	not pass away until all these things have **h**.	*1181*
Lk	2:15	to Bethlehem and see this thing that has **h**,	*1181*
	8:34	those tending the pigs saw what had **h**,	*1181*
	8:35	and the people went out to see what had **h**.	*1181*
	8:56	not to tell anyone what had **h**.	*1181*
	10:31	A priest **h** to be going down the same road,	*2848+5175*
	21:32	not pass away until all these things have **h**.	*1181*
	23:47	The centurion, seeing what had **h**,	*1181*
	24:12	wondering to himself what had **h**.	*1181*
	24:14	with each other about everything that had **h**.	*5201*
	24:18	and do not know the things that have **h** there	*1181*
	24:35	Then the two told what had **h** on the way,	*NIG*
Jn	1:28	This all **h** at Bethany on the other side of	*1181*
	9: 3	"but this **h** so that the work of God might	*NIG*
	18: 9	This **h** so that the words he had spoken	*1181*
	18:32	This **h** so that the words Jesus had spoken	*NIG*
	19:24	This **h** that the scripture might be	*NIG*
	19:36	These things **h** so that the scripture would	*1181*
	21: 1	It **h** this way:	*NIG*
Ac	3:10	with wonder and amazement at what had **h**	*5201*
	4:21	people were praising God for what had **h**.	*1181*
	5: 5	great fear seized all who heard what had **h**.	*NIG*
	5: 7	not knowing what had **h**.	*1181*
	7:40	we don't know what *has* **h** to him!'	*1181*
	10: 8	He told them everything that had **h**	*NIG*
	10:16	This **h** three times,	*1181*
	10:37	You know what *has* **h** throughout Judea,	*1181*
	11: 4	to them precisely **as it had h**:	*2759*
	11:10	This **h** three times,	*1181*
	11:28	(This **h** during the reign of Claudius),	*1181*
	12: 3	*This* **h** during the Feast of Unleavened	*1639*
	13:12	When the proconsul saw what had **h**,	*1181*
	17:17	by day with those who **h** to be there.	*4193*
	19:21	After all this *had* **h**, Paul decided to go	*4444*
	28: 9	*When* this had **h**, the rest of the sick	*1181*
1Co	10:11	These things **h** to them as examples	*5201*
2Co	1: 9	But **this h** that we might not rely	*2671*
Gal	4:15	What *has* **h** to all your joy?	*NIG*
Php	1:12	**what** *has* **h** to me has really served to	*2848+3836*
	1:19	what *has* **h** to me will turn out for my	*609*
2Ti	3:11	what kinds of things **h** to me in Antioch,	*1181*

Lk	1:20	and not able to speak until the day this **h,**	1181
Jn	13:19	"I am telling you now before it **h,**	1181
	14:29	I have told you now before *it* **h,**	1181
Php	1:27	**Whatever h,** conduct yourselves in a	3668

HAPPIER (3) [HAPPY]

Ecc	4: 2	who had already died, are **h** than the living,	NIH
Mt	18:13	*he is* **h** about that one sheep than	3437+5897
1Co	7:40	she is **h** if she stays as she is—	3421

HAPPINESS (6) [HAPPY]

Dt	24: 5	to be free to stay at home and **bring h** to	8523
Est	8:16	For the Jews it was a **time of h** and joy,	245
Job	7: 7	my eyes will never see **h** again.	3202
Ecc	2:26	God gives wisdom, knowledge and **h,**	8525
Mt	25:21	Come and share your master's **h!'**	5915
	25:23	Come and share your master's **h!'**	5915

HAPPIZZEZ (1)

1Ch	24:15	the eighteenth to **H,**	2204

HAPPY (24) [HAPPIER, HAPPINESS]

Ge	30:13	Then Leah said, "How **h** I am!	891
	30:13	The women *will* **call me h."**	887
1Ki	4:20	they ate, they drank and they were **h.**	8524
	10: 8	**How h** your men must be!	897
	10: 8	**How h** your officials,	897
2Ch	9: 7	**How h** your men must be!	897
	9: 7	**How h** your officials,	897
Est	5: 9	Haman went out that day **h** and	8524
	5:14	go with the king to the dinner and be **h."**	8524
Ps	10: 6	I'll always be **h** and never have trouble."	890
	68: 3	*may* they be **h** and joyful.	8464
	113: 9	in her home as a **h** mother of children.	8524
	137: 8	**h** is he who repays you for what you have	897
Pr	15:13	A **h** heart makes the face cheerful,	8524
Ecc	3:12	to be **h** and do good while they live.	8523
	5:19	to accept his lot and *be* **h** in his work—	8523
	7:14	When times are good, be **h;**	3202
	11: 9	*Be* **h,** young man, while you are young,	8523
Jnh	4: 6	and Jonah *was* very **h** about the vine.	8523+8525
Zec	8:19	and glad occasions and **h** festivals	3202
1Co	7:30	those who *are* **h,** as if they were not;	5897
2Co	7: 9	yet now *I am* **h,** not because you were	5897
	7:13	delighted to see how **h** Titus was.	5915
Jas	5:13	*Is* anyone **h?** Let him sing songs of praise.	2313

HARA (1)

1Ch	5:26	Habor, **H** and the river of Gozan,	2217

HARADAH (2)

Nu	33:24	They left Mount Shepher and camped at **H.**	3011
	33:25	They left **H** and camped at Makheloth.	3011

HARAM See BETH HARAM

HARAN (21) [BETH HARAN]

Ge	11:26	the father of Abram, Nahor and **H.**	2237
	11:27	the father of Abram, Nahor and **H.**	2237
	11:27	And **H** became the father of Lot.	2237
	11:28	**H** died in Ur of the Chaldeans,	2237
	11:29	she was the daughter of **H,**	2237
	11:31	his grandson Lot son of **H,**	2237
	11:31	But when they came to **H,** they settled there.	3059
	11:32	Terah lived 205 years, and he died in **H.**	3059
	12: 4	when he set out from **H.**	3059
	12: 5	and the people they had acquired in **H,**	3059
	27:43	Flee at once to my brother Laban in **H.**	3059
	28:10	Jacob left Beersheba and set out for **H.**	3059
	29: 4	"We're from **H,"** they replied.	3059
2Ki	19:12	the gods of Gozan, **H,**	3059
1Ch	2:46	Ephah was the mother of **H,**	3060
	2:46	**H** was the father of Gazez.	3060
	23: 9	Shelomoth, Haziel and **H**—three in all.	2237
Isa	37:12	the gods of Gozan, **H,**	3059
Eze	27:23	" **'H,** Canneh and Eden and merchants	3059
Ac	7: 2	before he lived in **H.**	5924
	7: 4	the land of the Chaldeans and settled in **H.**	5924

HARARITE (5)

2Sa	23:11	to him was Shammah son of Agee the **H.**	2240
	23:33	son of Shammah the **H,**	2240
	23:33	Ahiam son of Sharar the **H,**	2240
1Ch	11:34	Jonathan son of Shagee the **H,**	2240
	11:35	Ahiam son of Sacar the **H,**	2240

HARASHIM See GE HARASHIM

HARASS (2) [HARASSED]

Dt	2: 9	not **h** the Moabites or provoke them to war,	7444
	2:19	*do* not **h** them or provoke them to war,	7444

HARASSED (2) [HARASS]

Mt	9:36	because they were **h** and helpless,	5035
2Co	7: 5	but *we were* **h** at every turn—	2567

HARBONA (2)

Est	1:10	Mehuman, Biztha, **H,** Bigtha, Abagtha,	3002
	7: 9	Then **H,** one of the eunuchs attending	3003

HARBOR (10) [HARBORED, HARBORS]

Dt	15: 9	Be careful not *to* **h** this wicked thought:	2118+4222+6640
Job	36:13	"The godless in heart **h** resentment;	8492
Ps	28: 3	with their neighbors but **h** malice **in**	928
	103: 9	nor *will* he **h** *his* **anger** forever;	5757
Isa	23: 1	and left without house or **h.**	995
	23:10	for you no longer have a **h.**	4651
Jer	4:14	How long *will you* **h** wicked thoughts?	928+4328+7931
Ac	27:12	Since the **h** was unsuitable to winter in,	3348
	27:12	This was a **h** in Crete,	3348
Jas	3:14	if *you* **h** bitter envy and selfish ambition	2400

HARBORED (1) [HARBOR]

Eze	35: 5	" 'Because you **h** an ancient hostility	2118+4200

HARBORS (1) [HARBOR]

Pr	26:24	but in his heart *he* **h** deceit.	8883

HARD (65) [HARDEN, HARDENED, HARDENING, HARDENS, HARDER, HARDEST, HARDSHIP, HARDSHIPS]

Ge	18:14	*Is* anything too **h** for the LORD?	7098
	33:13	If they *are* **driven h** just one day,	1985
Ex	1:14	They made their lives bitter with **h** labor	7997
	1:14	in all their **h** labor the Egyptians used them	NIH
	2:11	and watched them at their **h** labor.	6026
	7:13	Yet Pharaoh's heart *became* **h** and he would	2616
	7:22	and Pharaoh's heart *became* **h;**	2616
	8:19	But Pharaoh's heart *was* **h** and he would	2616
	9:35	So Pharaoh's heart *was* **h** and he would	2616
Dt	1:17	Bring me any case too **h** for you,	7996
	8:15	He brought you water out of **h** rock.	2734
	26: 6	made us suffer, putting us to **h** labor.	7997
1Sa	13: 6	and that their army *was* **h** pressed,	5601
	31: 2	The Philistines **pressed h after** Saul	1815
1Ki	10: 1	she came to test him with **h questions.**	2648
	10: 3	nothing was too **h** for the king to explain	6623
1Ch	10: 2	The Philistines **pressed h after** Saul	1815
2Ch	9: 1	to Jerusalem to test him with **h questions.**	2648
	9: 2	nothing *was* too **h** for him to explain to her.	6623
	32: 5	Then *he* **worked h** repairing all	2616
Job	7: 1	"Does not man have **h** service on earth?	7372
	14:14	of my **h** service I will wait for my renewal	7372
	37:18	**h** as a mirror of cast bronze?	2617
	38:30	*when* the waters **become h** as stone,	2461
	38:38	when the dust *becomes* **h**	2021+3668+4200+4607
	41:24	His chest *is* **h** as rock,	3668
	41:24	**h** as a lower millstone.	3668
Ps	114: 8	the **h** rock into springs of water.	2734
Pr	13:15	but the way of the unfaithful is **h.**	419
	14:23	All **h work** brings a profit,	6776
Ecc	8: 1	a man's face and changes its **h** appearance.	6437
Isa	40: 2	that her **h** service has been completed,	7372
Jer	32:17	Nothing *is* too **h** for you.	7098
	32:27	*Is* anything too **h** for me?	7098
Eze	29:18	of Babylon drove his army in a **h** campaign	1524
Zec	7:12	They made their hearts **as h as** flint	9032
Mt	19: 8	because your **hearts** were **h.**	5016
	19:23	it is **h** for a rich man to enter the kingdom	1552
	25:24	he said, 'I knew that you are a **h** man,	5017
Mk	10: 5	"It was because your **hearts** were **h**	5016
	10:23	How **h** it is for the rich to enter the kingdom	1552
	10:24	how **h** it is to enter the kingdom of God!	1551
Lk	5: 5	we've **worked h** all night	3159
	12:58	**try** to be reconciled to him on the way,	1443+2238
	18:24	How **h** it is for the rich to enter the kingdom	1552
	19:21	because you are a **h** man.	893
	19:22	You knew, did you, that I am a **h** man,	893
Jn	4:38	Others *have done* the **h work,**	3159
	6:60	"This is a **h** teaching.	5017
Ac	20:35	that by this kind of **h work** we must help	3159
	26:14	It is **h** for you to kick against the goads.'	5017
Ro	16: 6	Greet Mary, who worked very **h** for you.	4498
	16:12	those women who **work h** in the Lord.	3159
	16:12	another woman who *has* **worked** very **h** in	3159
1Co	4:12	We **work h** with our own hands.	2237+3159
2Co	4: 8	We are **h** pressed on every side,	2567
	6: 5	in **h work,** sleepless nights and hunger;	3160
	8:13	while you are **h** pressed,	2568
Col	4:13	he *is* working **h** for you and for those	2400+4498
1Th	5:12	to respect those who **work h** among you,	3159
2Ti	1:17	he searched **h** for me until he found me.	5081
Heb	5:11	but *it is* **h to explain** because you are slow	1549
1Pe	4:18	And, "If it is **h** for the righteous to be saved,	3660
2Pe	3:16	some things that are **h to understand,**	1554
Rev	2: 2	your **h work** and your perseverance.	3160

HARDEN (11) [HARD]

Ex	4:21	But I *will* **h** his heart so that he will not let	2616
	7: 3	But I *will* **h** Pharaoh's heart,	7996
	14: 4	And *I will* **h** Pharaoh's heart,	2616
	14:17	I *will* **h** the hearts of the Egyptians so	2616
1Sa	6: 6	Why *do you* **h** your hearts as the Egyptians	3877
Ps	95: 8	*do* not **h** your hearts as you did at Meribah,	7996
Isa	63:17	from your ways and **h** our hearts so we do	7998
Ro	9:18	and he hardens whom he wants to **h.**	NIG
Heb	3: 8	not **h** your hearts as you did in the rebellion,	5020
	3:15	if you hear his voice, *do* not **h** your hearts	5020
	4: 7	if you hear his voice, *do* not **h** your hearts."	5020

HARDENED (19) [HARD]

Ex	8:15	he **h** his heart and would not listen to Moses	3877
	8:32	also Pharaoh **h** his heart and would not let	3877
	9:12	the LORD **h** Pharaoh's heart and he would	2616
	9:34	He and his officials **h** their hearts.	3877
	10: 1	for I *have* **h** his heart and the hearts	2616
	10:20	But the LORD **h** Pharaoh's heart,	2616
	10:27	But the LORD **h** Pharaoh's heart,	2616
	11:10	but the LORD **h** Pharaoh's heart,	2616
	14: 8	The LORD **h** the heart of Pharaoh king	2616
Jos	11:20	the LORD himself *who* **h** their hearts	2616
2Ch	36:13	He became stiff-necked and **h** his heart	599
Jer	6:28	They are all **h** rebels,	6073+6253
Eze	3: 7	house of Israel is **h** and obstinate.	2617+5195
	3: 8	I will make you as unyielding and **h**	2617+5195
Da	5:20	his heart became arrogant and **h** with pride,	10772
Mk	6:52	their hearts were **h.**	4800
	8:17	*Are* your hearts **h?**	2400+4800
Ro	11: 7	The others *were* **h,**	4800
Heb	3:13	none of you *may be* **h** by sin's deceitfulness.	5020

HARDENING (2) [HARD]

Ro	11:25	Israel has experienced a **h** in part until	4801
Eph	4:18	of the ignorance that is in them due to the **h**	4801

HARDENS (2) [HARD]

Pr	28:14	but he who **h** his heart falls into trouble.	7996
Ro	9:18	and *he* **h** whom he wants to harden.	5020

HARDER (6) [HARD]

Ex	5: 9	**Make** the work **h** for the men so	3877
Jer	5: 3	*They* **made** their faces **h** than stone	2616
Eze	3: 9	like the hardest stone, **h** than flint.	2617
Jn	5:18	For this reason the Jews tried **all the h**	3437
1Co	15:10	No, I worked **h than** all of them—	4358
2Co	11:23	I have worked **much h,**	4359

HARDEST (1) [HARD]

Eze	3: 9	I will make your forehead like the **h** stone,	9032

HARDHEARTED (1) [HEART]

Dt	15: 7	*do* not *be* **h** or tightfisted toward your poor brother.	599+906+4222

HARDLY (8)

Ge	48:10	and he could **h** see.	4202
Job	2:12	they could **h** recognize him;	4202
Da	10:17	My strength is gone and I **can h** breathe."	4202+5972+8636
Mt	13:15	they **h** hear with their ears,	977
Mk	7:32	a man who was deaf and **could h** talk,	3652
Lk	11:46	down with burdens *they can* **h** carry,	1546
Ac	27:16	we were **h** able to make the lifeboat secure.	3660
	28:27	they **h** hear with their ears,	977

HARDSHIP (12) [HARD]

Ge	31:42	But God has seen my **h** and the toil	6715
Dt	15:18	not consider it a **h** to set your servant free,	7996
Ne	9:32	not let all this **h** seem trifling in your eyes—	9430
	9:32	the **h** that has come upon us,	NIH
Job	5: 6	For **h** does not spring from the soil,	224
Isa	30: 6	Through a land of **h** and distress,	7650
La	3: 5	and surrounded me with bitterness and **h.**	9430
Ro	8:35	or **h** or persecution or famine or nakedness	5103
1Th	2: 9	you remember, brothers, our toil and **h;**	3677
2Ti	2: 3	Endure **h** with us **like** a good soldier	6055
	4: 5	keep your head in all situations, **endure h,**	2802
Heb	12: 7	Endure **h** as discipline;	NIG

HARDSHIPS (11) [HARD]

Ex	18: 8	about all the **h** they had met along the way	9430
Nu	11: 1	Now the people complained about their **h** in	8273
	20:14	You know about all the **h** that have come	9430
1Ki	2:26	**shared** all my father's **h."**	889+928+6700+6700
Ps	132: 1	remember David and all *the* **h** he endured.	6700
Ac	14:22	"We must go through many **h** to enter	2568
	20:23	that prison and **h** are facing me.	2568
2Co	1: 8	the **h** we suffered in the province of Asia.	2568
	6: 4	in troubles, and distresses;	340
	12:10	I delight in weaknesses, in insults, in **h,**	340
Rev	2: 3	You have persevered and *have* **endured h**	1002

HARDWORKING (1) [WORK]

2Ti	2: 6	The **h** farmer should be the first to receive	3159

HARE (KJV) See RABBIT

HAREM (8)

Est	2: 3	bring all these beautiful girls into the **h**	851+1074
	2: 8	who had charge of the **h.**	851
	2: 9	her maids into the best place in the **h.**	851+1074
	2:11	near the courtyard of the **h** to find out	851+1074
	2:13	with her from the **h** to the king's palace.	851+1074
	2:14	morning return to another part of the **h.**	851+1074
	2:15	king's eunuch who was in charge of the **h,**	851
Ecc	2: 8	and a **h** as well—	2256+8721+8721

HAREPH (1)

1Ch	2:51	and **H** the father of Beth Gader.	3073

HARESETH   See KIR HARESETH

HARETH   (KJV) See HERETH

HARHAIAH   (1)
Ne   3: 8   Uzziel son of H, one of the goldsmiths,   3015

HARHAS   (1)
2Ki 22:14   the son of H, keeper of the wardrobe.   3030

HARHUR   (2)
Ezr   2:51   Bakbuk, Hakupha, H,   3028
Ne   7:53   Bakbuk, Hakupha, H,   3028

HARIM   (10) [HARIM'S]
1Ch 24: 8   the third to H, the fourth to Seorim,   3053
Ezr   2:32   of H 320   3053
    2:39   of H 1,017   3053
  10:21   From the descendants of H: 3053
  10:31   From the descendants of H: 3053
Ne   3:11   Malkijah son of H and Hasshub son   3053
    7:35   of H 320   3053
    7:42   of H 1,017   3053
  10: 5   H, Meremoth, Obadiah,   3053
  10:27   Malluch, H and Baanah.   3053

HARIM'S   (1) [HARIM]
Ne 12:15   of H, Adna; of Meremoth's, Helkai;   3053

HARIPH   (2)
Ne   7:24   of H 112   3040
  10:19   H, Anathoth, Nebai,   3040

HARLOT   (KJV) See also PROSTITUTE

HARLOT   (2) [HARLOTS]
Isa   1:21   See how the faithful city has become a h!   2390
Na   3: 4   all because of the wanton lust of a h,   2390

HARLOTS   (1) [HARLOT]
Hos   4:14   because the men themselves consort with h   2390

HARM   (73) [HARMED, HARMFUL, HARMING, HARMLESS, HARMS]
Ge 26:29   that you will do us no h,   8288
  31: 7   However, God has not allowed him to h me.   8317
  31:29   I have the power to h you;   6913+8273
  31:52   not go past this heap to your side to h you   NIH
  31:52   past this heap and pillar to my side to h me.   8288
  42: 4   he was afraid that h might come to him.   656
  42:38   If h comes to him on the journey   656
  44:29   from me too and h comes to him,   656
  48:16   the Angel who has delivered me from all h   8273
  50:20   You intended to h me,   8288
Nu   5:19   that brings a curse not h you.   4946+5927
  35:23   and he did not intend to h him,   8288
Jdg 15: 3   I will really h them.   6913+8288
1Sa 20: 7   be sure that he is determined to h me.   8288
  20: 9   that my father was determined to h you,   8288
  20:13   But if my father is inclined to h you,   8288
  25:26   and all who intend to h my master be   8288
  26:21   I will not try to h you again.   8317
2Sa 18:32   the king and all who rise up to h you be like   8288
  20: 6   Sheba son of Bicri will do us more h than
       Absalom did.   8317
2Ki   8:12   "Because I know the h you will do to   8288
1Ch   4:10   and keep me from h so that I will be free   8288
  16:22   do my prophets no h."   8317
Ne   6: 2   But they were scheming to h me;   6913+8288
Job 16:19   in seven no h will befall you.   8273
Ps 38:12   those who would h me talk of my ruin;   8288
  56: 5   they are always plotting to h me,   8273
  71:13   to h me be covered with scorn and disgrace.   8288
  71:24   for those who wanted to h me have been put   8288
  91:10   then no h will befall you,   8288
  105:15   do my prophets no h."   8317
  121: 6   the sun will not h you by day,   5782
  121: 7   The LORD will keep you from all h—   8273
Pr   1:33   and be at ease, without fear of h."   8288
  3:29   Do not plot h against your neighbor,   8288
  3:30   when he has done you no h.   8288
  12:21   No h befalls the righteous,   224
  13:20   but a companion of fools suffers h.   8317
  31:12   She brings him good, not h,   8273
Ecc   5:13   wealth hoarded to the h of its owner,   8288
  8: 5   to no h, and the wise heart will know   1821+8273
Isa 11: 9   They will neither h nor destroy   8317
  27: 3   and night so that no one may h it.   7212
  65:25   They will neither h nor destroy   8317
Jer   5:12   No h will come to us;   8288
  7: 6   you do not follow other gods to your own h,   8273
  10: 5   they can do no h nor can they do any good."   8317
  21:10   I have determined to do this city h and   8288
  23:17   'No h will come to you.'   8288
  25: 6   Then I will not h you."   8317
  25: 7   and you have brought h to yourselves."   8273
  29:11   "plans to prosper you and not to h you,   8288
  39:12   don't h him but do for him whatever   6913+8273
  44:17   of food and were well off and suffered no h.   8288

Jer 44:27   For I am watching over them for h,   8288
  44:29   'so that you will know that my threats of h   8288
Zep   3:15   never again will you fear any h.   8273
Lk 10:19   nothing will h you.   92
Ac   9:13   about this man and all the h he has done   2805
  16:28   But Paul shouted, "Don't h yourself!   2805+4556
  18:10   and no one is going to attack and h you,   2808
Ro 13:10   Love does no h to its neighbor.   2805
1Co 11:17   for your meetings do more h than good.   2482
2Ti   4:14   the metalworker did me a great deal of h.   2805
1Pe   3:13   Who is going to h you if you are eager   2808
2Pe   2:13   with h for the harm they have done.   94
  2:13   with harm for the h they have done.   92
1Jn   5:18   and the evil one cannot h him.   721
Rev   7: 2   power to h the land and the sea: 92
  7: 3   "Do not h the land or the sea or the trees   92
  9: 4   not to h the grass of the earth or any plant   92
  11: 5   If anyone tries to h them,   92
  11: 5   how anyone who wants to h them must die.   92

HARMED   (3) [HARM]
Ru   2:22   in someone else's field you might be h."   7003
Da   3:27   saw that the fire had not h their bodies,   10715
2Co   7: 9   and so were not h in any way by us.   2423

HARMFUL   (3) [HARM]
2Ki   4:41   And there was nothing h in the pot.   8273
Ps 52: 4   You love every h word,   1184
1Ti   6: 9   a trap and into many foolish and h desires   1054

HARMING   (3) [HARM]
1Sa 24: 9   'David is bent on h you'?   8288
  25:34   lives, who has kept me from h you,   8317
Jer   7:19   Are they not rather h themselves,   NIH

HARMLESS   (2) [HARM]
Lev 13:39   a h rash that has broken out on the skin;   993
Pr   1:11   let's waylay some h soul;   2855+5929

HARMON   (1)
Am   4: 3   and you will be cast out toward H,"   2236

HARMONY   (4)
Zec   6:13   And there will be h between the two.'   6783+8934
Ro 12:16   Live in h with one another.   899+3836+5858
2Co   6:15   What h is there between Christ and Belial?   5245
1Pe   3: 8   all of you, live in h with one another;   3939

HARMS   (1) [HARM]
Pr   8:36   But whoever fails to find me h himself;   2803

HARNEPHER   (1)
1Ch   7:36   The sons of Zophah: Suah, H, Shual, Beri,   3062

HARNESS   (4) [HARNESSED]
Job 39:10   Can you hold him to the furrow with a h?   6310
Ps 50:19   for evil and h your tongue to deceit.   7537
Jer 46: 4   Harness the horses, mount the steeds!   673
Mic   1:13   h the team to the chariot.   8412

HARNESSED   (1) [HARNESS]
SS   1: 9   a mare h to one of the chariots of Pharaoh.   928

HAROD   (1) [HARODITE]
Jdg   7: 1   and all his men camped at the spring of H.   3008

HARODITE   (2) [HAROD]
2Sa 23:25   Shammah the H, Elika the Harodite,   3012
  23:25   Shammah the Harodite, Elika the H,   3012

HAROEH   (1)
1Ch   2:52   H, half the Manahathites,   2218

HARORITE   (1)
1Ch 11:27   Shammoth the H, Helez the Pelonite,   2229

HAROSHETH HAGGOYIM   (3)
Jdg   4: 2   who lived in H.   3099
  4:13   from H to the Kishon River.   3099
  4:16   and army as far as H.   3099

HARP   (32) [HARPIST, HARPISTS, HARPS]
Ge   4:21   the father of all who play the h and flute.   4036
1Sa 16:16   to search for someone who can play the h.   4036
  16:18   who knows how to play the h.   5594
  16:23   David would take his h and play.   4036
  18:10   while David was playing the h,   928+3338+5594
  19: 9   While David was playing the h,   928+3338+5594
1Ch 25: 3   the h in thanking and praising the LORD.   4036
Job 21:12   to the music of tambourine and h;   4036
  30:31   My h is tuned to mourning,   4036
Ps 33: 2   Praise the LORD with the h;   4036
  43: 4   I will praise you with the h, O God,   4036
  49: 4   with the h I will expound my riddle;   4036
  57: 8   Awake, h and lyre!   4036
  71:22   with the h for your faithfulness, O my God;   5575
  81: 2   play the melodious h and lyre,   4036

Ps 92: 3   and the melody of the h.   4036
  98: 5   make music to the LORD with the h,   4036
  98: 5   with the h and the sound of singing,   4036
  108: 2   Awake, h and lyre! I will awaken the dawn.   4036
  147: 7   make music to our God on the h.   4036
  149: 3   to him with tambourine and h.   4036
  150: 3   praise him with the h and lyre,   4036
Isa 16:11   My heart laments for Moab like a h,   4036
  23:16   "Take up a h, walk through the city,   4036
  23:16   play the h well, sing many a song,   5594
  24: 8   the joyful h is silent.   4036
Da   3: 5   zither, lyre, h, pipes and all kinds of music,   10590
  3: 7   flute, zither, lyre, h and all kinds of music,   10590
  3:10   the sound of the horn, flute, zither, lyre, h,   10590
  3:15   zither, lyre, h, pipes and all kinds of music,   10590
1Co 14: 7   such as the flute or h,   3067
Rev   5: 8   a h and they were holding golden bowls full   3067

HARPIST   (2) [HARP]
2Ki   3:15   But now bring me a h."   5594
  3:15   While the h was playing,   5594

HARPISTS   (2) [HARP]
Rev 14: 2   like that of h playing their harps.   3069
  18:22   The music of h and musicians,   3069

HARPOONS   (1)
Job 41: 7   Can you fill his hide with h or his head   8496

HARPS   (25) [HARP]
Ge 31:27   to the music of tambourines and h?   4036
1Sa 10: 5   flutes and h being played before them,   4036
2Sa   6: 5   with songs and h, lyres, tambourines,   4036
1Ki 10:12   and to make h and lyres for the musicians.   4036
1Ch 13: 8   with songs and h, lyres, tambourines,   4036
  15:16   lyres, h and cymbals.   4036
  15:21   Jeiel and Azaziah were to play the h,   4036
  15:28   and the playing of lyres and h.   4036
  16: 5   They were to play the lyres and h,   4036
  25: 1   accompanied by h, lyres and cymbals.   4036
  25: 6   with cymbals, lyres and h.   4036
2Ch   5:12   in fine linen and playing cymbals, h   4036
  9:11   and to make h and lyres for the musicians.   4036
  20:28   to the temple of the LORD with h and lutes   5575
  29:25   h and lyres in the way prescribed by David   4036
Ne 12:27   and with the music of cymbals, h and lyres.   4036
Ps 137: 2   There on the poplars we hung our h,   4036
Isa   5:12   They have h and lyres at their banquets,   4036
  14:11   along with the noise of your h;   5575
  30:32   be to the music of tambourines and h,   4036
Eze 26:13   the music of your h will be heard no more.   4036
Am   5:23   I will not listen to the music of your h.   5575
  6: 5   You strum away on your h like David   5575
Rev 14: 2   like that of harpists playing their h,   3067
  15: 2   They held h given them by God   3067

HARROW   (KJV) See TILL

HARROWING   (1)
Isa 28:24   Does he keep on breaking up and h the soil?   8440

HARSH   (13) [HARSHLY]
Dt 28:59   h and prolonged disasters,   1524
1Ki 12: 4   the h labor and the heavy yoke he put on us,   7997
2Ch 10: 4   the h labor and the heavy yoke he put on us,   7997
Pr 15: 1   but a h word stirs up anger.   6776
Isa 66: 4   so I also will choose h treatment for them   9500
La   1: 3   After affliction and h labor,   8044
Da   2:15   "Why did the king issue such a h decree?"   10280
Mal   2:17   "You have said h things against me,"   2616
2Co 13:10   not have to be h in my use of authority—   705
Col   2:23   their false humility and their h treatment of   910
  3:19   love your wives and do not be h with them.   4393
1Pe   2:18   but also to those who are h.   5021
Jude   1:15   the h words ungodly sinners have spoken   5017

HARSHA   (2) [TEL HARSHA]
Ezr   2:52   Bazluth, Mehida, H,   3095
Ne   7:54   Bazluth, Mehida, H,   3095

HARSHLY   (13) [HARSH]
Ge 42: 7   to be a stranger and spoke h to them.   7997
  42:30   over the land spoke to us and treated us as   7997
Ex 10: 2   and grandchildren how I dealt h with   6618
1Sa   6: 6   When he treated them h,   6618
  20:10   if your father answers you h?"   7997
2Sa 19:43   men of Judah responded even more h than   7996
1Ki 12:13   The king answered the people h,   7997
2Ch 10:13   The king answered them h,   7997
Job 39:16   She treats her young h,   7996
Pr 18:23   but a rich man answers h.   6434
Eze 34: 4   You have ruled them h and brutally.   928+2622
Mk 14: 5   And they rebuked her h.   1839
1Ti   5: 1   Do not rebuke an older man h,   2159

HART   (KJV) See DEER, STAG

HARUM   (1)
1Ch   4: 8   and of the clans of Aharhel son of H.   2227

HARUMAPH (1)

Ne   3:10   of H made repairs opposite his house,   3018

HARUPHITE (1)

1Ch 12: 5   Bealiah, Shemariah and Shephatiah the H;   3020

HARUZ (1)

2Ki 21:19   His mother's name was Meshullemeth
        daughter of H;   3027

HARVEST (96) [HARVESTED, HARVESTERS, HARVESTING, HARVESTS]

Ge	8:22	long as the earth endures, seedtime and h,	7907
	30:14	During wheat h, Reuben went out into	7907
	41:34	of the h of Egypt during the seven years	NIH
Ex	23:10	to sow your fields and h the crops,	665
	23:16	Feast of H with the firstfruits of the crops	7907
	34:21	the plowing season and h you must rest.	7907
	34:22	Feast of Weeks with the firstfruits of the	
		wheat h,	7907
Lev	19: 9	" 'When you reap the h of your land,	7907
	19: 9	or gather the gleanings of your h.	7907
	19:25	In this way your h will be increased.	9311
	23:10	to give you and you reap its h,	7907
	23:10	to the priest a sheaf of the first grain you h.	7907
	23:22	" 'When you reap the h of your land,	7907
	23:22	or gather the gleanings of your h.	7907
	25: 5	not reap what grows of itself or h the grapes	1305
	25:11	and do not reap what grows of itself or h	1305
	25:20	if we do not plant or h our crops?"	665
	25:22	and will continue to eat from it until the h	9311
	26: 5	Your threshing will continue until grape h	1292
	26: 5	and the grape h will continue until planting,	1292
	26:10	still be eating last year's h when you	3823+3824
Nu	18:12	the LORD as the firstfruits of their h.	8040
Dt	16:15	in all your h and in all the work	9311
	24:21	When you h the grapes in your vineyard,	1305
	28:38	in the field but you will h little,	665
Jos	3:15	the Jordan is at flood stage all during h.	7907
Jdg	8: 2	the full grape h of Abiezer?	1292
	15: 1	Later on, at the time of wheat h,	7907
Ru	1:22	in Bethlehem as the barley h was beginning.	7907
1Sa	8:12	others to plow his ground and reap his h,	7907
	12:17	Is it not wheat h now?	7907
2Sa	21: 9	to death during the first days of the h,	7907
	21: 9	just as the barley h was beginning.	7907
	21:10	the beginning of the h till the rain poured	7907
	23:13	During h time, three of the thirty chief	7907
2Ch	32:28	also made buildings to store the h of grain,	9311
Ne	9:37	its abundant h goes to the kings	9311
Job	5: 5	The hungry consume his h,	7907
	31:12	it would have uprooted my h.	9311
Ps	67: 6	Then the land will yield its h, and God,	3292
	85:12	and our land will yield its h.	3292
	107:37	that yielded a fruitful h;	9311
Pr	6: 8	in summer and gathers its food at h.	7907
	10: 5	he who sleeps during h is a disgraceful son.	7907
	14: 4	the strength of an ox comes an abundant h.	9311
	18:20	with the h from his lips he is satisfied.	9311
	20: 4	so at h time he looks but finds nothing.	7907
	25:13	Like the coolness of snow at h time is	7907
	26: 1	Like snow in summer or rain in h,	7907
Isa	9: 3	before you as people rejoice at the h,	7907
	17:11	yet the h will be as nothing in the day	7907
	18: 4	like a cloud of dew in the heat of h."	7907
	18: 5	For, before the h, when the blossom is gone	7907
	23: 3	the h of the Nile was the revenue of Tyre,	7907
	24:13	as when gleanings are left after the grape h.	1292
	28: 4	will be like a fig ripe before h—	7811
	32:10	the grape h will fail,	1292
	32:10	and the h of fruit will not come.	668
	62: 9	but those who h it will eat it and praise	665
Jer	2: 3	the firstfruits of his h;	9311
	5:24	who assures us of the regular weeks of h.'	7907
	8:13	" 'I will take away their h,	658
	8:20	"The h is past, the summer has ended,	7907
	12:13	So bear the shame of your h because of	9311
	40:10	but you are to h the wine,	665
	50:16	and the reaper with his sickle at h.	7907
	51:33	the time to h her will soon come."	7907
Hos	6:11	"Also for you, Judah, a h is appointed.	7907
Joel	1:11	because the h of the field is destroyed.	7907
	3:13	Swing the sickle, for the h is ripe.	7907
Am	4: 7	when the h was still three months away.	7907
Mic	6:15	You will plant but not h;	7917
Mt	9:37	"The h is plentiful but the workers are few.	2546
	9:38	Ask the Lord of the h, therefore,	2546
	9:38	to send out workers into his h field."	2546
	13:30	Let both grow together until the h.	2546
	13:39	The h is the end of the age,	2546
	21:34	When the h time approached,	2843
	21:41	his share of the crop at h time."	NIG
	25:26	that I h where I have not sown and gather	2545
Mk	4:29	because the h has come.	2546
	12: 2	At h time he sent a servant to the tenants	NIG
Lk	10: 2	He told them, "The h is plentiful,	2546
	10: 2	Ask the Lord of the h, therefore,	2546
	10: 2	to send out workers into his h field.	2546
	20:10	At h time he sent a servant to the tenants	NIG
Jn	4:35	'Four months more and then the h'?	2546
	4:35	They are ripe for h.	2546
Ro	1:13	in order that I might have a h among you,	2843

1Co	9:10	to do so in the hope of sharing in the h.	NIG
	9:11	is it too much if we reap a material h	2545
2Co	9:10	of seed and will enlarge the h	1163
Gal	6: 9	at the proper time we will reap a h if we do	2545
Heb	12:11	it produces a h of righteousness and peace	2843
Jas	3:18	Peacemakers who sow in peace raise a h	2843
Rev	14:15	for the h of the earth is ripe."	2546

HARVESTED (5) [HARVEST]

Isa	33: 4	O nations, is h as by young locusts;	665
Jer	40:12	And they h an abundance of wine	665
Am	7: 1	after the king's share had been h and just as	1600
Hag	1: 6	You have planted much, but have h little.	995
Rev	14:16	and the earth was h.	2545

HARVESTERS (8) [HARVEST]

Ru	2: 3	to glean in the fields behind the h.	7917
	2: 4	from Bethlehem and greeted the h,	7917
	2: 5	Boaz asked the foreman of his h,	7917
	2: 7	among the sheaves behind the h.'	7917
	2:14	When she sat down with the h,	7917
Mt	13:30	At that time I will tell the h:	2547
	13:39	and the h are angels.	2547
Jas	5: 4	The cries of the h have reached the ears of	2545

HARVESTING (6) [HARVEST]

Lev	25:15	of the number of years left for h crops.	9311
Dt	24:19	When you are h in your field	7907+7917
Ru	2: 9	Watch the field where the men are h,	7917
	2:21	until they finish h all my grain.' "	7907
1Sa	6:13	of Beth Shemesh were h their wheat	7907+7917
Mt	25:24	h where you have not sown and gathering	2545

HARVESTS (6) [HARVEST]

Dt	32:22	It will devour the earth and its h	3292
Ru	2:23	until the barley and wheat h were finished.	7907
Isa	16: 9	and over your h have been stilled.	7907
	17: 5	a reaper gathers the standing grain and h	7917
Jer	5:17	They will devour your h and food,	7907
Jn	4:36	even now he h the crop for eternal life,	5251

HAS (266 of 2407) [HAVE] See Index of Articles Etc. for an Exhaustive Listing (See Introduction, page x)

Ge	31:32	But if you find anyone who h your gods—	6640
	38:23	Then Judah said, "Let her keep what she h,	4200
Ex	21: 3	but if he h a wife when he comes,	1251
	21: 8	He h no right to sell her to foreigners,	5440
	21:16	still h him when he is caught must be	928+3338
	22: 3	but if he h nothing, he must be sold	4200
	22:19	h sexual relations with an animal	6640+8886
	32:24	I told them, 'Whoever h any gold jewelry,	4200
Lev	11:34	but h water on it from such a pot is unclean,	995
	13: 2	"When anyone h a swelling or a rash or	2118
	13: 9	anyone h an infectious skin disease,	928+2118
	13:18	"When someone h a boil on his skin	928+2118
	13:24	"When someone h a burn on his skin and	2118
	13:29	If a man or woman h a sore on the head	928+2118
	13:38	a man or woman h white spots on the skin,	2118
	13:42	if he h a reddish-white sore on his bald head	2118
	13:46	as he h the infection he remains unclean.	928
	13:52	that h the contamination in it, because	2118
	13:57	and whatever h the mildew must be burned	928
	14:32	for anyone who h an infectious skin disease	928
	15: 2	'When any man h a bodily discharge,	2118
	15:16	" 'When a man h an emission of semen,	3655
	15:17	Any clothing or leather that h semen	2118
	15:19	a woman h her regular flow of blood,	2118
	15:25	a woman h a discharge of blood	2307+2308
	20:15	h sexual relations with an animal,	5989+8888
	20:18	h sexual relations with her,	906+1655+6872
	21: 3	on him since she h no husband—	2118+4200
	21:17	who h a defect may come near to offer	928+2118
	21:18	No man who h any defect may come near:	928
	21:20	or who h any eye defect,	928
	21:20	or who h festering or running sores	NIH
	21:21	the priest who h any defect is to come near	928
	21:21	He h a defect;	928
	22: 4	h an infectious skin disease or	7665
	22: 4	or by anyone who h an emission of semen,	3655
	22:13	widow or is divorced, yet h no children,	4200
	25:26	a man h no one to redeem it for him	2118+4200
Nu	5: 2	anyone who h an infectious skin disease	7665
	5: 8	But if that person h no close relative	4200
	14:24	my servant Caleb h a different spirit	2118+6640
	24:16	h knowledge from the Most High,	1981+3359
	27: 9	If he h no daughter,	4200
	27:10	If he h no brothers,	4200
	35:17	anyone h a stone in his hand that could kill,	928
	35:18	Or if anyone h a wooden object in his hand	928
Dt	14: 9	you may eat any that h fins and scales.	4200
	15:21	If an animal h a defect, is lame or blind,	928+2118
	15:21	is lame or blind, or h any serious flaw,	NIH
	17: 1	an ox or a sheep that h any defect or flaw	2118
	21:15	If a man h two wives,	2118+4200
	21:17	giving him a double share of all he h.	4200+5162
	21:18	If a man h a stubborn and rebellious	2118+4200
	26:19	He h declared that he will set you in praise,	NIH
	27:21	h sexual relations with any animal."	6640+8886
	28:55	It will be all he h left because of	4200
Jdg	18:14	that one of these houses h an ephod,	928+3780S
Ru	4: 4	For no one h the right to do it	1457S
	4:17	women living there said, "Naomi h a son."	3528

1Sa	2: 8	with princes and h them inherit a throne	5706
2Sa	6:12	of Obed-Edom and everything he h,	4200
	14:30	and he h barley there.	4200
	15: 4	Then everyone who h a complaint	2118+4200
	17: 5	so we can hear what he h to say."	928
2Ki	4: 2	"Your servant h nothing there at all,"	4200
	4:14	she h no son and her husband is old."	4200
2Ch	25: 8	God h the power to help or to overthrow."	928+3780
Job	1:10	and his household and everything he h?	4200
	1:11	and strike everything he h,	4200
	1:12	then, everything he h is in your hands,	4200
	2: 4	"A man will give all he h for his own life.	4200
	11: 6	for true wisdom h two sides.	4200
	18:17	he h no name in the land.	4200
	18:19	he h no offspring or descendants	4200
	20:23	When he h filled his belly,	2118
	38:37	Who h the wisdom to count the clouds?	928
	41:11	Who h a claim against me that I must pay?	7709
	41:26	The sword that reaches him h no effect,	7756
	42: 8	what is right, as my servant Job h."	NIH
Ps	41: 1	Blessed is he who h regard for the weak;	8505
	49:20	A man who h riches without understanding	928
	73:25	And earth h nothing I desire besides you.	928
	103:13	As a father h compassion on his children,	8163
	103:13	the LORD h compassion on those who fear	8163
	109:11	May a creditor seize all he h;	4200
	147: 5	his understanding h no limit.	4200
Pr	6: 7	It h no commander, no overseer or ruler,	4200
	14:26	the LORD h a secure fortress,	928
	18:21	The tongue h the power of life and death,	928
	21:20	but a foolish man devours all he h.	5647S
	23:24	he who h a wise son delights in him.	3528
	23:29	Who h woe?	4200
	23:29	Who h sorrow?	4200
	23:29	Who h strife?	4200
	23:29	Who h complaints?	4200
	23:29	Who h needless bruises?	4200
	23:29	Who h bloodshot eyes?	4200
	24:20	for the evil man h no future hope,	2118+4200
	30:15	"The leech h two daughters. 'Give!'	4200
	31:11	Her husband h full confidence in her	1053+4213
Ecc	1: 8	The eye never h enough of seeing,	8425
	1:16	in wisdom more than anyone who h ruled	2118
	5:10	Whoever loves money never h money enough;	8425
	5:14	when he h a son there is nothing left for him	3528
	6: 5	it h more rest than does that man—	4200
	6: 8	What advantage h a wise man over a fool?	4200
	9: 4	Anyone who is among the living h hope—	3780
SS	4: 2	Each h its twin; not one of them is alone.	9298
	6: 6	Each h its twin, not one of them is alone.	9298
Isa	2:12	The LORD Almighty h a day in store	4200
	10: 7	this is not what he h in mind;	3108+4222
	22: 5	h a day of tumult and trampling and terror	4200
	28: 2	the Lord h one who is powerful and strong.	4200
	34: 6	For the LORD h a sacrifice in Bozrah and	4200
	34: 8	For the LORD h a day of vengeance,	4200
	45: 9	Does your work say, 'He h no hands'?	4200
	49:10	He who h compassion on them	8163
	50:10	who h no light,	4200
	54: 1	of her who h a husband,"	1249
	54:10	says the LORD, who h compassion on you.	8163
Jer	6:25	for the enemy h a sword,	4200
	17: 8	It h no worries in a year of drought	1793
	23:28	the prophet who h a dream tell his dream,	907
	23:28	the one who h my word speak it faithfully.	907
	23:28	what h straw to do with grain?"	4200
	49: 1	"H Israel no sons?	4200
	49: 1	H she no heirs?	4200
	49:31	"a nation that h neither gates nor bars;	4200
	50:25	The Sovereign LORD Almighty h work to do	4200
Eze	9: 6	but do not touch anyone who h the mark.	6584
	18:10	"Suppose he h a violent son,	3528
	18:14	"But suppose this son h a son who sees all	3528
	33:13	none of the righteous things he h done will	NIH
Hos	4: 1	because the LORD h a charge to bring	4200
	8: 7	stalk h no head; it will produce no flour.	4200
	12: 2	The LORD h a charge to bring	4200
Joel	1: 6	it h the teeth of a lion, the fangs of a lioness.	4200
Am	3: 4	a lion roar in the thicket when he h no prey?	4200
Jnh	4:11	But Nineveh h more than a hundred	928+3780
Mic	6: 2	For the LORD h a case against his people;	4200
Zec	2: 8	"After he h honored me and has sent me	NIH
Mal	1:14	the cheat who h an acceptable male	3780
Mt	5:23	that your brother h something against you,	2400
	8:20	the Son of Man h no place to lay his head."	2400
	9: 6	Son of Man h authority on earth to forgive sins...."	2400
	11:15	He who h ears, let him hear.	2400
	11:18	and they say, 'He h a demon.'	2400
	12:11	of you h a sheep and it falls into a pit on	2400
	13: 9	He who h ears, let him hear."	2400
	13:12	Whoever h will be given more,	2400
	13:12	even what he h will be taken from him.	2400
	13:21	he h no root, he lasts only a short time.	2400
	13:43	He who h ears, let him hear.	2400
	16:27	according to what he h done.	4552
	25:28	and give it to the one who h the ten talents.	2400
	25:29	For everyone who h will be given more,	2400
	25:29	even what he h will be taken from him.	2400
Mk	2:10	Son of Man h authority on earth to forgive sins...."	2400
	3:26	he cannot stand; his end h come.	2400
	3:30	"He h an evil spirit."	2400
	4: 9	Then Jesus said, "He who h ears to hear,	2400
	4:23	If anyone h ears to hear, let him hear."	2400

Mk	4:25	Whoever **h** will be given more;	2400
	4:25	even what he **h** will be taken from him."	2400
Lk	1:61	among your relatives who **h** that name."	2813
	3:11	should share with him who **h** none,	2400
	3:11	the one who **h** food should do the same."	2400
	5:24	Son of Man **h** authority on earth to forgive sins...."	2400
	7:33	and you say, 'He **h** a demon.'	2400
	8:8	"He who **h** ears to hear, let him hear."	2400
	8:18	Whoever **h** will be given more;	2400
	8:18	what he thinks he **h** will be taken from him.	2400
	9:58	the Son of Man **h** no place to lay his head."	2400
	11:5	"Suppose one of you **h** a friend,	2400
	12:5	**h** power to throw you into hell.	2400
	14:28	to see if he **h** enough money to	1650+2400
	14:33	who does not give up everything he **h** cannot be my disciple.	3836+5639
	14:35	"He who **h** ears to hear, let him hear."	2400
	15:4	"Suppose one of you **h** a hundred sheep	2400
	15:8	a woman **h** ten silver coins and loses one.	2400
	15:27	'Your brother **h** come,' he replied,	2457
	15:27	the fattened calf because he **h** him **back** safe	655
	19:24	and give it to the one who **h** ten minas.'	2400
	19:25	" 'Sir,' they said, 'he already **h** ten!'	2400
	19:26	'I tell you that to everyone who **h**,	2400
	19:26	but as for the one who **h** nothing,	2400
	19:26	even what he **h** will be taken away.	2400
Jn	3:36	Whoever believes in the Son **h** eternal life,	2400
	4:44	a prophet **h** no honor in his own country.)	2400
	5:24	and believes him who sent me **h** eternal life	2400
	5:26	For as the Father **h** life in himself,	2400
	6:47	he who believes **h** everlasting life.	2400
	6:54	and drinks my blood **h** eternal life,	2400
	11:10	he stumbles, for he **h** no light."	1639
	14:21	Whoever **h** my commands and obeys them,	2400
	14:30	He **h** no hold on me,	2400
	15:13	Greater love **h** no one than this,	2400
	16:21	**h** pain because her time has come;	2400
Ac	23:17	he **h** something to tell him."	2400
	23:18	to you because he **h** something to tell you."	2400
Ro	6:9	death no longer **h mastery** over him.	3259
	8:24	Who hopes for what he already **h**?	1063[S]
	9:18	Therefore God **h mercy on** whomever he wants	1796
	12:4	of us **h** one body with many members,	2400
1Co	5:1	A man **h** his father's wife.	2400
	6:1	If any of you **h** a dispute with another,	2400
	7:7	But each man **h** his own gift from God;	2400
	7:7	one **h** this gift, another has that.	NIG
	7:7	one has this gift, another **h** that.	NIG
	7:12	If any brother **h** a wife who is not a believer	2400
	7:13	a woman **h** a husband who is not a believer	2400
	7:37	who is under no compulsion but **h** control	2400
	11:14	that if a man **h long hair**,	3150
	11:15	but that if a woman **h long hair**,	3150
	14:26	you come together, everyone **h** a hymn,	2400
	16:10	See to it that he **h** nothing to fear while he is	1181
	16:12	but he will go when he **h the opportunity.**	2320
2Co	8:12	gift is acceptable according to what one **h**,	2400
Gal	4:27	of the desolate woman than of her who **h**	2400
Eph	5:5	**h** any inheritance in the kingdom of Christ	2400
Php	1:12	that **what h happened to** me has really served	2848+3836
	1:12	to me he really **served** to advance the gospel.	2262
1Ti	4:8	but godliness **h** value for all things,	1639
	5:4	But if a widow **h** children or grandchildren,	2400
	5:16	If any woman who is a believer **h** widows	2400
	6:20	**what h been entrusted to** your care.	4146
2Ti	4:10	Crescens **h** gone to Galatia,	NIG
Phm	1:7	Your love **h given** me great joy	2400
Heb	3:3	the builder of a house **h** greater honor than	2400
	3:12	brothers, that none of you **h** a sinful,	1639
	3:15	As **h** just been said:	1877+3306+3836
	5:3	This is why he **h** to offer sacrifices	4053
	6:12	inherit **what h been promised.**	2039+3836
	7:24	he **h** a permanent priesthood.	2039
	10:36	you will receive what he **h promised.**	2039
Jas	2:14	a man claims to have faith but **h** no deeds?	2400
2Pe	3:4	on **as it h** since the beginning of creation."	4048
1Jn	2:16	**what he h** and does—	1050
	2:23	No one who denies the Son **h** the Father;	2400
	2:23	whoever acknowledges the Son **h**	2400
	3:3	Everyone who **h** this hope	2400
	3:15	that no murderer **h** eternal life in him.	2400
	3:17	If anyone **h** material possessions	2400
	3:17	brother in need but **h no pity**	3091+3836+5073
	4:16	we know and rely on the love God **h** for us.	2400
	4:18	because fear **h** to do with punishment.	2400
	5:10	the Son of God **h** this testimony in his heart.	2400
	5:12	He who **h** the Son has life;	2400
	5:12	He who has the Son **h** life;	2400
	5:20	We know also that the Son of God **h come**	2457
2Jn	1:9	the teaching **h** both the Father and the Son.	2400
Rev	2:7	He who **h** an ear, let him hear	2400
	2:11	He who **h** an ear, let him hear	2400
	2:12	These are the words of him who **h** the sharp,	2400
	2:17	He who **h** an ear, let him hear	2400
	2:29	He who **h** an ear, let him hear	2400
	3:6	He who **h** an ear, let him hear	2400
	3:13	He who **h** an ear, let him hear	2400
	3:22	He who **h** an ear, let him hear	2400
	13:9	He who **h** an ear, let him hear	2400
	13:18	If anyone **h** insight,	2400
	17:7	which **h** the seven heads and ten horns.	2400
	19:12	He **h** a name written on him	2400
	19:16	and on his thigh he **h** this name written:	2400
	20:6	The second death **h** no power over them.	2400
	22:12	to everyone according to what he **h** done.	1639

HASADIAH (1)

1Ch	3:20	Ohel, Berekiah, **H** and Jushab-Hesed.	2878

HASENUAH (KJV) See HASSENUAH

HASHABIAH (15)

1Ch	6:45	the son of **H**,	3116
	9:14	the son of Azrikam, the son of **H**,	3116
	25:3	Zeri, Jeshaiah, Shimei, **H** and Mattithiah,	3117
	25:19	the twelfth to **H**, his sons and relatives, 12	3116
	26:30	From the Hebronites: **H** and his relatives—	3117
	27:17	**H** son of Kemuel;	3116
2Ch	35:9	his brothers, and **H**, Jeiel and Jozabad,	3117
Ezr	8:19	and **H**, together with Jeshaiah from	3116
	8:24	**H** and ten of their brothers,	3116
Ne	3:17	**H**, ruler of half the district of Keilah,	3116
	10:11	Mica, Rehob, **H**,	3116
	11:15	the son of Azrikam, the son of **H**,	3116
	11:22	the son of **H**, the son of Mattaniah,	3116
	12:21	of Hilkiah's, **H**; of Jedaiah's, Nethanel.	3116
	12:24	And the leaders of the Levites were **H**,	3116

HASHABNAH (1)

Ne	10:25	Rehum, **H**, Maaseiah,	3118

HASHABNEIAH (2)

Ne	3:10	Hattush son of **H** made repairs next to him.	3119
	9:5	Jeshua, Kadmiel, Bani, **H**, Sherebiah,	3119

HASHBADDANAH (1)

Ne	8:4	Hashum, **H**, Zechariah and Meshullam.	3111

HASHEM (1)

1Ch	11:34	the sons of **H** the Gizonite,	2244

HASHMONAH (2)

Nu	33:29	They left Mithcah and camped at **H**.	3135
	33:30	They left **H** and camped at Moseroth.	3135

HASHUB (KJV) See HASSHUB

HASHUBAH (1)

1Ch	3:20	There were also five others: **H**, Ohel,	3112

HASHUM (5)

Ezr	2:19	of **H** 223	3130
	10:33	From the descendants of **H**:	3130
Ne	7:22	of **H** 328	3130
	8:4	Mishael, Malkijah, **H**, Hashbaddanah,	3130
	10:18	Hodiah, **H**, Bezai,	3130

HASHUPHA (KJV) See HASUPHA

HASN'T (7) [HAVE, NOT]

Ge	38:21	"There **h** been any shrine prostitute here,"	4202
	38:22	"There **h** been any shrine prostitute here.' "	4202
Nu	12:2	"H he also spoken through us?"	4202
1Sa	20:27	"Why **h** the son of Jesse come to the meal,	4202
2Sa	10:3	**H** David sent them to you to explore the city	4202
Ac	9:21	h he **come** here to take them as prisoners	AIT
	22:25	**h** even **been found guilty?"**	185

HASRAH (1)

2Ch	34:22	the son of **H**, keeper of the wardrobe.	2897

HASSENAAH (1)

Ne	3:3	The Fish Gate was rebuilt by the sons of **H**.	2189

HASSENUAH (2)

1Ch	9:7	the son of Hodaviah, the son of **H**;	2190
Ne	11:9	of **H** was over the Second District of	2190

HASSHUB (5)

1Ch	9:14	Shemaiah son of **H**, the son of Azrikam,	3121
Ne	3:11	Malkijah son of Harim and **H** son	3121
	3:23	and **H** made repairs in front of their house;	3121
	10:23	Hoshea, Hananiah, **H**,	3121
	11:15	Shemaiah son of **H**, the son of Azrikam,	3121

HASSOPHERETH (1)

Ezr	2:55	the descendants of Sotai, **H**, Peruda,	2191

HASTE (7) [HASTEN, HASTILY, HASTY]

Ex	12:11	Eat it in **h**; it is the LORD's Passover.	2906
Dt	16:3	because you left Egypt in **h**—	2906
Ps	68:12	"Kings and armies **flee in h**;	5610+5610
Pr	21:5	to profit as surely as **h** leads to poverty.	237
	29:20	Do you see a man who speaks **in h**?	237
Isa	52:12	But you will not leave in **h** or go in flight;	2906
Jer	46:5	They **flee in h** without looking back,	4960+5674

HASTEN (5) [HASTE]

Ps	70:1	**H**, O God, to save me;	NIH
	119:60	I will **h** and not delay	2590

Isa	5:19	let him **h** his work so we may see it.	2590
	49:17	Your sons **h** back,	4554
	55:5	nations that do not know you will **h** to you,	8132

HASTEN (KJV) See also HURRIED, HURRY, RUN, SWIFTLY

HASTILY (1) [HASTE]

Pr	25:8	do not bring **h** to court,	4554

HASTY (3) [HASTE]

Pr	19:2	nor to be **h** and miss the way.	237+928+8079
Ecc	5:2	do not be **h** in your heart to utter anything	4554
1Ti	5:22	Do not be **h** in the laying on of hands,	5441

HASUPHA (2)

Ezr	2:43	the descendants of Ziha, **H**, Tabbaoth,	3102
Ne	7:46	the descendants of Ziha, **H**, Tabbaoth,	3102

HATACH (KJV) See HATHACH

HATCH (2) [HATCHED, HATCHES]

Isa	34:15	she will **h** them, and care for her young	1324
	59:5	They **h** the eggs of vipers and spin	1324

HATCHED (1) [HATCH]

Isa	59:5	and when one is broken, an adder is **h**.	1324

HATCHES (1) [HATCH]

Jer	17:11	Like a partridge that **h** eggs it did not lay is	1842

HATCHETS (1) [HATCHET]

Ps	74:6	the carved paneling with their axes and **h**.	3965

HATE (80) [GOD-HATERS, HATED, HATES, HATING, HATRED]

Ex	18:21	trustworthy men who **h** dishonest gain—	8533
	20:5	and fourth generation of those who **h** me,	8533
Lev	19:17	" 'Do not **h** your brother in your heart.	8533
	26:17	those who **h** you will rule over you,	8533
Dt	5:9	and fourth generation of those who **h** me,	8533
	7:10	But those who **h** him he will repay	8533
	7:10	to repay to their face those who **h** him.	8533
	7:15	but he will inflict them on all who **h** you.	8533
	30:7	on your enemies who **h** and persecute you.	8533
	32:41	and repay those who **h** me.	8533
Jdg	11:7	"Didn't you **h** me and drive me	8533
	14:16	on him, sobbing, "You **h** me!	8533
2Sa	19:6	You love those who **h** you	8533
	19:6	and **h** those who love you.	8533
1Ki	22:8	but I **h** him because he never prophesies	8533
2Ch	18:7	but I **h** him because he never prophesies	8533
	19:2	and love those who **h** the LORD?	8533
Ps	5:5	you **h** all who do wrong.	8533
	25:19	and how fiercely they **h** me!	8533+8534
	31:6	I **h** those who cling to worthless idols;	8533
	35:19	let not those who **h** me	8533
	36:2	to detect or **h** his sin.	8533
	38:19	those who **h** me without reason	8533
	45:7	You love righteousness and **h** wickedness;	8533
	50:17	You **h** my instruction and cast my words	8533
	69:4	Those who **h** me without reason outnumber	8533
	69:14	deliver me from those who **h** me,	8533
	81:15	Those who **h** the LORD would cringe	8533
	97:10	Let those who love the LORD **h** evil,	8533
	101:3	The deeds of faithless men I **h**;	8533
	105:25	whose hearts he turned to **h** his people,	8533
	119:104	therefore I **h** every wrong path.	8533
	119:113	I **h** double-minded men,	8533
	119:128	I **h** every wrong path.	8533
	119:163	I **h** and abhor falsehood	8533
	120:6	among those who **h** peace.	8533
	129:5	all who **h** Zion be turned back in shame.	8533
	139:21	Do I not **h** those who hate you, O LORD,	8533
	139:21	Do I not hate those who **h** you, O LORD,	8533
Pr	1:22	in mockery and fools **h** knowledge?	8533
	8:13	To fear the LORD is to **h** evil;	8533
	8:13	I **h** pride and arrogance,	8533
	8:36	all who **h** me love death."	8533
	9:8	Do not rebuke a mocker or he will **h** you;	8533
	13:5	The righteous **h** what is false,	8533
	25:17	too much of you, and he will **h** you.	8533
	29:10	Bloodthirsty men **h** a man of integrity	8533
Ecc	3:8	a time to love and a time to **h**,	8533
	9:1	no man knows whether love or **h** awaits him	8534
	9:6	their **h** and their jealousy have long since	8534
Isa	61:8	I **h** robbery and iniquity.	8533
	66:5	"Your brothers who **h** you,	8533
Jer	12:8	She roars at me; therefore I **h** her.	8533
	44:4	'Do not do this detestable thing that I **h!'**	8533
Eze	23:28	I am about to hand you over to those you **h**,	8533
	35:6	Since you did not **h** bloodshed,	8533
Am	5:10	you **h** the one who reproves in court	8533
	5:15	**H** evil, love good;	8533
	5:21	"I **h**, I despise your religious feasts;	8533
Mic	3:2	you who **h** good and love evil;	8533
Zec	8:17	I **h** all this," declares the LORD.	8533
Mal	2:16	"I **h** divorce," says the LORD God	8533
	2:16	"and I **h** a man's covering himself	NIH
Mt	5:43	'Love your neighbor and **h** your enemy.'	3631

Mt	6:24	Either *he will* h the one and love the other,	3631
	10:22	All men *will* h *you* because of me,	1639+3631
	24:10	the faith and will betray and h each other,	3631
Mk	13:13	All men *will* h *you* because of me,	1639+3631
Lk	1:71	and from the hand of all who h us—	3631
	6:22	Blessed are you when men h you,	3631
	6:27	do good *to* those who h you,	3631
	14:26	to me and *does* not h his father and mother,	3631
	16:13	Either *he will* h the one and love the other,	3631
	21:17	All men *will* h *you* because of me.	1639+3631
Jn	7: 7	The world cannot h you,	3631
Ro	7:15	I do not do, but what *I* h I do.	3631
	12: 9	*You* h what is evil; cling to what is good.	696
Rev	2: 6	the practices of the Nicolaitans,	3631
	2: 6	of the Nicolaitans, which I also h.	3631
	17:16	The beast and the ten horns you saw *will* h	3631

HATED (29) [HATE]

Ge	37: 4	*they* h him and could not speak a kind word	8533
	37: 5	*they* h him all the more.	8533
	37: 8	And *they* h him all the more because	8534
Dt	9:28	and because he h them,	8533
Jdg	15: 2	"I was so sure *you* **thoroughly h** her,"	8533+8533
2Sa	13:15	Then Amnon h her *with* intense hatred.	8533
	13:15	In fact, he h her more than he had loved her.	8533
	13:22	he h Amnon because he had disgraced his sister Tamar.	8533
Est	9: 1	the upper hand over *those who* h them.	8533
	9: 5	did what they pleased to *those who* h them.	8533
Pr	1:29	Since *they* h knowledge and did not choose	8533
	5:12	You will say, "How *I* h discipline!	8533
	14:17	and a crafty man **is h**.	8533
Ecc	2:17	So *I* h life, because the work that is done	8533
	2:18	I h all the things I had toiled for under	8533
Isa	60:15	"Although you have been forsaken and h,	8533
Eze	16:37	those you loved as well as those *you* h.	8533
Hos	9:15	wickedness in Gilgal, *I* h them there.	8533
Mal	1: 3	but Esau *I* have h,	8130
Mt	24: 9	you will be h by all nations because of me.	3631
Lk	19:14	"But his subjects h him and sent	3631
Jn	15:18	keep in mind that *it* h me first.	3631
	15:24	and yet *they* have h both me and my Father.	3631
	15:25	'*They* h me without reason.'	3631
	17:14	and the world has h them,	3631
Ro	9:13	"Jacob I loved, but Esau *I* h."	3631
Eph	5:29	After all, no one ever h his own body,	3631
Tit	3: 3	being h and hating one another.	5144
Heb	1: 9	You have loved righteousness and h wickedness;	3631

HATEFUL (KJV) See DESTESTABLE, HATE, HATED

HATES (27) [HATE]

Ex	23: 5	the donkey of *someone who* h you fallen	8533
Dt	1:27	"The LORD h us; so he brought us out	8534
	12:31	kinds of detestable things the LORD **h**.	8533
	16:22	for these the LORD your God **h**.	8533
	19:11	But if a man h his neighbor and lies in wait	8533
Job	34:17	*Can he who* h justice govern?	8533
Ps	11: 5	and those who love violence his soul **h**.	8133
Pr	6:16	There are six things the LORD **h**,	8533
	12: 1	but *he who* h correction is stupid.	8533
	13:24	He who spares the rod h his son,	8533
	15:10	*he who* h correction will die.	8533
	15:27	but *he who* h bribes will live.	8533
	26:28	A lying tongue h those it hurts,	8533
	28:16	but *he who* h ill-gotten gain will enjoy	8533
Isa	1:14	and your appointed feasts my soul **h**.	8533
Jn	3:20	Everyone who does evil h the light,	3631
	7: 7	but *it* h me because I testify	3631
	12:25	while the man who h his life in this world	3631
	15:18	"If the world h you, keep in mind that	3631
	15:19	That is why the world h you.	3631
	15:23	He who h me hates my Father as well.	3631
	15:23	He who hates me h my Father as well.	3631
1Jn	2: 9	but h his brother is still in the darkness	3631
	2:11	But whoever h his brother is in the darkness	3631
	3:13	my brothers, if the world h you.	3631
	3:15	Anyone who h his brother is a murderer,	3631
	4:20	"I love God," yet h his brother, he is a liar.	3631

HATHACH (3)

Est	4: 5	Then Esther summoned **H**,	2251
	4: 6	So **H** went out to Mordecai in	2251
	4: 9	**H** went back and reported	2251

HATHATH (1)

1Ch	4:13	The sons of Othniel: **H** and Meonothai.	3171

HATING (2) [HATE]

Tit	3: 3	being hated and h one another.	3631
Jude	1:23	h even the clothing stained	3631

HATIPHA (2)

Ezr	2:54	Neziah and **H**	2640
Ne	7:56	Neziah and **H**	2640

HATITA (2)

Ezr	2:42	of Shallum, Ater, Talmon, Akkub, **H**	2638
Ne	7:45	of Shallum, Ater, Talmon, Akkub, **H**	2638

HATRED (11) [HATE]

2Sa	13:15	Then Amnon hated her with intense **h**.	8534
Ps	109: 3	With words of **h** they surround me;	8534
	109: 5	and **h** for my friendship.	8534
	139:22	*I* have nothing but **h** *for* them;	8533+8534
Pr	10:12	**H** stirs up dissension,	8534
	10:18	He who conceals his **h** has lying lips,	8534
	15:17	a fattened calf with **h**.	8534
Eze	23:29	They will deal with you in **h**	8534
	35:11	and jealousy you showed in your **h** of them	8534
Gal	5:20	**h**, discord, jealousy, fits of rage,	2397
Jas	4: 4	that friendship with the world is **h**	2397

HATTAAVAH   See KIBROTH HATTAAVAH

HATTICON   See HAZER HATTICON

HATTIL (2)

Ezr	2:57	**H**, Pokereth-Hazzebaim	2639
Ne	7:59	**H**, Pokereth-Hazzebaim	2639

HATTUSH (5)

1Ch	3:22	**H**, Igal, Bariah, Neariah and Shaphat—	2637
Ezr	8: 2	of the descendants of David, **H**	2637
Ne	3:10	and **H** son of Hashabneiah made repairs	2637
	10: 4	**H**, Shebaniah, Malluch,	2637
	12: 2	Amariah, Malluch, **H**,	2637

HAUGHTINESS (1) [HAUGHTY]

Jer	48:29	and arrogance and the **h** *of* her heart.	8124

HAUGHTY (15) [HAUGHTINESS]

2Sa	22:28	your eyes are on the **h** to bring them low.	8123
Job	41:34	He looks down on all *that* are **h**;	1469
Ps	10: 5	he is **h** and your laws are far from him;	5294
	18:27	but bring low *those* whose eyes *are* **h**.	8123
	101: 5	whoever has **h** eyes and a proud heart,	1468
	131: 1	O LORD, my eyes are not **h**;	8123
Pr	6:17	**h** eyes, a lying tongue, hands	8123
	16:18	a **h** spirit before a fall.	1470
	21: 4	**H** eyes and a proud heart,	8124
	30:13	so **h**, whose glances are so disdainful;	8123
Isa	3:16	"The women of Zion *are* **h**,	1467
	10:12	the willful pride of his heart and the **h** look	8124
	13:11	I will put an end to the arrogance of the **h**	2294
Eze	16:50	*They were* **h** and did detestable things	1467
Zep	3:11	Never again *will you be* **h** on my holy hill.	1467

HAUL (3)

1Ki	5: 9	My men *will* h them **down** from Lebanon	3718
Eze	32: 3	and *they will* h you **up** in my net.	6590
Jn	21: 6	they were unable *to* h the net **in** because of	1816

HAUNT (8) [HAUNTS]

Ps	44:19	and made us a **h** *for* jackals and covered us	5226
Isa	34:13	She will become a **h** *for* jackals,	5659
Jer	9:11	Jerusalem a heaps of ruins, a **h** of jackals;	5061
	10:22	towns of Judah desolate, a **h** of jackals.	5061
	49:33	"Hazor will become a **h** *of* jackals,	5061
	51:37	a **h** *of* jackals, an object of horror	5061
Rev	18: 2	She has become a home for demons and a **h**	5871
	18: 2	a **h** for every unclean and detestable bird.	5871

HAUNTS (3) [HAUNT]

Ps	74:20	because **h** *of* violence fill the dark places of	5661
SS	4: 8	from the lions' dens and the **mountain h** *of*	2215
Isa	35: 7	In the **h** where jackals once lay,	5659

HAURAN (2)

Eze	47:16	which is on the border of **H**.	2588
	47:18	the boundary will run between **H**	2588

HAVE (827 of 4313) [HAD, HASN'T, HAVE, HAVEN'T, HAVING] See Index of Articles Etc. for an Exhaustive Listing (See Introduction page x)

Ge	13: 8	not h any quarreling between you and me,	2118
	14:24	*Let* them h their share."	4374
	16:11	"You are now with child and *you will* h a son."	3528
	18:10	and Sarah your wife will h a son."	4200
	18:12	*will I* now h this pleasure?"	2118+4200
	18:13	'*Will I* really h **a child**,	3528
	18:14	and Sarah will h a son."	4200
	19: 5	to us so that *we can* h **sex with** them."	3359
	19: 8	I h two daughters who have never slept with	4200
	19:12	"Do you h anyone else here—	4200
	20:17	so *they could* h **children** again,	3528
	24:14	that *I may* h **a drink**,' and she says, 'Drink,	9272
	24:25	"We h plenty of straw and fodder,	6640
	24:33	**what I** h to say."	1821
	25:30	"Quick, *let* me h some of that red stew!	4358
	26:10	the men **might well h** slept with your wife,	3869+5071
	27:38	"Do you h only one blessing, my father?	4200
	31:14	"*Do we still* h any share in the inheritance	4200
	31:29	I h the power to harm you;	3780+4200
	32: 5	I h cattle and donkeys, sheep and	2118+4200
	33: 9	Esau said, "I *already* h plenty.	3780+4200
Ge	33: 9	Keep what you h for yourself."	4200
	33:11	to me and I h all I need."	3780+4200
	35:17	"Don't be afraid, for you h another son."	4200
	43: 7	'*Do you* h another brother?'	3780+4200
	44: 9	If any of your servants is found to h it,	907
	44:10	to h it will become my slave;	907
	44:16	the one who was found to h the cup."	928+3338
	44:17	to h the cup will become my slave.	928+3338
	44:19	'*Do you* h a father or a brother?'	3780+4200
	44:20	we answered, 'We h an aged father,	3780+4200
	45: 1	"**H** everyone **leave** my presence!"	3655
	45:10	your flocks and herds, and all you **h**.	4200
	47: 4	and your servants' flocks h no pasture.	4200
Ex	9:19	and everything you h in the field to a place	4200
	10: 5	They will devour what little you h left after	4200
	10:25	"You must allow us to h sacrifices	928+3338
	12:39	and *did not* h **time** to prepare food	3523+4538
	16:16	for each person you h in your tent.' "	889+4200
	16:18	he who gathered much *did not* h **too much**,	6369
	16:18	he who gathered little *did not* h **too little**.	2893
	18:16	Whenever they h a dispute,	2118+4200
	20: 3	You *shall* h no other gods before me.	2118+4200
	23: 7	**H** nothing to do with a false charge and do	8178
	25:20	*to* h their wings spread upward,	2118
	27: 9	be a hundred cubits long and is to h curtains	4200
	28: 1	"**H** Aaron your brother **brought** to you	278
	28: 7	*to* h two shoulder pieces attached to	2118+4200
	33:19	*I will* h **mercy** *on* whom I will have mercy,	2858
	33:19	I will have mercy on whom *I will* h **mercy**,	2858
	33:19	and *I will* h **compassion**	8163
	33:19	on whom *I will* h **compassion**.	8163
	35: 5	From what you **h**,	907
Lev	7:33	fat of the fellowship offering *shall* h	2118+4200
	11: 9	you may eat any that h fins and scales	4200
	11:10	or streams that do not h fins and scales—	4200
	11:12	the water that does not h fins and scales is	4200
	11:21	those that h jointed legs for hopping on	4200
	11:23	that h four legs you are to detest.	4200
	14:41	h all the inside walls of the house **scraped**	7909
	18: 6	close relative to h **sexual relations**.	1655+6872
	18: 7	*do not* h **relations with** her.	1655+6872
	18: 8	" '*Do not* h **sexual relations with**	1655+6872
	18: 9	" '*Do not* h **sexual relations with**	1655+6872
	18:10	" '*Do not* h **sexual relations with**	1655+6872
	18:11	" '*Do not* h **sexual relations with**	1655+6872
	18:12	" '*Do not* h **sexual relations with**	1655+6872
	18:13	" '*Do not* h **sexual relations with**	1655+6872
	18:14	" '*Do not* **dishonor** *your father's brother* by approaching his wife **to** h **sexual relations;**	1655+6872
	18:15	" '*Do not* h **sexual relations with**	1655+6872
	18:15	*do not* h **relations with** her.	1655+6872
	18:16	" '*Do not* h **sexual relations with**	1655+6872
	18:17	" '*Do not* h **sexual relations with**	1655+6872
	18:17	*Do not* h **sexual relations with**	1655+6872
	18:18	as a rival wife and h **sexual relations**	1655+6872
	18:19	a woman to h **sexual relations** during	1655+6872
	18:20	*Do not* h **sexual relations**	2446+4200+5989+8888
	18:23	not h **sexual relations** with an animal	5989+8888
	18:23	to an animal to h **sexual relations** *with* it;	8061
	19:10	**grapes that h fallen.**	7261
	19:30	and h **reverence for** my sanctuary.	3707
	20:16	to h **sexual relations with**	8061
	20:17	and *they* h **sexual relations,**	906+6872+8011
	20:19	" '*Do not* h **sexual relations with**	1655+6872
	22:25	because they are deformed and h **defects.**' "	928
	23:24	the seventh month you *are to* h a day;	2118+4200
	24:22	*are to* h the same law for the alien and	2118+4200
	25: 4	seventh year the land *is to* h a sabbath	2118+4200
	25: 5	The land *is to* h a year of rest.	2118+4200
	25: 9	Then h the trumpet **sounded** everywhere on	6296
	25:32	" 'The Levites always h the right	2118+4200
	26: 2	" 'Observe my Sabbaths and h **reverence**	3707
	26:35	the land *will* h the **rest** it did not have	8697
	26:35	not h during the sabbaths you lived in it.	8697S
Nu	5:16	" 'The priest shall bring her and h her **stand**	6641
	5:24	He shall h the woman **drink** the bitter water	9197
	5:26	he is to h the woman **drink** the water.	9197
	5:28	**be able to** h children.	2445+2446
	5:30	*to* h her **stand** before the LORD and is	6641
	8: 7	then h *them* **shave** their whole bodies	6296+9509
	8:13	H the Levites **stand** in front of Aaron	6641
	9:14	You *must* h the same regulations for	2118+4200
	11:16	**H** them **come** to the Tent of Meeting,	4374
	11:22	*Would* they h **enough** if flocks	5162
	11:22	*Would* they h **enough** if all the fish in	5162
	15:39	You *will* h these tassels to look at and	2118+4200
	16: 5	h that person **come near**	7928
	18: 9	*to* h the part of the most holy offerings	2118+4200
	18:20	"You *will* h no **inheritance** in their land,	5706
	18:20	nor *will you* h any share among them;	2118+4200
	18:24	'*They will* h no **inheritance** among	5706+5709
	23:22	they h the strength of a wild ox.	4200
	24: 7	their seed will h abundant water.	928
	24: 8	they h the strength of a wild ox.	4200
	25:13	and his descendants *will* h a covenant	2118+4200
	27:19	**H** him **stand** before Eleazar the priest and	6641
	32: 4	and your servants h livestock.	4200
	35: 3	Then they h towns to live in	2118+4200
	35: 5	They *will* h this area as pastureland	2118+4200
Dt	3:19	(I know you h much livestock) may stay	4200
	4: 7	as to h their gods near them the way	4200
	4: 8	as to h such righteous decrees and laws	4200
	4:33	as you h, and lived?	9048S
	5: 7	You *shall* h no other gods before me.	2118+4200
	5:26	as we h, and survived?	NIH
	8:13	and all you h is multiplied,	4200

Dt	10: 9	the Levites **h** no share or inheritance	2118+4200
	11: 8	so that *you may* **h** *the* **strength** to go in	2616
	12:12	who **h** no allotment or inheritance	4200
	12:26	and whatever you **h** vowed to give,	2118+4200
	13:17	he will show you mercy, **h** **compassion**	8163
	14:10	that does not **h** fins and scales you may	4200
	14:27	for they **h** no allotment or inheritance	4200
	14:29	so that the Levites (who **h** no allotment	4200
	18: 1	*to* **h** no allotment or inheritance with	2118+4200
	18: 2	They *shall* **h** no inheritance	2118+4200
	22: 7	with you and *you may* **h** *a* **long** life.	799
	23:13	equipment **h** something to dig with,	2118+4200
	25: 1	When men **h** a dispute,	1068+2118
	25: 2	down and **h** him **flogged** in his presence	5782
	25:13	not **h** two differing weights in your bag—	2118+4200
	25:14	*Do not* **h** two differing measures	2118+4200
	25:15	You *must* **h** accurate and honest weights	2118+4200
	28:33	and *you will* **h** nothing	2118
	28:40	You *will* **h** olive trees	2118+4200
	28:41	*You will* **h** sons and daughters but you will	3528
	28:54	among you *will* **h** **no compassion**	6524+8317
	30: 3	and **h** **compassion** on you	8163
	32:36	and **h** **compassion** on his servants	5714
	33: 9	'*I* **h** no **regard** for them.'	8011
Jos	17:16	in the plain **h** iron chariots,	928
	17:17	You *will* **h** not only one allotment	2118+4200
	17:18	though the Canaanites **h** iron chariots and	4200
	22:24	'What do you **h** to do with the LORD,	4200
	22:25	You **h** no share in the LORD.'	4200
	22:27	'You **h** no share in the LORD.'	4200
	23: 8	as *you* **h** until now.	6913^S
Jdg	3:19	"I **h** a secret message for you, O king."	4200
	3:20	"I **h** a message from God for you."	4200
	7: 2	"You **h** too many men for me	907
	8:24	And he said, "I do **h** one **request,**	8626+8629
	11:12	"What do you **h** against us	4200
	13: 3	but you are going to conceive and **h** a son.	3528
	15: 3	"This time / **h** a **right** to get even	5927
	18:24	What else do I **h**?	4200
	19:19	We **h** both straw and fodder for our donkeys	3780
	19:22	to your house so *we can* **h** **sex with** him."	3359
	21:17	The Benjamite survivors must **h** heirs,"	4200
Ru	1:11	Am I going to **h** any more sons,	928+5055
	1:12	I am too old *to* **h** another husband.	2118+4200
	2:13	though *I do not* **h** the standing of one	2118
	2:14	**H** some bread and dip it in	430^S
	4:11	*May you* **h** standing in Ephrathah and	6913
1Sa	9: 7	We **h** no gift to take to the man of God.	NIH
	9: 7	What do we **h**?"	907
	9: 8	I **h** a quarter of a shekel of silver.	928+3338+5162
	9:12	for the people **h** a sacrifice at the high place.	4200
	18:25	Saul's plan was to **h** David **fall** by	5877
	21: 3	then, what do you **h** **on hand?**	3338+3780+9393
	21: 4	**h** any ordinary bread **on hand,**	448+3338+9393
	21: 8	you **h** a spear or a sword here?	3338+3780+9393
	25:31	my master *will* not **h** on his conscience	2118+4200
	28:22	so you may eat and **h** the strength to go	928+2118
2Sa	1:21	may you **h** neither dew nor rain,	6584
	7:10	plant them so that *they can* **h** **a home**	8905+9393
	16:10	"What do you and I **h in common,**	4200
	18:18	"I **h** no son to carry on the memory	4200
	18:22	You don't **h** any news that will bring you	4200
	18:25	"If he is alone, he must **h** good news."	928+7023
	19:22	"What do you and I **h in common,**	4200
	19:26	'*I will* **h** my donkey **saddled** and will ride	2502
	19:28	So what right do I **h**	3780+4200
	19:43	"We **h** ten shares in the king;	4200
	19:43	**h** a greater **claim on** David than	928
	19:43	a greater claim on David than you **h.**	NIH
	20: 1	"We **h** no share in David,	4200
	21: 4	"We **h** no **right** to demand silver or gold	4200
	21: 4	nor do we **h** the **right** to put anyone in Israel	4200
1Ki	2: 4	you *will* never **fail to h** a man on	4162+4200
	2:14	he added, "I **h** something to say to you."	4200
	2:16	**h** one **request to make**	8626+8629
	2:20	**h** one small **request to make**	8626+8629
	3:13	so that in your lifetime you *will* **h** no equal	2118
	3:26	"Neither I nor you *shall* **h** him."	2118+4200
	5: 6	that we **h** no one so skilled in felling timber	928
	8:18	you did well *to* **h** this in your heart.	2118
	8:25	'You *shall* never **fail to h** a man to sit	4162+4200
	9: 5	'You *shall* never **fail to h** a man on	4162+4200
	11:32	he *will* **h** one tribe.	2118+4200
	11:36	that David my servant *may* always **h** a lamp	2118+4200
	12:16	"What share do we **h** in David,	4200
	13: 7	with me and **h something to eat,**	6184
	17:12	she replied, "I don't **h** any bread—	3780+4200
	17:13	for me from what you **h** and bring it to me,	NIH
	17:18	"What do you **h** against me, man of God?	4200
	18:18	"But you and your father's family **h.**	NIH
	20: 4	I and all I **h** are yours."	4200
	21: 2	"**Let** me **h** your vineyard to use for	5989
	21:10	and **h** *them* **testify** that he has cursed	6386
	22:17	'These people **h** no master.	4200
2Ki	1:13	please **h** **respect** for my life and	928+3700+6524
	1:14	But now **h** **respect** for my life!"	928+3700+6524
	1:16	Because you **h** done this,	NIH
	2:16	"we your servants **h** fifty able men.	907+3780
	3:13	"What do we **h** to do with each	2256+4200+4200
	3:14	if I did not **h** **respect** for the presence	5951
	3:23	"Those kings must **h** fought	2991+4200
	4: 2	Tell me, what do you **h** in your house?"	3780+4200
	4:13	"I **h** a **home** among my own people."	3782

2Ki	4:43	'They will eat and **h** *some* **left over.' "**	3855
	9: 5	"I **h** a message for you, commander,"	4200
	9:18	"What do you **h** to do with peace?"	4200
	9:19	"What do you **h** to do with peace?	4200
	10: 2	with you and you **h** chariots and horses,	907
	17:27	"**H** one of the priests you took captive from Samaria **go** back to live there	2143
	19: 7	and there *I will* **h** him **cut down** with	5877
	21:15	in my eyes and **h** provoked me to anger	2118
	22: 4	the high priest and **h** him **get ready**	9462
1Ch		but his brothers did not **h** many children;	4200
	17: 9	plant them so that *they can* **h** **a home**	8905+9393
	21:22	"*Let* me **h** the site of your threshing floor	5989
	22: 9	But you *will* **h** a son who will be a man	3528
	22:11	and *may you* **h** **success** and build the house	7503
	22:13	Then *you will* **h** **success** if you are careful	7503
	22:15	You **h** many workmen;	6640
	23:11	but Jeush and Beriah *did* not **h** many sons;	8049
2Ch	1: 2	and none after *you will* **h.**"	2118
	6: 8	you did well *to* **h** this in your heart.	2118
	6:16	You *shall* never **fail to h** a man to sit	4162+4200
	7:18	You *shall* never **fail to h** a man to rule	4162+4200
	10:16	"What share do we **h** in David,	4200
	18:16	'These people **h** no master.	4200
	20:12	For we **h** no power to face this vast army	928
	20:20	**H** faith in the LORD your God	586
	20:20	**h** faith in his prophets and you will	586
Ezr	4: 3	"You **h** no **part** with us in building a temple	4200
	7:20	of your God than *you may* **h** occasion	10484
	7:24	that you **h** no authority to impose taxes,	NIH
Ne	2: 7	*may I* **h** letters to the governors	4200+5989
	2: 8	And *may I* **h** a letter to Asaph,	NIH
Est	9:21	to **h** them celebrate annually the fourteenth	7756
Job	1: 5	Job would send and **h** them **purified.**	7727
	3:26	*I* **h** no **peace,** no quietness;	8922
	3:26	*I* **h** no **rest,** but only turmoil."	5663
	5:16	So the poor **h** hope, and injustice	2118+4200
	6: 8	"Oh, that I *might* **h** my request,	995
	6:10	Then I *would* still **h** this consolation—	2118
	6:13	Do I **h** any power to help myself,	928
	6:14	"A despairing man should **h** the devotion	4200
	7: 1	"Does not man **h** hard service on earth?	4200
	9:21	I am blameless, *I* **h** no **concern for** myself;	3359
	10: 4	Do you **h** eyes of flesh?	4200
	10:20	from me so *I can* **h** a moment's **joy**	1158
	12: 3	But I **h** a mind as well as you;	4200
	12: 5	at ease **h** contempt for misfortune as the fate	6953
	15: 3	with speeches that **h** no profit?	3603
	15: 9	What **insights** *do you* **h** that we do not	1067
	15: 9	that we do not **h?**	6640
	19:21	"**H** pity *on* me, my friends, have pity,	2858
	19:21	"Have pity on me, my friends, **h** pity,	2858
	20:20	he *will* **h** no respite from his craving;	3359
	21:14	*We* **h** no **desire** to know your ways.	2911
	24:22	*they* **h** no **assurance** of life.	586
	27:14	his offspring *will* never **h** enough to eat.	8425
	32:17	I too *will* **h** my **say;**	2750+6699
	33:32	If you **h** anything to say, answer me;	3780
	37:24	for *does* he not **h** regard for all the wise	8011
	38:28	*Does* the rain **h** a father?	3780+4200
	40: 5	I spoke once, but *I* **h** no **answer**—	6699
	40: 9	Do you **h** an arm like God's,	4200
Ps	9:13	**H** mercy, and lift me up from the gates	2858
	10: 6	I'll always be happy and never **h** trouble."	928
	16: 6	surely I **h** a delightful inheritance.	6584
	17:14	their sons **h** plenty,	8425
	32: 9	*which* **h** no **understanding** but must	1067
	37:16	the little that the righteous **h** than the wealth	4200
	38: 3	my bones **h** no soundness because	928
	41: 4	I said, "O LORD, **h** mercy on me;	2858
	41:10	But you, O LORD, **h** mercy on me;	2858
	50:16	"**What right h** you to recite my laws	3870+4200+4537
	51: 1	**H** mercy *on* me, O God,	2858
	57: 1	**H** mercy *on* me, O God, have mercy on me,	2858
	57: 1	Have mercy on me, O God, **h** **mercy** on me,	2858
	73: 4	They **h** no struggles;	4200
	73:11	Does the Most High **h** knowledge?"	928+3780
	73:25	Whom **h** I in heaven but you?	4200
	74:20	**H** **regard for** your covenant,	4200+5564
	81: 9	You *shall* **h** no foreign god among you;	2118
	84: 3	where *she may* **h** her young—	8883
	86: 3	**H** mercy *on* me, O Lord,	2858
	86:16	Turn to me and **h** mercy *on* me;	2858
	90:10	or eighty, if we **h** the strength;	2858
	90:13	**H** **compassion** on your servants.	5714
	101: 4	**h** nothing to do with	3359
	102:13	You will arise and **h** **compassion** on Zion,	8163
	111:10	all who follow his precepts **h** good understanding.	4200
	112: 7	*He will* **h** no **fear** of bad news;	3707
	112: 8	His heart is secure, *he will* **h** no **fear;**	3707
	115: 5	They **h** mouths, but cannot speak, eyes,	4200
	115: 6	they **h** ears, but cannot hear, noses,	4200
	115: 7	they **h** hands, but cannot feel, feet,	NIH
	119:99	*I* **h** more **insight** than all my teachers,	8505
	119:100	*I* **h** more **understanding** than the elders,	1067
	119:117	*I will* always **h regard** for your decrees.	9120
	119:132	Turn to me and **h** mercy *on* me,	2858
	119:165	Great peace **h** they who love your law,	4200
	123: 3	**H** mercy *on* us, O LORD, have mercy on us,	2858
	123: 3	O LORD, **h** mercy *on* us,	2858
	135:14	and **h** **compassion** on his servants.	5714
	135:16	They **h** mouths, but cannot speak,	4200
	135:17	they **h** ears, but cannot hear,	4200
	139:22	*I* **h** nothing but **hatred** *for* them;	8533+8534
	142: 4	I **h** no refuge; no one cares for my life.	6+4946

Pr	3:28	when you *now* **h** it with you.	3780
	4: 7	Though it cost all you **h,** get understanding.	7871
	7:14	"I **h** fellowship offerings at home;	6584
	8: 9	they are faultless to *those who* **h** knowledge.	5162
	8:14	I **h** understanding and power.	4200
	12: 9	a nobody and yet **h** a servant than pretend to	4200
	12: 9	to be somebody and **h** no food.	2894
	12:11	who works his land *will* **h** **abundant** food,	8425
	12:21	but the wicked **h** their **fill** of trouble.	4848
	14:32	but even in death the righteous **h** a **refuge.**	2879
	16:22	a fountain of life to *those who* **h** it,	1251
	17:21	To **h** a fool *for a* **son** brings grief;	3528
	20:13	stay awake and *you will* **h** food **to spare.**	8425
	22: 2	Rich and poor **h** this **in common:**	7008
	22:18	**h** all of them **ready**	3922
	28:19	who works his land *will* **h** **abundant** food,	8425
	28:19	one who chases fantasies *will* **h** his **fill**	8425
	29: 7	but the wicked **h** no *such* **concern.**	1067+1981
	29:13	and the oppressor **h** this **in common:**	7008
	30: 2	I do not **h** a man's understanding.	4200
	30: 3	nor **h** / **knowledge** *of* the Holy One.	1981+3359
	30: 9	*I may* **h** too much and disown you and say,	8425
	30:27	locusts **h** no king, yet they advance together	4200
Ecc	2:19	Yet *he will* **h** **control** over all the work	8948
	3:19	All **h** the same breath;	4200
	4: 1	and they **h** no comforter;	4200
	4: 1	and they **h** no comforter.	4200
	4: 9	they **h** a good return for their work:	3780+4200
	6: 3	A man *may* **h** a hundred **children**	3528
	9: 5	they **h** no further reward;	4200
	9: 6	never again will they **h** a part in anything	4200
SS	8: 8	We **h** a young sister,	4200
Isa	1:11	"I **h** more than enough of burnt offerings,	8425
	1:11	/ **h** no **pleasure** *in* the blood of bulls	2911
	3: 6	and say, "You **h** a cloak, you be our leader;	4200
	3: 7	in that day he will cry out, "I **h** no remedy.	2118
	3: 7	I **h** no food or clothing in my house;	NIH
	5:12	*They* **h** harps and lyres at their banquets,	2118
	5:12	but *they* **h** no **regard** for the deeds of	5564
	8:20	they **h** no light of dawn.	4200
	10:13	because / **h** understanding.	1067
	13:17	not care for silver and **h** no **delight** in gold.	2911
	13:18	*they will* **h** no **mercy** on infants	8163
	14: 1	The LORD *will* **h** **compassion** on Jacob;	8163
	17: 8	and *they will* **h** no **regard** for	8011
	22:11	or **h** **regard** for	8011
	26: 1	We **h** a strong city;	4200
	29:20	all who **h** an **eye** for evil will be cut down	9193
	30: 4	Though they **h** officials in Zoan	2118
	30:15	but *you* would **h** none of it.	14
	32: 9	hear what I **h** to say!	614
	37: 7	and there *I will* **h** him **cut down** with	5877
	40:11	he gently leads *those that* **h** young,	6402
	43: 8	Lead out those who **h** eyes but are blind,	3780
	43: 8	who **h** ears but are deaf.	4200
	49:15	the baby at her breast and **h** no **compassion**	8163
	52: 5	"And now what do I **h** here?"	4200
	54: 8	with everlasting kindness *I will* **h** **compassion** *on* you,"	8163
	55: 1	you who **h** no money, come, buy and eat!	4200
	55: 7	and *he will* **h** **mercy** on him,	8163
	56:11	*they* never **h** enough.	3359
Jer	2:19	the LORD your God and **h** no awe of me,"	448
	2:28	For you **h** as many gods as you have towns,	2118
	2:28	For you have as many gods as you **h** towns,	NIH
	3: 3	you **h** the brazen look of a prostitute;	2118+4200
	4:10	'You *will* **h** peace,'	2118+4200
	4:19	I **h** heard the battle cry.	NIH
	4:22	they **h** no **understanding.**	1067
	5:21	who **h** eyes but do not see,	4200
	5:21	who **h** ears but do not hear;	4200
	5:23	But these people **h** stubborn	2118+4200
	5:28	Their evil deeds **h** no **limit;**	6296
	6:15	**h** no **shame** at all;	1017+1017
	8: 8	for we **h** the law of the LORD,"	907
	8: 9	what kind of wisdom do they **h?**	4200
	8:12	No, *they* **h** no **shame at all;**	1017+1017
	11:13	You **h** as many gods as you have towns,	2118
	11:13	You have as many gods as you **h** towns,	NIH
	12:15	I will again **h** **compassion**	8163
	15: 5	"Who *will* **h** **pity** on you, O Jerusalem?	2798
	16: 2	and **h** sons or daughters in this place."	2118+4200
	22:15	a king *to* **h** **more and more** cedar?	3013
	22:15	*Did* not your father **h** food and drink?	430
	22:19	He *will* **h** the **burial** of a donkey—	7690+7699
	23:17	You *will* **h** peace.'	2118+4200
	25:35	The shepherds *will* **h** **nowhere** to flee,	6+4946
	27:18	If they are prophets and **h** the word of	907+3780
	29: 6	Marry and **h** sons and daughters;	3528
	29: 6	so that *they* too may **h** sons and daughters.	3528
	29: 8	dreams *you* encourage them to **h.**	2706+2731
	29:11	For I know the **plans** I **h** for you,"	3108+4742
	29:32	*will* **h** no one left among this people,	2118+4200
	30:10	Jacob will again **h** peace and security,	9200
	30:18	and **h** **compassion** on his dwellings;	8163
	31:20	I **h** **great compassion** for him,"	8163+8163
	32:25	**h** the transaction witnessed.' "	6332+6386
	33:17	'David *will* never **fail to h** a man to sit	4162+4200
	33:18	*ever* **fail to h** a man to stand	4162+4200
	33:21	David *will* no longer **h** a descendant	2118+4200
	33:26	and **h** **compassion** on them.' "	8163
	35: 7	you *must* never **h** any of these things,	2118+4200
	35:19	Recab *will* never **fail to h** a man	4162+4200
	36:30	*He will* **h** no one to sit on the throne	2118+4200
	41: 8	We **h** wheat and barley, oil and honey,	3780+4200
	42:12	so that *he will* **h** **compassion** on you	8163
	46:27	Jacob will again **h** peace and security,	9200

Eze 12: 2 They **h** eyes to see but do not see and ears 4200
12:22 what is this proverb you **h** in the land 4200
20:32 But what you **h** in mind will never happen. 6590
24:14 *I will* not **h** pity, nor will I relent. 2571
24:19 tell us what these things **h** to do with us? 4200
28:24 people of Israel **h** malicious neighbors who
are painful briers 2118+4200
34:15 and **h** them **lie down,** 8069
37:24 and they *will* all **h** one shepherd. 2118+4200
39:25 from captivity and *will* **h compassion** *on* all 8163
40:45 priests *who* **h charge** of the temple, 5466+9068
40:46 priests *who* **h charge** of the altar. 5466+9068
45: 7 " 'The prince will **h** the land bordering 4200
47:22 among you and who **h** children. 3528
Da 1:10 The king would then **h** my head because 4200
2:30 I **h** greater wisdom than other living men, 10029+10089
2:41 *it will* **h** some of the strength of iron in it, 10201
5:11 to **h** insight and intelligence and wisdom 10089
5:12 was found to **h** a keen mind and knowledge 10089
5:14 of the gods is in you and that you **h** insight, 10089
8:22 but will not **h** the same power. 928
9:26 be cut off and will **h** nothing. 4200
11:16 and will **h** the power to destroy it. 928+3338
Hos 4:10 "They will eat but not **h enough;** 8425
10: 3 "We **h** no king because we did not revere 4200
13:14 "I will **h no** compassion, 4946+6259+6524
14: 8 what more **h I** to do with idols? 4200
Joel 1:18 herds mill about because they **h** no pasture; 4200
2:14 He may turn and **h** pity and leave behind 5714
2:26 *You will* **h** plenty to eat, 430+430
Am 5: 3 **h** only a hundred **left;** 8636
5: 3 a hundred strong *will* **h** only ten **left."** 8636
5: 6 and Bethel *will* **h** no one to quench it. 4200
5:15 the LORD God Almighty *will* **h mercy** *on* 2858
5:22 *I will* **h** no regard for them. 5564
Jnh 4: 4 "**H** you **any right** to be angry?" 3512
4: 9 "Do you **h** a right to be angry about 3512
Mic 2: 5 Therefore you *will* **h** no one in 2118+4200
4: 9 **h** you no king? 928
6: 1 hear **what** you **h to say.** 7754
7:19 You will again **h compassion** *on* us; 8163
Na 1:14 "You *will* **h no descendants** 2445
Hab 1:14 like sea creatures that **h** no ruler. 928
Zep 1: 3 The wicked will **h** only heaps of rubble 907
Hag 1: 6 You eat, but never **h enough.** 8425
1: 6 You drink, but never **h** *your* **fill.** 8910
Zec 3: 7 and **h charge** of my courts, 9068
10: 6 I will restore them because *I* **h compassion** 8163
11: 6 For *I will* no longer **h** pity on the people 2798
14:17 Lord Almighty, they *will* **h** no rain. 2118+6584
14:18 they *will* **h** no rain. 6584
Mal 2:10 **H** we not all one Father? 4200
3: 3 LORD *will* **h** men who will bring 2118+4200
3:10 that you will not **h** room enough for it. 4200
Mt 3: 9 'We **h** Abraham as our father.' 2400
6: 1 *you will* **h** no reward from your Father 2400
8:20 "Foxes **h** holes and birds of 2400
8:20 and birds of the air **h** nests, NIG
9:27 "**H mercy** on us, Son of David!" 1796
10: 8 raise the dead, cleanse **those who h leprosy,** 3320
11: 5 *those who* **h leprosy** are cured, 3320
13: 5 where *it did* not **h** much soil. 2400
13:12 and he will **h an abundance.** 4355
13:12 Whoever *does* not **h,** 2400
14: 4 "It is not lawful for you to **h** her." 2400
14:17 "*We* **h** here only five loaves of bread 2400
15:22 "Lord, Son of David, **h mercy** on me! 1796
15:32 "*I* **h compassion** for these people, 5072
15:32 with me three days and **h** nothing to eat. 2400
15:34 "How many loaves *do you* **h?"** 2400
16:23 *you do* not **h in mind** the things of God, 5858
17: 9 "Don't tell anyone what **you h seen,** 3969
17:15 "Lord, **h mercy** on my son," he said. 1796
17:20 if you **h** faith as small as a mustard seed, 2400
18: 8 or crippled than *to* **h** two hands or two feet 2400
18: 9 to enter life with one eye than *to* **h** two eyes 2400
19:21 and *you will* **h** treasure in heaven. 2400
20:15 Don't I **h the right** to do what I want 2003
20:30 "Lord, Son of David, **h mercy** on us!" 1796
20:31 "Lord, Son of David, **h mercy** on us!" 1796
21:21 if you **h** faith and do not doubt, 2400
22:24 the widow and **h children** for him. 482+5065
23: 8 for you **h** only one Master 1639
23: 9 for you **h** one Father, and he is in heaven. 1639
23:10 for you **h** one Teacher, the Christ. 1639
23:23 But *you* **h neglected** 918
25:29 and he will **h an abundance.** 4355
25:29 Whoever *does* not **h,** 2400
26:11 The poor *you will* always **h** with you, 2400
26:11 but *you will* not always **h** me. 2400
26:35 Peter declared, "Even if I **h** to die with you, 1256
Mk 2:19 so long as they **h** him with them. 2400
3:15 and *to* **h** authority to drive out demons. 2400
4: 5 where *it did* not **h** much soil. 2400
4:17 *they* **h** no root, they last only a short time. 2400
4:25 whoever *does* not **h,** 2400
4:40 *Do you* still **h** no faith?" 2400
6:18 for you to **h** your brother's wife." 2400
6:31 and going that they did not even **h a chance** 2320
6:38 "How many loaves *do you* **h?"** 2400
6:39 **h** all the people **sit down** 369
8: 2 "*I* **h compassion** for these people 5072
8: 2 with me three days and **h** nothing to eat. 2400
8: 5 "How many loaves *do you* **h?"** 2400
8:16 "It is because *we* **h** no bread." 2400
8:18 Do you **h** eyes but fail to see, 2400

Mk 8:33 "*You do* not **h in mind** the things of God, 5858
9:45 to enter life crippled than *to* **h** two feet and 2400
9:47 of God with one eye than *to* **h** two eyes and 2400
9:50 **H** salt in yourselves. 2400
10:21 sell everything *you* **h** and give to the poor, 2400
10:21 and *you will* **h** treasure in heaven. 2400
10:47 "Jesus, Son of David, **h mercy** on me!" 1796
10:48 "Son of David, **h mercy** on me!" 1796
11:22 "**H** faith in God," Jesus answered. 2400
12:19 widow and **h children** for his brother. 1985+5065
14: 7 The poor *you will* always **h** with you, 2400
14: 7 But *you will* not always **h** me. 2400
14:31 "Even if I **h** to die with you, 1256
Lk 1:36 Even Elizabeth your relative *is going to* **h** 5197
1:57 for Elizabeth *to* **h** her baby, 5503
3: 8 '*We* **h** Abraham as our father.' 2400
6:31 Do to others as you would **h** them **do** to you 4472
7:22 *those who* **h leprosy** are cured, 3320
7:36 of the Pharisees invited Jesus to **h dinner** 2266
7:40 "Simon, *I* **h** something to tell you." 2400
8:13 but they **h** no root. 2400
8:18 whoever *does* not **h,** 2400
9:13 "We **h** only five loaves of bread 1639
9:58 "Foxes **h** holes and birds of 2400
9:58 and birds of the air **h** nests, NIG
11: 6 and *I* **h** nothing to set before him.' 2400
12:17 *I* **h** no place to store my crops.' 2400
12:19 "You **h** plenty of good things laid up 2400
12:24 they **h** no storeroom or barn; 1639
12:37 **h** them **recline at the table** 369
12:50 But *I* **h** a baptism to undergo, 2400
15:17 of my father's hired men **h** food **to spare,** 4355
15:23 Let's **h** a feast and celebrate. 2266
15:31 and everything I **h** is yours. 1847+3836
16:24 **h** pity on me and send Lazarus to dip the tip 1796
16:28 for *I* **h** five brothers. 2400
16:29 '*They* **h** Moses and the Prophets; 2400
17: 6 "If *you* **h** faith as small as a mustard seed, 2400
17:13 "Jesus, Master, **h pity** on us!" 1796
18:22 Sell everything *you* **h** and give to the poor, 2400
18:22 and *you will* **h** treasure in heaven. 2400
18:38 "Jesus, Son of David, **h mercy** on me!" 1796
18:39 "Son of David, **h mercy** on me!" 1796
19:20 *I* **h** kept it laid away in a piece of cloth. 2400
20:28 must marry the widow and **h children** for
his brother. 1985+5065
22:36 "But now *if you* **h** a purse, take it, 2400+3836
22:36 and *if you* don't **h** a sword, 2400+3836
24:26 not the Christ **h** to suffer these things and 1256
24:39 a ghost *does* not **h** flesh and bones, 2400
24:39 as you see I **h."** 2400
24:41 "*Do you* **h** anything here to eat?" 2400
Jn 2: 3 "*They* **h** no more wine." 2400
3:15 in him *may* **h** eternal life. 2400
3:16 in him shall not perish but **h** eternal life. 2400
4:11 "*you* **h** nothing to draw with and 2400
4:17 "*I* **h** no husband," she replied. 2400
4:17 when you say *you* **h** no husband. 2400
4:18 the man *you now* **h** is not your husband. 2400
4:32 "*I* **h** food to eat that you know nothing about 2400
5: 7 "*I* **h** no one to help me into the pool when 2400
5:26 he has granted the Son *to* **h** life in himself. 2400
5:36 "*I* **h** testimony weightier than that of John. 2400
5:40 yet you refuse to come to me to **h** life. 2400
5:42 I know that *you do* not **h** the love of God 2400
6: 7 not buy enough bread for each one *to* **h** 3284
6:10 Jesus said, "**H** the people sit down." 4472
6:40 and believes in him *shall* **h** eternal life, 2400
6:53 *you* **h** no life in you. 2400
6:68 *You* **h** the words of eternal life. 2400
8: 6 in order to **h** a basis for accusing him. 2400
8:12 but *will* **h** the light of life." 2400
8:26 "*I* **h** much to say in judgment of you. 2400
8:41 "The only Father *we* **h** is God himself." 2400
10:10 I have come that *they may* **h** life, 2400
10:10 and **h** it to the full. 2400
10:16 *I* **h** other sheep that are not 2400
10:18 *I* **h** authority to lay it down and authority 2400
12: 8 *You will* always **h** the poor among you, 2400
12: 8 but *you will* not always **h** me. 2400
12:35 "*You are going to* **h** the light just a little 1639
12:35 Walk while *you* **h** the light, 2400
12:36 Put your trust in the light while *you* **h** it, 2400
13: 8 *you* **h** no part with me." 2400
15:22 however, *they* **h** no excuse for their sin. 2400
16:12 "*I* **h** much more to say to you, 2400
16:33 so that in me *you may* **h** peace. 2400
16:33 In this world *you will* **h right** to execute anyone," 2400
17:10 All *I* **h** is yours, and all you have is 1847+3836
17:10 I have is yours, and all you **h** is mine. 3836+5050
17:13 that *they may* **h** the full measure of my joy 2400
18:31 "But we **h** no **right** to execute anyone," 2003
19: 7 The Jews insisted, "*We* **h** a law, 2400
19:10 "Don't you realize *I* **h power** either 2400
19:11 "*You would* **h** no power over me if it were 2400
19:15 "*We* **h** no king but Caesar," 2400
20:31 by believing *you may* **h** life in his name. 2400
21:25 the whole world *would* not **h room for** 6003
Ac 3: 6 Then Peter said, "Silver or gold *I do* not **h,** 5639
3: 6 but what *I* **h** I give you. 2400
8:21 You **h** no part or share in this ministry, 1639
10:33 that he could hear what *you* **h to say."** 4123+5148
13:15 if you **h** a message of encouragement for the 1639
17:28 in him we live and move and **h** our being.' 1639
18:10 because I **h** many people in this city." 1639
19:38 and his fellow craftsmen **h** a grievance 2400
21:23 There are four men with us *who* **h made** 2400

Ac 24:15 and *I* **h** the same hope in God as these men, 2400
24:19 and bring charges if *they* **h** anything 2400
25: 3 to **h** Paul **transferred** to Jerusalem. 3569
25:26 But *I* **h** nothing definite to write 2400
25:26 of this investigation *I may* **h** something 2400
Ro 1:13 in order that *I might* **h** a harvest among you, 2400
2: 1 You, therefore, **h** no excuse, 1639
2:14 when Gentiles, *who do* not **h** the law, 2400
2:14 *even though they do* not **h** the law, 2400
2:20 because *you* **h** in the law the embodiment 2400
3: 3 What if some *did* **not h faith?** 601
3:26 one who justifies those who **h faith** 1666+4411
5: 1 we **h** peace with God through our Lord 2400
5: 2 through whom *we* **h gained** access by faith 2400
7:18 For *I* **h** the desire to do what is good, 4154
8: 5 with the Spirit **h** their minds set on what NIG
8: 9 if anyone *does* not **h** the Spirit of Christ, 2400
8:12 brothers, *we* **h an obligation—** 1639+4050
8:23 who **h** the firstfruits of the Spirit, 2400
8:25 But if we hope for what *we do* not yet **h,** 1063S
9: 2 *I* **h** great sorrow and unceasing anguish 1639
9: 9 and Sarah *will* **h** a son. 1639
9:15 "*I will* **h mercy** on whom I have mercy, 1796
9:18 on whom he wants to **h** mercy, NIG
9:21 *Does* not the potter **h** the right to make out 2400
11:32 to disobedience so that *he may* **h mercy on** 1796
12: 4 and these members *do* not all **h** 2400
12: 6 *We* **h** different gifts, 2400
15: 4 of the Scriptures *we might* **h** hope. 2400
15:23 and since *I* **h** been longing for many years 2400
1Co 2:16 But we **h** the mind of Christ. 2400
4: 2 **h** been given a trust must prove faithful. 3874
4: 7 What *do you* **h** that you did not receive? 2400
4: 8 Already *you* **h** all you want! 1639+3170
4:15 Even though *you* **h** ten thousand guardians 2400
4:15 you *do* not **h** many fathers, NIG
5:10 that case *you would* **h** to leave this world. 4053
6: 4 if you **h** disputes about such matters, 2400
6: 7 The very fact that *you* **h** lawsuits 2400
6:19 whom *you* **h** received from God? 2400
7: 2 each man *should* **h** his own wife, 2400
7:25 *I* **h** no command from the Lord, 2400
7:29 From now on those who **h** wives should live 2400
7:40 and I think that I too **h** the Spirit of God. 2400
8:10 weak conscience sees you who **h** this
knowledge eating 2400
9: 4 Don't *we* **h** the right to food and drink? 2400
9: 5 Don't *we* **h** the right to take a believing wife 2400
9:12 If others **h** this right of support from you, 3576
9:12 shouldn't *we* **h** it all the more? NIG
9:17 If I preach voluntarily, *I* **h** a reward; 2400
10:21 you cannot **h a part** in both the Lord's table 3576
11:10 the woman ought *to* **h** a sign of authority 2400
11:16 we **h** no other practice— 2400
11:17 In the following directives *I* **h no praise** 2046
11:19 No doubt *there* **h** to be differences 1256
11:22 Don't *you* **h** homes to eat and drink in? 2400
11:22 of God and humiliate those who **h** nothing? 2400
11:25 but that its parts *should* **h** equal **concern** 3534
12:30 Do all **h** gifts of healing? 2400
13: 1 but **h** not love, 2400
13: 2 If *I* **h** the gift of prophecy 2400
13: 2 and if *I* **h** a faith that can move mountains, 2400
13: 2 but **h** not love, I am nothing. 2400
13: 3 but **h** not love, I gain nothing. 2400
14: 5 but I would rather **h** *you* **prophesy.** 4736
15:19 If only for this life *we* **h** hope in Christ, 1639+1827
2Co 3:12 since *we* **h** such a hope, we are very bold. 2400
4: 1 through God's mercy *we* **h** this ministry, 2400
4: 7 But *we* **h** this treasure in jars of clay to show 2400
5: 1 *we* **h** a building from God, 2400
7: 1 Since *we* **h** these promises, dear friends, 2400
7: 3 before that *you* **h** such a place in our hearts 2400
8:10 to give but also *to* **h** the desire to do so. 2527
8:12 not according to what *he does* not **h.** 2400
8:15 He who gathered much *did* not **h too much,** 4429
8:15 who gathered little *did* not **h too little."** 1782
11:27 **h** often **gone without sleep;** 71+1877
12:14 children *should* not **h** to save up 4053
12:15 **everything I h** and **expend** 1682
13: 7 even though we *may* seem *to* **h** failed. 99+1639
Gal 2: 4 to spy on the freedom *we* **h** in Christ Jesus 2400
3: 9 So those who **h faith** are blessed along 1666+4411
4:15 I can testify that, if you **could h done so,** 1543
4:27 you who **h no labor pains;** 6048
6:10 Therefore, as *we* **h** opportunity, 2400
Eph 1: 7 In him *we* **h** redemption through his blood, 2400
2:18 through him *we* both **h** access to the Father 2400
4:18 that *he may* **h** something to share with those 2400
Php 1: 7 since *I* **h** you in my heart; 2400
2:20 *I* **h** no one else like him, 2400
2:28 be glad and *I may* **h** less anxiety. 1639
3: 4 I myself **h** reasons for such confidence. 2400
4:18 I am amply supplied, now that *I* **h received** 1312
Col 1: 4 in Christ Jesus and of the love *you* **h** for all 2400
1:14 in whom *we* **h** redemption, 2400
1:18 in everything *he might* **h** the supremacy. 1181
2:23 regulations indeed **h** an appearance 1639+2400
3:13 and forgive whatever grievances *you may* **h** 2400
1Th 3: 6 that *you* always **h** pleasant memories of us 2400
3: 9 for all the **joy** *we* **h** in the presence 5897+5915
4:13 who **h** no hope. 2400
2Th 3: 9 because *we do* not **h** the right to such help, 2400
1Ti 2:12 a woman to teach or *to* **h authority over** 883
3: 7 also **h** a good reputation with outsiders, 2400

1Ti	5:14	*to* h **children,** to manage their homes and	5449
	6: 2	Those who h believing masters are not	2400
	6: 8	But *if we* h food and clothing,	2400
2Ti	2:23	**Don't** h anything to do with foolish and	4148
	3: 5	H nothing to do with them.	706
Tit	2: 8	be ashamed *because they* h nothing bad	
	3:13	h everything they need.	3309+3594
Phm	1:15	a little while was that *you might* h him **back**	600
Heb	2:14	Since the children h flesh and blood,	3125
	4:14	*since we* h a great high priest who has gone	2400
	4:15	For *we do not* h a high priest who is unable	2400
	4:15	but *we* h one who has been tempted	NIG
	5:14	who by constant use h trained themselves	2400
	6:19	*We* h this hope as an anchor for the soul,	2400
	8: 1	*We do* h such a high priest,	2400
	8: 3	for this one also *to* h something to offer.	2400
	10: 2	would no longer h felt guilty for their sins.	2400
	10: 7	*I* h come to do your will, O God.' "	2457
	10: 9	"Here I am, *I* h come to do your will."	2457
	10:19	*since we* h confidence to enter	2400
	10:21	we h a great priest over the house of God,	NIG
	11:32	*I do not* h time to tell about Gideon, Barak,	2142
	13: 5	of money and be content *with* what *you* h,	4205
	13:10	*We* h an altar from which those who	2400
	13:10	at the tabernacle h no right to eat.	2400
	13:14	For here *we do not* h an enduring city,	2400
	13:18	We are sure that *we* h a clear conscience	2400
Jas	2:14	if a man claims *to* h faith but has no deeds?	2400
	2:18	But someone will say, "You h faith;	2400
	2:18	"You have faith; I h **deeds.**	2400
	4: 2	but you cannot h what you want.	2209
	4: 2	*You do not* h, because you do not ask God.	2400
	5: 2	and **moths** h eaten your clothes.	1181+4963
1Pe	3:15	the reason for the hope that **you** h.	1877+5148
2Pe	1: 9	But *if* anyone *does not* h them,	4205
	1:12	in the truth *you now* h.	4205
	1:19	And *we* h the word of the prophets	2400
1Jn	1: 3	so that you also *may* h fellowship with us.	2400
	1: 6	If we claim *to* h fellowship with him	2400
	1: 7	*we* h fellowship with one another,	2400
	2: 1	*we* h one who speaks to the Father	2400
	2:20	But *you* h an anointing from the Holy One,	2400
	3:21	*we* h confidence before God	2400
	4:17	among us so that *we will* h confidence on	2400
	5:12	not h the Son of God *does not* h life,	2400
	5:12	not have the Son of God *does not* h life.	2400
	5:13	that you may know that *you* h eternal life.	2400
	5:14	the confidence *we* h in approaching God:	2400
	5:15	we know that *we* h what we asked of him.	2400
2Jn	1: 9	in the teaching of Christ *does not* h God;	2400
	1:12	*I* h much to write to you,	2400
3Jn	1: 4	*I* h no greater joy than to hear	2400
	1: 9	*will* h nothing *to do with* us.	2110
	1:13	*I* h much to write to you,	2400
Jude	1:19	and *do not* h the Spirit.	2400
Rev	2: 6	But *you* h this in your favor:	2400
	2:14	Nevertheless, *I* h a few things against you:	2400
	2:14	*You* h people there who hold to the teaching	2400
	2:15	also h those who hold to the teaching of	2400
	2:20	Nevertheless, *I* h this against you:	2400
	2:25	Only hold on to what *you* h until I come.	2400
	3: 1	*you* h a reputation of being alive,	2400
	3: 4	Yet *you* h a few people in Sardis who have	2400
	3: 8	I know that *you* h little strength,	2400
	3:11	Hold on to what *you* h,	2400
	9: 4	but only those people who *did not* h the seal	2400
	11: 6	These men h power to shut up the sky so	2400
	11: 6	and *they* h power to turn the waters	2400
	17:13	They h one purpose	2400
	20: 6	Blessed and holy are those who h part in	2400
	22:14	that they *may* h the right to the tree of life	1639

HAVEN (2)

Ge	49:13	by the seashore and become a h *for* ships;	2572
Ps	107:30	and he guided them to their desired h.	4685

HAVEN'T (19) [HAVE, NOT]

Ge	27:36	"H you reserved any blessing for me?"	4202
Nu	16:14	you h brought us into a land flowing	4202
Jdg	14:16	but you h told me the answer."	4202
	14:16	"I h even explained it to my father	4202
	16:15	a fool of me and h told me the secret	4202
1Sa	21: 8	I h brought my sword or any other weapon,	4202
2Sa	3: 8	I h handed you over to David.	4202
	11:10	"H you just come from a distance?"	4202
1Ki	18:13	H you heard, my lord,	4202
1Ch	19: 3	H his men come to you to explore	4202
2Ch	24: 6	"Why h you required the Levites to bring in	4202
Mt	12: 3	"H you read what David did when he	4024
	12: 5	Or h you read in the Law that on	4024
	19: 4	"H you read," he replied,	4024
Mk	12:10	H you read this scripture:	4028
Lk	5: 5	and h caught **anything.**	4029
	13: 7	for fruit on this fig tree and h found any.	4024
Jn	21: 5	"Friends, h *you* any fish?"	2400+3590
Ac	27:33	you h eaten **anything.**	3594

HAVENS See FAIR HAVENS

HAVILAH (7)

Ge	2:11	it winds through the entire land *of* H,	2564
	10: 7	Seba, H, Sabtah, Raamah and Sabteca.	2564
	10:29	Ophir, H and Jobab. All these were sons of Joktan.	2564

Ge	25:18	His descendants settled in the area from H	2564
1Sa	15: 7	the Amalekites all the way from H to Shur,	2564
1Ch	1: 9	Seba, H, Sabta, Raamah and Sabteca.	2564
	1:23	Ophir, H and Jobab. All these were sons of Joktan.	2564

HAVING (73) [HAVE]

Ge	16: 2	"The LORD has kept me from h **children.**	3528
	29:35	Then she stopped h children.	3528
	30: 2	who has kept you from *h* **children?**"	AIT
	30: 9	Leah saw that she had stopped h **children,**	3528
	31:35	I'm h my period."	4200
	35:17	as she *was* h **great** difficulty in childbirth,	7996
Ex	12: 4	h taken into account the number	NIH
Lev	9:22	And h **sacrificed** the sin offering,	AIT
	16:17	h **made atonement** for himself,	AIT
	18: 7	'*Do not* **dishonor** your father **by** h **sexual** relations with your mother.	1655+6872
Nu	10: 2	h the camps **set out.**	5023
Jdg	16:19	H put him **to sleep**	AIT
1Sa	24: 5	for h **cut off** a corner of his robe.	AIT
	25:31	or of h **avenged** himself.	NIH
1Ki	6:34	each h two leaves that turned in sockets.	AIT
1Ch	23:22	Eleazar died without h **sons:**	2118+4200
	29:28	h enjoyed long life, wealth and honor.	NIH
Ne	9: 1	fasting and wearing sackcloth and h dust	NIH
Est	3: 6	h **learned** who Mordecai's people were,	AIT
Job	21:25	never h **enjoyed** anything good.	AIT
Ps	65: 6	h **armed yourself** with strength,	AIT
Isa	22: 3	h **fled** while the enemy was still far away.	AIT
Eze	44:11	h **charge** of the gates of the temple	7213
Da	4:21	and h **nesting places** in its branches for	AIT
Am	1: 3	with **sledges** h iron teeth,	AIT
Zec	9: 9	righteous and h **salvation,**	3828
Mt	2:12	And h **been warned** in a dream not	AIT
	2:22	H *been* warned in a dream,	AIT
	4:24	the demon-possessed, those h **seizures,**	AIT
	9:10	*While* Jesus *was* h **dinner**	367
	16: 8	among yourselves about h no bread?	2400
	22:24	that if a man dies without h **children,**	2400
Mk	2:15	*While* Jesus *was* h **dinner** at Levi's house,	AIT
	8: 9	And h **sent** them **away,**	AIT
	8:17	"Why are you talking about h no bread?	2400
Lk	17:20	h *been* **asked** by the Pharisees when	AIT
Jn	4:54	h **come** from Judea to Galilee.	AIT
	7: 9	*H* **said** this, he stayed in Galilee.	AIT
	7:15	"How did this man get such learning without h **studied?**"	AIT
	9: 6	*H* **said** this, he spit on the ground,	AIT
	13: 1	h **loved** his own who were in the world,	AIT
Ac	5:27	*H* **brought** the apostles,	AIT
	7:45	*H* **received** the tabernacle,	AIT
	8:22	Perhaps he will forgive you for h such	NIG
	12:20	*H* **secured the support** of Blastus,	AIT
	16: 6	h *been* **kept** by the Holy Spirit from	AIT
	21:40	*H* **received** the commander's **permission,**	AIT
Ro	5:10	how much more, h *been* **reconciled,**	AIT
1Co	8: 7	of it as h *been* sacrificed to an idol,	NIG
	9:21	*To* those **not** h the law I became like one	491
	9:21	the law I became like one **not** h the law	491
	9:21	so as to win those **not** h the law.	491
	12:28	also those h gifts of healing,	NIG
2Co	6:10	h nothing, and yet possessing everything.	2400
	9: 4	would be ashamed of h been so confident.	NIG
	9: 8	h all that you need,	2400
Eph	1:11	h *been* **predestined** according to the plan	AIT
	1:13	*H* **believed,** you were marked in him with	AIT
	4:19	*H* **lost all** sensitivity,	AIT
Php	2: 2	h the same love,	2400
	3: 9	not h a righteousness of my own that comes	2400
Col	2:12	h *been* **buried** with him in baptism	AIT
	2:14	h **canceled** the written code,	AIT
	2:15	And h **disarmed** the powers and authorities,	AIT
2Ti	3: 5	h a form of godliness but denying its power.	2400
Tit	3: 7	h *been* **justified** by his grace,	AIT
	3: 7	we might become heirs h the hope	NIG
Heb	9:12	h **obtained** eternal redemption.	AIT
	10:22	h our hearts **sprinkled to cleanse**	AIT
	10:22	and h our bodies **washed** with pure water.	AIT
Rev	7: 2	h the seal of the living God.	2400
	9:19	h heads with which they inflict injury.	2400
	20: 1	h the key to the Abyss and holding	2400

HAVOC (3)

Isa	54:16	the destroyer to **work** h;	2472
Jer	48: 3	cries of great h and destruction.	8719
Ac	9:21	"Isn't he the man who **raised** h in Jerusalem	4514

HAVOCK (KJV) See DESTROY

HAVVOTH JAIR (4) [JAIR]

Nu	32:41	and called them H.	2596
Dt	3:14	so that to this day Bashan is called H.)	2596
Jdg	10: 4	which to this day are called H.	2596
1Ch	2:23	(But Geshur and Aram captured H,	2596

HAWK (3)

Lev	11:16	the screech owl, the gull, any kind of h,	5891
Dt	14:15	the screech owl, the gull, any kind of h,	5891
Job	39:26	"Does the h take flight by your wisdom	5891

HAY (2)

Pr	27:25	the h is removed and new growth appears	2945

1Co	3:12	silver, costly stones, wood, h or straw,	5965

HAZAEL (24)

1Ki	19:15	you get there, anoint H king over Aram,	2599
	19:17	to death any who escape the sword of H,	2599
2Ki	8: 8	he said to H, "Take a gift with you	2599
	8: 9	H went to meet Elisha,	2599
	8:11	with a fixed gaze until H felt ashamed.	NIH
	8:12	"Why is my lord weeping?" asked H.	2599
	8:13	H said, "How could your servant,	2599
	8:14	H left Elisha and returned to his master.	NIH
	8:14	H replied, "He told me	NIH
	8:15	Then H succeeded him as king.	2599
	8:28	against H king of Aram at Ramoth Gilead.	2599
	8:29	on him at Ramoth in his battle with H king	2599
	9:14	against H king of Aram,	2599
	9:15	on him in the battle with H king of Aram.)	2599
	10:32	H overpowered the Israelites	2599
	12:17	About this time H king of Aram went up	2599
	12:18	and he sent them to H king of Aram,	2599
	13: 3	of H king of Aram and Ben-Hadad his son.	2599
	13:22	H king of Aram oppressed Israel throughout	2599
	13:24	H king of Aram died,	2599
	13:25	of H the towns he had taken in battle	2599
2Ch	22: 5	of Ahab king of Israel to war against H king	2599
	22: 6	on him at Ramoth in his battle with H king	2599
Am	1: 4	upon the house of H that will consume	2599

HAZAIAH (1)

Ne	11: 5	the son of Col-Hozeh, the son of H,	2610

HAZAR ADDAR (1) [ADDAR]

Nu	34: 4	Then it will go to H and over	2960

HAZAR ENAN (4) [ENAN]

Nu	34: 9	continue to Ziphron and end at H.	2966
	34:10	run a line from H to Shepham.	2966
Eze	47:17	from the sea to H,	2965
	48: 1	H and the northern border	2966

HAZAR GADDAH (1)

Jos	15:27	H, Heshmon, Beth Pelet,	2961

HAZAR SHUAL (4) [SHUAL]

Jos	15:28	H, Beersheba, Biziothiah,	2967
	19: 3	H, Balah, Ezem,	2967
1Ch	4:28	in Beersheba, Moladah, H,	2967
Ne	11:27	in H, in Beersheba	2967

HAZAR SUSAH (1)

Jos	19: 5	Ziklag, Beth Marcaboth, H,	2963

HAZAR SUSIM (1)

1Ch	4:31	H, Beth Biri and Shaaraim.	2964

HAZARDED (KJV) See RISKED

HAZARHATTICON (KJV) See HAZER HATTICON

HAZARMAVETH (2)

Ge	10:26	the father of Almodad, Sheleph, H,	2975
1Ch	1:20	the father of Almodad, Sheleph, H,	2975

HAZAZON TAMAR (2) [EN GEDI, TAMAR]

Ge	14: 7	the Amorites who were living in H.	2954
2Ch	20: 2	It is already in H" (that is, En Gedi).	2954

HAZEL (KJV) See ALMOND

HAZELELPONI (KJV) See HAZZELELPONI

HAZER HATTICON (1)

Eze	47:16	as far as H,	2962

HAZERIM (KJV) See VILLAGE

HAZEROTH (5)

Nu	11:35	the people traveled to H and stayed there.	2972
	12:16	the people left H and encamped in	2972
	33:17	and camped at H.	2972
	33:18	They left H and camped at Rithmah.	2972
Dt	1: 1	Laban, H and Dizahab.	2972

HAZIEL (1)

1Ch	23: 9	Shelomoth, H and Haran—three in all.	2609

HAZO (1)

Ge	22:22	Kesed, H, Pildash, Jidlaph and Bethuel."	2605

HAZOR (18) [BAAL HAZOR, EN HAZOR, HAZOR HADATTAH, KERIOTH HEZRON]

Jos	11: 1	When Jabin king of H heard of this,	2937
	11:10	that time Joshua turned back and captured H	2937

Jos	11:10	**H** had been the head of all these kingdoms.) 2937
	11:11	and he burned up **H** itself. 2937
	11:13	except **H**, which Joshua burned. 2937
	12:19	the king of Madon one the king of **H** one 2937
	15:23	Kedesh, **H**, Ithnan, 2937
	15:25	Kerioth Hezron (that is, **H**), 2937
	19:36	Adamah, Ramah, **H**, 2937
Jdg	4: 2	a king of Canaan, who reigned in **H**. 2937
	4:17	of **H** and the clan of Heber the Kenite. 2937
1Sa	12: 9	the commander of the army of **H**, 2937
1Ki	9:15	the wall of Jerusalem, and **H**, 2937
2Ki	15:29	Abel Beth Maacah, Janoah, Kedesh and **H**. 2937
Ne	11:33	in **H**, Ramah and Gittaim, 2937
Jer	49:28	Concerning Kedar and the kingdoms of **H**, 2937
	49:30	Stay in deep caves, you who live in **H**," 2937
	49:33	"**H** will become a haunt of jackals, 2937

HAZOR HADATTAH (1) [HAZOR]

Jos 15:25 **H**, Kerioth Hezron   2939

HAZZELELPONI (1)

1Ch 4: 3 Their sister was named **H**.   2209

HAZZOBEBAH (1)

1Ch 4: 8 who was the father of Anub and **H** and of   2206

HAZZURIM See HELKATH HAZZURIM

HE (9660) [HE'S, HIM, HIS] See Index of Articles Etc.

HE'S (12) [BE, HE]

Ge	27:36	and now *h* taken my blessing!" AIT
Jdg	13:10	to tell her husband, "**H** here! NIH
1Sa	9:12	"**H** ahead of you. NIH
2Sa	18:27	"**H** a good man," the king said. 2296
Mt	27:42	**H** the King of Israel," 1639
	27:47	they said, "**H** calling Elijah." 4047
Mk	2: 7	like that? *H* **blaspheming!** AIT
	9:26	like a corpse that many said, "*H* dead." AIT
	10:49	*H* **calling** you." AIT
	15:35	they said, "Listen, *h* **calling** Elijah." AIT
Ac	20:10	be alarmed," he said. "**H** alive!" 899+1639+6034
	22:22	**H** not fit to live!" 899

HE-GOAT (1) [GOAT]

Pr 30:31 a **h**, and a king with his army around him.   9411

HEAD (335) [AHEAD, FIGUREHEAD, HEADED, HEADING, HEADS, HOTHEADED]

Ge	3:15	he will crush your **h**, and you will strike his 8031
	28:11	he put it **under** his **h** and lay down to sleep. 5265
	28:18	the stone he had placed **under** his **h** 5265
	40:13	up your **h** and restore you to your position, 8031
	40:16	On my **h** were three baskets of bread. 8031
	40:17	of the basket on my **h**." 8031
	40:19	three days Pharaoh will lift off your **h** 8031
	42:38	you will bring my **gray h** down to the grave 8484
	44:29	you will bring my **gray h** down to the grave 8484
	44:31	the **gray h** of our father down to the grave 8484
	48:14	and put it on Ephraim's **h**, 8031
	48:14	he put his left hand on Manasseh's **h**, 8031
	48:17	on Ephraim's **h** he was displeased; 8031
	48:17	from Ephraim's **h** to Manasseh's head. 8031
	48:17	from Ephraim's **head** to Manasseh's **h**. 8031
	48:18	put your right hand on his **h**." 8031
	49:26	Let all these rest on the **h** of Joseph, 8031
Ex	12: 9	**h**, legs and inner parts. 8031
	22: 1	he must pay back five *h* of **cattle** for AIT
	28:32	with an opening for the **h** in its center. 8031
	29: 6	on his **h** and attach the sacred diadem to 8031
	29: 7	and anoint him by pouring it on his **h**. 8031
	29:10	and his sons shall lay their hands on its **h**. 8031
	29:15	and his sons shall lay their hands on its **h**. 8031
	29:17	with the **h** and the other pieces. 8031
	29:19	and his sons shall lay their hands on its **h**. 8031
Lev	1: 4	He is to lay his hand on the **h** of 8031
	1: 8	including the **h** and the fat, 8031
	1:12	including the **h** and the fat, 8031
	1:15	wring off the **h** and burn it on the altar; 8031
	3: 2	on the **h** of his offering and slaughter it at 8031
	3: 8	the **h** of his offering and slaughter it in front 8031
	3:13	on its **h** and slaughter it in front of the Tent 8031
	4: 4	on its **h** and slaughter it before the LORD. 8031
	4:11	as well as the **h** and legs, 8031
	4:15	to lay their hands on the bull's **h** before 8031
	4:24	on the goat's **h** and slaughter it at the place 8031
	4:29	on the **h** of the sin offering and slaughter it 8031
	4:33	on its **h** and slaughter it for a sin offering at 8031
	5: 8	He is to wring its **h** from its neck, 8031
	8: 9	Then he placed the turban on Aaron's **h** 8031
	8:12	of the anointing oil on Aaron's **h** 8031
	8:14	Aaron and his sons laid their hands on its **h**. 8031
	8:18	Aaron and his sons laid their hands on its **h**. 8031
	8:20	He cut the ram into pieces and burned the **h**, 8031
	8:22	Aaron and his sons laid their hands on its **h**. 8031
	9:13	including the **h**, and he burned them on 8031
	13:12	the skin of the infected person from **h** 8031
	13:29	or woman has a sore on the **h** or on the chin, 8031
	13:30	an infectious disease of the **h** or chin. 8031

Lev	13:42	if he has a reddish-white sore on his **bald h** 7949
	13:42	an infectious disease breaking out on his **h** 7949
	13:43	on his **h** or forehead is reddish-white like 7949
	13:44	because of the sore on his **h**. 8031
	14: 9	he must shave his **h**, his beard, 8031
	14:18	in his palm the priest shall put on the **h** of 8031
	14:29	in his palm the priest shall put on the **h** of 8031
	16:21	the **h** of the live goat and confess over it all 8031
	16:21	and put them on the goat's **h**. 8031
	19:27	" 'Do not cut the hair at the sides of your **h** 8031
	20: 9	and his blood will be on his own **h**. NIH
	21:10	on his **h** and who has been ordained to wear 8031
	24:14	to lay their hands on his **h**, 8031
Nu	1: 4	each the **h** of his family, is to help you. 8031
	6: 5	of separation no razor may be used on his **h**. 8031
	6: 5	he must let the hair of his **h** grow long. 8031
	6: 7	symbol of his separation to God is on his **h**. 8031
	6: 9	he must shave his **h** on the day 8031
	6:11	That same day he is to consecrate his **h**. 8031
	17: 3	be one staff for the **h** of each ancestral tribe. 8031
Dt	19: 5	the **h** may fly off and hit his neighbor 1366
	21:12	into your home and have her shave her **h**, 8031
	28:13	The LORD will make you the **h**, 8031
	28:23	The sky over your **h** will be bronze, 8031
	28:35	the soles of your feet to the **top of** your **h**. 7721
	28:44	He will be the **h**, but you will be the tail. 8031
	33:16	Let all these rest on the **h** of Joseph, 8031
	33:20	tearing at arm or **h**. 7721
Jos	2:19	his blood will be on his own **h**; 8031
	2:19	his blood will be on our **h** if a hand is laid 8031
	11:10	the **h** of all these kingdoms.) 8031
	22:14	each the **h** of a family division among 8031
Jdg	5:26	She struck Sisera, she crushed his **h**, 8031
	8:28	the Israelites and did not raise its **h** again. 8031
	9:53	on his **h** and cracked his skull. 8031
	10:18	be the **h** of all those living in Gilead." 8031
	11: 8	and you will be our **h** over all who live 8031
	11: 9	will I really be your **h**?" 8031
	11:11	and the people made him **h** and commander 8031
	12: 1	to burn down your house over your **h**." NIH
	13: 5	No razor may be used on his **h**, 8031
	16:13	"If you weave the seven braids of my **h** into 8031
	16:13	Delilah took the seven braids of his **h**, 8031
	16:17	"No razor has ever been used on my **h**," 8031
	16:17	If my **h** were shaved, NIH
	16:22	But the hair on his **h** began to grow again 8031
1Sa	1:11	and no razor will ever be used on his **h**." 8031
	4:12	his clothes torn and dust on his **h**. 8031
	5: 4	His **h** and hands had been broken off 8031
	9: 2	a **h** taller than any of the others. 2025+2256+4946+5087+8900
	9:22	at the **h** of those who were invited— 8031
	10: 1	and poured it on Saul's **h** and kissed him, 8031
	10:23	among the people he was a **h** taller than any of the others. 2025+2256+4946+5087+8900
	14:45	not a hair of his **h** will fall to the ground, 8031
	15:17	not become the **h** of the tribes of Israel? 8031
	17: 5	He had a bronze helmet on his **h** and wore 8031
	17:38	on him and put a bronze helmet on his **h**. 8031
	17:46	and I'll strike you down and cut off your **h**. 8031
	17:51	he cut off his **h** with the sword. 8031
	17:54	David took the Philistine's **h** and brought it 8031
	17:57	with David still holding the Philistine's **h**. 8031
	19:13	and putting some goats' hair at the **h**, 5265
	19:16	and at the **h** was some goats' hair. 5265
	21: 7	the Edomite, Saul's **h** shepherd. 52
	25:39	wrongdoing down on his own **h**." 8031
	26: 7	in the ground **near** his **h**. 5265
	26:11	the spear and water jug that are **near** his **h**, 5265
	26:12	the spear and water jug **near** Saul's **h**, 5265
	26:16	and water jug that were **near** his **h**?" 5265
	31: 9	They cut off his **h** 8031
2Sa	1: 2	with his clothes torn and with dust on his **h**. 8031
	1:10	And I took the crown that was on his **h** and 8031
	1:16	"Your blood be on your own **h**. 8031
	2:16	by the **h** and thrust his dagger 8031
	3: 8	"Am I a dog's **h**—on Judah's side? 8031
	3:29	May his blood fall upon the **h** of Joab and 8031
	4: 7	they cut off his **h**. 8031
	4: 8	They brought the **h** of Ish-Bosheth to David 8031
	4: 8	"Here is the **h** of Ish-Bosheth son of Saul, 8031
	4:12	But they took the **h** of Ish-Bosheth 8031
	12:30	the crown from the **h** of their king— 8031
	12:30	and it was placed on David's **h**. 8031
	13:19	Tamar put ashes on her **h** and tore 8031
	13:19	She put her hand on her **h** and went away, 8031
	14:11	**hair of** your son's **h** 8553
	14:25	From the **top of** his **h** to the sole 7721
	14:26	Whenever he cut the hair of his **h**— 8031
	15:30	his **h** was covered and he was barefoot. 8031
	15:32	his robe torn and dust on his **h**. 8031
	16: 9	Let me go over and cut off his **h**." 8031
	18: 9	Absalom's **h** got caught in the tree. 8031
	20:21	"His **h** will be thrown to you from 8031
	20:22	and they cut off the **h** of Sheba son of Bicri 8031
	22:44	you have preserved me as the **h** of nations. 8031
1Ki	1:52	not a **hair** of his **h** will fall to the ground; 8553
	2: 6	not let his **gray h** go down to the grave 8484
	2: 9	Bring his **gray h** down to the grave 8484
	2:33	the guilt of their blood rest on the **h** of Joab 8031
	2:37	your blood will be on your own **h**." 8031
	4:23	ten *h* of stall-fed **cattle**, AIT
	8:32	down on their own **h** what he has done. AIT
	19: 6	there **by** his **h** was a cake of bread baked 5265
2Ki	4:19	"My **h**! My head!" he said to his father. 8031
	4:19	"My **head**! My **h**!" he said to his father. 8031
	6:25	that a donkey's **h** sold for eighty shekels 8031

2Ki	6:31	if the **h** of Elisha son of Shaphat remains 8031
	6:32	sending someone to cut off my **h**? 8031
	9: 3	Then take the flask and pour the oil on his **h** 8031
	9: 6	Then the prophet poured the oil on Jehu's **h** 8031
	19:21	The Daughter of Jerusalem tosses her **h** 8031
1Ch	5:15	the son of Guni, was **h** of their family. 8031
	10:10	They stripped him and took his **h** 8031
	10:10	the temple of their gods and hung up his **h** 1653
	15:22	the **h** Levite was in charge of the singing; 8569
	20: 2	the crown from the **h** of their king— 8031
	20: 2	and it was placed on David's **h**. 8031
	29:11	you are exalted as **h** over all. 8031
2Ch	6:23	down on his own **h** what he has done. 8031
	7: 5	of twenty-two thousand *h* of **cattle** and AIT
	15:11	to the LORD seven hundred *h* of **cattle** AIT
	20:21	as they went out **at the h** of the army, 4200+7156
	35: 9	and five hundred *h* of **cattle** for AIT
Ezr	9: 3	pulled hair from my **h** and beard and sat 8031
Ne	6: 8	you are just making it up out of your **h**." 4213
Est	2:17	on her **h** and made her queen instead 8031
	6: 8	one with a royal crest placed on its **h**. 8031
	6:12	with his **h** covered in grief, 8031
	9:25	the Jews should come back onto his own **h**, 8031
Job	1:20	up and tore his robe and shaved his **h**. 8031
	2: 7	the soles of his feet to the **top of** his **h**. 7721
	10:15	Even if I am innocent, I cannot lift my **h**, 8031
	10:16	If I **hold** my **h** high, 1448
	16: 4	against you and shake my **h** at you. 8031
	19: 9	and removed the crown from my **h**. 8031
	20: 6	to the heavens and his **h** touches the clouds, 8031
	29: 3	when his lamp shone above my **h** and 8031
	41: 7	Can you fill his hide with harpoons or his **h** 8031
Ps	3: 3	you bestow glory on me and lift up my **h**. 8031
	7:16	his violence comes down on his own **h**. 7721
	18:43	you have made me the **h** of nations; 8031
	21: 3	and placed a crown of pure gold on his **h**. 8031
	23: 5	You anoint my **h** with oil; 8031
	27: 6	Then my **h** will be exalted above 8031
	35:14	*I* **bowed** my **h** in grief as though weeping 8820
	40:12	They are more than the hairs of my **h**, 8031
	69:4	outnumber the hairs of my **h**; 8031
	110: 7	therefore he will lift up his **h**. 8031
	132:18	but the crown on his **h** will be resplendent." NIH
	133: 2	It is like precious oil poured on the **h**, 8031
	140: 7	who shields my **h** in the day of battle— 8031
	141: 5	let him rebuke me—it is oil on my **h**. 8031
	141: 5	My **h** will not refuse it. 8031
Pr	1: 9	They will be a garland to grace your **h** and 8031
	1:21	at the **h** of the noisy streets she cries out, in 8031
	4: 9	She will set a garland of grace on your **h** 8031
	10: 6	Blessings crown the **h** of the righteous, 8031
	25:22	you will heap burning coals on his **h**, 8031
Ecc	2:14	The wise man has eyes in his **h**, 8031
	9: 8	and always anoint your **h** with oil. 8031
SS	2: 6	His left arm is under my **h**, 8031
	5: 2	My **h** is drenched with dew, 8031
	5:11	His **h** is purest gold; 8031
	7: 5	Your **h** crowns you like Mount Carmel. 8031
	8: 3	under my **h** and his right arm embraces me. 8031
Isa	1: 5	Your whole **h** is injured, 8031
	1: 6	to the **top of** your **h** there is no soundness— 8031
	7: 8	for the **h** of Aram is Damascus, 8031
	7: 8	and the **h** of Damascus is only Rezin. 8031
	7: 9	The **h** of Ephraim is Samaria, 8031
	7: 9	the **h** of Samaria is only Remaliah's son. 8031
	7:20	to shave your **h** and the hair of your legs, 8031
	9:14	both **h** and tail, both palm branch and reed 8031
	9:15	the elders and prominent men are the **h**, 8031
	15: 2	Every **h** is shaved and every beard cut off. 8031
	19:15	**h** or tail, palm branch or reed. 8031
	28: 1	set on the **h** of a fertile valley— 8031
	28: 4	set on the **h** of a fertile valley, 8031
	37:22	The Daughter of Jerusalem tosses her **h** 8031
	51:20	they lie at the **h** of every street, 8031
	58: 5	Is it only for bowing one's **h** like a reed and 8031
	59:17	and the helmet of salvation on his **h**; 8031
	61:10	as a bridegroom **adorns** his **h** like a priest, 6996
Jer	2:16	have shaved the **crown of** your **h**. 7721
	2:37	that place with your hands on your **h**, for 8031
	9: 1	that my **h** were a spring of water 8031
	16: 6	and no one will cut himself or **shave** *his* **h** 7942
	47: 5	**shave** *her* **h** in mourning; 995+7947
	48:27	**shake** *your* **h** in scorn 5653
	48:37	Every **h** is shaved and every beard cut off; 8031
La	2:19	from hunger at the **h** of every street. 8031
	3:54	the waters closed over my **h**, 8031
	4: 1	The sacred gems are scattered at the **h** 8031
	5:16	The crown has fallen from our **h**. 8031
Eze	5: 1	as a barber's razor to shave your **h** 8031
	8: 3	like a hand and took me by the hair of my **h**. 8031
	10:11	in whatever direction the **h** faced, 8031
	16:12	and a beautiful crown on your **h**. 8031
	16:25	At the **h** of every street you built 8031
	16:31	When you built your mounds at the **h** 8031
	16:43	down on your **h** what you have done, 8031
	17:19	as I live, I will bring down on his **h** my oath 8031
	18:13	to death and his blood will be on his own **h**. NIH
	29:18	every **h** was rubbed bare 8031
	33: 4	his blood will be on his own **h**. 8031
	33: 5	his blood will be on his own **h**. NIH
Da	1:10	The king would then have my **h** because 8031
	2:32	The **h** of the statue was made of pure gold, 10646
	2:38	You are that **h** of gold. 10646
	7: 9	the hair of his **h** was white like wool. 10646
	7:20	on its **h** and about the other horn that came 10646
Hos	8: 7	The stalk has no **h**; it will produce no flour. 7542
Joel	2:11	The LORD thunders at the **h** of his army; 7156

Ob	1:15	your deeds will return upon your own **h**.	8031
Jnh	2: 5	seaweed was wrapped around my **h**	8031
	4: 6	up over Jonah to give shade for his **h**	8031
	4: 8	and the sun blazed on Jonah's **h** so	8031
Mic	2:13	the LORD at their **h**."	8031
Na	3:10	Her infants were dashed to pieces at the **h**	8031
Hab	3:13	you stripped him from **h** to foot.	7418
	3:14	With his own spear you pierced his **h**	8031
Zec	1:21	so that no one could raise his **h**,	8031
	3: 5	Then I said, "Put a clean turban on his **h**."	8031
	3: 5	a clean turban on his **h** and clothed him,	8031
	6:11	and set it on the **h** of the high priest.	8031
Mt	5:36	And do not swear by your **h**,	3051
	6:17	put oil on your **h** and wash your face,	3051
	8:20	the Son of Man has no place to lay his **h**."	3051
	10:25	**h** of the house has been called Beelzebub,	3867
	10:30	the very hairs of your **h** are all numbered.	3051
	14: 8	"Give me here on a platter the **h** of John	3051
	14:11	His **h** was brought in on a platter and given	3051
	26: 7	on his **h** as he was reclining at the table.	3051
	27:29	a crown of thorns and set it on his **h**.	3051
	27:30	and struck him on the **h** again and again.	3051
	27:37	Above his **h** they placed the written charge	3051
Mk	4:28	first the stalk, then the **h**,	5092
	4:28	then the head, then the full kernel in the **h**.	5092
	6:24	"The **h** of John the Baptist," she answered.	3051
	6:25	now the **h** of John the Baptist on a platter."	3051
	6:27	with orders to bring John's **h**.	3051
	6:28	and brought back his **h** on a platter.	3051
	12: 4	struck this man **on the h**	3052
	14: 3	the jar and poured the perfume on his **h**.	3051
	15:19	Again and again they struck him on the **h**	3051
Lk	7:46	You did not put oil on my **h**,	3051
	9:58	the Son of Man has no place to lay his **h**."	3051
	12: 7	the very hairs of your **h** are all numbered.	3051
	21:18	But not a hair of your **h** will perish.	3051
Jn	13: 9	"not just my feet but my hands and my **h**	3051
	19: 2	a crown of thorns and put it on his **h**,	3051
	19:30	he bowed his **h** and gave up his spirit.	3051
	20: 7	that had been around Jesus' **h**.	3051
	20:12	one at the **h** and the other at the foot.	3051
Ac	27:15	by the storm and could not **h into** the wind;	535
	27:34	of you will lose a single hair from his **h**."	3051
Ro	12:20	you will heap burning coals on his **h**."	3051
1Co	11: 3	to realize that the **h** of every man is Christ,	3051
	11: 3	and the **h** of the woman is man,	3051
	11: 3	and the **h** of Christ is God.	3051
	11: 4	with his **h** covered dishonors his head.	3051
	11: 4	with his head covered dishonors his **h**.	3051
	11: 5	*with* her uncovered dishonors her head—	3051
	11: 5	her head uncovered dishonors her **h**—	3051
	11: 5	it is just as though her **h** were shaved.	NIG
	11: 6	If a woman does not cover her **h**,	NIG
	11: 6	she should cover her **h**.	NIG
	11: 7	A man ought not to cover his **h**,	3051
	11:10	to have a sign of authority on her **h**.	3051
	11:13	to pray to God with her **h** uncovered?	NIG
	12:21	And the **h** cannot say to the feet,	3051
Eph	1:10	**bring** all things in heaven and on earth	
		together under one h,	368
	1:22	and appointed him to be **h** over everything	3051
	4:15	in all things grow up into him who is the **H**,	3051
	5:23	the husband is the **h** of the wife as Christ is	3051
	5:23	of the wife as Christ is the **h** of the church,	3051
Col	1:18	And he is the **h** of the body, the church;	3051
	2:10	the **h** over every power and authority.	3051
	2:19	He has lost connection with the **H**,	3051
2Ti	4: 5	But you, **keep** *your* **h** in all situations,	3768
Rev	1:14	His **h** and hair were white like wool,	3051
	10: 1	with a rainbow above his **h**;	3051
	12: 1	and a crown of twelve stars on her **h**.	3051
	13: 1	and on each **h** a blasphemous name.	3051
	14:14	a son of man" with a crown of gold on his **h**	3051
	19:12	and on his **h** are many crowns.	3051

HEADBAND (2) [HEADBANDS]

1Ki	20:38	He disguised himself with his **h** down	710
	20:41	Then the prophet quickly removed the **h**	710

HEADBANDS (5) [HEADBAND]

Ex	28:40	Make tunics, sashes and **h** for Aaron's sons,	4457
	29: 9	and put **h** on them. Then tie sashes on	4457
	39:28	the linen **h** and the undergarments	4457+6996
Lev	8:13	tied sashes around them and put **h** on them,	4457
Isa	3:18	the bangles and **h** and crescent necklaces,	8667

HEADDRESSES (1)

Isa	3:20	the **h** and ankle chains and sashes,	6996

HEADED (6) [HEAD]

Ge	31:21	he **h for** the hill country of Gilead.	7156+8492
Ex	9:31	the barley had **h** and the flax was in bloom.	26
Jos	15: 9	the hilltop the boundary **h** toward the spring	9305
	18:12	of Jericho and **h** west into the hill country,	6590
Jer	39: 4	and **h** toward the Arabah.	3655
Jnh	1: 3	But Jonah ran away from the LORD and **h**	NIH

HEADING (2) [HEAD]

Lk	9:53	because he was **h** for Jerusalem.	4513
Jn	6:21	the shore where *they were* **h**.	5632

HEADLONG (4)

2Ki	7:15	in their **h** flight.	2905

Job	27:22	*as he* **flees** from its power.	1368+1368
Hab	1: 8	Their cavalry **gallops** **h**;	7055
Ac	1:18	there he **fell h**, his body burst open	1181+4568

HEADS (177) [HEAD]

Ge	40:20	He lifted up the **h** of the chief cupbearer	8031
	41: 5	Seven **h of grain**, healthy and good,	8672
	41: 6	seven other **h of grain** sprouted—	8672
	41: 7	The thin **h of grain** swallowed up	8672
	41: 7	up the seven healthy, full **h**.	8672
	41:22	"In my dreams I also saw seven **h of grain**,	8672
	41:23	After them, seven other **h** sprouted—	8672
	41:24	The thin **h of grain** swallowed up	8672
	41:24	of grain swallowed up the seven good **h**.	8672
	41:26	the seven good **h of grain** are seven years;	8672
	41:27	the seven worthless **h of grain** scorched by	8672
Ex	6:14	These were the **h** of their families:	8031
	6:25	These were the **h** of the Levite families,	8031
Lev	2:14	offer crushed **h** of new grain roasted in	26
	20:11	their blood will be on their own **h**.	NIH
	20:12	their blood will be on their own **h**.	NIH
	20:13	their blood will be on their own **h**.	NIH
	20:16	their blood will be on their own **h**.	NIH
	20:27	their blood will be on their own **h**.' "	NIH
	21: 5	not shave their **h** or shave off the edges	8031
	26:13	and enabled you to walk **with h held high**.	7758
Nu	1:16	They were the **h** of the clans of Israel.	8031
	7: 2	the **h** of families who were the tribal leaders	8031
	8:12	Levites lay their hands on the **h** of the bulls,	8031
	10: 4	the **h** of the clans of Israel—	8031
	30: 1	Moses said to the **h** of the tribes of Israel:	8031
	31:26	and Eleazar the priest and the family **h** of	8031
	32:28	and Joshua son of Nun and to the family **h**	8031
	36: 1	The family **h** of the clan of Gilead son	8031
	36: 1	the **h** of the Israelite families.	8031
Dt	14: 1	shave the **front of** your **h** for the dead,	1068+6524
	32:42	the **h** of the enemy leaders."	8031
	33:21	When the **h** of the people assembled,	8031
Jos	7: 6	and sprinkled dust on their **h**.	8031
	14: 1	the **h** of the tribal clans of Israel allotted	8031
	19:51	the **h** of the tribal clans of Israel assigned	8031
	21: 1	Now the family **h** of the Levites	8031
	21: 1	the **h** of the other tribal families of Israel	8031
	22:21	the half-tribe of Manasseh replied to the **h**	8031
	22:30	the **h** of the clans of the Israelites—	8031
Jdg	7:25	and brought the **h** of Oreb and Zeeb to	8031
1Sa	29: 4	by taking the **h** of our own men?	8031
2Sa	15:30	All the people with him covered their **h** too	8031
1Ki	8: 1	all the **h** of the tribes and the chiefs of	8031
	20:31	around our waists and ropes around our **h**.	8031
	20:32	and ropes around their **h**, they went to	8031
2Ki	4:42	along with *some* **h of new grain**.	4152
	10: 6	the **h** of your master's sons and come to me	8031
	10: 7	They put their **h** in baskets and sent them	8031
	10: 8	"They have brought the **h** of the princes."	8031
1Ch	5:24	These were the **h** of their families:	8031
	5:24	famous men, and **h** of their families.	8031
	7: 2	**h** of their families.	8031
	7: 7	Jerimoth and Iri, **h** of families—five in all.	8031
	7: 9	Their genealogical record listed the **h**	8031
	7:11	All these sons of Jediael were **h** of families.	8031
	7:40	**h** of families, choice men,	8031
	8: 6	who were **h** of families of those living	8031
	8:10	These were his sons, **h** of families.	8031
	8:13	who were **h** of families of those living	8031
	8:28	All these were **h** of families,	8031
	9: 9	All these men were **h** of their families.	8031
	9:13	The priests, who were **h** of families,	8031
	9:33	**h** of Levite families,	8031
	9:34	All these were **h** of Levite families,	8031
	12:19	"It will cost us our **h** if he deserts	8031
	15:12	"You are the **h** of the Levitical families;	8031
	23: 9	These were the **h** of the families of Ladan.	8031
	23:24	the **h** of families as they were registered	8031
	24: 4	sixteen **h** of families	8031
	24: 4	from Eleazar's descendants and eight **h**	NIH
	24: 6	and the **h** of families of the priests and of	8031
	24:31	and the **h** of families of the priests and of	8031
	26:21	and who were **h** of families belonging	8031
	26:26	the **h** of families who were the commanders	8031
	26:32	who were able men and **h** of families,	8031
	27: 1	**h** of families, commanders of thousands	8031
2Ch	1: 2	the leaders in Israel, the **h** of families—	8031
	5: 2	all the **h** of the tribes and the chiefs of	8031
	19: 8	and **h** of Israelite families to administer	8031
	23: 2	the Levites and the **h** of Israelite families	8031
	29:30	and **bowed** *their* **h** and worshiped.	7702
Ezr	1: 5	Then the family **h** of Judah and Benjamin,	8031
	2:68	the **h** of the families gave freewill offerings	8031
	3:12	the older priests and Levites and family **h**,	8031
	4: 2	to Zerubbabel and to the **h** of the families	8031
	4: 3	of the **h** of the families of Israel answered,	8031
	8: 1	These are the family **h** and those registered	8031
	8:29	and the Levites and the family **h** of Israel."	8569
	9: 6	because our sins are higher than our **h**	8031
	10:16	the priest selected men who were family **h**,	8031
Ne	4: 4	Turn their insults back on their own **h**.	8031
	7:70	Some of the **h** of the families contributed to	8031
	7:71	the **h** of the families gave to the treasury for	8031
	8:13	the **h** of all the families,	8031
	9: 1	and having dust on their **h**.	NIH
	11:13	who were **h** of families—	8031
	11:16	two of the **h** of the Levites,	8031
	12:12	these were the **h** of the priestly families:	8031
	12:22	The family **h** of the Levites in the days	8031
	12:23	The family **h** among the descendants	8031

Job	2:12	and sprinkled dust on their **h**.	8031
	24:24	they are cut off like **h** of grain.	8031
Ps	22: 7	they hurl insults, shaking their **h**:	8031
	24: 7	Lift up your **h**, O you gates;	8031
	24: 9	Lift up your **h**, O you gates;	8031
	44:14	the peoples shake their **h** at us.	8031
	64: 8	*will* **shake** *their* **h in scorn.**	5653
	66:12	You let men ride over our **h**;	8031
	68:21	Surely God will crush the **h** of his enemies,	8031
	74:13	broke the **h** of the monster in the waters.	8031
	74:14	you who crushed the **h** of Leviathan and	8031
	83: 2	how your foes rear their **h**.	8031
	109:25	when they see me, they shake their **h**.	8031
	140: 9	the **h** of those who surround me be covered	8031
Isa	3:17	Therefore the Lord will bring sores on the **h**	7721
	17: 5	when a man gleans **h** of grain in the Valley	8672
	29:10	he has covered your **h** (the seers).	8031
	35:10	everlasting joy will crown their **h**.	8031
	51:11	everlasting joy will crown their **h**.	8031
Jer	13:18	your glorious crowns will fall from your **h**."	5265
	14: 3	dismayed and despairing, they cover their **h**.	8031
	14: 4	the farmers are dismayed and cover their **h**.	8031
	18:16	by will be appalled and will shake their **h**.	8031
	23:19	a whirlwind swirling down on the **h** of	8031
	30:23	a driving wind swirling down on the **h** of	8031
La	2:10	they have sprinkled dust on their **h** and put	8031
	2:10	of Jerusalem have bowed their **h** to	8031
	2:15	they scoff and shake their **h** at the Daughter	8031
Eze	1:22	Spread out above the **h** of	8031
	1:25	above the expanse over their **h** as they stood	8031
	1:26	over their **h** was what looked like a throne	8031
	7:18	be covered with shame and their **h** will	8031
	9:10	down on their own **h** what they have done."	8031
	10: 1	above the expanse that was over the **h** of	8031
	11:21	down on their own **h** what they have done,	8031
	13:18	and make veils of various lengths for their **h**	8031
	22:31	down on their own **h** all they have done,	8031
	23:15	and flowing turbans on their **h**;	8031
	23:42	and beautiful crowns on their **h**.	8031
	24:23	on your **h** and your sandals on your feet.	8031
	27:30	they will sprinkle dust on their **h** and roll	8031
	27:31	They will **shave** *their* **h** because of you	7942+7947
	32:27	whose swords were placed under their **h**?	8031
	44:18	They are to wear linen turbans on their **h**	8031
	44:20	not shave their **h** or let their hair grow long,	8031
	44:20	they are to keep the hair of their **h** trimmed.	8031
Da	3:27	nor was a hair of their **h** singed;	10646
	7: 6	This beast had four **h**,	10646
Joel	3: 4	return on your own **h** what you have done.	8031
	3: 7	return on your own **h** what you have done.	8031
Am	2: 7	They trample on the **h** of the poor as upon	8031
	8:10	of you wear sackcloth and shave your **h**.	8031
	9: 1	Bring them down on the **h** of all the people;	8031
Mic	1:16	**Shave** *your* **h** in mourning for the children	
			1605+7942
Mt	12: 1	to pick some **h** of grain and eat them.	5092
	13:26	When the wheat sprouted and formed **h**,	2843
	27:39	by hurled insults at him, shaking their **h**	3051
Mk	2:23	they began to pick some **h** of grain.	5092
	15:29	shaking their **h** and saying, "So!	3051
Lk	6: 1	his disciples began to pick some **h** of grain,	5092
	21:28	stand up and lift up your **h**,	3051
Ac	18: 6	"Your blood be on your own **h**!	3051
	21:24	so that they can have their **h** shaved.	3051
Rev	4: 4	in white and had crowns of gold on their **h**.	3051
	9: 7	On their **h** they wore something like crowns	3051
	9:17	The **h** of the horses resembled the heads	3051
	9:17	the horses resembled the **h** of lions,	3051
	9:19	having **h** with which they inflict injury.	3051
	12: 3	an enormous red dragon with seven **h**	3051
	12: 3	and ten horns and seven crowns on his **h**.	3051
	13: 1	He had ten horns and seven **h**,	3051
	13: 1	of the **h** of the beast seemed to have had	3051
	17: 3	with blasphemous names and had seven **h**	3051
	17: 7	which has the seven **h** and ten horns.	3051
	17: 9	The seven **h** are seven hills on which	3051
	18:19	They will throw dust on their **h**,	3051

HEADSTONE (KJV) See CAPSTONE

HEADWATERS (1) [WATER]

Ge	2:10	from there it was separated into four **h**.	8031

HEADWAY (1)

Ac	27: 7	*We* **made slow h** for many days	1095

HEADY (KJV) See RASH

HEAL (44) [HEALED, HEALING, HEALS]

Nu	12:13	"O God, please **h** her!"	8324
Dt	32:39	I have wounded and I *will* **h**,	8324
2Ki	20: 5	I *will* **h** you.	8324
	20: 8	the LORD *will* **h** me and that I will go up	8324
2Ch	7:14	and *will* **h** their land.	8324
Job	5:18	he injures, but his hands also **h**.	8324
Ps	6: 2	O LORD, **h** me, for my bones are in agony.	8324
	41: 4	**h** me, for I have sinned against you."	8324
Ecc	3: 3	a time to kill and a time to **h**,	8324
Isa	19:22	he will strike them and **h** them.	8324
	19:22	he will respond to their pleas and **h** them.	8324
	57:18	I have seen his ways, but *I will* **h** him;	8324
	57:19	"And *I will* **h** them."	8324
Jer	17:14	**H** me, O LORD, and I will be healed;	8324
	30:17	to health and **h** your wounds,'	8324

Jer	33: 6	*I will* **h** my people	8324
La	2:13	Who *can I* **h** you?	8324
Hos	5:13	not able *to* **h** your sores.	1564
	6: 1	He has torn us to pieces but *he will* **h** us;	8324
	7: 1	whenever I *would* **h** Israel,	8324
	14: 4	*"I will* **h** their waywardness	8324
Na	3:19	Nothing can **h** your wound;	3911
Zec	11:16	or **h** the injured, or feed the healthy,	8324
Mt	8: 7	Jesus said to him, "I *will* go and **h** him."	2543
	10: 1	and *to* **h** every disease and sickness.	2543
	10: 8	**H** the sick, raise the dead,	2543
	12:10	"Is it lawful *to* **h** on the Sabbath?"	2543
	13:15	and turn, and *I would* **h** them.'	2615
	17:16	but they could not **h** him."	2543
Mk	3: 2	to see if *he would* **h** him on the Sabbath.	2543
	6: 5	on a few sick people and **h** them.	2543
Lk	4:23	'Physician, **h** yourself!	2543
	5:17	the Lord was present for him *to* **h** the sick.	2615
	6: 7	to see if *he would* **h** on the Sabbath.	2615
	7: 3	asking him to come and **h** his servant.	1407
	8:43	but no one could **h** her.	2543
	9: 2	to preach the kingdom of God and *to* **h**	2615
	10: 9	**H** the sick who are there and tell them,	2543
	13:32	and **h** people today and tomorrow,	699+2543
	14: 3	"Is it lawful *to* **h** on the Sabbath or not?"	2543
Jn	4:47	and begged him *to* come and **h** his son,	2615
	12:40	nor turn—and *I would* **h** them."	2615
Ac	4:30	to **h** and perform miraculous signs	2617
	28:27	and turn, and *I would* **h** them.'	2615

HEALED (73) [HEAL]

Ge	20:17	and God **h** Abimelech,	8324
Ex	21:19	see that *he* is completely **h**.	8324+8324
Lev	13:37	the itch *is* **h**.	8324
	14: 3	If the person *has* been **h**	8324
Jos	5: 8	where they were in camp until they *were* **h**.	2649
1Sa	6: 3	Then *you will* be **h**,	8324
2Ki	2:21	'I have **h** this water.	8324
2Ch	30:20	the Lord heard Hezekiah and **h** the people.	8324
Ps	30: 2	I called to you for help and *you* **h** me.	8324
	107:20	He sent forth his word and **h** them;	8324
Isa	6:10	and turn and *be* **h**."	8324
	53: 5	and by his wounds we *are* **h**.	8324
Jer	14:19	so that we cannot be **h**?	5340
	17:14	Heal me, O Lord, and *I will* be **h**;	8324
	51: 8	Get balm for her pain; perhaps *she can* be **h**.	8324
	51: 9	" 'We would have **h** Babylon,	8324
	51: 9	but *she* cannot be **h**;	8324
Eze	34: 4	You have not strengthened the weak or **h**	8324
Hos	11: 3	they did not realize *it was* I who **h** them.	8324
Mt	4:24	and the paralyzed, and **h** them.	2543
	8: 8	and my servant *will be* **h**.	2615
	8:13	And his servant *was* **h** at that very hour.	2615
	8:16	the spirits with a word and **h** all the sick.	2543
	9:21	"If I only touch his cloak, *I will* be **h**."	5392
	9:22	daughter," he said, "your faith *has* **h** you."	5392
	9:22	And the woman was **h** from that moment.	5392
	12:15	Many followed him, and *he* **h** all their sick,	2543
	12:22	Jesus **h** him, so that he could both talk and	2543
	14:14	he had compassion on them and **h** their sick.	2543
	14:36	and all who touched him were **h**.	1407
	15:28	her daughter *was* **h** from that very hour.	2615
	15:30	laid them at his feet; and *he* **h** them.	2543
	17:18	and he *was* **h** from that moment.	2543
	19: 2	crowds followed him, and *he* **h** them there.	2543
	21:14	at the temple, and *he* **h** them.	2543
Mk	1:34	and Jesus **h** many who had various diseases.	2543
	3:10	For *he had* **h** many,	2543
	5:23	on her so that *she will* be **h** and live."	5392
	5:28	"If I just touch his clothes, *I will* be **h**."	5392
	5:34	"Daughter, your faith *has* **h** you.	5392
	6:13	many sick people with oil and **h** them.	2543
	6:56	and all who touched him were **h**.	5392
	10:52	"Go," said Jesus, "your faith *has* **h** you."	5392
Lk	4:40	laying his hands on each one, he **h** them.	2543
	5:15	to hear him and *to* be **h** of their sicknesses.	2543
	6:18	to hear him and *to* be **h** of their diseases.	2615
	7: 7	say the word, and my servant *will be* **h**.	2615
	8:47	and how *she had been* instantly **h**.	2615
	8:48	"Daughter, your faith *has* **h** you.	5392
	8:50	just believe, and *she will* be **h**."	5392
	9:11	and **h** those who needed healing.	2615
	9:42	**h** the boy and gave him back to his father.	2615
	13:14	because Jesus *had* **h** on the Sabbath,	2543
	13:14	So come and *be* **h** on those days,	2543
	14: 4	*he* **h** him and sent him away.	2615
	17:15	One of them, when he saw *he was* **h**,	2615
	18:42	your faith *has* **h** you."	5392
	22:51	And *he* touched the man's ear and **h** him.	2615
Jn	5:10	so the Jews said *to* the man who *had* been **h**,	2543
	5:13	The man who *was* **h** had no idea who it was,	2615
Ac	4: 9	to a cripple and are asked how he *was* **h**,	5392
	4:10	that this man stands before you **h**.	5618
	4:14	the man who *had* been **h** standing there	2543
	4:22	For the man who was miraculously **h** was	2617
	5:16	and all of them were **h**.	2543
	8: 7	and many paralytics and cripples were **h**.	2543
	14: 9	saw that he had faith *to* be **h**	3836+5392
	28: 8	placed his hands on him and **h** him.	2615
Heb	12:13	the lame may not be disabled, but rather **h**.	2615
Jas	5:16	pray for each other so that **you may be h**.	2615
1Pe	2:24	by his wounds *you have* been **h**.	2615
Rev	13: 3	but the fatal wound *had* been **h**.	2543
	13:12	whose fatal wound *had* been **h**.	2543

HEALING (28) [HEAL]

2Ch	28:15	food and drink, and **h** balm.	6057
Pr	12:18	but the tongue of the wise brings **h**.	5340
	13:17	but a trustworthy envoy brings **h**.	5340
	15: 4	The tongue that brings **h** is a tree of life,	5340
	16:24	sweet to the soul and **h** to the bones.	5340
Isa	58: 8	and your **h** will quickly appear;	776
Jer	8:15	for a time of **h** but there was only terror.	5340
	8:22	Why then is there no **h** for the wound	776
	14:19	for a time of **h** but there is only terror.	5340
	30:12	your injury beyond **h**.	2703
	30:13	no remedy for your sore, no **h** for you.	9499
	33: 6	I will bring health and **h** to it;	5340
	46:11	there is no **h** for you.	9499
Eze	30:21	not been bound up for **h** or put in	5989+8337
	47:12	for food and their leaves for **h**."	9559
Mal	4: 2	the sun of righteousness will rise with **h**	5340
Mt	4:23	and **h** every disease and sickness among	2543
	9:35	of the kingdom and **h** every disease	2543
Lk	6:19	power was coming from him and **h** them all.	2615
	9: 6	the gospel and **h** people everywhere.	2543
	9:11	and healed those who needed **h**.	2542
Jn	7:23	for **h** the whole man on the Sabbath?	4472+5618
Ac	3:16	through him that has given this complete **h**	3907
	10:38	and **h** all who were under the power of	2615
1Co	12: 9	to another gifts *of* **h** by that one Spirit,	2611
	12:28	also those having gifts *of* **h**,	2611
	12:30	Do all have gifts *of* **h**?	2611
Rev	22: 2	And the leaves of the tree are for the **h** of	2542

HEALS (6) [HEAL]

Ex	15:26	for I am the Lord, *who* **h** you."	8324
Lev	13:18	a boil on his skin and *it* **h**,	8324
Ps	103: 3	and **h** all your diseases,	8324
	147: 3	He **h** the brokenhearted and binds	8324
Isa	30:26	of his people and **h** the wounds he inflicted.	8324
Ac	9:34	Peter said to him, "Jesus Christ **h** you.	2615

HEALTH (11) [HEALTHIER, HEALTHY]

1Sa	25: 6	Good **h** to you and your household!	8934
	25: 6	And good **h** to all that is yours!	8934
Ps	38: 3	of your wrath there is no **h** in my body;	5507
	38: 7	there is no **h** in my body.	5507
Pr	3: 8	This will bring **h** to your body	8326
	4:22	to those who find them and **h** to	5340
	15:30	and good news **gives h** to the bones.	2014
Isa	38:16	*You* restored me to **h** and let me live.	2730
Jer	30:17	to **h** and heal your wounds,'	776
	33: 6	I will bring **h** and healing to it;	776
3Jn	1: 2	I pray that you *may* enjoy good **h** and	5617

HEALTHIER (1) [HEALTH]

Da	1:15	At the end of the ten days they looked **h**	3202

HEALTHY (7) [HEALTH]

Ge	41: 5	Seven heads of grain, **h** and good,	1374
	41: 7	of grain swallowed up the seven **h**,	1374
Ps	73: 4	their bodies are **h** and strong.	1374
Zec	11:16	or heal the injured, or feed the **h**,	5893
Mt	9:12	"It is not the **h** who need a doctor,	2710
Mk	2:17	"It is not the **h** who need a doctor,	2710
Lk	5:31	"It is not the **h** who need a doctor,	5617

HEAP (29) [HEAPED, HEAPING, HEAPS]

Ge	31:46	So they took stones and piled them in a **h**,	1643
	31:46	and they ate there by the **h**.	1643
	31:48	"This **h** is a witness between you	1643
	31:51	Laban also said to Jacob, "Here is this **h**,	1643
	31:52	This **h** is a witness,	1643
	31:52	not go past this **h** to your side to harm you	1643
	31:52	past this **h** and pillar to my side to harm me.	1643
Lev	4:12	and burn it in a wood fire on the ash **h**.	9162
Dt	32:23	"I *will* **h** calamities upon them	3578
Jos	3:13	be cut off and stand up in a **h**."	5603
	3:16	It piled up in a **h** a great distance away,	5603
	8:28	and made it a permanent **h** of ruins,	9424
1Sa	2: 8	the dust and lifts the needy from the ash **h**;	883
2Sa	18:17	in the forest and piled up a large **h** of rocks	1643
Ps	113: 7	the dust and lifts the needy from the ash **h**;	883
Pr	25:22	you *will* **h** burning coals on his head,	3149
Isa	3: 6	take charge of this **h of ruins**!"	4843
	17: 1	be a city but will become a **h** of ruins.	5075
	25: 2	You have made the city a **h** of rubble,	1643
Jer	9:11	"I will make Jerusalem a **h** of ruins,	1643
	26:18	Jerusalem will become a **h** of rubble,	6505
	51:37	Babylon will be a **h** of ruins,	1643
Eze	24:10	So **h** *on* the wood and kindle the fire.	8049
Mic	1: 6	I will make Samaria a **h** of rubble,	6505
	3:12	Jerusalem will become a **h** of rubble,	6505
Hag	2:16	anyone came to a **h** *of* twenty measures,	6894
Ro	12:20	you *will* **h** burning coals on his head."	5397
1Th	2:16	**h** up their sins to the limit.	405
1Pe	4: 4	and *they* **h** abuse on you.	1059

HEAP (Anglicized) See also PILE

HEAPED (6) [HEAP]

Jos	7:26	Over Achan *they* **h** up a large pile of rocks,	7756
2Ki	19:23	By your messengers *you have* **h** insults **on**	3070
Isa	37:24	By your messengers *you have* **h** insults **on**	3070
Zec	9: 3	she has **h up** silver like dust,	7392
Mt	27:44	with him also **h** insults **on** him.	3943

HEAPING (2) [HEAP]

Ps	110: 6	**h up** the dead and crushing the rulers of	4848
Isa	30: 1	but not by my Spirit, **h** sin upon sin;	3578

HEAPS (10) [HEAP]

Ex	8:14	They were piled into **h**,	2818+2818
2Ch	31: 6	and they piled them in **h**.	6894+6894
	31: 8	and his officials came and saw the **h**,	6894
	31: 9	the priests and Levites about the **h**;	6894
Ne	4: 2	the stones back to life from those **h**	6894
Job	27:16	Though *he* **h** up silver like dust and clothes	7392
Ps	39: 6	*he* **h up wealth**, not knowing who will get it	7392
Jer	50:26	pile her up like **h** of grain.	6894
La	4: 5	Those nurtured in purple now lie on ash **h**.	883
Zep	1: 3	The wicked will have only **h** of rubble	4843

HEAR (379) [HEARD, HEARERS, HEARING, HEARS, OVERHEARD]

Ge	4:23	wives of Lamech, **h** my words.	263
	41:15	*when you* **h** a dream you can interpret it."	9048
Ex	15:14	The nations *will* **h** and tremble;	NIH
	18: 9	Jethro was delighted to **h** about all	NIH
	19: 9	the people *will* **h** me speaking with you	9048
	22:23	I will certainly **h** their cry.	9048+9048
	22:27	When he cries out to me, *I will* **h**,	9048
	32:18	it is the sound of singing that I **h**."	9048
Nu	14:13	"Then the Egyptians *will* **h** *about* it!	9048
	23:18	**h** me, son of Zippor.	263
Dt	1:16	**H** the disputes between your brothers	9048
	1:17	**h** both small and great alike.	9048
	1:17	and *I will* **h** it.	9048
	2:25	*They will* **h** reports of you and will tremble	9048
	4: 1	**H** now, O Israel, the decrees and laws I am	9048
	4: 6	who *will* **h** *about* all these decrees	9048
	4:10	the people before me *to* **h** my words so	9048
	4:28	which cannot see or **h** or eat or smell.	9048
	4:36	From heaven he *made* you **h** his voice	9048
	5: 1	Moses summoned all Israel and said: **H**,	9048
	5:25	and we will die if we **h** the voice of	9048
	6: 3	**H**, O Israel, and be careful to obey so	9048
	6: 4	**H**, O Israel: The Lord our God,	9048
	9: 1	**H**, O Israel. You are now about to cross	9048
	13:11	Then all Israel *will* **h** and be afraid,	9048
	13:12	If *you* **h** it said about one of the towns	9048
	17:13	All the people *will* **h** and be afraid,	9048
	18:16	not **h** the voice of the Lord our God	9048
	19:20	of the people *will* **h** of this and be afraid.	9048
	20: 3	He shall say: "**H**, O Israel,	9048
	21:21	All Israel *will* **h** of it and be afraid.	9048
	29: 4	or eyes that see or ears that **h**.	9048
	31:13	*must* **h** it and learn to fear	9048
	32: 1	**h**, O earth, the words of my mouth.	9048
	33: 7	"**H**, O Lord, the cry of Judah;	9048
Jos	6: 5	When you **h** them sound a long blast on	9048
	7: 9	and the other people of the country *will* **h**	9048
	22:33	to **h** the report and praised God.	NIH
Jdg	5: 3	"**H** this, *you* kings!	9048
	5:16	Why did you stay among the campfires to **h**	9048
	14:13	"Let's **h** it."	9048
1Sa	2:23	I **h** from all the people	9048
	2:24	not a good report that I **h** spreading among	9048
	13: 3	"Let the Hebrews **h**!"	9048
	15:14	What is this lowing of cattle that I **h**?"	9048
	16: 2	Saul *will* **h** *about* it and kill me."	9048
	25: 7	" 'Now *I* **h** that it is sheep-shearing time.	9048
	25:24	**h** what your servant has to say.	9048
2Sa	15: 3	As soon as you **h** the sound of marching in	9048
	15: 3	no representative of the king *to* **h** you."	9048
	15:10	soon as you **h** the sound of the trumpets,	9048
	15:35	Tell them anything *you* **h** in the king's	9048
	15:36	Send them to me with anything *you* **h**."	9048
	16:21	Then all Israel *will* **h** that you have made	9048
	17: 5	so *we can* **h** what he has to say."	9048
	18:31	"My lord the king, **h** *the* good news!	1413
	19:35	Can *I* still **h** the voices of men	9048
	22:45	as soon as they **h** me, they obey me.	9048
1Ki	1:45	That's the noise *you* **h**.	9048
	8:28	**H** the cry and the prayer	9048
	8:29	so that *you will* **h** the prayer your servant	9048
	8:30	**H** the supplication of your servant and	9048
	8:30	**H** from heaven, your dwelling place,	9048
	8:30	your dwelling place, and when *you* **h**,	9048
	8:32	then **h** from heaven and act.	9048
	8:34	then **h** from heaven and forgive the sin	9048
	8:36	then **h** from heaven and forgive the sin	9048
	8:39	then **H** from heaven, your dwelling place.	9048
	8:42	for *men will* **h** *of* your great name	9048
	8:43	then **h** from heaven, your dwelling place,	9048
	8:45	**h** from heaven their prayer and their plea,	9048
	8:49	**h** their prayer and their plea,	9048
	8:52	before you and **h** your servant's plea	9048
	10:24	with Solomon to **h** the wisdom God had put	9048
	22:19	"Therefore **h** the word of the Lord:	9048
2Ki	7: 1	Elisha said, "**H** the word of the Lord.	9048
	7: 6	caused the Arameans *to* **h** the sound of	9048
	18:28	"**H** the word of the great king,	9048
	19: 4	the Lord your God *will* **h** all the words	9048
	19:16	Give ear, O Lord, and **h**;	9048
	20:16	"**H** the word of the Lord:	9048
1Ch	14:15	As soon as you **h** the sound of marching in	9048
2Ch	6:19	**H** the cry and the prayer that your servant	9048
	6:20	*May* you **h** the prayer your servant prays	9048

2Ch	6:21	H the supplications of your servant and	9048
	6:21	H from heaven, your dwelling place;	9048
	6:21	and when *you* h, forgive.	9048
	6:23	then h from heaven and act.	9048
	6:25	then h from heaven and forgive the sin	9048
	6:27	then h from heaven and forgive the sin	9048
	6:30	then h from heaven, your dwelling place.	9048
	6:33	then h from heaven, your dwelling place,	9048
	6:35	h from heaven their prayer and their plea,	9048
	6:39	h their prayer and their pleas,	9048
	7:14	then *will* I h from heaven	9048
	9: 7	before you and h your wisdom!	9048
	9:23	with Solomon to h the wisdom God had put	9048
	18:18	"Therefore h the word of the LORD.	9048
	20: 9	and *you will* h us and save us.'	9048
Ne	1: 6	to h the prayer your servant is praying	9048
	4: 4	H us, O our God, for we are despised.	9048
	4:20	Wherever *you* h the sound of the trumpet,	9048
	13:27	*Must we* h now that you too are doing	9048
Job	3:18	*they* no longer h the slave driver's shout.	9048
	5:27	So h it and apply it to yourself."	9048
	13: 6	H now my argument;	9048
	20: 3	*I* h a rebuke that dishonors me,	9048
	22:27	You will pray to him, and *he will* h you,	9048
	26:14	how faint the whisper *we* h of him!	9048
	31:35	that I had *someone* to h me!	9048
	34: 2	"H my words, you wise men;	9048
	34:16	"If you have understanding, h this;	9048
	34:34	wise men *who* h me say to me,	9048
	39: 7	*he does* not h a driver's shout.	9048
Ps	4: 1	be merciful to me and h my prayer.	9048
	4: 3	the LORD *will* h when I call to him.	9048
	5: 3	In the morning, O LORD, *you* h my voice;	9048
	10:17	*You* h, O LORD, the desire of the afflicted;	9048
	17: 1	H, O LORD, my righteous plea;	9048
	17: 6	give ear to me and h my prayer.	9048
	18:44	As soon as they h me, they obey me;	9051
	27: 7	H my voice when I call, O LORD;	9048
	28: 2	H my cry for mercy as I call to you for help,	9048
	30:10	H, O LORD, and be merciful to me;	9048
	31:13	For *I* h the slander of many;	9048
	34: 2	*let* the afflicted h and rejoice.	9048
	38:13	I am like a deaf man, *who* cannot h,	9048
	38:14	I have become like a man who *does* not h,	9048
	39:12	"H my prayer, O LORD, listen to my cry	9048
	49: 1	H this, all you peoples;	9048
	50: 7	"H, O my people, and I will speak, O Israel,	9048
	51: 8	Let me h joy and gladness;	9048
	54: 2	H my prayer, O God;	9048
	55: 2	h me and answer me.	7992
	55:19	*will* h them and afflict them—	9048
	59: 7	and they say, "Who *can* h us?"	9048
	61: 1	H my cry, O God; listen to my prayer.	9048
	64: 1	H me, O God, as I voice my complaint;	9048
	65: 2	O you *who* h prayer,	9048
	77: 1	I cried out to God to h me.	263
	78: 1	O my people, h my teaching;	263
	80: 1	H us, O Shepherd of Israel,	263
	81: 8	"H, O my people, and I will warn you—	9048
	84: 8	H my prayer, O LORD God Almighty;	9048
	86: 1	H, O LORD, and answer me,	265+5742
	86: 6	H my prayer, O LORD;	263
	94: 9	*Does he* who implanted the ear not h?	9048
	95: 7	Today, if *you* h his voice,	9048
	102: 1	H my prayer, O LORD;	9048
	102:20	to h the groans of the prisoners	9048
	115: 6	but cannot h, noses, but they cannot smell;	9048
	119:149	H my voice in accordance with your love;	9048
	130: 2	O Lord, h my voice.	9048
	135:17	but cannot h, nor is there breath	263
	138: 4	when *they* h the words of your mouth.	9048
	140: 6	H, O LORD, my cry for mercy.	263
	141: 1	H my voice when I call to you.	263
	143: 1	O LORD, h my prayer,	9048
Pr	20:12	Ears *that* h and eyes that see—	9048
Ecc	7:21	or *you may* h your servant cursing you—	9048
SS	2:14	show me your face, *let* me h your voice;	9048
	8:13	let me h your voice!	9048
Isa	1: 2	H, O heavens!	9048
	1:10	H the word of the LORD,	9048
	6:10	h with their ears,	9048
	7:13	Isaiah said, "H now, you house of David!	9048
	18: 3	and when a trumpet sounds, *you will* h it.	9048
	21: 3	I am staggered by *what* I h,	9048
	24:16	From the ends of the earth *we* h singing:	9048
	28:14	Therefore h the word of the LORD,	9048
	28:23	Listen and h my voice;	9048
	28:23	pay attention and h what I say.	9048
	29:18	In that day the deaf *will* h the words of	9048
	30:21	your ears *will* h a voice behind you,	9048
	30:30	The LORD *will cause* men to h his majestic voice	9048
	32: 3	and the ears of *those who* h will listen.	9048
	32: 9	h what I have to say!	263
	33:13	You who are far away, h what I have done;	9048
	34: 1	*Let* the earth h, and all that is in it,	9048
	36:13	"H the words of the great king,	9048
	37: 4	that the LORD your God *will* h the words	9048
	37:17	Give ear, O LORD, and h;	9048
	39: 5	"H the word of the LORD Almighty;	9048
	42:18	"H, *you* deaf; look, you blind, and see!	9048
	42:20	your ears are open, but *you* h nothing.	9048
	43: 9	so that *others may* h and say, "It is true."	9048
	49: 1	h me, you distant nations:	7992
	51: 1	"Listen to me, my people; h me, my nation:	263
	51: 7	"H me, you who know what is right,	9048
	51:21	Therefore h this, *you* afflicted one,	9048

Isa	55: 3	h me, that your soul may live.	9048
	59: 1	nor his ear too dull to h.	9048
	59: 2	so that *he will* not h.	9048
	65:24	while they are still speaking I *will* h.	9048
	66: 5	H the word of the LORD,	9048
	66: 6	H that uproar from the city,	7754
	66: 6	h that noise from the temple!	NIH
Jer	2: 4	H the word of the LORD,	9048
	4:21	the battle standard and the sound of	9048
	4:31	*I* h a cry as of a woman in labor,	9048
	5:21	H this, *you* foolish and senseless people,	9048
	5:21	who have ears but *do* not h:	9048
	6:10	Their ears are closed so they cannot h.	7992
	6:18	Therefore h, O nations;	9048
	6:19	H, O earth: I am bringing disaster on	9048
	7: 2	" 'H the word of the LORD,	9048
	9:20	Now, O women, h the word of the LORD;	9048
	10: 1	H what the LORD says to you,	9048
	13:15	H and pay attention, do not be arrogant,	9048
	17:20	Say to them, 'H the word of the LORD,	9048
	18:19	h what my accusers are saying!	9048
	19: 3	'H the word of the LORD,	9048
	20:10	*I* h many whispering,	9048
	20:16	*May he* h wailing in the morning,	9048
	21:11	'H the word of the LORD;	9048
	22: 2	'H the word of the LORD, O king	9048
	22:29	land, land, h the word of the LORD!	9048
	23:18	of the LORD to see or to h his word?	9048
	25:36	H the cry of the shepherds,	7754
	29:20	Therefore, h the word of the LORD,	9048
	31:10	"H the word of the LORD, O nations;	9048
	33: 9	and honor before all nations on earth that h	9048
	34: 4	" 'Yet h the promise of the LORD,	9048
	36: 3	of Judah h *about* every disaster I plan	9048
	38:25	If the officials h that I talked with you,	9048
	42: 2	"Please h our petition and pray	4200+5877+7156
	42:14	where we will not see war or h the trumpet	9048
	42:15	then h the word of the LORD,	9048
	44:24	"H the word of the LORD,	9048
	44:26	But h the word of the LORD,	9048
	46:12	The nations *will* h *of* your shame;	9048
	49:20	h what the LORD has planned	9048
	50:45	h what the LORD has planned	9048
Eze	3:17	so h the word I speak	9048
	6: 3	h the word of the Sovereign LORD.	9048
	12: 2	but do not see and ears to h but do not hear,	9048
	12: 2	but do not see and ears to hear but *do* not h,	9048
	13: 2	'H the word of the LORD!	9048
	16:35	you prostitute, h the word of the LORD!	9048
	18:25	H, O house of Israel: Is my way unjust?	9048
	20:47	'H the word of the LORD.	9048
	25: 3	'H the word of the Sovereign LORD.	9048
	33: 7	so h the word I speak	9048
	33:30	'Come and h the message that has come	9048
	33:32	for *they* h your words but do not put them	9048
	34: 7	you shepherds, h the word of the LORD:	9048
	34: 9	O shepherds, h the word of the LORD:	9048
	36: 1	h the word of the LORD.	9048
	36: 4	h the word of the Sovereign LORD:	9048
	36:15	No longer *will I make* you h the taunts of	9048
	37: 4	'Dry bones, h the word of the LORD!	9048
	37: 4	look with your eyes and h with your ears	9048
Da	3: 5	As soon as *you* h the sound of the horn,	10725
	3:15	Now when *you* h the sound of the horn,	10725
	5:23	which cannot see or h or understand.	10725
	9:17	h the prayers and petitions of your servant.	9048
	9:18	Give ear, O God, and h;	9048
	9:19	O Lord, h and act!	7992
Hos	4: 1	H the word of the LORD, you Israelites,	9048
	5: 1	"H this, *you* priests!	9048
	7:12	When I h them flocking together,	9051
Joel	1: 2	H this, you elders;	9048
Am	3: 1	H this word the LORD has spoken	9048
	3:13	"H this and testify against the house	9048
	4: 1	H this word, you cows of Bashan	9048
	5: 1	H this word, O house of Israel,	9048
	7:16	Now then, h the word of the LORD.	9048
	8: 4	H this, you who trample the needy	9048
Mic	1: 2	H, O peoples, all of you, listen,	9048
	3: 9	H this, you leaders of the house of Jacob,	9048
	6: 1	*let* the hills h what you have to say.	9048
	6: 2	H, O mountains, the LORD's accusation;	9048
	7: 7	my God will h me.	9048
Zec	8: 8	"You who now h these words spoken by	9048
Mt	11: 4	"Go back and report to John what *you* h	201
	11: 5	the deaf h, the dead are raised,	201
	11:15	He who has ears, *let him* h.	201
	12:19	no one will h his voice in the streets.	201
	13: 9	He who has ears, *let him* h."	201
	13:13	though hearing, *they do* not h or understand.	201
	13:15	*they* hardly h with their ears,	201
	13:15	might see with their eyes, h with their ears,	201
	13:16	and your ears because *they* h.	201
	13:17	and *to* h what you hear but did not hear it.	201
	13:17	and to hear what *you* h but did not hear it.	201
	13:17	and to hear what you hear but *did* not h it.	201
	13:43	He who has ears, *let him* h.	201
	21:16	*"Do you* h what these children are saying?"	201
	24: 6	You will h of wars and rumors of wars,	201
	27:13	Then Pilate asked him, "Don't *you* h	201
Mk	4: 9	Then Jesus said, "He who has ears *to* h,"	201
	4: 9	"He who has ears to hear, *let him* h."	201
	4:15	As soon as *they* h it,	201
	4:16	they h the word and at once receive it with joy.	201
	4:18	like seed sown among thorns, h the word;	201+1639+4047
	4:20	h the word, accept it, and produce a	201+4015

Mk	4:23	If anyone has ears *to* h, let him hear."	201
	4:23	If anyone has ears to hear, *let him* h."	201
	4:24	"Consider carefully what *you* h,"	201
	7:37	even makes the deaf h and the mute speak."	201
	8:18	and ears but fail to h?	201
	12:29	'H, O Israel, the Lord our God,	201
	13: 7	When *you* h of wars and rumors of wars,	201
	14:11	They were delighted *to* h this and promised	201
	15:44	to h that he was already dead.	NIG
Lk	5:15	so that crowds of people came *to* h him and	201
	6:18	*to* h him and to be healed of their diseases.	201
	6:27	"But I tell you who h me:	201
	7:22	the deaf h, the dead are raised,	201
	8: 8	"He who has ears *to* h, let him hear."	201
	8: 8	"He who has ears to hear, *let him* h."	201
	8:12	Those along the path are the ones who h,	201
	8:13	the word with joy when they h,	201
	8:14	among thorns stands for those who h,	201
	8:15	*who* h the word, retain it,	201
	8:21	and brothers are those who h God's word	201
	9: 9	Who, then, is this *I* h such things about?"	201
	10:24	and *to* h what you hear but did not hear it.	201
	10:24	and to hear what *you* h but did not hear it.	201
	10:24	and to hear what you hear but *did* not h it."	201
	11:28	"Blessed rather are those who h the word	201
	14:35	"He who has ears *to* h, let him hear."	201
	14:35	"He who has ears to hear, *let him* h."	201
	15: 1	were all gathering around *to* h him.	201
	16: 2	'What is this *I* h about you?	201
	21: 9	When *you* h of wars and revolutions,	201
	21:38	in the morning *to* h him at the temple.	201
Jn	3: 8	*You* h its sound, but you cannot tell where	201
	5:25	the dead *will* h the voice of the Son of God	201
	5:25	of the Son of God and those who h will live.	201
	5:28	in their graves *will* h his voice	201
	5:30	I judge only as *I* h,	201
	8:43	Because you are unable *to* h what I say.	201
	8:47	not h is that you do not belong to God."	201
	9:27	Why do you want *to* h it again?	201
	11:42	I knew that *you* always h me,	201
	14:24	These words *you* h are not my own;	201
Ac	2:11	*we* h them declaring the wonders of God	201
	2:33	and has poured out what you now see and h.	201
	10:22	*so that he could* h what you have to say."	201
	13: 7	and Saul because he wanted *to* h the word	201
	13:44	the whole city gathered to h the word of	201
	15: 7	that the Gentiles *might* h from my lips	201
	17:32	"*We want to* h you again on this subject."	201
	19:26	and h how this fellow Paul has convinced	201
	21:22	*They will* certainly h that you have come,	201
	22:14	to see the Righteous One and *to* h words	201
	23:35	"*I will* h your *case* when your accusers	1358
	24: 4	that you be kind enough *to* h us briefly.	201
	25:22	"I would like *to* h this man myself."	201
	25:22	He replied, "Tomorrow *you will* h him."	201
	28:22	But we want *to* h what your views are,	201
	28:27	*they* hardly h with their ears,	201
	28:27	h with their ears,	201
Ro	2:13	not those who h the law who are righteous	212
	10:14	how *can they* h without someone preaching	201
	10:18	But I ask: Did *they* not h?	201
	11: 8	not see and ears so that *they could* not h,	201
1Co	11:18	*I* h that when you come together as	201
Php	1:27	whether I come and see you or only h	201
	1:30	and now h that I still have.	201
2Th	3:11	*We* h that some among you are idle.	201
2Ti	4: 3	to say *what* their itching **ears want to h.**	NIG
	4:17	and all the Gentiles *might* h it.	201
Phm	1: 5	*because* I h about your faith in	201
Heb	3: 7	"Today, if *you* h his voice,	201
	3:15	"Today, if *you* h his voice,	201
	4: 7	"Today, if *you* h his voice,	201
3Jn	1: 4	to h that my children are walking in	201
Rev	1: 3	blessed are those who h it and take to heart	201
	2: 7	*let him* h what the Spirit says to the churches	201
	2:11	*let him* h what the Spirit says to the churches	201
	2:17	*let him* h what the Spirit says to the churches	201
	2:29	*let him* h what the Spirit says to the churches	201
	3: 6	*let him* h what the Spirit says to the churches	201
	3:13	*let him* h what the Spirit says to the churches	201
	3:22	*let him* h what the Spirit says to the churches	201
	9:20	idols that cannot see or h or walk.	201
	13: 9	He who has an ear, *let him* h.	201

HEARD (577) [HEAR]

Ge	3: 8	and his wife h the sound of the LORD God	9048
	3:10	He answered, "I h you in the garden,	9048
	14:14	When Abram h that his relative had been taken captive,	9048
	16:11	for the LORD *has* h of your misery.	9048
	17:20	And as for Ishmael, I have h you:	9048
	21:17	God h the boy crying,	9048
	21:17	God *has* h the boy crying as he lies there.	9048
	21:26	and I h *about* it only today."	9048
	24:30	*had* h Rebekah tell what the man said	9048
	24:52	When Abraham's servant h what they said,	9048
	27:34	When Esau h his father's words,	9048
	29:13	As soon as Laban h the news about Jacob,	9048
	29:33	"Because the LORD h that I am not loved,	9048
	31: 1	Jacob h that Laban's sons were saying,	9048
	34: 5	When Jacob h that his daughter Dinah had been defiled,	9048
	34: 7	as soon as they h what had happened.	9048
	35:22	and Israel h *of* it.	9048
	37:17	"*I* h them say, 'Let's go to Dothan.' "	9048
	37:21	When Reuben h this, he tried to rescue him	9048

Ge	39:15	When he **h** me scream for help, 9048
	39:19	When his master **h** the story his wife told 9048
	41:15	But I have **h** it said of you *that* 9048
	42:2	"*I have* **h** that there is grain in Egypt. 9048
	43:25	*they had* **h** that they were to eat there. 9048
	45:2	he wept so loudly that the Egyptians **h** him, 9048
	45:2	and Pharaoh's household **h** *about* it. 9048
Ex	2:15	When Pharaoh **h** of this, 9048
	2:24	God **h** their groaning 9048
	3:7	*I have* **h** them crying out because 9048
	4:31	when *they* **h** that the LORD was concerned 9048
	6:5	*I have* **h** the groaning of the Israelites. 9048
	16:7	he *has* **h** your grumbling against him. 9048
	16:8	he *has* **h** your grumbling against him. 9048
	16:9	for *he has* **h** your grumbling.' " 9048
	16:12	"*I have* **h** the grumbling of the Israelites. 9048
	18:1	**h** of everything God had done for Moses 9048
	20:18	the thunder and lightning and **h** the trumpet 7754
	23:13	*do not let them* be **h** on your lips. 9048
	28:35	of the bells *will* be **h** when he enters 9048
	32:17	Joshua **h** the noise of the people shouting, 9048
	33:4	When the people **h** these distressing words, 9048
Lev	10:20	When Moses **h** this, he was satisfied. 9048
	24:14	All those *who* **h** him are to lay their hands 9048
Nu	7:89	*he* **h** the voice speaking to him from 9048
	11:1	and when he **h** them his anger was aroused. 9048
	11:10	Moses **h** the people of every family wailing, 9048
	11:18	The LORD **h** you when you wailed, 265
	12:2	And the LORD **h** this. 9048
	14:14	*They have already* **h** that you, O LORD, 9048
	14:15	the nations who *have* **h** this report 9048
	14:27	*I have* **h** the complaints of these grumbling 9048
	14:28	do to you the very things I **h** you say: 265+928
	16:4	When Moses **h** this, he fell facedown. 9048
	20:16	*he* **h** our cry and sent an angel 9048
	21:1	**h** that Israel was coming along the road 9048
	22:36	When Balak **h** that Balaam was coming, 9048
	33:40	**h** that the Israelites were coming. 9048
Dt	1:34	When the LORD **h** what you said, 9048
	4:12	You **h** the sound of words but saw no form; 9048
	4:32	or *has* anything like it *ever* been **h** of? 9048
	4:33	*Has* any other people **h** the voice 9048
	4:36	and you **h** his words from out of the fire. 9048
	5:23	When you **h** the voice out of the darkness, 9048
	5:24	and *we have* **h** his voice from the fire. 9048
	5:26	For what mortal man *has* ever **h** the voice of 9048
	5:28	The LORD **h** you when you spoke to me 9048
	5:28	"*I have* **h** what this people said to you. 9048
	9:2	You know about them and *have* **h** it said: 9048
	26:7	the LORD **h** our voice and saw our misery, 9048
Jos	2:10	*We have* **h** how the LORD dried up 9048
	2:11	When *we* **h** of it, our hearts melted 9048
	5:1	along the coast how the LORD had dried 9048
	9:1	when all the kings west of the Jordan **h** 9048
	9:3	people of Gibeon **h** what Joshua had done 9048
	9:9	For *we have* **h** reports of him: 9048
	9:16	the Israelites **h** that they were neighbors, 9048
	10:1	of Jerusalem **h** that Joshua had taken Ai 9048
	11:1	When Jabin king of Hazor **h** of this, 9048
	14:12	*You* yourself **h** then that 9048
	22:11	And *when* the Israelites **h** that they had built 9048
	22:30	**h** what Reuben, Gad and Manasseh had 9048
	24:27	It *has* **h** all the words the LORD has said 9048
Jdg	7:15	When Gideon **h** the dream 9048
	9:30	of the city **h** what Gaal son of Ebed said, 9048
	9:47	Abimelech **h** that they had assembled there, 5583
	13:9	God **h** Manoah, and the angel 7754+9048
	17:2	about which I **h** you utter a curse— 265+606+928
	20:3	(The Benjamites **h** that the Israelites 9048
Ru	1:6	When *she* **h** in Moab that 9048
1Sa	1:13	but her voice *was* not **h.** 9048
	2:22	**h** about everything his sons were doing 9048
	4:14	Eli **h** the outcry and asked, 9048
	4:19	When *she* **h** the news that the ark 9048
	7:7	the Philistines **h** that Israel had assembled 9048
	7:7	And when the Israelites **h** of it, 9048
	8:21	When Samuel **h** all that the people said, 9048
	11:6	When Saul **h** their words, 9048
	13:3	and the Philistines **h** about it. 9048
	13:4	So all Israel **h** the news: 9048
	14:22	of Ephraim **h** that the Philistines were on 9048
	14:27	not **h** that his father had bound the people 9048
	17:23	shouted his usual defiance, and David **h** it. 9048
	17:28	**h** him speaking with the men, 9048
	22:1	and his father's household **h** *about* it, 9048
	22:6	Now Saul **h** that David and his men 9048
	23:10	your servant *has* **h definitely** 9048+9048
	23:11	as your servant *has* **h?** 9048
	23:25	When Saul **h** this, 9048
	25:4	*he* **h** that Nabal was shearing sheep. 9048
	25:35	*I have* **h** your words 9048
	25:39	When David **h** that Nabal was dead, he said, 9048
	31:11	When the people of Jabesh Gilead **h** of what 9048
2Sa	3:28	Later, when David **h** *about* this, he said, 9048
	4:1	of Saul **h** that Abner had died in Hebron, 9048
	5:17	When the Philistines **h** that David 9048
	5:17	but David **h** *about* it and went down to 9048
	7:22	as *we have* **h** with our own ears. 9048
	8:9	of Hamath **h** that David had defeated 9048
	11:26	Uriah's wife **h** that her husband was dead, 9048
	13:21	When King David **h** all this, he was furious. 9048
	18:5	And all the troops **h** the king giving orders 9048
	19:2	because on that day the troops **h** it said, 9048
	22:7	From his temple *he* **h** my voice; 9048
1Ki	1:11	"*Have you* not **h** that Adonijah, 9048
	1:41	and all the guests who were with him **h** it 9048
	3:28	all Israel **h** the verdict the king had given, 9048

1Ki	4:34	who *had* **h** of his wisdom. 9048
	5:1	When Hiram king of Tyre **h** 9048
	5:7	When Hiram **h** Solomon's message, 9048
	6:7	chisel or any other iron tool *was* **h** at 9048
	9:3	*I have* **h** the prayer and plea you have made 9048
	10:1	When the queen of Sheba **h** about the fame 9048
	10:6	"The report *I* **h** in my own country 9048
	10:7	you have far exceeded the report *I* **h.** 9048
	11:21	Hadad **h** that David rested with his fathers 9048
	12:2	of Nebat **h** this (he was still in Egypt, 9048
	12:20	the Israelites **h** that Jeroboam had returned, 9048
	13:4	When King Jeroboam **h** what the man 9048
	13:26	from his journey **h** *of* it, 9048
	14:6	when Ahijah **h** the sound of her footsteps at 9048
	15:21	When Baasha **h** this, 9048
	16:16	in the camp **h** that Zimri had plotted against 9048
	17:22	The LORD **h** Elijah's cry, 9048
	18:13	Haven't you **h,** my lord, 5583
	19:13	When Elijah **h** it, 9048
	20:12	Ben-Hadad **h** this message while he and 9048
	20:31	*we have* **h** that the kings of the house 9048
	21:15	as Jezebel **h** that Naboth had been stoned 9048
	21:16	When Ahab **h** that Naboth was dead, 9048
	21:27	When Ahab **h** these words, 9048
2Ki	3:21	the Moabites *had* **h** that the kings had come 9048
	5:8	When Elisha the man of God **h** that the king 9048
	6:30	When the king **h** the woman's words, 9048
	9:30	When Jezebel **h** about it, 9048
	11:13	When Athaliah **h** the noise made by 9048
	19:1	When King Hezekiah **h** this, 9048
	19:4	for the words the LORD your God *has* **h.** 9048
	19:6	Do not be afraid of what *you have* **h**— 9048
	19:8	When the field commander **h** that the king 9048
	19:11	Surely you *have* **h** what the kings 9048
	19:20	*I have* **h** your prayer 9048
	19:25	" '*Have you* not **h?** 9048
	20:5	*I have* **h** your prayer and seen your tears; 9048
	20:12	because *he had* **h** of Hezekiah's illness. 9048
	22:11	When the king **h** the words of the Book of 9048
	22:18	says concerning the words you **h:** 9048
	22:19	the LORD when you **h** what I have spoken 9048
	22:19	*I have* **h** you, declares the LORD. 9048
	25:23	When all the army officers and their men **h** 9048
1Ch	10:11	When all the inhabitants of Jabesh Gilead **h** 9048
	14:8	When the Philistines **h** 9048
	14:8	but David **h** *about* it and went out 9048
	17:20	as *we have* **h** with our own ears. 9048
	18:9	of Hamath **h** that David had defeated 9048
2Ch	7:12	"*I have* **h** your prayer 9048
	9:1	the queen of Sheba **h** *of* Solomon's fame, 9048
	9:5	"The report *I* **h** in my own country 9048
	9:6	you have far exceeded the report *I* **h.** 9048
	10:2	When Jeroboam son of Nebat **h** this 9048
	15:8	When Asa **h** these words and the prophecy 9048
	16:5	When Baasha **h** this, 9048
	20:29	the kingdoms of the countries when they **h** 9048
	23:12	When Athaliah **h** the noise of 9048
	30:20	LORD **h** Hezekiah and healed the people. 9048
	30:27	and God **h** them, for their prayer 7754+9048
	34:19	When the king **h** the words of the Law, 9048
	34:26	says concerning the words you **h:** 9048
	34:27	before God when you **h** what he spoke 9048
	34:27	*I have* **h** you, declares the LORD. 9048
Ezr	3:13	And the sound *was* **h** far away. 9048
	4:1	When the enemies of Judah and Benjamin **h** 9048
	9:3	When I **h** this, I tore my tunic and cloak, 9048
Ne	1:4	When I **h** these things, I sat down and wept. 9048
	2:10	the Ammonite official **h** *about* this, 9048
	2:19	and Geshem the Arab **h** *about* it, 9048
	4:1	When Sanballat **h** that we were rebuilding 9048
	4:7	the Ammonites and the men of Ashdod **h** 9048
	4:15	When our enemies **h** that we were aware 9048
	5:6	When *I* **h** their outcry and these charges, 9048
	6:16	When all our enemies **h** *about* this, 9048
	9:9	*you* **h** their cry at the Red Sea. 9048
	9:27	From heaven you **h** them, 9048
	9:28	you **h** from heaven, 9048
	12:43	*sound* of rejoicing in Jerusalem *could* be **h** 9048
	13:3	When the people **h** this law, 9048
Est	1:18	of the nobility who *have* **h** *about* 9048
Job	2:11	**h** *about* all the troubles that had come 9048
	3:7	*may* no shout of joy be **h** in it. 995S
	4:16	and *I* **h** a hushed voice: 9048
	13:1	my ears *have* **h** and understood it. 9048
	16:2	"*I have* **h** many things like these; 9048
	29:11	Whoever **h** me spoke well of me, 9048
	33:8	*I* **h** the very words— 9048
	34:28	so that he **h** the cry of the needy. 9048
	42:5	My ears *had* **h** *of* you but 9048+9051
Ps	6:8	for the LORD *has* **h** my weeping. 9048
	6:9	The LORD *has* **h** my cry for mercy; 9048
	18:6	From his temple *he* **h** my voice; 9048
	19:3	or language where their voice *is* not **h.** 9048
	28:6	for *he has* **h** my cry for mercy. 9048
	31:22	Yet *you* **h** my cry for mercy when I called 9048
	34:6	and the LORD **h** him; 9048
	40:1	he turned to me and **h** my cry. 9048
	44:1	*We have* **h** with our ears, O God; 9048
	48:8	As *we have* **h,** so have we seen in the city of 9048
	61:5	For *you have* **h** my vows, O God; 9048
	62:11	two things *have* I **h:** 9048
	66:8	*let* the sound of his praise *be* **h;** 9048
	66:19	but God has surely listened and **h** my voice 7992
	77:18	Your thunder was **h** in the whirlwind, 7754
	78:3	what *we have* **h** and known, 9048
	78:21	When the LORD **h** them, 9048
	78:59	When God **h** them, he was very angry; 9048

Ps	81:5	*we* **h** a language we did not understand. 9048
	92:11	my ears *have* **h** the rout of my wicked foes. 9048
	106:44	of their distress when he **h** their cry; 9048
	116:1	I love the LORD, for *he* **h** my voice; 9048
	116:1	he **h** my cry for mercy. NIH
	132:6	*We* **h** it in Ephrathah, 9048
Ecc	12:13	Now all *has been* **h;** 9048
SS	2:12	the cooing of doves *is* **h** in our land. 9048
Isa	5:7	for righteousness, but **h** cries of distress. 2180
	6:8	Then *I* **h** the voice of the Lord saying, 9048
	15:4	their voices *are* **h** all the way to Jahaz. 9048
	16:6	*We have* **h** of Moab's pride— 9048
	21:10	I tell you what *I have* **h** from 9048
	37:1	When King Hezekiah **h** this, 9048
	37:4	for the words the LORD your God *has* **h.** 9048
	37:6	Do not be afraid of what *you have* **h**— 9048
	37:8	When the field commander **h** that the king 9048
	37:9	When he **h** it, he sent messengers 9048
	37:11	Surely you *have* **h** what the kings 9048
	37:26	"*Have you* not **h?** 9048
	38:5	*I have* **h** your prayer and seen your tears; 9048
	39:1	because *he had* **h** of his illness and recovery. 9048
	40:21	*Have you* not **h?** 9048
	40:28	*Have you* not **h?** 9048
	41:26	no one **h** any words from you. 9048
	48:6	*You have* **h** these things; look at them all. 9048
	48:7	*you have* not **h** of them before today. 9048
	48:8	*You have* neither **h** nor understood; 9048
	52:15	they will see, and what *they* have not **h,** 9048
	58:4	and *expect* your voice to *be* **h** on high. 9048
	60:18	No longer *will* violence be **h** in your land, 9048
	64:4	Since ancient times *no one has* **h,** 9048
	65:19	and of crying *will* be **h** in it no more. 9048
	66:8	Who *has ever* **h** of such a thing? 9048
	66:19	and to the distant islands that *have* not **h** 9048
Jer	3:21	A cry *is* **h** on the barren heights, 9048
	4:19	For I *have* **h** the sound of the trumpet; 9048
	4:19	the battle cry. NIH
	6:24	*We have* **h** reports about them; 9048
	8:16	The snorting of the enemy's horses *is* **h** 9048
	9:10	and the lowing of cattle *is* not **h.** 9048
	9:19	The sound of wailing *is* **h** from Zion: 9048
	18:13	Who *has ever* **h** anything like this? 9048
	18:22	*Let* a cry *be* **h** from their houses 9048
	20:1	**h** Jeremiah prophesying these things, 9048
	22:20	*let* your voice *be* **h** in Bashan, 5989
	23:18	Who has listened and **h** his word? 9048
	23:25	"*I have* **h** what the prophets say 9048
	26:7	the people **h** Jeremiah speak these words in 9048
	26:10	the officials of Judah **h** *about* these things, 9048
	26:11	*You have* **h** it with your own ears!" 9048
	26:12	and this city all the things *you have* **h.** 9048
	26:21	and all his officers and officials **h** his words, 9048
	26:21	But Uriah **h** of it and fled in fear to Egypt. 9048
	30:5	" 'Cries of fear *are* **h**—terror, not peace. 9048
	31:7	**Make** your praises **h,** and say, 'O LORD, 9048
	31:15	"A voice *is* **h** in Ramah, 9048
	31:18	"I have **surely** **h** Ephraim's moaning: 9048+9048
	33:10	*there will be* **h** once more 9048
	36:11	**h** all the words of the LORD from 9048
	36:13	Micaiah told them everything *he had* **h**
		Baruch read 9048
	36:16	When they **h** all these words, 9048
	36:24	all his attendants who **h** all these words showed no fear, 9048
	37:5	Babylonians who were besieging Jerusalem **h** the report 9048
	38:1	of Malkijah **h** what Jeremiah was telling all 9048
	38:7	**h** that they had put Jeremiah into the cistern. 9048
	38:27	no *one had* **h** his conversation with the king. 9048
	40:7	in the open country **h** that the king 9048
	40:11	and all the other countries **h** that the king 9048
	41:11	the army officers who were with him **h** 9048
	42:4	"*I have* **h** you," replied Jeremiah 9048
	48:5	cries over the destruction *are* **h.** 9048
	48:29	"*We have* **h** of Moab's pride— 9048
	49:14	I *have* **h** a message from the LORD: 9048
	49:23	for *they have* **h** bad news. 9048
	50:43	king of Babylon *has* **h** reports about them, 9048
	51:46	or be afraid when rumors *are* **h** in the land; 9048
La	1:21	"*People have* **h** my groaning, 9048
	1:21	All my enemies *have* **h** of my distress, 9048
	3:56	*You* **h** my plea: 9048
	3:61	O LORD, *you have* **h** their insults, 9048
Eze	1:24	*I* **h** the sound of their wings, 9048
	1:28	and *I* **h** the voice of one speaking. 9048
	2:2	and *I* **h** him speaking to me. 9048
	3:12	and *I* **h** behind me a loud rumbling sound— 9048
	9:1	Then *I* **h** him call out in a loud voice, 265+928
	10:5	of the cherubim *could be* **h** as far away as 9048
	10:13	I **h** the wheels being called 265+928
	19:4	The nations **h** about him, 9048
	19:9	his roar *was* **h** no longer on the mountains 9048
	26:13	the music of your harps *will* be **h** no more. 9048
	33:5	Since he **h** the sound of the trumpet but did 9048
	35:12	that I the LORD *have* **h** all the contemptible 9048
	35:13	without restraint, and I **h** it. 9048
	43:6	I **h** someone speaking to me from inside 9048
Da	3:7	as soon as they **h** the sound of the horn, 10725
	5:14	*I have* **h** that the spirit of the gods is in you 10725
	5:16	Now I have **h** that you are able 10725
	6:14	When the king **h** this, 10725
	8:13	Then *I* **h** a holy one speaking, 9048
	8:16	I **h** a man's voice from the Ulai calling, 9048
	10:9	Then *I* **h** him speaking, 9048
	10:12	your words were **h,** and I have come 9048
	12:7	*I* **h** him swear by him who lives forever, 9048

Da	12: 8	I h, but I did not understand.	9048
Ob	1: 1	We have h a message from the LORD:	9048
Na	2:13	of your messengers will no longer be h."	9048
Hab	3: 2	LORD, I have h of your fame;	9048
	3:16	I h and my heart pounded.	9048
Zep	2: 8	"I have h the insults of Moab and the taunts	9048
Zec	8:23	because we have h that God is with you.' "	9048
Mal	3:16	and the LORD listened and h.	9048
Mt	2: 3	When King Herod h this he was disturbed,	201
	2: 9	After they had h the king,	201
	2:18	"A voice is h in Ramah,	201
	2:22	But when he h that Archelaus was reigning	201
	4:12	When Jesus h that John had been put	201
	5:21	"You have h that it was said to	201
	5:27	"You have h that it was said,	201
	5:33	you have h that it was said to	201
	5:38	"You have h that it was said, 'Eye for eye,	201
	5:43	"You have h that it was said,	201
	6: 7	for they think they will be h because	1653
	8:10	When Jesus h this, he was astonished	201
	11: 2	When John h in prison what Christ was doing,	201
	12:24	But when the Pharisees h this, they said,	201
	14: 1	At that time Herod the tetrarch h the reports	201
	14:13	When Jesus h what had happened,	201
	15:12	when they h this?"	201
	17: 6	When the disciples h this,	201
	19:22	When the young man h this,	201
	19:25	When the disciples h this,	201
	20:24	When the ten h about this,	201
	20:30	and when they h that Jesus was going by,	201
	21:45	and the Pharisees h Jesus' parables,	201
	22:22	When they h this, they were amazed.	201
	22:33	When the crowds h this,	201
	26:65	Look, now you have h the blasphemy.	201
	27:47	When some of those standing there h this,	201
Mk	2: 1	the people h that he had come home.	201
	3: 8	When they h all he was doing,	201
	3:21	When his family h about this,	201
	5:27	When she h about Jesus,	201
	6: 2	and many who h him were amazed.	201
	6:14	King Herod h about this,	201
	6:16	But when Herod h this, he said, "John,	201
	6:20	When Herod h John, he was greatly puzzled;	201
	6:55	the sick on mats to wherever they h he was.	201
	7:25	In fact, as soon as she h about him,	201
	10:41	When the ten h about this,	201
	10:47	When he h that it was Jesus of Nazareth,	201
	11:14	And his disciples h him say it.	201
	11:18	the law h this and began looking for a way	201
	12:28	of the law came and h them debating.	201
	14:58	"We h him say, 'I will destroy this	201
	14:64	"You have h the blasphemy.	201
	15:35	When some of those standing near h this,	201
	15:39	h his cry and saw how he died, he said,	NIG
	16:11	When they h that Jesus was alive and	201
Lk	1:13	your prayer has been h.	1653
	1:41	When Elizabeth h Mary's greeting,	201
	1:58	Her neighbors and relatives h that	201
	1:66	Everyone who h this wondered about it,	201
	2:18	and all who h it were amazed at what	201
	2:20	for all the things they had h and seen,	201
	2:47	Everyone who h him was amazed	201
	4:23	Do here in your hometown what we have h	201
	4:28	synagogue were furious when they h this.	201
	7: 3	The centurion h of Jesus	201
	7: 9	When Jesus h this, he was amazed at him,	201
	7:22	to John what you have seen and h:	201
	7:29	when they h Jesus' words,	201
	9: 7	the tetrarch h about all that was going on.	201
	12: 3	What you have said in the dark will be h in	201
	14:15	of those at the table with him h this,	201
	15:25	he h music and dancing.	201
	16:14	h all this and were sneering at Jesus.	201
	18:22	When Jesus h this, he said to him,	201
	18:23	When he h this, he became very sad,	201
	18:26	Those who h this asked,	201
	18:36	When he h the crowd going by,	201
	20:16	When the people h this, they said,	201
	22:71	We have h it from his own lips."	201
	23: 8	From what he had h about him,	201
Jn	1:37	When the two disciples h him say this,	201
	1:40	of the two who h what John had said	201
	3:32	He testifies to what he has seen and h,	201
	4: 1	The Pharisees h that Jesus was gaining	201
	4:42	now we have h for ourselves,	201
	4:47	When this man h that Jesus had arrived	201
	5:37	You have never h his voice	201
	7:32	The Pharisees h the crowd whispering such things about him.	201
	8: 9	those who h began to go away one at a time,	201
	8:26	what I have h from him I tell the world."	201
	8:38	you do what you have h from your father."	201
	8:40	a man who has told you the truth that I h	201
	9:32	Nobody has ever h of opening the eyes of	201
	9:35	Jesus h that they had thrown him out,	201
	9:40	with him h him say this and asked,	201
	11: 4	When he h this, Jesus said,	201
	11: 6	Yet when he h that Lazarus was sick,	201
	11:20	When Martha h that Jesus was coming,	201
	11:29	When Mary h this, she got up quickly	201
	11:41	"Father, I thank you that you have h me.	201
	12:12	that had come for the Feast h that Jesus was	201
	12:18	because they had h that he had given this	201
	12:29	that was there and h it said it had thundered;	201
	12:34	"We have h from the Law that the Christ	201
	14:28	"You h me say, 'I am going away	201
Jn	18:21	Ask those who h me.	201
	19: 8	When Pilate h this,	201
	19:13	When Pilate h this,	201
	21: 7	As soon as Simon Peter h him say,	201
Ac	1: 4	which you have h me speak about.	201
	1:19	Everyone in Jerusalem h about this,	1181+1196
	2: 6	When they h this sound,	1181+5889
	2: 6	because each one h them speaking	201
	2:37	When the people h this,	201
	4: 4	But many who h the message believed,	201
	4:20	about what we have seen and h."	201
	4:24	When they h this,	201
	5: 5	When Ananias h this, he fell down and died.	201
	5: 5	great fear seized all who h what had happened.	201
	5:11	the whole church and all who h about	201
	5:33	When they h this, they were furious	201
	6:11	"We have h Stephen speak words	201
	6:14	For we have h him say that this Jesus	201
	7:12	When Jacob h that there was grain in Egypt,	201
	7:29	When Moses h this, he fled to Midian,	3364
	7:31	he h the Lord's voice:	NIG
	7:34	I have h their groaning and have come	201
	7:54	When they h this, they were furious	201
	8: 6	When the crowds h Philip and saw	201
	8:14	in Jerusalem h that Samaria had accepted	201
	8:30	to the chariot and h the man reading Isaiah	201
	9: 4	to the ground and h a voice say to him,	201
	9: 7	they h the sound but did not see anyone.	201
	9:13	"I have h many reports about this man	201
	9:21	All those who h him were astonished	201
	9:38	when the disciples h that Peter was in Lydda,	201
	10:31	God has h your prayer	1653
	10:44	Holy Spirit came on all who h the message.	201
	10:46	For they h them speaking in tongues	201
	11: 1	and the brothers throughout Judea h that	201
	11: 7	Then I h a voice telling me, 'Get up, Peter.	201
	11:18	When they h this, they had no further	201
	13:48	When the Gentiles h this,	201
	14:14	the apostles Barnabas and Paul h of this,	201
	15:24	We have h that some went out from us	201
	16:38	and when they h that Paul	201
	17: 8	When they h this,	201
	17:32	When they h about the resurrection of	201
	18: 8	of the Corinthians who h him believed	201
	18:26	When Priscilla and Aquila h him,	201
	19: 2	not even h that there is a Holy Spirit."	201
	19:10	the province of Asia h the word of the Lord.	201
	19:28	When they h this, they were furious	201
	21:12	When we h this,	201
	21:20	When they h this, they praised God.	201
	22: 2	When they h him speak to them in Aramaic,	201
	22: 7	I fell to the ground and h a voice say to me,	201
	22:15	to all men of what you have seen and h.	201
	22:26	When the centurion h this,	201
	23:16	when the son of Paul's sister h of this plot,	201
	26:14	and I h a voice saying to me in Aramaic,	201
	28:15	brothers there had h that we were coming,	201
Ro	10:14	in the one of whom they have not h?	201
	10:17	the message is h through the word of Christ.	NIG
	15:21	and those who have not h will understand."	201
	16:19	Everyone has h about your obedience,	919
1Co	2: 9	"No eye has seen, no ear has h,	201
2Co	6: 2	he says, "In the time of my favor I h you,	2052
	12: 4	He h inexpressible things,	201
Gal	1:13	For you have h of my previous way of life	201
	1:23	They only h the report:	201+1639
	3: 2	or by believing what you h?	198
	3: 5	or because you believe what you h?	198
Eph	1:13	also were included in Christ when you h	201
	1:15	since I h about your faith in the Lord Jesus	201
	3: 2	Surely you have h about the administration	201
	4:21	Surely you h of him and were taught	201
Php	2:26	and is distressed because you h he was ill.	201
	4: 9	Whatever you have learned or received or h	201
Col	1: 4	h of your faith in Christ Jesus and of	201
	1: 5	that you have already h about in the word	4578
	1: 6	among you since the day you h it	201
	1: 9	since the day we h about you,	201
	1:23	that you h and that has been proclaimed	201
1Th	2:13	which you h from us,	198
2Ti	1:13	What you h from me,	201
	2: 2	And the things you have h me say in	201
Heb	2: 1	therefore, to what we have h,	201
	2: 3	was confirmed to us by those who h him.	201
	3:16	Who were they who h and rebelled?	201
	4: 2	the message they h was of no value to them,	198
	4: 2	those who h did not combine it with faith.	201
	5: 7	he was h because of his reverent submission	1653
	12:19	that those who h it begged	201
Jas	1:25	not forgetting what he has h, but doing	212+1181
	5:11	You have h of Job's perseverance	201
2Pe	1:18	We ourselves h this voice that came	201
	2: 8	by the lawless deeds he saw and h)—	198
1Jn	1: 1	which we have h, which we have seen	201
	1: 3	to you what we have seen and h,	201
	1: 5	the message we have h from him and	201
	2: 7	the message you have h.	201
	2:18	as you have h that the antichrist is coming,	201
	2:24	See that what you have h from	201
	3:11	the message you h from the beginning:	201
	4: 3	which you have h is coming and even	201
2Jn	1: 6	As you have h from the beginning,	201
Rev	1:10	I h behind me a loud voice like a trumpet,	201
	3: 3	therefore, what you have received and h;	201
	4: 1	And the voice I had first h speaking to me	201
Rev	5:11	I looked and h the voice of many angels,	201
	5:13	Then I h every creature in heaven and	201
	6: 1	Then I h one of the four living creatures	201
	6: 3	I h the second living creature say, "Come!"	201
	6: 5	I h the third living creature say, "Come!"	201
	6: 6	Then I h what sounded like a voice among	201
	6: 7	I h the voice of the fourth living creature	201
	7: 4	I h the number of those who were sealed:	201
	8:13	I h an eagle that was flying	201
	9:13	and I h a voice coming from the horns of	201
	9:16	I h their number.	201
	10: 4	but I h a voice from heaven say,	201
	10: 8	the voice that I had h from heaven spoke	201
	11:12	Then they h a loud voice	201
	12:10	Then I h a loud voice in heaven say:	201
	14: 2	And I h a sound from heaven like the roar	201
	14: 2	The sound I h was like that	201
	14:13	Then I h a voice from heaven say, "Write:	201
	16: 1	Then I h a loud voice from	201
	16: 5	I h the angel in charge of the waters say:	201
	16: 7	And I h the altar respond:	201
	18: 4	Then I h another voice from heaven say:	201
	18:22	will never be h in you again.	201
	18:22	of a millstone will never be h in you.	201
	18:23	of bridegroom and bride will never be h	201
	19: 1	After this I h what sounded like the roar of	201
	19: 6	I h what sounded like a great multitude,	201
	21: 3	I h a loud voice from the throne saying,	201
	22: 8	am the one who h and saw these things.	201
	22: 8	And when I had h and seen them,	201

HEARERS (1) [HEAR]

1Ti	4:16	you will save both yourself and your h.	201

HEARING (56) [HEAR]

Ge	23:10	in the h of all the Hittites who had come to	265
	23:13	and he said to Ephron in their h,	265
	23:16	for him the price he had named in the h of	265
Nu	11: 1	about their hardships in the h of	265
Dt	5: 1	and laws I declare in your h today.	265
	31:11	before them in their h.	265
	31:28	so that I can speak these words in their h	265
	31:30	of this song from beginning to end in the h	265
	32:44	and spoke all the words of this song in the h	265
Jdg	9:46	On h this, the citizens in the tower	9048
1Sa	4: 6	H the uproar, the Philistines asked,	9048
	17:11	On h the Philistine's words,	9048
2Sa	10: 7	On h this, David sent Joab out with	9048
	18:12	In our h the king commanded you	265
1Ki	1:41	On h the sound of the trumpet, Joab asked,	9048
2Ki	18:26	to us in Hebrew in the h of the people on	265
	23: 2	He read in their h all the words of the Book	265
1Ch	19: 8	On h this, David sent Joab out with	9048
	28: 8	and in the h of our God:	265
2Ch	34:30	He read in their h all the words of the Book	265
Ne	13: 1	the Book of Moses was read aloud in the h	265
Job	9:16	I do not believe he would give me a h.	263+7754
	33: 8	"But you have said in my h—	9048
Ecc	1: 8	nor the ear is full of h.	9048
Isa	5: 9	LORD Almighty has declared in my h:	265
	6: 9	" 'Be ever h, but never understanding;	9048+9048
	22:14	LORD Almighty has revealed this in my h:	265
	36:11	to us in Hebrew in the h of the people on	265
	49:20	yet say in your h, 'This place is too small	265
Jer	2: 2	"Go and proclaim in the h of Jerusalem	265
	26:15	to you to speak all these words in your h."	265
	28: 7	listen to what I have to say in your h and in	265
	28: 7	to say in your hearing and in the h of all	265
Da	9:	h the voices of the king and his nobles,	NIH
Am	8:11	but a famine of h the words of the LORD.	9048
Mt	9:12	On h this, Jesus said,	201
	13:13	though h, they do not hear or understand.	201
	13:14	be ever h but never understanding;	198+201
	14:13	H of this, the crowds followed him on foot	201
	22:34	H that Jesus had silenced the Sadducees,	201
Mk	2:17	On h this, Jesus said to them,	201
	4:12	and ever h but never understanding;	201+201
	6:29	On h of this, John's disciples came	201
Lk	4:21	"Today this scripture is fulfilled in your h."	4044
	7: 1	saying this in the h of the people,	198
	8:10	though h, they may not understand.'	201
	8:50	H this, Jesus said to Jairus, "Don't be afraid;	201
	23: 6	On h this, Pilate asked if the man was	201
Jn	6:60	On h it, many of his disciples said,	201
	7:40	On h his words, some of the people said,	201
	7:51	condemn anyone without first h him	201
Ac	5:24	On h this report,	201
	19: 5	On h this, they were baptized into the name	201
	28:26	be ever h but never understanding;	198+201
Ro	10:17	faith comes from h the message,	NIG
1Co	12:17	where would the sense of h be?	198

HEARKEN, HEARKENED, HEARKENETH, HEARKENING (KJV)

See AGREE, ANSWER, ATTENTION, FOLLOW, HEAR, HEARD, HEED, MARK WORDS, OBEYED, OBEYING

HEARS (52) [HEAR]

Ge	21: 6	and everyone who h about this will laugh	9048
Ex	17:14	make sure that Joshua h it,	265+928+8492
Lev	5: 1	he does not speak up when he h	7754+9048

Nu 24: 4	the oracle of *one who* h the words of God,	9048
24:16	the oracle of *one who* h the words of God,	9048
30: 4	and her father h *about* her vow or pledge	9048
30: 5	if her father forbids her when he h *about* it,	9048
30: 7	and her husband h *about* it	9048
30: 8	But if her husband forbids her when he h	9048
30:11	and her husband h *about* it	9048
30:12	But if her husband nullifies them when he h	9048
30:14	by saying nothing to her when he h	9048
30:15	he nullifies them some time after he h	9048
Dt 29:19	a person h the words of this oath,	9048
1Sa 3:11	that will make the ears of everyone *who* h	9048
2Sa 17: 9	whoever h *about* it will say,	9048+9048
2Ki 19: 7	to put such a spirit in him that when he h	9048
21:12	the ears of everyone *who* h *of* it will tingle.	9048
Ps 34:17	righteous cry out, and the LORD h them;	9048
55:17	and *he* h my voice.	9048
69:33	The LORD h the needy and does	9048
97: 8	Zion h and rejoices and the villages	9048
145:19	*he* h their cry and saves them.	9048
Pr 13: 8	but a poor man h no threat.	9048
15:29	The LORD is far from the wicked but *he* h	9048
25:10	or *he who* h it may shame you	9048
Isa 11: 3	or decide by *what* he h with his ears;	5461
30:19	As soon as he h, he will answer you.	9048
37: 7	in him so that *when he* h a certain report,	9048
Jer 19: 3	that will make the ears of everyone *who* h	9048
Eze 33: 4	then if *anyone* h the trumpet but	7754+9048+9048
Da 3:10	that everyone who h the sound of the horn,	10725
Na 3:19	Everyone *who* h the news	9048
Mt 7:24	"Therefore everyone who h these words	201
7:26	But everyone who h these words of mine	201
13:19	*When* anyone h the message about	201
13:20	on rocky places is the man who h the word	201
13:22	that fell among the thorns is the man who h	201
13:23	the man who h the word and understands it.	201
Lk 6:47	and h my words and puts them into practice.	201
6:49	But the one who h my words and does	201
Jn 3:29	of joy when he h the bridegroom's voice.	NIG
5:24	whoever h my word and believes him	201
8:47	He who belongs to God h what God says.	201
12:47	for the person who h my words but does	201
16:13	he will speak only what *he* h,	201
Ac 2: 8	of us h them in his own native language?	201
1Jn 5:14	according to his will, he h us.	201
5:15	And if we know that *he* h us—	201
Rev 3:20	If anyone h my voice and opens the door,	201
22:17	let him who h say, "Come!"	201
22:18	I warn everyone who h the words of	201

HEART (570) [BROKENHEARTED, DISHEARTENED, DOWNHEARTED, FAINTHEARTED, HARDHEARTED, HEART'S, HEARTACHE, HEARTLESS, HEARTS, HEARTS', KINDHEARTED, SIMPLEHEARTED, STOUTHEARTED, STUBBORN-HEARTED, WHOLEHEARTED, WHOLEHEARTEDLY]

Ge 6: 5	thoughts of his h was only evil all the time.	4213
6: 6	and his h was filled with pain.	4213
8:21	the pleasing aroma and said in his h:	4213
8:21	though every inclination of his h is evil	4213
24:45	"Before I finished praying in my h,	4213
34: 3	His h was drawn to Dinah daughter	5883
34: 8	"My son Shechem has his h set	5883
Ex 4:14	and his h will be glad when he sees you.	4213
4:21	But I will harden his h so that he will not let	4213
7: 3	But I will harden Pharaoh's h,	4213
7:13	Yet Pharaoh's h became hard and he would	4213
7:14	"Pharaoh's h is unyielding;	4213
7:22	and Pharaoh's h became hard;	4213
7:23	and did not take even this to h.	4213
8:15	he hardened his h and would not listen	4213
8:19	But Pharaoh's h was hard and he would	4213
8:32	But this time also Pharaoh hardened his h	4213
9: 7	Yet his h was unyielding and he would	4213
9:12	But the LORD hardened Pharaoh's h	4213
9:35	So Pharaoh's h was hard and he would	4213
10: 1	for I have hardened his h and the hearts	4213
10:20	But the LORD hardened Pharaoh's h,	4213
10:27	But the LORD hardened Pharaoh's h,	4213
11:10	but the LORD hardened Pharaoh's h,	4213
14: 4	And I will harden Pharaoh's h,	4213
14: 8	the h of Pharaoh king of Egypt,	4213
15: 8	deep waters congealed in the h *of* the sea.	4213
25: 2	from each man whose h prompts him	4213
28:29	the names of the sons of Israel over his h on	4213
28:30	be over Aaron's h whenever he enters	4213
28:30	the Israelites over his h before the LORD.	4213
35:21	and whose h moved him came and brought	4213
Lev 19:17	" 'Do not hate your brother in your h.	4222
Dt 1:28	Our brothers have made us lose h.	4222
2:30	and his h obstinate in order to give him	4222
4: 9	or let them slip from your h as long	4222
4:29	if you look for him with all your h and	4222
4:39	Acknowledge and take to h this day that	4222
6: 5	Love the LORD your God with all your h	4222
8: 2	in order to know what was in your h,	4222
8: 5	so in your h that as a man disciplines his son,	4222
8:14	then your h will become proud	4222
10:12	the LORD your God with all your h and	4222
11: 3	and the things he did in the h *of* Egypt, both	9348
11:13	with all your h and with all your soul—	4222

Dt 13: 3	with all your h and with all your soul.	4222
15:10	to him and do so without a grudging h;	4222
17:17	or his h will be led astray.	4222
26:16	carefully observe them with all your h and	4222
28:65	weary with longing, and a despairing h.	5883
29:18	among you today whose h turns away from	4222
30: 1	upon you and you take them to h wherever	4222
30: 2	with all your h and with all your soul and	4222
30: 6	that you may love him with all your h and	4222
30:10	to the LORD your God with all your h and	4222
30:14	in your h so you may obey it.	4222
30:17	your h turns away and you are not obedient,	4222
32:46	to h all the words I have solemnly declared	4222
Jos 22: 5	to him and to serve him with all your h	4222
23:14	with all your h and soul that not one of all	4222
Jdg 5: 9	My h is with Israel's princes,	4213
5:15	of Reuben there was much searching of h.	4213
5:16	of Reuben there was much searching of h.	4213
1Sa 1:13	Hannah was praying in her h,	4213
2: 1	"My h rejoices in the LORD;	4213
2:33	with tears and to grieve your h,	5883
2:35	who will do according to what is in my h	4222
4:13	because his h feared for the ark of God.	4213
9:19	and will tell you all that is in your h.	4222
10: 9	God changed Saul's h,	4213
12:20	but serve the LORD with all your h.	4222
12:24	and serve him faithfully with all your h;	4222
13:14	after his own h and appointed him leader	4222
14: 7	"Go ahead; I am with you h **and soul.**"	3869+4222
16: 7	but the LORD looks at the h."	4222
17:28	and how wicked your h is;	4222
17:32	"Let no one lose h on account of this	4213
21:12	words to h and was very much afraid	4222
25:37	his h failed him and he became like a stone.	4213
28: 5	he was afraid; terror filled his h.	4213
2Sa 3:21	you may rule over all that your h desires."	5883
6:16	she despised him in her h.	4213
13:20	Don't take this thing to h."	4213
14: 1	of Zeruiah knew that the king's h longed	4213
17:10	whose h is like the heart of a lion,	4213
17:10	whose heart is like the h *of* a lion,	4213
18:14	and plunged them into Absalom's h	4213
22:46	They all **lose** h; they come trembling	5570
1Ki 2: 4	before me with all their h and soul,	4222
2:44	"You know in your h all the wrong you did	4222
3: 6	to you and righteous and upright in h.	4222
3: 9	a discerning h to govern your people and	4222
3:12	I will give you a wise and discerning h,	4222
8:17	in his h to build a temple for the Name of	4222
8:18	'Because it was in your h to build a temple	4222
8:18	you did well to have this in your h.	4222
8:38	of his own h, and spreading out his hands	4222
8:39	since you know his h (for you alone know	4222
8:47	of h in the land where they are held captive,	4213
8:48	and if they turn back to you with all their h	4222
8:66	joyful and glad in h for all the good things	4222
9: 3	My eyes and my h will always be there.	4213
9: 4	before me in integrity of h and uprightness,	4222
10:24	to hear the wisdom God had put in his h.	4213
11: 4	his wives turned his h after other gods,	4222
11: 4	his h was not fully devoted to	4222
11: 4	as the h *of* David his father had been.	4222
11: 9	because his h had turned away from	4222
11:37	you will rule over all that your h desires;	5883
14: 8	and followed me with all his h,	4222
15: 3	his h was not fully devoted to the LORD	4222
15: 3	as the h *of* David his forefather had been.	4222
15:14	Asa's h was fully committed to the LORD	4222
2Ki 9:24	The arrow pierced his h and he slumped	4213
10:31	the God of Israel, with all his h.	4222
22:19	Because your h was responsive	4222
23: 3	and decrees with all his h and all his soul,	4213
23:25	with all his h and with all his soul and	4213
1Ch 15:29	she despised him in her h.	4213
22: 7	"My son, I had it in my h to build a house	4222
22:19	Now devote your h and soul to seeking	4222
28: 2	I had it in my h to build a house as a place	4222
28: 9	for the LORD searches every h	4222
29:17	you test the h and are pleased with integrity.	4222
2Ch 6: 7	in his h to build a temple for the Name of	4222
6: 8	'Because it was in your h to build a temple	4222
6: 8	you did well to have this in your h.	4222
6:30	since you know his h (for you alone know	4222
6:37	of h in the land where they are held captive,	4222
6:38	and if they turn back to you with all their h	4213
7:10	joyful and glad in h for the good things	4222
7:16	My eyes and my h will always be there.	4213
9:23	to hear the wisdom God had put in his h.	4222
12:14	He did evil because he had not set his h	4213
15:12	with all their h and soul.	4222
15:17	Asa's h was fully committed	4222
17: 6	His h was devoted to the ways of the LORD	4213
19: 3	of the Asherah poles and have set your h	4222
22: 9	who sought the LORD with all his h."	4222
30:19	who sets his h on seeking God—	4222
32:25	But Hezekiah's h was proud and he did	4213
32:26	Hezekiah repented of the pride of his h,	4213
32:31	and to know everything that was in his h.	4222
34:27	Because your h was responsive	4222
34:31	and decrees with all his h and all his soul,	4222
36:13	He became stiff-necked and hardened his h	4222
36:22	the LORD moved the h *of* Cyrus king	8120
Ezr 1: 1	the LORD moved the h *of* Cyrus king	8120
1: 5	everyone whose h God had moved—	8120
7:27	into the king's h to bring honor to the house	4213
Ne 2: 2	This can be nothing but sadness of h."	4213
2:12	in my h to do for Jerusalem.	4213

Ne 4: 6	for the people worked *with all* their h.	4213
7: 5	So my God put it into my h to assemble	4213
9: 8	You found his h faithful to you,	4213
Job 10:13	"But this is what you concealed in your h,	4222
11:13	"Yet if you devote your h to him	4213
15:12	Why has your h carried you away,	4213
17:11	and so are the desires of my h.	4222
19:27	How my h yearns within me!	4000
22:22	and lay up his words in your h.	4213
23:16	God has made my h faint;	4213
29:13	I made the widow's h sing.	4213
31: 7	if my h has been led by my eyes,	4213
31: 9	"If my h has been enticed by a woman,	4213
31:20	and his h did not bless me for warming him	2743
31:27	so that my h was secretly enticed	4213
31:33	by hiding my guilt in my h	2460
33: 3	My words come from an upright h;	4213
36:13	"The godless in h harbor resentment;	4213
37: 1	"At this my h pounds and leaps	4213
37:24	not have regard for all the wise in h?"	4213
38:36	the h with wisdom or gave understanding to	3219
Ps 4: 7	You have filled my h with greater joy than	4213
5: 9	their h is filled with destruction.	7931
7:10	who saves the upright in h.	4213
9: 1	I will praise you, O LORD, with all my h;	4213
10: 3	He boasts of the cravings of his h;	5883
11: 2	from the shadows at the upright in h.	4213
13: 2	and every day have sorrow in my h?	4222
13: 5	my h rejoices in your salvation.	4213
14: 1	The fool says in his h, "There is no God."	4213
15: 2	who speaks the truth from his h	4222
16: 7	even at night my h instructs me.	4000
16: 9	Therefore my h is glad	4213
17: 3	you probe my h and examine me at night,	4213
18:45	They all **lose** h;	5570
19: 8	giving joy to the h.	4213
19:14	of my mouth and the meditation of my h	4213
20: 4	of your h and make all your plans succeed.	4222
21: 2	of his h and have not withheld the request	4213
22:14	My h has turned to wax;	4213
24: 4	He who has clean hands and a pure h,	4222
25:17	The troubles of my h have multiplied;	4213
26: 2	and try me, examine my h and my mind;	4000
27: 3	an army besiege me, my h will not fear;	4213
27: 8	My h says of you, "Seek his face!"	4213
27:14	and **take** h and wait for the LORD.	599+4213
28: 7	my h trusts in him, and I am helped.	4213
28: 7	My h leaps for joy and I give thanks	4213
30:12	that my h may sing to you and not be silent.	3883
31:24	Be strong and **take** h!	599+4222
32:11	sing, all you who are upright in h!	4213
33:11	purposes of his h through all generations.	4213
36: 1	within my h concerning the sinfulness of	4213
36:10	your righteousness to the upright in h.	4213
37: 4	and he will give you the desires of your h.	4213
37:31	The law of his God is in his h;	4213
38: 8	I groan in anguish of h.	4213
38:10	My h pounds, my strength fails me;	4213
39: 3	My h grew hot within me,	4213
40: 8	your law is within my h."	5055
40:10	I do not hide your righteousness in my h;	4213
40:12	and my h fails within me.	4213
41: 6	while his h gathers slander;	4213
44:21	since he knows the secrets of the h?	4213
45: 1	My h is stirred by a noble theme	4213
46: 2	and the mountains fall into the h *of* the sea,	4213
49: 3	from my h will give understanding.	4213
51:10	Create in me a pure h, O God,	4213
51:17	a broken and contrite h,	4213
53: 1	The fool says in his h, "There is no God."	4213
54: 4	My h is in anguish within me;	4213
55:21	yet war is in his h.	4213
57: 7	My h is steadfast,	4213
57: 7	O God, my h is steadfast;	4213
58: 2	No, in your h you devise injustice.	4213
61: 2	I call as my h grows faint;	4213
62:10	do not set your h on them.	4213
64: 6	Surely the mind and h of man are cunning.	4213
64:10	let all the upright in h praise him!	4213
66:18	If I had cherished sin in my h,	4213
69:20	Scorn has broken my h	4213
73: 1	to those who are pure in h.	4222
73:13	Surely in vain have I kept my h pure;	4222
73:21	my h was grieved and my spirit embittered,	4222
73:26	My flesh and my h may fail,	4222
73:26	of my h and my portion forever.	4222
77: 6	My h mused and my spirit inquired:	4222
78:72	David shepherded them with integrity of h;	4222
84: 2	my h and my flesh cry out for	4213
86:11	give me an undivided h,	4222
86:12	O Lord my God, with all my h;	4222
89:50	I bear in my h the taunts of all the nations,	2668
90:12	that we may gain a h of wisdom.	4213
94:15	and all the upright in h will follow it.	4213
97:11	the righteous and joy on the upright in h.	4213
101: 2	I will walk in my house with blameless h.	4222
101: 4	Men of perverse h shall be far from me;	4222
101: 5	whoever has haughty eyes and a proud h,	4222
102: 4	My h is blighted and withered like grass;	4213
104:15	wine that gladdens the h *of* man,	4222
104:15	and bread that sustains his h.	4222
108: 1	My h is steadfast, O God;	4213
109:22	and my h is wounded within me.	4213
111: 1	I will extol the LORD with all my h	4222
112: 7	his h is steadfast, trusting in the LORD.	4213
112: 8	His h is secure, he will have no fear;	4213
119: 2	and seek him with all their h.	4213

Ps	119: 7	an upright h as I learn your righteous laws. 4222
	119:10	I seek you with all my h; 4213
	119:11	in my h that I might not sin against you. 4213
	119:30	*I have set* my h *on* your laws. 8751
	119:32	for you have set my h free. 4213
	119:34	and obey it with all my h. 4213
	119:36	Turn my h toward your statutes and not 4213
	119:58	I have sought your face with all my h; 4213
	119:69	I keep your precepts with all my h. 4213
	119:80	May my h be blameless 4213
	119:111	they are the joy of my h. 4213
	119:112	My h is set on keeping your decrees to 4213
	119:145	I call with all my h; 4213
	119:161	but my h trembles at your word. 4213
	125: 4	to those who are upright in h. 4213
	131: 1	My h is not proud, O LORD, 4213
	138: 1	I will praise you, O LORD, with all my h; 4213
	139:23	Search me, O God, and know my h; 4222
	141: 4	Let not my h be drawn to what is evil, 4213
	143: 4	my h within me is dismayed. 4213
	148:14	of Israel, the people **close** to his h. 7940
Pr	1:23	I would have poured out my h to you 8120
	2: 2	and applying your h to understanding, 4213
	2:10	For wisdom will enter your h, 4213
	3: 1	but keep my commands in your h, 4213
	3: 3	write them on the tablet of your h. 4213
	3: 5	Trust in the LORD with all your h and lean 4213
	4: 4	"Lay hold of my words with all your h; 4213
	4:21	keep them within your h; 4222
	4:23	Above all else, guard your h, 4213
	5:12	How my h spurned correction! 4213
	6:14	who plots evil with deceit in his h— 4213
	6:18	a h that devises wicked schemes, 4213
	6:21	Bind them upon your h forever; 4213
	6:25	Do not lust in your h after her beauty 4222
	7: 3	write them on the tablet of your h. 4213
	7:25	Do not let your h turn to her ways or stray 4213
	10: 8	The wise in h accept commands, 4213
	10:20	but the h of the wicked is of little value. 4213
	11:20	The LORD detests men of perverse h 4213
	12:23	but the h of fools blurts out folly. 4213
	12:25	An anxious h weighs a man down, 4213
	13:12	Hope deferred makes the h sick, 4213
	14:10	*Each* h knows its own bitterness, 4213
	14:13	Even in laughter the h may ache, 4213
	14:30	A h at peace gives life to the body, 4213
	14:33	Wisdom reposes in the h of the discerning 4213
	15:13	A happy h makes the face cheerful, 4213
	15:14	The discerning h seeks knowledge, 4213
	15:15	but the cheerful h has a continual feast. 4213
	15:28	The h of the righteous weighs its answers, 4213
	15:30	A cheerful look brings joy to the h, 4213
	16: 1	To man belong the plans of the h, 4213
	16: 5	The LORD detests all the proud of h. 4213
	16: 9	In his h a man plans his course, 4213
	16:21	The wise in h are called discerning, 4213
	16:23	A wise man's h guides his mouth, 4213
	17: 3	but the LORD tests the h. 4213
	17:20	A man of perverse h does not prosper, 4213
	17:22	A cheerful h is good medicine, 4213
	18:12	Before his downfall a man's h is proud, 4213
	18:15	h of the discerning acquires knowledge; 4213
	19: 3	yet his h rages against the LORD. 4213
	19:21	Many are the plans in a man's h, 4213
	20: 5	The purposes of a man's h are deep waters, 4213
	20: 9	Who can say, "I have kept my h pure; 4213
	21: 1	The king's h is in the hand of the LORD; 4213
	21: 2	but the LORD weighs the h. 4213
	21: 4	Haughty eyes and a proud h, 4213
	22:11	He who loves a pure h 4213
	22:15	Folly is bound up in the h of a child, 4213
	22:17	apply your h to what I teach, 4213
	22:18	when you keep them in your h and have all 1061
	23: 7	he says to you, but his h is not with you. 4213
	23:12	Apply your h to instruction and your ears 4213
	23:15	My son, if your h is wise, 4213
	23:15	if your heart is wise, then my h will be glad; 4213
	23:17	Do not let your h envy sinners, 4213
	23:19	and keep your h on the right path. 4213
	23:26	give me your h and let your eyes keep 4213
	24:12	does not he who weighs the h perceive it? 4213
	24:17	when he stumbles, do not let your h rejoice, 4213
	24:32	I applied my h to what I observed 4213
	25:20	is one who sings songs to a heavy h. 4213
	26:23	are fervent lips with an evil h. 4213
	26:24	but in his h he harbors deceit. 7931
	26:25	for seven abominations fill his h. 4213
	27: 9	Perfume and incense bring joy to the h, 4213
	27:11	Be wise, my son, and bring joy to my h; 4213
	27:19	so a man's h reflects the man. 4213
	28:14	but he who hardens his h falls into trouble. 4213
Ecc	2: 1	I thought in my h, "Come now, 4213
	2: 8	the **delights of the** h *of* man. 9503
	2:10	I refused my h no pleasure. 4213
	2:10	My h took delight in all my work, 4213
	2:15	Then I thought in my h, 4213
	2:15	I said in my h, "This too is meaningless." 4213
	2:20	So my h began to despair 4213
	3:17	I thought in my h, "God will bring to 4213
	5: 2	do not be hasty in your h to utter anything 4213
	5:20	God keeps him occupied with gladness of h. 5883
	6: 2	so that he lacks nothing his h desires, 5883
	7: 2	the living should take this to h. 4213
	7: 3	because a sad face is good for the h. 4213
	7: 4	h *of* the wise is in the house of mourning, 4213
	7: 4	the h *of* fools is in the house of pleasure. 4213
	7: 7	and a bribe corrupts the h. 4213

Ecc	7:22	for you know in your h that many times 4213
	7:26	whose h is a trap and whose hands are 4213
	8: 5	and the wise h will know the proper time 4213
	9: 7	and drink your wine with a joyful h, 4213
	10: 2	The h *of* the wise inclines to the right, 4213
	10: 2	but the h *of* the fool to the left. 4213
	11: 9	and let your h give you joy in the days 4213
	11: 9	of your h and whatever your eyes see, 4213
	11:10	banish anxiety from your h and cast off 4213
SS	3: 1	on my bed I looked for the one my h loves. 5883
	3: 2	I will search for the one my h loves. 5883
	3: 3	"Have you seen the one my h loves?" 5883
	3: 4	when I found the one my h loves. 5883
	3:11	the day his h rejoiced. 4213
	4: 9	*You have* **stolen** my h, my sister, my bride; 4220
	4: 9	*you have* **stolen** my h with one glance 4220
	5: 2	I slept but my h was awake. 4213
	5: 4	my h began to pound for him. 5055
	5: 6	My h sank at his departure. 5883
	8: 6	Place me like a seal over your h, 4213
Isa	1: 5	your whole h afflicted. 4222
	6:10	Make the h of this people calloused; 4213
	7: 4	Do not lose h because 4222
	9: 9	who say with pride and arrogance of h, 4222
	10:12	of Assyria for the willful pride of his h and 4222
	13: 7	every man's h will melt. 4222
	14:13	You said in your h, "I will ascend to heaven 4222
	15: 5	My h cries out over Moab; 4213
	16:11	My h laments for Moab like a harp, 5055
	19: 3	The Egyptians *will* **lose h**, 928+1327+7931+8120
	19:10	and all the wage earners will be sick at h. 5883
	19:19	be an altar to the LORD in the h of Egypt, 9348
	21: 4	My h falters, fear makes me tremble; 4222
	40:11	in his arms and carries them close to his h; 2668
	42:25	but they did not take it to h. 4213
	44:20	a deluded h misleads him; 4213
	46: 8	"Remember this, fix it in mind, take it to h, 4213
	49:21	Then you will say in your h, 4222
	57: 1	and no one ponders it in his h; 4213
	57:15	the lowly and to revive the h of the contrite. 4213
	60: 5	your h will throb and swell with joy; 4222
	63: 4	For the day of vengeance was in my h, 4213
	65:14	from anguish of h and wail in brokenness 4213
	66:14	your h will rejoice and you will flourish 4213
Jer	3:10	Judah did not return to me with all her h, 4213
	3:15	I will give you shepherds after my own h, 4213
	4: 9	"the king and the officials will lose h, 4213
	4:14	wash the evil from your h and be saved. 4213
	4:18	How it pierces to the h!" 4213
	4:19	Oh, the agony of my h! 4213
	4:19	My h pounds within me, 4213
	8:18	my h is faint within me. 4213
	9: 8	but in his h he sets a trap for him. 7931
	9:26	whole house of Israel is uncircumcised in h. 4213
	11:20	you who judge righteously and test the h 4213
	15: 1	my h would not go out to this people. 5883
	16:12	the stubbornness of his evil h instead 4213
	17: 5	and whose h turns away from the LORD. 4213
	17: 9	The h is deceitful above all things and 4213
	17:10	"I the LORD search the h and examine 4213
	18:12	the stubbornness of his evil h.' " 4213
	20: 9	his word is in my h like a fire, 4213
	20:12	the righteous and probe the h and mind, 4213
	22:17	and your h are set only on dishonest gain, 4213
	23: 9	My h is broken within me; 4213
	23:20	fully accomplishes the purposes of his h. 4213
	24: 7	I will give them a h to know me, 4213
	24: 7	for they will return to me with all their h. 4213
	29:13	when you seek me with all your h. 4222
	30:24	fully accomplishes the purposes of his h. 4213
	31:20	Therefore my h yearns for him; 5055
	32:39	I will give them singleness of h and action, 4213
	32:41	in this land with all my h and soul. 4213
	48:29	and arrogance and the haughtiness of her h. 4213
	48:36	"So my h laments for Moab like a flute; 4213
	48:41	of Moab's warriors will be like the h of 4213
	49:16	and the pride of your h has deceived you, 4213
	49:22	of Edom's warriors will be like the h of 4213
	51:46	Do not lose h or be afraid 4222
La	1:20	and in my h I am disturbed, 4213
	1:22	My groans are many and my h is faint." 4213
	2:11	my h is poured out on the ground 3879
	2:19	pour out your h like water in the presence of 4213
	3:13	He pierced my h with arrows 4000
Eze	3:10	and take to h all the words I speak to you. 4222
	11:19	an undivided h and put a new spirit in them; 4213
	11:19	from them their h *of* stone and give them 4213
	11:19	of stone and give them a h *of* flesh. 4213
	14: 4	in his h and puts a wicked stumbling block 4213
	14: 7	in his h and puts a wicked stumbling block 4213
	18:31	and get a new h and a new spirit. 4213
	21: 6	before them with broken h and bitter grief. 5516
	21: 7	Every h will melt and every hand go limp; 4213
	25: 6	rejoicing with all the malice of your h 5883
	27:25	You are filled with heavy cargo in the h *of* 4213
	27:26	to pieces in the h *of* the sea. 4213
	27:27	on board will sink into the h *of* the sea on 4213
	28: 2	" 'In the pride of your h you say, 4213
	28: 2	on the throne of a god in the h *of* the seas." 4213
	28: 5	of your wealth your h has grown proud. 4222
	28: 8	and you will die a violent death in the h *of* 4213
	28:17	Your h became proud on account 4213
	36:26	I will give you a new h and put a new spirit 4213
	36:26	I will remove from you your h *of* stone 4213
	36:26	of stone and give you a h *of* flesh. 4213
	44: 7	you brought foreigners uncircumcised in h 4213
	44: 9	in h and flesh is to enter my sanctuary, 4213

Da	5:20	when his h became arrogant and hardened 10381
	7: 4	and the h *of* a man was given to it. 10381
	11:28	his h will be set against the holy covenant. 4222
	11:30	and *he will* **lose h.** 3874
Hos	5: 4	A spirit of prostitution is in their h; 7931
	10: 2	Their h is deceitful. 4213
	11: 8	My h is changed within me; 4213
Joel	2:12	"return to me with all your h, 4222
	2:13	Rend your h and not your garments. 4222
Am	7:10	a conspiracy against you in the very h 7931
Ob	1: 3	The pride of your h has deceived you, 4213
Jnh	2: 3	into the very h of the seas, 4222
Hab	3:16	I heard and my h pounded, 1061
Zep	3:14	Be glad and rejoice with all your h, 4213
Mal	2: 2	if you do not set your h to honor my name," 4213
	2: 2	you have not set your h to honor me. 4213
Mt	5: 8	Blessed are the pure in h, 2840
	5:28	committed adultery with her in his h. 2840
	6:21	your treasure is, there your h will be also. 2840
	9: 2	"Take h, son; your sins are forgiven." 2510
	9:22	"Take h, daughter," he said, 2510
	11:29	for I am gentle and humble in h, 2840
	12:34	of the overflow *of* the h the mouth speaks. 2840
	12:40	three days and three nights in the h *of* 2840
	13:15	For this people's h has become calloused; 2840
	13:19	and snatches away what was sown in his h. 2840
	15:18	of the mouth come from the h, 2840
	15:19	For out of the h come evil thoughts, murder, 2840
	18:35	you forgive your brother from your h." 2840
	22:37	" 'Love the Lord your God with all your h 2840
Mk	7:19	it doesn't go into his h but into his stomach, 2840
	11:23	and does not doubt in his h but believes 2840
	12:30	Love the Lord your God with all your h and 2840
	12:33	To love him with all your h, 2840
Lk	2:19	and pondered them in her h. 2840
	2:51	But his mother treasured all these things in her h. 2840
	6:45	of the good stored up *in* his h, 2840
	6:45	of the evil stored up *in* his h. 2840
	6:45	of the overflow *of* his h his mouth speaks. 2840
	7:13	*his* h went out to her and he said, 5072
	8:15	for those with a noble and good h, 2840
	10:27	" 'Love the Lord your God with all your h 2840
	12:29	not *set your* h on what you will eat or drink; 2426
	12:34	your treasure is, there your h will be also. 2840
Jn	12:27	my h is troubled, and what shall I say? 6034
	16:33	But **take h!** I have overcome the world. 2510
Ac	1:24	they prayed, "Lord, you **know** everyone's h. 2841
	2:26	my h is glad and my tongue rejoices; 2840
	2:37	they were cut to the h and said to Peter and 2840
	4:32	All the believers were one *in* h and mind. 2840
	5: 3	how is it that Satan has so filled your h 2840
	8:21	because your h is not right before God. 2840
	8:22	for having such a thought *in* your h. 2840
	13:22	of Jesse a man after my own h; 2840
	15: 8	God, who **knows** the h, 2841
	16:14	The Lord opened her h to respond 2840
	21:13	Why are you weeping and breaking my h? 2840
	28:27	For this people's h has become calloused; 2840
Ro	1: 9	whom I serve with my whole h in preaching 4460
	2: 5	stubbornness and your unrepentant h, 2840
	2:29	and circumcision is circumcision *of* the h, 2840
	9: 2	and unceasing anguish *in* my h. 2840
	10: 6	"Do not say in your h, 'Who will ascend 2840
	10: 8	it is in your mouth and in your h," that is, 2840
	10: 9	and believe in your h that God raised him 2840
	10:10	For it is *with* your h that you believe 2840
	15: 6	that with one h and mouth you may glorify 3924
1Co	14:25	and the secrets *of* his h will be laid bare. 2840
2Co	2: 4	and anguish *of* h and with many tears, 2840
	4: 1	we have this ministry, we *do not* **lose h.** 1591
	4:16	Therefore *we do* not **lose h.** 1591
	5:12	rather than in what is in the h. 2840
	8:16	into the h of Titus the same concern I have 2840
	9: 7	what he has decided *in* his h to give, 2840
Eph	1:18	that the eyes of your h may be enlightened 2840
	5:19	Sing and make music in your h to the Lord, 2840
	6: 5	and with sincerity *of* h, 2840
	6: 6	doing the will of God from your h. 6034
Php	1: 7	since I have you in my h; 2840
Col	2: 2	that they may be encouraged in h and united 2840
	3:22	to win their favor, but with sincerity *of* h 2840
	3:23	Whatever you do, work at it with all your h, 6034
1Ti	1: 5	from a pure h and a good conscience and 2840
2Ti	2:22	who call on the Lord out of a pure h. 2840
Phm	1:12	I am sending him—who is my **very h**— 5073
	1:20	refresh my h in Christ. 5073
Heb	3:12	unbelieving h that turns away from 2840
	4:12	it judges the thoughts and attitudes *of* the h. 2840
	10:22	with a sincere h in full assurance of faith, 2840
	12: 3	so that you will not grow weary and **lose h.** 6034
	12: 5	and *do not* **lose h** when he rebukes you, 1725
1Pe	1:22	love one another deeply, from the h. 2840
1Jn	5:10	who believes in the Son of God has this testimony in his h. 1571
Rev	1: 3	and **take to h** what is written in it, 5498
	18: 7	In her h she boasts, 'I sit as queen; 2840

HEART'S (4) [HEART]

2Ch	1:11	"Since this is your h desire and you have 4222
Jer	15:16	they were my joy and my h delight, 4213
Eze	24:25	the delight of their eyes, their h desire, 5883
Ro	10: 1	my h desire and prayer to God for the Israelites is that they may be saved. 2840

HEARTACHE (1) [HEART]
Pr   15:13   but **h** crushes the spirit.   4213+6780

HEARTH (6)
Lev   6: 9   to remain on the altar **h** throughout   4612
Isa   29: 2   she will be to me like an **altar h.**   789
   30:14   from a **h** or scooping water out of a cistern."   3683
Eze   43:15   The **altar h** is four cubits high,   2219
   43:15   and four horns project upward from the **h.**   789
   43:16   The **altar h** is square,   789

HEARTILY (KJV) See WITH ALL HEART

HEARTLESS (2) [HEART]
La   4: 3   but my people have become **h** like ostriches   425
Ro   1:31   they are senseless, faithless, **h,** ruthless.   *845*

HEARTS (207) [HEART]
Ge   42:28   Their **h** sank and they turned   4213
Ex   9:34   He and his officials hardened their **h.**   4213
   10: 1   for I have hardened his heart and the **h**   4213
   14:17   the **h** of the Egyptians so that they will go   4213
Lev   26:36   I will make their **h** so fearful in the lands   4222
   26:41   when their uncircumcised **h** are humbled   4222
Nu   15:39   after the lusts of your own **h** and eyes.   4222
Dt   5:29   that their **h** would be inclined to fear me   4222
   6: 6   that I give you today are to be upon your **h.**   4222
   10:16   Circumcise your **h,** therefore,   4222
   11:18   Fix these words of mine in your **h**   4222
   28:67   because of the terror that will fill your **h** and   4222
   30: 6   The LORD your God will circumcise your **h**   4222
   30: 6   and the **h** of your descendants,   4222
Jos   2:11   our **h** melted and everyone's courage failed   4222
   5: 1   their **h** melted and they no longer had   4222
   7: 5   the **h** of the people melted and became   4222
   11:20   the LORD himself who hardened their **h**   4213
   14: 8   up with me made the **h** of the people melt   4213
   24:23   among you and yield your **h** to the LORD,   4222
1Sa   6: 6   Why do you harden your **h** as the Egyptians   4213
   7: 3   to the LORD with all your **h,**   4222
   10:26   by valiant men whose **h** God had touched.   4222
2Sa   15: 6   and so he stole the **h** of the men of Israel.   4213
   15:13   **h** of the men of Israel are with Absalom.   4213
   19:14   He won over the **h** of all the men of Judah   4213
1Ki   8:39   (for you alone know the **h** of all men),   4222
   8:58   May he turn our **h** to him,   4222
   8:61   But your **h** must be fully committed to   4222
   11: 2   because they will surely turn your **h**   4222
   18:37   and that you are turning their **h** back again."   4213
1Ch   16:10   the **h** of those who seek the LORD rejoice.   4213
   29:18   in the **h** of your people forever,   4222
   29:18   and keep their **h** loyal to you.   4222
2Ch   6:30   (for you alone know the **h** of men),   4222
   11:16   from every tribe of Israel who set their **h**   4222
   16: 9   to strengthen those whose **h** are fully committed to him.   4222
   20:33   not set their **h** on the God of their fathers.   4213
   29:31   all whose **h** were willing brought burnt offerings.   4213
Job   1: 5   and cursed God in their **h.**"   4222
Ps   4: 4   search your **h** and be silent.   4222
   7: 9   who searches minds and **h,**   4213
   17:10   They close up their **callous h,**   2693
   22:26   may your **h** live forever!   4222
   28: 3   but harbor malice in their **h.**   4222
   33:15   he who forms the **h** of all,   4213
   33:21   In him our **h** rejoice,   4213
   37:15   But their swords will pierce their own **h,**   4213
   44:18   Our **h** had not turned back;   4213
   45: 5   Let your sharp arrows pierce the **h** of   4213
   62: 4   but in their **h** they curse.   7931
   62: 8   pour out your **h** to him,   4222
   69:32   you who seek God, may your **h** live!   4222
   73: 7   From their **callous h** comes iniquity;   2693
   74: 8   They said in their **h,**   4213
   78: 8   whose **h** were not loyal to God,   4213
   78:37   their **h** were not loyal to him,   4213
   81:12   So I gave them over to their stubborn **h**   4213
   84: 5   who have set their **h** on pilgrimage.   4222
   95: 8   do not harden your **h** as you did at Meribah,   4222
   95:10   "They are a people whose **h** go astray,   4222
   105: 3   the **h** of those who seek the LORD rejoice.   4213
   105:25   whose **h** he turned to hate his people,   4213
   119:70   Their **h** are callous and unfeeling,   4213
   140: 2   who devise evil plans in their **h** and stir   4213
Pr   12:20   in the **h** of those who plot evil,   4213
   15: 7   not so the **h** of fools.   4213
   15:11   how much more the **h** of men!   4213
   24: 2   for their **h** plot violence,   4213
   25: 3   so the **h** of kings are unsearchable.   4213
Ecc   3:11   He has also set eternity in the **h** of men;   4213
   8:11   the **h** of the people are filled with schemes   4213
   9: 3   The **h** of men, moreover, are full of evil   4213
   9: 3   of evil and there is madness in their **h**   4222
Isa   6:10   hear with their ears, understand with their **h,**   4222
   7: 2   the **h** of Ahaz and his people were shaken,   4222
   15: 4   and their **h** are faint.   5883
   19: 1   the **h** of the Egyptians melt within them.   4222
   26: 8   and renown are the desire of our **h.**   5883
   29:13   but their **h** are far from me.   4213
   30:29   your **h** will rejoice as when people go up   4213
   35: 4   say to those with fearful **h,** "Be strong, do   4213
   51: 7   you people who have my law in your **h:**   4213
   57:11   nor pondered this in your **h?**   4213

Isa   59:13   uttering lies our **h** have conceived.   4213
   63:17   harden our **h** so we do not revere you?   4213
   65:14   servants will sing out of the joy of their **h,**   4213
Jer   3:17   the stubbornness of their evil **h.**   4213
   4: 4   circumcise **h,** you men of Judah   4222
   5:23   But these people have stubborn and rebellious **h;**   4213
   7:24   the stubborn inclinations of their evil **h.**   4213
   9:14   the stubbornness of their **h;**   4213
   11: 8   the stubbornness of their evil **h.**   4213
   12: 2   on their lips but far from their **h.**   4000
   13:10   stubbornness of their **h** and go after other   4213
   17: 1   on the tablets of their **h** and on the horns of   4213
   23:17   the stubbornness of their **h** they say,   4213
   23:26   How long will this continue in the **h**   4213
   31:33   in their minds and write it on their **h.**   4213
   48:41   In that day the **h** of Moab's warriors will be   4213
   49:22   In that day the **h** of Edom's warriors will be   4213
La   2:18   The **h** of the people cry out to the Lord.   4213
   3:41   up our **h** and our hands to God in heaven,   4222
   3:65   Put a veil over their **h,**   4213
   5:15   Joy is gone from our **h;**   4213
   5:17   Because of this our **h** are faint,   4213
Eze   6: 9   I have been grieved by their adulterous **h,**   4213
   11:21   But as for those whose **h** are devoted   4213
   14: 3   in their **h** and put wicked stumbling blocks   4213
   14: 5   to recapture the **h** of the people of Israel,   4213
   20:16   For their **h** were devoted to their idols.   4213
   21:15   So that **h** may melt and the fallen be many,   4213
   25:15   and took revenge with malice in their **h,**   5883
   32: 9   I will trouble the **h** of many peoples   4213
   33:31   but their **h** are greedy for unjust gain.   4213
   36: 5   with malice in their **h** they made my land   4222
Da   11:27   The two kings, with their **h** bent on evil,   4222
Hos   7: 6   Their **h** are like an oven;   4213
   7:14   to me from their **h** but wail upon their beds.   4213
Na   2:10   **H** melt, knees give way, bodies tremble,   4213
Zec   7:10   In your **h** do not think evil of each other.'   4222
   7:12   They made their **h** as hard as flint   4213
   10: 7   and their **h** will be glad as with wine.   4213
   10: 7   their **h** will rejoice in the LORD.   4213
   12: 5   the leaders of Judah will say in their **h,**   4213
Mal   4: 6   the **h** of the fathers to their children, and   4213
   4: 6   and the **h** of the children to their fathers;   4213
Mt   9: 4   "Why do you entertain evil thoughts in your **h?**   *2840*
   13:15   understand *with* their **h** and turn,   *2840*
   15: 8   but their **h** are far from me.   *2840*
   19: 8   because your **h** were **hard.**   *5016*
Mk   2: 8   what they were thinking in **their h,**   *1571*
   3: 5   deeply distressed at their stubborn **h,**   *2840*
   6:52   their **h** were hardened.   *2840*
   7: 6   but their **h** are far from me.   *2840*
   7:21   For from within, out of men's **h,**   *2840*
   8:17   Are your **h** hardened?   *2840*
   10: 5   "It was because your **h** were **hard**   *5016*
Lk   1:17   to turn the **h** of the fathers to their children   *2840*
   2:35   the thoughts of many **h** will be revealed.   *2840*
   3:15   wondering in their **h** if John might possibly   *2840*
   5:22   "Why are you thinking these things in your **h?**   *2840*
   8:12   and takes away the word from their **h,**   *2840*
   16:15   but God knows your **h.**   *2840*
   21:34   or your **h** will be weighed down   *2840*
   24:32   not our **h** burning within us while he talked   *2840*
Jn   5:42   not have the love of God in **your h.**   *1571*
   12:40   and deadened their **h,** so they can neither   *2840*
   12:40   nor understand *with* their **h,** nor turn—   *2840*
   14: 1   "Do not let your **h** be troubled.   *2840*
   14:27   Do not let your **h** be troubled and do not   *2840*
Ac   2:46   and ate together with glad and sincere **h,**   *2840*
   7:39   they rejected him and in their **h** turned back   *2840*
   7:51   with uncircumcised **h** and ears!   *2840*
   11:23   to remain true to the Lord *with* all their **h.**   *2840*
   14:17   plenty of food and fills your **h** with joy."   *2840*
   15: 9   for he purified their **h** by faith.   *2840*
   28:27   understand *with* their **h** and turn,   *2840*
Ro   1:21   and their foolish **h** were darkened.   *2840*
   1:24   over in the sinful desires *of* their **h**   *2840*
   2:15   of the law are written on their **h,**   *2840*
   5: 5   into our **h** by the Holy Spirit,   *2840*
   8:27   And he who searches our **h** knows the mind   *2840*
1Co   4: 5   and will expose the motives *of* men's **h.**   *2840*
   10: 6   to keep us from **setting** our **h** on evil things   *2122*
2Co   1: 9   in **our h** we felt the sentence of death.   *1571*
   1:22   and put his Spirit in our **h** as a deposit,   *2840*
   3: 2   written on our **h,** known and read by   *2840*
   3: 3   of stone but on tablets of human **h.**   *2840*
   3:15   when Moses is read, a veil covers their **h.**   *2840*
   4: 6   made his light shine in our **h** to give us   *2840*
   6:11   Corinthians, and opened wide our **h** to you.   *2840*
   6:13   open wide your **h** also.   NIG
   7: 2   Make room for us in your **h.**   NIG
   7: 3   in our **h** that we would live or die with you.   *2840*
   9:14   their **h** *will* go out to you,   *2160*
Gal   4: 6   God sent the Spirit of his Son into our **h,**   *2840*
Eph   3:17   Christ may dwell in your **h** through faith.   *2840*
   4:18   in them due to the hardening *of* their **h.**   *2840*
Php   4: 7   will guard your **h** and your minds   *2840*
Col   3: 1   **set** *your* **h** on things above,   *2426*
   3:15   Let the peace of Christ rule in your **h,**   *2840*
   3:16   and spiritual songs with gratitude in your **h**   *2840*
   4: 8   and that he may encourage your **h.**   *2840*
1Th   2: 4   but God, who tests our **h.**   *2840*
   3:13   May he strengthen your **h** so that you will   *2840*
2Th   2:17   encourage your **h** and strengthen you   *2840*
   3: 5   May the Lord direct your **h** into God's love   *2840*

Phm   1: 7   brother, have refreshed the **h** of the saints.   *5073*
Heb   3: 8   do not harden your **h** as you did in   *2840*
   3:10   and I said, 'Their **h** are always going astray,   *2840*
   3:15   if you hear his voice, do not harden your **h**   *2840*
   4: 7   if you hear his voice, do not harden your **h.**"   *2840*
   8:10   in their minds and write them on their **h.**   *2840*
   10:16   I will put my laws in their **h,**   *2840*
   10:22   having our **h** sprinkled to cleanse us from   *2840*
   13: 9   It is good for our **h** to be strengthened   *2840*
Jas   3:14   and selfish ambition in your **h,**   *2840*
   4: 8   and purify your **h,** you double-minded.   *2840*
1Pe   3:15   But in your **h** set apart Christ as Lord.   *2840*
2Pe   1:19   and the morning star rises in your **h.**   *2840*
1Jn   3:19   and how we set our **h** at rest in his presence   *2840*
   3:20   whenever our **h** condemn us.   *2840*
   3:20   For God is greater than our **h,**   *2840*
   3:21   Dear friends, if our **h** do not condemn us,   *2840*
Rev   2:23   that I am he who searches **h** and minds,   *2840*
   17:17   into their **h** to accomplish his purpose   *2840*

HEARTS' (1) [HEART]
Pr   13:25   The righteous eat to their **h'** content,   5883

HEARTY (KJV) See EARNEST

HEAT (32) [HEATED]
Ge   8:22   seedtime and harvest, cold and **h,**   2770
   18: 1   the entrance to his tent in the **h** of the day.   2770
   30:38   the flocks *were* in **h** and came to drink,   3501
   30:41   Whenever the stronger females *were* in **h,**   3501
   31:40   The **h** consumed me in the daytime and   2996
Dt   28:22   with **scorching h** and drought,   3031
1Sa   11:11   and slaughtered them until the **h** of the day.   2770
2Sa   4: 5   and they arrived there in the **h** of the day   2770
2Ki   23:26   the LORD did not turn away from the **h**   3019
Job   6:17   and in the **h** vanish from their channels.   2801
   24:19   As **h** and drought snatch away   2770
Ps   19: 6   nothing is hidden from its **h.**   2780
   32: 4   my strength was sapped as in the **h**   3001
   58: 9   Before your pots can feel [the **h** of]   NIH
Isa   4: 6   be a shelter and shade from the **h** of the day,   2996
   18: 4   like shimmering **h** in the sunshine,   2770
   18: 4   like a cloud of dew in the **h** of harvest."   2770
   21:15   from the bent bow and from the **h** of battle.   3880
   25: 4   from the storm and a shade from the **h.**   2996
   25: 5   and like the **h** of the desert.   2996
   25: 5   as **h** is reduced by the shadow of a cloud,   2996
   49:10   the **desert h** or the sun beat upon them.   9220
Jer   2:24   in her **h** who can restrain her?   9299
   17: 8   It does not fear when **h** comes;   2996
   36:30   be thrown out and exposed to the **h** by day   2996
Hos   13: 5   in the land of **burning h.**   9429
Mt   20:12   of the work and the **h of the day.'**   *3014*
Ac   28: 3   a viper, driven out by the **h,**   *2549*
Jas   1:11   the sun rises with **scorching h** and withers   *3014*
2Pe   3:12   and the elements will melt *in* the **h.**   *3012*
Rev   7:16   nor any **scorching h.**   *3008*
   16: 9   by the intense **h** and they cursed the name   *3008*

HEATED (1) [HEAT]
Da   3:19   the furnace **h** seven times hotter than usual   10015

HEATH (KJV) See BUSH

HEATHEN (1)
1Th   4: 5   not in passionate lust like the **h,** who do   *1620*

HEAVE [OFFERING] (KJV) See WAVE [OFFERING]

HEAVEN (422) [HEAVEN'S, HEAVENLY, HEAVENS, HEAVENWARD]
Ge   14:19   God Most High, Creator of **h** and earth.   9028
   14:22   God Most High, Creator of **h** and earth,   9028
   21:17   and the angel of God called to Hagar from **h**   9028
   22:11   of the LORD called out to him from **h,**   9028
   22:15   of the LORD called to Abraham from **h**   9028
   24: 3   the God of **h** and the God of earth,   9028
   24: 7   "The LORD, the God of **h,**   9028
   27:39   away from the dew of **h** above.   9028
   28:12   with its top reaching to **h,**   9028
   28:17   the house of God; this is the gate of **h.**"   9028
Ex   16: 4   "I will rain down bread from **h** for you.   9028
   17:14   the memory of Amalek from under **h.**"   9028
   20: 4   an idol in the form of anything in **h** above   9028
   20:22   that I have spoken to you from **h:**   9028
Dt   2:25   and fear of you on all the nations under **h**   9028
   3:24   in **h** or on earth who can do the deeds   9028
   4:19   to all the nations under **h.**   9028
   4:26   I call **h** and earth as witnesses   9028
   4:36   From **h** he made you hear his voice   9028
   4:39   to heart this day that the LORD is God in **h**   9028
   5: 8   an idol in the form of anything in **h** above   9028
   7:24   you will wipe out their names from under **h.**   9028
   9:14   and blot out their name from under **h.**   9028
   11:11   and valleys that drinks rain from **h.**   9028
   25:19   the memory of Amalek from under **h.**   9028
   26:15   Look down from **h,** your holy dwelling   9028
   29:20   LORD will blot out his name from under **h.**   9028
   30:12   It is not up in **h,** so that you have to ask,   9028
   30:12   ascend into **h** to get it and proclaim it to us   9028

Dt	30:19	This day I call **h** and earth as witnesses	9028
	31:28	and call **h** and earth to testify against them.	9028
	32:40	I lift my hand to **h** and declare:	9028
	33:13	the precious dew from **h** above and with	9028
Jos	2:11	the LORD your God is God in **h** above and	9028
Jdg	13:20	the flame blazed up from the altar toward **h**,	9028
1Sa	2:10	He will thunder against them from **h**;	9028
	5:12	and the outcry of the city went up to **h**.	9028
2Sa	22:14	The LORD thundered from **h**;	9028
1Ki	8:22	spread out his hands toward **h**	9028
	8:23	like you in **h** above or on earth below—	9028
	8:27	The heavens, even the **highest h**,	9028+9028
	8:30	Hear from **h**, your dwelling place,	9028
	8:32	then hear from **h** and act.	9028
	8:34	then hear from **h** and forgive the sin	9028
	8:36	from **h** and forgive the sin of your servants,	9028
	8:39	then hear from **h**, your dwelling place.	9028
	8:43	then hear from **h**, your dwelling place,	9028
	8:45	then hear from **h** their prayer and their plea,	9028
	8:49	then from **h**, your dwelling place,	9028
	8:54	with his hands spread out toward **h**.	9028
	22:19	on his throne with all the host of **h** standing	9028
2Ki	1:10	down from **h** and consume you	9028
	1:10	Then fire fell from **h** and consumed	9028
	1:12	down from **h** and consume you	9028
	1:12	of God fell from **h** and consumed him	9028
	1:14	from **h** and consumed the first two captains	9028
	2: 1	the LORD was about to take Elijah up to **h**	9028
	2:11	and Elijah went up to **h** in a whirlwind.	9028
	14:27	the name of Israel from under **h**,	9028
	19:15	You have made **h** and earth.	9028
1Ch	21:16	the angel of the LORD standing between **h**	9028
	21:26	the LORD answered him with fire from **h**	9028
	29:11	for everything in **h** and earth is yours.	9028
2Ch	2:12	the God of Israel, who made **h** and earth!	9028
	6:13	of Israel and spread out his hands toward **h**.	9028
	6:14	there is no God like you in **h** or on earth—	9028
	6:21	Hear from **h**, your dwelling place;	9028
	6:23	then hear from **h** and act.	9028
	6:25	then hear from **h** and forgive the sin	9028
	6:27	from **h** and forgive the sin of your servants,	9028
	6:30	then hear from **h**, your dwelling place,	9028
	6:33	then hear from **h**, your dwelling place,	9028
	6:35	then hear from **h** their prayer and their plea,	9028
	6:39	then from **h**, your dwelling place,	9028
	7: 1	from **h** and consumed the burnt offering and	9028
	7:14	from **h** and will forgive their sin	9028
	18:18	on his throne with all the host of **h** standing	9028
	20: 6	are you not the God who is in **h**?	9028
	28: 9	in a rage that reaches to **h**.	9028
	30:27	for their prayer reached **h**,	9028
	32:20	of Amoz cried out in prayer to **h** about this.	9028
	36:23	" 'The LORD, the God of **h**,	9028
Ezr	1: 2	" 'The LORD, the God of **h**,	9028
	5:11	the servants of the God of **h** and earth,	10723
	5:12	because our fathers angered the God of **h**,	10723
	6: 9	the God of **h**, salt, wine and oil,	10723
	6:10	of **h** and pray for the well-being of the king	10723
	7:12	a teacher of the Law of the God of **h**:	10723
	7:21	a teacher of the Law of the God of **h**,	10723
	7:23	Whatever the God of **h** has prescribed,	10723
	7:23	for the temple of the God of **h**.	10723
Ne	1: 4	and fasted and prayed before the God of **h**.	9028
	1: 5	Then I said: "O LORD, God of **h**,	9028
	2: 4	Then I prayed to the God of **h**,	9028
	2:20	"The God of **h** will give us success.	9028
	9: 6	and the multitudes of **h** worship you.	9028
	9:13	you spoke to them from **h**.	9028
	9:15	In their hunger you gave them bread from **h**	9028
	9:27	From **h** you heard them,	9028
	9:28	you heard from **h**,	9028
Job	16:19	my witness is in **h**; my advocate is on high.	9028
	22:12	"Is not God in the heights of **h**?	9028
	25: 2	he establishes order in the **heights of h**.	5294
	37: 3	the whole **h** and sends it to the ends of	9028
	41:11	Everything under **h** belongs to me.	9028
Ps	2: 4	The One enthroned in **h** laughs;	9028
	14: 2	The LORD looks down from **h** on the sons	9028
	18:13	The LORD thundered from **h**;	9028
	20: 6	he answers him from his holy **h** with	9028
	33:13	From the LORD looks down	9028
	53: 2	God looks down from **h** on the sons of men	9028
	57: 3	He sends from **h** and saves me,	9028
	69:34	Let **h** and earth praise him,	9028
	73: 9	Their mouths lay claim to **h**,	9028
	73:25	Whom have I in **h** but you?	9028
	75: 5	Do not lift your horns against **h**;	5294
	76: 8	From **h** you pronounced judgment,	9028
	78:24	he gave them the grain of **h**.	9028
	80:14	Look down from **h** and see!	9028
	85:11	and righteousness looks down from **h**.	9028
	89: 2	you established your faithfulness in **h** itself.	9028
	102:19	from **h** he viewed the earth,	9028
	103:19	The LORD has established his throne in **h**,	9028
	105:40	and satisfied them with the bread of **h**.	9028
	115: 3	Our God is in **h**; he does whatever he	9028
	115:15	the LORD, the Maker of **h** and earth.	9028
	121: 2	the LORD, the Maker of **h** and earth.	9028
	123: 1	to you whose throne is in **h**.	9028
	124: 8	the LORD, the Maker of **h** and earth.	9028
	134: 3	May the LORD, the Maker of **h** and earth,	9028
	136:26	Give thanks to the God of **h**.	9028
	146: 6	of **h** and earth, the sea, and everything	9028
Pr	30: 4	Who has gone up to **h** and come down?	9028
Ecc	1:13	by wisdom all that is done under **h**.	9028
	2: 3	for men to do under **h** during the few days	9028
	3: 1	and a season for every activity under **h**:	9028

Ecc	5: 2	God is in **h** and you are on earth,	9028
Isa	13:10	The stars of **h** and their constellations will	9028
	14:12	How you have fallen from **h**,	9028
	14:13	You said in your heart, "I will ascend to **h**;	9028
	37:16	You have made **h** and earth.	9028
	55:10	the rain and the snow come down from **h**,	9028
	63:15	from **h** and see from your lofty throne,	9028
	66: 1	"**H** is my throne, and the earth is my	9028
Jer	7:18	cakes of bread for the Queen of **H**.	9028
	23:24	"Do not I fill **h** and earth?"	9028
	33:25	and night and the fixed laws of **h** and earth,	9028
	44:17	We will burn incense to the Queen of **H**	9028
	44:18	Queen of **H** and pouring out drink offerings	9028
	44:19	we burned incense to the Queen of **H**	9028
	44:25	drink offerings to the Queen of **H**.'	9028
	51:48	Then **h** and earth and all that is in	9028
La	2: 1	down the splendor of Israel from **h** to earth;	9028
	3:41	up our hearts and our hands to God in **h**,	9028
	3:50	the LORD looks down from **h** and sees.	9028
Eze	8: 3	The Spirit lifted me up between earth and **h**	9028
Da	2:18	from the God of **h** concerning this mystery,	10723
	2:19	Then Daniel praised the God of **h**	10723
	2:28	there is a God in **h** who reveals mysteries.	10723
	2:37	of **h** has given you dominion and power	10723
	2:44	of **h** will set up a kingdom that will never	10723
	4:13	a holy one, coming down from **h**.	10723
	4:15	" 'Let him be drenched with the dew of **h**,	10723
	4:23	coming down from **h** and saying,	10723
	4:23	Let him be drenched with the dew of **h**;	10723
	4:25	and be drenched with the dew of **h**,	10723
	4:26	to you when you acknowledge that **H** rules.	10723
	4:31	on his lips when a voice came from **h**,	10723
	4:33	of **h** until his hair grew like the feathers of	10723
	4:34	Nebuchadnezzar, raised my eyes toward **h**,	10723
	4:35	the powers of **h** and the peoples of the earth	10723
	4:37	praise and exalt and glorify the King of **h**,	10723
	5:21	his body was drenched with the dew of **h**,	10723
	5:23	set yourself up against the Lord of **h**.	10723
	7: 2	the four winds of **h** churning up	10723
	7:13	a son of man, coming with the clouds of **h**.	10723
	7:27	under the whole **h** will be handed over to	10723
	8: 8	up toward the four winds of **h**.	9028
	9:12	the whole **h** nothing has ever been done	9028
	11: 4	and parceled out toward the four winds of **h**.	9028
	12: 7	and his left hand toward **h**,	9028
Jnh	1: 9	I worship the LORD, the God of **h**,	9028
Zec	2: 6	I have scattered you to the four winds of **h**,"	9028
	5: 9	and they lifted up the basket between **h**	9028
	6: 5	"These are the four spirits of **h**,	9028
Mal	3:10	if I will not throw open the floodgates of **h**	9028
Mt	3: 2	"Repent, for the kingdom **of h** is near."	4041
	3:16	At that moment **h** was opened,	4041
	3:17	And a voice from **h** said, "This is my Son,	4041
	4:17	"Repent, for the kingdom **of h** is near."	4041
	5: 3	for theirs is the kingdom **of h**.	4041
	5:10	for theirs is the kingdom **of h**.	4041
	5:12	because great is your reward in **h**,	4041
	5:16	and praise your Father in **h**.	4041
	5:18	until **h** and earth disappear,	4041
	5:19	be called least in the kingdom **of h**,	4041
	5:19	be called great in the kingdom **of h**.	4041
	5:20	certainly not enter the kingdom **of h**.	4041
	5:34	either by **h**, for it is God's throne;	4041
	5:45	that you may be sons of your Father in **h**.	4041
	6: 1	have no reward from your Father in **h**.	4041
	6: 9	" 'Our Father in **h**, hallowed be your name,	4041
	6:10	your will be done on earth as it is in **h**.	4041
	6:20	But store up for yourselves treasures in **h**,	4041
	7:11	Father in **h** give good gifts to those who ask	4041
	7:21	'Lord, Lord,' will enter the kingdom **of h**,	4041
	7:21	the will of my Father who is in **h**.	4041
	8:11	Isaac and Jacob in the kingdom **of h**.	4041
	10: 7	'The kingdom **of h** is near.'	4041
	10:32	before my Father in **h**.	4041
	10:33	I will disown him before my Father in **h**.	4041
	11:11	in the kingdom **of h** is greater than he.	4041
	11:12	kingdom **of h** has been forcefully advancing	4041
	11:25	"I praise you, Father, Lord **of h** and earth,	4041
	12:50	in **h** is my brother and sister and mother."	4041
	13:11	of the kingdom **of h** has been given to you,	4041
	13:24	**of h** is like a man who sowed good seed	4041
	13:31	"The kingdom **of h** is like a mustard seed,	4041
	13:33	"The kingdom **of h** is like yeast that	4041
	13:44	"The kingdom **of h** is like treasure hidden	4041
	13:45	the kingdom **of h** is like a merchant looking	4041
	13:47	the kingdom **of h** is like a net that was let	4041
	13:52	about the kingdom **of h** is like the owner of	4041
	14:19	and the two fish and looking up to **h**,	4041
	16: 1	by asking him to show them a sign from **h**.	4041
	16:17	to you by man, but by my Father in **h**.	4041
	16:19	will give you the keys of the kingdom **of h**;	4041
	16:19	you bind on earth will be bound in **h**,	4041
	16:19	you loose on earth will be loosed in **h**."	4041
	18: 1	"Who is the greatest in the kingdom **of h**?"	4041
	18: 3	you will never enter the kingdom **of h**.	4041
	18: 4	child is the greatest in the kingdom **of h**.	4041
	18:10	that their angels in **h** always see the face	4041
	18:10	the face of my Father in **h**.	4041
	18:14	the same way your Father in **h** is not willing	4041
	18:18	you bind on earth will be bound in **h**,	4041
	18:18	you loose on earth will be loosed in **h**.	4041
	18:19	it will be done for you by my Father in **h**.	4041
	18:23	the kingdom **of h** is like a king who wanted	4041
	19:12	because of the kingdom **of h**.	4041
	19:14	the kingdom **of h** belongs to such as these."	4041
	19:21	and you will have treasure in **h**.	4041
	19:23	for a rich man to enter the kingdom **of h**.	4041

Mt	20: 1	kingdom **of h** is like a landowner who went	4041
	21:25	Was it from **h**, or from men?"	4041
	21:25	"If we say, 'From **h**,' he will ask,	4041
	22: 2	kingdom **of h** is like a king who prepared	4041
	22:30	they will be like the angels in **h**.	4041
	23: 9	for you have one Father, and he is in **h**.	4039
	23:13	You shut the kingdom **of h** in men's faces.	4041
	23:22	by **h** swears by God's throne and by	4041
	24:35	**H** and earth will pass away,	4041
	24:36	not even the angels in **h**, nor the Son,	4041
	25: 1	"At that time the kingdom **of h** will be	4041
	26:64	and coming on the clouds of **h**."	4041
	28: 2	angel of the Lord came down from **h** and,	4041
	28:18	"All authority in **h** and on earth has been	4041
		given to me.	4041
Mk	1:10	he saw **h** being torn open and the Spirit	4041
	1:11	And a voice came from **h**:	4041
	6:41	and the two fish and looking up to **h**,	4041
	7:34	He looked up to **h** and with a deep sigh said	4041
	8:11	they asked him for a sign from **h**.	4041
	10:21	and you will have treasure in **h**.	4041
	11:25	your Father in **h** may forgive you your sins.	4041
	11:30	was it from **h**, or from men?	4041
	11:31	"If we say, 'From **h**,' he will ask,	4041
	12:25	they will be like the angels in **h**.	4041
	13:31	**H** and earth will pass away,	4041
	13:32	not even the angels in **h**, nor the Son,	4041
	14:62	and coming on the clouds of **h**."	4041
	16:19	into **h** and he sat at the right hand of God.	4041
Lk	1:78	the rising sun will come to us from **h**	5737
	2:15	the angels had left them and gone into **h**,	4041
	3:21	And as he was praying, **h** was opened	4041
	3:22	And a voice came from **h**:	4041
	6:23	because great is your reward in **h**,	4041
	9:16	and the two fish and looking up to **h**,	4041
	9:51	for him to be taken up to **h**,	NIG
	9:54	to call fire down from **h** to destroy them?"	4041
	10:18	"I saw Satan fall like lightning from **h**.	4041
	10:20	rejoice that your names are written in **h**."	4041
	10:21	"I praise you, Father, Lord of **h** and earth,	4041
	11:13	how much more will your Father in **h** give	4041
	11:16	by asking for a sign from **h**.	4041
	12:33	a treasure in **h** that will not be exhausted,	4041
	15: 7	rejoicing in **h** over one sinner who repents	4041
	15:18	I have sinned against **h** and against you.	4041
	15:21	I have sinned against **h** and against you.	4041
	16:17	It is easier for **h** and earth to disappear than	4041
	17:29	down from **h** and destroyed them all.	4041
	18:13	He would not even look up to **h**,	4041
	18:22	and you will have treasure in **h**.	4041
	19:38	"Peace in **h** and glory in the highest!"	4041
	20: 4	was it from **h**, or from men?"	4041
	20: 5	"If we say, 'From **h**,' we will ask,	4041
	21:11	and fearful events and great signs from **h**.	4041
	21:33	**H** and earth will pass away,	4041
	22:43	An angel from **h** appeared to him	4041
	24:51	he left them and was taken up into **h**.	4041
Jn	1:32	down from **h** as a dove and remain on him.	4041
	1:51	"I tell you the truth, you shall see **h** open,	4041
	3:13	No one has ever gone into **h** except	4041
	3:13	the one who came from **h**—	4041
	3:27	can receive only what is given him from **h**.	4041
	3:31	The one who comes from **h** is above all.	4041
	6:31	'He gave them bread from **h** to eat.' "	4041
	6:32	who has given you the bread from **h**,	4041
	6:32	who gives you the true bread from **h**.	4041
	6:33	down from **h** and gives life to the world."	4041
	6:38	from **h** not to do my will but to do the will	4041
	6:41	"I am the bread that came down from **h**."	4041
	6:42	can he now say, 'I came down from **h**'?"	4041
	6:50	here is the bread that comes down from **h**,	4041
	6:51	the living bread that came down from **h**.	4041
	6:58	This is the bread that came down from **h**.	4041
	12:28	Then a voice came from **h**,	4041
	17: 1	he looked toward **h** and prayed:	4041
Ac	1: 2	until the day he was taken up to **h**,	NIG
	1:11	who has been taken from you into **h**,	4041
	1:11	the same way you have seen him go into **h**."	4041
	2: 2	the blowing of a violent wind came from **h**	4041
	2: 5	from every nation under **h**.	4041
	2:19	in the **h** above and signs on the earth below,	4041
	2:34	For David did not ascend to **h**,	4041
	3:21	He must remain in **h** until the time comes	4041
	4:12	under **h** given to men by which we must	4041
	4:24	"you made the **h** and the earth and the sea,	4041
	7:49	" '**H** is my throne, and the earth	4041
	7:55	looked up to **h** and saw the glory of God,	4041
	7:56	"I see **h** open and the Son of Man standing	4041
	9: 3	suddenly a light from **h** flashed around him.	4041
	10:11	He saw **h** opened and something like	4041
	10:16	immediately the sheet was taken back to **h**.	4041
	11: 5	like a large sheet being let down from **h**	4041
	11: 9	"The voice spoke from **h** a second time,	4041
	11:10	and then it was all pulled up to **h** again.	4041
	14:15	who made **h** and earth and sea	4041
	14:17	by giving you rain **from h** and crops	4040
	17:24	the Lord **of h** and earth and does not live	4041
	19:35	and of her **image, which fell from h**?	1479
	22: 6	a bright light from **h** flashed around me.	4041
	26:13	I saw a light **from h**, brighter than the sun,	4040
	26:19	I was not disobedient *to* the vision from **h**.	4041
Ro	1:18	of God is being revealed from **h** against all	4041
	10: 6	'Who will ascend into **h**?' "	4041
1Co	8: 5	so-called gods, whether in **h** or on earth	4041
	15:47	dust of the earth, the second man from **h**.	2230
	15:48	and as is the *man from* **h**,	2230
	15:48	so also are those who are *of* **h**.	2230

1Co	15:49	we bear the likeness *of* the *man from* h.	2230
2Co	5: 1	an eternal house in h, not built by human	4041
	12: 2	was caught up to the third h.	4041
Gal	1: 8	even if we or an angel *from* h should preach	4041
Eph	1:10	to bring all things in h and on earth together	4041
	3:15	from whom his whole family in h and	4041
	6: 9	both their Master and yours is in h,	4041
Php	2:10	in h and on earth and under the earth,	2230
	3:20	But our citizenship is in h.	4041
Col	1: 5	for you in h and that you have already heard	4041
	1:16	created: things in h and on earth,	4041
	1:20	whether things on earth or things in h,	4041
	1:23	to every creature under h,	4041
	4: 1	you know that you also have a Master in h.	4041
1Th	1:10	to wait for his Son from h, whom he raised	4041
	4:16	the Lord himself will come down from h,	4041
2Th	1: 7	when the Lord Jesus is revealed from h	4041
Heb	1: 3	down at the right hand of the Majesty in h.	5734
	8: 1	of the throne of the Majesty in h,	4041
	8: 5	that is a copy and shadow of what *is* in h.	2230
	9:24	he entered h itself,	4041
	9:25	Nor did he enter h to offer himself again	NIG
	12:23	whose names are written in h.	4041
	12:25	from him who warns us from h?	4041
Jas	3:15	Such "wisdom" does not come down from h	NIG
	3:17	But the wisdom that comes from h is first	NIG
	5:12	not by h or by earth or by anything else.	4041
1Pe	1: 4	kept in h for you,	4041
	1:12	to you by the Holy Spirit sent from h.	4041
	3:22	into h and is at God's right hand—	4041
2Pe	1:18	that came from h when we were with him	4041
	3:13	to a new h and a new earth,	4041
Rev	3:12	which is coming down out of h	4041
	4: 1	before me was a door standing open in h.	4041
	4: 2	a throne in h with someone sitting on it.	4041
	5: 3	But no one in h or on earth or under	4041
	5:13	in h and on earth and under the earth and on	4041
	8: 1	silence in h for about half an hour.	4041
	10: 1	another mighty angel coming down from h.	4041
	10: 4	but I heard a voice from h say,	4041
	10: 5	and on the land raised his right hand to h.	4041
	10: 8	the voice that I had heard from h spoke	4041
	11:12	Then they heard a loud voice from h saying	4041
	11:12	And they went up to h in a cloud,	4041
	11:13	and gave glory to the God *of* h.	4041
	11:15	and there were loud voices in h, which said:	4041
	11:19	Then God's temple in h was opened,	4041
	12: 1	A great and wondrous sign appeared in h:	4041
	12: 3	Then another sign appeared in h:	4041
	12: 7	And there was war in h.	4041
	12: 8	and they lost their place in h.	4041
	12:10	Then I heard a loud voice in h say:	4041
	13: 6	and those who live in h.	4041
	13:13	to come down from h to earth in full view	4041
	14: 2	from h like the roar of rushing waters and	4041
	14:13	Then I heard a voice from h say, "Write:	4041
	14:17	Another angel came out of the temple in h,	4041
	15: 1	I saw in h another great and marvelous sign:	4041
	15: 5	After this I looked and in h the temple,	4041
	16:11	*of* h because of their pains and their sores,	4041
	18: 1	I saw another angel coming down from h.	4041
	18: 4	Then I heard another voice from h say:	4041
	18: 5	for her sins are piled up to h,	4041
	18:20	Rejoice over her, *O* h!	4041
	19: 1	the roar of a great multitude in h shouting:	4041
	19:11	I saw h standing open and there	4041
	19:14	The armies of h were following him,	4041
	20: 1	And I saw an angel coming down out of h,	4041
	20: 9	fire came down from h and devoured them.	4041
	21: 1	Then I saw a new h and a new earth,	4041
	21: 1	first h and the first earth had passed away,	4041
	21: 2	coming down out of h from God,	4041
	21:10	Jerusalem, coming down out of h from God.	4041

HEAVEN'S (1) [HEAVEN]

Ge	27:28	give you *of* h dew and of earth's richness—	9028

HEAVENLY (36) [HEAVEN]

Dt	4:19	the moon and the stars—all the h array—	9028
Ps	8: 5	the h **beings** and crowned him with glory	466
	11: 4	the Lord is on his h throne.	
	89: 6	like the Lord among the h **beings**?	446+1201
	103:21	Praise the Lord, all his h **hosts**,	7372
	148: 2	all his angels, praise him, all his h **hosts**.	7372
Mt	5:48	therefore, as your h Father is perfect.	4039
	6:14	your h Father will also forgive you.	4039
	6:26	and yet your h Father feeds them.	4039
	6:32	your h Father knows that you need them.	4039
	15:13	that my h Father has not planted will	4039
	18:35	"This is how my h Father will treat each	4039
	24:29	and the h bodies will be shaken.'	4041
	25:31	he will sit on his throne in h glory.	NIG
Mk	13:25	and the h bodies will be shaken.'	4041
Lk	2:13	a great company *of* the h host appeared	4039
	21:26	for the h **bodies** will be shaken.	1539+3836+4041
Jn	3:12	then will you believe if I speak of h **things**?	2230
Ac	7:42	over to the worship *of* the h bodies.	4041
1Co	15:40	also h bodies and there are earthly bodies,	2230
	15:40	but the splendor *of* the h bodies is one kind,	2230
2Co	5: 2	longing to be clothed with our h dwelling,	1666+4041
	5: 4	but to be clothed with our h dwelling,	NIG
Eph	1: 3	in the h realms with every spiritual blessing	2230
	1:20	at his right hand in the h realms,	2230
	2: 6	with him in the h realms in Christ Jesus,	2230

Eph	3:10	to the rulers and authorities in the h realms,	2230
	6:12	the spiritual forces of evil in the h realms.	2230
2Ti	4:18	and will bring me safely to his h kingdom.	2230
Heb	3: 1	holy brothers, who share in the h calling,	2230
	6: 4	who have tasted the h **gift**,	2230
	9:23	the copies of the h **things** to be	1877+3836+4041
	9:23	but the h **things** themselves	2230
	11:16	longing for a better country—a h *one*.	2230
	12:22	to Mount Zion, to the h Jerusalem,	2230
Jas	1:17	down from the Father of the h lights,	NIG

HEAVENS (173) [HEAVEN]

Ge	1: 1	In the beginning God created the h and	9028
	2: 1	Thus the h and the earth were completed	9028
	2: 4	the h and the earth when they were created.	9028
	2: 4	the Lord God made the earth and the h—	9028
	6:17	on the earth to destroy all life under the h,	9028
	7:11	and the floodgates of the h were opened.	9028
	7:19	under the entire h were covered.	9028
	8: 2	and the floodgates of the h had been closed,	9028
	11: 4	with a tower that reaches to the h,	9028
	15: 5	"Look up at the h and count the stars—	9028
	19:24	from the Lord out of the h.	9028
	49:25	who blesses you with blessings *of* the h	9028
Ex	20:11	For in six days the Lord made the h and	9028
	31:17	for in six days the Lord made the h and	9028
Dt	4:11	while it blazed with fire to the very h,	9028
	4:32	ask from one end of the h to the other.	9028
	10:14	To the Lord your God belong the h,	9028
	10:14	even the **highest** h, the earth and	9028+9028
	11:17	and he will shut the h so that it will not rain	9028
	11:21	as the days that the h are above the earth.	9028
	28:12	The Lord will open the h,	9028
	30: 4	to the most distant land under the h,	9028
	32: 1	O h, and I will speak;	9028
	33:26	on the h to help you and on the clouds	9028
	33:28	where the h drop dew.	9028
Jdg	5: 4	the earth shook, the h poured,	9028
	5:20	From the h the stars fought,	9028
2Sa	21:10	till the rain poured down from the h on	9028
	22: 8	the foundations of the h shook;	9028
	22:10	He parted the h and came down;	9028
1Ki	8:27	the h, even the highest heaven,	9028
	8:35	"When the h are shut up and there is no rain	9028
2Ki	7: 2	Lord should open the floodgates of the h,	9028
	7:19	Lord should open the floodgates of the h,	9028
1Ch	16:26	but the Lord made the h.	9028
	16:31	Let the h rejoice, let the earth be glad;	9028
2Ch	2: 6	since the h, even the highest heavens,	9028
	2: 6	the **highest** h, cannot contain him?	9028+9028
	6:18	The h, even the highest heavens,	9028
	6:18	The heavens, even the **highest** h,	9028+9028
	6:26	"When the h are shut up and there is no rain	9028
	7:13	I shut up the h so that there is no rain,	9028
Ezr	9: 6	and our guilt has reached to the h.	9028
Ne	9: 6	You made the h, even the highest heavens,	9028
	9: 6	made the heavens, even the **highest** h,	9028+9028
Job	9: 8	He alone stretches out the h and treads on	9028
	11: 8	They are higher than the h—	9028
	14:12	till the h are no more,	9028
	15:15	if even the h are not pure in his eyes,	9028
	20: 6	to the h and his head touches the clouds,	9028
	20:27	The h will expose his guilt;	9028
	22:14	as he goes about in the vaulted h.'	9028
	26:11	pillars of the h quake, aghast at his rebuke.	9028
	28:24	of the earth and sees everything under the h.	9028
	35: 5	Look up at the h and see;	9028
	38:29	Who gives birth to the frost from the h	9028
	38:33	Do you know the laws of the h?	9028
	38:37	Who can tip over the water jars of the h	9028
Ps	8: 1	You have set your glory above the h.	9028
	8: 3	When I consider your h,	9028
	18: 9	He parted the h and came down;	9028
	19: 1	The h declare the glory of God;	9028
	19: 4	In the h he has pitched a tent for the sun,	2157S
	19: 6	at one end of the h and makes its circuit to	9028
	33: 6	the word of the Lord were the h made,	9028
	36: 5	Your love, O Lord, reaches to the h,	9028
	50: 4	He summons the h above, and the earth,	9028
	50: 6	And the h proclaim his righteousness,	9028
	57: 5	Be exalted, O God, above the h;	9028
	57:10	For great is your love, reaching to the h;	9028
	57:11	Be exalted, O God, above the h;	9028
	68: 8	the h poured down rain, before God,	9028
	78:23	above and opened the doors of the h;	9028
	78:26	from the h and led forth the south wind	9028
	89: 5	The h praise your wonders,	9028
	89:11	The h are yours, and yours also the earth;	9028
	89:29	his throne as long as the h endure.	9028
	96: 5	but the Lord made the h.	9028
	96:11	Let the h rejoice, let the earth be glad;	9028
	97: 6	The h proclaim his righteousness,	9028
	102:25	and the h are the work of your hands.	9028
	103:11	For as high as the h are above the earth,	9028
	104: 2	he stretches out the h like a tent	9028
	107:26	They mounted up to the h and went down to	9028
	108: 4	For great is your love, higher than the h;	9028
	108: 5	Be exalted, O God, above the h,	9028
	113: 4	his glory above the h.	9028
	113: 6	who stoops down to look on the h and	9028
	115:16	The **highest** h belong to the Lord,	9028+9028
	119:89	it stands firm in the h.	9028
	135: 6	pleases him, in the h and on the earth,	9028
	136: 5	who by his understanding made the h,	9028
	139: 8	If I go up to the h, you are there;	9028
	144: 5	Part your h, O Lord, and come down;	9028

Ps	148: 1	Praise the Lord from the h,	9028
	148: 4	you **highest** h and you waters above	9028+9028
	148:13	his splendor is above the earth and the h.	9028
	150: 1	praise him in his mighty h.	8385
Pr	3:19	by understanding set the h in place;	9028
	8:27	I was there when he set the h in place,	9028
	8:28	As the h are high and the earth is deep,	9028
Isa	1: 2	Hear, O h! Listen, O earth!	9028
	13: 5	from the ends of the h—	9028
	13:13	Therefore I will make the h tremble;	9028
	24:18	The floodgates of the h are opened,	5294
	24:21	The Lord will punish the powers in the h	5294
	34: 4	the h will be dissolved and the sky rolled up	9028
	34: 5	My sword has drunk its fill in the h;	9028
	38:14	My eyes grew weak as I looked to the h.	5294
	40:12	the breadth of his hand marked off the h?	9028
	40:22	He stretches out the h like a canopy,	9028
	40:26	Lift your eyes and look to the h:	5294
	42: 5	the h and stretched them out,	9028
	44:23	Sing for joy, O h, for the Lord has done	9028
	44:24	who alone stretched out the h,	9028
	45: 8	"You h above, rain down righteousness;	9028
	45:12	My own hands stretched out the h;	9028
	45:18	he who created the h, he is God;	9028
	48:13	and my right hand spread out the h;	9028
	49:13	Shout for joy, O h; rejoice, O earth;	9028
	51: 6	Lift up your eyes to the h,	9028
	51: 6	the h will vanish like smoke,	9028
	51:13	the h and laid the foundations of the earth,	9028
	51:16	I who set the h in place,	9028
	55: 9	"As the h are higher than the earth,	9028
	64: 1	that you would rend the h and come down,	9028
	65:17	I will create new h and a new earth,	9028
	66:22	"As the new h and the new earth	9028
Jer	2:12	Be appalled at this, O h,	9028
	4:23	and at the h, and their light was gone.	9028
	4:28	Therefore the earth will mourn and the h	9028
	8: 2	and the moon and all the stars of the h,	9028
	10:11	who did not make the h and the earth,	10723
	10:11	from the earth and from under the h.' "	10723
	10:12	by his wisdom and stretched out the h	9028
	10:13	When he thunders, the waters in the h roar;	9028
	31:37	"Only if the h above can be measured and	9028
	32:17	the h and the earth by your great power	9028
	49:36	from the four quarters of the h;	9028
	51:15	by his wisdom and stretched out the h	9028
	51:16	When he thunders, the waters in the h roar;	9028
La	3:66	in anger and destroy them from under the h	9028
Eze	1: 1	h were opened and I saw visions of God.	9028
	32: 7	I will cover the h and darken their stars;	9028
	32: 8	All the shining lights in the h I will darken	9028
Da	6:27	he performs signs and wonders in the h and	10723
	8:10	It grew until it reached the host of the h,	9028
	12: 3	like the brightness of the h,	8385
Joel	2:30	I will show wonders in the h and on	9028
Am	9: 2	Though they climb up to the h,	9028
	9: 6	in the h and sets its foundation on the earth,	9028
Hab	3: 3	the h and his praise filled the earth.	9028
	3:11	Sun and moon stood still in the h at the glint	2292
Hag	1:10	of you the h have withheld their dew and	9028
	2: 6	a little while I will once more shake the h	9028
	2:21	that I will shake the h and the earth.	9028
Zec	8:12	and the h will drop their dew.	9028
	12: 1	The Lord, who stretches out the h,	9028
Mt	24:31	from one end *of* the h to the other.	4041
Mk	13:27	the ends of the earth to the ends *of* the h.	4041
Eph	4:10	who ascended higher than all the h,	4041
Heb	1:10	and the h are the work of your hands.	4041
	4:14	through the h, Jesus the Son of God,	4041
	7:26	set apart from sinners, exalted above the h.	4041
	12:26	not only the earth but also the h."	4041
Jas	5:18	Again he prayed, and the h gave rain,	4041
2Pe	3: 5	the h existed and the earth was formed out	4041
	3: 7	the present h and earth are reserved for fire,	4041
	3:10	The h will disappear with a roar;	4041
	3:12	about the destruction of the h by fire,	4041
Rev	10: 6	who created the h and all that is in them,	4041
	12:12	you h and you who dwell in them!	4041
	14: 7	Worship him who made the h, the earth,	4041

HEAVENWARD (1) [HEAVEN]

Php	3:14	the prize for which God has called me h	539

HEAVIER (6) [HEAVY]

1Ki	12:11	I *will* **make** it even h.	3578
	12:14	I *will* **make** it even h.	3578
2Ch	10:11	I *will* **make** it even h.	3578
	10:14	I *will* **make** it even h.	3578
Pr	27: 3	but provocation by a fool is h than both.	3878
Isa	28:22	or your chains *will* **become** h;	2616

HEAVILY (3) [HEAVY]

Ps	88: 7	Your wrath **lies** h upon me;	6164
Ecc	6: 1	and it **weighs** h on men:	8041
	8: 6	though a man's misery **weighs** h upon him.	8041

HEAVY (48) [HEAVIER, HEAVILY]

Ex	18:18	The work is too h for you;	3878
Nu	11:14	the burden is too h for me.	3878
Dt	1: 9	too h a burden for me to carry	3523+4202+5951
	25:13	in your bag,	1524
	32:15	filled with food, *he* became h and sleek.	6286
Jdg	20:34	so h that the Benjamites did not realize how	3877
1Sa	4:17	and the army has suffered h losses.	1524

1Sa	4:18	for he was an old man and **h.**	3878
	5: 6	The LORD's hand *was* **h** upon the people	3877
	5: 7	because his hand *is* **h** upon us and	7996
	5:11	God's hand *was* very **h** *upon* it.	3877
	6:19	The people mourned because of the **h** blow	1524
	23: 5	He inflicted **h** losses on the Philistines	1524
2Sa	14:26	to time when it became too **h** for him—	3878
1Ki	12: 4	"Your father *put a* **h** yoke on us,	7996
	12: 4	the harsh labor and the **h** yoke he put on us,	3878
	12:10	'Your father *put a* **h** yoke on us,	3877
	12:11	My father laid on you a **h** yoke;	3878
	12:14	"My father **made** your yoke **h**;	3877
	18:41	for there is the sound of a **h** rain."	2162
	18:45	a **h** rain came on and Ahab rode off	1524
	20:21	and inflicted **h** losses on the Arameans.	1524
2Ch	10: 4	"Your father *put a* **h** yoke on us,	7996
	10: 4	the harsh labor and the **h** yoke he put on us,	3878
	10:10	'Your father *put a* **h** yoke on us,	3877
	10:11	My father laid on you a **h** yoke;	3878
	10:14	"My father **made** your yoke **h**;	3877
	13:17	and his men inflicted **h** losses on them,	8041
	21:14	everything that is yours, with a **h** blow.	1524
	28: 5	who inflicted **h** casualties on him.	1524
Ne	5:15	**placed a h burden** on the people	3877
	5:18	the demands *were* **h** on these people.	3877
Job	23: 2	his hand *is* **h** in spite of my groaning.	3877
	33: 7	nor *should* my hand *be* **h** upon you.	3877
	39:11	Will you leave your **h** work to him?	3330
Ps	32: 4	day and night your hand *was* **h** upon me;	3877
	38: 4	like a burden too **h** to bear.	3877+3878
	144:14	our oxen *will* **draw h loads.**	6022
Pr	25:20	is one who sings songs to a **h** heart.	8273
	27: 3	Stone is **h** and sand a burden,	3880
Ecc	1:13	What a **h** burden God has laid on men!	8273
Isa	24:20	so **h** upon it *is* the guilt of its rebellion	3877
	47: 6	Even on the aged *you* **laid** a very **h** yoke.	3877
Eze	24:12	its **h** deposit has not been removed,	8041
	27:25	You are filled with **h** *cargo* in the	3877+4394
Mt	23: 4	They tie up **h** loads and put them on men's	987
	26:43	sleeping, because their eyes were **h.**	976
Mk	14:40	sleeping, because their eyes were **h.**	2852

HEBER (10) [HEBER'S, HEBERITE]

Ge	46:17	The sons of Beriah: **H** and Malkiel.	2491
Nu	26:45	through the Heberite clan;	2491
Jdg	4:11	**H** the Kenite had left the other Kenites,	2491
	4:17	the wife of **H** the Kenite,	2491
	4:17	of Hazor and the clan of **H** the Kenite.	2491
	5:24	the wife of **H** the Kenite,	2491
1Ch	4:18	**H** the father of Soco,	2491
	7:31	The sons of Beriah: **H** and Malkiel.	2491
	7:32	**H** was the father of Japhlet,	2491
	8:17	Zebadiah, Meshullam, Hizki, **H,**	2491

HEBER'S (1) [HEBER]

Jdg	4:21	**H** wife, picked up a tent peg and a hammer	2491

HEBERITE (1) [HEBER]

Nu	26:45	through Heber, the **H** clan;	2499

HEBRAIC (1) [HEBREW]

Ac	6: 1	among them complained against the **H** Jews	1578

HEBREW (25) [HEBRAIC, HEBREWS]

Ge	14:13	and reported this to Abram the **H.**	6303
	39:14	"this **H** has been brought to us to make sport	6303
	39:17	"That **H** slave you brought came to me	6303
	41:12	Now a young **H** was there with us,	6303
Ex	1:15	The king of Egypt said to the **H** midwives,	6303
	1:16	the **H** *women* in childbirth and observe them	6303
	1:19	"**H** women are not like Egyptian women;	6303
	2: 6	"This is one of the **H** babies," she said.	6303
	2: 7	of the **H** women to nurse the baby for you?"	6303
	2:11	He saw an Egyptian beating a **H,**	6303
	2:13	"Why are you hitting your fellow **H?"**	NIH
	21: 2	"If you buy a **H** servant,	6303
Dt	15:12	If a fellow **H,** *a man* or a woman,	6303
1Sa	4: 6	"What's all this shouting in the **H** camp?"	6303
2Ki	18:26	to us in **H** in the hearing of the people on	3376
	18:28	the commander stood and called out **in H:**	3376
2Ch	32:18	Then they called out **in H** to the people	3376
Isa	36:11	to us in **H** in the hearing of the people on	3376
	36:13	the commander stood and called out **in H,**	3376
Jer	34: 9	Everyone was to free his **H** slaves,	6303
	34:14	must free any fellow **H** who has sold	
		himself to you.	6303
Jnh	1: 9	"I am a **H** and I worship the LORD,	6303
Php	3: 5	of the tribe of Benjamin, a **H** of Hebrews;	1578
Rev	9:11	whose name **in H** is Abaddon, and in Greek,	1580
	16:16	to the place that **in H** is called Armageddon.	1580

HEBREWS (18) [HEBREW]

Ge	40:15	from the land of the **H,**	6303
	43:32	because Egyptians could not eat with **H,**	6303
Ex	2:13	and saw two **H** fighting.	6303
	3:18	The God of the **H,** has met with us.	6303
	5: 3	"The God of the **H** has met with us.	6303
	7:16	say to him, 'The LORD, the God of the **H,**	6303
	9: 1	'This is what the LORD, the God of the **H,**	6303
	9:13	'This is what the LORD, the God of the **H,**	6303
	10: 3	"This is what the LORD, the God of the **H,**	6303
1Sa	4: 9	Be men, or you will be subject to the **H,**	6303
	13: 3	"Let the **H** hear!"	6303

1Sa	13: 7	*Some* **H** even crossed the Jordan to the land	6303
	13:19	"Otherwise the **H** will make swords	6303
	14:11	"The **H** are crawling out of the holes	6303
	14:21	Those **H** who had previously been with	6303
	29: 3	"What about these **H?"**	6303
2Co	11:22	Are they **H?** So am I.	1578
Php	3: 5	of the tribe of Benjamin, a Hebrew of **H;**	1578

HEBRON (74) [HEBRONITE, HEBRONITES, KIRIATH ARBA]

Ge	13:18	to live near the great trees of Mamre at **H,**	2496
	23: 2	(that is, **H**) in the land of Canaan,	2496
	23:19	of Machpelah near Mamre (which is at **H**)	2496
	35:27	**H**), where Abraham and Isaac had stayed.	2496
	37:14	Then he sent him off from the Valley of **H.**	2496
Ex	6:18	The sons of Kohath were Amram, Izhar, **H**	2497
Nu	3:19	Amram, Izhar, **H** and Uzziel.	2497
	13:22	up through the Negev and came to **H,**	2496
	13:22	(**H** had been built seven years before Zoan	2496
Jos	10: 3	of Jerusalem appealed to Hoham king of **H,**	2496
	10: 5	the kings of Jerusalem, **H,** Jarmuth,	2496
	10:23	the kings of Jerusalem, **H,** Jarmuth,	2496
	10:36	up from Eglon to **H** and attacked it.	2496
	10:39	to Libnah and its king and to **H.**	2496
	11:21	from **H,** Debir and Anab,	2496
	12:10	the king of Jerusalem one the king of **H** one	2496
	14:13	and gave him **H** as his inheritance.	2496
	14:14	So **H** has belonged to Caleb son	2496
	14:15	**H** used to be called Kiriath Arba after Arba,	2496
	15:13	Kiriath Arba, that is, **H.**	2496
	15:14	From **H** Caleb drove out	9004S
	15:54	**H**) and Zior—nine towns and their villages.	2496
	20: 7	**H** in the hill country of Judah.	2496
	21:11	**H**), with its surrounding pastureland,	2496
	21:13	the priest they gave **H** (a city of refuge	2496
Jdg	1:10	in **H** (formerly called Kiriath Arba)	2496
	1:20	**H** was given to Caleb,	2496
	16: 3	to the top of the hill that faces **H.**	2496
1Sa	30:31	and **H;** and to those in all the other places	2496
2Sa	2: 1	"To **H,**" the LORD answered.	2496
	2: 3	and they settled in **H** and its towns.	2496
	2: 4	to **H** and there they anointed David king	NIH
	2:11	of time David was king in **H** over the house	2496
	2:32	and arrived at **H** by daybreak.	2496
	3: 2	Sons were born to David in **H:**	2496
	3: 5	These were born to David in **H.**	2496
	3:19	to **H** to tell David everything that Israel and	2496
	3:20	came to David at **H,**	2496
	3:22	But Abner was no longer with David in **H,**	2496
	3:27	Now when Abner returned to **H,**	2496
	3:32	They buried Abner in **H,**	2496
	4: 1	son of Saul heard that Abner had died in **H,**	2496
	4: 8	of Ish-Bosheth to David at **H** and said to	2496
	4:12	and hung the bodies by the pool in **H.**	2496
	4:12	and buried it in Abner's tomb at **H.**	2496
	5: 1	All the tribes of Israel came to David at **H**	2496
	5: 3	of Israel had come to King David at **H,**	2496
	5: 3	the king made a compact with them at **H**	2496
	5: 5	In **H** he reigned over Judah seven years	2496
	5:13	After he left **H,** David took more	2496
	15: 7	to **H** and fulfill a vow I made to the LORD.	2496
	15: 8	I will worship the LORD in **H.**' "	2496
	15: 9	So he went to **H.**	2496
	15:10	then say, 'Absalom is king in **H.'** "	2496
1Ki	2:11	in **H** and thirty-three in Jerusalem.	2496
1Ch	2:42	who was the father of **H.**	2497
	2:43	The sons of **H:**	2496
	3: 1	the sons of David born to him in **H:**	2496
	3: 4	These six were born to David in **H,**	2496
	6: 2	Amram, Izhar, **H** and Uzziel.	2497
	6:18	Amram, Izhar, **H** and Uzziel.	2497
	6:55	They were given **H** in Judah	2496
	6:57	So the descendants of Aaron were given **H**	2496
	11: 1	All Israel came together to David at **H**	2496
	11: 3	of Israel had come to King David at **H,**	2496
	11: 3	he made a compact with them at **H** before	2496
	12:23	at **H** to turn Saul's kingdom over to him, as	2496
	12:38	to **H** fully determined to make David king	2496
	15: 9	from the descendants of **H,** Eliel the leader	2497
	23:12	Amram, Izhar, **H** and Uzziel—four in all.	2497
	23:19	The sons of **H:**	2497
	24:23	The sons of **H:**	2497
	29:27	seven in **H** and thirty-three in Jerusalem.	2496
2Ch	11:10	Zorah, Aijalon and **H.** These were fortified	2496

HEBRONITE (1) [HEBRON]

Nu	26:58	the Libnite clan, the **H** clan,	2498

HEBRONITES (5) [HEBRON]

Nu	3:27	Izharites, **H** and Uzzielites;	2498
1Ch	26:23	the Izharites, the **H** and the Uzzielites,	2498
	26:30	From the **H:** Hashabiah	2498
	26:31	As for the **H,** Jeriah was their chief	2498
	26:31	among the **H** were found at Jazer in Gilead.	2157S

HEDGE (3) [HEDGED]

Job	1:10	not **put** a **h** around him and his household	8455
Isa	5: 5	I will take away its **h,**	5372
Mic	7: 4	the most upright worse than a **thorn h.**	5004

HEDGED (1) [HEDGE]

Job	3:23	whom God *has* **h** in?	6114

HEED (9) [HEEDED, HEEDS]

1Sa	15:22	and to **h** is better than the fat of rams.	7992
Ps	58: 5	that *will* not **h** the tune of the charmer,	9048
	94: 7	the God of Jacob **pays** no **h.**"	1067
	94: 8	Take **h,** *you* senseless ones among	1067
	107:43	*let him* **h** these things and consider	9068
Pr	1:24	when I called and no one **gave h**	7992
	16:20	*Whoever* **gives h** to instruction prospers,	8505
Ecc	7: 5	to **h** a wise man's rebuke than to listen to	9048
Mic	6: 9	"**H** the rod and the One who appointed it.	9048

HEEDED (2) [HEED]

Ecc	9:16	and his words *are* no longer **h.**	9048
	9:17	the wise *are* more to be **h** than the shouts of	9048

HEEDS (5) [HEED]

Pr	10:17	*He who* **h** discipline shows the way to life,	9068
	13: 1	A wise son **h** his father's instruction,	NIH
	13:18	but *whoever* **h** correction is honored.	9068
	15: 5	but *whoever* **h** correction shows prudence.	9068
	15:32	*whoever* **h** correction gains understanding.	9048

HEEL (6) [HEELS]

Ge	3:15	crush your head, and you will strike his **h.**"	6811
	25:26	with his hand grasping Esau's **h;**	6811
Job	18: 9	A trap seizes him by the **h;**	6811
Ps	41: 9	has lifted up his **h** against me.	6811
Hos	12: 3	**grasped** his brother's **h;**	6810
Jn	13:18	'He who shares my bread has lifted up his **h**	4761

HEELS (3) [HEEL]

Ge	49:17	that bites the horse's **h** so	6811
	49:19	but he will attack them at their **h.**	6811
La	5: 5	Those who pursue us are **at** our **h;**	6584+7418

HEGAI (4)

Est	2: 3	Let them be placed under the care of **H,**	2043
	2: 8	of Susa and put under the care of **H.**	2051
	2: 8	to the king's palace and entrusted to **H,**	2051
	2:15	she asked for nothing other than what **H,**	2051

HEIFER (15) [HEIFER'S]

Ge	15: 9	So the LORD said to him, "Bring me a **h,**	6320
Nu	19: 2	Tell the Israelites to bring you a red **h**	7239
	19: 5	While he watches, the **h** is to be burned—	7239
	19: 6	and throw them onto the burning **h.**	7239
	19: 9	up the ashes of the **h** and put them in	7239
	19:10	of the **h** must also wash his clothes,	7239
Dt	21: 3	town nearest the body shall take a **h**	1330+6320
	21: 6	the **h** whose neck was broken in the valley,	6320
Jdg	14:18	"If you had not plowed with my **h,**	6320
1Sa	16: 2	"Take a **h** with you and say,	1330+6320
Jer	46:20	"Egypt is a beautiful **h,**	6320
	50:11	a **h** threshing grain and neigh like stallions,	6320
Hos	4:16	Israelites are stubborn, like a stubborn **h.**	7239
	10:11	Ephraim is a trained **h** that loves to thresh;	6320
Heb	9:13	and bulls and the ashes *of* a **h** sprinkled	1239

HEIFER'S (1) [HEIFER]

Dt	21: 4	in the valley they are to break the **h** neck.	6320

HEIGHT (15) [HEIGHTS]

Nu	23: 3	Then he went off to a **barren h.**	9155
Jdg	6:26	to the LORD your God on the top of this **h.**	5057
1Sa	16: 7	not consider his appearance or his **h,**	1469+7757
1Ki	6:10	The **h** of each was five cubits,	7757
	6:26	The **h** of each cherub was ten cubits.	7757
Ne	4: 6	the wall till all of it **reached** half its **h,**	6330+8003
Isa	22:16	*on* the **h** and chiseling your resting place in	5294
Eze	19:11	for its **h** and for its many branches.	1470
	31:10	and because it was proud of its **h,**	1470
	31:14	so well-watered are ever to reach *such* a **h;**	1470
	43:13	And this is the **h** *of* the altar:	1470
Da	4:10	Its **h** was enormous.	10660
	8: 8	**h** of his **power** his large horn was broken	6793
Ro	8:39	neither **h** nor depth, nor anything else	5739
Rev	2: 5	the **h** from which you have fallen!	NIG

HEIGHTS (40) [HEIGHT]

Nu	21:28	the citizens of Arnon's **h.**	1195
	23: 9	from the **h** I view them.	1496
Dt	32:13	the **h** of the land and fed him with the fruit	1195
Jdg	5:18	so did Naphtali on the **h** of the field.	5294
2Sa	1:19	O Israel, lies slain on your **h.**	1195
	1:25	Jonathan lies slain on your **h.**	1195
	22:34	he enables me to stand on the **h.**	1195
2Ki	19:23	the **h** of the mountains,	5294
	19:23	the **utmost h** of Lebanon.	3752
Job	22:12	"Is not God in the **h** *of* heaven?	1470
	25: 2	he establishes order in the **h** of heaven.	5294
Ps	18:33	he enables me to stand on the **h.**	1195
	42: 6	the **h** of Hermon—from Mount Mizar.	3056
	48: 2	the **utmost h** of Zaphon is Mount Zion,	3752
	78:69	He built his sanctuary like the **h,**	8123
	148: 1	praise him in the **h above.**	
Pr	8: 2	On *the* **h** along the way,	5294+8031
Ecc	12: 5	when men are afraid of **h** and of dangers in	1469
Isa	7:11	depths or *in* the highest **h.**"	2025+4200+5089
	14:13	on the **utmost h** of the sacred mountain.	3752
	31: 4	to do battle on Mount Zion and on its **h.**	1496
	33:16	this is the man who will dwell **on the h,**	5294

Isa 37:24 the **h** *of* the mountains, 5294
37:24 the **utmost h** *of* Lebanon. 3752
37:24 I have reached its remotest **h**, 5294
41:18 I will make rivers flow on **barren h**, 9155
58:14 to ride on the **h** *of* the land and to feast on 1195
Jer 3: 2 "Look up to the **barren h** and see. 9155
3:21 A cry is heard on the **barren h**, 9155
4:11 "A scorching wind from the **barren h** in 9155
7:29 take up a lament on the **barren h**, 9155
12:12 Over all the **barren h** in the desert 9155
14: 6 on the **barren h** and pant like jackals; 9155
31:12 They will come and shout for joy on the **h** 5294
49:16 who occupy the **h** of the hill. 5294
Eze 17:23 On the mountain **h** *of* Israel I will plant it; 5294
34:14 and the mountain **h** *of* Israel will 5294
36: 2 The ancient **h** have become our possession. 1195
Ob 1: 3 of the rocks and make your home on the **h**, 5294
Hab 3:19 he enables me to go on the **h**. 1195

HEINOUS (KJV) See SHAMEFUL

HEIR (13) [INHERIT]
Ge 15: 3 so a servant in my household *will be* my **h**." 3769
15: 4 "This man *will* not *be* your **h**, 3769
15: 4 from your own body *will be* your **h**." 3769
2Sa 14: 7 then we will get rid of the **h** as well.' 3769
Ps 105:44 to what others had toiled for 3769
Mt 21:38 they said to each other, 'This is the **h**. 3101
Mk 12: 7 'This is the **h**. Come, let's kill him, 3101
Lk 20:14 'This is the **h**,' they said. 'Let's kill him, 3101
Ro 4:13 the promise that he would be **h** of the world, 3101
Gal 4: 1 What I am saying is that as long as the **h** is 3101
4: 7 you are a son, God has made you also an **h**. 3101
Heb 1: 2 whom he appointed **h** of all things, 3101
11: 7 and became **h** of the righteousness 3101

HEIRS (12) [INHERIT]
Jdg 21:17 The Benjamite survivors must have **h**," 3772
Jer 49: 1 "Has Israel no sons? Has she no **h**? 3769
Ac 3:25 And you are **h** of the prophets and of 5626
Ro 4:14 For if those who live by law are **h**, 3101
8:17 Now if we are children, then we are **h**— 3101
8:17 **h** of God and co-heirs with Christ, 3101
Gal 3:29 and **h** according to the promise. 3101
Eph 3: 6 the Gentiles are **h** together with Israel, 5169
Tit 3: 7 we might become **h** having the hope 3101
Heb 6:17 of his purpose very clear *to* the **h** 3101
11: 9 who *were* **h** with him of the same promise. 5169
1Pe 3: 7 as **h with** you of the gracious gift of life, 5169

HELAH (2)
1Ch 4: 5 of Tekoa had two wives, **H** and Naarah. 2690
4: 7 The sons of **H**: Zereth, Zohar, Ethnan, 2690

HELAM (2)
2Sa 10:16 they went to **H**, 2663
10:17 crossed the Jordan and went to **H**. 2663

HELBAH (1)
Jdg 1:31 or Ahlab or Aczib or **H** or Aphek or Rehob, 2695

HELBON (1)
Eze 27:18 in wine from **H** and wool from Zahar. 2696

HELD (83) [HOLD]
Ge 21: 8 on the day Isaac was weaned Abraham **h** 6913
27:41 Esau **h a grudge against** Jacob because of 8475
39:22 in charge of all those **h** in the prison, 659
40: 5 who *were* *being* **h** in prison— 673
41:36 This food should be **h** in reserve for 7214
Ex 17:11 As long as Moses **h** up his hands, 8123
17:12 Aaron and Hur **h** his hands **up**— 9461
21:19 *will* not be **h** responsible if the other gets 5927
21:28 of the bull will not be **h** responsible. 5929
Lev 5: 1 he *will be* **h** responsible. 5951+6411
5:17 he is guilty and *will be* **h** responsible. 5951+6411
7:18 of it *will be* **h** responsible. 5951+6411
17:16 he *will be* **h** responsible.' " 5951+6411
19: 8 Whoever eats *will be* **h** responsible 5951+6411
20:17 and *will be* **h** responsible. 5951+6411
20:19 both of you *would be* **h** responsible. 5951+6411
20:20 They *will be* **h** responsible; 2628+5951
24:15 he *will be* **h** responsible; 2628+5951
26:13 and enabled you to walk **with heads high**. 7758
Nu 28:16 the LORD's Passover is to be **h**. NIH
Dt 4: 1 but all of you who **h fast** to the LORD your 1816
Jos 8:18 So Joshua **h out** his javelin toward Ai. 5742
8:26 the hand that **h out** his javelin 5742
21:41 The towns of the Levites in the **territory** *h* AIT
Jdg 4: 5 She **h court** under the Palm of Deborah 3782
7:21 each man **h** his position around the camp, 6641
9:27 *they* **h** a festival in the temple of their god. 6913
16:26 Samson said to the servant who **h** his hand, 2616
1Sa 11:15 all the Israelites **h** a great **celebration**. 8523
2Sa 6:22 *I will* be **h** in honor." 3877
23:19 not **h** in greater **honor** than the Three? 3877
23:23 was **h** in greater **honor** than any of the 3877
1Ki 3:28 *they* **h** the king **in awe**, 3707
7:26 *It* **h** two thousand baths. 3920
8:47 in the land where *they* are **h** captive, 8647
11: 2 Solomon **h** fast to them in love. 1815
12:32 like the festival **h** in Judah, NIH

2Ki 18: 6 He **h** fast to the LORD and did not cease 1815
1Ch 11:25 was **h** in greater **honor** than any of the 3877
2Ch 4: 5 It **h** three thousand baths. 3920
6:37 in the land where *they* are **h** captive, 8647
7: 9 On the eighth day *they* **h** an assembly, 6913
Ne 4:17 with one hand and **h** a weapon in the other, 2616
Est 5: 2 and **h** out to her the gold scepter that was 3804
8:15 Susa **h** a **joyous celebration**. 7412
10: 3 **h** in high esteem by his many fellow Jews, 8354
Job 36: 8 **h** fast by cords of affliction, 4334
Ps 17: 5 My steps *have* **h** to your paths; 9461
106:46 to be pitied by all *who* **h** them **captive**. 8647
SS 3: 4 *I* **h** him and would not let him go 296
7: 5 the king *is* **h** captive by its tresses. 673
Isa 33:23 mast *is* not **h** secure, the sail is not spread. 2616
40:12 *Who has* **h** the dust of the earth in a basket, 3920
42:14 I have been quiet and **h** myself **back**. 706
65: 2 All day long *I* *have* **h** out 7298
Jer 2: 3 all who devoured her *were* **h** guilty, 870
Eze 31:15 *I* **h** back its streams, 4979
Mt 21:46 because the people **h** that he was a prophet. 2400
Mk 11:32 everyone **h** that John really was a prophet.) 2400
Lk 5:29 Then Levi **h** a great banquet for Jesus 4472
11:50 *be* **h** responsible **for** the blood of all 1699
11:51 this generation *will be* **h** responsible 1699
Ac 3:11 *While* the beggar **h** on to Peter and John, 3195
7:41 to it and **h** a celebration in honor 2370
19:17 the name of the Lord Jesus *was* **h** in high honor. 3486
25: 4 "Paul *is being* **h** at Caesarea, 5498
25:21 When Paul made his appeal *to be* **h** over 5498
25:21 I ordered him **h** until I could send him 5498
27:32 the soldiers cut the ropes that **h** the lifeboat NIG
27:40 and at the same time untied the ropes that **h** NIG
Ro 3:19 whole world **h accountable** to God. 1181+5688
10:21 "All day long *I* *have* **h** out my hands to 1736
Gal 3:23 we were **h** prisoners by the law, 5864
Eph 4:16 joined and **h together** by every supporting 5204
Col 1:23 from the hope **h** out in the gospel. NIG
2:19 and **h together** by its ligaments and sinews, 5204
2Ti 4:16 *May it* not be **h** against them. 3357
Heb 2:15 and free those who all their lives were **h** 1944
2Pe 2: 4 putting them into gloomy dungeons *to be* **h** 5498
Rev 1:16 In his right hand *he* **h** seven stars, 2400
6: 2 Its rider **h** a bow, and he was given a crown, 2400
15: 2 *They* **h** harps given them by God 2400
17: 1 *She* **h** a golden cup in her hand, 2400

HELDAI (3)
1Ch 27:15 was **H** the Netophathite, 2702
Zec 6:10 "Take [silver and gold] from the exiles **H**, 2702
6:14 The crown will be given to **H**, Tobijah, 2702

HELECH (1)
Eze 27:11 Men of Arvad and **H** manned your walls 2662

HELED (2)
2Sa 23:29 **H** son of Baanah the Netophathite, 2699
1Ch 11:30 **H** son of Baanah the Netophathite, 2699

HELEK (2) [HELEKITE]
Nu 26:30 through **H**, the Helekite clan; 2751
Jos 17: 2 the clans of Abiezer, **H**, Asriel, Shechem, 2751

HELEKITE (1) [HELEK]
Nu 26:30 through Helek, the **H** clan; 2757

HELEM (1)
1Ch 7:35 The sons of his brother **H**: 2152

HELEPH (1)
Jos 19:33 from **H** and the large tree in Zaanannim, 2738

HELEZ (5)
2Sa 23:26 **H** the Paltite, Ira son of Ikkesh from Tekoa, 2742
1Ch 2:39 Azariah the father of **H**, 2742
2:39 **H** the father of Eleasah, 2742
11:27 Shammoth the Harorite, **H** the Pelonite, 2742
27:10 for the seventh month, was **H** the Pelonite, 2742

HELI (1)
Lk 3:23 so it was thought, of Joseph, the son of **H**, 2459

HELIOPOLIS (1)
Eze 30:17 The young men of **H** and Bubastis will fall 225

HELKAI (1)
Ne 12:15 of Harim's, Adna; of Meremoth's, **H**; 2758

HELKATH (2) [HELKATH HAZZURIM]
Jos 19:25 Their territory included: **H**, Hali, Beten, 2762
21:31 **H** and Rehob, together 2762

HELKATH HAZZURIM (1) [HELKATH]
2Sa 2:16 in Gibeon was called **H**. 2763

HELL (14)
Mt 5:22 will be in danger of the fire of **h**. 1147

Mt 5:29 for your whole body to be thrown into **h**. 1147
5:30 for your whole body to go into **h**. 1147
10:28 both soul and body in **h**. 1147
18: 9 and be thrown into the fire *of* **h**. 1147
23:15 you make him twice as much a son of **h** 1147
23:33 will you escape being condemned to **h**? 1147
Mk 9:43 with two hands to go into **h**, 1147
9:45 to have two feet and be thrown into **h**, 1147
9:47 to have two eyes and be thrown into **h**, 1147
Lk 12: 5 has power to throw you into **h**. 1147
16:23 In **h**, where he was in torment, 87
Jas 3: 6 and is itself set on fire by **h**. 1147
2Pe 2: 4 when they sinned, but *sent* them to **h**, 5434

HELM (KJV) See RUDDER

HELMET (7) [HELMETS]
1Sa 17: 5 He had a bronze **h** on his head and wore 3916
17:38 of armor on him and a bronze **h** on his head. 7746
Ps 60: 7 Ephraim is my **h**, Judah my scepter. 5057+8031
108: 8 Ephraim is my **h**, Judah my scepter. 5057+8031
Isa 59:17 and the **h** of salvation on his head; 3916
Eph 6:17 Take the **h** of salvation and the sword of 4330
1Th 5: 8 and the hope of salvation as a **h**. 4330

HELMETS (5) [HELMET]
2Ch 26:14 Uzziah provided shields, spears, **h**, 3916
Jer 46: 4 Take your positions with **h** on! 3916
Eze 23:24 with large and small shields and with **h**. 7746
27:10 They hung their shields and **h** 3916
38: 5 all with shields and **h**, 3916

HELON (5)
Nu 1: 9 from Zebulun, Eliab son of **H**; 2735
2: 7 of the people of Zebulun is Eliab son of **H**. 2735
7:24 On the third day, Eliab son of **H**, 2735
7:29 This was the offering of Eliab son of **H**. 2735
10:16 and Eliab son of **H** was over the division of 2735

HELP (219) [HELPED, HELPER, HELPERS, HELPFUL, HELPING, HELPLESS, HELPS]
Ge 4: 1 "With the **h** of the LORD I have brought 907
39:15 When he heard me **scream for h**, he left his cloak 2256+7754+7924+8123
39:18 soon as I **screamed for h**, 2256+7754+7924+8123
Ex 1:16 the Hebrew women **in childbirth** 3528
2:23 and their **cry for h** because of their slavery 8784
4:12 I *will* **h** you speak and will teach you 2118+6640
4:15 I *will* **h** both of you speak 2118+6640
23: 1 *Do* not **h** a wicked man by being 3338+6640+8883
23: 5 be sure *you* **h** him with it. 6441+6641
31: 6 of the tribe of Dan, to **h** him. 907
Lev 25:35 **h** him as you would an alien or 2616
Nu 11:17 They will **h** you carry the burden of 907+2118
34:18 from each tribe to **h** assign the land. 5706
Dt 22: 4 **h** him get it to its feet. 6640
22:24 in a town and *did* not **scream for h**, 7590
32:38 Let them rise up to **h** you! 6468
33: 7 Oh, be his **h** against his foes!" 6469
33:26 on the heavens to **h** you and on the clouds 6469
Jos 1:14 *You are to* **h** your brothers 6468
10: 4 "Come up and **h** me attack Gibeon," 6468
10: 6 **h** us, because all the Amorite kings from 6468
10:33 up to **h** Lachish, but Joshua defeated him 6468
24: 7 But *they* **cried** to the LORD for **h**, 7590
Jdg 4: 3 *they* **cried for help**. 7590
5:23 because they did not come to **h** the LORD, 6476
5:23 to **h** the LORD against the mighty.' 6476
6: 6 *they* **cried out** to the LORD for **h**. 2410
10:12 *you* **cried** to me for **h**, 7590
12: 3 When I saw that you wouldn't **h**, 3828
1Sa 12: 8 *they* **cried** to the LORD for **h**, 2410
14:45 for he did this today **with God's h**." 6640
2Sa 3:12 will **h** you bring all Israel over to you. 3338+6640
8: 5 of Damascus came to **h** Hadadezer king 6468
10:19 So the Arameans were afraid to **h** 3828
14: 4 and she said, "**H** me, O king!" 3828
15:34 then you can **h** me by frustrating 4200
22:30 **With** your **h** I can advance against a troop; 928
22:42 *They* **cried** for **h**, but there was no one 8775
2Ki 4: 2 Elisha replied to her, "How can *I* **h** you? 4200+6913
6:26 a woman cried to him, "**H** me, 3828
6:27 "If the LORD *does* not **h** you, 3828
6:27 where *can* I *get* **h** for you? 3828
14:26 there was no *one* to **h** them. 6468
23:29 went up to the Euphrates River to **h** the king 6584
1Ch 12:17 "If you have come to me in peace, to **h** me, 6468
12:18 and success to *those who* **h** you, 6468
12:18 for your God *will* **h** you." 6468
12:19 *(He and his men did)* not **h** the Philistines 6468
12:22 Day after day men came to **h** David, 6468
12:33 to **h** David with undivided loyalty— 6370
18: 5 of Damascus came to **h** Hadadezer king 6468
19:19 not willing to **h** the Ammonites anymore. 3828
22:17 the leaders of Israel to **h** his son Solomon 6468
23:28 was to **h** Aaron's descendants in the 3338+4200
24: 3 **With the h** of Zadok a descendant of 2256
28:21 in any craft will **h** you in all the work. 6640
2Ch 14:11 there is no *one* like you to **h** the powerless 6468
14:11 **H** us, O LORD our God, for we rely on you, 6468
16:12 even in his illness *he did* not **seek h** *from* 2011

2Ch	19: 2	"Should you **h** the wicked	6468
	20: 4	people of Judah came together to **seek h**	1335
	25: 8	God has the power to **h** or to overthrow."	6468
	28:16	Ahaz sent to the king of Assyria for **h**.	6468
	28:20	but he gave him trouble instead of **h**.	2616
	28:21	but that did not **h** him	6476
	28:23	I will sacrifice to them so *they* will **h** me."	6468
	32: 8	with us is the LORD our God to **h** us and	6468
Ezr	4: 2	"Let us **h** you build because, like you,	6640
Ne	3:12	the next section who with his daughters	2256
	6:16	this work had been done **with the h of**	907+4946
Est	7: 9	who spoke up to **h** the king."	3202
Job	6:13	Do I have any power to **h** myself,	NIH
	6:21	Now you too have proved to be of no **h**;	NIH
	19: 7	though *I* **call for h**, there is no justice.	8775
	24:12	and the souls of the wounded **cry out for h**,	8775
	29:12	because I rescued the poor *who* **cried for h**,	8775
	30:24	a hand on a broken man when *he* **cries for h**	8780
	30:28	I stand up in the assembly and **cry for h**.	8775
	36:13	when he fetters *them, they* do not **cry for h**.	8775
Ps	5: 2	Listen to my **cry for h**,	7754+8776
	12: 1	**H**, LORD, for the godly are no more;	3828
	18: 6	*I* **cried** to my God for **h**.	8775
	18:29	**With your h** I can advance against a troop;	928
	18:41	*They* **cried for h**, but there was no one	8775
	20: 2	May he send you **h** from the sanctuary	6469
	22:11	for trouble is near and there is no *one* to **h**.	6468
	22:19	O my Strength, come quickly to **h** me.	6476
	22:24	from him but has listened to his **cry for h**.	8775
	28: 2	I **call** to you **for h**,	8775
	30: 2	*I* **called** to you **for h**	8775
	30:10	O LORD, be my **h**."	6468
	31:22	I **called** to you **for h**.	8775
	33:20	he is our **h** and our shield.	6469
	38:22	Come quickly to **h** me, O Lord my Savior.	6476
	39:12	O LORD, listen to my **cry for h**;	8784
	40:13	O LORD, come quickly to **h** me.	6476
	40:17	You are my **h** and my deliverer;	6476
	44:26	Rise up and **h** us;	6965
	46: 1	an ever-present **h** in trouble.	6476
	46: 5	God *will* **h** her at break of day.	6468
	54: 4	Surely God *is* my **h**;	6468
	56: 9	when *I* **call for h**.	7924
	59: 4	Arise to **h** me; look on my plight!	7925
	60: 5	Save us and **h** us with your right hand,	6699
	60:11	for the **h** of man is worthless.	9591
	63: 7	Because you are my **h**,	6476
	69: 3	I am worn out **calling for h**;	7924
	70: 1	O LORD, come quickly to **h** me.	6476
	70: 5	You are my **h** and my deliverer;	6469
	71:12	come quickly, O my God, to **h** me.	6476
	72:12	the afflicted who have no *one* to **h**.	6468
	77: 1	*I* **cried** out to God **for h**;	7590+7754
	79: 9	**H** us, O God our Savior,	6468
	88:13	But I **cry** to you **for h**, O LORD;	8775
	94:17	Unless the LORD had given me **h**,	6476
	102: 1	let my **cry for h** come to you.	8784
	107:12	they stumbled, and there was no *one* to **h**.	6468
	108: 6	Save us and **h** us with your right hand,	6699
	108:12	for the **h** of man is worthless.	9591
	109:26	**H** me, O LORD my God;	6468
	115: 9	he is their **h** and shield.	6469
	115:10	he is their **h** and shield.	6469
	115:11	he is their **h** and shield.	6469
	119:86	**h** me, for men persecute me without cause.	6468
	119:147	I rise before dawn and **cry for h**;	8775
	119:173	May your hand be ready to **h** me,	6468
	121: 1	where does my **h** come from?	6469
	121: 2	My **h** comes from the LORD,	6469
	124: 8	Our **h** is in the name of the LORD,	6469
	146: 5	Blessed is he whose **h** is the God of Jacob,	6469
Ecc	4:10	his friend *can* **h** him **up**.	7756
	4:10	and has no one to **h** him **up**!	7756
Isa	10: 3	To whom will you run for **h**?	6476
	20: 6	those we fled to for **h** and deliverance from	6476
	30: 2	*who* **look** to Pharaoh's protection,	6395
	30: 5	who bring neither **h** nor advantage,	6469
	30: 7	*whose* **h** is utterly useless.	6468
	30:19	How gracious he will be when you **cry for h**!	2410+7754
	31: 1	Woe to those who go down to Egypt for **h**,	6476
	31: 1	or **seek h** *from* the LORD.	2011
	31: 2	against *those who* **h** evildoers.	6476
	41:10	I will strengthen you and **h** you;	6468
	41:13	Do not fear; I *will* **h** you.	6468
	41:14	O little Israel, for I myself *will* **h** you,"	6468
	44: 2	and *who will* **h** you:	6468
	49: 8	and in the day of salvation *I* will **h** you;	6468
	57:13	When you **cry out for h**,	2410
	58: 9	*you* will **cry for h**, and he will say;	8775
	63: 5	I looked, but there was no *one* to **h**,	6468
	64: 5	**come** to the **h** of those who gladly do right,	7003
Jer	11:12	not **h** them **at all** when disaster strikes.	3828+3828
	47: 3	Fathers *will* not **turn** to **h** their children;	7155
	47: 4	to cut off all survivors *who could* **h** Tyre	6468
	50:32	and fall and no *one* will **h** her **up**;	7756
La	1: 7	there was no *one* to **h** her.	6468
	3: 8	Even when I call out or **cry for h**,	8775
	3:11	and mangled me and left me **without h**.	9037
	4: 6	in a moment without a hand turned to **h** her.	NIH
	4:17	our eyes failed, looking in vain for **h**;	6476
Eze	16:49	*they* did not **h** the poor and needy.	2616+3338
	17:17	and great horde *will be* of no **h** to him	6913
	29:16	of their sin in turning to her for **h**.	NIH
Da	11: 1	and **asking** God for **h**.	10274
	10:13	one of the chief princes, came to **h** me,	6468
	11:17	his plans will not succeed or **h** him.	2118+4200

Da	11:34	*they* will **receive** a little **h**,	6468+6469
	11:39	the mightiest fortresses **with the h of**	6640
	11:45	and no *one* will **h** him.	6468
Hos	5:13	**sent** to the great king **for h**.	8938
Jnh	2: 2	the depths of the grave / **called for h**,	8775
Hab	1: 2	How long, O LORD, *must I* **call for h**,	8775
Zec	6:15	and *h to* **build** the temple of the LORD,	AIT
Mt	8: 5	a centurion came to him, **asking for h**.	4151
	15: 5	**h** you might otherwise have received from	1565
	15:25	"Lord, **h** me!" she said.	1070
	25:44	sick or in prison, and *did not* **h** you?'	1354
Mk	7:11	**h** *you might* otherwise have **received**	6067
	9:22	take pity on us and **h** us."	1070
	9:24	**h** me overcome my unbelief!"	1070
	14: 7	you can **h** them any time you want.	2292+4472
Lk	4:38	and they asked Jesus to **h** her.	4309
	5: 7	in the other boat *to* come and **h** them,	5197
	7:16	"God has **come to h** his people."	2170
	10:40	Tell her *to* **h** me!"	5269
	11:46	not lift one finger to **h** them.	5845
Jn	5: 7	"I have no one *to* **h** me into the pool when	965
	12: 6	of the money bag, *he* used to **h** himself to	1002
Ac	2:23	and you, with the **h** of wicked men,	5931
	4:20	For we cannot **h speaking** about	3281+3590
	11:29	to provide **h** for the brothers living in Judea.	1355
	16: 9	"Come over to Macedonia and **h** us."	1070
	18:27	he *was* a great **h** to those who	5202
	20:35	that by this kind of hard work we must **h**	514
	21:28	"Men of Israel, **h** us!	1070
	26:22	But I have had God's **h** to this very day,	2135
Ro	16: 2	to give her any **h** she may need from you,	NIG
	16: 2	for she has been a great **h** to many people,	4706
1Co	12:28	**those able to h** others,	516
	16: 6	**h** me on my *journey*,	4636
2Co	1:11	*as* you **h** us by your prayers.	5348
	8:19	and to show our eagerness to **h**.	NIG
	9: 2	For I know your eagerness **to h**,	5642
Php	1:19	that through your prayers and the **h given**	2221
	2:30	to make up for the **h** you could not give me.	3311
	4: 3	**h** these women who have contended	5197
1Th	2: 2	but **with the h of** our God we dared	1877
	5:14	**h** the weak, be patient with everyone.	504
2Th	3: 9	because we do not have the right to such **h**,	NIG
1Ti	5: 5	**pray** and to ask God for **h**.	1255
	5:16	she should **h** them and not let the church	2064
	5:16	church can **h** those widows who are really	2064
2Ti	1:14	the **h** of the Holy Spirit who lives in us.	NIG
Tit	3:13	to **h** Zenas the lawyer and Apollos on *their way*	4636
Heb	2:18	to **h** those who are being tempted.	1070
	4:16	and find grace to **h** us in our time of need.	1069
	6:10	and *continue* to **h** them.	1354
1Pe	5:12	**With the h of** Silas,	1328
3Jn	1: 7	receiving no **h** from the pagans.	NIG

HELPED (31) [HELP]

Jdg	9:24	had **h** him murder his brothers.	906+2616+3338
1Sa	7:12	saying, "Thus far *has* the LORD **h** us."	6468
	23:16	to David at Horesh and **h** him **find strength**	906+2616+3338
2Ki	10:15	he did, and Jehu **h** him up into the chariot.	6590
1Ch	5:20	*They* were **h** in fighting them,	6468
	12: 1	among the warriors *who* **h** him *in* battle;	6468
	12:21	They **h** David against raiding bands,	6468
	15:26	Because God *had* **h** the Levites	6468
2Ch	18:31	cried out, and the LORD **h** him.	6468
	20:23	*they* to destroy one another.	6468
	26: 7	God **h** him against the Philistines and	6468
	26:15	he was greatly **h** until he became powerful.	6468
	28:23	the gods of the kings of Aram *have* **h** them,	6468
	29:34	so their kinsmen the Levites **h** them until	2616
	32: 3	and *they* **h** him.	6468
Est	9: 3	and the king's administrators **h** the Jews,	5951
Job	26: 2	"How you have **h** the powerless!	6468
	26: 4	Who has **h** you utter these words?	907
Ps	28: 7	my heart trusts in him, and *I* am **h**.	6468
	86:17	O LORD, *have* **h** me and comforted me.	6468
	118:13	about to fall, but the LORD **h** me.	6468
Isa	31: 3	he who is **h** will fall;	6468
Jer	2:37	*you* will not *be* **h** by them.	7503
Mk	1:31	he went to her, took her hand and **h** her **up**.	1586
Lk	1:54	He has **h** his servant Israel,	514
Ac	1586	Taking him by the right hand, *he* **h** him **up**,	1586
	9:41	by the hand and **h** her **to her feet**.	482
2Co	6: 2	and in the day of salvation *I* **h** you."	1070
2Ti	1:18	in how many ways *he* **h** me in Ephesus.	1354
Heb	6:10	*as you have* **h** his people and continue	1354
Rev	12:16	the earth **h** the woman by opening its mouth	1070

HELPER (11) [HELP]

Ge	2:18	I will make a **h** suitable for him."	6469
	2:20	But for Adam no suitable **h** was found.	6469
Ex	18: 4	for he said, "My father's God was my **h**;	6469
Dt	33:29	and **h** and your glorious sword.	6469
Ne	4:22	and his **h** stay inside Jerusalem at night,	5853
Ps	10:14	you are the **h** of the fatherless.	6468
	27: 9	you have been my **h**.	6476
	118: 7	The LORD is with me; *he is* my **h**.	6468
Hos	13: 9	because you are against me, against your **h**.	6468
Ac	13: 5	John was with them as their **h**.	5677
Heb	13: 6	"The Lord is my **h**; I will not be afraid.	1071

HELPERS (2) [HELP]

Eze	30: 8	I set fire to Egypt and all her **h** are crushed.	6468
Ac	19:22	He sent two *of* his **h**, Timothy and Erastus,	1354

HELPFUL (3) [HELP]

Ac	20:20	to preach anything that *would be* **h** to you	5237
Eph	4:29	but only what is **h** for building others up	19
2Ti	4:11	because he is **h** to me in my ministry.	2378

HELPING (8) [HELP]

Jos	14:12	but, the LORD **h** me, I will drive them out	907
Jdg	21:22	'Do us a kindness by **h** them,	NIH
Ezr	5: 2	prophets of God were with them, **h** them.	10514
Job	30:13	without *anyone's* **h** them.	6468
Lk	8: 3	These women *were* **h to support** them out	1354
Ac	9:36	who was always doing good and **h the poor.**	1797+4472
1Ti	5:10	**h** those in trouble and devoting herself	2064
Phm	1:13	in **h** me while I am in chains for the gospel.	1354

HELPLESS (9) [HELP]

Ps	10: 9	he lies in wait to catch the **h**;	6714
	10: 9	he catches the **h** and drags them off	6714
	10:12	Do not forget the **h**.	6705
	69:20	and *has left* me **h**;	5683
Pr	28:15	a wicked man ruling over a **h** people.	1924
Jer	48:45	the fugitives stand **h**, for a fire has	3946+4946
Da	10: 8	my face turned deathly pale and *I* was **h**.	3946+4202+6806
	10:16	my lord, and *I am* **h**.	3946+4202+6806
Mt	9:36	because they were harassed and **h**,	4849

HELPS (8) [HELP]

Ge	49:25	who **h** you, because of the Almighty,	6468
Ps	37:40	The LORD **h** them and delivers them;	6468
Isa	3: 3	*he who* **h** will stumble,	6468
	41: 6	each **h** the other and says to his brother,	6468
	50: 7	Because the Sovereign LORD **h** me,	6468
	50: 9	It is the Sovereign LORD *who* **h** me.	6468
Ro	8:26	the Spirit **h** us in our weakness.	5269
Heb	2:16	For surely it is not angels *he* **h**,	2138

HEM (10) [HEMMED]

Ex	28:33	and scarlet yarn around the **h** *of* the robe,	8767
	28:34	to alternate around the **h** *of* the robe.	8767
	39:24	and finely twisted linen around the **h** *of*	8767
	39:25	of pure gold and attached them around the **h**	8767
	39:26	the **h** *of* the robe to be worn for ministering,	8767
1Sa	15:27	Saul caught hold of the **h** *of* his robe,	4053
Ps	139: 5	You **h** me in—behind and before;	7443
Hab	1: 4	The wicked **h** in the righteous,	4193
Zec	8:23	of one Jew by the **h** *of his robe* and say,	4053
Lk	19:43	and encircle you and **h** you **in** on every side.	5309

HEMAN (16) [HEMAN'S]

1Ki	4:31	wiser than **H**, Calcol and Darda,	2124
1Ch	2: 6	Zimri, Ethan, **H**, Calcol and Darda—	2124
	6:33	**H**, the musician, the son of Joel;	2124
	15:17	So the Levites appointed **H** son of Joel;	2124
	15:19	The musicians **H**, Asaph and Ethan were	2124
	16:41	With them were **H** and Jeduthun and the	2124
	16:42	**H** and Jeduthun were responsible for	2124
	25: 1	**H** and Jeduthun for the ministry	2124
	25: 4	As for **H**, from his sons:	2124
	25: 5	All these were sons of **H** the king's seer.	2124
	25: 5	God gave **H** fourteen sons	2124
	25: 6	Jeduthun and **H** were under the supervision	2124
2Ch	5:12	**H**, Jeduthun and their sons and relatives—	2124
	29:14	the descendants of **H**, Jehiel and Shimei;	2124
	35:15	Asaph, **H** and Jeduthun the king's seer.	2124
Ps	88: T	A maskil of **H** the Ezrahite.	2124

HEMAN'S (1) [HEMAN]

1Ch	6:39	and **H** associate Asaph, who served	2257S

HEMATH (KJV) See HAMATH, HAMMATH

HEMDAN (2)

Ge	36:26	**H**, Eshban, Ithran and Keran.	2777
1Ch	1:41	**H**, Eshban, Ithran and Keran.	2777

HEMLOCK (KJV) See POISON, POISONOUS

HEMMED (1) [HEM]

Ex	14: 3	**h** in by the desert.'	6037

HEN (3)

Zec	6:14	and **H** son of Zephaniah as a memorial in	2835
Mt	23:37	as a **h** gathers her chicks under her wings,	3998
Lk	13:34	as a **h** gathers her chicks under her wings,	3998

HENA (3)

2Ki	18:34	are the gods of Sepharvaim, **H** and Ivvah?	2184
	19:13	Sepharvaim, or of **H** or Ivvah?"	2184
Isa	37:13	Sepharvaim, or of **H** or Ivvah?"	2184

HENADAD (4)

Ezr	3: 9	the sons of **H** and their sons and brothers—	2836
Ne	3:18	by their countrymen under Binnui son of **H**,	2836
	3:24	Binnui son of **H** repaired another section,	2836
	10: 9	Binnui of the sons of **H**, Kadmiel,	2836

HENCE (KJV) See AWAY, FROM HERE, LEAVE, PLACE, SOMEWHERE ELSE

HENNA (2)
SS	1:14	a cluster of **h** blossoms from the vineyards	4110
	4:13	with choice fruits, with **h** and nard,	4110

HENOCH (KJV) See ENOCH

HEPHER (9) [GATH HEPHER, HEPHERITE]
Nu	26:32	through **H**, the Hepherite clan.	2918
	26:33	(Zelophehad son of **H** had no sons;	2918
	27: 1	The daughters of Zelophehad son of **H**,	2918
Jos	12:17	the king of Tappuah one the king of **H** one	2919
	17: 2	Helek, Asriel, Shechem, **H** and Shemida.	2918
	17: 3	Now Zelophehad son of **H**,	2918
1Ki	4:10	and all the land of **H** were his);	2919
1Ch	4: 6	Naarah bore him Ahuzzam, **H**,	2918
	11:36	**H** the Mekerathite, Ahijah the Pelonite,	2918

HEPHERITE (1) [HEPHER]
Nu	26:32	through Hepher, the **H** clan.	2920

HEPHZIBAH (2)
2Ki	21: 1	His mother's name was **H**.	2915
Isa	62: 4	But you will be called **H**,	2915

HER (1669) [SHE] See Index of Articles Etc.

HERALD (4)
Da	3: 4	Then the **h** loudly proclaimed,	10370
Hab	2: 2	on tablets so that a **h** may run with it.	7924
1Ti	2: 7	And for this purpose I was appointed a **h**	3061
2Ti	1:11	And of this gospel I was appointed a **h** and	3061

HERBS (6)
Ex	12: 8	along with **bitter h**, and bread made	5353
Nu	9:11	with unleavened bread and **bitter h**.	5353
2Ki	4:39	the fields to gather **h** and found a wild vine.	246
Job	30: 4	In the brush they gathered **salt h**,	4865
La	3:15	He has filled me with **bitter h** and sated me	5353
Lk	11:42	rue and all other kinds of **garden h**,	3303

HERD (21) [HERDED, HERDING, HERDS, HERDSMEN]
Ge	18: 7	Then he ran to the **h** and selected a choice,	1330
	32:16	care of his servants, **each h** by itself,	6373+6373
Ex	34:19	whether from **h** or flock.	8802
Lev	1: 2	as your offering an animal from either the **h**	1330
	1: 3	the offering is a burnt offering from the **h**,	1330
	3: 1	and he offers an animal from the **h**,	1330
	22:21	from the **h** or flock a fellowship offering to	1330
	27:32	The entire tithe of the **h** and flock—	1330
Nu	15: 3	from the **h** or the flock,	1330
Dt	16: 2	an animal from your flock or **h** at the place	1330
	32:14	with curds and milk from **h** and flock and	1330
Jdg	6:25	"Take the second bull from your father's **h**,	8802
Ps	68:30	**h** of bulls among the calves of the nations.	6337
Jnh	3: 7	Do not let any man or beast, **h** or flock,	1330
Mt	8:30	from them a large **h** of pigs was feeding.	36
	8:31	send us into the **h** of pigs."	36
	8:32	and the whole **h** rushed down the steep bank	36
Mk	5:11	A large **h** of pigs was feeding on	36
	5:13	The **h**, about two thousand in number,	36
Lk	8:32	A large **h** of pigs was feeding there on	36
	8:33	and the **h** rushed down the steep bank into	36

HERDED (1) [HERD]
Isa	24:22	*They will* be **h together** like	665+669

HERDING (1) [HERD]
1Sa	25:16	around us all the time we were **h** our sheep	8286

HERDS (53) [HERD]
Ge	13: 5	also flocks and **h** and tents.	1330
	26:14	He had so many flocks and **h** and	1330+5238
	32: 7	and the flocks and **h** and camels as well.	1330
	32:16	and keep some space between the **h**."	6373
	32:19	and all the others who followed the **h**:	6373
	34:28	They seized their flocks and **h** and donkeys	1330
	45:10	your flocks and **h**, and all you have.	1330
	46:32	and **h** and everything they own.'	1330
	47: 1	and **h** and everything they own,	1330
	50: 8	and their flocks and **h** were left in Goshen.	1330
Ex	10: 9	and with our flocks and **h**,	1330
	10:24	only leave your flocks and **h** behind."	1330
	12:32	Take your flocks and **h**, as you have said,	1330
	12:38	both flocks and **h**.	1330
	34: 3	not even the flocks and **h** may graze in front	1330
Nu	11:22	if flocks and **h** were slaughtered for them?	1330
	31: 9	and children and took all the Midianite **h**,	989
	32: 1	who had very large **h and flocks**,	5238
	32:26	our flocks and **h** will remain here in	989
Dt	7:13	of your **h** and the lambs of your flocks in	546
	8:13	and when your flocks and **h** grow large	1330
	12: 6	and the firstborn of your **h** and flocks.	1330
	12:17	or the firstborn of your **h** and flocks,	1330
	12:21	the **h** and flocks the LORD has given you,	1330
	14:23	and the firstborn of your **h** and flocks in	1330
	15:19	of your **h** and flocks.	1330
	28: 4	of your **h** and the lambs of your flocks.	546
	28:18	of your **h** and the lambs of your flocks.	546
	28:51	nor any calves of your **h** or lambs	546
Jos	14: 4	with pasturelands for their flocks and **h**.	7871
	22: 8	with large **h of livestock**, with silver,	5238
1Sa	30:20	He took all the flocks and **h**,	1330
2Ki	5:26	flocks, **h**, or menservants and maidservants?	1330
1Ch	27:29	the Sharonite was in charge of the **h** grazing	1330
	27:29	Shaphat son of Adlai was in charge of the **h**	1330
2Ch	31: 6	also brought a tithe of their **h** and flocks and	1330
	32:29	and acquired great numbers of flocks and **h**,	1330
Ne	10:36	of our **h** and of our flocks to the house	1330
Job	1:10	that his **flocks and h** are spread throughout	5238
Ps	8: 7	all flocks and **h**, and the beasts of the field,	546
	107:38	and he did not let their **h** diminish.	989
Pr	27:23	give careful attention to your **h**;	6373
Ecc	2: 7	I also owned more **h** and flocks than anyone	1330
Isa	60: 6	**H** of camels will cover your land,	9180
	65:10	the Valley of Achor a resting place for **h**,	1330
Jer	3:24	their flocks and **h**, their sons and daughters.	1330
	5:17	they will devour your flocks and **h**,	1330
	31:12	the young of the flocks and **h**.	1330
	49:32	and their large **h** will be booty.	5238
Hos	5: 6	with their flocks and **h** to seek the LORD,	1330
Joel	1:18	**h** mill about because they have no pasture;	1330+6373
Zep	2:14	**Flocks and h** will lie down there,	6373
Jn	4:12	as did also his sons and his **flocks and h**?"	2576

HERDSMEN (6) [HERD]
Ge	13: 7	quarreling arose between Abram's **h**	5238+8286
	13: 7	Abram's herdsmen and the **h** of Lot.	5238+8286
	13: 8	or between your **h** and mine,	8286
	26:20	But the **h** of Gerar quarreled	8286
	26:20	of Gerar quarreled with Isaac's **h** and said,	8286
2Ch	14:15	the camps of the **h** and carried off droves	5238

HERE (398) [HERE'S, HEREBY]
Ge	3:12	"The woman you put **h** with me—	AIT
	12:19	Now then, **h** is your wife.	2180
	15:16	In the fourth generation your descendants	
		will come back **h**,	2025+2178
	19: 9	they said, "This fellow came **h** as an alien,	NIH
	19:12	"Do you have anyone else **h**—	7024
	19:12	Get them out of **h**,	2021+5226ˢ
	19:15	and your two daughters who *are* **h**,	5162
	19:20	Look, **h** is a town near enough to run to,	2296
	19:31	there is no man around **h** to lie with us	824+2021ˢ
	21:23	swear to me **h** before God that you will	2178
	22: 5	"Stay **h** with the donkey while I and	7024
	22: 7	"The fire and wood are **h**," Isaac said,	2180
	22:11	"**H** I am," he replied.	2180
	23: 4	for a burial site **h** so I can bury my dead."	6640
	24:31	"Why are you standing **out h**?	928+2021+2575
	24:51	**H** is Rebekah; take her	2180
	27: 1	"**H** I am," he answered.	2180
	27:26	Then his father Isaac said to him, "**Come h**,	5602
	29: 6	"and **h** comes his daughter Rachel with	2180
	29:19	**Stay h** with me.	AIT
	29:26	"It is not our custom **h** to give	928+5226ˢ
	30: 3	she said, "**H** is Bilhah, my maidservant,	2180
	31:11	I answered, '**H** I am.'	2180
	31:32	here is anything of yours **h** with me;	AIT
	31:37	Put it **h** in front of your relatives and mine,	3907
	31:51	Laban also said to Jacob, "**H** is this heap,	2180
	31:51	and **h** is this pillar I have set up	2180
	37:17	"They have moved on from **h**,"	2296
	37:19	"**H** comes that dreamer!"	2180
	37:22	Throw him into this cistern **h** in the desert,	889
	38:21	hasn't been any shrine prostitute **h**,"	928+2296
	38:22	hasn't been any shrine prostitute **h**.' "	928+2296
	39:14	He came in **h** to sleep with me,	NIH
	40:15	and even **h** I have done nothing	7024
	42:15	unless your youngest brother comes **h**.	2178
	42:19	let one of your brothers stay **h** in prison,	AIT
	42:28	"**H** it is in my sack."	2180
	42:33	Leave one of your brothers *h* with me,	AIT
	43: 7	'Bring your brother down **h**'?"	NIH
	43: 9	not bring him back to you and set him **h**	NIH
	43:18	"We were brought **h** because of the silver	NIH
	43:20	"we came down **h** the first time to buy food.	NIH
	44:33	please let your servant remain **h**	AIT
	45: 5	be angry with yourselves for selling me **h**,	2178
	45: 8	it was not you who sent me **h**, but God.	2178
	45:13	And bring my father down **h** quickly."	NIH
	46: 2	"**H** I am," he replied.	2180
	47: 4	"We have come to live **h** awhile,	824+928+2021ˢ
	47:23	**h** is seed for you so you can plant	2026
	48: 5	in Egypt before I came to you **h** will	2025+5213ˢ
	48: 5	They are the sons God has given me **h**,	928+2296
Ex	3: 4	And Moses said, "**H** I am."	2180
	8:25	"Go, sacrifice to your God **h** in the land."	NIH
	11: 1	After that, he will let you go from **h**,	2296
	24:12	up to me on the mountain and stay **h**,	9004
	24:14	"Wait **h** for us until we come back to	928+2296
	33:15	do not send us up from **h**.	2296
Lev	10: 4	and said to them, "**Come h**;	7928
Nu	5:21	**h** the priest is to put the woman	2256
	11:21	"**H** I am among six hundred thousand men	889
	11:23	flow with milk and honey!' **H** is its fruit.	2296
	14:33	children will be shepherds **h**	928+2021+4497ˢ
	14:35	in this desert; **h** they will die."	9004

Nu	20: 4	that we and our livestock should die **h**?	9004
	20:16	"Now we are **h** at Kadesh,	NIH
	20:18	"You may not pass through **h**;	3276ˢ
	22: 8	"Spend the night **h**," Balaam said to them,	7024
	22:19	Now stay **h** tonight as the others did,	928+2296
	22:32	I have come **h** to oppose you	2180
	23: 1	Balaam said, "Build me seven altars **h**,	928+2296
	23: 3	"Stay **h** beside your offering while I go	NIH
	23:15	"Stay **h** beside your offering while I meet	3907
	23:29	Balaam said, "Build me seven altars **h**,	928+2296
	32: 6	countrymen go to war while you sit **h**?	7024
	32:14	"And **h** you are, a brood of sinners,	2180
	32:16	to build pens **h** for our livestock and cities	7024
	32:26	our flocks and herds will remain **h** in	9004
	33: 1	**H** are the stages in the journey of	465
Dt	5: 3	with all of us who are alive **h** today.	7024
	5:31	But you stay **h** with me so	7024
	9: 4	"The LORD has brought me **h**	NIH
	9: 7	the day you left Egypt until you arrived **h**,	2021+2021+2296+5226ˢ
	9:12	LORD told me, "Go down from **h** at once,	2296
	12: 8	You are not to do as we do **h** today,	7024
	22:17	**h** is the proof of my daughter's virginity."	465
	29:12	You are standing **h** in order to enter into	NIH
	29:15	who are standing **h** with us today in	7024
	29:15	but also with those who are not **h** today.	7024
	29:16	through the countries on the way **h**.	NIH
Jos	1:11	the Jordan **h** to go in and take possession of	2296
	2: 2	the Israelites have come **h** tonight to spy out	2178
	3: 9	"Come **h** and listen to the words of	2178
	10:24	"**Come h** and put your feet on the necks	7928
	14:10	So **h** I am today, eighty-five years old!	2180
	18: 6	bring them **h** to me and I will cast lots	2178
	18: 8	and I will cast lots for you **h** at Shiloh in	7024
Jdg	4:20	by and asks you, 'Is anyone **h**?'	7024
	8:15	"**H** are Zebah and Zalmunna,	2180
	13:10	to tell her husband, "He's **h**!	2180
	14:15	Did you invite us **h** to rob us?"	NIH
	16: 2	people of Gaza were told, "Samson is **h**!"	2178
	18: 3	"Who brought you **h**?	2151
	18: 3	Why are you **h**?"	7024
	19: 9	Spend the night **h**; the day is nearly over.	2180
	19:24	Look, **h** is my virgin daughter,	NIH
Ru	2: 8	in another field and don't go away from **h**.	2296
	2: 8	Stay **h** with my servant girls.	3907
	2:14	to her, "**Come over h**.	2151
	3:13	Stay **h** for the night,	NIH
	3:13	Lie **h** until morning."	NIH
	4: 1	"**Come over h**, my friend, and sit down."	7024
	4: 2	"Sit **h**," and they did so.	7024
	4: 4	of these seated **h** and in the presence of	NIH
1Sa	1:16	I have been praying **h** out	2178+6330
	1:23	"Stay **h** until you have weaned him;	NIH
	1:26	woman who stood **h** beside you praying	928+2296
	3: 4	Samuel answered, "**H** I am."	2180
	3: 5	And he ran to Eli and said, "**H** I am;	2180
	3: 6	"**H** I am; you called me."	2180
	3: 8	"**H** I am; you called me."	2180
	3:16	Samuel answered, "**H** I am."	2180
	5: 7	"The ark of the god of Israel must not stay **h**	NIH
	6:20	To whom will the ark go up from **h**?	5646ˢ
	9:11	and they asked them, "Is the seer **h**?"	928+2296
	9:24	is what has been kept for you.	2180
	9:27	"but you stay **h** awhile,	NIH
	10:22	"Has the man come **h** yet?"	2151
	12: 2	and my sons are **h** with you.	2180
	12: 3	**H** I stand. Testify against me	2180
	12: 7	stand **h**, because I am going to confront you	NIH
	14:33	Now **h** is the king you have chosen,	2180
	14:33	"Roll a large stone over **h** at once."	3276ˢ
	14:34	and slaughter them **h** and eat them.	928+2296
	14:36	the priest said, "Let us inquire of God **h**."	2151
	14:38	Saul therefore said, "**Come h**,	2151
	14:40	I and Jonathan my son will stand **over h**."	285+4200+6298
	16: 6	"Surely the LORD's anointed stands **h**	NIH
	16:16	Let our lord command his servants **h**	4200+7156
	17:28	"Why have you come down **h**?	2296
	17:44	"Come **h**," he said, "and I'll give your flesh	448
	17:47	All those gathered **h** will know that it is not	NIH
	18:17	"**H** is my older daughter Merab.	2180
	20:21	bring them **h**,' then come, because,	NIH
	21: 4	there is some consecrated bread **h**—	NIH
	21: 8	"Don't you have a spear or a sword **h**?	7024
	21: 9	in the Valley of Elah, is **h**;	2180
	21: 9	there is no sword **h** but that one."	928+2296
	21:15	that you have to bring this fellow **h** to carry	NIH
	23: 3	"**H** in Judah we are afraid.	7024
	25:41	"**H** is your maidservant,	2180
	26:22	"**H** is the king's spear," David answered.	2180
	30:26	"**H** is a present for you from the plunder of	2180
2Sa	1:10	and have brought them **h** to my lord."	2178
	4: 8	"**H** is the head of Ish-Bosheth son of Saul,	2180
	5: 6	"You will not get in **h**;	2178
	5: 6	They thought, "David cannot get in **h**.	2178
	7: 2	"**H** I am, living in a palace of cedar,	8011
	11:12	said to him, "Stay **h** one more day,	928+2296
	13: 9	"Send everyone out of **h**," Amnon	3276+6584ˢ
	13:10	the food **h** into my bedroom so I may eat	NIH
	13:17	**Get** this woman out **h**	2021+2025+2575+8938
	13:35	"See, the king's sons *are* **h**;	995
	14:32	'Come **h** so I can send you to the king	2178
	18:30	The king said, "Stand aside and wait **h**."	3907
	19:20	but today I have come **h** as the first of	2180
	19:37	But **h** is your servant Kimham.	2180
	20: 4	and be **h** yourself."	7024
	20:16	Tell Joab to come **h** so I can speak to him."	2178

2Sa	24:22	**H** are oxen for the burnt offering,	8011
	24:22	and **h** are threshing sledges and ox yokes	NIH
1Ki	1:23	told the king, "Nathan the prophet is **h.**"	2180
	2:30	But he answered, "No, I will die **h.**	7024
	3: 8	Your servant is **h** among the people	NIH
	9:15	**H** is the account of the forced labor	2296
	11:22	"What have you lacked **h** that you	3276+6640S
	11:27	is the account of how he rebelled against	2296
	12:28	**H** are your gods, O Israel,	2180
	13: 2	who now make offerings **h,**	3870+6584S
	13: 8	nor would I eat bread or drink water **h.**	928+2021+2021+2296+5226S
	17: 3	"Leave **h,** turn eastward and hide in	2296
	18: 8	"Go tell your master, 'Elijah is **h.**'"	2180
	18:11	to go to my master and say, 'Elijah is **h.**'	2180
	18:14	to go to my master and say, 'Elijah is **h.**'	2180
	18:30	**"Come h** to me."	5602
	19: 9	"What are you doing **h,** Elijah?"	7024
	19:13	a voice said to him, "What are you doing **h,**	7024
	20:40	While your servant was busy **h** and there,	2178
	22: 7	of the LORD whom we can inquire of?"	7024
2Ki	2: 2	Elijah said to Elisha, "Stay **h;**	7024
	2: 4	Then Elijah said to him, "Stay **h,** Elisha;	7024
	2: 6	Then Elijah said to him, "Stay **h;**	7024
	3:11	"Is there no prophet of the LORD **h,**	7024
	3:11	Elisha son of Shaphat is **h.**	7024
	7: 3	"Why stay **h** until we die?	7024
	7: 4	And if we stay **h,** we will die.	7024
	7:13	be like that of all the Israelites left **h—**	928+2023S
	8: 7	of God has come all the way up **h,**"	2178
	9:12	Jehu said, "**H** is what he told me:	2256+2296+2296+3869+3869
	10:23	and see that no servants of the LORD are **h**	7024
	19:32	not enter this city or shoot an arrow **h.**	9004
1Ch	6:33	**H** are the men who served,	465
	11: 5	"You will not get in **h.**"	2178
	17: 1	he said to Nathan the prophet, "**H** I am,	2180
	22: 1	"The house of the LORD God is to be **h,**	2296
	25: 1	*H* is the list of the men who performed	AIT
	29:17	willingly your people who are **h** have given	7024
2Ch	18: 6	of the LORD **h** whom we can inquire of?"	7024
	20:10	"But now **h** are men from Ammon,	2180
	28:13	"You must not bring those prisoners **h,**"	2178
	34:28	on this place and on those who live **h.**'"	2257S
Ezr	4: 2	king of Assyria, who brought us **h.**"	7024
	9:15	**H** we are before you in our guilt,	2180
	10:13	But there are many people **h** and it is	NIH
Ne	13: 7	I learned about the evil thing	2256
Job	27:13	"**H** is the fate God allots to the wicked,	2296
	38:11	is where your proud waves halt'?	7024
	38:35	Do they report to you, '**H** we are'?	2180
Ps	40: 7	Then I said, "**H** I am, I have come—	2180
	52: 7	"**H** now is the man who did not make	2180
	132:14	**h** I will sit enthroned, for I have desired it—	7024
	132:17	"**H** I will make a horn grow for David	9004
Pr	9: 4	"Let all who are simple come in **h!**"	2178
	9:16	"Let all who are simple come in **h!**"	2178
	25: 7	"Come up **h,**" than for him to humiliate you	2178
Ecc	1:10	It was **h** already, long ago;	NIH
	1:10	it was **h** before our time.	NIH
	12:13	**h** is the conclusion of the matter:	NIH
SS	2: 8	**H** he comes, leaping across the mountains,	2296
Isa	5:26	**H** they come, swiftly and speedily!	2180
	6: 8	And I said, "**H** am I.	2180
	8:18	**H** am I, and the children	2180
	21: 9	**h** comes a man in a chariot with a team	2296
	22:16	What are you doing **h**	7024
	22:16	to cut out a grave for yourself **h,**	7024
	28:10	a little **h,** a little there."	9004
	28:13	a little **h,** a little there—	9004
	37:33	not enter this city or shoot an arrow **h.**	9004
	40: 9	say to the towns of Judah, "**H** is your God!"	2180
	41:27	the first to tell Zion, 'Look, **h** they are!'	2180
	42: 1	"**H** is my servant, whom I uphold,	2176
	47:14	**H** are no coals to warm anyone;	401
	47:14	**h** is no fire to sit by.	NIH
	52: 5	"And now what do I have **h?**"	7024
	57: 3	come **h,** you sons of a sorceress,	2178
	58: 9	and he will say: **H** am I.	2180
	65: 1	I said, '**H** am I, here am I.'	2180
	65: 1	I said, 'Here am I, **h** am I.'	2180
Jer	2:23	swift she-camel **running h** and there,	2006+8592
	8:14	"Why are we sitting **h?**	NIH
	19:12	to this place and to those who live **h,**	2257S
	28: 3	king of Babylon removed from **h** and took to Babylon.	2021+2021+2296+5226S
	38:10	"Take thirty men from **h** with you	2296
	43:10	over these stones I have buried **h;**	NIH
	48:47	**H** ends the judgment on Moab.	2178
	49: 3	**rush h and there** inside the walls,	8763
	51:64	The words of Jeremiah end **h.**	2178
La	4:15	"They can stay **h** no longer."	NIH
Eze	7:10	"The day is **h!**	2180
	8: 6	the house of Israel is doing **h,**	7024
	8: 9	and detestable things they are doing **h.**"	7024
	8:17	the detestable things they are doing **h?**	7024
	9: 1	"**Bring** the guards of the city **h,**	7928
	40: 4	for that is why you have been brought **h.**	2178
Da	3:26	of the Most High God, come out! Come **h!**"	NIH
	4: 9	**H** is my dream; interpret it for me.	8763
	12: 4	Many *will* go **h and there**	8763
Zec	3: 7	a place among these standing **h.**	NIH
	6:12	"**H** is the man whose name is the Branch,	2296
Mt	6:30	which is **h** today and tomorrow is thrown	NIG
	8:29	"Have you come **h** to torture us before	6045
	11:19	and they say, '**H** is a glutton and a drunkard,	2627
	12: 6	that one greater than the temple is **h.**	6045
Mt	12:18	"**H** is my servant whom I have chosen,	2627
	12:41	and now one greater than Jonah is **h.**	6045
	12:42	and now one greater than Solomon is **h.**	6045
	12:49	he said, "**H** are my mother and my brothers.	2627
	14: 8	"Give me **h** on a platter the head of John	6045
	14:17	"We have **h** only five loaves of bread	6045
	14:18	"Bring them **h** to me," he said.	6045
	16:28	some who are standing **h** will	6045
	17: 4	"Lord, it is good for us to be **h.**	6045
	17:17	Bring the boy **h** to me."	6045
	17:20	'Move **from h** to there' and it will move.	1925
	20: 6	standing **h** all day long doing nothing?'	6045
	22:12	get in **h** without wedding clothes?'	6045
	24: 2	not one stone **h** will be left on another;	6045
	24:23	'Look, **h** is the Christ!'	6045
	24:26	or, '**H** he is, in the inner rooms,'	2627
	25:25	See, **h** is what belongs to you.'	NIG
	26:36	"Sit **h** while I go over there and pray."	899
	26:38	Stay **h** and keep watch with me."	6045
	26:46	Rise, let us go! **H** comes my betrayer!"	2627
	28: 6	He is not **h;** he has risen, just as he said.	6045
Mk	3:34	"**H** are my mother and my brothers!	3972
	6: 3	Aren't his sisters **h** with us?"	6045
	9: 1	some who are standing **h** will not taste death	6045
	9: 5	"Rabbi, it is good for us to be **h.**	6045
	11: 2	Untie it and bring it **h.**	NIG
	11: 3	and will send it back **h** shortly.'"	6045
	13: 2	"Not one stone **h** will be left on another;	6045
	13:21	'Look, **h** is the Christ!'	6045
	14:32	"Sit **h** while I pray."	6045
	14:34	"Stay **h** and keep watch."	6045
	14:42	Rise! Let us go! **H** comes my betrayer!"	2627
	16: 6	He has risen! He is not **h.**	6045
Lk	4: 9	he said, "throw yourself down **from h.**	1949
	4:23	in your hometown what we have heard that you did in Capernaum.'"	6045
	7:34	'**H** *is* a glutton and a drunkard,	2627
	9:12	because we are in a remote place **h.**"	6045
	9:27	some who are standing **h** will	899
	9:33	"Master, it is good for us to be **h.**	6045
	9:41	Bring your son **h.**"	6045
	11:31	and now one greater than Solomon is **h.**	6045
	11:32	and now one greater than Jonah is **h.**	6045
	12:28	grass of the field, which is **h** today,	NIG
	15:17	and **h** I am starving to death!	6045
	16: 4	when I lose my job **h,**	NIG
	16:25	he is comforted **h** and you are in agony.	6045
	16:26	those who want to go **from h** to you cannot,	1925
	17:21	'**H** it is,' or 'There it is,'	6045
	17:23	'There he is!' or '**H** he is!'	2627
	19: 8	**H** and now I give half of my possessions to	NIG
	19:20	'Sir, **h** is your mina;	2627
	19:27	bring them **h** and kill them in front of me.'"	6045
	19:30	Untie it and bring it **h.**	NIG
	21: 6	for what *you* **see h,** the time will come	2555+4047
	22:38	"See, Lord, **h** are two swords."	6045
	23: 5	in Galilee and has come all the way **h.**"	6045
	24: 6	He is not **h;** he has risen!	6045
	24:41	"Do you have anything **h** to eat?"	1924
Jn	1:47	he said of him, "**H** is a true Israelite,	3972
	2:16	"Get these out of **h!**	1949
	4:15	and have to keep coming **h** to draw water."	1924
	5: 3	**H** a great number of disabled people	1877+4047
	6: 9	"**H** is a boy with five small barley loaves	6045
	6:25	"Rabbi, when did you get **h?**"	6045
	6:50	But **h** is the bread that comes down	4047
	7: 3	"You ought to leave **h** and go to Judea.	1949
	7:26	**H** *he is,* speaking publicly,	3972
	7:28	*I am* not **h** on my own,	2262
	8:13	The Pharisees challenged him, "**H** you are,	NIG
	8:42	for I came from God and *now* am **h.**	2457
	10:40	in the early days. **H** he stayed	1695
	11:21	Martha said to Jesus, "if you had been **h,**	6045
	11:28	"The Teacher is **h,**" she said,	4205
	11:32	"Lord, if you had been **h,**	6045
	11:42	for the benefit of the people **standing h,**	4325
	11:47	"**H** is this man performing many miraculous signs.	4022
	12: 2	**H** a dinner was given in Jesus' honor.	1695
	19: 5	Pilate said to them, "**H** is the man!"	2627
	19:14	"**H** is your king," Pilate said to the Jews.	3972
	19:18	**H** they crucified him, and	3963
	19:26	"Dear woman, **h** is your son,"	3972
	19:27	"**H** is your mother."	3972
	20:27	he said to Thomas, "Put your finger **h;**	6045
Ac	1:11	"why do you stand **h** looking into the sky?	NIG
	2:29	and his tomb is **h** to this day.	1609+1877
	7: 5	He gave him no inheritance **h,**	899+1877
	8:36	and the eunuch said, "Look, **h** is water.	NIG
	9:14	And he has come **h** with authority from	6045
	9:17	to you on the road as you were coming **h—**	NIG
	9:21	And hasn't he come **h** to take them	6045
	10:33	Now we are all **h** in the presence of God	4205
	16:28	"Don't harm yourself! We are all **h!**"	1924
	17: 6	over the world have now come	1924
	19:26	of people **h** in Ephesus and in practically	NIG
	19:37	You have brought these men **h,**	NIG
	23:15	We are ready to kill him before he **gets h.**"	1581
	23:35	when your accusers **get h.**"	4134
	24:19	*to be* **h** before you and bring charges	4205
	24:20	these **who are h** should state what crime	4047
	25:14	a man **h** whom Felix left as a prisoner.	NIG
	25:17	When they came **h** with me,	1924
	25:24	about him in Jerusalem and **h** in Caesarea,	1924
	26: 7	and so I stand **h** and testify to small	1924
Ro	13:12	night is nearly over; the day *is* **almost h.**	1581
	16:23	hospitality I and the whole church **h** enjoy,	NIG
1Co	16:20	All the brothers **h** send you greetings.	NIG
2Co	8:10	And **h** is my advice about what is best	1877+4047
Eph	4:14	and **blown h and there** by every wind	4367
Php	1:16	knowing that *I am* put **h** for the defense of	3023
Col	3:11	**H** there is no Greek or Jew,	3963
	4: 9	tell you everything that is happening **h.**	6045
1Ti	1:15	**H** is a trustworthy saying	NIG
	3: 1	**H** is a trustworthy saying:	NIG
2Ti	2:11	**H** is a trustworthy saying:	NIG
	4:21	Do your best *to* **get h** before winter.	2262
Heb	2:13	And again he says, "**H** am I,	2627
	9:11	of the good things that are already **h,**	NIG
	10: 1	Then I said, '**H** I am—	2627
	10: 9	Then he said, "**H** I am,	2627
	13:14	For **h** we do not have an enduring city,	6045
1Pe	1:17	your lives as strangers **h** in reverent fear.	NIG
3Jn	1:14	The friends **h** send their greetings.	NIG
Rev	3:20	**H** I am! I stand at the door and knock.	2627
	4: 1	to me like a trumpet said, "Come up **h,**	6045
	11:12	from heaven saying to them, "Come up **h.**"	6045

HERE'S (2) [BE, HERE]

Mt	25: 6	the cry rang out: '**H** the bridegroom!	2627
Jas	2: 3	"**H** a good seat for you,"	6045

HEREAFTER (KJV) See AFTER, AFTERWARD, FROM NOW ON, FUTURE, LATER, LONGER, TO COME

HEREBY (2) [HERE]

Ge	41:41	"*I* **h** put you in charge of the whole land	AIT
Ezr	6: 8	I **h** decree what you are to do	NIH

HEREIN (KJV) See HERE, ON CONDITION, THIS, THIS WAY, THUS

HERES (2)

Jdg	1:35	also to hold out in Mount **H,**	3065
	8:13	from the battle by the Pass of **H.**	3065

HERESH (1)

1Ch	9:15	**H,** Galal and Mattaniah son of Mica,	3090

HERESIES (1)

2Pe	2: 1	They will secretly introduce destructive **h,**	146

HERETH (1)

1Sa	22: 5	So David left and went to the forest of **H.**	3101

HERETICK (KJV) See DIVISIVE PERSON

HERETOFORE (KJV) See BEFORE, EARLIER, IN THE PAST

HERITAGE (7) [INHERIT]

Job	20:29	the **h** appointed for them by God."	5709
	27:13	the **h** a ruthless man receives from	5709
	31: 2	his **h** *from* the Almighty on high?	5709
Ps	61: 5	the **h** of those who fear your name.	3772
	119:111	Your statutes *are* my **h** forever;	5706
	127: 3	Sons are a **h** *from* the LORD,	5709
Isa	54:17	This is the **h** of the servants of the LORD,	5709

HERMAS (1)

Ro	16:14	Patrobas, **H** and the brothers with them.	2254

HERMES (2)

Ac	14:12	and Paul they called **H** because he was	2258
Ro	16:14	Greet Asyncritus, Phlegon, **H,** Patrobas,	2258

HERMOGENES (1)

2Ti	1:15	including Phygelus and **H.**	2259

HERMON (14) [BAAL HERMON, SENIR, SIRION, SIYON]

Dt	3: 8	from the Arnon Gorge as far as Mount **H.**	3056
	3: 9	(**H** is called Sirion by the Sidonians;	3056
	4:48	to Mount Siyon (that is, **H**),	3056
Jos	11: 3	and to the Hivites below **H** in the region	3056
	11:17	in the Valley of Lebanon below Mount **H.**	3056
	12: 1	from the Arnon Gorge to Mount **H,**	3056
	12: 5	He ruled over Mount **H,** Salecah,	3056
	13: 5	to the east, from Baal Gad below Mount **H**	3056
	13:11	all of Mount **H** and all Bashan as far	3056
1Ch	5:23	that is, to Senir (Mount **H**).	3056
Ps	42: 6	the **heights of H**—from Mount Mizar.	3056
	89:12	Tabor and **H** sing for joy at your name.	3056
	133: 3	if the dew of **H** were falling on Mount Zion.	3056
SS	4: 8	from the top of Senir, the summit of **H,**	3056

HERO (2) [HEROES]

1Sa	17:51	the Philistines saw that their **h** was dead,	1475
Isa	3: 2	the **h** and warrior, the judge and prophet,	1475

HEROD (43) [HEROD'S, HERODIANS]

Mt	2: 1	during the time of King **H**,	2476
	2: 3	When King **H** heard this he was disturbed,	2476
	2: 7	Then **H** called the Magi secretly	2476
	2:12	in a dream not to go back to **H**,	2476
	2:13	for **H** is going to search for the child	2476
	2:15	where he stayed until the death of **H**.	2476
	2:16	When **H** realized that he had been outwitted	2476
	2:19	After **H** died, an angel of the Lord appeared	2476
	2:22	in Judea in place of his father **H**,	2476
	14: 1	At that time **H** the tetrarch heard the reports	2476
	14: 3	Now **H** had arrested John and bound him	2476
	14: 5	**H** wanted to kill John,	NIG
	14: 6	of Herodias danced for them and pleased **H**	2476
Mk	6:14	King **H** heard about this,	2476
	6:16	But when **H** heard this, he said, "John,	2476
	6:17	For **H** himself had given orders	2476
	6:18	For John had been saying to **H**,	2476
	6:20	because he feared John and protected him,	2476
	6:20	When **H** heard John, he was greatly puzzled;	NIG
	6:21	On his birthday **H** gave a banquet	2476
	6:22	he pleased **H** and his dinner guests.	2476
	8:15	for the yeast of the Pharisees and that of **H**."	2476
Lk	1: 5	In the time of **H** king of Judea there was	2476
	3: 1	of Judea, **H** tetrarch of Galilee,	2476
	3:19	when John rebuked **H** the tetrarch because	2476
	3:20	**H** added this to them all:	2476
	9: 7	Now **H** the tetrarch heard about all	2476
	9: 9	But **H** said, "I beheaded John.	2476
	13:31	**H** wants to kill you."	2476
	23: 7	he sent him to **H**, who was also in Jerusalem	2476
	23: 8	When **H** saw Jesus, he was greatly pleased,	2476
	23:11	Then **H** and his soldiers ridiculed	2476
	23:12	That day **H** and Pilate became friends—	2476
	23:15	Neither has **H**, for he sent him back to us;	2476
Ac	4:27	Indeed **H** and Pontius Pilate met together	2476
	12: 1	that King **H** arrested some who belonged to	2476
	12: 4	**H** intended to bring him out for public trial	NIG
	12: 6	The night before **H** was to bring him to trial,	2476
	12:19	After **H** had a thorough search made for him	2476
	12:19	Then **H** went from Judea to Caesarea	NIG
	12:21	On the appointed day **H**,	2476
	12:23	because **H** did not give praise to God,	NIG
	13: 1	Manaen (who had been brought up with **H**	2476

HEROD'S (5) [HEROD]

Mt	14: 6	On **H** birthday the daughter	2476
Lk	8: 3	the manager of **H** household;	2476
	23: 7	that Jesus was under **H** jurisdiction,	2476
Ac	12:11	rescued me from **H** clutches and from	2476
	23:35	that Paul be kept under guard in **H** palace.	2476

HERODIANS (3) [HEROD]

Mt	22:16	to him along with the **H**.	2477
Mk	3: 6	to plot with the **H** how they might kill Jesus.	2477
	12:13	of the Pharisees and **H** to Jesus to catch him	2477

HERODIAS (6)

Mt	14: 3	and put him in prison because of **H**,	2478
	14: 6	of **H** danced for them and pleased Herod	2478
Mk	6:17	He did this because of **H**,	2478
	6:19	So **H** nursed a grudge against John	2478
	6:22	the daughter of **H** came in and danced,	2478
Lk	3:19	the tetrarch because of **H**,	2478

HERODION (1)

Ro	16:11	Greet **H**, my relative.	2479

HEROES (3) [HERO]

Ge	6: 4	They were the **h** of old, men of renown.	1475
Ne	3:16	as the artificial pool and the House of the **H**.	1475
Isa	5:22	Woe to those who are **h** at drinking wine	1475

HERON (2)

Lev	11:19	any kind of **h**, the hoopoe and the bat.	649
Dt	14:18	any kind of **h**, the hoopoe and the bat.	649

HERS (4) [SHE]

Ge	3:15	and between your offspring and **h**;	2023
Job	39:16	as if they were not **h**;	2023+4200
Pr	14: 1	the foolish one tears **h** down.	5647
La	1: 7	the treasures that were **h** in days of old.	2023

HERSELF (45) [SELF, SHE] See Index of Articles Etc.

HESED (KJV) See BEN-HESED

HESHBON (38)

Nu	21:25	and occupied them, including **H**	3114
	21:26	**H** was the city of Sihon king of	3114
	21:27	"Come to **H** and let it be rebuilt;	3114
	21:28	"Fire went out from **H**,	3114
	21:30	**H** is destroyed all the way to Dibon.	3114
	21:34	king of the Amorites, who reigned in **H**."	3114
	32: 3	Dibon, Jazer, Nimrah, **H**, Elealeh, Sebam,	3114
	32:37	And the Reubenites rebuilt **H**,	3114
Dt	1: 4	king of the Amorites, who reigned in **H**,	3114
	2:24	king of **H**, and his country.	3114
	2:26	to Sihon king of **H** offering peace	3114

Dt	2:30	king of **H** refused to let us pass through.	3114
	3: 2	of the Amorites, who reigned in **H**."	3114
	3: 6	as we had done with Sihon king of **H**,	3114
	4:46	in **H** and was defeated by Moses and	3114
	29: 7	of **H** and Og king of Bashan came out	3114
Jos	9:10	Sihon king of **H**, and Og king of Bashan,	3114
	12: 2	of the Amorites, who reigned in **H**,	3114
	12: 5	of Gilead to the border of Sihon king of **H**.	3114
	13:10	of the Amorites, who ruled in **H**,	3114
	13:17	to **H** and all its towns on the plateau,	3114
	13:21	of the Amorites, who ruled at **H**.	3114
	13:26	from **H** to Ramath Mizpah and Betonim,	3114
	13:27	with the rest of the realm of Sihon king of **H**	3114
	21:39	**H** and Jazer, together	3114
Jdg	11:19	who ruled in **H**, and said to him,	3114
	11:26	For three hundred years Israel occupied **H**,	3114
1Ch	6:81	**H** and Jazer, together with	3114
Ne	9:22	of **H** and the country of Og king of Bashan.	3114
SS	7: 4	the pools of **H** by the gate of Bath Rabbim.	3114
Isa	15: 4	**H** and Elealeh cry out,	3114
	16: 8	The fields of **H** wither,	3114
	16: 9	O **H**, O Elealeh, I drench you with tears!	3114
Jer	48: 2	in **H** men will plot her downfall:	3114
	48:34	"The sound of their cry rises from **H**	3114
	48:45	shadow of **H** the fugitives stand helpless,	3114
	48:45	for a fire has gone out from **H**,	3114
	49: 3	"Wail, O **H**, for Ai is destroyed!	3114

HESHMON (1)

Jos	15:27	Hazar Gaddah, **H**, Beth Pelet,	3132

HESITATE (4) [HESITATED, HESITATION]

Jdg	18: 9	Don't **h** to go there and take it over.	6788
Job	30:10	they do not **h** to spit in my face.	3104
Da	9:14	The LORD **did not h** to bring the disaster	9193
Ac	10:20	Do not **h** to go with them,	1359

HESITATED (3) [HESITATE]

Ge	19:16	When he **h**, the men grasped his hand and	4538
Ac	20:20	that I have not **h** to preach anything	5713
	20:27	not **h** to proclaim to you the whole will	5713

HESITATION (1) [HESITATE]

Ac	11:12	The Spirit told me to have no **h** about going	1359

HETHLON (2)

Eze	47:15	by the **H** road past Lebo Hamath to Zedad,	3158
	48: 1	it will follow the **H** road to Lebo Hamath;	3158

HEW (KJV) See CHISEL

HEWER (KJV) See WOODCUTTER

HEWING (1) [HEWN]

Isa	22:16	**h** your grave on the height	2933

HEWN (2) [HEWING]

Pr	9: 1	she has **h** out its seven pillars.	2933
Isa	51: 1	and to the quarry from which you were **h**;	5941

HEZEKI (KJV) See HIZKI

HEZEKIAH (123) [HEZEKIAH'S]

2Ki	16:20	And **H** his son succeeded him as king.	2625
	18: 1	**H** son of Ahaz king of Judah began to reign.	2625
	18: 5	**H** trusted in the LORD, the God of Israel.	NIH
	18:14	So **H** king of Judah sent this message to	2624
	18:14	from **H** king of Judah three hundred talents	2624
	18:15	So **H** gave him all the silver that was found	2624
	18:16	At this time **H** king of Judah stripped off	2624
	18:17	from Lachish to King **H** at Jerusalem.	2625
	18:19	The field commander said to them, "Tell **H**:	2625
	18:22	high places and altars **H** removed,	2625
	18:29	Do not let **H** deceive you.	2625
	18:30	Do not let **H** persuade you to trust in	2625
	18:31	"Do not listen to **H**.	2625
	18:32	"Do not listen to **H**,	2625
	18:37	of Asaph the recorder went to **H**,	2625
	19: 1	When King **H** heard this,	2625
	19: 3	They told him, "This is what **H** says:	2625
	19: 9	So he again sent messengers to **H**	2625
	19:10	"Say to **H** king of Judah:	2625
	19:14	**H** received the letter from the messengers	2625
	19:15	And **H** prayed to the LORD:	2625
	19:20	Isaiah son of Amoz sent a message to **H**:	2625
	19:29	"This will be the sign for you, O **H**:	NIH
	20: 1	In those days **H** became ill and was at	2625
	20: 2	**H** turned his face to the wall and prayed to	NIH
	20: 3	And **H** wept bitterly.	2625
	20: 5	"Go back and tell **H**, the leader	2625
	20: 8	**H** had asked Isaiah,	2625
	20:10	the shadow to go forward ten steps," said **H**.	3491
	20:12	of Baladan king of Babylon sent **H** letters	2625
	20:13	**H** received the messengers	2625
	20:13	or in all his kingdom that **H** did not show	2625
	20:14	Then Isaiah the prophet went to King **H**	2625
	20:14	"From a distant land," **H** replied.	2625
	20:15	everything in my palace," **H** said.	2625
	20:16	Then Isaiah said to **H**,	2625
	20:19	you have spoken is good," **H** replied.	2625

2Ki	20:21	**H** rested with his fathers.	2625
	21: 3	the high places his father **H** had destroyed;	2625
1Ch	3:13	Ahaz his son, **H** his son, Manasseh his son,	2625
	4:41	in the days of **H** king of Judah.	3491
2Ch	28:27	And **H** his son succeeded him as king.	3491
	29: 1	**H** was twenty-five years old	3491
	29:18	Then they went in to King **H** and reported:	2625
	29:20	Early the next morning King **H** gathered	3491
	29:27	**H** gave the order to sacrifice	2625
	29:30	King **H** and his officials ordered the Levites	3491
	29:31	Then **H** said, "You have now dedicated	3491
	29:36	**H** and all the people rejoiced	3491
	30: 1	**H** sent word to all Israel and Judah	3491
	30:18	But **H** prayed for them, saying,	3491
	30:20	the LORD heard **H** and healed the people.	3491
	30:22	**H** spoke encouragingly to all the Levites,	3491
	30:24	**H** king of Judah provided a thousand bulls	2625
	31: 2	**H** assigned the priests and Levites	3491
	31: 8	**H** and his officials came and saw the heaps,	3491
	31: 9	**H** asked the priests and Levites about	3491
	31:11	**H** gave orders to prepare storerooms in	3491
	31:13	of King **H** and Azariah the official in charge	3491
	31:20	This is what **H** did throughout Judah,	3491
	32: 1	After all that **H** had so faithfully done,	NIH
	32: 2	When **H** saw that Sennacherib had come	3491
	32: 8	the people gained confidence from what **H**	3491
	32: 9	with this message for **H** king of Judah and	3491
	32:11	**H** says, 'The LORD our God will save us	3491
	32:12	not **H** himself remove this god's high places	3491
	32:15	not let **H** deceive you and mislead you	2625
	32:16	the LORD God and against his servant **H**.	3491
	32:17	so the god of **H** will not rescue his people	3491
	32:20	King **H** and the prophet Isaiah son	3491
	32:22	So the LORD saved **H** and the people	3491
	32:23	for the LORD and valuable gifts for **H** king	3491
	32:24	In those days **H** became ill and was at	3491
	32:26	Then **H** repented of the pride of his heart,	3491
	32:26	not come upon them during the days of **H**.	3491
	32:27	**H** had very great riches and honor,	3491
	32:30	It was **H** who blocked the upper outlet of	3491
	32:33	**H** rested with his fathers and was buried on	3491
	33: 3	the high places his father **H** had demolished;	3491
Ezr		of Ater (through **H**) 98	3490
Ne	7:21	of Ater (through **H**) 98	2624
	10:17	Ater, **H**, Azzur,	2624
Pr	25: 1	copied by the men of **H** king of Judah:	2624
Isa	1: 1	Jotham, Ahaz and **H**, kings of Judah.	3491
	36: 2	with a large army from Lachish to King **H**	2625
	36: 4	The field commander said to them, "Tell **H**,	2625
	36: 7	high places and altars **H** removed,	2625
	36:14	Do not let **H** deceive you.	2625
	36:15	Do not let **H** persuade you to trust in	2625
	36:16	"Do not listen to **H**.	2625
	36:18	"Do not let **H** mislead you when he says,	2625
	36:22	Joah son of Asaph the recorder went to **H**,	2625
	37: 1	When King **H** heard this,	2625
	37: 3	They told him, "This is what **H** says:	2625
	37: 9	he sent messengers to **H** with this word:	2625
	37:10	"Say to **H** king of Judah:	2625
	37:14	**H** received the letter from the messengers	2625
	37:15	And **H** prayed to the LORD:	2625
	37:21	Isaiah son of Amoz sent a message to **H**:	2625
	37:30	"This will be the sign for you, O **H**:	NIH
	38: 1	In those days **H** became ill and was at	2625
	38: 2	**H** turned his face to the wall and prayed to	2625
	38: 3	And **H** wept bitterly.	2625
	38: 5	"Go and tell **H**, 'This is what the LORD,	2625
	38: 9	writing of **H** king of Judah after his illness	2625
	38:22	**H** had asked, "What will be the sign	2625
	39: 1	of Baladan king of Babylon sent **H** letters	2625
	39: 2	**H** received the envoys gladly	2625
	39: 2	or in all his kingdom that **H** did not show	2625
	39: 3	Then Isaiah the prophet went to King **H**	2625
	39: 3	"From a distant land," **H** replied.	2625
	39: 4	everything in my palace," **H** said.	2625
	39: 5	Then Isaiah said to **H**,	2625
	39: 8	you have spoken is good," **H** replied.	2625
Jer	15: 4	because of what Manasseh son of **H** king	3491
	26:18	in the days of **H** king of Judah.	2625
	26:19	"Did **H** king of Judah or anyone else	2625
	26:19	not **H** fear the LORD and seek his favor?	NIH
Hos	1: 1	Jotham, Ahaz and **H**, kings of Judah,	3490
Mic	1: 1	Ahaz and **H**, kings of Judah—	3490
Zep	1: 1	the son of Amariah, the son of **H**,	2624
Mt	1: 9	Ahaz the father of **H**,	1614
	1:10	**H** the father of Manasseh,	1614

HEZEKIAH'S (10) [HEZEKIAH]

2Ki	18: 9	In King **H** fourth year,	2625+4200
	18:10	Samaria was captured in **H** sixth year,	2624+4200
	18:13	In the fourteenth year of King **H** reign,	2624
	19: 5	When King **H** officials came to Isaiah,	2625
	20:12	because he had heard of **H** illness.	2625
	20:20	As for the other events of **H** reign,	2625
2Ch	32:25	But **H** heart was proud and he did	3491
	32:32	The other events of **H** reign and his acts	3491
Isa	36: 1	In the fourteenth year of King **H** reign,	2625
	37: 5	When King **H** officials came to Isaiah,	2625

HEZION (1)

1Ki	15:18	the son of **H**, the king of Aram,	2611

HEZIR (2)

1Ch	24:15	the seventeenth to **H**,	2615
Ne	10:20	Magpiash, Meshullam, **H**,	2615

HEZRAI (KJV) See HEZRO

HEZRO (2)
2Sa	23:35	H the Carmelite, Paarai the Arbite,	2968
1Ch	11:37	H the Carmelite, Naarai son of Ezbai,	2968

HEZRON (20) [HEZRONITE, KIRIOTH HEZRON]
Ge	46:9	Hanoch, Pallu, H and Carmi.	2969
	46:12	The sons of Perez: H and Hamul.	2969
Ex	6:14	of Israel were Hanoch and Pallu, H	2969
Nu	26:6	through H, the Hezronite clan;	2969
	26:21	through H, the Hezronite clan;	2969
Jos	15:3	Then it ran past H up to Addar and curved	2970
Ru	4:18	Perez was the father of H,	2969
	4:19	H the father of Ram,	2969
1Ch	2:5	The sons of Perez: H and Hamul.	2969
	2:9	The sons born to H were:	2969
	2:18	of H had children by his wife Azubah (and	2969
	2:21	H lay with the daughter of Makir the father	2969
	2:24	After H died in Caleb Ephrathah,	2969
	2:24	of H bore him Ashhur the father of Tekoa.	2969
	2:25	The sons of Jerahmeel the firstborn of H:	2969
	4:1	Perez, H, Carmi, Hur and Shobal.	2969
	5:3	Hanoch, Pallu, H and Carmi.	2969
Mt	1:3	Perez the father of H,	2272
	1:3	H the father of Ram,	2272
Lk	3:33	the son of H, the son of Perez,	2272

HEZRONITE (2) [HEZRON]
Nu	26:6	through Hezron, the H clan; through Carmi,	2971
	26:21	through Hezron, the H clan;	2971

HID (34) [HIDE]
Ge	3:8	and they h from the LORD God among	2461
	3:10	because I was naked; so I h."	2461
Ex	2:2	she h him for three months.	7621
	2:12	the Egyptian and h him in the sand.	3243
	3:6	At this, Moses h his face,	6259
Jos	6:17	because she h the spies we sent.	2461
	6:25	because she h the men Joshua had sent	2461
1Sa	13:6	they h in caves and thickets,	2461
	20:19	where you h when this trouble began,	6259
	20:24	So David h in the field,	6259
1Ki	18:13	I h a hundred of the LORD's prophets	2461
	20:30	And Ben-Hadad fled to the city and h in	995
2Ki	7:8	gold and clothes, and went off and h them.	3243
	7:8	from it and h them also.	3243
1Ch	29:11	sons who were with him h themselves.	2461
2Ch	22:11	she h the child from Athaliah so she could	6259
Ps	30:7	but when you h your face, I was dismayed.	6259
	35:7	Since they h their net for me without cause	3243
	35:8	may the net they h entangle them,	3243
Isa	49:2	in the shadow of his hand he h me;	2461
	54:8	a surge of anger I h my face from you for	6259
	57:17	I punished him, and h my face in anger,	6259
Jer	13:5	So I went and h it at Perath,	3243
Eze	39:23	So I h my face from them and handed them	6259
	39:24	and I h my face from them.	6259
Da	10:7	that they fled and h themselves.	2461
Mt	13:44	When a man found it, he h it again,	3221
	25:18	in the ground and h his master's money.	3221
	25:25	and went out and h your talent in	3221
Jn	8:59	but Jesus h himself,	3221
	12:36	Jesus left and h himself from them.	3221
Ac	1:9	and a cloud h him from their sight.	5696
Heb	11:23	By faith Moses' parents h him	3221
Rev	6:15	and every free man h in caves and among	3221

HIDDAI (1)
2Sa	23:30	H from the ravines of Gaash,	2068

HIDDEKEL (KJV) See TIGRIS

HIDDEN (82) [HIDE]
Ge	4:14	and I will be h from your presence;	6259
Nu	5:13	and this is h from her husband	6623
Dt	33:19	on the treasures h in the sand."	3243+8561
Jos	2:4	woman had taken the two men and h them.	7621
	2:6	up to the roof and h them under the stalks	3243
	7:21	They are h in the ground inside my tent,	3243
	7:22	h in his tent, with the silver underneath.	3243
	10:16	the five kings had fled and h in the cave	2461
Jdg	16:9	With men h in the room, she called to him,	741
	16:12	Then, with men h in the room,	741
1Sa	10:22	he has h himself among the baggage."	2461
	14:22	the Israelites who had h in the hill country	2461
2Sa	17:9	now, he is h in a cave or some other place.	2461
	18:13	and nothing is h from the king—	3948
1Ki	13:8	a hundred prophets and h them	2461
2Ki	4:27	but the LORD has h it from me and has	6623
	6:29	but she had h him."	2461
	11:3	He remained h with his nurse at the temple	2461
2Ch	22:12	He remained h with them at the temple	2461
Job	3:16	not h in the ground like a stillborn child,	3243
	3:21	who search for it more than for h treasure,	4759
	18:10	A noose is h for him on the ground;	3243
	28:7	No bird of prey knows that h path,	5985
	28:11	and brings h things to light.	9502
	28:21	It is h from the eyes of every living thing,	6623
Job	33:21	and his bones, once h, now stick out.	4202+8011
	40:21	h among the reeds in the marsh.	6260
Ps	9:15	their feet are caught in the net they have h.	3243
	19:6	nothing is h from its heat.	6259
	19:12	Forgive my h faults.	6259
	22:24	not h his face from him but has listened	6259
	38:9	my sighing is not h from you.	6259
	69:5	my guilt is not h from you.	6259
	78:2	I will utter h things, things from of old—	2648
	119:11	I have h your word in my heart that I might	7621
	139:15	My frame was not h from you	6259
	140:5	Proud men have h a snare for me;	3243
	142:3	In the path where I walk men have h a snare	3243
Pr	2:4	for silver and search for it as for h treasure,	4759
	27:5	Better is open rebuke than h love.	6259
Ecc	12:14	into judgment, including every h thing,	6623
Isa	30:20	your teachers will be h no more;	4052
	40:27	O Israel, "My way is h from the LORD;	6259
	42:22	of them trapped in pits or h away in prisons.	2461
	48:6	of h things unknown to you.	5915
	59:2	your sins have h his face from you,	6259
	64:7	for you have h your face from us	6259
	65:16	For the past troubles will be forgotten and h	6259
Jer	13:7	and took it from the place where I had h it,	3243
	16:17	they are not h from me,	6259
	18:22	to capture me and have h snares for my feet.	3243
	36:26	But the LORD had h them.	6259
	41:8	oil and honey, h in a field."	4759
Eze	28:3	Is no secret h from you?	6670
Da	2:22	He reveals deep and h things;	10519
Hos	5:3	Israel is not h from me.	3948
Ob	1:6	his h treasures pillaged!	5208
Hab	3:4	where his power was h.	2470
Mt	5:14	A city on a hill cannot be h.	3221
	10:26	or h that will not be made known.	3220
	11:25	because you have h these things from	3221
	13:35	I will utter things h since the creation of	3221
	13:44	"The kingdom of heaven is like treasure h	3221
Mk	4:22	For whatever is h is meant to be disclosed,	3220
Lk	8:17	there is nothing that will not be disclosed,	3220
	9:45	It was h from them,	4152
	10:21	because you have h these things from	648
	11:33	place where it will be h,	3219
	12:2	or h that will not be made known.	3220
	18:34	Its meaning was h from them,	3221
	19:42	but now it is h from your eyes.	3221
Ro	16:25	the revelation of the mystery h for long ages	4967
1Co	2:7	that has been h and that God destined	648
	4:5	He will bring to light what is h in darkness	3220
Eph	3:9	which for ages past was kept h in God,	648
Col	1:26	the mystery that has been kept h for ages	648
	2:3	in whom are h all the treasures of wisdom	649
	3:3	and your life is now h with Christ in God.	3221
1Ti	5:25	and even those that are not cannot be h.	3221
Heb	4:13	Nothing in all creation is h from	905
Rev	2:17	I will give some of the h manna.	3221

HIDE (74) [HID, HIDDEN, HIDES, HIDING]
Ge	18:17	"Shall I h from Abraham what I am about	4059
	47:18	"We cannot h from our lord the fact that	3948
Ex	2:3	But when she could h him no longer,	7621
	29:14	the bull's flesh and its h and its offal outside	6425
Lev	4:11	But the h of the bull and all its flesh,	6425
	7:8	a burnt offering for anyone may keep its h	6425
	8:17	But the bull with its h and its flesh	6425
	9:11	and the h he burned up outside the camp.	6425
	11:32	of wood, cloth, h or sackcloth.	6425
Nu	19:5	its h, flesh, blood and offal.	6425
Dt	7:20	among them until even the survivors who h	6259
	31:17	I will h my face from them,	6259
	31:18	And I will certainly h my face on	6259+6259
	32:20	"I will h my face from them," he said,	6259
Jos	2:16	H yourselves there three days	2461
	7:19	do not h it from me."	3948
Jdg	21:20	"Go and h in the vineyards	741
1Sa	3:17	"Do not h it from me.	3948
	3:17	if you h from me anything he told you."	3948
	20:2	Why would he h this from me?	6259
	20:5	and h in the field until the evening of	6259
1Ki	17:3	turn eastward and h in the Kerith Ravine,	6259
	22:25	on the day you go to h in an inner room."	2461
2Ki	7:12	so they have left the camp to h in	2461
	11:2	in a bedroom to h him from Athaliah;	6259
2Ch	18:24	on the day you go to h in an inner room."	2461
Job	3:10	on me to h trouble from my eyes.	6259
	13:20	O God, and then I will not h from you:	6259
	13:24	Why do you h your face	6259
	14:13	"If only you would h me in the grave	7621
	34:22	no deep shadow, where evildoers can h.	6259
	41:7	Can you fill his h with harpoons or his head	6425
Ps	10:1	Why do you h yourself in times of trouble?	6623
	13:1	How long will you h your face from me?	6259
	17:8	h me in the shadow of your wings	6259
	27:5	he will h me in the shelter of his tabernacle	6259
	27:9	Do not h your face from me,	6259
	31:20	In the shelter of your presence you h them	6259
	40:10	I do not h your righteousness in my heart;	4059
	44:24	Why do you h your face	6259
	51:9	H your face from my sins	6259
	55:12	I could h from him.	6259
	64:2	H me from the conspiracy of the wicked,	6259
	69:17	Do not h your face from your servant;	6259
	78:4	We will not h them from their children;	3948
	88:14	do you reject me and h your face from me?	6259
	89:46	Will you h yourself forever?	6259
	102:2	Do not h your face from me when I am	6259
Ps	104:29	When you h your face, they are terrified;	6259
	119:19	do not h your commands from me.	6259
	139:11	"Surely the darkness will h me and	8503
	143:7	Do not h your face from me or I will be	6259
	143:9	O LORD, for I h myself in you.	4059
Isa	1:15	I will h my eyes from you;	6623
	2:10	h in the ground from dread of the LORD	3243
	16:3	H the fugitives, do not betray the refugees.	6259
	26:20	h yourselves for a little while	2464
	29:15	to great depths to h their plans from	6259
	50:6	not h my face from mocking and spitting.	6259
	53:3	Like one from whom men h their faces he was despised,	5040
Jer	13:4	now to Perath and h it there in a crevice in	3243
	13:6	and get the belt I told you to h there."	3243
	23:24	Can anyone h in secret places so	6259
	33:5	I will h my face from this city because	6259
	36:19	"You and Jeremiah, go and h,	6259
	38:14	"Do not h anything from me."	3948
	38:25	do not h it from us or we will kill you,'	3948
	49:8	Turn and flee, h in deep caves,	3782
Eze	39:29	I will no longer h my face from them,	6259
Am	9:3	Though they h themselves on the top	2461
	9:3	Though they h from me at the bottom of	6259
Mic	7:3	At that time he will h his face from them	6259
Rev	6:16	on us and h us from the face of him who sits	3221

HIDES (18) [HIDE]
Ex	25:5	ram skins dyed red and h of sea cows;	6425
	26:14	and over that a covering of h of sea cows.	6425
	35:7	ram skins dyed red and h of sea cows;	6425
	35:23	or h of sea cows brought them.	6425
	36:19	and over that a covering of h of sea cows.	6425
	39:34	of h of sea cows and the shielding curtain;	6425
Lev	16:27	their h, flesh and offal are to be burned up.	6425
Nu	4:6	they are to cover this with h of sea cows,	6425
	4:8	that with h of sea cows and put its poles	6425
	4:10	in a covering of h of sea cows and put it on	6425
	4:11	to spread a blue cloth and cover that with h	6425
	4:12	cover that with h of sea cows and put them	6425
	4:14	of h of sea cows and put its poles in place.	6425
		and the outer covering of h of sea cows,	9391
Job	20:12	in his mouth and he h it under his tongue,	3948
	34:29	If he h his face, who can see him?	6259
Isa	45:15	Truly you are a God who h himself,	6259
Lk	8:16	a lamp and h it in a jar or puts it under	2821

HIDING (29) [HIDE]
Jos	10:17	the five kings had been found h in the cave	2461
	10:27	into the cave where they had been h.	2461
Jdg	9:5	of Jerub-Baal, escaped by h.	2461
	9:35	came out from their h place.	4422
1Sa	3:18	h nothing from him.	3948
	14:11	of the holes they were h in."	2461
	19:2	go into h and stay there.	6260
	23:19	"Is not David h among us in the strongholds	2461
	23:23	the h places he uses and come back to me	4676
	26:1	"Is not David h on the hill of Hakilah,	6259
2Ch	18:24	and his men captured him while he was h	2461
Job	15:18	h nothing received from their fathers	3948
	24:4	force all the poor of the land into h.	2461
	31:33	by h my guilt in my heart	3243
Ps	32:7	You are my h place;	6260
	54:T	"Is not David h among us?"	6259
	64:5	they talk about h their snares;	3243
Pr	28:12	the wicked rise to power, men go into h.	2924
	28:28	the wicked rise to power, people go into h;	6259
SS	2:14	in the h places on the mountainside,	6260
Isa	4:6	and a refuge and h place from the storm	5039
	8:17	who is h his face from the house of Jacob.	6259
	28:15	a lie our refuge and falsehood our h place."	6259
	28:17	and water will overflow your h place.	6260
Jer	49:10	I will uncover his h places,	5041
La	3:10	Like a bear lying in wait, like a lion in h,	5041
Am	6:10	of the house and asks anyone still h there,	NIH
Na	3:11	you will go into h and seek refuge from	6623
Hab	3:14	to devour the wretched who were in h.	5041

HIEL (1)
1Ki	16:34	In Ahab's time, H of Bethel rebuilt Jericho.	2647

HIERAPOLIS (1)
Col	4:13	for you and for those at Laodicea and H.	2631

HIGGAION (1)
Ps	9:16	by the work of their hands. H.	2053

HIGH (380) [HIGH-GRADE, HIGHBORN, HIGHER, HIGHEST, HIGHLY]
Ge	6:15	75 feet wide and 45 feet h.	7757
	7:17	as the waters increased they lifted the ark h	8123
	7:19	and all the h mountains under	1469
	14:18	He was priest of God Most H,	6610
	14:19	saying, "Blessed be Abram by God Most H,	6610
	14:20	And blessed be God Most H,	6610
	14:22	God Most H, Creator of heaven and earth,	6610
	29:7	"Look," he said, "the sun is still h;	1524
Ex	25:10	a cubit and a half h.	7757
	25:23	a cubit wide and a cubit and a half h.	7757
	27:1	an altar of acacia wood, three cubits h;	7757
	27:18	of finely twisted linen five cubits h,	7757
	30:2	a cubit wide, and two cubits h—	7757

Ref	Text	No.
Ex 37: 1	and a cubit and a half **h**.	7757
37:10	a cubit wide, and a cubit and a half **h**.	7757
37:25	and two cubits **h**—	7757
38: 1	of acacia wood, three cubits **h**;	7757
38:18	the curtains of the courtyard, five cubits **h**,	7757
Lev 16:32	to succeed his father as **h priest** is	3912
21:10	" 'The **h** priest, the one	1524
21:10	and enabled you to walk **with heads held h**.	7758
26:30	I will destroy your **h** places,	1195
Nu 14:40	up toward the **h** hill country.	8031
14:44	up toward the **h** hill country,	8031
24:16	who has knowledge from the **Most H**,	6610
33:52	and demolish all their **h** places.	1195
35:25	until the death of the **h** priest,	1524
35:28	of refuge until the death of the **h** priest;	1524
35:28	after the death of the **h** priest may he return	1524
35:32	before the death of the **h** priest.	NIH
Dt 3: 5	All these cities were fortified with **h** walls	1469
12: 2	on the **h** mountains and on the hills and	8123
26:19	fame and honor **h** above all	6609
28: 1	the LORD your God will set you **h**	6609
28:52	until the **h** fortified walls	1469
32: 8	**Most H** gave the nations their inheritance,	6610
33:29	and you will trample down their **h** places."	1195
Jos 20: 6	until the death of the **h** priest who is serving	1524
Jdg 16:25	they **were in h spirits**, they shouted,	3201+2213
1Sa 2: 1	in the LORD my horn **is lifted h**.	8123
9:12	the people have a sacrifice at the **h** place.	1195
9:13	before he goes up to the **h** place to eat.	1195
9:14	toward them on his way up to the **h** place.	1195
9:19	"Go up ahead of me to the **h** place,	1195
9:25	After they came down from the **h** place to	1195
10: 5	of prophets coming down from the **h** place	1195
10:13	he went to the **h** place.	1195
18: 5	**gave** him a **h** rank in in the army.	6584+8492
25:36	He **was in h spirits** and very drunk.	3201+2213
2Sa 13:28	When Amnon **is in h spirits**	3201+2213
22:14	the voice of the **Most H** resounded.	6610
22:17	"He reached down from **on h** and took hold	5294
23: 1	oracle of the man exalted by the **Most H**,	6583
1Ki 3: 2	were still sacrificing at the **h** places,	1195
3: 3	and burned incense on the **h** places.	1195
3: 4	for that was the most important **h** place,	1195
6: 2	twenty wide and thirty **h**.	7757
6:20	twenty wide and twenty **h**.	7757
6:23	each ten cubits **h**.	7757
7: 2	fifty wide and thirty **h**,	7757
7: 4	**windows** were **placed h**	9209
7:15	each eighteen cubits **h** and twelve cubits	7757
7:16	each capital was five cubits **h**	7757
7:19	in the shape of lilies, four cubits **h**.	NIH
7:23	from rim to rim and five cubits **h**.	7757
7:27	four wide and three **h**.	7757
11: 7	a **h** place for Chemosh the detestable god	1195
12:31	Jeroboam built shrines on **h places**	1195
12:32	at the **h** places he had made.	1195
13: 2	the **h** places who now make offerings here,	1195
13:32	and against all the shrines on the **h** places	1195
13:33	for the **h** places from all sorts of people.	1195
13:33	a priest he consecrated for the **h** places.	1195
14:23	They also set up for themselves **h** places,	1195
14:23	and Asherah poles on every **h** hill and	1469
15:14	Although he did not remove the **h** places,	1195
22:43	The **h** places, however, were not removed,	1195
2Ki 12: 3	The **h** places, however, were not removed;	1195
12:10	the royal secretary and the **h** priest came,	1524
14: 4	The **h** places, however, were not removed;	1195
15: 4	The **h** places, however, were not removed;	1195
15:35	The **h** places, however, were not removed;	1195
16: 4	and burned incense at the **h** places,	1195
17: 9	fortified city they built themselves **h** places	1195
17:10	and Asherah poles on every **h** hill and	1469
17:11	At every **h** place they burned incense,	1195
17:29	of Samaria had made at the **h** places.	1195
17:32	as priests in the shrines at the **h** places.	1195
18: 4	He removed the **h** places,	1195
18:22	isn't he the one whose **h** places	1195
21: 3	**h** places his father Hezekiah had destroyed;	1195
22: 4	the **h** priest have him get ready	1524
22: 8	the **h** priest said to Shaphan the secretary,	1524
23: 4	The king ordered Hilkiah the **h** priest,	1524
23: 5	of Judah to burn incense on the **h** places of	1195
23: 8	of Judah and desecrated the **h** places,	1195
23: 9	of the **h** places did not serve at the altar of	1195
23:13	the **h** places that were east of Jerusalem on	1195
23:15	the **h** place made by Jeroboam son	1195
23:15	even that altar and **h** place he demolished.	1195
23:15	the **h** place and ground it to powder,	1195
23:19	and defiled all the shrines at the **h** places	1195
23:20	the priests of those **h** places on the altars	1195
25:17	Each pillar was twenty-seven feet **h**.	7757
25:17	and a half feet **h** and was decorated with	7757
1Ch 16:39	the tabernacle of the LORD at the **h** place	1195
21:29	at that time on the **h** place at Gibeon.	1195
2Ch 1: 3	the whole assembly went to the **h** place	1195
1:13	to Jerusalem from the **h** place at Gibeon,	1195
3: 4	of the building and twenty cubits **h**.	1470
4: 1	twenty cubits wide and ten cubits **h**.	7757
4: 2	from rim to rim and five cubits **h**.	7757
6:13	five cubits wide and three cubits **h**,	7757
11:15	for the **h** places and for the goat	1195
14: 3	the foreign altars and the **h** places,	1195
14: 5	He removed the **h** places and incense altars	1195
15:17	Although he did not remove the **h** places,	1195
17: 6	furthermore, he removed the **h** places and	1195
20:33	The **h** places, however, were not removed,	1195
21:11	also built **h** places on the hills of Judah	1195

Ref	Text	No.
2Ch 28: 4	and burned incense at the **h** places,	1195
28:25	in Judah he built **h** places to burn sacrifices	1195
31: 1	They destroyed the **h** places and the altars	1195
32:12	Hezekiah himself remove this god's **h** places and altars,	1195
33: 3	rebuilt the **h** places his father Hezekiah had demolished;	1195
33:17	continued to sacrifice at the **h** places,	1195
33:19	the sites where he built **h** places and set	1195
34: 3	to purge Judah and Jerusalem of **h** places,	1195
34: 9	the **h** priest and gave him the money	1524
Ezr 6: 3	It is to be ninety feet **h** and ninety feet wide,	10660
Ne 3: 1	the **h** priest and his fellow priests went	1524
3:20	of the house of Eliashib the **h** priest.	1524
8: 4	on a **h** wooden **platform** built for	4463
13:28	the **h** priest was son-in-law to Sanballat	1524
Est 1:10	Xerxes *was* in **h** spirits from wine,	3201+2213
5: 9	that day happy and in **h** spirits.	3201+2213
5:14	"Have a gallows built, seventy-five feet **h**,	1469
7: 9	"A gallows seventy-five feet **h** stands	1469
10: 3	**held in h esteem** by his many fellow Jews,	8354
Job 5:11	The lowly he sets on **h**,	5294
10:16	If I **hold** my **head h**,	1448
16:19	my advocate is on **h**.	928+2021+5294
31: 2	his heritage from the Almighty on **h**?	4946+5294
31:28	I would have been unfaithful to God on **h**.	4946+5087
35: 5	gaze at the clouds *so* **h** above you.	1467
39:27	and **build** his nest on **h**?	8123
Ps 7: 7	Rule over them from on **h**;	2021+5294
7: 8	according to my integrity, O **Most H**.	6604
7:10	My shield is God **Most H**,	6583
7:17	to the name of the LORD **Most H**.	6610
9: 2	I will sing praise to your name, O **Most H**.	6610
18:13	the voice of the **Most H** resounded.	6610
18:16	He reached down from **on h** and took hold	5294
21: 7	the unfailing love of the **Most H** he will not	6610
27: 5	in the shelter of his tabernacle and **set me h**	8123
36: 7	Both **h** and low among men find refuge in	466
46: 4	the holy place where the **Most H** dwells.	6610
47: 2	How awesome is the LORD **Most H**,	6610
49: 2	both low and **h**, rich and poor alike:	408+1201
50:14	fulfill your vows to the **Most H**,	6610
57: 2	I cry out to God **Most H**, to God,	6610
68:18	When you ascended on **h**,	2021+4200+5294
73:11	Does the **Most H** have knowledge?"	6610
77:10	the years of the right hand of the **Most H**."	6610
78:17	rebelling in the desert against the **Most H**;	6610
78:35	that God **Most H** was their Redeemer.	6610
78:56	to the test and rebelled against the **Most H**;	6610
78:58	They angered him with their **h** places;	1195
82: 6	you are all sons of the **Most H**.'	6610
83:18	you alone are the **Most H** over all the earth.	6610
87: 5	and the **Most H** himself will establish her."	6610
91: 1	of the **Most H** will rest in the shadow of	6610
91: 9	If you make the **Most H** your dwelling—	6610
92: 1	and make music to your name, O **Most H**,	6610
93: 4	the LORD on **h** is mighty.	928+2021+5294
97: 9	O LORD, are the **Most H** over all the earth;	6610
102:19	down from his sanctuary on **h**,	5294
103:11	For as **h** as the heavens are above the earth,	1469
104:18	The **h** mountains belong to the wild goats;	1469
107:11	and despised the counsel of the **Most H**.	6610
107:25	and stirred up a tempest *that* **lifted h**	8123
112: 9	his horn *will be* **lifted h** in honor.	8123
113: 5	the *One* who sits enthroned on **h**,	1467
118:16	The LORD's right hand *is* **lifted h**;	8123
138: 6	Though the LORD *is* on **h**,	8123
144: 7	Reach down your hand from on **h**;	5294
Pr 17:19	he who **builds** a **h** gate invites destruction.	1467
23:34	You will be like one sleeping on the **h** seas,	3542+2213
24: 7	Wisdom *is too* **h** for a fool;	8123
25: 3	As the heavens are **h** and the earth is deep,	8124
30:19	the way of a ship on the **h** seas,	3542+2213
Ecc 10: 6	Fools are put in many **h** positions,	5294
Isa 2:14	the towering mountains and all the **h** hills,	5951
6: 1	**h** and exalted, and the train of his robe filled	8123
14:14	I will make myself like the **Most H**."	6610
15: 2	to its **h** places to weep;	1195
16: 3	Make your shadow like night—at **h** noon.	7416
16:12	When Moab appears at her **h** place,	1195
25:12	He will bring down your **h** fortified walls	5369
26: 5	He humbles those who dwell on **h**,	5294
26:11	O LORD, your hand *is* **lifted h**,	8123
30:13	this sin will become for you like a **h** wall,	8435
30:25	on every **h** mountain and every lofty hill.	1469
32:15	till the Spirit is poured upon us from on **h**,	5294
33: 5	The LORD is exalted, for he dwells on **h**;	5294
36: 7	isn't he the one whose **h** places	1195
40: 9	go up on a **h** mountain.	1469
57: 7	You have made your bed on a **h**	1469
57:15	For this is what the **h** and lofty One says—	8123
57:15	"I live in a **h** and holy place,	5294
58: 4	your voice to be heard on **h**.	928+2021+5294
Jer 2:20	on every **h** hill and under every spreading	1469
3: 6	She has gone up on every **h** hill and	1469
7:31	They have built the **h** places of Topheth in	1195
16: 6	"Both **h** and low will die in this land.	1524
17: 2	beside the spreading trees and on the **h** hills.	1469
17: 3	together with your **h** places,	1195
19: 5	the **h** places of Baal to burn their sons in	1195
25:30	" 'The LORD will roar from on **h**;	5294
32:35	They built **h** places for Baal in the Valley	1195
39: 3	a chief officer, Nergal-Sharezer a **h** official	8042
39:13	a **h** official and all the other officers of	8042
48:35	on the **h** places and burn incense	1195

Ref	Text	No.
Jer 49:16	**build** your nest as **h** as the eagle's,	1467
51: 9	*it rises* as **h** as the clouds.'	5951
51:58	be leveled and her **h** gates set on fire;	1469
52:21	Each of the pillars was eighteen cubits **h**	7757
52:22	on top of the one pillar was five cubits **h**	7757
La 1:13	"From on **h** he sent fire,	4791
3:35	to deny a man his rights before the **Most H**,	6610
3:38	from the mouth of the **Most H** that both calamities and good	6610
Eze 1:18	Their rims were **h** and awesome,	1470
1:26	and **h** above on the throne was a figure like that of a man.	2025+4200+4946+5087
6: 3	and I will destroy your **h** places.	1195
6: 6	be laid waste and the **h** places demolished,	1195
6:13	on every **h** hill and on all the mountaintops,	8123
16:16	of your garments to make gaudy **h** places,	1195
17:22	from its topmost shoots and plant it on a **h**	1469
17:24	It towered **h** above the thick foliage,	7757
20:28	and they saw any **h** hill or any leafy tree,	8123
20:29	What is this **h** place you go to?' "	1195
20:40	the **h** mountain of Israel,	5294
23:23	chariot officers and **men of h** rank,	7924
24: 9	I, too, *will* **pile** the wood **h**.	1540
27: 4	Your domain was on the **h** seas;	3542+2213
27:26	Your oarsmen take you out to the **h** seas,	8041
31: 3	it towered on **h**, its top above the thick	7757
31:10	Because it towered on **h**,	928+7757
31:14	are ever to tower proudly on **h**,	928+7757
34: 6	over all the mountains and on every **h** hill.	8123
40: 2	of Israel and set me on a very **h** mountain,	1469
40: 5	rod thick and one rod **h**.	7757
40:12	of each alcove was a wall one cubit **h**,	NIH
40:42	a cubit and a half wide and a cubit **h**.	1470
41:22	There was a wooden altar three cubits **h**	1469
43: 7	of their kings at their **h** places.	1195
43:14	up to the lower ledge it is two cubits **h** and	NIH
43:14	up to the larger ledge it is four cubits **h** and	NIH
43:15	The altar hearth is four cubits **h**,	NIH
Da 2:48	the king **placed** Daniel in a **h** position	10648
3: 1	ninety feet **h** and nine feet wide,	10660
3:26	servants of the **Most H** God, come out!	10546
4: 2	that the **Most H** God has performed for me.	10546
4:17	the **Most H** is sovereign over the kingdoms	10546
4:24	and this is the decree the **Most H** has issued	10546
4:25	the **Most H** is sovereign over the kingdoms	10546
4:32	the **Most H** is sovereign over the kingdoms	10546
4:34	Then I praised the **Most H**;	10546
5:18	the **Most H** God gave your father Nebuchadnezzar sovereignty—	10546
5:19	Because of the **h** position he gave him,	10650
5:21	that the **Most H** God is sovereign over	10546
7:18	But the saints of the **Most H** will receive	10548
7:22	in favor of the saints of the **Most H**,	10548
7:25	against the **Most H** and oppress his saints	10546
7:25	the people of the **Most H**.	10548
Hos 7:16	They do not turn to the **Most H**;	6583
10: 8	The **h** places of wickedness will	1195
11: 7	Even if they call to the **Most H**,	6583
Am 4:13	and treads the **h** places of the earth—	1195
7: 9	"The **h** places of Isaac will be destroyed	1195
Mic 1: 3	he comes down and treads the **h** places of	1195
1: 5	What is Judah's **h** place?	1195
Hab 2: 9	by unjust gain to set his nest on **h**,	5294
3:10	the deep roared and lifted its waves on **h**.	8125
Hag 1: 1	to Joshua son of Jehozadak, the **h** priest:	1524
1:12	Joshua son of Jehozadak, the **h** priest,	1524
1:14	of Jehozadak, the **h** priest, and the spirit of	1524
2: 2	to Joshua son of Jehozadak, the **h** priest,	1524
2: 4	O Joshua son of Jehozadak, the **h** priest.	1524
Zec 3: 1	the **h** priest standing before the angel of	1524
3: 8	O **h** priest Joshua and your associates seated	1524
6:11	and set it on the head of the **h** priest,	1524
Mt 4: 8	to a very **h** mountain and showed him all	5734
17: 1	led them up a **h** mountain by themselves.	5734
20:25	and their **h** officials exercise authority	3489
26: 3	in the palace of the **h** priest,	797
26: 9	a **h** price and the money given to the poor."	4498
26:51	and struck the servant of the **h** priest,	797
26:57	to Caiaphas, the **h** priest, where the teachers	797
26:58	right up to the courtyard of the **h** priest.	797
26:62	Then the **h** priest stood up and said to Jesus,	797
26:63	The **h** priest said to him,	797
26:65	Then the **h** priest tore his clothes and said,	797
Mk 2:26	In the days of Abiathar the **h** priest,	797
5: 7	Jesus, Son *of* the **Most H** God?	5736
6:21	a banquet *for* his **h** officials	3491
9: 2	with him and led them up a **h** mountain,	5734
10:42	and their **h** officials exercise authority	3489
14:47	and struck the servant *of* the **h** priest,	797
14:53	They took Jesus to the **h** priest,	797
14:54	right into the courtyard of the **h** priest.	797
14:60	Then the **h** priest stood up before them	797
14:61	Again the **h** priest asked him,	797
14:63	The **h** priest tore his clothes.	797
14:66	of the servant girls *of* the **h** priest came by.	797
Lk 1:32	and will be called the Son *of* the **Most H**.	5736
1:35	power of the **Most H** will overshadow you.	5736
1:76	will be called a prophet of the **Most H**;	5736
3: 2	the **h** priesthood of Annas and Caiaphas,	797
4: 5	a **h** place and showed him in an instant all	5734
4:38	was suffering *from* a **h** fever,	3489
6:35	and will be sons of the **Most H**.	5736
8:28	Jesus, Son *of* the **Most H** God?	5736
22:50	of them struck the servant *of* the **h** priest,	797
22:54	and took him into the house of the **h** priest.	797
24:49	with power from on **h**."	5737
Jn 11:49	Caiaphas, who was **h priest** that year,	797

Jn	11:51	but as **h priest** that year he prophesied	797
	18:10	drew it and struck the **h priest's** servant,	797
	18:13	Caiaphas, the **h priest** that year.	797
	18:15	this disciple was known *to* the **h priest,**	797
	18:15	with Jesus into the **h priest's** courtyard,	797
	18:16	who was known *to* the **h priest,** came back,	797
	18:19	the **h priest** questioned Jesus	797
	18:22	"Is this the way you answer the **h priest?"**	797
	18:24	still bound, to Caiaphas the **h priest.**	797
	18:26	One of the **h priest's** servants,	797
Ac	4: 6	Annas the **h priest** was there,	797
	4: 6	and the other men of the **h priest's** family.	796
	5:17	Then the **h priest** and all his associates,	797
	5:21	the **h priest** and his associates arrived,	797
	5:27	to be questioned by the **h priest.**	797
	7: 1	Then the **h priest** asked him,	797
	7:48	the **Most H** does not live in houses made	5736
	8:10	all the people, both **h** and low,	3489
	9: 1	He went to the **h priest**	797
	13:50	the God-fearing women of **h standing** and	2363
	16:17	servants of the **Most H** God,	5736
	19:17	the name of the Lord Jesus *was* held in **h** honor.	3486
	22: 5	the **h priest** and all the Council can testify.	797
	23: 2	the **h priest** Ananias ordered those standing	797
	23: 4	"You dare to insult God's **h priest?"**	797
	23: 5	I did not realize that he was the **h priest;**	797
	24: 1	the **h priest** Ananias went down to Caesarea	797
	25:23	the **h ranking officers** and the leading men	5941
Eph	3:18	how wide and long and **h** and deep is	5737
	4: 8	"When he ascended on **h,**	5737
Heb	2:17	a merciful and faithful **h priest** in service	797
	3: 1	the apostle and **h priest** whom we confess.	797
	4:14	since we have a great **h priest** who has gone	797
	4:15	For we do not have a **h priest** who is unable	797
	5: 1	Every **h priest** is selected from among men	797
	5: 5	the glory of becoming a **h priest.**	797
	5:10	and was designated by God to be **h priest** in	797
	6:20	He has become a **h priest** forever,	797
	7: 1	of Salem and priest of God **Most H.**	5736
	7:26	Such a **h priest** meets our need—	797
	7:27	Unlike the other **h priests,**	797
	7:28	as **h priests** men who are weak;	797
	8: 1	We do have such a **h priest,**	797
	8: 3	Every **h priest** is appointed to offer	797
	9: 7	only the **h priest** entered the inner room,	797
	9:11	When Christ came as **h priest** of	797
	9:25	the way the **h priest** enters	797
	13:11	The **h priest** carries the blood of animals	797
Jas	1: 9	to take pride in his **h position.**	5737
Rev	14:20	rising **as h as** the horses' bridles for	948
	21:10	in the Spirit to a mountain great and **h,**	5734
	21:12	It had a great, **h wall** with twelve gates,	5734
	21:16	and as wide and **h** as it is long.	5737

HIGH-GRADE (2) [HIGH]

| 1Ki | 7: 9 | of blocks of **h stone** cut to size and trimmed | 3701 |
| | 7:11 | Above were **h stones,** cut to size, | 3701 |

HIGHBORN (1) [BEAR, HIGH]

| Ps | 62: 9 | the **h** are but a lie; | 408+1201 |

HIGHER (16) [HIGH]

Dt	28:43	among you will rise above you **h**	2025+5087
	28:43	above you higher and **h,**	2025+5087
2Ki	25:28	gave him a seat of honor **h than** those	4946+6584
2Ch	33:14	he also made it much **h.**	1467
Ezr	9: 6	because our sins *are* **h than** our heads	2025+4200+5087+8049
Est	3: 1	seat of honor **h than** that of all the other nobles.	4946+6584
Job	11: 8	They are **h** *than* the heavens—	1470
Ps	61: 2	lead me to the rock *that is* **h than** I.	8123
	108: 4	For great is your love, **h than** the heavens;	4946+6584
Ecc	5: 8	for one official is eyed by a **h** one,	4946+6584
	5: 8	**over** them both are others **h**	6584
Isa	55: 9	"As the heavens *are* **h than** the earth,	1467
	55: 9	so *are* my ways **h than** your ways	1467
Jer	52:32	gave him a seat of honor **h than** those	4946+6584
Eze	31: 5	So it towered **h than** all the trees of	7757
Eph	4:10	the very one who ascended **h than** all	5645

HIGHEST (25) [HIGH]

Dt	10:14	even the **h heavens,**	9028+9028
1Ki	8:27	The heavens, even the **h heaven,**	9028+9028
2Ch	2: 6	the **h heavens,** cannot contain him?	9028+9028
	6:18	The heavens, even the **h heavens,**	9028+9028
Ne	9: 6	You made the heavens, even the **h heavens,**	9028+9028
Est	1:14	to the king and were **h** in the kingdom.	8037
Job	21:22	since he judges even the **h?**	8123
	22:12	And see how lofty are the **h stars!**	8031
Ps	115:16	The **h heavens** belong to the LORD,	
	137: 6	I do not consider Jerusalem my **h joy.**	6584+8031
	148: 4	you **h heavens** and you waters above	9028+9028
Pr	9: 3	she calls from the **h point** of the city,	1726+5294
	9:14	on a seat at the **h point** of the city,	5294
Isa	7:11	in the deepest depths or in the **h heights.**	1467
Da	5: 7	be made the **third h ruler** in the kingdom."	10761
	5:16	be made the **third h ruler** in the kingdom."	10761
	5:29	and he was proclaimed the **third h ruler** in	10761
Mt	4: 5	had him stand on the **h point** of the temple.	4762
	21: 9	"Hosanna in the **h!"**	5736

Mk	11:10	"Hosanna in the **h!"**	5736
Lk	2:14	"Glory to God in the **h,**	5736
	4: 9	had him stand on the **h point** of the temple.	4762
	19:38	"Peace in heaven and glory in the **h!"**	5736
Php	2: 9	God **exalted** him to the **h place**	5671
1Th	5:13	Hold them *in the* **h regard** in love because	5655

HIGHLY (23) [HIGH]

Ex	11: 3	and Moses himself was **h regarded** in Egypt	1524+4394
	15: 1	sing to the LORD, for *he is* **h exalted.**	1448+1448
	15:21	"Sing to the LORD, for *he is* **h exalted.**	1448+1448
Jdg	5:30	**h embroidered** garments for my neck—	8391
1Sa	9: 6	he *is* **h respected.**	3877
	22:14	captain of your bodyguard and **h respected**	3877
2Sa	14:25	In all Israel there was not a man **so h** praised	4394
1Ki	7:14	Huram *was* **h skilled** and experienced	4848
2Ki	5: 1	sight of his master and **h regarded,**	5951+7156
1Ch	14: 2	his kingdom had been **h exalted**	2025+4200+5087
	29:25	The LORD **h exalted** Solomon	2025+4200+5087
2Ch	32:23	he *was* **h regarded** by all the nations.	5951
Isa	32: 5	nor the scoundrel be **h respected.**	8777
	52:13	he will be raised and lifted up and **h exalted.**	4394
Da	9:23	for you are **h esteemed.**	2776
	10:11	He said, "Daniel, you who are **h esteemed,**	2776
	10:19	"Do not be afraid, O man **h esteemed,"**	2776
Lk	1:28	"Greetings, *you* who are **h favored!**	5923
	7: 2	whom his master **valued** h,	1639+1952
	16:15	is **h valued** among men is detestable	3836+5734
Ac	5:13	though they *were* **h regarded** by the people.	3486
	22:12	and **h** respected by all the Jews living there.	NIG
Ro	12: 3	*Do* not **think** of yourself more **h** than	5672

HIGHMINDED (KJV) See ARROGANT, CONCEITED

HIGHWAY (11) [HIGHWAYS]

Nu	20:17	along the king's **h** and not turn to the right	2006
	21:22	along the king's **h** until we have passed	2006
Pr	7:27	Her house is a **h** *to* the grave,	2006
	15:19	but the path of the upright **is a h.**	6148
	16:17	The **h** of the upright avoids evil;	
Isa	11:16	a **h** for the remnant of his people that is left	5019
	19:23	In that day there will be a **h** from Egypt	5019
	35: 8	And a **h** will be there;	5020
	40: 3	make straight in the wilderness a **h**	5019
	62:10	Build up, build up the **h!**	5019
Jer	31:21	Take note of the **h,** the road that you take.	5019

HIGHWAYS (2) [HIGHWAY]

| Isa | 33: 8 | **h** are deserted, no travelers are on the roads. | 5019 |
| | 49:11 | and my **h** will be raised up. | 5019 |

HILEN (1)

| 1Ch | 6:58 | **H,** Debir, | 2664 |

HILKIAH (31) [HILKIAH'S]

2Ki	18:18	Eliakim son of **H** the palace administrator,	2760
	18:26	Then Eliakim son of **H,**	2760
	18:37	Eliakim son of **H** the palace administrator,	2759
	22: 4	to **H** the high priest and have him get ready	2760
	22: 8	**H** the high priest said to Shaphan	2759
	22:10	"**H** the priest has given me a book."	2759
	22:12	He gave these orders to the **h** priest,	2759
	22:14	**H** the priest, Ahikam, Acbor,	2759
	23: 4	The king ordered **H** the high priest,	2759
	23:24	the book that **H** the priest had discovered in	2760
1Ch	6:13	Shallum the father of **H,**	2759
	6:13	the father of Azariah,	2759
	6:45	the son of Amaziah, the son of **H,**	2759
	9:11	Azariah son of **H,** the son of Meshullam,	2759
	26:11	**H** the second, Tabaliah the third	2759
2Ch	34: 9	They went to **H** the high priest and gave	2760
	34:14	the priest found the Book of the Law of	2760
	34:15	**H** said to Shaphan the secretary,	2760
	34:18	"**H** the priest has given me a book."	2760
	34:20	He gave these orders to **H,**	2760
	34:22	**H** and those the king had sent with him	2760
	35: 8	**H,** Zechariah and Jehiel,	2759
Ezr	7: 1	the son of Azariah, the son of **H,**	2759
Ne	8: 4	Shema, Anaiah, Uriah, **H** and Maaseiah;	2759
	11:11	Seraiah son of **H,**	2759
	12: 7	**H** and Jedaiah. These were the leaders of	2759
Isa	22:20	Eliakim son of **H.**	2760
	36: 3	Eliakim son of **H** the palace administrator,	2760
	36:22	Eliakim son of **H** the palace administrator,	2760
Jer	1: 1	The words of Jeremiah son of **H,**	2760
	29: 3	of Shaphan and to Gemariah son of **H,**	2759

HILKIAH'S (1) [HILKIAH]

| Ne | 12:21 | of **H,** Hashabiah; of Jedaiah's, Nethanel. | 2759 |

HILL (157) [FOOTHILLS, HILLS, HILLSIDE, HILLTOP, HILLTOPS]

Ge	10:30	lived in the eastern **h country.**	2215
	14: 6	and the Horites in the **h country** of Seir,	2215
	31:21	he headed for the **h country** of Gilead.	2215
	31:23	and caught up with him in the **h country**	2215
	31:25	Jacob had pitched his tent in the **h country**	2215
	31:54	He offered a sacrifice there in the **h country**	2215

Ge	36: 8	Edom) settled in the **h country** of Seir.	2215
	36: 9	the father of the Edomites in the **h country**	2215
Ex	17: 9	of the **h** with the staff of God in my hands."	1496
	17:10	Aaron and Hur went to the top of the **h.**	1496
Nu	13:17	the Negev and on into the **h country.**	2215
	13:29	and Amorites live in the **h country;**	2215
	14:40	up toward the high **h country.**	2215
	14:44	up toward the high **h country,**	2215
	14:45	in that **h country** came down	2215
Dt	1: 7	Break camp and advance into the **h country**	2215
	1:19	from Horeb and went toward the **h country**	2215
	1:20	"You have reached the **h country** of	2215
	1:24	They left and went up into the **h country,**	2215
	1:41	thinking it easy to go up into the **h country.**	2215
	1:43	up into the **h country.**	2215
	2: 1	around the **h country** of Seir.	2215
	2: 3	around this **h country** long enough;	2215
	2: 5	I have given Esau the **h country** of Seir	2215
	3:12	including half the **h country** of Gilead,	2215
	3:25	that fine **h country** and Lebanon."	2215
Jos	9: 1	those in the **h country,**	2215
	10: 6	from the **h country** have joined forces	2215
	10:40	including the **h country,** the Negev,	2215
	11: 3	Perizzites and Jebusites in the **h country;**	2215
	11:16	the **h country,** all the Negev,	2215
	11:21	the Anakites from the **h country:**	2215
	11:21	from all the **h country** of Judah,	2215
	11:21	and from all the **h country** of Israel.	2215
	12: 8	the **h country,** the western foothills,	2215
	13:19	Zereth Shahar on the **h** *in* the valley,	2215
	14:12	Now give me this **h country** that	2215
	15: 8	the top of the **h** west of the Hinnom Valley	2215
	15:48	In the **h country:** Shamir, Jattir, Socoh,	2215
	16: 1	the desert into the **h country** of Bethel.	2215
	17:15	if the **h country** of Ephraim is too small	2215
	17:16	"The **h country** is not enough for us,	2215
	17:18	but the forested **h country** as well.	2215
	18:12	and headed west into the **h country,**	2215
	18:13	down to Ataroth Addar on the **h** south	2215
	18:14	From the **h** facing Beth Horon on the south	2215
	18:16	down to the foot of the **h** facing the Valley	2215
	19:50	Timnath Serah in the **h country**	2215
	20: 7	in Galilee in the **h country** of Naphtali,	2215
	20: 7	Shechem in the **h country** of Ephraim,	2215
	20: 7	Hebron) in the **h country** of Judah.	2215
	21:11	in the **h country** of Judah.	2215
	21:21	In the **h country** of Ephraim	2215
	24: 4	I assigned the **h country** of Seir to Esau,	2215
	24:30	at Timnath Serah in the **h country**	2215
	24:33	to his son Phinehas in the **h country**	2215
Jdg	1: 9	the Canaanites living in the **h country,**	2215
	1:19	They took possession of the **h country,**	2215
	1:34	the Danites to the **h country,**	2215
	2: 9	at Timnath Heres in the **h country**	2215
	3:27	a trumpet in the **h country** of Ephraim,	2215
	4: 5	and Bethel in the **h country** of Ephraim.	2215
	7: 1	of them in the valley near the **h** of Moreh.	1496
	7:24	throughout the **h country** of Ephraim,	2215
	10: 1	in the **h country** of Ephraim.	2215
	12:15	in the **h country** of the Amalekites.	2215
	16: 3	to the top of the **h** that faces Hebron.	2215
	17: 1	a man named Micah from the **h country**	2215
	17: 8	to Micah's house in the **h country**	2215
	18: 2	The men entered the **h country** of Ephraim	2215
	18:13	on to the **h country** of Ephraim and came	2215
	19: 1	the **h country** of Ephraim took a concubine	2215
	19:16	an old man from the **h country** of Ephraim,	2215
	19:18	a remote area in the **h country** of Ephraim	2215
1Sa	1: 1	a Zuphite from the **h country** of Ephraim,	2215
	7: 1	They took it to Abinadab's house on the **h**	1496
	9: 4	the **h country** of Ephraim and through	2215
	9:11	As they were going up the **h** *to* the town,	5090
	13: 2	at Micmash and in the **h country** of Bethel,	2215
	14:22	in the **h country** of Ephraim heard that	2215
	17: 3	The Philistines occupied one **h** and	
	22: 6	was seated under the tamarisk tree on the **h**	8229
	23:19	on the **h** of Hakilah, south of Jeshimon?	1496
	26: 1	"Is not David hiding on the **h** of Hakilah,	1496
	26: 3	on the **h** of Hakilah facing Jeshimon,	1496
	26:13	on top of the **h** some distance away;	2215
2Sa	2:24	they came to the **h** of Ammah,	1496
	2:25	a group and took their stand on top of a **h.**	1496
	6: 3	house of Abinadab, which was on the **h.**	1496
	13:34	coming down the side of the **h.**	2215
	13:34	on the side of the **h."**	2215
	20:21	from the **h country** of Ephraim,	2215
	21: 9	who killed and exposed them on a **h** before	2215
1Ki	4: 8	in the **h country** of Ephraim;	2215
	11: 7	On a **h** east of Jerusalem,	2215
	12:25	the **h country** of Ephraim and lived there.	2215
	14:23	and Asherah poles on every high **h** and	1496
	16:24	He bought the **h** of Samaria from Shemer	2215
	16:24	of silver and built a city on the **h,**	2215
	16:24	the name of the former owner of the **h.**	2215
2Ki	1: 9	who was sitting on the top of a **h,**	2215
	5:22	to me from the **h country** of Ephraim.	2215
	5:24	When Gehazi came to the **h,**	6755
	17:10	and Asherah poles on every high **h** and	1496
	23:13	on the south of the **H** of Corruption—	2215
1Ch	4:42	invaded the **h country** of Seir.	2215
	6:67	In the **h country** of Ephraim	2215
2Ch	13: 4	in the **h country** of Ephraim, and said,	2215
	19: 4	the people from Beersheba to the **h country**	2215
	27: 3	on the wall at the **h of Ophel.**	6755
	32:33	and was buried on the **h** *where* the tombs	5090
	33:14	and encircling the **h of Ophel;**	6755
	33:15	as all the altars he had built on the temple **h**	2215

Ne	3:26	on the **h of Ophel** made repairs up to	6755
	8:15	into the **h country** and bring back branches	2215
	11:21	temple servants lived on the **h of Ophel,**	6755
Ps	2: 6	on Zion, my holy **h.**"	2215
	3: 4	and he answers me from his holy **h.**	2215
	15: 1	Who may live on your holy **h?**	2215
	24: 3	Who may ascend the **h** of the LORD?	2215
	78:54	to the **h country** his right hand had taken.	2215
SS	4: 6	mountain of myrrh and to the **h** of incense.	1496
Isa	10:32	at the **h** of Jerusalem.	1496
	30:17	like a banner on a **h.**"	1496
	30:25	on every high mountain and every lofty **h.**	1496
	40: 4	every mountain and **h** made low;	1496
	49: 9	and find pasture on every **barren h.**	9155
	57: 7	on a high and lofty **h;**	2215
Jer	2:20	on every high **h** and under every spreading	1496
	3: 6	She has gone up on every high **h** and	2215
	16:16	down on every mountain and **h** and from	1496
	17:26	from the **h country** and the Negev,	2215
	26:18	of rubble, the temple **h** a mound overgrown	2215
	31:39	from there straight to the **h** of Gareb and	1496
	32:44	of Judah and in the towns of the **h country,**	2215
	33:13	In the towns of the **h country,**	2215
	49:16	who occupy the heights of the **h.**	1496
	50: 6	and **h** and forgot their own resting place.	2215
Eze	6:13	on every high **h** and on all	1496
	20:28	and they saw any high **h** or any leafy tree,	1496
	34: 6	over all the mountains and on every high **h.**	1496
	34:26	and the places surrounding my **h.**	1496
Da	9:16	from Jerusalem, your city, your holy **h.**	2215
	9:20	to the LORD my God for his holy **h**—	2215
Joel	2: 1	sound the alarm on my holy **h.**	2215
	3:17	dwell in Zion, my holy **h.**	2215
Ob	1:16	Just as you drank on my holy **h,**	2215
Mic	3:12	the temple **h** a mound overgrown	2215
Zep	3:11	be haughty on my holy **h.**	2215
Mt	5:14	A city on a **h** cannot be hidden.	4001
Lk	1:39	and hurried to a town in the **h country**	3978
	1:65	and throughout the **h country** of Judea	3978
	3: 5	every mountain and **h** made low.	1090
	4:29	and took him to the brow of the **h** on which	4001
	19:29	at the **h** called the Mount of Olives,	4001
	21:37	night on the **h** called the Mount of Olives,	4001
Ac	1:12	from the **h** called the Mount of Olives,	4001

HILLEL (2)

Jdg	12:13	After him, Abdon son of **H,** from Pirathon,	2148
	12:15	Then Abdon son of **H** died,	2148

HILLS (80) [HILL]

Ge	12: 8	From there he went on toward the **h** east	2215
	14:10	into them and the rest fled to the **h.**	2215
	49:26	than the bounty of the age-old **h.**	1496
Dt	1:44	in those **h** came out against you;	2215
	2:37	nor that around the towns in the **h.**	2215
	8: 7	with springs flowing in the valleys and **h;**	2215
	8: 9	and you can dig copper out of the **h.**	2215
	12: 2	and on the **h** and under every spreading tree	1496
	33:15	and the fruitfulness of the everlasting **h;**	1496
Jos	2:16	to the **h** so the pursuers will not find you.	2215
	2:22	into the **h** and stayed there three days,	2215
	2:23	They went down out of the **h,**	2215
Jdg	3:27	Israelites went down with him from the **h,**	2215
	11:37	to roam the **h** and weep with my friends,	2215
	11:38	She and the girls went into the **h** and wept	2215
1Sa	23:14	in the desert strongholds and in the **h of**	2215
1Ki	5:15	and eighty thousand stonecutters in the **h,**	2215
	20:23	"Their gods are gods of the **h.**	2215
	20:28	a god of the **h** and not a god of the valleys,	2215
	22:17	on the **h** like sheep without a shepherd,	2215
2Ki	6:17	and he looked and saw the **h** full of horses	2215
2Ch	2: 2	and eighty thousand as stonecutters in the **h**	2215
	2:18	to be stonecutters in the **h,** with 3,600	2215
	15: 8	and from the towns he had captured in the **h**	2215
	18:16	on the **h** like sheep without a shepherd,	2215
	21:11	the **h** of Judah and had caused the people	2215
	26:10	in the **h** and in the fertile lands,	2215
	27: 4	He built towns in the Judean **h** and forts	2215
Job	15: 7	Were you brought forth before the **h?**	1496
	39: 8	He ranges the **h** for his pasture and searches	2215
	40:20	The **h** bring him their produce,	2215
Ps	50:10	and the cattle on a thousand **h.**	2215
	65:12	the **h** are clothed with gladness.	1496
	72: 3	the **h** the fruit of righteousness.	1496
	72:16	on the tops of the **h** may it sway.	2215
	114: 4	the **h** like lambs.	1496
	114: 6	that you skipped like rams, you **h,**	1496
	121: 1	I lift up my eyes to the **h**—	2215
	147: 8	with rain and makes grass grow on the **h.**	2215
	148: 9	you mountains and all **h,**	1496
Pr	8:25	before the **h,** I was given birth,	1496
	27:25	and the grass from the **h** is gathered in,	2215
SS	2: 8	bounding over the **h.**	1496
	2:17	or like a young stag on the rugged **h.**	2215
Isa	2: 2	it will be raised above the **h,**	1496
	2:14	the towering mountains and all the high **h,**	1496
	7:25	As for all the **h** once cultivated by the hoe,	2215
	17:13	driven before the wind like chaff on the **h,**	2215
	40:12	the mountains on the scales and the **h** in	1496
	41:15	and reduce the **h** to chaff.	1496
	42:15	I will lay waste the mountains and **h** and dry	1496
	54:10	mountains be shaken and the **h** be removed,	1496
	55:12	the mountains and **h** will burst into song	1496
	65: 7	on the mountains and defied me on the **h,**	1496
Jer	3:23	Surely the [idolatrous] commotion on the **h**	1496

Jer	4:15	proclaiming disaster from the **h** of Ephraim.	2215
	4:24	all the **h** were swaying.	1496
	13:16	your feet stumble on the darkening **h.**	2215
	13:27	I have seen your detestable acts on the **h.**	1496
	17: 2	the spreading trees and on the high **h.**	1496
	31: 5	Again you will plant vineyards on the **h**	2215
	31: 6	be a day when watchmen cry out on the **h**	2215
	50:19	his appetite will be satisfied on the **h**	2215
Eze	6: 3	to the mountains and **h,** to the ravines	1496
	35: 8	those killed by the sword will fall on your **h**	2215
	36: 4	to the mountains and **h,** to the ravines	1496
	36: 6	of Israel and say to the mountains and **h,** to	1496
Hos	4:13	and burn offerings on the **h,**	1496
	10: 8	and to the **h,** "Fall on us!"	1496
Joel	3:18	and the **h** will flow with milk;	1496
Am	9:13	from the mountains and flow from all the **h.**	1496
Mic	4: 1	it will be raised above the **h,**	1496
	6: 1	let the **h** hear what you have to say.	1496
Na	1: 5	before him and the **h** melt away.	1496
Hab	3: 6	and the age-old **h** collapsed.	1496
Zep	1:10	and a loud crash from the **h.**	1496
Mt	18:12	the ninety-nine on the **h** and go to look for	4001
Mk	5: 5	in the **h** he would cry out and cut himself	4001
Lk	23:30	and to the **h,** "Cover us!" '	1090
Rev	17: 9	The seven heads are seven **h** on which	4001

HILLSIDE (5) [HILL]

2Sa	16:13	along the **h** opposite him,	2215+7521
2Ki	23:16	he saw the tombs that were there on the **h,**	2215
Isa	5: 1	My loved one had a vineyard on a fertile **h.**	7967
Mk	5:11	of pigs was feeding on the nearby **h.**	4001
Lk	8:32	of pigs was feeding there on the **h.**	4001

HILLTOP (2) [HILL]

Jos	15: 9	From the **h** the boundary headed	2215+8031
Isa	13: 2	Raise a banner on a bare **h,** shout to them;	2215

HILLTOPS (3) [HILL]

Jdg	9:25	Shechem set men on the **h** to ambush	2215+8031
2Ki	16: 4	on the **h** and under every spreading tree.	1496
2Ch	28: 4	on the **h** and under every spreading tree.	1496

HIM (5427) [HE] See Index of Articles Etc.

HIMSELF (430) [HE, SELF] See Index of Articles Etc.

HIN (22)

Ex	29:40	a quarter of a **h** of oil from pressed olives,	2125
	29:40	a quarter of a **h** of wine as a drink offering.	2125
	30:24	and a **h** of olive oil.	2125
Lev	19:36	an honest ephah and an honest **h.**	2125
	23:13	its drink offering of a quarter of a **h** of wine.	2125
Nu	15: 4	of fine flour mixed with a quarter of a **h**	2125
	15: 5	a quarter of a **h** of wine as a drink offering.	2125
	15: 6	of fine flour mixed with a third of a **h**	2125
	15: 7	a third of a **h** of wine as a drink offering.	2125
	15: 9	of an ephah of fine flour mixed with half a **h**	2125
	15:10	bring half a **h** of wine as a drink offering.	2125
	28: 5	a quarter of a **h** of oil from pressed olives,	2125
	28: 7	of a **h** of fermented drink with each lamb.	2125
	28:14	to be a drink offering of half a **h** of wine;	2125
	28:14	with the ram, a third of a **h;**	2125
	28:14	and with each lamb, a quarter of a **h.**	2125
Eze	4:11	Also measure out a sixth of a **h** of water	2125
	45:24	along with a **h** of oil for each ephah.	2125
	46: 5	along with a **h** of oil for each ephah.	2125
	46: 7	along with a **h** of oil with each ephah.	2125
	46:11	along with a **h** of oil for each ephah.	2125
	46:14	a sixth of an ephah with a third of a **h** of oil	2125

HIND (KJV) See DOE, MOUNTAIN GOAT

HINDER (7) [HINDERED, HINDERS, HINDRANCE]

1Sa	14: 6	Nothing can **h** the LORD from saving,	5109
Job	15: 4	even undermine piety and **h** devotion	1757
Mt	19:14	and do not **h** them,	3266
Mk	10:14	and do not **h** them,	3266
Lk	18:16	and do not **h** them,	3266
1Co	9:12	put up with anything rather than **h** the gospel of Christ.	1443+1600
1Pe	3: 7	so that nothing will **h** your prayers.	1601

HINDERED (2) [HINDER]

Lk	11:52	and you have **h** those who were entering."	3266
Ro	15:22	This is why I have often been **h** from	1601

HINDERMOST (KJV) See IN THE REAR, LEAST

HINDERS (1) [HINDER]

Heb	12: 1	let us throw off everything that **h** and the sin	3839

HINDMOST (KJV) See LAST, LAGGING BEHIND, REAR

HINDQUARTERS (2)

1Ki	7:25	and their **h** were toward the center.	294
2Ch	4: 4	and their **h** were toward the center.	294

HINDRANCE (1) [HINDER]

Ac	28:31	and without **h** he preached the kingdom	219

HINGED (1) [HINGES]

Eze	41:24	two **h** leaves for each door.	6015

HINGES (1) [HINGED]

Pr	26:14	As a door turns on its **h,**	7494

HINNOM (3) [BEN HINNOM]

Jos	15: 8	to the top of the hill west of the **H** Valley at	2183
	18:16	down the **H** Valley along the southern slope	2183
Ne	11:30	the way from Beersheba to the Valley of **H.**	2183

HINT (1)

Eph	5: 3	among you there must not be even a **h** of	3951

HIP (5)

Ge	32:25	of Jacob's **h** so that his hip was wrenched	3751
	32:25	that his **h** was wrenched as he wrestled with	3751
	32:31	and he was limping because of his **h.**	3751
	32:32	the tendon attached to the socket of the **h,**	3751
	32:32	because the socket of Jacob's **h** was touched	3751

HIRAH (2)

Ge	38: 1	to stay with a man of Adullam named **H.**	2669
	38:12	his friend **H** the Adullamite went with him.	2669

HIRAM (23) [HIRAM'S]

2Sa	5:11	**H** king of Tyre sent messengers to David,	2671
1Ki	5: 1	When **H** king of Tyre heard	2671
	5: 2	Solomon sent back this message to **H:**	2671
	5: 7	When **H** heard Solomon's message,	2671
	5: 8	So **H** sent word to Solomon:	2671
	5:10	In this way **H** kept Solomon supplied	2670
	5:11	and Solomon gave **H** twenty thousand cors	2671
	5:11	Solomon continued to do this for **H** year	2671
	5:12	There were peaceful relations between **H**	2671
	5:18	of Solomon and **H** and the men of Gebal cut	2670
	9:11	in Galilee to **H** king of Tyre,	2671
	9:11	because **H** had supplied him with all	2671
	9:12	when **H** went from Tyre to see the towns	2671
	9:14	**H** had sent to the king 120 talents of gold.	2671
	9:27	And **H** sent his men—	2671
	10:22	at sea along with the ships of **H.**	2671
1Ch	14: 1	**H** king of Tyre sent messengers to David,	2671
2Ch	2: 3	Solomon sent this message to **H** king	2586
	2:11	**H** king of Tyre replied by letter to Solomon:	2586
	2:12	And **H** added: "Praise be to the LORD,	2586
	8: 2	the villages that **H** had given him,	2586
	8:18	And **H** sent him ships commanded	2586
	9:10	of **H** and the men of Solomon brought gold	2586

HIRAM'S (2) [HIRAM]

1Ki	10:11	(**H** ships brought gold from Ophir;	2671
2Ch	9:21	a fleet of trading ships manned by **H** men.	2586

HIRE (7) [HIRED, HIRES]

Ex	22:15	**money paid for** the **h** covers the loss.	8510
Jdg	9: 4	Abimelech used it to **h** reckless adventurers	8509
1Sa	2: 5	Those who were full **h themselves out**	8509
1Ch	19: 6	a thousand talents of silver to **h** chariots	8509
Isa	23:17	She will return to her **h** as a prostitute	924
	46: 6	they **h** a goldsmith to make it into a god,	8509
Mt	20: 1	to **h** men to work in his vineyard.	3636

HIRED (38) [HIRE]

Ge	30:16	"I have **h** you with my son's mandrakes."	8509+8509
Ex	12:45	a temporary resident and a **h** worker	8502
	22:15	If the animal was **h,** the money paid for	8502
Lev	19:13	hold back the wages of a **h** man overnight.	8502
	22:10	the guest of a priest or his **h** worker eat it.	8502
	25: 6	and maidservant, and the **h** worker	8502
	25:40	as a **h** worker or a temporary resident	8502
	25:50	on the rate paid to a **h** man for that number	8502
	25:53	to be treated as a **man h** from year to year;	8502
Dt	15:18	as much as that of a **h** hand.	8502
	23: 4	and they **h** Balaam son of Beor from Pethor	8509
	24:14	not take advantage of a **h** man who is poor	8502
Jdg	18: 4	and said, "He has **h** me and I am his priest."	8509
2Sa	10: 6	twenty thousand Aramean foot soldiers	8509
2Ki	7: 6	the king of Israel has **h** the Hittite	8509
1Ch	19: 7	They **h** thirty-two thousand chariots	8509
2Ch	24:12	They **h** masons and carpenters to restore	8509
	25: 6	He also **h** a hundred thousand fighting men	8509
Ezr	4: 5	They **h** counselors to work against them	6128
Ne	6:12	because Tobiah and Sanballat had **h** him.	8509
	6:13	He had been **h** to intimidate me so	8509
	13: 2	but had **h** Balaam to call a curse down on	8509
Job	7: 1	Are not his days like those of a **h** man?	8502
	7: 2	or a **h** man waiting eagerly for his wages,	8502
	14: 6	till he has put in his time like a **h** man.	8502
Isa	7:20	In that day the Lord will use a razor **h** from	8502
Mt	20: 7	" 'Because no one has **h** us,' they answered.	3636

Mt	20: 8	beginning with the last ones **h** and going on	*NIG*
	20: 9	"The workers who were **h** about	*NIG*
	20:10	So when those came who were **h** first,	*NIG*
	20:12	'These men who were **h** last worked only one hour,'	*NIG*
	20:14	to give the man who was **h** last the same	*NIG*
Mk	1:20	Zebedee in the boat with the **h** men and	3638
Lk	15:15	So *he* went and **h** himself **out** to a citizen	3140
	15:17	'How many of my father's **h** men have food	3634
	15:19	make me like one *of your* **h men.'**	3634
Jn	10:12	The **h** hand is not the shepherd who owns	3638
	10:13	because he is a **h** hand and cares nothing for the sheep.	3638

HIRELING (KJV) See HIRED, LABORERS, MAN, SERVANT

HIRES (1) [HIRE]

| Pr | 26:10 | wounds at random is *he who* **h** a fool | 8509 |

HIS (7165) [HE] See Index of Articles Etc.

HISS (2) [HISSES]

| Jer | 46:22 | Egypt will **h** like a fleeing serpent as | 7754 |
| Eze | 27:36 | The merchants among the nations **h** at you; | 9239 |

HISSES (1) [HISS]

| Job | 27:23 | It claps its hands in derision and **h** him out | 9239 |

HISTORIC (1) [HISTORY]

| Ne | 2:20 | in Jerusalem or any claim or **h** right to it." | 2355 |

HISTORY (1) [HISTORIC]

| Ezr | 4:19 | and it was found that this city has a **long h** of revolt against kings | 10317+10427+10550 |

HIT (7) [HITS, HITTING]

Ex	21:22	"If men who are fighting **h**	5597
Dt	19: 5	the head may fly off and **h** his neighbor	5162
1Ki	22:34	and **h** the king of Israel between the sections	5782
2Ch	18:33	and **h** the king of Israel between the sections	5782
Pr	23:35	"They **h** me," you will say, "but I'm not hurt!"	5782
Mt	26:68	"Prophesy to us Christ. Who **h** you?"	4091
Lk	22:64	"Prophesy! Who **h** you?"	4091

HITCH (3) [HITCHED]

1Sa	6: 7	**H** the cows to the cart,	673
1Ki	18:44	'**H up** your chariot and go down before	673
2Ki	9:21	"**H up** my chariot," Joram ordered.	673

HITCHED (2) [HITCH]

| 1Sa | 6:10 | They took two such cows and **h** them to | 673 |
| 2Ki | 9:21 | And when *it was* **h up,** | 673 |

HITHER (KJV) See BACK, HERE, RIGHT

HITHERTO (KJV) See ABUNDANTLY, IN THE PAST, THIS FAR, THUS FAR, TO THIS DAY, UNTIL NOW, UP TO

HITS (4) [HIT]

Ex	21:18	"If men quarrel and one **h** the other with	5782
	21:26	"If a man **h** a manservant or maidservant *in*	5782
Nu	35:18	and **h** someone so that he dies,	5782
	35:21	or if in hostility *he* **h** him with his fist so	5782

HITTING (1) [HIT]

| Ex | 2:13 | "Why *are you* **h** your fellow Hebrew?" | 5782 |

HITTITE (25) [HITTITES]

Ge	23:10	Ephron the **H** was sitting among his people	3153
	25: 9	in the field of Ephron son of Zohar the **H,**	3153
	26:34	he married Judith daughter of Beeri the **H,**	3153
	26:34	and also Basemath daughter of Elon the **H.**	3153
	27:46	with living because of these **H** women.	3147
	27:46	from **H** women like these,	3153
	36: 2	Adah daughter of Elon the **H,**	3153
	49:29	in the cave in the field of Ephron the **H,**	3153
	49:30	as a burial place from Ephron the **H,**	3153
	50:13	as a burial place from Ephron the **H,**	3153
Jos	1: 4	all the **H** country—	3153
1Sa	26: 6	David then asked Ahimelech the **H**	3153
2Sa	11: 3	of Eliam and the wife of Uriah the **H?"**	3153
	11: 6	"Send me Uriah the **H.**"	3153
	11:17	moreover, Uriah the **H** died.	3153
	11:21	'Also, your servant Uriah the **H** is dead.' "	3153
	11:24	your servant Uriah the **H** is dead."	3153
	12: 9	the **H** with the sword and took his wife to	3153
	12:10	the wife of Uriah the **H** to be your own.'	3153
	23:39	and Uriah the **H.**	3153
1Ki	15: 5	except in the case of Uriah the **H.**	3153
2Ki	7: 6	of Israel has hired the **H** and Egyptian kings	3153
1Ch	11:41	Uriah the **H,** Zabad son of Ahlai.	3153
Eze	16: 3	an Amorite and your mother a **H.**	3153
	16:45	Your mother was a **H** and your father	3153

HITTITES (36) [HITTITE]

Ge	10:15	Sidon his firstborn, and of the **H,**	3147
	15:20	**H,** Perizzites, Rephaites,	3153
	23: 3	his dead wife and spoke to the **H.**	1201+3147
	23: 5	The **H** replied to Abraham,	1201+3147
	23: 7	before the people of the land, the **H.**	1201+3147
	23:10	in the hearing of all the **H** who	1201+3147
	23:16	in the hearing of the **H:**	1201+3147
	23:18	in the presence of all the **H** who	1201+3147
	23:20	were deeded to Abraham by the **H** as	1201+3147
	25:10	field Abraham had bought from the **H.**	1201+3147
	49:32	cave in it were bought from the **H.**"	1201+3147
Ex	3: 8	the home of the Canaanites, **H,** Amorites,	3153
	3:17	**H,** Amorites, Perizzites,	3153
	13: 5	**H,** Amorites, Hivites and Jebusites—	3153
	23:23	**H,** Perizzites, Canaanites,	3153
	23:28	Canaanites and **H** out of your way.	3153
	33: 2	**H,** Perizzites, Hivites and Jebusites.	3153
	34:11	**H,** Perizzites, Hivites and Jebusites.	3153
Nu	13:29	The Amalekites live in the Negev; the **H,**	3153
Dt	7: 1	the **H,** Girgashites, Amorites, Canaanites,	3153
	20:17	the **H,** Amorites, Canaanites, Perizzites,	3153
Jos	3:10	**H,** Hivites, Perizzites, Girgashites,	3153
	9: 1	as far as Lebanon (the kings of the **H,**	3153
	11: 3	to the Amorites, **H,** Perizzites and Jebusites	3153
	12: 8	the lands of the **H,** Amorites, Canaanites,	3153
	24:11	Perizzites, Canaanites, **H,** Girgashites,	3153
Jdg	1:26	He then went to the land of the **H,**	3153
	3: 5	**H,** Amorites, Perizzites,	3153
1Ki	9:20	All the people left from the Amorites, **H,**	3153
	10:29	also exported them to all the kings of the **H**	3153
	11: 1	Ammonites, Edomites, Sidonians and **H.**	3153
1Ch	1:13	Sidon his firstborn, and of the **H,**	3147
2Ch	1:17	also exported them to all the kings of the **H**	3153
	8: 7	All the people left from the Amorites, **H,**	3153
Ezr	9: 1	like those of the Canaanites, **H,** Perizzites,	3153
Ne	9: 8	**H,** Amorites, Perizzites,	3153

HIVITE (2) [HIVITES]

| Ge | 34: 2 | When Shechem son of Hamor the **H,** | 2563 |
| | 36: 2 | and granddaughter of Zibeon the **H—** | 2563 |

HIVITES (23) [HIVITE]

Ge	10:17	**H,** Arkites, Sinites,	2563
Ex	3: 8	Amorites, Perizzites, **H** and Jebusites.	2563
	3:17	Amorites, Perizzites, **H** and Jebusites—	2563
	13: 5	Hittites, Amorites, **H** and Jebusites—	2563
	23:23	**H** and Jebusites, and I will wipe them out.	2563
	23:28	the hornet ahead of you to drive the **H,**	2563
	33: 2	Hittites, Perizzites, **H** and Jebusites.	2563
	34:11	Hittites, Perizzites, **H** and Jebusites.	2563
Dt	7: 1	Canaanites, Perizzites, **H** and Jebusites,	2563
	20:17	Canaanites, Perizzites, **H** and Jebusites—	2563
Jos	3:10	Hittites, **H,** Perizzites, Girgashites,	2563
	9: 1	Canaanites, Perizzites, **H** and Jebusites)—	2563
	9: 7	The men of Israel said to the **H,**	2563
	11: 3	and to the **H** below Hermon in the region	2563
	11:19	Except for the **H** living in Gibeon,	2563
	12: 8	Canaanites, Perizzites, **H** and Jebusites):	2563
	24:11	Hittites, Girgashites, **H** and Jebusites,	2563
Jdg	3: 3	and the **H** living in the Lebanon mountains	2563
	3: 5	Amorites, Perizzites, **H** and Jebusites.	2563
2Sa	24: 7	and all the towns of the **H** and the Canaanites.	2563
1Ki	9:20	**H** and Jebusites (these peoples were	2563
1Ch	1:15	**H,** Arkites, Sinites,	2563
2Ch	8: 7	**H** and Jebusites (these peoples were	2563

HIZKI (1)

| 1Ch | 8:17 | Zebadiah, Meshullam, **H,** Heber, | 2623 |

HIZKIAH (1)

| 1Ch | 3:23 | Elioenai, **H** and Azrikam—three in all. | 2624 |

HO (KJV) See COME

HOAR (KJV) See GRAY, THIN FLAKES

HOARD (1) [HOARDED, HOARDS]

| Am | 3:10 | "who **h** plunder and loot in their fortresses." | 732 |

HOARDED (3) [HOARD]

Ecc	5:13	wealth **h** to the harm of its owner,	9068
Isa	23:18	they will not be stored up or **h.**	2889
Jas	5: 3	You have **h** wealth in the last days.	2564

HOARDS (1) [HOARD]

| Pr | 11:26 | People curse the *man who* **h** grain, | 4979 |

HOARY (KJV) See AGED, GRAY HAIR, WHITE HAIR

HOBAB (2)

| Nu | 10:29 | Moses said to **H** son of Reuel the Midianite, | 2463 |
| Jdg | 4:11 | the descendants of **H,** | 2463 |

HOBAH (1)

| Ge | 14:15 | pursuing them as far as **H,** | 2551 |

HOBAIAH (2)

| Ezr | 2:61 | The descendants of **H,** | 2469 |
| Ne | 7:63 | the descendants of **H,** | 2469 |

HOD (1)

| 1Ch | 7:37 | **H,** Shamma, Shilshah, Ithran and Beera. | 2087 |

HODAIAH, HODEVAH (KJV) See HODAVIAH

HODAVIAH (6)

1Ch	3:24	The sons of Elioenai: **H,** Eliashib, Pelaiah,	2090
	5:24	Ishi, Eliel, Azriel, Jeremiah, **H** and Jahdiel.	2089
	9: 7	Sallu son of Meshullam, the son of **H,**	2089
Ezr	2:40	and Kadmiel (through the line of **H**) 74	2089
	3: 9	and his sons (descendants of **H**) and	2088
Ne	7:43	(through Kadmiel through the line of **H**) 74	2088

HODESH (1)

| 1Ch | 8: 9 | By his wife **H** he had Jobab, Zibia, Mesha, | 2545 |

HODIAH (5) [HODIAH'S]

Ne	8: 7	Shabbethai, **H,** Maaseiah, Kelita, Azariah,	2091
	9: 5	Kadmiel, Bani, Hashabneiah, Sherebiah, **H,**	2091
	10:10	Shebaniah, **H,** Kelita, Pelaiah, Hanan,	2091
	10:13	**H,** Bani and Beninu.	2091
	10:18	**H,** Hashum, Bezai,	2091

HODIAH'S (1) [HODIAH]

| 1Ch | 4:19 | The sons of **H** wife, the sister of Naham: | 2091 |

HODIJAH (KJV) See HODIAH

HODSHI See TAHTIM HODSHI

HOE (1)

| Isa | 7:25 | As for all the hills once cultivated by the **h,** | 5053 |

HOGLAH (4) [BETH HOGLAH]

Nu	26:33	whose names were Mahlah, Noah, **H,**	2519
	27: 1	Noah, **H,** Milcah and Tirzah.	2519
	36:11	Mahlah, Tirzah, **H,** Milcah and Noah—	2519
Jos	17: 3	whose names were Mahlah, Noah, **H,**	2519

HOHAM (1)

| Jos | 10: 3 | of Jerusalem appealed to **H** king of Hebron, | 2097 |

HOISED (KJV) See HOISTED

HOISTED (2)

| Ac | 27:17 | *When* the men *had* **h** it aboard, | *149* |
| | 27:40 | Then they **h** the foresail to the wind | *2048* |

HOLD (163) [HELD, HOLDING, HOLDS]

Ge	43: 9	**h** me personally **responsible**	1335+3338+4946
	48:17	so *he* took **h** of his father's hand to move it	9461
Ex	4: 4	and took **h** of the snake and it turned back	2616
	5: 1	so that *they may* **h** a festival to me in	2510
	9: 2	to let them go and continue *to* **h** them **back,**	2616
	12:16	On the first day **h** a sacred assembly,	2118
	13: 6	the seventh day **h** a festival to the LORD.	NIH
	20: 7	**h** anyone **guiltless** who misuses his name.	5927
	22:29	"Do not **h** back offerings from your granaries	336
	25:27	to the rim to **h** the poles used in carrying	1074
	26:29	and make gold rings to **h** the crossbars	1074
	30: 4	to **h** the poles used to carry it.	1074
	36:34	and made gold rings to **h** the crossbars,	1074
	37:14	to the rim to **h** the poles used in carrying	1074
	37:27	to **h** the poles used to carry it.	1074
	38: 5	They cast bronze rings to **h** the poles for	1074
Lev	19:13	" 'Do not **h** back the wages of a hired man **overnight.**	1332+4328+6330
	23: 7	On the first day **h** a sacred assembly	2118
	23: 8	And on the seventh day **h** a sacred assembly	NIH
	23:27	**H** a sacred assembly and deny yourselves,	2118
	23:36	and on the eighth day **h** a sacred assembly	2118
	25:24	the country that you **h** as a **possession,**	299
	25:33	that is, a house sold in any town they **h**—	299
Nu	12:11	*do not* **h** against us the sin we have	8883
	28:18	On the first day **h** a sacred assembly	NIH
	28:25	On the seventh day **h** a sacred assembly	2118
	28:26	Feast of Weeks, **h** a sacred assembly	2118
	29: 1	" 'On the first day of the seventh month **h**	2118
	29: 7	" 'On the tenth day of this seventh month **h**	2118
	29:12	of the seventh month, **h** a sacred assembly	2118
	29:35	" 'On the eighth day **h** an assembly	2118
Dt	5:11	**h** anyone **guilty** who misuses his name.	5927
	10:20	**H** fast to him and take your oaths	1815
	11:22	in all his ways and to **h** fast to him—	1815
	13: 4	serve him and **h** fast to him.	1815
	16: 8	and on the seventh day **h** an assembly to	NIH
	21: 8	and *do not* **h** your people guilty of the blood	5989
	21:19	his father and mother *shall* **take h** of him	9530
	30:20	listen to his voice, and **h** fast to him.	1815
Jos	8:18	"**H out** toward Ai the javelin that is	5742
	22: 5	to obey his commands, to **h** fast to him and	1815

Jos	23: 8	you are to **h** fast to the LORD your God,	1815
Jdg	1:35	the Amorites were determined also to **h** out	3782
	9: 9	to **h** sway over the trees?'	5675
	9:11	to **h** sway over the trees?'	5675
	9:13	to **h** sway over the trees?'	5675
	16: 3	up and took **h** of the doors of the city gate,	296
Ru	3:15	the shawl you are wearing and **h** it out."	296
1Sa	15:27	Saul caught **h** of the hem of his robe,	2616
	17:51	He took **h** of the Philistine's sword	4374
2Sa	1:11	David and all the men with him took **h**	2616
	6: 6	Uzzah reached out and took **h** of the ark	296
	15: 5	take **h** of him and kiss him.	2616
	19:19	"May my lord not **h** me guilty.	3108
	22:17	"He reached down from on high and took **h**	4374
1Ki	1:50	went and took **h** of the horns of the altar.	2616
	2:28	he fled to the tent of the LORD and took **h**	2616
	8:64	before the LORD was too small to **h**	3920
	11:30	and Ahijah took **h** of the new cloak	9530
	18:32	around it large enough to **h** two seahs	1074
2Ki	2:12	Then he took **h** of his own clothes	2616
	4:16	a son in your arms."	2485
	4:27	she took **h** of his feet.	2616
	6:32	shut the door and **h** it shut against him.	4315
	10:19	I am going to **h** a great sacrifice for Baal.	4200
	15:19	to gain his support and strengthen his own **h**	3338
2Ch	7: 7	the bronze altar he had made could not **h**	3920
Job	8:15	he clings to it, but it does not **h**.	7756
	9:28	for I know you will not **h** me innocent.	5927
	10:16	If I **h** my head high,	1448
	17: 9	the righteous will **h** to their ways,	296
	36:17	judgment and justice have taken **h** of you.	9461
	39:10	Can you **h** him to the furrow with	8003
Ps	18:16	He reached down from on high and took **h**	4374
	21: 8	Your hand will lay **h** on all your enemies;	5162
	73:23	you **h** me by my right hand.	296
	74:11	Why do you **h** back your hand,	8740
	75: 3	it is I who **h** its pillars firm.	9419
	79: 8	Do not **h** against us the sins of the fathers;	2349
	119:31	I **h** fast to your statutes, O LORD;	1815
	139:10	your right hand will **h** me fast.	296
Pr	3:18	those who lay **h** of her will be blessed.	9461
	4: 4	"Lay **h** of my words with all your heart;	9461
	4:13	**H** on to instruction, do not let it go;	2616
	5:22	the cords of his sin **h** him fast.	9461
	7:13	She took **h** of him and kissed him and with	2616
	20:16	**h** it in pledge if he does it for	2471
	24:11	**h** back those staggering toward slaughter.	3104
	27:13	**h** it in pledge if he does it for a wayward	2471
SS	7: 8	I will take **h** of its fruit."	296
Isa	4: 1	In that day seven women will take **h**	2616
	22:17	LORD is about to take firm **h** of you	6487+6487
	41:13	who takes **h** of your right hand and says	2616
	42: 6	I will take **h** of your hand.	2616
	43: 6	and to the south, 'Do not **h** them back.'	3973
	45: 1	whose right hand I take **h** of	2616
	48: 9	the sake of my praise I **h** it back from you,	2641
	54: 2	do not **h** back;	3104
	56: 4	who choose what pleases me and **h** fast	2616
	56: 6	without desecrating it and who **h** fast	2616
	58: 1	"Shout it aloud, do not **h** back.	3104
	64: 7	on your name or strives to lay **h** of you;	2616
	64:12	O LORD, will you **h** yourself back?	706
	65: 4	and whose pots **h** broth of unclean meat;	NIH
Jer	2:13	broken cisterns that cannot **h** water.	3920
	6:11	of wrath of the LORD, and I cannot **h** it in.	3920
	34: 9	**h** a fellow Jew in bondage.	6268
	34:10	and no longer **h** them in bondage.	6268
	50:33	All their captors **h** them fast,	2616
Eze	3:18	I will **h** you accountable for his blood.	1335+3338+4946
	3:20	I will **h** you accountable for his blood.	1335+3338+4946
	17: 3	Taking **h** of the top of a cedar,	4374
	24:14	I will not **h** back;	7277
	30: 9	Anguish will take **h** of them on the day	928+2118
	30:21	so as to become strong enough to **h** a sword.	9530
	33: 6	I will **h** the watchman accountable for his blood.'	2011+3338+4946
	33: 8	I will **h** you accountable for his blood.	1335+3338+4946
	34:10	and will **h** them accountable	2011+3338+4946
	37:20	**H** before their eyes the sticks	928+2118+3338
Da	4:35	No one can **h** back his hand or say to him:	10411
Jnh	1:14	Do not **h** us accountable for killing	5989+6584
Zec	8:23	and nations will take firm **h** of one Jew by	2616
Mt	11:12	and forceful men lay **h** of it.	773
	12:11	will you not take **h** of it and lift it out?	3195
	21:26	for they all **h** that John was a prophet."	2400
Mk	11:25	if you **h** anything against anyone,	2400
Lk	14: 4	So taking **h** of the man,	2138
Jn	8:31	Jesus said, "If you **h** to my teaching,	3531
	14:30	He has no **h** on me,	2400
	20:17	Jesus said, "Do not **h** on to me,	721
Ac	2:24	for death to keep its **h** on him.	3195
	7:60	"Lord, do not **h** this sin against them."	2705
	27: 7	wind did not allow us to **h** our course,	4661
	27:17	they passed ropes under the ship itself to **h** it together.	5690
Ro	13: 3	For rulers **h** no terror for those who do right,	1639+5832
1Co	15: 2	if you **h** firmly to the word I preached	2988
Php	2:16	as you **h** out the word of life—	2091
	3:12	but I press on to take **h** of that	2898
	3:12	of that for which Christ Jesus took **h** of me.	2898
	3:13	not consider myself yet to have taken **h** of	2898
Col	1:17	and in him all things **h** together.	5319
1Th	5:13	**H** them in the highest regard in love	2451

1Th	5:21	Test everything. **H** on to the good.	2988
2Th	2:15	stand firm and **h** to the teachings we passed	3195
1Ti	3: 9	They must keep **h** of the deep truths of	2400
	6:12	Take **h** of the eternal life	2138
	6:19	they may take **h** of the life that is truly life.	2138
Tit	1: 9	He must **h** firmly to the trustworthy message	504
Heb	3: 6	if we **h** on to our courage and the hope	2988
	3:14	to share in Christ if we **h** firmly till the end	2988
	4:14	let us **h** firmly to the faith we profess.	3195
	6:18	to take **h** of the hope offered to us may	3195
	10:23	Let us **h** unswervingly to the hope	2988
2Pe	2: 9	to rescue godly men from trials and to **h**	5498
Rev	1:18	And I **h** this against you:	2400
	2: 4	Yet I **h** this against you:	2400
	2:14	You have people there who **h** to the teaching of Balaam,	3195
	2:15	also have those who **h** to the teaching of	3195
	2:24	to you who do not **h** to her teaching	2400
	2:25	Only **h** on to what you have until I come.	3195
	3:11	**H** on to what you have,	3195
	12:17	and **h** to the testimony of Jesus.	2400
	19:10	with your brothers who **h** to the testimony	2400

HOLDING (24) [HOLD]

Ge	50:11	"The Egyptians are **h** a solemn ceremony	4200
Jdg	7:20	in their left hands and **h** in their right hands	NIH
1Sa	17:57	with David still **h** the Philistine's head.	928+3338
	25:36	he was in the house **h** a banquet like that of	4200
1Ki	7:38	each **h** forty baths	3920
Ne	4:21	the work with half the men **h** spears,	2616
Job	1: 4	to take turns **h** feasts in their homes,	6913
	2: 9	"Are you still **h** on to your integrity?	2616
Jer	20: 9	I am weary of **h** it in; indeed, I cannot.	3920
	34: 7	of Judah that were still **h** out—	3855
Mk	7: 3	**h** to the tradition of the elders.	3195
	7: 8	of the commands of God and are **h** on to	3195
Jn	2: 6	each **h** from twenty to thirty gallons.	6003
	8:44	not **h** to the truth, for there is no truth in him	2705
1Co	11: 2	in everything and for **h** to the teachings,	2988
2Th	2: 6	And now you know what is **h** him back,	2988
1Ti	1:19	**h** on to faith and a good conscience.	2400
	4: 8	**h** promise for both the present life and	2400
Rev	5: 8	a harp and they were **h** golden bowls full	NIG
	6: 5	Its rider was **h** a pair of scales in his hand.	2400
	7: 1	**h** back the four winds of the earth	3195
	7: 9	and were **h** palm branches in their hands.	NIG
	10: 2	He was **h** a little scroll,	2400
	20: 1	to the Abyss and **h** in his hand a great chain.	2093

HOLDS (22) [HOLD]

Ge	50:15	"What if Joseph **h** a grudge against us	8475
Nu	5:18	he himself **h** the bitter water	928+2118+3338
Job	12:15	If he **h** back the waters, there is drought;	6806
	18: 9	a snare **h** him fast.	2616
	37: 4	his voice resounds, he **h** nothing back.	6810
Pr	2: 7	He **h** victory in store for the upright,	7621
	3:35	but fools he **h** up to shame.	8123
	10:19	but he who **h** his tongue is wise.	3104
	11:12	but a man of understanding **h** his tongue.	3087
	17:28	and discerning if he **h** his tongue.	357
	31:19	In her hand she **h** the distaff and grasps	8938
Isa	41:23	tell us what the future **h**,	910
	56: 2	the man who **h** it fast,	2616
Eze	23:32	for it **h** so much.	3920
Da	5:23	But you did not honor the God who **h**	NIH
Am	1: 5	and the one who **h** the scepter in Beth Eden,	9461
	1: 8	and the one who **h** the scepter in Ashkelon.	9461
2Th	2: 7	but the one who now **h** it back will continue	2988
Heb	2:14	by his death he might destroy him who **h**	2400
Rev	2: 1	the words of him who **h** the seven stars	3195
	3: 1	of him who **h** the seven spirits of God and	2400
	3: 7	who **h** the key of David.	2400

HOLE (7) [HOLES]

Dt	23:13	dig a **h** and cover up your excrement.	2916
2Ki	12: 9	the priest took a chest and bored a **h**	2986
Ps	7:15	He who digs a **h** and scoops it out falls into	1014
Isa	11: 8	The infant will play near the **h** of the cobra,	2987
Eze	8: 7	I looked, and I saw a **h** in the wall.	2986
	12:12	and a **h** will be dug in the wall for him	NIH
Mt	25:18	dug a **h** in the ground	4002

HOLES (8) [HOLE]

1Sa	14:11	crawling out of the **h** they were hiding in."	2986
Job	30: 6	among the rocks and in **h** in the ground.	2986
Isa	2:19	the rocks and in **h** in the ground from dread	4704
	7:19	all the thornbushes and at all the water **h**.	5635
Hag	1: 6	only to put them in a purse with **h** in it."	5918
Mt	8:20	"Foxes have **h** and birds of the air have	5887
Lk	9:58	"Foxes have **h** and birds of the air have	5887
Heb	11:38	and in caves and **h** in the ground.	3956

HOLIDAY (1)

Est	2:18	He proclaimed a **h** throughout the provinces	2182

HOLIEST (1) [HOLY]

Nu	18:29	as the LORD's portion the best and **h** part	5219

HOLILY (KJV) See HOLY

HOLINESS (25) [HOLY]

Ex	15:11	Who is like you—majestic in **h**,	7731

Dt	32:51	because you did not uphold my **h** among	7727
1Ch	16:29	worship the LORD in the splendor of his **h**.	7731
2Ch	20:21	for the splendor of his **h** as they went out at	7731
Ps	29: 2	worship the LORD in the splendor of his **h**.	7731
	89:35	Once for all, I have sworn by my **h**—	7731
	93: 5	**h** adorns your house for endless days,	7731
	96: 9	Worship the LORD in the splendor of his **h**;	7731
Isa	29:23	they will acknowledge the **h** of the Holy One	7727
	35: 8	it will be called the Way of **H**.	7731
Eze	36:23	I will show the **h** of my great name,	7727
	38:23	And so I will show my greatness and my **h**,	7727
Am	4: 2	The Sovereign LORD has sworn by his **h**:	7731
Lk	1:75	in **h** and righteousness before him	4009
Ro	1: 4	through the Spirit of **h** was declared with	43
	6:19	in slavery to righteousness leading to **h**.	40
	6:22	the benefit you reap leads to **h**,	40
1Co	1:30	that is, our righteousness, **h** and redemption.	40
2Co	1:12	in the **h** and sincerity that are from God.	605
	7: 1	perfecting **h** out of reverence for God.	43
Eph	4:24	to be like God in true righteousness and **h**.	4009
1Ti	2: 2	and quiet lives in all godliness and **h**.	4949
	2:15	love and **h** with propriety.	40
Heb	12:10	that we may share in his **h**.	42
	12:14	without **h** no one will see the Lord.	4005S

HOLLOW (8)

Ex	27: 8	Make the altar **h**, out of boards.	5554
	38: 7	They made it **h**, out of boards.	5554
Jdg	15:19	Then God opened up the **h** place in Lehi,	4847
Pr	30: 4	up the wind in the **h** of his hands?	2908
Isa	40:12	the waters in the **h** of his hand,	9123
Jer	52:21	each was four fingers thick, and **h**.	5554
2Co	9: 3	in this matter should not prove **h**,	3033
Col	2: 8	to it that no one takes you captive through **h**	3031

HOLON (3)

Jos	15:51	Goshen, **H** and Giloh—	2708
	21:15	**H**, Debir,	2708
Jer	48:21	Judgment has come to the plateau—to **H**,	2708

HOLPEN (KJV) See HELPED, LEND STRENGTH

HOLY (584) [HALLOWED, HOLIEST, HOLINESS]

Ge	2: 3	God blessed the seventh day and made it **h**,	7727
Ex	3: 5	where you are standing is **h** ground."	7731
	15:13	you will guide them to your **h** dwelling.	7731
	16:23	a **h** Sabbath to the LORD.	7731
	19: 6	for me a kingdom of priests and a **h** nation.'	7705
	19:23	the mountain and set it apart as **h**.' "	7727
	20: 8	Remember the Sabbath day by keeping it **h**.	7727
	20:11	blessed the Sabbath day and made it **h**.	7727
	22:31	"You are to be my **h** people.	7731
	26:33	The curtain will separate the **H** Place from	7731
	26:33	Holy Place from the Most **H** Place.	7731+7731
	26:34	of the Testimony in the Most **H** Place.	7731+7731
	28:29	"Whenever Aaron enters the **H** Place,	7731
	28:35	be heard when he enters the **H** Place	7731
	28:36	as on a seal: **H** TO THE LORD.	7731
	28:43	the altar to minister in the **H** Place,	7731
	29:30	in the **H** Place is to wear them seven days.	7731
	29:37	Then the altar will be most **h**,	7731+7731
	29:37	and whatever touches it will be **h**.	7727
	30:10	It is most **h** to the LORD."	7731+7731
	30:29	so they will be most **h**,	7731+7731
	30:29	and whatever touches them will be **h**.	7727
	30:36	It shall be most **h** to you.	7731+7731
	30:37	consider it **h** to the LORD.	7731
	31:11	and fragrant incense for the **H** Place.	7731
	31:13	I am the LORD, who makes you **h**.	7727
	31:14	because it is **h** to you.	7731
	31:15	a Sabbath of rest, **h** to the LORD.	7731
	35: 2	but the seventh day shall be your **h** day,	7731
	39:30	inscription on a seal: **H** TO THE LORD.	7731
	40: 9	and it will be **h**.	7731
	40:10	the altar, and it will be most **h**.	7731+7731
Lev	2: 3	it is a most **h** part of the offerings	7731+7731
	2:10	it is a most **h** part of the offerings	7731+7731
	5:15	in regard to any of the LORD's **h** things,	7731
	5:16	to do in regard to the **h** things,	7705
	6:16	it is to be eaten without yeast in a **h** place;	7705
	6:17	and the guilt offering, it is most **h**.	7731+7731
	6:18	Whatever touches them will become **h**.' "	7727
	6:25	it is most **h**.	7731+7731
	6:26	it is to be eaten in a **h** place,	7705
	6:27	of the flesh will become **h**,	7727
	6:27	you must wash it in a **h** place.	7705
	6:29	it is most **h**.	7731+7731
	6:30	to make atonement in the **H** Place must not	7731
	7: 1	which is most **h**:	7731+7731
	7: 6	but it must be eaten in a **h** place;	7705
	7: 6	it is most **h**.	7731+7731
	10: 3	" 'Among those who approach me I will show myself **h**;	7727
	10:10	You must distinguish between the **h** and	7731
	10:12	for it is most **h**.	7731+7731
	10:13	Eat it in a **h** place,	7705
	10:17	It is most **h**;	7731+7731
	10:18	its blood was not taken into the **H** Place,	7731
	11:44	consecrate yourselves and be **h**,	7705
	11:44	and be holy, because I am **h**.	7705
	11:45	therefore be **h**, because I am holy.	7705

Lev 11:45 therefore be holy, because I am h. 7705
14:13 to slaughter the lamb in the h place where 7705
14:13 belongs to the priest; it is most h. 7731+7731
16: 2 into the Most H Place behind the curtain 7731
16:16 for the Most H Place because of 7731
16:17 in to make atonement in the Most H Place 7731
16:20 for the Most H Place, 7731
16:23 on before he entered the Most H Place, 7731
16:24 in a h place and put on his regular garments. 7705
16:27 the Most H Place to make atonement, 7731
16:33 make atonement for the Most H Place, 5219+7731
19: 2 'Be h because I, the LORD your God, 7705
19: 2 the LORD your God, am h. 7705
19: 8 because he has desecrated what is h to 7731
19:24 In the fourth year all its fruit will be h, 7731
20: 3 and profaned my h name. 7731
20: 7 " 'Consecrate yourselves and be h, 7705
20: 8 I am the LORD, who makes you h. 7727
20:26 You are to be h to me because I, 7705
20:26 be holy to me because I, the LORD, am h, 7705
21: 6 be h to their God and must not profane 7731
21: 6 the food of their God, they are to be h. 7731
21: 7 because priests are h to their God. 7705
21: 8 Regard them as h, 7727
21: 8 Consider them h, because I the LORD 7705
21: 8 because I the LORD am h— 7705
21: 8 I who make you h. 7727
21:15 I am the LORD, who makes him h.' " 7727
21:22 may eat the most h food of his God, 7731+7731
21:22 as well as the h food; 7731
21:23 I am the LORD, who makes them h.' " 7727
22: 2 so they will not profane my h name. 7731
22: 9 I am the LORD, who makes them h. 7727
22:16 I am the LORD, who makes them h.' " 7727
22:32 Do not profane my h name. 7731
22:32 I must be acknowledged as h by 7727
22:32 I am the LORD, who makes you h. 7727
24: 9 who are to eat it in a h place, 7705
24: 9 a most h part of their regular share of 7731+7731
25:12 For it is a jubilee and is to be h for you; 7731
27: 9 an animal given to the LORD becomes h. 7731
27:10 both it and the substitute become h. 7731
27:14 a man dedicates his house as something h 7731
27:21 it will become h, like a field devoted to 7731
27:23 on that day as something h to the LORD. 7731
27:28 so devoted is most h to the LORD. 7731+7731
27:30 belongs to the LORD; it is h to the LORD. 7731
27:32 will be h to the LORD. 7731
27:33 both the animal and its substitute become h 7731
Nu 4: 4 the care of the most h things. 7731+7731
4:15 the h furnishings and all the holy articles, 7731
4:15 the holy furnishings and all the h articles, 7731
4:15 not touch the h things or they will die. 7731
4:16 including its h furnishings and articles." 7731
4:19 near the most h things, do this for them 7731+7731
4:20 not go in to look at the h things, 7731
5:17 Then he shall take some h water in 7705
6: 5 be h until the period of his separation to 7705
6:20 they are h and belong to the priest, 7731
7: 9 to carry on their shoulders the h things, 7731
10:21 Kohathites set out, carrying the h things, 5219
16: 3 The whole community is h, 7705
16: 5 who belongs to him and who is h, 7705
16: 7 chooses will be the one who is h. 7705
16:37 for the censers are h— 7727
16:38 before the LORD and have become h. 7727
18: 8 the h offerings the Israelites give me I give 7731
18: 9 of the most h offerings that is kept 7731+7731
18: 9 the gifts they bring me as most h offerings, 7731+7731
18:10 Eat it as something most h; 7731+7731
18:10 You must regard it as h. 7731
18:17 or a goat; they are h. 7731
18:19 from the h offerings the Israelites present to 7731
18:32 not defile the h offerings of the Israelites, 7731
20:12 in me enough to honor me as h in the sight 7727
20:13 where he showed himself h among them. 7727
27:14 to honor me as h before their eyes." 7727
35:25 who was anointed with the h oil. 7731
Dt 5:12 "Observe the Sabbath day by keeping it h, 7727
7: 6 you are a people h to the LORD your God. 7705
14: 2 you are a people h to the LORD your God. 7705
14:21 you are a people h to the LORD your God. 7705
23:14 Your camp must be h, 7705
26:15 your h dwelling place, 7731
26:19 be a people h to the LORD your God, 7705
28: 9 LORD will establish you as his h people, 7705
33: 2 with myriads of h ones from the south, 7731
33: 3 all the h ones are in your hand. 7705
Jos 5:15 for the place where you are standing is h." 7731
24:19 He is a h God; he is a jealous God. 7705
24:26 up there under the oak near the h place of 5219
1Sa 2: 2 "There is no one like the LORD; 7705
6:20 in the presence of the LORD, this h God? 7705
21: 5 The men's things are h even on missions 7705
21: 5 even on missions that are not h. 2687
1Ki 6:16 inner sanctuary, the Most H Place, 7731+7731
7:50 innermost room, the Most H Place, 7731+7731
8: 6 of the temple, the Most H Place, 7731+7731
8: 8 the H Place in front of the inner sanctuary, 7731
8: 8 but not from outside the H Place; NIH
8:11 the priests withdrew from the h place, 7731
2Ki 4: 9 who often comes our way a h man of God. 7705
19:22 Against the H One of Israel! 7705
1Ch 6:49 all that was done in the Most H Place, 7731+7731
16:10 Glory in his h name; 7731
16:35 that we may give thanks to your h name, 7731

1Ch 23:13 to consecrate the most h things, 7731+7731
23:32 for the H Place and, 7731
29: 3 I have provided for this h temple: 7731
29:16 for building you a temple for your H Name, 7731
2Ch 3: 8 He built the Most H Place, 7731+7731
3:10 In the Most H Place he made a pair 7731+7731
4:22 the inner doors to the Most H Place, 7731+7731
5: 7 of the temple, the Most H Place, 7731+7731
5: 9 but not from outside the H Place; NIH
5:11 priests then withdrew from the H Place. 7731
8:11 the ark of the LORD has entered are h." 7731
30:27 heaven, his h dwelling place. 7731
31: 6 and a tithe of the h things dedicated to 7731
35: 5 in the h place with a group of Levites 7731
35:13 and the h offerings in pots, 7731
Ezr 9: 2 the h race with the peoples around them. 7731
Ne 9:14 You made known to them your h Sabbath 7731
10:31 from them on the Sabbath or on any h day. 7731
10:33 for the h offerings; for sin offerings 7731
11: 1 of every ten to live in Jerusalem, the h city, 7731
11:18 The Levites in the h city totaled 284. 7731
13:22 in order to keep the Sabbath day h. 7727
Job 5: 1 To which of the h ones will you turn? 7705
6:10 I had not denied the words of the H One. 7705
15:15 If God places no trust in his h ones, 7705
Ps 2: 6 on Zion, my h hill." 7731
3: 4 and he answers me from his h hill. 7731
5: 7 down toward your h temple. 7731
11: 4 The LORD is in his h temple; 7731
15: 1 Who may live on your h hill? 7731
16:10 nor will you let your H One see decay. 2883
20: 6 from his h heaven with the saving power 7731
22: 3 Yet you are enthroned as the H One; 7705
24: 3 Who may stand in his h place? 7731
28: 2 my hands toward your Most H Place. 1808+7731
30: 4 praise his h name. 7731
33:21 for we trust in his h name. 7731
43: 3 let them bring me to your h mountain, 7731
46: 4 the h place where the Most High dwells. 7731
47: 8 God is seated on his h throne. 7731
48: 1 in the city of our God, his h mountain. 7731
51:11 from your presence or take your H Spirit 7705
65: 4 of your house, of your h temple. 7705
68: 5 a defender of widows, is God in his h dwelling. 7731
71:22 O H One of Israel. 7705
77:13 Your ways, O God, are h. 7731
78:41 they vexed the H One of Israel. 7705
78:54 to the border of his h land, 7731
79: 1 they have defiled your h temple, 7731
87: 1 set his foundation on the h mountain; 7731
89: 5 in the assembly of the h ones. 7705
89: 7 of the h ones God is greatly feared, 7705
89:18 our king to the H One of Israel. 7705
97:12 and praise his h name. 7731
98: 1 and his h arm have worked salvation 7731
99: 3 and awesome name—he is h. 7705
99: 5 at his footstool; he is h. 7705
99: 9 and worship at his h mountain, 7731
99: 9 for the LORD our God is h. 7705
103: 1 all my inmost being, praise his h name. 7731
105: 3 Glory in his h name; 7731
105:42 he remembered his h promise given 7731
106:47 to your h name and glory in your praise. 7731
110: 3 Arrayed in h majesty, 7731
111: 9 h and awesome is his name. 7705
138: 2 I will bow down toward your h temple 7731
145:21 Let every creature praise his h name. 7731
Pr 9:10 knowledge of the H One is understanding. 7705
30: 3 nor have I knowledge of the H One. 7705
Ecc 8:10 and go from the h place and receive praise 7705
Isa 1: 4 the H One of Israel and turned their backs 7705
4: 3 who remain in Jerusalem, will be called h, 7705
5:16 and the h God will show himself holy 7731
5:16 and the holy God will show himself h 7727
5:19 let the plan of the H One of Israel come, 7705
5:24 spurned the word of the H One of Israel. 7705
6: 3 "H, holy, holy is the LORD Almighty; 7705
6: 3 "Holy, h, holy is the LORD Almighty; 7705
6: 3 "Holy, holy, h is the LORD Almighty; 7705
6:13 so the h seed will be the stump in the land." 7731
8:13 the one you are to regard as h, 7727
10:17 their H One a flame; 7705
10:20 on the H One of Israel. 7705
11: 9 nor destroy on all my h mountain, 7731
12: 6 for great is the H One of Israel among you." 7705
13: 3 I have commanded my h ones, 7727
17: 7 and turn their eyes to the H One of Israel. 7705
27:13 the LORD on the h mountain in Jerusalem. 7731
29:19 needy will rejoice in the H One of Israel. 7705
29:23 they will keep my name h; 7727
29:23 the holiness of the H One of Jacob, 7705
30:11 and stop confronting us with the H One 7705
30:12 this is what the H One of Israel says: 7705
30:15 the Sovereign LORD, the H One of Israel, 7705
30:29 as on the night you celebrate a h festival; 7727
31: 1 but do not look to the H One of Israel, 7705
37:23 Against the H One of Israel! 7705
40:25 says the H One. 7705
41:14 your Redeemer, the H One of Israel. 7705
41:16 the LORD and glory in the H One of Israel. 7705
41:20 that the H One of Israel has created it. 7705
43: 3 your God, the H One of Israel, your Savior; 7705
43:14 your Redeemer, the H One of Israel: 7705
43:15 I am the LORD, your H One, 7705
45:11 the H One of Israel, and its Maker: 7705
47: 4 is the H One of Israel. 7705

Isa 48: 2 of the h city and rely on the God of Israel— 7731
48:17 your Redeemer, the H One of Israel: 7705
49: 7 the Redeemer and H One of Israel— 7705
49: 7 the H One of Israel, who has chosen you." 7731
52: 1 O Jerusalem, the h city. 7731
52:10 The LORD will lay bare his h arm in 7731
54: 5 the H One of Israel is your Redeemer; 7705
55: 5 the LORD your God, the H One of Israel, 7705
56: 7 to my h mountain and give them joy 7731
57:13 the land and possess my h mountain." 7731
57:15 he who lives forever, whose name is h: 7705
57:15 "I live in a high and h place, 7705
58:13 and from doing as you please on my h day, 7731
58:13 and the LORD's h day honorable, 7731
60: 9 the LORD your God, the H One of Israel, 7705
60:14 Zion of the H One of Israel. 7705
62:12 They will be called the H People, 7731
63:11 is he who set his H Spirit among them, 7731
63:18 while your people possessed your h place, 7731
64:11 Our h and glorious temple, 7731
65:11 the LORD and forget my h mountain, 7731
65:25 nor destroy on all my h mountain," 7731
66:20 to my h mountain in Jerusalem as 7731
Jer 2: 3 Israel was h to the LORD, 7731
17:22 keep the Sabbath day h, 7727
17:24 keep the Sabbath day h 7727
17:27 keep the Sabbath day h 7727
23: 9 because of the LORD and his h words. 7731
25:30 from his h dwelling and roar mightily 7731
31:40 will be h to the LORD. 7731
50:29 defied the LORD, the H One of Israel. 7705
51: 5 of guilt before the H One of Israel. 7705
51:51 the h places of the LORD's house." 5219
Eze 20:12 that I the LORD made them h. 7727
20:20 Keep my Sabbaths h, 7727
20:39 to me and no longer profane my h name 7731
20:40 For on my h mountain, 7731
20:40 along with all your h sacrifices. 7731
20:41 and I will show myself h among you in 7727
22: 8 You have despised my h things 7731
22:26 to my law and profane my h things; 7731
22:26 they do not distinguish between the h and 7731
28:14 You were on the h mount of God; 7731
28:22 on her and show myself h within her. 7727
28:25 I will show myself h among them in 7727
36:20 the nations they profaned my h name, 7731
36:21 I had concern for my h name, 7731
36:22 but for the sake of my h name, 7731
36:23 when I show myself h through you 7727
37:28 that the LORD make Israel h, 7727
38:16 when I show myself h through you 7727
39: 7 " 'I will make known my h name 7731
39: 7 I will no longer let my h name be profaned, 7731
39: 7 that I the LORD am the H One in Israel. 7705
39:25 and I will be zealous for my h name. 7731
39:27 I will show myself h through them in 7727
41: 4 to me, "This is the Most H Place." 7731+7731
41:21 the front of the Most H Place was similar. 7731
41:23 and the Most H Place had double doors. 7731
42:13 LORD will eat the most h offerings. 7731+7731
42:13 they will put the most h offerings— 7731+7731
42:13 for the place is h. 7705
42:14 Once the priests enter the h precincts, 7731
42:14 for these are h. 7731
42:20 to separate the h from the common. 7731
43: 7 The house of Israel will never again defile my h name— 7731
43: 8 they defiled my h name by their detestable 7731
43:12 on top of the mountain will be most h. 7731+7731
44: 8 in regard to my h things, 7731
44:13 as priests or come near any of my h things 7731
44:13 holy things or my most h offerings; 7731+7731
44:23 the h and the common and show them how 7731
44:24 and they are to keep my Sabbaths h. 7727
45: 1 the entire area will be h. 7731
45: 3 the sanctuary, the Most H Place. 7731+7731
45: 4 a place for their houses as well as a h place 5219
48:12 of the land, a most h portion, 7731+7731
48:14 because it is h to the LORD. 7731
Da 4: 8 and the spirit of the h gods is in him.) 10620
4: 9 I know that the spirit of the h gods is in you 10620
4:13 a h one, coming down from heaven. 10620
4:17 the h ones declare the verdict, 10620
4:18 because the spirit of the h gods is in you." 10620
4:23 "You, O king, saw a messenger, a h one, 10620
5:11 the spirit of the h gods in him. 10620
8:13 Then I heard a h one speaking, 7705
8:13 and another h one said to him, 7705
8:24 the mighty men and the h people. 7705
9:16 your city, your h hill. 7731
9:20 to the LORD my God for his h hill— 7731
9:24 and your h city to finish transgression, 7731
9:24 prophecy and to anoint the most h. 7731+7731
11:28 his heart will be set against the h covenant. 7731
11:30 and vent his fury against the h covenant. 7731
11:30 to those who forsake the h covenant. 7731
11:45 the seas at the beautiful h mountain. 7731
12: 7 of the h people has been finally broken, 7705
Hos 11: 9 the H One among you. 7705
11:12 even against the faithful H One. 7705
Joel 1:14 Declare a h fast; call a sacred assembly. 7727
2: 1 sound the alarm on my h hill. 7731
2:15 Blow the trumpet in Zion, declare a h fast, 7727
3:17 dwell in Zion, my h hill. 7731
3:17 Jerusalem will be h; 7731

Am	2: 7	the same girl and so profane my **h** name.	7731
Ob	1:16	Just as you drank on my **h** hill,	7731
	1:17	it will be **h**, and the house of Jacob	7731
Jnh	2: 4	yet I will look again toward your **h** temple.'	7731
	2: 7	my prayer rose to you, to your **h** temple.	7731
Mic	1: 2	the Lord from his **h** temple.	7731
Hab	1:12	My God, my **H One**, we will not die.	7705
	2:20	But the LORD is in his **h** temple;	7731
	3: 3	the **H One** from Mount Paran.	7705
Zep	3:11	Never again will you be haughty on my **h** hill.	7731
Zec	2:12	the **h** land and will again choose Jerusalem.	7731
	2:13	he has roused himself from his **h** dwelling."	7731
	8: 3	be called the **H** Mountain."	7731
	14: 5	and all the **h** *ones* with him.	7705
	14:20	On that day **H TO THE LORD** will be	7731
	14:21	Every pot in Jerusalem and Judah will be **h**	7731
Mt	1:18	to be with child through the **H** Spirit.	41
	1:20	in her is from the **H** Spirit.	41
	3:11	He will baptize you with the **H** Spirit and	41
	4: 5	Then the devil took him to the **h** city	41
	12:32	anyone who speaks against the **H** Spirit will not be forgiven,	41
	24:15	"So when you see standing in the **h** place	41
	27:52	of many **h** people who had died were raised	41
	27:53	into the **h** city and appeared to many people.	41
	28:19	the Father and of the Son and of the **H** Spirit,	41
Mk	1: 8	but he will baptize you with the **H** Spirit."	41
	1:24	I know who you are—the **H** *One* of God!"	41
	3:29	whoever blasphemes against the **H** Spirit will never be forgiven;	41
	6:20	knowing him to be a righteous and **h** man.	41
	8:38	in his Father's glory with the **h** angels."	41
	12:36	David himself, speaking by the **H** Spirit,	41
	13:11	for it is not you speaking, but the **H** Spirit.	41
Lk	1:15	and he will be filled *with* the **H** Spirit even	41
	1:35	"The **H** Spirit will come upon you,	41
	1:35	the **h** one to be born will be called the Son	41
	1:41	and Elizabeth was filled *with* the **H** Spirit.	41
	1:49	**h** is his name.	41
	1:67	*with* the **H** Spirit and prophesied:	41
	1:70	he said through his **h** prophets of long ago),	41
	1:72	and to remember his **h** covenant.	41
	2:25	and the **H** Spirit was upon him.	41
	2:26	to him by the **H** Spirit that he would not die	41
	3:16	He will baptize you with the **H** Spirit and	41
	3:22	and the **H** Spirit descended on him	41
	4: 1	Jesus, full *of* the **H** Spirit,	41
	4:34	I know who you are—the **H** *One* of God!"	41
	9:26	the glory of the Father and *of* the **h** angels.	41
	10:21	full of joy through the **H** Spirit, said,	41
	11:13	the **H** Spirit to those who ask him!"	41
	12:10	anyone who blasphemes against the **H** Spirit will not be forgiven.	41
	12:12	for the **H** Spirit will teach you at	41
Jn	1:33	he who will baptize you with the **H** Spirit.'	41
	6:69	and know that you are the **H** *One* of God."	41
	14:26	But the Counselor, the **H** Spirit,	41
	17:11	**H** Father, protect them by the power	41
	20:22	"Receive the **H** Spirit.	41
Ac	1: 2	giving instructions through the **H** Spirit	41
	1: 5	you will be baptized with the **H** Spirit."	41
	1: 8	when the **H** Spirit comes on you;	41
	1:16	the **H** Spirit spoke long ago through	41
	2: 4	All of them were filled *with* the **H** Spirit	41
	2:27	nor will you let your **H** *One* see decay.	4008
	2:33	from the Father the promised **H** Spirit	41
	2:38	you will receive the gift *of* the **H** Spirit.	41
	3:14	You disowned the **H** and Righteous *One*	41
	3:21	through his **h** prophets.	41
	4: 8	Peter, filled *with* the **H** Spirit, said to them:	41
	4:25	You spoke by the **H** Spirit through	41
	4:27	to conspire against your **h** servant Jesus,	41
	4:30	through the name of your **h** servant Jesus."	41
	4:31	And they were all filled *with* the **H** Spirit	41
	5: 3	you have lied to the **H** Spirit	41
	5:32	so is the **H** Spirit, whom God has given	41
	6: 5	a man full of faith and of the **H** Spirit;	41
	6:13	against this **h** place and against the law.	41
	7:33	where you are standing is **h** ground.	41
	7:51	You always resist the **H** Spirit!	41
	7:55	But Stephen, full *of* the **H** Spirit,	41
	8:15	that they might receive the **H** Spirit,	41
	8:16	**H** Spirit had not yet come upon any of them	NIG
	8:17	and they received the **H** Spirit.	41
	8:19	on whom I lay my hands may receive the **H** Spirit."	41
	9:17	and be filled *with* the **H** Spirit."	41
	9:31	and encouraged *by* the **H** Spirit,	41
	10:22	A **h** angel told him to have you come	41
	10:38	of Nazareth *with* the **H** Spirit and power,	41
	10:44	the **H** Spirit came on all who heard the message.	41
	10:45	*of* the **H** Spirit had been poured out even on	41
	10:47	They have received the **H** Spirit just as we	41
	11:15	the **H** Spirit came on them as he had come	41
	11:16	but you will be baptized with the **H** Spirit.'	41
	11:24	full *of* the **H** Spirit and faith,	41
	13: 2	the **H** Spirit said, "Set apart for me Barnabas	41
	13: 4	sent on their way by the **H** Spirit,	41
	13: 9	filled *with* the **H** Spirit,	41
	13:34	**h** and sure **blessings promised** to David.'	4008
	13:35	" 'You will not let your **H** *One* see decay.'	4008
	13:52	with joy and *with* the **H** Spirit.	41
	15: 8	that he accepted them by giving the **H** Spirit	41
	15:28	It seemed good to the **H** Spirit and to us not	41
	16: 6	by the **H** Spirit from preaching the word in	41

Ac	19: 2	receive the **H** Spirit when you believed?"	41
	19: 2	not even heard that there is a **H** Spirit."	41
	19: 6	the **H** Spirit came on them,	41
	20:23	that in every city the **H** Spirit warns me	41
	20:28	the **H** Spirit has made you overseers.	41
	21:11	"The **H** Spirit says, 'In this way	41
	21:28	the temple area and defiled this **h** place."	41
	28:25	"The **H** Spirit spoke the truth	41
Ro	1: 2	through his prophets in the **H** Scriptures	41
	5: 5	his love into our hearts by the **H** Spirit,	41
	7:12	So then, the law is **h**,	41
	7:12	the law is holy, and the commandment is **h**,	41
	9: 1	my conscience confirms it in the **H** Spirit—	41
	11:16	of the dough offered as firstfruits is **h**, then	41
	11:16	then the whole batch is **h**;	NIG
	11:16	if the root is **h**, so are the branches.	41
	12: 1	living sacrifices, **h** and pleasing to God—	41
	14:17	peace and joy in the **H** Spirit,	41
	15:13	with hope by the power of the **H** Spirit.	41
	15:16	sanctified by the **H** Spirit.	41
	16:16	Greet one another with a **h** kiss.	41
1Co	1: 2	in Christ Jesus and called to be **h**, together	41
	6:19	that your body is a temple *of* the **H** Spirit,	41
	7:14	but as it is, they are **h**.	41
	12: 3	"Jesus is Lord," except by the **H** Spirit.	41
	16:20	Greet one another with a **h** kiss.	41
2Co	6: 6	in the **H** Spirit and in sincere love;	41
	13:12	Greet one another with a **h** kiss.	41
	13:14	fellowship *of* the **H** Spirit be with you all.	41
Eph	1: 4	the world to be **h** and blameless in his sight.	41
	1:13	the promised **H** Spirit,	41
	2:21	and rises to become a **h** temple in the Lord.	41
	3: 5	the Spirit to God's **h** apostles and prophets.	41
	4:30	And do not grieve the **H** Spirit of God,	41
	5: 3	these are improper *for* God's **h** people.	41
	5:26	to **make** her **h**, cleansing her by	39
	5:27	but **h** and blameless.	41
Col	1: 2	*To the* **h** and faithful brothers in Christ	41
	1:22	through death to present you **h** in his sight,	41
	3:12	as God's chosen people, **h** and dearly loved,	41
1Th	1: 5	with the **H** Spirit and with deep conviction,	41
	1: 6	with the joy *given* by the **H** Spirit.	41
	2:10	You are witnesses, and so is God, of how **h**,	4010
	3:13	**h** in the presence of our God and Father	43+1877
	3:13	Lord Jesus comes with all his **h** *ones*.	41
	4: 4	to control his own body in a way that is **h**	40
	4: 7	but to live a **h** life.	40
	4: 8	who gives you his **H** Spirit.	41
	5:26	Greet all the brothers with a **h** kiss.	41
2Th	1:10	in his **h** people and to be marveled at	41
1Ti	2: 8	I want men everywhere to lift up **h** hands	4008
2Ti	1: 9	who has saved us and called us *to a* **h** life—	41
	1:14	with the help *of* the **H** Spirit who lives in us.	41
	2:21	an instrument for noble purposes, **made h**,	39
	3:15	known the **h** Scriptures, which are able	2641
Tit	1: 8	upright, **h** and disciplined.	4008
	3: 5	of rebirth and renewal *by* the **H** Spirit,	41
Heb	2: 4	**H** Spirit distributed according to his will.	41
	2:11	Both the one who **makes** men **h**	39
	2:11	and those who *are* **made h** are of	39
	3: 1	Therefore, **h** brothers, who share in	41
	3: 7	So, as the **H** Spirit says:	41
	6: 4	who have shared in the **H** Spirit,	41
	7:26	one who is **h**, blameless, pure,	4008
	9: 2	this was called the **H** Place.	41
	9: 3	a room called the **Most H Place**,	41+41
	9: 8	The **H** Spirit was showing by this that	41
	9: 8	the Most **H** Place had not yet been disclosed	41
	9:12	but he entered the Most **H** Place once for all	41
	9:25	the Most **H** Place every year with blood	41
	10:10	we have been **made h** through the sacrifice of the body of Jesus Christ	39+1639
	10:14	by one sacrifice he has made perfect forever those who *are* being **made h**.	39
	10:15	The **H** Spirit also testifies to us about this.	41
	10:19	the Most **H** *Place* by the blood of Jesus,	41
	11: 7	in **h** fear built an ark to save his family.	2326
	12:14	to live in peace with all men and to be **h**;	40
	13:11	the blood of animals into the Most **H** *Place*	41
	13:12	**make** the people **h** through his own blood.	39
1Pe	1:12	to you by the **H** Spirit sent from heaven.	41
	1:15	But just as he who called you is **h**,	41
	1:15	so be **h** in all you do;	41
	1:16	for it is written: "Be **h**, because I am holy."	41
	1:16	for it is written: "Be holy, because I am **h**."	41
	2: 5	into a spiritual house to be a **h** priesthood,	41
	2: 9	a **h** nation, a people belonging to God,	41
	3: 5	the **h** women of the past who put their hope	41
2Pe	1:21	as they were carried along by the **H** Spirit.	41
	3: 2	by the prophets and the command given	41
	3:11	You ought to live **h** and godly *lives*	41
1Jn	2:20	But you have an anointing from the **H One**,	41
Jude	1:14	with thousands upon thousands of his **h** *ones*	41
	1:20	build yourselves up *in* your *most* **h** faith	41
	1:20	and pray in the **H** Spirit.	41
Rev	3: 7	These are the words of him who is **h**	41
	4: 8	Day and night they never stop saying: "**H**,	41
	4: 8	"Holy, holy, **h** is the Lord God Almighty,	41
	4: 8	"Holy, holy, **h** is the Lord God Almighty,	41
	6:10	"How long, Sovereign Lord, **h** and true,	41
	11: 2	They will trample on the **h** city	41
	14:10	in the presence *of* the **h** angels and of	41
	15: 4	For you alone are **h**.	4008
	16: 5	the **H** *One*, because you have so judged;	4008
	20: 6	Blessed and **h** are those who have part in	41
	21: 2	I saw the **H** City, the new Jerusalem,	41
	21:10	and showed me the **H** City, Jerusalem,	41

Rev	22:11	and let him who *is* **h** continue to be holy."	41
	22:11	and *let* him who is holy continue *to be* **h**."	39
	22:19	in the tree of life and in the **h** city,	41

HOLYDAY (KJV) See RELIGIOUS FESTIVAL

HOMAGE (3)

2Ch	24:17	the officials of Judah came and **paid h** to	2556
Job	31:27	hand **offered** them a **kiss** of **h**,	4200+5975+7023
Mk	15:19	Falling on their knees, *they* **paid h** to him.	4686

HOMAM (2)

Ge	36:22	The sons of Lotan: Hori and **H**.	2123
1Ch	1:39	The sons of Lotan: Hori and **H**.	2102

HOME (186) [HOMELAND, HOMELESS, HOMES]

Ge	18:33	he left, and Abraham returned **h**.	5226
	29:13	and kissed him and brought him to his **h**,	1074
	31:55	Then he left and returned **h**.	5226
	34: 5	so he kept quiet about it until they **came h**.	995
	35:27	Jacob **came h** to his father Isaac in Mamre,	995
	39:16	beside her until his master came **h**.	1074
	43:26	When Joseph came **h**,	1074
Ex	3: 8	the **h** *of* the Canaanites, Hittites, Amorites,	5226
	18:23	and all these people will go **h** satisfied."	5226
Lev	18: 9	**born in the same h** or elsewhere.	1074+4580
Nu	14:30	with uplifted hand to **make** your **h**,	8905
	15: 2	you enter the land I am giving you as a **h**	4632
	24:11	Now leave at once and go **h**!	5226
	24:25	Then Balaam got up and returned **h**	5226
Dt	6: 7	when you sit at **h** and when you walk along	1074
	11:19	when you sit at **h** and when you walk along	1074
	20: 5	Let him go **h**, or he may die in battle	1074
	20: 7	Let him go **h**, or he may die in battle	1074
	20: 8	Let him go **h** so that his brothers will	1074
	21:12	into your **h** and have her shave her head,	1074
	22: 2	take it **h** with you and keep it	1074
	24: 5	to be free to stay at **h** and bring happiness to	1074
Jos	9:12	when we packed it at **h** on the day we left	1074
	20: 6	Then he may go back to his own **h** in	1074
	22: 7	When Joshua sent them **h**, he blessed them,	185
Jdg	8:29	Jerub-Baal son of Joash went back **h** to live.	1074
	9: 5	He went to his father's **h** in Ophrah and	1074
	9:55	that Abimelech was dead, they went **h**.	5226
	11:34	When Jephthah returned to his **h** in Mizpah,	1074
	18:26	turned around and went back **h**.	1074
	19: 9	up and be on your way **h**."	185
	19:15	no one took them into his **h** for the night.	1074
	19:28	man put her on his donkey and set out for **h**.	5226
	19:29	When he reached **h**,	1074
	20: 8	saying, "None of us will go **h**.	185
	21:24	the Israelites left that place and went **h**	NIH
Ru	1: 6	to return **h** from there.	NIH
	1: 8	"Go back, each of you, to your mother's **h**.	1074
	1: 9	that each of you will find rest in the **h**	1074
	1:11	But Naomi said, "Return **h**, my daughters.	NIH
	1:12	Return **h**, my daughters;	NIH
	3: 1	should I not try to find a **h** for you,	4955
	4:11	the woman who is coming into your **h**	1074
1Sa	1:19	the LORD and then went back to their **h**	1074
	1:23	the woman **stayed at h** and nursed her son	3782
	2:11	Then Elkanah went **h** to Ramah,	1074
	2:20	Then they would go **h**.	5226
	7:17	went back to Ramah, where his **h** was,	1074
	10:25	each to his own **h**.	1074
	10:26	Saul also went to his **h** in Gibeah,	1074
	15:34	but Saul went up to his **h** *in* Gibeah of Saul.	1074
	18: 6	When the men were returning **h**	NIH
	23:18	Then Jonathan went **h**,	1074
	24:22	Then Saul returned **h**,	1074
	25: 1	and they buried him at his **h** in Ramah.	1074
	25:35	"Go **h** in peace.	1074
	26:25	and Saul returned **h**.	5226
2Sa	3:16	Then Abner said to him, "Go back **h**!"	NIH
	6:20	David returned **h** to bless his household,	NIH
	7:10	so that *they can* **have a h** of their own	8905+9393
	11: 4	Then she went back **h**.	1074
	11:10	When David was told, "Uriah did not go **h**,"	1074
	11:10	Why didn't you go **h**?"	1074
	11:13	he did not go **h**.	1074
	12:15	After Nathan had gone **h**,	1074
	14: 8	The king said to the woman, "Go **h**,	1074
	19:30	that my lord the king has arrived **h** safely."	1074
	19:39	and Barzillai returned to his **h**.	5226
	20:22	each returning to his **h**.	185
1Ki	1:53	and Solomon said, "Go to your **h**."	1074
	5:14	in Lebanon and two months at **h**.	1074
	8:66	They blessed the king and then went **h**,	185
	12:16	So the Israelites went **h**.	185
	12:24	Go **h**, every one of you,	1074
	12:24	the word of the LORD and **went h** again,	2143
	13: 7	"Come **h** with me and have something	1074
	13:15	"Come **h** with me and eat."	1074
	14:12	"As for you, go back **h**.	1074
	16: 9	getting drunk in the **h** of Arza,	1074
	17:12	a few sticks *to* **take h** and make a meal	995
	17:13	Go **h** and do as you have said.	995
	21: 4	So Ahab went **h**, sullen and angry	1074
	22:17	Let each one go **h** in peace.' "	1074
2Ki	4:13	"**I have a h** among my own people."	3782

2Ki 8:21 his army, however, fled back h. 185
14:10 Glory in your victory, but stay at h! 1074
14:12 and every man fled to his h. 185
1Ch 16:43 Then all the people left, each for his own h, 1074
16:43 and David returned h to bless his family. 6015
17: 9 so that they can have a h of their own 8905+9393
2Ch 10:16 So all the Israelites went h. 185
11: 4 Go h, every one of you, 1074
18:16 Let each one go h in peace.' " 1074
25:10 to him from Ephraim and sent them h. 5226
25:10 They were furious with Judah and left for h 5226
25:19 But stay at h! 1074
25:22 and every man fled to his h. 185
Ne 6:10 who was shut in at his h. NIH
Est 5:10 Haman restrained himself and went h. 1074
6:12 But Haman rushed h, 1074
Job 17:13 If the only h I hope for is the grave, 1074
39: 6 I gave him the wasteland as his h, 1074
Ps 84: 3 Even the sparrow has found a h, 1074
104:17 the stork has its h in the pine trees. 1074
113: 9 He settles the barren woman in her h as 1074
Pr 3:33 but he blesses the h of the righteous. 5659
7:11 her feet never stay at h; 1074
7:14 "I have fellowship offerings at h; NIH
7:19 My husband is not at h; 1074
7:20 and will not be h till full moon." 1074
15:31 to a life-giving rebuke will be at h among 4328
27: 8 a man who strays from his h. 5226
30:26 yet they make their h in the crags; 1074
Ecc 12: 5 to his eternal h and mourners go about 1074
Isa 3: 6 at his father's h, and say, "You have 1074
14:17 and would not let his captives go h?" 1074
34:13 a haunt for jackals, a h for owls. 2948
Jer 39:14 to take him back to his h. 1074
Eze 36: 8 for they will soon come h. 995
Da 4: 4 I, Nebuchadnezzar, was at h in my palace, 10103
6:10 he went h to his upstairs room where 10103
Ob 3 the clefts of the rocks and make your h on 8699
Jnh 4: 2 is this not what I said when I was still at h? 141
Mic 2: 2 They defraud a man of his h, 1074
Zep 3:20 at that time I will bring you h. 995
Hag 1: 9 What you brought h, I blew away. 1074
Mt 1:20 not be afraid to take Mary h as your wife, NIG
1:24 and took Mary h as his wife. NIG
8: 6 at h paralyzed and in terrible suffering." 3864
9: 6 "Get up, take your mat and go h." 3875
9: 7 And the man got up and went h. 3875
10:12 As you enter the h, give it your greeting. 3864
10:13 If the h is deserving, let your peace rest on 3864
10:14 the dust off your feet when you leave that h 3864
26: 6 the h of a man known as Simon the Leper, 3864
Mk 1:29 and John to the h of Simon and Andrew. 3864
2: 1 the people heard that he had come h. 3875
2:11 "I tell you, get up, take your mat and go h." 1650+3836+3875+5148
5:19 "Go to your family and tell them 3875
5:38 to the h of the synagogue ruler, 3875
7:30 She went h and found her child 899+3836+3875
8: 3 If I send them h hungry, 899+1650+3875
8:26 Jesus sent him h, saying, 899+1650+3875
10:29 "no one who has left h or brothers or sisters 3864
14: 3 the table in the h of a man known as Simon 3864
Lk 1:23 of service was completed, he returned h. 3875
1:40 where she entered Zechariah's h 3875
1:56 for about three months and then returned h. NIG
2:43 while his parents were returning h, NIG
4:38 the synagogue and went to the h of Simon. 3864
5:24 get up, take your mat and go h. 1650+3836+3875
5:25 and went h praising God. 899+1650+3836+3875
8:39 "Return h and tell how much God has done 3875+5148
10:38 a woman named Martha opened her h to 5685
15: 6 and goes h. Then he calls his friends 3875
15:30 with prostitutes comes h, 2262
18:14 went h justified before God. 899+3836+3875
18:29 "no one who has left h or wife or brothers 3864
19:15 however, and returned h. NIG
23:56 Then they went h and prepared spices 5715
Jn 7:53 Then each went to his own h. 3875
9: 7 man went and washed, and came h seeing. NIG
11:20 but Mary stayed at h. 3875
14:23 and we will come to him and make our h 3665
16:32 each to his own h. 2625+3836
19:27 this disciple took her into his h. 2625+3836
Ac 8:28 and on his way h was sitting 5715
10:32 He is a guest in the h of Simon the tanner, 3864
16:15 she invited us to her h. NIG
18:26 invited him to their h 4689
20:12 The people took the young man alive NIG
21: 6 and they returned h. 2625+3836
21:16 and brought us to the h of Mnason, NIG
28: 7 He welcomed us to his h and NIG
1Co 11:34 If anyone is hungry, he should eat at h, 3875
14:35 they should ask their own husbands at h; 3875
2Co 5: 6 that as long as we are at h in the body, 1897
5: 8 away from the body and at h with the Lord. 1897
5: 9 whether we are at h in the body or away 1897
Tit 2: 5 to be busy at h, to be kind, 3877
Phm 2 and to the church that meets in your h: 3875
Heb 11: 9 By faith he made his h in the promised land 4228
2Pe 3:13 and a new earth, the h of righteousness. 2997
Jude 6 of authority but abandoned their own h— 3863
Rev 18: 2 She has become a h for demons and a haunt 2999

HOMEBORN (KJV) See BY BIRTH, NATIVE BORN

HOMELAND (7) [HOME]
Ge 30:25 so I can go back to my own h. 824+5226
Ru 2:11 mother and your h and came to live 824+4580
2Sa 4:16 You are a foreigner, an exile from your h. 5226
2Ki 17:23 the people of Israel were taken from their h 141
Ps 79: 7 devoured Jacob and destroyed his h. 5659
Jer 2:15 that you might send them far from their h. 5659
Joel 3: 6 that you might send them far from their h. 1473

HOMELESS (1) [HOME]
1Co 4:11 we are brutally treated, we are h. 841

HOMER (10) [HOMERS]
Lev 27:16 fifty shekels of silver to a h of barley seed. 2818
Isa 5:10 a h of seed only an ephah of grain." 2818
Eze 45:11 of a h and the ephah a tenth of a homer; 2818
45:11 of a homer and the ephah a tenth of a h; 2818
45:11 the h is to be the standard measure for both. 2818
45:13 an ephah from each h of wheat and a sixth 2818
45:13 a sixth of an ephah from each h of barley. 2818
45:14 of ten baths or one h, 2818
45:14 for ten baths are equivalent to a h). 2818
Hos 3: 2 for fifteen shekels of silver and about a h 2818

HOMERS (1) [HOMER]
Nu 11:32 No one gathered less than ten h. 2818

HOMES (30) [HOME]
Ex 12:27 of the Israelites in Egypt and spared our h 1074
Nu 32:18 We will not return to our h 1074
Dt 32:25 in their h terror will reign. 2540
Jos 22: 4 to your h in the land that Moses the servant 185
22: 6 and they went to their h. 185
22: 8 "Return to your h with your great wealth— 185
1Sa 13: 2 The rest of the men he sent back to their h. 185
2Sa 6:19 And all the people went to their h. 1074
18:17 Meanwhile, all the Israelites fled to their h. 185
19: 8 Meanwhile, the Israelites had fled to their h. 185
2Ki 13: 5 So the Israelites lived in their own h 185
2Ch 7:10 he sent the people to their h, joyful 185
Ne 4:14 your wives and your h." 1074
5: 3 our vineyards and our h to get grain during 1074
5: 3 to take turns holding feasts in their h, 1074
Job 2:11 from their h and met together by agreement 5226
21: 9 Their h are safe and free from fear; 1074
36:20 to drag people away from their h. 9393
Ps 78:55 he settled the tribes of Israel in their h. 185
109:10 may they be driven from their ruined h. 2999
Isa 32:18 in secure h, in undisturbed places of rest. 5438
La 5: 2 to aliens, our h to foreigners. 1074
Hos 11:11 I will settle them in their h," 1074
Mic 2: 9 of my people from their pleasant h. 1074
Mk 10:30 as much in this present age (h, brothers, 3864
Jn 20:10 Then the disciples went back to their h, 899S
Ac 2:46 They broke bread in their h and ate together 2848+3875
1Co 11:22 Don't you have h to eat and drink in? 3864
1Ti 5:14 to manage their h and to give 3866
2Ti 3: 6 the kind who worm their way into h 3864

HOMETOWN (9) [TOWN]
1Sa 20: 6 to hurry to Bethlehem, his h, because 6551
2Sa 15:12 to come from Giloh, his h. 6551
17:23 and set out for his house in his h. 6551
Mt 13:54 Coming to his h, he began teaching 4258
13:57 in his h and in his own house is a prophet 4258
Mk 6: 1 Jesus left there and went to his h, 4258
6: 4 Jesus said to them, "Only in his h, 4258
Lk 4:23 in your h what we have heard that you did 4258
4:24 "no prophet is accepted in his h. 4258

HOMOSEXUAL (1)
1Co 6: 9 nor male prostitutes nor h offenders 780

HONEST (19) [HONESTLY, HONESTY]
Ge 42:11 Your servants are h men, not spies." 4026
42:19 If you are h men, 4026
42:31 But we said to him, 'We are h men; 4026
42:33 how I will know whether you are h men: 4026
42:34 that you are not spies but h men. 4026
Ex 23: 7 not put an innocent or h person to death, 7404
Lev 19:36 Use h scales and honest weights, 7406
19:36 Use honest scales and h weights, 7406
19:36 an h ephah and an honest hin. 7406
19:36 an honest ephah and an h hin. 7406
Dt 25:15 You must have accurate and h weights 7406
1Ch 29:17 and with h intent. 3841
Job 6:25 How painful are h words! 3841
31: 6 let God weigh me in h scales 7406
Pr 12:17 A truthful witness gives h testimony, 7406
16:11 H scales and balances are from the LORD; 5477
16:13 Kings take pleasure in h lips; 7406
24:26 An h answer is like a kiss on the lips. 5791
Lk 20:20 they sent spies, who pretended to be h 1465

HONESTLY (1) [HONEST]
Jer 5: 1 If you can find but one person who deals h 5477

HONESTY (3) [HONEST]
Ge 30:33 And my h will testify for me in the future, 7407
2Ki 12:15 because they acted with complete h. 575

Isa 59:14 in the streets, h cannot enter. 5791

HONEY (60) [HONEYCOMB]
Ge 43:11 a little balm and a little h, 1831
Ex 3: 8 a land flowing with milk and h— 1831
3:17 a land flowing with milk and h.' 1831
13: 5 a land flowing with milk and h, 1831
16:31 and tasted like wafers made with h. 1831
33: 3 Go up to the land flowing with milk and h. 1831
Lev 2:11 to burn any yeast or h in an offering made 1831
20:24 a land flowing with milk and h." 1831
Nu 13: 7 and it does flow with milk and h! 1831
14: 8 a land flowing with milk and h, 1831
16:13 of a land flowing with milk and h to kill us 1831
16:14 a land flowing with milk and h or given us 1831
Dt 6: 3 in a land flowing with milk and h; 1831
8: 8 pomegranates, olive oil and h; 1831
11: 9 a land flowing with milk and h. 1831
26: 9 a land flowing with milk and h; 1831
26:15 a land flowing with milk and h." 1831
27: 3 a land flowing with milk and h, 1831
31:20 into the land flowing with milk and h, 1831
32:13 He nourished him with h from the rock, 1831
Jos 5: 6 a land flowing with milk and h. 1831
Jdg 14: 8 In it was a swarm of bees and some h, 1831
14: 9 not tell them that he had taken the h from 1831
14:18 "What is sweeter than h? 1831
14:25 and there was h on the ground. 1831
1Sa 14:26 they saw the h oozing out, 1831
14:29 when I tasted a little of this h. 1831
14:43 "I merely tasted a little h with the end 1831
2Sa 17:29 h and curds, sheep, and cheese 1831
1Ki 14: 3 some cakes and a jar of h, and go to him. 1831
2Ki 18:32 a land of olive trees and h. 1831
2Ch 31: 5 oil and h and all that the fields produced. 1831
Job 20:17 the rivers flowing with h and cream. 1831
Ps 19:10 they are sweeter than h, 1831
19:10 than h from the comb. 5885
81:16 with h from the rock I would satisfy you." 1831
119:103 sweeter than h to my mouth! 1831
Pr 5: 3 For the lips of an adulteress drip h, 5885
24:13 Eat h, my son, for it is good; 1831
24:13 h from the comb is sweet to your taste. 5885
25:16 If you find h, eat just enough— 1831
25:27 It is not good to eat too much h, 1831
27: 7 He who is full loathes h, 5885
SS 4:11 milk and h are under your tongue. 1831
5: 1 I have eaten my honeycomb and my h; 1831
Isa 7:15 and h when he knows enough to reject 1831
7:22 in the land will eat curds and h. 1831
Jer 11: 5 a land flowing with milk and h'— 1831
32:22 a land flowing with milk and h, 1831
41: 8 We have wheat and barley, oil and h, 1831
Eze 3: 3 and it tasted as sweet as h in my mouth. 1831
16:13 Your food was fine flour, h and olive oil. 1831
16:19 olive oil and h I gave you to eat— 1831
20: 6 a land flowing with milk and h, 1831
20:15 a land flowing with milk and h, 1831
27:17 h, oil and balm for your wares. 1831
Mt 3: 4 His food was locusts and wild h. 3510
Mk 1: 6 and he ate locusts and wild h. 3510
Rev 10: 9 but in your mouth it will be as sweet as h." 3510
10:10 It tasted as sweet as h in my mouth, 3510

HONEYCOMB (4) [HONEY]
1Sa 14:27 in his hand and dipped it into the h. 1831+3626
Pr 16:24 Pleasant words are a h, 1831+7430
SS 4:11 Your lips drop sweetness as the h, my bride; 5885
5: 1 I have eaten my h and my honey; 3624

HONOR (174) [HONORABLE, HONORABLY, HONORED, HONORING, HONORS]
Ge 30:20 This time my husband will treat me with h, 2290
43:28 And they bowed low to pay him h. 2556
45:13 Tell my father about all the h I accorded me 3883
49: 3 the first sign of my strength, excelling in h, 8420
Ex 8: 9 leave to you the h of setting the time 6995
12:42 the Israelites are to keep vigil to h 4200
20:12 "H your father and your mother, 3877
28: 2 to give him dignity and h. 9514
28:40 to give them dignity and h. 9514
Nu 20:12 in me enough to h me as holy in the sight of 7727
25:11 as zealous as I am for my h among them, NIH
25:13 because he was zealous for the h of his God NIH
27:14 to h me as holy before their eyes." 7727
Dt 5:16 "H your father and your mother, 3877
26:19 fame and h high above all the nations 9514
Jdg 4: 9 the h will not be yours, 9514
13:17 we may h you when your word comes true? 3877
1Sa 2: 8 and has them inherit a throne of h. 3883
2:29 Why do you h your sons more than me 3877
2:30 Those who h me I will honor, 3877
2:30 Those who honor me I will h, 3877
6: 5 and pay h to Israel's god. 3883
15:12 up a monument in his own h and has turned 4200
15:30 But please h me before the elders 3877
2Sa 1: 2 he fell to the ground to pay him h. 2556
6:22 I will be held in h." 3877
9: 6 he bowed down to pay him h. 2556
14: 4 with her face to the ground to pay him h, 2556
14:22 with his face to the ground to pay him h, 2556
23:19 he not held in greater h than the Three? 3877

2Sa	23:23	*He* was held in greater **h** than any of	3877
1Ki	3:13	have not asked for—both riches and **h**—	3883
2Ki	10:20	"Call an assembly **in h** of Baal."	4200+7727
	25:28	and gave him a **seat of h** higher than those	4058
1Ch	11:25	*He* was held in greater **h** than any of	3877
	29:12	Wealth and **h** come from you;	3883
	29:28	having enjoyed long life, wealth and **h**	3883
2Ch	1:11	or, **h**, nor for the death of your enemies, and	3883
	1:12	I will also give you wealth, riches and **h**,	3883
	16:14	and they made a huge fire **in his h.**	4200
	17: 5	so that he had great wealth and **h.**	3883
	18: 1	Now Jehoshaphat had great wealth and **h**,	3883
	21:19	His people made no fire **in his h**,	4200
	32:27	Hezekiah had very great riches and **h**,	3883
Ezr	7:27	into the king's heart to **bring h** *to* the house	6995
Est	3: 1	and giving him a **seat of h** higher than that	4058
	3: 2	at the king's gate knelt down and **paid h**	2556
	3: 2	not kneel down or **pay him h.**	2556
	3: 5	not kneel down or **pay him h**,	2556
	6: 3	"What **h** and recognition has Mordecai received	3702
	6: 6	be done for the man the king delights to **h?**"	3702
	6: 6	that the king would rather **h** than me?"	3702+6913
	6: 7	"For the man the king delights to **h**,	3702
	6: 9	robe the man the king delights to **h**	3702
	6: 9	done for the man the king delights to **h!**' "	3702
	6:11	done for the man the king delights to **h!**"	3702
	8:16	a time of happiness and joy, gladness and **h.**	3702
Job	19: 9	He has stripped me of my **h** and removed	3883
	40:10	and clothe yourself in **h** and majesty.	2086
Ps	8: 5	and crowned him with glory and **h.**	2077
	22:23	All *you* descendants of Jacob, **h** him!	3877
	45:11	**h** him, for he is your lord.	2556
	50:15	I will deliver you, and *you will* **h** me."	3877
	62: 7	My salvation and my **h** depend on God;	3883
	71:21	You will increase my **h**	1525
	84:11	the Lord bestows favor and **h;**	3883
	91:15	I will deliver him and **h** him.	3877
	112: 9	his horn will be lifted high in **h.**	3883
	149: 5	the saints rejoice in this **h** and sing for joy	3883
Pr	3: 9	**H** the Lord with your wealth,	3877
	3:16	in her left hand are riches and **h.**	3883
	3:35	The wise inherit **h**,	3883
	4: 8	embrace her, and *she will* **h** you.	3877
	8:18	With me are riches and **h**,	3883
	15:33	and humility comes before **h.**	3883
	18:12	but humility comes before **h.**	3883
	20: 3	It is to a man's **h** to avoid strife,	3883
	21:21	and love finds life, prosperity and **h.**	3883
	22: 4	of the Lord bring wealth and **h** and life.	3883
	25:27	nor is it honorable to seek one's own **h.**	3883
	26: 1	**h** is not fitting for a fool.	3883
	26: 8	a stone in a sling is the giving of **h** to a fool.	3883
	29:23	but a man of lowly spirit gains **h.**	3883
Ecc	6: 2	a man wealth, possessions and **h**, so	3883
	10: 1	so a little folly outweighs wisdom and **h.**	3883
Isa	9: 1	the future *he will* **h** Galilee of the Gentiles,	3877
	22:23	be a seat of **h** for the house of his father.	3883
	25: 3	Therefore strong peoples *will* **h** you;	3877
	26:13	but your name alone *do we* **h.**	2349
	29:13	with their mouth and **h** me with their lips,	3877
	43:20	The wild animals **h** me,	3877
	45: 4	**bestow** *on* you a **title of h**,	4033
	58:13	and if *you* **h** it by not going your own way	3877
	60: 9	to the **h** *of* the Lord your God,	9005
Jer	3:17	and all nations will gather in Jerusalem to **h**	NIH
	13:11	for my renown and praise and **h.**	9514
	30:19	*I will* **bring** them **h**,	3877
	33: 9	and **h** before all nations on earth that hear	9514
	34: 5	As people made a **funeral fire** in **h**	AIT
	34: 5	they will make a fire in your **h** and lament,	4200
	52:32	and gave him a **seat of h** higher than those	4058
La	4:16	priests *are* **shown** no **h**, the elders no favor.	5951+7156
Da	2: 6	from me gifts and rewards and great **h.**	10331
	2:46	and **paid** him **h** and ordered that an offering	10504
	4:36	my **h** and splendor were returned to me for	10199
	5:23	But *you did not* **h** the God who holds	10198
	11:21	not been given the **h** *of* royalty.	2086
	11:38	*he will* **h** a god of fortresses;	3877
	11:38	to his fathers *he will* **h** with gold and silver,	3877
	11:39	will greatly **h** those who acknowledge him.	3883
Hab	1: 7	to themselves and promote their own **h.**	8420
Zep	3:19	I will give them praise and **h** in every land	9005
	3:20	I will give you **h** and praise among all	9005
Zec	12: 7	so that the **h** *of the* house of David and	9514
Mal	1: 6	If I am a father, where is the **h** *due* me?	3883
	2: 2	if you do not set your heart to **h** my name,"	3883+5989
	2: 2	you have not set your heart to **h** me.	NIH
Mt	13:57	in his own house is a prophet **without h.**"	872
	15: 4	'**H** your father and mother'	5506
	15: 6	*he is not to* '**h** his father' with it.	5506
	15: 8	" 'These people **h** me with their lips,	5506
	19:19	**h** your father and mother,'	5506
	23: 6	they love the **place of h** at banquets	4752
Mk	6: 4	in his own house is a prophet **without h.**"	872
	7: 6	" 'These people **h** me with their lips,	5506
	7:10	'**H** your father and your mother,' and,	5506
	10:19	do not defraud, **h** your father and mother.' "	5506
	12:39	in the synagogues and the **places of h**	4752
Lk	14: 7	guests picked the **places of h at the table**,	4752
	14: 8	do not take the **place of h**,	4752
	18:20	**h** your father and mother.' "	5506
	20:46	in the synagogues and the **places of h**	4752
Jn	4:44	that a prophet has no **h** in his own country.)	5507
	5:23	that all *may* **h** the Son just as they honor	5506

Jn	5:23	honor the Son just as *they* **h** the Father,	5506
	5:23	He who *does* not **h** the Son does not honor	5506
	5:23	not honor the Son *does* not **h** the Father,	5506
	7:18	He who speaks on his own does so to gain **h**	1518
	7:18	for the **h** of the one who sent him is a man	1518
	8:49	"but *I* **h** my Father and you dishonor me.	5506
	12: 2	Here a dinner was given in **Jesus'** *h.*	AIT
	12:26	My Father *will* **h** the one who serves me.	5506
Ac	7:41	in **h** of what their hands had made.	NIG
	19:17	name of the Lord Jesus *was* **held** in high **h.**	3486
Ro	2: 7	**h** and immortality, he will give eternal life.	5507
	2:10	and peace for everyone who does good:	5507
	12:10	**H** one another above yourselves.	5507
	13: 7	if respect, then respect; if **h**, then honor.	5507
	13: 7	if respect, then respect; if honor, then **h.**	5507
1Co	6:20	Therefore **h** God with your body.	1519
	12:23	that we think are less honorable we treat with special **h.**	5507
	12:24	the body and has given greater **h** to the parts	5507
2Co	8:19	in order to **h** the Lord himself and	1518
	8:23	of the churches and an **h** to Christ.	1518
Eph	6: 2	"**H** your father and mother"—	5506
Php	2:29	and **h** men like him,	1952+2400
1Ti	1:17	be **h** and glory for ever and ever.	5507
	5:17	of the church well are worthy of double **h**,	5507
	6:16	To him be **h** and might forever.	5507
Heb	2: 7	you crowned him *with* glory and **h**	5507
	2: 9	*with* glory and **h** because he suffered death,	5507
	3: 3	found worthy of greater **h** than Moses,	1518
	3: 3	as the builder of a house has greater **h** than	5507
	5: 4	No one takes this **h** upon himself;	5507
1Pe	1: 7	glory and **h** when Jesus Christ is revealed.	5507
	2:17	fear God, **h** the king.	5506
2Pe	1:17	For he received **h** and glory from God	5507
Rev	4: 9	**h** and thanks to him who sits on the throne	5507
	4:11	to receive glory and **h** and power,	5507
	5:12	and wealth and wisdom and strength and **h**	5507
	5:13	the throne and to the Lamb be praise and **h**	5507
	7:12	and **h** and power and strength be to our God	5507
	13:14	in **h** *of* **the beast** who was wounded by	AIT
	21:26	and **h** of the nations will be brought into it.	5507

HONORABLE (7) [HONOR]

1Ch	4: 9	Jabez was more **h** than his brothers.	3877
Ezr	4:10	and Ashurbanipal deported and settled in	10330
Pr	25:27	nor is it **h** to seek one's own honor.	3883
Isa	3: 5	the base against the **h.**	3877
	58:13	a delight and the Lord's holy day **h**,	3877
1Co	12:23	the parts that we think are **less h** we treat	872
1Th	4: 4	in a way that is holy and **h**,	5507

HONORABLY (3) [HONOR]

Jdg	9:16	if you have acted **h** and in good faith	622+928
	9:19	if then you have acted **h** and in good faith	622+928
Heb	13:18	a clear conscience and desire to live **h**	2822

HONORED (32) [HONOR]

Ge	34:19	the most **h** of all his father's household,	3877
Ex	20:24	**cause** my name **to be h**,	2349
Lev	10: 3	in the sight of all the people *I will* **be h.** ' "	3877
Jdg	9: 9	by which both gods and men *are* **h**,	3877
1Ch	11:21	*He* was doubly **h** above the Three	3877
2Ch	26:18	and you will not be **h** by the **Lord God.**"	3883
	32:33	and the people of Jerusalem **h** him	3883+6913
Est	3: 1	King Xerxes **h** Haman son of Hammedatha,	1540
	5:11	and all the ways the king *had* **h** him and	1540
Job	14:21	If his sons *are* **h**, he does not know it;	3877
	22: 8	an **h** *man*, living on it.	5951+7156
Ps	12: 8	about when what is vile *is* **h** among men.	8123
	45: 9	of kings are among your **h** *women;*	3701
Pr	13:18	but whoever heeds correction is **h.**	3877
	27:18	and he who looks after his master *will* **be h.**	3877
Isa	43: 4	Since you are precious and **h** in my sight,	3877
	43:23	nor **h** me *with* your sacrifices.	3877
	49: 5	and gather Israel to himself, for *I am* **h** in	3877
La	1: 8	All *who* **h** her despise her,	3877
Da	4:34	*I* **h** and glorified him who lives forever.	10693
Hag	1: 8	so that I may take pleasure in it and **be h**,"	3877
Zec	2: 8	"After he has **h** me and sent me against	3883
Mal	3:16	feared the Lord and **h** his name.	3108
Mt	6: 2	to be **h** by men.	1519
Lk	14:10	Then you will be **h** in the presence	1518
Ac	5:34	who was **h** by all the people,	5508
	13:48	were glad and **h** the word of the Lord;	1518
	28:10	They **h** us in many ways and	5506+5507
1Co	12:10	You are **h**, we are dishonored!	1902
	12:26	if one part is **h**, every part rejoices with it.	1519
2Th	3: 1	of the Lord may spread rapidly and *be* **h**,	1519
Heb	13: 4	Marriage should be **h** by all,	5508

HONORING (3) [HONOR]

2Sa	10: 3	"Do you think David *is* **h** your father	3877
1Ch	17:18	to you for **h** your servant?	3883
	19: 3	"Do you think David *is* **h** your father	3877

HONORS (4) [HONOR]

Ps	15: 4	a vile man but **h** those who fear the Lord,	3877
	50:23	He who sacrifices thank offerings **h** me,	3877
Pr	14:31	but whoever is kind to the needy **h** God.	3877
Mal	1: 6	son **h** his father, and a servant his master.	3877

HOOF (12) [HOOFS]

Ex	10:26	not a **h** is to be left behind.	7274

Lev	11: 3	a split **h** completely divided and that chews	7274
	11: 4	the cud or only have a split **h**,	7274
	11: 4	does not have a split **h;**	7274
	11: 5	does not have a split **h;**	7274
	11: 6	does not have a split **h;**	7274
	11: 7	though it has a split **h** completely divided,	7274
	11:26	**h** not completely divided or that does	7274
Dt	14: 6	a split **h** divided in two and that chews	7274
	14: 7	a split **h** completely divided you may	7274
	14: 7	they do not have a split **h;**	7274
	14: 8	although it has a split **h**,	7274

HOOFS (8) [HOOF]

Jdg	5:22	Then thundered the horses' **h**—	6811
Ps	69:31	more than a bull with its horns and **h.**	7271
Isa	5:28	their horses' **h** seem like flint,	7274
Jer	47: 3	at the sound of the **h** of galloping steeds,	7274
Eze	26:11	**h** of his horses will trample all your streets;	7274
	32:13	by the foot of man or muddied by the **h**	7274
Mic	4:13	I will give you **h** of bronze	7274
Zec	11:16	tearing off their **h.**	7274

HOOK (4) [FISHHOOK, FISHHOOKS, HOOKS]

2Ki	19:28	I will put my **h** in your nose and my bit	2626
2Ch	33:11	took Manasseh prisoner, put a **h** in his nose,	2560
Job	41: 2	or pierce his jaw with a **h?**	2560
Isa	37:29	I will put my **h** in your nose and my bit	2626

HOOKS (24) [HOOK]

Ex	26:32	Hang it with gold **h** on four posts	2260
	26:37	Make gold **h** for this curtain and five posts	2260
	27:10	and twenty bronze bases and with silver **h**	2260
	27:11	and twenty bronze bases and with silver **h**	2260
	27:17	the courtyard are to have silver bands and **h**,	2260
	36:36	They made gold **h** for them	2260
	36:38	and they made five posts with **h** for them.	2260
	38:10	and with silver **h** and bands *on* the posts.	2260
	38:11	with silver **h** and bands *on* the posts.	2260
	38:12	with silver **h** and bands *on* the posts.	2260
	38:17	The **h** and bands *on* the posts were silver,	2260
	38:19	Their **h** and bands were silver,	2260
	38:28	shekels to make the **h** for the posts,	2260
Isa	2: 4	and their spears into **pruning h.**	4661
	19: 8	all who cast **h** into the Nile;	2676
Eze	19: 4	They led him with **h** to the land of Egypt.	2626
	19: 9	With **h** they pulled him into a cage	2626
	29: 4	But I will put **h** in your jaws and make	2626
	38: 4	put **h** in your jaws and bring you out	2626
	40:43	And **double-pronged h**,	9191
Joel	3:10	into swords and your **pruning h** into spears.	4661
Am	4: 2	when you will be taken away with **h**,	7553
Mic	4: 3	and their spears into **pruning h.**	4661
Hab	1:15	The wicked foe pulls all of them up with **h**,	2676

HOOPOE (2)

Lev	11:19	any kind of heron, the **h** and the bat.	1871
Dt	14:18	any kind of heron, the **h** and the bat.	1871

HOPE (166) [HOPED, HOPELESS, HOPES, HOPING]

Ru	1:12	Even if I thought there was still **h** for me—	9536
1Ch	29:15	on earth are like a shadow, without **h.**	5223
Ezr	10: 2	But in spite of this, there is still **h** for Israel.	5223
Job	4: 6	and your blameless ways your **h?**	9536
	5:16	poor have **h**, and injustice shuts its mouth.	9536
	6: 8	that God would grant *what* I **h** *for*,	9536
	6:11	strength do I have, that *I should still* **h?**	3498
	6:19	the traveling merchants of Sheba **look** in **h.**	7747
	7: 6	and they come to an end without **h.**	9536
	8:13	so perishes the **h** *of* the godless.	9536
	11:18	You will be secure, because there is **h**;	9536
	11:20	their **h** will become a dying gasp."	9536
	13:15	Though he slay me, yet *will* I **h** in him;	3498
	14: 7	"At least there is **h** for a tree:	9536
	14:19	so you destroy man's **h.**	9536
	17:13	If the only home *I* **h** for is the grave,	7747
	17:15	where then is my **h?**	9536
	17:15	Who can see any **h** *for* me?	9536
	19:10	he uproots my **h** like a tree.	9536
	27: 8	what **h** has the godless when he is cut off,	9536
	41: 9	Any **h** of subduing him is false;	9347
Ps	9:18	nor the **h** *of* the afflicted ever perish.	9536
	25: 3	No one *whose* **h** *is* in you will ever be put to shame,	7747
	25: 5	and *my* **h** *is* in you all day long.	7747
	25:21	because *my* **h** *is* in you.	7747
	31:24	all you who **h** in the Lord.	3498
	33:17	A horse is a **vain h** for deliverance;	9214
	33:18	on those *whose* **h** is in his unfailing love,	3498
	33:20	We **wait** in **h** for the Lord;	2675
	33:22	O Lord, even as *we* **put** *our* **h** in you.	3498
	37: 9	but *those who* **h** in the Lord will inherit	7747
	39: 7	*My* **h** *is* in you.	3498
	42: 5	**Put** *your* **h** in God,	3498
	42:11	**Put** *your* **h** in God,	3498
	43: 5	**Put** *your* **h** in God,	3498
	52: 9	in your name *I will* **h**,	7747
	62: 5	my **h** comes from him.	9536
	65: 5	the **h** of all the ends of the earth and of	4440
	69: 6	May *those who* **h** in you not be disgraced	7747
	71: 5	For you have been my **h**,	9536
	71:14	But as for me, *I will* always **have h**;	3498

Ps	119:43	for *I* have **put** *my* h in your laws.	3498
	119:49	for *you* have **given** me h.	3498
	119:74	for *I* have **put** *my* h in your word.	3498
	119:81	but *I* have **put** *my* h in your word.	3498
	119:114	*I* have **put** *my* h in your word.	3498
	119:147	*I* have **put** *my* h in your word.	3498
	130: 5	my soul waits, and in his word *I* **put** *my* h.	3498
	130: 7	O Israel, **put** *your* h in the LORD,	3498
	131: 3	**put** *your* h in the LORD both now	3498
	146: 5	whose h is in the LORD his God,	8433
	147:11	who **put** *their* h in his unfailing love.	3498
Pr	11: 7	When a wicked man dies, his h perishes;	9536
	11:23	but the h *of* the wicked only in wrath.	9536
	13:12	**H** deferred makes the heart sick,	9347
	19:18	Discipline your son, for in that there is h;	9536
	23:18	There is surely a **future** h for you,	344
	23:18	and your h will not be cut off.	9536
	24:14	if you find it, there is a **future** h for you,	344
	24:14	and your h will not be cut off.	9536
	24:20	for the evil man has no **future** h,	344
	26:12	There is more h for a fool than for him.	9536
	29:20	There is more h for a fool than for him.	9536
Ecc	9: 4	Anyone who is among the living has h—	1059
Isa	19: 9	the weavers of fine linen will lose h.	NIH
	38:18	to the pit cannot h for your faithfulness.	8432
	40:31	but *those* who h in the LORD will renew	7747
	42: 4	In his law the islands *will* **put** *their* h."	3498
	49:23	those *who* h in me will not be disappointed.	7747
	51: 5	The islands will look to me and **wait in** h	3498
Jer	13:16	*You* h for light, but he will turn it	7747
	14: 8	O H *of* Israel, its Savior in times of distress,	5223
	14:22	Therefore *our* h is in you,	7747
	17:13	O LORD, the h *of* Israel,	5223
	29:11	plans to give you h and a future.	9536
	31:17	So there is h for your future,"	9536
	50: 7	the LORD, the h *of* their fathers.'	5223
La	3:21	this I call to mind and therefore *I* have h:	3498
	3:25	LORD is good to *those whose* h is in him,	7747
	3:29	there may yet be h.	9536
Eze	19: 5	"When she saw *her* h **unfulfilled,**	3498
	37:11	'Our bones are dried up and our h is gone;	9536
Hos	2:15	will make the Valley of Achor a door of h.	9536
Mic	7: 7	But as for me, *I* **watch in** h for the LORD,	7595
Zec	9: 5	and Ekron too, for her h will wither.	4438
	9:12	Return to your fortress, O prisoners of h;	9536
Mt	12:21	In his name the nations *will* **put** *their* h."	1827
Ac	2:26	my body also will live in h,	1828
	16:19	that their h of making money was gone,	1828
	23: 6	on trial because of my h in the resurrection	1828
	24:15	and I have the same h in God as these men,	1828
	26: 6	And now it is because *of* my h.	1828
	26: 7	*of* this h that the Jews are accusing me.	1828
	27:20	we finally gave up all h *of* being saved.	1828
	28:20	because of the h of Israel that I am bound	1828
Ro	4:18	Against **all** h, Abraham in hope believed	1828
	4:18	in h believed and so became the father	1828
	5: 2	And we rejoice in the h of the glory of God.	1828
	5: 4	perseverance, character; and character, h.	1828
	5: 5	And h does not disappoint us,	1828
	8:20	by the will of the one who subjected it, in h	1828
	8:24	For in this h we were saved.	1828
	8:24	But h that is seen is no hope at all.	1828
	8:24	But hope that is seen is no h at all.	1828
	8:25	But if *we* h for what we do not yet have,	1827
	11:14	**in the** h **that** I may somehow arouse my	1623
	12:12	Be joyful *in* h, patient in affliction,	1828
	15: 4	of the Scriptures we might have h.	1828
	15:12	the Gentiles *will* h in him."	1827
	15:13	The God of h fill you with all joy and peace	1828
	15:13	that you may overflow with h by the power	1828
	15:24	*I* h to visit you while passing through and	1827
1Co	9:10	to do so in the h of sharing in the harvest.	1828
	9:15	And I am not writing this **in the** h **that**	2671
	13:13	now these three remain: faith, h and love.	1828
	15:19	only for this life we **have** h in Christ,	1639+1827
	16: 7	*I* h to spend some time with you,	1827
2Co	1: 7	And our h for you is firm,	1828
	1:10	On him *we have* **set** *our* h	1827
	1:13	And *I* h that,	1827
	3:12	since we have such a h, we are very bold.	1828
	5:11	and *I* h it is also plain to your conscience.	1827
	10:15	Our h is that, as your faith continues to	1828
	11: 1	**I** h you will put up with a little	4054
Gal	5: 5	the Spirit the righteousness for which we h.	1828
Eph	1:12	we, who were the **first to** h in Christ,	4598
	1:18	in order that you may know the h	1828
	2:12	without and without God in the world.	1828
	4: 4	to one h when you were called—	1828
Php	1:20	I eagerly expect and h that I will in no way	1828
	2:19	*I* h in the Lord Jesus to send Timothy	1827
	2:23	*I*, therefore, to send him as soon as I see	1827
Col	1: 5	and love that spring from the h that is stored	1828
	1:23	from the h held out in the gospel.	1828
	1:27	which is Christ in you, the h of glory.	1828
1Th	1: 3	and your endurance *inspired by* h	1828
	2:19	For what is our h, our joy,	1828
	4:13	like the rest of men, who have no h.	1828
	5: 8	and the h of salvation as a helmet.	1828
2Th	2:16	gave us eternal encouragement and good h,	1828
1Ti	1: 1	and *of* Christ Jesus our h,	1828
	3:14	*Although I* h to come to you soon,	1827
	4:10	that *we* have **put** our h in the living God,	1827
	5: 5	in need and left all alone **puts** *her* h in God	1827
	6:17	to be arrogant nor *to* **put** their h in wealth,	1827
	6:17	but to put their h in God,	NIG
2Ti	2:25	**in the** h **that** God will grant them	3607
Tit	1: 2	a faith and knowledge resting on the h	1828

Tit	2:13	while we wait for the blessed h—	1828
	3: 7	we might become heirs having the h	1828
Phm	1:22	Prepare a guest room for me, because *I* h to	1827
Heb	3: 6	to our courage and the h of which we boast.	1828
	6:11	in order to make your h sure.	1828
	6:18	to take hold of the h offered to us may	1828
	6:19	We have **this** h as an anchor for the soul,	4005S
	7:19	and a better h is introduced,	1828
	10:23	hold unswervingly to the h we profess,	1828
	11: 1	*of what* we h **for** and certain of what we do	1827
1Pe	1: 3	into a living h through the resurrection	1828
	1:13	**set** *your* h fully on the grace to be given	1827
	1:21	and so your faith and h are in God.	1828
	3: 5	the holy women of the past who **put** *their* h	1828
	3:15	to give the reason for the h that you have.	1828
1Jn	3: 3	Everyone who has this h in him purifies	1828
2Jn	1:12	*I* h to visit you and talk with you face	1827
3Jn	1:14	*I* h to see you soon,	1827

HOPED (8) [HOPE]

Est	9: 1	On this day the enemies of the Jews *had* h	8432
Job	30:26	Yet *when I* h *for* good, evil came;	7747
Jer	8:15	We h for peace but no good has come,	7747
	14:19	We h for peace but no good has come,	7747
La	2:16	"My splendor is gone and *all that* I had h	7747
Lk	20:20	They h to catch Jesus in something he said	2671
	23: 8	*he* h to see him perform some miracle.	1827
	24:21	but we *had* h that he was	1827

HOPELESS (1) [HOPE]

Isa	57:10	but you would not say, '*It is* h.'	3286

HOPES (7) [HOPE]

2Ki	4:28	"Didn't I tell you, 'Don't **raise** my h'?"	8922
Ps	119:116	do not let my h be dashed.	8433
Pr	10:28	but the h of the wicked come to nothing.	9536
Jer	23:16	**fill** you **with false** h.	2038
Jn	5:45	on whom your h **are set.**	1827
Ro	8:24	Who h **for** what he already has?	1827
1Co	13: 7	It always protects, always trusts, always h,	1827

HOPHNI (5)

1Sa	1: 3	where **H** and Phinehas, the two sons of Eli,	2909
	2:34	**H** and Phinehas, will be a sign to you—	2909
	4: 4	And Eli's two sons, **H** and Phinehas,	2909
	4:11	and Eli's two sons, **H** and Phinehas, died.	2909
	4:17	your two sons, **H** and Phinehas, are dead,	2909

HOPHRA (1)

Jer	44:30	to hand Pharaoh **H** king of Egypt over	2922

HOPING (4) [HOPE]

Da	2: 9	h the situation will change.	10168+10527
Ac	24:26	At the same time *he was* h	1827
	26: 7	This is the promise our twelve tribes *are* h	1827
	27:12	h to reach Phoenix and winter there.	1623+4803

HOPPING (1)

Lev	11:21	that have jointed legs for h on the ground.	6001

HOR (12) [HOR HAGGIDGAD]

Nu	20:22	from Kadesh and came to Mount **H.**	2216
	20:23	At Mount **H,** near the border of Edom,	2216
	20:25	and take them up Mount **H.**	2216
	20:27	They went up Mount **H** in the sight of	2216
	21: 4	traveled from Mount **H** along the route	2216
	33:37	They left Kadesh and camped at Mount **H,**	2216
	33:38	Aaron the priest went up Mount **H,**	2216
	33:39	when he died on Mount **H.**	2216
	33:41	They left Mount **H** and camped	2216
	34: 7	run a line from the Great Sea to Mount **H**	2216
	34: 8	and from Mount **H** to Lebo Hamath.	2216
Dt	32:50	on Mount **H** and was gathered to his people.	2216

HOR HAGGIDGAD (2) [HOR]

Nu	33:32	and camped at **H.**	2988
	33:33	They left **H** and camped	2988

HORAM (1)

Jos	10:33	**H** king of Gezer had come up	2235

HORDE (4) [HORDES]

Nu	22: 4	"This h is going to lick up everything	7736
Eze	17:17	and great h will be of no help to him in war,	7736
	38: 4	and a great h with large and small shields,	7736
	38:15	all of them riding on horses, a great h,	7736

HORDES (21) [HORDE]

Isa	29: 5	the ruthless h like blown chaff.	2162
	29: 7	h of all the nations that fight against Ariel,	2162
	29: 8	So will it be with the h of all the nations	2162
Eze	30:10	" 'I will put an end to the h *of* Egypt by	2162
	30:15	and cut off the h *of* Thebes,	2162
	31: 2	say to Pharaoh king of Egypt and to his h:	2162
	31:18	" 'This is Pharaoh and all his h,	2162
	32:12	I will cause your h to fall by the swords	2162
	32:12	and all your h will be overthrown.	2162
	32:16	for Egypt and all her h they will chant it,	2162
	32:18	wail for the h *of* Egypt and consign to	2162

Eze	32:20	let her be dragged off with all her h.	2162
	32:24	with all her h around her grave.	2162
	32:25	with all her h around her grave.	2162
	32:26	with all their h around their graves.	2162
	32:31	be consoled for all his h that were killed by	2162
	32:32	Pharaoh and all his h will be laid among	2162
	38: 7	you and all the h gathered about you,	7736
	38:13	Have you gathered your h to loot,	7736
	39:11	Gog and all his h will be buried there.	2162
Hab	1: 9	Their h advance like a desert wind	4480

HOREB (17) [SINAI]

Ex	3: 1	to the far side of the desert and came to **H,**	2998
	17: 6	before you by the rock at **H.**	2998
	33: 6	So the Israelites stripped off their ornaments at Mount **H.**	2998
Dt	1: 2	to go from **H** to Kadesh Barnea by	2998
	1: 6	The LORD our God said to us at **H,**	2998
	1:19	from **H** and went toward the hill country of	2998
	4:10	before the LORD your God at **H,**	2998
	4:15	the LORD spoke to you at **H** out of the fire.	2998
	5: 2	our God made a covenant with us at **H.**	2998
	9: 8	At **H** you aroused the LORD's wrath so	2998
	18:16	of the LORD your God at **H** on the day of	2998
	29: 1	the covenant he had made with them at **H.**	2998
1Ki	8: 9	that Moses had placed in it at **H,**	2998
	19: 8	and forty nights until he reached **H,**	2998
2Ch	5:10	that Moses had placed in it at **H,**	2998
Ps	106:19	At **H** they made a calf and worshiped	2998
Mal	4: 4	and laws I gave him at **H** for all Israel.	2998

HOREM (1)

Jos	19:38	**H,** Beth Anath and Beth Shemesh.	3054

HORESH (4)

1Sa	23:15	While David was at **H** in the Desert of Ziph,	3092
	23:16	And Saul's son Jonathan went to David at **H**	3092
	23:18	but David remained at **H.**	3092
	23:19	among us in the strongholds at **H,**	3092

HORI (3) [HORITE, HORITES]

Ge	36:22	The sons of Lotan: **H** and Homam.	3036
Nu	13: 5	from the tribe of Simeon, Shaphat son of **H;**	3036
1Ch	1:39	The sons of Lotan: **H** and Homam.	3036

HORIMS (KJV) See HORITE, HORITES

HORITE (4) [HORI]

Ge	36:20	These were the sons of Seir the **H,**	3037
	36:21	These sons of Seir in Edom were **H** chiefs.	3037
	36:29	These were the **H** chiefs:	3037
	36:30	These were the **H** chiefs,	3037

HORITES (4) [HORI]

Ge	14: 6	and the **H** in the hill country of Seir,	3037
Dt	2:12	**H** used to live in Seir,	3037
	2:12	They destroyed **the H** from before them	4392S
	2:22	when he destroyed the **H** from before them.	3037

HORIZON (3)

Ne	1: 9	if your exiled people are at the farthest h,	9028
Job	26:10	He marks out the h on the face of the waters	2976
Pr	8:27	he marked out the h on the face of the deep,	2553

HORMAH (9)

Nu	14:45	and beat them down all the way to **H.**	3055
	21: 3	so the place was named **H.**	3055
Dt	1:44	down from Seir all the way to **H.**	3055
Jos	12:14	the king of **H** one the king of Arad one	3055
	15:30	Eltolad, Kesil, **H,**	3055
	19: 4	Eltolad, Bethul, **H,**	3055
Jdg	1:17	Therefore it was called **H.**	3055
1Sa	30:30	to those in **H,** Bor Ashan, Athach	3055
1Ch	4:30	Bethuel, **H,** Ziklag,	3055

HORN (38) [HORNED, HORNS, TWO-HORNED]

Ex	19:13	the **ram's** h sounds a long blast may they go	3413
	27: 2	Make a h at each of the four corners,	7967
	38: 2	They made a h at each of the four corners,	7967
1Sa	2: 1	in the LORD my h is lifted high.	7967
	2:10	to his king and exalt the h *of* his anointed."	7967
	16: 1	Fill your h with oil and be on your way;	7967
	16:13	Samuel took the h *of* oil and anointed him	7967
2Sa	22: 3	my shield and the h *of* my salvation,	7967
1Ki	1:39	Zadok the priest took the h *of* oil from	7967
Ps	18: 2	He is my shield and the h *of* my salvation,	7967
	81: 3	Sound the **ram's** h at the New Moon,	8795
	89:17	and by your favor you exalt our h.	7967
	89:24	and through my name his h will be exalted.	7967
	92:10	You have exalted my h like that of	7967
	98: 6	with trumpets and the blast of the **ram's** h	8795
	112: 9	his h will be lifted high in honor.	7967
	132:17	"Here I will make a h grow for David	7967
	148:14	He has raised up for his people a h,	7967
Jer	48:25	Moab's h is cut off;	7967
La	2: 3	In fierce anger he has cut off every h	7967
	2:17	he has exalted the h *of* your foes.	7967
Eze	29:21	that day I will make a h grow for the house	7967
Da	3: 5	As soon as you hear the sound of the h,	10641

Da	3: 7	as soon as they heard the sound of the **h**,	10641
	3:10	that everyone who hears the sound of the **h**,	10641
	3:15	Now when you hear the sound of the **h**,	10641
	7: 8	there before me was another **h**, a little one,	10641
	7: 8	This **h** had eyes like the eyes of a man and	10641
	7:11	of the boastful words the **h** was speaking.	10641
	7:20	the other **h** that came up, before which three	NIH
	7:20	the **h** that looked more imposing than	10641
	7:21	this **h** was waging war against the saints	10641
	8: 5	a prominent **h** between his eyes came from	7967
	8: 8	of his power his large **h** was broken off,	7967
	8: 9	Out of one of them came another **h**,	7967
	8:21	large **h** between his eyes is the first king.	7967
Hos	5: 8	the trumpet in Gibeah, the **h** in Ramah.	2956
Lk	1:69	He has raised up a **h** of salvation for us in	3043

HORNED (2) [HORN]

Lev	11:16	the **h** owl, the screech owl,	1426+3613
Dt	14:15	the **h** owl, the screech owl,	1426+3613

HORNET (3)

Ex	23:28	the **h** ahead of you to drive the Hivites,	7667
Dt	7:20	the LORD your God will send the **h**	7667
Jos	24:12	I sent the **h** ahead of you,	7667

HORNS (66) [HORN]

Ge	22:13	in a thicket he saw a ram caught by its **h**.	7967
Ex	27: 2	so that the **h** and the altar are of one piece,	7967
	29:12	of the bull's blood and put it on the **h** of	7967
	30: 2	its **h** of one piece with it.	7967
	30: 3	Overlay the top and all the sides and the **h**	7967
	30:10	a year Aaron shall make atonement on its **h**.	7967
	37:25	its **h** of one piece with it.	7967
	37:26	and all the sides and the **h** with pure gold,	7967
	38: 2	so that the **h** and the altar were of one piece,	7967
Lev	4: 7	the **h** of the altar of fragrant incense that is	7967
	4:18	the blood on the **h** of the altar that is before	7967
	4:25	on the **h** of the altar of burnt offering	7967
	4:30	the blood with his finger and put it on the **h**	7967
	4:34	on the **h** of the altar of burnt offering	7967
	8:15	and with his finger he put it on all the **h** of	7967
	9: 9	the blood and put it on the **h** of the altar;	7967
	16:18	of the goat's blood and put it on all the **h** of	7967
Dt	33:17	his **h** are the horns of a wild ox.	7967
	33:17	his horns are the **h** of a wild ox.	7967
Jos	6: 4	seven priests carry trumpets of **rams' h**	3413
1Ki	1:50	went and took hold of the **h** of the altar.	7967
	1:51	and is clinging to the **h** of the altar.	7967
	2:28	LORD and took hold of the **h** of the altar.	7967
	22:11	Zedekiah son of Kenaanah had made iron **h**	7967
1Ch	15:28	with the sounding of **rams' h** and trumpets,	8795
2Ch	15:14	with shouting and with trumpets and **h**,	8795
	18:10	Zedekiah son of Kenaanah had made iron **h**,	7967
Ps	22:21	save me from the **h** of the wild oxen.	7967
	69:31	more than a bull *with its* **h** and hoofs.	7966
	75: 4	and to the wicked, 'Do not lift up your **h**.	7967
	75: 5	Do not lift up your **h** against heaven;	7967
	75:10	I will cut off the **h** of all the wicked,	7967
	75:10	but the **h** of the righteous will be lifted up.	7967
	118:27	The festal procession up to the **h** of the altar.	7967
Jer	17: 1	of their hearts and on the **h** of their altars.	7967
Eze	34:21	butting all the weak sheep with your **h**	7967
	43:15	and four **h** project upward from the hearth.	7967
	43:20	and put it on the four **h** of the altar and on	7967
Da	7: 7	from all the former beasts, and it had ten **h**.	10641
	7: 8	"While I was thinking about the **h**,	10641
	7: 8	and three of the first **h** were uprooted	10641
	7:20	to know about the ten **h** on its head and	10641
	7:24	The ten **h** are ten kings who will come	10641
	8: 3	and there before me was a ram with *two* **h**,	7967
	8: 3	and the **h** were long.	7967
	8: 3	One of the **h** was longer than the other but	NIH
	8: 7	striking the ram and shattering his two **h**.	7967
	8: 8	and in its place four prominent **h** grew up	NIH
	8:22	The four **h** that replaced the one	NIH
Am	3:14	the **h** of the altar will be cut off and fall to	7967
Mic	4:13	for I will give you **h** of iron;	7967
Zec	1:18	and there before me were four **h**!	7967
	1:19	"These are the **h** that scattered Judah,	7967
	1:21	"These are the **h** that scattered Judah so	7967
	1:21	to terrify them and throw down these **h** of	7967
	1:21	of the nations who lifted up their **h** against	7967
Rev	5: 6	He had seven **h** and seven eyes,	3043
	9:13	the **h** of the golden altar that is before God.	3043
	12: 3	and ten **h** and seven crowns on his heads.	3043
	13: 1	He had ten **h** and seven heads,	3043
	13: 1	with ten crowns on his **h**,	3043
	13:11	He had two **h** like a lamb,	3043
	17: 3	and had seven heads and ten **h**.	3043
	17: 7	which has the seven heads and ten **h**.	3043
	17:12	"The ten **h** you saw are ten kings who have	3043
	17:16	The beast and the ten **h** you saw will hate	3043

HORON See BETH HORON

HORONAIM (5)

2Sa	13:34	"I see men in the direction of **H**,	2589
Isa	15: 5	the road to **H** they lament their destruction.	2589
Jer	48: 3	Listen to the cries from **H**,	2589
	48: 5	on the road down to **H** anguished cries over	2589
	48:34	as far as **H** and Eglath Shelishiyah,	2589

HORONITE (3) [BETH HORON]

Ne	2:10	When Sanballat the **H** and Tobiah	3061
	2:19	But when Sanballat the **H**,	3061
	13:28	son-in-law to Sanballat the **H**.	3061

HORRIBLE (8) [HORROR]

Dt	7:15	not inflict on you the **h** diseases you knew	8273
Jer	5:30	"A **h** and shocking thing has happened in	9014
	18:13	most **h** thing has been done by Virgin Israel	9137
	23:14	of Jerusalem I have seen **something h**:	9136
Eze	26:21	I will bring you to a **h** end and you will	1166
	27:36	you have come to a **h** end and will	1166
	28:19	you have come to a **h** end and will	1166
Hos	6:10	I have seen a **h** thing in the house of Israel.	9137

HORRIFIED (2) [HORROR]

Jer	4: 9	the priests *will be* **h**,	9037
	50:13	All who pass Babylon *will be* **h** and scoff	9037

HORROR (23) [HORRIBLE, HORRIFIED]

Dt	28:25	a **thing of h** to all the kingdoms on earth.	2400
	28:37	You will become a **thing of h** and an object	9014
2Ch	29: 8	he has made them an object of dread and **h**	9014
	30: 7	so that he made them an **object of h**,	9014
Job	18:20	men of the east are seized with **h**.	8550
Ps	55: 5	**h** has overwhelmed me.	7146
Isa	21: 4	the twilight I longed for has become a **h**	3010
Jer	2:12	O heavens, and shudder with great **h**,"	2990
	8:21	I mourn, and **h** grips me.	9014
	25: 9	and make them an **object of h** and scorn,	9014
	25:18	and an **object of h** and scorn and cursing,	9014
	29:18	of the earth and an object of cursing and **h**,	9014
	42:18	You will be an object of cursing and **h**,	9014
	44:12	an object of cursing and **h**,	9014
	48:39	an **object of h** to all those around her."	4745
	49:13	an **object of h**, of reproach and of cursing;	2997
	49:17	"Edom will become an **object of h**;	9014
	51:37	an **object of h** and scorn,	9014
	51:41	a **h** Babylon will be among the nations!	9014
Eze	5:15	a warning and an **object of h** to the nations	5457
	20:26	that I *might* fill them **with h**	9037
	27:35	with **h** and their faces are distorted	8550
	32:10	and their kings will shudder with **h** because	8550

HORSE (37) [HORSE'S, HORSEBACK, HORSEMAN, HORSEMEN, HORSES, HORSES', WAR-HORSES]

Ex	15: 1	The **h** and its rider he has hurled into	6061
	15:21	The **h** and its rider he has hurled into	6061
1Ki	10:29	and a **h** for a hundred and fifty.	6061
	20:25	**h** for horse and chariot for chariot—	6061
	20:25	horse for **h** and chariot for chariot—	6061
2Ki	14:20	He was brought back by **h** and was buried	6061
2Ch	1:17	and a **h** for a hundred and fifty.	6061
	23:15	as she reached the entrance of the **H** Gate on	6061
	25:28	He was brought back by **h** and was buried	6061
Ne	3:28	Above the **H** Gate, the priests made repairs,	6061
Est	6: 8	king has worn and a **h** the king has ridden,	6061
	6: 9	Then let the robe and **h** be entrusted to one	6061
	6: 9	on the **h** through the city streets,	6061
	6:10	and the **h** and do just as you have suggested	6061
	6:11	So Haman got the robe and the **h**.	6061
Job	39:18	she laughs at **h** and rider.	6061
	39:19	the **h** his strength or clothe his neck with	6061
Ps	32: 9	Do not be like the **h** or the mule,	6061
	33:17	A **h** is a vain hope for deliverance;	6061
	76: 6	O God of Jacob, both **h** and chariot lie still.	6061
	147:10	His pleasure is not in the strength of the **h**,	6061
Pr	21:31	The **h** is made ready for the day of battle,	6061
	26: 3	A whip for the **h**, a halter for the donkey,	6061
Isa	63:13	Like a **h** in open country,	6061
Jer	8: 6	like a **h** charging into battle.	6061
	31:40	the east as far as the corner of the **H** Gate,	6061
	51:21	with you I shatter **h** and rider,	6061
Zec	1: 8	there before me was a man riding a red **h**!	6061
	10: 3	and make them like a proud **h** in battle.	6061
	12: 4	On that day I will strike every **h** with panic	6061
Rev	6: 2	and there before me was a white **h**!	2691
	6: 4	Then another **h** came out, a fiery red one.	2691
	6: 5	and there before me was a black **h**!	2691
	6: 8	I looked, and there before me was a pale **h**!	2691
	19:11	and there before me was a white **h**,	2691
	19:19	against the rider on the **h** and his army,	2691
	19:21	of the mouth of the rider on the **h**,	2691

HORSE'S (1) [HORSE]

Ge	49:17	that bites the **h** heels so	6061

HORSEBACK (3) [HORSE]

1Ki	20:20	But Ben-Hadad king of Aram escaped on **h**	6061
Est	6:11	and led him on **h** through the city streets,	8206
Ecc	10: 7	I have seen slaves on **h**,	6061

HORSELEACH (KJV) See LEECH

HORSEMAN (4) [HORSE, MAN]

2Ki	9:17	"Get a **h**," Joram ordered.	8208
	9:18	The **h** rode off to meet Jehu and said,	6061+8206
	9:19	So the king sent out a second **h**.	6061+8206
Am	2:15	and the **h** will not save his life.	6061+8206

HORSEMEN (29) [HORSE, MAN]

Ge	50: 9	Chariots and **h** also went up with him.	7305
Ex	14: 9	on your **h** and donkeys and camels and	7305
	14:17	through his chariots and his **h**.	7305
	14:18	his chariots and his **h**."	7305
	14:23	and chariots and **h** followed them into	7305
	14:26	the Egyptians and their chariots and **h**."	7305
	14:28	and covered the chariots and **h**—	7305
	15:19	chariots and **h** went into the sea,	7305
Jos	24: 6	with chariots and **h** as far as the Red Sea.	7305
1Ki	20:20	on horseback with *some* of his **h**.	7305
2Ki	2:12	The chariots and **h** of Israel!"	7305
	13: 7	of the army of Jehoahaz except fifty **h**,	7305
	13:14	"The chariots and **h** of Israel!"	7305
	18:24	on Egypt for chariots and **h**?	7305
2Ch	12: 3	and sixty thousand **h** and	7305
	16: 8	with great numbers of chariots and **h**?	7305
Ezr	8:22	the king for soldiers and **h** to protect us	7305
Isa	22: 7	and **h** are posted at the city gates,	7305
	31: 1	and in the great strength of their **h**,	7305
	36: 9	on Egypt for chariots and **h**?	7305
Jer	4:29	the sound of **h** and archers every town takes	7305
Eze	23: 6	handsome young men, and mounted **h**.	7305
	23:12	mounted **h**, all handsome young men.	7305
	26: 7	with **h** and a great army.	7305
	38: 4	your horses, your **h** fully armed,	7305
Hos	1: 7	sword or battle, or by horses and **h**,	7305
Hab	1: 8	their **h** come from afar.	7305
Zec	10: 5	they will fight and overthrow the **h**.	6061+8206
Ac	23:23	seventy and two hundred spearmen to go	2689

HORSES (123) [HORSE]

Ge	47:17	he gave them food in exchange for their **h**,	6061
Ex	14: 9	all Pharaoh's **h** and chariots,	6061
	14:23	and all Pharaoh's **h** and chariots	6061
	15:19	When Pharaoh's **h**, chariots	6061
Dt	11: 4	Egyptian army, to its **h** and chariots,	6061
	17:16	not acquire great numbers of **h** for himself	6061
	20: 1	against your enemies and see **h** and chariots	6061
Jos	11: 4	with all their troops and a large number of **h**	6061
	11: 6	You are to hamstring their **h** and burn	6061
	11: 9	He hamstrung their **h** and burned their	6061
1Sa	8:11	make them serve with his chariots and **h**,	7304
2Sa	8: 4	but a hundred of the **chariot h**.	8207
	15: 1	a chariot and **h** and with fifty men to run	6061
1Ki	1: 5	So he got chariots and **h** ready,	7304
	4:26	Solomon had four thousand stalls for chariot **h**,	6061
	4:26	and twelve thousand **h**.	7304
	4:28	of barley and straw for the **chariot h** and	8224
	4:28	for the chariot horses and the other **h**.	6061
	9:19	the towns for his chariots and for his **h**—	7304
	10:25	weapons and spices, and **h** and mules.	6061
	10:26	Solomon accumulated chariots and **h**;	7304
	10:26	and twelve thousand **h**.	7304
	10:28	Solomon's **h** were imported from Egypt and	6061
	18: 5	Maybe we can find some grass to keep the **h**	6061
	20: 1	by thirty-two kings with their **h**	6061
	20:21	the **h** and chariots and inflicted heavy losses	6061
	22:21	my **h** as your horses."	6061
	22: 4	my horses as your **h**."	6061
2Ki	2:11	of fire and **h** of fire appeared and separated	6061
	3: 7	my **h** as your horses."	6061
	3: 7	my horses as your **h**."	6061
	5: 9	So Naaman went with his **h** and chariots	6061
	6:14	Then he sent **h** and chariots and	6061
	6:15	an army with **h** and chariots had surrounded	6061
	6:17	of **h** and chariots of fire all around Elisha.	6061
	7: 6	to hear the sound of chariots and **h** and	6061
	7: 7	and abandoned their tents and their **h**	6061
	7:10	only tethered **h** and donkeys,	6061
	7:13	"Have some men take five of the **h**	6061
	7:14	So they selected two chariots with their **h**,	6061
	9:33	and the **h** as they trampled her underfoot.	6061
	10: 2	with you and you have chariots and **h**,	6061
	11:16	as she reached the place where the **h** enter	6061
	18:23	I will give you two thousand **h**—	6061
	23:11	the **h** that the kings of Judah had dedicated	6061
1Ch	18: 4	but a hundred of the **chariot h**.	8207
2Ch	1:14	Solomon accumulated chariots and **h**;	7304
	1:14	and twelve thousand **h**,	7304
	1:16	Solomon's **h** were imported from Egypt and	6061
	8: 6	all the cities for his chariots and for his **h**—	7304
	9:24	weapons and spices, and **h** and mules.	6061
	9:25	Solomon had four thousand stalls for **h**	7304
	9:25	and twelve thousand **h**.	7304
	9:28	Solomon's **h** were imported from Egypt and	6061
Ezr	2:66	They had 736 **h**, 245 mules,	6061
Ne	7:68	There were 736 **h**, 245 mules,	NIH
Est	8:10	who rode fast **h** especially bred for	8224
	8:14	The couriers, riding the royal **h**, raced out,	8224
Ps	20: 7	Some trust in chariots and some in **h**,	6061
Isa	2: 7	Their land is full of **h**;	6061
	21: 7	When he sees chariots with teams of **h**,	7304
	21: 9	a man in a chariot with a team of **h**.	7304
	22: 6	with her charioteers and **h**;	7304
	28:28	his **h** do not grind it.	7304
	30:16	You said, 'No, we will flee on **h**.'	6061
	30:16	You said, 'We will ride off on swift **h**.'	NIH
	31: 1	go down to Egypt for help, who rely on **h**,	6061
	31: 3	their **h** are flesh and not spirit.	6061
	36: 8	I will give you two thousand **h**—	6061
	43:17	who drew out the chariots and **h**, the army	6061
	66:20	on **h**, in chariots and wagons,	6061

Jer	4:13	his **h** are swifter than eagles.	6061
	6:23	like the roaring sea as they ride on their **h**;	6061
	8:16	The snorting of the enemy's **h** is heard	6061
	12: 5	how can you compete with **h**?	6061
	17:25	in chariots and on **h**, accompanied by	6061
	22: 4	riding in chariots and on **h**,	6061
	46: 4	Harness the **h**, mount the steeds!	6061
	46: 9	Charge, O **h**! Drive furiously,	6061
	50:37	A sword against her **h** and chariots and all	6061
	50:42	like the roaring sea as they ride on their **h**;	6061
	51:27	send up **h** like a swarm of locusts.	6061
Eze	17:15	by sending his envoys to Egypt to get **h** and	6061
	23:20	and whose emission was like that of **h**.	6061
	23:23	men of high rank, all mounted on **h**.	6061
	26: 7	king of kings, with **h** and chariots,	6061
	26:10	His **h** will be so many that they will cover	6061
	26:10	will tremble at the noise of the **war h**,	7304
	26:11	hoofs of his **h** will trample all your streets;	6061
	27:14	of Beth Togarmah exchanged **work h**,	6061
	27:14	**war h** and mules for your merchandise.	7304
	38: 4	your **h**, your horsemen fully armed,	6061
	38:15	all of them riding on **h**, a great horde,	6061
	39:20	At my table you will eat your fill of **h**	6061
Hos	1: 7	sword or battle, or by **h** and horsemen.	6061
Joel	2: 4	They have the appearance of **h**;	6061
Am	4:10	along with your captured **h**.	6061
	6:12	Do **h** run on the rocky crags?	6061
Mic	5:10	"I will destroy your **h** from among you	6061
Na	3: 2	galloping **h** and jolting chariots!	6061
Hab	1: 8	Their **h** are swifter than leopards,	6061
	3: 8	against the sea when you rode with your **h**	6061
	3:15	You trampled the sea with your **h**,	6061
Hag	2:22	**h** and their riders will fall,	6061
Zec	1: 8	Behind him were red, brown and white **h**.	6061
	6: 2	The first chariot had red **h**,	6061
	6: 6	The one with the black **h** is going toward	6061
	6: 6	the one with the white **h** toward the west,	NIH
	6: 6	one with the dappled **h** toward the south."	NIH
	6: 7	When the powerful **h** went out,	NIH
	12: 4	but I will blind all the **h** of the nations.	6061
	14:15	A similar plague will strike the **h** and mules,	6061
	14:20	be inscribed on the bells of the **h**,	6061
Jas	3: 3	into the mouths of **h** to make them obey us,	2691
Rev	9: 7	The locusts looked like **h** prepared	2691
	9: 9	of many **h** and chariots rushing into battle.	2691
	9:17	The **h** and riders I saw in my vision looked	2691
	9:17	The heads of the **h** resembled the heads	2691
	9:19	The power of the **h** was in their mouths and	2691
	18:13	and sheep; **h** and carriages;	2691
	19:14	riding on white **h** and dressed in fine linen,	2691
	19:18	and mighty men, of **h** and their riders,	2691

HORSES' (3) [HORSE]

Jdg	5:22	Then thundered the **h'** hoofs—	6061
Isa	5:28	their **h'** hoofs seem like flint,	6061
Rev	14:20	rising as high as the **h'** bridles for a distance	2691

HOSAH (5)

Jos	19:29	turned toward **H** and came out at the sea in	2881
1Ch	16:38	Obed-Edom son of Jeduthun, and also **H**,	2880
	26:10	**H** the Merarite had sons:	2880
	26:11	The sons and relatives of **H** were 13 in all.	2880
	26:16	on the upper road fell to Shuppim and **H**.	2880

HOSANNA (6)

Mt	21: 9	"**H** to the Son of David!"	6057
	21: 9	"**H** in the highest!"	6057
	21:15	"**H** to the Son of David,"	6057
Mk	11: 9	and those who followed shouted, "**H**!"	6057
	11:10	"**H** in the highest!"	6057
Jn	12:13	and went out to meet him, shouting, "**H**!"	6057

HOSEA (5)

Hos	1: 1	The word of the LORD that came to **H** son	2107
	1: 2	the LORD began to speak through **H**,	2107
	1: 4	Then the LORD said to **H**,	2257S
	1: 6	Then the LORD said to **H**,	2257S
Ro	9:25	As he says in **H**: "I will call them	6060

HOSEN (KJV) See TROUSERS

HOSHAIAH (3)

Ne	12:32	**H** and half the leaders	2108
Jer	42: 1	of Kareah and Jezaniah son of **H**,	2108
	43: 2	Azariah son of **H** and Johanan son of Kareah	2108

HOSHAMA (1)

| 1Ch | 3:18 | Shenazzar, Jekamiah, **H** and Nedabiah. | 2106 |

HOSHEA (12) [JOSHUA]

Nu	13: 8	from the tribe of Ephraim, **H** son of Nun;	2107
	13:16	Moses gave **H** son of Nun the name Joshua.	2107
2Ki	15:30	Then **H** son of Elah conspired	2107
	17: 1	**H** son of Elah became king of Israel	2107
	17: 3	of Assyria came up to attack **H**,	2107
	17: 4	of Assyria discovered that **H** was a traitor,	2107
	17: 6	In the ninth year of **H**, the king of Assyria	2107
	18: 1	In the third year of **H** son of Elah king	2107
	18: 9	the seventh year of **H** son of Elah king	2107
	18:10	was the ninth year of **H** king of Israel.	2107
1Ch	27:20	**H** son of Azaziah;	2107

| Ne | 10:23 | **H**, Hananiah, Hasshub, | 2107 |

HOSPITABLE (2) [HOSPITALITY]

| 1Ti | 3: 2 | self-controlled, respectable, **h**, able to teach, | 5811 |
| Tit | 1: 8 | Rather he must be **h**, | 5811 |

HOSPITABLY (1) [HOSPITALITY]

| Ac | 28: 7 | and for three days entertained us **h**. | 5819 |

HOSPITALITY (5) [HOSPITABLE, HOSPITABLY]

Ro	12:13	God's people who are in need. Practice **h**.	5810
	16:23	whose **h** I and the whole church here enjoy,	3828
1Ti	5:10	**showing h**, washing the feet of the saints,	3827
1Pe	4: 9	Offer **h** to one another without grumbling.	5811
3Jn	1: 8	We ought therefore to **show h** to such men	5696

HOST (16) [HOSTS]

1Ki	22:19	the **h** of heaven standing around him	7372
2Ch	18:18	the **h** of heaven standing on his right and	7372
Ne	9: 6	and all their **starry h**,	7372
Ps	33: 6	their **starry h** by the breath of his mouth.	7372
Isa	34: 4	all the **starry h** will fall like withered leaves	7372
	40:26	He who brings out the **starry h** one by one,	7372
Da	8:10	It grew until it reached the **h** of the heavens,	7372
	8:10	the **starry h** down to the earth and trampled	7372
	8:11	up to be as great as the Prince of the **h**;	7372
	8:12	the **h** [of the saints] and the daily sacrifice	7372
	8:13	the surrender of the sanctuary and of the **h**	7372
Zep	1: 5	down on the roofs to worship the **starry h**,	7372
Lk	2:13	of the heavenly **h** appeared with the angel,	5131
	14: 9	the **h** who invited both of you will come	2813
	14:10	so that when your **h** comes,	2813
	14:12	Then Jesus said to his **h**,	2813

HOSTAGES (2)

| 2Ki | 14:14 | also took **h** and returned to Samaria. | 1201+9510 |
| 2Ch | 25:24 | with the palace treasures and the **h**, | 1201+9510 |

HOSTILE (13) [HOSTILITY]

Ge	26:27	since you were **h** to me and sent me away?"	8533
Lev	26:21	"If you remain **h** toward me and refuse	7950
	26:23	but continue to be **h** toward me,	7950
	26:24	be **h** toward you and will afflict you	7950
	26:27	to me but continue to be **h** toward me,	7950
	26:28	then in my anger I will be **h** toward you,	7950
	26:41	which made me **h** toward them so	7950
Nu	24: 8	They devour **h** nations	7640
Jdg	6:31	Joash replied to the **h** crowd around him,	NIH
1Ki	11:25	So Rezon ruled in Aram and was **h**	7762
Isa	11:13	nor Judah **h** toward Ephraim.	7675
Ro	8: 7	the sinful mind is **h** to God.	2397
1Th	2:15	They displease God and are **h** to all men	1885

HOSTILITY (15) [HOSTILE]

Ge	16:12	will live in **h** toward all his brothers."	6584+7156
	25:18	they lived in **h** toward all their brothers.	5877+6584+7156
	49:23	they shot at him with **h**.	8475
Lev	26:40	their treachery against me and their **h**	7950
Nu	35:21	in **h** he hits him with his fist or he dies,	368
	35:22	without **h** someone suddenly shoves another	368
2Ch	21:16	against Jehoram the **h** of the Philistines and	8120
Job	17: 2	my eyes must dwell on their **h**.	5286
Ps	78:49	his wrath, indignation and **h**—	7650
Eze	25:15	and with ancient **h** sought to destroy Judah,	368
	35: 5	an ancient **h** and delivered the Israelites	368
Hos	9: 7	your sins are so many and your **h** so great,	5378
	9: 8	and **h** in the house of his God.	5378
Eph	2:14	destroyed the barrier, the dividing wall of **h**,	2397
	2:16	by which he put to death their **h**.	2397

HOSTS (11) [HOST]

2Ki	17:16	They bowed down to all the starry **h**,	7372
	21: 3	to all the starry **h** and worshiped them.	7372
	21: 5	he built altars to all the starry **h**.	7372
	23: 4	for Baal and Asherah and all the starry **h**.	7372
	23: 5	to the constellations and to all the starry **h**.	7372
2Ch	33: 3	to all the starry **h** and worshiped them.	7372
	33: 5	he built altars to all the starry **h**.	7372
Ps	103:21	Praise the LORD, all his **heavenly h**,	7372
	148: 2	praise him, all his **heavenly h**.	7372
Isa	45:12	I marshaled their **starry h**.	7372
Jer	19:13	the starry **h** and poured out drink offerings	7372

HOT (21) [HOTLY, HOTTER]

Ge	36:24	the Anah who discovered the **h** springs	3553
Ex	11: 8	Then Moses, **h** with anger, left Pharaoh.	3034
	16:21	and when the sun grew **h**, it melted away.	2801
1Sa	11: 9	'By the time the sun is **h** tomorrow,	2801
	14:22	they joined the battle in **h** pursuit.	339
	21: 6	before the LORD and replaced by **h** bread	2770
1Ki	19: 6	a cake of bread **baked over h coals**,	8363
Ne	7: 3	not to be opened until the sun is **h**.	2801
Job	15: 2	or fill his belly with the **h east wind**?	7708
Ps	39: 3	My heart grew **h** within me,	2801
	78:49	He unleashed against them his **h** anger,	3019
Pr	6:28	on **h** coals without his feet being scorched?	1624
La	5:10	Our skin is **h** as an oven,	4023
Eze	24:11	the empty pot on the coals till it becomes **h**	2801
	38:18	my **h** anger will be aroused,	2779

Da	3:22	and the furnace so **h** that the flames of	10015
Hos	7: 7	All of them are **h** as an oven;	2801
Lk	12:55	you say, 'It's going to be **h**,' and it is.	3014
1Ti	4: 2	have been **seared as with a h iron**.	3013
Rev	3:15	that you are neither cold nor **h**.	2412
	3:16	you are lukewarm—neither **h** nor cold—	2412

HOT-TEMPERED (5) [TEMPER]

Jdg	18:25	or some **h** men will attack you,	5253+5883
Pr	15:18	A **h** man stirs up dissension,	2779
	19:19	A **h** man must pay the penalty;	1524+2779
	22:24	Do not make friends with a **h** man,	678
	29:22	and a **h** one commits many sins.	1251+2779

HOTHAM (2)

| 1Ch | 7:32 | Shomer and **H** and of their sister Shua. | 2598 |
| | 11:44 | Shama and Jeiel the sons of **H** the Aroerite, | 2598 |

HOTHEADED (1) [HEAD]

| Pr | 14:16 | but a fool is **h** and reckless. | 6297 |

HOTHIR (2)

| 1Ch | 25: 4 | Joshbekashah, Mallothi, **H** and Mahazioth, | 2110 |
| | 25:28 | the twenty-first to **H**, | 2110 |

HOTLY (2) [HOT]

| Ps | 56: 1 | O God, for men **h** pursue me; | 8634 |
| | 57: 3 | rebuking those who **h** pursue me; | 8634 |

HOTTER (1) [HOT]

| Da | 3:19 | the furnace heated seven times **h** than usual | 10015 |

HOUGH (KJV) See HAMSTRING

HOUND (1) [HOUNDED]

| Job | 19:28 | "If you say, 'How we will **h** him, | 8103 |

HOUNDED (2) [HOUND]

| Ps | 109:16 | but **h** to death the poor and the needy and | 8103 |
| Eze | 36: 3 | Because they ravaged and **h** you | 8635 |

HOUR (59) [HOURS]

Ecc	9:12	no man knows when his **h** will come:	6961
Mt	6:27	Who of you by worrying can add a single **h**	4388
	8:13	And his servant was healed at that very **h**.	6052
	15:28	her daughter was healed from that very **h**.	6052
	20: 3	"About the third **h** he went out	6052
	20: 5	about the sixth **h** and the ninth hour and did	NIG
	20: 5	about the sixth hour and the ninth **h** and did	6052
	20: 6	About the eleventh **h** he went out	NIG
	20: 9	the eleventh **h** came and each received	6052
	20:12	who were hired last worked only one **h**,'	6052
	24:36	"No one knows about that day or **h**,	6052
	24:44	because the Son of Man will come at an **h**	6052
	24:50	not expect him and at an **h** he is	6052
	25:13	because you do not know the day or the **h**.	6052
	26:40	not keep watch with me for one **h**?"	6052
	26:45	Look, the **h** is near,	6052
	27:45	From the sixth **h** until the ninth hour	6052
	27:45	the ninth **h** darkness came over all the land.	6052
	27:46	the ninth **h** Jesus cried out in a loud voice,	6052
Mk	13:32	"No one knows about that day or **h**,	6052
	14:35	and prayed that if possible the **h** might pass	6052
	14:37	Could you not keep watch for one **h**?	6052
	14:41	The **h** has come.	6052
	15:25	It was the third **h** when they crucified him.	6052
	15:33	At the sixth **h** darkness came over	1181+6052
	15:33	over the whole land until the ninth **h**.	6052
	15:34	the ninth **h** Jesus cried out in a loud voice,	6052
Lk	12:25	Who of you by worrying can add a single **h**	4388
	12:39	of the house had known at what **h**	6052
	12:40	because the Son of Man will come at an **h**	6052
	12:46	not expect him and at an **h** he is not aware	6052
	22:14	When the **h** came, Jesus and his apostles	6052
	22:53	But this is your **h**—when darkness reigns."	6052
	22:59	About an **h** later another asserted,	6052
	23:44	It was now about the sixth **h**,	6052
	23:44	over the whole land until the ninth **h**,	6052
Jn	1:39	It was about the tenth **h**.	6052
	4: 6	It was about the sixth **h**.	6052
	4:52	fever left him yesterday at the seventh **h**."	6052
	12:23	"The **h** has come for the Son of Man to	6052
	12:27	'Father, save me from this **h**'?	6052
	12:27	it was for this very reason I came to this **h**.	6052
	19:14	about the sixth **h**.	6052
Ac	10:30	in my house praying at this **h**,	6052
	16:33	At that **h** of the night the jailer took them	6052
Ro	13:11	The **h** has come for you to wake up	6052
1Co	4:11	To this very **h** we go hungry and thirsty,	6052
	15:30	why do we endanger ourselves every **h**?	6052
1Jn	2:18	Dear children, this is the last **h**;	6052
	2:18	This is how we know it is the last **h**.	6052
Rev	3:10	the **h** of trial that is going to come upon	6052
	8: 1	silence in heaven for about half an **h**.	2469
	9:15	for this very **h** and day and month	6052
	11:13	At that very **h** there was a severe earthquake	6052
	14: 7	because the **h** of his judgment has come.	6052
	17:12	but who for one **h** will receive authority	6052
	18:10	In one **h** your doom has come!'	6052
	18:17	In one **h** such great wealth has been brought	6052

Rev 18:19 *In one **h** she has been brought to ruin!* 6052

HOURS (3) [HOUR]
Jn 11: 9 "Are there not twelve **h** of daylight? 6052
Ac 5: 7 About three **h** later his wife came in, 6052
 19:34 they all shouted in unison for about two **h:** 6052

HOUSE (971) [HOUSEHOLD, HOUSEHOLDS, HOUSES, STOREHOUSE, STOREHOUSES]
Ge 19: 2 "please turn aside to your servant's **h.** 1074
 19: 3 that they did go with him and entered his **h.** 1074
 19: 4 both young and old—surrounded the **h.** 1074
 19:10 and pulled Lot back into the **h** and shut 1074
 19:11 the men who were at the door of the **h,** 1074
 24:23 in your father's **h** for us to spend the night?" 1074
 24:27 to the **h** of my master's relatives." 1074
 24:31 I have prepared a **h** and a place for 1074
 24:32 So the man went to the **h,** 1074
 27:15 which she had in the **h,** 1074
 28: 2 to the **h** of your mother's father Bethuel. 1074
 28:17 This is none other than the **h** of God; 1074
 28:21 so that I return safely to my father's **h,** 1074
 28:22 that I have set up as a pillar will be God's **h,** 1074
 31:30 to return to your father's **h.** 1074
 34:26 and took Dinah from Shechem's **h** and left. 1074
 38:11 "Live as a widow in your father's **h** 1074
 38:11 So Tamar went to live in her father's **h.** 1074
 39: 2 he lived in the **h** of his Egyptian master. 1074
 39: 5 both in the **h** and in the field. 1074
 39: 8 not concern himself with anything in the **h;** 1074
 39: 9 No one is greater in this **h** than I am. 1074
 39:11 One day he went into the **h** to attend 1074
 39:12 in her hand and ran out of the **h.** NIH
 39:13 in her hand and had run out of the **h,** NIH
 39:15 beside me and ran out of the **h,** NIH
 39:18 beside me and ran out of the **h."** NIH
 40: 3 in custody in the **h** of the captain of 1074
 40: 7 in custody with him in his master's **h,** 1074
 41:10 and the chief baker in the **h** of the captain 1074
 43:16 he said to the steward of his **h,** 1074
 43:16 "Take these men to my **h,** 1074
 43:17 and took the men to Joseph's **h.** 1074
 43:18 when they were taken to his **h.** 1074
 43:19 and spoke to him at the entrance to the **h.** 1074
 43:24 The steward took the men into Joseph's **h,** 1074
 43:26 to him the gifts they had brought into the **h,** 1074
 44: 1 to the steward of his **h:** 1074
 44: 8 steal silver or gold from your master's **h?** 1074
 44:14 the when Judah and his brothers came in, 1074
Ex 2: 1 of the **h** of Levi married a Levite woman, 1074
 3:22 and any woman living in her **h** for articles 1074
 12:22 Not one of you shall go out the door of his **h** 1074
 12:30 for there was not a **h** without someone dead. 1074
 12:46 "It must be eaten inside one **h;** 1074
 12:46 take none of the meat outside the **h.** 1074
 19: 3 to say to the **h** of Jacob and what you are 1074
 20:17 "You shall not covet your neighbor's **h.** 1074
 22: 7 and they are stolen from the neighbor's **h,** 1074
 22: 8 of the **h** must appear before the judges 1074
 23:19 the best of the firstfruits of your soil to the **h** 1074
 34:26 the best of the firstfruits of your soil to the **h** 1074
 40:38 of all the **h** of Israel during all their travels. 1074
Lev 10: 6 But your relatives, all the **h** of Israel, 1074
 14:34 I put a spreading mildew in a **h** in that land, 1074
 14:35 the owner of the **h** must go and tell 1074
 14:35 that looks like mildew in my **h.'** 1074
 14:36 to order the **h** to be emptied before he goes 1074
 14:36 in the **h** will be pronounced unclean. 1074
 14:36 the priest is to go in and inspect the **h.** 1074
 14:38 the priest shall go out the doorway of the **h** 1074
 14:39 the priest shall return to inspect the **h.** NIH
 14:41 the inside walls of the **h** scraped and 1074
 14:42 and take new clay and plaster the **h.** 1074
 14:43 the **h** after the stones have been torn out and 1074
 14:43 and the **h** scraped and plastered, 1074
 14:44 if the mildew has spread in the **h,** 1074
 14:44 the **h** is unclean. 1074
 14:46 the **h** while it is closed up will be unclean 1074
 14:47 or eats in the **h** must wash his clothes. 1074
 14:48 not spread after the **h** has been plastered, 1074
 14:48 he shall pronounce the **h** clean, 1074
 14:49 To purify the **h** he is to take two birds 1074
 14:51 and sprinkle the **h** seven times. 1074
 14:52 He shall purify the **h** with the bird's blood, 1074
 14:53 he will make atonement for the **h,** 1074
 14:55 for mildew in clothing or in a **h,** 1074
 22:13 and she returns to live in her father's **h** as 1074
 25:29 " 'If a man sells a **h** in a walled city, 1074+4632
 25:30 before a full year has passed, the **h** in 1074
 25:33 that is, a **h** sold in any town they hold— 1074
 27:14 a man dedicates his **h** as something holy to 1074
 27:15 If the man who dedicates his **h** redeems it, 1074
 27:15 and the **h** will again become his. NIH
Nu 12: 7 he is faithful in all my **h.** 1074
 17: 8 which represented the **h** of Levi, 1074
 20:29 the entire **h** of Israel mourned 1074
 30: 3 in her father's **h** makes a vow to the LORD 1074
 30:16 and his young daughter still living in his **h.** 1074
Dt 5:21 not set your desire on your neighbor's **h.** 1074
 7:26 Do not bring a detestable thing into your **h** 1074
 20: 5 "Has anyone built a new **h** and 1074
 21:13 in your **h** and mourned her father 1074
 22: 8 When you build a new **h,** 1074
 22: 8 not bring the guilt of bloodshed on your **h** 1074

Dt 22:21 the door of her father's **h** and there the men 1074
 22:21 while still in her father's **h.** 1074
 23:18 of a male prostitute into the **h** of the LORD 1074
 24: 1 gives it to her and sends her from his **h,** 1074
 24: 2 after she leaves his **h** she becomes the wife 1074
 24: 3 gives it to her and sends her from his **h,** 1074
 24:10 not go into his **h** to get what he is offering 1074
 25:14 not have two differing measures in your **h**— 1074
 26:13 from my **h** the sacred portion 1074
 28:30 You will build a **h,** 1074
Jos 2: 1 the **h** of a prostitute named Rahab 1074
 2: 3 to you and entered your **h,** 1074
 2:15 the **h** she lived in was part of the city wall. 1074
 2:18 and all your family into your **h.** 1074
 2:19 If anyone goes outside your **h** into 1074
 2:19 As for anyone who is in the **h** with you, 1074
 6:17 and all who are with her in her **h** shall 1074
 6:22 "Go into the prostitute's **h** and bring her out 1074
 6:24 into the treasury of the LORD's **h.** 1074
 9:23 as woodcutters and water carriers for the **h** 1074
 17:17 But Joshua said to the **h** of Joseph— 1074
 18: 5 the south and the **h** of Joseph in its territory 1074
 21:45 of all the LORD's good promises to the **h** 1074
Jdg 1:22 Now the **h** of Joseph attacked Bethel, 1074
 1:35 the power of the **h** of Joseph increased, 1074
 3:24 in the inner room of the **h.''** 5249
 10: 9 Benjamin and the **h** of Ephraim; 1074
 11: 7 and drive me from my father's **h?** 1074
 11:31 the door of my **h** to meet me when I return 1074
 12: 1 to burn down your **h** over your head." 1074
 14:19 he went up to his father's **h.** 1074
 17: 4 And they were put in Micah's **h.** 1074
 17: 8 to Micah's **h** in the hill country of Ephraim. 1074
 17:12 became his priest and lived in his **h.** 1074
 18: 2 of Ephraim and came to the **h** of Micah, 1074
 18: 3 When they were near Micah's **h,** 1074
 18:13 of Ephraim and came to Micah's **h.** 1074
 18:15 So they turned in there and went to the **h** of 1074
 18:18 into Micah's **h** and took the carved image, 1074
 18:22 from Micah's **h,** the men who lived 1074
 18:31 all the time the **h** of God was in Shiloh. 1074
 19: 2 She left him and went back to her father's **h** 1074
 19: 3 She took him into her father's **h,** 1074
 19:18 and now I am going to the **h** of the LORD. 1074
 19:18 No one has taken me into his **h.** 1074
 19:20 "You are welcome at my **h,"** NIH
 19:21 he took him into his **h** and fed his donkeys. 1074
 19:22 of the city surrounded the **h.** 1074
 19:22 to the old man who owned the **h,** 1074
 19:22 to your **h** so we can have sex with him." 1074
 19:23 The owner of the **h** went outside and said 1074
 19:26 At daybreak the woman went back to the **h** 1074
 19:27 in the morning and opened the door of the **h** 1074
 19:27 fallen in the doorway of the **h,** 1074
 20: 5 after me and surrounded the **h,** 1074
 20: 8 No, not one of us will return to his **h.** 1074
Ru 4:11 who together built up the **h** of Israel. 1074
1Sa 1: 7 Whenever Hannah went up to the **h** of 1074
 1:24 and brought him to the **h** of the LORD 1074
 2:27 to your father's **h** when they were in Egypt 1074
 2:28 I also gave your father's **h** all 1074
 2:30 'I promised that your **h** and your father's 1074
 2:30 and your father's **h** would minister 1074
 2:31 and the strength of your father's **h,** 1074
 2:35 I will firmly establish his **h,** 1074
 3:14 Therefore, I swore to the **h** of Eli, 1074
 3:14 'The guilt of Eli's **h** will never be atoned for 1074
 3:15 and then opened the doors of the **h** of 1074
 7: 1 They took it to Abinadab's **h** on the hill 1074
 7: 3 And Samuel said to the whole **h** of Israel, 1074
 9:18 where the seer's **h** is?" 1074
 9:25 with Saul on the **roof** of his **h.** 1511
 18: 2 and did not let him return to his father's **h.** 1074
 18:10 He was prophesying in his **h,** 1074
 19: 9 as he was sitting in his **h** with his spear 1074
 19:11 Saul sent men to David's **h** to watch it and 1074
 20:16 So Jonathan made a covenant with the **h** 1074
 21:15 Must this man come into my **h?"** 1074
 25:36 the **h** holding a banquet like that of a king. 1074
 28:24 The woman had a fattened calf at the **h,** 1074
2Sa 1:12 the army of the LORD and the **h** of Israel, 1074
 2: 4 anointed David king over the **h** of Judah. 1074
 2: 7 and the **h** of Judah has anointed me king 1074
 2:10 The **h** of Judah, however, followed David. 1074
 2:11 over the **h** of Judah was seven years 1074
 3: 1 the **h** of Saul and the house of David lasted 1074
 3: 1 the house of Saul and the **h** of David lasted 1074
 3: 1 the **h** of Saul grew weaker and weaker. 1074
 3: 6 During the war between the **h** of Saul and 1074
 3: 6 the house of Saul and the **h** of David, 1074
 3: 6 his own position in the **h** of Saul. 1074
 3: 8 the **h** of your father Saul and to his family 1074
 3:10 and transfer the kingdom from the **h** of Saul 1074
 3:19 and the whole **h** of Benjamin wanted to do. 1074
 3:29 the head of Joab and upon all his father's **h!** 1074
 3:29 May Joab's **h** never be without 1074
 4: 5 set out for the **h** of Ish-Bosheth, 1074
 4: 6 They went into the inner part of the **h** as if 1074
 4: 7 They had gone into the **h** while he was lying 1074
 4:11 in his own **h** and on his own bed— 1074
 6: 3 and brought it from the **h** of Abinadab, 1074
 6: 5 and the whole **h** of Israel were celebrating 1074
 6:10 he took it aside to the **h** of Obed-Edom 1074
 6:11 The ark of the LORD remained in the **h** 1074
 6:12 the ark of God from the **h** of Obed-Edom to 1074
 6:15 and the entire **h** of Israel brought up the ark 1074
 6:21 from his **h** when he appointed me ruler over 1074

2Sa 7: 5 Are you the one to build me a **h** to dwell in? 1074
 7: 6 in a **h** from the day I brought the Israelites 1074
 7: 7 "Why have you not built me a **h** of cedar?" 1074
 7:11 the LORD himself will establish a **h** for you: 1074
 7:13 the one who will build a **h** for my Name, 1074
 7:16 Your **h** and your kingdom will endure 1074
    forever before me; 1074
 7:19 about the future of the **h** of your servant. 1074
 7:25 concerning your servant and his **h.** 1074
 7:26 And the **h** of your servant David will 1074
 7:27 saying, 'I will build a **h** for you.' 1074
 7:29 be pleased to bless the **h** of your servant, 1074
 7:29 and with your blessing the **h** of your servant 1074
 9: 1 the **h** of Saul to whom I can show kindness 1074
 9: 3 "Is there no one still left of the **h** of Saul 1074
 9: 4 "He is at the **h** of Makir son of Ammiel 1074
 9: 5 from the **h** of Makir son of Ammiel. 1074
 11: 8 "Go down to your **h** and wash your feet." 1074
 11: 9 and did not go down to his **h.** 1074
 11:11 How could I go to my **h** to eat and drink 1074
 11:27 David had her brought to his **h,** 1074
 12: 8 I gave your master's **h** to you, 1074
 12: 8 I gave you the **h** of Israel and Judah. 1074
 12:10 the sword will never depart from your **h,** 1074
 12:16 He fasted and went into his **h** and spent NIH
 12:20 into the **h** of the LORD and worshiped. 1074
 12:20 Then he went to his own **h,** 1074
 13: 7 "Go to the **h** of your brother Amnon 1074
 13: 8 Tamar went to the **h** of her brother Amnon, 1074
 13:20 in her brother Absalom's **h,** 1074
 14:24 the king said, "He must go to his own **h;** 1074
 14:24 to his own **h** and did not see the face of 1074
 14:31 to Absalom's **h** and he said to him, 1074
 16: 3 because he thinks, 'Today the **h** 1074
 17:18 of them left quickly and went to the **h** of 1074
 17:20 to the woman at the **h,** 1074
 17:23 he saddled his donkey and set out for his **h** 1074
 17:23 He put his **h** in order and then hanged 1074
 19: 5 Joab went into the **h** to the king and said, 1074
 19:20 the first of the whole **h** of Joseph to come 1074
 20: 3 the palace and put them in a **h** under guard. 1074
 21: 1 on account of Saul and his blood-stained **h;** 1074
 23: 5 "Is not my **h** right with God? 1074
1Ki 2: 27 had spoken at Shiloh about the **h** of Eli. 1074
 2:31 so clear me and my father's **h** of the guilt of 1074
 2:33 and his descendants, his **h** and his throne, 1074
 2:36 "Build yourself a **h** in Jerusalem 1074
 3:17 this woman and I live in the same **h.** 1074
 3:18 there was no one in the **h** but the two of us. 1074
 8:43 that this **h** I have built bears your Name. 1074
 11:18 a **h** and land and provided him with food. 1074
 11:28 of the whole labor force of the **h** of Joseph. 1074
 12:16 Look after your own **h,** O David!" 1074
 12:19 So Israel has been in rebellion against the **h** 1074
 12:20 of Judah remained loyal to the **h** of David. 1074
 12:21 he mustered the whole **h** of Judah and 1074
 12:21 the **h** of Israel and to regain the kingdom 1074
 12:23 to the whole **h** of Judah and Benjamin, 1074
 12:26 now likely revert to the **h** of David. 1074
 13: 2 'A son named Josiah will be born to the **h** 1074
 13:18 with you to your **h** so that he may eat bread 1074
 13:19 with him and ate and drank in his **h.** 1074
 13:34 of the **h** of Jeroboam that led to its downfall 1074
 14: 4 and went to Ahijah's **h** in Shiloh. 1074
 14: 8 from the **h** of David and gave it to you, 1074
 14:10 to bring disaster on the **h** of Jeroboam. 1074
 14:10 up the **h** of Jeroboam as one burns dung, 1074
 14:13 the only one in the **h** of Jeroboam in whom 1074
 14:17 as she stepped over the threshold of the **h,** 1074
 15:27 of the **h** of Issachar plotted against him, 1074
 16: 3 So I am about to consume Baasha and his **h,** 1074
 16: 3 and I will make your **h** like that of Jeroboam 1074
 16: 7 of Hanani to Baasha and his **h,** because 1074
 16: 7 and becoming like the **h** of Jeroboam— 1074
 17:17 of the woman who owned the **h** became ill. 1074
 17:23 down from the room into the **h.** 1074
 20:31 that the kings of the **h** of Israel are merciful. 1074
 21:22 I will make your **h** like that of Jeroboam son 1074
 21:29 but I will bring it on his **h** in the days 1074
2Ki 4: 2 Tell me, what do you have in your **h?"** 1074
 4:32 When Elisha reached the **h,** 1074
 5: 9 and stopped at the door of Elisha's **h.** 1074
 5:24 the servants and put them away in the **h.** 1074
 6:32 Now Elisha was sitting in his **h,** 1074
 7:17 when the king came down to his **h.** NIH
 8: 3 to the king to beg for her **h** and land. 1074
 8: 5 to life came to beg the king for her **h** 1074
 8:18 as the **h** of Ahab had done, 1074
 8:27 in the ways of the **h** of Ahab and did evil in 1074
 8:27 as the **h** of Ahab had done, 1074
 9: 6 Jehu got up and went into the **h.** 1074
 9: 7 to destroy the **h** of Ahab your master, 1074
 9: 8 The whole **h** of Ahab will perish. 1074
 9: 9 I will make the **h** like the house 1074
 9: 9 the **h** of Jeroboam son of Nebat and like 1074
 9: 9 of Jeroboam son of Nebat and the **h** 1074
 10: 1 in Samaria seventy sons of the **h** of Ahab. NIH
 10: 3 Then fight for your master's **h."** 1074
 10:10 a word the LORD has spoken against the **h** 1074
 10:11 in Jezreel who remained of the **h** of Ahab, 1074
 10:30 and have done to the **h** of Ahab all I had 1074
 13: 6 not turn away from the sins of the **h** 1074
 15: 5 and he lived in a separate **h.** 1074
 17:21 He tore Israel away from the **h** of David, 1074
 19:30 of the **h** of Judah will take root below 1074
 20: 1 Put your **h** in order, because you are going 1074
 21:13 the plumb line used against the **h** of Ahab. 1074

1Ch	2:55	the father of the **h** of Recab.	1074
	6:31	in the **h** of the LORD after the ark came	1074
	6:48	of the tabernacle, the **h** of God.	1074
	9:11	the official in charge of the **h** of God;	1074
	9:13	responsible for ministering in the **h** of God.	1074
	9:23	in charge of guarding the gates of the **h** of	1074
	9:23	the **h** called the Tent.	1074
	9:26	the rooms and treasuries in the **h** of God.	1074
	9:27	the **h**, because they had to guard it;	1074
	10: 6	and all his **h** died together.	1074
	12:29	of whom had remained loyal to Saul's **h**	1074
	13: 7	of God from Abinadab's **h** on a new cart,	1074
	13:13	he took it aside to the **h** of Obed-Edom	1074
	13:14	of Obed-Edom in his **h** for three months,	1074
	15:25	the LORD from the **h** of Obed-Edom,	1074
	17: 4	not the one to build me a **h** to dwell in.	1074
	17: 5	in a **h** from the day I brought Israel up out	1074
	17: 6	"Why have you not built me a **h** of cedar?"	1074
	17:10	that the LORD will build a **h** for you:	1074
	17:12	He is the one who will build a **h** for me,	1074
	17:14	over my **h** and my kingdom forever;	1074
	17:17	you have spoken about the future of the **h**	1074
	17:23	concerning your servant and his **h**	1074
	17:24	And the **h** of your servant David will	1074
	17:25	to your servant that you will build a **h**	1074
	17:27	Now you have been pleased to bless the **h**	1074
	22: 1	"The **h** of the LORD God is to be here,	1074
	22: 2	to prepare dressed stone for building the **h**	1074
	22: 5	and the **h** to be built for the LORD should	1074
	22: 6	and charged him to build a **h** for	1074
	22: 7	"My son, I had it in my heart to build a **h**	1074
	22: 8	You are not to build a **h** for my Name,	1074
	22:10	the one who will build a **h** for my Name.	1074
	22:11	and may you have success and build the **h**	1074
	23:28	and the performance of other duties at the **h**	1074
	25: 6	for the ministry at the **h** of God.	1074
	26:20	in charge of the treasuries of the **h** of God	1074
	28: 2	in my heart to build a **h** as a place of rest for	1074
	28: 3	'You are not to build a **h** for my Name,	1074
	28: 4	from the **h** of Judah he chose my family,	1074
	28: 6	the one who will build my **h** and my courts,	1074
2Ch	6:33	that this **h** I have built bears your Name.	1074
	10:16	Look after your own **h**, O David!"	1074
	10:19	So Israel has been in rebellion against the **h**	1074
	11: 1	he mustered the **h** of Judah and Benjamin—	1074
	21: 6	as the **h** of Ahab had done,	1074
	21: 7	the LORD was not willing to destroy the **h**	1074
	21:13	just as the **h** of Ahab did.	1074
	21:13	members of your father's **h**,	1074
	22: 3	He too walked in the ways of the **h**	1074
	22: 4	as the **h** of Ahab had done,	1074
	22: 7	the LORD had anointed to destroy the **h**	1074
	22: 8	executing judgment on the **h** of Ahab,	1074
	22: 9	the **h** of Ahaziah powerful enough to retain	1074
	22:10	to destroy the whole royal family of the **h**	1074
	26:21	He lived in a separate **h**—	1074
	35:21	but the **h** with which I am at war.	1074
Ezr	1: 5	and build the **h** of the LORD in Jerusalem.	1074
	2:68	When they arrived at the **h** of the LORD	1074
	2:68	the rebuilding of the **h** of God on its site.	1074
	3: 8	of the second year after their arrival at the **h**	1074
	3: 8	and older to supervise the building of the **h**	1074
	3: 9	in supervising those working on the **h**	1074
	3:11	foundation of the **h** of the LORD was laid.	1074
	4:24	on the **h** of God in Jerusalem came to	10103
	5: 2	of Jozadak set to work to rebuild the **h**	10103
	5:13	King Cyrus issued a decree to rebuild this **h**	10103
	5:14	the gold and silver articles of the **h** of God,	10103
	5:15	And rebuild the **h** of God on its site.'	10103
	5:16	and laid the foundations of the **h** of God	10103
	5:17	to rebuild this **h** of God in Jerusalem.	10103
	6: 5	the gold and silver articles of the **h** of God,	10103
	6: 5	they are to be deposited in the **h** of God.	10103
	6: 7	Jews and the Jewish elders rebuild this **h**	10103
	6: 8	of the Jews in the construction of this **h**	10103
	6:11	pulled from his **h** and he is to be lifted up	10103
	6:11	for this crime his **h** is to be made a pile	10103
	6:16	celebrated the dedication of the **h** of God	10103
	6:17	the dedication of this **h** of God they offered	10103
	6:22	so that he assisted them in the work on the **h**	1074
	7:24	temple servants or other workers at this **h**	10103
	7:27	into the king's heart to bring honor to the **h**	1074
	8:17	attendants to us for the **h** of our God.	1074
	8:25	had donated for the **h** of our God.	1074
	8:29	of the **h** of the LORD in Jerusalem before	1074
	8:30	be taken to the **h** of our God in Jerusalem.	1074
	8:33	On the fourth day, in the **h** of our God,	1074
	8:36	to the people and to the **h** of God.	1074
	9: 9	He has granted us new life to rebuild the **h**	1074
	10: 1	the **h** of God, a large crowd of Israelites—	1074
	10: 6	before the **h** of God and went to the room	1074
	10: 9	in the square before the **h** of God,	1074
Ne	1: 6	including myself and my father's **h**,	1074
	3:10	of Harumaph made repairs opposite his **h**,	1074
	3:16	the artificial pool and the **H** of the Heroes.	1074
	3:20	from the angle to the entrance of the **h**	1074
	3:21	from the entrance of Eliashib's **h** to the end	1074
	3:23	made repairs in front of their **h**;	1074
	3:23	made repairs beside his **h**.	1074
	3:24	from Azariah's **h** to the angle and	1074
	3:28	each in front of his own **h**.	1074
	3:29	of Immer made repairs opposite his **h**.	1074
	3:31	as far as the **h** of the temple servants and	1074
	5:13	"In this way may God shake out of his **h**	1074
	6:10	One day I went to the **h** of Shemaiah son	1074
	6:10	He said, "Let us meet in the **h** of God,	1074
	8:16	the courts of the **h** of God and in the square	1074

Ne	10:32	of a shekel each year for the service of the **h**	1074
	10:33	and for all the duties of the **h** of our God.	1074
	10:34	to the **h** of our God at set times each year	1074
	10:35	the **h** of the LORD each year the firstfruits	1074
	10:36	of our herds and of our flocks to the **h**	1074
	10:37	we will bring to the storerooms of the **h**	1074
	10:38	a tenth of the tithes up to the **h** of our God,	1074
	10:39	"We will not neglect the **h** of our God."	1074
	11:11	supervisor in the **h** of God,	1074
	11:16	who had charge of the outside work of the **h**	1074
	11:22	for the service of the **h** of God.	1074
	12:37	the wall and passed above the **h** of David to	1074
	12:40	then took their places in the **h** of God;	1074
	13: 4	of the storerooms of the **h** of our God.	1074
	13: 7	a room in the courts of the **h** of God.	1074
	13: 9	into them the equipment of the **h** of God,	1074
	13:11	"Why is the **h** of God neglected?"	1074
	13:14	so faithfully done for the **h** of my God	1074
Est	4:13	because you are in the king's **h** you alone	1074
	7: 8	the queen while she is with me in the **h**?"	1074
	7: 9	"A gallows seventy-five feet high stands by	
		Haman's **h**.	1074
Job	1:13	and drinking wine at the oldest brother's **h**,	1074
	1:18	and drinking wine at the oldest brother's **h**,	1074
	1:19	and struck the four corners of the **h**.	1074
	5: 3	but suddenly his **h** was cursed.	5659
	7:10	He will never come to his **h** again;	1074
	20:28	A flood will carry off his **h**,	1074
	21:28	You say, 'Where now is the great man's **h**,	1074
	27:18	The **h** he builds is like a moth's cocoon,	1074
	29: 4	God's intimate friendship blessed my **h**,	185
	29:18	"I thought, 'I will die in my own **h**,	7860
	42:11	before came and ate with him in his **h**.	1074
Ps	5: 7	by your great mercy, will come into your **h**;	1074
	23: 6	I will dwell in the **h** of the LORD forever.	1074
	26: 8	I love the **h** where you live, O LORD,	1074
	27: 4	the **h** of the LORD all the days of my life,	1074
	36: 8	They feast on the abundance of your **h**;	1074
	42: 4	leading the procession to the **h** of God,	1074
	45:10	Forget your people and your father's **h**.	1074
	49:16	when the splendor of his **h** increases;	1074
	52: T	"David has gone to the **h** of Ahimelech."	1074
	52: 8	an olive tree flourishing in the **h** of God;	1074
	55:14	as we walked with the throng at the **h**	1074
	59: T	to watch David's **h** in order to kill him.	1074
	65: 4	with the good things of your **h**,	1074
	69: 9	for zeal for your **h** consumes me,	1074
	84: 4	Blessed are those who dwell in your **h**;	1074
	84:10	a doorkeeper in the **h** of my God than dwell	1074
	92:13	planted in the **h** of the LORD,	1074
	93: 5	holiness adorns your **h** for endless days,	1074
	98: 3	and his faithfulness to the **h** of Israel;	1074
	101: 2	I will walk in my **h** with blameless heart.	1074
	101: 7	No one who practices deceit will dwell in	
		my **h**;	1074
	112: 3	Wealth and riches are in his **h**,	1074
	114: 1	**h** of Jacob from a people of foreign tongue,	1074
	115: 9	O **h** of Israel, trust in the LORD—	NIH
	115:10	O **h** of Aaron, trust in the LORD—	1074
	115:12	He will bless the **h** of Israel,	1074
	115:12	he will bless the **h** of Aaron,	1074
	116:19	in the courts of the **h** of the LORD—	1074
	118: 3	Let the **h** of Aaron say:	1074
	118:26	From the **h** of the LORD we bless you.	1074
	122: 1	"Let us go to the **h** of the LORD."	1074
	122: 5	the thrones of the **h** of David.	1074
	122: 9	the sake of the **h** of the LORD our God,	1074
	127: 1	Unless the LORD builds the **h**,	1074
	128: 3	be like a fruitful vine within your **h**;	1074
	132: 3	"I will not enter my **h** or go to my bed	185+1074
	134: 1	the LORD who minister by night in the **h**	1074
	135: 2	you who minister in the **h** of the LORD,	1074
	135: 2	in the courts of the **h** of our God.	1074
	135:19	O **h** of Israel, praise the LORD;	1074
	135:19	O **h** of Aaron, praise the LORD;	1074
	135:20	O **h** of Levi, praise the LORD;	1074
Pr	2:18	For her **h** leads down to death and her paths	1074
	3:33	LORD's curse is on the **h** of the wicked,	1074
	4: 3	When I was a boy in my father's **h**,	NIH
	5: 8	do not go near the door of her **h**,	1074
	5:10	and your toil enrich another man's **h**.	1074
	6:31	though it costs him all the wealth of his **h**.	1074
	7: 6	At the window of my **h** I looked out through	1074
	7: 8	walking along in the direction of her **h**	1074
	7:27	Her **h** is a highway to the grave,	1074
	9: 1	Wisdom has built her **h**;	1074
	9:14	She sits at the door of her **h**,	1074
	12: 7	but the **h** of the righteous stands firm.	1074
	14: 1	The wise woman builds her **h**,	1074
	14:11	The **h** of the wicked will be destroyed,	1074
	15: 6	the **h** of the righteous contains great treasure,	1074
	15:25	The LORD tears down the proud man's **h**	1074
	17: 1	a dry crust with peace and quiet than a **h** full	1074
	17:13	evil will never leave his **h**.	1074
	21: 9	to live on a corner of the roof than share a **h**	1074
	21:12	the **h** of the wicked and brings the wicked	1074
	21:20	the **h** of the wise are stores of choice food	5659
	24: 3	By wisdom a **h** is built,	1074
	24:15	like an outlaw against a righteous man's **h**,	5659
	24:27	after that, build your **h**.	1074
	25:17	Seldom set foot in your neighbor's **h**—	1074
	25:24	to live on a corner of the roof than share a **h**	1074
	27:10	and do not go to your brother's **h**	1074
Ecc	5: 1	Guard your steps when you go to the **h**	1074
	7: 2	to a **h** of mourning than to go to a house	1074
	7: 2	of mourning than to go to a **h** of feasting,	1074

Ecc	7: 4	heart of the wise is in the **h** of mourning,	1074
	7: 4	but the heart of fools is in the **h** of pleasure.	1074
	10:18	if his hands are idle, the **h** leaks.	1074
SS	1:17	The beams of our **h** are cedars;	1074
	3: 4	till I had brought him to my mother's **h**,	1074
	8: 2	and bring you to my mother's **h**—	1074
	8: 7	If one were to give all the wealth of his **h**	1074
Isa	2: 3	to the **h** of the God of Jacob.	1074
	2: 5	Come, O **h** of Jacob,	1074
	2: 6	abandoned your people, the **h** of Jacob.	1074
	3: 7	I have no food or clothing in my **h**;	1074
	5: 7	of the LORD Almighty is the **h** of Israel,	1074
	5: 8	to you who add **h** to house and join field	1074
	5: 8	to you who add house to **h** and join field	1074
	7: 2	Now the **h** of David was told,	1074
	7:13	Isaiah said, "Hear now, you **h** of David!	1074
	7:17	on your people and on the **h** of your father	1074
	8:17	who is hiding his face from the **h** of Jacob.	1074
	10:20	the survivors of the **h** of Jacob,	1074
	14: 1	Aliens will join them and unite with the **h**	1074
	14: 2	And the **h** of Israel will possess the nations	1074
	16: 5	one from the **h** of David—	185
	22:18	you disgrace to your master's **h**!	1074
	22:21	to those who live in Jerusalem and to the **h**	1074
	22:22	I will place on his shoulder the key to the **h**	1074
	22:23	be a seat of honor for the **h** of his father.	1074
	23: 1	For Tyre is destroyed and left without **h**	1074
	24:10	the entrance to every **h** is barred.	1074
	29:22	says to the **h** of Jacob:	1074
	31: 2	He will rise up against the **h** of the wicked,	1074
	37:31	of the **h** of Judah will take root below	1074
	38: 1	Put your **h** in order, because you are going	1074
	38:12	Like a shepherd's tent my **h** has been pulled	1886
	46: 3	"Listen to me, O **h** of Jacob,	1074
	46: 3	all you who remain of the **h** of Israel,	1074
	48: 1	"Listen to this, O **h** of Jacob,	1074
	56: 7	and give them joy in my **h** of prayer.	1074
	56: 7	for my **h** will be called a house of prayer	1074
	56: 7	for my house will be called a **h** of prayer	1074
	58: 1	to my people their rebellion and to the **h**	1074
	63: 7	the many good things he has done for the **h**	1074
	66: 1	Where is the **h** you will build for me?	1074
Jer	2: 4	Hear the word of the LORD, O **h** of Jacob,	1074
	2: 4	all you clans of the **h** of Israel—	1074
	2:26	so the **h** of Israel is disgraced—	1074
	3:18	the **h** of Judah will join the house of Israel,	1074
	3:18	the house of Judah will join the **h** of Israel,	1074
	3:20	O **h** of Israel," declares the LORD.	1074
	5:11	The **h** of Israel and the house	1074
	5:11	the **h** of Judah have been utterly unfaithful	1074
	5:15	O **h** of Israel," declares the LORD,	1074
	5:20	to the **h** of Jacob and proclaim it in Judah:	1074
	7: 2	"Stand at the gate of the LORD's **h**	1074
	7:10	before me in this **h**, which bears my Name,	1074
	7:11	Has this **h**, which bears my Name,	1074
	7:14	what I did to Shiloh I will now do to the **h**	1074
	7:30	up their detestable idols in the **h**	1074
	9:26	even the whole **h** of Israel is uncircumcised	1074
	10: 1	what the LORD says to you, O **h** of Israel.	1074
	11:10	Both the **h** of Israel and the house	1074
	11:10	of Israel and the **h** of Judah have broken	1074
	11:17	because the **h** of Israel and the house	1074
	11:17	of Israel and the **h** of Judah have done evil	1074
	12: 7	"I will forsake my **h**,	1074
	12:14	from their lands and I will uproot the **h**	1074
	13:11	the whole **h** of Israel and the whole house	1074
	13:11	of Israel and the whole **h** of Judah to me,'	1074
	16: 5	not enter a **h** where there is a funeral meal;	1074
	16: 8	"And do not enter a **h** where there is	
		feasting	1074
	17:26	and thank offerings to the **h** of the LORD.	1074
	18: 2	"Go down to the potter's **h**,	1074
	18: 3	So I went down to the potter's **h**,	1074
	18: 6	"O **h** of Israel, can I not do with you as	1074
	18: 6	so are you in my hand, O **h** of Israel.	1074
	20: 6	and all who live in your **h** will go into exile	1074
	21:11	"Moreover, say to the royal **h** of Judah,	1074
	21:12	O **h** of David, this is what the LORD says:	1074
	26: 2	the LORD's **h** and speak to all the people	1074
	26: 2	of Judah who come to worship in the **h**	1074
	26: 6	then I will make this **h** like Shiloh	1074
	26: 7	these words in the **h** of the LORD.	1074
	26: 9	in the LORD's name that this **h** will be	1074
	26: 9	around Jeremiah in the **h** of the LORD.	1074
	26:10	to the **h** of the LORD and took their places	1074
	26:10	of the New Gate of the LORD's **h**.	NIH
	26:12	to prophesy against this **h** and this city all	1074
	27:16	from the LORD's **h** will be brought back	1074
	27:18	in the **h** of the LORD and in the palace of	1074
	27:21	says about the things that are left in the **h** of	1074
	28: 1	in the **h** of the LORD in the presence of	1074
	28: 3	the LORD's **h** that Nebuchadnezzar king	1074
	28: 5	the people who were standing in the **h**	1074
	28: 6	by bringing the articles of the LORD's **h**	1074
	29:26	in place of Jehoiada to be in charge of the **h**	1074
	31:27	the **h** of Israel and the house of Judah with	1074
	31:27	the house of Israel and the **h** of Judah with	1074
	31:31	the **h** of Israel and with the house of Judah.	1074
	31:31	the house of Israel and with the **h** of Judah.	1074
	31:33	"This is the covenant I will make with the **h**	1074
	32:34	They set up their abominable idols in the **h**	1074
	33:11	of those who bring thank offerings to the **h**	1074
	33:14	to the **h** of Israel and to the **h** of Judah.	1074
	33:14	to the house of Israel and to the **h** of Judah.	1074
	33:17	a man to sit on the throne of the **h** of Israel,	1074
	34:15	even made a covenant before me in the **h**	1074

Jer	35: 2	to come to one of the side rooms of the **h** *of*	1074
	35: 4	I brought them into the **h** *of* the LORD,	1074
	36: 6	So you go to the **h** *of* the LORD on a day	1074
	37:15	and had him beaten and imprisoned in the **h**	1074
	37:20	Do not send me back to the **h** *of* Jonathan	1074
	38:26	not to send me back to Jonathan's **h**	1074
	41: 5	with them to the **h** *of* the LORD.	1074
	48:13	as the **h** *of* Israel was ashamed	1074
	51:51	the holy places of the LORD's **h**."	1074
La	2: 7	a shout in the **h** *of* the LORD as on the day	1074
Eze	2: 5	for they are a rebellious **h**—	1074
	2: 6	though they are a rebellious **h.**	1074
	2: 8	Do not rebel like that rebellious **h;**	1074
	3: 1	then go and speak to the **h** *of* Israel."	1074
	3: 4	the **h** *of* Israel and speak my words to them.	1074
	3: 5	but to the **h** *of* Israel—	1074
	3: 7	the **h** *of* Israel is not willing to listen to you	1074
	3: 7	whole **h** *of* Israel is hardened and obstinate.	1074
	3: 9	though they are a rebellious **h.**"	1074
	3:17	I have made you a watchman for the **h**	1074
	3:24	"Go, shut yourself inside your **h.**	1074
	3:26	though they are a rebellious **h.**	1074
	3:27	for they are a rebellious **h.**	1074
	4: 3	This will be a sign to the **h** *of* Israel.	1074
	4: 4	on your left side and put the sin of the **h**	1074
	4: 5	for 390 days you will bear the sin of the **h**	1074
	4: 6	and bear the sin of the **h** *of* Judah.	1074
	5: 4	A fire will spread from there to the whole **h**	1074
	6:11	the wicked and detestable practices of the **h**	1074
	8: 1	in my **h** and the elders of Judah were sitting	1074
	8: 6	the utterly detestable things the **h**	1074
	8:10	and all the idols of the **h** *of* Israel.	1074
	8:11	of them stood seventy elders of the **h**	1074
	8:12	of the **h** *of* Israel are doing in the darkness,	1074
	8:14	to the entrance to the north gate of the **h** *of*	1074
	8:16	then brought me into the inner court of the **h**	1074
	8:17	Is it a trivial matter for the **h** *of* Judah to do	1074
	9: 9	"The sin of the **h** *of* Israel	1074
	10:19	to the east gate of the LORD's **h,**	1074
	11: 1	up and brought me to the gate of the **h** *of*	1074
	11: 5	That is what you are saying, O **h** *of* Israel,	1074
	11:15	and the whole **h** *of* Israel—	1074
	12: 3	though they are a rebellious **h.**	1074
	12: 6	I have made you a sign to the **h** *of* Israel."	1074
	12: 9	did not that rebellious **h** *of* Israel ask you,	1074
	12:10	and the whole **h** *of* Israel who are there.'	1074
	12:25	For in your days, you rebellious **h,**	1074
	12:27	the **h** *of* Israel is saying,	1074
	13: 5	to the breaks in the wall to repair it for the **h**	1074
	13: 9	or be listed in the records of the **h** *of* Israel,	1074
	14: 6	"Therefore say to the **h** *of* Israel,	1074
	17: 2	an allegory and tell the **h** *of* Israel a parable.	1074
	17:12	"Say to this rebellious **h,**	1074
	18: 6	or look to the idols of the **h** *of* Israel.	1074
	18:15	or look to the idols of the **h** *of* Israel.	1074
	18:25	Hear, O **h** *of* Israel: Is my way unjust?	1074
	18:29	Yet the **h** *of* Israel says,	1074
	18:29	Are my ways unjust, O **h** *of* Israel?	1074
	18:30	"Therefore, O **h** *of* Israel, I will judge you,	1074
	18:31	Why will you die, O **h** *of* Israel?	1074
	20: 5	the **h** *of* Jacob and revealed myself to them	1074
	20:30	"Therefore say to the **h** *of* Israel:	1074
	20:31	let you inquire of me, O **h** *of* Israel?	1074
	20:39	"'As for you, O **h** *of* Israel,	1074
	20:40	the land the entire **h** *of* Israel will serve me,	1074
	20:44	your corrupt practices, O **h** *of* Israel,	1074
	22:18	the **h** *of* Israel has become dross to me;	1074
	23:39	That is what they did in my **h.**	1074
	24: 3	Tell this rebellious **h** a parable and say	1074
	24:21	Say to the **h** *of* Israel, 'This is what	1074
	25: 8	'Because Moab and Seir said, "Look, the **h**	1074
	25:12	on the **h** *of* Judah and became very guilty	1074
	29: 6	"'You have been a staff of reed for the **h**	1074
	29:21	that day I will make a horn grow for the **h**	1074
	33: 7	I have made you a watchman for the **h**	1074
	33:10	"Son of man, say to the **h** *of* Israel,	1074
	33:11	Why will you die, O **h** *of* Israel?'	1074
	33:20	Yet, O **h** *of* Israel, you say,	1074
	34:30	am with them and that they, the **h** *of* Israel,	1074
	35:15	of the **h** *of* Israel became desolate,	1074
	36:10	even the whole **h** *of* Israel.	1074
	36:21	the **h** *of* Israel profaned among the nations	1074
	36:22	"Therefore say to the **h** *of* Israel,	1074
	36:22	It is not for your sake, O **h** *of* Israel,	1074
	36:32	disgraced for your conduct, O **h** *of* Israel!	1074
	36:37	Once again I will yield to the plea of the **h**	1074
	37:11	these bones are the whole **h** *of* Israel.	1074
	37:16	and all the **h** *of* Israel associated with him.'	1074
	39:12	the **h** *of* Israel will be burying them in order	1074
	39:22	that day forward the **h** *of* Israel will know	1074
	39:29	I will pour out my Spirit on the **h** *of* Israel,	1074
	40: 4	Tell the **h** *of* Israel everything you see."	1074
	43: 7	the **h** *of* Israel will never again defile my holy name"	1074
	44: 6	Say to the rebellious **h** *of* Israel,	1074
	44: 6	of your detestable practices, O **h** *of* Israel!	1074
	44:12	in the presence of their idols and made the **h**	1074
	45: 6	it will belong to the whole **h** *of* Israel.	1074
	45: 8	the **h** *of* Israel to possess the land according	1074
	45:17	at all the appointed feasts of the **h** *of* Israel.	1074
	45:17	to make atonement for the **h** *of* Israel.	1074
Da	1: 2	in Babylonia and put in the treasure **h**	1074
	2:17	Then Daniel returned to his **h** and explained	10103
Hos	1: 4	because I will soon punish the **h** *of* Jehu for	1074
	1: 6	for I will no longer show love to the **h**	1074
	1: 7	Yet I will show love to the **h** *of* Judah;	1074
	5: 1	Listen, O royal **h**! This judgment is against	1074

Hos	6:10	I have seen a horrible thing in the **h**	1074
	8: 1	An eagle is over the **h** *of* the LORD	1074
	9: 8	and hostility in the **h** *of* his God.	1074
	9:15	I will drive them out of my **h.**	1074
	11:12	the **h** *of* Israel with deceit.	1074
Joel	1: 9	and drink offerings are cut off from the **h** *of*	1074
	1:13	and drink offerings are withheld from the **h**	1074
	1:14	the land to the **h** *of* the LORD your God,	1074
	1:16	joy and gladness from the **h** *of* our God?	1074
	3:18	of the LORD's **h** and will water the valley	1074
Am	1: 4	upon the **h** *of* Hazael that will consume	1074
	2: 8	In the **h** *of* their god they drink wine taken	1074
	3:13	and testify against the **h** *of* Jacob,"	1074
	3:15	the winter **h** along with the summer house;	1074
	3:15	the winter house along with the summer **h;**	1074
	5: 1	Hear this word, O **h** *of* Israel,	1074
	5: 4	This is what the LORD says to the **h**	1074
	5: 6	or he will sweep through the **h** *of* Joseph	1074
	5:19	though he entered his **h** and rested his hand	1074
	5:25	forty years in the desert, O **h** *of* Israel?	1074
	6: 9	If ten men are left in one **h,**	1074
	6:10	comes to carry them out of the **h**	1074
	6:11	the great **h** into pieces and the small house	1074
	6:11	the great house into pieces and the small **h**	1074
	6:14	O **h** *of* Israel, that will oppress you	1074
	7: 9	with my sword I will rise against the **h**	1074
	7:16	and stop preaching against the **h** *of* Isaac.'	1074
	9: 8	I will not totally destroy the **h** *of* Jacob,"	1074
	9: 9	and I will shake the **h** *of* Israel among all	1074
Ob	1:17	the **h** *of* Jacob will possess its inheritance.	1074
	1:18	The **h** *of* Jacob will be a fire and the house	1074
	1:18	The house of Jacob will be a fire and the **h.**	1074
	1:18	the **h** *of* Esau will be stubble.	1074
	1:18	There will be no survivors from the **h**	1074
Mic	1: 5	because of the sins of the **h** *of* Israel.	1074
	2: 7	Should it be said, O **h** *of* Jacob:	1074
	3: 1	you rulers of the **h** *of* Israel.	1074
	3: 9	Hear this, you leaders of the **h** *of* Jacob,	1074
	3: 9	you rulers of the **h** *of* Israel,	1074
	4: 2	to the **h** *of* the God of Jacob.	1074
	6:10	Am I still to forget, O wicked **h,**	1074
	6:16	of Omri and all the practices of Ahab's **h,**	1074
Hab	2:10	shaming your own **h** and forfeiting your life	1074
Zep	2: 7	It will belong to the remnant of the **h**	1074
Hag	1: 2	yet come for the LORD's **h** to be built.' "	1074
	1: 4	while this **h** remains a ruin?"	1074
	1: 8	and bring down timber and build the **h,**	1074
	1: 9	"Because of my **h,** which remains a ruin,	1074
	1: 9	while each of you is busy with his own **h.**	1074
	1:14	to work on the **h** *of* the LORD Almighty,	1074
	2: 3	'Who of you is left who saw this **h**	1074
	2: 7	and I will fill this **h** with glory,'	1074
	2: 9	glory of this present **h** will be greater than	1074
	2: 9	be greater than the glory of the former **h,'**	NIH
Zec	1:16	and there my **h** will be rebuilt.	1074
	3: 7	then you will govern my **h** and have charge	1074
	5: 4	and it will enter the **h** *of* the thief and	1074
	5: 4	and the **h** *of* him who swears falsely	1074
	5: 4	It will remain in his **h** and destroy it,	1074
	5:11	the country of Babylonia to build a **h** for it.	1074
	6:10	Go the same day to the **h** *of* Josiah son	1074
	7: 3	the priests of the **h** *of* the LORD Almighty	1074
	8: 9	when the foundation was laid for the **h** *of*	1074
	9: 8	But I will defend my **h**	1074
	10: 3	for his flock, the **h** *of* Judah,	1074
	10: 6	"I will strengthen the **h** *of* Judah and save	1074
	10: 6	of Judah and save the **h** *of* Joseph.	1074
	11:13	and threw them into the **h** *of* the LORD to	1074
	12: 4	"I will keep a watchful eye over the **h**	1074
	12: 7	so that the honor of the **h** *of* David and	1074
	12: 8	and the **h** *of* David will be like God,	1074
	12:10	"And I will pour out on the **h** *of* David and	1074
	12:12	the clan of the **h** *of* David and their wives,	1074
	12:12	the clan of the **h** *of* Nathan and their wives,	1074
	12:13	the clan of the **h** *of* Levi and their wives,	1074
	13: 1	a fountain will be opened to the **h** *of* David	1074
	13: 6	'The wounds I was given at the **h**	1074
	14:20	and the cooking pots in the LORD's **h** will	1074
	14:21	in the **h** *of* the LORD Almighty.	1074
Mal	3:10	that there may be food in my **h.**	1074
Mt	2:11	On coming to the **h,** they saw the child	3864
	5:15	and it gives light to everyone in the **h.**	3864
	7:24	like a wise man who built his **h** on the rock.	3864
	7:25	and the winds blew and beat against that **h;**	3864
	7:26	like a foolish man who built his **h** on sand.	3864
	7:27	and the winds blew and beat against that **h,**	3864
	8:14	When Jesus came into Peter's **h,**	3864
	9:10	at Matthew's **h,** many tax collectors	3864
	9:23	the ruler's **h** and saw the flute players and	3864
	10:11	and stay **at his h** until you leave.	1695
	10:25	**head of the h** has been called Beelzebub,	3867
	12: 4	He entered the **h** *of* God,	3875
	12:29	how can anyone enter a strong man's **h**	3864
	12:29	Then he can rob his **h.**	3864
	12:44	Then it says, 'I will return to the **h** I left.'	3875
	12:44	When it arrives, it finds the **h** unoccupied,	3875
	13: 1	That same day Jesus went out of the **h**	3864
	13:36	Then he left the crowd and went into the **h.**	3864
	13:52	like the **owner of a h** who brings out	476+3867
	13:57	"Only in his hometown and in his own **h** is	3864
	17:25	When Peter came into the **h,**	3864
	21:13	" 'My **h** will be called a house of prayer,'	3875
	21:13	" 'My house will be called a house of prayer,'	3875
	23:38	Look, your **h** is left to you desolate.	3875
	24:17	Let no one on the **roof of** his **h** go down	1560
	24:17	down to take anything out of the **h.**	3864
	24:43	the **owner of the h** had known at what time	3867

Mt	24:43	and would not have let his **h** be broken into.	3864
	26:18	the Passover with my disciples at your **h.** "	NIG
Mk	1:35	left the **h** and went off to a solitary place,	NIG
	2:15	While Jesus was having dinner at Levi's **h,**	3864
	2:26	the **h** *of* God and ate the consecrated bread,	3875
	3:20	Then Jesus entered a **h,**	3875
	3:25	If a **h** is divided against itself,	3864
	3:25	that **h** cannot stand.	3864
	3:27	no one can enter a strong man's **h** and	3864
	3:27	Then he can rob his **h.**	3864
	5:35	some men came from the **h** *of* Jairus,	NIG
	6: 4	in his own **h** is a prophet without honor."	3864
	6:10	Whenever you enter a **h,**	3864
	7:17	the crowd and entered the **h,**	3875
	7:24	He entered a **h** and did not want anyone	3864
	9:33	When he was in the **h,** he asked them,	3864
	10:10	When they were in the **h** again,	3864
	11:17	" 'My **h** will be called a house of prayer	3875
	11:17	" 'My house will be called a house of prayer	3875
	13:15	the roof of his **h** go down or enter the house	3864
	13:15	the roof of his house go down or enter the **h**	NIG
	13:34	He leaves his **h** and puts his servants	3864
	13:35	when the owner *of* the **h** will come back—	3864
	14:14	Say *to* the **owner of the h** he enters,	3867
Lk	1:33	he will reign over the **h** *of* Jacob forever;	3875
	1:69	up a horn of salvation for us in the **h**	3875
	2: 4	because he belonged to the **h** and line	3875
	2:49	I had to be in my Father's **h?**"	3836
	5:18	and tried to take him into the **h** to lay him	NIG
	5:29	Levi held a great banquet for Jesus at his **h,**	3864
	6: 4	He entered the **h** *of* God,	3875
	6:48	He is like a man building a **h,**	3864
	6:48	torrent struck that **h** but could not shake it,	3864
	6:49	into practice is like a man who built a **h** on	3864
	6:49	The moment the torrent struck that **h,**	3864
	7: 6	the **h** when the centurion sent friends to say	3864
	7:10	the men who had been sent returned to the **h**	3875
	7:36	to the Pharisee's **h** and reclined at the table.	3875
	7:37	that Jesus was eating at the Pharisee's **h,**	3864
	7:44	I came into your **h.**	3864
	8:27	not worn clothes or lived in a **h,**	3864
	8:41	pleading with him to come to his **h**	3875
	8:49	someone came from the **h** *of* Jairus,	NIG
	8:51	When he arrived at the **h** *of* Jairus,	3864
	9: 4	Whatever **h** you enter, stay there until	3864
	10: 5	"When you enter a **h,** first say,	3864
	10: 5	first say, 'Peace *to* this **h.'**	3875
	10: 7	Stay in that **h,** eating and drinking whatever	3864
	10: 7	Do not move around from **h** to house.	3864
	10: 7	Do not move around from house to **h.**	3864
	11:17	and a **h** divided against itself will fall.	3864
	11:21	strong man, fully armed, guards his own **h,**	885
	11:24	Then it says, 'I will return to the **h** I left.'	3875
	11:25	it finds the **h** swept clean and put in order.	NIG
	12:39	the **owner of the h** had known at what hour	3867
	12:39	he would not have let his **h** be broken into.	3875
	13:25	Once the **owner of the h** gets up and closes	3867
	13:35	Look, your **h** is left to you desolate.	3875
	14: 1	to eat in the **h** *of* a prominent Pharisee,	3864
	14:21	Then the **owner of the h** became angry	3867
	14:23	so that my **h** will be full.	3875
	15: 8	the **h** and search carefully until she finds it?	3864
	15:25	When he came near the **h,**	3864
	16:27	father, send Lazarus to my father's **h,**	3875
	17:31	that day no one who is on the roof of his **h,**	3864
	19: 5	I must stay at your **h** today."	3875
	19: 9	"Today salvation has come *to* this **h,**	3875
	19:46	" 'My **h** will be a house of prayer';	3875
	19:46	" 'My house will be a house of prayer';	3875
	22:10	Follow him to the **h** that he enters,	3864
	22:11	to the owner of the **h,** 'The Teacher asks:	3864
	22:54	they led him away and took him into the **h**	3864
Jn	2:16	How dare you turn my Father's **h** into	3875
	2:17	"Zeal *for* your **h** will consume me."	3875
	11:31	the Jews who had been with Mary in the **h,**	3864
	12: 3	And the **h** was filled with the fragrance of	3864
	14: 2	In my Father's **h** are many rooms;	3864
	20:26	his disciples were in the **h** again,	NIG
Ac	2: 2	the whole **h** where they were sitting.	3875
	5:42	temple courts and **from h to house,**	2848+3875
	5:42	temple courts and **from house to h,**	2848+3875
	7:20	he was cared for in his father's **h.**	3875
	7:42	and offerings forty years in the desert, O **h**	NIG
	7:47	But it was Solomon who built the **h** for him.	3875
	7:49	What kind of **h** will you build for me?	3875
	8: 3	Going **from h to house,**	2848+3836+3875
	8: 3	Going **from house to h,**	2848+3836+3875
	9:11	the **h** *of* Judas on Straight Street and ask for	3864
	9:17	Then Ananias went to the **h** and entered it.	3864
	10: 6	Simon the tanner, whose **h** is by the sea."	3875
	10:17	where Simon's **h** was and stopped at	3864
	10:22	to his **h** so that he could hear what you have	3875
	10:23	Then Peter invited the men into the **h** to	NIG
	10:25	As Peter entered the **h,** Cornelius met him	NIG
	10:30	"Four days ago I was in my **h** praying	3875
	11: 3	"You went into the **h** *of* uncircumcised men	NIG
	11:11	to me from Caesarea stopped at the **h**	3864
	11:12	and we entered the man's **h.**	3875
	11:13	how he had seen an angel appear in his **h**	3875
	12:12	to the **h** *of* Mary the mother of John,	3864
	16:15	she said, "come and stay at my **h.**"	3875
	16:32	to him and to all the others in his **h.**	3864
	16:34	The jailer brought them into his **h** and set	3875
	16:40	they went to Lydia's **h,**	NIG
	17: 5	They rushed to Jason's **h** in search of Paul	3864
	17: 7	**welcomed** them **into** his **h.**	5685
	18: 7	and went next door to the **h** *of* Titius Justus,	3864

Ac	19:16	a beating that they ran out of the **h** naked	3875
	20:20	and **from h to house.**	2848+3875
	20:20	and **from house to h.**	2848+3875
	21: 8	and stayed at the **h** of Philip the evangelist,	3875
	28:30	Paul stayed there in his own **rented h**	3637
Ro	16: 5	Greet also the church that meets at their **h.**	3875
1Co	16:19	and so does the church that meets at their **h.**	3875
2Co	5: 1	an eternal **h** in heaven,	3864
Col	4:15	and to Nympha and the church in her **h.**	3875
1Ti	5:13	and going about **from h to house.**	3836+3864
	5:13	and going about **from house to h.**	3836+3864
2Ti	2:20	a large **h** there are articles not only of gold	3864
Heb	3: 2	just as Moses was faithful in all God's **h.**	3875
	3: 3	as the builder of a **h** has greater honor than	NIG
	3: 3	a house has greater honor than the **h** itself.	3875
	3: 4	For every **h** is built by someone,	3875
	3: 5	Moses was faithful as a servant in all God's **h,**	3875
	3: 6	But Christ is faithful as a son over God's **h.**	3875
	3: 6	And we are his **h,** if we hold on to our	3875
	8: 8	a new covenant with the **h** of Israel and with	3875
	8: 8	the house of Israel and with the **h** of Judah.	3875
	8:10	the covenant I will make **with** the **h** of Israel	3875
	10:21	we have a great priest over the **h** of God,	3875
1Pe	2: 5	into a spiritual **h** to be a holy priesthood.	
2Jn	1:10	not take him into your **h** or welcome him.	3864

HOUSEHOLD (116) [HOUSE]

Ge	12: 1	your people and your father's **h** and go to	1074
	12:17	and his **h** because of Abram's wife Sarai.	1074
	14:14	the 318 trained men born in his **h** and went	1074
	15: 3	so a servant in my **h** will be my heir."	1074
	17:12	including those born in your **h** or bought	1074
	17:13	in your **h** or bought with your money,	1074
	17:23	and all those born in his **h** or bought	1074
	17:23	every male in his **h,** and circumcised them,	1074
	17:27	And every male in Abraham's **h,**	1074
	17:27	including those born in his **h** or bought from	1074
	18:19	so that he will direct his children and his **h**	1074
	20:13	God had me wander from my father's **h,**	1074
	20:18	up every womb in Abimelech's **h** because	1074
	24: 2	He said to the chief servant in his **h,**	1074
	24: 7	who brought me out of my father's **h**	1074
	24:28	and told her mother's **h** about these things.	1074
	30:30	when may I do something for my own **h?"**	1074
	31:19	Rachel stole her father's **h** gods.	9572
	31:34	Now Rachel had taken the **h** gods	9572
	31:35	but could not find the **h** gods.	9572
	31:37	have you found that belongs to your **h?**	1074
	31:41	for the twenty years I was in your **h.**	1074
	34:19	the most honored of all his father's **h,**	1074
	34:30	I and my **h** will be destroyed."	1074
	35: 2	So Jacob said to his **h** and to all who were	1074
	36: 6	and daughters and all the members of his **h,**	1074
	39: 4	Potiphar put him in charge of his **h,**	1074
	39: 5	From the time he put him in charge of his **h**	1074
	39: 5	the LORD blessed the **h** of the Egyptian	1074
	39:11	and none of the **h** servants was inside.	1074
	39:14	she called her **h** servants.	1074
	41:51	all my trouble and all my father's **h."**	1074
	45: 2	and Pharaoh's **h** heard about it.	1074
	45: 8	lord of his entire **h** and ruler of all Egypt.	1074
	45:11	and your **h** and all who belong	1074
	46:31	to his brothers and to his father's **h,**	1074
	46:31	'My brothers and my father's **h,**	3864
	47:12	and his brothers and all his father's **h**	1074
	50: 8	the members of Joseph's **h** and his brothers	1074
	50: 8	and **those belonging to** his father's **h.**	1074
Ex	12: 3	a lamb for his family, one for each **h.**	1074
	12: 4	If any **h** is too small for a whole lamb,	1074
	12:48	the males in his **h** circumcised;	NIH
	23:12	and the **slave born in** your **h,**	563+1201
Lev	16: 6	to make atonement for himself and his **h.**	1074
	16:11	to make atonement for himself and his **h,**	1074
	16:17	his **h** and the whole community of Israel.	1074
	22:11	or if a slave is born in his **h,**	1074
Nu	18:11	Everyone in your **h** who is ceremonially clean may eat it.	1074
	18:13	Everyone in your **h** who is ceremonially clean may eat it.	1074
Dt	6:22	upon Egypt and Pharaoh and his whole **h.**	1074
	14:26	and your **h** shall eat there in the presence of	1074
	26:11	your God has given you and your **h.**	1074
Jos	24:15	me and my **h,** we will serve the LORD."	1074
Jdg	14:15	or we will burn you and your father's **h**	1074
	18:14	an ephod, other **h** gods, a carved image and	9572
	18:17	the other **h** gods and the cast idol while	9572
	18:18	the other **h** gods and the cast idol,	9572
	18:19	as priest rather than just one man's **h?"**	1074
	18:20	the other **h** gods and the carved image	9572
1Sa	22: 1	When his brothers and his father's **h** heard	1074
	22:14	and highly respected in your **h?**	1074
	25: 6	Good health to you and your **h!**	1074
	25:17	over our master and his whole **h.**	1074
2Sa	6:11	the LORD blessed him and his entire **h.**	1074
	6:12	the **h** of Obed-Edom and everything he has,	1074
	6:20	When David returned home to bless his **h,**	1074
	9: 2	there was a servant of Saul's **h** named Ziba.	1074
	9:12	of Ziba's **h** were servants of Mephibosheth.	1074
	12:11	of your own **h** I am going to bring calamity	1074
	12:17	of his **h** stood beside him to get him up	1074
	15:16	with his entire **h** following him;	1074
	16: 2	donkeys are for the king's **h** to ride on,	1074
	16: 8	for all the blood you shed in the **h** of Saul,	1074
	19:17	along with Ziba, the steward of Saul's **h,**	1074
	19:18	They crossed at the ford to take the king's **h**	1074

2Sa	19:41	steal the king away and bring him and his **h**	1074
1Ki	4: 7	for the king and the royal **h.**	1074
	5: 9	by providing food for your royal **h."**	1074
	5:11	of wheat as food for his **h,**	1074
	10:21	the **h** articles *in* the Palace of the Forest	3998
2Ki	23:24	and spiritists, the **h** gods, the idols and all	9572
1Ch	13:14	and the LORD blessed his **h** and everything	1074
2Ch	9:20	the **h** articles *in* the Palace of the Forest	3998
Ne	13: 8	and threw all Tobiah's **h** goods out of	1074
Est	1:22	every man should be ruler over his own **h.**	1074
Job	1:10	not put a hedge around him and his **h**	1074
	16: 7	you have devastated my entire **h.**	6337
	31:31	the men of my **h** have never said, 'Who has	185
Ps	105:21	He made him master of his **h,**	1074
Pr	31:21	When it snows, she has no fear for her **h;**	1074
	31:27	over the affairs of her **h** and does not eat	1074
Jer	23:34	I will punish that man and his **h.**	1074
Eze	44:30	so that a blessing may rest on your **h.**	1074
Mic	7: 6	the members of his own **h.**	1074
Mt	10:25	how much more the **members of** his **h!**	3865
	10:36	enemies will be the **members of** his own **h.**	3865
	12:25	or **h** divided against itself will not stand.	3864
	24:45	the **servants in** his **h** to give them their food	3859
Lk	8: 3	the manager of Herod's **h;**	NIG
Jn	4:53	So he and all his **h** believed.	3864
Ac	11:14	through which you and all your **h** will	3875
	16:15	and the **members of** her **h** were baptized,	3875
	16:31	and you will be saved—you and your **h."**	3875
	18: 8	and his entire **h** believed in the Lord;	3875
Ro	16:10	Greet those who belong to the **h**	3836
	16:11	Greet those in the **h** of Narcissus who are in	NIG
1Co	1:11	some from Chloe's **h** have informed me	3836
	1:16	(Yes, I also baptized the **h** of Stephanas;	3875
	16:15	the **h** of Stephanas were the first converts	3864
Eph	2:19	God's people and **members of** God's **h,**	3858
Php	4:22	especially those who belong to Caesar's **h.**	3864
1Ti	3:12	must manage his children and his **h** well.	3875
	3:15	to conduct themselves in God's **h,**	3875
2Ti	1:16	May the Lord show mercy *to* the **h**	3875
	4:19	and Aquila and the **h** of Onesiphorus.	3875

HOUSEHOLDS (7) [HOUSE]

Ge	42:19	and take grain back for your starving **h.**	1074
	42:33	and take food for your starving **h** and go.	1074
	47:24	and as food for yourselves and your **h**	1074
Nu	16:32	with their **h** and all Korah's men	1074
	18:31	and your **h** may eat the rest of it anywhere,	1074
Dt	11: 6	and swallowed them up with their **h,**	1074
Tit	1:11	because they are ruining whole **h**	3875

HOUSES (94) [HOUSE]

Ge	34:29	taking as plunder everything in the **h.**	1074
Ex	8: 3	the **h** of your officials and on your people,	1074
	8: 9	that you and your **h** may be rid of the frogs,	1074
	8:11	The frogs will leave you and your **h,**	1074
	8:13	The frogs died in the **h,**	1074
	8:21	on your people and into your **h.**	1074
	8:21	The **h** of the Egyptians will be full of flies,	1074
	8:24	into Pharaoh's palace and into the **h**	1074
	10: 6	They will fill your **h** and those	1074
	12: 7	the sides and tops of the doorframes of the **h**	1074
	12:13	be a sign for you on the **h** where you are;	1074
	12:15	the first day remove the yeast from your **h,**	1074
	12:19	no yeast is to be found in your **h.**	1074
	12:23	not permit the destroyer to enter your **h**	1074
	12:27	who passed over the **h** of the Israelites	1074
Lev	25:31	But **h** in villages outside walls	1074
	25:32	to redeem their **h** in the Levitical towns,	1074
	25:33	in the Jubilee, because the **h** in the towns of	1074
Dt	6: 9	Write them on the doorframes of your **h** and	1074
	6:11	**h** filled with all kinds of good things,	1074
	8:12	when you build fine **h** and settle down,	1074
	11:20	Write them on the doorframes of your **h** and	1074
	19: 1	and settled in their towns and **h,**	1074
Jdg	18:14	"Do you know that one of these **h** has	1074
1Ki	20: 6	to search your palace and the **h**	1074
2Ki	25: 9	the royal palace and all the **h** of Jerusalem.	1074
Ne	5:11	vineyards, olive groves and **h,**	1074
	7: 3	at their posts and some near their own **h."**	1074
	7: 4	and the **h** had not yet been rebuilt.	1074
	9:25	of **h** filled with all kinds of good things,	1074
Job	3:15	who filled their **h** with silver.	1074
	4:19	much more those who live in **h** of clay,	1074
	15:28	he will inhabit ruined towns and **h**	1074
	15:28	**h** crumbling to rubble.	889S
	20:19	he has seized **h** that did not build.	1074
	22:18	Yet it was he who filled their **h**	1074
	24:16	In the dark, men break into **h,**	1074
Ps	49:11	Their tombs will remain their **h** forever,	1074
Pr	1:13	and fill our **h** with plunder;	1074
	19:14	**H** and wealth are inherited from parents,	1074
Ecc	2: 4	I built **h** for myself and planted vineyards.	1074
Isa	3:14	the plunder from the poor is in your **h.**	1074
	5: 9	"Surely the great **h** will become desolate,	1074
	6:11	the **h** are left deserted and the fields ruined	1074
	8:14	but for both **h** of Israel he will be a stone	1074
	13:16	their **h** will be looted	1074
	13:21	jackals will fill her **h;**	1074
	22:10	the buildings in Jerusalem and tore down **h**	1074
	32:13	for all **h** of merriment and for this city	1074
	65:21	They will build **h** and dwell in them;	1074
	65:22	No longer will they build **h** and others live	NIH
Jer	5: 7	and thronged to the **h** of prostitutes.	1074
	5:27	their **h** are full of deceit;	1074
	6:12	Their **h** will be turned over to others,	1074

Jer	9:19	We must leave our land because our **h** are	5438
	17:22	of your **h** or do any work on the Sabbath,	1074
	18:22	Let a cry be heard from their **h**	1074
	19:13	The **h** in Jerusalem and those of the kings	1074
	19:13	all the **h** where they burned incense on	1074
	29: 5	"Build **h** and settle down;	1074
	29:28	Therefore build **h** and settle down;	1074
	32:15	**H,** fields and vineyards will again be bought	1074
	32:29	with the **h** where the people provoked me	1074
	33: 4	the **h** in this city and the royal palaces	1074
	35: 7	Also you must never build **h,**	1074
	35: 9	or built **h** to live in or had vineyards.	1074
	39: 8	to the royal palace and the **h** of the people	1074
	52:13	the royal palace and all the **h** of Jerusalem.	1074
Eze	7:24	of the nations to take possession of their **h;**	1074
	11: 3	'Will it not soon be time to build **h?**	1074
	16:41	down your **h** and inflict punishment on you	1074
	23:47	and daughters and burn down their **h.**	1074
	26:12	down your walls and demolish your fine **h**	1074
	28:26	and will build **h** and plant vineyards;	1074
	33:30	by the walls and at the doors of the **h,**	1074
	45: 4	a place for their **h** as well as a holy place for	1074
	48:15	for **h** and for pastureland.	4632
Da	2: 5	into pieces and your **h** turned into piles	10103
	3:29	and Abednego be cut into pieces and their **h**	10103
Hos	7: 1	They practice deceit, thieves break into **h,**	NIH
Joel	2: 9	They climb into the **h;**	1074
Am	3:15	the **h** *adorned with* ivory will be destroyed	1074
Mic	2: 2	They covet fields and seize them, and **h,**	1074
Zep	1:13	be plundered, their **h** demolished.	1074
	1:13	They will build **h** but not live in them;	1074
	2: 7	In the evening they will lie down in the **h**	1074
Hag	1: 4	to be living in your paneled **h,**	1074
Zec	14: 2	the city will be captured, the **h** ransacked,	1074
Mt	19:29	And everyone who has left **h** or brothers	3864
Mk	12:40	They devour widows' **h** and for a show	3864
Lk	16: 4	people will welcome me into their **h.'**	3875
	20:47	They devour widows' **h** and for a show	3864
Ac	4:34	those who owned lands or **h** sold them,	3864
	7:48	Most High does not live in **h** made by men.	NIG

HOVERING (2) [HOVERS]

Ge	1: 2	and the Spirit of God *was* **h** over the waters.	8173
Isa	31: 5	Like birds **h overhead,**	6414

HOVERS (1) [HOVERING]

Dt	32:11	that stirs up its nest and **h** over its young,	8173

HOW (729) [HOWEVER, SOMEHOW]

Ge	6: 5	The LORD saw **h** great man's wickedness	3954
	6:12	God saw **h corrupt** the earth *had* become,	AIT
	6:15	This is **h** you are to build it:	889
	15: 8	**h** can I know that I will gain possession	928+4537
	20: 9	I have I wronged you?	4537
	20:13	'This is **h** you can show your love to me:	889
	27:20	**H** did you find it so quickly, my son?	2296+4537
	28: 8	Esau then realized **h** displeasing	3954
	28:17	"**H** awesome is this place!	4537
	30:13	Then Leah said, "**H** happy I am!	928
	30:26	You know **h** much work I've done for you."	889
	30:29	"You know **h** I have worked for you and	889
	30:29	for you and **h** your livestock has fared	889
	38:29	"So this is **h** you have broken out!"	4537
	39: 9	**H** then could I do such a wicked thing	375
	39:19	saying, "**This is h** your slave treated me,"	465+1821+2021+2021+3869
	42:15	And **this is h** you will be tested:	928+2296
	42:21	We saw **h** distressed he was when he	AIT
	42:33	'This is **h** I will know whether you are	928+2296
	43: 7	**H** were we to know he would say,	AIT
	43:27	asked them **h** they were,	4200+8626+8934
	43:27	"**H** is your aged father you told me about?	8934
	44:16	**H** can we prove our innocence?	4537
	44:34	**H** can I go back to my father if the boy is	375
	47: 8	Pharaoh asked him, "**H** old are you?"	3869+4537
	49:15	When he sees **h** good is his resting place	3954
	49:15	how good is his resting place and **h**	3954
Ex	10: 2	and grandchildren **h** I dealt harshly with	889
	10: 2	the Egyptians and **h** I performed my signs	889
	10: 3	'**H long** will you refuse to humble yourself before me?	5503+6330
	10: 7	**H long** will this man be a snare to us?	5503+6330
	12:11	**This is h** you are to eat it:	3970
	16:28	"**H long** will you refuse	625+2025+6330
	18: 1	and **h** the LORD had brought Israel out	3954
	18: 8	the way and **h** the LORD had saved them.	NIH
	19: 4	and **h** I carried you on eagles' wings	NIH
	23: 9	you yourselves know **h** it feels to	5883
	32:22	"You know **h** prone these people are to evil.	3954
	33:16	**H** will anyone know that you are pleased with me	686+928+4537
	34:10	among will see **h** awesome is the work	3954
	36: 1	and ability to **know h** to carry out all	3359
Lev	5: 3	**This is h** his discharge will bring	2296
	16: 3	"**This is h** Aaron is to enter	928+2296
	18:24	because **this is h** the nations that I	465+928+3972
Nu	6:23	'**This is h** you are to bless the Israelites.	3907
	8: 4	**This is h** the lampstand was made:	2296
	8:26	**This, then, is h** you are to assign	3970
	9:16	**That is h** it continued to be;	4027
	11:15	If **this is h** you are going to treat me,	3970
	13:20	**h** is the soil?	4537
	14:11	**H long** will these people treat me	625+2025+6330
	14:11	**H long** will they refuse to believe in me,	625+2025+6330

Nu	14:27	"**H long** will this wicked community grumble against me?	5503+6330
	16:28	"**This is h** you will know that	928+2296
	23: 8	**H** can I curse those whom God has	4537
	23: 8	**H** can I denounce those whom	4537
	24: 5	"**H** beautiful are your tents,	4537
Dt	1:12	But **h** can I bear your problems	377
	1:31	There you saw **h** the LORD your God	889
	7:17	**H** can we drive them out?"	377
	8: 2	Remember **h** the LORD your God led you	889
	9: 7	Remember this and never forget **h**	889
	11: 4	**h** he overwhelmed them with the waters of	889
	11: 4	**h** the LORD brought lasting ruin on them.	NIH
	12:30	"**H** do these nations serve their gods?	377
	15: 2	This is **h** it is to be done:	1821
	18:21	"**H** can we know when a message has	377
	20:15	**This is h** you are to treat all the cities that	4027
	29:16	You yourselves know **h** we lived in Egypt	889
	29:16	and **h** we passed through the countries on	889
	31:27	For I know **h** rebellious and stiff-necked	NIH
	31:27	**h** much more will you rebel after I die!	677+2256+3954
	32:30	**H** could one man chase a thousand,	377
Jos	2:10	We have heard **h** the LORD dried up	889
	3:10	**This is h** you will know that	928+2296
	5: 1	the Canaanite kings along the coast heard **h**	889
	9: 7	**H** then can we make a treaty with you?"	375
	9:12	But now see **h** dry and moldy it is.	NIH
	9:13	but see **h** cracked they are.	NIH
	9:24	"Your servants were clearly told **h**	889
	18: 3	**H long** will you wait before you	625+2025+6330
	22:16	'**H** could you break faith with the God	4537
	22:16	**H** could you turn away from the LORD	NIH
	23: 4	Remember **h** I have allotted as	NIH
Jdg	1:24	"Show us **h to get into** the city	4427
	6:15	Gideon asked, "**h** can I save Israel?	928+4537
	13: 8	to teach us **h** to bring up the boy who is to	4537
	16: 5	and **h** we can overpower him	928+4537
	16: 5	great strength and **h** you can be tied	928+4537
	16:10	Come now, tell me **h** you can be tied."	928+4537
	16:13	Tell me **h** you can be tied."	928+4537
	16:15	Then she said to him, "**H** can you say,	375
	18: 8	"**H did you find things?**"	4537
	18:24	**H** can you ask, 'What's the matter	4537
	20: 3	"Tell us **h** this awful thing happened."	377
	20:34	that the Benjamites did not realize **h**	3954
	21: 7	"**H** can we provide wives for those who	4537
	21:16	**h** shall we provide wives for the men	4537
Ru	2:11	**h** you left your father and mother	2256
	2:18	her mother-in-law saw **h much** she had gathered.	889
	3:16	Naomi asked, "**H did it go,** my daughter?"	905+4769
1Sa	1:14	"**H long** will you keep on getting drunk?	5503+6330
	2:14	**This is h** they treated all the Israelites	3970
	2:22	to all Israel and **h** they slept with	889
	6: 2	Tell us **h** we should send it back	928+4537
	10:27	"**H** can this fellow save us?"	4537
	14:29	See **h** my eyes brightened when I tasted	3954
	14:30	**H much better** it would have been if	677+3954
	16: 1	"**H long** will you mourn for Saul,	5503+6330
	16: 2	But Samuel said, "**H** can I go?	375
	16:18	of Bethlehem *who* **knows h** to play the harp.	3359
	17:18	See **h** your brothers **are**	8934
	17:25	"Do you see **h** this man keeps coming out?	3954
	17:28	I know **h** conceited you are and	NIH
	17:28	and **h** wicked your heart is;	NIH
	18:15	When Saul saw **h** successful he was,	4394
	20: 1	I have I wronged your father,	
	21: 5	**H much more so** today!"	677+3954
	23: 3	**H much more,** then, if we go to Keilah	677
	24:10	your own eyes **h** the LORD has delivered	889
	29: 4	**H better** could he regain his master's favor than by taking the heads of	928+4537
2Sa	1: 5	"**H** do you know that Saul	375
	1:19	**H** the mighty have fallen!	375
	1:25	"**H** the mighty have fallen in battle!	375
	1:27	"**H** the mighty have fallen!	375
	2:22	**H** could I look your brother Joab in	375
	2:26	**H long** before you order your men	5503+6330
	4:11	**H much more**—when wicked men have killed an innocent man	677
	6: 9	"**H** can the ark of the LORD ever come	375
	6:20	said, "**H** the king of Israel has distinguished	4537
	7:22	"**H** great you are, O Sovereign LORD!	4027+6584
	11: 7	David asked him **h** Joab **was,**	4200+8934
	11: 7	**h** the soldiers **were** and how	4200+8934
	11: 7	**h** the war **was going.**	4200+8934
	11:11	*H could I go* to my house to eat and drink	AIT
	12:18	**H** can we tell him the child is dead?"	375
	16:11	**H much more,** then, this Benjamite!	677+3954
	16:23	**That was h** both David	4027
	19:19	Do not remember **h** your servant did wrong	889
	19:34	"**H many more** years will I live,	3869+4537
	20: 9	Joab said to Amasa, "**H are** you,	8934
	21: 3	**H** shall I make amends so that	928+4537
	24: 2	so that I may know **h many** there are."	5031
	24:13	think it over and decide **h** I should answer	4537
1Ki	1:12	let me advise you **h** you can save your own	2256
	2: 4	'If your descendants watch **h** they **live,**	2006
	2:30	"**This is h** Joab answered me."	3907
	3: 7	I am only a little child and *do* not **know h**	3359
	7:28	**h** the stands were **made:**	5126
	8:27	**H much less** this temple I have built!	677+3954
	10: 8	**H happy** your men must be!	897
	10: 8	**H happy** your officials,	897
1Ki	11:27	Here is the account of **h** he rebelled against	889
	11:28	Solomon saw **h well** the young man did	3954
	12: 6	"**H** would you advise me	375
	12: 9	**H** should we answer these people who say	NIH
	14:19	his wars and **h** he ruled,	889
	18:21	"**H long** will you waver	5503+6330
	19: 1	and **h** he had killed all the prophets with	889
	20: 7	"See **h** this man is looking for trouble!	3954
	21: 7	"Is this **h** you act as king over Israel?	NIH
	21:29	"Have you noticed **h** Ahab	3954
	22:16	"**H many** times must I make you swear to tell me nothing but the truth	3869+4537+6330
2Ki	4: 2	Elisha replied to her, "**H** can I help you?	4537
	4:43	"**H** can I set this before a hundred men?"	4537
	5: 7	See **h** he is trying to pick a quarrel	3954
	5:13	**H much more,** then, when he tells you,	677
	6:32	"Don't you see **h** this murderer	3954
	6: 5	the king **h** Elisha had restored the dead	889
	8:13	Hazael said, "**H** could your servant,	4537
	9:22	"**H** can there be peace," Jehu replied,	4537
	9:25	Remember **h** you and I were riding together	3954
	10: 4	"If two kings could not resist him, **h**	375
	13: 4	for he saw **h** severely the king	3954
	14:26	The LORD had seen **h** bitterly everyone	4394
	14:28	including **h** he recovered for Israel	889
	17:28	and taught them **h** to worship the LORD.	375
	18:24	**H** can you repulse one officer of the least	375
	18:35	**H** then can the LORD deliver Jerusalem	375
	19:27	and when you come and go and *h* you **rage**	AIT
	20: 3	**h** I have walked before you faithfully and	889
	20:20	all his achievements and **h** he made the pool	889
1Ch	13:12	"**H** can I ever bring the ark of God to me?"	2120
	15:13	We did not inquire of him about **h** to do it in	NIH
	21: 2	so that I may know **h many** there are."	5031
	21:12	decide **h** I should answer	4537
	29:17	And now I have seen with joy **h**	4537
2Ch	6:18	**H much less** this temple I have built!	677+3954
	9: 7	**H happy** your men must be!	897
	9: 7	**H happy** your officials,	897
	10: 6	"**H** would you advise me	375
	10: 9	**H** should we answer these people who say	NIH
	18:15	"**H many** times must I make you swear to tell me nothing but the truth	3869+4537+6330
	20:11	See **h** they *are* **repaying** us by coming	AIT
	20:29	when they heard **h** the LORD had fought	3954
	32:14	**H** then can your god deliver you	3954
	32:15	**H much less** will your god deliver you	677+3954+4202
	33:19	and **h** God was moved by his entreaty,	NIH
Ne	2: 6	"**H long** will your journey take,	5503+6330
	9:10	for you knew **h** arrogantly the Egyptians	3954
	13:24	not know **h** to speak the language of Judah.	5795
Est	2:11	of the harem to find out **h** Esther **was**	8934
	2:13	And **this is h** she would go to the king:	928+2296
	5:11	the ways the king had honored him and **h**	889
	8: 1	for Esther had told **h** he was related to her.	4537
	8: 6	For **h** can I bear to see disaster fall	379
	8: 6	**H** can I bear to see the destruction	379
Job	2:13	because they saw **h** great his suffering was.	3954
	4: 3	Think **h** you have instructed many,	NIH
	4: 3	**h** you have strengthened feeble hands.	NIH
	4:19	**h** much more those who live in houses	677
	6:25	**H** painful are honest words!	4537
	7: 4	'**H long** before I get up?'	5503
	8: 2	"**H long** will you say such things?	625+6330
	9: 2	But **h** can a mortal be righteous before God?	4537
	9:14	"**H** then can I dispute with him?	3954
	9:14	*H can I* **find** words to argue with him?	AIT
	11: 5	Oh, **h I wish** that God would speak,	4769+5989
	13:23	**H many** wrongs and sins have I committed?	3869+4537
	15:16	**h much less** man, who is vile and	677+3954
	19: 2	"**H long** will you torment me	625+2025+6330
	19:27	**H** my heart yearns within me!	NIH
	19:28	"If you say, '**H** we will hound him,	4537
	20: 4	"Surely you know **h** it has been from of old,	2296
	21:17	"Yet **h often** is the lamp of	3869+4537
	21:17	**H often** does calamity come upon them,	NIH
	21:18	**H often** are they like straw before the wind,	NIH
	21:34	**h** can you console me with your nonsense?	375
	22:12	And see **h** lofty are the highest stars!	3954
	25: 4	**H** then can a man be righteous before God?	4537
	25: 4	**H** can one born of woman be pure?	4537
	25: 6	**h much less** man, who is but a maggot—	677+3954
	26: 2	"**H** you have helped the powerless!	4537
	26: 2	**H** you have saved the arm that is feeble!	NIH
	26:14	**h** faint the whisper we hear of him!	4537
	29: 2	"**H I long for** the months gone by,	4769+5761+5989
	35: 6	If you sin, **h** does that affect him?	4537
	35:14	**H much less,** then, will he listen	677+3954
	36:26	*H* **great** is God—beyond our understanding!	AIT
	36:29	Who can understand **h** he spreads out	NIH
	36:29	**h** he thunders from his pavilion?	NIH
	36:30	See **h** he scatters his lightning about him,	NIH
	37:15	Do you know **h** God controls the clouds	NIH
	37:16	Do you know **h** the clouds hang poised,	6584
	40: 4	**h** can I reply to you?	4537
Ps	3: 1	O LORD, **h** many are my foes!	4537
	3: 1	**H** many rise up against me!	NIH
	4: 2	**H long,** O men, will you turn my glory	4537+6330
	4: 2	**h** long will you love delusions	NIH
	6: 3	**H long,** O LORD, how long?	5503+6330
	6: 3	How long, O LORD, how long?	NIH
	8: 1	**h** majestic is your name in all the earth!	4537
	8: 9	**h** majestic is your name in all the earth!	4537
	9:13	O LORD, see **h** my enemies persecute me!	NIH
Ps	11: 1	**H** *then* can you say to me:	375
	13: 1	**H long,** O LORD?	625+2025+6330
	13: 1	**H long** will you hide your face from me?	625+2025+6330
	13: 2	**H long** must I wrestle with my thoughts	625+2025+6330
	13: 2	**H long** will my enemy triumph over me?	625+2025+6330
	21: 1	**H** great is his joy in the victories you give!	4537
	25:19	See **h** my enemies have increased and	3954
	25:19	See how my enemies have increased and **h**	NIH
	31:19	**H** great is your goodness,	4537
	35:17	O Lord, **h long** will you look on?	3869+4537
	36: 7	**H** priceless is your unfailing love!	4537
	36:12	See **h** the evildoers lie fallen—	NIH
	39: 4	let me know **h** fleeting is my life.	4537
	42: 4	**h** I used to go with the multitude,	3954
	47: 2	**H** awesome is the LORD Most High,	3954
	59: 3	See **h** they lie in wait for me!	3954
	62: 3	**H long** will you assault a man?	625+2025+6330
	66: 3	Say to God, "**H** awesome are your deeds!	4537
	66: 5	*h* awesome his works in man's behalf!	AIT
	69:19	You know **h** I am scorned,	NIH
	73:11	They say, "**H** can God know?	377
	73:19	**H** suddenly are they destroyed,	NIH
	74: 1	none of us knows **h long** this will be.	4537+6330
	74:10	**H long** will the enemy mock you, O God?	5503+6330
	74:18	Remember **h** the enemy has mocked you,	2296
	74:18	**h** foolish people have reviled your name.	NIH
	74:22	remember **h** fools mock you all day long.	NIH
	78:40	**H often** they rebelled against him in	3869+4537
	79: 5	**H long,** O LORD?	4537+6330
	79: 5	**H long** will your jealousy burn like fire?	NIH
	80: 4	**h long** will your anger smolder against	5503+6330
	81:14	**h quickly** would I subdue their enemies	3869+5071
	82: 2	"**H long** will you defend the unjust	5503+6330
	83: 2	See **h** your enemies are astir,	NIH
	83: 2	**h** your foes rear their heads.	NIH
	84: 1	**H** lovely is your dwelling place,	4537
	89:46	**H long,** O LORD? Will you hide yourself forever?	4537+6330
	89:46	**H long** will your wrath burn like fire?	NIH
	89:47	Remember **h** fleeting is my life.	4537
	89:50	Lord, **h** your servant has been mocked,	NIH
	89:50	**h** I bear in my heart the taunts of all	NIH
	90:13	**H long** will it be?	5503+6330
	92: 5	**H** great are your works, O LORD,	4537
	92: 5	O LORD, **h** profound your thoughts!	4394
	94: 3	**H long** will the wicked, O LORD,	5503+6330
	94: 3	**h long** will the wicked be jubilant?	5503+6330
	103:14	for he **knows h** we are formed,	3359
	104:24	**H** many are your works, O LORD!	4537
	116:12	**H** can I repay the LORD	4537
	119: 9	**H** can a young man keep his way pure?	928+4537
	119:40	**H** I long for your precepts!	2180
	119:84	**H long** must your servant **wait?**	3427+3869+4537
	119:97	Oh, **h** I love your law!	4537
	119:103	**H** sweet are your words to my taste,	4537
	119:159	See **h** I love your precepts;	3954
	133: 1	**H** good and pleasant it is	4537
	137: 4	**H** can we sing the songs of the LORD	375
	139:17	**H** precious to me are your thoughts, O God!	4537
	139:17	**H** vast is the sum of them!	4537
	147: 1	**H** good it is to sing praises to our God,	3954
	147: 1	**h** pleasant and fitting to praise him!	3954
Pr	1:17	**H** useless to spread a net in full view of all	3954
	1:22	"**H long** will you simple ones love your simple ways?	5503+6330
	1:22	**H** long will mockers delight in mockery	NIH
	5:12	You will say, "**H** I hated discipline!	375
	5:12	**H** my heart spurned correction!	NIH
	6: 9	**H long** will you lie there, you sluggard?	5503+6330
	11:31	**h much more** the ungodly and the sinner!	677+3954
	15:11	**h much more** the hearts of men!	677+3954
	15:23	and **h** good is a timely word!	4537
	16:16	**H much** better to get wisdom than gold,	4537
	17: 7	**h much worse** lying lips to a ruler!	677+3954
	19: 7	**h much more** do his friends avoid him!	677+3954
	19:10	**h much worse** for a slave to rule over princes!	677+3954
	20:24	**H** then can anyone understand his own way?	4537
	21:27	**h much more so** when brought	677+3954
	24:10	**h** small is your strength!	NIH
Ecc	4:11	But **h** can one keep warm alone?	375
	4:13	but foolish king who no longer **knows h**	3359
	6: 3	yet no matter **h** long he lives,	8611
	6: 8	What does a poor man gain *by* **knowing h**	3359
	6:11	and **h** does that profit anyone?	4537
	10: 3	and shows everyone *h* **stupid** he is.	AIT
	11: 5	**h** the body is formed in a mother's womb,	3869
SS	1: 4	*H* **right** they are to adore you!	AIT
	1:15	**H** beautiful you are, my darling!	2180
	1:15	Oh, **h** beautiful!	2180
	1:16	**H** handsome you are, my lover!	2180
	1:16	Oh, **h** charming!	677
	4: 1	**H** beautiful you are, my darling!	2180
	4: 1	Oh, **h** beautiful!	2180
	4:10	**H** delightful is your love, my sister,	4537
	4:10	**H much more** pleasing is your love than wine,	4537
	5: 9	**H** is your beloved better than others,	4537
	5: 9	**H** is your beloved better than others,	4537

SS	7: 1	**H** beautiful your sandaled feet,	4537
	7: 6	**H** beautiful you are and how pleasing,	4537
	7: 6	How beautiful you are and **h** pleasing,	4537
Isa	1:21	**See h** the faithful city has become a harlot!	377
	6:11	Then I said, "For **h** long, O Lord?"	5503+6330
	8: 4	Before the boy **knows h** to say 'My father'	3359
	14: 4	**H** the oppressor has come to an end!	375
	14: 4	**H** his fury has ended!	NIH
	14:12	**H** you have fallen from heaven,	375
	19:11	**H** can you say to Pharaoh,	375
	20: 6	**H** then can we escape?' "	375
	29:12	answer, *"I don't know h to read."*	3359+6219
	30:19	*H gracious he will be* when you cry	AIT
	32:20	*h blessed* you will be,	AIT
	36: 9	**H** then can you repulse one officer of	375
	36:20	**H** then can the LORD deliver Jerusalem	3954
	37:28	and when you come and go and **h** you **rage**	AIT
	38: 3	**h** I have walked before you faithfully and	889
	47:11	and *you will not* **know h** to conjure it away.	3359
	48: 4	For I knew **h** stubborn you were;	3954
	48: 8	Well do I know **h treacherous** *you are;*	953+953
	48:11	**H** can I let myself be defamed?	375
	52: 7	**H** beautiful on the mountains are the feet	4537
	63:14	**This is h** you guided your people to make	4027
	64: 5	**H** then can we be saved?	NIH
Jer	1: 6	*I do not* **know h** to speak; I am only a child.	3359
	2: 2	" 'I remember the devotion of your youth, **h**	NIH
	2:19	and realize **h** evil and bitter it is for you	3954
	2:21	**H** then did you turn against me into	375
	2:23	**"H** can you say, 'I am not defiled;	375
	2:23	**See h** you **behaved** in the valley;	2006
	2:33	**H** skilled you are at pursuing love!	4537
	3: 5	**This is h** you talk,	2180
	3:19	" '**H gladly** would I treat you like sons	375
	4:10	**h** completely you have deceived this people	434
	4:14	**H long** will you harbor wicked thoughts?	
			5503+6330
	4:18	**H** bitter it is!	3954
	4:18	**H** it pierces to the heart!"	3954
	4:21	**H long** must I see the battle standard	5503+6330
	4:22	*they* **know** not **h** to do good.	3359
	6:15	*they do* not even **know h** to blush.	3359
	8: 8	" '**H** can you say, "We are wise,	377
	8:12	*they do* not even **know h** to blush.	3359
	9:19	'**H** ruined we are!	375
	9:19	**H** great is our shame!	NIH
	9:20	Teach your daughters **h** to wail;	NIH
	12: 4	**H long** will the land lie parched and	5503+6330
	12: 5	**h** can you compete with horses?	375
	12: 5	**h** will you manage in the thickets by	375
	13:27	**H long** will you be unclean?"	339+5503+6388
	15: 5	Who will stop to ask **h** you **are?**	8934
	15:15	think of **h** I **suffer** reproach for your sake.	AIT
	16:12	**See h** each of you is following	NIH
	22:23	**h** you will groan when pangs come	4537
	23:26	**H** long will this continue in the hearts	5503+6330
	30: 7	**H** awful that day will be!	3954
	31:22	**H long** will you wander,	5503+6330
	32:24	"See **h** the siege ramps are built up to take	NIH
	36:17	"Tell us, **h** did you come to write all this?	375
	38:28	**This is h** Jerusalem was taken:	889+3869
	47: 2	"See **h** the waters are rising in the north;	NIH
	47: 5	**h long** will you cut yourselves?	5503+6330
	47: 6	**'h long** till you rest?'	625+2025+6330
	47: 7	But **h** can it rest when the LORD	375
	48:14	**"H** can you say, 'We are warriors,	375
	48:17	say, **'H broken** is the mighty scepter,	377
	48:17	**h broken** the glorious staff!'	NIH
	48:39	**"H shattered** she is!	375
	48:39	**H** they wail!	375
	48:39	**H** Moab turns her back in shame!	NIH
	50:23	**H** broken and shattered is the hammer of	375
	50:23	**H** desolate is Babylon among the nations!	NIH
	50:28	declaring in Zion **h** the LORD our God	NIH
	51:41	**"H** Sheshach will be captured,	375
La	1: 1	**H** deserted lies the city,	377
	1: 1	**H** like a widow is she,	NIH
	1:20	"See, O LORD, **h** distressed I am!	3954
	2: 1	**H** the Lord has covered the Daughter	377
	4: 1	**H** the gold has lost its luster,	377
	4: 2	**H** the precious sons of Zion,	377
Eze	6: 9	**h** I have been grieved	889
	14:21	**H much worse** will it be when I send	677+3954
	15: 2	**h** is the wood of a vine better than that of	4537
	15: 5	**h much less** can it be made	677+3954
	16:30	" '**H weak-willed** you are,	4537
	22: 6	" 'See **h** each of the princes	NIH
	26:17	" '**H** you are destroyed, O city of renown,	375
	33:10	**H** then can we live?' "	375
	35:15	**that is h** I will treat you.	4027
	44:23	**show** them **h** to distinguish	3359
Da	4: 3	**H** great are his signs,	10341+10408
	4: 3	**h** mighty his wonders!	10341+10408
	8:13	**"H long** will it take *for* the vision to	5503+6330
	10:17	**H** can I, your servant, talk with you,	2120
	12: 6	**"H long** will it be	5503+6330
Hos	4:16	**H** then can the LORD pasture them	NIH
	8: 5	**H long** will they be incapable of purity?	5503
	11: 8	**"H** can I give you up, Ephraim?	375
	11: 8	**H** can I hand you over, Israel?	NIH
	11: 8	**H** can I treat you like Admah?	375
	11: 8	**H** can I make you like Zeboiim?	NIH
Joel	1:18	**H** the cattle moan!	4537
Am	3:10	*"They do* not **know h** to do right,"	3359
	5:12	For I know **h** many are your offenses and	NIH
	5:12	how many are your offenses and **h**	NIH
	7: 2	**H** can Jacob survive?	4769

Am	7: 5	**H** can Jacob survive?	4769
Ob	1: 6	But **h** Esau will be ransacked,	375
Jnh	1: 6	**"H** can you sleep?	4537
	3:10	and **h** they turned from their evil ways,	3954
Mic	6: 3	**H** have I burdened you?	4537
Hab	1: 2	**H long**, O LORD, must I call for help,	
			625+2025+6330
	2: 6	**H long** must this go on?'	5503+6330
Hag	2: 3	**H** does it look to you now?	4537
	2:15	consider **h** things were before one stone	NIH
Zec	1:12	**h long** will you withhold mercy	5503+6330
	2: 2	to find out how wide and how long it is."	3869+4537
	2: 2	to find out how wide and **h** long it is."	3869+4537
	7:14	This is **h** they made the pleasant land	NIH
	9:17	**H** attractive and beautiful they will be!	4537
Mal	1: 2	"But you ask, '**H** have you loved us?'	928+4537
	1: 6	'**H** have we shown contempt	928+4537
	1: 7	"But you ask, '**H** have we defiled you?'	928+4537
	2:17	**"H** have we wearied him?"	928+4537
	3: 7	"But you ask, '**H** are we to return?'	928+4537
	3: 8	"But you ask, '**H** do we rob you?'	928+4537
Mt	1:18	**This is h** the birth of Jesus Christ came	4048
	5:13	**h** can it be made salty again?	1877+5515
	6: 9	**"This**, then, **is h** you should pray:	4048
	6:23	**h great** is that darkness!	4531
	6:28	See **h** the lilies of the field grow.	4802
	6:30	If **that is h** God clothes the grass of	4048
	7: 4	**H can** you say to your brother,	4802
	7:11	know **h** to give good gifts to your children,	NIG
	7:11	**h much** more will your Father	4531
	9:14	**"H is it that** we and the Pharisees fast,	1328+5515
	9:15	**"H** can the guests of the bridegroom mourn	3590
	10:19	not worry about what to say or **h** to say it.	4802
	10:25	**h much** more the members of his	
		household!	4531
	12:12	**H much more** valuable is a man than a	
		sheep!	4531
	12:14	But the Pharisees went out and plotted **h**	3968
	12:26	**H** then can his kingdom stand?	4802
	12:29	**h** can anyone enter a strong man's house	4802
	12:34	**h** can you who are evil say anything good?	4802
	12:45	**That is h** it will be with this wicked	4048
	13:49	**This is h** it will be at the end of the age.	4048
	15:34	**"H many** loaves do you have?"	4531
	16: 3	*You* **know h** to interpret the appearance of	1182
	16: 9	and **h many** basketfuls you gathered?	4531
	16:10	and **h many** basketfuls you gathered?	4531
	16:11	**H** is it you don't understand that I was	4802
	17:17	**"h long** shall I stay with you?	2401+4536
	17:17	**H long** shall I put up with you?	2401+4536
	18:21	**h many times** shall I forgive my brother	4529
	18:35	**"This is h** my heavenly Father will treat	
		each of you unless you forgive	4048
	21:20	**"H** did the fig tree wither so quickly?"	4802
	22:12	'**h** did you get in here	4802
	22:43	He said to them, **"H** is it then that David,	4802
	22:45	**h** can he be his son?	4802
	23:33	**H** will you escape being condemned to hell?	4802
	23:37	**h often** I have longed to gather your	
		children together,	4529
	24:19	**H dreadful** it will be in those days	4026
	24:39	**That is h** it will be at the coming of the Son	4048
	26:54	But **h** then would the Scriptures be fulfilled	4802
	27:65	make the tomb as secure as you **know h.**"	
Mk	2:18	**"H is it that** John's disciples and	1328+5515
	2:19	**"H** can the guests of the bridegroom fast	3590
	3: 6	with the Herodians **h** they might kill Jesus.	3968
	3:23	**"H** can Satan drive out Satan?	4802
	4:13	**H** then will you understand any parable?	4802
	4:27	though he does not know **h.**	NIG
	5:19	and tell them **h much** the Lord has done	4012
	5:19	and **h** he has had mercy on you."	NIG
	5:20	in the Decapolis **h much** Jesus had done	4012
	6:38	**"H many** loaves do you have?"	4531
	8: 5	**"H many** loaves do you have?"	4531
	8:19	for the five thousand, **h many** basketfuls	4531
	8:20	for the four thousand, **h many** basketfuls	4531
	9:19	Jesus replied, "**H** long shall I stay with you?	2401
	9:19	**H** long shall I put up with you?	2401
	9:21	**"H** long has he been like this?"	2401
	9:50	**h** can you make it salty again?	1877+5515
	10:23	**"H** hard it is for the rich to enter	4802
	10:24	**h** hard it is to enter the kingdom of God!	4802
	12:26	**h** God said to him,	4802
	12:35	**"H is it that** the teachers of the law say that	4802
	12:37	**H** then **can** he be his son?	4470
	13:17	**H dreadful** it will be in those days	4026
	15: 4	See **h many** *things* they are accusing you of.	4531
	15:39	heard his cry and saw **h** he died, he said,	4048
Lk	1:18	**"H** can I be sure of this?	2848+5515
	1:34	**"H** will this be," Mary asked the angel,	4802
	6:23	**that is h** their fathers treated the prophets.	
			899+2848+3836
	6:26	for **that is h** their fathers treated	899+2848+3836
	6:42	**H** can you say to your brother, 'Brother,	4802
	8:18	Therefore consider carefully **h** you listen.	4802
	8:36	Those who had seen it told the people **h**	4802
	8:39	and tell **h much** God has done for you."	4012
	8:39	over town **h much** Jesus had done for him.	4012
	8:47	she told why she had touched him and **h**	6055
	9:41	**h** long shall I stay with you and put up	2401
	10:26	**"H** do you read it?"	NIG
	11:13	know **h** to give good gifts to your children,	NIG
	11:13	**h much** more will your Father in heaven	
		give the Holy Spirit	4531
	11:18	**h** can his kingdom stand?	4802
	12:11	about **h** you will defend yourselves	4802

Lk	12:21	**"This is h** it will be with anyone who stores	4048
	12:24	**h** much more valuable you are than birds!	4531
	12:27	"Consider **h** the lilies grow.	4802
	12:28	If **that is h** God clothes the grass of	4048
	12:28	**h** much more will he clothe you,	4531
	12:49	and **h** I wish it were already kindled!	NIG
	12:50	and **h** distressed I am until it is completed!	4802
	12:56	You know **h** to interpret the appearance of	NIG
	12:56	**H** is it that you don't know how	4802
	12:56	don't know **h** *to* **interpret** this present time?	1507
	13:34	**h often** I have longed to gather your	
		children together,	4529
	14: 7	When he noticed **h** the guests picked	4802
	14:34	**h** can it be made salty again?	1877+5515
	15:17	**H many** of my father's hired men have food	4531
	16: 5	'**H much** do you owe my master?'	4531
	16: 7	'And **h much** do you owe?'	4531
	18:24	**"H** hard it is for the rich to enter	4802
	20:41	**H is it** that they say the Christ is the Son	4802
	20:44	**H** then can he be his son?"	4802
	21: 5	of his disciples were remarking about **h**	4022
	21:14	up your mind not to worry beforehand **h**	NIG
	21:23	**H dreadful** it will be in those days	4026
	22: 4	the temple guard and discussed with them **h**	4802
	23:55	and saw the tomb and **h** his body was laid	6055
	24: 6	Remember **h** he told you,	6055
	24:25	He said to them, **"H foolish you are,**	485+6043
	24:25	and **h slow** of heart to believe all that	1096
	24:35	and **h** Jesus was recognized by them	6055
Jn	1:48	**"H** do you know me?"	4470
	2:16	**H dare you** turn my Father's house into	3590
	3: 4	**"H** can a man be born when he is old?"	4802
	3: 9	**"H** can this be?" Nicodemus asked.	4802
	3:12	**h** then will you believe if I speak	4802
	4: 9	**H** can you ask me for a drink?"	4802
	5:44	**H** can you believe if you accept praise	4802
	5:47	**h** are you going to believe what I say?"	4802
	6: 9	but **h far will they go** among so	1639+4047+5515
	6:42	**H can** he now say,	4802
	6:52	**"H** can this man give us his flesh to eat?"	4802
	7:15	**"H** did this man get such learning	4802
	7:41	**"H** can the Christ come from Galilee?	1142+3590
	8:33	**H** can you say that we shall be set free?"	4802
	9:10	**"H** then were your eyes opened?"	4802
	9:15	also asked him **h** he had received his sight.	4802
	9:16	**"H** can a sinner do such miraculous signs?"	4802
	9:19	**H** is it that now he can see?"	4802
	9:21	But **h** he can see now,	4802
	9:26	**H** did he open your eyes?"	4802
	9:34	**h dare** you lecture us!"	NIG
	10:24	**"H long** will you keep us in suspense?	2401+4536
	11:31	noticed **h** quickly she got up and went out,	4022
	11:36	Then the Jews said, "See **h** he loved him!"	4802
	12:19	Look **h** the whole world has gone	NIG
	12:34	so **h** can you say,	4802
	12:49	to say and **h** to say it.	5515
	14: 5	so **h** can we know the way?"	4802
	14: 9	**H** can you say, 'Show us the Father'?	4802
Ac	2: 8	Then **h** is it that each of us hears them	4802
	3:18	But **this is h** God fulfilled what he had	4048
	4: 9	cripple and are asked **h** he was healed,	1877+5515
	4:21	They could not decide **h** to punish them,	4802
	5: 3	**h** is it that Satan has so filled your heart	
		that you have lied to the Holy Spirit	1328+5515
	5: 9	**"H** could you agree to test the Spirit of the	
		Lord?	4022+5515
	8:31	**"H** can I," he said,	4802
	9:16	I will show him **h** much he must suffer	4012
	9:27	He told them **h** Saul on his journey had seen	4802
	9:27	and **h** in Damascus he had preached	4802
	10:34	"I now realize **h true** it is that God does	237+2093
	10:38	**h** God anointed Jesus of Nazareth with	6055
	10:38	and **h** he went around doing good	NIG
	11:13	He told us **h** he had seen an angel appear	4802
	12:17	for them to be quiet and described **h**	4802
	14:27	through them and **h** he had opened the door	4022
	15: 3	*they* **told h** the Gentiles had been converted.	1687
	15:14	to us **h** God at first showed his concern	2777
	15:36	of the Lord and see **h** they are doing."	4802
	19:26	and hear **h** this fellow Paul has convinced	4022
	20:18	"You know **h** I lived the whole time I was	4802
	21:20	**h many** thousands of Jews have believed,	4531
	25:20	I was at a loss **h** to investigate such matters;	NIG
Ro	1: 9	is my witness **h** constantly I remember you	6055
	3: 6	**h** could God judge the world?	4802
	5: 9	**h much** more shall we be saved	4498
	5:10	**h much** more, having been reconciled,	4498
	5:15	**h much** more did God's grace and the gift	4498
	5:17	**h** much more will those who receive God's	
		abundant provision	4498
	6: 2	**h** can we live in it any longer?	4802
	8:32	**h** will he not also, along with him,	4802
	9: 9	For this was **h** the promise was stated:	NIG
	10:14	**H**, then, can they call on the one they have	4802
	10:14	And **h** can they believe in the one	4802
	10:14	And **h** can they hear without someone	4802
	10:15	And **h** can they preach unless they are sent?	4802
	10:15	**"H** beautiful are the feet	6055
	11: 2	**h** he appealed to God against Israel:	6055
	11:12	**h much** greater riches will their fullness	
		bring!	4531
	11:24	**h** much more readily will these,	4531
	11:33	**H** unsearchable his judgments,	6055
	13:14	not think about **h** to gratify the desires of	NIG
1Co	3:10	But each one should be careful **h** he builds.	4802
	4: 8	**H** I wish that you really had become kings	4054
	4:19	not only **h** these arrogant people are talking,	NIG

1Co 6: 3 **H much more** the things of this life! 3615
  7:16 **H do you know**, wife, 5515
  7:16 Or, **h do you know**, husband, 5515
  7:32 **h** he can please the Lord. 4802
  7:33 **h** he can please his wife— 4802
  7:34 **h** she can please her husband. 4802
  14: 7 **h** will anyone know what tune 4802
  14: 9 **h** will anyone know what you are saying? 4802
  14:16 **h** can one who finds himself 4802
  15:12 **h** can some of you say 4802
  15:35 someone may ask, "**H** are the dead raised? 4802
  15:36 **H** foolish! What you sow does *NIG*
2Co 1:20 no matter **h many** promises God has made, 4012
  3: 9 **h** much more glorious is the ministry *NIG*
  3:11 **h** much **greater** is the glory of 3437
  7:12 **h** devoted to us you are. *NIG*
  7:13 delighted to see **h** happy Titus was, *NIG*
  12:13 **H** were you inferior to the other churches, 5515
Gal 1:13 **h** intensely I persecuted the church of God 4022
  2:14 **H is it**, then, that you force Gentiles 4802
  4: 9 **h is it** that you are turning back 4802
  4:20 **H** I wish I could be with you now *NIG*
Eph 3:18 to grasp **h** wide and long and high 5515
  5:15 Be very careful, then, **h** you live— 4802
  6:21 know **h** I am and what I am doing. 2848+3836
  6:22 that you may know **h** we are, 3836+4309
Php 1: 8 God can testify **h** I long for all of you with 6055
  2:23 to send him as soon as I see **h** things go 4048
  4: 1 **that is h** you should stand firm in the Lord, 4048
Col 2: 1 to know **h much** I am struggling for you 2462
  2: 5 in spirit and delight to see **h** orderly you are *NIG*
  2: 5 how orderly you are and **h** firm your faith *NIG*
  4: 6 that you may know **h** to answer everyone. 4802
1Th 1: 5 You know **h** we lived among you 3888
  1: 9 They tell **h** you turned to God from idols 4802
  2:10 You are witnesses, and so is God, of **h** holy, 6055
  3: 9 **H** can we thank God enough for you 5515
  4: 1 we instructed you **h** to live in order 4802
2Th 3: 7 For you yourselves know **h** you ought 4802
  3:17 **This is h** I write. 4048
1Ti 3: 5 not know **h** to manage his own family, *NIG*
  3: 5 **h** can he take care of God's church?) 4802
  3:15 you will know **h** people ought to conduct 4802
2Ti 1:18 in **h many** *ways* he helped me in Ephesus. 4012
  3:15 and **h** from infancy you have known 4022
Heb 2: 3 **h** shall we escape if we ignore such 4802
  7: 4 Just think **h great** he was: 4383
  9:14 **H much** more, then, will the blood of Christ 4531
  10:24 let us consider **h** we may spur one another *NIG*
  10:29 **H much** more severely do you think 4531
  12: 9 **H** much more should we submit to *NIG*
  12:25 **h** much less will we, if we turn away *NIG*
Jas 5: 7 **See h** the farmer waits for the land 2627
  5: 7 to yield its valuable crop and **h** patient he is *NIG*
1Pe 2:20 But **h is it** to your credit if you receive 4481
2Pe 2: 9 then the Lord knows **h** to rescue godly men *NIG*
1Jn 2: 5 **This is h** we know we are in him: 1877+4047
  2:18 **This is h** we know it is the last hour. 3854
  3: 1 **H great** is the love the Father has lavished 4534
  3:10 **This is h** we know who the children 1877+4047
  3:16 **This is h** we know what love is: 1877+4047
  3:17 **h** can the love of God be in him? 4802
  3:19 This then is **h** we know that we belong to 1877
  3:19 **h** we set our hearts at rest in his presence *NIG*
  3:24 And this is **h** we know that he lives in us: 1877
  4: 2 **This is h** you can recognize the Spirit 1877+4047
  4: 6 **This is h** we recognize the Spirit of truth
     and the spirit of falsehood. 1666+4047
  4: 9 **This is h** God showed his love among us: 1877+4047
  5: 2 **This is h** we know that we love the
     children of God: 1877+4047
3Jn 1: 3 and **h** you continue to walk in the truth. *NIG*
Rev 6:10 called out in a loud voice, "**H long**, 2401+4536
  11: 5 **This is h** anyone who wants to harm 4048

HOWBEIT (KJV) See ALTHOUGH, BUT, HOWEVER, NEVERTHELESS, THOUGH, YET

HOWEVER (145) [HOW]
Ge 15:10 the birds, **h**, he did not cut in half. 2256
  15:15 **h**, will go to your fathers in peace and 2256
  30:37 **h**, took fresh-cut branches from poplar, 2256
  31: 7 **H**, God has not allowed him to harm me. 2256
  33:17 Jacob, **h**, went to Succoth, 2256
  40:23 The chief cupbearer, **h**, did not remember 2256
  47:13 There was no food, **h**, in the whole region 2256
  47:22 **H**, he did not buy the land of the priests, 8370
Ex 1:17 **h**, feared God and did not do what the king 2256
  9:32 The wheat and spelt, **h**, were not destroyed, 2256
  16:20 **H**, some of them paid no attention to Moses; 2256
  21:13 **H**, if he does not do it intentionally, 2256
  21:19 **h**, he must pay the injured man for the loss 8370
  21:29 **h**, the bull has had the habit of goring and 2256
  21:30 **H**, if payment is demanded of him, *NIH*
  21:36 **H**, if it was known that the bull had *NIH*
  32:34 **H**, when the time comes for me to punish, 2256
Lev 5:11 "'If, **h**, he cannot afford two doves 2256
  7:16 "'If, **h**, his offering is the result of a vow 2256
  11:21 **h**, some winged creatures that walk 421
  11:36 A spring, **h**, or a cistern 421
  13:28 **h**, the spot is unchanged and has not spread 2256
  13:37 If, **h**, in his judgment it is unchanged 2256
  14:21 "If, **h**, he is poor and cannot afford these, 2256

Lev 19:21 **h**, must bring a ram to the entrance to 2256
  22:13 No unauthorized person, **h**, 2256
  22:23 **h**, present as a freewill offering an ox or 2256
  25:26 If, **h**, a man has no one to redeem it for him 2256
  27:20 If, **h**, he does not redeem the field, 2256
  27:26 **h**, may dedicate the firstborn of an animal, 421
Nu 1:53 The Levites, **h**, are to set up their tents 2256
  2:33 The Levites, **h**, were not counted along with 2256
  3: 4 and Abihu, **h**, fell dead before the LORD 2256
  5:28 If, **h**, the woman has not defiled herself 2256
  11:26 **H**, two men, whose names were Eldad 2256
  21:24 **h**, put him to the sword and took 2256
  26:11 The line of Korah, **h**, did not die out. 2256
  30:15 If, **h**, he nullifies them some time 2256
Dt 3:19 **H**, your wives, your children 8370
  14: 7 **H**, of those that chew the cud or that have 2256
  15: 4 **H**, there should be no poor among you, 700+3954
  20:16 **H**, in the cities of the nations 8370
  20:20 **H**, you may cut down trees 8370
  22:20 If, **h**, the charge is true and no proof of 2256
  23: 5 **H**, the LORD your God would not listen 2256
  25: 7 **H**, if a man does not want 2256
  28:15 **H**, if you do not obey the LORD your God 2256
Jos 9: 3 When the people of Gibeon 2256
  14: 8 I, **h**, followed the LORD my God
     wholeheartedly. 2256
  17:13 **H**, when the Israelites grew stronger, 2256
  18: 7 **h**, do not get a portion among you, 3954
Jdg 1:21 **h**, failed to dislodge the Jebusites, 2256
  4:17 Sisera, **h**, fled on foot to the tent of Jael, 2256
  9:51 Inside the city, **h**, was a strong tower, 2256
  11:20 **h**, did not trust Israel to pass 2256
  11:28 The king of Ammon, **h**, 2256
1Sa 2:25 did not listen to their father's rebuke, 2256
  21: 4 **h**, there is some consecrated bread here 561+3954
  26:19 If, **h**, men have done it, 2256
  30:22 **H**, each man may take his wife and 561+3954
2Sa 2:10 The house of Judah, **h**, followed David. 421
  3:16 Her husband, **h**, went with her, 2256
  24: 4 **h**, overruled Joab and 2256
1Ki 3: 2 **h**, were still sacrificing at the high places, 8370
  7: 1 It took Solomon thirteen years, **h**, 2256
  11: 1 Solomon, **h**, loved many foreign women 2256
  11:37 **H**, as for you, I will take you, 2256
  12:18 **h**, managed to get into his chariot 2256
  15:23 In his old age, **h**, his feet became diseased. 8370
  22:43 The high places, **h**, were not removed, 421
2Ki 8:21 his army, **h**, fled back home. 2256
  10:29 **h**, he did not turn away from the sins 8370
  12: 3 The high places, **h**, were not removed; 8370
  14: 4 The high places, **h**, were not removed; 8370
  14:11 Amaziah, **h**, would not listen, 2256
  15: 4 The high places, **h**, were not removed; 8370
  15:35 The high places, **h**, were not removed; 8370
  17:40 They would not listen, **h**, 2256
  25:25 In the seventh month, **h**, 2256
1Ch 21: 4 The king's word, **h**, overruled Joab; 2256
2Ch 10:18 **h**, managed to get into his chariot 2256
  12: 8 They will, **h**, become subject to him, 3954
  19: 3 There is, **h**, some good in you, 66
  20:33 The high places, **h**, were not removed, 421
  25:20 Amaziah, **h**, would not listen, 2256
  27: 2 people, **h**, continued their corrupt practices. 2256
  29:34 priests, **h**, were too few to skin all 8370
  33:17 **h**, continued to sacrifice at the high places, 66
  35:22 Josiah, **h**, would not turn away from him, 2256
Ezr 5:13 "**H**, in the first year of Cyrus king 10124
Ne 13: 2 **h**, turned the curse into a blessing.) 2256
Est 9:16 The Jews in Susa, **h**, had assembled 2256
Job 13: 4 You, **h**, smear me with lies; 219+2256
  27:14 **H** many his children, their fate is the sword; 561
Ps 58: 5 skillful the enchanter may be. *NIH*
Pr 6:35 he will refuse the bribe, **h** great it is. 3954
Ecc 12: 8 **H** many years a man may live, 561+3954
Jer 16:14 "**H**, the days are coming," 4027+4200
  26:15 Be assured, **h**, that if you put me to death, 421
  26:22 **h**, sent Elnathan son of Acbor to Egypt, 2256
  27: 8 "'If, **h**, any nation or kingdom will 2256
  29:29 Zephaniah the priest, **h**, read the letter 2256
  34:14 **h**, did not listen to me or pay attention 2256
  37: 3 **h**, sent Jehucal son of Shelemiah with 2256
  40: 5 **H**, before Jeremiah turned to go, 2256
  42:13 "**H**, if you say, 'We will not stay 2256
  46:26 **h**, Egypt will be inhabited as in times past," 2256
Eze 16:53 "**H**, I will restore the fortunes of Sodom 2256
  44:25 **h**, if the dead person was his father 3954
  46:17 **h**, he makes a gift from his inheritance 2256
Da 2:10 No king, **h**, great and mighty, *NIH*
  11:20 In a few years, **h**, he will be destroyed, *NIH*
Mt 25: 4 **h**, took oil in jars along with their lamps. 1254
Lk 10:20 **h**, do not rejoice that the spirits submit 4440
  18: 8 **H**, when the Son of Man comes, 4440
  19:15 He was made king, **h**, and returned home. *NIG*
  24:12 Peter, **h**, got up and ran to the tomb. 1254
Jn 7:10 **h**, after his brothers had left for the Feast, 1254
  15:22 Now, **h**, they have no excuse for their sin. 1254
Ac 2:13 Some, **h**, made fun of them and said, 1254
  6: 9 **h**, from members of the Synagogue of 1254
  7:48 "**H**, the Most High does not live 247
  8:40 **h**, appeared at Azotus and traveled about, 1254
  11:20 **h**, men from Cyprus and Cyrene, 1254
  20:24 **H**, I consider my life worth nothing to me, 247
  24:14 **H**, I worship the God 247
  25:11 If, **h**, I am guilty of anything 3525+4036
Ro 4: 5 **H**, to the man who does not work 1254
  8: 9 **h**, are controlled not by the sinful nature but 1254

Ro 15:25 Now, **h**, I am on my way to Jerusalem in 1254
1Co 2: 6 **h**, speak a message of wisdom among 1254
  2: 9 **H**, as it is written: 247
  8: 9 **h**, that the exercise of your freedom does 1254
  11:11 **h**, woman is not independent of man, 4440
  14:22 prophecy, **h**, is for believers, 1254
2Co 10:13 We, **h**, will not boast beyond proper limits, 1254
Gal 3:20 **h**, does not represent just one party; 1254
Eph 4:20 **h**, did not come to know Christ that way. 1254
  5:33 **H**, each one of you also must love his wife 4440
Col 2:17 the reality, **h**, is found in Christ. 1254
2Ti 3:10 You, **h**, know all about my teaching, 1254
Heb 7: 6 **h**, did not trace his descent from Levi, 1254
  12:11 **h**, it produces a harvest of righteousness 1254
1Pe 4:16 **H**, if you suffer as a Christian, 1254

HOWL (4) [HOWLING]
Ps 59:15 for food and **h** if not satisfied. 4296
Isa 13:22 Hyenas *will* **h** in her strongholds, 6702
  14:31 Wail, O gate! **H**, O city! 2410
Mic 1: 8 *I will* **h** like a jackal and moan like 5027+6913

HOWLING (1) [HOWL]
Dt 32:10 in a barren and **h** waste. 3537

HOWSOEVER (KJV) See COME WHAT MAY

HUBBAH (1)
1Ch 7:34 Ahi, Rohgah, **H** and Aram. 2465

HUBS (1)
1Ki 7:33 rims, spokes and **h** were all of cast metal. 3141

HUDDLED (1)
Job 30: 7 among the bushes and **h** in the undergrowth. 6202

HUG (1)
Job 24: 8 They are drenched by mountain rains and **h** 2485

HUGE (12)
Ge 41:49 Joseph stored up **h** quantities of grain, 4394
Jos 11: 4 a **h** army, as numerous as the sand on 8041
2Sa 21:20 a **h** man with six fingers on each hand 4500
  23:21 And he struck down a **h** Egyptian. 5260
1Ch 20: 6 a **h** man with six fingers on each hand 4500
2Ch 16:14 and they made a **h** fire in his honor.
       1524+4200+4394+6330
Ecc 9:14 surrounded it and built **h** siegeworks 1524
Da 2:35 that struck the statue became a **h** mountain 10647
  11:13 with a **h** army fully equipped. 1524
Mt 12:40 and three nights in the belly of *a* **h** fish, 3063
Rev 8: 8 and something like a **h** mountain, all ablaze, 3489
  16:21 From the sky **h** hailstones of about 3489

HUKKOK (1)
Jos 19:34 through Aznoth Tabor and came out at **H**. 2982

HUKOK (1)
1Ch 6:75 **H** and Rehob, together 2577

HUL (2)
Ge 10:23 Uz, **H**, Gether and Meshech. 2566
1Ch 1:17 Uz, **H**, Gether and Meshech. 2566

HULDAH (2)
2Ki 22:14 to speak to the prophetess **H**, 2701
2Ch 34:22 with him went to speak to the prophetess **H**, 2701

HUMAN (50) [HUMANITY]
Lev 5: 3 "'Or if he touches **h** uncleanness— 132
  7:21 whether **h** uncleanness or an unclean animal 132
  24:17 "'If anyone takes the life of a **h being**, 132
Nu 19:16 or anyone who touches a **h** bone or a grave, 132
  19:18 a **h** bone or a grave *NIH*
1Ki 13: 2 and **h** bones will be burned on you.'" 132
2Ki 23:14 and covered the sites with **h** bones. 132
  23:20 on the altars and burned **h** bones on them. 132
Job 34:20 the mighty are removed without **h** hand. *NIH*
Ps 73: 5 they are not plagued by **h** ills. 132
Isa 37:19 fashioned by **h** hands. 132
  52:14 his form marred beyond **h** likeness— 132+1201
Eze 4:12 using **h** excrement for fuel." 132
  4:15 over cow manure instead of **h** excrement." 132
  39:15 the land and one of them sees a **h** bone, 132
Da 2:34 a rock was cut out, but not by **h** hands. *NIH*
  2:45 but not by **h** hands— *NIH*
  5: 5 a **h** hand appeared and wrote on the plaster 10050
  8:25 he will be destroyed, but not by **h** power. *NIH*
Hos 11: 4 I led them with cords of **h** kindness, 132
  13: 2 "They offer **h** sacrifice and kiss 132
Jn 1:13 nor of **h** decision or a husband's will, 4922
  5:34 Not that I accept **h** testimony, 476
  8:15 You judge by **h standards**; 3836+4922
Ac 5:38 For if their purpose or activity is of **h** origin, 476
  14:11 "The gods have come down to us *in* **h** form!" 476
  14:15 We too are only men, **h** like you. 3926
  17:25 And he is not served by **h** hands, 474

Ro	1: 3	to his **h** nature was a descendant of David,	4922
	2: 9	distress for every **h being** who does evil:	476
	3: 5	(I am using a **h** argument.)	476+2848
	6:19	**I put this in h terms** because	474+3306
	9: 5	from them is traced the **h ancestry** of Christ	4922
1Co	1:17	not with words of **h** wisdom,	NIG
	1:26	Not many of you were wise by **h** standards;	4922
	2:13	not in words taught us by **h** wisdom but	474
	4: 3	if I am judged by you or by any **h** court;	474
	9: 8	from a **h** point of view?	476+2848
	15:32	in Ephesus for merely **h reasons,**	476
2Co	3: 3	of stone but on tablets of **h** hearts.	4921
	5: 1	house in heaven, **not built by h hands.**	942
Gal	3: 3	to attain your goal **by h effort?**	4922
	3:15	a **h** covenant that has been duly established,	476
Php	2: 7	being made in **h** likeness.	476
Col	2: 8	on **h** tradition and the basic principles	476
	2:22	because they are based on **h** commands	476
Heb	12: 9	we have all had fathers who disciplined us	4922
1Pe	4: 2	the rest of his earthly life for evil **h** desires,	476
2Pe	2:18	to the lustful desires of **sinful h nature,**	4922
Rev	9: 7	and their faces resembled **h** faces.	476

HUMANITY (1) [HUMAN]

Heb	2:14	he too shared in their **h** so that	NIG

HUMBLE (40) [HUMBLED, HUMBLES, HUMBLY, HUMILIATE, HUMILIATED, HUMILIATION, HUMILITY]

Ex	10: 3	'How long will you refuse to **h yourself**	6700
Nu	12: 3	(Now Moses was a very **h** man,	6705
	12: 3	more **h** than anyone else on the face of	NIH
Dt	8: 2	to **h** you and to test you in order	6700
	8:16	to **h** and to test you so that in	6700
2Sa	22:28	You save the **h,** but your eyes are on	6639+6714
1Ki	11:39	I will **h** David's descendants because	6700
2Ch	7:14	will **h themselves** and pray	4044
	33:23	he did not **h himself** before the LORD;	4044
	36:12	of the LORD his God and **did not h himself**	4044
Ezr	8:21	that we **might h ourselves** before our God	6700
Job	8: 7	Your beginnings will seem **h,**	5203
	40:12	look at every proud man and **h** him,	4044
Ps	18:27	You save the **h** but bring low	6639+6714
	25: 9	He guides the **h** in what is right	6705
	147: 6	The LORD sustains the **h** but casts the	6705
	149: 4	he crowns the **h** with salvation.	6705
Pr	3:34	but gives grace to the **h.**	6705
	6: 3	Go and **h yourself;**	8346
Isa	13:11	to the arrogance of the haughty and will **h**	9164
	23: 9	and to **h** all who are renowned on the earth.	7837
	29:19	Once more the **h** will rejoice in the LORD;	6705
	58: 5	only a day for a man to **h** himself?	6700
	66: 2	he who is **h** and contrite in spirit,	6714
Da	4:37	those who walk in pride he is able to **h.**	10737
	5:19	and those he wanted to **h,** he humbled.	NIH
	10:12	to gain understanding and to **h yourself**	6700
Zep	2: 3	Seek the LORD, all you **h** of the land,	6705
	3:12	But I will leave within you the meek and **h,**	1924
Mt	11:29	for I am gentle and **h** in heart,	5424
Lk	1:48	for he has been mindful of the **h state**	5428
	1:52	from their thrones but has lifted up the **h.**	5424
2Co	12:21	that when I come again my God will **h** me	5427
Eph	4: 2	Be completely **h** and gentle;	5425
Jas	1: 9	The brother **in h circumstances** ought	5424
	4: 6	the proud but gives grace to the **h.**"	5424
	4:10	**H** yourselves before the Lord,	5427
1Pe	3: 8	love as brothers, be compassionate and **h.**	5426
	5: 5	the proud but gives grace to the **h.**"	5424
	5: 6	**H** yourselves, therefore, under God's	5427

HUMBLED (34) [HUMBLE]

Lev	26:41	then when their uncircumcised hearts **are h**	4044
Dt	8: 3	He **h** you, causing you to hunger and	6700
1Ki	21:29	"Have you noticed how Ahab **has h himself**	4044
	21:29	Because he has **h** himself,	4044
2Ki	22:19	and you **h yourself** before the LORD	4044
2Ch	12: 6	leaders of Israel and the king **h themselves**	4044
	12: 7	the LORD saw that they **h themselves,**	4044
	12: 7	"Since they have **h themselves,**	4044
	12:12	Because Rehoboam **h** himself,	4044
	28:19	The LORD had **h** Judah because	4044
	30:11	Manasseh and Zebulun **h themselves**	4044
	33:12	of the LORD his God and **h himself** greatly	4044
	33:19	and idols before he **h himself—**	4044
	34:27	and you **h yourself** before God	4044
	34:27	and because you **h yourself** before me	4044
Ps	35:13	on sackcloth and **h** myself with fasting.	6700
	44: 9	But now you have rejected and **h** us;	4007
	68:30	**H,** may it bring bars of silver.	8346
	107:39	and they were **h** by oppression,	8820
Isa	2: 9	man will be brought low and mankind **h—**	9164
	2:11	The eyes of the arrogant man will be **h** and	9164
	2:12	for all that is exalted (and they will be **h),**	9164
	2:17	be brought low and the pride of men **h;**	9164
	5:15	So man will be brought low and mankind **h,**	9164
	5:15	the eyes of the arrogant **h,**	9164
	9: 1	past he **h** the land of Zebulun and the land	7837
	58: 3	Why have we **h** ourselves,	6700
Jer	44:10	To this day they have not **h themselves**	1917
Da	5:19	and those he wanted to humble, he **h.**	10737
	5:22	O Belshazzar, have not **h** yourself,	10737
Mt	23:12	For whoever exalts himself will be **h,**	5427
Lk	14:11	For everyone who exalts himself will be **h,**	5427
	18:14	For everyone who exalts himself will be **h,**	5427

HUMBLES (6) [HUMBLE]

1Sa	2: 7	he **h** and he exalts.	9164
Isa	26: 5	He **h** those who dwell on high,	8820
Mt	18: 4	whoever **h** himself like this child is	5427
	23:12	and whoever **h** himself will be exalted.	5427
Lk	14:11	and he who **h** himself will be exalted.	5427
	18:14	and he who **h** himself will be exalted."	5427

HUMBLY (4) [HUMBLE]

2Sa	16: 4	"I **h** bow," Ziba said.	2556
Isa	38:15	I will walk **h** all my years because	1844
Mic	6: 8	to love mercy and to walk **h** with your God.	7570
Jas	1:21	and **h** accept the word planted in you,	1877+4559

HUMILIATE (2) [HUMBLE]

Pr	25: 7	than for him to **h** you before a nobleman.	9164
1Co	11:22	of God and **h** those who have nothing?	2875

HUMILIATED (10) [HUMBLE]

2Sa	6:22	and I will be **h** in my own eyes.	9166
	10: 5	for they were greatly **h.**	4007
	19: 5	"Today you have **h** all your men,	1017
1Ch	19: 5	for they were greatly **h.**	4007
Isa	54: 4	Do not fear disgrace; you will not be **h.**	2917
Jer	15: 9	she will be disgraced and **h.**	2917
	31:19	I was ashamed and **h** because I bore	4007
Mal	2: 9	"So I have caused you to be despised and **h**	9166
Lk	13:17	When he said this, all his opponents were **h,**	2875
	14: 9	Then, **h,** you will have to take	158+3552

HUMILIATION (4) [HUMBLE]

Ezr	9: 7	and **h** at the hand of foreign kings,	1425+7156
Job	19: 5	above me and use my **h** against me,	3075
Eze	16:63	because of your **h,**	4009
Ac	8:33	In his **h** he was deprived of justice.	5428

HUMILITY (14) [HUMBLE]

Ps	45: 4	in behalf of truth, **h** and righteousness;	6708
Pr	11: 2	but with **h** comes wisdom.	7560
	15:33	and **h** comes before honor.	6708
	18:12	but **h** comes before honor.	6708
	22: 4	**H** and the fear of the LORD bring wealth	6708
Zep	2: 3	Seek righteousness, seek **h;**	6708
Ac	20:19	the Lord with **great h** and with tears,	4246+5425
Php	2: 3	in **h** consider others better than yourselves.	5425
Col	2:18	not let anyone who delights in false **h** and	5425
	2:23	their false **h** and their harsh treatment of	5425
	3:12	kindness, **h,** gentleness and patience.	5425
Tit	3: 2	and to show **true h** toward all men.	4559
Jas	3:13	by deeds done in the **h** that comes	4559
1Pe	5: 5	with **h** toward one another,	5425

HUMPS (1)

Isa	30: 6	their treasures on the **h** of camels,	1832

HUMTAH (1)

Jos	15:54	**H,** Kiriath Arba (that is, Hebron) and Zior—	2794

HUNCHBACKED (1)

Lev	21:20	or who is **h** or dwarfed,	1492

HUNDRED (291) [HUNDREDFOLD, HUNDREDS, HUNDREDTH, 100]

Ge	6: 3	his days will be a **h** and twenty years."	4395
	7: 6	Noah was six **h** years old when	4395
	7:24	flooded the earth for a **h** and fifty days.	4395
	8: 3	of the **h** and fifty days the water had gone	4395
	8:13	first month of Noah's six **h** and first year,	4395
	15:13	be enslaved and mistreated four **h** years.	4395
	17:17	"Will a son be born to a man a **h** years old?	4395
	21: 5	a **h** years old when his son Isaac was born	4395
	23: 1	to be a **h** and twenty-seven years old.	4395
	23:15	the land is worth four **h** shekels of silver,	4395
	23:16	four **h** shekels of silver,	4395
	25: 7	Abraham lived a **h** and seventy-five years.	4395
	25:17	Ishmael lived a **h** and thirty-seven years.	4395
	32: 6	and four **h** men are with him.	4395
	32:14	two **h** female goats and twenty male goats,	4395
	32:14	two **h** ewes and twenty rams,	4395
	33: 1	coming with his four **h** men;	4395
	33:19	For a **h** pieces of silver,	4395
	35:28	Isaac lived a **h** and eighty years.	4395
	45:22	but to Benjamin he gave three **h** shekels	4395
	47: 9	years of my pilgrimage are a **h** and thirty.	4395
	47:28	years of his life were a **h** and forty-seven.	4395
	50:22	He lived a **h** and ten years	4395
	50:26	So Joseph died at the age of a **h** and ten.	4395
Ex	12:37	There were about six **h** thousand men	4395
	14: 7	He took six **h** of the best chariots,	4395
	27: 9	be a **h** cubits long and is to have curtains	4395
	27:11	The north side shall also be a **h** cubits long	4395
	27:18	be a **h** cubits long and fifty cubits wide,	4395
	38: 9	The south side was a **h** cubits long	4395
	38:11	also a **h** cubits long and had twenty posts	4395
Lev	26: 8	Five of you will chase a **h,**	4395
	26: 8	and a **h** of you will chase ten thousand,	4395
Nu	7:13	silver plate weighing a **h** and thirty shekels,	4395
	7:19	silver plate weighing a **h** and thirty shekels,	4395

Nu	7:25	silver plate weighing a **h** and thirty shekels,	4395
	7:31	silver plate weighing a **h** and thirty shekels,	4395
	7:37	silver plate weighing a **h** and thirty shekels,	4395
	7:43	silver plate weighing a **h** and thirty shekels,	4395
	7:49	silver plate weighing a **h** and thirty shekels,	4395
	7:55	silver plate weighing a **h** and thirty shekels,	4395
	7:61	silver plate weighing a **h** and thirty shekels,	4395
	7:67	silver plate weighing a **h** and thirty shekels,	4395
	7:73	silver plate weighing a **h** and thirty shekels,	4395
	7:79	silver plate weighing a **h** and thirty shekels,	4395
	7:85	Each silver plate weighed a **h** and thirty	4395
	7:85	dishes weighing two thousand four **h** shekels	4395
	7:86	gold dishes weighed a **h** and twenty shekels.	4395
	11:21	"Here I am among six **h** thousand men	4395
	31:28	for the LORD one out of every five **h,**	4395
	33:39	a **h** and twenty-three years old when he died	4395
	35: 4	the Levites will extend six **fifteen h feet**	547+564
Dt	22:19	They shall fine him a **h** shekels of silver	4395
	31: 2	"I am now a **h** and twenty years old	4395
	34: 7	a **h** and twenty years old when he died,	4395
Jos	7:21	two **h** shekels of silver and a wedge	4395
	24:29	died at the age of a **h** and ten.	4395
	24:32	a **h** pieces of silver from the sons of Hamor,	4395
Jdg	2: 8	died at the age of a **h** and ten.	4395
	3:31	who struck down six **h** Philistines with	4395
	4: 3	Because he had nine **h** iron chariots	4395
	4:13	gathered together his nine **h** iron chariots	4395
	7: 6	Three **h** men lapped with their hands	4395
	7: 7	the three **h** men that lapped I will save you	4395
	7: 8	to their tents but kept the three **h,**	4395
	7:16	the three **h** men into three companies,	4395
	7:19	and the **h** men with him reached the edge of	4395
	7:22	When the three **h** trumpets sounded,	4395
	8: 4	Gideon and his three **h** men,	4395
	8:10	a **h** and twenty thousand swordsmen had	4395
	8:26	to **seventeen h** shekels,	547+2256+4395+8679
	11:26	For three **h** years Israel occupied Heshbon,	4395
	15: 4	and caught three **h** foxes and tied them tail	4395
	16: 5	will give you **eleven h** shekels	547+2256+4395
	17: 2	"The **eleven h** shekels of silver	547+2256+4395
	17: 3	the **eleven h** shekels of silver	547+2256+4395
	17: 4	and she took two **h** shekels of silver	4395
	18:11	six **h** men from the clan of the Danites,	4395
	18:16	The six **h** Danites, armed for battle,	4395
	18:17	the six **h** armed men stood at the entrance to	4395
	20: 2	four **h** thousand soldiers armed with swords.	4395
	20:10	We'll take ten men out of every **h** from all	4395
	20:10	and a **h** from a thousand,	4395
	20:15	to seven **h** chosen men from those living	4395
	20:16	seven **h** chosen men who were left-handed,	4395
	20:17	mustered four **h** thousand swordsmen,	4395
	20:47	But six **h** men turned and fled into	4395
	21:12	in Jabesh Gilead four **h** young women who had never slept with a man,	4395
1Sa	11: 8	men of Israel numbered three **h** thousand	4395
	13:15	They numbered about six **h.**	4395
	14: 2	With him were about six **h** men,	4395
	15: 4	two **h** thousand foot soldiers	4395
	17: 7	and its iron point weighed six **h** shekels.	4395
	18:25	for the bride than a **h** Philistine foreskins.	4395
	18:27	and killed two **h** Philistines.	4395
	22: 2	About four **h** men were with him.	4395
	23:13	David and his men, about six **h** in number,	4395
	25:13	About four **h** men went up with David,	4395
	25:13	while two **h** stayed with the supplies.	4395
	25:18	She took two **h** loaves of bread,	4395
	25:18	a **h** cakes of raisins and two hundred cakes	4395
	25:18	a hundred cakes of raisins and two **h** cakes	4395
	27: 2	the six **h** men with him left and went over	4395
	30: 9	David and the six **h** men with him came to	4395
	30:10	for two **h** men were too exhausted to cross	4395
	30:10	and four **h** men continued the pursuit.	4395
	30:17	except four **h** young men who rode off	4395
	30:21	the two **h** men who had been too exhausted	4395
2Sa	2:31	But David's men had killed three **h**	4395
	3:14	for the price of a **h** Philistine foreskins."	4395
	8: 4	but a **h** of the chariot horses.	4395
	10:18	and David killed seven **h** of their charioteers	4395
	14:26	and its weight was two **h** shekels by	4395
	15:11	Two **h** men from Jerusalem	4395
	15:18	the six **h** Gittites who had accompanied him	4395
	16: 1	and loaded with two **h** loaves of bread,	4395
	16: 1	a **h** cakes of raisins,	4395
	16: 1	a **h** cakes of figs and a skin of wine.	4395
	21:16	bronze spearhead weighed three **h** shekels	4395
	23: 8	he raised his spear against eight **h** men,	4395
	23:18	He raised his spear against three **h** men,	4395
	24: 3	the troops a **h** times over,	4395
	24: 9	In Israel there were eight **h** thousand able-bodied men who could handle	4395
	24: 9	and in Judah five **h** thousand.	4395
1Ki	4:23	twenty of pasture-fed cattle and a **h** sheep	4395
	5:16	as **thirty-three h** foremen who supervised	547+2256+4395+8993+8993
	6: 1	In the four **h** and eightieth year after	4395
	7: 2	of the Forest of Lebanon a **h** cubits long,	4395
	7:20	the two **h** pomegranates in rows all around.	4395
	7:42	the four **h** pomegranates for the two sets	4395
	8:63	a **h** and twenty thousand goats and goats.	4395
	10:16	King Solomon made two **h** large shields	4395
	10:16	six **h** bekas of gold went into each shield.	4395
	10:17	He also made three **h** small shields,	4395
	10:26	he had **fourteen h** chariots	547+752+2256+4395
	10:29	from Egypt for six **h** shekels of silver,	4395
	10:29	and a horse for a **h** and fifty.	4395
	11: 3	He had seven **h** wives of royal birth	4395
	11: 3	of royal birth and three **h** concubines,	4395

1Ki	12:21	a **h** and eighty thousand fighting men—	4395
	18: 4	a **h** prophets and hidden them in two caves,	4395
	18:13	a **h** of the LORD's prophets in two caves,	4395
	18:19	the four **h** and fifty prophets of Baal and	4395
	18:19	of Baal and the four **h** prophets of Asherah,	4395
	18:22	but Baal has four **h** and fifty prophets.	4395
	20:29	a **h** thousand casualties on the Aramean	4395
	22: 6	about four **h** men—	4395
2Ki	3: 4	with a **h** thousand lambs and with the wool	4395
	3: 4	and with the wool of a **h** thousand rams.	4395
	3:26	with him seven **h** swordsmen to break	4395
	4:43	"How can I set this before a **h** men?"	4395
	11: 4	for the commanders of **units of a h,**	4395
	11: 9	The commanders of **units of a h** did just	4395
	11:15	the commanders of **units of a h,** who were	4395
	14:13	a section **about six h** feet long. 564+752+4395	
	18:14	from Hezekiah king of Judah three **h** talents	4395
	18:14	of the LORD went out and put to death a **h**	4395
	19:35	of the LORD went out and put to death a **h**	4395
	23:33	of a **h** talents of silver and a talent of gold.	4395
1Ch	4:42	And five **h** of these Simeonites,	4395
	5:21	two **h** fifty thousand sheep	4395
	5:21	also took one **h** thousand people captive,	4395
	11:11	he raised his spear against three **h** men,	4395
	11:20	He raised his spear against three **h** men,	4395
	12:14	the least was a match for a **h,**	4395
	18: 4	but a **h** of the chariot horses.	4395
	21: 3	the LORD multiply his troops a **h** times over.	4395
	21: 5	In all Israel there were one million one **h**	
		thousand men who could handle a sword,	4395
	21: 5	including four **h** and seventy thousand	4395
	21:25	So David paid Araunah six **h** shekels	4395
	22:14	of the LORD a **h** thousand talents of gold,	4395
	26:30	**seventeen h** able men— 547+2256+4395+8679	
	26:32	Jeriah had **twenty-seven h** relatives,	
		547+2256+4395+8679	
	29: 7	of bronze and a thousand talents of iron.	4395
2Ch	1:14	he had **fourteen h** chariots 547+752+2256+4395	
	1:17	from Egypt for six **h** shekels of silver,	4395
	1:17	and a horse for a **h** and fifty.	4395
	2: 2	and **thirty-six h** as 547+2256+4395+8993+9252	
	3: 8	the inside with six **h** talents of fine gold.	4395
	3:16	a **h** pomegranates and attached them to	4395
	4: 8	He also made a **h** gold sprinkling bowls.	4395
	4:13	the four **h** pomegranates for the two sets	4395
	7: 5	of cattle and a **h** and twenty thousand sheep	4395
	8:10	two **h** and fifty officials supervising	4395
	8:18	and brought back four **h** and fifty talents	4395
	9:15	King Solomon made two **h** large shields	4395
	9:15	six **h** bekas of hammered gold went	4395
	9:16	He also made three **h** small shields	4395
	9:16	with three **h** bekas of gold in each shield.	4395
	11: 1	a **h** and eighty thousand fighting men—	4395
	12: 3	With **twelve h** chariots 547+2256+4395	
	13: 3	of four **h** thousand able fighting men,	4395
	13: 3	with eight **h** thousand able troops.	4395
	13:17	so that there were five **h** thousand casualties	4395
	14: 8	Asa had an army of three **h** thousand men	4395
	14: 8	two **h** and eighty thousand from Benjamin,	4395
	14: 9	with a vast army and three **h** chariots	4395
	15:11	to the LORD seven **h** head of cattle	4395
	17:11	seven thousand seven **h** rams	4395
	17:11	and seven thousand seven **h** goats.	4395
	18: 5	brought together the prophets—four **h** men	4395
	23: 1	with the commanders of **units of a h:**	4395
	23: 9	the commanders of **units of a h** the spears	4395
	23:14	the commanders of **units of a h,** who were	4395
	24:15	and he died at the age of a **h** and thirty.	4395
	25: 5	that there were three **h** thousand men ready	4395
	25: 6	a **h** thousand fighting men from Israel for	4395
	25: 6	from Israel for a **h** talents of silver.	4395
	25: 9	"But what about the **h** talents I paid	4395
	25:23	a section **about six h** feet long. 564+752+4395	
	27: 5	the Ammonites paid him a **h** talents	4395
	28: 6	a **h** and twenty thousand soldiers in Judah—	4395
	28: 8	from their kinsmen two **h** thousand wives,	4395
	29:32	a **h** rams and two hundred male lambs—	4395
	29:32	a hundred rams and two **h** male lambs—	4395
	29:33	to six **h** bulls and three thousand sheep	4395
	35: 8	the priests **twenty-six h** Passover offerings	
		547+2256+4395+9252	
	35: 8	and three **h** cattle.	4395
	35: 9	and five **h** head of cattle for the Levites.	4395
	36: 3	and imposed on Judah a levy of a **h** talents	4395
Ezr	6:17	of this house of God they offered a **h** bulls,	10395
	6:17	two **h** rams, four hundred male lambs and,	10395
	6:17	two hundred rams, four **h** male lambs and,	10395
	7:22	up to a **h** talents of silver,	10395
	7:22	a **h** cors of wheat, a hundred baths of wine,	10395
	7:22	a hundred cors of wheat, a **h** baths of wine,	10395
	7:22	a **h** baths of olive oil, and salt without limit.	10395
Ne	3: 1	building as far as the Tower of the **H,**	4396
	3:13	also repaired **five h** yards of the wall	547+564
	5:17	a **h** and fifty Jews and officials ate	4395
	12:39	of Hananel and the Tower of the **H,**	4396
Est	9: 6	the Jews killed and destroyed five **h** men.	4395
	9:12	and destroyed five **h** men and the ten sons	4395
	9:15	and they put to death in Susa three **h** men,	4395
Job	1: 3	five **h** yoke of oxen	4395
	1: 3	and five hundred donkeys,	4395
	42:16	After this, Job lived a **h** and forty years;	4395
Pr	17:10	of discernment more than a **h** lashes a fool.	4395
Ecc	6: 3	a **h** children and live many years;	4395
	8:12	Although a wicked man commits a **h** crimes	4395
SS	8:12	and two **h** are for those who tend its fruit.	4395
Isa	37:36	of the LORD went out and put to death a **h**	4395
	65:20	dies at a **h** will be thought a mere youth;	4395
	65:20	to reach a **h** will be considered accursed.	4395

Jer	52:23	above the surrounding network was a **h.**	4395
Eze	40:19	it was a **h** cubits on the east side as well as	4395
	40:23	it was a **h** cubits.	4395
	40:27	it was a **h** cubits.	4395
	40:47	a **h** cubits long and a hundred cubits wide.	4395
	40:47	a hundred cubits long and a **h** cubits wide.	4395
	41:13	it was a **h** cubits long,	4395
	41:13	with its walls were also a **h** cubits long.	4395
	41:14	was a **h** cubits.	4395
	41:15	it was a **h** cubits.	4395
	42: 2	a **h** cubits long and fifty cubits wide.	4395
	42: 4	and a **h** cubits long.	4395
	42: 8	the sanctuary was a **h** cubits long.	4395
	42:16	it was five **h** cubits.	4395
	42:17	it was five **h** cubits by the measuring rod.	4395
	42:18	it was five **h** cubits by the measuring rod.	4395
	42:19	it was five **h** cubits by the measuring rod.	4395
	42:20	five **h** cubits long	4395
	42:20	and five **h** cubits wide,	4395
	45:15	to be taken from every flock of two **h** from	4395
Am	5: 3	for Israel will have only a **h** left;	4395
	5: 3	a **h** strong will have only ten left."	4395
Jnh	4:11	**h** and twenty thousand** people who cannot	
		tell their right hand from 6926+8052+9109	
Mt	13: 8	a **h,** sixty or thirty times what was sown.	1669
	13:23	He produces a crop, yielding a **h,**	1669
	18:12	If a man owns a **h** sheep,	1669
	18:28	fellow servants who owed him a **h** denarii.	1669
	19:29	for my sake will receive a **h** times as much	1671
Mk	4: 8	multiplying thirty, sixty, or even a **h** times."	1669
	4:20	sixty or even a **h** times what was sown."	1669
	10:30	will fail to receive a **h** times as much	1671
Lk	7:41	One owed him **five h** denarii,	4296
	8: 8	a **h** times more than was sown.	1671
	15: 4	of you has a **h** sheep and loses one of them.	1669
	16: 6	" 'Eight h** gallons of olive oil,'	1004+1669
	16: 6	sit down quickly, and make it **four h.'**	4299
	16: 7	'Take your bill and make it **eight h.'**	3837
Jn	21: 8	not far from shore, about a **h** yards.	1357+4388
Ac	1:15	(a group numbering about a **h** and twenty)	1669
	5:36	about four **h** men rallied to him.	5484
	7: 6	be enslaved and mistreated four **h** years.	5484
	23:23	"Get ready a detachment of two **h** soldiers,	1357
	23:23	seventy horsemen and two **h** spearmen to go	1357
	27:28	a **h** and twenty feet deep.	1633+3976
Ro	4:19	since he was about a **h** years old—	1670
1Co	15: 6	to more than **five h** of the brothers at	4001
Rev	9:16	mounted troops was two **h** million.	1490+3689
	16:21	of about a **h** pounds each fell upon men.	5418

HUNDREDFOLD (1) [HUNDRED]

Ge	26:12	land and the same year reaped a **h,**	4395+9134

HUNDREDS (21) [HUNDRED]

Ex	18:21	appoint them as officials over thousands, **h,**	4395
	18:25	officials over thousands, **h,** fifties and tens.	4395
Nu	31:14	of thousands and commanders of **h—**	4395
	31:48	of thousands and commanders of **h—**	4395
	31:52	of **h** that Moses and Eleazar presented as	4395
	31:54	of **h** and brought it into the Tent of Meeting	4395
Dt	1:15	as commanders of thousands, of **h,**	4395
1Sa	22: 7	of thousands and commanders of **h?**	4395
	29: 2	with their **units of h** and thousands,	4395
2Sa	18: 1	of thousands and commanders of **h,**	4395
	18: 4	while all the men marched out in **units of h**	4395
2Ki	11:19	He took with him the commanders of **h,**	4395
1Ch	13: 1	of thousands and commanders of **h,**	4395
	26:26	of thousands and commanders of **h,**	4395
	27: 1	of thousands and commanders of **h,**	4395
	28: 1	of thousands and commanders of **h,**	4395
	29: 6	of thousands and commanders of **h,**	4395
2Ch	1: 2	and commanders of **h,** to the judges and	4395
	23:20	He took with him the commanders of **h,**	4395
	25: 5	of thousands and commanders of **h**	4395
Mk	6:40	So they sat down in groups of **h** and fifties.	1669

HUNDREDTH (2) [HUNDRED]

Ge	7:11	In the six **h** year of Noah's life,	4395
Ne	5:11	the **h** part of the money, grain,	4395

HUNG (16) [HANG]

Ex	40:21	the tabernacle and **h** the shielding curtain	8492
Dt	21:22	to death and his body is **h** on a tree,	9434
	21:23	who is **h** on a tree is under God's curse.	9434
Jos	8:29	He **h** the king of Ai on a tree and	9434
	10:26	the kings and **h** them on five trees,	9434
2Sa	4:12	and **h** the bodies by the pool in Hebron.	9434
	21:12	where the Philistines had **h** them	9428
1Ch	10:10	and **h** up his head in the temple of Dagon.	9546
Ps	137: 2	There on the poplars we **h** our harps,	9434
La	5:12	Princes have been **h** up by their hands;	9434
Eze	27:10	They **h** their shields and helmets	9434
	27:11	They **h** their shields around your walls;	9434
Mt	18: 6	be better for him to have a large millstone **h**	3203
Lk	19:48	because all the people **h** on his words.	1717
	23:39	of the criminals who **h** there hurled insults	3203
Gal	3:13	"Cursed is everyone who is **h** on a tree."	3203

HUNGER (22) [HUNGRY]

Dt	8: 3	**causing** you to **h** and then feeding you	8279
	28:48	therefore in **h** and thirst,	8280
1Sa	2: 5	but those who were hungry **h** no more.	NIH
2Ch	32:11	to let you die of **h** and thirst.	8280
Ne	9:15	In their **h** you gave them bread from heaven	8280

Job	30: 3	Haggard from want and **h,**	4103
	38:39	for the lioness and satisfy the **h** of the lions	4103
Ps	17:14	You still the **h** of those you cherish;	1061+4848
Pr	6:30	to satisfy his **h** when he is starving.	5883
	16:26	his **h** drives him on.	7023
Isa	5:13	of rank will die of **h** and their masses will	8280
	29: 8	but he awakens, and his **h** remains;	5883+8199
	49:10	They will neither **h** nor thirst,	8279
La	2:19	who faint from **h** at the head of every street.	8280
	4: 9	**racked with h,** they waste away for lack	1991
	5:10	Our skin is hot as an oven, feverish from **h.**	8280
Eze	7:19	not satisfy their **h** or fill their stomachs	5883
Mt	5: 6	Blessed are those who **h** and thirst	4277
Lk	6:21	Blessed are you who **h** now,	4277
2Co	6: 5	in hard work, sleepless nights and **h;**	3763
	11:27	I have known **h** and thirst,	3350
Rev	7:16	Never again will they **h;**	4277

HUNGRY (52) [HUNGER]

1Sa	2: 5	but those who were **h** hunger no more.	8281
2Sa	17:29	"The people have become **h** and tired	8281
Job	5: 5	The **h** consume his harvest,	8281
	18:12	Calamity is **h** for him;	8281
	22: 7	and you withheld food from the **h,**	8281
	24:10	they carry the sheaves, but still go **h.**	8281
Ps	17:12	They are like a lion **h** for prey,	4083
	34:10	The lions may grow weak and **h,**	8279
	50:12	If I were **h** I would not tell you,	8279
	107: 5	They were **h** and thirsty,	8281
	107: 9	and fills the **h** with good things.	5883+8281
	107:36	there he brought the **h** to live,	8281
	146: 7	of the oppressed and gives food to the **h.**	8281
Pr	10: 3	The LORD does not **let** the righteous go **h**	8279
	13:25	but the stomach of the wicked **goes h.**	2893
	19:15	and the shiftless man **goes h.**	8279
	25:21	If your enemy is **h,** give him food to eat;	8281
	27: 7	but to the **h** even what is bitter tastes sweet.	8281
Isa	8:21	Distressed and **h,** they will roam through	8281
	9:20	they will devour, but still be **h;**	8279
	29: 8	as when a **h** man dreams that he is eating,	8281
	32: 6	the **h** he leaves empty and from 5883+8281	
	44:12	He gets **h** and loses his strength;	8279
	58: 7	to share your food with the **h** and to provide	8281
	58:10	the **h** and satisfy the needs of the oppressed,	8281
	65:13	"My servants will eat, but you will go **h;**	8279
Jer	42:14	not see war or hear the trumpet or be **h**	8279
Eze	18: 7	to the **h** and provides clothing for the naked.	8281
	18:16	to the **h** and provides clothing for the naked.	8281
Mt	4: 2	and forty nights, he was **h.**	4277
	12: 1	His disciples were **h** and began	4277
	12: 3	when he and his companions were **h?**	4277
	15:32	I do not want to send them away **h,**	3765
	21:18	on his way back to the city, he was **h.**	4277
	25:35	I was **h** and you gave me something to eat,	4277
	25:37	'Lord, when did we see you **h** and feed you,	4277
	25:42	I was **h** and you gave me nothing to eat,	4277
	25:44	when did we see you **h** or thirsty or	4277
Mk	2:25	and his companions were **h** and in need?	4277
	8: 3	If I send them home **h,**	3765
	11:12	as they were leaving Bethany, Jesus was **h.**	4277
Lk	1:53	He has filled the **h** with good things	4277
	4: 2	and at the end of them he was **h.**	4277
	6: 3	when he and his companions were **h?**	4277
	6:25	who are well fed now, for you will go **h.**	4277
Jn	6:35	He who comes to me will never go **h,**	4277
Ac	10:10	He became **h** and wanted something to eat,	4698
Ro	12:20	"If your enemy is **h,** feed him;	4277
1Co	4:11	To this very hour we go **h** and thirsty,	4277
	11:21	One remains **h,** another gets drunk.	4277
	11:34	If anyone is **h,** he should eat at home,	4277
Php	4:12	whether well fed or **h,**	4277

HUNT (7) [HUNTED, HUNTER, HUNTERS, HUNTING, HUNTS]

Ge	27: 3	to the open country to **h** some wild game	7421
	27: 5	for the open country to **h** game	7421
	31:36	that you **h** me down?	1944
Job	38:39	"Do you **h** the prey for the lioness and	7421
Ps	140:11	may disaster **h** down men of violence.	
		4200+4511+7421	
Jer	16:16	and they will **h** them **down**	7421
Am	9: 3	there I will **h** them **down** and seize them.	2924

HUNTED (3) [HUNT]

Ge	27:33	then, that **h** game and brought it to me?	7421
Isa	13:14	Like a **h** gazelle,	5615
La	3:52	without cause **h** me like a bird.	7421+7421

HUNTER (4) [HUNT]

Ge	10: 9	He was a mighty **h** before the LORD;	7473
	10: 9	Nimrod, a mighty **h** before the LORD."	7473
	25:27	and Esau became a skillful **h,**	408+7473
Pr	6: 5	like a gazelle from the hand of the **h,**	NIH

HUNTERS (1) [HUNT]

Jer	16:16	After that I will send for many **h,**	7475

HUNTING (2) [HUNT]

Ge	27:30	his brother Esau came in from **h.**	7473
1Sa	24:11	but you are **h** me **down** to take my life.	7399

HUNTS (4) [HUNT]

Lev	17:13	among you who **h** any animal or bird	7421
1Sa	26:20	as *one* **h** a partridge in the mountains."	8103
Ps	10: 2	In his arrogance the wicked man **h down**	1944
Mic	7: 2	each **h** his brother with a net.	7421

HUPHAM (1) [HUPHAMITE]

Nu	26:39	through **H**, the Huphamite clan.	2573

HUPHAMITE (1) [HUPHAM]

Nu	26:39	through Hupham, the **H** clan.	2574

HUPHAMITES (KJV) See HUPHAM

HUPPAH (1)

1Ch	24:13	the thirteenth to **H**,	2904

HUPPIM (1)

Ge	46:21	Naaman, Ehi, Rosh, Muppim, **H** and Ard.	2907

HUPPITES (2)

1Ch	7:12	The Shuppites and **H** were the descendants	2907
	7:15	a wife from among the **H** and Shuppites.	2907

HUR (15) [BEN-HUR]

Ex	17:10	Aaron and **H** went to the top of the hill.	2581
	17:12	Aaron and **H** held his hands up—	2581
	24:14	Aaron and **H** are with you,	2581
	31: 2	the son of **H**, of the tribe of Judah,	2581
	35:30	the son of **H**, of the tribe of Judah,	2581
	38:22	(Bezalel son of Uri, the son of **H**,	2581
Nu	31: 8	Zur, **H** and Reba—the five kings of Midian.	2581
Jos	13:21	Evi, Rekem, Zur, **H** and Reba—	2581
1Ch	2:19	Caleb married Ephrath, who bore him **H**.	2581
	2:20	**H** was the father of Uri,	2581
	2:50	The sons of **H** the firstborn of Ephrathah:	2581
	4: 1	Perez, Hezron, Carmi, **H** and Shobal.	2581
	4: 4	These were the descendants of **H**,	2581
2Ch	1: 5	of **H**, had made was in Gibeon in front of	2581
Ne	3: 9	Rephaiah son of **H**,	2581

HURAI (1)

1Ch	11:32	**H** from the ravines of Gaash,	2584

HURAM (6)

1Ki	7:13	King Solomon sent to Tyre and brought **H**,	2671
	7:14	**H** was highly skilled and experienced	NIH
	7:40	So **H** finished all the work he had	2671
	7:45	that **H** made for King Solomon for	2671
1Ch	8: 5	Gera, Shephuphan and **H**.	2586
2Ch	4:11	So **H** finished the work he had undertaken	2586

HURAM-ABI (2)

2Ch	2:13	"I am sending you **H**, a man of great skill,	2587
	4:16	the objects that **H** made for King Solomon	2587

HURI (1)

1Ch	5:14	These were the sons of Abihail son of **H**,	2585

HURL (8) [HURLED, HURLS]

1Sa	25:29	the lives of your enemies he will **h away** as	7843
2Ch	26:15	to shoot arrows and **h** large stones.	NIH
Ps	22: 7	*they* **h insults**, shaking their heads:	
			928+7080+8557
Isa	22:17	take firm hold of you and **h** you **away**,	3214+3232
Jer	10:18	"At this time I *will* **h out** those who live	7843
	22:26	*I will* **h** you and and the mother who gave	3214
Eze	32: 4	and **h** you on the open field.	3214
Mic	7:19	and **h** all our iniquities into the depths of	8959

HURLED (23) [HURL]

Ex	15: 1	The horse and its rider he has **h** into the sea.	8227
	15: 4	Pharaoh's chariots and his army he has **h**	3721
	15:21	horse and its rider he has **h** into the sea."	8227
Jos	10:11	**h** large hailstones **down**	8959
1Sa	18:11	and he **h** it, saying to himself,	3214
	20:33	But Saul **h** his spear at him to kill him.	3214
	25:14	but *he* **h** insults at them.	6512
Ne	9:11	but *you* **h** their pursuers into the depths,	8959
Ps	79:12	the reproach *they* have **h** at you,	3070
Jer	22:28	Why *will* he and his children **be h out**,	3214
La	2: 1	*He has* **h down** the splendor of Israel	8959
Jnh	2: 3	*You* **h** me into the deep,	8959
Mt	27:39	Those who passed by **h** insults at him,	1059
Mk	15:29	Those who passed by **h** insults at him,	1059
Lk	23:39	the criminals who hung there **h insults at**	1059
Jn	9:28	Then *they* **h** insults at him and said,	3366
1Pe	2:23	*When* they **h** *their* **insults** at him,	3366
Rev	8: 5	and **h** it on the earth;	965
	8: 7	and *it was* **h** down upon the earth.	965
	12: 9	The great dragon *was* **h down**—	965
	12: 9	*He was* **h** to the earth, and his angels	965
	12:10	*has been* **h down**.	965
	12:13	When the dragon saw that *he had been* **h** to	965

HURLS (2) [HURL]

Job	27:22	It **h** *itself* against him without mercy	8959
Ps	147:17	*He* **h down** his hail like pebbles.	8959

HURRICANE (1)

Ac	27:14	Before very long, a wind **of h** force,	5607

HURRIED (25) [HURRY]

Ge	18: 2	*he* **h** from the entrance of his tent	8132
	18: 6	So Abraham **h** into the tent to Sarah.	4554
	18: 7	*who* **h** to prepare it.	4554
	24:17	The servant **h** to meet her and said,	8132
	24:29	and he **h** out to the man at the spring.	8132
	29:13	his sister's son, *he* **h** to meet him.	8132
	43:15	*They* **h** down to Egypt	7756
	43:30	Joseph **h** *out* and looked for a place	4554
Ex	9:20	of the LORD **h to bring** their slaves	5674
Jos	4:10	The people **h** over,	4554
	8:14	he and all the men of the city **h** out early in	4554
Jdg	13:10	The woman **h** to tell her husband,	4554
1Sa	4:14	The man **h** over to Eli,	4554
2Sa	4: 4	but as she **h** to leave,	2905
	19:16	**h** down with the men of Judah	4554
2Ki	5:21	So Gehazi **h** after Naaman.	8103
	9:13	*They* **h** and took their cloaks	4554
2Ch	26:20	so *they* **h** him out.	987
Est	6:14	and **h** Haman away to	987
Job	31: 5	in falsehood or my foot *has* **h** after deceit—	2590
Da	6:19	the king got up and **h** to the lions' den.	10097
Mt	28: 8	So the women **h away from** the tomb,	599+5444
Mk	6:25	the girl **h** in to the king with the request:	
			1656+3552+5082
Lk	1:39	Mary got ready and **h** to a town	3552+4513+5082
	2:16	*they* **h off** and found Mary and Joseph,	2262+5067

HURRIEDLY (1) [HURRY]

Jdg	9:54	**H** he called to his armor-bearer,	4559

HURRIES (1) [HURRY]

Ecc	1: 5	and **h back** to where it rises.	8634

HURRY (15) [HURRIED, HURRIES, HURRIEDLY, HURRYING]

Ge	19:14	He said, "**H** and get out of this place,	7756
	19:15	the angels urged Lot, saying, "**H!**	7756
	45: 9	Now **h** back to my father and say to him,	4554
Ex	12:33	the people to **h** and leave the country.	4554
Nu	16:46	**h** to the assembly to make atonement	2143+4559
1Sa	9:12	"He's ahead of you. **H** now;	4554
	17:17	for your brothers and **h** to their camp.	8132
	20: 6	'David earnestly asked my permission to **h**	8132
	20:38	Then he shouted, "**H!**	4559
2Ch	35:21	God has told me to **h**;	987
Ps	55: 8	*I would* **h** to my place of shelter,	2590
Ecc	8: 3	not *be* **in a h** to leave the king's presence.	987
SS	1: 4	Take me away with you—*let us* **h!**	8132
Isa	5:19	"*Let* God **h**, let him hasten his work	4554
Ac	20:16	for *he was* **in a h** to reach Jerusalem,	5067

HURRYING (1) [HURRY]

1Sa	23:26	**h** to get away from Saul.	2905

HURT (9) [HURTS]

Ps	69:26	and talk about the pain of *those* you **h**.	2728
Pr	23:35	you will say, "but *I'm* not **h!**	2703
Ecc	8: 9	a man lords it over others to his own **h**.	8273
Da	6:22	*They have* not **h** me,	10243
Mk	16:18	*it will* not **h** them at all;	1055
Jn	21:17	Peter *was* **h** because Jesus asked him	3382
Ac	7:26	why *do you* want to **h** each other?'	92
2Co	7: 8	I see that my letter **h** you,	3382
Rev	2:11	He who overcomes *will* not *be* **h** at all by	92

HURTLING (1)

Eze	13:11	and I will send hailstones **h down**,	5877

HURTS (2) [HURT]

Ps	15: 4	who keeps his oath even when *it* **h**,	8317
Pr	26:28	A lying tongue hates *those* it **h**,	1916

HUSBAND (116) [HUSBAND'S, HUSBANDS]

Ge	3: 6	She also gave some to her **h**,	408
	3:16	Your desire will be for your **h**,	408
	16: 3	and gave her to her **h** to be his wife.	408
	29:32	Surely my **h** will love me now."	408
	29:34	at last my **h** will become attached to me,	408
	30:15	that you took away my **h**?	408
	30:18	for giving my maidservant to my **h**."	408
	30:20	This time my **h** will treat me with honor,	408
Ex	21:22	be fined whatever the woman's **h** demands	1251
Lev	21: 3	on him since she has no **h**—	408
Nu	5:13	from her **h** and her impurity is undetected	408
	5:14	and if feelings of jealousy come over **her h**	2257S
	5:19	while married to your **h**,	408
	5:20	to your **h** and you have defiled yourself	408
	5:20	by sleeping with a man other than your **h**"	408
	5:27	to her **h**, then when she is made to drink	408
	5:29	and defiles herself while married to her **h**,	408
	5:31	The **h** will be innocent of any wrongdoing,	408
	30: 7	her **h** hears about it but says nothing to her,	408
	30: 8	if her **h** forbids her when he hears about it,	408
	30:10	with her **h** makes a vow or obligates herself	408
	30:11	and her **h** hears about it but says nothing	408

Nu	30:12	But if her **h** nullifies them when he hears	408
	30:12	he has nullified them,	408
	30:13	Her **h** may confirm or nullify any vow	408
	30:14	But if her **h** says nothing to her about it	408
Dt	21:13	and *be* her **h** and she shall be your wife.	1249
	24: 3	and her second **h** dislikes her and writes her	408
	24: 4	then her first **h**, who divorced her,	1251
	25:11	of one of them comes to rescue her **h**	408
	28:56	the **h** she loves and her own son or daughter	408
Jdg	13: 6	the woman went to her **h** and told him,	408
	13: 9	but her **h** Manoah was not with her.	408
	13:10	The woman hurried to tell her **h**,	408
	14:15	"Coax your **h** into explaining the riddle	408
	19: 3	her **h** went to her to persuade her to return.	408
	20: 4	the Levite, the **h** *of* the murdered woman,	408
Ru	1: 3	Now Elimelech, Naomi's **h**, died,	408
	1: 5	without her two sons and her **h**.	408
	1: 9	in the home of another **h**."	408
	1:12	I am too old to have another **h**.	408
	1:12	even if I had a **h** tonight and then gave birth	408
	2:11	since the death of your **h**—	408
1Sa	1: 8	Elkanah her **h** would say to her, "Hannah,	408
	1:22	She said to her **h**, "After the boy is weaned,	408
	1:23	Elkanah her **h** told her.	408
	2:19	to him when she went up with her **h** to offer	408
	4:19	that her father-in-law and her **h** were dead,	408
	4:21	the deaths of her father-in-law and her **h**.	408
	25: 3	but her **h**, a Calebite, was surly and mean	408
	25:19	But she did not tell her **h** Nabal.	408
2Sa	3:15	from her **h** Paltiel son of Laish.	408
	3:16	Her **h**, however, went with her,	408
	11:26	Uriah's wife heard that her **h** was dead,	408
	14: 5	"I am indeed a widow; my **h** is dead.	408
	14: 7	leaving my **h** neither name nor descendant	408
2Ki	4: 1	"Your servant my **h** is dead,	408
	4: 9	She said to her **h**,	408
	4:14	"Well, she has no son and her **h** is old."	408
	4:22	She called her **h** and said,	408
	4:26	Is your **h** all right?"	408
Pr	7:19	My **h** is not at home;	408
	31:11	Her **h** has full confidence in her	1251
	31:23	Her **h** is respected at the city gate,	1251
	31:28	her **h** also, and he praises her:	1251
Isa	54: 1	desolate woman than *of her who* **has a h**,"	1249
	54: 5	For your Maker *is* your **h**—	1249
Jer	3:14	declares the LORD, "for I *am* your **h**.	1249
	3:20	But like a woman unfaithful to her **h**,	8276
	6:11	both **h** and wife will be caught in it,	408
	31:32	though I *was a* **h** to them,"	1249
Eze	16:32	You prefer strangers to your own **h!**	408
	16:45	who despised her **h** and her children;	408
Hos	2: 2	for she is not my wife, and I am not her **h**.	408
	2: 7	'I will go back to my **h** as at first,	408
	2:16	"you will call me 'my **h**';	408
Joel	1: 8	in sackcloth grieving for the **h** *of* her youth.	1251
Mt	1:16	the **h** of Mary, of whom was born Jesus,	467
	1:19	Because Joseph her **h** was a righteous man	467
	19:10	"If this is the situation between a **h**	476
Mk	10:12	she divorces her **h** and marries another man,	467
Lk	2:36	with *her* **h** seven years after her marriage,	467
Jn	4:16	"Go, call your **h** and come back."	467
	4:17	"I have no **h**," she replied.	467
	4:17	"You are right when you say you have no **h**.	467
	4:18	and the man you now have is not your **h**.	467
Ac	5: 9	the men who buried your **h** are at the door,	467
	5:10	carried her out and buried her beside her **h**.	467
Ro	7: 2	a married woman is bound *to* her **h** as long	467
	7: 2	but if her **h** dies, she is released from the	467
	7: 3	if she marries another man while her **h** is	
		still alive,	467
	7: 3	But if her **h** dies, she is released from that	467
1Co	7: 2	and each woman her own **h**.	467
	7: 3	**h** should fulfill his marital duty to his wife,	467
	7: 3	and likewise the wife to her **h**.	467
	7: 4	not belong to her alone but also to her **h**.	467
	7:10	A wife must not separate from her **h**.	467
	7:11	or else be reconciled *to* her **h**.	467
	7:11	And a **h** must not divorce his wife.	467
	7:13	a **h** who is not a believer and he is willing	467
	7:14	For the unbelieving **h** has been sanctified	467
	7:14	sanctified through her believing **h**.	467
	7:16	wife, whether you will save your **h**?	467
	7:16	Or, how do you know, **h**,	467
	7:34	how she can please her **h**.	467
	7:39	woman is bound to her **h** as long as she lives.	467
	7:39	But if her **h** dies, she is free to marry	467
2Co	11: 2	I promised you *to* one **h**, to Christ,	467
Gal	4:27	desolate woman than *of* her who has a **h**."	467
Eph	5:23	For the **h** is the head of the wife as Christ is	467
	5:33	and the wife must respect her **h**.	
1Ti	3: 2	overseer must be above reproach, the **h** of	
		but one wife, temperate,	467
	3:12	A deacon must be the **h** of but one wife	467
	5: 9	has been **faithful to her h**,	467+1222+1651
Tit	1: 6	An elder must be blameless, the **h** of but	
		one wife,	467
Rev	21: 2	as a bride beautifully dressed *for* her **h**.	467

HUSBAND'S (7) [HUSBAND]

Dt	25: 5	Her **h brother** shall take her and marry her	3303
	25: 7	"My **h brother** refuses to carry	3303
Ru	2: 1	Now Naomi had a relative on her **h** side,	408
Pr	6:34	for jealousy arouses a **h** fury,	1505
	12: 4	A wife of noble character is her **h** crown.	1251
Jn	1:13	nor of human decision or a **h** will,	467
1Co	7: 4	the **h** body does not belong to him alone but	467

HUSBANDMAN (KJV) See FARMER, GARDENER, MAN OF THE SOIL

HUSBANDS (20) [HUSBAND]

Lev	21: 7	by prostitution or divorced from their **h,**	408
Ru	1:11	who could become your **h?**	408
Est	1:17	and so they will despise their **h** and say,	1251
	1:20	all the women will respect their **h,**	1251
Jer	44:19	not our **h** know that we were making cakes	408
Eze	16:45	who despised their **h** and their children.	408
Am	4: 1	and crush the needy and say to your **h,**	123
Jn	4:18	The fact is, you have had five **h,**	467
1Co	14:35	they should ask their own **h** at home;	467
Eph	5:22	Wives, submit *to* your **h** as to the Lord.	467
	5:24	so also wives should submit *to* their **h**	467
	5:25	**H,** love your wives, just as Christ loved	467
	5:28	**h** ought to love their wives	467
Col	3:18	Wives, submit *to* your **h,**	467
	3:19	**H,** love your wives and do not be harsh	467
Tit	2: 4	the younger women to **love their h**	5791
	2: 5	to be kind, and to be subject *to* their **h,**	467
1Pe	3: 1	in the same way be submissive *to* your **h** so	467
	3: 5	They were submissive *to* their own **h,**	467
	3: 7	**H,** in the same way be considerate	467

HUSH (1) [HUSHED]

| Am | 6:10 | and he says, "No," then he will say, **"H!** | 2187 |

HUSHAH (1)

| 1Ch | 4: 4 | and Ezer the father of **H.** | 2592 |

HUSHAI (12)

2Sa	15:32	**H** the Arkite was there to meet him,	2593
	15:37	So David's friend **H** arrived at Jerusalem	2593
	16:16	Then **H** the Arkite, David's friend,	2593
	16:17	Absalom asked **H,** "Is this the love you	2593
	16:18	**H** said to Absalom, "No,	2593
	17: 5	Absalom said, "Summon also **H** the Arkite,	2593
	17: 6	When **H** came to him, Absalom said,	2593
	17: 7	**H** replied to Absalom, "The advice	2593
	17:14	"The advice of **H** the Arkite is better than	2593
	17:15	**H** told Zadok and Abiathar, the priests,	2593
1Ki	4:16	Baana son of **H**—in Asher and in Aloth,	2593
1Ch	27:33	**H** the Arkite was the king's friend.	2593

HUSHAM (4)

Ge	36:34	**H** from the land of the Temanites	2595
	36:35	When **H** died, Hadad son of Bedad,	2595
1Ch	1:45	**H** from the land of the Temanites	2595
	1:46	When **H** died, Hadad son of Bedad,	2595

HUSHATHITE (5)

2Sa	21:18	At that time Sibbecai the **H** killed Saph,	3144
	23:27	Abiezer from Anathoth, Mebunnai the **H,**	3144
1Ch	11:29	Sibbecai the **H,** Ilai the Ahohite,	3144
	20: 4	At that time Sibbecai the **H** killed Sippai,	3144
	27:11	for the eighth month, was Sibbecai the **H,**	3144

HUSHED (4) [HUSH]

Job	4:16	and I heard a **h** voice:	1960
	29:10	the voices of the nobles were **h,**	2461
	37:17	when the land **lies h** under the south wind,	9200
Ps	107:29	the waves of the sea were **h.**	3120

HUSHIM (3)

Ge	46:23	The son of Dan: **H.**	3123
1Ch	8: 8	in Moab after he had divorced his wives **H**	2594
	8:11	By **H** he had Abitub and Elpaal.	2594

HUSHITES (1)

| 1Ch | 7:12 | and the **H** the descendants of Aher. | 3131 |

HUSK (KJV) See GRAIN, SKIN

HUT (3)

Job	27:18	like a **h** made by a watchman.	6109
Isa	1: 8	like a **h** in a field of melons,	4870
	24:20	it sways like a **h** in the wind;	4870

HUZ (KJV) See UZ

HUZOTH See KIRIATH HUZOTH

HUZZAB (KJV) See DECREED

HYENAS (3)

Isa	13:22	**H** will howl in her strongholds,	363
	34:14	Desert creatures will meet with **h,**	363
Jer	50:39	"So desert creatures and **h** will live there,	363

HYMENAEUS (2)

| 1Ti | 1:20 | Among them are **H** and Alexander, | 5628 |
| 2Ti | 2:17 | Among them are **H** and Philetus, | 5628 |

HYMN (4) [HYMNS]

Ps	40: 3	in my mouth, a **h of praise** to our God.	9335
Mt	26:30	*When they had* **sung a h,** they went out	5630
Mk	14:26	*When they had* **sung a h,** they went out	5630
1Co	14:26	When you come together, everyone has a **h,**	6011

HYMNS (4) [HYMN]

Ac	16:25	Silas *were* praying and **singing h** to God,	5630
Ro	15: 9	*I will* **sing h** to your name."	6010
Eph	5:19	psalms, **h** and spiritual songs.	5631
Col	3:16	psalms, **h** and spiritual songs with gratitude	5631

HYPOCRISY (6) [HYPOCRITE, HYPOCRITES, HYPOCRITICAL]

Mt	23:28	the inside you are full *of* **h** and wickedness.	5694
Mk	12:15	But Jesus knew their **h.**	5694
Lk	12: 1	the yeast of the Pharisees, which is **h.**	5694
Gal	2:13	The other Jews **joined** him **in** his **h,**	5347
	2:13	*by* their **h** even Barnabas was led astray.	5694
1Pe	2: 1	**h,** envy, and slander of every kind.	5694

HYPOCRITE (2) [HYPOCRISY]

| Mt | 7: 5 | *You* **h,** first take the plank out of your own | 5695 |
| Lk | 6:42 | *You* **h,** first take the plank out of your eye, | 5695 |

HYPOCRITES (16) [HYPOCRISY]

Ps	26: 4	nor do I consort with **h;**	6623
Mt	6: 2	as the **h** do in the synagogues and on	5695
	6: 5	"And when you pray, do not be like the **h,**	5695
	6:16	do not look somber as the **h** do,	5695
	15: 7	*You* **h!** Isaiah was right when he prophesied	5695
	22:18	Jesus, knowing their evil intent, said, *"You* **h,** why are you trying to trap me?	5695
	23:13	teachers of the law and Pharisees, *you* **h!**	5695
	23:15	teachers of the law and Pharisees, *you* **h!**	5695
	23:23	teachers of the law and Pharisees, *you* **h!**	5695
	23:25	teachers of the law and Pharisees, *you* **h!**	5695
	23:27	teachers of the law and Pharisees, *you* **h!**	5695
	23:29	teachers of the law and Pharisees, *you* **h!**	5695
	24:51	to pieces and assign him a place with the **h,**	5695
Mk	7: 6	when he prophesied about you **h;**	5695
Lk	12:56	**H!** You know how to interpret	5695
	13:15	The Lord answered him, *"You* **h!**	5695

HYPOCRITICAL (1) [HYPOCRISY]

| 1Ti | 4: 2 | Such teachings come through **h** liars, | 5694 |

HYSSOP (12)

Ex	12:22	Take a bunch of **h,** dip it in the blood	257
Lev	14: 4	and **h** be brought for the one to be cleansed.	257
	14: 6	the scarlet yarn and the **h,**	257
	14:49	scarlet yarn and **h.**	257
	14:51	Then he is to take the cedar wood, the **h,**	257
	14:52	the cedar wood, the **h** and the scarlet yarn.	257
Nu	19: 6	**h** and scarlet wool and throw them onto	257
	19:18	to take *some* **h,** dip it in the water	257
1Ki	4:33	the cedar of Lebanon to the **h** that grows out	257
Ps	51: 7	Cleanse me with **h,** and I will be clean;	257
Jn	19:29	put the sponge *on* a stalk of the **h plant,**	5727
Heb	9:19	scarlet wool and **branches of h,**	5727

I

I (8747) [I'LL, I'M, I'VE, ME, MINE, MYSELF] See Index of Articles Etc.

I AM (61 of 1036) See Index of Articles Etc. for Exhaustive Listings of I and AM (See Introduction, pages x-xi)

Ge	15: 1	"Do not be afraid, Abram. **I am** your shield, your very great reward."	644
	17: 1	"**I am** God Almighty; walk before me and be blameless.	638
Ex	3:14	God said to Moses, "**I AM WHO I AM.**	2118
	3:14	God said to Moses, "**I AM WHO I AM.**	2118
	3:14	This is what you are to say to the Israelites: '**I AM** has sent me to you.' "	2118
Ps	46:10	"Be still, and know that **I am** God;	644
Isa	41:10	So do not fear, for **I am** with you;	638
	41:10	do not be dismayed, for **I am** your God.	638
	43: 3	For **I am** the LORD, your God, the Holy One of Israel, your Savior;	638
	43:11	**I, even I, am** the LORD, and apart from me there is no savior.	644+644
	43:15	**I am** the LORD, your Holy One, Israel's Creator, your King."	638
	44: 6	**I am** the first and I am the last; apart from me there is no God.	638
	44: 6	I am the first and **I am** the last; apart from me there is no God.	638
	48:12	I am the first and **I am** the last.	638
	48:12	**I am** the first and I am the last.	638
Jer	3:14	"Return, faithless people," declares the LORD, "for **I am** your husband.	644
	32:27	"**I am** the LORD, the God of all mankind. Is anything too hard for me?	638
Mt	16:15	he asked. "Who do you say **I am**?"	1609+1639
	28:20	And surely **I am** with you always, to the very end of the age."	1609+1639
Mk	8:29	he asked. "Who do you say **I am**?"	1609+1639
	14:62	"**I am,**" said Jesus. "And you will see the Son of Man sitting at the right hand	1609+1639
Jn	6:35	Jesus declared, "**I am** the bread of life.	1609+1639
	6:41	because he said, "**I am** the bread that came down from heaven."	1609+1639
	6:48	**I am** the bread of life.	1609+1639
	6:51	**I am** the living bread that came down from heaven.	1609+1639
	8:12	"**I am** the light of the world.	1609+1639
	8:24	if you do not believe that **I am** [the one I claim to be], you will indeed die in your sins."	1609+1639
	8:28	said, "When you have lifted up the Son of Man, then you will know that **I am**	1609+1639
	8:58	"before Abraham was born, **I am**!"	1609+1639
	9: 5	**I am** the light of the world."	1639
	10: 7	**I am** the gate for the sheep.	1609+1639
	10: 9	**I am** the gate; whoever enters through me will be saved.	1609+1639
	10:11	"**I am** the good shepherd.	1609+1639
	10:14	"**I am** the good shepherd;	1609+1639
	10:36	Why then do you accuse me of blasphemy because I said, '**I am** God's Son'?	1639
	11:25	Jesus said to her, "**I am** the resurrection and the life.	1609+1639
	13:19	so that when it does happen you will believe that **I am** He.	1609+1639
	14: 6	Jesus answered, "**I am** the way and the truth and the life.	1609+1639
	14:10	Don't you believe that **I am** in the Father, and that the Father is in me?	1609
	14:11	Believe me when I say that **I am** in the Father and the Father is in me;	1609
	14:20	On that day you will realize that **I am** in my Father,	1609
	14:20	and you are in me, and **I am** in you.	1609
	15: 1	"**I am** the true vine, and my Father is the gardener.	1609+1639
	15: 5	"**I am** the vine; you are the branches.	1609+1639
	18: 5	"Jesus of Nazareth," they replied. "**I am** he," Jesus said.	1609+1639
	18: 6	When Jesus said, "**I am** he," they drew back and fell to the ground.	1609+1639
	18: 8	"I told you that **I am** he," Jesus	1609+1639
Ac	9: 5	"**I am** Jesus, whom you are persecuting," he replied.	1609+1639
	18:10	For **I am** with you, and no one is going to attack and harm you,	1609+1639
	22: 8	" '**I am** Jesus of Nazareth, whom you are persecuting,' he replied.	1609+1639
	26:15	" '**I am** Jesus, whom you are persecuting,' the Lord replied.	1609+1639
Rev	1: 8	"**I am** the Alpha and the Omega," says the Lord God, "who is, and who was, and who is to come, the Almighty."	1609+1639
	1:17	"Do not be afraid. **I am** the First and the Last.	1609+1639
	1:18	I am the Living One; I was dead, and behold **I am** alive for ever and ever!	1639
	3:11	*I am* **coming** soon.	AIT
	21: 6	**I am** the Alpha and the Omega, the Beginning and the End.	1609+1639
	22: 7	"Behold, *I am* **coming** soon!	AIT
	22:12	"Behold, *I am* **coming** soon!	AIT
	22:13	**I am** the Alpha and the Omega, the First and the Last, the Beginning and the End.	1609
	22:16	**I am** the Root and the Offspring of David, and the bright Morning Star."	1609+1639
	22:20	He who testifies to these things says, "Yes, *I am* **coming** soon." Amen. Come, Lord Jesus.	AIT

I'LL (38) [I, WILL] See Index of Articles Etc.

I'M (24) [BE, I] See Index of Articles Etc.

I'VE (9) [HAVE, I]

Ge	30:26	You know how much work **I** done	3276
	31: 6	You know that **I worked for** your father	AIT
Ru	2:11	"**I** been told all about what you have done	3276
1Ki	22:34	**I been wounded.**"	AIT
2Ch	18:33	**I been wounded.**"	AIT
Job	19: 7	"Though I cry, 'I been wronged!'	NIH
Pr	30:20	'**I done** nothing wrong.'	AIT
Lk	13: 7	'For three years now *I been* **coming**	AIT
	15:29	All these years *I been* **slaving** for you	AIT

IBEX (1)

| Dt | 14: 5 | the **i,** the antelope and the mountain sheep. | 1913 |

IBHAR (3)

2Sa	5:15	**I,** Elishua, Nepheg, Japhia,	3295
1Ch	3: 6	There were also **I,** Elishua, Eliphelet,	3295
	14: 5	**I,** Elishua, Elpelet,	3295

IBLEAM (3)

Jos	17:11	I and the people of Dor, Endor,	3300
Jdg	1:27	of Beth Shan or Taanach or Dor or I	3300
2Ki	9:27	in his chariot on the way up to Gur near I,	3300

IBNEIAH (1)

1Ch	9: 8	I son of Jeroham;	3307

IBNIJAH (1)

1Ch	9: 8	the son of Reuel, the son of I.	3308

IBRI (1)

1Ch	24:27	Beno, Shoham, Zaccur and I.	6304

IBSAM (1)

1Ch	7: 2	Rephaiah, Jeriel, Jahmai, I and Samuel—	3311

IBZAN (3)

Jdg	12: 8	After him, I of Bethlehem led Israel.	83
	12: 9	I led Israel seven years.	NIH
	12:10	Then I died, and was buried in Bethlehem.	83

ICE (4) [ICY]

Job	6:16	when darkened by thawing i and swollen	7943
	37:10	The breath of God produces i,	7943
	38:29	From whose womb comes the i?	7943
Eze	1:22	sparkling like i, and awesome.	7943

ICHABOD (1) [ICHABOD'S]

1Sa	4:21	She named the boy I, saying,	376

ICHABOD'S (1) [ICHABOD]

1Sa	14: 3	a son of I brother Ahitub son of Phinehas,	376

ICONIUM (6)

Ac	13:51	in protest against them and went to I.	2658
	14: 1	At I Paul and Barnabas went as usual into	2658
	14:19	Then some Jews came from Antioch and I	2658
	14:21	they returned to Lystra, I and Antioch,	2658
	16: 2	The brothers at Lystra and I spoke well	2658
2Ti	3:11	I and Lystra, the persecutions I endured.	2658

ICY (1) [ICE]

Ps	147:17	Who can withstand his i blast?	7938

IDALAH (1)

Jos	19:15	Nahalal, Shimron, I and Bethlehem.	3339

IDBASH (1)

1Ch	4: 3	Jezreel, Ishma and I.	3340

IDDO (13) [IDDO'S]

1Ki	4:14	Ahinadab son of I—in Mahanaim;	6333
1Ch	6:21	I his son, Zerah his son	6341
	27:21	I son of Zechariah;	3346
2Ch	9:29	the Shilonite and in the visions of I the seer	3587
	12:15	of Shemaiah the prophet and of I the seer	6341
	13:22	in the annotations of the prophet I.	6341
Ezr	5: 1	Zechariah the prophet, a descendant of I,	10529
	6:14	Zechariah, a descendant of I.	10529
	8:17	and I sent them to I,	120
	8:17	to say to I and his kinsmen,	120
Ne	12: 4	I, Ginnethon, Abijah,	6342
Zec	1: 1	Zechariah son of Berekiah, the son of I:	6341
	1: 7	Zechariah son of Berekiah, the son of I.	6342

IDDO'S (1) [IDDO]

Ne	12:16	of I, Zechariah; of Ginnethon's,	6342

IDEA (8) [IDEAS]

Nu	16:28	and that it was not my i:	4213+4946
Dt	1:23	The i seemed good to me;	1821
Est	3: 6	he scorned the i of killing only Mordecai.	928+1022+6524
Jn	5:13	man who was healed had no i who it was,	3857
	8:14	But you have no i where I come from or	3857
	18:34	"Is that your own i," Jesus asked,	NIG
Ac	12: 9	but he had no i that what the angel was	3857
2Pe	2:13	Their i of pleasure is to carouse	2451

IDEAS (3) [IDEA]

Ac	17:20	You are bringing some strange i	AIT
	17:21	about and listening to the latest i.)	5516S
1Ti	6:20	from godless chatter and the opposing i	509

IDENTICAL (2)

1Ki	6:25	the two cherubim were i in size and shape.	285
	7:37	in the same molds and were i in size	285

IDLE (11) [IDLENESS, IDLERS]

Dt	32:47	They are not just i words for you—	8199
Job	11: 3	Will your i talk reduce men to silence?	966
Ecc	10:18	if his hands are i, the house leaks.	9170
	11: 6	at evening let not your hands be i,	5663
Isa	58:13	as you please or speaking i words,	NIH

Col	2:18	unspiritual mind puffs up with i notions.	1632
1Th	5:14	warn those who are i, encourage the timid,	864
2Th	3: 6	to keep away from every brother who is i	865
	3: 7	We were not i when we were with you,	863
	3:11	We hear that some among you are i.	865+4344
1Ti	5:13	they get into the habit of being i and going	734

IDLENESS (1) [IDLE]

Pr	31:27	and does not eat the bread of i.	6791

IDLERS (1) [IDLE]

1Ti	5:13	And not only do they become i,	734

IDOL (39) [CALF-IDOL, CALF-IDOLS, IDOL'S, IDOLATER, IDOLATERS, IDOLATRIES, IDOLATROUS, IDOLATRY, IDOLS]

Ex	20: 4	"You shall not make for yourself an i in	7181
	32: 4	and made it into an i cast in the shape of	5011
	32: 8	and have made themselves an i cast in	5011
Dt	4:16	and make for yourselves an i,	7181
	4:23	do not make for yourselves an i in the form	7181
	4:25	and make any kind of i,	7181
	5: 8	for yourself an i in the form of anything	7181
	9:12	and have made a cast i for themselves."	5011
	9:16	you had made for yourselves an i cast in	5011
	27:15	the man who carves an image or casts an i—	5011
Jdg	17: 3	to make a carved image and a cast i.	5011
	17: 4	who made them into the image and the i.	5011
	18:14	a carved image and a cast i?	5011
	18:17	the other household gods and the cast i	5011
	18:18	the other household gods and the cast i,	5011
1Sa	19:13	Michal took an i and laid it on the bed,	9572
	19:16	the men entered, there was the i in the bed,	9572
Ps	24: 4	up his soul to an i or swear by what is false.	8736
	106:19	a calf and worshiped an i cast from metal.	5011
Isa	40:19	As for an i, a craftsman casts it,	7181
	40:20	a skilled craftsman to set up an i that will	7181
	41: 7	He nails down the i so it will not topple.	2084S
	44:10	Who shapes a god and casts an i,	7181
	44:12	he shapes an i with hammers,	2084S
	44:15	he makes an i and bows down to it.	7181
	44:17	From the rest he makes a god, his i;	7181
	66: 3	like one who worships an i.	224
Eze	8: 3	where the i that provokes to jealousy stood.	6166
	8: 5	the gate of the altar I saw this i of jealousy.	6166
	8:12	each at the shrine of his own i?	5381
Hos	3: 4	without ephod or i,	9572
	4:12	They consult a wooden i and are answered	6770
	9:10	to that shameful i and became as vile as	1425
Hab	2:18	"Of what value is an i,	7181
Ac	7:41	the time they made an i in the form of	NIG
1Co	8: 4	that an i is nothing at all in the world and	1631
	8: 7	of it as having been sacrificed to an i,	NIG
	10:19	that a sacrifice offered to an i is anything,	1628
	10:19	or that an i is anything?	1631

IDOL'S (1) [IDOL]

1Co	8:10	eating in an i temple,	1627

IDOLATER (2) [IDOL]

1Co	5:11	immoral or greedy, an i or a slanderer,	1629
Eph	5: 5	or greedy person—such a man is an i—	1629

IDOLATERS (5) [IDOL]

1Co	5:10	or the greedy and swindlers, or i.	1629
	6: 9	the sexually immoral nor i nor adulterers	1629
	10: 7	Do not be i, as some of them were;	1629
Rev	21: 8	practice magic arts, the i and all liars—	1629
	22:15	the i and everyone who loves and	1629

IDOLATRIES (1) [IDOL]

Jer	14:14	i and the delusions of their own minds.	496

IDOLATROUS (3) [IDOL]

Jer	3:23	Surely the [i] commotion on the hills	NIH
Hos	10: 5	and so will its i priests,	4024
Zep	1: 4	the names of the pagan and the i priests—	3913

IDOLATRY (8) [IDOL]

1Sa	15:23	and arrogance like the evil of i.	9572
2Ki	9:22	"as long as all the i and witchcraft	2393
Eze	14: 4	in keeping with his great i.	1658
	23:49	and bear the consequences of your sins of i.	1658
1Co	10:14	Therefore, my dear friends, flee from i.	1630
Gal	5:20	i and witchcraft; hatred,	1630
Col	3: 5	lust, evil desires and greed, which is i.	1630
1Pe	4: 3	orgies, carousing and detestable i.	1630

IDOLS (173) [IDOL]

Ex	34:17	"Do not make cast i.	466
Lev	17: 7	offer any of their sacrifices to the goat i	8539
	19: 4	not turn to i or make gods of cast metal	496
	26: 1	" 'Do not make i or set up an image or	496
	26:30	on the lifeless forms of your i,	1658
Nu	33:52	carved images and their cast i,	7512
Dt	7: 5	down their Asherah poles and burn their i	7178
	12: 3	the i of their gods and wipe out their names	7178
	29:17	among them their detestable images and i	1658

Dt	32:16	and angered him with their detestable i.	9359
	32:21	and angered me with their worthless i.	2039
Jdg	3:19	At the i near Gilgal he himself turned back	7178
	3:26	He passed by the i and escaped to Seirah.	7178
	17: 5	and some i and installed one of his sons	9572
	18:30	the Danites set up for themselves the i,	7181
	18:31	to use the i Micah had made.	7181
1Sa	12:21	Do not turn away after useless i.	9332
	31: 9	to proclaim the news in the temple of their i	6773
2Sa	5:21	The Philistines abandoned their i there,	6773
1Ki	14: 9	other gods, i made of metal;	5011
	15:12	and got rid of all the i his fathers had made.	1658
	16:13	to anger by their worthless i.	2039
	16:26	to anger by their worthless i.	2039
	21:26	in the vilest manner by going after i,	1658
2Ki	11:18	and i to pieces and killed Mattan the priest	7512
	17:12	They worshiped i, though	1658
	17:15	They followed worthless i.	2039
	17:16	and made for themselves two i cast in	5011
	17:41	they were serving their i.	7178
	21:11	and has led Judah into sin with his i.	1658
	21:21	the i his father had worshiped,	1658
	22:17	i their hands have made,	5126
	23:24	the i and all the other detestable things seen	1658
1Ch	10: 9	the news among their i and their people.	6773
	16:26	For all the gods of the nations are i,	496
2Ch	11:15	and for the goat and calf i he had made.	8539
	15: 8	the detestable i from the whole land	9199
	23:17	the altars and i and killed Mattan the priest	7512
	24:18	and worshiped Asherah poles and i.	6773
	28: 2	also made cast i for worshiping the Baals.	5011
	33: 9	and i before he humbled himself—	7178
	33:22	to all the i Manasseh had made.	7178
	34: 3	Asherah poles, carved i and cast images.	7178
	34: 4	the i and the images.	7178
	34: 7	and the Asherah poles and crushed the i	7178
	34:33	Josiah removed all the detestable i	9359
Ps	31: 6	I hate those who cling to worthless i;	2039+8736
	78:58	they aroused his jealousy with their i.	7178
	96: 5	For all the gods of the nations are i,	496
	97: 7	those who boast in i—	496
	106:36	They worshiped their i,	6773
	106:38	whom they sacrificed to the i of Canaan,	6773
	115: 4	But their i are silver and gold,	6773
	135:15	The i of the nations are silver and gold,	6773
Isa	2: 8	Their land is full of i;	496
	2:18	and the i will totally disappear.	496
	2:20	and bats their i of silver and idols of gold,	496
	2:20	and bats their idols of silver and i of gold,	496
	10:10	As my hand seized the kingdoms of the i,	496
	10:11	as I dealt with Samaria and her i?' "	496
	19: 1	The i of Egypt tremble before him,	496
	19: 3	they will consult the i and the spirits of	496
	30:22	Then you will defile your i overlaid	7178
	31: 7	in that day every one of you will reject the i	496
	41:22	"Bring in [your i] to tell us what is going	NIH
	42: 8	to another or my praise to i.	7178
	42:17	But those who trust in i,	7181
	44: 9	All who make i are nothing,	7181
	45:16	All the makers of i will be put to shame	7497
	45:20	Ignorant are those who carry about i	7181
	46: 1	their i are borne by beasts of burden.	6773
	48: 5	so that you could not say, 'My i did them;	6777
	48:14	Which of [the i] has foretold these things?	2157S
	57: 6	[The i] among the smooth stones of	NIH
	57:13	let your collection [of i] save you!	NIH
Jer	2: 5	They followed worthless i	2039
	2: 8	following worthless i.	3603+4202
	2:11	But my people have exchanged their Glory for worthless i.	3603+4202
	4: 1	"If you put your detestable i out	9199
	7:30	They have set up their detestable i	9199
	8:19	with their worthless foreign i?"	2039
	10: 5	their i cannot speak;	2156S
	10: 8	they are taught by worthless wooden i.	2039
	10:14	every goldsmith is shamed by his i.	7181
	14:22	of the worthless i of the nations bring rain?	2039
	16:18	with their detestable i."	9359
	16:19	worthless i that did them no good.	2039
	18:15	they burn incense to worthless i,	8736
	32:34	They set up their abominable i in the house	9199
	50: 2	be put to shame and her i filled with terror.'	1658
	50:38	For it is a land of i,	7178
	50:38	i that will go mad with terror.	NIH
	51:17	every goldsmith is shamed by his i.	7181
	51:47	when I will punish the i of Babylon;	7178
	51:52	"when I will punish her i,	7178
Eze	5: 9	Because of all your detestable i.	9359
	6: 4	I will slay your people in front of your i.	1658
	6: 5	of the Israelites in front of their i,	1658
	6: 6	your i smashed and ruined,	1658
	6: 9	which have lusted after their i.	1658
	6:13	when their people lie slain among their i	1658
	6:13	fragrant incense to all their i.	1658
	7:20	to make their detestable i and vile images.	7512
	8:10	and detestable animals and all the i of	1658
	11:18	remove all its vile images and detestable i.	9359
	11:21	to their vile images and detestable i,	9359
	14: 3	these men have set up i in their hearts	1658
	14: 4	When any Israelite sets up i in his heart	1658
	14: 5	who have all deserted me for their i.'	1658
	14: 6	Turn from your i and renounce all your	1658
	14: 7	from me and sets up i in his heart and puts	1658
	16:17	and you made for yourself male i	7512
	16:20	to me and sacrificed them as food to the i.	2157S
	16:21	and sacrificed them to the i.	2157S
	16:36	and because of all your detestable i,	1658

Eze	18: 6	at the mountain shrines or look to the *i of*	1658
	18:12	He looks to the **i.**	1658
	18:15	at the mountain shrines or look to the *i of*	1658
	20: 7	not defile yourselves with the *i of* Egypt.	1658
	20: 8	nor did they forsake the *i of* Egypt.	1658
	20:16	For their hearts were devoted to their **i.**	1658
	20:18	or defile yourselves with their **i.**	1658
	20:24	and their eyes [lusted] after their fathers' **i.**	1658
	20:31	to defile yourselves with all your **i**	1658
	20:39	Go and serve your **i,** every one of you!	1658
	20:39	with your gifts and **i.**	1658
	21:21	he will consult his **i,**	9572
	22: 3	and defiles herself by making **i,**	1658
	22: 4	by the **i** you have made.	1658
	23: 7	with all the *i of* everyone she lusted after.	1658
	23:30	the nations and defiled yourself with their **i.**	1658
	23:37	They committed adultery with their **i;**	1658
	23:39	to their **i,** they entered my sanctuary	1658
	30:13	" 'I will destroy the **i** and put an end to	1658
	33:25	with the blood still in it and look to your **i**	1658
	36:18	and because they had defiled it with their **i.**	1658
	36:25	and from all your **i.**	1658
	37:23	with their **i** and vile images or with any	1658
	43: 7	by their prostitution and the **lifeless i**	7007
	43: 9	and the **lifeless** *i of* their kings,	7007
	44:10	after their **i** must bear the consequences	1658
	44:12	the presence of their **i** and made the house	1658
Hos	4:17	Ephraim is joined to **i;** leave him alone!	6773
	5:11	trampled in judgment, intent on pursuing **i.**	7417
	8: 4	With their silver and gold they make **i**	6773
	10: 6	Israel will be ashamed of its **wooden i.**	6785
	13: 2	they make **i** for themselves	5011
	14: 8	what more have I to do with **i?**	6773
Am	5:26	the pedestal of your **i,**	7512
Jnh	2: 8	to worthless **i** forfeit the grace that could	8736
Mic	1: 7	All her **i** will be broken to pieces;	7178
Na	1:14	I will destroy the carved images and **cast i**	5011
Hab	2:18	he makes **i** that cannot speak.	496
Zec	10: 2	The **i** speak deceit, diviners see visions	9572
	13: 2	I will banish the names of the **i** from	6773
Ac	7:43	the **i** you made to worship.	5596
	15:20	to abstain from food polluted *by* **i,**	1631
	15:29	to abstain from **food sacrificed to i,**	1628
	17:16	to see that the city was **full of i.**	2977
	21:25	from **food sacrificed to i,**	1628
Ro	2:22	You who abhor **i,** do you rob temples?	1631
1Co	8: 1	Now about **food sacrificed to i:**	1628
	8: 4	So then, about eating food **sacrificed to i:**	1628
	8: 7	to **i** that when they eat such food they think	1631
	8:10	to eat what *has been* **sacrificed to i?**	1628
	12: 2	and led astray to mute **i.**	1631
2Co	6:16	between the temple of God and **i?**	1631
1Th	1: 9	They tell how you turned to God from **i**	1631
1Jn	5:21	Dear children, keep yourselves from **i.**	1631
Rev	2:14	to sin by eating **food sacrificed to i** and	1628
	2:20	and the eating of **food sacrificed to i.**	1628
	9:20	and **i** of gold, silver, bronze,	1631
	9:20	**i** that cannot see or hear or walk.	*NIG*

IDUMEA (1)

Mk	3: 8	from Judea, Jerusalem, **I,** and the regions	*2628*

IEZER (1) [IEZERITE]

Nu	26:30	through **I,** the Iezerite clan;	404

IEZERITE (1) [IEZER]

Nu	26:30	through Iezer, the **I** clan;	405

IF (1784)

Ge	4: 7	**I** you do what is right,	561
	4: 7	But **i** you do not do what is right,	561
	4:15	**i** anyone kills Cain, he will suffer vengeance	NIH
	4:24	**i** Cain is avenged seven times,	3954
	8: 8	a dove to see **i** the water had receded from	2022
	11: 6	"I as one people speaking	2176
	13: 9	**I** you go to the left, I'll go to the right;	561
	13: 9	**i** you go to the right, I'll go to the left."	561
	13:16	so that anyone could count the dust,	561
	15: 5	**i indeed** you can count them."	561
	17:18	"I only Ishmael might live under your	4273
	18: 3	He said, "I I have found favor in your eyes,	561
	18:21	and see **i** what they have done is as bad as	2022
	18:21	**I** not, I will know."	561
	18:24	**What i** there are fifty righteous people in	218
	18:26	"I I find fifty righteous people in the city	561
	18:28	**what i** the number of	218
	18:28	"I I find forty-five there," he said,	561
	18:29	**What i** only forty are found there?"	218
	18:30	**What i** only thirty can be found there?"	218
	18:30	"I will not do it **i** I find thirty there."	561
	18:31	**what i** only twenty can be found there?"	218
	18:32	**What i** only ten can be found there?"	218
	20: 7	But **i** you do not return her,	561
	23: 8	"I you are willing to let me bury my dead,	561
	23:13	"Listen to me, **i** you will.	561
	24: 5	"What **i** the woman is unwilling	218
	24: 8	**I** the woman is unwilling to come back	561
	24:39	'What **i** the woman will not come back	218
	24:41	be released from your oath even **i** they refuse	561
	24:42	God of my master Abraham, **i** you will,	561
	24:43	**i** a maiden comes out to draw water	NIH
	24:44	and **i** she says to me,	NIH
	24:49	Now **i** you will show kindness	561
	24:49	and **i** not, tell me, so I may know	561

Ge	27:12	**What i** my father touches me?	218
	27:46	**I** Jacob takes a wife from among	561
	28:20	"I God will be with me and will watch	561
	30:27	"I I have found favor in your eyes,	561
	30:31	"But **i** you will do this one thing for me,	561
	30:42	but **i** the animals were weak,	928
	31: 8	**I** he said, 'The speckled ones will	561+3907
	31: 8	and **i** he said, 'The streaked ones will	561+3907
	31:32	But **i** you find anyone who has your gods,	NIH
	31:32	and **i** so, take it."	NIH
	31:42	**I** the God of my father, the God of	
		Abraham and the Fear of Isaac, had **not**	4295
	31:50	**I** you mistreat my daughters or	561
	31:50	If you mistreat my daughters or **i**	561
	32: 8	"I Esau comes and attacks one group,	561
	33:10	"I I have found favor in your eyes,	561
	33:13	**i** they are driven hard just one day,	2256
	34:17	But **i** you will not agree to be circumcised,	561
	34:30	and **i** they **join forces** against me	AIT
	37:14	"Go and see **i** all is well with your brothers	561
	37:26	"What will we gain **i** we kill our brother	3954
	38:25	"See **i** you **recognize** whose seal and cord	AIT
	42:16	be tested to see **i** you are telling the truth.	2022
	42:16	**I** you are not,	561
	42:19	**I** you are honest men,	561
	42:37	to death **i** I do not bring him back to you.	561
	42:38	**I** harm comes to him on	2256
	43: 4	**I** you will send our brother along with us,	561
	43: 5	But **i** you will not send him,	561
	43: 9	**I** I do not bring him back to you	561
	43:10	As it is, **i** we had **not** delayed,	3954+4295
	43:11	"I it must be, then do this:	561
	43:14	**i** I am bereaved, I am bereaved."	889+3869
	44: 9	**I** any of your servants is found to have it,	NIH
	44:22	**i** he leaves him, his father will die.'	2256
	44:26	**Only i** our youngest brother is	561
	44:29	**I** you take this one from me too	2256
	44:30	**i** the boy is not with us when I go back	2256
	44:30	to your servant my father and **i** my father,	NIH
	44:32	I said, 'I I do not bring him back to you,	561
	44:34	How can I go back to my father **i** the boy is	2256
	47: 6	And **i** you know of any among them	561
	47:29	"I I have found favor in your eyes,	561
	50: 4	"I I have found favor in your eyes,	561
	50:15	"What **i** Joseph holds a grudge against us	4273
Ex	1:10	**i** war breaks out, will join our enemies,	3954
	1:16	**i** it is a boy, kill him;	561
	1:16	but **i** it is a girl, let her live."	561
	4: 1	"What **i** they do not believe me or listen	2176
	4: 8	"I they do not believe you or pay attention	561
	4: 9	But **i** they do not believe these two signs	561
	4:16	and it will be **as i** he were your mouth and	4200
	4:16	be as if he were your mouth and **as i**	4200
	4:18	to my own people in Egypt to see **i** any	2022
	6:12	"I the Israelites will not listen to me,	2176
	8: 2	**I** you refuse to let them go,	561
	8:21	**I** you do not let my people go,	561+3954
	8:26	And **i** we offer sacrifices that are detestable	2176
	9: 2	**I** you refuse to let them go and continue	561+3954
	10: 4	**I** you refuse to let them go,	561+3954
	10:10	**i** I let you go, along with your women	889+3869
	12: 4	**I** any household is too small for a whole	561
	12:10	**i** some is left till morning, you must burn it.	2256
	13:13	but **i** you do not redeem it, break its neck.	561
	13:17	For God said, "I they face war,	928
	15:26	"I you listen carefully to the voice of	561
	15:26	**i** you pay attention to his commands	2256
	16: 3	"I only we had died by the LORD's hand	4769+5989
	18:23	**I** you do this and God so commands,	561
	19: 5	Now **i** you obey me fully	561
	20:25	**I** you make an altar of stones for me,	561
	20:25	for you will defile it **i** you use a tool on it.	NIH
	21: 2	"I you buy a Hebrew servant,	3954
	21: 3	**I** he comes alone, he is to go free alone;	561
	21: 3	but **i** he has a wife when he comes,	561
	21: 4	**I** his master gives him a wife	561
	21: 5	"But **i** the servant declares,	561
	21: 7	"I a man sells his daughter as a servant,	3954
	21: 8	**I** she does not please	561
	21: 9	**I** he selects her for his son,	561
	21:10	**I** he marries another woman,	561
	21:11	**I** he does not provide her with these three	561
	21:13	However, **i** he does not do it intentionally,	NIH
	21:14	But **i** a man schemes and kills another	3954
	21:18	"I men quarrel and one hits the other with	3954
	21:19	not be held responsible **i** the other gets up	561
	21:20	"I a man beats his male or female slave	3954
	21:21	but he is not to be punished **i** the slave gets	561
	21:22	"I men who are fighting hit a pregnant	3954
	21:23	But **i** there is serious injury,	561
	21:26	"I a man hits a manservant or maidservant	3954
	21:27	And **i** he knocks out the tooth of	561
	21:28	"I a bull gores a man or a woman to death,	3954
	21:29	**I,** however, the bull has had the habit	561
	21:30	However, **i** payment is demanded of him,	561
	21:31	This law also applies **i** the bull gores a son	196
	21:32	**I** the bull gores a male or female slave,	561
	21:33	"I a man uncovers a pit or digs one	3954
	21:35	"I a man's bull injures the bull of another	3954
	21:36	**i** it was known that the bull had the habit	196
	22: 1	"I a man steals an ox or a sheep	3954
	22: 2	"I a thief is caught breaking in and is struck	561
	22: 3	but **i** it happens after sunrise,	561
	22: 3	but **i** he has nothing,	561
	22: 4	"I the stolen animal is found alive	561
	22: 5	"I a man grazes his livestock in a field	3954

Ex	22: 6	"I a fire breaks out and spreads	3954
	22: 7	"I a man gives his neighbor silver or goods	3954
	22: 7	**i** he is caught, must pay back double.	561
	22: 8	But **i** the thief is not found,	561
	22:10	"I a man gives a donkey, an ox,	3954
	22:12	**i** the animal was stolen from the neighbor,	561
	22:13	**I** it was torn to pieces by a wild animal,	561
	22:14	"I a man borrows an animal	3954
	22:15	But **i** the owner is with the animal,	561
	22:15	**I** the animal was hired,	561
	22:16	"I a man seduces a virgin who is not	3954
	22:17	**I** her father absolutely refuses to give her	561
	22:23	**I** you do and they cry out to me,	561
	22:25	"I you lend money to one of my people	561
	22:26	**I** you take your neighbor's cloak as	561
	23: 4	"I you come across your enemy's ox	3954
	23: 5	**I** you see the donkey of someone	561
	23:22	**I** you listen carefully to what he says	561+3954
	29:34	And **i** any of the meat of the ordination ram	561
	32:32	but **i** not, then blot me out of the book	561
	33: 5	**I** *I were to go* with you even for a moment	AIT
	33:13	**I** you are pleased with me,	561
	33:15	"I your Presence does not go with us,	561
	34: 9	**i** I have found favor in your eyes," he said,	561
	34:20	but **i** you do not redeem it, break its neck.	561
	40:37	but **i** the cloud did not lift, they did	561
Lev	1: 3	" 'I the offering is a burnt offering from	561
	1:10	" 'I the offering is a burnt offering from	561
	1:14	" 'I the offering to the LORD is	561
	2: 4	" 'I you bring a grain offering baked in	3954
	2: 5	**I** your grain offering is prepared on	561
	2: 7	**I** your grain offering is cooked in a pan,	561
	2:14	" 'I you bring a grain offering of firstfruits	3954
	3: 1	" 'I someone's offering is a fellowship	561
	3: 6	" 'I he offers an animal from the flock as	561
	3: 7	**I** he offers a lamb,	561
	3:12	" 'I his offering is a goat,	561
	4: 3	" 'I the anointed priest sins,	561
	4:13	" 'I the whole Israelite community sins	
		unintentionally	561
	4:27	" 'I a member of the community sins	
		unintentionally	561
	4:32	" 'I he brings a lamb as his sin offering,	561
	5: 1	" 'I a person sins because he does	3954
	5: 2	" 'Or **i** a person touches anything	
		ceremonially unclean—	889
	5: 3	" 'Or **i** he touches human uncleanness—	3954
	5: 4	" 'Or **i** a person thoughtlessly takes an oath	3954
	5: 7	" 'I he cannot afford a lamb,	561
	5:11	" 'I, however, he cannot afford two doves	561
	5:17	" 'I a person sins and does what is forbidden	561
	6: 2	" 'I anyone sins and is unfaithful to	3954
	6: 2	or **i** he cheats him,	NIH
	6: 3	or **i** he finds lost property and lies about it,	NIH
	6: 3	or **i** he swears falsely,	NIH
	6: 3	or **i** he commits any such sin	NIH
	6:27	and **i** any of the blood is spattered on	889
	6:28	but **i** it is cooked in a bronze pot,	561
	7:12	" 'I he offers it as an expression	561
	7:16	" 'I, however, his offering is the result of	561
	7:18	**I** any meat of the fellowship offering	561
	7:20	But **i** anyone who is unclean eats any meat	NIH
	7:21	**I** anyone touches something unclean—	3954
	7:27	**I** anyone eats blood,	NIH
	10:19	**i** I had eaten the sin offering today?"	2256
	11:33	**I** one of them falls into a clay pot,	2256
	11:37	**I** a carcass falls on any seeds that are to	3954
	11:38	But **i** water has been put on the seed and	3954
	11:39	" 'I an animal that you are allowed	3954
	12: 5	**I** she gives birth to a daughter,	561
	12: 8	**I** she cannot afford a lamb,	561
	13: 3	and **i** the hair in the sore has turned white	NIH
	13: 4	**I** the spot on his skin is white but does	561
	13: 5	and **i** he sees that the sore is unchanged	2180
	13: 6	and **i** the sore has faded and has not spread	2180
	13: 7	But **i** the rash does spread in his skin,	561
	13: 8	and **i** the rash has spread in the skin,	2180
	13: 9	and **i** there is a white swelling in the skin	2180
	13:10	the skin that has turned the hair white and **i**	NIH
	13:12	"I the disease breaks out all over his skin	561
	13:13	**i** the disease has covered his whole body,	2180
	13:17	and **i** the sores have turned white,	2180
	13:20	and **i** it appears to be more than skin deep	2180
	13:21	But **i,** when the priest examines it,	561
	13:22	**I** it is spreading in the skin,	561
	13:23	**i** the spot is unchanged and has not spread,	561
	13:25	and **i** the hair in it has turned white,	2180
	13:26	But **i** the priest examines it	561
	13:27	the spot and **i** it is not more than skin deep	NIH
	13:27	and **i** it is spreading in the skin,	561
	13:28	**I,** however, the spot is unchanged and has	561
	13:29	"I a man or woman has a sore on the head	3954
	13:30	and **i** it appears to be more than skin deep	2180
	13:31	But **i,** when the priest examines this kind	NIH
	13:32	and **i** the itch has not spread	2180
	13:34	and **i** it has not spread in the skin,	2180
	13:35	But **i** the itch does spread in the skin	561
	13:36	and **i** the itch has spread in the skin,	561
	13:37	**I,** however, in his judgment it is unchanged	561
	13:39	and **i** the spots are dull white,	2180
	13:41	**I** he has lost his hair from the front	561
	13:42	But **i** he has a reddish-white sore	3954
	13:43	and **i** the swollen sore on his head	2180
	13:47	"I any clothing is contaminated	3954
	13:49	and **i** the contamination in the clothing,	NIH
	13:51	and **i** the mildew has spread in the clothing,	3954
	13:53	"But **i,** when the priest examines it,	561

Lev 13:55	and i the mildew has not changed	2180	
13:56	I, when the priest examines it,	561	
13:57	But i it reappears in the clothing,	561	
14: 3	I the person has been healed	2180	
14:21	"I, however, he is poor	561	
14:37	and i it has greenish or reddish depressions	2180	
14:39	I the mildew has spread on the walls,	2180	
14:43	"I the mildew reappears in the house after	561	
14:44	i the mildew has spread in the house,	2180	
14:48	"But i the priest comes to examine it and	561	
15: 8	"I the man with the discharge spits	3954	
15:24	I a man lies with her	561	
17:16	But i he does not wash his clothes	561	
18:28	And i you defile the land,	928	
19: 7	I any of it is eaten on the third day,	561	
19:20	"'I a man sleeps with a woman who is	3954	
20: 4	I the people of the community close their	561	
20: 9	"'I anyone curses his father or mother,	3954	
20:10	"'I a man commits adultery	2256	
20:11	"'I a man sleeps with his father's wife,	2256	
20:12	"'I a man sleeps with his daughter-in-law,	2256	
20:13	"'I a man lies with a man as one lies with	2256	
20:14	"'I a man marries both a woman	2256	
20:15	"'I a man has sexual relations with	2256	
20:16	"'I a woman approaches an animal	2256	
20:17	"'I a man marries his sister,	2256	
20:18	"'I a man lies with a woman	2256	
20:20	"'I a man sleeps with his aunt,	2256	
20:21	"'I a man marries his brother's wife,	2256	
21: 9	"'I a priest's daughter defiles herself	3954	
22: 3	'For the generations to come, i any	889	
22: 4	"'I a descendant of Aaron has	NIH	
22: 4	be unclean i he touches something defiled	NIH	
22: 5	or i he touches any crawling thing	NIH	
22:11	But i a priest buys a slave with money,	3954	
22:11	or i a slave is born in his household,	NIH	
22:12	I a priest's daughter marries anyone other than a priest,	3954	
22:13	But i a priest's daughter becomes a widow	3954	
22:14	"'I anyone eats a sacred offering	3954	
22:18	'I any of you—either a Israelite or an alien	889	
22:15	I anyone curses his God,	3954	
22:17	"'I anyone takes the life of a human being,	3954	
24:19	I anyone injures his neighbor,	3954	
25:14	"'I you sell land to one of your countrymen	3954	
25:20	"What will we eat in the seventh year i	2176	
25:25	"'I one of your countrymen becomes poor	3954	
25:26	I, however, a man has no one to redeem it	3954	
25:28	But i he does not acquire the means	561	
25:29	"'I a man sells a house in a walled city,	3954	
25:30	I it is not redeemed before a full year	561	
25:35	"'I one of your countrymen becomes poor	3954	
25:39	"'I one of your countrymen becomes poor	3954	
25:47	"'I an alien or a temporary resident	3954	
25:49	Or i he prospers, he may redeem himself.	NIH	
25:51	I many years remain,	561	
25:52	I only a few years remain until the Year	561	
25:54	i he is not redeemed in any of these ways,	561	
26: 3	"'I you follow my decrees and are careful	561	
26:14	"'But i you will not listen to me	561	
26:15	and i you reject my decrees	561	
26:18	"'I after all this you will not listen to me,	561	
26:21	"'I you remain hostile toward me	561	
26:23	"'I in spite of these things you do	561	
26:27	"'I in spite of this you still do not listen	561	
26:40	"'But i they will confess their sins and	NIH	
27: 2	'I anyone makes a special vow	3954	
27: 4	and i it is a female,	561	
27: 5	I it is a person between the ages of five	561	
27: 6	I it is a person between one month	561	
27: 7	I it is a person sixty years old or more,	561	
27: 8	I anyone making the vow is too poor to pay	561	
27: 9	"'I what he vowed is an animal	561	
27:10	i he should substitute one animal	561	
27:11	I what he vowed is	561	
27:13	I the owner wishes to redeem the animal,	561	
27:14	"'I a man dedicates his house	3954	
27:15	I the man who dedicates his house redeems	561	
27:16	"'I a man dedicates to the LORD part	561	
27:17	I he dedicates his field during the Year	561	
27:18	But i he dedicates his field after the Jubilee,	561	
27:19	I the man who dedicates the field wishes	561	
27:20	I, however, he does not redeem the field,	561	
27:20	or i he has sold it to someone else,	561	
27:22	"'I a man dedicates to the LORD	561	
27:27	I it is one of the unclean animals,	561	
27:27	I he does not redeem it,	561	
27:31	I a man redeems any of his tithe,	561	
27:33	I he does make a substitution.	561	
Nu 5: 8	But i that person has no close relative	561	
5:12	'I a man's wife goes astray	3954	
5:14	and i feelings of jealousy come	NIH	
5:14	or i he is jealous and suspects her even	NIH	
5:19	"I no other man has slept with you	561	
5:20	But i you have gone astray while married	3954	
5:27	I she has defiled herself	561	
5:28	I, however, the woman has	561	
6: 2	'I a man or woman wants to make	3954	
6: 7	Even i his own father or mother or brother	928	
6: 9	"'I someone dies suddenly in his presence,	3954	
9:13	But i a man who is ceremonially clean and	NIH	
10: 4	I only one is sounded, the leaders	561	
10:32	I you come with us,	3954	
11: 4	"I only we had meat to eat!	4769	
11:15	I this is how you are going to treat me,	561	
11:15	i I have found favor in your eyes—	561	
11:18	"I only we had meat to eat!"	4769	

Nu 11:22	Would they have enough i flocks	2022	
11:22	Would they have enough i all the fish in	561	
12:14	"I her father had spit in her face,	2256	
14: 2	"I only we had died in Egypt!	4273	
14: 8	I the LORD is pleased with us,	561	
14:15	I you put these people to death all	2256	
15:22	"'Now i you unintentionally fail	3954	
15:24	and i this is done unintentionally without	561	
15:27	I just one person sins unintentionally,	561	
16:29	I these men die a natural death	561	
16:30	But i the LORD brings about something	561	
19:12	But i he does not purify himself on	561	
19:20	But i a person who is unclean does	2256	
20: 3	"I only we had died	561	
20:18	i you try, we will march out and attack you	7153	
20:19	"We will go along the main road, and i we	561	
21: 2	"I you will deliver these people	561	
22:18	"Even i Balak gave me his palace filled	561	
22:29	I I had a sword in my hand,	4273	
22:33	I she had not turned away,	218	
22:34	Now i you are displeased, I will go back."	561	
22:37	'Even i Balak gave me his palace filled	561	
27: 8	'I a man dies and leaves no son,	3954	
27: 9	I he has no daughter,	561	
27:10	I he has no brothers,	561	
27:11	I his father had no brothers,	561	
30: 5	I her father forbids her when he hears	561	
30: 6	"I she marries after she makes a vow or	561	
30: 8	But i her husband forbids her	561	
30:10	"I a woman living with her husband makes	561	
30:12	But i her husband nullifies them	561	
30:14	But i her husband says nothing to her	561	
30:15	I, however, he nullifies them some time	561	
32: 5	I we have found favor in your eyes,"	561	
32:15	I you turn away from following him,	3954	
32:20	Moses said to them, "I you will do this—	561	
32:20	i you will arm yourselves before	561	
32:21	and i all of you go armed over	NIH	
32:23	"But i you fail to do this,	561	
32:29	"I the Gadites and Reubenites,	561	
32:30	i they do not cross over with you armed,	561	
33:55	"'But i you do not drive out the inhabitants	561	
35:16	"I a man strikes someone with	561	
35:17	Or i anyone has a stone in his hand	561	
35:18	Or i anyone has a wooden object	NIH	
35:20	I anyone with malice aforethought shoves	561	
35:21	or i in hostility he hits him with his fist so	NIH	
35:22	"'But i without hostility	561	
35:26	"'But i the accused ever goes outside	561	
Dt 4:25	i you then become corrupt	2256	
4:29	But i from there you seek the LORD	NIH	
4:29	you will find him i you look for him	3954	
4:42	a person could flee i he had unintentionally	NIH	
5:24	a man can live even i God speaks with him.	NIH	
5:25	and we will die i we hear the voice of	561	
6:25	And i we are careful to obey all this law	3954	
7:12	I you pay attention to these laws	6813	
8:19	I you ever forget the LORD your God	561	
11:13	So i you faithfully obey	561	
11:22	I you carefully observe all these commands	561	
11:27	the blessing i you obey the commands of	889	
11:28	the curse i you disobey the commands of	561	
12:15	as i it were gazelle or deer,	3869	
12:21	the place where the LORD your God	3954	
13: 1	I a prophet, or one who foretells	3954	
13: 2	and i the sign or wonder	NIH	
13: 6	I your very own brother,	3954	
13:12	I you hear it said about one of the towns	3954	
13:14	And i it is true and it has been proved	2180	
14:24	But i that place is too distant	3954	
15: 5	i only you fully obey the LORD your God	561	
15: 7	I there is a poor man among your brothers	3954	
15:12	I a fellow Hebrew, a man or a woman,	3954	
15:16	But i your servant says to you,	3954	
15:21	I an animal has a defect, is lame or blind,	3954	
15:22	as i it were gazelle or deer.	3869	
17: 2	I a man or woman living among you in one	3954	
17: 4	I it is true and it has been proved	2180	
17: 8	I cases come before your courts	3954	
18: 6	I a Levite moves from one of your towns	3954	
18:19	I anyone does not listen to my words that	889	
18:22	I what a prophet proclaims in the name of	2256	
19: 6	overtake him i the distance is too great,	3954	
19: 8	I the LORD your God enlarges your territory,	561	
19:11	But i a man hates his neighbor and lies	3954	
19:16	I a malicious witness takes the stand	3954	
19:18	and i the witness proves to be a liar,	2180	
20:11	I they accept and open their gates,	561	
20:12	I they refuse to make peace	561	
21: 1	I a man is found slain,	3954	
21:11	i you notice among the captives	2256	
21:14	I you are not pleased with her,	561	
21:15	I a man has two wives,	3954	
21:18	I a man has a stubborn and rebellious son	3954	
21:22	I a man guilty of a capital offense is put	3954	
22: 1	I you see your brother's ox	NIH	
22: 2	I the brother does not live near you or	561	
22: 2	near you or i you do not know who he is,	NIH	
22: 3	the same i you find your brother's donkey	NIH	
22: 3	I you see your brother's donkey	NIH	
22: 6	I you come across a bird's nest beside	3954	
22: 8	of bloodshed on your house i someone falls	3954	
22: 9	i you do, not only the crops you plant but	7153	
22:13	I a man takes a wife and, after lying with	3954	
22:20	I, however, the charge is true and no proof	561	
22:22	I a man is found sleeping with another	3954	
22:23	I a man happens to meet in a town	3954	

Dt 22:25	But i out in the country a man happens	561	
22:28	I a man happens to meet a virgin who is	3954	
23:10	I one of your men is unclean because of	3954	
23:15	I a slave has taken refuge with you,	889	
23:21	I you make a vow to the LORD your God,	3954	
23:22	But i you refrain from making a vow,	3954	
23:24	I you enter your neighbor's vineyard,	3954	
23:25	I you enter your neighbor's grainfield,	3954	
24: 1	I a man marries a woman who becomes	3954	
24: 2	i after she leaves his house she becomes the wife of another	NIH	
24: 3	sends her from his house, or i he dies,	3954	
24: 5	I a man has recently married,	3954	
24: 7	I a man is caught kidnapping one	3954	
24:12	I the man is poor,	561	
25: 2	I the guilty man deserves to be beaten,	561	
25: 3	I he is flogged more than that,	7153	
25: 5	I brothers are living together and one	3954	
25: 7	I a man does not want to marry his brother's	561	
25: 8	I he persists in saying,	2256	
25:11	I two men are fighting and the wife of one	3954	
28: 1	I you fully obey the LORD your God	561	
28: 2	upon you and accompany you i you obey	3954	
28: 9	i you keep the commands of	3954	
28:13	I you pay attention to the commands of	3954	
28:15	i you do not obey the LORD your God	561	
28:58	I you do not carefully follow all the words	561	
28:67	"I only it were evening!"	4769+5989	
28:67	"I only it were morning!"—	4769+5989	
30: 4	Even i you have been banished to	561	
30:10	i you obey the LORD your God	3954	
30:17	But i your heart turns away and you are	561	
30:17	and i you are drawn away to bow down	NIH	
31:27	I you have been rebellious against	2176	
32:29	I only they were wise and would understand	4273	
Jos 2:14	"I you don't tell what we are doing,	561	
2:19	I anyone goes outside your house into	889	
2:19	be on our head i a hand is laid on him.	561	
2:20	But i you tell what we are doing,	561	
7: 7	I only we had been content to stay on	4273	
17:15	"I you are so numerous," Joshua answered,	561	
17:15	"and i the hill country of Ephraim is too	3954	
20: 5	I the avenger of blood pursues him,	3954	
22:18	"'I you rebel against the LORD today,	2256	
22:19	I the land you possess is defiled,	561	
22:22	I this has been in rebellion or disobedience	561	
22:23	I we have built our own altar to turn away	561	
22:28	"And we said, 'I they ever say this to us,	3954	
23:12	"But i you turn away and ally yourselves	561	
23:12	among you and i you intermarry with them	NIH	
23:16	I you violate the covenant of the LORD	928	
24:15	But i serving the LORD seems undesirable	561	
24:20	I you forsake the LORD and serve foreign	3954	
24:27	against you i you are untrue to your God."	7153	
Jdg 4: 8	Barak said to her, "I you go with me,	561	
4: 8	but i you don't go with me, I won't go."	561	
4:20	"I someone comes by and asks you,	561	
6:13	Gideon replied, "i the LORD is with us,	2256	
6:17	"I now I have found favor in your eyes,	561	
6:31	I Baal really is a god,	561	
6:36	"I you will save Israel by my hand	561	
6:37	I there is dew only on the fleece and all	561	
7: 4	I I say, 'This one shall go with you,'	889	
7: 4	but i I say, 'This one shall not go with you,'	889	
7:10	I you are afraid to attack,	561	
8:19	LORD lives, i you had spared their lives,	4273	
9:15	'I you really want to anoint me king	561	
9:15	but i not, then let fire come out of	561	
9:16	"Now i you have acted honorably and	561	
9:16	and i you have been fair to Jerub-Baal	561	
9:16	i you have treated him as he deserves—	561	
9:19	i then you have acted honorably and	561	
9:20	But i you have not, let fire come out	561	
9:29	I only this people were under my	4769+5989	
11:30	"I you give the Ammonites into my hands,	561	
12: 5	"Are you an Ephraimite?" He replied,	2256	
12: 6	I he said, "Sibboleth,"	2256	
13:16	But i you prepare a burnt offering,	561	
13:23	"I the LORD had meant to kill us,	4273	
14:12	"I you can give me the answer within	561	
14:12	I you can't tell me the answer,	561	
14:18	"I you had not plowed with my heifer,	4295	
16: 5	"See i you can lure him into showing	AIT	
16: 7	"I anyone ties me with seven fresh thongs	561	
16:11	"I anyone ties me securely with new ropes	561	
16:12	But he snapped the ropes off his arms as i	3869	
16:13	"I you weave the seven braids of my head	561	
16:17	I my head were shaved,	561	
Ru 1:12	Even i I thought there was still hope	3954	
1:12	even i I had a husband tonight and	NIH	
1:17	i anything but death separates you	3954	
2:15	"Even i she gathers among the sheaves,	1685	
3:13	and in the morning i he wants to redeem,	561	
3:13	But i he is not willing,	561	
4: 4	I you will redeem it, do so.	561	
4: 4	But i you will not, tell me, so I will know.	561	
1Sa 1:11	i you will only look upon your servant's	561	
2:16	I the man said to him,	2256	
2:16	i you don't, I'll take it by force."	561	
2:25	I a man sins against another man,	561	
2:25	but i a man sins against the LORD,	561	
3: 9	"Go and lie down, and i he calls you, say,	561	
3:17	i you hide from me anything he told you."	561	
6: 3	"I you return the ark of the god of Israel,	561	
6: 9	I it goes up to its own territory,	561	
6: 9	But i it does not, then we will know that	561	
7: 3	"I you are returning to the LORD	561	

1Sa	9: 7	Saul said to his servant, "**I** we go,	2180
	9: 9	**i** a man went to inquire of God,	928
	9:20	**i** not to you and all your father's family?"	2022
	11: 3	**i** no one comes to rescue us,	561
	12: 3	**I** I have done any of these,	NIH
	12:14	**I** you fear the LORD and serve	561
	12:14	and **i** both you and the king who reigns	NIH
	12:15	But **i** you do not obey the LORD,	561
	12:15	and **i** you rebel against his commands,	NIH
	12:25	Yet **i** you persist in doing evil,	561
	13:13	not kept the command the LORD your God	
		gave you; **i** you had,	3954
	14: 9	**I** they say to us, 'Wait there	561
	14:10	But **i** they say, 'Come up to us,'	561
	14:30	How much better it would have been **i**	4273
	14:39	even **i** it lies with my son Jonathan,	561
	14:44	be it ever so severely, **i** you do **not** die,	3954
	17: 9	**I** he is able to fight and kill me,	561
	17: 9	but **i** I overcome him and kill him,	561
	19:11	"**I** you don't run for your life tonight,	561
	20: 6	**I** your father misses me at all, tell him,	561
	20: 7	**I** he says, 'Very well,'	561
	20: 7	But **i** he loses his temper,	561
	20: 8	**I** I am guilty, then kill me yourself!	561
	20: 9	"**I** I had the least inkling	561+3954
	20:10	"Who will tell me **i** your father answers	196+4537
	20:12	**I** he is favorably disposed toward you,	2180
	20:13	But **i** my father is inclined to harm you,	3954
	20:13	**i** I do not let you know	2256
	20:21	**I** I say to him, 'Look,	561
	20:22	But **i** I say to the boy, 'Look,	561
	20:29	**I** I have found favor in your eyes,	561
	21: 9	**I** you want it, take it,'	561
	23: 3	**i** we go to Keilah against the Philistine	3954
	23:23	Then I will go with you; **i** he is in the area,	561
	25:22	**i** by morning I leave alive one male	561
	25:34	**i** you had **not** come quickly to meet	3954+4295
	26:19	The LORD has incited you against me,	561
	26:19	**I**, however, men have done it,	561
	27: 5	"**I** I have found favor in your eyes,	561
2Sa	2:27	**i** you had **not** spoken,	3954+4295
	3: 9	**i** I do not do for David what	3954
	3:35	**i** I taste bread or anything else	561+3954
	4: 6	of the house as **i** to get some wheat,	NIH
	7:19	And as **i** this were not enough in your sight,	NIH
	10:11	"**I** the Arameans are too strong for me,	561
	10:11	but **i** the Ammonites are too strong for you,	561
	11:21	**I** he asks you this, then say to him, 'Also,	NIH
	12: 8	And **i** all this had been too little,	561
	13:26	Then Absalom said, "**I** not,	2256
	14:10	"**I** anyone says anything to you,	561
	14:32	be better for me **i** I were still there!" '	NIH
	14:32	and **i** I am guilty of anything,	561
	15: 4	"**I** only I were appointed judge in	4769
	15: 8	'**I** the LORD takes me back to Jerusalem,	561
	15:25	**I** I find favor in the LORD's eyes,	561
	15:26	But **i** he says, 'I am not pleased with you,'	561
	15:33	David said to him, "**I** you go with me,	561
	15:34	**i** you return to the city and say to Absalom,	561
	16:10	**I** he is cursing because the LORD said	3954
	17: 6	**I** not, give us your opinion."	561
	17: 9	**I** he should attack your troops first,	3869
	17:13	**I** he withdraws into a city,	561
	18: 3	**i** we are forced to flee,	561+3954
	18: 3	Even **i** half of us die, they won't care;	561
	18:12	But the man replied, "Even **i**	4273
	18:13	And **i** I had put my life in jeopardy—	196
	18:25	The king said, "**I** he is alone,	561
	18:33	**I** only I had died instead of you—	4769+5989
	19: 6	be pleased **i** Absalom were alive today	4273
	19: 7	by the LORD that **i** you don't go out,	3954
	19: 7	**i** from now on you are not the commander	561
1Ki	1:52	"**I** he shows himself to be a worthy man,	561
	1:52	but **i** evil is found in him, he will die."	561
	2: 4	'**I** your descendants watch how they live,	561
	2: 4	how they live, and **i** they walk faithfully	NIH
	2: 5	shedding their **blood** in peacetime as **i**	AIT
	2:23	be it ever so severely, **i** Adonijah does **not**	3954
	3:14	And **i** you walk in my ways	561
	6:12	**i** you follow my decrees,	561
	8:25	**i** only your sons are careful in all they do	561
	8:47	and **i** they have a change of heart in	NIH
	8:48	and **i** they turn back to you	NIH
	9: 4	**i** you walk before me in integrity of heart	561
	9: 6	"But **i** you or your sons turn away from me	561
	11:38	**I** you do whatever I command you	561
	12: 7	"**I** today you will be a servant	561
	12:27	These people go up to offer sacrifices at	561
	13: 8	"Even **i** you were to give me half	561
	18:12	**I** I go and tell Ahab	2256
	18:21	**I** the LORD is God, follow him;	561
	18:21	but **i** Baal is God, follow him."	561
	19: 2	**i** by this time tomorrow I do **not** make your	3954
	20:10	**i** enough dust remains in Samaria	561
	20:18	He said, "**I** they have come out for peace,	561
	20:18	**i** they have come out for war,	561
	20:23	But **i** we fight them on the plains,	219
	20:39	**I** he is missing, it will be your life	561
	21: 2	or, **i** you prefer, I will pay you	561
	21: 6	or **i** you prefer, I will give you another	561
	22:28	Micaiah declared, "**I** you ever return safely,	561
2Ki	1: 2	to see **i** I will recover from this injury."	561
	1:10	"**I** I am a man of God,	561
	1:12	"**I** I am a man of God," Elijah replied,	561
	2:10	"yet **i** you see me when I am taken	561
	3:14	**i** I did **not** have respect for the	3954+4295
	4:29	**I** you meet anyone, do not greet him,	3954

2Ki	4:29	do not greet him, and **i** anyone greets you,	3954
	5: 3	"**I** only my master would see	332
	5:13	**i** the prophet had told you to do some	2022
	5:17	"**I** you will **not**," said Naaman,	2256
	6:27	"**I** the LORD does not help you,	NIH
	6:31	**i** the head of Elisha son of Shaphat remains	561
	7: 2	**i** the LORD should **open** the floodgates	AIT
	7: 4	**I** we say, 'We'll go into the city'—	561
	7: 4	And **i** we stay here, we will die.	561
	7: 4	**I** they spare us, we live;	561
	7: 4	**i** they kill us, then we die."	561
	7: 9	**I** we wait until daylight,	2256
	7:19	**i** the LORD should **open** the floodgates	AIT
	9:15	Jehu said, "**I** this is the way you feel,	561
	10: 4	"**I** two kings could not resist him,	2180
	10: 6	"**I** you are on my side and will obey me,	561
	10:15	"**I** so," said Jehu, "give me your hand."	2256
	10:24	"**I** one of you lets any of the men	NIH
	18:21	a man's hand and wounds him **i** he leans	889
	18:22	And **i** you say to me,	3954
	18:23	**i** you can put riders on them!	561
	21: 8	**i** only they will be careful	561
1Ch	12:17	"**I** you have come to me in peace,	561
	12:17	But **i** you have come to betray me	561
	12:19	"It will cost us our heads **i** he **deserts**	AIT
	13: 2	"**I** it seems good to you and if it is the will	561
	13: 2	"**I** it seems good to you and **i** it is the will	NIH
	17:17	And as **i** this were not enough in your sight,	NIH
	19:12	"**I** the Arameans are too strong for me,	561
	19:12	but **i** the Ammonites are too strong for you,	561
	22:13	Then you will have success **i** you are careful	561
	28: 7	I will establish his kingdom forever **i** he is	561
	28: 9	**I** you seek him, he will be found by you;	561
	28: 9	but **i** you forsake him,	561
2Ch	6:16	**i** only your sons are careful in all they do	NIH
	6:37	and **i** they have a change of heart in	NIH
	6:38	and **i** they turn back to you	NIH
	7:14	**i** my people, who are called by my name,	2256
	7:17	**i** you walk before me	561
	7:19	"But **i** you turn away and forsake	561
	10: 7	"**I** you will be kind to these people	561
	15: 2	**I** you seek him, he will be found by you,	561
	15: 2	but **i** you forsake him, he will forsake you.	561
	18:27	Micaiah declared, "**I** you ever return safely,	561
	20: 9	'**I** calamity comes upon us,	561
	25: 8	**i** you go and fight courageously in battle,	561
	30: 9	**I** you return to the LORD,	3954
	30: 9	not turn his face from you **i** you return	561
	30:19	even **i** he is not clean according to the rules	2256
	33: 8	**i** only they will be careful to do	561
Ezr	4:13	the king should know that **i** this city is built	10213
	4:16	We inform the king that **i** this city is built	10213
	5:17	Now **i** it pleases the king,	10213
	5:17	in the royal archives of Babylon to see **i**	10213
	6:11	I decree that **i** anyone changes this edict,	10168
Ne	1: 8	saying, '**I** you are unfaithful,	NIH
	1: 9	**i** you return to me and obey my commands,	NIH
	1: 9	then even **i** your exiled people are at	561
	2: 5	"**I** it pleases the king and	561
	2: 5	the king and **i** your servant has found favor	561
	2: 7	I also said to him, "**I** it pleases the king,	561
	4: 3	**i** even a fox climbed up on it,	561
	9:29	by which a man will live **i** he obeys them.	2256
	13:21	**I** you do this again,	561
Est	1:19	"Therefore, **i** it pleases the king,	561
	3: 9	**I** it pleases the king,	561
	4:14	For **i** you remain silent at this time,	561
	4:16	And **i** I perish, I perish."	889+3869
	5: 4	"**I** it pleases the king," replied Esther,	561
	5: 8	**I** the king regards me with favor and	561
	5: 8	and **i** it pleases the king to grant	561
	7: 3	"**I** I have found favor with you, O king,	561
	7: 3	O king, and **i** it pleases your majesty,	561
	7: 4	**I** we had merely been sold as male	467
	8: 5	"**I** it pleases the king," she said,	561
	8: 5	"and **i** he regards me with favor	561
	8: 5	and **i** he is pleased with me,	NIH
	9:13	"**I** it pleases the king," Esther answered,	561
Job	4: 2	"**I** someone ventures a word with you,	2022
	4:18	**I** God places no trust in his servants,	2176
	4:18	**i** he charges his angels with error,	NIH
	5: 1	"Call **i** you will,	5528
	5: 8	"But **i** it were I, I would appeal to God;	219
	6: 2	"**I** only my anguish could be weighed	4273
	7:20	**I** I have sinned, what have I done to you,	NIH
	8: 5	But **i** you will look to God and plead with	561
	8: 6	**i** you are pure and upright,	561
	9:12	**I** he snatches away, who can stop him?	2176
	9:16	Even **i** I summoned him and he responded,	561
	9:19	**I** it is a matter of strength, he is mighty!	561
	9:19	And **i** it is a matter of justice,	561
	9:20	Even **i** I were innocent,	561
	9:20	**i** I were blameless,	NIH
	9:24	**I** it is not he, then who is it?	561
	9:27	**I** I say, 'I will forget my complaint,	561
	9:30	Even **i** I washed myself with soap	561
	9:33	**I** only there were someone to arbitrate	4273
	10:14	**I** I sinned, you would be watching me	561
	10:15	**I** I am guilty—woe to me!	561
	10:15	Even **i** I am innocent, I cannot lift my head,	2256
	10:16	**I** I hold my head high,	561
	10:19	**I** only I had never come into being,	889+3869
	11:10	"**I** he comes along and confines you	561
	11:13	"Yet **i** you devote your heart to him	561
	11:14	**i** you put away the sin that is in your hand	561
	12:15	**I** he holds back the waters, there is drought;	2176
	12:15	**i** he lets them loose,	2256

Job	13: 5	**I** only you would be altogether silent!	4769+5989
	13: 9	Would it turn out well **i** he examined you?	3954
	13:10	rebuke you **i** you secretly showed partiality.	561
	13:19	**I** so, I will be silent and die.	3954+6964
	14: 7	**I** it is cut down, it will sprout again,	561
	14:13	**I** only you would hide me in the grave	4769+5989
	14:13	**I** only you would set me a time and	NIH
	14:14	**I** a man dies, will he live again?	561
	14:21	**I** his sons are honored, he does not know it;	NIH
	14:21	**i** they are brought low, he does not see it.	2256
	15:15	**I** God places no trust in his holy ones,	2176
	15:15	**i** even the heavens are not pure in his eyes,	4273
	16: 4	**i** you were in my place;	4273
	16: 6	"Yet **i** I speak, my pain is not relieved;	561
	16: 6	and **i** I refrain, it does not go away.	NIH
	17: 5	**I** a man denounces his friends for reward,	NIH
	17:13	**I** the only home I hope for is the grave,	561
	17:13	**i** I spread out my bed in darkness,	NIH
	17:14	**I** I say to corruption,	NIH
	19: 4	**I** it is true that I have gone astray,	677
	19: 5	**I** indeed you would exalt yourselves	561
	19:28	"**I** you say, 'How we will hound him,	561
	22: 3	What pleasure would it give the Almighty **i**	3954
	22: 3	What would he gain **i** your ways were	3954
	22:23	**I** you return to the Almighty,	561
	22:23	**I** you remove wickedness far	NIH
	23: 3	**I** only I knew where to find him;	4769+5989
	23: 3	**i** only I could go to his dwelling!	NIH
	23: 8	"But **i** I go to the east, he is not there;	2176
	23: 8	**i** I go to the west, I do not find him.	2256
	24:25	"**I** this is not so,	561
	25: 5	**I** even the moon is not bright and	2176
	30: 5	shouted at as **i** they were thieves.	3869
	31: 5	"**I** I have walked in falsehood	561
	31: 7	**i** my steps have turned from the path,	561
	31: 7	**i** my heart has been led by my eyes,	2256
	31: 7	or **i** my hands have been defiled,	NIH
	31: 9	"**I** my heart has been enticed by a woman,	561
	31: 9	or **i** I have lurked at my neighbor's door,	NIH
	31:13	"**I** I have denied justice to my menservants	561
	31:16	"**I** I have denied the desires of the poor	561
	31:17	**i** I have kept my bread to myself,	2256
	31:19	**i** I have seen anyone perishing for lack	561
	31:21	**i** I have raised my hand against	561
	31:24	"**I** I have put my trust in gold or said	561
	31:25	**i** I have rejoiced over my great wealth,	561
	31:26	**i** I have regarded the sun in its radiance or	561
	31:29	"**I** I have rejoiced at my enemy's misfortune	561
	31:31	**i** the men of my household have never said,	561
	31:33	**i** I have concealed my sin as men do,	561
	31:38	"**i** my land cries out against me	561
	31:39	**i** I have devoured its yield without payment	561
	32:22	for **i** I were skilled in flattery,	4202
	33: 5	Answer me then, **i** you can;	561
	33:23	"Yet **i** there is an angel on his side as	561
	33:32	**I** you have anything to say, answer me;	561
	33:33	But **i** not, then listen to me;	561
	34:14	**I** it were his intention	561
	34:16	"**I** you have understanding, hear this;	561
	34:29	**i** he remains silent, who can condemn him?	NIH
	34:29	**I** he hides his face, who can see him?	2256
	34:32	**i** I have done wrong,	561
	35: 6	**I** you sin, how does that affect him?	561
	35: 6	**I** your sins are many,	2256
	35: 7	**I** you are righteous,	561
	36: 8	But **i** men are bound in chains,	561
	36:11	**I** they obey and serve him,	561
	36:12	But **i** they do not listen,	561
	38: 4	Tell me, **i** you understand.	561
	38:18	Tell me, **i** you know all this.	561
	39:16	as **i** they were not hers;	4200
	41: 8	**I** you lay a hand on him,	NIH
Ps	7: 3	**i** I have done this and there is guilt	561
	7: 4	**i** I have done evil to him who is at peace	561
	7:12	**I** he does not relent,	561
	14: 2	to see **i** there are any who understand,	2022
	28: 1	For **i** you remain silent,	7153
	37:23	the LORD delights in a man's way,	2256
	44:20	**I** we had forgotten the name of our God	561
	50:12	**I** I were hungry I would not tell you,	561
	53: 2	to see **i** there are any who understand,	2022
	55:12	**I** an enemy were insulting me,	4273
	55:12	**i** a foe were raising himself against me,	4273
	59:15	and howl **i** not satisfied.	561
	62: 9	**i** weighed on a balance, they are nothing;	NIH
	66:18	**I** I had cherished sin in my heart,	561
	73:15	**I** I had said, "I will speak thus,"	561
	81: 8	**i** you would but listen to me, O Israel!	561
	81:13	"**I** my people would but listen to me,	4273
	81:13	**i** Israel would follow my ways,	NIH
	89:30	"**I** his sons forsake my law and do	561
	89:31	**i** they violate my decrees and fail	561
	90:10	or eighty, **i** we have the strength;	561
	91: 9	**I** you make the Most High your dwelling—	3954
	95: 7	Today, **i** you hear his voice,	561
	119:92	**I** your law had **not** been my delight,	4295
	124: 1	**I** the LORD had **not** been on our side—	4295
	124: 2	**i** the LORD had **not** been on our side	4295
	130: 3	**I** you, O LORD, kept a record of sins,	561
	132:12	**i** your sons keep my covenant and	561
	133: 3	It is as **i** the dew of Hermon were falling	3869
	137: 5	**I** I forget you, O Jerusalem,	561
	137: 6	of my mouth **i** I do not remember you,	561
	137: 6	**i** I do not hold my highest if my	561
	139: 8	**I** I go up to the heavens, you are there;	561
	139: 8	**i** I make my bed in the depths,	2256
	139: 9	**I** I rise on the wings of the dawn,	NIH

Ps 139: 9	i I settle on the far side of the sea,	NIH
139:11	I I say, "Surely the darkness will hide me	2256
139:19	I only you would slay the wicked, O God!	561
139:24	See i there is any offensive way in me,	561
Pr 1:10	My son, i sinners entice you,	561
1:11	I they say, "Come along with us;	561
1:23	I you had responded to my rebuke,	NIH
2: 1	i you accept my words and store	561
2: 3	and i you call out for insight and cry aloud	561
2: 4	and i you look for it as for silver and search	561
6: 1	i you have put up security	561
6: 1	i you have struck hands in pledge	NIH
6: 2	i you have been trapped by what you said,	NIH
6:30	a thief i he steals to satisfy his hunger	3954
6:31	Yet i he is caught, he must pay sevenfold,	NIH
9:12	I you are wise, your wisdom will reward	561
9:12	i you are a mocker, you alone will suffer."	2256
11:31	I the righteous receive their due on earth,	2176
17:13	I a man pays back evil for good,	NIH
17:28	a fool is thought wise i he keeps silent,	NIH
17:28	and discerning i he holds his tongue.	NIH
19:19	i you rescue him,	561+3954
20:16	hold it in pledge i he does it for	2256
20:18	i you wage war, obtain guidance.	2256
20:20	I a man curses his father or mother,	NIH
21:13	I a man shuts his ears to the cry of	NIH
22:27	i you lack the means to pay,	561
23: 2	to your throat i you are given to gluttony.	561
23:13	i you punish him with the rod,	3954
23:15	My son, i your heart is wise,	561
24:10	I you falter in times of trouble,	NIH
24:12	I you say, "But we knew nothing	3954
24:14	i you find it, there is a future hope for you,	561
25: 8	the end i your neighbor puts you to shame?	928
25: 9	I you argue your case with a neighbor,	NIH
25:16	I you find honey, eat just enough—	NIH
25:21	I your enemy is hungry,	561
25:21	i he is thirsty, give him water to drink.	561
26:27	I a man digs a pit, he will fall into it;	NIH
26:27	i a man rolls a stone,	NIH
27:13	hold it in pledge i he does it for	2256
27:14	I a man loudly blesses his neighbor early in	NIH
28: 9	I anyone turns a deaf ear to the law,	NIH
29: 9	I a wise man goes to court with a fool,	NIH
29:12	I a ruler listens to lies,	NIH
29:14	I a king judges the poor with fairness,	NIH
29:21	I a man pampers his servant from youth,	NIH
30: 4	Tell me i you know!	3954
30:32	"I you have played the fool	561
30:32	or i you have planned evil,	561
Ecc 3:21	Who knows i the spirit of man rises upward	NIH
3:21	and i the spirit of the animal goes down	NIH
4:10	I one falls down,	561+3954
4:11	Also, i two lie down together,	561
5: 8	I you see the poor oppressed in a district,	561
6: 3	i he cannot enjoy his prosperity and does	2256
6: 6	even i he lives a thousand years twice over	467
8:17	Even i a wise man claims he knows,	561
10: 4	I a ruler's anger rises against you,	561
10:10	I the ax is dull and its edge unsharpened,	561
10:11	I a snake bites before it is charmed,	561
10:18	I a man is lazy, the rafters sag;	928
10:18	i his hands are idle, the house leaks.	928
11: 3	I clouds are full of water,	561
SS 1: 8	I you do not know,	561
5: 8	i you find my lover, what will you tell him?	561
6:11	to see i the vines had budded or	2022
7:12	Let us go early to the vineyards to see i	561
7:12	i their blossoms have opened,	NIH
7:12	and i the pomegranates are in bloom—	NIH
8: 1	I only you were to me like a brother,	4769+5989
8: 1	Then, i I found you outside,	NIH
8: 7	I one were to give all the wealth	561
8: 9	I she is a wall, we will build towers	561
8: 9	I she is a door, we will enclose her	561
Isa 1:15	i you offer many prayers, I will not listen.	3954
1:19	I you are willing and obedient,	561
1:20	but i you resist and rebel,	561
5:30	And i one looks at the land,	NIH
7: 9	I you do not stand firm in your faith,	561
8:20	I they do not speak according to this word,	561
10:15	As i a rod were to wield him who lifts it up,	3869
21:12	I you would ask, then ask;	561
27: 4	I only there were briers	4769+5989
29:11	And i you give the scroll	NIH
29:12	Or i you give the scroll	NIH
29:16	as i the potter were thought to be like	561
33:12	The peoples will be burned as i to lime;	AIT
36: 6	a man's hand and wounds him i he leans	889
36: 7	And i you say to me,	3954
36: 8	i you can put riders on them!	561
41:25	He treads on rulers as i they were mortar,	AIT
41:25	as i he were a potter treading the clay.	AIT
48:18	I only you had paid attention	4273
54: 6	The LORD will call you back as i	3869
54:15	I anyone does attack you,	2176
58: 2	to know my ways, as i they were a nation	3869
58: 9	"I you do away with the yoke	561
58:10	and i you spend yourselves in behalf of	NIH
58:13	"I you keep your feet from breaking	561
58:13	i you call the Sabbath a delight and	NIH
58:13	i you honor it by not going your own way	NIH
59:10	At midday we stumble as i it were twilight;	3869
Jer 2:10	see i there has ever been anything like this:	2176
2:28	Let them come i they can save you	561
3: 1	"I a man divorces his wife	2176
4: 1	"I you will return, O Israel, return to me,"	561

Jer 4: 1	"I you put your detestable idols out	561
4: 2	and i in a truthful, just and righteous way	NIH
5: 1	I you can find but one person who deals	561
7: 5	I you really change your ways	561+3954
7: 6	i you do not oppress the alien,	NIH
7: 6	and i you do not follow other gods	NIH
12: 5	"I you have raced with men on foot	3954
12: 5	I you stumble in safe country,	2256
12:16	And i they learn well the ways	561
12:17	But i any nation does not listen,	561
13:12	And i they say to you,	NIH
13:17	But i you do not listen,	561
13:22	And i you ask yourself,	3954
14:18	I I go into the country,	561
14:18	i I go into the city,	561
15: 1	"Even i Moses and Samuel were to stand	561
15: 2	And i they ask you, 'Where shall we go?'	3954
15:19	"I you repent, I will restore you	561
15:19	i you utter worthy, not worthless, words,	561
17:24	But i you are careful to obey me,	561
17:27	But i you do not obey me to keep	561
18: 7	I at any time I announce that a nation	NIH
18: 8	i that nation I warned repents of its evil,	NIH
18: 9	And i at another time I announce that	NIH
18:10	and i it does evil in my sight and does	NIH
20: 9	But i I say, "I will not mention him	NIH
22: 4	For i you are careful to carry out	561
22: 5	But i you do not obey these commands,	561
22:24	I live," declares the LORD, "even i you,	561
22:30	"Record this man as i childless,	NIH
23:22	But i they had stood in my council,	561
23:34	I a prophet or a priest or anyone else claims	NIH
25:28	But i they refuse to take the cup	3954
26: 4	I you do not listen to me	561
26: 5	and i you do not listen to the words	NIH
26:15	however, that i you put me to death,	561
27: 8	" 'I, however, any nation or kingdom	NIH
27:11	But i any nation will bow its neck under	NIH
27:18	I they are prophets and have the word of	561
28: 9	as one truly sent by the LORD only i	561
29: 7	because i it prospers, you too will prosper."	928
31:36	"Only i these decrees vanish	561
31:37	"Only i the heavens above can	561
32: 5	I you fight against the Babylonians,	3954
33:20	'I you can break my covenant with the day	561
33:25	'I I have not established my covenant	561
37:10	Even i you were to defeat	561
38:15	"I I give you an answer,	3954
38:15	Even i I did give you counsel,	3954
38:17	'I you surrender to the officers of the king	561
38:18	But i you will not surrender to the officers	561
38:21	But i you refuse to surrender,	561
38:25	I the officials hear that I talked with you,	3954
40: 4	Come with me to Babylon, i you like,	561
40: 4	but i you do not want to, then don't come.	561
42: 5	be a true and faithful witness against us i	561
42:10	'I you stay in this land, I will build you up	561
42:13	i you say, 'We will not stay in this land,'	561
42:14	and i you say, 'No we will go	NIH
42:15	'I you are determined to go to Egypt	561
49: 9	I grape pickers came to you,	561
49: 9	I thieves came during the night,	561
49:12	"I those who do not deserve to drink	2180
51:53	Even i Babylon reaches the sky	3954
La 3:37	Who can speak and have it happen i	NIH
Eze 1:27	like glowing metal, as i full of fire,	3869
3: 6	Surely i I had sent you to them,	561
3:19	But i you do warn the wicked man	3954
3:21	But i you do warn the righteous man not	3954
14: 9	i the prophet is enticed to utter a prophecy,	3954
14:13	i a country sins against me	3954
14:14	even i these three men—Noah, Daniel and	2256
14:15	"Or i I send wild beasts through	4273
14:16	even i these three men were in it,	NIH
14:17	"Or i I bring a sword against that country	NIH
14:18	even i these three men were in it,	2256
14:19	"Or i I send a plague into that land	NIH
14:20	even i Noah, Daniel and Job were in it,	2256
15: 5	I it was not useful for anything	2180
17:10	Even i it is transplanted, will it thrive?	2180
18:21	"But i a wicked man turns away from all	3954
18:24	"But i a righteous man turns	928
18:26	I a righteous man turns	928
18:27	But i a wicked man turns away from	928
21:13	And what i the scepter [of Judah],	561
33: 4	then i anyone hears the trumpet but does	NIH
33: 5	I he had taken warning,	2256
33: 6	But i the watchman sees the sword coming	3954
33: 9	But i you do warn the wicked man to turn	3954
33:12	The righteous man, i he sins,	928+3427
33:13	I I tell the righteous man that he will	928
33:14	And i I say to the wicked man,	928
33:15	i he gives back what he took in pledge for	NIH
33:18	I a righteous man turns	928
33:19	And i a wicked man turns away	928
39:18	the princes of the earth as i they were rams	NIH
43:11	and i they are ashamed	561
44:25	i the dead person was his father or mother,	561
46:16	I the prince makes a gift	3954
46:17	I, however, he makes a gift	3954
Da 2: 5	I you do not tell me what my dream was	10213
2: 6	But i you tell me the dream and explain it,	10213
2: 9	I you do not tell me the dream,	10213
3:15	i you are ready to fall down and worship	10213
3:15	But i you do not worship it,	10213
3:17	I we are thrown into the blazing furnace,	10213
3:18	But even i he does not,	10213

Da 4:19	i only the dream applied to your enemies	NIH
5:16	I you can read this writing	10213
Hos 9: 6	Even i they escape from destruction,	3954
9:12	Even i they rear children,	561
9:16	Even i they bear children,	3954
10: 3	i we had a king, what could he do for us?"	NIH
11: 7	Even i they call to the Most High,	AIT
Joel 3: 4	I you are paying me back,	561
Am 2: 1	Because he burned, as i to lime,	NIH
6: 9	I ten men are left in one house,	561
6:10	And i a relative who is to burn	NIH
Ob 1: 5	"I thieves came to you,	561
1: 5	i robbers in the night—	561
1: 5	I grape pickers came to you,	561
1:16	and drink and be as i they had never been.	3869
Mic 2:11	I a liar and deceiver comes and says,	4273
3: 5	i one feeds them, they proclaim 'peace';	NIH
3: 5	i he does not, they prepare to wage war	2256
Hab 2: 3	not believe, even i you were told.	3954
Hag 2:12	I a person carries consecrated meat in	2176
2:13	"I a person defiled by contact with	561
Zec 3: 7	'I you will walk in my ways	561
6:15	This will happen i you diligently obey	561
11:12	I told them, "I you think it best,	561
11:12	but i not, keep it."	561
13: 3	And i anyone still prophesies,	3954
13: 6	I someone asks him,	2256
14:17	I any of the peoples of the earth do not go	889
14:18	I the Egyptian people do not go up	561
Mal 1: 6	I I am a father, where is the honor due me?	561
1: 6	I I am a master, where is the respect due	561
2: 2	I you do not listen,	561
2: 2	and i you do not set your heart	561
3:10	"and see i I will not throw open the	561
Mt 4: 3	"I you are the Son of God,	1623
4: 6	"I you are the Son of God," he said,	1623
4: 9	"i you will bow down and worship me."	1569
5:13	But i the salt loses its saltiness,	1569
5:23	i you are offering your gift at the altar	1569
5:29	I your right eye causes you to sin,	1623
5:30	And i your right hand causes you to sin,	1623
5:39	I someone strikes you on the right cheek,	247
5:40	And i someone wants to sue you	NIG
5:41	I someone forces you to go one mile,	2779
5:46	I you love those who love you,	1569
5:47	And i you greet only your brothers,	1569
6: 1	I you do, you will have no reward	1623
6:14	For i you forgive men when they sin	1569
6:15	But i you do not forgive men their sins,	1569
6:22	I your eyes are good, your whole body	1569
6:23	But i your eyes are bad, your whole body	1569
6:23	I then the light within you is darkness,	1623
6:30	I that is how God clothes the grass of	1623
7: 6	I you do, they may trample them	3607
7: 9	"Which of you, i his son asks for bread,	1569
7:10	i he asks for a fish, will give him a snake?	2779
7:11	I you, then, though you are evil,	1623
8: 2	i you are willing, you can make me clean."	1569
8:31	"I you drive us out,	1623
9:17	I they do, the skins will burst,	1623
9:21	"I I only touch his cloak, I will be healed."	1569
10:13	I the home is deserving, let your peace	1569
10:13	i it is not, let your peace return to you.	1569
10:14	I anyone will not welcome you or listen	323
10:25	I the head of the house has been called	1623
10:42	And i anyone gives even a cup of cold water	323
11: 8	I not, what did you go out to see?	247
11:14	And i you are willing to accept it,	1623
11:21	I the miracles that were performed	1623
11:21	I the miracles that were performed	1623
12: 7	I you had known what these words mean,	1623
12:11	"I any of you has a sheep and it falls into	1569
12:26	I Satan drives out Satan,	1623
12:27	And i I drive out demons by Beelzebub,	1623
12:27	i I drive out demons by the Spirit of God,	1623
14:28	"Lord, i it's you," Peter replied,	1623
15: 5	But you say that i a man says to his father	323
15:14	I a blind man leads a blind man,	1569
16:24	"I anyone would come after me,	1623
16:26	What good will it be for a man i he gains	1569
17: 4	I you wish, I will put up three shelters—	1623
17:20	i you have faith as small as a mustard seed,	1569
18: 6	But i anyone causes one of these little ones	323
18: 8	I your hand or your foot causes you to sin,	1623
18: 9	And i your eye causes you to sin,	1623
18:12	I a man owns a hundred sheep,	1569
18:13	And i he finds it, I tell you the truth,	1569
18:15	"I your brother sins against you,	1569
18:15	I he listens to you, you have won your	1569
18:16	But i he will not listen, take one or two	1569
18:17	I he refuses to listen to them, tell it to	1569
18:17	i he refuses to listen even to the church,	1569
18:19	I tell you that i two of you on earth agree	1569
19:10	"I this is the situation between a husband	1623
19:17	I you want to enter life, obey	1623
19:21	Jesus answered, "I you want to be perfect,	1623
21: 3	I anyone says anything to you,	1569
21:21	i you have faith and do not doubt,	1569
21:22	I you believe, you will receive whatever	323
21:24	I you answer me, I will tell you	1569
21:25	"I we say, 'From heaven,' he will ask,	1569
21:26	But i we say, 'From men'—	1569
22:24	that i a man dies without having children,	1569
22:45	I then David calls him 'Lord,'	1623
23:16	You say, 'I anyone swears by the temple,	323
23:16	i anyone swears by the gold of the temple,	323
23:18	'I anyone swears by the altar,	323

Mt	23:18	but i anyone swears by the gift on it,	323

Mt
23:18 but i anyone swears by the gift on it, — 323
23:30 'i we had lived in the days — 1623
24:22 I those days had not been cut short, — 1623
24:23 At that time i anyone says to you, 'Look, — 1569
24:24 i that were possible. — 1623
24:26 "So i anyone tells you, 'There he is, — 1569
24:43 I the owner of the house had known — 1623
26:15 to give me i I hand him over to you?" — 2779
26:24 be better for him i he had not been born. — 1623
26:33 "Even i all fall away on account of you, — 1623
26:35 "Even i I have to die with you, — 1569
26:39 "My Father, i it is possible, — 1623
26:42 i it is not possible for this cup to — 1623
26:63 Tell us i you are the Christ, — 1623
27:40 i you are the Son of God!" — 1623
27:43 Let God rescue him now i he wants him, — 1623
27:49 Let's see i Elijah comes to save him." — 1623
28:14 I this report gets to the governor, — 1569

Mk
1:40 "I you are willing, you can make me clean." — 1569
2:21 I he does, the new piece will pull away from the old, — 1254+1623+3590
2:22 I he does, the wine will burst the skins, — 1254+1623+3590
3: 2 to see i he would heal him on the Sabbath. — 1623
3:24 I a kingdom is divided against itself, — 1569
3:25 I a house is divided against itself, — 1569
3:26 I Satan opposes himself and is divided, — 1623
4:23 I anyone has ears to hear, let him hear." — 1623
4:38 "Teacher, don't you care i we drown?" — 4022
5:28 "I I just touch his clothes, I will be healed." — 1569
6:11 And i any place will not welcome you — 323+4005
7:11 But you say that i a man says to his father — 1569
8: 3 I I send them home hungry, — 1569
8:34 "I anyone would come after me, — 1623
8:38 I anyone is ashamed of me and my words — 1569
9:22 But i you can do anything, — 1623
9:23 " 'I you can'?" — 1623
9:35 "I anyone wants to be first, he must be — 1623
9:42 And i anyone causes one of these little ones — 323
9:43 I your hand causes you to sin, cut it off. — 1569
9:45 And i your foot causes you to sin, cut it off. — 1569
9:47 i your eye causes you to sin, pluck it out. — 1569
9:50 "Salt is good, but i it loses its saltiness, — 1569
10:12 And i she divorces her husband — 1569
11: 3 I anyone asks you, 'Why are you doing this — 1569
11:13 he went to find out i it had any fruit. — 1623
11:23 i anyone says to this mountain, 'Go, — 323
11:25 i you hold anything against anyone, — 1623
11:31 "I we say, 'From heaven,' he will ask, — 1569
11:32 But i we say, 'From men'...." — NIG
12:19 for us that i a man's brother dies and leaves — 1569
13:20 I the Lord had not cut short those days, — 1623
13:21 At that time i anyone says to you, 'Look, — 1569
13:22 deceive the elect—i that were possible. — 1623
13:36 I he comes suddenly, — 3590
14:21 be better for him i he had not been born. — 1623
14:29 Peter declared, "Even i all fall away, — 1623
14:31 "Even i I have to die with you, — 1569
14:35 to the ground and prayed that i possible — 1623
15:36 Let's see i Elijah comes to take him down," — 1623
15:44 he asked him i Jesus had already died. — 1623

Lk
3:15 and were all wondering in their hearts i — 3607
4: 3 "I you are the Son of God, — 1623
4: 7 So i you worship me, it will all be yours." — 1569
4: 9 "I you are the Son of God," he said, — 1623
5:12 i you are willing, you can make me clean." — 1569
5:36 I he does, he will have torn — 1623
5:37 I he does, the new wine will burst — 1623
6: 7 to see i he would heal on the Sabbath. — 1623
6:29 I someone strikes you on one cheek, — AIT
6:29 i someone takes your cloak, — AIT
6:30 and i anyone takes what belongs to you, — AIT
6:32 "I you love those who love you, — 1623
6:33 And i you do good to those who are good — 1569
6:34 And i you lend to those from whom you — 1569
7:25 I not, what did you go out to see? — 247
7:39 "I this man were a prophet, — 1623
9: 5 I people do not welcome you, — 323
9:23 "I anyone would come after me, — 1623
9:26 I anyone is ashamed of me and my words, — 323
10: 6 I a man of peace is there, — 1569
10: 6 i not, it will return to you. — 1623
10:13 For i the miracles that were performed — 1623
11:11 i your son asks for a fish, — AIT
11:12 Or i he asks for an egg, — AIT
11:13 I you then, though you are evil, — 1623
11:18 I Satan is divided against himself, — 1623
11:19 Now i I drive out demons by Beelzebub, — 1623
11:20 i I drive out demons by the finger of God, — 1623
11:36 i your whole body is full of light, — 1623
12:28 I that is how God clothes the grass of — 1623
12:38 even i he comes in the second or third — 1569
12:39 I the owner of the house had known — 1623
13: 9 I it bears fruit next year, fine! — 1569
13: 9 I not, then cut it down.' " — 1623
14: 5 "I one of you has a son or an ox that falls — NIG
14: 9 I so, the host who invited both — 2779
14:12 i you do, they may invite you back and — 3607
14:26 "I anyone comes to me and does — 1623
14:28 the cost to see i he has enough money — 1623
14:29 For i he lays the foundation and — 2671+3607
14:32 I he is not able, — 1623
14:34 "Salt is good, but i it loses its saltiness, — 1569
16:11 So i you have not been trustworthy — 1623
16:12 And i you have not been trustworthy — 1623
16:30 'but i someone from the dead goes to them, — 1569
16:31 'I they do not listen to Moses and — 1569

Lk
16:31 be convinced even i someone rises from — 1569
17: 3 "I your brother sins, rebuke him, — 1569
17: 3 rebuke him, and i he repents, forgive him. — 1569
17: 4 I he sins against you seven times in a day, — 1569
17: 6 "I you have faith as small as — 1623
19: 8 i I have cheated anybody out of anything, — 1623
19:31 I anyone asks you, 'Why are you untying — 1569
19:40 "I tell you," he replied, "i they keep quiet, — 1569
19:42 "I you, even you, had only known — 1569
20: 5 "I we say, 'From heaven,' he will ask, — 1569
20: 6 But i we say, 'From men,' — 1569
20:28 for us that i a man's brother dies and leaves — 1569
22:36 "But now i you have a purse, take it, — AIT
22:36 and i you don't have a sword, — AIT
22:42 i you are willing, take this cup from me; — 1623
22:67 "I you are the Christ," they said, "tell us. — 1623
22:67 Jesus answered, "I I tell you, — 1569
22:68 and i I asked you, you would not answer. — 1569
23: 6 Pilate asked i the man was a Galilean. — 1623
23:31 For i men do these things when — 1623
23:35 let him save himself i he is the Christ — 1623
23:37 "I you are the king of the Jews, — 1623
24:28 Jesus acted as i he were going farther. — 4701

Jn
1:25 "Why then do you baptize i you are not — 1623
3: 2 the miraculous signs you are doing i — 1569
3:12 how then will you believe i I speak — 1569
4:10 "I you knew the gift of God and who it is — 1623
5:31 "I I testify about myself, — 1569
5:43 but i someone else comes in his own name, — 1569
5:44 How can you believe i you accept praise — AIT
5:46 I you believed Moses, you would believe me, — 1623
6:51 I anyone eats of this bread, — 1569
6:62 What i you see the Son of Man ascend to — 1569
7:17 I anyone chooses to do God's will, — 1569
7:23 Now i a child can be circumcised on — 1623
7:37 "I anyone is thirsty, let him come to me — 1569
8: 7 "I any one of you is without sin, — NIG
8:14 "Even i I testify on my own behalf, — 1569
8:16 But i I do judge, my decisions are right, — 1569
8:19 "I you knew me, you would know my — 1623
8:24 i you do not believe that I am — 1569
8:31 Jesus said, "I you hold to my teaching, — 1569
8:36 So i the Son sets you free, you will be free — 1569
8:39 "I you were Abraham's children," — 1623
8:42 "I God were your Father, you would love — 1623
8:46 I I am telling the truth, — 1623
8:51 i anyone keeps my word, — 1569
8:52 yet you say that i anyone keeps your word, — 1569
8:54 Jesus replied, "I I glorify myself, — 1569
8:55 I I said I did not, I would be a liar like you, — 1569
9:33 I this man were not from God, — 1623
9:41 Jesus said, "I you were blind, — 1623
10:24 I you are the Christ, tell us plainly." — 1623
10:35 I he called them 'gods,' — 1623
10:38 But i I do it, even though you do not — 1623
11:12 His disciples replied, "Lord, i he sleeps, — 1623
11:21 Martha said to Jesus, "i you had been here, — 1623
11:32 "Lord, i you had been here, — 1623
11:40 "Did I not tell you that i you believed, — 1569
11:48 I we let him go on like this, — 1569
11:57 that i anyone found out where Jesus was, — 1569
12:24 But i it dies, it produces many seeds. — 1569
13:17 you will be blessed i you do them. — 1569
13:32 I God is glorified in him, — 1623
13:35 i you love one another." — 1569
14: 2 i it were not so, I would have told you. — 1623
14: 3 And i I go and prepare a place for you, — 1569
14: 7 I you really knew me, — 1623
14:15 "I you love me, you will obey what I — 1569
14:23 Jesus replied, "I anyone loves me, — 1569
14:28 I you loved me, you would be glad — 1623
15: 5 I a man remains in me and I in him, — AIT
15: 6 I anyone does not remain in me, — 1569
15: 7 I you remain in me and my words remain — 1569
15:10 I you obey my commands, — 1569
15:14 You are my friends i you do what I command. — 1569
15:18 "I the world hates you, — 1623
15:19 I you belonged to the world, — 1623
15:20 I they persecuted me, — 1623
15:20 I they obeyed my teaching, — 1623
15:22 I I had not come and spoken to them, — 1623
15:24 I I had not done among them what — 1623
16: 7 but i I go, I will send him to you. — 1623
18: 8 "I you are looking for me, — 1623
18:14 that it would be good i one man died for — AIT
18:23 "I I said something wrong," Jesus replied, — 1623
18:23 i I spoke the truth, why did you strike me?" — 1623
18:30 "I he were not a criminal," they replied, — 1623
18:36 I it were, my servants would fight — 1623
19:11 "You would have no power over me i — 1623
19:12 "I you let this man go, — 1569
20:15 she said, "Sir, i you have carried him away, — 1623
20:23 I you forgive anyone his sins, — 323
20:23 i you do not forgive them, — 323
21:22 "I I want him to remain alive until I return, — 1569
21:23 "I I want him to remain alive until I return, — 1569
21:25 I every one of them were written down, — 1569

Ac
3:12 you stare at us as i by our own power — 6055
4: 9 I we are being called to account today for — 1623
5:38 For i their purpose or activity is — 1569
5:39 But i it is from God, you will not be able — 1623
5:39 so that i he found any there who belonged — 1569
10:18 asking i Simon who was known — 1623
11:17 So i God gave them the same gift — 1623
13:15 i you have a message of encouragement for — 1623

Ac
13:41 even i someone told you.' " — 1569
16:15 "I you consider me a believer in the Lord," — 1623
17:11 to see i what Paul said was true. — 1623
17:25 as i he needed anything, — AIT
18:14 "I you Jews were making a complaint — 1623
18:21 "I will come back i it is God's will." — AIT
19:38 I, then, Demetrius and his fellow — 1623
19:39 I there is anything further you want — 1623
20:16 i possible, by the day of Pentecost. — 1623
20:24 i only I may finish the race and complete — 6055
23: 9 "What i a spirit or an angel has spoken — 1623
24:19 to be here before you and bring charges i — 1623
25: 5 i he has done anything wrong." — 1623
25:11 I, however, i am guilty — 1623
25:11 But i the charges brought against me — 1623
25:20 so I asked i he would be willing to go — 1623
26: 5 can testify, i they are willing. — 1569
26:32 "This man could have been set free i he had — 1623
27:39 to run the ship aground i they could. — 1623

Ro
2:17 Now you, i you call yourself a Jew; — 1623
2:17 i you rely on the law and brag — NIG
2:18 i you know his will and approve — NIG
2:19 i you are convinced that you are a guide for — NIG
2:25 Circumcision has value i you observe — 1569
2:25 but i you break the law, — 1569
2:26 I those who are not circumcised keep — 1569
2:28 not a Jew i he is only one outwardly, — NIG
2:29 No, a man is a Jew i he is one inwardly; — NIG
3: 3 What i some did not have faith? — 1623
3: 5 But i our unrighteousness brings out God's righteousness more clearly, — 1623
3: 6 I that were so, how could God judge — 2075
3: 7 Someone might argue, "I my falsehood — 1623
4: 2 I, in fact, Abraham was justified by works, — 1623
4:14 For i those who live by law are heirs, — 1623
5:10 For i, when we were God's enemies, — 1623
5:15 For i the many died by the trespass of — 1623
5:17 For i, by the trespass of the one man, — 1623
6: 5 I we have been united with him like this — 1623
6: 8 Now i we died with Christ, — 1623
7: 2 but i her husband dies, — 1569
7: 3 i she marries another man — 1569
7: 3 But i her husband dies, — 1569
7: 7 not have known what coveting really was i — 1623
7:16 And i I do what I do not want to do, — 1623
7:20 Now i I do what I do not want to do, — 1623
8: 9 i the Spirit of God lives in you. — 1642
8: 9 i anyone does not have the Spirit of Christ, — 1623
8:10 But i Christ is in you, — 1623
8:11 And i the Spirit of him who raised Jesus — 1623
8:13 i you live according to the sinful nature, — 1623
8:13 but i by the Spirit you put to death — 1623
8:17 Now i we are children, then we are heirs— — 1623
8:17 and co-heirs with Christ, i indeed we share — 1642
8:25 But i we hope for what we do not yet have, — 1623
8:31 I God is for us, who can be against us? — 1623
9:22 What i God, choosing to show his wrath — 1623
9:23 What i he did this to make the riches — NIG
9:32 Because they pursued it not by faith but as i — 6055
10: 9 That i you confess with your mouth, — 1569
11: 6 i by grace, then it is no longer by works; — 1623
11: 6 i it were, grace would no longer be grace. — 2075
11:12 But i their transgression means riches for — 1623
11:15 For i their rejection is the reconciliation of — 1623
11:16 I the part of the dough offered — 1623
11:16 i the root is holy, so are the branches. — 1623
11:17 I some of the branches have been broken off — 1623
11:18 I you do, consider this: — 1623
11:21 I God did not spare the natural branches, — 1623
11:23 And i they do not persist in unbelief, — 1569
11:24 i you were cut out of an olive tree — 1623
12: 6 I a man's gift is prophesying, — 1664
12: 7 I it is serving, let him serve; — 1664
12: 7 i it is teaching, let him teach; — 1664
12: 8 i it is encouraging, let him encourage; — 1664
12: 8 i it is contributing to the needs of others, — NIG
12: 8 i it is leadership, let him govern diligently; — NIG
12: 8 i it is showing mercy, let him do it — NIG
12:18 I it is possible, as far as it depends on you, — 1623
12:20 "I your enemy is hungry, feed him; — 1569
12:20 i he is thirsty, give him something to drink. — 1569
13: 4 But i you do wrong, be afraid, — 1569
13: 7 I you owe taxes, pay taxes; — NIG
13: 7 i revenue, then revenue; — NIG
13: 7 i respect, then respect; if honor, then honor. — NIG
13: 7 if respect, then respect; i honor, then honor. — NIG
14: 8 I we live, we live to the Lord; — 1569
14: 8 and i we die, we die to the Lord. — 1569
14:14 But i anyone regards something as unclean, — 1623
14:15 I your brother is distressed because — 1623
14:23 the man who has doubts is condemned i — 1569
15:15 as i to remind you of them again, — 6055
15:27 For i the Gentiles have shared in — 1623

1Co
1:16 I don't remember i I baptized anyone else.) — 1623
2: 8 for i they had, they would not have crucified — 1623
3:12 I any man builds on this foundation — 1623
3:14 I what he has built survives, — 1623
3:15 I it is burned up, he will suffer loss; — 1623
3:17 I anyone destroys God's temple, — 1623
3:18 I any one of you thinks he is wise by — 1623
4: 7 I care very little i I am judged by you or — 2671
4: 7 And i you did receive it, — 1623
4:18 as i I were not coming to you, — 6055
4:19 come to you very soon, i the Lord is willing, — 1569
5: 3 just as i I were present. — 4048
6: 1 I any of you has a dispute with another, — AIT
6: 2 And i you are to judge the world, — 1623

1Co	6: 4	i you have disputes about such matters,	1569
	7: 9	But i they cannot control themselves,	1623
	7:11	But i she does, she must remain unmarried	1569
	7:12	I any brother has a wife who is not	1623
	7:13	And i a woman has a husband who is not	1623
	7:15	But i the unbeliever leaves, let him do so.	1623
	7:21	i you can gain your freedom, do so.	1623
	7:28	But i you do marry, you have not sinned;	1569
	7:28	and i a virgin marries, she has not sinned.	1569
	7:29	on those who have wives should live as i	6055
	7:30	those who mourn, as i they did not;	6055
	7:30	those who are happy, as i they were not;	6055
	7:30	as i it were not theirs to keep;	6055
	7:31	as i not engrossed in them.	6055
	7:36	I anyone thinks he is acting improperly	1623
	7:36	and i she is getting along in years	1569
	7:39	But i her husband dies, she is free to marry	1569
	7:40	she is happier i she stays as she is—	1569
	8: 5	For even i there are so-called gods,	1642
	8: 8	we are no worse i we do not eat,	1569
	8: 8	and no better i we do.	1569
	8:10	For i anyone with a weak conscience	1569
	8:13	i what I eat causes my brother to fall	1623
	9:11	I we have sown spiritual seed among you,	1623
	9:11	is it too much i we reap a material harvest	1623
	9:12	I others have this right of support	1623
	9:16	Woe to me i I do not preach the gospel!	1569
	9:17	I I preach voluntarily, I have a reward;	1623
	9:17	i not voluntarily, I am simply discharging	1623
	10:12	So, i you think you are standing firm,	AIT
	10:27	I some unbeliever invites you to a meal	1623
	10:28	But i anyone says to you,	1569
	10:30	I I take part in the meal with thankfulness,	1623
	11: 6	I a woman does not cover her head,	1623
	11: 6	and i it is a disgrace for a woman	1623
	11:14	the very nature of things teach you that i	1569
	11:15	but that i a woman has long hair,	1569
	11:16	I anyone wants to be contentious	1623
	11:31	But i we judged ourselves,	1623
	11:34	I anyone is hungry, he should eat at home,	1623
	12:15	I the foot should say,	1569
	12:16	And i the ear should say,	1569
	12:17	I the whole body were an eye,	1623
	12:17	I the whole body were an ear,	1623
	12:19	I they were all one part,	1623
	12:26	I one part suffers, every part suffers with it;	1664
	12:26	i one part is honored,	1664
	13: 1	I I speak in the tongues of men and	1569
	13: 2	I I have the gift of prophecy	1569
	13: 2	i I have a faith that can move mountains,	1569
	13: 3	I I give all I possess to the poor	1569
	14: 6	i I come to you and speak in tongues,	1569
	14: 8	i the trumpet does not sound a clear call,	1569
	14:11	I then I do not grasp the meaning	1569
	14:14	For i I pray in a tongue, my spirit prays,	1569
	14:16	I you are praising God with your spirit,	1569
	14:23	So i the whole church comes together	1569
	14:24	But i an unbeliever or someone who does	1569
	14:27	I anyone speaks in a tongue, two—	1664
	14:28	I there is no interpreter,	1569
	14:30	And i a revelation comes to someone	1569
	14:35	I they want to inquire about something,	1623
	14:37	I anybody thinks he is a prophet	1623
	14:38	I he ignores this, he himself will be	1623
	15: 2	i you hold firmly to the word I preached	1623
	15:12	But i it is preached that Christ	1623
	15:13	I there is no resurrection of the dead,	1623
	15:14	And i Christ has not been raised,	1623
	15:15	not raise i in fact the dead are	726+1642
	15:16	For i the dead are not raised,	1623
	15:17	And i Christ has not been raised,	1623
	15:19	I only for this life we have hope in Christ,	1623
	15:29	Now i there is no resurrection,	2075
	15:29	I the dead are not raised at all,	1623
	15:32	I I fought wild beasts in Ephesus	1623
	15:32	I the dead are not raised,	1623
	15:44	I there is a natural body,	1623
	16: 4	I it seems advisable for me to go also,	1569
	16: 7	I hope to spend some time with you, i	1569
	16:10	I Timothy comes, see to it that	1569
	16:22	I anyone does not love the Lord—	1623
2Co	1: 6	I we are distressed, it is for your comfort	1664
	1: 6	i we are comforted, it is for your comfort,	1664
	2: 2	For i I grieve you, who is left to make me	1623
	2: 5	I anyone has caused grief,	1623
	2: 9	to see i you would stand the test and	1182
	2:10	I you forgive anyone, I also forgive him.	1254
	2:10	i there was anything to forgive—	1623
	3: 7	Now i the ministry that brought death,	1623
	3: 9	I the ministry that condemns men is glorious,	1623
	3:11	i what was fading away came with glory,	1623
	4: 3	And even i our gospel is veiled,	1623
	5: 1	Now we know that i the earthly tent we live	1569
	5:13	I we are out of our mind, it is for the sake of	1664
	5:13	i we are in our right mind, it is for you.	1664
	5:17	i anyone is in Christ, he is a new creation;	1623
	7: 8	Even i I caused you sorrow by my letter,	1623
	8:12	For i the willingness is there,	1569
	9: 4	For i any Macedonians come with me	1569
	10: 7	I anyone is confident that he belongs	1623
	10: 8	For even i I boast somewhat freely about	1569
	10:14	as would be the case i we had not come	NIG
	11: 4	For i someone comes to you and preaches	1569
	11: 4	or i you receive a different spirit from	NIG
	11:15	i his servants masquerade as servants	1623
	11:16	But i you do, then receive me just as	1623

2Co	11:30	I I must boast, I will boast of	1623
	12: 6	Even i I should choose to boast,	1569
	12:15	I I love you more, will you love me less?	1623
Gal	1: 8	But even i we or an angel	1569
	1: 9	I anybody is preaching to you	1623
	1:10	I I were still trying to please men,	1623
	2:17	"I, while we seek to be justified in Christ,	1623
	2:18	I I rebuild what I destroyed,	1623
	2:21	for i righteousness could be gained through	1623
	3: 4	i it really was for nothing?	1623
	3:18	For i the inheritance depends on the law,	1623
	3:21	For i a law had been given that could	1623
	3:29	I you belong to Christ,	1623
	4:14	you welcomed me as i I were an angel	6055
	4:14	as i I were Christ Jesus himself.	6055
	4:15	I can testify that, i you could have done so,	1623
	5: 2	that i you let yourselves be circumcised,	1569
	5:11	i I am still preaching circumcision,	1623
	5:15	I you keep on biting and devouring each	1623
	5:18	But i you are led by the Spirit,	1623
	6: 1	Brothers, i someone is caught in a sin,	1569
	6: 3	I anyone thinks he is something	1623
	6: 9	a harvest i we do not give up.	AIT
Eph	6: 8	as i you were serving the Lord, not men,	6055
Php	1:22	I I am to go on living in the body,	1623
	2: 1	I you have any encouragement	1623
	2: 1	i any comfort from his love,	1623
	2: 1	i any fellowship with the Spirit,	1623
	2: 1	i any tenderness and compassion,	1623
	2:17	But even i I am being poured out like	1623
	3: 4	I anyone else thinks he has reasons	1623
	3:15	And i on some point you think differently,	1623
	4: 8	i anything is excellent or praiseworthy—	1623
Col	1:23	i you continue in your faith,	1623
	4:10	i he comes to you, welcome him.)	1623
2Th	3:10	"I a man will not work, he shall not eat."	1623
	3:14	I anyone does not obey our instruction	1623
1Ti	1: 8	that the law is good i one uses it properly.	1569
	2:15	i they continue in faith, love and holiness	1569
	3: 1	I anyone sets his heart on being an overseer	1623
	3: 5	(I anyone does not know how to manage	1623
	3:10	and then i there is nothing against them,	AIT
	3:15	i I am delayed, you will know how	1569
	4: 4	nothing is to be rejected i it is received	AIT
	4: 6	I you point these things out	AIT
	4:16	Persevere in them, because i you do,	AIT
	5: 1	but exhort him as i he were your father.	6055
	5: 4	i a widow has children or grandchildren,	1623
	5: 8	I anyone does not provide for his relatives,	1623
	5:16	I any woman who is a believer has widows	1623
	6: 3	I anyone teaches false doctrines and does	1623
	6: 8	But i we have food and clothing,	AIT
2Ti	2: 5	Similarly, i anyone competes as an athlete,	1569
	2:11	I we died with him, we will also live with	1623
	2:12	i we endure, we will also reign	1623
	2:12	i we disown him, he will also disown us;	1623
	2:13	i we are faithless, he will remain faithful,	1623
	2:21	I a man cleanses himself from the latter,	1569
Phm	1:17	So i you consider me a partner,	1623
	1:18	I he has done you any wrong	1623
Heb	2: 2	For i the message spoken	1623
	2: 3	how shall we escape i we ignore such	AIT
	3: 6	i we hold on to our courage and the hope	1570
	3: 7	"Today, i you hear his voice,	1569
	3:14	to share in Christ i we hold firmly till	1570
	3:15	"Today, i you hear his voice,	1569
	3:18	that they would never enter his rest i not	1623
	4: 7	"Today, i you hear his voice,	1569
	4: 8	For i Joshua had given them rest,	1623
	6: 6	i they fall away, to be brought back	AIT
	7:11	I perfection could have been attained	1623
	7:15	And what we have said is even more clear i	1623
	8: 4	I he were on earth, he would not be a priest,	1623
	8: 7	For i there had been nothing wrong with	1623
	10: 2	I it could, would they not have stopped	2075
	10:26	I we deliberately keep on sinning	AIT
	10:38	And i he shrinks back, I will not be pleased	AIT
	11:15	I they had been thinking of the	1623+3525
	12: 8	I you are not disciplined	1623
	12:20	"I even an animal touches the mountain,	1569
	12:25	I they did not escape when they refused	1623
	12:25	i we turn away from him who warns us	AIT
	13: 3	Remember those in prison as i	6055
	13: 3	and those who are mistreated as i	6055
	13:23	I he arrives soon.	1569
Jas	1: 5	I any of you lacks wisdom, he should ask	1623
	1:26	I anyone considers himself religious and	1623
	2: 3	I you show special attention to the man	AIT
	2: 8	I you really keep the royal law found	1623
	2: 9	But i you show favoritism, you sin	1623
	2:11	I you do not commit adultery	1623
	2:14	i a man claims to have faith but has no	1569
	2:16	I one of you says to him, "Go,	AIT
	2:17	i it is not accompanied by action, is dead.	1569
	3: 2	I anyone is never at fault in what he says,	1623
	3: 4	But i your harbor bitter envy	1623
	4:15	you ought to say, "I it is the Lord's will,	1569
	5:15	I he has sinned, he will be forgiven.	1623
	5:19	i one of you should wander from the truth	1569
1Pe	2:19	For it is commendable i a man bears up	1623
	2:20	But how is it to your credit i you receive	1623
	2:20	But i you suffer for doing good	1623
	3: 1	i any of them do not believe the word,	1623
	3: 6	i you do what is right and do not give way	AIT
	3:13	Who is going to harm you i you are eager	1569
	3:14	even i you should suffer for what is right,	1623
	3:17	It is better, i it is God's will,	1623

1Pe	4:11	I anyone speaks, he should do it	1623
	4:11	I anyone serves, he should do it with	1623
	4:14	I you are insulted because of the name	1623
	4:15	I you suffer, it should not be as a murderer	1142
	4:16	However, i you suffer as a Christian,	1623
	4:17	and i it begins with us,	1623
	4:18	"I it is hard for the righteous to be saved,	1623
2Pe	1: 8	For i you possess these qualities	AIT
	1: 9	i anyone does not have them,	AIT
	1:10	For i you do these things,	AIT
	2: 4	I God did not spare angels	1623
	2: 5	i he did not spare the ancient world	NIG
	2: 6	i he condemned the cities of Sodom	NIG
	2: 7	and i he rescued Lot,	NIG
	2: 9	i this is so, then the Lord knows how	NIG
	2:20	I they have escaped the corruption of	1623
1Jn	1: 6	I we claim to have fellowship with him	1569
	1: 7	But i we walk in the light, as he is in	1569
	1: 8	I we claim to be without sin, we deceive	1569
	1: 9	I we confess our sins, he is faithful and just	1569
	1:10	I we claim we have not sinned,	1569
	2: 1	But i anybody does sin, we have one who	1569
	2: 3	come to know him i we obey his commands.	1569
	2: 5	But i anyone obeys his word,	323
	2:15	I anyone loves the world,	1569
	2:19	For i they had belonged to us,	1623
	2:24	I it does, you also will remain in the Son	1569
	2:29	I you know that he is righteous,	1569
	3:13	my brothers, i the world hates you.	1623
	3:17	I anyone has material possessions	323
	3:21	i our hearts do not condemn us,	1569
	4:12	but i we love one another,	1569
	4:15	I anyone acknowledges that Jesus is	1569
	4:20	I anyone says, "I love God,"	1569
	5:14	that i we ask anything according to his will,	1569
	5:15	And i we know that he hears us—	1569
	5:16	I anyone sees his brother commit a sin	1569
2Jn	1:10	I anyone comes to you and does not bring	1623
3Jn	1:10	So I come, I will call attention to what	1569
Rev	2: 5	I you do not repent, I will come to you	1623
	3: 3	But i you do not wake up, I will come like	1623
	3:20	I anyone hears my voice and opens	1569
	5: 6	a Lamb, looking as i it had been slain,	6055
	11: 5	I anyone tries to harm them,	1623
	13:10	I anyone is to go into captivity,	1623
	13:10	I anyone is to be killed with the sword,	1623
	13:18	I anyone has insight, let him calculate	AIT
	14: 9	"I anyone worships the beast and his image	1623
	20:15	I anyone's name was not found written in	1623
	22:18	I anyone adds anything to them,	1569
	22:19	And i anyone takes words away	1569

IGAL (3)

Nu	13: 7	from the tribe of Issachar, I son of Joseph;	3319
2Sa	23:36	I son of Nathan from Zobah,	3319
1Ch	3:22	Hattush, I, Bariah, Neariah and Shaphat—	3319

IGDALIAH (1)

| Jer | 35: 4 | the sons of Hanan son of I the man of God. | 3323 |

IGEAL (KJV) See IGAL

IGNOBLE (1)

| 2Ti | 2:20 | for noble purposes and some for i. | 871 |

IGNOMINY (KJV) See SHAME

IGNORANCE (7) [IGNORE]

Eze	45:20	who sins unintentionally or through i;	7344
Ac	3:17	"Now, brothers, I know that you acted in i,	53
	17:30	In the past God overlooked such i,	53
Eph	4:18	of the i that is in them due to the hardening	53
1Ti	1:13	I was shown mercy because I acted in i	51
Heb	9: 7	sins the people had committed in i.	52
1Pe	1:14	when you lived in i.	53

IGNORANT (12) [IGNORE]

Ps	73:22	I was senseless and i;	3359+4202
Pr	30: 2	"I am the most i of men;	1280
Isa	44: 9	they are i, to their own shame.	1153+3359
	45:20	I are those who carry about idols of wood,	3359+4202
Ro	11:25	I do not want you to be i of this mystery,	51
1Co	10: 1	For I do not want you to be i of the fact,	51
	12: 1	brothers, I do not want you to be i.	51
	15:34	for there are some who are i of God—	57+2400
1Th	4:13	to be i about those who fall asleep,	51
Heb	5: 2	with those who are i and are going astray,	51
1Pe	2:15	by doing good you should silence the i talk	57
2Pe	3:16	which i and unstable people distort,	276

IGNORE (10) [IGNORANCE, IGNORANT, IGNORED, IGNORES, IGNORING]

Dt	22: 1	do not i it but be sure to take it back to him.	6623
	22: 3	or anything he loses. Do not i it.	6623
	22: 4	or his ox fallen on the road, do not i it.	6623
Ps	9:12	he does not i the cry of the afflicted.	8894
	55: 1	O God, do not i my plea;	6623
	74:23	Do not i the clamor of your adversaries,	8894
	119:139	for my enemies i your words.	8894
Pr	8:33	to my instruction and be wise; do not i it.	7277

Hos	4: 6	I also *will* i your children.
Heb	2: 3	how shall we escape *if we* i such a great salvation?

8894
288

IGNORED (5) [IGNORE]

Ex	9:21	But those who i the word of	4202+4213+8492
Pr	1:25	since *you* i all my advice and would	7277
	2:17	who has left the partner of her youth and i	8894
Hos	4: 6	because *you have* i the law of your God,	8894
1Co	14:38	If he ignores this, *he himself will be* i.	51

IGNORES (4) [IGNORE]

Pr	10:17	but *whoever* i correction leads others astray.	6440
	13:18	He who i discipline comes to poverty	7277
	15:32	He who i discipline despises himself.	7277
1Co	14:38	If he i this, he himself will be ignored.	51

IGNORING (1) [IGNORE]

Mk	5:36	I what they said, Jesus told the synagogue	4159

IIM (1)

Jos	15:29	Baalah, I, Ezem,	6517

IJE-ABARIM (KJV) See IYE ABARIM

IJON (3)

1Ki	15:20	He conquered I, Dan, Abel Beth Maacah	6510
2Ki	15:29	of Assyria came and took I,	6510
2Ch	16: 4	They conquered I, Dan,	6510

IKKESH (3)

2Sa	23:26	Helez the Paltite, Ira son of I from Tekoa,	6837
1Ch	11:28	Ira son of I from Tekoa,	6837
	27: 9	was Ira the son of I the Tekoite.	6837

ILAI (1)

1Ch	11:29	Sibbecai the Hushathite, I the Ahohite,	6519

ILL (24) [ILLNESS, ILLNESSES, ILLS]

Ge	48: 1	"Your father is i."	2703
Dt	15: 9	*do* not show i will toward your needy brother	6524+8317
1Sa	19:14	Michal said, "He is i."	2703
	30:13	when *I* became i three days ago.	2703
2Sa	12:15	and he became i.	653
	13: 5	"Go to bed and **pretend to be** i,"	2703
	13: 6	So Amnon lay down and **pretended to be** i.	2703
1Ki	14: 1	that time Abijah son of Jeroboam *became* i,	2703
	14: 5	to ask you about her son, for he *is* i,	2703
	17:17	the woman who owned the house *became* i.	2703
2Ki	8: 7	and Ben-Hadad king of Aram *was* i.	2703
	20: 1	In those days Hezekiah *became* i and was at	2703
2Ch	21:15	be very i with a lingering disease of	2716
	32:24	In those days Hezekiah *became* i and was at	2703
Ne	2: 2	so sad when you *are* not i?	2703
Job	6: 7	I refuse to touch it; such food makes me i.	1867
Ps	35:13	Yet when they *were* i,	2703
Isa	33:24	No one living in Zion will say, *"I am* i";	2703
	38: 1	In those days Hezekiah *became* i and was at	2703
Da	8:27	was exhausted and **lay** i for several days.	2703
Mt	4:24	all who **were** i with various diseases,	2400+2809
Ac	28: 5	into the fire and suffered no i **effects.**	2805
Php	2:26	because you heard he was i.	820
	2:27	Indeed he was i, and almost died.	820

ILL-GOTTEN (5) [GET]

Pr	1:19	is the end of all *who* **go after** i **gain;**	1298+1299
	10: 2	I treasures are of no value,	8400
	28:16	he who hates i **gain** will enjoy a long life.	1299
Mic	4:13	You will devote their i **gains** to the LORD,	1299
	6:10	your i treasures and the short ephah,	8400

ILL-TEMPERED (1) [TEMPER]

Pr	21:19	a desert than with a quarrelsome and i wife.	4088

ILL-TREAT, ILL-TREATED, ILL-TREATING (Anglicized) See MISTREAT, MISTREATED, MISTREATING

ILLEGAL (1) [LEGAL]

Ex	22: 9	In all cases of i **possession** of an ox,	7322

ILLEGITIMATE (3)

Hos	5: 7	they give birth to i children.	2424
Jn	8:41	"We *are* not i children,"	1164+1666+4518
Heb	12: 8	then you are i children and not true sons.	3785

ILLICIT (1)

Eze	16:33	to you from everywhere for your i **favors.**	9373

ILLNESS (11) [ILL]

2Sa	13: 2	Amnon became frustrated to the point of i	2703
2Ki	8: 8	ask him, 'Will I recover from this i?' "	2716
	8: 9	'Will I recover from this i?' "	2716
	13:14	Now Elisha was suffering from the i	2716
	20:12	because he had heard of Hezekiah's i.	2703

2Ch	16:12	even in his i he did not seek help from	2716
Ps	41: 3	and restore him from his bed of i.	2716
Isa	38: 9	of Hezekiah king of Judah after his i	2703
	39: 1	because he had heard of *his* i and recovery.	2703
Gal	4:13	an i that I first preached the gospel to you.	819+3836+4922
	4:14	Even though my i was a trial to you,	NIG

ILLNESSES (3) [ILL]

Dt	28:59	and severe and lingering i.	2716
Ac	19:12	and their i were cured and	3798
1Ti	5:23	of your stomach and your frequent i.	819

ILLS (1) [ILL]

Ps	73: 5	they are not plagued by human i.	NIH

ILLUMINATED (1)

Rev	18: 1	and the earth *was* i by his splendor.	5894

ILLUSIONS (1)

Isa	30:10	Tell us pleasant things, prophesy i.	4562

ILLUSTRATION (1)

Heb	9: 9	This is an i for the present time,	4130

ILLYRICUM (1)

Ro	15:19	So from Jerusalem all the way around to I,	2665

IMAGE (47) [IMAGES]

Ge	1:26	Then God said, "Let us make man in our i,	7512
	1:27	So God created man in his own i,	7512
	1:27	in the i *of* God he created him;	7512
	5: 3	in his own i; and he named him Seth.	7512
	9: 6	for in the i of God has God made man.	7512
Lev	26: 1	up an i or a sacred stone for yourselves,	7181
Dt	4:16	an idol, an i *of* any shape,	9454
	27:15	"Cursed is the man who carves an i or casts	7181
Jdg	17: 3	the LORD for my son to make a **carved** i	7181
	17: 4	who made them into the i and the idol.	7181
	18:14	a **carved** i and a cast idol?	7181
	18:17	the land went inside and took the **carved** i,	7181
	18:18	into Micah's house and took the **carved** i,	7181
	18:20	the other household gods and the **carved** i	7181
2Ch	33: 7	He took the carved i he had made and put it	6166
	33:15	of the foreign gods and removed the i from	6166
Ne	9:18	when they cast for themselves an i of a calf	5011
Ps	106:20	They exchanged their Glory for an i of	9322
Isa	40:18	What i will you compare him to?	1952
	48: 5	my wooden i and metal god ordained	7181
Jer	44:19	that we were making cakes **like** her i	6771
Da	3: 1	King Nebuchadnezzar made an i of gold,	10614
	3: 2	to the dedication of the i he had set up.	10614
	3: 3	the i that King Nebuchadnezzar had set up,	10614
	3: 5	you must fall down and worship the i	10614
	3: 7	down and worshiped the i *of* gold	10614
	3:10	of music must fall down and worship the i	10614
	3:12	nor worship the i *of* gold you have set up."	10614
	3:14	or worship the i *of* gold I have set up?	10614
	3:15	to fall down and worship the i I made,	10614
	3:18	or worship the i *of* gold you have set up."	10614
Hab	2:18	Or an i that teaches lies?	5011
Ac	17:29	an i made by man's design and skill.	5916
	19:35	and of her i, **which fell from heaven?**	1479
1Co	11: 7	since he is the i and glory of God;	1635
2Co	4: 4	who is the i of God.	1635
Col	1:15	He is the i of the invisible God,	1635
	3:10	in knowledge in the i of its Creator.	1635
Rev	13:14	He ordered them to set up an i in honor of	1635
	13:15	He was given power to give breath *to* the i	1635
	13:15	and cause all who refused to worship the i	1635
	14: 9	the beast and his i and receives his mark on	1635
	14:11	for those who worship the beast and his i,	1635
	15: 2	and his i and over the number of his name.	1635
	16: 2	the mark of the beast and worshiped his i.	1635
	19:20	the mark of the beast and worshiped his i.	1635
	20: 4	They had not worshiped the beast or his i	1635

IMAGES (35) [IMAGE]

Nu	33:52	Destroy all their **carved** i	5381
Dt	7:25	i of their gods you are to burn in the fire.	7178
	29:17	among them their **detestable** i and idols	9199
2Ch	34: 3	Asherah poles, carved idols and **cast** i.	5011
	34: 4	Asherah poles, the idols and the i.	5011
Ps	97: 7	All who worship i are put to shame,	7181
Isa	10:10	kingdoms whose i excelled those	7178
	10:11	not deal with Jerusalem and her i as I dealt	6773
	21: 9	All the i *of* its gods lie shattered on	7178
	30:22	with silver and your i covered with gold;	5011
	41:29	their i are but wind and confusion.	5822
	42:17	But those who trust in idols, who say to i,	5011
	46: 1	i **that are carried about** are burdensome,	5953
Jer	8:19	they provoked me to anger with their i,	7178
	10:14	His i are a fraud;	5822
	16:18	with the lifeless forms of their **vile** i	9199
	50: 2	Her i will be put to shame.	6773
	51:17	His i are a fraud;	5822
Eze	5:11	with all your **vile** i and detestable practices,	9199
	7:20	to make their **detestable** idols and **vile** i.	9199
	11:18	to it and remove all its **vile** i	9199
	16:17	to their **vile** i and detestable idols,	9199
	20: 7	get rid of the **vile** i you have set your eyes	9199
	20: 8	of the **vile** i they had set their eyes on,	9199

Eze	20:30	and lust after their **vile** i?	9199
	30:13	and put an end to the i in Memphis.	496
	37:23	and **vile** i or with any of their offenses,	9199
Da	4: 5	the i and visions that passed	10217
	11: 8	their **metal** i and their valuable articles	5816
Hos	11: 2	to the Baals and they burned incense to i.	7178
	13: 2	from their silver, cleverly fashioned i,	6773
Mic	1: 7	I will destroy all her i.	6773
	5:13	I will destroy your **carved** i	7178
Na	1:14	I will destroy the **carved** i and cast idols	7181
Ro	1:23	the glory of the immortal God for i made	1635

IMAGINATION (2) [IMAGINE]

Eze	13: 2	to those who prophesy out of their own i:	4213
	13:17	who prophesy out of their own i.	4213

IMAGINATIONS (2) [IMAGINE]

Isa	65: 2	pursuing their own i—	4742
	66:18	"And I, because of their actions and their i,	4742

IMAGINE (4) [IMAGINATION, IMAGINATIONS]

Ps	41: 7	*they* i the worst for me, saying,	3108
Pr	18:11	they i it an unscalable wall.	928+5381
	23:33	and your mind i confusing things.	1819
Eph	3:20	or i, according to his power that is at work	3783

IMITATE (6) [IMITATED, IMITATORS]

Dt	18: 9	to i the detestable ways of the nations	3869+6913
Eze	23:48	may take warning and not i you.	3869+6913
1Co	4:16	Therefore I urge you to i me.	1181+3629
Heb	6:12	but to i those who through faith	3629
	13: 7	of their way of life and i their faith.	3628
3Jn	1:11	*do* not i what is evil but what is good.	3628

IMITATED (1) [IMITATE]

2Ki	17:15	They i the nations around them although	339

IMITATORS (3) [IMITATE]

Eph	5: 1	Be i of God, therefore,	3629
1Th	1: 6	You became i of us and of the Lord;	3629
	2:14	became i of God's churches in Judea,	3629

IMLAH (4)

1Ki	22: 8	He is Micaiah son of I."	3551
	22: 9	"Bring Micaiah son of I at once."	3551
2Ch	18: 7	He is Micaiah son of I"	3550
	18: 8	"Bring Micaiah son of I at once."	3550

IMMANUEL (3)

Isa	7:14	give birth to a son, and will call him I.	6672
	8: 8	the breadth of your land, O I!"	6672
Mt	1:23	I"—which means, "God with us."	1842

IMMEASURABLY (1) [MEASURE]

Eph	3:20	to do i more than all we ask or imagine,	5655

IMMEDIATE (1) [IMMEDIATELY]

1Ti	5: 8	and especially for his i **family,**	3858

IMMEDIATELY (55) [IMMEDIATE]

1Sa	28:20	I Saul fell full length on the ground,	4554
2Sa	15:14	*We must* leave i, or he will move quickly	4554
	17:16	Now send a message i and tell David,	4559
Ezr	4:23	they went i to the Jews in Jerusalem	10089+10096
Ne	5:11	Give back to them i their fields,	2021+3427+3869
Est	2: 9	I *he* provided her with her beauty treatments	987
Da	3: 6	and worship will i be thrown into a blazing furnace.	10002+10734
	3:15	you will be thrown i into a blazing furnace.	10191+10734
	4:33	I what had been said about	10002+10734
Mt	4:22	and i they left the boat and their father	2311
	8: 3	I he was cured of his leprosy	2311
	14:22	I Jesus made the disciples get into the boat	2311
	14:27	But Jesus i said to them: "Take courage!	2317
	14:31	I Jesus reached out his hand	2311
	20:34	I they received their sight	2311
	21:19	I the tree withered.	4202
	24:29	"I after the distress of those days	2311
	26:74	I a rooster crowed.	2311
	27:48	I one of them ran and got a sponge.	2311
Mk	1:42	I the leprosy left him and he was cured.	2311
	2: 8	I Jesus knew in his spirit that this was what	2317
	5:29	I her bleeding stopped and she felt	2317
	5:42	I the girl stood up and walked	2317
	6:27	So he i sent an executioner with orders	2317
	6:45	I Jesus made his disciples get into the boat	2317
	6:50	I he spoke to them and said,	2317
	9:20	it i threw the boy into a convulsion.	2317
	9:24	The boy's father exclaimed, "I do believe;	2317
	10:52	I he received his sight and followed Jesus	2317
	14:72	I the rooster crowed the second time.	2317
Lk	1:64	I his mouth was opened	4202
	5:13	And i the leprosy left him.	2311
	5:25	I he stood up in front of them,	4202
	8:44	and i her bleeding stopped.	4202
	12:36	when he comes and knocks they can i open	2311
	12:54	i you say, 'It's going to rain,' and it does.	2311

Lk 13:13 and i she straightened up and praised God. 4202
    14: 5 will you not i pull him out?" 2311
    18:43 I he received his sight and followed Jesus, 4202
    19: 5 "Zacchaeus, come down i. 5067
    20:19 for a way to arrest him i, 899+1877+3836+6052
Jn 6:21 and i the boat reached the shore 2311
Ac 9:18 I, something like scales fell from Saul's 2311
    9:34 I Aeneas got up. 2311
    10:16 and the sheet was taken back to heaven. 2317
    10:33 So I sent for you i, 1994
    12:23 I, because Herod did not give praise 4202
    13:11 I mist and darkness came over him, 4202
    16:33 then i he and all his family were baptized. 4202
    17:14 The brothers i sent Paul to the coast, 2311
    21:30 and i the gates were shut. 2311
    22:18 'Leave Jerusalem i, because they will 1877+5443
    22:29 about to question him withdrew i. 2311
Gal 1:17 but I went i into Arabia and later returned NIG
Jas 1:24 goes away and i forgets what he looks like. 2311

IMMENSE (1)
Eze 1: 4 an i cloud with flashing lightning 1524

IMMER (10)
1Ch 9:12 the son of Meshillemith, the son of I. 612
    24:14 the fifteenth to Bilgah, the sixteenth to I, 612
Ezr 2:37 of I 1,052 612
    2:59 Tel Harsha, Kerub, Addon and I, 613
    10:20 From the descendants of I: 612
Ne 3:29 of I made repairs opposite his house. 612
    7:40 of I 1,052 612
    7:61 Tel Harsha, Kerub, Addon and I, 613
    11:13 the son of Meshillemoth, the son of I, 612
Jer 20: 1 When the priest Pashhur son of I, 612

IMMORAL (10) [IMMORALITY]
Pr 6:24 keeping you from the i woman, 8273
1Co 5: 9 not to associate with sexually i people— 4521
    5:10 the people of this world who are i, 4521
    5:11 a brother but is sexually i or greedy, 4521
    6: 9 the sexually i nor idolaters nor adulterers 4521
Eph 5: 5 No i, impure or greedy person— 4521
Heb 12:16 See that no one is sexually i, 4521
    13: 4 the adulterer and all the sexually i. 4521
Rev 21: 8 the vile, the murderers, the sexually i, 4521
    22:15 the sexually i, the murderers, 4521

IMMORALITY (23) [IMMORAL]
Nu 25: 1 the men began to indulge in sexual i 2388
Jer 3: 9 Because Israel's i mattered so little to her, 2394
Mt 15:19 adultery, sexual i, theft, false testimony, 4518
Mk 7:21 come evil thoughts, sexual i, theft, 4518
Ac 15:20 from food polluted by idols, from sexual i, 4518
    15:29 of strangled animals and from sexual i, 4518
    21:25 of strangled animals and from sexual i." 4518
Ro 13:13 not in sexual i and debauchery, 3130
1Co 5: 1 It is actually reported that there is sexual i 4518
    6:13 The body is not meant for sexual i, 4518
    6:18 Flee from sexual i. 4518
    7: 2 But since there is so much i, 4518
    10: 8 We should not commit sexual i, 4519
Gal 5:19 sexual i, impurity and debauchery; 4518
Eph 5: 3 not be even a hint of sexual i, 4518
Col 3: 5 sexual i, impurity, lust, 4518
1Th 4: 3 that you should avoid sexual i; 4518
Jude 1: 4 the grace of our God into a license for i 816
    1: 7 gave themselves up to sexual i 1745
Rev 2:14 to idols and by committing sexual i. 4519
    2:20 into sexual i and the eating 4519
    2:21 I have given her time to repent of her i, 4518
    9:21 their sexual i or their thefts. 4518

IMMORTAL (3) [IMMORTALITY]
Ro 1:23 exchanged the glory of the i God for images 915
1Ti 1:17 Now to the King eternal, i, invisible, 915
    6:16 who alone is i and who lives 114

IMMORTALITY (5) [IMMORTAL]
Pr 12:28 along that path is i. 440+4638
Ro 2: 7 honor and i, he will give eternal life. 914
1Co 15:53 and the mortal with i, 114
    15:54 and the mortal with i, 114
2Ti 1:10 and has brought life and i to light through 914

IMMOVABLE (2)
Job 41:23 they are firm and i. 1153+4572
Zec 12: 3 I will make Jerusalem an i rock for all 5098

IMMUTABILITY, IMMUTABLE (KJV) See UNCHANGEABLE

IMNA (1)
1Ch 7:35 Zophah, I, Shelesh and Amal. 3557

IMNAH (4) [IMNITE]
Ge 46:17 I, Ishvah, Ishvi and Beriah. 3555
Nu 26:44 through I, the Imnite clan; 3555
1Ch 7:30 sons of Asher: I, Ishvah, Ishvi and Beriah. 3555
2Ch 31:14 Kore son of I the Levite, 3555

IMNITE (1) [IMNAH]
Nu 26:44 through Imnah, the I clan; 3555

IMPALED (1)
Ezr 6:11 and he is to be lifted up and i on it. 10411

IMPART (2) [IMPARTED, IMPARTS]
Ro 1:11 so that I may i to you some spiritual gift 3556
Gal 3:21 if a law had been given that could i life, 2443

IMPARTED (1) [IMPART]
Ecc 12: 9 but also he i knowledge to the people. 4340

IMPARTIAL (1) [IMPARTIALLY]
Jas 3:17 full of mercy and good fruit, i and sincere. 88

IMPARTIALLY (2) [IMPARTIAL]
1Ch 24: 5 divided them i by drawing lots, 465+465+6640
1Pe 1:17 on a Father who judges each man's work i, 719

IMPARTS (1) [IMPART]
Pr 29:15 The rod of correction i wisdom, 5989

IMPATIENT (3)
Nu 21: 4 But the people grew i on the way; 5883+7918
Job 4: 2 ventures a word with you, will you be i? 4206
    21: 4 Why should I not be i? 7918

IMPEDIMENT (KJV) See HARDLY TALK

IMPENITENT (KJV) See UNREPENTANT

IMPERFECT (1)
1Co 13:10 perfection comes, the i disappears. 1666+3538

IMPERIAL (13) [EMPIRE]
2Ki 25: 8 Nebuzaradan commander of the i guard, 3184
    25:10 under the commander of the i guard, 3184
    25:15 The commander of the i guard took away 3184
Jer 39: 9 of the i guard carried into exile to Babylon 3184
    39:11 commander of the i guard: 3184
    40: 1 of the i guard had released him at Ramah. 3184
    41:10 of the i guard had appointed Gedaliah son 3184
    43: 6 of the i guard had left with Gedaliah son 3184
    52:12 Nebuzaradan commander of the i guard, 3184
    52:14 under the commander of the i guard broke 3184
    52:19 The commander of the i guard took away 3184
    52:30 the commander of the i guard. 3184
Ac 27: 1 who belonged to the I Regiment. 4935

IMPERISHABLE (6)
1Co 15:42 that is sown is perishable, it is raised i; 914+1877
    15:50 nor does the perishable inherit the i. 914
    15:52 the dead will be raised i, 915
    15:53 the perishable must clothe itself with the i, 914
    15:54 with the i, and the mortal with immortality, 914
1Pe 1:23 not of perishable seed, but of i, 915

IMPETUOUS (2)
Job 6: 3 no wonder my words have been i. 4362
Hab 1: 6 that ruthless and i people, 4554

IMPLACABLE (KJV) See RUTHLESS

IMPLANTED (1) [PLANT]
Ps 94: 9 Does he who i the ear not hear? 5749

IMPLEAD (KJV) See PRESS CHARGES

IMPLORE (2)
Mal 1: 9 "Now i God to be gracious to us. 2704+7156
2Co 5:20 We i you on Christ's behalf: 1289

IMPORTANCE (1) [IMPORTANT]
1Co 15: 3 I passed on to you as of first i: 1877+4755

IMPORTANT (19) [IMPORTANCE]
Jos 10: 2 because Gibeon was an i city, 1524
1Ki 3: 4 for that was the most i high place, 1524
2Ki 25: 9 Every i building he burned down. 1524
Jer 52:13 Every i building he burned down. 1524
Jnh 3: 3 Now Nineveh was a very i city— 1524
Mt 6:25 Is not life more i than food, AIT
    6:25 and the body more i than clothes? NIG
    23: 6 and the most i seats in the synagogues; 4751
    23:23 But you have neglected the more i matters 987
    23:23 which is the most i? 4755
Mk 12:28 which is the most i?" 4755
    12:29 "The most i one," answered Jesus, "is this: 4755
    12:33 is more i than all burnt offerings 4358
    12:39 and have the most i seats in the synagogues 4751
Lk 11:43 because you love the most i seats in 4751
    14: 9 you will have to take the least i place. 2274
    20:46 and have the most i seats in the synagogues 4751
Ac 8:27 an i official in charge of all the treasury 1541

IMPORTED (7)
1Ki 10:12 So much almugwood has never been i 995
    10:28 Solomon's horses were i from Egypt and 4604
    10:29 They i a chariot from Egypt 2256+3655+6590
2Ch 1:16 Solomon's horses were i from Egypt and 4604
    1:17 They i a chariot from Egypt 2256+3655+6590
    9:28 Solomon's horses were i from Egypt and 3655
Isa 17:10 the finest plants and plant i vines, 2424

IMPORTUNITY (KJV) See BOLDNESS

IMPOSE (2) [IMPOSED, IMPOSING, SELF-IMPOSED]
Ezr 7:24 that you have no authority to i taxes, 10667
Rev 2:24 not i any other burden on you): 965

IMPOSED (5) [IMPOSE]
2Ki 23:33 and he i on Judah a levy of a hundred talents 5989
2Ch 24: 6 in from Judah and Jerusalem the tax i AIT
    36: 3 i on Judah a levy of a hundred talents 6740
Est 10: 1 King Xerxes i tribute throughout 8492
Jer 19: 9 during the stress of the siege i on them by 7439

IMPOSING (4) [IMPOSE]
Jos 22:10 and the half-tribe of Manasseh built an i altar 1524+4200+5260
1Ki 9: 8 And though this temple is now i, 6609
2Ch 7:21 And though this temple is now so i, 6609
Da 7:20 the horn that looked more i than the others 10647

IMPOSSIBLE (13)
Ge 11: 6 then nothing they plan to do will be i 1307
Jdg 6: 5 It was i to count the men and their camels; 401
2Sa 13: 2 it seemed i for him to do anything to her. 7098
Mt 17:20 Nothing will be i for you." 104
    19:26 "With man this is i, but with God all things 105
Mk 10:27 "With man this is i, but not with God; 105
Lk 1:37 For nothing is i with God." 104
    18:27 "What is i with men is possible with God." 105
Ac 2:24 i for death to keep its hold on him. 1543+4024
Heb 6: 4 It is i for those who have once been enlightened, 105
    6:18 by two unchangeable things in which it is i 105
    10: 4 because it is i for the blood of bulls 105
    11: 6 And without faith it is i to please God, 105

IMPOSTORS (2)
2Co 6: 8 genuine, yet regarded as i; 4418
2Ti 3:13 while evil men and i will go from bad 1200

IMPOTENT (KJV) See CRIPPLE, CRIPPLED, DISABLED, INVALID

IMPOVERISHED (1) [POOR]
Jdg 6: 6 Midian so i the Israelites that they cried out 1937

IMPRESS (1) [IMPRESSED, IMPRESSES, IMPRESSION, IMPRESSIVE]
Dt 6: 7 I them on your children. 9112

IMPRESSED (1) [IMPRESS]
Ecc 9:13 of wisdom that greatly i me: 448

IMPRESSES (1) [IMPRESS]
Pr 17:10 A rebuke i a man of discernment more than 5737

IMPRESSION (1) [IMPRESS]
Gal 6:12 to make a good i outwardly are trying 2349

IMPRESSIVE (1) [IMPRESS]
1Sa 9: 2 an i young man without equal among 3202

IMPRISON (1) [PRISON]
Ac 22:19 to another to i and beat those who believe 5872

IMPRISONED (4) [PRISON]
Ge 41:10 and he i me and the chief baker 928+5464+5989
1Sa 23: 7 for David has i himself by entering a town 6037
Jer 32: 3 Zedekiah king of Judah had i him there, 3973
    37:15 and had him beaten and i 657+1074+2021+5989

IMPRISONMENT (3) [PRISON]
Ezr 7:26 banishment, confiscation of property, or i. 10054
Ac 23:29 against him that deserved death or i 1301
    26:31 not doing anything that deserves death or i." 1301

IMPRISONMENTS (1) [PRISON]
2Co 6: 5 in beatings, i and riots; 5871

IMPRISONS (1) [PRISON]
Job 12:14 the man he i cannot be released. 6037

IMPROPER (1) [IMPROPERLY]
Eph 5: 3 because these are i for God's holy people.   NIG

IMPROPERLY (1) [IMPROPER]
1Co 7:36 If anyone thinks *he is* **acting** i toward   858

IMPROVISE (1)
Am 6: 5 like David and i on musical instruments.   3108

IMPUDENT (KJV) See BRAZEN, OBSTINATE, HARDENED

IMPURE (16) [IMPURITIES, IMPURITY]
Lev	7:18	for it is i; the person who eats any of it	7002
	19: 7	it is i and will not be accepted.	7002
Nu	5:14	and he suspects his wife and she *is* i—	3237
	5:14	and suspects her even though she *is* not i—	3237
	5:19	not gone astray and become i while married	3240
Dt	23: 9	keep away from everything i.	8273
Job	14: 4	Who can bring what is pure from the i?	3238
Ac	10:14	"I have never eaten anything i or unclean."	3123
	10:15	"*Do not* **call** anything i that God has made	3123
	10:28	that I should not call any man i or unclean.	3123
	11: 8	Nothing i or unclean has ever entered my	3123
	11: 9	'*Do not* **call** anything i that God has made	3123
Eph	5: 5	No immoral, i or greedy person—	176
1Th	2: 3	not spring from error or i motives,	174
	4: 7	For God did not call us **to be** i,	174+2093
Rev	21:27	Nothing i will ever enter it,	3123

IMPURITIES (3) [IMPURE]
Isa	1:25	and remove all your i.	975
Eze	24:11	and its copper glows so its i may be melted	3240
	36:25	from all your i and from all your idols.	3240

IMPURITY (16) [IMPURE]
Lev	15:19	i of her **monthly period**	5614
	20:21	marries his brother's wife, it is an **act of** i;	5614
Nu	5:13	from her husband and *her* i is undetected	3237
	5:28	not defiled herself and is **free from** i,	3196
Ezr	9:11	with their i from one end to the other.	3240
Eze	24:13	" 'Now your i is lewdness.	3240
	24:13	but you would not be cleansed from your i,	3240
Zec	13: 1	to cleanse them from sin and i.	5614
	13: 2	both the prophets and the spirit of i from	3240
Ro	1:24	of their hearts to **sexual** i for the degrading	174
	6:19	the parts of your body in slavery *to* i and	174
2Co	12:21	and have not repented of the i,	174
Gal	5:19	sexual immorality, i and debauchery;	174
Eph	4:19	so as to indulge in every kind *of* i,	174
	5: 3	or of any kind of i, or of greed,	174
Col	3: 5	sexual immorality, i, lust,	174

IMPUTE, IMPUTED, IMPUTETH, IMPUTING (KJV) See ACCUSE, COUNT, COUNTING, CREDIT, CREDITED, CREDITS, HOLD GUILTY, TAKEN INTO ACCOUNT

IMRAH (1)
1Ch 7:36 Suah, Harnepher, Shual, Beri, **I,**   3559

IMRI (2)
1Ch	9: 4	the son of Omri, the son of **I,**	617
Ne	3: 2	and Zaccur son of **I** built next to them.	617

IN (11277) [INASMUCH, INMOST, INNER, INNERMOST, INSIDE, WITHIN] See Index of Articles Etc.

INASMUCH (1) [IN]
Ro 11:13 **I as** I am the apostle to the Gentiles,   2093+3525+4012+4036

INCAPABLE (1)
Hos 8: 5 How long *will they be* i of purity?   3523+4202

INCENSE (150) [FRANKINCENSE, INCENSED]
Ex	25: 6	for the anointing oil and for the fragrant i;	7792
	30: 1	an altar of acacia wood for burning i.	7792
	30: 7	"Aaron must burn fragrant i on	7792
	30: 7	He must burn i again when he lights	5626ˢ
	30: 8	so i will burn regularly before the LORD	7792
	30: 9	Do not offer on this altar any other i	7792
	30:27	and its accessories, the altar of i,	7792
	30:35	and make a fragrant blend of i,	7792
	30:37	Do not make any i with this formula	7792
	31: 8	and all its accessories, the altar of i,	7792
	31:11	and the anointing oil and fragrant i for	7792
	35: 8	for the anointing oil and for the fragrant i;	7792
	35:15	the altar of i with its poles, the anointing oil	7792
	35:15	the anointing oil and the fragrant i;	7792
	35:28	for the anointing oil and for the fragrant i.	7792
	37:25	made the altar of i out of acacia wood.	7792
Ex	37:29	fragrant i—the work of a perfumer.	7792
	39:38	the anointing oil, the fragrant i,	7792
	40: 5	Place the gold altar of i in front of the ark	7792
	40:27	and burned fragrant i on it,	7792
Lev	2: 1	He is to pour oil on it, put i on it	4247
	2: 2	together with all the i,	4247
	2:15	Put oil and i on it; it is a grain offering.	4247
	2:16	together with all the i,	4247
	4: 7	on the horns of the altar of fragrant i that is	7792
	5:11	He must not put oil or i on it,	4247
	6:15	together with all the i on the grain offering,	4247
	10: 1	put fire in them and added i;	7792
	16:12	of finely ground fragrant i and take them	7792
	16:13	to put the i on the fire before the LORD,	7792
	16:13	of the i will conceal the atonement cover	7792
	24: 7	Along each row put *some* pure i as	4247
	26:30	cut down your i **altars**	2802
Nu	4:16	the fragrant i, the regular grain offering and	7792
	5:15	He must not pour oil on it or put i on it,	4247
	7:14	gold dish weighing ten shekels, filled with i;	7792
	7:20	gold dish weighing ten shekels, filled with i;	7792
	7:26	gold dish weighing ten shekels, filled with i;	7792
	7:32	gold dish weighing ten shekels, filled with i;	7792
	7:38	gold dish weighing ten shekels, filled with i;	7792
	7:44	gold dish weighing ten shekels, filled with i;	7792
	7:50	gold dish weighing ten shekels, filled with i;	7792
	7:56	gold dish weighing ten shekels, filled with i;	7792
	7:62	gold dish weighing ten shekels, filled with i;	7792
	7:68	gold dish weighing ten shekels, filled with i;	7792
	7:74	gold dish weighing ten shekels, filled with i;	7792
	7:80	gold dish weighing ten shekels, filled with i;	7792
	7:86	with i weighed ten shekels each,	7792
	16: 7	and tomorrow put fire and i in them before	7792
	16:17	Each man is to take his censer and put i	7792
	16:18	put fire and i in it,	7792
	16:35	the 250 men who were offering the i.	7792
	16:40	of Aaron should come to burn i before	7792
	16:46	"Take your censer and put i in it,	7792
	16:47	the i and made atonement for them.	7792
Dt	33:10	He offers i before you	7777
1Sa	2:28	to go up to my altar, to burn i,	7792
1Ki	3: 3	that he offered sacrifices and **burned** i on	7787
	9:25	**burning** i before the LORD along	7787
	11: 8	*who* **burned** i and offered sacrifices	7787
	22:43	to offer sacrifices and **burn** i there.	7787
2Ki	12: 3	to offer sacrifices and **burn** i there.	7787
	14: 4	to offer sacrifices and **burn** i there.	7787
	15: 4	to offer sacrifices and **burn** i there.	7787
	15:35	to offer sacrifices and **burn** i there.	7787
	16: 4	He offered sacrifices and **burned** i at	7787
	17:11	At every high place *they* **burned** i,	7787
	18: 4	that time the Israelites had been **burning** i	7787
	22:17	**burned** i to other gods and provoked me	7787
	23: 5	*to* **burn** i on the high places of the towns	7787
	23: 5	those *who* **burned** i to Baal,	7787
	23: 8	where the priests *had* **burned** i.	7787
1Ch	6:49	of i in connection with all that was done in	7792
	9:29	and the oil, i and spices.	4247
	28:18	of the refined gold for the altar of i.	7792
2Ch	2: 4	to dedicate it to him for burning fragrant i	7792
	13:11	and fragrant i to the LORD.	7792
	14: 5	the high places and i **altars** in every town	2802
	26:16	the LORD to **burn** i on the altar of incense.	7787
	26:16	to burn incense on the altar of i.	7792
	26:18	Uzziah, to **burn** i to the LORD.	7787
	26:18	who have been consecrated to **burn** i.	7787
	26:19	a censer in his hand ready to **burn** i,	7787
	26:19	before the i altar in the LORD's temple,	7792
	28: 4	He offered sacrifices and **burned** i	7787
	29: 7	not burn i or present any burnt offerings at	7792
	29:11	to minister before him and *to* **burn** i."	7787
	30:14	in Jerusalem and cleared away the i **altars**	5232
	34: 4	he cut to pieces the i **altars** that were	2802
	34: 7	to powder and cut to pieces all the i **altars**	2802
	34:25	**burned** i to other gods and provoked me	7787
Ne	13: 5	to store the grain offerings and i	4247
	13: 9	with the grain offerings and the i.	4247
Ps	141: 2	May my prayer be set before you like i;	7792
Pr	27: 9	Perfume and i bring joy to the heart,	7792
SS	3: 6	with myrrh and made from all the spices	4247
	4: 6	the mountain of myrrh and to the hill of i.	4247
	4:14	with every kind of i tree,	4247
Isa	1:13	Your i is detestable to me.	7792
	17: 8	and the i **altars** their fingers have made.	2802
	27: 9	no Asherah poles or i **altars** will	2802
	43:23	nor wearied you with demands for i.	4247
	60: 6	bearing gold and i and proclaiming	4247
	65: 3	offering sacrifices in gardens and **burning** i	7787
	66: 3	and whoever burns memorial i,	4247
Jer	1:16	*in* **burning** i to other gods and	7787
	6:20	about i from Sheba or sweet calamus from	4247
	7: 9	adultery and perjury, **burn** i to Baal	7787
	11:12	to the gods to whom *they* **burn** i,	7787
	11:13	up to **burn** i to that shameful god Baal are	7787
	11:17	and provoked me to anger by **burning** i	7787
	17:26	and thank offerings to the house of	4247
	18:15	*they* **burn** i to worthless idols,	7787
	19:13	the houses where *they* **burned** i on the roofs	7787
	32:29	to anger by **burning** i on the roofs to Baal	7787
	41: 5	and i with them to the house of the LORD.	4247
	44: 3	by **burning** i and by worshiping other gods	7787
	44: 5	from their wickedness or stop **burning** i	7787
	44: 8	**burning** i to other gods in Egypt,	7787
	44:15	that their wives *were* **burning** i	7787
	44:17	We *will* **burn** i to the Queen of Heaven	7787
	44:18	since we stopped **burning** i to the Queen	7787
	44:19	When we **burned** i to the Queen of Heaven	7787
Jer	44:21	and think about the i burned in the towns	7789
	44:23	Because *you have* **burned** i and have sinned	7787
	44:25	to **burn** i and pour out drink offerings to	7787
	48:35	on the high places and **burn** i to their gods,"	7787
Eze	6: 4	be demolished and your i **altars** will	2802
	6: 6	your i **altars** broken down,	2802
	6:13	places where they offered **fragrant** i	5767+8194
	8:11	and a fragrant cloud of i was rising.	7792
	16:18	and you offered my oil and i before them.	7792
	16:19	you offered as **fragrant** i before them.	5767+8194
	20:28	presented their **fragrant** i	5767+8194
	20:41	as **fragrant** i when I bring you out	5767+8194
	23:41	before it on which you had placed the i	7792
Da	2:46	that an offering and i be presented to him.	10478
Hos	2:13	I will punish her for the days *she* **burned** i	7787
		to the Baals;	7787
	11: 2	to the Baals and *they* **burned** i to images.	7787
Hab	1:16	to his net and **burns** i to his dragnet,	7787
Mal	1:11	In every place i and pure offerings will	5231
Mt	2:11	with gifts of gold and of i and of myrrh.	3337
Lk	1: 9	into the temple of the Lord and **burn** i.	2594
	1:10	when the time *for* the **burning** of i came.	2592
	1:11	standing at the right side of the altar *of* i.	2592
Heb	9: 4	which had the golden **altar** of i and	2593
Rev	5: 8	of i, which are the prayers of the saints.	2592
	8: 3	He was given much i to offer,	2592
	8: 4	smoke *of* the i, together with the prayers	2592
	18:13	of i, myrrh and frankincense,	2592

INCENSED (1) [INCENSE]
Ne 4: 1 he became angry and *was* greatly i.   4087

INCHES (1)
Ge 6:16 a roof for it and finish the ark to within **18** i   564

INCIDENT (1)
1Ki 21: 1 Some time later there was an i involving   NIH

INCITED (6) [INCITING]
1Sa	22: 8	that my son *has* i my servant to lie in wait	7756
	26:19	If the LORD *has* i you against me,	6077
2Sa	24: 1	and *he* i David against them, saying,	6077
1Ch	21: 1	against Israel and i David to take a census	6077
Job	2: 3	though *you* i me against him to ruin him	6077
Ac	13:50	But the Jews i the God-fearing women	4241

INCITING (2) [INCITED]
Jer	43: 3	son of Neriah *is* i you against us to hand us	6077
Lk	23:14	*who was* i the people **to rebellion.**	695

INCLINATION (2) [INCLINATIONS, INCLINED, INCLINES]
Ge	6: 5	and that every i *of* the thoughts	3671
	8:21	every i *of* his heart is evil from childhood.	3671

INCLINATIONS (1) [INCLINATION]
Jer 7:24 instead, they followed the stubborn i   4600

INCLINED (3) [INCLINATION]
Dt	5:29	that their hearts *would be* i to fear me	2118+2296
Jdg	9: 3	they *were* i to follow Abimelech,	4213+5742
1Sa	20:13	But if my father *is* i to harm you,	3512

INCLINES (1) [INCLINATION]
Ecc 10: 2 The heart of the wise i **to the right,**   4200

INCLOSE (KJV) See ENCLOSE

INCLUDE (18) [INCLUDED, INCLUDES, INCLUDING]
Nu	1:49	i them **in the census**	906+5951+8031
	28:22	I one male goat as a sin offering	2256
	28:30	I one male goat to make atonement for you.	NIH
	29: 5	I one male goat as a sin offering,	2256
	29:11	I one male goat as a sin offering,	NIH
	29:16	I one male goat as a sin offering,	2256
	29:19	I one male goat as a sin offering,	2256
	29:22	I one male goat as a sin offering,	2256
	29:25	I one male goat as a sin offering,	2256
	29:28	I one male goat as a sin offering,	2256
	29:31	I one male goat as a sin offering,	2256
	29:34	I one male goat as a sin offering,	2256
	29:38	I one male goat as a sin offering,	2256
	34: 3	" 'Your southern side *will* i some of	2118
Jos	17: 7	The boundary ran southward from there to i	448
1Ch	21: 6	not i Levi and Benjamin in the numbering,	928+9348
Eze	16:29	to i Babylonia, a land of merchants, but	448
1Co	15:27	it is clear that this does **not** i God himself,	1760

INCLUDED (18) [INCLUDE]
Dt	4:49	**and** i all the Arabah east of the Jordan,	2256
Jos	12: 5	This half of Gilead.	2256
	13: 9	**and** i the whole plateau of Medeba as far	2256
	13:11	It *also* i Gilead, the territory of the people	2256
	16: 9	It also i all the towns and their villages	NIH
	19: 2	It i: Beersheba (or Sheba), Moladah,	2118
	19:15	I were Kattath, Nahalal, Shimron,	2256
	19:18	Their territory i: Jezreel,	2118

Jos	19:25	Their territory i: Helkath,	2118
	19:41	The territory of their inheritance i:	2118
2Sa	23:19	even though *he was* not i among them,	995
	23:23	but *he was* not i among the Three.	995
1Ch	7:28	Their lands and settlements i Bethel	NIH
	11:21	even though *he was* not i among them,	995
	11:25	but *he was* not i among the Three.	995
2Ch	31:18	They i all the little ones, the wives,	NIH
Job	3: 6	*may it* not *be* i among the days of the year	2526
Eph	1:13	also were i in Christ when you heard	NIG

INCLUDES (1) [INCLUDE]

2Th	1:10	all those who have believed. This i you,	NIG

INCLUDING (66) [INCLUDE]

Ge	17:12	i those born in your household or bought	NIH
	17:27	i those born in his household or bought	NIH
	19:25	i all those living in the cities—	2256
Ex	10: 5	i every tree that is growing in your fields.	2256
	27:19	i all the tent pegs for it and those for	2256
	34:19	i all the firstborn males of your livestock,	2256
Lev	1: 8	i the head **and** the fat,	2256
	1:12	i the head and the fat,	2256
	9:13	i the head, and he burned them on the altar.	2256
Nu	3:39	i every male a month old or more,	NIH
	4:14	i the firepans, meat forks,	NIH
	4:16	i its holy furnishings and articles."	928
	21:25	and occupied them, i Heshbon	928
	31:11	i the people and animals,	928
Dt	3:12	i half the hill country of Gilead,	2256
Jos	8:35	i the women and children,	2256
	10: 7	i all the best fighting men.	2256
	10:40	i the hill country, the Negev,	2256
	12: 1	i all the eastern side of the Arabah:	2256
	13:17	i Dibon, Bamoth Baal, Beth Baal Meon,	NIH
	13:30	from Mahanaim and i all of Bashan,	NIH
	24: 2	i Terah the father of Abraham and Nahor,	NIH
	24:18	i the Amorites, who lived in the land.	2256
Jdg	20:48	the towns to the sword, i the animals	6330
	21:10	i the women and children.	2256
1Sa	30:18	i his two wives.	2256
1Ki	4:31	i Ethan the Ezrahite—	4946
	10:15	not i the revenues from merchants and traders	963+4200+4946
	14:26	i all the gold shields Solomon had made.	2256
	22:39	other events of Ahab's reign, i all he did,	2256
2Ki	8: 6	i all the income from her land from	2256
	13:12	i his war against Amaziah king of Judah,	889
	14:15	i his war against Amaziah king of Judah,	2256
	14:28	i how he recovered for Israel both	2256
	15:29	i all the land of Naphtali,	NIH
	21:17	and all he did, i the sin he committed,	2256
	24: 4	i the shedding of innocent blood.	1685+2256
1Ch	12:27	Jehoiada, leader of the family of Aaron,	2256
	21: 5	i four hundred and seventy thousand in	2256
2Ch	8:15	i that of the treasuries.	2256
	9:14	**not** i the revenues brought in by merchants	963+4200+4946
	12: 9	i the gold shields Solomon had made.	2256
	27: 7	i all his wars and the other things he did,	2256
	30:25	i the aliens who had come from Israel	2256
	33:18	i his prayer to his God and the words	2256
Ezr	7: 7	Some of the Israelites, i priests, Levites,	2256
	7:13	i priests and Levites,	10221
	9: 1	i the priests and the Levites,	2256
Ne	1: 6	i myself and my father's house,	2256
	10:39	The people of Israel, i the Levites,	2256
Est	4: 7	i the exact amount of money Haman had	2256
Ecc	12:14	deed into judgment, i every hidden thing,	6584
Jer	10:16	for he is the Maker of all things, i Israel,	2256
	13:13	i the kings who sit on David's throne,	2256
	42: 1	i Johanan son of Kareah and Jezaniah son	2256
	44:24	the people, i the women, "Hear the word of	2256
	51:19	i the tribe of his inheritance—	2256
Eze	12:22	Their entire bodies, i their backs,	2256
	41:14	the front of the temple,	2256
	41:15	i its galleries on each side;	2256
	41:16	and i the threshold was covered with wood.	NIH
Mt	8:33	i what had happened to	2779
Lk	23:27	i women who mourned and wailed for him.	2779
	23:49	i the women who had followed him	2779
Ro	16: 2	a great help to many people, i me.	2779
2Ti	1:15	i Phygelus and Hermogenes.	1639+4005

INCOME (6)

2Ki	8: 6	the i *from* her land from the day she left	9311
Pr	10:16	i *of* the wicked brings them punishment.	9311
	15: 6	but the i *of* the wicked brings them trouble.	9311
Ecc	5:10	whoever loves wealth is never satisfied with his i.	9311
Ac	19:25	"Men, you know we receive a **good** i	2345
1Co	16: 2	**in keeping with** *his* i,	1569+2338+4005+5516

INCOMPARABLE (1) [INCOMPARABLY]

Eph	2: 7	the coming ages he might show the i riches	5650

INCOMPARABLY (1) [INCOMPARABLE]

Eph	1:19	and his i great power for us who believe.	5650

INCOMPREHENSIBLE (1)

Isa	33:19	with their strange, i tongue.	401+1069

INCONTINENCY (KJV) See LACK OF SELF-CONTROL

INCORRUPTIBLE, INCORRUPTION
(KJV) See IMPERISHABLE, LAST FOREVER, NEVER PERISH

INCREASE (54) [EVER-INCREASING, INCREASED, INCREASES, INCREASING]

Ge	1:22	and i in number and fill the water in	8049
	1:22	and *let* the birds i on the earth."	8049
	1:28	"Be fruitful and i in number;	8049
	3:16	"I will greatly i your pains in childbearing;	8049+8049
	6: 1	men began to i in number on the earth	8045
	8:17	on the earth and be fruitful and i in **number**	8049
	9: 1	"Be fruitful and i in **number** and fill	8049
	9: 7	As for you, be fruitful and i in **number;**	8049
	9: 7	multiply on the earth and i upon it."	8049
	16:10	"I will so i your descendants that they	8049+8049
	17: 2	and you and *will* greatly i your **numbers."**	8049
	17:20	and *will* greatly i his **numbers.**	8049
	24:60	*may* you i to thousands upon thousands;	2118
	26:24	and *will* i **the number** *of* your descendants	8049
	28: 3	and make you fruitful and i your **numbers**	8049
	35:11	be fruitful and i in **number.**	8049
	48: 4	and *will* i your **numbers.**	8049
	48:16	and *may they* i greatly upon the earth."	1835
Lev	25:16	the years are many, *you are to* i the price,	8049
	26: 9	and make you fruitful and i your **numbers,**	8049
Dt	1:11	i you a thousand times and bless you	3578+6584
	6: 3	and that *you may* i greatly in a land flowing	8049
	7:13	and bless you and i your **numbers.**	8049
	8: 1	and i and may enter and possess the land	8049
	8:13	and gold i and all you have is multiplied,	8049
	13:17	on you, and i your **numbers,**	8049
	28:63	to make you prosper and i in **number,**	8049
	30:16	then you will live and i,	8049
Job	10:17	against me and i your anger toward me;	8049
Ps	6: 4	of those *will* i who run after other gods.	8049
	61: 6	I the days of the king's life,	3578
	62:10	though your riches i, do not set your heart	5649
	71:21	You will i my honor and comfort me	8049
	73:12	always carefree, *they* i in wealth.	8436
	115:14	May the LORD **make** you i,	3578
	144:13	Our sheep *will* i **by thousands,**	545
Pr	22:16	He who oppresses the poor to i his wealth	8049
Ecc	5: 9	The i *from* the land is taken by all;	3862
	5:11	As goods i, so do those who consume them.	8049
Isa	9: 7	Of the i *of* his government and peace	5269
Jer	23: 3	where they will be fruitful and i in **number.**	8049
	29: 6	I in **number** there; do not decrease.	8049
Eze	36:11	*I will* i **the number** *of* men and animals	8049
	36:30	*I will* i the fruit of the trees and the crops	8049
	37:26	I will establish them and i their **numbers,**	8049
Da	12: 4	and there *to* i knowledge."	8049
Hos	4:10	they will engage in prostitution but not i,	7287
Mt	24:12	Because of the i of wickedness,	4437
Lk	17: 5	The apostles said to the Lord, **"I**our faith!"	4707
Ac	12:24	word of God *continued to* i and spread.	889
Ro	5:20	law was added so that the trespass *might* i.	4429
	6: 1	go on sinning so that grace *may* i?	4429
2Co	9:10	for food will also supply and i your store	4437
1Th	3:12	May the Lord **make** your love i and	4429

INCREASED (32) [INCREASE]

Ge	7:17	and *as* the waters i they lifted the ark high	8049
	7:18	The waters rose and i greatly on the earth,	8049
	30:30	little you had before I came *has* i greatly,	7287
	47:27	and were fruitful and i greatly in **number.**	8049
Ex	1:20	the midwives and the people i and became	8049
	23:30	until *you have i enough* to take possession	7238
Lev	19:25	In this way your harvest *will be* i.	3578
Dt	1:10	The LORD your God *has* i your **numbers** so	8049
Jdg	1:35	when the power of the house of Joseph i,	3877
1Sa	14:19	tumult in the Philistine camp i **more and more.**	2143+2143+2256+8041
1Ch	4:38	Their families i greatly,	7287
	5: 9	because their livestock *had* i in Gilead.	8049
2Ch	33:23	Amon i his guilt.	8049
Ps	25:19	See how my enemies *have* i and	8045
	39: 2	even saying anything good, my anguish i.	6579
	107:38	and *their* **numbers** greatly i,	8049
	107:41	and i their families like flocks.	8492
Ecc	1:16	I have grown and i in wisdom more than	3578
Isa	9: 3	have enlarged the nation and i their joy;	1540
	26:15	with olive oil and i your perfumes.	8049
Jer	3:16	*your* **numbers** *have* i greatly	2256+7238+8049
Eze	16:29	Then *you* i your promiscuity	8049
	28: 5	in trading *you have* i your wealth,	8049
	31: 5	its boughs i and its branches grew long,	8049
Hos	8:11	The more the priests i,	8045
	10: 1	As his fruit i, he built more altars;	8044
Na	3:16	*You have* i **the number** *of* your merchants	8049
Lk	11:29	As the crowds i, Jesus said,	2044
Ac	6: 7	of disciples in Jerusalem i rapidly,	4437
	7:17	of our people in Egypt i greatly,	889+2779+4437
Ro	5:20	But where sin i, grace increased all the	4429
	5:20	where sin increased, grace i **all the more,**	5668

INCREASES (5) [INCREASE]

Ps	49:16	when the splendor of his house i;	8049

Pr	24: 5	and a man of knowledge i strength;	599
	28: 8	*He who* i his wealth by exorbitant interest	8049
Isa	40:29	to the weary and i the power of the weak.	8049
Ro	3: 7	and so i his glory, why am I still condemned	NIG

INCREASING (7) [INCREASE]

1Sa	15:12	and Absalom's following kept on i.	8041
Job	21: 7	growing old and i in power?	1504
Eze	16:25	offering your body *with* i promiscuity	8049
	16:26	to anger with your i promiscuity.	8049
Ac	6: 1	*when* the number of disciples *was* i,	4437
2Th	1: 3	of you has for each other *is* i.	4429
2Pe	1: 8	if you possess these qualities in i measure,	4429

INCREDIBLE (1)

Ac	26: 8	Why should any of you consider it i	603

INCUR (1) [INCURS]

Ex	28:43	so that *they will* not i guilt and die.	5951

INCURABLE (7)

2Ch	21:18	with an i disease of the bowels.	401+5340
Job	34: 6	his arrow inflicts an i **wound.'**	631
Isa	17:11	as nothing in the day of disease and i pain.	631
Jer	10:19	My wound *is* i!	2703
	15:18	and my wound grievous and i?	4412+8324
	30:12	" 'Your wound is i,	631
Mic	1: 9	For her wound is i; it has come to Judah.	631

INCURS (2) [INCUR]

Pr	9: 7	whoever rebukes a wicked man i abuse.	NIH
	14:35	but a shameful servant i his wrath.	2118

INDECENT (3)

Dt	23:14	that he will not see among you anything i	6872
	24: 1	because he finds something i about her,	6872
Ro	1:27	Men committed i **acts** with other men,	859

INDECISIVE (1)

2Ch	13: 7	and i and not strong enough to resist	4222+8205

INDEED (64)

Ge	15: 5	**if** i you can count them."	561
	27:33	**and** i he will be blessed!"	1685
Ex	3: 7	"I have i **seen** the misery of my people	8011+8011
Nu	22: 3	I, Moab was filled with dread because of	2256
Dt	9:13	and they are a stiff-necked people i!	2180
	18: 1	i the whole tribe of Levi—	NIH
Jdg	5:29	The wisest of her ladies answer her; i,	677
1Sa	21: 5	"I women have been kept from us,	561+3954
2Sa	3:36	i, everything the king did pleased them.	3869
	14: 5	She said, "I am i a widow,"	66
1Ki	8:13	*I have* i **built** a magnificent temple	1215+1215
	10: 7	I, not even half was told me;	2180
2Ki	14:10	*You have* i **defeated** Edom and	5782+5782
1Ch	16:19	When they were but few in number, few i,	3869
2Ch	9: 6	I, not even half the greatness	2180
	12:12	I, there was some good in Judah.	1685+2256
	13: 8	You are i a vast army and have with you	2256
	20: 4	i, they came from every town in Judah	1685
	26:20	I, he himself was eager to leave,	1685+2256
Job	9: 2	"I, I know that this is true.	597
	13:16	I, this will turn out for my deliverance,	1685
	19: 5	If i you would exalt yourselves above me	597
	35:13	I, God does not listen to their empty plea;	421
Ps	58: 1	Do you rulers i speak justly?	598
	85:12	The LORD will i give what is good,	1685
	87: 5	I, of Zion it will be said,	2256
	89:18	I, our shield belongs to the LORD,	3954
	105:12	When they were but few in number, few i,	NIH
	121: 4	i, he who watches over Israel	2180
Jer	2:20	I, on every high hill and	3954
	14:13	I, I will give you lasting peace	3954
	14:20	we have i sinned against you.	3954
	20: 9	I am weary of holding it in; i, I cannot.	2256
	23:32	I, I am against those	2180
	25:29	and *will* you i **go unpunished?**	5927+5927
	32:30	the people of Israel have done nothing	3954
	42:17	I, all who are determined to go to Egypt	2256
La	3: 3	i, he has turned his hand against me again	421
Eze	33:32	I, to them you are nothing more than one who sings love songs with a	2180
Hab	2; 5	wine betrays him;	677+2256+4309
Mt	20:23	"You will i **drink** from my cup,	3525
Lk	12: 7	I, the very hairs of your head	247+2779
	13:30	I there are those who are last who will	2627+2779
	18:25	I, it is easier for a camel to go through	1142
Jn	4:14	the water I give him will become in him	247
	8:24	you will i die in your sins."	NIG
	8:36	if the Son sets you free, you will be free i.	3953
Ac	3:24	**"I,** all the prophets from Samuel on,	1254+2089
	4:27	I Herod and Pontius Pilate met together	1142
	7:34	*I have* i **seen** the oppression of my people	3972+3972
Ro	2:14	(I, when Gentiles, who do not have the law	1142
	7: 7	I would not have known what sin was	247
	8:17	with Christ, if i we share in his sufferings	1642
	15:27	**and** i they owe it to them.	2779
1Co	3: 2	I, you are still not ready.	247
	4: 3	i, I do not even judge myself.	247
	8: 5	or on earth (**as** i there are many "gods"	6061
	14: 2	I, no one understands him;	1142

1Co	15:20	But Christ has **i** been raised from the dead,	3815
2Co	1: 9	**I**, in our hearts we felt the sentence	247
Php	2:27	**I** he was ill, and almost died.	1142
	4:10	**I**, you have been concerned,	2779
Col	2:23	Such regulations **i** have an appearance	3525
1Th	2:20	**I**, you are our glory and joy.	1142

INDEPENDENT (2)
1Co 11:11 however, woman is not **i** of man, — 6006
    11:11 nor is man **i** of woman. — NIG

INDESCRIBABLE (1)
2Co 9:15 Thanks be to God for his **i** gift! — 442

INDESTRUCTIBLE (1)
Heb 7:16 but on the basis of the power *of* an **i** life. — 186

INDIA (2)
Est 1: 1 over 127 provinces stretching from **I** — 2064
    8: 9 of the 127 provinces stretching from **I** — 2064

INDICATE (3) [INDICATED, INDICATING]
1Sa 16: 3 You are to anoint for me the one *I* **i**." — 606
Jn 21:19 Jesus said this *to* **i** the kind of death — 4955
Heb 12:27 The words "once more" **i** the removing — 1317

INDICATED (2) [INDICATE]
Nu 1:18 The people **i** *their* **ancestry** by their clans — 3528
2Ki 6:10 So the king of Israel checked on the place **i** — 606

INDICATING (2) [INDICATE]
Jn 18:32 that the words Jesus had spoken **i** the kind — 4955
Heb 9: 9 **i** that the gifts and sacrifices being — 2848+4005

INDICTMENT (1)
Job 31:35 let my accuser put his **i** in writing. — 6219

INDIGNANT (6) [INDIGNANTLY, INDIGNATION]
Mt 20:24 *they were* **i** with the two brothers. — 24
    21:15 to the Son of David," *they were* **i**. — 24
    26: 8 When the disciples saw this, *they were* **i**. — 24
Mk 10:14 When Jesus saw this, *he was* **i**. — 24
    10:41 they became **i** with James and John. — 24
Lk 13:14 **I** because Jesus had healed on the Sabbath, — 24

INDIGNANTLY (1) [INDIGNANT]
Mk 14: 4 Some of those present were **saying i** — 24

INDIGNATION (6) [INDIGNANT]
Ps 78:49 his wrath, **i** and hostility— — 2405
    90: 7 by your anger and terrified by your **i**. — 2779
    119:53 **I** grips me because of the wicked, — 2363
Jer 15:17 on me and you had filled me with **i**. — 2405
Na 1: 6 Who can withstand his **i**? — 2405
2Co 7:11 what eagerness to clear yourselves, what **i**, — 25

INDISPENSABLE (1)
1Co 12:22 of the body that seem to be weaker are **i**, — 338

INDIVIDUALLY (1)
1Ch 23:24 under their names and counted **i**, — 1653+4200

INDOORS (2)
Mt 9:28 When he had gone **i**, — 1650+3836+3864
Mk 9:28 After Jesus had gone **i**, — 1650+3875

INDULGE (7) [INDULGED, INDULGENCE, INDULGING, SELF-INDULGENCE]
Ex 32: 6 to eat and drink and got up to **i in revelry.** — 7464
Nu 25: 1 the men began to **i in sexual immorality** — 2388
Lk 7:25 those who wear expensive clothes and **i** — 5639
1Co 10: 7 and got up to **i in pagan revelry."** — 4089
Gal 5:13 not use your freedom to **i** the sinful nature; — 929
Eph 4:19 over to sensuality so as to **i** in every kind — 2238
2Ti 2:16 because *those who* **i** in it will become more — 4621

INDULGED (1) [INDULGE]
2Co 12:21 and debauchery in which *they have* **i**. — 4556

INDULGENCE (1) [INDULGE]
Col 2:23 they lack any value in restraining sensual **i**. — 4447

INDULGING (1) [INDULGE]
1Ti 3: 8 sincere, not **i** in much wine, — 4668

INEFFECTIVE (1)
2Pe 1: 8 they will keep you from being **i** — 734

INEXCUSABLE (KJV) See NO EXCUSE

INEXPERIENCED (2)
1Ch 22: 5 "My son Solomon is young and **i**, — 8205

1Ch 29: 1 one whom God has chosen, is young and **i**. — 8205

INEXPRESSIBLE (2)
2Co 12: 4 He heard **i** *things,* things that man is not — 777
1Pe 1: 8 you believe in him and are filled with an **i** — 443

INFALLIBLE (KJV) See CONVINCING

INFAMOUS (1) [INFAMY]
Eze 22: 5 O **i** city, full of turmoil. — 2021+3238+9005

INFAMY (1) [INFAMOUS]
Isa 44:11 they will be brought down to terror and **i**. — 1017

INFANCY (1) [INFANT]
2Ti 3:15 from **i** you have known the holy Scriptures, — *1100*

INFANT (7) [INFANCY, INFANT'S, INFANTS]
Nu 11:12 as a nurse carries an **i**, — 3437
    12:12 not let her be like a **stillborn i** coming — 3437
Job 3:16 like an **i** who never saw the light of day? — 6407
    24: 9 the **i** of the poor is seized for a debt. — 6403
Isa 11: 8 Their **i** will play near the hole of the cobra, — 3437
    65:20 be in it an **i** who lives but a few days, or — 6403
Heb 5:13 Anyone who lives on milk, being still an **i**, — 3758

INFANT'S (1) [INFANT]
La 4: 4 the **i** tongue sticks to the roof of its mouth; — 3437

INFANTS (15) [INFANT]
Dt 32:25 **i** and gray-haired men. — 3437
1Sa 15: 3 children and **i**, cattle and sheep, — 3437
    22:19 its men and women, its children and **i**, — 3437
Ps 8: 2 of children and **i** you have ordained praise — 3437
    137: 9 he who seizes your **i** and dashes them — 6408
Isa 13:16 Their **i** will be dashed to pieces — 6407
    13:18 they will have no mercy on **i** — 1061+7262
Jer 44: 7 the men and women, the children and **i**, — 3437
La 2:11 children and **i** faint in the streets of the city. — 3437
Na 3:10 Her **i** were dashed to pieces at the head — 6408
Mt 21:16 and you have ordained praise'?" — 2558
Ro 2:20 a teacher *of* **i**, because you have in the law — 3758
1Co 3: 1 but as worldly—mere **i** in Christ. — 3758
    14:20 In regard to evil be **i**, — 3757
Eph 4:14 Then we will no longer be **i**, — 3758

INFECTED (4) [INFECTION]
Lev 13: 4 the priest is to put the **i person** in isolation — 5596
    13:12 the skin of the **i person** from head to foot, — 5596
    13:17 shall pronounce the **i person** clean; — 5596
    13:31 is to put the **i person** in isolation — 5596+5999

INFECTION (1) [INFECTED, INFECTIOUS]
Lev 13:46 As long as he has the **i** he remains unclean. — 5596

INFECTIOUS (21) [INFECTION]
Lev 13: 2 that may become an **i** skin disease, — 5596
    13: 3 it is an **i** skin disease. — 5596
    13: 8 it is an **i disease.** — 7669
    13: 9 "When anyone has an **i** skin disease, — 5596
    13:15 raw flesh is unclean; he has an **i disease.** — 7669
    13:20 an **i** skin disease that has broken out where — 5596
    13:22 priest shall pronounce him unclean; it is **i**. — 5596
    13:25 an **i disease** that has broken out in the burn. — 7669
    13:25 it is an **i** skin disease. — 5596
    13:27 it is an **i** skin disease. — 5596
    13:30 it is an itch, an **i disease** *of* the head or chin. — 7669
    13:42 it is an **i disease** breaking out on his head — 7669
    13:43 like an **i skin disease,** — 7669
    13:45 The person with such an **i disease** must wear — 5596
    14: 3 of his **i** skin disease, — 5596
    14: 7 of the **i disease** and pronounce him clean. — 7669
    14:32 an **i** skin disease and who cannot afford — 5596
    14:54 the regulations for any **i** skin disease, — 5596
    14:57 **i skin diseases and mildew.** — 7669
    22: 4 a descendant of Aaron **has an i skin disease** — 7665
Nu 5: 2 anyone who **has an i skin disease** — 7665

INFERIOR (6)
Job 12: 3 I *am* not **i** to you. — 5877
    13: 2 I *am* not **i** to you. — 5877
Da 2:39 another kingdom will rise, **i** to yours. — 10075
2Co 11: 5 But I do not think *I am* in the least **i** to — 5728
    12:11 not in the least **i** to the "super-apostles," — 5728
    12:13 How were *you* **i** to the other churches, — 2273

INFIDEL (KJV) See UNBELIEVER

INFILTRATED (1)
Gal 2: 4 some false brothers *had* **i** *our* **ranks** — 4207+4209

INFINITE (KJV) See BOUNDLESS, ENDLESS, NO LIMIT

INFIRMITIES (2) [INFIRMITY]
Isa 53: 4 he took up our **i** and carried our sorrows, — 2716

Mt 8:17 "He took up our **i** and carried our diseases." — 819

INFIRMITY (1) [INFIRMITIES]
Lk 13:12 "Woman, you are set free *from* your **i**." — 819

INFLAMED (3) [INFLAMMATION]
Isa 5:11 up late at night *till they are* **i** with wine. — 1944
Hos 7: 5 the princes *become* **i** with wine, — 2703+2779
Ro 1:27 and *were* **i** with lust for one another. — 1706

INFLAMMATION (1) [INFLAMED]
Dt 28:22 with fever and **i**, with scorching heat — 1945

INFLICT (22) [INFLICTED, INFLICTS]
Dt 7:15 not **i** on you the horrible diseases you knew — 8492
    7:15 but *he will* **i** them on all who hate you, — 5989
    28:53 of the suffering that your enemy *will* **i** — 7439
    28:55 because of the suffering your enemy *will* **i** — 7439
    28:57 the distress that your enemy *will* **i** on you — 7439
Jdg 20:31 to **i** casualties on the Israelites as before, so — 5782
    20:39 The Benjamites had begun to **i** casualties — 5782
Ps 149: 7 to **i** vengeance on the nations — 6913
Jer 18: 8 and not **i** on it the disaster I had planned. — 6913
    36: 3 about every disaster I plan to **i** on them, — 6913
Eze 5: 8 and *I will* **i** punishment on you in — 6913
    5:10 I will **i** punishment on you — 6913
    5:15 when I **i** punishment on you in anger and — 6913
    11: 9 over to foreigners and **i** punishment on you. — 6913
    16:41 down your houses and **i** punishment on you — 6913
    25:11 and *I will* **i** punishment on Moab. — 6913
    28:22 when I **i** punishment on her — 6913
    28:26 they will live in safety when I **i** punishment — 6913
    30:14 to Zoan and **i** punishment on Thebes. — 6913
    30:19 So *I will* **i** punishment on Egypt, — 6913
    39:21 the nations will see the punishment *I* **i** and — 6913
Rev 9:19 having heads with which *they* **i injury.** — 92

INFLICTED (16) [INFLICT]
Ge 12:17 the Lord **i** serious diseases *on* Pharaoh — 5595
1Sa 14:47 he **i** punishment on them. — 8399
    14:47 He **i** heavy losses on the Philistines — 5782
2Sa 7:14 the rod of men, with **floggings** *i by* men. — AIT
1Ki 20:21 the horses and chariots and **i** heavy losses — 5782
    20:29 a hundred thousand **casualties** — 5782
2Ki 8:29 the wounds the Arameans *had* **i** *on* him — 5782
    9:15 the wounds the Arameans *had* **i** *on* him — 5782
2Ch 13:17 Abijah and his men **i** heavy losses on them, — 5782
    22: 6 the wounds *they had* **i** *on* him at Ramoth — 5782
    28: 5 *who* **i** heavy casualties on him. — 5782
Isa 30:26 of his people and heals the wounds he **i**. — 4804
Jer 42:10 for I am grieved over the disaster *I have* **i** — 6913
La 1:12 Is any suffering like my suffering that *was* **i** — 6618
Eze 23:10 and punishment *was* **i** on her. — 6913
2Co 2: 6 The punishment **i** on him by — NIG

INFLICTS (2) [INFLICT]
Job 34: 6 his arrow **i** an incurable wound.' — NIH
Zec 14:18 the plague *he* **i** on the nations that do not go — 5597

INFLUENCE (1) [INFLUENCED, INFLUENTIAL]
Job 31:21 knowing that I had **i** in court, — 6476

INFLUENCED (1) [INFLUENCE]
1Co 12: 2 somehow or other *you were* **i** and led astray — 72

INFLUENTIAL (1) [INFLUENCE]
1Co 1:26 not many were **i**; — *1543*

INFORM (8) [INFORMATION, INFORMED]
Ex 18:16 and I decide between the parties and *I* them — 3359
1Sa 27:11 for he thought, "They might **i** on us and say, — 5583
2Sa 15:28 until word comes from you to **i** me." — 5583
    17:17 A servant girl was to go and **i** them, — 5583
    17:21 of the well and went *to* **i** King David. — 5583
Ezr 4:14 we are sending this message *to* **i** the king, — 10313
    4:16 We **i** the king that if this city is built — 10313
Job 12: 8 or *let* the fish of the sea **i** you. — 6218

INFORMATION (4) [INFORM]
1Sa 23:23 and come back to me with **definite i**. — 3922
Ezr 5:10 down the names of their leaders *for* your **i**. — 10313
Ac 23:15 of wanting more accurate **i** about his case. — *1336*
    23:20 on the pretext of wanting more accurate **i** — 4785

INFORMED (6) [INFORM]
2Ki 22:10 Then Shaphan the secretary **i** the king, — 5583
2Ch 34:18 Then Shaphan the secretary **i** the king, — 5583
Da 1: 4 well **i**, quick to understand, — 1981+3359
Ac 21:21 They have been **i** that you teach all — 2994
    23:30 *When* I *was* **i** of a plot to be carried out — 3606
1Co 1:11 some from Chloe's household *have* **i** me — 1317

INGATHERING (2) [GATHER]
Ex 23:16 "Celebrate the Feast of **I** at the end of the year, — 658
    34:22 and the Feast of **I** at the turn of the year. — 658

INHABIT (2) [HABITAT, INHABITANT, INHABITANTS, INHABITED]

Job	15:28	he will i ruined towns and houses	8905
Ac	17:26	that *they should* i the whole earth;	2997

INHABITANT (3) [INHABIT]

Isa	6:11	"Until the cities lie ruined and without i,	3782
Jer	4: 7	Your towns will lie in ruins without i.	3782
	46:19	be laid waste and lie in ruins without i.	3782

INHABITANTS (41) [INHABIT]

Lev	18:25	and the land vomited out its i.	3782
	25:10	throughout the land to all its i.	3782
Nu	14:14	And they will tell the i *of* this land about it.	3782
	32:17	for protection from the i *of* the land.	3782
	33:52	drive out all the i *of* the land before you,	3782
	33:55	if you do not drive out the i *of* the land,	3782
Jos	9:24	the whole land and to wipe out all its i from	3782
	13: 6	"As for all the i *of* the mountain regions	3782
Jdg	1:32	of Asher lived among the Canaanite i *of*	3782
	1:33	among the Canaanite i *of* the land,	3782
1Ki	9:16	He killed its Canaanite i and then gave it	3782
2Ki	16: 9	He deported **its** i to Kir and put Rezin	2023S
1Ch	8:13	in Aijalon and who drove out the i *of* Gath.	3782
	10:11	the i *of* Jabesh Gilead heard of everything	NIH
	22:18	he has handed the i *of* the land over to me,	3782
2Ch	15: 5	the i *of* the lands were in great turmoil.	3782
	20: 7	the i *of* this land before your people Israel	3782
	34: 9	the people of Judah and Benjamin and the i	3782
Isa	9: 9	Ephraim and the i *of* Samaria—	3782
	24: 1	he will ruin its face and scatter its i—	3782
	24: 6	Therefore earth's i are burned up,	3782
	51: 6	like a garment and its i die like flies.	3782
Jer	25: 9	against this land and its i and against all	3782
	44:22	of cursing and a desolate waste without i,	3782
	48:18	O i *of* the Daughter of Dibon,	3782
	49: 3	Cry out, O i *of* Rabbah!	1426
	51:35	be upon Babylon," say the i *of* Zion.	3782
Mic	7:13	earth will become desolate because of its i,	3782
Zec	8:20	and the i *of* many cities will yet come,	3782
	8:21	the i *of* one city will go to another and say,	3782
	12: 7	of Jerusalem's i may not be greater than	3782
	12:10	the house of David and the i *of* Jerusalem	3782
	13: 1	the house of David and the i *of* Jerusalem,	3782
Rev	6:10	the i *of* the earth and avenge our blood?"	2997
	8:13	Woe *to* the i *of* the earth,	2997
	11:10	The i *of* the earth will gloat over them	2997
	13: 8	All i *of* the earth will worship the beast—	2997
	13:12	the earth and its i worship the first beast,	2997
	13:14	he deceived the i *of* the earth.	2997
	17: 2	and the i *of* the earth were intoxicated with	2997
	17: 8	The i *of* the earth whose names have	2997

INHABITED (16) [INHABIT]

Isa	13:20	*be* i or lived in through all generations;	3782
	44:26	who says of Jerusalem, *'It shall* **be** i,'	3782
	45:18	but formed it to *be* i—	3782
Jer	17:25	and this city will be i forever.	3782
	22: 6	like a desert, like towns not i.	3782
	33:10	i *by* neither men nor animals,	3782
	46:26	however, Egypt *will be* i as in times past,"	8905
	50:13	not *be* i but will be completely desolate.	3782
	50:39	*It will* never again *be* i or lived in	3782
Eze	12:20	The i towns will be laid waste and	3782
	26:19	like cities no longer i,	3782
	35: 9	your towns *will* not *be* i.	3782
	36:10	The towns *will* **be** i and the ruins rebuilt.	3782
	36:35	*are now* fortified and i."	3782
Joel	3:20	Judah *will be* i forever and Jerusalem	3782
Zec	14:11	It *will be* i; never again will it be destroyed.	3782

INHERIT (45) [CO-HEIRS, HEIR, HEIRS, HERITAGE, INHERITANCE, INHERITANCES, INHERITED, INHERITS]

Ge	15: 2	the **one who** will i my estate is Eliezer	1201+5479
	48: 6	the **territory** they i they will be reckoned	5709
Nu	14:24	and his descendants *will* i it.	3769
	32:32	but the property we i will be on this side of	5709
Dt	1:38	because he *will* **lead** Israel to i it.	5706
	3:28	across and *will* **cause** them to i the land	5706
	33:23	*he will* i southward to the lake."	3769
Jos	1: 6	*you will* **lead** these people to i	5706
1Sa	2: 8	He seats them with princes and has them i	5709
2Ki	2: 9	*Let me* i a double portion of your spirit,	448+2118
1Ch	28:8	of Canaan as the portion you will i."	5709
Job	13:26	and **make** me i the sins of my youth.	3769
Ps	25:13	and his descendants *will* i the land.	3769
	37: 9	those who hope in the LORD *will* i	3769
	37:11	But the meek *will* i the land	3769
	37:22	those the LORD blesses *will* i the land,	3769
	37:29	the righteous *will* i the land and dwell	3769
	37:34	He will exalt you to i the land;	3769
	69:36	the children of his servants *will* i it,	5706
	105:11	of Canaan as the portion you will i."	5709
Pr	3:35	The wise i honor,	5706
	11:29	trouble on his family *will* i only wind,	5706
	14:18	The simple i folly,	5157
Isa	14:21	not to rise *to* i the land and cover the earth	3769
	57:13	the man who makes me his refuge *will* i	5706
	61: 7	and so *they* will i a double portion	3769
	65: 9	my chosen people *will* i them,	3423
Zep	2: 9	survivors of my nation *will* i their **land**."	5706

Zec	2:12	The LORD *will* i Judah as his portion in	5706
Mt	5: 5	for they *will* i the earth.	3099
	19:29	as much and *will* i eternal life.	3099
Mk	10:17	he asked, "what must I do to i eternal life?"	3099
Lk	10:25	"what must I do *to* i eternal life?"	3099
	18:18	what must I do *to* i eternal life?"	3099
1Co	6: 9	the wicked *will* not i the kingdom of God?	3099
	6:10	nor swindlers *will* i the kingdom of God.	3099
	15:50	that flesh and blood cannot i the kingdom	3099
	15:50	nor *does* the perishable i the imperishable.	3099
Gal	5:21	like this *will* not i the kingdom of God.	3099
Heb	1:14	to serve those who will i salvation?	3099
	6:12	and patience i what has been promised.	3099
	12:17	when he wanted *to* i this blessing,	3099
Jas	2: 5	of the world to be rich in faith and to i	3101
1Pe	3: 9	to this you were called so that *you may* i	3099
Rev	21: 7	He who overcomes *will* i all this,	3099

INHERITANCE (238) [INHERIT]

Ge	21:10	slave woman's son *will* never **share in the** i	3769
	31:14	"Do we still have any share in the i	5709
Ex	15:17	and plant them on the mountain of your i—	5709
	32:13	and *it will be* their i forever.' "	5706
	34: 9	and **take** us **as** *your* i."	5706
Lev	20:24	I will give it to you as an i,	3769
Nu	16:14	or given us an i *of* fields and vineyards,	5709
	18:20	"You will **have** no i in their land,	5706
	18:20	I am your share and your i among	5159
	18:21	the Levites all the tithes in Israel as their i	5709
	18:23	*They will* **receive** no i among	5706+5709
	18:24	as their i the tithes that the Israelites present	5709
	18:24	*'They will* **have** no i among	5706+5709
	18:26	the Israelites the tithe I give you as your i,	5709
	26:53	as an i based on the number of names.	5159
	26:54	To a larger group give a larger i,	5159
	26:54	to receive its i according to the number	5159
	26:56	Each i is to be distributed by lot among	5159
	26:62	because they received no i among them.	5159
	27: 7	as an i among their father's relatives	5159
	27: 7	and turn their father's i over to them.	5159
	27: 8	turn his i over to his daughter.	5159
	27: 9	give his i to his brothers.	5159
	27:10	give his i to his father's brothers.	5159
	27:11	give his i to the nearest relative in his clan,	5159
	32:18	until every Israelite has received his i.	5157
	32:19	*We will* not **receive** *any* i with them on	5706
	32:19	because our i has come to us on	5159
	33:54	To a larger group give a larger i,	5157
	34: 2	to you as an i will have these boundaries:	5159
	34:13	"**Assign** this land by lot **as an** i.	5157
	34:14	of Manasseh have received their i	5159
	34:15	two and a half tribes have received their i	5157
	34:17	**assign** the land for you **as an** i:	5157
	34:29	the LORD commanded to **assign** *the* i *to*	5157
	35: 2	in from the i the Israelites will possess.	5159
	35: 8	in proportion to the i of each tribe;	5159
	36: 2	to give the land as an i to the Israelites	5157
	36: 2	to give the i of our brother Zelophehad	5159
	36: 3	then their i will be taken	5159
	36: 3	be taken from our ancestral i and added to	5157
	36: 3	of the i allotted *to* us will be taken away.	5159
	36: 4	their i will be added to that of the tribe	5159
	36: 4	from the tribal i *of* our forefathers."	5159
	36: 7	No i in Israel is to pass from tribe to tribe,	5159
	36: 8	so that every Israelite will possess the i	5159
	36: 9	No i may pass from tribe to tribe,	5159
	36:12	and their i remained in their father's clan	5159
Dt	4:20	to be the people of his i, as you now are.	5159
	4:21	and enter the good land the LORD your God is giving you as your i.	5159
	4:38	into their land to give it to you for your i,	5709
	9:26	your own i that you redeemed	5159
	9:29	your i that you brought out	5159
	10: 9	That is why the Levites have no share or i	5159
	10: 9	the LORD is their i,	5159
	12: 9	not yet reached the resting place and the i	5159
	12:10	the LORD your God *is* **giving** you **as an** i,	5157
	12:12	who have no allotment or i *of* their own.	5159
	14:27	they have no allotment or i *of* their own.	5159
	14:29	that the Levites (who have no allotment or i	5159
	15: 4	your God is giving you to possess as your i,	5159
	18: 1	are to have no allotment or i in Israel.	5159
	18: 1	for that is their i.	5159
	18: 2	They shall have no i among their brothers;	5159
	18: 2	the LORD is their i, as he promised them.	5159
	19: 3	the LORD your God *is* **giving** you **as an** i,	5157
	19:10	as your i, and so that you will not be guilty	5159
	19:14	by your predecessors in the i you receive in	5159
	20:16	the LORD your God is giving you as an i,	5159
	21:23	the LORD your God is giving you as an i.	5159
	24: 4	the LORD your God is giving you as an i.	5159
	25:19	the land he is giving you to possess as an i,	5159
	26: 1	the LORD your God is giving you as an i	5159
	29: 8	We took their land and gave it as an i to	5159
	31: 7	**divide** it *among* them as their i.	5157
	32: 8	the Most High **gave** the nations their i,	5157
	32: 9	Jacob his allotted i.	5159
Jos	11:23	and he gave it as an i to Israel according	5159
	12: 7	toward Seir (their lands Joshua gave as an i	3772
	13: 6	to allocate this land to Israel for an i,	5159
	13: 7	and divide it as an i among the nine tribes	5159
	13: 8	the i that Moses had given them east of	5159
	13:14	But to the tribe of Levi he gave no i,	5159
	13:14	are their i, as he promised them.	5159
	13:23	These towns and their villages were the i	5159
	13:28	and their villages were the i *of* the Gadites,	5159

Jos	13:32	This is *the* i Moses *had* **given** when he was	5706
	13:33	to the tribe of Levi, Moses had given no i;	5709
	13:33	the LORD, the God of Israel, is their i,	5709
	14: 1	the areas the Israelites **received as an** i in	5706
	14: 3	the two-and-a-half tribes their i east of	5709
	14: 3	not granted the Levites an i among the rest,	5709
	14: 9	be your i and that of your children forever,	5709
	14:13	and gave him Hebron as his i.	5709
	15:20	This is the i *of* the tribe of Judah,	5706
	16: 4	the descendants of Joseph, **received** *their* i.	5706
	16: 5	of their i went from Ataroth Addar in	5709
	16: 8	the i *of* the tribe of the Ephraimites,	5709
	16: 9	for the Ephraimites within the i *of*	5709
	17: 4	to give us an i among our brothers."	5159
	17: 4	an i along with the brothers of their father,	5159
	17: 6	of Manasseh received an i among the sons.	5159
	17:14	and one portion for an i?"	5159
	18: 2	not yet received their i.	5159
	18: 4	according to the i *of* each.	5159
	18: 7	the priestly service of the LORD is their i.	5159
	18: 7	of Manasseh have already received their i	5159
	18:20	the i of the clans of Benjamin on all sides.	5159
	18:28	This was the i *of* Benjamin for its clans.	5159
	19: 1	Their i lay within the territory of Judah.	5159
	19: 8	the i of the tribe of the Simeonites,	5159
	19: 9	The i *of* the Simeonites was taken from	5159
	19: 9	So the Simeonites **received** *their* i within	5706
	19:10	The boundary of their i went as far	5159
	19:16	These towns and their villages were the i	5159
	19:23	These towns and their villages were the i	5159
	19:31	These towns and their villages were the i	5159
	19:39	These towns and their villages were the i	5159
	19:41	The territory of their i included:	5159
	19:48	These towns and their villages were the i	5159
	19:49	the Israelites gave Joshua son of Nun an i	5159
	21: 3	and pasturelands out of their own i:	5159
	23: 4	Remember how I have allotted as an i	5307
	24:28	each to his own i.	5159
	24:30	And they buried him in the land of his i,	5159
	24:32	This became the i of Joseph's descendants.	5159
Jdg	2: 6	each to his own i.	5159
	2: 9	And they buried him in the land of his i,	5159
	11: 2	not *going to* **get** *any* i in our family,"	5157
	18: 1	because they had not yet come into an i	5159
	20: 6	to each region of Israel's i,	5159
	21:23	to their i and rebuilt the towns and settled	5159
	21:24	each to his own i.	5159
1Sa	10: 1	not the LORD anointed you leader over his i?	5159
	26:19	from my share in the LORD's i	5159
2Sa	14:16	and my son from the i God gave us.'	5159
	20:19	to swallow up the LORD's i?"	5159
	21: 3	so that you will bless the LORD's i?"	5159
1Ki	8:36	on the land you gave your people for an i.	5159
	8:51	for they are your people and your i,	5159
	8:53	the nations of the world to be your own i,	5159
	21: 3	that I should give you the i *of* my fathers."	5159
	21: 4	"I will not give you the i *of* my fathers."	5159
2Ki	21:14	the remnant of my i and hand them over	5159
1Ch	28: 8	and **pass** *it* **on as an** i to your descendants	5706
2Ch	6:27	on the land you gave your people for an i.	5159
	20:11	the possession *you* **gave** us **as an** i.	3769
Ezr	9:12	**leave** it to your children as an everlasting i.'	3769
Job	42:15	and their father granted them an i along	5159
Ps	2: 8	and I will make the nations your i,	5159
	16: 6	surely I have a delightful i.	5159
	28: 9	Save your people and bless your i;	5159
	33:12	the people he chose for his i.	5159
	37:18	and their i will endure forever.	5159
	47: 4	He chose our i for us, the pride of Jacob,	5159
	68: 9	you refreshed your weary i.	5159
	74: 2	the tribe of your i, whom you redeemed—	5159
	78:55	and allotted their lands to them as an i;	5159
	78:62	he was very angry with his i.	5159
	78:71	of his people Jacob, of Israel his i.	5159
	79: 1	O God, the nations have invaded your i;	5159
	82: 8	for all the nations *are* your i.	5157
	94: 5	they oppress your i.	5159
	94:14	he will never forsake his i.	5159
	106: 5	in the joy of your nation and join your i	5159
	106:40	with his people and abhorred his i.	5159
	135:12	and he gave their land as an i,	5159
	135:12	an i to his people Israel.	5159
	136:21	and gave their land as an i,	5159
	136:22	an i to his servant Israel;	5159
Pr	13:22	A good man **leaves an** i	5157
	17: 2	and will share the i as one of the brothers.	5159
	20:21	An i quickly gained at the beginning will	5159
	28:10	but the blameless *will* **receive** a good i.	5157
Ecc	7:11	Wisdom, like an i, is a good thing	5159
Isa	19:25	Assyria my handiwork, and Israel my i."	5159
	47: 6	with my people and desecrated my i;	5159
	58:14	the heights of the land and to feast on the i	5159
	61: 7	of disgrace they will rejoice in their i;	2750
	63:17	the tribes that are your i.	5159
Jer	2: 7	and made my i detestable.	5159
	3:18	**gave** your forefathers *as an* i.	5159
	3:19	the most beautiful i *of* any nation.'	5159
	10:16	including Israel, the tribe of his i—	5159
	12: 7	"I will forsake my house, abandon my i;	5159
	12: 8	My i has become to me like a lion in	5159
	12: 9	not my i become to me like a speckled bird	5159
	12:14	the i I gave my people Israel,	5159
	12:15	to his own i and his own country.	5159
	16:18	of their vile images and have filled my i	5159
	17: 4	the i I gave you.	5159
	50:11	you who pillage my i,	5159
	51:19	including the tribe of his i—	5159

La	5: 2	Our **i** has been turned over to aliens,	5709
Eze	35:15	Because you rejoiced when the **i** of	5709
	36:12	and you will be their **i**;	5709
	44:28	" 'I am to be the only **i** the priests have.	5709
	45: 1	" 'When you allot the land as an **i**,	5709
	46:16	If the prince makes a gift from his **i** to one	5709
	46:16	it is to be their property by **i**.	5709
	46:17	a gift from his **i** to one of his servants,	5709
	46:17	His **i** belongs to his sons only; it is theirs.	5709
	46:18	The prince must not take any of the **i** of	5709
	46:18	give his sons their **i** out of his own	5706
	47:13	**divide** the land **for an i** among the twelve	5706
	47:14	this land will become your **i**.	5709
	47:22	You are to allot it as an **i** for yourselves and	5709
	47:22	with you they are to be allotted an **i** among	5709
	47:23	there you are to give him his **i**,"	5709
	48:29	the land you are to allot as an **i** to the tribes	5709
Da	12:13	to receive your **allotted i**."	1598
Joel	2:17	Do not make your **i** an object of scorn,	5709
	3: 2	against them concerning my **i**,	5709
Ob	1:17	and the house of Jacob will possess its **i**.	4625
Mic	2: 2	a man of his home, a fellowman of his **i**.	5709
	7:14	the flock of your **i**, which lives by itself	5709
	7:18	the transgression of the remnant of his **i**?	5709
Zec	8:12	**give** all these things **as an i**	5706
Mal	1: 3	and left his **i** to the desert jackals."	5709
Mt	21:38	Come, let's kill him and take his **i**.'	3100
	25:34	**take** your **i**, the kingdom prepared for you	3099
Mk	12: 7	Come, let's kill him, and the **i** will be ours.'	3100
Lk	12:13	tell my brother to divide the **i** with me."	3100
	20:14	'Let's kill him, and the **i** will be ours.'	3100
Ac	7: 5	He gave him no **i** here,	3100
	13:19	**gave** their land to his people **as their i**.	2883
	20:32	which can build you up and give you an **i**	3100
Gal	3:18	For if the **i** depends on the law,	3100
	4:30	slave woman's son will never **share in the i**	3099
Eph	1:14	who is a deposit guaranteeing our **i** until	3100
	1:18	the riches of his glorious **i** in the saints,	3100
	5: 5	has any **i** in the kingdom of Christ and	3100
Col	1:12	who has qualified you to share **in** the **i** of	3102
	3:24	that you will receive an **i** from the Lord as	3100
Heb	9:15	may receive the promised eternal **i**—	3100
	11: 8	to a place he would later receive as his **i**,	3100
	12:16	sold his **rights as the oldest son.**	4757
1Pe	1: 4	an **i** that can never perish, spoil or fade—	3100

INHERITANCES (2) [INHERIT]

| Jos | 14: 2 | Their **i** were assigned by lot to | 5709 |
| Isa | 49: 8 | the land and to reassign its desolate **i**, | 5709 |

INHERITED (4) [INHERIT]

Lev	25:46	as **i** property and can make them slaves	3769
Nu	36: 7	the tribal **land i** from his forefathers.	5709
Pr	19:14	Houses and wealth are **i** from parents,	5709
Heb	1: 4	to the angels as the name he has **i** is superior	3099

INHERITS (3) [INHERIT]

Nu	26:55	What each group **i** will be according to	5706
	36: 8	Every daughter who **i** land in any	3769
	36: 9	every Israelite tribe is to keep the **land** it **i**."	5709

INIQUITIES (11) [INIQUITY]

Ps	78:38	he forgave their **i** and did not destroy them.	6411
	90: 8	You have set our **i** before you,	6411
	103:10	or repay us according to our **i**.	6411
	107:17	and suffered affliction because of their **i**.	6411
Isa	53: 5	he was crushed for our **i**;	6411
	53:11	and he will bear their **i**.	6411
	59: 2	your **i** have separated you from your God;	6411
	59:12	and we acknowledge our **i**:	6411
La	4:13	because of the sins of her prophets and the **i**	6411
Da	9:16	our fathers have made Jerusalem	6411
Mic	7:19	and hurl all our **i** into the depths of the sea.	2633

INIQUITY (14) [INIQUITIES]

Ps	25:11	O LORD, forgive my **i**, though it is great.	6411
	32: 5	to you and did not cover up my **i**.	6411
	38:18	I confess my **i**; I am troubled by my sin.	6411
	51: 2	Wash away all my **i** and cleanse me	6411
	51: 9	from my sins and blot out all my **i**.	6411
	73: 7	From their callous hearts comes **i**;	6411
	85: 2	You forgave the **i** of your people	6411
	89:32	their **i** with flogging;	6411
	109:14	the **i** of his fathers be remembered before	6411
Isa	53: 6	the LORD has laid on him the **i** of us all.	6411
	61: 8	I hate robbery and **i**.	6406
Hos	12: 8	not find in me any **i** or sin."	6411
Mic	2: 1	Woe to those who plan **i**,	224
Zec	5: 6	the **i** of the people throughout the land."	6411

INITIATIVE (1)

| 2Co | 8:17 | with much enthusiasm and **on** his own **i**. | 882 |

INJURE (1) [INJURED, INJURES, INJURING, INJURY]

| Zec | 12: 3 | who try to move it will **i themselves.** | 8581+8581 |

INJURED (16) [INJURE]

Ex	21:19	he must pay the **i man** for the loss	2257S
	22:10	and it dies or **is i** or is taken away	8689
	22:14	from his neighbor and it **is i** or dies while	8689

Lev	22:22	the blind, the **i** or the maimed,	8653
	24:20	As he has **i** the other, so he is to be injured.	
			4583+5989
	24:20	he has injured the other, so he **is** to **be i**.	5989
2Ki	1: 2	in Samaria and **i** himself.	2703
Ecc	10: 9	Whoever quarries stones may be **i** by them;	6772
Isa	1: 5	Your whole head is **i**,	2716
	28:13	**be i** and snared and captured.	8689
Eze	34: 4	or healed the sick or bound up the **i**.	8689
	34:16	I will bind up the **i** and strengthen	8689
Hos	6: 1	he has **i** us but he will bind up our wounds.	5782
Zec	11:16	or heal the **i**, or feed the healthy,	8689
Mal	1:13	"When you bring **i**, crippled or diseased	1608
2Co	7:12	the one who did the wrong or of the **i** party,	92

INJURES (3) [INJURE]

Ex	21:35	"If a man's bull **i** the bull of another	5597
Lev	24:19	If anyone **i** his neighbor,	4583+5989
Job	5:18	he **i**, but his hands also heal.	4730

INJURING (2) [INJURE]

| Ge | 4:23 | for wounding me, a young man for **i** me. | 2467 |
| Lk | 4:35 | before them all and came out without **i** him. | 1055 |

INJURY (7) [INJURE]

Ex	21:22	but there is no **serious i**,	656
	21:23	But if there is **serious i**,	656
2Ki	1: 2	to see if I will recover from this **i**."	2716
Jer	10:19	Woe to me because of my **i**!	8691
	30:12	your **i** beyond healing.	4804
Na	3:19	your **i** is fatal.	4804
Rev	9:19	having heads with which they **inflict i**.	92

INJUSTICE (10)

2Ch	19: 7	for with the LORD our God there is no **i**	6406
Job	5:16	the poor have hope, and **i** shuts its mouth.	6637
Ps	58: 2	No, in your heart you devise **i**,	6406
	64: 6	They plot **i** and say,	6406
Pr	13:23	but **i** sweeps it away.	4202+5477
	16: 8	righteousness than much gain with **i**.	4202+5477
Isa	58: 6	to loose the chains of **i** and untie the cords	8400
Jer	22:13	his upper rooms by **i**,	4202+5477
Eze	9: 9	of bloodshed and the city is full of **i**.	4754
Hab	1: 3	Why do you make me look at **i**?	224

INK (4)

Jer	36:18	and I wrote them in **i** on the scroll."	1902
2Co	3: 3	with **i** but with the Spirit of the living God,	3506
2Jn	1:12	but I do not want to use paper and **i**.	3506
3Jn	1:13	but I do not want to do so with pen and **i**.	3506

INKHORN (KJV) See WRITING KIT

INKLING (1)

| 1Sa | 20: 9 | "If I **had the least i** that my father | 3359+3359 |

INLAID (6)

1Ki	10:18	the king made a great **throne i** with ivory	AIT
	22:39	the palace he built and **i** with ivory,	NIH
2Ch	9:17	the king made a great **throne i** with ivory	AIT
SS	3:10	its interior lovingly **i** by the daughters	8362
Eze	27: 6	the coasts of Cyprus they made your deck, **i**	NIH
Am	6: 4	You lie on **beds i** with ivory and lounge	AIT

INMOST (10) [IN, MOST]

Ps	51: 6	you teach me wisdom in the **i** place.	6258
	103: 1	all my **i** being, praise his holy name.	7931
	139:13	For you created my **i** being;	4000
Pr	18: 8	they go down to a man's **i** parts.	1061+2540
	20:27	it searches out his **i** being.	1061+2540
	20:30	and beatings purge the **i** being.	1061+2540
	23:16	my **i** being will rejoice	4000
	26:22	they go down to a man's **i** parts.	1061+2540
Isa	16:11	my **i** being for Kir Hareseth.	7931
Lk	1:51	are proud in their **i** thoughts.	2840

INN (2) [INNKEEPER]

| Lk | 2: 7 | there was no room for them in the **i**. | 2906 |
| | 10:34 | took him to an **i** and took care of him. | 4106 |

INNER (84) [IN]

Ge	30:37	the bark and exposing the white **i** wood of	6584
Ex	12: 9	head, legs and **i** parts.	7931
	29:13	Then take all the fat around the **i** parts,	7931
	29:17	the ram into pieces and wash the **i** parts	7931
	29:22	the fat tail, the fat around the **i** parts,	7931
Lev	1: 9	to wash the **i** parts and the legs with water,	7931
	1:13	to wash the **i** parts and the legs with water,	7931
	3: 3	that covers the **i** parts or is connected	7931
	3: 9	that covers the **i** parts or is connected	7931
	3:14	that covers the **i** parts or is connected	7931
	4: 8	that covers the **i** parts or is connected	7931
	4:11	the **i** parts and offal—	7931
	7: 3	the fat that covers the **i** parts,	7931
	8:16	also took all the fat around the **i** parts,	7931
	8:21	He washed the **i** parts and the legs	7931
	8:25	the fat tail, all the fat around the **i** parts,	7931
	9:14	the **i** parts and the legs and burned them	7931
Dt	18: 3	the shoulder, the jowls and the **i** parts.	7687
Jdg	3:24	"He must be relieving himself in the **i room**	2540

2Sa	4: 6	They went into the **i** part of the house as if	9348
	18:24	between the **i** and outer gates,	9109S
1Ki	6: 5	and **i sanctuary** he built a structure around	1808
	6:16	to form within the temple an **i sanctuary**,	1808
	6:19	the **i sanctuary** within the temple to set	1808
	6:20	The **i sanctuary** was twenty cubits long,	1808
	6:21	across the front of the **i sanctuary**,	1808
	6:22	the altar that belonged to the **i sanctuary**.	1808
	6:23	the **i sanctuary** he made a pair of cherubim	1808
	6:29	in both the **i** and outer rooms,	4200+7156
	6:30	the **i** and outer rooms of the temple	4200+7163
	6:31	of the **i sanctuary** he made doors	1808
	6:36	the **i** courtyard of three courses	7164
	7: 9	and trimmed with a saw on their **i** and outer	1074
	7:12	the **i** courtyard of the temple of the LORD	7164
	7:49	in front of the **i sanctuary**);	1808
	8: 6	in the **i sanctuary** of the temple,	1808
	8: 8	the Holy Place in front of the **i sanctuary**,	1808
	20:30	to the city and hid in an **i room**.	928+2540+2540
	22:25	you go to hide in an **i room**."	928+2540+2540
2Ki	9: 2	and take him into an **i room**.	928+2540+2540
	10:25	the bodies out and then entered the **i shrine**	6551
1Ch	28:11	its **i** rooms and the place of atonement,	7164
2Ch	4:20	in front of the **i sanctuary** as prescribed;	1808
	4:22	the **i** doors to the Most Holy Place and	7164
	5: 7	in the **i sanctuary** of the temple,	1808
	5: 9	be seen from in front of the **i sanctuary**,	1808
	18:24	you go to hide in an **i room**."	928+2540+2540
Est	4:11	in the **i** court without being summoned	7164
	5: 1	on her royal robes and stood in the **i** court	7164
Ps	51: 6	Surely you desire truth in the **i** parts;	3219
Eze	8: 3	the entrance to the north gate of the **i** court,	7164
	8:16	into the court of the house of the LORD,	7164
	10: 3	and a cloud filled the **i** court.	7164
	40:19	to the outside of the **i** court;	7164
	40:23	a gate to the **i** court facing the north gate,	7164
	40:27	The **i** court also had a gate facing south,	7164
	40:28	into the **i** court through the south gate,	7164
	40:30	the **i** court were twenty-five cubits wide	NIH
	40:32	Then he brought me to the **i** court on	7164
	40:38	by the portico in each of the **i** gateways,	NIH
	40:44	Outside the **i** gate, within the inner court,	7164
	40:44	Outside the inner gate, within the **i** court,	6584
	41: 3	the **i sanctuary** and measured the jambs of	7163
	41: 4	he measured the length of the **i sanctuary**;	2257S
	41:15	the **i sanctuary** and the portico facing	7164
	41:17	of the entrance to the **i** sanctuary and on	7164
	41:17	around the **i** and outer **sanctuary**	7164
	42: 3	in the section twenty cubits from the **i** court	7164
	42: 4	an **i** passageway ten cubits wide and	7164
	43: 5	up and brought me into the **i** court,	7164
	44:17	" 'When they enter the gates of the **i** court,	7164
	44:17	the gates of the **i** court or inside the temple.	7164
	44:21	to drink wine when he enters the **i** court.	7164
	44:27	into the **i** court of the sanctuary to minister	7164
	45:19	the altar and on the gateposts of the **i** court.	7164
	46: 1	of the **i** court facing east is to be shut on	7164
Mt	24:26	or, 'Here he is, in the **i rooms**,'	5421
Lk	12: 3	in the **i rooms** will be proclaimed	5421
Ac	16:24	in the **i** cell and fastened their feet in	2278
Ro	7:22	For in my **i** being I delight in God's law;	2276
Eph	3:16	through his Spirit in your **i** being,	2276
Heb	6:19	It enters the **i sanctuary** behind the curtain,	2278
	9: 7	But only the high priest entered the **i room**,	1311
1Pe	3: 4	Instead, it should be that of your **i** self,	3220

INNERMOST (2) [IN, MOST]

| 1Ki | 6:27 | He placed the cherubim inside the **i** room of | 7164 |
| | 7:50 | the gold sockets for the doors of the **i** room, | 7164 |

INNKEEPER (1) [INN]

| Lk | 10:35 | two silver coins and gave them to the **i**. | 4107 |

INNOCENCE (6) [INNOCENT]

Ge	44:16	How can we prove our **i**?	7405
1Ki	8:32	and so establish his **i**.	7407
2Ch	6:23	not guilty and so establish his **i**.	7407
Ps	26: 6	I wash my hands in **i**,	5931
	73:13	in vain have I washed my hands in **i**.	5931
Isa	43:26	state the case for your **i**.	7405

INNOCENT (69) [INNOCENCE, INNOCENTLY]

Ge	20: 4	"Lord, will you destroy an **i** nation?	7404
Ex	23: 7	to do with a false charge and do not put an **i**	5929
Nu	5:31	The husband will be **i** of any wrongdoing,	5927
Dt	19:10	that **i** blood will not be shed in your land,	5929
	19:13	from Israel the guilt of shedding **i** blood,	5929
	21: 8	guilty of the blood of an **i** man."	5929
	21: 9	the guilt of shedding **i** blood,	5929
	25: 1	acquitting the **i** and condemning the guilty.	7404
	27:25	a bribe to kill an **i** person."	5929
Jdg	15: 3	and you are **i**, since you did not give	870
1Sa	19: 5	then would you do wrong to an **i man**	1947+5929
2Sa	3:28	"I and my kingdom are forever **i** before	5929
	4:11	when wicked men have killed an **i** man	7404
1Ki	2: 9	But now, do not **consider** him **i**.	5927
	2:31	of the guilt of the blood that Joab shed.	2855
	8:32	Declare the **i** not guilty,	7404
2Ki	10: 9	before all the people and said, "You are **i**.	7404
	21:16	so much **i** blood that he filled Jerusalem	5929
	24: 4	including the shedding of **i** blood,	5929
	24: 4	For he had filled Jerusalem with **i** blood,	5929
2Ch	6:23	Declare the **i** not guilty and	7404

Job	4: 7	Who, being i, has ever perished?	5929
	9:15	Though *I were* i, I could not answer him;	7405
	9:20	if *I were* i, my mouth would condemn me;	7405
	9:23	he mocks the despair of the i.	5929
	9:28	for I know *you* will not **hold** me i.	5927
	10:15	Even if *I am* i, I cannot lift my head,	7405
	17: 8	the i are aroused against the ungodly.	5929
	22:19	the i mock them, saying,	5929
	22:30	He will deliver even *one* who is not i,	5929
	27:17	and the i will divide his silver.	5929
	34: 5	"Job says, '*I am* i, but God denies me	7404
Ps	10: 8	from ambush he murders the i,	5929
	15: 5	and does not accept a bribe against the i.	5929
	19:13	will I be blameless, i of great transgression.	5927
	64: 4	They shoot from ambush at the i *man;*	9447
	94:21	the righteous and condemn the i to death.	5929
	106:38	They shed i blood, the blood of their sons	5929
Pr	6:17	a lying tongue, hands that shed i blood,	5929
	16: 2	All a man's ways seem i to him,	2341
	17:15	Acquitting the guilty and condemning the i	7404
	17:26	It is not good to punish an i *man,*	7404
	18: 5	to the wicked or to deprive the i of justice.	7404
	21: 8	but the conduct of the i is upright.	3838
	24:24	to the guilty, "You are i"—	7404
Isa	5:23	but deny justice to the i.	7404
	29:21	and with false testimony deprive the i	7404
	59: 7	they are swift to shed i blood.	5929
Jer	2:34	the lifeblood of the i poor,	5929
	2:35	'*I am* i; he is not angry with me.'	5927
	7: 6	or the widow and do not shed i blood	5929
	19: 4	with the blood of the i.	5929
	22: 3	and do not shed i blood in this place.	5929
	22:17	on shedding i blood and on oppression	5929
	26:15	of i blood on yourselves and on this city	5929
Da	6:22	because I was found i in his sight.	10229
Joel	3:19	in whose land they shed i blood.	5929
Jnh	1:14	not hold us accountable for killing an i *man,*	5929
Mt	10:16	be as shrewd as snakes and as i as doves.	193
	12: 5	the temple desecrate the day and yet are i?	360
	12: 7	you would not have condemned the i.	360
	27: 4	he said, "for I have betrayed i blood."	127
	27:19	"Don't have anything to do *with that* i *man,*	1465
	27:24	"I am i of this man's blood," he said.	127
Ac	20:26	to you today that I am i of the blood	2754
Ro	16:19	about what is good, and i about what is evil.	193
1Co	4: 4	but *does* not **make** me i.	1467
2Co	7:11	proved yourselves to be i in this matter.	54
Jas	5: 6	You have condemned and murdered i *men,*	1465

INNOCENTLY (1) [INNOCENT]

2Sa	15:11	invited as guests and went quite i,	4200+9448

INNUMERABLE (1)

2Ch	12: 3	and the i troops of Libyans,	401+5031

INORDINATE (KJV) See LUST

INQUIRE (37) [INQUIRED, INQUIRES, INQUIRING, INQUIRY]

Ge	25:22	So she went to i of the LORD.	2011
Dt	13:14	then *you* must i, probe and investigate it	2011
	17: 9	I of them and they will give you	2011
Jos	9:14	but *did* not i of the LORD.	906+7023+8626
Jdg	18: 5	"Please i of God to learn whether	928+8626
1Sa	9: 9	if a man went to i of God, he would say,	2011
	14:36	the priest said, "*Let us* i of God here."	448+7928
	28: 7	so I may go and i of her."	928+2011
1Ki	22: 7	LORD here whom *we can* i of?"	907+2011+4946
	22: 8	through whom *we can* i of the LORD,	2011
2Ki	3:11	that *we may* i of the LORD through him?"	2011
	22:13	"Go and i of the LORD for me and for	2011
	22:18	who sent you to i of the LORD,	2011
1Ch	10:14	and *did* not i of the LORD.	928+2011
	13: 3	*we did* not i of it during the reign of Saul."	2011
	15:13	*We did* not i of him *about* how to do it in	2011
	21:30	David could not go before it to i of God,	2011
2Ch	18: 6	of the LORD here whom *we can* i of?"	2011
	18: 7	through whom *we can* i of the LORD,	2011
	20: 3	Jehoshaphat resolved to i of the LORD,	2011+4200
	34:21	"Go and i of the LORD for me and for	2011
	34:26	who sent you to i of the LORD,	928+2011
Ezr	7:14	to i about Judah and Jerusalem with regard	10118
Isa	8:19	*should* not a people i of their God?	448+2011
Jer	10:21	The shepherds are senseless and *do* not i of	2011
	18:13	"I among the nations:	8626
	21: 2	"I now of the LORD for us	2011
	37: 7	who sent you to i of me, 'Pharaoh's army,	2011
Eze	14: 3	*Should I* let them i of **me at all?**	2011+2011+4200
	14: 7	and then goes to a prophet to i of me,	2011+8626
	20: 1	some of the elders of Israel came to i of	2011
	20: 3	Have you come to i of me?	2011
	20: 3	as I live, I will not let you i of me,	2011
	20:31	*Am* I to let you i of me, O house of Israel?	2011+4200
	20:31	*I* will not let you i of me.	2011+4200
Zep	1: 6	and neither seek the LORD nor i of him.	2011
1Co	14:35	If they want *to* i about something,	3443

INQUIRED (21) [INQUIRE]

Lev	10:16	When Moses i **about** the goat of	2011+2011
Jdg	13:17	Then Manoah i of the angel of the LORD,	448+606
	20:18	Israelites went up to Bethel and i of	928+8626
	20:23	and *they* i of the LORD.	928+8626

Jdg	20:27	And the Israelites i of the LORD.	928+8626
1Sa	10:22	So *they* i further **of** the LORD,	928+8626
	22:10	Ahimelech i of the LORD for him;	928+8626
	22:15	the first time I i of God for him?"	928+8626
	23: 2	he i of the LORD,	928+8626
	23: 4	Once again David i of the LORD,	928+8626
	28: 6	He i of the LORD,	928+8626
	30: 8	and David i of the LORD,	928+8626
2Sa	2: 1	David i of the LORD.	928+8626
	5:19	so David i of the LORD.	928+8626
	5:23	so David i of the LORD,	928+8626
1Ch	14:10	so David i of God:	928+8626
	14:14	so David i of God again,	928+8626
2Ch	1: 5	Solomon and the assembly i of him there.	2011
Ps	77: 6	My heart mused and my spirit i:	2924
Mt	19:18	"Which ones?" the man i.	3306
Jn	4:52	When *he* i as to the time when his son	4785

INQUIRES (1) [INQUIRE]

2Sa	16:23	like that of one *who* i of God.	928+1821+8626

INQUIRING (4) [INQUIRE]

Ex	33: 7	Anyone i of the LORD would go to	1335
Nu	27:21	obtain decisions for him by i *of* the Urim	5477
Dt	12:30	not to be ensnared *by* i about their gods,	2011
1Sa	22:13	him bread and a sword and i of God	928+8626

INQUIRY (1) [INQUIRE]

Job	34:24	Without i he shatters the mighty and sets	2984

INQUISITION (KJV) See AVENGES, INVESTIGATION

INSANE (5)

1Sa	21:13	*he* **pretended to be** i in their presence;	3248+9101
	21:14	"Look at the man! *He is* i!	8713
Ps	34: T	**pretended to be** i before Abimelech,	3248+9101
Ac	26:24	"Your great learning is driving you i."	3444
	26:25	"I am not i, most excellent Festus,	3419

INSATIABLE (1)

Eze	16:28	because *you were* i;	1194+8425

INSCRIBE (1) [INSCRIBED, INSCRIPTION]

Isa	30: 8	write it on a tablet for them, i it on a scroll,	2980

INSCRIBED (6) [INSCRIBE]

Ex	31:18	the tablets of stone i by the finger of God.	4180
	32:15	They *were* i on both sides, front and back.	4180
Dt	9:10	The LORD gave me two stone tablets i by	4180
Job	19:24	that they were i with an iron tool on lead,	NIH
Jer	17: 1	i with a flint point,	3086
Zec	14:20	be i on the bells of the horses,	AIT

INSCRIPTION (9) [INSCRIBE]

Ex	39:30	like an i *on* a seal:	4844+7334
Da	5:24	Therefore he sent the hand that wrote the i.	10375
	5:25	"This is the i that was written:	10375
Zec	3: 9	and I will engrave an i *on* it,'	7334
Mt	22:20	"Whose portrait is this? And whose i?"	2107
Mk	12:16	"Whose portrait is this? And whose i?"	2107
Lk	20:24	Whose portrait and i are on it?"	2107
Ac	17:23	I even found an altar with **this** i:	2108+4005
2Ti	2:19	sealed with this i: "The Lord knows who	NIG

INSECTS (2)

Lev	11:20	"'All flying i that walk on all fours are to	9238
Dt	14:19	All flying i **that swarm** are unclean to you;	9238

INSERT (1) [INSERTED]

Ex	25:14	I the poles into the rings on the sides of	995

INSERTED (6) [INSERT]

Ex	27: 7	*to* **be** i into the rings so they will be	995
	37: 5	And *he* i the poles into the rings on	995
	38: 7	*They* i the poles into the rings	995
	40:18	i the crossbars and set up the posts.	5989
1Ki	6: 6	the temple so that nothing *would be* i into	296
Eze	41: 6	so that the supports were not i **into** the wall	928

INSIDE (80) [IN]

Ge	6:14	and coat it with pitch i and out.	1074+4946
	9:21	he became drunk and lay uncovered i	928+9348
	19:10	the men i reached out and pulled Lot back	448
	31:34	the household gods and put them i	928
	39:11	of the household servants was i.	928+1074+2021
	44: 8	of Canaan the silver we found i the mouths	928
Ex	4: 6	LORD said, "Put your hand i your cloak."	928
	9:20	their slaves and their livestock i.	448+1074+2021
	12:46	"It must be eaten i one house;	928
	25:11	Overlay it with pure gold, both i and	1074+4946
	28:26	of the breastpiece on the i edge next to	1074+2025
	37: 2	with pure gold, both i and out,	1074+4946
	39:19	of the breastpiece on the i edge next to	1074+2025
Lev	14:41	the i walls of the house scraped and	1074
Nu	18: 7	at the altar and i the curtain.	1074+4200+4946
Jos	7:21	are hidden in the ground i my tent,	928+9348
Jdg	7:16	the hands of all of them, with torches i.	928+9348

Jdg	9:49	and set it on fire over the people i.	NIH
	9:51	I the city, however, was a strong tower,	928+9348
	18:17	went i and took the carved image,	2025+9004S
1Sa	26: 5	Saul was lying i the camp,	928
	26: 7	lying asleep i the camp with his spear stuck	928
2Sa	5: 8	in its place i the tent that David had	928+9348
	10:14	they fled before Abishai and **went** i the city.	995
1Ki	6:18	The i of the temple was cedar,	7163
	6:20	He overlaid the i with pure gold,	4200+7156
	6:21	Solomon covered the i of the temple	4946+7163
	6:27	the cherubim the innermost room of	928+9348
	7:31	On the i of the stand there was an opening	1074
2Ki	4: 4	Then **go** i and shut the door behind you	AIT
	6:20	and there they were, i Samaria.	928+9348
1Ch	16: 1	set it i the tent that David had pitched	928+9348
	19:15	before his brother Abishai and went i	2025
2Ch	3: 4	He overlaid the i with pure gold.	7163
	3: 8	He overlaid **the** i with six hundred talents	2084S
Ne	4:22	and his helper stay i Jerusalem at night,	928+9348
	6:10	i the temple, and let us close	448+9348
Job	30:27	The churning i me never stops;	5055
	32:19	i I am like bottled-up wine,	1061
Ps	78:28	He made them come down i their camp,	928+7931
Jer	21: 4	And I will gather them i this city.	448+9348
	49: 3	rush here and there i the walls,	928
La	1:20	i, there is only death.	928+1074+2021
Eze	3:24	"Go, shut yourself i your house.	928+9348
	5: 2	a third of the hair with fire i the city.	928+9348
	5:12	of the plague or perish by famine i you;	928+9348
	7:15	i are plague and famine;	1074+4946
	22:18	tin, iron and lead left i a furnace.	928+9348
	22:20	in my anger and my wrath and put you i	NIH
	22:21	and you will be melted i her.	928+9348
	22:22	so you will be melted i her,	928+9348
	40:10	I the east gate were three alcoves	NIH
	40:14	of the projecting walls all around the i of	NIH
	40:16	The alcoves and the projecting walls i	4200+7163
	40:19	the i of the lower gateway to the	4200+7156
	42:15	he had finished measuring what was i	7164
	43: 6	I heard someone speaking to me **from** i	4946
	44: 3	the only one who may sit i the gateway	928
	44:17	the gates of the inner court or i the temple.	2025
	46:23	Around the i of each of the four courts was	928
Jnh	1:17	and Jonah was i the fish three days	928+5055
	2: 1	From i the fish Jonah prayed to	5055
Mt	23:25	i they are full of greed and self-indulgence.	2277
	23:26	First clean the i of the cup and dish,	1955
	23:27	but **on the** i are full of dead men's bones	2277
	23:28	but **on the** i you are full of hypocrisy	2277
Mk	7:23	All these evils come **from** i and make	2277
Lk	11: 7	"Then the one i answers, 'Don't bother me.	2277
	11:39	but i you are full of greed and wickedness.	2277
	11:40	the one who made the outside make the i	2277
	11:41	But give what *is* i [the dish] to the poor,	1913
	17:31	on the roof of his house, with his goods i,	1877
Jn	18:33	Pilate then **went** back i the palace,	1656
	19: 9	and *he* **went** back i the palace.	1656
	20: 8	who had reached the tomb first, also **went** i.	1656
Ac	5:23	when we opened them, we found no one i."	2276
	10:27	Peter **went** i and found a large gathering	1656
1Co	5:12	Are you not to judge those i?	2276
Rev	5: 3	could open the scroll or even look i it.	NIG
	5: 4	worthy to open the scroll or look i.	NIG

INSIGHT (16) [INSIGHTS]

1Ki	4:29	gave Solomon wisdom and very great i,	9312
1Ch	27:32	was a counselor, a man of i and a scribe.	1067
Job	26: 3	And what great i you have displayed!	9370
	34:35	speaks without knowledge; his words lack i.	8505
Ps	119:99	*I have* more i than all my teachers,	8505
Pr	1: 2	for understanding words of i;	1069
	2: 3	for i and cry aloud for understanding,	1069
	5: 1	listen well to my **words of** i,	9312
	21:30	There is no wisdom, no i,	9312
Da	5:11	to have i and intelligence and wisdom like	10467
	5:14	of the gods is in you and that you have i,	10467
	9:22	now come to **give** you i and understanding.	8505
Eph	3: 4	be able to understand my i into the mystery	5304
Php	1: 9	and more in knowledge and depth of i,	151
2Ti	2: 7	for the Lord will give you i into all this.	5304
Rev	13:18	If anyone has i, let him calculate	3808

INSIGHTS (1) [INSIGHT]

Job	15: 9	What i *do you* **have** that we do not have?	1067

INSIST (3) [INSISTED, INSISTING, INSISTENTLY]

2Sa	24:24	i on paying you for	928+4697+7864+7864
1Ch	21:24	"No, *I* i on paying the full price.	7864+7864
Eph	4:17	So I tell you this, and i on it in the Lord,	3458

INSISTED (7) [INSIST]

Ge	19: 3	But *he* i so strongly that they did go	7210
	33:11	And because Jacob i, Esau accepted it.	7210
1Ki	3:22	But the first one i, "No!	606
Mk	14:31	But Peter i emphatically,	3281
Lk	23: 5	But they i, "He stirs up the people all	2196
Jn	9: 9	But he himself i, "I am the man."	3306
	19: 7	The Jews i, "We have a law,	646

INSISTENTLY (1) [INSIST]

Lk	23:23	with loud shouts they i demanded that he	2130

INSISTING (1) [INSIST]
Ac 12:15 When she kept **i that** it was so, they said,   1462

INSOLENCE (6) [INSOLENT]
2Ki	19:28	against me and your **i** has reached my ears,	8633
Isa	16: 6	her pride and her **i**—	6301
	37:29	and because your **i** has reached my ears,	8633
Jer	48:30	I know her **i** but it is futile,"	6301
Da	11:18	but a commander will put an end to his **i**	3075
	11:18	to his insolence and will turn his **i** back	3075

INSOLENT (3) [INSOLENCE]
Nu	16: 1	On son of Peleth—became **i**	3689
Hos	7:16	by the sword because of their **i** words.	2405
Ro	1:30	God-haters, **i**, arrogant and boastful;	5616

INSOMUCH (KJV) See AS A RESULT, BECAUSE, SO MUCH

INSPECT (2) [INSPECTED, INSPECTION]
Lev	14:36	the priest is to go in and **i** the house.	8011
	14:39	the seventh day the priest shall return to **i**	8011

INSPECTED (1) [INSPECT]
Ex 39:43 Moses **i** the work and saw that they had   8011

INSPECTION (1) [INSPECT]
Ne 3:31 opposite the **I** Gate, and as far as the room   5152

INSPIRE (2) [INSPIRED, INSPIRES]
Jer	32:40	and *I will* **i** them to fear me,	928+4222+5989
	49:16	The terror you **i** and the pride	NIH

INSPIRED (2) [INSPIRE]
Hos	9: 7	the **i** man a maniac.	8120
1Th	1: 3	and your endurance *i by* **hope**	AIT

INSPIRES (1) [INSPIRE]
Job 20: 3 and my understanding **i** me to reply.   8120

INSTALLED (5)
Jdg	17: 5	some idols and **i** one of his sons	906+3338+4848
	17:12	Then Micah **i** the Levite,	906+3338+4848
1Ki	12:32	And at Bethel *he* also **i** priests at	6641
Ezr	6:18	And *they* **i** the priests in their divisions and	10624
Ps	2: 6	"*I have* **i** my King on Zion, my holy hill."	5820

INSTANCE (1)
Dt 19: 5 **For i**, a man may go into the forest   2256

INSTANT (9) [INSTANTLY]
Job	7:19	or let me alone even **for an i**?	1180+6330+8371
	34:20	They die **in an i**, in the middle of the night;	8092
Pr	6:15	Therefore disaster will overtake him **in an i**;	7328
Isa	29: 5	like blown chaff. Suddenly, **in an i**,	7353
	30:13	that collapses suddenly, **in an i**.	7353
Jer	4:20	**In an i** my tents are destroyed,	7328
	49:19	I will chase Edom from its land *in an i*.	8088
	50:44	I will chase Babylon from its land **in an i**.	8088
Lk	4: 5	showed him in an **i** all the kingdoms	5117+5989

INSTANTLY (2) [INSTANT]
Lk	8:47	and how she had been **i** healed.	4202
Ac	3: 7	**i** the man's feet and ankles became strong.	4202

INSTEAD (102) [STEAD]
Ge	11: 3	They used brick **i of** stone,	4200
	22:13	sacrificed it as a burnt offering **i of** his son.	9393
Ex	7:23	**I**, he turned and went into his palace,	2256
Lev	17: 4	**i of** bringing it to the entrance to the Tent	4202
Nu	1:50	**I**, appoint the Levites to be in charge of	2256
	18:24	**I**, I give to the Levites as their inheritance	3954
Dt	12:18	**I**, you are to eat them in the presence of	561+3954
Jos	23:13	**I**, they will become snares and traps	2256
Jdg	15: 2	Take her **i**."	9393
2Sa	12: 4	he took it aside to the house	2256
	12: 4	**i**, he took the ewe lamb that belonged to	2256
	14:14	But God does not take away life; **i**,	2256
	18:33	If only I had died **i of** you—	9393
	23:16	**i**, he poured it out before the LORD.	2256
1Ch	11:18	**i**, he poured it out before the LORD.	2256
	13:13	**i**, he took it aside to the house	2256
2Ch	28:20	but he gave him trouble **i of** help.	4202
Ne	5:16	**I**, I devoted myself to the work	1685+2256
Est	2: 4	the girl who pleases the king be queen **i of**	9393
	2:17	on her head and made her queen **i of** Vashti.	9393
	3: 6	I Haman looked for a way to destroy all	2256
	4: 4	She sent clothes for him to put on **i of**	6073
Job	3:24	For sighing comes to me **i of** food;	4200+7156
	31:40	up **i of** wheat and weeds instead of barley."	9393
	31:40	instead of wheat and weeds **i of** barley."	9393
Pr	8:10	Choose my instruction **i of** silver,	440
	11: 8	and it comes on the wicked **i**,	9393
Ecc	6: 2	and a stranger enjoys them **i**.	3954
Isa	3:24	**I of** fragrance there will be a stench;	9393
	3:24	**i of** a sash, a rope;	9393
	3:24	**i of** well-dressed hair, baldness;	9393

Isa	3:24	**i of** fine clothing, sackcloth;	9393
	3:24	sackcloth; **I of** beauty,	9393
	55:13	**I** *of* the thornbush will grow the pine tree,	9393
	55:13	and **i of** briers the myrtle will grow.	9393
	60:17	**I of** bronze I will bring you gold,	9393
	60:17	**I of** wood I will bring you bronze,	9393
	61: 3	to bestow on them a crown of beauty **i of**	9393
	61: 3	the oil of gladness **i of** mourning,	9393
	61: 3	a garment of praise **i of** a spirit of despair.	9393
	61: 7	**I of** their shame my people will receive	9393
	61: 7	and **i of** disgrace they will rejoice	NIH
Jer	7:24	But they did not listen or pay attention; **i**,	2256
	9:14	**I**, they have followed the stubbornness	2256
	11: 8	But they did not listen or pay attention; **i**,	2256
	14:12	**I**, I will destroy them with the sword,	3954
	16:12	the stubbornness of his evil heart **i of**	1194+4200
	30: 9	**I**, they will serve the LORD their God	2256
	31:13	I will give them comfort and joy **i of**	4946
	31:30	**I**, everyone will die for his own sin;	561+3954
	36:26	the king commanded Jerahmeel,	2256
	37:14	But Irijah would not listen to him; **i**,	2256
	43: 5	**I**, Johanan son of Kareah and all	2256
Eze	4:15	over cow manure **i of** human excrement."	9393
	36:34	be cultivated **i of** lying desolate in	889+9393
	44: 8	**I of** carrying out your duty in regard	4202
Da	1:16	to drink and gave them vegetables **i**.	NIH
	5:23	you have set yourself up against the Lord	10221
	11:38	**I of** them, he will honor a god	4030+6584
Jnh	1:13	**I**, the men did their best to row back	2256
Hab	2:16	You will be filled with shame **i of** glory.	4946
Mt	5:15	**I** they put it on its stand,	247
	18:30	**I**, he went off and had the man thrown	247
	20:26	**I**, whoever wants to become great	247
	25: 9	**I**, go to those who sell oil and buy some	3437
	27:24	but that **i** an uproar was starting,	3437
Mk	1:45	**I** he went out and began to talk freely,	1254
	4:21	**I**, don't you put it on its stand?	NIG
	5:26	yet **i of** getting better she grew worse.	3437
	7: 5	according to the tradition of the elders **i of**	247
	10:43	**I**, whoever wants to become great	247
	15:11	the crowd to have Pilate release Barabbas **i**.	3437
Lk	8:16	**I**, he puts it on a stand,	247
	11:11	will give him a snake **i**?	505
	11:33	**I** he puts it on its stand,	247
	22:26	**I**, the greatest among you should be like	247
Jn	3:19	but men loved darkness **i of** light	2445+3437
	11:54	**I** he withdrew to a region near the desert,	247
	15:15	**I**, I have called you friends,	1254
	19:34	**I**, one of the soldiers pierced Jesus' side	247
	20:17	Go **i** to my brothers and tell them,	1254
Ac	7:39	**I**, they rejected him and	247
	15:20	**I** we should write to them,	247
	25:19	**I**, they had some points of dispute with him	1254
	27:11	**i of** listening to what Paul said,	2445+3437
Ro	14:13	**I**, make up your mind not to put any	247
1Co	6: 1	the ungodly for judgment **i of** before	2779+4049
	6: 6	But **i**, one brother goes to law against	247
	6: 8	**I**, you yourselves cheat and do wrong,	247
2Co	2: 7	Now **i**, you ought to forgive	1883+3437+3836
Gal	4:14	**I**, you welcomed me as if I were an angel	247
Eph	4:15	**I**, speaking the truth in love,	1254
	5:18	**I**, be filled with the Spirit.	247
	6: 4	Fathers, do not exasperate your children; **i**,	247
1Ti	5: 1	they are to serve them even better,	247+3437
2Ti	2:24	And the Lord's servant must not quarrel; **i**,	247
	4: 3	**I**, to suit their own desires,	247
Heb	11:16	**I**, they were longing for a better country—	1254+3814
Jas	4:15	**I**, you ought to say, "If it is the Lord's will,	505
1Pe	2:23	**I**, he entrusted himself to him who judges	1254
	3: 4	**i**, it should be that of your inner self,	247
2Jn	1:12	**I**, I hope to visit you and talk with you face	247

INSTINCT (2) [INSTINCTS]
2Pe	2:12	They are like brute beasts, **creatures of i**,	5879
Jude	1:10	and what things they do understand *by* **i**,	5880

INSTINCTS (1) [INSTINCT]
Jude 1:19 **follow mere natural i** and do not have   6035

INSTITUTED (5)
Nu	28: 6	the regular burnt offering **i** at Mount Sinai	6913
1Ki	12:32	He **i** a festival on the fifteenth day of	6913
	12:33	So he **i** the festival for the Israelites	6913
Ro	13: 2	is rebelling against what God has **i**,	1411
1Pe	2:13	for the Lord's sake to every authority **i**	NIG

INSTRUCT (12) [INSTRUCTED, INSTRUCTING, INSTRUCTION, INSTRUCTIONS, INSTRUCTOR, INSTRUCTORS, INSTRUCTS]
Dt	24: 8	who are Levites, **i**.	3723
Ne	9:20	You gave your good Spirit to **i** them.	8505
Job	8:10	*Will* they not **i** you and tell you?	3723
Ps	25:12	*He will* **i** him in the way chosen for him.	3723
	32: 8	*I will* **i** you and teach you in	8505
	105:22	to **i** his princes as he pleased	673
Pr	9: 9	**I** a wise man and he will be wiser still;	5989
Da	11:33	"Those who are wise *will* **i** many,	1067
Ro	15:14	and competent to **i** one another.	3805
1Co	2:16	the mind of the Lord that he *may* **i** him?"	5204
	14:19	to **i** others than ten thousand words in	2994
2Ti	2:25	Those who oppose him *he must* gently **i**,	4084

INSTRUCTED (33) [INSTRUCT]
Ge	32: 4	*He* **i** them: "This is what you are to say	7422
	32:17	*He* **i** the one in the lead:	7422
	32:19	*He* also **i** the second,	7422
Ex	12:35	The Israelites did as Moses **i** and asked	1821
Nu	5: 4	They did just as the LORD *had* **i** Moses.	1819
	27:23	as the LORD **i** through Moses.	1819
Jos	8:27	as the LORD *had* **i** Joshua.	7422
	13: 6	Israel for an inheritance, as *I have* **i** you,	7422
	13: 8	Joshua **i** them, "Go and make a survey of	7422
	20: 2	as *I* **i** you through Moses,	1819
Jdg	21:20	So *they* **i** the Benjamites, saying,	7422
2Sa	11:19	*He* **i** the messenger:	7422
	14:19	it was your servant Joab *who* **i** me to do this	7422
2Ki	12: 2	the years Jehoiada the priest **i** him.	3723
2Ch	26: 5	who **i** him in the fear of God.	1067
	35: 3	He said to the Levites, who **i** all Israel	1067
Ne	8: 7	**i** the people in the Law while	1067
Est	1: 8	for the king **i** all the wine stewards	3569
	4:10	Then she **i** him to say to Mordecai,	606
Job	4: 3	Think how *you have* **i** many,	3579
Pr	21:11	when a wise man *is* **i**, he gets knowledge.	8505
Isa	40:13	or **i** him as his counselor?	3359
	50: 4	an **i** tongue, to know the word that sustains	4341
Jer	9:12	Who *has been* **i** by the LORD	1819+7023
Da	9:22	*He* **i** me and said to me, "Daniel,	1067
Mt	13:52	*who has been* **i** about the kingdom of heaven	3411
	17: 9	coming down the mountain, Jesus **i** them,	1948
	21: 6	and did as Jesus *had* **i** them.	5332
	28:15	the money and did as *they were* **i**.	1438
Ac	18:25	He had been **i** in the way of the Lord,	2994
Ro	2:18	of what is superior *because you are* **i** by	2994
1Co	14:31	so that everyone *may be* **i** and encouraged.	3443
1Th	4: 1	we **i** *you* how to live in order	4161

INSTRUCTING (2) [INSTRUCT]
Ne	8: 9	and the Levites who *were* **i** the people said	1067
Mt	11: 1	Jesus had finished **i** his twelve disciples,	1411

INSTRUCTION (33) [INSTRUCT]
Ex	24:12	and commands I have written for their **i**."	3723
Dt	33: 3	and from you receive **i**,	1830
Ne	1: 8	the **i** you gave your servant Moses,	1821
Job	22:22	Accept **i** from his mouth and lay	9368
Ps	50:17	You hate my **i** and cast my words	4592
Pr	1: 8	Listen, my son, to your father's **i** and do	4592
	4: 1	Listen, my sons, to a father's **i**;	4592
	4:13	Hold on to **i**, do not let it go;	4592
	8:10	Choose my **i** instead of silver,	4592
	8:33	Listen to my **i** and be wise; do not ignore it.	4592
	13: 1	A wise son heeds his father's **i**,	4592
	13:13	He who scorns **i** will pay for it,	1821
	16:20	Whoever gives heed to **i** prospers,	1821
	16:21	and pleasant words promote **i**.	4375
	16:23	and his lips promote **i**.	4375
	19:20	Listen to advice and accept **i**,	4592
	19:27	Stop listening to **i**, my son,	4592
	23:12	to **i** and your ears to words of knowledge.	4592
	31:26	and faithful **i** is on her tongue.	9368
Isa	29:24	those who complain will accept **i**."	4375
	30: 9	to listen to the LORD's **i**.	9368
Mal	2: 6	True **i** was in his mouth	9368
	2: 7	and from his mouth men should seek **i**—	9368
1Co	14: 6	or knowledge or prophecy or word of **i**?	1439
	14:26	everyone has a hymn, or a word of **i**,	1439
Gal	6: 6	Anyone who **receives i** in the word	2994
Eph	6: 4	instead, bring them up in the training and **i**	3804
1Th	4: 8	he who rejects this **i** does not reject man	NIH
2Th	3:14	If anyone does not obey our **i** in this letter,	3364
1Ti	1:18	I give you this **i** in keeping with	4132
	6: 3	to the sound *of* our Lord Jesus Christ and	3364
2Ti	4: 2	with great patience and **careful i**.	1439
Heb	6: 2	**i** about baptisms, the laying on of hands,	1439

INSTRUCTIONS (31) [INSTRUCT]
Ge	44: 1	Now Joseph *gave these* **i** *to* the steward	7422
	49:29	Then *he gave them these* **i**:	7422
	49:33	Jacob had finished *giving* **i** *to* his sons,	7422
	50:16	"Your father *left these* **i** before he died:	7422
Ex	12:24	"Obey *these* **i** as a lasting ordinance for you	1821
	16: 4	and see whether they will follow my **i**.	9368
	16:28	to keep my commands and my **i**?	9368
Jos	8:33	when he gave **i** to bless the people of Israel.	NIH
Jdg	21:10	with **i** to go to Jabesh Gilead and put to	7422
1Sa	15:11	from me and has not carried out my **i**."	1821
	15:13	I have carried out the LORD's **i**."	1821
	15:24	the LORD's command and your **i**.	1821
	21: 2	about your mission and your **i**.'	7422
1Ch	23:27	According to the last **i** of David,	1821
	28:13	He gave him **i** for the divisions of	NIH
Est	2:20	for she continued to follow Mordecai's **i**	4411
	4:17	and carried out all of Esther's **i**.	7422
Jer	19:16	He who obeys it guards his life,	5184
	32:13	"In their presence *I gave* Baruch *these* **i**:	7422
	35:18	and have followed all his **i**	5184
Mt	10: 5	Jesus sent out with the following **i**:	4133
Mk	6: 8	These *were* his **i**: "Take nothing for the	4133
Ac	1: 2	*after giving* **i** through the Holy Spirit to	1948
	17:15	then left *with* **i** for Silas and Timothy	1953+3284
	19:33	and *some* of the crowd shouted **i** to him.	5204
Col	4:10	(You have received **i** about him;	1953
1Th	4: 2	For you know what **i** we gave you by	4132
1Ti	3:14	I am writing you these **i** so that,	NIG
	5: 7	**Give** the people these **i**,	4133

1Ti 5:21 to keep these **i** without partiality,   NIG
Heb 11:22 from Egypt and **gave i** about his bones.   1948

INSTRUCTOR (2) [INSTRUCT]

Ro   2:20 an **i** of the foolish, a teacher of infants,   4083
Gal 6: 6 word must share all good things *with* his **i**.   2994

INSTRUCTORS (1) [INSTRUCT]

Pr   5:13 not obey my teachers or listen to my **i**.   4340

INSTRUCTS (3) [INSTRUCT]

Ps 16: 7 even at night my heart **i**   3579
    25: 8 therefore *he* **i** sinners in his ways.   3723
Isa 28:26 His God **i** him and teaches him   3579

INSTRUMENT (3) [INSTRUMENTS]

Eze 33:32 with a beautiful voice and **plays an i** well,   5594
Ac   9:15 This man is my chosen **i** to carry my name   5007
2Ti 2:21 he will be an **i** for noble purposes,   5007

INSTRUMENTS (23) [INSTRUMENT]

1Ch 15:16 accompanied by musical **i**:   3998
    16:42 the playing of the other **i** *for* sacred song.   3998
    23: 5 with the *musical* **i** I have provided for   3998
2Ch 5:13 and other **i**, they raised their voices   3998+8877
     7: 6 the Levites with the LORD's musical **i**,   3998
    23:13 and singers with musical **i** were leading   3998
    29:26 So the Levites stood ready with David's **i**,   3998
    29:27 by trumpets and the **i** of David king   3998
    30:21 accompanied by the LORD's musical **i** of praise.   3998
    34:12 all who were skilled in playing musical **i**—   3998
Ne 12:36 with musical **i** [prescribed by] David   3998
Ps   4: T With **stringed i**.   5593
     6: T With **stringed i**.   5593
    54: T With **stringed i**.   5593
    55: T With **stringed i**.   5593
    61: T With **stringed i**.   5593
    67: T With **stringed i**.   5593
    76: T With **stringed i**.   5593
Isa 38:20 and we will sing with **stringed i** all the days   5593
Am   6: 5 like David and improvise on musical **i**.   3998
Hab 3:19 On my **stringed i**.   5593
Ro   6:13 parts of your body to sin, as **i** of wickedness,   3960
     6:13 of your body to him as **i** of righteousness.   3960

INSULT (15) [INSULTED, INSULTING, INSULTS]

2Ki 19:16 to the words Sennacherib has sent to **i**   3070
Ps 69: 9 the insults of *those who* **i** you fall on me.   3070
Pr   9: 7 "Whoever corrects a mocker invites **i**;   7830
    12:16 but a prudent man overlooks an **i**.   7830
Isa 37:17 to all the words Sennacherib has sent to **i**   3070
Jer 20: 8 the word of the LORD has brought me **i**   3075
Mt   5:11 "Blessed are you when *people* **i** you,   3943
Lk   6:22 and **i** you and reject your name as evil,   3943
    11:45 when you say these things, *you* **i** us also."   5614
    18:32 They will mock him, **i** *him*, spit on him,   5614
Ac   3: 4 "*You* dare to **i** God's high priest?"   3366
Ro 15: 3 "The insults *of those who* **i** you have fallen *to i* 3943
Heb 10:33 Sometimes you were publicly exposed *to* **i**   3944
1Pe 3: 9 Do not repay evil with evil or **i** with insult,   3367
     3: 9 Do not repay evil with evil or insult with **i**,   3367

INSULTED (8) [INSULT]

2Ki 19:22 Who is it *you have* **i** and blasphemed?   3070
Isa 37:23 Who is it *you have* **i** and blasphemed?   3070
Jer 51:51 we have been **i** and shame covers our faces,   3075
Zep 2: 8 who **i** my people and made threats   3070
1Th 2: 2 *We had* previously suffered and *been* **i**   5614
Heb 10:29 and who *has* **i** the Spirit of grace?   1964
Jas 2: 6 But you *have* **i** the poor.   869
1Pe 4:14 If *you are* **i** because of the name of Christ,   3943

INSULTING (4) [INSULT]

2Ch 32:17 The king also wrote letters **i** the LORD,   3070
Ps 55:12 If an enemy *were* **i** me, I could endure it;   3070
Zep 2:10 for **i** and mocking the people of   3070
Lk 22:65 And they said many other **i** things to him.   1059

INSULTS (21) [INSULT]

1Sa 25:14 but *he* **hurled i** at them.   6512
2Ki 19:23 By your messengers *you have* **heaped i** on   3070
Ne   4: 3 Turn their **i** back on their own heads.   3075
     4: 5 for *they have* **thrown i** in the face of   4087
Ps 22: 7 *they* **hurl i**, shaking their heads: 928+7080+8557
    69: 9 the **i** of those who insult you fall on me.   3075
Pr 22:10 quarrels and **i** are ended.   7830
Isa 37:24 By your messengers *you have* **heaped i** on   3070
    51: 7 of men or be terrified by their **i**.   1528
La   3:61 O LORD, you have heard their **i**,   3075
Eze 21:28 about the Ammonites and their **i**:   3075
Zep 2: 8 "I have heard the **i** of Moab and the taunts   3075
Mt 27:39 Those who passed by **hurled i** at him,   1059
    27:44 with him also **heaped i** on him.   3943
Mk 15:29 Those who passed by **hurled i** at him,   1059
    15:32 Those crucified with him also **heaped i** on   3943
Lk 23:39 of the criminals who hung there **hurled i** at   1059
Jn   9:28 Then *they* **hurled i** at him and said,   3366
Ro 15: 3 "The **i** of those who insult you have fallen   3944
2Co 12:10 I delight in weaknesses, in **i**, in hardships,   5615
1Pe 2:23 *When they* **hurled their i** at him,   3366

INSURRECTION (2) [INSURRECTIONISTS]

Lk 23:19 into prison for an **i** in the city,   5087
    23:25 into prison for **i** and murder,   5087

INSURRECTIONISTS (1) [INSURRECTION]

Mk 15: 7 with the **i** who had committed murder in   5086

INTACT (2)

Pr 15:25 **keeps** the widow's boundaries **i**.   5893
Zec 12: 6 but Jerusalem *will* remain **i** in her place.   3782

INTEGRITY (22)

Dt   9: 5 not because of your righteousness or your **i**
                                                           3841+4222
1Ki 9: 4 before me in **i** *of* heart and uprightness,   9448
1Ch 29:17 you test the heart and are pleased with **i**.   4797
Ne   7: 2 because he was a man of **i**   622
Job 2: 3 And he still maintains his **i**,   9450
     2: 9 "Are you still holding on to your **i**?   9450
     6:29 reconsider, for my **i** is at stake.   7406
    27: 5 till I die, I will not deny my **i**.   9450
Ps   7: 8 according to my **i**, O Most High.   9448
    25:21 May **i** and uprightness protect me,   9448
    41:12 In my **i** you uphold me and set me   9448
    78:72 David shepherded them with **i** *of* heart;   9448
Pr 10: 9 The man of **i** walks securely,   9448
    11: 3 The **i** of the upright guides them,   9450
    13: 6 Righteousness guards the **man of i**,   2006+9448
    17:26 or to flog officials for their **i**.   3841
    29:10 Bloodthirsty men hate a *man of* **i** and seek   9447
Isa 45:23 *in all* **i** a word that will not be revoked: 7407
    59: 4 no one pleads his case with **i**.   575
Mt 22:16 man *of* **i** and that you teach the way of God   239
Mk 12:14 "Teacher, we know you are a *man of* **i**.   239
Tit 2: 7 In your teaching show **i**,   917

INTELLIGENCE (5) [INTELLIGENT]

2Ch 2:12 endowed with **i** and discernment,   8507
Isa 29:14 the **i** *of* the intelligent will vanish."   1069
Da   5:11 to have insight and **i** and wisdom like that   10684
     5:14 **i** and outstanding wisdom.   10684
1Co 1:19 the **i** *of* the intelligent I will frustrate."   5304

INTELLIGENT (4) [INTELLIGENCE]

1Sa 25: 3 She was an **i** and beautiful woman,   3202+8507
Isa 29:14 the intelligence of the **i** will vanish.   1067
Ac 13: 7 The proconsul, an **i** man,   5305
1Co 1:19 the intelligence *of* the **i** I will frustrate."   5305

INTELLIGIBLE (2)

1Co 14: 9 you speak **i** words with your tongue,   2358
    14:19 in the church I would rather speak five **i**
                                                      1609+3808+3836
                words

INTEND (11) [INTENDED, INTENDING, INTENDS, INTENT, INTENTION, INTENTIONAL, INTENTIONALLY, INTENTLY]

Ge 37: 8 "*Do you* **i** to reign over us?   4887+4887
Nu 35:23 not his enemy and *he did* not **i** to harm him,   1335
1Sa 35:26 and all who **i** to harm my master be   1335
1Ki 5: 5 I **i**, therefore, to build a temple for the Name   606
2Ch 28:10 now you **i** to make the men and women   606
    28:13 *Do you* **i** to add to our sin and guilt?   606
    29:10 I **i** to make a covenant with the LORD,   4222+6640
Ps 62: 4 They fully **i** to topple him   3619
Jn   7:35 "Where *does* this man **i** to go   3516
    14:22 why *do you* **i** to show yourself to us and   3516
Ac   5:35 of Israel, consider carefully what *you* **i**   3516

INTENDED (14) [INTEND]

Ge 50:20 You **i** *to* harm me, but God intended it for   3108
    50:20 but God **i** it for good to accomplish what is   3108
Dt 19:19 then do to him as *he* **i** to do to his brother.   2372
1Sa 4: of the pass that Jonathan **i** to cross to reach   1335
    20:33 Then Jonathan knew that his father **i**   3983
2Ch 32: 2 that Sennacherib had come and that he **i**   7156
Jer 18:10 then I will reconsider the good *I had* **i** to do   606
Hos 2: 9 **i** to cover her nakedness.   NIH
Jn   6:15 that *they* **i** to come and make him king   3516
    12: 7 [**It was i**] *that* she should save this perfume   2671
Ac 12: 4 Herod **i** to bring him out for public trial   1089
    20: 7 *because* he **i** to leave the next day,   3516
Ro   7:10 was **i** to bring life actually brought death.   1650
2Co 7: 9 For you became sorrowful **as** God **i** and   2848

INTENDING (2) [INTEND]

Jdg 20: 5 surrounded the house, **i** to kill me.   1948
Ac 12: 1 Herod arrested some who belonged to the
                church, **i** to **persecute** them.   AIT

INTENDS (2) [INTEND]

Dt 28:57 For *she is* **i** to **eat** them secretly during   AIT
Isa 10: 7 But this is not what *he* **i**,   1948

INTENSE (3) [INTENSELY]

2Sa 13:15 Then Amnon hated him with **i** hatred.   1524+4394
1Th 2:17 out of our **i** longing we made every effort   4498
Rev 16: 9 the **i** heat and they cursed the name of God,   3489

INTENSELY (3) [INTENSE]

Gal 1:13 how **i** I persecuted the church of God   2848+5651
Jas 4: 5 the spirit he caused to live in us envies **i**?   2160
Rev 2:22 who commit adultery with her suffer **i**,   3489

INTENT (8) [INTEND]

Ex 32:12 with **evil i** that he brought them out,   8288
1Ch 29:17 given willingly and with honest **i**.   4222
Ps 139:20 They speak of you with **evil i**;   4659
Pr   7:10 dressed like a prostitute and with crafty **i**.   4213
    21:27 much more so when brought with **evil i**!   2365
Hos 5:11 trampled in judgment, **i** on pursuing idols.   3283
Mt 22:18 But Jesus, knowing their evil **i**, said,   NIG
Eph 3:10 His **i** was *that* now, through the church,   2671

INTENTION (2) [INTEND]

2Sa 13:32 This has been Absalom's expressed **i** ever   8461
Job 34:14 If *it were* his **i** and he withdrew his spirit
                                                           4213+8492

INTENTIONAL (1) [INTEND]

Nu 15:25 for it was **not i** and they have brought to   8705

INTENTIONALLY (2) [INTEND]

Ex 21:13 However, if he *does* not do it **i**,   7399
Nu 35:20 something at him **i** so that he dies   928+7402

INTENTLY (4) [INTEND]

Ac   1:10 They were **looking i** up into the sky   867
     6:15 in the Sanhedrin **looked i** at Stephen,   867
Jas 1:25 the man who **looks i** into the perfect law   4160
1Pe 1:10 **searched i** and with the greatest care,
                                                       1699+2001+2779

INTERCEDE (5) [INTERCEDED, INTERCEDES, INTERCEDING, INTERCESSION, INTERCESSOR]

Ge 23: 8 then listen to me and **i** with Ephron son   7003
1Sa 2:25 sins against the LORD, who *will* **i** for him?"   7137
     7: 5 at Mizpah and *I will* **i** with the LORD   7137
1Ki 13: 6 "**I** with the LORD your God and   906+2704+7156
Heb 7:25 because he always lives to **i** for them.   1961

INTERCEDED (1) [INTERCEDE]

1Ki 13: 6 the man of God **i** with the LORD,   906+2704+7156

INTERCEDES (2) [INTERCEDE]

Ro   8:26 but the Spirit himself **i** for us with groans   5659
     8:27 the Spirit **i** for the saints in accordance   1961

INTERCEDING (1) [INTERCEDE]

Ro   8:34 the right hand of God and *is* also **i** for us.   1961

INTERCESSION (2) [INTERCEDE]

Isa 53:12 and **made i** for the transgressors.   7003
1Ti 2: 1 **i** and thanksgiving be made for everyone—   1950

INTERCESSOR (1) [INTERCEDE]

Job 16:20 My **i** is my friend as my eyes pour out tears   4885

INTEREST (16) [INTERESTS]

Ex 22:25 charge him no **i**.   5968
Lev 25:36 Do not take **i** *of any kind* from   2256+5968+9552
    25:37 not lend him money at **i** or sell him food at   5968
Dt 23:19 *Do not* **charge** your brother **i**,   5967+5968
    23:19 or food or anything else that *may* **earn i**.   5967
    23:20 *You may* **charge** a foreigner **i**,   5967
Est 3: 8 it is not in the king's **best i**   8750
Pr 28: 8 his wealth by **exorbitant i**   2256+5968+9552
Eze 18: 8 not lend at usury or take **excessive i**.   9552
    18:13 He lends at usury and takes **excessive i**.   9552
    18:17 from sin and takes no usury or **excessive i**.   9552
    22:12 and **excessive i** and make unjust gain   9552
Mt 25:27 I would have received it back with **i**.   5527
Lk 19:23 I could have collected it with **i**?'   5527
Php 2:20 who **takes** a genuine **i** in your welfare.   3534
1Ti 6: 4 an unhealthy **i** in controversies and quarrels   4309

INTERESTS (5) [INTEREST]

Ezr 4:22 to the detriment of the **royal i**?   10421
1Co 7:34 and his **i** are divided. An unmarried   NIG
Php 2: 4 of you should look not only to your own **i**,   3836
     2: 4 but also to the **i** of others,   3836
     2:21 For everyone looks out for his own **i**,   3836

INTERFERE (1) [INTERFERED]

Ezr 6: 7 *Do* **not i** with the work on this temple   10697

INTERFERED (1) [INTERFERE]

1Ki 1: 6 (His father *had* never **i** with him by asking,   6772

INTERIOR (4)
1Ki	6:15	He lined its **i** walls with cedar	1074+2025+4946
	6:22	So he overlaid the whole **i** with gold.	1074
SS	3:10	its **i** lovingly inlaid by the daughters	9348
Ac	19: 1	Paul took the road through the **i** and	541+3538

INTERMARRY (5) [MARRY]
Ge	34: 9	**I** with us; give us your daughters	3161
Dt	7: 3	*Do* not **i** with them.	3161
Jos	23:12	if *you* **i** with them and associate with them,	3161
1Ki	11: 2	*"You must* not **i** with them,	995
Ezr	9:14	Shall we again break your commands and **i**	3161

INTERMEDDLE (KJV) See SHARE

INTERMITTENT (1)
Job	6:15	as undependable as **i** streams,	5707

INTERPRET (25) [INTERPRETATION, INTERPRETATIONS, INTERPRETED, INTERPRETER, INTERPRETERS, INTERPRETS]
Ge	40: 8	"but there is no *one* to **i** them."	7354
	41: 8	but no *one could* **i** them for him.	7354
	41:15	"I had a dream, and no *one can* **i** it.	7354
	41:15	that when you hear a dream *you can* **i** it."	7354
Da	2: 4	the dream, and *we will* **i** it."	10252+10600
	2: 5	not tell me what my dream was and **i** it,	10600
	2: 6	So tell me the dream and **i** it for me."	10600
	2: 7	the dream, and *we will* **i** it."	10252+10600
	2: 9	I will know that *you can* **i** it *for* me.	10252+10600
	2:16	that he *might* **i** the dream for him.	10252+10600
	2:24	and *I will* **i** his dream for him."	10252+10600
	2:26	in my dream and **i** it?"	10600
	2:36	and now *we will* **i** it to the king.	10042+10600
	4: 6	before me *to* **i** the dream for me.	10313+10600
	4: 7	but *they could* not **i** it for me.	10313+10600
	4: 9	Here is my dream; **i** it for me.	10042+10600
	4:18	wise men in my kingdom can **i** it	10313+10600
	5:12	and also the *ability to* **i** dreams,	10599
Mt	16: 3	You know how to **i** the appearance of	1359
	16: 3	but *you* cannot **i** the signs of the times.	NIG
Lk	12:56	how to **i** the appearance of the earth and	1507
	12:56	you don't know **how** to **i** this present time?	1507
1Co	12:30	Do all speak in tongues? Do all **i**?	1450
	14:13	that *he may* **i** what he says.	1450
	14:27	one at a time, and someone *must* **i**.	1450

INTERPRETATION (11) [INTERPRET]
Ge	40:16	that Joseph *had given* a favorable **i**, he said	7354
	40:22	**said** to them in his **i**.	7354
	41:12	*giving* each man *the* **i** of his dream.	7354
Jdg	7:15	When Gideon heard the dream and its **i**,	8694
Da	2:30	O king, may know the **i** and	10600
	2:45	The dream is true and the **i** is trustworthy."	10600
	4:24	"This is the **i**, O king,	10600
	7:16	and gave me the *i* of these things:	10600
1Co	12:10	and to still another the **i** of tongues.	2255
	14:26	a revelation, a tongue or an **i**.	2255
2Pe	1:20	about by the prophet's own **i**.	2146

INTERPRETATIONS (2) [INTERPRET]
Ge	40: 8	"Do not **i** belong to God?	7355
Da	5:16	able to **give i** and to solve difficult problems.	10599+10600

INTERPRETED (2) [INTERPRET]
Ge	41:12	and he **i** them for us,	7354
	41:13	things turned out exactly as he **i** them to us:	7354

INTERPRETER (2) [INTERPRET]
Ge	42:23	since he was using an **i**.	4885
1Co	14:28	If there is no **i**,	1449

INTERPRETERS (1) [INTERPRET]
Jer	27: 9	your diviners, your **i of dreams**,	2706

INTERPRETS (2) [INTERPRET]
Dt	18:10	**i omens**, engages in witchcraft,	5727
1Co	14: 5	unless *he* **i**, so that the church may	1450

INTERRUPTED (1)
Ac	26:24	At this point Festus **i** Paul's defense.	NIG

INTERSECTING (2)
Eze	1:16	appeared to be made like a wheel **i**	928+9348
	10:10	each was like a wheel **i** a wheel.	928+9348

INTERVALS (1)
Eze	41:17	the walls **at regular i** all around the inner	4500

INTERVENE (1) [INTERVENED]
Isa	59:16	he was appalled that there was no *one to* **i**;	7003

INTERVENED (1) [INTERVENE]
Ps	106:30	But Phinehas stood up and **i**,	7136

INTERWOVEN (3) [WEAVE]
1Ki	7:17	A network of **i chains** festooned the	5126+9249
2Ch	3:16	He made **i** chains and put them	928+2021+8054
Ps	45:13	her gown is **i** *with* gold.	5401

INTESTINES (2)
2Sa	20:10	and his **i** spilled out on the ground.	5055
Ac	1:18	his body burst open and all his **i** spilled out.	5073

INTIMATE (4)
1Ki	1: 4	had no **i relations with** her.	3359
Job	19:19	All my **i** friends detest me;	6051
	29: 4	when God's **i friendship** blessed my house,	6051
Hos	3: 3	you must not be a prostitute or be **i with**	4200

INTIMIDATE (3)
Ne	6:13	to **i** me so that I would commit a sin	3707
	6:14	the prophets who have been *trying to* **i** me.	3707
	6:19	And Tobiah sent letters to **i** me.	3707

INTO (1286)
Ge	2: 7	and breathed **i** his nostrils the breath of life,	928
	2:10	from there it was separated **i** four	4200
	2:21	**caused** the man **to fall i** a deep sleep;	AIT
	6:19	to bring **i** the ark two of all living creatures,	448
	7: 1	LORD then said to Noah, "Go **i** the ark,	448
	9: 2	they are given **i** your hands.	928
	10: 5	the maritime peoples spread out **i** their	928
	12: 2	"I will make you **i** a great nation.	4200
	12:15	and she **was taken i** his palace.	AIT
	14:10	of the men fell **i** them and the rest fled to	2025
	14:20	who delivered your enemies **i** your hand."	928
	15:12	Abram **fell i** a deep sleep,	AIT
	17:20	and I will make him **i** a great nation.	4200
	18: 6	So Abraham hurried **i** the tent to Sarah.	2025
	19:10	and pulled Lot back **i** the house and shut	2025
	20: 1	on from there **i** the region of the Negev	2025
	21:13	the son of the maidservant **i** a nation also,	4200
	21:18	for I will make him **i** a great nation."	4200
	24:20	So she quickly emptied her jar **i** the trough,	448
	24:67	Isaac brought her **i** the tent	2025
	30:14	Reuben went out **i** the fields	928
	31:33	So Laban went **i** Jacob's tent and	928
	31:33	into Jacob's tent and **i** Leah's tent and into	928
	31:33	into Jacob's tent and into Leah's tent and **i**	928
	32: 7	the people who were with him **i** two groups	4200
	37:20	and throw him **i** one of these cisterns	928
	37:22	Throw him **i** this cistern here in the desert,	448
	37:24	they took him and threw him **i** the cistern.	2025
	39:11	One day he went **i** the house to attend	2025
	40:10	and its clusters **ripened i** grapes.	AIT
	40:11	squeezed them **i** Pharaoh's cup and put	448
	40:21	he once again put the cup **i** Pharaoh's hand,	6584
	43:12	the silver that was put back **i** the mouths	928
	43:18	that was put back **i** our sacks the first time.	928
	43:24	The steward took the men **i** Joseph's house,	2025
	43:26	the gifts they had brought **i** the house,	2025
	43:30	He went **i** his private room and wept there.	2025
	45: 4	the one you sold **i** Egypt!	2025
	46: 3	for I will make you **i** a great nation there.	4200
	49:33	he drew his feet up **i** the bed,	448
Ex	1:22	"Every boy that is born you must throw **i**	2025
	3: 8	to bring them up out of that land **i** a good	448
	3:17	up out of your misery in Egypt **i** the land of	448
	3:18	Let us take a three-day journey **i** the desert	928
	4: 4	the snake and *it* **turned** *back* **i** a staff	2118+4200
	4: 6	So Moses put his hand **i** his cloak,	928
	4: 7	"Now put it back **i** your cloak," he said.	448
	4: 7	So Moses put his hand back **i** his cloak,	448
	4:27	"Go **i** the desert to meet Moses."	2025
	5: 3	Now let us take a three-day journey **i**	928
	7:15	hand the staff that was changed **i** a snake.	4200
	7:17	and it will be changed **i** blood.	4200
	7:20	and all the water was changed **i** blood.	4200
	7:23	Instead, he turned and went **i** his palace,	448
	8: 3	up **i** your palace and your bedroom	928
	8: 3	**i** the houses of your officials and	928
	8: 3	and **i** your ovens and kneading troughs.	928
	8:14	They *were* **piled i** heaps,	AIT
	8:21	on your people and **i** your houses.	928
	8:24	of flies poured **i** Pharaoh's palace and into	2025
	8:24	of flies poured into Pharaoh's palace and **i**	NIH
	8:27	We must take a three-day journey **i**	928
	9: 8	a furnace and have Moses toss **i** the air in	2025
	9:10	Moses tossed it **i** the air,	2025
	10: 4	I will bring locusts **i** your country	928
	10:19	the locusts and carried them **i** the Red Sea.	2025
	12: 4	having **taken i account** the number	4200
	12:11	**cloak tucked i** your belt,	2520+5516
	12:22	dip it **i** the blood in the basin and put some	928
	13: 5	When the LORD brings you **i** the land of	448
	13:11	"After the LORD brings you **i** the land of	448
	14:21	a strong east wind and turned it **i** dry land.	4200
	14:23	and horsemen followed them **i** the sea.	448+9348
	14:24	the Egyptian army and **threw** it **i confusion.**	2169
	14:27	and the LORD swept them **i** the sea.	928+9348
	14:28	of Pharaoh that had followed the Israelites **i**	928
	15: 1	The horse and its rider he has hurled **i**	928
	15: 4	and his army he has hurled **i** the sea.	928
	15:19	chariots and horsemen went **i** the sea,	928
	15:19	The horse and its rider he has hurled **i**	928
	15:22	the Red Sea and they went **i** the Desert	448
	15:25	He threw it **i** the water,	448
	16: 3	but you have brought us out **i** this desert	448
Ex	18: 7	They greeted each other and then went **i**	2025
	21:33	to cover it and an ox or a donkey falls **i** it,	2025
	22: 6	a fire breaks out and **spreads i** thornbushes	AIT
	23:23	and bring you **i** the land of the Amorites,	448
	23:27	**throw i confusion** every nation you encounter.	2169
	25:14	Insert the poles **i** the rings on the sides of	928
	26: 1	with cherubim **worked i** them *by*	AIT
	26: 9	five of the curtains together **i one set**	963+4200
	26: 9	one set and the other six **i another set.**	963+4200
	26:24	and fitted **i** a single ring;	448
	26:31	with cherubim **worked i** it *by*	AIT
	27: 7	to be inserted **i** the rings so they will be	928
	29:17	the ram **i** pieces and wash the inner parts	4200
	30:25	**Make** these **i** a sacred anointing oil,	AIT
	32: 4	and **made** it **i** an idol cast in the shape of	AIT
	32:10	Then I will make you **i** a great nation."	4200
	32:21	that *you* **led** them **i** such great sin?"	995
	32:24	and I threw it **i** the fire,	928
	33: 9	As Moses went **i** the tent,	2025
	36: 8	with cherubim **worked i** them *by*	AIT
	36:16	the curtains **i** one set and the other six	4200
	36:16	the curtains into one set and the other six **i**	4200
	36:29	the way to the top and fitted **i** a single ring;	448
	36:35	with cherubim **worked i** it *by*	AIT
	37: 5	the poles **i** the rings on the sides of the ark	928
	38: 7	the poles **i** the rings so they would be on	928
	39: 3	and cut strands to be worked **i** the blue,	928+9348
	40:21	Then he brought the ark **i** the tabernacle	448
Lev	1: 6	to skin the burnt offering and cut it **i** pieces.	4200
	1:12	He is to cut it **i** pieces,	4200
	4: 5	of the bull's blood and carry it **i** the Tent	448
	4: 6	He is to dip his finger **i** the blood	928
	4:16	to take some of the bull's blood **i** the Tent	448
	4:17	He shall dip his finger **i** the blood	4946
	6:30	any sin offering whose blood is brought **i**	448
	8:20	the ram **i** pieces and burned the head,	4200
	9: 9	and he dipped his finger **i** the blood	928
	9:23	and Aaron then went **i** the Tent of Meeting.	448
	10: 9	or other fermented drink whenever you go **i**	448
	10:18	its blood was not taken **i** the Holy Place,	448+7163
	11:33	If one of them falls **i** a clay pot,	448+9348
	14: 6	**i** the blood of the bird that was killed over	928
	14: 8	After this he may come **i** the camp,	448
	14:16	dip his right forefinger **i** the oil in his palm,	4946
	14:26	of the oil **i** the palm of his own left hand,	6584
	14:40	and thrown **i** an unclean place outside	448
	14:41	the material that is scraped off dumped **i**	448
	14:46	"Anyone who goes **i** the house	448
	14:51	dip them **i** the blood of the dead bird and	928
	16: 2	not to come whenever he chooses **i**	448
	16:10	by sending it **i** the desert as a scapegoat.	2025
	16:21	He shall send the goat away **i** the desert in	2025
	16:23	"Then Aaron is to go **i** the Tent of Meeting	448
	16:26	afterward he may come **i** the camp.	448
	16:27	whose blood was brought **i**	928
	16:28	afterward he may come **i** the camp.	448
	26:25	When you withdraw **i** your cities,	448
	26:25	and you will be given **i** enemy hands.	928
	26:31	*I will* **turn** your cities **i** ruins	5989
	26:41	toward them so that I sent them **i** the land	928
Nu	4:19	and his sons *are to* **go i** the sanctuary	995
	5:17	from the tabernacle floor **i** the water.	448
	5:23	and then wash them off **i** the bitter water.	448
	5:27	it will go **i** her and cause bitter suffering;	928
	10: 9	When *you* **go i** battle in your own land	995
	11: 8	They cooked it in a pot or **made** it **i** cakes.	AIT
	13:17	the Negev and **on i** the hill country.	AIT
	13:27	"We went **i** the land to which you sent us,	448
	14: 8	he will lead us **i** that land,	448
	14:12	but I will make you **i** a nation greater	4200
	14:16	not able to bring these people **i**	448
	14:24	I will bring him **i** the land he went to,	448
	16:14	you haven't brought us **i** a land flowing	448
	16:30	and they go down alive **i** the grave,	2025
	16:33	They went down alive **i** the grave,	2025
	16:38	**Hammer** the censers **i** sheets to overlay	AIT
	16:47	and ran **i** the midst of the assembly.	448
	19: 7	He may then come **i** the camp,	448
	19:17	from the burned purification offering **i** a jar	448
	20: 4	the LORD's **community i** this desert,	448
	20:12	you will not bring this community **i**	448
	20:15	Our forefathers went down **i** Egypt,	2025
	21: 2	"If you will deliver these people **i**	928
	21:13	in the desert extending **i** Amorite territory.	4946
	21:22	not turn aside **i** any field or vineyard,	928
	21:23	and marched out **i** the desert against Israel.	2025
	22:23	she turned off the road **i** a field.	928
	25: 8	and followed the Israelite **i** the tent.	448
	25: 8	the Israelite and **i** the woman's body.	448
	31: 4	Send **i** battle a thousand men from each of	4200
	31: 6	Moses sent them **i** battle,	4200
	31:21	the soldiers who had gone **i** battle, "This is	4200
	31:24	Then you may come **i** the camp."	448
	31:54	and brought it **i** the Tent of Meeting as	448
	32: 7	over **i** the land the LORD has given them?	448
	32:32	**cross over** before the LORD **i**	AIT
	33: 8	and passed through the sea **i** the desert,	2025
	33:51	'When you cross the Jordan **i** Canaan,	448
	35:10	'When you cross the Jordan **i** Canaan,	2025
	36: 3	added to that of the tribe *they* **marry i.**	2118+4200
	36: 4	that of the tribe **i** which *they* **marry**,	2118+4200
Dt	1: 7	Break camp and **advance i** the hill country	AIT
	1:24	They left and went up **i** the hill country,	2025
	1:27	to deliver us **i** the hands of the Amorites	928
	1:41	thinking it easy to go up **i** the hill country.	2025
	1:43	in your arrogance you marched up **i** the hill	2025

Dt
2:24 I have given i your hand Sihon 928
2:29 until we cross the Jordan i the land 448
2:30 in order to give him i your hands, 928
3: 3 also gave i our hands Og king of Bashan 928
4:19 *do not* be enticed i bowing down to them AIT
4:38 to bring you i their land to give it to you 995
4:42 He could flee i one of these cities 448
6:10 When the LORD your God brings you i 448
7: 1 When the LORD your God brings you i 448
7:23 throwing them i great confusion 2169+4539
7:24 He will give their kings i your hand, 448
7:26 not bring a detestable thing i your house 448
8: 7 For the LORD your God is bringing you i 448
9:14 And I will make you i a nation stronger 4200
9:21 as fine as dust and threw the dust i a stream 448
9:28 the LORD was not able to take them i 448
10:22 Your forefathers who went down i 2025
11:29 the LORD your God has brought you i 448
13:16 the town i the middle of the public square 448
15:17 and push it through his ear lobe i the door, 928
19: 3 Build roads to them and divide i three parts 8992
19: 5 a man may go i the forest with his neighbor 928
20: 2 When you are about to go i battle, 448
20: 3 "Hear, O Israel, today you are going i battle 4200
20:13 LORD your God delivers it i your hand, 928
21:10 and the LORD your God delivers them i 928
21:12 Bring her i your home 448+9348
23: 5 to Balaam but turned the curse i a blessing 4200
23:18 a female prostitute or of a male prostitute i NIH
24:10 not go i his house to get what he is offering 448
26: 5 a wandering Aramean, and he went down i 2025
27: 2 When you have crossed the Jordan i 448
28:24 turn the rain of your country i dust and 5989
28:41 because they will go i captivity. 928
29:12 You are standing here in order to enter i 928
29:28 from their land and thrust them i 448
30:12 "Who will ascend i heaven to get it 2025
31: 7 for you must go with this people i the land 448
31:20 When I have brought them i the land 448
31:21 even before I bring them i the land 448
31:23 the Israelites i the land I promised them 448
32:49 "Go up i the Abarim Range to Mount Nebo 448
34: 4 but you will not cross over i it." 2025

Jos
1: 2 to cross the Jordan River i the land I am 448
2:18 your brothers and all your family i your 2025
2:19 If anyone goes outside your house i the 2025
2:22 they went i the hills 2025
2:24 surely given the whole land i our hands; 928
3:11 the Lord of all the earth will go i the Jordan 928
4: 5 before the ark of the LORD your God i 448
6: 2 "See, I have delivered Jericho i your hands, 928
6:19 to the LORD and *must* go i his treasury." 995
6:22 "Go i the prostitute's house 995
6:24 put the silver and gold and the articles of
bronze and iron i AIT
7: 7 across the Jordan to deliver us i the hands 928
8: 1 For I have delivered i your hands the king 928
8: 7 The LORD your God will give it i your hand. 928
8:13 That night Joshua went i the valley. 928+9348
8:18 for i your hand I will deliver the city." 928
10: 8 I have given them i your hand. 928
10:10 threw them i confusion before Israel. 2169
10:19 for the LORD your God has given them i 928
10:27 from the trees and threw them i the cave 448
10:30 that city and its king i Israel's hand. 928
11: 8 the LORD gave them i the hand of Israel. 928
16: 1 and went up from there through the desert i 928
17:15 go up i the forest and clear land 2025
18: 5 You are to divide the land i seven parts. 4200
18:12 and headed west i the hill country, 928
18:18 of Beth Arabah and on down i the Arabah. 2025
19:49 When they had finished dividing the land i 4200
20: 4 Then they are to admit him i their city 2025
24: 8 but I gave them i your hands. 928
24:11 but I gave them i your hands. 928

Jdg
1: 2 I have given the land i their hands." 928
1: 3 "Come up with us i the territory allotted 928
1: 3 We in turn will go with you i yours." 928
1: 4 and Perizzites i their hands and they struck 928
1:24 "Show us how to get i the city 4427
1:28 they pressed the Canaanites i forced labor 4200
1:34 not allowing them to come down i 4200
1:35 they too were pressed i forced labor. 4200
2: 1 of Egypt and led you i the land that I swore 448
2:23 not drive them out at once by giving them i 928
3: 8 against Israel so that he sold them i 928
3:10 of Aram i the hands of Othniel, 928
3:21 from his right thigh and plunged it i 928
3:28 your enemy, i your hands. 928
4: 2 the LORD sold them i the hands of Jabin, 928
4: 7 to the Kishon River and give him i 928
4:14 the LORD has given Sisera i your hands. 928
4:21 the peg through his temple i the ground, 928
5:15 rushing after him i the valley. 928
6: 1 for seven years he gave them i the hands of 928
6:13 the LORD has abandoned us and put us i 928
6:35 and also i Asher, Zebulun and Naphtali, 928
7: 2 for me to deliver Midian i their hands. 928
7: 7 and give the Midianites i your hands. 928
7: 9 because I am going to give it i your hands. 928
7:13 of barley bread came tumbling i 928
7:14 the Midianites and the whole camp i 928
7:15 The LORD has given the Midianite camp i NIH
7:16 the three hundred men i three companies. NIH
8: 3 the Midianite leaders, i your hands. 928
8: 7 and Zalmunna i my hand, 928
8:27 Gideon made the gold i an ephod, 4200

Jdg
9:26 moved with his brothers i Shechem, 928
9:27 After *they* had gone out i the fields AIT
9:43 divided them i three companies and set 4200
9:46 the tower of Shechem went i the stronghold 448
10: 7 He sold them i the hands of the Philistines 928
11:21 gave Sihon and all his men i Israel's hands, 928
11:30 "If you give the Ammonites i my hands, 928
11:32 and the LORD gave them i his hands. 928
11:38 She and the girls went i the hills and wept 6584
13: 1 so the LORD delivered them i the hands 928
14:15 "Coax your husband i explaining AIT
15:18 Must I now die of thirst and fall i the hands 928
16: 5 "See if you can lure him i showing you AIT
16:13 :he seven braids of my head i the fabric [on 6640
16:13 wove them i the fabric 6640
16:23 our enemy, i our hands." 928
16:24 Our god has delivered our enemy i 928
17: 4 who made them i the image and the idol. AIT
18: 1 come i an inheritance among the tribes 928+5877
18:10 and a spacious land that God has put i 995
18:18 When these men went i Micah's house 995
19: 3 *She* took him i her father's house, 995
19:12 We won't go i an alien city, 448
19:15 no one took them i his home for the night. 2025
19:18 No one has taken me i his house. 2025
19:21 So he took him i his house 4200
19:29 i twelve parts and sent them into all 4200
19:29 and sent them i all the areas of Israel. 928
20: 6 cut her i pieces and sent one piece 5983
20:28 tomorrow I will give them i your hands." 928
20:37 in ambush made a sudden dash i Gibeah, 448
20:40 the smoke of the whole city going up i 2025
20:47 and fled i the desert to the rock of Rimmon, 2025

Ru
2: 7 *She* went i the field 995
3:15 poured i it six measures of barley 4499
4:11 the woman who is coming i your home 448

1Sa
2:14 He would plunge it i the pan or kettle 928
4: 5 of the LORD's covenant came i the camp, 448
4: 6 the ark of the LORD had come i the camp, 448
4: 7 "A god has come i the camp," they said. 448
4:19 *she* went i labor and gave birth, 4156
5: 2 Then they carried the ark i Dagon's temple AIT
5: 9 throwing it i a great panic. NIH
6:19 of them to death because they had looked i 928
7:10 threw them i such a panic 2169
9: 4 They went i the district of Shaalim, 928
9:22 Then Samuel brought Saul and his servant i 2025
10: 6 you will be changed i a different person. 4200
11: 7 He took a pair of oxen, cut them i pieces, 5983
11:11 The next day Saul separated his men i AIT
11:11 the last watch of the night they broke i 928+9348
12: 9 so he sold them i the hand of Sisera 928
12: 9 the commander of the army of Hazor, and i 928
14:10 the LORD has given them i our hands." 928
14:12 the LORD has given them i the hand 928
14:26 When they went i the woods, 448
14:27 the staff that was in his hand and dipped it i 928
14:37 Will you give them i Israel's hand?" 928
14:52 took him i his service. 665
17:47 and he will give all of you i our hands." 928
17:49 Reaching i his bag and taking out a stone, 448
17:49 The stone sank i his forehead, 928
19: 2 go i hiding and stay there. 928
19:10 as Saul drove the spear i the wall. 928
20: 8 for you have brought him i a covenant 928
20:11 Jonathan said, "let's go out i the field." AIT
21:15 Must this man come i my house?" 448
22: 5 Go i the land of Judah." 995
23: 4 for I am going to give the Philistines i 928
23:14 but God did not give David i his hands. 928
23:25 went i the Desert of Maon in pursuit AIT
24: 4 'I will give your enemy i your hands 928
24:10 how the LORD delivered you i my hands 928
24:18 the LORD delivered me i your hands, 928
25: 1 David moved i the Desert of Maon. 448
25:20 As she came riding her donkey i 928
26: 6 "Who will go down i the camp with me 448
26: 8 "Today God has delivered your enemy i 928
26:10 or he will go i battle and perish. 928
26:12 the LORD *had* put them i a deep sleep. AIT
26:23 The LORD delivered you i my hands today, 928
29: 4 He must not go with us i battle, 928
29: 9 'He must not go up with us i battle.' 928

2Sa
2:16 and thrust his dagger i his opponent's side, 928
2:23 the butt of his spear i Asahel's stomach, 448
2:25 They formed themselves i a group 4200
3:13 *Do* not come i my presence 906+7156+8011
3:27 Joab took him aside i the gateway, 448+9348
4: 6 They went i the inner part of the house as if 6330
4: 7 *They* had gone i the house 995
12: 8 and your master's wives i your arms. 928
12:16 He fasted and went i his house and spent 995
12:20 he went i the house of the LORD 995
13:10 "Bring the food here i my bedroom 995
14: 6 *They* got i a fight with each other in 5897
14:19 and who put all these words i the mouth 928
15:25 "Take the ark of God back i the city. AIT
15:31 turn Ahithophel's counsel i foolishness." 6118
17:11 with you yourself leading them i battle. 928
17:13 If he withdraws i a city, 448
17:18 and *they* climbed down i it. AIT
18: 6 The army marched i the field to fight Israel, 3655
18:12 if a thousand shekels were weighed out i 6584
18:14 and plunged them i Absalom's heart 928
18:17 threw him i a big pit in the forest and piled 448
19: 2 that day *was* turned i mourning, 2118+4200
19: 3 The men stole i the city that day 995+1704+4200

2Sa
19: 5 Joab went i the house to the king and said, 448
20:10 and Joab plunged it i his belly, 448
20:12 dragged him from the road i AIT
22:20 He brought me out i a spacious place; 4200
22:29 turns my darkness i light. 5585
23:20 also went down i a pit on a snowy day 928+9348
24:14 Let us fall i the hands of the LORD, 928
24:14 but do not let me fall i the hands of men." 928

1Ki
1:28 So she came i the king's presence and stood AIT
6: 6 so that nothing would be inserted i 928
8: 1 King Solomon summoned i his presence 448
10:16 six hundred bekas of gold went i 6584
11:30 the new cloak he was wearing and tore it i AIT
12:18 to get i his chariot and escape to Jerusalem. 928
15:15 *He* brought i the temple of the LORD 995
16:18 he went i the citadel of the royal palace 448
16:21 people of Israel were split i two factions; 4200
17:23 and carried him down from the room i 2025
18:23 and *let them* cut it i pieces and put it on 5983
18:33 cut the bull i pieces 5983
18:46 tucking his cloak i his belt, 5516+9113
19: 4 while he himself went a day's journey i 928
19: 9 There he went i a cave and spent the night. 448
20: 2 He sent messengers i the city to Ahab king 2025
20:13 I will give it i your hand today, 928
20:28 I will deliver this vast army i your hands, 928
20:33 Ahab had him come up i his chariot. 6584
20:39 "Your servant went i the thick of the battle, 928
22: 6 "for the Lord will give it i the king's hand." 928
22:12 the LORD will give it i the king's hand." 928
22:15 the LORD will give it i the king's hand." 928
22:20 'Who *will* entice Ahab i attacking AIT
22:30 of Israel disguised himself and went i 928

2Ki
2:21 to the spring and threw the salt i it, 9004S
4: 4 Pour oil i all the jars, and as each is filled, 6584
4:29 "Tuck your cloak i your belt, 2520+5516
4:39 of them went out i the fields to gather herbs 448
4:39 he cut them up i the pot of stew, 448
4:41 He put it i the pot and said, 448
6: 5 the iron axhead fell i the water. 448
7: 4 If we say, '*We'll* go i the city" 995
7:10 "We went i the Aramean camp and not 448
7:10 and then we will take them alive and get i 448
9: 1 "Tuck *your* cloak i your belt, 2520+5516
9: 2 from his companions and take him i 995
9: 2 Jehu got up and went i the house. 2025
9:16 he got i *his* chariot and rode to Jezreel, 8206
10:15 and Jehu helped him up i the chariot. 448
10:21 *They* crowded i the temple of Baal 995
10:23 of Recab went i the temple of Baal. 995
11:19 from the temple of the LORD and went i 995
12: 9 The priests who guarded the entrance put i 2025
12:10 counted the money that *had* been brought i AIT
12:10 the temple of the LORD and put it i bags. 7437
12:13 The money brought i the temple was 995
12:13 and sin offerings was not brought i 995
13:21 they threw the man's body i Elisha's tomb. 928
16: 6 then moved i Elath and have lived there 995
17:20 he afflicted them and gave them i the hands 928
17:23 taken from their homeland i exile 1655
18: 4 *He* broke i pieces the bronze snake 4198
18:30 be given i the hand of the king of Assyria.' 928
19: 1 and put on sackcloth and went i the temple 995
19:18 They have thrown their gods i the fire 928
19:25 turned fortified cities i piles of stone. 8615
20:20 and the tunnel by which he brought water i 2025
21:11 and *has* led Judah i sin with his idols. 2627
22: 4 that *has* been brought i the temple of 995
23:12 and threw the rubble i the Kidron Valley. 448
24:14 *He* carried i exile all Jerusalem: 1655+1655
25:11 the commander of the guard carried i exile 1655
25:21 So Judah went i captivity, 1655

1Ch
5: 6 king of Assyria took i exile. 1655
5:26 took the Reubenites, the Gadites and the
half-tribe of Manasseh i exile. 1655
6:15 sent Judah and Jerusalem i exile 1655
11:22 also went down i a pit on a snowy day 928+9348
21:13 Let me fall i the hands of the LORD, 928
21:13 but do not let me fall i the hands of men." 928
21:27 and he put his sword back i its sheath. 448
22:19 and the sacred articles belonging to God i 4200
23: 6 David divided the Levites i groups AIT
24: 3 David separated them i divisions 2745

2Ch
3:14 with cherubim worked i it. 6584
9:15 six hundred bekas of hammered gold went i 6584
10:18 to get i his chariot and escape to Jerusalem. 928
13: 3 Abijah went i battle with a force 673
13:16 and God delivered them i their hands. 928
15:12 They entered i a covenant to seek 928
15:18 *He* brought i the temple of God the silver 995
16: 8 he delivered them i your hand. 928
18: 5 "for God will give it i the king's hand." 928
18:11 the LORD will give it i the king's hand." 928
18:14 "for they will be given i your hand." 928
18:19 entice Ahab king of Israel i attacking AIT
18:29 of Israel disguised himself and went i 928
22: 1 who came with the Arabs i the camp, 4200
23:20 *They* went i the palace through 995
24: 7 wicked woman Athaliah had broken i 7287
24:10 dropping them i the chest until it was full. 4200
24:24 the LORD delivered i their hands 928
28: 5 also given i the hands of the king of Israel, 928
28: 9 he gave them i your hand. 928
29:16 The priests went i the sanctuary of 4200+7163
30:14 and threw them i the Kidron Valley. 4200
32:21 And when *he* went i the temple of his god, 995
34: 9 money that *had* been brought i the temple 995

2Ch	34:11	kings of Judah had **allowed to fall** i ruin. 8845
	34:14	the money that had **been taken** i the temple 995
	36:20	*He* **carried i exile** to Babylon the remnant, 1655
Ezr	7:27	who has put it i the king's heart 928
	8:33	and gold and the sacred articles i the hands 6584
Ne	6:11	like me go i the temple to save his life? 448
	7:5	So my God put it i my heart to assemble 448
	8:15	"Go out i the hill country AIT
	9:11	but you hurled their pursuers i the depths, 928
	9:11	like a stone i mighty waters. 928
	9:23	and you brought them i the land 448
	12:44	around the towns they were to bring i 928
	13:1	or Moabite should ever be admitted i 928
	13:2	however, turned the curse i a blessing.) 4200
	13:9	and then *I* **put back** i them the equipment AIT
	13:12	new wine and oil i the storerooms. 4200
	13:15	And *they were* **bringing** all this i Jerusalem 995
	13:26	even he *was* **led** i sin *by* foreign women. 2627
Est	2:3	to bring all these beautiful girls i the harem 448
	2:6	had **been carried i exile** from Jerusalem 1655
	2:9	and her maids the best place in the harem. 4200
	3:9	of silver i the royal treasury for 448
	4:1	and went out i the city, 928+9348
	4:7	of money Haman had promised to pay i 6584
	4:8	urge her to go i the king's **presence** to beg 448
	7:7	and went out i the palace garden. 448
	8:1	And Mordecai came i the presence of 4200
	9:22	the month when their sorrow was turned i 4200
	9:22	and their mourning i a day of celebration. 4200
Job	6:18	they go up i the wasteland and perish. 928
	9:24	a land falls i the hands of the wicked, 928
	9:31	you would plunge me i a slime pit so that 928
	10:19	If only *I* had never **come** i being, 2118+2118
	12:22	of darkness and brings deep shadows i 4200
	16:11	and thrown me i the clutches of the wicked. 6584
	17:12	These men turn night i day; 4200
	17:16	Will we descend together i the dust?" 6584
	18:8	His feet thrust him i a net and he wanders 928
	18:8	into a net and he wanders i its mesh. 6584
	18:18	from light i darkness and is banished from 448
	24:4	**force** all the poor of the land i **hiding**. 2461
	24:16	In the dark, *men* **break** i houses, 3168
	30:19	He throws me i the mud, 928
	39:21	and charges i the fray. 7925
Ps	4:2	O men, will you **turn** my glory i shame? 4200
	5:7	by your great mercy, *will* **come** i your house; 995
	7:15	and scoops it out falls i the pit he has made. 928
	9:15	nations have fallen i the pit they have dug; 928
	18:6	my cry came before him, i his ears. 928
	18:19	He brought me out i a spacious place; 4200
	18:28	my God **turns** my darkness i **light**. 5585
	19:4	Their voice goes out i all the earth, 928
	30:3	you spared me from **going down** i the pit. AIT
	30:9	in my going down i the pit? 448
	30:11	You turned my wailing i dancing; 4200
	31:5	I your hands I commit my spirit; 928
	33:7	He gathers the waters of the sea i jars; 3869
	33:7	he puts the deep i storehouses. 928
	35:8	may they fall i the pit, to their ruin. 928
	46:2	and the mountains fall i the heart of the sea, 928
	55:23	down the wicked i the pit of corruption; 4200
	57:T	When he had fled from Saul i the cave. 928
	57:6	but they have fallen i it themselves. 928+9348
	66:6	He turned the sea i dry land, 4200
	66:11	You brought us i prison and laid burdens 928
	68:17	Lord [has come] from Sinai i his sanctuary. 928
	68:24	Your procession *has* **come** i view, O God, 8011
	68:24	the procession of my God and King i 928
	69:2	I have come i the deep waters; 928
	73:24	and afterward *you will* **take** me i glory. AIT
	78:61	He sent [the ark of] his might i captivity, 4200
	78:61	his splendor i the hands of the enemy. 928
	79:12	Pay back i the laps 448
	96:8	bring an offering and come i his courts. 4200
	98:4	**burst** i jubilant song with music; AIT
	104:8	*they* **went down** i the valleys, AIT
	104:10	He makes springs pour water i the ravines; 928
	105:29	He turned their waters i blood, 4200
	105:30	up i the bedrooms of their rulers. 928
	105:32	*He* **turned** their rain i hail, 5989
	107:33	He turned rivers i a desert, 4200
	107:33	flowing springs i thirsty ground, 4200
	107:34	and fruitful land i a salt waste, 4200
	107:35	He turned the desert i pools of water and 4200
	107:35	and the parched ground i flowing springs; 4200
	109:18	it entered i his body like water, 928
	109:18	like water, i his bones like oil. 928
	114:8	who **turned** the rock i a pool, 2200
	114:8	the hard rock i springs of water. 4200
	135:9	He sent his signs and wonders i your midst, 928
	136:15	swept Pharaoh and his army i the Red Sea; 928
	140:10	may they be thrown i the fire, 928
	140:10	i miry pits, never to rise. 928
	141:10	Let the wicked fall i their own nets, 928
	143:2	Do not bring your servant i judgment, 928
	144:14	no **going** i captivity, 3448
Pr	1:16	for their feet rush i sin, 4200
	3:32	but takes the upright i his confidence. 907
	6:3	you have fallen i your neighbor's hands: 928
	6:18	feet that are quick to rush i evil, 4200
	6:27	Can a man scoop fire i his lap 928
	7:22	like a deer stepping i a noose 448
	7:23	like a bird darting i a snare, 448
	7:25	not let your heart turn to her ways or stray i 928
	8:3	beside the gates **leading** i the city, at 4200+7023
	13:17	A wicked messenger falls i trouble, 928
	16:33	The lot is cast i the lap, 928

Pr	17:20	he whose tongue is deceitful falls i trouble. 928
	18:16	for the giver and ushers him i the presence 4200
	22:14	under the LORD's wrath *will* **fall** i it. AIT
	26:27	If a man digs a pit, he will fall i it; 928
	28:10	along an evil path will fall i his own trap, 928
	28:12	the wicked rise to power, men **go** i **hiding**. 2924
	28:14	but he who hardens his heart falls i trouble. 928
	28:28	wicked rise to power, people **go** i **hiding**; 6259
Ecc	1:7	All streams flow i the sea, 448
	2:19	the work i **which** I have poured my effort AIT
	3:21	and if the spirit of the animal goes down i 4200
	5:6	Do not let your mouth **lead** you i **sin**. 2627
	7:7	Extortion **turns** a wise man i **a fool**, 2147
	10:8	Whoever digs a pit may fall i it; 928
	12:14	For God will bring every deed i judgment, 928
SS	1:4	*Let* the **king bring** me i his chambers. 995
	4:16	Let my lover come i his garden 4200
	5:1	I have come i my garden, my sister, 4200
Isa	2:4	They will beat their swords i plowshares 4200
	2:4	into plowshares and their spears i 4200
	2:10	Go i the rocks, hide in the ground 928
	3:14	The LORD enters i judgment against 928
	5:13	Therefore my people *will* **go** i **exile** 1655
	5:14	it will descend their nobles and masses 928
	8:8	and sweep on i Judah, 928
	8:22	and *they will* **be thrust** i utter darkness. AIT
	10:14	As one reaches i a nest, 3869
	11:8	young child put his hand i the viper's nest. 6584
	11:15	up i seven streams so that men can cross 4200
	14:7	*they* **break** i singing. AIT
	14:23	"I will turn her i a place for owls and 4200
	14:23	"I will turn her into a place for owls and i NIH
	19:8	all who cast hooks i the Nile; 928
	19:14	The LORD has poured i them a spirit 928+7931
	22:18	like a ball and throw you i a large country. 448
	22:23	I will drive him like a peg i a firm place; 928
	22:25	peg driven i the firm place will give way; 928
	23:13	and turned it i a ruin. 4200
	24:18	at the sound of terror will fall i a pit; 448
	28:15	"*We have* **entered** i a covenant with death, AIT
	29:17	will not Lebanon be turned i a fertile field 4200
	34:9	Edom's streams will be turned i pitch, 4200
	34:9	her dust i burning sulfur; 4200
	35:2	it will **burst** i bloom; 7255+7255
	36:15	be given i the hand of the king of Assyria.' AIT
	37:1	and put on sackcloth and **went** i the temple 995
	37:19	They have thrown their gods i the fire 928
	37:26	**turned** fortified cities i piles of stone. 8615
	41:15	"See, I will make you i a threshing sledge, 4200
	41:18	I will turn the desert i pools of water, 4200
	41:18	and the parched ground i springs. 4200
	42:9	before *they* **spring** i being I announce them 7541
	42:15	I will turn rivers i islands and dry up 4200
	42:16	I will turn the darkness i light before them 4200
	44:23	**Burst** i song, *you* mountains, AIT
	44:25	of the wise and **turns** it i **nonsense**, 6118
	45:16	they will go off i disgrace together. 928
	46:2	they themselves go off i captivity. 928
	46:6	they hire a goldsmith to **make** it i a god, AIT
	47:5	"Sit in silence, go i darkness, 928
	47:6	I gave them i your hand, 928
	49:2	he made me i a polished arrow 4200
	49:11	I will turn all my mountains i roads, 4200
	49:13	**burst** i song, O mountains! AIT
	50:2	*I* **turn** rivers i a desert; 8492
	51:23	I will put it i the hands of your tormentors, 928
	52:9	**Burst** i songs of joy together, AIT
	54:1	**burst** i song, shout for joy, AIT
	54:16	the blacksmith *who* **fans** the coals i flame AIT
	55:12	the mountains and hills *will* **burst** i song AIT
	57:2	Those who walk uprightly **enter** i peace; AIT
	57:8	*you* **climbed** i it and opened it wide; AIT
	59:7	Their feet rush i sin; 4200
	59:8	**turned** them i **crooked** AIT
	65:6	I will pay it back i their laps— 6584
	65:7	I will measure i their laps the full payment 448
	66:2	and so they **came** i **being**?" 2118
	66:7	"Before *she* **goes** i labor, she gives birth; 2655
	66:17	and purify themselves to go i the gardens, 448
Jer	1:3	when the people of Jerusalem **went** i **exile**. 1655
	2:7	I brought you i a fertile land to eat its fruit 448
	2:21	then *did you* **turn** against me i a corrupt, 2200
	4:29	Some go i the thickets; 928
	8:6	like a horse charging i battle. 928
	12:7	the one I love i the hands of her enemies. 928
	12:10	they will turn my pleasant field i 4200
	13:19	All Judah *will* **be carried** i **exile**, 1655
	14:16	be thrown out i the streets of Jerusalem 928
	14:18	If *I* **go** i the country, 3655
	14:18	if *I* **go** i the city, 995
	16:13	So I will throw you out of this land i 6584
	18:4	so the potter **formed** it i another pot, AIT
	20:6	in your house will go i exile to Babylon. 928
	21:10	It will be given i the hands of the king 928
	22:7	up your fine cedar beams and throw them i 6584
	22:22	and your allies will go i exile. 928
	22:26	and the mother who gave you birth i 6584
	22:28	cast i a land they do not know? 6584
	24:1	the artisans of Judah *were* **carried** i **exile** 1655
	26:23	down with a sword and his body thrown i 448
	27:20	**carried** Jehoiachin son of Jehoiakim king of Judah i **exile** 1655
	29:1	people Nebuchadnezzar had **carried** i **exile** 1655
	29:2	the craftsmen and the artisans had gone i NIH
	29:4	says to all those *I* **carried** i **exile** 1655
	29:7	to which *I have* **carried** you i **exile**, 1655
	29:14	from which *I* **carried** you i **exile**." 1655

Jer	29:16	your countrymen who did not go with you i 928
	29:26	like a prophet i the stocks and neck-irons. 448
	30:16	all your enemies will go i exile. 928
	31:13	I will turn their mourning i gladness; 4200
	32:18	the fathers' sins i the laps of their children 448
	34:10	the officials and people who entered i 928
	35:4	I brought them i the house of the LORD, NIH
	35:4	i the room of the sons of Hanan son 448
	36:23	with a scribe's knife and threw them i 448
	37:15	which they had made i a prison. 4200
	37:16	Jeremiah was put i a vaulted cell in 448
	38:6	and put him i the cistern of Malkijah, 448
	38:6	They lowered Jeremiah by ropes i 928
	38:6	and Jeremiah sank down i the mud. 928
	38:7	that they had put Jeremiah i the cistern. 448
	38:9	They have thrown him i a cistern, 448
	39:9	of the imperial guard **carried** i **exile** 1655
	40:1	and Judah who *were* **being carried** i **exile** 1655
	40:7	and who had not **been carried** i **exile** 1655
	41:7	When they went i the city, 448+9348
	41:7	and threw them i a cistern. 448+9348
	42:16	the famine you dread *will* **follow** you i AIT
	43:3	so they may kill us or **carry** us i **exile** 1655
	48:7	and Chemosh will go i exile, 928
	48:11	she has not gone i exile. 928
	48:44	"Whoever flees from the terror will fall i 448
	48:46	your sons are taken i exile 928
	48:46	into exile and your daughters i captivity. 928
	49:3	for Molech will go i exile, 928
	51:34	*he has* **thrown** us i confusion, 2169
	51:63	stone to it and throw it i the Euphrates. 448+9348
	52:15	of the guard **carried** i **exile** some of 1655
	52:27	So Judah **went** i **captivity**, 1655
	52:28	the people Nebuchadnezzar **carried** i **exile**: 1655
	52:30	745 Jews **taken** i **exile** by Nebuzaradan 1655
La	1:3	Judah *has* **gone** i **exile**. 1655
	1:5	Her children *have* **gone** i exile, AIT
	1:7	When her people fell i enemy hands, 928
	1:13	sent it down i my bones. 928
	1:14	"My sins *have* **been bound** i a yoke; AIT
	1:18	My young men and maidens have gone i 928
	2:9	Her gates have sunk i the ground; 928
Eze	2:2	the Spirit came i me and raised me 928
	3:24	Spirit came i me and raised me to my feet. 928
	5:4	throw them i the fire and burn them up. 448+9348
	7:11	Violence has grown i a rod 4200
	7:14	no one will go i battle, 4200
	7:19	They will throw their silver i the streets, 928
	7:19	for it has made them **stumble** i sin. AIT
	7:20	Therefore I will turn these i 4200
	8:8	"Son of man, now dig i the wall." 928
	8:8	I dug i the wall and saw a doorway there. 928
	8:16	He then brought me i the inner court of 448
	10:7	He took up some of it and put it i the hands 448
	12:4	go out like *those who* **go** i exile. AIT
	12:11	They will go i exile as captives. 928
	14:19	a plague i that land and pour out my wrath 448
	15:5	be made i something useful when 4200
	16:5	you were thrown out i the open field, 448
	16:8	I gave you my solemn oath and entered i 928
	19:9	With hooks they pulled him i a cage 928
	20:6	that I would bring them out of Egypt i 448
	20:10	of Egypt and brought them i the desert. 448
	20:15	in the desert that I would not bring them i 448
	20:28	When I brought them i the land I had sworn 448
	20:35	I will bring you i the desert of the nations 448
	20:37	I will bring you i the bond of the covenant. 928
	20:42	when I bring you i the land of Israel, 448
	21:22	I his right hand will come the lot 448
	22:19	I will gather you i Jerusalem. 448+9348
	22:20	lead and tin i a furnace to melt it with 448+9348
	23:31	so I will put her cup i your hand. 928
	24:3	put it on and pour water i it. 928
	24:4	Put i it the pieces of meat, 448
	25:3	the people of Judah when they went i exile, 928
	25:5	I will turn Rabbah i a pasture for camels 4200
	25:5	for camels and Ammon i a resting place 4200
	26:12	timber and rubble i the sea. 928+9348
	27:27	on board will sink i the heart of the sea on 928
	30:17	the cities themselves will go i captivity. 928
	30:18	and her villages will go i captivity. 928
	30:25	when I put my sword i the hand of the king 928
	33:31	but *they do not* **put** them i **practice**. 6913
	33:32	but *do not* **put** them i **practice**. 6913
	34:13	and I will bring them i their own land. 448
	35:4	*I will* **turn** your towns i ruins 8492
	36:24	from all the countries and bring you back i 448
	37:9	O breath, and breathe i these slain, 928
	37:17	Join them together i one stick so 4200
	37:21	from all around and bring them back i 448
	37:22	or be divided i two kingdoms. 4200
	38:10	On that day thoughts will come i your mind 6584
	39:23	that the people of Israel **went** i **exile** 1655
	39:28	I **sent** them i **exile** among the nations, 1655
	40:17	Then he brought me i the outer court. 448
	40:20	**leading** i the outer court. 4200
	40:28	Then he brought me i the inner court 448
	41:3	Then he went i the inner sanctuary 4200
	41:6	the supports were not **inserted** i the wall of 928
	42:1	the man led me northward i the outer court 448
	42:14	not to go i the outer court until they leave 448
	43:5	the Spirit lifted me up and brought me i 448
	44:7	in heart and flesh i my sanctuary, 928
	44:12	**made** the house of Israel **fall** i AIT
	44:19	When they go out i the outer court where 448
	44:27	On the day he goes i the inner court of 448
	46:20	to avoid bringing them i the outer court 448

Eze	47: 8	toward the eastern region and goes down **i**	6584
	47: 8	When it empties **i** the Sea,	448
	48:14	of the land and *must* not **pass i other hands,**	6296
Da	1: 2	Jehoiakim king of Judah **i** his hand,	928
	2: 5	and interpret it, I *will* **have you cut i**	10522
	2: 5	into pieces and your houses **turned i** piles	10682
	3: 6	will immediately be thrown **i** a	10135+10378
	3:11	and worship will be thrown **i** a	10135+10378
	3:15	immediately **i** a blazing furnace.	10135+10378
	3:17	If we are thrown **i** the blazing furnace,	NIH
	3:20	Meshach and Abednego and throw them **i**	10378
	3:21	and thrown **i** the blazing furnace.	10135+10378
	3:23	tied, fell **i** the blazing furnace.	10378
	3:24	we tied up and threw **i** the fire?"	10135+10378
	3:29	Meshach and Abednego **be cut i** pieces	10522
	3:29	their houses **be turned i** piles of rubble,	10702
	4: 8	Daniel **came i** my presence and I told him	10549
	5:10	came **i** the banquet hall.	10378
	6: 7	O king, shall be thrown **i** the lions' den.	10378
	6:12	O king, would be thrown **i** the lions' den?"	10378
	6:16	and they brought Daniel and threw him **i**	10378
	6:24	in and thrown **i** the lions' den,	10378
	7:11	and its body destroyed and thrown **i**	10378
	7:13	of Days and was led **i** his **presence.**	10621
	10: 9	*I* **fell i a deep sleep,**	8101
Hos	2: 3	turn her **i** a parched land,	3869
	2:14	I will lead her **i** the desert	NIH
	7: 1	They practice deceit, thieves **break i** houses,	995
	9: 4	not **come i** the temple of the LORD.	995
	9: 9	*They have* **sunk deep i** corruption,	AIT
	10: 5	**taken** from them **i exile.**	1655
Joel	2: 9	They climb **i** the houses;	928
	2:20	pushing it **i** a parched and barren land,	448
	2:20	its front columns going **i** the eastern sea	448
	2:20	sea and those in the rear **i** the westsern sea.	448
	3: 2	There *I will* **enter i judgment**	9149
	3:10	Beat your plowshares **i** swords	4200
	3:10	and your pruning hooks **i** spears.	4200
	3:12	let them advance **i** the Valley	448
Am	1: 5	The people of Aram *will* **go i exile**	1655
	1:15	Her king will go **i** exile,	928
	3: 5	Does a bird fall **i** a trap on the ground	1655
	5: 5	For Gilgal *will* **surely go i exile,**	1655+1655
	5: 7	You who turn justice **i** bitterness	4200
	5: 8	who turns blackness **i** dawn	4200
	5: 8	and **darkens** day *i* night, who calls for	AIT
	5:27	Therefore *I will* **send** you **i exile**	1655
	6: 7	be among the first to **go i exile;**	1655+1655
	6:11	**smash** the great house *i* bits.	AIT
	6:11	into pieces and the small house **i** bits.	NIH
	6:12	But you have turned justice **i** poison and	4200
	6:12	and the fruit of righteousness **i** bitterness—	4200
	7:11	and Israel *will* **surely go i exile,**	1655+1655
	7:17	Israel *will* **certainly go i exile,**	1655+1655
	8:10	I will turn your religious feasts **i** mourning	4200
	8:10	into mourning and all your singing **i**	4200
	9: 4	Though they are driven **i** exile	928
Jnh	1: 5	the cargo **i** the sea to lighten the ship.	448
	1: 5	lay down and **fell i a deep sleep.**	8101
	1:12	"Pick me up and throw me **i** the sea,"	448
	2: 3	You hurled me **i** the deep,	NIH
	2: 3	**i** the very heart of the seas,	928
	3: 4	On the first day, Jonah started **i** the city.	928
Mic	1: 6	I will pour her stones **i** the valley	4200
	1:16	**go** from you **i exile.**	1655
	4: 3	They shall beat their swords **i** plowshares	4200
	4: 3	into plowshares and their spears **i**	4200
	5: 6	when he invades our land and marches **i**	928
	7: 9	He will bring me out **i** the light;	4200
	7:19	and hurl all our iniquities **i** the depths of	928
Na	3:10	he will pursue his foes **i** darkness.	NIH
	3:10	Yet she was taken captive and went **i** exile.	928
	3:11	*you will* **go i** hiding and seek refuge from	AIT
	3:12	the figs fall **i** the mouth of the eater.	6584
Hab	3:16	decay crept **i** my bones,	928
Hag	1: 8	**Go up** *i* the mountains and bring	AIT
Zec	5: 8	and he pushed her back **i** the basket	448+9348
	11:13	the thirty pieces of silver and **threw** them *i*	AIT
	13: 9	This third I will bring **i** the fire;	928
	14: 2	Half of the city will go **i** exile,	928
Mal	1: 3	**turned** his mountains **i** a wasteland	8492
	3:10	Bring the whole tithe **i** the storehouse,	448
Mt	3:10	be cut down and thrown **i** the fire.	1650
	3:12	gathering his wheat **i** the barn and burning	1650
	4: 1	Then Jesus was led by the Spirit **i** the desert	1650
	4:18	They were casting a net **i** the lake,	1650
	5:25	and you may be thrown **i** prison.	1650
	5:29	for your whole body to be thrown **i** hell.	1650
	5:30	for your whole body to go **i** hell.	1650
	6: 6	But when you pray, **go** *i* your room,	1656
	6:13	And **lead** us not **i** temptation,	1662
	6:30	and tomorrow is thrown **i** the fire,	1650
	7:19	down and thrown **i** the fire.	1650
	7:24	of mine and **puts** them **i practice** is like	4472
	7:26	and *does* not **put** them **i practice** is like	4472
	8:12	**i** the darkness, where there will be weeping	1650
	8:14	When Jesus came **i** Peter's house,	1650
	8:23	Then he got **i** the boat	1650
	8:31	send us **i** the herd of pigs."	1650
	8:32	So they came out and went **i** the pigs,	1650
	8:32	down the steep bank **i** the lake and died in	1650
	8:33	went **i** the town and reported all this,	1650
	9: 1	Jesus stepped **i** a boat,	1650
	9:17	Neither do men pour new wine **i** old	1650
	9:17	No, they pour new wine **i** new wineskins,	1650
	9:38	to send out workers **i** his harvest field."	1650
	11: 7	"What did you go out **i** the desert to see?	1650

Mt	12: 9	he went **i** their synagogue,	1650
	12:11	"If any of you has a sheep and it falls **i** a pit	1650
	13: 2	around him that he got **i** a boat and sat in it,	1650
	13:30	the wheat and bring it **i** my barn.' "	1650
	13:33	a woman took and mixed **i** a large amount	1650
	13:36	he left the crowd and went **i** the house.	1650
	13:42	They will throw them **i** the fiery furnace,	1650
	13:47	down **i** the lake and caught all kinds of fish.	1650
	13:50	and throw them **i** the fiery furnace,	1650
	14:22	the disciples get **i** the boat and go on ahead	1650
	14:32	And when they climbed **i** the boat,	1650
	15:11	What **goes i** a man's mouth does not	1656
	15:14	both will fall **i** a pit."	1650
	15:17	the mouth goes **i** the stomach and then out	1650
	15:39	*he* **got i** the boat and went to the vicinity	1832
	17:15	He often falls **i** the fire or into the water.	1650
	17:15	He often falls into the fire or **i** the water.	1650
	17:22	of Man is going to be betrayed **i** the hands	1650
	17:25	When Peter came **i** the house,	1650
	18: 8	or two feet and be thrown **i** eternal fire.	1650
	18: 9	to have two eyes and be thrown **i** the fire	1650
	18:30	the man thrown **i** prison until he could pay	1650
	19: 1	he left Galilee and went **i** the region	1650
	20: 2	for the day and sent them **i** his vineyard.	1650
	21:21	'Go, throw yourself **i** the sea,'	1650
	22:10	So the servants went out **i** the streets	1650
	22:13	and throw him outside, **i** the darkness,	1650
	24:43	not have let his house *be* **broken i.**	1482
	25:30	**i** the darkness, where there will be weeping	1650
	25:41	**i** the eternal fire prepared for the devil	1650
	26:18	"Go **i** the city to a certain man and tell him,	1650
	26:23	"The one who has dipped his hand **i**	1877
	26:32	I will go ahead of you **i** Galilee."	1650
	26:41	so that *you will* not **fall i** temptation.	1656
	26:45	and the Son of Man is betrayed **i** the hands	1650
	27: 5	So Judas threw the money **i** the temple	1650
	27: 6	against the law to put this **i** the treasury,"	1650
	27:27	Then the governor's soldiers took Jesus **i**	1650
	27:53	and after Jesus' resurrection *they* **went i**	1656
	28: 7	from the dead and is going ahead of you **i**	1650
	28:11	of the guards went **i** the city and reported to	1650
Mk	1:12	At once the Spirit sent him out **i** the desert,	1650
	1:14	Jesus went **i** Galilee,	1650
	1:16	and his brother Andrew casting a net **i**	1877
	1:21	Jesus went **i** the synagogue and began	1656
	2:22	no one pours new wine **i** old wineskins.	1650
	2:22	No, he pours new wine **i** new wineskins."	1650
	3: 1	Another time *he* **went i** the synagogue,	1656
	4: 1	around him was so large that he got **i** a boat	1650
	4:22	to be brought out **i** the open.	1650
	5:12	allow *us to* **go i** them."	1656
	5:13	the evil spirits came out and **went i** the pigs.	1656
	5:13	the steep bank **i** the lake and were drowned.	1650
	5:18	As Jesus was getting **i** the boat,	1650
	6:45	Immediately Jesus made his disciples get **i**	1650
	6:51	Then he climbed **i** the boat with them,	1650
	6:56	And wherever *he* **went—i** villages,	1660
	7:15	a man can make him 'unclean' *by* **going i**	1660
	7:19	For *it* doesn't **go i** his heart but	1660
	7:19	For it doesn't go into his heart but **i**	NIG
	7:31	and the region of the Decapolis.	324+3545
	7:33	Jesus put his fingers **i** the man's ears.	1650
	8:10	he got **i** the boat with his disciples and went	1650
	8:13	got back **i** the boat and crossed to	1650
	8:26	saying, "Don't **go i** the village."	1656
	9:20	**threw** the boy **i a convulsion.**	5360
	9:22	"It has often thrown him **i** fire or water	1650
	9:31	of Man is going to be betrayed **i** the hands	1650
	9:42	it would be better for him to be thrown **i**	1650
	9:43	with two hands to go **i** hell,	1650
	9:45	to have two feet and be thrown **i** hell.	1650
	9:47	to have two eyes and be thrown **i** hell,	1650
	10: 1	and went **i** the region of Judea and across	1650
	11:23	'Go, throw yourself **i** the sea,'	1650
	12:41	the crowd putting their money **i**	1650
	12:43	this poor widow has put more **i**	1650
	14:13	telling them, "Go **i** the city,	1650
	14:16	went **i** the city and found things just	1650
	14:20	"one who dips bread **i** the bowl with me.	1650
	14:28	I will go ahead of you **i** Galilee."	1650
	14:38	Watch and pray so that you will not fall **i**	1650
	14:41	of Man is betrayed **i** the hands of sinners.	1650
	14:54	**right i** the courtyard of the high	1650+2276+2401
	14:68	he said, and went out **i** the entryway.	1650
	16: 7	'He is going ahead of you **i** Galilee.	1650
	16:15	"Go **i** all the world and preach	1650
	16:19	up **i** heaven and he sat at the right hand	1650
Lk	1: 9	to **go i** the temple of the Lord	1656
	1:79	to guide our feet **i** the path of peace."	1650
	2:15	the angels had left them and gone **i** heaven,	1650
	2:27	he went **i** the temple courts.	1650
	3: 3	He went **i** all the country around	1650
	3: 9	be cut down and thrown **i** the fire."	1650
	3:17	and to gather the wheat **i** his barn,	1650
	4:16	on the Sabbath day *he* **went i** the synagogue	1656
	5: 3	He got **i** one of the boats,	1650
	5: 4	he said to Simon, "Put out **i** deep water,	1650
	5:18	and tried *to* **take** him **i** the house to lay him	1662
	5:19	through the tiles **i** the middle of the crowd,	1650
	5:37	no one pours new wine **i** old wineskins.	1650
	5:38	new wine must be poured **i** new wineskins.	1650
	6: 6	On another Sabbath he **went i**	1650
	6:38	will be poured **i** your lap.	1650
	6:39	Will they not both fall **i** a pit?	1650
	6:47	and **puts** them **i practice** is like	4472
	6:49	and *does* not **put** them **i practice** is like	4472

Lk	7:24	"What did you go out **i** the desert to see?	1650
	7:44	*I* **came i** your house.	1656
	8:17	not be known or brought out **i** the open.	1650
	8:21	and **put** it **i practice."**	4472
	8:22	So they got **i** a boat and set out.	1650
	8:29	and had been driven by the demon **i**	1650
	8:30	because many demons *had* **gone i** him.	1656
	8:31	not to order them to go **i** the Abyss.	1650
	8:32	The demons begged Jesus to let them **go i**	1656
	8:33	*they* **went i** the pigs,	1656
	8:33	the steep bank **i** the lake and was drowned.	1650
	8:37	So he got **i** the boat and left.	1650
	9:39	**throws** him **i convulsions**	5057
	9:44	of Man is going to be betrayed **i** the hands	1650
	9:52	who **went i** a Samaritan village	1656+4513
	10: 2	to send out workers **i** his harvest field.	1650
	10:10	go **i** its streets and say,	1650
	10:30	**fell i the hands of** robbers.	4346
	10:36	a neighbor to the man who fell **i** the hands	1650
	11: 4	And **lead** us not **i** temptation.' "	1662
	12: 5	has power to throw you **i** hell.	1650
	12:28	and tomorrow is thrown **i** the fire,	1650
	12:39	would not have let his house *be* **broken i.**	1482
	12:58	and the officer throw you **i** prison.	1650
	13:21	a woman took and mixed **i** a large amount	1650
	14: 5	"If one of you has a son or an ox that falls **i**	1650
	14:21	'Go out quickly **i** the streets and alleys of	1650
	16: 4	people will welcome me **i** their houses.'	1650
	16: 9	you will be welcomed **i** eternal dwellings.	1650
	16:16	and everyone is forcing his way **i** it.	1650
	17: 2	to be thrown **i** the sea with a millstone tied	1650
	17:12	*As he was* **going i** a village,	1656
	21: 1	Jesus saw the rich putting their gifts **i**	1650
	22:40	that *you will* not **fall i** temptation."	1656
	22:46	so that *you will* not **fall i** temptation."	1656
	22:54	they led him away and **took** him **i** the house	1652
	23:19	(Barabbas had been thrown **i** prison for	1877
	23:25	He released the man who had been thrown **i**	1650
	23:42	when you come **i** your kingdom."	1650
	23:46	"Father, **i** your hands I commit my spirit."	1650
	24: 7	be delivered **i** the hands of sinful men,	1650
	24:51	he left them and was taken up **i** heaven.	1650
Jn	1: 9	that gives light to every man was coming **i**	1650
	2: 9	the water *that had* **been turned i** wine.	1181
	2:16	**turn** my Father's house **i** a market!"	4472
	3: 4	**enter** a second time **i** his mother's womb	1656
	3:13	No one has ever gone **i** heaven except	1650
	3:17	For God did not send his Son **i** the world	1650
	3:19	Light has come **i** the world,	1650
	3:20	and will not come **i** the light for fear	4639
	3:21	But whoever lives by the truth comes **i**	4639
	3:22	Jesus and his disciples went out **i**	1650
	4: 8	(His disciples had gone **i** the town	1650
	4:46	where *he had* **turned** the water **i** wine.	4472
	5: 7	"I have no one to help me **i** the pool when	1650
	5:13	for Jesus had slipped away **i** the crowd	NIG
	6:14	"Surely this is the Prophet who is to come **i**	1650
	6:17	where they got **i** a boat and set off across	1650
	6:21	they were willing to take him **i** the boat,	1650
	6:24	they got **i** the boats and went to Capernaum	1650
	7:52	**Look i** it, and you will find that	2236
	9:39	"For judgment I have come **i** this world,	1650
	10:36	as his very own and sent **i** the world?	1650
	11:27	who was to come **i** the world."	1650
	12: 6	he used to help himself to what was put **i** it.	NIG
	12:46	I have come **i** the world as a light,	1650
	13: 5	he poured water **i** a basin and began	1650
	13:27	Satan **entered i** him.	1656
	15: 6	thrown **i** the fire and burned.	1650
	16:13	comes, he will guide you **i** all truth.	1877
	16:21	of her joy that a child is born **i** the world.	1650
	17:18	As you sent me **i** the world,	1650
	17:18	I have sent them **i** the world.	1650
	18: 1	and he and his disciples **went i** it.	1656
	18:15	*he* **went** with Jesus **i** the high priests'	5291
	18:37	and for this I came **i** the world,	1650
	19:23	**dividing** them **i four shares,**	3538+4472
	19:27	this disciple took her **i** his home.	1650
	20: 6	arrived and **went i** the tomb.	1656
	20:11	she bent over to look **i** the tomb	1650
	20:25	and put my hand **i** his side,	1650
	20:27	Reach out your hand and put it **i** my side.	1650
	21: 3	So they went out and **got i** the boat,	1832
	21: 7	(for he had taken it off) and jumped **i**	1650
Ac	1:10	They were looking intently up **i** the sky	1650
	1:10	"why do you stand here looking **i** the sky?	1650
	1:11	who has been taken from you **i** heaven,	1650
	1:11	in the same way you have seen him go **i**	1650
	3: 2	to beg from those **going i** the temple courts.	1660
	3: 8	Then *he* **went i** the temple courts,	1656
	5:15	the sick **i** the streets and laid them on beds	1650
	7: 9	they sold him as a slave **i** Egypt.	1650
	7:43	Therefore *I will* **send** you **i exile'**	3579
	7:53	that was **put i effect** through angels	1408
	8:16	they had simply been baptized **i** the name	1650
	8:38	down **i** the water and Philip baptized him.	1650
	9: 6	"Now get up and **go i** the city,	1650
	9: 8	**led** him by the hand **i** Damascus.	1650
	10:10	he **fell i a trance.**	1181+1749+2093
	10:23	Then Peter invited the men **i** the house to	NIG
	11: 3	"You **went i** the house of uncircumcised	1656
	11: 6	I looked **i** it and saw four-footed animals of	1650
	14: 1	Paul and Barnabas **went** as usual **i**	1656
	14:14	they tore their clothes and rushed out **i**	1650
	14:20	*he* got up and **went** back **i** the city.	1656
	14:24	they came **i** Pamphylia,	1650
	15: 2	Paul and Barnabas **i** sharp dispute and	NIG

Ac	16:19	and dragged them i the marketplace to face	1650
	16:20	**throwing** our city i **an uproar**	1752
	16:23	they were thrown i prison,	1650
	16:34	The jailer brought them i his house and set	1650
	16:37	and threw us i prison.	1650
	17: 2	Paul **went** i the synagogue,	1656
	17: 7	**welcomed** them i *his* **house.**	5685
	17: 8	the city officials *were* **thrown** i turmoil.	5429
	18:12	a united attack on Paul and brought him i	2093
	18:19	He himself **went** i the synagogue	1656
	19: 5	they were baptized i the name of	1650
	19:29	and rushed as one man i the theater.	1650
	19:31	a message begging him not to venture i	1650
	20: 9	who was sinking *i* a **deep sleep**	AIT
	20:18	the first day I came i the province of Asia.	1650
	21:28	*he has* **brought** Greeks i the temple area	1652
	21:29	Paul had **brought** him i the temple area.	1652
	21:34	he ordered that Paul be taken i the barracks.	1650
	21:37	As the soldiers were about to **take** Paul i	1652
	21:38	and led four thousand terrorists out i	1650
	22: 4	both men and women and throwing them i	1650
	22:10	the Lord said, 'and go i Damascus.	1650
	22:11	My companions led me by the hand i	1650
	22:17	I fell i a trance	1877
	22:23	and flinging dust i the air,	1650
	22:24	the commander ordered Paul *to be* **taken** i	1652
	23:10	by force and bring him i the barracks.	1650
	23:16	he **went** i the barracks and told Paul.	1656
	27:15	by the storm and could not **head** i the wind;	535
	27:30	the sailors let the lifeboat down i the sea,	1650
	27:38	the ship by throwing the grain i the sea.	1650
	28: 5	But Paul shook the snake off i the fire	1650
Ro	5: 2	by faith i this grace in which we now stand.	1650
	5: 5	because God has poured out his love i	1877
	5:13	not **taken** i **account** when there is no law.	1824
	6: 3	that all of us who were baptized i Christ	1650
	6: 3	into Christ Jesus were baptized i his death?	1650
	6: 4	with him through baptism i death in order	1650
	8:21	to decay and brought i the glorious freedom	1650
	10: 6	'Who will ascend i heaven?' "	1650
	10: 7	"or 'Who will descend i the deep?' "	1650
	10:18	"Their voice has gone out i all the earth,	1650
	11:24	and contrary to nature were grafted i	1650
	11:24	*be* grafted i their own olive tree!	1596
1Co	1: 9	who has called you i fellowship	1650
	1:13	Were you baptized i the name of Paul?	1650
	1:15	no one can say that you were baptized i my	1650
		brother *to* **fall i sin**,	4997
	8:13	**causes** my brother *to* **fall i sin,**	4997
	9:25	in the games **goes** i strict **training.**	1603
	10: 2	They were all baptized i Moses in the cloud	1650
	12:13	For we were all baptized by one Spirit i	1650
	14: 9	You will just be speaking i the air.	1650
2Co	1: 5	as the sufferings of Christ flow over i	1650
	3:18	*are being* **transformed** i his likeness	3565
	7: 5	For when we came i Macedonia,	1650
	8:16	who put i the heart of Titus	1877
	11:29	Who *is* **led i sin,** and I do not inwardly	4997
Gal	1: 7	**throwing** you i **confusion**	5429
	1:17	but I went immediately i Arabia	1650
	3:19	The law *was* **put i effect** through angels	1411
	3:27	for all of you who were baptized i	1650
	4: 6	God sent the Spirit of his Son i our hearts,	1650
	5:10	the one who *is* **throwing** you i **confusion**	5429
Eph	1:10	to be **put i effect** when the times	3873
	3: 4	you will be able to understand my insight i	1877
	4:15	we will in all things grow up i him who is	1650
Php	4: 9	**put it i practice.**	4556
Col	1:13	the dominion of darkness and brought us i	1650
	2:18	**goes i great detail about** what he has seen	1836
	4:12	who calls you i his kingdom and glory.	1650
1Th	3: 5	the Lord direct your hearts i God's love	1650
2Th	3: 5	the Lord direct your hearts i God's love	1650
1Ti	1: 3	As I urged you when I went i Macedonia,	1650
	1:15	Christ Jesus came i the world	1650
	3: 7	not fall i disgrace and into the devil's trap.	1650
	3: 7	not fall into disgrace and i the devil's trap.	NIG
	5: 4	**put** *their* **religion i practice** by caring for	2355
	5:13	**get i the habit of being** idle	3443
	6: 7	For *we* **brought** nothing i the world,	1662
	6: 9	to get rich fall i temptation and a trap and	1650
	6: 9	and i many foolish and harmful desires	NIG
	6: 9	and harmful desires that plunge men i ruin	1650
2Ti	1: 6	*to* **fan i flame** the gift of God,	351
	2: 7	for the Lord will give you insight i all this.	1877
	3: 6	They are the kind who worm their way i	1650
Heb	1: 6	God **brings** his firstborn i the world,	1650+1652
	9: 6	the priests **entered** regularly i the outer	1655
	9: 8	that the way i the Most Holy Place had not	NIG
	9:18	even the first covenant *was* not **put i effect**	1590
	10: 5	*when* Christ **came** i the world, he said:	1656
	10:31	It is a dreadful thing to fall i the hands of	1650
	13:11	the blood of animals i the Most Holy Place	1650
Jas	1:25	But the man who looks intently i	1650
	2: 2	a man **comes** i your meeting wearing	1656
	2: 6	not the ones who are dragging you i court?	1650
	3: 3	When we put bits i the mouths of horses	1650
1Pe	1: 3	he has given us new birth i a living hope	1650
	1: 4	and i an inheritance that can never perish,	1650
	1:12	Even angels long to look i these things.	1650
	2: 5	are being built i a spiritual house to be	NIG
	2: 9	of him who called you out of darkness i	1650
	3:22	who has gone i heaven and is	1650
	4: 4	with them i the same flood of dissipation,	1650
2Pe	2:11	and you will receive a rich **welcome** i	1658
	2: 2	**bring** the way of truth i **disrepute.**	1059
	2: 4	**putting** them i gloomy dungeons to	4140
1Jn	4: 1	many false prophets have gone out i	1650
	4: 9	and only Son i the world that we might live	1650

2Jn	1: 7	have gone out i the world.	1650
	1:10	not take him i your house or welcome him.	1650
Jude	1: 4	of our God i a license for immorality	1650
	1:11	for profit i Balaam's **error;**	AIT
Rev	2:20	By her teaching she misleads my servants i	NIG
	5: 6	the seven spirits of God sent out i all	1650
	8: 8	all ablaze, was thrown i the sea.	1650
	8: 8	A third of the sea **turned i** blood,	1181
	9: 9	of many horses and chariots rushing i	1650
	11: 6	the waters i blood and to strike the earth	1650
	12: 6	The woman fled i the desert to	1650
	13:10	If anyone is to go i captivity,	1650
	13:10	i captivity he will go.	1650
	14:10	which has been poured full strength i	1877
	14:19	and threw them i the great winepress	1650
	16: 3	*it* **turned i** blood like that of a dead man,	1181
	16:10	and his kingdom *was* **plunged** i darkness,	1181
	16:17	The seventh angel poured out his bowl i	2093
	16:19	The great city split i three parts,	1650
	17: 3	the angel carried me away in the Spirit i	1650
	17:17	For God has put it i their hearts	1650
	18:21	the size of a large millstone and threw it i	1650
	19:20	of them were thrown alive i the fiery lake	1650
	20: 3	He threw him i the Abyss,	1650
	20:10	was thrown i the lake of burning sulfur,	1650
	20:14	and Hades were thrown i the lake of fire.	1650
	20:15	he was thrown i the lake of fire.	1650
	21:24	of the earth will bring their splendor i it.	1650
	21:26	and honor of the nations will be brought i	1650
	22:14	and *may* **go** through the gates i the city.	1656

INTOXICATED (1)
Rev	17: 2	and the inhabitants of the earth *were* i with	3499

INTREAT, INTREATED, INTREATIES, INTREATY (KJV) See ANSWER, ANSWERED, ASK, CURRY FAVOR, ENTREATY, EXHORT, INTERCEDE, INTERCEDED, PRAY, PRAYED, SEEK, URGE

INTRIGUE (3) [INTRIGUES]
Da	8:23	a stern-faced king, a master of i, will arise.	2648
	11:21	and he will seize it through i.	2761
Hos	7: 6	they approach him with i.	744

INTRIGUES (2) [INTRIGUE]
Ps	5:10	Let their i be their downfall.	4600
	31:20	of your presence you hide them from the i	8222

INTRODUCE (1) [INTRODUCED, INTRODUCTION]
2Pe	2: 1	They *will* **secretly** i destructive heresies,	4206

INTRODUCED (4) [INTRODUCE]
2Ki	17: 8	as the practices that the kings of Israel *had* i.	6913
	17:19	They followed the practices Israel *had* i.	6913
Gal	3:17	The law, i 430 years later,	1181
Heb	7:19	and a better hope is i,	2081

INTRODUCTION (1) [INTRODUCE]
1Co	16: 3	of i to the men you approve and send them	NIG

INVADE (14) [INVADED, INVADER, INVADERS, INVADES, INVADING]
Dt	12:29	the nations you *are about to* i	995+2025+9004
1Sa	7:13	and *did* not i Israelite territory again.	928+995
2Ch	20:10	not allow Israel to i when they came	928+995
Isa	7: 6	"Let us i Judah;	928+6590
Eze	38: 8	In future years *you* will i a land	448+995
	38:11	"I will i a land of unwalled villages;	6584+6590
Da	11: 9	the king of the North *will* i the realm	928+995
	11:21	He will i the kingdom	995
	11:24	*he will* i them	995
	11:29	"At the appointed time *he will* i	928+995
	11:40	He will i many countries and sweep	928+995
	11:41	He will also i the Beautiful Land.	928+995
Joel	3:17	never again *will* foreigners i her.	928+6296
Na	1:15	No more *will* the wicked i you;	6296

INVADED (15) [INVADE]
Ex	10:14	they i all Egypt and settled down	6584+6590
Jdg	6: 3	other eastern peoples i the country.	6584+6590
	6: 5	*they* i the land to ravage it.	928+6590
2Ki	3:24	the Israelites i the land and slaughtered	928+995
	15:19	Then Pul king of Assyria i the land,	995+6584
	17: 5	The king of Assyria i the entire land,	928+995
	24: 1	Nebuchadnezzar king of Babylon i	6590
1Ch	4:42	sons of Ishi, i the hill country of Seir.	2143+4200
2Ch	21:17	i it and carried off all the goods found in	1324
	24:23	*it* i Judah and Jerusalem and killed all	448+995
	32: 1	of Assyria came and i Judah.	928+995
Ps	79: 1	O God, the nations *have* i your inheritance;	928+995
Jer	35:11	of Babylon i this land,	448+6590
	48:15	Moab will be destroyed and her towns i;	6590
Joel	1: 6	A nation *has* i my land,	6584+6590

INVADER (2) [INVADE]			
Isa	21: 1	an i comes from the desert,	AIT
Da	11:16	The i will do as he pleases;	448+995

INVADERS (1) [INVADE]
Jer	18:22	when you suddenly bring i against them,	1522

INVADES (2) [INVADE]
Mic	5: 5	When the Assyrian i our land and	928+995
	5: 6	from the Assyrian when *he* i our land	928+995

INVADING (2) [INVADE]
2Ch	20:22	and Mount Seir who *were* i Judah,	995+4200
Hab	3:16	of calamity to come on the nation i us.	1574

INVALID (2)
Jn	5: 5	One who was there had been an i	819
	5: 7	the i replied, "I have no one to help me into	820

INVENT (1) [INVENTED]
Ro	1:30	they i ways of doing evil;	2388

INVENTED (1) [INVENT]
2Pe	1:16	We did not follow **cleverly** i stories	5054

INVENTORY (1)
Ezr	1: 9	This was the i:	5031

INVESTIGATE (6) [INVESTIGATED, INVESTIGATION]
Ex	9: 7	Pharaoh sent men to i and found that not	NIH
Dt	13:14	probe and i it thoroughly.	8626
	17: 4	then *you* must i it thoroughly.	2011
Ezr	10:16	of the tenth month they sat down to i	2011
Ecc	7:25	to i and to search out wisdom and	9365
Ac	25:20	I was at a loss how to i such matters;	2428

INVESTIGATED (3) [INVESTIGATE]
Jdg	6:29	When *they* **carefully** i,	1335+2011+2256
Est	2:23	when the report **was** i and found to be true,	1335
Lk	1: 3	since *I* myself *have* carefully i everything	4158

INVESTIGATION (2) [INVESTIGATE]
Dt	19:18	The judges *must* **make** *a* thorough i,	2011
Ac	25:26	as a result *of* this i I may have something	374

INVISIBLE (5)
Ro	1:20	creation of the world God's i *qualities*—	548
Col	1:15	He is the image of the i God,	548
	1:16	things in heaven and on earth, visible and i,	548
1Ti	1:17	Now to the King eternal, immortal, i,	548
Heb	11:27	because he saw him who *is* i.	548

INVITATION (1) [INVITE]
2Sa	11:13	At David's i, he ate and drank with him,	7924

INVITE (15) [INVITATION, INVITED, INVITES, INVITING]
Ex	2:20	i him to have something to eat."	7924
	34:15	and sacrifice to them, *they will* i you	7924
Jdg	14:15	*Did you* i us here to rob us?"	7924
1Sa	16: 3	I Jesse to the sacrifice,	7924
1Ki	1:10	not i Nathan the prophet or Benaiah or	7924
	1:10	and your servant Solomon *he did* not i.	7924
Job	1: 4	and *they would* i their three sisters to eat	2256+7924+8938
Jer	35: 2	to the Recabite family and i them to come	1819
Zec	3:10	that day each of you *will* i his neighbor	7924
Mt	22: 9	and i to the banquet anyone you find.'	2813
	25:38	a stranger and i you in,	5251
	25:43	I was a stranger and *you did* not i me **in,**	5251
Lk	14:12	*do* not i your friends,	5888
	14:12	they *may* i you **back** and so you will	511
	14:13	But when you give a banquet, i the poor,	2813

INVITED (37) [INVITE]
Ge	31:54	in the hill country and i his relatives to	7924
Nu	25: 2	*who* i them to the sacrifices to their gods.	7924
1Sa	9:13	afterward, those *who are* i will eat.	7924
	9:22	at the head of those *who* were i—	7924
	9:24	from the time I said, 'I have i guests.' "	7924
	16: 5	and his sons and i them to the sacrifice.	7924
2Sa	13:23	he i all the king's sons to come there.	7924
	15:11	They had **been** i as guests	7924
1Ki	1: 9	*He* i all his brothers, the king's sons,	7924
	1:19	and sheep, and *has* i all the king's sons,	7924
	1:19	but *he has* not i Solomon your servant.	7924
	1:25	*He has* i all the king's sons,	7924
Est	5:12	"I'm the only person Queen Esther i	995
	5:12	And she *has* i me along with	7924
Zep	1: 7	he has consecrated *those* he has i.	7924
Mt	22: 3	He sent his servants to those who *had been* i	2813
	22: 4	'Tell those *who have been* i	2813
	22: 8	but those I *did not deserve* to come.	2813
	22:14	"For many are i, but few are chosen."	3105
	25:35	I was a stranger and *you* i me **in,**	5251
Lk	7:36	of the Pharisees i Jesus to have dinner	2263

Lk	7:39	When the Pharisee who *had* **i** him saw this,	2813
	11:37	a Pharisee **i** him to eat with him;	2263
	14: 8	distinguished than you may have been **i**.	2813
	14: 9	**host who i** both of you will come and say	2813
	14:10	But when *you are* **i**, take the lowest place,	2813
	14:16	a great banquet and **i** many guests.	2813
	14:17	to tell those who *had been* **i**,	2813
	14:24	not one of those men who *were* **i** will get	2813
Jn	2: 2	and Jesus and his disciples *had* also *been* **i**	2813
Ac	8:31	So he **i** Philip to come up and sit with him.	4151
	10:23	Then Peter **i** the men into the house to	1657
	13:42	the *people* **i** them to speak further	4151
	16:15	*she* **i** us to her home.	4151
	18:26	**i** him **to** *their* **home**	4689
	28:14	There we found some brothers who **i** *us*	4151
Rev	19: 9	'Blessed are those who *are* **i** to	2813

INVITES (6) [INVITE]

Pr	9: 7	"Whoever corrects a mocker **i** insult;	4374
	10:14	but the mouth of a fool **i** ruin.	7940
	17:19	he who builds a high gate **i** destruction.	1335
	18: 6	and his mouth **i** a beating.	7924
Lk	14: 8	"When someone **i** you to a wedding feast,	2813
1Co	10:27	If some unbeliever **i** you to a meal	2813

INVITING (1) [INVITE]

2Ch	30: 1	**i** them to come to the temple of the LORD	NIH

INVOKE (6) [INVOKED, INVOKES, INVOKING]

Ex	23:13	*Do* not **i** the names of other gods;	2349
Jos	23: 7	*do* not **i** the names of their gods or swear	2349
2Sa	14:11	"Then *let* the king **i** the LORD his God	2349
Isa	48: 1	in the name of the LORD and **i** the God	2349
Jer	44:26	Egypt *will* ever again **i** my name 928+7023+7924
Ac	19:13	to **i the name** of the Lord Jesus 3950+3951

INVOKED (1) [INVOKE]

Hos	2:17	no longer *will* their names **be i**.	2349

INVOKES (2) [INVOKE]

Dt	29:19	he **i a blessing on himself**	1385
Isa	65:16	Whoever **i a blessing** in the land will do so	1385

INVOKING (1) [INVOKE]

Job	31:30	not allowed my mouth to sin by **i** a curse	8626

INVOLVE (1) [INVOLVED, INVOLVES, INVOLVING]

Jn	2: 4	"Dear woman, **why** do you **i** me?" 2779+5515

INVOLVED (7) [INVOLVE]

Ex	24:14	and anyone **i** in a dispute can go to them."	1251
	28:38	and he will bear the **guilt** *i in*	AIT
Nu	15:26	because all the people were **i in**	928
Dt	19:17	the two men **i** in the dispute must stand in	4200
Ac	23:13	More than forty men were **i in** this plot.	4472
	24:18	nor was I **i in** any disturbance.	3552
2Ti	2: 4	as a soldier *gets* **i in** civilian affairs—	1861

INVOLVES (1) [INVOLVE]

Ac	18:15	since it **i** questions about words and names	1639

INVOLVING (2) [INVOLVE]

2Sa	3: 8	of an **offense** *i* this woman!	AIT
1Ki	21: 1	Some time later there was an incident **i**	NIH

INWARD (2) [INWARDLY]

2Sa	5: 9	from the supporting terraces **i**. 1074+2025
Eze	40:16	the openings all around faced **i**.	7163

INWARDLY (5) [INWARD]

Mt	7:15	but **i** they are ferocious wolves.	2277
Ro	2:29	a man is a Jew if he is one **i**; 1877+3220+3836
	8:23	groan **i** as we wait eagerly for our adoption as sons, 1571+1877
2Co	4:16	yet **i** we are being renewed day by day. 2276+3836
	11:29	Who is led into sin, and I do not **i burn?**	4792

INWARDS (KJV) See INNER PARTS

IPHDEIAH (1)

1Ch	8:25	**I** and Penuel were the sons of Shashak.	3635

IPHTAH (1) [IPHTAH EL]

Jos	15:43	**I**, Ashnah, Nezib,	3652

IPHTAH EL (2) [IPHTAH]

Jos	19:14	and ended at the Valley of **I**.	3654
	19:27	touched Zebulun and the Valley of **I**,	3654

IR (1)

1Ch	7:12	and Huppites were the descendants of **I**,	6553

IR NAHASH (1) [NAHASH]

1Ch	4:12	and Tehinnah the father of **I**.	6560

IR SHEMESH (1)

Jos	19:41	Zorah, Eshtaol, **I**,	6561

IRA (6)

2Sa	20:26	and **I** the Jairite was David's priest.	6562
	23:26	**I** son of Ikkesh from Tekoa,	6562
	23:38	**I** the Ithrite, Gareb the Ithrite	6562
1Ch	11:28	**I** son of Ikkesh from Tekoa,	6562
	11:40	**I** the Ithrite, Gareb the Ithrite,	6562
	27: 9	was **I** the son of Ikkesh the Tekoite.	6562

IRAD (2)

Ge	4:18	To Enoch was born **I**,	6563
	4:18	and **I** was the father of Mehujael,	6563

IRAM (2)

Ge	36:43	and **I**. These were the chiefs of Edom,	6566
1Ch	1:54	and **I**. These were the chiefs of Edom.	6566

IRI (1)

1Ch	7: 7	Ezbon, Uzzi, Uzziel, Jerimoth and **I**,	6565

IRIJAH (2)

Jer	37:13	whose name was **I** son of Shelemiah,	3713
	37:14	But **I** would not listen to him;	3713

IRON (95) [IRON-SMELTING, IRONS, NECK-IRONS]

Ge	4:22	of tools out of bronze and **i**.	1366
Lev	26:19	and make the sky above you like **i** and	1366
Nu	31:22	Gold, silver, bronze, **i**, tin, lead	1366
	35:16	" 'If a man strikes someone with an **i** object	1366
Dt	3:11	of **i** and was more than thirteen feet long	1366
	8: 9	the rocks are **i** and you can dig copper out	1366
	27: 5	Do not use any **i tool** upon them.	1366
	28:23	the ground beneath you **i**.	1366
	28:48	He will put an **i** yoke on your neck	1366
	33:25	bolts of your gates will be **i** and bronze,	1366
Jos	6:19	and **i** are sacred to the LORD and must go	1366
	6:24	the articles of bronze and **i** into the treasury	1366
	8:31	on which no **i tool** had been used.	1366
	17:16	in the plain have **i** chariots,	1366
	17:18	though the Canaanites have **i** chariots and	1366
	19:38	**I**, Migdal El, Horem, Beth Anath	3712
	22: 8	with silver, gold, bronze and **i**,	1366
Jdg	1:19	because they had **i** chariots.	1366
	4: 3	Because he had nine hundred **i** chariots	1366
	4:13	Sisera gathered together his nine hundred **i** chariots	1366
1Sa	17: 7	and its **i** point weighed six hundred shekels.	1366
2Sa	12:31	with saws and with **i** picks and axes,	1366
	23: 7	Whoever touches thorns uses a **tool of i**	1366
1Ki	6: 7	chisel or any other **i** tool was heard at	1366
	22:11	of Kenaanah had made **i** horns	1366
2Ki	6: 5	the **i axhead** fell into the water.	1366
	6: 6	and made the **i** float.	1366
1Ch	20: 3	with saws and with **i** picks and axes.	1366
	22: 3	a large amount of **i** to make nails for	1366
	22:14	of bronze and **i** too great to be weighed,	1366
	22:16	bronze and **i**—craftsmen beyond number.	1366
	29: 2	**i** for the iron and wood for the wood,	1366
	29: 2	iron for the **i** and wood for the wood,	1366
	29: 7	and a hundred thousand talents of **i**.	1366
2Ch	2: 7	bronze and **i**, and in purple,	1366
	2:14	bronze and **i**, stone and wood,	1366
	18:10	of Kenaanah had made **i** horns,	1366
	24:12	and also workers in **i** and bronze to repair	1366
Job	19:24	they were inscribed with an **i** tool on lead,	1366
	20:24	Though he flees from an **i** weapon,	1366
	28: 2	**I** is taken from the earth,	1366
	40:18	his limbs like rods of **i**.	1366
	41:27	**I** he treats like straw and bronze	1366
Ps	2: 9	You will rule them with an **i** scepter;	1366
	107:10	prisoners suffering in **i chains**,	1366
	107:16	of bronze and cuts through bars of **i**.	1366
	149: 8	their nobles with shackles of **i**,	1366
Pr	27:17	As **i** sharpens iron, so one man sharpens	1366
	27:17	As iron sharpens **i**, so one man sharpens	1366
Isa	45: 2	of bronze and cut through bars of **i**.	1366
	48: 4	the sinews of your neck were **i**,	1366
	60:17	and silver in place of **i**.	1366
	60:17	and **i** in place of stones.	1366
Jer	1:18	an **i** pillar and a bronze wall to stand	1366
	6:28	They are bronze and **i**;	1366
	15:12	"Can a man break **i**—	1366
	15:12	**i** from the north—or bronze?	1366
	17: 1	"Judah's sin is engraved with an **i** tool,	1366
	28:13	but in its place you will get a yoke of **i**.	1366
	28:14	an **i** yoke on the necks of all these nations	1366
Eze	4: 3	Then take an **i** pan,	1366
	4: 3	as an **i** wall between you and the city	1366
	22:18	tin, **i** and lead left inside a furnace.	1366
	22:20	As men gather silver, copper, **i**,	1366
	27:12	they exchanged silver, **i**,	1366
	27:19	they exchanged wrought **i**,	1366
Da	2:33	its legs of **i**, its feet partly of iron	10591
	2:33	its feet partly of **i** and partly of baked clay.	10591
	2:34	on its feet of **i** and clay and smashed them.	10591

Da	2:35	Then the **i**, the clay, the bronze,	10591
	2:40	there will be a fourth kingdom, strong as **i**	10591
	2:40	**i** breaks and smashes everything—	10591
	2:40	and as **i** breaks things to pieces,	10591
	2:41	of baked clay and partly of **i**, so this will be	10591
	2:41	it will have some of the strength of **i** in it,	10591
	2:41	even as you saw **i** mixed with clay.	10591
	2:42	As the toes were partly **i** and partly clay,	10591
	2:43	as you saw the **i** mixed with baked clay,	10591
	2:43	any more than **i** mixes with clay.	10591
	2:45	a rock that broke the **i**, the bronze, the clay,	10591
	4:15	bound with **i** and bronze,	10591
	4:23	bound with **i** and bronze,	10591
	5: 4	of bronze, **i**, wood and stone,	10591
	5:23	of bronze, **i**, wood and stone,	10591
	7: 7	It had large **i** teeth;	10591
	7:19	with its **i** teeth and bronze claws—	10591
Am	1: 3	with sledges having **i** teeth,	1366
Mic	4:13	for I will give you horns of **i**;	1366
Ac	12:10	and came to the **i** gate leading to the city.	4969
1Ti	4: 2	**seared as with a hot i**.	3013
Rev	2:27	'He will rule them with an **i** scepter;	4969
	9: 9	They had breastplates like breastplates of **i**,	4969
	12: 5	the nations with an **i** scepter.	4969
	18:12	costly wood, bronze, **i** and marble;	4970
	19:15	"He will rule them with an **i** scepter."	4969

IRON-SMELTING (3) [IRON]

Dt	4:20	and brought you out of the **i** furnace,	1366
1Ki	8:51	out of Egypt, out of that **i** furnace.	1366
Jer	11: 4	out of Egypt, out of the **i** furnace.'	1366

IRONS (2) [IRON]

Ps	105:18	his neck was put in **i**,	1366
Mk	5: 4	the chains apart and broke the **i on his feet**.	4267

IRPEEL (1)

Jos	18:27	Rekem, **I**, Taralah,	3761

IRRELIGIOUS (1)

1Ti	1: 9	the ungodly and sinful, the unholy and **i**;	1013

IRRESISTIBLE (1)

Da	11:10	on like an **i** flood and carry the battle as far	6296

IRREVERENT (1)

2Sa	6: 7	burned against Uzzah because of his **i act**;	8915

IRREVOCABLE (1)

Ro	11:29	for God's gifts and his call are **i**.	294

IRRIGATED (1) [IRRIGATE]

Dt	11:10	and **i** it by foot as in a vegetable garden.	9197

IRRITATE (1)

1Sa	1: 6	rival kept provoking her in order to **i** her.	8307

IRU (1)

1Ch	4:15	The sons of Caleb son of Jephunneh: **I**,	6564

IS (7214) [BE] See Index of Articles Etc.

ISAAC (132) [ISAAC'S]

Ge	17:19	and you will call him **I**.	3663
	17:21	But my covenant I will establish with **I**,	3663
	21: 3	the name **I** to the son Sarah bore him.	3663
	21: 4	When his son **I** was eight days old,	3663
	21: 5	when his son **I** was born to him.	3663
	21: 8	and on the day **I** was weaned Abraham held	3663
	21:10	in the inheritance with my son **I**."	3663
	21:12	through **I** that your offspring will	3663
	22: 2	God said, "Take your son, your only son, **I**,	3663
	22: 3	with him two of his servants and his son **I**.	3663
	22: 6	and placed it on his son **I**,	3663
	22: 7	**I** spoke up and said to his father Abraham,	3663
	22: 7	"The fire and wood are here," **I** said,	NIH
	22: 9	He bound his son **I** and laid him on	3663
	24: 4	and get a wife for my son **I**."	3663
	24:14	the one you have chosen for your servant **I**.	3663
	24:62	Now **I** had come from Beer Lahai Roi,	3663
	24:64	Rebekah also looked up and saw **I**.	3663
	24:66	Then the servant told **I** all he had done.	3663
	24:67	**I** brought her into the tent	3663
	24:67	**I** was comforted after his mother's death.	3663
	25: 5	Abraham left everything he owned to **I**.	3663
	25: 6	and sent them away from his son **I** to	3663
	25: 9	His sons **I** and Ishmael buried him in	3663
	25:11	God blessed his son **I**,	3663
	25:19	This is the account of Abraham's son **I**.	3663
	25:19	Abraham became the father of **I**,	3663
	25:20	and **I** was forty years old	3663
	25:21	**I** prayed to the LORD on behalf	3663
	25:26	**I** was sixty years old	3663
	25:28	**I**, who had a taste for wild game,	3663
	26: 1	and **I** went to Abimelech king of	3663
	26: 2	The LORD appeared to **I** and said,	2257S
	26: 6	So **I** stayed in Gerar.	3663
	26: 8	When **I** had been there a long time,	2257S
	26: 8	and saw **I** caressing his wife Rebekah.	3663

Ge	26: 9	So Abimelech summoned I and said,	3663
	26: 9	'She is my sister'?" I answered him,	3663
	26:12	I planted crops in that land and	3663
	26:16	Abimelech said to I, "Move away from us;	3663
	26:17	So I moved away from there and encamped	3663
	26:18	I reopened the wells that had been dug in	3663
	26:25	I built an altar there and called on the name	NIH
	26:27	I asked them, "Why have you come to me,	3663
	26:30	I then made a feast for them,	NIH
	26:31	Then I sent them on their way,	3663
	26:35	a source of grief to I and Rebekah.	3663
	27: 1	When I had grown old and his eyes were so weak	3663
	27: 2	I said, "I am now an old man	NIH
	27: 5	Now Rebekah was listening as I spoke	3663
	27:20	I asked his son, "How did you find it	3663
	27:21	Then I said to Jacob,	3663
	27:22	Jacob went close to his father I,	3663
	27:26	Then his father I said to him, "Come here,	3663
	27:27	When I caught the smell of his clothes,	NIH
	27:30	After I finished blessing him	3663
	27:32	His father I asked him, "Who are you?"	3663
	27:33	I trembled violently and said, "Who was it,	3663
	27:37	I answered Esau, "I have made him lord	3663
	27:39	His father I answered him,	3663
	27:46	Then Rebekah said to I,	3663
	28: 1	So I called for Jacob and blessed him	3663
	28: 5	Then I sent Jacob on his way,	3663
	28: 6	Now Esau learned that I had blessed Jacob	3663
	28: 8	the Canaanite women were to his father I;	3663
	28:13	of your father Abraham and the God of I.	3663
	31:18	to go to his father I in the land of Canaan.	3663
	31:42	the God of Abraham and the Fear of I,	3663
	31:53	in the name of the Fear of his father I.	3663
	32: 9	God of my father I, O LORD,	3663
	35:12	to Abraham and I I also give to you,	3663
	35:27	Jacob came home to his father I in Mamre,	3663
	35:27	Hebron), where Abraham and I had stayed.	3663
	35:28	I lived a hundred and eighty years.	3663
	46: 1	to the God of his father I.	3663
	48:15	before whom my fathers Abraham and I walked,	3663
	48:16	the names of my fathers Abraham and I,	3663
	49:31	there I and his wife Rebekah were buried,	3663
	50:24	the land he promised on oath to Abraham, I	3663
Ex	2:24	with Abraham, with I and with Jacob.	3663
	3: 6	the God of I and the God of Jacob."	3663
	3:15	the God of Abraham, the God of I and Jacob—	3663
	3:16	the God of Abraham, I and Jacob—	3663
	4: 5	the God of I and the God of Jacob—	3663
	6: 3	to I and to Jacob as God Almighty,	3663
	6: 8	give to Abraham, to I and to Jacob.	3663
	32:13	I and Israel, to whom you swore	3663
	33: 1	the land I promised on oath to Abraham, I	3663
Lev	26:42	and my covenant with I and my covenant	3663
Nu	32:11	the land I promised on oath to Abraham, I	3663
Dt	1: 8	to Abraham, I and Jacob—	3663
	6:10	to Abraham, I and Jacob, to give you—	3663
	9: 5	to Abraham, I and Jacob.	3663
	9:27	Remember your servants Abraham, I and	3663
	29:13	Abraham, I and Jacob.	3663
	30:20	Abraham, I and Jacob.	3663
	34: 4	Abraham, I and Jacob when I said,	3663
Jos	24: 3	gave him many descendants. I gave him I,	3663
	24: 4	and to I I gave Jacob and Esau.	3663
1Ki	18:36	"O LORD, God of Abraham, I and Israel,	3663
2Ki	13:23	of his covenant with Abraham, I and Jacob.	3663
1Ch	1:28	The sons of Abraham: I and Ishmael.	3663
	1:34	Abraham was the father of I.	3663
	1:34	The sons of I: Esau and Israel.	3663
	16:16	the oath he swore to I.	3663
	29:18	God of our fathers Abraham, I and Israel,	3663
2Ch	30: 6	the God of Abraham, I and Israel,	3663
Ps	105: 9	the oath he swore to I.	3773
Jer	33:26	to rule over the descendants of Abraham, I	3773
Am	7: 9	"The high places of I will be destroyed and	3663
	7:16	and stop preaching against the house of I.'	3663
Mt	1: 2	Abraham was the father of I,	2693
	1: 2	I the father of Jacob,	2693
	8:11	I and Jacob in the kingdom of heaven.	2693
	22:32	the God of I, and the God of Jacob'?	2693
Mk	12:26	'I am the God of Abraham, the God of I,	2693
Lk	3:34	the son of I, the son of Abraham,	2693
	13:28	I and Jacob and all the prophets in	2693
	20:37	and the God of I, and the God of Jacob.'	2693
Ac	3:13	The God of Abraham, I and Jacob,	2693
	7: 8	And Abraham became the father of I	2693
	7: 8	Later I became the father of Jacob,	2693
	7:32	the God of Abraham, I and Jacob.'	2593
Ro	9: 7	"It is through I that your offspring will	2693
	9:10	and the same father, our father I.	2693
Gal	4:28	Now you, brothers, like I,	2693
Heb	11: 9	he lived in tents, as did I and Jacob,	2693
	11:17	offered I as a sacrifice.	2693
	11:18	"It is through I that your offspring will	2693
	11:19	he did receive I back from death.	899S
	11:20	By faith I blessed Jacob and Esau in regard	2693
Jas	2:21	for what he did when he offered his son I	2693

ISAAC'S (3) [ISAAC]

Ge	26:19	I servants dug in the valley and discovered	3663
	26:20	of Gerar quarreled with I herdsmen	3663
	26:32	That day I servants came and told him	3663

ISAIAH (53)

2Ki	19: 2	to the prophet I son of Amoz.	3833

2Ki	19: 5	When King Hezekiah's officials came to I,	3833
	19: 6	I said to them, "Tell your master,	3833
	19:20	I son of Amoz sent a message to Hezekiah:	3833
	20: 1	The prophet I son of Amoz went to him	3833
	20: 4	Before I had left the middle court,	3833
	20: 7	Then I said, "Prepare a poultice of figs."	3833
	20: 8	Hezekiah had asked I,	3833
	20: 9	I answered, "This is the LORD's sign	3833
	20:11	Then the prophet I called upon the LORD,	3833
	20:14	Then I the prophet went to King Hezekiah	3833
	20:16	Then I said to Hezekiah,	3833
2Ch	26:22	are recorded by the prophet I son of Amoz.	3833
	32:20	and the prophet I son of Amoz cried out	3833
	32:32	of the prophet I son of Amoz in the book of	3833
Isa	1: 1	concerning Judah and Jerusalem that I son	3833
	2: 1	This is what I son of Amoz saw	3833
	7: 3	Then the LORD said to I, "Go out,	3833
	7:13	I said, "Hear now, you house of David!	NIH
	13: 1	An oracle concerning Babylon that I son	3833
	20: 2	at that time the LORD spoke through I son	3833
	20: 3	"Just as my servant I has gone stripped	3833
	37: 2	to the prophet I son of Amoz.	3833
	37: 5	When King Hezekiah's officials came to I,	3833
	37: 6	I said to them, "Tell your master,	3833
	37:21	I son of Amoz sent a message to Hezekiah:	3833
	38: 1	The prophet I son of Amoz went to him	3833
	38: 4	Then the word of the LORD came to I:	3833
	38:21	I had said, "Prepare a poultice of figs	3833
	39: 3	Then I the prophet went to King Hezekiah	3833
	39: 5	Then I said to Hezekiah,	3833
Mt	3: 3	spoken of through the prophet I:	2480
	4:14	what was said through the prophet I:	2480
	8:17	what was spoken through the prophet I:	2480
	12:17	what was spoken through the prophet I:	2480
	13:14	In them is fulfilled the prophecy of I:	2480
	15: 7	I was right when he prophesied about you:	2480
Mk	1: 2	It is written in I the prophet:	2480
	7: 6	I was right when he prophesied	2480
Lk	3: 4	As is written in the book of the words of I	2480
	4:17	The scroll of the prophet I was handed	2480
Jn	1:23	John replied in the words of I the prophet,	2480
	12:38	to fulfill the word of I the prophet:	2480
	12:39	because, as I says elsewhere:	2480
	12:41	I said this because he saw Jesus' glory	2480
Ac	8:28	in his chariot reading the book of I	2480
	8:30	to the chariot and heard the man reading I	2480
	28:25	to your forefathers when he said through I	2480
Ro	9:27	I cries out concerning Israel:	2480
	9:29	It is just as I said previously:	2480
	10:16	For I says, "Lord, who have believed our	2480
	10:20	And I boldly says, "I was found	2480
	15:12	I says, "The Root of Jesse will spring up,	2480

ISCAH (1)

Ge	11:29	the father of both Milcah and I.	3576

ISCARIOT (11)

Mt	10: 4	Simon the Zealot and Judas I,	2697
	26:14	the one called Judas I—	2697
Mk	3:19	and Judas I, who betrayed him.	2697
	14:10	Then Judas I, one of the Twelve,	2697
Lk	6:16	and Judas I, who became a traitor.	2697
	22: 3	Then Satan entered Judas, called I,	2697
Jn	6:71	(He meant Judas, the son of Simon I, who,	2697
	12: 4	But one of his disciples, Judas I,	2697
	13: 2	the devil had already prompted Judas I,	2697
	13:26	he gave it to Judas I, son of Simon.	2697
	14:22	Then Judas (not Judas I) said, "But, Lord,	2697

ISH-BOSHETH (14) [ESH-BAAL]

2Sa	2: 8	had taken I son of Saul and brought him	410
	2:10	I son of Saul was forty years old	410
	2:12	together with the men of I son of Saul,	410
	2:15	twelve men for Benjamin and I son of Saul,	410
	3: 7	And I said to Abner,	NIH
	3: 8	because of what I said and he answered,	410
	3:11	I did not dare to say another word	NIH
	3:14	David sent messengers to I son of Saul,	410
	3:15	So I gave orders and had her taken away	410
	4: 1	When I son of Saul heard	NIH
	4: 5	set out for the house of I,	410
	4: 8	the head of I to David at Hebron and said	410
	4: 8	"Here is the head of I son of Saul,	410
	4:12	the head of I and buried it in Abner's tomb	410

ISHBAH (1)

1Ch	4:17	Shammai and I the father of Eshtemoa.	3786

ISHBAK (2)

Ge	25: 2	Jokshan, Medan, Midian, I and Shuah.	3791
1Ch	1:32	Jokshan, Medan, Midian, I and Shuah.	3791

ISHBI-BENOB (1)

2Sa	21:16	And I, one of the descendants of Rapha,	3787

ISHHOD (1)

1Ch	7:18	His sister Hammoleketh gave birth to I,	412

ISHI (4)

1Ch	2:31	I, who was the father of Sheshan.	3831
	4:20	The descendants of I:	3831
	4:42	Rephaiah and Uzziel, the sons of I,	3831

1Ch	5:24	Epher, I, Eliel, Azriel, Jeremiah,	3831

ISHIAH (KJV) See ISSHIAH

ISHIJAH (1)

Ezr	10:31	From the descendants of Harim: Eliezer, I,	3807

ISHMA (1)

1Ch	4: 3	Jezreel, I and Idbash.	3816

ISHMAEL (47) [ISHMAELITE, ISHMAELITES]

Ge	16:11	You shall name him I,	3817
	16:15	the name I to the son she had borne.	3817
	16:16	when Hagar bore him I.	3817
	17:18	"If only I might live under your blessing!"	3817
	17:20	And as for I, I have heard you:	3817
	17:23	On that very day Abraham took his son I	3817
	17:25	and his son I was thirteen;	3817
	17:26	and his son I were both circumcised on	3817
	25: 9	His sons Isaac and I buried him in the cave	3817
	25:12	This is the account of Abraham's son I,	3817
	25:13	These are the names of the sons of I,	3817
	25:13	Nebaioth the firstborn of I, Kedar, Adbeel,	3817
	25:16	These were the sons of I,	3817
	25:17	I lived a hundred and thirty-seven years.	3817
	28: 9	so he went to I and married Mahalath,	3817
	28: 9	the sister of Nebaioth and daughter of I son	3817
	36: 3	also Basemath daughter of I and sister	3817
2Ki	25:23	I son of Nethaniah, Johanan son of Kareah,	3817
	25:25	I son of Nethaniah, the son of Elishama,	3817
1Ch	1:28	The sons of Abraham: Isaac and I.	3817
	1:29	Nebaioth the firstborn of I, Kedar, Adbeel,	3817
	1:31	These were the sons of I.	3817
	8:38	Azrikam, Bokeru, I, Sheariah,	3817
	9:44	Azrikam, Bokeru, I, Sheariah,	3817
2Ch	19:11	and Zebadiah son of I,	3817
	23: 1	I son of Jehohanan, Azariah son of Obed,	3817
Ezr	10:22	Elioenai, Maaseiah, I, Nethanel,	3817
Jer	40: 8	I son of Nethaniah,	3817
	40:14	the Ammonites has sent I son of Nethaniah	3817
	40:15	"Let me go and kill I son of Nethaniah.	3817
	40:16	What you are saying about I is not true."	3817
	41: 1	In the seventh month I son of Nethaniah,	3817
	41: 2	I son of Nethaniah and	3817
	41: 3	I also killed all the Jews who were	3817
	41: 6	I son of Nethaniah went out from Mizpah	3817
	41: 7	I son of Nethaniah and the men who were	3817
	41: 8	But ten of them said to I, "Don't kill us!	3817
	41: 9	I son of Nethaniah filled it with the dead.	3817
	41:10	I made captives of all the rest of	3817
	41:10	I son of Nethaniah took them captive	3817
	41:11	with him heard about all the crimes I son	3817
	41:12	and went to fight I son of Nethaniah.	3817
	41:13	the people I had with him saw Johanan son	3817
	41:14	All the people I had taken captive	3817
	41:15	But I son of Nethaniah and eight	3817
	41:16	from I son of Nethaniah	3817
	41:18	They were afraid of them because I son	3817

ISHMAELITE (2) [ISHMAEL]

1Ch	2:17	whose father was Jether the I.	3818
	27:30	Obil the I was in charge of the camels.	3818

ISHMAELITES (6) [ISHMAEL]

Ge	37:25	a caravan of I coming from Gilead.	3818
	37:27	let's sell him to the I and not lay our hands	3818
	37:28	for twenty shekels of silver to the I,	3818
	39: 1	from the I who had taken him from there.	3818
Jdg	8:24	the custom of the I to wear gold earrings.)	3818
Ps	83: 6	the tents of Edom and the I,	3818

ISHMAIAH (2)

1Ch	12: 4	and I the Gibeonite, a mighty man among	3819
	27:19	I son of Obadiah;	3820

ISHMEELITE, ISHMEELITES (KJV) See ISHMAELITE, ISHMAELITES

ISHMERAI (1)

1Ch	8:18	I, Izliah and Jobab were the sons of Elpaal.	3821

ISHOD (KJV) See ISHHOD

ISHPAH (1)

1Ch	8:16	I and Joha were the sons of Beriah.	3834

ISHPAN (1)

1Ch	8:22	I, Eber, Eliel,	3836

ISHTOB (KJV) See MEN OF TOB

ISHUAH (KJV) See ISHVAH

ISHUAI (KJV) See ISHUI, ISHVI

ISHUI (KJV) See ISHVI

ISHVAH (2)

Ge	46:17	Imnah, I, Ishvi and Beriah.	3796
1Ch	7:30	sons of Asher: Imnah, I, Ishvi and Beriah.	3796

ISHVI (4) [ISHVITE]

Ge	46:17	Imnah, Ishvah, I and Beriah.	3798
Nu	26:44	through I, the Ishvite clan;	3798
1Sa	14:49	Saul's sons were Jonathan, I and	3798
1Ch	7:30	sons of Asher: Imnah, Ishvah, I and Beriah.	3798

ISHVITE (1) [ISHVI]

Nu	26:44	through Ishvi, the I clan;	3799

ISLAND (13) [ISLANDERS, ISLANDS]

Isa	23: 2	you people of the i and you merchants	362
	23: 6	wail, you people of the i.	362
Ac	13: 6	the whole i until they came to Paphos.	3762
	27:14	swept down from the i.	899S
	27:16	to the lee of a small i called Cauda,	3761
	27:26	we must run aground on some i.'	3762
	28: 1	we found out that the i was called Malta.	3762
	28: 7	the chief official of the i.	3762
	28: 9	of the sick on the i came and were cured.	3762
	28:11	to sea in a ship that had wintered in the i.	3762
Rev	1: 9	was on the i of Patmos because of the word	3762
	6:14	and every mountain and i was removed	3762
	16:20	Every i fled away and the mountains could	3762

ISLANDERS (2) [ISLAND]

Ac	28: 2	The i showed us unusual kindness.	975
	28: 4	the i saw the snake hanging from his hand,	975

ISLANDS (15) [ISLAND]

Isa	11:11	from Hamath and from the i of the sea.	362
	24:15	the God of Israel, in the i of the sea.	362
	40:15	the i as though they were fine dust.	362
	41: 1	"Be silent before me, you i!	362
	41: 5	The i have seen it and fear;	362
	42: 4	In his law the i will put their hope."	362
	42:10	you i, and all who live in them.	362
	42:12	the Lord and proclaim his praise in the i.	362
	42:15	I will turn rivers into i and dry up the pools.	362
	49: 1	Listen to me, you i;	362
	51: 5	The i will look to me and wait in hope	362
	59:18	he will repay the i their due.	362
	60: 9	Surely the i look to me;	362
	66:19	the distant i that have not heard of my fame	362
Eze	26:18	the i in the sea are terrified	362

ISMACHIAH (KJV) See ISMAKIAH

ISMAIAH (KJV) See ISHMAIAH

ISMAKIAH (1)

2Ch	31:13	Nahath, Asahel, Jerimoth, Jozabad, Eliel, I,	3577

ISN'T (32) [BE, NOT] See Index of Articles Etc.

ISOLATE (2) [ISOLATION]

Lev	13:50	The priest is to examine the mildew and i	6037
	13:54	Then he is to i it for another seven days.	6037

ISOLATION (7) [ISOLATE]

Lev	13: 4	priest is to put the infected person in i	6037
	13: 5	he is to keep him in i another seven days.	6037
	13:11	He is not to put him in i,	6037
	13:21	priest is to put him in i for seven days.	6037
	13:26	priest is to put him in i for seven days.	6037
	13:31	priest is to put the infected person in i	6037
	13:33	to keep him in i another seven days.	6037

ISPAH (KJV) See ISHPAH

ISRAEL (1840) [ISRAEL'S, ISRAELITE, ISRAELITES, ISRAELITES']

Ge	32:28	"Your name will no longer be Jacob, but I,	3776
	34: 7	in I by lying with Jacob's daughter—	3776
	35:10	your name will be I."	3776
	35:10	So he named him I.	3776
	35:21	I moved on again and pitched his tent	3776
	35:22	While I was living in that region,	3776
	35:22	and I heard of it.	3776
	37: 3	Now I loved Joseph more than any	3776
	37:13	and I said to Joseph,	3776
	43: 6	I asked, "Why did you bring this trouble	3776
	43: 8	Then Judah said to I his father,	3776
	43:11	Then their father I said to them,	3776
	45:21	So the sons of I did this.	3776
	45:28	And I said, "I'm convinced!	3776

Ge	46: 1	So I set out with all that was his,	3776
	46: 2	God spoke to I in a vision at night and said,	3776
	46: 8	These are the names of the sons of I (Jacob	3776
	46:29	and went to Goshen to meet his father I.	3776
	46:30	I said to Joseph, "Now I am ready to die,	3776
	47:29	When the time drew near for I to die,	3776
	47:31	and I worshiped as he leaned on the top	3776
	48: 2	I rallied his strength and sat up on the bed.	3776
	48: 8	When I saw the sons of Joseph, he asked,	3776
	48: 9	Then I said, "Bring them to me	NIH
	48:11	I said to Joseph, "I never expected to see	3776
	48:14	But I reached out his right hand and put it	3776
	48:20	In your name will I pronounce this blessing:	3776
	48:21	Then I said to Joseph, "I am about to die,	3776
	49: 2	listen to your father I.	3776
	49: 7	in Jacob and disperse them in I.	3776
	49:16	for his people as one of the tribes of I.	3776
	49:24	because of the Shepherd, the Rock of I,	3776
	49:28	All these are the twelve tribes of I,	3776
	50: 2	in his service to embalm his father I.	3776
	50:25	And Joseph made the sons of I swear	3776
Ex	1: 1	of I who went to Egypt with Jacob, each	3776
	3:16	assemble the elders of I and say to them,	3776
	3:18	"The elders of I will listen to you.	3776
	4:22	I is my firstborn son,	3776
	5: 1	"This is what the Lord, the God of I,	3776
	5: 2	that I should obey him and let I go?	3776
	5: 2	the Lord and I will not let I go."	3776
	6:14	the firstborn son of I were Hanoch	3776
	9: 4	a distinction between the livestock of I and	3776
	11: 7	a distinction between Egypt and I.	3776
	12: 3	Tell the whole community of I that on	3776
	12: 6	of the community of I must slaughter them	3776
	12:15	through the seventh must be cut off from I.	3776
	12:19	be cut off from the community of I,	3776
	12:21	Then Moses summoned all the elders of I	3776
	12:47	whole community of I must celebrate it.	3776
	13:19	the sons of I swear an oath.	3776
	14:20	coming between the armies of Egypt and I.	3776
	14:30	the Lord saved I from the hands of	3776
	14:30	and I saw the Egyptians lying dead on	3776
	15:22	Then Moses led I from the Red Sea	3776
	16:31	The people of I called the bread manna.	3776
	17: 5	with you some of the elders of I and take	3776
	17: 6	in the sight of the elders of I.	3776
	18: 1	for Moses and for his people I,	3776
	18: 1	the Lord had brought I out of Egypt.	3776
	18: 9	the Lord had done for I in rescuing them	3776
	18:11	to those who had treated I arrogantly."	2157S
	18:12	of I to eat bread with Moses' father-in-law	3776
	18:25	from all I and made them leaders of	3776
	19: 2	and I camped there in the desert in front of	3776
	19: 3	and what you are to tell the people of I:	3776
	24: 1	and seventy of the elders of I.	3776
	24: 4	the twelve tribes of I.	3776
	24: 9	and the seventy elders of I went up	3776
	24:10	and saw the God of I.	3776
	28: 9	on them the names of the sons of I	3776
	28:11	the sons of I on the two stones the way	3776
	28:12	as memorial stones for the sons of I.	3776
	28:21	one for each of the names of the sons of I,	3776
	28:29	the names of the sons of I over his heart on	3776
	32: 4	Then they said, "These are your gods, O I,	3776
	32: 8	O I, who brought you up out of Egypt.'	3776
	32:13	Isaac and I, to whom you swore	3776
	32:27	"This is what the Lord, the God of I,	3776
	34:23	the Sovereign Lord, the God of I.	3776
	34:27	a covenant with you and with I."	3776
	39: 6	like a seal with the names of the sons of I.	3776
	39: 7	as memorial stones for the sons of I,	3776
	39:14	one for each of the names of the sons of I,	3776
	40:38	of all the house of I during all their travels.	3776
Lev	9: 1	and his sons and the elders of I.	3776
	10: 6	But your relatives, all the house of I,	3776
	16:17	and the whole community of I.	3776
	19: 2	to the entire assembly of I and say	1201+3776
	20: 2	or any alien living in I who gives any	3776
	22:18	either an Israelite or an alien living in I—	3776
Nu	1: 3	in I twenty years old or more who are able	3776
	1:16	They were the heads of the clans of I.	3776
	1:20	of Reuben the firstborn son of I:	3776
	1:44	and Aaron and the twelve leaders of I,	3776
	3:13	I set apart for myself every firstborn in I,	3776
	3:45	the Levites in place of all the firstborn of I,	1201+3776
	4:46	and the leaders of I counted all the Levites	3776
	7: 2	Then the leaders of I,	3776
	8:17	Every firstborn male in I,	1201+3776
	8:18	in place of all the firstborn sons in I.	1201+3776
	10: 4	the heads of the clans of I—	3776
	10:29	The Lord has promised good things to I."	3776
	10:36	O Lord, to the countless thousands of I."	3776
	11:30	Then Moses and the elders of I returned to	3776
	16: 9	for you that the God of I has separated you	3776
	16:25	and the elders of I followed him.	3776
	18:14	in I that is devoted to the Lord is yours.	3776
	18:21	the tithes in I as their inheritance in return	3776
	19:13	That person must be cut off from I.	3776
	20:14	"This is what your brother I says:	3776
	20:21	I turned away from them.	3776
	20:29	of I mourned for him thirty days.	3776
	21: 1	heard that I was coming along the road	3776
	21: 2	Then I made this vow to the Lord:	3776
	21:17	Then I sang this song: "Spring up, O well!	3776
	21:21	I sent messengers to say to Sihon king of	3776
	21:23	not let I pass through his territory.	3776
	21:23	and marched out into the desert against I.	3776

Nu	21:23	When he reached Jahaz, he fought with I.	3776
	21:24	I, however, put him to the sword and took	3776
	21:25	I captured all the cities of the Amorites	3776
	21:31	So I settled in the land of the Amorites.	3776
	22: 2	of Zippor saw all that I had done to	3776
	23: 7	for me; come, denounce I.'	3776
	23:10	of Jacob or number the fourth part of I?	3776
	23:21	no misery observed in I.	3776
	23:23	no divination against I.	3776
	23:23	It will now be said of Jacob and of I,	3776
	24: 1	that it pleased the Lord to bless I,	3776
	24: 2	and saw I encamped tribe by tribe,	3776
	24: 5	O Jacob, your dwelling places, O I!	3776
	24:17	a scepter will rise out of I.	3776
	24:18	will be conquered, but I will grow strong.	3776
	25: 1	While I was staying in Shittim,	3776
	25: 3	So I joined in worshiping the Baal of Peor.	3776
	25: 4	Lord's fierce anger may turn away from I."	3776
	25: 6	Moses and the whole assembly of I	1201+3776
	26: 2	to serve in the army of I."	3776
	26: 5	the firstborn son of I, were:	3776
	26:51	total number of the men of I was 601,730.	3776
	30: 1	said to the heads of the tribes of I:	1201+3776
	31: 4	from each of the tribes of I."	3776
	31: 5	were supplied from the clans of I.	3776
	32: 4	the Lord subdued before the people of I—	3776
	32:13	against I and he made them wander in	3776
	32:14	the Lord even more angry with I.	3776
	32:22	to the Lord and to I.	3776
	36: 7	No inheritance in I is to pass from	1201+3776
Dt	1: 1	These are the words Moses spoke to all I in	3776
	1:38	because he will lead I to inherit it.	3776
	2:12	as I did in the land the Lord gave them	3776
	4: 1	now, O I, the decrees and laws I am about	3776
	5: 1	Moses summoned all I and said:	3776
	5: 1	Hear, O I, the decrees and laws I declare	3776
	6: 3	Hear, O I, and be careful to obey so	3776
	6: 4	Hear, O I: The Lord our God, the Lord is one.	3776
	9: 1	Hear, O I. You are now about to cross	3776
	10:12	O I, what does the Lord your God ask	3776
	11: 6	the middle of all I and swallowed them up	3776
	13:11	Then all I will hear and be afraid.	3776
	17: 4	that this detestable thing has been done in I,	3776
	17:12	You must purge the evil from I.	3776
	17:20	a long time over his kingdom in I.	3776
	18: 1	to have no allotment or inheritance with I.	3776
	18: 6	from one of your towns anywhere in I	3776
	19:13	You must purge from I the guilt	3776
	20: 3	He shall say: "Hear, O I,	3776
	21: 8	Accept this atonement for your people I,	3776
	21:21	All I will hear of it and be afraid.	3776
	22:21	in I by being promiscuous while still	3776
	22:22	You must purge the evil from I.	3776
	25: 6	that his name will not be blotted out from I.	3776
	25: 7	to carry on his brother's name in I as	3776
	25:10	That man's line shall be known in I as	3776
	26:15	and bless your people I and	3776
	27: 1	and the elders of I commanded the people:	3776
	27: 9	said to all I, "Be silent, O Israel, and listen!	3776
	27: 9	said to all Israel, "Be silent, O I, and listen!	3776
	27:14	to all the people of I in a loud voice:	3776
	29:10	and all the other men of I,	3776
	29:21	from all the tribes of I for disaster,	3776
	31: 1	and spoke these words to all I:	3776
	31: 7	and said to him in the presence of all I,	3776
	31: 9	and to all the elders of I.	3776
	31:11	when all I comes to appear before	3776
	31:30	in the hearing of the whole assembly of I:	3776
	32: 8	according to the number of the sons of I.	3776
	32:45	When Moses finished reciting all these words to all I,	3776
	32:52	the land I am giving to the people of I."	3776
	33: 5	along with the tribes of I.	3776
	33:10	to Jacob and your law to I.	3776
	33:21	and his judgments concerning I."	3776
	33:28	So I will live in safety alone;	3776
	33:29	Blessed are you, O I!	3776
	34:10	no prophet has risen in I like Moses,	3776
	34:12	that Moses did in the sight of all I.	3776
Jos	3: 7	to exalt you in the eyes of all I,	3776
	3:12	choose twelve men from the tribes of I,	3776
	3:17	while all I passed by until	3776
	4: 7	be a memorial to the people of I forever."	3776
	4:14	in the sight of all I;	3776
	4:22	'I crossed the Jordan on dry ground.'	3776
	6:18	of I liable to destruction and bring trouble	3776
	6:23	in a place outside the camp of I.	3776
	7: 1	So the Lord's anger burned against I.	1201+3776
	7: 6	The elders of I did the same,	3776
	7: 8	now that I has been routed by its enemies?	3776
	7:11	I has sinned; they have violated my covenant,	3776
	7:13	this is what the Lord, the God of I, says:	3776
	7:13	That which is devoted is among you, O I.	3776
	7:15	and has done a disgraceful thing in I!'"	3776
	7:16	next morning Joshua had I come forward	3776
	7:19	give glory to the Lord, the God of I,	3776
	7:20	sinned against the Lord, the God of I.	3776
	7:24	Then Joshua, together with all I,	3776
	7:25	Then all I stoned him,	3776
	8:10	the leaders of I marched before them to Ai.	3776
	8:14	in the morning to meet I in battle at	3776
	8:15	and all I let themselves be driven back	3776
	8:17	in Ai or Bethel who did not go after I.	3776
	8:17	the city open and went in pursuit of I.	3776
	8:21	and all I saw that the ambush had taken	3776

Jos	8:22	I cut them down,	NIH
	8:24	When I had finished killing all the men	3776
	8:27	But I did carry off for themselves	3776
	8:30	an altar to the LORD, the God of I,	3776
	8:33	All I, aliens and citizens alike,	3776
	8:33	to bless the people of I.	3776
	8:35	not read to the whole assembly of I,	3776
	9: 2	to make war against Joshua and I.	3776
	9: 6	at Gilgal and said to him and the men of I,	3776
	9: 7	The men of I said to the Hivites,	3776
	9:14	The men of I sampled their provisions	NIH
	9:18	an oath to them by the LORD, the God of I.	3776
	9:19	our oath by the LORD, the God of I,	3776
	10: 1	of peace with I and were living near them.	3776
	10:10	threw into confusion before I,	3776
	10:10	I pursued them along the road going up	NIH
	10:11	before I on the road down from Beth Horon	3776
	10:12	the LORD gave the Amorites over to I,	1201+3776
	10:12	to the LORD in the presence of I:	3776
	10:14	Surely the LORD was fighting for I!	3776
	10:15	Then Joshua returned with all I to the camp	3776
	10:24	he summoned all the men of I and said to	3776
	10:29	Then Joshua and all I with him moved on	3776
	10:31	Then Joshua and all I with him moved on	3776
	10:32	The LORD handed Lachish over to I,	3776
	10:34	and all I with him moved on from Lachish	3776
	10:36	Then Joshua and all I with him went up	3776
	10:38	Then Joshua and all I with him turned	3776
	10:40	just as the LORD, the God of I,	3776
	10:42	because the God of I,	3776
	10:42	the God of Israel, fought for I.	3776
	10:43	Then Joshua returned with all I to the camp	3776
	11: 5	at the Waters of Merom, to fight against I.	3776
	11: 6	I will hand all of them over to I,	3776
	11: 8	the LORD gave them into the hand of I.	3776
	11:13	Yet I did not burn any of the cities built	3776
	11:16	and the mountains of I with their foothills,	3776
	11:20	to wage war against I,	3776
	11:21	and from all the hill country of I.	3776
	11:23	to I according to their tribal divisions.	3776
	12: 7	an inheritance to the tribes of I according	3776
	13: 6	to allocate this land to I for an inheritance,	3776
	13:14	the God of I, are their inheritance,	3776
	13:33	the LORD, the God of I,	3776
	14: 1	heads of the tribal clans of I allotted	1201+3776
	14: 1	while I moved about in the desert.	3776
	14:14	the God of I, wholeheartedly.	3776
	19:51	heads of the tribal clans of I assigned	1201+3776
	21: 1	heads of the other tribal families of I	1201+3776
	21:43	So the LORD gave I all the land he had	3776
	21:45	good promises to the house of I failed;	3776
	22:12	assembly of I gathered at Shiloh	1201+3776
	22:14	one for each of the tribes of I,	3776
	22:16	with the God of I like this?	3776
	22:18	be angry with the whole community of I.	3776
	22:20	upon the whole community of I?	3776
	22:21	to the heads of the clans of I:	3776
	22:22	And let I know!	3776
	22:24	have to do with the LORD, the God of I?	3776
	23: 1	and the LORD had given I rest	3776
	23: 2	summoned all I—their elders,	3776
	24: 1	Then Joshua assembled all the tribes of I	3776
	24: 1	leaders, judges and officials of I,	3776
	24: 2	"This is what the LORD, the God of I,	3776
	24: 9	prepared to fight against I,	3776
	24:23	hearts to the LORD, the God of I."	3776
	24:31	I served the LORD throughout the lifetime	3776
	24:31	the LORD had done for I.	3776
Jdg	1:28	When I became strong,	3776
	2: 7	the great things the LORD had done for I.	3776
	2:10	the LORD nor what he had done for I.	3776
	2:14	against I the LORD handed them over	3776
	2:15	Whenever I went out to fight,	NIH
	2:20	the LORD was very angry with I and said,	3776
	2:22	to test I and see whether they will keep	3776
	3: 8	The anger of the LORD burned against I	3776
	3:12	gave Eglon king of Moab power over I.	3776
	3:13	Eglon came and attacked I,	3776
	3:30	That day Moab was made subject to I,	3776
	3:31	He too saved I.	3776
	4: 4	was leading I at that time.	3776
	4: 6	the God of I, commands you:	3776
	5: 2	"When the princes in I take the lead, when	3776
	5: 3	to the LORD, the God of I.	3776
	5: 5	before the LORD, the God of I.	3776
	5: 7	Village life in I ceased, ceased until I,	3776
	5: 7	Deborah, arose, arose a mother in I.	3776
	5: 8	among forty thousand in I.	3776
	5:11	the righteous acts of his warriors in I.	3776
	6: 4	and did not spare a living thing for I,	3776
	6: 8	"This is what the LORD, the God of I,	3776
	6:14	"Go in the strength you have and save I out	3776
	6:15	Gideon asked, "how can I save I?	3776
	6:36	"If you will save I by my hand	3776
	6:37	then I will know that you will save I	3776
	7: 2	In order that I may not boast against I	3776
	7:15	He returned to the camp of I and called out,	3776
	8:27	All I prostituted themselves	3776
	9:22	Abimelech had governed I three years,	3776
	10: 1	the son of Dodo, rose to save I.	3776
	10: 2	He led I twenty-three years;	3776
	10: 3	who led I twenty-two years.	3776
	10: 9	and I was in great distress.	3776
	11: 4	when the Ammonites made war on I,	3776
	11:13	"When I came up out of Egypt,	3776
	11:15	I did not take the land of Moab or the land	3776
	11:16	I went through the desert to the Red Sea	3776

Jdg	11:17	I sent messengers to the king of Edom,	3776
	11:17	So I stayed at Kadesh.	3776
	11:19	"Then I sent messengers to Sihon king of	3776
	11:20	did not trust I to pass through his territory.	3776
	11:20	and encamped at Jahaz and fought with I.	3776
	11:21	"Then the LORD, the God of I,	3776
	11:21	I took over all the land of the Amorites	3776
	11:23	"Now since the LORD, the God of I,	3776
	11:23	the Amorites out before his people I,	3776
	11:25	Did he ever quarrel with I or fight	3776
	11:26	three hundred years I occupied Heshbon,	3776
	11:33	Thus I subdued Ammon.	1201+3776
	11:40	that each year the young women of I go out	3776
	12: 7	Jephthah led I six years.	3776
	12: 8	After him, Ibzan of Bethlehem led I.	3776
	12: 9	Ibzan led I seven years.	3776
	12:11	Elon the Zebulunite led I ten years.	3776
	12:13	Abdon son of Hillel, from Pirathon, led I.	3776
	12:14	He led I eight years.	3776
	13: 5	and he will begin the deliverance of I from	3776
	14: 4	for at that time they were ruling over I.)	3776
	15:20	Samson led I for twenty years in the days	3776
	16:31	He had led I twenty years.	3776
	17: 6	In those days I had no king;	3776
	18: 1	In those days I had no king.	3776
	18: 1	into an inheritance among the tribes of I.	3776
	18:19	that you serve a tribe and clan in I	3776
	18:29	who was born to I—	3776
	19: 1	In those days I had no king.	3776
	19:29	and sent them into all the areas of I.	3776
	20: 2	of I took their places in the assembly of	3776
	20: 6	and disgraceful act in I.	3776
	20:10	of every hundred from all the tribes of I,	3776
	20:10	for all this vileness done in I."	3776
	20:11	So all the men of I got together and united	3776
	20:12	The tribes of I sent men throughout	3776
	20:13	to death and purge the evil from I."	3776
	20:17	I, apart from Benjamin, mustered	408+3776
	20:20	of I went out to fight the Benjamites	3776
	20:22	of I encouraged one another and again took	3776
	20:29	Then I set an ambush around Gibeah.	3776
	20:33	All the men of I moved from their places	3776
	20:35	The LORD defeated Benjamin before I,	3776
	20:36	men of I had given way before Benjamin,	3776
	20:38	of I had arranged with the ambush	3776
	20:39	then the men of I would turn in the battle.	3776
	20:39	to inflict casualties on the men of I	3776
	20:41	Then the men of I turned on them,	3776
	20:42	of I who came out of the towns cut them	NIH
	20:48	of I went back to Benjamin and put all	3776
	21: 1	The men of I had taken an oath at Mizpah:	3776
	21: 3	"O LORD, the God of I," they cried,	3776
	21: 3	they cried, "why has this happened to I?	3776
	21: 3	should one tribe be missing from I today?"	3776
	21: 5	the tribes of I has failed to assemble before	3776
	21: 6	"Today one tribe is cut off from I,"	3776
	21: 8	of the tribes of I failed to assemble before	3776
	21:15	LORD had made a gap in the tribes of I.	3776
	21:17	"so that a tribe of I will not be wiped out.	3776
	21:25	In those days I had no king;	3776
Ru	2:12	rewarded by the LORD, the God of I,	3776
	4: 7	(Now in earlier times in I,	3776
	4: 7	the method of legalizing transactions in I.)	3776
	4:11	who together built up the house of I.	3776
	4:14	May he become famous throughout I!	3776
1Sa	1:17	of I grant you what you have asked	3776
	2:22	to all I and how they slept with	3776
	2:28	I chose your father out of all the tribes of I	3776
	2:29	of every offering made by my people I?'	3776
	2:30	"Therefore the LORD, the God of I,	3776
	2:32	Although good will be done to I,	3776
	3:11	to do something in I that will make the ears	3776
	3:20	And all I from Dan to Beersheba	3776
	4: 1	And Samuel's word came to all I.	3776
	4: 2	Philistines deployed their forces to meet I,	3776
	4: 2	I was defeated by the Philistines.	3776
	4: 3	the elders of I asked,	3776
	4: 5	all I raised such a great shout that	3776
	4:10	I lost thirty thousand foot soldiers.	3776
	4:17	"I fled before the Philistines.	3776
	4:18	He had led I forty years.	3776
	4:21	saying, "The glory has departed from I"—	3776
	4:22	She said, "The glory has departed from I,	3776
	5: 7	"The ark of the god of I must not stay here	3776
	5: 8	with the ark of the god of I?"	3776
	5: 8	the ark of the god of I moved to Gath."	3776
	5: 8	So they moved the ark of the God of I.	3776
	5:10	of I around to us to kill us and our people."	3776
	5:11	"Send the ark of the god of I away;	3776
	6: 3	"If you return the ark of the god of I,	3776
	7: 2	and all the people of I mourned and sought	3776
	7: 3	And Samuel said to the whole house of I,	3776
	7: 5	"Assemble all I at Mizpah	3776
	7: 6	Samuel was leader of I at Mizpah.	1201+3776
	7: 7	Philistines heard that I had assembled	1201+3776
	7:10	the Philistines drew near to engage I	3776
	7:11	of I rushed out of Mizpah and pursued	3776
	7:14	from I were restored to her,	3776
	7:14	and I delivered the neighboring territory	3776
	7:14	And there was peace between I and	3776
	7:15	as judge over I all the days of his life.	3776
	7:16	judging I in all those places.	3776
	7:17	and there he also judged I.	3776
	8: 1	he appointed his sons as judges for I.	3776
	8: 4	of I gathered together and came to Samuel	3776
	8:22	Then Samuel said to the men of I,	3776
	9: 9	(Formerly in I, if a man went to inquire	3776

1Sa	9:16	Anoint him leader over my people I;	3776
	9:20	And to whom is all the desire of I turned,	3776
	9:21	from the smallest tribe of I,	3776
	10:17	the people of I to the LORD at Mizpah	NIH
	10:18	"This is what the LORD, the God of I,	3776
	10:18	'I brought I up out of Egypt,	3776
	10:20	Samuel brought all the tribes of I near,	3776
	11: 2	of you and so bring disgrace on all I."	3776
	11: 3	so we can send messengers throughout I;	3776
	11: 7	the pieces by messengers throughout I,	3776
	11: 8	of I numbered three hundred thousand and	3776
	11:13	for this day the LORD has rescued I."	3776
	12: 1	Samuel said to all I,	3776
	13: 1	and he reigned over I [forty-]two years.	3776
	13: 2	Saul chose three thousand men from I,	3776
	13: 4	So all I heard the news:	3776
	13: 4	I has become a stench to the Philistines."	3776
	13: 5	The Philistines assembled to fight I,	3776
	13: 6	of I saw that their situation was critical and	3776
	13:13	over I for all time.	3776
	13:19	be found in the whole land of I,	3776
	13:20	So all I went down to the Philistines	3776
	14:12	into the hand of I."	3776
	14:23	So the LORD rescued I that day,	3776
	14:24	Now the men of I were in distress that day,	3776
	14:39	surely as the LORD who rescues I lives,	3776
	14:41	Saul prayed to the LORD, the God of I,	3776
	14:45	about this great deliverance in I?	3776
	14:47	After Saul had assumed rule over I,	3776
	14:48	delivering I from the hands	3776
	15: 1	to anoint you king over his people I;	3776
	15: 2	to I when they waylaid them as they came	3776
	15:17	not become the head of the tribes of I?	3776
	15:17	The LORD anointed you king over I.	3776
	15:26	the LORD has rejected you as king over I!"	3776
	15:28	of I from you today and has given it to one	3776
	15:29	He who is the Glory of I does not lie	3776
	15:30	the elders of my people and before I;	3776
	15:35	that he had made Saul king over I.	3776
	16: 1	since I have rejected him as king over I?	3776
	17: 8	Goliath stood and shouted to the ranks of I,	3776
	17:10	"This day I defy the ranks of I!	3776
	17:19	with Saul and all the men of I in the Valley	3776
	17:21	I and the Philistines were drawing	3776
	17:25	He comes out to defy I.	3776
	17:25	exempt his father's family from taxes in I."	3776
	17:26	and removes this disgrace from I?	3776
	17:45	the LORD Almighty, the God of the armies of I,	3776
	17:46	will know that there is a God in I.	3776
	17:52	of I and Judah surged forward with a shout	3776
	18: 6	from all the towns of I to meet King Saul	3776
	18:16	But all I and Judah loved David,	3776
	18:18	what is my family or my father's clan in I,	3776
	19: 5	The LORD won a great victory for all I,	3776
	20:12	"By the LORD, the God of I,	3776
	23:10	David said, "O LORD, God of I,	3776
	23:11	O LORD, God of I, tell your servant."	3776
	23:17	You will be king over I,	3776
	24: 2	from all I and set out to look for David	3776
	24:14	"Against whom has the king of I come out?	3776
	24:20	that the kingdom of I will be established	3776
	25: 1	and all I assembled and mourned for him;	3776
	25:30	and has appointed him leader over I,	3776
	25:32	"Praise be to the LORD, the God of I,	3776
	25:34	as surely as the LORD, the God of I,	3776
	26: 2	with his three thousand chosen men of I,	3776
	26:15	And who is like you in I?	3776
	26:20	The king of I has come out to look for	3776
	27: 1	up searching for me anywhere in I,	3776
	28: 1	gathered their forces to fight against I.	3776
	28: 3	and all I had mourned for him	3776
	28:19	The LORD will hand over both I and you	3776
	28:19	over the army of I to the Philistines."	3776
	29: 1	and I camped by the spring in Jezreel.	3776
	29: 3	who was an officer of Saul king of I?	3776
	30:25	a statute and ordinance for I from that day	3776
	31: 1	Now the Philistines fought against I;	3776
2Sa	1:12	the army of the LORD and the house of I,	3776
	1:19	O I, lies slain on your heights.	3776
	1:24	"O daughters of I, weep for Saul,	3776
	2: 9	and also over Ephraim, Benjamin and all I.	3776
	2:10	when he became king over I,	3776
	2:17	and Abner and the men of I were defeated	3776
	2:28	they no longer pursued I,	3776
	3:10	of Saul and establish David's throne over I	3776
	3:12	and I will help you bring all I over to you."	3776
	3:17	Abner conferred with the elders of I	3776
	3:18	'By my servant David I will rescue my people I	3776
	3:19	to Hebron to tell David everything that I	3776
	3:21	and assemble all I for my lord the king,	3776
	3:37	So on that day all the people and all I knew	3776
	3:38	and a great man has fallen in I this day?	3776
	4: 1	he lost courage, and all I became alarmed.	3776
	5: 1	All the tribes of I came to David at Hebron	3776
	5: 2	you were the one who led I	3776
	5: 2	'You will shepherd my people I,	3776
	5: 3	of I had come to King David at Hebron,	3776
	5: 3	and they anointed David king over I.	3776
	5: 5	over all I and Judah thirty-three years.	3776
	5:12	as king over I and had exalted his kingdom	3776
	5:12	for the sake of his people I.	3776
	5:17	that David had been anointed king over I,	3776
	6: 1	brought together out of I chosen men,	3776
	6: 5	and the whole house of I were celebrating	3776
	6:15	and the entire house of I brought up the ark	3776

2Sa	6:20	king of I has distinguished himself today, 3776
	6:21	ruler over the LORD's people I— 3776
	7: 7	to shepherd my people I, 3776
	7: 8	the flock to be ruler over my people I. 3776
	7:10	a place for my people I and will plant them 3776
	7:11	I appointed leaders over my people I. 3776
	7:23	And who is like your people I— 3776
	7:24	You have established your people I 3776
	7:26	'The LORD Almighty is God over I!' 3776
	7:27	"O LORD Almighty, God of I, 3776
	8:15	David reigned over all I, 3776
	10: 9	so he selected some of the best troops in I 3776
	10:15	that they had been routed by I, 3776
	10:17	David was told of this, he gathered all I, 3776
	10:18	But they fled before I, 3776
	10:19	that they had been defeated by I, 3776
	11:11	ark and I and Judah are staying in tents, 3776
	12: 7	This is what the LORD, the God of I, 3776
	12: 7	'I anointed you king over I, 3776
	12: 8	I gave you the house of I and Judah. 3776
	12:12	in broad daylight before all I.'" 3776
	13:12	Such a thing should not be done in I! 3776
	13:13	be like one of the wicked fools in I. 3776
	14:25	In all I there was not a man 3776
	15: 2	Your servant is from one of the tribes of I. 3776
	15: 6	and so he stole the hearts of the men of I. 3776
	15:10	throughout the tribes of I to say, 3776
	15:13	hearts of the men of I are with Absalom." 3776
	16: 3	the house of I will give me back my grandfather's kingdom.'" 3776
	16:15	and all the men of I came to Jerusalem, 3776
	16:18	by these people, and by all the men of I— 3776
	16:21	Then all I will hear 3776
	16:22	in the sight of all I. 3776
	17: 4	to Absalom and to all the elders of I. 3776
	17:10	for all I knows that your father is a fighter 3776
	17:11	Let all I, from Dan to Beersheba— 3776
	17:13	then all I will bring ropes to that city, 3776
	17:14	Absalom and all the men of I said, 3776
	17:15	and the elders of I to do such and such, 3776
	17:24	the Jordan with all the men of I. 3776
	18: 6	The army marched into the field to fight I, 3776
	18: 7	of I was defeated by David's men, and 3776
	18:16	and the troops stopped pursuing I, 3776
	19: 9	Throughout the tribes of I, 3776
	19:11	throughout I has reached the king 3776
	19:22	Should anyone be put to death in I today? 3776
	19:22	not know that today I am king over I?" 3776
	19:40	of Judah and half the troops of I had taken 3776
	19:41	of I were coming to the king and saying 3776
	19:42	the men of Judah answered the men of I, 3776
	19:43	the men of I answered the men of Judah, 3776
	19:43	even more harshly than the men of I. 3776
	20: 1	Every man to his tent, O I!" 3776
	20: 2	of I deserted David to follow Sheba son 3776
	20:14	the tribes of I to Abel Beth Maacah and 3776
	20:19	We are the peaceful and faithful in I. 3776
	20:19	to destroy a city that is a mother in I. 3776
	21: 2	the Gibeonites were not a part of I 1201+3776
	21: 2	but Saul in his zeal for I and Judah 1201+3776
	21: 4	nor do we have the right to put anyone in I 3776
	21: 5	and have no place anywhere in I, 3776
	21:15	a battle between the Philistines and I. 3776
	21:17	that the lamp of I will not be extinguished." 3776
	21:21	When he taunted I, 3776
	23: 3	The God of I spoke, 3776
	23: 3	the Rock of I said to me: 3776
	23: 9	Then the men of I retreated, 3776
	24: 1	the anger of the LORD burned against I, 3776
	24: 1	"Go and take a census of I and Judah." 3776
	24: 2	"Go throughout the tribes of I from Dan 3776
	24: 4	of the king to enroll the fighting men of I. 3776
	24: 9	In I there were eight hundred thousand able-bodied men who could handle 3776
	24:15	on I from that morning until the end of 3776
	24:25	and the plague on I was stopped. 3776
1Ki	1: 3	Then they searched throughout I for 3776
	1:20	the eyes of all I are on you, 3776
	1:30	the God of I: 3776
	1:34	the prophet anoint him king over I. 3776
	1:35	I have appointed him ruler over I 3776
	1:48	'Praise be to the LORD, the God of I, 3776
	2: 4	to have a man on the throne of I.' 3776
	2:11	He had reigned forty years over I— 3776
	2:15	All I looked to me as their king. 3776
	3:28	all I heard the verdict the king had given, 3776
	4: 1	So King Solomon ruled over all I. 3776
	4: 7	over all I, who supplied provisions for 3776
	4:20	and I were as numerous as the sand on 3776
	4:25	During Solomon's lifetime Judah and I, 3776
	5:13	Solomon conscripted laborers from all I— 3776
	6: 1	the fourth year of Solomon's reign over I, 3776
	6:13	and will not abandon my people I." 3776
	8: 1	at Jerusalem the elders of I, 3776
	8: 2	of I came together to King Solomon at 3776
	8: 3	When all the elders of I had arrived, 3776
	8: 5	the entire assembly of I that had gathered 3776
	8:14	whole assembly of I was standing there, 3776
	8:15	"Praise be to the LORD, the God of I, 3776
	8:16	the day I brought my people I out of Egypt, 3776
	8:16	of I to have a temple built for my Name 3776
	8:16	I have chosen David to rule my people I.' 3776
	8:17	I swore to you by the LORD, the God of I. 3776
	8:20	and now I sit on the throne of I, 3776
	8:20	for the Name of the LORD, the God of I. 3776
	8:22	in front of the whole assembly of I, 3776
	8:23	"O LORD, God of I, 3776

1Ki	8:25	"Now LORD, God of I, 3776
	8:25	a man to sit before me on the throne of I, 3776
	8:26	And now, O God of I, 3776
	8:30	and of your people I when they pray 3776
	8:33	"When your people I have been defeated 3776
	8:34	of your people I and bring them back to 3776
	8:36	the sin of your servants, your people I. 3776
	8:38	or plea is made by any of your people I— 3776
	8:41	not belong to your people I but has come 3776
	8:43	as do your own people I, 3776
	8:52	and to the plea of your people I, 3776
	8:55	the whole assembly of I in a loud voice, 3776
	8:56	who has given rest to his people I just 3776
	8:59	of his servant and the cause of his people I 3776
	8:62	and all I with him offered sacrifices before 3776
	8:65	and all I with him— 3776
	8:66	for his servant David and his people I. 3776
	9: 5	I will establish your royal throne over I forever, 3776
	9: 5	to have a man on the throne of I.' 3776
	9: 7	then I will cut off I from 3776
	9: 7	I will then become a byword and an object 3776
	10: 9	in you and placed you on the throne of I. 3776
	10: 9	Because of the LORD's eternal love for I, 3776
	11: 9	the LORD, the God of I, 3776
	11:25	in Aram and was hostile toward I. 3776
	11:31	for this is what the LORD, the God of I, 3776
	11:32	of all the tribes of I, 3776
	11:37	you will be king over I. 3776
	11:38	as the one I built for David and will give I 3776
	11:42	in Jerusalem over all I forty years. 3776
	12: 3	the whole assembly of I went to Rehoboam 3776
	12:16	When all I saw that the king refused 3776
	12:16	To your tents, O I! 3776
	12:18	but all I stoned him to death. 3776
	12:19	So I has been in rebellion against the house 3776
	12:20	the assembly and made him king over all I. 3776
	12:21	the house of I and Judah to regain the kingdom 3776
	12:28	Here are your gods, O I, 3776
	14: 7	what the LORD, the God of I, says: 3776
	14: 7	and made you a leader over my people I. 3776
	14:10	from Jeroboam every last male in I— 3776
	14:13	All I will mourn for him and bury him. 3776
	14:13	the God of I, has found anything good. 3776
	14:14	for himself a king over I who will cut off 3776
	14:15	And the LORD will strike I, 3776
	14:15	He will uproot I from this good land 3776
	14:16	And he will give I up because of 3776
	14:16	and has caused I to commit." 3776
	14:18	and all I mourned for him, 3776
	14:19	in the book of the annals of the kings of I. 3776
	14:21	the tribes of I in which to put his Name. 3776
	15: 9	In the twentieth year of Jeroboam king of I, 3776
	15:16	between Asa and Baasha king of I 3776
	15:17	Baasha king of I went up against Judah 3776
	15:19	with Baasha king of I so he will withdraw 3776
	15:20	of his forces against the towns of I. 3776
	15:25	Nadab son of Jeroboam became king of I 3776
	15:25	and he reigned over I two years. 3776
	15:26	which he had caused I to commit. 3776
	15:27	while Nadab and all I were besieging it. 3776
	15:30	and had caused I to commit, 3776
	15:30	provoked the LORD, the God of I, to anger. 3776
	15:31	in the book of the annals of the kings of I? 3776
	15:32	between Asa and Baasha king of I 3776
	15:33	Baasha son of Ahijah became king of all I 3776
	15:34	which he had caused I to commit. 3776
	16: 2	and made you leader of my people I, 3776
	16: 2	of Jeroboam and caused my people I to sin 3776
	16: 5	in the book of the annals of the kings of I? 3776
	16: 8	Elah son of Baasha became king of I, 3776
	16:13	and had caused I to commit, 3776
	16:13	provoked the LORD, the God of I, to anger 3776
	16:14	in the book of the annals of the kings of I? 3776
	16:16	king over I that very day there in the camp. 3776
	16:19	the sin he had committed and had caused I 3776
	16:20	in the book of the annals of the kings of I? 3776
	16:21	the people of I were split into two factions; 3776
	16:23	Omri became king of I, 3776
	16:26	which he had caused I to commit, 3776
	16:26	provoked the LORD, the God of I, to anger 3776
	16:27	in the book of the annals of the kings of I? 3776
	16:29	Ahab son of Omri became king of I, 3776
	16:29	in Samaria over I twenty-two years. 3776
	16:33	provoke the LORD, the God of I, to anger 3776
	16:33	to anger than did all the kings of I 3776
	17: 1	"As the LORD, the God of I, lives, 3776
	17:14	this is what the LORD, the God of I, says: 3776
	18:17	"Is that you, you troubler of I?" 3776
	18:18	"I have not made trouble for I," 3776
	18:19	Now summon the people from all over I 3776
	18:20	So Ahab sent word throughout all I 1201+3776
	18:31	saying, "Your name shall be I." 3776
	18:36	"O LORD, God of Abraham, Isaac and I, 3776
	18:36	let it be known today that you are God in I 3776
	19:16	anoint Jehu son of Nimshi king over I, 3776
	19:18	Yet I reserve seven thousand in I— 3776
	20: 2	into the city to Ahab king of I, 3776
	20: 4	The king of I answered, "Just as you say, 3776
	20: 7	The king of I summoned all the elders of 3776
	20:11	The king of I answered, "Tell him: 3776
	20:13	of I and announced, "This is what 3776
	20:21	of I advanced and overpowered the horses 3776
	20:22	the prophet came to the king of I and said, 3776
	20:25	so we can fight I on the plains. 4392S
	20:26	and went up to Aphek to fight against I. 3776
	20:28	up and told the king of I, "This is what 3776

1Ki	20:31	the kings of the house of I are merciful. 3776
	20:31	Let us go to the king of I with sackcloth 3776
	20:32	they went to the king of I and said, 3776
	20:40	"That is your sentence," the king of I said. 3776
	20:41	of I recognized him as one of the prophets. 3776
	20:43	the king of I went to his palace in Samaria. 3776
	21: 7	"Is this how you act as king over I?" 3776
	21:18	"Go down to meet Ahab king of I, 3776
	21:21	cut off from Ahab every last male in I— 3776
	21:22	to anger and have caused I to sin.' 3776
	21:26	the LORD drove out before I.) 1201+3776
	22: 1	there was no war between Aram and I. 3776
	22: 2	of Judah went down to see the king of I. 3776
	22: 3	The king of I had said to his officials, 3776
	22: 4	Jehoshaphat replied to the king of I, 3776
	22: 5	But Jehoshaphat also said to the king of I, 3776
	22: 6	king of I brought together the prophets— 3776
	22: 8	The king of I answered Jehoshaphat, 3776
	22: 9	So the king of I called one of his officials 3776
	22:10	the king of I and Jehoshaphat king 3776
	22:17	"I saw all I scattered on the hills like sheep 3776
	22:18	The king of I said to Jehoshaphat, 3776
	22:26	The king of I then ordered, 3776
	22:29	of I and Jehoshaphat king of Judah went up 3776
	22:30	The king of I said to Jehoshaphat, 3776
	22:30	So the king of I disguised himself and went 3776
	22:31	small or great, except the king of I." 3776
	22:32	they thought, "Surely this is the king of I." 3776
	22:33	not the king of I and stopped pursuing him. 3776
	22:34	and hit the king of I between the sections 3776
	22:39	in the book of the annals of the kings of I? 3776
	22:41	in the fourth year of Ahab king of I. 3776
	22:44	also at peace with the king of I. 3776
	22:51	of Ahab became king of I in Samaria in 3776
	22:51	and he reigned over I two years. 3776
	22:52	Jeroboam son of Nebat, who caused I to sin. 3776
	22:53	provoked the LORD, the God of I, to anger, 3776
2Ki	1: 1	Ahab's death, Moab rebelled against I. 3776
	1: 3	'Is it because there is no God in I 3776
	1: 6	Is it because there is no God in I 3776
	1:16	Is it because there is no God in I for you 3776
	1:18	in the book of the annals of the kings of I? 3776
	2:12	The chariots and horsemen of I!" 3776
	3: 1	Joram son of Ahab became king of I 3776
	3: 3	which he had caused I to commit; 3776
	3: 4	of I with a hundred thousand lambs and 3776
	3: 5	of Moab rebelled against the king of I. 3776
	3: 6	from Samaria and mobilized all I. 3776
	3: 9	the king of I set out with the king of Judah 3776
	3:10	exclaimed the king of I. 3776
	3:11	An officer of the king of I answered, 3776
	3:12	the king of I and Jehoshaphat and the king 3776
	3:13	Elisha said to the king of I, 3776
	3:13	"No," the king of I answered, 3776
	3:24	when the Moabites came to the camp of I, 3776
	3:27	The fury against I was great; 3776
	5: 2	had taken captive a young girl from I, 824+3776
	5: 4	told him what the girl from I had said. 824+3776
	5: 5	"I will send a letter to the king of I." 3776
	5: 6	The letter that he took to the king of I read: 3776
	5: 7	As soon as the king of I read the letter, 3776
	5: 8	that the king of I had torn his robes, 3776
	5: 8	that there is a prophet in I." 3776
	5:12	better than any of the waters of I? 3776
	5:15	in all the world except in I. 3776
	6: 8	Now the king of Aram was at war with I. 3776
	6: 9	The man of God sent word to the king of I: 3776
	6:10	the king of I checked on the place indicated 3776
	6:11	of us is on the side of the king of I?" 3776
	6:12	"but Elisha, the prophet who is in I, 3776
	6:12	tells the king of I the very words you speak 3776
	6:21	When the king of I saw them, 3776
	6:26	the king of I was passing by on the wall, 3776
	7: 6	the king of I has hired the Hittite 3776
	8:16	of Joram son of Ahab king of I, 3776
	8:18	He walked in the ways of the kings of I, 3776
	8:25	of Joram son of Ahab king of I, 3776
	8:26	a granddaughter of Omri king of I. 3776
	9: 3	I anoint you king over I.' 3776
	9: 6	"This is what the LORD, the God of I, 3776
	9: 6	over the LORD's people I. 3776
	9: 8	from Ahab every last male in I— 3776
	9:12	I anoint you king over I.' " 3776
	9:14	all I had been defending Ramoth Gilead 3776
	9:21	of I and Ahaziah king of Judah rode out, 3776
	10:21	Then he sent word throughout I, 3776
	10:28	So Jehu destroyed Baal worship in I. 3776
	10:29	which he had caused I to commit— 3776
	10:30	on the throne of I to the fourth generation." 3776
	10:31	the God of I, with all his heart. 3776
	10:31	which he had caused I to commit. 3776
	10:32	the LORD began to reduce the size of I. 3776
	10:34	in the book of the annals of the kings of I? 3776
	10:36	over I in Samaria was twenty-eight years. 3776
	13: 1	Jehoahaz son of Jehu became king of I 3776
	13: 2	which he had caused I to commit, 3776
	13: 3	So the LORD's anger burned against I, 3776
	13: 4	the king of Aram was oppressing I. 3776
	13: 5	The LORD provided a deliverer for I, 3776
	13: 6	which he had caused I to commit; 3776
	13: 8	in the book of the annals of the kings of I? 3776
	13:10	Jehoash son of Jehoahaz became king of I 3776
	13:11	which he had caused I to commit; 3776
	13:12	in the book of the annals of the kings of I? 3776
	13:13	in Samaria with the kings of I. 3776
	13:14	Jehoash king of I went down to see him 3776
	13:14	"The chariots and horsemen of I!" 3776

2Ki 13:16	he said to the king of I.	3776
13:22	of Aram oppressed I throughout the reign	3776
14: 1	of Jehoash son of Jehoahaz king of I,	3776
14: 8	king of I, with the challenge:	3776
14: 9	of I replied to Amaziah king of Judah:	3776
14:11	so Jehoash king of I attacked.	3776
14:12	Judah was routed by I,	3776
14:13	Jehoash king of I captured Amaziah king	3776
14:15	in the book of the annals of the kings of I?	3776
14:16	in Samaria with the kings of I.	3776
14:17	of Jehoash son of Jehoahaz king of I.	3776
14:23	of Jehoash king of I became king	3776
14:24	which he had caused I to commit.	3776
14:25	the boundaries of I from Lebo Hamath to	3776
14:25	the word of the LORD, the God of I,	3776
14:26	in I, whether slave or free, was suffering;	3776
14:27	not said he would blot out the name of I	3776
14:28	how he recovered for I both Damascus	3776
14:28	in the book of the annals of the kings of I?	3776
14:29	rested with his fathers, the kings of I.	3776
15: 1	of Jeroboam king of I,	3776
15: 8	of Jeroboam became king of I in Samaria,	3776
15: 9	which he had caused I to commit.	3776
15:11	in the book of the annals of the kings of I.	3776
15:12	on the throne of I to the fourth generation."	3776
15:15	in the book of the annals of the kings of I.	3776
15:17	Menahem son of Gadi became king of I	3776
15:18	which he had caused I to commit.	3776
15:20	Menahem exacted this money from I.	3776
15:21	in the book of the annals of the kings of I?	3776
15:23	of Menahem became king of I in Samaria,	3776
15:24	which he had caused I to commit.	3776
15:26	in the book of the annals of the kings of I.	3776
15:27	of Remaliah became king of I in Samaria,	3776
15:28	which he had caused I to commit.	3776
15:29	In the time of Pekah king of I,	3776
15:31	in the book of the annals of the kings of I?	3776
15:32	of Pekah son of Remaliah king of I,	3776
16: 3	He walked in the ways of the kings of I and	3776
16: 5	of I marched up to fight against Jerusalem	3776
16: 7	of the king of Aram and of the king of I,	3776
17: 1	Hoshea son of Elah became king of I	3776
17: 2	not like the kings of I who preceded him.	3776
17: 8	that the kings of I had introduced.	3776
17:13	The LORD warned I and Judah	3776
17:18	So the LORD was very angry with I	3776
17:19	the practices I had introduced.	3776
17:20	the LORD rejected all the people of I;	3776
17:21	he tore I away from the house of David,	3776
17:21	Jeroboam enticed I away from following	3776
17:23	of I were taken from their homeland	3776
17:34	descendants of Jacob, whom he named I.	3776
18: 1	of Hoshea son of Elah king of I,	3776
18: 5	Hezekiah trusted in the LORD, the God of I.	3776
18: 9	of Hoshea son of Elah king of I,	3776
18:10	the ninth year of Hoshea king of I.	3776
18:11	The king of Assyria deported I to Assyria	3776
19:15	"O LORD, God of I,	3776
19:20	"This is what the LORD, the God of I,	3776
19:22	Against the Holy One of I!	3776
21: 3	as Ahab king of I had done.	3776
21: 7	chosen out of all the tribes of I,	3776
21:12	the LORD, the God of I, says:	3776
22:15	"This is what the LORD, the God of I,	3776
22:18	'This is what the LORD, the God of I,	3776
23:13	the ones Solomon king of I had built	3776
23:15	who had caused I to sin—	3776
23:19	the high places that the kings of I had built	3776
23:22	Not since the days of the judges who led I,	3776
23:22	throughout the days of the kings of I and	3776
23:27	also from my presence as I removed I,	3776
24:13	that Solomon king of I had made for	3776
1Ch 1:34	The sons of Isaac: Esau and I.	3776
2: 1	These were the sons of I:	3776
2: 7	who brought trouble on I by violating	3776
4:10	Jabez cried out to the God of I, "Oh,	3776
5: 1	the firstborn of I (he was the firstborn, but	3776
5: 1	to the sons of Joseph son of I;	3776
5: 3	the sons of Reuben the firstborn of I:	3776
5:17	of Judah and Jeroboam king of I.	3776
5:26	the God of I stirred up the spirit of Pul king	3776
6:38	the son of Levi, the son of I;	3776
6:49	making atonement for I,	3776
7:29	The descendants of Joseph son of I lived	3776
9: 1	All I was listed in the genealogies recorded	3776
9: 1	in the book of the kings of I.	3776
10: 1	Now the Philistines fought against I;	3776
11: 1	All I came together to David at Hebron	3776
11: 2	you were the one who led I	3776
11: 2	'You will shepherd my people I,	3776
11: 3	of I had come to King David at Hebron,	3776
11: 3	and they anointed David king over I,	3776
11:10	they, together with all I,	3776
12:32	the times and knew what I should do—	3776
12:38	to make David king over all I.	3776
12:40	oil, cattle and sheep, for there was joy in I.	3776
13: 2	He then said to the whole assembly of I,	3776
13: 2	throughout the territories of I,	3776
14: 2	established him as king over I and	3776
14: 2	for the sake of his people I.	3776
14: 8	over all I, they went up in full force	3776
15: 3	David assembled all I in Jerusalem to bring	3776
15:12	up the ark of the LORD, the God of I,	3776
15:14	the ark of the LORD, the God of I.	3776
15:25	the elders of I and the commanders of units	3776
15:28	So all I brought up the ark of the covenant	3776
16: 4	and to praise the LORD, the God of I:	3776
1Ch 16:13	O descendants of I his servant,	3776
16:17	to I as an everlasting covenant:	3776
16:36	Praise be to the LORD, the God of I,	3776
16:40	law of the LORD, which he had given I.	3776
17: 5	in a house from the day I brought I up out	3776
17: 7	to be ruler over my people I.	3776
17: 9	a place for my people I and will plant them	3776
17:10	I appointed leaders over my people I.	3776
17:21	And who is like your people I—	3776
17:22	You made your people I your very own	3776
	forever,	3776
17:24	'The LORD Almighty, the God over I,	3776
18:14	David reigned over all I,	3776
19:10	so he selected some of the best troops in I	3776
19:16	that they had been routed by I,	3776
19:17	he gathered all I and crossed the Jordan;	3776
19:18	But they fled before I,	3776
19:19	that they had been defeated by I,	3776
20: 7	When he taunted I,	3776
21: 1	against I and incited David to take a census	3776
21: 1	and incited David to take a census of I.	3776
21: 3	Why should he bring guilt on I?"	3776
21: 4	and went throughout I and then came back	3776
21: 5	In all I there were one million one hundred	
	thousand men who could handle a sword,	3776
21: 7	evil in the sight of God, so he punished I.	3776
21:12	angel of the LORD ravaging every part of I.	3776
21:14	So the LORD sent a plague on I,	3776
21:14	and seventy thousand men of I fell dead.	3776
22: 1	and also the altar of burnt offering for I."	3776
22: 2	to assemble the aliens living in I,	824+3776
22: 6	a house for the LORD, the God of I.	3776
22: 9	and I will grant I peace and quiet	3776
22:10	the throne of his kingdom over I forever.'	3776
22:12	when he puts you in command over I,	3776
22:13	and laws that the LORD gave Moses for I.	3776
22:17	the leaders of I to help his son Solomon.	3776
23: 1	he made his son Solomon king over I.	3776
23: 2	also gathered together all the leaders of I,	3776
23:25	"Since the LORD, the God of I,	3776
24:19	the God of I, had commanded him.	3776
26:29	as officials and judges over I.	3776
26:30	in I west of the Jordan for all the work of	3776
27:16	The officers over the tribes of I:	3776
27:22	These were the officers over the tribes of I.	3776
27:23	to make I as numerous as the stars in	3776
27:24	on I on account of this numbering,	3776
28: 1	The officials of I to assemble at Jerusalem:	3776
28: 4	"Yet the LORD, the God of I,	3776
28: 4	to be king over I forever.	3776
28: 4	to make me king over all I.	3776
28: 5	of the kingdom of the LORD over I.	3776
28: 8	now I charge you in the sight of all I and of	3776
29: 6	the officers of the tribes of I,	3776
29:10	O LORD, God of our father I,	3776
29:18	God of our fathers Abraham, Isaac and I,	3776
29:21	and other sacrifices in abundance for all I.	3776
29:23	He prospered and all I obeyed him.	3776
29:25	in the sight of all I and bestowed	3776
29:25	as no king over I ever had before.	3776
29:26	David son of Jesse was king over all I.	3776
29:27	He ruled over I forty years—	3776
29:30	that surrounded him and I and	3776
2Ch 1: 2	Then Solomon spoke to all I—	3776
1: 2	to the judges and to all the leaders in I,	3776
1:13	And he reigned over I.	3776
2: 4	This is a lasting ordinance for I.	3776
2:12	"Praise be to the LORD, the God of I,	3776
2:17	a census of all the aliens who were in I,	824+3776
5: 2	to Jerusalem the elders of I,	3776
5: 3	of I came together to the king at the time of	3776
5: 4	When all the elders of I had arrived,	3776
5: 6	the entire assembly of I that had gathered	3776
6: 3	whole assembly of I was standing there,	3776
6: 4	"Praise be to the LORD, the God of I,	3776
6: 5	of I to have a temple built for my Name to	3776
6: 5	to be the leader over my people I.	3776
6: 6	I have chosen David to rule my people I.'	3776
6: 7	for the Name of the LORD, the God of I.	3776
6:10	and now I sit on the throne of I,	3776
6:10	for the Name of the LORD, the God of I.	3776
6:11	that he made with the people of I."	3776
6:12	in front of the whole assembly of I	3776
6:13	down before the whole assembly of I	3776
6:14	He said: "O LORD, God of I,	3776
6:16	"Now LORD, God of I,	3776
6:16	a man to sit before me on the throne of I,	3776
6:17	And now, O LORD, God of I,	3776
6:21	and of your people I when they pray	3776
6:24	"When your people I have been defeated	3776
6:25	of your people I and bring them back to	3776
6:27	the sin of your servants, your people I.	3776
6:29	or plea is made by any of your people I—	3776
6:32	not belong to your people I but has come	3776
6:33	as do your own people I,	3776
7: 8	and all I with him—a vast assembly	3776
7:10	and Solomon and for his people I.	3776
7:18	to have a man to rule over I.'	3776
7:20	then I will uproot I from my land,	4392S
8:11	not live in the palace of David king of I,	3776
9: 8	for I and his desire to uphold them forever,	3776
9:30	in Jerusalem over all I forty years.	3776
10: 3	and all I went to Rehoboam and said	3776
10:16	When all I saw that the king refused	3776
10:16	To your tents, O I!	3776
10:19	So I has been in rebellion against the house	3776
11: 1	against I and to regain the kingdom	3776
2Ch 11:13	from all their districts throughout I sided	3776
11:16	from every tribe of I who set their hearts	3776
11:16	seeking the LORD, the God of I,	3776
12: 1	he and all I with him abandoned the law of	3776
12: 6	of I and the king humbled themselves	3776
12:13	the tribes of I in which to put his Name.	3776
13: 4	and said, "Jeroboam and all I, listen to me!	3776
13: 5	know that the LORD, the God of I,	3776
13: 5	of I to David and his descendants forever	3776
13:12	Men of I, do not fight against the LORD,	3776
13:15	and all I before Abijah and Judah.	3776
13:18	of I were subdued on that occasion,	3776
15: 3	For a long time I was without the true God,	3776
15: 4	the LORD, the God of I, and sought him,	3776
15: 9	over to him from I when they saw that	3776
15:13	the God of I, were to be put to death,	3776
15:17	not remove the high places from I,	3776
16: 1	of Asa's reign Baasha king of I went up	3776
16: 3	with Baasha king of I so he will withdraw	3776
16: 4	of his forces against the towns of I.	3776
16:11	in the book of the kings of Judah and I.	3776
17: 1	as king and strengthened himself against I.	3776
17: 4	rather than the practices of I.	3776
18: 3	Ahab king of I asked Jehoshaphat king	3776
18: 4	But Jehoshaphat also said to the king of I,	3776
18: 5	king of I brought together the prophets—	3776
18: 7	The king of I answered Jehoshaphat,	3776
18: 8	So the king of I called one of his officials	3776
18: 9	the king of I and Jehoshaphat king	3776
18:16	"I saw all I scattered on the hills like sheep	3776
18:17	The king of I said to Jehoshaphat,	3776
18:19	of I into attacking Ramoth Gilead	3776
18:25	The king of I then ordered,	3776
18:28	of I and Jehoshaphat king of Judah went up	3776
18:29	The king of I said to Jehoshaphat,	3776
18:29	So the king of I disguised himself and went	3776
18:30	small or great, except the king of I."	3776
18:31	they thought, "This is the king of I."	3776
18:32	that he was not the king of I,	3776
18:33	and hit the king of I between the sections	3776
18:34	and the king of I propped himself up	3776
20: 7	before your people I and give it forever to	3776
20:10	whose territory you would not allow I	3776
20:19	the God of I, with very loud voice.	3776
20:29	LORD had fought against the enemies of I.	3776
20:34	in the book of the kings of I.	3776
20:35	an alliance with Ahaziah king of I,	3776
21: 2	of Jehoshaphat king of I.	3776
21: 4	along with some of the princes of I.	3776
21: 6	He walked in the ways of the kings of I,	3776
21:13	in the ways of the kings of I,	3776
22: 5	with Joram son of Ahab king of I to war	3776
24: 5	the money due annually from all I,	3776
24: 6	of the LORD and by the assembly of I for	3776
24: 9	the servant of God had required of I in	3776
24:16	because of the good he had done in I	3776
25: 6	a hundred thousand fighting men from I for	3776
25: 7	from I must not march with you, for	3776
25: 7	for the LORD is not with I—	3776
25:17	king of I: "Come, meet me face to face."	3776
25:18	of I replied to Amaziah king of Judah:	3776
25:21	So Jehoash king of I attacked.	3776
25:22	Judah was routed by I,	3776
25:23	Jehoash king of I captured Amaziah king	3776
25:25	of Jehoash son of Jehoahaz king of I.	3776
25:26	in the book of the kings of Judah and I?	3776
27: 7	are written in the book of the kings of I	3776
28: 2	He walked in the ways of the kings of I and	3776
28: 5	also given into the hands of the king of I,	3776
28:13	and his fierce anger rests on I."	3776
28:19	because of Ahaz king of I,	3776
28:23	and the downfall of all I.	3776
28:26	in the book of the kings of Judah and I.	3776
28:27	not placed in the tombs of the kings of I.	3776
29: 7	at the sanctuary to the God of I.	3776
29:10	covenant with the LORD, the God of I,	3776
29:24	the altar for a sin offering to atone for all I,	3776
29:24	and the sin offering for all I.	3776
29:27	and the instruments of David king of I.	3776
30: 1	Hezekiah sent word to all I and Judah and	3776
30: 1	Passover to the LORD, the God of I.	3776
30: 5	to send a proclamation throughout I,	3776
30: 5	Passover to the LORD, the God of I,	3776
30: 6	throughout I and Judah with letters from	3776
30: 6	"People of I, return to the LORD,	3776
30: 6	the God of Abraham, Isaac and I,	3776
30:25	and all who had assembled from I,	3776
30:25	the aliens who had come from I	824+3776
30:26	of David king of I there had been nothing	3776
31: 6	of I and Judah who lived in the towns	3776
31: 8	the LORD and blessed his people I.	3776
32:17	the God of I, and saying this against him:	3776
32:32	in the book of the kings of Judah and I.	3776
33: 7	of all the tribes of I,	3776
33:16	to serve the LORD, the God of I.	3776
33:18	the name of the LORD, the God of I,	3776
33:18	are written in the annals of the kings of I.	3776
34: 7	the incense altars throughout I,	824+3776
34: 9	Ephraim and the entire remnant of I and	3776
34:21	the LORD for me and for the remnant in I	3776
34:23	"This is what the LORD, the God of I,	3776
34:26	'This is what the LORD, the God of I,	3776
34:33	and he had all who were present in I serve	3776
35: 3	the Levites, who instructed all I	3776
35: 3	that Solomon son of David king of I built.	3776
35: 3	the LORD your God and his people I.	3776
35: 4	to the directions written by David king of I	3776

2Ch 35:18	in I since the days of the prophet Samuel;	3776
35:18	of the kings of I had ever celebrated such	3776
35:18	and all Judah and I who were there with	3776
35:25	in I and are written in the Laments.	3776
35:27	are written in the book of the kings of I	3776
36: 8	are written in the book of the kings of I	3776
36:13	would not turn to the LORD, the God of I.	3776
Ezr 1: 3	the God of I, the God who is in Jerusalem.	3776
2: 2	The list of the men of the people of I:	3776
2:59	that their families were descended from I:	3776
3: 2	of the LORD to sacrifice burnt offerings	3776
3:10	as prescribed by David king of I.	3776
3:11	his love to I endures forever."	3776
4: 1	a temple for the LORD, the God of I,	3776
4: 3	of the heads of the families of I answered,	3776
4: 3	the LORD, the God of I, as King Cyrus,	3776
5: 1	and Jerusalem in the name of the God of I,	10335
5:11	one that a great king of I built and finished.	10335
6:14	according to the command of the God of I	10335
6:16	Then the people of I—	10335
6:17	as a sin offering for all I,	10335
6:17	one for each of the tribes of I.	10335
6:21	to seek the LORD, the God of I.	3776
6:22	the house of God, the God of I.	3776
7: 6	which the LORD, the God of I, had given.	3776
7:10	and to teaching its decrees and laws in I.	3776
7:11	and decrees of the LORD for I:	3776
7:15	advisers have freely given to the God of I,	10335
7:28	and gathered leading men from I to go up	3776
8:18	the son of I, and Sherebiah's sons	3776
8:25	and all I present there had donated for	3776
8:29	and the Levites and the family heads of I."	3776
8:35	offerings to the God of I:	3776
8:35	twelve bulls for all I, ninety-six rams,	3776
9: 1	"The people of I, including the priests	3776
9: 4	the God of I gathered around me because	3776
9:15	O LORD, God of I, you are righteous!	3776
10: 2	But in spite of this, there is still hope for I.	3776
10: 5	the leading priests and Levites and all I	3776
Ne 1: 6	for your servants, the people of I.	3776
7: 7	The list of the men of I:	3776+6639
7:61	that their families were descended from I:	3776
8: 1	which the LORD had commanded for I.	3776
10:33	for sin offerings to make atonement for I;	3776
10:39	The people of I, including the Levites,	3776
12:47	all I contributed the daily portions for	3776
13: 3	from I all who were of foreign descent.	3776
13:18	up more wrath against I by desecrating	3776
13:26	like these that Solomon king of I sinned?	3776
13:26	and God made him king over all I,	3776
Ps 14: 7	that salvation for I would come out	3776
14: 7	let Jacob rejoice and I be glad!	3776
22: 3	you are the praise of I.	3776
22:23	Revere him, all you descendants of I!	3776
25:22	Redeem I, O God, from all their troubles!	3776
41:13	Praise be to the LORD, the God of I,	3776
50: 7	O my people, and I will speak, O I,	3776
53: 6	salvation for I would come out of Zion!	3776
53: 6	let Jacob rejoice and I be glad!	3776
59: 5	O LORD God Almighty, the God of I,	3776
68: 8	the One of Sinai, before God, the God of I.	3776
68:26	praise the LORD in the assembly of I.	3776
68:34	whose majesty is over I,	3776
68:35	of I gives power and strength to his people.	3776
69: 6	be put to shame because of me, O God of I.	3776
71:22	O Holy One of I.	3776
72:18	Praise be to the LORD God, the God of I,	3776
73: 1	Surely God is good to I,	3776
76: 1	his name is great in I.	3776
78: 5	for Jacob and established the law in I,	3776
78:21	and his wrath rose against I,	3776
78:31	cutting down the young men of I.	3776
78:41	they vexed the Holy One of I.	3776
78:55	he settled the tribes of I in their homes.	3776
78:59	he rejected I completely.	3776
78:71	of I his inheritance.	3776
80: 1	Hear us, O Shepherd of I,	3776
81: 4	this is a decree for I,	3776
81: 8	if you would but listen to me, O I!	3776
81:11	I would not submit to me.	3776
81:13	if I would follow my ways,	3776
83: 4	the name of I be remembered no more."	10335
89:18	our king to the Holy One of I.	3776
98: 3	and his faithfulness to the house of I;	3776
99: 8	you were to I a forgiving God,	2157S
103: 7	his deeds to the people of I:	3776
105:10	to I as an everlasting covenant:	3776
105:23	Then I entered Egypt;	3776
105:37	He brought out I,	4392S
105:38	because dread of I had fallen on them.	4392S
106:48	Praise be to the LORD, the God of I,	3776
114: 1	When I came out of Egypt,	3776
114: 2	Judah became God's sanctuary, I his dominion.	3776
115: 9	O house of I, trust in the LORD—	3776
115:12	He will bless the house of I.	3776
118: 2	Let I say: "His love endures forever."	3776
121: 4	he who watches over I will neither slumber	3776
122: 4	according to the statute given to I.	3776
124: 1	on our side—let I say—	3776
125: 5	Peace be upon I.	3776
128: 6	Peace be upon I.	3776
129: 1	oppressed me from my youth—let I say—	3776
130: 7	O I, put your hope in the LORD,	3776
130: 8	He himself will redeem I	3776
131: 3	O I, put your hope in the LORD both now	3776
135: 4	I to be his treasured possession.	3776

Ps 135:12	an inheritance to his people I.	3776
135:19	O house of I, praise the LORD;	3776
136:11	and brought I out from	3776
136:14	and brought I through the midst of it,	3776
136:22	an inheritance to his servant I;	3776
147: 2	he gathers the exiles of I.	3776
147:19	his laws and decrees to I.	3776
148:14	of I, the people close to his heart.	1201+3776
149: 2	Let I rejoice in their Maker;	3776
Pr 1: 1	of Solomon son of David, king of I:	3776
Ecc 1:12	the Teacher, was king over I in Jerusalem.	3776
SS 3: 7	escorted by sixty warriors, the noblest of I,	3776
Isa 1: 3	but I does not know,	3776
1: 4	the Holy One of I and turned their backs	3776
1:24	the LORD Almighty, the Mighty One of I,	3776
5: 7	be the pride and glory of the survivors in I.	3776
5: 7	of the LORD Almighty is the house of I,	3776
5:19	let the plan of the Holy One of I come,	3776
5:24	and spurned the word of the Holy One of I.	3776
7: 1	of I marched up to fight against Jerusalem,	3776
8:14	but for both houses of I he will be a stone	3776
8:18	We are signs and symbols that I from	3776
9: 8	it will fall on I.	3776
9:12	have devoured I with open mouth.	3776
9:14	from I both head and tail, both palm branch	3776
10:17	The Light of I will become a fire,	3776
10:20	In that day the remnant of I,	3776
10:20	rely on the LORD, the Holy One of I.	3776
10:22	Though your people, O I,	3776
11:12	for the nations and gather the exiles of I;	3776
11:16	as there was for I when they came up	3776
12: 6	for great is the Holy One of I among you."	3776
14: 1	once again he will choose I	3776
14: 2	of I will possess the nations as menservants	3776
17: 6	declares the LORD, the God of I.	3776
17: 7	and turn their eyes to the Holy One of I.	3776
19:24	In that day I will be the third,	3776
19:25	and I my inheritance."	3776
21:10	the LORD Almighty, from the God of I.	3776
21:17	The LORD, the God of I, has spoken.	3776
24:15	exalt the name of the LORD, the God of I,	3776
27: 6	I will bud and blossom and fill all	3776
29:19	the needy will rejoice in the Holy One of I.	3776
29:23	and will stand in awe of the God of I.	3776
30:11	stop confronting us with the Holy One of I!	3776
30:12	this is what the Holy One of I says:	3776
30:15	the Holy One of I, says:	3776
30:29	mountain of the LORD, to the Rock of I.	3776
31: 1	but do not look to the Holy One of I,	3776
37:16	God of I, enthroned between the cherubim,	3776
37:21	"This is what the LORD, the God of I,	3776
37:23	Against the Holy One of I!	3776
40:27	"My way is hidden from the LORD;	3776
41: 8	"But you, O I, my servant, Jacob,	3776
41:14	Do not be afraid, O worm Jacob, O little I,	3776
41:14	your Redeemer, the Holy One of I.	3776
41:16	the LORD and glory in the Holy One of I.	3776
41:17	I, the God of I, will not forsake them.	3776
41:20	that the Holy One of I has created it.	3776
42:24	and I to the plunderers?	3776
43: 1	O Jacob, he who formed you, O I:	3776
43: 3	your God, the Holy One of I, your Savior;	3776
43:14	your Redeemer, the Holy One of I:	3776
43:22	not wearied yourselves for me, O I.	3776
43:28	to destruction and I to scorn.	3776
44: 1	"But now listen, O Jacob, my servant, I,	3776
44: 5	'The LORD's,' and will take the name I.	3776
44:21	O Jacob, for you are my servant, O I.	3776
44:21	O I, I will not forget you.	3776
44:23	he displays his glory in I.	3776
45: 3	the God of I, who summons you by name.	3776
45: 4	sake of Jacob my servant, of I my chosen,	3776
45:11	the Holy One of I, and its Maker:	3776
45:15	O God and Savior of I.	3776
45:17	But I will be saved by the LORD with	3776
45:25	of I will be found righteous and will exult.	3776
46: 3	all you who remain of the house of I,	3776
46:13	my splendor to I.	3776
47: 4	is the Holy One of I.	3776
48: 1	by the name of I and come from the line	3776
48: 1	of the LORD and invoke the God of I—	3776
48: 2	of the holy city and rely on the God of I—	3776
48:12	"Listen to me, O Jacob, I,	3776
48:17	your Redeemer, the Holy One of I:	3776
49: 3	He said to me, "You are my servant, I,	3776
49: 5	and gather to himself, for I am honored in	3776
49: 6	and bring back those of I I have kept.	3776
49: 7	the Redeemer and Holy One of I—	3776
49: 7	the Holy One of I, who has chosen you."	3776
52:12	the God of I will be your rear guard.	3776
54: 5	the Holy One of I is your Redeemer;	3776
55: 5	the LORD your God, the Holy One of I,	3776
56: 8	he who gathers the exiles of I."	3776
57:19	on the lips of the mourners in I.	2257S
60: 9	the LORD your God, the Holy One of I,	3776
60:14	Zion of the Holy One of I.	3776
63: 7	for the house of I,	3776
63:16	not know us or I acknowledge us;	3776
Jer 2: 3	I was holy to the LORD,	3776
2: 4	all you clans of the house of I.	3776
2:14	Is I a servant, a slave by birth?	3776
2:26	so the house of I is disgraced—	3776
2:31	a desert to I or a land of great darkness?	3776
3: 6	"Have you seen what faithless I has done?	3776
3: 8	I gave faithless I her certificate of divorce	3776
3:11	"Faithless I is more righteous than unfaithful Judah.	3776

Jer 3:12	" 'Return, faithless I,' declares the LORD,	3776
3:18	the house of Judah will join the house of I,	3776
3:20	O house of I," declares the LORD.	3776
3:21	weeping and pleading of the people of I,	3776
3:23	in the LORD our God is the salvation of I.	3776
4: 1	"If you will return, O I, return to me,"	3776
5:11	The house of I and the house	3776
5:15	O house of I," declares the LORD,	3776
6: 9	the remnant of I as thoroughly as a vine;	3776
7: 3	the LORD Almighty, the God of I, says:	3776
7:12	because of the wickedness of my people I.	3776
7:21	the LORD Almighty, the God of I, says:	3776
9:15	the LORD Almighty, the God of I, says:	3776
9:26	even the whole house of I is uncircumcised	3776
10: 1	the LORD says to you, O house of I.	3776
10:16	including I, the tribe of his inheritance—	3776
11: 3	the LORD, the God of I, says:	3776
11:10	of I and the house of Judah have broken	3776
11:17	of I and the house of Judah have done evil	3776
12:14	the inheritance I gave my people I,	3776
13:11	of I and the whole house of Judah to me,'	3776
13:12	'This is what the LORD, the God of I,	3776
14: 8	O Hope of I, its Savior in times of distress,	3776
16: 9	the LORD Almighty, the God of I, says:	3776
17:13	O LORD, the hope of I,	3776
18: 6	"O house of I, can I not do with you as	3776
18: 6	so are you in my hand, O house of I.	3776
18:13	A most horrible thing has been done by Virgin I.	3776
19: 3	LORD Almighty, the God of I, says: Listen!	3776
19:15	LORD Almighty, the God of I, says: 'Listen!	3776
21: 4	the LORD the God of I, says	3776
23: 2	the LORD the God of I, says to	3776
23: 6	be saved and I will live in safety.	3776
23: 8	who brought the descendants of I up	1074+3776
23:13	by Baal and led my people I astray.	3776
24: 5	the LORD, the God of I, says:	3776
25:15	This is what the LORD, the God of I,	3776
25:27	the LORD Almighty, the God of I, says:	3776
27: 4	the LORD, the God of I, says:	3776
27:21	the LORD Almighty, the God of I, says	3776
28: 2	the God of I, says:	3776
28:14	the LORD Almighty, the God of I, says:	3776
29: 4	the LORD Almighty, of I, says	3776
29: 8	the LORD Almighty, the God of I, says:	3776
29:21	God of I, says about Ahab son of Kolaiah	3776
29:23	For they have done outrageous things in I;	3776
29:25	the LORD Almighty, the God of I, says:	3776
30: 2	the LORD, the God of I, says:	3776
30: 3	'when I will bring my people I	3776
30: 4	the LORD spoke concerning I and Judah:	3776
30:10	do not be dismayed, O I,'	3776
31: 1	"I will be the God of all the clans of I,	3776
31: 2	I will come to give rest to I."	3776
31: 4	and you will be rebuilt, O Virgin I.	3776
31: 7	save your people, the remnant of I.'	3776
31:10	'He who scattered I will gather them	3776
31:21	Return, O Virgin I, return to your towns.	3776
31:23	the LORD Almighty, the God of I, says:	3776
31:27	the house of I and the house of Judah with	3776
31:31	the house of I and with the house of Judah.	3776
31:33	with the house of I after that time,"	3776
31:36	"will the descendants of I ever cease to be	3776
31:37	of I because of all they have done,"	3776
32:14	the LORD Almighty, the God of I, says:	3776
32:15	the LORD Almighty, the God of I, says:	3776
32:20	both in I and among all mankind,	3776
32:21	You brought your people I out of Egypt	3776
32:30	of I and Judah have done nothing but evil	3776
32:30	indeed, the people of I have done nothing	3776
32:32	of I and Judah have provoked me by all	3776
32:36	but this is what the LORD, the God of I,	3776
33: 4	For this is what the LORD, the God of I,	3776
33: 7	I will bring Judah and I back from captivity	3776
33:14	to the house of I and to the house of Judah.	3776
33:17	a man to sit on the throne of the house of I,	3776
34: 2	the LORD, the God of I, says:	3776
34:13	the LORD, the God of I, says:	3776
35:13	the LORD Almighty, the God of I, says:	3776
35:17	LORD Almighty, the God of I, says: 'Listen!	3776
35:18	the LORD Almighty, the God of I, says:	3776
35:19	the LORD Almighty, the God of I, says:	3776
36: 2	to you concerning I, Judah and all	3776
37: 7	the LORD, the God of I, says:	3776
38:17	the LORD Almighty, the God of I, says:	3776
39:16	the LORD Almighty, the God of I, says:	3776
41: 9	of his defense against Baasha king of I.	3776
42: 9	"This is what the LORD, the God of I,	3776
42:15	the LORD Almighty, the God of I, says:	3776
42:18	the LORD Almighty, the God of I, says:	3776
43:10	the LORD Almighty, the God of I, says:	3776
44: 2	the LORD Almighty, the God of I, says:	3776
44: 7	the LORD Almighty, the God of I, says:	3776
44:11	the LORD Almighty, the God of I, says:	3776
44:25	the LORD Almighty, the God of I, says:	3776
45: 2	the LORD, the God of I, says to you, Baruch:	3776
46:25	The LORD Almighty, the God of I, says:	3776
46:27	do not be dismayed, O I.	3776
48: 1	the LORD Almighty, the God of I, says:	3776
48:13	house of I was ashamed when they trusted	3776
48:27	Was not I the object of your ridicule?	3776
49: 1	"Has I no sons?	3776
49: 2	I will drive out those who drove her out,"	3776
50: 4	"the people of I and the people	3776
50:17	"I is a scattered flock	3776
50:18	the LORD Almighty, the God of I, says:	3776
50:19	But I will bring I back to his own pasture	3776

Jer	50:29	the LORD, the Holy One of I.	3776
	50:33	"The people of I are oppressed,	3776
	51: 5	For I and Judah have not been forsaken	3776
	51: 5	of guilt before the Holy One of I.	3776
	51:33	the LORD Almighty, the God of I, says:	3776
La	2: 1	the splendor of I from heaven to earth;	3776
	2: 3	fierce anger he has cut off every horn of I.	3776
	2: 5	he has swallowed up I.	3776
Eze	3: 1	then go and speak to the house of I."	3776
	3: 4	the house of I and speak my words to them.	3776
	3: 5	but to the house of I—	3776
	3: 7	the house of I is not willing to listen to you	3776
	3: 7	whole house of I is hardened and obstinate.	3776
	3:17	a watchman for the house of I.	3776
	4: 3	This will be a sign to the house of I.	3776
	4: 4	the sin of the house of I upon yourself.	3776
	4: 5	the sin of the house of I.	3776
	4:13	of I will eat defiled food among the nations	3776
	5: 4	from there to the whole house of I.	3776
	6: 2	set your face against the mountains of I;	3776
	6: 3	'O mountains of I,	3776
	6:11	and detestable practices of the house of I,	3776
	7: 2	the Sovereign LORD says to the land of I:	3776
	8: 4	before me was the glory of the God of I,	3776
	8: 6	the house of I is doing here,	3776
	8:10	and all the idols of the house of I.	3776
	8:11	elders of the house of I,	3776
	8:12	of the house of I are doing in the darkness,	3776
	9: 3	of I went up from above the cherubim,	3776
	9: 8	the entire remnant of I in this outpouring	3776
	9: 9	of I and Judah is exceedingly great;	3776
	10:19	the glory of the God of I was above them.	3776
	10:20	the God of I by the Kebar River,	3776
	11: 5	That is what you are saying, O house of I,	3776
	11:10	on you at the borders of I.	3776
	11:11	on you at the borders of I.	3776
	11:13	the remnant of I?"	3776
	11:15	and the whole house of I—	3776
	11:17	the land of I again.'	3776
	11:22	the glory of the God of I was above them.	3776
	12: 6	I have made you a sign to the house of I."	3776
	12: 9	did not that rebellious house of I ask you,	3776
	12:10	and the whole house of I who are there.'	3776
	12:19	in Jerusalem and in the land of I:	3776
	12:22	proverb you have in the land of I,	3776
	12:23	and they will no longer quote it in I.'	3776
	12:24	among the people of I.	3776
	12:27	the house of I is saying,	3776
	13: 2	the prophets of I who are now prophesying.	3776
	13: 4	O I, are like jackals among ruins.	3776
	13: 5	of I so that it will stand firm in the battle on	3776
	13: 9	or be listed in the records of the house of I,	3776
	13: 9	nor will they enter the land of I.	3776
	13:16	those prophets of I who prophesied	3776
	14: 1	Some of the elders of I came to me and sat	3776
	14: 5	to recapture the hearts of the people of I,	3776
	14: 6	"Therefore say to the house of I,	3776
	14: 7	or any alien living in I separates himself	3776
	14: 9	and destroy him from among my people I.	3776
	14:11	people of I will no longer stray from me,	3776
	17: 2	set forth an allegory and tell the house of I.	3776
	17:23	On the mountain heights of I I will plant it;	3776
	18: 2	by quoting this proverb about the land of I:	3776
	18: 3	you will no longer quote this proverb in I.	3776
	18: 6	or look to the idols of the house of I.	3776
	18:15	or look to the idols of the house of I.	3776
	18:25	Hear, O house of I: Is my way unjust?	3776
	18:29	Yet the house of I says,	3776
	18:29	Are my ways unjust, O house of I?	3776
	18:30	"Therefore, O house of I, I will judge you,	3776
	18:31	Why will you die, O house of I?	3776
	19: 1	up a lament concerning the princes of I	3776
	19: 9	on the mountains of I.	3776
	20: 1	some of the elders of I came to inquire of	3776
	20: 3	speak to the elders of I and say to them,	3776
	20: 5	On the day I chose I,	3776
	20:13	" 'Yet the people of I rebelled against me	3776
	20:27	speak to the people of I and say to them,	3776
	20:30	"Therefore say to the house of I:	3776
	20:31	let you inquire of me, O house of I?	3776
	20:38	yet they will not enter the land of I.	3776
	20:39	" 'As for you, O house of I,	3776
	20:40	my holy mountain, the high mountain of I,	3776
	20:40	the entire house of I will serve me,	3776
	20:42	when I bring you into the land of I,	3776
	20:44	your corrupt practices, O house of I,	3776
	21: 2	Prophesy against the land of I	3776
	21:12	it is against all the princes of I.	3776
	21:25	" 'O profane and wicked prince of I,	3776
	22: 6	" 'See how each of the princes of I who are	3776
	22:18	the house of I has become dross to me;	3776
	24:21	Say to the house of I, 'This is what	3776
	25: 3	over the land of I when it was laid waste	3776
	25: 6	of your heart against the land of I,	3776
	25:14	the hand of my people I, and they will deal	3776
	27:17	" 'Judah and I traded with you;	824+3776
	28:24	the people of I have malicious neighbors	3776
	28:25	When I gather the people of I from	3776
	29: 6	a staff of reed for the house of I.	3776
	29:16	of confidence for the people of I but will be	3776
	29:21	a horn grow for the house of I,	3776
	33: 7	a watchman for the house of I;	3776
	33:10	"Son of man, say to the house of I,	3776
	33:11	Why will you die, O house of I?"	3776
	33:20	Yet, O house of I, you say,	3776
	33:24	in those ruins in the land of I are saying,	3776
	33:28	the mountains of I will become desolate so	3776

Eze	34: 2	prophesy against the shepherds of I;	3776
	34: 2	to the shepherds of I who only take care	3776
	34:13	I will pasture them on the mountains of I,	3776
	34:14	and the mountain heights of I will	3776
	34:14	in a rich pasture on the mountains of I.	3776
	34:30	am with them and that they, the house of I,	3776
	35:12	against the mountains of I,	3776
	35:15	of the house of I became desolate,	3776
	36: 1	prophesy to the mountains of I and say,	3776
	36: 1	'O mountains of I, hear the word of	3776
	36: 4	O mountains of I, hear the word of	3776
	36: 6	of I and say to the mountains and hills, to	3776
	36: 8	" 'But you, O mountains of I,	3776
	36: 8	and fruit for my people I.	3776
	36:10	even the whole house of I.	3776
	36:12	I will cause people, my people I,	3776
	36:17	people of I were living in their own land,	3776
	36:21	the house of I profaned among the nations	3776
	36:22	"Therefore say to the house of I,	3776
	36:22	It is not for your sake, O house of I,	3776
	36:32	disgraced for your conduct, O house of I!	3776
	36:37	to the plea of the house of I and do this	3776
	37:11	these bones are the whole house of I.	3776
	37:12	I will bring you back to the land of I.	3776
	37:16	and all the house of I associated with him.'	3776
	37:22	on the mountains of I.	3776
	37:28	that I the LORD make I holy,	3776
	38: 8	from many nations to the mountains of I,	3776
	38:14	when my people I are living in safety,	3776
	38:16	against my people I like a cloud that covers	3776
	38:17	by my servants the prophets of I?	3776
	38:18	When Gog attacks the land of I,	3776
	38:19	be a great earthquake in the land of I.	3776
	39: 2	and send you against the mountains of I.	3776
	39: 4	On the mountains of I you will fall,	3776
	39: 7	my holy name among my people I.	3776
	39: 7	that I the LORD am the Holy One in I.	3776
	39: 9	of I will go out and use the weapons	3776
	39:11	that day I will give Gog a burial place in I,	3776
	39:12	the house of I will be burying them in order	3776
	39:17	the great sacrifice on the mountains of I.	3776
	39:22	that day forward the house of I will know	3776
	39:23	the people of I went into exile for their sin,	3776
	39:25	have compassion on all the people of I,	3776
	39:29	I will pour out my Spirit on the house of I,	3776
	40: 2	of I and set me on a very high mountain,	3776
	40: 4	Tell the house of I everything you see."	3776
	43: 2	and I saw the glory of the God of I coming	3776
	43: 7	of I will never again defile my holy name—	3776
	43:10	describe the temple to the people of I,	3776
	44: 2	the God of I, has entered through it.	3776
	44: 6	Say to the rebellious house of I,	3776
	44: 6	of your detestable practices, O house of I!	3776
	44:10	when I went astray and who wandered	3776
	44:12	of their idols and made the house of I fall	3776
	44:28	I am to give them no possession in I;	3776
	44:29	In I devoted to the LORD will belong	3776
	45: 6	it will belong to the whole house of I.	3776
	45: 8	This land will be his possession in I.	3776
	45: 8	the house of I to possess the land according	3776
	45: 9	You have gone far enough, O princes of I!	3776
	45:15	from the well-watered pastures of I.	3776
	45:16	for the use of the prince in I.	3776
	45:17	at all the appointed feasts of the house of I.	3776
	45:17	to make atonement for the house of I.	3776
	47:13	an inheritance among the twelve tribes of I,	3776
	47:18	between Gilead and the land of I,	3776
	47:21	according to the tribes of I.	3776
	47:22	an inheritance among the tribes of I.	3776
	48:19	from all the tribes of I.	3776
	48:29	to allot as an inheritance to the tribes of I,	3776
	48:31	the city will be named after the tribes of I.	3776
Da	9: 7	of Judah and people of Jerusalem and all I,	3776
	9:11	All I has transgressed your law	3776
	9:20	of my people I and making my request to	3776
Hos	1: 1	of Jeroboam son of Jehoash king of I:	3776
	1: 4	I will put an end to the kingdom of I.	1074+3776
	1: 6	no longer show love to the house of I,	3776
	1:11	and the people of I will be reunited,	3776
	4:15	"Though you commit adultery, O I,	3776
	5: 3	I is not hidden from me.	3776
	5: 3	to prostitution; I is corrupt.	3776
	5: 9	the tribes of I I proclaim what is certain.	3776
	6:10	a horrible thing in the house of I.	3776
	6:10	to prostitution and I is defiled.	3776
	7: 1	whenever I would heal I,	3776
	8: 2	I cries out to me, 'O our God,	3776
	8: 3	But I has rejected what is good;	3776
	8: 6	They are from I!	3776
	8: 8	I is swallowed up;	3776
	8:14	I has forgotten his Maker and built palaces;	3776
	9: 1	Do not rejoice, O I;	3776
	9: 7	Let I know this. Because your sins are so	3776
	9:10	"When I found I, it was like finding grapes	3776
	10: 1	I was a spreading vine;	3776
	10: 6	I will be ashamed of its wooden idols.	3776
	10: 8	it is the sin of I.	3776
	10: 9	the days of Gibeah, you have sinned, O I,	3776
	10:15	the king of I will be completely destroyed.	3776
	11: 1	"When I was a child, I loved him,	3776
	11: 2	But the more I called I,	2157S
	11: 8	How can I hand you over, I?	3776
	11:12	the house of I with deceit.	3776
	12:12	I served to get a wife,	3776
	12:13	The LORD used a prophet to bring I up	3776
	13: 1	he was exalted in I.	3776
	13: 9	"You are destroyed, O I,	3776

Hos	14: 1	Return, O I, to the LORD your God.	3776
	14: 5	I will be like the dew to I;	3776
Joel	2:27	Then you will know that I am in I,	3776
	3: 2	my people I, for they scattered my people	3776
	3:16	a stronghold for the people of I.	3776
Am	1: 1	what he saw concerning I two years before	3776
	1: 1	of Jehoash was king of I.	3776
	2: 6	"For three sins of I, even for four,	3776
	2:11	Is this not true, people of I?"	3776
	3: 1	O people of I—against the whole family	3776
	3:14	"On the day I punish I for her sins,	3776
	4:12	"Therefore this is what I will do to you, I,	3776
	4:12	prepare to meet your God, O I."	3776
	5: 1	Hear this word, O house of I,	3776
	5: 2	"Fallen is Virgin I, never to rise again,	3776
	5: 3	a thousand strong for I will have only	1074+3776
	5: 4	the LORD says to the house of I:	3776
	5:25	O house of I?	3776
	6: 1	to whom the people of I come!	3776
	6:14	O house of I,	3776
	7: 8	a plumb line among my people I;	3776
	7: 9	be destroyed and the sanctuaries of I will	3776
	7:10	a message to Jeroboam king of I:	3776
	7:10	against you in the very heart of I.	1074+3776
	7:11	and I will surely go into exile,	3776
	7:15	'Go, prophesy to my people I.'	3776
	7:16	You say, " 'Do not prophesy against I,	3776
	7:17	And I will certainly go into exile,	3776
	8: 2	"The time is ripe for my people I;	3776
	9: 7	"Did I not bring I up from Egypt,	3776
	9: 9	and I will shake the house of I among all	3776
	9:14	I will bring back my exiled people I;	3776
	9:15	I will plant I in their own land,	4392S
Mic	1: 5	because of the sins of the house of I.	3776
	1:13	the transgressions of I were found in you.	3776
	1:14	will prove deceptive to the kings of I.	3776
	1:15	the glory of I will come to Adullam.	3776
	2:12	surely bring together the remnant of I.	3776
	3: 1	you rulers of the house of I.	3776
	3: 8	to Jacob his transgression, to I his sin.	3776
	3: 9	you rulers of the house of I,	3776
	5: 2	for me one who will be ruler over I,	3776
	5: 3	Therefore I will be abandoned until	4392S
	6: 2	he is lodging a charge against I.	3776
Na	2: 2	the splendor of Jacob like the splendor of I,	3776
Zep	2: 9	the God of I, "surely Moab will become	3776
	3:13	The remnant of I will do no wrong;	3776
	3:14	shout aloud, O I!	3776
	3:15	The LORD, the King of I, is with you;	3776
Zec	1:19	that scattered Judah, I and Jerusalem."	3776
	8:13	O Judah and I, so will I save you,	1074+3776
	9: 1	and all the tribes of I are on the LORD—	3776
	11:14	the brotherhood between Judah and I.	3776
	12: 1	the word of the LORD concerning I.	3776
Mal	1: 1	word of the LORD to I through Malachi.	3776
	1: 5	even beyond the borders of I!"	3776
	2:11	A detestable thing has been committed in I	3776
	2:16	"I hate divorce," says the LORD God of I,	3776
	4: 4	and laws I gave him at Horeb for all I.	3776
Mt	2: 6	be the shepherd of my people I.' "	2702
	2:20	and his mother and go to the land of I,	2702
	2:21	and his mother and went to the land of I.	2702
	8:10	not found anyone in I with such great faith.	2702
	9:33	"Nothing like this has ever been seen in I."	2702
	10: 6	Go rather to the lost sheep of I	2702+3875
	10:23	not finish going through the cities of I	2702
	15:24	I was sent only to the lost sheep of I.	2702+3875
	15:31	And they praised the God of I.	2702
	19:28	judging the twelve tribes of I.	2702
	27: 9	price set on him by the people of I,	2702+5626
	27:42	He's the King of I!	2702
Mk	12:29	'Hear, O I, the Lord our God,	2702
	15:32	Let this Christ, this King of I,	2702
Lk	1:16	Many of the people of I will he bring back	2702
	1:54	He has helped his servant I,	2702
	1:68	"Praise be to the Lord, the God of I,	2702
	1:80	in the desert until he appeared publicly to I.	2702
	2:25	He was waiting for the consolation of I,	2702
	2:32	the Gentiles and for glory to your people I."	2702
	2:34	to cause the falling and rising of many in I,	2702
	4:25	that there were many widows in I	2702
	4:27	And there were many in I with leprosy in	2702
	7: 9	I have not found such great faith even in I."	2702
	22:30	judging the twelve tribes of I.	2702
	24:21	the one who was going to redeem I.	2702
Jn	1:31	that he might be revealed to I."	2702
	1:49	you are the King of I."	2702
	12:13	"Blessed is the King of I!"	2702
Ac	1: 6	to restore the kingdom to I?"	2702
	2:22	"Men of I, listen to this:	2703
	2:36	"Therefore let all I be assured of this:	2702+3875
	3:12	"Men of I, why does this surprise you?	2703
	4:10	you and all the people of I:	2702
	4:27	the Gentiles and the people of I in this city	2702
	5:21	the full assembly of the elders of I—	2702+5626
	5:31	and forgiveness of sins to I.	2702
	5:35	Then he addressed them: "Men of I,	2703
	7:42	in the desert, O house of I?	2702
	9:15	and their kings and before the people of I.	2702
	10:36	the message God sent to the people of I,	2702
	13:16	"Men of I and you Gentiles who worship God,	2703
	13:17	God of the people of I chose our fathers;	2703
	13:23	God has brought to I the Savior Jesus,	2702
	13:24	and baptism to all the people of I.	2702
	21:28	"Men of I, help us!	2703
	28:20	because of the hope of I that I am bound	2702

Ro	9: 4	the people of I. Theirs is the adoption as	2703
	9: 6	not all who are descended from I are Israel.	2702
	9: 6	not all who are descended from Israel are I.	2702
	9:27	Isaiah cries out concerning I:	2702
	9:31	but I, who pursued a law of righteousness	2702
	10:19	Again I ask: Did I not understand?	2702
	10:21	But concerning I he says,	2702
	11: 2	how he appealed to God against I:	2702
	11: 7	What I sought so earnestly it did not obtain,	2702
	11:11	come to the Gentiles to make I envious.	899S
	11:25	I has experienced a hardening in part until	2702
	11:26	And so all I will be saved, as it is written:	2702
1Co	10:18	Consider the people of I:	2702
Gal	6:16	even to the I of God.	2702
Eph	2:12	in I and foreigners to the covenants of	2702
	3: 6	the Gentiles are heirs together with I,	NIG
Php	3: 5	of the people of I, of the tribe of	2702
Heb	8: 8	the house of I and with the house of Judah.	2702
	8:10	with the house of I after that time,	2702
	11:28	not touch the firstborn of I.	NIG
Rev	7: 4	144,000 from all the tribes of I.	2702+5626
	21:12	the names of the twelve tribes of I.	2702+5626

ISRAEL'S (44) [ISRAEL]

Ge	42: 5	So I sons were among those who went	3776
	46: 5	and I sons took their father Jacob	3776
	48:10	I eyes were failing because of old age,	3776
	48:12	Then Joseph removed them from I knees	2257S
	48:13	toward I left hand and Manasseh on his left	3776
	48:13	on his left toward I right hand,	3776
Ex	14:19	who had been traveling in front of I army,	3776
	18: 8	to Pharaoh and the Egyptians for I sake and	3776
Nu	1:45	able to serve in I army were counted	928+3776
	11:16	of I elders who are known to you as leaders	3776
	21: 3	The LORD listened to I plea and gave	3776
	25: 5	So Moses said to I judges,	3776
Jos	10:30	also gave that city and its king into I hand.	3776
Jdg	3:10	so that he became I judge and went to war.	3776
	5: 9	My heart is with I princes,	3776
	10:16	And he could bear I misery no longer.	3776
	11:21	gave Sihon and all his men into I hands,	3776
	20: 6	to each region of I inheritance,	3776
	20:34	Then ten thousand of I finest men made	3776
1Sa	6: 5	and pay honor to I god.	3776
	7: 9	He cried out to the LORD on I behalf,	3776
	14:37	Will you give them into I hand?"	3776
2Sa	20:23	Joab was over I entire army;	3776
	23: 1	by the God of Jacob, I singer of songs:	3776
	23:11	I troops fled from them.	2021S
1Ki	2: 5	to the two commanders of I armies,	3776
	2:32	Abner son of Ner, commander of I army,	3776
	11:25	Rezon was I adversary as long	3776+4200
2Ki	6:23	from Aram stopped raiding I territory.	3776
1Ch	17:24	the God over Israel, is I God!'	3776+4200
2Ch	13:17	casualties among I able men.	3776
Ezr	10:10	married foreign women, adding to I guilt.	3776
Isa	43:15	I am the LORD, your Holy One, I Creator,	3776
	44: 6	I King and Redeemer, the LORD Almighty	3776
	56:10	I watchmen are blind,	2257S
Jer	3: 9	I immorality mattered so little to her,	2023S
	31: 9	because I am I father,	3776+4200
	50:20	"search will be made for I guilt,	3776
	51:49	"Babylon must fall because of I slain,	3776
Hos	1: 5	In that day I will break I bow in the Valley	3776
	5: 5	I arrogance testifies against them;	3776
	5: 5	I arrogance testifies against him,	3776
Mic	5: 1	They will strike I ruler on the cheek with	3776
Jn	3:10	"You are I teacher," said Jesus,	2702

ISRAELITE (96) [ISRAEL]

Ge	36:31	in Edom before any I king reigned:	1201+3776
Ex	5:14	The I foremen appointed	1201+3776
	5:15	I foremen went and appealed to Pharaoh:	1201+3776
	5:19	The I foremen realized they were in trouble	1201+3776
	12:40	the I people lived in Egypt was 430 years.	1201+3776
	16: 1	whole I community set out from Elim	1201+3776
	16: 9	"Say to the entire I community,	1201+3776
	16:10	to the whole I community,	1201+3776
	17: 1	The whole I community set out from	1201+3776
	24: 5	Then he sent young I men,	1201+3776
	35: 1	Moses assembled the whole I community	1201+3776
	35: 4	Moses said to the whole I community,	1201+3776
	35:20	Then the whole I community withdrew	1201+3776
	35:29	All the I men and women who were	1201+3776
Lev	4:13	the whole I community sins unintentionally	3776
	16: 5	From the I community he is	1201+3776
	17: 3	I who sacrifices an ox,	408+1074+3776+4946
	17: 8	Any I or any alien living	408+1074+3776+4946
	17:10	Any I or any alien living	408+1074+3776+4946
	17:13	Any I or any alien living	408+1201+3776+4946
	20: 2	Any I or any alien living	408+1201+3776+4946
	22:18	an I or an alien living in	408+1074+3776+4946
	24:10	Now the son of an I mother and	3778
	24:10	the camp between him and an I.	408+2021+3778
	24:11	son of the I woman blasphemed the Name	3778
Nu	1: 2	"Take a census of the whole I community	1201+3776
	1:53	that wrath will not fall on the I community.	1201+3776
	3:12	first male offspring of every I woman.	1201+3776
	3:40	firstborn I males who are a month old	1201+3776

Nu	7:84	the I leaders for the dedication of the altar	3776
	8: 9	and assemble the whole I community.	1201+3776
	8:16	first male offspring from every I woman.	1201+3776
	8:20	Aaron and the whole I community did	1201+3776
	10:28	for the I divisions as they set out.	1201+3776
	13:26	the whole I community at Kadesh in	1201+3776
	14: 5	the whole I assembly gathered there.	1201+3776
	14: 7	and said to the entire I assembly,	1201+3776
	15:25	for the whole I community,	1201+3776
	15:26	The whole I community and	1201+3776
	15:29	he is a native-born I or an alien.	928+1201+3776
	16: 2	With them were 250 I men,	1201+3776
	16: 9	of the I community and brought you	3776
	16:41	the whole I community grumbled	1201+3776
	19: 9	the I community for use in the water	1201+3776
	20: 1	the whole I community arrived at	1201+3776
	20:22	The whole I community set out	1201+3776
	25: 6	an I man brought to his family	1201+3776+4946
	25: 8	and followed the I into the tent.	408+3776
	25: 8	the I and into the woman's body.	408+3776
	25:14	The name of the I who was killed with	408+3776
	26: 2	"Take a census of the whole I community	1201+3776
	27:20	the whole I community will obey him.	1201+3776
	31:12	priest and the I assembly at their camp	1201+3776
	32:18	until every I has received his inheritance.	1201+3776
	32:28	and to the family heads of the I tribes.	1201+3776
	36: 1	the heads of the I families.	1201+3776
	36: 3	from other I tribes;	1201+3776
	36: 7	for every I shall keep	1201+3776
	36: 8	in any I tribe must marry someone	1201+3776
	36: 8	every I will possess the inheritance	1201+3776
	36: 9	for each I tribe is to keep	1201+3776
Dt	15: 2	the loan he has made to his fellow I.	8276
	15: 2	not require payment from his fellow I	8276
	17:15	one who is not a brother I.	3870S
	22:19	this man has given an I virgin a bad name.	3776
	23:17	No I man or woman is to become	3776+4946
	23:20	but not a brother I,	278
	24:14	whether he is a brother I or an alien living	278
Jos	11:22	No Anakites were left in I territory;	1201+3776
	18: 2	but there were still seven I tribes who	1201+3776
	22:11	Geliloth near the Jordan on the I side,	1201+3776
	22:14	of a family division among the I clans.	3776
Jdg	7:14	sword of Gideon son of Joash, the I.	408+3776
	11:39	From this comes the I custom	928+3776
	20:33	and the I ambush charged out of its place	3776
1Sa	7:13	and did not invade I territory again.	3776
	31: 7	the Jordan saw that the I army had fled and	3776
2Sa	1: 3	"I have escaped from the I camp."	3776
	11: 1	with the king's men and the whole I army.	3776
	17:25	an I who had married Abigail,	3778
1Ki	8: 1	tribes and the chiefs of the I families,	1201+3776
2Ki	13:25	and so he recovered the I towns.	3776
1Ch	1:43	before any I king reigned:	1201+3776+4200
	16: 3	a cake of raisins to each I man and	408+3776
2Ch	5: 2	tribes and the chiefs of the I families,	1201+3776
	19: 8	priests and heads of I families to administer	3776
	23: 2	the heads of I families from all the towns.	3776
	25: 9	for these I troops?"	3776
Ne	9: 2	of I descent had separated themselves	3776
Eze	14: 4	When any I sets up idols in his heart	408+1074+3776+4946
	14: 7	When any I or any alien	408+1074+3776+4946
	37:19	and of the I tribes associated with him,	3776
	44:22	may marry only virgins of I descent	1074+3776
Ob	1:20	of I exiles who are in Canaan	1201+3776
Jn	1:47	he said of him, "Here is a true I,	2703
Ro	11: 1	I am an I myself, a descendant of Abraham,	2703

ISRAELITES (611) [ISRAEL]

Ge	32:32	the I do not eat the tendon attached to	1201+3776
	47:27	I settled in Egypt in the region of Goshen.	3776
Ex	1: 7	I were fruitful and multiplied greatly	1201+3776
	1: 9	I have become much too numerous for us.	1201+3776+6639
	1:12	so the Egyptians came to dread the I	1201+3776
	2:23	The I groaned in their slavery	1201+3776
	2:25	So God looked on the I and was concerned about them.	1201+3776
	3: 9	now the cry of the I has reached me,	1201+3776
	3:10	Pharaoh to bring my people the I out	1201+3776
	3:11	Pharaoh and bring the I out of Egypt?	1201+3776
	3:13	Suppose I go to the I and say to them,	1201+3776
	3:14	This is what you are to say to the I:	1201+3776
	3:15	God also said to Moses, "Say to the I,	1201+3776
	4:29	the elders of the I,	1201+3776
	6: 5	I have heard the groaning of the I,	1201+3776
	6: 6	"Therefore, say to the I:	1201+3776
	6: 9	Moses reported this to the I,	1201+3776
	6:11	to let the I go out of his country."	1201+3776
	6:12	"If the I will not listen to me,	1201+3776
	6:13	to Moses and Aaron about the I	1201+3776
	6:13	he commanded them to bring the I out	1201+3776
	6:26	the I out of Egypt by their divisions."	1201+3776
	6:27	about bringing the I out of Egypt.	1201+3776
	7: 2	to tell Pharaoh to let the I go out	1201+3776
	7: 4	my people the I,	1201+3776
	7: 5	against Egypt and bring the I out of it.	1201+3776
	9: 4	no animal belonging to the I will die.	1201+3776
	9: 6	not one animal belonging to the I had died.	1201+3776
	9: 7	even one of the animals of the I had died.	3776
	9:26	Goshen, where the I were.	1201+3776
	9:35	and he would not let the I go,	1201+3776

Ex	10:20	and he would not let the I go.	1201+3776
	10:23	Yet all the I had light in the places	1201+3776
	11: 7	the I not a dog will bark at any man	1201+3776
	11:10	not let the I go out of his country.	1201+3776
	12:27	the I in Egypt and spared our homes	1201+3776
	12:28	The I did just what the LORD	1201+3776
	12:31	Leave my people, you and the I!	1201+3776
	12:35	The I did as Moses instructed and	1201+3776
	12:37	The I journeyed from Rameses to	1201+3776
	12:42	I are to keep vigil to honor the LORD	1201+3776
	12:50	All the I did just what	1201+3776
	12:51	very day the LORD brought the I out	1201+3776
	13: 2	first offspring of every womb among the I belongs to me,	1201+3776
	13:18	The I went up out of Egypt armed	1201+3776
	14: 2	"Tell the I to turn back and encamp	1201+3776
	14: 3	'The I are wandering around the land	1201+3776
	14: 4	So the I did this.	NIH
	14: 5	the I go and have lost their services!"	3776
	14: 8	so that he pursued the I,	1201+3776
	14: 9	pursued the I and overtook them	2157S
	14:10	Pharaoh approached, the I looked up,	1201+3776
	14:15	Tell the I to move on.	1201+3776
	14:16	the I can go through the sea on dry ground.	1201+3776
	14:22	the I went through the sea on dry ground,	1201+3776
	14:25	"Let's get away from the I!	3776
	14:28	of Pharaoh that had followed the I into	2157S
	14:29	the I went through the sea on dry ground,	1201+3776
	14:31	And when the I saw the great power	3776
	15: 1	Then Moses and the I sang this song to	1201+3776
	15:19	the I walked through the sea on dry ground.	1201+3776
	16: 3	The I said to them,	1201+3776
	16: 6	So Moses and Aaron said to all the I,	1201+3776
	16:12	"I have heard the grumbling of the I.	1201+3776
	16:15	When the I saw it, they said to each	1201+3776
	16:17	The I did as they were told;	1201+3776
	16:35	The I ate manna forty years,	1201+3776
	17: 7	and Meribah because the I quarreled	1201+3776
	17: 8	The Amalekites came and attacked the I	3776
	17:11	the I were winning,	3776
	19: 1	the third month after the I had fled	1201+3776
	19: 6	the words you are to speak to the I."	1201+3776
	20:22	the LORD said to Moses, "Tell the I	1201+3776
	24:11	against these leaders of the I;	1201+3776
	24:17	the I the glory of the LORD looked like	1201+3776
	25: 2	"Tell the I to bring me an offering.	1201+3776
	25:22	give you all my commands for the I.	1201+3776
	27:20	the I to bring you clear oil of pressed olives	1201+3776
	27:21	the I for the generations to come.	1201+3776
	28: 1	to you from among the I,	1201+3776
	28:30	decisions for the I over his heart	1201+3776
	28:38	in the sacred gifts the I consecrate,	1201+3776
	29:28	the regular share from the I for Aaron	1201+3776
	29:28	It is the contribution the I are to make	1201+3776
	29:43	there also I will meet with the I,	1201+3776
	29:45	I will dwell among the I and be their God.	1201+3776
	30:12	take a census of the I to count them,	1201+3776
	30:16	the atonement money from the I and	1201+3776
	30:16	a memorial for the I before the LORD,	1201+3776
	30:31	Say to the I,	1201+3776
	31:13	"Say to the I,	1201+3776
	31:16	The I are to observe the Sabbath,	1201+3776
	31:17	a sign between me and the I forever,	1201+3776
	32:20	on the water and made the I drink it.	1201+3776
	33: 5	LORD had said to Moses, "Tell the I,	1201+3776
	33: 6	So the I stripped off their ornaments	1201+3776
	34:30	When Aaron and all the I saw Moses,	1201+3776
	34:32	Afterward all the I came near him,	1201+3776
	34:34	the I what he had been commanded,	1201+3776
	35:30	Then Moses said to the I, "See,	1201+3776
	36: 3	offerings the I had brought to	1201+3776
	39:32	The I did everything just as	1201+3776
	39:42	The I had done all the work just as	1201+3776
	40:36	In all the travels of the I,	1201+3776
Lev	1: 2	"Speak to the I and say to them:	1201+3776
	4: 2	"Say to the I:	1201+3776
	7:23	"Say to the I:	1201+3776
	7:29	"Say to the I:	1201+3776
	7:34	From the fellowship offerings of the I	1201+3776
	7:34	as their regular share from the I.' "	1201+3776
	7:36	the I give this to them as their regular share	1201+3776
	7:38	I to bring their offerings to the LORD,	1201+3776
	9: 3	Then say to the I:	1201+3776
	10:11	you must teach the I all the decrees	1201+3776
	11: 2	"Say to the I,	1201+3776
	12: 2	"Say to the I,	1201+3776
	15: 2	"Speak to the I and say to them:	1201+3776
	15:31	" 'You must keep the I separate	1201+3776
	16:16	the uncleanness and rebellion of the I,	1201+3776
	16:19	from the uncleanness of the I.	1201+3776
	16:21	the wickedness and rebellion of the I	1201+3776
	16:34	a year for all the sins of the I."	1201+3776
	17: 2	to Aaron and his sons and to all the I	1201+3776
	17: 5	This is so the I will bring to the LORD	1201+3776
	17:12	Therefore I say to the I,	1201+3776
	17:14	That is why I have said to the I,	1201+3776
	18: 2	"Speak to the I and say to them:	1201+3776
	20: 2	"Say to the I:	1201+3776
	21:24	to Aaron and his sons and to all the I.	1201+3776
	22: 2	sacred offerings the I consecrate to	1201+3776

Lev	22: 3	sacred offerings that the I consecrate	1201+3776
	22:15	the sacred offerings the I present to	1201+3776
	22:18	to Aaron and his sons and to all the I	1201+3776
	22:32	I must be acknowledged as holy by the I.	1201+3776
	23: 2	"Speak to the I and say to them:	1201+3776
	23:10	"Speak to the I and say to them:	1201+3776
	23:24	"Say to the I:	1201+3776
	23:34	"Say to the I:	1201+3776
	23:42	All native-born I are to live in booths	3776
	23:43	that I had the I live in booths	1201+3776
	23:44	the I the appointed feasts of the LORD.	1201+3776
	24: 2	"Command the I to bring you clear oil of pressed olives	1201+3776
	24: 8	after Sabbath, on behalf of the I,	1201+3776
	24:10	went out among the I,	1201+3776
	24:15	Say to the I:	1201+3776
	24:23	Then Moses spoke to the I,	1201+3776
	24:23	The I did as the LORD commanded	1201+3776
	25: 2	"Speak to the I and say to them:	1201+3776
	25:33	Levites are their property among the I.	1201+3776
	25:42	Because the I are my servants,	2156S
	25:46	not rule over your fellow I ruthlessly.	1201+3776
	25:55	for the I belong to me as servants.	1201+3776
	26:46	Sinai between himself and the I	1201+3776
	27: 2	"Speak to the I and say to them:	1201+3776
	27:34	on Mount Sinai for the I.	1201+3776
Nu	1: 1	of the second year after the I came out	4392S
	1:45	All the I twenty years old	1201+3776
	1:49	them in the census of the other I.	1201+3776
	1:52	I are to set up their tents by divisions,	1201+3776
	1:54	The I did all this just as	1201+3776
	2: 2	"The I are to camp around the Tent	1201+3776
	2:32	These are the I,	1201+3776
	2:33	not counted along with the other I,	1201+3776
	2:34	So the I did everything	1201+3776
	3: 8	fulfilling the obligations of the I by	1201+3776
	3: 9	are the I who are to be given wholly	1201+3776
	3:12	"I have taken the Levites from among the I	1201+3776
	3:38	of the sanctuary on behalf of the I.	1201+3776
	3:41	in place of all the firstborn of the I,	1201+3776
	3:41	the firstborn of the livestock of the I.	1201+3776
	3:42	So Moses counted all the firstborn of the I,	1201+3776
	3:46	273 firstborn I who exceed the number	1201+3776
	3:48	the redemption of the additional I to Aaron	2157S
	3:50	firstborn of the I he collected silver	1201+3776
	5: 2	"Command the I to send away from	1201+3776
	5: 4	The I did this;	1201+3776
	5: 6	"Say to the I:	1201+3776
	5: 9	All the sacred contributions the I bring	1201+3776
	5:12	"Speak to the I and say to them:	1201+3776
	6: 2	"Speak to the I and say to them:	1201+3776
	6:23	'This is how you are to bless the I.	1201+3776
	6:27	"So they will put my name on the I,	1201+3776
	8: 6	the Levites from among the other I	1201+3776
	8:10	the I are to lay their hands on them.	1201+3776
	8:11	LORD as a wave offering from the I,	1201+3776
	8:14	set the Levites apart from the other I,	1201+3776
	8:16	are the I who are to be given wholly	1201+3776
	8:19	Of all the I,	1201+3776
	8:19	the I and to make atonement for them	1201+3776
	8:19	so that no plague will strike the I	1201+3776
	9: 2	"Have the I celebrate the Passover at	1201+3776
	9: 4	told the I to celebrate the Passover,	1201+3776
	9: 5	The I did everything just as	1201+3776
	9: 7	the LORD's offering with the other I at	1201+3776
	9:10	"Tell the I: 'When any of you	1201+3776
	9:17	from above the Tent, the I set out;	1201+3776
	9:17	the cloud settled, the I encamped.	1201+3776
	9:18	At the LORD's command the I set out,	1201+3776
	9:19	the I obeyed the LORD's order and did	1201+3776
	9:22	the I would remain in camp and not	1201+3776
	10:12	the I set out from the Desert of Sinai	1201+3776
	11: 4	again the I started wailing and said,	1201+3776
	13: 2	which I am giving to the I.	1201+3776
	13: 3	All of them were leaders of the I.	1201+3776
	13:24	cluster of grapes the I cut off there.	1201+3776
	13:32	they spread among the I a bad report	1201+3776
	14: 2	I grumbled against Moses and Aaron,	1201+3776
	14:10	at the Tent of Meeting to all the I.	1201+3776
	14:27	the complaints of these grumbling I.	1201+3776
	14:39	When Moses reported this to all the I,	1201+3776
	15: 2	"Speak to the I and say to them:	1201+3776
	15:18	"Speak to the I and say to them:	1201+3776
	15:32	While the I were in the desert,	1201+3776
	15:38	"Speak to the I and say to them:	1201+3776
	16:34	At their cries, all the I around them fled,	3776
	16:38	Let them be a sign to the I."	1201+3776
	16:40	to remind the I that no one except	1201+3776
	17: 2	the I and get twelve staffs from them,	1201+3776
	17: 5	grumbling against you by the I."	1201+3776
	17: 6	So Moses spoke to the I,	1201+3776
	17: 9	from the LORD's presence to all the I.	1201+3776
	17:12	The I said to Moses, "We will die!	1201+3776
	18: 5	that wrath will not fall on the I again.	1201+3776
	18: 6	from among the I as a gift to you,	1201+3776
	18: 8	all the holy offerings the I give me	1201+3776
	18:11	gifts of all the wave offerings of the I.	1201+3776
	18:19	the I present to the LORD I give to you	1201+3776
	18:20	and your inheritance among the I.	1201+3776
	18:22	the I must not go near the Tent of Meeting,	1201+3776
	18:23	receive no inheritance among the I.	1201+3776
	18:24	tithes that the I present as an offering	1201+3776
	18:24	will have no inheritance among the I.	1201+3776
Nu	18:26	'When you receive from the I	1201+3776
	18:28	all the tithes you receive from the I.	1201+3776
	18:32	not defile the holy offerings of the I,	1201+3776
	19: 2	Tell the I to bring you a red heifer	1201+3776
	19:10	a lasting ordinance both for the I and	1201+3776
	20:12	honor me as holy in the sight of the I,	1201+3776
	20:13	the I quarreled with the LORD and	1201+3776
	20:19	The I replied: "We will go along the	1201+3776
	20:24	He will not enter the land I give the I,	1201+3776
	21: 1	he attacked the I and captured some	3776
	21: 6	they bit the people and many I died.	3776+4946
	21:10	The I moved on and camped at Oboth	1201+3776
	21:32	the I captured its surrounding settlements	NIH
	22: 1	the I traveled to the plains of Moab	1201+3776
	22: 3	with dread because of the I.	1201+3776
	25: 8	the plague against the I was stopped;	1201+3776
	25:11	has turned my anger away from the I;	1201+3776
	25:13	God and made atonement for the I."	1201+3776
	26: 4	were the I who came out of Egypt:	1201+3776
	26:62	not counted along with the other I	1201+3776
	26:63	the I on the plains of Moab by the	1201+3776
	26:64	when they counted the I in the Desert	1201+3776
	26:65	For the LORD had told those I they would	2157S
	27: 8	"Say to the I,	1201+3776
	27:11	is to be a legal requirement for the I,	1201+3776
	27:12	and see the land I have given the I.	1201+3776
	27:21	entire community of the I will go out,	1201+3776
	28: 2	"Give this command to the I and say	1201+3776
	29:40	I all that the LORD commanded him.	1201+3776
	31: 2	on the Midianites for the I.	1201+3776
	31: 9	The I captured the Midianite women	1201+3776
	31:16	were the means of turning the I away	1201+3776
	31:42	The half belonging to the I,	1201+3776
	31:54	of Meeting as a memorial for the I	1201+3776
	32: 7	do you discourage the I from going	1201+3776
	32: 9	they discouraged the I from entering	1201+3776
	32:17	of the I until we have brought them	1201+3776
	33: 1	journey of the I when they came out	1201+3776
	33: 3	The I set out from Rameses on	1201+3776
	33: 5	The I left Rameses and camped at	1201+3776
	33:38	the fortieth year after the I came out	1201+3776
	33:40	heard that the I were coming.	1201+3776
	33:51	"Speak to the I and say to them:	1201+3776
	34: 2	"Command the I and say to them:	1201+3776
	34:13	Moses commanded the I:	1201+3776
	34:29	inheritance to the I in the land	1201+3776
	35: 2	the I to give the Levites towns	1201+3776
	35: 2	in from the inheritance the I will possess.	4392S
	35: 8	the land the I possess are to be given	1201+3776
	35:10	"Speak to the I and say to them:	1201+3776
	35:15	be a place of refuge for I,	1201+3776
	35:34	for I, the LORD, dwell among the I.' "	1201+3776
	36: 2	give the land as an inheritance to the I	1201+3776
	36: 4	the Year of Jubilee for the I comes,	1201+3776
	36: 5	Moses gave this order to the I:	1201+3776
	36:13	the LORD gave through Moses to the I	1201+3776
Dt	1: 3	Moses proclaimed to the I all that	1201+3776
	1:16	between brother I or between one of them	278
	3:18	cross over ahead of your brother I.	1201+3776
	4:44	This is the law Moses set before the I.	1201+3776
	4:46	and was defeated by Moses and the I	1201+3776
	10: 6	(The I traveled from the wells of	1201+3776
	24: 7	of his brother I and treats him as a slave	1201+3776+4946
	29: 1	to make with the I in Moab,	1201+3776
	29: 2	Moses summoned all the I and said	3776
	31:19	this song and teach it to the I	1201+3776
	31:22	that day and taught it to the I	1201+3776
	31:23	you will bring the I into the land I promised them on oath,	1201+3776
	32:49	the I as their own possession.	1201+3776
	32:51	the I at the waters of Meribah Kadesh	1201+3776
	32:51	not uphold my holiness among the I.	1201+3776
	33: 1	the man of God pronounced on the I	1201+3776
	34: 8	The I grieved for Moses in the plains	1201+3776
	34: 9	So the I listened to him and did what	1201+3776
Jos	1: 2	to give to them—to the I.	1201+3776
	2: 2	Some of the I have come here tonight to spy out	1201+3776
	3: 1	and all the I set out from Shittim and	1201+3776
	3: 9	Joshua said to the I,	1201+3776
	4: 4	men he had appointed from the I,	1201+3776
	4: 5	to the number of the tribes of the I,	1201+3776
	4: 8	So the I did as Joshua commanded	1201+3776
	4: 8	of the I, as the LORD had told Joshua;	1201+3776
	4:12	armed, in front of the I,	1201+3776
	4:21	He said to the I,	1201+3776
	5: 1	before the I until we had crossed	1201+3776
	5: 1	the courage to face the I.	1201+3776
	5: 2	and circumcise the I again."	1201+3776
	5: 3	circumcised the I at Gibeath Haaraloth	1201+3776
	5: 6	The I had moved about in	1201+3776
	5:10	the I celebrated the Passover.	1201+3776
	5:12	was no longer any manna for the I,	1201+3776
	6: 1	shut up because of the I.	1201+3776
	6:25	and she lives among the I to this day.	3776
	7: 1	the I acted unfaithfully in regard to	1201+3776
	7: 5	They chased the I from the city gate as far	4392S
	7:12	I cannot stand against their enemies;	1201+3776
	7:23	brought them to Joshua and all the I	1201+3776
	8:20	for the I who had been fleeing toward	6639S
	8:22	with I on both sides.	3776
	8:24	all the I returned to Ai	3776
	8:31	of the LORD had commanded the I.	1201+3776
	8:32	There, in the presence of the I,	1201+3776
	9:16	the I heard that they were neighbors,	NIH
	9:17	the I set out and on the third day came	1201+3776
Jos	9:18	But the I did not attack them,	1201+3776
	9:26	So Joshua saved them from the I,	1201+3776
	10: 4	made peace with Joshua and the I."	1201+3776
	10:11	by the swords of the I.	1201+3776
	10:20	the I destroyed them completely—	1201+3776
	10:21	no one uttered a word against the I.	1201+3776
	11:14	The I carried off for themselves all	1201+3776
	11:19	city made a treaty of peace with the I,	1201+3776
	12: 1	of the land whom the I had defeated	1201+3776
	12: 6	and the I conquered them.	1201+3776
	12: 7	land that Joshua and the I conquered	1201+3776
	13: 6	will drive them out before the I.	1201+3776
	13:13	the I did not drive out the people of Geshur	1201+3776
	13:13	so they continue to live among the I	3776
	13:22	the I had put to the sword Balaam son	1201+3776
	14: 1	areas the I received as an inheritance	1201+3776
	14: 5	So the I divided the land,	1201+3776
	17:13	However, when the I grew stronger,	1201+3776
	18: 1	I gathered at Shiloh and set up the Tent of Meeting	1201+3776
	18: 3	So Joshua said to the I:	1201+3776
	18:10	I according to their tribal divisions.	1201+3776
	19:49	the I gave Joshua son of Nun	1201+3776
	20: 2	the I to designate the cities of refuge,	1201+3776
	20: 9	Any of the I or any alien living	1201+3776
	21: 3	the I gave the Levites the following	1201+3776
	21: 8	I allotted to the Levites these towns	1201+3776
	21:41	the territory held by the I were	1201+3776
	22: 9	of Manasseh left the I at Shiloh	1201+3776
	22:11	the I heard that they had built the altar	1201+3776
	22:13	So the I sent Phinehas son of Eleazar,	1201+3776
	22:30	the heads of the clans of the I—	3776
	22:31	Now you have rescued the I from	1201+3776
	22:32	in Gilead and reported to the I.	1201+3776
	24:32	the I had brought up from Egypt,	1201+3776
Jdg	1: 1	the I asked the LORD,	1201+3776
	2: 4	to all the I,	1201+3776
	2: 6	After Joshua had dismissed the I,	1201+3776
	2:11	the I did evil in the eyes of the LORD	1201+3776
	3: 1	the LORD left to test all those I who had	3776
	3: 2	to the descendants of the I who had	1201+3776
	3: 4	to test the I to see whether they would obey	3776
	3: 5	The I lived among the Canaanites,	1201+3776
	3: 7	The I did evil in the eyes of the LORD;	1201+3776
	3: 8	the I were subject for eight years.	1201+3776
	3:12	The I did evil in the eyes of the LORD,	1201+3776
	3:14	I were subject to Eglon king of Moab	1201+3776
	3:15	Again the I cried out to the LORD,	1201+3776
	3:15	The I sent him with tribute to Eglon	1201+3776
	3:27	I went down with him from the hills,	1201+3776
	4: 1	the I once again did evil in the eyes of	1201+3776
	4: 3	and had cruelly oppressed the I	1201+3776
	4: 5	and the I came to her	1201+3776
	4:23	the Canaanite king, before the I.	1201+3776
	4:24	And the hand of the I grew stronger	1201+3776
	6: 1	the I did evil in the eyes of the LORD,	1201+3776
	6: 2	the I prepared shelters for themselves	1201+3776
	6: 3	Whenever the I planted their crops,	3776
	6: 6	so impoverished the I that they cried out to	3776
	6: 7	When the I cried to the LORD because	1201+3776
	7: 8	the rest of the I to their tents but kept	408+3776
	7:23	I from Naphtali, Asher	408+3776
	8:22	The I said to Gideon, "Rule over us—	408+3776
	8:28	Thus Midian was subdued before the I	1201+3776
	8:33	the I again prostituted themselves to	1201+3776
	9:55	the I saw that Abimelech was dead,	408+3776
	10: 6	the I did evil in the eyes of the LORD.	1201+3776
	10: 6	And because the I forsook the LORD	NIH
	10: 8	eighteen years they oppressed all the I	1201+3776
	10:10	Then the I cried out to the LORD,	1201+3776
	10:15	I said to the LORD, "We have sinned.	1201+3776
	10:17	I assembled and camped at Mizpah.	1201+3776
	11:27	the dispute this day between the I	1201+3776
	13: 1	the I did evil in the eyes of the LORD,	1201+3776
	19:12	whose people are not I.	1201+3776+4946
	19:30	the day the I came up out of Egypt.	1201+3776
	20: 1	Then all the I from Dan to Beersheba	1201+3776
	20: 3	Benjamites heard that the I had gone	1201+3776
	20: 3	Then the I said,	1201+3776
	20: 7	you I, speak up and give your verdict.	1201+3776
	20:13	not listen to their fellow I.	1201+3776
	20:14	at Gibeah to fight against the I.	1201+3776
	20:18	The I went up to Bethel and inquired	1201+3776
	20:19	the I got up and pitched camp	1201+3776
	20:21	and cut down twenty-two thousand I on	3776
	20:23	I went up and wept before the LORD	1201+3776
	20:24	I drew near to Benjamin the second	1201+3776
	20:25	cut down another eighteen thousand I,	1201+3776
	20:26	Then the I, all the people,	1201+3776
	20:27	And the I inquired of the LORD.	1201+3776
	20:31	the I as before, so that about thirty men fell	6639S
	20:32	the I were saying,	1201+3776
	20:35	on that day the I struck down 25,100	1201+3776
	20:42	So they fled before the I in the direction	408+3776
	20:45	the I cut down five thousand men along	NIH
	21: 5	Then the I asked,	1201+3776
	21: 6	I grieved for their brothers, the Benjamites.	1201+3776
	21:18	since we I have taken this oath:	1201+3776
	21:24	the I left that place and went home	1201+3776
1Sa	2:14	This is how they treated all the I who came	3776
	2:28	the offerings made with fire by the I.	1201+3776
	4: 1	I went out to fight against the Philistines.	3776
	4: 1	I camped at Ebenezer,	NIH
	4:10	and the I were defeated and every man fled	3776
	6: 6	did they not send the I out so they could go	4392S

Column 1

1Sa	7: 4	the I put away their Baals and	1201+3776
	7: 7	And when the I heard of it,	1201+3776
	7:10	a panic that they were routed before the I.	3776
	9: 2	without equal among the I—	1201+3776
	11:15	and all the I held a great celebration.	408+3776
	14:18	(At that time it was with the I.)	1201+3776
	14:21	to the I who were with Saul and Jonathan.	3776
	14:22	the I who had hidden in the hill country	408+3776
	14:31	after the I had struck down the Philistines	6639S
	14:40	Saul then said to all the I,	3776
	15: 6	the I when they came up out of Egypt	1201+3776
	17: 2	I he assembled and camped in the	408+3776
	17: 3	occupied one hill and the I another,	3776
	17:11	and all the I were dismayed and terrified.	3776
	17:24	When the I saw the man,	408+3776
	17:25	Now the I had been saying,	408+3776
	17:53	the I returned from chasing the Philistines,	1201+3776
	27:12	the I, that he will be my servant forever."	3776
	28: 4	while Saul gathered all the I and set	3776
	31: 1	the I fled before them,	408+3776
	31: 7	the I along the valley and those across	408+3776
2Sa	6:19	to each person in the whole crowd of I,	3776
	7: 6	from the day I brought the I up out	1201+3776
	7: 7	Wherever I have moved with all the I,	1201+3776
	10:19	with the I and became subject to them.	3776
	15: 6	in this way toward all the I who came to	3776
	17:26	The I and Absalom camped in the land	3776
	18:17	Meanwhile, all the I fled to their homes.	3776
	19: 8	Meanwhile, the I had fled to their homes.	3776
	21: 2	the I had sworn to [spare] them,	1201+3776
1Ki	6: 1	after the I had come out of Egypt,	1201+3776
	6:13	And I will live among the I and will	1201+3776
	8: 9	covenant with the I after they came	1201+3776
	8:63	king and all the I dedicated the temple	1201+3776
	9:20	Jebusites (these peoples were not I),	1201+3776
	9:21	whom the I could not exterminate—	1201+3776
	9:22	not make slaves of any of the I;	1201+3776
	11: 2	about which the LORD had told the I,	1201+3776
	11:16	and all the I stayed there for six months,	3776
	12: 1	all the I had gone there to make him king.	3776
	12:16	So the I went home.	3776
	12:17	the I who were living in the towns of Judah,	1201+3776
	12:20	the I heard that Jeroboam had returned,	3776
	12:24	up to fight against your brothers, the I.	1201+3776
	12:33	So he instituted the festival for the I	1201+3776
	14:24	the LORD had driven out before the I.	1201+3776
	16:16	When the I in the camp heard	6639S
	16:17	Then Omri and all the I with him withdrew	3776
	19:10	The I have rejected your covenant,	1201+3776
	19:14	The I have rejected your covenant,	1201+3776
	20:15	Then he assembled the rest of the I,	1201+3776
	20:20	The Arameans fled, with the I in pursuit.	3776
	20:27	the I were also mustered and given	1201+3776
	20:27	The I camped opposite them	1201+3776
	20:29	I inflicted a hundred thousand casualties on the Aramean foot soldiers	1201+3776
2Ki	3:24	the I rose up and fought them	3776
	3:24	And the I invaded the land and slaughtered	NIH
	7:13	be like that of all the I left here—	3776
	7:13	be like all these I who are doomed.	3776
	8:12	the harm you will do to the I,"	1201+3776
	10:32	the I throughout their territory	3776
	13: 5	So the I lived in their own homes	1201+3776
	13:21	Once while some I were burying a man,	2156S
	16: 3	the LORD had driven out before the I.	1201+3776
	17: 6	and deported the I to Assyria.	3776
	17: 7	took place because the I had sinned	1201+3776
	17: 9	The I secretly did things against	1201+3776
	17:22	I persisted in all the sins of Jeroboam	1201+3776
	17:24	the towns of Samaria to replace the I.	1201+3776
	17:35	the LORD made a covenant with the I,	4392S
	18: 4	the I had been burning incense to it.	1201+3776
	21: 2	the LORD had driven out before the I.	1201+3776
	21: 8	not again make the feet of the I wander	3776
	21: 9	the LORD had destroyed before the I.	3776
1Ch	6:64	So the I gave the Levites these towns	3776
	6:70	of Manasseh the I gave Aner and Bileam,	NIH
	9: 2	in their own towns were some I,	3776
	10: 1	the I fled before them,	3776
	10: 7	When all the I in the valley saw that	408+3776
	11: 4	and all the I marched to Jerusalem (that is,	3776
	12:38	All the rest of the I were also of one mind	3776
	13: 5	So David assembled all the I,	3776
	13: 6	and all the I with him went to Baalah	3776
	13: 8	the I were celebrating with all their might	3776
	17: 6	Wherever I have moved with all the I,	3776
	21: 2	and count the I from Beersheba to Dan.	3776
	27: 1	This is the list of the I—	1201+3776
2Ch	5:10	covenant with the I after they came	1201+3776
	7: 3	all the I saw the fire coming down	1201+3776
	7: 6	and all the I were standing.	3776
	8: 2	and settled I in them.	1201+3776
	8: 7	and Jebusites (these peoples were not I),	3776
	8: 8	whom the I had not destroyed—	3776
	8: 9	Solomon did not make slaves of the I	1201+3776
	10: 1	all the I had gone there to make him king.	3776
	10:16	So all the I went home.	3776
	10:17	as for the I who were living in the towns of Judah,	1201+3776
	10:18	but the I stoned him to death.	3776
	11: 3	of Solomon king of Judah and to all the I	3776
	13:16	The I fled before Judah,	3776
	28: 3	the LORD had driven out before the I.	1201+3776
	28: 8	The I took captive from their kinsmen	1201+3776
	30:21	The I who were present	3776

Column 2

2Ch	31: 1	the I who were there went out to the towns	3776
	31: 1	the I returned to their own towns	1201+3776
	31: 5	the I generously gave the firstfruits	1201+3776
	33: 2	the LORD had driven out before the I.	1201+3776
	33: 8	I will not again make the feet of the I leave	3776
	33: 9	the LORD had destroyed before the I.	1201+3776
	34:33	all the territory belonging to the I,	1201+3776
	35:17	The I who were present celebrated	1201+3776
Ezr	2:70	and the rest of the I settled in their towns.	3776
	3: 1	and the I had settled in their towns,	1201+3776
	6:21	the I who had returned from the exile	1201+3776
	7: 7	Some of the I, including priests,	1201+3776
	7:13	that any of the I in my kingdom,	10335+10553
	10: 1	a large crowd of I—	3776
	10:25	And among the other I:	1201+3776
Ne	1: 6	I confess the sins we I,	1201+3776
	2:10	to promote the welfare of the I.	1201+3776
	7:73	of the people and the rest of the I,	3776
	7:73	and the I had settled in their towns,	1201+3776
	8:14	the I were to live in booths during the	1201+3776
	8:17	the I had not celebrated it like this.	3776
	9: 1	the I gathered together,	1201+3776
	11: 3	who settled in Jerusalem (now some I,	3776
	11:20	The rest of the I,	3776
	13: 2	they had met the I with food	1201+3776
Isa	17: 3	Aram will be like the glory of the I,"	1201+3776
	17: 9	which they left because of the I,	1201+3776
	27:12	O I, will be gathered up one by one.	1201+3776
	31: 6	so greatly revolted against, O I.	1201+3776
	66:20	as the I bring their grain offerings,	1201+3776
Jer	16:14	who brought the I up out of Egypt,'	1201+3776
	16:15	the I up out of the land of the north	1201+3776
	23: 7	who brought the I up out of Egypt,'	1201+3776
Eze	2: 3	Son of man, I am sending you to the I,	1201+3776
	6: 5	I will lay the dead bodies of the I in	1201+3776
	20: 9	to the I by bringing them out of Egypt.	2157S
	35: 5	delivered the I over to the sword	1201+3776
	36: 5	'Belonging to Judah and the I	1201+3776
	37:21	I will take the I out of the nations	1201+3776
	43: 7	where I will live among the I forever.	1201+3776
	44: 9	the foreigners who live among the I.	1201+3776
	44:15	when the I went astray from me,	1201+3776
	47:22	to consider them as native-born I;	1201+3776
	48:11	the Levites did when the I went astray.	1201+3776
Da	1: 3	some of the I from the royal family	1201+3776
Hos	1:10	the I will be like the sand on the seashore,	1201+3776
	3: 1	Love her as the LORD loves the I,	1201+3776
	3: 4	the I will live many days without king	1201+3776
	3: 5	Afterward the I will return and seek	1201+3776
	4: 1	Hear the word of the LORD, you I,	1201+3776
	4:16	The I are stubborn, like a stubborn heifer.	3776
	5: 1	Pay attention, you I!	1074+3776
	5: 5	the I, even Ephraim, stumble in their sin;	3776
Am	3:12	so will the I be saved,	1201+3776
	4: 5	boast about them, you I,	1201+3776
	9: 7	you I the same to me as the Cushites?	1201+3776
Mic	5: 3	rest of his brothers return to join the I.	1201+3776
Ac	7:23	he decided to visit his fellow I.	2702+3836+5526
	7:26	Moses came upon two I who were fighting.	899S
	7:37	"This is that Moses who told the I,	2702+5626
Ro	9:27	the number of the I be like the sand by the sea,	2702+5626
	10: 1	and prayer to God for the I is that they may	899S
	10:16	But not all the I accepted the good news.	NIG
2Co	3: 7	the I could not look steadily at the face of Moses because of its glory,	2702+5626
	3:13	veil over his face to keep the I from	2702+5626
	11:22	Are they I? So am I.	2703
Heb	11:22	about the exodus of the I from Egypt	2702+5626
Rev	2:14	who taught Balak to entice the I	2702+5626

ISRAELITES' (3) [ISRAEL]

Lev	10:14	share of the I' fellowship offerings.	1201+3776
Nu	31:30	From the I' half, select one out of	1201+3776
	31:47	From the I' half, Moses selected one	1201+3776

ISSACHAR (43)

Ge	30:18	So she named him I.	3779
	35:23	Simeon, Levi, Judah, I and Zebulun.	3779
	46:13	The sons of I:	3779
	49:14	"I is a rawboned donkey lying down	3779
Ex	1: 3	I, Zebulun and Benjamin;	3779
Nu	1: 8	from I, Nethanel son of Zuar;	3779
	1:28	From the descendants of I:	3779
	1:29	The number from the tribe of I was 54,400.	3779
	2: 5	The tribe of I will camp next to them.	3779
	2: 5	of the people of I is Nethanel son of Zuar.	3779
	7:18	the leader of I, brought his offering.	3779
	10:15	over the division of the tribe of I,	1201+3779
	13: 7	from the tribe of I, Igal son of Joseph;	3779
	26:23	The descendants of I by their clans were:	3779
	26:25	These were the clans of I;	3779
	34:26	the leader from the tribe of I;	1201+3779
Dt	27:12	Simeon, Levi, Judah, I,	3779
	33:18	in your going out, and you, I, in your tents.	3779
Jos	17:10	and bordered Asher on the north and I on	3779
	17:11	Within I and Asher,	3779
	19:17	The fourth lot came out for I, clan by	1201+3779
	19:23	the inheritance of the tribe of I,	1201+3779
	21: 6	from the clans of the tribes of I,	3779
	21:28	from the tribe of I, Kishion, Daberath,	3779
Jdg	5:15	The princes of I were with Deborah;	3779
	5:15	yes, I was with Barak,	3779
	10: 1	After the time of Abimelech a man of I,	3779

Column 3

1Ki	4:17	Jehoshaphat son of Paruah—in I;	3779
	15:27	of the house of I plotted against him,	3779
1Ch	2: 1	Reuben, Simeon, Levi, Judah, I, Zebulun,	3779
	6:62	from the tribes of I,	3779
	6:72	from the tribe of I they received Kedesh,	3779
	7: 1	The sons of I:	3779
	7: 5	to all the clans of I,	3779
	12:32	men of I, who understood the times	3779
	12:40	Also, their neighbors from as far away as I,	3779
	26: 5	I the seventh and Peullethai the eighth.	3779
	27:18	a brother of David; over I:	3779
2Ch	30:18	I and Zebulun had not purified themselves,	3779
Eze	48:25	"I will have one portion;	3779
	48:26	it will border the territory of I from east	3779
	48:33	the gate of I and the gate of Zebulun.	3779
Rev	7: 7	from the tribe of I 12,000,	2704

ISSHIAH (6)

1Ch	7: 3	Michael, Obadiah, Joel and I.	3807
	12: 6	I, Azarel, Joezer and Jashobeam	3808
	23:20	Micah the first and I the second.	3807
	24:21	for Rehabiah, from his sons: I was the first.	3807
	24:25	I; from the sons of Isshiah: Zechariah.	3807
	24:25	from the sons of I: Zechariah.	3807

ISSUE (10) [ISSUED, ISSUES, ISSUING]

Ex	22:11	the i between them will be settled by	NIH
2Sa	14: 8	and I will i an order in your behalf."	7422
Ezr	4:21	Now i an order to these men to stop work,	10682
	5:17	to see if King Cyrus did in fact i a decree	10682
Est	1:19	let him i a royal decree and let it	3655
Isa	10: 1	to those who i oppressive decrees,	4180+4180
Da	2:15	did the king i such a harsh decree?"	10427+10621
	6: 7	that the king should i an edict and enforce	10624
	6: 8	i the decree and put it in writing so	10624
	6:26	"I i a decree that in every part	10682

ISSUED (19) [ISSUE]

1Ki	15:22	Then King Asa i an order to all Judah—	9048
2Ch	24: 9	A proclamation was then i in Judah	5989
Ezr	4:19	I i an order and a search was made,	10682
	5:13	King Cyrus i a decree to rebuild this house	10682
	6: 1	King Darius then i an order,	10682
	6: 3	the king i a decree concerning the temple	10682
	10: 7	then i throughout Judah and Jerusalem	6296
Est	3: 9	let a decree be i to destroy them,	4180
	3:14	A copy of the text of the edict was to be i	5989
	3:15	and the edict was i in the citadel of Susa.	5989
	8:13	A copy of the text of the edict was to be i	5989
	8:14	the edict was also i in the citadel of Susa.	5989
	9:14	An edict was i in Susa,	5989
	9:25	he i written orders that the evil scheme	606
Da	2:13	decree was i to put the wise men to death,	10485
	3:10	You have i a decree, O king,	10413
	4:24	and this is the decree the Most High has i	10413
Jnh	3: 7	Then he i a proclamation in Nineveh:	2410
Lk	2: 1	In those days Caesar Augustus i a decree	2002

ISSUES (1) [ISSUE]

| Da | 6:15 | or edict that the king i can be changed." | 10624 |

ISSUING (1) [ISSUE]

| Da | 9:25 | From the i of the decree to restore and | 4604 |

ISUAH (KJV) See ISHUAH

ISUI (KJV) See ISHUI

IT (5147) [IT'S, ITS, ITSELF] See Index of Articles Etc.

IT'S (20) [BE, IT] See Index of Articles Etc.

ITALIAN (1) [ITALY]

| Ac | 10: 1 | in what was known as the I Regiment. | 2713 |

ITALY (4) [ITALIAN]

Ac	18: 2	who had recently come from I	2712
	27: 1	that we would sail for I,	2712
	27: 6	an Alexandrian ship sailing for I and put us	2712
Heb	13:24	Those from I send you their greetings.	2712

ITCH (8) [ITCHING]

Lev	13:30	it is an i, an infectious disease	5999
	13:32	and if the i has not spread	5999
	13:34	the priest is to examine the i,	5999
	13:35	But if the i does spread in the skin	5999
	13:36	and if the i has spread in the skin,	5999
	13:37	the i is healed. He is clean,	5999
	14:54	for any infectious skin disease, for an i,	5999
Dt	28:27	festering sores and the i,	3063

ITCHING (1) [ITCH]

| 2Ti | 4: 3 | teachers to say what their i ears want to hear | 3117 |

ITHAI (2)

| 2Sa | 23:29 | I son of Ribai from Gibeah in Benjamin, | 915 |
| 1Ch | 11:31 | I son of Ribai from Gibeah in Benjamin, | 416 |

ITHAMAR (19) [ITHAMAR'S]

Ex	6:23	and Abihu, Eleazar and I.	418
	28: 1	Eleazar and I, so they may serve me	418
	38:21	by the Levites under the direction of I son	418
Lev	10: 6	to Aaron and his sons Eleazar and I,	418
	10:12	Eleazar and I, "Take the grain offering left	418
	10:16	he was angry with Eleazar and I,	418
Nu	3: 2	the firstborn and Abihu, Eleazar and I.	418
	3: 4	and I served as priests during the lifetime	418
	4:28	to be under the direction of I son of Aaron,	418
	4:33	of Meeting under the direction of I son	418
	7: 8	They were all under the direction of I son	418
	26:60	of Nadab and Abihu, Eleazar and I.	418
1Ch	6: 3	Nadab, Abihu, Eleazar and I.	418
	24: 1	of Aaron were Nadab, Abihu, Eleazar and I.	418
	24: 2	so Eleazar and I served as the priests.	418
	24: 3	and Ahimelech a descendant of I,	418
	24: 5	the descendants of both Eleazar and I.	418
	24: 6	from Eleazar and then one from I.	418
Ezr	8: 2	of the descendants of I, Daniel;	418

ITHAMAR'S (2) [ITHAMAR]

1Ch	24: 4	among Eleazar's descendants than among I,	418
	24: 4	of families from I descendants.	418

ITHIEL (3)

Ne	11: 7	the son of Maaseiah, the son of I,	417
Pr	30: 1	This man declared to I,	417
	30: 1	to I and to Ucal:	417

ITHLAH (1)

Jos	19:42	Shaalabbin, Aijalon, I,	3849

ITHMAH (1)

1Ch	11:46	and Joshaviah the sons of Elnaam, I	3850

ITHNAN (1)

Jos	15:23	Kedesh, Hazor, I,	3854

ITHRAN (3)

Ge	36:26	Hemdan, Eshban, I and Keran.	3864
1Ch	1:41	Hemdan, Eshban, I and Keran.	3864
	7:37	Hod, Shamma, Shilshah, I and Beera.	3864

ITHREAM (2)

2Sa	3: 5	I the son of David's wife Eglah.	3865
1Ch	3: 3	and the sixth, I, by his wife Eglah.	3865

ITHRITE (4) [ITHRITES]

2Sa	23:38	Ira the I, Gareb the Ithrite	3863
	23:38	Ira the Ithrite, Gareb the I	3863
1Ch	11:40	Ira the I, Gareb the Ithrite,	3863
	11:40	Ira the Ithrite, Gareb the I,	3863

ITHRITES (1) [ITHRITE]

1Ch	2:53	the I, Puthites, Shumathites and Mishraites.	3863

ITS (1008) [IT] See Index of Articles Etc.

ITSELF (53) [IT, SELF] See Index of Articles Etc.

ITTAH-KAZIN (KJV) See ETH KAZIN

ITTAI (7)

2Sa	15:19	The king said to I the Gittite,	915
	15:21	But I replied to the king,	915
	15:22	David said to I, "Go ahead, march on."	915
	15:22	So I the Gittite marched on	915
	18: 2	and a third under I the Gittite.	915
	18: 5	The king commanded Joab, Abishai and I,	915
	18:12	and Abishai and I,	915

ITUREA (1)

Lk	3: 1	brother Philip tetrarch *of* I and Traconitis,	*2714*

IVAH (KJV) See IVVAH

IVORY (13)

1Ki	10:18	the king made a great throne inlaid with i	9094
	10:22	silver and i, and apes and baboons.	9105
	22:39	the palace he built and inlaid with i,	9094
2Ch	9:17	the king made a great throne inlaid with i	9094
	9:21	silver and i, and apes and baboons.	9105
Ps	45: 8	from palaces adorned with i the music of	9094
SS	5:14	like polished i decorated with sapphires.	9094
	7: 4	Your neck is like an i tower.	9094
Eze	27: 6	Cyprus they made your deck, inlaid with i.	9094
	27:15	they paid you with i tusks and ebony.	9094
Am	3:15	the houses adorned with i will be destroyed	9094
	6: 4	You lie on beds inlaid with i and lounge	9094
Rev	18:12	and articles of every kind *made of* i,	*1804*

IVVAH (3)

2Ki	18:34	are the gods of Sepharvaim, Hena and I?	6394
	19:13	Sepharvaim, or of Hena or I?"	6394
Isa	37:13	Sepharvaim, or of Hena or I?"	6394

IYE ABARIM (2) [ABARIM]

Nu	21:11	from Oboth and camped in I,	6516
	33:44	They left Oboth and camped at I,	6516

IYIM (1)

Nu	33:45	They left I and camped at Dibon Gad.	6517

IZEHAR (KJV) See IZHAR

IZEHARITES (KJV) See IZHARITES

IZHAR (9) [IZHARITES]

Ex	6:18	The sons of Kohath were Amram, I,	3659
	6:21	The sons of I were Korah,	3659
Nu	3:19	Amram, I, Hebron and Uzziel.	3659
	16: 1	Korah son of I, the son of Kohath,	3659
1Ch	6: 2	Amram, I, Hebron and Uzziel.	3659
	6:18	Amram, I, Hebron and Uzziel.	3659
	6:38	of I, the son of Kohath, the son of Levi,	3659
	23:12	Amram, I, Hebron and Uzziel—four in all.	3659
	23:18	The sons of I: Shelomith was the first.	3659

IZHARITES (4) [IZHAR]

Nu	3:27	I, Hebronites and Uzzielites;	3660
1Ch	24:22	From the I: Shelomoth;	3660
	26:23	From the Amramites, the I,	3660
	26:29	From the I: Kenaniah	3660

IZLIAH (1)

1Ch	8:18	I and Jobab were the sons of Elpaal.	3468

IZRAHIAH (2)

1Ch	7: 3	The son of Uzzi: I.	3474
	7: 3	The sons of I: Michael, Obadiah, Joel	3474

IZRAHITE (1)

1Ch	27: 8	was the commander Shamhuth the I.	3473

IZRI (1)

1Ch	25:11	the fourth to I, his sons and relatives, 12	3673

IZZIAH (1)

Ezr	10:25	Ramiah, I, Malkijah, Mijamin, Eleazar,	3466

J

JAAKAN   See BENE JAAKAN

JAAKANITES (1) [BENE JAAKAN]

Dt	10: 6	from the wells of the J to Moserah.	1201+3622

JAAKOBAH (1)

1Ch	4:36	J, Jeshohaiah, Asaiah, Adiel, Jesimiel,	3621

JAALA (2)

Ezr	2:56	J, Darkon, Giddel,	3608
Ne	7:58	J, Darkon, Giddel,	3606

JAALAM (KJV) See JALAM

JAAN   See DAN JAAN

JAANAI (KJV) See JANAI

JAAR (1)

Ps	132: 6	we came upon it in the fields of J:	3625

JAARE-OREGIM (1)

2Sa	21:19	of J the Bethlehemite killed Goliath	3629

JAARESHIAH (1)

1Ch	8:27	J, Elijah and Zicri were the sons	3631

JAASAU (KJV) See JAASU

JAASIEL (2)

1Ch	11:47	Eliel, Obed and J the Mezobaite.	3634
	27:21	J son of Abner;	3634

JAASU (1)

Ezr	10:37	Mattaniah, Mattenai and J.	3632

JAAZANIAH (5)

2Ki	25:23	J the son of the Maacathite, and their men.	3280
Jer	35: 3	So I went to get J son of Jeremiah,	3279
	40: 8	and J the son of the Maacathite,	3471
Eze	8:11	and J son of Shaphan was standing	3280
	11: 1	and I saw among them J son of Azzur	3279

JAAZER (KJV) See JAZER

JAAZIAH (2)

1Ch	24:26	The son of J: Beno,	3596
	24:27	from J: Beno, Shoham, Zaccur and Ibri.	3596

JAAZIEL (1)

1Ch	15:18	Zechariah, J, Shemiramoth, Jehiel, Unni,	3595

JABAL (1)

Ge	4:20	Adah gave birth to J;	3299

JABBOK (7)

Ge	32:22	and crossed the ford of the J.	3309
Nu	21:24	over his land from the Arnon to the J,	3309
Dt	2:37	the J nor that around the towns in the hills.	3309
	3:16	(the border) and out to the J River,	3309
Jos	12: 2	the middle of the gorge—to the J River,	3309
Jdg	11:13	from the Arnon to the J,	3309
	11:22	to the J and from the desert to the Jordan.	3309

JABESH (11) [JABESH GILEAD]

1Sa	11: 1	And all the men of J said to him,	3315
	11: 3	The elders of J said to him,	3315
	11: 5	to him what the men of J had said.	3315
	11: 9	and reported this to the men of J,	3315
	31:12	from the wall of Beth Shan and went to J,	3315
	31:13	and buried them under a tamarisk tree at J,	3315
2Ki	15:10	of J conspired against Zechariah.	3314
	15:13	of J became king in the thirty-ninth year	3314
	15:14	He attacked Shallum son of J in Samaria,	3314
1Ch	10:12	and his sons and brought them to J.	3315
	10:12	under the great tree in J,	3315

JABESH GILEAD (12) [GILEAD, JABESH]

Jdg	21: 8	from J had come to the camp for	3316
	21: 9	of the people of J were there.	3316
	21:10	with instructions to go to J and put	3316
	21:12	in J four hundred young women who had never slept with a man,	3316
	21:14	the women of J who had been spared.	3316
1Sa	11: 1	the Ammonite went up and besieged J.	3316
	11: 9	"Say to the men of J,	3316
	31:11	When the people of J heard of what	3316
2Sa	2: 4	the men of J who had buried Saul,	3316
	2: 5	he sent messengers to the men of J	3316
	21:12	from the citizens of J.	3316
1Ch	10:11	When all the inhabitants of J heard	3316

JABEZ (4)

1Ch	2:55	and the clans of scribes who lived at J:	3583
	4: 9	J was more honorable than his brothers.	3584
	4: 9	His mother had named him J, saying,	3584
	4:10	J cried out to the God of Israel, "Oh,	3584

JABIN (6) [JABIN'S]

Jos	11: 1	When J king of Hazor heard of this,	3296
Jdg	4: 2	the LORD sold them into the hands of J,	3296
	4:17	between J king of Hazor and the clan	3296
	4:23	On that day God subdued J,	3296
	4:24	and stronger against J,	3296
Ps	83: 9	you did to Sisera and J at the river Kishon.	3296

JABIN'S (1) [JABIN]

Jdg	4: 7	the commander of J army,	3296

JABNEEL (2)

Jos	15:11	along to Mount Baalah and reached J.	3305
	19:33	and J to Lakkum and ending at the Jordan.	3305

JABNEH (1)

2Ch	26: 6	down the walls of Gath, J and Ashdod.	3306

JACAN (1)

1Ch	5:13	Michael, Meshullam, Sheba, Jorai, J,	3602

JACHIN, JACHINITES (KJV) See JAKIN, JAKINITE

JACINTH (3)

Ex	28:19	the third row a j, an agate and an amethyst;	4385
	39:12	the third row a j, an agate and an amethyst;	4385
Rev	21:20	the eleventh j, and the twelfth amethyst.	*5611*

JACKAL (2) [JACKALS]

Ne	2:13	through the Valley Gate toward the J Well	9490
Mic	1: 8	I will howl like a j and moan like an owl.	9478

JACKALS (17) [JACKAL]

Job	30:29	I have become a brother of j,	9478
Ps	44:19	and made us a haunt for j and covered us	9478
	63:10	over to the sword and become food for j.	8785
Isa	13:21	j will fill her houses;	280
	13:22	j in her luxurious palaces.	9478
	34:13	She will become a haunt for j,	9478
	35: 7	In the haunts where j once lay,	9478
	43:20	wild animals honor me, the j and the owls,	9478
Jer	9:11	a haunt of j;	9478
	10:22	a haunt of j.	9478
	14: 6	on the barren heights and pant like j;	9478
	49:33	"Hazor will become a haunt of j,	9478
	51:37	a haunt of j, an object of horror and scorn,	9478
La	4: 3	j offer their breasts to nurse their young,	9478
	5:18	with j prowling over it.	8785
Eze	13: 4	O Israel, are like j among ruins.	8785
Mal	1: 3	and left his inheritance to the desert j."	9478

JACOB (363) [JACOB'S]

Ge	25:26	so he was named J.	3620
	25:27	while J was a quiet man,	3620
	25:28	loved Esau, but Rebekah loved J.	3620
	25:29	Once when J was cooking some stew,	3620
	25:30	He said to J, "Quick, let me have some	3620
	25:31	J replied, "First sell me your birthright."	3620
	25:33	But J said, "Swear to me first."	3620
	25:33	selling his birthright to J.	3620
	25:34	Then J gave Esau some bread	3620
	27: 6	Rebekah said to her son J.	3620
	27:11	J said to Rebekah his mother,	3620
	27:15	and put them on her younger son J.	3620
	27:17	to her son J the tasty food and	3620
	27:19	J said to his father, "I am Esau	3620
	27:21	Then Isaac said to J, "Come near so I can	3620
	27:22	J went close to his father Isaac,	3620
	27:22	"The voice is the voice of J, but the hands	3620
	27:25	J brought it to him and he ate;	NIH
	27:30	J had scarcely left his father's presence,	3620
	27:36	Esau said, "Isn't he rightly named J?	3620
	27:41	Esau held a grudge against J because of	3620
	27:41	then I will kill my brother J."	3620
	27:42	she sent for her younger son J and said	3620
	27:46	If J takes a wife from among the women	3620
	28: 1	So Isaac called for J and blessed him	3620
	28: 5	Then Isaac sent J on his way,	3620
	28: 5	who was the mother of J and Esau.	3620
	28: 6	Now Esau learned that Isaac had blessed J	3620
	28: 7	that J had obeyed his father and mother	3620
	28:10	J left Beersheba and set out for Haran.	3620
	28:16	When J awoke from his sleep, he thought,	3620
	28:18	Early the next morning J took the stone	3620
	28:20	Then J made a vow, saying,	3620
	29: 1	Then J continued on his journey and came	3620
	29: 4	J asked the shepherds, "My brothers,	3620
	29: 6	Then J asked them, "Is he well?"	NIH
	29:10	When J saw Rachel daughter of Laban,	3620
	29:11	J kissed Rachel and began to weep aloud.	3620
	29:13	As soon as Laban heard the news about J,	3620
	29:13	and there J told him all these things.	NIH
	29:14	After J had stayed with him for	NIH
	29:18	J was in love with Rachel and said,	3620
	29:20	So J served seven years to get Rachel,	3620
	29:21	Then J said to Laban, "Give me my wife.	3620
	29:23	his daughter Leah and gave her to J,	2257S
	29:23	and J lay with her.	NIH
	29:25	So J said to Laban, "What is this you have	NIH
	29:28	And J did so.	NIH
	29:30	J lay with Rachel also, and he loved Rachel	NIH
	30: 1	that she was not bearing J any children,	3620
	30: 1	So she said to J, "Give me children,	3620
	30: 2	J became angry with her and said,	3620
	30: 4	Bilhah as a wife. J slept with her,	3620
	30: 7	and bore a second son.	3620
	30: 9	Zilpah and gave her to J as a wife.	3620
	30:10	Leah's servant Zilpah bore J a son.	3620
	30:12	Leah's servant Zilpah bore J a second son.	3620
	30:16	J came in from the fields that evening,	3620
	30:17	and she became pregnant and bore	3620
	30:19	Leah conceived again and bore J	3620
	30:25	J said to Laban, "Send me on my way	3620
	30:29	J said to him, "You know how I	NIH
	30:31	"Don't give me anything," J replied.	3620
	30:36	between himself and J,	3620
	30:36	while J continued to tend the rest	3620
	30:37	J, however, took fresh-cut branches	3620
	30:40	J set apart the young of the flock	3620
	30:41	J would place the branches in the troughs	3620
	30:42	to Laban and the strong ones to J.	3620
	31: 1	J heard that Laban's sons were saying,	NIH
	31: 1	"J has taken everything our father owned	3620
	31: 2	And J noticed that Laban's attitude	3620
	31: 3	Then the LORD said to J, "Go back	3620
	31: 4	So J sent word to Rachel and Leah	3620
	31:11	of God said to me in the dream, 'J.'	3620
	31:17	J put his children and his wives on camels,	3620
	31:20	J deceived Laban the Aramean by	3620
	31:22	Laban was told that J had fled.	3620
	31:23	he pursued J for seven days and caught up	2257S
	31:24	"Be careful not to say anything to J,	3620
	31:25	J had pitched his tent in the hill country	3620
Ge	31:26	Laban said to J, "What have you done?	3620
	31:29	'Be careful not to say anything to J,	3620
	31:31	J answered Laban, "I was afraid,	3620
	31:32	Now J did not know that Rachel had stolen	3620
	31:36	J was angry and took Laban to task.	3620
	31:43	Laban answered J, "The women are my daughters,	3620
	31:45	So J took a stone and set it up as a pillar.	3620
	31:47	and J called it Galeed.	3620
	31:51	Laban also said to J, "Here is this heap,	3620
	31:53	So J took an oath in the name of the Fear	3620
	32: 1	J also went on his way,	3620
	32: 2	When J saw them, he said,	3620
	32: 3	J sent messengers ahead of him	3620
	32: 4	'Your servant J says, I have been staying	3620
	32: 6	When the messengers returned to J,	3620
	32: 7	J divided the people who were with him	3620
	32: 9	Then J prayed, "O God of my father	3620
	32:18	'They belong to your servant J.	3620
	32:20	'Your servant J is coming behind us.' "	3620
	32:22	That night J got up and took his two wives	NIH
	32:24	So J was left alone,	3620
	32:26	But J replied, "I will not let you go	NIH
	32:27	"J," he answered.	NIH
	32:28	man said, "Your name will no longer be J,	3620
	32:29	J said, "Please tell me your name."	3620
	32:30	So J called the place Peniel, saying,	3620
	33: 1	J looked up and there was Esau.	3620
	33: 4	But Esau ran to meet J and embraced him;	2257S
	33: 5	J answered, "They are the children	NIH
	33:10	"No, please!" said J.	3620
	33:11	And because I insisted, Esau accepted it.	NIH
	33:13	But J said to him, "My lord knows	NIH
	33:15	"But why do that?" J asked.	NIH
	33:17	J, however, went to Succoth,	3620
	33:18	After J came from Paddan Aram,	3620
	34: 1	Dinah, the daughter Leah had borne to J,	3620
	34: 3	His heart was drawn to Dinah daughter of J,	3620
	34: 5	When J heard that his daughter Dinah had been defiled,	3620
	34: 6	Hamor went out to talk with J.	3620
	34:27	of J came upon the dead bodies and looted	3620
	34:30	Then J said to Simeon and Levi,	3620
	35: 1	Then God said to J, "Go up to Bethel	3620
	35: 2	So J said to his household and	3620
	35: 4	So they gave J all the foreign gods	3620
	35: 4	J buried them under the oak at Shechem.	3620
	35: 6	J and all the people with him came to Luz	3620
	35: 9	After J returned from Paddan Aram,	3620
	35:10	God said to him, "Your name is J,	3620
	35:10	but you will no longer be called J;	3620
	35:14	J set up a stone pillar at the place	3620
	35:15	J called the place where God had talked	3620
	35:20	Over her tomb J set up a pillar,	3620
	35:22	J had twelve sons:	3620
	35:23	Reuben the firstborn of J, Simeon, Levi,	3620
	35:26	These were the sons of J,	3620
	35:27	J came home to his father Isaac in Mamre,	3620
	35:29	And his sons Esau and J buried him.	3620
	36: 6	to a land some distance from his brother J.	3620
	37: 1	J lived in the land where his father had	3620
	37: 2	This is the account of J.	3620
	37:34	Then J tore his clothes,	3620
	42: 1	J learned that there was grain in Egypt,	3620
	42: 4	But J did not send Benjamin,	3620
	42:29	to their father J in the land of Canaan,	3620
	42:36	Their father J said to them,	3620
	42:38	But J said, "My son will not go	NIH
	45:25	up out of Egypt and came to their father J	3620
	45:26	J was stunned; he did not believe them.	2257S
	45:27	the spirit of their father J revived.	3620
	46: 2	to Israel in a vision at night and said, "J!	3620
	46: 2	at night and said, "Jacob! J!"	3620
	46: 5	Then J left Beersheba,	3620
	46: 5	and Israel's sons took their father J	3620
	46: 6	and J and all his offspring went to Egypt.	3620
	46: 8	of Israel (J and his descendants) who went	3620
	46: 8	Reuben the firstborn of J.	3620
	46:15	the sons Leah bore to J in Paddan Aram,	3620
	46:18	to J by Zilpah, whom Laban had given	3620
	46:22	the sons of Rachel who were born to J—	3620
	46:25	These were the sons born to J by Bilhah,	3620
	46:26	All those who went to Egypt with J—	3620
	46:28	Now J sent Judah ahead of him to Joseph	NIH
	47: 7	Then Joseph brought his father J in	3620
	47: 7	After J blessed Pharaoh,	3620
	47: 9	And J said to Pharaoh,	3620
	47:10	Then J blessed Pharaoh and went out	3620
	47:28	J lived in Egypt seventeen years,	3620
	48: 2	When J was told, "Your son Joseph has	3620
	48: 3	J said to Joseph, "God Almighty appeared	3620
	49: 1	Then J called for his sons and said:	3620
	49: 2	"Assemble and listen, sons of J;	3620
	49: 7	I will scatter them in J and disperse them	3620
	49:24	of the hand of the Mighty One of J,	3620
	49:33	When J had finished giving instructions	3620
	50:24	on oath to Abraham, Isaac and J."	3620
Ex	1: 1	of Israel who went to Egypt with J, each	3620
	1: 5	The descendants of J numbered seventy	3620
	2:24	with Isaac and J.	3620
	3: 6	the God of Isaac and the God of J."	3620
	3:15	the God of Isaac and the God of J—	3620
	3:16	the God of Abraham, Isaac and J—	3620
	4: 5	the God of Isaac and the God of J—	3620
	6: 3	to Isaac and J, the God Almighty,	3620
	6: 8	give to Abraham, to Isaac and to J,	3620
	19: 3	to say to the house of J and what you are	3620
Ex	33: 1	Isaac and J, saying, 'I will give it	3620
Lev	26:42	I will remember my covenant with J	3620
Nu	23: 7	'Come,' he said, 'curse J for me;	3620
	23:10	of J or number the fourth part of Israel?	3620
	23:21	"No misfortune is seen in J,	3620
	23:23	There is no sorcery against J,	3620
	23:23	It will now be said of J and of Israel,	3620
	24: 5	O J, your dwelling places, O Israel!	3620
	24:17	A star will come out of J;	3620
	24:19	of J and destroy the survivors of the city."	3620
	32:11	on oath to Abraham, Isaac and J—	3620
Dt	1: 8	to Abraham, Isaac and J—	3620
	6:10	to Abraham, Isaac and J, to give you—	3620
	9: 5	to Abraham, Isaac and J.	3620
	9:27	Remember your servants Abraham, Isaac and J.	3620
	29:13	Abraham, Isaac and J.	3620
	30:20	Abraham, Isaac and J.	3620
	32: 9	J his allotted inheritance.	3620
	33: 4	the possession of the assembly of J.	3620
	33:10	He teaches your precepts to J and your law	3620
	34: 4	Abraham, Isaac and J when I said,	3620
Jos	24: 4	and to Isaac I gave J and Esau.	3620
	24: 4	but J and his sons went down to Egypt.	3620
	24:32	that J bought for a hundred pieces of silver	3620
1Sa	12: 8	"After J entered Egypt,	3620
2Sa	23: 1	the man anointed by the God of J,	3620
	23: 1	for each of the tribes descended from J,	3620
2Ki	13:23	with Abraham, Isaac and J.	3620
	17:34	that the LORD gave the descendants of J,	3620
1Ch	16:13	O sons of J, his chosen ones.	3620
	16:17	He confirmed it to J as a decree,	3620
Ps	14: 7	let J rejoice and Israel be glad!	3620
	20: 1	may the name of the God of J protect you.	3620
	22:23	All you descendants of J, honor him!	3620
	24: 6	who seek your face, O God of J.	3620
	44: 4	who decrees victories for J.	3620
	46: 7	the God of J is our fortress.	3620
	46:11	the God of J is our fortress.	3620
	47: 4	the pride of J, whom he loved.	3620
	53: 6	let J rejoice and Israel be glad!	3620
	59:13	the ends of the earth that God rules over J.	3620
	75: 9	I will sing praise to the God of J.	3620
	76: 6	At your rebuke, O God of J,	3620
	77:15	the descendants of J and Joseph.	3620
	78: 5	He decreed statutes for J and established	3620
	78:21	his fire broke out against J,	3620
	78:71	to be the shepherd of his people J,	3620
	79: 7	for they have devoured J	3620
	81: 1	shout aloud to the God of J!	3620
	81: 4	an ordinance of the God of J.	3620
	84: 8	listen to me, O God of J.	3620
	85: 1	you restored the fortunes of J.	3620
	87: 2	of Zion more than all the dwellings of J.	3620
	94: 7	the God of J pays no heed."	3620
	99: 4	in J you have done what is just and right.	3620
	105: 6	O sons of J, his chosen ones.	3620
	105:10	He confirmed it to J as a decree,	3620
	105:23	J lived as an alien in the land of Ham.	3620
	114: 1	J from a people of foreign tongue,	3620
	114: 7	at the presence of the God of J,	3620
	132: 2	and made a vow to the Mighty One of J:	3620
	132: 5	a dwelling for the Mighty One of J."	3620
	135: 4	the LORD has chosen J to be his own,	3620
	146: 5	Blessed is he whose help is the God of J,	3620
	147:19	He has revealed his word to J,	3620
Isa	2: 3	to the house of the God of J.	3620
	2: 5	Come, O house of J, let us walk in the	3620
	2: 6	abandoned your people, the house of J.	3620
	8:17	who is hiding his face from the house of J;	3620
	9: 8	The Lord has sent a message against J;	3620
	10:20	the survivors of the house of J,	3620
	10:21	of J will return to the Mighty God.	3620
	14: 1	The LORD will have compassion on J;	3620
	14: 1	and unite with the house of J.	3620
	17: 4	"In that day the glory of J will fade;	3620
	27: 6	In days to come J will take root,	3620
	29:22	says to the house of J:	3620
	29:22	"No longer will J be ashamed;	3620
	29:23	the holiness of the Holy One of J,	3620
	40:27	Why do you say, O J, and complain,	3620
	41: 8	"But you, O Israel, my servant,	3620
	41:14	Do not be afraid, O worm J, O little Israel,	3620
	42:24	Who handed J over to become loot,	3620
	43: 1	he who created you, O J,	3620
	43:22	"Yet you have not called upon me, O J,	3620
	43:28	and I will consign J to destruction	3620
	44: 1	"But now listen, O J, my servant, Israel,	3620
	44: 2	Do not be afraid, O J, my servant,	3620
	44: 5	another will call himself by the name of J;	3620
	44:21	"Remember these things, O J,	3620
	44:23	for the LORD has redeemed J.	3620
	45: 4	For the sake of J my servant,	3620
	46: 3	"Listen to me, O house of J,	3620
	48: 1	"Listen to this, O house of J,	3620
	48:12	"Listen to me, O J, Israel,	3620
	48:20	"The LORD has redeemed his servant J."	3620
	49: 5	the womb to be his servant to bring J back	3620
	49: 6	to be my servant to restore the tribes of J	3620
	49:26	your Redeemer, the Mighty One of J."	3620
	58: 1	and to the house of J their sins.	3620
	58:14	to feast on the inheritance of your father J."	3620
	59:20	to those in J who repent of their sins,"	3620
	60:16	your Redeemer, the Mighty One of J.	3620
	65: 9	I will bring forth descendants from J,	3620
Jer	2: 4	Hear the word of the LORD, O house of J,	3620
	5:20	to the house of J and proclaim it in Judah:	3620

Jer	10:16	He who is the Portion of **J** is not like these,	3620
	10:25	For they have devoured **J**;	3620
	30: 7	It will be a time of trouble for **J**,	3620
	30:10	" 'So do not fear, O **J** my servant;	3620
	30:10	**J** will again have peace and security,	3620
	31: 7	"Sing with joy for **J**;	3620
	31:11	For the LORD will ransom **J**	3620
	33:26	the descendants of **J** and David my servant	3620
	33:26	the descendants of Abraham, Isaac and **J**.	3620
	46:27	"Do not fear, O **J** my servant;	3620
	46:27	**J** will again have peace and security,	3620
	46:28	Do not fear, O **J** my servant,	3620
	51:19	He who is the Portion of **J** is not like these,	3620
La	1:17	for **J** that his neighbors become his foes;	3620
	2: 2	up all the dwellings of **J**;	3620
	2: 3	He has burned in **J** like a flaming fire	3620
Eze	20: 5	the house of **J** and revealed myself to them	3620
	28:25	which I gave to my servant **J**.	3620
	37:25	in the land I gave to my servant **J**,	3620
	39:25	I will now bring **J** back from captivity	3620
Hos	10:11	and **J** must break up the ground.	3620
	12: 2	he will punish **J** according to his ways	3620
	12:12	**J** fled to the country of Aram;	3620
Am	3:13	and testify against the house of **J**,"	3620
	6: 8	the pride of **J** and detest his fortresses;	3620
	7: 2	How can **J** survive?	3620
	7: 5	How can **J** survive?	3620
	8: 7	The LORD has sworn by the Pride of **J**:	3620
	9: 8	I will not totally destroy the house of **J**,"	3620
Ob	1:10	of the violence against your brother **J**,	3620
	1:17	the house of **J** will possess its inheritance.	3620
	1:18	The house of **J** will be a fire and the house	3620
Mic	2: 7	Should it be said, O house of **J**:	3620
	2:12	"I will surely gather all of you, O **J**;	3620
	3: 1	Then I said, "Listen, you leaders of **J**,	3620
	3: 8	to declare to **J** his transgression,	3620
	3: 9	Hear this, you leaders of the house of **J**,	3620
	4: 2	to the house of the God of **J**.	3620
	5: 7	of **J** will be in the midst of many peoples	3620
	5: 8	The remnant of **J** will be among	3620
	7:20	You will be true to **J**,	3620
Na	2: 2	The LORD will restore the splendor of **J**	3620
Mal	1: 2	"Yet I have loved **J**,	3620
	2:12	the LORD cut him off from the tents of **J**—	3620
	3: 6	So you, O descendants of **J**,	3620
Mt	1: 2	Isaac the father of **J**,	2609
	1: 2	**J** the father of Judah and his brothers,	2609
	1:15	Matthan the father of **J**,	2609
	1:16	and **J** the father of Joseph,	2609
	8:11	Isaac and **J** in the kingdom of heaven.	2609
	22:32	the God of Isaac, and the God *of* **J**'?	2609
Mk	12:26	the God of Isaac, and the God *of* **J**.	2609
Lk	1:33	he will reign over the house *of* **J** forever;	2609
	3:34	the son *of* **J**, the son of Isaac,	2609
	13:28	**J** and all the prophets in the kingdom	2609
	20:37	and the God of Isaac, and the God *of* **J**.'	2609
Jn	4: 5	of ground **J** had given to his son Joseph.	2609
	4:12	Are you greater than our father **J**,	2609
Ac	3:13	The God of Abraham, Isaac and **J**,	2609
	7: 8	Later Isaac became the father of **J**,	2609
	7: 8	and **J** became the father of the twelve	2609
	7:12	When **J** heard that there was grain	2609
	7:14	for his father **J** and his whole family,	2609
	7:15	Then **J** went down to Egypt,	2609
	7:32	the God *of* Abraham, Isaac and **J**.'	2609
	7:46	a dwelling place for the God *of* **J**.	2609
Ro	9:13	"**J** I loved, but Esau I hated."	2609
	11:26	he will turn godlessness away from **J**.	2609
Heb	11: 9	he lived in tents, as did Isaac and **J**,	2609
	11:20	By faith Isaac blessed **J** and Esau in regard	2609
	11:21	By faith **J**, when he was dying,	2609

JACOB'S (21) [JACOB]

Ge	31:33	into **J** tent and into Leah's tent and into	3620
	32:21	So **J** gifts went on ahead of him,	2021S
	32:25	of **J** hip so that his hip was wrenched	3620
	32:32	because the socket of **J** hip was touched	3620
	34: 7	Now **J** sons had come in from the fields	3620
	34: 7	in Israel by lying with **J** daughter—	3620
	34:13	**J** sons replied deceitfully as they spoke	3620
	34:19	because he was delighted with **J** daughter.	3620
	34:25	two of **J** sons, Simeon and Levi,	3620
	46:19	The sons of **J** wife Rachel.	3620
	46:27	the members of **J** family,	3620
	50:12	So **J** sons did as he had commanded them:	2257S
Dt	33:28	**J** spring is secure in a land of grain	3620
Isa	27: 9	By this, then, will **J** guilt be atoned for,	3620
	41:21	"Set forth your arguments," says **J** King.	3620
	45:19	I have not said to **J** descendants,	3620
Jer	30:18	" 'I will restore the fortunes of **J** tents	3620
Mic	1: 5	All this is because of **J** transgression,	3620
	1: 5	What is **J** transgression?	3620
Mal	1: 2	"Was not Esau **J** brother?"	3620+4200
Jn	4: 6	**J** well was there, and Jesus,	2609

JADA (2)

1Ch	2:28	The sons of Onam: Shammai and **J**.	3360
	2:32	The sons of **J**, Shammai's brother:	3360

JADAH (2)

1Ch	9:42	Ahaz was the father of **J**,	3586
	9:42	**J** was the father of Alemeth,	3586

JADAU (KJV) See JADDAI

JADDAI (1)

Ezr	10:43	Jeiel, Mattithiah, Zabad, Zebina, **J**,	3350

JADDUA (3)

Ne	10:21	Meshezabel, Zadok, **J**,	3348
	12:11	and Jonathan the father of **J**.	3348
	12:22	Joiada, Johanan and **J**,	3348

JADON (1)

Ne	3: 7	Melatiah of Gibeon and **J** of Meronoth—	3347

JAEL (6)

Jdg	4:17	however, fled on foot to the tent of **J**,	3605
	4:18	**J** went out to meet Sisera and said to him,	3605
	4:21	But **J**, Heber's wife, picked up a tent peg	3605
	4:22	and **J** went out to meet him.	3605
	5: 6	in the days of **J**, the roads were abandoned;	3605
	5:24	"Most blessed of women be **J**,	3605

JAGGED (1)

Job	41:30	His undersides are **j** potsherds,	2529

JAGUR (1)

Jos	15:21	of Edom were: Kabzeel, Eder, **J**,	3327

JAH (KJV) See †LORD

JAHATH (7)

1Ch	4: 2	Reaiah son of Shobal was the father of **J**,	3511
	4: 2	and **J** the father of Ahumai and Lahad.	3511
	6:43	of **J**, the son of Gershon, the son of Levi;	3511
	23:10	sons of Shimei: **J**, Ziza, Jeush and Beriah.	3511
	23:11	**J** was the first and Ziza the second,	3511
	24:22	from the sons of Shelomoth: **J**.	3511
2Ch	34:12	to direct them were **J** and Obadiah,	3511

JAHAZ (7)

Nu	21:23	When he reached **J**, he fought with Israel.	3403
Dt	2:32	to meet us in battle at **J**,	3403
Jos	13:18	**J**, Kedemoth, Mephaath,	3403
	21:36	from the tribe of Reuben, Bezer, **J**,	3403
Jdg	11:20	and encamped at **J** and fought with Israel.	3403
Isa	15: 4	their voices are heard all the way to **J**.	3403
Jer	48:34	from Heshbon to Elealeh and **J**,	3403

JAHAZA, JAHAZAH (KJV) See JAHAZ

JAHAZIAH (KJV) See JAHZEIAH

JAHAZIEL (6)

1Ch	12: 4	Jeremiah, **J**, Johanan,	3487
	16: 6	and Benaiah and **J** the priests were to blow	3487
	23:19	**J** the third and Jekameam the fourth.	3487
	24:23	**J** the third and Jekameam the fourth.	3487
2Ch	20:14	the LORD came upon **J** son of Zechariah,	3487
Ezr	8: 5	of **J**, and with him 300 men;	3487

JAHDAI (1)

1Ch	2:47	The sons of **J**:	3367

JAHDIEL (1)

1Ch	5:24	Eliel, Azriel, Jeremiah, Hodaviah and **J**.	3484

JAHDO (1)

1Ch	5:14	the son of Jeshishai, the son of **J**,	3482

JAHLEEL (2) [JAHLEELITE]

Ge	46:14	The sons of Zebulun: Sered, Elon and **J**.	3499
Nu	26:26	through **J**, the Jahleelite clan.	3499

JAHLEELITE (1) [JAHLEEL]

Nu	26:26	through Jahleel, the **J** clan.	3500

JAHMAI (1)

1Ch	7: 2	Uzzi, Rephaiah, Jeriel, **J**,	3503

JAHZAH (2)

1Ch	6:78	Jericho they received Bezer in the desert, **J**,	3404
Jer	48:21	to Holon, **J** and Mephaath,	3404

JAHZEEL (1) [JAHZEELITE]

Nu	26:48	through **J**, the Jahzeelite clan;	3505

JAHZEELITE (1) [JAHZEEL]

Nu	26:48	through Jahzeel, the **J** clan;	3506

JAHZEIAH (1)

Ezr	10:15	Only Jonathan son of Asahel and **J** son	3488

JAHZERAH (1)

1Ch	9:12	and Maasai son of Adiel, the son of **J**,	3492

JAHZIEL (2)

Ge	46:24	**J**, Guni, Jezer and Shillem.	3505
1Ch	7:13	**J**, Guni, Jezer and Shillem—	3507

JAIL (7) [JAILER, JAILERS]

Ac	4: 3	they put them in **j** until the next day.	5499
	5:18	the apostles and put them in the public **j**.	5499
	5:19	the doors *of* the **j** and brought them out.	5871
	5:21	and sent to the **j** for the apostles.	1303
	5:22	But on arriving at the **j**,	5871
	5:23	"We found the **j** securely locked, with	1303
	5:25	The men you put in **j** are standing in	5871

JAILER (7) [JAIL]

Ac	16:23	**j** was commanded to guard them carefully.	1302
	16:27	The **j** woke up, and when he saw the	1302
	16:29	The **j** called for lights,	NIG
	16:33	the **j** took them and washed their wounds;	NIG
	16:34	The **j** brought them into his house and set	NIG
	16:35	the magistrates sent their officers to the **j**	NIG
	16:36	The **j** told Paul, "The magistrates have	1302

JAILERS (1) [JAIL]

Mt	18:34	turned him over *to* the **j** to be tortured,	991

JAIR (9) [JAIRITE, HAVVOTH JAIR]

Nu	32:41	**J**, a descendant of Manasseh,	3281
Dt	3:14	**J**, a descendant of Manasseh,	3281
Jos	13:30	all the settlements of **J** in Bashan,	3281
Jdg	10: 3	He was followed by **J** of Gilead.	3281
	10: 5	When **J** died, he was buried in Kamon.	3281
1Ki	4:13	in Ramoth Gilead (the settlements of **J** son	3281
1Ch	2:22	Segub was the father of **J**,	3281
	20: 5	Elhanan son of **J** killed Lahmi the brother	3600
Est	2: 5	named Mordecai son of **J**,	3281

JAIRITE (1) [JAIR]

2Sa	20:26	and Ira the **J** was David's priest.	3285

JAIRUS (6)

Mk	5:22	one of the synagogue rulers, named **J**,	2608
	5:35	some men came from the house of **J**,	NIG
Lk	8:41	a man named **J**, a ruler of the synagogue,	2608
	8:49	someone came from the house of **J**,	NIG
	8:50	Hearing this, Jesus said *to* **J**,	899S
	8:51	When he arrived at the house of **J**,	NIG

JAKAN (KJV) See AKAN

JAKEH (1)

Pr	30: 1	The sayings of Agur son of **J**—	3681

JAKIM (2)

1Ch	8:19	**J**, Zicri, Zabdi,	3691
	24:12	the eleventh to Eliashib, the twelfth to **J**,	3691

JAKIN (8) [JAKINITE]

Ge	46:10	Jemuel, Jamin, Ohad, **J**,	3520
Ex	6:15	of Simeon were Jemuel, Jamin, Ohad, **J**,	3520
Nu	26:12	through **J**, the Jakinite clan;	3520
1Ki	7:21	to the south he named **J** and the one to	3521
1Ch	9:10	Of the priests: Jedaiah; Jehoiarib; **J**;	3520
	24:17	the twenty-first to **J**,	3520
2Ch	3:17	to the south he named **J** and the one to	3521
Ne	11:10	the son of Joiarib; **J**;	3520

JAKINITE (1) [JAKIN]

Nu	26:12	through Jakin, the **J** clan;	3522

JALAM (4)

Ge	36: 5	and Oholibamah bore Jeush, **J** and Korah.	3609
	36:14	Jeush, **J** and Korah.	3609
	36:18	Chiefs Jeush, **J** and Korah.	3609
1Ch	1:35	Eliphaz, Reuel, Jeush, **J** and Korah.	3609

JALON (1)

1Ch	4:17	Jether, Mered, Epher and **J**.	3534

JAMBRES (1)

2Ti	3: 8	Just as Jannes and **J** opposed Moses,	2612

JAMBS (12)

1Ki	6:31	of olive wood with five-sided **j**.	382+4647
	6:33	In the same way he made four-sided **j**	4647
Eze	40: 9	and its **j** were two cubits thick.	382
	40:24	He measured its **j** and its portico,	382
	40:31	palm trees decorated its **j**,	382
	40:34	palm trees decorated the **j** on either side,	382
	40:37	palm trees decorated the **j** on either side,	382
	40:48	of the temple and measured the **j** *of*	382
	40:49	and there were pillars on each side of the **j**.	382
	41: 1	to the outer sanctuary and measured the **j**;	382
	41: 1	width of the **j** was six cubits on each side.	NIH
	41: 3	into the inner sanctuary and measured the **j**	382

JAMES (42)

Mt	4:21	J son of Zebedee and his brother John.	2610
	10: 2	J son of Zebedee, and his brother John;	2610
	10: 3	J son of Alphaeus, and Thaddaeus;	2610
	13:55	and aren't his brothers J, Joseph,	2610
	17: 1	J and John the brother of James,	2610
	17: 1	James and John the brother of J,	899S
	27:56	Mary the mother of J and Joses,	2610
Mk	1:19	he saw J son of Zebedee	2610
	1:29	they went with J and John to the home	2610
	3:17	J son of Zebedee and his brother John	2610
	3:18	Thomas, J son of Alphaeus, Thaddaeus,	2610
	5:37	J and John the brother of James.	2610
	5:37	James and John the brother of J.	2610
	6: 3	Isn't this Mary's son and the brother of J,	2610
	9: 2	J and John with him and led them up	2610
	10:35	Then J and John; the sons of Zebedee,	2610
	10:41	they became indignant with J and John.	2610
	13: 3	J, John and Andrew asked him privately,	2610
	14:33	He took Peter, J and John along with him,	2610
	15:40	the mother of J the younger and of Joses,	2610
	16: 1	Mary Magdalene, Mary the mother of J,	2610
Lk	5:10	and so were J and John,	2610
	6:14	his brother Andrew, J, John, Philip,	2610
	6:15	Thomas, J son of Alphaeus,	2610
	6:16	Judas son of J, and Judas Iscariot,	2610
	8:51	in with him except Peter, John and J, and	2610
	9:28	John and J with him and went up onto	2610
	9:54	When the disciples J and John saw this,	2610
	24:10	Joanna, Mary the mother of J,	2610
Ac	1:13	present were Peter, John, J and Andrew;	2610
	1:13	J son of Alphaeus and Simon the Zealot,	2610
	1:13	and Judas son of J.	2610
	12: 2	He had J, the brother of John,	2610
	12:17	"Tell J and the brothers about this,"	2610
	15:13	When they finished, J spoke up:	2610
	21:18	and the rest of us went to see J,	2610
1Co	15: 7	Then he appeared to J, then to all the	2610
Gal	1:19	only J, the Lord's brother.	2610
	2: 9	J, Peter and John, those reputed to	2610
	2:12	Before certain men came from J,	2610
Jas	1: 1	J, a servant of God and of the Lord Jesus	2610
Jude	1: 1	servant of Jesus Christ and a brother of J,	2610

JAMIN (6) [JAMINITE]

Ge	46:10	The sons of Simeon: Jemuel, J, Ohad,	3546
Ex	6:15	The sons of Simeon were Jemuel, J, Ohad,	3546
Nu	26:12	through J, the Jaminite clan;	3546
1Ch	2:27	Maaz, J and Eker.	3546
	4:24	Nemuel, J, Jarib, Zerah and Shaul;	3546
Ne	8: 7	The Levites—Jeshua, Bani, Sherebiah, J,	3546

JAMINITE (1) [JAMIN]

Nu	26:12	through Jamin, the J clan;	3547

JAMLECH (1)

1Ch	4:34	Meshobab, J, Joshah son of Amaziah,	3552

JANAI (1)

1Ch	5:12	Shapham the second, then J and Shaphat,	3614

JANGLING (KJV) See TALK

JANIM (1)

Jos	15:53	J, Beth Tappuah, Aphekah,	3565

JANNAI (1)

Lk	3:24	the son of J, the son of Joseph,	2613

JANNES (1)

2Ti	3: 8	Just as J and Jambres opposed Moses,	2614

JANOAH (3)

Jos	16: 6	passing by it to J on the east.	3562
	16: 7	Then it went down from J to Ataroth	3562
2Ki	15:29	Abel Beth Maacah, J, Kedesh and Hazor.	3562

JANUM (KJV) See JANIM

JAPHETH (12)

Ge	5:32	he became the father of Shem, Ham and J.	3651
	6:10	Noah had three sons: Shem, Ham and J.	3651
	7:13	and J, together with his wife and the wives	3651
	9:18	of the ark were Shem, Ham and J.	3651
	9:23	But Shem and J took a garment and laid it	3651
	9:27	May God extend the territory of J;	3651
	9:27	may J live in the tents of Shem,	NIH
	10: 1	This is the account of Shem, Ham and J,	3651
	10: 2	The sons of J: Gomer, Magog, Madai,	3651
	10:21	whose older brother was J;	3651
1Ch	1: 4	The sons of Noah: Shem, Ham and J.	3651
	1: 5	The sons of J: Gomer, Magog, Madai,	3651

JAPHIA (5)

Jos	10: 3	J king of Lachish and Debir king of Eglon.	3644
	19:12	and went on to Daberath and up to J.	3643
2Sa	5:15	Ibhar, Elishua, Nepheg, J,	3644
1Ch	3: 7	Nogah, Nepheg, J,	3644
	14: 6	Nogah, Nepheg, J,	3644

JAPHLET (2) [JAPHLET'S, JAPHLETITES]

1Ch	7:32	Heber was the father of J,	3646
	7:33	The sons of J:	3646

JAPHLET'S (1) [JAPHLET]

1Ch	7:33	These were J sons.	3646

JAPHLETITES (1) [JAPHLET]

Jos	16: 3	to the territory of the J as far as the region	3647

JAPHO (KJV) See JOPPA

JAR (37) [JARS]

Ge	24:14	'Please let down your j that I may have	3902
	24:15	Rebekah came out with her j	3902
	24:16	filled her j and came up again.	3902
	24:17	"Please give me a little water from your j."	3902
	24:18	the j to her hands and gave him a drink.	3902
	24:20	she quickly emptied her j into the trough,	3902
	24:43	a little water from your j,"	3902
	24:45	with her j on her shoulder.	3902
	24:46	"She quickly lowered her j	3902
Ex	16:33	"Take a j and put an omer of manna in it.	7573
Nu	5:17	in a clay j and put some dust from	3998
	19:17	into a j and pour fresh water over them.	3998
1Ki	14: 3	some cakes and a j of honey,	1318
	17:10	a little water in a j so I may have a drink?"	3998
	17:12	only a handful of flour in a j and a little oil	3902
	17:14	'The j of flour will not be used up and	3902
	17:16	the j of flour was not used up and the jug	3902
	19: 6	bread baked over hot coals, and a j of water.	7608
2Ki	4: 6	But he replied, "There is not a j left."	3998
Jer	19: 1	"Go and buy a clay j from a potter.	1318
	19:10	"Then break the j while those who go	1318
	19:11	as this potter's j is smashed and cannot	3998
	32:14	and put them in a clay j so they will last	3998
	48:11	not poured from one j to another—	3998
	48:38	for I have broken Moab like a j	3998
	51:34	he has made us an empty j.	3998
Eze	4: 9	in a storage j and use them to make bread	3998
Mt	26: 7	an alabaster j of very expensive perfume,	223
Mk	14: 3	an alabaster j of very expensive perfume,	223
	14: 3	the j and poured the perfume on his head.	223
	14:13	a man carrying a j of water will meet you.	3040
Lk	7:37	she brought an alabaster j of perfume,	223
	8:16	a lamp and hides it in a j or puts it under	5007
	22:10	a man carrying a j of water will meet you.	3040
Jn	4:28	Then, leaving her water j,	5620
	19:29	A j of wine vinegar was there,	5007
Heb	9: 4	This ark contained the gold j of manna,	5085

JAREB (KJV) See GREAT

JARED (7)

Ge	5:15	he became the father of J.	3719
	5:16	And after he became the father of J,	3719
	5:18	When J had lived 162 years,	3719
	5:19	J lived 800 years and had other sons	3719
	5:20	Altogether, J lived 962 years,	3719
1Ch	1: 2	Kenan, Mahalalel, J,	3719
Lk	3:37	the son of J, the son of Mahalalel,	2616

JARESIAH (KJV) See JAARESHIAH

JARHA (2)

1Ch	2:34	He had an Egyptian servant named J.	3739
	2:35	in marriage to his servant J,	3739

JARIB (3)

1Ch	4:24	Nemuel, Jamin, J, Zerah and Shaul;	3743
Ezr	8:16	Shemaiah, Elnathan, J, Elnathan, Nathan,	3743
	10:18	Maaseiah, Eliezer, J and Gedaliah.	3743

JARKON See ME JARKON

JARMUTH (7)

Jos	10: 3	Piram king of J,	3754
	10: 5	the kings of Jerusalem, Hebron, J,	3754
	10:23	the kings of Jerusalem, Hebron, J,	3754
	12:11	the king of J one the king of Lachish one	3754
	15:35	J, Adullam, Socoh, Azekah,	3754
	21:29	J and En Gannim, together	3754
Ne	11:29	in En Rimmon, in Zorah, in J,	3754

JAROAH (1)

1Ch	5:14	the son of J, the son of Gilead,	3726

JARS (23) [JAR]

Ex	7:19	even in the wooden buckets and stone j."	AIT
Nu	4: 7	and the j for drink offerings;	7987
	4: 9	and all its j for the oil used to supply it.	3998
Jdg	7:16	and empty j in the hands of all of them,	3902
	7:19	They blew their trumpets and broke the j	3902
	7:20	the trumpets and smashed the j.	3902
Ru	2: 9	from the water j the men have filled."	3998
1Ki	18:33	"Fill four large j with water and pour it	3902
2Ki	4: 3	and ask all your neighbors for empty j.	3998
	4: 4	Pour oil into all the j, and as each is filled,	3998

JASHAR (2)

Jos	10:13	as it is written in the Book of J.	3839
2Sa	1:18	of the bow (it is written in the Book of J):	3839

JASHEN (1)

2Sa	23:32	the sons of J,	3826

JASHER (KJV) See JASHAR

JASHOBEAM (3)

1Ch	11:11	J, a Hacmonite, was chief of the officers;	3790
	12: 6	Azarel, Joezer and J the Korahites;	3790
	27: 2	for the first month, was J son of Zabdiel.	3790

JASHUB (4) [JASHUBITE]

Ge	46:13	Tola, Puah, J and Shimron.	3793
Nu	26:24	through J, the Jashubite clan;	3793
1Ch	7: 1	Tola, Puah, J and Shimron—four in all.	3793
Ezr	10:29	Meshullam, Malluch, Adaiah, J,	3793

JASHUBI LEHEM (1)

1Ch	4:22	who ruled in Moab and J.	3788

JASHUBITE (1) [JASHUB]

Nu	26:24	through Jashub, the J clan;	3795

JASIEL (KJV) See JAASIEL

JASON (4) [JASON'S]

Ac	17: 6	they dragged J and some other brothers	2619
	17: 7	and J has welcomed them into his house.	2619
	17: 9	Then they made J and the others post bond	2619
Ro	16:21	as do Lucius, J and Sosipater,	2619

JASON'S (1) [JASON]

Ac	17: 5	They rushed to J house in search of Paul	2619

JASPER (8)

Ex	28:20	an onyx and a j.	3835
	39:13	an onyx and a j.	3835
Job	28:18	Coral and j are not worthy of mention;	1486
Eze	28:13	topaz and emerald, chrysolite, onyx and j,	3835
Rev	4: 3	the appearance of j and carnelian.	2618
	21:11	like a j, clear as crystal.	2618+3345
	21:18	The wall was made of j,	2618
	21:19	The first foundation was j,	2618

JATHNIEL (1)

1Ch	26: 2	Zebadiah the third, J the fourth,	3853

JATTIR (4)

Jos	15:48	In the hill country: Shamir, J, Socoh,	3848
	21:14	J, Eshtemoa,	3848
1Sa	30:27	Ramoth Negev and J;	3848
1Ch	6:57	and Libnah, J, Eshtemoa,	3848

JAVAN (4)

Ge	10: 2	Gomer, Magog, Madai, J, Tubal,	3430
	10: 4	The sons of J: Elishah, Tarshish,	3430
1Ch	1: 5	Gomer, Magog, Madai, J, Tubal,	3430
	1: 7	The sons of J: Elishah, Tarshish,	3430

JAVELIN (7) [JAVELINS]

Jos	8:18	toward Ai the j that is in your hand,	3959
	8:18	So Joshua held out his j toward Ai.	3959
	8:26	not draw back the hand that held out his j	3959
1Sa	17: 6	and a bronze j was slung on his back.	3959
	17:45	against me with sword and spear and j,	3959
Job	41:26	nor does the spear or the dart or the j.	9233
Ps	35: 3	and j against those who pursue me.	6038

JAVELINS (1) [JAVELIN]

2Sa	18:14	So he took three j in his hand	8657

JAW (2) [JAWBONE, JAWS]

Job	41: 2	a cord through his nose or pierce his j with	4305
Ps	3: 7	Strike all my enemies on the j;	4305

JAWBONE (4) [JAW]

Jdg	15:15	Finding a fresh j of a donkey,	4305
	15:16	a donkey's j I have made donkeys of them.	4305
	15:16	With a donkey's j I have killed	4305

(Third column top, before JASHAR:)

2Ki	4: 5	the j to her and she kept pouring.	NIH
	4: 6	When all the j were full,	3998
Job	38:37	Who can tip over the water j of the heavens	5574
Ps	33: 7	He gathers the waters of the sea into j;	5532
Isa	22:24	from the bowls to all the j.	5574
Jer	14: 3	They return with their j unfilled;	3998
	40:10	and put them in your storage j,	3998
	48:12	"when I will send men who pour from j,	NIH
	48:12	they will empty her j and smash her jugs.	3998
Mt	25: 4	took oil in j along with their lamps.	31
Jn	2: 6	Nearby stood six stone water j,	5620
	2: 7	"Fill the j with water";	5620
2Co	4: 7	But we have this treasure in j of clay	5007

Jdg 15:17 he threw away the **j**; 4305

JAWS (5) [JAW]

Job 36:16	"He is wooing you from the **j** of distress to	7023
Pr 30:14	and whose **j** are set with knives to devour	5506
Isa 30:28	he places in the **j** of the peoples a bit	4305
Eze 29: 4	But I will put hooks in your **j** and make	4305
38: 4	put hooks in your **j** and bring you out	4305

JAZER (13)

Nu 21:32	After Moses had sent spies to **J**,	3597
32: 1	that the lands of **J** and Gilead were suitable	3597
32: 3	**J**, Nimrah, Heshbon, Elealeh, Sebam,	3597
32:35	Atroth Shophan, **J**, Jogbehah,	3597
Jos 13:25	The territory of **J**, all the towns of Gilead	3597
21:39	and **J**, together with their pasturelands—	3597
2Sa 24: 5	and then went through Gad and on to **J**.	3597
1Ch 6:81	Heshbon and **J**, together	3597
26:31	the Hebronites were found at **J** in Gilead.	3597
Isa 16: 8	which once reached **J** and spread toward	3597
16: 9	So I weep, as **J** weeps,	3597
Jer 48:32	I weep for you, as **J** weeps,	3597
48:32	they reached as far as the sea of **J**.	3597

JAZIZ (1)

1Ch 27:31	**J** the Hagrite was in charge of the flocks.	3467

JEALOUS (28) [JEALOUSY]

Ge 30: 1	she became **j** of her sister.	7861
37:11	His brothers were **j** of him,	7861
Ex 20: 5	for I, the LORD your God, am a **j** God,	7862
34:14	whose name is **J**, is a jealous God.	7862
34:14	whose name is Jealous, is a **j** God.	7862
Nu 5:14	or if he is **j** and suspects her even though	
	she is not impure—	6296+6584+7863+8120
11:29	But Moses replied, "Are you **j** for my sake?	7861
Dt 4:24	your God is a consuming fire, a **j** God.	7862
5: 9	for I, the LORD your God, am a **j** God,	7862
6:15	is a **j** God and his anger will burn	7862
32:16	They made him **j** with their foreign gods	7861
32:21	They made me **j** by what is no god	7861
Jos 24:19	He is a holy God; he is a **j** God.	7868
1Sa 18: 9	Saul kept a **j** eye on David.	6523
1Ki 14:22	they stirred up his **j** anger more than	7861
Isa 11:13	Ephraim will not be **j** of Judah,	7861
Eze 16:38	of my wrath and **j** anger.	7863
16:42	and my **j** anger will turn away from you;	7863
23:25	I will direct my **j** anger against you,	7863
36: 6	in my **j** wrath because you have suffered	7863
Joel 2:18	Then the LORD will be **j** for his land	7861
Na 1: 2	The LORD is a **j** and avenging God;	7868
Zep 3: 8	be consumed by the fire of my **j** anger.	7863
Zec 1:14	'I am very **j** for Jerusalem and Zion,	7861+7863
8: 2	"I am very **j** for Zion;	7861+7863
Ac 7: 9	"Because the patriarchs were **j** of Joseph,	2420
17: 5	But the Jews were **j**;	2420
2Co 11: 2	I am **j** for you with a godly jealousy.	2420

JEALOUSY (26) [JEALOUS]

Nu 5:14	and if feelings of **j** come over her husband	7863
5:15	because it is a grain offering for **j**,	7863
5:18	the grain offering for **j**,	7863
5:25	from her hands the grain offering for **j**,	7863
5:29	is the law of **j** when a woman goes astray	7863
5:30	or when feelings of **j** come over a man	7863
Ps 78:58	they aroused his **j** with their idols.	7861
79: 5	How long will your **j** burn like fire?	7863
Pr 6:34	for **j** arouses a husband's fury,	7863
27: 4	but who can stand before **j**?	7863
Ecc 4: 4	and their **j** have long since vanished,	7863
SS 8: 6	its **j** unyielding as the grave.	7863
Isa 11:13	Ephraim's **j** will vanish,	7863
Eze 8: 3	where the idol that provokes to **j** stood.	7861
8: 5	of the gate of the altar I saw this idol of **j**.	7863
35:11	the anger and **j** you showed in your hatred	7863
Zep 1:18	of his **j** the whole world will be consumed,	7863
Zec 8: 2	I am burning with **j** for her."	7861
Ac 5:17	of the Sadducees, were filled with **j**.	2419
13:45	they were filled with **j** and talked abusively	2419
Ro 13:13	not in dissension and **j**.	2419
1Co 3: 3	since there is **j** and quarreling among you,	2419
10:22	Are we trying to arouse the Lord's **j**?	4143
2Co 11: 2	I am jealous for you with a godly **j**.	2419
12:20	I fear that there may be quarreling, **j**,	2419
Gal 5:20	hatred, discord, **j**, fits of rage,	2419

JEARIM (1) [KESALON, KIRIATH JEARIM]

Jos 15:10	ran along the northern slope of Mount **J**	3630

JEATHERAI (1)

1Ch 6:21	Iddo his son, Zerah his son and **J** his son.	3290

JEBERECHIAH (KJV) See JEBEREKIAH

JEBEREKIAH (1)

Isa 8: 2	in Uriah the priest and Zechariah son of **J**	3310

JEBUS (3) [JEBUSITE, JEBUSITES, JERUSALEM]

Jdg 19:10	and went toward **J** (that is, Jerusalem),	3293

Jdg 19:11	near **J** and the day was almost gone,	3293
1Ch 11: 4	to Jerusalem (that is, **J**).	3293

JEBUSI (KJV) See JEBUSITES

JEBUSITE (9) [JEBUS]

Jos 15: 8	the southern slope of the **J** city (that is,	3294
18:16	along the southern slope of the **J** city and	3294
18:28	Haeleph, the **J** city (that is, Jerusalem),	3294
2Sa 24:16	at the threshing floor of Araunah the **J**.	3294
24:18	on the threshing floor of Araunah the **J**."	3294
1Ch 21:15	at the threshing floor of Araunah the **J**.	3294
21:18	on the threshing floor of Araunah the **J**.	3294
21:28	on the threshing floor of Araunah the **J**,	3294
2Ch 3: 1	on the threshing floor of Araunah the **J**,	3294

JEBUSITES (33) [JEBUS]

Ge 10:16	**J**, Amorites, Girgashites,	3294
15:21	Amorites, Canaanites, Girgashites and **J**."	3294
Ex 3: 8	Amorites, Perizzites, Hivites and **J**.	3294
3:17	Amorites, Perizzites, Hivites and **J**.	3294
13: 5	Hittites, Amorites, Hivites and **J**—	3294
23:23	Hivites and **J**, and I will wipe them out.	3294
33: 2	Hittites, Perizzites, Hivites and **J**.	3294
34:11	Hittites, Perizzites, Hivites and **J**.	3294
Nu 13:29	**J** and Amorites live in the hill country;	3294
Dt 7: 1	Canaanites, Perizzites, Hivites and **J**,	3294
20:17	Canaanites, Perizzites, Hivites and **J**,	3294
Jos 3:10	Perizzites, Girgashites, Amorites and **J**.	3294
9: 1	Canaanites, Perizzites, Hivites and **J**)—	3294
11: 3	Perizzites and **J** in the hill country;	3294
12: 8	Canaanites, Perizzites, Hivites and **J**):	3294
15:63	Judah could not dislodge the **J**,	3294
15:63	to this day the **J** live there with the people	3294
24:11	Hittites, Girgashites, Hivites and **J**,	3294
Jdg 1:21	however, failed to dislodge the **J**,	3294
1:21	the **J** live there with the Benjamites.	3294
3: 5	Amorites, Perizzites, Hivites and **J**.	3294
19:11	at this city of the **J** and spend the night."	3294
2Sa 5: 6	to Jerusalem to attack the **J**,	3294
5: 6	The **J** said to David,	NIH
5: 8	"Anyone who conquers the **J** will have	3294
1Ki 9:20	and **J** (these peoples were not Israelites)—	3294
1Ch 1:14	**J**, Amorites, Girgashites,	3294
11: 4	The **J** who lived there	3294
11: 6	the **J** will become commander-in-chief."	3294
2Ch 8: 7	and **J** (these peoples were not Israelites),	3294
Ezr 9: 1	Perizzites, **J**, Ammonites, Moabites,	3294
Ne 9: 8	Amorites, Perizzites, **J** and Girgashites.	3294
Zec 9: 7	and Ekron will be like the **J**.	3294

JECAMIAH (KJV) See JEKAMIAH

JECHOLIAH (KJV) See JECOLIAH

JECHONIAS (KJV) See JECONIAH

JECOLIAH (2)

2Ki 15: 2	His mother's name was **J**;	3525
2Ch 26: 3	His mother's name was **J**;	3524

JECONIAH (2)

Mt 1:11	the father of **J** and his brothers at the time	2651
1:12	**J** was the father of Shealtiel,	2651

JEDAIAH (11) [JEDAIAH'S]

1Ch 4:37	the son of **J**, the son of Shimri,	3355
9:10	Of the priests: **J**; Jehoiarib; Jakin;	3361
24: 7	the second to **J**,	3361
Ezr 2:36	the descendants of **J** (through the family	3361
Ne 3:10	Adjoining this, **J** son of Harumaph	3355
7:39	the descendants of **J** (through the family	3361
11:10	From the priests: **J**; the son of Joiarib;	3361
12: 6	Shemaiah, Joiarib, **J**,	3361
12: 7	Amok, Hilkiah and **J**.	3361
Zec 6:10	from the exiles Heldai, Tobijah and **J**,	3361
6:14	**J** and Hen son of Zephaniah as a memorial	3361

JEDAIAH'S (2) [JEDAIAH]

Ne 12:19	of Joiarib's, Mattenai; of **J**, Uzzi;	3361
12:21	of Hilkiah's, Hashabiah; of **J**, Nethanel.	3361

JEDIAEL (6)

1Ch 7: 6	Bela, Beker and **J**.	3356
7:10	The son of **J**: Bilhan.	3356
7:11	All these sons of **J** were heads of families.	3356
11:45	**J** son of Shimri,	3356
12:20	Adnah, Jozabad, **J**, Michael, Jozabad,	3356
26: 2	Zechariah the firstborn, **J** the second,	3356

JEDIDAH (1)

2Ki 22: 1	His mother's name was **J** daughter of	3352

JEDIDIAH (1)

2Sa 12:25	through Nathan the prophet to name him **J**.	3354

JEDUTHUN (16)

1Ch 9:16	the son of Galal, the son of **J**;	3349

1Ch 16:38	Obed-Edom son of **J**, and also Hosah,	3357
16:41	With them were Heman and **J** and the rest	3349
16:42	and **J** were responsible for the sounding of	3349
16:42	The sons of **J** were stationed at the gate.	3349
25: 1	and **J** for the ministry of prophesying,	3349
25: 3	As for **J**, from his sons:	3349
25: 3	under the supervision of their father, **J**,	3349
25: 6	**J** and Heman were under the supervision	3349
2Ch 5:12	Heman, **J** and their sons and relatives—	3349
29:14	from the descendants of **J**,	3349
35:15	Asaph, Heman and **J** the king's seer.	3349
Ne 11:17	the son of Galal, the son of **J**.	3349
Ps 39: T	For the director of music. For **J**.	3349
62: T	For the director of music. For **J**.	3349
77: T	For the director of music. For **J**.	3349

JEER (1) [JEERED, JEERS]

Job 16:10	Men open their mouths to **j** at me;	NIH

JEERED (1) [JEER]

2Ki 2:23	some youths came out of the town and **j**	7840

JEERS (1) [JEER]

Heb 11:36	Some faced **j** and flogging,	1849

JEEZER (KJV) See IEZER

JEEZERITES (KJV) See IEZERITE

JEGAR SAHADUTHA (1)

Ge 31:47	Laban called it **J**, and Jacob called it Galeed	3337

JEHALLELEL (2)

1Ch 4:16	The sons of **J**:	3401
2Ch 29:12	Kish son of Abdi and Azariah son of **J**;	3401

JEHATH (1)

1Ch 6:20	Libni his son, **J** his son, Zimmah his son,	3511

JEHDEIAH (2)

1Ch 24:20	from the sons of Shubael: **J**.	3485
27:30	**J** the Meronothite was in charge of	3485

JEHEZKEL (1)

1Ch 24:16	the twentieth to **J**,	3489

JEHIAH (1)

1Ch 15:24	and **J** were also to be doorkeepers for	3496

JEHIEL (14)

1Ch 15:18	Zechariah, Jaaziel, Shemiramoth, **J**, Unni,	3493
15:20	Aziel, Shemiramoth, **J**, Unni, Eliab,	3493
16: 5	then Jeiel, Shemiramoth, **J**, Mattithiah,	3493
23: 8	**J** the first, Zetham and Joel—three in all.	3493
27:32	**J** son of Hacmoni took care of	3493
29: 8	in the custody of **J** the Gershonite.	3493
2Ch 21: 2	the sons of Jehoshaphat, were Azariah, **J**,	3493
29:14	the descendants of Heman, **J** and Shimei;	3493
31:13	**J**, Azaziah, Nahath, Asahel, Jerimoth,	3493
35: 8	Hilkiah, Zechariah and **J**,	3493
Ezr 8: 9	Obadiah son of **J**, and with him 218 men;	3493
10: 2	Then Shecaniah son of **J**,	3493
10:21	Maaseiah, Elijah, Shemaiah, **J** and Uzziah.	3493
10:26	Mattaniah, Zechariah, **J**, Abdi,	3493

JEHIELI (2)

1Ch 26:21	to Ladan the Gershonite, were **J**,	3494
26:22	the sons of **J**,	3494

JEHIZKIAH (1)

2Ch 28:12	of Meshillemoth, **J** son of Shallum,	3491

JEHOADDAH (2)

1Ch 8:36	Ahaz was the father of **J**,	3389
8:36	**J** was the father of Alemeth,	3389

JEHOADDIN (2)

2Ki 14: 2	His mother's name was **J**;	3390
2Ch 25: 1	His mother's name was **J**;	3391

JEHOAHAZ (22)

2Ki 10:35	And **J** his son succeeded him as king.	3370
13: 1	**J** son of Jehu became king of Israel	3370
13: 4	Then **J** sought the LORD's favor,	3370
13: 7	of the army of **J** except fifty horsemen,	3370
13: 8	As for the other events of the reign of **J**,	3370
13: 9	**J** rested with his fathers and was buried	3370
13:10	Jehoash son of **J** became king of Israel	3370
13:22	throughout the reign of **J**.	3370
13:25	of **J** recaptured from Ben-Hadad son	3370
13:25	in battle from his father's.	3370
14: 1	In the second year of Jehoash son of **J** king	3407
14: 8	to Jehoash son of **J**, the son of Jehu, king	3370
14:17	after the death of Jehoash son of **J**	3370
23:30	the people of the land took **J** son of Josiah	3370
23:31	**J** was twenty-three years old	3370

2Ki 23:34 But he took J and carried him off to Egypt, 3370
2Ch 25:17 he sent this challenge to Jehoash son of J, 3370
    25:25 after the death of Jehoash son of J king 3370
    36: 1 the people of the land took J son of Josiah 3370
    36: 2 J was twenty-three years old 3407
    36: 4 made Eliakim, a brother of J, king over 2257S
    36: 4 But Neco took Eliakim's brother J 3407

JEHOASH (28) [JOASH]

2Ki 13: 9 And J his son succeeded him as king. 3409
    13:10 son of Jehoahaz became king of Israel 3371
    13:12 As for the other events of the reign of J, 3409
    13:13 J rested with his fathers, 3409
    13:13 J was buried in Samaria with the kings 3409
    13:14 J king of Israel went down to see him 3409
    13:25 Then J son of Jehoahaz recaptured 3371
    13:25 Three times J defeated him, 3409
    14: 1 the second year of J son of Jehoahaz king 3409
    14: 8 to J son of Jehoahaz, the son of Jehu, king 3371
    14: 9 But J king of Israel replied 3371
    14:11 so J king of Israel attacked. 3371
    14:13 J king of Israel captured Amaziah king 3371
    14:13 Then J went to Jerusalem and broke down NIH
    14:15 As for the other events of the reign of J, 3371
    14:16 J rested with his fathers and was buried 3371
    14:17 after the death of J son of Jehoahaz king 3371
    14:23 of J king of Israel became king in Samaria, 3409
    14:27 by the hand of Jeroboam son of J. 3409
2Ch 25:17 he sent this challenge to J son of Jehoahaz, 3409
    25:18 But J king of Israel replied 3409
    25:20 that he might hand them over to [J], NIH
    25:21 So J king of Israel attacked. 3409
    25:23 J king of Israel captured Amaziah king 3409
    25:23 Then J brought him to Jerusalem 3409
    25:25 after the death of J son of Jehoahaz king 3409
Hos 1: 1 during the reign of Jeroboam son of J king 3409
Am 1: 1 and Jeroboam son of J was king of Israel. 3409

JEHOHANAN (9)

1Ch 26: 3 J the sixth and Eliehoenai the seventh, 3380
2Ch 17:15 next, J the commander, with 280,000; 3380
    23: 1 Azariah son of Jeroham, Ishmael son of J, 3380
    28:12 Azariah son of J, Berekiah son 3380
Ezr 10: 6 and went to the room of J son of Eliashib. 3380
    10:28 J, Hananiah, Zabbai and Athlai. 3380
Ne 6:18 and his son J had married the daughter 3380
    12:13 of Ezra's, Meshullam; of Amariah's, J; 3380
    12:42 Eleazar, Uzzi, J, Malkijah, Elam and Ezer. 3380

JEHOIACHIN (26) [JEHOIACHIN'S]

2Ki 24: 6 And J his son succeeded him as king. 3382
    24: 8 J was eighteen years old when he became 3382
    24:12 J king of Judah, his mother, his attendants, 3382
    24:12 he took J prisoner. 2257S
    24:15 Nebuchadnezzar took J captive 3382
    25:27 of the exile of J king of Judah, 3382
    25:27 he released J from prison 3382
    25:29 So J put aside his prison clothes and for NIH
    25:30 the king gave J a regular allowance as long 2257S
1Ch 3:16 J his son, and Zedekiah. 3526
    3:17 The descendants of J the captive: 3526
2Ch 36: 8 And J his son succeeded him as king. 3382
    36: 9 J was eighteen years old whe he became 3382
Est 2: 6 among those taken captive with J king 3526
Jer 22:24 J son of Jehoiakim king of Judah, 4037
    22:28 Is this man J a despised, broken pot, 4037
    24: 1 After J son of Jehoiakim king of Judah 3527
    27:20 when he carried J son of Jehoiakim king 3526
    28: 4 I will also bring back to this place J son 3526
    29: 2 after King J and the queen mother, 3526
    37: 1 he reigned in place of J son of Jehoiakim. 4037
    52:31 of the exile of J king of Judah, 3382
    52:31 he released J king of Judah and freed him 3382
    52:33 So J put aside his prison clothes and for NIH
    52:34 Day by day the king of Babylon gave J 2257S
Eze 1: 2 it was the fifth year of the exile of King J— 3422

JEHOIACHIN'S (2) [JEHOIACHIN]

2Ki 24:17 He made Mattaniah, J uncle, 2257S
2Ch 36:10 and he made J uncle, Zedekiah, 2257S

JEHOIADA (53)

2Sa 8:18 Benaiah son of J was over the Kerethites 3381
    20:23 Benaiah son of J was over the Kerethites 3381
    23:20 of J was a valiant fighter from Kabzeel, 3381
    23:22 the exploits of Benaiah son of J; 3381
1Ki 1: 8 But Zadok the priest, Benaiah son of J, 3381
    1:26 and Benaiah son of J, 3381
    1:32 Nathan the prophet and Benaiah son of J." 3381
    1:36 Benaiah son of J answered the king, 3381
    1:38 Nathan the prophet, Benaiah son of J, 3381
    1:44 Nathan the prophet, Benaiah son of J, 3381
    2:25 to Benaiah son of J, 3381
    2:29 Then Solomon ordered Benaiah son of J 3381
    2:34 So Benaiah son of J went up and struck 3381
    2:35 of J over the army in Joab's position 3381
    2:46 king gave the order to Benaiah son of J, 3381
    4: 4 Benaiah son of J— 3381
2Ki 11: 4 In the seventh year J sent for 3381
    11: 9 a hundred did just as J the priest ordered. 3381
    11: 9 and came to J the priest. 3381
    11:12 J brought out the king's son and put NIH
    11:15 the priest ordered the commanders 3381
    11:17 J then made a covenant between 3381

2Ki 11:18 Then J the priest posted guards at NIH
    12: 2 in the eyes of the LORD all the years J 3381
    12: 7 Therefore King Joash summoned J 3381
    12: 9 J the priest took a chest and bored a hole 3381
1Ch 11:22 of J was a valiant fighter from Kabzeel, 3381
    11:24 the exploits of Benaiah son of J; 3381
    11:27 including J, leader of the family of Aaron, 3381
    18:17 Benaiah son of J was over the Kerethites 3381
    27: 5 was Benaiah son of J the priest. 3381
    27:34 by J son of Benaiah and by Abiathar. 3381
2Ch 22:11 of King Jehoram and wife of the priest J, 3381
    23: 1 In the seventh year J showed his strength. 3381
    23: 3 J said to them. "The king's son shall reign, NIH
    23: 8 of Judah did just as J the priest ordered. 3381
    23: 8 for the priest had not released any of 3381
    23:11 J and his sons brought out the king's son 3381
    23:14 J the priest sent out the commanders 3381
    23:16 J then made a covenant that he and 3381
    23:18 Then J placed the oversight of the temple 3381
    24: 2 in the eyes of the LORD all the years of J 3381
    24: 3 J chose two wives for him, 3381
    24: 6 the king summoned J the chief priest 3381
    24:12 and J gave it to the men who carried out 3381
    24:14 and J, and with it were made articles for 3381
    24:14 As long as J lived, burnt offerings were 3381
    24:15 Now J was old and full of years, 3381
    24:17 After the death of J, the officials of Judah 3381
    24:20 of God came upon Zechariah son of J 3381
    24:22 Joash did not remember the kindness
    24:22 Zechariah's father J had shown him 3381
    24:25 against him for murdering the son of J 3381
Jer 29:26 in place of J to be in charge of the house 3381

JEHOIAKIM (34) [ELIAKIM, JEHOIAKIM'S]

2Ki 23:34 and changed Eliakim's name to J. 3383
    23:35 J paid Pharaoh Neco the silver 3383
    23:36 J was twenty-five years old 3383
    24: 1 and J became his vassal for three years. 3383
    24: 6 J rested with his fathers. 3383
    24:19 just as J had done. 3383
1Ch 3:15 Johanan the firstborn, J the second son, 3383
    3:16 The successors of J: 3383
2Ch 36: 4 and changed Eliakim's name to J. 3383
    36: 5 J was twenty-five years old 3383
Jer 1: 3 the reign of J son of Josiah king of Judah, 3383
    22:18 the LORD says about J son of Josiah king 3383
    22:24 Jehoiachin son of J king of Judah, 3383
    24: 1 After Jehoiachin son of J king of Judah 3383
    25: 1 in the fourth year of J son of Josiah king 3383
    26: 1 the reign of J son of Josiah king of Judah, 3383
    26:21 When King J and all his officers 3383
    26:22 King J, however, sent Elnathan son 3383
    26:23 of Egypt and took him to King J, 3383
    27:20 when he carried Jehoiachin son of J king 3383
    28: 4 J king of Judah and all the other exiles 3383
    35: 1 from the LORD during the reign of J son 3383
    36: 1 In the fourth year of J son of Josiah king 3383
    36: 9 the ninth month of the fifth year of J son 3383
    36:28 which J king of Judah burned up. 3383
    36:29 Also tell J king of Judah, 3383
    36:30 this is what the LORD says about J king 3383
    36:32 that J king of Judah had burned in the fire. 3383
    37: 1 he reigned in place of Jehoiachin son of J. 3383
    45: 1 in the fourth year of J son of Josiah king 3383
    46: 2 in the fourth year of J son of Josiah king 3383
    52: 2 just as J had done. 3383
Da 1: 1 In the third year of the reign of J king 3383
    1: 2 And the Lord delivered J king of Judah 3383

JEHOIAKIM'S (3) [JEHOIAKIM]

2Ki 24: 1 During J reign, Nebuchadnezzar king 2257S
    24: 5 As for the other events of J reign, 3383
2Ch 36: 8 The other events of J reign. 3383

JEHOIARIB (2)

1Ch 9:10 Of the priests: Jedaiah; J; Jakin; 3384
    24: 7 The first lot fell to J, 3384

JEHONADAB (3)

2Ki 10:15 he left there, he came upon J son of Recab, 3386
    10:15 "I am," J answered. 3386
    10:23 and J son of Recab went into the temple 3386

JEHONATHAN (2)

2Ch 17: 8 J, Adonijah, Tobijah and Tob-Adonijah— 3387
Ne 12:18 of Bilgah's, Shammua; of Shemaiah's, J; 3387

JEHORAM (29) [JEHORAM'S, JORAM]

1Ki 22:50 And J his son succeeded him. 3393
2Ki 1:17 of J son of Jehoshaphat king of Judah. 3393
    8:16 J son of Jehoshaphat began his reign 3393
    8:20 In the time of J, Edom rebelled 2257S
    8:21 So J went to Zair with all his chariots. 3456
    8:24 J rested with his fathers and was buried 3456
    8:25 Ahaziah son of J king of Judah began 3393
    8:29 Then Ahaziah son of J king of Judah went 3393
    11: 2 daughter of King J and sister of Ahaziah, 3456
    12:18 Jehoshaphat, and Ahaziah, 3393
1Ch 3:11 J his son, Ahaziah his son, Joash his son, 3456
2Ch 17: 8 and the priests Elishama and J. 3393
    21: 1 And J his son succeeded him as king. 3393
    21: 3 to J because he was his firstborn son. 3393
    21: 4 When J established himself firmly 3393

2Ch 21: 5 J was thirty-two years old 3393
    21: 8 In the time of J, Edom rebelled 2257S
    21: 9 So J went there with his officers 3393
    21:10 because J had forsaken the LORD. NIH
    21:12 J received a letter from Elijah the prophet, 2257S
    21:16 against J the hostility of the Philistines and 3393
    21:18 the LORD afflicted J with an incurable 2257S
    21:20 J was thirty-two years old NIH
    22: 1 So Ahaziah son of J king of Judah began 3393
    22: 6 Then Ahaziah son of J king of Judah went 3393
    22:11 But Jehosheba, the daughter of King J, NIH
    22:11 of King J and wife of the priest Jehoiada, 3393
Mt 1: 8 Jehoshaphat the father of J, 2732
    1: 8 J the father of Uzziah, 2732

JEHORAM'S (3) [JEHORAM]

2Ki 8:23 As for the other events of J reign, 3456
2Ch 21: 2 J brothers, the sons of Jehoshaphat, 2257S
    22: 1 J youngest son, king in his place, 2257S

JEHOSHAPHAT (85) [JEHOSHAPHAT'S]

2Sa 8:16 J son of Ahilud was recorder; 3398
    20:24 J son of Ahilud was recorder; 3398
1Ki 4: 3 J son of Ahilud—recorder; 3398
    4:17 J son of Paruah—in Issachar; 3398
    15:24 And J his son succeeded him as king. 3398
    22: 2 But in the third year J king of Judah went 3398
    22: 4 So he asked J, 3398
    22: 4 J replied to the king of Israel, 3398
    22: 5 But J also said to the king of Israel, 3398
    22: 7 But J asked, "Is there not a prophet of 3398
    22: 8 The king of Israel answered J, 3398
    22: 8 "The king should not say that," J replied. 3398
    22:10 of Israel and J king of Judah were sitting 3398
    22:18 The king of Israel said to J, 3398
    22:29 the king of Israel and J king of Judah went 3398
    22:30 the king of Israel said to J, 3398
    22:32 When the chariot commanders saw J, 3398
    22:32 but when J cried out, 3398
    22:41 J son of Asa became king of Judah in 3398
    22:42 J was thirty-five years old 3398
    22:44 J was also at peace with the king of Israel. 3398
    22:48 Now J built a fleet of trading ships to go 3398
    22:49 that time Ahaziah son of Ahab said to J, 3398
    22:49 with your men," but J refused. 3398
    22:50 Then J rested with his fathers 3398
    22:51 in the seventeenth year of J king of Judah, 3398
2Ki 1:17 the second year of Jehoram son of J king 3398
    3: 1 in Samaria in the eighteenth year of J king 3398
    3: 7 also sent this message to J king of Judah: 3398
    3:11 J asked, "Is there no prophet of the LORD 3398
    3:12 J said, "The word of the LORD is 3398
    3:12 of Israel and J and the king of Edom went 3398
    3:14 not have respect for the presence of J king 3398
    8:16 J was king of Judah. 3398
    8:16 Jehoram son of J began his reign as king 3398
    9: 2 you get there, look for Jehu son of J, 3398
    9:14 So Jehu son of J, the son of Nimshi, 3398
    12:18 J, Jehoram and Ahaziah, 3398
1Ch 3:10 Abijah his son, Asa his son, J his son, 3398
    18:15 J son of Ahilud was recorder; 3398
2Ch 17: 1 J his son succeeded him as king 3398
    17: 3 with J because in his early years he walked 3398
    17: 5 and all Judah brought gifts to J, 3398
    17:10 so that they did not make war with J. 3398
    17:11 Some Philistines brought J gifts and silver 3398
    17:12 J became more and more powerful; 3398
    18: 1 Now J had great wealth and honor, 3398
    18: 3 Ahab king of Israel asked J king of Judah, 3398
    18: 3 J replied, "I am as you are, NIH
    18: 4 But J also said to the king of Israel, 3398
    18: 6 J asked, "Is there not a prophet of the LORD 3398
    18: 7 The king of Israel answered J, 3398
    18: 7 "The king should not say that," J replied. 3398
    18: 9 of Israel and J king of Judah were sitting 3398
    18:17 The king of Israel said to J, 3398
    18:28 the king of Israel and J king of Judah went 3398
    18:29 The king of Israel said to J, 3398
    18:31 When the chariot commanders saw J, 3398
    18:31 they turned to attack him, but J cried out, 3398
    19: 1 When J king of Judah returned safely 3398
    19: 4 J lived in Jerusalem, 3398
    19: 8 J appointed some of the Levites, 3398
    20: 1 of the Meunites came to make war on J. 3398
    20: 2 Some men came and told J, 3398
    20: 3 J resolved to inquire of the LORD, 3398
    20: 5 Then J stood up in the assembly of Judah 3398
    20:15 "Listen, King J and all who live in Judah 3398
    20:18 J bowed with his face to the ground, 3398
    20:20 As they set out, J stood and said, 3398
    20:21 J appointed men to sing to the LORD and NIH
    20:25 So J and his men went 3398
    20:27 Then, led by J, all the men of Judah 3398
    20:30 And the kingdom of J was at peace, 3398
    20:31 So J reigned over Judah. 3398
    20:35 J king of Judah made an alliance 3398
    20:37 of Mareshah prophesied against J, 3398
    21: 1 Then J rested with his fathers 3398
    21: 2 Jehoram's brothers, the sons of J, 3398
    21: 2 All these were sons of J king of Israel. 3398
    21:12 in the ways of your father J or of Asa king 3398
    22: 9 for they said, "He was a son of J, 3398
Joel 3: 2 and bring them down to the Valley of J, 3399
    3:12 let them advance into the Valley of J, 3399
Mt 1: 8 Asa the father of J, 2734

Mt 1: 8 J the father of Jehoram,   2734

JEHOSHAPHAT'S (2) [JEHOSHAPHAT]

1Ki 22:45 As for the other events of J reign,   3398
2Ch 20:34 The other events of J reign,   3398

JEHOSHEBA (3)

2Ki 11: 2 But J, the daughter of King Jehoram   3394
2Ch 22:11 But J, the daughter of King Jehoram,   3395
   22:11 Because J, the daughter of King Jehoram   3395

JEHOSHUA, JEHOSHUAH (KJV) See JOSHUA

JEHOVAH (KJV) See †LORD

JEHOVAH-JIREH (KJV) See †LORD WILL PROVIDE

JEHOVAH-NISSI (KJV) See †LORD IS MY BANNER

JEHOVAH-SHALOM (KJV) See †LORD IS PEACE

JEHOZABAD (4)

2Ki 12:21 of Shimeath and J son of Shomer.   3379
1Ch 26: 4 Shemaiah the firstborn, J the second,   3379
2Ch 17:18 J, with 180,000 men armed for battle.   3379
   24:26 and J, son of Shimrith a Moabite woman.   3379

JEHOZADAK (8)

1Ch 6:14 and Seraiah the father of J.   3392
   6:15 J was deported when the LORD sent Judah   3392
Hag 1: 1 governor of Judah, and to Joshua son of J,   3392
   1:12 Joshua son of J, the high priest,   3392
   1:14 and the spirit of Joshua son of J,   3392
   2: 2 governor of Judah, to Joshua son of J,   3392
   2: 4 'Be strong, O Joshua son of J,   3392
Zec 6:11 Joshua son of J.   3392

JEHU (74) [JEHU'S]

1Ki 16: 1 word of the LORD came to J son of Hanani   3369
   16: 7 the prophet J son of Hanani to Baasha   3369
   16:12 against Baasha through the prophet J—   3369
   19:16 anoint J son of Nimshi king over Israel,   3369
   19:17 J will put to death any who escape   3369
   19:17 to death any who escape the sword of J.   3369
2Ki 9: 2 look for J son of Jehoshaphat,   3369
   9: 5 "For which of us?" asked J.   3369
   9: 6 J got up and went into the house.   NIH
   9:11 When J went out to his fellow officers,   3369
   9:11 and the sort of things he says," J replied.   NIH
   9:12 J said, "Here is what he told me: NIH
   9:13 the trumpet and shouted, "J is king!"   3369
   9:14 So J son of Jehoshaphat,   3369
   9:15 J said, "If this is the way you feel,   3369
   9:18 The horseman rode off to meet J and said,   2257S
   9:18 do you have to do with peace?" J replied.   3369
   9:19 J replied, "What do you have to do   3369
   9:20 The driving is like that of J son   3369
   9:21 each in his own chariot, to meet J.   3369
   9:22 When Joram saw J he asked,   3369
   9:22 "Have you come in peace, J?"   3369
   9:22 "How can there be peace," J replied,   NIH
   9:24 Then J drew his bow and shot Joram   3369
   9:25 J said to Bidkar, his chariot officer,   NIH
   9:27 J chased him, shouting, "Kill him too!"   3369
   9:30 Then J went to Jezreel.   3369
   9:31 As J entered the gate, she asked,   3369
   9:33 "Throw her down!" J said.   NIH
   9:34 J went in and ate and drank.   NIH
   9:36 They went back and told J, who said,   2257S
   10: 1 J wrote letters and sent them to Samaria,   3369
   10: 5 and the guardians sent this message to J: 3369
   10: 6 Then J wrote them a second letter, saying,   NIH
   10: 7 in baskets and sent them to J in Jezreel.   2257S
   10: 8 When the messenger arrived, he told J,   2257S
   10: 8 Then J ordered, "Put them in two piles at   NIH
   10: 9 The next morning J went out.   NIH
   10:11 So J killed everyone in Jezreel who   3369
   10:12 J then set out and went toward Samaria.   NIH
   10:15 J greeted him and said,   NIH
   10:15 "If so," said J, "give me your hand."   NIH
   10:15 and J helped him up into the chariot.   NIH
   10:16 J said, "Come with me and see my zeal for   NIH
   10:17 When J came to Samaria,   NIH
   10:18 Then J brought all the people together   3369
   10:18 J will serve him much.   3369
   10:19 But J was acting deceptively in order   3369
   10:20 J said, "Call an assembly in honor   3369
   10:22 And J said to the keeper of the wardrobe,   NIH
   10:23 Then J and Jehonadab son of Recab went   3369
   10:23 J said to the ministers of Baal,   NIH
   10:24 Now J had posted eighty men outside   3369
   10:25 As soon as J had finished making   3369
   10:28 So J destroyed Baal worship in Israel.   3369
   10:30 The LORD said to J,   3369
   10:31 Yet J was not careful to keep the law of   3369

2Ki 10:35 J rested with his fathers and was buried   3369
   10:36 The time that J reigned over Israel   3369
   12: 1 In the seventh year of J,   3369
   13: 1 Jehoahaz son of J became king of Israel   3369
   14: 8 the son of J, king of Israel,   3369
   15:12 of the LORD spoken to J was fulfilled: 3369
1Ch 2:38 Obed the father of J,   3369
   2:38 J the father of Azariah,   3369
   4:35 J son of Joshibiah, the son of Seraiah,   3369
   12: 3 Beracah, J the Anathothite,   3369
2Ch 19: 2 J the seer, the son of Hanani, went out   3369
   20:34 are written in the annals of J son   3369
   22: 7 he went out with Joram to meet J son   3369
   22: 8 While J was executing judgment on   3369
   22: 9 He was brought to J and put to death.   3369
   25:17 the son of J, king of Israel: 3369
Hos 1: 4 the house of J for the massacre at Jezreel,   3369

JEHU'S (3) [JEHU]

2Ki 9: 6 Then the prophet poured the oil on J head   2257S
   9:17 in Jezreel saw J troops approaching,   3369
   10:34 As for the other events of J reign,   3369

JEHUBBAH (KJV) See HUBBAH

JEHUCAL (2)

Jer 37: 3 sent J son of Shelemiah with the priest   3385
   38: 1 J son of Shelemiah, and Passhur son of   3426

JEHUD (1)

Jos 19:45 J, Bene Berak, Gath Rimmon,   3372

JEHUDI (4)

Jer 36:14 all the officials sent J son of Nethaniah,   3375
   36:21 The king sent J to get the scroll,   3375
   36:21 and J brought it from the room   3375
   36:23 Whenever J had read three or four columns   3375

JEHUDIJAH (KJV) See JUDEAN

JEHUSH (KJV) See JEUSH

JEIEL (13)

1Ch 5: 7 J the chief, Zechariah,   3599
   8:29 J the father of Gibeon lived in Gibeon.   3599
   9:35 J the father of Gibeon lived in Gibeon.   3599
   11:44 J the sons of Hotham the Aroerite,   3599
   15:18 Eliphelehu, Mikneiah, Obed-Edom and J,   3599
   15:21 J and Azaziah were to play the harps,   3599
   16: 5 Zechariah second, then J, Shemiramoth,   3599
   16: 5 Eliab, Benaiah, Obed-Edom and J.   3599
2Ch 20:14 the son of J, the son of Mattaniah,   3599
   26:11 by J the secretary and Maaseiah the officer   3599
   29:13 of Elizaphan, Shimri and J;   3599
   35: 9 and Jozabad, the leaders of the Levites,   3599
Ezr 10:43 J, Mattithiah, Zabad, Zebina, Jaddai,   3599

JEKABZEEL (1)

Ne 11:25 in J and its villages,   3677

JEKAMEAM (2)

1Ch 23:19 Jahaziel the third and J the fourth.   3694
   24:23 Jahaziel the third and J the fourth.   3694

JEKAMIAH (3)

1Ch 2:41 Shallum the father of J,   3693
   2:41 and J the father of Elishama.   3693
   3:18 Shenazzar, J, Hoshama and Nedabiah.   3693

JEKUTHIEL (1)

1Ch 4:18 and J the father of Zanoah.)   3688

JEMIMAH (1)

Job 42:14 The first daughter he named J,   3544

JEMUEL (2)

Ge 46:10 The sons of Simeon: J, Jamin, Ohad,   3543
Ex 6:15 The sons of Simeon were J, Jamin, Ohad,   3543

JEOPARDED (KJV) See RISKED

JEOPARDY (2)

2Sa 18:13 And if I had put my life in j—   6913+9214
Job 13:14 Why do I put myself in j and take my life   928+1414+5951+9094

JEPHTHAE (KJV) See JEPHTHAH

JEPHTHAH (23) [JEPHTHAH'S]

Jdg 11: 1 J the Gileadite was a mighty warrior.   3653
   11: 2 they drove J away.   3653
   11: 3 So J fled from his brothers and settled in   3653
   11: 5 the elders of Gilead went to get J from   3653
   11: 7 J said to them, "Didn't you hate me   3653
   11: 9 J answered, "Suppose you take me back   3653
   11:11 So J went with the elders of Gilead,   3653

Jdg 11:12 Then J sent messengers to the Ammonite   3653
   11:14 J sent back messengers to the Ammonite   3653
   11:15 "This is what J says: 3653
   11:28 to the message J sent him.   3653
   11:29 the Spirit of the LORD came upon J.   3653
   11:30 And J made a vow to the LORD: 3653
   11:32 Then J went over to fight the Ammonites,   3653
   11:34 When J returned to his home in Mizpah,   3653
   11:40 to commemorate the daughter of J   3653
   12: 1 crossed over to Zaphon and said to J,   3653
   12: 2 J answered, "I and my people were   3653
   12: 4 J then called together the men of Gilead   3653
   12: 7 J led Israel six years.   3653
   12: 7 Then J the Gileadite died,   3653
1Sa 12:11 Barak, J and Samuel,   3653
Heb 11:32 J, David, Samuel and the prophets,   2650

JEPHTHAH'S (1) [JEPHTHAH]

Jdg 11:13 of the Ammonites answered J messengers,   3653

JEPHUNNEH (16)

Nu 13: 6 from the tribe of Judah, Caleb son of J;   3648
   14: 6 Joshua son of Nun and Caleb son of J,   3648
   14:30 except Caleb son of J and Joshua son   3648
   14:38 of Nun and Caleb son of J survived.   3648
   26:65 of them was left except Caleb son of J   3648
   32:12 of J the Kenizzite and Joshua son of Nun,   3648
   34:19 Caleb son of J, from the tribe of Judah;   3648
Dt 1:36 except Caleb son of J.   3648
Jos 14: 6 Caleb son of J the Kenizzite said to him,   3648
   14:13 Then Joshua blessed Caleb son of J   3648
   14:14 to Caleb son of J the Kenizzite ever since,   3648
   15:13 Joshua gave to Caleb son of J a portion   3648
   21:12 the city they had given to Caleb son of J   3648
1Ch 4:15 The sons of Caleb son of J: 3648
   6:56 the city were given to Caleb son of J   3648
   7:38 The sons of Jether: J, Pispah and Ara.   3648

JERAH (2)

Ge 10:26 Sheleph, Hazarmaveth, J,   3733
1Ch 1:20 Sheleph, Hazarmaveth, J,   3733

JERAHMEEL (9) [JERAHMEELITES]

1Sa 27:10 "Against the Negev of J" or   3738
1Ch 2: 9 The sons born to Hezron were: J,   3737
   2:25 The sons of J the firstborn of Hezron   3737
   2:26 J had another wife,   3737
   2:27 The sons of Ram the firstborn of J: 3737
   2:33 These were the descendants of J.   3737
   2:42 The sons of Caleb the brother of J: 3737
   24:29 From Kish: the son of Kish: J.   3737
Jer 36:26 Instead, the king commanded J,   3737

JERAHMEELITES (1) [JERAHMEEL]

1Sa 30:29 in the towns of the J and the Kenites;   3738

JERED (1)

1Ch 4:18 (His Judean wife gave birth to J the father   3719

JEREMAI (1)

Ezr 10:33 Mattenai, Mattattah, Zabad, Eliphelet, J,   3757

JEREMIAH (145) [JEREMIAH'S]

2Ki 23:31 mother's name was Hamutal daughter of J;   3759
   24:18 mother's name was Hamutal daughter of J;   3759
1Ch 5:24 Epher, Ishi, Eliel, Azriel, J,   3758
   12: 4 J, Jahaziel, Johanan, Jozabad   3758
   12:10 Mishmannah the fourth, J the fifth,   3758
   12:13 J the tenth and Macbannai the eleventh.   3759
2Ch 35:25 J composed laments for Josiah,   3759
   36:12 not humble himself before the prophet,   3759
   36:21 of the word of the LORD spoken by J.   3759
   36:22 the word of the LORD spoken by J,   3759
Ezr 1: 1 the word of the LORD spoken by J,   3758
Ne 10: 2 Seraiah, Azariah, J,   3758
   12: 1 with Jeshua: Seraiah, J,   3758
   12:34 Judah, Benjamin, Shemaiah, J,   3758
Jer 1: 1 The words of J son of Hilkiah,   3759
   1:11 "What do you see, J?"   3759
   7: 1 the word that came to J from the LORD: 3759
   11: 1 the word that came to J from the LORD: 3759
   14: 1 of the LORD to J concerning the drought: 3759
   18: 1 the word that came to J from the LORD: 3759
   18:18 "Come, let's make plans against J;   3759
   19:14 J then returned from Topheth,   3759
   20: 1 heard J prophesying these things,   3759
   20: 2 he had J the prophet beaten and put in   3759
   20: 3 J said to him, "The LORD's name for you   3759
   21: 1 The word came to J from the LORD   3759
   21: 3 But J answered them, "Tell Zedekiah,   3759
   24: 3 LORD asked me, "What do you see, J?"   3759
   25: 1 to J concerning all the people of Judah in   3759
   25: 2 So J the prophet said to all the people   3759
   25:13 and prophesied by J against all the nations.   3759
   26: 7 the people heard J speak these words in   3759
   26: 8 But as soon as J finished telling all   3759
   26: 9 the people crowded around J in the house   3759
   26:12 J said to all the officials and all the people: 3759
   26:20 against this city and this land as J did.   3759
   26:24 Ahikam son of Shaphan supported J,   3759
   27: 1 this word came to J from the LORD: 3758
   28: 5 Then the prophet J replied to   3758

Jer	28:10	the neck of the prophet J and broke it,	3758
	28:11	At this, the prophet J went on his way.	3758
	28:12	the yoke off the neck of the prophet J,	3758
	28:12	the word of the LORD came to J:	3758
	28:15	the prophet J said to Hananiah the prophet,	3758
	29: 1	the text of the letter that the prophet J sent	3758
	29:27	So why have you not reprimanded J	3759
	29:29	however, read the letter to J the prophet.	3759
	29:30	Then the word of the LORD came to J:	3759
	30: 1	the word that came to J from the LORD:	3759
	32: 1	the word that came to J from the LORD	3759
	32: 2	and J the prophet was confined in	3759
	32: 6	J said, "The word of the LORD came	3759
	32:26	Then the word of the LORD came to J:	3759
	33: 1	While J was still confined in the courtyard	3759
	33:19	The word of the LORD came to	3759
	33:23	The word of the LORD came to J:	3759
	34: 1	this word came to J from the LORD:	3759
	34: 6	Then J the prophet told all this	3759
	34: 8	The word came to J from the LORD	3759
	34:12	Then the word of the LORD came to J:	3759
	35: 1	the word that came to J from the LORD	3759
	35: 3	So I went to get Jaazaniah son of J,	3759
	35:12	the word of the LORD came to J, saying:	3759
	35:18	Then J said to the family of the Recabites,	3759
	36: 1	this word came to J from the LORD:	3759
	36: 4	So J called Baruch son of Neriah,	3759
	36: 4	and while J dictated all the words	3759
	36: 5	Then J told Baruch, "I am restricted;	3759
	36: 8	Baruch son of Neriah did everything J	3759
	36:10	the LORD's temple the words of J from	3759
	36:17	Did J dictate it?"	2257S
	36:19	the officials said to Baruch, "You and J,	3759
	36:26	of Abdeel to arrest Baruch the scribe and J	3759
	36:27	the word of the LORD came to J:	3759
	36:32	So J took another scroll and gave it to	3759
	36:32	and as J dictated, Baruch wrote on it	3759
	37: 2	the LORD had spoken through J	3759
	37: 3	the priest Zephaniah son of Maaseiah to J	3759
	37: 4	Now J was free to come and go among	3759
	37: 6	word of the LORD came to J the prophet:	3759
	37:12	J started to leave the city to go to	3759
	37:14	"That's not true!" J said.	3759
	37:14	instead, he arrested J and brought him to	3759
	37:15	with J and had him beaten and imprisoned	3759
	37:16	J was put into a vaulted cell in a dungeon,	3759
	37:17	J replied, "you will be handed over to	3759
	37:18	Then J said to King Zedekiah,	3759
	37:21	King Zedekiah then gave orders for J to	3759
	37:21	J remained in the courtyard of the guard.	3759
	38: 1	of Malkijah heard what J was telling all	3759
	38: 6	So they took J and put him into the cistern	3759
	38: 6	They lowered J by ropes into the cistern;	3759
	38: 6	only mud, and J sank down into the mud.	3759
	38: 7	heard that they had put J into the cistern.	3759
	38: 9	in all they have done to J the prophet.	3759
	38:10	and lift J the prophet out of the cistern	3759
	38:11	and let them down with ropes to J in	3759
	38:12	Ebed-Melech the Cushite said to J,	3759
	38:12	to pad the ropes." J did so,	3759
	38:13	J remained in the courtyard of the guard.	3759
	38:14	Then King Zedekiah sent for J the prophet	3759
	38:14	the king said to J. "Do not hide anything	3759
	38:15	J said to Zedekiah, "If I give you an answer	3759
	38:16	Zedekiah swore this oath secretly to J:	3759
	38:17	Then J said to Zedekiah, "This is what	3759
	38:19	King Zedekiah said to J,	3759
	38:20	"They will not hand you over," J replied.	3759
	38:24	Then Zedekiah said to J,	3759
	38:27	All the officials did come to J	3759
	38:28	And J remained in the courtyard of	3759
	39:11	of Babylon had given these orders about J	3759
	39:14	sent and had J taken out of the courtyard	3759
	39:15	While J had been confined in	3759
	40: 1	The word came to J from the LORD	3759
	40: 1	He had found J bound in chains among all	2257S
	40: 2	the commander of the guard found J,	3759
	40: 5	However, before J turned to go,	5647S
	40: 6	So J went to Gedaliah son of Ahikam	3759
	42: 2	J the prophet and said to him,	3759
	42: 4	"I have heard you," replied J the prophet.	3759
	42: 5	Then they said to J,	3759
	42: 7	the word of the LORD came to J.	3759
	43: 1	When J finished telling the people all	3759
	43: 2	and all the arrogant men said to J,	3759
	43: 6	J the prophet and Baruch son of Neriah.	3759
	43: 8	the word of the LORD came to J:	3759
	44: 1	This word came to J concerning all	3759
	44:15	in Lower and Upper Egypt, said to J,	3759
	44:20	Then J said to all the people,	3759
	44:24	Then J said to all the people,	3759
	45: 1	This is what J the prophet told Baruch son	3759
	45: 1	on a scroll the words J was then dictating:	3759
	46: 1	of the LORD that came to J the prophet	3759
	46:13	This is the message the LORD spoke to J	3759
	47: 1	to J the prophet concerning the Philistines	3759
	49:34	to J the prophet concerning Elam, early in	3759
	50: 1	through J the prophet concerning Babylon	3759
	51:59	This is the message J gave to the staff	3759
	51:60	J had written on a scroll about all the	
		disasters that would come upon Babylon	3759
	51:64	The words of J end here.	
	52: 1	mother's name was Hamutal daughter of J;	3759
Da	9: 2	of the LORD given to J the prophet.	3758
Mt	2:17	through the prophet J was fulfilled:	2635
	16:14	and still others, J or one of the prophets."	2635
	27: 9	by J the prophet was fulfilled:	2635

JEREMIAH'S (2) [JEREMIAH]

Ne	12:12	Meraiah; of J, Hananiah;	3758
Jer	36:27	that Baruch had written at J dictation,	3759

JEREMIAS, JEREMY (KJV) See
JEREMIAH

JEREMOTH (5)

1Ch	7: 8	Zemirah, Joash, Eliezer, Elioenai, Omri, J,	3756
	8:14	Ahio, Shashak, J,	3756
Ezr	10:26	Zechariah, Jehiel, Abdi, J and Elijah.	3756
	10:27	Elioenai, Eliashib, Mattaniah, J,	3756
	10:29	Malluch, Adaiah, Jashub, Sheal and J.	3756

JERIAH (4)

1Ch	23:19	J the first, Amariah the second,	3746
	24:23	J the first, Amariah the second,	3746
	26:31	J was their chief according to	3745
	26:32	J had twenty-seven hundred relatives,	2257S

JERIBAI (1)

1Ch	11:46	J and Joshaviah the sons of Elnaam,	3744

JERICHO (62)

Nu	22: 1	along the Jordan across from J.	3735
	26: 3	plains of Moab by the Jordan across from J,	3735
	26:63	plains of Moab by the Jordan across from J.	3735
	31:12	by the Jordan across from J.	3735
	33:48	plains of Moab by the Jordan across from J.	3735
	33:50	the Jordan across from J the LORD said	3735
	34:15	on the east side of the Jordan of J,	3735
	35: 1	plains of Moab by the Jordan across from J.	3735
	36:13	plains of Moab by the Jordan across from J.	3735
Dt	32:49	across from J, and view Canaan.	3735
	34: 1	to the top of Pisgah, across from J.	3735
	34: 3	and the whole region from the Valley of J,	3735
Jos	2: 1	look over the land," he said, "especially J."	3735
	2: 2	The king of J was told, "Look!	3735
	2: 3	the king of J sent this message to Rahab:	3735
	3:16	So the people crossed over opposite J.	3735
	4:13	over before the LORD to the plains of J	3735
	4:19	at Gilgal on the eastern border of J.	3735
	5:10	while camped at Gilgal on the plains of J,	3735
	5:13	Now when Joshua was near J,	3735
	6: 1	Now J was tightly shut up because of	3735
	6: 2	"See, I have delivered J into your hands,	3735
	6:25	the men Joshua had sent as spies to J—	3735
	6:26	who undertakes to rebuild this city, J:	3735
	7: 2	Now Joshua sent men from J to Ai,	3735
	8: 2	and its king as you did to J and its king,	3735
	9: 3	what Joshua had done to J and Ai,	3735
	10: 1	to Ai and its king as he had done to J	3735
	10:28	as he had done to the king of J.	3735
	10:30	to its king as he had done to the king of J.	3735
	12: 9	of J one the king of Ai (near Bethel) one	3735
	13:32	of Moab across the Jordan east of J.	3735
	16: 1	for Joseph began at the Jordan of J,	3735
	16: 1	east of the waters of J,	3735
	16: 7	touched J and came out at the Jordan.	3735
	18:12	of J and headed west into the hill country,	3735
	18:21	J, Beth Hoglah, Emek Keziz,	3735
	20: 8	of the Jordan of J they designated Bezer in	3735
	24:11	you crossed the Jordan and came to J.	3735
	24:11	The citizens of J fought against you,	3735
2Sa	10: 5	"Stay at J till your beards have grown,	3735
1Ki	16:34	In Ahab's time, Hiel of Bethel rebuilt J.	3735
2Ki	2: 4	the LORD has sent me to J."	3735
	2: 4	So they went to J.	3735
	2: 5	The company of the prophets at J went up	3735
	2:15	The company of the prophets from J,	3735
	2:18	who was staying in J, he said to them,	3735
	25: 5	and overtook him in the plains of J	3735
1Ch	6:78	the Jordan east of J they received Bezer in	3735
	19: 5	"Stay at J till your beards have grown,	3735
2Ch	28:15	to their fellow countrymen at J,	3735
Ezr	2:34	of J 345	3735
Ne	3: 2	The men of J built the adjoining section,	3735
	7:36	of J 345	3735
Jer	39: 5	and overtook Zedekiah in the plains of J.	3735
	52: 8	and overtook him in the plains of J.	3735
Mt	20:29	As Jesus and his disciples were leaving J,	2637
Mk	10:46	Then they came to J.	2637
Lk	10:30	man was going down from Jerusalem to J,	2637
	18:35	As Jesus approached J,	2637
	19: 1	Jesus entered J and was passing through.	2637
Heb	11:30	By faith the walls of J fell,	2637

JERIEL (1)

1Ch	7: 2	The sons of Tola: Uzzi, Rephaiah, J,	3741

JERIJAH (KJV) See JERIAH

JERIMOTH (9)

1Ch	7: 7	Ezbon, Uzzi, Uzziel, J and Iri,	3748
	12: 5	J, Bealiah, Shemariah and Shephatiah	3748
	23:33	The sons of Mushi: Mahli, Eder and J.	3756
	24:30	And the sons of Mushi: Mahli, Eder and J.	3748
	25: 4	Mattaniah, Uzziel, Shubael and J;	3748
	25:22	the fifteenth to J, his sons and relatives, 12	3756
	27:19	J son of Azriel;	3748
2Ch	11:18	who was the daughter of David's son J	3748

2Ch	31:13	Jehiel, Azaziah, Nahath, Asahel, J,	3748

JERIOTH (1)

1Ch	2:18	by his wife Azubah (and by J).	3750

JEROBOAM (95) [JEROBOAM'S]

1Ki	11:26	J son of Nebat rebelled against the king.	3716
	11:28	Now J was a man of standing,	3716
	11:29	that time J was going out of Jerusalem,	3716
	11:31	Then he said to J, "Take ten pieces	3716
	11:40	Solomon tried to kill J, but Jeroboam fled	3716
	11:40	but J fled to Egypt, to Shishak the king,	3716
	12: 2	When J son of Nebat heard this	3716
	12: 3	So they sent for J.	3716
	12:12	Three days later J and all the people	3716
	12:15	the word the LORD had spoken to J son	3716
	12:20	the Israelites heard that J had returned,	3716
	12:25	Then J fortified Shechem in the hill	3716
	12:26	J thought to himself,	3716
	12:31	J built shrines on high places	NIH
	13: 1	as J was standing by the altar to make	3716
	13: 4	When King J heard what the man	3716
	13:33	after this, J did not change his evil ways,	3716
	13:34	This was the sin of the house of J that led	3716
	14: 1	At that time Abijah son of J became ill,	3716
	14: 2	and J said to his wife, "Go, disguise	3716
	14: 2	you won't be recognized as the wife of J.	3716
	14: 6	he said, "Come in, wife of J.	3716
	14: 7	Go, tell J that this is what the LORD,	3716
	14:10	to bring disaster on the house of J.	3716
	14:10	I will cut off from J every last male	3716
	14:10	up the house of J as one burns dung,	3716
	14:11	Dogs will eat those belonging to J who die	3716
	14:13	He is the only one belonging to J who will	3716
	14:13	the only one in the house of J in whom	3716
	14:14	who will cut off the family of J.	3716
	14:16	up because of the sins J has committed	3716
	14:30	warfare between Rehoboam and J.	3716
	15: 1	In the eighteenth year of the reign of J son	3716
	15: 6	There was war between Rehoboam and J	3716
	15: 7	There was war between Abijah and J.	3716
	15: 9	In the twentieth year of J king of Israel,	3716
	15:25	Nadab son of J became king of Israel in	3716
	15:29	He did not leave J anyone that breathed,	3716
	15:30	because of the sins J had committed	3716
	15:34	walking in the ways of J and in his sin,	3716
	16: 2	of J and caused my people Israel to sin and	3716
	16: 3	like that of J son of Nebat.	3716
	16: 7	and becoming like the house of J—	3716
	16:19	the LORD and walking in the ways of J	3716
	16:26	the ways of J son of Nebat and in his sin,	3716
	16:31	to commit the sins of J son of Nebat,	3716
	21:22	of J son of Nebat and that of Baasha son	3716
	22:52	and mother and in the ways of J son	3716
2Ki	3: 3	he clung to the sins of J son of Nebat,	3716
	9: 9	the house of Ahab like the house of J son	3716
	10:29	he did not turn away from the sins of J son	3716
	10:31	He did not turn away from the sins of J,	3716
	13: 2	the LORD by following the sins of J son	3716
	13: 6	the house of J, which he had caused Israel	3716
	13:11	not turn away from any of the sins of J son	3716
	13:13	and succeeded him on the throne.	3716
	14:16	And J his son succeeded him as king.	3716
	14:23	son of Jehoash king of Israel	3716
	14:24	not turn away from any of the sins of J son	3716
	14:27	he saved them by the hand of J son	3716
	14:29	J rested with his fathers,	3716
	15: 1	the twenty-seventh year of J king of Israel,	3716
	15: 8	Zechariah son of J became king of Israel	3716
	15: 9	not turn away from the sins of J son	3716
	15:18	not turn away from the sins of J son	3716
	15:24	not turn away from the sins of J son	3716
	15:28	not turn away from the sins of J son	3716
	17:21	they made J son of Nebat their king.	3716
	17:21	J enticed Israel away from following	3716
	17:22	The Israelites persisted in all the sins of J	3716
	23:15	the high place made by J son of Nebat,	3716
1Ch		of Jotham king of Judah and J king	3716
2Ch	9:29	the seer concerning J son of Nebat?	3716
	10: 2	When J son of Nebat heard this (he was	3716
	10: 3	So they sent for J.	3716
	10:12	Three days later J and all Israel went to	3716
	10:15	the word the LORD had spoken to J	3716
	11: 4	and turned back from marching against J.	3716
	11:14	because J and his sons had rejected them	3716
	12:15	warfare between Rehoboam and J.	3716
	13: 1	In the eighteenth year of the reign of J,	3716
	13: 2	There was war between Abijah and J.	3716
	13: 3	and J drew up a battle line against him	3716
	13: 4	and said, "J and all Israel, listen to me!	3716
	13: 6	Yet J son of Nebat, an official of Solomon	3716
	13: 8	with you the golden calves that J made to	3716
	13:13	Now J had sent troops around to the rear,	3716
	13:15	God routed J and all Israel before Abijah	3716
	13:19	Abijah pursued J and took from him	3716
	13:20	J did not regain power during the time	3716
Hos	1: 1	during the reign of J son of Jehoash king	3716
Am	1: 1	when Uzziah was king of Judah and J son	3716
	7: 9	against the house of J."	3716
	7:10	of Bethel sent a message to J king	3716
	7:11	" 'J will die by the sword,	3716

JEROBOAM'S (6) [JEROBOAM]

1Ki	14: 4	So J wife did what he said and went	3716
	14: 5	"J wife is coming to ask you	3716

1Ki	14:17	J wife got up and left and went to Tirzah.	3716
	14:19	The other events of J reign,	3716
	15:29	he killed J whole family.	3716
2Ki	14:28	As for the other events of J reign,	3716

JEROHAM (10)

1Sa	1: 1	whose name was Elkanah son of J,	3736
1Ch	6:27	J his son, Elkanah his son	3736
	6:34	the son of J, the son of Eliel,	3736
	8:27	Elijah and Zicri were the sons of J.	3736
	9: 8	Ibneiah son of J;	3736
	9:12	Adaiah son of J, the son of Pashhur,	3736
	12: 7	and Zebadiah the sons of J from Gedor.	3736
	27:22	Azarel son of J.	3736
2Ch	23: 1	Azariah son of J,	3736
Ne	11:12	Adaiah son of J, the son of Pelaliah,	3736

JERUB-BAAL (11) [GIDEON, JERUB-BAAL'S, JERUB-BESHETH]

Jdg	6:32	So that day they called Gideon "J," saying,	3715
	7: 1	Early in the morning, J (that is, Gideon)	3715
	8:29	J son of Joash went back home to live.	3715
	8:35	to show kindness to the family of J	3715
	9: 1	of J went to his mother's brothers	3715
	9: 5	murdered his seventy brothers, the sons of J	3715
	9: 5	But Jotham, the youngest son of J,	3715
	9:16	if you have been fair to J and his family,	3715
	9:19	toward J and his family today,	3715
	9:57	The curse of Jotham son of J came	3715
1Sa	12:11	Then the LORD sent J, Barak,	3715

JERUB-BAAL'S (3) [JERUB-BAAL]

Jdg	9: 2	to have all seventy of J sons rule over you,	3715
	9:24	that the crime against J seventy sons,	3715
	9:28	Isn't he J son, and isn't Zebul his deputy?	3715

JERUB-BESHETH (1) [JERUB-BAAL]

| 2Sa | 11:21 | Who killed Abimelech son of J? | 3717 |

JERUEL (1)

| 2Ch | 20:16 | at the end of the gorge in the Desert of J. | 3725 |

JERUSALEM (804) [JEBUS, JERUSALEM'S]

Jos	10: 1	king of J heard that Joshua had taken Ai	3731
	10: 3	king of J appealed to Hoham king of Hebron,	3731
	10: 5	the kings of J, Hebron, Jarmuth,	3731
	10:23	the kings of J, Hebron, Jarmuth,	3731
	12:10	the king of J one the king of Hebron one	3731
	15: 8	of the Jebusite city (that is, J).	3731
	15:63	who were living in J.	3731
	18:28	Haeleph, the Jebusite city (that is, J),	3731
Jdg	1: 7	They brought him to J, and he died there.	3731
	1: 8	men of Judah attacked J also and took it.	3731
	1:21	who were living in J;	3731
	19:10	(that is, J), with his two saddled donkeys	3731
1Sa	17:54	the Philistine's head and brought it to J,	3731
2Sa	5: 5	and in J he reigned over all Israel	3731
	5: 6	The king and his men marched to J	3731
	5:13	David took more concubines and wives in J,	3731
	8: 7	of Hadadezer and brought them to J.	3731
	9:13	And Mephibosheth lived in J,	3731
	10:14	the Ammonites and came to J.	3731
	11: 1	But David remained in J.	3731
	11:12	Uriah remained in J that day and the next.	3731
	12:31	David and his entire army returned to J.	3731
	14:23	to Geshur and brought Absalom back to J	3731
	14:28	in J without seeing the king's face.	3731
	15: 8	'If the LORD takes me back to J,	3731
	15:11	from J had accompanied Absalom.	3731
	15:14	to all his officials who were with him in J,	3731
	15:29	and Abiathar took the ark of God back to J	3731
	15:37	at J as Absalom was entering the city.	3731
	16: 3	Ziba said to him, "He is staying in J,	3731
	16:15	and all the men of Israel came to J,	3731
	17:20	so they returned to J.	3731
	19:19	on the day my lord the king left J.	3731
	19:25	When he came from J to meet the king,	3731
	19:33	over with me and stay with me in J,	3731
	19:34	that I should go up to J with the king?	3731
	20: 2	the way from the Jordan to J.	3731
	20: 3	When David returned to his palace in J,	3731
	20: 7	from J to pursue Sheba son of Bicri.	3731
	20:22	And Joab went back to the king in J.	3731
	24: 8	they came back to J at the end	3731
	24:16	angel stretched out his hand to destroy J,	3731
1Ki	2:11	in Hebron and thirty-three in J.	3731
	2:36	"Build yourself a house in J and live there,	3731
	2:38	And Shimei stayed in J for a long time.	3731
	2:41	that Shimei had gone from J to Gath	3731
	3: 1	temple of the LORD, and the wall around J.	3731
	3:15	He returned to J,	3731
	8: 1	into his presence at J the elders of Israel,	3731
	9:15	the supporting terraces, the wall of J,	3731
	9:19	whatever he desired to build in J,	3731
	10: 2	Arriving at J with a very great caravan—	3731
	10:26	in the chariot cities and also with him in J.	3731
	10:27	The king made silver as common in J	3731
	11: 7	hill east of J, Solomon built a high place	3731
	11:13	of David my servant and for the sake of J,	3731
	11:29	that time Jeroboam was going out of J,	3731

1Ki	11:32	sake of my servant David and the city of J,	3731
	11:36	may always have a lamp before me in J,	3731
	11:42	in J over all Israel forty years.	3731
	12:18	to get into his chariot and escape to J.	3731
	12:21	When Rehoboam arrived in J,	3731
	12:27	at the temple of the LORD in J,	3731
	12:28	"It is too much for you to go up to J.	3731
	14:21	and he reigned seventeen years in J,	3731
	14:25	Shishak king of Egypt attacked J.	3731
	15: 2	and he reigned in J three years.	3731
	15: 4	in J by raising up a son to succeed him and	3731
	15: 4	to succeed him and by making J strong.	3731
	15:10	and he reigned in J forty-one years.	3731
	22:42	and he reigned in J twenty-five years.	3731
2Ki	8:17	and he reigned in J eight years.	3731
	8:26	and he reigned in J one year.	3731
	9:28	His servants took him by chariot to J	3731
	12: 1	and he reigned in J forty years.	3731
	12:17	Then he turned to attack J.	3731
	12:18	who then withdrew from J.	3731
	14: 2	and he reigned in J twenty-nine years.	3731
	14: 2	Jehoaddin; she was from J.	3731
	14:13	J and broke down the wall of Jerusalem	3731
	14:13	to Jerusalem and broke down the wall of J	3731
	14:19	They conspired against him in J,	3731
	14:20	and was buried in J with his fathers,	3731
	15: 2	and he reigned in J fifty-two years.	3731
	15: 2	Jecoliah; she was from J.	3731
	15:33	and he reigned in J sixteen years.	3731
	16: 2	and he reigned in J sixteen years.	3731
	16: 5	up to fight against J and besieged Ahaz,	3731
	18: 2	and he reigned in J twenty-nine years.	3731
	18:17	from Lachish to King Hezekiah at J.	3731
	18:17	up to J and stopped at the aqueduct of	3731
	18:22	saying to Judah and J,	3731
	18:22	"You must worship before this altar in J"?	3731
	18:35	can the LORD deliver J from my hand?"	3731
	19:10	when he says, 'J will not be handed over	3731
	19:21	Daughter of J tosses her head as you flee.	3731
	19:31	For out of J will come a remnant,	3731
	21: 1	and he reigned in J fifty-five years.	3731
	21: 4	"In J I will put my Name."	3731
	21: 7	"In this temple and in J,	3731
	21:12	to bring such disaster on J and Judah that	3731
	21:13	over J the measuring line used	3731
	21:13	I will wipe out J as one wipes a dish,	3731
	21:16	so much innocent blood that he filled J	3731
	21:19	and he reigned in J two years.	3731
	22: 1	and he reigned in J thirty-one years.	3731
	22:14	She lived in J, in the Second District.	3731
	23: 1	the elders of Judah and J.	3731
	23: 2	of J, the priests and the prophets—	3731
	23: 4	He burned them outside J in the fields of	3731
	23: 5	the towns of Judah and on those around J—	3731
	23: 6	the LORD to the Kidron Valley outside J	3731
	23: 9	not serve at the altar of the LORD in J,	3731
	23:13	that were east of J on the south of the Hill	3731
	23:20	Then he went back to J.	3731
	23:23	Passover was celebrated to the LORD in J.	3731
	23:24	detestable things seen in Judah and J,	3731
	23:27	and I will reject J, the city I chose,	3731
	23:30	to J and buried him in his own tomb.	3731
	23:31	and he reigned in J three months.	3731
	23:33	of Hamath so that he might not reign in J,	3731
	23:36	and he reigned in J eleven years.	3731
	24: 4	For he had filled J with innocent blood,	3731
	24: 8	and he reigned in J three months.	3731
	24: 8	daughter of Elnathan; she was from J.	3731
	24:10	of Babylon advanced on J and laid siege	3731
	24:14	He carried into exile all J:	3731
	24:15	from J to Babylon the king's mother,	3731
	24:18	and he reigned in J eleven years.	3731
	24:20	that all this happened to J and Judah,	3731
	25: 1	against J with his whole army.	3731
	25: 8	of the king of Babylon, came to J.	3731
	25: 9	the royal palace and all the houses of J.	3731
	25:10	broke down the walls around J.	3731
1Ch	3: 4	David reigned in J thirty-three years,	3731
	6:10	in the temple Solomon built in J,	3731
	6:15	the LORD sent Judah and J into exile by	3731
	6:32	the temple of the LORD in J.	3731
	8:28	and they lived in J.	3731
	8:32	They too lived near their relatives in J.	3731
	9: 3	and Manasseh who lived in J were:	3731
	9:34	and they lived in J.	3731
	9:38	They too lived near their relatives in J.	3731
	11: 4	all the Israelites marched to J (that is, Jebus)	3731
	14: 3	In J David took more wives and became	3731
	15: 3	David assembled all Israel in J to bring up	3731
	18: 7	of Hadadezer and brought them to J.	3731
	19:15	So Joab went back to J.	3731
	20: 1	but David remained in J.	3731
	20: 3	David and his entire army returned to J.	3731
	21: 4	throughout Israel and then came back to J.	3731
	21:15	And God sent an angel to destroy J.	3731
	21:16	in his hand extended over J.	3731
	23:25	and has come to dwell in J forever,	3731
	28: 1	the officials of Israel to assemble at J:	3731
	29:27	seven in Hebron and thirty-three in J.	3731
2Ch	1: 4	because he had pitched a tent for it in J.	3731
	1:13	to J from the high place at Gibeon,	3731
	1:14	in the chariot cities and also with him in J.	3731
	1:15	and gold as common in J as stones,	3731
	2: 7	in Judah and J with my skilled craftsmen,	3731
	2:16	You can then take them up to J."	3731
	3: 1	to build the temple of the LORD in J	3731
	5: 2	Then Solomon summoned to J the elders	3731

	6: 6	I have chosen J for my Name to be there,	3731
	8: 6	whatever he desired to build in J	3731
	9: 1	to J to test him with hard questions.	3731
	9:25	in the chariot cities and also with him in J.	3731
	9:27	The king made silver as common in J	3731
	9:30	in J over all Israel forty years.	3731
	10:18	to get into his chariot and escape to J.	3731
	11: 1	When Rehoboam arrived in J,	3731
	11: 5	Rehoboam lived in J and built up towns	3731
	11:14	to Judah and J because Jeroboam	3731
	11:16	followed the Levites to J to offer sacrifices	3731
	12: 2	Shishak king of Egypt attacked J in	3731
	12: 4	of Judah and came as far as J.	3731
	12: 5	of Judah who had assembled in J for fear	3731
	12: 7	not be poured out on J through Shishak.	3731
	12: 9	When Shishak king of Egypt attacked J,	3731
	12:13	in J and continued as king.	3731
	12:13	and he reigned seventeen years in J,	3731
	13: 2	and he reigned in J three years.	3731
	14:15	Then they returned to J.	3731
	15:10	at J in the third month of the fifteenth year	3731
	17:13	also kept experienced fighting men in J.	3731
	19: 1	of Judah returned safely to his palace in J,	3731
	19: 4	Jehoshaphat lived in J,	3731
	19: 8	In J also, Jehoshaphat appointed some of	3731
	19: 8	And they lived in J.	3731
	20: 5	of Judah and J at the temple of the LORD	3731
	20:15	and all who live in Judah and J!	3731
	20:17	the LORD will give you, O Judah and J.	3731
	20:18	and all the people of Judah and J fell down	3731
	20:20	"Listen to me, Judah and people of J!	3731
	20:27	the men of Judah and J returned joyfully	3731
	20:27	and Jerusalem returned joyfully to J,	3731
	20:28	They entered J and went to the temple of	3731
	20:31	and he reigned in J twenty-five years.	3731
	21: 5	and he reigned in J eight years.	3731
	21:11	of Judah and had caused the people of J	3731
	21:13	and you have led Judah and the people of J	3731
	21:20	and he reigned in J eight years.	3731
	22: 1	The people of J made Ahaziah,	3731
	22: 2	and he reigned in J one year.	3731
	23: 2	When they came to J,	3731
	24: 1	and he reigned in J forty years.	3731
	24: 6	the Levites to bring in from Judah and J	3731
	24: 9	and J that they should bring to the LORD	3731
	24:18	God's anger came upon Judah and J.	3731
	24:23	it invaded Judah and J and killed all	3731
	25: 1	and he reigned in J twenty-nine years.	3731
	25: 1	Jehoaddin; she was from J.	3731
	25:23	to J and broke down the wall of Jerusalem	3731
	25:23	to Jerusalem and broke down the wall of J	3731
	25:27	they conspired against him in J and he fled	3731
	26: 3	and he reigned in J fifty-two years.	3731
	26: 3	Jecoliah; she was from J.	3731
	26: 9	Uzziah built towers in J at the Corner Gate,	3731
	26:15	In J he made machines designed	3731
	27: 1	and he reigned in J sixteen years.	3731
	27: 8	and he reigned in J sixteen years.	3731
	28: 1	and he reigned in J sixteen years.	3731
	28:10	and women of Judah and J your slaves.	3731
	28:24	and set up altars at every street corner in J.	3731
	28:27	and was buried in the city of J,	3731
	29: 1	and he reigned in J twenty-nine years.	3731
	29: 8	of the LORD has fallen on Judah and J;	3731
	30: 1	the LORD in J and celebrate the Passover	3731
	30: 2	decided to celebrate the Passover in	3731
	30: 3	and the people had not assembled in J.	3731
	30: 5	to come to J and celebrate the Passover to	3731
	30:11	humbled themselves and went to J.	3731
	30:13	of people assembled in J to celebrate	3731
	30:14	in J and cleared away the incense altars	3731
	30:21	in J celebrated the Feast	3731
	30:26	There was great joy in J,	3731
	30:26	there had been nothing like this in J.	3731
	31: 4	He ordered the people living in J to give	3731
	32: 2	and that he intended to make war on J,	3731
	32: 9	he sent his officers to J with this message	3731
	32:10	that you remain in J under siege?	3731
	32:12	saying to Judah and J,	3731
	32:18	in Hebrew to the people of J who were on	3731
	32:19	They spoke about the God of J as they did	3731
	32:22	of J from the hand of Sennacherib king	3731
	32:23	to J for the LORD and valuable gifts	3731
	32:25	on him and on Judah and J.	3731
	32:26	as did the people of J;	3731
	32:33	the people of J honored him when he died.	3731
	33: 1	and he reigned in J fifty-five years.	3731
	33: 4	"My Name will remain in J forever."	3731
	33: 7	"In this temple and in J,	3731
	33: 9	and the people of J astray,	3731
	33:13	so he brought him back to J and	3731
	33:15	on the temple hill and in J;	3731
	33:21	and he reigned in J two years.	3731
	34: 1	and he reigned in J thirty-one years.	3731
	34: 3	to purge Judah and J of high places,	3731
	34: 5	and so he purged Judah and J.	3731
	34: 7	Then he went back to J.	3731
	34: 9	and Benjamin and the inhabitants of J.	3731
	34:22	She lived in J, in the Second District.	3731
	34:29	the elders of Judah and J.	3731
	34:30	of J, the priests and the Levites—	3731
	34:32	in J and Benjamin pledge themselves to it;	3731
	34:32	the people of J did this in accordance with	3731
	35: 1	the Passover to the LORD in J,	3731
	35:18	who were there with the people of J.	3731
	35:24	and brought him to J, where he died.	3731
	35:24	and all Judah and J mourned for him.	3731

2Ch	36: 1	of Josiah and made him king in J in place	3731
	36: 2	and he reigned in J three months.	3731
	36: 3	of Egypt dethroned him in J and imposed	3731
	36: 4	king over Judah and J and changed	3731
	36: 5	and he reigned in J eleven years.	3731
	36: 9	he reigned in J three months and ten days.	3731
	36:10	Zedekiah, king over Judah and J.	3731
	36:11	and he reigned in J eleven years.	3731
	36:14	which he had consecrated in J.	3731
	36:19	and broke down the wall of J;	3731
	36:23	to build a temple for him at J in Judah.	3731
Ezr	1: 2	to build a temple for him at J in Judah.	3731
	1: 3	with him, and let him go up to J in Judah	3731
	1: 3	the God of Israel, the God who is in J	3731
	1: 4	for the temple of God in J.' "	3731
	1: 5	up and build the house of the LORD in J.	3731
	1: 7	from J and had placed in the temple	3731
	1:11	the exiles came up from Babylon to J.	3731
	2: 1	to Babylon (they returned to J and Judah,	3731
	2:68	at the house of the LORD in J,	3731
	3: 1	the people assembled as one man in J.	3731
	3: 8	after their arrival at the house of God in J,	3731
	3: 8	from the captivity to J) began the work,	3731
	4: 6	against the people of Judah and J.	3731
	4: 8	a letter against J to Artaxerxes the king	10332
	4:12	to J and are rebuilding that rebellious	10332
	4:20	J has had powerful kings ruling over	10332
	4:23	the Jews in J and compelled them by force	10332
	4:24	the work on the house of God in J came to	10332
	5: 1	to the Jews in Judah and J in the name of	10332
	5: 2	to work to rebuild the house of God in J.	10332
	5:14	in J and brought to the temple in Babylon.	10332
	5:15	and go and deposit them in the temple in J.	10332
	5:16	the foundations of the house of God in J.	10332
	5:17	a decree to rebuild this house of God in J.	10332
	6: 3	concerning the temple of God in J:	10332
	6: 5	the temple in J and brought to Babylon,	10332
	6: 5	to their places in the temple in J;	10332
	6: 9	as requested by the priests in J—	10332
	6:12	or to destroy this temple in J.	10332
	6:18	in their groups for the service of God at J,	10332
	7: 7	also came up to J in the seventh year	3731
	7: 8	in J in the fifth month of the seventh year	3731
	7: 9	in J on the first day of the fifth month,	3731
	7:13	who wish to go to J with you, may go.	10332
	7:14	to inquire about Judah and J with regard to	10332
	7:15	whose dwelling is in J.	10332
	7:16	for the temple of their God in J.	10332
	7:17	on the altar of the temple of your God in J.	10332
	7:19	to the God of J all the articles entrusted	10332
	7:27	to the house of the LORD in J in this way	3731
	8:29	the LORD in J before the leading priests	3731
	8:30	to be taken to the house of our God in J.	3731
	8:31	from the Ahava Canal to go to J.	3731
	8:32	So we arrived in J, where we rested	3731
	9: 9	a wall of protection in Judah and J.	3731
	10: 7	then issued throughout Judah and J for all	3731
	10: 7	of the exiles to assemble in J.	3731
	10: 9	of Judah and Benjamin had gathered in J.	3731
Ne	1: 2	that survived the exile, and also about J.	3731
	1: 3	The wall of J is broken down,	3731
	2:11	I went to J, and after staying there three	3731
	2:12	God had put in my heart to do for J.	3731
	2:13	examining the walls of J, which had been	3731
	2:17	J lies in ruins, and its gates have been	3731
	2:17	Come, let us rebuild the wall of J,	3731
	2:20	in J or any claim or historic right to it."	3731
	3: 8	They restored as far as the Broad Wall.	3731
	3: 9	ruler of a half-district of J,	3731
	3:12	ruler of a half-district of J,	3731
	4: 8	against J and stir up trouble against it.	3731
	4:22	and his helper stay inside J at night,	3731
	6: 7	to make this proclamation about you in J:	3731
	7: 2	I put in charge of J my brother Hanani,	3731
	7: 3	"The gates of J are not to be opened until	3731
	7: 3	Also appoint residents of J as guards,	3731
	7: 6	(they returned to J and Judah,	3731
	8:15	throughout their towns and in J:	3731
	11: 1	Now the leaders of the people settled in J,	3731
	11: 1	to bring one out of every ten to live in J,	3731
	11: 2	the men who volunteered to live in J.	3731
	11: 3	the provincial leaders who settled in J	3731
	11: 4	from both Judah and Benjamin lived in J):	3731
	11: 6	who lived in J totaled 468 able men.	3731
	11:22	of the Levites in J was Uzzi son of Bani,	3731
	12:27	At the dedication of the wall of J,	3731
	12:27	and were brought to J to celebrate joyfully	3731
	12:28	from the region around J—	3731
	12:29	built villages for themselves around J.	3731
	12:43	of rejoicing in J could be heard far away.	3731
	13: 6	while all this was going on, I was not in J,	3731
	13: 7	and came back to J.	3731
	13:15	And they were bringing all this into J on	3731
	13:16	from Tyre who lived in J were bringing	2023S
	13:16	in J on the Sabbath to the people of Judah.	3731
	13:19	on the gates of J before the Sabbath,	3731
	13:20	all kinds of goods spent the night outside J.	3731
Est	2: 6	into exile from J by Nebuchadnezzar king	3731
Ps	51:18	build up the walls of J.	3731
	68:29	at J kings will bring you gifts.	3731
	79: 1	they have reduced J to rubble.	3731
	79: 3	poured out blood like water all around J,	3731
	102:21	be declared in J and his praise in	3731
	116:19	in your midst, O J.	3731
	122: 2	Our feet are standing at your gates, O J.	3731
	122: 3	J is built like a city that is closely	3731
	122: 6	Pray for the peace of J: "May those who	3731
Ps	125: 2	As the mountains surround J,	3731
	128: 5	may you see the prosperity of J;	3731
	135:21	to him who dwells in J.	3731
	137: 5	If I forget you, O J,	3731
	137: 6	if I do not consider J my highest joy.	3731
	137: 7	what the Edomites did on the day J fell.	3731
	147: 2	The LORD builds up J;	3731
	147:12	Extol the LORD, O J;	3731
Ecc	1: 1	the Teacher, son of David, king in J:	3731
	1:12	I, the Teacher, was king over Israel in J.	3731
	1:16	anyone who has ruled over J before me;	3731
	2: 7	and flocks than anyone in J before me.	3731
	2: 9	I became greater by far than anyone in J	3731
SS	1: 5	Dark am I, yet lovely, O daughters of J,	3731
	2: 7	Daughters of J, I charge you by the gazelles	3731
	3: 5	Daughters of J, I charge you by the gazelles	3731
	3:10	by the daughters of J.	3731
	5: 8	O daughters of J, I charge you—	3731
	5:16	this my friend, O daughters of J.	3731
	6: 4	my darling, as Tirzah, lovely as J,	3731
	8: 4	Daughters of J, I charge you:	3731
Isa	1: 1	and J that Isaiah son of Amoz saw during	3731
	2: 1	of Amoz saw concerning Judah and J:	3731
	2: 3	the word of the LORD from J.	3731
	3: 1	from J and Judah both supply and support:	3731
	3: 8	J staggers, Judah is falling;	3731
	4: 3	who remain in J, will be called holy,	3731
	4: 3	all who are recorded among the living in J,	3731
	4: 4	from J by a spirit of judgment and a spirit	3731
	5: 3	"Now you dwellers in J and men of Judah,	3731
	7: 1	of Israel marched to fight against J,	3731
	8:14	people of J he will be a trap and a snare.	3731
	10:10	excelled those of J and Samaria—	3731
	10:11	not deal with J and her images as I dealt	3731
	10:12	against Mount Zion and J,	3731
	10:32	the Daughter of Zion, at the hill of J.	3731
	22:10	the buildings in J and tore down houses	3731
	22:21	He will be a father to those who live in J	3731
	24:23	on Mount Zion and in J,	3731
	27:13	the LORD on the holy mountain in J.	3731
	28:14	you scoffers who rule this people in J.	3731
	30:19	O people of Zion, who live in J,	3731
	31: 5	the LORD Almighty will shield J;	3731
	31: 9	whose furnace is in J.	3731
	33:20	your eyes will see J, a peaceful abode,	3731
	36: 2	from Lachish to King Hezekiah at J.	3731
	36: 7	saying to Judah and J,	3731
	36:20	can the LORD deliver J from my hand?"	3731
	37:10	when he says, 'J will not be handed over	3731
	37:22	Daughter of J tosses her head as you flee.	3731
	37:32	For out of J will come a remnant,	3731
	40: 2	Speak tenderly to J, and proclaim to her	3731
	40: 9	You who bring good tidings to J,	3731
	41:27	I gave to J a messenger of good tidings.	3731
	44:26	who says of J, 'It shall be inhabited,'	3731
	44:28	he will say of J, "Let it be rebuilt,"	3731
	51:17	O J, you who have drunk from the hand of	3731
	52: 1	Put on your garments of splendor, O J,	3731
	52: 2	rise up, sit enthroned, O J.	3731
	52: 9	into songs of joy together, you ruins of J,	3731
	52: 9	comforted his people, he has redeemed J.	3731
	62: 6	O J; they will never be silent day or night.	3731
	62: 7	and give him no rest till he establishes J	3731
	64:10	even Zion is a desert, J a desolation.	3731
	65:18	for I will create J to be a delight	3731
	65:19	over J and take delight in my people;	3731
	66:10	"Rejoice with J and be glad for her,	3731
	66:13	and you will be comforted over J."	3731
	66:20	to my holy mountain in J as an offering to	3731
Jer	1: 3	when the people of J went into exile.	3731
	1:15	in the entrance of the gates of J.	3731
	2: 2	"Go and proclaim in the hearing of J:	3731
	3:17	they will call J The Throne of the LORD,	3731
	3:17	and all nations will gather in J to honor	3731
	4: 3	to the men of Judah and to J:	3731
	4: 4	you men of Judah and people of J,	3731
	4: 5	"Announce in Judah and proclaim in J	3731
	4:10	and J by saying, 'You will have peace,'	3731
	4:14	O J, wash the evil from your heart and	3731
	4:16	"Tell this to the nations, proclaim it to J:	3731
	5: 1	"Go up and down the streets of J,	3731
	6: 1	Flee from J! Sound the trumpet	3731
	6: 6	the trees and build siege ramps against J.	3731
	6: 8	O J, or I will turn away from you	3731
	7:17	the towns of Judah and in the streets of J?	3731
	7:34	in the towns of Judah and the streets of J,	3731
	8: 1	of J will be removed from their graves.	3731
	8: 5	Why does J always turn away?	3731
	9:11	"I will make J a heap of ruins,	3731
	11: 2	of Judah and to those who live in J.	3731
	11: 6	the towns of Judah and in the streets of J:	3731
	11: 9	of Judah and those who live in J.	3731
	11:12	and the people of J will go and cry out to	3731
	11:13	as many as the streets of J—	3731
	13: 9	the pride of Judah and the great pride of J.	3731
	13:13	the prophets and all those living in J,	3731
	13:27	Woe to you, O J!	3731
	14: 2	and a cry goes up from J.	3731
	14:16	be thrown out into the streets of J because	3731
	15: 4	son of Hezekiah king of Judah did in J.	3731
	15: 5	"Who will have pity on you, O J?	3731
	17:19	stand also at all the other gates of J,	3731
	17:20	living in J who come through these gates.	3731
	17:21	or bring it through the gates of J.	3731
	17:25	by the men of Judah and those living in J,	3731
	17:26	towns of Judah and the villages around J,	3731
Jer	17:27	through the gates of J on the Sabbath day,	3731
	17:27	of J that will consume her fortresses.' "	3731
	18:11	the people of Judah and those living in J,	3731
	19: 3	O kings of Judah and people of J.	3731
	19: 7	the plans of Judah and J.	3731
	19:13	in J and those of the kings of Judah will	3731
	21:13	I am against you, [J,]	NIH
	22:19	and thrown outside the gates of J."	3731
	23:14	of J I have seen something horrible:	3731
	23:14	the people of J are like Gomorrah."	2023S
	23:15	the prophets of J ungodliness has spread	3731
	24: 1	of Judah were carried into exile from J	3731
	24: 8	his officials and the survivors from J,	3731
	25: 2	of Judah and to all those living in J:	3731
	25:18	J and the towns of Judah, its kings	3731
	26:18	J will become a heap of rubble,	3731
	27: 3	through the envoys who have come to J	3731
	27:18	the palace of the king of Judah and in J not	3731
	27:20	of Judah into exile from J to Babylon,	3731
	27:20	along with all the nobles of Judah and J—	3731
	27:21	in the palace of the king of Judah and in J,	3731
	29: 1	that the prophet Jeremiah sent from J to	3731
	29: 1	into exile from J to Babylon.	3731
	29: 2	and the leaders of Judah and J,	3731
	29: 2	the artisans had gone into exile from J.)	3731
	29: 4	says to all those I carried into exile from J	3731
	29:20	sent them away from J to Babylon.	3731
	29:25	in your own name to all the people in J,	3731
	32: 2	the king of Babylon was then besieging J,	3731
	32:32	the men of Judah and the people of J.	3731
	32:44	in the villages around J,	3731
	33:10	in the towns of Judah and the streets of J	3731
	33:13	in the villages around J and in the towns	3731
	33:16	be saved and J will live in safety.	3731
	34: 1	the empire he ruled were fighting against J	3731
	34: 6	to Zedekiah king of Judah, in J,	3731
	34: 7	the king of Babylon was fighting against J	3731
	34: 8	in J to proclaim freedom for the slaves.	3731
	34:19	The leaders of Judah and J,	3731
	35:11	we must go to J to escape the Babylonian	3731
	35:11	So we have remained in J."	3731
	35:13	the men of Judah and the people of J,	3731
	35:17	in J every disaster I pronounced	3731
	36: 9	the people in J and those who had come	3731
	36:31	I will bring on them and those living in J	3731
	37: 5	Babylonians who were besieging J heard	3731
	37: 5	they withdrew from J.	3731
	37:11	from J because of Pharaoh's army,	3731
	38:28	of the guard until the day J was captured.	3731
	38:28	This is how J was taken:	3731
	39: 1	against J with his whole army	3731
	39: 8	the people and broke down the walls of J.	3731
	40: 1	from J and Judah who were being carried	3731
	42:18	on those who lived in J,	3731
	44: 2	the great disaster I brought on J and on all	3731
	44: 6	the towns of Judah and the streets of J	3731
	44: 9	in the land of Judah and the streets of J?	3731
	44:13	famine and plague, as I punished J,	3731
	44:17	the towns of Judah and in the streets of J,	3731
	44:21	the towns of Judah and the streets of J	3731
	51:35	on those who live in Babylonia," says J.	3731
	51:50	in a distant land, and think on J."	3731
	52: 1	and he reigned in J eleven years.	3731
	52: 3	that all this happened to J and Judah,	3731
	52: 4	against J with his whole army.	3731
	52:12	the king of Babylon, came to J.	3731
	52:13	the royal palace and all the houses of J.	3731
	52:14	broke down all the walls around J.	3731
	52:29	832 people from J;	3731
La	1: 7	J remembers all the treasures that were hers	3731
	1: 8	J has sinned greatly and so has become	3731
	1:17	J has become an unclean thing	3731
	2:10	of J have bowed their heads to the ground.	3731
	2:13	what can I compare you, O Daughter of J?	3731
	2:15	and shake their heads at the Daughter of J:	3731
	4:12	and foes could enter the gates of J.	3731
Eze	4: 1	put it in front of you and draw the city of J	3731
	4: 7	the siege of J and with bared arm prophesy	3731
	4:16	I will cut off the supply of food in J.	3731
	5: 5	This is J, which I have set in the center of	3731
	5: 8	I myself am against you, J,	NIH
	8: 3	and in visions of God he took me to J,	3731
	9: 4	throughout the city of J and put a mark on	3731
	9: 8	in this outpouring of your wrath on J?"	3731
	11:15	of J have said, 'They are far away from	3731
	12:10	This oracle concerns the prince in J and	3731
	12:19	about those living in J and in the land	3731
	13:16	to J and saw visions of peace for her	3731
	14:21	against J my four dreadful judgments—	3731
	14:22	the disaster I have brought upon J—	3731
	15: 6	so will I treat the people living in J.	3731
	16: 2	confront J with her detestable practices	3731
	16: 3	the Sovereign LORD says to J:	3731
	17:12	'The king of Babylon went to J	3731
	21: 2	against J and preach against the sanctuary.	3731
	21:20	and another against Judah and fortified J.	3731
	21:22	Into his right hand will come the lot for J,	3731
	22:19	I will gather you into J.	3731
	23: 4	Oholah is Samaria, and Oholibah is J.	3731
	24: 2	has laid siege to J this very day.	3731
	26: 2	because Tyre has said of J, 'Aha!	3731
	33:21	a man who had escaped from J came to me	3731
	36:38	as numerous as the flocks for offerings at J	3731
Da	1: 1	king of Babylon came to J and besieged it.	3731
	5: 2	had taken from the temple in J,	10332
	5: 3	taken from the temple of God in J,	10332
	6:10	where the windows opened toward J.	10332

Da	9: 2	desolation of **J** would last seventy years.	3731
	9: 7	of Judah and people of **J** and all Israel,	3731
	9:12	like what has been done to **J**.	3731
	9:16	and your wrath from **J**,	3731
	9:16	the iniquities of our fathers have made **J**	3731
	9:25	of the decree to restore and rebuild **J** until	3731
Joel	2:32	Zion and in **J** there will be deliverance,	3731
	3: 1	when I restore the fortunes of Judah and **J**,	3731
	3: 6	the people of Judah and **J** to the Greeks,	3731
	3:16	from Zion and thunder from **J**;	3731
	3:17	**J** will be holy; never again will foreigners	3731
	3:20	Judah will be inhabited forever and **J**	3731
Am	1: 2	from Zion and thunders from **J**;	3731
	2: 5	that will consume the fortresses of **J**."	3731
Ob	1:11	entered his gates and cast lots for **J**,	3731
	1:20	from **J** who are in Sepharad will possess	3731
Mic	1: 1	concerning Samaria and **J**.	3731
	1: 5	What is Judah's high place? Is it not **J**?	3731
	1: 9	the very gate of my people, even to **J** itself.	3731
	1:12	come from the LORD, even to the gate of **J**.	3731
	3:10	and **J** with wickedness.	3731
	3:12	**J** will become a heap of rubble,	3731
	4: 2	the word of the LORD from **J**.	3731
	4: 8	kingship will come to the Daughter of **J**."	3731
Zep	1: 4	against Judah and against all who live in **J**.	3731
	1:12	At that time I will search **J** with lamps	3731
	3:14	rejoice with all your heart, O Daughter of **J**!	3731
	3:16	On that day they will say to **J**,	3731
Zec	1:12	how long will you withhold mercy from **J**	3731
	1:14	'I am very jealous for **J** and Zion,	3731
	1:16	"I will return to **J** with mercy,	3731
	1:16	measuring line will be stretched out over **J**,'	3731
	1:17	LORD will again comfort Zion and choose **J**.	3731
	1:19	the horns that scattered Judah, Israel and **J**."	3731
	2: 2	He answered me, "To measure **J**,	3731
	2: 4	"Run, tell that young man, '**J** will be a city	3731
	2:12	in the holy land and will again choose **J**.	3731
	3: 2	The LORD, who has chosen **J**,	3731
	7: 7	when **J** and its surrounding towns were	3731
	8: 3	"I will return to Zion and dwell in **J**.	3731
	8: 3	Then **J** will be called the City of Truth,	3731
	8: 4	of ripe old age will sit in the streets of **J**,	3731
	8: 8	I will bring them back to live in **J**;	3731
	8:15	to do good again to **J** and Judah.	3731
	8:22	to **J** to seek the LORD Almighty and	3731
	9: 9	Shout, Daughter of **J**!	3731
	9:10	from Ephraim and the war-horses from **J**,	3731
	12: 2	"I am going to make **J** a cup that sends all	3731
	12: 2	Judah will be besieged as well as **J**.	3731
	12: 3	I will make **J** an immovable rock for all	3731
	12: 5	'The people of **J** are strong,	3731
	12: 6	but **J** will remain intact in her place.	3731
	12: 8	the LORD will shield those who live in **J**,	3731
	12: 9	to destroy all the nations that attack **J**.	3731
	12:10	the house of David and the inhabitants of **J**	3731
	12:11	On that day the weeping in **J** will be great,	3731
	13: 1	of David and the inhabitants of **J**,	3731
	14: 2	I will gather all the nations to **J** to fight	3731
	14: 4	of **J**, and the Mount of Olives will be split	3731
	14: 8	that day living water will flow out from **J**,	3731
	14:10	south of **J**, will become like the Arabah.	3731
	14:10	**J** will be raised up and remain in its place,	NIH
	14:11	**J** will be secure.	3731
	14:12	the nations that fought against **J**:	3731
	14:14	Judah too will fight at **J**.	3731
	14:16	the nations that have attacked **J** will go	3731
	14:17	the peoples of the earth do not go up to **J**	3731
	14:21	Every pot in **J** and Judah will be holy to	3731
Mal	2:11	has been committed in Israel and in **J**:	3731
	3: 4	and **J** will be acceptable to the LORD,	3731
Mt	2: 1	Magi from the east came to **J**	2647
	2: 3	he was disturbed, and all **J** with him.	2647
	3: 5	from **J** and all Judea and the whole region	2647
	4:25	from Galilee, the Decapolis, **J**, Judea and	2647
	5:35	or by **J**, for it is the city of the Great King.	2647
	15: 1	teachers of the law came to Jesus from **J**	2647
	16:21	to **J** and suffer many things at the hands of	2647
	20:17	Now as Jesus was going up to **J**,	2647
	20:18	"We are going up to **J**,	2647
	21: 1	As they approached **J** and came	2647
	21:10	When Jesus entered **J**,	2647
	23:37	"O **J**, Jerusalem, you who kill the prophets	2647
	23:37	**J**, you who kill the prophets and stone those	2647
Mk	1: 5	and all the **people of J** went out to him.	2643
	3: 8	many people came to him from Judea, **J**,	2647
	3:22	teachers of the law who came down from **J**	2647
	7: 1	teachers of the law who had come from **J**	2647
	10:32	They were on their way up to **J**,	2647
	10:33	"We are going up to **J**," he said,	2647
	11: 1	As they approached **J** and came	2647
	11:11	Jesus entered **J** and went to the temple.	2647
	11:15	On reaching **J**, Jesus entered	2647
	11:27	They arrived again in **J**,	2647
	15:41	had come up with him to **J** were also there.	2647
Lk	2:22	and Mary took him to **J** to present him to	2647
	2:25	Now there was a man in **J** called Simeon,	2647
	2:38	looking forward to the redemption of **J**.	2647
	2:41	Every year his parents went to **J** for	2647
	2:43	the boy Jesus stayed behind in **J**,	2647
	2:45	they went back to **J** to look for him.	2647
	4: 9	to **J** and had him stand on the highest point	2647
	5:17	of Galilee and from Judea and **J**,	2647
	6:17	of people from all over Judea, from **J**, and	2647
	9:31	about to bring to fulfillment at **J**.	2647
	9:51	Jesus resolutely set out for **J**.	2647
	9:53	because he was heading for **J**.	2647
	10:30	"A man was going down from **J** to Jericho,	2647

Lk	13: 4	more guilty than all the others living in **J**?	2647
	13:22	teaching as he made his way to **J**.	2647
	13:33	for surely no prophet can die outside **J**!	2647
	13:34	"O **J**, Jerusalem, you who kill the prophets	2647
	13:34	**J**, you who kill the prophets and stone those	2647
	17:11	Now on his way to **J**,	2647
	18:31	"We are going up to **J**,	2647
	19:11	near **J** and the people thought that	2647
	19:28	he went on ahead, going up to **J**.	2647
	19:41	As he approached **J** and saw the city,	NIG
	21:20	"When you see **J** being surrounded	2647
	21:24	**J** will be trampled on by the Gentiles until	2647
	23: 7	who was also in **J** at that time.	2647
	23:28	"Daughters of **J**, do not weep for me;	2647
	24:13	Emmaus, about seven miles from **J**.	2647
	24:18	Are you only a visitor to **J** and do not know	2647
	24:33	They got up and returned at once to **J**.	2647
	24:47	in his name to all nations, beginning at **J**.	2647
	24:52	Then they worshiped him and returned to **J**	2647
Jn	1:19	when the Jews of **J** sent priests and Levites	2647
	2:13	Jesus went up to **J**.	2647
	2:23	while he was in **J** at the Passover Feast,	2647
	4:20	the place where we must worship is in **J**."	2647
	4:21	neither on this mountain nor in **J**.	2647
	4:45	that he had done in **J** at the Passover Feast,	2647
	5: 1	Jesus went up to **J** for a feast of the Jews.	2647
	5: 2	there is in **J** near the Sheep Gate a pool,	2647
	7:25	that point some of the **people of J** began	2643
	10:22	Then came the Feast of Dedication at **J**.	2647
	11:18	Bethany was less than two miles from **J**,	2647
	11:55	to **J** for their ceremonial cleansing before	2647
	12:12	that Jesus was on his way to **J**.	2647
Ac	1: 4	"Do not leave **J**, but wait for the gift	2647
	1: 8	and you will be my witnesses in **J**,	2647
	1:12	Then they returned to **J** from the hill called	2647
	1:19	Everyone in **J** heard about this,	2647
	2: 5	in **J** God-fearing Jews from every nation	2647
	2:14	"Fellow Jews and all of you who live in **J**,	2647
	4: 5	elders and teachers of the law met in **J**.	2647
	4:16	in **J** knows they have done an outstanding	2647
	5:16	also from the towns around **J**,	2647
	5:28	"Yet you have filled **J** with your teaching	2647
	6: 7	number of disciples in **J** increased rapidly,	2647
	8: 1	broke out against the church at **J**,	2647
	8:14	in **J** heard that Samaria had accepted	2647
	8:25	Peter and John returned to **J**,	2647
	8:26	that goes down from **J** to Gaza."	2647
	8:27	This man had gone to **J** to worship,	2647
	9: 2	he might take them as prisoners to **J**.	2647
	9:13	the harm he has done to your saints in **J**.	2647
	9:21	in **J** among those who call on this name?	2647
	9:26	When he came to **J**, he tried to join	2647
	9:28	with them and moved about freely in **J**,	2647
	10:39	in the country of the Jews and in **J**.	2647
	11: 2	So when Peter went up to **J**,	2647
	11:22	of this reached the ears of the church at **J**,	2647
	11:27	prophets came down from **J** to Antioch.	2647
	12:25	they returned from **J**, taking with them John	2647
	13:13	where John left them to return to **J**.	2647
	13:27	The people of **J** and their rulers did	2647
	13:31	traveled with him from Galilee to **J**.	2647
	15: 2	to go up to **J** to see the apostles and elders	2647
	15: 4	When they came to **J**, they were welcomed	2647
	16: 4	the apostles and elders in **J** for the people	2647
	19:21	Paul decided to go to **J**,	2647
	20:16	for he was in a hurry to reach **J**.	2647
	20:22	compelled by the Spirit, I am going to **J**,	2647
	21: 4	Spirit they urged Paul not to go on to **J**.	2647
	21:11	Jews of **J** will bind the owner of this belt	2647
	21:12	pleaded with Paul not to go up to **J**.	2647
	21:13	to die in **J** for the name of the Lord Jesus."	2647
	21:15	After this, we got ready and went up to **J**.	2647
	21:31	that the whole **city of J** was in an uproar.	2647
	22: 5	to bring these people as prisoners to **J** to	2647
	22:17	"When I returned to **J** and was praying at	2647
	22:18	'Leave **J** immediately, because they will not	2647
	23:11	As you have testified about me in **J**,	2647
	24:11	I went up to **J** to worship.	2647
	24:17	to **J** to bring my people gifts for the poor	NIG
	25: 1	Festus went up from Caesarea to **J**,	2647
	25: 3	to have Paul transferred to **J**,	2647
	25: 7	had come down from **J** stood around him,	2647
	25: 9	up to **J** and stand trial before me there	2647
	25:15	When I went to **J**, the chief priests and	2647
	25:20	so I asked if he would be willing to go to **J**	2647
	25:24	about him in **J** and here in Caesarea,	2647
	26: 4	in my own country, and also in **J**.	2647
	26:10	And that is just what I did in **J**.	2647
	26:20	then to those in **J** and in all Judea,	2647
	28:17	I was arrested in **J** and handed over to	2647
Ro	15:19	So from **J** all the way around to Illyricum,	2647
	15:25	I am on my way to **J** in the service of	2647
	15:26	for the poor among the saints in **J**.	2647
	15:31	and that my service in **J** may be acceptable	2647
1Co	16: 3	and send them with your gift to **J**.	2647
Gal	1:17	up to **J** to see those who were apostles	2647
	1:18	I went up to **J** to get acquainted with Peter	2647
	2: 1	Fourteen years later I went up again to **J**,	2647
	4:25	and corresponds to the present **city of J**,	2647
	4:26	But the **J** that is above is free,	2647
Heb	12:22	to Mount Zion, to the heavenly **J**,	2647
Rev	3:12	the new **J**, which is coming down out of	
		heaven from my God;	2647
	21: 2	I saw the Holy City, the new **J**,	2647
	21:10	the Holy City, **J**, coming down out of	
		heaven from God.	2647

JERUSALEM'S (3) [JERUSALEM]

Ne	4: 7	that the repairs to **J** walls had gone ahead	3731
Isa	62: 1	for **J** sake I will not remain quiet,	3731
Zec	12: 7	of **J** inhabitants may not be greater than	3731

JERUSHA (2)

2Ki	15:33	His mother's name was **J** daughter	3729
2Ch	27: 1	His mother's name was **J** daughter	3730

JESAIAH (KJV) See JESHAIAH

JESARELAH (1)

1Ch	25:14	the seventh to **J**, his sons and relatives, 12	3777

JESHAIAH (7)

1Ch	3:21	Pelatiah and **J**, and the sons of Rephaiah,	3832
	25: 3	Gedaliah, Zeri, **J**, Shimei,	3833
	25:15	the eighth to **J**, his sons and relatives, 12	3833
	26:25	Rehabiah his son, **J** his son, Joram his son,	3833
Ezr	8: 7	**J** son of Athaliah, and with him 70 men;	3832
	8:19	with **J** from the descendants of Merari,	3832
Ne	11: 7	the son of Ithiel, the son of **J**,	3832

JESHANAH (3)

2Ch	13:19	and took from him the towns of Bethel, **J**	3827
Ne	3: 6	The **J** Gate was repaired by Joiada son	3827
	12:39	the **J** Gate, the Fish Gate,	3827

JESHARELAH (KJV) See JESARELAH

JESHEBEAB (1)

1Ch	24:13	the fourteenth to **J**,	3784

JESHER (1)

1Ch	2:18	**J**, Shobab and Ardon.	3840

JESHIMON (4)

1Sa	23:19	on the hill of Hakilah, south of **J**?	3810
	23:24	in the Arabah south of **J**.	3810
	26: 1	on the hill of Hakilah, which faces **J**?"	3810
	26: 3	the road on the hill of Hakilah facing **J**,	3810

JESHIMOTH   See BETH JESHIMOTH

JESHISHAI (1)

1Ch	5:14	the son of Michael, the son of **J**,	3814

JESHOHAIAH (1)

1Ch	4:36	Jaakobah, **J**, Asaiah, Adiel, Jesimiel,	3797

JESHUA (29)

1Ch	24:11	the ninth to **J**, the tenth to Shecaniah,	3800
2Ch	31:15	Eden, Miniamin, **J**, Shemaiah,	3800
Ezr	2: 2	**J**, Nehemiah, Seraiah, Reelaiah, Mordecai,	3800
	2: 6	of Pahath-Moab (through the line of **J**	3800
	2:36	of Jedaiah (through the family of **J**) 973	3800
	2:40	the descendants of **J** and Kadmiel (through	3800
	3: 2	Then **J** son of Jozadak	3800
	3: 8	**J** son of Jozadak and the rest	3800
	3: 9	**J** and his sons and brothers and Kadmiel	3800
	4: 3	**J** and the rest of the heads of the families	3800
	5: 2	and **J** son of Jozadak set to work to rebuild	10336
	8:33	and so were the Levites Jozabad son of **J**	3800
	10:18	From the descendants of **J** son of Jozadak,	3800
Ne	3:19	Next to him, Ezer son of **J**,	3800
	7: 7	**J**, Nehemiah, Azariah, Raamiah,	3800
	7:11	of Pahath-Moab (through the line of **J**	3800
	7:39	of Jedaiah (through the family of **J**) 973	3800
	7:43	of **J** (through Kadmiel through the line	3800
	8: 7	The Levites—**J**, Bani, Sherebiah, Jamin,	3800
	9: 4	**J**, Bani, Kadmiel, Shebaniah, Bunni,	3800
	9: 5	**J**, Kadmiel, Bani, Hashabneiah, Sherebiah,	3800
	10: 9	The Levites: **J** son of Azaniah,	3800
	11:26	in **J**, in Moladah, in Beth Pelet,	3801
	12: 1	of Shealtiel and with **J**:	3800
	12: 7	and their associates in the days of **J**.	3800
	12: 8	The Levites were **J**, Binnui, Kadmiel,	3800
	12:10	**J** was the father of Joiakim,	3800
	12:24	**J** son of Kadmiel, and their associates,	3800
	12:26	in the days of Joiakim son of **J**,	3800

JESHURUN (4)

Dt	32:15	**J** grew fat and kicked;	3843
	33: 5	He was king over **J** when the leaders of	3843
	33:26	"There is no one like the God of **J**,	3843
Isa	44: 2	Do not be afraid, O Jacob, my servant, **J**,	3843

JESIAH (KJV) See ISSHIAH

JESIMIEL (1)

1Ch	4:36	Jaakobah, Jeshohaiah, Asaiah, Adiel, **J**,	3774

JESSE (42) [JESSE'S]

Ru	4:17	He was the father of **J**, the father of David.	3805
	4:22	Obed the father of **J**,	3805
	4:22	and **J** the father of David.	3805

1Sa	16: 1	I am sending you to J of Bethlehem.	3805
	16: 3	Invite J to the sacrifice,	3805
	16: 5	Then he consecrated J and his sons	3805
	16: 8	Then J called Abinadab and had him pass	3805
	16: 9	J then had Shammah pass by,	3805
	16:10	J had seven of his sons pass before Samuel,	3805
	16:11	So he asked J, "Are these all the sons you	3805
	16:11	"There is still the youngest," J answered,	NIH
	16:18	of J of Bethlehem who knows how to play	3805
	16:19	Then Saul sent messengers to J and said,	3805
	16:20	So J took a donkey loaded with bread,	3805
	16:22	Then Saul sent word to J, saying,	3805
	17:12	the son of an Ephrathite named J,	3805
	17:12	J had eight sons, and in Saul's time	2257S
	17:17	Now J said to his son David,	3805
	17:20	loaded up and set out, as J had directed.	3805
	17:58	the son of your servant J of Bethlehem."	3805
	20:27	"Why hasn't the son of J come to	3805
	20:30	sided with the son of J to your own shame	3805
	20:31	As long as the son of J lives on this earth,	3805
	22: 7	Will the son of J give all of you fields and	3805
	22: 8	a covenant with the son of J.	3805
	22: 9	"I saw the son of J come to Ahimelech son	3805
	22:13	conspired against me, you and the son of J,	3805
	25:10	Who is this son of J?	3805
2Sa	23: 1	"The oracle of David son of J,	3805
1Ch	2:12	of Obed and Obed the father of J.	3805
	2:13	J was the father of Eliab his firstborn;	414
	10:14	the kingdom over to David son of J.	3805
	12:18	We are with you, O son of J!	3805
	29:26	David son of J was king over all Israel.	3805
Ps	72:20	the prayers of David son of J.	3805
Isa	11: 1	A shoot will come up from the stump of J;	3805
	11:10	the Root of J will stand as a banner for the peoples;	3805
Mt	1: 5	Obed the father of J,	2649
	1: 6	and J the father of King David.	2649
Lk	3:32	the son of J, the son of Obed,	2649
Ac	13:22	'I have found David son of J a man	2649
Ro	15:12	Isaiah says, "The Root of J will spring up,	2649

JESSE'S (5) [JESSE]

1Sa	17:13	J three oldest sons had followed Saul to	3805
2Sa	20: 1	have no share in David, no part in J son!	3805
1Ki	12:16	do we have in David, what part in J son?	3805
2Ch	10:16	do we have in David, what part in J son?	3805
	11:18	the daughter of J son Eliab.	3805

JESTING (KJV) See COARSE JOKING

JESUI, JESUITES (KJV) See ISHVI, ISHVITE

JESURUN (KJV) See JESHURUN

JESUS (1241) [JESUS']

Mt	1: 1	A record of the genealogy of J Christ	2652
	1:16	of whom was born J, who is called Christ.	2652
	1:18	how the birth of J Christ came about:	2652
	1:21	and you are to give him the name J.	2652
	1:25	And he gave him the name J.	2652
	2: 1	After J was born in Bethlehem in Judea,	2652
	3:13	Then J came from Galilee to the Jordan to	2652
	3:15	J replied, "Let it be so now;	2652
	3:16	As soon as J was baptized,	2652
	4: 1	Then J was led by the Spirit into the desert	2652
	4: 4	J answered, "It is written:	1254+3836S
	4: 7	J answered him, "It is also written:	2652
	4:10	J said to him, "Away from me, Satan!	2652
	4:12	When J heard that John had been put	NIG
	4:17	From that time on J began to preach,	2652
	4:18	As J was walking beside the Sea	NIG
	4:19	"Come, follow me," J said,	NIG
	4:21	preparing their nets. J called them,	NIG
	4:23	J went throughout Galilee.	NIG
	7:28	When J had finished saying these things,	2652
	8: 3	J reached out his hand and touched	NIG
	8: 4	Then J said to him, "See that you don't tell	2652
	8: 5	When J had entered Capernaum,	899S
	8: 7	J said to him, "I will go and heal him."	NIG
	8:10	When J heard this, he was astonished	2652
	8:13	Then J said to the centurion, "Go!	2652
	8:14	When J came into Peter's house,	2652
	8:18	When J saw the crowd around him,	2652
	8:20	J replied, "Foxes have holes and birds of	2652
	8:22	But J told him, "Follow me,	2652
	8:24	But J was sleeping.	899S
	8:31	The demons begged J,	899S
	8:34	Then the whole town went out to meet J.	2652
	9: 1	J stepped into a boat, crossed over	2652
	9: 2	When J saw their faith, he said	2652
	9: 4	Knowing their thoughts, J said,	2652
	9: 9	As J went on from there,	2652
	9:10	While J was having dinner	NIG
	9:12	On hearing this, J said,	3836S
	9:15	J answered, "How can the guests of	2652
	9:19	J got up and went with him,	2652
	9:22	J turned and saw her.	2652
	9:23	When J entered the ruler's house and saw	2652
	9:27	As J went on from there,	2652
	9:30	J warned them sternly, "See that no one	2652
	9:32	and could not talk was brought to J.	899S
	9:35	J went through all the towns and villages,	2652

Mt	10: 5	These twelve J sent out with the following	2652
	11: 1	After J had finished instructing his twelve disciples,	2652
	11: 4	J replied, "Go back and report	2652
	11: 7	J began to speak to the crowd about John:	2652
	11:20	Then J began to denounce the cities	2652
	11:25	At that time J said, "I praise you, Father,	2652
	12: 1	that time J went through the grainfields on	2652
	12:10	Looking for a reason to accuse J,	899S
	12:14	and plotted how they might kill J.	899S
	12:15	Aware of this, J withdrew from that place.	2652
	12:22	J healed him, so that he could both talk and	NIG
	12:25	J knew their thoughts and said to them,	NIG
	12:46	While J was still talking to the crowd,	899S
	13: 1	That same day J went out of the house	2652
	13:24	J told them another parable:	NIG
	13:34	J spoke all these things to the crowd	2652
	13:51	"Have you understood all these things?" J asked.	2652
	13:53	When J had finished these parables,	2652
	13:57	But J said to them, "Only in his hometown	2652
	14: 1	Herod the tetrarch heard the reports about J,	2652
	14:12	Then they went and told J.	2652
	14:13	When J heard what had happened,	2652
	14:14	When J landed and saw a large crowd,	NIG
	14:16	J replied, "They do not need to go away.	2652
	14:22	Immediately J made the disciples get into	NIG
	14:25	the fourth watch of the night J went out	NIG
	14:27	But J immediately said to them:	NIG
	14:29	walked on the water and came toward J.	2652
	14:31	Immediately J reached out his hand	NIG
	14:35	when the men of that place recognized J,	899S
	15: 1	of the law came to J from Jerusalem	2652
	15: 3	J replied, "And why do you break	1254+3836S
	15:10	J called the crowd to him and said,	NIG
	15:16	"Are you still so dull?" J asked then.	1254+3836S
	15:21	J withdrew to the region of Tyre	2652
	15:23	J did not answer a word.	1254+3836S
	15:28	J answered, "Woman, you have great faith!	2652
	15:29	J left there and went along the Sea	2652
	15:32	J called his disciples to him and said,	2652
	15:34	"How many loaves do you have?" J asked.	2652
	15:39	After J had sent the crowd away,	NIG
	16: 1	and Sadducees came to J and tested him	NIG
	16: 4	J then left them and went away.	NIG
	16: 6	"Be careful," J said to them.	2652
	16: 8	Aware of their discussion, J asked,	2652
	16:13	When J came to the region of Caesarea	2652
	16:17	J replied, "Blessed are you,	2652
	16:21	J began to explain to his disciples that	2652
	16:23	J turned and said to Peter, "Get behind me, Satan!	1254+3836S
	16:24	Then J said to his disciples,	2652
	17: 1	After six days J took with him Peter,	2652
	17: 3	Moses and Elijah, talking with J.	899S
	17: 4	Peter said to J, "Lord, it is good for us	2652
	17: 7	But J came and touched them.	2652
	17: 8	they saw no one except J.	2652
	17: 9	down the mountain, J instructed them,	2652
	17:11	J replied, "To be sure, Elijah comes	1254+3836S
	17:14	a man approached J and knelt before him.	899S
	17:17	J replied, "how long shall I stay with you?	2652
	17:18	J rebuked the demon, and it came out	2652
	17:19	disciples came to J in private and asked,	2652
	17:24	After J and his disciples arrived	899S
	17:25	J was the first to speak.	2652
	17:26	"Then the sons are exempt," J said to him.	2652
	18: 1	At that time the disciples came to J	2652
	18:21	Then Peter came to J and asked, "Lord,	899S
	18:22	J answered, "I tell you, not seven times,	2652
	19: 1	When J had finished saying these things,	2652
	19: 8	J replied, "Moses permitted you	NIG
	19:11	J replied, "Not everyone can accept this word,	1254+3836S
	19:13	to J for him to place his hands on them	899S
	19:14	J said, "Let the little children come to me,	2652
	19:16	Now a man came up to J and asked,	899S
	19:17	about what is good?" J replied.	1254+3836S
	19:18	J replied, " 'Do not murder,	2652
	19:21	J answered, "If you want to be perfect, go,	2652
	19:23	Then J said to his disciples,	2652
	19:26	J looked at them and said,	2652
	19:28	J said to them, "I tell you the truth,	2652
	20:17	Now as J was going up to Jerusalem,	2652
	20:20	of Zebedee's sons came to J with her sons	899S
	20:22	what you are asking," J said to them.	2652
	20:23	J said to them, "You will indeed drink	NIG
	20:25	J called them together and said,	2652
	20:29	As J and his disciples were leaving Jericho,	899S
	20:30	and when they heard that J was going by,	NIG
	20:32	J stopped and called them.	2652
	20:34	J had compassion on them	2652
	21: 1	J sent two disciples,	2652
	21: 6	went and did as J had instructed them.	2652
	21: 7	their cloaks on them, and J sat on them.	NIG
	21:10	When J entered Jerusalem,	899S
	21:11	The crowds answered, "This is J,	2652
	21:12	J entered the temple area and drove out	2652
	21:16	"Yes," replied J, "have you never read,	2652
	21:21	J replied, "I tell you the truth,	2652
	21:23	J entered the temple courts, and,	899S
	21:24	J replied, "I will also ask you one question.	2652
	21:27	So they answered J, "We don't know."	2652
	21:31	J said to them, "I tell you the truth,	2652
	21:42	J said to them, "Have you never read in	2652
	22: 1	J spoke to them again in parables, saying:	2652
	22:18	But J, knowing their evil intent, said,	2652

Mt	22:29	J replied, "You are in error because you do	2652
	22:34	Hearing that J had silenced the Sadducees,	NIG
	22:37	J replied: " 'Love the Lord your God with all your heart	1254+3836S
	22:41	Pharisees were gathered together, J asked	2652
	23: 1	J said to the crowds and to his disciples:	2652
	24: 1	J left the temple and was walking away	2652
	24: 3	As J was sitting on the Mount of Olives,	899S
	24: 4	J answered: "Watch out that no one	2652
	26: 1	When J had finished saying all these things,	2652
	26: 4	to arrest J in some sly way and kill him.	2652
	26: 6	While J was in Bethany in the home of	2652
	26:10	Aware of this, J said to them,	2652
	26:17	the disciples came to J and asked,	2652
	26:19	So the disciples did as J had directed them	2652
	26:20	J was reclining at the table with	NIG
	26:23	J replied, "The one who has dipped his hand into the bowl with me	1254+3836S
	26:25	J answered, "Yes, it is you."	NIG
	26:26	While they were eating, J took bread,	2652
	26:31	Then J told them, "This very night you will	2652
	26:34	"I tell you the truth," J answered,	2652
	26:36	Then J went with his disciples to a place	2652
	26:49	Going at once to J, Judas said, "Greetings,	2652
	26:50	J replied, "Friend, do what you came for."	2652
	26:50	seized J and arrested him.	2652
	26:52	sword back in its place," J said to him,	2652
	26:55	At that time J said to the crowd,	2652
	26:57	Those who had arrested J took him	2652
	26:59	against J so that they could put him	2652
	26:62	the high priest stood up and said to J,	899S
	26:63	But J remained silent.	2652
	26:64	"Yes, it is as you say," J replied.	2652
	26:69	"You also were with J of Galilee,"	2652
	26:71	"This fellow was with J of Nazareth."	2652
	26:75	Peter remembered the word J had spoken:	2652
	27: 1	of the people came to the decision to put J	2652
	27: 3	saw that J was condemned,	NIG
	27:11	Meanwhile J stood before the governor,	2652
	27:11	"Yes, it is as you say," J replied.	2652
	27:14	But J made no reply,	NIG
	27:17	Barabbas, or J who is called Christ?"	2652
	27:18	of envy that they had handed J over	899S
	27:20	for Barabbas and to have J executed.	2652
	27:22	then, with J who is called Christ?"	2652
	27:26	But he had J flogged,	2652
	27:27	Then the governor's soldiers took J into	2652
	27:34	There they offered J wine to drink,	899S
	27:37	THIS IS J, THE KING OF THE JEWS.	2652
	27:46	the ninth hour J cried out in a loud voice,	2652
	27:48	and offered it to J to drink.	899S
	27:50	when J had cried out again in a loud voice,	2652
	27:54	with him who were guarding J saw	2652
	27:55	They had followed J from Galilee to care	2652
	27:57	who had himself become a disciple of J.	2652
	28: 5	for I know that you are looking for J,	2652
	28: 9	Suddenly J met them.	2652
	28:10	Then J said to them, "Do not be afraid.	2652
	28:16	the mountain where J had told them to go.	2652
	28:18	Then J came to them and said,	2652
Mk	1: 1	beginning of the gospel about J Christ,	2652
	1: 9	that time J came from Nazareth in Galilee	2652
	1:10	As J was coming up out of the water,	NIG
	1:14	J went into Galilee, proclaiming the good	2652
	1:16	As J walked beside the Sea of Galilee,	NIG
	1:17	"Come, follow me," J said,	2652
	1:21	J went into the synagogue and began	NIG
	1:24	"What do you want with us, J of Nazareth?	2652
	1:25	said sternly. "Come out of him!"	2652
	1:30	and they told J about her.	899S
	1:32	after sunset the people brought to J all	899S
	1:34	J healed many who had various diseases.	NIG
	1:35	while it was still dark, J got up,	NIG
	1:38	J replied, "Let us go somewhere else—	NIG
	1:41	J reached out his hand and touched	NIG
	1:43	J sent him away at once with a strong	NIG
	1:45	J could no longer enter a town openly	899S
	2: 1	when J again entered Capernaum,	NIG
	2: 4	Since they could not get him to J because	899S
	2: 4	they made an opening in the roof above J	NIG
	2: 5	When J saw their faith, he said	2652
	2: 8	Immediately J knew in his spirit	2652
	2:13	Once again J went out beside the lake.	NIG
	2:14	"Follow me," J told him,	NIG
	2:15	While J was having dinner	899S
	2:17	On hearing this, J said to them,	2652
	2:18	Some people came and asked J,	899S
	2:19	J answered, "How can the guests of	2652
	2:23	One Sabbath J was going through	899S
	3: 2	looking for a reason to accuse J,	899S
	3: 3	J said to the man with the shriveled hand,	NIG
	3: 4	Then he asked them, "Which is lawful on	NIG
	3: 6	with the Herodians how they might kill J.	899S
	3: 7	J withdrew with his disciples to the lake,	2652
	3:13	J went up on a mountainside and called	NIG
	3:20	Then J entered a house,	NIG
	3:23	So J called them and spoke to them	NIG
	4: 1	Again J began to teach by the lake.	NIG
	4: 9	Then J said, "He who has ears to hear,	NIG
	4:13	Then J said to them, "Don't you understand	NIG
	4:33	With many similar parables J spoke	NIG
	4:38	J was in the stern, sleeping on a cushion.	899S
	5: 2	When J got out of the boat,	899S
	5: 6	When he saw J from a distance,	2652
	5: 7	"What do you want with me, J,	2652
	5: 8	For J had said to him, "Come out of him,	NIG
	5: 9	Then J asked him, "What is your name?"	NIG

Mk	5:10	And he begged J again and again not — 899S
	5:12	The demons begged J, "Send us among — 899S
	5:15	When they came to J, they saw the man — 2652
	5:17	Then the people began to plead with J — 899S
	5:18	As J was getting into the boat, — 899S
	5:19	J did not let him, but said, — NIG
	5:20	in the Decapolis how much J had done — 2652
	5:21	When J had again crossed over by boat to — 2652
	5:22	Seeing J, he fell at his feet — 899S
	5:24	So J went with him. — NIG
	5:27	When she heard about J, she came up — 2652
	5:30	At once J realized that power had gone out — 2652
	5:32	But J kept looking around to see who — NIG
	5:35	While J was still speaking, — 899S
	5:36	told the synagogue ruler, — 2652
	5:38	J saw a commotion, with people crying — NIG
	6:1	J left there and went to his hometown, — NIG
	6:4	J said to them, "Only in his hometown, — 2652
	6:6	Then J went around teaching from village — NIG
	6:30	The apostles gathered around J — 2652
	6:34	When J landed and saw a large crowd, — NIG
	6:39	Then J directed them to have all — NIG
	6:45	Immediately J made his disciples get into — NIG
	6:54	of the boat, people recognized J. — 899S
	7:1	from Jerusalem gathered around J and — 899S
	7:5	Pharisees and teachers of the law asked J, — 899S
	7:14	Again J called the crowd to him and said, — NIG
	7:19	(In saying this, J declared all foods "clean.") — NIG
	7:24	J left that place and went to the vicinity — NIG
	7:26	She begged J to drive the demon out — 899S
	7:31	Then J left the vicinity of Tyre and went — NIG
	7:33	J put his fingers into the man's ears. — NIG
	7:36	J commanded them not to tell anyone. — NIG
	8:1	J called his disciples to him and said, — NIG
	8:5	"How many loaves do you have?" J asked. — NIG
	8:11	Pharisees came and began to question J. — 899S
	8:15	"Be careful," J warned them. — NIG
	8:17	Aware of their discussion, J asked them: — 2652
	8:22	a blind man and begged J to touch him. — 899S
	8:23	J asked, "Do you see anything?" — NIG
	8:25	Once more J put his hands on the man's eyes — NIG
	8:26	J sent him home, saying, — NIG
	8:27	J and his disciples went on to the villages — 2652
	8:30	J warned them not to tell anyone — NIG
	8:33	when J turned and looked at his disciples, — 3836S
	9:2	After six days J took Peter, — 2652
	9:4	Elijah and Moses, who were talking with J. — 2652
	9:5	Peter said to J, "Rabbi, it is good for us — 2652
	9:8	no longer saw anyone with them except J. — 2652
	9:9	J gave them orders not to tell anyone — NIG
	9:12	J replied, "To be sure, Elijah does — 1254+3836S
	9:15	As soon as all the people saw J, — 1254+3836S
	9:19	"O unbelieving generation," J replied — 1254+3836S
	9:20	When the spirit saw J, it immediately — 899S
	9:21	J asked the boy's father, — NIG
	9:23	" 'If you can'?" said J. — 2652
	9:25	When J saw that a crowd was running to — 2652
	9:27	But J took him by the hand and lifted him — 2652
	9:28	After J had gone indoors, — 899S
	9:30	J did not want anyone to know — NIG
	9:35	Sitting down, J called the Twelve and said, — NIG
	9:39	"Do not stop him," J said. — 2652
	10:1	J then left that place and went into — NIG
	10:5	that Moses wrote you this law," J replied. — 2652
	10:10	the disciples asked J about this. — 899S
	10:13	People were bringing little children to J — 899S
	10:14	When J saw this, he was indignant. — 2652
	10:17	As J started on his way, — 899S
	10:18	"Why do you call me good?" J answered. — 2652
	10:21	J looked at him and loved him. — 2652
	10:23	J looked around and said to his disciples, — 2652
	10:24	But J said again, "Children, how hard it is — 2652
	10:27	J looked at them and said, "With man this is — 2652
	10:29	"I tell you the truth," J replied, — 2652
	10:32	to Jerusalem, with J leading the way, — 2652
	10:38	don't know what you are asking," J said. — NIG
	10:39	J said to them, "You will drink the cup — 2652
	10:42	J called them together and said, — 2652
	10:46	As J and his disciples, — 899S
	10:47	he heard that it was J of Nazareth, — 2652
	10:47	"J, Son of David, have mercy on me!" — 2652
	10:49	J stopped and said, "Call him." — 2652
	10:50	he jumped to his feet and came to J. — 2652
	10:51	do want me to do for you?" J asked him. — 2652
	10:52	"Go," said J, "your faith has healed you." — 2652
	10:52	and followed J along the road. — 899S
	11:1	J sent two of his disciples, — NIG
	11:6	They answered as J had told them to, — 2652
	11:7	the colt to J and threw their cloaks over it, — 2652
	11:11	J entered Jerusalem and went to — NIG
	11:12	they were leaving Bethany, J was hungry. — NIG
	11:15	J entered the temple area and began — NIG
	11:21	Peter remembered and said to J, "Rabbi, — 899S
	11:22	"Have faith in God," J answered. — 2652
	11:27	while J was walking in the temple courts, — 899S
	11:29	J replied, "I will ask you one question. — 2652
	11:33	So they answered J, "We don't know." — 2652
	11:33	J said, "Neither will I tell you — 2652
	12:13	of the Pharisees and Herodians to J — 899S
	12:15	But J knew their hypocrisy. — 3836S
	12:17	Then J said to them, "Give to Caesar — 2652
	12:24	J replied, "Are you not in error — 2652
	12:28	that J had given them a good answer, — NIG
	12:29	"The most important one," J answered, — 2652
	12:34	When J saw that he had answered wisely, — 2652
	12:35	While J was teaching in the temple courts, — 2652
	12:38	As he taught, J said, "Watch out for — NIG
Mk	12:41	J sat down opposite the place where — NIG
	12:43	Calling his disciples to him, J said, — NIG
	13:2	you see all these great buildings?" replied J. — 2652
	13:3	As J was sitting on the Mount — 899S
	13:5	J said to them: "Watch out that no one — NIG
	14:1	for some sly way to arrest J and kill him. — 899S
	14:6	"Leave her alone," said J. — 2652
	14:10	to the chief priests to betray J to them. — 899S
	14:16	and found things just as J had told them. — NIG
	14:17	J arrived with the Twelve. — NIG
	14:22	While they were eating, J took bread, — 2652
	14:27	"You will all fall away," J told them, — 2652
	14:30	"I tell you the truth," J answered, "today— — 2652
	14:32	and J said to his disciples, — NIG
	14:45	Going at once to J, Judas said, "Rabbi!" — 899S
	14:46	The men seized J and arrested him. — 899S
	14:48	"Am I leading a rebellion," said J, — 2652
	14:51	but a linen garment, was following J. — 899S
	14:53	They took J to the high priest, — 2652
	14:55	against J so that they could put him — 2652
	14:60	up before them and asked J, — 2652
	14:61	But J remained silent and gave no answer. — 3836S
	14:62	"I am," said J. — 2652
	14:67	"You also were with that Nazarene, J," — 2652
	14:72	the word J had spoken to him: — 2652
	15:1	They bound J, led him away — 2652
	15:2	"Yes, it is as you say," J replied. — 1254+3836S
	15:5	But J still made no reply, — 2652
	15:10	the chief priests had handed J over to him. — 899S
	15:15	He had J flogged, and handed him over — 2652
	15:16	The soldiers led J away into the palace — 899S
	15:22	brought J to the place called Golgotha — 899S
	15:34	the ninth hour J cried out in a loud voice, — 2652
	15:36	and offered it to J to drink. — 899S
	15:37	With a loud cry, J breathed his last. — 2652
	15:39	centurion, who stood there in front of J, — 899S
	15:44	he asked him if J had already died. — NIG
	16:6	"You are looking for J the Nazarene, — 2652
	16:9	When J rose early on the first day of — NIG
	16:11	that J was alive and that she had seen him, — NIG
	16:12	Afterward J appeared in a different form — NIG
	16:14	Later J appeared to the Eleven — NIG
	16:19	After the Lord J had spoken to them, — 2652
Lk	1:31	and you are to give him the name J. — NIG
	2:21	he was named J, the name the angel had — 2652
	2:27	the child J to do for him what the custom — 2652
	2:43	the boy J stayed behind in Jerusalem, — 2652
	2:52	And J grew in wisdom and stature, — 2652
	3:21	J was baptized too. — NIG
	3:23	Now J himself was about thirty years old — 2652
	4:1	J, full of the Holy Spirit, returned from — 2652
	4:4	J answered, "It is written: — 2652
	4:8	J answered, "It is written: — 2652
	4:12	J answered, "It says: — 2652
	4:14	J returned to Galilee in the power of — 2652
	4:23	J said to them, "Surely you will quote — NIG
	4:34	What do you want with us, J of Nazareth? — 2652
	4:35	J said sternly. "Come out of him!" — 2652
	4:38	J left the synagogue and went to the home — NIG
	4:38	and they asked J to help her. — 899S
	4:40	to J all who had various kinds of sickness, — 899S
	4:42	At daybreak J went out to a solitary place. — NIG
	5:1	One day as J was standing by the Lake — 899S
	5:10	Then J said to Simon, "Don't be afraid; — 2652
	5:12	While J was in one of the towns, — 899S
	5:12	When he saw J, he fell with his face to — 2652
	5:13	J reached out his hand and touched — 899S
	5:14	Then J ordered him, "Don't tell anyone, — 899S
	5:16	But J often withdrew to lonely places — 899S
	5:18	into the house to lay him before J. — 899S
	5:19	middle of the crowd, right in front of J. — 2652
	5:20	When J saw their faith, he said, "Friend, — NIG
	5:22	J knew what they were thinking — 2652
	5:27	J went out and saw a tax collector by — NIG
	5:27	"Follow me," J said to him, — NIG
	5:29	Then Levi held a great banquet for J — 899S
	5:31	J answered them, "It is not the healthy — 2652
	5:34	J answered, "Can you make the guests of — 2652
	6:1	One Sabbath J was going through — 899S
	6:3	J answered them, "Have you never read — 2652
	6:5	Then J said to them, "The Son of Man is — NIG
	6:7	looking for a reason to accuse J, — 899S
	6:8	But J knew what they were thinking — 899S
	6:9	Then J said to them, "I ask you, — 2652
	6:11	with one another what they might do to J. — 2652
	6:12	of those days J went out to a mountainside — 899S
	7:1	When J had finished saying all this in — 899S
	7:3	of J and sent some elders of the Jews — 2652
	7:4	When they came to J, they pleaded — 2652
	7:6	So J went with them. — 2652
	7:9	When J heard this, he was amazed at him, — 2652
	7:11	J went to a town called Nain, — NIG
	7:15	and J gave him back to his mother. — NIG
	7:17	about J spread throughout Judea and — 899S
	7:20	When the men came to J, they said, — 899S
	7:21	very time J cured many who had diseases, — NIG
	7:24	J began to speak to the crowd about John: — NIG
	7:36	of the Pharisees invited J to have dinner — 899S
	7:37	that J was eating at the Pharisee's house, — NIG
	7:40	J answered him, "Simon, I have something — 2652
	7:43	"You have judged correctly," J said. — 1254+3836S
	7:48	J said to her, "Your sins are forgiven." — NIG
	7:50	J said to the woman, "Your faith has saved — NIG
	8:1	J traveled about from one town and village — 899S
	8:4	and people were coming to J from town — 899S
	8:22	One day J said to his disciples, — NIG
	8:27	When J stepped ashore, he was met by — NIG
Lk	8:28	When he saw J, he cried out and fell at — 2652
	8:28	"What do you want with me, J, — 2652
	8:29	For J had commanded the evil spirit — NIG
	8:30	J asked him, "What is your name?" — 2652
	8:32	The demons begged J to let them go — 899S
	8:35	When they came to J, they found the man — 2652
	8:37	of the Gerasenes asked J to leave them, — 899S
	8:38	but J sent him away, saying, — NIG
	8:39	over town how much J had done for him. — 2652
	8:40	Now when J returned, a crowd welcomed — 2652
	8:42	As J was on his way, — 899S
	8:45	"Who touched me?" J asked. — 2652
	8:46	But J said, "Someone touched me; — 899S
	8:49	While J was still speaking, — 899S
	8:50	Hearing this, J said to Jairus, — 2652
	8:52	"Stop wailing," J said. — 1254+3836S
	8:55	J told them to give her something to eat. — NIG
	9:1	When J had called the Twelve together, — NIG
	9:10	they reported to J what they had done. — 899S
	9:18	Once when J was praying in private — 899S
	9:21	J strictly warned them not to tell this — 1254+3836S
	9:28	About eight days after J said this, — NIG
	9:31	in glorious splendor, talking with J. — 899S
	9:33	As the men were leaving J, — 2652
	9:36	they found that J was alone. — 2652
	9:41	J replied, "how long shall I stay with you — 2652
	9:42	But J rebuked the evil spirit, healed the boy — 2652
	9:43	was marveling at all that J did, — NIG
	9:47	J, knowing their thoughts, — 2652
	9:50	"Do not stop him," J said, — 2652
	9:51	resolutely set out for Jerusalem. — 899S
	9:55	But J turned and rebuked them, — NIG
	9:58	J replied, "Foxes have holes and birds of — 2652
	9:60	J said to him, "Let the dead bury their own — NIG
	9:62	J replied, "No one who puts his hand to — 2652
	10:21	J, full of joy through the Holy Spirit — NIG
	10:25	an expert in the law stood up to test J. — 899S
	10:28	"You have answered correctly," J replied. — NIG
	10:29	he asked J, "And who is my neighbor?" — 2652
	10:30	In reply J said: "A man was going down — 2652
	10:37	J told him, "Go and do likewise." — 2652
	10:38	As J and his disciples were on their way, — 899S
	11:1	One day J was praying in a certain place. — 899S
	11:14	J was driving out a demon that was mute. — NIG
	11:17	J knew their thoughts and said to them: — 899S
	11:27	As J was saying these things, — 899S
	11:29	As the crowds increased, J said, — NIG
	11:37	When J had finished speaking, — NIG
	11:38	that J did not first wash before the meal, — NIG
	11:46	J replied, "And you experts in the law — 1254+3836S
	11:53	When J left there, the Pharisees and the — 899S
	12:1	J began to speak first to his disciples, — NIG
	12:14	J replied, "Man, who appointed me — 1254+3836S
	12:22	Then J said to his disciples: — NIG
	13:1	some present at that time who told J about — 899S
	13:2	J answered, "Do you think that these — NIG
	13:10	On a Sabbath J was teaching in one of — NIG
	13:12	When J saw her, he called her forward — 2652
	13:14	because J had healed on the Sabbath, — 2652
	13:18	Then J asked, "What is the kingdom — NIG
	13:22	J went through the towns and villages, — NIG
	13:31	At that time some Pharisees came to J — 899S
	14:1	when J went to eat in the house of — 899S
	14:3	J asked the Pharisees and experts in — 2652
	14:12	Then J said to his host, "When you give a — NIG
	14:15	he said to J, "Blessed is the man who will — 899S
	14:16	J replied: "A certain man was preparing a great banquet — 1254+3836S
	14:25	Large crowds were traveling with J, — 899S
	15:3	Then J told them this parable: — NIG
	15:11	J continued: "There was a man who had two sons. — NIG
	16:1	J told his disciples: "There was a rich man — NIG
	16:14	heard all this and were sneering at J. — 899S
	17:1	J said to his disciples: — NIG
	17:11	J traveled along the border — 899S
	17:13	"J, Master, have pity on us!" — 2652
	17:17	J asked, "Were not all ten cleansed? — 2652
	17:20	J replied, "The kingdom of God does — NIG
	18:1	Then J told his disciples a parable — NIG
	18:9	J told this parable: — NIG
	18:15	People were also bringing babies to J — 899S
	18:16	But J called the children to him and said, — 2652
	18:19	"Why do you call me good?" J answered. — 2652
	18:22	When J heard this, he said to him, — 2652
	18:24	J looked at him and said, "How hard it is — 2652
	18:27	J replied, "What is impossible — 1254+3836S
	18:29	"I tell you the truth," J said to them, — 1254+3836S
	18:31	J took the Twelve aside and told them, — NIG
	18:35	As J approached Jericho, — 899S
	18:37	"J of Nazareth is passing by." — 2652
	18:38	He called out, "J, Son of David, — 2652
	18:40	J stopped and ordered the man to — 2652
	18:40	When he came near, J asked him, — NIG
	18:42	J said to him, "Receive your sight; — 2652
	18:43	he received his sight and followed J, — 899S
	19:1	J entered Jericho and was passing through. — NIG
	19:3	He wanted to see who J was, — 2652
	19:4	since J was coming that way. — NIG
	19:5	When J reached the spot, — 2652
	19:9	J said to him, "Today salvation has come — 2652
	19:28	After J had said this, he went on ahead, — NIG
	19:35	They brought it to J, — 2652
	19:35	threw their cloaks on the colt and put J — 2652
	19:39	of the Pharisees in the crowd said to J, — 899S
	20:8	J said, "Neither will I tell you — 2652
	20:17	J looked directly at them and asked, — 1254+3836S

Lk	20:20	to catch J in something he said so	899S
	20:27	came to J with a question.	899S
	20:34	J replied, "The people of this age marry	2652
	20:41	Then J said to them, "How is it that they say	NIG
	20:45	J said to his disciples,	NIG
	21: 1	J saw the rich putting their gifts into	NIG
	21: 5	with gifts dedicated to God. But J said,	NIG
	21:37	Each day J was teaching at the temple,	NIG
	22: 2	looking for some way to get rid of J,	899S
	22: 4	with them how he might betray J,	899S
	22: 6	for an opportunity to hand J over to them	899S
	22: 8	J sent Peter and John, saying,	NIG
	22:13	and found things just as J had told them.	NIG
	22:14	J and his apostles reclined at the table.	899S
	22:25	J said to them, "The kings of	1254+3836S
	22:34	J answered, "I tell you, Peter,	1254+3836S
	22:35	Then J asked them, "When I sent you	NIG
	22:39	J went out as usual to the Mount of Olives,	NIG
	22:47	He approached J to kiss him,	2652
	22:48	but J asked him, "Judas, are you betraying	2652
	22:51	But J answered, "No more of this!"	2652
	22:52	Then J said to the chief priests,	2652
	22:63	The men who were guarding J began mocking and beating him.	899S
	22:66	met together, and J was led before them.	899S
	22:67	J answered, "If I tell you,	NIG
	23: 3	So Pilate asked J, "Are you the king of	899S
	23: 3	"Yes, it is as you say," J replied.	1254+3836S
	23: 7	that J was under Herod's jurisdiction,	NIG
	23: 8	When Herod saw J, he was greatly pleased,	2652
	23: 9	but J gave him no answer.	899S
	23:20	Wanting to release J, Pilate appealed to	2652
	23:25	and surrendered J to their will.	2652
	23:26	on him and made him carry it behind J.	2652
	23:28	J turned and said to them, "Daughters of	2652
	23:34	J said, "Father, forgive them,	2652
	23:42	"J, remember me when you come	2652
	23:43	J answered him, "I tell you the truth,	NIG
	23:46	J called out with a loud voice, "Father,	2652
	23:55	with J from Galilee followed Joseph	NIG
	24: 3	they did not find the body of the Lord J.	2652
	24:15	J himself came up and walked along	2652
	24:19	"About J of Nazareth," they replied.	2652
	24:28	J acted as if he were going farther.	899S
	24:35	and how J was recognized by them	NIG
	24:36	J himself stood among them and said	899S
Jn	1:17	grace and truth came through J Christ.	2652
	1:29	The next day John saw J coming toward	2652
	1:36	When he saw J passing by, he said, "Look,	2652
	1:37	When the two disciples heard him say this, they followed J.	2652
	1:38	J saw them following and asked,	2652
	1:40	what John had said and who had followed J.	899S
	1:42	And he brought him to J.	2652
	1:42	J looked at him and said, "You are Simon	2652
	1:43	next day J decided to leave for Galilee.	NIG
	1:45	J of Nazareth, the son of Joseph."	2652
	1:47	When J saw Nathanael approaching,	2652
	1:48	J answered, "I saw you while you were	2652
	1:50	J said, "You believe because I told you	2652
	2: 2	J and his disciples had also been invited	2652
	2: 4	why do you involve me?" J replied.	2652
	2: 7	J said to the servants, "Fill the jars with	2652
	2:11	J performed at Cana in Galilee.	2652
	2:13	J went up to Jerusalem.	2652
	2:19	J answered them, "Destroy this temple,	2652
	2:22	and the words that J had spoken.	2652
	2:24	J would not entrust himself to them,	899+2652
	3: 2	He came to J at night and said, "Rabbi,	899S
	3: 3	In reply J declared, "I tell you the truth,	2652
	3: 5	J answered, "I tell you the truth,	2652
	3:10	"You are Israel's teacher," said J,	2652
	3:22	J and his disciples went out into the Judean	2652
	4: 1	The Pharisees heard that J was gaining	2652
	4: 2	although in fact it was not J who baptized,	2652
	4: 6	Jacob's well was there, and J,	2652
	4: 7	J said to her, "Will you give me a drink?"	2652
	4:10	J answered her, "If you knew the gift	2652
	4:13	J answered, "Everyone who drinks this water will be thirsty again,	2652
	4:17	J said to her, "You are right when you say	2652
	4:21	J declared, "Believe me, woman,	2652
	4:26	J declared, "I who speak to you am he."	2652
	4:34	said J, "is to do the will of him who sent me	2652
	4:44	(Now J himself had pointed out that	2652
	4:47	that J had arrived in Galilee from Judea,	2652
	4:48	J told him, "you will never believe."	2652
	4:50	J replied, "You may go.	2652
	4:50	The man took J at his word and departed.	2652
	4:53	the exact time at which J had said to him,	2652
	4:54	that J performed, having come from Judea	2652
	5: 1	J went up to Jerusalem for a feast of	2652
	5: 6	When J saw him lying there and learned	2652
	5: 8	Then J said to him, "Get up!	2652
	5:13	for J had slipped away into the crowd	2652
	5:14	Later J found him at the temple and said	2652
	5:15	that it was J who had made him well.	2652
	5:16	J was doing these things on the Sabbath,	2652
	5:17	J said to them, "My Father is always at work	2652
	5:19	J gave them this answer:	2652
	6: 1	J crossed to the far shore of the Sea	2652
	6: 3	Then J went up on a mountainside and sat	2652
	6: 5	When J looked up and saw a great crowd	2652
	6:10	J said, "Have the people sit down."	2652
	6:11	J then took the loaves, gave thanks,	2652
	6:14	people saw the miraculous sign that J did,	NIG
	6:15	J, knowing that they intended to come	2652

Jn	6:17	and J had not yet joined them.	2652
	6:19	they saw J approaching the boat,	2652
	6:22	that J had not entered it with his disciples,	2652
	6:24	that neither J nor his disciples were there,	2652
	6:24	and went to Capernaum in search of J.	2652
	6:26	J answered, "I tell you the truth,	2652
	6:29	J answered, "The work of God is this:	2652
	6:32	J said to them, "I tell you the truth,	2652
	6:35	Then J declared, "I am the bread of life.	2652
	6:42	"Is this not J, the son of Joseph,	2652
	6:43	among yourselves," J answered.	2652
	6:53	J said to them, "I tell you the truth,	2652
	6:61	J said to them, "Does this offend you?	2652
	6:64	For J had known from the beginning	2652
	6:67	to leave too, do you?" J asked the Twelve.	2652
	6:70	Then J replied, "Have I not chosen you,	2652
	7: 1	After this, J went around in Galilee,	2652
	7: 6	Therefore J told them, "The right time	2652
	7:14	until halfway through the Feast did J go up	2652
	7:16	J answered, "My teaching is not my own.	2652
	7:21	J said to them, "I did one miracle,	2652
	7:28	Then J, still teaching in the temple courts,	2652
	7:33	J said, "I am with you for only a short time,	2652
	7:37	J stood and said in a loud voice,	2652
	7:39	since J had not yet been glorified.	2652
	7:43	the people were divided because of J.	899S
	7:50	to J earlier and who was one	899S
	8: 1	But J went to the Mount of Olives.	2652
	8: 4	said to J, "Teacher, this woman was caught	899S
	8: 6	But J bent down and started to write on	2652
	8: 9	the older ones first, until only J was left,	NIG
	8:10	J straightened up and asked her, "Woman,	2652
	8:11	neither do I condemn you," J declared.	2652
	8:12	When J spoke again to the people, he said,	2652
	8:14	J answered, "Even if I testify	2652
	8:19	not know me or my Father," J replied.	2652
	8:21	Once more J said to them, "I am going	NIG
	8:25	"Just what I have been claiming all along," J replied.	2652
	8:28	So J said, "When you have lifted up	2652
	8:31	To the Jews who had believed him, J said,	2652
	8:34	J replied, "I tell you the truth,	2652
	8:39	"If you were Abraham's children," said J,	2652
	8:42	J said to them, "If God were your Father,	2652
	8:49	"I am not possessed by a demon," said J,	2652
	8:54	J replied, "If I glorify myself,	2652
	8:58	"I tell you the truth," J answered,	2652
	8:59	but J hid himself, slipping away from	2652
	9: 3	said J, "but this happened so that the work	2652
	9:11	"The man they call J made some mud	2652
	9:14	on which J had made the mud and opened	2652
	9:22	that anyone who acknowledged that J was	899S
	9:35	J heard that they had thrown him out,	2652
	9:37	J said, "You have now seen him;	2652
	9:39	J said, "For judgment I have come	2652
	9:41	J said, "If you were blind,	2652
	10: 6	J used this figure of speech,	2652
	10: 7	Therefore J said again,	2652
	10:23	and J was in the temple area walking	2652
	10:25	J answered, "I did tell you,	2652
	10:32	but J said to them, "I have shown you many	2652
	10:34	J answered them, "Is it not written	2652
	10:40	J went back across the Jordan to	NIG
	10:42	And in that place many believed in J.	899S
	11: 3	So the sisters sent word to J, "Lord,	899S
	11: 4	When he heard this, J said,	2652
	11: 5	J loved Martha and her sister and Lazarus.	2652
	11: 9	J answered, "Are there not twelve hours	2652
	11:13	J had been speaking of his death,	2652
	11:17	J found that Lazarus had already been in	2652
	11:20	When Martha heard that J was coming,	2652
	11:21	"Lord," Martha said to J,	2652
	11:23	J said to her, "Your brother will rise again."	2652
	11:25	J said to her, "I am the resurrection and	2652
	11:30	Now J had not yet entered the village,	2652
	11:32	When Mary reached the place where J was	2652
	11:33	When J saw her weeping,	2652
	11:35	J wept.	2652
	11:38	J, once more deeply moved, came to	2652
	11:40	Then J said, "Did I not tell you that	2652
	11:41	Then J looked up and said, "Father,	2652
	11:43	J called in a loud voice, "Lazarus, come out!"	NIG
	11:44	J said to them, "Take off the grave clothes	2652
	11:45	to visit Mary, and had seen what J did,	NIG
	11:46	and told them what J had done.	2652
	11:51	that year he prophesied that J would die	2652
	11:54	Therefore J no longer moved about publicly	2652
	11:56	They kept looking for J,	2652
	11:57	that if anyone found out where J was,	NIG
	12: 1	J arrived at Bethany, where Lazarus lived,	2652
	12: 1	whom J had raised from the dead.	2652
	12: 7	"Leave her alone," J replied.	2652
	12: 9	of Jews found out that J was there	NIG
	12:11	over to J and putting their faith in him.	2652
	12:12	for the Feast heard that J was on his way	2652
	12:14	J found a young donkey and sat upon it,	2652
	12:16	Only after J was glorified did they realize	2652
	12:21	"Sir," they said, "we would like to see J."	2652
	12:21	Andrew and Philip in turn told J.	2652
	12:23	J replied, "The hour has come for the Son	2652
	12:30	J said, "This voice was for your benefit,	2652
	12:35	Then J told them, "You are going to have	2652
	12:36	J left and hid himself from them.	2652
	12:37	after J had done all these miraculous signs	899S
	12:44	Then J cried out, "When a man believes	2652
	13: 1	J knew that the time had come for him	2652

Jn	13: 2	Judas Iscariot, son of Simon, to betray J.	899S
	13: 3	J knew that the Father had put all things	NIG
	13: 7	J replied, "You do not realize now what	2652
	13: 8	J answered, "Unless I wash you,	2652
	13:10	J answered, "A person who has had	2652
	13:21	J was troubled in spirit and testified,	2652
	13:23	One of them, the disciple whom J loved,	2652
	13:25	Leaning back against J, he asked him,	2652
	13:26	J answered, "It is the one to whom I will	2652
	13:27	you are about to do, do quickly," J told him,	2652
	13:28	at the meal understood why J said this	NIG
	13:29	some thought J was telling him	2652
	13:31	When he was gone, J said,	2652
	13:36	J replied, "Where I am going,	2652
	13:38	Then J answered, "Will you really lay	2652
	14: 6	J answered, "I am the way and the truth	2652
	14: 9	J answered: "Don't you know me,	2652
	14:23	J replied, "If anyone loves me,	2652
	16:19	J saw that they wanted to ask him	2652
	16:31	"You believe at last!" J answered.	2652
	17: 1	After J said this, he looked toward heaven	2652
	17: 3	and J Christ, whom you have sent.	2652
	18: 1	J left with his disciples and crossed	2652
	18: 2	J had often met there with his disciples.	2652
	18: 4	J, knowing all that was going to happen	2652
	18: 5	"J of Nazareth," they replied.	2652
	18: 5	"I am he," J said.	NIG
	18: 6	When J said, "I am he,"	NIG
	18: 7	And they said, "J of Nazareth."	2652
	18: 8	"I told you that I am he," J answered.	2652
	18:11	J commanded Peter, "Put your sword away!	2652
	18:12	and the Jewish officials arrested J.	2652
	18:15	and another disciple were following J,	2652
	18:15	with J into the high priest's courtyard,	2652
	18:19	the high priest questioned J	2652
	18:20	have spoken openly to the world," J replied.	2652
	18:22	When J said this, one of the officials	899S
	18:23	"If I said something wrong," J replied,	2652
	18:28	the Jews led J from Caiaphas to the palace	2652
	18:32	the words J had spoken indicating the kind	2652
	18:33	summoned J and asked him,	2652
	18:34	"Is that your own idea," J asked,	2652
	18:36	J said, "My kingdom is not of this world.	2652
	18:37	J answered, "You are right in saying I am	2652
	19: 1	Then Pilate took J and had him flogged.	2652
	19: 5	When J came out wearing the crown	2652
	19: 9	he asked J, but Jesus gave him no answer.	2652
	19: 9	he asked Jesus, but J gave him no answer.	2652
	19:11	J answered, "You would have no power	2652
	19:12	From then on, Pilate tried to set J free,	899S
	19:13	he brought J out and sat down on	2652
	19:16	So the soldiers took charge of J.	2652
	19:18	one on each side and J in the middle.	2652
	19:19	J OF NAZARETH, THE KING OF THE JEWS.	2652
	19:20	the place where J was crucified was near	2652
	19:23	When the soldiers crucified J,	2652
	19:25	Near the cross of J stood his mother,	2652
	19:26	When J saw his mother there,	2652
	19:28	J said, "I am thirsty."	2652
	19:30	When he had received the drink, J said,	2652
	19:32	man who had been crucified with J,	899S
	19:33	to J and found that he was already dead,	2652
	19:38	asked Pilate for the body of J.	2652
	19:38	Now Joseph was a disciple of J,	2652
	19:39	the man who earlier had visited J at night.	899S
	19:41	At the place where J was crucified,	NIG
	19:42	the tomb was nearby, they laid J there.	2652
	20: 2	other disciple, the one J loved, and said,	2652
	20: 9	not understand from Scripture that J had	899S
	20:14	turned around and saw J standing there,	2652
	20:14	but she did not realize that it was J.	2652
	20:16	J said to her, "Mary."	2652
	20:17	J said, "Do not hold on to me,	2652
	20:19	J came and stood among them and said,	2652
	20:21	Again J said, "Peace be with you!	2652
	20:24	was not with the disciples when J came.	2652
	20:26	J came and stood among them and said,	2652
	20:29	J told him, "Because you have seen me,	2652
	20:30	J did many other miraculous signs in	2652
	20:31	that you may believe that J is the Christ,	2652
	21: 1	Afterward J appeared again	2652
	21: 4	Early in the morning, J stood on the shore,	2652
	21: 4	the disciples did not realize that it was J.	2652
	21: 7	the disciple whom J loved said to Peter,	2652
	21:10	J said to them, "Bring some of the fish	2652
	21:12	J said to them, "Come and have breakfast."	2652
	21:13	J came, took the bread and gave it to them,	2652
	21:14	the third time J appeared to his disciples	2652
	21:15	J said to Simon Peter, "Simon son of John,	2652
	21:15	J said, "Feed my lambs."	NIG
	21:16	Again J said, "Simon son of John,	NIG
	21:16	J said, "Take care of my sheep."	NIG
	21:17	Peter was hurt because J asked him	NIG
	21:17	J said, "Feed my sheep.	2652
	21:19	J said this to indicate the kind of death	NIG
	21:20	disciple whom J loved was following them.	2652
	21:20	the one who had leaned back against J at	899S
	21:22	J answered, "If I want him to remain alive	2652
	21:23	But J did not say that he would not die;	2652
	21:25	J did many other things as well.	2652
Ac	1: 1	about all that J began to do and to teach	2652
	1:11	This same J, who has been taken from you	2652
	1:14	the women and Mary the mother of J,	2652
	1:16	as guide for those who arrested J—	2652
	1:21	the whole time the Lord J went in and out	2652
	1:22	to the time when J was taken up from us.	NIG
	2:22	J of Nazareth was a man accredited	2652

Ac 2:32 God has raised this **J** to life, 2652
2:36 God has made this **J**, whom you crucified, 2652
2:38 in the name of **J** Christ for the forgiveness 2652
3: 6 In the name of **J** Christ of Nazareth, 2652
3:13 has glorified his servant **J**. 2652
3:16 By faith in the name of **J**, 899S
3:20 who has been appointed for you—even **J** 2652
4: 2 and proclaiming in **J** the resurrection of 2652
4:10 It is by the name of **J** Christ of Nazareth, 2652
4:13 that these men had been with **J**. 2652
4:18 to speak or teach at all in the name of **J** 2652
4:27 to conspire against your holy servant **J**, 2652
4:30 through the name of your holy servant **J**." 2652
4:33 to testify to the resurrection of the Lord **J** 2652
5:30 of our fathers raised **J** from the dead— 2652
5:40 not to speak in the name of **J** 2652
5:42 and proclaiming the good news that **J** is 2652
6:14 For we have heard him say that this **J** 2652
7:55 and **J** standing at the right hand of God. 2652
7:59 "Lord **J**, receive my spirit." 2652
8:12 of God and the name of **J** Christ. 2652
8:16 baptized into the name of the Lord **J**. 2652
8:35 and told him the good news about **J**. 2652
9: 5 "I am **J**, whom you are persecuting," 2652
9:17 **J**, who appeared to you on the road 2652
9:20 in the synagogues that **J** is the Son of God. 2652
9:22 in Damascus by proving that **J** is 4047S
9:27 preached fearlessly in the name of **J**. 2652
9:34 Peter said to him, "**J** Christ heals you. 2652
10:36 the good news of peace through **J** Christ, 2652
10:38 how God anointed **J** of Nazareth with 2652
10:48 be baptized in the name of **J** Christ. 2652
11:17 who believed in the Lord **J** Christ, 2652
11:20 the good news about the Lord **J**. 2652
13:23 God has brought to Israel the Savior **J**, 2652
13:24 Before the coming of **J**, 899S
13:27 and their rulers did not recognize **J**, 4047S
13:33 their children, by raising up **J**. 2652
13:38 to know that through **J** the forgiveness 4047S
15:11 the grace of our Lord **J** that we are saved, 2652
15:26 for the name of our Lord **J** Christ. 2652
16: 7 the Spirit of **J** would not allow them to. 2652
16:18 "In the name of **J** Christ I command you 2652
16:31 They replied, "Believe in the Lord **J**, 2652
17: 3 "This **J** I am proclaiming to you is 2652
17: 7 that there is another king, one called **J**." 2652
17:18 about **J** and the resurrection. 2652
18: 5 testifying to the Jews that **J** was the Christ. 2652
18:25 and taught about **J** accurately, 2652
18:28 from the Scriptures that **J** was the Christ. 2652
19: 4 in the one coming after him, that is, in **J**." 2652
19: 5 baptized into the name of the Lord **J**. 2652
19:13 to invoke the name of the Lord **J** 2652
19:13 They would say, "In the name of **J**, 2652
19:15 "**J** I know, and I know about Paul, 2652
19:17 name of the Lord **J** was held in high honor. 2652
20:21 in repentance and have faith in our Lord **J**. 2652
20:24 the task the Lord **J** has given me— 2652
20:35 the words the Lord **J** himself said: 2652
21:13 in Jerusalem for the name of the Lord **J**." 2652
22: 8 'I am **J** of Nazareth, whom you are persecuting,' 2652
24:24 to him as he spoke about faith in Christ **J**. 2652
25:19 about a dead man named **J** who Paul claimed was alive. 2652
26: 9 that was possible to oppose the name of **J** 2652
26:15 " 'I am **J**, whom you are persecuting,' 2652
28:23 of God and tried to convince them about **J** 2652
28:31 of God and taught about the Lord **J** Christ. 2652

Ro 1: 1 Paul, a servant of Christ **J**, 2652
1: 4 from the dead: **J** Christ our Lord. 2652
1: 6 called to *belong to* **J** Christ. 2652
1: 7 and from the Lord **J** Christ. 2652
1: 8 I thank my God through **J** Christ for all 2652
2:16 when God will judge men's secrets through **J** Christ, 2652
3:22 from God comes through faith *in* **J** Christ 2652
3:24 the redemption that came by Christ **J**. 2652
3:26 one who justifies those who have faith *in* **J**. 2652
4:24 in him who raised **J** our Lord from 2652
5: 1 with God through our Lord **J** Christ, 2652
5:11 in God through our Lord **J** Christ, 2652
5:15 **J** Christ, overflow to the many! 2652
5:17 in life through the one man, **J** Christ. 2652
5:21 through **J** Christ our Lord. 2652
6: 3 into Christ **J** were baptized into his death? 2652
6:11 to sin but alive to God in Christ **J**. 2652
6:23 of God is eternal life in Christ **J** our Lord. 2652
7:25 through **J** Christ our Lord! 2652
8: 1 for those who are in Christ **J**, 2652
8: 2 through Christ **J** the law of the Spirit 2652
8:11 of him who raised **J** from the dead is living 2652
8:34 Christ **J**, who died—more than that, 2652
8:39 love of God that is in Christ **J** our Lord. 2652
10: 9 with your mouth, "**J** is Lord," and believe 2652
13:14 clothe yourselves with the Lord **J** Christ, 2652
14:14 As one who is in the Lord **J**, 2652
15: 5 among yourselves as you follow Christ **J**, 2652
15: 6 the God and Father of our Lord **J** Christ. 2652
15:16 to be a minister of Christ **J** to the Gentiles 2652
15:17 I glory in Christ **J** in my service to God. 2652
15:30 by our Lord **J** Christ and by the love of 2652
16: 3 my fellow workers in Christ **J**. 2652
16:20 The grace of our Lord **J** be with you. 2652
16:25 and the proclamation of **J** Christ, 2652
16:27 be glory forever through **J** Christ! 2652

1Co 1: 1 an apostle of Christ **J** by the will of God, 2652
1: 2 to those sanctified in Christ **J** and called to 2652
1: 2 on the name *of* our Lord **J** Christ— 2652
1: 3 God our Father and the Lord **J** Christ. 2652
1: 4 because of his grace given you in Christ **J**. 2652
1: 7 as you eagerly wait for our Lord **J** Christ 2652
1: 8 on the day of our Lord **J** Christ. 2652
1: 9 with his Son **J** Christ our Lord, 2652
1:10 brothers, in the name of our Lord **J** Christ, 2652
1:30 that you are in Christ **J**, who has become 2652
2: 2 while I was with you except **J** Christ 2652
3:11 one already laid, which is **J** Christ. 2652
4:15 in Christ **J** I became your father through 2652
4:17 of my way of life in Christ **J**, 2652
5: 4 the name of our Lord **J** and I am with you 2652
5: 4 and the power of our Lord **J** is present, 2652
6:11 in the name of the Lord **J** Christ and by 2652
8: 6 and there is but one Lord, **J** Christ, 2652
9: 1 Have I not seen **J** our Lord? 2652
11:23 The Lord **J**, on the night he was betrayed, 2652
12: 3 "**J** be cursed," and no one can say, 2652
12: 3 "**J** is Lord," except by the Holy Spirit. 2652
15:31 as I glory over you in Christ **J** our Lord. 2652
15:57 the victory through our Lord **J** Christ. 2652
16:23 The grace of the Lord **J** be with you. 2652
16:24 My love to all of you in Christ **J**. Amen. 2652

2Co 1: 1 an apostle of Christ **J** by the will of God, 2652
1: 2 God our Father and the Lord **J** Christ. 2652
1: 3 the God and Father of our Lord **J** Christ, 2652
1:14 of you in the day of the Lord **J**. 2652
1:19 For the Son of God, **J** Christ, 2652
4: 5 not preach ourselves, but **J** Christ as Lord, 2652
4:10 carry around in our body the death of **J**, 2652
4:10 life of **J** may also be revealed in our body. 2652
4:14 the Lord **J** from the dead will also raise us 2652
4:14 from the dead will also raise us with **J** 2652
8: 9 you know the grace of our Lord **J** Christ, 2652
11: 4 other than the **J** we preached, 2652
11: 4 a Jesus other than the **J** we preached, 4005S
11:31 The God and Father of the Lord **J**, 2652
13: 5 Do you not realize that Christ **J** is in you— 2652
13:14 May the grace of the Lord **J** Christ, 2652

Gal 1: 1 but by **J** Christ and God the Father, 2652
1: 3 God our Father and the Lord **J** Christ, 2652
1:12 I received it by revelation *from* **J** Christ. 2652
2: 4 to spy on the freedom we have in Christ **J** 2652
2:16 observing the law, but by faith *in* **J** Christ. 2652
2:16 have put our faith in Christ **J** that we may 2652
3: 1 Before your very eyes **J** Christ was clearly portrayed as crucified. 2652
3:14 might come to the Gentiles through Christ **J** 2652
3:22 being given through faith *in* **J** Christ, 2652
3:26 all sons of God through faith in Christ **J**, 2652
3:28 for you are all one in Christ **J**. 2652
4:14 angel of God, as if I were Christ **J** himself. 2652
5: 6 For in Christ **J** neither circumcision 2652
5:24 *to* Christ **J** have crucified the sinful nature 2652
6:14 in the cross of our Lord **J** Christ, 2652
6:17 for I bear on my body the marks of **J**. 2652
6:18 of our Lord **J** Christ be with your spirit. 2652

Eph 1: 1 an apostle of Christ **J** by the will of God, 2652
1: 1 the faithful in Christ **J**: 2652
1: 2 God our Father and the Lord **J** Christ. 2652
1: 3 the God and Father *of* our Lord **J** Christ, 2652
1: 5 as his sons through **J** Christ, in accordance 2652
1:15 since I heard about your faith in the Lord **J** 2652
1:17 that the God *of* our Lord **J** Christ, 2652
2: 6 in the heavenly realms in Christ **J**, 2652
2: 7 expressed in his kindness to us in Christ **J**. 2652
2:10 created in Christ **J** to do good works, 2652
2:13 in Christ **J** you who once were far away have been brought near 2652
2:20 Christ **J** himself as the chief cornerstone. 2652
3: 1 of Christ **J** for the sake of you Gentiles— 2652
3: 6 sharers together in the promise in Christ **J**. 2652
3:11 accomplished in Christ **J** our Lord. 2652
3:21 and in Christ **J** throughout all generations, 2652
4:21 in accordance with the truth that is in **J**. 2652
5:20 in the name of our Lord **J** Christ. 2652
6:23 from God the Father and the Lord **J** Christ. 2652
6:24 Grace to all who love our Lord **J** Christ 2652

Php 1: 1 Paul and Timothy, servants *of* Christ **J**, 2652
1: 1 To all the saints in Christ **J** at Philippi, 2652
1: 2 God our Father and the Lord **J** Christ. 2652
1: 6 on to completion until the day of Christ **J**. 2652
1: 8 of you all with the affection of Christ **J**. 2652
1:11 righteousness that comes through **J** Christ— 2652
1:19 the help given by the Spirit of **J** Christ, 2652
1:26 in Christ **J** will overflow on account of me. 2652
2: 5 be the same as that of Christ **J**: 2652
2:10 at the name of **J** every knee should bow, 2652
2:11 every tongue confess that **J** Christ is Lord, 2652
2:19 in the Lord **J** to send Timothy to you soon, 2652
2:21 his own interests, not those of **J** Christ. 2652
3: 3 glory in Christ **J**, and put no confidence 2652
3: 8 of knowing Christ **J** my Lord, 2652
3:12 of that for which Christ **J** took hold of me. 2652
3:14 the prize for which God has called me heavenward in Christ **J**. 2652
3:20 a Savior from there, the Lord **J** Christ, 2652
4: 7 your hearts and your minds in Christ **J** 2652
4:19 according to his glorious riches in Christ **J**. 2652
4:21 Greet all the saints in Christ **J**. 2652
4:23 The grace of the Lord **J** Christ be with your spirit. 2652

Col 1: 1 an apostle of Christ **J** by the will of God, 2652
1: 3 God, the Father *of* our Lord **J** Christ, 2652
1: 4 we have heard of your faith in Christ **J** 2652
2: 6 then, just as you received Christ **J** as Lord, 2652
3:17 do it all in the name of the Lord **J**, 2652
4:11 **J**, who is called Justus, also sends 2652
4:12 one of you and a servant of Christ **J**, 2652

1Th 1: 1 in God the Father and the Lord **J** Christ: 2652
1: 3 inspired by hope in our Lord **J** Christ. 2652
1:10 **J**, who rescues us from the coming wrath. 2652
2:14 churches in Judea, which are in Christ **J**: 2652
2:15 who killed the Lord **J** and the prophets and 2652
2:19 presence of our Lord **J** when he comes? 2652
3:11 and Father himself and our Lord **J** clear 2652
3:13 God and Father when our Lord **J** comes 2652
4: 1 and urge you in the Lord **J** to do this more 2652
4: 2 by the authority of the Lord **J**. 2652
4:14 We believe that **J** died and rose again and 2652
4:14 with **J** those who have fallen asleep 899S
5: 9 salvation through our Lord **J** Christ. 2652
5:18 for this is God's will for you in Christ **J**. 2652
5:23 at the coming of our Lord **J** Christ. 2652
5:28 grace of our Lord **J** Christ be with you. 2652

2Th 1: 1 in God our Father and the Lord **J** Christ: 2652
1: 2 from God the Father and the Lord **J** Christ. 2652
1: 7 when the Lord **J** is revealed from heaven 2652
1: 8 and do not obey the gospel of our Lord **J** 2652
1:12 the name of our Lord **J** may be glorified 2652
1:12 the grace of our God and the Lord **J** Christ. 2652
2: 1 the coming of our Lord **J** Christ 2652
2: 8 the Lord **J** will overthrow with the breath 2652
2:14 in the glory of our Lord **J** Christ. 2652
2:16 May our Lord **J** Christ himself 2652
3: 6 In the name of the Lord **J** Christ, 2652
3:12 the Lord **J** Christ to settle down and earn 2652
3:18 grace of our Lord **J** Christ be with you all. 2652

1Ti 1: 1 an apostle of Christ **J** by the command 2652
1: 1 God our Savior and of Christ **J** our hope, 2652
1: 2 God the Father and Christ **J** our Lord. 2652
1:12 I thank Christ **J** our Lord, 2652
1:14 with the faith and love that are in Christ **J**. 2652
1:15 Christ **J** came into the world to save 2652
1:16 Christ **J** might display his unlimited patience as an example 2652
2: 5 between God and men, the man Christ **J**, 2652
3:13 assurance in their faith in Christ **J**. 2652
4: 6 you will be a good minister of Christ **J**, 2652
5:21 of God and Christ **J** and the elect angels, 2652
6: 3 the sound instruction of our Lord **J** Christ 2652
6:13 and of Christ **J**, who while testifying 2652
6:14 until the appearing of our Lord **J** Christ, 2652

2Ti 1: 1 an apostle of Christ **J** by the will of God, 2652
1: 1 to the promise of life that is in Christ **J**, 2652
1: 2 God the Father and Christ **J** our Lord. 2652
1: 9 This grace was given us in Christ **J** before 2652
1:10 the appearing of our Savior, Christ **J**, 2652
1:13 with faith and love in Christ **J**. 2652
2: 1 be strong in the grace that is in Christ **J**. 2652
2: 3 with us like a good soldier of Christ **J**. 2652
2: 8 Remember **J** Christ, raised from the dead, 2652
2:10 the salvation that is in Christ **J**, 2652
3:12 a godly life in Christ **J** will be persecuted, 2652
3:15 for salvation through faith in Christ **J**. 2652

Tit 1: 1 In the presence of God and of Christ **J**, 2652
1: 1 a servant of God and an apostle of **J** Christ 2652
1: 4 God the Father and Christ **J** our Savior. 2652
2:13 of our great God and Savior, **J** Christ, 2652
3: 6 generously through **J** Christ our Savior, 2652

Phm 1: 1 Paul, a prisoner *of* Christ **J**, 2652
1: 3 God our Father and the Lord **J** Christ. 2652
1: 5 I hear about your faith in the Lord **J** 2652
1: 9 and now also a prisoner of Christ **J**— 2652
1:23 Epaphras, my fellow prisoner in Christ **J**, 2652
1:25 The grace of the Lord **J** Christ be with your spirit. 2652

Heb 2: 9 But we see **J**, who was made a little lower 2652
2:11 So **J** is not ashamed to call them brothers. NIG
3: 1 fix your thoughts on **J**, the apostle and 2652
3: 3 **J** has been found worthy of greater honor 4047S
4:14 through the heavens, **J** the Son of God, 2652
6:20 where **J**, who went before us, has entered 2652
7:22 **J** has become the guarantee of a better covenant. 2652
7:24 but because **J** lives forever, 899S
8: 6 the ministry **J** has received is as superior NIG
10:10 the sacrifice of the body *of* **J** Christ once 2652
10:19 the Most Holy Place by the blood *of* **J**, 2652
12: 2 Let us fix our eyes on **J**, the author 2652
12:24 *to* **J** the mediator of a new covenant, 2652
13: 8 **J** Christ is the same yesterday and today 2652
13:12 And so **J** also suffered outside the city gate 2652
13:15 Through **J**, therefore, let us continually 899S
13:20 brought back from the dead our Lord **J**, 2652
13:21 to him, through **J** Christ, to whom be glory 2652

Jas 1: 1 a servant of God and of the Lord **J** Christ, 2652
2: 1 as believers in our glorious Lord **J** Christ, 2652

1Pe 1: 1 Peter, an apostle of **J** Christ, 2652
1: 2 for obedience *to* **J** Christ and sprinkling 2652
1: 3 the God and Father of our Lord **J** Christ! 2652
1: 3 the resurrection *of* **J** Christ from the dead, 2652
1: 7 glory and honor when **J** Christ is revealed. 2652
1:13 to be given you when **J** Christ is revealed. 2652
2: 5 acceptable to God through **J** Christ. 2652
3:21 saves you by the resurrection *of* **J** Christ, 2652
4:11 God be praised through **J** Christ. 2652

2Pe 1: 1 Peter, a servant and apostle of **J** Christ, 2652
1: 1 and Savior **J** Christ have received a faith 2652
1: 2 the knowledge of God and of **J** our Lord. 2652
1: 8 in your knowledge of our Lord **J** Christ. 2652
1:11 of our Lord and Savior **J** Christ. 2652

2Pe	1:14	as our Lord J Christ has made clear to me.	2652
	1:16	and coming of our Lord J Christ,	2652
	2:20	by knowing our Lord and Savior J Christ	2652
	3:18	of our Lord and Savior J Christ.	2652
1Jn	1: 3	with the Father and with his Son, J Christ.	2652
	1: 7	and the blood of J, his Son,	2652
	2: 1	J Christ, the Righteous One.	2652
	2: 6	to live in him must walk as J did.	1697S
	2:22	the man who denies that J is the Christ.	2652
	3:16	**J Christ** laid down his life for us.	1697S
	3:23	to believe in the name of his Son, J Christ,	2652
	4: 2	that acknowledges that J Christ has come	2652
	4: 3	not acknowledge J is not from God.	2652
	4:15	If anyone acknowledges that J is the Son	2652
	5: 1	that J is the Christ is born of God,	2652
	5: 5	Only he who believes that J is the Son	2652
	5: 6	who came by water and blood—J Christ.	2652
	5:20	even in his Son J Christ.	2652
2Jn	1: 3	from God the Father and from J Christ,	2652
	1: 7	not acknowledge J Christ as coming in	2652
Jude	1: 1	servant of J Christ and a brother of James,	2652
	1: 1	by God the Father and kept by J Christ:	2652
	1: 4	and deny J Christ our only Sovereign	2652
	1:17	the apostles of our Lord J Christ foretold.	2652
	1:21	for the mercy of our Lord J Christ	2652
	1:25	through J Christ our Lord, before all ages,	2652
Rev	1: 1	The revelation of J Christ,	2652
	1: 2	word of God and the testimony of J Christ.	2652
	1: 5	J Christ, who is the faithful witness	2652
	1: 9	and patient endurance that are ours in J,	2652
	1: 9	of the word of God and the testimony of J.	2652
	12:17	and hold to the testimony of J.	2652
	14:12	and remain faithful to J.	2652
	17: 6	of those who bore testimony to J.	2652
	19:10	who hold to the testimony of J.	2652
	19:10	testimony of J is the spirit of prophecy."	2652
	20: 4	of their testimony for J and because of	2652
	22:16	I, have sent my angel to give you this	2652
	22:20	Come, Lord J.	2652
	22:21	grace of the Lord J be with God's people.	2652

JESUS' (33) [JESUS]

Mt	21:45	and the Pharisees heard J' parables,	899S
	26:51	of J' companions reached for his sword,	899S
	27:53	and after J' resurrection they went into	899S
	27:58	Going to Pilate, he asked for J' body,	2652
Mk	3:31	Then J' mother and brothers arrived.	899S
	6:14	for J' name had become well known.	899S
	14:12	J' disciples asked him,	899S
	15:43	to Pilate and asked for J' body.	2652
	16: 1	so that they might go to anoint **J' body.**	899S
Lk	5: 8	he fell at J' knees and said,	2652
	7:29	when they heard J' words,	NIG
	8:19	J' mother and brothers came to see him,	899S
	8:35	at J' feet, dressed and in his right mind;	2652
	8:41	came and fell at J' feet,	2652
	17:16	at J' feet and thanked him—	2652
	22:49	J' **followers** saw what was going	1254+3836S
	23:52	Going to Pilate, he asked for J' body.	2652
Jn	2: 1	J' mother was there,	2652
	2: 3	J' mother said to him, "They have no more	2652
	7: 3	J' brothers said to him, "You ought to	899S
	12: 2	Here a dinner was given in J' honor.	899S
	12: 3	on J' feet and wiped his feet with her hair.	2652
	12:41	Isaiah said this because he saw J' glory	899S
	16:29	Then J' disciples said, "Now you are	899S
	19:29	hyssop plant, and lifted it to J' lips.	3836S
	19:34	of the soldiers pierced J' side with a spear,	899S
	19:40	Taking J' body, the two of them wrapped	2652
	20: 7	burial cloth that had been around J' head.	899S
	20:12	seated where J' body had been,	2652
Ac	3:16	It is J' name and the faith that comes	899S
2Co	4: 5	and ourselves as your servants for J' sake.	2652
	4:11	being given over to death for J' sake,	2652
Heb	5: 7	During the days of J' life on earth,	899S

JETHER (10)

Jdg	8:20	Turning to J, his oldest son, he said,	3858
	8:20	But J did not draw his sword,	2021+5853S
2Sa	17:25	Amasa was the son of a man named J,	3859
1Ki	2: 5	Abner son of Ner and Amasa son of J.	3858
	2:32	and Amasa son of J.	3858
1Ch	2:17	whose father was J the Ishmaelite.	3858
	2:32	Shammai's brother: J and Jonathan.	3858
	2:32	J died without children.	3858
	4:17	J, Mered, Epher and Jalon.	3858
	7:38	The sons of J: Jephunneh, Pispah and Ara.	3858

JETHETH (2)

Ge	36:40	and regions: Timna, Alvah, J,	3867
1Ch	1:51	of Edom were: Timna, Alvah, J,	3867

JETHLAH (KJV) See ITHLAH

JETHRO (11)

Ex	3: 1	tending the flock of J his father-in-law,	3861
	4:18	to J his father-in-law and said to him,	3858
	4:18	J said, "Go, and I wish you well."	3861
	18: 1	Now J, the priest of Midian	3861
	18: 2	his father-in-law J received her	3861
	18: 5	J, Moses' father-in-law, together with	3861
	18: 6	J had sent word to him, "I, your	NIH
	18: 6	"I, your father-in-law J, am coming	3861
	18: 9	J was delighted to hear about all the good	3861

Ex	18:12	Then J, Moses' father-in-law, brought a	3861
	18:27	and J returned to his own country.	2257S

JETUR (3)

Ge	25:15	Hadad, Tema, J, Naphish and Kedemah.	3515
1Ch	1:31	J, Naphish and Kedemah.	3515
	5:19	They waged war against the Hagrites, J,	3515

JEUEL (2)

1Ch	9: 6	Of the Zerahites: J.	3590
Ezr	8:13	J and Shemaiah, and with them 60 men;	3590

JEUSH (9)

Ge	36: 5	and Oholibamah bore J,	3593
	36:14	she bore to Esau: J, Jalam and	3593
	36:18	Chiefs J, Jalam and Korah.	3593
1Ch	1:35	Eliphaz, Reuel, J, Jalam and Korah.	3593
	7:10	The sons of Bilhan: J, Benjamin, Ehud,	3593
	8:39	J the second son and Eliphelet the third.	3593
	23:10	sons of Shimei: Jahath, Ziza, J and Beriah.	3593
	23:11	but J and Beriah did not have many sons;	3593
2Ch	11:19	J, Shemariah and Zaham.	3593

JEUZ (1)

1Ch	8:10	J, Sakia and Mirmah.	3591

JEW (32) [JEWESS, JEWISH, JEWS, JEWS', JUDAISM]

Est	2: 5	Now there was in the citadel of Susa a J of	3374
	3: 4	for he had told them he was a J.	3374
	5:13	that J Mordecai sitting at the king's gate."	3374
	6:10	as you have suggested for Mordecai the J,	3374
	8: 7	to Queen Esther and to Mordecai the J,	3374
	9:29	along with Mordecai the J,	3374
	9:31	the J and Queen Esther had decreed	3374
	10: 3	the J was second in rank to King Xerxes,	3374
Jer	34: 9	no one was to hold a fellow J in bondage.	3374
Zec	8:23	and nations will take firm hold of one J by	3374
Jn	3:25	of John's disciples and a certain J over	2681
	4: 9	"You are a J and I am a Samaritan woman.	2681
	18:35	"Am I a J?" Pilate replied.	2681
Ac	10:28	a J to associate with a Gentile or visit	467+2681
	18: 2	There he met a J named Aquila,	2681
	18:24	Meanwhile a J named Apollos.	2681
	19:34	But when they realized he was a J,	2681
	21:39	Paul answered, "I am a J, from Tarsus	476+2681
	22: 3	"I am a J, born in Tarsus of Cilicia,	467+2681
Ro	1:16	first for the J, then for the Gentile;	2681
	2: 9	first for the J, then for the Gentile;	2681
	2:10	first for the J, then for the Gentile;	2681
	2:17	Now you, if you call yourself a J;	2681
	2:28	not a J if he is only one outwardly,	2681
	2:29	No, a man is a J if he is one inwardly;	2681
	3: 1	advantage, then, is there in being a J,	2681
	10:12	For there is no difference between J	2681
1Co	9:20	To the Jews I became like a J,	2681
Gal	2:14	"You are a J, yet you live like a Gentile	2681
	2:14	yet you live like a Gentile and not **like a J.**	2680
	3:28	There is neither J nor Greek,	2681
Col	3:11	Here there is no Greek or J,	2681

JEWEL (4) [JEWELRY, JEWELS]

Pr	20:15	but lips that speak knowledge are a rare j.	3998
SS	4: 9	with one j of your necklace.	6736
Isa	13:19	Babylon, the j of kingdoms,	7382
Rev	21:11	brilliance was like that of a very precious j,	3345

JEWELRY (13) [JEWEL]

Ge	24:53	the servant brought out gold and silver j	3998
Ex	32:24	So I told them, 'Whoever has any gold j,	NIH
	35:22	came and brought gold j of all kinds:	3998
Jer	2:32	Does a maiden forget her j,	6344
Eze	7:20	They were proud of their **beautiful j**	6344+7382
	16:11	I adorned you with j:	6344
	16:17	You also took the fine j I gave you,	3998
	16:17	the j made of my gold and silver,	NIH
	16:39	and take your fine j and leave you naked	3998
	23:26	of your clothes and take your fine j.	3998
	23:40	painted your eyes and **put on** your j.	6335+6344
Hos	2:13	she decked herself with rings and j,	2719
1Pe	3: 3	as braided hair and the wearing of **gold j**	5992

JEWELS (9) [JEWEL]

Job	28:17	nor can it be had for j of gold.	3998
SS	1:10	your neck with **strings of** j.	3016
	5:12	washed in milk, **mounted like** j	3782+4859+6584
	7: 1	Your graceful legs are like j,	2717
Isa	54:12	your gates of **sparkling j,**	74+734
	61:10	and as a bride adorns herself with her j.	3998
Jer	4:30	Why dress yourself in scarlet and put on j	6344
Eze	16: 7	and became the **most beautiful of** j.	6344+6344
Zec	9:16	They will sparkle in his land like j in	74

JEWESS (2) [JEW]

Ac	16: 1	whose mother was a J and a believer,	2681
	24:24	his wife Drusilla, who was a J.	2681

JEWISH (27) [JEW]

Ezr	6: 7	the J elders rebuild this house of God	10316
Ne	1: 2	and I questioned them about the J remnant	3374

Ne	5: 1	a great outcry against their J brothers.	3374
	5: 8	bought back our J brothers who were sold	3374
Est	6:13	is of J origin, you cannot stand	3374
Jn	2:13	it was almost time for the J Passover,	2681
	3: 1	a member of the J ruling council.	2681
	6: 4	The J Passover Feast was near.	2681
	7: 2	when the J Feast of Tabernacles was near,	2681
	11:51	that Jesus would die for the J nation,	NIG
	11:55	it was almost time for the J Passover,	2681
	18:12	and the J officials arrested Jesus.	2681
	19:40	in accordance with J burial customs.	2681
	19:42	Because it was the J day of Preparation	2681
Ac	10:22	who is respected by all the J people.	2681
	12:11	the J people were anticipating."	2681
	13: 5	the word of God in the J synagogues.	2681
	13: 6	they met a J sorcerer named Bar-Jesus,	2681
	14: 1	went as usual into the J synagogue.	2681
	17: 1	where there was a J synagogue.	2681
	17:10	they went to the J synagogue.	2681
	19:14	Seven sons of Sceva, a J chief priest,	2681
	25: 2	the chief priests and J leaders appeared	2681
	25:24	whole J **community** has petitioned me	2681+4436
	26: 3	with all the J customs and controversies.	2681
Gal	2:14	force Gentiles to **follow J customs?**	2678
Tit	1:14	and will pay no attention to J myths or to	2679

JEWRY (KJV) See JUDAH, JUDEA

JEWS (243) [JEW]

Ezr	4:12	The king should know that the J who came	10316
	4:23	to the J in Jerusalem and compelled them	10316
	5: 1	prophesied to the J in Judah and Jerusalem	10316
	5: 5	over the elders of the J and	10316
	6: 7	Let the governor of the J and	10316
	6: 8	for these elders of the J in the construction	10316
	6:14	the J continued to build and prosper under	10316
	7:18	You and your **brother** J may	10017
Ne	2:16	to the J or the priests or nobles or officials	3374
	4: 1	He ridiculed the J,	3374
	4: 2	he said, "What are those feeble J doing?	3374
	4:12	Then the J who lived near them came	3374
	5:17	and fifty J and officials ate at my table,	3374
	6: 6	that you and the J are plotting to revolt,	3374
Est	3: 6	to destroy all Mordecai's people, the J,	3374
	3:10	the Agagite, the enemy of the J.	3374
	3:13	kill and annihilate all the J—	3374
	4: 3	there was great mourning among the J,	3374
	4: 7	for the destruction of the J.	3374
	4:13	you alone of all the J will escape.	3374
	4:14	relief and deliverance for the J will arise	3374
	4:16	gather together all the J who are in Susa,	3374
	8: 1	Haman, the enemy of the J.	3374
	8: 3	which he had devised against the J.	3374
	8: 5	to destroy the J in all the king's provinces.	3374
	8: 7	"Because Haman attacked the J,	3374
	8: 8	the J as seems best to you, and seal it with	3374
	8: 9	to the J, and to the satraps, governors	3374
	8: 9	to the J in their own script and language.	3374
	8:11	The king's edict granted the J in every city	3374
	8:12	for the J to do this in all the provinces	NIH
	8:13	so that the J would be ready on that day	3374
	8:16	the J it was a time of happiness and joy,	3374
	8:17	there was joy and gladness among the J,	3374
	8:17	of other nationalities **became** J because fear	3366
	8:17	because fear of the J had seized them.	3374
	9: 1	On this day the enemies of the J had hoped	3374
	9: 1	now the tables were turned and the J got	3374
	9: 2	The J assembled in their cities in all	3374
	9: 3	and the king's administrators helped the J,	3374
	9: 5	The J struck down all their enemies with	3374
	9: 6	J killed and destroyed five hundred men.	3374
	9:10	son of Hammedatha, the enemy of the J,	3374
	9:12	"The J have killed and destroyed	3374
	9:13	"give the J in Susa permission to carry out	3374
	9:15	The J in Susa came together on the	3374
	9:16	of the J who were in the king's provinces	3374
	9:18	The J in Susa, however, had assembled	3374
	9:19	That is why rural J—	3374
	9:20	and he sent letters to all the J throughout	3374
	9:22	when the J got relief from their enemies,	3374
	9:23	So the J agreed to continue the celebration	3374
	9:24	the Agagite, the enemy of all the J,	3374
	9:24	against the J to destroy them and had cast	3374
	9:25	the J should come back onto his own head,	3374
	9:27	the J took it upon themselves to establish	3374
	9:28	never cease to be celebrated by the J,	3374
	9:30	the J in the 127 provinces of the kingdom	3374
	10: 3	preeminent among the J, and held in high	3374
	10: 3	in high esteem by his many **fellow** J,	278
	10: 3	and spoke up for the welfare of all the J.	2446S
Jer	32:12	the J sitting in the courtyard of the guard.	3374
	38:19	"I am afraid of the J who have gone over	3374
	40:11	When all the J in Moab, Ammon,	3374
	40:15	the J who are gathered around you to	3373
	41: 3	the J who were with Gedaliah at Mizpah,	3374
	43: 9	"While the J are watching,	3374
	44: 1	to Jeremiah concerning all the J living	3374
	44:26	all J living in Egypt:	3373
	44:27	the J in Egypt will perish by sword	3373
	52:28	in the seventh year, 3,023 J;	3374
	52:30	745 J taken into exile by Nebuzaradan	3374
Da	3: 8	came forward and denounced the J.	10316
	3:12	But there are some J whom you have set	10316
Mt	2: 2	the one who has been born king of the J?	2681
	27:11	"Are you the king of the J?"	2681

Mt	27:29	"Hail, king of the J!"	2681
	27:37	THIS IS JESUS, THE KING OF THE J.	2681
	28:15	among the J to this very day.	2681
Mk	7: 3	(The Pharisees and all the J do not eat	2681
	15: 2	"Are you the king of the J?"	2681
	15: 9	to release to you the king of the J?"	2681
	15:12	with the one you call the king of the J?"	2681
	15:18	"Hail, king of the J!"	2681
	15:26	THE KING OF THE J.	2681
Lk	7: 3	and sent some elders of the J to him,	2681
	23: 3	"Are you the king of the J?"	2681
	23:37	"If you are the king of the J,	2681
	23:38	THIS IS THE KING OF THE J.	2681
Jn	1:19	Now this was John's testimony when the J	2681
	2: 6	kind used by the J for ceremonial washing,	2681
	2:18	Then the J demanded of him,	2681
	2:20	The J replied, "It has taken forty-six years	2681
	4: 9	(For J do not associate with Samaritans.)	2681
	4:20	but you claim that the place where we	NIG
	4:22	for salvation is from the J.	2681
	5: 1	went up to Jerusalem for a feast of the J.	2681
	5:10	the J said to the man who had been healed,	2681
	5:15	The man went away and told the J	2681
	5:16	things on the Sabbath, the J persecuted him.	2681
	5:18	For this reason the J tried all the harder	2681
	6:41	At this the J began to grumble about him	2681
	6:52	Then the J began to argue sharply	2681
	7: 1	the J there were waiting to take his life.	2681
	7:11	the J were watching for him and asking,	2681
	7:13	anything publicly about him for fear of the J	2681
	7:15	The J were amazed and asked,	2681
	7:35	The J said to one another,	2681
	8:22	This made the J ask, "Will he kill himself?	2681
	8:31	To the J who had believed him, Jesus said,	2681
	8:48	The J answered him, "Aren't we right	2681
	8:52	At this the J exclaimed, "Now we know	2681
	8:57	The J said to him, "and you have seen	2681
	9:18	The J still did not believe	2681
	9:22	because they were afraid of the J,	2681
	9:22	for already the J had decided that	2681
	10:19	At these words the J were again divided.	2681
	10:24	The J gathered around him, saying,	2681
	10:31	Again the J picked up stones to stone him,	2681
	10:33	replied the J, "but for blasphemy,	2681
	11: 8	"a short while ago the J tried to stone you,	2681
	11:19	and many J had come to Martha and Mary	2681
	11:31	J who had been with Mary in the house,	2681
	11:33	and the J who had come along with her	2681
	11:36	Then the J said, "See how he loved him!"	2681
	11:45	many of the J who had come to visit Mary,	2681
	11:54	moved about publicly among the J.	2681
	12: 9	Meanwhile a large crowd of J found out	2681
	12:11	on account of him many of the J were going over	2681
	13:33	and just as I told the J, so I tell you now:	2681
	18:14	the J that it would be good if one man died	2681
	18:20	where all the J come together.	2681
	18:28	the J led Jesus from Caiaphas to the palace	NIG
	18:28	to avoid ceremonial uncleanness the J did	899S
	18:31	to execute anyone," the J objected.	2681
	18:33	"Are you the king of the J?"	2681
	18:36	to prevent my arrest by the J.	2681
	18:38	With this he went out again to the J	2681
	18:39	to release 'the king of the J'?"	2681
	19: 3	saying, "Hail, king of the J!"	2681
	19: 4	Pilate came out and said to the J,	899S
	19: 7	The J insisted, "We have a law,	2681
	19:12	to set Jesus free, but the J kept shouting,	2681
	19:14	"Here is your king," Pilate said to the J.	2681
	19:19	JESUS OF NAZARETH, THE KING OF THE J.	2681
	19:20	Many of the J read this sign,	2681
	19:21	The chief priests of the J protested	2681
	19:21	"Do not write 'The King of the J,'	2681
	19:21	that this man claimed to be king of the J."	2681
	19:31	Because the J did not want the bodies left	2681
	19:38	but secretly because he feared the J.	2681
	20:19	with the doors locked for fear of the J,	2681
Ac	2: 5	in Jerusalem God-fearing J from every	2681
	2:11	(both J and converts to Judaism);	2681
	2:14	"Fellow J and all of you who live	467+2681
	6: 1	the Grecian J among them complained	1821
	6: 1	against the Hebraic J because their widows	1578
	6: 9	J of Cyrene and Alexandria as well as	NIG
	9:22	and more powerful and baffled the J living	2681
	9:23	the J conspired to kill him,	2681
	9:29	He talked and debated with the Grecian J,	1821
	10:39	in the country of the J and in Jerusalem.	2681
	11:19	telling the message only to J.	2681
	12: 3	When he saw that this pleased the J,	2681
	13:43	many of the J and devout converts	2681
	13:45	When the J saw the crowds,	2681
	13:50	But the J incited the God-fearing women	2681
	14: 1	a great number of J and Gentiles believed.	2681
	14: 2	But the J who refused to believe stirred up	2681
	14: 4	were divided; some sided with the J,	2681
	14: 5	a plot afoot among the Gentiles and J,	2681
	14:19	Then some J came from Antioch	2681
	16: 3	because of the J who lived in that area,	2681
	16:20	"These men are J, and are throwing our city	2681
	17: 4	of the J were persuaded and joined Paul	899S
	17: 5	But the J were jealous,	2681
	17:12	Many of the J believed,	899S
	17:13	When the J in Thessalonica learned	2681
	17:17	with the J and the God-fearing Greeks,	2681
	18: 2	because Claudius had ordered all the J	2681
	18: 4	trying to persuade J and Greeks.	2681
	18: 5	testifying to the J that Jesus was the Christ.	2681
	18: 6	the J opposed Paul and became abusive,	899S

Ac	18:12	the J made a united attack on Paul	2681
	18:14	Gallio said to the J, "If you Jews were	2681
	18:14	"If you J were making a complaint	2681
	18:19	the synagogue and reasoned with the J.	2681
	18:28	For he vigorously refuted the J	2681
	19:10	the J and Greeks who lived in the province	2681
	19:13	Some J who went around driving out	2681
	19:17	to the J and Greeks living in Ephesus,	2681
	19:33	The J pushed Alexander to the front,	2681
	20: 3	Because the J made a plot against him just	2681
	20:19	severely tested by the plots of the J.	2681
	20:21	to both J and Greeks that they must turn	2681
	21:11	'In this way the J of Jerusalem will bind	2681
	21:20	how many thousands of J have believed,	2681
	21:21	that you teach all the J who live among	2681
	21:21	some J from the province of Asia saw Paul	2681
	22:12	highly respected by all the J living there.	2681
	22:30	by the J, he released him and ordered	2681
	23:12	The next morning the J formed	2681
	23:20	"The J have agreed to ask you	2681
	23:27	by the J and they were about to kill him,	2681
	24: 5	a riots among the J all over the world.	2681
	24: 9	The J joined in the accusation,	2681
	24:19	But there are some J from the province	2681
	24:27	Felix wanted to grant a favor to the J,	2681
	25: 7	the J who had come down from Jerusalem	2681
	25: 8	the law of the J or against the temple or	2681
	25: 9	Festus, wishing to do the J a favor,	2681
	25:10	I have not done any wrong to the J,	2681
	25:11	against me by these J are not true,	NIG
	25:15	of the J brought charges against him	2681
	26: 2	against all the accusations of the J,	2681
	26: 4	"The J all know the way I have lived ever	2681
	26: 7	of this hope that the J are accusing me.	2681
	26:21	the J seized me in the temple courts	2681
	28:17	he called together the leaders of the J.	2681
	28:19	But when the J objected,	2681
Ro	3: 9	the charge that J and Gentiles alike are all	2681
	3:29	Is God the God of J only?	2681
	9:24	only from the J but also from the Gentiles?	2681
	15: 8	a servant of the J on behalf of God's truth,	4364
	15:27	they owe it to the J to share with them	NIG
1Co	1:22	J demand miraculous signs	2681
	1:23	a stumbling block to J and foolishness	2681
	1:24	God has called, both J and Greeks,	2681
	9:20	To the J I became like a Jew,	2681
	9:20	I became like a Jew, to win the J.	2681
	10:32	whether J, Greeks or the church of God—	2681
	12:13	whether J or Greeks, slave or free—	2681
2Co	11:24	from the J the forty lashes minus one.	2681
Gal	1:14	advancing in Judaism beyond many J of my own age	1169+1609+1877+3836
	2: 7	just as Peter had been to the J.	4364
	2: 8	of Peter as an apostle to the J,	4364
	2: 9	should go to the Gentiles, and they to the J.	4364
	2:13	The other J joined him in his hypocrisy,	2681
	2:15	"We who are J by birth and not	2681
Col	4:11	the only J among my fellow workers	1666+4364
1Th	2:14	things those churches suffered from the J,	2681
Rev	2: 9	of those who say they are J and are not,	2681
	3: 9	who claim to be J though they are not,	2681

JEWS' (1) [JEW]
Ro	15:27	have shared in the J' spiritual blessings,	899S

JEZANIAH (1)
Jer	42: 1	including Johanan son of Kareah and J son	3470

JEZEBEL (19) [JEZEBEL'S]
1Ki	16:31	also married J daughter of Ethbaal king of	374
	18: 4	J was killing off the LORD's prophets,	374
	18:13	what I did while J was killing the prophets	374
	19: 1	Ahab told J everything Elijah had done	374
	19: 2	So J sent a messenger to Elijah to say,	374
	21: 5	His wife J came in and asked him,	374
	21: 7	J his wife said, "Is this how you act as king	374
	21:11	as J directed in the letters she had written	374
	21:14	Then they sent word to J:	374
	21:15	as J heard that Naboth had been stoned	374
	21:23	"And also concerning J the LORD says:	374
	21:23	'Dogs will devour J by the wall	374
	21:25	urged on by J his wife.	374
2Ki	9: 7	of all the LORD's servants shed by J.	374
	9:10	As for J, dogs will devour her on the plot	374
	9:22	and witchcraft of your mother J abound?"	374
	9:30	When J heard about it, she painted her eyes	374
	9:37	that no one will be able to say, 'This is J.'"	374
Rev	2:20	You tolerate that woman J,	2630

JEZEBEL'S (3) [JEZEBEL]
1Ki	18:19	prophets of Asherah, who eat at J table."	374
2Ki	9:36	at Jezreel dogs will devour J flesh.	374
	9:37	J body will be like refuse on the ground in	374

JEZER (3) [JEZERITE]
Ge	46:24	Jahziel, Guni, J and Shillem.	3672
Nu	26:49	through J, the Jezerite clan;	3672
1Ch	7:13	Jahziel, Guni, J and Shillem—	3672

JEZERITE (1) [JEZER]
Nu	26:49	through Jezer, the J clan;	3673

JEZIAH (KJV) See IZZIAH

JEZIEL (1)
1Ch	12: 3	J and Pelet the sons of Azmaveth;	3465

JEZLIAH (KJV) See IZLIAH

JEZOAR (KJV) See ZOHAR

JEZRAHIAH (1)
Ne	12:42	The choirs sang under the direction of J.	3474

JEZREEL (41) [JEZREELITE]
Jos	15:56	J, Jokdeam, Zanoah,	3476
	17:16	and those in the Valley of J."	3476
	19:18	Their territory included: J, Kesulloth,	3476
Jdg	6:33	the Jordan and camped in the Valley of J.	3476
1Sa	25:43	David had also married Ahinoam of J,	3477
	27: 3	Ahinoam of J and Abigail of Carmel,	3477
	29: 1	and Israel camped by the spring in J.	3476
	29:11	and the Philistines went up to J.	3476
	30: 5	Ahinoam of J and Abigail,	3477
2Sa	2: 2	Ahinoam of J and Abigail,	3477
	2: 9	Ashuri and J, and also over Ephraim,	3476
	3: 2	the son of Ahinoam of J;	3477
1Ki	4:12	of Beth Shan next to Zarethan below J,	3476
	18:45	heavy rain came on and Ahab rode off to J.	3476
	18:46	he ran ahead of Ahab all the way to J.	3476
	21: 1	The vineyard was in J, close to the palace	3476
	21:23	'Dogs will devour Jezebel by the wall of J.'	3476
2Ki	8:29	so King Joram returned to J to recover	3476
	8:29	of Judah went down to J to see Joram son	3476
	9:10	on the plot of ground at J,	3476
	9:15	but King Joram had returned to J	3476
	9:15	of the city to go and tell the news in J."	3476
	9:16	Then he got into his chariot and rode to J,	3476
	9:17	in J saw Jehu's troops approaching,	3476
	9:30	Then Jehu went to J.	3476
	9:36	at J dogs will devour Jezebel's flesh.	3476
	9:37	like refuse on the ground in the plot at J,	3476
	10: 1	to the officials of J, to the elders	3476
	10: 6	of your master's sons and come to me in J	3476
	10: 7	in baskets and sent them to Jehu in J,	3476
	10:11	So Jehu killed everyone in J who remained	3476
1Ch	3: 1	Amnon the son of Ahinoam of J;	3477
	4: 3	These were the sons of Etam: J,	3475
2Ch	22: 6	so he returned to J to recover from	3476
	22: 6	of Judah went down to J to see Joram son	3476
Hos	1: 4	the LORD said to Hosea, "Call him J,	3475
	1: 4	the house of Jehu for the massacre at J,	3476
	1: 5	break Israel's bow in the Valley of J."	3476
	1:11	for great will be the day of J.	3476
	2:22	and they will respond to J.	3476

JEZREELITE (7) [JEZREEL]
1Ki	21: 1	a vineyard belonging to Naboth the J.	3477
	21: 4	and angry because Naboth the J had said,	3477
	21: 6	"Because I said to Naboth the J,	3477
	21: 7	I'll get you the vineyard of Naboth the J."	3477
	21:15	of Naboth the J that he refused to sell you.	3477
2Ki	9:21	that had belonged to Naboth the J.	3477
	9:25	on the field that belonged to Naboth the J.	3477

JEZREELITESS (KJV) See JEZREELITE

JIBSAM (KJV) See IBSAM

JIDLAPH (1)
Ge	22:22	Kesed, Hazo, Pildash, J and Bethuel."	3358

JIMNA, JIMNAH (KJV) See IMNAH

JIMNITES (KJV) See IMNITE

JINGLING (1)
Isa	3:16	with ornaments j on their ankles.	6576

JIPHTAH (KJV) See IPHTAH

JIPHTHAH-EL (KJV) See IPHTAH EL

JOAB (141) [JOAB'S, ATROTH BETH JOAB]
2Sa	2:13	J son of Zeruiah and David's men went out	3405
	2:14	Then Abner said to J, "Let's have some of	3405
	2:14	"All right, let them do it." J said.	3405
	2:18	J, Abishai and Asahel.	3405
	2:22	How could I look your brother J in	3405
	2:24	But J and Abishai pursued Abner,	3405
	2:26	Abner called out to J, "Must the sword	3405
	2:27	J answered, "As surely as God lives,	3405
	2:28	So J blew the trumpet,	3405
	2:30	Then J returned from pursuing Abner	3405
	2:32	Then J and his men marched all night	3405
	3:22	Just then David's men and J returned from	3405
	3:23	J and all the soldiers with him arrived,	3405
	3:24	So J went to the king and said,	3405

2Sa	3:26	J then left David and sent messengers	3405

2Sa 3:26 J then left David and sent messengers — 3405
3:27 J took him aside into the gateway, — 3405
3:27 J stabbed him in the stomach, and he died. — NIH
3:29 May his blood fall upon the head of J and — 3405
3:30 (J and his brother Abishai murdered Abner — 3405
3:31 Then David said to J and all the people — 3405
8:16 J son of Zeruiah was over the army; — 3405
10:7 David sent J out with the entire army — 3405
10:9 J saw that there were battle lines in front — 3405
10:11 J said, "If the Arameans are too strong — NIH
10:13 Then J and the troops with him advanced — 3405
10:14 So J returned from fighting — 3405
11:1 David sent J out with the king's men and — 3405
11:6 So David sent this word to J: — 3405
11:6 And J sent him to David. — 3405
11:7 David asked him how J was, — 3405
11:11 and my master J and my lord's men — 3405
11:14 In the morning David wrote a letter to J — 3405
11:16 So while J had the city under siege, — 3405
11:17 of the city came out and fought against J, — 3405
11:18 J sent David a full account of the battle. — 3405
11:22 he told David everything J had sent him — 3405
11:25 David told the messenger, "Say this to J: — 3405
11:25 Say this to encourage J." — 2084S
12:26 Meanwhile J fought against Rabbah of — 3405
12:27 J then sent messengers to David, saying, — 3405
14:1 J son of Zeruiah knew that — 3405
14:2 So J sent someone to Tekoa and had — 3405
14:3 And J put the words in her mouth. — 3405
14:19 "Isn't the hand of J with you in all this?" — 3405
14:19 it was your servant J who instructed me — 3405
14:20 Your servant J did this to change — 3405
14:21 The king said to J, "Very well, I will do it. — 3405
14:22 J fell with his face to the ground — 3405
14:22 J said, "Today your servant knows — 3405
14:23 Then J went to Geshur — 3405
14:29 for J in order to send him to the king, — 3405
14:29 but J refused to come to him. — NIH
14:31 Then J did go to Absalom's house — 3405
14:32 Absalom said to J, "Look, — 3405
14:33 So J went to the king and told him this. — 3405
17:25 over the army in place of J. — 3405
17:25 and sister of Zeruiah the mother of J. — 3405
18:2 a third under the command of J, — 3405
18:5 The king commanded J, Abishai and Ittai, — 3405
18:10 When one of the men saw this, he told J, — 3405
18:11 J said to the man who had told him this, — 3405
18:14 J said, "I'm not going to wait like this — 3405
18:16 Then J sounded the trumpet, — 3405
18:16 stopped pursuing Israel, for J halted them. — 3405
18:20 to take the news today," J told him. — 3405
18:21 Then J said to a Cushite, "Go, — 3405
18:21 The Cushite bowed down before J — 3405
18:22 Ahimaaz son of Zadok again said to J, — 3405
18:22 But J replied, "My son, why do you want — NIH
18:23 So J said, "Run!" — NIH
18:29 "I saw great confusion just as J was about — 3405
19:1 J was told, "The king is weeping — 3405
19:5 J went into the house to the king and said, — 3405
19:13 the commander of my army in place of J.' " — 3405
20:8 J was wearing his military tunic, — 3405
20:9 J said to Amasa, "How are you, — 3405
20:9 Then J took Amasa by the beard — 3405
20:10 and J plunged it into his belly, — NIH
20:10 Amasa died. Then J and his brother — 3405
20:11 "Whoever favors J, and whoever is — 3405
20:11 whoever is for David, let him follow J!" — 3405
20:13 on with J to pursue Sheba son of Bicri. — 3405
20:15 the troops with J came and besieged Sheba — 3405
20:16 Tell J to come here so I can speak to him." — 3405
20:17 and she asked, "Are you J?" — 3405
20:20 J replied, "Far be it from me to swallow — 3405
20:21 The woman said to J, "His head will be — 3405
20:22 head of Sheba son of Bicri and threw it to J. — 3405
20:22 And J went back to the king in Jerusalem. — 3405
20:23 J was over Israel's entire army; — 3405
23:18 of J son of Zeruiah was chief of the Three. — 3405
23:24 Asahel the brother of J, — 3405
23:37 the armor-bearer of J son of Zeruiah, — 3405
24:2 to J and the army commanders with him, — 3405
24:3 But J replied to the king, — 3405
24:4 overruled J and the army commanders; — 3405
24:9 J reported the number of the fighting men — 3405
1Ki 1:7 Adonijah conferred with J son of Zeruiah — 3405
1:19 Abiathar the priest and J the commander — 3405
1:41 the sound of the trumpet, J asked, "What's — 3405
2:5 "Now you yourself know what J son — 3405
2:22 and for Abiathar the priest and J son — 3405
2:28 When the news reached J, — 3405
2:29 King Solomon was told that J had fled to — 3405
2:30 the tent of the LORD and said to J, — 2257S
2:30 "This is how J answered me." — 3405
2:31 the guilt of the innocent blood that J shed. — 3405
2:33 the head of J and his descendants forever. — 3405
2:34 of Jehoiada went up and struck down J — 2257S
11:15 J the commander of the army, — 3405
11:16 J and all the Israelites stayed there — 3405
11:21 and that J the commander of the army was — 3405
1Ch 2:16 Zeruiah's three sons were Abishai, J and Asahel. — 3405
4:14 Seraiah was the father of J, — 3405
11:6 J son of Zeruiah went up first, — 3405
11:8 while J restored the rest of the city. — 3405
11:20 the brother of J was chief of the Three. — 3405
11:26 Asahel the brother of J, — 3405
11:39 the armor-bearer of J son of Zeruiah, — 3405
18:15 J son of Zeruiah was over the army; — 3405

1Ch 19:8 David sent J out with the entire army — 3405
19:10 J saw that there were battle lines in front — 3405
19:12 J said, "If the Arameans are too strong — NIH
19:14 Then J and the troops with him advanced — 3405
19:15 So J went back to Jerusalem. — 3405
20:1 J led out the armed forces. — 3405
20:1 J attacked Rabbah and left it in ruins. — 3405
21:2 So David said to J and the commanders of — 3405
21:3 But J replied, "May the LORD multiply his — 3405
21:4 The king's word, however, overruled J; — 3405
21:4 so J left and went throughout Israel and — 3405
21:5 J reported the number of the fighting men — 3405
21:6 But J did not include Levi and Benjamin — 3405
26:28 Abner son of Ner and J son of Zeruiah. — 3405
27:7 was Asahel the brother of J; — 3405
27:24 J son of Zeruiah began to count the men — 3405
27:34 J was the commander of the royal army. — 3405
Ezr 2:6 (through the line of Jeshua and J) 2,812 — 3405
8:9 of the descendants of J, Obadiah son — 3405
Ne 7:11 (through the line of Jeshua and J) 2,818 — 3405
Ps 60:T and when J returned and struck — 3405

JOAB'S (9) [JOAB]
1Sa 26:6 of Zeruiah, J brother, "Who will go down — 3405
2Sa 3:29 May J house never be without someone — 3405
14:30 "Look, J field is next to mine, — 3405
18:2 under J brother Abishai son of Zeruiah, — 3405
18:15 J armor-bearers surrounded Absalom, — 3405
20:7 So J men and the Kerethites and Pelethites — 3405
20:10 on his guard against the dagger in J hand, — 3405
20:11 of J men stood beside Amasa and said, — 3405
1Ki 2:35 of Jehoiada over the army in J position — 2257S

JOAH (11)
2Ki 18:18 and J son of Asaph the recorder went out — 3406
18:26 Shebna and J said to the field commander, — 3406
18:37 Shebna the secretary and J son of Asaph — 3406
1Ch 6:21 J his son, Iddo his son, Zerah his son — 3406
26:4 Jehozabad the second, J the third, — 3406
2Ch 29:12 J son of Zimmah and Eden son of Joah; — 3406
29:12 Joah son of Zimmah and Eden son of J; — 3406
34:8 with J son of Joahaz, the recorder, — 3406
Isa 36:3 and J son of Asaph the recorder went out — 3406
36:11 Shebna and J said to the field commander, — 3406
36:22 and J son of Asaph the recorder went — 3406

JOAHAZ (1)
2Ch 34:8 with Joah son of J, the recorder, — 3407

JOANAN (1)
Lk 3:27 the son of J, — 2720

JOANNA (2)
Lk 8:3 J the wife of Cuza, the manager — 2721
24:10 It was Mary Magdalene, J, — 2721

JOASH (42) [JEHOASH]
Jdg 6:11 under the oak in Ophrah that belonged to J — 3409
6:29 they were told, "Gideon son of J did it." — 3409
6:30 The men of the town demanded of J, — 3409
6:31 J replied to the hostile crowd around him, — 3409
7:14 the sword of Gideon son of J, — 3409
8:13 of J then returned from the battle by — 3409
8:29 Jerub-Baal son of J went back home — 3409
8:32 of J died at a good old age and was buried — 3409
8:32 of his father J in Ophrah of the Abiezrites. — 3409
1Ki 22:26 the ruler of the city and to J the king's son — 3409
2Ki 11:2 took J son of Ahaziah and stole him away — 3409
11:21 J was seven years old when he began — 3371
12:1 In the seventh year of Jehu, J became king, — 3371
12:2 J did what was right in the eyes of the LORD — 3371
12:4 J said to the priests, "Collect all the money — 3371
12:6 of King J the priests still had not repaired — 3371
12:7 Therefore King J summoned Jehoiada — 3371
12:18 But J king of Judah took all — 3371
12:19 As for the other events of the reign of J, — 3409
13:1 of J son of Ahaziah king of Judah, — 3409
13:10 the thirty-seventh year of J king of Judah, — 3409
14:1 Amaziah son of J king of Judah began — 3409
14:3 the example of his father J. — 3409
14:13 the son of J, the son of Ahaziah, — 3371
14:17 of J king of Judah lived for fifteen years — 3409
14:23 the fifteenth year of Amaziah son of J king — 3409
1Ch 3:11 Ahaziah his son, J his son, — 3409
4:22 the men of Cozeba, and J and Saraph, — 3409
7:8 The sons of Beker: Zemirah, J, Eliezer, — 3447
12:3 and J the sons of Shemaah the Gibeathite; — 3409
27:28 J was in charge of the supplies of olive oil. — 3447
2Ch 18:25 the ruler of the city and to J the king's son, — 3409
22:11 took J son of Ahaziah and stole him away — 3409
24:1 J was seven years old — 3409
24:2 J did what was right in the eyes of the LORD — 3409
24:4 Some time later J decided to restore — 3409
24:22 King J did not remember — 3409
24:23 the army of Aram marched against J; — 2257S
24:24 judgment was executed on J. — 3409
24:25 they left J severely wounded. — 2257S
25:23 the son of J, the son of Ahaziah, — 3409
25:25 of J king of Judah lived for fifteen years — 3409

JOATHAM (KJV) See JOTHAM

JOB (55) [JOB'S]
2Ch 34:13 and supervised all the workers from j — 6275
34:13 the workers from job to j. — 6275
Job 1:1 a man whose name was J. — 373
1:5 J would send and have them purified. — 373
1:8 "Have you considered my servant J? — 373
1:9 "Does J fear God for nothing?" — 373
1:14 a messenger came to J and said, — 373
1:20 J got up and tore his robe — 373
1:22 J did not sin by charging God — 373
2:3 "Have you considered my servant J? — 373
2:7 the presence of the LORD and afflicted J — 373
2:8 Then J took a piece of broken pottery — 2257S
2:10 In all this, J did not sin in what he said. — 373
3:1 J opened his mouth and cursed the day — 373
6:1 Then J replied: — 373
9:1 Then J replied: — 373
12:1 Then J replied: — 373
16:1 Then J replied: — 373
19:1 Then J replied: — 373
21:1 Then J replied: — 373
23:1 Then J replied: — 373
26:1 Then J replied: — 373
27:1 And J continued his discourse: — 373
29:1 J continued his discourse: — 373
31:40 The words of J are ended. — 373
32:1 So these three men stopped answering J, — 373
32:2 became very angry with J — 373
32:3 because they had found no way to refute J, — 373
32:4 so J because they were older than he. — 373
32:12 But not one of you has proved J wrong; — NIH
32:14 J has not marshaled his words against me, — 373
33:1 "But now, J, listen to my words; — 373
33:31 "Pay attention, J, and listen to me; — 373
34:5 "J says, 'I am innocent, — 373
34:7 What man is like J, — 373
34:35 'J speaks without knowledge; — 373
34:36 that J might be tested to the utmost — 373
35:16 So J opens his mouth with empty talk; — 373
37:14 J; stop and consider God's wonders. — 373
38:1 the LORD answered J out of the storm. — 373
40:1 The LORD said to J: — 373
40:3 Then J answered the LORD: — 373
40:6 the LORD spoke to J out of the storm: — 373
42:1 Then J replied to the LORD: — 373
42:7 the LORD had said these things to J, — 373
42:7 of me what is right, as my servant J has. — 373
42:8 and seven rams and go to my servant J — 373
42:8 My servant J will pray for you, — 373
42:8 of me what is right, as my servant J has." — 373
42:10 After J had prayed for his friends, — 373
42:16 J lived a hundred and forty years; — 373
Eze 14:14 Noah, Daniel and J— — 373
14:20 even if Noah, Daniel and J were in it, — 373
Lk 16:3 My master is taking away my j. — 3873
16:4 when I lose my j here, — 3873

JOB'S (8) [JOB]
Job 1:5 This was J regular custom. — 373
1:13 when J sons and daughters were feasting — 2257S
2:11 When J three friends, Eliphaz the — 373
31:31 'Who has not had his fill of J meat?'— — 2257S
42:9 and the LORD accepted J prayer. — 373
42:12 the latter part of J life more than the first. — 373
42:15 as beautiful as J daughters, — 373
Jas 5:11 of J perseverance and have seen what — 2724

JOBAB (9)
Ge 10:29 Ophir, Havilah and J. — 3411
36:33 J son of Zerah from Bozrah succeeded him — 3412
36:34 When J died, Husham from the land of — 3412
Jos 11:1 he sent word to J king of Madon, — 3412
1Ch 1:23 Ophir, Havilah and J. — 3411
1:44 J son of Zerah from Bozrah succeeded him — 3412
1:45 When J died, Husham from the land of — 3412
8:9 By his wife Hodesh he had J, Zibia, — 3412
8:18 Izliah and J were the sons of Elpaal. — 3412

JOCHEBED (2)
Ex 6:20 Amram married his father's sister J, — 3425
Nu 26:59 the name of Amram's wife was J, — 3425

JODA (1)
Lk 3:26 the son of Josech, the son of J, — 2726

JOED (1)
Ne 11:7 Sallu son of Meshullam, the son of J, — 3444

JOEL (21)
1Sa 8:2 The name of his firstborn was J and — 3408
1Ch 4:35 J, Jehu son of Joshibiah, the son — 3408
5:4 The descendants of J: — 3408
5:8 the son of Shema, the son of J. — 3408
5:12 J was the chief, — 3408
6:28 J the firstborn and Abijah the second son. — 3408
6:33 Heman, the musician, the son of J, — 3408
6:36 the son of J, the son of Azariah, — 3408
7:3 Michael, Obadiah, J and Isshiah. — 3408
11:38 J the brother of Nathan, — 3408
15:7 J the leader and 130 relatives; — 3408
15:11 and Uriel, Asaiah, J, Shemaiah, — 3408
15:17 So the Levites appointed Heman son of J; — 3408

1Ch	23: 8	Jehiel the first, Zetham and J—three in all.	3408
	26:22	Zetham and his brother J.	3408
	27:20	J son of Pedaiah;	3408
2Ch	29:12	Mahath son of Amasai and J son	3408
Ezr	10:43	Zabad, Zebina, Jaddai, J and Benaiah.	3408
Ne	11: 9	J son of Zicri was their chief officer,	3408
Joel	1: 1	The word of the LORD that came to J son	3408
Ac	2:16	this is what was spoken by the prophet J:	2727

JOELAH (1)
1Ch	12: 7	and J and Zebadiah the sons of Jeroham	3443

JOEZER (1)
1Ch	12: 6	Azarel, J and Jashobeam the Korahites;	3445

JOGBEHAH (2)
Nu	32:35	Atroth Shophan, Jazer, J,	3322
Jdg	8:11	and J and fell upon the unsuspecting army.	3322

JOGLI (1)
Nu	34:22	Bukki son of J, the leader from the tribe	3332

JOHA (2)
1Ch	8:16	Ishpah and J were the sons of Beriah.	3418
	11:45	his brother J the Tizite,	3418

JOHANAN (24)
2Ki	25:23	Ishmael son of Nethaniah, J son	3419
1Ch	3:15	J the firstborn, Jehoiakim the second son,	3419
	3:24	Hodaviah, Eliashib, Pelaiah, Akkub, J,	3419
	6: 9	Azariah the father of J,	3419
	6:10	J the father of Azariah (it was he who	3419
	12: 4	Jeremiah, Jahaziel, J,	3419
	12:12	J the eighth, Elzabad the ninth,	3419
Ezr	8:12	J son of Hakkatan, and with him 110 men;	3419
Ne	12:22	the days of Eliashib, Joiada, J and Jaddua,	3419
	12:23	the time of J son of Eliashib were recorded	3419
Jer	40: 8	J and Jonathan the sons of Kareah,	3419
	40:13	J son of Kareah and all the army officers	3419
	40:15	Then J son of Kareah said privately	3419
	40:16	But Gedaliah son of Ahikam said to J son	3419
	41:11	When J son of Kareah and all	3419
	41:13	the people Ishmael had with him saw J son	3419
	41:14	at Mizpah turned and went over to J son	3419
	41:15	of his men escaped from J and fled to	3419
	41:16	Then J son of Kareah and all the army	3419
	42: 1	including J son of Kareah	3419
	42: 8	So he called together J son of Kareah	3419
	43: 2	of Hoshaiah and J son of Kareah and all	3419
	43: 4	So J son of Kareah and all the army	3419
	43: 5	J son of Kareah and all the army officers	3419

JOHN (138) [JOHN'S]
Mt	3: 1	In those days J the Baptist came,	2722
	3:13	to the Jordan to be baptized by J.	2722
	3:14	But J tried to deter him, saying,	2722
	3:15	Then J consented.	NIG
	4:12	When Jesus heard that J had been put	2722
	4:21	James son of Zebedee and his brother J.	2722
	10: 2	James son of Zebedee, and his brother J;	2722
	11: 2	J heard in prison what Christ was doing,	2722
	11: 4	"Go back and report to J what you hear	2722
	11: 7	Jesus began to speak to the crowd about J:	2722
	11:11	not risen anyone greater than J the Baptist;	2722
	11:12	From the days of J the Baptist until now,	2722
	11:13	and the Law prophesied until J.	2722
	11:18	For J came neither eating nor drinking,	2722
	14: 2	"This is J the Baptist;	2722
	14: 3	Now Herod had arrested J and bound him	2722
	14: 4	for J had been saying to him:	2722
	14: 5	Herod wanted to kill J,	899S
	14: 8	"Give me here on a platter the head of J	2722
	14:10	and had J beheaded in the prison.	2722
	16:14	They replied, "Some say J the Baptist;	2722
	17: 1	James and J the brother of James,	2722
	17:13	that he was talking to them about J	2722
	21:26	for they all hold that J was a prophet."	2722
	21:32	For J came to you to show you the way	2722
Mk	1: 4	And so J came, baptizing in the desert	2722
	1: 6	J wore clothing made of camel's hair,	2722
	1: 9	and was baptized by J in the Jordan.	2722
	1:14	After J was put in prison,	2722
	1:19	of Zebedee and his brother J in a boat,	2722
	1:29	and J to the home of Simon and Andrew.	2722
	3:17	James son of Zebedee and his brother J	2722
	5:37	James and J the brother of James.	2722
	6:14	"J the Baptist has been raised from	2722
	6:16	But when Herod heard this, he said, "J,	2722
	6:17	had give orders to have J arrested,	2722
	6:18	For J had been saying to Herod,	2722
	6:19	a grudge against J and wanted to kill him.	899S
	6:20	because Herod feared and protected him,	2722
	6:20	When Herod heard J, he was greatly	899S
	6:24	"The head of J the Baptist," she answered.	2722
	6:25	the head of J the Baptist on a platter."	2722
	6:27	The man went, beheaded J in the prison,	899S
	8:28	They replied, "Some say J the Baptist;	2722
	9: 2	James and J with him and led them up	2722
	9:38	said J, "we saw a man driving out demons	2722
	10:35	Then James and J, the sons of Zebedee,	2722
	10:41	they became indignant with James and J.	2722
	11:32	everyone held that J really was a prophet.)	2722
Mk	13: 3	James, J and Andrew asked him privately,	2722
	14:33	James and J along with him,	2722
Lk	1:13	and you are to give him the name J."	2722
	1:60	He is to be called J."	2722
	1:63	"His name is J."	2722
	3: 2	word of God came to J son of Zechariah in	2722
	3: 7	J said to the crowds coming out to	NIG
	3:11	J answered, "The man with two tunics	NIG
	3:15	if J might possibly be the Christ.	2722
	3:16	J answered them all, "I baptize you with	2722
	3:18	And with many other words J exhorted	NIG
	3:19	when J rebuked Herod the tetrarch because	899S
	3:20	He locked J up in prison.	2722
	5:10	and so were James and J,	2722
	6:14	his brother Andrew, James, J, Philip,	2722
	7:20	"J the Baptist sent us to you to ask,	2722
	7:22	to J what you have seen and heard:	2722
	7:24	Jesus began to speak to the crowd about J:	2722
	7:28	of women there is no one greater than J;	2722
	7:29	because they had been baptized by J,	2722
	7:30	because they had not been baptized by J.)	899S
	7:33	For J the Baptist came neither eating bread	2722
	8:51	in with him except Peter, J and James, and	2722
	9: 7	that J had been raised from the dead,	2722
	9: 9	But Herod said, "I beheaded J.	2722
	9:19	They replied, "Some say J the Baptist;	2722
	9:28	J and James with him and went up onto	2722
	9:49	said J, "we saw a man driving out demons	2722
	9:54	When the disciples James and J saw this,	2722
	11: 1	just as J taught his disciples."	2722
	16:16	and the Prophets were proclaimed until J.	2722
	20: 6	they are persuaded that J was a prophet."	2722
	22: 8	Jesus sent Peter and J, saying,	2722
Jn	1: 6	who was sent from God; his name was J.	2722
	1:15	J testifies concerning him.	2722
	1:23	I replied in the words of Isaiah	NIG
	1:26	"I baptize with water," J replied,	2722
	1:28	side of the Jordan, where J was baptizing.	2722
	1:29	The next day J saw Jesus coming	NIG
	1:32	Then J gave this testimony:	2722
	1:35	The next day J was there again with two	2722
	1:40	of the two who heard what J had said	2722
	1:42	"You are Simon son of J.	2722
	3:23	J also was baptizing at Aenon near Salim,	2722
	3:24	(This was before J was put in prison.)	2722
	3:26	They came to J and said to him, "Rabbi,	2722
	3:27	To this J replied, "A man can receive only	2722
	4: 1	and baptizing more disciples than J,	2722
	5:33	"You have sent to J and he has testified to	2722
	5:35	J was a lamp that burned and gave light,	1697S
	5:36	"I have testimony weightier than that of J.	2722
	10:40	to the place where J had been baptizing in	2722
	10:41	"Though J never performed	2722
	10:41	all that J said about this man was true."	2722
	21:15	"Simon son of J, do you truly love me?	2722
	21:16	Again Jesus said, "Simon son of J,	2722
	21:17	"Simon son of J, do you love me?"	2722
Ac	1: 5	For J baptized with water,	2722
	1:13	Those present were Peter, J,	2722
	3: 1	One day Peter and J were going up to	2722
	3: 3	When he saw Peter and J about to enter,	2722
	3: 4	Peter looked straight at him, as did J.	2722
	3:11	While the beggar held on to Peter and J,	2722
	4: 1	to Peter and J while they were speaking to	899S
	4: 3	They seized Peter and J,	899S
	4: 6	and so were Caiaphas, J, Alexander and	2722
	4: 7	They had Peter and J brought before them	899S
	4:13	When they saw the courage of Peter and J	2722
	4:19	But Peter and J replied, "Judge for	2722
	4:23	Peter and J went back to their own people	NIG
	8:14	they sent Peter and J to them.	2722
	8:17	Peter and J placed their hands on them,	NIG
	8:25	Peter and J returned to Jerusalem,	3525+3836S
	10:37	after the baptism that J preached—	2722
	11:16	'J baptized with water,	2722
	12: 2	He had James, the brother of J,	2722
	12:12	to the house of Mary the mother of J,	2722
	12:25	taking with them J, also called Mark.	2722
	13: 5	J was with them as their helper.	2722
	13:13	where J left them to return to Jerusalem,	2722
	13:24	J preached repentance and baptism to all	2722
	13:25	As J was completing his work, he said:	2722
	15:37	Barnabas wanted to take J,	2722
	18:25	though he knew only the baptism of J.	2722
Gal	2: 9	Peter and J, those reputed to be pillars,	2722
Rev	1: 1	by sending his angel to his servant J,	2722
	1: 4	J, To the seven churches in the province	2722
	1: 9	J, your brother and companion in	2722
	22: 8	J, am the one who heard and saw	2722

JOHN'S (19) [JOHN]
Mt	3: 4	J clothes were made of camel's hair,	899+2722
	9:14	Then J disciples came and asked him,	2722
	11: 7	As J disciples were leaving,	4047S
	14:12	J disciples came and took his body	899S
	21:25	J baptism—where did it come from?	2722
Mk	2:18	J disciples and the Pharisees were fasting.	2722
	2:18	"How is it that J disciples and the disciples	2722
	6:27	an executioner with orders to bring J head.	899S
	6:29	J disciples came and took his body	899S
	11:30	J baptism—was it from heaven,	2722
Lk	5:33	"J disciples often fast and pray,	2722
	7:18	told John about all these things.	2722
	7:24	After J messengers left,	2722
	20: 4	J baptism—was it from heaven,	2722
Jn	1:19	Now this was J testimony when the Jews	2722
	3:25	of J disciples and a certain Jew over	2722
Ac	1:22	beginning from J baptism to the time	2722
	19: 3	"J baptism," they replied.	2722
	19: 4	"J baptism was a baptism of repentance.	2722

JOIADA (5)
Ne	3: 6	The Jeshanah Gate was repaired by J son	3421
	12:10	Eliashib the father of J,	3421
	12:11	J the father of Jonathan,	3421
	12:22	J, Johanan and Jaddua,	3421
	13:28	One of the sons of J son of Eliashib	3421

JOIAKIM (4)
Ne	12:10	Jeshua was the father of J,	3423
	12:10	J the father of Eliashib.	3423
	12:12	In the days of J, these were the heads of	3423
	12:26	They served in the days of J son of Jeshua,	3423

JOIARIB (4) [JOIARIB'S]
Ezr	8:16	who were leaders, and J and Elnathan,	3424
Ne	11: 5	the son of J, the son of Zechariah,	3424
	11:10	From the priests: Jedaiah; the son of J;	3424
	12: 6	Shemaiah, J, Jedaiah,	3424

JOIARIB'S (1) [JOIARIB]
Ne	12:19	of J, Mattenai; of Jedaiah's, Uzzi;	3424

JOIN (42) [ADJOINING, JOINED, JOINING, JOINS, JUNCTION, REJOINED]
Ge	34:30	if they j forces against me and attack me,	665
	49: 6	let me not j their assembly,	3479
Ex	1:10	if war breaks out, will j our enemies,	3578
	26: 3	J five of the curtains together,	2489
	26: 9	J five of the curtains together	2489
Nu	18: 2	from your ancestral tribe to j you	4277
	18: 4	to j you and be responsible for the care of	4277
	34: 5	j the Wadi of Egypt and end at the Sea.	2025
Jdg	3:13	the Ammonites and Amalekites to j him,	665
	21:21	When the girls of Shiloh come out to j in	2565
1Sa	13: 4	people were summoned to j Saul at Gilgal.	339
	22:20	escaped and fled to j David.	339
2Sa	3:21	the king and his officials please j me?"	2143+6640
1Ki	1: 8	David's special guard did not j Adonijah.	6640
1Ch	13: 2	towns and pasturelands, to come and j us.	7695
2Ch	18: 3	we will j you in the war."	6640
Ne	4:20	the sound of the trumpet, j us there.	7695
	10:29	these now j their brothers the nobles,	2616+6584
Est	9:27	and all who j them should	4277
Job	37:18	can you j him in spreading out the skies,	6640
Ps	49:19	he will j the generation of his fathers,	995+6330
	50:18	When you see a thief, you j with him;	8354
	106: 5	and j your inheritance in giving praise.	6640
	118:27	j in the festal procession up to the horns of	673
Pr	23:20	Do not j those who drink too much wine	928+2118
	24:21	my son, and do not j with the rebellious;	6843
Ecc	9: 3	and afterward they j the dead.	448
Isa	5: 8	to you who add house to house and j field	7928
	14: 1	Aliens will j them and unite with	4277
	14:20	you will not j them in burial,	3479
Jer	3:18	In those days the house of Judah will j	2143+6584
Eze	37:17	j them together into one stick so	7928
	37:19	and j it to Judah's stick,	5989
Da	11:34	and many who are not sincere will j them.	4277
Mic	5: 3	of his brothers return to j the Israelites.	NIH
Ac	5:13	No one else dared j them,	3140
	9:26	he tried to j the disciples.	3140
	17:15	Timothy to j him as soon as possible.	2262+4639
	21:24	j in their purification rites	5250
Ro	15:30	j me in my struggle by praying to God	5253
Php	3:17	J with others in following my example,	1181+5213
2Ti	1: 8	j with me in suffering for the gospel,	5155

JOINED (34) [JOIN]
Ge	14: 3	All these latter kings j forces in the Valley	2489
Ex	36:10	They j five of the curtains together and did	2489
	36:16	They j five of the curtains into one set and	2489
Nu	25: 3	So Israel j in worshiping the Baal of Peor.	7537
	25: 5	of your men who have j in worshiping	7537
Jos	10: 5	Jarmuth, Lachish and Eglon—j forces.	665
	10: 6	the hill country have j forces against us."	7695
	11: 5	All these kings j forces	3585
	15: 4	along to Azmon and j the Wadi of Egypt,	3655
Jdg	6:33	and other eastern peoples j forces	665+3481
1Sa	10:10	and he j in their prophesying.	928+9348
	14:22	they j the battle in hot pursuit.	1815
	28:23	his men j the woman in urging him,	1685+2256
1Ki	20:29	and on the seventh day the battle was j.	7928
2Ch	5:13	The trumpeters and singers j in unison,	2118
Ezr	3:	j together in supervising those	285+3869+6641
Job	41:17	They are j fast to one another;	1815
	41:23	The folds of his flesh are tightly j;	1815
Ps	83: 8	Even Assyria has j them to lend strength to	4277
Hos	4:17	Ephraim is j to idols; leave him alone!	2489
Zec	2:11	"Many nations will be j with the LORD	4277
Mt	19: 6	Therefore what God has j together,	5183
Mk	10: 9	Therefore what God has j together,	5183
Jn	6:17	and Jesus had not yet j them.	2262+4639
Ac		j together constantly in prayer, along with	4674
	12:20	now j together and sought an audience	3924
	16:22	The crowd j in the attack against Paul	5308
	17: 4	of the Jews were persuaded and j Paul	4677

Ac 20: 6 five days later **j** the others at Troas,   2262+4639
24: 9 The Jews **j in the accusation,**   5298
Gal 2:13 **j** him **in** his **hypocrisy,**   5347
Eph 2:21 the whole building is **j together** and rises   5274
4:16 the whole body, **j** and held together   5274

JOINING (1) [JOIN]
Eze 31:17 **j** those killed by the sword.   448

JOINS (2) [JOIN]
Hos 7: 5 and he **j** hands with the mockers.   5432
1Co 16:16 as these and *to* everyone who **j in the work,**   5300

JOINT (2) [JOINTED, JOINTS]
Job 31:22 let it be broken off at the **j.**   7866
Ps 22:14 and all my bones *are* out of **j.**   7233

JOINTED (1) [JOINT]
Lev 11:21 that have **j** legs for hopping on the ground.   4200+4946+5087+8079

JOINTS (1) [JOINT]
Heb 4:12 to dividing soul and spirit, **j** and marrow;   765

JOISTS (1)
2Ch 34:11 for **j** and beams for the buildings that   4677

JOKDEAM (1)
Jos 15:56 Jezreel, **J,** Zanoah,   3680

JOKIM (1)
1Ch 4:22 **J,** the men of Cozeba, and Joash   3451

JOKING (3)
Ge 19:14 But his sons-in-law thought he was **j.**   7464
Pr 26:19 "I *was* only **j!**"   8471
Eph 5: 4 foolish talk or **coarse j,**   2365

JOKMEAM (2)
1Ki 4:12 to Abel Meholah across to **J;**   3695
1Ch 6:68 **J,** Beth Horon,   3695

JOKNEAM (4)
Jos 12:22 the king of **J** in Carmel one   3696
19:11 and extended to the ravine near **J.**   3696
21:34 from the tribe of Zebulun, **J,** Kartah,   3696
1Ch 6:77 From the tribe of Zebulun they received,   3696

JOKSHAN (4)
Ge 25: 2 She bore him Zimran, **J,** Medan, Midian,   3705
25: 3 **J** was the father of Sheba and Dedan;   3705
1Ch 1:32 Zimran, **J,** Medan, Midian,   3705
1:32 The sons of **J:** Sheba and Dedan.   3705

JOKTAN (6)
Ge 10:25 his brother was named **J.**   3690
10:26 **J** was the father of Almodad, Sheleph,   3690
10:29 All these were sons of **J.**   3690
1Ch 1:19 his brother was named **J.**   3690
1:20 **J** was the father of Almodad, Sheleph,   3690
1:23 All these were sons of **J.**   3690

JOKTHEEL (2)
Jos 15:38 Dilean, Mizpah, **J,**   3706
2Ki 14: 7 calling it **J,** the name it has to this day.   3706

JOLTING (1)
Na 3: 2 galloping horses and **j** chariots!   8376

JONA (KJV) See JOHN

JONADAB (12)
2Sa 13: 3 Now Amnon had a friend named **J** son   3432
13: 3 **J** was a very shrewd man.   3432
13: 5 "Go to bed and pretend to be ill," **J** said.   3386
13:32 But **J** son of Shimeah, David's brother,   3432
13:35 **J** said to the king, "See,   3432
Jer 35: 6 because our forefather **J** son   3432
35: 8 We have obeyed everything our forefather
J son of Recab commanded   3386
35:10 fully obeyed everything our forefather **J**   3432
35:14 '**J** son of Recab ordered his sons not to
drink wine   3386
35:16 of **J** son of Recab have carried out   3386
35:18 obeyed the command of your forefather **J**   3386
35:19 '**J** son of Recab will never fail to have   3432

JONAH (28) [JONAH'S]
2Ki 14:25 through his servant **J** son of Amittai,   3434
Jnh 1: 1 of the LORD came to **J** son of Amittai: 3434
1: 3 But **J** ran away from the LORD   3434
1: 5 But **J** had gone below deck,   3434
1: 7 They cast lots and the lot fell on **J.**   3434
1:15 they took **J** and threw him overboard,   3434
1:17 LORD provided a great fish to swallow **J,**   3434
1:17 and **J** was inside the fish three days   3434

Jnh 2: 1 From inside the fish **J** prayed to the LORD   3434
2:10 and it vomited **J** onto dry land.   3434
3: 1 Then the word of the LORD came to **J**   3434
3: 3 **J** obeyed the word of the LORD and went   3434
3: 4 On the first day, **J** started into the city.   3434
4: 1 But **J** was greatly displeased   3434
4: 5 **J** went out and sat down at a place east of   3434
4: 6 and make it grow up over **J** to give shade   3434
4: 6 and **J** was very happy about the vine.   3434
4: 9 But God said to **J,**   3434
Mt 12:39 the sign *of* the prophet **J.**   2731
12:40 For as **J** was three days and three nights in   2731
12:41 for they repented at the preaching *of* **J,**   2731
12:41 and now one greater than **J** is here.   2731
16: 4 none will be given it except the sign *of* **J.**"   2731
16:17 "Blessed are you, Simon **son of J,**   980
Lk 11:29 none will be given it except the sign *of* **J.**   2731
11:30 For as **J** was a sign to the Ninevites,   2731
11:32 for they repented at the preaching *of* **J,**   2731
11:32 and now one greater than **J** is here.   2731

JONAH'S (1) [JONAH]
Jnh 4: 8 sun blazed on **J** head so that he grew faint.   3434

JONAM (1)
Lk 3:30 the son *of* **J,** the son of Eliakim,   2729

JONAN (KJV) See JONAM

JONAS (KJV) See JONAH

JONATHAN (112) [JONATHAN'S]
Jdg 18:30 and **J** son of Gershom, the son of Moses,   3387
1Sa 13: 2 of Bethel, and a thousand were with **J**   3440
13: 3 **J** attacked the Philistine outpost at Geba,   3440
13:16 Saul and his son **J** and the men   3440
13:22 the battle not a soldier with Saul and **J** had   3440
13:22 only Saul and his son **J** had them.   3440
14: 1 One day **J** son of Saul said to   3440
14: 3 No one was aware that **J** had left.   3440
14: 4 of the pass that **J** intended to cross to reach   3440
14: 6 **J** said to his young armor-bearer, "Come,   3387
14: 8 **J** said, "Come, then;   3387
14:12 The men of the outpost shouted to **J**   3440
14:12 So **J** said to his armor-bearer,   3440
14:13 **J** climbed up, using his hands and feet,   3440
14:13 The Philistines fell before **J,**   3440
14:14 In that first attack **J** and his armor-bearer   3440
14:17 it was **J** and his armor-bearer who were   3440
14:21 to the Israelites who were with Saul and **J.**   3440
14:27 But **J** had not heard that his father   3440
14:29 **J** said, "My father has made trouble for   3440
14:39 even if it lies with my son **J,** he must die."   3440
14:40 I and my son will stand over here."   3440
14:41 And **J** and Saul were taken by lot,   3440
14:42 "Cast the lot between me and **J** my son."   3440
14:42 And **J** was taken.   3440
14:43 Then Saul said to **J,** "Tell me what you   3440
14:43 So **J** told him, "I merely tasted a little   3440
14:44 be it ever so severely, if you do not die, **J.**"   3440
14:45 But the men said to Saul, "Should **J** die—   3440
14:45 So the men rescued **J,**   3440
14:49 Saul's sons were **J,** Ishvi and Malki-Shua.   3440
18: 1 **J** became one in spirit with David,   3387
18: 3 And **J** made a covenant with David   3387
18: 4 **J** took off the robe he was wearing   3387
19: 1 Saul told his son **J** and all the attendants   3440
19: 1 But **J** was very fond of David   3387
19: 4 **J** spoke well of David to Saul his father   3387
19: 6 Saul listened to **J** and took this oath: 3387
19: 7 So **J** called David and told him   3387
20: 1 from Naioth at Ramah and went to **J**   3387
20: 2 "Never!" **J** replied. "You are not going to   NIH
20: 3 '**J** must not know this or he will   3387
20: 4 **J** said to David, "Whatever you want me   3387
20: 9 "Never!" **J** said. "If I had the least inkling   3387
20:11 **J** said, "let's go out into the field."   3387
20:12 Then **J** said to David: 3387
20:16 So **J** made a covenant with the house   3387
20:17 And **J** had David reaffirm his oath out   3387
20:18 Then **J** said to David: 3387
20:25 opposite **J,** and Abner sat next to Saul,   3387
20:27 Then Saul said to his son **J,**   3387
20:28 **J** answered, "David earnestly asked me   3387
20:30 Saul's anger flared up at **J** and he said   3387
20:32 What has he done?" **J** asked his father.   3387
20:33 Then **J** knew that his father intended   3387
20:34 **J** got up from the table in fierce anger;   3387
20:35 In the morning **J** went out to the field   3387
20:37 **J** called out after him,   3387
20:39 only **J** and David knew.)   3387
20:40 **J** gave his weapons to the boy and said,   3387
20:41 and bowed down before **J** three times,   NIH
20:42 **J** said to David, "Go in peace,   3387
20:42 David left, and **J** went back to the town.   3387
23:16 And Saul's son **J** went to David at Horesh   3387
23:18 Then **J** went home,   3387
31: 2 and they killed his sons **J,** Abinadab and   3387
2Sa 1: 4 And Saul and his son **J** are dead."   3387
1: 5 that Saul and his son **J** are dead?"   3387
1:12 till evening for Saul and **J** his son,   3387
1:17 concerning Saul and his son **J,**   3387
1:22 the bow of **J** did not turn back,   3387
1:23 "Saul and **J**—in life they were loved   3387

2Sa 1:25 **J** lies slain on your heights.   3387
1:26 I grieve for you, **J** my brother;   3387
4: 4 (**J** son of Saul had a son who was lame in   3387
4: 4 when the news about Saul and **J** came   3387
9: 3 "There is still a son of **J;**   3387
9: 6 When Mephibosheth son of **J,**   3387
9: 7 for the sake of your father **J.**   3387
15:27 with your son Ahimaaz and **J** son   3387
15:36 Ahimaaz son of Zadok and **J** son   3387
17:17 **J** and Ahimaaz were staying at En Rogel;   3387
17:20 they asked, "Where are Ahimaaz and **J?**"   3387
21: 7 The king spared Mephibosheth son of **J,**   3387
21: 7 the LORD between David and **J** son   3387
21:12 and took the bones of Saul and his son **J**   3387
21:13 the bones of Saul and his son **J** from there,   3387
21:14 the bones of Saul and his son **J** in the tomb   3387
21:21 When he taunted Israel, **J** son of Shimea,   3387
23:32 the Shaalbonite, the sons of Jashen,   3387
1Ki 1:42 **J** son of Abiathar the priest arrived.   3440
1:43 "Not at all!" **J** answered.   3440
1Ch 2:32 Shammai's brother: Jether and **J.**   3440
2:33 The sons of **J:** Peleth and Zaza.   3440
8:33 and Saul the father of **J,** Malki-Shua,   3387
8:34 The son of **J:** Merib-Baal,   3387
9:39 and Saul the father of **J,** Malki-Shua,   3387
9:40 The son of **J:** Merib-Baal;   3387
10: 2 and they killed his sons **J,** Abinadab   3440
11:34 **J** son of Shagee the Hararite,   3440
20: 7 When he taunted Israel, **J** son of Shimea,   3387
27:25 **J** son of Uzziah was in charge of   3387
27:32 **J,** David's uncle, was a counselor,   3387
Ezr 8: 6 Ebed son of **J,** and with him 50 men;   3440
10:15 Only **J** son of Asahel and Jahzeiah son   3440
Ne 12:11 Joiada the father of **J,**   3440
12:11 and **J** the father of Jaddua.   3440
12:14 of Malluch's, **J;** of Shecaniah's, Joseph;   3440
12:35 and also Zechariah son of **J,**   3440
Jer 37:15 and imprisoned in the house of **J**   3387
37:20 Do not send me back to the house of **J**   3387
40: 8 Johanan and **J** the sons of Kareah,   3440

JONATHAN'S (3) [JONATHAN]
1Sa 20:37 to the place where **J** arrow had fallen,   3387
2Sa 9: 1 to whom I can show kindness for **J** sake?"   3387
Jer 38:26 to send me back to **J** house to die there.' "   3387

JOPPA (14)
Jos 19:46 with the area facing **J.**   3639
2Ch 2:16 will float them in rafts by sea down to **J.**   3639
Ezr 3: 7 bring cedar logs by sea from Lebanon to **J,**   3639
Jnh 1: 3 He went down to **J,** where he found a ship   3639
Ac 9:36 In **J** there was a disciple named Tabitha   2673
9:38 Lydda was near **J;**   2673
9:42 This became known all over **J,**   2673
9:43 Peter stayed in **J** for some time with   2673
10: 5 Now send men to **J** to bring back   2673
10: 8 that had happened and sent them to **J.**   2673
10:23 some of the brothers from **J** went along.   2673
10:32 Send to **J** for Simon who is called Peter.   2673
11: 5 "I was in the city *of* **J** praying,   2673
11:13 'Send to **J** for Simon who is called Peter.   2673

JORAH (1)
Ezr 2:18 of **J** 112   3454

JORAI (1)
1Ch 5:13 Michael, Meshullam, Sheba, **J,** Jacan,   3455

JORAM (28) [JEHORAM]
2Sa 8:10 he sent his son **J** to King David   3456
8:10 **J** brought with him articles of silver   NIH
2Ki 1:17 **J** succeeded him as king in the second year   3393
3: 1 **J** son of Ahab became king of Israel   3393
3: 6 at that time King **J** set out from Samaria   3393
8:16 In the fifth year of **J** son of Ahab king   3456
8:25 In the twelfth year of **J** son of Ahab king   3456
8:28 Ahaziah went with **J** son of Ahab to war   3456
8:28 The Arameans wounded **J;**   3456
8:29 so King **J** returned to Jezreel to recover   3456
8:29 of Judah went down to Jezreel to see **J** son   3456
9:14 the son of Nimshi, conspired against **J.**   3456
9:14 against Joram. (Now **J** and all Israel   3456
9:15 but King **J** had returned to Jezreel   3393
9:16 because **J** was resting there   3456
9:17 "Get a horseman," **J** ordered.   3393
9:21 "Hitch up my chariot," **J** ordered.   3393
9:21 **J** king of Israel and Ahaziah king   3393
9:22 When **J** saw Jehu he asked,   3393
9:23 **J** turned about and fled,   3393
9:24 Then Jehu drew his bow and shot **J**   3393
9:29 (In the eleventh year of **J** son of Ahab,   3456
1Ch 26:25 Jeshaiah his son, **J** his son,   3456
2Ch 22: 5 with **J** son of Ahab king of Israel to war   3393
22: 5 The Arameans wounded **J;**   3456
22: 6 of Judah went down to Jezreel to see **J** son   3393
22: 7 Through Ahaziah's visit to **J,**   3456
22: 7 he went out with Jehu to meet **J** son   3393

JORDAN (193) [JORDAN'S]
Ge 13:10 the whole plain of the **J** was well watered,   3720
13:11 the whole plain of the **J** and set out toward   3720
32:10 I had only my staff when I crossed this **J,**   3720
50:10 the **J,** they lamented loudly and bitterly;   3720

Ge	50:11	near the **J** is called Abel Mizraim.	3720
Nu	13:29	near the sea and along the **J**."	3720
	22: 1	the plains of Moab and camped along the **J**	3720
	26: 3	So on the plains of Moab by the **J** *across*	3720
	26:63	of Moab by the **J** *across from* Jericho.	3720
	31:12	by the **J** *across from* Jericho.	3720
	32: 5	Do not make us cross the **J**."	3720
	32:19	with them on the other side of the **J**,	3720
	32:19	to us on the east side of the **J**."	3720
	32:21	and if all of you will go armed over the **J**	3720
	32:29	over the **J** with you before the LORD,	3720
	32:32	be on this side of the **J**."	3720
	33:48	and camped on the plains of Moab by the **J**	3720
	33:49	the **J** from Beth Jeshimoth to Abel Shittim.	3720
	33:50	the **J** *across from* Jericho the LORD said	3720
	33:51	'When you cross the **J** into Canaan,	3720
	34:12	down along the **J** and end at the Salt Sea.	3720
	34:15	on the east side of the **J** of Jericho,	3720
	35: 1	On the plains of Moab by the **J** *across*	3720
	35:10	'When you cross the **J** into Canaan,	3720
	35:14	Give three on this side of the **J** and three	3720
	36:13	of Moab by the **J** *across from* Jericho.	3720
Dt	1: 1	to all Israel in the desert east of the **J**—	3720
	1: 5	East of the **J** in the territory of Moab,	3720
	2:29	until we cross the **J** into the land	3720
	3: 8	of the Amorites the territory east of the **J**,	3720
	3:17	Its western border was the **J** in the Arabah,	3720
	3:20	land that the LORD your God is giving	
		them, across the **J**.	3720
	3:25	over and see the good land beyond the **J**—	3720
	3:27	since you are not going to cross this **J**.	3720
	4:14	you are crossing **the J** to possess.	2025+9004S
	4:21	not cross the **J** and enter the good land	3720
	4:22	I will not cross the **J**;	3720
	4:26	from the land that you are crossing the **J**	3720
	4:41	Moses set aside three cities east of the **J**,	3720
	4:46	in the valley near Beth Peor east of the **J**,	3720
	4:47	the two Amorite kings east of the **J**,	3720
	4:49	and included all the Arabah east of the **J**,	3720
	6: 1	you are crossing **the J** to possess,	2025+9004S
	9: 1	You are now about to cross the **J** to go in	3720
	11: 8	the land that you are crossing **the J**	2025+9004S
	11:11	But the land you are crossing **the J**	2025+9004S
	11:30	these mountains are across the **J**,	3720
	11:31	to cross the **J** to enter and take possession	3720
	12:10	But you will cross the **J** and settle in	3720
	27: 2	When you have crossed the **J** into the land	3720
	27: 4	And when you have crossed the **J**,	3720
	27:12	When you have crossed the **J**,	3720
	30:18	in the land you are crossing the **J** to enter	3720
	31: 2	'You shall not cross the **J**.'	3720
	31:13	the land you are crossing the **J** to possess."	3720
	32:47	the land you are crossing the **J** to possess."	3720
Jos	1: 2	the **J** River into the land I am about to give	3720
	1:11	from now you will cross the **J** here to go in	3720
	1:14	the land that Moses gave you east of the **J**,	3720
	1:15	the LORD gave you east of the **J** toward	3720
	2: 7	on the road that leads to the fords of the **J**,	3720
	2:10	of the Amorites east of the **J**,	3720
	3: 1	from Shittim and went to the **J**,	3720
	3:11	the Lord of all the earth will go into the **J**	3720
	3:13	set foot in the **J**, its waters flowing	3720
	3:14	the people broke camp to cross the **J**,	3720
	3:15	the **J** is at flood stage all during harvest.	3720
	3:15	the ark reached the **J** and their feet touched	3720
	3:17	on dry ground in the middle of the **J**,	3720
	4: 1	finished crossing the **J**, the LORD said	3720
	4: 3	of the **J** from right where the priests stood	3720
	4: 5	into the middle of the **J**.	3720
	4: 7	the flow of the **J** was cut off before the ark	3720
	4: 7	When it crossed the **J**, the waters	3720
	4: 7	the waters of the **J** were cut off.	3720
	4: 8	the **J**, according to the number of the tribes	3720
	4: 9	in the middle of the **J** at the spot where	3720
	4:10	in the middle of the **J** until everything	3720
	4:16	of the Testimony to come up out of the **J**."	3720
	4:17	"Come up out of the **J**."	3720
	4:18	the waters of the **J** returned to their place	3720
	4:19	the people went up from the **J** and camped	3720
	4:20	twelve stones they had taken out of the **J**,	3720
	4:22	'Israel crossed the **J** on dry ground.'	3720
	4:23	For the LORD your God dried up the **J**	3720
	4:23	the **J** just what he had done to the Red Sea	NIH
	5: 1	of the **J** and all the Canaanite kings along	3720
	5: 1	how the LORD had dried up the **J** before	3720
	7: 7	across the **J** to deliver us into the hands of	3720
	7: 7	to stay on the other side of the **J**!	3720
	9: 1	when all the kings west of the **J** heard	3720
	9:10	the two kings of the Amorites east of the **J**	3720
	12: 1	over east of the **J**, from the Arnon Gorge	3720
	12: 7	on the west side of the **J**, from Baal Gad in	3720
	13: 8	that Moses had given them east of the **J**,	3720
	13:23	of the Reubenites was the bank of the **J**.	3720
	13:27	of Heshbon (the east side of the **J**,	3720
	13:32	in the plains of Moab across the **J** east	3720
	14: 3	of the **J** but had not granted the Levites	3720
	15: 5	the Salt Sea as far as the mouth of the **J**.	3720
	15: 5	the bay of the sea at the mouth of the **J**.	3720
	16: 1	The allotment for Joseph began at the **J**	3720
	16: 7	touched Jericho and came out at the **J**.	3720
	17: 5	and Bashan east of the **J**,	3720
	18: 7	on the east side of the **J**.	3720
	18:12	the **J**, passed the northern slope of Jericho	3720
	18:19	at the mouth of the **J** in the south.	3720
	18:20	The **J** formed the boundary on the eastern	3720
	19:22	and ended at the **J**.	3720
	19:33	to Lakkum and ending at the **J**.	3720

Jos	19:34	Asher on the west and the **J** on the east.	3720
	20: 8	of the **J** of Jericho they designated Bezer	3720
	22: 4	on the other side of the **J**.	3720
	22: 7	the west side of the **J** with their brothers.)	3720
	22:10	When they came to Geliloth near the **J** in	3720
	22:10	an imposing altar there by the **J**.	3720
	22:11	the border of Canaan at Geliloth near the **J**	3720
	22:25	the **J** a boundary between us and you—	3720
	23: 4	the **J** and the Great Sea in the west.	3720
	24: 8	of the Amorites who lived east of the **J**.	3720
	24:11	you crossed the **J** and came to Jericho.	3720
Jdg	3:28	taking possession of the fords of the **J**	3720
	5:17	Gilead stayed beyond the **J**.	3720
	6:33	the **J** and camped in the Valley of Jezreel.	NIH
	7:24	the Midianites and seize the waters of the **J**	3720
	7:24	the waters of the **J** as far as Beth Barah.	3720
	7:25	to Gideon, who was by the **J**.	3720
	8: 4	came to the **J** and crossed it.	3720
	10: 8	the Israelites on the east side of the **J**	3720
	10: 9	The Ammonites also crossed the **J** to fight	3720
	11:13	all the way to the **J**.	3720
	11:22	from the Jabbok and from the desert to the **J**.	3720
	12: 5	the fords of the **J** leading to Ephraim,	3720
	12: 6	and killed him at the fords of the **J**.	3720
1Sa	13: 7	even crossed the **J** to the land of Gad	3720
	31: 7	along the valley and those across the **J** saw	3720
2Sa	2:29	They crossed the **J**, continued through	3720
	10:17	crossed the **J** and went to Helam.	3720
	17:22	with him set out and crossed the **J**.	3720
	17:22	no one was left who had not crossed the **J**.	3720
	17:24	and Absalom crossed the **J** with all	3720
	19:15	the king returned and went as far as the **J**.	3720
	19:15	the king and bring him across the **J**.	3720
	19:17	They rushed to the **J**, where the king was.	3720
	19:18	When Shimei son of Gera crossed the **J**,	3720
	19:31	from Rogelim to cross the **J** with the king	3720
	19:36	the **J** with the king for a short distance,	3720
	19:39	So all the people crossed the **J**,	3720
	19:41	and his household across the **J**,	3720
	20: 2	by their king all the way from the **J**.	3720
	24: 5	After crossing the **J**, they camped	3720
1Ki	2: 8	When he came down to meet me at the **J**,	3720
	7:46	of the **J** between Succoth and Zarethan.	3720
	17: 3	in the Kerith Ravine, east of the **J**.	3720
	17: 5	east of the **J**, and stayed there.	3720
2Ki	2: 6	the LORD has sent me to the **J**."	3720
	2: 7	and Elisha had stopped at the **J**.	3720
	2:13	and stood on the bank of the **J**.	3720
	5:10	"Go, wash yourself seven times in the **J**,	3720
	5:14	and dipped himself in the **J** seven times,	3720
	6: 2	Let us go to the **J**, where each of us can get	3720
	6: 4	to the **J** and began to cut down trees.	3720
	7:15	They followed them as far as the **J**,	3720
	10:33	the **J** in all the land of Gilead (the region	3720
1Ch	6:78	the **J** east of Jericho they received Bezer in	3720
	12:15	It was they who crossed the **J** in	3720
	12:37	from east of the **J**, men of Reuben, Gad	3720
	19:17	he gathered all Israel and crossed the **J**;	3720
	26:30	of the **J** for all the work of the LORD and	3720
2Ch	4:17	of the **J** between Succoth and Zarethan.	3720
Job	40:23	the **J** should surge against his mouth.	3720
Ps	42: 6	the land of the **J**, the heights of Hermon—	3720
	114: 3	The sea looked and fled, the **J** turned back;	3720
	114: 5	Why was it, O sea, that you fled, O **J**,	3720
Isa	9: 1	by the way of the sea, along the **J**—	3720
Jer	12: 5	in the thickets by the **J**?	3720
Eze	47:18	along the **J** between Gilead and the land	3720
Zec	11: 3	the lush thicket of the **J** is ruined!	3720
Mt	3: 5	and the whole region of the **J**.	2674
	3: 6	they were baptized by him in the **J** River	2674
	3:13	Then Jesus came from Galilee to the **J** to	2674
	4:15	along the **J**, Galilee of the Gentiles—	2674
	4:25	and the region across the **J** followed him.	2674
	19: 1	of Judea to the other side of the **J**.	2674
Mk	1: 5	they were baptized by him in the **J** River.	2674
	1: 9	and was baptized by John in the **J**.	2674
	3: 8	the regions across the **J** and around Tyre	2674
	10: 1	into the region of Judea and across the **J**.	2674
Lk	3: 3	He went into all the country around the **J**,	2674
	4: 1	from the **J** and was led by the Spirit in	2674
Jn	1:28	at Bethany on the other side of the **J**,	2674
	3:26	with you on the other side of the **J**—	2674
	10:40	Then Jesus went back across the **J** to	2674

JORDAN'S (3) [JORDAN]

Jos	3: 8	'When you reach the edge of the **J** waters,	3720
Jer	49:19	"Like a lion coming up from **J** thickets to	3720
	50:44	Like a lion coming up from **J** thickets to	3720

JORIM (1)

Lk	3:29	the son *of* **J**, the son of Matthat,	*2733*

JORKEAM (1)

1Ch	2:44	and Raham the father of **J**.	3767

JORKOAM (KJV) See JORKEAM

JOSABAD (KJV) See JOZABAD

JOSAPHAT (KJV) See JEHOSHAPHAT

JOSE (KJV) See JOSHUA

JOSECH (1)

Lk	3:26	the son of Semein, the son *of* **J**,	*2738*

JOSEDECH (KJV) See JEHOZADAK

JOSEPH (237) [JOSEPH'S]

Ge	30:24	She named him **J**, and said,	3441
	30:25	After Rachel gave birth to **J**,	3441
	33: 2	and Rachel and **J** in the rear.	3441
	33: 7	Last of all came **J** and Rachel.	3441
	35:24	The sons of Rachel: **J** and Benjamin.	3441
	37: 2	**J**, a young man of seventeen,	3441
	37: 3	Now Israel loved **J** more than any	3441
	37: 5	**J** had a dream, and when he told it to	3441
	37:13	and Israel said to **J**, "As you know,	3441
	37:14	When **J** arrived at Shechem,	NIH
	37:17	So **J** went after his brothers	3441
	37:23	So when **J** came to his brothers,	3441
	37:28	his brothers pulled **J** up out of the cistern	3441
	37:29	to the cistern and saw that **J** was not there,	3441
	37:33	**J** has surely been torn to pieces."	3441
	37:36	the Midianites sold **J** in Egypt to Potiphar,	2257S
	39: 1	Now **J** had been taken down to Egypt.	3441
	39: 2	The LORD was with **J** and he prospered,	3441
	39: 4	**J** found favor in his eyes	3441
	39: 5	of the Egyptian because of **J**.	3441
	39: 6	with **J** in charge, he did not concern himself	2257S
	39: 6	Now **J** was well-built and handsome,	3441
	39: 7	a while his master's wife took notice of **J**	3441
	39:10	And though she spoke to **J** day after day,	3441
	39:20	But while **J** was there in the prison,	NIH
	39:22	the warden put **J** in charge of all those held	3441
	39:23	because the LORD was with **J**	2257S
	40: 3	in the same prison where **J** was confined.	3441
	40: 4	of the guard assigned them to **J**,	3441
	40: 6	When **J** came to them the next morning,	3441
	40: 8	Then **J** said to them,	3441
	40: 9	So the chief cupbearer told **J** his dream.	3441
	40:12	"This is what it means," **J** said to him.	3441
	40:16	When the chief baker saw that **J** had given	NIH
	40:16	he said to **J**, "I too had a dream:	3441
	40:18	"This is what it means," **J** said.	3441
	40:22	as **J** had said to them in his interpretation.	3441
	40:23	did not remember **J**; he forgot him.	3441
	41:14	So Pharaoh sent for **J**.	3441
	41:15	Pharaoh said to **J**, "I had a dream,	3441
	41:16	"I cannot do it," **J** replied to Pharaoh,	3441
	41:25	Then **J** said to Pharaoh, "The dreams of	3441
	41:39	Then Pharaoh said to **J**, "Since God has	3441
	41:41	So Pharaoh said to **J**, "I hereby put you	3441
	41:44	Then Pharaoh said to **J**, "I am Pharaoh,	3441
	41:45	Pharaoh gave **J** the name Zaphenath-Paneah	3441
	41:45	And **J** went throughout the land of Egypt.	3441
	41:46	**J** was thirty years old when he entered	3441
	41:46	And **J** went out from Pharaoh's presence	3441
	41:48	**J** collected all the food produced	NIH
	41:49	**J** stored up huge quantities of grain,	3441
	41:50	to **J** by Asenath daughter of Potiphera,	3441
	41:51	**J** named his firstborn Manasseh and said,	3441
	41:54	years of famine began, just as **J** had said.	3441
	41:55	"Go to **J** and do what he tells you."	3441
	41:56	**J** opened the storehouses and sold grain to	3441
	41:57	to Egypt to buy grain from **J**,	3441
	42: 6	Now **J** was the governor of the land,	3441
	42: 7	As soon as **J** saw his brothers,	3441
	42: 8	Although **J** recognized his brothers,	3441
	42:14	**J** said to them, "It is just as I told you:	3441
	42:18	On the third day, **J** said to them,	3441
	42:23	not realize that **J** could understand them,	3441
	42:25	**J** gave orders to fill their bags with grain,	3441
	42:36	**J** is no more and Simeon is no more,	3441
	43:15	to Egypt and presented themselves to **J**.	3441
	43:16	When **J** saw Benjamin with them,	3441
	43:17	The man did as **J** told him and took	3441
	43:26	When **J** came home,	3441
	43:30	**J** hurried out and looked for a place	3441
	44: 1	Now **J** gave these instructions to	NIH
	44: 2	And he did as **J** said.	3441
	44: 4	from the city when **J** said to his steward,	3441
	44:14	**J** was still in the house when Judah	3441
	44:15	**J** said to them, "What is this you have done?	3441
	44:17	But **J** said, "Far be it from me to do such	NIH
	45: 1	Then **J** could no longer control himself	3441
	45: 1	with **J** when he made himself known	3441
	45: 3	**J** said to his brothers, "I am **J**!	3441
	45: 3	Joseph said to his brothers, "I am **J**!	3441
	45: 4	**J** said to his brothers, "Come close to me."	3441
	45: 4	he said, "I am your brother **J**,	3441
	45: 9	'This is what your son **J** says:	3441
	45:17	Pharaoh said to **J**, "Tell your brothers,	3441
	45:21	**J** gave them carts, as Pharaoh had	3441
	45:26	They told him, "**J** is still alive!	3441
	45:27	when they told him everything **J** had said	3441
	45:27	the carts **J** had sent to carry him back,	3441
	45:28	My son **J** is still alive.	3441
	46:19	of Jacob's wife Rachel: **J** and Benjamin.	3441
	46:20	to **J** by Asenath daughter of Potiphera,	3441
	46:28	With the two sons who had been born to **J**	3441
	46:28	Now Jacob sent Judah ahead of him to **J**	3441
	46:29	**J** had his chariot made ready and went	3441
	46:29	As soon as **J** appeared before him,	NIH
	46:30	Israel said to **J**, "Now I am ready to die,	3441
	46:31	Then **J** said to his brothers and	3441
	47: 1	**J** went and told Pharaoh,	3441

Ge	47: 5	Pharaoh said to J, "Your father and	3441

Ge 47: 5 Pharaoh said to J, "Your father and 3441
47: 7 Then J brought his father Jacob in 3441
47:11 So J settled his father and his brothers 3441
47:12 J also provided his father and his brothers 3441
47:14 J collected all the money that was to 3441
47:15 all Egypt came to J and said, 3441
47:16 "Then bring your livestock," said J. 3441
47:17 So they brought their livestock to J, 3441
47:20 J bought all the land in Egypt for Pharaoh. 3441
47:21 and J reduced the people to servitude, NIH
47:23 J said to the people, "Now that I have 3441
47:26 So J established it as a law 3441
47:29 he called for his son J and said to him, 3441
47:31 Then J swore to him, and Israel NIH
48: 1 Some time later J was told, 3441
48: 2 "Your son J has come to you," 3441
48: 3 Jacob said to J, "God Almighty appeared 3441
48: 8 When Israel saw the sons of J, he asked, 3441
48: 9 J said to his father. 3441
48:10 So J brought his sons close to him, NIH
48:11 Israel said to J, "I never expected to see 3441
48:12 Then J removed them from Israel's knees 3441
48:13 And J took both of them, 3441
48:15 Then he blessed J and said, 3441
48:17 J saw his father placing his right hand 3441
48:18 J said to him, "No, my father, 3441
48:21 Then Israel said to J, "I am about to die. 3441
49:22 "J is a fruitful vine, a fruitful vine near a 3441
49:26 Let all these rest on the head of J, 3441
50: 1 J threw himself upon his father and wept 3441
50: 2 Then J directed the physicians 3441
50: 4 J said to Pharaoh's court, 3441
50: 7 So J went up to bury his father. 3441
50:10 and there J observed a seven-day period NIH
50:14 burying his father, J returned to Egypt, 3441
50:15 "What if J holds a grudge against us 3441
50:16 So they sent word to J, saying, 3441
50:17 'This is what you are to say to J: 3441
50:17 When their message came to him, J wept. 3441
50:19 But J said to them, "Don't be afraid. 3441
50:22 J stayed in Egypt, along with all 3441
50:24 J said to his brothers, "I am about to die. 3441
50:25 And J made the sons of Israel swear 3441
50:26 So J died at the age of a hundred and ten. 3441
Ex 1: 5 J was already in Egypt. 3441
1: 6 Now J and all his brothers and all 3441
1: 8 a new king, who did not know about J, 3441
13:19 of J with him because Joseph had made 3441
13:19 of Joseph with him because J had made NIH
Nu 1:10 from the sons of J: 3441
1:32 From the sons of J: 3441
13: 7 from the tribe of Issachar, Igal son of J; 3441
13:11 from the tribe of Manasseh (a tribe of J), 3441
26:28 of J by their clans through Manasseh 3441
26:37 the descendants of J by their clans. 3441
27: 1 to the clans of Manasseh son of J. 3441
32:33 and the half-tribe of Manasseh son of J 3441
34:23 from the tribe of Manasseh son of J; 3441
34:24 leader from the tribe of Ephraim son of J; NIH
36: 1 from the clans of the descendants of J, 3441
36: 5 of the descendants of J is saying is right. 3441
36:12 of the descendants of Manasseh son of J, 3441
Dt 27:12 Levi, Judah, Issachar, J and Benjamin. 3441
33:13 About J he said: "May the LORD bless 3441
33:16 Let all these rest on the head of J, 3441
Jos 14: 4 for the sons of J had become two tribes— 3441
16: 1 allotment for J began at the Jordan 1201+3441
16: 4 the descendants of J, 3441
17: 2 of Manasseh son of J by their clans. 3441
17:14 The people of J said to Joshua, 3441
17:16 The people of J replied, 3441
17:17 But Joshua said to the house of J— 3441
18: 5 the south and the house of J in its territory 3441
18:11 between the tribes of Judah and J: 1201+3441
Jdg 1:22 Now the house of J attacked Bethel, 3441
1:35 the power of the house of J increased, 3441
2Sa 19:20 as the first of the whole house of J to come 3441
1Ki 11:28 of the whole labor force of the house of J. 3441
1Ch 2: 2 J, Benjamin, Naphtali, Gad and Asher. 3441
5: 1 as firstborn were given to the sons of J 3441
5: 2 the rights of the firstborn belonged to J)— 3441
7:29 The descendants of J son of Israel lived 3441
25: 2 Zaccur, J, Nethaniah and Asarelah. 3441
25: 9 fell to J, his sons and relatives, 3441
Ezr 10:42 Shallum, Amariah and J. 3441
Ne 12:14 of Malluch's, Jonathan; of Shecaniah's, J; 3441
Ps 77:15 the descendants of Jacob and J. 3441
78:67 Then he rejected the tents of J, 3441
80: 1 you who lead J like a flock; 3441
81: 5 for J when he went out against Egypt, 3388
105:17 sent a man before them—J, sold as a slave. 3441
Eze 37:16 to J and all the house of Israel associated 3441
37:19 I am going to take the stick of J— 3441
47:13 with two portions for J. 3441
48:32 the gate of J, the gate of Benjamin, 3441
Am 5: 6 or he will sweep through the house of J 3441
5:15 have mercy on the remnant of J. 3441
6: 6 but you do not grieve over the ruin of J. 3441
Ob 1:18 of Jacob will be a fire and the house of J 3441
Zec 10: 6 of Judah and save the house of J. 3441
Mt 1:16 and Jacob the father of J 2737
1:18 Mary was pledged to be married to J, 2737
1:19 Because J her husband was a righteous man 2737
1:20 "J son of David, do not be afraid to take 2737
1:24 When J woke up, he did what the angel 2737
2:13 angel of the Lord appeared to J in a dream. 2737
2:19 angel of the Lord appeared in a dream to J 2737

Mt 13:55 and aren't his brothers James, J, 2737
27:57 a rich man from Arimathea, named J, 2737
27:59 J took the body, wrapped it in a clean linen 2737
Mk 6: 3 and the brother of James, J, Judas 2736
15:43 J of Arimathea, a prominent member of 2737
15:45 he gave the body to J. 2737
15:46 So J bought some linen cloth, NIG
Lk 1:27 pledged to be married to a man named J, 2737
2: 4 So J also went up from the town 2737
2:16 So they hurried off and found Mary and J, 2737
2:22 J and Mary took him to Jerusalem NIG
2:39 When J and Mary had done everything NIG
3:23 He was the son, so it was thought, of J, 2737
3:24 the son of Jannai, the son of J, 2737
3:30 the son of J, the son of Jonam, 2737
23:50 Now there was a man named J, 2737
23:55 from Galilee followed J and saw the tomb 899S
Jn 1:45 Jesus of Nazareth, the son of J." 2737
4: 5 of ground Jacob had given to his son J. 2737
6:42 They said, "Is this not Jesus, the son of J, 2737
19:38 J of Arimathea asked Pilate for the body 2737
19:38 Now J was a disciple of Jesus, NIG
Ac 1:23 J called Barsabbas (also known as Justus) 2737
4:36 a Levite from Cyprus, 2737
7: 9 "Because the patriarchs were jealous of J, 2737
7:10 He gave J wisdom and enabled him 899S
7:13 J told his brothers who he was, 2737
7:14 J sent for his father Jacob 2737
7:18 another king, who knew nothing about J, 2737
Heb 11:22 By faith J, when his end was near, 2737
Rev 7: 8 from the tribe of J 12,000, 2737

JOSEPH'S (24) [JOSEPH]

Ge 37:31 Then they got J robe, 3441
39: 6 So he left in J care everything he had; 3441
39:20 J master took him and put him in prison, 3441
39:23 to anything under J care, 2257S
41:42 from his finger and put it on J finger. 3441
42: 3 of J brothers went down to buy grain 3441
42: 4 Jacob did not send Benjamin, J brother, 3441
42: 6 So when J brothers arrived, 3441
43:17 and took the men to J house. 3441
43:19 So they went up to J steward and spoke 3441
43:24 The steward took the men into J house, 3441
43:25 They prepared their gifts for J arrival 3441
43:34 portions were served to them from J table, 2257S
45:16 that J brothers had come, 3441
46: 4 And J own hand will close your eyes." 3441
50: 8 besides all the members of J household 3441
50:15 J brothers saw that their father was dead, 3441
50:23 were placed at birth on J knees. 3441
Jos 17: 1 for the tribe of Manasseh as J firstborn. 3441
24:32 And J bones, which the Israelites had brought up from Egypt, 3441
24:32 the inheritance of J descendants. 3441
Lk 4:22 "Isn't this J son?" 2737
Ac 7:13 and Pharaoh learned about J family. 2737
Heb 11:21 blessed each of J sons, 2737

JOSES (3)

Mt 27:56 Mary the mother of James and J, 2736
Mk 15:40 the mother of James the younger and of J, 2736
15:47 the mother of J saw where he was laid. 2736

JOSHAH (1)

1Ch 4:34 Meshobab, Jamlech, J son of Amaziah, 3459

JOSHAPHAT (2)

1Ch 11:43 Hanan son of Maacah, J the Mithnite, 3461
15:24 Shebaniah, J, Nethanel, Amasai, 3461

JOSHAVIAH (1)

1Ch 11:46 Jeribai and J the sons of Elnaam, 3460

JOSHBEKASHAH (2)

1Ch 25: 4 J, Mallothi, Hothir and Mahazioth, 3792
25:24 the seventeenth to J, 3792

JOSHEB-BASSHEBETH (1)

2Sa 23: 8 J, a Tahkemonite, was chief of the Three; 3783

JOSHIBIAH (1)

1Ch 4:35 Jehu son of J, the son of Seraiah, 3458

JOSHUA (218) [HOSHEA]

Ex 17: 9 Moses said to J, "Choose some of our men 3397
17:10 So J fought the Amalekites 3397
17:13 So J overcame the Amalekite army with 3397
17:14 and make sure that J hears it, 3397
24:13 Then Moses set out with J his aide. 3397
32:17 J heard the noise of the people shouting, 3397
33:11 but his young aide J son of Nun did 3397
Nu 11:28 J son of Nun, who had been Moses' aide 3397
13:16 Moses gave Hoshea son of Nun the name J. 3397
14: 6 J son of Nun and Caleb son of Jephunneh, 3397
14:30 except Caleb son of Jephunneh and J son 3397
14:38 only J son of Nun and Caleb son 3397
26:65 of Jephunneh and J son of Nun. 3397
27:18 "Take J son of Nun, a man in whom 3397
27:22 He took J and had him stand 3397
32:12 of Jephunneh the Kenizzite and J son 3397

Nu 32:28 to Eleazar the priest and J son of Nun and 3397
34:17 Eleazar the priest and J son of Nun. 3397
Dt 1:38 your assistant, J son of Nun, will enter it. 3397
3:21 At that time I commanded J: 3397
3:28 But commission J, and encourage 3397
31: 3 J also will cross over ahead of you, 3397
31: 7 Then Moses summoned J and said to him 3397
31:14 Call J and present yourselves at the Tent 3397
31:14 J came and presented themselves at 3397
31:23 The LORD gave this command to J son 3397
32:44 with J son of Nun and spoke all the words 2107
34: 9 Now J son of Nun was filled with 3397
Jos 1: 1 the LORD said to J son of Nun, 3397
1:10 So J ordered the officers of the people: 3397
1:12 and the half-tribe of Manasseh, J said, 3397
1:16 Then they answered J, 3397
2: 1 Then J son of Nun secretly sent two spies 3397
2:23 forded the river and came to J son of Nun 3397
2:24 to J, "The LORD has surely given 3397
3: 1 the morning J and all the Israelites set out 3397
3: 5 J told the people, "Consecrate yourselves, 3397
3: 6 J said to the priests, "Take up the ark 3397
3: 7 And the LORD said to J, "Today I will begin 3397
3: 9 J said to the Israelites, "Come here and 3397
4: 1 crossing the Jordan, the LORD said to J, 3397
4: 4 So J called together the twelve men 3397
4: 8 the Israelites did as J commanded them. 3397
4: 9 J set up the twelve stones that had been in 3397
4:10 the LORD had commanded J was done 3397
4:10 just as Moses had directed J. 3397
4:14 That day the LORD exalted J in the sight 3397
4:15 Then the LORD said to J, 3397
4:17 So J commanded the priests, 3397
4:20 And J set up at Gilgal the twelve stones 3397
5: 2 At that time the LORD said to J, 3397
5: 3 So J made flint knives and circumcised 3397
5: 7 and these were the ones J circumcised. 3397
5: 9 Then the LORD said to J, 3397
5:13 Now when J was near Jericho, 3397
5:13 J went up to him and asked, 3397
5:14 J fell facedown to the ground in reverence, 3397
5:15 And J did so. 3397
6: 2 Then the LORD said to J, "See, 3397
6: 6 So J son of Nun called the priests and said 3397
6: 8 When J had spoken to the people, 3397
6:10 But J had commanded the people, 3397
6:12 J got up early the next morning and 3397
6:16 J commanded the people, "Shout! 3397
6:22 J said to the two men who had spied out 3397
6:25 But J spared Rahab the prostitute, 3397
6:25 the men J had sent as spies to Jericho— 3397
6:27 that time J pronounced this solemn oath: 3397
6:27 So the LORD was with J, 3397
7: 2 Now J sent men from Jericho to Ai, 3397
7: 3 When they returned to J, they said, 3397
7: 6 Then J tore his clothes and fell facedown 3397
7: 7 And J said, "Ah, Sovereign LORD, 3397
7:10 The LORD said to J, "Stand up! 3397
7:16 next morning J had Israel come forward 3397
7:18 J had his family come forward man NIH
7:19 Then J said to Achan, "My son, 3397
7:22 So J sent messengers, 3397
7:23 brought them to J and all the Israelites 3397
7:24 Then J, together with all Israel, 3397
7:25 J said, "Why have you brought this trouble 3397
8: 1 the LORD said to J, "Do not be afraid; 3397
8: 3 So J and the whole army moved out 3397
8: 9 Then J sent them off, 3397
8: 9 but J spent that night with the people. 3397
8:10 the next morning J mustered his men, 3397
8:12 J had taken about three thousand men NIH
8:13 That night J went into the valley. 3397
8:15 J and all Israel let themselves 3397
8:16 and they pursued J and were lured away 3397
8:18 Then the LORD said to J, 3397
8:18 So J held out his javelin toward Ai. 3397
8:21 For when J and all Israel saw that 3397
8:23 the king of Ai alive and brought him to J. 3397
8:26 For J did not draw back the hand 3397
8:27 as the LORD had instructed J. 3397
8:28 So J burned Ai and made it a permanent 3397
8:29 J ordered them to take his body from 3397
8:30 Then J built on Mount Ebal an altar to 3397
8:32 J copied on stones the law of Moses, NIH
8:34 J read all the words of the law— NIH
8:35 that J did not read to the whole assembly 3397
9: 2 they came together to make war against J 3397
9: 3 of Gibeon heard what J had done 3397
9: 6 Then they went to J in the camp at Gilgal 3397
9: 8 "We are your servants," they said to J. 3397
9: 8 But J asked, "Who are you and 3397
9:15 Then J made a treaty of peace with them 3397
9:22 Then J summoned the Gibeonites and said, 3397
9:24 They answered J, "Your servants were 3397
9:26 J saved them from the Israelites, NIH
10: 1 that J had taken Ai and totally destroyed it, 3397
10: 4 "because it has made peace with J and 3397
10: 6 then sent word to J in the camp at Gilgal: 3397
10: 7 So J marched up from Gilgal, 3397
10: 8 The LORD said to J, 3397
10: 9 J took them by surprise. 3397
10:12 J said to the LORD in the presence 3397
10:15 Then J returned with all Israel to the camp 3397
10:17 When J was told that the five kings 3397
10:20 So J and the Israelites destroyed them completely— 3397

Jos	10:21	The whole army then returned safely to J	3397
	10:22	J said, "Open the mouth of the cave	3397
	10:24	When they had brought these kings to J,	3397
	10:25	J said to them, "Do not be afraid;	3397
	10:26	Then J struck and killed the kings	3397
	10:27	At sunset J gave the order	3397
	10:28	That day J took Makkedah.	3397
	10:29	Then J and all Israel with him moved on	3397
	10:30	and everyone in it J put to the sword.	NIH
	10:31	Then J and all Israel with him moved on	3397
	10:32	and J took it on the second day.	NIH
	10:33	but J defeated him and his army—	3397
	10:34	Then J and all Israel with him moved on	3397
	10:36	Then J and all Israel with him went up	3397
	10:38	Then J and all Israel with him turned	3397
	10:40	So J subdued the whole region,	3397
	10:41	J subdued them from Kadesh Barnea	3397
	10:42	All these kings and their lands J conquered	3397
	10:43	Then J returned with all Israel to the camp	3397
	11: 6	The LORD said to J, "Do not be afraid	3397
	11: 7	So J and his whole army came	3397
	11: 9	J did to them as the LORD had directed:	3397
	11:10	that time J turned back and captured Hazor	3397
	11:12	J took all these royal cities and their kings	3397
	11:13	except Hazor, which J burned.	3397
	11:15	so Moses commanded J, and Joshua did it;	3397
	11:15	so Moses commanded Joshua, and J did it;	3397
	11:16	So J took this entire land:	3397
	11:18	J waged war against all these kings for	3397
	11:21	At that time J went and destroyed	3397
	11:21	J totally destroyed them and their towns.	3397
	11:23	So J took the entire land,	3397
	12: 7	the land that J and the Israelites conquered	3397
	12: 7	which rises toward Seir (their lands J gave	3397
	13: 1	J was old and well advanced in years,	3397
	14: 1	son of Nun and the heads of	3397
	14: 6	the men of Judah approached J at Gilgal,	3397
	14:13	Then J blessed Caleb son of Jephunneh	3397
	15:13	J gave to Caleb son of Jephunneh	3397
	17: 4	son of Nun, and the leaders and said,	3397
	17: 4	So J gave them an inheritance along with	NIH
	17:14	The people of Joseph said to J,	3397
	17:15	"If you are so numerous," J answered,	3397
	17:17	But J said to the house of Joseph—	3397
	18: 3	So J said to the Israelites:	3397
	18: 8	the land, J instructed them, "Go and make	3397
	18: 9	and returned to J in the camp at Shiloh.	3397
	18:10	J then cast lots for them in Shiloh in	3397
	19:49	the Israelites gave J son of Nun	3397
	19:51	son of Nun and the heads of	3397
	20: 1	Then the LORD said to J:	3397
	21: 1	Eliezer the priest, J son of Nun,	3397
	22: 1	Then J summoned the Reubenites,	3397
	22: 6	Then J blessed them and sent them away,	3397
	22: 7	to the other half of the tribe J gave land on	3397
	22: 7	When J sent them home, he blessed them,	3397
	23: 1	J, by then old and well advanced in years,	3397
	24: 1	Then J assembled all the tribes of Israel	3397
	24: 2	J said to all the people, "This is what	3397
	24:19	J said to the people, "You are not able to	3397
	24:21	But the people said to J, "No!	3397
	24:22	Then J said, "You are witnesses	3397
	24:23	said J, "throw away the foreign gods	NIH
	24:24	And the people said to J,	3397
	24:25	that day J made a covenant for the people,	3397
	24:26	And J recorded these things in the Book of	3397
	24:28	Then J sent the people away,	3397
	24:29	After these things, J son of Nun,	3397
	24:31	Israel served the LORD throughout the lifetime of J	3397
Jdg	1: 1	After the death of J, the Israelites asked	3397
	2: 6	After J had dismissed the Israelites,	3397
	2: 7	The people served the LORD throughout the lifetime of J	3397
	2: 8	J son of Nun, the servant of the LORD,	3397
	2:21	before them any of the nations J left	3397
	2:23	at once by giving them into the hands of J.	3397
1Sa	6:14	to the field of J of Beth Shemesh,	3397
	6:18	is a witness to this day in the field of J	3397
1Ki	16:34	the word of the LORD spoken by J son	3397
2Ki	23: 8	at the entrance to the Gate of J,	3397
1Ch	7:27	Nun his son and J his son.	3397
Ne	8:17	the days of J son of Nun until that day,	3800
Hag	1: 1	and to J son of Jehozadak, the high priest:	3397
	1:12	J son of Jehozadak, the high priest,	3397
	1:14	and the spirit of J son of Jehozadak,	3397
	2: 2	governor of Judah, to J son of Jehozadak,	3397
	2: 4	'Be strong, O J son of Jehozadak.	3397
Zec	3: 1	Then he showed me J the high priest	3397
	3: 3	Now J was dressed in filthy clothes	3397
	3: 4	Then he said to J, "See, I have taken	2257S
	3: 6	of the LORD gave this charge to J:	3397
	3: 8	O high priest J and your associates seated	3397
	3: 9	See, the stone I have set in front of J!	3397
	6:11	J son of Jehozadak.	3397
Lk	3:29	the son of J, the son of Eliezer,	2652
Ac	7:45	our fathers under J brought it with them	2652
Heb	4: 8	For if J had given them rest,	2652

JOSIAH (56) [JOSIAH'S]

1Ki	13: 2	'A son named J will be born to the house	3288
2Ki	21:24	and they made J his son king in his place.	3288
	21:26	And J his son succeeded him as king.	3288
	22: 1	J was eight years old when he became king	3288
	22: 3	King J sent the secretary,	3288
	23: 8	J brought all the priests from the towns	NIH

2Ki	23:11	J then burned the chariots dedicated to	NIH
	23:14	J smashed the sacred stones and cut down	NIH
	23:16	Then J looked around, and when he saw	3288
	23:19	J removed and defiled all the shrines at	3288
	23:20	J slaughtered all the priests	NIH
	23:23	But in the eighteenth year of King J,	3288
	23:24	J got rid of the mediums and spiritists,	3288
	23:25	Neither before nor after J was there a king	2257S
	23:29	While J was king, Pharaoh Neco of Egypt	2257S
	23:29	King J marched out to meet him in battle,	3288
	23:30	of J and anointed him and made him king	3288
	23:34	Pharaoh Neco made Eliakim son of J king	3288
	23:34	of Josiah king in place of his father J	3288
1Ch	3:14	Amon his son, J his son.	3288
	3:15	The sons of J: Johanan the firstborn,	3288
2Ch	33:25	and they made J his son king in his place.	3288
	34: 1	J was eight years old when he became king	3288
	34:33	J removed all the detestable idols from all	3288
	35: 1	J celebrated the Passover to the LORD	3288
	35: 7	J provided for all the lay people	3288
	35:16	as King J had ordered.	3288
	35:18	celebrated such a Passover as did J,	3288
	35:20	all this, when J had set the temple in order,	3288
	35:20	and J marched out to meet him in battle.	3288
	35:22	J, however, would not turn away	3288
	35:23	Archers shot King J, and he told his officers	3288
	35:25	Jeremiah composed laments for J,	3288
	35:25	and women singers commemorate J in	3288
	36: 1	of J and made him king in Jerusalem	3288
Jer	1: 2	the reign of J son of Amon king of Judah,	3288
	1: 3	of Jehoiakim son of J king of Judah,	3288
	1: 3	of Zedekiah son of J king of Judah,	3288
	3: 6	During the reign of King J,	3288
	22:11	the LORD says about Shallum son of J,	3288
	22:18	about Jehoiakim son of J king of Judah:	3288
	25: 1	the fourth year of Jehoiakim son of J king	3288
	25: 3	the thirteenth year of J son of Amon king	3288
	26: 1	of J king of Judah, this word came from	3288
	27: 1	in the reign of Zedekiah son of J king	3288
	35: 1	of Jehoiakim son of J king of Judah:	3288
	36: 1	the fourth year of Jehoiakim son of J king	3288
	36: 2	to you in the reign of J till now.	3288
	36: 9	of the fifth year of Jehoiakim son of J king	3288
	37: 1	Zedekiah son of J was made king of Judah	3288
	45: 1	the fourth year of Jehoiakim son of J king	3288
	46: 2	the fourth year of Jehoiakim son of J king	3288
Zep	1: 1	the reign of J son of Amon king of Judah:	3288
Zec	6:10	Go the same day to the house of J son	3287
Mt	1:10	Amon the father of J,	2739
	1:11	and J the father of Jeconiah	2739

JOSIAH'S (5) [JOSIAH]

2Ki	23:28	As for the other events of J reign,	3288
	23:30	J servants brought his body in a chariot	2257S
2Ch	34: 8	In the eighteenth year of J reign,	2257S
	35:19	In the eighteenth year of J reign.	3288
	35:26	The other events of J reign and his acts	3288

JOSIAS (KJV) See JOSIAH

JOSIBIAH (KJV) See JOSHIBIAH

JOSIPHIAH (1)

Ezr	8:10	of J, and with him 160 men;	3442

JOSTLE (1) [JOSTLED]

Joel	2: 8	They do not j each other;	1895

JOSTLED (1) [JOSTLE]

Ge	25:22	The babies j each other within her,	8368

JOT (KJV) See SMALLEST LETTER

JOTBAH (1)

2Ki	21:19	daughter of Haruz; she was from J.	3513

JOTBATH (KJV) See JOTBATHAH

JOTBATHAH (3)

Nu	33:33	They left Hor Haggidgad and camped at J.	3514
	33:34	They left J and camped at Abronah.	3514
Dt	10: 7	to Gudgodah and on to J,	3514

JOTHAM (27) [JOTHAM'S]

Jdg	9: 5	But J, the youngest son of Jerub-Baal	3462
	9: 7	When J was told about this,	3462
	9:21	Then J fled, escaping to Beer,	3462
	9:57	The curse of J son of Jerub-Baal came	3462
2Ki	15: 5	J the king's son had charge of the palace	3462
	15: 7	And J his son succeeded him as king.	3462
	15:30	in the twentieth year of J son of Uzziah.	3462
	15:32	J son of Uzziah king of Judah began	3462
	15:35	J rebuilt the Upper Gate of the temple of	2085S
	15:38	J rested with his fathers and was buried	3462
	16: 1	Ahaz son of J king of Judah began	3462
1Ch	2:47	The sons of Jahdai: Regem, J, Geshan,	3462
	3:12	Azariah his son, J his son,	3462
	5:17	of J king of Judah and Jeroboam king	3462
2Ch	26:21	J his son had charge of the palace	3462
	26:23	And J his son succeeded him as king.	3462

2Ch	27: 1	J was twenty-five years old	3462
	27: 3	J rebuilt the Upper Gate of the temple of	2085S
	27: 5	J made war on the king of the Ammonites	2085S
	27: 6	J grew powerful because he walked	3462
	27: 9	J rested with his fathers and was buried in	3462
Isa	1: 1	J, Ahaz and Hezekiah, kings of Judah.	3462
	7: 1	When Ahaz son of J, the son of Uzziah,	3462
Hos	1: 1	J, Ahaz and Hezekiah, kings of Judah,	3462
Mic	1: 1	of J, Ahaz and Hezekiah, kings of Judah—	3462
Mt	1: 9	Uzziah the father of J,	2718
	1: 9	J the father of Ahaz,	2718

JOTHAM'S (2) [JOTHAM]

2Ki	15:36	As for the other events of J reign,	3462
2Ch	27: 7	The other events in J reign,	3462

JOURNEY (56) [JOURNEYED, JOURNEYS]

Ge	24:21	or not the LORD had made his j successful.	2006
	24:27	the LORD has led me on the j to	2006
	24:40	with you and make your j a success,	2006
	24:42	to the j on which I have come.	2006
	24:56	the LORD has granted success to my j.	2006
	28:20	on this j I am taking and will give me food	2006
	29: 1	Then Jacob continued on his j and	5951+8079
	30:36	Then he put a three-day j between himself	2006
	42:25	and to give them provisions for their j.	2006
	42:38	harm comes to him on the j you are taking,	2006
	45:21	he also gave them provisions for their j.	2006
	45:23	and bread and other provisions for his j.	2006
Ex	3:18	Let us take a three-day j into the desert	2006
	5: 3	Now let us take a three-day j into	2006
	8:27	We must take a three-day j into the desert	2006
Nu	9:10	because of a dead body or are away on a j,	2006
	9:13	not on a j fails to celebrate the Passover,	2006
	33: 1	Here are the stages in the j of the Israelites	5023
	33: 2	Moses recorded the stages in their j.	5023
	33: 2	This is their j by stages:	5023
Dt	1:33	who went ahead of you on your j,	2006
	2: 7	over your j through this vast desert.	2143
	25:18	they met you on your j	2006
	28:68	on a j I said you should never make again.	2006
Jos	5: 5	the desert during the j from Egypt had not.	2006
	9:11	'Take provisions for your j;	2006
	9:13	worn out by the very long j."	2006
	24:17	on our entire j and among all the nations	2006
Jdg	18: 5	to learn whether our j will be successful."	2006
	18: 6	Your j has the LORD's approval."	2006
1Ki	13:26	who had brought him back from his j	2006
	19: 4	he himself went a day's j into the desert.	2006
	19: 7	for the j is too much for you."	2006
Ezr	7: 9	He had begun his j from Babylon on the	5092
	8:21	before our God and ask him for a safe j	2006
Ne	2: 6	asked me, "How long will your j take,	4544
Job	16:22	A few years will pass before I go on the j	784
Pr	7:19	he has gone on a long j.	2006
Isa	35: 8	The unclean will not j on it;	6296
Am	5: 5	do not go to Gilgal, do not j to Beersheba.	6296
Mic	6: 5	Remember [your j] from Shittim to Gilgal,	NIH
Mt	10:10	the j, or extra tunic, or sandals or a staff;	3847
	21:33	to some farmers and went away on a j.	623
	25:14	"Again, it will be like a man going on a j,	623
	25:15	Then he went on his j.	623
Mk	6: 8	"Take nothing for the j except a staff—	3847
	12: 1	to some farmers and went away on a j.	623
Lk	9: 3	He told them: "Take nothing for the j—	3847
	11: 6	a friend of mine on a j has come to me,	3847
Jn	4: 6	and Jesus, tired as he was from the j,	3845
Ac	9: 3	As he neared Damascus on his j,	1877+4513
	9:27	He told them how Saul on his j had seen	3847
	10: 9	the following day as they were on their j	3844
	16: 3	Paul wanted to take him along on the j,	NIG
Ro	15:24	to have you assist me on my j there,	4636
1Co	16: 6	so that you can help me on my j,	4636

JOURNEYED (3) [JOURNEY]

Ex	12:37	The Israelites j from Rameses to Succoth.	5825
1Sa	31:12	all their valiant men j through the night	2143
Job	38:16	"Have you j to the springs of the sea	995

JOURNEYS (1) [JOURNEY]

Ac	26:12	"On one of these j I was going to Damascus	4005S

JOWLS (1)

Dt	18: 3	the shoulder, the j and the inner parts.	4305

JOY (218) [ENJOY, ENJOYED, ENJOYING, ENJOYMENT, ENJOYS, JOYFUL, JOYOUS, JOYFULLY, OVERJOYED, REJOICE, REJOICED, REJOICES, REJOICING]

Ge	31:27	so I could send you away with j	8525
Lev	9:24	they shouted for j and fell facedown.	8264
Dt	16:15	and your j will be complete.	8524
Jdg	9:19	may Abimelech be your j,	8523
1Ch	12:40	cattle and sheep, for there was j in Israel.	8525
	16:27	strength and j in his dwelling place.	2530
	16:33	they will sing for j before the LORD,	8264
	29:17	And now I have seen with j	8525
	29:22	with great j in the presence of the LORD	8525
2Ch	30:26	There was great j in Jerusalem,	8525
Ezr	3:12	while many others shouted for j.	8525

Ezr	3:13	the sound of the shouts of **j** from the sound	8525
	6:16	the dedication of the house of God with **j**.	10250
	6:22	with **j** the Feast of Unleavened Bread,	8525
	6:22	because the LORD had **filled** them with **j**	8523
Ne	8:10	for the **j** of the LORD is your strength."	2530
	8:12	of food and to celebrate with great **j**,	8525
	8:17	And their **j** was very great.	8525
	12:43	because God had given them great **j**.	8523+8525
Est	8:16	the Jews it was a time of happiness and **j**,	8525
	8:17	there was **j** and gladness among the Jews,	8525
	9:17	and made it a day of feasting and **j**.	8525
	9:18	and made it a day of feasting and **j**.	8525
	9:19	of the month of Adar as a day of **j**	8525
	9:22	when their sorrow was turned into **j**	8525
	9:22	of feasting and **j** and giving presents	8525
Job	3: 7	may no **shout of j** be heard in it.	8265
	6:10	my **j** in unrelenting pain—	6134
	8:21	and your lips with **shouts of j**.	9558
	9:25	they fly away without a glimpse of **j**.	3208
	10:20	from me so I can **have** a moment's	1158
	20: 5	the **j** of the godless lasts but a moment.	8525
	33:26	he sees God's face and **shouts for j**;	9558
	38: 7	and all the angels **shouted for j**?	8131
Ps	4: 7	You have filled my heart with greater **j**	8525
	5:11	let them ever sing for **j**;	8264
	16:11	you will fill me with **j** in your presence,	8525
	19: 8	**giving j** to the heart.	8523
	20: 5	We will **shout for j** when you are victorious	8264
	21: 1	How great is his **j** in the victories you give!	1635
	21: 6	made him glad with the **j** of his presence.	8525
	27: 6	I will sacrifice with **shouts of j**;	9558
	28: 7	My heart **leaps for j**	6600
	30:11	and clothed me with **j**,	8525
	33: 3	play skillfully, and **shout for j**.	9558
	35:27	in my vindication shout for **j** and gladness;	8264
	42: 4	with **shouts of j** and thanksgiving	7754+8262
	43: 4	to God, my **j** and my delight.	8525
	45: 7	by anointing you with the oil of **j**.	8607
	45:15	They are led in with **j** and gladness;	8525
	47: 1	shout to God with cries of **j**.	8262
	47: 5	God has ascended amid **shouts of j**,	9558
	48: 2	the **j** of the whole earth.	5375
	51: 8	Let me hear **j** and gladness;	8607
	51:12	Restore to me the **j** of your salvation.	8607
	65: 8	you **call forth songs of j**.	8264
	65:13	they **shout for j** and sing.	8131
	66: 1	**Shout with j** to God, all the earth!	8131
	67: 4	May the nations be glad and **sing for j**,	8264
	71:23	My lips will **shout for j**	8264
	81: 1	**Sing for j** to God our strength;	8264
	86: 4	**Bring j** to your servant, for to you,	8523
	89:12	Tabor and Hermon **sing for j** at your name.	8264
	90:14	we may **sing for j** and be glad all our days.	8264
	92: 4	I **sing for j** at the works of your hands.	8264
	94:19	your consolation **brought j** to my soul.	9130
	95: 1	Come, let us **sing for j** to the LORD;	8264
	96:12	all the trees of the forest will **sing for j**;	8264
	97:11	the righteous and **j** on the upright in heart.	8525
	98: 4	**Shout for j** to the LORD, all the earth,	8131
	98: 6	**shout for j** before the LORD, the King.	8131
	98: 8	let the mountains **sing together for j**;	8264
	100: 1	**Shout for j** to the LORD, all the earth.	8131
	105:43	his chosen ones with **shouts of j**;	8262
	106: 5	that I may **share** in the **j** of your nation	8523+8525
	107:22	and tell of his works with **songs of j**.	8262
	118:15	**Shouts of j** and victory resound in the tents	8262
	119:111	they are the **j** of my heart.	8607
	126: 2	our tongues with **songs of j**.	8262
	126: 3	and we are **filled with j**.	8524
	126: 5	in tears will reap with **songs of j**.	8262
	126: 6	will return with **songs of j**,	8262
	132: 9	may your saints **sing for j**."	8264
	132:16	and her saints will **ever sing for j**.	8264+8264
	137: 3	our tormentors demanded songs of **j**;	8525
	137: 6	I do not consider Jerusalem my highest **j**.	8525
	149: 5	in this honor and **sing for j** on their beds.	8264
Pr	10: 1	A wise son **brings j** to his father,	8523
	10:28	The prospect of the righteous is **j**,	8525
	11:10	the wicked perish, there are **shouts of j**.	8262
	12:20	but **j** for those who promote peace.	8525
	14:10	and no one else can share its **j**.	8525
	14:13	and **j** may end in grief.	8525
	15:20	A wise son **brings j** to his father,	8523
	15:23	A man finds **j** in giving an apt reply—	8525
	15:30	A cheerful look **brings j** to the heart,	8523
	17:21	there is no **j** for the father of a fool.	8523
	21:15	it brings **j** to the righteous but terror	8525
	23:24	father of a righteous man has great **j**;	1635+1635
	27: 9	Perfume and incense **bring j** to the heart,	8523
	27:11	Be wise, my son, and **bring j** to my heart;	8523
	29: 3	A man who loves wisdom **brings j**	8055
Ecc	8:15	Then I will accompany him in his work all	2085S
	11: 9	and let your heart **give** you **j** in the days	3512
Isa	9: 3	the nation and increased their **j**;	8525
	12: 3	With **j** you will draw water from the wells	8607
	12: 6	Shout aloud and **sing for j**, people of Zion,	8264
	16: 9	The **shouts of j** over your ripened fruit and	2116
	16:10	**J** and gladness are taken away from	8525
	22:13	But see, there is **j** and revelry,	8607
	24:11	all **j** turns to gloom,	8525
	24:14	They raise their voices, they **shout for j**;	8264
	26:19	wake up and **shout for j**.	8264
	35: 2	it will rejoice greatly and **shout for j**.	8264
	35: 6	and the mute tongue **shout for j**.	8264
	35:10	everlasting **j** will crown their heads.	8525
	35:10	Gladness and **j** will overtake them,	8525
	42:11	Let the people of Sela **sing for j**;	8264

Isa	44:23	**Sing for j**, O heavens,	8264
	48:20	with **shouts of j** and proclaim it.	7754+8262
	49:13	**Shout for j**, O heavens;	8264
	51: 3	**J** and gladness will be found in her,	8607
	51:11	everlasting **j** will crown their heads.	8525
	51:11	Gladness and **j** will overtake them,	8525
	52: 8	together they **shout for j**.	8264
	52: 9	Burst into **songs of j** together,	8264
	54: 1	burst into song, **shout for j**,	7412
	55:12	You will go out in **j** and be led forth	8525
	56: 7	and **give** them **j** in my house of prayer.	8523
	58:14	then you will **find** your **j** in the LORD,	6695
	60: 5	your heart will throb and **swell with j**;	8143
	60:15	the everlasting pride and the **j**	5375
	61: 7	and everlasting **j** will be theirs.	8525
	65:14	My servants will sing out of the **j**	3206
	65:18	to be a delight and its people a **j**.	5375
	66: 5	that we may see your **j**!'	8525
Jer	7:34	bring an end to the sounds of **j** and gladness	8607
	15:16	they were my **j** and my heart's delight.	8607
	16: 9	bring an end to the sounds of **j** and gladness	8607
	25:10	from them the sounds of **j** and gladness,	8607
	31: 7	"Sing with **j** for Jacob;	8525
	31:12	and **shout for j** on the heights of Zion;	8264
	31:13	I will give them comfort and **j** instead	8523
	33: 9	Then this city will bring me renown, **j**,	8607
	33:11	the sounds of **j** and gladness, the voices	8607
	48:33	**J** and gladness are gone from the orchards	8525
	48:33	no one treads with **shouts of j**.	2116
	48:33	there are shouts, there are no **shouts of j**.	2116
	51:48	in them will **shout for j** over Babylon.	8264
La	2:15	the **j** of the whole earth?"	5375
	5:15	**J** is gone from our hearts;	5375
Eze	7: 7	there is panic, not **j**, upon the mountains.	2059
	24:25	their **j** and glory, the delight of their eyes,	5375
Joel	1:12	Surely the **j** of mankind is withered away.	8607
	1:16	**j** and gladness from the house of our God?	8525
Mt	13: 3	the word and at once receives it with **j**,	5915
	13:44	and then in his **j** went and sold all he had	5915
	28: 8	afraid yet **filled with j**,	3489+5915
Mk	4:16	hear the word and at once receive it with **j**.	5915
Lk	1:14	He will be a **j** and delight to you,	5915
	1:44	the baby in my womb leaped for **j**.	21
	1:58	and they **shared** her **j**.	5176
	2:10	I bring you good news of great **j** that will	5915
	6:23	"Rejoice in that day and **leap for j**,	5015
	8:13	the ones who receive the word with **j**	5915
	10:17	The seventy-two returned with **j** and said,	5915
	10:21	**full of j** through the Holy Spirit, said,	22
	24:41	not believe it because of **j** and amazement,	5915
	24:52	and returned to Jerusalem with great **j**.	5915
Jn	3:29	and is **full of j** when he hears	5897+5915
	3:29	That **j** is mine, and it is now complete.	5915
	15:11	I have told you this so that my **j** may be	5915
	15:11	be in you and that your **j** may be complete.	5915
	16:20	but your grief will turn to **j**.	5915
	16:21	of her **j** that a child is born into the world.	5915
	16:22	and no one will take away your **j**.	5915
	16:24	and your **j** will be complete.	5915
	17:13	the full measure of my **j** within them.	5915
Ac	2:28	you will fill me with **j** in your presence.'	2372
	8: 8	So there was great **j** in that city.	5915
	13:52	the disciples were filled with **j** and with	5915
	14:17	**fills** your hearts with **j**."	2372
	16:34	he was **filled with j** because he had come	22
Ro	14:17	peace and **j** in the Holy Spirit,	5915
	15:13	with all **j** and peace as you trust in him,	5915
	15:32	with **j** and together with you be refreshed.	5915
	16:19	so I am **full of j** over you;	5897
2Co	1:24	but we work with you for your **j**,	5915
	2: 3	that you would all share my **j**.	5915
	7: 4	in all our troubles my **j** knows no bounds.	5915
	7: 7	so that my **j** was greater than ever.	5897
	8: 2	of the most severe trial, their overflowing **j**	5915
Gal	4:15	What has happened to all your **j**?	3422
	5:22	But the fruit of the Spirit is love, **j**, peace,	5915
Php	1: 4	I always pray with **j**	5915
	1:25	of you for your progress and **j** in the faith,	5915
	1:26	through my being with you again your **j**	3017
	2: 2	make my **j** complete by being like-minded,	5915
	2:29	Welcome him in the Lord with great **j**,	5915
	4: 1	my **j** and crown,	5915
1Th	1: 6	with the **j** given by the Holy Spirit.	5915
	2:19	For what is our hope, our **j**,	5915
	2:20	Indeed, you are our glory and **j**.	5915
2Ti	1: 4	so that I may be filled with **j**.	5915
Phm	1: 7	Your love has given me great **j**	5915
Heb	1: 9	by anointing you with the oil of **j**."	21
	12: 2	for the **j** set before him endured the cross,	5915
	13:17	Obey them so that their work will be a **j**,	5915
Jas	1: 2	Consider it pure **j**, my brothers,	5915
	4: 9	to mourning and your **j** to gloom.	5915
1Pe	1: 8	**filled with** an inexpressible and glorious **j**,	22+5915
1Jn	1: 4	We write this to make our **j** complete.	5915
2Jn	1: 4	It has given me great **j** to find some	5897
	1:12	so that our **j** may be complete.	5915
3Jn	1: 3	It gave me great **j** to have some brothers	5897
	1: 4	I have no greater **j** than to hear	5915
Jude	1:24	without fault and with **great j**—	21

JOYFUL (16) [JOY]

Dt	16:14	Be **j** at your Feast—	8523
1Sa	18: 6	with **j songs** and with tambourines	8525
1Ki	8:66	**j** and glad in heart for all the good things	8524

1Ch	15:16	as singers to sing **j** songs, accompanied	8525
2Ch	7:10	**j** and glad in heart for the good things	8524
Ps	68: 3	may they be happy and **j**.	8525
	100: 2	come before him with **j** songs.	8265
Ecc	9: 7	and drink your wine with a **j** heart,	3202
Isa	24: 8	the **j** harp is silent.	5375
Jer	31: 4	and go out to dance with the **j**.	8471
Hab	3:18	I will be **j** in God my Savior.	1635
Zec	8:19	seventh and tenth months will become **j**	8607
	10: 7	Their children will see it and be **j**;	8523
Ro	12:12	Be **j** in hope, patient in affliction,	5897
1Th	5:16	Be **j** always;	5897
Heb	12:22	upon thousands of angels in **j assembly**,	4108

JOYFULLY (11) [JOY]

Dt	28:47	you did not serve the LORD your God **j**	928+8525
2Ch	20:27	men of Judah and Jerusalem returned **j**	928+8525
	30:23	so for another seven days they celebrated **j**.	8525
Ne	12:27	to Jerusalem to celebrate **j** the dedication	8525
Job	39:13	"The wings of the ostrich **flap j**,	6632
Ps	33: 1	**Sing j** to the LORD, you righteous;	8264
	145: 7	and **j sing** of your righteousness.	8264
Lk	15: 5	he **j** puts it on his shoulders	5897
	19:37	the whole crowd of disciples began **j**	5897
Col	1:11	great endurance and patience, and **j**	3552+5915
Heb	10:34	**j** accepted the confiscation of your	3552+5915

JOYOUS (1) [JOY]

| Est | 8:15 | And the city of Susa held a **j** celebration. | 8523 |

JOZABAD (11)

2Ki	12:21	The officials who murdered him were **J** son	3416
1Ch	12: 4	Jahaziel, Johanan, **J** the Gederathite,	3416
	12:20	Adnah, **J**, Jediael, Michael, Jozabad,	3416
	12:20	Adnah, Jozabad, Jediael, Michael, **J**,	3416
2Ch	31:13	Azaziah, Nahath, Asahel, Jerimoth, **J**,	3416
	35: 9	his brothers, and Hashabiah, Jeiel and **J**,	3416
Ezr	8:33	and so were the Levites **J** son of Jeshua	3416
	10:22	Ishmael, Nethanel, **J** and Elasah.	3416
	10:23	**J**, Shimei, Kelaiah (that is, Kelita),	3416
Ne	8: 7	Kelita, Azariah, **J**, Hanan and Pelaiah—	3416
	11:16	Shabbethai and **J**, two of the heads of	3416

JOZACHAR (KJV) See JEHOZABAD

JOZADAK (5)

Ezr	3: 2	Then Jeshua son of **J** and his fellow priests	3449
	3: 8	of **J** and the rest of their brothers	3449
	5: 2	and Jeshua son of **J** set to work to rebuild	10318
	10:18	From the descendants of Jeshua son of **J**,	3449
Ne	12:26	Joiakim son of Jeshua, the son of **J**,	3449

JUBAL (1)

| Ge | 4:21 | His brother's name was **J**; | 3415 |

JUBILANT (5)

1Ch	16:32	let the fields be **j**;	6636
Ps	94: 3	how long will the wicked be **j**?	6600
	96:12	let the fields be **j**;	6600
	98: 4	all the earth, burst into **j song** with music;	8264
Hos	9: 1	do not be **j** like the other nations.	1637

JUBILEE (21)

Lev	25:10	It shall be a **j** for you;	3413
	25:11	The fiftieth year shall be a **j** for you;	3413
	25:12	For it is a **j** and is to be holy for you;	3413
	25:13	" 'In this Year of **J** everyone is to return	3413
	25:15	of the number of years since the **J**.	3413
	25:28	of the buyer until the Year of **J**;	3413
	25:28	It will be returned in the **J**,	3413
	25:30	It is not to be returned in the **J**.	3413
	25:31	and they are to be returned in the **J**.	3413
	25:33	and is to be returned in the **J**,	3413
	25:40	he is to work for you until the Year of **J**.	3413
	25:50	up to the Year of **J**.	3413
	25:52	a few years remain until the Year of **J**,	3413
	25:54	he is to be released in the Year of **J**,	3413
	27:17	he dedicates his field during the Year of **J**,	3413
	27:18	But if he dedicates his field after the **J**,	3413
	27:18	that remain until the next Year of **J**,	3413
	27:21	When the field is released in the **J**,	3413
	27:23	determine its value up to the Year of **J**,	3413
	27:24	In the Year of **J** the field will revert to	3413
Nu	36: 4	the **Year of J** for the Israelites comes,	3413

JUDAH (828) [JUDAH'S, JUDEA, JUDEAN]

Ge	29:35	So she named him **J**.	3373
	35:23	Simeon, Levi, **J**, Issachar and Zebulun.	3373
	37:26	**J** said to his brothers, "What will we gain	3373
	38: 1	**J** left his brothers and went down to stay	3373
	38: 2	There **J** met the daughter of a Canaanite	3373
	38: 6	**J** got a wife for Er, his firstborn,	3373
	38: 8	Then **J** said to Onan,	3373
	38:11	**J** then said to his daughter-in-law Tamar,	3373
	38:12	When **J** had recovered from his grief,	3373
	38:15	When **J** saw her, he thought she was a	3373
	38:20	Meanwhile **J** sent the young goat	3373
	38:22	So he went back to **J** and said,	3373
	38:23	Then **J** said, "Let her keep what she has,	3373
	38:24	About three months later **J** was told,	3373
	38:24	**J** said, "Bring her out and have her burned	3373

Ref	Text	Strong's
Ge 38:26	J recognized them and said,	3373
43: 3	But J said to him, "The man warned us	3373
43: 8	Then J said to Israel his father,	3373
44:14	the house when J and his brothers came in,	3373
44:16	"What can we to my lord?" J replied.	3373
44:18	Then J went up to him and said:	3373
46:12	The sons of J: Er, Onan, Shelah,	3373
46:28	Now Jacob sent J ahead of him to Joseph	3373
49: 8	"J, your brothers will praise you;	3373
49: 9	You are a lion's cub, O J;	3373
49:10	The scepter will not depart from J,	3373
Ex 1: 2	Reuben, Simeon, Levi and J;	3373
31: 2	the son of Hur, of the tribe of J,	3373
35:30	the son of Hur, of the tribe of J,	3373
38:22	the son of Hur, of the tribe of J.	3373
Nu 1: 7	from J, Nahshon son of Amminadab;	3373
1:26	From the descendants of J,	3373
1:27	number from the tribe of J was 74,600.	3373
2: 3	of J are to encamp under their standard.	3373
2: 3	of J is Nahshon son of Amminadab.	3373
2: 9	All the men assigned to the camp of J,	3373
7:12	of Amminadab of the tribe of J.	3373
10:14	divisions of the camp of J went first,	1201+3373
13: 6	the tribe of J, Caleb son of Jephunneh;	3373
26:19	Er and Onan were sons of J.	3373
26:20	The descendants of J by their clans were:	3373
26:22	These were the clans of J;	3373
34:19	from the tribe of J;	3373
Dt 27:12	Simeon, Levi, J, Issachar,	3373
33: 7	And this he said about J:	3373
33: 7	"Hear, O LORD, the cry of J;	3373
34: 2	all the land of J as far as the western sea,	3373
Jos 7: 1	of the tribe of J, took some of them.	3373
7:16	came forward by tribes, and J was taken.	3373
7:17	The clans of J came forward,	3373
7:18	the son of Zerah, of the tribe of J,	3373
11:21	from all the hill country of J,	3373
14: 6	the men of J approached Joshua at Gilgal,	3373
15: 1	The allotment for the tribe of J,	1201+3373
15:12	the boundaries around the people of J	3373
15:13	Caleb son of Jephunneh a portion in J	1201+3373
15:20	the inheritance of the tribe of J,	1201+3373
15:63	southernmost towns of the tribe of J	1201+3373
15:63	J could not dislodge the Jebusites,	1201+3373
15:63	with the people of J.	3373
18: 5	J is to remain in its territory on the south	3373
18:11	between the tribes of J and Joseph:	3373
18:14	Kiriath Jearim), a town of the people of J	3373
19: 1	within the territory of J.	1201+3373
19: 9	from the share of J,	1201+3373
19: 9	within the territory of J.	4392S
20: 7	Hebron) in the hill country of J.	3373
21: 4	from the tribes of J,	3373
21: 9	tribes of J and Simeon they allotted	1201+3373
21:11	in the hill country of J.	3373
Jdg 1: 2	The LORD answered, "J is to go;	3373
1: 3	of J said to the Simeonites their brothers,	3373
1: 4	When J attacked, the LORD gave	3373
1: 8	of J attacked Jerusalem also and took it.	3373
1: 9	the men of J went down to fight against	3373
1:16	with the men of J to live among the people	3373
1:16	to live among the people of the Desert of J	3373
1:17	Then the men of J went with	3373
1:18	The men of J also took Gaza,	3373
1:19	The LORD was with the men of J.	3373
10: 9	the Jordan to fight against J, Benjamin and	3373
15: 9	The Philistines went up and camped in J,	3373
15:10	The men of J asked,	3373
15:11	from J went down to the cave in the rock	3373
17: 7	A young Levite from Bethlehem in J,	3373
17: 7	who had been living within the clan of J,	3373
17: 9	"I'm a Levite from Bethlehem in J,"	3373
18:12	up camp near Kiriath Jearim in J.	3373
19: 1	a concubine from Bethlehem in J.	3373
19: 2	to her father's house in Bethlehem, J.	3373
19:18	"We are on our way from Bethlehem in J	3373
19:18	to Bethlehem in J and now I am going to	3373
20:18	The LORD replied, "J shall go first.	3373
Ru 1: 1	and a man from Bethlehem in J,	3373
1: 2	They were Ephrathites from Bethlehem, J.	3373
1: 7	that would take them back to the land of J.	3373
4:12	Perez, whom Tamar bore to J."	3373
1Sa 11: 8	and the men of J thirty thousand.	3373
15: 4	and ten thousand men from J.	3373
17: 1	for war and assembled at Socoh in J.	3373
17:12	who was from Bethlehem in J.	3373
17:52	of Israel and J surged forward with a shout	3373
18:16	But all Israel and J loved David,	3373
22: 5	Go into the land of J."	3373
23: 3	"Here in J we are afraid.	3373
23:23	down among all the clans of J."	3373
27: 6	belonged to the kings of J ever since.	3373
27:10	David would say, "Against the Negev of J"	3373
30:14	the territory belonging to J and the Negev	3373
30:16	from the land of the Philistines and from J.	3373
30:26	of the plunder to the elders of J.	3373
2Sa 1:18	that the men of J be taught this lament of	3373
2: 1	"Shall I go up to one of the towns of J?"	3373
2: 4	Then the men of J came to Hebron	3373
2: 4	anointed David king over the house of J.	3373
2: 7	and the house of J has anointed me king	3373
2:10	The house of J, however, followed David.	3373
2:11	of J was seven years and six months.	3373
3:10	over Israel and J from Dan to Beersheba."	3373
5: 5	In Hebron he reigned over J seven years	3373
5: 5	over all Israel and J thirty-three years.	3373
6: 2	of J to bring up from there the ark of God,	3373
2Sa 11:11	ark and Israel and J are staying in tents,	3373
12: 8	I gave you the house of Israel and J.	3373
19:11	"Ask the elders of J,	3373
19:14	the men of J as though they were one man.	3373
19:15	of J had come to Gilgal to go out and meet	3373
19:16	with the men of J to meet King David.	3373
19:40	of J and half the troops of Israel had taken	3373
19:41	"Why did our brothers, the men of J,	3373
19:42	the men of J answered the men of Israel,	3373
19:43	the men of Israel answered the men of J	3373
19:43	of J responded even more harshly than	3373
20: 2	of J stayed by their king all the way from	3373
20: 4	"Summon the men of J to come to me	3373
20: 5	But when Amasa went to summon J,	3373
21: 2	in his zeal for Israel and J had tried	3373
24: 1	"Go and take a census of Israel and J."	3373
24: 7	on to Beersheba in the Negev of J.	3373
24: 9	and in J five hundred thousand.	3373
1Ki 1: 9	all the men of J who were royal officials,	3373
1:35	appointed him ruler over Israel and J."	3373
4:20	of J and Israel were as numerous as	3373
4:25	During Solomon's lifetime J and Israel,	3373
12:17	living in the towns of J,	3373
12:20	of J remained loyal to the house of David.	3373
12:21	he mustered the whole house of J and	3373
12:23	to Rehoboam son of Solomon king of J,	3373
12:23	to the whole house of J and Benjamin,	3373
12:27	Rehoboam king of J.	3373
12:32	like the festival held in J,	3373
13: 1	of the LORD a man of God came from J	3373
13:12	the man of God from J had taken.	3373
13:14	the man of God who came from J?"	3373
13:21	to the man of God who had come from J,	3373
14:21	Rehoboam son of Solomon was king in J.	3373
14:22	J did evil in the eyes of the LORD.	3373
14:29	the book of the annals of the kings of J?	3373
15: 1	Abijah became king of J,	3373
15: 7	the book of the annals of the kings of J?	3373
15: 9	Asa became king of J,	3373
15:17	Baasha king of Israel went up against J	3373
15:17	or entering the territory of Asa king of J.	3373
15:22	Then King Asa issued an order to all J—	3373
15:23	the book of the annals of the kings of J?	3373
15:25	in the second year of Asa king of J,	3373
15:28	in the third year of Asa king of J and	3373
15:33	In the third year of Asa king of J,	3373
16: 1	In the twenty-sixth year of Asa king of J,	3373
16:10	the twenty-seventh year of Asa king of J,	3373
16:15	the twenty-seventh year of Asa king of J,	3373
16:23	In the thirty-first year of Asa king of J,	3373
16:29	In the thirty-eighth year of Asa king of J,	3373
19: 3	When he came to Beersheba in J,	3373
22: 2	the third year Jehoshaphat king of J went	3373
22:10	and Jehoshaphat king of J were sitting	3373
22:29	of Israel and Jehoshaphat king of J went	3373
22:41	of Asa became king of J in the fourth year	3373
22:45	the book of the annals of the kings of J?	3373
22:51	year of Jehoshaphat king of J,	3373
2Ki 1:17	of Jehoram son of Jehoshaphat king of J,	3373
3: 1	year of Jehoshaphat king of J,	3373
3: 7	to Jehoshaphat king of J:	3373
3: 9	the king of Israel set out with the king of J	3373
3:14	for the presence of Jehoshaphat king of J,	3373
8:16	when Jehoshaphat was king of J,	3373
8:16	of Jehoshaphat began his reign as king of J.	3373
8:19	the LORD was not willing to destroy J.	3373
8:20	against J and set up its own king.	3373
8:22	in rebellion against J.	3373
8:23	the book of the annals of the kings of J?	3373
8:25	Ahaziah son of Jehoram king of J began	3373
8:29	of J went down to Jezreel to see Joram son	3373
9:16	and Ahaziah king of J had gone down	3373
9:21	of Israel and Ahaziah king of J rode out,	3373
9:27	Ahaziah king of J saw what had happened,	3373
9:29	Ahaziah had become king of J.)	3373
10:13	he met some relatives of Ahaziah king of J	3373
12:18	of J took all the sacred objects dedicated	3373
12:18	Jehoram and Ahaziah, the kings of J—	3373
12:19	the book of the annals of the kings of J?	3373
13: 1	of Joash son of Ahaziah king of J,	3373
13:10	the thirty-seventh year of Joash king of J,	3373
13:12	against Amaziah king of J,	3373
14: 1	Amaziah son of Joash king of J began	3373
14: 9	of Israel replied to Amaziah king of J:	3373
14:10	your own downfall and that of J also?"	3373
14:11	and Amaziah king of J faced each other	3373
14:11	at Beth Shemesh in J.	3373
14:12	J was routed by Israel,	3373
14:13	of Israel captured Amaziah king of J	3373
14:15	against Amaziah king of J,	3373
14:17	of J lived for fifteen years after the death	3373
14:18	the book of the annals of the kings of J?	3373
14:21	Then all the people of J took Azariah,	3373
14:22	to J after Amaziah rested with his fathers.	3373
14:23	of Amaziah son of Joash king of J,	3373
15: 1	Azariah son of Amaziah king of J began	3373
15: 6	the book of the annals of the kings of J?	3373
15: 8	the thirty-eighth year of Azariah king of J,	3373
15:13	the thirty-ninth year of Uzziah king of J,	3373
15:17	the thirty-ninth year of Azariah king of J,	3373
15:23	In the fiftieth year of Azariah king of J,	3373
15:27	the fifty-second year of Azariah king of J,	3373
15:32	Jotham son of Uzziah king of J began	3373
15:36	the book of the annals of the kings of J?	3373
15:37	and Pekah son of Remaliah against J.)	3373
16: 1	Ahaz son of Jotham king of J began	3373
16: 6	for Aram by driving out the men of J.	3374
2Ki 16:19	the book of the annals of the kings of J?	3373
17: 1	In the twelfth year of Ahaz king of J,	3373
17:13	and J through all his prophets and seers:	3373
17:18	Only the tribe of J was left,	3373
17:19	and even J did not keep the commands of	3373
18: 1	Hezekiah son of Ahaz king of J began	3373
18: 5	like him among all the kings of J,	3373
18:13	the fortified cities of J and captured them.	3373
18:14	So Hezekiah king of J sent this message to	3373
18:14	of J three hundred talents of silver	3373
18:16	Hezekiah king of J stripped off the gold	3373
18:22	saying to J and Jerusalem,	3373
19:10	"Say to Hezekiah king of J:	3373
19:30	of the house of J will take root below	3373
20:20	the book of the annals of the kings of J?	3373
21:11	of J has committed these detestable sins.	3373
21:11	and has led J into sin with his idols.	3373
21:12	and that the ears of everyone who hears	3373
21:16	the sin that he had caused J to commit,	3373
21:17	the book of the annals of the kings of J?	3373
21:25	the book of the annals of the kings of J?	3373
22:13	for all J about what is written in this book	3373
22:16	in the book the king of J has read.	3373
22:18	Tell the king of J, who sent you to inquire	3373
23: 1	the king called together all the elders of	3373
23: 2	the LORD with the men of J, the people	3373
23: 5	of J to burn incense on the high places of	3373
23: 8	on the high places of the towns of J and	3373
23: 8	of J and desecrated the high places,	3373
23:11	the horses that the kings of J had dedicated	3373
23:12	the kings of J had erected on the roof near	3373
23:17	of God who came from J and pronounced	3373
23:22	of the kings of Israel and the kings of	3373
23:24	all the other detestable things seen in J	824+3373
23:26	which burned against J because of all	3373
23:27	"I will remove J also from my presence	3373
23:28	the book of the annals of the kings of J?	3373
23:33	J a levy of a hundred talents of silver	824+2021S
24: 2	He sent them to destroy J,	3373
24: 3	to J according to the LORD's command,	3373
24: 5	the book of the annals of the kings of J?	3373
24:12	Jehoiachin king of J, his mother,	3373
24:20	that all this happened to Jerusalem and J,	3373
25:21	So J went into captivity,	3373
25:22	over the people he had left behind in J.	824+3373
25:22	and also the men of J and	3374
25:27	of the exile of Jehoiachin king of J,	3373
1Ch 2: 1	Reuben, Simeon, Levi, J, Issachar,	3373
2: 3	The sons of J: Er, Onan and Shelah.	3373
2: 4	J had five sons in all.	3373
2:10	the leader of the people of J.	3373
4: 1	The descendants of J: Perez, Hezron,	3373
4:21	The sons of Shelah son of J:	3373
4:27	as numerous as the people of J.	3373
4:41	in the days of Hezekiah king of J.	3373
5: 2	though J was the strongest of his brothers	3373
5:17	of Jotham king of J and Jeroboam king	3373
6:15	the LORD sent J and Jerusalem into exile	3373
6:55	in J with its surrounding pasturelands.	824+3373
6:65	From the tribes of J,	1201+3373
9: 1	The people of J were taken captive	3373
9: 3	Those from J, from Benjamin,	1201+3373
9: 4	a descendant of Perez son of J.	3373
9: 6	the **people from** J numbered 690.	278+2157
12:16	and some men from J also came to David	3373
12:24	men of J, carrying shield and spear—	3373
13: 6	of J (Kiriath Jearim) to bring up from there	3373
21: 5	and seventy thousand in J,	3373
27:18	over J: Elihu, a brother of David;	3373
28: 4	He chose J as leader,	3373
28: 4	from the house of J he chose my family,	3373
2Ch 2: 7	to work in J and Jerusalem	3373
9:11	like them had ever been seen in J.)	824+3373
10:17	living in the towns of J,	3373
11: 1	the house of J and Benjamin—	3373
11: 3	to Rehoboam son of Solomon king of J	3373
11: 3	and to all the Israelites in J and Benjamin,	3373
11: 5	and built up towns for defense in J:	3373
11:10	These were fortified cities in J	3373
11:12	So J and Benjamin were his.	3373
11:14	to J and Jerusalem because Jeroboam	3373
11:17	They strengthened the kingdom of J	3373
11:23	throughout the districts of J and Benjamin,	3373
12: 4	the fortified cities of J and came as far	3373
12: 5	and to the leaders of J who had assembled	3373
12:12	Indeed, there was some good in J.	3373
13: 1	Abijah became king of J,	3373
13:13	in front of J the ambush was behind them.	3373
13:14	J turned and saw that they were	3373
13:15	and the men of J raised the battle cry.	3373
13:15	and all Israel before Abijah and J.	3373
13:16	The Israelites fled before J,	3373
13:18	of J were victorious because they relied on	3373
14: 4	He commanded J to seek the LORD,	3373
14: 5	and incense altars in every town in J,	3373
14: 6	He built up the fortified cities of J,	3373
14: 7	"Let us build up these towns," he said to J,	3373
14: 8	of three hundred thousand men from J,	3373
14:12	down the Cushites before Asa and J.	3373
14:13	of J carried off a large amount of plunder.	NIH
15: 2	"Listen to me, Asa and all J and Benjamin	3373
15: 8	from the whole land of J and Benjamin	3373
15: 9	Then he assembled all J and Benjamin and	3373
15:15	All J rejoiced about the oath	3373
16: 1	up against J and fortified Ramah	3373
16: 1	or entering the territory of Asa king of J.	3373
16: 6	Then King Asa brought all the men of J,	3373

2Ch 16: 7	the seer came to Asa king of J and said	3373
16:11	are written in the book of the kings of J	3373
17: 2	the fortified cities of J and put garrisons	3373
17: 2	and put garrisons in J and in the towns	824+3373
17: 5	and all J brought gifts to Jehoshaphat,	3373
17: 6	and the Asherah poles from J.	3373
17: 7	and Micaiah to teach in the towns of J.	3373
17: 9	They taught throughout J,	3373
17: 9	to all the towns of J and taught the people.	3373
17:10	the kingdoms of the lands surrounding J,	3373
17:12	he built forts and store cities in J	3373
17:13	and had large supplies in the towns of J.	3373
17:14	From J, commanders of units of 1,000:	3373
17:19	in the fortified cities throughout J.	3373
18: 3	of Israel asked Jehoshaphat king of J,	3373
18: 9	and Jehoshaphat king of J were sitting	3373
18:28	of Israel and Jehoshaphat king of J went	3373
19: 1	of J returned safely to his palace	3373
19: 5	in each of the fortified cities of J.	3373
19:11	the leader of the tribe of J,	3373
20: 3	and he proclaimed a fast for all J.	3373
20: 4	The people of J came together to seek help	3373
20: 4	indeed, they came from every town in J	3373
20: 5	up in the assembly of J and Jerusalem at	3373
20:13	All the men of J, with their wives and	3373
20:15	King Jehoshaphat and all who live in J	3373
20:17	the LORD will give you, O J	3373
20:18	and all the people of J and Jerusalem fell	3373
20:20	"Listen to me, J and people of Jerusalem!	3373
20:22	and Mount Seir who were invading J,	3373
20:24	When the men of J came to the place	3373
20:27	of J and Jerusalem returned joyfully	3373
20:31	So Jehoshaphat reigned over J	3373
20:31	when he became king of J,	NIH
20:35	of J made an alliance with Ahaziah king	3373
21: 3	as well as fortified cities in J,	3373
21: 8	Edom rebelled against J and set up its own	3373
21:10	Edom has been in rebellion against J.	3373
21:11	on the hills of J and had caused the people	3373
21:11	and had led J astray.	3373
21:12	Jehoshaphat or of Asa king of J.	3373
21:13	and you have led J and the people	3373
21:17	They attacked J, invaded it	3373
22: 1	of Jehoram king of J began to reign.	3373
22: 6	of J went down to Jezreel to see Joram son	3373
22: 8	of J and the sons of Ahaziah's relatives,	3373
22:10	the whole royal family of the house of J.	3373
23: 2	throughout J and gathered the Levites and	3373
23: 8	of J did just as Jehoiada the priest ordered.	3373
24: 5	of J and collect the money due annually	3373
24: 6	in from J and Jerusalem the tax imposed	3373
24: 9	in J and Jerusalem that they should bring	3373
24:17	the officials of J came and paid homage to	3373
24:18	God's anger came upon J and Jerusalem.	3373
24:23	it invaded J and Jerusalem and killed all	3373
24:24	Because J had forsaken the LORD,	NIH
25: 5	the people of J together and assigned them	3373
25: 5	and commanders of hundreds for all J	3373
25:10	They were furious with J and left for home	3373
25:12	of J also captured ten thousand men alive,	3373
25:17	Amaziah king of J consulted his advisers,	3373
25:18	of Israel replied to Amaziah king of J:	3373
25:19	your own downfall and that of J also?"	3373
25:21	and Amaziah king of J faced each other	3373
25:21	at Beth Shemesh in J.	3373
25:22	J was routed by Israel,	3373
25:23	of Israel captured Amaziah king of J.	3373
25:25	of J lived for fifteen years after the death	3373
25:26	not written in the book of the kings of J	3373
25:28	with his fathers in the City of J.	3373
26: 1	Then all the people of J took Uzziah,	3373
26: 2	of J after Amaziah rested with his fathers.	3373
27: 7	in the book of the kings of Israel and J.	3373
28: 6	and twenty thousand soldiers in J—	3373
28: 6	because J had forsaken the LORD,	4392S
28: 9	the God of your fathers, was angry with J,	3373
28:10	to make the men and women of J	1201+3373
28:17	and attacked and carried away prisoners,	3373
28:18	in the foothills and in the Negev of J.	3373
28:19	The LORD had humbled J because	3373
28:19	for he had promoted wickedness in J	3373
28:25	in J he built high places to burn sacrifices	3373
28:26	are written in the book of the kings of J	3373
29: 8	the LORD has fallen on J and Jerusalem;	3373
29:21	for the sanctuary and for J.	3373
30: 1	Hezekiah sent word to all Israel and J and	3373
30: 6	throughout Israel and J with letters from	3373
30:12	in the hand of God was on the people	3373
30:24	of J provided a thousand bulls	3373
30:25	The entire assembly of J rejoiced,	3373
30:25	from Israel and those who lived in J.	3373
31: 1	went out to the towns of J,	3373
31: 1	the high places and the altars throughout J	3373
31: 6	of Israel and Judah who lived in the towns of Judah	3373
31: 6	and Judah who lived in the towns of J	3373
31:20	This is what Hezekiah did throughout J,	3373
32: 1	of Assyria came and invaded J.	3373
32: 8	from what Hezekiah the king of J said.	3373
32: 9	with this message for Hezekiah king of J	3373
32: 9	and for all the people of J who were there:	3373
32:12	saying to J and Jerusalem,	3373
32:23	and valuable gifts for Hezekiah king of J	3373
32:25	the LORD's wrath was on him and on J	3373
32:32	in the book of the kings of J and Israel.	3373
32:33	All J and the people of Jerusalem	3373
33: 9	But Manasseh led J and the people	3373
33:14	in all the fortified cities in J.	3373
2Ch 33:16	and told J to serve the LORD,	3373
34: 3	to purge J and Jerusalem of high places,	3373
34: 5	and so he purged J and Jerusalem.	3373
34: 9	from all the people of J and Benjamin and	3373
34:11	the kings of J had allowed to fall into ruin.	3373
34:21	for me and for the remnant in Israel and J	3373
34:24	in the presence of the king of J,	3373
34:26	Tell the king of J, who sent you to inquire	3373
34:29	the king called together all the elders of J	3373
34:30	the LORD with the men of J, the people	3373
35:18	and all J and Israel who were there with	3373
35:21	between you and me, O king of J?	3373
35:24	and all J and Jerusalem mourned for him.	3373
35:27	in the book of the kings of Israel and J.	3373
36: 3	J a levy of a hundred talents of silver	824+2021S
36: 4	king over J and Jerusalem	3373
36: 8	in the book of the kings of Israel and J.	3373
36:10	Zedekiah, king over J and Jerusalem.	3373
36:23	to build a temple for him at Jerusalem in J.	3373
Ezr 1: 2	to build a temple for him at Jerusalem in J.	3373
1: 3	up to Jerusalem in J and build the temple	3373
1: 5	Then the family heads of J and Benjamin,	3373
1: 8	to Sheshbazzar the prince of J.	3373
2: 1	they returned to Jerusalem and J,	3373
4: 1	the enemies of J and Benjamin heard that	3373
4: 4	the people of J and make them afraid to go	3373
4: 6	against the people of J and Jerusalem.	3373
5: 1	the Jews in J and Jerusalem in the name of	10315
5: 8	that we went to the district of J,	10315
7:14	and his seven advisers to inquire about J	10315
9: 9	a wall of protection in J and Jerusalem.	3373
10: 7	then issued throughout J and Jerusalem	3373
10: 9	the men of J and Benjamin had gathered	3373
10:23	Kelita), Pethahiah, J and Eliezer.	3373
Ne 1: 2	came from J with some other men,	3373
2: 5	to the city in J where my fathers are buried	3373
2: 7	provide me safe-conduct until I arrive in J?	3373
4:10	Meanwhile, the people in J said,	3373
4:16	behind all the people of J	3373
5:14	to be their governor in the land of J,	3373
6: 7	'There is a king in J!'	3373
6:17	of J were sending many letters to Tobiah,	3373
6:18	For many in J were under oath to him,	3373
7: 6	they returned to Jerusalem and J,	3373
11: 3	lived in the towns of J,	3373
11: 4	both J and Benjamin lived in Jerusalem):	3373
11: 4	From the descendants of J:	3373
11: 9	and J son of Hassenuah was over	3373
11: 9	were in all the towns of J,	3373
11:24	one of the descendants of Zerah son of J,	3373
11:25	the people of J lived in Kiriath Arba	3373
11:36	of the divisions of the Levites of J settled	3373
12: 8	Sherebiah, J, and also Mattaniah, who,	3373
12:31	the leaders of J go up on top of the wall.	3373
12:32	and half the leaders of J followed them,	3373
12:34	J, Benjamin, Shemaiah, Jeremiah,	3373
12:36	Gilalai, Maai, Nethanel, and Hanani—	3373
12:44	for J was pleased with	3373
13:12	All J brought the tithes of grain,	3373
13:15	in J treading winepresses on the Sabbath	3373
13:16	on the Sabbath to the people of J.	3373
13:17	I rebuked the nobles of J and said to them,	3373
13:23	I saw **men of J** who had married women	3374
13:24	how to speak the **language of J**.	3376
Est 2: 6	taken captive with Jehoiachin king of J.	3373
Ps 48:11	of J are glad because of your judgments.	3373
60: 7	Ephraim is my helmet, J my scepter.	3373
63: T	When he was in the Desert of J.	3373
69:35	and rebuild the cities of J.	3373
76: 1	In J God is known;	3373
78:68	but he chose the tribe of J,	3373
97: 8	and rejoices and the villages of J are glad	3373
108: 8	Ephraim is my helmet, J my scepter.	3373
114: 2	J became God's sanctuary,	3373
Pr 25: 1	copied by the men of Hezekiah king of J:	3373
Isa 1: 1	concerning J and Jerusalem that Isaiah son	3373
1: 1	Jotham, Ahaz and Hezekiah, kings of J.	3373
2: 1	of Amoz saw concerning J and Jerusalem:	3373
3: 1	to take from Jerusalem and J both supply	3373
3: 8	Jerusalem staggers, J is falling;	3373
5: 3	in Jerusalem and men of J,	3373
5: 7	the men of J are the garden of his delight.	3373
7: 1	the son of Uzziah, was king of J,	3373
7: 6	"Let us invade J;	3373
7:17	since Ephraim broke away from J—	3373
8: 8	and sweep on into J,	3373
9:21	together they will turn against J.	3373
11:12	he will assemble the scattered people of J	3373
11:13	Ephraim will not be jealous of J	3373
11:13	nor J hostile toward Ephraim.	3373
19:17	land of J will bring terror to the Egyptians;	3373
19:17	to whom J is mentioned will be terrified,	2023S
22: 8	the defenses of J are stripped away.	3373
22:21	in Jerusalem and to the house of J.	3373
26: 1	be sung in the land of J:	3373
36: 1	the fortified cities of J and captured them.	3373
36: 7	saying to J and Jerusalem,	3373
37:10	"Say to Hezekiah king of J:	3373
37:31	of the house of J will take root below	3373
38: 9	of Hezekiah king of J after his illness	3373
40: 9	say to the towns of J, "Here is your God!"	3373
44:26	'It shall be inhabited,' of the towns of J	3373
48: 1	from the line of J, you who take oaths in	3373
65: 9	those who will possess my mountains,	3373
Jer 1: 2	the reign of Josiah son of Amon king of J,	3373
1: 3	of Jehoiakim son of Josiah king of J,	3373
1: 3	of Zedekiah son of Josiah king of J,	3373
Jer 1:15	and against all the towns of J.	3373
1:18	against the kings of J, its officials,	3373
2:28	as many gods as you have towns, O J.	3373
3: 7	and her unfaithful sister J saw it.	3373
3: 8	that her unfaithful sister J had no fear;	3373
3:10	her unfaithful sister J did not return to me	3373
3:11	"Faithless Israel is more righteous than unfaithful J.	3373
3:18	the house of J will join the house of Israel,	3373
4: 3	the LORD says to the men of J and	3373
4: 4	you men of J and people of Jerusalem,	3373
4: 5	"Announce in J and proclaim in Jerusalem	3373
4:16	raising a war cry against the cities of J.	3373
5:11	the house of J have been utterly unfaithful	3373
5:20	to the house of Jacob and proclaim it in J:	3373
7: 2	the LORD, all you people of J who come	3373
7:17	of J and in the streets of Jerusalem?	3373
7:30	" 'The people of J have done evil	3373
7:34	the towns of J and the streets of Jerusalem,	3373
8: 1	the bones of the kings and officials of J,	3373
9:11	the towns of J so no one can live there."	3373
9:26	J, Edom, Ammon, Moab and all who live	3373
10:22	It will make the towns of J desolate,	3373
11: 2	of J and to those who live in Jerusalem.	3373
11: 6	"Proclaim all these words in the towns of J	3373
11: 9	among the people of J and those who live	3373
11:10	of Israel and the house of J have broken	3373
11:12	of J and the people of Jerusalem will go	3373
11:13	as many gods as you have towns, O J;	3373
11:17	of Israel and the house of J have done evil	3373
12:14	and I will uproot the house of J from	3373
13: 9	the same way I will ruin the pride of J and	3373
13:11	of Israel and the whole house of J to me,'	3373
13:19	All J will be carried into exile,	3373
14: 2	"J mourns, her cities languish;	3373
14:19	Have you rejected J completely?	3373
15: 4	of Hezekiah king of J did in Jerusalem.	3373
17:19	through which the kings of J go in and out;	3373
17:20	O kings of J and all people of Judah	3373
17:20	and all people of J and everyone living	3373
17:25	the men of J and those living in Jerusalem,	3373
17:26	People will come from the towns of J and	3373
18:11	"Now therefore say to the people of J	3373
19: 3	O kings of J and people of Jerusalem.	3373
19: 4	nor the kings of J ever knew,	3373
19: 7	" 'In this place I will ruin the plans of J	3373
19:13	and those of the kings of J will be defiled	3373
20: 4	I will hand all J over to the king	3373
20: 5	and all the treasures of the kings of J.	3373
21: 7	I will hand over Zedekiah king of J,	3373
21:11	"Moreover, say to the royal house of J,	3373
22: 1	"Go down to the palace of the king of J	3373
22: 2	of J, you who sit on David's throne—	3373
22: 6	about the palace of the king of J	3373
22:11	as king of J but has gone from this place:	3373
22:18	about Jehoiakim son of Josiah king of J:	3373
22:24	Jehoiachin son of Jehoiakim king of J,	3373
22:30	the throne of David or rule anymore in J."	3373
23: 6	In his days J will be saved	3373
24: 1	of Jehoiakim king of J and the officials,	3373
24: 1	and the artisans of J were carried into exile	3373
24: 5	I regard as good the exiles from J,	3373
24: 8	'so will I deal with Zedekiah king of J,	3373
25: 1	to Jeremiah concerning all the people of J	3373
25: 1	of Jehoiakim son of Josiah king of J,	3373
25: 2	to all the people of J and to all those living	3373
25: 3	of Amon king of J until this very day—	3373
25:18	and the towns of J, its kings and officials,	3373
26: 1	of Josiah king of J, this word came from	3373
26: 2	of the towns of J who come to worship in	3373
26:10	the officials of J heard about these things,	3373
26:18	in the days of Hezekiah king of J.	3373
26:18	He told all the people of J,	3373
26:19	"Did Hezekiah king of J or anyone else	3373
26:19	or anyone else in J put him to death?	3373
27: 1	of J, this word came to Jeremiah from	3373
27: 3	to Jerusalem to Zedekiah king of J.	3373
27:12	the same message to Zedekiah king of J.	3373
27:18	the king of J and in Jerusalem not be taken	3373
27:20	of J into exile from Jerusalem to Babylon,	3373
27:20	with all the nobles of J and Jerusalem,	3373
27:21	and in the palace of the king of J and	3373
28: 1	early in the reign of Zedekiah king of J,	3373
28: 4	of Jehoiakim king of J and all	3373
28: 4	and all the other exiles from J who went	3373
29: 2	the court officials and the leaders of J	3373
29: 3	of J sent to King Nebuchadnezzar	3373
29:22	all the exiles from J who are in Babylon	3373
30: 3	and J back from captivity and restore them	3373
30: 4	the LORD spoke concerning Israel and J:	3373
31:23	from captivity, the people in the land of J	3373
31:24	People will live together in J	3373
31:27	the house of Israel and the house of J with	3373
31:31	the house of Israel and with the house of J	3373
32: 1	in the tenth year of Zedekiah king of J,	3373
32: 2	of the guard in the royal palace of J.	3373
32: 3	king of J had imprisoned him there,	3373
32: 4	Zedekiah king of J will not escape out of	3373
32:30	of Israel and J have done nothing but evil	3373
32:32	of Israel and J have provoked me by all	3373
32:32	the men of J and the people of Jerusalem.	3373
32:35	a detestable thing and so make J sin.	3373
32:44	of J and in the towns of the hill country,	3373
33: 4	the royal palaces of J that have been torn	3373
33: 7	I will bring J and Israel back	3373
33:10	the towns of J and the streets of Jerusalem	3373
33:13	around Jerusalem and in the towns of J,	3373

Jer	33:14	to the house of Israel and to the house of J.	3373
	33:16	In those days J will be saved	3373
	34: 2	Go to Zedekiah king of J and tell him,	3373
	34: 4	O Zedekiah king of J.	3373
	34: 6	told all this to Zedekiah king of J,	3373
	34: 7	against Jerusalem and the other cities of J	3373
	34: 7	the only fortified cities left in J.	3373
	34:19	The leaders of J and Jerusalem,	3373
	34:21	"I will hand Zedekiah king of J	3373
	34:22	the towns of J so no one can live there."	3373
	35: 1	of Jehoiakim son of Josiah king of J:	3373
	35:13	the men of J and the people of Jerusalem,	3373
	35:17	to bring on J and on everyone living	3373
	36: 1	of J, this word came to Jeremiah from	3373
	36: 2	J and all the other nations from	3373
	36: 3	of J hear about every disaster I plan	3373
	36: 6	Read them to all the people of J who come	3373
	36: 9	of Jehoiakim son of Josiah king of J.	3373
	36: 9	who had come from the towns of J.	3373
	36:28	which Jehoiakim king of J burned up.	3373
	36:29	Also tell Jehoiakim king of J:	3373
	36:30	about Jehoiakim king of J:	3373
	36:31	the people of J every disaster I pronounced	3373
	36:32	scroll that Jehoiakim king of J had burned	3373
	37: 1	Zedekiah son of Josiah was made king of J	3373
			824+3373
	37: 7	Tell the king of J, who sent you to inquire	3373
	38:22	of J will be brought out to the officials of	3373
	39: 1	In the ninth year of Zedekiah king of J,	3373
	39: 4	of J and all the soldiers saw them,	3373
	39: 6	and also killed all the nobles of J.	3373
	39:10	the guard left behind in the land of J some	3373
	40: 1	and J who were being carried into exile	3373
	40: 5	has appointed over the towns of J.	3373
	40:11	the king of Babylon had left a remnant in J	3373
	40:12	they all came back to the land of J.	3373
	40:15	to be scattered and the remnant of J	3373
	42:15	O remnant of J,	3373
	42:19	"O remnant of J, the LORD has told you,	3373
	43: 4	to stay in the land of J.	3373
	43: 5	of J who had come back to live in the land	3373
	43: 5	to live in the land of J from all the nations	3373
	44: 2	on Jerusalem and on all the towns of J.	3373
	44: 6	the towns of J and the streets of Jerusalem	3373
	44: 7	by cutting off from J the men and women,	3373
	44: 9	of J and the wickedness committed by you	3373
	44: 9	by you and your wives in the land of J and	3373
	44:11	on you and to destroy all J.	3373
	44:12	of J who were determined to go to Egypt	3373
	44:14	of the remnant of J who have gone to live	3373
	44:14	to J, to which they long to return and live;	3373
	44:17	and our officials did in the towns of J and	3373
	44:21	the towns of J and the streets of Jerusalem	3373
	44:24	all you people of J in Egypt.	3373
	44:26	'that no one from J living anywhere	3373
	44:28	and return to the land of J from Egypt will	3373
	44:28	the whole remnant of J who came to live	3373
	44:30	just as I handed Zedekiah king of J over	3373
	45: 1	of J, after Baruch had written on a scroll	3373
	46: 2	of Jehoiakim son of Josiah king of J:	3373
	49:34	early in the reign of Zedekiah king of J:	3373
	50: 4	the people of J together will go in tears	3373
	50:20	and for the sins of J,	3373
	50:33	and the people of J as well.	3373
	51: 5	and J have not been forsaken by their God,	3373
	51:59	with Zedekiah king of J in the fourth year	3373
	52: 3	that all this happened to Jerusalem and J,	3373
	52:10	he also killed all the officials of J.	3373
	52:27	So J went into captivity,	3373
	52:31	of the exile of Jehoiachin king of J,	3373
	52:31	of J and freed him from prison on	3373
La	1: 3	J has gone into exile.	3373
	1:15	has trampled the Virgin Daughter of J.	3373
	2: 2	down the strongholds of the Daughter of J.	3373
	2: 5	and lamentation for the Daughter of J.	3373
	5:11	and virgins in the towns of J.	3373
Eze	4: 6	and bear the sin of the house of J.	3373
	8: 1	and the elders of J were sitting before me,	3373
	8:17	Is it a trivial matter for the house of J to do	3373
	9: 9	of Israel and J is exceedingly great;	3373
	21:10	in the scepter of my son [J]?	NIH
	21:13	And what if the scepter [of J],	NIH
	21:20	of the Ammonites and another against J	3373
	25: 3	the people of J when they went into exile,	3373
	25: 8	of J has become like all the other nations,"	3373
	25:12	on the house of J and became very guilty	3373
	25:15	with ancient hostility sought to destroy J,	NIH
	27:17	"'J and Israel traded with you;	3373
	37:16	to J and the Israelites associated	3373
	48: 7	"J will have one portion;	3373
	48: 8	the territory of J from east to west will be	3373
	48:22	the prince will lie between the border of J	3373
	48:31	the gate of J and the gate of Levi.	3373
Da	1: 1	of the reign of Jehoiakim king of J,	3373
	1: 2	the Lord delivered Jehoiakim king of J	3373
	1: 6	Among these were some from J:	3373
	2:25	among the exiles from J who can tell	10315
	5:13	the king brought from J?	10315
	6:13	"Daniel, who is one of the exiles from J,	10315
	9: 7	of J and people of Jerusalem and all Israel,	3373
Hos	1: 1	Jotham, Ahaz and Hezekiah, kings of J,	3373
	1: 7	Yet I will show love to the house of J;	3373
	1:11	people of J and the people of Israel will	3373
	4:15	O Israel, let not J become guilty.	3373
	5: 5	J also stumbles with them.	3373
	5:12	like rot to the people of J.	3373
	5:13	Ephraim saw his sickness, and J his sores,	3373

Hos	5:14	like a great lion to J.	1074+3373
	6: 4	What can I do with you, J?	3373
	6:11	"Also for you, J, a harvest is appointed.	3373
	8:14	J has fortified many towns.	3373
	10:11	I will drive Ephraim, J must plow,	3373
	11:12	And J is unruly against God,	3373
Joel	3: 1	I restore the fortunes of J and Jerusalem,	3373
	3: 6	You sold the people of J and Jerusalem to	3373
	3: 8	and daughters to the people of J,	3373
	3:18	all the ravines of J will run with water.	3373
	3:19	of violence done to the people of J,	3373
	3:20	J will be inhabited forever and Jerusalem	3373
Am	1: 1	the earthquake, when Uzziah was king of J	3373
	2: 4	"For three sins of J, even for four,	3373
	2: 5	I will send fire upon J that will consume	3373
	7:12	Go back to the land of J.	3373
Ob	1:12	nor rejoice over the people of J in the day	3373
Mic	1: 1	Ahaz and Hezekiah, kings of J—	3373
	1: 9	her wound is incurable; it has come to J.	3373
	5: 2	you are small among the clans of J,	3373
Na	1:12	Although I have afflicted you, [O J,]	NIH
	1:15	Celebrate your festivals, O J,	3373
Zep	1: 1	the reign of Josiah son of Amon king of J:	3373
	1: 4	"I will stretch out my hand against J and	3373
	2: 7	to the remnant of the house of J;	3373
Hag	1: 1	of J, and to Joshua son of Jehozadak,	3373
	1:14	governor of J, and the spirit of Joshua son	3373
	2: 2	governor of J, to Joshua son of Jehozadak,	3373
	2:21	of J that I will shake the heavens and	3373
Zec	1:12	from Jerusalem and from the towns of J,	3373
	1:19	"These are the horns that scattered J,	3373
	1:21	"These are the horns that scattered J,	3373
	1:21	against the land of J to scatter its people."	3373
	2:12	The LORD will inherit J as his portion in	3373
	8:13	O J and Israel, so will I save you,	1074+3373
	8:15	to do good again to Jerusalem and J.	1074+3373
	8:19	and happy festivals for J.	1074+3373
	9: 7	to our God and become leaders in J,	3373
	9:13	I will bend J as I bend my bow and fill it	3373
	10: 3	for his flock, the house of J,	3373
	10: 4	From J will come the cornerstone,	5647S
	10: 6	"I will strengthen the house of J and save	3373
	11:14	the brotherhood between J and Israel.	3373
	12: 2	J will be besieged as well as Jerusalem.	3373
	12: 4	a watchful eye over the house of J,	3373
	12: 5	the leaders of J will say in their hearts,	3373
	12: 6	"On that day I will make the leaders of J	3373
	12: 7	will save the dwellings of J first,	3373
	12: 7	not be greater than that of J.	3373
	14: 5	in the days of Uzziah king of J.	3373
	14:14	J too will fight at Jerusalem.	3373
	14:21	Every pot in Jerusalem and J will be holy	3373
Mal	2:11	J has broken faith.	3373
	2:11	J has desecrated the sanctuary	3373
	3: 4	and the offerings of J and Jerusalem will	3373
Mt	1: 2	Jacob the father of J and his brothers,	2683
	1: 3	J the father of Perez and Zerah,	2683
	2: 6	Bethlehem, in the land of J,	2683
	2: 6	by no means least among the rulers of J;	2683
Lk	3:30	the son of J, the son of Joseph,	2683
	3:33	the son of Perez, the son of J,	2683
Heb	7:14	it is clear that our Lord descended from J,	2683
	8: 8	of Israel and with the house of J.	2683
Rev	5: 5	See, the Lion of the tribe of J,	2683
	7: 5	From the tribe of J 12,000 were sealed,	2683

JUDAH'S (13) [JUDAH]

Ge	38: 7	But Er, J firstborn, was wicked in	3373
	38:12	After a long time J wife,	3373
Jos	19: 9	J portion was more than they needed.	1201+3373
2Sa	3: 8	"Am I a dog's head—on J side?	3373
1Ki	2:32	Amasa son of Jether, commander of J army	3373
1Ch	2: 3	Er, J firstborn, was wicked in	3373
	2: 4	Tamar, J daughter-in-law,	2257S
Ps	68:27	there the great throng of J princes,	3373
Isa	11:13	and J enemies will be cut off;	3373
Jer	17: 1	"J sin is engraved with an iron tool,	3373
Eze	37:19	and join it to J stick, making them a single	3373
Hos	5:10	J leaders are like those who move	3373
Mic	1: 5	What is J high place? Is it not Jerusalem?	3373

JUDAISM (5) [JEW]

Ac	2:11	(both Jews and converts to J);	4670
	6: 5	Nicolas from Antioch, a convert to J.	4670
	13:43	and devout converts to J followed Paul	4670
Gal	1:13	heard of my previous way of life in J,	2682
	1:14	I was advancing in J beyond many Jews	2682

JUDAS (41)

Mt	10: 4	Simon the Zealot and J Iscariot,	2683
	13:55	Joseph, Simon and J?	2683
	26:14	the one called J Iscariot—	2683
	26:16	From then on J watched for an opportunity	NIG
	26:25	Then J, the one who would betray him,	2683
	26:47	While he was still speaking, J,	2683
	26:49	Going at once to Jesus, J said, "Greetings,	NIG
	27: 3	When J, who had betrayed him,	2683
	27: 5	J threw the money into the temple and left.	NIG
Mk	3:19	and J Iscariot, who betrayed him.	2683
	6: 3	Joseph, J and Simon?	2683
	14:10	Then J Iscariot, one of the Twelve,	2683
	14:43	Just as he was speaking, J,	2683
	14:45	Going at once to Jesus, J said, "Rabbi!"	NIG
Lk	6:16	J son of James, and Judas Iscariot,	2683

Lk	6:16	and J Iscariot, who became a traitor.	2683
	22: 3	Then Satan entered J, called Iscariot,	2683
	22: 4	And J went to the chief priests and	NIG
	22:47	and the man who was called J,	2683
	22:48	but Jesus asked him, "J, are you betraying	2683
Jn	6:71	(He meant J, the son of Simon Iscariot,	2683
	12: 4	But one of his disciples, J Iscariot,	2683
	13: 2	the devil had already prompted J Iscariot,	2683
	13:26	he gave it to J Iscariot, son of Simon.	2683
	13:27	As soon as J took the bread,	NIG
	13:29	Since J had charge of the money,	2683
	13:30	As soon as J had taken the bread,	1697S
	14:22	Then J (not Judas Iscariot) said, "But,	2683
	14:22	Then Judas (not J Iscariot) said, "But,	NIG
	18: 2	Now J, who betrayed him, knew the place,	2683
	18: 3	So J came to the grove,	2683
	18: 5	(And J the traitor was standing there	2683
Ac	1:13	and J son of James.	2683
	1:16	through the mouth of David concerning J,	2683
	1:18	J bought a field,	4047S
	1:25	which J left to go where he belongs."	2683
	5:37	J the Galilean appeared in the days of	2683
	9:11	of J on Straight Street and ask for a man	2683
	15:22	They chose J (called Barsabbas) and Silas,	2683
	15:27	Therefore we are sending J and Silas	2683
	15:32	J and Silas, who themselves were prophets,	2683

JUDE (1)

Jude	1: 1	J, a servant of Jesus Christ and a brother	2683

JUDEA (44) [JUDAH]

Mt	2: 1	After Jesus was born in Bethlehem in J,	2677
	2: 5	"In Bethlehem in J," they replied,	2677
	2:22	that Archelaus was reigning in J in place	2677
	3: 1	preaching in the Desert of J	2677
	3: 5	to him from Jerusalem and all J and	2677
	4:25	J and the region across the Jordan	2677
	19: 1	into the region of J to the other side of	2677
	24:16	then let those who are in J flee to	2677
Mk	3: 8	many people came to him from J,	2677
	10: 1	into the region of J and across the Jordan.	2677
	13:14	then let those who are in J flee to	2677
Lk	1: 5	of J there was a priest named Zechariah,	2677
	1:39	to a town in the hill country of J,	2683
	1:65	the hill country of J people were talking	2677
	2: 4	from the town of Nazareth in Galilee to J,	2677
	3: 1	when Pontius Pilate was governor of J,	2677
	4:44	on preaching in the synagogues of J.	2677
	5:17	from every village of Galilee and from J	2677
	6:17	a great number of people from all over J,	2677
	7:17	This news about Jesus spread throughout J	2677
	21:21	Then let those who are in J flee to	2677
	23: 5	up the people all over J by his teaching.	2677
Jn	4: 3	he left J and went back once more	2677
	4:47	that Jesus had arrived in Galilee from J,	2677
	4:54	having come from J to Galilee.	2677
	7: 1	purposely staying away from J because	2677
	7: 3	"You ought to leave here and go to J,	2677
	11: 7	"Let us go back to J."	2677
Ac	1: 8	and in all J and Samaria,	2677
	2: 9	J and Cappadocia, Pontus and Asia,	2677
	8: 1	the apostles were scattered throughout J	2677
	9:31	Then the church throughout J,	2677
	10:37	throughout J, beginning in Galilee after	2677
	11: 1	and the brothers throughout J heard that	2677
	11:29	to provide help for the brothers living in J.	2677
	12:19	Then Herod went from J to Caesarea	2677
	15: 1	down from J to Antioch and were teaching	2677
	21:10	prophet named Agabus came down from J.	2677
	26:20	then to those in Jerusalem and in all J,	2677
	28:21	"We have not received any letters from J	2677
Ro	15:31	in J and that my service in Jerusalem may	2677
2Co	1:16	then to have you send me on my way to J.	2677
Gal	1:22	to the churches of J that are in Christ.	2677
1Th	2:14	became imitators of God's churches in J,	2677

JUDEAN (6) [JUDAH]

1Ch	4:18	(His J wife gave birth to Jered the father	3374
2Ch	25:13	in the war raided J towns from Samaria	3373
	27: 4	He built towns in J hills and forts	3373
Mk	1: 5	The whole J countryside and all the people	2677
Lk	23:51	He came from the J town of Arimathea	2681
Jn	3:22	went out into the J countryside,	2681

JUDGE (153) [JUDGE'S, JUDGED, JUDGES, JUDGING, JUDGMENT, JUDGMENTS]

Ge	16: 5	May the LORD j between you and me."	9149
	18:25	Will not the J of all the earth do right?"	9149
	19: 9	and now he wants to play the j!	9149+9149
	31:37	and let them j between the two of us.	3519
	31:53	the God of their father, j between us."	9149
Ex	2:14	"Who made you ruler and j over us?"	9149
	5:21	the LORD look upon you and j you!	9149
	18:13	to serve as j for the people,	9149
	18:14	Why do you alone sit as j,	3782
Lev	19:15	but j your neighbor fairly.	9149
	27:12	who will j its quality as good or bad.	6885
	27:14	the priest will j its quality as good	6885
Nu	35:24	the assembly must j between him and	9149
Dt	1:16	between your brothers and j fairly.	9149
	16:18	and they shall j the people fairly.	5477+9149
	17: 8	that are too difficult for you to j—	5477

Dt	17: 9	and to the j who is **in office**	9149
	17:12	The man who shows contempt for the j or	9149
	25: 2	the j shall make him lie down	9149
	32:36	The LORD will j his people	1906
Jdg	2:18	the LORD raised up a j for them, he was	9149
	2:18	with the j and saved them out of the hands	9149
	2:18	of their enemies as long as the j lived;	9149
	2:19	But when the j died,	9149
	3:10	that *he became* Israel's j and went to war.	9149
	11:27	Let the LORD, the J, decide the dispute	9149
1Sa	2:10	the LORD will j the ends of the earth.	1906
	3:13	that I *would* j his family forever because of	9149
	7:15	Samuel *continued as* j over Israel all	9149
	24:12	May the LORD j between you and me.	9149
	24:15	May the LORD be our j and decide	1908
2Sa	15: 4	"If only I were appointed j in the land!	9149
1Ki	7: 7	the Hall of Justice, where *he was to* j,	9149
	8:32	J *between* your servants,	9149
1Ch	12:17	the God of our fathers see it and j you."	3519
	16:33	for he comes to j the earth.	9149
2Ch	6:23	J *between* your servants,	9149
	19: 7	J carefully, for with the LORD our God there is no injustice	6913S
	20:12	O our God, *will you* not j them?	9149
Job	9:15	I could only plead with my J for mercy.	9149
	22:13	*Does he* j through such darkness?	9149
	23: 7	I would be delivered forever from my j.	9149
Ps	7: 8	*let the* LORD j the peoples.	1906
	7: 8	J me, O LORD, according	9149
	7:11	God is a righteous j,	9149
	9: 8	He *will* j the world in righteousness;	9149
	50: 4	and the earth, that he *may* j his people:	1906
	50: 6	for God himself *is* j.	9149
	51: 4	when you speak and justified when you j.	9149
	58: 1	*Do you* j uprightly among men?	9149
	72: 2	He *will* j your people in righteousness,	1906
	75: 2	it is I *who* j uprightly.	9149
	76: 9	when you, O God, rose up to j,	5477
	82: 8	Rise up, O God, j the earth,	9149
	94: 2	Rise up, O J *of* the earth;	9149
	96:10	He will j the peoples with equity.	1906
	96:13	for he comes, he comes to j the earth.	9149
	96:13	He will j the world in righteousness and	9149
	98: 9	for he comes to j the earth.	9149
	98: 9	He will j the world in righteousness and	9149
	110: 6	He will j the nations,	1906
Pr	20: 8	When a king sits on his throne to j,	1907
	31: 9	Speak up and j fairly;	9149
Isa	2: 4	He *will* j between the nations	9149
	3: 2	the j and prophet, the soothsayer and elder,	9149
	3:13	he rises to j the people.	1906
	5: 3	j between me and my vineyard.	9149
	11: 3	not j by what he sees with his eyes,	9149
	11: 4	but with righteousness *he will* j the needy,	9149
	33:22	For the LORD *is* our j,	9149
Jer	11:20	you *who* j righteously and test the heart	9149
Eze	7: 3	*I will* j you according to your conduct	9149
	7: 8	*I will* j you according to your conduct	9149
	7:27	and by their own standards *I will* j them.	9149
	18:30	O house of Israel, *I will* j you,	9149
	20: 4	"*Will you* j them? Will you judge them,	9149
	20: 4	*Will you* j them, son of man?	9149
	20:36	so *I will* j you, declares the Sovereign	9149
	21:30	in the land of your ancestry, *I will* j you.	9149
	22: 2	*will you* j her? Will you judge this city	9149
	22: 2	*Will you* j this city of bloodshed?	9149
	23:36	*will you* j Oholah and Oholibah?	9149
	33:20	But *I will* j each of you according	9149
	34:17	*I will* j between one sheep and another,	9149
	34:20	See, I myself *will* j between the fat sheep	9149
	34:22	*I will* j between one sheep and another.	9149
	35:11	known among them when *I* j you.	9149
Joel	3:12	of Jehoshaphat, for there I will sit to j all	9149
Mic	3:11	Her leaders j for a bribe,	9149
	4: 3	*He will* j between many peoples	9149
	7: 3	ruler demands gifts, the j accepts bribes,	9149
Mt	5:25	or he may hand you over *to the* j,	3216
	5:25	and the j may hand you over to the officer,	3216
	7: 1	"Do not j, or you too will be judged.	3212
	7: 2	For in the same way *you* j others,	3212
Lk	6:37	"Do not j, and you will not be judged.	3212
	12:14	who appointed me a j or an arbiter	3216
	12:57	"Why don't *you* j for yourselves	3212
	12:58	or he may drag you off to the j,	3216
	12:58	and the j turn you over to the officer,	3216
	18: 2	a j who neither feared God nor cared	3216
	18: 6	"Listen to what the unjust j says.	3216
	19:22	'*I will* j you by your own words,	3212
Jn	5:27	And he has given him authority *to* j	3213+4472
	5:30	I j only as I hear, and my judgment is just,	3212
	8:15	You j by human standards;	3212
	8:16	But if I *do* j, my decisions are right,	3212
	8:50	there is one who seeks it, and he is the j.	3212
	12:47	but does not keep them, I *do not* j him.	3212
	12:47	I did not come to j the world, but to save it.	3212
	12:48	There is a j for the one who rejects me and does not accept my words;	2400+3212+3836
	18:31	"Take him yourselves and j him	3212
Ac	4:19	"J *for yourselves* whether it is right	3212
	7:27	'Who made you ruler and j over us?	1471
	7:35	'Who made you ruler and j?'	1471
	10:42	that he is the one whom God appointed as j	3216
	17:31	a day when he will j the world with justice	3212
	18:15	I will not be a j of such things."	3216
	23: 3	You sit there *to* j me according to the law,	3212
	24:10	of years you have been a j over this nation;	3216
Ro	2: 1	for at whatever point *you* j the other,	3212
Ro	2:16	on the day when God *will* j men's secrets	3212
	3: 4	when you speak and prevail when you j."	3212
	3: 6	how *could* God j the world?	3212
	14: 4	Who are you *to* j someone else's servant?	3212
	14:10	You, then, why *do you* j your brother?	3212
1Co	4: 3	indeed, *I* do not even j myself.	373
	4: 5	j nothing before the appointed time;	3212
	5:12	of mine *to* j those outside the church?	3212
	5:12	*Are you* not *to* j those inside?	3212
	5:13	God *will* j those outside.	3212
	6: 2	not know that the saints *will* j the world?	3212
	6: 2	And if you are to j the world,	3212
	6: 2	are you not competent *to* j trivial **cases?**	3215
	6: 3	Do you not know that *we will* j angels?	3212
	6: 5	among you wise enough *to* j a dispute	1359
	10:15	j for yourselves what I say.	3212
	11:13	J for yourselves: Is it proper	3212
Gal	2: 6	not j by external appearance—	476+3284+4725
Col	2:16	not *let* anyone j you by what you eat	3212
2Ti	4: 1	who will j the living and the dead,	3212
	4: 8	which the Lord, the righteous J,	3216
Heb	10:30	and again, "The Lord *will* j his people."	3212
	12:23	You have come to God, the j of all men,	3216
	13: 4	for God *will* j the adulterer and all	3212
Jas	4:11	When *you* j the law, you are not keeping it,	3212
	4:12	There is only one Lawgiver and J,	3216
	4:12	But you—who are you *to* j your neighbor?	3212
	5: 9	The J is standing at the door!	3216
1Pe	4: 5	to give account to him who is ready *to* j	3212
Jude	1:15	*to* j everyone, and to convict all	3213+4472
Rev	6:10	**until** *you* j the inhabitants of the earth	3212+4024
	20: 4	those who had been given authority *to* j.	3210

JUDGE'S (2) [JUDGE]

| Mt | 27:19 | While Pilate was sitting on the j **seat,** | 1037 |
| Jn | 19:13 | sat down on the j **seat** at a place known as | 1037 |

JUDGED (25) [JUDGE]

1Sa	7:17	and there he also j Israel.	9149
Job	31:11	would have been shameful, a sin **to be** j.	7132
	31:28	then these also would be sins **to be** j,	7132
Ps	9:19	*let the* nations **be** j in your presence.	9149
Eze	20:36	As I your fathers in the desert of the land	9149
	24:14	You *will be* j according to your conduct	9149
	36:19	I j them according to their conduct	9149
Mt	7: 1	"Do not judge, or you too will be j.	3212
	7: 2	same way you judge others, *you will be* j,	3212
Lk	6:37	"Do not judge, and *you will* not **be** j.	3212
	7:43	"*You have* j correctly," Jesus said.	3212
Ro	2:12	who sin under the law *will be* j by the law.	3212
1Co	4: 3	if *I am* j by you or by any human court;	373
	10:29	For why *should* my freedom be j	3212
	11:31	But if *we* j ourselves, we would not come	1359
	11:32	*When we are* j by the Lord,	3212
	14:24	that he is a sinner and *will be* j by all,	373
Jas	2:12	as those who are going to *be* j by the law	3212
	3: 1	we who teach *will be* j more strictly.	3210+3284
	5: 9	brothers, or *you will be* j.	3212
1Pe	4: 6	so that *they might be* j according to men	3212
Rev	16: 5	the Holy One, because *you have* so j;	3212
	18:20	God *has* j her for the way she treated you.'	3212
	20:12	The dead *were* j according to what	3212
	20:13	and each person *was* j according to what	3212

JUDGES (53) [JUDGE]

Ex	18:22	*Have them* serve as j *for* the people	9149
	18:26	*They* served as j *for* the people at all times.	9149
	21: 6	then his master must take him before the j.	466
	22: 8	of the house must appear before the j	466
	22: 9	parties are to bring their cases before the j	466
	22: 9	the j declare guilty must pay back double	466
Nu	25: 5	So Moses said to Israel's j,	9149
Dt	1:16	And I charged your j at that time:	9149
	16:18	Appoint j and officials for each	9149
	19:17	and the j who are **in office**	9149
	19:18	The j must make a thorough investigation,	9149
	21: 2	and j shall go out and measure the distance	9149
	25: 1	to take it to court and *the j will* **decide**	9149
Jos	8:33	with their elders, officials and j,	9149
	23: 2	their elders, leaders, j and officials—	9149
	24: 1	leaders, j and officials of Israel,	9149
Jdg	2:16	Then the LORD raised up j,	9149
	2:17	to their j but prostituted themselves	9149
Ru	1: 1	In the days when the j ruled,	9149
1Sa	8: 1	he appointed his sons as j for Israel.	9149
2Ki	23:22	Not since the days of the j who led Israel,	9149
1Ch	23: 4	and six thousand are to be officials and j.	9149
	26:29	as officials and j over Israel.	9149
2Ch	1: 2	to the j and to all the leaders in Israel,	9149
	19: 5	He appointed j in the land,	9149
Ezr	4: 9	j and officials over the men from Tripolis,	10171
	4:10	and j to administer justice to all the people	10171
	10:14	along with the elders and j of each town,	9149
Job	9:24	he blindfolds its j.	9149
	12:17	and makes fools of j.	9149
	21:22	since he j even the highest?	9149
Ps	58:11	surely there is a God *who* j the earth."	9149
	75: 7	But it is God *who* j.	9149
Pr	29:14	If a king j the poor with fairness,	9149
Isa	1:26	I will restore your j as in days of old,	9149
Eze	18: 8	and j fairly between man and man.	5477+6913
	44:24	the priests are to serve as j and decide it	9149
Da	3: 2	prefects, governors, advisers, treasurers, j,	10188
	3: 3	prefects, governors, advisers, treasurers, j,	10188
Mt	12:27	So then, they will be your j.	3216
Lk	11:19	So then, they will be your j.	3216
Jn	5:22	Moreover, the Father j no one,	3212
Ac	13:20	God gave them j until the time of Samuel	3216
1Co	4: 4	It is the Lord *who* j me.	373
	6: 4	**appoint as** j even men of little account in	2767
Heb	4:12	it j the thoughts and attitudes of the heart.	3217
Jas	2: 4	and become j with evil thoughts?	3216
	4:11	against his brother or j him speaks against	3212
	4:11	against the law and j it.	3212
1Pe	1:17	Father who j each man's work impartially,	3212
	2:23	he entrusted himself to him who j justly.	3212
Rev	18: 8	for mighty is the Lord God who j her.	3212
	19:11	With justice he j and makes war.	3212

JUDGING (10) [JUDGE]

Dt	1:17	Do not show partiality in j;	5477
1Sa	7:16	j Israel in all those places.	9149
2Ch	19: 6	*you are* not j for man but for the LORD,	9149
Ps	9: 4	you have sat on your throne, j righteously.	9149
Pr	24:23	To show partiality in j is not good:	5477
Isa	16: 5	*in* j seeks justice and speeds the cause	9149
Mt	19:28	j the twelve tribes of Israel.	3212
Lk	22:30	j the twelve tribes of Israel.	3212
Jn	7:24	Stop j by mere appearances,	3212
Rev	11:18	The time has come *for* j the dead,	3212

JUDGMENT (132) [JUDGE]

Ex	6: 6	outstretched arm and with mighty **acts of** j.	9150
	7: 4	with mighty **acts of** j I will bring out my divisions,	9150
	12:12	and I will bring j on all the gods of Egypt.	9150
Lev	13:37	If, however, in his j it is unchanged	6524
Nu	33: 4	for the LORD had brought j on their gods.	9150
Dt	1:17	for j belongs to God.	5477
	32:41	and my hand grasps it in j,	5477
1Sa	25:33	May you be blessed for your **good** j and	3248
2Ch	20: 9	whether the sword of j	9144
	22: 8	While Jehu was **executing** j on the house	9149
	24:24	j was executed on Joash.	9150
Job	14: 3	Will you bring him before you for j?	5477
	19:29	and then you will know that there is j."	8723
	24: 1	the Almighty not set times for j?	NIH
	34:23	that they should come before him for j.	5477
	36:17	you are laden with the j *due* the wicked;	1907
	36:17	j and justice have taken hold of you.	1907
Ps	1: 5	the wicked will not stand in the j,	5477
	9: 7	he has established his throne for j.	5477
	76: 8	From heaven you pronounced j,	1907
	82: 1	he *gives* j among the "gods":	9149
	94:15	J will again be founded on righteousness,	5477
	119:66	Teach me knowledge and good j,	3248
	122: 5	There the thrones for j stand,	5477
	143: 2	Do not bring your servant into j,	5477
Pr	3:21	My son, preserve **sound** j and discernment,	9370
	6:32	But a man who commits adultery lacks j;	4213
	7: 7	a youth who lacked j.	4213
	8:14	Counsel and **sound** j are mine;	9370
	9: 4	she says to those who lack j,	4213
	9:16	she says to those who lack j.	4213
	10:13	a rod is for the back of him who lacks j.	4213
	10:21	but fools die for lack of j.	4213
	11:12	A man who lacks j derides his neighbor,	4213
	12:11	but he who chases fantasies lacks j.	4213
	15:21	Folly delights a man who lacks j,	4213
	17:18	A man lacking in j strikes hands in pledge	4213
	18: 1	he defies all **sound** j.	9370
	24:30	past the vineyard of the man who lacks j;	4213
	28:16	A tyrannical ruler lacks j,	9312
Ecc	3:16	In the place of j—wickedness was there	5477
	3:17	"God *will* **bring to** j both the righteous	9149
	11: 9	for all these things God will bring you to j.	5477
	12:14	For God will bring every deed into j,	5477
Isa	3:14	The LORD enters into j against the elders	5477
	4: 4	from Jerusalem by a spirit of j and a spirit	5477
	28: 6	be a spirit of justice to him who sits in j,	5477
	34: 5	see, it descends in j on Edom,	5477
	41: 1	let us meet together at the **place of** j.	5477
	53: 8	By oppression and j he was taken away.	5477
	66:16	with his sword the LORD will **execute** j	9149
Jer	2:35	But I *will* **pass** j on you because you say,	9149
	10:15	when their j comes, they will perish.	7213
	25:31	he *will* **bring** j on all mankind and put	9149
	48:21	J has come to the plateau—	5477
	48:47	Here ends the j *on* Moab.	5477
	51: 9	for her j reaches to the skies,	5477
	51:18	when their j comes, they will perish.	7213
Eze	5: 8	and *I will* **execute** j against you at the borders	9149
	11:11	*I will* **execute** j on you at the borders	9149
	17:20	I will bring him to Babylon and **execute** j	9149
	20:35	face to face, *I will* **execute** j upon you	9149
	38:22	*I will* **execute** j upon him with plague	9149
Da	7:22	of Days came and pronounced j in favor of	10170
Hos	5: 1	This j is against you:	5477
	5:11	Ephraim is oppressed, trampled in j,	5477
Joel	3: 2	There I will **enter into** j against them	9149
Am	7: 4	The Sovereign LORD was calling for j	8189
Hab	1:12	you have appointed them to execute j;	5477
Zec	8:16	**render** true and sound j	5477+9149
Mal	3: 5	"So I will come near to you for j.	5477
Mt	5:21	anyone who murders will be subject *to* j.'	3213
	5:22	with his brother will be subject *to* j.	3213
	10:15	and Gomorrah on the day *of* j than for	3213
	11:22	for Tyre and Sidon on the day *of* j than	3213
	11:24	for Sodom on the day *of* j than for you."	3213
	12:36	to give account on the day *of* j	3213

Mt	12:41	the **j** with this generation and condemn it;	3213
	12:42	the **j** with this generation and condemn it;	3213
Lk	10:14	for Tyre and Sidon at the **j** than for you.	3213
	11:31	of the South will rise at the **j** with the men	3213
	11:32	the **j** with this generation and condemn it;	3213
Jn	5:22	but has entrusted all **j** to the Son,	3213
	5:30	I judge only as I hear, and my **j** is just,	3213
	7:24	and **make** a right **j.**"	3212+3213
	8:15	by human standards; I **pass j** on no one.	3212
	8:26	"I have much to say in **j** of you.	3212
	9:39	"For **j** I have come into this world,	3210
	12:31	Now is the time for **j** on this world;	3212
	16: 8	in regard to sin and righteousness and **j:**	3213
	16:11	and in regard to **j,** because the prince of this	3213
Ac	15:19	"It is my **j,** therefore, **that** we should	3212
	24:25	self-control and the **j** to come,	3210
Ro	2: 1	you who **pass j** on someone else,	3212
	2: 1	because you who **pass j** do the same things,	3212
	2: 2	Now we know that God's **j** against those	3210
	2: 3	**pass j** on them and yet do the same things,	3212
	2: 3	do you think you will escape God's **j?**	3210
	2: 5	when his **righteous j** will be revealed.	1464
	5:16	The **j** followed one sin and brought	3210
	12: 3	but rather think of yourself with **sober j,**	5404
	13: 2	and those who do so will bring **j**	3210
	14: 1	without **passing j** on disputable matters.	1360
	14:10	For we will all stand before God's **j seat.**	1037
	14:13	**let** us stop **passing j** on one another.	3212
1Co	2:15	he himself **is** not subject to any man's **j:**	373
	5: 3	And I have already **passed j** on	3212
	6: 1	**take** it before the ungodly **for j**	3212
	7:25	from the Lord, but I give a **j** as one who by	1191
	7:40	In my **j,** she is happier if she stays	1191
	9: 3	This is my defense **to** those who **sit in j** on	373
	11:29	of the Lord eats and drinks **j** on himself.	3210
	11:31	**we** would not **come under j.**	3210
	11:34	you meet together it may not result in **j.**	3210
2Co	5:10	For we must all appear before the **j seat**	1037
2Th	1: 5	All this is evidence that God's **j** is right,	3213
1Ti	3: 6	and fall under the same **j** as the devil.	3210
	5:12	Thus they bring **j** on themselves,	3210
	5:24	reaching the place of **j** ahead of them;	3213
Heb	6: 2	the resurrection of the dead, and eternal **j.**	3210
	9:27	to die once, and after that to face **j,**	3213
	10:27	a fearful expectation **of j** and of raging fire	3213
Jas	2:13	because **j** without mercy will be shown	3213
	2:13	Mercy triumphs over **j!**	3213
	4:11	you are not keeping it, but **sitting in j** on it.	3216
1Pe	4:17	For it is time for **j** to begin with the family	3210
2Pe	2: 4	into gloomy dungeons to be held for **j;**	3213
	2: 9	to hold the unrighteous for the day **of j,**	3213
	3: 7	being kept for the day **of j** and destruction	3213
1Jn	4:17	have confidence on the day **of j,**	3213
Jude	1: 6	bound with everlasting chains for **j** on	3213
Rev	14: 7	because the hour **of** his **j** has come.	3213

JUDGMENTS (18) [JUDGE]

Dt	33:21	and his **j** concerning Israel."	5477
1Ch	16:12	his miracles, and the **j** he pronounced,	5477
	16:14	his **j** are in all the earth.	5477
Ps	48: 1	villages of Judah are glad because of your **j.**	5477
	97: 8	villages of Judah are glad because of your **j,**	5477
	105: 5	his miracles, and the **j** he pronounced,	5477
	105: 7	his **j** are in all the earth.	5477
Isa	26: 9	When your **j** come upon the earth,	5477
Jer	1:16	I will pronounce my **j** on my people	5477
	4:12	Now I pronounce my **j** against them."	5477
Eze	14:21	against Jerusalem my four dreadful **j**—	9150
Da	9:11	"Therefore the curses and **sworn j** written	8652
Hos	6: 5	my **j** flashed like lightning upon you.	5477
Ro	11:33	How unsearchable his **j,**	3210
1Co	2:15	The spiritual man **makes j about** all things,	373
Rev	16: 5	"You are just in these **j,**	NIG
	16: 7	true and just are your **j.**"	3213
	19: 2	for true and just are his **j.**	3213

JUDITH (1)

Ge	26:34	he married **J** daughter of Beeri the Hittite,	3377

JUG (6) [JUGS]

1Sa	26:11	the spear and water **j** that are near his head,	7608
	26:12	the spear and water **j** near Saul's head,	7608
	26:16	Where are the king's spear and water **j**	7608
1Ki	17:12	of flour in a jar and a little oil in a **j.**	7608
	17:14	be used up and the **j** of oil will not run dry	7608
	17:16	the jar of flour was not used up and the **j**	7608

JUGS (1) [JUG]

Jer	48:12	they will empty her jars and smash her **j.**	5574

JUICE (3)

Nu	6: 3	not drink grape **j** or eat grapes or raisins,	5489
	18:27	the threshing floor or **j** from the winepress.	4852
Isa	65: 8	when **j** is still found in a cluster of grapes	9408

JULIA (1)

Ro	16:15	Greet Philologus, **J,** Nereus and his sister,	2684

JULIUS (2)

Ac	27: 1	over **to** a centurion named **J,**	2685
	27: 3	The next day we landed at Sidon; and **J,**	2685

JUMP (1) [JUMPED, JUMPING]

Ac	27:43	to **j** overboard first and get to land.	681

JUMPED (5) [JUMP]

Mk	10:50	he **j** to **his feet** and came to Jesus.	403
Jn	21: 7	and **j** into the water.	965+1571
Ac	3: 8	He **j** to his feet and began to walk.	1982
	14:10	At that, the **man j up** and began to walk.	256
	19:16	Then the man who had the evil spirit **j** on	2383

JUMPING (1) [JUMP]

Ac	3: 8	walking and **j,** and praising God.	256

JUNCTION (1) [JOIN]

Eze	21:21	at the **j** of the two roads, to seek an omen:	8031

JUNIAS (1)

Ro	16: 7	Greet Andronicus and **J,**	2687

JUPITER (KJV) See ZEUS

JURISDICTION (1)

Lk	23: 7	that Jesus was under Herod's **j,**	2026

JUSHAB-HESED (1)

1Ch	3:20	Ohel, Berekiah, Hasadiah and **J.**	3457

JUST (393) [JUSTICE, JUSTIFICATION, JUSTIFIED, JUSTIFIES, JUSTIFY, JUSTIFYING, JUSTLY]

Ge	6:22	Noah did everything **j as** God had	3869
	9: 3	**J as** I gave you the green plants,	3869
	18:19	of the LORD by doing what is right and **j,**	5477
	18:32	but let me speak **j** once more.	421
	26:29	**j as** we did not molest you	889+3869
	27: 9	**j** the **way** he likes it.	889+3869
	27:13	I do what I say; go and get them for me."	421
	27:14	the **way** his father liked it.	889+3869
	27:33	I ate it **j before** you came	928+3270
	29:15	"**J because** you are a relative of mine,	3954
	33:13	If they are driven hard **j** one day,	NIH
	33:15	"I let me **find** favor in the eyes	AIT
	38:11	"He may die too, **j, like** his brothers."	3869
	40:13	**j as** you used to do	3869
	40:22	**j as** Joseph had said to them	889+3869
	41:21	they looked **j as** ugly as before.	889+3869
	41:28	"It is **j as** I said to Pharaoh:	889
	41:54	**j as** Joseph had said.	889+3869
	42: 1	**j keep looking** at each other?"	AIT
	42:14	Joseph said to them, "It is **j as** I told you:	889
	46:34	**j as** our fathers did."	1685
	47: 3	"**j as** our fathers were."	1685
	48: 5	**j as** Reuben and Simeon are mine.	3869
Ex	5:13	**j as** when you had straw."	889+3869
	7: 6	Moses and Aaron did **j as**	889+3869+4027
	7:10	Aaron went to Pharaoh and did **j as** the LORD commanded.	889+3869+4027
	7:13	**j as** the LORD had said.	889+3869
	7:20	Moses and Aaron did **j as**	889+3869+4027
	7:22	**j as** the LORD had said.	889+3869
	8:15	**j as** the LORD had said.	889+3869
	8:19	**j as** the LORD had said.	889+3869
	9:12	**j as** the LORD had said to Moses.	889+3869
	9:35	**j as** the LORD had said through Moses.	889+3869
	10: 8	"But **j** who will be going?"	2256+4769+4769
	10:29	"**J as** you say," Moses replied,	4027
	12:28	The Israelites did **j what**	889+3869+4027
	12:50	All the Israelites did **j what**	889+3869+4027
	27: 8	be made **j as** you were shown on	889+3869
	28:27	to the seam **j above** the waistband of	4946+5087
	31:11	them **j as** I commanded you."	889+3869+3972
	36: 1	**j as** the LORD has commanded."	889+3972+4200
	39:20	to the seam **j above** the waistband of	4946+5087
	39:32	The Israelites did everything **j as**	889+3869+4027
	39:42	The Israelites had done all the work **j as** the LORD had commanded	889+3869+4027
	39:43	saw that they had done it **j as**	889+3869+4027
	40:15	Anoint them **j as** you anointed their father,	889+3869
	40:16	Moses did everything **j as**	889+3869+4027
Lev	4:10	**j as** the fat is removed from	889+3869
	4:20	this bull **j as** he did with the bull	889+3869+4027
	4:31	**j as** the fat is removed from the	889+3869
	4:35	**j as** the fat is removed from the lamb of	889+3869
	12: 2	**j as** she is unclean during her monthly	3869
	15:25	**j as** in the days of her period.	3869
Nu	1:54	The Israelites did all this **j as**	889+3869+4027
	5: 4	They did **j as** the LORD had	889+3869+4027
	8: 3	**j as** the LORD commanded Moses.	889+3869
	8:20	the Levites **j as** the LORD	889+3869+3972+4027
	8:22	They did with the Levites **j as**	889+3869
	9: 5	The Israelites did everything **j as**	889+3869+4027
	11:19	You will not eat it for **j** one day,	NIH
	14:17	**j as** you have declared;	889+3869
	14:19	**j as** you have pardoned them from	889+3869
	15:27	"But if **j** one person sins unintentionally,	NIH
	17:11	Moses did **j as** the LORD	889+3869+4027
	18:18	**j as** the breast of the wave offering and	3869
	20: 9	**j as** he commanded him.	3869
	22:38	"But can I say **j** anything?	NIH
Nu	32:27	**j as** our lord says."	889+3869
Dt	2:12	**j as** Israel did in the land	889+3869
	6: 3	**j as** the LORD, the God of your fathers,	889+3869
	27: 3	**j as** the LORD, the God of your fathers,	889+3869
	28:63	**j as** it pleased the LORD	889+3869
	30: 9	**j as** he delighted in your fathers,	889+3869
	32: 4	and all his ways are **j.**	5477
	32: 4	upright and **j** is he.	3838
	32:47	They are not **j** idle words for you—	3954
	32:50	**j as** your brother Aaron died on Mount Hor	889+3869
Jos	1:17	**J as** we fully obeyed Moses,	3869
	4:10	**j as** Moses had directed Joshua.	889+3869+3972
	4:14	**j as** they had revered Moses.	889+3869
	4:23	to the Jordan **j** what he had done to	889+3869
	8:34	**j as** it is written in the Book of the Law.	3869
	10:32	**j as** he had done to Libnah.	889+3869+3972
	10:35	**j as** they had done to Lachish.	889+3869+3972
	10:37	**J as** at Eglon, they totally	889+3869+3972
	10:40	**j as** the LORD, the God of Israel,	889+3869
	11:23	**j as** the LORD had directed	889+3869+3972
	14: 5	**j as** the LORD had commanded	889+3869+4027
	14:10	"Now then, **j as** the LORD promised,	889+3869
	14:11	I'm **j as** vigorous to go out to battle now	3869
	14:12	I will drive them out **j as** he said."	889+3869
	21:44	**j as** he had sworn to their forefathers.	889+3869+3972
	23:10	fights for you, **j as** he promised.	889+3869
	23:15	But **j as** every good promise of	889+3869
Jdg	2:15	**j as** he had sworn to them.	889+3869
	6:39	Let me make **j** one more request.	421
	7:13	Gideon arrived **j as** a man was telling	2180
	7:19	**j after** they had changed the guard.	421
	8: 7	Then Gideon replied, "**J for that,**	4027+4200
	9: 2	sons rule over you, or **j** one man?'	NIH
	9:35	the entrance to the city gate **j as** Abimelech	2256
	11:36	Do to me **j as** you promised,	889+3869
	16:28	O God, please strengthen me **j** once more,	421
	18: 19	priest rather than **j** one man's household?"	NIH
Ru	2: 4	**J then** Boaz arrived from Bethlehem	2180+2256
1Sa	4:16	"I **have j come** from the battle line;	AIT
	9:12	he has **j** come to our town today,	3954
	11: 5	**J then** Saul was returning from the fields,	2180
	13:10	**J as** he finished making the offering,	3869
	24:18	You have **j now** told me of	2021+3427
	25:21	David had **j** said, "It's been useless—	AIT
	25:25	is **j** like his name—his name is Fool,	3869+4027
2Sa	3:22	**J then** David's men and Joab returned	2180+2256
	8:15	doing what was **j** and right for all	5477
	10: 2	**j as** his father showed kindness to me."	889+3869
	11:10	"Haven't you **j come** from a distance?	AIT
	13:35	has happened **j as** your servant said."	3869+4027
	16:19	**J as** I served your father,	889+3869
	18:10	"I **j** saw Absalom hanging in an oak tree."	2180
	18:29	"I saw great confusion **j** as Joab was about	NIH
	19: 5	your men, who have **j** saved your life	2021+3427
	21: 9	**j as** the barley harvest was beginning.	928
1Ki	5:12	**j as** he had promised him.	889+3869
	8:20	**j as** the LORD promised,	889+3869
	8:53	as you declared through your	889+3869
	8:56	rest to his people Israel **j as**	889+3869+3972
	20: 4	The king of Israel answered, "**J as** you say,	3869
	22:53	to anger, **j as** his father had done.	889+3869+3972
2Ki	4: 3	Don't ask for **j** a few.	5070
	4:17	**j as** Elisha had told her.	889
	5:22	company of the prophets have **j** come	2296+6964
	7:10	and the tents left **j as** they were."	889+3869
	7:17	**j as** the man of God had foretold when	889+3869
	8: 5	**J as** Gehazi was telling the king	2256
	11: 9	of a hundred did **j as** Jehoiada	889+3869+3972
	15: 3	**j as** his father Amaziah had done.	889+3869+3972
	15:34	**j as** his father Uzziah had done.	889+3869+3972
	16:16	did **j as** King Ahaz had ordered.	889+3869+3972
	18: 3	**j as** his father David had done.	889+3869+3972
	23:19	**J as** he had done at Bethel,	3869+3972
	23:32	**j as** his fathers had done.	889+3869+3972
	23:37	**j as** his fathers had done.	889+3869+3972
	24: 9	**j as** his father had done.	889+3869+3972
	24:19	**j as** Jehoiakim had done.	889+3869+3972
1Ch	9:19	for guarding the thresholds of the Tent **j as**	2256
	18:14	doing what was **j** and right for all	5477
	24:31	**j as** their brothers the descendants	4200+6645
	26:12	**j as** their relatives had.	4200+6645
2Ch	6:10	**j as** the LORD promised,	889+3869
	12: 6	"The LORD is **j.**"	7404
	21:13	as the house of Ahab did.	3869
	23: 8	men of Judah did **j as** Jehoiada	889+3869+3972
	26: 4	**j as** his father Amaziah had done.	889+3869+3972
	27: 2	**j as** his father Uzziah had done.	889+3869+3972
	29: 2	**j as** his father David had done.	889+3869+3972
	32:17	"**J as** the gods of the peoples of the other	3869
Ne	6: 8	you are **j** making it up out of your head."	3954
	9:13	and laws that are **j** and right,	3838
	9:33	all that has happened to us, you have been **j;**	7404
Est	2:20	nationality **j as** Mordecai had told her	889+3869
	6: 4	Now Haman had **j entered** the outer court	AIT
	6:10	and do **j as** you have suggested	889+3869+4027
	7: 8	**J as** the king returned from	2256
Job	33: 6	I am **j like** you before God;	3869+7023
	34:17	Will you condemn the **j** and mighty One?	7404
	35: 2	"Do you think this is **j?**	5477
Ps	35:25	"Aha, **j what we wanted!"**	5883
	37:28	the **j** and will not forsake his faithful ones.	5477
	37:30	and his tongue speaks **what** is **j.**	5477
	90: 4	like a day that has **j** gone by,	AIT
	99: 4	in Jacob you have done **what** is **j** and right.	5477
	111: 7	The works of his hands are faithful and **j;**	5477

Ps	119:121	I have done what is righteous and j;	5477
Pr	1: 3	doing what is right and j and fair;	5477
	2: 8	the course of the j and protects the way	5477
	2: 9	what is right and j and fair—	5477
	8: 8	All the words of my mouth are j;	7406
	8:15	and rulers make laws that are j;	7406
	12: 5	The plans of the righteous are j,	5477
	21: 3	what is right and j is more acceptable to	5477
	25:16	If you find honey, eat j enough—	1896
Ecc	2:13	j as light is better than darkness.	3869
	12:10	Teacher searched to find j the right words,	2914
SS	4: 2	Your teeth are like a flock of sheep j shorn,	7892
Isa	20: 3	"J as my servant Isaiah has gone stripped and barefoot	889+3869
	28: 9	to those j taken from the breast?	AIT
	32: 7	even when the plea of the needy is j.	5477
	52:14	J as there were many who were appalled at him—	889+3869
	58: 2	for j decisions and seem eager for God	7406
Jer	4: 2	Have you not j called to me:	4946+6964
	4: 2	j and righteous way you swear,	5477
	7:15	j as I did all your brothers,	889+3869
	7:22	I did not j give them commands	AIT
	19:11	will smash this nation and this city as j	889+3869
	22: 3	Do what is just,	5477
	22:15	He did what was right and j,	7407
	23: 5	and do what is j and right in the land.	5477
	23:27	j as their fathers forgot my name	889+3869
	31:28	J as I watched over them to uproot	889+3869
	32: 8	"Then, j as the LORD had said,	3869
	33:15	he will do what is j and right in the land.	5477
	40: 3	he has done j as he said he would.	889+3869
	44:11	will pour out drink offerings to her j as	889+3869
	44:30	j as I handed Zedekiah king of Judah	889+3869
	51:49	j as the slain in all the earth have fallen	1685
	52: 2	j as Jehoiakim had done.	889+3869+3972
Eze	18: 5	a righteous man who does what is j	5477
	18:19	Since the son has done what is j and right	5477
	18:21	and keeps all my decrees and does what is j	5477
	18:25	you say, 'The way of the Lord is not j.'	9419
	18:27	and does what is j and right,	5477
	18:29	'The way of the Lord is not j.'	9419
	20:49	'Isn't he j telling parables?'"	AIT
	23:18	j as I had turned away from her sister.	889+3869
	24:24	you will do j as he has done.	889+3869+3972
	33:14	from his sin and does what is j and right—	5477
	33:16	He has done what is j and right;	5477
	33:17	'The way of the Lord is not j.'	9419
	33:19	from his wickedness and does what is j	5477
	33:20	you say, 'The way of the Lord is not j.'	9419
	40:23	j as there was on the east.	2256
	45: 9	and oppression and do what is j and right.	5477
Da	2: 9	there is j one penalty for you.	NIH
	2:41	J as you saw the feet and toes were	10168
	2:43	And j as you saw the iron mixed	10168
	4:37	and all his ways are j.	10170
	6:10	j as he had done before.	10168+10353+10619
	9:13	J as it is written in the Law of Moses,	889+3869
Am	5:14	j as you say he is.	889+3869+4027
	7: 1	and j as the second crop was coming up.	928
Ob	1:16	J as you drank on my holy hill,	889+3869
Mic	2:11	he would be j the prophet for this people!	NIH
Zec	1: 6	j as he determined to do.'"	889+3869
	7: 6	were you not j feasting for yourselves?	AIT
	8:14	"J as I had determined to bring disaster	889+3869
Mal	3:17	j as in compassion a man spares his	889+3869
Mt	8: 8	But j say the word, and my servant will be	3667
	8:13	It will be done j as you believed it would."	6055
	9:18	"My daughter has j died.	785
	9:20	J then a woman who had been subject	2627+2779
	12:13	j as sound as the other.	6055
	14:36	to let the sick j touch the edge of his cloak,	3668
	17: 3	J then there appeared before them Moses	2627
	18:15	j between the two of you.	3668
	18:33	on your fellow servant j as I had on you?'	6055
	20:28	j as the Son of Man did not come to	6061
	26:24	Son of Man will go j as it is written about	2777
	28: 6	He is not here; he has risen, j as he said.	2777
Mk	1:23	J then a man in their synagogue	2317
	4:36	they took him along, j as he was,	6055
	5:28	If I j touch his clothes, I will be healed	1569+2779
	5:36	"Don't be afraid; j believe."	3668
	9:13	j as it is written about him."	2777
	11: 2	and j as you enter it, you will find	2317
	13:11	J say whatever is given you at the time,	247
	14:16	and found things j as Jesus had told them.	2777
	14:21	Son of Man will go j as it is written about	2777
	14:43	J as he was speaking, Judas,	2285+2317
	16: 2	j after sunrise, they were on their way to the tomb.	422+2463+3836
	16: 7	There you will see him, j as he told you.'"	2777
Lk	1: 2	j as they were handed down to us	2777
	2:20	which were j as they had been told.	NIG
	6:36	Be merciful, j as your Father is merciful.	2777
	8:50	j believe, and she will be healed."	3668
	11: 1	j as John taught his disciples.	2777
	14:18	The first said, 'I have j bought a field,	NIG
	14:19	'I have j bought five yoke of oxen,	NIG
		"Still another said, 'I j got married,	NIG
	17:26	"J as it was in the days of Noah,	2777
	17:30	"It will be j like this on the day the Son of Man is revealed.	899+2848+3836
	19:32	and found it j as he had told them.	2777
	22:13	and found things j as Jesus had told them.	2777
	22:29	j as my Father conferred one on me,	2777
	22:60	J as he was speaking, the rooster crowed.	4202
Lk	24:24	and found it j as the women had said,	2777+4048
Jn	3:14	J as Moses lifted up the snake in	2777
	4:18	What you have j said is quite true."	NIG
	4:27	J then his disciples returned	2093+4047
	4:42	"We no longer believe j because	NIG
	5:21	For j as the Father raises the dead	6061
	5:23	that all may honor the Son j as they honor	2777
	5:30	and my judgment is j,	1465
	6:57	J as the living Father sent me and I live	2777
	8:25	"J what I have been claiming all along,"	NIG
	8:28	but speak j what the Father has taught me.	2777
	10:15	j as the Father knows me and I know	2777
	12:35	"You are going to have the light j a little	NIG
	12:50	whatever I say is j what the Father told me	2777
	13: 1	It was j before the Passover Feast.	NIG
	13: 9	"not j my feet but my hands and my head	3667
	13:33	and j as I told the Jews, so I tell you now:	2777
	14:10	The words I say to you are not j my own.	NIG
	15:10	j as I have obeyed my Father's commands	2777
	17:21	Father, j as you are in me and I am in you.	2777
	21:10	some of the fish you have j caught.	3814
Ac	7:51	You are j like your fathers:	6055
	10:47	They have received the Holy Spirit j	6055
	14:13	whose temple was j outside the city,	4574
	15: 8	the Holy Spirit to them, j as he did to us.	6055
	15:11	we are saved, j as they are."	2848+4005+5573
	18:14	J as Paul was about to speak,	1254
	20: 3	a plot against him j as he was about to sail	NIG
	22: 3	of our fathers and was j as zealous for God	NIG
	26:10	And that is j what I did in Jerusalem.	2777
	27:25	happen j as he told me.	2848+4005+4048+5573
	27:33	J before dawn Paul urged them all	948+4005
Ro	1:13	j as I have had among the other Gentiles.	2777
	1:17	j as it is written: "The righteous will live by	2777
	3:26	so as to be j and the one who justifies	1465
	4:18	j as it had been said to him,	2848
	5: 6	at j the right time, when we were	2789+2848
	5:12	j as sin entered the world through one man,	6061
	5:18	as the result of one trespass was	6061
	5:19	For j as through the disobedience of the one	6061
	5:21	j as sin reigned in death,	6061
	6: 4	j as Christ was raised from the dead	6061
	6:19	J as you used to offer the parts of your body	6061
	9:13	J as it is written: "Jacob I loved,	2777
	9:29	j as Isaiah said previously: "Unless	2777
	11:30	J as you who were at one time disobedient	6061
	12: 4	j as each of us has one body	2749
	15: 7	then, j as Christ accepted you,	2777
1Co	5: 3	j as if I were present.	4048
	9:18	then is my reward? J this: that in preaching	NIG
	11: 2	j as I passed them on to you.	2777
	11: 5	it is j as though her head were shaved.	899+1651+2779+3836
	12:11	j as he determines.	2777
	12:18	j as he wanted them to be.	2777
	14: 9	You will j be speaking into the air.	NIG
	15:31	I mean that, brothers—j as surely	3755
	15:37	but j a seed, perhaps of wheat or	NIG
	15:49	And j as we have borne the likeness of	2777
	16:10	carrying on the work of the Lord, j as I am.	6055
2Co	1: 5	For j as the sufferings of Christ flow over	2777
	1: 7	because we know that j as you share	6055
	1:14	of us j as we will boast of you in the day of	2749
	7:14	j as everything we said to you was true,	6055
	8: 7	But j as you excel in everything—	6061
	10: 7	that we belong to Christ j as much as he.	2777
	11: 3	But I am afraid that j as Eve was deceived	6055
	11:16	then receive me j as you would a fool,	6055
Gal	2: 7	j as Peter had been to the Jews.	2777
	3: 2	like to learn j one thing from you:	3668+4047
	3:15	J as no one can set aside or add to	3940
	3:20	however, does not represent j one party;	NIG
	4: 8	so always and j when I am with you.	3667
Eph	4: 4	j as you were called to one hope	2777
	4:32	j as in Christ God forgave you.	2777
	5: 2	j as Christ loved us and gave himself up	2777
	5:25	j as Christ loved the church	2777
	5:29	j as Christ does the church—	2777+2779
	6: 5	j as you would obey Christ.	6055
Col	1: 6	j as it has been doing among you since	2777
	2: 6	j as you received Christ Jesus as Lord,	6055
1Th	3: 6	But Timothy has j now come to us	785
	3: 6	j as we also long to see you.	2749
	3:12	j as ours does for you.	2749
	4:11	to work with your hands, j as we told you,	2777
	5:11	j as in fact you are doing.	2777
2Th	1: 6	God is j: He will pay back trouble to those	1465
	3: 1	j as it was with you.	2777
2Ti	3: 8	J as Jannes and Jambres opposed Moses,	4005+5573
Heb	2: 2	disobedience received its j punishment,	1899
	3: 2	j as Moses was faithful in all God's house.	6055
	3: 3	j as the builder of a house has	2848+4012
	3:15	As has j been said: "Today, if	1877+3306+3836
	4: 2	preached to us, j as they did;	2749
	4: 3	j as God has said, "So I declared on oath	2777
	4:10	from his own work, j as God did from his.	6061
	4:15	j as we are—yet was without sin.	2848
	5: 4	he must be called by God, j as Aaron was.	2778
	7: 4	J think how great he was:	1254
	9:27	J as man is destined to die once,	2848+4012
	10:37	For in j a very little while,	NIG
Jas	2:10	at j one point is guilty of breaking all of it.	NIG
	5:17	Elijah was a man j like us.	3926
1Pe	1:15	But j as he who called you is holy,	2848
2Pe	2: 1	j as there will be false teachers among you.	6055
	2:18	they entice people who are j escaping	3903
2Pe	3:15	j as our dear brother Paul also wrote you	2777
1Jn	1: 9	and j and will forgive us our sins	1465
	2:27	j as it has taught you, remain in him.	2777
	3: 3	purifies himself, j as he is pure.	2777
	3: 7	right is righteous, j as he is righteous.	2777
2Jn	1: 4	j as the Father commanded us.	2777
Rev	2:27	j as I have received authority from my Father.	6055
	3:21	j as I overcame and sat down with my Father on his throne.	6055
	10: 7	j as he announced to his servants	6055
	15: 3	J and true are your ways, King of the ages.	1465
	16: 5	"You are j in these judgments,	1465
	16: 7	true and j are your judgments."	1465
	19: 2	for true and j are his judgments.	1465

JUSTICE (134) [JUST]

Ge	49:16	"Dan will provide j for his people as one	1906
Ex	23: 2	do not pervert j by siding with the crowd,	NIH
	23: 6	"Do not deny j to your poor people	5477
Lev	19:15	" 'Do not pervert j;	5477
Dt	16:19	Do not pervert j or show partiality.	5477
	16:20	Follow j and justice alone,	7406
	16:20	Follow justice and j alone,	7406
	24:17	not deprive the alien or the fatherless of j,	5477
	27:19	"Cursed is the man who withholds j from	5477
1Sa	8: 3	and accepted bribes and perverted j.	5477
2Sa	15: 4	see that he gets j."	7405
	15: 6	to the king asking for j,	5477
1Ki	3:11	but for discernment in administering j,	5477
	3:28	he had wisdom from God to administer j.	5477
	7: 7	He built the throne hall, the Hall of J,	5477
	7: 7	to maintain j and righteousness.	5477
2Ch	9: 8	to maintain j and righteousness."	5477
Ezr	7:25	and judges to administer j to all the people	10169
Est	1:13	to consult experts in matters of law and j,	1907
Job	8: 3	Does God pervert j?	5477
	9:19	And if it is a matter of j,	5477
	19: 7	though I call for help, there is no j.	5477
	27: 2	who has denied me j, the Almighty,	5477
	29:14	j was my robe and my turban.	5477
	31:13	"If I have denied j to my menservants	5477
	34: 5	'I am innocent, but God denies me j.	5477
	34:12	that the Almighty would pervert j.	5477
	34:17	Can he who hates j govern?	5477
	36: 3	I will ascribe j to my Maker.	7406
	36:17	judgment and j have taken hold of you.	5477
	37:23	in his j and great righteousness,	5477
	40: 8	"Would you discredit my j?	5477
Ps	7: 6	Awake, my God; decree j.	5477
	9: 8	he will govern the peoples with j.	4797
	9:16	The LORD is known by his j;	5477
	11: 7	For the LORD is righteous, he loves j;	7407
	33: 5	The LORD loves righteousness and j;	5477
	36: 6	your j like the great deep.	5477
	37: 6	the j of your cause like the noonday sun.	5477
	45: 6	of j will be the scepter of your kingdom.	4793
	72: 1	Endow the king with your j, O God,	5477
	72: 2	your afflicted ones with j.	5477
	89:14	and are the foundation of your throne;	5477
	97: 2	righteousness and j are the foundation	5477
	99: 4	The King is mighty, he loves j—	5477
	101: 1	I will sing of your love and j;	5477
	103: 6	The LORD works righteousness and j	5477
	106: 3	Blessed are they who maintain j,	5477
	112: 5	who conducts his affairs with j.	5477
	140:12	that the LORD secures j for the poor	1907
Pr	8:20	along the paths of j,	5477
	16:10	and his mouth should not betray j.	5477
	17:23	a bribe in secret to pervert the course of j.	5477
	18: 5	the wicked or to deprive the innocent of j.	5477
	19:28	A corrupt witness mocks at j,	5477
	21:15	When j is done, it brings joy to the	5477
	28: 5	Evil men do not understand j,	5477
	29: 4	By a king gives a country stability,	5477
	29: 7	The righteous care about j for the poor,	1907
	29:26	but it is from the LORD that man gets j.	5477
Ecc	3:16	wickedness was there, in the place of j—	7406
	5: 8	and j and rights denied,	5477
Isa	1:17	Seek j, encourage the oppressed.	5477
	1:21	She once was full of j;	5477
	1:27	Zion will be redeemed with j,	5477
	5: 7	And he looked for j, but saw bloodshed;	5477
	5:16	LORD Almighty will be exalted by his j,	5477
	5:23	but deny j to the innocent.	7407
	9: 7	with j and righteousness from that time on	5477
	10: 2	the poor of their rights and withhold j from	5477
	11: 4	with j he will give decisions for the poor of	4793
	16: 5	in judging seeks j and speeds the cause	5477
	28: 6	be a spirit of j to him who sits in judgment,	5477
	28:17	I will make j the measuring line	5477
	29:21	false testimony deprive the innocent of j.	NIH
	30:18	For the LORD is a God of j.	5477
	32: 1	in righteousness and rulers will rule with j.	5477
	32:16	J will dwell in the desert	5477
	33: 5	he will fill Zion with j and righteousness,	5477
	42: 1	on him and he will bring j to the nations.	5477
	42: 3	In faithfulness he will bring forth j;	5477
	42: 4	or be discouraged till he establishes j	5477
	51: 4	my j will become a light to the nations.	5477
	51: 5	and my arm will bring j to the nations.	9149
	56: 1	"Maintain j and do what is right,	5477
	59: 4	No one calls for j;	7406
	59: 8	there is no j in their paths.	5477
	59: 9	So j is far from us,	5477
	59:11	We look for j, but find none;	5477

Isa 59:14 So **j** is driven back, 5477
    59:15 and was displeased that there was no **j**. 5477
    61: 8 "For I, the LORD, love **j**; 5477
Jer 9:24 **j** and righteousness on earth, 5477
    10:24 Correct me, LORD, but only with **j**— 5477
    12: 1 Yet I would speak with you about your **j**: 5477
    21:12 " 'Administer **j** every morning; 5477
    30:11 I will discipline you but only with **j**; 5477
    46:28 I will discipline you but only with **j**; 5477
La 3:36 to deprive a man of **j**— 8190
Eze 22:29 and mistreat the alien, denying them **j**. 5477
    34:16 I will shepherd the flock with **j**. 5477
Hos 2:19 I will betroth you in righteousness and **j**, 5477
    12: 6 maintain love and **j**, 5477
Am 2: 7 of the ground and deny **j** to the oppressed. 2006
    5: 7 You who turn **j** into bitterness 5477
    5:12 **deprive** the poor of **j** in the courts. 5742
    5:15 maintain **j** in the courts. 5477
    5:24 But let **j** roll on like a river, 5477
    6:12 But you have turned **j** into poison and 5477
Mic 3: 1 Should you not know **j**, 5477
    3: 8 and with **j** and might, 5477
    3: 9 who despise **j** and distort all that is right; 5477
Hab 1: 4 and **j** never prevails. 5477
    1: 4 so that **j** is perverted. 5477
Zep 3: 5 Morning by morning he dispenses his **j**, 5477
Zec 7: 9 "This is what the LORD Almighty says:
       'Administer true **j**; 5477
Mal 2:17 or "Where is the God of **j**?" 5477
    3: 5 and **deprive** aliens of **j**, 5742
Mt 12:18 and he will proclaim **j** to the nations. 3213
    12:20 till he leads **j** to victory. 3213
    23:23 **j**, mercy and faithfulness. 3213
Lk 11:42 but you neglect **j** and the love of God. 3213
    18: 3 'Grant me **j** against my adversary.' 1688
    18: 5 I will **see that** she gets **j**, 1688
    18: 7 not God bring about **j** for his chosen ones, 1689
    18: 8 I tell you, he will see that they get **j**, 1689
Ac 8:33 In his humiliation he was deprived of **j**. 3213
    17:31 a day when he will judge the world with **j** 1466
    28: 4 **J** has not allowed him to live." 1472
Ro 3:25 He did this to demonstrate his **j**, 1466
    3:26 to demonstrate his **j** at the present time, 1466
2Co 7:11 **readiness to see j** done. 1689
Heb 11:33 through faith conquered kingdoms,
       administered **j**, 1466
Rev 19:11 With **j** he judges and makes war. 1466

JUSTIFICATION (4) [JUST]
Eze 16:52 you have **furnished** some **j** for your sisters. 7136
Ro 4:25 for our sins and was raised to life for our **j**. 1470
    5:16 but the gift followed many trespasses and
       brought **j**, 1468
    5:18 the result of one act of righteousness was **j** 1470

JUSTIFIED (22) [JUST]
Ps 51: 4 when you speak and **j** when you judge. 2342
Lk 18:14 went home **j** before God. 1467
Ac 13:39 Through him everyone who believes is **j** 1467
    13:39 from everything you could not be **j** from 1467
Ro 3:24 and are **j** freely by his grace through 1467
    3:28 a man is **j** by faith apart from observing 1467
    4: 2 If, in fact, Abraham was **j** by works, 1467
    5: 1 since we have been **j** through faith, 1467
    5: 9 Since we have now been **j** by his blood, 1467
    8:30 those he called, he also **j**; 1467
    8:30 those he **j**, he also glorified. 1467
    10:10 your heart that you believe and **are j**, 1466+1650
1Co 6:11 you were **j** in the name of the Lord Jesus 1467
Gal 2:16 that a man is not **j** by observing the law, 1467
    2:16 be **j** by faith in Christ and not by observing 1467
    2:16 by observing the law no one will be **j**. 1467
    2:17 "If, while we seek to be **j** in Christ, 1467
    3:11 Clearly no one is **j** before God by the law, 1467
    3:24 to lead us to Christ that we might be **j** 1467
    5: 4 trying to be **j** by law have been alienated 1467
Tit 3: 7 having been **j** by his grace, 1467
Jas 2:24 You see that a person is **j** by what he does 1467

JUSTIFIES (3) [JUST]
Ro 3:26 the one who **j** those who have faith in Jesus. 1467
    4: 5 not work but trusts God who **j** the wicked, 1467
    8:33 It is God who **j**. 1467

JUSTIFY (7) [JUST]
Est 7: 4 no such distress would **j** disturbing 8750
Job 40: 8 Would you condemn me to **j** yourself? 7405
Isa 53:11 by his knowledge my righteous servant will
       j many, 7405
Lk 10:29 But he wanted to **j** himself, 1467
    16:15 "You are the ones who **j** yourselves in 1467
Ro 3:30 who will **j** the circumcised by faith and 1467
Gal 3: 8 The Scripture foresaw that God would **j** 1467

JUSTIFYING (1) [JUST]
Job 32: 2 angry with Job for **j** himself rather than God 7405

JUSTLE (KJV) See RUSHING

JUSTLY (6) [JUST]
Ps 58: 1 Do you rulers indeed speak **j**? 7406
    67: 4 the peoples **j** and guide the nations of 4793

Jer 7: 5 and deal with each other **j**, 5477
Mic 6: 8 To act **j** and to love mercy and 5477
Lk 23:41 We are punished **j**, 1469
1Pe 2:23 he entrusted himself to him who judges **j**. 1469

JUSTUS (3) [BARSABBAS, JESUS, TITIUS]
Ac 1:23 Joseph called Barsabbas (also known as **J**) 2688
    18: 7 to the house of Titius **J**, 2688
Col 4:11 Jesus, who is called **J**, 2688

JUTTAH (3)
Jos 15:55 Maon, Carmel, Ziph, **J**, 3420
    21:16 **J** and Beth Shemesh, together 3420
1Ch 6:59 **J** and Beth Shemesh, 3420

K

KABZEEL (3)
Jos 15:21 toward the boundary of Edom were: **K**, 7696
2Sa 23:20 of Jehoiada was a valiant fighter from **K**, 7696
1Ch 11:22 of Jehoiada was a valiant fighter from **K**, 7696

KADESH (14) [EN MISHPAT, KADESH BARNEA, MERIBAH KADESH]
Ge 14: 7 went to En Mishpat (that is, **K**), 7729
    16:14 it is still there, between **K** and Bered. 7729
    20: 1 the Negev and lived between **K** and Shur. 7729
Nu 13:26 and the whole Israelite community at **K** in 7729
    20: 1 and they stayed at **K**. 7729
    20:14 Moses sent messengers from **K** to the king 7729
    20:16 "Now we are here at **K**, 7729
    20:22 from **K** and came to Mount Hor. 7729
    33:36 They left Ezion Geber and camped at **K**, 7729
    33:37 They left **K** and camped at Mount Hor, 7729
Dt 1:46 And so you stayed in **K** many days— 7729
Jdg 11:16 the desert to the Red Sea and on to **K**. 7729
    11:17 So Israel stayed at **K**. 7729
Ps 29: 8 the LORD shakes the Desert of **K**. 7729

KADESH BARNEA (10) [KADESH]
Nu 32: 8 when I sent them from **K** to look 7732
    34: 4 on to Zin and go south of **K**, 7732
Dt 1: 2 to **K** by the Mount Seir road.) 7732
    1:19 and so we reached **K**. 7732
    2:14 from the time we left **K** until we crossed 7732
    9:23 the LORD sent you out from **K**, 7732
Jos 10:41 Joshua subdued them from **K** 7732
    14: 6 said to Moses the man of God at **K** about 7732
    14: 7 the servant of the LORD sent me from **K** 7732
    15: 3 and went over to the south of **K**. 7732

KADMIEL (8)
Ezr 2:40 the descendants of Jeshua and **K** (through 7718
    3: 9 Jeshua and his sons and brothers and **K** 7718
Ne 7:43 of Jeshua (through **K** through the line 7718
    9: 4 Jeshua, Bani, **K**, Shebaniah, Bunni, 7718
    9: 5 Jeshua, Bani, Hashabneiah, Sherebiah, 7718
    10: 9 Binnui of the sons of Henadad, **K**, 7718
    12: 8 The Levites were Jeshua, Binnui, **K**, 7718
    12:24 Jeshua son of **K**, and their associates, 7718

KADMONITES (1)
Ge 15:19 the land of the Kenites, Kenizzites, **K**, 7720

KAIN (1)
Jos 15:57 **K**, Gibeah and Timnah— 7805

KALLAI (1)
Ne 12:20 of Sallu's, **K**; of Amok's, Eber; 7834

KAMAI See LEB KAMAI

KAMON (1)
Jdg 10: 5 When Jair died, he was buried in **K**. 7852

KANAH (3)
Jos 16: 8 the border went west to the **K** Ravine 7867
    17: 9 boundary continued south to the **K** Ravine. 7867
    19:28 It went to Abdon, Rehob, Hammon and **K**, 7867

KAREAH (14)
2Ki 25:23 of Nethaniah, Johanan son of **K**, 7945
Jer 40: 8 Johanan and Jonathan the sons of **K**, 7945
    40:13 son of **K** and all the army officers still in 7945
    40:15 of **K** said privately to Gedaliah in Mizpah, 7945
    40:16 of Ahikam said to Johanan son of **K**, 7945
    41:11 son of **K** and all the army officers who were 7945
    41:13 son of **K** and the army officers who were 7945
    41:14 and went over to Johanan son of **K**. 7945

Jer 41:16 son of **K** and all the army officers who were 7945
    42: 1 son of **K** and Jezaniah son of Hoshaiah, 7945
    42: 8 son of **K** and all the army officers who were 7945
    43: 2 of Hoshaiah and Johanan son of **K** and all 7945
    43: 4 son of **K** and all the army officers and all 7945
    43: 5 of **K** and all the army officers led away all 7945

KARKA (1)
Jos 15: 3 up to Addar and curved around to **K**. 7978

KARKOR (1)
Jdg 8:10 Now Zebah and Zalmunna were in **K** with 7980

KARNAIM (1)
Am 6:13 "Did we not take **K** by our own strength?" 7969

KARTAH (2)
Jos 21:34 from the tribe of Zebulun, Jokneam, **K**, 7985
1Ch 6:77 **K**, Rimmono and Tabor, 7985

KARTAN (1)
Jos 21:32 and **K**, together with their pasturelands— 7986

KATTATH (1)
Jos 19:15 Included were **K**, Nahalal, Shimron, 7793

KATYDID (1)
Lev 11:22 Of these you may eat any kind of locust, **k**, 6155

KAZIN See ETH KAZIN

KEBAR (8)
Eze 1: 1 I was among the exiles by the **K** River, 3894
    1: 3 the **K** River in the land of the Babylonians. 3894
    3:15 at Tel Abib near the **K** River. 3894
    3:23 like the glory I had seen by the **K** River, 3894
    10:15 I had seen by the **K** River. 3894
    10:20 the God of Israel by the **K** River, 3894
    10:22 as those I had seen by the **K** River. 3894
    43: 3 like the visions I had seen by the **K** River, 3894

KEDAR (11) [KEDAR'S]
Ge 25:13 Nebaioth the firstborn of Ishmael, **K**, 7723
1Ch 1:29 Nebaioth the firstborn of Ishmael, **K**, 7723
Ps 120: 5 that I live among the tents of **K**! 7723
SS 1: 5 dark like the tents of **K**, 7723
Isa 21:16 all the pomp of **K** will come to an end. 7723
    21:17 the warriors of **K**, will be few." 1201+7723
    42:11 let the settlements where **K** lives rejoice. 7723
Jer 2:10 send to **K** and observe closely; 7723
    49:28 Concerning **K** and the kingdoms of Hazor, 7723
    49:28 attack **K** and destroy the people of the East. 7723
Eze 27:21 the princes of **K** were your customers; 7723

KEDAR'S (1) [KEDAR]
Isa 60: 7 All **K** flocks will be gathered to you, 7723

KEDEMAH (2)
Ge 25:15 Hadad, Tema, Jetur, Naphish and **K**. 7715
1Ch 1:31 and **K**. These were the sons of Ishmael. 7715

KEDEMOTH (4)
Dt 2:26 From the desert of **K** I sent messengers 7717
Jos 13:18 Jahaz, **K**, Mephaath, 7717
    21:37 **K** and Mephaath, together 7717
1Ch 6:79 **K** and Mephaath, together 7717

KEDESH (11)
Jos 12:22 the king of **K** one 7730
    15:23 **K**, Hazor, Ithnan, 7730
    19:37 **K**, Edrei, En Hazor, 7730
    20: 7 So they set apart **K** in Galilee in 7730
    21:32 **K** in Galilee (a city of refuge) 7730
Jdg 4: 6 She sent for Barak son of Abinoam from **K** 7730
    4: 9 So Deborah went with Barak to **K**, 7730
    4:11 by the great tree in Zaanannim near **K**. 7730
2Ki 15:29 Abel Beth Maacah, Janoah, **K** and Hazor. 7730
1Ch 6:72 from the tribe of Issachar they received **K**, 7730
    6:76 from the tribe of Naphtali they received **K** 7730

KEDORLAOMER (5)
Ge 14: 1 **K** king of Elam and Tidal king of Goiim 3906
    14: 4 twelve years they had been subject to **K**, 3906
    14: 5 **K** and the kings allied with him went out 3906
    14: 9 against **K** king of Elam, Tidal king 3906
    14:17 After Abram returned from defeating **K** and 3906

KEEN (1)
Da 5:12 **k** mind and knowledge and understanding, 10339

KEEP (325) [KEEPER, KEEPERS, KEEPING, KEEPS, KEPT, SAFEKEEPING]
Ge 6:19 to **k** them **alive** with you. 2649
    7: 3 to **k** their various kinds **alive** 2649
    14:21 the people and **k** the goods for yourself." 4374
    17: 9 "As for you, you must **k** my covenant, 9068

Ref		
Ge	17:10	the covenant *you are to* **k:**	9068
	18:19	and his household after him *to* **k** the way of	9068
	31:49	the Lord **k watch** between you and me	7595
	32:16	and **k** some space between the herds.	8492
	33: 9	**K** what you have for yourself."	2118
	38: 9	the ground to **k from** producing offspring	1194
	38:23	Then Judah said, "*Let her* **k** what she has,	4374
	42: 1	"Why *do you* **k looking at each other?**"	AIT
Ex	47:24	other four-fifths you may **k** as seed for	2118+4200
	5: 9	so that *they* **k working** and pay no attention	AIT
	5:17	That is why *you* **k saying,**	AIT
	12:42	on this night all the Israelites are to **k vigil**	4200
	13:10	*You must* **k** this ordinance at the appointed	9068
	15:26	to his commands and **k** all his decrees,	9068
	16:19	"No one *is to* **k** any of it until morning."	3855
	16:23	Save whatever is left and **k** it until morning.	5466
	16:28	to **k** my commands and my instructions?	9068
	16:32	of manna and **k** it for the generations	5466
	19: 5	if you obey me fully and **k** my covenant,	9068
	20: 6	and **k** my commandments.	9068
	20:20	will be with you to **k** you **from** sinning."	1194
	21:36	yet the owner *did* not **k** it **penned up,**	9068
	27:21	*to* **k** the lamps burning before the Lord	6885
Lev	7: 8	a burnt offering for anyone *may* **k** its hide	2118
	13: 5	to **k** him **in isolation** another seven days.	6037
	13:33	*to* **k** him **in isolation** another seven days.	6037
	15:31	**k** the Israelites **separate** from things that	5692
	18: 5	**K** my decrees and laws,	9068
	18:26	But you *must* **k** my decrees and my laws.	9068
	18:30	**K** my requirements and do not follow any	9068
	19:19	" '**K** my decrees.	9068
	19:37	" '**K** all my decrees and all my laws	9068
	20: 8	**K** my decrees and follow them.	9068
	20:22	" '**K** all my decrees and laws	9068
	22: 9	" 'The priests *are to* **k** my requirements so	9068
	22:31	"**K** my commands and follow them.	9068
	26: 9	and *I will* **k** my covenant with you.	7756
Nu	6:24	" ' "The Lord bless you and **k** you;	9068
	11:13	*They* **k wailing** to me,	AIT
	15:22	" 'Now if *you* unintentionally fail *to* **k** any	6913
	22:16	not *let anything* **k** you from coming to me,	4979
	36: 7	for every Israelite *shall* **k** the tribal land	1815
	36: 9	for each Israelite tribe *is to* **k** the land	1815
Dt	4: 2	but **k** the commands of the Lord	9068
	4:40	**K** his decrees and commands,	9068
	5:10	and **k** my commandments.	9068
	5:29	to fear me and **k** all my commands always,	9068
	6:17	**Be sure to k** the commands of	9068+9068
	7: 9	of those who love him and **k** his commands.	9068
	7:12	the Lord your God *will* **k** his covenant	9068
	7:15	Lord *will* **k** you **free** from every disease.	6073
	8: 2	whether or not *you would* **k** his commands.	9068
	11: 1	and **k** his requirements,	9068
	13: 4	**K** his commands and obey him;	9068
	22: 2	with you and **k** it until he comes looking	2118
	23: 9	**k** away from everything impure.	9068
	26:17	that you *will* **k** his decrees,	9068
	26:18	and that *you are to* **k** all his commands.	9068
	27: 1	"**K** all these commands	9068
	28: 9	if *you* **k** the commands of the Lord	9068
	28:41	and daughters but you *will* not **k** them,	2118+4200
	30:10	the Lord your God and **k** his commands	9068
	30:16	to walk in his ways, and to **k** his commands,	9068
Jos	3: 4	But **k** a distance of about a thousand yards	2118
	6:18	But **k** away from the devoted things,	9068
	7:11	which I commanded them to **k.**	NIH
Jdg	2:22	to test Israel and see whether they *will* **k**	9068
	6:11	in a winepress to **k** it from the Midianites.	5674
1Sa	1:14	"How long *will you* **k on getting drunk?**	8910
	2: 3	"*Do* not **k** talking so proudly	8049
	6: 9	but **k watching** it.	AIT
2Sa	7:25	**k** forever the promise you have made	7756
	13:13	not **k** me from being married to you."	4979
	14:18	"*Do* not **k** from me the answer	3948
1Ki	1: 1	not *k* **warm** even when they put covers	AIT
	1: 2	so that our lord the king *may* **k warm.**"	AIT
	2: 3	and **k** his decrees and commands,	9068
	2: 4	that the Lord *may* **k** his promise to me:	7756
	2:43	then *did you* not **k** your oath to the Lord	9068
	6:12	and **k** all my commands and obey them,	9068
	8:23	you who **k** your covenant of love	9068
	8:25	**k** for your servant David my father	9068
	8:58	in all his ways and to **k** the commands,	9068
	11:10	Solomon did not **k** the Lord's command.	9068
	15: 5	*had* not **failed to k** any of the Lord's	4946+6073
	18: 5	**k** the horses and mules **alive**	2649
2Ki	10:31	Yet Jehu was not careful to **k** the law of	928+2143
	17:19	and even Judah *did* not **k** the commands of	9068
	17:37	You must always be careful to **k** the decrees	6913
	21: 8	and *will* **k** the whole Law	NIH
	23: 3	to follow the Lord and **k** his commands,	9068
1Ch	10:13	*he did* not **k** the word of the Lord and	9068
	22:12	so that you *may* **k** the law of the Lord	9068
	29:18	**k** this desire in the hearts	9068
	29:18	and **k** their hearts **loyal** to you.	3922
	29:19	wholehearted devotion to **k** your commands	9068
2Ch	2:18	foremen over them to **k** the people **working**	6268
	6:14	you who **k** your covenant of love	9068
	6:16	**k** for your servant David my father	9068
	23: 4	on the Sabbath are to **k watch** *at* the doors,	8788
	34:31	to follow the Lord and **k** his commands,	9068
Ne	5:13	*who does* not **k** this promise.	7756
	13:22	**k** the Sabbath day **holy.**	7727
Est	3:11	"**K** the money," the king said to Haman,	5989
Job	4: 2	But who can **k** from speaking?	6806

Ref		
Job	7:11	"Therefore I *will* not **k silent;**	3104+7023
	13:13	"*K* **silent** and let me speak;	AIT
	13:27	you **k close watch on** all my paths	9068
	14:16	but not **k track of** my sin.	9068
	16: 3	What ails you that *you* **k on arguing?**	AIT
	22:15	*Will you* **k** to the old path	9068
	30:10	They detest me and **k** *their* **distance;**	8178
	33:17	to turn man from wrongdoing and **k** him	4059
	34:30	to **k** a godless man from ruling,	NIH
	36: 6	*He does* not **k** the wicked **alive** but gives	2649
	41: 3	*Will he* **k** begging you for mercy?	8049
Ps	12: 7	you *will* **k** us **safe** and protect us	9068
	16: 1	**K** me **safe,** O God, for in you I take refuge.	9068
	17: 8	**K** me as the apple of your eye;	9068
	18:28	You, O Lord, **k** my lamp **burning;**	239
	19:13	**K** your servant also from willful sins;	3104
	22:29	*those who* cannot **k** themselves **alive.**	2649
	25:10	and faithful for *those who* **k** the demands	5915
	27: 5	of trouble *he will* **k** me **safe** in his dwelling;	7621
	31:20	in your dwelling *you* **k** them **safe**	7621
	33:19	from death and **k** them **alive** in famine.	2649
	34:13	**k** your tongue from evil and your lips	5915
	37:34	Wait for the Lord and **k** his way.	9068
	39: 1	"I will watch my ways and **k** my tongue	NIH
	78: 7	but *would* **k** his commands.	5915
	78:10	*they did* not **k** God's covenant and refused	9068
	78:56	*they did* not **k** his statutes.	9068
	83: 1	O God, do not **k** silent;	NIH
	89:31	and fail to **k** my commands,	9068
	103:18	with *those who* **k** his covenant	9068
	105:45	that *they might* **k** his precepts	9068
	106:23	in the breach before him to **k** his wrath	8740
	119: 2	Blessed are *they who* **k** his statutes	5915
	119: 9	How *can* a young man **k** his way **pure?**	2342
	119:22	for *I* **k** your statutes.	5915
	119:29	**K** me from deceitful ways;	6073
	119:33	then *I will* **k** them to the end.	5915
	119:34	and *I will* **k** your law and obey it	5915
	119:55	O Lord, and *I will* **k** your law.	9068
	119:69	I **k** your precepts with all my heart.	5915
	119:115	that *I may* **k** the commands of my God!	5915
	119:146	save me and *I will* **k** your statutes.	9068
	121: 7	The Lord *will* **k** you from all harm—	9068
	132:12	if your sons **k** my covenant and	9068
	140: 4	**K** me, O Lord, from the hands of	9068
	141: 3	**k** watch over the door of my lips.	NIH
	141: 9	**K** me from the snares they have laid for me,	9068
Pr	2:20	the ways of good men and *k* to the paths of	9068
	3: 1	but **k** my commands *in* your heart,	5915
	3:26	be your confidence and *will* **k** your foot	9068
	4: 4	**k** my commands and you will live.	9068
	4:21	**k** them within your heart;	9068
	4:24	**k** corrupt talk **far** from your lips.	8178
	4:27	**k** your foot from evil.	6073
	5: 8	**K** to a path **far** from her,	8178
	6:20	**k** your father's commands and do not	5915
	7: 1	**k** my words and store up my commands	9068
	7: 2	**K** my commands and you will live;	9068
	7: 5	they *will* **k** you from the adulteress,	9068
	8:32	blessed are *those who* **k** my ways.	9068
	15:24	for the wise to **k** him from going down to	6073
	20:28	Love and faithfulness **k** a king **safe;**	5915
	22: 3	but the simple *k* **going** and suffer for it.	AIT
	22:12	of the Lord **k watch over** knowledge,	5915
	22:18	when *you* **k** them in your heart and have all	9068
	23:19	**k** your heart on the **right**	886
	23:26	give me your heart and *let* your eyes **k** to	5915
	27:12	but the simple *k* **going** and suffer for it.	AIT
	28: 4	but *those who* **k** the law resist them.	9068
	30: 8	**K** falsehood and lies **far** from me;	8178
Ecc	3: 6	a time to **k** and a time to throw away,	9068
	4:11	if two lie down together, they *will* **k warm.**	AIT
	4:11	But how *can* one **k warm** alone?	AIT
	12:13	Fear God and **k** his commandments,	9068
Isa	7: 4	"*Be* careful, *k* **calm** and don't be afraid.	AIT
	7:21	a man *will* **k alive** a young cow	2649
	19:21	to the Lord and **k** them.	8966
	26: 3	*You will* **k** *in* perfect peace him whose mind	5915
	28:24	*Does* he **k on breaking up** and harrowing	AIT
	29:23	*they will* **k** my name **holy;**	7727
	42: 6	*I will* **k** you and will make you to be	5915
	47:12	"**K on,** then, with your magic spells and	6641
	49: 8	*I will* **k** you and will make you to be	5915
	56: 4	"To the eunuchs who **k** my Sabbaths,"	9068
	56: 6	all *who* **k** the Sabbath without desecrating it	9068
	58:13	"If *you* **k** your feet from breaking	8740
	62: 1	For Zion's sake *I will* not **k silent,**	AIT
	64:12	*Will you* **k silent** and punish us	AIT
	65: 5	say, '**K away;** don't come near	448+3870+7928
	65: 6	*I will* not **k silent** but will pay back	AIT
Jer	4:19	*I cannot* **k silent,**	AIT
	11: 8	to follow but that *they did* not **k.'** "	6913
	13:14	or mercy or compassion to **k** me **from**	4946
	14:13	the prophets **k telling** them,	AIT
	15: 6	"*You* **k on** backsliding.	2143
	16:11	They forsook me and *did* not **k** my law.	9068
	17:15	*They* **k saying** to me,	AIT
	17:18	but **k** me from **shame;**	AIT
	17:18	let them be terrified, but **k** me from **terror.**	AIT
	17:22	**k** the Sabbath day **holy,**	7727
	17:24	**k** the Sabbath day **holy**	7727
	17:27	**k** the Sabbath day **holy**	7727
	23:17	*They* **k saying** to those who despise me,	606+606
	23:37	This is what *you* **k saying** to a prophet:	AIT
	42: 4	the Lord says and *will* **k nothing back**	4979
	44:25	**K** your vows!'	7756+7756
	50: 2	**k** nothing **back,** but say,	3948

Ref		
La	1:11	for food to **k** themselves **alive.**	5883+8740
	1:19	food *to* **k** themselves **alive**	906+4392+5883+8740
Eze	11:20	and be careful *to* **k** my laws.	6913
	18:19	and has been careful *to* **k** all my decrees,	6913
	20: 7	I did what would **k** it **from** being profaned	1194
	20:14	I did what would **k** it **from** being profaned	1194
	20:18	the statutes of your fathers or **k** their laws	9068
	20:19	and be careful *to* **k** my laws.	6913
	20:20	**K** my Sabbaths **holy,**	7727
	20:21	they were not careful *to* **k** my laws—	6913
	20:22	or my name I did what would **k** it **from**	1194
	24:17	**K** your turban **fastened**	AIT
	24:23	You will **k** your turbans on your heads	NIH
	36:27	and be careful *to* **k** my laws.	6913
	37:24	and be careful *to* **k** my decrees.	6913
	44:20	**k** *the* **hair** of their heads **trimmed.**	4080+4080
	44:24	*They are to* **k** my requirements,	9068
	44:24	and *they are to* **k** my Sabbaths **holy.**	7727
	46:17	the servant *may* **k** it until the year	2118+4200
Da	5:17	"You *may* **k** your gifts for yourself	10201
Hab	1:17	Is he to **k on** emptying his net,	9458
Zec	3: 7	in my ways and **k** my requirements,	9068
	11:12	give me my pay; but if not, **k** it."	2532
	12: 4	"*I will* **k** a **watchful** eye over the house	7219
Mt	5:33	but **k** the oaths you have made to the Lord.'	625
	6: 7	*do* not **k on** babbling like pagans,	AIT
	10:10	for the worker is worth his **k.**	5575
	24:42	"Therefore **k watch,** because you do	1213
	25:13	"Therefore **k watch,** because you do	1213
	26:38	Stay here and **k watch with me.**"	1213
	26:40	"Could you men not **k watch** with me	1213
	28:14	we will satisfy him and **k** you out	4472
Mk	3: 9	to **k** the people **from** crowding him.	2671+3590
	7:24	yet he could not **k** his presence **secret.**	3291
	13:34	and tells the one at the door to **k watch.**	1213
	13:35	"Therefore **k watch** because you do	1213
	14:34	"Stay here and **k watch.**"	1213
	14:37	Could you not **k watch** for one hour?	1213
Lk	4:42	*they* tried to **k** him from leaving them.	2988
	12:35	**k** your lamps **burning,**	AIT
	13:33	I must **k going** today and tomorrow and	AIT
	17:33	Whoever tries to **k** his life will lose it,	4347
	18: 7	**k putting** them **off?**	AIT
	19:40	"I tell you," he replied, "if they **k quiet,**	AIT
Jn	4:15	and have *to* **k coming** here to draw water."	AIT
	8:55	but I do know him and his word.	5498
	9:16	for he does not **k** the Sabbath."	5498
	10:24	"How long *will you* **k** us **in suspense?**	149+3836+6034
	12:25	in this world *will* **k** it for eternal life.	5875
	12:47	hears my words but *does* not **k** them,	5875
	15:18	**k** in mind that it hated me first.	1182
	18:18	around a fire they had made to **k warm.**	2548
Ac	2:24	for death to **k** its **hold on** him.	AIT
	10:47	"Can anyone **k** these people **from**	3266
	18: 9	**k on speaking,** do not be silent.	AIT
	20:28	**K watch over** yourselves and all the flock	4668
	24:16	So I strive always *to* **k** my conscience clear	2400
	24:23	the centurion to **k** Paul **under guard** but	5498
	27:22	But now I urge you *to* **k up** your **courage,**	2313
	27:25	So **k up** your **courage,** men,	2313
Ro	2:26	not circumcised **k** the law's requirements,	5875
	7:19	this I **k on doing.**	AIT
	12:11	**k** your spiritual **fervor,**	AIT
	14:22	about these things **k** between yourself	2400
	16:17	**K away** from them.	AIT
1Co	1: 8	He *will* **k** you **strong** to the end,	1011
	5: 8	Therefore *let us* **k** the Festival,	2037
	7:30	as if *it were* not theirs to **k;**	2988
	10: 6	to **k** us from setting our hearts on evil things	1639
	14:28	the speaker *should* **k quiet** in the church	AIT
2Co	9: 4	to **k** the Israelites **from**	3590+3836+4639
	11:12	And I will **k on** doing what I am doing	AIT
	12: 7	To **k** me **from** becoming conceited because	3590
Gal	5:15	If *you* **k** on biting and devouring	AIT
	5:25	*let us* **k in step** with the Spirit.	5123
Eph	1:17	I **k** asking that the God of our Lord Jesus	NIG
	4: 3	to **k** the unity of the Spirit through the bond	5498
	6:18	and always **k on** praying for all the saints.	4675
1Th	2:16	in their effort to **k** us from speaking to the Gentiles so	3266
2Th	3: 6	to **k away** from every brother who is idle	5097
1Ti	3: 9	They must **k hold of** the deep truths of	2400
	5:21	to **k** these instructions without partiality,	5875
	5:22	**K** yourself pure.	5498
	6:14	*to* **k** this command without spot or blame	5498
2Ti	1:13	**k** as the pattern of sound teaching,	2400
	2:14	**K** reminding them **of** these things.	AIT
	4: 5	But you, **k** your **head** in all situations,	3768
Phm	1:13	I would have liked *to* **k** him with me so	2988
Heb	9:20	which God *has* **commanded** you *to* **k.**"	1948
	10:26	*If* we deliberately **k on** sinning	AIT
	13: 1	**K on** loving each other as brothers.	3531
	13: 5	**K** your lives free from the love of money	NIG
	13:17	They **k watch** over you	70
Jas	1:26	not **k** a **tight rein on** his tongue,	5902
	1:27	and *to* **k** oneself from being polluted by	5498
	2: 8	If *you* really **k** the royal law found	5464
	2:16	**k warm** and **well fed,**	AIT
	3: 2	**k** his whole body **in check.**	5902
1Pe	3:10	and see good days *must* **k** his tongue	4264
2Pe	1: 8	*they will* **k** you from being ineffective	2770
1Jn	5:21	Dear children, **k** yourselves from idols.	5875
Jude	1: 6	And the angels who *did* not **k** their positions	5498
	1:21	**K** yourselves in God's love as you wait for	5498
	1:24	To him who is able *to* **k** you **from** falling	5875
Rev	3:10	I will also **k** you from the hour of trial	5498
	20: 3	to **k** him **from** deceiving the nations	3590

Rev 22: 9 and *of* all who **k** the words of this book. 5498

KEEPER (8) [KEEP]
Ge 4: 9 "Am I my brother's **k?**" 9068
1Sa 17:22 David left his things with the **k** of supplies, 9068
2Ki 10:22 Jehu said to the **k** of the wardrobe, 889+6584S
22:14 the son of Harhas, **k** of the wardrobe. 9068
2Ch 31:14 the Levite, **k** of the East Gate, 8788
34:22 the son of Hasrah, **k** of the wardrobe. 9068
Ne 2: 8 Asaph, **k** of the king's forest, 9068
Jn 12: 6 as **k** of the **money bag**, he used to 1186+2400

KEEPERS (1) [KEEP]
Ecc 12: 3 when the **k** of the house tremble, and 9068

KEEPING (39) [KEEP]
Ge 41:49 it was so much that he stopped **k records** 6218
Ex 20: 8 "Remember the Sabbath day by **k** it **holy.** 7727
Dt 5:12 "Observe the Sabbath day by **k** it **holy,** 7727
6: 2 as long as you live by **k** all his decrees 9068
7: 9 the faithful God, **k** his covenant of love to 9068
13:18 **k** all his commands that I am giving you 9068
Jdg 8: 4 exhausted yet **k** up the **pursuit,** AIT
1Sa 6:12 **k** on the road and lowing **all the way;** 2143+2143
17:34 "Your servant has been **k** his father's sheep. 8286
25:33 and for **k** me from bloodshed this day and 3973
1Ki 11:38 in my eyes by **k** my statutes and commands, 9068
17:16 in **k** with the word of the LORD spoken 3869
2Ki 7: 9 of good news and we *are* **k** it to ourselves. 3120
2Ch 8:14 In **k** with the ordinance of his father David, 3869
Est 1: 7 in **k** with the king's liberality. 3869
Ps 19:11 in **k** them there is great reward. 9068
119:112 My heart is set on **k** your decrees to 6913
Pr 6:24 **k** you from the immoral woman, 9068
15: 3 **k** watch *on* the wicked and the good. 7595
Isa 65: 4 and spend their nights **k** secret **vigil;** 5915
Eze 14: 4 LORD will answer him myself in **k** with 928
17:14 surviving only by **k** his treaty. 9068
22:26 they shut their eyes to the **k** of my Sabbaths, NIH
Da 9:16 O Lord, in **k** with all your righteous acts, 3869
Zec 9:12 for now I *am* **k** watch. 928+6524+8011
Mt 3: 8 Produce fruit in **k** with repentance. 545
Lk 2: 8 **k** watch over their flocks at night. 5871+5875
2:24 to offer a sacrifice in **k** with what is said 2848
3: 8 Produce fruit in **k** with repentance. 545
20:20 **K a close watch** on him, they sent spies, 4190
Ac 14:18 *they* had difficulty **k** the crowd from 2924
1Co 7:19 **K** God's commands is what counts. 5499
16: 2 in **k** with his income, 1569+2338+4005+5516
2Co 8: 5 and then to us in **k** with God's will. 1328
1Ti 1:18 I give you this instruction in **k** with 2848
Jas 4:11 When you judge the law, you are not **k** it, 4475
1Pe 3:16 **k** a clear conscience. 2400
2Pe 3: 9 The Lord is not slow in **k** his promise, NIG
3:13 But in **k** with his promise we are looking 2848

KEEPS (44) [KEEP]
Jdg 5:29 indeed, she **k** saying to herself, 609+8740
1Sa 17:25 "Do you see how this man **k** coming out? AIT
Ne 1: 5 and awesome God, who **k** his covenant 9068
9:32 who **k** his covenant of love, 9068
Job 20:13 though he cannot bear to let it go and **k** it 4979
24:15 and *he* **k** his face concealed. 8492
33:11 *he* **k** close watch *on* all my paths.' 9068
34: 8 He **k** company with evildoers; 782+2495+4200
Ps 15: 4 who **k** his oath even when it hurts, 4202+4614
Pr 11:13 but a trustworthy man **k** a secret. 4059
12:23 prudent man **k** his knowledge *to himself,* 4059
15:21 a man of understanding **k** a straight course. 3837
15:25 **k** the widow's boundaries **intact.** 5893
17:24 A discerning man **k** wisdom in view, NIH
17:28 Even a fool is thought wise if *he* **k** silent, 3087
18:18 **k** strong opponents **apart.** 7233
21:23 and his tongue **k** himself from calamity. 9068
28: 7 *He who* **k** the law is a discerning son, 5915
29:11 but a wise man *himself* **k** under control. 8656
29:18 but blessed is he *who* **k** the law. 9068
Ecc 5:20 God **k** him **occupied** with gladness of heart. 6701
Isa 26: 2 nation may enter, the nation *that* **k** faith. 9068
33:15 and **k** his hand from accepting bribes, 5850
56: 2 who **k** the Sabbath without desecrating it, 9068
56: 2 and **k** his hand from doing any evil." 9068
65: 5 a fire *that* **k** **burning** all day. AIT
Jer 23:35 of *you* **k** on **saying** to his friend or relative: AIT
48:10 on him who **k** his sword from bloodshed! 4979
Eze 18: 9 my decrees and faithfully **k** my laws. 9068
18:17 *He* **k** my laws and follows my decrees, 6913
18:21 and **k** all my decrees and does what is just 9068
Da 9: 4 and awesome God, who **k** his covenant 9068
Am 5:13 the prudent man **k** quiet in such times, 1957
Mt 15:23 for *she* **k crying out** after us." AIT
Lk 18: 5 yet because this widow **k** **bothering** me, AIT
Jn 7:19 Yet not one of you **k** the law. 4472
8:51 I tell you the truth, if anyone **k** my word, 5498
8:52 yet you say that if anyone **k** your word, 5498
1Co 13: 5 it **k** no **record** of wrongs. AIT
Jas 2:10 For whoever **k** the whole law and 5498
1Jn 3: 6 No one who lives in him **k** on **sinning.** AIT
5:18 the one who was born of God **k** him **safe,** 5498
Rev 16:15 and **k** his clothes with him, 5498
22: 7 Blessed is he who **k** the words of 5498

KEHELATHAH (2)
Nu 33:22 They left Rissah and camped at **K.** 7739

Nu 33:23 They left **K** and camped at Mount Shepher. 7739

KEILAH (18)
Jos 15:44 **K,** Aczib and Mareshah— 7881
1Sa 23: 1 the Philistines are fighting against **K** 7881
23: 2 "Go, attack the Philistines and save **K.**" 7881
23: 4 if we go to **k** against the Philistine forces!" 7881
23: 4 "Go down to **K,** for I am going to give 7881
23: 5 So David and his men went to **K,** 7881
23: 5 the Philistines and saved the people of **K.** 7881
23: 6 with him when he fled to David at **K.)** 7881
23: 7 Saul was told that David had gone to **K,** 7881
23: 8 down to **K** to besiege David and his men. 7881
23:10 that Saul plans to come to **K** and destroy 7881
23:11 Will the citizens of **K** surrender me to him? 7881
23:12 the citizens of **K** surrender me and my men 7881
23:13 left **K** and kept moving from place to place. 7881
23:13 that David had escaped from **K,** 7881
1Ch 4:19 the father of **K** the Garmite, 7881
Ne 3:17 Hashabiah, ruler of half the district of **K.** 7881
3:18 ruler of the other half-district of **K.** 7881

KELAIAH (1) [KELITA]
Ezr 10:23 Jozabad, Shimei, **K** (that is, Kelita), 7835

KELAL (1)
Ezr 10:30 Adna, **K,** Benaiah, Maaseiah, Mattaniah, 4006

KELITA (3) [KELAIAH]
Ezr 10:23 Jozabad, Shimei, Kelaiah (that is, **K),** 7836
Ne 8: 7 Shabbethai, Hodiah, Maaseiah, **K,** Azariah, 7836
10:10 Shebaniah, Hodiah, **K,** Pelaiah, Hanan, 7836

KELUB (2)
1Ch 4:11 **K,** Shuhah's brother, was the father 3991
27:26 Ezri son of **K** was in charge of 3991

KELUHI (1)
Ezr 10:35 Benaiah, Bedeiah, **K,** 3988

KEMUEL (3)
Ge 22:21 Buz his brother, **K** (the father of Aram) 7851
Nu 34:24 **K** son of Shiphtan, the leader from the tribe 7851
1Ch 27:17 Hashabiah son of **K;** 7851

KENAANAH (5)
1Ki 22:11 of **K** had made iron horns and he declared, 4049
22:24 of **K** went up and slapped Micaiah in 4049
1Ch 7:10 Jeush, Benjamin, Ehud, **K,** Zethan, 4049
2Ch 18:10 Zedekiah son of **K** had made iron horns, 4049
18:23 of **K** went up and slapped Micaiah in 4049

KENAN (7)
Ge 5: 9 he became the father of **K.** 7809
5:10 And after he became the father of **K,** 7809
5:12 When **K** had lived 70 years, 7809
5:13 **K** lived 840 years and had other sons 7809
5:14 Altogether, **K** lived 910 years, 7809
1Ch 1: 2 **K,** Mahalalel, Jared, 7809
Lk 3:37 the son of Mahalalel, the son *of* **K,** 2783

KENANI (1)
Ne 9: 4 Shebaniah, Bunni, Sherebiah, Bani and **K—** 4039

KENANIAH (3)
1Ch 15:22 **K** the head Levite was in charge of 4041
15:27 and as were the singers, and **K,** 4040
26:29 **K** and his sons were assigned duties away 4041

KENATH (2)
Nu 32:42 And Nobah captured **K** 7875
1Ch 2:23 as **K** with its surrounding settlements— 7875

KENAZ (11)
Ge 36:11 Teman, Omar, Zepho, Gatam and **K.** 7869
36:15 Chiefs Teman, Omar, Zepho, **K,** 7869
36:42 **K,** Teman, Mibzar, 7869
Jos 15:17 Othniel son of **K,** Caleb's brother, took it; 7869
Jdg 1:13 Othniel son of **K,** Caleb's younger brother, 7869
3: 9 Othniel son of **K,** Caleb's younger brother, 7869
3:11 until Othniel son of **K** died. 7869
1Ch 1:36 Teman, Omar, Zepho, Gatam and **K;** 7869
1:53 **K,** Teman, Mibzar, 7869
4:13 The sons of **K:** Othniel and Seraiah. 7869
4:15 The son of Elah: **K.** 7869

KENEZITE (KJV) See KENIZZITE

KENITE (5) [KENITES]
Jdg 1:16 the **k,** went up from the City of Palms with 7808
4:11 Heber the **K** had left the other Kenites, 7808
4:17 the wife of Heber the **K,** 7808
4:17 of Hazor and the clan of Heber the **K.** 7808
5:24 the wife of Heber the **K,** 7808

KENITES (9) [KENITE]
Ge 15:19 the land of the **K,** Kenizzites, Kadmonites, 7808

Nu 24:21 Then he saw the **K** and uttered his oracle: 7808
24:22 yet you **K** will be destroyed 7804
Jdg 4:11 Now Heber the Kenite had left the other **K,** 7804
1Sa 15: 6 So he said to the **K,** "Go away, 7808
15: 6 So the **K** moved away from the Amalekites. 7808
27:10 or "Against the Negev of the **K.**" 7808
30:29 the towns of the Jerahmeelites and the **K;** 7808
1Ch 2:55 These are the **K** who came from Hammath, 7808

KENIZZITE (3) [KENIZZITES]
Nu 32:12 of Jephunneh the **K** and Joshua son of Nun, 7870
Jos 14: 6 Caleb son of Jephunneh the **K** said to him, 7870
14:14 to Caleb son of Jephunneh the **K** ever since, 7870

KENIZZITES (1) [KENIZZITE]
Ge 15:19 the land of the Kenites, **K,** Kadmonites, 7870

KEPHAR AMMONI (1)
Jos 18:24 **K,** Ophni and Geba— 4112

KEPHIRAH (4)
Jos 9:17 Gibeon, **K,** Beeroth and Kiriath Jearim. 4098
18:26 Mizpah, **K,** Mozah, 4098
Ezr 2:25 of Kiriath Jearim, **K** and Beeroth 743 4098
Ne 7:29 of Kiriath Jearim, **K** and Beeroth 743 4098

KEPT (178) [KEEP]
Ge 4: 2 Abel **k** flocks, and Cain worked the soil. 8286
6:20 the ground will come to you to be **k** alive. 2649
7:17 For forty days the flood **k** **coming** on AIT
8: 7 and it **k** **flying** back and forth until AIT
16: 2 "The LORD has **k** me from having children. 6806
19: 9 They **k** **bringing pressure** on Lot 4394+7210
20: 6 so I have **k** you from sinning against me. 3104
26: 5 and **k** my requirements, 9068
30: 2 who has **k** you from having children?" 4979
34: 5 he **k** quiet *about* it until they came home. 3087
37:11 his father **k** the matter *in mind.* 9068
39:16 She **k** his cloak beside her 5663
41:35 *to be* **k** in the cities *for* food. 9068
42:16 the rest of you *will* be **k** in prison, 673
Ex 5:13 The slave drivers **k** **pressing** them, saying, AIT
12:42 Because the LORD **k** vigil that night 4200
16:20 *they* **k** part of it until morning, 3855
16:33 Then place it before the LORD to be **k** for 5466
16:34 in front of the Testimony, that it might be **k.** 5466
21:29 *has not* **k** it **penned up** and it kills a man 9068
23:18 of my festival offerings *must not* be **k** 4328
27:20 so that the lamps may be **k** **burning.** 9458
Lev 6: 9 and the fire *must* be **k** **burning** on the altar. 3678
6:12 The fire on the altar *must* be **k** **burning;** 3678
6:13 The fire *must* be **k** **burning** on the altar 3678
24: 2 the lamps *must* be **k** **burning** continually. 6590
Nu 9: 7 *should we* be **k** **from** presenting 1194+1757+4200
15:34 and *they* **k** him in custody, 5663
17:10 to be **k** as a sign to the rebellious. 5466
18: 9 of the most holy offerings that is **k from** 4946
19: 9 *They shall be* **k** by the Israelite community 2118
24:11 the LORD has **k** you from being rewarded 4979
Dt 6:24 we might always prosper and be **k** alive, 2649
7: 8 and **k** the oath he swore to your forefathers 9068
32:34 "Have I not **k** this **in reserve** and sealed in 4022
33:21 the leader's portion *was* **k** for him. 6211
Jos 6:13 while the trumpets **k** sounding. 2143
9:21 promise to them *was* **k.** AIT
14:10 he has **k** me **alive** for forty-five years since 2649
Jdg 2: 7 the rest of the Israelites to their tents but **k** 2616
20:45 *They* **k** **pressing** after the Benjamites as far AIT
1Sa 1: 6 her rival **k provoking** her 1685+4087+4088
1:12 As she **k** on praying to the LORD, 8049
9:24 "Here is what has **been k** for you. 8636
10:27 But Saul **k** silent. 2118
13:13 "You have not **k** the command 9068
13:14 you have not **k** the LORD's command." 9068
17:41 **k** **coming** closer to David. 2143+2143
18: 2 that day Saul **k** David with him and did 4374
18: 9 Saul **k** a jealous eye on David. 6523
21: 4 the men have **k** themselves from women." 9068
21: 5 "Indeed women *have* **been k** from us, 6806
23:13 **k** moving from place to place. AIT
25:26 "Now since the LORD *has* **k** you, 4979
25:34 lives, who *has* **k** me from harming you, 4979
25:39 He *has* **k** his servant from doing wrong 3104
2Sa 15:12 and Absalom's following **k** on increasing. 2143
18: 9 while the mule he was riding **k** on going. 6296
18:13 you *would have* **k** your **distance** *from me.*" 3656+4946+5584
20: 3 They were **k** in confinement till the day 7674
22:22 For I *have* **k** the ways of the LORD; 9068
22:22 before him and *have* **k** myself from sin. 9068
1Ki 5:10 In this way Hiram **k** Solomon **supplied** AIT
8:20 "The LORD *has* **k** the promise he made: 7756
8:24 You have **k** your promise 9068
10:26 and twelve thousand horses, which *he* **k** in 5663
11:11 not **k** my covenant and my decrees, 9068
11:33 nor **k** my statutes and laws as David, NIH
13:21 of the LORD and *have* not **k** the command 9068
14: 8 who **k** my commands and followed me 9068
2Ki 4: 5 the jars to her and she **k** **pouring.** AIT
13: 3 for a long time *he* **k** them under the power 5989
18: 6 *he* **k** the commands the LORD had given 9068
25: 2 The city *was* **k** under siege until 995
1Ch 4:33 And *they* **k** a **genealogical record.** 3509
2Ch 1:14 and twelve thousand horses, which *he* **k** in 5663

2Ch	6:10	"The LORD *has* **k** the promise he made.	7756
	6:15	You *have* **k** your promise	9068
	9:25	which *he* **k** in the chariot cities and also	5663
	17:13	He also **k** experienced fighting men	NIH
	34:21	because our fathers *have* not **k** the word of	9068
Ezr	9: 1	*have* not **k** themselves **separate** from	976
Ne	5: 8	They **k quiet,** because they could not find	AIT
	6:17	and replies from Tobiah **k coming** to them.	AIT
	6:19	*they* **k** reporting to me his good deeds and	2118
	9: 8	You *have* **k** your promise	7756
	10:39	where the articles for the sanctuary are **k**	NIH
	11:19	who **k watch** at the gates—172 men.	9068
Est	2:20	Esther *had* **k secret** her family background	
		and nationality	401+5583
	7: 4	*I would have* **k quiet,** because no such	AIT
Job	21:32	and **watch** *is* **k** over his tomb.	9193
	23:11	*I have* **k** to his way without turning aside.	9068
	31:17	if *I have* **k** my bread to myself,	430
	31:34	that *I* **k silent** and would not go outside	AIT
Ps	17: 4	*I have* **k** *myself from* the ways of the violent.	9068
	18:21	For *I have* **k** the ways of the LORD;	9068
	18:23	before him and *have* **k myself** from sin.	9068
	32: 3	When *I* **k silent,** my bones wasted away	AIT
	50:21	These things you *have* done *and I* **k silent;**	AIT
	66: 9	he has preserved our lives and **k** our feet	5989
	73:13	Surely in vain *have I* **k** my heart **pure;**	2342
	77: 4	**k** my eyes **from closing;**	296+9073
	78:32	In spite of all this, they **k on** sinning;	6388
	99: 7	*they* **k** his statutes and the decrees	9068
	119:101	*I have* **k** my feet from every evil path so	3973
	130: 3	If *you,* O LORD, **k a record** *of* sins,	9068
Pr	20: 9	Who can say, "*I have* **k** my heart **pure;**	2342
	28:18	He whose walk is blameless *is* **k safe,**	3828
	28:26	but he who walks in wisdom *is* **k safe.**	4880
	29:25	but whoever trusts in the LORD *is* **k safe.**	8435
Isa	38:17	**In** your love you **k** me from the pit	3137
	42:14	"For a long time *I have* **k silent,**	AIT
	49: 6	and bring back *those of* Israel I *have* **k.**	5915
	57:17	yet *he* **k on** in his willful ways.	2143+8743
Jer	5:25	Your wrongdoings *have* **k** these **away;**	5742
	35:14	to drink wine and this command *has* been **k.**	7756
	52: 5	The city *was* **k** under siege until	995
Eze	5: 7	not followed my decrees or **k** my laws.	6913
	11:12	not followed my decrees or **k** my laws	6913
Da	7:11	*I* **k** looking until the beast was slain	10201
	7:28	but *I* **k** the matter to myself."	10476
	9:10	not obeyed the LORD our God or **k**	928+2143
Hos	13:12	his sins *are* **k on record.**	7621
Am	2: 4	of the LORD and *have* not **k** his decrees,	9068
Mal	3: 7	from my decrees and *have* not **k** them.	9068
Mt	19:20	"All these *I have* **k,"** the young man said.	5875
	24:43	thief was coming, *he* would *have* **k watch**	1213
	27:36	sitting down, *they* **k watch over** him there.	5498
Mk	5:32	But Jesus **k looking around**	AIT
	7:36	the more they **k talking about** it.	AIT
	9:10	*They* **k** the matter to themselves,	3195
	9:34	But *they* **k quiet** because on the way	AIT
	10:20	"all these *I have* **k** since I was a boy."	5875
Lk	1:22	for *he* **k making signs** to them	AIT
	4:44	And *he* **k on** preaching in the synagogues	1639
	8:29	and foot and **k under guard,**	5875
	9:36	The disciples **k this to themselves,**	4967
	13:16	whom Satan *has* **k bound**	AIT
	18: 3	a widow in that town *who* **k coming** to him	AIT
	18:21	"All these *I have* **k** since I was a boy,"	5875
	19:20	*I have* **k** it laid away in a piece of cloth.	2400
	23:21	But *they* **k shouting,** "Crucify him!	AIT
	24:16	but they *were* **k** from recognizing him.	3195
Jn	8: 7	When *they* **k on** questioning him,	2152
	11:37	*have* **k** this man from dying?"	4472
	11:56	*They* **k looking for** Jesus,	AIT
	16:18	*They* **k asking,** "What does he mean by	AIT
	17:12	and **k** them **safe** by that name you gave me.	5875
	19:12	but the Jews **k shouting,**	AIT
Ac	5: 2	*he* **k back** part of the money for himself,	3802
	5: 3	and *have* **k** for yourself some of the money	3802
	9:24	Day and night *they* **k close watch on**	4190
	12: 5	So Peter *was* **k** in prison,	5498
	12:15	When she **k insisting that** it was so,	AIT
	12:16	But Peter **k on** knocking,	2152
	16: 6	**k** by the Holy Spirit **from** preaching	3266
	16:18	*She* **k this up** for many days.	4472
	20: 7	**k on** talking until midnight.	4189
	21:36	The crowd that followed **k shouting,**	AIT
	23:35	he ordered that Paul *be* **k under guard**	5875
	27:43	and **k** them **from** carrying out their plan.	3266
2Co	11: 9	*I have* **k** myself from being a burden to you	5498
Gal	5: 7	and you **from** obeying the truth?	3590
Eph	3: 9	which for ages past *was* **k hidden** in God,	AIT
Col	1:26	the mystery that *has* been **k hidden for** ages	648
1Th	1: 1	*we* **k telling** you that we would	AIT
	5:23	soul and body *be* **k** blameless at the coming	5498
2Ti	4: 7	I have finished the race, *I have* **k** the faith.	5498
Heb	11:28	By faith he **k** the Passover and	4472
	13: 4	and the marriage bed **k pure,**	NIG
1Pe	1: 4	**k** in heaven for you,	5498
2Pe	3: 7	*being* **k** for the day of judgment	5498
Jude	1: 1	by God the Father and by Jesus Christ;	5498
	1: 6	these *he has* **k** in darkness;	5498
Rev	3: 8	yet *you have* **k** my word and have	5498
	3:10	Since you have **k** my command	5498
	9:15	And the four angels who *had been* **k ready**	2286
	14: 4	for they **k** themselves **pure.**	NIG

KERAMIM See ABEL KERAMIM

KERAN (2)

Ge	36:26	Hemdan, Eshban, Ithran and **K.**	4154
1Ch	1:41	Hemdan, Eshban, Ithran and **K.**	4154

KERCHIEFS (KJV) See VEILS

KEREN-HAPPUCH (1)

Job	42:14	the second Keziah and the third **K.**	7968

KERETHITE (1) [KERETHITES]

Zep	2: 5	to you who live by the sea, O **K** people;	4165

KERETHITES (10) [KERETHITE]

1Sa	30:14	the **K** and the territory belonging to Judah	4165
2Sa	8:18	of Jehoiada was over the **K** and Pelethites;	4165
	15:18	along with all the **K** and Pelethites;	4165
	20: 7	So Joab's men and the **K** and Pelethites,	4165
	20:23	of Jehoiada was over the **K** and Pelethites;	4165
1Ki	1:38	the **K** and the Pelethites went down	4165
	1:44	the **K** and the Pelethites,	4165
1Ch	18:17	of Jehoiada was over the **K** and Pelethites;	4165
Eze	25:16	the **K** and destroy those remaining along	4165
Zep	2: 6	The land by the sea, where the **K** dwell,	4165

KERIOTH (3)

Jer	48:24	to **K** and Bozrah—to all the towns of Moab	7954
	48:41	**K** will be captured and the strongholds	7954
Am	2: 2	that will consume the fortresses of **K.**	7954

KERIOTH HEZRON (1) [HAZOR, HEZRON]

Jos	15:25	Hazor Hadattah, **K** (that is, Hazor),	7955

KERITH (2)

1Ki	17: 3	turn eastward and hide in the **K** Ravine,	4134
	17: 5	He went to the **K** Ravine,	4134

KERNEL (2) [KERNELS]

Mk	4:28	then the head, then the full **k** in the head.	4992
Jn	12:24	a **k** of wheat falls to the ground and dies,	3133

KERNELS (3) [KERNEL]

Dt	23:25	you may pick **k** with your hands,	4884
	32:14	with choice rams of Bashan and the finest **k**	4000
Lk	6: 1	rub them in their hands and eat the **k.**	NIG

KEROS (2)

Ezr	2:44	**K,** Siaha, Padon,	7820
Ne	7:47	**K,** Sia, Padon,	7820

KERUB (2)

Ezr	2:59	Tel Harsha, **K,** Addon and Immer,	4132
Ne	7:61	Tel Harsha, **K,** Addon and Immer,	4132

KESALON (1) [JEARIM]

Jos	15:10	of Mount Jearim (that is, **K**), continued	4076

KESED (1)

Ge	22:22	**K,** Hazo, Pildash, Jidlaph and Bethuel."	4168

KESIL (1)

Jos	15:30	Eltolad, **K,** Hormah,	4069

KESULLOTH (1)

Jos	19:18	Their territory included: Jezreel, **K,**	4063

KETTLE (1) [KETTLES]

1Sa	2:14	He would plunge it into the pan or **k**	1857

KETTLES (1) [KETTLE]

Mk	7: 4	as the washing of cups, pitchers and **k.**)	5908

KETURAH (4)

Ge	25: 1	took another wife, whose name was **K.**	7778
	25: 4	All these were descendants of **K.**	7778
1Ch	1:32	The sons born to **K,** Abraham's concubine,	7778
	1:33	All these were descendants of **K.**	7778

KEY (8) [KEYS]

Jdg	3:25	they took a **k** and unlocked them.	5158
1Ch	9:27	of the **k** for **opening** it each morning.	5158
Isa	22:22	on his shoulder the **k** to the house of David;	5158
	33: 6	fear of the LORD is **the k** to this treasure.	2085S
Lk	11:52	you have taken away the **k** to knowledge.	3090
Rev	3: 7	who holds the **k** of David.	3090
	9: 1	The star was given the **k** to the shaft of	3090
	20: 1	the **k** to the Abyss and holding in his hand	3090

KEYS (2) [KEY]

Mt	16:19	I will give you the **k** of the kingdom	3090
Rev	1:18	And I hold the **k** of death and Hades.	3090

KEZIAH (1)

Job	42:14	the second **K** and the third Keren-Happuch.	7905

KEZIB (1)

Ge	38: 5	It was at **K** that she gave birth to him.	3945

KEZIZ See EMEK KEZIZ

KIBROTH HATTAAVAH (5)

Nu	11:34	Therefore the place was named **K,**	7701
	11:35	From **K** the people traveled to Hazeroth	7701
	33:16	left the Desert of Sinai and camped at **K.**	7701
	33:17	They left **K** and camped at Hazeroth.	7701
Dt	9:22	LORD angry at Taberah, at Massah and at **K.**	7701

KIBZAIM (1)

Jos	21:22	**K** and Beth Horon, together	7698

KICK (1) [KICKED, KICKING]

Ac	26:14	It is hard for you *to* **k** against the goads.'	3280

KICKED (1) [KICK]

Dt	32:15	Jeshurun grew fat and **k;**	1246

KICKING (2) [KICK]

Eze	16: 6	" 'Then I passed by and saw you **k about**	1008
	16:22	**k about** in your blood.	1008

KIDNAPPER (1) [KIDNAPPING, KIDNAPS]

Dt	24: 7	as a slave or sells him, the **k** must die.	1705

KIDNAPPING (1) [KIDNAPPER]

Dt	24: 7	If a man is caught **k** one of his brother	1704+5883

KIDNAPS (1) [KIDNAPPER]

Ex	21:16	"Anyone who **k** another and either sells him	1704

KIDNEYS (18)

Ex	29:13	and both **k** with the fat on them,	4000
	29:22	both **k** with the fat on them,	4000
Lev	3: 4	both **k** with the fat on them near the loins,	4000
	3: 4	which he will remove with the **k.**	4000
	3:10	both **k** with the fat on them near the loins,	4000
	3:10	which he will remove with the **k.**	4000
	3:15	both **k** with the fat on them near the loins,	4000
	3:15	which he will remove with the **k.**	4000
	4: 9	both **k** with the fat on them near the loins,	4000
	4: 9	which he will remove with the **k**—	4000
	7: 4	both **k** with the fat on them near the loins,	4000
	7: 4	which is to be removed with the **k.**	4000
	8:16	and both **k** and their fat,	4000
	8:25	both **k** and their fat and the right thigh.	4000
	9:10	the **k** and the covering of the liver from	4000
	9:19	the **k** and the covering of the liver—	4000
Job	16:13	he pierces my **k** and spills my gall on	4000
Isa	34: 6	fat from the **k** *of* rams.	4000

KIDON (1)

1Ch	13: 9	they came to the threshing floor of **K,**	3961

KIDRON (11)

2Sa	15:23	The king also crossed the **K** Valley,	7724
1Ki	2:37	The day you leave and cross the **K** Valley,	7724
	15:13	down and burned it in the **K** Valley.	7724
2Ki	23: 4	the **K** Valley and took the ashes to Bethel.	7724
	23: 6	to the **K** Valley outside Jerusalem	7724
	23:12	and threw the rubble into the **K** Valley.	7724
2Ch	15:16	broke it up and burned it in the **K** Valley.	7724
	29:16	and carried it out to the **K** Valley.	7724
	30:14	and threw them into the **K** Valley.	7724
Jer	31:40	the **K** Valley on the east as far as the corner	7724
Jn	18: 1	with his disciples and crossed the **K** Valley.	3022

KILEAB (1)

2Sa	3: 3	**K** the son of Abigail the widow of Nabal	3976

KILION (3)

Ru	1: 2	names of his two sons were Mahlon and **K.**	4002
	1: 5	both Mahlon and **K** also died,	4002
	4: 9	the property of Elimelech, **K** and Mahlon.	4002

KILL (186) [KILLED, KILLING, KILLS]

Ge	4:14	and whoever finds me *will* **k** me."	2222
	4:15	so that no one who found me *would* **k** him.	5782
	12:12	Then *they* **k** me but will let you live.	2222
	18:25	to **k** the righteous with the wicked,	4637
	20:11	and *they will* **k** me because of my wife.'	2222
	26: 7	of this place might **k** me on account	2222
	27:41	then *I will* **k** my brother Jacob."	2222
	37:18	they plotted to **k** him.	4637
	37:20	*let's* **k** him and throw him into one	2222
	37:26	if *we* **k** our brother and cover up his blood?	2222
Ex	1:16	if it is a boy, **k** him; but if it is a girl,	4637
	2:15	Pharaoh heard of this, he tried to **k** Moses,	2222
	4:19	all the men who **wanted to k** you are dead."	906+1335+5883

Ex	4:23	so I will k your firstborn son.' "	2222
	4:24	and was about to k him.	4637
	5:21	and have put a sword in their hand to k us."	2222
	22:24	and I will k you with the sword;	2222
	32:12	to k them in the mountains and	2222
Lev	14:50	He shall k one of the birds over fresh water	8821
	20:15	and you must k the animal.	2222
	20:16	k both the woman and the animal.	2222
Nu	16:13	a land flowing with milk and honey to k us	4637
	22:29	I would k you right now."	2222
	25: 4	and expose them in broad daylight	3697
	25:17	the Midianites as enemies and k them,	5782
	31:17	Now k all the boys.	2222
	31:17	And k every woman who has slept with	2222
	35:17	anyone has a stone in his hand that could k,	4637
	35:18	a wooden object in his hand that could k,	4637
	35:23	drops a stone on him that could k him,	4637
	35:27	the avenger of blood may k the accused	8357
Dt	19: 5	and hit his neighbor and k him.	4637
	19: 6	and k him even though he is not deserving of death,	5782+5883
	27:25	"Cursed is the man who accepts a bribe to k an innocent person."	5782+5883
Jos	9:26	and they did not k them.	2222
Jdg	8:18	"What kind of men did you k at Tabor?"	2222
	8:19	I would not k you."	2222
	8:20	his oldest son, he said, "K them!"	2222
	9:54	"Draw your sword and k me,	4637
	13:23	"If the LORD had meant to k us,	4637
	15:12	to me that you won't k me yourselves."	7003
	15:13	We will not k you.	4637+4637
	16: 2	saying, "At dawn we'll k him."	2222
	20: 5	surrounded the house, intending to k me.	2222
	21:11	"K every male and every woman who is not	3049
1Sa	5:10	ark of the god of Israel around to us to k us	4637
	5:11	or it will k us and our people."	4637
	16: 2	Saul will hear about it and k me."	2222
	17: 9	If he is able to fight and k me,	5782
	17: 9	but if I overcome him and k him,	5782
	19: 1	and all the attendants to k David.	4637
	19: 2	Saul is looking for a chance to k you.	4637
	19:11	to David's house to watch it and to k him in	4637
	19:15	up to me in his bed so that I may k him.	4637
	19:17	Why should I k you?' "	4637
	20: 8	If I am guilty, then k me yourself!	4637
	20:33	But Saul hurled his spear at him to k him.	5782
	20:33	that his father intended to k David.	4637
	22:17	"Turn and k the priests of the LORD,	2222
	24:10	Some urged me to k you, but I spared you;	2222
	24:11	the corner of your robe but did not k you.	2222
	24:18	but you did not k me.	4637
	30:15	to me before God that you will not k me	4637
2Sa	1: 9	he said to me, 'Stand over me and k me!	4637
	13:28	'Strike Amnon down,' then k him.	4637
	21:16	said he would k David.	5782
1Ki	3:26	Don't k him!"	4637+4637
	3:27	Do not k him; she is his mother."	4637+4637
	11:40	Solomon tried to k Jeroboam,	4637
	12: 7	They will k me and return to King	2222
	17:18	to remind me of my sin and k my son?"	4637
	18: 5	not have to k any of our animals."	4162
	18:12	and doesn't find you, he will k me.	2222
	18:14	He will k me!"	2222
	19:10	and now they are trying to k me too."	4374+5883
	19:14	and now they are trying to k me too."	4374+5883
	20:36	as soon as you leave me a lion will k you."	5782
2Ki	5: 7	Can I k and bring back to life?	4637
	6:21	he asked Elisha, "Shall I k them,	5782
	6:21	Shall I k them?"	5782
	6:22	"Do not k them," he answered.	5782
	6:22	"Would you k men you have captured	5782
	7: 4	if they k us, then we die."	4637
	8:12	k their young men with the sword,	2222
	9:27	Jehu chased him, shouting, "K him too!"	5782
	10:25	"Go in and k them; let no one escape."	5782
2Ch	22:11	from Athaliah so she could not k him.	4637
	30:17	the Levites had to k the Passover lambs	8824
Ne	4:11	be right there among them and will k them	2222
	6:10	because men are coming to k you—	2222
	6:10	by night they are coming to k you."	2222
Est	3:13	destroy, k and annihilate all the Jews—	2222
	8:11	to destroy, k and annihilate any armed force	2222
Job	20:16	the fangs of an adder will k him.	2222
Ps	59: T	to watch David's house in order to k him.	4637
	59:11	But do not k them, O Lord our shield,	2222
	71:10	those who wait to k me conspire together.	5883+9068
Pr	1:32	waywardness of the simple will k them,	2222
	29:10	a man of integrity and seek to k the upright.	5883
Ecc	3: 3	a time to k and a time to heal,	2222
Jer	15: 3	"the sword to k and the dogs to drag away	2222
	18:23	O LORD, all their plots to k me.	4638
	20:17	For he did not k me in the womb,	4637
	38:15	will you not k me?	4637+4637
	38:16	I will neither k you nor hand you over	4637
	40:15	do not hide it from us or we will k you,'	4637
	41: 2	"Let me go and k Ishmael son of Nethaniah,	5782
	41: 8	ten of them said to Ishmael, "Don't k us!	4637
	41: 8	So he let them alone and did not k them	4637
	43: 3	so they may k us or carry us into exile	4637
	50:21	Pursue, k and completely destroy them,"	2991
	50:27	K all her young bulls;	2991
Eze	9: 5	"Follow him through the city and k,	5782
	9: 6	upon it and k its men and their animals,	4162
	14:17	and I k its men and their animals,	4162
	14:21	to k its men and their animals!	4162
	22:27	and k people to make unjust gain.	6

Eze	23:47	they will k their sons and daughters	2222
	25:13	and k its men and their animals.	4162
	26:11	he will k your people with the sword,	2222
	28: 9	in the presence of those who k you?	2222
	29: 8	a sword against you and k your men	4162
Am	2: 3	I will destroy her ruler and k all her officials	2222
	9: 1	those who are left I will k with the sword.	2222
Na	2:12	filling his lairs with the k and his dens with	3272
Mt	2:13	to search for the child to k him."	660+3836
	2:16	and he gave orders to k all the boys	359
	10:28	Do not be afraid of those who k the body	650
	10:28	of those who kill the body but cannot k	650
	12:14	and plotted how they might k Jesus.	660
	14: 5	Herod wanted to k John,	650
	17:23	They will k him, and on the third day	650
	21:38	let's k him and take his inheritance.'	650
	23:34	Some of them you will k and crucify;	650
	23:37	you who k the prophets and stone those sent	650
	26: 4	to arrest Jesus in some sly way and k him.	650
Mk	3: 4	to save life or to k?"	650
	3: 6	with the Herodians how they might k Jesus.	660
	6:19	a grudge against John and wanted to k him.	2309
	9:22	thrown him into fire or water to k him.	660
	9:31	They will k him, and after three days	650
	10:34	spit on him, flog him and k him.	650
	11:18	and began looking for a way to k him,	660
	12: 7	let's k him, and the inheritance will	650
	12: 9	He will come and k those tenants and give	660
	14: 1	for some sly way to arrest Jesus and k him.	650
Lk	11:49	some of whom they will k and others	650
	12: 4	be afraid of those who k the body and after	650
	13:31	Herod wants to k you."	650
	13:34	you who k the prophets and stone those sent	650
	15:23	Bring the fattened calf and k it.	2604
	15:30	you k the fattened calf for him!'	2604
	18:32	insult him, spit on him, flog him and k him.	650
	19:27	bring them here and k them in front	2956
	19:47	among the people were trying to k him.	660
	20:14	'Let's k him, and the inheritance will	650
	20:16	He will come and k those tenants and give	660
Jn	5:18	the Jews tried all the harder to k him;	650
	7:19	Why are you trying to k me?"	650
	7:20	"Who is trying to k you?"	650
	7:25	"Isn't this the man they are trying to k?	650
	8:22	This made the Jews ask, "Will he k himself?	650
	8:37	Yet you are ready to k me,	650
	8:40	As it is, you are determined to k me,	650
	10:10	thief comes only to steal and k and destroy;	2604
	12:10	So the chief priests made plans to k Lazarus	650
Ac	7:28	Do you want to k me as you killed	359
	9:23	the Jews conspired to k him,	359
	9:24	on the city gates in order to k him.	359
	9:29	but they tried to k him.	359
	10:13	"Get up, Peter. K and eat."	2604
	11: 7	'Get up, Peter. K and eat.'	2604
	16:27	about to k himself because he thought	650
	21:31	While they were trying to k him,	650
	23:15	We are ready to k him before he gets here."	359
	23:27	by the Jews and they were about to k him,	359
	25: 3	an ambush to k him along the way.	359
	26:21	in the temple courts and tried to k me.	1429
	27:42	to k the prisoners to prevent any of them	650
Ro	11: 3	and they are trying to k me"?	2426+3836+6034
1Ti	1: 9	for those who k their fathers or mothers,	4260
Jas	4: 2	You k and covet,	5839
Rev	6: 8	over a fourth of the earth to k by sword,	650
	9: 5	They were not given power to k them,	650
	9:15	and month and year were released to k	650
	11: 7	and overpower and k them.	650

KILLED (211) [KILL]

Ge	4: 8	Cain attacked his brother Abel and k him.	2222
	4:23	I have k a man for wounding me,	2222
	4:25	child in place of Abel, since Cain k him."	2222
	49: 6	for they have k men in their anger	2222
Ex	2:12	he k the Egyptian and hid him in the sand.	5782
	2:14	Are you thinking of killing me as you k	2222
	13:15	the LORD k every firstborn in Egypt,	2222
Lev	14: 5	that one of the birds be k over fresh water in	8821
	14: 6	of the bird that was k over the fresh water.	8821
Nu	16:41	"You have k the LORD's people,"	4637
	19:16	open who touches someone who has been k	2728
	19:18	or a grave or someone who has been k	2728
	22:33	I would certainly have k you,	2022
	25:14	The name of the Israelite who was k	5782
	25:18	the woman who was k when the plague	5782
	31: 7	LORD commanded Moses, and k every man.	2222
	31: 8	also k Balaam son of Beor with the sword.	2222
	31:19	"All of you who have k anyone	2222
	31:19	touched anyone who was k must stay outside	2728
	35: 6	a person who has k someone may flee.	8357
	35:11	person who has k someone accidentally may flee.	5782+8357
	35:15	anyone who has k another accidentally can flee there.	5782
Dt	4:42	to which anyone who had k a person could flee	8357
	4:42	if he had unintentionally k his neighbor	8357
	21: 1	and it is not known who k him,	5782
Jos	7: 5	who k about thirty-six of them.	5782
	8:24	Israelites returned to Ai and those who were in it.	2995+4200+5782+7023
	10:11	the hailstones than were k by the swords	2222
	10:26	and k the kings and hung them on five trees,	4637
	20: 5	because he k his neighbor unintentionally	5782

Jos	20: 9	who k someone accidentally could flee	5782
	20: 9	and not be k by the avenger of blood prior	4637
Jdg	7:25	They k Oreb at the rock of Oreb,	2222
	8:17	also pulled down the tower of Peniel and k	2222
	8:21	So Gideon stepped forward and k them,	2222
	9:45	until he had captured it and k its people.	2222
	9:54	so that they can't say, 'A woman k him.' "	2222
	12: 6	they seized him and k him at the fords of	8821
	12: 6	Forty-two thousand Ephraimites were k at	5877
	15:16	With a donkey's jawbone I have k	5782
	16:30	Thus he k many more when he died than	4637
1Sa	4: 2	who k about four thousand of them on	5782
	14:13	and his armor-bearer followed and k	4637
	14:14	and his armor-bearer killed some twenty men in	5782
	17:35	I seized it by its hair, struck it and k it.	4637
	17:36	Your servant has k both the lion and	5782
	17:50	down the Philistine and k him.	4637
	17:51	he k him, he cut off his head with the sword	4637
	18: 6	k the Philistine.	5782
	18:27	and k two hundred Philistines.	5782
	19: 5	He took his life in his hands when he k	5782
	19:11	tomorrow you'll be k."	4637
	20:14	so that I may not be k,	4637
	21: 9	whom you k in the Valley of Elah,	5782
	22:18	That day he k eighty-five men who wore	4637
	22:21	He told David that Saul had k the priests of	2222
	30: 2	They k none of them,	4637
	31: 2	and they k his sons Jonathan,	5782
2Sa	1:10	"So I stood over him and k him,	4637
	1:16	'I k the LORD's anointed.' "	4637
	2:31	But David's men had k three hundred	4637+5782
	3:30	because he had k their brother Asahel in	4637
	4: 7	After they stabbed him and	4637
	4:11	when wicked men have k an innocent man	2222
	4:12	gave an order to his men, and they k them.	2222
	10:18	and David k seven hundred of their	2222
	11:21	Who k Abimelech son of Jerub-Besheth?	5782
	12: 9	You k him with the sword of the	2222
	13:32	"My lord should not think that they k all	4637
	14: 6	One struck the other and k him.	4637
	14: 7	for the life of his brother whom he k;	2222
	18:15	Absalom, struck him and k him.	4637
	21: 6	to us to be k and exposed before the LORD	3697
	21: 9	who k and exposed them on a hill before	3697
	21:13	who had been k and exposed were gathered	3697
	21:17	he struck the Philistine down and k him,	4191
	21:18	that time Sibbecai the Hushathite k Saph,	5782
	21:19	of Jaare-Oregim the Bethlehemite k Goliath	5782
	21:21	David's brother, k him.	2222
	23: 8	whom he k in one encounter.	2728
	23:18	against three hundred men, whom he k,	2728
	23:20	down into a pit on a snowy day and k a lion.	5782
	23:21	from the Egyptian's hand and k him	2222
1Ki	2: 5	He k them, shedding their blood	2222
	2:32	and k them with the sword.	2222
	2:34	up and struck down Joab and k him,	4637
	2:46	and struck Shimei down and k him.	4637
	9:16	He k its Canaanite inhabitants and	2222
	13:24	a lion met him on the road and k him.	4637
	13:26	which has mauled him and k him,	4637
	15:28	Baasha k Nadab in the third year	4191
	15:29	he k Jeroboam's whole family.	5782
	16:10	down and k him in the twenty-seventh year	4637
	16:11	he k off Baasha's whole family.	5782
	19: 1	he had k all the prophets with the sword.	2222
	20:36	a lion found him and k him.	5782
2Ki	10: 9	against my master and k him,	2222
	10: 9	but who k all these?	5782
	10:11	So Jehu k everyone in Jezreel who remained	5782
	10:17	he k all who were left there of Ahab's	5782
	11: 2	so he was not k.	4191
	11:18	and k Mattan the priest of Baal	2222
	14:19	after him to Lachish and k him there.	4637
	15:25	So Pekah k Pekahiah and succeeded him	4191
	17:25	among them and k some of the people.	2026
	21:24	the people of the land k all who had plotted	5782
	23:29	but Neco faced him and k him at Megiddo.	4191
	25: 7	They k the sons of Zedekiah	8821
1Ch	4:43	They k the remaining Amalekites who had	5782
	7:21	and Elead were k by the native-born men	2222
	10: 2	and they k his sons Jonathan,	5782
	11:11	whom he k in one encounter.	2728
	11:20	whom he k, and so he became as famous as	2728
	11:22	down into a pit on a snowy day and k a lion.	5782
	11:23	from the Egyptian's hand and k him	2222
	19:18	and David k seven thousand	2222
	19:18	He also k Shophach the commander	4637
	20: 4	that time Sibbecai the Hushathite k Sippai,	5782
	20: 5	Elhanan son of Jair k Lahmi the brother	5782
	20: 7	David's brother, k him.	2222
2Ch	22: 1	had k all the older sons.	2222
	22: 8	been attending Ahaziah, and he k them.	2222
	23:17	the altars and idols and k Mattan the priest	2222
	24:22	but k his son, who said as he lay dying,	2222
	24:23	it invaded Judah and Jerusalem and k all	8845
	24:25	and they k him in his bed.	2222
	25:11	where he k ten thousand men of Seir.	5782
	25:13	They k three thousand people	5221
	25:27	after him to Lachish and k him there.	4637
	28: 6	In one day Pekah son of Remaliah k	2026
	33:25	the people of the land k all who had plotted	5782
	36:17	who k their young men with the sword in	2222
Ne	9:26	They k your prophets,	2222
Est	9: 6	the Jews k and destroyed five hundred men.	2222
	9: 7	They also k Parshandatha, Dalphon,	2222
	9:12	"The Jews have k and destroyed	2222

Est	9:16	They **k** seventy-five thousand of them	2222
Ps	135:10	down many nations and **k** mighty kings—	2222
	136:18	**k** mighty kings—His love endures forever.	2222
Isa	14:20	destroyed your land and **k** your people.	2222
	22: 2	Your slain were not **k** *by* the sword,	2728
	27: 7	*Has she been* **k** as those were killed who	2222
	27: 7	killed as *those* were killed **k** her?	2223
	27: 7	killed as *those* were killed *who* **k** her?	2222
Jer	39: 6	of Zedekiah before his eyes and also **k** all	8821
	41: 3	also **k** all the Jews who were with Gedaliah	5782
	41: 9	of the men *he had* **k** along with Gedaliah	5782
	41:18	Nethaniah *had* **k** Gedaliah son of Ahikam,	5782
	52:10	*he* also **k** all the officials of Judah.	8821
La	2:20	and prophet be **k** in the sanctuary of	2222
	4: 9	*Those* **k** *by* the sword are better off than	2728
Eze	11: 6	You have **k** many *people* in this city	2728
	13:19	you *have* **k** those who should not have died	4637
	23:10	took away her sons and daughters and **k** her	2222
	31:17	joining *those* **k** *by* the sword.	2728
	31:18	with *those* **k** *by* the sword.	2728
	32:20	They will fall among *those* **k** *by* the sword.	2728
	32:21	with *those* **k** *by* the sword.'	2728
	32:25	are uncircumcised, **k** *by* the sword	2728
	32:26	are uncircumcised, **k** *by* the sword	2726
	32:28	with *those* **k** *by* the sword	2728
	32:29	they are laid with *those* **k** *by* the sword.	2728
	32:30	They lie uncircumcised with *those* **k** *by*	2728
	32:31	for all his hordes *that* were **k** *by* the sword,	2728
	32:32	with *those* **k** *by* the sword,	2728
	35: 8	*those* **k** *by* the sword will fall on your hills	2728
Da	3:22	flames of the fire **k** the soldiers who took	10625
Hos	6: 5	*I* **k** you with the words of my mouth;	2222
Am	4:10	*I* **k** your young men with the sword,	2222
Na	2:12	The lion **k** enough for his cubs	3271
Mt	16:21	and that he must *be* **k** and on the third day	650
	21:35	they beat one, **k** another, and stoned a third.	650
	21:39	of the vineyard and **k** him.	650
	22: 6	mistreated them and **k** them.	650
Mk	8:31	he must *be* **k** and after three days rise again.	650
	12: 5	He sent still another, and that one *they* **k**.	650
	12: 5	some of them *they* beat, others *they* **k**.	650
	12: 8	So *they* took him and **k** him,	650
Lk	9:22	*be* **k** and on the third day *be* raised to life."	650
	11:47	and it was your forefathers who **k** them.	650
	11:48	they **k** the prophets,	650
	11:51	who *was* **k** between the altar and	660
	15:27	'and your father *has* **k** the fattened calf	2604
	20:15	of the vineyard and **k** him.	650
Ac	3:13	You handed him over to *be* **k**,	NIG
	3:15	*You* **k** the author of life, but God raised him	650
	5:30	whom *you had* **k** by hanging him on a tree.	1429
	5:36	He *was* **k**, all his followers were dispersed.	359
	5:37	He too *was* **k**, and all his followers were	660
	7:28	as *you* **k** the Egyptian yesterday?'	359
	7:52	even *k* those who predicted the coming of	650
	10:39	*They* **k** him by hanging him on a tree,	359
	23:12	not to eat or drink until *they had* **k** Paul.	650
	23:14	not to eat anything until we *have* **k** Paul.	650
	23:21	not to eat or drink until *they have* **k** him.	359
Ro	11: 3	they have **k** your prophets and torn down	650
1Co	10: 9	some of them did—and *were* **k** by snakes.	660
	10:10	and *were* **k** by the destroying angel.	660
2Co	6: 9	beaten, and yet not **k**;	2506
1Th	2:15	who **k** the Lord Jesus and the prophets and	650
Heb	11:31	*was* not **k** with those who were disobedient.	5272
Rev	6:11	to be **k** as they had been was completed.	650
	9:18	third of mankind *was* **k** by the three plagues	650
	9:20	not **k** by these plagues still did not repent of	650
	11:13	Seven thousand people *were* **k** in	650
	13:10	If anyone *is* to be **k** with the sword,	650
	13:10	with the sword he *will* be **k**.	650
	13:15	refused to worship the image to *be* **k**.	650
	18:24	and of all who *have* been **k** on the earth."	5377
	19:21	*were* **k** with the sword that came out of	650

KILLING (21) [KILL]

Ge	27:42	with the thought of **k** you.	2222
	34:25	the unsuspecting city, **k** every male.	2222
Ex	2:14	Are you thinking of **k** me as you killed	2222
	32:27	each **k** his brother and friend	2222
Jos	8:24	When Israel had finished **k** all the men	2222
1Sa	17:57	as David returned from **k** the Philistine,	5782
	24: 7	to an innocent man like David by **k** him	4637
1Ki	18: 4	Jezebel *was* **k** off the Lord's prophets,	4162
	18:13	what I did while Jezebel *was* **k** the prophets	2222
2Ki	17:26	lions among them, which *are* **k** them off,	4637
Est	3: 6	the idea of **k** only Mordecai. 928+3338+8938	
	9: 5	with the sword, and destroying them,	2223
Isa	22:13	slaughtering of cattle and **k** of sheep,	8821
Jer	41: 2	**k** the one whom the king of Babylon	4637
Eze	9: 7	So they went out and *began* **k** throughout	5782
	9: 8	While they *were* **k** and I was left alone,	5782
	14:19	**k** its men and their animals,	4162
Jnh	1:14	Do not hold us accountable for **k** an	1947
Lk	12: 5	Fear him who, after the **k** of the body,	650
Ac	7:24	to his defense and avenged him *by* **k**	4250
	22:20	the clothes *of* those who *were* **k** him.'	359

KILLS (21) [KILL]

Ge	4:15	if anyone **k** Cain, he will suffer vengeance	2222
Ex	21:12	"Anyone who strikes a man and **k** him shall	4637
	21:14	and **k** another man deliberately,	2222
	21:29	but has not kept it penned up and *it* **k**	4637
Lev	24:21	*Whoever* **k** an animal must make restitution,	5782
	24:21	but *whoever* **k** a man must be put to death.	5782

Nu	35:30	" 'Anyone *who* **k** a person is to be put	5782
Dt	19: 3	so that anyone *who* **k** a man may flee there.	8357
	19: 4	the rule concerning the *man who* **k** another	8357
	19: 4	*one* who **k** his neighbor unintentionally,	5782
	19:11	assaults and **k** him, 2256+4637+5782+5883	
	27:24	the man *who* **k** his neighbor secretly."	5782
Jos	20: 3	so that anyone *who* **k** a person accidentally	5782
1Sa	17:25	great wealth to the man who **k** him.	5782
	17:26	be done for the man who **k** this Philistine	5782
	17:27	be done for the man who **k** him."	5782
Job	5: 2	Resentment **k** a fool,	2222
	24:14	murderer rises up and **k** the poor and needy;	7779
Isa	66: 3	like *one who* **k** a man, and whoever offers	5782
Jn	16: 2	anyone who **k** you will think he is offering	650
2Co	3: 6	for the letter **k**, but the Spirit gives life.	650

KILMAD (1)

Eze	27:23	Asshur and **K** traded with you.	4008

KIMHAM (3) [GERUTH KIMHAM]

2Sa	19:37	But here is your servant **K**.	4016
	19:38	The king said, "**K** shall cross over with me,	4016
	19:40	**K** crossed with him.	4016

KIN (1) [KINSMAN, KINSMEN]

Ru	3:12	Although it is true that I *am* **near of k**,	1457

KINAH (1)

Jos	15:22	**K**, Dimonah, Adadah,	7807

KIND (112) [KINDEST, KINDHEARTED, KINDLY, KINDNESS, KINDNESSES, KINDS]

Ge	1:21	and every winged bird according to its **k**.	4786
	1:24	and wild animals, each according to its **k**."	4786
	6:20	Two of every **k** of bird,	4786
	6:20	of every **k** of animal and of every kind	4786
	6:20	and of every **k** of creature that moves along	4786
	6:21	to take every **k** of food that is to be eaten	AIT
	7: 2	with you seven of every **k** of clean animal,	AIT
	7: 2	and two of every **k** of unclean animal,	NIH
	7: 3	and also seven of every **k** of bird,	NIH
	7:14	every wild animal according to its **k**,	4786
	7:14	the ground according to its **k** and every bird	4786
	7:14	to its kind and every bird according to its **k**,	4786
	8:17	Bring out every **k** of living creature that is	AIT
	8:19	came out of the ark, **one k after another**.	AIT
	9:15	and you and all living creatures of every **k**. 2157+4200+5476	1414
	9:16	and all living creatures of every **k** on	1414
	27: 4	the **k** of tasty food I like and bring it 889+3469	
	37: 4	and could not speak a **k** word to him.	8934
Ex	1:20	So God *was* **k** to the midwives and	3512
Lev	7:14	He is to bring one of **each k** as an offering,	AIT
	11:14	the red kite, any **k** of black kite,	4786
	11:15	any **k** of raven,	4786
	11:16	the screech owl, the gull, any **k** of hawk,	4786
	11:19	any **k** of heron, the hoopoe and the bat.	4786
	11:22	Of these you may eat any **k** of locust,	4786
	11:29	the weasel, the rat, any **k** of great lizard,	4786
	13:31	if, when the priest examines **this k** of sore, 2021+5596+5999	
	19:23	" 'When you enter the land and plant **any k**	AIT
	25:36	Do not take **interest of any k** 2256+5968+9552	
Nu	5: 2	or a discharge *of* **any k**,	AIT
	13:19	**What** *k* of land do they live in?	AIT
	13:19	**What** *k* of towns do they live in?	AIT
	28: 8	along with the **same** *k* of grain offering	AIT
Dt	4:15	*of* **any** *k* the day the Lord spoke to you	AIT
	4:25	if you then become corrupt and make any **k**	9454
	14:13	the red kite, the black kite, any **k** *of* falcon,	4786
	14:14	any **k** *of* raven,	4786
	14:15	the screech owl, the gull, any **k** *of* hawk,	4786
	14:18	any **k** *of* heron, the hoopoe and the bat.	4786
	24:10	you make a loan of **any k** to your neighbor,	4399
	28:61	The Lord will also bring on you **every** *k*	AIT
Jdg	6:26	a **proper k** of altar to the Lord your God	5120
	8:18	"What **k** of men did you kill at Tabor?"	NIH
2Sa	13:18	for this was the **k** *of* garment	4027
1Ki	9:13	"What **k** of towns are these you have given	NIH
2Ki	1: 7	"What **k** of man was it who came	5477
1Ch	22:15	as well as men skilled in **every** *k* of work	AIT
2Ch	2:14	be **k** to these people and please them	3202
	15: 6	troubling them with **every** *k* of distress.	AIT
Job	24:21	"But now **be so k as** to look at me.	3283
Ps	144:13	Our barns will be filled with **every** *k* of provision. 448+2385+2385+4946	
Pr	11:17	A **k** man benefits himself,	2876
	12:25	but a **k** word cheers him up.	3202
	14:21	but blessed is he *who is* **k** to the needy.	2858
	14:31	but *whoever is* **k** to the needy honors God.	2858
	19:17	*He who is* **k** to the poor lends to the Lord,	2858
	21: 3	the **k** of man who is always thinking about	4017
	28: 8	*who will* be **k** to the poor.	2858
SS	4:14	with **every** *k* of incense tree,	AIT
Isa	44:11	He and his **k** will be put to shame;	2492
	58: 5	Is this the **k** of fast I have chosen,	3869
	58: 6	"Is not this the **k** of fasting I have chosen:	NIH
Jer	8: 9	**what** *k* of wisdom do they have?	4537
Eze	17:23	Birds of **every** *k* will nest in it;	AIT
	39:17	to **every** *k* of bird and all the wild animals:	4053S
	39:20	mighty men and soldiers of **every** *k*,'	AIT
Da	1: 4	showing aptitude for **every** *k* of learning,	AIT

Da	4:27	and your wickedness by *being* **k** *to*	10274
Zep	2:14	will lie down there, creatures of every **k**.	1580
Zec	1:13	the Lord spoke **k** and comforting words	3202
Mt	8:27	"**What k** *of man* is this?	4534
Mk	9:29	"This **k** can come out only by prayer."	1169
Lk	1:29	and wondered **what k** of greeting this might	4534
	6:35	he is **k** to the ungrateful and wicked.	5982
	7:39	and **what k** of woman she is—	4534
	16: 8	with their own **k** than are the people of	1155
Jn	2: 6	**k** used by the Jews for ceremonial washing,	NIG
	4:23	for **they are the k** of worshipers	5525
	12:33	to show the **k** of death he was going to die.	
	16:25	will no longer use **this k** of language 1877+4231S	
	18:32	the **k** of death he was going to die would	4481
	21:19	Jesus said this to indicate the **k** of death	4481
Ac	7:49	**What k** of house will you build for me?	4481
	20:35	that *by this* **k** of hard work we must help	4048
	24: 2	that you be **k** enough to hear us briefly.	2116
Ro	1:29	They have become filled *with* **every** *k*	AIT
	7: 8	produced in me **every** *k* of covetous desire.	AIT
1Co	5: 1	and of a **k** that does not occur even	5525
	13: 4	Love is patient, love *is* **k**.	5980
	15:35	With **what k** of body will they come?"	4481
	15:38	to **each k** of seed he gives its own body.	AIT
	15:39	Men have one **k** of flesh,	NIG
	15:40	of the heavenly bodies is one **k**,	NIG
	15:41	The sun has one **k** of splendor,	NIG
Gal	5:8	That **k** of persuasion does not come from	NIG
Eph	4:19	to sensuality so as to indulge in **every** *k*	AIT
	4:32	Be **k** and compassionate to one another,	5982
	5: 3	or of **any** *k* of impurity, or of greed,	AIT
1Th	1: 9	for they themselves report **what k** of	3961
	5:15	to be **k** to each other and to everyone else.	19
	5:22	Avoid **every k** of evil.	1626
2Ti	2:24	instead, he must be **k** to everyone,	2473
	3: 6	They are the **k** who worm their way 1666+4047	
Tit	2: 5	to be **k**, and to be subject to their husbands,	19
Jas	1:18	be a **k** of firstfruits of all he created.	5516
1Pe	2: 1	hypocrisy, envy, and slander of **every** *k*.	AIT
	4:15	not be as a murderer or thief or any other **k**	NIG
	5: 9	the world are undergoing the **same** *k*	AIT
2Pe	3:11	**what k** of *people* ought you to be?	4534
Rev	11: 6	to strike the earth with **every** *k* of plague	AIT
	18:12	and articles of every **k** made of ivory,	5007
	21:19	the city walls were decorated *with* **every** *k*	AIT

KINDEST (1) [KIND]

Pr	12:10	but the **k** acts *of* the wicked are cruel.	8171

KINDHEARTED (1) [KIND, HEART]

Pr	11:16	A **k** woman gains respect,	2834

KINDLE (5) [KINDLED, KINDLES, KINDLING]

Jer	15:14	for my anger *will* **k** a fire that will burn	7706
	17:27	then *I will* **k** an unquenchable fire in	3675
	21:14	*I will* **k** a fire in your forests	3675
	50:32	*I will* **k** a fire in her towns	3675
Eze	24:10	So heap on the wood and **k** the fire.	1944

KINDLED (7) [KINDLE]

Dt	32:22	For a fire *has been* **k** by my wrath,	7706
Isa	10:16	a fire *will be* **k** like a blazing flame.	3678
Jer	17: 4	for *you have* **k** my anger, 836+7706	
La	4:11	He **k** a fire in Zion	3675
Eze	20:48	that I the Lord *have* **k** it;	1277
Lk	12:49	and how I wish *it were* already **k**!	409
	22:55	But *when they had* **k** a fire in the middle of	4312

KINDLES (1) [KINDLE]

Isa	44:15	he **k** a fire and bakes bread.	5956

KINDLING (1) [KINDLE]

Pr	26:21	so is a quarrelsome man for **k** strife.	3081

KINDLY (6) [KIND]

Ge	50:21	And he reassured them and spoke **k** to them.	4213
Jos	2:14	we will treat you **k** and faithfully when	2876
Ru	2:14	*have* **spoken k** to your servant. 1819+4213+6584	
2Ki	25:28	He spoke **k** to him and gave him a seat	3208
Jer	52:32	He spoke **k** to him and gave him a seat	3208
1Co	4:13	when we are slandered, *we* **answer k**.	4151

KINDNESS (64) [KIND]

Ge	19:19	and you have shown great **k** to me	2876
	21:23	an alien the same **k** I have shown to you."	2876
	24:12	and show **k** to my master Abraham.	2876
	24:14	By this I will know that you have shown **k**	2876
	24:27	not abandoned his **k** and faithfulness	2876
	24:49	Now if you will show **k** and faithfulness	2876
	32:10	I am unworthy of all the **k**	2876
	39:21	he showed him **k** and granted him favor in	2876
	40:14	remember me and show me **k**;	2876
	47:29	that you will show me **k** and faithfulness.	2876
Jos	2:12	to me by the Lord that you will show **k**	2876
	2:12	because I have shown **k** to you.	2876
Jdg	8:35	They also failed to show **k** to the family	2876
	21:22	'Do us a **k** by helping them,	2858
Ru	1: 8	May the Lord show **k** to you,	2876
	2:20	not stopped showing his **k** to the living and	2876
	3:10	"This **k** is greater than that which you	2876

1Sa	15: 6	for you showed **k** to all the Israelites	2876
	20: 8	As for you, show **k** to your servant,	2876
	20:14	But show me **unfailing k** like that of	2876
	20:15	not ever cut off your **k** from my family—	2876
2Sa	2: 5	"The LORD bless you for showing this **k**	2876
	2: 6	May the LORD now show you **k**	2876
	9: 1	to whom I can show **k** for Jonathan's sake?"	2876
	9: 3	of Saul to whom I can show God's **k?"**	2876
	9: 7	"for I will surely show you **k** for the sake	2876
	10: 2	"I will show **k** to Hanun son of Nahash,	2876
	10: 2	just as his father showed **k** to me."	2876
	15:20	May **k** and faithfulness be with you."	2876
	22:51	he shows **unfailing k** to his anointed,	2876
1Ki	2: 7	"But show **k** to the sons of Barzillai	2876
	3: 6	"You have shown great **k** to your servant,	2876
	3: 6	You have continued this great **k** to him	2876
1Ch	19: 2	"I will show **k** to Hanun son of Nahash,	2876
	19: 2	because his father showed **k** to me."	2876
2Ch	1: 8	"You have shown great **k**	2876
	24:22	**k** Zechariah's father Jehoiada had shown	2876
	32:25	and he did not respond to the **k** shown him;	1691
Ezr	9: 9	He has shown us **k** in the sight of the kings	2876
Job	10:12	You gave me life and showed me **k,**	2876
	24:21	and to the widow **show** no **k.**	3512
Ps	18:50	he shows **unfailing k** to his anointed,	2876
	109:12	May no one extend **k** to him or take pity	2876
	109:16	For he never thought of doing a **k,**	2876
	141: 5	Let a righteous man strike me—it is a **k;**	2876
Isa	54: 8	with everlasting **k** I will have compassion	2876
Jer	9:24	that I am the LORD, who exercises **k,**	2876
Hos	11: 4	I led them with cords of human **k,**	NIH
Ac	4: 9	an **act of k shown to** a cripple	2307
	14:17	He has **shown k** by giving you rain	
	27: 3	and Julius, **in k** to Paul,	5793+5968
	28: 2	The islanders showed us unusual **k.**	5792
Ro	2: 4	for the riches of his **k,**	5983
	2: 4	that God's **k** leads you toward repentance?	5982
	11:22	Consider therefore the **k** and sternness	5983
	11:22	sternness to those who fell, but **k** to you,	5983
	11:22	provided that you continue in his **k.**	5983
2Co	6: 6	understanding, patience and **k;**	5983
Gal	5:22	peace, patience, **k,** goodness, faithfulness,	5983
Eph	2: 7	expressed in his **k** to us in Christ Jesus.	5983
Col	3:12	clothe yourselves with compassion, **k,**	5983
Tit	3: 4	the **k** and love of God our Savior appeared,	5983
2Pe	1: 7	and to godliness, **brotherly k;**	5789
	1: 7	and to **brotherly k,** love.	5789

KINDNESSES (3) [KIND]

Ps	106: 7	they did not remember your many **k,**	2876
Isa	63: 7	I will tell of the **k** of the LORD,	2876
	63: 7	according to his compassion and many **k.**	2876

KINDRED, KINDREDS (KJV) See
BLOOD RELATIVES, CLAN, FAMILY,
KINSMAN, KINSMEN, NATIVE, PEOPLE,
RELATIVES, TRIBE

KINDS (77) [KIND]

Ge	1:11	according to their **various k."**	4786
	1:12	according to their **k** and trees bearing fruit	4786
	1:12	with seed in it according to their **k.**	4786
	1:21	according to their **k,**	4786
	1:24	according to their **k:**	4786
	1:25	the wild animals according to their **k,**	4786
	1:25	the livestock according to their **k,**	4786
	1:25	along the ground according to their **k.**	4786
	2: 9	And the LORD God made all **k**	AIT
	4:22	who forged all **k** of tools out of bronze	AIT
	7: 3	to keep their **various k** alive throughout	2446
	7:14	all livestock according to their **k,**	4786
	24:10	taking with him all **k** of good things	AIT
	40:17	top basket were all **k** of baked goods	3972+4946
Ex	1:14	and mortar and with all **k** of work in	AIT
	31: 3	and knowledge in all **k** of crafts—	AIT
	31: 5	and to engage in all **k** of craftsmanship.	AIT
	35:22	came and brought gold jewelry of all **k:**	AIT
	35:31	and knowledge in all **k** of crafts—	AIT
	35:33	to engage in all **k** of artistic craftsmanship.	4856
	35:35	He has filled them with skill to do all **k**	AIT
Lev	19:19	"Do not mate **different k** of animals.	3977
	19:19	not plant your field with **two k** of seed.	3977
	19:19	"Do not wear clothing woven of **two k**	3977
Dt	6:11	with all **k** of good things you did	AIT
	12:31	they do all **k** of detestable things	AIT
	22: 9	Do not plant **two k** of seed in your vineyard;	3977
1Sa	4: 8	the Egyptians with all **k** of plagues in	AIT
1Ki	7:14	in all **k** of bronze work.	AIT
1Ch	18:10	Hadoram brought all **k** of articles	AIT
	28:14	be used in **various k of service,**	2256+6275+6275
	28:14	be used in **various k of service:**	2256+6275+6275
	29: 2	and all **k** of fine stone and marble—	AIT
2Ch	2:14	He is experienced in all **k** of engraving	AIT
	32:27	spices, shields and all **k** of valuables.	3998
	32:28	made stalls for various **k of cattle,**	989+989+2256
Ne	5:18	an abundant supply of wine of all **k.**	AIT
	9:25	houses filled with all **k** of good things,	AIT
	13:15	grapes, figs and all **other k** of loads.	AIT
	13:16	in fish and all **k** of merchandise	AIT
	13:20	and sellers of all **k** of goods spent	AIT
Ecc	2: 5	and parks and planted all **k** of fruit trees	AIT
Jer	15: 3	"I will send four **k** of destroyers	5476
Eze	8:10	and I saw portrayed all over the walls all **k**	9322
	27:22	of all **k** of spices and precious stones,	AIT

Eze	39: 4	as food to all **k** of carrion birds and to	4053S
	47:10	The fish will be of many **k—**	4786
	47:12	of all **k** will grow on both banks of	AIT
Da	1:17	and understanding of **all k** of literature	AIT
	1:17	understand visions and dreams of **all k.**	AIT
	3: 5	zither, lyre, harp, pipes and all **k** of music,	10235
	3: 7	flute, zither, lyre, harp and all **k** of music,	10235
	3:10	pipes and all **k** of music must fall down	10235
	3:15	zither, lyre, harp, pipes and all **k** of music,	10235
Mt	13:47	down into the lake and caught all **k** of fish.	1169
Lk	4:40	who had **various k** of sickness,	4476
	11:42	rue and **all** other **k** of garden herbs,	AIT
	12:15	Be on your guard against all **k** of greed;	AIT
Ac	10:12	It contained all **k** of four-footed animals,	AIT
	13:10	full of all **k** of deceit and trickery.	AIT
1Co	12: 4	There are **different k** of gifts,	AIT
	12: 5	There are **different k** of service,	AIT
	12: 6	There are **different k** of working,	AIT
	12:10	to another speaking in different **k**	1169
	12:28	those speaking in different **k** of tongues.	1169
Eph	6:18	in the Spirit on all occasions with **all k**	AIT
2Th	2: 9	the work of Satan displayed in all **k**	AIT
1Ti	5:10	in trouble and devoting herself to **all k**	AIT
	6:10	love of money is a root of **all k** of evil.	AIT
2Ti	3: 6	and are swayed by **all k** of evil desires,	4476
	3:11	**what k** of things happened to me	3888
Tit	3: 3	by **all k** of passions and pleasures.	4476
Heb	13: 9	Do not be carried away by **all k** of	4476
Jas	1: 2	whenever you face trials of **many k,**	4476
	3: 7	All **k** of animals, birds,	5882
1Pe	1: 6	to suffer grief in **all k** of trials.	4476

KINE (KJV) See COW, COWS

KING (2314) [KING'S, KINGDOM, KINGDOMS, KINGS, KINGS', KINGSHIP]

Ge	14: 1	At this time Amraphel **k** of Shinar,	4889
	14: 1	Arioch **k** of Ellasar,	4889
	14: 1	Kedorlaomer **k** of Elam and Tidal king	4889
	14: 1	Kedorlaomer king of Elam and Tidal **k**	4889
	14: 2	went to war against Bera **k** of Sodom,	4889
	14: 2	Birsha **k** of Gomorrah,	4889
	14: 2	Shinab **k** of Admah,	4889
	14: 2	Shemeber **k** of Zeboiim,	4889
	14: 2	and the **k** of Bela (that is, Zoar).	4889
	14: 8	Then the **k** of Sodom,	4889
	14: 8	the king of Sodom, the **k** of Gomorrah,	4889
	14: 8	the king of Gomorrah, the **k** of Admah,	4889
	14: 8	the **k** of Zeboiim and the king of Bela	4889
	14: 8	the king of Zeboiim and the **k** of Bela	4889
	14: 9	against Kedorlaomer **k** of Elam, Tidal king	4889
	14: 9	Tidal **k** of Goiim, Amraphel king of Shinar	4889
	14: 9	Amraphel **k** of Shinar and Arioch king	4889
	14: 9	Amraphel king of Shinar and Arioch **k**	4889
	14:17	**k** of Sodom came out to meet him in	4889
	14:18	Then Melchizedek **k** of Salem	4889
	14:21	The **k** of Sodom said to Abram,	4889
	14:22	But Abram said to the **k** of Sodom,	4889
	20: 2	Then Abimelech **k** of Gerar sent for Sarah	4889
	26: 1	to Abimelech **k** of the Philistines in Gerar.	4889
	26: 8	Abimelech **k** of the Philistines looked down	4889
	36:31	in Edom before any Israelite **k** reigned:	4889
	36:32	Bela son of Beor became **k** of Edom.	4887
	36:33	of Zerah from Bozrah succeeded him as **k.**	4887
	36:34	of the Temanites succeeded him as **k.**	4887
	36:35	succeeded him as **k.**	4887
	36:36	Samlah from Masrekah succeeded him as **k.**	4887
	36:37	on the river succeeded him as **k.**	4887
	36:38	son of Acbor succeeded him as **k.**	4887
	36:39	Hadad succeeded him as **k.**	4887
	40: 1	and the baker of the **k** of Egypt offended	4889
	40: 1	offended their master, the **k** of Egypt.	4889
	40: 5	cupbearer and the baker of the **k** of Egypt,	4889
	41:46	when he entered the service of Pharaoh **k**	4889
	49:20	he will provide delicacies fit for a **k.**	4889
Ex	1: 8	Then a new **k,** who did not know about	4889
	1:15	**k** of Egypt said to the Hebrew midwives,	4889
	1:17	not do what the **k** of Egypt had told them	4889
	1:18	the **k** of Egypt summoned the midwives	4889
	2:23	that long period, the **k** of Egypt died.	4889
	3:18	Then you and the elders are to go to the **k**	4889
	3:19	the **k** of Egypt will not let you go unless	4889
	5: 4	But the **k** of Egypt said, "Moses and Aaron,	4889
	6:11	"Go, tell Pharaoh **k** of Egypt to let	4889
	6:13	about the Israelites and Pharaoh **k** of Egypt,	4889
	6:27	They were the ones who spoke to Pharaoh **k**	4889
	6:29	Pharaoh **k** of Egypt everything I tell you."	4889
	14: 5	When the **k** of Egypt was told that	4889
	14: 8	hardened the heart of Pharaoh **k** of Egypt,	4889
Nu	20:14	from Kadesh to the **k** of Edom, saying:	4889
	21: 1	When the Canaanite **k** of Arad,	4889
	21:21	Israel sent messengers to say to Sihon **k** of	4889
	21:26	the city of Sihon **k** of the Amorites,	4889
	21:26	against the former **k** of Moab and had taken	4889
	21:29	and his daughters as captives to Sihon **k** of	4889
	21:33	and Og **k** of Bashan and his whole army	4889
	21:34	Do to him what you did to Sihon **k** of	4889
	22: 4	who was **k** of Moab at that time,	4889
	22:10	"Balak son of Zippor, **k** of Moab,	4889
	23: 7	the **k** of Moab from the eastern mountains.	4889
	23:21	the shout of the **K** is among them.	4889
	24: 7	"Their **k** will be greater than Agag;	4889
	32: 7	the kingdom of Sihon **k** of the Amorites	4889
	32:33	of the Amorites and the kingdom of Og **k**	4889S

Nu	33:40	The Canaanite **k** of Arad,	4889
Dt	1: 4	This was after he had defeated Sihon **k** of	4889
	1: 4	and at Edrei had defeated Og **k** of Bashan,	4889
	2:24	**k** of Heshbon, and his country.	4889
	2:26	of Kedemoth I sent messengers to Sihon **k**	4889
	2:30	But Sihon **k** of Heshbon refused	4889
	3: 1	and Og **k** of Bashan and his whole army	4889
	3: 2	Do to him what you did to Sihon **k** of	4889
	3: 3	also gave into our hands Og **k** of Bashan	4889
	3: 6	as we had done with Sihon **k** of Heshbon,	4889
	3:11	(Only Og **k** of Bashan was left of	4889
	4:46	in the land of Sihon **k** of the Amorites,	4889
	4:47	of his land and the land of Og **k** of Bashan,	4889
	7: 8	from the power of Pharaoh **k** of Egypt.	4889
	11: 3	both to Pharaoh **k** of Egypt and	4889
	17:14	a **k** over us like all the nations around us,"	4889
	17:15	the **k** the LORD your God chooses.	4889
	17:16	The **k,** moreover, must not acquire great	NIH
	28:36	the **k** you set over you to a nation unknown	4889
	29: 7	Sihon **k** of Heshbon and Og king of	4889
	29: 7	of Heshbon and Og **k** of Bashan came out	4889
	33: 5	He was **k** over Jeshurun when the leaders of	4889
Jos	2: 2	The **k** of Jericho was told, "Look!	4889
	2: 3	the **k** of Jericho sent this message to Rahab:	4889
	6: 2	along with its **k** and its fighting men.	4889
	8: 1	For I have delivered into your hands the **k**	4889
	8: 2	and its **k** as you did to Jericho and its king,	4889
	8: 2	and its king as you did to Jericho and its **k,**	4889
	8:14	When the **k** of Ai saw this,	4889
	8:23	the **k** of Ai alive and brought him	4889
	8:29	the **k** of Ai on a tree and left him there	4889
	9:10	Sihon **k** of Heshbon,	4889
	9:10	and Og **k** of Bashan,	4889
	10: 1	Now Adoni-Zedek **k** of Jerusalem heard	4889
	10: 1	to Ai and its **k** as he had done to Jericho	4889
	10: 1	as he had done to Jericho and its **k,**	4889
	10: 3	So Adoni-Zedek **k** of Jerusalem appealed	4889
	10: 3	Jerusalem appealed to Hoham **k** of Hebron,	4889
	10: 3	Piram **k** of Jarmuth,	4889
	10: 3	Japhia **k** of Lachish and Debir king of	4889
	10: 3	king of Lachish and Debir **k** of Eglon.	4889
	10:28	He put the city and its **k** to the sword	4889
	10:28	to the **k** of Makkedah as he had done to	4889
	10:28	of Makkedah as he had done to the **k** of	4889
	10:30	The LORD also gave that city and its **k**	4889
	10:30	And he did to its **k** as he had done to	4889
	10:30	as he had done to the **k** of Jericho.	4889
	10:33	Horam **k** of Gezer had come up	4889
	10:37	to the sword, together with its **k,**	4889
	10:39	They took the city, its **k** and its villages,	4889
	10:39	They did to Debir and its **k** as they had done	4889
	10:39	as they had done to Libnah and its **k** and	4889
	11: 1	When Jabin **k** of Hazor heard of this,	4889
	11: 1	he sent word to Jobab **k** of Madon,	4889
	11:10	and captured Hazor and put its **k** to	4889
	12: 2	Sihon **k** of the Amorites,	4889
	12: 4	And the territory of Og **k** of Bashan,	4889
	12: 5	and half of Gilead to the border of Sihon **k**	4889
	12: 9	the **k** of Jericho one the king of Ai	4889
	12: 9	of Jericho one the **k** of Ai (near Bethel) one	4889
	12:10	**k** of Jerusalem one the king of Hebron one	4889
	12:10	king of Jerusalem one the **k** of Hebron one	4889
	12:11	**k** of Jarmuth one the king of Lachish one	4889
	12:11	king of Jarmuth one the **k** of Lachish one	4889
	12:12	the **k** of Eglon one the king of Gezer one	4889
	12:12	the king of Eglon one the **k** of Gezer one	4889
	12:13	the **k** of Debir one the king of Geder one	4889
	12:13	the king of Debir one the **k** of Geder one	4889
	12:14	the **k** of Hormah one the king of Arad one	4889
	12:14	the king of Hormah one the **k** of Arad one	4889
	12:15	**k** of Libnah one the king of Adullam one	4889
	12:15	king of Libnah one the **k** of Adullam one	4889
	12:16	**k** of Makkedah one the king of Bethel one	4889
	12:16	king of Makkedah one the **k** of Bethel one	4889
	12:17	**k** of Tappuah one the king of Hepher one	4889
	12:17	king of Tappuah one the **k** of Hepher one	4889
	12:18	**k** of Aphek one the king of Lasharon one	4889
	12:18	king of Aphek one the **k** of Lasharon one	4889
	12:19	the **k** of Madon one the king of Hazor one	4889
	12:19	the king of Madon one the **k** of Hazor one	4889
	12:20	the **k** of Shimron Meron one the king	4889
	12:20	the king of Shimron Meron one the **k**	4889
	12:21	**k** of Taanach one the king of Megiddo one	4889
	12:21	king of Taanach one the **k** of Megiddo one	4889
	12:22	the **k** of Kedesh one the king of Jokneam	4889
	12:22	the king of Kedesh one the **k** of Jokneam	4889
	12:23	the **k** of Dor (in Naphoth Dor) one the king	4889
	12:23	the king of Dor (in Naphoth Dor) one the **k**	4889
	12:24	the **k** of Tirzah one thirty-one kings in all.	4889
	13:10	all the towns of Sihon **k** of the Amorites,	4889
	13:21	the entire realm of Sihon **k** of the Amorites,	4889
	13:27	the rest of the realm of Sihon **k** of Heshbon	4889
	13:30	the entire realm of Og **k** of Bashan—	4889
	24: 9	When Balak son of Zippor, the **k** of Moab,	4889
Jdg	3: 8	into the hands of Cushan-Rishathaim **k**	4889
	3:10	The LORD gave Cushan-Rishathaim **k**	4889
	3:12	the LORD gave Eglon **k** of Moab power	4889
	3:14	to Eglon **k** of Moab for eighteen years.	4889
	3:15	with tribute to Eglon **k** of Moab.	4889
	3:17	He presented the tribute to Eglon **k**	4889
	3:19	"I have a secret message for you, O **k."**	4889
	3:19	The **k** said, "Quiet!"	NIH
	3:20	As the **k** rose from his seat,	NIH
	4: 2	a **k** of Canaan, who reigned in Hazor.	4889
	4:17	between Jabin **k** of Hazor and the clan	4889
	4:23	the Canaanite **k,** before the Israelites.	4889
	4:24	the Canaanite **k,** until they destroyed him.	4889

Ref	Text	Num
Jdg 9: 6	in Shechem to crown Abimelech **k**.	4889
9: 8	One day the trees went out to anoint a **k**	4889
9: 8	They said to the olive tree, '*Be* our **k**.'	4887
9:10	'Come and *be* our **k**.'	4887
9:12	trees said to the vine, 'Come and *be* our **k**.'	4887
9:14	'Come and *be* our **k**.'	4887
9:15	'If you really want to anoint me **k** over you,	4887
9:16	in good faith when *you* **made** Abimelech **k**,	4887
9:18	**made** Abimelech, the son of his slave girl, **k**	4887
11:12	to the Ammonite **k** with the question:	4889
11:13	**k** of the Ammonites answered Jephthah's	4889
11:14	messengers to the Ammonite **k**,	4889
11:17	Israel sent messengers to the **k** *of* Edom,	4889
11:17	but the **k** *of* Edom would not listen.	4889
11:17	They sent also to the **k** *of* Moab,	4889
11:19	"Then Israel sent messengers to Sihon **k** *of*	4889
11:25	of Zippor, **k** *of* Moab?	4889
11:28	The **k** *of* Ammon, however,	4889
17: 6	In those days Israel had no **k**;	4889
18: 1	In those days Israel had no **k**.	4889
19: 1	In those days Israel had no **k**.	4889
21:25	In those days Israel had no **k**;	4889
1Sa 2:10	to his **k** and exalt the horn of his anointed."	4889
8: 5	now appoint a **k** to lead us,	4889
8: 6	when they said, "Give us a **k** to lead us,"	4889
8: 7	but they have rejected me as their **k**.	4887
8: 9	the **k** who will reign over them will do."	4889
8:10	to the people who were asking him for a **k**.	4889
8:11	the **k** who will reign over you will do:	4889
8:18	for relief from the **k** you have chosen,	4889
8:19	"We want a **k** over us.	4889
8:20	with a **k** to lead us and to go out before us	4889
8:22	"Listen to them and **give** them a **k**."	4887+4889
10:19	And you have said, 'No, set a **k** over us.'	4889
10:24	Then the people shouted, "Long live the **k**!"	4889
11:15	and **confirmed** Saul as **k** in the presence of	4887
12: 1	to me and *have* **set** a **k** over you.	4887+4889
12: 2	Now you have a **k** as your leader.	4889
12: 9	into the hands of the Philistines and the **k**	4889
12:12	"But when you saw that Nahash **k** *of*	4889
12:12	'No, we want a **k** to rule over us'—	4889
12:12	though the LORD your God was your **k**.	4889
12:13	Now here is the **k** you have chosen,	4889
12:13	see, the LORD has set a **k** over you.	4889
12:14	and the **k** who reigns over you follow	4889
12:17	of the LORD when you asked for a **k**."	4889
12:19	the evil of asking for a **k**."	4889
12:25	both you and your **k** will be swept away."	4889
13: 1	when he *became* **k**, and he reigned over	4887
15: 1	the one the LORD sent to anoint you **k**	4889
15: 8	He took Agag **k** *of* the Amalekites alive,	4889
15:11	I am grieved that *I have* **made** Saul **k**,	4887+4889
15:17	The LORD anointed you **k** over Israel.	4889
15:20	and brought back Agag their **k**.	4889
15:23	he has rejected you as **k**."	4889
15:26	LORD has rejected you as **k** over Israel!"	4889
15:32	"Bring me Agag **k** *of* the Amalekites."	4889
15:35	that he *had* **made** Saul **k** over Israel.	4887
16: 1	since I have rejected him as **k** over Israel?	4887
16: 1	I have chosen one of his sons to be **k**."	4889
17:25	The **k** will give great wealth to the man	4889
17:55	Abner replied, "As surely as you live, O **k**,	4889
17:56	The **k** said, "Find out whose son this young man is."	4889
18: 6	from all the towns of Israel to meet **K** Saul	4889
18:22	'Look, the **k** is pleased with you,	4889
18:25	'The **k** wants no other price for	4889
18:27	and presented the full number to the **k** so	4889
19: 4	not the **k** do wrong to his servant David;	4889
20: 5	and I am supposed to dine with the **k**;	4889
20:24	the **k** sat down to eat.	4889
21: 2	"The **k** charged me with a certain matter	4889
21:10	from Saul and went to Achish **k** *of* Gath.	4889
21:11	"Isn't this David, the **k** *of* the land?	4889
21:12	was very much afraid of Achish **k** *of* Gath.	4889
22: 3	to Mizpah in Moab and said to the **k**	4889
22: 4	So he left them with the **k** *of* Moab,	4889
22:11	the **k** sent for the priest Ahimelech son	4889
22:11	and they all came to the **k**.	4889
22:14	Ahimelech answered the **k**,	4889
22:15	Let not the **k** accuse your servant or any	4889
22:16	But the **k** said, "You will surely die,	4889
22:17	Then the **k** ordered the guards at his side:	4889
22:18	The **k** then ordered Doeg,	4889
23:17	You *will be* **k** over Israel,	4887
23:20	O **k**, come down whenever it pleases you	4889
23:20	for handing him over to the **k**."	4889
24: 8	"My lord the **k**!"	4889
24:14	"Against whom has the **k** *of* Israel	4889
24:20	I know that *you will* **surely** be **k** and	4887+4887
25:36	the house holding a banquet like that of a **k**.	4889
26:14	"Who are you who calls to the **k**?"	4889
26:15	Why didn't you guard your lord the **k**?	4889
26:15	Someone came to destroy your lord the **k**.	4889
26:17	David replied, "Yes it is, my lord the **k**."	4889
26:19	the **k** listen to his servant's words.	4889
26:20	The **k** *of* Israel has come out to look for	4889
27: 2	and went over to Achish son of Maoch **k**	4889
28:13	The **k** said to her, "Don't be afraid.	4889
29: 3	who was an officer of Saul **k** *of* Israel?	4889
29: 8	against the enemies of my lord the **k**?"	4889
2Sa 2: 4	to Hebron and there they anointed David **k**	4889
2: 7	and the house of Judah has anointed me **k**	4889
2: 9	*He* **made** him **k** over Gilead,	4887
2:10	when he *became* **k** over Israel,	4887
2:11	The length of time David was **k** in Hebron	4889
3: 3	of Maacah daughter of Talmai **k** *of* Geshur;	4889

Ref	Text	Num
2Sa 3:17	have wanted to make David your **k**.	4889
3:21	and assemble all Israel for my lord the **k**,	4889
3:23	to the **k** and that the king had sent him away	4889
3:23	to the king and that the **k** had sent him away	NIH
3:24	So Joab went to the **k** and said,	4889
3:31	**K** David himself walked behind the bier.	4889
3:32	and he wept aloud at Abner's tomb.	4889
3:33	The **k** sang this lament for Abner:	4889
3:36	indeed, everything the **k** did pleased them.	4889
3:37	and all Israel knew that the **k** had no part in	4889
3:38	Then the **k** said to his men,	4889
3:39	And today, though I am the anointed **k**,	4889
4: 8	to David at Hebron and said to the **k**,	4889
4: 8	the LORD has avenged my lord the **k**	4889
5: 2	In the past, while Saul was **k** over us,	4889
5: 3	of Israel had come to **K** David at Hebron,	4889
5: 3	the **k** made a compact with them at Hebron	4889
5: 3	and they anointed David **k** over Israel.	4889
5: 4	thirty years old when he *became* **k**,	4887
5: 6	The **k** and his men marched to Jerusalem	4889
5:11	Hiram **k** *of* Tyre sent messengers to David,	4889
5:12	that the LORD had established him as **k**	4889
5:17	that David had been anointed **k** over Israel,	4889
6:12	Now **K** David was told,	4889
6:16	when she saw **K** David leaping and dancing	4889
6:20	**k** *of* Israel has distinguished himself today,	4889
7: 1	After the **k** was settled in his palace and	4889
7: 3	Nathan replied to the **k**,	4889
7:18	**K** David went in and sat before the LORD,	4889
8: 3	of Rehob, **k** *of* Zobah, when he went	4889
8: 5	of Damascus came to help Hadadezer **k**	4889
8: 8	**K** David took a great quantity of bronze.	4889
8: 9	When Tou **k** *of* Hamath heard	4889
8:10	he sent his son Joram to **K** David	4889
8:11	**K** David dedicated these articles to	4889
8:12	from Hadadezer son of Rehob, **k** *of* Zobah.	4889
9: 2	and the **k** said to him, "Are you Ziba?"	4889
9: 3	The **k** asked, "Is there no one still left of	4889
9: 3	Ziba answered the **k**, "There is still a son	4889
9: 4	"Where is he?" the **k** asked.	4889
9: 5	**K** David had him brought from Lo Debar,	4889
9: 9	Then the **k** summoned Ziba, Saul's servant,	4889
9:11	Then Ziba said to the **k**,	4889
9:11	the **k** commands his servant to do."	4889
10: 1	the **k** *of* the Ammonites died,	4889
10: 1	and his son Hanun succeeded him as **k**.	4887
10: 5	The **k** said, "Stay at Jericho	4889
10: 6	as the **k** *of* Maacah with a thousand men,	4889
11: 8	and a gift from the **k** was sent after him.	4889
11:19	the **k** this account of the battle,	4889
12: 7	'I anointed you **k** over Israel,	4889
12:30	He took the crown from the head of their **k**	4889
13: 6	When the **k** came to see him,	4889
13:13	Please speak to the **k**;	4889
13:18	the virgin daughters of the **k** wore.	4889
13:21	**K** David heard all this, he was furious.	4889
13:24	Absalom went to the **k** and said,	4889
13:24	Will the **k** and his officials please join me?"	4889
13:25	"No, my son," the **k** replied.	4889
13:26	Then he asked him, "Why should he go	4889
13:31	The **k** stood up, tore his clothes and lay	4889
13:33	My lord the **k** should not be concerned	4889
13:34	The watchman went and told the **k**,	4889
13:35	Jonadab said to the **k**, "See,	4889
13:36	wailing loudly. The **k**, too, and all	4889
13:37	Talmai son of Ammihud, the **k** *of* Geshur.	4889
13:37	**K** David mourned for his son every day.	NIH
13:39	the spirit of the **k** longed to go to Absalom,	4889
14: 3	go to the **k** and speak these words to him."	4889
14: 4	the woman from Tekoa went to the **k**,	4889
14: 4	and she said, "Help me, O **k**!"	4889
14: 5	The **k** asked her, "What is troubling you?"	4889
14: 8	The **k** said to the woman, "Go home,	4889
14: 9	"My lord the **k**, let the blame rest on me	4889
14: 9	let the **k** and his throne be without guilt."	4889
14:10	The **k** replied, "If anyone says anything	4889
14:11	the **k** invoke the LORD his God to prevent	4889
14:12	speak a word to my lord the **k**."	4889
14:13	When the **k** says this,	4889
14:13	**k** has not brought back his banished son?	4889
14:15	to say this to my lord the **k** because	4889
14:15	'I will speak to the **k**;	4889
14:16	the **k** will agree to deliver his servant from	4889
14:17	the word of my lord the **k** bring me rest,	4889
14:17	for my lord the **k** is like an angel of God	4889
14:18	Then the **k** said to the woman,	4889
14:18	"Let my lord the **k** speak," the woman said.	4889
14:19	The **k** asked, "Isn't the hand of Joab	4889
14:19	"As surely as you live, my lord the **k**,	4889
14:19	to the left from anything my lord the **k** says.	4889
14:21	The **k** said to Joab, "Very well, I will do it.	4889
14:22	to pay him honor, and he blessed the **k**.	4889
14:22	favor in your eyes, my lord the **k**,	4889
14:22	the **k** has granted his servant's request."	4889
14:24	the **k** said, "He must go to his own house;	4889
14:24	and did not see the face of the **k**.	4889
14:29	for Joab in order to send him to the **k**,	4889
14:32	'Come here so I can send you to the **k**	4889
14:33	So Joab went to the **k** and told him this.	4889
14:33	Then the **k** summoned Absalom,	4889
14:33	with his face to the ground before the **k**.	4889
14:33	And the **k** kissed Absalom.	4889
15: 2	with a complaint to be placed before the **k**	4889
15: 3	but there is no representative of the **k**	4889
15: 6	the Israelites who came to the **k** asking	4889
15: 7	Absalom said to the **k**,	4889
15: 9	The **k** said to him, "Go in peace."	4889

Ref	Text	Num
2Sa 15:10	then say, 'Absalom *is* **k** in Hebron.' "	4887
15:15	to do whatever our lord the **k** chooses."	4889
15:16	The **k** set out, with his entire household	4889
15:17	So the **k** set out, with all the people	4889
15:18	from Gath marched before the **k**.	4889
15:19	The **k** said to Ittai the Gittite,	4889
15:19	Go back and stay with **K** Absalom.	4889
15:21	But Ittai replied to the **k**,	4889
15:21	and as my lord the **k** lives,	4889
15:21	wherever my lord the **k** may be,	4889
15:23	The **k** also crossed the Kidron Valley,	4889
15:25	Then the **k** said to Zadok,	4889
15:27	The **k** also said to Zadok the priest,	4889
15:34	'I will be your servant, O **k**;	4889
16: 2	The **k** asked Ziba,	4889
16: 3	The **k** then asked,	4889
16: 4	Then the **k** said to Ziba,	4889
16: 4	find favor in your eyes, my lord the **k**."	4889
16: 5	As **K** David approached Bahurim,	4889
16: 9	Then Abishai son of Zeruiah said to the **k**,	4889
16: 9	"Why should this dead dog curse my lord the **k**?	4889
16:10	But the **k** said,	4889
16:14	The **k** and all the people with him arrived	4889
16:16	"Long live the **k**!	4889
16:16	Long live the **k**!"	4889
17: 2	I would strike down only the **k**	4889
17:16	over without fail, or the **k** and all the people	4889
17:17	and they were to go and tell **K** David,	4889
17:21	of the well and went to inform **K** David.	4889
18: 2	The **k** told the troops,	4889
18: 4	**k** answered, "I will do whatever seems best	4889
18: 4	So the **k** stood beside the gate while all	4889
18: 5	The **k** commanded Joab, Abishai and Ittai,	4889
18: 5	And all the troops heard the **k** giving orders	4889
18:12	the **k** commanded you and Abishai and Ittai,	4889
18:13	and nothing is hidden from the **k**—	4889
18:19	"Let me run and take the news to the **k** that	4889
18:21	"Go, tell the **k** what you have seen."	4889
18:25	The watchman called out to the **k**.	4889
18:25	The **k** said, "If he is alone,	4889
18:26	The **k** said, "He must be bringing good	4889
18:27	"He's a good man," the **k** said.	4889
18:28	Ahimaaz called out to the **k**, "All is well!"	4889
18:28	He bowed down before the **k** with his face	4889
18:28	lifted their hands against my lord the **k**."	4889
18:29	The **k** asked, "Is the young man Absalom safe?"	4889
18:30	The **k** said, "Stand aside and wait here."	4889
18:31	"My lord the **k**, hear the good news!	4889
18:32	The **k** asked the Cushite,	4889
18:32	the **k** and all who rise up to harm you be	4889
18:33	The **k** was shaken.	4889
19: 1	"The **k** is weeping and mourning	4889
19: 2	"The **k** is grieving for his son."	4889
19: 4	The **k** covered his face and cried aloud,	4889
19: 5	Joab went into the house to the **k** and said,	4889
19: 8	**k** got up and took his seat in the gateway.	4889
19: 8	"The **k** is sitting in the gateway,"	4889
19: 9	"The **k** delivered us from the hand	4889
19:10	about bringing the **k** back?"	4889
19:11	**K** David sent this message to Zadok	4889
19:11	be the last to bring the **k** back to his palace,	4889
19:11	throughout Israel has reached the **k**	4889
19:12	be the last to bring back the **k**?'	4889
19:14	They sent word to the **k**, "Return,	4889
19:15	the **k** returned and went as far as the Jordan.	4889
19:15	to go out and meet the **k** and bring him	4889
19:16	with the men of Judah to meet **K** David.	4889
19:17	They rushed to the Jordan, where the **k** was.	4889
19:18	he fell prostrate before the **k**	4889
19:19	on the day my lord the **k** left Jerusalem.	4889
19:19	May the **k** put it out of his mind.	4889
19:20	to come down and meet my lord the **k**."	4889
19:22	not know that today I am **k** over Israel?"	4889
19:23	So the **k** said to Shimei, "You shall not die."	4889
19:23	And the **k** promised him on oath.	4889
19:24	also went down to meet the **k**.	4889
19:24	or washed his clothes from the day the **k** left	4889
19:25	from Jerusalem to meet the **k**,	4889
19:25	the **k** asked him, "Why didn't you go with	4889
19:26	He said, "My lord the **k**,	4889
19:26	ride on it, so I can go with the **k**.'	4889
19:27	slandered your servant to my lord the **k**.	4889
19:27	My lord the **k** is like an angel of God;	4889
19:28	but death from my lord the **k**,	4889
19:28	to make any more appeals to the **k**?"	4889
19:29	The **k** said to him, "Why say more?	4889
19:30	Mephibosheth said to the **k**,	4889
19:30	that my lord the **k** has arrived home safely."	4889
19:31	from Rogelim to cross the Jordan with the **k**	4889
19:32	He had provided for the **k** during his stay	4889
19:33	The **k** said to Barzillai,	4889
19:34	But Barzillai answered the **k**,	4889
19:34	I should go up to Jerusalem with the **k**?	4889
19:35	be an added burden to my lord the **k**?	4889
19:36	the Jordan with the **k** for a short distance.	4889
19:36	why should the **k** reward me in this way?	4889
19:37	Let him cross over with my lord the **k**.	4889
19:38	The **k** said, "Kimham shall cross over	4889
19:39	and then the **k** crossed over.	4889
19:39	The **k** kissed Barzillai and gave him	4889
19:40	When he crossed over to Gilgal,	4889
19:40	the troops of Israel had taken the **k** over.	4889
19:41	of Israel were coming to the **k** and said	4889
19:41	the **k** away and bring him and his household	4889
19:42	"We did this because the **k** is closely related	4889

Ref	Text	#
2Sa 19:43	"We have ten shares in the **k**;	4889
19:43	the first to speak of bringing back our **k**?"	4889
20: 2	of Judah stayed by their **k** all the way from	4889
20: 4	Then the **k** said to Amasa,	4889
20: 5	he took longer than the time the **k** had set	NIH
20:21	has lifted up his hand against the **k**,	4889
20:22	And Joab went back to the **k** in Jerusalem.	4889
21: 2	The **k** summoned the Gibeonites and spoke	4889
21: 5	They answered the **k**,	4889
21: 6	So the **k** said, "I will give them to you."	4889
21: 7	The **k** spared Mephibosheth son	4889
21: 8	But the **k** took Armoni and Mephibosheth,	4889
21:14	and did everything the **k** commanded.	4889
22:51	He gives his **k** great victories;	4889
24: 2	So the **k** said to Joab and	4889
24: 3	But Joab replied to the **k**,	4889
24: 3	and may the eyes of my lord the **k** see it.	4889
24: 3	But why does my lord the **k** want to do such	4889
24: 4	of the **k** to enroll the fighting men of Israel.	4889
24: 9	the number of the fighting men to the **k**:	4889
24:20	the **k** and his men coming toward him,	4889
24:20	and bowed down before the **k** with his face	4889
24:21	"Why has my lord the **k** come	4889
24:22	the **k** take whatever pleases him	4889
24:23	O **k**, Araunah gives all this to the king.	4889
24:23	O king, Araunah gives all this to the **k**."	4889
24:24	But the **k** replied to Araunah, "No,	4889
1Ki 1: 1	When **K** David was old and well advanced	4889
1: 2	a young virgin to attend the **k** and take care	4889
1: 2	so that our lord the **k** may keep warm."	4889
1: 3	a Shunammite, and brought her to the **k**.	4889
1: 4	she took care of the **k** and waited on him,	4889
1: 4	but the **k** had no intimate relations with her.	4889
1: 5	put himself forward and said, "I *will be* **k**."	4887
1:11	Adonijah, the son of Haggith, *has become* **k**	4887
1:13	Go in to **K** David and say to him,	4889
1:13	the **k**, did you not swear to me your servant	4889
1:13	"Surely Solomon your son *shall be* **k**	4887
1:13	Why then *has* Adonijah *become* **k**?'	4887
1:14	While you are still there talking to the **k**,	4889
1:15	So Bathsheba went to see the aged **k**	4889
1:16	and knelt before the **k**.	4889
1:16	"What is it your want?" the **k** asked.	4889
1:17	'Solomon your son *shall be* **k** after me,	4887
1:18	But now Adonijah *has become* **k**, and you,	4887
1:18	my lord the **k**, do not know about it.	4889
1:20	My lord the **k**, the eyes of all Israel are on	4889
1:20	on the throne of my lord the **k** after him.	4889
1:21	as soon as my lord the **k** is laid to rest	4889
1:22	While she was still speaking with the **k**,	4889
1:23	And they told the **k**,	4889
1:23	before the **k** and bowed with his face to	4889
1:24	Nathan said, "Have you, my lord the **k**,	4889
1:24	declared that Adonijah *shall be* **k** after you,	4887
1:25	'Long live **K** Adonijah!'	4889
1:27	Is this something my lord the **k** has done	4889
1:27	on the throne of my lord the **k** after him?"	4889
1:28	Then **K** David said, "Call in Bathsheba."	4889
1:29	The **k** then took an oath:	4889
1:30	Solomon your son *shall be* **k** after me,	4889
1:31	kneeling before the **k**, said,	4889
1:31	said, "May my lord **K** David live forever!"	4889
1:32	**K** David said, "Call in Zadok the priest,	4889
1:32	When they came before the **k**,	4889
1:34	and Nathan the prophet anoint him **k**	4889
1:34	'Long live **K** Solomon!'	4889
1:36	Benaiah son of Jehoiada answered the **k**,	4889
1:36	May the LORD, the God of my lord the **k**,	4889
1:37	As the LORD was with my lord the **k**,	4889
1:37	the throne of my lord **K** David!"	4889
1:38	down and put Solomon on **K** David's mule	4889
1:39	"Long live **K** Solomon!"	4889
1:43	"Our lord King David has **made** Solomon king.	4889
1:43	Our lord King David *has* **made** Solomon **k**.	4887
1:44	The **k** has sent with him Zadok the priest,	4889
1:45	and Nathan the prophet have anointed him **k**	4889
1:47	to congratulate our lord **K** David,	4889
1:47	And the **k** bowed in worship on his bed	4889
1:51	of **K** Solomon and is clinging to the horns	4889
1:51	'Let **K** Solomon swear to me today	4889
1:53	Then **K** Solomon sent men,	4889
1:53	and bowed down to **K** Solomon,	4889
2:15	All Israel looked to me as their **k**	4887
2:17	So he continued, "Please ask **K** Solomon—	4889
2:18	"I will speak to the **k** for you."	4889
2:19	to **K** Solomon to speak for him for Adonijah,	4889
2:19	the **k** stood up to meet her,	4889
2:20	The **k** replied, "Make it, my mother;	4889
2:22	**K** Solomon answered his mother,	4889
2:23	Then **K** Solomon swore by the LORD:	4889
2:25	So **K** Solomon gave orders to Benaiah son	4889
2:26	To Abiathar the priest the **k** said,	4889
2:29	**K** Solomon was told that Joab had fled to	4889
2:30	"The **k** says, 'Come out!' "	4889
2:30	Benaiah reported to the **k**,	4889
2:31	the **k** commanded Benaiah, "Do as he says.	4889
2:35	The **k** put Benaiah son of Jehoiada over	4889
2:36	Then the **k** sent for Shimei and said to him,	4889
2:38	Shimei answered the **k**,	4889
2:38	as my lord the **k** has said."	4889
2:39	**k** of Gath, and Shimei was told,	4889
2:42	the **k** summoned Shimei and said to him,	4889
2:44	The **k** also said to Shimei,	4889
2:45	But **K** Solomon will be blessed,	4889
2:46	**k** gave the order to Benaiah son of Jehoiada,	4889
3: 1	Solomon made an alliance with Pharaoh **k**	4889
3: 4	The **k** went to Gibeon to offer sacrifices,	4889

Ref	Text	#
1Ki 3: 7	you *have* **made** your servant **k** in place	4887
3:16	Now two prostitutes came to the **k**	4889
3:22	And so they argued before the **k**.	4889
3:23	The **k** said, "This one says,	4889
3:24	Then the **k** said, "Bring me a sword."	4889
3:24	So they brought a sword for the **k**.	4889
3:26	for her son and said to the **k**,	4889
3:27	Then the **k** gave his ruling:	4889
3:28	all Israel heard the verdict the **k** had given,	4889
3:28	they held the **k** in awe,	4889
4: 1	So **K** Solomon ruled over all Israel.	4889
4: 5	a priest and personal adviser to the **k**;	4889
4: 7	who supplied provisions for the **k** and	4889
4:19	(the country of Sihon **k** of the Amorites and	4889
4:19	of the Amorites, and the country of Og **k**	4889
4:27	for **K** Solomon and all who came to	4889
5: 1	When Hiram **k** of Tyre heard	4889
5: 1	that Solomon had been anointed **k**	4889
5:13	**K** Solomon conscripted laborers	4889
6: 2	The temple that **K** Solomon built for	4889
7:13	**K** Solomon sent to Tyre and brought Huram	4889
7:14	to **K** Solomon and did all the work assigned	4889
7:40	for **K** Solomon in the temple of the LORD:	4889
7:45	that Huram made for **K** Solomon for	4889
7:46	The **k** had them cast in clay molds in	4889
7:51	When all the work **K** Solomon had done for	4889
8: 1	Then **K** Solomon summoned into his	4889
8: 2	to **K** Solomon at the time of the festival in	4889
8: 5	and **K** Solomon and the entire assembly	4889
8:14	the **k** turned around and blessed them.	4889
8:62	Then the **k** and all Israel	4889
8:63	So the **k** and all the Israelites dedicated	4889
8:64	the **k** consecrated the middle part of	4889
8:66	They blessed the **k** and then went home,	4889
9:11	**K** Solomon gave twenty towns in Galilee	4889
9:11	in Galilee to Hiram **k** of Tyre,	4889
9:14	Hiram had sent to the **k** 120 talents of gold.	4889
9:15	of the forced labor **K** Solomon conscripted	4889
9:16	(Pharaoh **k** of Egypt had attacked	4889
9:26	**K** Solomon also built ships at Ezion Geber,	4889
9:28	which they delivered to **K** Solomon.	4889
10: 3	nothing was too hard for the **k** to explain	4889
10: 6	She said to the **k**, "The report I heard	4889
10: 9	eternal love for Israel, he has made you **k**,	4889
10:10	And she gave the **k** 120 talents of gold,	4889
10:10	the queen of Sheba gave to **K** Solomon.	4889
10:12	The **k** used the almugwood	4889
10:13	**K** Solomon gave the queen of Sheba	4889
10:16	**K** Solomon made two hundred large shields	4889
10:17	The **k** put them in the Palace of the Forest	4889
10:18	the **k** made a great throne inlaid with ivory	4889
10:21	All **K** Solomon's goblets were gold,	4889
10:22	The **k** had a fleet of trading ships at sea	4889
10:23	**K** Solomon was greater in riches	4889
10:27	The **k** made silver as common in Jerusalem	4889
11: 1	**K** Solomon, however, loved many foreign	
	women besides Pharaoh's daughter—	4889
11:18	they went to Egypt, to Pharaoh **k** of Egypt,	4889
11:23	Hadadezer **k** of Zobah.	4889
11:26	Jeroboam son of Nebat rebelled against	
	the **k**.	4889
11:27	of how he rebelled against the **k**:	4889
11:37	you will be **k** over Israel.	4889
11:40	to Shishak the **k**, and stayed there	4889
11:43	And Rehoboam his son succeeded him *as* **k**.	4887
12: 1	the Israelites had gone there to **make** him **k**.	4887
12: 2	where he had fled from **K** Solomon),	4889
12: 6	Then **K** Rehoboam consulted	4889
12:12	as the **k** had said,	4889
12:13	The **k** answered the people harshly,	4889
12:15	So the **k** did not listen to the people,	4889
12:16	When all Israel saw that the **k** refused	4889
12:16	they answered the **k**:	4889
12:18	**K** Rehoboam sent out Adoniram,	4889
12:18	Rehoboam, however, managed to get	4889
12:20	assembly and **made** him **k** over all Israel.	4889
12:23	to Rehoboam son of Solomon **k** of Judah,	4889
12:27	Rehoboam **k** of Judah.	4889
12:27	and return to **K** Rehoboam."	4889
12:28	the **k** made two golden calves,	4889
13: 4	When **K** Jeroboam heard what the man	4889
13: 6	Then the **k** said to the man of God,	4889
13: 7	The **k** said to the man of God,	4889
13: 8	But the man of God answered the **k**,	4889
13:11	told their father what he had said to the **k**.	4889
14: 2	the one who told me I would be **k**	4889
14:14	for himself a **k** over Israel who will cut off	4889
14:20	And Nadab his son succeeded him *as* **k**.	4887
14:21	Rehoboam son of Solomon *was* **k** in Judah.	4887
14:21	forty-one years old when he *became* **k**,	4887
14:25	In the fifth year of **K** Rehoboam,	4889
14:25	Shishak **k** of Egypt attacked Jerusalem.	4889
14:27	So **K** Rehoboam made bronze shields	4889
14:28	the **k** went to the LORD's temple,	4889
14:31	And Abijah his son succeeded him *as* **k**.	4887
15: 1	Abijah *became* **k** of Judah,	4887
15: 8	And Asa his son succeeded him *as* **k**.	4887
15: 9	the twentieth year of Jeroboam **k** of Israel,	4889
15: 9	Asa *became* **k** of Judah,	4887+4889
15:16	There was war between Asa and Baasha **k**	4889
15:17	Baasha **k** of Israel went up against Judah	4889
15:17	or entering the territory of Asa **k** of Judah.	4889
15:18	the son of Hezion, the **k** of Aram,	4889
15:19	with Baasha **k** of Israel so he will withdraw	4889
15:20	Ben-Hadad agreed with **K** Asa and sent	4889
15:22	Then **K** Asa issued an order to all Judah—	4889
15:22	With them **K** Asa built up Geba	4889

Ref	Text	#
1Ki 15:24	Jehoshaphat his son succeeded him *as* **k**.	4887
15:25	Nadab son of Jeroboam *became* **k** of Israel	4887
15:25	in the second year of Asa **k** of Judah,	4889
15:28	of Asa **k** of Judah and succeeded him	4889
15:28	of Judah and succeeded him *as* **k**.	4887
15:32	There was war between Asa and Baasha **k**	4889
15:33	In the third year of Asa **k** of Judah,	4889
15:33	Baasha son of Ahijah *became* **k** of all Israel	4887
16: 6	And Elah his son succeeded him *as* **k**.	4887
16: 8	In the twenty-sixth year of Asa **k** of Judah,	4889
16: 8	Elah son of Baasha *became* **k** of Israel,	4887
16:10	the twenty-seventh year of Asa **k** of Judah.	4889
16:10	Then *he* succeeded him *as* **k**.	4887
16:15	the twenty-seventh year of Asa **k** of Judah,	4889
16:16	that Zimri had plotted against the **k**	4889
16:16	**proclaimed** Omri, the commander of the	
	army, **k** over Israel	4887
16:21	half supported Tibni son of Ginath for **k**,	4887
16:22	So Tibni died and Omri *became* **k**.	4887
16:23	In the thirty-first year of Asa **k** of Judah,	4889
16:23	Omri *became* **k** of Israel,	4887
16:28	And Ahab his son succeeded him *as* **k**.	4887
16:29	In the thirty-eighth year of Asa **k** of Judah,	4889
16:29	Ahab son of Omri *became* **k** of Israel,	4887
16:31	also married Jezebel daughter of Ethbaal **k**	4889
19:15	you get there, anoint Hazael **k** over Aram.	4889
19:16	anoint Jehu son of Nimshi **k** over Israel,	4889
20: 1	Now Ben-Hadad **k** of Aram	4889
20: 2	He sent messengers into the city to Ahab **k**	4889
20: 4	The **k** of Israel answered, "Just as you say,	4889
20: 4	"Just as you say, my lord the **k**,	4889
20: 7	The **k** of Israel summoned all the elders of	4889
20: 9	"Tell my lord the **k**,	4889
20:11	The **k** of Israel answered, "Tell him:	4889
20:13	Meanwhile a prophet came to Ahab **k**	4889
20:20	But Ben-Hadad **k** of Aram escaped	4889
20:21	The **k** of Israel advanced and overpowered	4889
20:22	the prophet came to the **k** of Israel and said,	4889
20:22	the **k** of Aram will attack you again."	4889
20:23	the officials of the **k** of Aram advised him,	4889
20:28	up and told the **k** of Israel, "This is what	4889
20:31	Let us go to the **k** of Israel with sackcloth	4889
20:32	they went to the **k** of Israel and said,	4889
20:32	The **k** answered, "Is he still alive?	NIH
20:33	"Go and get him," the **k** said.	NIH
20:38	and stood by the road waiting for the **k**.	4889
20:39	As the **k** passed by,	4889
20:40	"That is your sentence," the **k** of Israel said.	4889
20:41	and the **k** of Israel recognized him as one of	4889
20:42	He said to the **k**,	2257
20:43	**k** of Israel went to his palace in Samaria.	4889
21: 1	close to the palace of Ahab **k** of Samaria.	4889
21: 7	"Is this how you act as **k** over Israel?	4867
21:10	that he has cursed both God and the **k**.	4889
21:13	"Naboth has cursed both God and the **k**."	4889
21:18	"Go down to meet Ahab **k** of Israel,	4889
22: 2	the third year Jehoshaphat **k** of Judah went	4889
22: 2	of Judah went down to see the **k** of Israel.	4889
22: 3	The **k** of Israel had said to his officials,	4889
22: 3	to retake it from the **k** of Aram?"	4889
22: 4	Jehoshaphat replied to the **k** of Israel,	4889
22: 5	But Jehoshaphat also said to the **k** of Israel,	4889
22: 6	**k** of Israel brought together the prophets—	4889
22: 8	The **k** of Israel answered Jehoshaphat,	4889
22: 8	"The **k** should not say that,"	4889
22: 9	So the **k** of Israel called one of his officials	4889
22:10	the **k** of Israel and Jehoshaphat king	4889
22:10	and Jehoshaphat **k** of Judah were sitting	4889
22:13	prophets are predicting success for the **k**.	4889
22:15	When he arrived, the **k** asked him,	4889
22:16	The **k** said to him,	4889
22:18	The **k** of Israel said to Jehoshaphat,	4889
22:26	The **k** of Israel then ordered,	4889
22:27	'This is what the **k** says:	4889
22:29	So the **k** of Israel and Jehoshaphat king	4889
22:29	of Israel and Jehoshaphat **k** of Judah went	4889
22:30	The **k** of Israel said to Jehoshaphat,	4889
22:30	the **k** of Israel disguised himself and went	4889
22:31	Now the **k** of Aram had ordered his	4889
22:31	small or great, except the **k** of Israel."	4889
22:32	"Surely this is the **k** of Israel."	4889
22:33	the **k** of Israel and stopped pursuing him.	4889
22:34	and hit the **k** of Israel between the sections	4889
22:34	The **k** told his chariot driver,	NIH
22:35	the **k** was propped up in his chariot facing	4889
22:37	So the **k** died and was brought to Samaria,	4889
22:40	And Ahaziah his son succeeded him *as* **k**.	4887
22:41	of Asa *became* **k** of Judah in the fourth year	4887
22:41	in the fourth year of Ahab **k** of Israel.	4889
22:42	thirty-five years old when he *became* **k**,	4887
22:44	Jehoshaphat was also at peace with the **k**	4889
22:47	There was then no **k** in Edom;	4889
22:51	of Ahab *became* **k** of Israel in Samaria in	4887
22:51	in the seventeenth year of Jehoshaphat **k**	4889
2Ki 1: 3	"Go up and meet the messengers of the **k**	4889
1: 5	When the messengers returned to the **k**,	2257S
1: 6	to the **k** who sent you and tell him,	4889
1: 7	The **k** asked them, "What kind of man	NIH
1: 8	The **k** said, "That was Elijah the Tishbite.	NIH
1: 9	"Man of God, the **k** says, 'Come down!' "	4889
1:11	At this the **k** sent to Elijah another captain	NIH
1:11	"Man of God, this is what the **k** says,	4889
1:13	the **k** sent a third captain with his fifty men.	NIH
1:15	up and went down with him to the **k**.	4889
1:16	He told the **k**, "This is what	2257S
1:17	*as* **k** in the second year of Jehoram son	4887
1:17	of Jehoram son of Jehoshaphat **k** of Judah.	4889

2Ki		
3: 1	of Ahab *became* **k** of Israel in Samaria in	4887
3: 1	in the eighteenth year of Jehoshaphat **k**	4889
3: 4	Now Mesha **k** *of* Moab raised sheep,	4889
3: 4	and he had to supply the **k** of Israel with	4889
3: 5	the **k** *of* Moab rebelled against the king	4889
3: 5	of Moab rebelled against the **k** *of* Israel.	4889
3: 6	at that time **K** Joram set out from Samaria	4889
3: 7	He also sent this message to Jehoshaphat **k**	4889
3: 7	"The **k** of Moab has rebelled against me.	4889
3: 9	So the **k** of Israel set out with the king	4889
3: 9	with the **k** of Judah and the king of Edom.	4889
3: 9	with the king of Judah and the **k** of Edom.	4889
3:10	exclaimed the **k** of Israel.	4889
3:11	An officer of the **k** of Israel answered,	4889
3:12	the **k** of Israel and Jehoshaphat and the king	4889
3:12	the king of Israel and Jehoshaphat and the **k**	4889
3:13	Elisha said to the **k** of Israel,	4889
3:13	"No," the **k** of Israel answered,	4889
3:14	for the presence of Jehoshaphat **k** of Judah,	4889
3:26	the **k** of Moab saw that the battle had gone	4889
3:26	to break through to the **k** of Edom,	4889
3:27	who *was* to succeed him *as* **k,**	4887
4:13	on your behalf to the **k** or the commander of	4889
5: 1	of the army of the **k** of Aram.	4889
5: 5	"By all means, go," the **k** of Aram replied.	4889
5: 5	"I will send a letter to the **k** of Israel."	4889
5: 6	that he took to the **k** of Israel read:	4889
5: 7	As soon as the **k** of Israel read the letter,	4889
5: 8	that the **k** of Israel had torn his robes,	4889
6: 8	Now the **k** of Aram was at war with Israel.	4889
6: 9	of God sent word to the **k** of Israel:	4889
6:10	So the **k** of Israel checked on	4889
6:10	Time and again Elisha warned **the k,**	2257S
6:11	This enraged the **k** of Aram.	4889
6:11	of us is on the side of the **k** of Israel?"	4889
6:12	"None of us, my lord the **k,**"	4889
6:12	the **k** of Israel the very words you speak	4889
6:13	"Go, find out where he is," the **k** ordered,	NIH
6:21	When the **k** of Israel saw them,	4889
6:24	Some time later, Ben-Hadad **k**	4889
6:26	the **k** of Israel was passing by on the wall,	4889
6:26	"Help me, my lord the **k!**"	4889
6:27	The **k** replied, "If the LORD does	NIH
6:30	When the **k** heard the woman's words,	4889
6:32	**The k** sent a messenger ahead,	2257S
6:33	**k]** said, "This disaster is from the LORD.	NIH
7: 2	the **k** was leaning said to the man of God,	4889
7: 6	the **k** of Israel has hired the Hittite	4889
7:12	The **k** got up in the night and said	4889
7:14	the **k** sent them after the Aramean army.	4889
7:15	messengers returned and reported to the **k.**	4889
7:17	Now the **k** had put the officer	4889
7:17	of God had foretold when the **k** came down	4889
7:18	as the man of God had said to the **k:**	4889
8: 3	the land of the Philistines and went to the **k**	4889
8: 4	The **k** was talking to Gehazi,	4889
8: 5	the **k** how Elisha had restored the dead	4889
8: 5	to life came to beg the **k** for her house	4889
8: 5	"This is the woman, my lord the **k,**	4889
8: 6	The **k** asked the woman about it,	4889
8: 7	and Ben-Hadad **k** of Aram was ill.	4889
8: 7	When the **k** was told,	2257S
8: 9	"Your son Ben-Hadad **k** of Aram	4889
8:13	that you will become **k** of Aram,"	4889
8:15	Then Hazael succeeded him *as* **k.**	4887
8:16	In the fifth year of Joram son of Ahab **k**	4889
8:16	when Jehoshaphat was **k** of Judah,	4889
8:16	of Jehoshaphat began his reign as **k**	4889
8:17	thirty-two years old when he *became* **k,**	4887
8:20	and **set up** its own **k.**	4887+4889
8:24	And Ahaziah his son succeeded him *as* **k.**	4887
8:25	In the twelfth year of Joram son of Ahab **k**	4889
8:25	Ahaziah son of Jehoram **k** of Judah began	4889
8:26	twenty-two years old when he *became* **k,**	4887
8:26	a granddaughter of Omri **k** of Israel.	4889
8:28	of Ahab to war against Hazael **k** of Aram	4889
8:29	so **K** Joram returned to Jezreel to recover	4889
8:29	at Ramoth in his battle with Hazael **k**	4889
8:29	of Jehoram **k** of Judah went down	4889
9: 3	I anoint you **k** over Israel.'	4889
9: 6	'I anoint you **k** over the LORD's people	4889
9:12	I anoint you **k** over Israel.' "	4889
9:13	the trumpet and shouted, "Jehu *is* **k!**"	4887
9:14	against Hazael **k** of Aram,	4889
9:15	but **K** Joram had returned to Jezreel	4889
9:15	in the battle with Hazael **k** of Aram.)	4889
9:16	and Ahaziah **k** of Judah had gone down	4889
9:18	"This is what the **k** says:	4889
9:19	So the **k** sent out a second horseman.	NIH
9:19	"This is what the **k** says:	4889
9:21	Joram **k** of Israel and Ahaziah king	4889
9:21	of Israel and Ahaziah **k** of Judah rode out,	4889
9:27	When Ahaziah **k** of Judah	4889
9:27	Ahaziah *had become* **k** of Judah.)	4887
10: 5	*We will* not **appoint** anyone **as k;**	4887
10:13	he met some relatives of Ahaziah **k**	4889
10:13	down to greet the families of the **k** and of	4889
10:35	And Jehoash his son succeeded him *as* **k.**	4887
11: 2	the daughter of **K** Jehoram and sister	4889
11: 7	to guard the temple for the **k.**	4889
11: 8	Station yourselves around the **k,**	4889
11: 8	Stay close to the **k** wherever he goes."	4889
11:10	that had belonged to **K** David and that were	4889
11:11	stationed themselves around the **k—**	4889
11:12	of the covenant and **proclaimed** him **k.**	4887
11:12	"Long live the **k!**"	4889
11:14	She looked and there was the **k,**	4889

2Ki		
11:14	and the trumpeters were beside the **k,**	4889
11:17	between the LORD and the **k** and people	4889
11:17	He also made a covenant between the **k** and	4889
11:19	and together they brought the **k** down from	4889
11:19	**k** then took his place on the royal throne,	NIH
12: 1	In the seventh year of Jehu, Joash *became* **k,**	NIH
12: 6	of **K** Joash the priests still had not repaired	4889
12: 7	Therefore **K** Joash summoned Jehoiada	4889
12:17	About this time Hazael **k** of Aram went up	4889
12:18	But Joash **k** of Judah took all	4889
12:18	and he sent them to Hazael **k** of Aram,	4889
12:21	And Amaziah his son succeeded him *as* **k.**	4887
13: 1	of Joash son of Ahaziah **k** of Judah,	4889
13: 1	Jehoahaz son of Jehu *became* **k** of Israel	4887
13: 3	under the power of Hazael **k** of Aram	4889
13: 4	the **k** of Aram was oppressing Israel.	4889
13: 7	for the **k** of Aram had destroyed the rest	4889
13: 9	And Jehoash his son succeeded him *as* **k.**	4887
13:10	the thirty-seventh year of Joash **k** of Judah,	4889
13:10	Jehoash son of Jehoahaz *became* **k** of Israel	4887
13:12	including his war against Amaziah **k**	4889
13:14	Jehoash **k** of Israel went down to see him	4889
13:16	he said to the **k** of Israel.	4889
13:18	"Take the arrows," and the **k** took them.	4889
13:22	Hazael **k** of Aram oppressed Israel	4889
13:24	Hazael **k** of Aram died,	4889
13:24	and Ben-Hadad his son succeeded him *as* **k.**	4887
14: 1	of Jehoash son of Jehoahaz **k** of Israel,	4889
14: 1	Amaziah son of Joash **k** of Judah began	4889
14: 2	twenty-five years old when he *became* **k,**	4887
14: 5	he executed the officials who had murdered	
	his father the **k.**	4889
14: 8	**k** of Israel, with the challenge:	4889
14: 9	But Jehoash **k** of Israel replied	4889
14: 9	of Israel replied to Amaziah **k** of Judah:	4889
14:11	so Jehoash **k** of Israel attacked.	4889
14:11	and Amaziah **k** of Judah faced each other	4889
14:13	Jehoash **k** of Israel captured Amaziah king	4889
14:13	Jehoash king of Israel captured Amaziah **k**	4889
14:15	including his war against Amaziah **k**	4889
14:16	And Jeroboam his son succeeded him *as* **k.**	4887
14:17	of Joash **k** of Judah lived for fifteen years	4889
14:17	after the death of Jehoash son of Jehoahaz **k**	4889
14:21	and **made** him **k** in place of his father	4887
14:23	the fifteenth year of Amaziah son of Joash **k**	4889
14:23	of Jehoash **k** of Israel became king	4889
14:23	of Jehoash king of Israel *became* **k**	4887
14:29	And Zechariah his son succeeded him *as* **k.**	4887
15: 1	In the twenty-seventh year of Jeroboam **k**	4889
15: 1	Azariah son of Amaziah **k** of Judah began	4889
15: 2	was sixteen years old when he *became* **k,**	4887
15: 5	The LORD afflicted the **k** with leprosy	4889
15: 7	And Jotham his son succeeded him *as* **k.**	4887
15: 8	the thirty-eighth year of Azariah **k** of Judah,	4889
15: 8	of Jeroboam *became* **k** of Israel in Samaria.	4887
15:10	assassinated him and succeeded him *as* **k.**	4887
15:13	of Jabesh *became* **k** in the thirty-ninth year	4887
15:13	the thirty-ninth year of Uzziah **k** of Judah,	4889
15:14	assassinated him and succeeded him *as* **k.**	4887
15:17	the thirty-ninth year of Azariah **k** of Judah,	4889
15:17	Menahem son of Gadi *became* **k** of Israel,	4887
15:19	Then Pul **k** of Assyria invaded the land,	4889
15:20	of silver to be given to the **k** of Assyria.	4889
15:20	So the **k** of Assyria withdrew and stayed in	4889
15:22	And Pekahiah his son succeeded him *as* **k.**	4887
15:23	In the fiftieth year of Azariah **k** of Judah,	4889
15:23	of Menahem *became* **k** of Israel in Samaria,	4887
15:25	killed Pekahiah and succeeded him *as* **k.**	4887
15:27	the fifty-second year of Azariah **k** of Judah,	4889
15:27	of Remaliah *became* **k** of Israel in Samaria,	4887
15:29	In the time of Pekah **k** of Israel,	4889
15:29	Tiglath-Pileser **k** of Assyria came	4889
15:30	*as* **k** in the twentieth year of Jotham son	4889
15:32	the second year of Pekah son of Remaliah **k**	4889
15:32	Jotham son of Uzziah **k** of Judah began	4889
15:33	twenty-five years old when he *became* **k,**	4887
15:37	the LORD began to send Rezin **k** of Aram	4889
15:38	And Ahaz his son succeeded him *as* **k.**	4887
16: 1	Ahaz son of Jotham **k** of Judah began	4889
16: 2	twenty years old when he *became* **k,**	4887
16: 5	Then Rezin **k** of Aram and Pekah son	4889
16: 5	of Remaliah **k** of Israel marched up to fight	4889
16: 6	Rezin **k** of Aram recovered Elath for Aram	4889
16: 7	to say to Tiglath-Pileser **k** of Assyria,	4889
16: 7	of the **k** of Aram and of the king of Israel,	4889
16: 7	of the hand of the king of Aram and of the **k**	4889
16: 8	the royal palace and sent it as a gift to the **k**	4889
16: 9	The **k** of Assyria complied by attacking	4889
16:10	Then **K** Ahaz went to Damascus	4889
16:10	to Damascus to meet Tiglath-Pileser **k**	4889
16:11	with all the plans that **K** Ahaz had sent	4889
16:11	and finished it before **K** Ahaz returned.	4889
16:12	the **k** came back from Damascus and saw	4889
16:15	**K** Ahaz then gave these orders to Uriah	4889
16:16	the priest did just as **K** Ahaz had ordered.	4889
16:17	**K** Ahaz took away the side panels	4889
16:18	in deference to the **k** of Assyria.	4889
16:20	And Hezekiah his son succeeded him *as* **k.**	4887
17: 1	In the twelfth year of Ahaz **k** of Judah,	4889
17: 1	Hoshea son of Elah *became* **k** of Israel	4887
17: 3	Shalmaneser **k** of Assyria came up	4889
17: 4	But the **k** of Assyria discovered	4889
17: 4	for he had sent envoys to So **k** of Egypt,	4889
17: 4	and he no longer paid tribute to the **k**	4889
17: 5	The **k** of Assyria invaded the entire land,	4889
17: 6	the **k** of Assyria captured Samaria	4889
17: 7	of Egypt from under the power of Pharaoh **k**	4889

2Ki		
17:21	**made** Jeroboam son of Nebat *their* **k.**	4887
17:24	The **k** of Assyria brought people	4889
17:26	It was reported to the **k** of Assyria:	4889
17:27	Then the **k** of Assyria gave this order:	4889
18: 1	In the third year of Hoshea son of Elah **k**	4889
18: 1	Hezekiah son of Ahaz **k** of Judah began	4889
18: 2	twenty-five years old when he *became* **k,**	4887
18: 7	He rebelled against the **k** of Assyria and did	4889
18: 9	In **K** Hezekiah's fourth year,	4889
18: 9	the seventh year of Hoshea son of Elah **k**	4889
18: 9	Shalmaneser **k** of Assyria marched	4889
18:10	which was the ninth year of Hoshea **k**	4889
18:11	The **k** of Assyria deported Israel to Assyria	4889
18:13	the fourteenth year of **K** Hezekiah's reign,	4889
18:13	Sennacherib **k** of Assyria attacked all	4889
18:14	So Hezekiah **k** of Judah sent this message	4889
18:14	of Judah sent this message to the **k**	4889
18:14	The **k** of Assyria exacted from Hezekiah	4889
18:14	exacted from Hezekiah **k** of Judah	4889
18:16	At this time Hezekiah **k** of Judah	4889
18:16	and gave it to the **k** of Assyria.	4889
18:17	**k** of Assyria sent his supreme commander,	4889
18:17	from Lachish to **K** Hezekiah at Jerusalem.	4889
18:18	They called for the **k;**	4889
18:19	" 'This is what the great **k,**	4889
18:19	the **k** of Assyria, says:	4889
18:21	Such is Pharaoh **k** of Egypt	4889
18:23	bargain with my master, the **k** of Assyria:	4889
18:28	"Hear the word of the great **k,**	4889
18:28	the word of the great king, the **k** of Assyria!	4889
18:29	This is what the **k** says:	4889
18:30	be given into the hand of the **k** of Assyria.'	4889
18:31	This is what the **k** of Assyria says:	4889
18:33	from the hand of the **k** of Assyria?	4889
18:36	because the **k** had commanded,	4889
19: 1	When **K** Hezekiah heard this,	4889
19: 4	whom his master, the **k** of Assyria,	4889
19: 5	**K** Hezekiah's officials came to Isaiah	4889
19: 6	of the **k** of Assyria have blasphemed me.	4889
19: 8	When the field commander heard that the **k**	4889
19: 8	and found the **k** fighting against Libnah.	NIH
19: 9	Tirhakah, the Cushite **k** [of Egypt],	4889
19:10	"Say to Hezekiah **k** of Judah:	4889
19:10	'Jerusalem will not be handed over to the **k**	4889
19:13	Where is the **k** of Hamath,	4889
19:13	is the king of Hamath, the **k** of Arpad,	4889
19:13	the **k** of the city of Sepharvaim,	4889
19:20	concerning Sennacherib **k** of Assyria.	4889
19:32	the LORD says concerning the **k**	4889
19:36	So Sennacherib **k** of Assyria broke camp	4889
19:37	Esarhaddon his son succeeded him *as* **k.**	4887
20: 6	and this city from the hand of the **k**	4889
20:12	Merodach-Baladan son of Baladan **k** of	4889
20:14	the prophet went to **K** Hezekiah and asked,	4889
20:18	in the palace of the **k** of Babylon."	4889
20:21	And Manasseh his son succeeded him *as* **k.**	4887
21: 1	twelve years old when he *became* **k,**	4887
21: 3	as Ahab **k** of Israel had done.	4889
21:11	"Manasseh **k** of Judah has committed	4889
21:18	And Amon his son succeeded him *as* **k.**	4887
21:19	twenty-two years old when he *became* **k,**	4887
21:23	and assassinated the **k** in his palace.	4889
21:24	killed all who had plotted against **K** Amon,	4889
21:24	**made** Josiah his son **k** in his place.	4887
21:26	And Josiah his son succeeded him *as* **k.**	4887
22: 1	eight years old when he *became* **k,**	4887
22: 3	**K** Josiah sent the secretary,	4889
22: 9	Then Shaphan the secretary went to the **k**	4889
22:10	Then Shaphan the secretary informed the **k,**	4889
22:10	from it in the presence of the **k.**	4889
22:11	**k** heard the words of the Book of the Law,	4889
22:16	to everything written in the book the **k**	4889
22:18	Tell the **k** of Judah,	4889
22:20	So they took her answer back to the **k.**	4889
23: 1	the **k** called together all the elders of Judah	4889
23: 3	The **k** stood by the pillar and renewed	4889
23: 4	The **k** ordered Hilkiah the high priest,	4889
23:13	The **k** also desecrated the high places	4889
23:13	the ones Solomon **k** of Israel had built	4889
23:17	The **k** asked, "What is that tombstone	NIH
23:21	The **k** gave this order to all the people:	4889
23:23	But in the eighteenth year of **K** Josiah,	4889
23:25	Neither before nor after Josiah was there a **k**	4889
23:29	While Josiah was **k,** Pharaoh Neco	NIH
23:29	Pharaoh Neco **k** of Egypt went up to	4889
23:29	up to the Euphrates River to help the **k**	4889
23:29	**K** Josiah marched out to meet him in battle,	4889
23:30	of Josiah and anointed him and **made** him **k**	4887
23:31	twenty-three years when he *became* **k,**	4887
23:34	**made** Eliakim son of Josiah **k** in place of	4887
23:36	twenty-five years old when he *became* **k,**	4887
24: 1	Nebuchadnezzar **k** of Babylon invaded	4889
24: 6	And Jehoiachin his son succeeded him *as* **k.**	4887
24: 7	The **k** of Egypt did not march out	4889
24: 7	the **k** of Babylon had taken all his territory,	4889
24: 8	eighteen years old when he *became* **k,**	4887
24:10	of Nebuchadnezzar **k** of Babylon advanced	4889
24:12	Jehoiachin **k** of Judah, his mother,	4889
24:12	In the eighth year of the reign of the **k**	4889
24:13	that Solomon **k** of Israel had made for the	4889
24:16	The **k** of Babylon also deported to Babylon	4889
24:17	**made** Mattaniah, Jehoiachin's uncle, **k**	4887
24:18	twenty-one years old when he *became* **k,**	4887
24:20	Zedekiah rebelled against the **k** of Babylon.	4889
25: 1	Nebuchadnezzar **k** of Babylon marched	4889
25: 2	until the eleventh year of **K** Zedekiah.	4889
25: 5	but the Babylonian army pursued the **k**	4889

2Ki 25: 6 He was taken to the **k** of Babylon at Riblah, 4889
25: 8 in the nineteenth year of Nebuchadnezzar **k** 4889
25: 8 an official of the **k** of Babylon, 4889
25:11 and those who had gone over to the **k** 4889
25:20 and brought them to the **k** of Babylon 4889
25:21 the **k** had them executed. 4889
25:22 Nebuchadnezzar **k** of Babylon 4889
25:23 the **k** of Babylon had appointed Gedaliah 4889
25:24 "Settle down in the land and serve the **k** 4889
25:27 of the exile of Jehoiachin **k** of Judah, 4889
25:27 in the year Evil-Merodach *became* **k** 4887
25:30 the **k** gave Jehoiachin a regular allowance 4889
1Ch 1:43 in Edom before any Israelite **k** reigned: 4889
1:44 of Zerah from Bozrah succeeded him *as* **k.** 4887
1:45 of the Temanites succeeded him *as* **k.** 4887
1:46 succeeded him *as* **k.** 4887
1:47 Samlah from Masrekah succeeded him *as* **k.** 4887
1:48 on the river succeeded him *as* **k.** 4887
1:49 son of Acbor succeeded him *as* **k.** 4887
1:50 Hadad succeeded him *as* **k.** 4887
3: 2 of Maacah daughter of Talmai **k** of Geshur; 4889
4:23 they stayed there and worked for the **k.** 4889
4:41 in the days of Hezekiah **k** of Judah. 4889
5: 6 whom Tiglath-Pileser **k** of Assyria took 4889
5:17 of Jotham **k** of Judah and Jeroboam king 4889
5:17 of Jotham king of Judah and Jeroboam **k** 4889
5:26 stirred up the spirit of Pul **k** of Assyria 4889
5:26 Tiglath-Pileser **k** *of* Assyria), 4889
11: 2 In the past, even while Saul was **k,** 4889
11: 3 of Israel had come to **K** David at Hebron, 4889
11: 3 and they anointed David **k** over Israel, 4889
12:31 by name to come and **make** David **k**— 4887
12:38 Hebron fully determined to **make** David **k** 4887
12:38 also of one mind to **make** David **k.** 4887
14: 1 Hiram **k** of Tyre sent messengers to David, 4889
14: 2 that the LORD had established him as **k** 4889
14: 8 that David had been anointed **k** 4889
15:29 she saw **K** David dancing and celebrating, 4889
17:16 David went in and sat before the LORD, 4889
18: 3 David fought Hadadezer **k** of Zobah, 4889
18: 5 of Damascus came to help Hadadezer **k** 4889
18: 9 When Tou **k** of Hamath heard 4889
18: 9 the entire army of Hadadezer **k** of Zobah, 4889
18:10 he sent his son Hadoram to **K** David 4889
18:11 **K** David dedicated these articles to 4889
19: 1 Nahash **k** of the Ammonites died, 4889
19: 1 and his son succeeded him *as* **k.** 4887
19: 5 The **k** said, "Stay at Jericho 4889
19: 7 as well as the **k** of Maacah with his troops, 4889
20: 2 the crown from the head of their **k**— 4889
21: 3 My lord the **k,** are they not all my lord's 4889
21:23 Let my lord the **k** do whatever pleases him. 4889
21:24 But **K** David replied to Araunah, "No, 4889
23: 1 *he* **made** his son Solomon **k** over 4887
24: 6 in the presence of the **k** and of the officials: 4889
24:31 in the presence of **K** David and of Zadok, 4889
25: 6 under the supervision of the **k.** 4889
26:26 for the things dedicated by **K** David, 4889
26:32 and **K** David put them in charge of 4889
26:32 to God and for the affairs of the **k.** 4889
27: 1 and their officers, who served the **k** in all 4889
27:24 in the book of the annals of **K** David. 4889
27:31 in charge of **K** David's property. 4889
28: 1 of the divisions in the service of the **k,** 4889
28: 1 and livestock belonging to the **k** 4889
28: 2 **K** David rose to his feet and said: 4889
28: 4 chose me from my whole family to be **k** 4889
28: 4 to **make** me **k** over all Israel. 4887
29: 1 Then **K** David said to the whole assembly: 4889
29: 9 David the **k** also rejoiced greatly. 4889
29:20 before the LORD and the **k.** 4889
29:22 **acknowledged** Solomon son of David **as k** 4887
29:23 on the throne of the LORD as **k** in place 4889
29:24 as well as all of **K** David's sons, 4889
29:24 pledged their submission to **K** Solomon. 4889
29:25 as no **k** over Israel ever had before. 4889
29:26 David son of Jesse *was* **k** over all Israel. 4887
29:28 His son Solomon succeeded him *as* **k.** 4887
29:29 As for the events of **K** David's reign, 4889
2Ch 1: 8 to David my father and *have* **made** me **k** 4887
1: 9 for you *have* **made** me **k** over 4887
1:11 over whom *I have* **made** you **k,** 4887
1:12 such as no **k** who was before you ever had 4889
1:15 The **k** made silver and gold as common 4889
2: 3 Solomon sent this message to Hiram **k** 4889
2:11 Hiram **k** of Tyre replied by letter 4889
2:11 he has made you their **k."** 4889
2:12 He has given **K** David a wise son, 4889
4:11 the work he had undertaken for **K** Solomon 4889
4:16 that Huram-Abi made for **K** Solomon for 4889
4:17 The **k** had them cast in clay molds in 4889
5: 3 of Israel came together to the **k** at the time 4889
5: 6 and **K** Solomon and the entire assembly 4889
6: 3 the **k** turned around and blessed them. 4889
7: 4 the **k** and all the people offered sacrifices 4889
7: 5 And **K** Solomon offered a sacrifice 4889
7: 5 So the **k** and all the people dedicated 4889
7: 6 which **K** David had made for praising 4889
8:10 also **K** Solomon's chief officials— 4889
8:11 not live in the palace of David **k** of Israel, 4889
8:18 which they delivered to **K** Solomon. 4889
9: 5 She said to the **k,** "The report I heard 4889
9: 8 and placed you on his throne as **k** to rule for 4889
9: 8 he has made you **k** over them, 4889
9: 9 Then she gave the **k** 120 talents of gold, 4889
9: 9 the queen of Sheba gave to **K** Solomon. 4889
9:11 The **k** used the algumwood to make steps 4889

2Ch 9:12 **K** Solomon gave the queen of Sheba 4889
9:15 **K** Solomon made two hundred large shields 4889
9:16 The **k** put them in the Palace of the Forest 4889
9:17 the **k** made a great throne inlaid with ivory 4889
9:20 All **K** Solomon's goblets were gold, 4889
9:21 The **k** had a fleet of trading ships manned 4889
9:22 **K** Solomon was greater in riches 4889
9:27 The **k** made silver as common in Jerusalem 4889
9:31 And Rehoboam his son succeeded him *as* **k.** 4887
10: 1 the Israelites had gone there to make him **k.** 4887
10: 2 where he had fled from **K** Solomon), 4887
10: 6 Then **K** Rehoboam consulted the elders 4889
10:12 as the **k** had said, 4889
10:13 The **k** answered them harshly. 4889
10:15 So the **k** did not listen to the people, 4889
10:16 When all Israel saw that the **k** refused 4889
10:16 they answered the **k:** 4889
10:18 **K** Rehoboam sent out Adoniram, 4889
10:18 **K** Rehoboam, however, managed to get 4889
11: 3 to Rehoboam son of Solomon **k** *of* Judah 4889
11:22 in order to **make** him **k.** 4887
12: 1 Rehoboam's **position as k** was established 4895
12: 2 Shishak **k** of Egypt attacked Jerusalem in 4889
12: 2 in the fifth year of **K** Rehoboam. 4889
12: 6 and the **k** humbled themselves and said, 4889
12: 9 Shishak **k** of Egypt attacked Jerusalem; 4889
12:10 So **K** Rehoboam made bronze shields 4889
12:11 the **k** went to the LORD's temple, 4889
12:13 **K** Rehoboam established himself firmly 4889
12:13 in Jerusalem and *continued as* **k.** 4889
12:13 forty-one years old when he *became* **k,** 4887
12:16 And Abijah his son succeeded him *as* **k.** 4887
13: 1 Abijah *became* **k** of Judah, 4887
14: 1 Asa his son succeeded him *as* **k,** 4887
15:16 **K** Asa also deposed his grandmother 4889
Maacah from her position
16: 1 the thirty-sixth year of Asa's reign Baasha **k** 4889
16: 1 or entering the territory of Asa **k** of Judah. 4889
16: 2 and sent it to Ben-Hadad **k** of Aram, 4889
16: 3 with Baasha **k** of Israel so he will withdraw 4889
16: 4 Ben-Hadad agreed with **K** Asa and sent 4889
16: 6 Then **K** Asa brought all the men of Judah, 4889
16: 7 At that time Hanani the seer came to Asa **k** 4889
16: 7 "Because you relied on the **k** of Aram and 4889
16: 7 the **k** of Aram has escaped from your hand. 4889
17: 1 Jehoshaphat his son succeeded him *as* **k** 4889
17:19 These were the men who served the **k,** 4889
18: 3 Ahab **k** of Israel asked Jehoshaphat king 4889
18: 3 Ahab king of Israel asked Jehoshaphat **k** 4889
18: 4 But Jehoshaphat also said to the **k** of Israel, 4889
18: 5 **k** of Israel brought together the prophets— 4889
18: 7 The **k** of Israel answered Jehoshaphat, 4889
18: 7 "The **k** should not say that," 4889
18: 8 So the **k** of Israel called one of his officials 4889
18: 9 the **k** of Israel and Jehoshaphat king 4889
18: 9 and Jehoshaphat **k** of Judah were sitting 4889
18:12 prophets are predicting success for the **k.** 4889
18:14 When he arrived, the **k** asked him, 4889
18:15 The **k** said to him, "How many times 4889
18:17 The **k** of Israel said to Jehoshaphat, 4889
18:19 'Who will entice Ahab **k** of Israel 4889
18:25 The **k** of Israel then ordered, 4889
18:26 'This is what the **k** says: 4889
18:28 So the **k** of Israel and Jehoshaphat king 4889
18:28 of Israel and Jehoshaphat **k** of Judah went 4889
18:29 The **k** of Israel said to Jehoshaphat, 4889
18:29 the **k** of Israel disguised himself and went 4889
18:30 Now the **k** of Aram had ordered 4889
18:30 small or great, except the **k** of Israel." 4889
18:31 they thought, "This is the **k** of Israel." 4889
18:32 that he was not the **k** of Israel, 4889
18:33 and hit the **k** of Israel between the sections 4889
18:33 The **k** told the chariot driver, NIH
18:34 and the **k** of Israel propped himself up 4889
19: 1 When Jehoshaphat **k** of Judah 4889
19: 2 went out to meet him and said to the **k,** 4889
19:11 be over you in any matter concerning the **k,** 4889
20:15 **K** Jehoshaphat and all who live in Judah 4889
20:31 when he *became* **k** of Judah, 4887
20:35 Jehoshaphat **k** of Judah made an alliance 4889
20:35 of Judah made an alliance with Ahaziah **k** 4889
21: 1 And Jehoram his son succeeded him *as* **k.** 4887
21: 2 All these were sons of Jehoshaphat **k** 4889
21: 5 thirty-two years old when he *became* **k,** 4887
21: 8 and **set up** its own **k.** 4887+4889
21:12 of your father Jehoshaphat or of Asa **k** 4889
21:20 when he *became* **k,** 4887
22: 1 **made** Ahaziah, Jehoram's youngest son, **k** 4887
22: 1 of Jehoram **k** of Judah began to reign. 4889
22: 2 thirty-two years old when he *became* **k,** 4887
22: 5 with Joram son of Ahab **k** of Israel to war 4889
22: 5 of Israel to war against Hazael **k** of Aram 4889
22: 6 at Ramoth in his battle with Hazael **k** 4889
22: 6 of Joram **k** of Judah went down 4889
22:11 But Jehosheba, the daughter of **K** Jehoram, 4889
22:11 the daughter of **K** Jehoram and wife of 4889
23: 3 a covenant with the **k** at the temple of God. 4889
23: 7 to station themselves around the **k,** 4889
23: 7 Stay close to the **k** wherever he goes." 4889
23: 9 that had belonged to **K** David and that were 4889
23:10 with his weapon in his hand, around the **k**— 4889
23:11 of the covenant and **proclaimed** him **k.** 4889
23:11 "Long live the **k!"** 4889
23:12 of the people running and cheering the **k,** 4889
23:13 She looked, and there was the **k,** 4889
23:13 and the trumpeters were beside the **k,** 4889
23:16 that he and the people and the **k** would be 4889

2Ch 23:20 the **k** down from the temple of the LORD. 4889
23:20 through the Upper Gate and seated the **k** on 4889
24: 1 seven years old when he *became* **k,** 4887
24: 6 the **k** summoned Jehoiada the chief priest 4889
24:12 The **k** and Jehoiada gave it to 4889
24:14 the rest of the money to the **k** and Jehoiada, 4889
24:17 of Judah came and paid homage to the **k,** 4889
24:21 by order of the **k** they stoned him to death 4889
24:22 **K** Joash did not remember the kindness 4889
24:23 the plunder to their **k** in Damascus. 4889
24:27 And Amaziah his son succeeded him *as* **k.** 4887
25: 1 twenty-five years old when he *became* **k,** 4887
25: 3 he executed the officials who had murdered 4889
his father the **k.** 4889
25: 7 a man of God came to him and said, "O **k,** 4889
25:16 the **k** said to him, NIH
25:16 appointed you an adviser to the **k?** NIH
25:17 Amaziah **k** of Judah consulted his advisers, 4889
25:17 **k** of Israel: "Come, meet me face to face." 4889
25:18 But Jehoash **k** of Israel replied 4889
25:18 of Israel replied to Amaziah **k** of Judah: 4889
25:21 So Jehoash **k** of Israel attacked. 4889
25:21 and Amaziah **k** of Judah faced each other 4889
25:23 Jehoash **k** of Israel captured Amaziah king 4889
25:23 Jehoash king of Israel captured Amaziah **k** 4889
25:25 of Joash **k** of Judah lived for fifteen years 4889
25:25 after the death of Jehoash son of Jehoahaz **k** 4889
26: 1 **made** him **k** in place of his father Amaziah. 4887
26: 3 sixteen years old when he *became* **k,** 4887
26:13 to support the **k** against his enemies. 4889
26:21 **K** Uzziah had leprosy until the day he died. 4889
26:23 And Jotham his son succeeded him *as* **k.** 4887
27: 1 twenty-five years old when he *became* **k,** 4887
27: 5 Jotham made war on the **k** of 4889
27: 8 twenty-five years old when he *became* **k,** 4887
27: 9 And Ahaz his son succeeded him *as* **k.** 4887
28: 1 twenty years old when he *became* **k,** 4887
28: 5 over to the **k** of Aram. 4889
28: 5 also given into the hands of the **k** of Israel, 4889
28: 7 and Elkanah, second to the **k.** 4889
28:16 that time **K** Ahaz sent to the king of Assyria 4889
28:16 At that time King Ahaz sent to the **k** 4889
28:19 because of Ahaz **k** of Israel, 4889
28:20 Tiglath-Pileser **k** of Assyria came to him, 4889
28:21 and presented them to the **k** of Assyria, 4889
28:22 In his time of trouble **K** Ahaz became 4889
28:27 And Hezekiah his son succeeded him *as* **k.** 4887
29: 1 twenty-five years old *when he became* **k,** 4887
29:15 as the **k** had ordered, 4889
29:18 they went in to **K** Hezekiah and reported: 4889
29:19 that **K** Ahaz removed in his unfaithfulness 4889
29:19 in his unfaithfulness while he was **k.** 4895
29:20 the next morning **K** Hezekiah gathered 4889
29:21 The **k** commanded the priests, NIH
29:23 the sin offering were brought before the **k** 4889
29:24 because the **k** had ordered the burnt offering 4889
29:27 by trumpets and the instruments of David **k** 4889
29:29 the **k** and everyone present with him knelt 4889
29:30 **K** Hezekiah and his officials ordered 4889
30: 2 The **k** and his officials and 4889
30: 4 The plan seemed right both to the **k** and to 4889
30: 6 the **k** and from his officials, which read: 4889
30:12 the **k** and his officials had ordered, 4889
30:24 Hezekiah **k** of Judah provided 4889
30:26 of David **k** of Israel there had been nothing 4889
31: 3 The **k** contributed from his own possessions 4889
31:13 by appointment of **K** Hezekiah and Azariah 4889
32: 1 Sennacherib **k** of Assyria came 4889
32: 7 or discouraged because of the **k** of Assyria 4889
32: 9 from what Hezekiah the **k** of Judah said. 4889
32: 9 when Sennacherib **k** of Assyria 4889
32: 9 with this message for Hezekiah **k** of Judah 4889
32:10 "This is what Sennacherib **k** 4889
32:11 from the hand of the **k** of Assyria,' 4889
32:17 **k** also wrote letters insulting the LORD, NIH
32:20 **K** Hezekiah and the prophet Isaiah son 4889
32:21 and officers in the camp of the Assyrian **k.** 4889
32:22 from the hand of Sennacherib **k** of Assyria 4889
32:23 and valuable gifts for Hezekiah **k** of Judah. 4889
32:33 And Manasseh his son succeeded him *as* **k.** 4887
33: 1 twelve years old when he *became* **k,** 4887
33:11 against them the army commanders of the **k** 4889
33:20 And Amon his son succeeded him *as* **k.** 4887
33:21 twenty-two years old when he *became* **k,** 4887
33:25 killed all who had plotted against **K** Amon, 4889
33:25 **made** Josiah his son **k** 4887
34: 1 eight years old when he *became* **k,** 4887
34:16 the book to the **k** and reported to him: 4889
34:18 Then Shaphan the secretary informed the **k,** 4889
34:18 from it in the presence of the **k.** 4889
34:19 When the **k** heard the words of the Law, 4889
34:22 the **k** had sent with him went to speak to 4889
34:24 that has been read in the presence of the **k** 4889
34:26 Tell the **k** of Judah, 4889
34:28 So they took her answer back to the **k.** 4889
34:29 the **k** called together all the elders of Judah 4889
34:31 The **k** stood by his pillar and renewed 4889
35: 3 that Solomon son of David **k** of Israel built. 4889
35: 4 the directions written by David **k** of Israel 4889
35:10 in their divisions as the **k** had ordered. 4889
35:16 as **K** Josiah had ordered. 4889
35:20 Neco **k** of Egypt went up to fight 4889
35:21 O **k** of Judah? It is not you I am attacking 4889
35:23 Archers shot **K** Josiah, 4889
36: 1 of Josiah and **made** him **k** in Jerusalem 4887
36: 2 twenty-three years old when he *became* **k,** 4887
36: 3 The **k** of Egypt dethroned him in Jerusalem 4889

2Ch	36: 4	The k of Egypt made Eliakim,	4889
	36: 4	made Eliakim, a brother of Jehoahaz, k	4887
	36: 5	twenty-five years old when he became k,	4887
	36: 6	Nebuchadnezzar k of Babylon attacked him	4889
	36: 8	And Jehoiachin his son succeeded him as k.	4887
	36: 9	eighteen years old when he became k,	4887
	36:10	K Nebuchadnezzar sent for him	4889
	36:10	made Jehoiachin's uncle, Zedekiah, k	4887
	36:11	twenty-one years old when he became k,	4887
	36:13	also rebelled against K Nebuchadnezzar,	4889
	36:17	up against them the k of the Babylonians,	4889
	36:18	and the treasures of the k her royal officials.	4889
	36:22	In the first year of Cyrus k of Persia,	4889
	36:22	the LORD moved the heart of Cyrus k	4889
	36:23	"This is what Cyrus k of Persia says:	4889
Ezr	1: 1	In the first year of Cyrus k of Persia,	4889
	1: 1	the LORD moved the heart of Cyrus k	4889
	1: 2	"This is what Cyrus k of Persia says:	4889
	1: 7	K Cyrus brought out the articles belonging	4889
	1: 8	Cyrus k of Persia had them brought	4889
	2: 1	Nebuchadnezzar k of Babylon had taken	4889
	3: 7	as authorized by Cyrus k of Persia.	4889
	3:10	as prescribed by David k of Israel.	4889
	4: 2	since the time of Esarhaddon k of Assyria,	4889
	4: 3	as K Cyrus, the king of Persia,	4889
	4: 3	the k of Persia, commanded us."	4889
	4: 5	during the entire reign of Cyrus k of Persia	4889
	4: 5	and down to the reign of Darius k of Persia.	4889
	4: 7	And in the days of Artaxerxes k of Persia,	4889
	4: 8	against Jerusalem to Artaxerxes the k	10421
	4:11	To K Artaxerxes, From your servants,	10421
	4:12	The k should know that the Jews who came	10421
	4:13	the k should know that if this city is built	10421
	4:14	not proper for us to see the k dishonored,	10421
	4:14	sending this message to inform the k,	10421
	4:16	We inform the k that if this city is built	10421
	4:17	The k sent this reply:	10421
	4:23	of the letter of K Artaxerxes was read	10421
	4:24	the second year of the reign of Darius k	10421
	5: 6	sent to K Darius,	10421
	5: 7	To K Darius: Cordial greetings.	10421
	5: 8	The k should know that we went to	10421
	5:11	that a great k of Israel built and finished.	10421
	5:12	k of Babylon, who destroyed this temple	10421
	5:13	in the first year of Cyrus k of Babylon,	10421
	5:13	K Cyrus issued a decree	10421
	5:14	"Then K Cyrus gave them to	10421
	5:17	Now if it pleases the k,	10421
	5:17	to see if K Cyrus did in fact issue a decree	10421
	5:17	let the k send us his decision in this matter.	10421
	6: 1	K Darius then issued an order,	10421
	6: 3	In the first year of K Cyrus, the king issued	10421
	6: 3	the k issued a decree concerning the temple	10421
	6:10	for the well-being of the k and his sons.	10421
	6:12	overthrow any k or people who lifts a hand	10421
	6:13	because of the decree K Darius had sent,	10421
	6:15	in the sixth year of the reign of K Darius.	10421
	6:22	by changing the attitude of the k of Assyria,	4889
	7: 1	during the reign of Artaxerxes k of Persia,	4889
	7: 6	The k had granted him everything he asked,	4889
	7: 7	in the seventh year of K Artaxerxes.	4889
	7: 8	the fifth month of the seventh year of the k.	4889
	7:11	of the letter K Artaxerxes had given to Ezra	4889
	7:12	k of kings, To Ezra the priest,	4889
	7:14	You are sent by the k and his seven advisers	10421
	7:15	that the k and his advisers have freely given	10421
	7:21	K Artaxerxes, order all the treasurers	10421
	7:23	against the realm of the k and of his sons?	10421
	7:26	of the k must surely be punished by death,	10421
	7:28	to me before the k and his advisers and all	4889
	8: 1	during the reign of K Artaxerxes:	4889
	8:22	I was ashamed to ask the k for soldiers	4889
	8:22	because we had told the k,	4889
	8:25	of silver and gold and the articles that the k,	4889
Ne	1:11	I was cupbearer to the k.	4889
	2: 1	in the twentieth year of K Artaxerxes,	4889
	2: 1	I took the wine and gave it to the k.	4889
	2: 2	so the k asked me, "Why does your face	4889
	2: 3	but I said to the k, "May the king live	4889
	2: 3	"May the k live forever!	4889
	2: 4	The k said to me, "What is it you want?"	4889
	2: 5	and I answered the k,	4889
	2: 5	the k and if your servant has found favor	4889
	2: 6	Then the k, with the queen sitting	4889
	2: 6	It pleased the k to send me; so I set a time.	4889
	2: 7	I also said to him, "If it pleases the k,	4889
	2: 8	the k granted my requests.	4889
	2: 9	The k had also sent army officers	4889
	2:18	of my God upon me and what the k had said	4889
	2:19	"Are you rebelling against the k?"	4889
	5:14	from the twentieth year of K Artaxerxes,	4889
	6: 6	reports that you are about to become their k	4889
	6: 6	'There is a k in Judah!'	4889
	6: 7	Now this report will get back to the k;	4889
	7: 6	of the exiles whom Nebuchadnezzar k	4889
	9:22	over the country of Sihon k of Heshbon and	4889
	9:22	of Heshbon and the country of Og k	4889
	13: 6	for in the thirty-second year of Artaxerxes k	4889
	13: 6	to Babylon I had returned to the k.	4889
	13:26	like these that Solomon k of Israel sinned?	4889
	13:26	many nations there was no k like him.	4889
	13:26	and God made him k over all Israel,	4889
Est	1: 2	At that time K Xerxes reigned	4889
	1: 5	the k gave a banquet, lasting seven days,	4889
	1: 8	for the k instructed all the wine stewards	4889
	1: 9	the women in the royal palace of K Xerxes.	4889
	1:10	K Xerxes was in high spirits from wine,	4889
Est	1:12	k became furious and burned with anger.	4889
	1:13	for the k to consult experts in matters of law	4889
	1:14	and were closest to the k—	2257S
	1:14	and Media who had special access to the k	4889
	1:15	not obeyed the command of K Xerxes that	4889
	1:16	in the presence of the k and the nobles,	4889
	1:16	against the k but also against all the nobles	4889
	1:16	of all the provinces of K Xerxes.	4889
	1:17	'K Xerxes commanded Queen Vashti to	4889
	1:19	"Therefore, if it pleases the k,	4889
	1:19	to enter the presence of K Xerxes.	4889
	1:19	Also let the k give her royal position	4889
	1:21	The k and his nobles were pleased	4889
	1:21	so the k did as Memucan proposed.	4889
	2: 1	when the anger of K Xerxes had subsided,	4889
	2: 2	for beautiful young virgins for the k.	4889
	2: 3	Let the k appoint commissioners	4889
	2: 4	the girl who pleases the k be queen instead	4889
	2: 4	This advice appealed to the k,	4889
	2: 6	from Jerusalem by Nebuchadnezzar k	4889
	2: 6	with Jehoiachin k of Judah.	4889
	2:12	a girl's turn came to go in to K Xerxes,	4889
	2:13	And this is how she would go to the k:	4889
	2:14	not return to the k unless he was pleased	4889
	2:15	of his uncle Abihail) to go to the k,	4889
	2:16	to K Xerxes in the royal residence in	4889
	2:17	Now the k was attracted to Esther more than	4889
	2:18	And the k gave a great banquet,	4889
	2:21	and conspired to assassinate K Xerxes.	4889
	2:22	who in turn reported it to the k,	4889
	2:23	of the annals in the presence of the k.	4889
	3: 1	K Xerxes honored Haman son	4889
	3: 2	the k had commanded this concerning him.	4889
	3: 7	In the twelfth year of K Xerxes,	4889
	3: 8	Then Haman said to K Xerxes,	4889
	3: 9	If it pleases the k,	4889
	3:10	So the k took his signet ring from his finger	4889
	3:11	"Keep the money," the k said to Haman,	4889
	3:12	in the name of K Xerxes himself and sealed	4889
	3:15	The k and Haman sat down to drink,	4889
	4: 3	to which the edict and order of the k came,	4889
	4:11	or woman who approaches the k in	4889
	4:11	the k has but one law:	2257S
	4:11	to this is for the k to extend the gold scepter	4889
	4:11	since I was called to go to the k."	4889
	4:16	When this is done, I will go to the k,	4889
	5: 1	The k was sitting on his royal throne in	4889
	5: 3	the k asked, "What is it, Queen Esther?	4889
	5: 4	"If it pleases the k," replied Esther,	4889
	5: 4	"let the k, together with Haman,	4889
	5: 5	"Bring Haman at once," the k said,	4889
	5: 5	So the k and Haman went to	4889
	5: 6	the k again asked Esther,	4889
	5: 8	the k regards me with favor and if it pleases	4889
	5: 8	and if it pleases the k to grant my petition	4889
	5: 8	let the k and Haman come tomorrow to	4889
	5:11	and all the ways the k had honored him and	4889
	5:12	to accompany the k to the banquet she gave.	4889
	5:12	along with the k tomorrow.	4889
	5:14	and ask the k in the morning	4889
	5:14	go with the k to the dinner and be happy."	4889
	6: 1	That night the k could not sleep;	4889
	6: 2	who had conspired to assassinate K Xerxes.	4889
	6: 3	Mordecai received for this?" the k asked.	4889
	6: 4	The k said, "Who is in the court?"	4889
	6: 4	to speak to the k about hanging Mordecai	4889
	6: 5	"Bring him in," the k ordered.	4889
	6: 6	When Haman entered, the k asked him,	4889
	6: 6	for the man the k delights to honor?"	4889
	6: 6	that the k would rather honor than me?"	4889
	6: 7	So he answered the k,	4889
	6: 7	"For the man the k delights to honor,	4889
	6: 8	have them bring a royal robe the k has worn	4889
	6: 8	and a horse the k has ridden,	4889
	6: 9	Let them robe the man the k delights	4889
	6: 9	for the man the k delights to honor!'"	4889
	6:10	"Go at once," the k commanded Haman.	4889
	6:11	for the man the k delights to honor!"	4889
	7: 1	So the k and Haman went to dine	4889
	7: 2	the k again asked, "Queen Esther,	4889
	7: 3	"If I have found favor with you, O k,	4889
	7: 4	because no such distress would justify	4889
	7: 4	disturbing the k."	4889
	7: 5	K Xerxes asked Queen Esther, "Who is he?	4889
	7: 6	Haman was terrified before the k and queen.	4889
	7: 7	The k got up in a rage,	4889
	7: 7	that the k had already decided his fate,	4889
	7: 8	as the k returned from the palace garden to	4889
	7: 8	The k exclaimed, "Will he even molest	4889
	7: 9	one of the eunuchs attending the k, said,	4889
	7: 9	who spoke up to help the k."	4889
	7: 9	The k said, "Hang him on it!"	4889
	8: 1	That same day K Xerxes gave Queen Esther	4889
	8: 1	into the presence of the k,	4889
	8: 2	The k took off his signet ring,	4889
	8: 3	Esther again pleaded with the k,	4889
	8: 4	the k extended the gold scepter to Esther	4889
	8: 5	"If it pleases the k," she said,	4889
	8: 7	K Xerxes replied to Queen Esther and	4889
	8:10	Mordecai wrote in the name of K Xerxes,	4889
	8:10	rode fast horses especially bred for the k.	350
	8:12	of K Xerxes was the thirteenth day of	4889
	8:17	wherever the edict of the k went,	4889
	9: 1	the edict commanded by the k was to	4889
	9: 2	in all the provinces of K Xerxes	4889
	9:11	of Susa was reported to the k that same day.	4889
	9:12	The k said to Queen Esther,	4889
Est	9:13	"If it pleases the k," Esther answered,	4889
	9:14	So the k commanded that this be done.	4889
	9:20	throughout the provinces of K Xerxes,	4889
	10: 1	K Xerxes imposed tribute throughout	4889
	10: 2	of Mordecai to which the k had raised him,	4889
	10: 3	the Jew was second in rank to K Xerxes,	4889
Job	15:24	like a k poised to attack,	4889
	18:14	and marched off to the k of terrors.	4889
	29:25	I dwelt as a k among his troops,	4889
	41:34	he is k over all that are proud."	4889
Ps	2: 6	"I have installed my K on Zion,	4889
	5: 2	my K and my God, for to you I pray.	4889
	10:16	The LORD is K for ever and ever;	4889
	18:50	He gives his k great victories;	4889
	20: 9	O LORD, save the k!	4889
	21: 1	O LORD, the k rejoices in your strength.	4889
	21: 7	For the k trusts in the LORD;	4889
	24: 7	that the K of glory may come in.	4889
	24: 8	Who is this K of glory?	4889
	24: 9	that the K of glory may come in.	4889
	24:10	Who is he, this K of glory?	4889
	24:10	LORD Almighty—he is the K of glory.	4889
	29:10	the LORD is enthroned as K forever.	4889
	33:16	No k is saved by the size of his army;	4889
	44: 4	You are my K and my God,	4889
	45: 1	as I recite my verses for the k;	4889
	45:11	The k is enthralled by your beauty;	4889
	45:14	In embroidered garments she is led to the k;	4889
	45:15	they enter the palace of the k.	4889
	47: 2	the great K over all the earth!	4889
	47: 6	sing praises to our K, sing praises.	4889
	47: 7	For God is the K of all the earth;	4889
	48: 2	the city of the Great K.	4889
	63:11	But the k will rejoice in God;	4889
	68:24	the procession of my God and K into	4889
	72: 1	Endow the k with your justice, O God,	4889
	74:12	But you, O God, are my k from of old;	4889
	84: 3	O LORD Almighty, my K and my God.	4889
	89:18	our k to the Holy One of Israel.	4889
	95: 3	the great K above all gods.	4889
	98: 6	shout for joy before the LORD, the K.	4889
	99: 4	The K is mighty, he loves justice—	4889
	105:20	The k sent and released him,	4889
	135:11	Sihon k of the Amorites, Og king	4889
	135:11	Og k of Bashan and all the kings	4889
	136:19	Sihon k of the Amorites	4889
	136:20	Og k of Bashan—	4889
	145: 1	I will exalt you, my God the K;	4889
	149: 2	let the people of Zion be glad in their K.	4889
Pr	1: 1	The proverbs of Solomon son of David, k	4889
	14:35	A k delights in a wise servant,	4889
	16:10	The lips of a k speak as an oracle,	4889
	20: 8	When a k sits on his throne to judge,	4889
	20:26	A wise k winnows out the wicked;	4889
	20:28	Love and faithfulness keep a k safe;	4889
	22:11	will have the k for his friend.	4889
	24:21	Fear the LORD and the k, my son,	4889
	25: 1	copied by the men of Hezekiah k of Judah:	4889
	29: 4	By justice a k gives a country stability,	4889
	29:14	If a k judges the poor with fairness,	4889
	30:22	a servant who becomes k,	4887
	30:27	locusts have no k, yet they advance together	4889
	30:31	and a k with his army around him.	4889
	31: 1	The sayings of K Lemuel—	4889
Ecc	1: 1	son of David, k in Jerusalem:	4889
	1:12	the Teacher, was k over Israel in Jerusalem.	4889
	4:13	an old but foolish k who no longer knows	4889
	5: 9	the k himself profits from the fields.	4889
	9:14	And a powerful k came against it,	4889
	10:16	O land whose k was a servant	4889
	10:17	O land whose k is of noble birth	4889
	10:20	Do not revile the k even in your thoughts,	4889
SS	1: 4	Let the k bring me into his chambers.	4889
	1:12	While the k was at his table,	4889
	3: 9	K Solomon made for himself the carriage;	4889
	3:11	and look at K Solomon wearing the crown,	4889
	7: 5	the k is held captive by its tresses.	4889
Isa	6: 1	In the year that K Uzziah died,	4889
	6: 5	and my eyes have seen the K,	4889
	7: 1	the son of Uzziah, was k of Judah,	4889
	7: 1	K Rezin of Aram and Pekah son	4889
	7: 1	of Remaliah k of Israel marched up to fight	4889
	7: 6	and make the son of Tabeel k	4887+4889
	7:17	he will bring the k of Assyria."	4889
	7:20	the k of Assyria—	4889
	8: 4	of Samaria will be carried off by the k	4889
	8: 7	the k of Assyria with all his pomp.	4889
	8:21	will curse their k and their God.	4889
	10:12	the k of Assyria for the willful pride	4889
	14: 4	you will take up this taunt against the k	4889
	14:28	This oracle came in the year K Ahaz died:	4889
	19: 4	and a fierce k will rule over them,"	4889
	20: 1	sent by Sargon k of Assyria,	4889
	20: 4	so the k of Assyria will lead away stripped	4889
	20: 6	and deliverance from the k of Assyria!'	4889
	30:33	it has been made ready for the k.	4889
	32: 1	a k will reign in righteousness	4889
	33:17	Your eyes will see the k in his beauty	4889
	33:22	the LORD is our k; it is he who will save us.	4889
	36: 1	the fourteenth year of K Hezekiah's reign,	4889
	36: 1	Sennacherib k of Assyria attacked all	4889
	36: 2	the k of Assyria sent his field commander	4889
	36: 2	from Lachish to K Hezekiah at Jerusalem.	4889
	36: 4	"Tell Hezekiah, ' This is what the great k,	4889
	36: 4	the k of Assyria, says:	4889
	36: 6	Such is Pharaoh k of Egypt	4889
	36: 8	bargain with my master, the k of Assyria:	4889

Isa	36:13	"Hear the words of the great **k**,	4889
	36:13	the great king, the **k** of Assyria!	4889
	36:14	This is what the **k** says:	4889
	36:15	be given into the hand of the **k** of Assyria.'	4889
	36:16	This is what the **k** of Assyria says:	4889
	36:18	from the hand of the **k** of Assyria?	4889
	36:21	because the **k** had commanded,	4889
	37: 1	When **K** Hezekiah heard this,	4889
	37: 4	whom his master, the **k** of Assyria,	4889
	37: 5	**K** Hezekiah's officials came to Isaiah,	4889
	37: 6	of the **k** of Assyria have blasphemed me.	4889
	37: 8	When the field commander heard that the **k**	4889
	37: 8	and found the **k** fighting against Libnah.	NIH
	37: 9	Tirhakah, the Cushite **k** [of Egypt],	4889
	37:10	"Say to Hezekiah **k** of Judah:	4889
	37:10	'Jerusalem will not be handed over to the **k**	4889
	37:13	Where is the **k** of Hamath,	4889
	37:13	is the king of Hamath, the **k** of Arpad,	4889
	37:13	the **k** of the city of Sepharvaim,	4889
	37:21	to me concerning Sennacherib **k** of Assyria,	4889
	37:33	the LORD says concerning the **k**	4889
	37:37	So Sennacherib **k** of Assyria broke camp	4889
	37:38	Esarhaddon his son succeeded him *as* **k**.	4887
	38: 6	and this city from the hand of the **k**	4889
	38: 9	of Hezekiah **k** of Judah after his illness	4889
	39: 1	Merodach-Baladan son of Baladan **k**	4889
	39: 3	the prophet went to **K** Hezekiah and asked,	4889
	39: 7	in the palace of the **k** of Babylon."	4889
	41:21	"Set forth your arguments," says Jacob's **K**.	4889
	43:15	your Holy One, Israel's Creator, your **K**."	4889
	44: 6	Israel's King and Redeemer,	4889
Jer	1: 2	the reign of Josiah son of Amon **k** of Judah,	4889
	1: 3	of Jehoiakim son of Josiah **k** of Judah,	4889
	1: 3	of Zedekiah son of Josiah **k** of Judah,	4889
	3: 6	During the reign of **K** Josiah,	4889
	4: 9	"the **k** and the officials will lose heart,	4889
	8:19	Is her **K** no longer there?"	4889
	10: 7	O **K** of the nations?	4889
	10:10	he is the living God, the eternal **K**.	4889
	13:18	Say to the **k** and to the queen mother,	4889
	15: 4	of Hezekiah **k** of Judah did in Jerusalem.	4889
	20: 4	I will hand all Judah over to the **k**	4889
	21: 1	when **K** Zedekiah sent to him Pashhur son	4889
	21: 2	for us because Nebuchadnezzar **k**	4889
	21: 4	which you are using to fight the **k**	4889
	21: 7	I will hand over Zedekiah **k** of Judah,	4889
	21: 7	to Nebuchadnezzar **k** of Babylon and	4889
	21:10	be given into the hands of the **k** of Babylon,	4889
	22: 1	"Go down to the palace of the **k** of Judah	4889
	22: 2	O **k** of Judah, you who sit	4889
	22: 6	the LORD says about the palace of the **k**	4889
	22:10	not weep for the dead [**k**] or mourn his loss;	NIH
	22:11	*as* **k** of Judah but has gone from this place:	4887
	22:15	*"Does it make you a* **k** *to have more*	4887
	22:18	about Jehoiakim son of Josiah **k** of Judah:	4889
	22:24	Jehoiachin son of Jehoiakim **k** of Judah,	4889
	22:25	to Nebuchadnezzar **k** of Babylon and to	4889
	23: 5	a **K** who will reign wisely	4889
	24: 1	of Jehoiakim **k** of Judah and the officials,	4889
	24: 1	by Nebuchadnezzar **k** of Babylon,	4889
	24: 8	'so will I deal with Zedekiah **k** of Judah,	4889
	25: 1	the fourth year of Jehoiakim son of Josiah **k**	4889
	25: 1	the first year of Nebuchadnezzar **k**	4889
	25: 3	the thirteenth year of Josiah son of Amon **k**	4889
	25: 9	the north and my servant Nebuchadnezzar **k**	4889
	25:11	and these nations will serve the **k**	4889
	25:12	the **k** of Babylon and his nation,	4889
	25:19	Pharaoh **k** of Egypt,	4889
	25:26	the **k** of Sheshach will drink it too.	4889
	26: 1	of Josiah **k** of Judah, this word came from	4889
	26:18	in the days of Hezekiah **k** of Judah.	4889
	26:19	"Did Hezekiah **k** of Judah or anyone else	4889
	26:21	When **K** Jehoiakim and all his officers	4889
	26:21	the **k** sought to put him to death.	4889
	26:22	**K** Jehoiakim, however, sent Elnathan	4889
	26:23	of Egypt and took him to **K** Jehoiakim,	4889
	27: 1	in the reign of Zedekiah son of Josiah **k**	4889
	27: 3	to Jerusalem for **k** of Judah.	4889
	27: 6	over to my servant Nebuchadnezzar **k**	4889
	27: 8	not serve Nebuchadnezzar **k** of Babylon	4889
	27: 9	'You will not serve the **k** of Babylon.'	4889
	27:11	the yoke of the **k** of Babylon and serve him,	4889
	27:12	the same message to Zedekiah **k** of Judah.	4889
	27:12	"Bow your neck under the yoke of the **k**	4889
	27:13	that will not serve the **k** of Babylon?	4889
	27:14	'You will not serve the **k** of Babylon,'	4889
	27:17	Serve the **k** of Babylon, and you will live.	4889
	27:18	of the LORD and in the palace of the **k**	4889
	27:20	which Nebuchadnezzar **k** of Babylon did	4889
	27:20	of Jehoiakim **k** of Judah into exile	4889
	27:21	of the LORD and in the palace of the **k**	4889
	28: 1	early in the reign of Zedekiah **k** of Judah,	4889
	28: 2	'I will break the yoke of the **k** of Babylon.	4889
	28: 3	the LORD's house that Nebuchadnezzar **k**	4889
	28: 4	to this place Jehoiachin son of Jehoiakim **k**	4889
	28: 4	I will break the yoke of the **k** of Babylon.' "	4889
	28:11	of Nebuchadnezzar **k** of Babylon off	4889
	28:14	to make them serve Nebuchadnezzar **k**	4889
	29: 2	after **K** Jehoiachin and the queen mother,	4889
	29: 3	whom Zedekiah **k** of Judah sent	4889
	29: 3	of Judah sent to **K** Nebuchadnezzar	4889
	29:16	the **k** who sits on David's throne and all	4889
	29:21	"I will hand them over to Nebuchadnezzar **k**	4889
	29:22	whom the **k** of Babylon burned in the fire.'	4889
	30: 9	the LORD their God and David their **k**,	4889
	32: 1	the LORD in the tenth year of Zedekiah **k**	4889
	32: 2	The army of the **k** of Babylon was	4889

Jer	32: 3	Now Zedekiah **k** of Judah	4889
	32: 3	to hand this city over to the **k** of Babylon,	4889
	32: 4	Zedekiah **k** of Judah will not escape out of	4889
	32: 4	but will certainly be handed over to the **k**	4889
	32:28	the Babylonians and to Nebuchadnezzar **k**	4889
	32:36	and plague it will be handed over to the **k**	4889
	34: 1	While Nebuchadnezzar **k** of Babylon	4889
	34: 2	Go to Zedekiah **k** of Judah and tell him,	4889
	34: 2	to hand this city over to the **k** of Babylon,	4889
	34: 3	the **k** of Babylon with your own eyes,	4889
	34: 4	O Zedekiah **k** of Judah.	4889
	34: 6	the prophet told all this to Zedekiah **k**	4889
	34: 7	the army of the **k** of Babylon was fighting	4889
	34: 8	the LORD after **K** Zedekiah had made	4889
	34:21	"I will hand Zedekiah **k** of Judah	4889
	34:21	to the army of the **k** of Babylon,	4889
	35: 1	of Jehoiakim son of Josiah **k** of Judah:	4889
	35:11	But when Nebuchadnezzar **k**	4889
	36: 1	the fourth year of Jehoiakim son of Josiah **k**	4889
	36: 9	the fifth year of Jehoiakim son of Josiah **k**	4889
	36:16	"We must report all these words to the **k**."	4889
	36:20	they went to the **k** in the courtyard	4889
	36:21	The **k** sent Jehudi to get the scroll,	4889
	36:21	the secretary and read it to the **k** and all	4889
	36:22	It was the ninth month and the **k** was sitting	4889
	36:23	the **k** cut them off with a scribe's knife	NIH
	36:24	The **k** and all his attendants who heard all	
		these words showed no fear,	4889
	36:25	Delaiah and Gemariah urged the **k** not	4889
	36:26	Instead, the **k** commanded Jerahmeel	4889
	36:26	Jerahmeel, a son of the **k**,	4889
	36:27	the **k** burned the scroll containing the words	4889
	36:28	which Jehoiakim **k** of Judah burned up.	4889
	36:29	Also tell Jehoiakim **k** of Judah,	4889
	36:29	that the **k** of Babylon would certainly come	4889
	36:30	the LORD says about Jehoiakim **k**	4889
	36:32	that Jehoiakim **k** of Judah had burned in	4889
	37: 1	Zedekiah son of Josiah *was* made **k** of	
		Judah	4887
	37: 1	of Judah by Nebuchadnezzar **k** of Babylon;	4889
	37: 3	**K** Zedekiah, however, sent Jehucal son	4889
	37: 7	Tell the **k** of Judah,	4889
	37:17	Then **K** Zedekiah sent for him	4889
	37:17	be handed over to the **k** of Babylon."	4889
	37:18	Then Jeremiah said to **K** Zedekiah,	4889
	37:19	'The **k** of Babylon will not attack you	4889
	37:20	But now, my lord the **k**, please listen.	4889
	37:21	**K** Zedekiah then gave orders for Jeremiah	4889
	38: 3	over to the army of the **k** of Babylon,	4889
	38: 4	Then the officials said to the **k**,	4889
	38: 5	**K** Zedekiah answered.	4889
	38: 5	"The **k** can do nothing to oppose you."	4889
	38: 7	the **k** was sitting in the Benjamin Gate,	4889
	38: 9	"My lord the **k**, these men have acted	4889
	38:10	k commanded Ebed-Melech the Cushite,	4889
	38:14	Then **K** Zedekiah sent for Jeremiah	4889
	38:14	he said to Jeremiah.	4889
	38:16	But **K** Zedekiah swore this oath secretly	4889
	38:17	of the **k** of Babylon, your life will be spared	4889
	38:18	the **k** of Babylon, this city will be handed	4889
	38:19	**K** Zedekiah said to Jeremiah,	4889
	38:22	All the women left in the palace of the **k**	4889
	38:22	be brought out to the officials of the **k**	4889
	38:23	but will be captured by the **k** of Babylon;	4889
	38:25	'Tell us what you said to the **k** and what	4889
	38:25	to the king and what the **k** said to you;	4889
	38:26	with the **k** not to send me back	4889
	38:27	he had ordered him to say.	4889
	38:27	had heard his conversation with the **k**.	NIH
	39: 1	In the ninth year of Zedekiah **k** of Judah,	4889
	39: 1	Nebuchadnezzar **k** of Babylon marched	4889
	39: 3	of the **k** of Babylon came and took seats in	4889
	39: 3	the other officials of the **k** of Babylon.	4889
	39: 4	When Zedekiah **k** of Judah and all	4889
	39: 5	to Nebuchadnezzar **k** of Babylon at Riblah	4889
	39: 6	at Riblah the **k** of Babylon slaughtered	4889
	39:11	Now Nebuchadnezzar **k** of Babylon	4889
	39:13	the other officers of the **k** of Babylon	4889
	40: 5	whom the **k** of Babylon has appointed over	4889
	40: 7	in the open country heard that the **k**	4889
	40: 9	"Settle down in the land and serve the **k**	4889
	40:11	and all the other countries heard that the **k**	4889
	40:14	"Don't you know that Baalis **k** of	4889
	41: 2	the **k** of Babylon had appointed as governor	4889
	41: 9	with Gedaliah was the one **K** Asa had made	4889
	41: 9	of his defense against Baasha **k** of Israel.	4889
	41:18	the **k** of Babylon had appointed as governor	4889
	42:11	Do not be afraid of the **k** of Babylon,	4889
	43:10	for my servant Nebuchadnezzar **k**	4889
	44:30	to hand Pharaoh Hophra **k** of Egypt over	4889
	44:30	just as I handed Zedekiah **k** of Judah over	4889
	44:30	over to Nebuchadnezzar **k** of Babylon,	4889
	45: 1	the fourth year of Jehoiakim son of Josiah **k**	4889
	46: 2	the army of Pharaoh Neco **k** of Egypt,	4889
	46: 2	the Euphrates River by Nebuchadnezzar **k**	4889
	46: 2	the fourth year of Jehoiakim son of Josiah **k**	4889
	46:13	about the coming of Nebuchadnezzar **k**	4889
	46:17	'Pharaoh **k** of Egypt is only a loud noise;	4889
	46:18	"As surely as I live," declares the **K**,	4889
	46:26	to Nebuchadnezzar **k** of Babylon	4889
	48:15	down in the slaughter," declares the **K**,	4889
	49:28	which Nebuchadnezzar **k** of Babylon	4889
	49:30	"Nebuchadnezzar **k** of Babylon has plotted	4889
	49:34	early in the reign of Zedekiah **k** of Judah:	4889
	49:38	in Elam and destroy her **k** and officials,"	4889
	50:17	first to devour him was the **k** of Assyria;	4889
	50:17	to crush his bones was Nebuchadnezzar **k**	4889

Jer	50:18	"I will punish the **k** of Babylon and his land	4889
	50:18	and his land as I punished the **k** of Assyria.	4889
	50:43	**k** of Babylon has heard reports about them,	4889
	51:31	to announce to the **k** of Babylon	4889
	51:34	"Nebuchadnezzar **k** of Babylon	4889
	51:57	and not awake," declares the **K**,	4889
	51:59	with Zedekiah **k** of Babylon in the fourth year	4889
	52: 1	twenty-one years old when he *became* **k**,	4887
	52: 3	Zedekiah rebelled against the **k** of Babylon.	4889
	52: 4	Nebuchadnezzar **k** of Babylon marched	4889
	52: 5	until the eleventh year of **K** Zedekiah.	4889
	52: 8	the Babylonian army pursued **K** Zedekiah	4889
	52: 9	He was taken to the **k** of Babylon at Riblah	4889
	52:10	at Riblah the **k** of Babylon slaughtered	4889
	52:12	in the nineteenth year of Nebuchadnezzar **k**	4889
	52:12	who served the **k** of Babylon,	4889
	52:15	and those who had gone over to the **k**	4889
	52:20	which **K** Solomon had made for the temple	4889
	52:26	and brought them to the **k** of Babylon	4889
	52:27	the **k** had them executed.	4889
	52:31	of the exile of Jehoiachin **k** of Judah,	4889
	52:31	in the year Evil-Merodach **became k**	4895
	52:31	he released Jehoiachin **k** of Judah	4889
	52:34	by day the **k** of Babylon gave Jehoiachin	4889
La	2: 6	in his fierce anger he has spurned both **k**	4889
	2: 9	Her **k** and her princes are exiled among	4889
Eze	1: 2	the fifth year of the exile of **K** Jehoiachin—	4889
	7:27	The **k** will mourn, the prince will be	4889
	17:12	'The **k** of Babylon went to Jerusalem	4889
	17:12	and carried off her **k** and her nobles,	4889
	17:15	But the **k** rebelled against him	NIH
	17:16	the land of the **k** who put him on the throne,	4889
	19: 9	and brought him to the **k** of Babylon.	4889
	21:19	for the sword of the **k** of Babylon to take,	4889
	21:21	For the **k** of Babylon will stop at the fork in	4889
	24: 2	because the **k** of Babylon has laid siege	4889
	26: 7	against Tyre Nebuchadnezzar **k** of Babylon,	4889
	26: 7	**k** of kings, with horses and chariots,	4889
	28:12	a lament concerning the **k** of Tyre and say	4889
	29: 2	against Pharaoh **k** of Egypt and prophesy	4889
	29: 3	" 'I am against you, Pharaoh **k** of Egypt,	4889
	29:18	Nebuchadnezzar **k** of Babylon	4889
	29:19	to give Egypt to Nebuchadnezzar **k**	4889
	30:10	the hand of Nebuchadnezzar **k** of Babylon.	4889
	30:21	I have broken the arm of Pharaoh **k**	4889
	30:22	I am against Pharaoh **k** of Egypt.	4889
	30:24	of the **k** of Babylon and put my sword	4889
	30:25	I will strengthen the arms of the **k**	4889
	30:25	when I put my sword into the hand of the **k**	4889
	31: 2	to Pharaoh **k** of Egypt and to his hordes:	4889
	32: 2	up a lament concerning Pharaoh **k** of Egypt	4889
	32:11	" 'The sword of the **k** of Babylon will come	4889
	37:22	There will be one **k** over all of them	4889
	37:24	" 'My servant David will be **k** over them,	4889
Da	1: 1	In the third year of the reign of Jehoiakim **k**	4889
	1: 1	Nebuchadnezzar **k** of Babylon came	4889
	1: 2	the Lord delivered Jehoiakim **k** of Judah	4889
	1: 3	Then the **k** ordered Ashpenaz,	4889
	1: 5	The **k** assigned them a daily amount of food	4889
	1:10	"I am afraid of my lord the **k**,	4889
	1:10	The **k** would then have my head because	4889
	1:18	of the time set by the **k** to bring them in,	4889
	1:19	The **k** talked with them,	4889
	1:20	about which the **k** questioned them,	4889
	1:21	until the first year of **K** Cyrus.	4889
	2: 2	So the **k** summoned the magicians,	4889
	2: 2	When they came in and stood before the **k**,	4889
	2: 4	the astrologers answered the **k** in Aramaic,	4889
	2: 4	the king in Aramaic, "O **k**,	10421
	2: 5	The **k** replied to the astrologers,	10421
	2: 7	"Let the **k** tell his servants the dream,	10421
	2: 8	Then the **k** answered, "I am certain	10421
	2:10	The astrologers answered the **k**,	10421
	2:10	a man on earth who can do what the **k** asks!	10421
	2:10	No **k**, however great and mighty,	10421
	2:11	What the **k** asks is too difficult.	10421
	2:11	No one can reveal it to the **k** except	10421
	2:12	the **k** so angry and furious that he ordered	10421
	2:15	"Why did the **k** issue such a harsh decree?"	10421
	2:16	Daniel went in to the **k** and asked for time,	10421
	2:23	to us the dream of the **k**."	10421
	2:24	the **k** had appointed to execute the wise men	10421
	2:24	Take me to the **k**,	10421
	2:25	Arioch took Daniel to the **k** at once	10421
	2:25	the **k** what his dream means."	10421
	2:26	k asked Daniel (also called Belteshazzar),	10421
	2:27	to the **k** the mystery he has asked about,	10421
	2:28	**K** Nebuchadnezzar what will happen	10421
	2:29	O **k**, your mind turned to things to come,	10421
	2:30	but so that you, O **k**, may know	10421
	2:31	O **k**, and there before you stood	10421
	2:36	and now we will interpret it to the **k**.	10421
	2:37	You, O **k**, are the king of kings.	10421
	2:37	You, O king, are the **k** of kings.	10421
	2:45	the **k** what will take place in the future.	10421
	2:46	Then Nebuchadnezzar fell prostrate	10421
	2:47	The **k** said to Daniel,	10421
	2:48	Then the **k** placed Daniel in a high position	10421
	2:49	the **k** appointed Shadrach, Meshach	10421
	3: 1	**K** Nebuchadnezzar made an image of gold,	10421
	3: 3	the image that **K** Nebuchadnezzar had set	10421
	3: 5	of gold that **K** Nebuchadnezzar has set up.	10421
	3: 7	of gold that **K** Nebuchadnezzar had set up.	10421
	3: 9	They said to **K** Nebuchadnezzar, "O king,	10421
	3: 9	They said to King Nebuchadnezzar, "O **k**,	10421
	3:10	You have issued a decree, O **k**,	10421
	3:12	who pay no attention to you, O **k**.	10421

Da	3:13	So these men were brought before the **k**,	10421
	3:16	Meshach and Abednego replied to the **k**,	10421
	3:17	and he will rescue us from your hand, O **k**.	10421
	3:18	if he does not, we want you to know, O **k**,	10421
	3:24	Then **K** Nebuchadnezzar leaped to his feet	10421
	3:24	They replied, "Certainly, O **k**."	10421
	3:30	Then the **k** promoted Shadrach,	10421
	4: 1	**K** Nebuchadnezzar, To the peoples,	10421
	4:18	**K** Nebuchadnezzar, had.	10421
	4:19	So the **k** said, "Belteshazzar,	10421
	4:22	O **k**, are that tree!	10421
	4:23	"You, O **k**, saw a messenger, a holy one,	10421
	4:24	"This is the interpretation, O **k**,	10421
	4:24	against my lord the **k**:	10421
	4:27	O **k**, be pleased to accept my advice:	10421
	4:28	All this happened to **K** Nebuchadnezzar.	10421
	4:29	as the **k** was walking on the roof of	NIH
	4:31	for you, **K** Nebuchadnezzar:	10421
	4:37	and exalt and glorify the **K** of heaven,	10421
	5: 1	**K** Belshazzar gave a great banquet for	10421
	5: 2	so that the **k** and his nobles,	10421
	5: 3	and the **k** and his nobles,	10421
	5: 5	The **k** watched the hand as it wrote.	10421
	5: 7	The **k** called out for the enchanters,	10421
	5: 8	the writing or tell the **k** what it meant.	10421
	5: 9	So **K** Belshazzar became even more	10421
	5:10	hearing the voices of the **k** and his nobles,	10421
	5:10	"O **k**, live forever!"	10421
	5:11	**K** Nebuchadnezzar your father—	10421
	5:11	your father the **k**, I say—	10421
	5:12	whom the **k** called Belteshazzar,	10421
	5:13	So Daniel was brought before the **k**,	10421
	5:13	and the **k** said to him, "Are you Daniel,	10421
	5:13	one of the exiles my father the **k** brought	10421
	5:17	Then Daniel answered the **k**,	10421
	5:17	for the **k** and tell him what it means.	10421
	5:18	"O **k**, the Most High God gave your father	
		Nebuchadnezzar sovereignty	10421
	5:19	Those the **k** wanted to put to death,	NIH
	5:30	**k** of the Babylonians, was slain,	10421
	6: 2	to them so that the **k** might not suffer loss.	10421
	6: 3	that the **k** planned to set him over	10421
	6: 6	and the satraps went as a group to the **k**	10421
	6: 6	"O **K** Darius, live forever!	10421
	6: 7	that the **k** should issue an edict and enforce	10421
	6: 7	O **k**, shall be thrown into the lions' den.	10421
	6: 8	O **k**, issue the decree and put it in writing so	10421
	6: 9	So **K** Darius put the decree in writing.	10421
	6:12	So they went to the **k** and spoke to him	10421
	6:12	O **k**, would be thrown into the lions' den?"	10421
	6:12	The **k** answered, "The decree stands—	10421
	6:13	Then they said to the **k**, "Daniel,	10421
	6:13	O **k**, or to the decree you put in writing.	10421
	6:14	When the **k** heard this,	10421
	6:15	the men went as a group to the **k** and said	10421
	6:15	O **k**, that according to the law of the Medes	10421
	6:15	or edict that the **k** issues can be changed."	10421
	6:16	So the **k** gave the order,	10421
	6:16	The **k** said to Daniel, "May your God,	10421
	6:17	and the **k** sealed it with his own signet ring	10421
	6:18	Then the **k** returned to his palace and spent	10421
	6:19	the **k** got up and hurried to the lions' den.	10421
	6:21	Daniel answered, "O **k**, live forever!	10421
	6:22	Nor have I ever done any wrong before	
		you, O **k**."	10421
	6:23	The **k** was overjoyed and gave orders	10421
	6:25	Then **K** Darius wrote to all the peoples,	10421
	7: 1	In the first year of Belshazzar **k** of Babylon,	10421
	7:24	After them another **k** will arise,	NIH
	8: 1	In the third year of **K** Belshazzar's reign, I,	4889
	8:21	The shaggy goat is the **k** of Greece,	4889
	8:21	large horn between his eyes is the first **k**.	4889
	8:23	a stern-faced **k**, a master of intrigue,	4889
	10: 1	In the third year of Cyrus **k** of Persia.	4889
	10:13	I was detained there with the **k** of Persia.	4889
	11: 3	Then a mighty **k** will appear,	4889
	11: 5	"The **k** of the South will become strong,	4889
	11: 6	of the **k** of the South will go to the king of	4889
	11: 6	of the king of the South will go to the **k** of	4889
	11: 7	of the **k** of the North and enter his fortress;	4889
	11: 8	For some years he will leave the **k** of	4889
	11: 9	the **k** of the North will invade the realm of	NIH
	11: 9	the North will invade the realm of the **k** of	4889
	11:11	"Then the **k** of the South will march out in	4889
	11:11	a rage and fight against the **k** of the North,	4889
	11:12	the **k** of the South will be filled with pride	2257S
	11:13	**k** of the North will muster another army,	4889
	11:14	"In those times many will rise against the **k**	4889
	11:14	the **k** of the North will come and build	4889
	11:17	alliance with **the k of the South.**	2257S
	11:25	up his strength and courage against the **k** of	4889
	11:25	The **k** of the South will wage war with	4889
	11:28	The **k** of the North will return	NIH
	11:36	"The **k** will do as he pleases.	4889
	11:40	the **k** of the South will engage him in battle,	4889
	11:40	and the **k** of the North will storm out	4889
Hos	1: 1	of Jeroboam son of Jehoash **k** of Israel:	4889
	3: 4	the Israelites will live many days without **k**	4889
	3: 5	the LORD their God and David their **k**.	4889
	5:13	and sent to the great **k** for help.	4889
	7: 3	"They delight the **k** with their wickedness,	4889
	7: 5	of our **k** the princes become inflamed	4889
	8:10	under the oppression of the mighty **k**.	4889
	10: 3	"We have no **k** because we did not revere	4889
	10: 3	if we had a **k**, what could he do for us?"	4889
	10: 6	to Assyria as tribute for the great **k**.	4889
	10: 7	Samaria and its **k** will float away like a twig	4889

Hos	10:15	**k** of Israel will be completely destroyed.	4889
	13:10	Where is your **k**, that he may save you?	4889
	13:10	'Give me a **k** and princes'?	4889
	13:11	So in my anger I gave you a **k**,	4889
Am	1: 1	before the earthquake, when Uzziah was **k**	4889
	1: 1	and Jeroboam son of Jehoash was **k**	4889
	1: 5	I will destroy the **k** who is in the Valley	3782
	1: 8	the **k** of Ashdod and the one who holds	3782
	1:15	Her **k** will go into exile,	4889
	2: 1	as if to lime, the bones of Edom's **k**,	4889
	5:26	You have lifted up the shrine of your **k**,	4889
	7:10	of Bethel sent a message to Jeroboam **k**	4889
Jnh	3: 6	When the news reached the **k** of Nineveh,	4889
	3: 7	"By the decree of the **k** and his nobles:	4889
Mic	2:13	Their **k** will pass through before them,	4889
	4: 9	Why do you cry aloud—have you no **k**?	4889
	6: 5	remember what Balak **k** of Moab counseled	4889
Na	3:18	O **k** of Assyria, your shepherds slumber;	4889
Zep	1: 1	the reign of Josiah son of Amon **k** of Judah:	4889
	3:15	The LORD, the **k** of Israel, is with you;	4889
Hag	1: 1	In the second year of **K** Darius,	4889
	1:15	in the second year of **K** Darius.	4889
Zec	7: 1	In the fourth year of **K** Darius,	4889
	9: 5	Gaza will lose her **k** and Ashkelon will	4889
	9: 9	See, your **k** comes to you,	4889
	11: 6	over to his neighbor and his **k**.	4889
	14: 5	from the earthquake in the days of Uzziah **k**	4889
	14: 9	The LORD will be **k** over the whole earth.	4889
	14:16	up year after year to worship the **K**,	4889
	14:17	not go up to Jerusalem to worship the **K**,	4889
Mal	1:14	For I am a great **k**,"	4889
Mt	1: 6	and Jesse the father of **K** David.	995
	2: 1	during the time of **K** Herod,	995
	2: 2	is the one who has been born **k** of the Jews?	995
	2: 3	When **K** Herod heard this he was disturbed,	995
	2: 9	After they had heard the **k**,	995
	5:35	for it is the city of the Great **K**.	995
	14: 9	The **k** was distressed,	995
	18:23	like a **k** who wanted to settle accounts	476+995
	21: 5	'See, your **k** comes to you,	995
	22: 2	like a **k** who prepared a wedding banquet	476+995
	22: 7	The **k** was enraged.	995
	22:11	"But when the **k** came in to see the guests,	995
	22:13	"Then the **k** told the attendants,	995
	25:34	"Then the **k** will say to those on his right,	995
	25:40	"The **k** will reply, 'I tell you the truth,	995
	27:11	"Are you the **k** of the Jews?"	995
	27:29	"Hail, **k** of the Jews!"	995
	27:37	THIS IS JESUS, THE **K** OF THE JEWS.	995
	27:42	He's the **K** of Israel!	995
Mk	6:14	**K** Herod heard about this,	995
	6:22	The **k** said to the girl,	995
	6:25	the girl hurried in to the **k** with the request:	995
	6:26	The **k** was greatly distressed,	995
	15: 2	"Are you the **k** of the Jews?"	995
	15: 9	"Do you want me to release to you the **k** of	995
	15:12	with the one you call the **k** of the Jews?"	995
	15:18	"Hail, **k** of the Jews!"	995
	15:26	THE **K** OF THE JEWS.	995
	15:32	Let this Christ, this **K** of Israel,	995
Lk	1: 5	In the time of Herod **k** of Judea there was	995
	14:31	"Or suppose a **k** is about to go to war	995
	14:31	about to go to war *against* another **k**.	995
	19:12	to have himself appointed **k** and then	993
	19:14	'We don't want this man *to be* our **k**.'	996
	19:15	"He *was* made **k**, however,	993+3284+3836
	19:27	of mine who did not want me *to be* **k**	996
	19:38	"Blessed is the **k** who comes in the name of	995
	23: 2	to Caesar and claims to be Christ, a **k**."	995
	23: 3	"Are you the **k** of the Jews?"	995
	23:37	"If you are the **k** of the Jews,	995
	23:38	THIS IS THE **K** OF THE JEWS.	995
Jn	1:49	you are the **K** of Israel."	995
	6:15	that they intended to come and make him **k**	995
	12:13	"Blessed is the **K** of Israel!"	995
	12:15	see, your **k** is coming,	995
	18:33	"Are you the **k** of the Jews?"	995
	18:37	"You are a **k**, then!"	995
	18:37	"You are right in saying I am a **k**.	995
	18:39	Do you want me to release 'the **k** of	995
	19: 3	saying, "Hail, **k** of the Jews!"	995
	19:12	to be a **k** opposes Caesar."	995
	19:14	"Here is your **k**," Pilate said to the Jews.	995
	19:15	"Shall I crucify your **k**?"	995
	19:15	"We have no **k** but Caesar,"	995
	19:19	JESUS OF NAZARETH, THE **K** OF THE JEWS.	995
	19:21	"Do not write 'The **K** of the Jews,'	995
	19:21	that this man claimed to be **k** of the Jews."	995
Ac	7:10	to gain the goodwill of Pharaoh **k** of Egypt;	995
	7:18	Then another **k**, who knew nothing about	995
	12: 1	that **K** Herod arrested some who belonged	995
	12:20	a trusted personal servant of the **k**,	995
	13:21	Then the people asked for a **k**,	995
	13:22	he made David their **k**.	995
	17: 7	saying that there is another **k**,	995
	25:13	A few days later **K** Agrippa	995
	25:14	Festus discussed Paul's case *with* the **k**.	995
	25:24	Festus said: "**K** Agrippa,	995
	25:26	and especially before you, **K** Agrippa,	995
	26: 2	"**K** Agrippa, I consider myself fortunate	995
	26: 7	O **k**, it is because of this hope that	995
	26:13	About noon, O **k**, as I was on the road,	995
	26:19	"So then, **K** Agrippa, I was not disobedient	995
	26:26	is familiar with these things,	995
	26:27	**K** Agrippa, do you believe the prophets?"	995
	26:30	The **k** rose, and with him the governor	995
2Co	11:32	the governor *under* **K** Aretas had the city of	995

1Ti	1:17	Now *to* the **K** eternal, immortal, invisible,	995
	6:15	the **K** of kings and Lord of lords,	995
Heb	7: 1	This Melchizedek was **k** of Salem and priest	995
	7: 2	First, his name means "**k** of righteousness";	995
	7: 2	"**k** of Salem" means "king of peace."	995
	7: 2	"king of Salem" means "**k** of peace."	995
1Pe	2:13	whether *to* the **k**, as the supreme authority,	995
	2:17	fear God, honor the **k**.	995
Rev	9:11	as **k** over them the angel of the Abyss,	995
	15: 3	Just and true are your ways, **K** of the ages.	995
	17:11	and now is not, is an eighth **k**.	NIG
	17:14	because he is Lord of lords and **K**	995
	19:16	**K** OF KINGS AND LORD OF LORDS.	995

KING'S (197) [KING]

Ge	14:17	the Valley of Shaveh (that is, the **K** Valley).	4889
	39:20	where the **k** prisoners were confined.	4889
Nu	20:17	the **k** highway and not turn to the right or to	4889
	21:22	along the **k** highway until we have passed	4889
Jdg	3:21	and plunged it into **the k** belly.	2257
1Sa	18:18	I should become the **k** son-in-law?"	4200+4889
	18:23	matter to become the **k** son-in-law?	928+4889
	18:26	pleased to become the **k** son-in-law.	928+4889
	18:27	that he might become the **k** son-in-law.	928+4889
	20:29	That is why he has not come to the **k** table."	4889
	21: 8	because the **k** business was urgent."	4889
	22:14	the **k** son-in-law, captain of your bodyguard	4889
	22:17	But the **k** officials were not willing to raise	4889
	26:16	Where are the **k** spear and water jug	4889
	26:22	"Here is the **k** spear," David answered.	4889
2Sa	9:11	at David's table like one of the **k** sons.	4889
	9:13	because he always ate at the **k** table,	4889
	11: 1	**the k** men and the whole Israelite army.	2257S
	11:20	the **k** anger may flare up,	4889
	11:24	and some of the **k** men died.	4889
	13: 4	He asked Amnon, "Why do you, the **k** son,	4889
	13:23	he invited all the **k** sons to come there.	4889
	13:27	with him Amnon and the rest of the **k** sons.	4889
	13:29	Then all the **k** sons got up,	4889
	13:30	"Absalom has struck down all the **k** sons;	4889
	13:33	about the report that all the **k** sons are dead.	4889
	13:35	"See, the **k** sons are here;	4889
	13:36	As he finished speaking, the **k** sons came in,	4889
	14: 1	of Zeruiah knew that the **k** heart longed	4889
	14:28	in Jerusalem without seeing the **k** face.	4889
	14:32	Now then, I want to see the **k** face,	4889
	15:15	The **k** officials answered him,	4889
	15:35	Tell them anything you hear in the **k** palace.	4889
	16: 2	donkeys are for the **k** household to ride on,	4889
	16: 6	He pelted David and all the **k** officials	4889
	18:12	I would not lift my hand against the **k** son.	4889
	18:18	in the **K** Valley as a monument to himself,	4889
	18:20	because the **k** son is dead."	4889
	18:29	as Joab was about to send the **k** servant	4889
	19:18	at the ford to take the **k** household over and	4889
	19:42	Have we eaten any of the **k** provisions?	4889
	24: 4	The **k** word, however, overruled Joab and	4889
1Ki	1: 9	He invited all his brothers, the **k** sons,	4889
	1:19	and sheep, and has invited all the **k** sons,	4889
	1:25	He has invited all the **k** sons,	4889
	1:28	So she came into the **k** presence and stood	4889
	1:44	and they have put him on the **k** mule,	4889
	2:19	He had a throne brought for the **k** mother,	4889
	4:27	and all who came to the **k** table.	4889
	5:17	At the **k** command they removed from	4889
	13: 6	and the **k** hand was restored and became	4889
	22: 6	"for the Lord will give it into the **k** hand."	4889
	22:12	the LORD will give it into the **k** hand."	4889
	22:15	the LORD will give it into the **k** hand."	4889
2Ki	8:15	the ruler of the city and to Joash the **k** son	4889
	8:15	in water and spread it over **the k** face,	2257S
	9:34	"and bury her, for she was a **k** daughter."	4889
	11: 4	Then he showed them the **k** son.	4889
	11:12	Jehoiada brought out the **k** son and put	4889
	13:16	Elisha put his hands on the **k** hands.	4889
	15: 5	Jotham the **k** son had charge of the palace	4889
	16:15	the **k** burnt offering and his grain offering,	4889
	22:12	the secretary and Asaiah the **k** attendant:	4889
	24:15	from Jerusalem to Babylon the **k** mother,	4889
	25: 4	between the two walls near the **k** garden,	4889
	25:29	of his life ate regularly at the **k** table.	2257S
1Ch	9:18	being stationed at the **K** Gate on the east,	4889
	18:17	sons were chief officials at the **k** side.	4889
	21: 4	The **k** word, however, overruled Joab;	4889
	21: 6	the **k** command was repulsive to him.	4889
	25: 2	who prophesied under the **k** supervision.	4889
	25: 5	All these were sons of Heman the **k** seer.	4889
	26:30	of the LORD and for the **k** service.	4889
	27:32	of Hacmoni took care of the **k** sons.	4889
	27:33	Ahithophel was the **k** counselor.	4200+4889
	27:33	Hushai the Arkite was the **k** friend.	4889
	29: 6	in charge of the **k** work gave willingly.	4889
2Ch	8:15	They did not deviate from the **k** commands	4889
	18: 5	"for God will give it into the **k** hand,"	4889
	18:11	the LORD will give it into the **k** hand."	4889
	18:25	the ruler of the city and to Joash the **k** son,	4889
	21:17	the goods found in the **k** palace,	4889
	23: 3	"The **k** son shall reign,	4889
	23:11	Jehoiada and his sons brought out the **k** son	4889
	24: 8	At the **k** command,	4889
	24:11	the **k** officials and they saw that there was	4889
	28: 7	killed Maaseiah the **k** son,	4889
	29:25	and Gad the **k** seer and Nathan the prophet;	4889
	30: 6	At the **k** command, couriers went	4889
	34:20	the secretary and Asaiah the **k** attendant:	4889
	35: 7	all from the **k** own possessions.	4889

2Ch	35:15	Asaph, Heman and Jeduthun the **k** seer.	4889
Ezr	7:27	into the **k** heart to bring honor to the house	4889
	7:28	and all the **k** powerful officials.	4889
	8:36	the **k** orders to the royal satraps and to	4889
Ne	2: 8	Asaph, keeper of the **k** forest,	4200+4889
	2: 9	and gave them the **k** letters.	4889
	2:14	the **K** Pool, but there was not enough room	4889
	3:15	Pool of Siloam, by the **K** Garden,	4889
	5: 4	to pay the **k** tax on our fields and vineyards.	4889
	11:23	The singers were under the **k** orders,	4889
	11:24	was the **k** agent in all affairs relating to	4889
Est	1: 5	in the enclosed garden of the **k** palace,	4889
	1: 7	in keeping with the **k** liberality.	4889
	1: 8	By the **k** command each guest was allowed	NIH
	1:12	the attendants delivered the **k** command,	4889
	1:18	to all the **k** nobles in the same way.	4889
	1:20	Then when the **k** edict is proclaimed	4889
	2: 2	Then the **k** personal attendants proposed,	4889
	2: 3	**k** eunuch, who is in charge of the women;	4889
	2: 8	the **k** order and edict had been proclaimed,	4889
	2: 8	also was taken to the **k** palace and entrusted	4889
	2: 9	the **k** palace and moved her and her maids	4889
	2:13	with her from the harem to the **k** palace.	4889
	2:14	the **k** eunuch who was in charge of	4889
	2:15	**k** eunuch who was in charge of the harem,	4889
	2:19	Mordecai was sitting at the **k** gate,	4889
	2:21	the time Mordecai was sitting at the **k** gate,	4889
	2:21	of the **k** officers who guarded the doorway,	4889
	3: 2	the royal officials at the **k** gate knelt down	4889
	3: 3	royal officials at the **k** gate asked Mordecai,	4889
	3: 3	"Why do you disobey the **k** command?"	4889
	3: 8	and who do not obey the **k** laws;	4889
	3: 8	not in the **k** best interest to tolerate them.	4889
	3:12	Haman's orders to the **k** satraps,	4889
	3:13	the **k** provinces with the order to destroy,	4889
	3:15	Spurred on by the **k** command,	4889
	4: 2	But he went only as far as the **k** gate,	4889
	4: 5	one of the **k** eunuchs assigned to attend her,	4889
	4: 6	of the city in front of the **k** gate.	4889
	4: 8	to urge her to go into the **k** presence to beg	4889
	4:11	"All the **k** officials and the people of	4889
	4:13	because you are in the **k** house you alone	4889
	5: 1	in front of the **k** hall.	4889
	5: 8	Then I will answer the **k** question."	4889
	5: 9	the **k** gate and observed that he neither rose	4889
	5:13	that Jew Mordecai sitting at the **k** gate."	4889
	6: 2	**k** officers who guarded the doorway,	4889
	6: 9	to one of the **k** most noble princes.	4889
	6:10	Mordecai the Jew, who sits at the **k** gate.	4889
	6:12	Afterward Mordecai returned to the **k** gate.	4889
	6:14	the **k** eunuchs arrived and	4889
	7: 8	As soon as the word left the **k** mouth,	4889
	7:10	Then the **k** fury subsided.	4889
	8: 5	to destroy the Jews in all the **k** provinces.	4889
	8: 8	Now write another decree in the **k** name	4889
	8: 8	and seal it with the **k** signet ring—	4889
	8: 8	in the **k** name and sealed with his ring can	4889
	8:10	sealed the dispatches with the **k** signet ring,	4889
	8:11	The **k** edict granted the Jews in every city	4889
	8:14	raced out, spurred on by the **k** command.	4889
	8:15	the **k** presence wearing royal garments	4889
	9: 3	the **k** administrators helped the Jews,	4200+4889
	9:12	in the rest of the **k** provinces?	4889
	9:16	of the Jews who were in the **k** provinces	4889
	9:25	But when the plot came to the **k** attention,	4889
Ps	45: 5	the hearts of the **k** enemies.	4889
	61: 6	Increase the days of the **k** life,	4889
Pr	14:28	A large population is a **k** glory,	4889
	16:14	A **k** wrath is a messenger of death,	4889
	16:15	When a **k** face brightens, it means life;	4889
	19:12	A **k** rage is like the roar of a lion,	4889
	20: 2	A **k** wrath is like the roar of a lion;	4889
	21: 1	The **k** heart is in the hand of the LORD;	4889
	25: 5	remove the wicked from the **k** presence,	4889
	25: 6	Do not exalt yourself in the **k** presence,	4889
Ecc	2:12	What more can the **k** successor do than	4889
		what has already been done?	
	4:15	sun followed the youth, the **k** successor.	2257S
	8: 2	Obey the **k** command, I say,	4889
	8: 3	not be in a hurry to leave the **k** presence.	2257S
	8: 4	Since a **k** word is supreme,	4889
Isa	23:15	seventy years, the span of a **k** life.	4889
Jer	38: 6	the **k** son, which was in the courtyard of	4889
	39: 4	the city at night by way of the **k** garden,	4889
	41: 1	and had been one of the **k** officers,	4889
	41:10	the **k** daughters along with all	4889
	43: 6	and the **k** daughters whom Nebuzaradan	4889
	52: 7	between the two walls near the **k** garden,	4889
	52:33	of his life ate regularly at the **k** table.	2257S
Da	1: 4	and qualified to serve in the **k** palace.	4889
	1: 5	of food and wine from the **k** table.	4889
	1: 5	after that they were to enter the **k** service.	4889
	1:19	so they entered the **k** service.	4889
	2:14	Arioch, the commander of the **k** guard,	10421
	2:15	He asked the **k** officer,	10421
	3:22	The **k** command was so urgent and	10421
	3:28	and defied the **k** command and were willing	10421
	5: 8	Then all the **k** wise men came in,	10421
	6:24	At the **k** command, the men who had	10421
	8:27	I got up and went about the **k** business.	4889
	11:26	Those who eat from the **k** provisions will	2257S
Am	7: 1	after the **k** *share* had been harvested and	4889
	7:13	because this is the **k** sanctuary and	4889
Zep	1: 8	the princes and the **k** sons and all those clad	4889
Ac	12:20	because they depended on the **k** country	997
Heb	11:23	and they were not afraid of the **k** edict.	995
	11:27	not fearing the **k** anger;	995

KINGDOM (302) [KING]

Ge	10:10	The first centers of his **k** were Babylon,	4930
	20: 9	upon me and my **k**?	4930
Ex	19: 6	be for me a **k** *of* priests and a holy nation.'	4930
Nu	24: 7	their **k** will be exalted.	4895
	32:33	the **k** *of* Sihon king of the Amorites and	4930
	32:33	of Sihon king of the Amorites and the **k**	4930
Dt	3: 4	whole region of Argob, Og's **k** in Bashan.	4930
	3:10	towns of Og's **k** in Bashan.	4930
	3:13	all of Bashan, the **k** *of* Og,	4930
	17:18	When he takes the throne of his **k**,	4930
	17:20	a long time over his **k** in Israel.	4930
Jos	13:12	the whole **k** *of* Og in Bashan.	4931
1Sa	13:13	he would have established your **k**	4930
	13:14	But now your **k** will not endure;	4930
	15:28	"The LORD has torn the **k** *of* Israel	4931
	18: 8	What more can he get but the **k**?"	4867
	20:31	neither you nor your **k** will be established.	4895
	24:20	surely be king and that the **k** *of* Israel will	4930
	28:17	the **k** out of your hands and given it to one	4930
2Sa	3:10	and transfer the **k** from the house of Saul	4930
	3:28	"I and my **k** are forever innocent before	4930
	5:12	as king over Israel and had exalted his **k** for	4930
	7:12	and I will establish his **k**.	4930
	7:13	I will establish the throne of his **k** forever.	4930
	7:16	Your house and your **k** will endure forever	4930
	8: 6	He put garrisons in the **Aramean k**	806
	16: 3	Israel will give me back my grandfather's **k**.	4931
	16: 8	The LORD has handed the **k** over	4867
1Ki	2:15	"As you know," he said, "the **k** was mine.	4867
	2:15	and the **k** has gone to my brother;	4867
	2:22	You might as well request the **k** for him—	4867
	2:46	The **k** was now firmly established	4930
	10:20	like it had ever been made for any other **k**.	4930
	11:11	the **k** away from you and give it to one	4930
	11:13	Yet I will not tear the whole **k** from him,	4930
	11:31	to tear the **k** out of Solomon's hand	4930
	11:34	" 'But I will not take the whole **k** out	4930
	11:35	I will take the **k** from his son's hands	4867
	12:21	and to regain the **k** for Rehoboam son	4867
	12:26	"The **k** will now likely revert to the house	4930
	14: 8	I tore the **k** away from the house of David	4930
	18:10	or **k** where my master has not sent someone	4930
	18:10	a nation or **k** claimed you were not there,	4930
2Ki	14: 5	After the **k** was firmly in his grasp,	4930
	15:19	and strengthen his own hold on the **k**.	4930
	20:13	or in all his **k** that Hezekiah did	4939
1Ch	10:14	and turned the **k** over to David son of Jesse.	4867
	12:23	at Hebron to turn Saul's **k** over to him, as	4895
	14: 2	and that his **k** had been highly exalted for	4895
	16:20	nation to nation, from one **k** to another.	4930
	17:11	and I will establish his **k**.	4895
	17:14	over my house and my **k** forever;	4895
	18: 6	He put garrisons in the **Aramean k**	806
	22:10	the throne of his **k** over Israel forever."	4895
	28: 5	to sit on the throne of the **k** *of* the LORD	4895
	28: 7	I will establish his **k** forever	4867
	29:11	Yours, O LORD, is the **k**;	4930
2Ch	1: 1	over his **k**, for the LORD his God was	4895
	9:19	like it had ever been made for any other **k**.	4930
	11: 1	and to regain the **k** for Rehoboam.	4930
	11:17	They strengthened the **k** *of* Judah	4895
	13: 8	now you plan to resist the **k** *of* the LORD,	4930
	14: 5	and the **k** was at peace under him.	4930
	17: 5	The LORD established the **k**	4930
	20:30	And the **k** *of* Jehoshaphat was at peace,	4895
	21: 3	but he had given the **k** to Jehoram	4930
	21: 4	Jehoram established himself firmly over his	
		father's **k**,	4930
	22: 9	of Ahaziah powerful enough to retain the **k**.	4930
	25: 3	After the **k** was firmly in his control,	4930
	29:21	as a sin offering for the **k**,	4930
	32:15	for no god of any nation or **k** has been able	4930
	33:13	to Jerusalem and to his **k**.	4895
	36:20	and his sons until the **k** *of* Persia came	4895
Ezr	7:13	I decree that any of the Israelites in my **k**,	10424
Ne	9:35	Even while they were in their **k**,	4895
Est	1: 4	the vast wealth of his **k** and the splendor	4895
	1:14	to the king and were highest in the **k**.	4895
	1:22	He sent dispatches to all parts of the **k**,	4889
	3: 6	throughout the whole **k** *of* Xerxes.	4895
	3: 8	of your **k** whose customs are different	4930
	5: 3	Even up to half the **k**, it will be given you."	4895
	5: 6	Even up to half the **k**, it will be granted."	4895
	7: 2	Even up to half the **k**, it will be granted."	4895
	9:30	to all the Jews in the 127 provinces of the **k**	4895
Ps	45: 6	of justice will be the scepter of your **k**.	4895
	103:19	and his **k** rules over all.	4895
	105:13	from *one* **k** to another.	4930
	145:11	the glory of your **k** and speak of your might,	4895
	145:12	and the glorious splendor of your **k**.	4895
	145:13	Your **k** is an everlasting kingdom,	4895
	145:13	Your kingdom is an everlasting **k**,	4895
Ecc	4:14	born in poverty within his **k**.	4895
Isa	9: 7	on David's throne and over his **k**,	4930
	19: 2	city against city, **k** against kingdom.	4930
	19: 2	city against city, kingdom against **k**.	4930
	34:12	have nothing there to be called a **k**,	4867
	39: 2	or in all his **k** that Hezekiah did	4939
	60:12	or **k** that will not serve you will perish;	4930
Jer	18: 7	at any time I announce that a nation or **k** is	4930
	18: 9	a nation or **k** is to be built up and planted,	4930
	27: 8	or **k** will not serve Nebuchadnezzar king	4930
La	2: 2	He has brought her **k** and its princes down	4930
Eze	17:14	so that the **k** would be brought low,	4930
	29:14	There they will be a lowly **k**.	4930

Da	1:20	and enchanters in his whole **k**.	4895
	2:39	"After you, another **k** will rise,	10424
	2:39	Next, a third **k**, one of bronze,	10424
	2:40	Finally, there will be a fourth **k**,	10424
	2:41	so this will be a divided **k**;	10424
	2:42	**k** will be partly strong and partly brittle.	10424
	2:44	of heaven will set up a **k** that will never	10424
	4: 3	His **k** is an eternal kingdom;	10424
	4: 3	His kingdom is an eternal **k**;	10424
	4:18	of the wise men in my **k** can interpret it	10424
	4:26	the tree with its roots means that your **k**	10424
	4:34	**k** endures from generation to generation.	10424
	4:36	to me for the glory of my **k**.	10424
	5: 7	be made the third highest ruler in the **k**."	10424
	5:11	your **k** who has the spirit of the holy gods	10424
	5:16	be made the third highest ruler in the **k**."	10424
	5:28	Your **k** is divided and given to the Medes	10424
	5:29	the third highest ruler in the **k**.	10424
	5:31	and Darius the Mede took over the **k**,	10424
	6: 1	to rule throughout the **k**,	10424
	6: 3	to set him over the whole **k**.	10424
	6:26	that in every part of my **k** people must fear	10424
	6:26	his **k** will not be destroyed,	10424
	7:14	his **k** is one that will never be destroyed.	10424
	7:18	of the Most High will receive the **k**	10424
	7:22	the time came when they possessed the **k**.	10424
	7:23	a fourth **k** that will appear on earth.	10424
	7:24	The ten horns are ten kings who will come	
		from this **k**.	10424
	7:27	His **k** will be an everlasting kingdom,	10424
	7:27	His kingdom will be an everlasting **k**,	10424
	9: 1	who was made ruler over the Babylonian **k**	4895
	10:13	the Persian **k** resisted me twenty-one days.	4895
	11: 2	up everyone against the **k** *of* Greece.	4895
	11: 5	and will rule his own **k** with great power.	4939
	11:17	with the might of his entire **k** and will make	4895
	11:17	in marriage in order to overthrow the **k**,	2023S
	11:21	the **k** when its people feel secure,	4895
Hos	1: 4	and I will put an end to the **k** *of* Israel.	4931
Am	7:13	and the temple of the **k**."	4930
	9: 8	of the Sovereign LORD are on the sinful **k**	4930
Ob	1:21	And the **k** will be the LORD's.	4867
Mt	3: 2	"Repent, for the **k** of heaven is near."	993
	4:17	"Repent, for the **k** of heaven is near."	993
	4:23	preaching the good news *of* the **k**,	993
	5: 3	for theirs is the **k** of heaven.	993
	5:10	for theirs is the **k** of heaven.	993
	5:19	to do the same will be called least in the **k**	993
	5:19	be called great in the **k** of heaven.	993
	5:20	you will certainly not enter the **k** of heaven.	993
	6:10	your **k** come, your will be done on earth	993
	6:33	But seek first his **k** and his righteousness,	993
	7:21	'Lord, Lord,' will enter the **k** of heaven,	993
	8:11	Isaac and Jacob in the **k** of heaven.	993
	8:12	the subjects of the **k** will be thrown outside,	993
	9:35	*of* the **k** and healing every disease	993
	10: 7	'The **k** of heaven is near.'	993
	11:11	in the **k** of heaven is greater than he.	993
	11:12	of heaven has been forcefully advancing,	993
	12:25	"Every **k** divided against itself will	993
	12:26	How then can his **k** stand?	993
	12:28	then the **k** of God has come upon you.	993
	13:11	*of* the **k** of heaven has been given to you,	993
	13:19	*about* the **k** and does not understand it,	993
	13:24	"The **k** of heaven is like a man who	993
	13:31	"The **k** of heaven is like a mustard seed,	993
	13:33	"The **k** of heaven is like yeast that	993
	13:38	the good seed stands for the sons *of* the **k**.	993
	13:41	and they will weed out of his **k** everything	993
	13:43	the righteous will shine like the sun in the **k**	993
	13:44	**k** of heaven is like treasure hidden in a field.	993
	13:45	the **k** of heaven is like a merchant looking	993
	13:47	the **k** of heaven is like a net that was let	993
	13:52	*about* the **k** of heaven is like the owner of	993
	16:19	I will give you the keys *of* the **k** of heaven;	993
	16:28	the Son of Man coming in his **k**."	993
	18: 1	"Who is the greatest in the **k** of heaven?"	993
	18: 3	you will never enter the **k** of heaven.	993
	18: 4	like this child is the greatest in the **k**	993
	18:23	the **k** of heaven is like a king who wanted	993
	19:12	because of the **k** of heaven.	993
	19:14	the **k** of heaven belongs to such as these."	993
	19:23	for a rich man to enter the **k** of heaven.	993
	19:24	of a needle than for a rich man to enter the **k**	993
	20: 1	"For the **k** of heaven is like a landowner	993
	20:21	and the other at your left in your **k**."	993
	21:31	and the prostitutes are entering the **k** of God	993
	21:43	"Therefore I tell you that the **k** of God will	993
	22: 2	"The **k** of heaven is like a king who	993
	23:13	You shut the **k** of heaven in men's faces.	993
	24: 7	and **k** against kingdom.	993
	24: 7	and kingdom against **k**.	993
	24:14	the **k** will be preached in the whole world as	993
	25: 1	"At that time the **k** of heaven will be	993
	25:34	the **k** prepared for you since the creation of	993
	26:29	with you in my Father's **k**."	993
Mk	1:15	"The **k** of God is near.	993
	3:24	If a **k** is divided against itself,	993
	3:24	against itself, that **k** cannot stand.	993
	4:11	"The secret *of* the **k** of God has been given	993
	4:26	"This is what the **k** of God is like.	993
	4:30	"What shall we say the **k** of God is like,	993
	6:23	I will give you, up to half my **k**."	993
	9: 1	not taste death before they see the **k**	993
	9:47	It is better for you to enter the **k** of God	993
	10:14	for the **k** of God belongs to such as these.	993
	10:15	anyone who will not receive the **k** of God	993

Mk	10:23	hard it is for the rich to enter the k of God!"	993
	10:24	how hard it is to enter the k of God!	993
	10:25	of a needle than for a rich man to enter the k	993
	11:10	the coming k of our father David!"	993
	12:34	"You are not far from the k of God."	993
	13: 8	and k against kingdom.	993
	13: 8	and kingdom against k.	993
	14:25	until that day when I drink it anew in the k	993
	15:43	who was himself waiting for the k of God.	993
Lk	1:33	his k will never end."	993
	4:43	of the k of God to the other towns also,	993
	6:20	for yours is the k of God.	993
	7:28	in the k of God is greater than he."	993
	8: 1	proclaiming the good news of the k of God.	993
	8:10	of the k of God has been given to you, but	993
	9: 2	and he sent them out to preach the k of God	993
	9:11	and spoke to them about the k of God,	993
	9:27	not taste death before they see the k	993
	9:60	but you go and proclaim the k of God."	993
	9:62	and looks back is fit for service in the k	993
	10: 9	'The k of God is near you.'	993
	10:11	Yet be sure of this: The k of God is near.'	993
	11: 2	hallowed be your name, your k come.	993
	11:17	"Any k divided against itself will be ruined,	993
	11:18	how can his k stand?	993
	11:20	then the k of God has come to you.	993
	12:31	But seek his k, and these things will be	993
	12:32	pleased to give you the k.	993
	13:18	Jesus asked, "What is the k of God like?	993
	13:20	"What shall I compare the k of God to?	993
	13:28	Isaac and Jacob and all the prophets in the k	993
	13:29	at the feast in the k of God	993
	14:15	the man who will eat at the feast in the k	993
	16:16	of the k of God is being preached,	993
	17:20	when the k of God would come,	993
	17:20	"The k of God does not come	993
	17:21	because the k of God is within you."	993
	18:16	for the k of God belongs to such as these.	993
	18:17	anyone who will not receive the k of God	993
	18:24	hard it is for the rich to enter the k of God!	993
	18:25	of a needle than for a rich man to enter the k	993
	18:29	or parents or children for the sake of the k	993
	19:11	the k of God was going to appear at once.	993
	21:10	and k against kingdom.	993
	21:10	and kingdom against k.	993
	21:31	you know that the k of God is near.	993
	22:16	until it finds fulfillment in the k of God."	993
	22:18	of the vine until the k of God comes."	993
	22:29	And I confer on you a k,	993
	22:30	at my table in my k and sit on thrones,	993
	23:42	remember me when you come into your k."	993
	23:51	of Arimathea and he was waiting for the k	993
Jn	3: 3	the k of God unless he is born again."	993
	3: 5	the k of God unless he is born of water and	993
	18:36	Jesus said, "My k is not of this world.	993
	18:36	But now my k is from another place."	993
Ac	1: 3	a period of forty days and spoke about the k	993
	1: 6	at this time going to restore the k to Israel?"	993
	8:12	the good news of the k of God and the name	993
	14:22	through many hardships to enter the k of God	993
	19: 8	arguing persuasively about the k of God.	993
	20:25	the k will ever see me again.	993
	28:23	and declared to them the k of God and tried	993
	28:31	without hindrance he preached the k of God	993
Ro	14:17	For the k of God is not a matter of eating	993
1Co	4:20	For the k of God is not a matter of talk but	993
	6: 9	the wicked will not inherit the k of God?	993
	6:10	nor swindlers will inherit the k of God.	993
	15:24	when he hands over the k to God the Father	993
	15:50	flesh and blood cannot inherit the k of God,	993
Gal	5:21	like this will not inherit the k of God.	993
Eph	2: 2	of this world and of the ruler of the k of	2026
	5: 5	has any inheritance in the k of Christ and	993
Col	1:12	the inheritance of the saints in the k of light.	NIG
	1:13	of darkness and brought us into the k of	993
	4:11	among my fellow workers for the k of God,	993
1Th	2:12	who calls you into his k and glory.	993
2Th	1: 5	a result you will be counted worthy of the k	993
2Ti	4: 1	and in view of his appearing and his k,	993
	4:18	and will bring me safely to his heavenly k.	993
Heb	1: 8	righteousness will be the scepter of your k.	993
	12:28	we are receiving a k that cannot be shaken,	993
Jas	2: 5	the k he promised those who love him?	993
2Pe	1:11	a rich welcome into the eternal k	993
Rev	1: 6	and has made us to be a k and priests	993
	1: 9	in the suffering and k and patient endurance	993
	5:10	You have made them to be a k and priests	993
	11:15	"The k of the world has become	993
	11:15	the world has become the k of our Lord and	NIG
	12:10	the salvation and the power and the k	993
	16:10	and his k was plunged into darkness.	993
	17:12	ten kings who have not yet received a k,	993

KINGDOMS (61) [KING]

Dt	3:21	to all the k over there where you are going.	4930
	28:25	a thing of horror to all the k on earth.	4930
Jos	11:10	(Hazor had been the head of all these k.)	4930
1Sa	10:18	of Egypt and all the k that oppressed you.'	4930
1Ki	4:21	over all the k from the River to the land of	4930
	4:24	For he ruled over all the k west of the River,	4889
2Ki	19:15	you alone are God over all the k of	4930
	19:19	that all k on earth may know that you,	4930
1Ch	29:30	and Israel and of all the k of the other lands.	
2Ch	17:10	on all the k of the lands surrounding Judah,	4930
	20: 6	You rule over all the k of the nations.	4930
	20:29	of God came upon all the k of the countries	4930

2Ch	36:23	the k of the earth and he has appointed me	4930
Ezr	1: 2	the k of the earth and he has appointed me	4930
Ne	9:22	"You gave them k and nations,	4930
Ps	46: 6	Nations are in uproar, k fall;	4930
	68:32	Sing to God, O k of the earth,	4930
	79: 6	the k that do not call on your name;	4930
	102:22	and the k assemble to worship the LORD.	4930
Isa	10:10	As my hand seized the k of the idols,	4930
	10:10	k whose images excelled those of Jerusalem	NIH
	13: 4	Listen, an uproar among the k,	4930
	13:19	Babylon, the jewel of k,	4930
	23:11	over the sea and made its k tremble.	4930
	23:11	and will ply her trade with all the k on	4930
	37:16	you alone are God over all the k	4930
	37:20	that all k on earth may know that you alone,	4930
	47: 5	no more will you be called queen of k.	4930
Jer	1:10	over nations and k to uproot and tear down,	4930
	1:15	the peoples of the northern k,"	4930
	10: 7	of the nations and in all their k,	4895
	15: 4	I will make them abhorrent to all the k of	4930
	24: 9	and an offense to all the k of the earth,	4930
	25:26	all the k on the face of the earth.	4930
	28: 8	against many countries and great k.	4930
	29:18	and will make them abhorrent to all the k of	4930
	33:24	the two k he chose"?	5476
	34: 1	and all his army and all the k and peoples in	4930
	34:17	I will make you abhorrent to all the k of	4930
	49:28	Concerning Kedar and the k of Hazor,	4930
	51:20	with you I destroy k,	4930
	51:27	summon against her these k:	4930
Eze	29:15	of k and will never again exalt itself above	4930
	37:22	be two nations or be divided into two k.	4930
Da	2:44	It will crush all those k and bring them to	10424
	4:17	that the Most High is sovereign over the k	10424
	4:25	that the Most High is sovereign over the k	10424
	4:32	that the Most High is sovereign over the k	10424
	5:21	the Most High God is sovereign over the k	10424
	7:17	'The four great beasts are four k	10421
	7:23	the other k and will devour the whole earth,	10424
	7:27	of the k under the whole heaven will	10424
	8:22	the one that was broken off represent four k	4895
Am	6: 2	Are they better off than your two k?	4930
Na	3: 5	and the k your shame.	4930
Zep	3: 8	the k and to pour out my wrath on them—	4930
Hag	2:22	and shatter the power of the foreign k.	4930
Mt	4: 8	and showed him all the k of the world	993
Lk	4: 5	and showed him in an instant all the k of	993
Heb	11:33	who through faith conquered k,	993

KINGS (324) [KING]

Ge	14: 3	All these latter k joined forces in the Valley	NIH
	14: 5	k allied with him went out and defeated	4889
	14: 9	four k against five.	4889
	14:10	when the k of Sodom and Gomorrah fled,	4889
	14:11	The four k seized all the goods of Sodom	NIH
	14:17	and the k allied with him,	4889
	17: 6	and k will come from you.	4889
	17:16	k of peoples will come from her."	4889
	35:11	and k will come from your body.	4889
	36:31	These were the k who reigned in Edom	4889
Nu	31: 8	the five k of Midian.	4889
Dt	3: 8	So at that time we took from these two k of	4889
	3:21	LORD your God has done to these two k.	4889
	4:47	the two Amorite k east of the Jordan.	4889
	7:24	He will give their k into your hand,	4889
	31: 4	Sihon and Og, the k of the Amorites,	4889
Jos	2:10	the two k of the Amorites east of	4889
	5: 1	when all the Amorite k west of the Jordan	4889
	5: 1	of the Jordan and all the Canaanite k along	4889
	9: 1	when all the k west of the Jordan heard	4889
	9: 1	of the Great Sea as far as Lebanon (the k of	NIH
	9:10	that he did to the two k of the Amorites east	4889
	10: 5	Then the five k of the Amorites—	4889
	10: 5	the k of Jerusalem, Hebron, Jarmuth,	4889
	10: 6	because all the Amorite k from	4889
	10:16	the five k had fled and hidden in the cave	4889
	10:17	the five k had been found hiding in the cave	4889
	10:22	the cave and bring those five k out to me."	4889
	10:23	So they brought the five k out of the cave—	4889
	10:23	the k of Jerusalem, Hebron, Jarmuth,	4889
	10:24	When they had brought these k to Joshua,	4889
	10:24	and put your feet on the necks of these k."	4889
	10:26	killed the k and hung them on five trees,	4392S
	10:40	together with all their k.	4889
	10:42	All these k and their lands Joshua	4889
	11: 1	to the k of Shimron and Acshaph,	4889
	11: 2	the northern k who were in the mountains,	4889
	11: 5	All these k joined forces	4889
	11:12	Joshua took all these royal cities and their k	4889
	11:17	He captured all their k and struck them	4889
	11:18	Joshua waged war against all these k for	4889
	12: 1	These are the k of the land whom	4889
	12: 7	These are the k of the land that Joshua and	4889
	12:24	the king of Tirzah one thirty-one k in all.	4889
	24:12	also the two Amorite k.	4889
Jdg	1: 7	"Seventy k with their thumbs	4889
	5: 3	"Hear this, you k!	4889
	5:19	"K came, they fought;	4889
	5:19	the k of Canaan fought at Taanach by	4889
	8: 5	and Zalmunna, the k of Midian."	4889
	8:12	Zebah and Zalmunna, the two k of Midian,	4889
	8:26	by the k of Midian or the chains that were	4889
1Sa	14:47	Edom, the k of Zobah, and the Philistines.	4889
	27: 6	belonged to the k of Judah ever since.	4889

2Sa	10:19	the k who were vassals of Hadadezer saw	4889
	11: 1	at the time when k go off to war,	4889
1Ki	3:13	in your lifetime you will have no equal among k.	4889
	4:34	sent by all the k of the world,	4889
	10:15	the Arabian k and the governors of the land.	4889
	10:23	in riches and wisdom than all the k of the	4889
	10:29	the k of the Hittites and of the Arameans.	4889
	14:19	are written in the book of the annals of the k	4889
	14:29	in the book of the annals of the k of Judah?	4889
	15: 7	in the book of the annals of the k of Judah?	4889
	15:23	in the book of the annals of the k of Judah?	4889
	15:31	in the book of the annals of the k of Israel?	4889
	16: 5	in the book of the annals of the k of Israel?	4889
	16:14	in the book of the annals of the k of Israel?	4889
	16:20	in the book of the annals of the k of Israel?	4889
	16:27	in the book of the annals of the k of Israel?	4889
	16:33	to anger than did all the k of Israel	4889
	20: 1	by thirty-two k with their horses	4889
	20:12	and the k were drinking in their tents,	4889
	20:16	while Ben-Hadad and the 32 k allied	4889
	20:24	Remove all the k from their commands	4889
	20:31	the k of the house of Israel are merciful.	4889
	22:39	in the book of the annals of the k of Israel?	4889
	22:45	in the book of the annals of the k of Judah?	4889
2Ki	1:18	in the book of the annals of the k of Israel?	4889
	3:10	the LORD called us three k together only	4889
	3:13	the LORD who called us three k together	4889
	3:21	the Moabites had heard that the k had come	4889
	3:23	"Those k must have fought	4889
	7: 6	the Hittite and Egyptian k to attack us!"	4889
	8:18	He walked in the ways of the k of Israel,	4889
	8:23	in the book of the annals of the k of Judah?	4889
	10: 4	"If two k could not resist him,	4889
	10:34	in the book of the annals of the k of Israel?	4889
	12:18	Jehoram and Ahaziah, the k of Judah—	4889
	12:19	in the book of the annals of the k of Judah?	4889
	13: 8	in the book of the annals of the k of Israel?	4889
	13:12	in the book of the annals of the k of Israel?	4889
	13:13	Jehoash was buried in Samaria with the k	4889
	14:15	in the book of the annals of the k of Israel?	4889
	14:16	and was buried in Samaria with the k	4889
	14:18	in the book of the annals of the k of Judah?	4889
	14:28	in the book of the annals of the k of Israel?	4889
	14:29	rested with his fathers, the k of Israel.	4889
	15: 6	in the book of the annals of the k of Israel.	4889
	15:11	in the book of the annals of the k of Israel.	4889
	15:15	are written in the book of the annals of the k	4889
	15:21	in the book of the annals of the k of Israel?	4889
	15:26	are written in the book of the annals of the k	4889
	15:31	in the book of the annals of the k of Israel?	4889
	15:36	in the book of the annals of the k of Judah?	4889
	16: 3	the k of Israel and even sacrificed his son in	4889
	16:19	in the book of the annals of the k of Judah?	4889
	17: 2	not like the k of Israel who preceded him.	4889
	17: 8	that the k of Israel had introduced.	4889
	18: 5	There was no one like him among all the k	4889
	19:11	Surely you have heard what the k	4889
	19:17	the Assyrian k have laid waste these nations	4889
	20:20	in the book of the annals of the k of Judah?	4889
	21:17	in the book of the annals of the k of Judah?	4889
	21:25	in the book of the annals of the k of Judah?	4889
	23: 5	with the pagan priests appointed by the k	4889
	23:11	that the k of Judah had dedicated to the sun.	4889
	23:12	the k of Judah had erected on the roof near	4889
	23:19	the high places that the k of Israel had built	4889
	23:22	throughout the days of the k of Israel and	4889
	23:22	of the kings of Israel and the k of Judah,	4889
	23:28	in the book of the annals of the k of Judah?	4889
	24: 5	the other k who were with him in Babylon.	4889
	25:28	These were the k who reigned in Edom	4889
1Ch	1:43	in the book of the k of Israel.	4889
	9: 1	for their sake he rebuked k:	4889
	16:21	the k who had come were by themselves in	4889
	19: 9	at the time when k go off to war,	4889
	20: 1	the k of the Hittites and of the Arameans.	4889
2Ch	1:17	Also all the k of Arabia and the governors	4889
	9:14	in riches and wisdom than all the other k of	4889
	9:23	All the k of the earth sought audience	4889
	9:26	over all the k from the River to the land of	4889
	12: 8	between serving me and serving the k	4930
	16:11	are written in the book of the k of Judah	4889
	20:34	which are recorded in the book of the k	4889
	21: 6	He walked in the ways of the k of Israel,	4889
	21:13	But you have walked in the ways of the k	4889
	21:20	but not in the tombs of the k.	4889
	24:16	He was buried with the k in the City	4889
	24:25	but not in the tombs of the k.	4889
	24:27	in the annotations on the book of the k.	4889
	25:26	not written in the book of the k of Judah	4889
	26:23	in a field for burial that belonged to the k,	4889
	27: 7	are written in the book of the k of Israel	4889
	28: 2	of the k of Israel and also made cast idols	4889
	28:23	gods of the k of Aram have helped them,	4889
	28:26	are written in the book of the k of Judah	4889
	28:27	but he was not placed in the tombs of the k	4889
	30: 6	who have escaped from the hand of the k	4889
	32: 4	the k of Assyria come and find plenty	4889
	32:32	in the book of the k of Judah and Israel.	4889
	34:11	the k of Judah had allowed to fall into ruin.	4889
	35:18	of the k of Israel had ever celebrated such	4889
	35:27	are written in the book of the k of Israel	4889
	36: 8	are written in the book of the k of Israel	4889
Ezr	4:15	troublesome to k and provinces,	10421
	4:19	against k and has been a place of rebellion	10421

Ezr	4:20	Jerusalem has had powerful **k** ruling over	10421
	6:14	Darius and Artaxerxes, **k** of Persia.	10421
	7:12	king of **k**, To Ezra the priest,	10421
	9: 7	we and our **k** and our priests	4889
	9: 7	and humiliation at the hand of foreign **k**,	4889
	9: 9	in the sight of the **k** of Persia:	4889
Ne	9:24	to them, along with their **k** and the peoples	4889
	9:32	upon our **k** and leaders,	4889
	9:32	and all your people, from the days of the **k**	4889
	9:34	Our **k**, our leaders, our priests	4889
	9:37	to the **k** you have placed over us.	4889
Est	10: 2	of the annals of the **k** of Media and Persia?	4889
Job	3:14	with **k** and counselors of the earth,	4889
	12:18	the shackles put on by **k** and ties a loincloth	4889
	34:18	Is he not the One who says to **k**,	4889
	36: 7	with **k** and exalts them forever.	4889
Ps	2: 2	The **k** of the earth take their stand and	4889
	2:10	Therefore, you **k**, be wise;	4889
	45: 9	of **k** are among your honored women;	4889
	47: 9	for the **k** of the earth belong to God;	4482
	48: 4	When the **k** joined forces,	4889
	68:12	"**K** and armies flee in haste;	4889
	68:14	the Almighty scattered the **k** in the land,	4889
	68:29	at Jerusalem **k** will bring you gifts.	4889
	72:10	The **k** of Tarshish and of distant shores	4889
	72:10	**k** of Sheba and Seba will present him gifts.	4889
	72:11	All **k** will bow down to him	4889
	76:12	he is feared by the **k** of the earth.	4889
	89:27	the most exalted of the **k** of the earth.	4889
	102:15	all the **k** of the earth will revere your glory.	4889
	105:14	for their sake he rebuked **k**:	4889
	110: 5	he will crush **k** on the day of his wrath.	4889
	119:46	of your statutes before **k** and will not be put	4889
	135:10	down many nations and killed mighty **k**—	4889
	135:11	of Bashan and all the **k** of Canaan—	4930
	136:17	who struck down great **k**,	4889
	136:18	killed mighty **k**—His love endures forever.	4889
	138: 4	May all the **k** of the earth praise you,	4889
	144:10	to the One who gives victory to **k**,	4889
	148:11	**k** of the earth and all nations,	4889
	149: 8	to bind their **k** with fetters,	4889
Pr	8:15	By me **k** reign and rulers make laws	4889
	16:12	**K** detest wrongdoing, for a throne is	4889
	16:13	**K** take pleasure in honest lips;	4889
	22:29	He will serve before **k**;	4889
	25: 2	to search out a matter is the glory of **k**.	4889
	25: 3	so the hearts of **k** are unsearchable.	4889
	31: 3	your vigor on those who ruin **k**.	4889
	31: 4	"It is not for **k**, O Lemuel—	4889
	31: 4	not for **k** to drink wine,	4889
Ecc	2: 8	and the treasure of **k** and provinces.	4889
Isa	1: 1	Jotham, Ahaz and Hezekiah, **k** of Judah.	4889
	7:16	of the two **k** you dread will be laid waste.	4889
	10: 8	'Are not my commanders all **k**?' he says.	4889
	10:13	like a mighty one I subdued their **k**.	3782
	14: 9	all *those* who were **k** over the nations.	4889
	14:18	All the **k** of the nations lie in state,	4889
	19:11	a disciple of the ancient **k**"?	4889
	24:21	the powers in the heavens above and the **k**	4889
	37:11	Surely you have heard what the **k**	4889
	37:18	Assyrian **k** have laid waste all these peoples	4889
	41: 2	He hands nations over to him and subdues **k**	4889
	45: 1	to subdue nations before him and to strip **k**	4889
	49: 7	"**K** will see you and rise up,	4889
	49:23	**K** will be your foster fathers,	4889
	52:15	and **k** will shut their mouths because of him.	4889
	60: 3	and **k** to the brightness of your dawn.	4889
	60:10	and their **k** will serve you.	4889
	60:11	their **k** led in triumphal procession.	4889
	62: 2	and all **k** your glory;	4889
Jer	1:15	"Their **k** will come and set up their thrones	408S
	1:18	against the **k** of Judah, its officials,	4889
	2:26	they, their **k** and their officials,	4889
	8: 1	the bones of the **k** and officials of Judah,	4889
	13:13	including the **k** who sit on David's throne,	4889
	17:19	through which the **k** of Judah go in and out;	4889
	17:20	O **k** of Judah and all people of Judah	4889
	17:25	then **k** who sit on David's throne will come	4889
	19: 3	O **k** of Judah and people of Jerusalem	4889
	19: 4	that neither they nor their fathers nor the **k**	4889
	19:13	The houses in Jerusalem and those of the **k**	4889
	20: 5	all its valuables and all the treasures of the **k**	4889
	22: 4	then **k** who sit on David's throne will come	4889
	25:14	be enslaved by many nations and great **k**;	4889
	25:18	its **k** and officials, to make them a ruin and	4889
	25:20	the foreign people there; all the **k** of Uz;	4889
	25:20	the **k** of the Philistines (those of Ashkelon,	4889
	25:22	all the **k** of Tyre and Sidon;	4889
	25:22	the **k** of the coastlands across the sea;	4889
	25:24	all the **k** of Arabia and all the kings of	4889
	25:24	and all the **k** of the foreign people who live	4889
	25:25	all the **k** of Zimri, Elam and Media;	4889
	25:26	and all the **k** of the north, near and far, one	4889
	27: 3	Then send word to the **k** of Edom, Moab,	4889
	27: 7	and great **k** will subjugate him.	4889
	32:32	they, their **k** and officials,	4889
	34: 5	the former **k** who preceded you,	4889
	44: 9	by your fathers and by the **k** and queens	4889
	44:17	and our fathers, our **k** and our officials did	4889
	44:21	your **k** and your officials and the people of	4889
	46:25	on Egypt and her gods and her **k**,	4889
	50:41	a great nation and many **k** are being stirred	4889
	51:11	LORD has stirred up the **k** of the Medes,	4889
	51:28	the **k** of the Medes, their governors	4889
	52:32	the other **k** who were with him in Babylon.	4889
La	4:12	The **k** of the earth did not believe,	4889
Eze	26: 7	king of **k**, with horses and chariots,	4889

Eze	27:33	and your wares you enriched the **k** of	4889
	27:35	their **k** shudder with horror	4889
	28:17	I made a spectacle of you before **k**.	4889
	32:10	and their **k** will shudder with horror because	4889
	32:29	"Edom is there, her **k** and all her princes;	4889
	43: 7	neither they nor their **k**—	4889
	43: 7	and the lifeless idols of their **k**	4889
	43: 9	and the lifeless idols of their **k**,	4889
Da	2:21	he sets up **k** and deposes them.	10421
	2:37	You, O king, are the king of **k**.	10421
	2:44	"In the time of those **k**,	10421
	2:47	God of **k** and a revealer of mysteries,	10421
	7:24	The ten horns are ten **k** who will come	10421
	7:24	he will subdue three **k**.	10421
	8:20	that you saw represents the **k** of Media	4889
	9: 6	who spoke in your name to our **k**,	4889
	9: 8	O LORD, we and our **k**,	4889
	11: 2	Three more **k** will appear in Persia.	4889
	11:27	The two **k**, with their hearts bent on evil,	4889
Hos	1: 1	Jotham, Ahaz and Hezekiah, **k** of Judah,	4889
	7: 7	All their **k** fall,	4889
	8: 4	They **set up k** without my consent;	4887
Mic	1: 1	Ahaz and Hezekiah, **k** of Judah—	4889
	1:14	of Aczib will prove deceptive to the **k**	4889
Hab	1:10	They deride **k** and scoff at rulers.	4889
Mt	10:18	before governors and **k** as witnesses to them	995
	17:25	the **k** of the earth collect duty and taxes—	995
Mk	13: 9	of me you will stand before governors and **k**	995
Lk	10:24	and **k** wanted to see what you see but did	995
	21:12	you will be brought before **k** and governors,	995
	22:25	"The **k** of the Gentiles lord it over them;	995
Ac	4:26	The **k** of the earth take their stand and	995
	9:15	and their **k** and before the people of Israel.	995
1Co	4: 8	*You* have become **k**—and that without us!	996
	4: 8	How I wish that *you* really *had* become **k** so	996
	4: 8	so that we *might be* **k** with you!	5203
1Ti	2: 2	for **k** and all those in authority,	995
	6:15	the King *of* **k** and Lord of lords,	996
Heb	7: 1	from the defeat *of* the **k** and blessed him,	995
Rev	1: 5	and the ruler *of* the **k** of the earth.	995
	6:15	Then the **k** of the earth, the princes,	995
	10:11	nations, languages and **k**."	995
	16:12	to prepare the way *for* the **k** from the East.	995
	16:14	and they go out to the **k** of the whole world,	995
	16:16	Then they gathered **the k** together to	899S
	17: 2	the **k** of the earth committed adultery and	995
	17:10	They are also seven **k**.	995
	17:12	"The ten horns you saw are ten **k** who have	995
	17:12	for one hour will receive authority as **k**	995
	17:14	because he is Lord of lords and King *of* **k**—	995
	17:18	the great city that rules over the **k** of	995
	18: 3	The **k** of the earth committed adultery	995
	18: 9	the **k** of the earth who committed adultery	995
	19:16	KING OF **K** AND LORD OF LORDS.	995
	19:18	so that you may eat the flesh *of* **k**,	995
	19:19	Then I saw the beast and the **k** of the earth	995
	21:24	the **k** of the earth will bring their splendor	995

KINGS' (2) [KING]

Pr	30:28	yet it is found in **k'** palaces.	4889
Mt	11: 8	who wear fine clothes in **k'** palaces.	995

KINGSHIP (7) [KING]

1Sa	10:16	not tell his uncle what Samuel had said about the **k**.	4867
	10:25	to the people the regulations of the **k**.	4867
	11:14	let us go to Gilgal and there reaffirm the **k**."	4867
1Ch	11:10	gave his **k** strong support to extend it over	4895
2Ch	13: 5	has given the **k** of Israel to David	4930
Ecc	4:14	youth may have come from prison to the **k**,	4887
Mic	4: 8	**k** will come to the Daughter of Jerusalem."	4930

KINNERETH (7)

Nu	34:11	along the slopes east of the Sea of **K**.	4055
Dt	3:17	from **K** to the Sea of the Arabah	4055
Jos	11: 2	in the Arabah south of **K**,	4054
	12: 3	of **K** to the Sea of the Arabah (the Salt Sea)	4054
	13:27	the territory up to the end of the Sea of **K**).	4055
	19:35	Zer, Hammath, Rakkath, **K**,	4055
1Ki	15:20	Abel Beth Maacah and all **K** in addition	4054

KINSMAN (2) [KIN]

Ru	3: 2	you have been, a **k** of ours?	4531
Pr	7: 4	and call understanding your **k**;	4530

KINSMAN-REDEEMER (7) [REDEEM]

Ru	3: 9	since you *are* a **k**."	1457
	3:12	there is a **k** nearer than I.	1457
	4: 1	When the **k** he had mentioned came along,	1457
	4: 1	Then he said to the **k**, "Naomi,	1457
	4: 6	At this, the **k** said, "Then I cannot redeem	1457
	4: 8	So the **k** said to Boaz, "Buy it yourself."	1457
	4:14	who this day has not left you without a **k**.	1457

KINSMAN-REDEEMERS (1) [REDEEM]

Ru	2:20	our close relative; he is one of our **k**."	1457

KINSMEN (6) [KIN]

1Ch	5: 2	they were **k** of Saul from the tribe	278
	12:29	men of Benjamin, Saul's **k**—	278
2Ch	28: 8	from their **k** two hundred thousand wives,	278
	29:34	so their **k** the Levites helped them until	278

Ezr	8:17	I told them what to say to Iddo and his **k**,	278
Job	19:14	My **k** have gone away;	7940

KIOS (1)

Ac	20:15	from there and arrived off **K**.	5944

KIR (5) [KIR HARESETH]

2Ki	16: 9	He deported its inhabitants to **K**	7817
Isa	15: 1	**K** in Moab is ruined, destroyed in a night!	7816
	22: 6	**K** uncovers the shield.	7817
Am	1: 5	people of Aram will go into exile to **K**,"	7817
	9: 7	from Caphtor and the Arameans from **K**?	7817

KIR HARESETH (5) [KIR]

2Ki	3:25	Only **K** was left with its stones	7819
Isa	16: 7	and grieve for the men of **K**.	7819
	16:11	my inmost being for **K**.	7818
Jer	48:31	I moan for the men of **K**.	7818
	48:36	like a flute for the men of **K**.	7818

KIR-HARASETH, KIR-HARESH, KIR-HERES (KJV) See KIR HARESETH

KIRIATH (1)

Jos	18:28	(that is, Jerusalem), Gibeah and **K**—	7956

KIRIATH ARBA (9) [ARBA, HEBRON]

Ge	23: 2	She died at **K** (that is, Hebron)	7957
	35:27	near **K** (that is, Hebron),	7959
Jos	14:15	(Hebron used to be called **K** after Arba,	7957
	15:13	**K**, that is, Hebron.	7957
	15:54	**K** (that is, Hebron) and Zior—	7957
	20: 7	at **K** (that is, Hebron)	7957
	21:11	They gave them **K** (that is, Hebron)	7957
Jdg	1:10	in Hebron (formerly called **K**)	7957
Ne	11:25	in **K** and its surrounding settlements,	7959

KIRIATH BAAL (2) [BAAL, KIRIATH JEARIM]

Jos	15:60	**K** (that is, Kiriath Jearim)	7958
	18:14	the western side and came out at **K**	7958

KIRIATH HUZOTH (1) [HUZOTH]

Nu	22:39	Balaam went with Balak to **K**.	7960

KIRIATH JEARIM (19) [BAALAH, JEARIM, KIRIATH BAAL]

Jos	9:17	Gibeon, Kephirah, Beeroth and **K**.	7961
	15: 9	down toward Baalah (that is, **K**).	7961
	15:60	(that is, **K**) and Rabbah—	7961
	18:14	(that is, **K**), a town of the people of Judah.	7961
	18:15	at the outskirts of **K** on the west,	7961
Jdg	18:12	up camp near **K** in Judah.	7961
	18:12	of **K** is called Mahaneh Dan	7961
1Sa	6:21	messengers to the people of **K**,	7961
	7: 1	So the men of **K** came and took up	7961
	7: 2	that the ark remained at **K**,	7961
1Ch	2:50	Shobal the father of **K**,	7961
	2:52	of Shobal the father of **K** were:	7961
	2:53	and the clans of **K**:	7961
	13: 5	to bring the ark of God from **K**.	7961
	13: 6	Baalah of Judah (**K**) to bring up from there	7961
2Ch	1: 4	from **K** to the place he had prepared	7961
Ezr	2:25	of **K**, Kephirah and Beeroth 743	7961
Ne	7:29	of **K**, Kephirah and Beeroth 743	7961
Jer	26:20	from **K** was another man who prophesied	7961

KIRIATH SANNAH (1) [DEBIR, SANNAH]

Jos	15:49	Dannah, **K** (that is, Debir),	7962

KIRIATH SEPHER (4) [SEPHER]

Jos	15:15	living in Debir (formerly called **K**).	7963
	15:16	the man who attacks and captures **K**."	7963
Jdg	1:11	living in Debir (formerly called **K**).	7963
	1:12	the man who attacks and captures **K**."	7963

KIRIATHAIM (6) [SHAVEH KIRIATHAIM]

Nu	32:37	Reubenites rebuilt Heshbon, Elealeh and **K**,	7964
Jos	13:19	**K**, Sibmah, Zereth Shahar on the hill in	7964
1Ch	6:76	in Galilee, Hammon and **K**, together	7964
Jer	48: 1	**K** will be disgraced and captured;	7964
	48:23	to **K**, Beth Gamul and Beth Meon,	7964
Eze	25: 9	Beth Jeshimoth, Baal Meon and **K**—	7964

KIRIOTH (KJV) See KERIOTH

KIRJATH (KJV) See KIRIATH

KIRJATH-ARBA (KJV) See KIRIATH ARBA

KIRJATH-ARIM (KJV) See KIRIATH ARIM

KIRJATH-BAAL (KJV) See KIRIATH BAAL

KIRJATH-HUZOTH (KJV) See KIRIATH HUZOTH

KIRJATH-JEARIM (KJV) See KIRIATH JEARIM

KIRJATH-SANNAH (KJV) See KIRIATH SANNAH

KIRJATH-SEPHER (KJV) See KIRIATH SEPHER

KIRJATHAIM (KJV) See KIRIATHAIM

KISH (22)

1Sa	9: 1	whose name was **K** son of Abiel,	7821
	9: 3	to Saul's father **K** were lost,	7821
	9: 3	and **K** said to his son Saul,	7821
	10:11	that has happened to the son of **K**?	7821
	10:21	Finally Saul son of **K** was chosen.	7821
	14:51	Saul's father **K** and Abner's father Ner	7821
2Sa	21:14	in the tomb of Saul's father **K**,	7821
1Ch	8:30	followed by Zur, **K**, Baal, Ner, Nadab,	7821
	8:33	Ner was the father of **K**,	7821
	8:33	**K** the father of Saul,	7821
	9:36	followed by Zur, **K**, Baal, Ner, Nadab,	7821
	9:39	Ner was the father of **K**,	7821
	9:39	**K** the father of Saul,	7821
	12: 1	the presence of Saul son of **K** (they were	7821
	23:21	The sons of Mahli: Eleazar and **K**.	7821
	23:22	Their cousins, the sons of **K**, married them.	7821
	24:29	From **K**: the son of Kish: Jerahmeel.	7821
	24:29	From Kish: the son of **K**: Jerahmeel.	7821
	26:28	by Samuel the seer and by Saul son of **K**,	7821
2Ch	29:12	from the Merarites, **K** son of Abdi	7821
Est	2: 5	the son of Shimei, the son of **K**,	7821
Ac	13:21	and he gave them Saul son *of* **K**,	3078

KISHI (1)

1Ch	6:44	Ethan son of **K**, the son of Abdi,	7823

KISHION (2)

Jos	19:20	Rabbith, **K**, Ebez,	8002
	21:28	from the tribe of Issachar, **K**, Daberath,	8002

KISHON (6)

Jdg	4: 7	and his troops to the **K** River and give him	7822
	4:13	from Harosheth Haggoyim to the **K** River.	7822
	5:21	The river **K** swept them away,	7822
	5:21	the age-old river, the river **K**.	7822
1Ki	18:40	down to the **K** Valley and slaughtered there.	7822
Ps	83: 9	you did to Sisera and Jabin at the river **K**,	7822

KISLEV (2)

Ne	1: 1	In the month of **K** in the twentieth year,	4075
Zec	7: 1	the ninth month, the month of **K**.	4075

KISLON (1)

Nu	34:21	of **K**, from the tribe of Benjamin;	4077

KISLOTH TABOR (1) [TABOR]

Jos	19:12	of **K** and went on to Daberath and up	4079

KISON (KJV) See KISHON

KISS (22) [KISSED, KISSES, KISSING]

Ge	27:26	"Come here, my son, and **k** me."	5975
	31:28	**k** my grandchildren and my daughters **good-by.**	5975
2Sa	15: 5	take hold of him and **k** him.	5975
	20: 9	by the beard with his right hand to **k** him.	5975
1Ki	19:20	**k** my father and mother **good-by**,"	5975
Job	31:27	**offered** them a **k** of homage,	4200+5975+7023
Ps	2:12	**K** the Son, lest he be angry and you	5975
	85:10	righteousness and peace **k** *each other*.	5975
Pr	24:26	An honest answer *is* like a **k** *on* the lips.	5975
SS	1: 2	*Let him* **k** me with the kisses	5975
	8: 1	if I found you outside, *I would* **k** you,	5975
Hos	13: 2	offer human sacrifice and **k** the calf-idols."	5975
Mt	26:48	"The one *I* **k** is the man; arrest him."	5797
Mk	14:44	"The one *I* **k** is the man; arrest him and	5797
Lk	7:45	You did not give me a **k**, but this woman,	5799
	22:47	He approached Jesus *to* **k** him,	5797
	22:48	the Son of Man *with* a **k**?"	5799
Ro	16:16	Greet one another with a holy **k**.	5799
1Co	16:20	Greet one another with a holy **k**.	5799
2Co	13:12	Greet one another with a holy **k**.	5799
1Th	5:26	Greet all the brothers with a holy **k**.	5799
1Pe	5:14	Greet one another with a **k** of love.	5799

KISSED (23) [KISS]

Ge	27:27	So he went to him and **k** him.	5975
	29:11	Jacob **k** Rachel and began to weep aloud.	5975
	29:13	and **k** him and brought him to his home,	5975
	31:55	the next morning Laban **k** his grandchildren	5975
	33: 4	around his neck and **k** him.	5975

Ge	45:15	he **k** all his brothers and wept over them.	5975
	48:10	and his father **k** them and embraced them.	5975
	50: 1	and wept over him and **k** him.	5975
Ex	4:27	at the mountain of God and **k** him.	5975
	18: 7	and bowed down and **k** him.	5975
Ru	1: 9	Then *she* **k** them and they wept aloud	5975
	1:14	**k** her mother-in-law **good-by**,	5975
1Sa	10: 1	and poured it on Saul's head and **k** him,	5975
	20:41	Then *they* **k** each other and wept together—	5975
2Sa	14:33	And the king **k** Absalom.	5975
	19:39	The king **k** Barzillai and gave him his	5975
1Ki	19:18	and all whose mouths *have* not **k** him."	5975
Pr	7:13	and **k** him and with a brazen face she said:	5975
Mt	26:49	Judas said, "Greetings, Rabbi!" and **k** him.	2968
Mk	14:45	Judas said, "Rabbi!" and **k** him.	2968
Lk	7:38	**k** them and poured perfume on them.	2968
	15:20	threw his arms around him and **k** him.	2968
Ac	20:37	as they embraced him and **k** him.	2968

KISSES (2) [KISS]

Pr	27: 6	but an enemy multiplies **k**.	5965
SS	1: 2	Let him kiss me with the **k** *of* his mouth—	5965

KISSING (1) [KISS]

Lk	7:45	has not stopped **k** my feet.	2968

KIT (3)

Eze	9: 2	a man clothed in linen who had a writing **k**	7879
	9: 3	in linen who had the writing **k** at his side	7879
	9:11	the **writing k** at his side brought back word,	7879

KITCHENS (1)

Eze	46:24	the **k** where those who minister	1074+1418

KITE (4)

Lev	11:14	the red **k**, any kind of black kite,	1798
	11:14	the red kite, any kind of **black k**,	370
Dt	14:13	the **red k**, the black kite, any kind of falcon,	8012
	14:13	the **black k**, any kind of falcon,	370

KITLISH (1)

Jos	15:40	Cabbon, Lahmas, **K**,	4186

KITRON (1)

Jdg	1:30	the Canaanites living in **K** or Nahalol,	7790

KITTIM (4)

Ge	10: 4	Elishah, Tarshish, the **K** and the Rodanim.	4183
Nu	24:24	Ships will come from the shores of **K**;	4183
1Ch	1: 7	Elishah, Tarshish, the **K** and the Rodanim.	4183
Jer	2:10	Cross over to the coasts of **K** and look,	4183

KNEAD (2) [KNEADED, KNEADING, WELL-KNEADED]

Ge	18: 6	of fine flour and **k** it and bake some bread."	4297
Jer	7:18	and the women **k** the dough and make cakes	4297

KNEADED (2) [KNEAD]

1Sa	28:24	**k** it and baked bread without yeast.	4297
2Sa	13: 8	She took some dough, **k** it,	4297

KNEADING (5) [KNEAD]

Ex	8: 3	and into your ovens and **k troughs**.	5400
	12:34	on their shoulders in **k troughs** wrapped	5400
Dt	28: 5	Your basket and your **k trough** will	5400
	28:17	Your basket and your **k trough** will	5400
Hos	7: 4	not stir from the **k** *of* the dough till it rises.	4297

KNEE (6) [KNEE-DEEP, KNEES]

Isa	45:23	Before me every **k** will bow;	1386
Eze	7:17	and every **k** will become as weak as water.	1386
	21: 7	and every **k** become as weak as water.'	1386
Ro	11: 4	not bowed the **k** to Baal."	1205
	14:11	says the Lord, 'every **k** will bow before me;	1205
Php	2:10	at the name of Jesus every **k** should bow,	1205

KNEE-DEEP (1) [KNEE]

Eze	47: 4	and led me through water that was **k**.	1386

KNEEL (7) [KNEELING, KNELT]

Ge	24:11	He had the camels **k down**	1384
Jdg	7: 5	a dog from those who **k** down to drink."	1386
Est	3: 2	But Mordecai would not **k down**	4156
	3: 5	that Mordecai *would* not **k down**	4156
Ps	22:29	down to the dust *will* **k** before him—	4156
	95: 6	*let us* **k** before the LORD our Maker;	1384
Eph	3:14	this reason *I* **k** before the Father,	1205+2828+3836

KNEELING (3) [KNEEL]

1Ki	1:31	and, **k** before the king, said,	2556
	8:54	where he had been **k**	1386+4156+6584
Mt	20:20	and, **k down,** asked a favor of him.	4686

KNEES (28) [KNEE]

Ge	48:12	Then Joseph removed them from Israel's **k**	1386
	50:23	were placed at birth on Joseph's **k**.	1386

Dt	28:35	The LORD will afflict your **k** and legs	1386
Jdg	7: 6	All the rest got down on their **k** to drink.	1386
1Ki	18:42	the ground and put his face between his **k**.	1386
	19:18	all whose **k** have not bowed down to Baal	1386
2Ki	1:13	This third captain went up and fell on his **k**	1386
Ezr	9: 5	and fell on my **k** with my hands spread out	1386
Job	4: 3	Why were there to receive me and breasts	1386
	4: 4	you have strengthened faltering **k**.	1386
Ps	20: 8	They *are* **brought to** *their* **k** and fall,	4156
	109:24	My **k** give way from fasting;	1386
Isa	35: 3	steady the **k** that give way;	1386
	66:12	be carried on her arm and dandled on her **k**.	1386
Da	5: 6	so frightened that his **k** knocked together	10072
	6:10	Three times a day he got down on his **k**	10123
	6:10	and set me trembling on my hands and **k**.	1386
Na	2:10	Hearts melt, **k** give way, bodies tremble.	1386
Mt	18:26	"The servant fell **on** *his* **k before** him.	4686
	18:29	"His fellow servant fell to his **k**	NIG
Mk	1:40	to him and begged him **on his k,**	1206
	5: 6	he ran and **fell on k in front of**	4686
	10:17	ran up to him and **fell on** his **k before**	1206
	15:19	Falling on their **k**, they paid homage to him.	1205
Lk	5: 8	he fell at Jesus' **k** and said,	1205
Ac	7:60	Then he fell on his **k** and cried out, "Lord,	1205
	9:40	then he got down on **k** and prayed.	1205
Heb	12:12	strengthen your feeble arms and weak **k**.	1205

KNELT (13) [KNEEL]

1Ki	1:16	Bathsheba bowed low and **k** before	2556
2Ch	6:13	and then **k down** before the whole assembly	1384+1386+6584
	7: 3	*they* **k** on the pavement with their faces to	4156
	29:29	and everyone present with him **k down**	4156
Est	3: 2	the royal officials at the king's gate **k down**	4156
Mt	8: 2	A man with leprosy came and **k before** him	4686
	9:18	a ruler came and **k before** him and said,	4686
	15:25	The woman came and **k before** him.	4686
	17:14	a man approached Jesus and **k before** him.	1206
	27:29	They put a staff in his right hand and **k**	1206
Lk	22:41	beyond them, **k down** and prayed,	1205+5502
Ac	20:36	he **k down** with all of them and prayed.	1205+3836+5502
	21: 5	there on the beach *we* **k** to pray.	1205+3836+5502

KNEW (83) [KNOW]

Ge	8:11	Then Noah **k** that the water had receded	3359
	16: 4	When *she* **k** she was pregnant,	8011
	38: 9	Onan **k** that the offspring would not be his;	3359
Dt	7:15	the horrible diseases *you* **k** in Egypt,	3359
	34:10	whom the LORD **k** face to face,	3359
Jdg	2:10	who **k** neither the LORD	3359
1Sa	3:13	because of the sin *he* **k** about;	3359
	20:33	Then Jonathan **k** that his father intended	3359
	20:39	(The boy **k** nothing *of* all this;	3359
	20:39	only Jonathan and David **k**.)	3359
	22:17	*They* **k** he was fleeing,	3359
	22:22	*I* **k** he would be sure to tell Saul.	3359
	26:12	No one saw or **k** about it,	3359
	28:14	Then Saul **k** it was Samuel,	3359
2Sa	1:10	and killed him, because *I* **k** that	3359
	3:37	So on that day all the people and all Israel **k**	3359
	5:12	And David **k** that the LORD had established	3359
	11:16	where *he* **k** the strongest defenders were.	3359
	14: 1	of Zeruiah **k** that the king's heart longed	3359
	17:19	No *one* **k** anything *about* it.	3359
1Ki	9:27	sailors who **k** the sea—	3359
2Ki	4:39	though no *one* **k** what they were.	3359
1Ch	12:32	the times and **k** what Israel should do—	3359
	14: 2	And David **k** that the LORD had established	3359
2Ch	8:18	men who **k** the sea.	3359
	33:13	Then Manasseh **k** that the LORD is God.	3359
Ne	9:10	for *you* **k** how arrogantly the Egyptians	3359
Job	23: 3	If only *I* **k** where to find him;	3359
Ps	31: 7	for you saw my affliction and **k** the anguish	3359
Pr	24:12	If you say, "But *we* **k** nothing *about* this,"	3359
Ecc	9: 1	Though it never saw the sun or **k** anything,	3359
Isa	48: 4	For I **k** how stubborn you were;	3359
	48: 7	So you cannot say, 'Yes, *I* **k** of them.'	3359
Jer	1: 5	"Before I formed you in the womb *I* **k** you,	3359
	11:18	the LORD revealed their plot to me, *I* **k** it,	3359
	19: 4	nor the kings of Judah *ever* **k**,	3359
	32: 8	"*I* **k** that this was the word of the LORD;	3359
	41: 4	before anyone **k** about it,	3359
	44: 3	nor you nor your fathers *ever* **k**.	3359
	44:15	Then all the men who **k** that their wives	3359
	50:24	and you were caught before you **k** it;	3359
Eze	19: 7	the nations *who* **k** you are appalled at you;	3359
Da	5:22	though *you* **k** all this.	10313
Jnh	1:10	(They **k** he was running away from	3359
	4: 2	*I* **k** that you are a gracious and compassionate God,	3359
Zec	11:11	of the flock who were watching me **k** it was	3359
Mt	7:23	'*I* never **k** you. Away from me,	1182
	12:25	Jesus **k** their thoughts and said to them,	3857
	21:45	*they* **k** he was talking about them.	1182
	24:39	and *they* **k** nothing **about** what would	1182
	25:24	he said, '*I* **k** that you are a hard man,	1182
	25:26	So *you* **k** that I harvest where I have	3857
	27:18	For *he* **k** it was out of envy	3857
Mk	1:34	because *they* **k** who he **was**.	3857
	2: 8	Immediately Jesus **k** in his spirit	2105
	12:12	to arrest him because *they* **k** he had spoken	1182
	12:15	But Jesus **k** their hypocrisy.	1182
Lk	4:41	because *they* **k** he was the Christ.	3857
	5:22	Jesus **k** what they were thinking and asked,	2105

Lk	6: 8	But Jesus k what they were thinking	3857
	11:17	Jesus k their thoughts and said to them:	3857
	19:22	You k, did you, that I am a hard man,	3857
	20:19	because they k he had spoken this parable	1182
	23:49	But all those who k him,	1196
Jn	2: 9	the servants who had drawn the water k.	3857
	2:24	not entrust himself to them, for he k all men	1182
	2:25	for he k what was in a man.	1182
	4:10	"If you k the gift of God and who it is	3857
	8:19	"If you k me, you would know my Father	3857
	11:42	I k that you always hear me,	3857
	13: 1	Jesus k that the time had come for him	3857
	13: 3	Jesus k that the Father had put all things	3857
	13:11	For he k who was going to betray him,	3857
	14: 7	If you really k me, you would know my	1182
	17: 8	They k with certainty that I came from you,	1182
	18: 2	Now Judas, who betrayed him, k the place,	3857
	21:12	They k it was the Lord.	3857
Ac	2:30	a prophet and k that God had promised him	3857
	7:18	another king, who k nothing about Joseph,	3857
	16: 3	for they all k that his father was a Greek.	3857
	18:25	though he k only the baptism of John.	2179
Ro	1:21	For although they k God,	1182
Heb	10:34	because you k that you yourselves had	1182

KNIFE (6) [KNIVES]

Ge	22: 6	and he himself carried the fire and the k.	4408
	22:10	Then he reached out his hand and took the k	4408
Ex	4:25	But Zipporah took a flint k,	7644
Jdg	19:29	he took a k and cut up his concubine,	4408
Pr	23: 2	and put a k to your throat if you are given	8501
Jer	36:23	a scribe's k and threw them into the firepot,	9509

KNIT (2) [CLOSE-KNIT, KNITTED]

Job	10:11	and k me together with bones and sinews?	6115
Ps	139:13	you k me together in my mother's womb.	6115

KNITTED (9) [KNIT]

Lev	13:48	or k material of linen or wool, any leather	6849
	13:49	or leather, or woven or k material,	6849
	13:51	or the woven or k material, or the leather,	6849
	13:52	the woven or k material of wool or linen,	6849
	13:53	or the woven or k material,	6849
	13:56	or the leather, or the woven or k material.	6849
	13:57	or in the woven or k material,	6849
	13:58	The clothing, or the woven or k material,	6849
	13:59	woven or k material, or any leather article,	6849

KNIVES (4) [KNIFE]

Jos	5: 2	"Make flint k and circumcise	2995
	5: 3	So Joshua made flint k and circumcised	2995
Pr	30:14	with k to devour the poor from the earth,	4408
Isa	18: 5	he will cut off the shoots with pruning k,	4661

KNOCK (3) [KNOCKED, KNOCKING, KNOCKS]

Mt	7: 7	k and the door will be opened to you.	3218
Lk	11: 9	k and the door will be opened to you.	3218
Rev	3:20	Here I am! I stand at the door and k.	3218

KNOCKED (3) [KNOCK]

Da	5: 6	so frightened that his knees k together	10491
	8: 7	the goat k him to the ground and trampled	8959
Ac	12:13	Peter k at the outer entrance,	3218

KNOCKING (3) [KNOCK]

SS	5: 2	My lover is k: "Open to me,	1985
Lk	13:25	you will stand outside and pleading,	3218
Ac	12:16	But Peter kept on k, and when they opened	3218

KNOCKS (4) [KNOCK]

Ex	21:27	And if he k out the tooth of a manservant	5877
Mt	7: 8	and to him who k, the door will be opened.	3218
Lk	11:10	and to him who k, the door will be opened.	3218
	12:36	and k they can immediately open the door	3218

KNOP, KNOPS (KJV) See BUD, BUDS

KNOTTED (1) [KNOT]

Eze	27:24	with cords twisted and tightly k.	775

KNOW (852) [FOREKNEW, FOREKNOWLEDGE, KNEW, KNOWING, KNOWLEDGE, KNOWN, KNOWS, WELL-KNOWN]

Ge	4: 9	"I don't k," he replied.	3359
	4:10	"I k what a beautiful woman you are.	3359
	15: 8	how can I k that I will gain possession	3359
	15:13	"K for certain that your descendants	3359+3359
	18:21	If not, I will k."	3359
	20: 6	I k you did this with a clear conscience,	3359
	21:26	"I don't k who has done this.	3359
	22:12	Now I k that you fear God,	3359
	24:14	By this I will k that you have shown	3359
	24:49	k which way to turn."	AIT
	27: 2	an old man and don't k the day of my death.	3359
	27:21	to k whether you really are my son Esau	NIH
	29: 5	He said to them, "Do you k Laban,	3359
Ge	29: 5	"Yes, we k him," they answered.	3359
	30:26	You k how much work I've done for you."	3359
	30:29	"You k how I have worked for you and	3359
	31: 6	You k that I've worked for your father	3359
	31:32	Now Jacob did not k that Rachel had stolen	3359
	37:13	"As you k, your brothers are grazing	2022+4202
	42:33	how I will k whether you are honest men:	3359
	42:34	to me so I will k that you are not spies	3359
	43: 7	How were we to k he would say,	3359+3359
	43:22	We don't k who put our silver in our sacks."	3359
	44:15	Don't you k that a man like me can find	3359
	44:27	'You k that my wife bore me two sons.	3359
	47: 6	And if you k of any among them	3359
	48:19	But his father refused and said, "I k,	3359
	48:19	"I know, my son, I k.	3359
Ex	1: 8	a new king, who did not k about Joseph,	3359
	3:19	But I k that the king of Egypt will	3359
	4:14	I k he can speak well.	3359
	5: 2	I do not k the Lord and I will	3359
	6: 7	you will k that I am the Lord your God,	3359
	7: 5	the Egyptians will k that I am the Lord	3359
	7:17	By this you will k that I am the Lord:	3359
	8:10	so that you may k there is no one like	3359
	8:22	so that you will k that I, the Lord,	3359
	9:14	so you may k that there is no one like me	3359
	9:29	so you may k that the earth is the Lord's.	3359
	9:30	But I k that you and your officials still do	3359
	10: 2	and that you may k that I am the Lord."	3359
	10:26	not k what we are to use to worship	3359
	11: 7	Then you will k that the Lord makes	3359
	14: 4	Egyptians will k that I am the Lord.	3359
	14:18	The Egyptians will k that I am the Lord	3359
	16: 6	"In the evening you will k that it was	3359
	16: 8	"You will k that it was the Lord	NIH
	16:12	Then you will k that I am the Lord your	3359
	16:15	For they did not k what it was.	3359
	18:11	Now I k that the Lord is greater than all	3359
	23: 9	you yourselves k how it feels to be aliens,	3359
	29:46	They will k that I am the Lord their God,	3359
	31:13	so you may k that I am the Lord,	3359
	32: 1	we don't k what has happened to him."	3359
	32:22	"You k how prone these people are to evil.	3359
	32:23	we don't k what has happened to him.'	3359
	33:12	not let me k whom you will send with me.	3359
	33:12	'I k you by name and you have found favor	3359
	33:13	so I may k you and continue to find favor	3359
	33:16	How will anyone k that you are pleased	3359
	33:17	because I am pleased with you and I k you	3359
	36: 1	ability to k how to carry out all the work	3359
Lev	5:17	even though he does not k it,	3359
	23:43	so your descendants will k that I had	3359
Nu	10:31	You k where we should camp in the desert,	3359
	14:34	suffer for your sins and k what it is like	3359
	16:28	"This is how you will k that	3359
	16:30	then you will k that these men	3359
	20:14	You k about all the hardships	3359
	22: 6	For I k that those you bless are blessed,	3359
Dt	1:39	your children who do not yet k good	3359
	3:19	(I k you have much livestock) may stay	3359
	4:35	so that you might k that the Lord is God;	3359
	7: 9	K therefore that the Lord your God is God;	3359
	8: 2	and to test you in order to k what was	3359
	8: 5	K then in your heart that as	3359
	9: 2	You k about them and have heard it said:	3359
	11:30	As you k, these mountains are across	2022+4202
	18:21	"How can we k when a message has	3359
	20:20	that you k are not fruit trees and use them	3359
	22: 2	near you or if you do not k who he is,	3359
	28:33	that you do not k will eat what your land	3359
	29: 6	I did this so that you might k that I am	3359
	29:16	You yourselves k how we lived in Egypt	3359
	29:26	gods they did not k, gods he had not given	3359
	31:13	Their children, who do not k this law,	3359
	31:21	I k what they are disposed to do,	3359
	31:27	I k how rebellious and stiff-necked you are	3359
	31:29	For I k that after my death you are sure	3359
Jos	2: 4	but I did not k where they had come from.	3359
	2: 9	I don't k which way they went.	3359
	2: 9	"I k that the Lord has given this land	3359
	3: 4	Then you will k which way to go,	3359
	3: 7	so they may k that I am with you as I was	3359
	3:10	how you will k that the living God is	3359
	4:24	that all the peoples of the earth might k that	3359
	8:14	not k that an ambush had been set	3359
	14: 6	"You k what the Lord said to Moses	3359
	22:22	And let Israel k!	3359
	22:31	"Today we k that the Lord is with us,	3359
	23:14	You k with all your heart and soul that	3359
Jdg	6:37	then I will k that you will save Israel	3359
	14: 4	(His parents did not k that this was from	3359
	16:20	he did not k that the Lord had left him.	3359
	17:13	I k that the Lord will be good to me,	3359
	18:14	"Do you k that one of these houses has	3359
	18:14	Now you k what to do."	3359
Ru	2:11	to live with a people you did not k before.	3359
	3: 3	but don't let him k you are there	3359
	3:11	All my fellow townsmen k that you are	3359
	4: 4	But if you will not, tell me, so I will k.	3359
1Sa	3: 7	Now Samuel did not yet k the Lord:	3359
	3:21	and you will k why his hand has	3359
	6: 3	then we will k that it was not his hand	3359
	8: 9	and let them k what the king who will reign	5583
	17:28	I k how conceited you are and	3359
	17:46	the whole world will k that there is a God	3359
	17:47	All those gathered here will k that it is not	3359
	17:55	"As surely as you live, O king, I don't k."	3359
	20: 3	'Jonathan must not k this or he will	3359
1Sa	20:12	I not send you word and let you k?	265+906+1655
	20:13	not let you k and send you away	265+906+1655
	20:30	Don't I k that you have sided with the son	3359
	21: 2	to k anything about your mission	3359
	24:20	I k that you will surely be king and that	3359
	28: 9	"Surely you k what Saul has done.	3359
	29: 9	"I k that you have been as pleasing	3359
2Sa	1: 5	"How do you k that Saul	3359
	3:25	You k Abner son of Ner;	3359
	3:26	But David did not k it.	3359
	7:20	you k your servant, O Sovereign Lord.	3359
	11:20	Didn't you k they would shoot arrows from	3359
	15:20	when I do not k where I am going?	889+2143+2143+6584
	17: 8	You k your father and his men;	3359
	18:29	your servant, but I don't k what it was."	3359
	19:20	For I your servant k that I have sinned,	3359
	19:22	not k that today I am king over Israel?"	3359
	22:44	People I did not k are subject to me,	3359
	24: 2	so that I may k how many there are."	3359
1Ki	1:18	my lord the king, do not k about it.	3359
	1:27	letting his servants k who should sit on	3359
	2: 5	"Now you yourself k what Joab son	3359
	2: 9	you will k what to do to him.	3359
	2:15	"As you k," he said, "the kingdom was	3359
	2:44	"You k in your heart all the wrong you did	3359
	3: 7	But I am only a little child and do not k how	3359
	5: 3	"You k that because of the wars waged	3359
	5: 6	You k that we have no one so skilled	3359
	8:39	since you k his heart (for you alone know	3359
	8:39	since you know his heart (for you alone k	3359
	8:43	of the earth may k your name and fear you,	3359
	8:43	as do your own people Israel, and may k	3359
	8:60	so that all the peoples of the earth may k	3359
		that the Lord is God	3359
	17:24	"Now I k that you are a man of God and	3359
	18:12	I don't k where the Spirit of	3359
	18:37	answer me, so these people will k that you,	3359
	20:13	then you will k that I am the Lord.' "	3359
	20:28	and you will k that I am the Lord.' "	3359
	22: 3	"Don't you k that Ramoth Gilead belongs	3359
2Ki	2: 3	"Do you k that the Lord is going	3359
	2: 3	"Yes, I k," Elisha replied,	3359
	2: 5	"Do you k that the Lord is going	3359
	2: 5	"Yes, I k," he replied,	3359
	4: 1	and you k that he revered the Lord.	3359
	4: 9	to her husband, "I k that this man	3359
	5: 8	to me and he will k that there is a prophet	3359
	5:15	"Now I k that there is no God in all	3359
	7:12	They k we are starving;	3359
	8:12	"Because I k the harm you will do to	3359
	9:11	"You k the man and the sort of things he	3359
	10:10	K then, that not a word the Lord has	3359
	17:26	not k what the god of that country requires.	3359
	17:26	the people do not k what he requires."	3359
	19:19	all kingdoms on earth may k that you alone,	3359
	19:27	" 'But I k where you stay and	3359
1Ch	17:18	For you k your servant,	3359
	21: 2	to me so that I may k how many there are."	3359
	29:17	I k, my God, that you test the heart	3359
2Ch	2: 8	for I k that your men are skilled	3359
	6:30	since you k his heart (for you alone know	3359
	6:30	since you know his heart (for you alone k	3359
	6:33	of the earth may k your name and fear you,	3359
	6:33	as do your own people Israel, and may k	3359
	13: 5	Don't you k that the Lord,	3359
	20:12	We do not k what to do,	3359
	25:16	I k that God has determined to destroy you,	3359
	32:13	not k what I and my fathers have done to all	3359
	32:31	God left him to test him and to k everything	3359
Ezr	4:12	The king should k that the Jews who came	10313
	4:13	the king should k that if this city is built	10313
	5: 8	The king should k that we went to	10313
	7:24	also to k that you have no authority	10313
	7:25	all who k the laws of your God.	10313
	7:25	you are to teach any who do not k them.	10313
Ne	2:16	not k where I had gone or what I was doing,	3359
	4:11	"Before they k it or see us,	3359
	13:24	not k how to speak the language of Judah.	5795
Est	4:11	and the people of the royal provinces that k	3359
Job	5:24	You will k that your tent is secure;	3359
	5:25	You will k that your children will be many,	3359
	7:10	his place will k him no more.	5795
	8: 9	we were born only yesterday and k nothing,	3359
	9: 2	I k that this is true.	3359
	9:28	for I k you will not hold me innocent.	3359
	10: 7	though you k that I am not guilty and	1981
	10:13	and I k that this was in your mind:	3359
	11: 6	for true wisdom has two sides, k this:	3359
	11: 8	depths of the grave—what can you k?	3359
	12: 3	Who does not k all these things?	907
	12: 9	Which of all these does not k that the hand	3359
	13: 2	What you k, I also know;	1981
	13: 2	What you know, I also k;	3359
	13:18	I k I will be vindicated.	3359
	14:21	If his sons are honored, he does not k it;	3359
	15: 9	What do you k that we do not know?	3359
	15: 9	What do you know that we do not k?	3359
	19: 6	then k that God has wronged me	3359
	19:25	I k that my Redeemer lives,	3359
	19:29	then you will k that there is judgment.	3359
	20: 4	"Surely you k how it has been from of old,	3359
	20: 9	We have no desire to k your ways.	1981
	21:19	so that he will k it!	3359
	21:27	"I k full well what you are thinking,	3359
	22:13	Yet you say, 'What does God k?	3359
	24: 1	Why must those who k him look in vain	3359

Job	24:13	who do not **k** its ways or stay in its paths.	5795
	30:23	I **k** you will bring me down to death,	3359
	31: 6	and he will **k** that I am blameless—	3359
	32: 6	not daring to tell you **what I k.**	1976
	32:10	I too will tell you **what I k.**	1976
	32:17	I too will tell **what I k.**	1976
	33: 3	my lips sincerely speak **what I k.**	1981
	34:33	so tell me what you **k.**	3359
	37: 7	that all men he has made may **k** his work,	3359
	37:15	Do you **k** how God controls the clouds	3359
	37:16	Do you **k** how the clouds hang poised,	3359
	38: 5	marked off its dimensions? Surely you **k!**	3359
	38:18	Tell me, if you **k** all this.	3359
	38:20	Do you **k** the paths to their dwellings?	1067
	38:21	Surely you **k,** for you were already born!	3359
	38:33	Do you **k** the laws of the heavens?	3359
	39: 1	"Do you **k** when the mountain goats	3359
	39: 2	Do you **k** the time they give birth?	3359
	42: 2	"I **k** that you can do all things;	3359
	42: 3	things too wonderful for me **to k.**	3359
Ps	4: 3	**K** that the LORD has set apart the godly	3359
	9:10	Those who **k** your name will trust in you,	3359
	9:20	let the nations **k** they are but men.	3359
	18:43	people I did not **k** are subject to me.	3359
	20: 6	I **k** that the LORD saves his anointed;	3359
	35:11	on things I **k** nothing **about.**	3359
	36:10	Continue your love to those who **k** you,	3359
	39: 4	let me **k** how fleeting is my life.	3359
	40: 9	I do not seal my lips, as you **k,** O LORD.	3359
	41:11	I **k** that you are pleased with me,	3359
	46:10	"Be still, and **k** that I am God;	3359
	50:11	I **k** every bird in the mountains,	3359
	51: 3	For I **k** my transgressions,	3359
	56: 9	By this I will **k** that God is for me.	3359
	69: 5	You **k** my folly, O God;	3359
	69:19	You **k** how I am scorned;	3359
	71:15	though I **k** not its measure.	3359
	73: 7	the evil conceits of their minds **k no limits.**	6296
	78: 6	so the next generation would **k** them,	3359
	82: 5	"They **k** nothing, they understand nothing.	3359
	83:18	Let them **k** that you,	3359
	92: 6	The senseless man does not **k,**	3359
	100: 3	**K** that the LORD is God.	3359
	109:27	Let them **k** that it is your hand, that you,	3359
	119:75	I **k,** O LORD, that your laws are righteous,	3359
	135: 5	I **k** that the LORD is great,	3359
	139: 1	you have searched me and you **k** me.	3359
	139: 2	You **k** when I sit and when I rise;	3359
	139: 4	on my tongue you **k** it completely,	3359
	139:14	your works are wonderful, I **k** that full well.	3359
	139:23	Search me, O God, and **k** my heart;	3359
	139:23	test me and **k** my anxious thoughts.	3359
	140:12	I **k** that the LORD secures justice for	3359
	142: 3	it is you who **k** my way.	3359
	145:12	that all men may **k** of your mighty acts and	3359
	147:20	they do not **k** his laws.	3359
Pr	4:19	they do not **k** what makes them stumble.	3359
	9:18	But little do they **k** that the dead are there,	3359
	10:32	The lips of the righteous **k** what is fitting,	3359
	24:12	Does not he who guards your life **k** it?	3359
	24:14	know also that wisdom is sweet to your soul;	3359
	27: 1	you do not **k** what a day may bring forth.	3359
	27:23	**Be sure** you **k** the condition of your flocks,	3359+3359
	30: 4	the name of his son? Tell me if you **k!**	3359
Ecc	3:12	I **k** that there is nothing better for men than	3359
	3:14	I **k** that everything God does will endure forever;	3359
	5: 1	who do not **k** that they do wrong.	3359
	7:22	for you **k** in your heart that many times	3359
	8: 5	and the wise heart will **k** the proper time	3359
	8:12	I **k** that it will go better with God-fearing	3359
	8:16	When I applied my mind to **k** wisdom and	3359
	9: 5	For the living **k** that they will die,	3359
	9: 5	but the dead **k** nothing;	3359
	10:15	he does not **k** the way to town.	3359
	11: 2	for you do not **k** what disaster may come	3359
	11: 5	As you do not **k** the path of the wind,	3359
	11: 6	for you do not **k** which will succeed,	3359
	11: 9	and whatever your eyes see, but **k** that	3359
SS	1: 8	If you do not **k,** most beautiful of women,	3359
Isa	1: 3	but Israel does not **k,**	3359
	5:19	so we may **k** it."	3359
	9: 9	All the people will **k** it—	3359
	29:12	will answer, "I don't **k how to read."**	3359+6219
	29:15	"Who sees us? Who will **k?"**	3359
	32: 4	of the rash will **k** and understand,	3359
	37:20	all kingdoms on earth may **k** that you alone,	3359
	37:28	"But I **k** where you stay and	3359
	40:21	Do you not **k?** Have you not heard?	3359
	40:28	Do you not **k?** Have you not heard?	3359
	41:20	so that people may see and **k,**	3359
	41:22	and their final outcome.	3359
	41:23	so we may **k** that you are gods.	3359
	41:26	so we could **k,** or beforehand,	3359
	43:10	so that you may **k** and believe me	3359
	44: 8	No, there is no other Rock; I **k** not one."	3359
	44:18	They **k** nothing, they understand nothing;	3359
	45: 3	so that you may **k** that I am the LORD,	3359
	45: 6	men may **k** there is none besides me.	3359
	47:11	and you will not **k how** to conjure it away.	3359
	48: 8	Well do I **k** how treacherous you are;	3359
	49:23	Then you will **k** that I am the LORD;	3359
	49:26	Then all mankind will **k** that I, the LORD,	3359
	50: 4	to **k** the word that sustains the weary.	3359
	50: 7	and I **k** I will not be put to shame.	3359

Isa	51: 7	"Hear me, you who **k** what is right,	3359
	52: 6	Therefore my people will **k** my name;	3359
	52: 6	therefore in that day they will **k**	NIH
	55: 5	Surely you will summon nations you **k** not,	3359
	55: 5	nations that do not **k** you will hasten to you,	3359
	58: 2	they seem eager to **k** my ways,	1981
	59: 8	The way of peace they do not **k;**	3359
	59: 8	no one who walks in them will **k** peace.	3359
	60:16	Then you will **k** that I, the LORD,	3359
	63:16	not **k** us or Israel acknowledge us;	3359
Jer	1: 6	"I do not **k how** to speak; I am only a child.	3359
	2: 8	Those who deal with the law did not **k** me;	3359
	4:22	"My people are fools; they do not **k** me.	3359
	4:22	they **k** not **how** to do good."	3359
	5: 4	for they do not **k** the way of the LORD,	3359
	5: 5	surely they **k** the way of the LORD,	3359
	5:15	a people whose language you do not **k,**	3359
	6:15	they do not even **k how** to blush.	3359
	8: 7	But my people do not **k** the requirements of	3359
	8:12	they do not even **k how** to blush.	3359
	10:23	I **k,** O LORD, that a man's life is	3359
	12: 3	Yet you **k** me, O LORD;	3359
	13:12	'Don't we **k** that every wineskin	3359+3359
	14:18	and priest have gone to a land they **k** not.'"	3359
	15:14	to your enemies in a land you do not **k,**	3359
	16:21	Then they will **k** that my name is the LORD	3359
	17: 4	to your enemies in a land you do not **k,**	3359
	17:16	you **k** I have not desired the day of despair.	3359
	18:23	you **k,** O LORD, all their plots to kill me.	3359
	22:16	Is that not what it means to **k** me?"	1981
	22:28	cast into a land they do not **k?**	3359
	24: 7	I will give them a heart to **k** me,	3359
	29:11	For I **k** the plans I have for you,"	3359
	29:23	I **k** it and am a witness to it,"	3359
	31:34	saying, "**K** the LORD,'	3359
	31:34	because they will all **k** me,	3359
	33: 3	and unsearchable things you do not **k.'**	3359
	36:19	Don't let anyone **k** where you are.	3359
	38:24	not let anyone **k** about this conversation,	3359
	40:14	"Don't you **k** that Baalis king of	3359+3359
	40:15	and no one will **k.**	NIH
	44:19	did not our husbands **k** that we were	NIH
	44:28	in Egypt will **k** whose word will stand—	3359
	44:29	'so that you will **k** that my threats of harm	3359
	48:17	all who live around her, all who **k** her fame;	3359
	48:30	I **k** her insolence but it is futile,"	3359
Eze	2: 5	they will **k** that a prophet has been	3359
	5:13	they will **k** that I the LORD have spoken	3359
	6: 7	and you will **k** that I am the LORD.	3359
	6:10	And they will **k** that I am the LORD;	3359
	6:13	And they will **k** that I am the LORD,	3359
	6:14	Then they will **k** that I am the LORD.'"	3359
	7: 4	Then you will **k** that I am the LORD.	3359
	7: 9	Then you will **k** that it is I	3359
	7:27	Then they will **k** that I am the LORD."	3359
	11: 5	but I **k** what is going through your mind.	3359
	11:10	then you will **k** that I am the LORD.	3359
	11:12	And you will **k** that I am the LORD,	3359
	12:15	"They will **k** that I am the LORD,	3359
	12:16	Then they will **k** that I am the LORD.	3359
	12:20	Then you will **k** that I am the LORD.'"	3359
	13: 9	you will **k** that I am the Sovereign LORD.	3359
	13:14	and you will **k** that I am the LORD.	3359
	13:21	Then you will **k** that I am the LORD.	3359
	13:23	then you will **k** that I am the LORD.'"	3359
	14: 8	Then you will **k** that I am the LORD.	3359
	14:23	for you will **k** that I have done nothing	3359
	15: 7	you will **k** that I am the LORD.	3359
	16:62	and you will **k** that I am the LORD.	3359
	17:12	'Do you not **k** what these things mean?'	3359
	17:21	you will **k** that I the LORD have spoken.	3359
	17:24	of the field will **k** that I the LORD bring	3359
	20:12	so they would **k** that I the LORD made them	3359
	20:20	Then you will **k** that I am the LORD.	3359
	20:26	so they would **k** that I am the LORD.'	3359
	20:38	Then you will **k** that I am the LORD.	3359
	20:42	Then you will **k** that I am the LORD,	3359
	20:44	You will **k** that I am the LORD,	3359
	21: 5	Then all people will **k** that I the LORD have	3359
	22:16	you will **k** that I am the LORD.'"	3359
	22:22	and you will **k** that I the LORD have poured	3359
	23:49	you will **k** that I am the Sovereign LORD.	3359
	24:24	you will **k** that I am the Sovereign LORD.	3359
	24:27	and they will **k** that I am the LORD."	3359
	25: 5	Then you will **k** that I am the LORD.	3359
	25: 7	and you will **k** that I am the LORD.'"	3359
	25:11	Then they will **k** that I am the LORD.'"	3359
	25:14	they will **k** my vengeance,	3359
	25:17	Then they will **k** that I am the LORD,	3359
	26: 6	Then they will **k** that I am the LORD.	3359
	28:22	They will **k** that I am the LORD,	3359
	28:23	Then they will **k** that I am the LORD,	3359
	28:24	they will **k** that I am the Sovereign LORD.	3359
	28:26	they will **k** that I am the LORD their God.	3359
	29: 6	Then all who live in Egypt will **k** that I am	3359
	29: 9	Then they will **k** that I am the LORD.	3359
	29:16	they will **k** that I am the Sovereign LORD.	3359
	29:21	Then they will **k** that I am the LORD."	3359
	30: 8	Then they will **k** that I am the LORD,	3359
	30:19	and they will **k** that I am the LORD.'"	3359
	30:25	Then they will **k** that I am the LORD,	3359
	30:26	Then they will **k** that I am the LORD.'"	3359
	32:15	then they will **k** that I am the LORD.'	3359
	33:33	then they will **k** that a prophet has been	3359
	34:27	They will **k** that I am the LORD,	3359
	34:30	they will **k** that I, the LORD their God,	3359

Eze	35: 4	Then you will **k** that I am the LORD.	3359
	35: 9	Then you will **k** that I am the LORD.	3359
	35:12	Then you will **k** that I the LORD have heard	3359
	35:15	Then they will **k** that I am the LORD.'"	3359
	36:11	Then you will **k** that I am the LORD.	3359
	36:23	the nations will **k** that I am the LORD,	3359
	36:32	to **k** that I am not doing this for your sake,	3359
	36:36	the nations around you that remain will **k**	3359
	36:38	Then they will **k** that I am the LORD."	3359
	37: 3	I said, "O Sovereign LORD, you alone **k."**	3359
	37: 6	Then you will **k** that I am the LORD.'"	3359
	37:13	my people, will **k** that I am the LORD,	3359
	37:14	you will **k** that I the LORD have spoken,	3359
	37:28	the nations will **k** that I the LORD made	3359
	38:16	so that the nations may **k** me	3359
	38:23	Then they will **k** that I am the LORD.'	3359
	39: 6	and they will **k** that I am the LORD.	3359
	39: 7	and the nations will **k** that I the LORD am	3359
	39:22	that day forward the house of Israel will **k**	3359
	39:23	And the nations will **k** that the people	3359
	39:28	they will **k** that I am the LORD their God,	3359
Da	2: 3	and I want to **k what it means."**	3359
	2: 9	I will **k** that you can interpret it for me."	10313
	2:30	may **k** the interpretation and that you	10313
	3:18	But even if he does not, we want you to **k,**	10313
	4: 9	I **k** that the spirit of the holy gods is in you,	10313
	4:17	so that the living may **k** that the Most High	10313
	7:19	to **k the true meaning** of the fourth beast,	10326
	7:20	to **k** about the ten horns on its head and	NIH
	9:25	"**K** and understand this: From the issuing	3359
	10:20	said, "Do you **k** why I have come to you?	3359
	11:32	but people who **k** their God will firmly resist him.	3359
Hos	5: 3	I **k all about** Ephraim; Israel is not hidden	3359
	9: 7	Let Israel **k** this. Because your sins are so	3359
Joel	2:27	Then you will **k** that I am in Israel,	3359
	3:17	"Then you will **k** that I, the LORD your God,	3359
Am	3:10	"They do not **k how** to do right,"	3359
	5:12	For I **k** how many are your offenses and	3359
Jnh	1:12	I **k** that it is my fault that this great storm	3359
Mic	3: 1	Should you not **k** justice,	3359
	4:12	they do not **k** the thoughts of the LORD;	3359
	6: 5	that you may **k** the righteous acts of	3359
Zep	3: 5	yet the unrighteous **k** no shame.	3359
Zec	2: 9	Then you will **k** that the LORD Almighty	3359
	2:11	I will live among you and you will **k** that	3359
	4: 5	"Do you not **k** what these are?"	3359
	4: 9	Then you will **k** that the LORD Almighty	3359
	4:13	He replied, "Do you not **k** what these are?"	3359
	6:15	and you will **k** that the LORD Almighty	3359
Mal	2: 4	And you will **k** that I have sent you this	3359
Mt	6: 3	not let your left hand **k** what your right hand is doing,	1182
	7:11	**k** how to give good gifts to your children,	3857
	9: 6	But so that you may **k** that the Son of Man	3857
	15:12	"Do you **k** that the Pharisees were offended	3857
	16: 3	You **k how** to interpret the appearance of	1182
	20:22	"You don't **k** what you are asking,"	3857
	20:25	"You **k** that the rulers of the Gentiles lord it	3857
	21:27	So they answered Jesus, "We don't **k."**	3857
	22:16	"we **k** you are a man of integrity and	3857
	22:29	not **k** the Scriptures or the power of God.	3857
	24:32	you **k** that summer is near.	1182
	24:33	you see all these things, you **k** that it is near,	1182
	24:42	not **k** on what day your Lord will come.	3857
	25:12	'I tell you the truth, I don't **k** you.'	3857
	25:13	because you do not **k** the day or the hour.	3857
	26: 2	you **k,** the Passover is two days away—	3857
	26:70	"I don't **k** what you're talking about,"	3857
	26:72	"I don't **k** the man!"	3857
	26:74	"I don't **k** the man!"	3857
	27:65	make the tomb as secure as you **k** how."	3857
	28: 5	for I **k** that you are looking for Jesus,	3857
Mk	1:24	I **k** who you are—the Holy One of God!"	3857
	2:10	But that you may **k** that the Son of Man	3857
	4:27	though he does not **k** how.	3857
	5:43	not to let anyone **k about** this,	1182
	7:24	a house and did not want anyone to **k** it;	1182
	9: 6	(He did not **k** what to say,	3857
	9:30	not want anyone to **k** where they were,	1182
	10:19	You **k** the commandments:	3857
	10:38	"You don't **k** what you are asking,"	3857
	10:42	"You **k** that those who are regarded as rulers	3857
	11:33	So they answered Jesus, "We don't **k."**	3857
	12:14	"Teacher, we **k** you are a man of integrity.	3857
	12:24	in error because you do not **k** the Scriptures	3857
	13:28	you **k** that summer is near.	1182
	13:29	you **k** that it is near, right at the door.	1182
	13:33	You do not **k** when that time will come.	3857
	13:35	because you do not **k** when the owner of	3857
	14:40	They did not **k** what to say to him.	1182
	14:68	"I don't **k** or understand what you're talking	3857
	14:71	"I don't **k** this man you're talking about."	3857
Lk	1: 4	so that you may **k** the certainty of the things	2105
	2:49	"Didn't you **k** I had to be in my Father's	3857
	4:34	I **k** who you are—the Holy One of God!"	3857
	5:24	But that you may **k** that the Son of Man	3857
	7:39	he would **k** who is touching him	1182
	8:46	I **k that** power has gone out from me."	1182
	9:33	(He did not **k** what he was saying.)	3857
	11:13	**k** how to give good gifts to your children,	3857
	12:48	But the one who does not **k**	1182
	12:56	You **k how** to interpret the appearance of	3857
	12:56	How is it that you do not **k**	1182
	13:25	'I don't **k** you or where you come from.'	3857
	13:27	'I don't **k** you or where you come from.	3857
	16: 4	I **k** what I'll do so that, when I lose my job	1182

Lk	18:20	*You* **k** the commandments:	3857
	18:34	they did not **k** what he was talking about.	1182
	20: 7	*"We don't* **k** where it was from."	3857
	20:21	we **k** that you speak and teach what is right,	3857
	21:20	you will **k** that its desolation is near.	1182
	21:30	for yourselves and **k** that summer is near.	1182
	21:31	you **k** that the kingdom of God is near.	1182
	22:34	you will deny three times that *you* **k** me."	3857
	22:57	*"Woman, I don't* **k** him," he said.	3857
	22:60	*I* don't **k** what you're talking about!"	3857
	23:34	for *they* do not **k** what they are doing."	3857
	24:18	visitor to Jerusalem and *do* not **k** the things	1182
Jn	1:26	"but among you stands one you *do* not **k.**	3857
	1:31	I myself *did* not **k** him,	3857
	1:48	*"How do you* **k** me?"	1182
	3: 2	we **k** you are a teacher who has come	3857
	3:11	I tell you the truth, we speak of what *we* **k,**	3857
	4:22	You Samaritans worship what *you do* not **k;**	3857
	4:22	we worship what *we do* **k,**	3857
	4:25	The woman said, *"I* **k** that the Messiah"	3857
	4:32	to eat that you **k** nothing about."	3857
	4:42	and *we* **k** that this man really is the Savior	3857
	5:32	*I* **k** that his testimony about me is valid.	3857
	5:42	but *I* **k** you. I know that you do not have	1182
	5:42	I **k** that you do not have the love of God	NIG
	6:42	whose father and mother we **k?**	3857
	6:69	We believe and **k** that you are the Holy One	1182
	7:27	But *we* **k** where this man is from;	3857
	7:27	no one *will* **k** where he is from."	1182
	7:28	you **k** me, and you know where I am from.	3857
	7:28	you know me, and *you* **k** where I am from.	3857
	7:28	You *do* not **k** him,	3857
	7:29	but I **k** him because I am from him	3857
	8:14	for *I* **k** where I came from and	3857
	8:19	*"You do* not **k** me or my Father,"	3857
	8:19	you would **k** my Father also."	3857
	8:28	then *you will* **k** that I am [the one I claim	1182
	8:32	Then *you will* **k** the truth,	1182
	8:37	*I* **k** you are Abraham's descendants.	3857
	8:52	"Now *we* **k** that you are demon-possessed!	1182
	8:55	Though *you do* not **k** him, I know him.	3857
	8:55	Though you do not know him, I **k** him.	3857
	8:55	but *I do* **k** him and keep his word.	3857
	9:12	*"I* don't **k,"** he said.	3857
	9:20	*"We* **k** he is our son," the parents answered,	3857
	9:20	"and *we* he was born blind.	NIG
	9:21	or who opened his eyes, we don't **k.**	3857
	9:24	*"We* **k** this man is a sinner."	3857
	9:25	"Whether he is a sinner or not, *I* don't **k.**	3857
	9:25	One thing *I do* **k.** I was blind but now I see!	3857
	9:29	We **k** that God spoke to Moses,	3857
	9:29	we don't even **k** where he comes from."	3857
	9:30	You don't **k** where he comes from,	3857
	9:31	We **k** that God does not listen to sinners.	3857
	10: 4	because *they* **k** his voice.	3857
	10:14	*I* **k** my sheep and my sheep know me—	1182
	10:14	I know my sheep and my sheep **k** me—	1182
	10:15	as the Father knows me and I **k** the Father—	1182
	10:27	I **k** them, and they follow me.	1182
	10:38	that *you may* **k** and understand that	1182
	11:22	But *I* **k** that even now God will give you	3857
	11:24	*"I* **k** he will rise again in the resurrection at	3857
	11:49	spoke up, "You **k** nothing at all!	1182
	12:35	The man who walks in the dark *does* not **k**	3857
	12:50	*I* **k** that his command leads to eternal life.	3857
	13:17	Now that *you* **k** these things,	3857
	13:18	I **k** those I have chosen.	3857
	13:22	at a loss to **k** which of them he meant.	NIG
	13:35	By this all men *will* **k** that you are my	
		disciples, if you love one another."	1182
	14: 4	*You* **k** the way to the place	3857
	14: 5	"Lord, we don't **k** where you are going,	3857
	14: 5	so how can *we* **k** the way?"	3857
	14: 7	*you would* **k** my Father as well.	1182
	14: 7	you *do* **k** him and have seen him."	1182
	14: 9	Jesus answered: "Don't *you* **k** me, Philip,	1182
	14:17	But you **k** him, for he lives with you	1182
	15:15	a servant *does* not **k** his master's business.	3857
	15:21	for *they* do not **k** the One who sent me.	3857
	16:30	Now we can see that you **k** all things and	3857
	17: 3	Now this is eternal life: that *they may* **k** you,	1182
	17: 7	Now *they* **k** that everything you have given	
		me comes from you.	1182
	17:23	to let the world **k** that you sent me	1182
	17:25	though the world *does* not **k** you,	1182
	17:25	not know you, *I* **k** you, and they know	1182
	17:25	and they **k** that you have sent me.	1182
	18:21	Surely they **k** what I said."	3857
	19: 4	to let *you* **k** that I find no basis for a charge	1182
	20: 2	and we don't **k** where they have put him!"	3857
	20:13	"and *I* don't **k** where they have put him."	3857
	21:15	Lord," he said, "you **k** that I love you."	3857
	21:16	"Yes, Lord, you **k** that I love you."	3857
	21:17	He said, "Lord, you **k** all things;	3857
	21:17	you **k** that I love you."	1182
	21:24	*We* **k** that his testimony is true.	3857
Ac	1: 7	to **k** the times or dates the Father has set	1182
	1:24	they prayed, "Lord, you **k** everyone's **heart.**	2841
	2:22	through him, as *you yourselves* **k.**	1182
	3:16	man whom you see and **k** was made strong.	3857
	3:17	brothers, *I* **k** that you acted in ignorance,	3857
	4:10	**k** *this,* you and all the people of Israel:	1196+1639
	7:40	we don't **k** what has happened to him!'	3857
	10:36	You **k** the message God sent to the people	NIG
	10:37	You **k** what has happened throughout Judea,	3857
	12:11	"Now *I* **k** without a doubt that	3857
	13:38	to **k** that through Jesus the forgiveness	1196

Ac	15: 7	you **k** that some time ago God made	2179
	17:19	"May we **k** what this new teaching is	1182
	17:20	and we want *to* **k** what they mean."	1182
	19:15	"Jesus *I* **k,** and I know about Paul,	1182
	19:15	and *I* **k** about Paul, but who are you?"	2179
	19:25	"Men, *you* **k** we receive a good income	2179
	19:32	not even **k** why they were there.	1182
	19:35	of Ephesus, doesn't all the world **k** that	1182
	20:18	"You **k** how I lived the whole time I was	2179
	20:20	You **k** that I have not hesitated	NIG
	20:23	I only **k** that in every city the Holy Spirit	NIG
	20:25	"Now I **k** that none of you	3857
	20:29	I **k** that after I leave, savage wolves will	1182
	20:34	*You yourselves* **k** that these hands	1182
	21:24	Then everybody *will* **k** there is no truth	1182
	22:14	of our fathers has chosen you *to* **k** his will	1182
	22:19	'these men that I went from me	2179
	23:28	I wanted *to* **k** why they were accusing him,	2105
	24:10	*"I* **k** that for a number of years	2179
	25:10	as *you* yourself **k** very well.	2105
	26: 4	"The Jews all **k** the way I have lived ever	3857
	26:27	do you believe the prophets? *I* **k** you do."	3857
	28:22	**k** that people everywhere are talking	1196+1639
	28:28	*to* **k** that God's salvation has been sent	1196+1639
Ro	1:32	Although they **k** God's righteous decree	2105
	2: 2	Now we **k** that God's judgment against	3857
	2:18	if you **k** his will and approve of what	1182
	3:17	and the way of peace *they* do not **k."**	1182
	3:19	Now we **k** that whatever the law says,	3857
	5: 3	we **k** that suffering produces perseverance;	3857
	6: 3	Or **don't** *you* **k** that all of us who	51
	6: 6	For we **k** that our old self was crucified	1182
	6: 9	For *we* **k** that since Christ was raised from	1182
	6:16	Don't *you* **k** that when you offer yourselves	1182
	7: 1	Do *you* not **k,** brothers—	51
	7: 1	for I am speaking *to men who* **k** the law—	1182
	7:14	*We* **k** that the law is spiritual;	3857
	7:18	*I* **k** that nothing good lives in me, that is,	3857
	8:22	*We* **k** that the whole creation has been	
		groaning as in the pains of childbirth	3857
	8:26	*We do* not **k** what we ought to pray for,	3857
	8:28	And *we* **k** that in all things God works for	3857
	10: 3	*Since they* did **not k** the righteousness	51
	11: 2	Don't *you* **k** what the Scripture says in	3857
	15:29	*I* **k** that when I come to you,	3857
1Co	1:21	the world through its wisdom *did* not **k** him,	1182
	2: 2	For I resolved *to* **k** nothing while I was	3857
	3:16	Don't *you* **k** that you yourselves are God's	
		temple	3857
	5: 6	Don't *you* **k** that a little yeast works	3857
	6: 2	not **k** that the saints will judge the world?	3857
	6: 2	*Do you* not **k** that we will judge angels?	3857
	6: 9	not **k** that the wicked will not inherit	3857
	6:15	*Do you* not **k** that your bodies are members	3857
	6:16	*Do you* not **k** that he who unites himself	3857
	6:19	*Do you* not **k** that your body is a temple of	3857
	7:16	How do *you* **k,** wife, whether you will save	3857
	7:16	Or, how do *you* **k,** husband, whether you	3857
	8: 1	We **k** that we all possess knowledge.	3857
	8: 2	not yet **k** as he ought to know.	1182
	8: 2	not yet know as he ought *to* **k.**	1182
	8: 4	We **k** that an idol is nothing at all in	3857
	9:13	Don't *you* **k** that those who work in	3857
	9:24	not **k** that in a race all the runners run,	3857
	12: 2	*You* **k** that when you were pagans,	1182
	13: 9	For *we* **k** in part and we prophesy in part,	1182
	13:12	Now *I* **k** in part; than I shall know fully	1182
	13:12	then *I shall* **k fully,** even as I am fully	2105
	14: 7	*will* anyone **k** what tune is being played	1182
	14: 9	how *will* anyone **k** what you are saying?	1182
	14:16	since *he does* not **k** what you are saying?	1182
	15:58	*because you* **k** that your labor is	3857
	16:15	*You* **k** that the household of Stephanas were	3857
2Co	1: 7	we **k** that just as you share in our sufferings,	3857
	2: 4	not to grieve you but to let *you* **k** the depth	1182
	4:14	*because we* **k** that the one who raised	3857
	5: 1	Now *we* **k** that if the earthly tent we live	3857
	5: 6	Therefore *we* are always confident and	3857
	5:11	then, *we* **k** what it is to fear the Lord,	3857
	8: 1	to **k about** the grace that God has given	1192
	8: 9	*you* **k** the grace of our Lord Jesus Christ,	1182
	9: 2	For *I* **k** your eagerness to help,	3857
	12: 2	*I* **k** a man in Christ who	3857
	12: 2	in the body or out of the body *I do* not **k—**	3857
	12: 3	And *I* **k** that this man—	3857
	12: 3	from the body *I do* not **k,** but God knows—	3857
Gal	1:11	*I want* you to **k,** brothers, that the gospel	1192
	2:16	**k** that a man is not justified by observing	3857
	4: 8	Formerly, *when you did* not **k** God,	1182
	4: 9	But now *that you* **k** God—	1182
	4:13	As *you* **k,** it was because of an illness	3857
Eph	1:17	so that you may **k** him **better.**	2106
	1:18	be enlightened in order that you *may* **k**	1182
	3:19	*to* **k** this love that surpasses knowledge—	1182
	4:20	however, *did* not *come* to **k** Christ that way.	3443
	6: 8	*because* you **k** that the Lord will reward	3857
	6: 9	*since* you **k** that he who is both their Master	3857
	6:21	also *may* **k** how I am and what I am doing.	3857
	6:22	that you *may* **k** how we are,	1182
Php	1:12	Now I want you to **k,** brothers,	1182
	1:19	for *I* **k** that through your prayers and	3857
	1:22	Yet what shall I choose? *I do* not **k!**	1192
	1:25	Convinced of this, *I* **k** that I will remain,	3857
	1:27	or *I* **k** that you stand firm in one spirit,	NIG
	2:22	But *you* **k** that Timothy has proved himself,	1182
	3:10	*I want* to **k** Christ and the power	1182
	4:12	*I* **k** what it is to be in need,	3857

Php	4:12	and *I* **k** what it is to have plenty.	3857
	4:15	Moreover, as you Philippians **k,**	3857
Col	2: 1	*to* **k** how much I am struggling for you and	3857
	2: 2	in order that they may **k** the mystery	2106
	3:24	*since you* **k** that you will receive	3857
	4: 1	*because you* **k** that you also have a Master	3857
	4: 6	*so that you may* **k** how to answer everyone.	3857
	4: 8	that *you may* **k** about our circumstances and	1182
1Th	1: 4	For *we* **k,** brothers loved by God,	3857
	1: 5	*You* **k** how we lived among you	3857
	2: 1	You **k,** brothers, that our visit to you was	3857
	2: 2	and been insulted in Philippi, as *you* **k,** but	3857
	2: 5	*You* **k** we never used flattery,	3857
	2:11	For you **k** that we dealt with each of you as	3857
	3: 3	You **k** quite well that we were destined	3857
	3: 4	And it turned out that way, as *you* well **k.**	3857
	4: 2	For you **k** what instructions we gave you by	3857
	4: 5	who *do* not **k** God;	3857
	5: 2	for you **k** very well that the day of the Lord	3857
2Th	1: 8	He will punish those who *do* not **k** God	3857
	2: 6	And now *you* **k** what is holding him back,	3857
	3: 7	For *you yourselves* **k** how you ought	3857
1Ti	1: 7	but *they* do not **k** what they are talking	3783
	1: 8	*We* **k** that the law is good if one uses	3857
	1: 9	also **k** that law is made not for the righteous	3857
	3: 5	not **k** how to manage his own family,	3857
	3:15	*you will* **k** how people ought to conduct	3857
	4: 3	by those who believe and who **k** the truth.	2105
2Ti	1:12	because *I* **k** whom I have believed,	3857
	1:15	*You* **k** that everyone in the province	3857
	1:18	You **k** very well in how many ways	1182
	2:23	*because you* **k** they produce quarrels,	3857
	3:10	You, however, **k all** *about* my teaching,	4158
	3:14	you **k** those from whom you learned it,	3857
Tit	1:16	They claim *to* **k** God, but by their actions	3857
Heb	8:11	or a man his brother, saying, '**K** the Lord,'	1182
	8:11	because *they will* all **k** me, from the least	1182
	10:30	we **k** him who said, "It is mine to avenge;	1182
	11: 8	*though he did* not **k** where he was going.	2179
	12:17	as *you* **k,** when he wanted to inherit	3857
	13:23	*I want you* to **k** that our brother Timothy	1182
Jas	1: 3	*because you* **k** that the testing of your faith	1182
	3: 1	*because you* **k** that we who teach will	3857
	4: 4	don't *you* **k** that friendship with the world	3857
	4:14	not even **k** what will happen tomorrow.	2179
	5:11	As *you* **k,** we consider blessed those who	
		have persevered.	2627
1Pe	1:18	*For you* **k** that it was not with perishable	3857
	5: 9	*because you* **k** that your brothers	3857
2Pe	1:12	even though *you* **k** them	3857
	1:14	*because I* **k** that I will soon put it aside,	3857
	3:17	dear friends, *since* you **already k** this,	4589
1Jn	2: 3	*We* **k** that we have come to know him	1182
	2: 3	We know that *we have come* to **k** him	1182
	2: 4	The man who says, *"I* **k** him,"	1182
	2: 5	This is how *we* **k** we are in him:	1182
	2:11	he *does* not **k** where he is going,	3857
	2:18	This is how *we* **k** it is the last hour.	1182
	2:20	and all of *you* **k** the truth.	1182
	2:21	I do not write to you because *you do* not **k**	3857
	2:21	but because *you do* **k** it and	3857
	2:29	If *you* **k** that he is righteous,	3857
	2:29	If you know that he is righteous, *you* **k**	1182
	3: 1	The reason the world *does* not **k** us is	1182
	3: 1	not know us is that *it did* not **k** him.	1182
	3: 2	But *we* **k** that when he appears,	3857
	3: 5	But *you* **k** that he appeared so	3857
	3:10	how we **k** who the children of God are	1639+5745
	3:14	We **k** that we have passed from death	3857
	3:15	and *you* **k** that no murderer has eternal life	3857
	3:16	This is how *we* **k** what love is:	1182
	3:19	then is how *we* **k** that we belong to the truth,	1182
	3:24	And this is how *we* **k** that he lives in us:	1182
	3:24	We **k** it by the Spirit he gave us.	NIG
	4: 8	Whoever *does* not **k** *does* not **k** God,	1182
	4:13	*We* **k** that we live in him and he in us,	1182
	4:16	so we **k** and rely on the love God has for us.	1182
	5: 2	how *we* **k** that we love the children of God:	1182
	5:13	so that *you may* **k** that you have eternal life.	3857
	5:15	And if *we* **k** that he hears us—	3857
	5:15	*we* **k** that we have what we asked of him.	3857
	5:18	*We* **k** that anyone born of God does not	3857
	5:19	*We* **k** that we are children of God,	3857
	5:20	*We* **k** also that the Son of God has come	3857
	5:20	so that *we may* **k** him who is true.	1182
2Jn	1: 1	not I only, but also all who **k** the truth—	1182
3Jn	1:12	and *you* **k** that our testimony is true.	3857
Jude	1: 5	**Though** you already **k** all this,	3857
Rev	2: 2	*I* **k** your deeds, your hard work and	3857
	2: 2	*I* **k** that you cannot tolerate wicked men,	NIG
	2: 9	*I* **k** your afflictions and your poverty—	3857
	2: 9	*I* **k** the slander of those who say they are	NIG
	2:13	*I* **k** where you live—where Satan has his	3857
	2:19	*I* **k** your deeds, your love and faith,	3857
	2:23	Then all the churches *will* **k** that I am he	1182
	3: 1	*I* **k** your deeds; you have a reputation	3857
	3: 3	not **k** at what time I will come to you.	1182
	3: 8	*I* **k** your deeds. See, I have placed before	3857
	3: 8	*I* **k** that you have little strength,	NIG
	3:15	*I* **k** your deeds, that you are neither cold	3857
	7:14	I answered, "Sir, you **k."**	3857

KNOWING (28) [KNOW]

Ge	3: 5	and you will be like God, **k** good and evil."	3359
	3:22	has become like one of us, **k** good and evil.	3359
2Sa	15:11	**k** nothing **about** the matter.	3359

1Ki	1:11	without our lord David's **k** it?	3359
Job	9: 5	He moves mountains without *their* **k** it	3359
	31:21	**k** that I had influence in court,	8011
Ps	39: 6	He heaps up wealth, not **k** who will get it.	3359
Pr	7:23	little **k** it will cost him his life.	3359
Ecc	6: 8	poor man gain *by* **k** how to conduct himself	3359
Mt	9: 4	**K** their thoughts, Jesus said,	3857
	22:18	But Jesus, **k** their evil intent, said,	1182
Mk	5:33	the woman, **k** what had happened to her,	3857
	6:20	**k** him to be a righteous and holy man.	3857
	15:10	**k** it was out of envy that the chief priests	1182
Lk	8:53	They laughed at him, **k** that she was dead.	3857
	9:47	Jesus, **k** their thoughts,	3857
	11:44	which men walk over without **k** it."	3857
Jn	6:15	**k** that they intended to come	1182
	18: 4	Jesus, **k** all that was going to happen to him,	3857
	19:28	Later, **k** that all was now completed,	3857
Ac	5: 7	not **k** what had happened.	3857
	20:22	not **k** what will happen to me there.	3857
	23: 6	**k** that some of them were Sadducees and	1182
Php	1:16	**k** that I am put here for the defense of	3857
	3: 8	*of* **k** Christ Jesus my Lord,	1194
Phm	1:21	**k** that you will do even more than I ask.	3857
Heb	13: 2	people have entertained angels **without** it.	3291
2Pe	2:20	the corruption of the world by **k** our Lord	2106

KNOWLEDGE (132) [KNOW]

Ge	2: 9	the tree of life and the tree of the **k** *of* good	1981
	2:17	but you must not eat from the tree of the **k**	1981
Ex	31: 3	ability and **k** in all kinds of crafts—	1981
	35:31	ability and **k** in all kinds of crafts—	1981
Nu	24:16	who has **k** from the Most High,	1981+3359
1Ki	2:32	because without the **k** of my father David	3359
2Ch	1:10	Give me wisdom and **k**,	4529
	1:11	but for wisdom and **k** to govern my people	4529
	1:12	therefore wisdom and **k** will be given you.	4529
Job	21:22	"Can anyone teach **k** to God,	1981
	34:35	'Job speaks without **k**;	1981
	35:16	without **k** he multiplies words."	1981
	36: 3	I get my **k** from afar;	1976
	36: 4	one perfect in **k** is with you.	1978
	36:12	by the sword and die without **k**.	1981
	37:16	those wonders of him who is perfect in **k**?	1976
	38: 2	darkens my counsel with words without **k**?	1981
	42: 3	that obscures my counsel without **k**?'	1981
Ps	19: 2	night after night they display **k**.	1981
	73:11	Does the Most High have **k**?"	1978
	94:10	Does he who teaches man lack **k**?	1981
	119:66	Teach me **k** and good judgment,	1981
	139: 6	*Such* **k** is too wonderful for me,	1981
Pr	1: 4	**k** and discretion to the young—	1981
	1: 7	fear of the LORD is the beginning of **k**,	1981
	1:22	in mockery and fools hate **k**?	1981
	1:29	Since they hated **k** and did not choose	1981
	2: 5	fear of the LORD and find the **k** *of* God.	1981
	2: 6	from his mouth come **k** and understanding.	1981
	2:10	and **k** will be pleasant to your soul.	1981
	3:20	by his **k** the deeps were divided,	1981
	5: 2	and your lips may preserve **k**.	1981
	8: 9	they are faultless to those who have **k**.	1981
	8:10	**k** rather than choice gold,	1981
	8:12	I possess **k** and discretion.	1981
	9:10	and **k** of the Holy One is understanding.	1981
	9:13	she is undisciplined and without **k**.	3359
	10:14	Wise men store up **k**,	1981
	11: 9	but through **k** the righteous escape.	1981
	12: 1	Whoever loves discipline loves **k**,	1981
	12:23	A prudent man keeps his **k** to himself,	1981
	13:16	Every prudent man acts out of **k**,	1981
	14: 6	but **k** comes easily to the discerning.	1981
	14: 7	for you will not find **k** on his lips.	1981
	14:18	but the prudent are crowned with **k**.	1981
	15: 2	The tongue of the wise commends **k**,	1981
	15: 7	The lips of the wise spread **k**;	1981
	15:14	The discerning heart seeks **k**,	1981
	17:27	A **man of k** uses words with restraint,	1981+3359
	18:15	The heart of the discerning acquires **k**;	1981
	19: 2	It is not good to have zeal without **k**,	1981
	19:25	rebuke a discerning man, and he will gain **k**.	1981
	19:27	and you will stray from the words of **k**.	1981
	20:15	but lips that speak **k** are a rare jewel.	1981
	21:11	when a wise man is instructed, he gets **k**.	1981
	22:12	The eyes of the LORD keep watch over **k**,	1981
	22:20	sayings of counsel and **k**,	1981
	23:12	to instruction and your ears to words of **k**.	1981
	24: 4	through **k** its rooms are filled with rare	1981
	24: 5	and a man of **k** increases strength;	1981
	28: 2	of understanding and **k** maintains order.	3359
	30: 3	nor have *I* **k** of the Holy One.	1981+3359
Ecc	1:16	I have experienced much of wisdom and **k**."	1981
	1:18	the more **k**, the more grief.	1981
	2:21	For a man may do his work with wisdom, **k**	1981
	2:26	God gives wisdom, **k** and happiness,	1981
	7:12	but the advantage of **k** is this:	1981
	9:10	there is neither working nor planning nor **k**	1981
	12: 9	but also he imparted **k** *to* the people.	1981
Isa	11: 2	Spirit of **k** and of the fear of the LORD—	1981
	11: 9	the earth will be full of the **k** of the LORD	1978
	33: 6	a rich store of salvation and wisdom and **k**;	1981
	40:14	that taught him **k** or showed him the path	1981
	44:19	no one has the **k** or understanding to say,	1981
	47:10	and **k** mislead you when you say	1981
	53:11	by his **k** my righteous servant will justify many,	1981
	56:10	Israel's watchmen are blind, they all lack **k**;	3359
Jer	3:15	with **k** and understanding.	1978

Jer	10:14	Everyone is senseless and without **k**;	1981
	51:17	"Every man is senseless and without **k**;	1981
Da	1:17	To these four young men God gave **k**	4529
	2:21	He gives wisdom to the wise and **k** to	10430
	5:12	a keen mind and **k** and understanding,	10430
	12: 4	Many will go here and there to increase **k**."	1981
Hos	4: 6	my people are destroyed from lack of **k**.	1981
	4: 6	"Because you have rejected **k**,	1981
Hab	2:14	For the earth will be filled with the **k** of	3359
Mal	2: 7	"For the lips of a priest ought to preserve **k**,	1981
Mt	13:11	"The **k** of the secrets of the kingdom	1182
Lk	1:77	to give his people the **k** of salvation through	1194
	8:10	"The **k** of the secrets of the kingdom	1182
	11:52	because you have taken away the key to **k**.	1194
Ac	5: 2	*With* his wife's **full k** he kept back part	5323
	18:24	with a thorough **k** of the Scriptures.	NIG
Ro	1:28	not think it worthwhile to retain the **k** of	2106
	2:20	in the law the embodiment of **k** and truth—	1194
	10: 2	but their zeal is not based on **k**.	2106
	11:33	the depth of the riches of the wisdom and **k**	1194
	15:14	*in* **k** and competent to instruct one another.	1194
1Co	1: 5	in all your speaking and in all your **k**—	1194
	8: 1	We know that we all possess **k**.	1194
	8: 1	**K** puffs up, but love builds up.	1194
	8:10	weak conscience sees you who have this **k** eating in an idol's temple,	1194
	8:11	is destroyed by your **k**.	1194
	12: 8	to another the message *of* **k** by means of	1194
	13: 2	and can fathom all mysteries and all **k**,	1194
	13: 8	where there is **k**, it will pass away.	1194
	14: 6	or **k** or prophecy or word of instruction?	1194
2Co	2:14	the fragrance of the **k** of him.	1194
	4: 6	in our hearts to give us the light of the **k** of	1194
	8: 7	in faith, in speech, *in* **k**,	1194
	10: 5	that sets itself up against the **k** of God,	1194
	11: 6	not be a trained speaker, but I do have **k**.	1194
Eph	3:19	and to know this love that surpasses **k**—	1194
	4:13	the **k** of the Son of God and become mature,	2106
Php	1: 9	and more in **k** and depth of insight,	2106
Col	1: 9	and asking God to fill you with the **k**	2106
	1:10	growing in the **k** of God,	2106
	2: 3	the treasures *of* wisdom and **k**.	1194
	3:10	which is being renewed in **k** in the image	2106
1Ti	2: 4	to be saved and to come to a **k** of the truth.	2106
	6:20	*of* what is falsely called **k**,	1194
2Ti	2:25	repentance leading to a **k** of the truth,	2106
Tit	1: 1	the **k** of the truth that leads to godliness—	2106
	1: 2	and a resting on the hope of eternal life,	NIG
Heb	10:26	on sinning after we have received the **k** of	2106
2Pe	1: 2	be yours in abundance through the **k** of God	2106
	1: 3	for life and godliness through our **k**	2106
	1: 5	and to goodness, **k**;	1194
	1: 6	and to **k**, self-control;	1194
	2:20	in your **k** of our Lord Jesus Christ.	2106
	3:18	and **k** of our Lord and Savior Jesus Christ.	1194

KNOWN (147) [KNOW]

Ge	41:39	"Since God has **made** all this **k** to you,	3359
	45: 1	when he **made himself k** to his brothers.	3359
Ex	2:14	"What I did *must have* **become k**."	3359
	6: 3	the LORD *I did* not **make myself k** to them.	3359
	21:36	if *it* was **k** that the bull had the habit	3359
Nu	11:16	of Israel's elders whom **k** *to you*	3359
Dt	3:13	of Argob in Bashan *used* to be **k** as a land	7924
	8: 3	which neither *you* nor your fathers had **k**,	3359
	8:16	something your fathers had never **k**,	3359
	9:24	against the LORD ever since I have **k** you.	3359
	11:28	other gods, which *you* have not **k**.	3359
	13: 2	not **k**) "and let us worship them,"	3359
	13: 6	that neither you nor your fathers have **k**,	3359
	13:13	worship other gods" (gods *you have* not **k**),	3359
	21: 1	and *it* is not **k** who killed him,	3359
	25:10	man's line *shall* be **k** in Israel as	7924+9005
	28:64	which neither you nor your fathers have **k**.	3359
	32:17	gods *they* had not **k**,	3359
Ru	3:14	"Don't *let it* be **k** that a woman came to	3359
1Sa	10:11	When all *those who* had formerly **k** him saw him prophesying	3359
	18:23	I'm only a poor man and **little k**."	7829
	18:30	and his name **became well k**.	3700+4394
2Sa	7:21	have done this great thing and **made** it **k**	3359
1Ki	18:36	*let* it be **k** today that you are God in Israel	3359
1Ch	16: 8	**make k** among the nations what he has done.	3359
	17:19	and **made k** all these great promises.	3359
Ne	8:12	the words that *had been* **made k** to them.	3359
	9:14	*You* **made k** to them your holy Sabbath	3359
Est	1:17	the queen's conduct *will* **become k** to all	3655
	2: 7	This girl, who was also **k** as Esther,	NIH
	3:14	**made k** to the people of every nationality	1655
	8:13	**made k** to the people of every nationality	1655
Job	36:33	even the cattle make **k** its approach.	NIH
	42:11	and everyone *who had* **k** him before came	3359
Ps	9:16	The LORD is **k** *by* his justice;	3359
	16:11	*You have* **made k** to me the path of life;	3359
	25:14	he makes his covenant **k** *to* them.	3359
	37:18	days of the blameless *are* **k** *to* the LORD,	3359
	59:13	be **k** to the ends of the earth that God rules	3359
	67: 2	that your ways *may be* **k** on earth,	3359
	76: 1	In Judah God is **k**;	3359
	78: 3	what we have heard and **k**,	3359
	79:10	**make k** among the nations that you avenge	3359
	88:12	Are your wonders **k** in the place	3359
	89: 1	I **make** your faithfulness **k**	3359
	95:10	and they *have* not **k** my ways."	3359
	98: 2	The LORD *has* **made** his salvation **k**	3359

Ps	103: 7	*He* **made k** his ways to Moses,	3359
	105: 1	**make k** among the nations what he has done.	3359
	106: 8	**make** his mighty power **k**.	3359
	119:168	for all my ways are **k** to you.	5584
Pr	1:23	to you and **made** my thoughts **k** *to* you.	3359
	14:33	even among fools *she* **lets** *herself* **be k**.	3359
	20:11	Even a child **is k** by his actions,	5795
	24: 8	He who plots evil *will be* **k** as a schemer.	7924
Ecc	6:10	and what man is *has* **been k**;	3359
Isa	12: 4	**make k** among the nations what he has done,	3359
	12: 5	*let* this *be* **k** to all the world.	3359
	19:12	Let them show you and **make k** what	3359
	19:21	So the LORD *will* **make himself k** to	3359
	42:16	the blind by ways *they have* not **k**,	3359
	46:10	I **make k** the end from the beginning,	5583
	48: 3	and *I* **made** them **k**;	9048
	61: 9	Their descendants *will be* **k** among	3359
	64: 2	down to **make** your name **k** to your enemies	3359
	66:14	the LORD *will* *be* **made k** to his servants,	3359
Jer	7: 9	and follow other gods *you have* not **k**,	3359
	9:16	that neither they nor their fathers *have* **k**,	3359
	16:13	a land neither you nor your fathers have **k**,	3359
Eze	20:11	I gave them my decrees and **made k**	3359
	32: 9	among lands *you have* not **k**.	3359
	35:11	and *I will* **make myself k** among them	3359
	38:23	and *I will* **make myself k** in the sight	3359
	39: 7	" 'I will **make k** my holy name	3359
	43:11	**make k** *to* them the design of the temple—	3359
Da	2:23	*you have* **made k** to me what we asked	10313
	2:23	of you, *you have* **made k** to us the dream of	10313
Hab	3: 2	in our time **make** them **k**;	3359
Zec	14: 7	a day **k** to the LORD.	3359
Mt	10:26	or hidden that *will not be* **made k**.	1182
	12: 7	If *you had* **k** what these words mean,	1182
	24:43	If the owner of the house *had* **k** at what time	3857
	26: 6	in the home of a man **k** as Simon the Leper,	NIG
Mk	6:14	for Jesus' name had become **well k**.	5745
	14: 3	reclining at the table in the home of a man	NIG
Lk	8:17	and nothing concealed that *will not be* **k**,	1182
	12: 2	or hidden that *will not be* **made k**.	1182
	12:39	If the owner of the house *had* **k** at what hour	3857
	19:42	and said, "If *you*, even you, *had only* **k**	1182
Jn	1:18	who is at the Father's side, *has* **made** him **k**.	2007
	1:33	I *would not have* **k** him,	3857
	6:64	For Jesus *had* **k** from the beginning which	3857
	15:15	I learned from my Father *I have* **made k**	1192
	16: 3	because *they have* not **k** the Father or me.	1182
	16:14	taking from what is mine and **making** it **k**	334
	16:15	from what is mine and **make** it **k** to you.	334
	17:26	*I have* **made** you **k** to them,	1192
	17:26	and *will continue to* **make** you **k** in order	1192
	18:15	this disciple was **k** to the high priest,	1196
	18:16	who *was* **k** to the high priest, came back,	1196
	19:13	at a place **k** as the Stone Pavement	3306
Ac	1:23	Joseph called Barsabbas (also **k** as Justus)	2813
	2:28	*You have* **made k** to me the paths of life;	1192
	6: 3	among you *who are* **k** to be full of the Spirit	3455
	8:10	the divine power **k** as the Great Power."	2813
	9:42	This became **k** all over Joppa,	1196
	10: 1	in what *was* **k** as the Italian Regiment.	2813
	10:18	asking if Simon who *was* **k** as Peter	2126
	15:18	*that have been* **k** for ages.	1196
	19:17	When this became **k** to the Jews	1196
	26: 5	*They have* **k** me for a long time	4589
Ro	1:19	what may be **k** about God is plain to them,	1196
	3:21	apart from law, *has been* **made k**,	5746
	7: 7	not *have* **k** what sin was except through	1182
	7: 7	not *have* **k** what coveting really was if	3857
	9:22	to show his wrath and **make** his power **k**,	1192
	9:23	**make** the riches of his glory **k**	1192
	11:34	"Who *has* **k** the mind of the Lord?	1182
	15:20	to preach the gospel where Christ *was not* **k**,	3951
	16:26	and **made k** through the prophetic writings	1192
1Co	2:16	"For who *has* **k** the mind of the Lord	1182
	8: 3	But the man who loves God *is* **k** by God.	1182
	13:12	I shall know fully, even as *I am* **fully k**.	2105
2Co	2:16	on our hearts, **k** and read by everybody.	1182
	6: 9	**k**, yet regarded as unknown;	2105
	11:27	I have **k** hunger and thirst	NIG
Gal	4: 9	or rather *are* **k** by God—	1182
Eph	1: 9	And he *made* **k** to us the mystery of his will	1192
	3: 3	the mystery *made* **k** to me by revelation,	1192
	3: 5	not **made k** to men in other generations	1192
	3:10	*be* **made k** to the rulers and authorities in	1192
	6:19	so that I will fearlessly **make k** the mystery	1192
Col	1:27	To them God has chosen to **make k** among	1192
1Th	1: 8	your faith in God *has* **become k** everywhere.	2002
1Ti	5:10	and *is* **well k** for her good deeds,	3455
2Ti	3:15	and how from infancy *you have* **k**	3857
Heb	3:10	and *they have* not **k** my ways.'	1182
	11:24	*to be* **k** as the son of Pharaoh's daughter.	3306
2Pe	2:21	not *to have* **k** the way of righteousness,	2105
	2:21	than *to have* **k** it and then to turn their backs	2105
1Jn	2:13	*you have* **k** him who is from the beginning.	1182
	2:13	because *you have* **k** the Father.	1182
	2:14	*you have* **k** him who is from the beginning.	1182
	3: 2	what we *will be has not yet been* **made k**.	5746
	3: 6	to sin has either seen him or **k** him.	1182
Rev	1: 1	*He* **made** it **k** by sending his angel	4955
	2:17	**k** only to him who receives it.	3857

KNOWS (91) [KNOW]

Ge	3: 5	"For God **k** that when you eat	3359
	16: 5	and now that *she* **k** she is pregnant,	8011

Ge	33:13	"My lord k that the children are tender and	3359
Dt	34: 6	but to this day no one k where his grave is.	3359
Jos	22:22	The Mighty One, God, the LORD! He k!	3359
1Sa	2: 3	for the LORD is a God who k,	1978
	16:18	of Bethlehem who k how to play the harp.	3359
	20: 3	"Your father k very well	3359+3359
	22:15	for your servant k nothing at all	3359
	23:17	Even my father Saul k this."	3359
	25:11	give it to men coming from who k where?"	3359
2Sa	12:22	I thought, 'Who k?	3359
	14:20	he k everything that happens in the land."	3359
	14:22	"Today your servant k that he has found	3359
	17:10	for all Israel k that your father is a fighter	3359
Est	4:14	And who k but that you have come	3359
Job	15:23	he k the day of darkness is at hand.	3359
	18:21	such is the place of one who k not God."	3359
	23:10	But he k the way that I take;	3359
	28: 7	No bird of prey k that hidden path,	3359
	28:23	the way to it and he alone k where it dwells,	3359
Ps	37:13	for he k their day is coming.	8011
	44:21	since he k the secrets of the heart?	3359
	74: 9	and none of us k how long this will be.	3359
	90:11	Who k the power of your anger?	3359
	94:11	The LORD k the thoughts of man;	3359
	94:11	he k that they are futile.	NIH
	103:14	for he k how we are formed,	3359
	104:19	and the sun k when to go down.	3359
	138: 6	but the proud he k from afar.	3359
Pr	5: 6	her paths are crooked, but she k it not.	3359
	14:10	Each heart k its own bitterness,	3359
	24:22	and who k what calamities they can bring?	3359
Ecc	2:19	And who k whether he will be a wise man	3359
	3:21	Who k if the spirit of man rises upward and	3359
	4:13	old but foolish king who no longer k how	3359
	6:12	For who k what is good for a man in life,	3359
	8: 1	Who k the explanation of things?	3359
	8: 7	Since no man k the future,	3359
	8:17	Even if a wise man claims he k,	3359
	9: 1	no man k whether love or hate awaits him.	3359
	9:12	no man k when his hour will come;	3359
	10:14	No one k what is coming—	3359
Isa	1: 3	The ox k his master,	3359
	7:15	when he k enough to reject the wrong and	3359
	7:16	before the boy k enough to reject the wrong	3359
	8: 4	Before the boy k how to say 'My father'	3359
	29:16	the pot say of the potter, "He k nothing"?	1067
Jer	8: 7	the stork in the sky k her appointed seasons,	3359
	9:24	that he understands and k me,	3359
Da	2:22	he k what lies in darkness,	10313
Joel	2:14	Who k? He may turn and have pity	3359
Jnh	3: 9	Who k? God may yet relent	3359
Na	3:17	and no one k where.	3359
Mt	6: 8	for your Father k what you need	3857
	6:32	your heavenly Father k that you need them.	3857
	9:30	"See that no one k about this."	1182
	11:27	No one k the Son except the Father,	2105
	11:27	and no one k the Father except the Son	2105
	24:36	"No one k about that day or hour,	3857
Mk	13:32	"No one k about that day or hour,	3857
Lk	10:22	No one k who the Son is except the Father,	1182
	10:22	and no one k who the Father is except	NIG
	12:30	and your Father k that you need them.	3857
	12:47	"That servant who k his master's will	1182
	16:15	but God k your hearts.	1182
Jn	7:49	But this mob that k nothing of the law—	1182
	10:15	as the Father k me and I know the Father—	1182
	14:17	because it neither sees him nor k him.	1182
	19:35	He k that he tells the truth,	3857
Ac	4:16	living in Jerusalem k they have done	5745
	15: 8	God, who k the heart,	2841
Ro	8:27	And he who searches our hearts k the mind	3857
1Co	2:11	among men k the thoughts of a man except	3857
	2:11	In the same way no one k the thoughts	1182
	3:20	"The Lord k that the thoughts of	1182
	8: 2	The man who thinks he k something does	1182
	8: 7	But not everyone k this.	1194
2Co	7: 4	in all our troubles my joy k no bounds.	5668
	11:11	Because I do not love you? God k I do!	3857
	11:31	k that I am not lying.	3857
	12: 2	of the body I do not know—God k.	3857
	12: 3	from the body I do not know, but God k—	3857
2Ti	2:19	"The Lord k those who are his," and,	1182
Jas	4:17	who k the good he ought to do	3857
2Pe	2: 9	then the Lord k how to rescue godly men	3857
1Jn	3:20	and he k everything.	1182
	4: 6	and whoever k God listens to us;	1182
	4: 7	who loves has been born of God and k God.	1182
Rev	12:12	because he k that his time is short."	3857
	19:12	He has a name written on him that no one k	3857

KOA (1)

| Eze | 23:23 | the men of Pekod and Shoa and K, | 7760 |

KOHATH (19) [KOHATH'S, KOHATHITE, KOHATHITES]

Ge	46:11	The sons of Levi: Gershon, K and Merari.	7740
Ex	6:16	Gershon, K and Merari.	7740
	6:18	The sons of K were Amram, Izhar,	7740
	6:18	K lived 133 years.	7740
Nu	3:17	Gershon, K and Merari.	7740
	3:27	To K belonged the clans of the Amramites,	7740
	16: 1	Korah son of Izhar, the son of K,	7740
	26:57	through K, the Kohathite clan;	7740
	26:58	(K was the forefather of Amram,	7740
1Ch	6: 1	The sons of Levi: Gershon, K and Merari.	7740

1Ch	6: 2	The sons of K: Amram, Izhar, Hebron	7740
	6:16	The sons of Levi: Gershon, K and Merari.	7740
	6:18	The sons of K: Amram, Izhar, Hebron	7740
	6:22	The descendants of K:	7740
	6:38	the son of K, the son of Levi,	7740
	15: 5	From the descendants of K, Uriel the leader	7740
	23: 6	Gershon, K and Merari.	7740
	23:12	The sons of K: Amram, Izhar, Hebron	7740
2Ch	34:12	and Meshullam, descended from K.	7741

KOHATH'S (2) [KOHATH]

| Jos | 21: 5 | of K descendants were allotted ten towns | 7740 |
| 1Ch | 6:61 | of K descendants were allotted ten towns | 7740 |

KOHATHITE (16) [KOHATH]

Nu	3:19	The K clans: Amram, Izhar,	1201+7741
	3:27	these were the K clans.	7741
	3:29	K clans were to camp on the south	1201+7740
	3:30	of the K clans was Elizaphan son of Uzziel.	7741
	4: 2	K branch of the Levites by their clans	1201+7740
	4:18	The K tribal clans are not cut off from	7741
	4:37	of all those in the K clans who served in	7741
	26:57	through Kohath, the K clan;	7741
Jos	21:10	from the K clans of the Levites, because	7741
	21:20	The rest of the K clans of	1201+7740
	21:26	to the rest of the K clans.	1201+7740
1Ch	6:54	from the K clan, because the first lot was	7741
	6:60	which were distributed among the K clans,	2157S
	6:66	Some of the K clans were given	1201+7740
	6:70	to the rest of the K clans.	1201+7740
	9:32	of their K brothers were in charge	1201+7741

KOHATHITES (12) [KOHATH]

Nu	3:28	The K were responsible for the care of	NIH
	4: 4	work of the K in the Tent of Meeting:	1201+7740
	4:15	The K are to come to do the carrying.	7740
	4:15	The K are to carry those things	1201+7740
	4:20	K must not go in to look at the holy things,	NIH
	4:34	counted the K by their clans	7741
	7: 9	But Moses did not give any to the K,	1201+7740
	10:21	the K set out, carrying the holy things.	7741
Jos	21: 4	The first lot came out for the K,	7741
1Ch	6:33	with their sons: From the K:	7741
2Ch	20:19	K and Korahites stood up and praised	1201+7740
	29:12	these Levites set to work: from the K,	1201+7741

KOLAIAH (2)

| Ne | 11: 7 | the son of K, the son of Maaseiah, | 7755 |
| Jer | 29:21 | says about Ahab son of K and Zedekiah son | 7755 |

KORAH (35) [KORAH'S, KORAHITE, KORAHITES]

Ge	36: 5	and Oholibamah bore Jeush, Jalam and K.	7946
	36:14	Jeush, Jalam and K.	7946
	36:16	K, Gatam and Amalek.	7946
	36:18	Chiefs Jeush, Jalam and K.	7946
Ex	6:21	The sons of Izhar were K,	7946
	6:24	The sons of K were Assir,	7946
Nu	16: 1	K son of Izhar, the son of Kohath,	7946
	16: 5	Then he said to K and all his followers:	7946
	16: 6	K, and all your followers are to do this:	7946
	16: 8	Moses also said to K, "Now listen,	7946
	16:16	to K, "You and all your followers are	7946
	16:19	When K had gathered all his followers	7946
	16:24	'Move away from the tents of K,	7946
	16:27	So they moved away from the tents of K,	7946
	16:40	he would become like K and his followers.	7946
	16:49	to those who had died because of K,	7946
	26:11	The line of K, however, did not die out.	7946
1Ch	1:35	Eliphaz, Reuel, Jeush, Jalam and K.	7946
	2:43	K, Tappuah, Rekem and Shema.	7946
	6:22	Amminadab his son, K his son,	7946
	6:37	the son of Ebiasaph, the son of	7946
	9:19	the son of Ebiasaph, the son of K,	7946
	26:19	the gatekeepers who were descendants of K	7948
Ps	42: T	A maskil of the Sons of K.	7946
	44: T	Of the Sons of K.	7946
	45: T	Of the Sons of K.	7946
	46: T	Of the Sons of K.	7946
	47: T	Of the Sons of K.	7946
	48: T	A song. A psalm of the Sons of K.	7946
	49: T	Of the Sons of K.	7946
	84: T	Of the Sons of K.	7946
	85: T	Of the Sons of K.	7946
	87: T	Of the Sons of K. A psalm. A song.	7946
	88: T	A psalm of the Sons of K.	7946

KORAH'S (4) [KORAH]

Nu	16:32	all K men and all their possessions.	4200+7946
	26: 9	and Aaron and were among K followers	7946
	27: 3	He was not among K followers,	7946
Jude	1:11	they have been destroyed in K rebellion.	3169

KORAHITE (3) [KORAH]

Ex	6:24	These were the K clan,	7948
Nu	26:58	the Mushite clan, the K clan.	7948
1Ch	9:31	the firstborn of Shallum the K,	7948

KORAHITES (4) [KORAH]

| 1Ch | 9:19 | from his family (the K) were responsible | 7948 |

1Ch	12: 6	Azarel, Joezer and Jashobeam the K;	7948
	26: 1	of the gatekeepers: From the K:	7948
2Ch	20:19	Kohathites and K stood up and praised	1201+7948

KORATHITES, KORHITES (KJV) See KORAHITE, KORAHITES

KORAZIN (2)

| Mt | 11:21 | "Woe to you, K! | 5960 |
| Lk | 10:13 | "Woe to you, K! | 5960 |

KORE (3)

1Ch	9:19	Shallum son of K, the son of Ebiasaph,	7927
	26: 1	Meshelemiah son of K,	7927
2Ch	31:14	K son of Imnah the Levite,	7927

KOUM (1)

| Mk | 5:41 | by the hand and said to her, "Talitha k!" | 3182 |

KOZ (1)

| 1Ch | 4: 8 | and K, who was the father of Anub | 7766 |

KUE (4)

1Ki	10:28	from Egypt and from K—	7750
	10:28	royal merchants purchased them from K.	7750
2Ch	1:16	from Egypt and from K—	7745
	1:16	royal merchants purchased them from K.	7745

KUSHAIAH (1)

| 1Ch | 15:17 | the Merarites, Ethan son of K; | 7773 |

L

LAADAH (1)

| 1Ch | 4:21 | L the father of Mareshah and the clans of | 4355 |

LAADAN (KJV) See LADAN

LABAN (49) [LABAN'S]

Ge	24:29	Now Rebekah had a brother named L,	4238
	24:33	"Then tell us," [L] said.	NIH
	24:50	L and Bethuel answered,	4238
	25:20	from Paddan Aram and sister of L	4238
	27:43	Flee at once to my brother L in Haran.	4238
	28: 2	from among the daughters of L,	4238
	28: 5	to L son of Bethuel the Aramean,	4238
	29: 5	He said to them, "Do you know L,	4238
	29:10	When Jacob saw Rachel daughter of L,	4238
	29:13	As soon as L heard the news about Jacob,	4238
	29:14	Then L said to him, "You are my own flesh	4238
	29:15	L said to him, "Just because you are a	4238
	29:16	Now L had two daughters;	4238
	29:19	L said, "It's better that I give her	4238
	29:21	Then Jacob said to L, "Give me my wife.	4238
	29:22	So L brought together all the people of	4238
	29:24	And L gave his servant girl Zilpah	4238
	29:25	So Jacob said to L, "What is this you have	4238
	29:26	L replied, "It is not our custom here	4238
	29:28	and then L gave him his daughter Rachel	NIH
	29:29	L gave his servant girl Bilhah	4238
	29:30	And he worked for L another seven years.	2257S
	30:25	Jacob said to L, "Send me on my way	4238
	30:27	But L said to him, "If I have found favor	4238
	30:34	said L. "Let it be as you have said."	4238
	30:40	dark-colored animals that belonged to L.	4238
	30:42	So the weak animals went to L and	4238
	31:12	for I have seen all that L has been doing	4238
	31:19	When L had gone to shear his sheep,	4238
	31:20	Jacob deceived L the Aramean by	4238
	31:22	On the third day L was told	4238
	31:24	to L the Aramean in a dream at night	4238
	31:25	of Gilead when L overtook him,	4238
	31:25	and L and his relatives camped there too.	4238
	31:26	L said to Jacob, "What have you done?	4238
	31:31	Jacob answered L, "I was afraid,	4238
	31:33	So L went into Jacob's tent and	4238
	31:34	L searched through everything in the tent	4238
	31:36	Jacob was angry and took L to task.	4238
	31:36	he asked L, "What sin have I committed	4238
	31:43	L answered Jacob, "The women are my daughters,	4238
	31:47	L called it Jegar Sahadutha,	4238
	31:48	L said, "This heap is a witness	4238
	31:51	L also said to Jacob, "Here is this heap,	4238
	31:55	next morning L kissed his grandchildren	4238
	32: 4	with L and have remained there till now.	4238
	46:18	whom L had given to his daughter Leah—	4238
	46:25	whom L had given to his daughter Rachel	4238
Dt	1: 1	between Paran and Tophel, L,	4239

LABAN'S (5) [LABAN]

Ge	29:10	his mother's brother, and L sheep,	4238
	30:36	to tend the rest of L flocks.	4238
	30:40	and did not put them with L animals.	4238
	31: 1	Jacob heard that L sons were saying,	4238
	31: 2	And Jacob noticed that L attitude	4238

LABOR (93) [LABORED, LABORER, LABORER'S, LABORERS, LABORING, LABORS]

Ge	5:29	the l and painful toil of our hands caused	5126
	49:15	to the burden and submit to forced l.	4989
Ex	1:11	over them to oppress them with forced l,	6026
	1:14	They made their lives bitter with hard l	6275
	1:14	in all their hard l the Egyptians used them	6275
	2:11	and watched them at their hard l.	6026
	5: 4	the people away from their l?	5126
	20: 9	Six days you shall l and do all your work,	6268
	34:21	"Six days you shall l, but on the seventh	6268
Dt	5:13	Six days you shall l and do all your work,	6268
	20:11	the people in it shall be subject to forced l	4989
	26: 6	made us suffer, putting us to hard l.	6275
	28:33	and I produce, and you will have nothing	3330
Jos	16:10	but are required to do forced l.	4989
	17:13	they subjected the Canaanites to forced l	4989
Jdg	1:28	they pressed the Canaanites into forced l	4989
	1:30	but they did subject them to forced l	4989
	1:35	they too were pressed into forced l.	4989
1Sa	4:19	she went into l and gave birth.	4156
	4:19	but was overcome by her l pains.	7496
2Sa	12:31	consigning them to l with saws and with	8492
	20:24	Adoniram was in charge of forced l;	4989
1Ki	4: 6	son of Abda—in charge of forced l.	4989
	5:14	Adoniram was in charge of the forced l.	4989
	9:15	of the forced l King Solomon conscripted	4989
	9:21	Solomon conscripted for his slave l force,	4989
	11:28	the whole l force of the house of Joseph.	6023
	12: 4	the harsh l and the heavy yoke he put	6275
	12:18	who was in charge of forced l	4989
1Ch	20: 3	consigning them to l with saws and with	8492
2Ch	8: 8	Solomon conscripted for his slave l force,	4989
	10: 4	the harsh l and the heavy yoke he put	6275
	10:18	who was in charge of forced l,	4989
Job	24: 5	the poor go about their l of foraging food;	7189
	37: 7	he stops every man from his l	3338
	39: 3	their l pains are ended.	2477
	39:16	she cares not that her l was in vain,	3330
Ps	48: 6	pain like that of a woman in l.	3528
	104:23	to his l until evening.	6275
	107:12	So he subjected them to bitter l;	6662
	109:11	may strangers plunder the fruits of his l.	3330
	127: 1	its builders l in vain.	6662
	128: 2	You will eat the fruit of your l;	3330+4090
Pr	12:24	but laziness ends in slave l.	4989
Ecc	1: 3	from all his l at which he toils under	6662
	2:10	and this was the reward for all my l.	6662
	2:20	to despair over all my toilsome l under	6661
	4: 4	that all l and all achievement spring	6662
	5:15	from his l that he can carry in his hand.	6662
	5:18	to find satisfaction in his toilsome l under	6661
	8:16	to know wisdom and to observe man's l	6721
	9: 9	and in your toilsome l under the sun.	6662
SS	8: 5	there she who was in l gave you birth.	2473
Isa	13: 8	they will writhe like a woman in l.	3528
	21: 3	pangs seize me, like those of a woman in l;	3528
	23: 4	"I have neither been in l nor given birth;	2655
	31: 8	their young men will be put to forced l.	4989
	54: 1	shout for joy, you who were never in l;	2655
	55: 2	and your l on what does not satisfy?	3330
	66: 7	"Before she goes into l, she gives birth;	2655
	66: 8	no sooner is Zion in l than she gives birth	2655
Jer	3:24	fruits of our fathers' l—their flocks and	3330
	4:31	I hear a cry as of a woman in l,	2655
	6:24	pain like that of a woman in l.	3528
	13:21	like that of a woman in l?	4156
	22:13	not paying them for their l.	7189
	22:23	pain like that of a woman in l!	3528
	30: 6	on his stomach like a woman in l,	3528
	31: 8	expectant mothers and women in l.	3528
	48:41	be like the heart of a woman in l.	7674
	49:22	be like the heart of a woman in l.	7674
	49:24	pain like that of a woman in l.	3528
	50:43	pain like that of a woman in l.	3528
	51:58	the nations' l is only fuel for the flames."	3615
La	1: 3	After affliction and harsh l,	6275
Mic	4: 9	pain seizes you like that of a woman in l?	3528
	4:10	O Daughter of Zion, like a woman in l,	3528
	5: 3	the time when she who is in l gives birth	3528
Hab	3:17	that the people's l is only fuel for the fire,	3333
Hag	1:11	and on the l of your hands."	3330
Mt	6:28	They do not l or spin.	3159
Lk	12:27	They do not l or spin.	3159
Jn	4:38	you have reaped the benefits of their l."	3160
1Co	3: 8	be rewarded according to his own l.	3160
	15:58	that your l in the Lord is not in vain.	3160
Gal	4:27	you who have no l pains;	6048
Php	1:22	this will mean fruitful l for me.	2240
	2:16	on the day of Christ that I did not run or l	3159
Col	1:29	To this end I l, struggling with all his energy	3159
1Th	1: 3	your l prompted by love,	3160
	5: 3	as l pains on a pregnant woman,	6047
1Ti	4:10	(and for this we l and strive),	3159
Rev	14:13	says the Spirit, "they will rest from their l,	3160

LABORED (4) [LABOR]

Isa	47:12	which you have l at since childhood.	3333
	47:15	these you have l with and trafficked with	3333
	49: 4	But I said, "I have l to no purpose;	3333
2Co	11:27	I have l and toiled and have often gone	3160

LABORER (1) [LABOR]

Ecc	5:12	The sleep of a l is sweet,	6268

LABORER'S (1) [LABOR]

Pr	16:26	The l appetite works for him;	6664

LABORERS (5) [LABOR]

Jdg	1:33	and Beth Anath became forced l for them.	4989
1Ki	5:13	King Solomon conscripted l from all Israel	4989
2Ch	34:13	of the l and supervised all the workers	6025
Ne	4:10	"The strength of the l is giving out,	6025
Mal	3: 5	against those who defraud l	8502

LABORING (1) [LABOR]

2Th	3: 8	l and toiling so that we would not be	3160

LABORS (2) [LABOR]

Ecc	2:22	and anxious striving with which he l	6665
1Co	16:16	who joins in the work, and l at it.	3159

LACE (KJV) See CORD

LACHISH (24)

Jos	10: 3	Japhia king of L and Debir king of Eglon.	4337
	10: 5	Jarmuth, L and Eglon—joined forces.	4337
	10:23	Hebron, Jarmuth, L and Eglon.	4337
	10:31	with him moved on from Libnah to L;	4337
	10:32	The LORD handed L over to Israel,	4337
	10:33	up to help L, but Joshua defeated him	4337
	10:34	and all Israel with him moved on from L	4337
	10:35	just as they had done to L.	4337
	12:11	the king of Jarmuth one the king of L one	4337
	15:39	L, Bozkath, Eglon,	4337
2Ki	14:19	against him in Jerusalem and he fled to L,	4337
	14:19	after him to L and killed him there.	4337
	18:14	to the king of Assyria at L:	4337
	18:17	from L to King Hezekiah at Jerusalem.	4337
	19: 8	that the king of Assyria had left L,	4337
2Ch	11: 9	Adoraim, L, Azekah.	4337
	25:27	against him in Jerusalem and he fled to L,	4337
	25:27	after him to L and killed him there.	4337
	32: 9	and all his forces were laying siege to L,	4337
Ne	11:30	in L and its fields,	4337
Isa	36: 2	from L to King Hezekiah at Jerusalem.	4337
	37: 8	that the king of Assyria had left L,	4337
Jer	34: 7	that were still holding out—L and Azekah.	4337
Mic	1:13	You who live in L, harness the team to	4337

LACK (40) [LACKED, LACKING, LACKS]

Dt	8: 9	not be scarce and you will l nothing;	2893
Job	4:11	The lion perishes for l of prey,	1172
	24: 8	by mountain rains and hug the rocks for l	1172
	31:19	if I have seen anyone perishing for l of	1172
	34:35	his words l insight.'	928+4202
	38:41	to God and wander about for l of food?	1172
Ps	34: 9	for those who fear him l nothing.	4728
	34:10	who fear the LORD l no good thing.	2893
	94:10	Does he who teaches man l knowledge?	NIH
Pr	5:23	He will die for l of discipline,	401
	9: 4	she says to those who l judgment.	2894
	9:16	she says to those who l judgment.	2894
	10:21	but fools die for l of judgment.	2894
	11:14	For l of guidance a nation falls,	401
	15:22	Plans fail for l of counsel,	401
	22:27	if you l the means to pay,	401+4200
	28:27	He who gives to the poor will l nothing,	4728
Isa	5:13	into exile for l of understanding,	1172
	34:16	not one will l her mate.	7212
	50: 2	Do I l the strength to rescue you?	401+928
	50: 2	their fish rot for l of water and die	401
	51:14	nor will they l bread.	2893
	56:10	they all l knowledge;	4202
	56:11	They are shepherds who l understanding;	4202
Jer	14: 6	their eyesight fails for l of pasture."	401
La	4: 9	with hunger, they waste away for l of	4946
Hos	4: 6	people are destroyed from l of knowledge.	1172
Am	4: 6	in every city and l of bread in every town,	2896
Zec	10: 2	like sheep oppressed for l of a shepherd.	401
Mt	13:58	because of their l of faith.	602
	19:20	"What do I still l?"	5728
Mk	6: 6	And he was amazed at their l of faith.	602
	10:21	"One thing you l," he said.	5728
	16:14	he rebuked them for their l of faith	602
Lk	18:22	he said to him, "You still l one thing.	3309
	22:35	bag or sandals, did you l anything?"	5728
Ro	3: 3	their l of faith nullify God's faithfulness?	602
1Co	1: 7	not l any spiritual gift as you eagerly wait	5728
	7: 5	because of your l of self-control.	202
Col	2:23	but they l any value in restraining sensual	4024

LACKED (6) [LACK]

Dt	2: 7	and you have not l anything.	2893
Jdg	18: 7	their land l nothing, they were prosperous.	4007
1Ki	11:22	"What have you l here that you want	2894
Ne	9:21	they l nothing, their clothes did not wear out	2893

LACKING (10) [LACK]

1Ki	4:27	saw to it that nothing was l.	6372
Job	24: 7	L clothes, they spend the night naked;	1172+4946
	24:10	L clothes, they go about naked;	1172
Pr	17:18	A man l in judgment strikes hands in pledge	2894
Ecc	1:15	what is l cannot be counted.	2898
Ro	12:11	Never be l in zeal,	3891
1Co	16:17	they have supplied what was l from you.	5729
Col	1:24	fill up in my flesh what is still l in regard	5729
1Th	3:10	and supply what is l in your faith.	5729
Jas	1: 4	be mature and complete, not l anything.	3309

LACKS (16) [LACK]

Jdg	18:10	a land that l nothing whatever."	4728
2Sa	3:29	or who falls by the sword or who l food."	2894
Pr	6:32	a man who commits adultery l judgment;	2894
	10:13	rod is for the back of him who l judgment.	2894
	11:12	man who l judgment derides his neighbor,	2894
	12:11	but he who chases fantasies l judgment.	2894
	15:21	Folly delights a man who l judgment,	2894
	24:30	the vineyard of the man who l judgment;	2894
	25:28	broken down is a man who l self-control.	401
	28:16	A tyrannical ruler l judgment,	2894
	31:11	in her and l nothing of value.	2893
Ecc	6: 2	so that he l nothing his heart desires,	2894
	10: 3	the fool l sense and shows everyone	2893
SS	7: 2	that never l blended wine.	2893
Eze	34: 2	because my flock l a shepherd and	401
Jas	1: 5	If any of you l wisdom,	3309

LAD (KJV) See BOY, SERVANT, YOUNG MAN

LADAN (7)

1Ch	7:26	L his son, Ammihud his son,	4356
	23: 7	to the Gershonites: L and Shimei.	4356
	23: 8	The sons of L:	4356
	23: 9	These were the heads of the families of L.	4356
	26:21	The descendants of L,	4356
	26:21	who were Gershonites through L	4356
	26:21	of families belonging to L the Gershonite,	4356

LADE, LADED, LADING (KJV) See LAID, LOAD

LADEN (3) [LOAD]

Job	36:16	to the comfort of your table l with	4848
	36:17	But now you are l with the judgment due	4848
Ps	105:37	He brought out Israel, l with silver and gold,	928

LADIES (1) [LADY]

Jdg	5:29	The wisest of her l answer her;	8576

LADY (2) [LADIES]

2Jn	1: 1	elder, To the chosen l and her children,	3257
	1: 5	And now, dear l, I am not writing you	3257

LAEL (1)

Nu	3:24	of the Gershonites was Eliasaph son of L.	4210

LAGGING (1)

Dt	25:18	and cut off all who were l behind;	3129

LAHAD (1)

1Ch	4: 2	and Jahath the father of Ahumai and L.	4262

LAHAI-ROI (KJV) See BEER LAHAI ROI

LAHMAS (1)

Jos	15:40	Cabbon, L, Kitlish,	4314

LAHMI (1)

1Ch	20: 5	Elhanan son of Jair killed L the brother	4313

LAID (147) [LAY]

Ge	9:23	a garment and l it across their shoulders;	8492
	22: 9	He bound his son Isaac and l him on	8492
Ex	19:13	not a hand is to be l on him.	5595
	22: 8	to determine whether he has l his hands on	8938
Lev	8:14	and his sons l their hands on its head.	6164
	8:18	and his sons l their hands on its head.	6164
	8:22	and his sons l their hands on its head.	6164
	9:20	these they l on the breasts,	8492
	26:33	Your land will be l waste,	9039
Nu	27:23	Then he l his hands on him	6164
Dt	24: 5	not be sent to war or have any other duty l	6296
	34: 9	of wisdom because Moses had l his hands	6164
Jos	2: 6	the stalks of flax she had l out on the roof.)	6885
	2:19	his blood will be on our head if a hand is l	NIH
Jdg	2:20	that I l down for their forefathers and has	7422
	16:24	the one who l waste our land	2990
Ru	4:16	l him in her lap and cared for him.	8883
1Sa	19:13	Michal took an idol and l it on the bed,	8492
2Sa	22:16	and the foundations of the earth l bare at	1655

1Ki	1:21	as soon as my lord the king *is* l to rest 8886
	6:37	**The foundation** of the temple of the LORD was l
	7:10	**The foundations were** l with large stones 3569
	12:11	My father l on you a heavy yoke; 6673
	13:29	l it on the donkey, 5663
	13:30	Then *he* l the donkey in his own tomb, 5663
	16:17	from Gibbethon and l **siege** to Tirzah. 7443
	16:34	*He* l its **foundations** at the cost of his 3569
	17:19	and l him on his bed. 8899
	18:33	the bull into pieces and l it on the wood. 8492
2Ki	4:21	on the bed of the man of God, 8886
	4:31	on ahead and l the staff on the boy's face, 8492
	6:24	marched up and l **siege** to Samaria. 7443
	17:5	marched against Samaria and l **siege** to it 7443
	18:9	against Samaria and l **siege** to it. 7443
	19:17	Assyrian kings *have* l **waste** these nations 2990
	22:19	they would become accursed and l **waste**, 9014
	24:10	Jerusalem and l **siege** to it, 928+995+2021+5189
1Ch	6:32	according to the **regulations** l down AIT
	20:1	*He* l **waste** the land of the Ammonites 8845
2Ch	3:3	**The foundation** Solomon l for building 3569
	8:16	**foundation** *of* the temple of the LORD was l 4586
	10:11	My father l on you a heavy yoke; 6673
	16:14	*They* l him on a bier covered with spices 8886
	29:23	and *they* l their hands on them. 6164
	32:1	*He* l **siege** to the fortified cities, 2837+6584
Ezr	3:6	the **foundation** of the LORD's temple *had* not *yet* been l. 3569
	3:10	When the builders l **the foundation** *of* 3569
	3:11	**the foundation** *of* the house of the LORD was l. 3569
	3:12	**the foundation** *of* this temple *being* l, 3569
	5:16	and l the **foundations** of the house of God 10314
	6:3	and *let* its **foundations** be l. 10502
Ne	3:3	They l its **beams** and put its doors and bolts 7936
	3:6	They l its **beams** and put its doors and bolts 7936
Job	14:10	But man dies and *is* l **low**; 2764
	16:18	may my cry never be l to rest! NIH
	38:4	l the earth's **foundation**? 3569
	38:6	or who l its **cornerstone**— 3721
Ps	18:15	and the foundations of the earth l **bare** 1655
	66:11	You brought us into prison and l **burdens** 8492
	102:25	In the beginning *you* l the **foundations** of 3569
	119:4	You have l **down** precepts that are to 7422
	119:25	I *am* l **low** in the dust; 1815
	119:138	statutes *you* have l **down** are righteous; 7422
	139:5	*you* have l your hand upon me. 8883
	141:9	Keep me from the snares *they* have l 3704
Pr	3:19	l the earth's **foundations**, 3569
Ecc	1:13	What a heavy burden God *has* l on men! 5989
	3:10	I have seen the burden God *has* l on men. 5989
Isa	1:7	l **waste** as when overthrown by strangers. 9039
	6:13	it will again be l **waste**. 1278
	7:16	the two kings you dread *will* be l **waste**. 6440
	14:8	"Now that *you have been* l **low**, 8886
	14:12	*you* who once l **low** the nations! 2765
	24:3	The earth *will* be **completely** l **waste** 1327+1327
	28:1	the pride of *those* l **low** by wine! 2150
	37:18	Assyrian kings *have* l **waste** all these peoples 2990
	44:28	"*Let its* **foundations** be l." ' 3569
	47:6	on the aged *you* l a very **heavy** yoke; 3877
	48:13	My own hand l the **foundations** of 3569
	49:17	*those* who l you **waste** depart from you. 2238+2256+2990
	49:19	and made desolate and your land l waste, NIH
	51:13	and l **the foundations** *of* the earth, 3569
	51:16	who l **the foundations** *of* the earth, 3569
	53:6	LORD *has* l on him the iniquity of us all. 7003
Jer	2:15	*They have* l **waste** his land; 8883
	9:12	Why has the land been ruined and l **waste** 5898
	12:11	the whole land *will* be l **waste** 9037
	18:16	Their land *will* be l **waste**, 8492
	25:37	The peaceful meadows *will* be l **waste** 1959
	39:1	with his whole army and l **siege** to it. 7443
	46:15	Why *will* your warriors be l **low**? 6085
	46:19	for Memphis will be l **waste** and lie 9014
	48:8	salt on Moab, for *she* will be l **waste**; 5898+5898
La	1:10	The enemy l hands on all her treasures; 7298
	2:6	*He has* l **waste** his dwelling like a garden; 2803
	3:28	for the LORD *has* l it on him. 5747
Eze	6:6	*be* l **waste** and the high places demolished, 2990
	6:6	so that your altars *will be* l **waste** 2990
	12:20	The inhabited towns *will be* l **waste** and 2990
	13:14	so that its foundation *will be* l **bare**. 1655
	21:29	*be* l on the necks of the wicked who are to 5989
	24:2	because the king of Babylon *has* l **siege** 6164
	25:3	over the land of Israel when *it* was l **waste** 9037
	32:19	down and *be* l among the uncircumcised.' 8886
	32:25	*they are* l among the slain. 5989
	32:29	*they are* l with those killed by the sword. 5989
	32:32	Pharaoh and all his hordes *will be* l 8886
	35:12	"*They have been* l **waste** 9037
	36:35	"This land that was l **waste** has become 9037
Hos	5:9	be l **waste** on the day of reckoning. 9014
Joel	1:7	*It has* l **waste** my vines 8492
Mic	5:1	l for a siege is laid against us. 8492
Na	2:2	though destroyers *have* l them **waste**, 1327
Hag	2:15	how things were before one stone *was* l 8492
	2:18	the **foundation** of the LORD's temple was l. 3569
Zec	4:9	of Zerubbabel *have* l **the foundation** 3569
	8:9	when **the foundation was** l *for* the house 3569
Mt	5:30	and l them at his feet; and he healed them. 4849
	22:15	the Pharisees went out and l **plans** 3284+5206
Mk	6:29	and took his body and l it in a tomb. 5502
	15:47	the mother of Joses saw where *he* was l. 5502

Mk	16:6	See the place where *they* l him. 5502
Lk	6:48	who dug down deep and l the foundation 5502
	12:19	"You have plenty of good things l **up** 3023
	16:20	At his gate *was* l a beggar named Lazarus, 965
	19:20	I have kept it l **away** in a piece of cloth. 641
	23:53	one in which no one had yet been l. 3023
	23:55	and saw the tomb and how his body *was* l 5502
Jn	7:30	but no one l a hand **on** him, 2095
	7:44	but no one l a hand **on** him. 2095
	11:34	"Where *have* you l him?" 5502
	11:38	a cave with a stone l **across** the entrance. 2130
	19:41	in which no one had ever been l. 5502
	19:42	the tomb was nearby, *they* l Jesus there. 5502
Ac	5:15	the sick into the streets and l them on beds 5502
	6:6	who prayed and l their hands **on** them. 2202
	7:58	the witnesses l their clothes at the feet of 700
	8:17	down from the tree and l him in a tomb. 5502
1Co	3:10	*I* l a foundation as an expert builder, 5502
	3:11	foundation other than the one already l, 3023
	14:25	and the secrets of his heart will be l **bare**. 5745
1Ti	4:14	when the body of elders l their hands **on** 2120
Heb	1:10	you l **the foundations** of the earth, 2530
	4:13	and l **bare** before the eyes of him 5548
2Pe	3:10	earth and everything in it *will be* l **bare**. 2351
1Jn	3:16	Jesus Christ l **down** his life for us. 5502
Rev	21:16	The city *was* l **out** like a square, 3023

LAIN (2) [LAY]

Ge	24:16	no man *had ever* l **with** her. 3359
1Sa	26:5	the commander of the army, *had* l **down**. 8886

LAIR (3) [LAIRS]

Jer	4:7	A lion has come out of his l; 6020
	25:38	Like a lion he will leave his l, 6108
Zep	2:15	a l for wild beasts! 5271

LAIRS (1) [LAIR]

Na	2:12	filling his l with the kill and his dens with 2986

LAISH (6) [DAN]

Jdg	18:7	So the five men left and came to L, 4332
	18:14	the land of L said to their brothers, 4332
	18:27	and his priest, and went on to L, 4332
	18:29	though the city used to be called L. 4332
1Sa	25:44	to Paltiel son of L, who was from Gallim. 4331
2Sa	3:15	from her husband Paltiel son of L. 4331

LAISHAH (1)

Isa	10:30	Listen, O L! 4333

LAKE (39)

Dt	33:23	he will inherit southward to the l." 3542
Mt	4:13	which was **by the** l in the area of Zebulun 4144
	4:18	They were casting a net into the l, 2498
	8:18	to cross to the other side of the l, NIG
	8:24	a furious storm came up on the l, 2498
	8:32	down the steep bank into the l and died in 2498
	13:1	of the house and sat by the l. 2498
	13:47	into the l and caught all kinds of fish. 2498
	14:25	Jesus went out to them, walking on the l, 2498
	14:26	the disciples saw him walking on the l, 2498
	16:5	When they went across the l, NIG
	17:27	go to the l and throw out your line. 2498
Mk	1:16	Andrew casting a net into the l. 2498
	2:13	Once again Jesus went out beside the l. 2498
	3:7	Jesus withdrew with his disciples to the l, 2498
	4:1	Again Jesus began to teach by the l. 2498
	4:1	into a boat and sat in it out *on the* l, 2498
	5:1	across the l to the region of the Gerasenes. 2498
	5:13	rushed down the steep bank into the l 2498
	5:21	over by boat to the other side of the l, NIG
	5:21	around him while he was by the l. 2498
	6:47	the boat was in the middle *of* the l, 2498
	6:48	he went out to them, walking on the l, 2498
	6:49	but when they saw him walking on the l, 2498
Lk	5:1	One day as Jesus was standing by the l 3349
	5:1	"Let's go over to the other side of the l." 3349
	8:22	A squall came down on the l, 3349
	8:23	which is across the l from Galilee. NIG
	8:33	the steep bank into the l and was drowned. 3349
Jn	6:16	his disciples went down to the l, 2498
	6:17	and set off across the l for Capernaum. 2498
	6:22	on the opposite shore of the l realized 2498
	6:25	on the other side of the l, 2498
Rev	19:20	of them were thrown alive into the fiery l 3349
	20:10	was thrown into the l of burning sulfur, 3349
	20:14	and Hades were thrown into the l of fire. 3349
	20:14	The l of fire is the second death. 3349
	20:15	he was thrown into the l of fire. 3349
	21:8	be in the fiery l of burning sulfur. 3349

LAKKUM (1)

Jos	19:33	and Jabneel to L and ending at the Jordan. 4373

LAMA (2)

Mt	27:46	"Eloi, Eloi, l sabachthani?"— 3316
Mk	15:34	"Eloi, Eloi, l sabachthani?"— 3316

LAMB (103) [LAMB'S, LAMBS]

Ge	22:7	"but where is the l for the burnt offering?" 8445
	22:8	"God himself will provide the l for 8445

Ge	30:32	every dark-colored l and 928+2021+4166+8445
	30:33	or any l that is not dark-colored, 4166
Ex	12:3	of this month each man is to take a l 8445
	12:4	any household is too small for a *whole* l, 8445
	12:4	the amount of l needed in accordance 8445
	12:21	and slaughter the **Passover** l. 7175
	13:13	Redeem with a l every firstborn donkey, 8445
	29:40	With the first l offer a tenth of an ephah 3897
	29:41	Sacrifice the other l at twilight with 3897
	34:20	Redeem the firstborn donkey with a l, 8445
Lev	3:7	If he offers a l, he is to present it 4166
	4:32	" 'If he brings a l as his sin offering, 3897
	4:35	just as the fat is removed from the l *of* 4166
	5:6	he must bring to the LORD a female l 4167
	5:7	" 'If he cannot afford a l, he is to bring 8445
	9:3	a calf and a l—both a year old and without 3897
	12:6	to the Tent of Meeting a year-old l for 3897
	12:8	If she cannot afford a l, she is to bring 8445
	14:10	and one **ewe** l a year old, 3898
	14:13	to slaughter the l in the holy place where 3897
	14:21	he must take one **male** l as a guilt offering 3897
	14:24	to take the l *for* the guilt offering 3897
	14:25	the l *for* the guilt offering and take some 3897
	17:3	a l or a goat in the camp or outside of it 4166
	22:27	"When a calf, a l or a goat is born, 4166
	23:12	to the LORD a l a year old without defect, 3897
Nu	6:12	a year-old **male** l as a guilt offering. 3897
	6:14	a year-old **male** l without defect for 3897
	6:14	for a burnt offering, a year-old **ewe** l 3898
	7:15	one ram and one **male** l a year old, 3897
	7:21	one ram and one **male** l a year old, 3897
	7:27	one ram and one **male** l a year old, 3897
	7:33	one ram and one **male** l a year old, 3897
	7:39	one ram and one **male** l a year old, 3897
	7:45	one ram and one **male** l a year old, 3897
	7:51	one ram and one **male** l a year old, 3897
	7:57	one ram and one **male** l a year old, 3897
	7:63	one ram and one **male** l a year old, 3897
	7:69	one ram and one **male** l a year old, 3897
	7:75	one ram and one **male** l a year old, 3897
	7:81	one ram and one **male** l a year old, 3897
	9:11	They are to eat **the** l, 2084S
	15:5	With each l for the burnt offering or 3897
	15:11	Each bull or ram, each l or young goat, 928+2021+3897+8445
	28:4	Prepare one l in the morning and the other 3897
	28:7	of a hin of fermented drink with each l. 3897
	28:8	Prepare the second l at twilight, 3897
	28:13	and with each l, a grain offering of a tenth 3897
	28:14	and with each l, a quarter of a hin. 3897
1Sa	7:9	a suckling l and offered it up as 3231
2Sa	12:3	poor man had nothing except one little **ewe** l he had bought. 3898
	12:4	the **ewe** l *that belonged to* the poor man 3898
	12:6	He must pay for that l four times over, 3898
2Ch	30:15	the **Passover** l on the fourteenth day of 7175
	35:1	and the **Passover** l was slaughtered on 7175
Ezr	6:20	The Levites slaughtered the **Passover** l 7175
Isa	11:6	The wolf will live with the l, 3897
	53:7	he was led like a l to the slaughter, 8445
	65:25	The wolf and the l will feed together, 3231
	66:3	and whoever offers a l, 8445
Jer	11:19	like a gentle l led to the slaughter; 3897
Eze	46:13	to provide a year-old l without defect for 3897
	46:15	So the l and the grain offering and 3897
Mk	14:12	to sacrifice the **Passover** l, 4247
Lk	22:7	the **Passover** l had to be sacrificed. 4247
Jn	1:29	"Look, the L of God, who takes away the sin 303
	1:36	he said, "Look, the L of God!" 303
Ac	8:32	and as a l before the shearer is silent, 303
1Co	5:7	For Christ, our **Passover** l, 4247
1Pe	1:19	a l without blemish or defect. 303
Rev	5:6	I saw a L, looking as if it had been slain, 768
	5:8	twenty-four elders fell down before the L. 768
	5:12	"Worthy is the L, who was slain, 768
	5:13	and *to* the L be praise and honor and glory 768
	6:1	as the L opened the first of the seven seals. 768
	6:3	When the L opened the second seal, NIG
	6:5	When the L opened the third seal, NIG
	6:7	When the L opened the fourth seal, NIG
	6:16	on the throne and from the wrath *of the* L! 768
	7:9	before the throne and in front of the L. 768
	7:10	who sits on the throne, and *to the* L." 768
	7:14	made them white in the blood of the L. 768
	7:17	For the L at the center of the throne will 768
	12:11	They overcame him by the blood of the L 768
	13:8	*to* the L that was slain from the creation of 768
	13:11	He had two horns like a l, 768
	14:1	I looked, and there before me was the L, 768
	14:4	They follow the L wherever he goes. 768
	14:4	and offered as firstfruits to God and the L. 768
	14:10	of the holy angels and of the L. 768
	15:3	the servant of God and the song of the L: 768
	17:14	They will make war against the L, 768
	17:14	but the L will overcome them 768
	19:7	For the wedding of the L has come, 768
	19:9	to the wedding supper of the L!" " 768
	21:9	show you the bride, the wife of the L." 768
	21:14	the names of the twelve apostles of the L. 768
	21:22	Lord God Almighty and the L are its temple. 768
	21:23	of God gives it light, and the L is its lamp. 768
	22:1	from the throne of God and of the L 768
	22:3	The throne of God and *of* the L will be in 768

LAMB'S (1) [LAMB]

Rev	21:27	names are written in the L book of life. 768

LAMBS (92) [LAMB]

Ge	21:28	Abraham set apart seven ewe l *from*	3898
	21:29	of these seven ewe l you have set apart	3898
	21:30	"Accept these seven l from my hand as	3898
	30:35	on them) and all the dark-colored l,	4166
Ex	12: 7	of the houses where they eat the l.	2257S
	29:38	regularly each day: two l a year old,	3897
Lev	14:10	the eighth day he must bring two male l	3897
	14:12	the male l and offer it as a guilt offering,	3897
	23:18	Present with this bread seven male l,	3897
	23:19	for a sin offering and two l,	3897
	23:20	to wave the two l before the LORD as	3897
Nu	7:17	five male goats and five male l a year old,	3897
	7:23	five male goats and five male l a year old,	3897
	7:29	five male goats and five male l a year old,	3897
	7:35	five male goats and five male l a year old,	3897
	7:41	five male goats and five male l a year old,	3897
	7:47	five male goats and five male l a year old,	3897
	7:53	five male goats and five male l a year old,	3897
	7:59	five male goats and five male l a year old,	3897
	7:65	five male goats and five male l a year old,	3897
	7:71	five male goats and five male l a year old,	3897
	7:77	five male goats and five male l a year old,	3897
	7:83	five male goats and five male l a year old,	3897
	7:87	twelve rams and twelve male l a year old,	3897
	7:88	sixty male goats and sixty male l	3897
	28: 3	two l a year old without defect,	3897
	28: 9	make an offering of two l a year old	3897
	28:11	one ram and seven male l a year old,	3897
	28:19	one ram and seven male l a year old,	3897
	28:21	and with each of the seven l, one-tenth.	3897
	28:27	one ram and seven male l a year old as	3897
	28:29	and with each of the seven l, one-tenth.	3897
	29: 2	one ram and seven male l a year old,	3897
	29: 4	and with each of the seven l, one-tenth.	3897
	29: 8	one ram and seven male l a year old,	3897
	29:10	and with each of the seven l, one-tenth.	3897
	29:13	two rams and fourteen male l a year old,	3897
	29:15	and with each of the fourteen l, one-tenth.	3897
	29:17	two rams and fourteen male l a year old,	3897
	29:18	With the bulls, rams and l,	3897
	29:20	two rams and fourteen male l a year old,	3897
	29:21	With the bulls, rams and l,	3897
	29:23	two rams and fourteen male l a year old,	3897
	29:24	With the bulls, rams and l,	3897
	29:26	two rams and fourteen male l a year old,	3897
	29:27	With the bulls, rams and l,	3897
	29:29	two rams and fourteen male l a year old,	3897
	29:30	With the bulls, rams and l,	3897
	29:32	two rams and fourteen male l a year old,	3897
	29:33	With the bulls, rams and l,	3897
	29:36	one ram and seven male l a year old,	3897
	29:37	With the bull, the ram and the l,	3897
Dt	7:13	of your herds and the l *of* your flocks in	6957
	28: 4	of your herds and the l *of* your flocks.	6957
	28:18	of your herds and the l *of* your flocks.	6957
	28:51	or l *of* your flocks until you are ruined.	6957
	32:14	and flock and with fattened l and goats,	4119
1Sa	15: 9	the fat calves and l—	4119
2Ki	3: 4	a hundred thousand l and with the wool of	4119
1Ch	29:21	a thousand rams and a thousand male l,	3897
2Ch	29:21	seven male l and seven male goats as	3897
	29:22	the l and sprinkled their blood on the altar.	3897
	29:32	a hundred rams and two hundred male l—	3897
	30:17	the Passover l for all those who were	7175
	30:17	not consecrate [their l] to the LORD.	NIH
	35: 6	Slaughter the Passover l,	7175
	35: 6	consecrate yourselves and prepare [the l]	NIH
	35:11	The Passover l were slaughtered,	7175
Ezr	6: 9	male l for burnt offerings to the God	10043
	6:17	four hundred male l and,	10043
	7:17	to buy bulls, rams and male l,	10043
	8:35	seventy-seven male l—	3897
Ps	114: 4	skipped like rams, the hills like l.	1201+7366
	114: 6	skipped like rams, you hills, like l?	1201+7366
Pr	27:26	the l will provide you with clothing,	3897
Isa	1:11	in the blood of bulls and l and goats.	3897
	5:17	l will feed among the ruins of the rich.	1531
	16: 1	Send l as tribute to the ruler of the land,	4119
	34: 6	the blood of l and goats,	4119
	40:11	the l in his arms and carries them close	3231
Jer	51:40	"I will bring them down like l to	4119
Eze	27:21	they did business with you in l,	4119
	39:18	if they were rams and l, goats and bulls—	4119
	46: 4	on the Sabbath day is to be six male l and	3897
	46: 5	with the l is to be as much as he pleases,	3897
	46: 6	six l and a ram, all without defect.	3897
	46: 7	with the l as much as he wants to give,	3897
	46:11	and with the l as much as one pleases,	3897
Hos	4:16	then can the LORD pasture them like l in	3897
Am	6: 4	You dine on choice l and fattened calves.	4119+4946+7366
Lk	10: 3	I am sending you out like l among wolves.	748
Jn	21:15	Jesus said, "Feed my l."	768

LAME (26)

Lev	21:18	no man who is blind or l,	7177
Dt	15:21	If an animal has a defect, is l or blind,	7177
2Sa	4: 4	(Jonathan son of Saul had a son who was l	5783
	5: 6	the blind and the l can ward you off."	7177
	5: 8	to use the water shaft to reach those 'l	7177
	5: 8	'blind and l' will not enter the palace."	7177
	19:26	since your servant am l, I said,	7177
Job	29:15	I was eyes to the blind and feet to the l.	7177
Pr	25:19	Like a bad tooth or a l foot is reliance on	5048

Pr	26: 7	Like a l *man's* legs that hang limp is	7177
Isa	33:23	and even the l will carry off plunder.	7177
	35: 6	Then will the l leap like a deer,	7177
Jer	31: 8	Among them will be the blind and the l,	7177
Mic	4: 6	declares the LORD, "I will gather the l;	7519
	4: 7	I will make the l a remnant,	7519
Zep	3:19	I will rescue the l and gather those	7519
Mt	11: 5	The blind receive sight, the l walk,	6000
	15:30	Great crowds came to him, bringing the l,	6000
	15:31	the l walking and the blind seeing.	6000
	21:14	and the l came to him at the temple,	6000
Lk	7:22	The blind receive sight, the l walk,	6000
	14:13	invite the poor, the crippled, the l,	6000
	14:21	the crippled, the blind and the l.'	6000
Jn	5: 3	the blind, the l, the paralyzed.	6000
Ac	14: 8	crippled in his feet, who was l from birth	6000
Heb	12:13	so that the l may not be disabled.	6000

LAMECH (12)

Ge	4:18	and Methushael was the father of L.	4347
	4:19	L married two women,	4347
	4:23	L said to his wives, "Adah and Zillah,	4347
	4:23	wives of L, hear my words.	4347
	4:24	then L seventy-seven times."	4347
	5:25	he became the father of L.	4347
	5:26	And after he became the father of L,	4347
	5:28	When L had lived 182 years, he had a son.	4347
	5:30	L lived 595 years and had other sons	4347
	5:31	Altogether, L lived 777 years,	4347
1Ch	1: 3	Enoch, Methuselah, L, Noah.	4347
Lk	3:36	the son of Noah, the son *of* L,	3285

LAMENT (29) [LAMENTATION, LAMENTED, LAMENTS]

2Sa	1:17	David took up this l concerning Saul	7801+7806
	1:18	the men of Judah be taught this l of the bow	NIH
	3:33	The king sang *this* l for Abner:	7801
Ps	56: 8	Record my l; list my tears on your	5654
	102: T	When he is faint and pours out his l before	8490
Isa	3:26	The gates of Zion *will* l and mourn;	627
	15: 5	to Horonaim *they* l their destruction.	2411+6424
	16: 7	L and grieve for the men of Kir Hareseth.	2047
	19: 8	The fishermen will groan and l,	61
	29: 2	she will mourn and l,	640
Jer	4: 8	So put on sackcloth, l and wail,	6199
	7:29	take up a l on the barren heights,	7806
	9:10	and wail for the mountains and take up a l	7806
	9:20	teach one another a l,	7806
	34: 5	they will make a fire in your honor and l,	6199
La	2: 8	made ramparts and walls l;	61
Eze	2:10	On both sides of it were written words of l	7806
	9: 4	on the foreheads of those who grieve and l	650
	19: 1	up a l concerning the princes of Israel	7806
	19:14	This is a l and is to be used as a lament."	7806
	19:14	This is a lament and is to be used as a l."	7806
	24:16	Yet do not l or weep or shed any tears.	6199
	26:17	Then they will take up a l concerning you	7806
	27: 2	"Son of man, take up a l concerning Tyre.	7806
	27:32	*they* will take up a l concerning you:	7801
	28:12	up a l concerning the king of Tyre and say	7806
	32: 2	up a l concerning Pharaoh king of Egypt	7806
	32:16	"This is the l they will chant for her.	7806
Am	5: 1	this l I take up concerning you:	7806

LAMENTATION (3) [LAMENT]

Est	9:31	in regard to their times of fasting and l.	2411
Isa	15: 8	their l as far as Beer Elim.	3538
La	2: 5	He has multiplied mourning and l for	640

LAMENTATIONS (KJV) See LAMENTS

LAMENTED (1) [LAMENT]

Ge	50:10	the Jordan, *they* l loudly and bitterly;	5027+6199

LAMENTS (6) [LAMENT]

2Ch	35:25	Jeremiah composed l for Josiah,	7801
	35:25	women singers commemorate Josiah in the l	7806
	35:25	in Israel and are written in the L.	7806
Isa	16:11	My heart l for Moab like a harp,	2159
Jer	48:36	"So my heart l for Moab like a flute;	2159
	48:36	it l like a flute for the men of Kir Hareseth.	2159

LAMP (35) [LAMPS, LAMPSTAND, LAMPSTANDS]

1Sa	3: 3	The l *of* God had not yet gone out,	5944
2Sa	21:17	the l of Israel will not be extinguished."	5944
	22:29	You are my l, O LORD;	5944
1Ki	11:36	a l before me in Jerusalem,	5775
	15: 4	a l in Jerusalem by raising up a son	5775
2Ki	4:10	a chair and a l for him.	4963
	8:19	He had promised to maintain a l for David	5775
2Ch	21: 7	He had promised to maintain a l for him	5775
Job	18: 5	"The l of the wicked is snuffed out;	240
	18: 6	the l beside him goes out.	5944
	21:17	the l *of* the wicked snuffed out?	5944
	29: 3	when his l shone upon my head and	5944
Ps	18:28	You, O LORD, keep my l burning;	5944
	119:105	Your word is a l to my feet and a light	5944
	132:17	a horn grow for David and set up a l	5944
Pr	6:23	For these commands are a l,	5944
	13: 9	but the l *of* the wicked is snuffed out.	5944
	20:20	his l will be snuffed out in pitch darkness.	5944

Pr	20:27	The l *of* the LORD searches the spirit of	5944
	21: 4	the l *of* the wicked, are sin!	5775
	24:20	the l *of* the wicked will be snuffed out.	5944
	31:18	and her l does not go out at night.	5944
Jer	25:10	sound of millstones and the light of the l.	5944
Mt	5:15	Neither do people light a l and put it under	3394
	6:22	"The eye is the l of the body.	3394
Mk	4:21	"Do you bring in a l to put it under a bowl	3394
Lk	8:16	a l and hides it in a jar or puts it under	3394
	11:33	"No one lights a l and puts it in a place	3394
	11:34	Your eye is the l of your body.	3394
	11:36	as when the light of a l shines on you."	3394
	15: 8	Does she not light a l,	3394
Jn	5:35	John was a l that burned and gave light,	3394
Rev	18:23	of a l will never shine in you again.	3394
	21:23	God gives it light, and the Lamb is its l.	3394
	22: 5	not need the light *of* a l or the light of	3394

LAMPS (33) [LAMP]

Ex	25:37	"Then make its seven l and set them up	5944
	27:20	the light so that the l may be kept burning.	5944
	27:21	to keep the l burning before the LORD	2257S
	30: 7	when he tends the l.	5944
	30: 8	when he lights the l at twilight	5944
	35:14	l and oil for the light;	5944
	37:23	They made its seven l,	5944
	39:37	*of* l and all its accessories, and the oil for	5944
	40: 4	bring in the lampstand and set up its l.	5944
	40:25	and set up the l before the LORD.	5944
Lev	24: 2	that the l may be kept burning continually.	5944
	24: 3	Aaron is to tend the l before the LORD	2257S
	24: 4	The l on the pure gold lampstand before	5944
Nu	4: 9	together with its l,	5944
	8: 2	'When you set up the seven l,	5944
	8: 3	he set up the l so that they faced forward	5944
1Ki	7:49	the gold floral work and l and tongs;	5944
1Ch	28:15	for the gold lampstands and their l, with	5944
	28:15	the weight for each lampstand and its l;	5944
	28:15	for each silver lampstand and its l,	5944
2Ch	4:20	of pure gold with their l, to burn in front	5944
	4:21	and tongs (they were solid gold);	5944
	13:11	the ceremonially clean table and light the l	5944
	29: 7	the doors of the portico and put out the l.	5944
Zep	1:12	At that time I will search Jerusalem with l	5944
Mt	25: 1	be like ten virgins who took their l	3286
	25: 3	The foolish ones took their l but did	3286
	25: 4	took oil in jars along with their l.	3286
	25: 7	the virgins woke up and trimmed their l.	3286
	25: 8	some of your oil; our l are going out.'	3286
Lk	12:35	for service and keep your l burning,	3394
Ac	20: 8	There were many l in the upstairs room	3286
Rev	4: 5	Before the throne, seven l were blazing.	3286

LAMPSTAND (37) [LAMP]

Ex	25:31	"Make a l of pure gold and hammer it out,	4963
	25:32	to extend from the sides of the l—	4963
	25:33	for all six branches extending from the l.	4963
	25:34	on the l there are to be four cups shaped	4963
	25:35	the l, a second bud under the second pair,	4963
	25:36	be of one piece with the l,	5626S
	25:39	A talent of pure gold is to be used for the l	NIH
	26:35	and put the l opposite it on the south side.	4963
	30:27	the l and its accessories,	4963
	31: 8	the pure gold l and all its accessories,	4963
	35:14	the l that is *for* light with its accessories,	4963
	37:17	the l of pure gold and hammered it out,	4963
	37:18	from the sides of the l—	4963
	37:19	for all six branches extending from the l.	4963
	37:20	And on the l were four cups shaped	4963
	37:21	of branches extending from the l,	5626S
	37:22	of one piece with the l,	5626S
	37:24	They made the l and all its accessories	2023S
	39:37	the pure gold l with its row of lamps,	4963
	40: 4	Then bring in the l and set up its lamps.	4963
	40:24	the l in the Tent of Meeting opposite	4963
Lev	24: 4	on the pure gold l before the LORD must	4963
Nu	3:31	the table, the l, the altars,	4963
	4: 9	to take a blue cloth and cover the l that is	4963
	8: 2	they are to light the area in front of the l.' "	4963
	8: 3	so that they faced forward on the l,	4963
	8: 4	This is how the l was made:	4963
	8: 4	The l was made exactly like the pattern	4963
1Ch	28:15	with the weight for each l and	2256+4963+4963
	28:15	for each silver l and its lamps,	4963+4963
	28:15	according to the use of each l;	2256+4963+4963
2Ch	13:11	the lamps on the gold l every evening.	4963
Da	5: 5	near the l in the royal palace.	10456
Zec	4: 2	"I see a solid gold l with a bowl at the top	4963
	4:11	on the right and the left of the l?"	4963
Heb	9: 2	In its first room were the l,	3393
Rev	2: 5	to you and remove your l from its place.	3393

LAMPSTANDS (11) [LAMP]

1Ki	7:49	the l of pure gold (five on the right	4963
1Ch	28:15	weight of gold for the gold l and their lamps,	4963
2Ch	4: 7	He made ten gold l according to	4963
	4:20	the l of pure gold with their lamps, to burn	4963
Jer	52:19	censers, sprinkling bowls, pots, l,	4963
Rev	1:12	And when I turned I saw seven golden l,	3393
	1:13	and among the l was someone "like a son of man,"	3393
	1:20	and of the seven golden l is this:	3393
	1:20	and the seven l are the seven churches.	3393
	2: 1	and walks among the seven golden l:	3393
	11: 4	the two olive trees and the two l that stand	3393

LANCE (2)

Job	39:23	along with the flashing spear and l.	3959
	41:29	he laughs at the rattling of the l.	3959

LANCETS (KJV) See SPEARS

LAND (1462) [BORDERLAND, GRASSLANDS, LAND'S, LANDED, LANDOWNER, LANDS, MAINLAND, SHORELANDS, WASTELAND, WASTELANDS]

Ge	1:10	God called the dry ground "l,"	824
	1:11	God said, "Let the l produce vegetation:	824
	1:11	and trees on the l that bear fruit with seed	824
	1:12	The l produced vegetation:	824
	1:24	and the l produce living creatures according	824
	2:11	it winds through the entire l of Havilah,	824
	2:12	(The gold of that l is good;	824
	2:13	it winds through the entire l of Cush.	824
	4:14	Today you are driving me from the l,	141
	4:16	the LORD's presence and lived in the l	824
	7:22	Everything on **dry** l that had the breath	3000
	10:11	From that l he went to Assyria,	824
	11:28	in the l of his birth.	824
	12: 1	and go to the l I will show you.	824
	12: 5	and they set out for the l of Canaan,	824
	12: 6	Abram traveled through the l as far as	824
	12: 6	At that time the Canaanites were in the l.	824
	12: 7	"To your offspring I will give this l."	824
	12:10	Now there was a famine in the l,	824
	13: 6	But the l could not support them	824
	13: 7	and Perizzites were also living in the l at	824
	13: 9	Is not the whole l before you?	824
	13:10	like the l of Egypt, toward Zoar.	824
	13:12	Abram lived in the l of Canaan,	824
	13:15	All the l that you see I will give to you	824
	13:17	through the length and breadth of the l,	824
	15: 7	to give you this l to take possession of it."	824
	15:18	"To your descendants I give this l,	824
	15:19	the l of the Kenites,	NIH
	17: 8	The whole l of Canaan,	824
	19:23	the sun had risen over the l.	824
	19:25	and also the vegetation in the l.	141
	19:28	toward all the l of the plain,	824
	19:28	and he saw dense smoke rising from the l,	824
	20:15	And Abimelech said, "My l is before you;	824
	21:32	his forces returned to the l of the Philistines.	824
	21:34	in the l of the Philistines for a long time.	824
	23: 2	Hebron) in the l of Canaan,	824
	23: 7	down before the people of the l,	824
	23:12	down before the people of the l	824
	23:15	l is worth four hundred shekels of silver,	824
	23:19	near Mamre (which is at Hebron) in the l	824
	24: 5	to come back with me to this l?	824
	24: 7	of my father's household and my native l	824
	24: 7	'To your offspring I will give this l'—	824
	24:37	Canaanites, in whose l I live,	824
	25: 6	from his son Isaac to the l of the east.	824
	26: 1	Now there was a famine in the l—	824
	26: 2	live in the l where I tell you to live.	824
	26: 3	Stay in this l for a while,	824
	26:12	in that l and the same year reaped	824
	26:22	and we will flourish in the l."	824
	27:46	a wife from among the women of this l,	824
	28: 4	so that you may take possession of the l	824
	28: 4	**the** l God gave to Abraham."	889S
	28:13	I will give you and your descendants the l	824
	28:15	and I will bring you back to this l.	141
	29: 1	and came to the l of the eastern peoples.	824
	31: 3	the l of your fathers and to your relatives,	824
	31:13	Now leave this l at once and go back	824
	31:13	at once and go back to your native l.' "	824
	31:18	to his father Isaac in the l of Canaan.	824
	32: 3	of him to his brother Esau in the l of Seir.	824
	34: 1	went out to visit the women of the l.	824
	34:10	settle among us; the l is open to you.	824
	34:21	"Let them live in our l and trade in it;	824
	34:21	the l has plenty of room for them.	824
	34:30	the people living in this l.	824
	35: 6	Bethel) in the l of Canaan.	824
	35:12	I l gave to Abraham and Isaac I	824
	35:12	and I will give this l to your descendants	824
	36: 6	a l some distance from his brother Jacob.	824
	36: 7	The l where they were staying could	824
	36:30	in the l of Seir.	824
	36:34	the l of the Temanites succeeded him	824
	36:43	to their settlements in the l they occupied.	824
	37: 1	in the l where his father had stayed,	824
	37: 1	his father had stayed, the l of Canaan.	824
	40:15	For I was forcibly carried off from the l	824
	41:19	such ugly cows in all the l of Egypt.	824
	41:29	coming throughout the l of Egypt,	824
	41:30	and the famine will ravage the l.	824
	41:31	in the l will not be remembered,	824
	41:33	and put him in charge of the l of Egypt.	824
	41:34	the l to take a fifth of the harvest of Egypt	824
	41:41	"I hereby put you in charge of the whole l	824
	41:43	Thus he put him in charge of the whole l	824
	41:45	Joseph went throughout the l of Egypt.	824
	41:47	of abundance the l produced plentifully.	824
	41:52	because God has made me fruitful in the l	824
	41:54	in the whole l of Egypt there was food.	824
	42: 5	the famine was in the l of Canaan also.	824

Ge	42: 6	Now Joseph was the governor of the l,	824
	42: 7	"From the l of Canaan," they replied,	824
	42: 9	to see where our l is unprotected."	824
	42:12	to see where our l is unprotected."	824
	42:13	who lives in the l of Canaan.	824
	42:29	to their father Jacob in the l of Canaan,	824
	42:30	the l spoke harshly to us and treated us as	824
	42:30	as though we were spying on the l.	824
	42:33	the man who is lord over the l said to us,	824
	42:34	and you can trade in the l.' "	824
	43: 1	Now the famine was still severe in the l.	824
	43:11	of the l in your bags and take them down	824
	44: 8	the l of Canaan the silver we found inside	824
	45: 6	now there has been famine in the l,	824
	45:17	Load your animals and return to the l	824
	45:18	I will give you the best of the l of Egypt	824
	45:18	and you can enjoy the fat of the l.'	824
	45:25	to their father Jacob in the l of Canaan.	824
	46:12	and Onan had died in the l of Canaan).	824
	46:31	who were living in the l of Canaan,	824
	47: 1	the l of Canaan and are now in Goshen."	824
	47: 6	and the l of Egypt is before you;	824
	47: 6	and your brothers in the best part of the l.	824
	47:11	in the best part of the l,	824
	47:18	for our lord except our bodies and our l.	141
	47:19	we and our l as well?	141
	47:19	Buy us and our l in exchange for food,	141
	47:19	with our l will be in bondage to Pharaoh.	141
	47:19	the l that l may not become desolate."	141
	47:20	So Joseph bought all the l in Egypt	141
	47:20	The l became Pharaoh's,	824
	47:22	he did not buy the l of the priests,	141
	47:22	That is why they did not sell their l.	141
	47:23	that I have bought you and your l today	141
	47:26	as a law concerning l in Egypt—	141
	47:26	It was only the l of the priests that did	141
	48: 3	to me at Luz in the l of Canaan,	824
	48: 4	I will give this l as an everlasting possession	824
	48: 7	in the l of Canaan while we were still on	824
	48:21	and take you back to the l of your fathers.	824
	48:22	the **ridge** of l I took from the Amorites	8900
	49:15	and how pleasant is his l,	824
	50: 5	in the tomb I dug for myself in the l	824
	50:13	to the l of Canaan and buried him in	824
	50:24	to your aid and take you up out of this l to	824
	50:24	to the l he promised on oath to Abraham,	824
Ex	1: 7	so that the l was filled with them.	824
	2:22	"I have become an alien in a foreign l."	824
	3: 8	to bring them up out of that l into a good	824
	3: 8	into a good and spacious l, a land flowing	824
	3: 8	a l flowing with milk and honey—	824
	3:17	up out of your misery in Egypt into the l	824
	3:17	a l flowing with milk and honey.'	824
	5: 5	the people of the l are now numerous,	824
	6: 4	with them to give them the l of Canaan,	824
	6: 8	to the l I swore with uplifted hand to give	824
	8: 5	make frogs come up on the l of Egypt.' "	824
	8: 6	and the frogs came up and covered the l.	824
	8: 7	they also made frogs come up on the l."	824
	8:14	and throughout the l of Egypt	824
	8:16	and the l reeked of them.	824
	8:17	throughout the l of Egypt became gnats.	824
	8:22	that day I will deal differently with the l	824
	8:22	know that I, the LORD, am in this l.	824
	8:24	and throughout Egypt the l was ruined by	824
	8:25	"Go, sacrifice to your God here in the l."	824
	9: 5	the LORD will do this in the l."	824
	9: 9	It will become fine dust over the whole l	824
	9: 9	on men and animals throughout the l."	824
	9:23	the LORD rained hail on the l of Egypt;	824
	9:24	in all the l of Egypt since it had become	824
	9:26	The only place it did not hail was the l	824
	9:33	the rain no longer poured down on the l.	824
	10: 6	the day they settled in this l till now.' "	141
	10:12	over the l and devour everything growing	824
	10:13	an east wind blow across the l all that day	824
	10:15	on tree or plant in all the l of Egypt.	824
	12:23	the LORD goes through the l to strike	NIH
	12:25	the l that the LORD will give you	824
	12:48	he may take part like one born in the l.	824
	13: 3	out of Egypt, out of the l of slavery,	1074
	13: 5	When the LORD brings you into the l of	
	13: 5	the l he swore to your forefathers	889S
	13: 5	a l flowing with milk and honey—	824
	13:11	the l of the Canaanites and gives it to you,	824
	13:14	out of Egypt, out of the l of slavery.	1074
	14: 3	'The Israelites are wandering around the l	824
	14:21	a strong east wind and turned it into **dry** l.	3000
	16:35	until they came to a l that was settled;	824
	18: 3	"I have become an alien in a foreign l";	824
	20: 2	out of Egypt, out of the l of slavery.	1074
	20:12	the l the LORD your God is giving you.	141
	23:11	the seventh year let **the** l lie unplowed	5626S
	23:23	and bring you into the l of the Amorites,	NIH
	23:26	none will miscarry or be barren in your l.	824
	23:29	because the l would become desolate and	824
	23:30	to take possession of the l.	824
	23:31	over to you the people who live in the l	824
	23:33	Do not let them live in your l,	824
	32:13	I will give your descendants all this l I	824
		promised them,	824
	33: 1	to the l I promised on oath to Abraham,	824
	33: 3	up to the l flowing with milk and honey.	824
	34:12	a treaty with those who live in the l	824
	34:15	a treaty with those who live in the l;	824
	34:24	and no one will covet your l when you go	824
Lev	11: 2	'Of all the animals that live on l,	824

Lev	14:34	"When you enter the l of Canaan,	824
	14:34	a spreading mildew in a house in that l,	824
	18: 3	and you must not do as they do in the l	824
	18:25	Even the l was defiled;	824
	18:25	and the l vomited out its inhabitants.	824
	18:27	the people who lived in the l before you,	824
	18:27	and the l became defiled.	824
	18:28	And if you defile the l,	824
	19: 9	" 'When you reap the harvest of your l,	824
	19:23	the l and plant any kind of fruit tree,	824
	19:29	the l will turn to prostitution and be filled	824
	19:33	" 'When an alien lives with you in your l,	824
	20:22	the l where I am bringing you to live may	824
	20:24	I said to you, "You will possess their l;	141
	20:24	a l flowing with milk and honey."	824
	22:24	You must not do this in your own l,	824
	23:10	'When you enter the l I am going	824
	23:22	" 'When you reap the harvest of your l,	824
	23:39	after you have gathered the crops of the l,	824
	25: 2	you enter the l I am going to give you,	824
	25: 2	the l itself must observe a sabbath to	824
	25: 4	the seventh year the l is to have a sabbath	824
	25: 5	The l is to have a year of rest.	824
	25: 6	the l yields during the sabbath year will	824
	25: 7	and the wild animals in your l.	824
	25: 7	Whatever **the** l produces may be eaten.	2023S
	25: 9	the trumpet throughout your l.	824
	25:10	throughout the l to all its inhabitants.	824
	25:14	If *you* **sell** l to one of your countrymen	4835+4928
	25:18	and you will live safely in the l.	824
	25:19	Then the l will yield its fruit,	824
	25:21	that the l will yield enough for three years.	NIH
	25:23	" 'The l must not be sold permanently,	824
	25:23	the l is mine and you are but aliens	824
	25:24	for the redemption of the l.	824
	25:38	of Egypt to give you the l of Canaan and	824
	26: 1	not place a carved stone in your l to bow	824
	26: 5	and live in safety in your l.	824
	26: 6	" 'I will grant peace in the l,	824
	26: 6	I will remove savage beasts from the l,	824
	26:20	nor will the trees of your l yield their fruit.	824
	26:32	I will lay waste the l,	824
	26:33	Your l will be laid waste,	824
	26:34	Then the l will enjoy its sabbath years all	824
	26:34	then the l will rest and enjoy its sabbaths.	824
	26:35	the l will have the rest it did not have	NIH
	26:38	the l of your enemies will devour you.	824
	26:41	toward them so that I sent them into the l	824
	26:42	and I will remember the l.	824
	26:43	For the l will be deserted by them	824
	26:44	when they are in the l of their enemies,	824
	27:16	of his **family** l, its value is to be set	299+8441
	27:22	which is not part of his **family** l,	299+8441
	27:24	the one whose l it was.	299+824
	27:28	whether man or animal or **family** l—	299+8441
	27:30	" 'A tithe of everything from the l,	824
Nu	10: 9	When you go into battle in your own l	824
	10:30	to my own l and my own people."	824
	11:12	to the l you promised on oath	141
	13: 2	"Send some men to explore the l	824
	13:16	of the men Moses sent to explore the l.	824
	13:18	See what the l is like and whether	824
	13:19	What kind of l do they live in?	824
	13:20	to bring back some of the fruit of the l."	824
	13:21	and explored the l from the Desert of Zin	824
	13:25	they returned from exploring the l.	824
	13:26	and showed them the fruit of the l.	824
	13:27	"We went into the l to which you sent us,	824
	13:30	up and take possession of the l,	2023S
	13:32	a bad report about the l they had explored.	824
	13:32	l we explored devours those living in it.	824
	14: 3	to this l only to let us fall by the sword?	824
	14: 6	among those who had explored the l,	824
	14: 7	"The l we passed through and explored	824
	14: 8	he will lead us into that l,	824
	14: 8	a l flowing with milk and honey,	824
	14: 9	do not be afraid of the people of the l,	824
	14:14	And they will tell the inhabitants of this l	824
	14:16	into the l he promised them on oath;	824
	14:23	of them will ever see the l I promised	824
	14:24	I will bring him into the l he went to,	824
	14:30	Not one of you will enter the l I swore	824
	14:31	in to enjoy the l you have rejected.	824
	14:34	of the forty days you explored the l—	824
	14:36	the men Moses had sent to explore the l,	824
	14:37	about the l were struck down and died of	824
	14:38	Of the men who went to explore the l,	824
	15: 2	you enter the l I am giving you as a home	824
	15:18	you enter the l to which I am taking you	824
	15:19	and you eat the food of the l,	824
	16:13	up out of a l flowing with milk and honey	824
	16:14	you haven't brought us into a l flowing	824
	18:20	"You will have no inheritance in their l,	824
	20:12	this community into the l I give them."	824
	20:24	He will not enter the l I give the Israelites,	824
	21:24	over his l from the Arnon to the Jabbok,	824
	21:26	of Moab and had taken from him all his l	824
	21:31	So Israel settled in the l of the Amorites.	824
	21:34	with his whole army and his l.	824
	21:35	And they took possession of his l.	824
	22: 5	near the River, in his native l.	824
	22: 5	cover the face of the l and have settled next	824
	22:11	come out of Egypt covers the face of the l.	824
	26:53	"The l is to be allotted to them as	824
	26:55	Be sure that the l is distributed by lot.	824
	27:12	and see the l I have given the Israelites.	824
	32: 4	the l the LORD subdued before the people	824

Nu	32: 5	"let this l be given to your servants	824
	32: 7	the Israelites from going over into the l	824
	32: 8	from Kadesh Barnea to look over the l.	824
	32: 9	to the Valley of Eshcol and viewed the l,	824
	32: 9	the l the LORD had given them.	824
	32:11	of Egypt will see the l I promised on oath	141
	32:17	protection from the inhabitants of the l.	824
	32:22	when the l is subdued before the LORD,	824
	32:22	And this I will be your possession before	824
	32:29	the l of Gilead as their possession.	824
	32:29	then when the l is subdued before you,	824
	32:33	the whole l with its cities and the territory	824
	33:52	drive out all the inhabitants of the l	824
	33:53	Take possession of the l and settle in it,	824
	33:53	for I have given you the l to possess.	824
	33:54	Distribute the l by lot,	824
	33:55	not drive out the inhabitants of the l,	824
	33:55	They will give you trouble in the l	824
	34: 2	'When you enter Canaan, the l that will	824
	34:12	" 'This will be your l,	824
	34:13	"Assign this l by lot as an inheritance.	824
	34:17	the men who are to assign the l for you as	824
	34:18	from each tribe to help assign the l.	824
	34:29	the inheritance to the Israelites in the l	824
	35: 8	The towns you give the Levites from the l	NIH
	35:32	and live on his own l before the death of	824
	35:33	" 'Do not pollute the l where you are.	824
	35:33	Bloodshed pollutes the l,	824
	35:33	and atonement cannot be made for the l	824
	35:34	the l where you live and where I dwell,	824
	36: 2	the l as an inheritance to the Israelites	824
	36: 7	the tribal l inherited from his forefathers.	5709
	36: 8	Every daughter who inherits l in any	5709
	36: 9	tribe is to keep the l it inherits."	5709
Dt	1: 7	to the l of the Canaanites and to Lebanon,	824
	1: 8	See, I have given you this l.	824
	1: 8	the l that the LORD swore he would give	824
	1:21	the LORD your God has given you the l.	824
	1:22	the l for us and bring back a report about	824
	1:25	with them some of the fruit of the l,	824
	1:25	"It is a good l that the LORD our God	824
	1:35	the good l I swore to give your forefathers.	824
	1:36	and his descendants the l he set his feet	824
	1:39	they will enter the l.	2025+9004S
	2: 5	for I will not give you any of their l,	824
	2: 9	for I will not give you any part of their l.	824
	2:12	in the l the LORD gave them	824
	2:19	of any l belonging to the Ammonites.	824
	2:20	too was considered a l of the Rephaites,	824
	2:29	the l the LORD our God is giving us."	824
	2:31	Now begin to conquer and possess his l."	824
	2:37	you did not encroach on any of the l of	824
	2:37	the l along the course of the Jabbok nor	NIH
	3: 2	over to you with his whole army and his l.	824
	3:12	Of the l that we took over at that time,	824
	3:13	in Bashan used to be known as a l of	824
	3:18	"The LORD your God has given you this l	824
	3:20	and they too have taken over the l that	824
	3:25	Let me go over and see the good l beyond	824
	3:27	Look at the l with your own eyes,	NIH
	3:28	across and will cause them to inherit the l	824
	4: 1	and may go in and take possession of the l	824
	4: 5	in the l you are entering to take possession	824
	4:10	to revere me as long as they live in the l	141
	4:14	in the l that you are crossing the Jordan	824
	4:21	not cross the Jordan and enter the good l	824
	4:22	I will die in this l; I will not cross the Jordan	824
	4:22	over and take possession of that good l.	824
	4:25	and grandchildren and have lived in the l	824
	4:26	from the l that you are crossing the Jordan	824
	4:38	to bring you into their l to give it to you	824
	4:40	in the l your God gives you	141
	4:46	in the l of Sihon king of the Amorites,	824
	4:47	of his l and the land of Og king of Bashan,	824
	4:47	They took possession of his land and the l	824
	4:48	This l extended from Aroer on the rim of	NIH
	5: 6	out of Egypt, out of the l of slavery.	1074
	5:16	the l the LORD your God is giving you.	141
	5:21	on your neighbor's house or l,	8441
	5:31	in the l I am giving them to possess."	824
	5:33	and prosper and prolong your days in the l	824
	6: 1	in the l that you are crossing the Jordan	824
	6: 3	in a l flowing with milk and honey,	824
	6:10	into the l he swore to your fathers,	824
	6:10	a l with large, flourishing cities	NIH
	6:12	out of Egypt, out of the l of slavery.	1074
	6:15	he will destroy you from the face of the l.	141
	6:18	over the good l that he promised you	824
	6:23	and give us the l that he promised on oath	824
	7: 1	into the l you are entering to possess	824
	7: 8	and redeemed you from the l of slavery,	1074
	7:13	the crops of your l—your grain, new wine	141
	7:13	in the l that he swore to your forefathers	141
	8: 1	the l that the LORD promised on oath	824
	8: 7	into a good l—a land with streams	824
	8: 7	a l with streams and pools of water,	824
	8: 8	a l with wheat and barley, vines	824
	8: 9	a l where bread will not be scarce	824
	8: 9	a l where the rocks are iron	824
	8:10	your God for the good l he has given you.	824
	8:14	out of Egypt, out of the l of slavery,	1074
	8:15	that thirsty and waterless l,	NIH
	9: 4	of this l because of my righteousness."	824
	9: 5	in to take possession of their l;	824
	9: 6	LORD your God is giving you this good l	824
	9:23	take possession of the l I have given you."	824
	9:28	into the l he had promised them,	824

Dt	10: 7	a l with streams of water.	824
	10:11	so that they may enter and possess the l	824
	11: 8	in and take over the l that you are crossing	824
	11: 9	and so that you may live long in the l that	141
	11: 9	a l flowing with milk and honey.	824
	11:10	The l you are entering to take over is not	824
	11:10	to take over is not like the l of Egypt,	824
	11:11	But the l you are crossing the Jordan	824
	11:11	to take possession of is a l of mountains	824
	11:12	It is a l the LORD your God cares for;	824
	11:14	I will send rain on your l in its season,	824
	11:17	from the good l the LORD is giving you.	824
	11:21	of your children may be many in the l that	141
	11:25	the terror and fear of you on the whole l,	824
	11:29	into the l you are entering to possess,	824
	11:31	to follow in the l that the LORD, the God	824
	12: 1	to follow in the l that the LORD, the God	824
	12: 1	as long as you live in the l.	141
	12:10	the l the LORD your God is giving you	824
	12:19	the Levites as long as you live in your l.	141
	12:29	driven them out and settled in their l,	824
	13: 5	and redeemed you from the l of slavery;	1074
	13: 7	from one end of the l to the other),	824
	13:10	out of Egypt, out of the l of slavery.	1074
	15: 4	the l the LORD your God is giving you	824
	15: 7	in any of the towns of the l that	824
	15:11	There will always be poor people in the l.	824
	15:11	and toward the poor and needy in your l.	824
	16: 4	be found in your possession in all your l	1473
	16:20	the l the LORD your God is giving you.	824
	17:14	the l the LORD your God is giving you	824
	18: 9	the l the LORD your God is giving you,	824
	19: 1	the nations whose l he is giving you,	824
	19: 2	the l the LORD your God is giving you	824
	19: 3	the l the LORD your God is giving you	824
	19: 8	gives you the whole l he promised you,	824
	19:10	innocent blood will not be shed in your l,	824
	19:14	the l the LORD your God is giving you	824
	21: 1	the l the LORD your God is giving you	141
	21:23	the l the LORD your God is giving you	141
	23:20	to in the l you are entering to possess.	824
	24: 4	the l the LORD your God is giving you	824
	25:15	the l the LORD your God is giving you	141
	25:19	in the l he is giving you to possess as	824
	26: 1	the l the LORD your God is giving you	824
	26: 2	the l the LORD your God is giving you	824
	26: 3	the l the LORD swore to our forefathers	824
	26: 9	and gave us this l, a land flowing	824
	26: 9	a l flowing with milk and honey;	824
	26:15	the l you have given us as you promised	141
	26:15	a l flowing with milk and honey."	824
	27: 2	the l the LORD your God is giving you,	824
	27: 3	when you have crossed over to enter the l	824
	27: 3	a l flowing with milk and honey,	824
	28: 4	and the crops of your l and the young	141
	28: 8	bless you in the l he is giving you.	824
	28:11	in the l he swore to your forefathers	141
	28:12	to send rain on your l in season and	824
	28:18	will be cursed, and the crops of your l,	141
	28:21	from the l you are entering to possess.	141
	28:33	that you do not know will eat what your l	141
	28:42	over all your trees and the crops of your l.	141
	28:51	the crops of your l until you are destroyed.	141
	28:52	to all the cities throughout your l until	824
	28:52	the l the LORD your God is giving you.	824
	28:63	be uprooted from the l you are entering	141
	29: 2	to all his officials and to all his l.	824
	29: 8	We took their l and gave it as	824
	29:19	This will bring disaster on the watered l	8116
	29:22	the calamities that have fallen on the l and	824
	29:23	The whole l will be a burning waste	824
	29:24	"Why has the LORD done this to this l?	824
	29:27	the LORD's anger burned against this l,	824
	29:28	the LORD uprooted them from their l	141
	29:28	and thrust them into another l,	824
	30: 4	to the most distant l under the heavens,	7895
	30: 5	He will bring you into the l that belonged	824
	30: 9	of your livestock and the crops of your l.	141
	30:16	in the l you are entering to possess.	824
	30:18	the l you are crossing the Jordan to enter	141
	30:20	in the l he swore to give to your fathers,	141
	31: 3	and you will take possession of their l.	NIH
	31: 4	whom he destroyed along with their l.	824
	31: 7	for you must go with this people into the l	824
	31:13	as you live in the l you are crossing	141
	31:16	the foreign gods of the l they are entering.	824
	31:20	into the l flowing with milk and honey,	141
	31:20	the l I promised on oath	889S
	31:21	into the l I promised them on oath."	824
	31:23	the Israelites into the l I promised them	824
	32:10	In a desert l he found him,	824
	32:13	He made him ride on the heights of the l	824
	32:43	and make atonement for his l and people.	141
	32:47	in the l you are crossing the Jordan	141
	32:49	the l I am giving the Israelites	824
	32:52	you will see the l only from a distance;	824
	32:52	the l I am giving to the people of Israel."	824
	33:13	"May the LORD bless his l with	824
	33:21	He chose the best l for himself;	NIH
	33:28	Jacob's spring is secure in a l of grain	824
	34: 1	There the LORD showed him the whole l—	824
	34: 2	all the l of Judah as far as the western sea,	824
	34: 4	the l I promised on oath to Abraham,	824
	34:11	and to all his officials and to his whole l.	824
Jos	1: 2	to cross the Jordan River into the l I am	824
	1: 6	to inherit the l I swore to their forefathers	824
	1:11	the l the LORD your God is giving you	824

Jos	1:13	and has granted you this l.'	824
	1:14	and your livestock may stay in the l	824
	1:15	taken possession of the l that the LORD	824
	1:15	you may go back and occupy your own l,	824
	2: 1	"Go, look over the l," he said,	824
	2: 2	tonight to spy out the l."	824
	2: 3	they have come to spy out the whole l."	824
	2: 9	"I know that the LORD has given this l	824
	2:14	when the LORD gives us the l."	824
	2:18	when we enter the l,	824
	2:24	"The LORD has surely given the whole l	824
	5: 6	to them that they would not see the l	824
	5: 6	a l flowing with milk and honey.	824
	5:11	they ate some of the produce of the l:	824
	5:12	the day after they ate this food from the l;	824
	6:22	to the two men who had spied out the l,	824
	6:27	and his fame spread throughout the l.	824
	8: 1	his people, his city and his l.	824
	9:24	his servant Moses to give you the whole l	824
	11:16	So Joshua took this entire l:	824
	11:23	So Joshua took the entire l,	824
	11:23	Then the l had rest from war.	824
	12: 1	of the l whom the Israelites had defeated	824
	12: 6	the LORD gave their l to the Reubenites,	2023S
	12: 7	These are the kings of the l that Joshua	824
	13: 1	and there are still very large areas of l to	824
	13: 2	"This is the l that remains:	824
	13: 4	all the l of the Canaanites,	824
	13: 6	Be sure to allocate this l to Israel for	2023S
	13:12	and taken over their l.	NIH
	14: 1	as an inheritance in the l of Canaan.	824
	14: 4	The Levites received no share of the l	824
	14: 5	So the Israelites divided the l,	824
	14: 7	from Kadesh Barnea to explore the l.	824
	14: 9	So on that day Moses swore to me, 'The l	824
	14:15	Then the l had rest from war.	824
	15:19	Since you have given me l in the Negev,	824
	17: 5	of ten tracts of l besides Gilead	824
	17: 6	The l of Gilead belonged to the rest of	824
	17: 8	(Manasseh had the l of Tappuah,	824
	17:10	On the south the l belonged to Ephraim,	NIH
	17:15	the forest and clear l for yourselves there	1345
	17:15	and clear land for yourselves there in the l	824
	18: 3	to take possession of the l that the LORD	824
	18: 4	a survey of the l and write a description	824
	18: 5	You are to divide the l into seven parts.	2023S
	18: 6	descriptions of the seven parts of the l,	824
	18: 8	on their way to map out the l,	824
	18: 8	"Go and make a survey of the l and write	824
	18: 9	So the men left and went through the l.	824
	18:10	and there he distributed the l to the Israelites	824
	19:49	When they had finished dividing the l	824
	19:51	And so they finished dividing the l.	824
	21:43	the l he had sworn to give their forefathers,	824
	22: 4	return to your homes in the l that Moses	299+824
	22: 7	half-tribe of Manasseh Moses had given l	NIH
	22: 7	the other half of the tribe Joshua gave l on	NIH
	22: 9	Canaan to return to Gilead, their own l,	299+824
	22:10	near the Jordan in the l of Canaan,	824
	22:13	the priest, to the l of Gilead—	824
	22:19	If the l you possess is defiled,	824
	22:19	come over to the LORD's l,	299+824
	22:19	and share the l with us.	NIH
	23: 4	as an inheritance for your tribes all the l of	NIH
	23: 5	and you will take possession of their l,	824
	23:13	until you perish from this good l,	141
	23:15	from this good l he has given you.	141
	23:16	from the good l he has given you."	824
	24: 3	from the l beyond the River and led him	6298
	24: 8	to the l of the Amorites who lived east of	824
	24: 8	and you took possession of their l.	824
	24:13	So I gave you a l on which you did	824
	24:15	the Amorites, in whose l you are living.	824
	24:17	out of Egypt, from that l of slavery,	1074
	24:18	including the Amorites, who lived in the l.	824
	24:30	they buried him in the l of his inheritance,	1473
	24:32	were buried at Shechem in the tract of l	8441
Jdg	1: 2	I have given the l into their hands."	824
	1:15	Since you have given me l in the Negev,	824
	1:26	He then went to the l of the Hittites,	824
	1:27	Canaanites were determined to live in that l.	824
	1:32	among the Canaanite inhabitants of the l.	824
	1:33	among the Canaanite inhabitants of the l,	824
	2: 1	and led you into the l that I swore to give	824
	2: 2	a covenant with the people of this l,	824
	2: 6	they went to take possession of the l,	824
	2: 9	they buried him in the l of his inheritance,	1473
	3:11	So the l had peace for forty years,	824
	3:30	and the l had peace for eighty years.	824
	5: 4	when you marched from the l of Edom,	8441
	5:31	Then the l had peace forty years.	824
	6: 4	on the l and ruined the crops all the way	824
	6: 5	they invaded the l to ravage it.	824
	6: 8	out of Egypt, out of the l of slavery.	1074
	6: 9	from before you and gave you their l.	824
	6:10	the Amorites, in whose l you live.'	824
	8:28	the l enjoyed peace forty years.	824
	9:37	down from the center of the l,	824
	10: 8	the l of the Amorites.	824
	11: 3	from his brothers and settled in the l	824
	11: 5	went to get Jephthah from the l of Tob.	824
	11:13	they took away my l from the Arnon to	824
	11:15	not take the l of Moab or the land of	824
	11:15	the land of Moab or the l of the Ammonites.	824
	11:21	over all the l of the Amorites who lived in	824
	12:12	and was buried in Aijalon in the l	824
	16:24	the one who laid waste our l	824

Ref		Text	Strong's
Jdg	18: 2	and Eshtaol to spy out the l and explore it.	824
	18: 2	They told them, "Go, explore the l."	824
	18: 7	And since their l lacked nothing,	824
	18: 9	We have seen that the l is very good.	824
	18:10	an unsuspecting people and a spacious l	824
	18:10	a l that lacks nothing whatever."	5226
	18:14	Then the five men who had spied out the l	824
	18:17	who had spied out the l went inside and	824
	18:30	until the time of the captivity of the l.	824
	20: 1	from the l of Gilead came out as one man	824
	21:21	from the girls of Shiloh and go to the l	824
Ru	1: 1	there was a famine in the l,	824
	1: 7	that would take them back to the l	824
	4: 3	is selling the piece of l that belonged	8441
	4: 5	"On the day you buy the l from Naomi	8441
1Sa	6: 5	from you and your gods and your l.	824
	9:16	a man from the l of Benjamin.	824
	13: 3	the trumpet blown throughout the l	824
	13: 7	even crossed the Jordan to the l of Gad	824
	13:19	be found in the whole l of Israel,	824
	14:46	and they withdrew to their own l.	5226
	21:11	"Isn't this David, the king of the l?	824
	22: 5	Go into the l of Judah."	824
	23:27	The Philistines are raiding the l."	824
	27: 1	to escape to the l of the Philistines.	824
	27: 8	in the l extending to Shur and Egypt.)	824
	28: 3	the mediums and spiritists from the l.	824
	28: 9	the mediums and spiritists from the l.	824
	29:11	up early in the morning to go back to the l	824
	30:16	of plunder they had taken from the l of	824
	31: 9	and they sent messengers throughout the l	824
2Sa	3:12	to say to David, "Whose l is it?	824
	9: 7	I will restore to you all the l that belonged	8441
	9:10	and your servants are to farm the l for him	141
	10: 2	When David's men came to the l of	824
	14:20	he knows everything that happens in the l."	824
	15: 4	"If only I were appointed judge in the l!	824
	17:26	and Absalom camped in the l of Gilead.	824
	21:14	God answered prayer in behalf of the l.	824
	24: 8	After they had gone through the entire l,	824
	24:13	upon you three years of famine in your l?	824
	24:13	Or three days of plague in your l?	824
	24:25	the LORD answered prayer in behalf of the l,	824
1Ki	2:34	he was buried on his own l in the desert.	1074
	4:10	and all the l of Hepher were his);	824
	4:21	from the River to the l of the Philistines,	824
	8:34	and bring them back to the l you gave	141
	8:36	on the l you gave your people for	824
	8:37	"When famine or plague comes to the l,	824
	8:40	in the l you gave our fathers.	141
	8:41	from a distant l because of your name—	824
	8:46	who takes them captive to his own l,	824
	8:47	and if they have a change of heart in the l	824
	8:47	and repent and plead with you in the l	824
	8:48	to you with all their heart and soul in the l	824
	8:48	toward the l you gave their fathers, toward	824
	9: 7	from the l I have given them	141
	9: 8	the LORD done such a thing to this l and	824
	9:13	And he called them the L of Cabul,	824
	9:18	and Tadmor in the desert, within his l,	824
	9:21	their descendants remaining in the l,	824
	10:15	and the governors of the l.	824
	11:18	a house and l and provided him with food.	824
	14:15	He will uproot Israel from this good l	141
	14:24	even male shrine prostitutes in the l;	824
	15:12	the male shrine prostitutes from the l	824
	17: 7	up because there had been no rain in the l.	824
	17:14	the day the LORD gives rain on the l.' "	141
	18: 1	and I will send rain on the l."	141
	18: 5	through the l to all the springs and valleys.	824
	18: 6	So they divided the l they were to cover,	824
	20: 7	of Israel summoned all the elders of the l	824
	22:36	everyone to his l!"	824
	22:46	He rid the l of the rest of the male shrine	824
2Ki	2:19	water is bad and the l is unproductive."	824
	2:21	or make the l unproductive.' "	NIH
	3:20	And the l was filled with water.	824
	3:24	the Israelites invaded the l and slaughtered	2023S
	3:27	they withdrew and returned to their own l.	824
	8: 1	the LORD has decreed a famine in the l	824
	8: 2	in the l of the Philistines seven years.	824
	8: 3	the seven years she came back from the l	824
	8: 3	to the king to beg for her house and l.	8441
	8: 5	to beg the king for her house and l.	8441
	8: 6	including all the income from her l from	8441
	10:33	in all the l of Gilead (the region of Gad,	824
	11: 3	for six years while Athaliah ruled the l.	824
	11:14	the l were rejoicing and blowing trumpets.	824
	11:18	All the people of the l went to the temple	824
	11:19	the guards and all the people of the l,	824
	11:20	and all the people of the l rejoiced.	824
	15: 5	and governed the people of the l.	824
	15:19	Then Pul king of Assyria invaded the l.	824
	15:20	and stayed in the l no longer.	824
	15:29	including all the l of Naphtali,	824
	16:15	burnt offering of all the people of the l,	824
	17: 5	The king of Assyria invaded the entire l,	824
	17:27	the people what the god of the l requires."	824
	18:32	and take you to a l like your own,	824
	18:32	a l of grain and new wine,	824
	18:32	a l of bread and vineyards,	824
	18:32	a l of olive trees and honey.	824
	18:33	the god of any nation ever delivered his l	824
	18:35	has been able to save his l from me?	824
	19:37	and they escaped to the l of Ararat.	824
	20:14	"From a distant l," Hezekiah replied.	824
	21: 8	from the l I gave their forefathers,	141
2Ki	21:24	of the l killed all who had plotted	824
	23:30	And the people of the l took Jehoahaz son	824
	23:33	the l of Hamath so that he might not reign	824
	23:35	the l and exacted the silver and gold from	824
	23:35	of the l according to their assessments.	824
	24: 1	king of Babylon invaded the l,	NIH
	24:14	Only the poorest people of the l were left.	824
	24:15	his officials and the leading men of the l.	824
	25:12	behind some of the poorest people of the l	824
	25:19	the l and sixty of his men who were found	824
	25:21	There at Riblah, in the l of Hamath,	824
	25:21	Judah went into captivity, away from her l.	141
	25:24	"Settle down in the l and serve the king	824
1Ch	1:45	the l of the Temanites succeeded him	824
	4:40	and the l was spacious, peaceful and quiet.	824
	5: 9	the east they occupied the l up to the edge	NIH
	5:22	And they occupied the l until the exile.	9393S
	5:23	in the l from Bashan to Baal Hermon,	824
	5:25	to the gods of the peoples of the l,	824
	10: 9	and sent messengers throughout the l of	824
	11:10	to extend it over the whole l, as	3776S
	14:17	David's fame spread throughout every l,	824
	16:18	"To you I will give the l of Canaan as	824
	19: 2	to Hanun in the l of the Ammonites	824
	20: 1	He laid waste the l of the Ammonites	824
	21:12	days of plague in the l, with the angel of	824
	22:18	For he has handed the inhabitants of the l	824
	22:18	and the l is subject to the LORD and	824
	27:26	of the field workers who farmed the l	141
	28: 8	that you may possess this good l	824
2Ch	6:25	to the l you gave to them and their fathers.	141
	6:27	on the l you gave your people for	824
	6:28	"When famine or plague comes to the l,	824
	6:31	in the l you gave our fathers.	141
	6:32	a distant l because of your great name	824
	6:36	who takes them captive to a l far away	824
	6:37	and if they have a change of heart in the l	824
	6:37	and repent and plead with you in the l	824
	6:38	to you with all their heart and soul in the l	824
	6:38	toward the l you gave their fathers, toward	824
	7:13	the l or send a plague among my people,	824
	7:14	forgive their sin and will heal their l.	824
	7:20	then I will uproot Israel from my l,	141
	7:21	the LORD done such a thing to this l and	824
	8: 8	their descendants remaining in the l,	824
	9:14	the l brought gold and silver to Solomon.	824
	9:26	from the River to the l of the Philistines,	824
	14: 6	since the l was at peace.	824
	14: 7	The l is still ours, because we have sought	824
	15: 8	from the whole l of Judah and Benjamin	824
	19: 3	for you have rid the l of the Asherah poles	824
	19: 5	He appointed judges in the l,	824
	20: 7	not drive out the inhabitants of this l	824
	22:12	for six years while Athaliah ruled the l.	824
	23:13	the l were rejoicing and blowing trumpets,	824
	23:20	of the l and brought the king down from	824
	23:21	and all the people of the l rejoiced.	824
	26:21	and governed the people of the l.	824
	30: 9	and will come back to this l,	824
	32: 4	and the stream that flowed through the l	824
	32:13	of those nations ever able to deliver their l	824
	32:21	So he withdrew to his own l in disgrace.	824
	32:31	miraculous sign that had occurred in the l,	824
	33: 8	of the Israelites leave the l I assigned	141
	33:25	people of the l killed all who had plotted	824
	34: 8	to purify the l and the temple,	824
	36: 1	And the people of the l took Jehoahaz son	824
	36:21	The l enjoyed its sabbath rests;	824
Ezr	9:11	'The l you are entering to possess is	824
	9:11	to possess is a l polluted by the corruption	824
	9:12	be strong and eat the good things of the l	824
Ne	4: 4	over as plunder in a l of captivity.	824
	5:14	to be their governor in the l of Judah,	824
	5:16	we did not acquire any l.	8441
	9: 8	to his descendants the l of the Canaanites,	824
	9:10	and all the people of his l,	824
	9:15	of the l you had sworn with uplifted hand	824
	9:23	the l that you told their fathers to enter	824
	9:24	in and took possession of the l.	824
	9:24	the Canaanites, who lived in the l;	824
	9:24	with their kings and the peoples of the l,	824
	9:25	They captured fortified cities and fertile l;	141
	9:35	the spacious and fertile l you gave them,	824
	9:36	slaves in the l you gave our forefathers	824
	10:31	the l and will cancel all debts.	NIH
Job	1: 1	In the l of Uz there lived a man	824
	1:10	and herds are spread throughout the land.	824
	9:24	a l falls into the hands of the wicked,	824
	10:21	to the l of gloom and deep shadow,	824
	10:22	to the l of deepest night,	824
	12:15	if he lets them loose, they devastate the l.	824
	15:19	the l was given when no alien passed	824
	15:29	nor will his possessions spread over the l.	824
	18:17	he has no name in the l.	2575
	22: 8	owning l—an honored man, living on it.	824
	24: 4	and force all the poor of the l into hiding.	824
	24:18	their portion of the l is cursed,	824
	28:13	it cannot be found in the l of the living.	824
	30: 3	the parched l in desolate wastelands	7480
	30: 8	they were driven out of the l.	824
	31:38	"if my l cries out against me	141
	37:17	the l lies hushed under the south wind,	824
	38:26	to water a l where no man lives,	824
	42:15	the l were there found women as beautiful	824
Ps	10:16	the nations will perish from his l.	824
	16: 3	As for the saints who are in the l,	824
	25:13	and his descendants will inherit the l.	824
Ps	27:13	goodness of the LORD in the l of the living.	824
	35:20	against those who live quietly in the l.	824
	37: 3	dwell in the l and enjoy safe pasture.	824
	37: 9	who hope in the LORD will inherit the l.	824
	37:11	But the meek will inherit the l	824
	37:22	those the LORD blesses will inherit the l,	824
	37:27	then you will dwell in the l forever.	NIH
	37:29	the righteous will inherit the l and dwell	824
	37:34	He will exalt you to inherit the l;	824
	41: 2	in the l and not surrender him to the desire	824
	42: 6	therefore I will remember you from the l	824
	44: 3	not by their sword that they won the l,	824
	45:16	you will make them princes throughout the l.	824
	52: 5	will uproot you from the l of the living.	824
	60: 2	You have shaken the l and torn it open;	824
	63: 1	a dry and weary l where there is no water.	824
	65: 9	You care for the l and water it;	824
	66: 6	He turned the sea into dry l,	3317
	67: 6	Then the l will yield its harvest, and God,	824
	68: 6	but the rebellious live in a sun-scorched l.	7461
	68:14	the Almighty scattered the kings in the l,	2023S
	72:16	Let grain abound throughout the l;	824
	74: 8	where God was worshiped in the l.	824
	74:20	of violence fill the dark places of the l.	824
	76: 8	and the l feared and was quiet—	824
	76: 9	to save all the afflicted of the l.	824
	78:12	the sight of their fathers in the l of Egypt,	824
	78:54	to the border of his holy l,	NIH
	80: 9	and it took root and filled the l.	824
	85: 1	You showed favor to your l, O LORD;	824
	85: 9	that his glory may dwell in our l.	824
	85:12	and our l will yield its harvest.	824
	88:12	your righteous deeds in the l of oblivion?	824
	95: 5	and his hands formed the dry l.	3318
	101: 6	My eyes will be on the faithful in the l,	824
	101: 8	to silence all the wicked in the l;	824
	105:11	"To you I will give the l of Canaan as	824
	105:16	on the l and destroyed all their supplies	824
	105:23	Jacob lived as an alien in the l of Ham.	824
	105:27	his wonders in the l of Ham.	824
	105:28	He sent darkness and made the l dark—	NIH
	105:30	Their l teemed with frogs,	824
	105:32	with lightning throughout their l;	824
	105:35	they ate up every green thing in their l,	824
	105:36	he struck down all the firstborn in their l,	824
	106:22	in the l of Ham and awesome deeds by	824
	106:24	Then they despised the pleasant l;	824
	106:38	and the l was desecrated by their blood.	824
	107:34	and fruitful l into a salt waste,	824
	112: 2	His children will be mighty in the l;	824
	116: 9	that I may walk before the LORD in the l	824
	125: 3	over the l allotted to the righteous,	AIT
	135:12	and he gave their l as an inheritance,	824
	136:21	and gave their l as an inheritance,	824
	137: 4	of the LORD while in a foreign l?	141
	140:11	Let slanderers not be established in the l;	824
	142: 5	my portion in the l of the living."	824
	143: 6	my soul thirsts for you like a parched l.	824
Pr	2:21	For the upright will live in the l,	824
	2:22	but the wicked will be cut off from the l,	824
	10:30	but the wicked will not remain in the l.	824
	12:11	He who works his l will have abundant food,	141
	25:25	is good news from a distant l.	824
	28:19	He who works his l will have abundant food,	141
	30:16	l, which is never satisfied with water,	824
	31:23	he takes his seat among the elders of the l.	824
Ecc	5: 9	The increase from the l is taken by all;	824
	10:16	Woe to you, O l whose king was a servant	824
	10:17	Blessed are you, O l whose king is of noble birth	824
	11: 2	not know what disaster may come upon the l.	824
SS	2:12	the cooing of doves is heard in our l.	824
Isa	1:19	you will eat the best from the l;	824
	2: 7	Their l is full of silver and gold;	824
	2: 7	Their l is full of horses;	824
	2: 8	Their l is full of idols; they bow down to	824
	4: 2	of the l will be the pride and glory of	824
	5: 8	and you live alone in the l.	824
	5:30	And if one looks at the l,	824
	6:12	and the l is utterly forsaken.	824
	6:13	And though a tenth remains in the l,	2023S
	6:13	so the holy seed will be the stump in the l."	2023S
	7:16	the l of the two kings you dread will	141
	7:18	and for bees from the l of Assyria.	824
	7:22	All who remain in the l will eat curds	824
	7:24	l will be covered with briers and thorns.	824
	8: 8	cover the breadth of your l, O Immanuel!"	824
	8:21	they will roam through the l;	2023S
	9: 1	the l of Zebulun and the land of Naphtali,	824
	9: 1	the land of Zebulun and the l of Naphtali,	824
	9: 2	on those living in the l of the shadow	824
	9:19	the l will be scorched and the people will	824
	10:23	the destruction decreed upon the whole l.	824
	13:13	the l desolate and destroy the sinners	824
	13:14	each will flee to his native l.	824
	14: 1	and will settle them in their own l.	141
	14: 2	and maidservants in the LORD's l.	141
	14:20	for you have destroyed your l	824
	14:21	and cover the earth with their cities.	824
	14:25	I will crush the Assyrian in my l;	824
	15: 9	and upon those who remain in the l,	141
	16: 1	Send lambs as tribute to the ruler of the l,	824
	16: 4	the aggressor will vanish from the l.	824
	18: 2	to the l of whirring wings along the rivers	824
	18: 2	whose l is divided by rivers	824
	18: 7	whose l is divided by rivers—	824
	19:17	And the l of Judah will bring terror to	141

Isa	19:20	to the LORD Almighty in the l of Egypt.	824
	21: 1	comes from the desert, from a l of terror.	824
	23: 1	From the l of Cyprus word has come	824
	23:10	Till your l as along the Nile,	824
	23:13	Look at the l of the Babylonians,	824
	26: 1	In that day this song will be sung in the l	824
	26:10	in a l of uprightness they go on doing evil	824
	26:15	you have extended all the borders of the l.	824
	28:22	destruction decreed against the whole l.	824
	30: 6	Through a l of hardship and distress,	824
	30:23	the food that comes from the l will be rich	141
	32: 2	the shadow of a great rock in a thirsty l.	824
	32:13	for the l of my people, a land overgrown	141
	32:13	a l overgrown with thorns and briers—	NIH
	33: 9	The l mourns and wastes away,	824
	33:17	the king in his beauty and view a l	824
	34: 7	Their l will be drenched with blood,	824
	34: 9	her l will become blazing pitch!	824
	35: 1	The desert and the **parched** l will be glad;	7480
	36:10	have I come to attack and destroy this l	824
	36:17	and take you to a l like your own—	824
	36:17	a l of grain and new wine,	824
	36:17	a l of bread and vineyards.	824
	36:18	the god of any nation ever delivered his l	824
	36:20	has been able to save his l from me?	824
	37:38	and they escaped to the l of Ararat.	824
	38:11	the LORD, in the l of the living;	824
	39: 3	"From a distant l," Hezekiah replied.	824
	44: 3	For I will pour water on the thirsty l,	NIH
	45:19	from somewhere in a l of darkness;	824
	46:11	from a far-off l, a man to fulfill my purpose.	824
	49: 8	a covenant for the people, to restore the l	824
	49:19	and made desolate and your l laid waste,	824
	53: 8	he was cut off from the l of the living;	824
	57:13	the l and possess my holy mountain."	824
	58:11	satisfy your needs in a **sun-scorched** l	7463
	58:14	to ride on the heights of the l and to feast	824
	60: 6	Herds of camels will cover your l,	NIH
	60:18	No longer will violence be heard in your l,	824
	60:21	and they will possess the l forever.	824
	61: 7	inherit a double portion in their l,	824
	62: 4	call you Deserted, or name your l Desolate.	824
	62: 4	called Hephzibah, and your l Beulah;	824
	62: 4	and your l will be married.	824
	65:16	a blessing in the l will do so by the God	824
	65:16	he who takes an oath in the l will swear	824
Jer	1:14	be poured out on all who live in the l.	824
	1:18	a bronze wall to stand against the whole l—	824
	1:18	its priests and the people of the l.	824
	2: 2	through the desert, through a l not sown.	824
	2: 6	through a l of deserts and rifts,	824
	2: 6	a l of drought and darkness,	824
	2: 6	a l where no one travels and no one lives?'	824
	2: 7	I brought you into a fertile l to eat its fruit	824
	2: 7	But you came and defiled my l	824
	2:15	They have laid waste his l;	824
	2:31	a desert to Israel or a l of great darkness?	824
	3: 1	Would not the l be completely defiled?	824
	3: 2	You have defiled the l with your prostitution	824
	3: 9	she defiled the l and committed adultery	824
	3:16	numbers have increased greatly in the l,"	824
	3:18	they will come from a northern l to	824
	3:18	to the l I gave your forefathers as	824
	3:19	like sons and give you a desirable l,	824
	4: 5	'Sound the trumpet throughout the l!'	824
	4: 7	He has left his place to lay waste your l.	824
	4:16	besieging army is coming from a distant l,	824
	4:20	the whole l lies in ruins.	824
	4:26	I looked, and the **fruitful** l was a desert;	4149
	4:27	"The whole l will be ruined,	824
	5:19	and served foreign gods in your own l,	824
	5:19	so now you will serve foreigners in a l	824
	5:30	and shocking thing has happened in the l:	824
	6: 8	away from you and make your l desolate	824
	6:12	against those who live in the l,"	824
	6:20	or sweet calamus from a distant l?	824
	6:22	an army is coming from the l of the north;	824
	7: 7	in the l I gave your forefathers for ever	824
	7:34	for the l will become desolate.	824
	8:16	of their stallions the whole l trembles.	824
	8:16	to devour the l and everything in it,	824
	8:19	to the cry of my people from a l far away:	824
	9: 3	it is not by truth that they triumph in the l.	824
	9:12	Why has the l been ruined and laid waste	824
	9:19	We must leave our l because our houses	824
	10:17	Gather up your belongings to leave the l,	824
	10:18	I will hurl out those who live in this l;	824
	10:22	a great commotion from the l of the north!	824
	11: 5	a l flowing with milk and honey'—	824
	11: 5	the l you possess today."	NIH
	11:19	let us cut him off from the l of the living,	824
	12: 4	How long will the l lie parched and	824
	12:11	the whole l will be laid waste	824
	12:12	from one end of the l to the other;	824
	13:13	with drunkenness all who live in this l,	824
	14: 2	they wail for the l, and a cry goes up from	824
	14: 4	because there is no rain in the l;	824
	14: 8	why are you like a stranger in the l,	824
	14:15	'No sword or famine will touch this l.'	824
	14:18	and priest have gone to a l they know not.' "	824
	15: 7	a winnowing fork at the city gates of the l.	824
	15:10	a man with whom the whole l strives	824
	15:14	to your enemies in a l you do not know,	824
	16: 3	shame and daughters born in this l	5226
	16: 6	"Both high and low will die in this l.	824
	16:13	So I will throw you out of this l into	824
	16:13	into a l neither you nor your fathers have	824

Jer	16:15	who brought the Israelites up out of the l	824
	16:15	to the l I gave their forefathers.	141
	16:18	because they have defiled my l with	824
	17: 3	My mountain in the l and your wealth	8441
	17: 4	to your enemies in a l you do not know,	824
	17: 6	in a salt l where no one lives.	824
	18:16	Their l will be laid waste,	824
	22:10	nor see his native l again.	824
	22:12	he will not see this l again."	824
	22:27	to the l you long to return to."	824
	22:28	cast into a l they do not know?	824
	22:29	O l, land, land, hear the word of the LORD!	824
	22:29	l, land, hear the word of the LORD!	824
	22:29	land, l, hear the word of the LORD!	824
	23: 5	and do what is just and right in the l.	824
	23: 8	the descendants of Israel up out of the l of	824
	23: 8	Then they will live in their own l."	141
	23:10	The l is full of adulterers;	824
	23:10	because of the curse the l lies parched and	824
	23:15	ungodliness has spread throughout the l.'"	824
	24: 5	whom I sent away from this place to the l	824
	24: 6	and I will bring them back to this l.	824
	24: 8	whether they remain in this l or live	824
	24:10	until they are destroyed from the l I gave	141
	25: 5	and you can stay in the l the LORD gave	141
	25: 9	against this l and its inhabitants and	824
	25:12	the l of the Babylonians, for their guilt,"	824
	25:13	upon that l all the things I have spoken	824
	25:30	and roar mightily against his l.	5659
	25:38	and their l will become desolate because	824
	26:17	of the elders of the l stepped forward	824
	26:20	against this city and this l as Jeremiah did.	824
	27: 7	until the time for his l comes;	824
	27:11	that nation remain in its own l to till it and	141
	30: 3	to the l I gave their forefathers to possess,'	824
	30:10	your descendants from the l of their exile.	824
	31: 8	I will bring them from the l of the north	824
	31:16	"They will return from the l of the enemy.	824
	31:17	"Your children will return to their own l.	1473
	31:23	from captivity, the people in the l	824
	32:15	vineyards will again be bought in this l.'	824
	32:22	You gave them this l you had sworn	824
	32:22	a l flowing with milk and honey.	824
	32:41	and will assuredly plant them in this l	824
	32:43	Once more fields will be bought in this l	824
	33:11	the fortunes of the l as they were before,'	824
	33:15	he will do what is just and right in the l.	824
	34:13	out of Egypt, out of the l of slavery.	1074
	34:19	and all the people of the l	824
	35: 7	Then you will live a long time in the l	141
	35:11	king of Babylon invaded this l,	824
	35:15	Then you will live in the l I have given	141
	36:29	and destroy this l and cut off both men	824
	37: 2	nor the people of the l paid any attention	824
	37: 7	will go back to its own l, to Egypt.	824
	37:19	of Babylon will not attack you or this l'?	824
	39: 5	of Babylon at Riblah in the l of Hamath,	824
	39:10	in the l of Judah some of the poor people,	824
	40: 6	the people who were left behind in the l.	824
	40: 7	over the l and had put him in charge of	824
	40: 7	and children who were the poorest in the l	824
	40: 9	"Settle down in the l and serve the king	824
	40:12	they all came back to the l of Judah,	824
	41: 2	had appointed as governor over the l.	824
	41:18	had appointed as governor over the l.	824
	42:10	'If you stay in this l, I will build you up	824
	42:12	on you and restore you to your l."	141
	42:13	if you say, 'We will not stay in this l,'	824
	43: 4	the LORD's command to stay in the l	824
	43: 5	in the l of Judah from all the nations	824
	44: 9	by you and your wives in the l of Judah	824
	44:14	or survive to return to the l of Judah,	824
	44:21	and the people of the l?	824
	44:22	your l became an object of cursing and	824
	44:28	the sword and return to the l of Judah	824
	45: 4	uproot what I have planted, throughout the l.	824
	46:10	will offer sacrifice in the l of the north by	824
	46:27	your descendants from the l of their exile.	824
	47: 2	They will overflow the l and everything	824
	47: 2	all who dwell in the l will wail	824
	49:19	I will chase Edom from **its** l in an instant.	2023S
	50: 1	the prophet concerning Babylon and the l	824
	50: 3	and lay waste her l.	824
	50: 8	leave the l of the Babylonians,	824
	50: 9	an alliance of great nations from the l of	824
	50:12	a wilderness, a **dry** l, a desert.	7480
	50:16	let everyone flee to his own l.	824
	50:18	of Babylon and his l as I punished	824
	50:21	the l of Meratham and those who live	824
	50:22	The noise of battle is in the l,	824
	50:25	to do in the l of the Babylonians.	824
	50:34	so that he may bring rest to their l,	824
	50:38	For it is a l of idols,	824
	50:44	I will chase Babylon from **its** l in	2023S
	50:45	what he has purposed against the l of	824
	51: 2	to winnow her and to devastate her l;	824
	51: 5	though their l is full of guilt before	824
	51: 9	let us leave her and each go to his own l,	824
	51:27	"Lift up a banner in the l!	824
	51:29	The l trembles and writhes,	824
	51:29	to lay waste the l of Babylon so	824
	51:43	towns will be desolate, a dry and desert l,	824
	51:43	a l where no one lives,	NIH
	51:46	be afraid when rumors are heard in the l;	824
	51:46	the next, rumors of violence in the l and	824
	51:47	her whole l will be disgraced	824
	51:50	Remember the LORD in a **distant** l,	AIT

Jer	51:52	throughout her l the wounded will groan.	824
	51:54	the sound of great destruction from the l	824
	52: 9	of Babylon at Riblah in the l of Hamath,	824
	52:16	of the l to work the vineyards and fields.	824
	52:25	the l and sixty of his men who were found	824
	52:27	There at Riblah, in the l of Hamath,	824
	52:27	Judah went into captivity, away from her l.	141
La	3:34	To crush underfoot all prisoners in the l,	824
	4:21	you who live in the l of Uz.	824
Eze	1: 3	the Kebar River in the l of the Babylonians.	824
	6:14	and make the l a desolate waste from	824
	7: 2	the Sovereign LORD says to the l	141
	7: 2	upon the four corners of the l.	824
	7: 7	you who dwell in the l.	824
	7:13	not recover the l he has **sold** as long as	4928
	7:23	because the l is full of bloodshed and	824
	7:27	hands of the people of the l will tremble.	824
	8:12	the LORD has forsaken the l.' "	824
	8:17	Must they also fill the l with violence	824
	9: 9	the l is full of bloodshed and	824
	9: 9	'The LORD has forsaken the l;	824
	11:15	this l was given to us as our possession.'	824
	11:17	and I will give you back the l	141
	12: 6	so that you cannot see the l,	824
	12:12	so that he cannot see the l.	824
	12:13	the l of the Chaldeans,	824
	12:19	Say to the people of the l:	824
	12:19	in Jerusalem and in the l of Israel:	141
	12:19	for their l will be stripped of everything	824
	12:20	be laid waste and the l will be desolate.	824
	12:22	what is this proverb you have in the l	141
	13: 9	nor will they enter the l of Israel.	824
	14:16	but the l would be desolate.	824
	14:17	'Let the sword pass throughout the l,'	824
	14:19	a plague into that l and pour out my wrath	824
	15: 8	I will make the l desolate	824
	16: 3	and birth were in the l of the Canaanites;	824
	16:29	Babylonia, a l of merchants,	824
	17: 4	and carried it away to a l of merchants,	824
	17: 5	the seed of your l and put it in fertile soil.	824
	17:13	also carried away the leading men of the l,	824
	17:16	in the l of the king who put him on	5226
	18: 2	by quoting this proverb about the l	141
	19: 4	They led him with hooks to the l	824
	19: 7	The l and all who were in it were terrified	824
	19:13	in the desert, in a dry and thirsty l.	824
	20: 6	into a l I had searched out for them,	824
	20: 6	a l flowing with milk and honey,	NIH
	20:15	into the l I had given them—	824
	20:15	a l flowing with milk and honey,	NIH
	20:28	into the l I had sworn to give them	824
	20:36	in the desert of the l of Egypt,	824
	20:38	Although I will bring them out of the l	824
	20:38	yet they will not enter the l of Israel.	141
	20:40	there in the l the entire house of Israel will	824
	20:42	when I bring you into the l of Israel,	141
	20:42	the l I had sworn with uplifted hand	824
	21: 2	Prophesy against the l of Israel	141
	21:30	in the l of your ancestry, I will judge you.	824
	21:32	your blood will be shed in your l,	824
	22:24	say to **the** l, 'You are a land that has had	2023S
	22:24	a l that has had no rain or showers on	824
	22:29	The people of the l practice extortion	824
	22:30	of the l so I would not have to destroy it,	824
	23: 3	In **that** l their breasts were fondled	9004S
	23:48	"So I will put an end to lewdness in the l,	824
	25: 3	over the l of Israel when it was laid waste	141
	25: 6	the malice of your heart against the l	141
	25: 9	and Kiriathaim—the glory of that l.	824
	26:20	or take your place in the l of the living.	824
	28:25	Then they will live in their own l,	141
	29:10	the l of Egypt a ruin and desolate waste	824
	29:12	I will make the l of Egypt desolate	824
	29:14	to Upper Egypt, the l of their ancestry.	824
	29:19	and plunder **the** l as pay for his army.	2023S
	30: 5	the covenant l will fall by the sword along	824
	30:11	will be brought in to destroy the l.	824
	30:11	against Egypt and fill the l with the slain.	824
	30:12	up the streams of the Nile and sell the l	824
	30:12	of foreigners will lay waste the l.	824
	30:13	and I will spread fear throughout the l.	824
	31:12	lay broken in all the ravines of the l.	824
	32: 4	I will throw you on the l and hurl you on	824
	32: 6	the l with your flowing blood all the way	824
	32: 8	I will bring darkness over your l,	824
	32:15	and strip the l of everything in it,	824
	32:23	All who had spread terror in the l of	824
	32:24	All who had spread terror in the l of	824
	32:25	Because their terror had spread in the l of	824
	32:26	because they spread their terror in the l of	824
	32:27	of these warriors had stalked through the l	824
	32:32	Although I had him spread terror in the l	824
	33: 2	'When I bring the sword against a l,	824
	33: 2	a land, and the people of the l choose one	824
	33: 3	the sword coming against the l and blows	824
	33:24	in those ruins in the l of Israel are saying,	141
	33:24	yet he possessed the l.	824
	33:24	l has been given to us as our possession.'	824
	33:25	should you then possess the l?	824
	33:26	Should you then possess the l?'	824
	33:28	I will make the l a desolate waste,	824
	33:29	when I have made the l a desolate waste	824
	34:13	and I will bring them into their own l.	141
	34:13	and in all the settlements in the l.	824
	34:14	heights of Israel will be their **grazing** l.	5659
	34:14	they will lie down in good **grazing** l,	5659
	34:25	the l of wild beasts so that they may live	824

Eze	34:27	the people will be secure in their l.	141
	34:29	I renowned **for** its **crops,**	4760
	34:29	in the l or bear the scorn of the nations.	824
	36: 5	hearts they made my l their own possession	824
	36: 6	the l *of* Israel and say to the mountains	141
	36:17	people of Israel were living in their own l,	141
	36:18	because they had shed blood in the l and	824
	36:20	and yet they had to leave his l.'	824
	36:24	and bring you back into your own l.	141
	36:28	in the l I gave your forefathers;	824
	36:34	The desolate l will be cultivated instead	824
	36:35	"This l that was laid waste has become	824
	37:12	I will bring you back to the l *of* Israel.	141
	37:14	and I will settle you in your own l.	141
	37:21	and bring them back into their own l.	141
	37:22	I will make them one nation in the l,	824
	37:25	in the l I gave to my servant Jacob,	824
	37:25	**the** l where your fathers lived.	2023ˢ
	38: 2	against Gog, the l *of* Magog,	824
	38: 8	In future years you will invade a l	824
	38: 9	you will be like a cloud covering the l.	824
	38:11	"I will invade a l *of* unwalled villages;	824
	38:12	living at the center of the l."	824
	38:16	like a cloud that covers the l.	824
	38:16	O Gog, I will bring you against my l,	824
	38:18	When Gog attacks the l *of* Israel,	141
	38:19	be a great earthquake in the l *of* Israel.	141
	39:12	be burying them in order to cleanse the l.	824
	39:13	All the people of the l will bury them,	824
	39:14	be regularly employed to cleanse **the** l.	2023ˢ
	39:14	Some will go throughout the l and,	824
	39:15	The l and one of them sees a human bone,	824
	39:16	And so they will cleanse the l.'	824
	39:26	in their l with no one to make them afraid.	141
	39:28	I will gather them to their own l,	141
	40: 2	In visions of God he took me to the l	824
	43: 2	and the l was radiant with his glory.	824
	45: 1	" 'When you allot the l as an inheritance	824
	45: 1	to present to the LORD a portion of the l	824
	45: 2	with 50 cubits around it for **open** l.	4494
	45: 4	the sacred portion of the l for the priests,	824
	45: 7	the l bordering each side of the area	NIH
	45: 8	This l will be his possession in Israel.	824
	45: 8	to possess the l according to their tribes.	824
	45:16	The l will participate in this special gift for	824
	45:22	for himself and for all the people of the l.	824
	46: 3	of the l are to worship in the presence of	824
	46: 9	" 'When the people of the l come before	824
	47:13	to divide the l for an inheritance among	824
	47:14	this l will become your inheritance.	824
	47:15	"This is to be the boundary of the l:	824
	47:18	along the Jordan between Gilead and the l	824
	47:21	to distribute this l among yourselves	824
	48:12	to them from the sacred portion of the l,	824
	48:14	This is the best of the l and must not pass	824
	48:29	the l you are to allot as an inheritance to	824
Da	4:10	a tree in the middle of the l.	10075
	6:25	of every language throughout the l:	10075
	8: 9	and to the east and toward the Beautiful **L.**	NIH
	9: 6	and to all the people of the l.	824
	11:16	in the Beautiful **L** and will have the power	824
	11:39	over many people and will distribute the l	141
	11:41	He will also invade the Beautiful **L.**	824
Hos	1: 2	the l is guilty of the vilest adultery	824
	1:11	and will come up out of the l,	824
	2: 3	turn her into a parched l,	824
	2:18	sword and battle I will abolish from the l,	824
	2:23	I will plant her for myself in the l;	824
	4: 1	to bring against you who live in the l,	824
	4: 1	no acknowledgment of God in the l.	824
	4: 3	Because of this the l mourns,	824
	7:16	For this they will be ridiculed in the l	824
	9: 3	They will not remain in the LORD'S l;	824
	10: 1	as his l prospered, he adorned his sacred	
		stones.	824
	13: 5	in the desert, in the l *of* burning heat.	824
Joel	1: 2	listen, all who live in the l.	824
	1: 6	A nation has invaded my l,	824
	1:14	the l to the house of the LORD your God,	824
	2: 1	Let all who live in the l tremble,	824
	2: 3	Before them the l is like the garden	824
	2:18	Then the LORD will be jealous for his l,	824
	2:20	pushing it into a parched and barren l,	824
	2:21	Be not afraid, O l; be glad and rejoice.	141
	3: 2	among the nations and divided up my l.	824
	3:19	in whose l they shed innocent blood.	824
Am	2:10	to give you the l *of* the Amorites.	824
	3:11	"An enemy will overrun the l;	824
	5: 2	never to rise again, deserted in her own l,	141
	5: 8	and pours them over the face of the l—	824
	6: 2	Is their l larger than yours?	1473
	7: 2	When they had stripped the l clean,	824
	7: 4	up the great deep and devoured the l.	2750
	7:10	The l cannot bear all his words.	824
	7:11	away from their **native** l.' "	141
	7:12	Go back to the l *of* Judah.	824
	7:17	Your l will be measured and divided up,	141
	7:17	go into exile, away from their **native** l.' "	141
	8: 4	and do away with the poor of the l,	824
	8: 8	"Will not the l tremble for this,	824
	8: 8	The whole l will rise like the Nile;	2023ˢ
	8:11	"when I will send a famine through the l—	824
	9: 5	the whole l rises like the Nile,	2023ˢ
	9: 6	and pours them out over the face of the l—	824
	9:15	I will plant Israel in their own l,	141
	9:15	from the l I have given them,"	141
Ob	1:19	from the foothills will possess the l *of*	NIH

Ob	1:20	in Canaan will possess [the l] as far as	NIH
Jnh	1: 9	who made the sea and the l."	3317
	1:13	the men did their best to row back to l.	3317
	2:10	and it vomited Jonah onto **dry** l.	3317
Mic	2: 5	the assembly of the LORD to divide the l	2475
	5: 5	the Assyrian invades our l and marches	824
	5: 6	They will rule the l *of* Assyria with	824
	5: 6	the l *of* Nimrod with drawn sword.	824
	5: 6	from the Assyrian when he invades our l	824
	5:11	I will destroy the cities of your l and tear	824
	6: 4	and redeemed you from the l *of* slavery.	1074
	7: 2	The godly have been swept from the l;	824
Na	3:13	of your l are wide open to your enemies;	824
	3:16	but like locusts they strip the l and	NIH
Hab	3:13	the leader of the l *of* wickedness.	1074
Zep	2: 3	Seek the LORD, all you humble of the l,	824
	2: 5	O Canaan, l *of* the Philistines.	824
	2: 6	The l *by* the sea, where the Kerethites	2475
	2: 8	and made threats against their l.	1473
	2: 9	of my nation *will* **inherit** their l."	5706
	2:11	when he destroys all the gods of the l.	824
	2:11	every one in its own l.	5226
	3:19	and honor in every l *where* they were put	824
Hag	2: 4	Be strong, all you people of the l,'	824
	2: 6	and the earth, the sea, and the **dry** l.	3000
Zec	1:21	up their horns against the l *of* Judah	824
	2: 6	Flee from the l *of* the north,"	824
	2:12	inherit Judah as his portion in the holy l	141
	3: 9	'and I will remove the sin of this l in	824
	5: 3	that is going out over the whole l;	824
	5: 6	the iniquity of the people throughout the l."	824
	6: 8	given my Spirit rest in the l *of* the north."	824
	7: 5	The people of the l and the priests,	824
	7:14	The l was left so desolate behind them	824
	7:14	how they made the pleasant l desolate.' "	824
	9: 1	of the LORD is against the l *of* Hadrach	824
	9:16	They will sparkle in his l like jewels in	141
	11: 6	no longer have pity on the people of the l,"	824
	11: 6	They will oppress the l,	824
	11:16	a shepherd over the l who will not care for	824
	12:12	The l will mourn, each clan by itself,	824
	13: 2	the names of the idols from the l,	824
	13: 2	and the spirit of impurity from the l.	824
	13: 5	the l has been my livelihood since my youth.	141
	13: 8	In the whole l," declares the LORD,	824
	14:10	The whole l, from Geba to Rimmon,	824
Mal	1: 4	They will be called the Wicked **L,**	1473
	3:12	for yours will be a delightful l,"	824
	4: 6	or else I will come and strike the l with	824
Mt	2: 6	Bethlehem, in the l *of* Judah,	1178
	2:20	and his mother and go to the l *of* Israel,	1178
	2:21	and his mother and went to the l *of* Israel.	1178
	4:15	"L *of* Zebulun and land of Naphtali,	1178
	4:15	of Zebulun and l *of* Naphtali, the way to	1178
	4:16	on those living in the l *of* the shadow	6001
	14:24	a considerable distance from l,	1178
	23:15	over l and sea to win a single convert,	3831
	27:45	the ninth hour darkness came over all the l.	1178
Mk	6:47	and he was alone on l.	1178
	15:33	over the whole l until the ninth hour.	1178
Lk	4:25	a severe famine throughout the l.	1178
	21:23	in the l and wrath against this people.	1178
	23:44	and darkness came over the whole l until	1178
Ac	5: 3	of the money you received for the l?	6005
	5: 8	the price you and Ananias got for the l?"	6005
	7: 3	'and go to the l I will show you.'	1178
	7: 4	left the l of the Chaldeans and settled	1178
	7: 4	God sent him to this l where you are	1178
	7: 5	after him would possess the l,	899ˢ
	7:45	with them when they took the l from	NIG
	7:45	It remained in the l until the time	NIG
	13:19	in Canaan and gave their l to his people	1178
	27:27	sailors sensed they were approaching l.	6001
	27:39	they did not recognize the l,	1178
	27:43	to jump overboard first and get to l.	1178
	27:44	In this way everyone reached l in safety.	1178
Heb	6: 7	L that drinks in the rain often falling on it	1178
	6: 8	But l that produces thorns and thistles	NIG
	11: 9	home in the promised l like a stranger in	1178
	11:29	passed through the Red Sea as on dry l;	1178
Jas	5: 7	for the l to yield its valuable crop and	1178
	5:17	not rain on the l for three and a half years.	1178
Rev	7: 1	to prevent any wind from blowing on the l	1178
	7: 2	given power to harm the l and the sea:	1178
	7: 3	"Do not harm the l or the sea or the trees	1178
	10: 2	on the sea and his left foot on the l,	1178
	10: 5	the sea and on the l raised his right hand	1178
	10: 8	standing on the sea and on the l."	1178
	16: 2	and poured out his bowl on the l,	1178

LAND'S (1) [LAND]

Nu	18:13	All the l firstfruits that they bring to	824+928

LANDMARK (KJV) See BOUNDARY STONE

LANDED (11) [LAND]

Mt	14:14	*When* Jesus l and saw a large crowd,	2002
	14:34	*they* l at Gennesaret.	1178+2093+2262+3836
Mk	6:34	*When* Jesus l and saw a large crowd,	2002
	6:53	*they* l at Gennesaret and had	1178+2093+2262+3836
Jn	6:23	Then some boats from Tiberias l near	2262
	21: 9	When *they* l, they saw a	609+1178+1650+3836
Ac	18:22	*When he* l at Caesarea, he went up	2982

Ac	21: 3	*We* l at Tyre, where our ship was to unload	2982
	21: 7	We continued our voyage from Tyre and l	2918
	27: 3	The next day *we* l at Sidon;	2864
	27: 5	*we* l at Myra in Lycia.	2982

LANDOWNER (3) [LAND]

Mt	20: 1	a l who went out early in the morning	476+3867
	20:11	they began to grumble against the l.	3867
	21:33	There was a l who planted a vineyard.	476+3867

LANDS (50) [LAND]

Ge	26: 3	your descendants I will give all these l	824
	26: 4	in the sky and will give them all these l,	824
	41:54	There was famine in all the other l,	824
Lev	26:36	in the l *of* their enemies that the sound of	824
	26:39	in the l *of* their enemies because	824
Nu	32: 1	the l *of* Jazer and Gilead were suitable	824
Dt	29:22	from distant l will see the calamities	824
Jos	10:42	and their l Joshua conquered	824
	12: 7	toward Seir (**their** l Joshua gave as	2023ˢ
	12: 8	the l *of* the Hittites, Amorites, Canaanites,	NIH
Jdg	11:18	skirted the l *of* Edom and Moab,	824
2Ki	19:17	have laid waste these nations and their l.	824
	19:24	I have dug wells in **foreign** l and drunk	AIT
1Ch	7:28	Their l and settlements included Bethel	299
	29:30	and the kingdoms of all the other l.	824
2Ch	12: 8	and serving the kings of other l."	824
	13: 9	of your own as the peoples of other l do?	824
	15: 5	for all the inhabitants of the l were	824
	17:10	the kingdoms of the l surrounding Judah,	824
	26:10	in the hills and in the **fertile** l,	4149
	31:19	on the farm l around their towns or	8441
	32:13	to all the peoples of the other l?	824
	32:17	the gods of the peoples of the other l did	824
Ps	49:11	though they had named l after themselves.	141
	76:11	the **neighboring** l bring gifts to the One to	AIT
	78:55	and allotted their l to them as an inheritance	2475
	105:44	he gave them the l *of* the nations,	824
	106:27	and scatter them throughout the l.	824
	107: 3	those he gathered from the l,	824
	111: 6	giving them the l *of* other nations.	5709
Isa	8: 9	Listen, all you distant l.	824
	13: 5	They come from faraway l,	824
	14: 7	All the l are at rest and at peace;	824
	23: 7	have taken her to settle in far-off l?	NIH
	37:18	have laid waste all these peoples and their l.	824
	37:25	I have dug wells in foreign l and drunk	NIH
Jer	12:14	from their l and I will uproot the house	141
	27:10	to remove you far from your l;	141
	32:37	I will surely gather them from all the l	824
	46:16	to our own people and our native l,	824
Eze	6: 8	when you are scattered among the l	824
	20: 6	the most beautiful of all l.	824
	20:15	most beautiful of all l—	824
	29:12	land of Egypt desolate among devastated l,	824
	30: 7	" 'They will be desolate among desolate l,	824
	32: 9	among l you have not known.	824
Hab	2: 8	you have destroyed l and cities	824
	2:17	you have destroyed l and cities	824
Zec	10: 9	yet in **distant** l they will remember me.	5305
Ac	4:34	For from time to time those who owned l	6005

LANES (1)

Lk	14:23	and **country** l and make them come in,	5850

LANGUAGE (41) [LANGUAGES]

Ge	10: 5	within their nations, each with its own l.)	4383
	11: 1	Now the whole world had one l and	8557
	11: 6	the same l they have begun to do this,	8557
	11: 7	down and confuse their l so they will	8557
	11: 9	because there the LORD confused the l	8557
Dt	28:49	a nation whose l you will not understand,	4383
Ezr	4: 7	in Aramaic script and in the Aramaic l.	9553
Ne	13:24	of their children spoke the l *of* **Ashdod** or	848
	13:24	Ashdod or the l *of* one of the other peoples	4383
	13:24	not know how to speak the l *of* **Judah.**	3376
Est	1:22	and to each people in its own l	4383
	3:12	the l *of* each people all Haman's orders to	4383
	8: 9	of each province and the l *of* each people	4383
	8: 9	also to the Jews in their own script and l.	4383
Ps	19: 3	or l where their voice is not heard.	1821
	81: 5	where we heard a l we did not understand.	8557
Isa	19:18	cities in Egypt will speak the l *of* Canaan	8557
Jer	5:15	a people whose l you do not know,	4383
Eze	3: 5	and difficult l, but to the house of Israel—	4383
	3: 6	of obscure speech and difficult l,	4383
Da	1: 4	He was to teach them the l and literature	4383
	3: 4	O peoples, nations and men of every l:	10392
	3: 7	nations and **men of every** l fell down	10392
	3:29	or l who say anything against the God	10392
	4: 1	nations and **men of every** l,	10392
	5:19	and nations and men of every l dreaded	10392
	6:25	and **men of every** l throughout the land:	10392
	7:14	nations and **men of every** l worshiped him.	10392
Jn	8:43	Why is my l not clear to you?	3282
	8:44	When he lies, he speaks **his native** l,	1666+2625+3836
	16:25	I *will* no longer **use** this kind of l	3281
Ac	1:19	they called that field *in* their l Akeldama,	1365
	2: 6	each one heard them speaking *in* his own l.	1365
	2: 8	each of us hears them *in* his own native l?	1365
	14:11	they shouted *in* **the** Lycaonian l,	3378
Col	3: 8	slander, and **filthy** l from your lips.	155
Rev	5: 9	for God from every tribe and l and people	1185

Rev 7: 9 from every nation, tribe, people and l, *1185*
11: 9 l and nation will gaze on their bodies *1185*
13: 7 over every tribe, people, l and nation. *1185*
14: 6 to every nation, tribe, l and people. *1185*

LANGUAGES (6) [LANGUAGE]
Ge 10:20 the sons of Ham by their clans and l, *4383*
10:31 the sons of Shem by their clans and l, *4383*
Zec 8:23 from all l and nations will take firm hold *4383*
1Co 14:10 Undoubtedly there are all sorts of l in *5889*
Rev 10:11 nations, and kings." *1185*
17:15 are peoples, multitudes, nations and l. *1185*

LANGUISH (2) [LANGUISHES]
Isa 24: 4 the exalted of the earth l. *581*
Jer 14: 2 "Judah mourns, her cities l; *581*

LANGUISHES (1) [LANGUISH]
Isa 24: 4 the world l and withers, *581*

LANTERNS (1)
Jn 18: 3 They were carrying torches, l and weapons. *3286*

LAODICEA (6) [LAODICEANS]
Col 2: 1 for you and for those at L, *3293*
4:13 for you and for those at L and Hierapolis. *3293*
4:15 Give my greetings to the brothers at L, *3293*
4:16 and that you in turn read the letter from L. *3293*
Rev 1:11 Thyatira, Sardis, Philadelphia and L." *3293*
3:14 "To the angel of the church in L write: *3293*

LAODICEANS (1) [LAODICEA]
Col 4:16 of the L and that you in turn read the letter *3294*

LAPIDOTH (KJV) See LAPPIDOTH

LAP (8) [LAPPED, LAPS]
Jdg 7: 5 "Separate those who l the water *4379*
16:19 Having put him to sleep on her l, *1386*
Ru 4:16 laid him in her l and cared for him. *2668*
2Ki 4:20 the boy sat on her l until noon, *1386*
Pr 6:27 Can a man scoop fire into his l *2668*
16:33 The lot is cast into the l, *2668*
Ecc 7: 9 for anger resides in the l of fools. *2668*
Lk 6:38 will be poured into your l. *3146*

LAPPED (2) [LAP]
Jdg 7: 6 Three hundred men l with their hands *4379*
7: 7 men that l I will save you and give *4379*

LAPPIDOTH (1)
Jdg 4: 4 Deborah, a prophetess, the wife of L, *4366*

LAPS (4) [LAP]
Ps 79:12 into the l of our neighbors seven times *2668*
Isa 65: 6 I will pay it back into their l— *2668*
65: 7 I will measure into their l the full payment *2668*
Jer 32:18 the fathers' sins into the l of their children *2668*

LAPWING (KJV) See HOOPOE

LARGE (154) [ENLARGE, ENLARGED, ENLARGES, LARGER, LARGEST]
Ge 29: 2 stone over the mouth of the well was l. *1524*
30:43 and came to own l flocks, *8041*
50: 9 It was a very l company. *3878*
Ex 12:38 as well as l droves of livestock, *3878+4394*
Nu 13:28 and the cities are fortified and very l. *1524*
20:20 against them with a l and powerful army. *3878*
32: 1 who had very l herds and flocks, *8041*
Dt 1:28 the cities are l, with walls up to the sky. *1524*
6:10 a land with l, flourishing cities *1524*
8:13 and when your herds and flocks grow l *8049*
9: 1 with l cities that have walls up to the sky. *1524*
17:17 accumulate l amounts of silver and *4394+8049*
25:14 measures in your house—one l, one small. *1524*
27: 2 set up some l stones and coat them *1524*
Jos 7:26 Over Achan they heaped up a l pile *1524*
8:29 And they raised a l pile of rocks over it, *1524*
10:11 the LORD hurled l hailstones down *1524*
10:18 "Roll l rocks up to the mouth of the cave, *1524*
10:27 the mouth of the cave they placed l rocks, *1524*
11: 4 and a l number of horses and chariots— *4394*
13: 1 and there are still very l areas of land to *2221*
14:12 and their cities were l and fortified, *1524*
19:33 from Heleph and the l tree in Zaanannim, *471*
22: 8 with l herds of livestock, with silver, *4394+8041*
24:26 a l stone and set it up there under the oak *1524*
1Sa 6:14 and there it stopped beside a l rock. *1524*
6:15 and placed them on the l rock. *1524*
6:18 The l rock, on which they set the ark of *1524*
14:33 "Roll a l stone over here at once." *1524*
2Sa 12: 2 The rich man had a very l number of sheep *2221*
18: 9 under the thick branches of a l oak, *1524*
18:17 pit in the forest and piled up a l heap *1524+4394*
1Ki 4:13 in Bashan and its sixty l walled cities *1524*
5:17 from the quarry l blocks of quality stone *1524*
7:10 The foundations were laid with l stones *1524*

1Ki 10: 2 l quantities of gold, and precious stones— *4394*
10:10 l quantities of spices, and precious stones. *4394*
10:16 King Solomon made two hundred l shields *7558*
18:32 he dug a trench around it l enough *3869*
18:33 "Fill four l jars with water and pour it on *3902*
2Ki 4:38 "Put on the l pot and cook some stew *1524*
12:10 that there was a l amount of money in *8041*
16:15 "On the l new altar, offer the morning burnt *1524*
18:17 and his field commander with a l army, *3878*
1Ch 22: 3 a l amount of iron to make nails for *4200+8044*
22: 4 Tyrians had brought l numbers of *4200+8044*
29: 2 all of these in l quantities. *4200+8044*
2Ch 2: 9 temple I build must be l and magnificent. *1524*
4: 9 and the l court and the doors for the court, *1524*
9: 1 l quantities of gold, and precious *4200+8044*
9: 9 l quantities of spices, and precious stones. *4394*
9:15 King Solomon made two hundred l shields *7558*
14: 8 equipped with l shields and with spears, *7558*
14:13 carried off a l amount of plunder. *2221+4394*
15: 9 for l numbers had come over to him *4200+8044*
17:13 and had l supplies in the towns of Judah. *8041*
23: 9 the l and small shields that had belonged *4482S*
24:11 and they saw that there was a l amount *8041*
26:15 to shoot arrows and hurl l stones. *1524*
30: 5 not been celebrated in l numbers *4200+8044*
30:13 A very l crowd of people assembled *8041*
32: 4 A l force of men assembled, *1524*
32: 5 He also made l numbers of weapons *4200+8044*
36:18 from the temple of God, both l and small, *1524*
Ezr 5: 8 are building it with l stones and *10006+10146*
6: 4 with three courses of l stones and *10006+10146*
10: 1 a l crowd of Israelites—men, women *4394+8041*
Ne 5: 7 So I called together a l meeting to deal *1524*
7: 4 Now the city was l and spacious, *1524*
12:31 I also assigned two l choirs to give thanks. *1524*
13: 5 with a l room formerly used to store *1524*
Est 8:15 a l crown of gold and a purple robe *1524*
Job 1: 3 and had a l number of servants. *4394*
36:18 do not let a l bribe turn you aside. *8044*
Ps 104:25 living things both l and small. *1524*
Pr 14:28 A l population is a king's glory, *8044*
Isa 8: 1 "Take a l scroll and write on it with *1524*
22:18 a ball and throw you into a l country. *3338+8146*
36: 2 a l army from Lachish to King Hezekiah *3878*
Jer 22:14 So he makes l windows in it, *7973*
43: 9 take some l stones with you *1524*
44:15 women who were present—a l assembly, *1524*
46: 3 both l and small, and march out for battle! *7558S*
49:32 and their l herds will be booty. *2162*
Eze 17:15 to Egypt to get horses and a l army. *8041*
23:24 with l and small shields and with helmets, *7558S*
23:32 drink your sister's cup, a cup l and deep; *8146*
38: 4 and a great horde with l and small shields, *7558S*
39: 9 burn them up—the small and l shields, *7558S*
47: 9 There will be l numbers of fish, *4394*
Da 2:31 and there before you stood a l statue— *10678*
4:11 The tree grew l and strong *10648*
4:20 The tree you saw, which grew l and strong, *10648*
7: 7 It had l iron teeth; it crushed and *10647*
8: 8 of his power his l horn was broken off, *1524*
8:21 l horn between his eyes is the first king. *1524*
11:11 who will raise a l army, *8041*
11:25 "With a l army he will stir up his strength *1524*
11:25 of the South will wage war with a l *1524*
Joel 2: 2 the mountains a l and mighty army comes, *8041*
Mt 4:25 L crowds from Galilee, the Decapolis, *4498*
8: 1 l crowds followed him. *4498*
8:30 from them a l herd of pigs was feeding. *4498*
13: 2 Such l crowds gathered around him *4498*
13:33 into a l amount of flour until it worked all *5552*
14:14 When Jesus landed and saw a l crowd, *4498*
18: 6 a l millstone hung around his neck *3685+3948*
19: 2 L crowds followed him, *4498*
20:29 a l crowd followed him. *4498*
21: 8 A very l crowd spread their cloaks on *4498*
26:47 a l crowd armed with swords and clubs, *4498*
28:12 they gave the soldiers a l sum of money, *2653*
Mk 2:13 A l crowd came to him, *NIG*
3: 7 and a l crowd from Galilee followed. *4498*
4: 1 around him was such a l crowd that he got into a boat *4498*
5:11 A l herd of pigs was feeding on *3489*
5:21 a l crowd gathered around him *4498*
5:24 A l crowd followed and pressed *4498*
6:34 When Jesus landed and saw a l crowd, *4498*
8: 1 During those days another l crowd gathered. *4498*
9:14 a l crowd around them and the teachers of *4498*
9:42 with a l millstone tied around his neck. *3948*
10:46 together with a l crowd, *2653*
12:37 The l crowd listened to him with delight. *4498*
12:41 Many rich people threw in l amounts. *4498*
14:15 He will show you a l upper room, *3489*
16: 4 they saw that the stone, which was very l, *3489*
Lk 5: 6 a l number of fish that their nets began *4498*
5:29 and a l crowd of tax collectors *4498*
6:17 A l crowd of his disciples was there and *4498*
7:11 and his disciples and a l crowd went along *4498*
7:12 a l crowd from the town was with her. *2653*
8: 4 While a l crowd was gathering *4498*
8:32 A l herd of pigs was feeding there on *2653*
9:37 a l crowd met him. *4498*
13:21 amount of flour until it *236+4929+5552*
14:25 L crowds were traveling with Jesus, *4498*
22:12 He will show you a l upper room, *3489*
23:27 A l number of people followed him, *4498*
Jn 12: 9 Meanwhile a l crowd of Jews found out *4498*
21: 6 the net in because of the l number of fish. *4436*
21:11 It was full of fish, 153, *3489*

Ac 6: 7 and a l number of priests became obedient *4498*
10:11 and something like a l sheet being let *3489*
10:27 Peter went inside and found a l gathering *4498*
11: 5 like a l sheet being let down from heaven *3489*
14:21 that city and won a l number of disciples. *2653*
17: 4 a l number of God-fearing Greeks and not *4498*
19:26 led astray l numbers of people here *2653+4063*
Gal 6:11 See what l letters I use as I write to you *4383*
2Ti 2:20 In a l house there are articles not only *3489*
Jas 3: 4 Although they are so l and are driven *5496*
Rev 6: 4 To him was given a l sword. *3489*
18:21 the size of a l millstone and threw it into *3489*

LARGER (15) [LARGE]
Lev 25:51 he must pay for his redemption a l share of *4946*
Nu 26:54 To a l group give a larger inheritance, *8041*
26:54 To a larger group give a l inheritance, *8049*
26:56 by lot among the l and smaller groups." *8041*
33:54 To a l group give a larger inheritance, *8041*
33:54 To a larger group give a l inheritance, *8049*
Dt 7: 1 seven nations l and stronger than you— *8041*
11:23 and you will dispossess nations l *1524*
Jos 22: 10 it was l than Ai, and all its men *1524*
1Ch 24: 4 A l number of leaders were found *8041*
2Ch 24:24 into their hands a much l army. *4200+8044*
Eze 43:14 up to the l ledge it is four cubits high and *1524*
Da 11:13 will muster another army, l than the first; *8041*
Am 6: 2 Is their land l than yours? *8041*
Ac 28:23 and came in even l numbers to the place *4498*

LARGEST (2) [LARGE]
Mt 13:32 the l of garden plants and becomes a tree, *3505*
Mk 4:32 and becomes the l of all garden plants, *3505*

LASCIVIOUSNESS (KJV) See
DEBAUCHERY, IMMORALITY,
LEWDNESS, SENSUALITY

LASEA (1)
Ac 27: 8 called Fair Havens, near the town of L. *3297*

LASH (2) [LASHED, LASHES]
Job 5:21 be protected from the l of the tongue, *8765*
Isa 10:26 The LORD Almighty will l them with *6424*

LASHA (1)
Ge 10:19 Admah and Zeboiim, as far as L. *4388*

LASHARON (1)
Jos 12:18 the king of Aphek one the king of L one *4389*

LASHED (1) [LASH]
Isa 54:11 l by storms and not comforted, *6192*

LASHES (4) [LASH]
Dt 25: 2 with the number of l his crime deserves, *NIH*
25: 3 he must not give him more than forty l. *5782*
Pr 17:10 more than a hundred l a fool. *5782*
2Co 11:24 from the Jews the forty l minus one. *NIG*

LAST (113) [LASTED, LASTING, LASTS, LATTER]
Ge 19:34 "L night I lay with my father. *621*
25: 8 Then Abraham breathed his l and died at *1588*
25:17 He breathed his l and died, *1588*
29:34 at l my husband will become attached *2021+7193*
31:29 l night the God of your father said to me, *621*
31:42 and l night he rebuked you." *621*
33: 7 L of all came Joseph and Rachel, *339*
35:18 As she breathed her l— *3655+5883*
35:29 Then he breathed his l and died *1588*
49:33 breathed his l and was gathered *1588*
Ex 14:24 During the l watch of the night *874+1332*
Lev 8:33 for your ordination will l seven days. *NIH*
15:19 of her monthly period will l seven days, *2118*
26:10 will still be eating l year's harvest *3823+3824*
Nu 2:31 They will set out l, under their standards. *340*
14:33 the l of your bodies lies in the desert. *9448*
24:20 but he will come to ruin at l." *344*
Dt 31:29 when the l of these fighting men among *9462*
Jos 12: 4 one of the l of the Rephaites, *3856*
13:12 and had survived as one of the l of the *3856*
1Sa 9:19 the l to bring the king back to his palace, *874+1332+2021*
15:16 the LORD said to me l night." *2021+4326*
2Sa 9:11 the l to bring the king back to his palace, *340*
19:12 So why should you be the l to bring back *340*
23: 1 These are the l words of David: *340*
1Ki 14:10 I will cut off from Jeroboam every l male *928+7815+8874*
21:21 cut off from Ahab every l male *928+7815+8874*
2Ki 8: 1 in the land that will l seven years." *995*
9: 8 I will cut off from Ahab every l male *928+7815+8874*
1Ch 23:27 According to the l instructions of David, *340*
Ezr 8:13 the l ones, whose names were Eliphelet, *340*
Ne 8:18 Day after day, from the first day to the l, *340*
Job 14:10 he breathes his l and is no more. *1588*
Ps 45: 6 O God, will l for ever and ever; *NIH*
76: 5 men lie plundered, they sleep their l sleep; *NIH*

Ps	81:15	and their punishment *would* l forever.	2118
	119:152	that you established them to l forever.	NIH
Isa	2: 2	In the l days the mountain of the LORD's	344
	41: 4	with the first of them and with the l—	340
	44: 6	I am the first and I am the l;	340
	48:12	I am the first and I am the l.	340
	51: 6	But my salvation *will* l forever,	2118
	51: 8	But my righteousness *will* l forever,	2118
Jer	15: 9	will grow faint and **breathe** her l.	5870+5883
	32:14	and put them in a clay jar so *they will* l	6641
	50:17	l to crush his bones was Nebuchadnezzar	340
Da	9: 2	of Jerusalem *would* l seventy years.	4848
	11: 6	and *he* and his power *will* not l.	6641
Hos	3: 5	and to his blessings in the l days.	344
Am	1: 8	till the l *of* the Philistines is dead,"	8642
	4: 2	the l *of* you with fishhooks.	344
Mic	4: 1	In the l days the mountain of the LORD's	344
Mt	5:26	until you have paid the l penny.	2274
	19:30	But many who are first will be l,	2274
	19:30	and many who are l will be first.	2274
	20: 8	beginning with the l *ones* hired and going	2274
	20:12	'These men who were hired l worked only	2274
	20:14	to give the man who was hired l the same	2274
	20:16	l will be first, and the first will be last."	2274
	20:16	the l will be first, and the first will be l."	2274
	21:37	**L** of all, he sent his son to them.	5731
	27:64	This l deception will be worse than	2274
Mk	4:17	they have no root, *they* l only a short time.	1639
	9:35	wants to be first, he must be the very l,	2274
	10:31	But many who are first will be l,	2274
	10:31	first will be last, and the l first."	2274
	12: 6	He sent him l **of all,** saying,	2274
	12:22	**L** of all, the woman died too.	2274
	15:37	With a loud cry, Jesus **breathed his l.**	1743
Lk	12:59	until you have paid the l penny."	2274
	13:30	Indeed there are *those who are* l who will	2274
	13:30	and first who will be **l.**"	2274
	23:46	When he had said this, *he* **breathed** *his* l.	1743
Jn	6:39	but raise them up at the l day."	2274
	6:40	and I will raise him up at the l day."	2274
	6:44	and I will raise him up at the l day.	2274
	6:54	and I will raise him up *at* the l day.	2274
	7:37	On the l and greatest day of the Feast,	2274
	11:24	rise again in the resurrection at the l day."	2274
	12:48	will condemn him at the l day.	2274
	15:16	go and bear fruit—fruit that *will* l.	3531
	16:31	"You believe **at l!**" Jesus answered.	785
Ac	2:17	" 'In the l days, God says, I will pour out	2274
	27:23	**L night** an angel of the God	3816+3836+4047
	27:33	"For the l fourteen days," he said,	1412
Ro	1:10	that **now** at l by God's will the way	2453+4537
	1:17	is by **faith from first to l,**	1650+4411+4411
1Co	9:25	They do it to get a crown that will **not l;**	5778
	9:25	we do it to get a crown that will l **forever.**	915
	15: 8	and l of all he appeared to me also,	2274
	15:26	The l enemy to be destroyed is death.	2274
	15:45	the l Adam, a life-giving spirit.	2274
	15:52	in the twinkling of an eye, at the l trumpet.	2274
2Co	8:10	**L year** you were the first not only to give	4373
	9: 2	that since l **year** you in Achaia were ready	4373
Php	4:10	**at** l you have renewed your concern	2453+4537
1Th	2:16	of God has come upon them at l.	5465
2Ti	3: 1	There will be terrible times in the l days.	2274
Heb	1: 2	but in these l days he has spoken to us	2274
	1: 8	O God, will l for ever and ever,	NIG
Jas	5: 3	You have hoarded wealth in the l days.	2274
1Pe	1: 5	that is ready to be revealed in the l time.	2274
	1:20	but was revealed in these l times	2274
2Pe	3: 3	that in the l days scoffers will come,	2274
1Jn	2:18	Dear children, this is the l hour;	2274
	2:18	This is how we know it is the l hour.	2274
Jude	1:18	"In the l times there will be scoffers	2274
Rev	1:17	I am the First and the **L.**	2274
	2: 8	of him who is the First and the **L,**	2274
	15: 1	seven angels with the seven l plagues—	2274
	15: 1	l, because with them God's wrath is completed.	NIG
	21: 9	the seven bowls full of the seven l plagues	2274
	22:13	the First and the **L,** the Beginning and	2274

LASTED (2) [LAST]

2Sa	3: 1	the house of Saul and the house of David l	2118
2Ki	6:25	the siege l **so long** that a donkey's head	6330

LASTING (35) [LAST]

Ex	12:14	to the LORD—a l ordinance.	6409
	12:17	a l ordinance for the generations to come.	6409
	12:24	these instructions as a l ordinance	6330+6409
	27:21	be a l ordinance among the Israelites for	6409
	28:43	"This is to be a l ordinance for Aaron	6409
	29: 9	The priesthood is theirs by a l ordinance.	6409
	30:21	This is to be a l ordinance for Aaron	6409
	31:16	the generations to come as a l covenant.	6409
Lev	3:17	" 'This is a l ordinance for the generations	6409
	10: 9	a l ordinance for the generations to come.	6409
	16:29	"This is to be a l ordinance for you:	6409
	16:31	must deny yourselves; it is a l ordinance.	6409
	16:34	"This is to be a l ordinance for you:	6409
	17: 7	This is to be a l ordinance for them and	6409
	23:14	a l ordinance for the generations to come,	6409
	23:21	a l ordinance for the generations to come,	6409
	23:31	a l ordinance for the generations to come.	6409
	23:41	a l ordinance for the generations to come;	6409
	24: 3	a l ordinance for the generations to come.	6409
	24: 8	on behalf of the Israelites, as a l covenant.	6409
Nu	10: 8	a l ordinance for you and the generations	6409
	15:15	a l ordinance for the generations to come.	6409
	18:23	a l ordinance for the generations to come.	6409
	19:10	a l ordinance both for the Israelites and for	6409
	19:21	This is a l ordinance for them.	6409
	25:13	a covenant of a l priesthood,	6409
Dt	11: 4	how the LORD brought l ruin on them.	2021+2021+2296+3427+6330
1Sa	25:28	a l dynasty for my master,	586
2Ch	2: 4	This is a l ordinance for Israel.	4200+6409
Est	1: 5	the king gave a banquet, l seven days,	NIH
Jer	31: 3	I will give you l peace in this place.' "	622
	18:16	will be laid waste, an object of l scorn;	AIT
Eze	45:21	Passover, a **feast** l seven days,	AIT
	46:14	to the LORD is a l ordinance.	6409+9458
Heb	10:34	you yourselves had better and l possessions.	3531

LASTS (7) [LAST]

Lev	23:34	Tabernacles begins, and it l for seven days.	NIH
Job	20: 5	the joy of the godless l but a moment.	6330
Ps	30: 5	For his anger l only a moment,	NIH
	30: 5	but his favor l a lifetime;	NIH
Pr	12:19	but a lying tongue l only a moment.	6330
Mt	13:21	since he has no root, *he* l only a short time.	1639
2Co	3:11	much greater is the glory of that which l!	3531

LATCH-OPENING (1)

SS	5: 4	My lover thrust his hand through the l;	2986

LATCHET (KJV) See THONGS

LATE (8) [LATELY, LATER, LATEST]

Ps	127: 2	In vain you rise early and stay up l,	336
Isa	5:11	*who* **stay up** l at night till they are inflamed	336
Mt	14:15	and it's already getting l.	6052
Mk	6:35	By this time it was l **in the day,**	4498+6052
	6:35	they said, "and it's already **very** l.	4498+6052
	11:11	but since it was already l,	4070
Lk	9:12	**L** in the **afternoon** the Twelve	806+2465+3111
Rev	6:13	as l figs drop from a fig tree when shaken	3913

LATELY (2) [LATE]

Isa	52: 4	l, Assyria has oppressed them.	700+928
Mic	2: 8	L my people have risen up like an enemy.	919

LATER (82) [LATE]

Ge	4: 2	L she gave birth to his brother Abel.	3578
	10:18	L the Canaanite clans scattered	339
	22: 1	**Some time** l God tested Abraham.	339+465+1821+2021+2021
	22:20	**Some time** l Abraham was told, "Milcah is also a mother;	339+465+1821+2021+2021
	30:21	**Some time** l she gave birth to a daughter	339
	32:20	l, when I see him, perhaps he will	339+4027
	34:25	Three days l, while all of them were still	928
	38:24	About three months l Judah was told,	4946
	40: 1	**Some time** l, the cupbearer and the baker of the king of Egypt	339+465+1821+2021+2021
	48: 1	**Some time** l Joseph was told, "Your father is ill.	339+465+1821+2021+2021
Ex	9:32	were not destroyed, because they **ripen** l.)	689
Dt	4:30	then in l days you will return to	344
	29:22	in l generations and foreigners who come	340
Jdg	11: 4	**Some time** l, when the Ammonites made war on Israel,	3427+4946
	14: 8	**Some time** l, when he went back	3427+4946
	15: 1	**L** on, at the time of wheat harvest,	3427+4946
	16: 4	**Some time** l, he fell in love with a woman	339+4027
1Sa	25:38	About ten days l, the LORD struck Nabal	NIH
2Sa	3:28	**L,** when David heard about this,	339+4027+4946
	13:23	Two years l, when Absalom's sheepshearers were at Baal Hazor	4200
1Ki	2:39	But three years l, two of Shimei's	4946+7891
	12:12	Three days l Jeroboam and all the people	928
	17: 7	Some time l the brook dried up	4946+7891
	17:17	**Some time** l the son of the woman	339+465+1821+2021+2021
	21: 1	**Some time** l there was an incident involving a vineyard	339+465+1821+2021+2021
2Ki	6:24	**Some time** l, Ben-Hadad king	339+4027
1Ch	2:21	**L,** Hezron lay with the daughter of Makir	339
2Ch	10:12	Three days l Jeroboam and all the people	928
	18: 2	**Some years** l he went down to visit Ahab in Samaria.	4200+7891+9102
	20:35	**L,** Jehoshaphat king of Judah made	339+4027
	24: 4	**Some time** l Joash decided to restore	339+4027
	32: 9	**L,** when Sennacherib king of Assyria	339+2296
Ne	13: 6	Some time l I asked his permission	4200+7891
Est	2: 1	**L** when the anger of King Xerxes had subsided,	339+465+1821+2021+2021
Pr	3:28	not say to your neighbor, "Come back l;	NIH
	20:25	rashly and only l to consider his vows.	339
Ecc	4:16	But those *who* came l were not pleased	340
Jer	13: 6	Many days l the LORD said to me,	4200+7891
	42: 7	Ten days l the word of the LORD came	4946+7891
	46:26	**L,** however, Egypt will be inhabited as	339+4027
Eze	16: 8	" 'L I passed by, and when I looked at you	2256
Da	4:29	Twelve months l, as the king was walking on the roof	10378+10636
	8: 3	the other but grew up l.	340+928+2021
	8:19	to tell you what will happen l **in the time**	344+928
Mt	21:29	but l he changed his mind and went.	5731

Mt	25:11	"**L** the others also came.	5731
Mk	2: 1	A few days l, when Jesus again entered	NIG
	10:34	Three days l he will rise."	3552
	12:13	**L** they sent some of the Pharisees	2779
	16:14	**L** Jesus appeared to the Eleven	5731
Lk	22:58	A little l someone else saw him and said,	3552
	22:59	About an hour l another asserted,	1460
Jn	5: 1	**Some time** l, Jesus went up to Jerusalem for a feast	3552+4047
	5:14	**L** Jesus found him at the temple and	3552+4047
	6:71	one of the Twelve, *was* l to betray him.)	3516
	7:39	whom those who believed in him were l	3516
	12: 4	Judas Iscariot, who *was* l to betray him,	3516
	13: 7	but l you will understand."	3552+4047
	13:36	but you will follow l."	5731
	19:28	**L,** knowing that all was now completed,	3552+4047
	19:38	**L,** Joseph of Arimathea asked Pilate	3552+4047
	20:26	**A week** l his disciples were in	2465+3552+3893
Ac	5: 7	About three hours l his wife came in,	1404
	7: 8	**L** Isaac became the father of Jacob,	2779
	15:36	Some time l Paul said to Barnabas,	3552
	20: 6	and five days l joined the others at Troas,	948
	24: 1	Five days l the high priest Ananias went	3552
	24:24	Several days l Felix came with his wife	3552
	25:13	A few days l King Agrippa and Bernice	1335
	27:28	A short time l they took soundings again	NIG
	28:17	Three days l he called together the leaders	3552
Gal	1:17	into Arabia and l returned to Damascus.	4099
	1:21	**L** I went to Syria and Cilicia.	2083
	2: 1	Fourteen years l I went up again	2083
	3:17	The law, introduced 430 years l,	3552
1Ti	4: 1	that in l times some will abandon the faith	5731
Heb	4: 7	**when** a long time l he spoke through David,	3552
	4: 8	not have spoken l about another day.	3552+4047
	11: 8	to go to a place *he would* l receive	3516
	12:11	**L on,** however, it produces a harvest	5731
Jude	1: 5	but l destroyed those who did not believe.	1309
Rev	1:19	what is now and what will take place l.	3552+4047

LATEST (1) [LATE]

Ac	17:21	about and listening to the l ideas.)	2785

LATIN (1)

Jn	19:20	and the sign was written in Aramaic, L	4872

LATRINE (1)

2Ki	10:27	and people have used it for a l to this day.	4738

LATTER (7) [LAST]

Ge	14: 3	All these l kings joined forces in	NIH
Job	42:12	The LORD blessed l **part of** Job's **life**	344
Da	8:23	"In the l part *of* their reign,	344
Mt	23:23	You should have practiced **the l,**	4047S
Lk	11:42	You should have practiced **the l**	4047S
Php	1:16	The l do so in love, knowing that I	3525
2Ti	2:21	If a man cleanses himself from **the l,**	4047S

LATTICE (4)

Jdg	5:28	behind the l she cried out,	876
2Ki	1: 2	Now Ahaziah had fallen through the l	8422
Pr	7: 6	of my house I looked out through the l.	876
SS	2: 9	peering through the l.	3048

LAUD (KJV) See SING PRAISES

LAUGH (13) [LAUGHED, LAUGHINGSTOCK, LAUGHS, LAUGHTER]

Ge	18:13	"Why did Sarah l and say,	7464
	18:15	so she lied and said, "*I did* not l."	7464
	18:15	But he said, "Yes, *you did* l."	7464
	21: 6	and everyone who hears about this *will* l	7464
Job	5:22	*You will* l at destruction and famine,	8471
Ps	52: 6	*they will* l at him, saying,	8471
	59: 8	But you, O LORD, l at them;	8471
Pr	1:26	I in turn *will* l at your disaster;	8471
	31:25	*she can* l at the days to come.	8471
Ecc	3: 4	a time to weep and a time to l,	8471
Hab	1:10	They l at all fortified cities;	8471
Lk	6:21	are you who weep now, for *you will* l.	1151
	6:25	Woe to you who l now,	1151

LAUGHED (6) [LAUGH]

Ge	17:17	*he* l and said to himself, "Will a son be	7464
	18:12	So Sarah l to herself as she thought,	7464
La	1: 7	Her enemies looked at her and l.	8471
Mt	9:24	But *they* l at him.	2860
Mk	5:40	But *they* l at him.	2860
Lk	8:53	*They* l at him, knowing that she was dead.	2860

LAUGHINGSTOCK (6) [LAUGH]

Ge	38:23	or we will become a l.	997
Ex	32:25	and so become a l to their enemies.	9067
Job	12: 4	"I have become a l to my friends,	8468
	12: 4	a mere l, though righteous and blameless!	8468
La	3:14	I became the l of all my people;	8468
Eze	22: 4	to the nations and a l to all the countries.	7842

LAUGHS (6) [LAUGH]

Job	39: 7	He l at the commotion in the town;	8471

Job	39:18	*she* l at horse and rider.	8471
	39:22	*He* l at fear, afraid of nothing;	8471
	41:29	*he* l at the rattling of the lance.	8471
Ps	2: 4	The One enthroned in heaven l;	8471
	37:13	but the Lord l at the wicked,	8471

LAUGHTER (10) [LAUGH]

Ge	21: 6	Sarah said, "God has brought me l,	7465
Job	8:21	He will yet fill your mouth with l	8468
Ps	126: 2	Our mouths were filled with l,	8468
Pr	14:13	Even in l the heart may ache,	8468
Ecc	2: 2	"L," I said, "is foolish.	8468
	7: 3	Sorrow is better than l,	8468
	7: 6	so is the l of fools.	8468
	10:19	A feast is made for l,	8468
Jer	51:39	so that *they* shout with l—	6600
Jas	4: 9	Change your l to mourning and your joy	*1152*

LAUNCH (1)

Jdg	10:18	"Whoever *will* l the attack against	2725

LAUNDERER'S (1)

Mal	3: 2	he will be like a refiner's fire or a l soap.	3891

LAVER (KJV) See BASIN

LAVISHED (6)

Isa	43:24	or l on me the fat of your sacrifices.	8115
Eze	16:15	*You* l your favors on anyone who passed	9161
Da	2:48	in a high position and l many gifts on him.	10314
Hos	2: 8	*who* l on her the silver and gold—	8049
Eph	1: 8	that *he* l on us with all wisdom	*4355*
1Jn	3: 1	How great is the love the Father *has* l	*1443*

LAW (467) [LAW'S, LAWFUL, LAWGIVER, LAWS, LAWYER]

Ge	47:26	as a l concerning land in Egypt—	2976
Ex	12:49	The same l applies to the native-born and	9368
	13: 9	and a reminder on your forehead that the l	9368
	15:25	There the LORD made a decree and a l	5477
	21:31	This l also applies if the bull gores a son	5477
	24:12	with the l and commands I have written	9368
Lev	7: 7	"The same l applies to both	9368
	24:22	You are to have the same l for the alien	5477
Nu	5:29	the l of jealousy when a woman goes astray	9368
	5:30	the LORD and is to apply this entire l	9368
	6:13	"'Now this is the l *for* the Nazirite when	9368
	6:21	"'This is the l of the Nazirite	9368
	6:21	according to the l *of* the Nazirite.'"	9368
	15:29	One and the same l applies	9368
	19: 2	of the l that the LORD has commanded:	9368
	19:14	the l that applies when a person dies in	9368
	31:21	of the l that the LORD gave Moses:	9368
Dt	1: 5	Moses began to expound this l, saying:	9368
	4:44	the l Moses set before the Israelites.	9368
	6:25	if we are careful to obey all this l before	5184
	17:11	Act according to the l they teach you and	9368
	17:18	for himself on a scroll a copy of this l,	9368
	17:19	and follow carefully all the words of this l	9368
	17:20	and turn from the l to the right or to	5184
	27: 3	the words of this l when you have crossed	9368
	27: 8	of this l on these stones you have set up."	9368
	27:26	the words of this l by carrying them out."	9368
	28:58	not carefully follow all the words of this l,	9368
	28:61	not recorded in this Book of the L,	9368
	29:21	the covenant written in this Book of the L.	9368
	29:29	that we may follow all the words of this l.	9368
	30:10	of the L and turn to the LORD your God	9368
	31: 9	So Moses wrote down this l and gave it to	9368
	31:11	you shall read this l before them	9368
	31:12	follow carefully all the words of this l.	9368
	31:13	Their children, who do not know this l,	NIH
	31:24	the words of this l from beginning to end,	9368
	31:26	of the L and place it beside the ark of	9368
	32:46	to obey carefully all the words of this l.	9368
	33: 4	the l that Moses gave us,	9368
	33:10	to Jacob and your l to Israel.	9368
Jos	1: 7	the l my servant Moses gave you;	9368
	1: 8	Do not let this Book of the L depart	9368
	8:31	to what is written in the Book of the L	9368
	8:32	Joshua copied on stones the l *of* Moses,	9368
	8:34	Joshua read all the words of the l—	9368
	8:34	just as it is written in the Book of the L.	9368
	22: 5	the commandment and the l that Moses	9368
	23: 6	that is written in the Book of the L	9368
	24:26	in the Book of the L *of* God.	9368
1Ki	2: 3	as written in the L of Moses,	9368
2Ki	10:31	Yet Jehu was not careful to keep the l *of*	9368
	14: 6	with what is written in the Book of the L	9368
	17:13	the entire L that I commanded your fathers	9368
	21: 8	and will keep the whole L	9368
	22: 8	of the L in the temple of the LORD."	9368
	22:11	the words of the Book of the L,	9368
	23:24	to fulfill the requirements of the l written	9368
	23:25	in accordance with all the L *of* Moses.	9368
1Ch	16:40	with everything written in the L *of*	9368
	22:12	the l of the LORD your God.	9368
2Ch	6:16	to walk before me according to my l,	9368
	12: 1	and all Israel with him abandoned the l *of*	9368
	15: 3	without a priest to teach and without the l.	9368
	17: 9	taking with them the Book of the L *of*	9368
	19: 8	the l *of* the LORD and to settle disputes.	5477
	19:10	the l, commands, decrees or ordinances—	9368

2Ch	23:18	the LORD as written in the L of Moses,	9368
	25: 4	with what is written in the L, in the Book	9368
	30:16	as prescribed in the L of Moses the man	9368
	31: 3	and appointed feasts as written in the L *of*	9368
	31: 4	so they could devote themselves to the L	9368
	31:21	of God's temple and in obedience to the l	9368
	34:14	Hilkiah the priest found the Book of the L	9368
	34:15	Book of the L in the temple of the LORD."	9368
	34:19	When the king heard the words of the L,	9368
	35:26	according to what is written in the L *of*	9368
Ezr	3: 2	in accordance with what is written in the L	9368
	7: 6	a teacher well versed in the L *of* Moses,	9368
	7:10	and observance of the L of the LORD,	9368
	7:12	a teacher of the L of the God of heaven:	10186
	7:14	and Jerusalem with regard to the L	10186
	7:21	a teacher of the L of the God of heaven,	10186
	7:26	Whoever does not obey the l of your God	10186
	7:26	not obey the law of your God and the l *of*	10186
	10: 3	Let it be done according to the L.	9368
Ne	8: 1	to bring out the Book of the L *of* Moses.	9368
	8: 2	the priest brought the L before	9368
	8: 3	listened attentively to the Book of the L.	9368
	8: 7	the L while the people were standing there.	9368
	8: 8	They read from the Book of the L *of* God,	9368
	8: 9	as they listened to the words of the L.	9368
	8:13	to give attention to the words of the L.	9368
	8:14	They found written in the L,	9368
	8:18	Ezra read from the Book of the L *of* God.	9368
	9: 3	the Book of the L of the LORD their God	9368
	9:26	they put your l behind their backs.	9368
	9:29	"You warned them to return to your l,	9368
	9:34	and our fathers did not follow your l;	9368
	10:28	of the L *of* God, together with their wives	9368
	10:29	and an oath to follow the L *of* God given	9368
	10:34	as it is written in the L.	9368
	10:36	"As it is also written in the L,	9368
	12:44	by the L for the priests and the Levites,	9368
	13: 3	When the people heard this l,	9368
Est	1:13	the king to consult experts in matters *of* l	2017
	1:15	"According to l, what must be done	2017
	3:14	as l in every province and made known to	2017
	4:11	the king has but one l:	2017
	4:16	even though it is against the l.	2017
	8:13	as l in every province and made known to	2017
Ps	1: 2	But his delight is in the l of the LORD,	9368
	1: 2	and on his l he meditates day and night.	9368
	19: 7	The l *of* the LORD is perfect,	9368
	37:31	The l of his God is in his heart;	9368
	40: 8	your l is within my heart."	9368
	78: 5	for Jacob and established the l in Israel,	9368
	78:10	and refused to live by his l.	9368
	89:30	"If his sons forsake my l and do	9368
	94:12	the man you teach from your l;	9368
	119: 1	according to the l of the LORD.	9368
	119:18	that I may see wonderful things in your l.	9368
	119:29	be gracious to me through your l.	9368
	119:34	and I will keep your l and obey it	9368
	119:44	I will always obey your l,	9368
	119:51	but I do not turn from your l.	9368
	119:53	who have forsaken your l.	9368
	119:55	O LORD, and I will keep your l.	9368
	119:61	I will not forget your l.	9368
	119:70	but I delight in your l.	9368
	119:72	The l *from* your mouth is more precious	9368
	119:77	for your l is my delight.	9368
	119:85	contrary to your l.	9368
	119:92	If your l had not been my delight,	9368
	119:97	Oh, how I love your l!	9368
	119:109	I will not forget your l.	9368
	119:113	but I love your l.	9368
	119:126	O LORD; your l is being broken.	9368
	119:136	for your l is not obeyed.	9368
	119:142	and your l is true.	9368
	119:150	but they are far from your l.	9368
	119:153	for I have not forgotten your l.	9368
	119:163	and abhor falsehood but I love your l.	9368
	119:165	Great peace have they who love your l,	9368
	119:174	O LORD, and your l is my delight.	9368
Pr	28: 4	Those who forsake the l praise the wicked,	9368
	28: 4	but those who keep the l resist them.	9368
	28: 7	He who keeps the l is a discerning son,	9368
	28: 9	If anyone turns a deaf ear to the l,	9368
	29:18	but blessed is he who keeps the l.	9368
	31: 5	and forget what the l decrees,	NIH
Isa	1:10	listen to the l of our God,	9368
	2: 3	The l will go out from Zion,	9368
	5:24	the l of the LORD Almighty and spurned	9368
	8:16	Bind up the testimony and seal up the l	9368
	8:20	To the l and to the testimony!	9368
	42: 4	In his l the islands will put their hope."	9368
	42:21	of his righteousness to make his l great	9368
	42:24	they did not obey his l.	9368
	51: 4	The l will go out from me;	9368
	51: 7	you people who have my l in your hearts;	9368
Jer	2: 8	Those who deal with the l did not know me;	9368
	6:19	to my words and have rejected my l.	9368
	8: 8	for we have the l of the LORD,"	9368
	9:13	"It is because they have forsaken my l,	9368
	9:13	they have not obeyed me or followed **my l**.	2023S
	16:11	They forsook me and did not keep my l.	9368
	18:18	**the teaching of** the l by the priest will not	9368
	26: 4	you do not listen to me and follow my l,	9368
	31:33	"I will put my l in their minds and write it	9368
	32:23	they did not obey you or follow your l,	9368
	44:10	nor have they followed my l and	9368
	44:23	and have not obeyed him or followed his l	9368
La	2: 9	the l is no more,	9368

Eze	7:26	the **teaching of the** l by the priest will	9368
	22:26	to my l and profane my holy things;	9368
	43:12	"This is the l of the temple:	9368
	43:12	Such is the l of the temple.	9368
Da	6: 5	unless it has something to do with the l	10186
	6:15	the l of the Medes and Persians no decree	10186
	9:11	All Israel has transgressed your l	9368
	9:11	and sworn judgments written in the L	9368
	9:13	Just as it is written in the L of Moses,	9368
Hos	4: 6	you have ignored the l of your God,	9368
	8: 1	and rebelled against my l.	9368
	8:12	I wrote for them the many things of my l,	9368
Am	2: 4	Because they have rejected the l *of*	9368
Mic	4: 2	The l will go out from Zion,	9368
Hab	1: 7	they are a l to themselves	5477
Zep	3: 4	the sanctuary and do violence to the l.	9368
Hag	2:11	'Ask the priests what the l says:	9368
Zec	7:12	as flint and would not listen to the l or to	9368
Mal	2: 9	shown partiality in **matters of the l.**"	9368
	4: 4	"Remember the l of my servant Moses,	9368
Mt	2: 4	chief priests and **teachers of the l**	1208
	5:17	not think that I have come to abolish the L	3795
	5:18	will by any means disappear from the L	3795
	5:20	of the Pharisees and the **teachers of the l**,	1208
	7:12	for this sums up the L and the Prophets.	3795
	7:29	and not as their **teachers of the l**.	1208
	8:19	a **teacher of the** l came to him and said,	1208
	9: 3	*of* the **teachers of the l** said to themselves,	1208
	11:13	For all the Prophets and the L prophesied	3795
	12: 5	in the L that on the Sabbath the priests in	3795
	12:38	of the Pharisees and **teachers of the l** said	1208
	13:52	"Therefore every **teacher of the** l who has been instructed	1208
	15: 1	and **teachers of the** l came to Jesus	1208
	16:21	chief priests and **teachers of the l**,	1208
	17:10	"Why then do the **teachers of the l** say	1208
	20:18	the chief priests and the **teachers of the l**.	1208
	21:15	and the **teachers of the l** saw	1208
	22:35	One of them, an **expert in the l**,	3788
	22:36	the greatest commandment in the L?"	3795
	22:40	All the L and the Prophets hang	3795
	23: 2	"The **teachers of the** l and the Pharisees sit	1208
	23:13	**teachers of the** l and Pharisees,	1208
	23:15	**teachers of the** l and Pharisees,	1208
	23:23	**teachers of the** l and Pharisees,	1208
	23:23	the more important **matters** *of* the l—	3795
	23:25	**teachers of the** l and Pharisees,	1208
	23:27	**teachers of the** l and Pharisees,	1208
	23:29	**teachers of the** l and Pharisees,	1208
	26:57	where the **teachers of the** l and	1208
	27: 6	against the l to put this into the treasury,	2003
	27:41	the **teachers of the** l and	1208
Mk	1:22	not as the **teachers of the l**.	1208
	2: 6	some **teachers of the** l were sitting there,	1208
	2:16	**teachers of the** l who were Pharisees saw him eating	1208
	3:22	And the **teachers of the** l who came down	1208
	7: 1	*of* the **teachers of the** l who had come	1208
	7: 5	and **teachers of the** l asked Jesus,	1208
	8:31	chief priests and **teachers of the l**,	1208
	9:11	"Why do the **teachers of the** l say	1208
	9:14	the **teachers of the** l arguing with them.	1208
	10: 5	that Moses wrote you this l,"	1953
	10:33	*to* the chief priests and **teachers of the l**.	1208
	11:18	and the **teachers of the** l heard this	1208
	11:27	the **teachers of the** l and the elders came	1208
	12:28	One *of* the **teachers of the** l came	1208
	12:35	the **teachers of the** l say that the Christ is	1208
	12:38	"Watch out for the **teachers of the l**.	1208
	14: 1	and the **teachers of the** l were looking	1208
	14:43	the **teachers of the l**, and the elders.	1208
	14:53	elders and **teachers of the** l came together.	1208
	15: 1	the **teachers of the** l and the whole	1208
	15:31	and the **teachers of the** l mocked him	1208
Lk	2:22	to the L of Moses had been completed,	3795
	2:23	(as it is written in the L of the Lord,	3795
	2:24	in keeping with what is said in the L *of*	3795
	2:27	for him what the custom *of* the L required,	3795
	2:39	everything required by the L of the Lord,	3795
	5:17	Pharisees and **teachers of the l**,	3791
	5:21	and the **teachers of the** l began thinking	1208
	5:30	and the **teachers of the** l who belonged	1208
	6: 7	and the **teachers of the** l were looking for	1208
	7:30	and **experts in the** l rejected God's purpose	3788
	9:22	chief priests and **teachers of the l**,	1208
	10:25	On one occasion an **expert in the** l stood	3788
	10:26	"What is written in the L?"	3795
	10:37	**The expert in the** l replied,	1254+3836S
	11:45	One of the **experts in the** l answered him,	3788
	11:46	Jesus replied, "And you **experts in the l**,	3788
	11:52	"Woe to you **experts in the l**,	3788
	11:53	and the **teachers of the** l began	1208
	14: 3	the Pharisees and **experts in the l**,	3788
	15: 2	and the **teachers of the** l muttered	1208
	16:16	"The L and the Prophets were proclaimed	3795
	16:17	least stroke of a pen to drop out of the L.	3795
	19:47	the **teachers of the** l and the leaders among	1208
	20: 1	the chief priests and the **teachers of the l**	1208
	20:19	The **teachers of the** l and the chief priests	1208
	20:39	Some *of* the **teachers of the** l responded,	1208
	20:46	"Beware of the **teachers of the l**.	1208
	22: 2	and the **teachers of the** l were looking	1208
	22:66	both the chief priests and **teachers of the l**,	1208
	23:10	the **teachers of the** l were standing there,	1208
	24:44	that is written about me in the L of Moses,	3795
Jn	1:17	For the l was given through Moses;	3795

Jn	1:45	the one Moses wrote about in the L, and	3795
	5:10	**the l forbids** you to carry your mat."	2003+4024
	7:19	Has not Moses given you the l?	3795
	7:19	Yet not one of you keeps the l.	3795
	7:23	the Sabbath so that the l of Moses may not	3795
	7:49	But this mob that knows nothing of the l—	3795
	7:51	"Does our l condemn anyone	3795
	8: 3	The **teachers of the l** and the Pharisees	1208
	8: 5	In the L Moses commanded us to stone such	3795
	8:17	In your own L it is written that	3795
	10:34	"Is it not written in your L,	3795
	12:34	the L that the Christ will remain forever,	3795
	15:25	this is to fulfill what is written in their L:	3795
	18:31	and judge him by your own l."	3795
	19: 7	The Jews insisted, "We have a l,	3795
	19: 7	and according to that l he must die,	3795
Ac	4: 5	and **teachers of the l** met in Jerusalem.	1208
	5:34	Gamaliel, a **teacher of the l**,	3791
	6:12	the elders and the **teachers of the l**.	1208
	6:13	against this holy place and against the l.	3795
	7:53	you who have received the l that was put	3795
	10:28	that it is **against** our l for a Jew	116
	13:15	the reading *from* the L and the Prophets,	3795
	13:39	not be justified from by the l of Moses.	3795
	15: 5	be circumcised and required to obey the l	3795
	18:13	to worship God in ways contrary to the l."	3795
	18:15	about words and names and your own l—	3795
	21:20	and all of them are zealous *for* the l.	3795
	21:24	are living in obedience to the l.	3795
	21:28	against our people and our l and this place.	3795
	22: 3	the l of our fathers and was just as zealous	3795
	22:12	He was a devout **observer of** the l	2848+3795
	23: 3	to judge me according to the l,	3795
	23: 3	yet you yourself **violate the l**	4174
	23: 9	**teachers of the l** who were Pharisees stood	1208
	23:29	to do with questions *about* their l,	3795
	24:14	that agrees with the L and that is written in	3795
	25: 8	"I have done nothing wrong against the l	3795
	28:23	about Jesus from the L of Moses and from	3795
Ro	2:12	All who sin **apart from** the l will also perish	3795
	2:12	the law will also perish **apart from the l**,	492
	2:12	and all who sin under the l will be judged	3795
	2:12	under the law will be judged by the l.	3795
	2:13	not those who hear the l who are righteous	3795
	2:13	but it is those who obey the l who will	3795
	2:14	when Gentiles, who do not have the l,	3795
	2:14	do by nature things *required by* the l,	3795
	2:14	they are a l for themselves,	3795
	2:14	even though they do not have the l,	3795
	2:15	that the requirements *of* the l are written	3795
	2:17	on the l and brag about your relationship	3795
	2:18	because you are instructed by the l;	3795
	2:20	because you have in the l the embodiment	3795
	2:23	You who brag about the l,	3795
	2:23	do you dishonor God by breaking the l?	3795
	2:25	has value if you observe the l,	3795
	2:25	but if you break the l, you become as though	3795
	2:27	yet obeys the l will condemn you who,	3795
	3:19	Now we know that whatever the l says,	3795
	3:19	it says *to* those who are under the l,	3795
	3:20	in his sight by observing the l;	3795
	3:20	through the l we become conscious of sin.	3795
	3:21	a righteousness from God, apart from l,	3795
	3:21	to which the L and the Prophets testify.	3795
	3:27	On that of observing the l?	NIG
	3:28	by faith apart from observing the l.	3795
	3:31	Do we, then, nullify the l by this faith?	3795
	3:31	Rather, we uphold the l.	3795
	4:13	It was not through l that Abraham and his	3795
	4:14	For if those who live by l are heirs,	3795
	4:15	because l brings wrath.	3795
	4:15	there is no l there is no transgression.	3795
	4:16	not only *to* those who are of the l but also	3795
	5:13	for before the l was given, sin was in the	3795
	5:13	not taken into account when there is no l.	3795
	5:20	The l was added so that the trespass	3795
	6:14	because you are not under l, but under grace	3795
	6:15	Shall we sin because we are not under l	3795
	7: 1	for I am speaking to men who know the l—	3795
	7: 1	the l has authority over a man only as long	3795
	7: 2	*by* l a married woman is bound to her	3795
	7: 2	she is released from the l of marriage.	3795
	7: 3	she is released from that l and is not	3795
	7: 4	you also died *to* the l through the body	3795
	7: 5	the sinful passions aroused by the l were	3795
	7: 6	from the l so that we serve in the new way	3795
	7: 7	Is the l sin? Certainly not!	3795
	7: 7	I would not have known what sin was except through the l.	3795
	7: 7	if the l had not said, "Do not covet."	3795
	7: 8	For apart from l, sin is dead.	3795
	7: 9	Once I was alive apart from l;	3795
	7:12	So then, the l is holy, and the commandment	3795
	7:14	We know that the l is spiritual.	3795
	7:16	I agree that the l is good.	3795
	7:21	So I find this l at work:	3795
	7:22	in my inner being I delight *in* God's l;	3795
	7:23	but I see another l at work in the members	3795
	7:23	against the l of my mind and making me	3795
	7:23	the l of sin at work within my members.	3795
	7:25	in my mind am a slave to God's l,	3795
	7:25	in the sinful nature a slave *to* the l of sin.	3795
	8: 2	the l of the Spirit of life set me free from	3795
	8: 2	of the Spirit of life set me free from the l	3795
	8: 3	For what the l was powerless to do in	3795
	8: 4	the righteous requirements *of* the l might	3795
	8: 7	It does not submit *to* God's l,	3795

Ro	9: 4	the covenants, the **receiving of the l**	3792
	9:31	who pursued a l of righteousness,	3795
	10: 4	*of* the l so that there may be righteousness	3795
	10: 5	the righteousness that is by the l:	3795
	13: 8	who loves his fellowman has fulfilled the l.	3795
	13:10	Therefore love is the fulfillment *of* the l.	3795
1Co	6: 6	one brother **goes to** l against another—	3212
	9: 8	Doesn't the L say the same thing?	3795
	9: 9	For it is written in the L of Moses:	3795
	9:20	To those under the l I became like one	3795
	9:20	under the l (though I myself am not under	3795
	9:20	(though I myself am not under the l),	3795
	9:20	so as to win those under the l.	3795
	9:21	*To* those **not having the l** I became	491
	9:21	the law I became like one **not having the l**	491
	9:21	the law (though I am not **free from** God's l	491
	9:21	from God's law but am **under** Christ's l),	1937
	9:21	so as to win those **not having the l**.	491
	14:21	In the L it is written:	3795
	14:34	but must be in submission, as the L says.	3795
	15:56	and the power of sin is the l.	3795
Gal	2:16	a man is not justified by observing the l,	3795
	2:16	faith in Christ and not by observing the l,	3795
	2:16	by observing the l no one will be justified.	3795
	2:19	the l I died to the law so that I might live	3795
	2:19	the law I died *to* the l so that I might live	3795
	2:21	righteousness could be gained through the l,	3795
	3: 2	Did you receive the Spirit by observing the l	3795
	3: 5	among you because you observe the l,	3795
	3:10	All who rely on observing the l are under	3795
	3:10	everything written in the Book *of* the L."	3795
	3:11	no one is justified before God by the l,	3795
	3:12	The l is not based on faith;	3795
	3:13	Christ redeemed us from the curse *of* the l	3795
	3:17	The l, introduced 430 years later,	3795
	3:18	For if the inheritance depends on the l,	3795
	3:19	What, then, was the purpose of the l?	3795
	3:19	The l was put into effect through angels	NIG
	3:21	the l, therefore, opposed to the promises	3795
	3:21	a l had been given that could impart life,	3795
	3:21	then righteousness would certainly have come by the l.	3795
	3:23	we were held prisoners by the l,	3795
	3:24	the l was put in charge to lead us to Christ	3795
	3:25	under the supervision of the l.	NIG
	4: 4	born of a woman, born under l,	3795
	4: 5	to redeem those under l,	3795
	4:21	Tell me, you who want to be under the l,	3795
	4:21	are you not aware of what the l says?	3795
	5: 3	that he is obligated to obey the whole l.	3795
	5: 4	to be justified by l have been alienated	3795
	5:14	The entire l is summed up in a single	3795
	5:18	led by the Spirit, you are not under l.	3795
	5:23	Against such things there is no l.	3795
	6: 2	in this way you will fulfill the l of Christ.	3795
	6:13	the l, yet they want you to be circumcised	3795
Eph	2:15	in his flesh the l with its commandments	3795
Php	3: 5	in regard to the l, a Pharisee;	3795
	3: 9	from the l, but that which is through faith	3795
1Ti	1: 7	They want to be **teachers of the l**,	3791
	1: 8	that the l is good if one uses it properly.	3795
	1: 9	that l is made not for the righteous but	3795
Tit	3: 9	and arguments and quarrels **about** the l,	3788
Heb	7: 5	Now the l requires the descendants	3795
	7:11	(for on the basis of it the l **was given** to	3793
	7:12	there must also be a change *of* the l.	3795
	7:19	(for the l made nothing perfect),	3795
	7:28	For the l appoints as high priests men who	3795
	7:28	but the oath, which came after the l,	3795
	8: 4	the gifts prescribed by the l.	3795
	9:19	commandment of the l to all the people,	3795
	9:22	the l requires that nearly everything	3795
	10: 1	The l is only a shadow of the good things	3795
	10: 8	(although the l required them to be made).	3795
	10:28	Anyone who rejected the l of Moses died	3795
Jas	1:25	into the perfect l that gives freedom,	3795
	2: 8	If you really keep the royal l found	3795
	2: 9	and are convicted by the l as lawbreakers.	3795
	2:10	For whoever keeps the whole l and	3795
	2:12	to be judged by the l that gives freedom,	3795
	4:11	or judges him speaks against the l.	3795
	4:11	When you judge the l, you are not keeping it	3795
1Jn	3: 4	Everyone who sins **breaks** the l;	490+4472

LAW'S (1) [LAW]

Ro	2:26	not circumcised keep the l requirements,	3795

LAWBREAKER (3) [BREAK]

Ro	2:27	written code and circumcision, are a l.	3795+4127
Gal	2:18	I prove that I am a l.	4127
Jas	2:11	you have become a l.	3795+4127

LAWBREAKERS (2) [BREAK]

1Ti	1: 9	not for the righteous but *for* l and rebels,	491
Jas	2: 9	you sin and are convicted by the law as l.	4127

LAWFUL (12) [LAW]

Mt	12: 4	which was not l for them to do,	2003
	12:10	"Is it l to heal on the Sabbath?"	2003
	12:12	*it is* l to do good on the Sabbath."	2003
	14: 4	"It is not l for you to have her."	2003
	19: 3	"Is it l for a man to divorce his wife	2003
Mk	2:26	which *is* l only **for** priests to eat.	2003+4024
	3: 4	"Which *is* l on the Sabbath:	2003

Mk	6:18	not l for you to have your brother's wife."	2003
	10: 2	"*Is it* l for a man to divorce his wife?"	2003
Lk	6: 4	he ate what *is* l only **for** priests to eat.	2003
	6: 9	"I ask you, which *is* l on the Sabbath:	2003
	14: 3	"*Is it* l to heal on the Sabbath or not?"	2003

LAWGIVER (2) [LAW]

Isa	33:22	LORD is our judge, the LORD *is* our l,	2980
Jas	4:12	There is only one L and Judge,	3794

LAWLESS (7) [LAWLESSNESS]

2Sa	3:33	"Should Abner have died as the l die?	5572
2Th	2: 8	And then the l **one** will be revealed,	491
	2: 9	*of* the l **one** will be in accordance with	4005S
Heb	10:17	and l **acts** I will remember no more."	490
2Pe	2: 7	distressed by the filthy lives *of* l men	118
	2: 8	in his righteous soul *by* the l deeds he saw	491
	3:17	not be carried away by the error *of* l men	118

LAWLESSNESS (3) [LAWLESS]

2Th	2: 3	and the man *of* l is revealed,	490
	2: 7	the secret power *of* l is already at work;	490
1Jn	3: 4	who sins breaks the law; in fact, sin is l.	490

LAWS (113) [LAW]

Ge	26: 5	my commands, my decrees and my l."	9368
Ex	18:16	and inform them of God's decrees and l."	9368
	18:20	Teach them the decrees and l,	9368
	21: 1	the l you are to set before them:	5477
	24: 3	the people all the LORD's words and l,	5477
Lev	18: 4	You must obey my l and be careful	5477
	18: 5	Keep my decrees and l,	5477
	18:26	But you must keep my decrees and my l.	5477
	19:37	" 'Keep all my decrees and all my l	5477
	20:22	" 'Keep all my decrees and my l	5477
	25:18	and be careful to obey my l,	5477
	26:15	if you reject my decrees and abhor my l	5477
	26:43	for their sins because they rejected my l	5477
	26:46	the l and the regulations that	5477
Nu	15:16	The same l and regulations will apply	9368
Dt	4: 1	the decrees and l I am about to teach you.	5477
	4: 5	I have taught you decrees and l as	5477
	4: 8	as to have such righteous decrees and l	5477
	4: 8	and laws as this body of l I am setting	9368
	4:14	to teach you the decrees and l you are	5477
	4:45	decrees and l Moses gave them	5477
	5: 1	Hear, O Israel, the decrees and l I declare	5477
	5:31	and l you are to teach them to follow in	5477
	6: 1	and l the LORD your God directed me	5477
	6:20	of the stipulations, decrees and l	5477
	7:11	decrees and l I give you today.	5477
	7:12	to these l and are careful to follow them,	5477
	8:11	his l and his decrees	5477
	11: 1	his l and his commands always.	5477
	11:32	and l I am setting before you today.	5477
	12: 1	and l you must be careful to follow in	5477
	19: 9	you carefully follow all these l I command	5184
	26:16	to follow these decrees and l;	5477
	26:17	commands and l, and	5477
	30:16	and to keep his commands, decrees and l;	5477
Jos	24:25	up for them decrees and l.	5477
2Sa	22:23	All his l are before me;	5477
1Ki	2: 3	his l and requirements,	5477
	9: 4	and observe my decrees and l,	5477
	11:33	nor kept my statutes and l as David,	5477
2Ki	17:34	the l and commands that the LORD gave	9368
	17:37	the l and commands he wrote for you.	9368
1Ch	22:13	and l that the LORD gave Moses	5477
	28: 7	in carrying out my commands and l,	5477
2Ch	7:17	and observe my decrees and l,	5477
	14: 4	and to obey his l and commands.	9368
	33: 8	concerning all the l, decrees and	9368
Ezr	7:10	and to teaching its decrees and l in Israel.	5477
	7:25	all who know the l *of* your God.	10186
Ne	1: 7	and l you gave our servant Moses.	5477
	9:13	You gave them regulations and l	9368
	9:14	decrees and l through your servant Moses.	9368
Est	1:19	a royal decree and let it be written in the l	2017
	3: 8	and who do not obey the king's l;	2017
Job	38:33	Do you know the l *of* the heavens?	2978
Ps	10: 5	he is haughty and your l are far from him;	5477
	18:22	All his l are before me;	5477
	50:16	"What right have you to recite my l	2976
	105:45	keep his precepts and observe his l.	9368
	119: 7	as I learn your righteous l.	5477
	119:13	With my lips I recount all the l *that come*	5477
	119:20	with longing for your l at all times.	5477
	119:30	I have set my heart on your l.	5477
	119:39	for your l are good.	5477
	119:43	for I have put my hope in your l.	5477
	119:52	I remember your ancient l, O LORD,	5477
	119:62	to give you thanks for your righteous l.	5477
	119:75	O LORD, that your l are righteous,	5477
	119:91	Your l endure to this day,	5477
	119:102	I have not departed from your l,	5477
	119:106	that I will follow your righteous l.	5477
	119:108	and teach me your l.	5477
	119:120	I stand in awe of your l.	5477
	119:137	O LORD, and your l are right.	5477
	119:149	O LORD, according to your l.	5477
	119:156	preserve my life according to your l.	5477
	119:160	all your righteous l are eternal.	5477
	119:164	a day I praise you for your righteous l.	5477
	119:175	and may your l sustain me.	5477

Ps 147:19 his l and decrees to Israel. 5477
147:20 they do not know his l. 5477
Pr 8:15 By me kings reign and rulers **make l** 2980
Isa 10: 1 Woe to those *who* **make** unjust l, 2976+2980
24: 5 they have disobeyed the l, 9368
26: 8 LORD, walking in the way of your l, 5477
Jer 33:25 and the **fixed** l *of* heaven and earth, 2978
Eze 5: 6 against my l and decrees more than 5477
5: 6 She has rejected my l and has 5477
5: 7 not followed my decrees or kept my l. 5477
11:12 not followed my decrees or kept my l. 5477
11:20 and be careful to keep my l. 5477
18: 9 and faithfully keeps my l. 5477
18:17 He keeps my l and follows my decrees. 5477
20:11 and made known to them my l, 5477
20:13 not follow my decrees but rejected my l— 5477
20:16 because they rejected my l and did 5477
20:18 the statutes of your fathers or keep their l 5477
20:19 and be careful to keep my l. 5477
20:21 they were not careful to keep my l— 5477
20:24 because they had not obeyed my l, 5477
20:25 not good and I they could not live by; 5477
36:27 and be careful to keep my l, 5477
37:24 They will follow my l and be careful 5477
43:11 and all its regulations and l. 9368
44:24 They are to keep my l and my decrees 9368
Da 6: 8 in accordance with the l *of* the Medes 10186
6:12 in accordance with the l *of* the Medes 10186
7:25 and try to change the set times and the l. 10186
9: 5 turned away from your commands and l. 5477
9:10 the l he gave us through his servants 9368
Mal 4: 4 and l l gave him at Horeb for all Israel. 5477
Heb 8:10 I will put my l in their minds 3795
10:16 I will put my l in their hearts, 3795

LAWSUIT (2) [LAWSUITS]

Ex 23: 2 When you give testimony in a l, 8190
23: 3 not show favoritism to a poor man in his l. 8190

LAWSUITS (4) [LAWSUIT]

Ex 23: 6 to your poor people in their l. 8190
Dt 17: 8 whether bloodshed, l or assaults 1907+1907+4200
Hos 10: 4 therefore l spring up like poisonous weeds 5477
1Co 6: 7 The very fact that you have l 3210

LAWYER (2) [LAW]

Ac 24: 1 of the elders and a l named Tertullus, 4842
Tit 3:13 Do everything you can to help Zenas the l 3788

LAX (1)

Jer 48:10 "A curse on him who is l in doing 8244

LAY (168) [LAID, LAIN, LAYER, LAYING, LAYS]

Ge 4: 1 Adam l **with** his wife Eve, 3359
4:17 Cain l **with** his wife, 3359
4:25 Adam l **with** his wife again, 3359
9:21 he became drunk and l **uncovered** AIT
19:33 older daughter went in and l **with** him. 907+8886
19:33 He was not aware of it when she l **down** or 8886
19:34 "Last night l l **with** my father. 907+8886
19:35 younger daughter went in and l **with** him. 6640+8886
19:35 of it when she l **down** or when she got up. 8886
22:12 "Do not l a hand on the boy," he said. 8938
28:11 under his head and l **down to sleep.** 8886
29:23 and Jacob l **with** her. 448+995
29:30 Jacob l **with** Rachel also, 448+995
37:22 but don't l a hand on him." 8938
37:27 to the Ishmaelites and l not our hands 2118
38: 2 He married her and l **with** her; 448+995
38: 9 so whenever *he* l **with** his brother's wife, 448+995
Ex 7: 4 Then *I* **will** l my hand on Egypt and 5989
22:11 not l hands on the other person's property. 8938
29:10 and Aaron and his sons *shall* l their hands 6164
29:15 and Aaron and his sons *shall* l their hands 6164
29:19 and Aaron and his sons *shall* l their hands 6164
Lev 1: 4 *He is to* l his hand on the head of 6164
3: 2 *to* l his hand on the head of his offering 6164
3: 8 *to* l his hand on the head of his offering 6164
3:13 *to* l his hand on its head and slaughter it 6164
4: 4 *to* l his hand on its head and slaughter it 6164
4:15 their hands on the bull's head before 6164
4:24 *He is to* l his hand on the goat's head 6164
4:29 *He is to* l his hand on the head of 6164
4:33 *to* l his hand on its head and slaughter it 6164
16:21 *He is to* l both hands on the head of 6164
24:14 *to* l their hands on his head, 6164
26:31 into ruins and l **waste** your sanctuaries. 9037
26:32 I *will* l **waste** the land, 9037
Nu 8:10 the Israelites *are to* l their hands on them. 6164
8:12 the Levites l their hands on the heads of 6164
22:27 *she* l **down** under Balaam, and he was 8069
27:18 and l your hand on him. 6164
Dt 9:25 *I* l **prostrate** before the LORD 5877
20:12 l **siege** to that city. 7443
20:19 When *you* l **siege** to a city for a long time, 7443
28:52 *They will* l **siege** to all the cities 7674
Jos 2: 8 Before the spies l **down** for the night, 8886
6:26 his firstborn son *will he* l its **foundations;** 3569
8: 9 of ambush and l **in wait** between Bethel 3782
18:11 Their allotted territory l between the tribes 3655
19: 1 Their inheritance l within the territory 2118
Jdg 4:21 to him while he l **fast asleep,** 8101

Jdg 4:22 and there l Sisera with the tent peg 5877
5:27 At her feet he sank, he fell; there *he* l. 8886
7: 8 camp of Midian l below him in the valley. 2118
16: 2 So they surrounded the place and l **in wait** 741
16: 3 But Samson l there only until the middle 8886
19:26 at the door and l there until daylight. NIH
19:27 there l his concubine, fallen in the doorway NIH
Ru 3: 7 uncovered his feet and l **down.** 8886
3:14 So *she* l at his feet until morning, 8886
1Sa 1:19 Elkanah l **with** Hannah his wife, 3359
3: 5 So he went and l **down.** 8886
3: 9 So Samuel went and l **down** in his place. 8886
3:15 Samuel l **down** until morning and 8886
9:23 the one I told you *to* l aside." 8492
19:24 *He* l that way all that day and night. 5877
23:17 "My father Saul *will* not l a hand **on** you. 5162
26: 9 Who *can* l a hand on the LORD's anointed 8938
26:11 the LORD forbid that I *should* l a hand 8938
26:23 not l a hand on the LORD's anointed. 8938
2Sa 12:24 and he went to her and l **with** her. 6640+8886
13: 6 So Amnon l **down** and pretended to be ill. 8886
13:31 tore his clothes and l **down** on the ground; 8886
16:22 and he l **with** his father's concubines in 448+995
20:12 Amasa l **wallowing** in his blood in 1670
1Ki 3:19 woman's son died because *she* l on him. 8886
13:31 l my bones beside his bones. 5663
19: 5 *he* l **down** under the tree and fell asleep. 8886
19: 6 He ate and drank and then l **down** again. 8886
21: 4 *He* l on his bed sulking and refused to eat. 8886
21:27 *He* l in sackcloth and went around meekly. 8886
2Ki 4:11 he went up to his room and l **down** there. 8886
4:29 l my staff on the boy's face." 8492
4:34 he got on the bed and l upon the boy, 8886
1Ch 2:21 Hezron l **with** the daughter of Makir 448+995
7:23 Then *he* l **with** his wife again, 448+995
2Ch 24:22 killed his son, who said as he l dying, NIH
35: 5 your fellow countrymen, the l **people.** 1201+6639
35: 7 for all the l **people** who were there 1201+6639
Ne 13:21 do this again, *I will* l hands on you." 8938
Est 4: 3 Many l in sackcloth and ashes. 3667
9:10 *they did* not l their hands on the plunder. 8938
9:15 *they did* not l their hands on the plunder. 8938
9:16 but *did* not l their hands on the plunder. 8938
Job 1:12 but on the man himself *do* not l a finger." 8938
5: 8 *I would* l my cause before him. 8492
to l his hand upon us both, 8883
22:22 from his mouth and l **up** his words 8492
30:12 *they* l **snares** for my feet, 8938
41: 8 If *you* l a hand on him, you will remember 8492
Ps 5: 3 in the morning *I* l my requests before you 6885
21: 8 Your hand *will* l **hold** on all your enemies; 5162
22:15 *you* l me in the dust of death. 9189
73: 9 Their mouths l **claim** to heaven, 9286
Pr 3:18 *those who* l **hold** *of* her will be blessed. 9461
4: 4 "l **hold** *of* my words *with* all your heart; 9461
Ecc 10: 4 calmness *can* l great errors **to rest.** 5663
Isa 11:14 They *will* l hands on Edom and Moab, 5447
21: 2 Elam, attack! Media, l **siege!** 7443
24: 1 the LORD *is going to* l **waste** the earth 1327
25:12 your high fortified walls and l *them* **low;** 9164
28:16 "See, I l a stone in Zion, a tested stone, 3569
34:15 The owl will nest there and l **eggs,** 4880
35: 7 In the haunts **where** jackals once l, 8070
42:15 I *will* l **waste** the mountains and hills 2990
43:17 and *they* l there, never to rise again, 8886
44: 7 and l **out** before me what has happened 6885
52:10 The LORD *will* l **bare** his holy arm in 3106
64: 7 on your name or strives to l **hold** of you; 2616
Jer 2:20 and under every spreading tree you l **down** 7579
4: 7 He has left his place to l **waste** your land. 8492
4:26 all its towns l **in ruins** before the LORD, 5997
9:11 and *I will* l **waste** the towns of Judah 5989
15: 6 *I will* l hands on you and destroy you; 5742
17:11 a partridge that hatches eggs *it did* not l 3528
34:22 And *I will* l **waste** the towns of Judah 5989
50: 3 and l **waste** her land. 8883
51:29 to l **waste** the land of Babylon so 8492
La 51:29 over the mountains and l **in wait** for us in 741
Eze 4: 2 Then l **siege** to it: 5989
6: 5 *I will* l the dead bodies of the Israelites 5989
16: 6 as you l there in your blood I said to you, NIH
19: 2 *She* l **down** among the young lions 8069
25:13 *I will* l it waste, 5989
26:16 from their thrones and l **aside** their robes 6073
30:12 by the hand of foreigners *I will* l **waste** 9037
30:14 *I will* l **waste** Upper Egypt, 9037
31:12 its branches l **broken** in all the ravines of AIT
39:21 the punishment I inflict and the hand *I* l 8492
Da 2:28 that passed through your mind as you l NIH
8:27 was exhausted and l **ill** for several days. 2703
Jnh 1: 5 where *he* l **down** and fell into a deep sleep. 8886
Mic 1: 6 into the valley and l **bare** her foundations. 1655
7:16 *They will* l their hands on their mouths 8492
Mt 8:20 Son of Man has no place to l his head." 3111
11:12 and forceful men l **hold** of it. 773
28: 6 Come and see the place where *he* l. 3023
Mk 6: 5 except l his hands **on** a few sick people 2202
Lk 5:18 into the house *to* l him before Jesus." 5502
9:58 Son of Man has no place to l his head." 3111
21:12 *they will* l hands **on** you 2095
22:53 and *you* did not l a hand on me. 1753
Jn 4:46 a certain royal official whose son l **sick** 820
10:15 and *I* l **down** my life for the sheep. 5502
10:17 Father loves me is that *I* l **down** my life— 5502
10:18 but l l it **down** of my own accord. 5502
10:18 I have authority *to* l it **down** and authority 5502
11: 2 whose brother Lazarus now l **sick,** 820

Jn 13:37 *I will* l **down** my life for you." 5502
13:38 "*Will you* really l **down** your life for me? 5502
15:13 that he l **down** his life for his friends. 5502
Ac 8:19 everyone **on** whom *I* l my hands may receive the Holy Spirit." 2202
Ro 9:33 "See, *I* l in Zion a stone that causes men 5502
1Co 3:11 no one can l any foundation other than 5502
7:17 **the rule** *I* l **down** in all the churches. 1411
1Ti 6:19 In this way *they* will l **up** treasure 631
1Pe 2: 6 "See, *I* l a stone in Zion, 5502
1Jn 3:16 *to* l **down** our lives for our brothers. 5502
Rev 4:10 *They* l their crowns before the throne 965
10: 2 a little scroll, *which* l **open** in his hand. 487

LAYER (2) [LAY]

Ex 16:13 the morning there was a l *of* dew around 8887
Lev 9:19 the fat tail, the l *of* fat, 4833

LAYING (8) [LAY]

2Ch 32: 9 and all his forces were l siege to Lachish, NIH
Job 34:30 from l snares for the people. NIH
Lk 4:40 and l his hands **on** each one, 2202
Ac 8:18 the Spirit was given at the l **on** of the apostles' hands, 2120
1Ti 5:22 *Do* not be hasty in the l **on** of hands, 2202
2Ti 1: 6 in you through the l **on** of my hands. 2120
Heb 6: 1 not l again the foundation of repentance 2850
6: 2 about baptisms, the l **on** of hands, 2120

LAYS (10) [LAY]

Job 27:17 what *he* l **up** the righteous will wear, 3922
28: 9 and l **bare** the roots of the mountains. 2200
30:24 "Surely no one l a hand on a broken man 8938
39:14 *She* l her eggs on the ground 6440
Ps 104: 3 and l *the* **beams** *of* his upper chambers 7936
Isa 26: 5 l the lofty city **low;** 9164
30:32 Every stroke the LORD l on them 5663
Zec 12: 1 *who* l **the foundation** *of* the earth, 3569
Lk 14:29 For if he l the foundation and is not able 5502
Jn 10:11 The good shepherd l **down** his life for 5502

LAZARUS (18)

Lk 16:20 At his gate was laid a beggar named L, 3276
16:23 saw Abraham far away, with L by his side. 3276
16:24 have pity on me and send L to dip the tip 3276
16:25 while L received bad things, 3276
16:27 father, send L to my father's house, 899S
Jn 11: 1 Now a man named L was sick. 3276
11: 2 This Mary, whose brother L now lay sick, 3276
11: 5 Jesus loved Martha and her sister and L. 3276
11: 6 Yet when he heard that L was sick, NIG
11:11 "Our friend L has fallen asleep; 3276
11:14 So then he told them plainly, "L is dead, 3276
11:17 Jesus found that L had already been in 899S
11:43 Jesus called in a loud voice, "L, 3276
12: 1 Jesus arrived at Bethany, where L lived, 3276
12: 2 while L was among those reclining at 3276
12: 9 not only because of him but also to see L, 3276
12:10 chief priests made plans to kill L as well, 3276
12:17 with him when he called L from the tomb 3276

LAZINESS (2) [LAZY]

Pr 12:24 but l ends in slave labor. 8244
19:15 L brings on deep sleep, 6790

LAZY (10) [LAZINESS]

Ex 5: 8 don't reduce the quota. They *are* l; 8332
5:17 Pharaoh said, "L, that's what you are— 8332
5:17 that's what you are—l! 8332
Pr 10: 4 L hands make a man poor, 8244
12:27 The l *man* does not roast his game, 4206
26:15 *he is too* l to bring it back to his mouth. 8244
Ecc 10:18 If a man is l, the rafters sag; 6792
Mt 25:26 'You wicked, l servant! 3891
Tit 1:12 always liars, evil brutes, l gluttons." 734
Heb 6:12 We do not want you to become l, 3821

LEAD (89) [LEADER, LEADER'S, LEADERS, LEADERS', LEADERSHIP, LEADING, LEADS, LED, RINGLEADER]

Ge 32:17 He instructed the **one in the l:** 8037
Ex 13:17 God *did* not l them *on* the road through 5697
15:10 They sank like l in the mighty waters. 6769
15:13 "In your unfailing love *you will* l 5697
32:34 l the people to the place I spoke of, 5697
33:12 'L these people,' but you have 6590
34:16 l your sons **to do the same.** 339+466+2177+2388S
Nu 14: 8 he *will* l us into that land, 995
21:15 the ravines that l to the site of Ar and lie 5742
27:17 *one* who *will* l them **out** and bring them 3655
27:17 *one* who *will* l them **out** and bring them 3655
Dt 1:38 because he *will* l Israel **to inherit** it. 5706
3:28 for he *will* l this people **across** 4200+6296+7156
10:11 "and l the people on their way, 2143+4200+7156
21: 4 and l her **down** to a valley that has 3718
21: 4 and I am no longer able to l you, 995+2256+3655
Jos 1: 6 because *you will* l these people **to inherit** 5706
Jdg 4: 6 of Naphtali and Zebulun and l **the way** 5432
5: 2 "When the princes *in* Israel **take the l,** 7276
7:17 "**Follow my l.** 4027+6913
1Sa 8: 5 now appoint a king to l us, 9149
8: 6 when they said, "Give us a king to l us," 9149

1Sa	8:20	with a king *to* l us and to go out before us	9149
	30:15	"*Can you* l me **down** to this raiding party?"	3718
2Ki	4:24	and said to her servant, "**L** on;	2143+2256+5627
	6:19	and *I will* l you to the man you are looking	2143
2Ch	1:10	wisdom and knowledge, that *I may* l this people,	995+2256+3655+4200+7156
	8:14	and the Levites to l the praise and to assist	5466
Est	6: 9	and l him on the horse through	8206
Job	19:24	they were inscribed with an iron tool on l,	6769
	38:32	the constellations in their seasons or l out	5697
Ps	5: 8	**L** me, O LORD, in your righteousness	5697
	26:11	But I l a blameless **life**;	928+2143
	27:11	l me in a straight path because	5697
	31: 3	for the sake of your name l and guide me.	5697
	60: 9	Who will l me to Edom?	5697
	61: 2	l me to the rock that is higher than I.	5697
	80: 1	you *who* l Joseph like a flock;	5627
	101: 2	I will be careful to l a blameless life—	NIH
	108:10	Who will l me to Edom?	5697
	139:24	and l me in the way everlasting.	5697
	143:10	*may* your good Spirit l me on level ground.	5697
Pr	4:11	of wisdom and l you along straight paths.	2005
	5: 5	her steps l **straight** *to* the grave.	9461
	21: 5	The plans of the diligent l to profit as	4200
Ecc	5: 6	Do not let your mouth l you **into sin.**	2627
SS	8: 2	*I would* l you and bring you my mother's	5627
Isa	3:12	O my people, your guides l you **astray;**	9494
	11: 6	and a little child *will* l them.	5627
	20: 4	the king of Assyria will l **away** stripped	5627
	42:16	*I will* l the blind by ways they have	2143
	43: 8	**L** out those who have eyes but are blind,	3655
	49:10	on them will guide them and l them	5633
	60: 9	in the l are the ships of Tarshish,	8037
Jer	3:15	*who will* l you *with* knowledge	8286
	6:29	the l with fire, but the refining goes on	6769
	23:32	"They tell them and l my people **astray**	9494
	31: 9	*I will* l them beside streams of water on	2143
	31:32	by the hand to l them **out** of Egypt,	3655
	50: 8	and be like the goats that l the flock.	4200+7156
Eze	13:10	" 'Because *they* l my people **astray,**	3246
	22:18	tin, iron and l left inside a furnace	6769
	22:20	l and tin into a furnace to melt it with	6769
	27:12	iron, tin and l for your merchandise.	6769
Da	12: 3	l many **to righteousness**	7405
Hos	2:14	*I will* l her into the desert	2143
Mic	5: 8	Raise the battle cry in Beth Aven; l **on,**	339+2143
	3: 5	for the prophets *who* l my people **astray,**	9494
	6: 4	I sent Moses to l you,	7156
Zec	5: 7	Then the cover of l was raised,	6769
	5: 8	the basket and pushed the l cover down	6769
Mt	6:13	And l us not **into** temptation,	1662
Mk	14:44	arrest him and l him **away** under guard."	552
Lk	6:39	"Can a blind man l a blind man?	3842
	11: 4	And l us not **into** temptation."	1662
	13:15	from the stall and l it **out** to give it water?	552
Jn	21:18	someone **to** l him **by the hand.**	5770
Ac	13:11	someone **to** l him **by the hand.**	5933
Gal	3:24	law *was* **put in charge to** l us to Christ	4080
1Th	4:11	Make it your ambition *to* l **a quiet life,**	2483
Heb	6: 1	of repentance from acts that l to death,	NIG
	8: 9	by the hand *to* l them **out** of Egypt,	1974
	9:14	cleanse our consciences from acts that l	NIG
1Jn	2:26	who *are trying to* l you **astray.**	4414
	3: 7	*do not let* anyone l you **astray.**	4414
	5:16	a sin that does not l **to death,**	4639
	5:16	I refer to those whose sin does not l **to**	4639
	5:17	and there is sin that does not l **to death.**	4639
Rev	7:17	*he will* l them to springs of living water.	3842

LEADER (79) [LEAD]

Lev	4:22	" 'When a l sins unintentionally	5954
Nu	2: 3	The l of the people of Judah is Nahshon	5954
	2: 5	The l of the people of Issachar is Nethanel	5954
	2: 7	The l of the people of Zebulun is Eliab	5954
	2:10	The l of the people of Reuben is Elizur	5954
	2:12	The l of the people of Simeon is Shelumiel	5954
	2:14	The l of the people of Gad is Eliasaph	5954
	2:18	The l of the people of Ephraim is Elishama	5954
	2:20	The l of the people of Manasseh is Gamaliel	5954
	2:22	The l of the people of Benjamin is Abidan	5954
	2:25	The l of the people of Dan is Ahiezer	5954
	2:27	The l of the people of Asher is Pagiel	5954
	2:29	The l of the people of Naphtali is Ahira	5954
	3:24	The l *of* the families of the Gershonites	5954
	3:30	The l *of* the families of the Kohathite	5954
	3:32	The **chief** l *of* the Levites was Eleazar	5954+5954
	3:35	The l *of* the families of the Merarite clans	5954
	7: 3	ox from each l and a cart from every two.	5954
	7:11	"Each day one l is to bring his offering for	5954
	7:18	the l of Issachar, brought his offering.	5954
	7:24	the l of the people of Zebulun	5954
	7:30	the l of the people of Reuben	5954
	7:36	the l of the people of Simeon	5954
	7:42	the l of the people of Gad,	5954
	7:48	the l of the people of Ephraim,	5954
	7:54	the l of the people of Manasseh,	5954
	7:60	the l of the people of Benjamin,	5954
	7:66	the l of the people of Dan,	5954
	7:72	the l of the people of Asher,	5954
	7:78	the l of the people of Naphtali,	5954
	14: 4	"We should choose a l and go back	8031
	17: 2	from the l *of* each of their ancestral tribes.	5954
	17: 6	for the l of each of their ancestral tribes,	5954
	25:14	the l of a Simeonite family.	5954
	25:18	the daughter of a Midianite l,	5954
	34:18	And appoint one l from each tribe	5954

Nu	34:22	the l from the tribe of Dan;	5954
	34:23	the l from the tribe of Manasseh son	5954
	34:24	l from the tribe of Ephraim son of Joseph;	5954
	34:25	the l from the tribe of Zebulun;	5954
	34:26	the l from the tribe of Issachar;	5954
	34:27	the l from the tribe of Asher;	5954
	34:28	the l from the tribe of Naphtali."	5954
1Sa	7: 6	And Samuel *was* l of Israel at Mizpah.	9149
	9:16	Anoint him l over my people Israel;	5592
	10: 1	"Has not the LORD anointed you l	5592
	12: 2	Now you have a king *as* your l.	2143+4200+7156
	12: 2	*have been* your l from my youth	2143+4200+7156
	13:14	after his own heart and appointed him l	5592
	19:20	with Samuel standing there *as* their l,	5893
	22: 2	gathered around him, and he became their l.	8569
	25:30	concerning him and has appointed him l	5592
1Ki	11:24	around him and became the l of a band	8569
	14: 7	from among the people and made you a l	5592
	16: 2	and made you l of my people Israel,	5592
2Ki	20: 5	Hezekiah, the l of my people,	5592
1Ch	2:10	Nahshon, the l of the people of Judah.	5954
	5: 6	Beerah was a l of the Reubenites.	5954
	12: 4	who was a l of the Thirty;	6584
	12:27	l of the family of Aaron, with 3,700 men,	5592
	15: 5	Uriel the l and 120 relatives;	8569
	15: 6	Asaiah the l and 220 relatives;	8569
	15: 7	Joel the l and 130 relatives;	8569
	15: 8	Shemaiah the l and 200 relatives;	8569
	15: 9	Eliel the l and 80 relatives;	8569
	15:10	Amminadab the l and 112 relatives;	8569
	27: 4	Mikloth was the l of his division.	5954
	28: 4	He chose Judah as l,	5592
2Ch	6: 5	nor have I chosen anyone to be the l	5592
	13:12	God is with us; he is our l.	8031
	19:11	the l of the tribe of Judah,	5592
Ezr	8:17	Iddo, the l in Casiphia.	8031
Ne	9:17	in their rebellion appointed a l in order	8031
Isa	3: 7	and say, "You have a cloak, you be our l;	7903
	3: 7	do not make me the l of the people."	7903
	55: 4	a l and commander of the peoples.	5592
Jer	30:21	Their l will be one of their own;	129
Hos	1:11	and they will appoint one l and will come	8031
Hab	3:13	the l of the land of wickedness,	8031

LEADER'S (1) [LEAD]

Dt	33:21	the l portion was kept for him.	2980

LEADERS (120) [LEAD]

Ex	15:15	l of Moab will be seized with trembling,	380
	16:22	and the l of the community came	5954
	18:25	from all Israel and made them l of	8031
	24:11	not raise his hand against these l of	722
	34:31	the l of the community came back to him,	5954
	35:27	The l brought onyx stones and other gems	5954
Nu	1:16	the l of their ancestral tribes.	5954
	1:44	by Moses and Aaron and the twelve l	5954
	4:34	and the l *of* the community counted	5954
	4:46	and the l *of* Israel counted all the Levites	5954
	7: 2	Then the l of Israel, the heads of families	5954
	7: 2	the heads of families who were the tribal l	5954
	7:10	the l brought their offerings	5954
	7:84	These were the offerings of the Israelite l	5954
	10: 4	If only one is sounded, the l—	5954
	11:16	to you as l and officials among the people.	2418
	13: 2	From each ancestral tribe send one of its l."	5954
	13: 3	All of them were l of the Israelites.	408+8031
	16: 2	well-known community l who had been	5954
	17: 6	and their l gave him twelve staffs,	5954
	25: 4	"Take all the l of these people,	8031
	27: 2	the l and the whole assembly, and said,	5954
	31:13	and all the l of the community went	5954
	32: 2	the priest and to the l of the community,	5954
	36: 1	came and spoke before Moses and the l,	5954
Dt	29:10	your l and chief men, your elders and	8031
	32:42	the heads of the enemy l."	7278
	33: 5	He was king over Jeshurun when the l of	8031
Jos	8:10	the l of Israel marched before them to Ai.	2418
	9:15	the l of the assembly ratified it by oath.	5954
	9:18	because the l of the assembly had sworn	5954
	9:18	The whole assembly grumbled against the l,	5954
	9:19	but all the l answered,	5954
	17: 4	Joshua son of Nun, and the l and said,	5954
	22:30	the priest and the l of the community—	5954
	22:32	and the l returned to Canaan	5954
	23: 2	their elders, l, judges and officials—	8031
	24: 1	He summoned the elders, l,	8031
Jdg	7:25	They also captured two of the Midianite l,	8569
	8: 3	God gave Oreb and Zeeb, the Midianite l,	8569
	10:18	The l of the people of Gilead said	8569
	20: 2	The l of all the people of the tribes	7157
1Sa	14:38	all you who are l of the army,	7157
2Sa	7:11	since the time I appointed l	9149
1Ch	4:38	The men listed above by name were l	5954
	7:40	brave warriors and outstanding l.	5954
	12:18	So David received them and made them l	8031
	12:20	l of units of a thousand in Manasseh.	8031
	15:16	David told the l of the Levites	8569
	17: 6	to any of their l whom I commanded	9149
	17:10	since the time I appointed l	9149
	22:17	the l of Israel to help his son Solomon.	8569
	23: 2	also gathered together all the l of Israel,	8569
	24: 4	A larger number of l were found	8031
	26: 6	who were l in their father's family	4938
	29: 6	Then the l of families, the officers	8569

1Ch	29: 9	at the willing response of **their** l,	4392S
2Ch	1: 2	to the judges and to all the l in Israel,	5954
	12: 5	and to the l of Judah who had assembled	8569
	12: 6	The l of Israel and the king humbled	8569
	24:23	and Jerusalem and killed all the l of	8569
	26:12	The total number of family l over	8031
	28:12	Then some of the l in Ephraim—	8031
	32:21	the fighting men and the l and officers in	5592
	35: 9	Jeiel and Jozabad, the l of the Levites,	8569
	36:14	all the l of the priests and	8569
Ezr	5:10	the names of their l for your information.	10646
	8:16	Zechariah and Meshullam, *who* were l,	8031
	9: 1	the l came to me and said,	8569
	9: 2	And the l and officials have led the way	8569
Ne	9:32	upon our kings and l,	8569
	9:34	our l, our priests and our fathers did	8569
	9:38	putting it in writing, and our l,	8569
	10:14	The l of the people:	8031
	11: 1	the l of the people settled in Jerusalem,	8569
	11: 3	the provincial l who settled in Jerusalem	8031
	12: 7	the l of the priests and their associates in	8031
	12:24	And the l of the Levites were Hashabiah,	8031
	12:31	the l of Judah go up on top of the wall.	8569
	12:32	and half the l of Judah followed them,	8569
Est	1: 3	the **military** l *of* Persia and Media,	2657
Job	12:24	the l of the earth of their reason;	6639+8031
Isa	3:14	against the elders and l of his people:	8569
	14: 9	all *those* who were l in the world;	6966
	19:13	the l of Memphis are deceived;	8569
	22: 3	All your l have fled together;	7903
Jer	2: 8	the l rebelled against me.	8286
	5: 5	So I will go to the l and speak to them;	1524
	25:34	roll in the dust, you l of the flock.	129
	25:35	the l of the flock no place to escape.	129
	25:36	the wailing of the l of the flock,	129
	29: 2	the court officials and the l of Judah	8569
	34:19	The l of Judah and Jerusalem,	8569
Eze	11: 1	l of the people.	8569
	32:21	the grave the mighty l will say of Egypt	1475
Da	11:41	and the l of Ammon will be delivered	8040
Hos	5:10	Judah's l are like those who move boundary	8569
	7:16	Their l will fall by the sword because	8569
	9:15	all their l are rebellious.	8569
Mic	3: 1	Then I said, "Listen, you l of Jacob,	8031
	3: 9	Hear this, you l of the house of Jacob,	8031
	3:11	Her l judge for a bribe,	8031
	5: 5	even eight l *of* men.	5817
Zec	9: 7	to our God and become l in Judah,	477
	10: 3	and I will punish the l;	6966
	12: 5	the l of Judah will say in their hearts,	477
	12: 6	the l of Judah like a firepot in a woodpile,	477
Lk	19:47	the teachers of the law and the l among	4755
Jn	12:42	even among the l believed in him.	807
Ac	3:17	you acted in ignorance, as did your l.	807
	14: 5	together with their l, to mistreat them	807
	15:22	two men *who were* l among the brothers.	2451
	25: 2	the chief priests and Jewish l appeared	4755
	25: 5	of your l come with me and press charges	1543
	28:17	later he called together the l of	1639+4755
Gal	2: 2	*to* those who seemed **to be** l,	1506
Heb	13: 7	Remember your l, who spoke the word	2451
	13:17	Obey your l and submit to their authority.	2451
	13:24	Greet all your l and all God's people.	2451

LEADERS' (1) [LEAD]

Jos	9:21	So the l' promise to them was kept.	5954

LEADERSHIP (4) [LEAD]

Nu	33: 1	by divisions under the l *of* Moses	3338
Ps	109: 8	*may* another take his **place of** l.	7213
Ac	1:20	and, " 'May another take his **place of** l.'	2175
Ro	12: 8	if it is l, let him govern diligently;	4613

LEADING (38) [LEAD]

Dt	1:15	So I took the l **men** *of* your tribes,	8031
	5:23	all the l **men** *of* your tribes	8031
Jdg	3:27	from the hills, with him l them.	4200+7156
	4: 4	*was* l Israel at that time.	9149
	12: 5	the fords of the Jordan l to Ephraim,	4200
	20:31	the one l to Bethel and the other	6590
2Sa	10:16	of Hadadezer's army l them.	4200+7156
	15: 2	and stand by the side of the **road** l *to* the	AIT
	17:11	with you yourself l them into battle.	2143
2Ki	10: 6	were with the l **men** *of* the city,	1524
	19: 2	Shebna the secretary and the l priests,	2418
	24:15	his officials and the l **men** *of* the land.	380
1Ch	19:16	of Hadadezer's army l them.	4200+7156
2Ch	23:13	with musical instruments *were* l	3359
Ezr	7:28	and gathered l **men** from Israel to go up	8031
	8:24	Then I set apart twelve of the l priests,	8569
	8:29	before the l priests and the Levites and	8569
	10: 5	The l priests and Levites and all Israel	8569
Ps	42: 4	l the procession to the house of God,	1844
	68:27	the little tribe of Benjamin, l them, there	8097
Pr	7:27	l **down** to the chambers of death.	3718
	8: 3	beside the gates l **into** the city, at	4200+7023
Isa	37: 2	and the l priests, all wearing sackcloth,	2418
Eze	17:13	He also carried away the l **men** *of* the land,	380
	40:20	l **into** the outer court.	4200
Mt	26:55	Jesus said to the crowd, "Am I l **a rebellion,**	3334
Mk	6:21	and military commanders and the l **men**	4755
	10:32	up to Jerusalem, with Jesus l the way,	4575
	14:48	"Am I l **a rebellion,**" said Jesus,	3334
Lk	22:47	Judas, one of the Twelve, *was* l them.	4601
	22:52	"Am I l **a rebellion,** that you have come	3334

Ac	12:10	and came to the iron gate l to the city.	5770
	13:50	of high standing and l men of the city.	4755
	16:12	the l city of that district of Macedonia.	4755
	25:23	the high ranking officers and the l men of	2029
Ro	6:19	in slavery to righteousness l to holiness.	1650
	15:18	through me in l the Gentiles to obey God	1650
2Ti	2:25	God will grant them repentance l them to	1650

LEADS (40) [LEAD]

Dt	27:18	"Cursed is the man who l the blind astray	8706
Jos	2:7	in pursuit of the spies on the road that l to	6584
1Ch	11:6	"Whoever l the attack on	928+2021+8037
Job	12:17	He l counselors away stripped	2143
	12:19	He l priests away stripped	2143
Ps	23:2	he l me beside quiet waters,	5633
	37:8	do not fret—it l only to evil.	8317
	68:6	he l forth the prisoners with singing;	3655
Pr	2:18	For her house l down to death	8755
	10:17	whoever ignores correction l others astray.	9494
	12:26	but the way of the wicked l them astray.	9494
	14:12	but in the end it l to death.	2006
	14:23	but mere talk l only to poverty.	4200
	15:24	of life l upward for the wise to keep him	NIH
	16:25	but in the end it l to death.	2006
	16:29	and l him down a path that is not good.	2143
	19:23	The fear of the LORD l to life:	4200
	20:7	The righteous man l a blameless life;	2143
	21:5	to profit as surely as haste l to poverty.	4200
	28:10	He who l the upright along	8706
Isa	30:28	of the peoples a bit that l them astray.	9494
	40:11	he gently l those that have young.	5633
Hos	4:12	A spirit of prostitution l them astray;	9494
Mt	7:13	and broad is the road that l to destruction,	552
	7:14	the gate and narrow the road that l to life,	552
	12:20	till he l justice to victory.	1675
	15:14	If a blind man l a blind man,	3842
Jn	10:3	by name and l them out.	1974
	12:50	I know that his command l to eternal life.	1639
Ro	2:4	not realizing that God's kindness l you	72
	6:16	which l to death, or to obedience,	1650
	6:16	or to obedience, which l to righteousness?	1650
	6:22	the benefit you reap l to holiness,	1650
	14:19	therefore make every effort to do what l	NIG
2Co	2:14	l us in triumphal procession	2581
	7:10	Godly sorrow brings repentance that l to	1650
Eph	5:18	Do not get drunk on wine, which l to debauchery,	1639
Tit	1:1	knowledge of the truth that l to godliness—	2848
1Jn	5:16	There is a sin that l to death.	4639
Rev	12:9	Satan, who l the whole world astray.	4414

LEAF (7) [LEAFY, LEAVES]

Ge	8:11	in its beak was a freshly plucked olive l!	6591
Lev	26:36	the sound of a windblown l will put them	6591
Job	13:25	Will you torment a windblown l?	6591
Ps	1:3	in season and whose l does not wither.	6591
Pr	11:28	but the righteous will thrive like a green l.	6591
Isa	64:6	we all shrivel up like a l,	6591
Mk	11:13	Seeing in the distance a fig tree in l,	2400+5877

LEAFY (4) [LEAF]

Lev	23:40	and palm fronds, l branches and poplars,	6290
Eze	6:13	every spreading tree and every l oak—	6290
	17:6	produced branches and put out l boughs.	6997
	20:28	and they saw any high hill or any l tree,	6290

LEAGUE (KJV) See TREATY

LEAH (29) [LEAH'S]

Ge	29:16	the name of the older was L,	4207
	29:17	L had weak eyes, but Rachel was lovely	4207
	29:23	he took his daughter L and gave her	4207
	29:25	When morning came, there was L!	4207
	29:28	He finished the week with L,	2296S
	29:30	and he loved Rachel more than L.	4207
	29:31	the LORD saw that L was not loved,	4207
	29:32	L became pregnant and gave birth to a son.	4207
	30:9	L saw that she had stopped having children,	4207
	30:11	Then L said, "What good fortune!"	4207
	30:13	Then L said, "How happy I am!	4207
	30:14	which he brought to his mother L.	4207
	30:14	Rachel said to L, "Please give me some of	4207
	30:16	L went out to meet him.	4207
	30:17	God listened to L, and she became pregnant	4207
	30:18	Then L said, "God has rewarded me	4207
	30:19	L conceived again and bore Jacob	4207
	30:20	Then L said, "God has presented me with	4207
	31:4	to Rachel and L to come out to the fields	4207
	31:14	Then Rachel and L replied,	4207
	33:1	so he divided the children among L,	4207
	33:2	L and her children next,	4207
	33:7	L and her children came and bowed down.	4207
	34:1	Dinah, the daughter L had borne to Jacob,	4207
	35:23	The sons of L: Reuben the firstborn	4207
	46:15	the sons L bore to Jacob in Paddan Aram,	4207
	46:18	whom Laban had given to his daughter L—	4207
	49:31	and there I buried L.	4207
Ru	4:11	into your home like Rachel and L,	4207

LEAH'S (5) [LEAH]

Ge	30:10	L servant Zilpah bore Jacob a son.	4207
	30:12	L servant Zilpah bore Jacob a second son.	4207
	31:33	into Jacob's tent and into L tent and into	4207
	31:33	After he came out of L tent,	4207
	35:26	The sons of L maidservant Zilpah:	4207

LEAKS (1) [LEAK]

Ecc	10:18	if his hands are idle, the house l.	1940

LEAN (7) [LEANED, LEANING, LEANS]

Ge	41:19	scrawny and very ugly and l.	1414+8369
	41:20	The l, ugly cows ate up the seven fat cows	8369
	41:27	The seven l, ugly cows that came	8369
Jdg	16:26	so that I may l against them."	9128
Pr	3:5	in the LORD with all your heart and l not	9128
Eze	34:20	between the fat sheep and the l sheep.	8136
Mic	3:11	Yet they l upon the LORD and say,	9128

LEANED (5) [LEAN]

Ge	47:31	and Israel worshiped as he l on the top	2556
2Ki	7:17	the officer on whose arm he l in charge of	9128
Eze	29:7	when they l on you, you broke	9128
Jn	21:20	the one who had l back against Jesus at	404
Heb	11:21	worshiped as he l on the top of his staff.	NIG

LEANFLESHED (KJV) See GAUNT, LEAN

LEANING (6) [LEAN]

2Sa	1:6	"and there was Saul, l on his spear,	9128
2Ki	5:18	of Rimmon to bow down and he is l	9128
	7:2	the king was l said to the man of God,	9128
Ps	62:3	this l wall, this tottering fence?	5742
SS	8:5	Who is this coming up from the desert l	8345
Jn	13:25	L back against Jesus, he asked him, "Lord,	404

LEANNOTH (1)

Ps	88:T	According to mahalath l.	4361

LEANS (4) [LEAN]

2Sa	3:29	or leprosy or who l on a crutch or who falls	2616
2Ki	18:21	a man's hand and wounds him if he l on it!	6164
Job	8:15	He l on his web, but it gives way;	9128
Isa	36:6	a man's hand and wounds him if he l on it!	6164

LEAP (6) [LEAPED, LEAPING, LEAPS]

Job	39:20	Do you make him l like a locust,	8321
Isa	13:21	and there the wild goats will l about.	8376
	35:6	Then will the lame l like a deer,	1925
Joel	2:5	of chariots they l over the mountaintops,	8376
Mal	4:2	and l like calves released from the stall.	7055
Lk	6:23	"Rejoice in that day and l for joy,	5015

LEAPED (3) [LEAP]

Da	3:24	Then King Nebuchadnezzar l to his feet	10624
Lk	1:41	the baby l in her womb,	5015
	1:44	the baby in my womb l for joy.	5015

LEAPING (2) [LEAP]

2Sa	6:16	when she saw King David l and dancing	7060
SS	2:8	Here he comes, l across the mountains,	1925

LEAPS (2) [LEAP]

Job	37:1	"At this my heart pounds and l	6001
Ps	28:7	My heart l for joy and I will give thanks	6600

LEARN (42) [LEARNED, LEARNING, LEARNS]

Ge	24:21	the man watched her closely to l whether	3359
Dt	4:10	so that they may l to revere me as long	4340
	5:1	L them and be sure to follow them.	4340
	14:23	so that you may l to revere the LORD your	4340
	17:19	that he may l to revere the LORD his God	4340
	18:9	do not l to imitate the detestable ways of	4340
	31:12	and l to fear the LORD your God	4340
	31:13	and l to fear the LORD your God as long	4340
Jdg	18:5	of God to l whether our journey will	3359
1Sa	22:3	with you until I l what God will do	3359
1Ki	1:20	to l from you who will sit on the throne	5583
2Ch	12:8	l the difference between serving me and	3359
Job	34:4	let us l together what is good.	3359
Ps	34:4	Will evildoers never l—	3359
	53:4	Will the evildoers never l—	3359
	119:7	an upright heart as I l your righteous laws.	4340
	119:71	be afflicted so that I might l your decrees.	4340
	119:73	give me understanding to l your commands.	4340
	141:6	and the wicked will l that my words were	9048
Pr	19:25	and the simple will l prudence;	6891
	22:25	or you may l his ways and get yourself	544
Isa	1:17	l to do right! Seek justice, encourage the	4340
	26:9	the people of the world l righteousness.	4340
	26:10	they do not l righteousness;	4340
Jer	2:33	the worst of women can l from your ways.	4340
	10:2	not l the ways of the nations or be terrified	4340
	12:16	if they l well the ways of my people	4340+4340
	35:13	'Will you not l a lesson and obey my words	4374
Mt	9:13	But go and l what this means:	3443
	11:29	Take my yoke upon you and l from me,	3443
	24:32	"Now l this lesson from the fig tree:	3443
Mk	13:28	"Now l this lesson from the fig tree:	3443
Jn	14:31	but the world must l that I love the Father	1182
Ac	24:8	be able to l the truth about all these charges	2105
1Co	4:6	so that you may l from us the meaning of	3443

Gal	3:2	I would like to l just one thing from you:	3443
1Th	4:4	of you should l to control his own body in	3857
1Ti	2:11	A woman should l in quietness	3443
	2:11	these should l first of all	3443
Tit	3:14	Our people must l to devote themselves	3443
Heb	5:11	to explain because you are slow to l.	198
Rev	14:3	No one could l the song except	3443

LEARNED (49) [LEARN]

Ge	28:6	Now Esau l that Isaac had blessed Jacob	8011
	30:27	I have l by divination that the LORD has	5727
	42:1	Jacob l that there was grain in Egypt,	8011
Lev	5:3	something he has seen or l about, he will	3359
Nu	20:29	whole community l that Aaron had died,	8011
1Sa	4:6	When they l that the ark of the LORD	3359
	23:9	When David l that Saul was plotting	3359
	23:15	he l that Saul had come out	8011
	26:4	and l that Saul had definitely arrived.	3359
Ezr	7:11	a man l in matters concerning	6221
Ne	13:7	Here I l about the evil thing Eliashib	1067
	13:10	I also l that the portions assigned to	3359
Est	3:6	having l who Mordecai's people were,	4200+5583
	4:1	Mordecai l of all that had been done,	3359
Job	8:8	and find out what their fathers l,	2984
Ps	89:15	Blessed are those who have l	3359
	119:152	Long ago I l from your statutes	3359
Pr	24:32	to what I observed and l a lesson	4374
	30:3	I have not l wisdom,	4340
Ecc	1:17	I l that this, too, is a chasing after the wind.	3359
	9:11	or wealth to the brilliant or favor to the l;	3359
Eze	19:3	He l to tear the prey and he devoured men.	4340
	19:6	He l to tear the prey and he devoured men.	4340
Da	6:10	Now when Daniel l that the decree	10313
Mt	2:8	in accordance with the time he had l from	208
	11:25	from the wise and l,	5305
Mk	15:45	When he l from the centurion that it was so,	1182
Lk	7:37	in that town l that Jesus was eating at	2105
	9:11	the crowds l about it and followed him.	1182
	10:21	hidden these things from the wise and l,	5305
	23:7	When he l that Jesus was eating at	2105
Jn	4:3	When the Lord l of this,	1182
	5:6	and l that he had been in this condition for	1182
	15:15	for everything that I l from my Father	201
Ac	7:13	Joseph's family.	1181+5745
	9:24	but Saul l of their plan.	1182
	9:30	When the brothers l of this,	2105
	17:13	in Thessalonica l that Paul was preaching	1182
	18:24	He was a l man, with a thorough knowledge	3360
	23:27	for I had l that he is a Roman citizen.	3443
Ro	16:17	contrary to the teaching you have l.	3443
Php	4:9	Whatever you have l or received or heard	3443
	4:11	for I have l to be content whatever	3443
	4:12	I have l the secret of being content in any	3679
Col	1:7	You l it from Epaphras,	3443
2Ti	3:14	continue in what you have l	3443
	3:14	you know those from whom you l it,	3443
Heb	5:8	he l obedience from what he suffered	3443
Rev	2:24	not l Satan's so-called deep secrets	1182

LEARNING (12) [LEARN]

Ezr	8:16	Joiarib and Elnathan, who were men of l,	1067
Job	34:2	listen to me, you men of l.	3359
Pr	1:5	the wise listen and add to their l, and let	4375
	4:2	I give you sound l,	4375
	9:9	a righteous man and he will add to his l.	4375
Isa	44:25	who overthrows the l of the wise	1981
Da	1:4	showing aptitude for every kind of l,	2683
	1:17	of all kinds of literature and l.	2683
Jn	7:15	"How did this man get such l	1207+3857
Ac	23:34	l that he was from Cilicia.	4785
	26:24	"Your great l is driving you insane."	1207
2Ti	3:7	always l but never able to acknowledge	3443

LEARNS (3) [LEARN]

Lev	5:3	when he l of it he will be guilty.	3359
	5:4	of it, in any case when he l of it he will	3359
Jn	6:45	to the Father and l from him comes to me.	3443

LEASH (1)

Job	41:5	or put him on a l for your girls?	8003

LEASING (KJV) See FALSE GODS, LIES

LEAST (41) [LESS]

Jdg	6:15	and I am the l in my family."	7582
1Sa	9:21	and is not my clan the l of all the clans of	7582
	20:9	"If I had the l inkling that	3359+3359
2Ki	18:24	How can you repulse one officer of the l	7783
	23:2	all the people from the l to the greatest.	7785
	25:26	all the people from the l to the greatest,	7785
1Ch	12:14	the l was a match for a hundred,	7783
2Ch	34:30	all the people from the l to the greatest,	7785
Est	1:5	all the people from the l to the greatest	7783
	1:20	from the l to the greatest."	7783
Job	8:7	"At l there is hope for a tree.	3954
	35:15	not take the l notice of wickedness.	4394
Isa	36:9	then can you repulse one officer of the l	7783
	60:22	The l of you will become a thousand,	7785
Jer	6:13	"From the l to the greatest,	7783
	8:10	From the l to the greatest,	7785
	23:32	not benefit these people in the l,"	3603+3603
	31:34	from the l of them to the greatest,"	7783
	42:1	from the l to the greatest approached	7785

Jer	42: 8	with him and all the people from the l to	7785
	44:12	From the l to the greatest,	7785
	50:12	She will be the l *of* the nations—	344
Jnh	3: 5	and all of them, from the greatest to the l,	7783
Mt	2: 6	by no means l among the rulers of Judah;	1788
	5:18	not the l **stroke of a pen,**	3037
	5:19	of the l of these commandments	1788
	5:19	the same will be called l in the kingdom	1788
	11:11	yet he who is l in the kingdom	3625
	25:40	for one of the l of these brothers of mine,	1788
	25:45	whatever you did not do for one of the l	1788
Lk	7:28	yet the one who is l in the kingdom	3625
	9:48	For he who is l among you all—	3625
	14: 9	to take the l **important** place.	2274
	16:17	than for the l **stroke of a pen,**	3037
Jn	14:11	**or** at l believe on the evidence	1254+1623+3590
Ac	5:15	so that **at** l Peter's shadow might fall	1569+2779
1Co	15: 9	For I am the l of the apostles and do not	1788
2Co	11: 5	**not** think I am **in the** l inferior to	3594
	12:11	for I am **not in the** l inferior to	4029
Eph	3: 8	I am *less than* the l of all God's people,	1788
Heb	8:11	from the l of them to the greatest.	3625

LEATHER (17)

Lev	13:48	any l or anything made of leather—	6425
	13:48	any leather or anything made of l—	6425
	13:49	or l, or woven or knitted material,	6425
	13:49	or any l article, is greenish or reddish,	6425
	13:51	or the woven or knitted material, or the l,	6425
	13:52	or any l article that has the contamination	6425
	13:53	woven or knitted material, or the l article,	6425
	13:56	or the l, or the woven or knitted material.	6425
	13:57	or in the l article, it is spreading,	6425
	13:58	or any l article that has been washed	6425
	13:59	woven or knitted material, or any l article,	6425
	13:17	or l that has semen on it must be washed	6425
Nu	31:20	as well as everything made of l,	6425
2Ki	1: 8	of hair and with a l belt around his waist."	6425
Eze	16:10	an embroidered dress and put l sandals	9391
Mt	3: 4	and he had a l belt around his waist.	1294
Mk	1: 6	with a l belt around his waist,	1294

LEATHERN (KJV) See LEATHER

LEAVE (207) [LEAVES, LEAVING]

Ge	2:24	a man *will* l his father and mother and	6440
	12: 1	Abram, "L your country, your people	2143+4946
	18:16	When the men got up to l,	4946+9004
	28:15	*I will* not l you until I have done what	6440
	31:13	Now l this land at once and go back	3655
	33:15	*let me* l some of my men with you."	3657
	42:15	*you will* not l this place unless	3655
	42:33	L one of your brothers here with me,	5663
	44:22	'The boy cannot l his father;	6440
	45: 1	"**Have** everyone l my presence!"	3655
Ex	1:10	fight against us and l the country."	4946+6590
	2:20	"Why *did you* l him?	6440
	3:21	so that when *you* l you will	2143
	8: 9	I *to you* **the honor** of setting the time	6995
	8:11	The frogs *will* l you and your houses,	6073
	8:29	Moses answered, "As soon as I l you,	3655
	8:29	the flies *will* l Pharaoh and his officials	6073
	10:23	or l his place for three days.	4946+7756
	10:24	l your flocks and herds **behind."**	3657
	11: 8	After that *I will* l."	3655
	12:10	*Do* not l any of it till morning;	3855
	12:31	L my people, you and the Israelites!	3655
	12:33	the people to hurry and l the country.	8938
	14:12	L us alone; let us serve the Egyptians	2532+4946
	23: 5	do not l it there; be sure you help him	6440
	23:11	and the wild animals may eat *what* they l.	3856
	32:10	Now l me **alone** so that my anger	5663
	33: 1	the LORD said to Moses, "L this place,	2143+4946
	33:11	Joshua son of Nun *did* not l the tent.	4631
	34: 7	not l **the guilty unpunished;**	5927+5927
Lev	2:13	*Do* not l the salt of the covenant	8697
	7:15	*he must* l none of it till morning.	5663
	8:33	not l the entrance to the Tent of Meeting	3655
	10: 7	not l the entrance to the Tent of Meeting	3655
	16:23	and *he is to* l them there.	5663
	19:10	L them for the poor and the alien.	6440
	21:12	nor l the sanctuary of his God	3655
	22:30	l none of it till morning.	3855
	23:22	L them for the poor and the alien.	6440
Nu	9:12	not l any of it till morning or break any	8636
	10:31	But Moses said, "Please *do not* l us.	6440
	11:20	saying, "Why *did we ever* l Egypt?" '"	3655
	14:18	not l **the guilty unpunished;**	5927+5927
	24:11	Now l at once and go home!	1368
	32:15	he will again l all this people in the desert,	5663
Dt	15:16	"*I do* not *want* to l you,"	3655
	20:16	*do* not l *alive* anything that breathes.	2649
	21:23	l his body on the tree **overnight.**	4328
	24:19	L it for the alien,	2118
	24:20	L what remains for the alien,	2118
	24:21	L what remains for the alien,	2118
	28:51	*They will* l you no grain,	8636
	31: 6	*he will* never l you nor forsake you."	8332
	31: 8	*he will* never l you nor forsake you.	8332
Jos	1: 5	*I will* never l you nor forsake you.	8332
Jdg	7: 3	may turn back and l Mount Gilead.' "	7629
	16:17	head were shaved, my strength *would* l me,	6073
	19: 5	up early and he prepared to l, but	2143
	19: 9	got up to l, his father-in-law,	2143
Ru	1:16	"Don't urge you to l you or to turn back	6440

Ru	2:16	the bundles and l them for her to pick up,	6440
1Sa	10: 2	When you l me today,	2143+4946+6643
	10: 9	As Saul turned to l Samuel,	2143+4946+6640
	14:36	*let us* not l one of them **alive."**	8636
	15: 6	I the Amalekites so that I do	3718+4946+9348
	15:27	As Samuel turned to l,	2143
	16:23	and the evil spirit *would* l him,	6073
	17:28	And with whom *did you* l those few sheep	5759
	25:22	if by morning *I* l *alive* one male	8636
	27: 9	*he did* not l a man or woman **alive,**	2649
	27:11	*He did* not l a man or woman *alive*	2649
	29:10	and l in the morning as soon as it is light."	2143
2Sa	4: 4	but as she hurried to l,	5674
	15:14	We must l immediately,	2143
	16:11	this Benjamite! L him **alone;**	5663
1Ki	2:37	The day you l and cross the Kidron Valley	3655
	2:42	'On the day you l to go anywhere else,	3655
	8:57	*may he* never l us nor forsake us.	6440
	15:29	not l Jeroboam anyone that breathed,	8636
	17: 3	"L here, turn eastward and hide in	2143+4946
	18:12	where the Spirit of the LORD may carry you when I l you.	907+2143+4946
	20:36	as you l me a lion will kill you."	907+2143+4946
2Ki	1: 4	*will* not l the bed you are lying on.	3718+4946
	1: 6	*will* not l the bed you are lying on.	3718+4946
	1:16	*will* never l the bed you are lying on.	3718+4946
	2: 2	*I will* not l you."	6440
	2: 4	*I will* not l you."	6440
	2: 6	*I will* not l you."	6440
	4:27	but the man of God said, "L her alone!	8332
	4:30	*I will* not l you."	6440
	23:18	"L it alone," he said.	5663
2Ch	26:18	to burn incense. L the sanctuary,	3655
	26:20	Indeed, he himself was eager to l,	3655
	33: 8	**make** the feet of the Israelites l	6073
	35:15	at each gate *did* not *need* to l their posts,	6073
Ezr	9:12	l it to your children **as an** everlasting inheritance.'	3769
Ne	6: 3	the work stop while *I* l it and go down	8332
Job	21:14	Yet they say to God, 'L us **alone!**	4946+6073
	22:17	They said to God, 'L us **alone!**	4946+6073
	39: 4	*they* l and do not return.	3655
	39:11	*Will you* l your heavy work to him?	6440
Ps	35:12	for good and l my soul forlorn.	NIH
	37:33	the LORD *will* not l them in their power	6440
	49:10	and l their wealth to others.	4631
	55:11	threats and lies never l its streets.	4631
	119:121	*do* not l me to my oppressors.	5663
Pr	2:13	who l the straight paths to walk	6440
	3: 3	*Let* love and faithfulness never l you;	6440
	9: 6	L your simple ways and you will live;	6440
	17:13	evil will never l his house.	4631
Ecc	2:18	because *I* must l them to the one who comes	5663
	2:21	and then *he must* l all he owns to someone	5989
	8: 3	Do not be in a hurry *to* l the king's presence.	2143+4946
	10: 4	anger rises against you; *do* not l your post;	5663
Isa	6:13	and oak l stumps when they are cut down,	928
	10: 3	Where *will you* l your riches?	6440
	30:11	L this way, get off this path,	6073
	48:20	L Babylon, flee from the Babylonians!	3655
	52:12	*you will* not l in haste or go in flight;	3655
	65:15	You will l your name to my chosen ones	5663
Jer	2:37	You will also l that place with your hands	3655
	9: 2	so that *I might* l my people and go away	6440
	9:19	We must l our land because our houses	6440
	10:17	Gather up your belongings to l the land,	4946
	25:38	Like a lion *he will* l his lair,	6440
	37: 9	'The Babylonians *will* **surely** l us.'	2143+2143+4946+6584
	37:12	Jeremiah *started to* l the city to go to	3655
	44: 7	and so l yourselves without a remnant?	3855
	49: 9	*would they* not l a few grapes?	8636
	49:11	L your orphans; I will protect their lives.	6440
	50: 8	l the land of the Babylonians,	3655
	50:26	and l her no remnant.	2118
	51: 9	*let us* l her and each go to his own land,	6440
	51:50	and do not linger!	2143
Eze	5:17	and *they* will l you **childless.**	8897
	10:16	the wheels *did* not l their side.	4946+6015
	12:12	on his shoulder at dusk and l,	3655
	14:15	that country and *they* l it **childless**	8897
	16:39	and l you naked and bare.	5663
	23:29	*They will* l you naked and bare,	6440
	29: 5	*I will* l you in the desert,	5759
	36:20	and yet *they* l his land.'	3655
	42:14	not to go into the outer court until *they* l	5663
	44:19	in and *are to* l them in the sacred rooms,	5663
Da	4:23	and destroy it, but l the stump,	10697
	4:26	The command to l the stump of the tree	10697
	11: 8	l the king of the North alone.	4946+6641
Hos	4:17	Ephraim is joined to idols; l him **alone!**	5663
	12:14	his Lord *will* l upon him the guilt	5759
Joel	2:14	He may turn and have pity and l behind	8636
	2:16	*Let* the bridegroom l his room and	3655
Ob	1: 5	*would they* not l a few grapes?	8636
Mic	4:10	for now you *must* l the city to camp in	3655
Na	1: 3	not l **the guilty unpunished.**	5927+5927
	2:13	*I will* l you **no** prey on the earth.	4162
Zep	3: 3	who l nothing for the morning.	1750
	3:12	But *I will* l within you the meek	8636
Mt	5:24	l your gift there in front of the altar.	918
	8:34	they pleaded with him to l their region.	3553
	10:14	and stay at his house until you l	2002
	10:14	shake the dust off your feet *when you* l	2002+2032
	15:14	L them; they are blind guides.	918
	18:12	*will he* not l the ninety-nine on the hills	918

Mt	19: 5	'For this reason a man *will* l his father	2901
	27:49	The rest said, "Now l him **alone.**	918
Mk	5:17	to plead with Jesus *to* l their region.	599
	6:10	stay there until *you* l that town.	2002
	6:11	shake the dust off your feet *when you* l,	1744
	10: 7	'For this reason a man *will* l his father	2901
	14: 6	"L her **alone,"** said Jesus.	918
	15:36	"Now l him **alone."**	918
Lk	8:37	of the Gerasenes asked Jesus *to* l them,	599
	9: 4	stay there until *you* l that town.	2002
	9: 5	*when you* l their town,	2002
	13: 8	'l it **alone** for one more year,	918
	13:31	"L this place and go somewhere else.	2002
	15: 4	not l the ninety-nine in the open country	2901
	19:44	*They will* not l one stone on another,	918
Jn	1:43	next day Jesus decided *to* l for Galilee.	2002
	6:67	"You do not want *to* l too, do you?"	5632
	7: 3	"*You ought to* l here and go to Judea,	3553
	8:11	"Go now and l your life of sin."	279+3600
	12: 7	"L her **alone,"** Jesus replied.	918
	13: 1	the time had come for *him to* l this world	3553
	14:18	*I will* not l you as orphans;	918
	14:27	Peace *I* l with you; my peace I give you.	918
	14:31	"Come now; *let us* l.	72+1949
	16:32	*You will* l me all alone.	918
Ac	1: 4	"*Do* not l Jerusalem,	6004
	5:38	L these men **alone!**	923
	7: 3	'L your country and your people,'	2002
	16:10	we got ready at once to l for Macedonia,	2002
	16:36	Now *you can* l.	2002
	16:39	requesting them *to* l the city.	599
	18: 2	had ordered all the Jews *to* l Rome.	6004
	20: 7	because he intended to l the next day,	1996
	20:29	I know that after I l, savage wolves	922
	22:18	'L Jerusalem immediately,	2002
	24:25	"That's enough for now! *You may* l.	4513
	28:25	among themselves and began to l	668
Ro	12:19	my friends, but l room for God's wrath,	1443
1Co	5:10	that case you would have *to* l this world.	2002
Eph	5:31	"For this reason a man *will* l his father	2901
Heb	6: 1	Therefore let us l the elementary teachings	918
	13: 5	"Never *will I* l you; never will I forsake you.	479
Rev	3:12	Never again *will he* l it.	2002+2032
	17:16	They will bring her to ruin and l her naked;	NIG

LEAVED (KJV) See DOORS

LEAVEN (KJV) See YEAST

LEAVENED (1)

Am	4: 5	Burn l **bread** as a thank offering and brag	2809

LEAVES (36) [LEAF, LEAVE]

Ge	3: 7	so they sewed fig l together	6591
	44:22	if *he* l him, his father will die.'	6440
Nu	27: 8	'If a man dies and l no son,	4200
Dt	24: 2	after *she* l his house she becomes the wife	3655
1Ki	6:34	each having two l that turned in sockets.	7521
Job	21:21	does he care about the family he l **behind**	339
	41:32	Behind him he l a **glistening** wake;	239
Pr	13:22	A good man l **an inheritance**	5706
	15:10	Stern discipline awaits *him who* l the path;	6440
	28: 3	like a driving rain that l no crops.	NIH
Isa	1:30	You will be like an oak with fading l,	6591
	32: 6	the hungry he l **empty** and from	8197
	33: 9	and Bashan and Carmel **drop** *their* l.	5850
	34: 4	all the starry host will fall like withered l	6591
Jer	3: 1	"If a man divorces his wife and *she* l him	907+2143+4946
	8:13	and their l will wither.	6591
	17: 8	its l are always green.	6591
Eze	41:24	Each door had two l—	1946
	41:24	two hinged l for each door.	1946
	47:12	Their l will not wither,	6591
	47:12	Their fruit will serve for food and their l	6591
Da	4:12	Its l were beautiful, its fruit abundant,	10564
	4:14	strip off its l and scatter its fruit.	10564
	4:21	with beautiful l and abundant fruit,	10564
Mt	21:19	up to it but found nothing on it except l.	5877
	24:32	as its twigs get tender and its l come out,	5877
Mk	11:13	he found nothing but l,	5877
	12:19	that if a man's brother dies and l a wife	2901
	13:28	as its twigs get tender and its l come out,	5877
	13:34	*He* l his house and puts his servants	918
Lk	9:39	It scarcely ever l him and is destroying him.	713
	20:28	if a man's brother dies and l a wife	1222+2400
	21:30	When *they* sprout l, you can see	4582
1Co	7:15	But if the unbeliever l, let him do so.	6004
2Co	7:10	that leads to salvation and l no regret,	NIG
Rev	22: 2	And the l of the tree are for the healing of	5877

LEAVING (44) [LEAVE]

Ge	45:24	and *as they were* l he said to them,	2143
Ex	13: 4	Today, in the month of Abib, you *are* l.	3655
	13:20	After l Succoth they camped at Etham	4946+5825
Nu	21:35	l them no survivors.	8636
Dt	3: 3	We struck them down, l no survivors.	8636
Jos	5: 4	died in the desert on the way after l Egypt.	3655
	8:22	l them neither survivors nor fugitives.	8636
2Sa	14: 7	l my husband neither name nor descendant	8492
	15:24	all the people had finished l the city.	4946+6296
1Ki	15:17	from l or entering the territory of Asa king	3655
2Ki	10:11	and his priests, l him no survivor.	8636
2Ch	16: 1	from l or entering the territory of Asa king	3655

Ezr	9: 8	in l us a remnant and giving us a firm place	8636
	9:14	l us no remnant or survivor?	NIH
Job	22: 6	of their clothing, l them naked.	NIH
	41:30	l a trail in the mud like a threshing sledge.	8331
Isa	17: 6	l two or three olives on the topmost	NIH
Eze	39:28	to their own land, not l any behind.	3855
Da	2:35	The wind swept them away without l	10708
Joel	1: 7	l their branches white.	4235
Zep	2:13	l Nineveh utterly desolate and dry as	8492
Mt	4:13	L Nazareth, he went and lived	2901
	11: 7	As John's disciples were l,	4513
	15:21	L that place, Jesus withdrew to the region	2002
	20:29	As Jesus and his disciples were l Jericho,	1744
Mk	4:36	L the crowd behind, they took him along,	918
	6:33	many who saw them l recognized them	5632
	6:46	After l them, he went up on	698
	10:46	were l the city, a blind man,	1744
	11:12	The next day as they were l Bethany,	2002
	12:20	and died without l any children.	918
	12:21	but he also died, l no child.	2901
	13: 1	As he was l the temple,	1744
	14:52	he fled naked, l his garment behind.	2901
Lk	4:42	they tried to keep him from l them.	608+4513
	9:33	As the men were l Jesus, Peter said to him,	1431
	10:30	beat him and went away, l him half dead.	918
	11:42	the latter without l the former undone.	4205
	20:31	the seven died, l no children.	2901
Jn	4:28	Then, l her water jar, the woman went back	918
	16:28	now l am l the world and going back to	918
Ac	13:42	and Barnabas were l the synagogue,	1996
	21: 8	L the next day, we reached Caesarea	2002
1Pe	2:21	l you an example, that you should follow	5701

LEB KAMAI (1)

Jer	51: 1	and the people of L.	4214

LEBANA (1)

Ne	7:48	L, Hagaba, Shalmai,	4245

LEBANAH (1)

Ezr	2:45	L, Hagabah, Akkub,	4245

LEBANON (70)

Dt	1: 7	to the land of the Canaanites and to L,	4248
	3:25	that fine hill country and L."	4248
	11:24	extend from the desert to L,	4248
Jos	1: 4	the desert to L, and from the great river,	4248
	9: 1	the entire coast of the Great Sea as far as L	4248
	11:17	in the Valley of L below Mount Hermon.	4248
	12: 7	in the Valley of L to Mount Halak,	4248
	13: 5	and all L to the east,	4248
	13: 6	of the mountain regions from L	4248
Jdg	3: 3	the L mountains from Mount Baal Hermon	4248
	9:15	and consume the cedars of L!'	4248
1Ki	4:33	the cedar of L to the hyssop that grows out	4248
	5: 6	give orders that cedars of L be cut for me.	4248
	5: 9	My men will haul them down from L to	4248
	5:14	to L in shifts of ten thousand a month,	4248
	5:14	so that they spent one month in L	4248
	7: 2	of the Forest of L a hundred cubits long,	4248
	9:19	in Jerusalem, in L and throughout all	4248
	10:17	in the Palace of the Forest of L.	4248
	10:21	Palace of the Forest of L were pure gold.	4248
2Ki	14: 9	in L sent a message to a cedar in Lebanon,	4248
	14: 9	in Lebanon sent a message to a cedar in L,	4248
	14: 9	a wild beast in L came along and trampled	4248
	19:23	the utmost heights of L.	4248
2Ch	2: 8	pine and algum logs from L,	4248
	2:16	from L that you need and will float them	4248
	8: 6	in Jerusalem, in L and throughout all	4248
	9:16	in the Palace of the Forest of L.	4248
	9:20	Palace of the Forest of L were pure gold.	4248
	25:18	in L sent a message to a cedar in Lebanon,	4248
	25:18	in Lebanon sent a message to a cedar in L,	4248
	25:18	a wild beast in L came along and trampled	4248
Ezr	3: 7	by sea from L to Joppa,	4248
Ps	29: 5	in pieces the cedars of L.	4248
	29: 6	He makes L skip like a calf,	4248
	72:16	Let its fruit flourish like L;	4248
	92:12	they will grow like a cedar of L;	4248
	104:16	the cedars of L that he planted.	4248
SS	3: 9	he made it of wood from L.	4248
	4: 8	Come with me from L, my bride,	4248
	4: 8	my bride, come with me from L.	4248
	4:11	of your garments is like that of L.	4248
	4:15	of flowing water streaming down from L.	4248
	5:15	His appearance is like L,	4248
	7: 4	the tower of L looking toward Damascus.	4248
Isa	2:13	for all the cedars of L,	4248
	10:34	L will fall before the Mighty One.	4248
	14: 8	and the cedars of L exult over you and say,	4248
	29:17	will not L be turned into a fertile field and	4248
	33: 9	L is ashamed and withers;	4248
	35: 2	The glory of L will be given to it,	4248
	37:24	the utmost heights of L.	4248
	40:16	L is not sufficient for altar fires,	4248
	60:13	"The glory of L will come to you, the pine,	4248
Jer	18:14	of L ever vanish from its rocky slopes?	4248
	22: 6	like the summit of L,	4248
	22:20	"Go up to L and cry out,	4248
	22:23	You who live in 'L,'	4248
Eze	17: 3	of varied colors came to L.	4248
	27: 5	they took a cedar from L to make a mast	4248
	31: 3	Consider Assyria, once a cedar in L,	4248

Eze	31:15	Because of it I clothed L with gloom,	4248
	31:16	the choicest and best of L,	4248
Hos	14: 5	a cedar of L he will send down his roots;	4248
	14: 6	his fragrance like a cedar of L.	4248
	14: 7	and his fame will be like the wine from L.	4248
Na	1: 4	and the blossoms of L fade.	4248
Hab	2:17	to L will overwhelm you,	4248
Zec	10:10	I will bring them to Gilead and L,	4248
	11: 1	Open your doors, O L,	4248

LEBAOTH (1) [BETH LEBAOTH]

Jos	15:32	L, Shilhim, Ain and Rimmon—	4219

LEBBAEUS (KJV) See THADDAEUS

LEBO HAMATH (12)

Nu	13:21	of Zin as far as Rehob, toward L.	4217
	34: 8	and from Mount Hor to L.	4217
Jos	13: 5	from Baal Gad below Mount Hermon to L.	4217
Jdg	3: 3	from Mount Baal Hermon to L.	4217
1Ki	8:65	a vast assembly, people from L to	4217
2Ki	14:25	the boundaries of Israel from L to	4217
1Ch	13: 5	the Shihor River in Egypt to L,	4217
2Ch	7: 8	a vast assembly, people from L to	4217
Eze	47:15	the Hethlon road past L to Zedad,	4217
	47:20	to a point opposite L.	4217
	48: 1	the Hethlon road to L;	4217
Am	6:14	oppress you all the way from L to	4217

LEBONAH (1)

Jdg	21:19	and to the south of L."	4228

LECAH (1)

1Ch	4:21	Er the father of L,	4336

LECTURE (2)

Jn	9:34	how dare you l us!"	1438
Ac	19: 9	and had discussions daily in the l hall	5391

LED (153) [LEAD]

Ge	19:16	of his two daughters and l them safely out	3655
	24:27	The LORD has l me on the journey to	5697
	24:48	who had l me on the right road to get	5697
Ex	3: 1	and he l the flock to the far side of	5627
	13:18	So God l the people around by	6015
	15:22	Then Moses l Israel from the Red Sea	5825
	19:17	Then Moses l the people out of the camp	3655
	32:21	that you l them into such great sin?"	995
Dt	8: 2	the LORD your God l you all the way in	2143
	8:15	He l you through the vast	2143
	13:13	l the people of their town astray,	5615
	17:17	or his heart will be l astray.	6073
	29: 5	the forty years that l l you through	2143
	32:12	The LORD alone l him;	5697
Jos	24: 3	from the land beyond the River and l him	2143
Jdg	2: 1	and l you into the land that I swore to give	995
	3:28	of the fords of the Jordan that l to Moab,	4200
	9:39	So Gaal l out the citizens of Shechem	3655+4200+7156
	10: 2	He l Israel twenty-three years;	9149
	10: 3	Jair of Gilead, who l Israel twenty-two years	9149
	12: 7	Jephthah l Israel six years.	9149
	12: 8	After him, Ibzan of Bethlehem l Israel.	9149
	12: 9	Ibzan l Israel seven years.	9149
	12:11	Elon the Zebulunite l Israel ten years.	9149
	12:13	Abdon son of Hillel, from Pirathon, l Israel.	9149
	12:14	He l Israel eight years.	9149
	15:13	with two new ropes and l him up from	6590
	15:20	Samson l Israel for twenty years in	9149
	16:31	He had l Israel twenty years.	9149
1Sa	4:18	He had l Israel forty years.	9149
	18:13	David l the troops in their campaigns.	995+2256+3655+4200+7156
	18:16	because he l them in their campaigns.	995+2256+3655+4200+7156
	30:16	He l David down, and there they were,	3718
2Sa	5: 2	l Israel on their military campaigns.	995+2256+3655
1Ki	6: 8	a stairway l up to the middle level and	AIT
	11: 3	and his wives l him astray.	4213+5742
	13:34	of Jeroboam that l to its downfall and	3948
2Ki	15:15	And he l them to Samaria.	2143
	21: 9	Manasseh l them astray,	9494
	21:11	and has l Judah into sin with his idols.	2627
	23:22	since the days of the judges who l Israel,	9149
1Ch	4:42	l by Pelatiah, Neariah,	928+8031
	11: 2	l Israel on their military campaigns.	995+2256+3655
	20: 1	Joab l out the armed forces.	5627
2Ch	20:27	Then, l by Jehoshaphat,	928+8031
	21:11	and had l Judah astray.	5615
	21:13	l Judah and the people of Jerusalem to prostitute themselves,	2388
	25:11	then marshaled his strength and l his army	5627
	26:16	his pride l to his downfall.	6330
Ezr	9: 2	and officials have l the way	2118+3338+8037
Ne	9:12	By day you l them with a pillar of cloud,	5697
	11:17	who l l in thanksgiving and prayer;	3344+9378
	12:36	Ezra the scribe l the procession.	4200+7156
	13:26	even he was l into sin by foreign women.	2627

Est	6:11	l him on horseback through the city streets,	8206
Job	31: 7	if my heart has been l by my eyes,	339+2143
Ps	26: 1	O LORD, for I have l a blameless life;	928+2143
	45:14	In embroidered garments she is l to	3297
	45:15	They are l in with joy and gladness;	3297
	68:18	l captives in your train;	8647
	77:19	Your path l through the sea,	NIH
	77:20	You l your people like a flock by the hand	5697
	78:13	He divided the sea and l them through;	6296
	78:26	and l forth the south wind by his power.	5627
	78:52	he l them like sheep through the desert.	5627
	78:72	with skillful hands he l them.	5697
	106: 9	he l them through the depths as through	2143
	107: 7	He l them by a straight way to a city	2005
	136:16	to him who l his people through the desert,	2143
Pr	5:23	l astray by his own great folly.	8706
	7:21	With persuasive words she l him astray;	5742
	20: 1	whoever is l astray by them is not wise.	8706
	24:11	Rescue those being l away to death;	4374
Isa	9:16	and those who are guided are l astray.	1182
	19:13	of her peoples have l Egypt astray.	9494
	48:21	They did not thirst when he l them through	2143
	53: 7	he was l like a lamb to the slaughter,	3297
	55:12	You will go out in joy and be l forth	3297
	60:11	l in triumphal procession.	5627
	63:13	who l them through the depths?	2143
Jer	2: 6	who brought us up out of Egypt and l us	2143
	2:17	the LORD your God when he l you in	2143
	11:19	like a gentle lamb l to the slaughter;	3297
	22:12	the place where they have l him captive;	1655
	23:13	l my people Israel astray.	9494
	29:31	and has l you to believe a lie,	1053
	41:16	with him l away all the survivors	4374
	43: 5	the army officers l away all the remnant	4374
	43: 6	They also l away all the men,	NIH
	50: 6	their shepherds have l them astray	9494
Eze	19: 4	They l him with hooks to the land	995
	20:10	Therefore l l them out of Egypt	3655
	29:18	from the campaign he l against Tyre.	6268
	37: 2	He l me back and forth among them,	6296
	40:22	Seven steps l up to it,	6590
	40:24	Then he l me to the south side and I saw	2143
	40:26	Seven steps l up to it,	6590
	40:31	and eight steps l up to it.	6590
	40:34	and eight steps l up to it.	6590
	40:37	and eight steps l up to it.	6590
	42: 1	Then the man l me northward into	3655
	42:15	he l me out by the east gate and measured	3655
	46:21	and l me around to its four corners,	6296
	47: 2	the north gate and l me around the outside	6015
	47: 3	a thousand cubits and then l me	6296
	47: 4	and l me through water that was knee-deep.	6296
	47: 4	and l me through water that was up to	6296
	47: 6	then he l me back to the bank of the river.	2143
Da	7:13	Ancient of Days and was l into his presence	10638
Hos	11: 4	l l them with cords of human kindness,	5432
	11: 4	they have been l astray by false gods,	9494
Am	2:10	and l l you forty years in the desert	2143
Mt	4: 1	Then Jesus was l by the Spirit into	343
	17: 1	l them up a high mountain by themselves.	429
	27: 2	l him away and handed him over to Pilate,	552
	27:31	Then they l him away to crucify him.	552
Mk	8:23	by the hand and l him outside the village.	1766
	9: 2	with him and l them up a high mountain,	429
	15: 1	l him away and handed him over to Pilate.	708
	15:16	The soldiers l Jesus away into the palace	552
	15:20	Then they l him out to crucify him.	1974
Lk	4: 1	from the Jordan and was l by the Spirit in	72
	4: 5	The devil l him up to a high place	343
	4: 9	The devil l him to Jerusalem	72
	18:39	Those who l the way rebuked him	4575
	22:54	they l him away and took him into	72
	22:66	met together, and Jesus was l before them.	552
	23: 1	the whole assembly rose and l him off	72
	23:26	As they l him away, they seized Simon from	552
	23:32	were also l out with him to be executed.	72
	24:50	When he had l them out to the vicinity	1974
Jn	18:28	Then the Jews l Jesus from Caiaphas to	72
Ac	5:37	and l a band of people in revolt.	923
	7:36	He l them out of Egypt and did wonders	1974
	7:40	As for this fellow Moses who l us out	1974
	8:32	"He was l like a sheep to the slaughter,	72
	9: 8	l him by the hand into	1652
	13:17	with mighty power he l them out of	1974
	19:26	and l astray large numbers of people here	3496
	21:38	l four thousand terrorists out	1974
	22:11	l me by the hand into Damascus.	5932
Ro	8:14	because those who are l by the Spirit	72
1Co	12: 2	or other you were influenced and l astray	552
2Co	7: 9	because your sorrow l you to repentance.	1650
	11: 3	your minds may somehow be l astray	5780
	11:29	Who is l into sin, and I do not inwardly	4997
Gal	2:13	even Barnabas was l astray.	5270
Eph	4: 8	l captives in his train and gave gifts	168+169
Heb	3:16	Were they not all those Moses l out	2002
Rev	18:23	the nations were l astray.	4414

LEDGE (10) [LEDGES]

Ex	27: 5	the l of the altar so that it is halfway up	4136
	38: 4	to be under its l, halfway up the altar.	4136
Eze	43:14	up to the lower l it is two cubits high and	6478
	43:14	and from the smaller l to the larger	6478
	43:14	up to the larger l it is four cubits high and	6478
	43:17	The upper l also is square,	6478
	43:20	on the four corners of the upper l and all	6478

Eze 45:19 the four corners of the upper l of the altar 6478
46:23 of each of the four courts was a l of stone, 3215
46:23 for fire built all around under the l. 3227

LEDGES (2) [LEDGE]

1Ki 6: 6 He made offset l around the outside of 4492
Eze 41: 6 There were l all around the wall of 995

LEE (3)

Ac 27: 4 passed to the l of Cyprus 5709
27: 7 sailed to the l of Crete, 5709
27:16 passed to the l of a small island called 5720

LEECH (1)

Pr 30:15 "The l has two daughters. 'Give!' 'Give!' 6598

LEEKS (1)

Nu 11: 5 also the cucumbers, melons, l, 2946

LEES (KJV) See AGED, DREGS

LEFT (556) [LEFT-HANDED, LEFTOVER]

Ge 7:23 Only Noah was l, and those with him 8636
12: 4 So Abram l, as the LORD had told him; 2143
13: 9 If you go to the l, I'll go to the right; 8520
13: 9 if you go to the right, I'll go to the l." 8521
18:33 he l, and Abraham returned home. 2143
19:30 Lot and his two daughters l Zoar and 4946+6590
24:10 of his master's camels and l, 2143
24:61 So the servant took Rebekah and l. 2143
25: 5 Abraham l everything he owned to Isaac. 5989
25:34 He ate and drank, and then got up and l. 2143
26:31 and they l him in peace. 2143
27: 5 When Esau l for the open country 2143
27:30 Jacob had scarcely l his father's 3655+3655
28:10 Jacob l Beersheba and set out for Haran. 3655
31:55 Then he l and returned home. 2143
32: 8 the group that is l may escape." 8636
32:24 So Jacob was l alone, 3855
34:26 from Shechem's house and l. 3855
38: 1 Judah l his brothers and went down 907+4946
38:19 After she l, she took off her veil and put 2143
39: 6 So he l in Joseph's care everything he had; 6440
39:12 But he l his cloak in her hand and ran out 6440
39:13 When she saw that he had l his cloak 6440
39:15 he l his cloak beside me and ran out of 6440
39:18 he l his cloak beside me and ran out of 6440
42:26 loaded their grain on their donkeys and l. 2143
42:38 and he is the only one l. 8636
44:20 he is the only one of his mother's sons l, 3855
46: 1 Then Jacob l Beersheba, 4946+7756
47:18 there is nothing l for our lord except 8636
48:13 toward Israel's l hand and Manasseh 8520
48:13 on his l toward Israel's right hand, 8520
48:14 he put his l hand on Manasseh's head, 8520
50: 8 and their flocks and herds were l 6440
50:16 "Your father l these instructions 7422
Ex 5:20 When they l Pharaoh, 3655
8:12 After Moses and Aaron l Pharaoh, 3655
8:30 Then Moses l Pharaoh and prayed to 3655
8:31 The flies l Pharaoh and his officials 6073
9:21 of the LORD l their slaves and livestock 6440
9:33 Moses l Pharaoh and went out of the city. 3655
10: 5 They will devour what little you have l 3856+7129+8636
10: 6 Then Moses turned and l Pharaoh. 3655
10:12 everything l by the hail." 8636
10:15 They devoured all that was l after 3855
10:18 then l Pharaoh and prayed to the LORD. 3655
10:19 Not a locust was l anywhere in Egypt. 8636
10:26 not a hoof is to be l behind. 8636
11: 8 Then Moses, hot with anger, l Pharaoh. 3655
12:10 some is l till morning, you must burn it. 3855
12:41 the LORD's divisions l Egypt. 3655
13:22 nor the pillar of fire by night l its place 4631
14:22 of water on their right and on their l. 8520
14:29 of water on their right and on their l. 8520
16:23 Save whatever is l and keep it 6369
19: 1 after the Israelites l Egypt— 3655
26:12 that is l is to hang down at the rear 6369
26:13 what is l will hang over the sides of 6369
29:34 the ordination ram or any bread is l over 3855
36: 4 the work on the sanctuary l their work 995+4946
Lev 6: 2 about something entrusted to him or l 9582
7:16 but anything l over may be eaten on 3855
7:17 the sacrifice l over till the third day must 3855
10:12 "Take the grain offering l over from 3855
14:15 pour it in the palm of his own l hand, 8522
14:26 of the oil into the palm of his own l hand, 8522
19: 6 anything l over until the third day must 3855
25:15 to you on the basis of the number of years l AIT
26:36 " 'As for those of you who are l, 8636
26:39 Those of you who are l will waste away in 8636
Nu 12: 9 LORD burned against them, and he l them. 2143
12:16 the people l Hazeroth and encamped 4946+5825
14:19 from the time they l Egypt until now." NIH
20:17 the right or to the l until we have passed 8520
22: 7 The elders of Moab and Midian l, 2143
22:26 either to the right or to the l. 8520
25: 7 saw this, he l the assembly, 4946+7756+9348
26:65 not one of them was l except Caleb son 4946+7756
27: 3 he died for his own sin and l no sons. 2118+4200
33: 5 The Israelites l Rameses and camped 5825

Nu 33: 6 They l Succoth and camped at Etham, 5825
33: 7 They l Etham, turned back to Pi Hahiroth, 5825
33: 8 They l Pi Hahiroth and passed through 5825
33: 9 They l Marah and went to Elim, 5825
33:10 They l Elim and camped by the Red Sea. 5825
33:11 They l the Red Sea and camped in 5825
33:12 They l the Desert of Sin and camped 5825
33:13 They l Dophkah and camped at Alush. 5825
33:14 They l Alush and camped at Rephidim, 5825
33:15 They l Rephidim and camped in 5825
33:16 They l the Desert of Sinai and camped 5825
33:17 They l Kibroth Hattaavah and camped 5825
33:18 They l Hazeroth and camped at Rithmah. 5825
33:19 They l Rithmah and camped 5825
33:20 They l Rimmon Perez and camped 5825
33:21 They l Libnah and camped at Rissah. 5825
33:22 They l Rissah and camped at Kehelathah. 5825
33:23 They l Kehelathah and camped at 5825
33:24 They l Mount Shepher and camped 5825
33:25 They l Haradah and camped at Makheloth. 5825
33:26 They l Makheloth and camped at Tahath. 5825
33:27 They l Tahath and camped at Terah. 5825
33:28 They l Terah and camped at Mithcah. 5825
33:29 They l Mithcah and camped 5825
33:30 They l Hashmonah and camped 5825
33:31 They l Moseroth and camped 5825
33:32 They l Bene Jaakan and camped 5825
33:33 They l Hor Haggidgad and camped 5825
33:34 They l Jotbathah and camped at Abronah. 5825
33:35 They l Abronah and camped 5825
33:36 They l Ezion Geber and camped 5825
33:37 They l Kadesh and camped at Mount Hor, 5825
33:41 They l Mount Hor and camped 5825
33:42 They l Zalmonah and camped at Punon. 5825
33:43 They l Punon and camped at Oboth. 5825
33:44 They l Oboth and camped at Iye Abarim, 5825
33:45 They l Iyim and camped at Dibon Gad. 5825
33:46 They l Dibon Gad and camped 5825
33:47 They l Almon Diblathaim and camped in 5825
33:48 They l the mountains of Abarim 5825
Dt 1:24 They l and went up into the hill country, 7155
2:14 from the time we l Kadesh Barnea 2143+4946
2:27 not turn aside to the right or to the l. 8520
2:34 We l no survivors. 8636
3:11 Og king of Bashan was l of the remnant 3855
5:32 do not turn aside to the right or to the l. 8520
9: 7 From the day you l Egypt 3655
16: 3 because you l Egypt in haste— 3655
17:11 to the right or to the l. 8520
17:20 from the law to the right or to the l. 8520
28:14 to the right or to the l, following other gods 8520
28:55 It will be all he has l because of 8636
28:62 as the stars in the sky will be l but few 8636
32:36 and no one is l, slave or free. NIH
Jos 1: 7 do not turn from it to the right or to the l, 8520
2: 5 to close the city gate, the men l. 3655
2:22 When they l, they went into the hills 2143
5: 6 of military age when they l Egypt had died, 3655
8:17 They l the city open and went in pursuit 6440
8:29 the king of Ai on a tree and l him there NIH
9:12 at home on the day we l to come to you. 3655
10:20 few who were l reached their fortified cities. 8572
10:26 and they were l hanging on the trees AIT
10:28 He l no survivors. 8636
10:30 He l no survivors there. 8636
10:33 until no survivors were l. 8636
10:37 They l no survivors. 8636
10:39 He l no survivors. 8636
10:40 He l no survivors. 8636
11: 8 until no survivors were l. 8636
11:15 he l nothing undone of all that 6073
11:22 No Anakites were l in Israelite territory; 3855
18: 9 So the men l and went through the land. 2143
19:27 passing Cabul on the l. 8520
22: 9 the half-tribe of Manasseh l the Israelites at Shiloh 907+2143+4946
23: 6 turning aside to the right or to the l. 8520
Jdg 2:21 before them any of the nations Joshua l 6440
3: 1 These are the nations the LORD l 5663
3: 4 They were l to test the Israelites 2118
3:19 And all his attendants l him. 3655
3:21 Ehud reached with his l hand, 8520
4:11 Heber the Kenite had l the other Kenites, 7233
4:16 not a man was l. 8636
5:13 men who were l came down to the nobles; 8586
7: 3 So twenty-two thousand men l, 8740
7:20 the torches in their l hands and holding 8520
8:10 all that were l of the armies of 3855
16:19 And his strength l him. 6073
16:20 he did not know that the LORD had l him. 6073
16:29 his right hand on the one and his l hand on 8520
17: 8 that town in search of some other 2143+4946
18: 7 So the five men l and came to Laish, 2143
18:21 they turned away and l. 2143
19: 2 She l him and went back 907+2143+4946
19:10 the man l and went toward Jebus (that is, 2143
21: 7 can we provide wives for those who are l, 3855
21:16 for the men who are l? 3855
21:24 Israelites l that place and went home 2143+4946
Ru 1: 3 and she was l with her two sons. 8636
1: 5 and Naomi was l without her two sons 8636
1: 7 With her two daughters-in-law she 3655
2:11 how you l your father and mother 6440
2:14 She ate all she wanted and had some l over. 3855
2:18 and gave her what had l over 3855
4:14 not l you without a kinsman-redeemer. 8697
1Sa 2:36 Then everyone l in your family line 3855

1Sa 6:12 they did not turn to the right or to the l. 8520
11:11 so that no two of them were l together. 8636
13:15 Then Samuel l Gilgal and went up 4946+7756
14: 3 No one was aware that Jonathan had l. 2143
14:17 "Muster the forces and see who has l us." 2143+4946+6640
15:34 Then Samuel l for Ramah, 2143
17:20 Early in the morning David l the flock 5759
17:22 David l his things with the keeper 5759
18:12 the LORD was with David but had l Saul. 6073
19:22 he himself l for Ramah and went to 2143
20:42 Then David l, and Jonathan went back to 2143
22: 1 David l Gath and escaped to the cave 2143+4946
22: 4 So he l them with the king of Moab, 5663
22: 5 David l and went to the forest of Hereth. 2143
23:13 l Keilah kept moving from place 3855
24: 7 And Saul l the cave and went his way. 4946+7756
25:34 belonging to Nabal would have been l alive 3855
26:12 near Saul's head, and they l. 2143
27: 2 the six hundred men with him l and went 7756
28:25 That same night they got up and l. 2143
29: 3 and from the day he l Saul until now, 5877
30: 4 until they had no strength l to weep. NIH
30:21 and who were l behind at the Besor Ravine. 8740
2Sa 2:12 l Mahanaim and went to Gibeon. 3655
2:19 to the right nor to the l as he pursued him. 8520
2:21 "Turn aside to the right or to the l; 8520
3:26 Joab then l David and sent messengers 3655
5:13 After he l Hebron, 995+4946
9: 1 "Is there anyone still l of the house 3855
9: 3 "Is there no one still l of the house of Saul NIH
11: 8 So Uriah l the palace, 3655
13: 9 So everyone l him. 3655
13:30 not one of them is l." 3855
14: 7 the only burning coal I have l, 8636
14:19 the right or to the l from anything my lord 8521
15:16 but he l ten concubines to take care of 6440
16: 6 special guard were on David's right and l. 8520
16:21 with your father's concubines whom he l 5663
17:12 nor any of his men will be l alive. 3855
17:18 of them l quickly and went to the house of 2143
17:22 no one was l who had not crossed 6372
18: 9 He was l hanging in midair, 5989
19: 7 not a man will be l with you by nightfall. 4328
19:19 on the day my lord the king l Jerusalem. 3655
19:24 the king l until the day he returned safely. 2143
20: 3 the ten concubines he had l to take care of 5663
24: 4 so they l the presence of the king to enroll 3655
1Ki 7:47 l all these things unweighed, 5663
7:49 on the l, in front of the inner sanctuary); 8520
9:20 All the people l from the Amorites, 3855
10:13 Then she l and returned with her retinue 7155
14:17 Then Jeroboam's wife got up and l 2143
15:18 then took all the silver and gold that was l 3855
18:22 the only one of the LORD's prophets l, 3855
19: 3 he l his servant there, 5663
19:10 I am the only one l, 3855
19:14 I am the only one l, 3855
19:20 Elisha then l his oxen and ran after Elijah. 6440
19:21 So Elisha l him and went back. 339+4946
20: 9 They l and took the answer back 2143
22:19 around him on his right and on his l. 8520
2Ki 2:14 to the right and to the l, 2178S
2:14 it divided to the right and to the l, 2178S
3:25 Only Kir Haraseth was l with its stones 8636
4: 5 She l him and afterward shut the 907+2143+4946
4: 6 But he replied, "There is not a jar l." 6388
4: 7 You and your sons can live on what is l." 3855
4:43 'They will eat and have some l over.' 3855
4:44 and they ate and had some l over, 3855
5: 5 So Naaman l, taking with him ten talents 2143
5:24 He sent the men away and they l. 2143
7: 7 They l the camp as it was and ran NIH
7:10 and the tents l just as they were." NIH
7:12 so they have l the camp to hide in 3655
7:13 of the horses that are l in the city. 8636
7:13 be like that of all the Israelites l here— 8636
8: 6 from the day she l the country until now." 6440
8:14 Hazael l Elisha and returned to 907+2143+4946
10:14 He l no survivor. 8636-
10:15 After he l there, 2143+4946
10:17 he killed all who were l there of Ahab's 8636
13: 7 Nothing had been l of the army 8636
17:18 Only the tribe of Judah was l, 8636
19: 8 that the king of Assyria had l Lachish. 5825
20: 4 Before Isaiah had l the middle court, 3655
20:17 Nothing will be l, says the LORD. 3855
22: 2 not turning aside to the right or to the l. 8520
23: 8 which is on the l of the city gate. 8520
24:14 Only the poorest people of the land were l. 8636
25:12 But the commander l behind some of 8636
25:22 over the people he had l behind in Judah. 8636
1Ch 6:44 the Merarites, at his l hand: 8520
16:37 David l Asaph and his associates before 6440
16:38 He also l Obed-Edom NIH
16:39 David l Zadok the priest NIH
16:43 Then all the people l, 2143
20: 1 Joab attacked Rabbah and l it in ruins. 2238
21: 4 so Joab l and went throughout Israel and 3655
21:21 he l the threshing floor and bowed down 3655
2Ch 8: 7 All the people l from the Hittites, 3855
9:12 Then she l and returned with her retinue 2200
18:18 on his right and on his l. 8520
20:20 Early in the morning they l for the Desert 3655
21:17 Not a son was l to him except Ahaziah, 8636
24:25 they l Joash severely wounded. 6440
25:10 with Judah and l for home in a great rage. 8740

2Ch	30: 6	that he may return to you who are l,	8636
	31:10	and this great amount is l over."	3855
	32:31	God l him to test him and to know	6440
	34: 2	not turning aside to the right or to the l.	8520
Ezr	4:16	you will be l with nothing	10029+10378
	9:15	We are l this day as a remnant.	8636
Ne	6: 1	the wall and not a gap was l in it—	3855
	8: 4	and on his l were Pedaiah, Mishael,	8520
Est	7: 7	l his wine and went out into the palace	4946
	7: 8	As soon as the word l the king's mouth,	3655
	8:15	Mordecai the king's presence wearing royal garments of blue	3655
Job	20:19	the poor and l them destitute;	6440
	20:21	Nothing is l for him to devour;	8586
	20:26	and devour what is l in his tent.	8586
	21:34	Nothing is l of your answers	8636
Ps	34: T	who drove him away, and he l.	2143
	69:20	and has l me helpless;	AIT
	74: 9	no prophets are l,	6388
	105:38	Egypt was glad when they l,	3655
Pr	2:17	who has l the partner of her youth	6440
	3:16	in her l hand are riches and honor.	8520
	4:27	Do not swerve to the right or the l;	8520
	29:15	a child l to himself disgraces his mother.	8938
Ecc	5:14	that when he has a son there is nothing l	NIH
	10: 2	but the heart of the fool to the l.	8520
SS	2: 6	His l arm is under my head,	8520
	5: 6	I opened for my lover, but my lover had l;	2811
	8: 3	His l arm is under my head	8520
Isa	1: 8	The Daughter of Zion is l like a shelter in	3855
	1: 9	LORD Almighty had l us some survivors,	3855
	4: 3	Those who are l in Zion,	8636
	5: 8	to field till no space is l and you live alone	NIH
	5: 9	the fine mansions l without occupants.	NIH
	6:11	until the houses are l deserted and	NIH
	9:20	on the l they will eat, but not be satisfied.	8520
	11:11	that is l of his people from Assyria	8636
	11:16	for the remnant of his people that is l	8636
	15: 6	vegetation is gone and nothing green is l	2118
	17: 2	The cities of Aroer will be deserted and l	2118
	17: 9	which they l because of the Israelites,	6440
	18: 6	They will all be l to the mountain birds	6440
	21:11	"Watchman, what is l of the night?	4946
	21:11	Watchman, what is l of the night?"	4946
	23: 1	For Tyre is destroyed and l without house	NIH
	24: 6	and very few are l.	8636
	24:12	The city is l in ruins,	8636
	24:13	gleanings are l after the grape harvest.	NIH
	27: 9	or incense altars will be l standing.	AIT
	30:17	till you are l like a flagstaff on	3855
	30:21	Whether you turn to the right or to the l,	8521
	37: 8	that the king of Assyria had l Lachish.	5825
	39: 6	Nothing will be l, says the LORD.	3855
	44:19	a detestable thing from what is l?	3856
	49:21	I was l all alone, but these—	8636
	54: 3	to the right and to the l;	8520
Jer	4: 7	He has l his place to lay waste your land.	3655
	7:25	From the time your forefathers l Egypt	3655
	10:20	no one is l now to pitch my tent or to set	6388
	11:23	Not even a remnant will be l to them.	2118
	25:20	Gaza, Ekron, and the people l at Ashdod);	8642
	27:19	the other furnishings that are l in this city,	3855
	27:21	about the things that are l in the house of	3855
	29:32	He will have no one l among this people,	3782
	34: 7	These were the only fortified cities l	8636
	37:10	and only wounded men were l	8636
	38: 4	He is discouraging the soldiers who are l	8636
	38:22	All the women l in the palace of the king	8636
	39: 4	they l the city at night by way of	3655
	39:10	the commander of the guard l behind in	8636
	40: 6	the people who were l behind in the land.	8636
	40:11	that the king of Babylon had l a remnant	5989
	41:10	along with all the others who were l there,	8636
	42: 2	now only a few are l.	8636
	43: 6	the imperial guard had l with Gedaliah son	5663
	48:11	like wine l on its dregs,	9200
	52: 7	They l the city at night through the gate	3655
	52:16	But Nebuzaradan l behind the rest of	8636
La	3:11	from the path and mangled me and l me	8492
Eze	1:10	and on the l the face of an ox;	8520
	4: 4	on your l side and put the sin of the house	8522
	7:11	none of the people will be l,	NIH
	9: 8	and I was l alone,	8636
	19:14	No strong branch is l on it fit for	2118
	21:16	O sword, slash to the right, then to the l,	8521
	22:18	tin, iron and lead l inside a furnace.	NIH
	23:25	of you who are l will fall by the sword.	344
	23:25	of you who are l will be consumed by fire.	344
	24:21	and daughters you l behind will fall by	6440
	31:12	of foreign nations cut it down and l it.	5759
	31:12	from under its shade and l it.	5759
	33:27	those who are l in the ruins will fall by	NIH
	39: 3	I will strike your bow from your l hand	8520
	47:11	they will be l for salt.	5989
Da	2:44	nor will it be l to another people.	10697
	7: 7	and trampled underfoot whatever was l.	10692
	7:19	and trampled underfoot whatever was l	10692
	10: 8	I was l alone, gazing at this great vision;	8636
	10: 8	I had no strength l,	8636
	12: 7	lifted his right hand and his l hand	8520
Joel	1: 4	What the locust swarm has l	3856
	1: 4	what the great locusts have l	3856
	1: 4	young locusts have l other locusts have	3856
Am	5: 3	will have only a hundred l;	8636
	5: 3	a hundred strong will have only ten l."	8636
	6: 9	If ten men are l in one house,	3855
	9: 1	those who are l I will kill with the sword.	344

Jnh	4:11	from their l, and many cattle	8520
Hab	2: 8	the peoples who are l will plunder you.	3856
Zep	1:12	who are like wine l on its dregs,	NIH
	2: 4	Gaza will be abandoned and Ashkelon l	NIH
	2: 5	"I will destroy you, and none will be l."	3782
	3: 6	I have l their streets deserted,	2990
	3: 6	no one will be l at all.	3782
Hag	2: 3	'Who of you is l who saw this house	8636
	2:19	Is there yet any seed l in the barn?	NIH
Zec	2: 3	Then the angel who was speaking to me l,	3655
	4: 3	the right of the bowl and the other on its l."	8520
	4:11	on the right and l of the lampstand?"	8520
	7:14	The land was l so desolate behind them	9037
	9: 7	Those who are l will belong to our God	8636
	11: 9	Let those who are l eat one another's flesh."	8636
	12: 6	and l all the surrounding peoples,	8520
	13: 8	yet one-third will be l in it.	3855
Mal	1: 3	and l his inheritance to the desert jackals."	NIH
	4: 1	"Not a root or a branch will be l to them.	6440
Mt	2:14	and his mother during the night and l	432
	4:11	Then the devil l him,	918
	4:20	At once they l their nets and followed him.	918
	4:22	and immediately they l the boat	918
	6: 3	do not let your l hand know what your right hand is doing,	754
	8:15	He touched her hand and the fever l her,	918
	12:44	it says, 'I will return to the house I l.'	2002
	13:36	he l the crowd and went into the house.	918
	14:20	of broken pieces that were l over.	4355
	15:29	Jesus l there and went along the Sea	1696+3553
	15:37	of broken pieces that were l	4355
	16: 4	Jesus then l them and went away.	2901
	19: 1	he l Galilee and went into the region	3558
	19:27	"We have l everything to follow you!	918
	19:29	And everyone who has l houses	918
	20:21	and the other at your l in your kingdom."	2381
	20:23	but to sit at my right or l is not for me	2381
	21:17	And he l them and went out of the city	2901
	22:22	So they l him and went away.	918
	22:25	he l his wife to his brother.	918
	23:38	Look, your house is l to you desolate.	918
	24: 1	Jesus l the temple and was walking away	2002
	24: 2	not one stone here will be l on another;	918
	24:40	one will be taken and the other l.	918
	24:41	one will be taken and the other l.	918
	25:33	on his right and the goats on his l.	2381
	25:41	"Then he will say to those on his l,	2381
	26:44	So he l them and went away once more	918
	27: 5	the money into the temple and l,	432
	27:38	one on his right and one on his l.	2381
Mk	1:18	At once they l their nets and followed him.	918
	1:20	and they l their father Zebedee in the boat	918
	1:29	As soon as they l the synagogue,	2002
	1:31	The fever l her and she began to wait	918
	1:35	the house and went off to a solitary place,	2002
	1:42	the leprosy l him and he was cured.	599
	2: 2	that there was no room l,	NIG
	6: 1	Jesus l there and went to his hometown,	2002
	7:17	After he had l the crowd and entered	608
	7:24	Jesus l that place and went to	1696
	7:29	the demon has l your daughter."	2002
	7:31	Then Jesus l the vicinity of Tyre and went	2002
	8: 8	of broken pieces that were l over.	4354
	8:13	Then he l them, got back into the boat	918
	9:30	They l that place and passed through	2002
	10: 1	then l that place and went into the region	482
	10:28	"We have l everything to follow you!"	918
	10:29	"no one who has l home or brothers	918
	10:37	and the other at your l in your glory."	754
	10:40	but to sit at my right or l is not for me	2381
	12: 6	"He had one l to send, a son,	2285
	12:12	so they l him and went away.	918
	12:22	In fact, none of the seven l any children.	918
	13: 2	"Not one stone here will be l on another;	2002
	14:16	The disciples l, went into the city	2002
	15:27	one on his right and one on his l.	2381
Lk	1:38	Then the angel l her.	599
	2:15	When the angels had l them and gone	599
	2:37	She never l the temple	918
	4:13	he l him until an opportune time.	923
	4:38	Jesus l the synagogue and went to	482+608
	4:39	rebuked the fever, and it l her.	918
	5: 2	l there by the fishermen,	609
	5:11	l everything and followed him.	918
	5:13	And immediately the leprosy l him.	599
	5:28	l everything and followed him.	2901
	7:24	After John's messengers l,	599
	8:37	So he got into the boat and l.	5715
	9:17	of broken pieces that were l over.	4355
	10:40	that my sister has l me to do the work	2901
	11:14	When the demon l, the man who had been	2002
	11:24	it says, 'I will return to the house I l.'	2002+3854
	11:53	When Jesus l there,	2002
	13:35	Look, your house is l to you desolate.	918
	17:29	But the day Lot l Sodom,	2002
	17:34	one will be taken and the other l."	918
	17:35	one will be taken and the other l."	918
	18:28	"We have l all we had to follow you!"	918
	18:29	"no one who has l home or wife	918
	21: 6	when not one stone will be l on another;	918
	22:13	They l and found things just as Jesus had	599
	23:33	one on his right, the other on his l.	754
	24:51	he l them and was taken up into heaven.	1460
Jn	4: 3	he l Judea and went back once more	2002
	4:43	After the two days he l for Galilee.	1696+2002
	4:52	"The fever l him yesterday at	918
	6:12	"Gather the pieces that are l over.	4355

Jn	6:13	the pieces of the five barley loaves l over	4355
	7:10	after his brothers had l for the Feast,	326
	8: 9	the older ones first, until only Jesus was l,	2901
	8:29	he has not l me alone,	918
	12:36	Jesus l and hid himself from them.	599
	18: 1	Jesus l with his disciples and crossed	2002
	19:31	the Jews did not want the bodies l on	3531
Ac	1:25	which Judas l to go where he belongs."	4124
	5:41	The apostles l the Sanhedrin,	4513
	7:13	"So he l the land of the Chaldeans	2002
	12:10	suddenly the angel l him.	923
	12:17	he said, and then he l for another place.	4513
	13:13	where John l them to return to Jerusalem;	713
	14:17	Yet he has not l himself without testimony:	918
	14:20	The next day he and Barnabas l for Derbe.	2002
	15:40	but Paul chose Silas and l,	2002
	16:18	At that moment the spirit l her.	2002
	16:40	and encouraged them. Then they l.	2002
	17:15	then l with instructions for Silas and	1996
	17:33	At that, Paul l the Council.	2002
	18: 1	this, Paul l Athens and went to Corinth.	6004
	18: 7	Then Paul l the synagogue	3553
	18:18	he l the brothers and sailed for Syria,	698
	18:19	where Paul l Priscilla and Aquila.	2901
	18:21	But as he l, he promised,	698
	19: 9	So Paul l them.	923
	19:12	were cured and the evil spirits l them.	1744
	20:11	After talking until daylight, he l.	2002
	21: 5	we l and continued on our way,	2002
	24:27	a favor to the Jews, l Paul in prison.	2901
	25:14	a man here whom Felix l as a prisoner	2901
	26:31	They l the room, and while talking	432
	27:40	they l them in the sea and at the same time	1572
Ro	3:25	he had l the sins committed beforehand unpunished—	4217
	9:29	the Lord Almighty had l us descendants,	1593
	11: 3	I am the only one l,	5699
2Co	1:10	who is l to make me glad but you	NIG
	6: 7	in the right hand and in the l;	754
1Th	3: 1	we thought it best to be l by ourselves	2901
	4:15	who are l till the coming of the Lord,	4335
	4:17	and are l will be caught up together	4335
1Ti	5: 5	in need and l all alone puts her hope	3670
2Ti	4:13	the cloak that l with Carpus at Troas,	657
	4:20	and l Trophimus sick in Miletus.	657
Tit	1: 5	The reason l l you in Crete was	657
	1: 5	might straighten out what was l unfinished	3309
Heb	2: 8	God l nothing that is not subject to him.	918
	10:26	no sacrifice for sins is l,	657
	11:15	of the country they had l,	1674
	11:27	By faith he l Egypt, not fearing the king's	2901
2Pe	2:15	They have l the straight way	2901
Rev	10: 2	on the sea and his l foot on the land,	2381

LEFT-HANDED (3) [HAND]

Jdg	3:15	Ehud, a l man, the son of Gera	360+3338+3545
	20:16	Among all these soldiers there were seven hundred chosen men who were l,	360+3338+3545
1Ch	12: 2	or to sling stones right-handed or l;	8521

LEFTOVER (1) [LEFT]

Ru	2: 2	and pick up the l grain behind anyone	8672

LEG (3) [LEGS]

1Sa	9:24	the l with what was on it and set it in front	8797
Eze	24: 4	the choice pieces—the l and the shoulder.	3751
Am	3:12	from the lion's mouth only two bones or	4157

LEGAL (4) [ILLEGAL, LEGALISTIC, LEGALIZING]

Nu	27:11	to be a l requirement for the Israelites,	5477
	35:29	"These are to be l requirements for you	5477
Ac	19:39	it must be settled in a l assembly.	1937
	22:25	"Is it l for you to flog a Roman citizen	2003

LEGALISTIC (1) [LEGAL]

Php	3: 6	as for l righteousness, faultless.	1877+3795

LEGALIZING (1) [LEGAL]

Ru	4: 7	the method of l transactions in Israel.)	9496

LEGALLY MADE OVER (Anglicized) See DEEDED

LEGION (3) [LEGIONS]

Mk	5: 9	"My name is L," he replied,	3305
	5:15	the l of demons, sitting there, dressed and	3305
Lk	8:30	"What is your name?" "L," he replied,	3305

LEGIONS (1) [LEGION]

Mt	26:53	at my disposal more than twelve l	3305

LEGS (28) [LEG]

Ex	12: 9	head, l and inner parts.	4157
	25:26	where the four l are.	8079
	29:17	and wash the inner parts and the l,	4157
	37:13	where the four l were.	8079
Lev	1: 9	He is to wash the inner parts and the l	4157
	1:13	He is to wash the inner parts and the l	4157
	4:11	as well as the head and l,	4157

Lev	8:21	the l with water and burned the whole ram	4157
	9:14	the inner parts and the l and burned them	4157
	11:21	those that have jointed l for hopping on	4157
	11:23	that have four l you are to detest.	8079
Dt	28:35	The LORD will afflict your knees and l	8797
1Sa	17: 6	on his l he wore bronze greaves,	8079
Ps	147:10	nor his delight in the l of a man;	8797
Pr	26: 7	a lame man's l that hang limp is a proverb	8797
SS	5:15	His l are pillars of marble set on bases	8797
	7: 1	Your graceful l are like jewels,	3751
Isa	7:20	to shave your head and the hair of your l,	8079
	47: 2	Lift up your skirts, bare your l,	8797
Eze	1: 7	Their l were straight;	8079
Da	2:33	its l of iron, its feet partly of iron	10741
	5: 6	and his l gave way.	10284+10626
	10: 6	and l like the gleam of burnished bronze,	5274
Hab	3:16	into my bones, and my l trembled.	9393
Jn	19:31	they asked Pilate to have the l broken and	5003
	19:32	came and broke the l of the first man	5003
	19:33	they did not break his l.	5003
Rev	10: 1	and his l were like fiery pillars.	4546

LEHABITES (2)

Ge	10:13	Anamites, L, Naphtuhites,	4260
1Ch	1:11	Anamites, L, Naphtuhites,	4260

LEHEM See JASHUBI LEHEM

LEHI (4) [RAMATH LEHI]

Jdg	15: 9	spreading out near L.	4306
	15:14	As he approached L, the Philistines	4306
	15:19	God opened up the hollow place in L,	4306
	15:19	and it is still there in L.	4306

LEISURE (KJV) See CHANCE

LEMUEL (2)

Pr	31: 1	The sayings of King L—	4345
	31: 4	"It is not for kings, O L—	4345

LEND (14) [LENDER, LENDING, LENDS, LENT, MONEYLENDER]

Ex	22:25	"If you l money to one of my people	4278
Lev	25:37	You must not l him money at interest	5989
Dt	15: 6	and you will l to many nations	6292
	15: 8	and freely l him whatever he needs.	6292+6292
	28:12	You will l to many nations	4278
	28:44	He will l to you, but you will not lend	4278
	28:44	but you will not l to him.	4278
Ps	37:26	They are always generous and l freely;	4278
	83: 8	to l strength to the descendants of Lot.	2118
Eze	18: 8	not l at usury or take excessive interest.	5989
Lk	6:34	if you l to those from whom you expect	1247
	6:34	Even 'sinners' l to 'sinners,'	1247
	6:35	and l to them without expecting	1247
	11: 5	'Friend, l me three loaves of bread,	3079

LENDER (2) [LEND]

Pr	22: 7	and the borrower is servant to the l.	4278
Isa	24: 2	for borrower as for l,	4278

LENDING (1) [LEND]

Ne	5:10	and my men are also l the people money	5957

LENDS (4) [LEND]

Ps	15: 5	who l his money without usury and does	5989
	112: 5	to him who is generous and l freely,	4278
Pr	19:17	He who is kind to the poor l to the LORD,	4278
Eze	18:13	He l at usury and takes excessive interest.	5989

LENGTH (27) [LONG]

Ge	13:17	walk through the l and breadth of the land,	802
Ex	12:40	the l of time the Israelite people lived	4632
	26:12	As for the additional l of the tent curtains,	6245
Lev	19:35	when measuring l, weight or	4500
1Sa	28:20	Immediately Saul fell full l on the ground,	7757
2Sa	2:11	The l of time David was king in Hebron	5031
	8: 2	and measured them off with a l of cord.	2475
	8: 2	and the third l was allowed to live.	2475
2Ch	3: 8	its l corresponding to the width of	802
Ps	21: 4	l of days, for ever and ever.	802
	90:10	The l of our days is seventy years—	3427+9102
Pr	10:27	The fear of the LORD adds l to life,	3578
Eze	40: 5	The l of the measuring rod in	NIH
	40:11	and its l was thirteen cubits.	802
	40:20	the l and width of the gate facing north,	802
	41: 4	he measured the l of the inner sanctuary;	802
	41: 8	It was the l of the rod, six long cubits.	4850
	41:12	and its l was ninety cubits.	802
	41:15	the l of the building facing the courtyard	802
	42:10	along the l of the wall of the outer court,	8145
	42:11	they had the same l and width,	802
	48: 8	and its l from east to west will equal one	802
	48:13	Its total l will be 25,000	802
	48:18	The sacred portion and running the l of it,	802
	48:21	the l of the tribal portions will belong	4200+6645
Ac	12:10	When they had walked the l of one street,	AIT
Rev	21:16	and found it to be 12,000 stadia in l, and	NIG

LENGTHEN (2) [LONG]

Ecc	8:13	and their days will not l like a shadow.	799
Isa	54: 2	l your cords, strengthen your stakes.	799

LENGTHS (2) [LONG]

2Sa	8: 2	Every two l of them were put to death,	2475
Eze	13:18	and make veils of various l for their heads	7757

LENGTHWISE (1) [LONG]

Eze	45: 7	running l from the western to	802

LENGTHY (2) [LONG]

Mk	12:40	and for a show make l prayers.	3431
Lk	20:47	and for a show make l prayers.	3431

LENT (1) [LEND]

Jer	15:10	I have neither l nor borrowed,	5957

LENTIL (1) [LENTILS]

Ge	25:34	gave Esau some bread and some l stew.	6378

LENTILS (3) [LENTIL]

2Sa	17:28	flour and roasted grain, beans and l,	6378
	23:11	at a place where there was a field full of l,	6378
Eze	4: 9	"Take wheat and barley, beans and l,	6378

LEOPARD (6) [LEOPARDS]

Isa	11: 6	the l will lie down with the goat,	5807
Jer	5: 6	a l will lie in wait near their towns to tear	5807
	13:23	or the l its spots?	5807
Da	7: 6	one that looked like a l.	10480
Hos	13: 7	like a l I will lurk by the path.	5807
Rev	13: 2	The beast I saw resembled a l,	4203

LEOPARDS (2) [LEOPARD]

SS	4: 8	and the mountain haunts of the l.	5807
Hab	1: 8	Their horses are swifter than l,	5807

LEPER (2) [LEPROSY]

Mt	26: 6	the home of a man known as Simon the L,	3320
Mk	14: 3	the home of a man known as Simon the L,	3320

LEPROSY (26) [LEPER, LEPROUS]

Nu	12:10	toward her and saw that she had l;	7665
2Sa	3:29	or l or who leans on a crutch or who falls	7665
2Ki	5: 1	He was a valiant soldier, but he had l.	7665
	5: 3	He would cure him of his l."	7669
	5: 6	to you so that you may cure him of his l."	7669
	5: 7	to me to cure me of his l?	7669
	5:11	over the spot and cure me of my l.	7665
	5:27	Naaman's l will cling to you and	7669
	7: 3	with l at the entrance of the city gate.	7665
	7: 8	The men who had l reached the edge of	7665
	15: 5	The LORD afflicted the king with l until	7665
2Ch	26:19	l broke out on his forehead.	7669
	26:20	they saw that he had l on his forehead,	7665
	26:21	King Uzziah had l until the day he died.	7665
	26:23	for people said, "He had l."	7665
Mt	8: 2	A man with l came and knelt before him	3320
	8: 3	Immediately he was cured of his l.	3319
	10: 8	cleanse those who have l, drive out demons	3320
	11: 5	the lame walk, those who have l are cured,	3320
Mk	1:40	A man with l came to him and begged him	3320
	1:42	the l left him and he was cured.	3319
Lk	4:27	And there were many in Israel with l in	3320
	5:12	along who was covered with l.	3319
	5:13	And immediately the l left him.	3319
	7:22	the lame walk, those who have l are cured,	3320
	17:12	ten men who had l met him.	3320

LEPROUS (5) [LEPROSY]

Ex	4: 6	and when he took it out, it was l,	7665
Nu	12:10	there stood Miriam—l,	7665
Dt	24: 8	of l diseases be very careful to do exactly	7669
2Ki	7: 3	from Elisha's presence and he was l,	7665
2Ch	26:21	He lived in a separate house—l,	7665

LESHEM (2) [DAN]

Jos	19:47	so they went up and attacked L, took it,	4386
	19:47	They settled in L and named it Dan	4386

LESS (23) [LEAST, LESSER]

Ge	18:28	number of the righteous is five l than	2893
Ex	30:15	the poor are not to give l when you make	5070
Nu	11:32	No one gathered l than ten homers.	5070
1Ki	8:27	How much l this temple I have built!	677+3954
1Ch	27:23	of the men twenty years old or l,	4752
2Ch	6:18	How much l this temple I have built!	677+3954
	32:15	How much l will your god deliver you	677+3954+4202
Ezr	9:13	you have punished us l than our sins have deserved	3104+4200+4752
Job	15:16	how much l man, who is vile and	677+3954
	25: 6	how much l man, who is but a maggot—677+3954
	35:14	How much l, then, will he listen	677+3954
Ecc	6:11	more the words, the l the meaning,	2039+8049
Isa	40:17	by him as worthless and l than nothing.	4946
	41:24	But you are l than nothing	4946

Eze	15: 5	how much l can it be made into	677+3954
Jn	3:30	He must become greater; I must become l.	1783
	11:18	Bethany was l than two miles from Jerusalem	NIG
1Co	12:23	parts that we think are l honorable we treat	872
2Co	12:15	If I love you more, will you love me l?	2482
Eph	3: 8	I am l than the least of all God's people,	AIT
Php	2:28	be glad and I may have l anxiety.	267
1Ti	6: 2	not to show l respect for them	2969
Heb	12:25	how much l will we, if we turn away	3437

LESSER (3) [LESS]

Ge	1:16	to govern the day and the l light to govern	7785
Isa	22:24	all its l vessels, from the bowls to all the	7783
Heb	7: 7	And without doubt the l person is blessed	1781

LESSON (6)

Jdg	8:16	taught the men of Succoth a l	3359
1Sa	14:12	"Come up to us and we'll teach you a l."	1821
Pr	24:32	to what I observed and learned a l	4592
Jer	35:13	people of Jerusalem, 'Will you not learn a l	4592
Mt	24:32	"Now learn this l from the fig tree:	4130
Mk	13:28	"Now learn this l from the fig tree:	4130

LEST (10)

Ex	20:26	l your nakedness be exposed on it.'	889+4202
Dt	32:27	l the adversary misunderstand and say,	7153
2Sa	1:20	l the daughters of the Philistines be glad,	7153
	1:20	l the daughters of the uncircumcised rejoice.	7153
Ps	2:12	l he be angry and you be destroyed	7153
Pr	5: 9	l you give your best strength to others	7153
	5:10	l strangers feast on your wealth	7153
	31: 5	l they drink and forget what	7153
Jer	10:24	in your anger, l you reduce me to nothing.	7153
1Co	1:17	human wisdom, l the cross of Christ	2671+3590

LET (1045) [LET'S, LETS, LETTING]

Ge	1: 3	And God said, "L there be light,"	AIT
	1: 6	"L there be an expanse between the waters	AIT
	1: 9	"L the water under the sky be gathered	AIT
	1: 9	and l dry ground appear."	AIT
	1:11	God said, "L the land produce vegetation:	AIT
	1:14	"L there be lights in the expanse of the sky	AIT
	1:14	and l them serve as signs to mark seasons	AIT
	1:15	and l them be lights in the expanse of	AIT
	1:20	"L the water teem with living creatures,	AIT
	1:20	and l birds fly above the earth across	AIT
	1:22	and l the birds increase on the earth."	AIT
	1:24	"L the land produce living creatures	AIT
	1:26	God said, "L us make man in our image,	AIT
	1:26	and l them rule over the fish of the sea and	AIT
	11: 4	"Come, l us build ourselves a city,	AIT
	11: 7	l us go down and confuse their language	AIT
	12:12	they will kill me but will l you live.	2649
	14:24	L them have their share."	AIT
	18: 4	L a little water be brought,	AIT
	18: 5	L me get you something to eat,	AIT
	18:30	"May the Lord not be angry, but l me speak.	AIT
	18:32	but l me speak just once more.	AIT
	19: 8	L me bring them out	AIT
	19:20	L me flee to it—it is very small, isn't it?	AIT
	20: 6	That is why I did not l you touch her.	5989
	23: 8	"If you are willing to l me bury my dead,	AIT
	24:14	'Please l down your jar that I may have	5742
	24:14	l her be the one you have chosen	NIH
	24:43	to her, "Please l me drink a little water	9197
	24:44	l her be the one the LORD has chosen	NIH
	24:51	l her become the wife of your master's son,	AIT
	24:55	"L the girl remain with us ten days or so;	AIT
	25:30	"Quick, l me have some of that red stew!	4358
	26:28	L us make a treaty with you	AIT
	27:13	"My son, l the curse fall on me.	NIH
	30:32	L me go through all your flocks today	AIT
	30:34	"L it be as you have said.	4273
	31:28	even l me kiss my grandchildren	5759
	31:37	and l them judge between the two of us.	AIT
	31:44	and l it serve as a witness between us."	AIT
	32:26	man said, "L me go, for it is daybreak."	8938
	32:26	"I will not l you go unless you bless me."	8938
	33:12	"L us be on our way;	AIT
	33:14	l my lord go on ahead of his servant,	AIT
	33:15	l me leave some of my men with you."	AIT
	33:15	"Just l me find favor in the eyes	AIT
	34:11	"L me find favor in your eyes,	AIT
	34:21	"L them live in our land and trade in it;	AIT
	34:23	l us give our consent to them,	AIT
	35: 3	Then come, l us go up to Bethel,	AIT
	38:16	"Come now, l me sleep with you."	AIT
	38:23	Then Judah said, "L her keep what she has,	AIT
	41:33	"And now l Pharaoh look for a discerning	AIT
	41:34	L Pharaoh appoint commissioners over	AIT
	42:19	l one of your brothers stay here in prison,	AIT
	43:14	l your other brother and Benjamin come back with you.	AIT
	44:10	then," he said, "l it be as you say.	2085+4027
	44:18	l your servant speak a word to my lord.	AIT
	44:33	please l your servant remain here	AIT
	44:33	and l the boy return with his brothers.	AIT
	44:34	Do not l me see the misery that would come	AIT
	47: 4	l your servants settle in Goshen."	AIT
	47: 6	L them live in Goshen.	AIT
	49: 6	L me not enter their council,	AIT
	49: 6	l me not join their assembly,	AIT
	49:26	L all these rest on the head of Joseph,	AIT
	50: 5	Now l me go up and bury my father;	AIT

Ex
1:16 but if it is a girl, l her **live."** AIT
1:17 *they* l the boys **live.** 2649
1:18 Why *have you* l the boys **live?"** 2649
1:22 but l every girl **live."** 2649
3:18 *L us* **take** a three-day journey into AIT
3:19 the king of Egypt *will* not l you go unless 5989
3:20 After that, *he will* l you **go.** 8938
4:18 "*L me* **go** back to my own people in Egypt AIT
4:21 so that *he will* not l the people **go.** 8938
4:23 "*L my* son **go,** so he may worship me." 8938
4:23 But you refused to l him **go;** 8938
4:26 So the LORD l him **alone.** 8332
5: 1 '**L my** people **go,** 8938
5: 2 that I should obey him and l Israel **go?** 8938
5: 2 the LORD and *I will* not l Israel **go.** 8938
5: 3 Now *l us* **take** a three-day journey into AIT
5: 7 l them **go** and gather their own straw. AIT
5: 8 '*L us* **go** and sacrifice to our God.' AIT
5:17 '*L us* **go** and sacrifice to the LORD.' AIT
6: 1 of my mighty hand *he will* l them go 8938
6:11 to l the Israelites **go** out of his country." 8938
7: 2 to tell Pharaoh to l the Israelites **go** out 8938
7:14 he refuses to l the people **go.** 8938
7:16 **L** my people **go,** 8938
8: 1 **L** my people **go,** 8938
8: 2 If you refuse to l them **go,** 8938
8: 8 and *I will* l your people **go** 8938
8:20 **L** my people **go,** 8938
8:21 If you *do* not l my people **go,** 8938
8:28 "I will l you **go** to offer sacrifices to 8938
8:32 and *would* not l the people **go.** 8938
9: 1 "**L** my people **go,** 8938
9: 2 If you refuse to l them **go** and continue 8938
9: 7 and *he would* not l the people **go.** 8938
9:13 **L** my people **go,** 8938
9:17 and *will* not l them **go.** 8938
9:28 *I will* l you **go;** 8938
9:35 and *he would* not l the Israelites **go,** 8938
10: 3 **L** my people **go,** 8938
10: 4 If you refuse to l them **go,** 8938
10: 7 **L** the people **go,** 8938
10:10 if *I* l you **go,** 8938
10:20 and *he would* not l the Israelites **go.** 8938
10:27 and he was not willing to l them **go.** 8938
11: 1 After that, *he will* l you **go** from here, 8938
11:10 not l the Israelites **go** out of his country. 8938
13:15 Pharaoh stubbornly refused to l us **go,** 8938
13:17 When Pharaoh l the people **go,** 8938
14: 5 *We have* l the Israelites **go** 8938
14:12 *l us* **serve** the Egyptians'? AIT
21: 8 he must l her **be redeemed.** 7009
21:26 he must l the servant **go free** 8938
21:27 he must l the servant **go free** 8938
22:30 **L** them **stay** with their mothers AIT
23:11 l the land **lie unplowed** AIT
23:13 *do* not l them **be heard** on your lips. AIT
23:33 *Do* not l them **live** in your land, AIT
32:25 Aaron had l them **get out of control** AIT
33:12 not l me **know** whom you will send 3359
34: 9 he said, "then l the Lord go with us. AIT
34:25 not l *any* of the sacrifice from the Passover
Feast **remain** AIT

Lev
10: 6 "*Do* not l your hair *become* **unkempt,** AIT
13:45 l his hair **be unkempt,** AIT
21:10 l his hair *become* **unkempt** AIT

Nu
6: 5 l the hair of his head **grow long.** AIT
11:15 and *do* not l *me* **face** my own ruin." AIT
12:12 *Do* not l *her* be like a stillborn infant AIT
14: 3 to this land only to l *us* **fall** by AIT
16:38 **L** them **be** a sign to the Israelites." AIT
20:17 Please l *us* **pass** through your country. AIT
20:21 to l them go through their territory, 5989
21:22 "*L us* **pass** through your country. AIT
21:23 not l Israel pass through his territory. 5989
21:27 "Come to Heshbon and l *it* **be rebuilt;** AIT
21:27 l Sihon's city **be restored.** AIT
22:13 LORD has refused to l me go with you." 5989
22:16 *Do* not l *anything* **keep** *you* from coming AIT
23:10 **L** me **die** the death of the righteous, AIT
23:27 "Come, l *me* **take** you to another place. AIT
23:27 to l *you* **curse** them for me from there." AIT
24:14 l *me* **warn** you of what this people will do AIT
32: 5 "*l* this land **be given** AIT

Dt
1:22 "*L us* **send** men ahead to spy out the land AIT
2:27 "*L us* **pass** through your country. AIT
2:28 Only l *us* **pass through** on foot— AIT
2:30 of Heshbon refused to l us **pass** through. 6296
3:25 **L** me **go over** and see the good land beyond AIT
4: 9 or l *them* **slip** from your heart as long AIT
9:14 **L** me **alone,** so that I may destroy them 8332
13: 2 "*L us* **follow** other gods" (gods you have AIT
13: 2 not known) "and *l us* **worship** them," AIT
13: 6 "*L us* **go** and worship other gods" (gods AIT
13:13 astray, saying, "*L us* **go** and worship other AIT
15:12 the seventh year *you must* l him **go free.** 8938
16: 4 **L** no yeast **be found** AIT
16: 4 not l *any* of the meat you sacrifice on the
evening of the first day **remain** AIT
17:14 "*L us* **set** a king over us like all the nations AIT
18:10 **L** no *one* **be found** among you who AIT
18:16 "*L us* not **hear** the voice of the LORD AIT
20: 5 **L** him **go** home, or he may die in battle AIT
20: 7 **L** him **go** home, or he may die in battle AIT
20: 8 l him **go** home so that his brothers will not AIT
21:14 l her **go** wherever she wishes. 8938
22: 7 **be sure to** l the mother **go,** 8938+8938

Dt
23:16 *L* him **live** among you wherever he likes AIT
24:11 l the man to whom you are making the loan
bring the pledge **out** AIT
32: 2 **L** my teaching **fall** like rain AIT
32:38 *L them* **rise up** to help you! AIT
32:38 *L them* **give** you **shelter!** AIT
33: 6 "**L** Reuben **live** and not die, AIT
33:12 "**L** the beloved of the LORD **rest** AIT
33:16 *L all* these **rest** on the head of Joseph, AIT
33:24 l him **be** favored by his brothers, AIT
33:24 and l him **bathe** his feet in oil. AIT
34: 4 I have l you **see** it with your eyes, 8011

Jos
1: 8 *Do* not l this Book of the Law **depart** AIT
2:15 So *she* l them **down** by a rope through 3718
2:18 the window through which *you* l us **down,** 3718
2:21 "**L** it be as you say." NIH
8:15 l themselves **be driven back** before them, 5595
9:15 of peace with them to l them **live,** 2649
9:20 *We will* l them **live,** 2649
9:21 They continued, "**L** them **live,** AIT
9:21 but l them **be** woodcutters AIT
10:19 the rear and don't l them reach their cities, 5989
22:22 And l Israel **know!** AIT
22:26 '*L us* **get ready** and build an altar— AIT

Jdg
6:32 saying, "**L** Baal **contend** with him," AIT
6:39 *L me* **make** just one more **request.** AIT
7: 7 **L** all the other men **go,** AIT
9:15 if not, then l fire **come out** of the thornbush AIT
9:20 l fire **come out** from Abimelech AIT
9:20 and l fire **come out** from you, AIT
10:14 **L** them **save** you when you are in trouble!" AIT
11:19 '*L us* **pass** through your country AIT
11:27 **L** the LORD, the Judge, **decide** *the* **dispute** AIT
11:38 And *he* l her **go** for two months. 8938
12: 5 "*L me* **cross over,**" AIT
13: 8 l the man of God you sent to us **come** AIT
14:12 "*L me* **tell** you a riddle," AIT
15: 1 But her father *would* not l him go in. 5989
15: 5 and l the foxes loose in the standing grain 8938
16:28 l *me* with one blow **get revenge** AIT
16:30 "*L me* **die** with the Philistines!" AIT
19:20 "**L** me **supply** whatever you need. NIH
19:25 and at dawn *they* l her **go.** 8938

Ru
2: 2 "*L me* **go** to the fields and pick up AIT
2: 7 'Please l *me* **glean** and gather among AIT
3: 3 but don't l him **know** *you* are there 3359
3:13 to l him, good; l him **redeem.** AIT
3:14 "Don't l *it* **be known** that a woman came to AIT

1Sa
2: 3 or l *your* mouth **speak** such arrogance, AIT
2:16 "**L** the fat **be burned up** AIT
2:18 l him **do** what is good in his eyes." AIT
2:19 l *none* of his words **fall** to the ground. 5877
4: 3 *L us* **bring** the ark of the LORD's AIT
5:11 l it **go back** to its own place, AIT
8: 9 and l them **know** what the king 5583
9: 9 he would say, "Come, l *us* **go** to the seer," AIT
9:19 and in the morning *I will* l you **go** 8938
11:14 l *us* **go** to Gilgal and there reaffirm AIT
13: 3 "**L** the Hebrews **hear!**" AIT
14: 8 over toward the men and l them **see** *us.* 1655
14:36 "*L us* **go down** after the Philistines by night AIT
14:36 l *us* not **leave** one of them alive. AIT
14:36 the priest said, "*L us* **inquire** of God here." AIT
14:38 l *us* **find out** what sin has been committed AIT
15:16 "*L me* **tell** you what the LORD said AIT
16:16 **L** our lord **command** his servants here AIT
17:10 Give me a man and l *us* **fight** each other." AIT
17:32 "*L* no *one* **lose** heart on account AIT
18: 2 not l him return to his father's house. 5989
18:17 **L** the Philistines **do that!**" AIT
19: 4 "**L** not the king **do wrong** AIT
19:12 Michal l David **down** through a window, 3718
19:17 He said to me, '**L** me **get away,** 8938
20: 5 but l me **go** and hide in the field until 8938
20:12 send you word and l you **know?** 265+906+1655
20:13 if *I do* not l you **know** and 265+906+1655
20:29 He said, '**L** me **go,** 8938
20:29 l *me* **get away** to see my brothers.' 4880
22: 3 l *my* father and mother **come** AIT
22:15 **L** not the king **accuse** your servant AIT
24:19 his enemy, *does he* l him **get away**
unharmed? 928+2006+8938
25:24 "My lord, l the blame be on me alone. NIH
25:24 Please l *your* servant **speak** to you; AIT
25:27 l this gift, which your servant has brought
to my master, **be given** AIT
25:28 **L** no wrongdoing **be found** AIT
26: 8 Now l *me* **pin** him to the ground AIT
26:19 l my lord the king **listen** AIT
26:20 not l my blood **fall** to the ground far AIT
26:22 "**L** one of your young men **come over** AIT
27: 5 l a place be **assigned** AIT
28:22 and l *me* **give** you some food AIT

2Sa
2:14 "**All right,** l them **do it,**" AIT
3:21 l *me* **go** at once and assemble all Israel AIT
3:24 Why *did you* l him **go?** 8938
10:12 and l *us* **fight bravely** for our people and AIT
11:25 'Don't l this **upset** you; AIT
12:22 be gracious to me and l the child **live.'** AIT
13: 5 l her **prepare** the food in my sight AIT
13:26 l my brother Amnon **come** AIT
14: 9 l the blame rest on me and NIH
14: 9 l the king and his throne be without guilt." NIH
14:11 "Then l the king **invoke** AIT
14:12 l *your* servant **speak** a word to my lord AIT
14:18 "*L* my lord the king **speak,**" AIT
14:32 l him **put me** to death." AIT

2Sa
15: 7 "*L me* **go** to Hebron and fulfill a vow AIT
15:25 he will bring me back and l me **see** it 8011
15:26 l him **do** to me whatever seems good AIT
16: 9 *L me* **go over** and cut off his head." AIT
16:11 Leave him alone; l him **curse,** AIT
17:11 *L* all Israel, from Dan to Beersheba—as
numerous as the sand on the seashore—**be
gathered** AIT
18:19 "*L me* **run** and take the news to the king AIT
18:22 please l me **run** behind the Cushite." AIT
19:30 "*L* him **take** everything, AIT
19:37 *L* your servant **return,** AIT
19:37 *L* him **cross over** with my lord the king. AIT
20:11 l him follow Joab!" NIH
21: 6 l seven of his male descendants **be given** AIT
21:10 not l the birds of the air touch them 5989
24:14 *L us* **fall** into the hands of the LORD, AIT
24:14 *do* not l *me* **fall** into the hands of men." AIT
24:17 *L* your hand **fall** upon me AIT
24:22 *L* my lord the king **take** AIT

1Ki
1: 2 "*L us* **look for** a young virgin to attend AIT
1:12 *l me* **advise** you how you can save your own AIT
1:51 '*L* King Solomon **swear** to me AIT
2: 6 l his gray head **go down** 3718
2: 7 the sons of Barzillai of Gilead and l them **be** AIT
2:21 "*L* Abishag the Shunammite **be given in
marriage** AIT
8:26 l your word that you promised your servant
David my father **come true.** AIT
11:21 Then Hadad said to Pharaoh, "**L** me **go,** 8938
11:22 Hadad replied, "but *do* l me **go!**" 8938+8938
15:19 "**L** there be a treaty between me and you," NIH
18:23 l them **choose** one for themselves, AIT
18:23 l them **cut** it **into pieces** AIT
18:36 l *it* **be known** today that you are God AIT
18:40 *Don't* l anyone **get away!**" 4880
19:20 "*L me* **kiss** my father and mother **good-by,**" AIT
20:31 *L us* **go** to the king of Israel AIT
20:32 '*Please* l me **live.'** AIT
20:34 he made a treaty with him, and l him **go.** 8938
21: 2 "*L me* **have** your vineyard to use for 5989
22:13 *L* your word **agree** with theirs, AIT
22:17 *L* each one go home in peace.' " AIT
22:49 "*L* my men **sail** with your men," AIT

2Ki
2: 9 *L* me **inherit** a double portion of your spirit, AIT
2:16 *L* them **go** and look for your master. AIT
5:17 l *me,* your servant, **be given** as much AIT
6: 2 *L us* **go** to the Jordan, AIT
6: 2 l *us* **build** a place there for us to live." AIT
7:13 l *us* **send** them to find out what happened." AIT
9:15 *don't* l anyone **slip out** of the city to go AIT
10:25 l no one **escape.**" AIT
12: 5 **L** every priest **receive** the money AIT
12: 5 l *it* **be used to repair** whatever damage AIT
18:29 *Do* not l Hezekiah **deceive** you. 5958
18:30 *Do* not l Hezekiah **persuade** you to trust 1053
19:10 *Do* not l the god you depend on **deceive** 5958
23:18 "*Don't* l anyone **disturb** his bones." AIT

1Ch
4:10 l your hand **be** with me, AIT
13: 2 l *us* **send word** far and wide to the rest AIT
13: 3 *L us* **bring** the ark of our God **back** AIT
16:10 l the hearts of those who seek the LORD
rejoice. AIT
16:31 **L** the heavens **rejoice,** AIT
16:31 l the earth *be* **glad;** AIT
16:31 l *them* **say** among the nations, AIT
16:32 **L** the sea **resound,** and all that is in it; AIT
16:32 l the fields *be* **jubilant,** AIT
17:23 l the promise you have made concerning
your servant and his house **be established** AIT
19:13 and l *us* **fight bravely** for our people and AIT
21:13 **L** me **fall** into the hands of the LORD, AIT
21:13 *do* not l *me* **fall** into the hands of men." AIT
21:17 l your hand **fall** upon me and my family, AIT
21:17 but *do* not l this plague remain on your
people." NIH
21:22 "*L me* **have** the site of your threshing floor AIT
21:23 *L* my lord the king **do** whatever pleases AIT

2Ch
1: 9 l your promise to my father David **be
confirmed,** AIT
2:15 "Now l my lord **send** his servants the wheat AIT
6:17 l your word that you promised your servant
David **come true.** AIT
14: 7 "*L us* **build up** these towns," AIT
14:11 *do* not l *man* **prevail** against you." AIT
16: 3 "**L** there be a treaty between me and you," NIH
18:12 *L* your word **agree** with theirs, AIT
18:16 *L* each one go home in peace.' " AIT
19: 7 l the fear of the LORD *be* upon you. AIT
32:11 l *you* die of hunger and thirst. 5989
32:15 Now *do* not l Hezekiah **deceive** you AIT
36:23 his God be with him, and l him **go up.'** " AIT

Ezr
1: 3 may his God be with him, and l him **go up** AIT
4: 2 "*L us* **help** you **build** AIT
4:22 Why l this threat **grow,** AIT
5:17 l *a* **search be made** in the royal archives AIT
5:17 Then l the king **send** us his decision AIT
6: 3 l the temple **be rebuilt** AIT
6: 3 l its foundations **be laid.** AIT
6: 7 **L** the governor of the Jews and the Jewish
elders **rebuild** AIT
6:12 *L it* **be carried out** with diligence. AIT
7:23 l it **be done** with diligence for the temple AIT
10: 3 Now l *us* **make** a covenant before our God AIT
10: 3 *L it* **be done** according to the Law. AIT
10:14 **L** our officials **act** for the whole assembly. AIT

Ezr	10:14	*l* everyone in our towns who has married a foreign woman **come** at a set time,	AIT
Ne	1: 6	*l* your ear **be attentive** and your eyes open	AIT
	1:11	*l* your ear **be** attentive to the prayer	AIT
	2: 5	*l* him **send** me to the city in Judah	AIT
	2:17	Come, *l us* **rebuild** the wall of Jerusalem,	AIT
	2:18	They replied, "*L us* **start** rebuilding."	AIT
	5:10	*l* the exacting of usury **stop!**	AIT
	6: 2	*l us* **meet** together in one of the villages on	AIT
	6: 7	so come, *l us* **confer** together."	AIT
	6:10	He said, "*L us* **meet** in the house of God,	AIT
	6:10	and *l us* **close** the temple doors,	AIT
	9:32	do not *l* all this hardship *seem* **trifling**	AIT
Est	1:19	*l* him **issue** a royal decree and let it	AIT
	1:19	and *l it* **be written** in the laws of Persia	AIT
	1:19	Also *l* the king **give** her royal position	AIT
	2: 2	"*L* a **search be made for** beautiful young	AIT
	2: 3	*L* the king **appoint** commissioners	AIT
	2: 3	*l* them **be placed** under the care of Hegai,	NIH
	2: 3	*l* beauty treatments **be given**	AIT
	2: 4	*l* the girl who pleases the king **be queen**	AIT
	3: 9	*l* a **decree be issued** to destroy them,	AIT
	5: 4	"*l* the king, together with Haman, **come**	AIT
	5: 8	*l* the king and Haman **come**	AIT
	6: 9	*l* the robe and horse **be entrusted**	AIT
	6: 9	*L* them **robe** the man the king delights	AIT
	8: 5	*l* an **order be written** overruling	AIT
	9:13	*l* Haman's ten sons **be hanged**	AIT
Job	6: 9	to *l* **loose** his hand and cut me off!	6000
	7:16	**L** me **alone**; my days have no meaning.	2532
	7:19	or *l* me **alone** even for an instant?	8332
	9:18	He would not *l* me regain my breath	5989
	10:14	and *would* not *l* my offense **go unpunished.**	5927
	12: 8	*l* the fish of the sea **inform** you.	AIT
	13:13	"Keep silent and *l* me **speak;**	AIT
	13:13	then *l* **come** to me what may.	AIT
	13:17	**l** your ears take in what I say.	NIH
	13:22	or *l* me **speak**, and you reply.	AIT
	14: 6	So look away from him and *l* him **alone,**	2532
	15:17	*l* me **tell** you what I have seen,	AIT
	15:31	*L* him not **deceive** himself	AIT
	17: 4	therefore *you will* not *l* them **triumph.**	8123
	20:13	to *l* it **go** and keeps it in his mouth,	AIT
	21: 2	*l* this **be** the consolation you give me.	AIT
	21:19	*L* him **repay** the man himself,	AIT
	21:20	*L* his own eyes **see** his destruction.	AIT
	21:20	*l* him **drink** of the wrath of the Almighty.	AIT
	24:23	He may *l* them rest in a feeling of security,	5989
	27: 6	and never *l* **go** of it;	8332
	31: 6	*l* God **weigh** me in honest scales	AIT
	31:16	*l* the eyes of the widow **grow weary,**	AIT
	31:22	then *l* my arm **fall** from the shoulder,	AIT
	31:22	*l* it **be broken off** at the joint.	AIT
	31:35	*l* the Almighty **answer**	AIT
	31:35	*l* my accuser **put** *his* indictment **in writing.**	AIT
	31:40	then *l* **briers come up** instead of wheat	AIT
	32:13	*l* God **refute** him, not man.'	AIT
	34: 4	*L us* **discern** for ourselves what is right;	AIT
	34: 4	*l us* **learn** together what is good.	AIT
	36:18	*l* a large bribe **turn** you **aside.**	AIT
	39: 5	"Who *l* the wild donkey **go free?**	8938
	40: 2	*L* him who accuses God **answer**	AIT
Ps	2: 3	"*L us* **break** their chains," they say,	AIT
	4: 6	*L* the light of your face **shine**	5951
	5:10	*L* their intrigues **be** their **downfall.**	AIT
	5:11	*l* all who take refuge in you **be glad;**	AIT
	5:11	*l* them ever **sing for joy.**	AIT
	7: 5	then *l* my enemy **pursue** and overtake me;	AIT
	7: 5	*l* him **trample** my life to the ground	AIT
	7: 7	*L* the assembled peoples **gather around**	AIT
	7: 8	*l* the LORD **judge** the peoples.	AIT
	9:19	Arise, O LORD, *l* not man **triumph;**	AIT
	9:19	*l* the nations **be judged**	AIT
	9:20	*l* the nations **know** they are but men.	AIT
	14: 7	*l* Jacob **rejoice** and Israel be glad!	AIT
	16:10	nor *will you l* your Holy One see decay.	5989
	22: 8	*l* the LORD **rescue** him.	AIT
	22: 8	*L* him **deliver** him,	AIT
	25: 2	*l* me be **put to shame,**	AIT
	25: 2	nor *l* my enemies **triumph** over me.	AIT
	25:20	*l* me not be **put to shame,**	AIT
	30: 1	and *did* not *l* my enemies **gloat**	8523
	31: 1	*l* me never be **put to shame,**	AIT
	31:16	*L* your face **shine** on your servant;	AIT
	31:17	*L* me not be **put to shame,**	AIT
	31:17	*l* the wicked *be* **put to shame**	AIT
	31:18	*L* their lying lips **be silenced,**	AIT
	32: 6	*l* everyone who is godly **pray**	AIT
	33: 8	*L* all the earth **fear** the LORD;	AIT
	33: 8	*l* all the people of the world **revere** him.	AIT
	34: 2	*l* the afflicted **hear** and rejoice.	AIT
	34: 3	*l us* **exalt** his name together.	AIT
	35:19	*L* not *those* who **gloat** over me	AIT
	35:19	*l* not those who hate me without reason **maliciously wink**	AIT
	35:24	*do* not *l* them **gloat** over me.	AIT
	35:25	Do not *l* them **think**, "Aha,	AIT
	37:33	in their power or *l* them be **condemned**	8399
	38:16	"Do not *l* them **gloat** or exalt themselves	AIT
	39: 4	*l* me **know** how fleeting my life is.	AIT
	43: 3	and your truth, *l* them **guide** me;	AIT
	43: 3	*l* them **bring** me to your holy mountain,	AIT
	45: 4	*l* your right hand **display** awesome deeds.	AIT
	45: 5	*L* your sharp arrows pierce the hearts of	NIH
	45: 5	*l* the nations **fall** beneath your feet.	AIT
	51: 8	*L* me **hear** joy and gladness;	9048
	51: 8	*l* the bones you have crushed **rejoice.**	AIT

Ps	53: 6	*l* Jacob **rejoice** and Israel be glad!	AIT
	54: 5	*L* evil **recoil** on those who slander me;	AIT
	55:15	*L* death **take** my enemies **by surprise;**	AIT
	55:15	*l* them **go down** alive *to* the grave,	AIT
	55:22	he will never *l* the righteous fall.	5989
	56: 7	On no account *l* them **escape;**	7117
	57: 5	*l* your glory be over all the earth.	NIH
	57:11	*l* your glory be over all the earth.	NIH
	58: 7	*L* them **vanish** like water that flows away;	AIT
	58: 7	*l* their arrows **be blunted.**	AIT
	59:10	before me and *will l* me **gloat**	8011
	59:12	*l* them **be caught** in their pride.	AIT
	64:10	*L* the righteous **rejoice**	AIT
	64:10	*l* all the upright in heart **praise**	AIT
	66: 6	come, *l us* **rejoice** in him.	AIT
	66: 7	*l* not the rebellious **rise up**	AIT
	66: 8	*l* the sound of his praise **be heard;**	9048
	66:12	You *l* men **ride** over our heads;	8206
	66:16	*l* me **tell** you what he has done for me.	AIT
	69:14	Rescue me from the mire, *do* not *l* me **sink;**	AIT
	69:15	Do not *l* the floodwaters **engulf** me	AIT
	69:24	*l* your fierce anger **overtake** them.	AIT
	69:25	*l* there **be** no one to dwell in their tents.	AIT
	69:27	do not *l* them **share** in your salvation.	AIT
	69:34	*L* heaven and earth **praise** him,	AIT
	70: 4	"*L* God **be exalted!**"	AIT
	71: 1	*l* me never be **put to shame.**	AIT
	72:16	*L* grain **abound** throughout the land;	AIT
	72:16	*L* its fruit **flourish** like Lebanon;	AIT
	72:16	*l it* **thrive** like the grass of the field.	AIT
	74:21	*l* the oppressed **retreat** in disgrace;	AIT
	76:11	*l* all the neighboring lands **bring** gifts	AIT
	78:26	He *l* loose the east wind from the heavens	5825
	80:17	*L* your hand **rest** on the man at your right	AIT
	83: 4	they say, "*l us* **destroy** them as a nation,	AIT
	83:12	"*L us* **take possession** of the pasturelands	AIT
	83:18	*L* them **know** that you,	AIT
	85: 8	but *l* them not **return** to folly.	AIT
	95: 1	*l us* **sing for joy**	AIT
	95: 1	*l us* **shout aloud** to the Rock	AIT
	95: 2	*L us* **come** before him with thanksgiving	AIT
	95: 6	Come, *l us* **bow down** in worship,	AIT
	95: 6	*l us* **kneel** before the LORD our Maker;	AIT
	96:11	*L* the heavens **rejoice,**	AIT
	96:11	*l* the earth **be glad;**	AIT
	96:11	*l* the sea **resound,** and all that is in it;	AIT
	96:12	*l* the fields **be jubilant,**	AIT
	97: 1	*l* the earth **be glad;**	AIT
	97: 1	*l* the distant shores **rejoice.**	AIT
	97:10	*L* those who **love** the LORD hate evil,	AIT
	98: 7	*L* the sea **resound,** and everything in it,	AIT
	98: 8	*L* the rivers **clap** their hands,	AIT
	98: 8	*l* the mountains **sing** together **for joy;**	AIT
	98: 9	*l* them sing before the LORD,	NIH
	99: 1	*l* the nations **tremble;**	AIT
	99: 1	between the cherubim, *l* the earth **shake.**	AIT
	99: 3	*L* them **praise** your great and awesome name	AIT
	102: 1	*l* my cry for help **come** to you.	AIT
	102:18	*L* this **be written** for a future generation,	AIT
	105: 3	*l* the hearts of those who seek the LORD **rejoice.**	AIT
	106:48	*L* all the people **say,**	AIT
	107: 2	*L* the redeemed of the LORD **say**	AIT
	107: 8	*L* them **give thanks** to the LORD	AIT
	107:15	*L* them **give thanks** to the LORD	AIT
	107:21	*L* them **give thanks** to the LORD	AIT
	107:22	*L* them **sacrifice** thank offerings and tell	AIT
	107:31	*L* them **give thanks** to the LORD	AIT
	107:32	*L* them **exalt** him in the assembly of	AIT
	107:38	and *he did* not *l* their herds **diminish.**	5070
	107:43	*l* him **heed** these things and consider	AIT
	108: 5	and *l* your glory be over all the earth.	NIH
	109: 6	*l* an accuser **stand** at his right hand.	AIT
	109: 7	When he is tried, *l* him be **found** guilty,	AIT
	109:27	*L* them **know** that it is your hand, that you,	AIT
	113: 2	*L* the name of the LORD **be praised,**	AIT
	118: 2	*L* Israel **say:** "His love endures forever."	AIT
	118: 3	*L* the house of Aaron **say:**	AIT
	118: 4	*L* those who fear the LORD **say:**	AIT
	118:24	*l us* **rejoice** and be glad in it.	AIT
	119:10	do not *l* me **stray** from your commands.	8706
	119:27	*L* me **understand** the teaching	1067
	119:31	do not *l* me be **put to shame.**	1017
	119:77	*L* your compassion **come** to me	AIT
	119:116	do not *l* my hopes **be dashed.**	1017
	119:122	*l* not the arrogant **oppress**	AIT
	119:133	*l* no sin **rule** over me.	8948
	119:175	*L* me **live** that I may praise you,	AIT
	121: 3	He will not *l* your foot slip—	5989
	122: 1	"*L us* **go** *to* the house of the LORD."	AIT
	124: 1	on our side—*l* Israel **say—**	AIT
	124: 6	who *has* not *l us* be torn by their teeth.	5989
	129: 1	from my youth—*l* Israel **say—**	AIT
	130: 2	*L* your ears **be** attentive to my cry	AIT
	132: 7	"*L us* **go** to his dwelling place;	AIT
	132: 7	*l us* **worship** at his footstool—	AIT
	140: 8	do not *l* their plans **succeed,**	7049
	140: 9	*L* the heads of those who surround me *be* **covered** with the trouble	AIT
	140:10	*L* burning coals **fall** upon them;	4572
	140:11	*L* slanderers not **be established** in the land;	AIT
	141: 4	*L* not my heart **be drawn** to what is evil,	5742
	141: 4	*l* me not **eat** of their delicacies.	AIT
	141: 5	*L* a righteous man **strike** me—	AIT
	141: 5	*l* him **rebuke** me—it is oil on my head.	AIT
	141:10	*L* the wicked **fall** into their own nets,	AIT
	143: 8	*L* the morning **bring** me word	AIT

Ps	145:21	*L* every creature **praise** his holy name	AIT
	148: 5	*L* them **praise** the name of the LORD,	AIT
	148:13	*L* them **praise** the name of the LORD,	AIT
	149: 2	*L* Israel **rejoice** in their Maker;	AIT
	149: 2	*l* the people of Zion **be glad**	AIT
	149: 3	*L* them **praise** his name with dancing	AIT
	149: 5	*L* the saints **rejoice** in this honor and sing	AIT
	150: 6	*L* everything that has breath **praise**	AIT
Pr	1: 5	*l* the wise **listen** and add to their learning,	AIT
	1: 5	and *l* the discerning **get guidance—**	AIT
	3: 3	*L* love and faithfulness never **leave** you;	AIT
	3:20	and the clouds *l* **drop** the dew.	8319
	3:21	do not *l* them **out** of your sight;	4279
	4:13	Hold on to instruction, do not *l* it **go;**	8332
	4:21	Do not *l* them **out** of your sight,	4279
	4:25	*L* your eyes **look** straight ahead,	5564
	5:17	*L* them **be** yours alone,	AIT
	6:25	after her beauty or *l* her **captivate** you	AIT
	7:25	not *l* your heart **turn** to her ways or stray	AIT
	9: 4	"*L* all who are simple **come in**	AIT
	9:16	"*L* all who are simple **come in**	AIT
	10: 3	*l* does not *l* the righteous **go hungry**	8279
	23:17	Do not *l* your heart **envy** sinners,	AIT
	23:26	give me your heart and *l* your eyes **keep**	AIT
	24:17	do not *l* your heart **rejoice,**	AIT
	27: 2	*L* another **praise** you, and	AIT
	28:17	*l* no one **support** him.	AIT
	31: 7	*l* them **drink** and forget their poverty	AIT
	31:31	*l* her works **bring** her **praise**	AIT
Ecc	5: 2	so *l* your words **be few.**	AIT
	5: 6	Do not *l* your mouth lead you into sin.	5989
	7:18	It is good to grasp the one and not *l* **go** of the other.	906+3338+5663
	11: 6	and at evening *l* not your hands **be idle,**	5663
	11: 8	*l* him **enjoy** them all.	AIT
	11: 8	But *l* him **remember** the days of darkness,	AIT
	11: 9	*l* your heart **give** you **joy**	AIT
SS	1: 2	*L* him **kiss** me with the kisses of his mouth	AIT
	1: 4	Take me away with you—*l us* **hurry!**	AIT
	1: 4	*L* the king **bring** me **into** his chambers.	AIT
	2:14	show me your face, *l* me **hear** your voice;	9048
	3: 4	I held him and *would* not *l* him **go**	8332
	4:16	*L* my lover **come** into his garden	AIT
	7:11	my lover, *l us* **go** to the countryside,	AIT
	7:11	*l us* **spend the night** in the villages.	AIT
	7:12	*L us* **go** early to the vineyards to see if	AIT
	8:11	he *l* **out** his vineyard to tenants.	5989
	8:13	*l* me **hear** your voice!	9048
Isa	1:18	"Come now, *l us* **reason together,**"	AIT
	2: 3	*l us* **go up** to the mountain of the LORD.	AIT
	2: 5	*l us* **walk** in the light of the LORD.	AIT
	4: 1	only *l us* be **called** *by* your name.	AIT
	5:19	"*L* God **hurry,** let him hasten his work	AIT
	5:19	*l* him **hasten** his work so we may see it.	AIT
	5:19	*L* it **approach,** let the plan of	AIT
	5:19	*l* the plan of the Holy One of Israel **come,**	AIT
	7: 6	"*l us* **invade** Judah;	AIT
	7: 6	*l us* **tear** it **apart** and divide it	AIT
	12: 5	*l* this **be known** to all the world.	AIT
	14:17	and *would* not *l* his captives **go home?**"	AIT
	16: 4	*l* the Moabite fugitives **stay** with you;	AIT
	19:12	*L* them **show** you and make known what	AIT
	21: 7	*l* him **be alert,** fully alert."	AIT
	22: 4	*l* me **weep bitterly.**	AIT
	22:13	"*L us* **eat** and drink," you say,	AIT
	25: 9	*l us* **rejoice** and be glad in his salvation."	AIT
	26:11	*L* them **see** your zeal for your people and	AIT
	26:11	*l* the fire reserved for your enemies **consume** them.	AIT
	27: 5	Or else *l* them **come** to me for refuge;	AIT
	27: 5	*l* them **make** peace with me, yes,	AIT
	27: 5	yes, *l* them **make** peace with me."	AIT
	28:12	"This is the resting place, *l* the weary **rest**";	AIT
	29: 1	*l* your **cycle** of festivals **go on.**	AIT
	34: 1	*L* the earth **hear,** and all that is in it,	AIT
	36:14	Do not *l* Hezekiah **deceive** you.	5958
	36:15	Do not *l* Hezekiah **persuade** you **to trust**	1053
	36:15	not *l* Hezekiah **mislead** you when he says,	6077
	37:10	Do not *l* the god you depend on **deceive**	5958
	38:16	You restored me to health and *l* me **live.**	2649
	41: 1	*L* the nations **renew** their strength!	2736
	41: 1	*L* them **come forward** and speak;	AIT
	41: 1	*l us* **meet** together at the place	AIT
	42:11	*L* the desert and its towns **raise**	AIT
	42:11	*l* the settlements where Kedar lives **rejoice.**	AIT
	42:11	*L* the people of Sela **sing for joy;**	AIT
	42:11	*l* them **shout** from the mountaintops.	AIT
	42:12	*L* them **give** glory to the LORD	AIT
	43: 9	*L* them **bring** in their witnesses;	AIT
	43:26	*l us* **argue** *the matter* together;	AIT
	44: 7	*L* him **proclaim** it.	AIT
	44: 7	*L* him **declare** and lay out	AIT
	44: 7	yes, *l* him **foretell** what will come.	AIT
	44:11	*L* them all **come together**	AIT
	44:14	He *l* it **grow** among the trees of the forest,	599
	44:28	he will say of Jerusalem, "*L* it **be rebuilt,**"	AIT
	44:28	"*L its* **foundations be laid.**"'	AIT
	45: 8	*l* the clouds **shower** it **down.**	AIT
	45: 8	*L* the earth **open wide,**	AIT
	45: 8	*l* salvation **spring up,**	AIT
	45: 8	*l* righteousness **grow** with it;	AIT
	45:21	*l* them **take counsel** together.	AIT
	47:13	*L* your astrologers **come forward,**	AIT
	47:13	*l* them **save** you from what is coming	AIT
	48:11	How *can I l* myself **be defamed?**	AIT
	50: 8	*L us* **face** each other!	AIT
	50: 8	*L* him **confront** me!	AIT

Isa 50:10 *L* him who walks in the dark, who has no light, **trust** in the name — AIT
55: 7 *L* the wicked **forsake** his way and — AIT
55: 7 *L* him **turn** to the LORD, — AIT
56: 3 *L* no foreigner who has bound himself to the LORD **say**, — AIT
56: 3 *l* not any eunuch **complain**, — AIT
56:12 "Come," each one cries, "*l* me **get** wine! — AIT
56:12 *L* us **drink** our **fill** — AIT
57:13 *l* your collection [of idols] **save** you! — AIT
66: 5 '*L* the LORD be **glorified**, — AIT

Jer 2:28 *L* them **come** if they can save you — AIT
3:25 *L* us **lie down** in our shame, — AIT
3:25 and *l* our disgrace **cover** us. — AIT
4: 5 *L* us **flee** to the fortified cities!' — AIT
5:13 *l* what they say **be done** — AIT
5:24 '*L* us **fear** the LORD our God, — AIT
6: 4 Arise, *l* us **attack** at noon! — AIT
6: 5 *l* us **attack** at night — AIT
6: 9 "*L* them **glean** the remnant of Israel as **thoroughly** as a vine; — AIT
7: 3 *l will l* you **live** in this place, — 8905
7: 7 then *l will l* you **live** in this place, — 8905
8:14 *L* us **flee** to the fortified cities — AIT
9:18 *L* them **come** quickly and wail over us — AIT
9:23 "*L* not the wise man **boast** — AIT
9:24 but *l* him who **boasts** boast about this: — AIT
11:19 saying, "*L* us **destroy** the tree and its fruit; — AIT
11:19 *l* us **cut** him **off** from the land of the living, — AIT
11:20 *l* me **see** your vengeance upon them, — AIT
13: 1 but *do* not *l* it **touch** water." — 928+995
14:17 " '*L* my eyes **overflow** with tears — AIT
15: 1 *L* them **go!** — AIT
15:19 *L* this people **turn** to you, — AIT
17:15 *L* it now be **fulfilled!**" — AIT
17:18 *L* my persecutors be **put to shame**, — AIT
17:18 *l* them be **terrified**, — AIT
18:21 *L* their wives be **made** childless and widows; — AIT
18:21 *l* their men **be put** to death, — AIT
18:22 *L* a cry **be heard** from their houses — AIT
18:23 *L* them **be** overthrown before you; — AIT
20:12 *l* me **see** your vengeance upon them, — AIT
22:20 *l* your voice **be heard** in Bashan, — 5989
23:28 *L* the prophet who has a dream **tell** — AIT
23:28 *l* the one who has my word **speak** — AIT
27:11 *L will l* that nation **remain** in its own land — 5663
27:18 *l* them **plead** with the LORD Almighty — AIT
29: 8 *Do* not *l* the prophets and diviners among you **deceive** you. — AIT
30:11 *l* you go entirely unpunished.' — 5927+5927
31: 6 'Come, *l* us **go up** to Zion, — AIT
32:37 to this place and *l* them **live** in safety. — 3782
33: 6 and *will l* them **enjoy** abundant peace — 1655
34:14 you must *l* him **go** free.' — 8938
36:19 Don't *l* anyone **know** where you are." — AIT
37:20 *L* me **bring** my petition before you; — AIT
38:11 and *l* them **down** with ropes to Jeremiah in — 8938
38:24 not *l* anyone **know** about this conversation, — AIT
40: 5 and a present and *l* him **go**. — 8938
40:15 "*L* me **go** and kill Ishmael son of Nethaniah, — AIT
41: 8 So *he l* them **alone** and did not kill them — 2532
45: 5 but wherever you go *l will l* you escape — 5989
46:16 *l* us **go back** to our own people — AIT
46:28 *l* you **go** entirely unpunished." — 5927+5927
48: 2 *l* us **put an end** to that nation.' — AIT
48:26 *L* Moab **wallow** in her vomit; — AIT
48:26 *l* her **be** an object of ridicule. — AIT
50:16 of the oppressor *l* everyone **return** — AIT
50:16 *l* everyone **flee** to his own land. — AIT
50:27 *l* them **go down** to the slaughter! — AIT
50:29 Encamp all around her; *l* no one escape. — 2118
50:33 refusing to *l* them **go**. — 8938
51: 3 *L* not the archer **string** his bow, — AIT
51: 3 nor *l* him **put on** his armor. — AIT
51: 9 *l* us **leave** her and each go — AIT
51:10 come, *l* us **tell** in Zion what — AIT

La 1:22 "*L* all their wickedness **come** — AIT
2:17 he has *l* the enemy **gloat** over you, — 8523
2:18 *l* your tears **flow** like a river day — 3718
3:28 *L* him **sit** alone in silence, — AIT
3:29 *L* him **bury** his face in the dust— — AIT
3:30 *L* him **offer** his cheek to the one — AIT
3:30 and *l* him **be filled** with disgrace. — AIT
3:40 *L* us **examine** our ways and test them, — AIT
3:40 and *l* us **return** to the LORD. — AIT
3:41 *L* us **lift up** our hearts and our hands — AIT

Eze 3:27 Whoever will listen *l* him **listen**, — AIT
3:27 and whoever will refuse *l* him **refuse**; — AIT
4:15 "*l will l* you bake your bread — 5989
7:12 *L* not the buyer **rejoice** — AIT
14: 3 *l* them **inquire** of *me* at all? — 2011+2011+4200
14:17 '*L* the sword **pass** throughout the land,' — AIT
20: 3 as I live, *l will* not *l* you **inquire** of *me*, — 2011
20:26 *l I them* become defiled through their gifts — 3237
20:31 *Am I to l* you **inquire** of *me*. — 2011+4200
20:31 *I will* not *l* you **inquire** of *me*. — 2011+4200
21:14 *L* the sword **strike** twice, — AIT
23:43 *l* them **use** her **as** a prostitute, — AIT
24:10 *l* the bones **be charred**. — AIT
32: 4 *l* all the birds of the air **settle** — 8905
32:14 Then *I will l* her waters **settle** — 9205
32:20 *l* her **be dragged off** — AIT
39: 7 *l* my holy name be **profaned**, — 2725
43: 9 Now *l* them **put away** — AIT
43:10 *L* them **consider** the plan, — AIT
44:20 or *l* their hair **grow** long, — 8938

Da 2: 7 "*L* the king **tell** his servants the dream, — AIT

Da 4:14 *L* the animals **flee** from under it and — AIT
4:15 *l* the stump and its roots, bound with iron and bronze, **remain** — AIT
4:15 *L* him be **drenched** with the dew — AIT
4:15 and *l* him live with the animals among — NIH
4:16 *L* his mind **be changed** — AIT
4:16 and *l* him be given the mind of an animal, — AIT
4:19 *l* the dream or its meaning **alarm** — AIT
4:23 *L* him be **drenched** with the dew of heaven; — AIT
4:23 *l* him live like the wild animals, — NIH

Hos 2: 2 *L* her **remove** the adulterous look — AIT
4: 4 *l* no man **bring** a charge, — AIT
4: 4 *l* no man **accuse** another, — AIT
4:15 *l* not Judah **become** guilty. — AIT
6: 1 "Come, *l* us **return** to the LORD. — AIT
6: 3 *L* us **acknowledge** the LORD; — AIT
6: 3 *l* us **press on** to acknowledge him. — AIT
9: 7 *L* Israel **know** this. — AIT

Joel 1: 3 and *l* your children tell it to their children, — NIH
2: 1 *L* all who live in the land **tremble**, — AIT
2:16 *L* the bridegroom **leave** his room — AIT
2:17 *L* the priests, who minister before the LORD, **weep** — AIT
2:17 *L* them **say**, "Spare your people, O LORD. — AIT
3: 9 *L* all the fighting men **draw near**. — AIT
3:10 *L* the weakling **say**, "I am strong!" — AIT
3:12 "*L* the nations **be roused**; — AIT
3:12 *l* them **advance** into the Valley — AIT

Am 5:24 But *l* justice **roll on** like a river, — AIT
Ob 1: 1 and *l* us **go** against her for battle"— — AIT
Jnh 1: 7 *l* us **cast** lots to find out — AIT
1:14 not *l* us **die** for taking this man's life. — AIT
3: 7 *l* any man or beast, herd or flock, **taste** — AIT
3: 7 *do* not *l* them **eat** or drink. — AIT
3: 8 *l* man and beast **be covered** — AIT
3: 8 *L* everyone **call** urgently on God. — AIT
3: 8 *L* them **give up** their evil ways — AIT

Mic 4: 2 *l* us **go up** to the mountain of the LORD, — AIT
4:11 They say, "*L* her be **defiled**, — AIT
4:11 *l* our eyes **gloat** over Zion!" — AIT
6: 1 *l* the hills **hear** what you have to say. — AIT
7:14 *L* them **feed** in Bashan and Gilead as — AIT

Hab 2:20 *l* all the earth **be silent** — AIT
Zep 3:16 *do* not *l* your hands **hang limp**. — AIT
Zec 8: 9 *l* your hands **be strong** — AIT
8:13 *l* your hands **be strong.** — AIT
8:21 '*L* us **go** at once to entreat the LORD — AIT
8:23 '*L* us **go** with you, — AIT
11: 9 *L* the dying **die**, and the perishing perish. — AIT
11: 9 *L* those who are left **eat** one another's — AIT

Mt 3:15 Jesus replied, "*L* it be so now; — 918
5:16 *l* your light **shine** before men, — AIT
5:37 Simply *l* your 'Yes' be 'Yes,' — AIT
5:40 *l* him have your cloak as well. — 918
6: 3 *do* not *l* your left hand **know** what — AIT
7: 4 '*L* me take the speck out of your eye,' — 918
8:21 "Lord, first *l* me go and bury my father." — 2205
8:22 and *l* the dead bury their own dead." — 918
10:13 *l* your peace **rest** on it; — AIT
10:13 if it is not, *l* your peace **return** to you. — AIT
11:15 He who has ears, *l* him **hear.** — AIT
13: 9 He who has ears, *l* him **hear.**" — AIT
13:30 *L* both grow together until the harvest. — 918
13:43 He who has ears, *l* him **hear.** — AIT
13:47 of heaven is like a net that *was l* **down** into — 965
14:36 and begged him to *l* the sick just touch — 2671
18:27 canceled the debt and *l* him go. — 668
19: 6 God has joined together, *l* man not **separate**. — AIT
19:14 "*L* the little children come to me, — 918
23:13 *will l* you those enter who are trying to. — 918
24:15 *l* the reader **understand**— — AIT
24:16 *l* those who are in Judea **flee** — AIT
24:17 *l* no one on the roof of his house **go down** — AIT
24:18 *L* no one in the field **go back** — AIT
24:43 not *have l* his house be broken into. — 1572
26:46 Rise, *l* us **go!** Here comes my betrayer!" — AIT
27:25 "*L* his blood be on us and — NIG
27:42 *L* him **come down** now from the cross, — AIT
27:43 *L* God **rescue** him now if he wants him, — AIT

Mk 1:34 but *he would* not *l* the demons speak — 918
1:38 Jesus replied, "*L* us **go** somewhere else— — AIT
4: 9 "He who has ears to hear, *l* him **hear.**" — AIT
4:23 If anyone has ears to hear, *l* him **hear.**" — AIT
4:35 "*L* us **go over** to the other side." — AIT
5:19 Jesus *did* not *l* him, but said, — 918
5:37 not *l* anyone follow him except Peter, — 918
5:43 not to *l* anyone know about this, — 2671
6:56 They begged him to *l* them touch even — 2671
7: 9 You have *l* **go** of the commands of God — 918
7:12 then *you* no longer *l* him do anything — 918
7:27 "First *l* the children eat all they want," — 918
9: 5 *L* us **put up** three shelters— — AIT
10: 9 God has joined together, *l* man not **separate**. — AIT
10:14 "*L* the little children come to me, — 918
10:37 "*L* one of us sit at your right and the other — 1443
11: 6 and the *people l* them go. — 918
12:15 "Bring me a denarius and *l* me look at it." — 2671
13:14 *l* the reader **understand**— — AIT
13:14 *l* those who are in Judea **flee** — AIT
13:15 *L* no one on the roof of his house **go down** — AIT
13:16 *L* no one in the field **go back** — AIT
13:36 *do* not *l* him find you sleeping. — NIG
14:42 Rise! *L* us **go!** Here comes my betrayer!" — AIT
15:32 *L* this Christ, this King of Israel, **come down** — AIT

Lk 5: 4 and *l* **down** the nets for a catch." — 5899
5: 5 you say so, *l will l* **down** the nets." — 5899

Lk 6:42 *l* me take the speck out of your eye,' — 918
8: 8 "He who has ears to hear, *l* him **hear.**" — AIT
8:32 The demons begged Jesus to *l* them go — 2205
8:51 not *l* anyone go in with him except Peter, — 918
9:33 *L* us **put up** three shelters— — AIT
9:59 "Lord, first *l* me go and bury my father." — 2205
9:60 "*L* the dead bury their own dead, — 918
9:61 but first *l* me go back and say good-by — 2205
12:39 not *have l* his house be broken into. — 918
14:35 "He who has ears to hear, *l* him **hear.**" — AIT
16:28 *L* him **warn** them, — AIT
16:29 *l* them **listen** to them.' — AIT
18:16 "*L* the little children come to me, — 918
21:21 *l* those who are in Judea **flee** — AIT
21:21 *l* those in the city **get out**, — AIT
21:21 *l* those in the country not **enter** — AIT
23:35 *l* him **save** himself if he is the Christ — AIT

Jn 6:12 *L* nothing be wasted." — 2671
7:37 *l* him **come** to me and drink. — AIT
8: 7 *l* him be the first to **throw** — AIT
11: 7 "*L* us **go** back to Judea." — AIT
11:15 But *l* us **go** to him." — AIT
11:16 "*L* us also **go**, that we may die with him." — AIT
11:44 "Take off the grave clothes and *l* him go. — 918
11:48 If *we l* him **go** on like this, — 918
14: 1 not *l* your hearts **be troubled**. Trust in God; — AIT
14:27 *Do* not *l* your hearts **be troubled** — AIT
14:31 "Come now; *l* us **leave**. — AIT
17:23 to complete unity to *l* the world know — 2671
18: 8 then *l* these men **go**." — 918
19: 4 to you to *l* you know that I find no basis — 2671
19:12 "If *you l* this man **go**, — 668

Ac 1:20 *l* there be no one to dwell in it,' and, — AIT
2:14 *l* me **explain** this to you; — AIT
2:27 nor *will you l* your Holy One see decay. — 1443
2:36 *l* all Israel **be assured** — AIT
3:13 though he had decided to *l* him go. — AIT
4:21 After further threats they *l* them **go**. — 668
5:38 *L* them **go!** — 918
5:40 and *l* them **go**. — 668
10:11 like a large sheet *being l* **down** to earth — 2768
11: 5 a large sheet *being l* **down** from heaven — 2768
13:35 not *l* your Holy One see decay.' — 1443
14:16 he *l* all nations go their own way. — 1572
15:36 "*L* us **go** back and **visit** — AIT
16:37 *L* them **come** themselves and **escort** us **out**." — AIT
17: 9 and the others post bond and *l* them **go**. — 668
19:30 but the disciples *would* not *l* him. — 1572
21:39 Please *l* me speak to the people." — 2205
23:32 The next day *they l* the cavalry go on — 1572
25: 5 *L* some of your leaders come with me and **press charges against** the man — AIT
27:17 *l* the ship **be driven** along. — 5770
27:30 the sailors *l* the lifeboat **down** into the sea, — 5899
27:32 that held the lifeboat and *l* it fall away. — 1572

Ro 3: 4 *L* God **be true**, and every man a liar. — AIT
3: 8 "*L* us **do** evil that good may result"? — AIT
6:12 not *l* sin **reign** in your mortal body so — AIT
12: 6 *l* him use it in proportion to his faith. — NIG
12: 7 If it is serving, *l* him **serve**; — NIG
12: 7 if it is teaching, *l* him **teach**; — NIG
12: 8 if it is encouraging, *l* him **encourage**; — NIG
12: 8 if it is giving generously; — NIG
12: 8 if it is leadership, *l* him **govern** diligently; — NIG
12: 8 *l* him **do** it cheerfully. — NIG
13: 8 *L* no **debt** remain outstanding, — AIT
13:12 *l* us **put aside** the deeds of darkness and — AIT
13:13 *L* us **behave** decently, as in the daytime, — AIT
14:13 *l* us stop **passing judgment** on — AIT
14:19 *L* us therefore **make every effort** — AIT

1Co 1:31 "*L* him who boasts **boast** — AIT
5: 8 *l* us **keep** the Festival, — AIT
7:15 But if the unbeliever leaves, *l* him **do** so. — AIT
7:21 Don't *l* it **trouble** you— — AIT
10:13 he *will* not *l* you be tempted — 1572
14:37 *l* him **acknowledge** that what I am writing — AIT
15:32 *L* us **eat** and **drink**, — AIT
15:58 *L* nothing move you. — NIG

2Co 2: 4 to grieve you but to *l* you know the depth — 2671
4: 6 who said, "*L* light **shine** out of darkness," — AIT
7: 1 *l* us **purify** ourselves from everything — AIT
10:17 But, "*L* him who **boasts** boast in the Lord." — AIT
11:16 *L* no one **take** me **for** — AIT

Gal 1: 8 *l* him be eternally condemned! — AIT
1: 9 *l* him be eternally condemned! — AIT
3:15 *l* me **take an example** — AIT
5: 1 *l* yourselves **be burdened** — AIT
5: 2 *l* yourselves **be circumcised**, — AIT
5:25 *l* us not **become conceited**, — AIT
6: 9 *L* us not **become weary** — AIT
6:10 *l* us **do** good to all people, — 2237
6:17 Finally, *l* no one **cause** me trouble, — AIT

Eph 4:26 *l* the sun **go down** — AIT
4:29 *l* any unwholesome talk **come out** — AIT
5: 6 *L* no one **deceive** you with empty words, — AIT

Php 3:16 Only *l* us **live up** — NIG
4: 5 *L* your gentleness **be evident** — AIT

Col 2:16 not *l* anyone **judge** you by what you eat — AIT
2:18 *l* anyone who delights in false humility and the worship of angels **disqualify** you **for the prize**. — AIT
3:15 *L* the peace of Christ **rule** in your hearts, — AIT
3:16 *L* the word of Christ **dwell in** — AIT
4: 6 *L* your conversation be always full — NIG

1Th 5: 6 *l* us not be like others, who are **asleep**, — AIT

1Th	5: 6	*l us* be **alert** and **self-controlled.**	AIT
	5: 8	*l us* be **self-controlled,**	AIT
2Th	2: 3	Don't *l* anyone **deceive** you in any way,	AIT
1Ti	3:10	*l them* **serve as deacons.**	AIT
	4:12	Don't *l* anyone **look down on** you	AIT
	5:16	not *l* the church **be burdened** with them,	AIT
Tit	2:15	*Do not l* anyone **despise** you.	AIT
Heb	1: 6	"*L* all God's angels **worship**	AIT
	4: 1	*l us* be **careful** that none of you be found	AIT
	4:11	*L us,* therefore, **make every effort**	AIT
	4:14	*l us* **hold firmly to** the faith we profess.	AIT
	4:16	*L us* then **approach** the throne of grace	AIT
	6: 1	*l us* leave the elementary teachings about Christ and **go on**	AIT
	10:22	*L us* **draw near** to God with a sincere heart	AIT
	10:23	*L us* **hold** unswervingly **to** the hope	AIT
	10:24	And *l us* **consider** how we may spur one	AIT
	10:25	*L us* not **give up** meeting together,	AIT
	10:25	but *l us* encourage one another—	NIG
	12: 1	*l us* **throw off** everything that hinders and	AIT
	12: 1	and *l us* **run** with perseverance	AIT
	12: 2	*L us* **fix** *our* **eyes** on Jesus	AIT
	12:28	*l us* be **thankful,**	AIT
	13:13	*L us,* then, **go** to him outside the camp,	AIT
	13:15	*l us* continually **offer** to God	AIT
Jas	3:13	*L him* **show** it by his good life,	AIT
	5:12	*L* your "**Yes**" be yes, and your "**No,**" no,	1639
	5:13	*L him* **sing songs of praise.**	AIT
1Jn	3: 7	*do not l* anyone **lead** you **astray.**	AIT
	3:18	*l us* not **love** with words or tongue but	AIT
	4: 7	Dear friends, *l us* **love** one another,	AIT
Rev	2: 7	*l him* **hear** what the Spirit says to	AIT
	2:11	*l him* **hear** what the Spirit says to	AIT
	2:17	*l him* **hear** what the Spirit says to	AIT
	2:29	*l him* **hear** what the Spirit says to	AIT
	3: 6	*l him* **hear** what the Spirit says to	AIT
	3:13	*l him* **hear** what the Spirit says to	AIT
	3:22	*l him* **hear** what the Spirit says to	AIT
	13: 9	He who has an ear, *l him* **hear.**	AIT
	13:18	*l him* **calculate** the number of the beast,	AIT
	19: 7	*L us* **rejoice** and **be glad** and **give**	AIT
	22:11	*L* him who does wrong continue *to do* **wrong;**	AIT
	22:11	*l* him who is vile continue *to be* **vile;**	AIT
	22:11	*l* him who does right continue *to do*	AIT
	22:11	*l* him who is holy continue *to be* **holy."**	AIT
	22:17	*l* him who hears **say,**	AIT
	22:17	Whoever is thirsty, *l* him **come;**	AIT
	22:17	*l* him **take** the free gift of the water of life.	AIT

LET (Anglicized) See also HAVE

LET'S (48) [LET, WE]

Ge	4: 8	"*L* go out *to* the field."	AIT
	11: 3	*l* **make bricks** and bake them thoroughly."	AIT
	13: 8	"*L* not **have** any quarreling between you	AIT
	13: 9	*L* **part company.**	AIT
	19:32	*L* **get** our father **to drink** wine	AIT
	19:34	*L* **get** him **to drink** wine	AIT
	24:57	"*L* **call** the girl and ask her about it."	AIT
	31:44	Come now, *l* **make** a covenant, you and I,	AIT
	37:17	"I heard them say, '*L* **go** to Dothan.' "	AIT
	37:20	*l* **kill** him and throw him into one	AIT
	37:21	"*L* not **take** his life," he said.	AIT
	37:27	*l* **sell** him to the Ishmaelites and	AIT
Ex	14:25	"*L* **get away** from the Israelites!	AIT
Jdg	14:13	"*L* **hear** it."	AIT
	18: 9	They answered, "Come on, *l* **attack** them!	AIT
	19:11	*l* **stop** at this city of the Jebusites	AIT
	19:13	*l try to* **reach** Gibeah or Ramah and spend	AIT
	19:28	He said to her, "Get up; *l* **go.**"	AIT
	20:32	"*L* **retreat** and draw them away from	AIT
1Sa	9: 5	*l* **go back,** or my father will stop thinking	AIT
	9: 6	*L* **go** there now.	AIT
	9:10	"Come, *l* **go.**"	AIT
	14: 1	*l* **go over** to the Philistine outpost on	AIT
	14: 6	*l* **go over** to the outpost	AIT
	20:11	Jonathan said, "*l* **go out** *into* the field."	AIT
	26:11	that are near his head, and *l* **go.**"	AIT
2Sa	2:14	"*L* **have** some of the young men **get up**	AIT
2Ki	4:10	*L* **make** a small room on the roof and put	AIT
	7: 4	So *l* **go over** to the camp of the Arameans	AIT
	7: 9	*L* **go at once** and report this to	AIT
Pr	1:11	*l* **lie in wait** for someone's **blood,**	AIT
	1:11	*l* **waylay** some harmless **soul;**	AIT
	1:12	*l* **swallow** them **alive,** like the grave,	AIT
	7:18	Come, *l* **drink deep** *of* love till morning;	AIT
	7:18	*l* **enjoy ourselves** with love!	AIT
Jer	18:18	"Come, *l* **make plans** against Jeremiah;	AIT
	18:18	*l* **attack** him with our tongues	AIT
	20:10	*L* **report him!**"	AIT
Mt	21:38	*l* **kill** him and take his inheritance.'	AIT
	27:49	*L* **see** if Elijah comes to save him."	AIT
Mk	12: 7	*l* **kill** him, and the inheritance will	AIT
	15:36	*L* **see** if Elijah comes to take him down,"	AIT
Lk	2:15	"*L* **go** to Bethlehem and see this thing	AIT
	8:22	"*L* **go over** to the other side of the lake."	AIT
	15:23	*L* **have** a feast and **celebrate.**	AIT
	20:14	'*L* **kill** him, and the inheritance will	AIT
Jn	19:24	"*L* not **tear** it," they said to one another.	AIT
	19:24	"*L* **decide by lot** who will get it."	AIT

LETHEK (1)

| Hos | 3: 2 | and about a homer and a *l* *of* barley. | 4390 |

LETS (7) [LET]

Ex	21:13	but God *l* it **happen,**	628+3338+4200
	22: 5	in a field or vineyard and *l them* **stray**	8938
2Ki	10:24	of you *l* any of the men I am placing	NIH
Job	12:15	if *he l* them **loose,** they devastate the land.	8938
	39:14	on the ground and *l them* **warm** in the sand,	2801
Pr	14:33	even among fools *she l herself* **be known.**	3359
Gal	5: 3	*l himself* be **circumcised**	AIT

LETTER (49) [LETTERS]

2Sa	11:14	In the morning David wrote a *l* to Joab	6219
2Ki	5: 5	"I will send a *l* to the king of Israel."	6219
	5: 6	The *l* that he took to the king	6219
	5: 6	"With this *l* I am sending my servant Naaman	6219
	5: 7	As soon as the king of Israel read the *l,*	6219
	10: 2	"As soon as this *l* reaches you,	6219
	10: 6	Then Jehu wrote them a second *l,* saying,	6219
	10: 7	When the *l* arrived,	6219
	19:14	the *l* from the messengers and read it.	6219
2Ch	2:11	of Tyre replied by *l* to Solomon:	4181
	21:12	a *l* from Elijah the prophet, which said:	4844
Ezr	4: 7	of his associates wrote a *l* to Artaxerxes.	NIH
	4: 7	The *l* was written in Aramaic script and in	10496
	4: 8	the secretary wrote a *l* against Jerusalem	10007
	4:11	(This is a copy of the *l* they sent him.)	10007
	4:18	The *l* you sent us has been read	10496
	4:23	of the *l* of King Artaxerxes was read	10496
	5: 6	This is a copy of the *l* that Tattenai,	10007
	7:11	of the *l* King Artaxerxes had given to Ezra	10496
Ne	2: 8	And may I have a *l* to Asaph,	115
	6: 5	and in his hand was an unsealed *l*	115
Est	9:26	Because of everything written in this *l* and	115
	9:29	with full authority to confirm this second *l*	115
Isa	37:14	the *l* from the messengers and read it.	6219
Jer	29: 1	of the *l* that the prophet Jeremiah sent	6219
	29: 3	the *l* to Elasah son of Shaphan and	NIH
	29:29	read the *l* to Jeremiah the prophet.	6219
Mt	5:18	not the **smallest** *l,*	2740
Ac	15:23	With them *they* **sent** the following *l:*	1211
	15:30	the church together and delivered the *l.*	2186
	23:25	He wrote a *l* as follows:	2186
	23:33	the *l* to the governor and handed Paul over	2186
	23:34	The governor read the *l*	NIG
Ro	16:22	I, Tertius, who wrote down this *l,*	2186
1Co	5: 9	I have written you in my *l* not to associate	2186
2Co	3: 2	You yourselves are our *l,*	2186
	3: 3	You show that you are a *l* from Christ,	2186
	3: 6	not *of* the *l* but of the Spirit;	1207
	3: 6	for the *l* kills, but the Spirit gives life.	1207
	7: 8	Even if I caused you sorrow by my *l,*	2186
	7: 8	I see that my *l* hurt you,	2186
Col	4:16	After this *l* has been read to you,	2186
	4:16	that you in turn read the *l* from Laodicea.	NIG
1Th	5:27	before the Lord to have this *l* read to all	2186
2Th	2: 2	or *l* supposed to have come from us,	2186
	2:15	whether by word of mouth or by *l.*	2186
	3:14	not obey our instruction in this *l,*	2186
Heb	13:22	for I have written you only a short *l.*	NIG
2Pe	3: 1	this is now my second *l* to you.	2186

LETTERS (29) [LETTER]

1Ki	21: 8	So she wrote *l* in Ahab's name,	6219
	21: 9	In those *l* she wrote:	6219
	21:11	as Jezebel directed in the *l* she had written	6219
2Ki	10: 1	So Jehu wrote *l* and sent them to Samaria:	6219
	20:12	of Babylon sent Hezekiah *l* and a gift,	6219
2Ch	30: 1	also wrote *l* to Ephraim and Manasseh,	115
	30: 6	throughout Israel and Judah with *l* from	115
	32:17	king also wrote *l* insulting the LORD,	6219
Ne	2: 7	may I have *l* to the governors	115
	2: 9	and gave them the king's *l.*	115
	6:17	of Judah were sending many *l* to Tobiah,	115
	6:19	And Tobiah sent *l* to intimidate me.	115
Est	9:20	and he sent *l* to all the Jews throughout	6219
	9:30	And Mordecai sent *l* to all the Jews in	6219
Isa	39: 1	of Babylon sent Hezekiah *l* and a gift,	6219
Jer	29:25	You sent *l* in your own name to all	6219
Ac	9: 2	asked him for *l* to the synagogues	2186
	22: 5	I even obtained *l* from them	2186
	28:21	"We have not received any *l* from Judea	1207
1Co	16: 3	I will give *l* of introduction to	2186
2Co	3: 1	*l* of recommendation to you or from you?	2186
	3: 7	which was engraved in *l* on stone,	1207
	10: 9	to be trying to frighten you with my *l.*	2186
	10:10	some say, "His *l* are weighty and forceful,	2186
	10:11	or *l* when we are absent,	2186
Gal	6:11	See what large *l* I use as I write to you	1207
2Th	3:17	the distinguishing mark in all my *l.*	2186
2Pe	3:16	He writes the same way in all his *l,*	2186
	3:16	His *l* contain some things that are hard	NIG

LETTING (4) [LET]

Ex	8:29	by not *l* the people **go** to offer sacrifices to	8938
1Sa	21:13	of the gate and *l* saliva **run down** his beard.	3718
1Ki	1:27	without *l* his servants **know** who should sit	3359
Isa	32:20	*l* your cattle and donkeys **range free.**	8079+8938

LETUSHITES (1)

| Ge | 25: 3 | the **L** and the Leummites. | 4322 |

LEUMMITES (1)

| Ge | 25: 3 | the Letushites and the **L.** | 4212 |

LEVEL (15) [LEVELED, LEVELS]

1Ki	6: 8	to the **middle** *l* and from there to the third.	AIT
Ps	26:12	My feet stand on **l ground;**	4793
	65:10	You drench its furrows and *l* its ridges;	5737
	143:10	may your good Spirit lead me on *l* ground.	4793
Pr	4:26	**Make** *l* paths for your feet	7142
Isa	26: 7	The path of the righteous is *l;*	4797
	40: 4	the rough ground shall become *l,*	4793
	45: 2	before you and *will l* the mountains;	3837
Jer	31: 9	on a *l* path where they will not stumble,	3838
Eze	13:14	with whitewash and *l* it to the ground,	5595
	41: 6	one above another, thirty on *each l.*	7193
	41: 7	temple were wider **at each successive l.** 2025+2025+4200+4200+5087+5087	
Zec	4: 7	Zerubbabel you will become **l ground.**	4793
Lk	6:17	down with them and stood on a *l* place.	4268
Heb	12:13	"Make *l* paths for your feet,"	3981

LEVELED (3) [LEVEL]

Isa	28:25	When *he has l* the surface,	8750
	32:19	the forest and the city *is l* **completely,** 928+2021+9164+9168	
Jer	51:58	"Babylon's thick wall *will be l*	6910+6910

LEVELS (3) [LEVEL]

Isa	26: 5	*he l* it to the ground and casts it down to	9164
Eze	41: 6	The side rooms were on three *l,*	NIH
	42: 3	gallery faced gallery at the **three** *l.*	AIT

LEVI (59) [LEVI'S, LEVITE, LEVITES, LEVITICAL]

Ge	29:34	So he was named **L.**	4290
	34:25	two of Jacob's sons, Simeon and **L,**	4290
	34:30	Then Jacob said to Simeon and **L,**	4290
	35:23	Reuben the firstborn of Jacob, Simeon, **L,**	4290
	46:11	The sons of **L:** Gershon, Kohath and	4290
	49: 5	"Simeon and **L** are brothers—	4290
Ex	1: 2	Reuben, Simeon, **L** and Judah;	4290
	2: 1	of the house of **L** married a Levite woman,	4290
	6:16	of the sons of **L** according to their records:	4290
	6:16	**L** lived 137 years.	4290
	6:19	the clans of **L** according to their records.	4290
Nu	1:47	The families of the tribe of **L,** however,	4291
	1:49	the tribe of **L** or include them in the census	4290
	3: 6	of **L** and present them to Aaron the priest	4290
	3:17	These were the names of the sons of **L:**	4290
	16: 1	the son of **L,** and certain Reubenites—	4290
	17: 3	On the staff of **L** write Aaron's name,	4290
	17: 8	which represented the house of **L,**	4290
	26:59	Jochebed, a descendant of **L,**	4290
Dt	10: 8	the LORD set apart the tribe of **L** to carry	4290
	18: 1	indeed the whole tribe of **L**—	4290
	21: 5	The priests, the sons of **L,**	4290
	27:12	Simeon, **L,** Judah, Issachar,	4290
	31: 9	the priests, the sons of **L,**	4290
	33: 8	About **L** he said:	4290
Jos	13:14	to the tribe of **L** he gave no inheritance.	4291
	13:33	But to the tribe of **L,**	4291
1Ch	2: 1	Reuben, Simeon, **L,** Judah, Issachar,	4290
	6: 1	sons of **L:** Gershon, Kohath and Merari.	4290
	6:16	sons of **L:** Gershon, Kohath and Merari.	4290
	6:38	the son of Kohath, the son of **L,**	4290
	6:43	the son of Gershon, the son of **L;**	4290
	6:47	the son of Merari, the son of **L.**	4290
	12:26	men of **L**—4,600,	4291
	21: 6	But Joab did not include **L** and Benjamin	4290
	23: 6	into groups corresponding to the sons of **L:**	4290
	23:14	as part of the tribe of **L.**	4290
	23:24	the descendants of **L** by their families—	4290
	24:20	As for the rest of the descendants of **L:**	4290
	27:17	over **L:** Hashabiah son of Kemuel;	4290
Ezr		from the descendants of Mahli son of **L,**	4291
Ne	12:23	among the descendants of **L** up to the time	4290
Ps	135:20	O house of **L,** praise the LORD;	4290
Eze	48:31	the gate of Judah and the gate of **L,**	4290
Zec	12:13	the clan of the house of **L** and their wives,	4290
Mal	2: 4	that my covenant with **L** may continue,"	4290
	2: 8	you have violated the covenant with **L,**"	4290
Mk	2:14	he saw **L** son of Alphaeus sitting at	3322
	2:14	and **L** got up and followed him.	NIG
Lk	3:24	the son *of* **L,** the son of Melki,	3322
	3:29	the son of Matthat, the son *of* **L,**	3322
	5:27	by the name *of* **L** sitting at his tax booth.	3322
	5:28	and **L** got up, left everything and followed	NIG
	5:29	Then **L** held a great banquet for Jesus	3322
Heb	7: 5	of **L** who become priests to collect a tenth	3322
	7: 6	however, did not trace his descent from **L,**	899S
	7: 9	One might even say that **L,**	3322
	7:10	**L** was still in the body of his ancestor.	NIG
Rev	7: 7	from the tribe *of* **L** 12,000,	3322

LEVI'S (1) [LEVI]

| Mk | 2:15 | While Jesus was having dinner at **L** house, | 899S |

LEVIATHAN (6)

Job	3: 8	those who are ready to rouse **L.**	4293
	41: 1	"Can you pull in **L** with a fishhook	4293
Ps	74:14	of **L** and gave him as food to the creatures	4293
	104:26	There the ships go to and fro, and the *l,*	4293
Isa	27: 1	**L** the gliding serpent,	4293
	27: 1	**L** the coiling serpent;	4293

LEVITE (30) [LEVI]

Ex	2: 1	of the house of Levi married a L woman,	4290
	4:14	"What about your brother, Aaron the L?	4291
	6:25	These were the heads of the L families,	4291
Nu	3:20	These were the L clans,	4291
	26:58	These also were L clans.	4290
Dt	18: 6	If a L moves from one of your towns	4291
	26:12	you shall give it to the L, the alien,	4291
	26:13	and have given it to the L.	4291
Jos	21:27	The L clans of the Gershonites were given:	4291
Jdg	17: 7	A young L from Bethlehem in Judah,	4291
	17: 9	"I'm a L from Bethlehem in Judah,"	4291
	17:11	So the L agreed to live with him,	4291
	17:12	Then Micah installed the L,	4291
	17:13	since this L has become my priest."	4291
	18: 3	they recognized the voice of the young L;	4291
	18:15	the house of the young L at Micah's place	4291
	19: 1	Now a L who lived in a remote area in	4291
	20: 4	So the L, the husband of the murdered	4291
1Ch	9:31	A L named Mattithiah,	4291
	9:33	heads of L families,	4291
	9:34	All these were heads of L families,	4291
	15:22	the head L was in charge of the singing;	4291
	24: 6	The scribe Shemaiah son of Nethanel, a L,	4291
2Ch	20:14	a L and a descendant of Asaph,	4291
	31:12	a L, was in charge of these things,	4291
	31:14	Kore son of Imnah the L,	4291
Ezr	10:15	by Meshullam and Shabbethai the L,	4291
Ne	13:13	and a L named Pedaiah in charge of	4291
Lk	10:32	So too, a L, when he came to the place	3324
Ac	4:36	Joseph, a L from Cyprus,	3324

LEVITES (282) [LEVI]

Ex	32:26	And all the L rallied to him.	1201+4290
	32:28	The L did as Moses commanded,	1201+4290
	38:21	by the L under the direction of Ithamar son	4291
Lev	25:32	" 'The L always have the right	4291
	25:33	So the property of the L is redeemable—	4291
	25:33	in the towns of the L are their property	4291
Nu	1:50	the L to be in charge of the tabernacle of	4291
	1:51	the L are to take it down,	4291
	1:51	the L shall do it.	4291
	1:53	The L, however, are to set up their tents	4291
	1:53	The L are to be responsible for the care of	4291
	2:17	of the L will set out in the middle of	4291
	2:33	The L, however, were not counted along	4291
	3: 9	Give the L to Aaron and his sons;	4291
	3:12	the L from among the Israelites in place of	4291
	3:12	The L are mine,	4291
	3:15	"Count the L by their families and	1201+4290
	3:32	The chief leader of the L was Eleazar son	4291
	3:39	of L counted at the LORD's command	4291
	3:41	the L for me in place of all the firstborn of	4291
	3:41	and the livestock of the L in place of all	4291
	3:45	the L in place of all the firstborn of Israel,	4291
	3:45	of the L in place of their livestock.	4291
	3:45	The L are to be mine.	4291
	3:46	the number of the L,	4291
	3:49	the number redeemed by the L.	4291
	4: 2	of the Kohathite branch of the L	1201+4290
	4:18	not cut off from the L.	4291
	4:46	and the leaders of Israel counted all the L	4291
	7: 5	to the L as each man's work requires."	4291
	7: 6	the carts and oxen and gave them to the L.	4291
	8: 6	the L from among the other Israelites	4291
	8: 9	the L to the front of the Tent of Meeting	4291
	8:10	You are to bring the L before the LORD,	4291
	8:11	to present the L before the LORD as	4291
	8:12	L lay their hands on the heads of the bulls,	4291
	8:12	to make atonement for the L.	4291
	8:13	the L stand in front of Aaron and his sons	4291
	8:14	In this way you are to set the L apart from	4291
	8:14	and the L will be mine.	4291
	8:15	"After you have purified the L	4291
	8:18	the L in place of all the firstborn sons	4291
	8:19	the L as gifts to Aaron and his sons to do	4291
	8:20	with the L just as the LORD commanded	4291
	8:21	The L purified themselves	4291
	8:22	the L came to do their work at the Tent	4291
	8:22	They did with the L just as	4291
	8:24	"This applies to the L:	4291
	8:26	to assign the responsibilities of the L."	4291
	16: 7	You L have gone too far!"	1201+4290
	16: 8	said to Korah, "Now listen, you L!	1201+4290
	16:10	has brought you and all your fellow L	1201+4290
	18: 2	Bring your fellow L from your	4290+4751
	18: 6	I myself have selected your fellow L from	4291
	18:21	"I give to the L all the tithes in Israel	1201+4290
	18:23	the L who are to do the work at the Tent	4291
	18:24	to the L as their inheritance the tithes that	4291
	18:26	"Speak to the L and say to them:	4291
	18:30	"Say to the L: 'When you present	4291
	26:57	the L who were counted by their clans:	4291
	26:59	who was born to the L in Egypt.	4290
	26:62	All the male L a month old	NIH
	31:30	Give them to the L,	4291
	31:47	and gave them to the L,	4291
	35: 2	the L towns to live in from the inheritance	4291
	35: 4	the L will extend out fifteen hundred feet	4291
	35: 6	of the towns you give the L will be cities	4291
	35: 7	the L forty-eight towns.	4291
	35: 8	The towns you give the L from the land	4291
Dt	10: 9	the L have no share or inheritance	4290
	12:12	and the L from your towns,	4291
	12:18	and the L from your towns—	4291

Dt	12:19	not to neglect the L as long as you live	4291
	14:27	do not neglect the L living in your towns,	4291
	14:29	so that the L (who have no allotment	4291
	16:11	the L in your towns, and the aliens,	4291
	16:14	and the L, the aliens,	4291
	17: 9	Go to the priests, who are L,	4291
	17:18	taken from that of the priests, who are L.	4291
	18: 1	The priests, who are L—	4291
	18: 7	like all his fellow L who serve there in	4291
	24: 8	who are L, instruct you.	4291
	26:11	And you and the L and the aliens	4291
	27: 9	Then Moses and the priests, who are L,	4291
	27:14	The L shall recite to all the people of Israel	4291
	31:25	the L who carried the ark of the covenant	4291
Jos	3: 3	and the priests, who are L, carrying it,	4291
	8:33	the priests, who were L.	4291
	14: 3	but had not granted the L an inheritance	4291
	14: 4	The L received no share of the land	4291
	18: 7	The L, however, do not get a portion	4291
	21: 1	of the L approached Eleazar the priest,	4291
	21: 3	the L the following towns	4291
	21: 4	The L who were descendants of Aaron	4291
	21: 8	the Israelites allotted to the L these towns	4291
	21:10	from the Kohathite clans of the L,	1201+4290
	21:20	of the L were allotted towns from the tribe	4291
	21:34	(the rest of the L) were given:	4291
	21:40	were the rest of the L, were twelve.	4291+5476
	21:41	The towns of the L in the territory held by	4291
1Sa	6:15	The L took down the ark of the LORD.	4291
2Sa	15:24	the L who were with him were carrying	4291
1Ki	8: 4	The priests and L carried them up,	4291
	12:31	even though they were not L.	1201+4290
1Ch	6:19	of the L listed according to their fathers:	4291
	6:48	Their fellow L were assigned to all	4291
	6:64	the L these towns and their pasturelands.	4291
	6:77	(the rest of the L) received the following:	NIH
	9: 2	priests, L and temple servants.	4291
	9:14	Of the L: Shemaiah son of Hasshub,	1201+4290
	9:18	to the camp of the L.	4291
	9:26	four principal gatekeepers, who were L,	4291
	13: 2	also to the priests and L who are with them	4291
	15: 2	"No one but the L may carry the ark	4291
	15: 4	the descendants of Aaron and the L:	4291
	15:11	Shemaiah, Eliel and Amminadab the L.	4291
	15:12	you and your **fellow** L are to consecrate	278
	15:13	It was because you, the L,	NIH
	15:14	the priests and L consecrated themselves	4291
	15:15	the L carried the ark of God with	1201+4291
	15:16	of the L to appoint their brothers as singers	4291
	15:17	So the L appointed Heman son of Joel;	4291
	15:26	the L who were carrying the ark of	4291
	15:27	were all the L who were carrying the ark,	4291
	16: 4	He appointed some of the L to minister	4291
	23: 2	as well as the priests and L.	4291
	23: 3	The L thirty years old or more	4291
	23: 6	David divided **the** L into groups	4392S
	23:26	the L no longer need to carry	4291
	23:27	the L were counted	1201+4290
	23:28	of **the** L was to help Aaron's descendants	4392S
	23:32	The L carried out their responsibilities for	NIH
	24: 6	of families of the priests and of the L—	4291
	24:30	These were the L,	1201+4290
	24:31	of families of the priests and of the L.	4291
	26:17	There were six L a day on the east,	4291
	26:20	Their fellow L were in charge of	4291
	28:13	for the divisions of the priests and L,	4291
	28:21	the priests and L are ready for all the work	4291
2Ch	5: 4	the L took up the ark.	4291
	5: 5	The priests, who were L, carried them up;	4291
	5:12	All the L who were musicians	4291
	7: 6	as did the L with the LORD's musical	4291
	7: 6	Opposite **the** L, the priests blew their	4392S
	8:14	and the L to lead the praise and to assist	4291
	8:15	to the priests or to the L in any matter,	4291
	11:13	The priests and L from all their districts	4291
	11:14	The L even abandoned their pasturelands	4291
	11:16	followed **the** L to Jerusalem	2157S
	13: 9	the sons of Aaron, and the L,	4291
	13:10	and the L assist them.	4291
	17: 8	With them were certain L—	4291
	19: 8	Jehoshaphat appointed some of the L,	4291
	19:11	the L will serve as officials before you.	4291
	20:19	Then some L from the Kohathites	4291
	23: 2	throughout Judah and gathered the L and	4291
	23: 4	of you priests and L who are going on duty	4291
	23: 6	of the LORD except the priests and L	4291
	23: 7	The L are to station themselves around	4291
	23: 8	The L and all the men of Judah did just	4291
	23:18	in the hands of the priests, who were L,	4291
	24: 5	He called together the priests and L	4291
	24: 5	But the L did not act at once.	4291
	24: 6	to bring in from Judah and Jerusalem	4291
	24:11	the L to the king's officials and they saw	4291
	29: 4	He brought in the priests and the L,	4291
	29: 5	"Listen to me, L!	4291
	29:12	Then these L set to work:	4291
	29:16	The L took it and carried it out to	4291
	29:25	He stationed the L in the temple of	4291
	29:26	L stood ready with David's instruments,	4291
	29:30	the L to praise the LORD with the words	4291
	29:34	so their kinsmen the L helped them until	4291
	29:34	for the L had been more conscientious	4291
	30:15	The priests and the L were ashamed	4291
	30:16	the blood handed to them by the L.	4291
	30:17	the L had to kill the Passover lambs	4291
	30:21	while the L and priests sang to	4291
	30:22	Hezekiah spoke encouragingly to all the L,	4291

2Ch	30:25	and L and all who had assembled	4291
	30:27	The priests and the L stood to bless	4291
	31: 2	Hezekiah assigned the priests and L	4291
	31: 2	according to their duties as priests or L—	4291
	31: 4	and L so they could devote themselves to	4291
	31: 9	Hezekiah asked the priests and L about	4291
	31:17	and likewise to the L twenty years old	4291
	31:19	in the genealogies of the L.	4291
	34: 9	which the L who were the doorkeepers	4291
	34:12	L descended from Merari,	4291
	34:12	descended from Kohath. The L—	4291
	34:13	Some of the L were secretaries,	4291
	34:30	the priests and the L—	4291
	35: 3	He said to the L, who instructed all Israel	4291
	35: 5	"Stand in the holy place with a group of L	4291
	35: 8	to the people and the priests and L.	4291
	35: 9	Jeiel and Jozabad, the leaders of the L,	4291
	35: 9	and five hundred head of cattle for the L.	4291
	35:10	in their places with the L in their divisions	4291
	35:11	while the L skinned the animals.	4291
	35:14	So the L made preparations for themselves	4291
	35:15	their fellow L made the preparations	4291
	35:18	as did Josiah, with the priests, the L	4291
Ezr	1: 5	and the priests and L—	4291
	2:40	The L: the descendants of Jeshua	4291
	2:70	The priests, the L, the singers,	4291
	3: 8	and the L and all who had returned from	4291
	3: 8	appointing L twenty years of age and older	4291
	3: 9	and their sons and brothers—all L—	4291
	3:10	the L (the sons of Asaph) with cymbals,	4291
	3:12	the older priests and L and family heads,	4291
	6:16	priests, the L and the rest of the exiles—	10387
	6:18	the L in their groups for the service of God	10387
	6:20	The priests and L had purified themselves	4291
	6:20	The L slaughtered the Passover lamb	NIH
	7: 7	including priests, L, singers,	4291
	7:13	including priests and L,	10387
	7:24	tribute or duty on any of the priests, L,	10387
	8:15	I found no L there.	1201+4291
	8:20	the officials had established to assist the L.	4291
	8:29	and the L and the family heads of Israel."	4291
	8:30	Then the priests and L received the silver	4291
	8:33	and so were the L Jozabad son of Jeshua	4291
	9: 1	including the priests and the L,	4291
	10: 5	the leading priests and L and all Israel	4291
	10:23	Among the L: Jozabad,	4291
Ne	3:17	by the L under Rehum son of Bani.	4291
	7: 1	and the singers and the L were appointed.	4291
	7:43	The L: the descendants of Jeshua	4291
	7:73	The priests, the L, the gatekeepers,	4291
	8: 7	The L—Jeshua, Bani, Sherebiah,	4291
	8: 9	the L who were instructing the people said	4291
	8:11	The L calmed all the people, saying,	4291
	8:13	along with the priests and the L,	4291
	9: 4	Standing on the stairs were the L—	4291
	9: 5	And the L—Jeshua, Kadmiel,	4291
	9:38	in writing, and our leaders, our L	4291
	10: 9	The L: Jeshua son of Azaniah,	4291
	10:28	"The rest of the people—priests, L,	4291
	10:34	"We—the priests, the L and the people—	4291
	10:37	we will bring a tithe of our crops to the L,	4291
	10:37	the L who collect the tithes in all the towns	4291
	10:38	to accompany the L when they receive	4291
	10:38	the L are to bring a tenth of the tithes up to	4291
	10:39	The people of Israel, including the L,	1201+4291
	11: 3	L, temple servants and descendants	4291
	11:15	From the L: Shemaiah son of Hasshub,	4291
	11:16	two of the heads of the L,	4291
	11:18	The L in the holy city totaled 284.	4291
	11:20	with the priests and L,	4291
	11:22	the L in Jerusalem was Uzzi son of Bani,	4291
	11:36	of the divisions of the L of Judah settled	4291
	12: 1	These were the priests and L who returned	4291
	12: 8	The L were Jeshua, Binnui, Kadmiel,	4291
	12:22	The family heads of the L in the days	4291
	12:24	And the leaders of the L were Hashabiah,	4291
	12:27	the L were sought out from	4291
	12:30	L had purified themselves ceremonially,	4291
	12:44	by the Law for the priests and the L,	4291
	12:44	with the ministering priests and L.	4291
	12:47	also set aside the portion for the other L,	4291
	12:47	and the L set aside the portion for	4291
	13: 5	new wine and oil prescribed for the L,	4291
	13:10	that the portions assigned to the L had	4291
	13:10	and that all the L and singers responsible	4291
	13:22	the L to purify themselves and go	4291
	13:29	of the priesthood and of the L.	4291
	13:30	the priests and the L of everything foreign,	4291
Isa	66:21	of them also to be priests and L,"	4291
Jer	33:18	who are L, ever fail to have a man to stand	4291
	33:21	with the L who are priests ministering	4291
	33:22	the L who minister before me as countless	4291
Eze	40:46	the only L who may draw near to	1201+4290
	43:19	who are L, of the family of Zadok,	4291
	44:10	" 'The L who went far from me	4291
	44:15	who are L and descendants of Zadok	4291
	45: 5	cubits wide will belong to the L,	4291
	48:11	the L did when the Israelites went astray.	4291
	48:12	bordering the territory of the L.	4291
	48:13	the L will have an allotment 25,000	4291
	48:22	So the property of the L and the property	4291
Mal	3: 3	the L and refine them like gold and	1201+4290
Jn	1:19	the Jews of Jerusalem sent priests and L	3324

LEVITICAL (3) [LEVI]

Lev	25:32	to redeem their houses in the L towns,	4291

1Ch 15:12 "You are the heads of the **L** families; 4291
Heb 7:11 through the **L** priesthood (for on the basis *3325*

LEVY (2)

2Ki 23:33 on Judah a **l** of a hundred talents of silver 6741
2Ch 36: 3 **imposed** on Judah a **l** of a hundred talents 6740

LEWD (4) [LEWDNESS]

Jdg 20: 6 **l** and disgraceful **act** in Israel. 2365
Eze 16:27 who were shocked by your **l** conduct. 2365
22: 9 the mountain shrines and commit **l acts.** 2365
23:44 so they slept with those **l** women, 2365

LEWDNESS (11) [LEWD]

Eze 16:43 Did you not add **l** to all your other 2365
16:58 bear the **consequences of** your **l** 2365
23:21 So you longed for the **l** *of* your youth, 2365
23:27 the **l** and prostitution you began in Egypt. 2365
23:29 Your **l** and promiscuity 2365
23:35 bear the **consequences of** your **l** 2365
23:48 "So I will put an end to **l** in the land, 2365
23:49 You will suffer the **penalty for** your **l** 2365
24:13 " 'Now your impurity is **l**. 2365
Hos 2:10 So now I will expose her **l** before the eyes 5578
Mk 7:22 **l**, envy, slander, arrogance and folly. *816*

LIABLE (2)

Jos 6:18 of Israel **l** to destruction and bring trouble 4200
7:12 and run because they have been made **l** to 4200

LIAR (14) [LIE]

Dt 19:18 and if the witness proves to be a **l**, 9214
Job 34: 6 Although I am right, *I am* **considered a l**; 3941
Pr 17: 4 a **l** pays attention to a malicious tongue. 3941
19:22 better to be poor than a **l**. 408+3942
30: 6 or he will rebuke you and **prove** *you* **a l**. 3941+8120
Mic 2:11 If a **l** and deceiver comes and says, 3941+8120
Jn 8:44 for he is a **l** and the father of lies. 6026
8:55 If I said I did not, I would be a **l** like you, 6026
Ro 3: 4 Let God be true, and every man a **l**, 6026
1Jn 1:10 make him out to be a **l** and his word 6026
2: 4 but does not do what he commands is a **l**, 6026
2:22 Who is the **l**? It is the man who denies 6026
4:20 yet hates his brother, he is a **l**. 6026
5:10 God has made him out to be a **l**, 6026

LIARS (9) [LIE]

Ps 63:11 while the mouths of **l** will be silenced. 1819+9214
116:11 And in my dismay I said, "All men *are* **l**." 3941
Isa 57: 4 the offspring of **l**? 9214
Mic 2:11 her people *are* **l** and their tongues 1819+9214
1Ti 1:10 *for* slave traders and **l** and perjurers— 6026
2: 4 Such teachings come through hypocritical **l**, 6016
Tit 1:12 "Cretans are always **l**, evil brutes, 6026
Rev 3: 9 to be Jews though *they* are not, but **are l**— 6017
21: 8 the idolaters and all **l**— 6014

LIBATIONS (1)

Ps 16: 4 I will not pour out their **l** of blood or take 5821

LIBERAL (1) [LIBERALITY, LIBERALLY]

2Co 8:20 of the way we administer this **l** gift. *103*

LIBERALITY (2) [LIBERAL]

Est 1: 7 in keeping with the king's **l**. 3338
2:18 and distributed gifts with royal **l**. 3338

LIBERALLY (1) [LIBERAL]

Dt 15:14 **Supply** him **l** from your flock, 6735+6735

LIBERATED (1) [LIBERTY]

Ro 8:21 that the creation itself *will be* **l** *1802*

LIBERTINES (KJV) See FREEDMEN

LIBERTY (1) [LIBERATED]

Lev 25:10 Consecrate the fiftieth year and proclaim **l** 2002

LIBNAH (17) [LIBNITE, LIBNITES]

Nu 33:20 They left Rimmon Perez and camped at **L**. 4243
33:21 They left **L** and camped at Rissah. 4243
Jos 10:29 with him moved on from Makkedah to **L** 4243
10:31 and all Israel with him moved on from **L** 4243
10:32 just as he had done to **L**. 4243
10:39 to Debir and its king as they had done to **L** 4243
12:15 the king of **L** one the king of Adullam one 4243
15:42 **L**, Ether, Ashan, 4243
21:13 of refuge for one accused of murder), **L**, 4243
2Ki 8:22 **L** revolted at the same time. 4243
19: 8 and found the king fighting against **L**. 4243
23:31 daughter of Jeremiah; she was from **L**. 4243
24:18 daughter of Jeremiah; she was from **L**. 4243
1Ch 6:57 and **L**, Jattir, Eshtemoa, 4243
2Ch 21:10 **L** revolted at the same time, 4243
Isa 37: 8 and found the king fighting against **L**. 4243
Jer 52: 1 daughter of Jeremiah; she was from **L**. 4243

LIBNATH   See SHIHOR LIBNATH

LIBNI (5)

Ex 6:17 by clans, were **L** and Shimei. 4249
Nu 3:18 of the Gershonite clans: **L** and Shimei. 4249
1Ch 6:17 of Gershon: **L** and Shimei. 4249
6:20 **L** his son, Jehath his son, Zimmah his son, 4249
6:29 Mahli, **L** his son, Shimei his son, 4249

LIBNITE (1) [LIBNAH]

Nu 26:58 These also were Levite clans: the **L** clan, 4250

LIBNITES (1) [LIBNAH]

Nu 3:21 To Gershon belonged the clans of the **L** 4250

LIBYA (3) [LIBYANS]

Eze 30: 5 **L** and the people of the covenant 4275
Na 3: 9 Put and **L** were among her allies. 4275
Ac 2:10 Egypt and the parts of **L** near Cyrene; *3340*

LIBYANS (4) [LIBYA]

2Ch 12: 3 and the innumerable troops of **L**, 4275
16: 8 and **L** a mighty army with great numbers 4275
Isa 66:19 to the **L** and Lydians (famous as archers), 4275
Da 11:43 with the **L** and Nubians in submission. 4275

LICE (KJV) See GNAT

LICENSE (1)

Jude 1: 4 grace of our God into a **l for immorality** *816*

LICK (6) [LICKED, LICKS]

Nu 22: 4 "This horde *is going to* **l** up everything 4308
1Ki 21:19 dogs *will* **l** up your blood— 4379
Ps 72: 9 before him and his enemies *will* **l** 4308
Isa 5:24 of fire **l** up straw and as dry grass sinks 430
49:23 *they will* **l** the dust at your feet. 4308
Mic 7:17 *They will* **l** dust like a snake, 4308

LICKED (4) [LICK]

1Ki 18:38 and also **l** up the water in the trench. 4308
21:19 the place where dogs **l** up Naboth's blood, 4379
22:38 and the dogs **l** up his blood, 4379
Lk 16:21 Even the dogs came and **l** his sores. *2143*

LICKS (1) [LICK]

Nu 22: 4 as an ox **l** up the grass of the field." 4308

LID (2)

Nu 19:15 without a **l** fastened on it will be unclean. 7544
2Ki 12: 9 a chest and bored a hole in its **l**. 1946

LIE (140) [LIAR, LIARS, LIED, LIES, LYING]

Ge 19:31 there is no man around here to **l with** us 995+6584
19:32 to drink wine and then **l with** him 6640+8886
19:34 and you go in and **l with** him 6640+8886
19:21 and *I want to* **l with** her." 448+995
38: 8 "**L with** your brother's wife 448+995
Ex 23:11 the seventh year *let the land* **l unplowed** 9023
Lev 18:22 " 'Do not **l with** a man as one lies with a woman; 907+8886
19:11 " 'Do not **l**. 3950
26: 6 and *you will* **l down** and no one will 8886
26:33 and your cities *will* **l** in ruins. 2118
Nu 21:15 the ravines that lead to the site of Ar and **l** 9128
23:19 God is not a man, that *he should* **l**, 3941
24: 9 Like a lion *they* crouch and **l down**, 8886
Dt 6: 7 when you **l down** and when you get up. 8886
11:19 when you **l down** and when you get up. 8886
25: 2 the judge *shall* **make** him **l down** 5877
33:13 and with the deep waters *that* **l** below; 8069
Jdg 9:32 and your men should come and **l in wait** 741
Ru 3: 4 Then go and uncover his feet and **l down**. 8886
3: 7 to **l down** at the far end of the grain pile. 8886
3:13 **L** here until morning." 8886
1Sa 3: 5 go back and **l down**." 8886
3: 6 go back and **l down**." 8886
3: 9 So Eli told Samuel, "Go and **l down**, 8886
15:29 He who is the Glory of Israel *does* not **l** 9213
22: 8 to **l in wait** for me," 741
2Sa 8: 2 *He made* them **l down** on the ground 8886
11:11 my house to eat and drink and **l with** 6640+8886
12:11 and *he will* **l with** your wives 6640+8886
16:21 Ahithophel answered, "**L with** 448+995
20: 3 but *did* not **l with** them. 448+995
23: 7 they are burned up where they **l**." 8699
1Ki 1: 2 She can **l** beside him so that our lord 8886
Job 6:28 Would I **l** to your face? 3941
7: 4 When *I* **l down** I think, 8886
7:21 For *I will* soon **l down** in the dust; 8886
11:19 You will **l down**, 8069
20:11 *will* **l** with him in the dust. 8886
21:26 Side by side they **l** in the dust, 8886
29:19 dew *will* **l** all night on my branches. 4328
38:40 when they crouch in their dens or **l** in wait 3782
Ps 3: 5 I **l down** and sleep; 8886
4: 8 I *will* **l down** and sleep in peace, 8886
23: 2 *He makes* me **l down** in green pastures, 8069
31:17 the wicked be put to shame and *l* silent in AIT

Ps 36:12 See how the evildoers **l fallen**— 5877
37:32 The wicked **l** in wait for the righteous, 7595
38: 9 All my longings **l** open before you, NIH
57: 4 *I* **l** among ravenous beasts— 8886
59: 3 See how *they* **l in wait** for me! 741
62: 9 the highborn are but a **l**; 3942
76: 5 Valiant men *l* **plundered**, AIT
76: 6 both horse and chariot **l** still. 8101
88: 5 like the slain *who* **l** in the grave, 8905
89:35 and *I* will not **l** to David— 3941
102: 7 *I* **l awake**; I have become like a 9193
104:22 they return and **l down** in their dens. 8069
Pr 1:11 *let's* **l in wait** for someone's blood, 741
1:18 These men **l in wait** for their own blood; 741
3:24 when *you* **l down**, you will not be afraid; 8886
3:24 *you* **l down**, your sleep will be sweet. 8886
6: 9 How long *will you* **l** there, 8886
12: 6 words of the wicked **l in wait** *for* blood, 741
15:11 Death and Destruction **l** open before NIH
22: 5 In the paths of the wicked **l** thorns NIH
24:15 *Do* not **l in wait** like an outlaw against 741
Ecc 4:11 two **l down** together, they will keep warm. 8886
11: 3 in the place where it falls, there *will* it **l**. 2093
Isa 6:11 the cities **l ruined** and without inhabitant, 8615
11: 6 the leopard *will* **l down** with the goat, 8069
11: 7 their young *will* **l down** together, 8069
13:21 But desert creatures *will* **l** there, 8069
14:18 the kings of the nations **l in state**, 928+3883+8886
14:30 and the needy *will* **l down** in safety. 8069
17: 2 *which will* **l down**, with no one to 8069
21: 9 All the images of its gods *l* **shattered** on AIT
27:10 there the calves graze, there *they* **l down**; 8069
28:15 for we have made **l** our refuge 3942
28:17 hail will sweep away your refuge, the **l**, 3942
34:10 to generation *it will* **l desolate**; AIT
44:20 "Is not this thing in my right hand a **l**?" 9214
50:11 You will **l down** in torment. 8886
51:20 *they* **l** at the head of every street, 8886
56:10 *they* **l around** and dream, 8886
57: 2 they find rest as they **l in death**. 5435
Jer 3:25 Let us **l down** in our shame, 8886
4: 7 Your towns *will* **l in ruins** 5898
5: 6 a leopard *will* **l in wait** near their towns 9193
5:26 "Among my people are wicked men *who* **l in wait** 8800
9: 5 They have taught their tongues *to* **l**; 1819+9214
9:22 " 'The dead bodies of men *will* **l** 5877
12: 4 How long *will* the land **l parched** and AIT
23:14 They commit adultery and live a **l**. 9214
29:31 and has led you to believe a **l**, 9214
44: 2 Today they **l deserted** and in ruins AIT
46:19 and **l in ruins** without inhabitant. 5898
51:47 and her slain *will* all **l fallen** 5877
La 2:21 "Young and old **l** *together* in the dust of 8886
4: 5 Those nurtured in purple now **l** on ash heaps 2485
Eze 4: 4 "Then **l** on your left side and put the sin of 8886
4: 4 for the number of days *you* **l** on your side. 8886
4: 6 you have finished this, **l down** again, 8886
4: 9 You are to eat it during the 390 days you **l** 8886
6:13 when their people **l** slain among 2118
13: 6 and their divinations a **l**. 3942
18: 6 not defile his neighbor's wife or **l with** 448+7928
29:12 and her cities *will* **l** desolate forty years 2118
30: 7 their cities *will* **l** among ruined cities. 2118
31:18 *you will* **l** among the uncircumcised, 8886
32:21 down and *they* **l with** the uncircumcised, 8886
32:27 *Do they* not **l with** the other uncircumcised, 8886
32:28 and *will* **l** among the uncircumcised, 8886
32:29 They **l** with the uncircumcised, 8886
32:30 *They* **l uncircumcised** with those killed by 8886
34:14 There *they* *will* **l down** 8069
34:15 and have them **l down**, 8069
48:22 of the city *will* **l** in the center of the area 2118
48:22 The area belonging to the prince *will* **l** 2118
Da 11:27 at the same table and **l** to each other, 1819+3942
Hos 2:18 so that all *may* **l down** in safety. 8886
6: 9 As marauders **l in ambush** *for* a man, 2675
Am 2: 8 *They* **l down** beside every altar 5742
6: 4 You **l** on beds inlaid with ivory and lounge 8886
Mic 7: 2 All men **l in wait** to shed blood; 741
Na 3:18 your nobles **l down to rest**. 8905
Zep 2: 7 In the evening *they will* **l down** in 8069
2:14 Flocks and herds *will* **l down** there, 8069
3:13 They will eat and **l down** 8069
Zec 10: 2 diviners see visions that **l**; 9214
Jn 3:20 of disabled people *used to* **l**— 2879
Ro 1:25 They exchanged the truth of God for a **l**, 6022
Gal 1:20 that what I am writing you *is* no **l**. 6017
Col 3: 9 *Do* not **l** to each other, 6017
2Th 2:11 so that they will believe the **l** 6022
Tit 1: 2 which God, who *does* not **l**, 950
Heb 6:18 in which it is impossible for God *to* **l**, 6017
1Jn 1: 6 we **l** and do not live by the truth. 6017
2:21 and because no **l** comes from the truth. 6022
Rev 11: 9 Their bodies will **l** in the street of NIG
14: 5 No **l** was found in their mouths; 6022

LIED (6) [LIE]

Ge 18:15 Sarah was afraid, so *she* **l** and said, 3950
Jos 7:11 they have stolen, *they have* **l**, 3950
Jdg 16:10 made a fool of me; *you* **l** to me. 1819+3942
Jer 5:12 *They have* **l** about the LORD; 3950
Ac 5: 3 heart *that you* **l** *have* **l** to the Holy Spirit 6017
5: 4 *You have* not **l** to men but to God." 6017

LIEN (KJV) See SLEEP, SLEPT, RAVISHED

LIES (106) [LIE]

Ge	21:17	the boy crying as he l there.	NIH
	49: 9	Like a lion he crouches and l down,	8069
	49:25	blessings of the deep that l below,	8069
Ex	5: 9	and pay no attention to l."	1821+9214
Lev	6: 3	or if he finds lost property and l about it,	3950
	15: 4	" 'Any bed the man with a discharge l	8886
	15:18	When a man l with a woman and	907+8886
	15:20	" 'Anything she l on during her period	8886
	15:24	" 'If a man l with her and her	907+8886+8886
	15:24	any bed he l on will be unclean.	8886
	15:26	Any bed she l on while her discharge	8886
	15:33	and for a man who l with a woman	6640+8886
	18:22	not lie with a man as one l with a woman;	5435
	20:13	'If a man l with a man as one lies with	907+8886
	20:13	'If a man lies with a man as one l with	5435
	20:18	'If a man l with a woman during her	907+8886
	26:34	the time that it l desolate and you are in	9037
	26:35	All the time that it l desolate,	9037
	26:43	while it l desolate without them.	9037
Nu	14:33	until the last of your bodies l in the desert.	NIH
Dt	19:11	if a man hates his neighbor and l in wait	741
Ru	3: 4	When he l down, note the place where	8886
1Sa	14:39	even if it l with my son Jonathan,	3780
	22:13	against me and l in wait for me,	741
2Sa	1:19	O Israel, l slain on your heights.	NIH
	1:25	Jonathan l slain on your heights.	NIH
Ne	2: 3	where my fathers are buried l in ruins,	NIH
	2:17	Jerusalem l in ruins,	NIH
Job	13: 4	You, however, smear me with l;	9214
	14:12	so man l down and does not rise;	8886
	18:10	a trap l in his path.	NIH
	19:28	since the root of the trouble l in him,'	5162
	20:26	total darkness l in wait for his treasures.	3243
	26: 6	Destruction l uncovered.	NIH
	27:19	He l down wealthy, but will do so no more;	8886
	37:17	the land l hushed under the south wind,	9200
	40:21	Under the lotus plants he l,	8886
Ps	5: 6	You destroy those who tell l;	3942
	10: 7	His mouth is full of curses and l	5327
	10: 8	He l in wait near the villages;	3782
	10: 9	He l in wait like a lion in cover;	741
	10: 9	he l in wait to catch the helpless;	741
	12: 2	Everyone l to his neighbor;	1819+8736
	34:13	from evil and your lips from speaking l.	5327
	41: 8	up from the place where he l."	8886
	55:11	threats and l never leave its streets.	5327
	58: 3	the womb they are wayward and speak l.	3942
	59:12	For the curses and l they utter,	3951
	62: 4	they take delight in l.	3942
	88: 7	Your wrath l heavily upon me;	6164
	119:69	the arrogant have smeared me with l,	9214
	144: 8	whose mouths are full of l,	8736
	144:11	of foreigners whose mouths are full of l,	8736
Pr	6:19	a false witness who pours out l and	3942
	12:17	but a false witness tells l.	5327
	14: 5	but a false witness pours out l.	3942
	19: 5	and he who pours out l will not go free.	3942
	19: 9	and he who pours out l will perish.	3942
	23:28	Like a bandit she l in wait,	741
	29:12	If a ruler listens to l,	1821+9214
	30: 8	Keep falsehood and l far from me;	1821+3942
Isa	9:15	the prophets who teach l are the tail.	9214
	24:10	The ruined city l desolate;	AIT
	32: 7	to destroy the poor with l,	609+9214
	59: 3	Your lips have spoken l,	9214
	59: 4	on empty arguments and speak l;	8736
	59:13	uttering l our hearts have conceived.	1821+9214
	64:11	and all that we treasured l in ruins.	2118
Jer	4:20	the whole land l in ruins.	8720
	5:31	The prophets prophesy l,	9214
	9: 3	ready their tongue like a bow, to shoot l;	9214
	14:14	prophets are prophesying l in my name.	9214
	20: 6	to whom you have prophesied l.'	9214
	23:10	because of the curse the land l parched and	AIT
	23:25	the prophets say who prophesy l	9214
	23:32	lead my people astray with their reckless l,	9214
	27:10	They prophesy l to you	9214
	27:14	for they are prophesying l to you.	9214
	27:15	'They are prophesying l in my name.	9214
	27:16	They are prophesying l to you.	9214
	28:15	persuaded this nation to trust in l.	9214
	29: 9	They are prophesying l to you	9214
	29:21	who are prophesying l to you in my name:	9214
	29:23	and in my name have spoken l.'	9214
	40: 4	Look, the whole country l before you;	NIH
La	1: 1	deserted the city, once so full of people!	3782
	5:18	which l desolate, with jackals prowling	9037
Eze	13:19	By lying to my people, who listen to l,	3942
	13:22	disheartened the righteous with your l,	9214
	26: 2	now that she l in ruins I will prosper,'	2990
	32:23	of the pit and her army l around her grave.	2118
	47:16	and Sibraim (which l on the border	NIH
Da	2:22	he knows what l in darkness,	NIH
Hos	7: 3	the princes with their l.	3951
	7:13	I long to redeem them but they speak l	3942
	11:12	Ephraim has surrounded me with l,	3951
	12: 1	the east wind all day and multiplies l	3942
Mic	7: 5	with her who l in your embrace be careful	8886
Na	1: 1	Woe to the city of blood, full of l,	3951
Hab	2:18	Or an image that teaches l?	9214
Zep	3:13	they will speak no l,	3942
Zec	13: 3	because you have told l in the LORD's name	9214

Mt	8: 6	"my servant l at home paralyzed and	965
Jn	8:44	When he l, he speaks his native language,	3281+3836+6022
	8:44	for he is a liar and the father of l.	899S
Rev	10: 8	"Go, take the scroll that l open in the hand	AIT

LIEUTENANTS (KJV) See SATRAP

LIFE (589) [LIVE]

Ge	1:30	everything that has the breath of l in it—	2645
	2: 7	into his nostrils the breath of l,	2644
	2: 9	of l and the tree of the knowledge of good	2644
	3:14	you will eat dust all the days of your l.	2644
	3:17	you will eat of it all the days of your l.	2644
	3:22	and take also from the tree of l and eat,	2644
	3:24	and forth to guard the way to the tree of l.	2644
	6:17	to destroy all l under the heavens,	1414
	6:17	every creature that has the breath of l in it.	2644
	7:11	In the six hundredth year of Noah's l,	2644
	7:15	of all creatures that have the breath of l.	2644
	7:22	that had the breath of l in its nostrils died.	2644
	9: 5	an accounting for the l of his fellow man.	5883
	9:11	Never again will all l be cut off by	1414
	9:15	the waters become a flood to destroy all l.	1414
	9:17	between me and all l on the earth."	1414
	12:13	be treated well for your sake and my l will	5883
	19:19	great kindness to me in sparing my l.	5883
	19:20	Then my l will be spared."	5883
	26: 9	"Because I thought I might lose my l	4637
	27:46	my l will not be worth living."	2644+4200+4537
	32:30	and yet my l was spared."	5883
	37:21	"Let's not take his l," he said.	5883
	42:21	with us for his l, but we would not listen;	5883
	43: 9	I will bear the blame before you all my l.	3427
	44:30	whose l is closely bound up with	5883
	44:30	closely bound up with the boy's l,	5883
	44:32	blame before you, my father, all my l!'	3427
	47:28	of his l were a hundred and forty-seven.	2644
	48:15	God who has been my shepherd all my l	4946+6388
Ex	21: 6	Then he will be his servant for l.	4200+6409
	21:23	you are to take l for life,	5883
	21:23	you are to take life for l,	5883
	21:30	he may redeem his l by paying whatever	5883
	23:26	I will give you a full l span.	3427+5031
	30:12	for his l at the time he is counted.	5883
Lev	17:11	For the l of a creature is in the blood,	5883
	17:11	that makes atonement for one's l.	5883
	17:14	the l of every creature is its blood.	5883
	17:14	the l of every creature is its blood;	5883
	19:16	Do not do anything that endangers your neighbor's l.	1947+6584+6641
	24:17	If anyone takes the l of a human being	5782+5883
	24:18	Anyone who takes the l of someone's	5782+5883
	24:18	animal must make restitution—l for life.	5883
	24:18	animal must make restitution—life for l.	5883
	25:46	and can make them slaves for l,	6409
	26:16	and drain away your l.	5883
Nu	35:31	" 'Do not accept a ransom for the l of	5883
Dt	4:42	into one of these cities and save his l.	2649
	6: 2	and so that you may enjoy long l.	799+3427
	12:23	because the blood is the l,	5883
	12:23	and you must not eat the l with the meat.	5883
	15:17	and he will become your servant for l.	6409
	16: 3	the days of your l you may remember	2644
	17:19	and he is to read it all the days of his l so	2644
	19: 4	and flees there to save his l.	2649
	19: 5	to one of these cities and save his l.	2649
	19:21	l for life, eye for eye, tooth for tooth,	5883
	19:21	life for l, eye for eye, tooth for tooth,	5883
	22: 7	with you and you may have a long l.	3427
	28:66	never sure of your l.	2644
	30:15	I set before you today l and prosperity,	2644
	30:19	that I have set before you l and death,	2644
	30:19	Now choose l, so that you	2644
	30:20	For the LORD is your l,	2644
	32:39	I put to death and I bring to l,	2649
	32:47	not just idle words for you—they are your l.	2644
Jos	1: 5	up against you all the days of your l.	2644
	4:14	and they revered him all the days of his l,	2644
Jdg	5: 7	Village l in Israel ceased,	7251
	9:17	risked his l to rescue you from the hand	5883
	12: 3	I took my l in my hands and crossed over	5883
	13:12	to be the rule for the boy's l and work?"	NIH
Ru	1:20	the Almighty has made my l very bitter.	3276
	4:15	He will renew your l and sustain you	5883
1Sa	1:11	to the LORD for all the days of his l,	2644
	1:28	For his whole l he will be given	889+2118+3427
	2:33	descendants will die in the prime of l.	408
	7:15	as judge over Israel all the days of his l.	2644
	19: 5	He took his l in his hands when he killed	5883
	19:11	"If you don't run for your l tonight,	5883
	20: 1	that he is trying to take my l?"	5883
	22:23	who is seeking your l is seeking mine also.	5883
	23:15	that Saul had come out to take his l.	5883
	24:11	but you are hunting me down to take my l.	5883
	25: 6	Say to him: 'Long l to you!	2021+2644+4200
	25:29	someone is pursuing you to take your l,	5883
	25:29	the l of my master will be bound securely	5883
	26:21	you considered my l precious today,	5883
	26:24	As surely as I valued your l today,	5883
	26:24	the LORD value my l and deliver me	5883
	28: 2	make you my bodyguard for l."	2021+3427+3972
	28: 9	Why have you set a trap for my l to bring	5883
	28:21	I took my l in my hands	5883

2Sa	1:23	in l they were loved and gracious,	2644
	4: 8	your enemy, who tried to take your l.	5883
	14: 7	so that we may put him to death for the l	5883
	14:14	But God does not take away l;	5883
	15:21	whether it means l or death,	2644
	16:11	is trying to take my l.	5883
	18:13	And if I had put my l in jeopardy—	5883
	19: 5	who have just saved your l and the lives	5883
1Ki	1:12	how you can save your own life and the l	5883
	1:12	how you can save your own life and the l	5883
	2:23	if Adonijah does not pay with his l!	5883
	3:11	and not for long l or wealth for yourself,	3427
	3:14	I will give you a long l."	3427
	4:21	and were Solomon's subjects all his l.	
	4:33	He described plant l,	6770
	11:34	I have made him ruler all the days of his l	2644
	15: 5	LORD's commands all the days of his l—	2644
	15:14	to the LORD all his l.	3427
	17:21	let this boy's l return to him!"	5883
	17:22	and the boy's l returned to him,	5883
	19: 2	not make your l like that of one of them."	5883
	19: 3	Elijah was afraid and ran for his l.	5883
	19: 4	he said. "Take my l;	5883
	20:31	Perhaps he will spare your l."	5883
	20:39	he is missing, it will be your l for his life,	5883
	20:39	he is missing, it will be your life for his l,	5883
	20:42	Therefore it is your l for his life,	5883
	20:42	Therefore it is your life for his l,	5883
2Ki	1:13	"please have respect for my l and the lives	5883
	1:14	But now have respect for my l!"	5883
	5: 7	Can I kill and bring back to l?	2649
	8: 1	the woman whose son he had restored to l,	2649
	8: 5	restored the dead to l,	2649
	8: 5	the woman whose son Elisha had brought back to l came	2649
	8: 5	this is her son whom Elisha restored to l."	2649
	10:24	it will be your l for his life."	5883
	10:24	it will be your life for his l."	5883
	13:21	the man came to l and stood up	2649
	18:32	Choose l and not death!	2649
	20: 6	I will add fifteen years to your l.	3427
	25:29	of his l ate regularly at the king's table.	2644
1Ch	29:28	having enjoyed long l, wealth and	3427+8428
2Ch	1:11	and since you have not asked for a long l	3427
	15:17	committed [to the LORD] all his l.	3427
Ezr	9: 9	He has granted us new l to rebuild	4695
Ne	4: 2	bring the stones back to l	2649
	6:11	like me go into the temple to save his l?	2649
	9: 6	You give l to everything,	2649
Est	4:11	the gold scepter to him and spare his l.	2649
	7: 3	grant me my l—this is my petition.	5883
	7: 7	behind to beg Queen Esther for his l.	5883
Job	2: 4	"A man will give all he has for his own l.	5883
	2: 6	but you must spare his l."	5883
	3:20	and l to the bitter of soul,	2644
	3:23	Why is l given to a man whose way	NIH
	7: 7	O God, that my l is but a breath;	2644
	7:16	I despise my l; I would not live forever.	NIH
	8:19	Surely its l withers away,	2006
	9:21	I despise my own l.	2644
	10: 1	"I loathe my very l;	2644
	10:12	You gave me l and showed me kindness,	2644
	11:17	L will be brighter than noonday,	2698
	12:10	In his hand is the l of every creature and	5883
	12:12	Does not long l bring understanding?	3427
	13:14	in jeopardy and take my l in my hands?	5883
	24:22	they have no assurance of l.	2644
	27: 3	as long as I have l within me,	5972
	27: 8	when God takes away his l?	5883
	30:16	"And now my l ebbs away;	5883
	31:30	to sin by invoking a curse against his l—	5883
	33: 4	the breath of the Almighty gives me l.	2649
	33:18	his l from perishing by the sword,	2652
	33:22	and his l to the messengers of death.	2652
	33:30	that the light of l may shine on him.	2644
	41: 4	for you to take him as your slave for l?	6409
	42:12	LORD blessed the latter part of Job's l	344
Ps	7: 5	let him trample my l to the ground	2644
	16:11	have made known to me the path of l;	2644
	17:14	of this world whose reward is in this l.	2645
	21: 4	He asked you for l,	2644
	22:20	Deliver my l from the sword,	5883
	22:20	my precious l from the power of the dogs.	3495
	23: 6	love will follow me all the days of my l,	2644
	25:20	Guard my l and rescue me;	5883
	26: 1	O LORD, for I have led a blameless l;	928+2143
	26: 9	my l with bloodthirsty men,	2644
	26:11	But I lead a blameless l;	928+2143
	27: 1	The LORD is the stronghold of my l—	2644
	27: 4	of the LORD all the days of my l,	2644
	31:10	My l is consumed by anguish	2644
	31:13	against me and plot to take my l.	5883
	34:12	Whoever of you loves l and desires	2644
	35: 4	May those who seek my l be disgraced	5883
	35:17	Rescue my l from their ravages,	5883
	35:17	my precious l from these lions.	3495
	36: 9	For with you is the fountain of l;	2644
	38:12	Those who seek my l set their traps,	5883
	39: 4	let me know how fleeting is my l.	638
	39: 5	Each man's l is but a breath.	5893
	40:14	May all who seek to take my l be put	5883
	41: 2	LORD will protect him and preserve his l;	2649
	42: 8	a prayer to the God of my l.	2644
	49: 7	the l of another or give to God a ransom	NIH
	49: 8	a l is costly, no payment is ever enough—	5883
	49:15	But God will redeem my l from the grave;	5883
	49:19	who will never see the light [of l].	NIH

Ps	54: 3	ruthless men seek my l— 5883
	56: 6	they watch my steps, eager to take my l. 5883
	56:13	I may walk before God in the light of l. 2644
	61: 6	Increase the **days of** the king's l, 3427
	63: 3	Because your love is better than l, 2644
	63: 9	They who seek my l will be destroyed; 5883
	64: 1	protect my l from the threat of the enemy. 2644
	69:28	May they be blotted out of the book of l 2644
	70: 2	May those who seek my l be put to shame 5883
	71:20	*you will* **restore** my l again; 2649
	74:19	over the l of your dove to wild beasts; 5883
	86: 2	Guard my l, for I am devoted to you. 5883
	86:14	a band of ruthless men seeks my l— 5883
	88: 3	of trouble and my l draws near the grave. 2644
	89:47	Remember how **fleeting** is my l. 2698
	91:16	With long l I will satisfy him 3427
	101: 2	I will be careful to lead a blameless l— 2006
	102:23	the **course of** my l he broke my strength; 2006
	103: 4	who redeems your l from the pit 2644
	104:33	I will sing to the LORD all my l; 2644
	109:31	to save his l from those who condemn him. 5883
	119:25	**preserve** my l according to your word. 2649
	119:37	**preserve** my l according to your word. 2649
	119:40	**Preserve** my l in your righteousness. 2649
	119:50	Your promise **preserves** my l. 2649
	119:88	**Preserve** my l according to your love, 2649
	119:93	for by them *you have* **preserved** my l. 2649
	119:107	I have suffered much; **preserve** my l, 2649
	119:109	I constantly take my l in my hands, 5883
	119:149	**preserve** my l, O LORD, 2649
	119:154	**preserve** my l according to your promise. 2649
	119:156	**preserve** my l according to your laws. 2649
	119:159	**preserve** my l, O LORD, 2649
	121: 7	he will watch over your l; 5883
	128: 5	from Zion all the days of your l; 2644
	133: 3	For there the LORD bestows his blessing, even l forevermore. 2644
	138: 7	*you* **preserve** my l; 2649
	142: 4	I have no refuge; no one cares for my l. 5883
	143:11	O LORD, **preserve** my l; 2649
	146: 2	I will praise the LORD all my l; 2644
Pr	1: 3	and **prudent** l, doing what is right and just AIT
	2:19	to her return or attain the paths of l. 2644
	3: 2	for they will prolong your l many years 2644
	3:16	Long l is in her right hand; 3427
	3:18	a tree of l to those who embrace her; 2644
	3:22	they will be l for you, 2644
	4:10	and the years of your l will be many. 2644
	4:13	guard it well, for it is your l. 2644
	4:22	for they are l to those who find them 2644
	4:23	for it is the wellspring of l. 2644
	5: 6	She gives no thought to the way of l; 2644
	5:11	At the **end of** your l you will groan, 344
	6:23	corrections of discipline are the way to l, 2644
	6:26	and the adulteress preys upon your very l. 5883
	7:23	little knowing it will cost him his l. 5883
	8:35	For whoever finds me finds l 2644
	9:11	and years will be added to your l. 2644
	10:11	mouth of the righteous is a fountain of l, 2644
	10:16	The wages of the righteous bring them l, 2644
	10:17	who heeds discipline shows the way to l, 2644
	10:27	The fear of the LORD adds length to l, 3427
	11:19	The truly righteous man attains l, 2644
	11:30	The fruit of the righteous is a tree of l, 2644
	12:28	In the way of righteousness there is l; 2644
	13: 3	He who guards his lips guards his l, 5883
	13: 8	A man's riches may ransom his l, 5883
	13:12	but a longing fulfilled is a tree of l. 2644
	13:14	The teaching of the wise is a fountain of l, 2644
	14:27	The fear of the LORD is a fountain of l, 2644
	14:30	A heart at peace gives l *to* the body, 2644
	15: 4	tongue that brings healing is a tree of l, 2644
	15:24	of l leads upward for the wise to keep him 2644
	16:15	When a king's face brightens, it means l; 2644
	16:17	he who guards his way guards his l. 5883
	16:22	a fountain of l to those who have it, 2644
	16:31	it is attained by a righteous l. 2006
	18:21	The tongue has the power of l and death, 2644
	19: 3	A man's own folly ruins his l, 2006
	19:16	He who obeys instructions guards his l, 5883
	19:23	The fear of the LORD leads to l: 2644
	20: 2	he who angers him forfeits his l. 5883
	20: 7	The righteous man **leads a** blameless l; 2143
	21:21	and love finds l, prosperity and honor. 2644
	22: 4	the LORD bring wealth and honor and l. 2644
	23:22	Listen to your father, who **gave** you l, 3528
	24:12	Does not he who guards your l know it? 5883
	28:16	he who hates ill-gotten gain *will* **enjoy a long** l. 799+3427
	31:12	not harm, all the days of her l. 2644
Ecc	2:17	So I hated l, because the work that is done 2644
	5:18	the few days of l God has given him— 2644
	5:20	He seldom reflects on the days of his l, 2644
	6:12	who knows what is good for a man in l, 2644
	7:12	wisdom **preserves** *the* l of its possessor. 2649
	7:15	In this meaningless l of mine I have seen 3427
	8:15	So I commend the enjoyment of l, NIH
	8:15	the days of their l God has given him under 2644
	9: 9	Enjoy l with your wife, whom you love, 2644
	9: 9	all the days of this meaningless l 2644
	9: 9	in l and in your toilsome labor under 2644
	10:19	and wine makes l merry. 2644
Isa	23:15	seventy years, the **span** of a king's l. 3427
	38: 5	I will add fifteen years to your l. 3427
	38:10	"In the prime of my l I must go through 3427
	38:12	Like a weaver I have rolled up my l, 2644
	38:16	and my spirit finds l in them too. 2644

Isa	42: 5	and l to those who walk on it: 8120
	43: 4	and people in exchange for your l. 5883
	53:10	the LORD makes his l a guilt offering, 5883
	53:11	he will see the light [of l] and be satisfied; NIH
	53:12	because he poured out his l unto death, 5883
Jer	4:30	Your lovers despise you; they seek your l. 5883
	4:31	my l is given over to murderers." 5883
	8: 3	of this evil nation will prefer death to l, 2644
	10:23	O LORD, that a man's l is not his own; 2006
	11:21	of Anathoth who are seeking your l 5883
	17:11	When his l is half gone, 3427
	20:13	the l of the needy from the hands of 5883
	21: 8	See, I am setting before you the way of l 2644
	21: 9	he will escape with his l. 5883
	22:25	to those who seek your l, those you fear— 5883
	38: 2	He will escape with his l; he will live.' 5883
	38:16	over to those who are seeking your l." 5883
	38:17	your l will be spared and this city will not 5883
	38:20	and your l will be spared. 5883
	39:18	by the sword but will escape with your l, 5883
	40:14	of Nethaniah to take your l?" 5883
	40:15	Why should he take your l and cause all 5883
	44:30	over to his enemies who seek his l, 5883
	44:30	the enemy who was seeking his l.' " 5883
	45: 5	I will let you escape with your l.' " 5883
	52:33	rest of his l ate regularly at the king's table. 2644
La	3:53	to end my l in a pit and threw stones 2644
	3:58	you redeemed my l. 2644
	4:20	The LORD's anointed, our very l **breath** 678+8120
Eze	3:18	from his evil ways in order to **save** his l, 2649
	7:13	not one of them will preserve his l. 2652
	18:27	he will save his l. 5883
	32:10	of them will tremble every moment for his l, 5883
	33: 4	and the sword comes and **takes** his l, 4374
	33: 6	the sword comes and takes the l of one 5883
	33:15	follows the decrees that give l, 2644
	37: 5	and *you will* **come to** l. 2649
	37: 6	and *you will* **come to** l. 2649
	37:10	*they* **came to** l and stood up 2649
Da	5:23	the God who holds in his hand your l 10494
	12: 2	will awake: some to everlasting l, 2644
Am	2:14	and the warrior will not save his l. 5883
	2:15	and the horseman will not save his l. 5883
Jnh	1:14	not let us die for taking this man's l. 5883
	2: 6	But you brought my l up from the pit, 2644
	2: 7	"When my l was ebbing away, 5883
	4: 3	Now, O LORD, take away my l, 5883
Hab	2:10	your own house and forfeiting your l. 2644
	2:19	to him who says to wood, 'Come to l!' 7810
Mal	2: 5	a covenant of l and peace, 2644
Mt	2:20	to take the child's l are dead." 6034
	6:25	I tell you, do not worry about your l, 6034
	6:25	Is not l more important than food, 6034
	6:27	by worrying can add a single hour to his l? 2461
	7:14	and narrow the road that leads to l, 2437
	10:39	Whoever finds his l will lose it, 6034
	10:39	and whoever loses his l for my sake 6034
	13:22	the worries of this l and the deceitfulness 172
	16:21	and on the third day *be* **raised to** l. 1586
	16:25	whoever wants to save his l will lose it, 6034
	16:25	but whoever loses his l for me will find l. 6034
	17:23	on the third day *he will be* **raised to** l." 1586
	18: 8	for you to enter l maimed or crippled than 2437
	18: 9	for you to enter l with one eye than 2437
	19:16	good thing must I do to get eternal l?" 2437
	19:17	If you want to enter l, 2437
	19:29	as much and will inherit eternal l. 2437
	20:19	On the third day *he will be* **raised to** l!" 1586
	20:28	and to give his l as a ransom for many." 6034
	25:46	but the righteous to eternal l." 2437
	27:52	holy people who had died *were* **raised to** l. 1586
Mk	3: 4	to save l or to kill?" 6034
	4:19	but the worries of this l, 1050
	8:35	whoever wants to save his l will lose it, 6034
	8:35	but whoever loses his l for me and for 6034
	9:43	It is better for you to enter l maimed than 2437
	9:45	It is better for you to enter l crippled than 2437
	10:17	"what must I do to inherit eternal l?" 2437
	10:30	and in the age to come, eternal l. 2437
	10:45	and to give his l as a ransom for many." 6034
Lk	6: 9	to save l or to destroy it?" 6034
	7:37	When a woman who had lived a **sinful** l, 283
	9: 8	of long ago *had* **come back to** l, 482
	9:19	of long ago *has* **come back to** l." 482
	9:22	and on the third day *be* **raised to** l." 1586
	9:24	whoever wants to save his l will lose it, 6034
	9:24	but whoever loses his l for me will save it. 6034
	10:25	"what must I do to inherit eternal l?" 2437
	12:15	a man's l does not consist in the abundance 2437
	12:19	**Take l easy;** eat, drink and be merry." ' 399
	12:20	This very night your l will be demanded 6034
	12:22	do not worry about your l, 6034
	12:23	L is more than food, 6034
	12:25	by worrying can add a single hour to his l? 2461
	14:26	yes, even his own l— 6034
	17:33	Whoever tries to keep his l will lose it, 6034
	17:33	and whoever loses his l will preserve it. NIG
	18:18	what must I do to inherit eternal l?" 2437
	18:30	in the age to come, eternal l." 2437
	21:19	By standing firm you will gain l. 6034
	21:34	drunkenness and the anxieties of l, 1053
Jn	1: 4	In him was l, and that life was the light 2437
	1: 4	and that l was the light of men. 2437
	3:15	who believes in him may have eternal l. 2437
	3:16	in him shall not perish but have eternal l. 2437
	3:36	Whoever believes in the Son has eternal l, 2437
	3:36	but whoever rejects the Son will not see l, 2437

Jn	4:14	a spring of water welling up to eternal l." 2437
	4:36	now he harvests the crop for eternal l, 2437
	5:21	the Father raises the dead and **gives** them l, 2443
	5:21	so the Son **gives** l to whom he is pleased 2443
	5:24	believes him who sent me has eternal l 2437
	5:24	he has crossed over from death to l. 2437
	5:26	For as the Father has l in himself, 2437
	5:26	so he has granted the Son to have l 2437
	5:39	that by them you possess eternal l. 2437
	5:40	yet you refuse to come to me to have l. 2437
	6:27	but for food that endures to eternal l, 2437
	6:33	from heaven and gives l to the world." 2437
	6:35	Then Jesus declared, "I am the bread *of* l. 2437
	6:40	and believes in him shall have eternal l, 2437
	6:47	he who believes has everlasting l. 2437
	6:48	I am the bread *of* l. 2437
	6:51	which I will give for the l of the world." 2437
	6:53	you have no l in you. 2437
	6:54	and drinks my blood has eternal l, 2437
	6:63	The Spirit **gives** l; 1639+2443
	6:63	to you are spirit and they are l. 2437
	6:68	You have the words of eternal l. 2437
	7: 1	the Jews there were waiting *to* **take** his l. 650
	8:11	"Go now and **leave your l** of sin." 279+3600
	8:12	but will have the light of l." 2437
	9: 3	of God might be displayed in his l. NIG
	10:10	I have come that they may have l, 2437
	10:11	The good shepherd lays down his l for 6034
	10:15	and I lay down my l for the sheep. 6034
	10:17	my Father loves me is that I lay down my l 6034
	10:28	I give them eternal l, and they shall never 2437
	11:25	"I am the resurrection and the l. 2437
	11:53	from that day on they plotted to **take** *his* l. 650
	12:25	The man who loves his l will lose it, 6034
	12:25	while the man who hates his l 6034
	12:25	in this world will keep it for eternal l. 2437
	12:50	that his command leads to eternal l. 2437
	13:37	I will lay down my l for you." 6034
	13:38	"Will you really lay down your l for me? 6034
	14: 6	"I am the way and the truth and the l. 2437
	15:13	that he lay down his l for his friends. 6034
	17: 2	over all people that he might give eternal l 2437
	17: 3	this is eternal l: that they may know you, 2437
	20:31	by believing you may have l in his name. 2437
Ac	2:28	made known to me the paths of l; 2437
	2:32	God has **raised** this Jesus to l, 482
	3:15	You killed the author *of* l, 2437
	5:20	the people the full message *of* this new l." 2437
	8:33	For his l was taken from the earth." 2437
	11:18	granted even the Gentiles repentance unto l. 2437
	13:46	not consider yourselves worthy of eternal l, 2437
	13:48	appointed for eternal l believed. 2437
	17:25	because he himself gives all men l 2437
	20:24	I consider my l worth nothing to me, 6034
	26: 4	the beginning of my l in my own country, NIG
	27:43	But the centurion wanted to spare Paul's l NIG
Ro	2: 7	he will give eternal l. 2437
	4:17	the God who **gives** l to the dead 2443
	4:25	and *was* **raised to** l for our justification. 1586
	5:10	shall we be saved through his l! 2437
	5:17	the gift of righteousness reign in l through 2437
	5:18	*that* **brings** l for all men. 2437
	5:21	through righteousness to bring eternal l 2437
	6: 4	we too may live a new l. 2437
	6:10	but **the** l he lives, he lives to God. 4005S
	6:13	**brought** from death to l; 2409
	6:22	and the result is eternal l. 2437
	6:23	the gift of God is eternal l in Christ Jesus 2437
	7: 9	sin **sprang to** l and I died. 348
	7:10	to bring l actually brought death. 2437
	8: 2	of the Spirit *of* l set me free from the law 2437
	8: 6	but the mind controlled by the Spirit is l 2437
	8:11	also **give** l to your mortal bodies 2443
	8:34	more than that, who *was* **raised to** l— 1586
	8:38	I am convinced that neither death nor l, 2437
	11:15	what will their acceptance be but l from 2437
	14: 9	and **returned to** l so that he might be 2409
1Co	3:22	or the world or l or death or the present or 2437
	4:17	He will remind you of my **way of** l 3847
	6: 3	How much more the *things of* this l! 1053
	7:17	**retain the place in** l that the Lord assigned 4344
	7:28	who marry will face many troubles in this l, 4922
	15:19	If only for this l we have hope in Christ, 2437
	15:36	What you sow *does* not **come to** l 2443
2Co	1: 8	so that we despaired even of l. 2409
	2:16	to the other, the fragrance of l. 2437
	3: 6	for the letter kills, but the Spirit **gives** l. 2443
	4:10	so that the l of Jesus may also be revealed 2437
	4:11	his l may be revealed in our mortal body. 2437
	4:12	but l is at work in you. 2437
	5: 4	what is mortal may be swallowed up by l. 2437
Gal	1:13	of my previous **way of** l in Judaism, 419
	2:20	**The** l I live in the body, 4005S
	3:15	me take an example **from everyday** l. 476+2848
	3:21	a law had been given that could **impart** l, 2443
	6: 8	from the Spirit will reap eternal l. 2437
Eph	4: 1	I urge you *to* **live a** l worthy of 4344
	4:18	and separated *from* the l of God because of 2437
	4:22	with regard to your former **way of** l, 419
	5: 2	and **live a** l of love, 4344
	6: 3	*you may* **enjoy long** l on the earth." 1639+3432
Php	1:20	whether by l or by death. 2437
	2:16	as you hold out the word of l— 2437
	2:30	risking his l to make up for the help you 6034
	4: 3	whose names are in the book *of* l. 2437
Col	1:10	*that* you *may* **live a** l worthy of the Lord 4344
	3: 3	your l is now hidden with Christ in God. 2437

Col	3: 4	When Christ, who is your l, appears,	2437
	3: 7	in the l you once lived.	4005^S
1Th	4: 7	impure, but to live a holy l.	40
	4:11	Make it your ambition to **lead a quiet l**,	2483
	4:12	so that *your* **daily l** may win the respect	4344
1Ti	1:16	believe on him and receive eternal l.	2437
	4: 8	holding promise for both the present l and	2437
	4: 8	for both the present life and the l to come.	NIG
	4:12	in l, in love, in faith and in purity.	419
	4:16	Watch **your** l and doctrine closely.	4932
	6:12	*of* the eternal l to which you were called	2437
	6:13	God, who **gives** l to everything,	2441
	6:19	so that they may take hold of the l	2437
	6:19	may take hold of the life that is truly l.	NIG
2Ti	1: 1	to the promise *of* l that is in Christ Jesus,	2437
	1: 9	who has saved us and called us *to a* **holy l**—	3104
	1:10	who has destroyed death and has brought l	2437
	3:10	know all about my teaching, my **way of l**,	73
	3:12	everyone who wants to live a **godly l**,	2357
Tit	1: 2	knowledge resting on the hope of eternal l.	2437
	3: 7	heirs having the hope of eternal l.	2437
Heb	7: 3	During the days of Jesus' **l on earth**,	4922
	7: 3	without beginning of days or end of l,	2437
	7:16	of the power of an indestructible l.	2437
	11: 5	By faith Enoch was taken from this l,	NIG
	11:35	received back their dead, **raised to l again.**	414
	13: 7	of their **way of l** and imitate their faith.	419
Jas	1:12	the crown *of* l that God has promised	2437
	1:20	about the **righteous** l that God desires.	1466
	3: 6	sets the whole course of his l on fire,	1161
	3:13	Let him show it by his good l,	419
	3:14	What is your l?	2437
1Pe	1:18	the empty **way of l** handed down to you	419
	3: 7	as heirs with you of the gracious gift *of* l,	2437
	3:10	**Whoever** would love l and see good days	2437
	4: 2	he does not live the rest of his earthly l	5989
2Pe	1: 3	for l and godliness through our knowledge	2437
1Jn	1: 1	concerning the Word of l.	2437
	1: 2	The l appeared; we have seen it	2437
	1: 2	and we proclaim to you the eternal l,	2437
	2:25	And this is what he promised us—even eternal l.	2437
	3:14	that we have passed from death to l,	2437
	3:15	that no murderer has eternal l in him.	2437
	3:16	Jesus Christ laid down his l for us.	6034
	5:11	God has given us eternal l,	2437
	5:11	and this l is in his Son.	2437
	5:12	He who has the Son has l;	2437
	5:12	not have the Son of God does not have l.	2437
	5:13	you may know that you have eternal l.	2437
	5:16	he should pray and God will give him l.	2437
	5:20	He is the true God and eternal l.	2437
Jude	1:21	to bring you to eternal l.	2437
Rev	2: 7	the right to eat from the tree *of* l,	2437
	2: 8	who died and **came to l** again.	2409
	2:10	and I will give you the crown of l.	2437
	3: 5	never blot out his name from the book *of* l	2437
	11:11	after the three and a half days a breath of l	2437
	13: 8	*of* l belonging to the Lamb that was slain	2437
	17: 8	book *of* l from the creation of the world will	2437
	20: 4	They **came to l** and reigned with Christ	2409
	20: 5	(The rest of the dead *did not* **come to l**	2409
	20:12	which is the book of l.	2437
	20:15	not found written in the book of l,	2437
	21: 6	from the spring of the water of l.	2437
	21:27	names are written in the Lamb's book of l.	2437
	22: 1	the river of the water of l,	2437
	22: 2	of the river stood the tree of l,	2437
	22:14	the tree *of* l and may go through the gates	2437
	22:17	let him take the free gift of the water *of* l.	2437
	22:19	from him his share in the tree of l and in	2437

LIFE'S (2) [LIVE]

| Ps | 39: 4 | **my** l end and the number of my days; | 3276 |
| Lk | 8:14 | on their way they are choked by l worries, | 1050 |

LIFE-GIVING (2) [GIVE]

| Pr | 15:31 | to a l rebuke will be at home among | 2644 |
| 1Co | 15:45 | the last Adam, a l spirit. | 2443 |

LIFEBLOOD (3) [BLOOD]

Ge	9: 4	not eat meat that has its l still in it.	1947+5883
	9: 5	l I will surely demand an accounting.	1947+5883
Jer	2:34	On your clothes men find the l *of*	1947+5883

LIFEBOAT (3) [BOAT]

Ac	27:16	we were hardly able to make the l secure.	5002
	27:30	the sailors let the l down into the sea,	5002
	27:32	So the soldiers cut the ropes that held the l	5002

LIFELESS (7) [LIVE]

Lev	26:30	and pile your dead bodies on the l forms	7007
Ps	106:28	and ate sacrifices offered to l gods;	4637
Jer	16:18	with the l forms *of* their vile images	5577
Eze	43: 7	by their prostitution and the l idols	7007
	43: 9	from me their prostitution and the l idols	7007
Hab	2:19	Or to l stone, 'Wake up!'	1876
1Co	14: 7	in the case of l *things* that make sounds,	953

LIFETIME (17) [LIVE]

Nu	3: 4	and Ithamar served as priests during the l	7156
Jos	24:31	Israel served the LORD throughout the l	3427
Jdg	2: 7	the LORD throughout the l *of* Joshua	3427
Jdg	8:28	During Gideon's l, the land enjoyed peace	3427
1Sa	7:13	Throughout Samuel's l, the hand of the LORD was against	3427
2Sa	18:18	During his l Absalom had taken a pillar	2644
1Ki	3:13	that in your l you will have no equal	3427+3972
	4:25	During Solomon's l Judah and Israel,	3427
	11:12	I will not do it during your l.	3427
	12: 6	had served his father Solomon during his l.	2645
	15: 6	and Jeroboam throughout [Abijah's] l.	2644+3427
2Ki	20:19	not be peace and security in my l?"	3427
2Ch	10: 6	had served his father Solomon during his l.	2645
Ps	30: 5	but his favor lasts a l;	2644
Isa	39: 8	"There will be peace and security in my l."	3427
Jer	22:30	a man who will not prosper in his l,	3427
Lk	16:25	in your l you received your good things,	2437

LIFT (73) [LIFTED, LIFTING, LIFTS, UPLIFTED]

Ge	13:14	"**L** up your eyes from where you are	5951
	21:18	**L** the boy **up** and take him by the hand,	5951
	40:13	Within three days Pharaoh *will* l **up**	5951
	40:19	Within three days Pharaoh *will* l **off** your head	5951
	41:44	but without your word no one *will* l hand	8123
Ex	40:37	the cloud *did* not l, they did not set out—	6590
Dt	28:32	powerless to l a hand.	NIH
	32:40	*I* l my hand to heaven and declare:	5951
1Sa	6: 5	Perhaps *he* will l his hand from you	7837
	24: 6	or l my hand against him;	8938
	24:10	'*I will* not l my hand against my master,	8938
2Sa	18:12	"Why were you not afraid to l your hand	8938
	18:12	not l my hand against the king's son.	8938
2Ki	6: 7	"**L** it **out**," he said.	8123
Ezr	9: 6	I am too ashamed and disgraced to l **up**	8123
Job	10:15	if I am innocent, *I* cannot l my head,	5951
	11:15	then *you* will l **up** your face	5951
	22:26	in the Almighty and *will* l **up** your face	5951
	22:29	and you say, '**L** them **up!**'	1575
Ps	3: 3	you bestow glory on me and l **up**	8123
	9:13	Have mercy and l me **up** from the gates	8123
	10:12	**L up** your hand, O God.	5951
	20: 5	and *will* l **up** *our* **banners** in the name	1839
	24: 4	who *does* not l **up** his soul to an idol	5951
	24: 7	**L up** your heads, O you gates;	5951
	24: 9	**L up** your heads, O you gates;	5951
	24: 9	l them **up**, *you* ancient doors,	5951
	25: 1	To you, O LORD, *I* l **up** my soul;	5951
	28: 2	as I l **up** my hands toward your Most Holy	5951
	63: 4	and in your name *I will* l **up** my hands.	5951
	75: 4	'*Do* not l **up** your horns.	8123
	75: 5	*Do* not l your horns against heaven;	8123
	76: 4	not one of the warriors *can* l his hands.	5162
	86: 4	for to you, O Lord, *I* l **up** my soul.	5951
	91:12	*they will* l you **up** in their hands,	5951
	110: 7	therefore *he will* l **up** his head.	8123
	116:13	*I will* l **up** the cup of salvation and call	5951
	119:48	*I* l **up** my hands to your commands,	5951
	121: 1	*I* l **up** my eyes to the hills—	5951
	123: 1	*I* l **up** my eyes to you,	5951
	134: 2	**L up** your hands in the sanctuary	5951
	142: 1	I l **up** my voice to the LORD for mercy.	2858
	143: 8	for to you *I* l **up** my soul.	5951
Isa	10:24	who beat you with a rod and l **up** a club	5951
	40: 9	l **up** your voice with a shout, lift it up,	8123
	40: 9	lift up your voice with a shout, l it **up**,	8123
	40:26	**L** your eyes and look to the heavens;	5951
	46: 7	*They* l it to their shoulders and carry it;	5951
	47: 2	**L up** your skirts, bare your legs,	3106
	49:18	**L up** your eyes and look around;	5951
	49:22	*I will* l **up** my banner to the peoples;	8123
	51: 6	**L up** your eyes to the heavens,	5951
	52: 8	Your watchmen l **up** their voices;	5951
	60: 4	"**L up** your eyes and look about you:	5951
Jer	13:20	**L up** your eyes and see those who are	5951
	38:10	and l Jeremiah the prophet out of the cistern	6590
	50: 2	l **up** a banner and proclaim it;	5951
	51:12	**L up** a banner against the walls	5951
	51:27	"**L up** a banner in the land!	5951
La	2:19	**L up** your hands to him for the lives	5951
	3:41	*Let us* l **up** our hearts and our hands	5951
Da	6:23	and gave orders to l Daniel **out** of	10513
Am	5: 2	with no *one* to l her **up**."	7756
Na	3: 5	"*I will* l your skirts over your face.	1655
Mt	4: 6	and *they will* l you **up** in their hands,	149
	12:11	will you not take hold of it and l it **out?**	1586
	23: 4	not willing to l a **finger** to move them.	1235
Lk	4:11	*they will* l you **up** in their hands,	149
	11:46	and *you* yourselves *will* not l one finger	4718
	21:28	stand up and l **up** your heads,	2048
1Ti	2: 8	I want men everywhere to l **up** holy hands	2048
Jas	4:10	and *he will* l you **up.**	5738
1Pe	5: 6	that *he may* l you **up** in due time.	5738

LIFTED (71) [LIFT]

Ge	7:17	as the waters increased *they* l the ark high	5951
	40:20	*He* l the heads of the chief cupbearer	5951
Ex	17:16	"For hands were l **up** to the throne of	NIH
	40:36	the cloud l from above the tabernacle,	6590
	40:37	they did not set out—until the day it l.	6590
Lev	9:22	Then Aaron l his hands toward the people	5951
Nu	9:17	Whenever the cloud l from above	6590
	9:21	and when it l in the morning, they set out.	6590
	9:21	whenever the cloud l, they set out.	6590
	9:22	but when it l, they would set out.	6590
	10:11	the cloud l from above the tabernacle of	6590
Nu	12:10	When the cloud l from above the Tent,	6073
Jdg	9:48	which *he* l to his shoulders.	5951
	16: 3	*He* l them to his shoulders	8492
1Sa	2: 1	in the LORD my horn *is* l **high.**	8123
	6: 3	why his hand *has* not *been* l from you."	6073
2Sa	18:28	the men who l their hands against my lord	5951
	20:21	*has* l **up** his hand against the king,	5951
1Ki	16: 2	"*I* l you **up** from the dust	8123
2Ki	4:20	the servant *had* l him **up** and carried him	5951
	19:22	and l your eyes in pride?	5951
Ezr	6:11	and *he is to be* l **up** and impaled on it.	10238
Ne	8: 6	all the people l their hands and responded,	5089
Job	5:11	and those who mourn *are* l to safety.	8435
Ps	24: 7	be l **up**, *you* ancient doors,	5951
	30: 1	I l me **out of the depths**	1926
	40: 2	*He* l me out of the slimy pit,	6590
	41: 9	*has* l **up** his heel against me.	1540
	75:10	the horns of the righteous *will be* l **up.**	8123
	93: 3	The seas *have* l **up**, O LORD,	5951
	93: 3	O LORD, the seas *have* l **up** their voice;	5951
	93: 3	the seas *have* l **up** their pounding waves.	5951
	107:25	and stirred up a tempest *that* l **high**	8123
	107:41	But *he* l the needy out of their affliction	8435
	112: 9	his horn *will be* l **high** in honor.	8123
	118:16	The LORD's right hand *is* l **high;**	8123
Isa	10:27	their burden *will be* l from your shoulders,	6073
	26:11	O LORD, your hand *is* l **high,**	8123
	33:10	will I be exalted; now *will I be* l **up.**	5951
	37:23	and l your eyes in pride?	5951
	52:13	be raised and l **up** and highly exalted.	5951
	63: 9	*he* l them **up** and carried them all the days	5747
Jer	38:13	with the ropes and l him **up** out of the cistern	6590
Eze	3:12	Then the Spirit l me **up,**	5951
	3:14	Spirit then l me **up** and took me away,	5951
	8: 3	The Spirit l me **up** between earth	5951
	11: 1	Then the Spirit l me **up** and brought me to	5951
	11:24	The Spirit l me **up** and brought me to	5951
	43: 5	Then the Spirit l me **up** and brought me	5951
Da	6:23	And when Daniel *was* l from the den,	10513
	7: 4	until its wings were torn off and *it was* l	10475
	12: 7	l his right hand and his left hand	8123
Hos	11: 4	I l the yoke from their neck and bent	8123
Am	5:26	You have l **up** the shrine of your king,	5951
Mic	5: 9	be l **up** in triumph over your enemies,	8123
Hab	3:10	the deep roared and l its waves on high.	5951
Zec	1:21	of the nations who l **up** their horns against	5951
	5: 9	and *they* l **up** the basket between heaven	5951
Mt	11:23	*will you* be l **up** to the skies?	5738
Mk	9:27	But Jesus took him by the hand and l him	1586
Lk	1:52	down rulers from their thrones but *has* l **up**	5738
	10:15	*will you* be l **up** to the skies?	5738
	24:50	he l **up** his hands and blessed them.	2048
Jn	3:14	Just as Moses l **up** the snake in the desert,	5738
	3:14	so the Son of Man must *be* l **up,**	5738
	8:28	"When *you* have l **up** the Son of Man,	5738
	12:32	But I, when *I am* l **up** from the earth,	5738
	12:34	'The Son of Man must *be* l **up**'?	5738
	13:18	'He who shares my bread *has* l **up** his heel	2048
	19:29	and l it to Jesus' lips.	4712
Ac	7:43	You have l **up** the shrine of Molech and	377

LIFTING (3) [LIFT]

Ps	141: 2	may the l **up** of my hands be like	5368
Eze	31:10	l its top above the thick foliage,	5989
	31:14	l their tops above the thick foliage.	5989

LIFTS (8) [LIFT]

1Sa	2: 8	and the needy from the ash heap;	8123
Ezr		overthrow any king or people who l	10714
Ps	46: 6	*he* l his voice, the earth melts.	5989
	113: 7	and the needy from the ash heap;	8123
	145:14	and l **up** all who are bowed down.	2422
	146: 8	the LORD l **up** those who are bowed down,	2422
Isa	5:26	*He* l **up** a banner for the distant nations,	5951
	10:15	As if a rod were to wield *him who* l it **up,**	8123

LIGAMENT (1) [LIGAMENTS]

| Eph | 4:16 | and held together by every supporting l, | 913 |

LIGAMENTS (1) [LIGAMENT]

| Col | 2:19 | and held together by its l and sinews, | 913 |

LIGHT (232) [DAYLIGHT, ENLIGHTEN, ENLIGHTENED, LIGHTED, LIGHTEN, LIGHTENED, LIGHTER, LIGHTING, LIGHTLY, LIGHTS, LIT, SUNLIGHT, TWILIGHT]

Ge	1: 3	And God said, "Let there be l,"	240
	1: 3	"Let there be light," and there was l.	240
	1: 4	God saw that the l was good,	240
	1: 4	and he separated the l from the darkness.	240
	1: 5	God called the l "day,"	240
	1:15	in the expanse of the sky to **give** l on	239
	1:16	the greater l to govern the day and	4401
	1:16	and the lesser l to govern the night.	4401
	1:17	in the expanse of the sky to **give** l on	239
	1:18	and to separate l from darkness.	240
Ex	10:23	Yet all the Israelites had l in the places	240
	13:21	by night in a pillar of fire to **give** them l,	239
	14:20	to the one side and l *to* the other side;	239
	25: 6	olive oil for the l;	4401
	25:37	on it so that *they* l the space in front of it.	239

Ex 27:20 of pressed olives for the l so that   4401
35: 3 *Do* not l a fire in any of your dwellings on   1277
35: 8 olive oil for the l;   4401
35:14 for l with its accessories, lamps and oil for   4401
35:14 accessories, lamps and oil for the l;   4401
35:28 also brought spices and olive oil for the l   4401
39:37 and the oil for the l;   4401
Lev 24: 2 of pressed olives for the l so that   4401
Nu 4: 9 and cover the lampstand that is for l,   4401
4:16 is to have charge of the oil for the l.'   4401
8: 2 *to* l the area in front of the lampstand."   239
Dt 25:13 weights in your bag—one heavy, one l.   7783
1Sa 29:10 leave in the morning as soon as *it is* l."   239
2Sa 22:29 turns my darkness into l.   5585
23: 4 he is like the l of morning at sunrise on   240
1Ki 3:21 I looked at him closely in the morning l,   1332
18:25 but do not l the fire."   8492
2Ch 13:11 on the ceremonially clean table and l   1277
Ezr 9: 8 and so our God gives l to our eyes and   239
Ne 4:21 first l of dawn till the stars came out.   6590+8840
9:12 by night with a pillar of fire to give them l   239
Job 3: 4 may no l shine upon it.   5644
3: 5 may blackness overwhelm its l.   3427
3:16 an infant who never saw the l of day?   240
3:20 "Why is l given to those in misery,   240
9: 7 he seals off the l of the stars.   NIH
10:22 where even the l is like darkness."   3649
12:22 and brings deep shadows into the l.   240
12:25 They grope in darkness with no l;   240
17:12 the face of darkness they say, 'L is near.'   240
18: 6 The l in his tent becomes dark;   240
18:18 from l into darkness and is banished from   240
22:28 and I will shine on your ways.   240
24:13 "There are those who rebel against the l,   240
24:16 they want nothing to do with the l.   240
25: 3 Upon whom does his l not rise?   240
26:10 for a boundary between l and darkness.   240
28:11 of the rivers and brings hidden things to l.   240
29: 3 and by his l I walked through darkness!   240
29:24 the l of my face was precious to them.   240
30:26 when I looked for l, then came darkness.   240
33:28 and I will live to enjoy the l.'   240
33:30 that the l of life may shine on him.   240
38:15 The wicked are denied their l,   240
38:19 "What is the way to the abode of l?   240
41:18 His snorting throws out flashes of l;   240
Ps 4: 6 Let the l of your face shine upon us,   240
13: 3 Give l to my eyes,   239
18:28 my God turns my darkness into l.   5585
19: 8 giving l to the eyes.   239
27: 1 The LORD is my l and my salvation—   240
36: 9 in your l we see light.   240
36: 9 in your light we see l.   240
38:10 even the l has gone from my eyes.   240
43: 3 Send forth your l and your truth,   240
44: 3 your arm, and the l of your face,   240
49:19 who will never see the l [of life].   240
56:13 I may walk before God in the l of life.   240
76: 4 You *are* resplendent with l,   239
78:14 by day and with l *from* the fire all night.   240
89:15 who walk in the l of your presence,   240
90: 8 our secret sins in the l of your presence.   4401
97:11 L is shed upon the righteous and joy on   240
104: 2 He wraps himself in l as with a garment;   240
105:39 and a fire to give l at night.   239
112: 4 Even in darkness l dawns for the upright,   240
118:27 and *he has* made *his* l shine upon us.   239
119:105 word is a lamp to my feet and a l for my path   240
119:130 The unfolding of your words gives l;   239
139:11 and the l become night around me,"   239
139:12 for darkness is as l to you.   245
Pr 4:18 shining ever brighter till the full l of day.   NIH
6:23 commands are a lamp, this teaching is a l,   240
13: 9 The l of the righteous shines brightly,   240
Ecc 2:13 just as l is better than darkness.   240
11: 7 L is sweet, and it pleases the eyes to see   240
12: 2 before the sun and the l and the moon and   240
Isa 2: 5 let us walk in the l of the LORD.   240
5:20 who put darkness for l and light   240
5:20 who put darkness for light and l   240
5:30 even the l will be darkened by the clouds.   240
8:20 they have no l of dawn.   8840
9: 2 in darkness have seen a great l;   240
9: 2 of the shadow of death a l has dawned.   240
10:17 The L of Israel will become a fire,   240
13:10 constellations will not show their l.   240
13:10 and the moon will not give its l.   240
30:26 like the l of seven full days,   240
42: 6 a covenant for the people and a l for the Gentiles,   240
42:16 I will turn the darkness into l before them   240
45: 7 I form the l and create darkness,   240
49: 6 I will also make you a l for the Gentiles,   240
50:10 who walks in the dark, who has no l,   5586
50:11 all you who l fires and provide yourselves   7706
50:11 walk in the l of your fires and of   241
51: 4 my justice will become a l to the nations.   240
53:11 he will see the l [of life] and be satisfied;   NIH
57: 9 In the l of these things, should I relent?   6584
58: 8 Then your l will break forth like the dawn,   240
58:10 then your l will rise in the darkness,   240
59: 9 We look for l, but all is darkness;   240
60: 1 "Arise, shine, for your l has come,   240
60: 3 Nations will come to your l,   240
60:19 The sun will no more be your l by day,   240
60:19 for the LORD will be your everlasting l,   240
60:20 the LORD will be your everlasting l,   240

Jer 4:23 and at the heavens, and their l was gone.   240
7:18 children gather wood, the fathers l the fire,   1277
13:16 You hope for l, but he will turn it to thick   240
25:10 sound of millstones and the l of the lamp.   240
La 3: 2 in darkness rather than l;   240
Eze 1: 4 and surrounded by brilliant l.   5586
1:27 and brilliant l surrounded him.   5586
32: 7 and the moon *will* not give its l.   239+240
Da 2:22 and l dwells with him.   10466
6:19 At the first l of dawn,   10459
Am 5:18 That day will be darkness, not l.   240
5:20 the day of the LORD be darkness, not l—   240
Mic 2: 1 At morning's l they carry it out   240
7: 8 I sit in darkness, the LORD will be my l.   240
7: 9 He will bring me out into the l;   240
Zec 14: 6 On that day there will be no l,   240
14: 7 When evening comes, there will be l.   240
Mal 1:10 *you would* not l useless **fires** *on* my altar!   239
Mt 4:16 in darkness have seen a great l;   5890
4:16 of the shadow of death a l has dawned."   5890
5:14 "You are the l of the world.   5890
5:15 Neither *do people* l a lamp and put it under   2794
5:15 and *it* gives l to everyone in the house.   3290
5:16 let your l shine before men,   5890
6:22 your whole body will be full of l.   5893
6:23 If then the l within you is darkness,   5890
11:30 For my yoke is easy and my burden is l."   1787
17: 2 and his clothes became as white as the l.   5890
24:29 and the moon will not give its l;   5766
Mk 13:24 and the moon will not give its l;   5766
Lk 2:32 a l for revelation to the Gentiles and   5890
8:16 so that those who come in can see the l.   5890
11:33 so that those who come in may see the l.   5890
11:34 your whole body also is full of l.   5893
11:35 then, that the l within you is not darkness.   5890
11:36 if your whole body is full of l,   5893
11:36 as when the l of a lamp shines on you."   847
15: 8 *Does she* not l a lamp,   721
16: 8 than are the people of the l.   5890
Jn 1: 4 and that life was the l of men.   5890
1: 5 The l shines in the darkness,   5890
1: 7 as a witness to testify concerning that l,   5890
1: 8 He himself was not the l;   5890
1: 8 he came only as a witness to the l.   5890
1: 9 The true l that gives light   5890
1: 9 that gives l to every man was coming into   5894
3:19 L has come into the world,   5890
3:19 but men loved darkness instead of l   5890
3:20 Everyone who does evil hates the l,   5890
3:20 into the l for fear that his deeds will   5890
3:21 by the truth comes into the l,   5890
5:35 John was a lamp that burned and gave l,   5743
5:35 and you chose for a time to enjoy his l.   5890
8:12 he said, "I am the l of the world.   5890
8:12 but will have the l of life."   5890
9: 5 I am in the world, I am the l of the world."   5890
11: 9 for he sees by this world's l.   5890
11:10 he stumbles, for he has no l."   5890
12:35 "You are going to have the l just a little   5890
12:35 Walk while you have the l,   5890
12:36 Put your trust in the l while you have it,   5890
12:36 so that you may become sons of l."   5890
12:46 I have come into the world as a l,   5890
Ac 9: 3 a l from heaven flashed around him.   5890
12: 7 of the Lord appeared and a l shone in   5890
13:11 for a time you will be unable to see the l"   NIG
13:47 " 'I have made you a l for the Gentiles,   5890
22: 6 a bright l from heaven flashed around me.   5890
22:11 the brilliance of the l had blinded me.   5890
26:13 I saw a l from heaven,   5890
26:18 and turn them from darkness to l,   5890
26:23 would proclaim l to his own people and to   5890
Ro 2:19 a l for those who are in the dark,   5890
13:12 of darkness and put on the armor of l.   5890
1Co 3:13 because the Day *will* bring it to l.   1317
4: 5 He *will* bring to l what is hidden   5894
2Co 4: 4 so that they cannot see the l of the gospel   5895
4: 6 who said, "Let l shine out of darkness,"   5890
4: 6 made his l shine in our hearts to give us   NIG
4: 6 the l of the knowledge of the glory of God   5895
4:17 For our l and momentary troubles are   1787
6:14 what fellowship can l have with darkness?   5890
11:14 Satan himself masquerades as an angel of l.   5890
Eph 5: 8 but now you are l in the Lord.   5890
5: 8 Live as children of l   5890
5: 9 the fruit *of the* l consists in all goodness,   5890
5:13 everything exposed by the l becomes visible,   5890
5:14 for it is l that makes everything visible.   5890
Col 1:12 inheritance of the saints in the kingdom of l.   5890
1Th 5: 5 You are all sons of the l and sons of the day.   5890
1Ti 6:16 and who lives in unapproachable l,   5890
2Ti 1:10 brought life and immortality to l   5894
Tit 1: 3 brought his word to l through the preaching   5746
Heb 10:32 *after* you had **received** the l,   5894
12: 5 *do* not **make** l of the Lord's discipline,   3902
1Pe 2: 9 you out of darkness into his wonderful l.   5890
2Pe 1:19 as *to a* l shining in a dark place,   3394
1Jn 1: 5 and declare to you: God is l;   5890
1: 7 But if we walk in the l, as he is in the light,   5890
1: 7 if we walk in the l, as he is in the light,   5890
2: 8 and the true l is already shining.   5890
2: 9 be in the l but hates his brother is still in   5890
2:10 Whoever loves his brother lives in the l,   5890
Rev 8:12 A third of the day *was* without l,   3590+5743
18:23 The l of a lamp will never shine   5890
21:23 for the glory of God gives it l,   5894

Rev 21:24 The nations will walk by its l,   5890
22: 5 not need the l of a lamp or the light of   5890
22: 5 the light of a lamp or the l of the sun,   5890
22: 5 for the Lord God *will* give them l.   5894

LIGHTED (1) [LIGHT]
Lk 11:36 it will be completely l,   5893

LIGHTEN (5) [LIGHT]
1Ki 12: 4 but now l the harsh labor and   7837
12: 9 'L the yoke your father put on us'?"   7837
2Ch 10: 4 but now l the harsh labor and   7837
10: 9 'L the yoke your father put on us'?"   7837
Jnh 1: 5 And they threw the cargo into the sea to l   7837

LIGHTENED (1) [LIGHT]
Ac 27:38 *they* l the ship by throwing the grain into   3185

LIGHTER (3) [LIGHT]
Ex 18:22 *That will* **make** your load l,   7837
1Ki 12:10 heavy yoke on us, but **make** our yoke l'—   7837
2Ch 10:10 heavy yoke on us, but **make** our yoke l'—   7837

LIGHTING (1) [LIGHT]
Mt 3:16 Spirit of God descending like a dove and l   2262

LIGHTLY (1) [LIGHT]
2Co 1:17 When I planned this, did I do it l?   1786

LIGHTNING (46)
Ex 9:23 and l flashed down to the ground,   836
9:24 hail fell and l flashed back and forth.   836
19:16 of the third day there was thunder and l,   1398
20:18 the thunder and l and heard the trumpet   4365
2Sa 22:13 of his presence bolts of l blazed forth.   836
22:15 **bolts of** l and routed them.   1398
Job 36:30 See how he scatters his l about him,   240
36:32 with l and commands it to strike its mark.   240
37: 3 He unleashes his l beneath the whole heaven   240
37:11 he scatters his l through them.   240
37:15 the clouds and makes his l flash?   240
38:24 to the place where the l is dispersed,   240
38:35 Do you send the l **bolts** on their way?   1398
Ps 18:12 with hailstones and bolts of l.   836
18:14 great **bolts of** l and routed them.   1398
29: 7 voice of the LORD strikes with flashes of l.   836
77:18 your l lit up the world;   1398
78:48 their livestock to **bolts of** l.   8404
97: 4 His l lights up the world;   1398
105:32 with l throughout their land;   836+4259
135: 7 he sends l with the rain and brings out   1398
144: 6 **Send forth** l and scatter [the enemies];   1397+1398
148: 8 l and hail, snow and clouds, stormy winds   836
Jer 10:13 He sends l with the rain and brings out   1398
51:16 He sends l with the rain and brings out   1398
Eze 1: 4 an immense cloud with flashing l   836
1:13 it was bright, and l flashed out of it.   1398
1:14 and forth like **flashes of** l.   1027
21:10 polished to **flash like** l!   1398
21:15 It is made to **flash like** l,   1398
21:28 polished to consume and to **flash like** l!   1398
Da 10: 6 his face like l, his eyes like flaming torches,   1398
Hos 6: 5 my judgments flashed like l upon you.   240
Na 2: 4 they dart about like l.   1398
Hab 3:11 at the l of your flashing spear.   1398
Zec 9:14 his arrow will flash like l.   1398
Mt 24:27 For as l that comes from the east is visible   847
28: 3 His appearance was like l,   847
Lk 9:29 as bright as a **flash of** l.   1993
10:18 "I saw Satan fall like l from heaven.   847
17:24 Son of Man in his day will be like the l,   847
24: 4 in clothes **that gleamed like** l stood   848
Rev 4: 5 From the throne came **flashes of** l,   847
8: 5 **flashes of** l and an earthquake.   847
11:19 And there came **flashes of** l, rumblings,   847
16:18 Then there came **flashes of** l, rumblings,   847

LIGHTS (14) [LIGHT]
Ge 1:14 be l in the expanse of the sky to separate   4401
1:15 and let them be l in the expanse of the sky   4401
1:16 God made two great l—   4401
Ex 30: 8 He must burn incense again when he l   6590
Ps 97: 4 His lightning l **up** the world;   239
136: 7 who made the great l—   240
Eze 32: 8 the shining l in the heavens I will darken   4401
Zec 4: 2 with a bowl at the top and seven l on it,   5944
4: 2 with seven channels to the l.   5944
Lk 8:16 "No one l a lamp and hides it in a jar   721
11:33 "No one l a lamp and puts it in a place   721
17:24 and l **up** the sky from one end to the other.   3290
Ac 16:29 The jailer called for l,   5890
Jas 1:17 down from the Father of the heavenly l,   5890

LIGURE (KJV) See JACINTH

LIKE (1532) [ALIKE, LIKE-MINDED, LIKED, LIKELY, LIKEN, LIKENESS, LIKES, LIKEWISE]
Ge 3: 5 and you will be l God, knowing good and   3869
3:22 "The man has now become l one of us,   3869

Ge
10:9 that is why it is said, "L Nimrod, — 3869
13:10 l the garden of the LORD, — 3869
13:10 l the land of Egypt, toward Zoar. — 3869
13:16 I will make your offspring l the dust of — 3869
19:8 you can do what you l with them. — 928+3202+6524
19:28 l smoke from a furnace. — 3869
20:15 live wherever you l." — 928+3202+6524
25:25 and his whole body was l a hairy garment; — 3869
27:4 of tasty food / I and bring it to me to eat, — 170
27:23 his hands were hairy l those of his brother — 3869
27:27 of my son is l the smell of a field that — 3869
27:46 from Hittite women l these, — 3869
28:14 Your descendants will be l the dust of — 3869
29:20 but they seemed l only a few days to him — 3869
31:26 and you've carried off my daughters l — 3869
31:41 It was l this for the twenty years I was — AIT
32:12 and will make your descendants l the sand — 3869
33:10 For to see your face is l seeing the face — 3869
34:12 Make the price for the bride and the gift l
    am to bring as great as you l, — 4394+8049
34:15 that you become l us by circumcising all — 4017
34:31 "Should he have treated our sister l — 3869
38:11 "He may die too, just l his brothers." — 3869
41:38 "Can we find anyone l this man, — 3869
41:49 quantities of grain, l the sand of the sea; — 3869
44:7 from your servants to do anything l that! — 3869
44:15 that a man l me can find things out — 4017
48:20 'May God make you l Ephraim — 3869
49:9 L a lion he crouches and lies down, — 3869
49:9 l a lioness—who dares to rouse him? — 3869

Ex
1:19 "Hebrew women are not l Egyptian — 3869
4:6 it was leprous, l snow. — 3869
4:7 it was restored, l the rest of his flesh. — 3869
7:1 "See, I have made you l God to Pharaoh, — NIH
8:10 you may know there is no one l the LORD — 3869
9:14 so you may know that there is no one l me — 4017
12:48 then he may take part l one born in — 3869
13:9 This observance will be for you l a sign — 4200
13:16 And it will be l a sign on your hand and — 4200
15:5 they sank to the depths l a stone. — 4017
15:7 it consumed them l stubble. — 3869
15:8 The surging waters stood firm l a wall; — 4017
15:10 They sank l lead in the mighty waters. — 3869
15:11 "Who among the gods l you, — 4017
15:11 Who is l you—majestic in holiness, — 4017
16:14 thin flakes l frost on the ground appeared — 3869
16:31 It was white l coriander seed and tasted — 3869
16:31 and tasted l wafers made with honey. — 3869
19:18 The smoke billowed up from it l smoke — 3869
22:25 do not be l a moneylender; — 3869
24:10 Under his feet was something l a pavement — 3869
24:17 of the LORD looked l a consuming fire — 3869
25:9 all its furnishings exactly l — 889+3869+3972+4027
25:33 cups shaped l almond flowers — 5481
25:34 cups shaped l almond flowers — 5481
26:24 both shall be l that. — 4027
28:8 skillfully woven waistband is to be l — 3869+5126
28:14 and two braided chains of pure gold, l — 5126
28:15 Make it l the ephod: — 3869+5126
28:21 each engraved / a seal with the name — AIT
28:22 braided chains of pure gold, l a rope. — 5126
28:32 There shall be a woven edge l a collar — 3869
30:33 Whoever makes perfume l it — 4017
30:38 Whoever makes any l it — 4017
34:1 "Chisel out two stone tablets l — 3869
34:4 So Moses chiseled out two stone tablets l — 3869
37:19 cups shaped l almond flowers — 5481
37:20 cups shaped l almond flowers — 5481
38:18 l the curtains of the courtyard, — 4200+6645
39:5 skillfully woven waistband was l it— — 3869+5126
39:6 and engraved them / a seal with the names — AIT
39:8 They made it l the ephod; — 3869
39:14 each engraved / a seal with the name — AIT
39:15 braided chains of pure gold, l a rope. — 5126
39:23 with an opening in the center of the robe l — 3869
39:30 l an inscription on a seal: — NIH

Lev
6:17 L the sin offering and the guilt offering, — 3869
13:43 his head or forehead is reddish-white l — 3869+5260
14:13 L the sin offering, the guilt offering — 3869
14:35 'I have seen something that looks l — 3869
26:19 and make the sky above you l iron and — 3869
26:19 like iron and the ground beneath you l — 3869
27:21 l a field devoted to the LORD; — 3869

Nu
8:4 The lampstand was made exactly l — 3869+4027
9:15 the cloud above the tabernacle looked l — 3869
9:16 and at night it looked / fire. — AIT
11:7 The manna was l coriander seed — 3869
11:7 l coriander seed and looked l resin. — 3869
11:8 it tasted l something made with olive oil. — 3869
12:10 there stood Miriam—leprous, l snow. — 3869
12:12 not let her be l a stillborn infant coming — 3869
13:18 See what the land is l and — 4537
13:33 We seemed l grasshoppers — 3869
14:34 know what it is l to have me against you.' — 3359
16:40 or he would become l Korah — 3869
23:10 and may my end be l theirs!" — 4017
23:24 The people rise l a lioness; — 3869
23:24 they rouse themselves l a lion that does — 3869
24:6 "L valleys they spread out, — 3869
24:6 l gardens beside a river, — 3869
24:6 l aloes planted by the LORD, — 3869
24:6 l cedars beside the waters. — 3869
24:9 L a lion they crouch and lie down, — 3869
24:9 l a lioness—who dares to rouse him? — 3869
27:17 the LORD's people will not be l sheep — 3869
32:16 "We would l to build pens here — AIT

Dt
1:44 they chased you l a swarm of bees — 889+3869
2:11 L the Anakites, they too were considered
    Rephaites, — 3869
4:16 whether formed / a man or a woman, — AIT
4:17 or l any animal on earth or any bird — NIH
4:18 or l any creature that moves along — NIH
4:32 or has anything l it ever been heard of? — 4017
4:34 l all the things the LORD your God did — 3869
7:26 l it, will be set apart for destruction. — 4017
8:20 L the nations the LORD destroyed — 3869
9:3 the one who goes across ahead of you l — NIH
10:1 "Chisel out two stone tablets l — 3869
10:3 and chiseled out two stone tablets l — 3869
11:10 to take over is not l the land of Egypt, — 3869
12:16 pour it out on the ground l water. — 3869
12:20 "I would l some meat," — 430
12:24 pour it out on the ground l water. — 3869
14:26 Use the silver to buy whatever you l: — 203
15:23 pour it out on the ground l water. — 3869
17:14 a king over us l all the nations around us," — 3869
18:7 in the name of the LORD his God l — 3869
18:15 up for you a prophet l me from — 4017
18:18 I will raise up for them a prophet l you — 4017
22:26 This case is l that of someone — 889+3869+4027
28:29 At midday you will grope about l — 889+3869
28:49 l an eagle swooping down, — 889+3869
29:23 It will be l the destruction of Sodom — 3869
32:2 Let my teaching l fall rain — 3869
32:2 like rain and my words descend l dew, — 3869
32:2 l showers on new grass, — 3869
32:2 l abundant rain on tender plants. — 3869
32:11 l an eagle that stirs up its nest and hovers — 3869
32:31 For their rock is not l our Rock, — 3869
33:17 In majesty he is l a firstborn bull; — NIH
33:20 Gad lives there l a lion, — 3869
33:26 "There is no one l the God of Jeshurun, — 3869
33:29 Who is l you, a people saved by the LORD? — 4017
34:10 no prophet has risen in Israel l Moses, — 3869

Jos
7:5 of the people melted and became l water. — 4200
10:2 l one of the royal cities; — 3869
10:14 There has never been a day l it before or — 3869
22:16 with the God of Israel l this? — 889

Jdg
5:31 be l the sun when it rises in its strength." — 3869
6:5 up with their livestock and their tents l — 3869
7:5 the water with their tongues l a dog — 889+3869
8:1 "Why have you treated us l this? — NIH
8:18 "Men l you," they answered, — 4017
13:6 He looked l an angel of God, — 3869
13:15 "We would l you to stay until we prepare — AIT
15:7 "Since you've acted l this, — 3869
15:14 on his arms became l charred flax, — 889+3869
17:11 young man was to him l one of his sons. — 3869
18:7 l the Sidonians, unsuspecting and — 3869+5477

Ru
4:11 into your home l Rachel and Leah, — 3869
4:12 may your family be l that of Perez, — 3869

1Sa
2:2 "There is no one holy l the LORD; — 3869
2:2 there is no Rock l our God. — 3869
4:7 Nothing l this has happened before. — 3869
8:20 Then we will be l all the other nations, — 3869
10:24 There is no one l him among all — 4017
15:23 For rebellion is l the sin of divination, — NIH
15:23 and arrogance l the evil of idolatry. — NIH
17:7 His spear shaft was l a weaver's rod, — 3869
17:36 this uncircumcised Philistine will be l one — 3869
18:22 and his attendants all l you, — 170
19:5 to an innocent man l David by killing him — NIH
19:17 "Why did you deceive me l this — 3970
20:14 But show me unfailing kindness l that of — AIT
21:9 David said, "There is none l it; — 4017
21:13 he was in their hands he acted l a madman, — 2147
21:15 to bring this fellow here to carry on l this — NIH
25:25 is just l his name—his name is Fool, — 3869+4027
25:26 and all who intend to harm my master be l — 3869
25:36 he was in the house holding a banquet l — 3869
25:37 and his heart failed him and he became l — 4200
26:15 And who is l you in Israel? — 4017
26:21 Surely I have acted l a fool — 6118
28:14 "What does he look l?" — 9307

2Sa
7:9 l the names of the greatest men of the earth. — 3869
7:22 There is no one l you, and there is no God — 4017
7:23 And who is l your people Israel— — 3869
9:8 that you should notice a dead dog l me?" — 4017
9:11 at David's table l one of the king's sons. — 3869
13:1 l a daughter to him. — 3869
13:5 'I would l my sister Tamar to come — 5528
13:6 "I would l my sister Tamar to come — 5528
13:13 You would be l one of the wicked fools — 3869
14:2 Act l a woman who has spent many days
    grieving for — 3869
14:13 "Why then have you devised a thing l this — 3869
14:14 L water spilled on the ground, — 3869
14:17 for my lord the king is l an angel of God — 3869
14:20 My lord has wisdom l that of an angel — 3869
16:23 the advice Ahithophel gave was l that — 3869
17:10 whose heart is l the heart of a lion, — 3869
18:14 "I'm not going to wait l this for you." — 4027
18:27 to me that the first one runs l Ahimaaz son — 3869
18:32 up to harm you l that young man." — 3869
19:27 My lord the king is l an angel of God; — 3869
21:19 a spear with a shaft l a weaver's rod. — 3869
22:34 He makes my feet l the feet of a deer; — 3869
22:43 and trampled them l mud in the streets. — 3869
23:3 he is l the light of morning at sunrise on — 3869
23:4 l the brightness after rain that brings — 4946
23:4 l evil men are all to be cast aside l thorns, — 3869

1Ki
1:42 A worthy man l you must — NIH
3:12 there will never have been anyone l you, — 4017
7:8 a palace l this hall for Pharaoh's daughter, — 3869
7:26 and its rim was l the rim of a cup, — 3869+5126
7:26 l a lily blossom. — NIH
7:33 wheels were made l chariot wheels; — 3869+5126
8:23 of Israel, there is no God l you in heaven — 4017
10:20 Nothing l it had ever been made — 4027
12:32 l the festival held in Judah, — 3869
14:8 but you have not been l my servant David, — 3869
14:15 it will be l a reed swaying in the water. — 889+3869
16:3 and I will make your house l that — 3869
16:7 and becoming l the house of Jeroboam— — 3869
19:2 not make your life l that of one of them." — 3869
20:11 not boast l one who takes it off.' " — 3869
20:25 also raise an army l the one you lost— — 3869
20:27 The Israelites camped opposite them l — 3869
21:22 I will make your house l that — 3869
21:25 (There was never a man l Ahab, — 3869
21:26 l the Amorites the LORD drove — 889+3869+3972
22:17 on the hills l sheep without a shepherd, — 3869

2Ki
3:22 the water looked red—l blood. — 3869
5:14 and became clean l that of a young boy. — 3869
7:13 be l that of all the Israelites left here— — 3869
7:13 be l all these Israelites who are doomed. — 3869
9:9 I will make the house of Ahab l the house — 3869
9:9 of Jeroboam son of Nebat and l the house — 3869
9:20 The driving is l that of Jehu son of Nimshi — 3869
9:20 he drives l a madman." — 928
9:37 be l refuse on the ground in the plot — 3869
13:7 the rest and made them l the dust — 3869
13:18 l the kings of Israel who preceded him. — 3869
18:5 There was no one l him among all — 4017
18:27 who, l you, will have to eat their own filth — 6640
18:32 until I come and take you to a land l — 3869
19:26 They are l plants in the field, — NIH
19:26 l tender green shoots, — NIH
19:26 l grass sprouting on the roof, — NIH
23:25 before nor after Josiah was there a king l — 4017

1Ch
11:23 the Egyptian had a spear l a weaver's rod — 3869
12:22 l the army of God. — 3869
17:8 Now I will make your name l the names — 3869
17:20 "There is no one l you, O LORD, — 4017
17:21 And who is l your people Israel— — 3869
20:5 a spear with a shaft l a weaver's rod. — 3869
29:15 Our days on earth are l a shadow, — 3869

2Ch
4:5 and its rim was l the rim of a cup, — 3869+5126
4:5 l a lily blossom. — NIH
6:14 of Israel, there is no God l you in heaven — 4017
9:11 Nothing l them had ever been seen — 3869
9:19 Nothing l it had ever been made — 4027
14:11 there is no one l you to help the powerless — 6640
18:16 on the hills l sheep without a shepherd, — 3869
30:7 Do not be l your fathers and brothers, — 3869
30:26 of Israel there had been nothing l this — 3869
32:15 and mislead you l this. — 3869
35:18 The Passover had not been observed l this — 4017

Ezr
4:2 "Let us help you build because, l you, — 3869
9:1 l those of the Canaanites, Hittites, — 4200
9:13 and have given us a remnant l this. — 3869

Ne
5:15 of reverence for God l did not act l that. — 4027
6:8 l what you are saying is happening; — 3869
6:11 But I said, "Should a man l me run away? — 4017
6:11 Or should one l me go into the temple — 4017
8:17 the Israelites had not celebrated it l this. — 4027
9:11 l a stone into mighty waters. — 4017
13:26 Was it not because of marriages l these — NIH
13:26 the many nations there was no king l him. — 4017

Job
1:8 There is no one on earth l him; — 4017
2:3 There is no one on earth l him; — 4017
2:10 "You are talking l a foolish woman. — 3869
3:16 Or why was I not hidden in the ground l — 3869
3:16 l an infant who never saw the light — 3869
3:24 my groans pour out l water. — 3869
5:25 your descendants l the grass of the earth. — 3869
5:26 l sheaves gathered in season. — 3869
7:1 Are not his days l those of a hired man? — 3869
7:2 L a slave longing for the evening shadows, — 3869
8:16 l a well-watered plant in the sunshine, — NIH
9:26 They skim past l boats of papyrus, — 6640
9:26 l eagles swooping down on their prey. — 3869
9:32 not a man l me that I might answer him, — 4017
10:5 Are your days l those of a mortal — 3869
10:5 like those of a mortal or your years l those — 3869
10:9 Remember that you molded me l clay. — 3869
10:10 not pour me out l milk and curdle me — 3869
10:10 not pour me out like milk and curdle me l — 3869
10:16 you stalk me l a lion — 3869
10:22 where even the light is l darkness." — 4017
11:17 and darkness will become l morning. — 3869
12:25 he makes them stagger l drunkards. — 3869
13:28 "So man wastes away l something rotten, — 3869
13:28 l a garment eaten by moths. — 3869
14:2 up l a flower and withers away; — 3869
14:2 l a fleeting shadow, he does not endure. — 3869
14:6 till he has put in his time l a hired man. — 3869
14:9 of water it will bud and put forth shoots l — 4017
15:16 who drinks up evil l water! — 3869
15:24 l a king poised to attack, — 3869
15:33 be l a vine stripped of its unripe grapes, — 3869
15:33 l an olive tree shedding its blossoms. — 3869
16:2 "I have heard many things l these; — 3869
16:4 I also could speak l you, — 3869
16:14 he rushes at me l a warrior. — 3869
19:10 he uproots my hope l a tree. — 3869
20:7 l his own dung; — 3869
20:8 L a dream he flies away, — 3869
20:8 banished l a vision of the night. — 3869
21:18 often are they l straw before the wind, — 3869
21:18 l chaff swept away by a gale? — 3869

Job	24: 5	L wild donkeys in the desert,	NIH
	24:14	in the night he steals forth l a thief.	3869
	24:20	but are broken l a tree.	3869
	24:24	they are brought low and gathered up l	3869
	24:24	they are cut off l heads of grain.	3869
	27: 7	"May my enemies be l the wicked,	3869
	27: 7	my adversaries l the unjust!	3869
	27:16	up silver l dust and clothes like piles	3869
	27:16	up silver like dust and clothes l piles	3869
	27:18	The house he builds is l a moth's cocoon,	3869
	27:18	l a hut made by a watchman.	3869
	27:20	Terrors overtake him l a flood;	3869
	29:25	I was l one who comforts mourners.	889+3869
	30:15	my safety vanishes l a cloud.	3869
	30:18	In his great power [God] **becomes** l	2924
	30:18	he binds me l the neck of my garment.	3869
	31:36	I would put it on l a crown.	NIH
	31:37	l a prince I would approach him.)—	4017
	32:19	inside I am l bottled-up wine,	3869
	32:19	l new wineskins ready to burst.	3869
	33: 6	I am **just** l you before God;	3869+7023
	33:25	then his flesh is renewed l a child's;	4946
	34: 7	What man is l Job,	3869
	34: 7	who drinks scorn l water?	3869
	34:36	the utmost for answering l a wicked man!	928
	35: 4	"I *would* l *to* reply *to* you and	AIT
	35: 8	Your wickedness affects only a man l	4017
	36:22	Who is a teacher l him?	4017
	38: 3	Brace yourself l a man;	3869
	38:14	The earth takes shape l clay under a seal;	3869
	38:14	its features stand out l those of a garment.	4017
	39:20	Do you make him leap l a locust,	3869
	40: 7	"Brace yourself l a man;	3869
	40: 9	Do you have an arm l God's,	3869
	40: 9	and can your voice thunder l his?	4017
	40:15	along with you and which feeds on grass l	3869
	40:17	His tail sways l a cedar;	4017
	40:18	his limbs l rods of iron.	3869
	41: 5	a pet of him l a bird or put him on a leash	3869
	41:18	his eyes are l the rays of dawn.	3869
	41:27	Iron he treats l straw and bronze	4200
	41:27	Iron he treats like straw and bronze l	4200
	41:28	slingstones are l chaff to him.	4200
	41:30	a trail in the mud l a threshing sledge.	NIH
	41:31	the depths churn l a boiling caldron	3869
	41:31	like a boiling caldron and stirs up the sea l	3869
Ps	1: 3	He is l a tree planted by streams of water,	3869
	1: 4	They are l chaff that the wind blows away.	3869
	2: 9	you will dash them to pieces l pottery."	3869
	7: 2	or they will tear me l a lion and rip me	3869
	10: 9	He lies in wait l a lion in cover;	3869
	11: 1	"Flee l a bird to your mountain.	NIH
	12: 6	l silver refined in a furnace of clay,	NIH
	17:12	They are l a lion hungry for prey,	1955
	17:12	a great lion crouching in cover.	3869
	18:33	He makes my feet l the feet of a deer;	3869
	18:42	I poured them out l mud in the streets.	3869
	19: 5	which is l a bridegroom coming forth	3869
	19: 5	l a champion rejoicing to run his course.	3869
	21: 9	of your appearing you will make them l	3869
	22:14	I am poured out l water,	3869
	22:15	My strength is dried up l a potsherd,	3869
	28: 1	*I will* **be** l those who have gone down to	5439
	29: 6	He makes Lebanon skip l a calf,	4017
	29: 6	Sirion l a young wild ox.	4017
	31:12	I have become l broken pottery.	3869
	32: 9	Do not be l the horse or the mule,	3869
	35: 5	May they be l chaff before the wind,	3869
	35:10	"Who is l you, O LORD?	4017
	35:16	l the ungodly they maliciously mocked;	3869
	36: 6	Your righteousness is l the mighty mountains,	3869
	36: 6	your justice l the great deep.	NIH
	37: 2	for l the grass they will soon wither,	3869
	37: 2	l green plants they will soon die away.	3869
	37: 6	He will make your righteousness shine l	3869
	37: 6	of your cause l the noonday sun.	3869
	37:20	The LORD's enemies will be l the beauty of	3869
	37:20	they will vanish—vanish l smoke.	928
	37:35	and ruthless man flourishing l a green tree	3869
	38: 4	My guilt has overwhelmed me l a burden	3869
	38:13	I am l a deaf man, who cannot hear,	3869
	38:13	l a mute, who cannot open his mouth;	3869
	38:14	I have become l a man who does not hear,	3869
	39:11	you consume their wealth l a moth—	3869
	44:11	be devoured l sheep and have scattered us	3869
	48: 2	L the utmost heights of Zaphon.	NIH
	48: 6	pain l that of a woman in labor.	3869
	48: 7	You destroyed them l ships of Tarshish	NIH
	48:10	L your name, O God, your praise reaches	3869
	49:12	*he* **is** l the beasts that perish.	5439
	49:14	L sheep they are destined for the grave,	3869
	49:20	without understanding **is** l the beasts	5439
	50:21	you thought I was altogether l you.	4017
	52: 2	it is l a sharpened razor,	3869
	52: 8	But I am l an olive tree flourishing in	3869
	55:13	But it is you, a man l myself,	3869+6886
	58: 4	Their venom is l the venom of a snake,	1952+3869
	58: 4	l that of a cobra that has stopped its ears,	4017
	58: 7	Let them vanish l water that flows away;	3869
	58: 8	L a slug melting away as it moves along,	4017
	58: 8	l a stillborn child,	NIH
	59: 6	snarling l dogs, and prowl about the city.	3869
	59:14	snarling l dogs, and prowl about the city.	3869
	64: 3	They sharpen their tongues l swords	3869
	64: 3	and aim their words l deadly arrows.	NIH
	66:10	you refined us l silver.	3869

Ps	68:14	*it was* l **snow fallen** on Zalmon.	AIT
	71: 7	I have become l a portent to many,	3869
	71:19	Who, O God, is l you?	4017
	72: 6	He will be l rain falling on a mown field,	3869
	72: 6	l showers watering the earth.	3869
	72:16	Let its fruit flourish l Lebanon;	3869
	72:16	let it thrive l the grass of the field.	3869
	73:12	This is what the wicked are l—	NIH
	74: 5	They behaved l men wielding axes to cut	3869
	77:20	You led your people l a flock by the hand	3869
	78: 8	They would not be l their forefathers—	3869
	78:13	he made the water stand firm l a wall.	4017
	78:16	a rocky crag and made water flow down l	3869
	78:27	He rained meat down on them l dust,	3869
	78:27	flying birds l sand on the seashore.	3869
	78:52	But he brought his people out l a flock;	3869
	78:52	he led them l sheep through the desert.	3869
	78:57	L their fathers they were disloyal	3869
	78:69	He built his sanctuary l the heights,	4017
	78:69	l the earth that he established forever.	3869
	79: 3	They have poured out blood l water all	3869
	79: 5	How long will your jealousy burn l fire?	4017
	80: 1	you who lead Joseph l a flock;	3869
	82: 7	But you will die l mere men;	3869
	82: 7	you will fall l every other ruler."	3869
	83:10	who perished at Endor and became l	NIH
	83:11	Make their nobles l Oreb and Zeeb,	3869
	83:11	all their princes l Zebah and Zalmunna,	3869
	83:13	Make them l tumbleweed, O my God,	3869
	83:13	O my God, l chaff before the wind.	3869
	86: 8	Among the gods there is none l you,	4017
	88: 4	I am l a man without strength.	3869
	88: 5	l the slain who lie in the grave,	3869
	88:17	All day long they surround me l a flood;	3869
	89: 6	*Who* is l the LORD among the heavenly	1948
	89: 8	O LORD God Almighty, who is l you?	4017
	89:10	You crushed Rahab l one of the slain;	3869
	89:36	and his throne endure before me l the sun;	3869
	89:37	it will be established forever l the moon,	3869
	89:46	How long will your wrath burn l fire?	4017
	90: 4	in your sight are l a day that has just gone	3869
	90: 4	or l a watch in the night.	NIH
	90: 5	they are l the new grass of the morning—	3869
	92: 7	that though the wicked spring up l grass	4017
	92:10	You have exalted my horn l that of	3869
	92:12	The righteous will flourish l a palm tree,	3869
	92:12	they will grow l a cedar of Lebanon;	3869
	97: 5	mountains melt l wax before the LORD,	3869
	102: 3	For my days vanish l smoke;	928
	102: 3	my bones burn l glowing embers.	3869
	102: 4	My heart is blighted and withered l grass;	3869
	102: 6	I **am** l a desert owl,	1948
	102: 6	l an owl among the ruins.	3869
	102: 7	I have become l a bird alone on a roof.	3869
	102:11	My days are l the evening shadow;	3869
	102:11	I wither away l grass.	3869
	102:26	they will all wear out l a garment.	3869
	102:26	L clothing you will change them	3869
	103: 5	that your youth is renewed l the eagle's.	3869
	103:15	As for man, his days are l grass,	3869
	103:15	he flourishes l a flower of the field;	3869
	104: 2	he stretches out the heavens l a tent	3869
	105:41	l a river it flowed in the desert.	NIH
	107:27	They reeled and staggered l drunken men;	3869
	107:41	and increased their families l flocks.	3869
	109:18	it entered into his body l water,	3869
	109:18	into his bones l oil.	3869
	109:19	May it be l a cloak wrapped about him,	3869
	109:19	l a belt tied forever around him.	4200
	109:23	I fade away l an evening shadow;	3869
	109:23	I am shaken off l a locust.	3869
	113: 5	Who is l the LORD our God,	3869
	114: 4	the mountains skipped l rams,	3869
	114: 4	skipped like rams, the hills l lambs.	3869
	114: 6	that you skipped l rams, you hills,	3869
	114: 6	skipped like rams, you hills, l lambs?	3869
	115: 8	Those who make them will be l them,	4017
	118:12	They swarmed around me l bees,	3869
	119:83	Though I am l a wineskin in the smoke,	3869
	119:119	All the wicked of the earth you discard l	NIH
	119:162	I rejoice in your promise l one who finds	3869
	119:176	I have strayed l a lost sheep.	3869
	122: 3	Jerusalem is built l a city	3869
	124: 7	We have escaped l a bird out of	3869
	125: 1	Those who trust in the LORD are l	3869
	126: 1	we were l men who dreamed.	3869
	126: 4	O LORD, l streams in the Negev.	3869
	127: 4	L arrows in the hands of a warrior	3869
	128: 3	l a fruitful vine within your house;	3869
	128: 3	be l olive shoots around your table.	3869
	129: 6	May they be l grass on the roof,	3869
	131: 2	I a weaned child with its mother,	3869
	131: 2	l a weaned child is my soul within me.	3869
	133: 2	It is l precious oil poured on the head,	3869
	135:18	Those who make them will be l them,	4017
	139:12	the night will shine l the day,	3869
	141: 2	May my prayer be set before you l	NIH
	141: 2	up of my hands be l the evening sacrifice.	NIH
	143: 3	he makes me dwell in darkness l	3869
	143: 6	my soul thirsts for you l a parched land.	3869
	143: 7	not hide your face from me or *I will* **be** l	5439
	144: 4	Man *is* l a breath;	1948
	144: 4	his days l a fleeting shadow.	3869
	144:12	Then our sons in their youth will be l	3869
	144:12	and our daughters will be l pillars carved	3869
	147:16	He spreads the snow l wool and scatters	3869
	147:16	and scatters the frost l ashes.	3869

Ps	147:17	He hurls down his hail l pebbles.	3869
Pr	1:12	l the grave, and whole,	3869
	1:12	l those who go down to the pit;	3869
	1:27	when calamity overtakes you l a storm,	3869
	1:27	disaster sweeps over you l a whirlwind,	3869
	4:18	the righteous is l the first gleam of dawn,	3869
	4:19	the way of the wicked is l deep darkness;	3869
	6: 5	l a gazelle from the hand of the hunter,	3869
	6: 5	l a bird from the snare of the fowler.	3869
	6:11	and poverty will come on you l a bandit	3869
	6:11	like a bandit and scarcity l an armed man.	3869
	7:10	**dressed** l a prostitute and with crafty intent.	AIT
	7:22	All at once he followed her l an ox going	3869
	7:22	l a deer stepping into a noose	3869
	7:23	l a bird darting into a snare,	3869
	11:22	L a gold ring in a pig's snout is	NIH
	11:28	but the righteous will thrive l a green leaf.	3869
	12: 4	a disgraceful wife is l decay in his bones.	3869
	12:18	Reckless words pierce l a sword,	3869
	16:15	his favor is l a rain cloud in spring.	3869
	16:27	and his speech is l a scorching fire.	3869
	17:14	Starting a quarrel is l breaching a dam;	NIH
	18: 8	words of a gossip are l choice morsels;	3869
	18:19	disputes are l the barred gates of a citadel.	3869
	19:12	A king's rage is l the roar of a lion,	3869
	19:12	but his favor is l dew on the grass.	3869
	19:13	quarrelsome wife is l a constant dripping.	NIH
	20: 2	A king's wrath is l the roar of a lion;	3869
	21: 1	he directs it l a watercourse wherever he	NIH
	23: 5	sprout wings and fly off to the sky l an eagle	3869
	23:28	L a bandit she lies in wait,	3869
	23:32	the end it bites l a snake and poisons like	3869
	23:32	bites like a snake and poisons l a viper.	3869
	23:34	be l one sleeping on the high seas,	3869
	24:15	Do not lie in wait l an outlaw against	NIH
	24:26	An honest answer is l a kiss on the lips.	NIH
	24:34	and poverty will come on you l a bandit	NIH
	24:34	like a bandit and scarcity l an armed man.	3869
	25:11	A word aptly spoken is l apples of gold	NIH
	25:12	L an earring of gold or an ornament	NIH
	25:13	L the coolness of snow at harvest time is	3869
	25:14	L clouds and wind without rain is	NIH
	25:18	L a club or a sword or a sharp arrow is	NIH
	25:19	L a bad tooth or a lame foot is reliance on	NIH
	25:20	L one who takes away a garment on	NIH
	25:20	or l vinegar poured on soda,	NIH
	25:25	L cold water to a weary soul is good news	NIH
	25:26	L a muddied spring or a polluted well is	NIH
	25:28	L a city whose walls are broken down is	NIH
	26: 1	L snow in summer or rain in harvest,	3869
	26: 2	L a fluttering sparrow or	3869
	26: 4	or *you will* **be** l him yourself.	8750
	26: 6	L cutting off one's feet	NIH
	26: 7	L a lame man's legs that hang limp is	NIH
	26: 8	L tying a stone in a sling is the giving	3869
	26: 9	L a thornbush in a drunkard's hand is	NIH
	26:10	L an archer who wounds at random	NIH
	26:17	L one who seizes a dog by the ears is	NIH
	26:18	L a madman shooting firebrands	3869
	26:22	words of a gossip are l choice morsels;	3869
	26:23	L a coating of glaze over earthenware	3869
	27: 8	L a bird that strays from its nest is	3869
	27:15	A quarrelsome wife **is** l a constant dripping	8750
	27:16	restraining her is l restraining the wind	NIH
	27:22	grinding him l grain with a pestle,	928+9348
	28: 3	A ruler who oppresses the poor is l a	NIH
	28:15	L a roaring lion or a charging bear is	3869
	31:14	She is l the merchant ships,	3869
Ecc	2:16	For the wise man, l the fool, will not be	6640
	2:16	L the fool, the wise man too must die!	NIH
	3:18	they may see that they are l the animals.	4200
	3:19	Man's fate is l that of the animals;	NIH
	6:12	and meaningless days he passes through l	3869
	7: 6	L the crackling of thorns under the pot,	3869
	7:11	Wisdom, l an inheritance, is a good thing	6640
	8: 1	Who is l the wise man?	3869
	8:13	their days will not lengthen l a shadow.	3869
	10: 7	while princes go on foot l slaves.	3869
	12:11	The words of the wise are l goads,	3869
	12:11	their collected sayings l firmly embedded	3869
SS	1: 3	your name is l perfume poured out.	NIH
	1: 5	dark l the tents of Kedar,	3869
	1: 5	l the tent curtains of Solomon.	3869
	1: 7	Why should I be l a veiled woman beside	3869
	2: 2	L a lily among thorns is my darling among	3869
	2: 3	L an apple tree among the trees of	3869
	2: 9	My lover **is** l a gazelle or a young stag.	1948
	2:17	and be l a gazelle or like a young stag on	1948
	2:17	and be like a gazelle or l a young stag on	NIH
	3: 6	up from the desert l a column of smoke,	3869
	4: 1	Your hair is l a flock of goats descending	3869
	4: 2	Your teeth are l a flock of sheep just shorn,	3869
	4: 3	Your lips are l a scarlet ribbon;	3869
	4: 3	Your temples behind your veil are l	3869
	4: 4	Your neck is l the tower of David,	3869
	4: 5	Your two breasts are l two fawns,	3869
	4: 5	l twin fawns of a gazelle that browse	NIH
	4:11	The fragrance of your garments is l that	3869
	5:12	His eyes are l doves by the water streams,	3869
	5:12	in milk, **mounted** l jewels.	3782+4859+6584
	5:13	His cheeks are l beds of spice	3869
	5:13	His lips are l lilies dripping with myrrh.	NIH
	5:14	His body is l polished ivory decorated	NIH
	5:15	His appearance is l Lebanon,	3869
	6: 5	Your hair is l a flock of goats descending	3869
	6: 6	Your teeth are l a flock of sheep coming	3869
	6: 7	Your temples behind your veil are l	3869

SS 6:10 Who is this that appears l the dawn, 4017
7: 1 Your graceful legs are l jewels, 4017
7: 3 Your breasts are l two fawns, 3869
7: 4 Your neck is l an ivory tower. 3869
7: 4 Your nose is l the tower of Lebanon 3869
7: 5 Your head crowns you l Mount Carmel. 3869
7: 5 Your hair is l royal tapestry; 3869
7: 7 Your stature is l that of the palm, 1948
7: 7 and your breasts l clusters of fruit. NIH
7: 8 May your breasts be l the clusters of 3869
7: 8 the fragrance of your breath l apples, 3869
7: 9 and your mouth l the best wine. 3869
8: 1 If only you were to me l a brother, 3869
8: 6 Place me l a seal over your heart, 3869
8: 6 l a seal on your arm; 3869
8: 6 It burns l blazing fire, like a mighty flame. NIH
8: 6 It burns like blazing fire, l a mighty flame. NIH
8:10 I am a wall, and my breasts are l towers. 3869
8:10 in his eyes l one bringing contentment. 3869
8:14 and be l a gazelle or like a young stag on 1948
8:14 and be like a gazelle or l a young stag on NIH
Isa 1: 8 The Daughter of Zion is left l a shelter in 3869
1: 8 l a hut in a field of melons, 3869
1: 8 l a city under siege. 3869
1: 9 we would have become l Sodom, 3869
1: 9 we would have been l Gomorrah. 1948
1:18 "Though your sins are l scarlet, 3869
1:18 sins are like scarlet, they shall be l wool. 3869
1:30 You will be l an oak with fading leaves, 3869
1:30 l a garden without water. 3869
2: 6 they practice divination l the Philistines 3869
3: 9 they parade their sin l Sodom; 3869
5:24 and their flowers blow away l dust; 3869
5:25 the dead bodies are l refuse in the streets. 3869
5:28 their horses' hoofs seem l flint, 3869
5:28 their chariot wheels l a whirlwind. 3869
5:29 Their roar is l that of the lion, 3869
5:29 they roar l young lions; 3869
5:30 that day they will roar over it l the roaring 3869
9:18 Surely wickedness burns l a fire; 3869
10: 6 to trample them down l mud in the streets. 3869
10: 9 'Has not Calno fared l Carchemish? 3869
10: 9 Is not Hamath l Arpad, 3869
10: 9 and Samaria l Damascus? 3869
10:13 I a mighty one l subdued their kings. 3869
10:16 a fire will be kindled l a blazing flame. 3869
10:22 O Israel, be l the sand by the sea, 3869
11: 7 and the lion will eat straw l the ox, 3869
13: 4 l that of a great multitude! 1952
13: 4 l nations massing together! NIH
13: 6 it will come l destruction from 3869
13: 8 they will writhe l a woman in labor. 3869
13:14 L a hunted gazelle, 3869
13:14 l sheep without a shepherd, 3869
13:19 will be overthrown by God l Sodom 3869
14:10 you have become l us." 5439
14:14 I will make myself l the Most High." 1948
14:19 But you are cast out of your tomb l 3869
14:19 L a corpse trampled underfoot, 3869
16: 2 L fluttering birds pushed from the nest, 3869
16: 3 Make your shadow l night—at high noon. 3869
16:11 My heart laments for Moab l a harp, 3869
17: 3 the remnant of Aram will be l the glory of 3869
17: 9 will be l places abandoned to thickets 3869
17:12 they rage l the raging sea! 3869
17:12 they roar l the roaring of great waters! 3869
17:13 peoples roar l the roar of surging waters, 3869
17:13 driven before the wind l chaff on the hills, 3869
17:13 l tumbleweed before a gale. 3869
18: 4 l shimmering heat in the sunshine, 3869
18: 4 l a cloud of dew in the heat of harvest." 3869
19:16 In that day the Egyptians will be l women. 3869
21: 1 L whirlwinds sweeping through 3869
21: 3 l those of a woman in labor; 3869
22:18 roll you up tightly l a ball and throw you 3869
22:23 I will drive him l a peg into a firm place; NIH
24:20 The earth reels l a drunkard, 3869
24:20 it sways l a hut in the wind; 3869
24:22 be herded together l prisoners bound in NIH
25: 4 of the ruthless is l a storm driving against 3869
25: 5 and l the heat of the desert. 3869
26:19 Your dew is l the dew of the morning; NIH
27: 9 When he makes all the altar stones to be l 3869
27:10 forsaken l the desert; 3869
28: 2 L a hailstorm and a destructive wind, 3869
28: 2 l a driving rain and a flooding downpour, 3869
28: 4 will be l a fig ripe before harvest— 3869
28: 4 she will be to me l an altar hearth. 3869
29: 2 But your many enemies will become l 3869
29: 5 the ruthless hordes l blown chaff. 3869
29:16 if the potter were thought to be l the clay! 3869
29:17 a fertile field and the fertile field seem l 4200
30:13 this sin will become for you l a high wall, 3869
30:14 It will break in pieces l pottery, 3869
30:17 till you are left l a flagstaff on 3869
30:17 l a banner on a hill." 3869
30:22 you will throw them away l a menstrual 4017
30:26 The moon will shine l the sun, 3869
30:26 l the light of seven full days, 3869
30:28 His breath is l a rushing torrent, 3869
30:33 l a stream of burning sulfur, sets it ablaze. 3869
31: 5 L birds hovering overhead, 3869
32: 2 Each man will be l a shelter from the wind 3869
32: 2 l streams of water in the desert and 3869
32:15 and the fertile field seems l a forest. 4200
33: 4 l a swarm of locusts men pounce on it. 3869
33: 9 Sharon is l the Arabah, 3869

Isa 33:12 I cut thornbushes they will be set ablaze." NIH
33:21 be l a place of broad rivers and streams. NIH
34: 4 and the sky rolled up l a scroll; 3869
34: 4 the starry host will fall l withered leaves 3869
34: 4 l shriveled figs from the fig tree. 3869
35: 1 and blossom. L the crocus, 3869
35: 6 Then will the lame leap l a deer, 3869
36:12 who, l you, will have to eat their own filth 6640
36:17 until I come and take you to a land l 3869
37:27 They are l plants in the field, NIH
37:27 l tender green shoots, NIH
37:27 l grass sprouting on the roof, NIH
38:12 L a shepherd's tent my house has been 3869
38:12 L a weaver I have rolled up my life, 3869
38:13 but l a lion he broke all my bones; 3869
38:14 I cried l a swift or thrush, 3869
38:14 I moaned l a mourning dove. 3869
40: 6 "All men are l grass, NIH
40: 6 all their glory is l the flowers of the field. 3869
40:11 He tends his flock l a shepherd: 3869
40:15 Surely the nations are l a drop in a bucket; 3869
40:22 and its people are l grasshoppers. 3869
40:22 He stretches out the heavens l a canopy, 3869
40:22 and spreads them out l a tent to live in. 3869
40:24 a whirlwind sweeps them away l chaff. 3869
40:31 They will soar on wings l eagles; 3869
42:13 LORD will march out l a mighty man, 3869
42:13 a warrior he will stir up his zeal; 3869
42:14 But now, l a woman in childbirth, 3869
42:19 and deaf l the messenger I send? 3869
42:19 Who is blind l the one committed to me, 3869
42:19 blind l the servant of the LORD? 3869
43:17 extinguished, snuffed out l a wick; 3869
44: 4 They will spring up l grass in a meadow, NIH
44: 4 l poplar trees by flowing streams. 3869
44: 7 Who then is l me? 4017
44:22 I have swept away your offenses l a cloud, 3869
44:22 your sins l the morning mist. 3869
46: 9 I am God, and there is none l me. 4017
47:14 Surely they are l stubble; 3869
48:18 your peace would have been l a river, 3869
48:18 your righteousness l the waves of the sea. 3869
48:19 Your descendants would have been l 3869
48:19 your children l its numberless grains; 3869
49: 2 He made my mouth l a sharpened sword, 3869
49:18 you will put them on, l a bride. 3869
50: 4 to listen l one being taught. 3869
50: 7 Therefore have I set my face l flint, 3869
50: 9 They will all wear out l a garment; 3869
51: 3 he will make her deserts l Eden, 3869
51: 3 her wastelands l the garden of the LORD. 3869
51: 6 the heavens will vanish l smoke, 3869
51: 6 like smoke, the earth will wear out l 3869
51: 6 a garment and its inhabitants die l flies. 4017
51: 8 For the moth will eat them up l a garment; 3869
51: 8 the worm will devour them l wool. 3869
51:20 l antelope caught in a net. 3869
51:23 And you made your back l the ground, 3869
51:23 l a street to be walked over." 3869
53: 2 He grew up before him l a tender shoot, 3869
53: 2 and l a root out of dry ground. 3869
53: 3 L one from whom men hide their faces he was despised, 3869
53: 7 he was led l a lamb to the slaughter, 3869
54: 9 "To me this is l the days of Noah, 3869
56:12 And tomorrow will be l today, 3869
57:20 But the wicked are l the tossing sea, 3869
58: 1 Raise your voice l a trumpet. 3869
58: 5 Is it only for bowing one's head l a reed 3869
58: 8 your light will break forth l the dawn, 3869
58:10 and your night will become l the noonday. 3869
58:11 You will be l a well-watered garden, 3869
58:11 l a spring whose waters never fail. 3869
59:10 L the blind we grope along the wall, 3869
59:10 feeling our way l men without eyes. 3869
59:10 among the strong, we are l the dead. 3869
59:11 We all growl l bears; 3869
59:11 we moan mournfully l doves. 3869
59:19 For he will come l a pent-up flood that 3869
60: 8 "Who are these that fly along l clouds, 3869
60: 8 l doves to their nests? 3869
61:10 as a bridegroom adorns his head l a priest, AIT
62: 1 till her righteousness shines out l the dawn, 3869
62: 1 her salvation l a blazing torch. 3869
63: 2 l those of one treading the winepress? 3869
63:13 L a horse in open country, 3869
63:14 l cattle that go down to the plain, 3869
64: 6 of us have become l one who is unclean, 3869
64: 6 and all our righteous acts are l filthy rags; 3869
64: 6 we all shrivel up l a leaf, 3869
64: 6 and l the wind our sins sweep us away. 3869
65:25 and the lion will eat straw l the ox, 3869
66: 3 sacrifices a bull is l one who kills a man, NIH
66: 3 l one who breaks a dog's neck; NIH
66: 3 whoever makes a grain offering is l NIH
66: 3 l one who worships an idol. NIH
66:12 "I will extend peace to her l a river, 3869
66:12 the wealth of nations l a flooding stream; 3869
66:14 and you will flourish l grass; 3869
66:15 and his chariots are l a whirlwind; 3869
Jer 2:10 see if there has ever been anything l this: 3869
2:21 I had planted you l a choice vine of sound NIH
2:30 Your sword has devoured your prophets l 3869
3: 2 sat l a nomad in the desert. 3869
3:19 " 'How gladly would I treat you l sons 928
3:20 But l a woman unfaithful to her husband, NIH

Jer 4: 4 or my wrath will break out and burn l fire 3869
4:13 He advances l the clouds, 3869
4:13 his chariots come l a whirlwind, 3869
4:17 They surround her l men guarding a field, 3869
5:16 Their quivers are l an open grave; 3869
5:26 in wait l men who snare birds and 3869
5:26 and l those who set traps to catch men. NIH
5:27 L cages full of birds, 3869
6: 9 l one gathering grapes." 3869
6:23 They sound l the roaring sea as they ride 3869
6:23 they come l men in battle formation 3869
6:24 pain l that of a woman in labor. 3869
8: 2 but will be l refuse lying on the ground. 4200
8: 6 pursues his own course l a horse charging 3869
9: 3 "They make ready their tongue l a bow, NIH
9:12 the land been ruined and laid waste l 3869
9:22 " 'The dead bodies of men will lie l refuse 3869
9:22 l cut grain behind the reaper, 3869
10: 5 L a scarecrow in a melon patch, 3869
10: 6 No one is l you, O LORD; 4017
10: 7 there is no one l you. 4017
10:16 of Jacob is not l these, for he is the Maker 3869
11:19 I had been l a gentle lamb led to 3869
12: 3 Drag them off l sheep to be butchered! 3869
12: 8 My inheritance has become to me l a lion 3869
12: 9 Has not my inheritance become to me l NIH
13:10 will be l this belt—completely useless! 3869
13:21 Will not pain grip you l that of a woman 4017
13:24 "I will scatter you l chaff driven by 3869
14: 6 on the barren heights and pant l jackals; 3869
14: 8 why are you l a stranger in the land, 3869
14: 8 l a traveler who stays only a night? 3869
14: 9 Why are you l a man taken by surprise, 3869
14: 9 l a warrior powerless to save? 3869
15:18 Will you be to me l a deceptive brook, 4017
15:18 l a spring that fails? NIH
16: 4 but will be l refuse lying on the ground. 4200
17: 6 He will be l a bush in the wastelands; 3869
17: 8 He will be l a tree planted by the water 3869
17:11 L a partridge that hatches eggs it did NIH
18: 6 "L clay in the hand of the potter, 3869
18:13 Who has ever heard anything l this? 3869
18:17 L a wind from the east, 3869
19:12 I will make this city l Topheth, 3869
19:13 of the kings of Judah will be defiled l 3869
20: 9 his word is in my heart l a fire, 3869
20:11 the LORD is with me l a mighty warrior; 3869
20:16 be l the towns the LORD overthrew 3869
21:12 or my wrath will break out and burn l fire 3869
22: 6 "Though you are l Gilead to me, NIH
22: 6 l the summit of Lebanon, NIH
22: 6 I will surely make you l a desert, NIH
22: 6 like a desert, l towns not inhabited. NIH
22:23 pain l that of a woman in labor! 3869
23: 9 I am l a drunken man, 3869
23: 9 l a man overcome by wine, 3869
23:14 They are all l Sodom to me; 3869
23:14 the people of Jerusalem are l Gomorrah." 3869
23:29 "Is not my word l fire," 3869
23:29 l a hammer that breaks a rock in pieces? 3869
24: 2 l those that ripen early; 3869
24: 5 'L these good figs, 3869
24: 8 " 'But l the poor figs, 3869
25:30 He will shout l those who tread 3869
25:33 but will be l refuse lying on the ground. 4200
25:34 you will fall and be shattered l 3869
25:38 L a lion he will leave his lair, 3869
26: 6 then I will make this house l Shiloh 3869
26: 9 be l Shiloh and this city will be desolate 3869
26:18 "Zion will be plowed l a field, NIH
29:17 and I will make them l poor figs that are 3869
29:22 'The LORD treat you l Zedekiah 3869
29:26 you should put any madman who acts l a prophet into the stocks 5547
30: 6 hands on his stomach l a woman in labor, 3869
30: 7 None will be l it. 4017
31:10 and will watch over his flock l 3869
31:12 They will be l a well-watered garden, 3869
31:18 'You disciplined me l an unruly calf, 3869
31:32 It will not be l the covenant I made 3869
34:18 l the calf they cut in two and AIT
40: 4 with me to Babylon, if you l, 928+3202+6524
44:19 that we were making cakes l her image 6771
46: 7 "Who is this that rises l the Nile, 3869
46: 7 l rivers of surging waters? 3869
46: 8 Egypt rises l the Nile, 3869
46: 8 l rivers of surging waters. 3869
46:18 "one will come who is l Tabor among 3869
46:18 l Carmel by the sea. 3869
46:21 mercenaries in her ranks are l fattened 3869
46:22 Egypt will hiss l a fleeing serpent as 3869
46:22 l men who cut down trees. 3869
48: 6 become l a bush in the desert. 3869
48:11 l wine left on its dregs, NIH
48:28 Be l a dove that makes its nest at the mouth 3869
48:36 "So my heart laments for Moab l a flute; 3869
48:36 it laments l a flute for the wealth of 3869
48:38 for I have broken Moab l a jar 3869
48:41 Moab's warriors will be l the heart of 3869
49:19 "L a lion coming up from Jordan's thickets 3869
49:19 Who is l me and who can challenge me? 4017
49:22 of Edom's warriors will be l the heart of 3869
49:23 troubled l the restless sea. 3869
49:24 pain l that of a woman in labor. 3869
50: 9 and be l the goats that lead the flock. 3869
50: 9 be l skilled warriors who do 3869
50:11 because you frolic l a heifer threshing grain 3869

Ref	Text	Num
Jer 50:11	like a heifer threshing grain and neigh l	3869
50:26	pile her up l heaps of grain.	4017
50:42	They sound l the roaring sea as they ride	3869
50:42	they come l men in battle formation	3869
50:43	pain l that of a woman in labor.	3869
50:44	L a lion coming up from Jordan's thickets	3869
50:44	Who is l me and who can challenge me?	4017
51:19	of Jacob is not l these, for he is the Maker	3869
51:27	send up horses l a swarm of locusts.	3869
51:30	they have become l women.	4200
51:33	of Babylon is l a threshing floor at the time	3869
51:34	L a serpent he has swallowed us	3869
51:38	Her people all roar l young lions,	3869
51:38	they growl l lion cubs.	3869
51:40	"I will bring them down l lambs to	3869
51:40	l rams and goats.	3869
51:55	[of enemies] will rage l great waters;	3869
La 1: 1	How l a widow is she,	3869
1: 6	Her princes are l deer that find no pasture;	3869
1:12	Is any suffering l my suffering	3869
1:21	so they may become l me.	4017
2: 3	He has burned in Jacob l a flaming fire	3869
2: 4	L an enemy he has strung his bow;	3869
2: 4	L a foe he has slain all who were pleasing	3869
2: 4	he has poured out his wrath l fire on	3869
2: 5	The Lord is l an enemy;	3869
2: 6	He has laid waste his dwelling l a garden;	3869
2:12	as they faint l wounded men in the streets	3869
2:18	let your tears flow l a river day and night;	3869
2:19	pour out your heart l water in the presence	3869
2:20	Whom have you ever treated l **this?**	3907
3: 6	He has made me dwell in darkness l	3869
3:10	L a bear lying in wait, like a lion in hiding,	NIH
3:10	l a lion in hiding,	NIH
3:52	without cause hunted me l a bird.	3869
4: 3	but my people have become heartless l	3869
4: 7	their appearance l sapphires.	NIH
4:14	through the streets l men who are blind.	NIH
5: 3	our mothers l widows.	3869
Eze 1: 4	of the fire looked l glowing metal,	3869
1: 5	and in the fire was *what* **looked l**	1952
1: 7	their feet were l those of a calf	3869
1: 7	and gleamed l burnished bronze.	3869+6524
1:10	Their faces **looked l** this:	1952
1:13	of the living creatures was l burning coals	1952
1:13	like burning coals of fire or l torches.	3869
1:14	The creatures sped back and forth l	3869
1:16	They sparkled l chrysolite,	3869
1:16	be made l a wheel intersecting a wheel.	889+3869
1:22	of the living creatures was *what* **looked l**	1952
1:22	sparkling l ice, and awesome.	3869
1:24	l the roar of rushing waters,	3869
1:24	l the voice of the Almighty,	3869
1:24	l the tumult of an army.	NIH
1:26	over their heads was what looked l	1952
1:26	on the throne was a figure l that of a man.	3869
1:27	be his waist up he looked l glowing metal,	3869
1:27	and that from there down he looked l fire;	3869
1:28	L the appearance of a rainbow in	3869
2: 8	Do not rebel l that rebellious house;	3869
3: 9	I will make your forehead the hardest	3869
3:23	l the glory I had seen by the Kebar River,	3869
7:16	moaning l doves of the valleys,	3869
8: 2	and I saw a figure l that of a man.	3869
8: 2	to be his waist down he was l fire,	NIH
8: 3	He stretched out *what* **looked l** a hand	9322
10: 5	l the voice of God Almighty	3869
10: 8	be seen *what* **looked l** the hands of a man.)	9322
10: 9	the wheels sparkled l chrysolite.	3869
10:10	each was l a wheel intersecting a wheel.	889+3869
10:21	and under their wings was *what* **looked l**	1952
12: 4	go out l those who go into exile.	3869
13: 4	O Israel, are l jackals among ruins.	3869
13:20	with which you ensnare people l birds	4200
13:20	I will set free the people that you ensnare l	4200
16: 7	I made you grow l a plant of the field.	3869
16:30	**acting** l a brazen prostitute!	AIT
16:44	"L mother, like daughter."	3869
16:44	"Like mother, l daughter."	NIH
17: 5	He planted it l a willow by abundat water,	NIH
19:10	'Your mother was l a vine in your vineyard	3869
20:32	" 'You say, "We want to be l the nations,	3869
20:32	l the peoples of the world,	3869
21:10	polished to **flash l lightning!**	1398
21:15	It is made to **flash l lightning,**	1398
21:23	It will seem l a false omen	3869
21:28	to consume and **flash l lightning!**	1398
22:25	within her l a roaring lion tearing its prey;	3869
22:27	within her are l wolves tearing their prey;	3869
23:15	all of them looked l Babylonian chariot	1952
23:20	whose genitals were l those of donkeys	NIH
23:20	of donkeys and whose emission was l that	NIH
25: 8	Judah has become l all the other nations,"	3869
26: 3	l the sea casting up its waves.	3869
26:19	l cities no longer inhabited,	3869
27:32	"Who was ever silenced l Tyre,	3869
30:24	before him l a mortally wounded man.	NIH
32: 2	" 'You are l a lion among the nations;	1948
32: 2	you are l a monster in the seas thrashing	3869
32:14	and make her streams flow l oil,	3869
36:17	Their conduct was l a woman's monthly	3869
36:35	waste has become l the garden of Eden;	3869
38: 9	advancing l a storm;	3869
38: 9	you will be l a cloud covering the land.	3869
38:16	against my people Israel l a cloud	3869
40: 2	that looked l a city.	3869
40: 3	and I saw a man whose appearance was l	3869

Ref	Text	Num
Eze 40:25	l the openings of the others.	3869
41:25	palm trees l those carved on the walls,	889+3869
42:11	These were l the rooms on the north;	3869+5260
43: 2	His voice was l the roar of rushing waters,	3869
43: 3	The vision I saw was l the vision I had seen	3869
43: 3	and l the visions I had seen by the Kebar	3869
47:10	l the fish of the Great Sea.	3869
Da 2:35	and became l chaff on a threshing floor in	10341
3:25	and the fourth looks l a son of the gods."	10179
4:23	let him live l the wild animals,	10554
4:25	you will eat grass l cattle and be drenched	10341
4:32	you will eat grass l cattle.	10341
4:33	from people and ate grass l cattle.	10341
4:33	of heaven until his hair grew l the feathers	10341
4:33	an eagle and his nails l the claws of a bird.	10341
5:11	and intelligence and wisdom l that of	10341
5:21	the wild donkeys and ate grass l cattle;	10341
7: 4	"The first was l a lion,	10341
7: 4	the ground so that it stood on two feet l	10341
7: 5	which **looked l** a bear.	10179
7: 6	one that looked l a leopard.	10341
7: 6	And on its back it had four wings l those	NIH
7: 8	This horn had eyes l the eyes of a man	10341
7: 9	the hair of his head was white l wool.	10341
7:13	and there before me was one l a son	10341
8:15	before me stood one who looked l a man.	3869
9:12	whole heaven nothing has ever been done l	3869
9:26	The end will come l a flood:	928
10: 6	His body was l chrysolite,	3869
10: 6	his face l lightning,	3869+5260
10: 6	his eyes l flaming torches,	3869
10: 6	and legs l the gleam of burnished bronze,	3869
10: 6	and his voice l the sound of a multitude.	3869
10:16	one who looked l a man touched my lips,	3869
10:18	the one who looked l a man touched me	3869
11:10	which will sweep on l an irresistible flood	NIH
11:40	and sweep through them l a flood.	NIH
12: 3	who are wise will shine l the brightness	3869
12: 3	l the stars for ever and ever.	3869
Hos 1:10	"Yet the Israelites will be l the sand on	3869
2: 3	I will make her l a desert,	3869
4: 4	your people are l those who bring charges	3869
4: 9	And it will be: L people, like priests.	3869
4: 9	And it will be: Like people, l priests.	3869
4:16	l a stubborn heifer.	3869
4:16	then can the LORD pasture them l lambs	3869
5:10	Judah's leaders are l those who move	3869
5:10	I will pour out my wrath on them l a flood	3869
5:12	I am l a moth to Ephraim,	3869
5:12	l rot to the people of Judah.	3869
5:14	For I will be l a lion to Ephraim,	3869
5:14	l a great lion to Judah.	3869
6: 3	he will come to us l the winter rains,	3869
6: 3	l the spring rains that water the earth."	3869
6: 4	Your love is l the morning mist,	3869
6: 4	l the early dew that disappears.	3869
6: 5	my judgments flashed l lightning	NIH
6: 7	L Adam, they have broken the covenant—	3869
7: 4	burning l an oven whose fire	4017
7: 6	Their hearts are l an oven;	3869
7: 6	in the morning it blazes l a flaming fire.	3869
7:11	"Ephraim is l a dove,	3869
7:12	I will pull them down l birds of the air.	3869
7:16	they are l a faulty bow.	3869
8: 8	among the nations l a worthless thing.	3869
8: 9	gone up to Assyria l a donkey wandering	NIH
9: 1	do not be jubilant l the other nations.	3869
9: 4	Such sacrifices will be to them l the bread	3869
9:10	it was l finding grapes in the desert;	3869
9:10	when I saw your fathers, it was l seeing	3869
9:11	Ephraim's glory will fly away l a bird—	3869
9:13	I have seen Ephraim, l Tyre,	889+3869
10: 4	up l poisonous weeds in a plowed field.	3869
10: 7	and its king will float away l a twig on	3869
11: 8	How can I treat you l Admah?	3869
11: 8	How can I make you l Zeboiim?	3869
11:10	he will roar l a lion.	3869
11:11	They will come trembling l birds	3869
11:11	l doves from Assyria.	3869
12:11	Their altars will be l piles of stones on	3869
13: 3	Therefore they will be l the morning mist,	3869
13: 3	l the early dew that disappears,	3869
13: 3	l chaff swirling from a threshing floor,	3869
13: 3	l smoke escaping through a window.	3869
13: 7	So I will come upon them l a lion,	4017
13: 7	l a leopard I will lurk by the path.	3869
13: 8	L a bear robbed of her cubs,	3869
13: 8	L a lion I will devour them;	3869
14: 5	I will be l the dew to Israel;	3869
14: 5	he will blossom l a lily.	3869
14: 5	L a cedar of Lebanon he will send	3869
14: 6	His splendor will be l an olive tree,	3869
14: 6	his fragrance l a cedar of Lebanon.	3869
14: 7	He will flourish l the grain.	NIH
14: 7	He will blossom l a vine,	3869
14: 7	his fame will be l the wine from Lebanon.	3869
14: 8	I am l a green pine tree;	3869
Joel 1: 2	Has anything l this ever happened	NIH
1: 8	Mourn l a virgin in sackcloth grieving for	3869
1:15	come l destruction from the Almighty.	3869
2: 2	l dawn spreading across the mountains	3869
2: 3	Before them the land is l the garden	3869
2: 4	They have the appearance of horses; l cavalry.	3869
2: 5	With a noise l that of chariots they leap	3869
2: 5	l a crackling fire consuming stubble,	3869
2: 5	l a mighty army drawn up for battle.	3869
2: 7	They charge l warriors;	3869

Ref	Text	Num
Joel 2: 7	they scale walls l soldiers.	3869
2: 9	l thieves they enter through the windows.	3869
Am 4:11	You were l a burning stick snatched from	3869
5: 6	through the house of Joseph l a fire;	3869
5:24	But let justice roll on l a river,	3869
5:24	righteousness l a never-failing stream!	3869
6: 5	You strum away on your harps l David	3869
8: 8	The whole land will rise l the Nile;	3869
8: 8	be stirred up and then sink l the river	3869
8:10	that time l mourning for an only son and	3869
8:10	an only son and the end of it l a bitter day.	3869
9: 5	the whole land rises l the Nile,	3869
9: 5	then sinks l the river of Egypt—	3869
Ob 1: 4	Though you soar l the eagle	3869
1:11	you were l one of them.	3869
Mic 1: 4	l wax before the fire,	3869
1: 4	l water rushing down a slope.	3869
1: 8	I will howl l a jackal and moan l	3869
1: 8	like a jackal and moan l an owl.	3869
2: 8	Lately my people have risen up l	4200
2: 8	l men returning from battle.	NIH
2:12	I will bring them together l sheep in a pen,	3869
2:12	l a flock in its pasture;	3869
3: 3	who chop them up l meat for the pan,	889+3869
3: 3	l flesh for the pot?"	3869
3:12	Zion will be plowed l a field,	NIH
4: 9	that pain seizes you l that of a woman	3869
4:10	O Daughter of Zion, l a woman in labor,	3869
4:12	he who gathers them l sheaves to	3869
5: 7	of many peoples l dew from the LORD,	3869
5: 7	l showers on the grass,	3869
5: 8	l a lion among the beasts of the forest,	3869
5: 8	l a young lion among flocks of sheep,	3869
7: 1	I am l one who gathers summer fruit at	3869
7: 4	The best of them is l a brier,	3869
7:10	even now she will be trampled underfoot l	3869
7:17	They will lick dust l a snake,	3869
7:17	l creatures that crawl on the ground.	3869
7:18	Who is a God l you, who pardons sin	4017
Na 1: 6	His wrath is poured out l fire;	3869
1:10	they will be consumed l dry stubble.	3869
2: 2	the splendor of Jacob l the splendor	3869
2: 4	They look l flaming torches;	3869
2: 4	they dart about l lightning.	3869
2: 7	Its slave girls moan l doves and beat	3869
2: 8	Nineveh is l a pool,	3869
3:12	All your fortresses are l fig trees	NIH
3:15	and, l grasshoppers, consume you.	3869
3:15	Multiply l grasshoppers,	3869
3:15	like grasshoppers, multiply l locusts!	3869
3:16	but l locusts they strip the land and	NIH
3:17	Your guards are l locusts,	3869
3:17	your officials l swarms of locusts	3869
Hab 1: 8	They fly l a vulture swooping to devour;	3869
1: 9	Their hordes advance l a desert wind	NIH
1: 9	a desert wind and gather prisoners l sand.	3869
1:11	they sweep past l the wind and go on—	NIH
1:14	You have made men l fish in the sea,	3869
1:14	l sea creatures that have no ruler.	3869
2: 5	Because he is as greedy as the grave and l	3869
3: 4	His splendor was l the sunrise;	3869
3:19	he makes my feet l the feet of a deer,	3869
Zep 1:12	who are l wine left on its dregs,	NIH
1:17	the people and they will walk l blind men,	3869
1:17	be poured out l dust and their entrails	3869
1:17	and their entrails l filth.	3869
2: 2	and that day sweeps on l chaff,	3869
2: 9	"surely Moab will become l Sodom,	3869
2: 9	the Ammonites l Gomorrah—	3869
Hag 2: 3	Does it not seem to you l nothing?	3869
2:23	'and I will make you l my signet ring,	3869
Zec 1: 4	Do not be l your forefathers,	3869
5: 9	They had wings l those of a stork,	3869
9: 3	she has heaped up silver l dust,	3869
9: 3	and gold l the dirt of the streets.	3869
9: 7	and Ekron will be l the Jebusites.	3869
9:13	and make you l a warrior's sword.	3869
9:14	his arrow will flash l lightning.	3869
9:15	be full l a bowl used for sprinkling	3869
9:16	They will sparkle in his land l jewels in	NIH
10: 2	the people wander l sheep oppressed	4017
10: 3	and make them l a proud horse in battle.	3869
10: 5	be l mighty men trampling	3869
10: 7	The Ephraimites will become l	3869
12: 6	that day I will make the leaders of Judah l	3869
12: 6	l a flaming torch among sheaves.	3869
12: 8	the feeblest among them will be l David,	3869
12: 8	and the house of David will be l God,	3869
12: 8	l the Angel of the LORD going	3869
12:11	the weeping of Hadad Rimmon in	3869
13: 9	I will refine them l silver and test them	3869
13: 9	like silver and test them l gold.	3869
14:10	will become l the Arabah.	3869
14:20	be l the sacred bowls in front of the altar.	3869
Mal 3: 2	be l a refiner's fire or a launderer's soap.	3869
3: 3	the Levites and refine them l gold	3869
3:14	going about l mourners before the LORD	NIH
4: 1	the day is coming; it will burn l a furnace.	3869
4: 2	and leap l calves released from the stall.	3869
Mt 3:16	the Spirit of God descending l a	6059
6: 5	when you pray, do not be l the hypocrites,	6055
6: 7	do not keep on babbling l pagans,	6061
6: 8	*Do not be* l them, for your Father knows	3929
6:29	his splendor was dressed l one of these.	6055
7:24	puts them into practice *is* l a wise man who	3929
7:26	does not put them into practice *is* l a foolish	3929
9:33	"Nothing l this has ever been seen	4048

Mt	9:36	I sheep without a shepherd.	6059
	10:16	I am sending you out I sheep	6055
	10:25	It is enough for the student to be I	6055
	10:25	and the servant I his master.	6055
	11:16	are I children sitting in the marketplaces	3927
	13:24	"The kingdom of heaven *is* I a man who	3929
	13:31	kingdom of heaven is I a mustard seed,	3927
	13:33	"The kingdom of heaven is I yeast that	3927
	13:43	Then the righteous will shine I the sun in	6055
	13:44	of heaven is I treasure hidden in a field.	3927
	13:45	of heaven is I a merchant looking	3927
	13:47	of heaven is I a net that was let down into	3927
	13:52	the kingdom of heaven is I the owner of	3927
	17: 2	His face shone I the sun,	6055
	18: 3	you change and become I little children,	6055
	18: 4	whoever humbles himself I this child is	6055
	18: 5	welcomes a little child I **this** in my name	5525
	18:23	kingdom of heaven is I a king who wanted	3929
	20: 1	kingdom of heaven is I a landowner who	3927
	22: 2	kingdom of heaven is I a king who prepared	3929
	22:30	they will be I the angels in heaven.	3927
	22:39	And the second is I it:	3927
	23:27	*You are* I whitewashed tombs,	4234
	25: 1	the kingdom of heaven *will be* I ten virgins	3929
	25:14	it will be I a man going on a journey,	6061
	28: 3	His appearance was I lightning,	6055
	28: 4	that they shook and became I dead men.	6055
Mk	1:10	and the Spirit descending on him I a dove.	6055
	2: 7	"Why does this fellow talk I **that?**	4048
	2:12	"We have never seen anything I **this!**"	4048
	4:15	Some people are I seed along the path,	NIG
	4:16	Others, I seed sown on rocky places,	3931
	4:18	Still others, I seed sown among thorns,	NIG
	4:20	Others, I seed sown on good soil,	NIG
	4:26	"This is what the kingdom of God is I.	6055
	4:30	*shall we* **say** the kingdom of God **is I,**	3929
	4:31	It is I a mustard seed,	6055
	6:15	I one of the prophets of long ago."	6055
	6:34	they were I sheep without a shepherd.	6055
	7:13	And you do many things I that."	4235
	8:24	they look I trees walking around."	6055
	9:21	"How long has he been I this?"	6055
	9:26	The boy **looked so much** I a corpse	1181+6059
	10:15	of God I a little child will never enter it."	6055
	12:25	they will be I the angels in heaven.	6055
	12:38	*They* I to walk around in flowing robes	2527
	13:34	It's I a man going away:	6055
Lk	1:62	to find out what *he* would I to name	2527
	2:48	"Son, why have you treated us I this?	4048
	3:22	descended on him in bodily form I a dove.	6055
	6:40	but everyone who is fully trained will be I	6055
	6:47	I will show you what he is I who comes	3927
	6:48	He is I a man building a house,	6055
	6:49	into practice is I a man who built a house	3927
	7:31	What are they I?	3927
	7:32	are I children sitting in the marketplace	3927
	10: 3	I am sending you out I lambs	6055
	10:18	"I saw Satan fall I lightning from heaven.	6055
	11:44	because you are I unmarked graves,	6055
	12:27	in all his splendor was dressed I one	6055
	12:36	I men waiting for their master to return	3927
	13:18	"What is the kingdom of God I?	3927
	13:19	It is I a mustard seed,	3927
	13:21	It is I yeast that a woman took and mixed	3927
	15:19	make me I one of your hired men.'	6055
	17:24	of Man in his day will be I the lightning,	6061
	17:30	"It will be **just** I **this** on the day the Son of Man is revealed.	899+2848+3836
	18:11	I thank you that I am not I other men—	6061
	18:11	or even I this tax collector.	6055
	18:17	of God I a little **child** will never enter it."	6055
	20:36	for they are I the **angels.**	2694
	20:46	They I to walk around in flowing robes	2527
	21:34	that day will close on you unexpectedly I	6055
	22:26	But you are not to be I **that.**	4048
	22:26	among you should be I the youngest,	6055
	22:26	the one who rules I the one who serves.	6055
	22:44	and his sweat was I drops of blood falling	6059
	24: 4	**that gleamed** I **lightning** stood beside them.	848
	24:11	their words seemed to them I nonsense.	6059
Jn	1:44	Philip, I Andrew and Peter, was from	NIG
	8:55	If I said I did not, I would be a liar I you,	3927
	9: 9	Others said, "No, *he* only **looks** I him."	1639+3927
	11:48	If we let him go on I **this,**	4048
	12:21	"Sir," they said, "*we would* I to see Jesus."	2527
	15: 6	he is I a branch that is thrown away	6055
Ac	2: 2	Suddenly a sound I the blowing of	6061
	3:22	raise up for you a prophet I me from	6055
	6:15	and they saw that his face was I the face	6059
	7:37	a prophet I me from your own people.'	6055
	7:51	You are **just** I your fathers:	6055
	8:32	"He was led I a sheep to the slaughter,	6055
	9:18	something I scales fell from Saul's eyes,	6055
	10:11	He saw heaven opened and something I	6055
	11: 5	I saw something I a large sheet being let	6055
	14:15	We too are only men, **human** I you.	3926
	17:29	not think that the divine being is I gold	3927
	22:24	the people were shouting at him I this.	4048
	25:22	"*I would* I to hear this man myself."	1089
Ro	1:23	for images made to **look** I mortal man	3930
	5:15	But the gift is not I the trespass.	4048
	5:16	not I the result of the one man's sin:	6055
	6: 5	If we have been united with him I this	3930
	9:20	'Why did you make me I **this?**'"	4048
	9:27	"Though the number of the Israelites be I	6055
	9:29	we would have become I Sodom,	6055
	9:29	*we would have been* I Gomorrah."	3929

1Co	3: 3	Are you not acting I mere men?	2848
	4: 9	I men condemned to die in the arena.	6055
	7:32	*I would* I you to be free from concern.	2527
	9:20	To the Jews I became I a Jew,	6055
	9:20	To those under the law I became I one	6055
	9:21	the law I became I one not having the law	6055
	9:26	I do not run I a man running aimlessly;	6055
	9:26	I do not fight I a man beating the air.	6055
	13:11	When I was a child, I talked I a child,	6055
	13:11	I thought I a child, I reasoned like a child.	6055
	13:11	like a child, I reasoned I a child.	6055
	14: 5	*I would* I every one of you to speak	2527
	14:20	Brothers, stop thinking I **children.**	AIT
2Co	2:17	I men sent from God.	6055
	3: 1	Or do we need, I some people,	6055
	3:13	We are not I Moses, who would put a veil	2749
	11:23	(I am out of my mind to talk I this.)	NIG
	12: 5	I will boast about a **man** I **that,**	5525
Gal	2:14	you live I **a Gentile** and not like a Jew.	1619
	2:14	yet you live like a Gentile and not I **a Jew.**	2680
	3: 2	*I would* I to learn just one thing	2527
	4:12	I plead with you, brothers, become I me,	6055
	4:12	become like me, for I became I you.	6055
	4:28	Now you, brothers, I Isaac,	2848
	5:21	drunkenness, orgies, and the I.	3927+4047
	5:21	that those who live I **this** will not inherit	5525
Eph	1:19	That power is I the working	2848
	2: 3	L the rest, we were by nature objects	6055
	4:24	created to be I God in true righteousness	2848
	6: 6	but I slaves of Christ,	6055
Php	2:15	in which you shine I stars in the universe	6055
	2:17	**poured out** I **a drink offering**	5064
	2:20	I have no one else I *him,*	2701
	2:29	and honor **men** I **him,**	5525
	3:10	**becoming** I him in his death,	5214
	3:21	so that they will be I his glorious body.	5215
1Th	2: 7	I a mother caring for her little children	1569+6055
	4: 5	in passionate lust I the heathen, who do	2749
	4:13	or to grieve I the rest of men,	2777
	5: 2	that the day of the Lord will come I a thief	6055
	5: 4	that this day should surprise you I a thief.	6055
	5: 2	So then, let us not be I others,	6055
2Ti	2: 3	Endure **hardship** with us I a good soldier	6055
	2: 9	to the point of being chained I a criminal.	6055
	2:17	Their teaching will spread I gangrene.	6055
	4: 6	**poured out** I **a drink offering,**	5064
Heb	1:11	they will all wear out I a garment.	6055
	1:12	You will roll them up I a robe;	6059
	1:12	I a garment they will be changed.	6055
	2:17	*to be* **made** I his brothers in every way,	3929
	6: 9	Even though we speak I **this,** dear friends,	4048
	7: 3	I the Son of God he remains a priest forever.	926
	7:15	if another priest I Melchizedek appears,	3928
	8: 9	It will not be I the covenant I made	2848
	9: 6	When everything had been arranged I **this,**	4048
	11: 9	in the promised land I a stranger in	6055
	12:16	or is godless I Esau,	6055
Jas	1: 6	he who doubts is I a wave of the sea,	2036
	1:10	because he will pass away I a wild flower.	6055
	1:17	who does not change I shifting shadows.	NIG
	1:23	the word but does not do what it says is I	2036
	1:24	and immediately forgets what *he* **looks** I.	1639
	5: 3	against you and eat your flesh I fire.	6055
	5:17	Elijah was a man **just** I us.	3926
1Pe	1:24	For, "All men are I grass,	6055
	1:24	all their glory is I the flowers of the field;	6055
	2: 2	L newborn babies, crave pure spiritual milk,	6055
	2: 5	also, I living stones, are being built into	6055
	2:25	For you were I sheep going astray,	6055
	3: 6	I Sarah, who obeyed Abraham	5613
	5: 8	Your enemy the devil prowls around I	6055
2Pe	2:12	They are I brute beasts,	6055
	2:12	and I beasts they too will perish.	NIG
	3: 8	With the Lord a day is I a thousand years,	6055
	3: 8	and a thousand years are I a day.	6055
	3:10	the day of the Lord will come I a thief.	6055
1Jn	3: 2	when he appears, we shall be I him,	3927
	3:12	Do not be I Cain, who belonged to the evil	2777
	3:17	because in this world we are I him.	2777
Jude	1:10	I unreasoning animals—	6055
Rev	1:10	a loud voice I a trumpet,	6055
	1:13	lampstands was someone "I a son of man,"	3927
	1:14	His head and hair were white I wool,	6055
	1:14	and his eyes were I blazing fire.	6055
	1:15	His feet were I bronze glowing in	3927
	1:15	his voice was I the sound of rushing waters.	6055
	1:16	His face was I the sun shining	6055
	2:18	Son of God, whose eyes are I blazing fire	6055
	2:18	and whose feet are I burnished bronze.	3927
	2:27	he will dash them to pieces I pottery'—	6055
	3: 3	you do not wake up, I will come I a thief,	6055
	3: 5	He who overcomes will, I them,	4048
	4: 1	speaking to me I a trumpet said,	6055
	4: 6	before the throne there was what **looked** I	6055
	4: 7	The first living creature was I a lion,	3927
	4: 7	the second was I an ox,	3927
	4: 7	the third had a face I a man,	6055
	4: 7	the fourth was I a flying eagle.	3927
	6: 1	four living creatures say in a voice I thunder	6055
	6: 6	Then I heard what sounded I a voice	6055
	6:12	The sun turned black I sackcloth made	6055
	6:14	The sky receded I a scroll, rolling up,	6055
	6:14	and something I a huge mountain,	6055
	8:10	and a great star, blazing I a torch,	6055
	9: 2	smoke rose from it I the smoke from a	6055
	9: 3	and were given power I **that of** scorpions	6055
	9: 5	And the agony they suffered was I **that of**	6055

Rev	9: 7	The locusts **looked** I horses prepared	3927+3930
	9: 7	they wore something I crowns of gold,	3927
	9: 8	Their hair was I women's hair,	6055
	9: 8	and their teeth were I lions' teeth.	6055
	9: 9	They had breastplates I breastplates	6055
	9: 9	of their wings was I the thundering	6055
	9:10	They had tails and stings I scorpions,	3927
	9:17	and riders I saw in my vision looked I **this:**	4048
	9:19	for their tails were I snakes,	3927
	10: 1	his face was I the sun,	6055
	10: 1	and his legs were I fiery pillars,	6055
	10: 3	he gave a loud shout I the roar of a lion.	6061
	11: 1	a reed I a measuring rod and was told,	3927
	12:15	from his mouth the serpent spewed water I	6055
	13: 2	but had feet I those of a bear and a mouth	6055
	13: 2	like those of a bear and a mouth I that of	6055
	13: 4	"Who is I the beast?	3927
	13:11	He had two horns I a lamb,	3927
	13:11	but he spoke I a dragon.	6055
	14: 2	from heaven I the roar of rushing waters	6055
	14: 2	rushing waters and I a loud peal of thunder.	6055
	14: 2	The sound I heard was I that of harpists	6055
	14:14	on the cloud was one "I a son of man"	3927
	15: 2	And I saw what looked I a sea of glass	6055
	16: 3	it turned into blood I that of a dead man,	6055
	16:13	I saw three evil spirits that looked I frogs;	6055
	16:15	"Behold, I come I a thief!	6055
	16:18	No earthquake I *it* has ever occurred	3888
	18:18	'Was there ever a city I this great city?'	3927
	19: 1	After this I heard **what sounded** I the roar	6055
	19: 6	I heard what sounded I a great multitude,	6055
	19: 6	I the roar of rushing waters and	6055
	19: 6	rushing waters and I loud peals of thunder,	6055
	19:12	His eyes are I blazing fire,	6055
	20: 8	number they are I the sand on the seashore.	6055
	21:11	brilliance was I that of a very precious jewel	3927
	21:11	I a jasper, clear as crystal.	6055
	21:16	The city was laid out I a square,	NIG
	21:21	of pure gold, I transparent glass.	6055

LIKE-MINDED (1) [LIKE, MIND]

Php	2: 2	then make my joy complete by being I,	899+3836+5858

LIKED (5) [LIKE]

Ge	27:14	tasty food, just the way his father I it.	170
Jdg	14: 7	with the woman, and he I her.	928+3837+6524
1Sa	16:21	Saul I him very much, and David became	170
Mk	6:20	yet he I to listen to him.	2452
Phm	1:13	*I would have* I to keep him with me so	1089

LIKELY (1) [LIKE]

1Ki	12:26	"The kingdom *will now* I **revert** to	AIT

LIKEN (3) [LIKE]

SS	1: 9	*I* I you, my darling, to a mare harnessed	1948
Isa	46: 5	To whom *will you* I me that we may	5439
La	2:13	To what *can I* I you, that I may comfort you,	8750

LIKENESS (14) [LIKE]

Ge	1:26	"Let us make man in our image, in our I,	1952
	5: 1	he made him in the I of God.	1952
	5: 3	he had a son in his own I,	1952
Ps	17:15	I will be satisfied with seeing your I.	9454
Isa	52:14	and his form marred beyond human I—	NIH
Eze	1:28	appearance of the I of the glory of the LORD	1952
	10: 1	and I saw the I of a throne of sapphire	1952
Ro	8: 3	in the I of sinful man to be a sin offering.	3930
	8:29	also predestined to be conformed *to* the I	1635
1Co	15:49	as we have borne the I of the earthly man,	1635
	15:49	so shall we bear the I of the man	1635
2Co	3:18	into his I with ever-increasing glory,	1635
Php	2: 7	being made in human I.	3930
Jas	3: 9	who have been made in God's I.	3932

LIKES (2) [LIKE]

Ge	27: 9	food for your father, just the way *he* I it.	170
Dt	23:16	Let him live among you wherever he I and	928+2021+3202+4200

LIKEWISE (11) [LIKE]

Jdg	11:24	L, whatever the LORD our God has given us,	2256
2Ch	31:17	**and** I to the Levites twenty years old or	2256
Mt	7:17	L every good tree bears good fruit,	4048
Lk	10:37	Jesus told him, "Go and do I."	3931
	17:31	L, no one in the field should go back	3931
1Co	7: 3	and I the wife to her husband.	3931
2Co	13: 4	L, we are weak in him,	1142+2779
1Ti	3: 8	I, are to be men worthy of respect,	6058
Tit	2: 3	L, teach the older women to be reverent in	6058
Jas	3: 5	L the tongue is a small part of the	2779+4048
Rev	2:15	L you also have those who hold to	4048

LIKHI (1)

1Ch	7:19	Ahian, Shechem, L and Aniam.	4376

LILIES (13) [LILY]

1Ki	7:19	in the portico were in the shape of I,	8808
	7:22	The capitals on top were in the shape of I.	8808
Ps	45: T	To [the tune of] "L."	8808
	69: T	To [the tune of] "L."	8808

Ps 80: T   To [the tune of] "The **L** of the Covenant."   8808
SS 2:16   he browses among the **l**.   8808
    4: 5   of a gazelle that browse among the **l**.   8808
    5:13   His lips are like **l** dripping with myrrh.   8808
    6: 2   to browse in the gardens and to gather **l**.   8808
    6: 3   he browses among the **l**.   8808
    7: 2   a mound of wheat encircled by **l**.   8808
Mt 6:28   See how the **l** of the field grow.   *3211*
Lk 12:27   "Consider how the **l** grow.   *3211*

LILY (6) [LILIES]

1Ki 7:26   a cup, like a **l** blossom.   8808
2Ch 4: 5   a cup, like a **l** blossom.   8808
Ps 60: T   To [the tune of] "The **L** of the Covenant."   8808
SS 2: 1   I am a rose of Sharon, a **l** of the valleys.   8808
    2: 2   a **l** among thorns is my darling among   8808
Hos 14: 5   he will blossom like a **l**.   8808

LIMB (2) [LIMBS]

Jdg 19:29   **l** by limb, into twelve parts and sent them   NIH
    19:29   limb by **l**, into twelve parts and sent them   6795

LIMBER (1)

Ge 49:24   his strong arms *stayed* **l**,   7060

LIMBS (3) [LIMB]

Job 18:13   death's firstborn devours his **l**.   963
    40:18   his **l** like rods of iron.   1752
    41:12   "I will not fail to speak of his **l**,   963

LIME (2)

Isa 33:12   The peoples will be burned as if to **l**;   8487
Am 2: 1   Because he burned, as if to **l**,   8487

LIMIT (8) [LIMITS]

Ezr 7:22   olive oil, and salt without **l**.   10375
Job 15: 8   *Do you* **l** wisdom to yourself?   1757
Ps 119:96   To all perfection I see a **l**;   7891
    147: 5   his understanding has no **l**.   5031
Isa 5:14   and opens its mouth without **l**;   2976
Jer 5:28   Their evil deeds **have no l**;   6296
Jn 3:34   for God gives the Spirit without **l**.   *3586*
1Th 2:16   **heap up** their sins **to the l**.   *405*

LIMITS (10) [LIMIT]

Ex 19:12   **Put l** *for* the people around the mountain   1487
    19:23   'Put **l** around the mountain   1487
Nu 35:26   if the accused ever goes outside the **l** of   1473
Jos 17:18   Clear it, and its **farthest l** will be yours;   9362
Job 11: 7   Can you probe the **l** *of* the Almighty?   9417
    14: 5   and have set **l** he cannot exceed.   2976
    38:10   when I fixed **l** for it and set its doors   2976
Ps 73: 7   the evil conceits of their minds **know no l**.   6296
2Co 10:13   will not boast **beyond** proper **l**,   296+1650+3836
    10:15   we go **beyond** our **l** by boasting   296+1650+3836

LIMP (9) [LIMPING]

Pr 26: 7   a lame man's legs *that* hang **l** is a proverb   1927
Isa 13: 7   Because of this, all hands *will* **go l**,   8332
Jer 6:24   and our hands **hang l**.   8332
    47: 3   their hands **will hang l**.   8342
    50:43   and his hands **hang l**.   8332
Eze 7:17   Every hand *will* **go l**,   8332
    21: 7   and every hand **go l**;   8332
    30:25   but the arms of Pharaoh *will* **fall l**.   5877
Zep 3:16   *do* not *let* your hands **hang l**.   8332

LIMPING (1) [LIMP]

Ge 32:31   and he *was* **l** because of his hip.   7519

LINE (55) [LINED, LINES]

Ge 5: 1   written **account of** Adam's **l**.   9352
    19:32   with him and preserve our **family l**   2446
    19:34   with him so we can preserve our **family l**   2446
Nu 26:11   The **l** of Korah, however, did not die out.   1201
    34: 7   **run a l** from the Great Sea to Mount Hor   9292
    34:10   **run a l** from Hazar Enan to Shepham.   204
Dt 25: 9   not build up his brother's **family l**."   1074
    25:10   **That man's l** shall be known in Israel as   2257[S]
Ru 4: 4   and I am **next in l**."   339
    4:18   This, then, is the **family l** of Perez: 9352
1Sa 2:31   not be an old man in your **family l**   1074
    2:32   in your **family l** there will never be   1074
    2:36   in your **family l** will come and bow down   1074
    4:12   from the **battle l** and went to Shiloh   5120
    4:16   "I have just come from the **battle l**;   5120
    17: 2   **drew up** their battle **l** to meet the Philistines   6885
    17: 8   "Why do you come out and **l** up   6885
    17:48   David ran quickly toward the **battle l**   5120
2Sa 11:15   "Put Uriah **in the front l** where   448+4578+7156
1Ki 7:15   and twelve cubits around, *by* **l**.   2562
    7:23   a **l** of thirty cubits to measure around it.   7742
    11:14   from the royal **l** of Edom.   2446
2Ki 21:13   the **measuring l** *used against* Samaria and   7742
    21:13   and the **plumb l** *used against* the house   5487
2Ch 4: 2   a **l** of thirty cubits to measure around it.   7742
    13: 3   Jeroboam **drew up** *a* battle **l** against him   6885
Ezr 2: 6   of Pahath-Moab (through the **l** *of* Jeshua   1201
    2:40   of Jeshua and Kadmiel (through the **l** *of*   1201
Ne 7:11   of Pahath-Moab (through the **l** *of* Jeshua   1201

Ne 7:43   of Jeshua (through Kadmiel through the **l**   1201
Job 38: 5   Who stretched a **measuring l** across it?   7742
Ps 89: 4   'I will establish your **l** forever   2446
    89:29   I will establish his **l** forever,   2446
    89:36   that his **l** will continue forever   2446
Isa 28:17   I will make justice the **measuring l**   7742
    28:17   and righteousness the **plumb l**;   5487
    34:11   over Edom the **measuring l** of chaos and   7742
    34:11   of chaos and the **plumb l** of desolation.   74
    44:13   a **l** and makes an outline with a marker;   7742
    48: 1   by the name of Israel and come from the **l**   5055
Jer 31:39   The measuring **l** will stretch from there   7742
    33:15   a righteous Branch sprout from **David's l**;   1858
La 2: 8   He stretched out a **measuring l** and did   7742
Eze 47: 3   the man went eastward with a **measuring l**   7742
Da 11: 7   "One from her **family l** will arise   5916+9247
Joel 2: 7   They all march in **l**,   2006
Am 7: 7   with a **plumb l** in his hand.   643
    7: 8   "A **plumb l**," I replied.   643
    7: 8   a **plumb l** among my people Israel;   643
Zec 1:16   And the **measuring l** will be stretched out   7742
    2: 1   before me was a man with a measuring **l**   2475
    4:10   the **plumb l** in the hand of Zerubbabel.   74+974
Mt 17:27   go to the lake and throw out your **l**.   *45*
Lk 2: 4   he belonged to the house and **l** of David.   *4255*
Gal 2:14   When I saw that *they were* not **acting in l**   *3980*

LINEAGE (KJV) See LINE

LINED (1) [LINE]

1Ki 6:15   *He* **l** its interior walls with cedar boards,   1215

LINEN (105) [LINENS]

Ge 41:42   He dressed him in robes of **fine l** and put   9254
Ex 25: 4   purple and scarlet yarn and **fine l**;   9254
    26: 1   with ten curtains of finely twisted **l**,   9254
    26:31   and scarlet yarn and finely twisted **l**,   9254
    26:36   and scarlet yarn and finely twisted **l**—   9254
    27: 9   and is to have curtains of finely twisted **l**,   9254
    27:16   and scarlet yarn and finely twisted **l**—   9254
    27:18   of finely twisted **l** five cubits high,   9254
    28: 5   purple and scarlet yarn, and **fine l**—   9254
    28: 6   and of finely twisted **l**—   9254
    28: 8   and with finely twisted **l**.   9254
    28:15   and of finely twisted **l**.   9254
    28:39   of **fine l** and make the turban of fine linen   9254
    28:39   fine linen and make the turban of the **fine l**.   9254
    28:42   "Make **l** undergarments as a covering for   965
    35: 6   purple and scarlet yarn and **fine l**,   9254
    35:23   purple or scarlet yarn or **fine l**,   9254
    35:25   blue, purple or scarlet yarn or **fine l**.   9254
    35:35   purple and scarlet yarn and **fine l**,   9254
    36: 8   with ten curtains of finely twisted **l**,   9254
    36:35   and scarlet yarn and finely twisted **l**,   9254
    36:37   and scarlet yarn and finely twisted **l**—   9254
    38: 9   and had curtains of finely twisted **l**,   9254
    38:16   the courtyard were of finely twisted **l**.   9254
    38:18   and scarlet yarn and finely twisted **l**—   9254
    38:23   purple and scarlet yarn and **fine l**.)   9254
    39: 2   and of finely twisted **l**.   9254
    39: 3   purple and scarlet yarn and **fine l**—   9254
    39: 5   and with finely twisted **l**,   9254
    39: 8   and of finely twisted **l**.   9254
    39:24   and finely twisted **l** around the hem of   NIH
    39:27   they made tunics of **fine l**—   9254
    39:28   and the turban of **fine l**,   9254
    39:28   the **l** headbands and the undergarments   965
    39:28   and the undergarments of finely twisted **l**.   9254
    39:29   The sash was of finely twisted **l** and blue,   9254
Lev 6:10   The priest shall then put on his **l** clothes,   965
    6:10   with **l** undergarments next to his body,   965
    13:47   any woolen or **l** clothing,   7324
    13:48   of **l** or wool, any leather or anything made   7324
    13:52   of wool or **l**, or any leather article that has   7324
    13:59   by mildew in woolen or **l** clothing,   7324
    16: 4   He is to put on the sacred **l** tunic,   965
    16: 4   with **l** undergarments next to his body;   965
    16: 4   he is to tie the **l** sash around him and put   965
    16: 4   around him and put on the **l** turban.   965
    16:23   the **l** garments he put on before he entered   965
    16:32   He is to put on the sacred **l** garments   965
Dt 22:11   of wool and **l** woven together.   7324
Jdg 14:12   I will give you thirty **l garments**   6041
    14:13   you must give me thirty **l garments**   6041
1Sa 2:18   a boy wearing a **l** ephod.   965
    22:18   That day he killed eighty-five men who   965
         wore the **l** ephod.   965
2Sa 6:14   David, wearing a **l** ephod, danced before   965
1Ch 4:21   of Mareshah and the clans of the **l** workers   1009
    15:27   David was clothed in a robe of **fine l**,   1009
    15:27   David also wore a **l** ephod.   965
2Ch 2:14   and blue and crimson yarn and **fine l**.   1009
    3:14   purple and crimson yarn and **fine l**,   1009
    5:12   dressed in **fine l** and playing cymbals,   1009
Est 1: 6   **hangings** of white and blue **l**.   4158
    1: 6   with cords of **white l** and purple material   1009
    8:15   of gold and a purple robe of **fine l**.   1009
Pr 31:22   she is clothed in **fine l** and purple.   9254
    31:24   She makes **l garments** and sells them,   6041
Isa 3:23   and the **l garments** and tiaras and shawls.   6041
    19: 9   the weavers of **fine l** will lose hope.   2583
Jer 13: 1   a **l** belt and put it around your waist,   7324
Eze 9: 2   a man clothed in **l** who had a writing kit   965
    9: 3   the man clothed in **l** who had the writing kit   965
    9:11   Then the man in **l** with the writing kit   965

Eze 10: 2   The LORD said to the man clothed in **l**,   965
    10: 6   the LORD commanded the man in **l**,   965
    10: 7   and put it into the hands of the man in **l**,   965
    16:10   I dressed you in **fine l** and covered you   9254
    16:13   your clothes were of **fine l**   9254
    27: 7   **Fine** embroidered **l** from Egypt   9254
    27:16   purple fabric, embroidered work, **fine l**,   1009
    40: 3   a **l** cord and a measuring rod in his hand.   7324
    44:17   they are to wear **l** clothes;   7324
    44:18   They are to wear **l** turbans on their heads   7324
    44:18   and **l** undergarments around their waists.   7324
Da 10: 5   before me was a man dressed in **l**,   965
    12: 6   One of them said to the man clothed in **l**,   965
    12: 7   The man clothed in **l**, who was above   965
Hos 2: 5   my wool and my **l**, my oil and my drink.'   7324
    2: 9   I will take back my wool and my **l**,   7324
Mt 27:59   wrapped it in a clean **l cloth**,   *4984*
Mk 14:51   wearing nothing but a **l garment**,   *4984*
    15:46   So Joseph bought some **l cloth**,   *4984*
    15:46   took down the body, wrapped it in the **l**,   *4984*
Lk 16:19   and **fine l** and lived in luxury every day.   *1116*
    23:53   *in* **l cloth** and placed it in a tomb cut in   *4984*
    24:12   he saw the **strips of l** lying by themselves,   *3856*
Jn 11:44   and feet wrapped *with* **strips of l**,   *3024*
    19:40   with the spices, *in* **strips of l**.   *3856*
    20: 5   and looked in at the **strips of l** lying there   *3856*
    20: 6   He saw the **strips of l** lying there,   *3856*
    20: 7   folded up by itself, separate from the **l**.   *3856*
Rev 15: 6   shining **l** and wore golden sashes   *3351*
    18:12   **fine l**, purple, silk and scarlet cloth;   *1115*
    18:16   Woe, O great city, dressed in **fine l**,   *1115*
    19: 8   **Fine l**, bright and clean,   *1115*
    19: 8   (**Fine l** stands for the righteous acts of the   saints.)   *1115*
    19:14   on white horses and dressed in **fine l**,   *1115*

LINENS (1) [LINEN]

Pr 7:16   I have covered my bed with colored **l**   355

LINES (13) [LINE]

Ge 10:32   according to their **l of descent**,   9352
    14: 8   **drew up** their battle **l** in the Valley of   6885
1Sa 17:21   drawing up their **l** facing each other.   5120
    17:22   to the **battle l** and greeted his brothers.   5120
    17:23   from his **l** and shouted his usual defiance,   5120
2Sa 2:25   Joab saw that there were **battle l** in front   4878
    10:17   The Arameans **formed** *their* **battle l**   6885
    23:16   mighty men broke through the Philistine **l**,   4722
1Ch 11:18   the Three broke through the Philistine **l**,   4722
    19:10   Joab saw that there were **battle l** in front   4878
    19:17   and **formed** *his* **battle l** opposite them.   6885
    19:17   David **formed** *his* **l** to meet the Arameans   6885
Ps 16: 6   The **boundary l** have fallen for me   2475

LINGER (5) [LINGERING]

Jdg 5:17   And Dan, why *did* he **l** by the ships?   1591
Pr 23:30   Those *who* **l** over wine,   336
Jer 51:50   leave and *do* not **l**!   6641
Mic 5: 7   not wait for man or **l** for mankind.   3498
Hab 2: 3   Though *it* **l**, wait for it;   4538

LINGERING (2) [LINGER]

Dt 28:59   and severe and **l** illnesses.   586
2Ch 21:15   ill with a **l** disease of the bowels,   3427+3427+6584

LINTEL (KJV) See TOP

LINUS (1)

2Ti 4:21   Eubulus greets you, and so do Pudens, **L**,   *3352*

LION (86) [LION'S, LIONESS, LIONESSES, LIONS, LIONS']

Ge 49: 9   Like a **l** he crouches and lies down,   793
Nu 23:24   they rouse themselves like a **l** that does   787
    24: 9   Like a **l** they crouch and lie down,   787
Dt 33:20   Gad lives there like a **l**,   4233
Jdg 14: 5   a **young l** came roaring toward him.   787+4097
    14: 6   that he tore the **l** apart with his bare hands   2084[S]
    14:18   What is stronger than a **l**?"   787
1Sa 17:34   a **l** or a bear came and carried off a sheep   787
    17:36   Your servant has killed both the **l** and   787
    17:37   from the paw of the **l** and the paw of   787
2Sa 17:10   whose heart is like the heart of a **l**,   793
    23:20   into a pit on a snowy day and killed a **l**.   787
1Ki 10:19   with a **l** standing beside each of them.   787
    13:24   a **l** met him on the road and killed him,   793
    13:24   with both the donkey and the **l** standing   793
    13:25   with the **l** standing beside the body,   793
    13:26   The LORD has given him over to the **l**,   793
    13:28   the donkey and the **l** standing beside it.   793
    13:28   The **l** had neither eaten the body   793
    20:36   as soon as you leave me a **l** will kill you."   793
    20:36   a **l** found him and killed him.   793
1Ch 11:22   into a pit on a snowy day and killed a **l**.   787
2Ch 9:18   with a **l** standing beside each of them.   787
Job 4:11   The **l** perishes for lack of prey,   4330
    10:16   a **l** and again display your awesome power   8828
    28: 8   and no **l** prowls there.   8828
Ps 7: 2   like a **l** and rip me to pieces with no one   793
    10: 9   He lies in wait like a **l** in cover;   793
    17:12   They are like a **l** hungry for prey,   793
    17:12   like a **great l** crouching in cover.   4097

Ps 91:13 You will tread upon the l and the cobra; 8828
91:13 you will trample the **great** l and 4097
Pr 19:12 A king's rage is like the roar of a l, 4097
20: 2 A king's wrath is like the roar of a l; 4097
22:13 The sluggard says, "There is a l outside!" 787
26:13 sluggard says, "There is a l in the road, 8828
26:13 a **fierce** l roaming the streets!" 787
28: 1 but the righteous are as bold as a l. 4097
28:15 Like a roaring l or a charging bear is 787
30:30 a l, mighty among beasts, who retreats 4330
Ecc 9: 4 even a live dog is better off than a dead l! 793
Isa 5:29 Their roar is like that of the l, 4233
11: 6 and the l and the yearling together; 4097
11: 7 and the l will eat straw like the ox. 793
15: 9 a l upon the fugitives of Moab and 793
31: 4 a l growls, a great lion over his prey— 793
31: 4 a lion growls, a **great** l over his prey 4097
35: 9 No l will be there, 793
38:13 but like a l he broke all my bones; 787
65:25 and the l will eat straw like the ox, 793
Jer 2:30 devoured your prophets like a ravening l. 793
4: 7 A l has come out of his lair; 793
5: 6 a l from the forest will attack them, 793
12: 8 My inheritance has become to me like a l 793
25:38 Like a l he will leave his lair, 4097
49:19 a l coming up from Jordan's thickets to 793
50:44 Like a l coming up from Jordan's thickets 793
51:38 they growl like l cubs. 787
La 3:10 like a l in hiding, 787
Eze 1:10 on the right side each had the face of a l, 793
10:14 the third the face of a l, 793
19: 3 and he became a **strong** l. 4097
19: 5 of her cubs and made him a **strong** l. 4097
19: 6 for he was now a **strong** l. 4097
22:25 within her like a roaring l tearing its prey; 787
32: 2 " 'You are like a l among the nations; 4097
41:19 and the face of a l toward the palm tree on 4097
Da 7: 4 "The first was like a l, 10069
Hos 5:14 For I will be like a l to Ephraim, 8828
5:14 like a **great** l to Judah. 4097
11:10 he will roar like a l. 793
13: 7 So I will come upon them like a l, 8828
13: 8 Like a l I will devour them; 4233
Joel 1: 6 it has the teeth of a l, 793
Am 3: 4 Does a l roar in the thicket 793
3: 8 The l has roared—who will not fear? 793
5:19 as though a man fled from a l only to meet 787
Mic 5: 8 like a l among the beasts of the forest, 793
5: 8 like a **young** l among flocks of sheep, 4097
Na 2:11 where the l and lioness went, 793
2:12 The l killed enough for his cubs 793
1Pe 5: 8 a roaring l looking for someone to devour. 3329
Rev 4: 7 The first living creature was like a l, 3329
5: 5 See, the L of the tribe of Judah, 3329
10: 3 he gave a loud shout like the roar of a l. 3329
13: 2 of a bear and a mouth like that of a l. 3329

LION'S (6) [LION]
Ge 49: 9 You are a l cub, O Judah; 793
Dt 33:22 "Dan is a l cub, springing out of Bashan." 793
Jdg 14: 8 he turned aside to look at the l carcass. 793
14: 9 the honey from the l carcass. 793
Am 3:12 the mouth only two leg bones or a piece 787
2Ti 4:17 And I was delivered from the l mouth. 3329

LIONESS (8) [LION]
Ge 49: 9 like a l—who dares to rouse him? 4233
Nu 23:24 The people rise like a l; 4233
24: 9 like a l—who dares to rouse them? 4233
Job 4:11 and the cubs of the l are scattered. 4233
38:39 for the l and satisfy the hunger of the lions 4233
Eze 19: 2 a l was your mother among the lions! 4234
Joel 1: 6 it has the teeth of a lion, the fangs of a l. 4233
Na 2:11 where the lion and l went, and the cubs, 4233

LIONESSES (1) [LION]
Isa 30: 6 of hardship and distress, of lions and l, 4330

LIONLIKE (KJV) See BEST

LIONS (36) [LION]
2Sa 1:23 they were stronger than l. 787
1Ki 7:29 the uprights were l, bulls and cherubim— 787
7:29 and below the l and bulls were wreaths 787
7:36 l and palm trees on the surfaces of 787
10:20 Twelve l stood on the six steps, 787
2Ki 17:25 so he sent l among them 787
17:26 He has sent l among them, 787
1Ch 12: 8 Their faces were the faces of l, 793
2Ch 9:19 Twelve l stood on the six steps, 787
Job 4:10 The l may roar and growl, 793
4:10 yet the teeth of the **great** l are broken. 4097
38:39 the lioness and satisfy their hunger of l 4097
Ps 22:13 Roaring l tearing their prey open their 793
22:21 Rescue me from the mouth of the l; 793
34:10 The l may grow weak and hungry, 4097
35:17 my precious life from these l. 4097
57: 4 I am in the midst of l; 4216
58: 6 tear out, O LORD, the fangs of the l! 4097
104:21 The l roar for their prey 4097
Isa 5:29 they roar like **young** l; 4097
30: 6 a land of hardship and distress, of l 4233
Jer 2:15 L have roared; they have growled at him. 4097
50: 17 a scattered flock that l have chased away. 787

Jer 51:38 Her people all roar like **young** l, 4097
Eze 19: 2 a lioness was your mother among the l! 787
19: 2 among the **young** l and reared her cubs. 4097
19: 6 He prowled among the l, 787
Da 6:20 been able to rescue you from the l?" 10069
6:22 shut the mouths of the l. 10069
6:24 the l overpowered them and crushed all 10069
6:27 rescued Daniel from the power of the l. 10069
Na 2:11 and the sword will devour your **young** l. 4097
Zep 3: 3 Her officials are roaring l, 787
Zec 11: 3 Listen to the roar of the l; 4097
Heb 11:33 who shut the mouths of l, *3329*
Rev 9:17 of the horses resembled the heads of l, *3329*

LIONS' (8) [LION]
SS 4: 8 from the l' dens and the mountain haunts 787
Da 6: 7 O king, shall be thrown into the l' den. 10069
6:12 O king, would be thrown into the l' den?" 10069
6:16 and threw him into the l' den. 10069
6:19 the king got up and hurried to the l' den. 10069
6:24 brought in and thrown into the l' den, 10069
Na 2:11 Where now is the l' den, 787
Rev 9: 8 and their teeth were like l' teeth. *3329*

LIPS (125)
Ex 6:12 since I speak with faltering l?" 8557
6:30 "Since I speak with faltering l, 8557
13: 9 the law of the LORD is to be on your l. 7023
23:13 do not let them be heard on your l. 7023
Nu 30: 6 after she makes a vow or after her l utter 8557
30:12 or pledges that came from her l will stand. 8557
Dt 23:23 Whatever your l utter you must be sure 8557
1Sa 1:13 and her l were moving but her voice was 8557
Job 6:30 Is there any wickedness on my l? 4383
8:21 laughter and your l with shouts of joy. 8557
11: 5 that he would open his l against you 8557
12:20 He silences the l of trusted advisers 8557
13: 6 listen to the plea of my l. 8557
15: 6 your own l testify against you. 8557
16: 5 comfort from my l would bring you relief. 8557
23:12 not departed from the commands of his l; 8557
27: 4 my l will not speak wickedness, 8557
32:20 I must open my l and reply. 8557
33: 3 my l sincerely speak what I know. 8557
Ps 8: 2 From the l of children and infants 7023
12: 2 their flattering l speak with deception. 8557
12: 3 May the LORD cut off all flattering l 8557
12: 4 we own our l—who is our master?" 8557
16: 4 of blood or take up their names on my l. 8557
17: 1 it does not rise from deceitful l. 8557
17: 4 by the word of your l I have kept myself 8557
21: 2 and have not withheld the request of his l. 8557
31:18 Let their lying l be silenced, 8557
34: 1 his praise will always be on my l. 8557
34:13 from evil and your l from speaking lies. 8557
40: 9 I do not seal my l, as you know, 8557
45: 2 your l have been anointed with grace, 8557
50:16 or take my covenant on your l? 7023
51:15 O Lord, open my l, 8557
59: 7 they spew out swords from their l, 8557
59:12 for the words of their l, 8557
63: 3 my l will glorify you. 8557
63: 5 with singing l my mouth will praise you. 8557
66:14 vows my l promised and my mouth spoke 8557
71:23 My l will shout for joy when I sing praise 8557
89:34 or alter what my l have uttered. 8557
106:33 and rash words came from Moses' l. 8557
119:13 With my l I recount all the laws that come 8557
119:171 May my l overflow with praise, 8557
120: 2 from lying l and from deceitful tongues. 8557
140: 3 the poison of vipers is on their l. 8557
140: 9 with the trouble their l have caused. 8557
141: 3 keep watch over the door of my l. 8557
Pr 4:24 keep corrupt talk far from your l. 8557
5: 2 and your l may preserve knowledge. 8557
5: 3 For the l of an adulteress drip honey, 8557
8: 6 I open my l to speak what is right. 8557
8: 7 for my l detest wickedness. 8557
10:13 Wisdom is found on the l of the discerning, 8557
10:18 He who conceals his hatred has lying l, 8557
10:21 The l of the righteous nourish many, 8557
10:32 l of the righteous know what is fitting, 8557
12:14 of his l a man is filled with good things as 7023
12:19 Truthful l endure forever, 8557
12:22 The LORD detests lying l, 8557
13: 2 the fruit of his l a man enjoys good things, 7023
13: 3 He who guards his l guards his life, 7023
14: 3 but the l of the wise protect them. 8557
14: 7 for you will not find knowledge on his l. 8557
15: 7 The l of the wise spread knowledge; 8557
16:10 The l of a king speak as an oracle, 8557
16:13 Kings take pleasure in honest l; 8557
16:23 and his l promote instruction. 8557
16:30 he who purses his l is bent on evil. 8557
17: 4 A wicked man listens to evil l; 8557
17: 7 Arrogant l are unsuited to a fool— 8557
17: 7 how much worse lying l to a ruler! 8557
18: 6 A fool's l bring him strife, 8557
18: 7 and his l are a snare to his soul. 8557
18:20 with the harvest from his l he is satisfied. 8557
19: 1 a fool whose l are perverse. 8557
20:15 l that speak knowledge are a rare jewel. 8557
22:18 and have all of them ready on your l. 8557
23:16 when your l speak what is right. 8557
24: 2 and their l talk about making trouble. 8557

Pr 24:26 An honest answer is like a kiss on the l. 8557
24:28 or use your l to deceive. 8557
26:23 earthenware are fervent l with an evil heart. 8557
26:24 malicious man disguises himself with his l, 8557
27: 2 someone else, and not your own l. 8557
Ecc 10:12 but a fool is consumed by his own l. 8557
SS 4: 3 Your l are like a scarlet ribbon; 8557
4:11 Your l drop sweetness as the honeycomb, 8557
5:13 His l are like lilies dripping with myrrh. 8557
7: 9 flowing gently over l and teeth. 8557
Isa 6: 5 For I am a man of unclean l, 8557
6: 5 and I live among a people of unclean l, 8557
6: 7 "See, this has touched your l; 8557
11: 4 the breath of his l he will slay the wicked. 8557
28:11 Very well then, with foreign l 8557
29:13 and honor me with their l, 8557
30:27 his l are full of wrath, 8557
57:19 creating praise on the l of the mourners 8557
59: 3 Your l have spoken lies. 8557
Jer 7:28 it has vanished from their l. 7023
12: 2 on their l but far from their hearts. 7023
17:16 What passes my l is open before you. 8557
Da 4:31 on his l when a voice came from heaven, 10588
10: 3 no meat or wine touched my l, 7023
10:16 one who looked like a man touched my l, 8557
Hos 2:17 the names of the Baals from her l; 7023
8: 1 "Put the trumpet to your l! 2674
14: 2 that we may offer the fruit of our l. 8557
Joel 1: 5 for it has been snatched from your l. 7023
Hab 3:16 my l quivered at the sound; 8557
Zep 3: 9 "Then will I purify the l of the peoples, 8557
Mal 2: 6 and nothing false was found on his l. 8557
2: 7 l of a priest ought to preserve knowledge, 8557
Mt 15: 8 " 'These people honor me with their l, 5927
21:16 " 'From the l of children and infants 5125
Mk 7: 6 " 'These people honor me with their l, 5927
Lk 4:22 the gracious words that came from his l. 5125
22:71 We have heard it from his own l." 5125
Jn 19:29 and lifted it to Jesus' l. 5125
Ac 11: 3 that the Gentiles might hear from my l 5125
Ro 3:13 "The poison of vipers is on their l." 5927
1Co 14:21 through the l of foreigners I will speak 5927
Col 3: 8 slander, and filthy language from your l. 5125
Heb 13:15 the fruit of l that confess his name. 5927
1Pe 3:10 from evil and his l from deceitful speech. 5927

LIQUID (2)
Ex 30:23 500 shekels of l myrrh, 2001
Lev 11:34 and any l that could be drunk 5482

LIQUOR (KJV) See BLENDED WINE, JUICE

LIST (10) [LISTED, LISTING]
Nu 3:40 or more and make a l of their names. 5031
Jos 17:11 (the third in the l is Naphoth). NIH
1Ch 11:11 this is the l of David's mighty men: 5031
25: 1 Here is the l of the men who performed this 5031
27: 1 This is the l of the Israelites— 5031
Ezr 2: 2 The l of the men of the people of Israel: 5031
Ne 7: 7 The l of the men of Israel: 5031
Ps 56: 8 l my tears on your scroll— 8492
1Ti 5: 9 No widow *may be* put on the l of widows unless *2899*
5:11 As for younger widows, *do not put* them **on such a l.** *4148*

LISTED (35) [LIST]
Ge 25:13 of Ishmael, l in the order of their birth: AIT
Nu 1:18 the men twenty years old or more were l 5031
1:20 to serve in the army were l by name, 5031
1:22 in the army were counted and l by name, 5031
1:24 to serve in the army were l by name, 5031
1:26 to serve in the army were l by name, 5031
1:28 to serve in the army were l by name, 5031
1:30 to serve in the army were l by name, 5031
1:32 to serve in the army were l by name, 5031
1:34 to serve in the army were l by name, 5031
1:36 to serve in the army were l by name, 5031
1:38 to serve in the army were l by name, 5031
1:40 to serve in the army were l by name, 5031
1:42 to serve in the army were l by name, 5031
3:43 l by name, was 22,273. 5031
11:26 They **were** l among the elders, 4180
26:54 according to the number of those l. 7212
1Ch 4:38 The men l above by name were leaders 995
4:41 The men whose names l came in 4180
5: 1 could not **be** l **in the genealogical record** 3509
5: 7 l according to their genealogical records: 3509
6:19 of the Levites according to their fathers: NIH
7: 2 the descendants of Tola l as fighting men 5031
7: 5 Issachar, as l in their **genealogy,** 3509
7: 7 **genealogical record** l 22,034 fighting men. 3509
7: 9 Their genealogical record l the heads 3509
7:40 as l in their **genealogy,** was 26,000. 3509
8:28 chiefs as l in their **genealogy,** 9352
9: 1 All Israel **was** l **in the genealogies** 3509
9: 1 as l in their **genealogy,** numbered 956. 9352
9:34 chiefs as l in their **genealogy,** 9352
2Ch 31:18 l in *these* **genealogical records.** 3509
Ps 69:28 of life and not **be** l with the righteous. 4180
Eze 13: 9 or **be** l in the records of the house of Israel; 4180
48: 1 "These are the tribes, l by name: NIH

LISTEN (352) [LISTENED, LISTENING, LISTENS]

Ge	4:10	"What have you done? L!	7754
	4:23	"Adah and Zillah, l to me;	9048
	21:12	L to whatever Sarah tells you,	9048
	23: 6	"Sir, l to us. You are a mighty prince among	9048
	23: 8	then l to me and intercede with Ephron	9048
	23:11	he said. "L to me;	9048
	23:13	"L to me, if you will.	9048
	23:15	"L to me, my lord;	9048
	27: 8	l carefully and do what I tell you:	928+7754+9048
	37: 6	He said to them, "L to this dream I had:	9048
	37: 9	"L," he said, "I had another dream,	2180
	42:21	but we would not l!	9048
	42:22	But you wouldn't l!	9048
	49: 2	"Assemble and l, sons of Jacob;	9048
	49: 2	sons of Jacob; l to your father Israel.	9048
Ex	3:18	"The elders of Israel will l to you.	9048
	4: 1	"What if they do not believe me or l to me	9048
	4: 9	if they do not believe these two signs or l	9048
	6: 9	but they did not l to him because	9048
	6:12	"If the Israelites will not l to me,	9048
	6:12	why would Pharaoh l to me,	9048
	6:30	why would Pharaoh l to me?"	9048
	7: 4	he will not l to you.	9048
	7:13	heart became hard and he would not l to	9048
	7:22	hard; he would not l to Moses and Aaron,	9048
	8:15	he hardened his heart and would not l	9048
	8:19	heart was hard and he would not l,	9048
	9:12	and he would not l to Moses and Aaron,	9048
	11: 9	"Pharaoh will refuse to l to you—	9048
	15:26	"If you l carefully to the voice of	9048+9048
	18:19	L now to me and I will give you some	9048
	20:19	"Speak to us yourself and we will l.	9048
	23:21	Pay attention to him and l to what he says.	9048
	23:22	If you l carefully to what he says	9048+9048
Lev	26:14	" 'But if you will not l to me	9048
	26:18	" 'If after all this you will not l to me,	9048
	26:21	toward me and refuse to l to me,	9048
	26:27	in spite of this you still do not l to me	9048
Nu	12: 6	"L to my words:	9048
	16: 8	Moses also said to Korah, "Now l,	9048
	20:10	of the rock and Moses said to them, "L,	9048
	23:18	"Arise, Balak, and l;	9048
Dt	1:43	So I told you, but you would not l.	9048
	3:26	with me and would not l to me.	9048
	5:27	and l to all that the LORD our God says.	9048
	5:27	We will l and obey.	9048
	13: 3	not l to the words of that prophet	9048
	13: 8	do not yield to him or l to him.	9048
	18:14	The nations you will dispossess l	9048
	18:15	You must l to him.	9048
	18:19	not l to my words that the prophet speaks	9048
	21:18	not l to them when they discipline him,	9048
	23: 5	not l to Balaam but turned the curse into	9048
	27: 9	"Be silent, O Israel, and l!	9048
	30:20	l to his voice, and hold fast to him.	9048
	31:12	so they can l and learn to fear	9048
	32: 1	L, O heavens, and I will speak;	263
Jos	3: 9	"Come here and l to the words of	9048
	8: 4	with these orders: "L carefully.	8011
	24:10	But I would not l to Balaam.	9048
Jdg	2:17	Yet they would not l to their judges	9048
	5: 3	L, you rulers!	263
	7:11	and l to what they are saying.	9048
	9: 7	"L to me, citizens of Shechem,	9048
	9: 7	so that God may l to you.	9048
	11:17	but the king of Edom would not l.	9048
	19:25	But the men would not l to him.	9048
	20:13	But the Benjamites would not l	9048
Ru	2: 8	Boaz said to Ruth, "My daughter, l to me.	9048
1Sa	2:25	however, did not l to their father's rebuke,	9048
	8: 7	"L to all that the people are saying to you;	9048
	8: 9	Now l to them; but warn them solemnly	9048
	8:19	But the people refused to l to Samuel.	9048
	8:22	"L to them and give them a king."	9048
	15: 1	so l now to the message from the LORD.	9048
	22: 7	Saul said to them, "L, men of Benjamin!	9048
	22:12	Saul said, "L now, son of Ahitub."	9048
	24: 9	"Why do you l when men say,	9048
	26:19	the king l to his servant's words.	9048
	28:22	Now please l to your servant	9048
	30:24	Who will l to what you say?	9048
2Sa	12:18	we spoke to David but he would not l	9048
	13:14	But he refused to l to her,	9048
	13:16	But he refused to l to her.	9048
	13:28	Absalom ordered his men, "L!	8011
	20:16	a wise woman called from the city, "L!	9048
	20:16	from the city, "Listen! L!	9048
	20:17	"L to what your servant has to say."	9048
1Ki	4:34	Men of all nations came to l	9048
	8:52	and may you l to them whenever they cry	9048
	12:15	So the king did not l to the people,	9048
	12:16	to l to them, they answered the king:	9048
	20: 8	"Don't l to him or agree to his demands."	9048
2Ki	14:11	Amaziah, however, would not l,	9048
	17:14	But they would not l and were	9048
	17:40	They would not l, however,	9048
	18:31	"Do not l to Hezekiah,	9048
	18:32	"Do not l to Hezekiah,	9048
	19: 7	L! I am going to put such a spirit in him	2180
	19:16	l to the words Sennacherib has sent	9048
	21: 9	But the people did not l.	9048
1Ch	28: 2	"L to me, my brothers and my people.	9048
2Ch	10:15	So the king did not l to the people,	9048
	10:16	to l to them, they answered the king:	9048
2Ch	13: 4	"Jeroboam and all Israel, l to me!	9048
	15: 2	to meet Asa and said to him, "L to me,	9048
	20:15	"L, King Jehoshaphat and all who live	7992
	20:20	"L to me, Judah and people of Jerusalem!	9048
	24:19	they would not l.	263
	25:20	Amaziah, however, would not l,	9048
	28:11	Now l to me!	9048
	29: 5	and said: "L to me,	9048
	35:22	He would not l to what Neco had said	9048
Ne	9:17	They refused to l and failed to remember	9048
	9:29	became stiff-necked and refused to l.	9048
Job	13: 6	l to the plea of my lips.	7992
	13:17	L carefully to my words;	9048+9048
	15: 8	Do you l in on God's council?	9048
	15:17	"L to me and I will explain to you;	9048
	21: 2	"L carefully to my words;	9048+9048
	27: 9	Does God l to his cry when distress comes	9048
	32:10	L to me; I too will tell you what I know.	9048
	33: 1	"But now, Job, l to my words;	9048
	33:31	"Pay attention, Job, and l to me;	9048
	33:33	But if not, then l to me;	9048
	34: 2	l to me, you men of learning.	263
	34:10	"So l to me, you men of understanding.	263
	34:16	hear this; l to what I say.	263
	35:13	God does not l to their empty plea;	9048
	35:14	will he l when you say that you do	NIH
	36:10	He makes them l to correction	265+1655
	36:12	But if they do not l,	9048
	37: 2	L! Listen to the roar of his voice,	9048
	37: 2	Listen! L to the roar of his voice,	9048
	37:14	"L to this, Job;	263
	42: 4	'L now, and I will speak;	9048
Ps	5: 2	l to my cry for help,	7992
	10:17	and you l to their cry,	265+7992
	17: 1	l to my cry. Give ear to my prayer—	7992
	34:11	Come, my children, l to me;	9048
	39:12	O LORD, l to my cry for help;	263
	45:10	L, O daughter, consider and give ear:	9048
	49: 1	Hear this, all you peoples; l,	263
	54: 2	l to the words of my mouth.	263
	55: 1	L to my prayer, O God,	263
	61: 1	Hear my cry, O God; l to my prayer.	7992
	66:16	Come and l, all you who fear God;	9048
	78: 1	l to the words of my mouth.	265+5742
	81: 8	if you would but l to me, O Israel!	9048
	81:11	"But my people would not l to me;	9048
	81:13	"If my people would but l to me,	9048
	84: 8	l to me, O God of Jacob.	263
	85: 8	I will l to what God	9048
	86: 6	l to my cry for mercy.	7992
	142: 6	L to my cry, for I am in desperate need;	7992
	143: 1	hear my prayer, l to my cry for mercy;	263
Pr	1: 5	let the wise l and add to their learning,	9048
	1: 8	L, my son, to your father's instruction	9048
	4: 1	L, my sons, to a father's instruction;	9048
	4:10	L, my son, accept what I say,	9048
	4:20	l closely to my words.	265+5742
	5: 1	l well to my words of insight,	265+5742
	5: 7	Now then, my sons, l to me;	9048
	5:13	I would not obey my teachers or l to my	265+5742
	7:24	Now then, my sons, l to me;	9048
	8: 6	L, for I have worthy things to say;	9048
	8:32	"Now then, my sons, l to me;	9048
	8:33	L to my instruction and be wise;	9048
	13: 1	but a mocker does not l to rebuke.	9048
	19:20	L to advice and accept instruction,	9048
	22:17	Pay attention and l to the sayings of	9048
	23:19	L, my son, and be wise,	9048
	23:22	L to your father, who gave you life,	9048
Ecc	5: 1	near to l rather than to offer the sacrifice	9048
	7: 5	a wise man's rebuke than to l to the song	9048
SS	2: 8	L! My lover! Look! Here he comes,	7754
	5: 2	but my heart was awake. L!	7754
Isa	1: 2	L, O earth!	263
	1:10	l to the law of our God,	263
	1:15	if you offer many prayers, I will not l.	9048
	8: 9	L, all you distant lands.	263
	10:30	L, O Laishah!	7992
	13: 4	L, a noise on the mountains,	7754
	13: 4	L, an uproar among the kingdoms,	7754
	28:12	but they would not l.	9048
	28:23	L and hear my voice;	263
	30: 9	to l to the LORD's instruction.	9048
	32: 3	and the ears of those who hear will l.	7992
	32: 9	rise up and l to me;	7754+9048
	34: 1	Come near, you nations, and l;	9048
	36:16	"Do not l to Hezekiah.	9048
	37: 7	L! I am going to put such a spirit in him	2180
	37:17	l to all the words Sennacherib has sent	9048
	42:23	Which of you will l to this	263
	44: 1	"But now l, O Jacob, my servant, Israel,	9048
	46: 3	"L to me, O house of Jacob,	9048
	46:12	L to me, you stubborn-hearted,	9048
	47: 8	"Now then, l, you wanton creature,	9048
	48: 1	"L to this, O house of Jacob,	9048
	48:12	"L to me, O Jacob, Israel:	9048
	48:14	"Come together, all of you, and l:	9048
	48:16	"Come near me and l to this:	9048
	49: 1	L to me, you islands;	9048
	50: 4	wakens my ear to l like one being taught.	9048
	51: 1	"L to me, you who pursue righteousness	9048
	51: 4	"L to me, my people;	7992
	52: 8	L! Your watchmen lift up their	7754
	55: 2	l, listen to me, and eat what is good,	9048
	55: 3	Listen, l to me, and eat what is good,	9048
	65:12	I spoke but you did not l.	9048
Jer	6:10	Who will l to me?	9048
Jer	6:17	'L to the sound of the trumpet!'	7992
	6:17	But you said, 'We will not l.'	7992
	7:13	but you did not l;	9048
	7:16	for I will not l to you.	9048
	7:24	But they did not l or pay attention,	9048
	7:26	But they did not l to me or pay attention.	9048
	7:27	they will not l to you;	9048
	8:19	L to the cry of my people from	7754
	10:22	L! The report is coming—	7754
	11: 2	'L to the terms of this covenant	9048
	11: 6	'L to the terms of this covenant	9048
	11: 8	But they did not l or pay attention;	9048
	11:10	who refused to l to my words.	9048
	11:11	I will not l to them.	9048
	11:14	because I will not l when they call to me	9048
	12:17	But if any nation does not l,	9048
	13:10	who refuse to l to my words,	9048
	13:17	But if you do not l,	9048
	14:12	they fast, I will not l to their cry;	9048
	17:23	Yet they did not l or pay attention.	9048
	17:23	and would not l or respond to discipline.	9048
	18:19	L to me, O LORD;	7992
	19: 3	the God of Israel, says: L!	2180
	19:15	the God of Israel, says: 'L!	2180
	19:15	and would not l to my words.'	9048
	22:21	but you said, 'I will not l!'	9048
	23:16	not l to what the prophets are prophesying	9048
	25: 7	"But you did not l to me,	9048
	26: 3	Perhaps they will l and each will turn	9048
	26: 4	If you do not l to me and follow my law,	9048
	26: 5	if you do not l to the words of my servants	9048
	27: 9	So do not l to your prophets,	9048
	27:14	not l to the words of the prophets who say	9048
	27:16	Do not l to the prophets who say,	9048
	27:17	Do not l to them.	9048
	28: 7	to what I have to say in your hearing	9048
	28:15	to Hananiah the prophet, "L,	9048
	29: 8	Do not l to the dreams	9048
	29:12	and I will l to you.	9048
	32:33	they would not l or respond to discipline.	9048
	34:14	did not l to me or pay attention to me.	9048
	35:17	the God of Israel, says: 'L!	2180
	35:17	I spoke to them, but they did not l;	9048
	36:25	he would not l.	9048
	37:14	But Irijah would not l to him;	9048
	37:20	But now, my lord the king, please l.	9048
	38:15	you would not l to me."	9048
	44: 5	But they did not l or pay attention;	9048
	44:16	not l to the message you have spoken	9048
	48: 3	L to the cries from Horonaim,	7754
	50:28	L to the fugitives and refugees	7754
La	1:18	L, all you peoples;	9048
Eze	2: 5	And whether they l or fail to listen—	9048
	2: 5	And whether they listen or fail to l—	NIH
	2: 7	whether they l or fail to listen,	9048
	2: 7	whether they listen or fail to l,	NIH
	2: 8	you, son of man, l to what I say to you.	9048
	3: 7	But the house of Israel is not willing to l	9048
	3: 7	to you because they are not willing to l	9048
	3:10	l carefully and take to heart all	265+928+9048
	3:11	whether they l or fail to listen."	9048
	3:11	whether they listen or fail to l."	NIH
	3:27	Whoever will l let him listen,	9048
	3:27	Whoever will listen let him l,	9048
	8:18	I will not l to them."	9048
	13:19	By lying to my people, who l to lies,	9048
	20: 8	against me and would not l to me;	9048
	20:39	But afterward you will surely l to me	9048
	33:31	and sit before you to l to your words,	9048
	33:31	l closely and give attention	265+928+9048
Da	9:19	O Lord, l! O Lord, forgive!	9048
Hos	5: 1	L, O royal house!	263
Joel	1: 2	l, all who live in the land.	263
Am	5:23	I will not l to the music of your harps.	9048
Mic	1: 2	Hear, O peoples, all of you, l,	7992
	3: 1	Then I said, "L, you leaders of Jacob,	9048
	6: 1	L to what the LORD says:	9048
	6: 2	l, you everlasting foundations of the earth.	NIH
	6: 9	L! The LORD is calling to the	NIH
Hab	1: 2	must I call for help, but you do not l?	9048
Zep	1:14	near and coming quickly. L!	NIH
Zec	1: 4	But they would not l or pay attention	9048
	3: 8	"L, O high priest Joshua	9048
	7:12	as hard as flint and would not l to the law	9048
	7:13	" 'When I called, they did not l;	9048
	7:13	so when they called, I would not l,'	9048
	11: 3	L to the wail of the shepherds;	7754
	11: 3	L to the roar of the lions;	7754
Mal	2: 2	If you do not l, and if you do not set your	9048
Mt	10:14	If anyone will not welcome you or l to your	201
		words,	201
	12:42	of the earth to l to Solomon's wisdom,	201
	13:18	"L then to what the parable of the sower	201
	15:10	to him and said, "L and understand.	201
	17: 5	with him I am well pleased. L to him!"	201
	18:16	But if he will not l,	201
	18:17	If he refuses to l to them,	4159
	18:17	and if he refuses to l even to the church,	4159
	21:33	"L to another parable:	201
Mk	4: 3	"L! A farmer went out to sow his seed.	201
	6:11	if any place will not welcome you or l to	201
	6:20	yet he liked to l to him.	201
	7:14	"L to me, everyone, and understand this.	201
	9: 7	"This is my Son, whom I love. L to him!"	201
	15:35	they said, "L, he's calling Elijah."	3972
Lk	8:18	Therefore consider carefully how you l.	201
	9:35	whom I have chosen; l to him."	201

Lk | 9:44 | **"L carefully** *to* what I am about to tell you: | 1650+3836+4044+5148+5148+5502
| 11:31 | ends of the earth *to* **l** Solomon's wisdom, | 201
| 16:29 | Moses and the Prophets; *let them* **l** to them.' | 201
| 16:31 | *they* do not **l** to Moses and the Prophets, | 201
| 18: 6 | **"L** to what the unjust judge says. | 201
Jn | 9:27 | told you already and *you did* not **l**. | 201
| 9:31 | We know that God *does* not **l** to sinners. | 201
| 10: 3 | and the sheep **l** to his voice. | 201
| 10: 8 | but the sheep *did* not **l** to them. | 201
| 10:16 | *They* too *will* **l** to my voice, | 201
| 10:20 | Why **l** to him?" | 201
| 10:27 | My sheep **l** to my voice; | 201
Ac | 2:14 | **l carefully** to what I say. | 1969
| 2:22 | "Men of Israel, **l** to this: | 201
| 3:22 | *you must* **l** to everything he tells you. | 201
| 3:23 | not **l** to him will be completely cut off | 201
| 7: 2 | "Brothers and fathers, **l** to me! | 201
| 10:33 | in the presence of God to **l** to everything | 201
| 13:16 | and you Gentiles who worship God, **l** | 201
| 15:13 | "Brothers, **l** to me. | 201
| 18:14 | it would be reasonable for *me* to **l** to you. | 462
| 22: 1 | **l** now to my defense." | 201
| 26: 3 | Therefore, I beg *you* to **l** to me patiently. | 201
| 28:28 | sent to the Gentiles, and *they will* **l!"** | 201
1Co | 14:21 | but even then *they* will not **l** to me," | 1653
| 15:51 | **L,** I tell you a mystery: | 2627
2Co | 13:11 | Aim for perfection, **l** to my appeal, | 4151
Eph | 4:29 | that it may benefit those who **l**. | 201
2Ti | 2:14 | and only ruins those who **l**. | 201
Jas | 1:19 | Everyone should be quick to **l,** | 201
| 1:22 | Do not merely **l** to the word, | 212
| 2: 5 | **L,** my dear brothers: Has not God chosen | 201
| 4:13 | Now **l,** you who say, "Today or tomorrow | 72
| 5: 1 | Now **l,** you rich people, weep and wail | 72
1Jn | 4: 6 | whoever is not from God *does* not **l** to us. | 201

LISTENED (52) [LISTEN]

Ge | 3:17 | "Because *you* **l** to your wife and ate from | 9048
| 30: 6 | *he has* **l** to my plea and given me a son." | 9048
| 30:17 | God **l** to Leah, and she became pregnant | 9048
| 30:22 | he **l** to her and opened her womb. | 9048
Ex | 7:16 | But until now *you have* not **l**. | 9048
| 18:24 | Moses **l** to his father-in-law | 9048
Nu | 21: 3 | The LORD **l** to Israel's plea and gave | 9048
Dt | 9:19 | But again the LORD **l** to me. | 9048
| 10:10 | and the LORD **l** to me at this time also. | 9048
| 34: 9 | So the Israelites **l** to him and did what | 9048
Jos | 10:14 | a day when the LORD **l** to a man. | 9048
Jdg | 2:20 | for their forefathers and *has* not **l** to me, | 9048
| 6:10 | But *you have* not **l** to me." | 9048
1Sa | 12: 1 | "*I have* **l** to everything you said to me | 9048
| 19: 6 | Saul **l** to Jonathan and took this oath: | 9048
| 28:23 | in urging him, and *he* **l** to them. | 9048
2Ki | 13: 4 | and the LORD **l** to him, for he saw how | 9048
| 18:12 | *They* neither **l** to the commands nor | 9048
2Ch | 24:17 | paid homage to the king, and he **l** to them. | 9048
| 25:16 | because you have done this and *have* not **l** | 9048
| 33:13 | by his entreaty and **l** to his plea; | 9048
Ne | 8: 3 | the people **l attentively to** the Book of | 265+448
| 8: 9 | the people had been weeping as they **l** to | 9048
Job | 29:21 | "*Men* **l** to me expectantly, | 9048
| 32:11 | **l** to your reasoning; | 263
Ps | 22:24 | not hidden his face from him but *has* **l** | 9048
| 66:18 | the Lord *would* not *have* **l**; | 9048
| 66:19 | but God *has* surely **l** and heard my voice | 9048
Isa | 66: 4 | no one answered, when I spoke, no *one* **l**. | 9048
Jer | 6:19 | of their schemes, because *they have* not **l** | 7992
| 8: 6 | *I have* **l** attentively, | 9048
| 13:11 | But *they have* not **l.'** | 7992
| 23:18 | Who *has* **l** and heard his word? | 7992
| 25: 3 | but *you have* not **l**. | 9048
| 25: 4 | *you have* not **l** or paid any attention. | 9048
| 25: 8 | "Because *you have* not **l** to my words, | 9048
| 26: 5 | and again (though *you have* not **l),** | 9048
| 29:19 | For *they have* not **l** to my words," | 9048
| 29:19 | And *you* exiles *have* not **l** either," | 9048
| 35:15 | But *you have* not paid attention or **l** to me. | 9048
| 36:31 | because *they have* not **l.' "** | 9048
Eze | 3: 6 | *they would have* **l** to you. | 9048
| 9: 5 | As **l l**, he said to the others, | 265+928
Da | 9: 6 | not **l** to your servants the prophets, | 9048
| 10: 9 | I heard him speaking, and as **l l** to him, | 9048
Jnh | 2: 2 | and *you* **l** to my cry. | 9048
Mal | 3:16 | and the LORD **l** and heard. | 7992
Mk | 12:37 | The large crowd **l** to him with delight. | 201
Ac | 14: 9 | He **l** to Paul as he was speaking, | 201
| 15:12 | as *they* **l** to Barnabas and Paul telling | 201
| 22:22 | The crowd **l** to Paul until he said this. | 201
| 24:24 | He sent for Paul and **l** to him as he spoke | 201

LISTENING (18) [LISTEN]

Ge | 18:10 | Sarah *was* **l** *at* the entrance to the tent, | 9048
| 27: 5 | Now Rebekah *was* **l** as Isaac spoke | 9048
1Sa | 3: 9 | 'Speak, LORD, for your servant *is* **l**.' " | 9048
| 3:10 | "Speak, for your servant *is* **l**." | 9048
2Sa | 20:17 | "I'm **l,**" he said. | 9048
Pr | 18:13 | He who answers before **l—** | 9048
| 19:27 | Stop **l** *to* instruction, my son, | 9048
| 25:12 | a wise man's rebuke to a **l** ear. | 9048
Lk | 2:46 | **l** *to* them and asking them questions. | 201
| 5: 1 | the people crowding around him and **l** *to* | 201
| 10:39 | at the Lord's feet *to* what he said. | 201
| 19:11 | *While* they *were* **l** to this, | 201
| 20:45 | *While* all the people *were* **l,** | 201

Ac | 16:14 | of those **l** was a woman named Lydia, | 201
| 16:25 | and the other prisoners *were* **l** to them, | 2053
| 17:21 | but talking about and **l** *to* the latest ideas.) | 201
| 26:29 | that not only you but all who *are* **l** | 201
| 27:11 | centurion, instead of **l** *to* what Paul said, | 4275

LISTENS (17) [LISTEN]

Pr | 1:33 | but *whoever* **l** to me will live in safety and | 9048
| 8:34 | Blessed is the man *who* **l** to me, | 9048
| 12:15 | but a wise man **l** to advice. | 9048
| 15:31 | *He who* **l** *to* a life-giving rebuke will be | 265+9048
| 17: 4 | A wicked man **l** to evil lips; | 7992
| 21:28 | and whoever **l** to him will be destroyed | 9048
| 29:12 | If a ruler **l** to lies, all his officials | 7992
Mt | 18:15 | If *he* **l** *to* you, you have won your brother | 201
Lk | 10:16 | "He who **l** to you listens to me; | 201
| 10:16 | "He who listens to you **l** *to* me; | 201
Jn | 3:29 | the bridegroom waits and **l** for him, | 201
| 6:45 | Everyone who **l** to the Father and learns | 201
| 9:31 | *He* **l** to the godly man who does his will. | 201
| 18:37 | Everyone on the side of truth **l** to me." | 201
Jas | 1:23 | Anyone who **l** *to* the word but does | 212+1639
1Jn | 4: 5 | and the world **l** to them. | 201
| 4: 6 | and whoever knows God **l** *to* us; | 201

LISTETH (KJV) See PLEASES, WANTS

LISTING (1) [LIST]

Nu | 1: 2 | **l** every man by name, one by one. | 5031

LIT (2) [LIGHT]

Jdg | 15: 5 | **l** the torches and let the foxes loose in | 836+1277
Ps | 77:18 | your lightning **l up** the world; | 239

LITERATURE (2)

Da | 1: 4 | He was to teach them the language and **l** | 6219
| 1:17 | and understanding of all kinds of **l** | 6219

LITTERS (KJV) See WAGONS

LITTLE (171)

Ge | 18: 4 | Let a **l** water be brought, | 5071
| 24:17 | "Please give me a **l** water from your jar." | 5071
| 24:43 | to her, "Please let me drink a **l** water | 5071
| 30:30 | The **l** you had before I came has increased | 5071
| 43: 2 | "Go back and buy us a **l** more food." | 5071
| 43:11 | a **l** balm and a little honey, | 5071
| 43:11 | a little balm and a **l** honey, | 5071
| 44:25 | 'Go back and buy a **l** more food.' | 5071
| 48: 7 | a **l distance** from Ephrath. | 824+3896
Ex | 10: 5 | will devour what **l** you have **left** | 3856+7129+8636
| 16:17 | some gathered much, some **l**, | 5070
| 16:18 | he *who* **gathered** much did not have too little. | 5070
| 16:18 | he who gathered little *did* not **have too l.** | 2893
| 23:30 | **L** by little **l** will drive them out before you, | 5071
| 23:30 | Little by **l l** will drive them out before you, | 5071
Lev | 11:17 | the **l owl**, the cormorant, the great owl, | 3927
Nu | 16:27 | and **l ones** at the entrances to their tents. | 3251
Dt | 1:39 | And the **l ones** that you said would | 3251
| 7:22 | drive out those nations before you, **l** *by* little | 5071
| 7:22 | drive out those nations before you, little by **l** | 5071
| 14:16 | the **l owl**, the great owl, the white owl, | 3927
| 28:38 | in the field but you will harvest **l**, | 5071
Jdg | 18:21 | Putting their **l children**, their livestock | 3251
1Sa | 2:19 | a **l** robe and took it to him when she went | 7785
| 14:29 | how my eyes brightened when I tasted a **l** | 5071
| 14:43 | "I merely tasted a **l** honey with the end | 5071
| 14:23 | I'm only a poor man and **l known.'** | 7829
2Sa | 12: 3 | man had nothing except one **l** ewe lamb | 7783
| 12: 8 | And if all this had been too **l**, | 5071
1Ki | 3: 7 | But I am only a **l** child and do not know | 7785
| 10:21 | silver was considered of **l value** | 4202+4399
| 12:10 | 'My **l finger** is thicker than my father's waist. | 7782
| 17:10 | a **l** water in a jar so I may have a drink?" | 5071
| 17:12 | only a handful of flour in a jar and a **l** oil | 5071
2Ki | 4: 2 | she said, "except a **l** oil." | 655ˢ
| 8:12 | dash their **l children** to the ground, | 6407
| 10:18 | "Ahab served Baal a **l;** | 5071
2Ch | 9:20 | because silver was considered of **l value** | 4399
| 10:10 | 'My **l finger** is thicker than my father's waist. | 7782
| 20:13 | with their wives and children and **l ones,** | 3251
| 31:18 | They included all the **l ones**, the wives, | 3251
Ezr | 9: 8 | to our eyes and a **l** relief in our bondage. | 5071
Est | 3:13 | young and old, women and **l children—** | 3251
Job | 19:18 | Even the **l boys** scorn me; | 6396
| 21:11 | their **l ones** dance about. | 3529
| 24:24 | For a **l while** they are exalted, | 5071
| 36: 2 | with me a **l longer** and I will show you | 10236
Ps | 8: 5 | a **l** lower than the heavenly beings | 5071
| 37:10 | A **l while**, and the wicked will be no | 5071+6388
| 37:16 | Better the **l** that the righteous have than | 5071
| 68:27 | There is the **l** tribe of Benjamin, | 7582
Pr | 6:10 | A **l** sleep, a little slumber, | 5071
| 6:10 | A little sleep, a **l** slumber, | 5071
| 6:10 | a **l** folding of the hands to rest— | 5071
| 7:23 | **l** knowing it will cost his life. | 4202
| 9:18 | But **l** do they know that the dead are there, | 4202
| 10:20 | the heart of the wicked is of **l value**. | 3869+5071
| 13:11 | he who gathers money **l by little** makes it grow. | 3338+6584

Pr | 13:11 | he who gathers money **little by l** makes it grow. | 3338+6584
| 15:16 | Better a **l** with the fear of the LORD than | 5071
| 16: 8 | Better a **l** with righteousness than much | 5071
| 23: 8 | You will vomit up the **l** you have eaten | 7326
| 24:33 | A **l** sleep, a little slumber, a little folding | 5071
| 24:33 | a **l** slumber, a little folding of the hands | 5071
| 24:33 | a **l** folding of the hands to rest— | 5071
| 30:25 | of **l** strength, yet they store up their food | 4202
| 30:26 | of **l** power, yet they make their home in | 4202
Ecc | 5:12 | whether he eats **l** or much, | 5071
| 10: 1 | so a **l** folly outweighs wisdom and honor. | 5071
SS | 2:15 | the **l** foxes that ruin the vineyards, | 7783
Isa | 11: 6 | and a **l** child will lead them. | 7785
| 26:20 | a **l while** until his wrath has passed by. | 5071+8092
| 28:10 | a **l** here, a little there. | 10236
| 28:10 | a little here, a **l** there." | 10236
| 28:13 | a **l** here, a little there— | 10236
| 28:13 | a little here, a **l** there— | 10236
| 32:10 | **In more than** a year you who feel | 3427+6584
| 41:14 | O **l** Israel, for I myself will help you," | 5493
| 63:18 | For a **l while** you people possessed | 5203
Jer | 3: 9 | Israel's immorality mattered so **l** to her, | 7825
| 48: 4 | her **l ones** will cry out. | 7582
Eze | 11:16 | the countries, yet *for* a **l while** I have been | 5071
Da | 7: 8 | there before me was another horn, a **l** *one*, | 10236
| 11:34 | When they fall, they will receive a **l** help, | 5071
Hos | 13:16 | their **l ones** will be dashed to the ground, | 6407
Hag | 1: 6 | planted much, but have harvested **l**. | 5071
| 1: 9 | but see, it turned out to be **l**. | 5071
| 2: 6 | 'In a **l while** I will once more shake | 5071
Zec | 1:15 | I was **only a l** angry, | 5071
| 13: 7 | and I will turn my hand against the **l ones.** | 7592
Mt | 6:30 | O you of **l faith?** | 3899
| 8:26 | He replied, "You of **l faith,** | 3899
| 10:42 | *of* these **l** ones because he is my disciple, | 3625
| 11:25 | and revealed them *to* **l children.** | 3758
| 14:31 | "You of **l faith,"** he said, | 3899
| 16: 8 | Jesus asked, "You of **l faith,** | 3899
| 17:20 | He replied, "Because you have so **l faith**. | 3898
| 18: 2 | a **l child** and had him stand among them. | 4086
| 18: 3 | you change and become like **l children,** | 4086
| 18: 5 | "And whoever welcomes a **l child** | 4086
| 18: 6 | of these **l ones** who believe in me to sin, | 3625
| 18:10 | not look down on one *of* these **l ones**. | 3625
| 18:14 | that any of these **l** ones should be lost. | 3625
| 19:13 | Then **l children** were brought to Jesus | 4086
| 19:14 | "Let the **l children** come to me, | 4086
| 26:39 | Going a **l** farther, he fell with his face to | 3625
| 26:73 | After a **l while**, those standing there | 3625
Mk | 1:19 | When he had gone a **l** farther, | 3900
| 5:23 | "My **l daughter** is dying. | 2589
| 5:41 | (which means, "**L girl**, I say to you, | 3166
| 7:25 | a woman whose **l daughter** was possessed | 2589
| 9:36 | a **l child** and had him stand among them. | 4086
| 9:37 | welcomes one *of* these **l children** in my | 4086
| 9:42 | *of* these **l** ones who believe in me to sin, | 3625
| 10:13 | People were bringing **l children** to Jesus | 4086
| 10:14 | "Let the **l children** come to me, | 4086
| 10:15 | of God like a **l child** will never enter it." | 4086
| 14:35 | Going a **l** farther, he fell to the ground | 3625
| 14:70 | After a **l** *while,* those standing near said | 3625
Lk | 5: 3 | and asked him to put out a **l** from shore. | 3900
| 7:47 | he who has been forgiven **l** loves little." | 3900
| 7:47 | he who has been forgiven little loves **l."** | 3900
| 9:47 | a **l child** and had him stand beside him. | 4086
| 9:48 | "Whoever welcomes this **l child** | 4086
| 10:21 | and revealed them *to* **l children.** | 3758
| 12:26 | Since you cannot do this **very l thing,** | 1788
| 12:28 | O you of **l faith!** | 3899
| 12:32 | "Do not be afraid, **l** flock, | 3625
| 16:10 | with **very l** can also be trusted with much, | 1788
| 16:10 | and whoever is dishonest with **very l** will | 1788
| 17: 2 | for him to cause one of these **l ones** | 3625
| 18:16 | "Let the **l children** come to me, | 4086
| 18:17 | of God like a **l child** will never enter it." | 4086
| 22:58 | A **l** later someone else saw him and said, | 1099
Jn | 12:35 | "You are going to have the light just a **l** | 3625
| 13:33 | I will be with you only a **l** longer. | 3625
| 16:16 | "*In a* **l while** you will see me no more, | 3625
| 16:16 | and then after a **l while** you will see me." | 3625
| 16:17 | '*In a* **l while** you will see me no more, | 3625
| 16:17 | and then after a **l while** you will see me,' | 3625
| 16:18 | "What does he mean by '**a l while'**? | 3625
| 16:19 | '*In a* **l while** you will see me no more, | 3625
| 16:19 | and then after a **l while** you will see me'? | 3625
Ac | 5:34 | that the men be put outside **for a l while.** | 1099
| 19:22 | while *he* **stayed** in the province of Asia a **l longer.** | 2091+5989
| 19:24 | brought in no **l** business for the craftsmen. | 3900
1Co | 4: 3 | I **care very l** if I am judged by | 1639+1650+1788
| 5: 6 | a **l** yeast works through the whole batch | 2024
| 6: 4 | appoint as judges even men **of l account** | 2024
2Co | 7: 8 | but only for a **l while—** | 6052
| 8:15 | he who gathered **l** did not have too little." | 3900
| 8:15 | he who gathered little *did* not **have too l."** | 1782
| 11: 1 | I hope you will put up with a **l** of my | 3625
| 11:16 | so that I may do a **l** boasting. | 3625
Gal | 5: 9 | "A **l** yeast works through the whole batch | 3625
1Th | 2: 7 | like a mother caring for her **l** children. | NIG
1Ti | 5:23 | and use a **l** wine because of your stomach | 3900
Phm | 1:15 | separated from you **for a l while,** | 4639+6052
Heb | 2: 7 | You made him a **l** lower than the angels; | 1099
| 2: 9 | who was made a **l** lower than the angels, | 1099
| 10:37 | For in just a **very l while,** | 3625
| 12:10 | Our fathers disciplined us for a **l while** | 3900
Jas | 4:14 | You are a mist that appears for a **l while** | 3900

1Pe	1: 6	a **l** while you may have had to suffer grief	3900
	5:10	after you have suffered a **l** while,	3900
Rev	3: 8	I know that you have **l** strength,	3625
	6:11	and they were told to wait a **l** longer,	3625
	10: 2	He was holding a **l** scroll,	1044
	10: 9	and asked him to give me the **l** scroll.	1044
	10:10	I took the **l** scroll from the angel's hand	1044
	17:10	he must remain for a **l** while.	3900

LIVE (650) [ALIVE, LIFE, LIFE'S, LIFELESS, LIFETIME, LIVED, LIVES, LIVING, OUTLIVED]

Ge	3:22	the tree of life and eat, and **l** forever."	2649
	4:20	of *those who* **l** in tents and raise livestock.	3782
	9:27	*may* Japheth **l** in the tents of Shem,	8905
	12:10	went down to Egypt to **l** there **for a while**	1591
	12:12	they will kill me but *will* let you **l**.	2649
	13:18	So Abram moved his tents and went to **l**	3782
	16:12	against him, and *he will* **l** in hostility	8905
	17:18	only Ishmael *might* **l** under your blessing!"	2649
	20: 7	and he will pray for you and *you will* **l**.	2649
	20:15	**l** wherever you like."	3782
	24:37	Canaanites, in whose land **l l**,	3782
	26: 2	**l** in the land where I tell you to live.	8905
	26: 2	live in the land where I tell you to.	NIH
	27:40	*You will* **l** by the sword and you will serve	2649
	28: 4	of the land where you now **l as an alien,**	4472
	31:32	has your gods, *he shall not* **l**.	2649
	34:10	**L** in it, trade in it,	3782
	34:21	"Let them **l** in our land and trade in it;	3782
	34:22	But the men will consent to **l** with us	3782
	38:11	"**L** as a widow **in** your father's house.	3782
	38:11	So Tamar went to **l** in her father's house.	3782
	42: 2	so that *we may* **l** and not die."	2649
	42:18	"Do this and *you will* **l**, for I fear God:	2649
	43: 8	so that we and you and our children *may* **l**	2649
	45:10	*You shall* **l** in the region of Goshen and	3782
	47: 4	"We have come to **l** here **awhile,**	1591
	47: 6	*Let them* **l** in Goshen.	3782
	47:19	Give us seed so that *we may* **l** and not die,	2649
	49:13	"Zebulun *will* **l** by the seashore	8905
Ex	1:16	but if it is a girl, *let her* **l**."	2649
	1:17	*they* let the boys **l**.	2649
	1:18	Why have you let the boys **l**?"	2649
	1:22	but *let* every girl **l**."	2649
	2:15	from Pharaoh and went to **l** in Midian,	3782
	8:22	the land of Goshen, where my people **l**;	6641
	12:20	Wherever you **l**, you must eat unleavened	4632
	18:20	and show them the way to **l**	2143
	19:13	*he shall not be* permitted to **l**.'	2649
	20:12	so that *you may* **l long** in the land	799+3427
	21:35	to sell the **l** one and divide both the money	2645
	22:18	"Do not **allow** a sorceress to **l**.	2649
	23:31	I will hand over to you the *people who* **l in**	3782
	23:33	*Do not let* them **l** in your land,	3782
	33:20	for no one may see me and **l**."	2649
	34:10	The people you **l** among will see	NIH
	34:12	not to make a treaty with *those who* **l in**	3782
	34:15	not to make a treaty with *those who* **l in**	3782
Lev	7: 2	the generations to come, wherever you **l**:	4632
	7:26	And wherever you **l**,	4632
	11: 2	'Of all the animals that **l** on land,	NIH
	13:46	*He must* **l** alone;	3782
	13:46	he must **l** outside the camp.	4632
	14: 4	the priest shall order that two **l** clean birds	2645
	14: 6	He is then to take the **l** bird and dip it,	2645
	14: 7	to release the **l** bird in the open fields	2645
	14:51	the hyssop, the scarlet yarn and the **l** bird,	2645
	14:52	the fresh water, the **l** bird, the cedar wood,	2645
	14:53	the **l** bird in the open fields outside	2645
	16:20	he shall bring forward the **l** goat.	2645
	16:21	to lay both hands on the head of the **l** goat	2645
	18: 3	in Egypt, where you *used to* **l**,	3782
	18: 5	the man who obeys them *will* **l** by them.	2649
	20:22	the land where I am bringing you to may **l**	3782
	20:23	*You must* not according to the customs	2143
	22:13	to **l** in her father's house as in her youth,	NIH
	23: 3	wherever you **l**, it is a Sabbath to	4632
	23:14	the generations to come, wherever you **l**.	4632
	23:17	From *wherever* you **l**,	4632
	23:21	the generations to come, wherever you **l**.	4632
	23:31	the generations to come, wherever you **l**.	4632
	23:42	**L** in booths for seven days:	3782
	23:42	All native-born Israelites *are to* **l**	3782
	23:43	that *I* had the Israelites **l** in booths	3782
	25: 6	and temporary resident who **l** among you,	1591
	25:18	and *you will* **l** safely in the land.	3782
	25:19	you will eat your fill and **l** there in safety.	3782
	25:35	so *he can continue to* **l** among you.	2649
	25:36	that your countryman *may continue to* **l**	2649
	26: 5	the food you want and **l** in safety	3782
	26:32	your enemies who **l** there will be appalled.	3782
Nu	4:19	So that *they may* **l** and not die	2649
	13:18	the people who **l** there are strong or weak,	3782
	13:19	What kind of land *do* they **l** in?	3782
	13:19	What kind of towns *do* they **l** in?	3782
	13:28	But the people who **l** there are powerful,	3782
	13:29	The Amalekites **l** in the Negev;	3782
	13:29	the Hittites, Jebusites and Amorites **l** in	3782
	13:29	the Canaanites **l** near the sea and along	3782
	14:21	Nevertheless, **as surely as** I **l**	2644
	14:28	'As surely as I **l**, declares the LORD,	2644
	21: 8	anyone who is bitten can look at it and **l**."	2649
	23: 9	I see a people *who* **l** apart and do	8905
	24:23	"Ah, who *can* **l** when God does this?	2649
Nu	31:15	"Have you **allowed** all the women to **l**?"	2649
	32:17	and children *will* **l** in fortified cities,	3782
	33:55	in the land where you *will* **l**.	3782
	35: 2	to give the Levites towns to **l** in from	3782
	35: 3	to **l** in and pasturelands for their cattle,	3782
	35:29	the generations to come, wherever you **l**.	4632
	35:32	and **l** on his own land before the death of	3782
	35:34	the land where I **l** and where I dwell,	3782
Dt	2: 4	the descendants of Esau, who **l** in Seir.	3782
	2: 8	the descendants of Esau, who **l** in Seir.	3782
	2:10	(The Emites used to **l** there—	3782
	2:12	Horites used to **l** in Seir,	3782
	2:20	Rephaites, who used to **l** there;	3782
	2:29	the descendants of Esau, who **l** in Seir,	3782
	2:29	and the Moabites, who **l** in Ar,	3782
	4: 1	Follow them so that *you may* **l** and may go	2649
	4: 9	from your heart as long as you **l**.	2644
	4:10	to revere me as long as they **l** in the land	2645
	4:26	not **l** there **long** but will certainly	799+3427
	4:40	after you and that you may **l long** in	799+3427
	5:16	so that you *may* **l long** and	799+3427
	5:24	Today we have seen that a man *can* **l** even	2649
	5:33	so that *you may* **l** and prosper	2649
	6: 2	as long as you **l** by keeping all his decrees	2644
	8: 1	that *you may* **l** and increase and may enter	2649
	8: 3	not **l** on bread alone but on every word	2649
	11: 9	so that *you may* **l long** in the land that	799+3427
	12: 1	as long as you **l** in the land.	2645
	12:10	around you so that *you will* **l** in safety.	3782
	12:19	as long as you **l** in your land.	3427+3972
	13:12	the LORD your God is giving you to **l** in	3782
	13:15	put to the sword all *who* **l** in that town.	3782
	14:29	the fatherless and the widows who **l**	NIH
	16:14	and the widows who **l** in your towns.	NIH
	16:20	so that *you may* **l** and possess the land	2649
	18: 1	*They shall* **l** on the offerings made to	430
	22: 2	If the brother does not **l** near you or	NIH
	22: 9	**as long as** you **l**.	3427+3972+4200+6409
	23:16	*Let him* **l** among you wherever he likes	3782
	25:15	so that *you may* **l long** in the land	799+3427
	28:30	but you will not **l** in it.	3782
	28:66	You will **l** in constant suspense,	2644
	30: 6	and with all your soul, and **l**,	2644
	30:16	then *you will* **l** and increase,	2649
	30:18	not **l long** in the land you are crossing	799+3427
	30:19	so that you and *your children may* **l**	2649
	31:13	the LORD your God as long as you **l** in	2645
	32:40	**As surely as** I **l** forever,	2645
	32:47	By them you will **l long** in the land	799+3427
	33: 6	"Let Reuben **l** and not die,	2649
	33:28	So Israel will **l** in safety alone;	8905
Jos	2: 9	so that all *who* **l** in this country are melting	3782
	9: 7	"But perhaps you **l** near us.	3782
	9:15	a treaty of peace with them to **let** them **l**,	2649
	9:20	*We will* **let** them **l**,	2649
	9:21	They continued, "*Let them* **l**,	2649
	9:22	'We **l** a long way from you,'	3782
	9:22	while actually you **l** near us?	NIH
	13:13	to **l** among the Israelites to this day.	3782
	14: 4	of the land but only towns to **l in,**	3782
	15:63	to this day the Jebusites **l** there with	3782
	16:10	to this day the Canaanites **l** among	3782
	17:12	for the Canaanites were determined to **l** in	3782
	17:16	and all the Canaanites **l** in the plain	3782
	20: 4	into their city and give him a place to **l**	3782
	21: 2	that you give us towns to **l in,**	3782
	24:13	and you **l** in them and eat from vineyards	3782
Jdg	1:16	the men of Judah *to* **l** among the people	3782
	1:21	the Jebusites **l** there with the Benjamites.	3782
	1:27	for the Canaanites were determined to **l**	3782
	1:29	but the Canaanites *continued to* **l** there	3782
	6:10	Amorites, in whose land you **l**.'	3782
	8:29	of Joash went back home to **l**.	3782
	11: 8	and you will be our head over all *who* **l in**	3782
	17:10	"**L** with me and be my father and priest,	3782
	17:11	So the Levite agreed to **l** with him,	3782
	19:18	in the hill country of Ephraim where I **l**.	NIH
Ru	1: 1	to **l** for a while in the country of Moab.	1591
	2:11	and your homeland and came to **l** with	NIH
1Sa	1:22	and he will **l** there always."	3782
	1:26	"**As surely as** you **l**, my lord,	2644+5883
	10:24	the people shouted, "**Long** **l** the king!"	2649
	17:55	"**As surely as** you **l**, O king,	2644
	20: 3	as surely as the LORD lives and **as you l**,	2644
	20:14	like that of the LORD as long as I **l**,	2644
	25:26	as surely as the LORD lives and as you **l**,	2644
	25:28	be found in you as long as you **l**.	3427
	27: 5	one of the country towns, that *I may* **l** there.	3782
	27: 5	Why *should* your servant **l** in the royal city	3782
2Sa	8: 2	and the third length *was* **allowed** to **l**.	2649
	11:11	**As surely as** you **l**,	2256+2644+2644+5883
	12:22	be gracious to me and *let* the child **l**.'	2649
	14:19	"**As surely as** you **l**, my lord the king,	2644+5883
	16:16	"**Long** **l** the king!	2649
	16:16	**Long** **l** the king!"	2649
	19:34	How many more years will I **l**	2644
1Ki	1:25	'**Long** **l** King Adonijah!'	2649
	1:31	said, "May my lord King David **l** forever!"	2649
	1:34	'**Long** **l** King Solomon!'	2649
	1:39	'**Long** **l** King Solomon!"	2649
	2: 4	'If your descendants watch how they **l**,	2006
	2:36	a house in Jerusalem and **l** there,	3782
	3:17	this woman and I **l** in the same house.	3782
	6:13	and *I will* **l** among the Israelites	8905
	7: 8	And the palace in which *he was to* **l**,	3782
	8:36	Teach them the right way to **l**,	2143
	8:40	that they will fear you all the time they **l**	2645
1Ki	8:61	the LORD our God, to **l** by his decrees	2143
	20:32	'Please let me **l**.'"	2649
2Ki	2: 2	surely as the LORD lives and **as you l**,	2644
	2: 4	surely as the LORD lives and **as you l**,	2644
	2: 6	surely as the LORD lives and **as you l**,	2644
	4: 7	You and your sons *can* **l** on what is left."	2649
	4:30	surely as the LORD lives and **as you l**,	2644
	6: 2	and let us build a place there for us to **l**."	3782
	7: 4	If they spare us, we **l**;	2649
	10:19	to come will no longer **l**."	2649
	11:12	"**Long** **l** the king!"	2649
	17:27	from Samaria go back *to* **l** there and teach	3782
	17:28	*to* **l** in Bethel and taught them how	3782
2Ch	2: 3	to build a palace to **l** in.	3782
	6:27	Teach them the right way to **l**,	2143
	6:31	and walk in your ways all the time they **l**	2645
	8:11	not **l** in the palace of David king of Israel,	3782
	19:10	from your fellow countrymen who **l** in	3782
	20:15	"Listen, King Jehoshaphat and all *who* **l in**	3782
	23:11	"**Long** **l** the king!	2649
	34:28	on this place and on *those who* **l** here.'"	3782
Ne	2: 3	"*May* the king live forever!	2649
	8:14	the Israelites *were to* **l** in booths during	3782
	9:29	by which a man *will* **l** if he obeys them.	2649
	11: 1	bring one out of every ten to **l** in Jerusalem,	3782
	11: 2	the men who volunteered to **l** in Jerusalem.	3782
Job	4:19	much more *those who* **l** in houses of clay,	8905
	7:16	I despise my life; *I* would not **l** forever.	2649
	14:14	If a man dies, *will he* **l again**?	2649
	21: 7	Why *do* the wicked **l on**,	2649
	26: 5	beneath the waters and *all that* **l** in them.	8905
	27: 6	will not reproach me as long as I **l**.	3427+4946
	30: 6	to **l** in the dry stream beds,	8905
	33:28	and I will **l** to enjoy the light.'	2652
Ps	15: 1	Who may **l** on your holy hill?	8905
	22:26	*may* your hearts **l** forever!	2649
	24: 1	the world, and *all who* **l** in it;	3782
	26: 8	I love the house **where** you **l**, O LORD,	5061
	33:14	dwelling place he watches all *who* **l** on earth	3782
	35:20	against *those who* **l quietly** in the land.	8091
	49: 1	listen, *all who* **l** in this world,	2649
	49: 9	he should **l** on forever and not see decay.	2649
	55:23	not **l** out half their days.	2936
	63: 4	I will praise you as long as I **l**,	2644
	65: 4	and bring near *to* **l** in your courts!	8905
	68: 6	but the rebellious **l** in a sun-scorched land.	8905
	69:32	you who seek God, *may* your hearts **l**!	2649
	72:15	**Long** may he **l**!	2649
	78:10	God's covenant and refused to **l** by his law.	2143
	89:48	What man *can* **l** and not see death,	2649
	98: 7	the world, and *all who* **l** in it.	3782
	102:28	of your servants *will* **l** in your presence;	8905
	104:33	sing praise to my God **as long as** I **l**.	928+6388
	107:36	there he **brought** the hungry to **l**,	3782
	116: 2	I will call on him as long as I **l**.	3427
	118:17	I will not die but **l**,	2649
	119:17	Do good to your servant, and *I will* **l**;	2649
	119:77	your compassion come to me that *I may* **l**,	2649
	119:116	according to your promise and *I will* **l**;	2649
	119:144	give me understanding that *I may* **l**.	2649
	119:175	*Let* me **l** that I may praise you,	2649
	120: 5	that *I* **l** among the tents of Kedar!	8905
	128: 6	*may* you **l** to see your children's children.	NIH
	133: 1	*when* brothers **l** together in unity!	3782
	140:13	and the upright *will* **l** before you.	3782
	146: 2	sing praise to my God **as long as** I **l**.	928+6388
Pr	1:33	but whoever listens to me will **l** in safety	8905
	2:21	For the upright *will* **l** in the land,	8905
	4: 4	keep my commands and *you will* **l**.	2649
	7: 2	Keep my commands and *you will* **l**;	2649
	9: 6	Leave your simple ways and *you will* **l**;	2649
	15:27	but he who hates bribes *will* **l**.	2649
	16: 1	makes even his enemies **l at peace** with him	8966
	19:10	It is not fitting for a fool to **l in luxury**—	9503
	21: 9	Better *to* **l** on a corner of the roof than share	3782
	21:19	Better *to* **l** in a desert than with a	3782
	25:24	Better *to* **l** on a corner of the roof than share	3782
Ecc	3:12	to be happy and do good while they **l**.	2644
	6: 3	a hundred children and **l** many years;	2649
	9: 3	in their hearts while they **l**,	2644
	9: 4	even a **l** dog is better off than a dead lion!	2645
	11: 8	However many years a man *may* **l**,	2649
Isa	5: 8	to field till no space is left and you **l** alone	3782
	6: 5	and I **l** among a people of unclean lips,	3782
	6: 6	of the seraphs flew to me with a **l coal**	8365
	10:24	"O my people who **l** in Zion,	3782
	11: 6	The wolf *will* **l** with the lamb,	1591
	18: 3	you who **l** on the earth,	8905
	20: 6	the people who **l** on this coast will say,	3782
	21:14	you who **l** in Tema,	3782
	22:21	be a father to *those who* **l** in Jerusalem and	3782
	23:18	Her profits will go to *those who* **l** before	3782
	26:14	They are now dead, they **l** no more;	2649
	26:19	your dead *will* **l**; their bodies will rise.	2649
	30:19	O people of Zion, *who* **l** in Jerusalem,	3782
	32:16	and righteousness **l** in the fertile field.	3782
	32:18	My people *will* **l** in peaceful dwelling places	3782
	38:16	Lord, by such things men **l**;	2649
	38:16	You restored me to health and *let* me **l**.	2649
	40:22	and spreads them out like a tent to **l** in.	3782
	42:10	you islands, and *all who* **l** in them.	3782
	49:18	**As surely as** I **l**," declares the LORD,	2644
	49:20	give us more space *to* **l** in."	3782
	51:13	that *you* **l** in constant **terror** every day	7064
	52: 4	my people went down to Egypt to **l**;	1591
	55: 3	hear me, that your soul *may* **l**.	2649
	57:15	"*I* **l** in a high and holy place,	8905

Isa	65: 9	and there *will* my servants **l**.	8905
	65:20	an old man who *does* not **l** *out* his years;	4848
	65:22	they build houses and others **l** *in* them,	3782
Jer	1:14	be poured out on all *who* **l** *in* the land.	3782
	6: 8	so no *one* can **l** *in* it."	3782
	6:12	against *those who* **l** *in* the land,"	3782
	7: 3	and *I will* let you **l** *in* this place.	8905
	7: 7	then *I will* let you **l** *in* this place,	8905
	8:16	the city and *all who* **l** *there*."	3782
	9: 6	You **l** *in* the midst of deception;	3782
	9:11	the towns of Judah so no *one* can **l** *there*."	3782
	9:26	Moab and all *who* **l** *in* the desert	3782
	10:17	you *who* **l** under siege.	3782
	10:18	"At this time I will hurl out *those who* **l** *in*	3782
	11: 2	of Judah and to *those who* **l** *in* Jerusalem.	3782
	11: 9	of Judah and *those who* **l** *in* Jerusalem.	3782
	12: 1	Why *do* all the faithless **l** *at* ease?	8922
	12: 4	Because *those who* **l** *in* it are wicked,	3782
	13:13	with drunkenness all *who* **l** *in* this land,	3782
	19:12	to this place and to *those who* **l** *here*,	3782
	20: 6	and all *who* **l** *in* your house will go	3782
	21: 6	I will strike down *those who* **l** *in*	3782
	21: 9	Babylonians who are besieging you *will* **l**;	2649
	21:13	you *who* **l** *above* this valley *on*	3782
	22:23	You *who* **l** *in* 'Lebanon,'	3782
	22:24	"**As surely as** I **l**," declares the Lord,	2644
	23: 6	be saved and Israel *will* **l** *in* safety.	8905
	23: 8	Then *they will* **l** *in* their own land."	3782
	23:14	They commit adultery and **l** a lie.	928+2143
	24: 8	whether they remain *in* this land or **l**	3782
	25:24	of the foreign people who **l** *in* the desert;	8905
	25:29	down a sword *upon* all *who* **l** *on* the earth,	3782
	25:30	shout against all *who* **l** *on* the earth.	3782
	26:15	and on this city and on *those who* **l** *in* it,	3782
	27:11	in its own land to till it and to **l** *there*,	3782
	27:12	serve him and his people, and *you will* **l**.	2649
	27:17	Serve the king of Babylon, and *you will* **l**.	2649
	31:24	*People will* **l** together in Judah	3782
	32:37	to this place and let them **l** *in* safety.	3782
	33:16	be saved and Jerusalem *will* **l** *in* safety.	8905
	34:22	the towns of Judah so no *one* can **l** *there*."	3782
	35: 7	but *must* always **l** *in* tents.	3782
	35: 7	Then *you will* **l** a long time in the land	2649
	35: 9	or built houses to **l** *in* or had vineyards,	3782
	35:15	Then *you will* **l** *in* the land I have given	3782
	38: 2	goes over to the Babylonians *will* **l**.	2649
	38: 2	He will escape with his life; *he will* **l**.'	2649
	38:17	you and your family *will* **l**.	2649
	40: 5	and **l** *with* him among the people,	3782
	40:10	and **l** *in* the towns you have taken over."	3782
	42:14	'No, we will go and **l** *in* Egypt,	3782
	43: 5	of Judah who had come back to **l** *in*	1591
	44: 8	where you have come to **l**?	1591
	44:13	I will punish *those who* **l** *in* Egypt with	3782
	44:14	the remnant of Judah who have gone to **l**	1591
	44:14	to which they long to return and **l**;	3782
	44:28	the whole remnant of Judah who came to **l**	1591
	46:18	"**As surely as** I **l**," declares the King,	2644
	46:19	you *who* **l** *in* Egypt,	3782
	47: 2	the towns and *those who* **l** *in* them.	3782
	48: 9	with no *one* to **l** *in* them."	3782
	48:17	Mourn for her, all *who* **l** *around* her,	NIH
	48:19	*you who* **l** *in* Aroer.	3782
	48:28	you *who* **l** *in* Moab.	3782
	49: 1	Why *do* his people **l** *in* its towns?	3782
	49: 8	hide in deep caves, you *who* **l** *in* Dedan,	3782
	49:16	you *who* **l** *in* the clefts of the rocks,	8905
	49:18	says the Lord, "so no one *will* **l** *there*;	3782
	49:20	against *those who* **l** *in* Teman:	3782
	49:30	Stay in deep caves, you *who* **l** *in* Hazor,"	3782
	49:31	neither gates nor bars, its *people* **l** alone.	8905
	49:33	No one *will* **l** *there*; no man will dwell in it.	3782
	50: 3	No one *will* **l** *in* it; both men and animals	3782
	50:21	the land of Merathaim and *those who* **l** *in*	3782
	50:34	but unrest to *those who* **l** *in* Babylon.	3782
	50:35	"against *those who* **l** *in* Babylon and	3782
	50:39	and hyenas *will* **l** *there*,	3782
	50:40	"so no one *will* **l** *there*;	3782
	51:13	*You who* **l** by many waters and are rich	8905
	51:24	and all *who* **l** *in* Babylonia for all	3782
	51:29	of Babylon so that no *one* *will* **l** *there*.	3782
	51:35	"May our blood be on *those who* **l** *in*	3782
	51:62	that neither man nor animal *will* **l** *in* it;	3782
La	4:20	that under his shadow *we would* **l** among	2649
	4:21	you *who* **l** *in* the land of Uz.	3782
Eze	2: 6	around you and you **l** among scorpions.	3782
	3:21	he will **surely** **l** because he took warning,	2649+2649
	5:11	**as surely as** I **l**, declares the Sovereign	2644
	6: 6	Wherever you **l**, the towns will	4632
	6:14	to Diblah—wherever they **l**.	4632
	7:13	as long as both of them **l**,	928+2021+2644
	12:19	because of the violence of all who **l** *there*.	3782
	13:19	and have spared *those who* *should* not **l**.	2649
	14:16	**as surely as** I **l**, declares the Sovereign	2644
	14:18	**as surely as** I **l**, declares the Sovereign	2644
	14:20	**as surely as** I **l**, declares the Sovereign	2644
	16: 6	lay there in your blood I said to you, "**L**!"	2649
	16:48	**As surely as** I **l**, declares the Sovereign	2644
	17:16	" '**As surely as** I **l**, declares the Sovereign	2644
	17:19	the Sovereign Lord says: **As surely as** I **l**,	2644
	18: 3	"**As surely as** I **l**, declares the Sovereign	2644
	18: 9	That man is righteous; *he will* **surely** **l**,	2649+2649
	18:13	*Will such a man* **l**?	2649
	18:17	for his father's sin; *he will* **surely** **l**.	2649+2649
	18:19	keep all my decrees, *he will* **surely** **l**.	2649+2649
	18:21	*he will* **surely** **l**; he will not die.	2649+2649

Eze	18:22	the righteous things he has done, *he will* **l**.	2649
	18:23	when they turn from their ways and **l**?	2649
	18:24	the wicked man does, *will he* **l**?	2649
	18:28	*he will* **surely** **l**; he will not die.	2649+2649
	18:32	Repent and **l**!	2649
	20: 3	**As surely as** I **l**, I will not let you inquire	2644
	20:11	the man who obeys them *will* **l** by them.	2649
	20:13	man who obeys them *will* **l** by them—	2649
	20:21	although the man who obeys them *will* **l**	2649
	20:25	not good and laws *they could* not **l** by;	2649
	20:31	**As surely as** I **l**, declares the Sovereign	2644
	20:33	**As surely as** I **l**, declares the Sovereign	2644
	27:35	All *who* **l** *in* the coastlands are appalled	3782
	28:25	Then *they will* **l** *in* their own land,	3782
	28:26	**They** *will* **l** *there* in safety.	3782
	28:26	*they will* **l** *in* safety.	3782
	29: 6	Then all *who* **l** *in* Egypt will know	3782
	29:11	no *one* *will* **l** *there* for forty years.	3782
	32:15	when I strike down all *who* **l** *there*,	3782
	33:10	How then *can we* **l**?" '	2649
	33:11	'**As surely as** I **l**, declares the Sovereign	2644
	33:11	rather that they turn from their ways and **l**.	2649
	33:12	to **l** because of his former righteousness.'	2649
	33:13	the righteous man that *he will* **surely** **l**,	2649+2649
	33:15	and does no evil, *he will* **surely** **l**;	2649+2649
	33:16	what is just and right; *he will* **surely** **l**.	2649+2649
	33:19	just and right, *he will* **l** by doing so.	2649
	33:27	the Sovereign Lord says: **As surely as** I **l**,	2644
	34: 8	**As surely as** I **l**, declares the Sovereign	2644
	34:25	so that *they may* **l** *in* the desert and sleep in	3782
	34:28	*They will* **l** *in* safety.	3782
	35: 6	**as surely as** I **l**, declares the Sovereign	2644
	35:11	**as surely as** I **l**, declares the Sovereign	2644
	36:28	*You will* **l** *in* in the land I gave	3782
	37: 3	"Son of man, *can* these bones **l**?"	2649
	37: 9	into these slain, that *they may* **l**.' "	2649
	37:14	I will put my Spirit in you and *you will* **l**,	2649
	37:25	*They will* **l** *in* the land I gave	3782
	37:25	their children's children *will* **l** *there* forever,	3782
	38: 8	and now all of them **l** *in* safety.	3782
	39: 6	on *those who* **l** *in* safety **in** the coastlands,	3782
	39: 9	" 'Then *those who* **l** *in* the towns	3782
	43: 7	This is where *I will* **l** among	8905
	43: 9	and *I will* **l** among them forever.	8905
	44: 9	the foreigners who **l** among the Israelites.	NIH
	45: 5	as their possession for towns to **l** *in*.	3782
	47: 9	of living creatures *will* **l** wherever	2649
	47: 9	where the river flows everything *will* **l**.	2644
Da	2: 4	the king in Aramaic, "O king, **l** forever!	10262
	2:11	and they do not **l** among men."	10407
	2:38	Wherever *they* **l**, has made you ruler	10163
	3: 9	King Nebuchadnezzar, "O king, **l** forever!	10262
	4: 1	who **l** *in* all the world:	10163
	4:15	and let him **l** *with* the animals among	10269
	4:23	let him **l** like the wild animals,	10269
	4:25	be driven away from people and will **l**	10403
	4:32	be driven away from people and will **l**	10403
	5:10	"O king, **l** forever!"	10262
	6: 6	"O King Darius, **l** forever!	10262
	6:21	Daniel answered, "O king, **l** forever!	10262
	7:12	but were allowed to **l** for a period of time.)	10073+10089+10261
Hos	3: 3	"You are to **l** *with* me many days;	3782
	3: 3	and I will **l** *with* you."	NIH
	3: 4	For the Israelites *will* **l** many days	3782
	4: 1	to bring against *you who* **l** *in* the land:	3782
	4: 3	and all *who* **l** *in* it waste away;	3782
	6: 2	that *we may* **l** *in* his presence.	2649
	10: 5	The **people who** **l** *in* Samaria fear for	8907
	12: 9	I *will* **make** you **l** *in* tents again,	3782
Joel	1: 2	listen, all *who* **l** *in* the land.	3782
	1:14	and all *who* **l** *in* the house of	3782
	2: 1	Let all *who* **l** *in* the land tremble,	3782
Am	5: 4	"Seek me and **l**;	2649
	5: 6	Seek the Lord and **l**,	2649
	5:11	*you will* not **l** *in* them;	3782
	5:14	Seek good, not evil, that *you may* **l**.	2649
	8: 8	and all *who* **l** *in* it?	3782
	9: 5	and all *who* **l** *in* it mourn—	3782
	9:14	they will rebuild the ruined cities and **l** *in*	3782
Ob	1: 3	you *who* **l** *in* the clefts of the rocks,	8905
Jnh	4: 3	for it is better for me to die than to **l**."	2644
	4: 8	"It would be better for me to die than to **l**."	2644
Mic	1:11	*you who* **l** *in* Shaphir.	3782
	1:11	*Those who* **l** *in* Zaanan will not come out.	3782
	1:12	*Those who* **l** *in* Maroth writhe in pain,	3782
	1:13	*You who* **l** *in* Lachish.	3782
	1:15	a conqueror against *you who* **l** *in*	3782
	5: 4	And *they will* **l** *securely*,	3782
Na	1: 5	the world and all *who* **l** *in* it.	3782
Hab	2: 4	but the righteous *will* **l** by his faith—	2649
Zep	1: 4	against Judah and against all *who* **l** *in*	3782
	1:11	Wail, *you who* **l** *in* the market district;	3782
	1:13	They will build houses but not **l** *in* them;	3782
	1:18	a sudden end of all *who* **l** *in* the earth."	3782
	2: 5	Woe to you *who* **l** by the sea,	3782
	2: 9	**as surely as** I **l**," declares the Lord	2644
Zec	1: 5	And the prophets, *do they* **l** forever?	2649
	2: 7	*you who* **l** *in* the Daughter of Babylon!"	3782
	2:10	I am coming, and *I will* **l** among you,"	8905
	2:11	*I will* **l** among you and you will know	8905
	8: 1	I will bring them back to **l** *in* Jerusalem;	8905
	12: 8	the Lord will shield *those who* **l** *in*	3782
Mt	4: 4	'Man *does* not **l** on bread alone.' "	2409
	9:18	put your hand on her, and *she will* **l**."	2409
	12:45	and they go in and **l** *there*.	2997
Mk	5:23	on her so that she will be healed and **l**."	2409

Mk	7: 5	"Why don't your disciples **l** according to	4344
	12:44	put in everything—all she had to **l** on."	1050
Lk	4: 4	'Man *does* not **l** on bread alone.' "	2409
	10:28	"Do this and *you will* **l**."	2409
	11:26	and *they* go in and **l** *there*.	2997
	21: 4	of her poverty put in all she had to **l** on."	1050
	21:35	For it will come upon all those who **l** on	2764
Jn	4:50	Your son *will* **l**."	2409
	4:53	"Your son *will* **l**."	2409
	5:25	Son of God and those who hear *will* **l**.	2409
	5:29	those who have done good will rise to **l**,	2437
	6:51	eats of this bread, *will* **l** forever.	2409
	6:57	the living Father sent me and I **l** because	2409
	6:57	the one who feeds on me *will* **l** because	2409
	6:58	he who feeds on this bread *will* **l** forever."	2409
	7:35	**people** **l** **scattered among** the Greeks,	1402+3836
	11:25	He who believes in me *will* **l**,	2409
	14:19	Because I **l**, you also will live.	2409
	14:19	Because I live, you also *will* **l**.	2409
Ac	2:14	"Fellow Jews and all of you who **l** *in*	2997
	2:26	my body also *will* **l** *in* hope,	2942
	7:48	the Most High *does* not **l** *in* houses made	2997
	17:24	and *does* not **l** *in* temples built by hands.	2997
	17:26	and the exact places where they should **l**.	3000
	17:28	in him *we* **l** and move and have our being."	2409
	21:21	that you teach all the Jews who **l** among	NIG
	21:21	to circumcise their children or **l** according	4344
	22:22	He's not fit to **l**!"	2409
	25:24	shouting that he ought not *to* **l** any longer.	2409
	28: 4	Justice has not allowed him *to* **l**."	2409
	28:16	Paul was allowed to **l** by himself,	3531
Ro	1:17	"The righteous *will* **l** by faith."	2409
	4:14	For if those who **l** by law are heirs,	NIG
	6: 2	how *can we* **l** *in* it any longer?	2409
	6: 4	we too *may* **l** a new life.	4344
	6: 8	we believe that *we will* also **l** **with** him.	5182
	8: 4	who *do* not **l** according to the sinful nature	4344
	8: 5	Those who **l** according to the sinful nature	1639
	8: 5	but those who **l** *in* accordance with	NIG
	8:12	not to the sinful nature, *to* **l** according to it.	2409
	8:13	For if *you* **l** according to the sinful nature,	2409
	8:13	the misdeeds of the body, *you will* **l**,	2409
	10: 5	"The man who does these things *will* **l**	2409
	12:16	**L** **in harmony** with one another.	899+3836+5858
	12:18	**l** **at peace** with everyone.	1644
	14: 8	If *we* **l**, we live to the Lord;	2409
	14: 8	If we live, *we* **l** to the Lord;	2409
	14: 8	So, whether *we* **l** or die,	2409
	14:11	" '**As surely as** I **l**,' says the Lord,	1609+2409
1Co	7: 1	wife who is not a believer and she is willing	
		to **l** with him, he must not divorce her.	3861
	7:13	husband who is not a believer and he is	
		willing *to* **l** with her, she must not divorce	3861
	7:15	God has called us to **l** *in* peace.	NIG
	7:29	now on those who have wives *should* **l** as	1639
	7:35	but that you may **l** *in* a right way	NIG
	8: 6	and for whom *we* **l**;	NIG
	8: 6	and through whom *we* **l**.	NIG
2Co	5: 1	that if the earthly tent we **l** *in* is destroyed,	3864
	5: 7	*We* **l** by faith, not by sight.	4344
	5:15	that those who **l** should no longer live	2409
	5:15	that those who live should no longer **l**	2409
	6: 9	dying, and yet *we* **l** on;	2409
	6:16	"I will **l** **with** them and walk among them,	1940
	7: 3	a place in our hearts that we *would* **l**	5182
	10: 2	toward some people who think that we **l**	4344
	10: 3	For *though* we **l** *in* the world,	4344
	13: 4	yet by God's power *we will* **l** *with* him	2409
	13:11	be of one mind, **l** *in* peace.	1644
Gal	2:14	*you* **l** like a Gentile and not like a Jew.	2409
	2:19	the law I died to the law so that *I might* **l**	2409
	2:20	with Christ and I no longer **l**,	2409
	2:20	The life *I* **l** *in* the body,	2409
	2:20	*I* **l** by faith in the Son of God,	2409
	3:11	because, "The righteous *will* **l** by faith."	2409
	3:12	"The man who does these things *will* **l**."	2409
	5:16	So I say, **l** by the Spirit,	4344
	5:21	that those who **l** like this will not inherit	4556
	5:25	Since *we* **l** by the Spirit,	2409
Eph	2: 2	in which *you* used to **l** when you followed	4344
	4: 1	I urge you to **l** a life worthy of	4344
	4:17	you *must* no longer **l** as the Gentiles do,	4344
	5: 2	and **l** a life of love,	4344
	5: 8	**L** as children of light	4344
	5:15	Be very careful, then, how *you* **l**—	4344
Php	1:21	For to me, *to* **l** is Christ and *to* die is gain.	2409
	3:16	Only let us **l** *up* to what we have already	5123
	3:17	and take note of those who **l** according to	4344
	3:18	many **l** as enemies of the cross of Christ.	4344
Col	1:10	*that you may* **l** a life worthy of the Lord	4344
	2: 6	Christ Jesus as Lord, *continue to* **l** *in* him,	4344
1Th	2:12	and urging you to **l** *lives* worthy of God,	4344
	3: 8	For now *we* really **l**, since you are standing	2409
	4: 1	we instructed you how *to* **l** *in* order	4344
	4: 7	but to **l** a holy life.	NIG
	5:10	*we may* **l** together with him.	2409
	5:13	**L** *in* peace with each other.	1644
2Th	3: 6	and *does* not **l** according to the teaching	4344
1Ti	2: 2	that *we may* **l** peaceful and quiet lives	1341
2Ti	2:11	If we died with him, *we will* also **l** **with** him;	5182
	3:12	everyone who wants *to* **l** a godly life	2409
Tit	2:12	to be reverent in the **way** they **l**,	2949
	2:12	and *to* **l** self-controlled, upright and godly	2409
	3:14	and not **l** unproductive lives.	1639
Heb	10:38	But my righteous one *will* **l** by faith.	2409
	12: 9	to the Father of our spirits and **l**!	2409
	12:14	to **l** *in* peace with all men and to be holy;	NIG

Heb	13:18	and desire *to* l honorably in every way.	418
Jas	4: 5	the spirit he caused to l in us envies	3001
	4:15	*we will* l and do this or that."	2409
1Pe	1:17	l your lives as strangers here	418
	2:12	L such good lives among the pagans that,	2400
	2:16	L as free men, but do not use your	NIG
	2:16	l as servants of God.	NIG
	2:24	*we might* die to sins and l for righteousness;	2409
	3: 7	be considerate *as you* l with your wives,	5324
	3: 8	all of you, l in harmony with one another;	3939
	4: 2	he does not l the rest of his earthly life	1051
	4: 6	l according to God in regard to the spirit.	2409
2Pe	1:13	to refresh your memory as long as *I* l in	1639
	2:18	from those who l in error.	418
	3:11	You ought to l holy and godly lives	419
1Jn	1: 6	we lie and *do not* l by the truth.	4472
	2: 6	Whoever claims *to* l in him must walk	3531
	3:24	Those who obey his commands l in him,	3531
	4: 9	and only Son into the world that *we might* l	2409
	4:13	We know that *we* l in him and he in us,	3531
Rev	2:13	I know where *you* l—	2997
	3:10	to test those who l on the earth.	2997
	11:10	these two prophets had tormented those who l on the earth.	2997
	13: 6	dwelling place and those who l in heaven.	5012
	14: 6	to proclaim to those who l on the earth—	2764
	21: 3	is with men, and *he will* l with them.	5012

LIVED (247) [LIVE]

Ge	4:16	LORD's presence and l in the land of Nod,	3782
	5: 3	When Adam *had* l 130 years,	2649
	5: 4	Adam l 800 years and had other sons	2118+3427
	5: 5	Altogether, Adam l 930 years,	2649
	5: 6	When Seth *had* l 105 years,	2649
	5: 7	Seth l 807 years and had other sons	2649
	5: 8	Altogether, Seth l 912 years,	2118+3427
	5: 9	When Enosh *had* l 90 years,	2649
	5:10	Enosh l 815 years and had other sons	2649
	5:11	When Kenan *had* l 70 years,	2649
	5:12	Kenan l 840 years and had other sons	2649
	5:13	Kenan l 840 years and had other sons	2649
	5:14	When Mahalalel l 910 years,	2118+3427
	5:15	When Mahalalel *had* l 65 years,	2649
	5:16	Mahalalel l 830 years and had other sons	2649
	5:17	Altogether, Mahalalel l 895 years,	2118+3427
	5:18	When Jared *had* l 162 years,	2649
	5:19	Jared l 800 years and had other sons	2649
	5:20	Altogether, Jared l 962 years,	2118+3427
	5:21	When Enoch *had* l 65 years,	2649
	5:23	Altogether, Enoch l 365 years.	2118+3427
	5:25	When Methuselah *had* l 187 years,	2649
	5:26	Methuselah l 782 years and had other sons	2649
	5:27	Altogether, Methuselah l 969 years,	2118+3427
	5:28	Lamech *had* l 182 years, he had a son.	2649
	5:30	Lamech l 595 years and had other sons	2649
	5:31	Altogether, Lamech l 777 years,	2118+3427
	9:28	After the flood Noah l 350 years.	2649
	9:29	Altogether, Noah l 950 years,	2118+3427
	10:30	The **region where** they l stretched	4632
	11:11	Shem l 500 years and had other sons	2649
	11:12	When Arphaxad *had* l 35 years,	2649
	11:13	Arphaxad l 403 years and had other sons	2649
	11:14	When Shelah *had* l 30 years,	2649
	11:15	Shelah l 403 years and had other sons	2649
	11:16	When Eber *had* l 34 years,	2649
	11:17	Eber l 430 years and had other sons	2649
	11:18	When Peleg *had* l 30 years,	2649
	11:19	Peleg l 209 years and had other sons	2649
	11:20	When Reu *had* l 32 years,	2649
	11:21	Reu l 207 years and had other sons	2649
	11:22	When Serug *had* l 30 years,	2649
	11:23	Serug l 200 years and had other sons	2649
	11:24	When Nahor *had* l 29 years,	2649
	11:25	Nahor l 119 years and had other sons	2649
	11:26	After Terah *had* l 70 years,	2649
	11:32	Terah l 205 years, and he died in	2118+3427
	13:12	Abram l in the land of Canaan,	3782
	13:12	while Lot l among the cities of the plain	3782
	19:29	that overthrew the cities where Lot had l.	3782
	19:30	He and his two daughters l in a cave.	3782
	20: 1	Negev and l between Kadesh and Shur.	3782
	21:20	He l in the desert and became an archer.	3782
	23: 1	Sarah l to be a hundred and twenty-seven	2644
	25: 7	Abraham l a hundred and seventy-five years	2649
	25:11	who then l near Beer Lahai Roi.	3782
	25:17	Ishmael l a hundred and thirty-seven	2644
	25:18	l in hostility toward all their	5877+6584+7156
	35:28	Isaac l a hundred and eighty years.	2118+3427
	37: 1	Jacob l in the land where his father had	3782
	38:21	He asked the men *who* l there,	AIT
	38:22	Besides, the **men** *who* l there said,	AIT
	39: 2	he l in the house of his Egyptian master.	2118
	47:28	Jacob l in Egypt seventeen years,	2649
	50:11	When the Canaanites *who* l there saw	3782
	50:22	He l a hundred and ten years	2649
Ex	6: 4	land of Canaan, **where** they l as aliens.	4472
	6:16	Levi l 137 years.	2644
	6:18	Kohath l 133 years.	2644
	6:20	Amram l 137 years.	2644
	10:23	in the **places where** they l.	4632
	12:40	the length of time the Israelite people l	3782
Lev	18:27	the people who l in the land before you,	NIH
	26:35	not have during the sabbaths you l in it.	3782
Nu	13:22	the descendants of Anak, l.	NIH
	14:45	the Amalekites and Canaanites who l in	3782
	20:15	and *we* l there many years.	3782

Nu	21: 1	king of Arad, *who* l in the Negev,	3782
	21: 9	and looked at the bronze snake, he l.	2649
	33:40	who l in the Negev of Canaan,	3782
Dt	1:44	The Amorites who l in those hills	3782
	2:22	descendants of Esau, who l in Seir,	3782
	2:22	and *have* l in their place to this day.	3782
	2:23	Avvites who l in villages as far as Gaza,	3782
	4:25	l in the land **a long time—**	3823
	4:33	speaking out of fire, as you have, and l?	2649
	21:13	After *she has* l in your house	3782
	23: 7	because *you* l as an alien in his country.	2118
	26: 5	with a few people and l there and became	1591
	29:16	You yourselves know how *we* l in Egypt	3782
Jos	2:15	house she l was part of the city wall.	3782
	8:26	until he had destroyed all *who* l in Ai.	3782
	8:35	and the aliens who l among them.	2143
	13:21	allied with Sihon—*who* l in that country.	3782
	22:33	where the Reubenites and the Gadites l.	3782
	24: 2	the father of Abraham and Nahor, l	3782
	24: 7	Then you l in the desert for a long time.	3782
	24: 8	of the Amorites who l east of the Jordan.	3782
	24:18	including the Amorites, *who* l in the land.	3782
Jdg	1:32	and because of this the people of Asher l	3782
	1:33	but the Naphtalites too l among	3782
	2:18	of their enemies as long as the judge l;	3427
	3: 5	The Israelites l among the Canaanites,	3782
	4: 2	who l in Harosheth Haggoyim.	3782
	8:31	His concubine, who l in Shechem,	NIH
	9:21	and he l there because he was afraid	3782
	10: 1	He l in Shamir, in the hill country	3782
	11:21	over all the land of the Amorites *who* l in	3782
	16:30	when he died than while he l.	2644
	17:12	the young man became his priest and l	2118
	18: 7	they l a long way from the Sidonians	NIH
	18:22	the men who l near Micah	928+1074+2021
	18:28	to rescue them because they l a long way	NIH
	19: 1	Now a Levite *who* l in a remote area in	1591
Ru	1: 4	And they went to Moab and l there.	2118
	1: 4	After *they had* l there about ten years,	3782
	2:23	And she l with her mother-in-law.	3782
1Sa	4: 6	A man who l there answered,	4946
	12:11	so that *you* l securely.	3782
	23:29	And David went up from there and l in	3782
	27: 7	David l in Philistine territory a year	3782
	27: 8	(From ancient times these peoples *had* l in	3782
	27:11	And such was his practice as long as he l	3782
2Sa	4: 3	of Beeroth fled to Gittaim and *have* l there	2118
	5: 6	to attack the Jebusites, who l there.	3782
	9:13	And Mephibosheth l in Jerusalem,	3782
	13:20	And Tamar l in her brother Absalom's	3782
	14:28	Absalom l two years in Jerusalem	3782
1Ki	4:25	from Dan to Beersheba, l in safety,	3782
	11:20	Genubath l with Pharaoh's own children.	2118
	11:25	adversary **as long as** Solomon l,	3427+3972
	12:25	in the hill country of Ephraim and l there.	3782
	13:25	in the city where the old prophet l.	3782
	14: 9	You have done more evil than all who l	2118
	17:22	the boy's life returned to him, and he l.	2649
	21: 8	and nobles who l in Naboth's city	3782
	21:11	and nobles who l in Naboth's city did	3782
2Ki	13: 5	So the Israelites l in their own homes	3782
	14:17	of Judah l for fifteen years after the death	2649
	15: 5	and he l in a separate house.	3782
	16: 6	then moved into Elath and l there	3782
	17:24	They took over Samaria and l in its towns.	3782
	17:25	When they first l there,	3782
	22:14	She l in Jerusalem, in the Second District.	3782
	25:30	a regular allowance as long as he l.	2644
1Ch	2:55	and the clans of scribes *who* l at Jabez:	3782
	4:23	the potters *who* l at Netaim and Gederah;	3782
	4:28	*They* l in Beersheba, Moladah,	3782
	4:40	Some Hamites *had* l there formerly.	3782
	4:43	and *they have* l there to this day.	3782
	5:11	The Gadites l next to them in Bashan,	3782
	5:16	The Gadites l in Gilead,	3782
	7:29	The descendants of Joseph son of Israel l	3782
	8:28	and they l in Jerusalem.	3782
	8:29	Jeiel the father of Gibeon l in Gibeon.	3782
	8:32	They too l near their relatives	3782
	9: 3	and Manasseh *who* l in Jerusalem were:	3782
	9:16	who l in the villages of the Netophathites.	3782
	9:34	and they l in Jerusalem.	3782
	9:35	Jeiel the father of Gibeon l in Gibeon.	3782
	9:38	They too l near their relatives	3782
	11: 4	the Jebusites *who* l there	3782
2Ch	11: 1	Rehoboam l in Jerusalem and built	3782
	19: 4	Jehoshaphat l in Jerusalem,	3782
	19: 8	And *they* l in Jerusalem.	3782
	20: 2	*They have* l in it and have built in it	3782
	21:16	the Philistines and of the Arabs who l near	NIH
	24:14	**As long as** Jehoiada l,	3427+3972
	25:25	of Judah l for fifteen years after the death	2649
	26: 7	the Philistines and against the Arabs who l	3782
	26:21	He l in a separate house—	3782
	30:25	from Israel and those *who* l in Judah.	3782
	31: 6	and Judah who l in the towns of Judah	3782
	31:19	who l on the farm lands	NIH
	34:22	She l in Jerusalem, in the Second District.	3782
	34:33	**As long as** he l, they did not fail to	3427+3972
Ne	4:12	Then the Jews who l near them came	3782
	8:17	from exile built booths and l there.	3782
	9:24	the Canaanites, *who* l in the land;	3782
	11: 3	and descendants of Solomon's servants l	3782
	11: 6	both Judah and Benjamin l in Jerusalem):	3782
	11: 6	The descendants of Perez who l	3782
	11:21	The temple servants l on the hill of Ophel	3782
	11:25	of the people of Judah l in Kiriath Arba	3782

Ne	11:31	the Benjamites from Geba l in Micmash,	NIH
	12:27	from **where** they l and were brought	5226
	13:16	Men from Tyre *who* l in Jerusalem	3782
Job	1: 1	of Uz *there* l a man whose name was Job.	2118
	18:19	no survivor where once he l.	4472
	21:28	the tents where wicked men l?'	5438
	38:21	You have l so many years!	NIH
	42:16	After this, Job l a hundred and forty years;	2649
Ps	49:18	while he l he counted himself blessed—	2644
	105:23	Jacob l as an alien in the land of Ham.	1591
	107:34	of the wickedness of *those who* l there.	3782
	120: 6	Too long have l l among those who hate	8905
Ecc	4:15	I saw that all who l and walked under	2645
	4:15	*there* l in that city a man poor but wise,	5162
Isa	13:20	She will never be inhabited or l in	8905
Jer	3: 1	But you have l as a **prostitute**	AIT
	35:10	*We have* l in tents and have fully obeyed	3782
	42:18	poured out on *those who* l in Jerusalem,	3782
	50:39	It will never again be inhabited or l in	8905
	52:34	a regular allowance as long as he l,	2644
La	2:16	*we have* l to see it."	5162
Eze	3:15	I came to the exiles who l at Tel Abib near	3782
	16:46	who l to the north of you	3782
	16:46	and your younger sister, who l to	3782
	20: 9	the eyes of the nations they l among and	NIH
	26:17	you put your terror on all *who* l there.	3782
	31: 6	all the great nations l in its shade.	3782
	31:17	Those *who* l in its shade,	3782
	37:25	the land where your fathers l.	3782
	39:26	when they l in safety in their land	3782
Da	4:12	and the birds of the air l in its branches;	10163
	5:21	he l with the wild donkeys and ate grass	10403
Zep	2:15	This is the carefree city that l in safety.	3782
Mt	2:23	he went and l in a town called Nazareth.	2997
	4:13	he went and l in Capernaum,	2997
	23:30	'If *we had* l in the days of our forefathers,	1639
Mk	5: 3	This man l in the tombs,	2400+2998+3836
Lk	1:80	and he l in the desert until he appeared	1639
	2:36	*she had* l with her husband seven years	2409
	7:37	When a woman *who had* l a sinful life in	1639
	8:27	not worn clothes or l in a house,	3531
	8:27	but had l in the tombs.	NIG
	16:19	and fine linen and l in luxury every day.	2370
Jn	7:42	the town where David l?"	1639
	12: 1	Jesus arrived at Bethany, where Lazarus l,	1639
Ac	7: 2	before he l in Haran.	2997
	9:35	All those who l in Lydda and Sharon	2997
	16: 1	where a disciple named Timothy l,	1639+1695
	16: 3	because of the Jews who l in that area,	1639
	17:21	foreigners who l **there** spent their time	2111
	19:10	the Jews and Greeks who l in the province	2997
	20:18	"You know how *I* l the whole time I was	1181
	26: 4	"The Jews all know the **way** I have l ever	1052
	26: 5	I l as a Pharisee.	2409
Eph	2: 3	All of us also l among them at one time,	418
Col	3: 7	in these ways, in the life you once l.	2409
1Th	2: 5	how *we* l among you for your sake.	1181
2Ti	1: 5	which first l in your grandmother Lois and	1940
Tit	3: 3	*We* l in malice and envy,	1341
Heb	11: 9	he l in tents, as did Isaac and Jacob,	2997
Jas	5: 5	l on earth **in luxury** and self-indulgence.	5587
1Pe	1:14	to the evil desires you had when you l	NIG
Rev	13:14	wounded by the sword and yet l.	2409

LIVELIHOOD (2)

Dt	24: 6	that would be taking a man's l as security.	5883
Zec	13: 5	the land has been my l since my youth.'	7871

LIVELY (KJV) See LIVING, VIGOROUS

LIVER (14)

Ex	29:13	the covering of the l,	3879
	29:22	the covering of the l,	3879
Lev	3: 4	and the covering of the l,	3879
	3:10	and the covering of the l,	3879
	3:15	and the covering of the l,	3879
	4: 9	and the covering of the l,	3879
	7: 4	and the covering of the l,	3879
	8:16	the covering of the l,	3879
	8:25	the covering of the l,	3879
	9:10	the covering of the l from the sin offering,	3879
	9:19	the kidneys and the covering of the l—	3879
Job	20:25	the gleaming point out of his l.	5355
Pr	7:23	till an arrow pierces his l,	3879
Eze	21:21	he will examine the l.	3879

LIVES (192) [LIVE]

Ge	9: 3	Everything that l and moves will be food	2645
	19:17	one of them said, "Flee for your l!	5883
	42:13	who l in the land of Canaan.	NIH
	42:15	**As surely as** Pharaoh l,	2644
	42:16	**as surely as** Pharaoh l,	2644
	45: 5	because it was to **save** l that God sent me	4695
	45: 7	and to **save** your l by a great deliverance.	2649
	47:25	"You have **saved** our l," they said.	2649
	50:20	now being done, the saving of many l.	6639
Ex	1:14	They made their l bitter with hard labor	2644
	30:15	offering to the LORD to atone for your l.	5883
	30:16	making atonement for your l."	5883
Lev	19:33	" 'When an alien l with you in your land,	1591
Nu	16:38	the men who sinned at the cost of their l.	5883
Dt	22:19	not divorce her **as long as** he l.	3427+3972
	22:29	never divorce her **as long as** he l.	3427+3972
	28:43	The alien who l among you will rise	NIH

```
Dt   33:20  Gad I there like a lion,                                     8905
Jos   2:13  that you will spare the I of my father                       2649
      2:14  "Our I for your lives!"                                      5883
      2:14  "Our lives for your I!"                                       NIH
      6:25  and she I among the Israelites to this day.                  3782
      9:24  So we feared for our I because of you,                       5883
Jdg   5:18  The people of Zebulun risked their very I;                   5883
      8:19  As surely as the LORD I,                                     2644
      8:19  the LORD lives, if you had spared their I,                   2649
     18:25  and you and your family will lose your I."                   5883
Ru    3:13  as surely as the LORD I                                      2644
1Sa  14:39  As surely as the LORD who rescues Israel I,                  2644
     14:45  As surely as the LORD I,                                     2644
     19: 6  "As surely as the LORD I                                     2644
     20: 3  as surely as the LORD I                                      2644
     20:21  as surely as the LORD I                                      2644
     20:31  As long as the son of Jesse I on this earth,                 2644
     25:26  as surely as the LORD I                                      2644
     25:29  the I of your enemies he will hurl away as                   5883
     25:34  as surely as the LORD, the God of Israel, I,                 2644
     26:10  As surely as the LORD I,"                                    2644
     26:16  As surely as the LORD I,                                     2644
     28:10  "As surely as the LORD I,                                    2644
     29: 6  "As surely as the LORD I,                                    2644
2Sa   2:27  "As surely as God I,                                         2644
      4: 9  "As surely as the LORD I,                                    2644
     12: 5  "As surely as the LORD I,                                    2644
     14:11  "As surely as the LORD I,"                                   2644
     15:21  "As surely as the LORD I,                                    2644
     15:21  as my lord the king I,                                       2644
     18: 8  the forest claimed more I that day than                      6639
     19: 5  and the I of your sons and daughters and                     5883
     19: 5  and the I of your wives and concubines.                      5883
     22:47  "The LORD I! Praise be to my Rock!                           2644
     23:17  of men who went at the risk of their I?"                     5883
1Ki   1:29  "As surely as the LORD I,                                    2644
      2:24  as surely as the LORD I—                                     2644
     17: 1  "As the LORD, the God of Israel, I,                          2644
     17:12  "As surely as the LORD your God I,"                          2644
     18:10  As surely as the LORD your God I,                            2644
     18:15  "As the LORD Almighty,                                       2644
     22:14  "As surely as the LORD I,                                    2644
2Ki   1:13  "please have respect for my life and the I                   5883
      2: 2  "As surely as the LORD I                                     2644
      2: 4  "As surely as the LORD I                                     2644
      2: 6  "As surely as the LORD I                                     2644
      3:14  "As surely as the LORD Almighty I,                           2644
      4:30  "As surely as the LORD I,                                    2644
      5:16  "As surely as the LORD I,                                    2644
      5:20  As surely as the LORD I,                                     2644
      7: 7  left the camp as it was and ran for their I.                 5883
1Ch  11:19  these men who went at the risk of their I?"                  5883
     11:19  they risked their I to bring it back,                        5883
2Ch  18:13  "As surely as the LORD I,                                    2644
Job  15:28  and houses where no one I,                                   3782
     19:25  I know that my Redeemer I,                                   2645
     27: 2  "As surely as God I, who has denied me                       2644
     38:26  to water a land where no man I,                               NIH
Ps   18:46  The LORD I! Praise be to my Rock!                           2644
     37:32  seeking their very I;                                        4637
     66: 9  he has preserved our I and kept our feet                     5883
     74:19  the I of your afflicted people forever.                      2652
     97:10  for he guards the I of his faithful ones                     5883
    107: 5  and their I ebbed away.                                      5883
Pr    1:19  it takes away the I of those who get it.                     5883
      3:29  your neighbor, who I trustfully near you.                    3782
     14:25  A truthful witness saves I,                                  5883
Ecc   2: 3  during the few days of their I.                              2644
      6: 3  yet no matter how long he I,                            3427+9102
      6: 6  if he I a thousand years twice over but fails               2649
      8:12  a hundred crimes and still I a long time,                    799
Isa  38:20  of our I in the temple of the LORD.                          2644
     42:11  let the settlements where Kedar I rejoice.                   3782
     57:15  he who I forever, whose name is holy:                        8905
     65:20  be in it an infant who I but a few days, or                   NIH
Jer   2: 6  where no one travels and no one I?'                          3782
      4: 2  'As surely as the LORD I,'                                   2644
      4:29  towns are deserted; no one I in them.                        3782
      5: 2  'As surely as the LORD I,'                                   2644
     12:16  'As surely as the LORD I'—                                   2644
     16:14  'As surely as the LORD I,                                    2644
     16:15  'As surely as the LORD I,                                    2644
     17: 6  in a salt land where no one I.                               3782
     19: 7  at the hands of those who seek their I,                      5883
     19: 9  on them by the enemies who seek their I.'                    5883
     21: 7  and to their enemies who seek their I,                       5883
     23: 7  'As surely as the LORD I,                                    2644
     23: 8  'As surely as the LORD I,                                    2644
     34:20  over to their enemies who seek their I.                      5883
     34:21  over to their enemies who seek their I,                      5883
     38:16  "As surely as the LORD I,                                    2644
     44:26  "As surely as the Sovereign LORD."                           2644
     46:26  hand them over to those who seek their I,                    5883
     48: 6  Run for your I; become like a bush in the                    5883
     49:11  I will protect their I.                                      2649
     49:31  a nation at ease, which I in confidence,"                    3782
     49:37  before those who seek their I;                               5883
     51: 6  Run for your I!                                              5883
     51:37  a place where no one I.                                      3782
     51:43  a land where no one I,                                       3782
     51:45  Run for your I!                                              5883
La    2:12  as their I ebb away in their mothers' arms.                  5883
      2:19  Lift up your hands to him for the I                          5883
      5: 9  of our I because of the sword in the desert.                 5883
Eze  13:18  the I of my people but preserve your own?                    5883
     13:22  from their evil ways and so save their I,                    2649
     17:17  siege works erected to destroy many I.                       5883

Da    3:28  willing to give up their I rather than serve               10151
      4:34  I honored and glorified him who I forever.                  10261
     12: 7  I heard him swear by him who I forever,                      2645
Hos   4:15  'As surely as the LORD I!'                                   2644
Am    8:14  'As surely as your god I,                                    2644
      8:14  'As surely as the god of Beersheba I'—                       2644
Mic   7:14  which I by itself in a forest,                               8905
Hab   1:16  for by his net he I in luxury and enjoys                     2750
Jn    3:21  But whoever I by the truth comes into                       4472
     11:26  and whoever I and believes                                   2409
     14:17  for he I with you and will be in you.                        3531
Ac   10:32  Simon the tanner, who I by the sea.'                          NIG
     15:26  men who have risked their I for the name                     6034
     27:10  loss to ship and cargo, and to our own I also.               6034
     27:24  and God has graciously given you the I of                     NIG
Ro    6:10  but the life he I, he lives to God.                          2409
      6:10  but the life he lives, he I to God.                          2409
      7: 1  over a man only as long as he I?                             2409
      7:18  I know that nothing good I in me, that is,                   3861
      8: 9  if the Spirit of God I in you.                               3861
      8:11  through his Spirit, who I in you.                            1940
     14: 7  For none of us I to himself alone and none                   2409
     16: 4  They risked their I for me.                             5549+5719
1Co   3:16  and that God's Spirit I in you?                              3861
      7:39  bound to her husband as long as he I.                        2409
2Co   1: 5  the sufferings of Christ flow over into our I,                NIG
     13: 4  yet he I by God's power.                                     2409
Gal   2:20  I no longer live, but Christ I in me.                        2409
Eph   2:22  a dwelling in which God I by his Spirit.                      NIG
Col   1:19  For in Christ all the fullness of the Deity I                2997
1Th   2: 8  not only the gospel of God but our I as                      6034
      2:12  and urging you to live I worthy of God,                      4344
1Ti   2: 2  and quiet I in all godliness and holiness.                   1050
      5: 6  But the widow who I for pleasure is dead                     5059
      5: 6  for pleasure is dead even while she I.                       2409
      6:16  immortal and who I in unapproachable light                   3861
2Ti   1: 5  I am persuaded, now I in you also.                            NIG
      1:14  with the help of the Holy Spirit who I in us.                1940
Tit   2:12  upright and godly I in this present age,                      AIT
      3:14  and not live unproductive I.                                  NIG
Heb   2:15  and free those who all their I were held                     2409
      5:13  Anyone who I on milk, being still an infant,                 3576
      7:24  because Jesus I forever,                                     3531
      7:25  because he always I to intercede for them.                   2409
     13: 5  Keep your I free from the love of money                      5573
1Pe   1:17  live your I as strangers here                                5989
      2:12  Live such good I among the pagans that                  419+3836
      3: 2  the purity and reverence of your I.                          419
2Pe   2: 7  who was distressed by the filthy I                           419
      3:11  You ought to live holy and godly I                            AIT
1Jn   1:10  a liar and his word has no place in our I.                    NIG
      2:10  Whoever loves his brother I in the light,                    3531
      2:14  and the word of God I in you,                                3531
      2:17  man who does the will of God I forever.                      3531
      3: 6  No one who I in him keeps on sinning.                        3531
      3:16  to lay down our I for our brothers.                          6034
      3:24  And this is how we know that he I in us:                     3531
      4:12  God I in us and his love is made complete                    3531
      4:15  God I in him and he in God,                                  3531
      4:16  Whoever I in love lives in God,                              3531
      4:16  Whoever lives in love I in God,                              3531
2Jn   1: 2  which I in us and will be with us forever:                   3531
Rev   2:13  in your city—where Satan I.                                  2997
      4: 9  on the throne and who I for ever and ever,                   2409
      4:10  and worship him who I for ever and ever.                     2409
     10: 6  he swore by him who I for ever and ever,                     2409
     12:11  not love their I so much as to shrink                        6034
     15: 7  who I for ever and ever.                                     2409
```

LIVESTOCK (88)

```
Ge    1:24  I, creatures that move along the ground,                     989
      1:25  the I according to their kinds,                              989
      1:26  over the I, over all the earth,                              989
      2:20  So the man gave names to all the I,                          989
      3:14  above all the I and all the wild animals!                    989
      4:20  of those who live in tents and raise I.                      5238
      7:14  all I according to their kinds,                              989
      7:21  birds, I, wild animals,                                      989
      8: 1  and the I that were with him in the ark,                     989
      9:10  the birds, the I and all the wild animals,                   989
     13: 2  Abram had become very wealthy in I and                       5238
     30:29  and how your I has fared under my care.                      5238
     31: 9  So God has taken away your father's I                        5238
     31:18  and he drove all his I ahead of him,                         5238
     33:17  for himself and made shelters for his I.                     5238
     34: 5  his sons were in the fields with his I;                      5238
     34:23  Won't their I, their property                                5238
     36: 6  as well as his I and all his other animals                   5238
     36: 7  not support them both because of their I.                    5238
     46: 6  They also took with them their I and                         5238
     46:32  men are shepherds; they tend I,              408+2118+5238
     46:34  'Your servants have tended I,                408+2118+5238
     47: 6  put them in charge of my own I."                             5238
     47:16  "Then bring your I," said Joseph.                            5238
     47:16  sell you food in exchange for your I,                        5238
     47:17  So they brought their I to Joseph,                           5238
     47:17  with food in exchange for all their I.                       5238
     47:18  Our money is gone and our I belongs              989+5238
Ex    9: 3  a terrible plague on your I in the field—                    5238
      9: 4  between the I of Israel and that of Egypt,                   5238
      9: 6  All the I of the Egyptians died,                             5238
      9:19  to bring your I and everything you have in                   5238
      9:20  to bring his slaves and their I inside.                      5238
      9:21  left their slaves and I in the field.                        5238
     10:26  Our I too must go with us;                                   5238
     12:29  and the firstborn of all the I as well.                      989
```

```
Ex   12:38  as well as large droves of I,                                5238
     13:12  All the firstborn males of your I belong to                  989
     17: 3  to make us and our children and I die                        5238
     22: 5  a man grazes his I in a field or vineyard                    1248
     34:19  including all the firstborn males of your I,                 5238
Lev   5: 2  of unclean wild animals or of unclean I or                   989
     25: 7  as well as for your I and the wild animals                   989
Nu    3:41  and the I of the Levites in place of all                     989
      3:41  in place of all the firstborn of the I of                    989
      3:45  and the I of the Levites in place                            989
      3:45  of the Levites in place of their I.                          989
     20: 4  that we and our I should die here?                           1248
     20: 8  so they and their I can drink."                              1248
     20:11  and the community and their I drank.                         1248
     20:19  and if we or our I drink any of your water,                  5238
     32: 1  of Jazer and Gilead were suitable for I.                     5238
     32: 4  are suitable for I, and your servants have                   5238
     32: 4  and your servants have I.                                    5238
     32:16  like to build pens here for our I and cities                 5238
     35: 3  flocks and all their other I.                                2651
Dt    2:35  But the I and the plunder from the towns                     989
      3: 7  But all the I and the plunder from their                     989
      3:19  your I (I know you have much livestock)                      5238
      3:19  (I know you have much I) may stay in                         5238
      7:14  nor any of your I without young.                             989
     13:15  both its people and its I.                                   989
     20:14  the I and everything else in the city,                       989
     28: 4  crops of your land and the young of your I                   989
     28:11  of your I and the crops of your ground—                      989
     28:51  They will devour the young of your I and                     989
     30: 9  of your I and the crops of your land.                        989
Jos   1:14  your children and your I may stay in                         5238
      8: 2  that you may carry off their plunder and I                   989
      8:27  for themselves the I and plunder                             989
     11:14  for themselves all the plunder and I                         989
     21: 2  with pasturelands for our I."                                989
     22: 8  with large herds of I, with silver, gold,                    5238
Jdg  18:21  their I and their possessions in front                       5238
1Sa  23: 5  the Philistines and carried off their I.                     5238
     30:20  his men drove them ahead of the other I,                     5238
1Ch   5: 9  because their I had increased in Gilead.                     5238
      5:21  They seized the I of the Hagrites—                           5238
      7:21  when they went down to seize their I.                        5238
     28: 1  and I belonging to the king and his sons,                    5238
2Ch  26:10  because he had much I in the foothills and                   5238
Ezr   1: 4  with silver and gold, with goods and I,                      989
      1: 6  with goods and I, and with valuable gifts,                   989
Ps   78:48  their I to bolts of lightning.                               5238
Eze  38:12  from the nations, rich in I and goods,                       5238
     38:13  to take away I and goods and                                 5238
Zec   2: 4  because of the great number of men and I                     989
```

LIVING (323) [LIVE]

```
Ge    1:20  "Let the water teem with I creatures,                        2645
      1:21  and every I and moving thing with which                      2645
      1:24  the land produce I creatures according                       2645
      1:28  and over every I creature that moves on                      2651
      2: 7  and the man became a I being.                                2645
      2:19  whatever the man called each I creature,                     2645
      3:20  she would become the mother of all the I.                    2645
      6:19  to bring into the ark two of all I creatures,                2644
      7: 4  the earth every I creature I have made.                      3685
      7:16  in were male and female of every I thing,                    1414
      7:21  Every I thing that moved on the earth                        1414
      7:23  Every I thing on the face of the earth                       3685
      8:17  Bring out every kind of I creature that is                   2651
      8:21  never again will I destroy all I creatures,                  2645
      9:10  with every I creature that was with you—                     2651
      9:10  every I creature on earth.                                   2651
      9:12  and every I creature with you, a covenant                    2651
      9:15  and you and all I creatures of every kind.                   2651
      9:16  and all I creatures of every kind on                         2651
     13: 7  The Canaanites and Perizzites were also I                    3782
     14: 7  as well as the Amorites who were I                           3782
     14:12  since he was I in Sodom.                                      3782
     14:13  Now Abram was I near the great trees                         8905
     16: 3  Abram had been I in Canaan ten years,                        3782
     19:25  including all those I in the cities—                         3782
     21:21  While he was I in the Desert of Paran,                       3782
     21:23  the country where you are I as an alien                      1591
     24: 3  the Canaanites, among whom I am I,                           3782
     24:62  for he was I in the Negev.                                   3782
     25: 6  But while he was still I,                                    2645
     27:46  with I because of these Hittite women.                       2645
     27:46  life will not be worth I."                       2644+4200+4537
     34:30  and Perizzites, the people I in this land.                   3782
     35:22  While Israel was I in that region,                          8905
     36:20  who were I in the region:                                    3782
     43: 7  'Is your father still I?'                                    2645
     43:27  Is he still I?"                                              2645
     45: 3  Is my father still I?"                                       2645
     46:31  who were I in the land of Canaan,                             AIT
Ex    3:22  and any woman I in her house for articles                    1591
     12:48  "An alien I among you who wants                              1591
     12:49  to the native-born and to the alien I                        1591
Lev  11: 9  the creatures I in the water of the seas and                  NIH
     11:10  or among all the other I creatures in                        2651
     11:12  Anything I in the water that does                             NIH
     11:46  every I thing that moves in the water                        2651
     11:47  between I creatures that may be eaten                        2651
     16:29  whether native-born or an alien I                            1591
     17: 8  or any alien I among them who offers                         1591
     17:10  " 'Any Israelite or any alien I                              1591
     17:12  nor may an alien I among you eat blood."                     1591
     17:13  " 'Any Israelite or any alien I                              1591
```

Lev	18:18	with her while your wife is l.	2644
	18:26	the aliens l among you must not do any	1591
	19:34	The alien l with you must be treated	1591
	20: 2	or any alien l in Israel who gives any	1591
	22:18	either an Israelite or an alien l in Israel—	NIH
	25:45	also buy some of the temporary residents l	1591
	25:47	and sells himself to the alien l among you	9369
Nu	9:14	" 'An alien l among you who wants	1591
	13:32	land we explored devours those l in it.	3782
	14:25	Since the Amalekites and Canaanites are l	3782
	15:14	or anyone else l among you presents	1591
	15:15	the same rules for you and for the alien l	1591
	15:16	to you and to the alien l among you.' "	1591
	15:26	the aliens l among them will be forgiven,	1591
	16:48	He stood between the l and the dead,	2645
	19:10	both for the Israelites and for the aliens l	1591
	30: 3	"When a young woman still l	NIH
	30:10	a woman l with her husband makes a vow	1074
	30:16	and his young daughter still l in his house.	NIH
	35:15	and any other people l among them,	9369
Dt	5:26	the voice of the l God speaking out of fire,	2645
	11: 6	their tents and every l thing that belonged	3685
	11:30	in the territory of those Canaanites l in	3782
	11:31	you have taken it over and are l there,	3782
	14: 9	Of all the creatures l in the water,	NIH
	14:21	You may give it to an alien l in any	NIH
	14:27	do not neglect the Levites l in your towns,	NIH
	16:11	the aliens, the fatherless and the widows l	NIH
	17: 2	If a man or woman l among you in one of	NIH
	18: 6	in Israel where he is l,	1591
	24:14	a brother Israelite or an alien l in one	NIH
	25: 5	If brothers are l together and one	3782
	29:11	and the aliens l in your camps	NIH
	31:12	and the aliens l in your towns—	NIH
Jos	3:10	how you will know that the l God is	2645
	6:21	with the sword every l thing in it—	889S
	9:11	and all those l in our country said to us,	3782
	9:16	that they were neighbors, l near them.	3782
	10: 1	of peace with Israel and were l near them.	2118
	11:19	Except for the Hivites l in Gibeon,	3782
	15:15	against the people l in Debir	3782
	15:63	who were l in Jerusalem;	3782
	16:10	not dislodge the Canaanites l in Gezer;	3782
	17: 7	to include the people l at En Tappuah.	3782
	20: 9	Any of the Israelites or any alien l	1591
	24:15	Amorites, in whose land you are l.	3782
Jdg	1: 1	down to fight against the Canaanites l in	3782
	1:10	They advanced against the Canaanites l	3782
	1:11	against the people l in Debir	3782
	1:17	and attacked the Canaanites l in Zephath,	3782
	1:21	the Jebusites, who were l in Jerusalem;	3782
	1:29	the Canaanites l in Gezer,	3782
	1:30	the Canaanites l in Kitron or Nahalol,	3782
	1:31	Nor did Asher drive out those l in Acco	3782
	1:33	Neither did Naphtali drive out those l in	3782
	1:33	of the land, and those l in Beth Shemesh	3782
	3: 3	the Hivites l in the Lebanon mountains	3782
	6: 4	and did not spare a l thing for Israel,	4695
	10:18	be the head of all those l in Gilead."	3782
	17: 7	who had been l within the clan of Judah,	1591
	18: 7	where they saw that the people were l	3782
	19:16	who was l in Gibeah (the men of the place	1591
	20:15	chosen men from those l in Gibeah.	3782
	21:10	and put to the sword those l there,	3782
	21:12	They found among the people l in	3782
Ru	1: 7	the place where she had been l and set out	2118
	2:20	not stopped showing his kindness to the l	2645
	4:17	women l there said, "Naomi has a son."	8907
1Sa	17:26	he should defy the armies of the l God?"	2645
	17:36	he has defied the armies of the l God.	2645
	25:29	be bound securely in the bundle of the l	2645
2Sa	7: 2	"Here I am, l in a palace of cedar,	3782
	12:18	"While the child was still l,	2645
	15: 8	While your servant was l at Geshur	3782
	20: 3	in confinement till the day of their death, l	2654
1Ki	3:22	The l one is my son;	2645
	3:22	The dead one is yours; the l one is mine."	2645
	3:25	the l child in two and give half to one	2645
	3:26	"Please, my lord, give her the l baby!	2645
	3:27	"Give the l baby to the first woman.	2645
	12:17	for the Israelites who were l in the towns	3782
	13:11	there was a certain old prophet l in Bethel,	3782
2Ki	19: 4	has sent to ridicule the l God,	2645
	19:16	Sennacherib has sent to insult the l God.	2645
1Ch	8: 6	who were heads of families of those l in	3782
	8:13	who were heads of families of those l in	3782
	12:15	and they put to flight everyone l in	AIT
	17: 1	"Here I am, l in a palace of cedar,	3782
	22: 2	to assemble the aliens l in Israel,	928
2Ch	10:17	for the Israelites who were l in the towns	3782
	31: 4	He ordered the people l in Jerusalem	3782
Ezr	1: 4	now be l are to provide him with silver	1591
	4:17	the rest of their associates l in Samaria	10338
Ne	3:26	and the temple servants l on the hill	3782
	3:30	made repairs opposite his l quarters.	5969
	11:30	So they were l all the way from Beersheba	2837
Est	9:19	rural Jews—those l in villages—	3782
Job	22: 8	an honored man, l on it.	3782
	28:13	it cannot be found in the land of the l.	2645
	28:21	It is hidden from the eyes of every l thing,	2645
	30:23	to the place appointed for all the l.	2645
Ps	27:13	of the LORD in the land of the l.	2645
	42: 2	My soul thirsts for God, for the l God.	2645
	52: 5	he will uproot you from the land of the l.	2645
	65: 4	Those l far away fear your wonders;	3782
	84: 2	and my flesh cry out for the l God.	2645
	104:25	l things both large and small.	2651
Ps	116: 9	before the LORD in the land of the l.	2645
	119: 9	By l according to your word.	9068
	142: 5	my portion in the land of the l."	2645
	143: 2	for no one l is righteous before you.	2645
	145:16	and satisfy the desires of every l thing.	2645
Ecc	4: 2	are happier than the l, who are still alive.	2645
	7: 2	The living take this to heart.	2645
	7:15	a wicked man l long in his wickedness.	799
	9: 4	Anyone who is among the l has hope—	2645
	9: 5	For the l know that they will die,	2645
Isa	4: 3	all who are recorded among the l	2645
	8:19	Why consult the dead on behalf of the l?	2645
	9: 2	on those l in the land of the shadow	3782
	33:24	No one l in Zion will say, "I am ill";	8907
	37: 4	has sent to ridicule the l God,	2645
	37:17	Sennacherib has sent to insult the l God.	2645
	38:11	the LORD, in the land of the l;	2645
	38:19	The l, the living—they praise you,	2645
	38:19	The living, the l—they praise you,	2645
	53: 8	For he was cut off from the land of the l;	2645
Jer	2:13	forsaken me, the spring of l water,	2645
	10:10	he is the l God, the eternal King.	2645
	11:19	let us cut him off from the land of the l,	2645
	13:13	the prophets and all those l in Jerusalem.	3782
	17:13	forsaken the LORD, the spring of l water.	2645
	17:20	and all people of Judah and everyone l in	3782
	17:25	by the men of Judah and those l in	3782
	18:11	and those l in Jerusalem, 'This is what	3782
	23:36	and so you distort the words of the l God,	2645
	25: 2	of Judah and to all those l in Jerusalem:	3782
	35:17	to bring on Judah and on everyone l in	3782
	36:31	and those l in Jerusalem and the people	3782
	44: 1	to Jeremiah concerning all the Jews l	3782
	44:15	the people l in Lower and Upper Egypt,	3782
	44:26	all Jews l in Egypt:	3782
	44:26	'that no one from Judah l anywhere	NIH
La	3:39	Why should any l man complain	2645
Eze	1: 5	what looked like four l creatures.	2651
	1:13	of the l creatures was like burning coals	2651
	1:15	As I looked at the l creatures,	2651
	1:19	When the l creatures moved,	2651
	1:19	the l creatures rose from the ground,	2651
	1:20	spirit of the l creatures was in the wheels.	2651
	1:21	spirit of the l creatures was in the wheels.	2651
	1:22	of the l creatures was what looked like	2651
	3:13	the l creatures brushing against each other	2651
	3:15	And there, where they were l,	3782
	10:15	These were the l creatures I had seen by	2651
	10:17	the spirit of the l creatures was in them.	2651
	10:20	the l creatures I had seen beneath the God	2651
	12: 2	you are l among a rebellious people.	3782
	12:19	about those l in Jerusalem and in the land	3782
	14: 7	or any alien l in Israel separates himself	1591
	15: 6	so will I treat the people l in Jerusalem,	3782
	18: 4	For every l soul belongs to me,	5883
	20:38	of the land where they are l,	4472
	26:20	or take your place in the land of the l,	2645
	32:23	in the land of the l are slain,	2645
	32:24	the land of the l went down uncircumcised	2645
	32:25	their terror had spread in the land of the l	2645
	32:26	spread their terror in the land of the l.	2645
	32:27	stalked through the land of the l.	2645
	32:32	I had him spread terror in the land of the l,	2645
	33:24	the people l in those ruins in the land	3782
	36:17	people of Israel were l in their own land,	3782
	38:11	of them l without walls and without gates	3782
	38:12	l at the center of the land."	3782
	38:14	when my people Israel are l in safety,	3782
	47: 9	Swarms of l creatures will live wherever	2651
Da	2:30	I have greater wisdom than other l men,	10261
	4:17	so that the l may know that the Most High	10261
	6:20	servant of the l God, has your God,	10261
	6:26	he is the l God and he endures forever;	10261
Hos	1:10	they will be called 'sons of the l God.'	2645
Hag	1: 4	"Is it a time for you yourselves to be l	3782
Zec	14: 8	On that day l water will flow out	2645
Mt	4:16	the people l in darkness have seen	2764
	4:16	on those l in the land of the shadow	2764
	16:16	the Son of the l God."	2409
	22:32	He is not the God of the dead but of the l."	2409
	26:63	I charge you under oath by the l God:	2409
Mk	12:27	He is not the God of the dead, but of the l.	2409
Lk	1:79	on those l in darkness and in the shadow	NIG
	2: 8	And there were shepherds l out in	64
	13: 4	the others l in Jerusalem?	2997
	15:13	and there squandered his wealth in wild l.	2409
	20:38	He is not the God of the dead, but of the l,	2409
	24: 5	"Why do you look for the l among	2409
Jn	4:10	and he would have given you l water."	2409
	4:11	Where can you get this l water?	2409
	4:51	with the news that his boy was l.	2409
	6:51	I am the l bread that came down from heaven.	2409
	6:57	the l Father sent me and I l because of	2409
	7:38	of l water will flow from within him."	2409
	14:10	Rather, it is the Father, l in me,	3531
Ac	4:16	"Everybody l in Jerusalem knows they have done an outstanding miracle,	2997
	7: 4	to this land where you are now l.	2997
	7:38	and he received l words to pass on to us.	2409
	9:22	and more powerful and baffled the Jews l	2997
	9:31	l in the fear of the Lord.	4513
	10:42	as judge of the l and the dead.	2409
	11:29	to provide help for the brothers l in Judea.	2997
	14:15	from these worthless things to the l God,	2409
	19:17	to the Jews and Greeks l in Ephesus,	2997
	21:24	you yourself are l in obedience to the law.	5123
Ac	22:12	highly respected by all the Jews l there.	2997
Ro	7:17	but it is sin l in me.	3861
	7:20	but it is sin l in me that does it.	3861
	8:11	who raised Jesus from the dead is l in you,	3861
	9:26	they will be called 'sons of the l God.' "	2409
	12: 1	to offer your bodies as l sacrifices,	2409
	14: 9	be the Lord of both the dead and the l.	2409
1Co	9: 6	I and Barnabas who must work for a l?	2237
	9:14	should receive their l from the gospel.	2409
	15: 6	most of whom are still l,	3531
	15:45	"The first man Adam became a l being";	2409
2Co	3: 3	with ink but with the Spirit of the l God,	2409
	6:16	For we are the temple of the l God.	2409
Php	1:22	If I am to go on l in the body,	2409
	4:12	whether l in plenty or in want.	4355
1Th	1: 9	from idols to serve the l and true God,	2409
	4: 1	as in fact you are l.	4344
1Ti	3:15	which is the church of the l God,	2409
	4:10	that we have put our hope in the l God,	2409
2Ti	4: 1	who will judge the l and the dead,	2409
Heb	3:12	that turns away from the l God.	2409
	4:12	For the word of God is l and active.	2409
	7: 8	by him who is declared to be l.	2409
	9:14	so that we may serve the l God!	2409
	9:17	while the one who made it is l.	2409
	10:20	by a new and l way opened for us through	2409
	10:31	to fall into the hands of the l God.	2409
	11:13	All these people were still l by faith	NIG
	12:22	heavenly Jerusalem, the city of the l God.	2409
1Pe	1: 3	into a l hope through the resurrection	2409
	1:23	through the l and enduring word of God.	2409
	2: 4	As you come to him, the l Stone—	2409
	2: 5	also, like l stones, are being built into	2409
	4: 3	l in debauchery, lust, drunkenness, orgies,	4513
	4: 5	to him who is ready to judge the l and	2409
2Pe	2: 8	among them day after day,	1594
Rev	1:18	I am the L One; I was dead, and behold	2409
	4: 6	around the throne, were four l creatures,	2442
	4: 7	The first l creature was like a lion,	2442
	4: 8	Each of the four l creatures had six wings	2442
	4: 9	Whenever the l creatures give glory,	2442
	5: 6	by the four l creatures and the elders.	2442
	5: 8	the four l creatures and the twenty-four	2442
	5:11	and the l creatures and the elders.	2442
	5:14	The four l creatures said, "Amen,"	2442
	6: 1	of the four l creatures say in a voice	2442
	6: 3	I heard the second l creature say,	2442
	6: 5	I heard the third l creature say, "Come!"	2442
	6: 6	like a voice among the four l creatures,	2442
	6: 7	the voice of the fourth l creature say,	2442
	7: 2	having the seal of the l God.	2409
	7:11	around the elders and the four l creatures.	2442
	7:17	he will lead them to springs of l water.	2437
	8: 9	a third of the creatures in the sea died,	2400+3836+6034
	14: 3	before the four l creatures and the elders.	2442
	15: 7	Then one of the four l creatures gave to	2442
	16: 3	and every l thing in the sea died,	2437
	18:17	and all who earn their l from the sea,	2237
	19: 4	and the four l creatures fell down	2442

LIZARD (4)

Lev	11:29	the weasel, the rat, any kind of great l,	7370
	11:30	the monitor l, the wall lizard,	3947
	11:30	the wall l, the skink and the chameleon.	4321
Pr	30:28	a l can be caught with the hand,	8532

LO DEBAR (4)

2Sa	9: 4	house of Makir son of Ammiel in L."	4274
	9: 5	King David had him brought from L,	4274
	17:27	and Makir son of Ammiel from L,	4203
Am	6:13	in the conquest of L and say,	4203

LO-AMMI (1)

Hos	1: 9	Then the LORD said, "Call him L,	4204

LO-RUHAMAH (2)

Hos	1: 6	the LORD said to Hosea, "Call her L,	4205
	1: 8	After she had weaned L,	4205

LOAD (12) [CAMEL-LOADS, LADEN, LOADED, LOADING, LOADS, SPICE-LADEN]

Ge	45:17	L your animals and return to the land	3250
Ex	18:22	That will make your l lighter,	6584
	23: 5	down under its l, do not leave it there;	5362
Ne	13:19	the gates so that no l could be brought in	5362
Job	35: 9	"Men cry out under a l of oppression,	8044
Isa	22:25	and the l hanging on it will be cut down."	5362
Jer	17:21	a l on the Sabbath day or bring it through	5362
	17:22	a l out of your houses or do any work on	5362
	17:24	and bring no l through the gates	5362
	17:27	the Sabbath day holy by not carrying any l	5362
Lk	11:46	woe to you, because you people down	5844
Gal	6: 5	for each one should carry his own l.	5845

LOADED (13) [LOAD]

Ge	37:25	Their camels were l with spices,	5951
	42:26	they l their grain on their donkeys	5951
	44:13	Then they all l their donkeys and returned	6673
	45:23	ten donkeys l with the best things	5951
	45:23	and ten female donkeys l with grain	5951

Jos 9: 4 as a delegation whose donkeys *were* l 4374
1Sa 16:20 So Jesse took a **donkey** l with bread, AIT
    17:20 l **up** and set out, as Jesse had directed. 5951
    25:18 and l them on donkeys. 8492
2Sa 16: 1 and l with two hundred loaves of bread, 6584
Isa 1: 4 Ah, sinful nation, a people l with guilt, 3878
Am 2:13 I will crush you as a cart crushes when l 4849
2Ti 3: 6 *who are* l **down** with sins and are swayed *5397*

LOADING (1) [LOAD]
Ne 13:15 and bringing in grain and l it on donkeys, 6673

LOADS (5) [LOAD]
Ne 13:15 grapes, figs and all other kinds of l. 5362
Job 37:11 *He* l the clouds with moisture; 3267
Ps 144:14 our oxen *will* **draw heavy** l. 6022
La 5:13 boys stagger under l of wood. 6770
Mt 23: 4 They tie up heavy l and put them *5845*

LOAF (9) [LOAVES]
Ex 29:23 which is before the LORD, take a l, 3971+4312
Lev 24: 5 using two-tenths of an ephah for each l. 2705
Jdg 7:13 "A **round** l of barley bread came tumbling 7501
2Sa 6:19 Then he gave a l of bread, 2705
1Ch 16: 3 Then he gave a l of bread, 3971
Pr 6:26 the prostitute reduces you to a l of bread, 3971
Mk 8:14 for one l they had with them in the boat. 788
1Co 10:17 Because there is one l, we, who are many, 788
    10:17 for we all partake of the one l. 788

LOAN (6)
Dt 15: 2 *the* l *he has* **made** to his fellow Israelite. 5957
  24:10 When *you* **make a** l of any kind to your
      neighbor, 5394+5957
  24:11 to whom *you are* **making** *the* l bring 5957
Eze 18: 7 but returns what he took in pledge for a l. 2550
  18:16 or **require** a pledge for a l. 2471+2478
  33:15 gives back **what** he **took in pledge** for a l, 2478

LOATHE (5) [LOATHED, LOATHES, LOATHING, LOATHSOME]
Nu 11:20 comes out of your nostrils and you l it— 2426
Job 10: 1 "I l my very life; 7752
Eze 6: 9 *They will* l themselves for the evil 7752
  20:43 and *you will* l yourselves for all the evil 7752
  36:31 and *you will* l yourselves for your sins 7752

LOATHED (1) [LOATHE]
Ps 107:18 They l all food and drew near the gates 9493

LOATHES (2) [LOATHE]
Job 33:20 and his soul l the choicest meal. NIH
Pr 27: 7 He who is full l honey, 1008

LOATHING (1) [LOATHE]
Ps 119:158 I look on the faithless *with* l, 7752

LOATHSOME (5) [LOATHE]
Job 19:17 *I am* l to my own brothers. 2859
Ps 38: 5 and *are* l because of my sinful folly. 944
Isa 66:24 and they will be l to all mankind." 1994
Jer 6:15 Are they ashamed of their l conduct? 9359
  8:12 Are they ashamed of their l conduct? 9359

LOAVES (32) [LOAF]
Lev 23:17 bring two l made of two-tenths of an ephah 4312
  24: 5 and bake twelve l **of bread,** 2705
1Sa 10: 3 another three l of bread. 3971
  10: 4 They will greet you and offer you two l NIH
  17:17 and these ten l **of bread** for your brothers 4312
  21: 3 Give me five l **of bread,** 4312
  25:18 She took two hundred l **of bread,** 4312
2Sa 16: 1 and loaded with two hundred l **of bread,** 4312
1Ki 14: 3 Take ten l **of bread** with you, 4312
2Ki 4:42 of God twenty l of barley **bread** baked 4312
Mt 14:17 "We have here only five l **of bread** 788
  14:19 the five l and the two fish and looking up 788
  14:19 he gave thanks and broke the l. 788
  15:34 "How many l do you have?" 788
  15:36 Then he took the seven l and the fish, 788
  16: 9 Don't you remember the five l for the five 788
  16:10 Or the seven l for the four thousand, 788
Mk 6:38 "How many l do you have?" 788
  6:41 the five l and the two fish and looking up 788
  6:41 he gave thanks and broke the l. 788
  6:52 for they had not understood about the l; 788
  8: 5 "How many l do you have?" 788
  8: 6 When he had taken the seven l and 788
  8:19 I broke the five l for the five thousand, 788
  8:20 I broke the seven l for the four thousand, NIG
Lk 9:13 "We have only five l **of bread** 788
  9:16 the five l and the two fish and looking up 788
  11: 5 'Friend, lend me three l **of bread,** 788
Jn 6: 9 "Here is a boy with five small barley l 788
  6:11 Jesus then took the l, gave thanks, 788
  6:13 with the pieces of the five barley l left 788
  6:26 but because you ate the l and had your fill. 788

LOBE (6) [LOBES]
Lev 8:23 and put it on the l of Aaron's right ear, 9483
  14:14 of the guilt offering and put it on the l of 9483
  14:17 the oil remaining in his palm on the l of 9483
  14:25 on the l of the right ear of the one to 9483
  14:28 on the l of the right ear of the one to 9483
Dt 15:17 and push it through his **ear** l into the door, 265

LOBES (2) [LOBE]
Ex 29:20 take some of its blood and put it on the l 9483
Lev 8:24 of the blood on the l of their right ears, 9483

LOCAL (2)
Mt 10:17 they will hand you over to the l **councils** 5284
Mk 13: 9 You will be handed over to the l councils NIG

LOCATED (1) [LOCATIONS]
Dt 19: 2 three cities **centrally** l in the land 928+9348

LOCATIONS (1) [LOCATED]
1Ch 6:54 the l of their settlements allotted 3227

LOCK (1) [LOCKED]
SS 5: 5 on the handles of the l. 4980

LOCKED (11) [LOCK]
Jdg 3:23 of the upper room behind him and l them. 5835
  3:24 and found the doors of the upper room l. 5835
  9:51 *They* l themselves in and climbed up on 6037
SS 4:12 You are a garden l **up,** my sister, 5835
Lk 3:20 *He* l John up in prison. 2881
  11: 7 The door *is* already l, 3091
Jn 20:19 with the doors l for fear of the Jews, 3091
  20:26 *Though* the doors *were* l, Jesus came and 3091
Ac 5:23 "We found the jail securely l, with 3091
Gal 3:23 l **up** until faith should be revealed. 5168
Rev 20: 3 Abyss, and l and sealed it over him, 3091

LOCKS (KJV) See BOLTS, BRAIDS, HAIR, VEIL

LOCUST (9) [LOCUSTS]
Ex 10:19 Not a l was left anywhere in Egypt. 746
Lev 11:22 Of these you may eat any kind of l, 746
Job 39:20 Do you make him leap like a l, 746
Ps 78:46 their produce to the l. 746
  109:23 I am shaken off like a l. 746
Joel 1: 4 What the l **swarm** has left 1612
  2:25 the **great** l and the young locust, 746
  2:25 the great locust and the **young** l, 3540
  2:25 the other locusts and the l **swarm**— 1612

LOCUSTS (36) [LOCUST]
Ex 10: 4 I will bring l into your country tomorrow. 746
  10:12 over Egypt so that l will swarm over 746
  10:13 By morning the wind had brought the l; 746
  10:14 before had there been such a plague of l, 746
  10:19 the l and carried them into the Red Sea. 746
Dt 28:38 because l will devour it. 746
  28:42 **Swarms of** l will take over all your trees 7526
Jdg 6: 5 and their tents like swarms of l. 746
  7:12 had settled in the valley, thick as l. 746
1Ki 8:37 or blight or mildew, l or grasshoppers, 746
2Ch 6:28 or blight or mildew, l or grasshoppers, 746
  7:13 or command l to devour the land or send 2506
Ps 105:34 He spoke, and the l came, 746
Pr 30:27 l have no king, yet they advance together 746
Isa 33: 4 O nations, is harvested as by **young** l; 2885
  33: 4 like a swarm of l men pounce on it. 1466
Jer 46:23 They are more numerous than l, 746
  51:14 fill you with men, as with a **swarm of** l, 3540
  51:27 send up horses like a swarm of l. 3540
Joel 1: 4 swarm has left the **great** l have eaten; 746
  1: 4 what the **great** l have left 746
  1: 4 the **young** l have eaten; 3540
  1: 4 **young** l have left other locusts have eaten. 3540
  1: 4 young locusts have eaten other l have eaten. 2885
  2:25 for the years the l have eaten— NIH
  2:25 the other l and the locust swarm— 2885
Am 4: 9 l devoured your fig and olive trees, 1612
  7: 1 He was preparing **swarms of** l after 1479
Na 3:15 like grasshoppers, multiply like l! 746
  3:16 but like l they strip the land and 3540
  3:17 Your guards are like l, 746
  3:17 of l that settle in the walls on a cold day— 1479
Mt 3: 4 His food was l and wild honey. 210
Mk 1: 6 and he ate l and wild honey. 210
Rev 9: 3 out of the smoke l came down upon the earth 210
  9: 7 The l looked like horses prepared for battle. 210

LOD (4)
1Ch 8:12 and L with its surrounding villages, 4254
Ezr 2:33 of L, Hadid and Ono 725 4254
Ne 7:37 of L, Hadid and Ono 721 4254
  11:35 in L and Ono, 4254

LODGE (1) [LODGED, LODGING]
Ps 119:54 the theme of my song wherever I l. 1074+4472

LODGED (1) [LODGE]
Ezr 4: 6 they l an accusation against the people 4180

LODGING (6) [LODGE]
Ex 4:24 At a l place on the way, 4869
Ps 55:15 for evil finds l among them. 4472
Jer 9: 2 I had in the desert a l place for travelers, 4869
Mic 6: 2 *he is* l a **charge** against Israel. 3519
Lk 9:12 and countryside and find food and l, 2907
Jas 2:25 for what she did *when she* **gave** l to *5685*

LOFT (KJV) See STORY, UPPER ROOM

LOFTINESS (1) [LOFTY]
Ps 48: 2 It is beautiful in its l, 5679

LOFTY (19) [LOFTINESS]
Job 22:12 And see how l *are* the highest stars! 8123
Ps 62: 4 to topple him from his l **place;** 8420
  139: 6 too wonderful for me, too l for me to attain. 8435
Isa 2:12 a day in store for all the proud and l, 8123
  2:13 tall and l, and all the oaks of Bashan, 5951
  2:15 for every l tower and every fortified wall, 1469
  10:33 The l trees will be felled, 7757+8123
  26: 5 he lays the l city low; 8435
  30:25 on every high mountain and every l hill. 5951
  57: 7 made your bed on a high and l hill; 5951
  57:15 For this is what the high and l One says— 5951
  63:15 from heaven and see from your l **throne,** 2292
Jer 51:53 the sky and fortifies her l stronghold, 5294
Eze 16:24 and made a l **shrine** in every public square. 8229
  16:25 of every street you built your l **shrines** 8229
  16:31 of every street and made your l **shrines** 8229
  16:39 and destroy your l **shrines.** 8229
  17:22 and plant it on a high and l mountain. 9435
Am 9: 6 he who builds his l **palace** in the heavens 5092

LOG (5) [LOGS]
Lev 14:10 for a grain offering, and one l of oil, 4253
  14:12 as a guilt offering, along with the l of oil; 4253
  14:15 priest shall then take some of the l of oil, 4253
  14:21 for a grain offering, a l of oil, 4253
  14:24 guilt offering, together with the l of oil, 4253

LOGS (10) [LOG]
2Sa 5:11 along with cedar l and carpenters 6770
1Ki 5: 8 in providing the cedar and pine l. 6770
  5:10 with all the cedar and pine l he wanted, 6770
1Ch 14: 1 messengers to David, along with cedar l, 6770
  22: 4 He also provided more cedar l than could 6770
2Ch 2: 3 "Send me cedar l as you did NIH
  2: 8 pine and algum l from Lebanon, 6770
  2:16 and we will cut all the l from Lebanon 6770
Ezr 3: 7 so that they would bring cedar l by sea 6770
Ecc 10: 9 whoever splits l may be endangered 6770

LOINCLOTH (1)
Job 12:18 on by kings and ties a l around their waist. 258

LOINS (7)
Lev 3: 4 with the fat on them near the l, 4072
  3:10 with the fat on them near the l, 4072
  3:15 with the fat on them near the l, 4072
  4: 9 on them near the l, and the covering of 4072
  7: 4 with the fat on them near the l, 4072
Dt 33:11 the l *of* those who rise up against him; 5516
Job 40:16 What strength he has in his l, 5516

LOIS (1)
2Ti 1: 5 which first lived in your grandmother L *3396*

LONELY (4) [ALONE]
Ps 25:16 for I am l and afflicted. 3495
  68: 6 God sets the l in families, 3495
Mk 1:45 but stayed outside in l places. 2245
Lk 5:16 But Jesus often withdrew to l **places** *2245*

LONG (434) [LENGTH, LENGTHEN, LENGTHS, LENGTHWISE, LENGTHY, LONGED, LONGER, LONGING, LONGINGS, LONGS]
Ge 6:15 The ark is to be 450 feet l, 802
  8:22 "As l as the earth endures, 3972+6388
  21:34 in the land of the Philistines for a l time. 8041
  26: 8 When Isaac *had been* there a l time, 799
  38:12 After a l time Judah's wife, 8049
  46:29 around his father and wept *for a* l **time.** 6388
Ex 10: 3 During that l period, the king of Egypt died. 8041
  10: 3 '**How** l will you refuse to humble yourself
      before me? 5503+6330
  10: 7 "**How** l will this man be a snare to us? 5503+6330
  14:20 neither went near the other **all** night l. AIT
  16:28 "**How** l will you refuse to keep 625+2025+6330
  17:11 **As** l **as** Moses held up his hands, 889+3869
  19:13 ram's horn **sounds** a l **blast** may they go 5432
  20:12 so that you *may* **live** l in the land 799+3427
  25:10 two and a half cubits l, 802
  25:17 a half cubits l and a cubit and a half wide. 802

Ex 25:23 two cubits l, a cubit wide and a cubit and 802
26: 2 twenty-eight cubits l and four cubits wide. 802
26: 8 thirty cubits l and four cubits wide. 802
26:16 Each frame is to be ten cubits l and a cubit 802
27: 1 five cubits l and five cubits wide. 802
27: 9 The south side shall be a hundred cubits l 802
27:11 a hundred cubits l and is to have curtains, 802
27:14 Curtains fifteen cubits l are to be NIH
27:15 and curtains fifteen cubits l are to be on NIH
27:16 provide a curtain twenty cubits l, of blue, 802
27:18 The courtyard shall be a hundred cubits l 802
28:16 a span l and a span wide— 802
30: 2 a cubit l and a cubit wide, 802
32: 1 that Moses was so l in coming down from 1018
36: 9 twenty-eight cubits l and four cubits wide. 802
36:15 thirty cubits l and four cubits wide. 802
36:21 Each frame was ten cubits l and a cubit 802
37: 1 two and a half cubits l, 802
37: 6 a half cubits l and a cubit and a half wide. 802
37:10 two cubits l, a cubit wide. 802
37:25 It was square, a cubit l and a cubit wide, 802
38: 1 five cubits l and five cubits wide. 802
38: 9 The south side was a hundred cubits l NIH
38:11 The north side was also a hundred cubits l NIH
38:14 Curtains fifteen cubits l were on one side NIH
38:15 and curtains fifteen cubits l were on NIH
38:18 It was twenty cubits l and, 802
39: 9 a span l and a span wide— 802
Lev 13:46 As l as he has the infection he remains 3427+3972
15:25 unclean as l as she has the discharge, 3427+3972
Nu 6: 4 As l as he is a Nazirite, 3427+3972
6: 5 he must let the hair of his head grow l. 1540
9:18 As l as the cloud stayed over 3427+3972
9:19 cloud remained over the tabernacle a l time, 8041
14:11 "How l will these people treat me with contempt? 625+2025+6330
14:11 How l will they refuse to believe in me, 625+2025+6330
14:27 "How l will this wicked community grumble against me? 5503+6330
36: 9 They may marry anyone they please as l as 421
Dt 1: 6 "You have stayed l enough 8041
2: 1 For a l time we made our way around 8041
2: 3 around this hill country l enough; 8041
3:11 of iron and was more than thirteen feet l 802
4: 9 or let them slip from your heart as l as 3427+3972
4:10 so that they may learn to revere me as l as they live in the land 2021+3427+3972
4:25 and have lived in the land a l time— 3823
4:26 not live there l but will certainly 799+3427
4:32 the former days, l before your time, NIH
4:40 that you may live l in the land 799+3427
5:16 so that you may live l and 799+3427
6: 2 the LORD your God as l as you live 3427+3972
6: 2 and so that you may enjoy l life. 799+3427
11: 9 so that you may live l in the land that 799+3427
12: 1 as l as you live in the land. 2021+3427+3972
12:19 as l as you live in your land. 3427+3972
17:20 and his descendants will reign a l time 799
20:19 When you lay siege to a city for a l time, 8041
22: 7 with you and you may have a l life. 799
22:19 not divorce her as l as he lives. 3427+3972
22:29 never divorce her as l as he lives. 3427+3972
23: 6 with them as l as you live. 3427+3972+4200+6409
25:15 so that you may live l in the land 799+3427
30:18 not live l in the land you are crossing 799+3427
31:13 fear the LORD your God as l as you live in the land 2021+3427+3972
32: 7 consider the generations l past. 1887+1887+2256+9102
32:47 By them you will live l in the land 799+3427
33:12 for he shields him all day l, AIT
Jos 6: 5 When you hear them sound a l blast on 5432
9:13 worn out by the very l journey." 8044
9:22 'We live a l way from you,' 4394+8158
11:18 against all these kings for a l time. 8041
18: 3 "How l will you wait before you 625+2025+6330
22: 3 For a l time now— 8041
23: 1 After a l time had passed and 8041
24: 2 'L ago your forefathers, 4946+6409
24: 7 Then you lived in the desert for a l time. 8041
Jdg 2:18 of their enemies as l as the judge lived; 3972
3:16 sword about a foot and a half l, 802
5:28 'Why is his chariot so l in coming? 1018
18: 7 they lived a l way from the Sidonians 8158
18:28 to rescue them because they lived a l way 8158
1Sa 1:14 How l will you keep on getting drunk? 5503+6330
7: 2 It was a l time, twenty years in all, 8049
10:24 the people shouted, "L live the king!" 2649
16: 1 "How l will you mourn for Saul, 5503+6330
20:14 like that of the LORD as l as I live, 561+6388
20:31 As l as the son of Jesse lives on this earth, 2021+3427+3972
22: 4 they stayed with him as l as David 3427+3972
25: 6 Say to him: 'L life to you! 2021+2644+4200
25:28 Let no wrongdoing be found in you as l as 4946
27:11 And such was his practice as l as he lived 2021+3427+3972
2Sa 2:26 How l before you order your men 5503+6330
3: 1 and the house of David lasted a l time. 801
16:16 "L live the king! 2649
16:16 L live the king!" 2649
20:18 "L ago they used to say, 928+2021+8037
1Ki 1:25 'L live King Adonijah!' 2649
1:34 'L live King Solomon!' 2649
1:39 'L live King Solomon!" 2649
2:38 Shimei stayed in Jerusalem for a l time. 8041

1Ki 3:11 and not for l life or wealth for yourself, 8041
3:14 I will give you a l life." 799
6: 2 for the LORD was sixty cubits l, 802
6:17 in front of this room was forty cubits l. NIH
6:20 The inner sanctuary was twenty cubits l, 802
6:24 of the first cherub was five cubits l, and NIH
7: 2 the Forest of Lebanon a hundred cubits l, 802
7: 6 a colonnade fifty cubits l and thirty wide. 802
7:27 each was four cubits l, 802
8: 8 These poles were so l that their ends could 799
11:25 adversary as l as Solomon lived, 3427+3972
18: 1 After a l time, in the third year, 8041
18:21 "How l will you waver 5503+6330
22:35 All day l the battle raged, 928+2021+2021+2085+3427
2Ki 6:25 the siege lasted so l that 6330
9:22 "as l as all the idolatry and witchcraft 6330
11:12 "L live the king!" 2649
13: 3 for a l time he kept them under the power 3972
14:13 a section about six hundred feet l. NIH
19:25 L ago I ordained it. 4200+4946+8158
25:30 a regular allowance as l as he lived. 3427+3972
1Ch 29:28 enjoyed l life, wealth and honor. 3427+8428
2Ch 1:11 for a l life but for wisdom and knowledge 8041
3: 3 the temple of God was sixty cubits l 802
3: 4 the front of the temple was twenty cubits l 802
3: 8 twenty cubits l and twenty cubits wide. NIH
3:11 of the first cherub was five cubits l NIH
3:11 while its other wing, also five cubits l, NIH
3:12 of the second cherub was five cubits l, NIH
3:12 and its other wing, also five cubits l, NIH
3:15 which [together] were thirty-five cubits l, 802
4: 1 He made a bronze altar twenty cubits l, 802
5: 9 These poles were so l that their ends, 799
6:13 a bronze platform, five cubits l, 802
15: 3 a l time Israel was without the true God, 8041
18:34 All day l the battle raged, 928+2021+2021+2085+3427
23:11 "L live the king!" 2649
24:14 As l as Jehoiada lived, burnt offerings 3427+3972
25:23 a section about six hundred feet l. NIH
26: 5 As l as he sought the LORD, God gave 928+3427
34:33 As l as he lived, they did not fail 3427+3972
Ezr 4:19 city has a l history of revolt 10317+10427+10550
Ne 2: 6 "How l will your journey take, 5503+6330
12:46 For l ago, in the days of David 4946+7710
Est 5:13 gives me no satisfaction as l as 928+3972+6961
Job 3:21 to those who l for death that does 2675
7: 4 I lie down I think, 'How l before I get up?' 5503
8: 2 "How l will you say such things? 625+6330
12:12 Does not l life bring understanding? 802
12:19 and overthrows men l established. 419
14:15 you will l for the creature your hands have 4083
19: 2 "How l will you torment me and 625+2025+6330
27: 3 as l as I have life within me, 3972+6388
27: 6 will not reproach me as l as I live. 3427+4946
29: 2 How l for the months gone by, 4769+5761+5989
36:20 Do not l for the night, 8634
Ps 4: 2 How l, O men, will you turn my glory 4537+6330
4: 2 How l will you love delusions NIH
6: 3 How l, O LORD, how long? 5503+6330
6: 3 How long, O LORD, how l? NIH
6: 6 all night l I flood my bed with weeping AIT
13: 1 How l, O LORD? 625+2025+6330
13: 1 How l will you hide your face from me? 625+2025+6330
13: 2 How l must I wrestle with my thoughts 625+2025+6330
13: 2 How l will my enemy triumph over me? 625+2025+6330
25: 5 and my hope is in you all day l. AIT
32: 3 through my groaning all day l. AIT
35:17 O Lord, how l will you look on? 3869+4537
35:28 and of your praises all day l. AIT
38: 6 all day l I go about mourning. AIT
38:12 all day l they plot deception. AIT
39: 1 I will put a muzzle on my mouth as l as 928+6388
42: 3 while men say to me all day l, AIT
42:10 saying to me all day l, AIT
44: 1 in their days, in days l ago. 7710
44: 8 In God we make our boast all day l, AIT
44:15 My disgrace is before me all day l, AIT
44:22 Yet for your sake we face death all day l; AIT
52: 1 Why do you boast all day l, AIT
56: 1 all day l they press their attack. AIT
56: 2 My slanderers pursue me all day l; AIT
56: 5 All day l they twist my words; AIT
61: 4 I l to dwell in your tent forever AIT
62: 3 How l will you assault a man? 625+2025+6330
63: 4 I will praise you as l as I live, 928
71: 8 declaring your splendor all day l. AIT
71:15 of your salvation all day l, AIT
71:24 of your righteous acts all day l, AIT
72: 5 He will endure as l as the sun, 6640
72: 5 as long as the sun, as l as the moon, 4200+7156
72:15 L may he live! 2649
72:15 for him and bless him all day l. AIT
72:17 may it continue as l as the sun. 4200+7156
73:14 All day l I have been plagued; AIT
74: 1 none of us knows how l this will be. 4537+6330
74:10 How l will the enemy mock you, O God? 5503+6330
74:22 remember how fools mock you all day l. AIT
77: 5 the former days, the years l ago; 6409
77:11 I will remember your miracles of l ago. 7710
79: 5 How l, O LORD? 4537+6330
79: 5 How l will your jealousy burn like fire? NIH

Ps 80: 4 how l will your anger smolder against 5503+6330
82: 2 "How l will you defend the unjust 5503+6330
86: 3 O Lord, for I call to you all day l. AIT
88:17 All day l they surround me like a flood; AIT
89:16 They rejoice in your name all day l; AIT
89:29 as l as the heavens endure. 3427+3869
89:46 How l, O LORD? Will you hide yourself forever? 4537+6330
89:46 How l will your wrath burn like fire? NIH
90:13 How l will it be? 5503+6330
91:16 With l life will I satisfy him 802
93: 2 Your throne was established l ago; 255+4946
94: 3 How l will the wicked, O LORD, 5503+6330
94: 3 how l will the wicked be jubilant? 5503+6330
102: 8 All day l my enemies taunt me; AIT
104:33 sing praise to my God as l as I live. 928+6388
116: 2 I will call on him as l as I live. 928
119:40 How I l for your precepts! 9289
119:84 "How l must your servant wait? 3427+3869+4537
119:97 I meditate on it all day l. AIT
119:152 L ago I learned from your statutes 7710
119:174 I l for your salvation, O LORD, 9289
120: 6 Too l have I lived among those who hate 8041
129: 3 and made their furrows l. 799
143: 3 in darkness like those l dead. 6409
143: 5 I remember the days of l ago; 7710
146: 2 sing praise to my God as l as I live. 928+6388
Pr 1:22 "How l will you simple ones love your simple ways? 5503+6330
1:22 How l will mockers delight in mockery NIH
3:16 L life is in her right hand; 802
6: 9 How l will you lie there, you sluggard? 5503+6330
7:19 he has gone on a l journey. 4946+8158
21:26 All day l he craves for more, AIT
28:16 he who hates ill-gotten gain will enjoy a l life. 799+3427
Ecc 1:10 It was here already, l ago; 4200+6409
2:16 the fool, will not be l remembered; 4200+6409
6: 3 yet no matter how l he lives, 8041
7:15 a wicked man living l in his wickedness. 799
8:12 a hundred crimes and still lives a l time, 799
9: 6 and their jealousy have l since vanished; 3893
SS 3: 1 All night l on my bed I looked 928+2021+4326
Isa 6:11 Then I said, "For how l, O Lord?" 5503+6330
6:11 for the One who planned it l ago. 4946+8158
25: 1 things planned l ago. 4946+8158
30:33 Topheth has l been prepared; 919+4946
33: 2 O LORD, be gracious to us; we l for you. 7747
37:26 L ago I ordained it. 4200+4946+8158
42:14 "For a l time I have kept silent, 6409
44: 8 not proclaim this and foretell it l ago? 255+4946
45:21 Who foretold this l ago, 4946+7710
46: 9 Remember the former things, those of l ago; 6409
48: 3 I foretold the former things, 255+4946
48: 5 Therefore I told you these things l ago; 255+4946
48: 7 They are created now, and not l ago; 255+4946
52: 5 all day l my name is constantly blasphemed. AIT
57:11 because I have been silent that you 4946+6409
61: 4 and restore the places l devastated; 8037
65: 2 All day l I have held out my hands to AIT
65:22 my chosen ones will l enjoy the works 1162
Jer 2:20 "L ago you broke off your yoke 4946+6409
4:14 How l will you harbor wicked thoughts? 5503+6330
4:21 How l must I see the battle standard 5503+6330
6: 4 and the shadows of evening grow l. 5742
12: 4 How l will the land lie parched and 5503+6330
13:27 How l will you be unclean?" 339+5503+6388
20: 7 I am ridiculed all day l; AIT
20: 8 brought me insult and reproach all day l. AIT
22:27 to the land you l to return to." 5883+5951
23:26 How l will this continue in the hearts 5503+6330
29:28 It will be a l time. 801
31:22 How l will you wander, 5503+6330
32:14 in a clay jar so they will last a l time. 8041
35: 7 Then you will live a l time in the land 8041
37:16 where he remained a l time. 8041
44:14 to which they l to return and live; 5883+5951
47: 5 how l will you cut yourselves? 5503+6330
47: 6 'how l till you rest? 625+2025+6330
52:34 a regular allowance as l as he lived, 3427+3972
La 1:13 He made me desolate, faint all the day l. AIT
2:17 which he decreed l ago. 3427+4946+7710
3: 3 against me again and again, all day l. AIT
3: 6 in darkness like those l dead. 6409
3:14 they mock me in song all day l. AIT
3:62 and mutter against me all day l. AIT
5:20 Why do you forsake us so l? 802+3427
Eze 7:13 not recover the land he has sold as l as 6388
17: 3 with powerful wings, l feathers 800
26:20 to the people of l ago. 6409
31: 5 and its branches grew l, 799
38: 8 which had l been desolate. 9458
40: 5 rod in the man's hand was six cubits, 564
40: 7 The alcoves for the guards were one rod l 802
40:18 and was as wide as they were l; 802
40:25 It was fifty cubits l and twenty-five cubits 802
40:29 It was fifty cubits l and twenty-five cubits 802
40:33 It was fifty cubits l and twenty-five cubits 802
40:36 It was fifty cubits l and twenty-five cubits 802
40:42 each a cubit and a half l, 802
40:43 each a handbreadth l, NIH
40:47 a square—a hundred cubits l and 802
41: 2 it was forty cubits l 802
41: 8 It was the length of the rod, six cubits. 723
41:13 it was a hundred cubits l, 802

Eze	41:13	also a hundred cubits **l**.	802

Eze 41:13 also a hundred cubits **l**. 802
42: 2 a hundred cubits **l** and fifty cubits wide. 802
42: 4 and a hundred cubits **l**. 2006
42: 8 to the outer court was fifty cubits **l**, 802
42: 8 the sanctuary was a hundred cubits **l**. NIH
42:20 five hundred cubits **l** 802
43:13 the measurements of the altar in **l cubits**. 564
43:16 twelve cubits **l** and twelve cubits wide. 802
43:17 fourteen cubits **l** and fourteen cubits wide, 802
44:20 or let their **hair** grow **l**, 7279
45: 1 25,000 cubits **l** and 20,000 cubits wide; 802
45: 3 25,000 cubits **l** and 10,000 cubits wide. 802
45: 5 An area 25,000 cubits **l** and 10,000 802
45: 6 25,000 cubits **l**, adjoining the sacred portion; 802
46:22 forty cubits **l** and thirty cubits wide; 802
48: 9 25,000 cubits **l** and 10,000 cubits wide. 802
48:10 It will be 25,000 cubits **l** on the north side. NIH
48:10 25,000 cubits **l** on the south side. 802
48:13 25,000 cubits **l** and 10,000 cubits wide. 802
48:15 5,000 cubits wide and 25,000 cubits **l**, NIH
48:30 which is 4,500 cubits **l**, 4500
48:32 "On the east side, which is 4,500 cubits **l**, NIH
48:34 "On the west side, which is 4,500 cubits **l**, NIH
Da 8: 3 and the horns were **l**. 1469
8:13 "How **l** will it take *for* the vision to 5503+6330
12: 6 "How **l** will it be before these 5503+6330
Hos 7:13 **l l** *to* redeem them but they speak lies AIT
8: 5 How **l** will they be incapable of purity? 5503
Am 5:18 to *you* who **l** for the day of the LORD! 203
5:18 Why do you **l** for the day of the LORD? 2296S
Mic 7:14 in Bashan and Gilead as in days **l ago**. 6409
7:20 on oath to our fathers in days **l ago**. 7710
Hab 1: 2 How **l**, O LORD, must I call for help, 625+2025+6330
2: 6 How **l** must this go on?' 5503+6330
Zec 1:12 how **l** will you withhold mercy 5503+6330
2: 2 to find out how wide and how **l** it is." 802
5: 2 thirty feet **l** and fifteen feet wide." 802
Mt 5:21 that it was said *to* the **people l ago**, 792
5:33 that it was said *to* the **people l ago**, 792
11:21 they would have repented **l ago** 4093
17:17 Jesus replied, "how **l** shall I stay with you? 2401+4536
17:17 How **l** shall I put up with you? 2401+4536
20: 6 'Why have you been standing here all **day l** AIT
23: 5 and the tassels on their **garments l**; 3486
24:48 'My master *is* **staying away a l time**,' 5988
25: 5 The bridegroom *was* a **l time in coming**, 5988
25:19 "After a **l** time the master 4498
Mk 2:19 so **l** as they have him with them. 4012+5989
6:15 like one of the prophets of **l** ago." NIG
8: 3 some of them have come a **l distance**." 3427
9:19 "how **l** shall I stay with you? 4536
9:19 How **l** shall I put up with you? 4536
9:21 "How **l** has he been like this?" 5989
Lk 1:21 and wondering why he **stayed so l** in 5988
1:70 through his holy prophets of **l ago**), 172
8:27 *For* a **l** time this man had not worn clothes 2653
9: 8 of the prophets of **l ago** had come back 792
9:19 of the prophets of **l ago** has come back 792
9:41 "how **l** shall I stay with you and put up 4536
10:13 they would have repented **l ago**, 4093
12:45 'My master *is* **taking a l time** in coming,' 5988
13:16 Satan has kept bound for eighteen **l**ong years, NIG
14:32 the other is still a **l way off** and will ask 4522
15:13 "Not **l** after that, the younger son 2465+4498
15:20 "But while he was still a **l way off**, 3426
17:22 when *you* will **l** to see one of the days of 2121
20: 9 and went away for a **l** time. 2653
23: 8 a **l** time he had been wanting to see him. 2653
Jn 5: 6 in this condition *for* a **l** time, 4498
9: 4 As **l** as it is day, we must do the work of 2401
10:24 "How **l** will you keep us in suspense? 2401+4536
14: 9 I have been among you such a **l** time? NIG
14:19 Before **l**, the world will not see me 2285+3625
Ac 1:16 the Holy Spirit **spoke l ago** through 4625
3:21 as he promised **l ago** through his holy 172+608
8:11 because he had amazed them *for* a **l** time 2653
14:28 And they stayed there a **l** time 3900+4024+5989
24: 2 "We have enjoyed a **l period** of peace 4498
26: 5 They have known me **for** a **l** time 540
26:29 Paul replied, "Short time or **l**— 3489
27:14 Before very **l**, a wind of 3552+4024+4498
27:21 the men had gone a **l** time without food, 4498
28: 6 but after waiting a **l** time 2093+4498
Ro 1:11 **l l** to see you so that I may impart 2160
7: 1 over a man only as **l** as he lives? 2093+4012+5989
7: 2 bound to her husband **l** *as* he is, AIT
8:36 "For your sake we face death all **day l**; AIT
10:21 "**All day l** I have held out my hands to 3910
16:25 of the mystery hidden for **l** ages past, 5989
1Co 7:39 bound to her husband **as l as** 2093+4012+5989
11:14 of things teach you that if a man **has l hair**, 3150
11:15 but that if a woman **has l hair**, 3150
11:15 For **l hair** is given to her as a covering. 3151
2Co 5: 2 as **l** *as we are* **at home** in the body AIT
Gal 4: 1 that as **l** as the heir is a child, 2093+4012+5989
Eph 3:18 how wide and **l** and high and deep is 3601
6: 3 and that *you may* **enjoy l life** on 1639+3432
Php 1: 8 how **l l** for all of you with the affection 2160
4: 1 my brothers, you whom I love and **l for**, 2162
1Th 3: 6 and that *you* **l** to see us, just as we also 2160
3: 6 just as we also **l** to see you. NIG
2Ti 1: 4 Recalling your tears, **l l** to see you, 2160
Heb 3:13 **as l as** it is called Today, 948+4005
4: 7 a **l** time later he spoke through David, 5537
9: 8 **as l as** the first tabernacle was **still** 2285

1Pe 1:12 Even angels **l** to look into these things. 2121
3:20 who disobeyed **l ago** when God waited NIG
2Pe 1:13 refresh your memory **as l as** I live in 2093+4012
2: 3 Their condemnation has **l** been hanging 1732
3: 5 But they deliberately forget that **l ago** 1732
Jude 1: 4 written about **l ago** have secretly slipped in 4093
Rev 6:10 called out in a loud voice, "How **l**, 2401+4536
9: 6 *they will* **l** to die, but death will elude them. 2121
21:16 like a square, as **l** as it was wide. 3601
21:16 and as wide and high as it is **l**. 3601

LONG-SUFFERING (1) [SUFFER]
Jer 15:15 You are **l**—do not take me away; 678+800

LONG-WINDED (1) [WIND]
Job 16: 3 Will your **l** speeches never end? 8120

LONGED (13) [LONG]
Ge 31:30 Now you have gone off because *you* **l** 4083+4083
2Sa 13:39 the spirit of the king **l** to go to Absalom, 3983
14: 1 knew that the king's heart **l** for Absalom. 6584
23:15 David **l** for water and said, "Oh, 203
1Ch 11:17 David **l** for water and said, "Oh, 203
Isa 21: 4 the twilight I **l** for has become a horror 3139
Eze 23:21 So *you* **l** for the lewdness of your youth, 7212
Mt 13:17 and righteous men **l** to see what you see 2121
23:37 how often I *have* **l** to gather your children 2527
Lk 13:34 how often I *have* **l** to gather your children 2527
15:16 *He* **l** to fill his stomach with the pods that 2121
2Ti 4: 8 also *to* all who *have* **l** for his appearing. 26
Rev 18:14 'The fruit you **l** for is gone from you. 2123

LONGER (197) [LONG]
Ge 4:12 it will no **l** yield its crops for you. 3578
17: 5 No **l** will you be called Abram; 6388
17:15 you are **no l** to call her Sarai; AIT
27: 1 so weak *that* he could no **l** see, AIT
27:45 When your brother *is* no **l** angry with you 8740
32:28 man said, "Your name will no **l** be Jacob, 6388
35:10 but you will no **l** be called Jacob; 6388
45: 1 Then Joseph could **no l** control himself AIT
49: 4 you will **no l** excel, AIT
Ex 2: 3 But when she could hide him no **l**, 6388
5: 7 "*You are* no **l** to supply the people 3578
9:28 you don't have to stay **any l**." 3578
9:33 and the rain no **l poured down** on the land. AIT
26:13 The tent curtains will be a cubit **l** on 802
Lev 17: 7 They must no **l** offer any of their sacrifices 6388
26:13 **so that** you would no **l** be slaves AIT
Nu 8:25 from their regular service and work no **l**. 6388
Dt 1:11 the voice of the LORD our God **any l**. 3578+6388
10:16 therefore, and do not be stiff-necked **any l**. 6388
31: 2 and I am no **l** able to lead you. 6388
32: 5 to their shame they are **no l** his children, AIT
Jos 5: 1 and they no **l** had the courage to face 6388
5:12 there was no **l** any manna for the Israelites, 6388
23:13 the LORD your God *will* no **l** drive out these nations 3578
Jdg 2:14 whom they were no **l** able to resist. 6388
2:21 I *will* no **l** drive out before them any of 3578
10: 6 forsook the LORD and **no l** served him, AIT
10:13 so *I will* no **l** save you. 3578
10:16 And he could **bear** Israel's misery no **l**. 7918
1Sa 1:18 and her face was no **l downcast**. 6388
27: 4 he no **l** searched for him. 3578+6388
28:15 He no **l** answers me, 6388
2Sa 1:21 the shield of Saul—**no l** rubbed with oil. 1172
2:28 *they* no **l** pursued Israel, 6388
3:22 But Abner *was* no **l** with David in Hebron, AIT
7:10 a home of their own and no **l** be disturbed. 6388
20: 5 *he took* **l** than the time the king had set 336
1Ki 21:15 He **is no l** alive, but dead." AIT
2Ki 6:33 Why should I wait for the LORD **any l**?" 6388
10:19 Anyone who fails to come *will* no **l live**." AIT
15:20 and **stayed** in the land no **l**. AIT
17: 4 he no **l paid** tribute to the king of Assyria, AIT
1Ch 17: 9 a home of their own and no **l** be disturbed. 6388
23:26 the Levites no **l** *need* to **carry** AIT
Ne 2:17 and we will no **l** be in disgrace." 6388
13:21 From that time on they no **l** came on AIT
Job 3:18 they no **l** hear the slave driver's shout. AIT
7: 8 eye that now sees me will see me no **l**; AIT
11: 9 Their measure is **l** than the earth 801
15:29 He will no **l** be rich and his wealth will AIT
17:20 evil men are no **l** remembered 6388
36: 2 with me a **little l** and I will show you 10236
Ps 44: 9 you no **l** go out with our armies. AIT
60:10 you who have rejected us and no **l** go out AIT
108:11 you who have rejected us and **no l** go out AIT
Ecc 4:13 an old but foolish king who no **l** knows 6388
9:16 and his words are no **l** heeded. AIT
12: 5 along and desire no **l** is stirred. 7296
Isa 7:25 you will no **l** go there for fear of the briers AIT
10:20 *will* no **l** rely on him who struck them 3578+6388
17: 1 "See, Damascus *will* no **l** be a city 4946+6073
23:10 for you no **l** have a harbor. 6388
24: 9 **No l** do they drink wine with a song; AIT
26:21 she will conceal her slain no **l**. AIT
29:22 "No **l** will Jacob be ashamed; 6964
29:22 no **l** will their faces grow pale. 6964
32: 5 No **l** will the fool be called noble nor 6388
32: 5 of those who are no **l be closed**, AIT
38:11 no **l** will I look on mankind, 6388
60:18 No **l** will violence be heard in your land, 6388

Isa 62: 4 No **l** will they call you Deserted, 6388
62:12 the City No **L** Deserted. AIT
65:22 No **l** will they build houses and others live AIT
Jer 3:12 'I will frown on you no **l**, AIT
3:16 declares the LORD, "men will no **l** say, 6388
3:17 No **l** will they follow the stubbornness 6388
4: 1 of my sight and no **l** go astray, AIT
7:32 when people will no **l** call it Topheth or 6388
8:19 **Is her King no l** there?" AIT
15: 6 **I can no l** show compassion. 4206
16:14 "when men will no **l** say, 6388
19: 6 people will no **l** call this place Topheth 6388
23: 4 and they will no **l** be afraid or terrified, 6388
23: 7 "when people will no **l** say, 6388
30: 8 no **l** will foreigners enslave them. 6388
31:29 "In those days people will no **l** say, 6388
31:34 No **l** will a man teach his neighbor, 6388
33:20 and night no **l come** at their appointed time, AIT
33:21 can be broken and David will **no l** have AIT
33:24 and no **l** regard them as a nation. 6388
34:10 and female slaves and no **l** hold them 6388
38: 9 when there is no **l** any bread in the city." 6388
44:22 LORD could no **l** endure your wicked actions 6388
49: 7 "Is there no **l** wisdom in Teman? 6388
51:44 The nations will no **l** stream to him. 6388
La 2: 9 and her prophets **no l** find visions from AIT
4:15 "They can stay here no **l**." 3578
4:16 he no **l** watches over them. 3578
Eze 12:23 and they will no **l** quote it in Israel.' 6388
12:28 None of my words will be delayed **any l**; 6388
13:21 and they will no **l** fall prey to your power. 6388
13:23 therefore you will no **l** see false visions 6388
14:11 people of Israel will no **l** stray from me, 6388
16:41 and you will no **l** pay your lovers. 6388
16:42 I will be calm and no **l** angry. 6388
18: 3 you will no **l** quote this proverb in Israel. 6388
19: 9 so his roar was heard no **l** on the mountains 6388
20:39 to me and no **l** profane my holy name 6388
24:27 speak with him and will no **l** be silent. 6388
26:19 like cities **no l** inhabited, AIT
28:24 " 'No **l** will the people of Israel have 6388
29:16 Egypt will no **l** be a source of confidence 6388
30:13 No **l** will there be a prince in Egypt, 6388
32:13 beside abundant waters no **l** be stirred 6388
33:22 and I was no **l** silent. 6388
34:10 the shepherds can no **l** feed themselves. 6388
34:10 and it will **no l** be food for them. AIT
34:22 and they will no **l** be plundered. 6388
34:28 They will no **l** be plundered by 6388
34:29 and they will no **l** be victims of famine in 6388
36:14 therefore you will no **l** devour men 6388
36:15 No **l** will I make you hear the taunts of 6388
36:15 and no **l** will you suffer the scorn of 6388
36:30 that you will no **l** suffer disgrace among 6388
37:23 They will no **l** defile themselves 6388
39: 7 I will no **l** let my holy name be profaned, 6388
39:29 I will no **l** hide my face from them, 6388
45: 8 my princes will no **l** oppress my people 6388
Da 8: 3 of the horns was **l** than the other but grew 1469
Hos 1: 6 for I will no **l** show love to the house 3578+6388
2:16 you will no **l** call me 'my master.' 6388
2:17 no **l** will their names be invoked, 6388
9:15 I will no **l** love them; 3578
Joel 2:10 and the stars **no l shine**. 665+5586
3:15 and the stars **no l shine**. 665+5586
Am 7: 8 I will spare them no **l**. 3578+6388
8: 2 I will spare them no **l**. 3578+6388
Mic 2: 3 You will **no l** walk proudly, AIT
5:12 and you will no **l** cast spells. NIH
5:13 you will no **l** bow down to the work 6388
Na 2:13 The voices of your messengers will no **l** 6388
Zec 11: 6 For I will no **l** have pity on the people of 6388
14:21 on that day there will no **l** be a Canaanite 6388
Mal 2:13 and wail because he no **l** pays attention 6388
Mt 5:13 It is no **l** good for anything, 2285
19: 6 So they are no **l** two, but one. 4033
Mk 1:45 Jesus could no **l** enter a town openly 3600
7:12 then you no **l** let him do anything 4033
9: 8 they no **l** saw anyone with them 4033
10: 8 So they are no **l** two, but one. 4033
Lk 15:19 I am no **l** worthy to be called your son; 4033
15:21 I am no **l** worthy to be called your son.' 4033
16: 2 because you cannot be manager **any l**.' 2285
20:36 and they can no **l** die; 2285
Jn 4:42 "We no **l** believe just because of what you 4033
6:66 disciples turned back and no **l** followed him. 4033
11:54 Therefore Jesus no **l** moved about publicly 4033
12:35 to have the light just a little while **l**. 2285
13:33 I will be with you only a little while **l**. 2285
14:30 I will **not** speak with you much **l**, 4033
15:15 I no **l** call you servants, 4033
16:10 where you can see me no **l**; 4033
16:23 In that day you will no **l** ask me anything. NIG
16:25 when I will no **l** use this kind of language 4033
17:11 I will remain in the world no **l**, 4033
Ac 4:17 we must warn these men to speak no **l** 3600
19:22 while *he* **stayed** in the province of Asia **a little l**. 2091+5989
25:24 shouting that he ought not to live **any l**. 3600
Ro 6: 2 how can we live in it **any l**? 2285
6: 6 that we should no **l** be slaves to sin— 3600
6: 6 death no **l** has mastery over him. 4033
7:17 As it is, it is no **l** I myself who do it, 4033
7:20 is no **l** I who do it, but it is sin living in me 4033
11: 6 And if by grace, then it is no **l** by works; 4033
11: 6 if it were, grace would no **l** be grace. 4033
12: 2 *Do not* **conform** any **l** to the pattern of AIT

Ro	14:15	you are **no l** acting in love.	4033
2Co	5:15	that those who live should **no l** live for	3600
	5:16	regarded Christ in this way, we do so **no l.**	4033
Gal	2:20	crucified with Christ and I **no l** live,	4033
	3:18	then it **no l** depends on a promise;	4033
	3:25	we are **no l** under the supervision of the law	4033
	4: 7	So you are **no l** a slave, but a son;	4033
Eph	2:19	you are **no l** foreigners and aliens,	3600
	4:14	Then we will **no l** be infants,	3600
	4:17	that you must **no l** live as the Gentiles do,	3600
	4:28	He who has been stealing must steal **no l,**	3600
1Th	3: 1	So when we could stand it **no l,**	3600
	3: 5	For this reason, when I could stand it **no l,**	3600
1Ti	1: 3	not to teach false doctrines any **l**	NIG
Phm	1:16	**no l** as a slave, but better than a slave,	4033
Heb	8:11	**No l** will a man teach his neighbor,	3590+4024
	10: 2	would no I have felt guilty for their sins.	2285
	10:18	there is **no l** any sacrifice for sin.	4033
Rev	6:11	and they were told to wait a little **l,**	2285+5989
	21: 1	and there was no l any sea.	2285
	22: 3	No I will there be any curse.	2285

LONGING (15) [LONG]

Dt	28:65	eyes **weary with l,** and a despairing heart.	4001
Job	7: 2	Like a slave **l for** the evening shadows,	8634
Ps	119:20	My soul is consumed with **l for** your laws	9291
	119:81	My soul **faints with l for** your salvation,	3983
	119:131	**l for** your commands.	3277
Pr	13:12	but a **l** fulfilled is a tree of life.	9294
	13:19	A **l** fulfilled is sweet to the soul,	9294
Eze	23:27	not **look** on these things **with l**	5951+6524
Lk	16:21	and I to eat what fell from the rich man's	2121
Ro	15:23	I have been **l for** many years to see you,	2163
2Co	5: 2	I to be clothed with our heavenly dwelling,	2160
	7: 7	He told us about your **l for** me,	2161
	7:11	what indignation, what alarm, what **l,**	2161
1Th	2:17	out of our intense **l** we made every effort	2123
Heb	11:16	Instead, *they were* **l for** a better country—	3977

LONGINGS (2) [LONG]

Ps	38: 9	All my **l** lie open before you, O Lord;	9294
	112:10	the **l** *of* the wicked will come to nothing.	9294

LONGS (4) [LONG]

Ps	63: 1	my body **l for** you, in a dry and weary land	4014
Isa	26: 9	in the morning my spirit **l for** you.	8838
	30:18	Yet the LORD **l** to be gracious to you;	2675
Php	2:26	For *he* **l for** all of you and is distressed	1639+2160

LONGSUFFERING (KJV) See PATIENCE

LOOK (325) [FINE-LOOKING, LOOKED, LOOKING, LOOKOUT, LOOKOUTS, LOOKS]

Ge	4: 5	and his offering *he did* not **l with favor.**	9120
	13:14	from where you are and **l** north and south,	8011
	15: 5	"**L** up at the heavens and count the stars—	5564
	19: 8	**L,** I have two daughters who have never	2180
	19:17	Don't **l** back, and don't stop anywhere in	5564
	19:20	**L,** here is a town near enough to run to,	2180
	25:32	"**L,** I am about to die," Esau said.	2180
	27: 6	"**L,** I overheard your father say	2180
	29: 7	"**L,**" he said, "the sun is still high;	2176
	31:12	'**L** up and see that all the male goats	6524
	39:14	"**L,**" she said to them,	8011
	41:33	"And now *let* Pharaoh **l for** a discerning	8011
	49:18	"I **l for** your deliverance, O LORD.	7747
Ex	1: 9	"**L,**" he said to his people,	2180
	3: 4	the LORD saw that he had gone over to **l,**	8011
	3: 6	because he was afraid to **l** at God.	5564
	5: 5	Then Pharaoh said, "**L,** the people	2176
	5:21	the LORD **l** upon you and judge you!	8011
Lev	13:36	priest *does* not *need to* **l** for yellow hair;	1329
	26: 9	" '**I will l** on you **with favor**	7155
Nu	4:20	But the Kohathites must not go in to **l** at	8011
	15:39	You will have these tassels *to* **l** at and	8011
	21: 8	anyone who is bitten *can* **l** at and live."	8011
	32: 8	from Kadesh Barnea to **l** over the land.	8011
Dt	3:27	Pisgah and **l** west and north and south	5951+6524
	3:27	**L** at the land with your own eyes,	8011
	4:19	when you **l** up to the sky and see the sun,	6524
	4:29	if *you* **l for** him with all your heart and	2011
	7:16	*Do* not **l** on them **with pity**	2571+6524
	26:15	**L down** from heaven,	9207
Jos	2: 1	"Go, **l** over the land," he said,	8011
	2: 2	The king of Jericho was told, "**L!**	2180
	22:28	**L** at the replica of the LORD's altar,	8011
Jdg	6:37	**l,** I will place a wool fleece on	2180
	9:36	Gaal saw them, he said to Zebul, "**L,**	2180
	9:37	But Gaal spoke up again: "**L,**	2180
	14: 8	he turned aside to **l** at the lion's carcass.	8011
	19: 9	said, "Now **l,** it's almost evening.	2180
	19:24	**L,** here is my virgin daughter,	2180
	21:19	But **l,** there is the annual festival of	2180
Ru	1:15	"**L,**" said Naomi, "your sister-in-law is	2180
1Sa	1:11	"O LORD Almighty, *if you will only* **l**	8011+8011
	9: 3	the servants with you and go and **l for**	1335
	9: 6	But the servant replied, "**L,**	2180
	9: 8	"**L,**" he said, "I have a quarter of a shekel	2180
	10: 2	'The donkeys you set out to **l for**	1335
	14:11	to the Philistine outpost. "**L!**"	2180
	14:33	Then someone said to Saul, "**L,**	2180
	16: 7	LORD does not **l** at the things man looks at.	NIH

1Sa	18:22	"Speak to David privately and say, '**L,**	2180
	20: 2	**L,** my father doesn't do anything,	2180
	20: 5	"**L,** tomorrow is the New Moon festival,	2180
	20:21	If I say to him, '**L,**	2180
	20:22	But if I say to the boy, '**L,**	2180
	21:14	Achish said to his servants, "**L** at the man!	8011
	23: 1	When David was told, "**L,**	2180
	24: 1	to **l for** David and his men near the Crags	1335
	24:11	**l** at this piece of your robe in my hand!	8011
	26:16	**L around** you.	8011
	26:20	The king of Israel has come out to **l for**	1335
	28:14	"What does he **l like?**"	9307
	28:21	"**L,** your maidservant has obeyed you.	2180
2Sa	2:22	I your brother Joab **in the face?**"	448+5951+7156
	3:24	**L,** Abner came to you.	2180
	13: 4	I so haggard morning after morning?	NIH
	13:10	Then he said to his servants, "**L,**	8011
	14:32	Absalom said to Joab, "**L,**	2180
	15: 3	Then Absalom would say to him, "**L,**	8011
	18:26	and he called down to the gatekeeper, "**L,**	2180
1Ki	1: 2	"*Let us* **l for** a young virgin to attend	1335
	2:19	**L** after your own house, O David!"	8011
	17:23	He gave him to his mother and said, "**L,**	8011
	18:10	not sent someone to **l for** you.	1335
	18:43	"Go and **l** toward the sea,"	5564
	20:31	His officials said to him, "**L,**	2180
	22:13	to summon Micaiah said to him, "**L,**	2180
2Ki	2:16	"**L,**" they said, "we your servants have fifty	2180
	2:16	Let them go and **l for** your master.	1335
	2:19	The men of the city said to Elisha, "**L,**	2180
	3:14	*I would* not **l** at you or even notice you.	5564
	4:25	man of God said to his servant Gehazi, "**L!**	2180
	6: 1	the prophets said to Elisha, "**L,** the place	2180
	6:32	**L,** when the messenger comes,	8011
	7: 2	"**L,** even if the LORD should open	2180
	7: 6	so that they said to one another, "**L,**	2180
	7:19	"**L,** even if the LORD should open	2180
	9: 2	**l for** Jehu son of Jehoshaphat,	8011
	10:23	"**L around** and see that no servants of	2924
	18:21	**L** now, you are depending on Egypt,	2180
1Ch	16:11	**L** to the LORD and his strength;	2011
	21:23	**L,** I will give the oxen for	8011
2Ch	10:16	**L** after your own house, O David!"	8011
	18:12	to summon Micaiah said to him, "**L,**	2180
Ne	2: 2	"Why does your face **l** *so* **sad**	8273
	2: 3	Why *should* my face not **l sad** when	8317
Est	1:11	for she was lovely to **l** at.	5260
Job	6:19	The caravans of Tema **l for** water,	5564
	6:19	the traveling merchants of Sheba **l in hope.**	7747
	6:28	"But now be so kind as *to* **l** at me.	7155
	7: 8	you will **l** for me, but I will be no more.	6524
	7:19	*Will you* never **l** away from me,	9120
	8: 5	But if you *will* **l** to God and plead with	8838
	11:18	*you will* **l about** you and take your rest	2916
	14: 6	So **l** away from him and let him alone,	9120
	19:15	they **l** upon me as an alien.	928+6524
	20: 9	his place will **l** on him no more.	8800
	21: 5	**L** at me and be astonished;	7155
	24: 1	Why *must* those who know him **l** in vain	2600
	30:20	I stand up, but *you merely* **l** at me.	1067
	31: 1	with my eyes not *to* **l lustfully** at a girl.	1067
	35: 5	**L** up at the heavens and see;	5564
	37:21	Now no *one* can **l** at the sun,	8011
	40:11	**l** at every proud man and bring him low,	8011
	40:12	**l** at every proud man and humble him,	8011
	40:15	"**L** at the behemoth,	2180
Ps	11: 2	For **l,** the wicked bend their bows;	2180
	13: 3	**L** on me and answer, O LORD my God.	5564
	25:18	**L** upon my affliction and my distress	8011
	34: 5	*Those who* **l** to him are radiant;	5564
	35:17	O Lord, how long will you **l** on?	8011
	37:10	*you* **l** for them, they will not be found.	1067
	39: 7	"But now, Lord, what *do I* **l for?**	7747
	39:13	**L** away from me,	9120
	40: 4	*who does* not **l** to the proud,	7155
	59: 4	Arise to help me; **l** on my plight!	8011
	80:14	**L down** from heaven and see!	5564
	84: 9	**L** upon our shield, O God;	5564
	84: 9	**l with favor** *on* your anointed one.	5564+7156
	104:27	These all **l** to you to give them their food	8432
	105: 4	**L** to the LORD and his strength;	2011
	112: 8	in the end he will **l** in triumph on his foes.	8011
	113: 6	who stoops down to **l** on the heavens and	8011
	118: 7	I will **l** in triumph on my enemies.	8011
	119:153	**L** upon my suffering and deliver me,	8011
	119:158	**I** *on* the faithless with loathing,	8011
	123: 2	of slaves **l** to the hand of their master,	NIH
	123: 2	of a maid **l** to the hand of her mistress,	NIH
	123: 2	so our eyes **l** to the LORD our God,	NIH
	142: 4	**L** to my right and see;	5564
	145:15	The eyes of all **l** to you,	8432
Pr	1:28	*they will* **l for** me but will not find me.	8838
	2: 4	and if *you* **l for** it as for silver and search	1335
	4:25	**Let** your eyes **l** straight ahead,	5564
	15:30	A cheerful **l** brings joy to the heart,	6524
Ecc	1:10	one can say, "**L!** This is something new"?	8011
	1:16	I thought to myself, "**L,** I have grown in	2180
	7:27	"**L,**" says the Teacher,	8011
SS	2: 8	My lover! **L!** Here he comes,	2180
	2: 9	or a young stag. **L!**	2180
	3: 7	**L!** It is Solomon's carriage,	2180
	3:11	and **l** at King Solomon wearing the crown,	8011
	6: 1	that *we may* **l for** him with you?	1335
	6:11	I went down to the grove of nut trees to **l**	8011
Isa	3: 9	The **l** *on* their faces testifies against them;	2129
	8:22	Then *they will* **l** toward the earth	5564
	10:12	of his heart and the haughty **l** in his eyes.	9514

Isa	13: 8	*They will* **l aghast** at each other,	9449
	13:18	nor *will* they **l with compassion**	2571+6524
	17: 7	In that day men *will* **l** to their Maker	9120
	17: 8	*They will* not **l** to the altars,	9120
	18: 4	and will **l** on from my dwelling place,	5564
	21: 9	**L,** here comes a man in a chariot with	2180
	22:11	but *you did* not **l** to the One who made it,	5564
	23:13	**L** at the land of the Babylonians,	2176
	30: 2	*who* **l for help** to Pharaoh's protection,	6395
	31: 1	but *do* not **l** to the Holy One of Israel,	9120
	33: 7	**L,** their brave men cry aloud in the streets;	2176
	33:20	**L** upon Zion, the city of our festivals;	2600
	34:16	**L** in the scroll of the LORD and read:	2011
	36: 6	**L** now, you are depending on Egypt,	2180
	38:11	no longer *will I* **l** on mankind,	5564
	40:26	Lift your eyes and **l** to the heavens:	8011
	41:27	I was the first to tell Zion, '**L,**	2180
	41:28	**l** but there is no one—	8011
	42:18	"Hear, you deaf; **l,** *you* blind, and see!	5564
	48: 6	**l** at them all. Will you not admit them?	2600
	49:18	Lift up your eyes and **l** around;	8011
	51: 1	**L** to the rock from which you were cut and	5564
	51: 2	**l** to Abraham, your father, and	5564
	51: 3	and *will* **l with compassion** on all her ruins;	5714
	51: 5	The islands *will* **l** to me and wait in hope.	7747
	51: 6	**l** at the earth beneath;	5564
	59: 9	*We* **l** for light, but all is darkness;	7747
	59:11	*We* **l** for justice, but find none;	7747
	60: 4	"Lift up your eyes and **l** about you:	8011
	60: 5	Then *you will* **l** and be radiant,	8011
	60: 9	Surely the islands **l** to me;	7747
	63:15	**L down** from heaven and see	5564
	64: 9	Oh, **l** upon us, we pray,	5564
	66:24	"And they will go out and **l** upon	8011
Jer	2:10	Cross over to the coasts of Kittim and **l,**	8011
	3: 2	"**L** up to the barren heights and see.	6524
	3: 3	Yet you have the **brazen l** *of* a prostitute;	5195
	4:13	He advances like the	2180
	5: 1	**l around** and consider,	8011
	5: 3	O LORD, do not your eyes **l for** truth?	NIH
	6:16	"Stand at the crossroads and **l;**	8011
	6:22	This is what the LORD says: "**L,**	2180
	7: 8	But **l,** you are trusting in deceptive words	2180
	8:11	'This is what the LORD says: **L!**	2180
	25:32	This is what the LORD Almighty says: "**L!**	2180
	39:12	"Take him and **l** after him;	6524+6584+8492
	40: 4	and I *will* **l** after you;	6524+6584+8492
	40: 4	**L,** the whole country lies before you;	8011
	48:40	This is what the LORD says: "**L!**	2180
	49:22	**L!** An eagle will soar and swoop down,	2180
	50:41	"**L!** An army is coming from the north;	2180
La	1: 9	"**L,** O LORD, *on* my affliction,	8011
	1:11	"**L,** O LORD, and consider,	8011
	1:12	**L around** and see.	5564
	1:18	**l** upon my suffering.	8011
	2:20	"**L,** O LORD, and consider:	8011
	3:63	**L** at them!	5564
	5: 1	**l,** and see our disgrace.	5564
Eze	5:11	*I will* not **l** on you **with pity**	2571+6524
	7: 4	*I will* not **l** on you **with pity**	2571+6524
	7: 9	*I will* not **l** on you **with pity**	2571+6524
	8: 5	"Son of man, **l** toward the north."	8011
	8:17	**L** at them putting the branch to their nose!	2180
	8:18	*I will* not **l** on them **with pity**	2571+6524
	9:10	*I will* not **l** on them **with pity**	2571+6524
	18: 6	or **l** to the idols of the house of Israel.	5951+6524
	18:15	or **l** to the idols of the house of Israel.	5951+6524
	23:27	**l** on these things **with longing**	5951+6524
	25: 8	'Because Moab and Seir said, "**L,**	2180
	33:25	the blood still in it and **l** to your idols	5951+6524
	34:11	for my sheep and **l** after them.	1329
	34:12	so *will I* **l** after my sheep.	1329
	36: 9	and *will I* **l** on you **with favor;**	7155
	40: 4	**l** with your eyes and hear with your ears	8011
	44: 5	"Son of man, **l carefully,**	928+6524+8011
Da	2:13	*to* **l for** Daniel and his friends to put them	10114
	3:25	He said, "**L!** I see four men walking around	10194
	3:25	Don't be alarmed! Don't **l** *so* **pale!**	10228+10731
	9:17	**l with favor** on your desolate sanctuary.	239+7156
Hos	2: 2	the **adulterous l** from her face and	2393
	2: 7	*she will* **l for** them but not find them.	1335
Am	6: 2	Go to Calneh and **l** at it;	8011
	7: 8	Then the Lord said, "**L,** I am setting	2180
Ob	1:12	*You should* not **l down on** your brother in	8011
	1:13	nor **l down on** them in their calamity in	8011
Jnh	2: 4	I will again toward your holy temple.'	5564
Mic	1: 3	**L!** The LORD is coming from his dwelling	2180
Na	1:15	**L,** there on the mountains,	2180
	2: 4	They **l** like flaming torches;	5260
	3:13	**L** at your troops—they are all women!	2180
Hab	1: 3	Why *do you* **make** me **l** at injustice?	8011
	1: 5	"**L** at the nations and watch—	8011
	1:13	Your eyes are too pure *to* **l** on evil;	8011
	2: 1	*I will* **l** to see what he will say to me,	7595
Hag	2: 3	How *does* it **l** to you now?	8011
Zec	5: 5	"**L** up and see what this is	6524
	6: 8	Then he called to me, "**L,** those going	8011
	12:10	*They will* **l** on me, the one they have pierced	5564
Mt	6:16	*do* not **l somber** as the hypocrites do,	1181+5034
	6:26	**L** at the birds of the air;	1838
	7: 3	"Why *do you* **l** at the speck of sawdust	1063
	12: 2	they said to him, "**L!** Your disciples are	2627
	18:10	not **l down on** one of these little ones.	2969
	18:12	and go *to* **l for** the one that wandered off?	2426
	23:27	which **l** beautiful on the outside but on the	5743
	23:38	**L,** your house is left to you desolate.	2627
	24:23	At that time if anyone says to you, '**L,**	2627

Mt	25:43	and in prison and *you did* not **l** *after* me.'	2170
	26:45	**L**, the hour is near, the Son of Man	2627
	26:65	**L**, now you have heard the blasphemy.	3972
	28: 1	and the other Mary went to **l** at the tomb.	2555
Mk	1:36	Simon and his companions *went* to **l** for	2870
	2:24	The Pharisees said to him, "**L**,	3972
	8:24	they **l** like trees walking around."	3972
	11:21	and said to Jesus, "Rabbi, **l**!	3972
	12:15	"Bring me a denarius and let *me* **l** at it."	3972
	13: 1	one of his disciples said to him, "**L**,	3972
	13:21	At that time if anyone says to you, '**L**,	3972
	13:21	or, '**L**, there he is!'	3972
	14:41	**L**, the Son of Man is betrayed into	2627
Lk	2:45	they went back to Jerusalem to **l** for him.	349
	6:41	"Why *do you* **l** at the speck of sawdust	1063
	9:38	"Teacher, I beg you to **l** at my son,	2098
	10:35	'**L** after him,' he said, 'and when I return,	2150
	13: 6	and he went to **l** for fruit on it,	2426
	13: 7	now I've been coming to **l** for fruit	2426
	13:35	**L**, your house is left to you desolate.	2627
	15:29	But he answered his father, '**L**!	2627
	18:13	would not even **l** up to heaven,	2048+3836+4057
	19: 8	Zacchaeus stood up and said to the Lord, "**L**	2627
	21:29	"**L** at the fig tree and all the trees.	3972
	24: 5	"Why *do you* **l** for the living among	2426
	24:39	**L** at my hands and my feet.	3972
Jn	1:29	**L**, the Lamb of God, who takes away the sin	3972
	1:36	he said, "**L**, the Lamb of God!"	3972
	4:35	open your eyes and **l** at the fields!	2517
	7:34	*You will* **l** for me, but you will not find me;	2426
	7:36	*'You will* **l** for me, but you will not find me,	2426
	7:52	**L** into it, and you will find that	2236
	8:21	and *you will* **l** for me,	2426
	12:19	**L** how the whole world has gone after him!	3972
	13:33	*You will* **l** for me, and just as I told the Jews,	2426
	19: 4	the Jews, "**L**, I am bringing him out to you	3972
	19:37	*"They will* **l** on the one they have pierced."	3972
	20:11	she *bent over* to **l** into the tomb	4160
Ac	3: 4	Then Peter said, "**L** at us!"	1063
	5: 9	**L**! The feet of the men who buried your	2627
	5:25	Then someone came and said, "**L**!	2627
	7:31	As he went over to **l** more closely,	2917
	7:32	with fear and did not dare to **l**.	2917
	7:56	"**L**," he said, "I see heaven open and	2627
	8:36	the eunuch said, "**L**, here is water.	2627
	11:25	Barnabas went to Tarsus to **l** for Saul,	349
	13:41	" '**L**, you scoffers, wonder and perish,	3972
Ro	1:23	for images made to **l** like mortal man	3930
	14: 3	not **l** down on him who does not,	2024
	14:10	Or why *do you* **l** down on your brother?	2024
1Co	1:22	miraculous signs and Greeks **l** for wisdom,	2426
	7:27	Are you unmarried? *Do* not **l** for a wife.	2426
2Co	3: 7	so that the Israelites could not **l** steadily	867
Php	2: 4	Each of you *should* **l** not only to	5023
1Ti	4:12	Don't *let* anyone **l** down on you	2969
Jas	1:27	to **l** after orphans and widows	2170
	5: 4	**L**! The wages you failed to pay	2627
1Pe	1:12	Even angels long to **l** into these things.	4160
2Pe	3:12	*as you* **l** forward to the day of God	4659
Rev	1: 7	**L**, he is coming with the clouds,	2627
	5: 3	could open the scroll or even **l** inside it.	1063
	5: 4	worthy *to* open the scroll or **l** inside.	1063

LOOKED (208) [LOOK]

Ge	4: 4	The LORD **l** *with favor* on Abel	9120
	13:10	Lot **l** up and saw that the whole plain of	6524
	18: 2	Abraham **l** up and saw three men standing	6524
	18:16	*they* **l** down toward Sodom,	9207
	19:26	But Lot's wife **l** back,	5564
	19:28	He **l** down toward Sodom and Gomorrah,	9207
	22: 4	On the third day Abraham **l** up and saw	6524
	22:13	Abraham **l** up and there in a thicket	6524
	24:63	and *as* he **l** up, he saw camels approaching.	6524
	24:64	Rebekah also **l** up and saw Isaac.	6524
	26: 8	Abimelech king of the Philistines **l** down	9207
	31:10	a dream in which I **l** up and saw that	6524
	33: 1	Jacob **l** up and there was Esau,	6524
	33: 5	Then Esau **l** up and saw the women	6524
	37:25	they **l** up and saw a caravan	6524
	41:21	they **l** just as ugly as before.	5260
	43:29	**l** about and saw his brother Benjamin,	5951+6524
	43:30	Joseph hurried out and **l** for a place	1335
	43:33	**l** at each other *in astonishment.*	9449
Ex	2:25	God **l** on the Israelites and was concerned	8011
	4:10	Pharaoh approached, the Israelites **l** up,	6524
	14:24	the LORD **l** down from the pillar of fire	9207
	16:10	*they* **l** toward the desert,	7155
	24:17	To the Israelites the glory of the LORD **l**	5260
Nu	9:15	the cloud above the tabernacle **l** like fire.	5260
	9:16	and at night it **l** like fire.	5260
	11: 7	The manna was like coriander seed and **l**	6524
	11:33	and *we* **l** the same *to* them."	928+2118+6524
	17: 9	*They* **l** at them, and each man took his own	8011
	21: 9	when anyone was bitten by a snake and **l**	5564
	24: 2	When Balaam **l** out and saw Israel	6524
Dt	9:16	When *I* **l**, I saw that you had sinned	8011
Jos	5:13	he **l** up and saw a man standing in front	6524
	8:20	The men of Ai **l** back and saw the smoke	8011
Jdg	13: 6	He **l** like an angel of God, very awesome.	5260
	19:17	*he* **l** and saw the traveler in the city	5951+6524
1Sa	6:13	and when they **l** up and saw the ark,	6524
	6:19	because *they had* **l** into the ark of the LORD.	8011
	9:16	I have **l** my people,	8011
	10:21	*they* **l** for him, he was not to be found.	1335
	17:42	He **l** David *over* and saw that he was only	5564
	24: 8	When Saul **l** behind him, David bowed	5564

2Sa	2:20	Abner **l** behind him and asked,	7155
	13:34	Now the man standing watch **l** up	906+6524
	18:24	As he **l** out, he saw a man running alone.	6524
	24:20	When Araunah **l** and saw the king	6524
1Ki	2:15	All Israel **l** to me as their king.	7156+8492
	3:21	*I* **l** at him *closely* in the morning light,	1067
	18:43	And he went up and **l**.	5564
	19: 6	He **l** around, and there by his head was	5564
2Ki	2:24	**l** at them and called down a curse	8011
	3:22	the water **l** red—like blood.	8011
	6:17	and *he* **l** and saw the hills full of horses	8011
	6:20	the LORD opened their eyes and *they* **l**,	8011
	6:30	As he went along the wall, the people **l**,	8011
	9:30	arranged her hair and **l** out of a window.	9207
	9:32	He **l** up at the window and called out,	7156
	9:32	Two or three eunuchs **l** down at him.	9207
	11:14	*She* **l** and there was the king,	8011
	23:16	Then Josiah **l** around,	7155
1Ch	17:17	*You have* **l** on me as though I were	8011
	21:16	David **l** up and saw the angel of	6524
	21:21	and when Araunah **l** and saw him,	5564
2Ch	20:24	to the place that overlooks the desert and **l**	7155
	23:13	*She* **l**, and there was the king,	8011
	26:20	the chief priest and all the other priests **l**	7155
Ne	4:14	After *I* **l** *things over,* I stood up and said	8011
Est	3: 6	Instead Haman **l** *for* a way to destroy all	1335
Job	28:27	then *he* **l** at wisdom and appraised it;	8011
	30:26	when *I* **l** for light, then came darkness.	3498
Ps	37:36	though *I* **l** for him, he could not be found.	1335
	54: 7	and my eyes *have* **l** in triumph on my foes.	8011
	69:20	*I* **l** for sympathy, but there was none,	7747
	102:19	"The LORD **l** down from his sanctuary	9207
	114: 3	The sea **l** and fled, the Jordan turned back;	8011
Pr	7: 6	the window of my house *I* **l** out through	9207
	7:15	*I* **l** for you and have found you!	8838
Ecc	4: 1	Again *I* **l** and saw all the oppression	NIH
SS	3: 1	on my bed *I* **l** for the one my heart loves;	1335
	3: 1	*I* **l** for him but did not find him.	1335
	3: 2	So *I* **l** for him but did not find him.	1335
	5: 6	*I* **l** for him but did not find him.	1335
Isa	5: 2	Then *he* **l** for a crop of good grapes,	7747
	5: 4	*When I* **l** for good grapes,	7747
	5: 7	And *he* **l** for justice, but saw bloodshed;	7747
	22: 8	And *you* **l** in that day to the weapons in	5564
	38:14	My eyes grew weak as I **l** to the heavens.	NIH
	57: 8	and *you* **l** on their nakedness.	2600
	59:15	The LORD **l** and was displeased	8011
	63: 5	*I* **l**, but there was no one to help,	5564
Jer	4:23	*I* **l** at the earth, and it was formless and	8011
	4:24	*I* **l** at the mountains, and they were quaking,	8011
	4:25	*I* **l**, and there were no people;	8011
	4:26	*I* **l**, and the fruitful land was a desert;	8011
	31:26	At this I awoke and **l** *around.*	8011
	36:16	*they* **l** at each other *in fear*	7064
La	1: 7	Her enemies **l** at her and laughed	8011
Eze	1: 4	*I* **l**, and I saw a windstorm coming out of	8011
	1: 4	The center of the fire **l** like glowing metal,	6524
	1: 5	and in the fire was *what* **l** like four living	1952
	1:10	Their faces **l** like this:	1952
	1:15	As *I* **l** at the living creatures,	8011
	1:16	and all four **l** alike.	1952
	1:22	of the living creatures was *what* **l** like	1952
	1:26	over their heads was what **l** like a throne	5260
	1:27	from what appeared to be his waist up he **l**	6524
	1:27	and that from there down he **l** like fire;	5260
	2: 9	*I* **l**, and I saw a hand stretched out to me.	8011
	8: 2	*I* **l**, and I saw a figure like that of a man.	8011
	8: 3	He stretched out *what* **l** like a hand	9322
	8: 5	So I **l**, and in the entrance north of	5951+6524
	8: 7	*I* **l**, and I saw a hole in the wall.	8011
	8:10	So I went in and **l**,	8011
	10: 1	*I* **l**, and I saw the likeness of a throne	8011
	10: 8	of the cherubim could be seen *what* **l** like	9322
	10: 9	*I* **l**, and I saw beside the cherubim	8011
	10:10	their appearance, the four of them **l** alike;	1952
	10:21	and under their wings was *what* **l** like	1952
	16: 5	No one **l** on you *with pity*	2571+6524
	16: 8	and when *I* **l** at you and saw	8011
	20:17	Yet *I* **l** on them *with pity*	2571+6524
	22:30	"*I* **l** for a man among them who would	1335
	23:15	of them **l** like Babylonian chariot officers,	5260
	34: 6	and no one searched or **l** for them.	1335
	37: 8	*I* **l**, and tendons and flesh appeared	8011
	40: 2	some buildings that **l** like a city.	NIH
	44: 4	*I* **l** and saw the glory of the LORD	8011
Da	1:15	the end of the ten days they **l** healthier	5260+8011
	2:31	"You **l**, O king, and there before you	10255
	4:10	I **l**, and there stood a tree in	10255
	4:13	I **l**, and there before me was a messenger,	10255
	7: 2	Daniel said: "In my vision at night *I* **l**,	10255
	7: 5	second beast, which **l** like a bear.	10179
	7: 6	I **l**, and there before me was another beast,	10255
	7: 6	one that **l** like a leopard.	NIH
	7: 7	"After that, in my vision at night I **l**,	10255
	7: 9	"As I **l**, "thrones were set in place,	10255
	7:13	"In my vision at night I **l**,	10255
	7:20	that **l** more imposing than the others and	10256
	8: 3	I **l** up, and there before me was a ram	6524
	8:15	before me stood one who **l** like a man.	5260
	10: 5	I **l** up and there before me was	6524
	10:16	one who **l** like a man touched my lips,	1952
	10:18	the one who **l** like a man touched me	5260
	12: 5	**l**, and there before me stood two others,	8011
Hab	3: 6	*he* **l**, and made the nations tremble.	8011
Zec	1:18	Then I **l** up—and there before me were	6524
	2: 1	Then I **l** up—and there before me was	6524
	5: 1	I **l** again—and there before me was	5951+6524

Zec	5: 9	Then I **l** up—and there before me were	6524
	6: 1	I **l** up again—and there before me were	6524
Mt	17: 8	*When they* **l** up, they saw	2048+3836+4057
	19:26	Jesus **l** at them and said,	1838
	21:46	*They* **l** *for a way* to arrest him,	2426
	25:36	I was sick and *you* **l** after me,	2170
Mk	3: 5	He **l** around at them in anger and,	4315
	3:34	Then he **l** at those seated in a circle	4315
	7:34	He **l** up to heaven with a deep sigh	329
	8:24	He **l** up and said, "I see people;	329
	8:33	*when* Jesus turned and **l** at his disciples,	3972
	9: 8	Suddenly, *when they* **l** around,	4315
	9:26	The boy **l** *so much like* a corpse	1181+6059
	10:21	Jesus **l** at him and loved him.	1838
	10:23	Jesus **l** around and said to his disciples,	4315
	10:27	Jesus **l** at them and said,	1838
	11:11	He **l** around at everything,	4315
	12:12	Then *they* **l** *for a way* to arrest him	2426
	14:67	*she* **l** *closely* at him.	1838
	16: 4	But *when they* **l** up, they saw that the stone,	329
Lk	6:10	He **l** around at them all,	4315
	16:23	he **l** up and saw Abraham far	2048+3836+4057
	18: 9	and **l** down on everybody else,	2024
	18:24	Jesus **l** at him and said, "How hard it is	3972
	19: 5	*he* **l** up and said to him, "Zacchaeus,	329
	20:17	Jesus **l** *directly* at them and asked,	1838
	20:19	of the law and the chief priests **l** *for a way*	2426
	21: 1	*As he* **l** up, Jesus saw the rich	329
	22:56	She **l** *closely* at him and said,	867
	22:61	The Lord turned and **l** *straight* at Peter.	1838
Jn	1:42	Jesus **l** at him and said, "You are Simon	1838
	6: 5	*When* Jesus **l** up and saw	2048+3836+4057
	11:41	Then Jesus **l** up and said, "Father,	149+3836+4057
	17: 1	he **l** toward heaven and prayed:	2048+3836+4057
	20: 5	and **l** in at the strips of linen lying there	1063
Ac	3: 4	Peter **l** *straight* at him, as did John.	867
	6:15	in the Sanhedrin **l** *intently* at Stephen,	867
	7:55	**l** up to heaven and saw the glory of God,	867
	11: 6	*I* **l** into it and saw four-footed animals	867+2917
	13: 9	**l** *straight* at Elymas and said,	867
	14: 9	Paul **l** *directly* at him,	867
	17:23	around and **l** *carefully* at your objects	355
	23: 1	Paul **l** *straight* at the Sanhedrin and said,	867
1Jn	1: 1	which *we have* **l** at and our hands have	2517
Rev	4: 1	After this *I* **l**, and there before me was a	3972
	4: 6	throne there was *what* **l** *like* a sea of glass,	6055
	5:11	*I* **l** and heard the voice of many angels,	3972
	6: 2	*I* **l**, and there before me was a white horse!	3972
	6: 5	*I* **l**, and there before me was a black horse!	3972
	6: 8	*I* **l**, and there before me was a pale horse!	3972
	7: 9	After this *I* **l** and there before me was	3972
	9: 7	The locusts **l** *like* horses prepared	3927+3930
	9:17	The horses and riders I saw in my vision **l**	NIG
	11:12	while their enemies **l** on.	2555
	14: 1	Then *I* **l**, and there before me was	3972
	14:14	*I* **l**, and there before me was	3972
	15: 2	And I saw what **l** *like* a sea of glass mixed	NIG
	15: 5	After this *I* **l** and in heaven the temple,	3972
	16:13	I saw three evil spirits that **l** *like* frogs;	NIG

LOOKING (67) [LOOK]

Ge	37:15	"What *are you* **l** for?"	1335
	37:16	He replied, "I'm **l** for my brothers.	1335
	42: 1	"Why *do you just keep* **l** at each other?"	8011
Ex	22:10	or is taken away *while no one is* **l**,	8011
	25:20	face each other, **l** toward the cover.	7156
	37: 9	faced each other, **l** toward the cover.	7156
Dt	22: 2	with you and keep it until he *comes* **l** for it.	2011
Jdg	4:22	"I will show you the man *you're* **l** for."	1335
	17: 9	he said, "and I'm **l** for a place to stay."	5162
1Sa	10:14	"**L** for the donkeys," he said.	1335
	19: 2	"My father Saul *is* **l** for a chance	1335
1Ki	20: 7	"See how this man *is* **l** for trouble!	1335
2Ki	6:19	I will lead you to the man *you are* **l** for."	1335
Ps	69: 3	My eyes fail, **l** for my God.	3498
	119:82	My eyes fail, **l** for your promise;	NIH
	119:123	My eyes fail, **l** for your salvation,	NIH
	119:123	**l** for your righteous promise.	NIH
Ecc	12: 3	those **l** through the windows grow dim;	8011
SS	7: 4	the tower of Lebanon **l** toward Damascus.	7595
Isa	8:21	they will become enraged and, **l** upward,	7155
Jer	46: 5	They flee in haste without **l** *back,*	7155
La	4:17	our eyes failed, **l** in vain for help;	NIH
Da	1:10	Why should he see you **l** *worse* than	2407
	7:11	I kept **l** until the beast was slain	10255
Mt	12:10	**L** for a reason to accuse Jesus,	NIG
	13:45	kingdom of heaven is like a merchant **l** for	2426
	14:19	the five loaves and the two fish and **l** up	329
	26:59	and the whole Sanhedrin *were* **l** for	2426
	28: 5	for I know that *you are* **l** for Jesus,	2426
Mk	1:37	"Everyone *is* **l** for you!"	2426
	3: 2	Some of them *were* **l** for a reason	NIG
	3:32	and brothers *are outside* **l** for you."	2426
	5:32	But Jesus *kept* **l** around	4315
	6:41	the five loaves and the two fish and **l** up	329
	11:18	the law heard this and *began* **l** for a way	2426
	14: 1	and the teachers of the law *were* **l** for	2426
	14:55	the whole Sanhedrin *were* **l** for evidence	2426
	16: 6	"*You are* **l** for Jesus the Nazarene,	2426
Lk	2:38	the child to all who *were* **l** *forward to*	4657
	2:44	then *they began* **l** for	349
	4:42	The people *were* **l** for him and	2118
	6: 7	*were* **l** for a reason to accuse Jesus,	2351+4057
	9:16	the five loaves and the two fish and **l** up	329
	17: 7	a servant plowing or **l** *after* the *sheep.*	4477

Lk	22: 2	of the law were l for some way to get rid	2426
Jn	6:26	"I tell you the truth, you are l for me,	2426
	11:56	They kept l for Jesus,	2426
	18: 8	you are l for me, then let these men go."	2426
	20:15	Who is it you are l for?"	2426
Ac	1:10	They were l intently up into the sky	867
	1:11	"why do you stand here l into the sky?	1838
	10:19	"Simon, three men are l for you.	2426
	10:21	"I'm the one you're l for.	2426
2Co	10: 7	You are l only on the surface of things.	1063
Php	4:17	Not that I am l for a gift,	2118
	4:17	but I am l for what may be credited	2118
1Th	2: 6	We were not l for praise from men,	2426
Heb	11:10	For he was l forward to the city	1683
	11:14	that they are l for a country of their own.	2118
	11:26	because he was l ahead to his reward.	611
	13:14	but we are l for the city that is to come.	2118
Jas	1:24	after l at himself, goes away and	2917
1Pe	5: 8	like a roaring lion l for someone to devour.	2426
2Pe	3:13	with his promise we are l forward to	4659
	3:14	since you are l forward to this,	4659
Rev	5: 6	I saw a Lamb, l as if it had been slain,	NIG

LOOKINGGLASSES (KJV) See MIRROR

LOOKOUT (5) [LOOK]
2Ki	9:17	When the l standing on the tower	7595
	9:18	The l reported, "The messenger has	7595
	9:20	The l reported, "He has reached them,	7595
Isa	21: 6	post a l and have him report what he sees.	7595
	21: 8	And the l shouted, "Day after day,	8011

LOOKOUTS (1) [LOOK]
1Sa	14:16	Saul's l at Gibeah in Benjamin saw	7595

LOOKS (33) [LOOK]
Lev	14:35	'I have seen something that l like mildew	NIH
1Sa	16: 7	not look at the things man l at.	8011
	16: 7	Man l at the outward appearance,	8011
	16: 7	but the LORD l at the heart."	8011
Ezr	8:22	"The gracious hand of our God is on everyone who l to him,	1335
Job	8:17	and l for a place among the stones.	2600
	41:34	He l down on all that are haughty;	8011
Ps	14: 2	The LORD l down from heaven on	9207
	33:13	the LORD l down and sees all mankind;	5564
	53: 2	God l down from heaven on the sons	9207
	85:11	and righteousness l down from heaven.	9207
	104:32	he who l at the earth,	5564
	138: 6	LORD is on high, he l upon the lowly,	8011
Pr	20: 4	so at harvest time he l but finds nothing.	8626
	25:23	so a sly tongue brings angry l.	7156
	27:18	he who l after his master will be honored.	9068
Ecc	11: 4	whoever l at the clouds will not reap.	8011
Isa	5:30	And if one l at the land,	5564
	40:20	He l for a skilled craftsman to set up	1335
La	3:50	the LORD l down from heaven and sees.	9207
Eze	18: l	He l to the idols.	5951+6524
	34:12	As a shepherd l after his scattered flock	1333
Da	3:25	and the fourth l like a son of the gods."	10657
Mt	5:28	But I tell you that anyone who l at	1063
	16: 4	A wicked and adulterous generation l for	2118
Lk	9:62	and l back is fit for service in the kingdom	1063
Jn	6:40	that everyone who l to the Son and believes	2555
	9: 9	Others said, "No, he only l like him."	1639+3927
	12:45	he l at me, he sees the one who sent me.	2555
Php	2:21	For everyone l out for his own interests,	2426
Jas	1:23	not do what it says is like a man who l at	2917
	1:24	and immediately forgets what he l like.	1639
	1:25	the man who l intently into the perfect law	4160

LOOM (3) [LOOMS]
Jdg	16:13	the fabric [on the l] and tighten it with	NIH
	16:14	and pulled up the pin and the l,	756
Isa	38:12	and he has cut me off from the l;	1929

LOOMS (1) [LOOM]
Jer	6: 1	For disaster l out of the north,	9207

LOOPS (11)
Ex	26: 4	Make l of blue material along the edge of	4339
	26: 5	Make fifty l on one curtain and fifty loops	4339
	26: 5	Make fifty loops on one curtain and fifty l	4339
	26: 5	with the l opposite each other.	4339
	26:10	Make fifty l along the edge of	4339
	26:11	in the l to fasten the tent together as a unit.	4339
	36:11	Then they made l of blue material along	4339
	36:12	They also made fifty l on one curtain	4339
	36:12	and fifty l on the end curtain of	4339
	36:12	with the l opposite each other.	4339
	36:17	Then they made fifty l along the edge of	4339

LOOSE (13) [LOOSED, LOOSEN, LOOSENED]
Jdg	15: 5	and let the foxes l in the standing grain	8938
	16: 3	and tore them l, bar and all.	5825
Job	6: 9	to let l his hand and cut me off!	6000
	12:15	if he lets them l, they devastate the land.	8938
	38:31	Can you l the cords of Orion?	7337
Ps	78:26	He let l the east wind from the heavens	5825
Isa	7:25	places where cattle are turned l	5448

Isa	33:23	Your rigging hangs l:	5759
	58: 6	to l the chains of injustice and untie	7337
Mt	16:19	whatever you l on earth will be loosed in heaven."	3395
	18:18	whatever you l on earth will be loosed in heaven.	3395
Ac	16:26	and everybody's chains came l.	479
	27:40	Cutting l the anchors,	4311

LOOSED (3) [LOOSE]
Mt	16:19	you loose on earth will be l in heaven."	3395
	18:18	you loose on earth will be l in heaven.	3395
Lk	1:64	his mouth was opened and his tongue was l,	NIG

LOOSEN (1) [LOOSE]
Nu	5:18	he shall l her hair and place in her hands	7277

LOOSENED (2) [LOOSE]
Isa	5:27	not a belt is l at the waist,	7337
Mk	7:35	his tongue was l and he began to speak	3395

LOOT (13) [LOOTED, LOOTER, LOOTING]
Isa	10: 6	to seize l and snatch plunder,	8965
	17:14	This is the portion of those who l us,	9115
	21: 2	The traitor betrays, the looter takes l.	8720
	42:22	they have been made l,	5468
	42:24	Who handed Jacob over to become l,	5468
Eze	7:21	over as plunder to foreigners and as l to	8965
	26:12	and l your merchandise;	1024
	29:19	He will l and plunder the land as pay	8964+8965
	38:12	I will plunder and l and turn my hand	1020+1024
	38:13	Have you gathered your hordes to l,	1020+1024
	39:10	and l those who looted them,	1024
Da	11:24	l and wealth among his followers.	8965
Am	3:10	who hoard plunder and l in their fortresses.	8719

LOOTED (5) [LOOT]
Ge	34:27	of Jacob came upon the dead bodies and l	1024
2Ki	21:14	be l and plundered by all their foes,	1020
Isa	13:16	their houses will be l and their wives	9116
	42:22	But this is a people plundered and l,	9115
Eze	39:10	and loot those who l them,	1024

LOOTER (1) [LOOT]
Isa	21: 2	The traitor betrays, the l takes loot.	8720

LOOTING (1) [LOOT]
1Sa	23: 1	and are l the threshing floors,"	9115

LOP (1)
Isa	10:33	will l off the boughs with great power.	6188

*LORD (933) [*LORD'S, LORDED, LORDING, LORDS]
Ge	18: 3	"If I have found favor in your eyes, my l,	123
	18:27	so bold as to speak to the L,	151
	18:30	Then he said, "May the L not be angry,	151
	18:31	so bold as to speak to the L,	151
	18:32	Then he said, "May the L not be angry,	151
	20: 4	"L, will you destroy an innocent nation?	151
	23:11	"No, my l," he said.	123
	23:15	"Listen to me, my l;	123
	24:18	"Drink, my l," she said,	123
	27:29	Be l over your brothers,	1484
	27:37	"I have made him l over you	1484
	31:35	"Don't be angry, my l,	123
	32: 5	Now I am sending this message to my l,	123
	32:18	They are a gift sent to my l Esau,	123
	33: 8	"To find favor in your eyes, my l," he said.	123
	33:13	"My l knows that the children are tender	123
	33:14	So let my l go on ahead of his servant,	123
	33:14	until I come to my l in Seir."	123
	33:15	"Just let me find favor in the eyes of my l."	123
	42:10	"No, my l," they answered.	123
	42:30	"The man who is l over the land spoke	123
	42:33	the man who is l over the land said to us,	123
	44: 7	"Why does my l say such things?	123
	44:16	"What can we say to my l?	123
	44:18	"Please, my l, let your servant speak	123
	44:18	let your servant speak a word to my l.	123
	44:19	My l asked his servants,	123
	44:22	And we said to my l,	123
	44:24	we told him what my l had said.	123
	45: 8	l of his entire household and ruler	123
	45: 9	God has made me l of all Egypt.	123
	47:18	"We cannot hide from our l the fact that	123
	47:18	left for our l except our bodies and our land.	123
	47:25	"May we find favor in the eyes of our l;	123
Ex	4:10	Moses said to the LORD, "O L,	151
	4:13	But Moses said, "O L, please send someone	151
	5:22	"O L, why have you brought trouble	151
	15:17	O L, your hands established.	151
	32:22	"Do not be angry, my l," Aaron answered.	123
	34: 9	"O L, if I have found favor in your eyes,"	151
	34: 9	he said, "then let the L go with us.	151
Nu	11:28	spoke up and said, "Moses, my l,	123
	12:11	and he said to Moses, "Please, my l, do	123
	16:13	And now you also want to l it over us?	8606+8606
	32:25	your servants will do as our l commands.	123
	32:27	fight before the LORD, just as our l says."	123
	36: 2	"When the LORD commanded my l	123

Dt	10:17	the LORD your God is God of gods and L of lords,	123
Jos	3:11	the ark of the covenant of the L of all	123
	3:13	ark of the LORD—the L of all the earth—	123
	5:14	"What message does my L have	151
	7: 6	O L, what can I say,	151
Jdg	3:25	There they saw their l fallen to the floor,	123
	4:18	"Come, my l, come right in.	123
	6:15	"But L," Gideon asked,	151
	13: 8	"O L, I beg you, let the man of God	151
Ru	2:13	to find favor in your eyes, my l,"	123
1Sa	1:15	"Not so, my l," Hannah replied,	123
	1:26	"As surely as you live, my l,	123
	16:16	Let our l command his servants here	123
	22:12	"Yes, my l," he answered.	123
	24: 8	"My l the king!"	123
	25:24	"My l, let the blame be on me alone.	123
	25:25	May my l pay no attention to that wicked	123
	26:15	Why didn't you guard your l the king?	123
	26:15	Someone came to destroy your l the king.	123
	26:17	David replied, "Yes it is, my l the king."	123
	26:18	"Why is my l pursuing his servant?	123
	26:19	Now let my l the king listen	123
	29: 8	against the enemies of my l the king?"	123
2Sa	1:10	and have brought them here to my l."	123
	3:21	and assemble all Israel for my l the king,	123
	4: 8	This day the LORD has avenged my l	123
	9:11	"Your servant will do whatever my l	123
	10: 3	Ammonite nobles said to Hanun their l,	123
	13:32	"My l should not think that they killed all	123
	13:33	My l the king should not be concerned	123
	14: 9	"My l the king, the blame rest on me	123
	14:12	"Let your servant speak a word to my l	123
	14:15	"And now I have come to say this to my l	123
	14:17	the word of my l the king bring me rest,	123
	14:17	for my l the king is like an angel of God	123
	14:18	"Let my l the king speak,"	123
	14:19	"As surely as you live, my l the king,	123
	14:19	from anything my l the king says.	123
	14:20	My l has wisdom like that of an angel	123
	14:22	found favor in your eyes, my l the king,	123
	15:15	to do whatever our l the king chooses."	123
	15:21	and as my l the king lives,	123
	15:21	wherever my l the king may be,	123
	16: 4	find favor in your eyes, my l the king."	123
	16: 9	"Why should this dead dog curse my l	123
	18:28	against my l the king."	123
	18:31	"My l the king, hear the good news!	123
	18:32	of my l the king and all who rise up	123
	19:19	"May my l not hold me guilty.	123
	19:19	on the day my l the king left Jerusalem.	123
	19:20	to come down and meet my l the king."	123
	19:26	He said, "My l the king,	123
	19:27	And he has slandered your servant to my l	123
	19:27	My l the king is like an angel of God;	123
	19:28	but death from my l the king,	123
	19:30	now that my l the king has arrived home	123
	19:35	be an added burden to my l the king?	123
	19:37	Let him cross over with my l the king.	123
	24: 3	and may the eyes of my l the king see it.	123
	24: 3	But why does my l the king want	123
	24:21	Why has my l the king come to his servant?	123
	24:22	to David, "Let my l the king take whatever	123
1Ki	1: 2	so that our l the king may keep warm."	123
	1:11	without our l David's knowing it?	123
	1:13	'My l the king, did you not swear	123
	1:17	He said to him, "My l, you yourself swore	123
	1:18	my l the king, do not know about it.	123
	1:20	My l the king, the eyes of all Israel are on	123
	1:20	on the throne of my l the king after him.	123
	1:21	as soon as my l the king is laid to rest	123
	1:24	Nathan said, "Have you, my l the king,	123
	1:27	Is this something my l the king has done	123
	1:27	on the throne of my l the king after him?"	123
	1:31	said, "May my l King David live forever!"	123
	1:36	the God of my l the king, so declare it.	123
	1:37	As the LORD was with my l the king,	123
	1:37	the throne of my l King David!"	123
	1:43	"Our l King David has made Solomon king.	123
	1:47	to congratulate our l King David,	123
	2:38	Your servant will do as my l the king	123
	3:10	The L was pleased that Solomon had asked	151
	3:26	One of them said, "My l, this woman and I	123
	3:26	"Please, my l, give her the living baby!	123
	12:27	to their l, Rehoboam king of Judah.	123
	18: 7	and said, "Is it really you, my l Elijah?"	123
	18:13	Haven't you heard, my l,	123
	20: 4	"Just as you say, my l the king,	123
	20: 9	"Tell my l the king,	123
	22: 6	the L will give it into the king's hand."	151
2Ki	2:19	"Look, our l, this town is well situated,	123
	4:16	"No, my l," she objected.	123
	4:28	"Did I ask you for a son, my l?"	123
	6: 5	"Oh, my l," he cried out,	123
	6:12	"None of us, my l the king,"	123
	6:15	"Oh, my l, what shall we do?"	123
	6:26	"Help me, my l the king!"	123
	7: 6	for the L had caused the Arameans to hear	151
	8: 5	"This is the woman, my l the king,	123
	8:12	"Why is my l weeping?"	123
	19:23	you have heaped insults on the L.	151
1Ch	21: 3	My l the king, are they not all my lord's	123
	21: 3	Why does my l want to do this?	123
	21:23	Let my l the king do whatever pleases him.	123
2Ch	2:14	and with those of my l,	123
	2:15	"Now let my l send his servants the wheat	123
Ezr	10: 3	the counsel of my l and of those who fear	123

*LORD distinguishes the words translated "Lord" and "lord" from the proper name of God, Yahweh, indicated in the NIV by "LORD" and indexed under the heading †LORD, pages 686-707.

Ne 1:11 O L, let your ear be attentive to the prayer 151
4:14 Remember the L, who is great 151
8:10 This day is sacred to our L. 151
10:29 and decrees of the LORD our L. 151
Job 28:28 And he said to man, 'The fear of the L— 151
Ps 2:4 the L scoffs at them. 151
8:1 our L, how majestic is your name in all 123
8:9 our L, how majestic is your name in all 123
16:2 I said to the LORD, "You are my L; 151
22:30 future generations will be told about the L. 151
30:8 to the L I cried for mercy; 151
35:17 O L, how long will you look on? 151
35:22 Do not be far from me, O L. 151
35:23 Contend for me, my God and L. 151
37:13 but the L laughs at the wicked, 151
38:9 All my longings lie open before you, O L; 151
38:15 you will answer, O L my God. 151
38:22 Come quickly to help me, O L my Savior. 151
39:7 "But now, L, what do I look for? 151
40:17 may the L think of me. 151
44:23 Awake, O L! Why do you sleep? 151
45:11 honor him, for he is your L. 123
51:15 O L, open my lips, 151
54:4 the L is the one who sustains me. 151
55:9 Confuse the wicked, O L, 151
57:9 I will praise you, O L, among the nations; 151
59:11 But do not kill them, O L our shield, 151
62:12 and that you, O L, are loving. 151
66:18 the L would not have listened; 151
68:11 The L announced the word, 151
68:17 the L [has come] from Sinai 151
68:19 Praise be to the L to God our Savior. 151
68:22 The L says, "I will bring them 151
68:32 sing praise to the L, 151
69:6 O L, the LORD Almighty; 151
73:20 O L, you will despise them as fantasies. 151
77:2 When I was in distress, I sought the L; 151
77:7 "Will the L reject forever? 151
78:65 Then the L awoke as from sleep, 151
79:12 the reproach they have hurled at you, O L. 151
86:3 Have mercy on me, O L, 151
86:4 Bring joy to your servant, for to you, O L, 151
86:5 You are forgiving and good, O L, 151
86:8 O L; no deeds can compare with yours. 151
86:9 O L; they will bring glory to your name. 151
86:12 I will praise you, O L my God, 151
86:15 But you, O L, are a compassionate 151
89:49 O L, where is your former great love, 151
89:50 L, how your servant has been mocked, 151
90:1 L, you have been our dwelling place 151
90:17 the favor of the L our God rest upon us; 151
97:5 before the L of all the earth. 123
110:1 The LORD says to my L: 151
110:5 The L is at your right hand; 151
114:7 Tremble, O earth, at the presence of the L, 123
130:2 O L, hear my voice. 151
130:3 you, O LORD, kept a record of sins, O L, 151
130:6 for the L more than watchmen wait for 151
135:5 that our L is greater than all gods. 151
136:3 Give thanks to the L of lords; 151
147:5 Great is our L and mighty in power; 151
Isa 1:24 Therefore the L, the LORD Almighty, 123
3:1 See now, the L, the LORD Almighty, 123
3:15 declares the L, the LORD Almighty. 151
3:17 Therefore the L will bring sores on 151
3:18 day the L will snatch away their finery: 151
4:4 The L will wash away the filth of 151
6:1 I saw the L seated on a throne, 151
6:8 Then I heard the voice of the L saying, 151
6:11 Then I said, "For how long, O L?" 151
7:14 Therefore the L himself will give you 151
7:20 that day the L will use a razor hired from 151
8:7 therefore the L is about to bring 151
9:8 The L has sent a message against Jacob; 151
9:17 Therefore the L will take no pleasure in 151
10:12 When the L has finished all his work 151
10:16 Therefore, the L, the LORD Almighty, 123
10:23 The L, the LORD Almighty, 151
10:24 Therefore, this is what the L, 151
10:33 See, the L, the LORD Almighty, 151
11:11 In that day the L will reach out his hand 151
19:4 declares the L, the LORD Almighty. 123
21:6 This is what the L says to me: 151
21:8 the lookout shouted, "Day after day, my l, 123
21:16 This is what the L says to me: 151
22:5 The L, the LORD Almighty, 151
22:12 The L, the LORD Almighty, 151
22:15 says the L, the LORD Almighty. 151
22:15 This is what the L, the LORD Almighty, 151
28:2 the L has one who is powerful and strong. 151
28:22 the L, the LORD Almighty, 151
29:13 The L says: "These people come near to 151
30:20 Although the L gives you the bread 151
37:24 you have heaped insults on the L. 151
38:14 I am troubled; O L, come to my aid!" 151
38:16 L, by such things men live; 151
49:14 the L has forgotten me." 151
Jer 2:19 declares the L, the LORD Almighty. 151
37:20 But now, my l my king, please listen. 123
38:9 "My l my king, these men have acted 123
46:10 But that day belongs to the L, 151
46:10 For the L, the LORD Almighty, 151
49:5 declares the L, the LORD Almighty, 151
50:31 declares the L, the LORD Almighty, 151
La 1:14 and the L has sapped my strength. 151
1:15 "The L has rejected all the warriors 151
1:15 In his winepress the L has trampled 151

La 2:1 How the L has covered the Daughter of Zion 151
2:2 Without pity the L has swallowed up all 151
2:5 The L is like an enemy; 151
2:7 The L has rejected his altar 151
2:18 The hearts of the people cry out to the L. 151
2:19 like water in the presence of the L. 151
2:20 be killed in the sanctuary of the L? 151
3:31 For men are not cast off by the L forever. 151
3:36 would not the L see such things? 151
3:37 and have it happen if the L has 151
3:58 O L, you took up my case; 151
Eze 18:25 you say, 'The way of the L is not just.' 151
18:29 'The way of the L is not just.' 151
21:9 prophesy and say, 'This is what the L says: 151
33:17 'The way of the L is not just.' 151
33:20 you say, 'The way of the L is not just.' 151
Da 1:2 And the L delivered Jehoiakim king 151
1:10 "I am afraid of my l the king, 123
2:47 the L of kings and a revealer of mysteries, 10437
4:19 Belteshazzar answered, "My l, 10437
4:24 the Most High has issued against my l 10437
5:23 you have set yourself up against the L 10437
9:3 So I turned to the L God and pleaded 151
9:4 "O L, the great and awesome God, 151
9:7 "L, you are righteous, 151
9:9 The L our God is merciful and forgiving, 151
9:15 "Now, O L our God, who brought your 151
9:16 O L, in keeping with all your righteous 151
9:17 For your sake, O L, look with favor 151
9:19 O L, listen! 151
9:19 O L, forgive! 151
9:19 O L, hear and act! 151
10:16 my l, and I am helpless. 123
10:17 your servant, talk with you, my l? 123
10:19 my l, since you have given me strength." 123
12:8 So I asked, "My l, what will the outcome 123
Hos 12:14 his L will leave upon him the guilt 151
Am 3:13 declares the L, the LORD God Almighty. 151
5:16 Therefore this is what the L, 151
7:7 The L was standing by a wall 151
7:8 Then the L said, "Look, I am setting 151
9:1 I saw the L standing by the altar, 151
9:5 The L, the LORD Almighty, 151
Mic 1:2 the L from his holy temple. 151
4:13 their wealth to the L of all the earth. 123
Zec 4:4 I asked, "What are these, my l?" 123
4:4 "What are these, my l?" 123
4:5 "No, my l," I replied. 123
4:13 "No, my l," I said. 123
4:14 the two who are anointed to serve the L 123
6:4 "What are these, my l?" 123
6:5 the presence of the L of the whole world. 123
9:4 But the L will take away her possessions 151
Mal 1:14 sacrifices a blemished animal to the L. 151
3:1 the L you are seeking will come 123
Mt 1:20 an angel of the L appeared to him in a dream 3261
1:22 to fulfill what the L had said through 3261
1:24 the angel of the L had commanded him 3261
2:13 of the L appeared to Joseph in a dream 3261
2:15 And so was fulfilled what the L had said 3261
2:19 an angel of the L appeared in a dream to Joseph 3261
3:3 'Prepare the way for the L, 3261
4:7 'Do not put the L your God to the test.' " 3261
4:10 For it is written: 'Worship the L your God, 3261
5:33 keep the oaths you have made to the L.' 3261
7:21 "Not everyone who says to me, 'L, Lord,' 3261
7:21 "Not everyone who says to me, 'Lord, L, 3261
7:22 Many will say to me on that day, 'L, Lord, 3261
7:22 Many will say to me on that day, 'Lord, L, 3261
8:2 "L, if you are willing, you can make me 3261
8:6 "L," he said, "my servant lies at home 3261
8:8 The centurion replied, "L, I do not deserve 3261
8:21 Another disciple said to him, "L, 3261
8:25 and woke him, saying, "L, save us! 3261
9:28 "Yes, L," they replied. 3261
9:38 Ask the L of the harvest, therefore, 3261
11:25 Father, L of heaven and earth, 3261
12:8 For the Son of Man is L of the Sabbath." 3261
14:28 "L, if it's you," Peter replied, 3261
14:30 beginning to sink, cried out, "L, save me!" 3261
15:22 "L, Son of David, have mercy on me! 3261
15:25 "L, help me!" she said. 3261
15:27 "L," she said, "but even the dogs eat 3261
16:22 began to rebuke him. "Never, L!" 3261
17:4 Peter said to Jesus, "L, it is good for us 3261
17:15 "L, have mercy on my son," he said. 3261
18:21 Then Peter came to Jesus and asked, "L, 3261
20:25 the rulers of the Gentiles l it over them, 2894
20:30 "L, Son of David, have mercy on us!" 3261
20:31 "L, Son of David, have mercy on us!" 3261
20:33 "L," they answered, "we want our sight." 3261
21:3 tell him that the L needs them, 3261
21:9 he who comes in the name of the L!" 3261
21:42 the L has done this, and it is marvelous 3261
22:37 " 'Love the L your God with all your heart 3261
22:43 speaking by the Spirit, calls him 'L'? 3261
22:44 " 'The L said to my Lord: 3261
22:44 " 'The Lord said to my L: 3261
22:45 If then David calls him 'L,' 3261
23:39 he who comes in the name of the L.' " 3261
24:42 not know on what day your L will come. 3261
25:37 "Then the righteous will answer him, 'L, 3261
25:44 "They also will answer, 'L, 3261
26:22 after the other, "Surely not I, L?" 3261
27:10 potter's field, as the L commanded me." 3261
28:2 an angel of the L came down from heaven 3261

Mk 1:3 'Prepare the way for the L, 3261
2:28 the Son of Man is L even of the Sabbath." 3261
5:19 and tell them how much the L has done 3261
7:28 L," she replied, "but even the dogs under 3261
10:42 as rulers of the Gentiles l it over them, 2894
11:3 'The L needs it and will send it back here 3261
11:9 he who comes in the name of the L!" 3261
12:11 the L has done this, and it is marvelous 3261
12:29 'Hear, O Israel, the L our God, 3261
12:29 O Israel, the Lord our God, the L is one. 3261
12:30 Love the L your God with all your heart 3261
12:36 " 'The L said to my Lord: 3261
12:36 " 'The Lord said to my L: 3261
12:37 David himself calls him 'L.' 3261
13:20 If the L had not cut short those days, 3261
16:19 After the L Jesus had spoken to them, 3261
16:20 and the L worked with them 3261
Lk 1:9 into the temple of the L and burn incense. 3261
1:11 Then an angel of the L appeared to him, 3261
1:15 for he will be great in the sight of the L. 3261
1:16 will he bring back to the L their God. 3261
1:17 And he will go on before the L, 899S
1:17 to make ready a people prepared for the L." 3261
1:25 "The L has done this for me," she said. 3261
1:28 The L is with you." 3261
1:32 The L God will give him the throne 3261
1:43 the mother of my l should come to me? 3261
1:45 that what the L has said to her will 3261
1:46 And Mary said: "My soul glorifies the L 3261
1:58 that the L had shown her great mercy, 3261
1:68 "Praise be to the L, the God of Israel 3261
1:76 on before the L to prepare the way for him, 3261
2:9 An angel of the L appeared to them, 3261
2:9 and the glory of the L shone around them, 3261
2:11 has been born to you; he is Christ the L. 3261
2:15 which the L has told us about." 3261
2:22 to Jerusalem to present him to the L 3261
2:23 (as it is written in the Law of the L, 3261
2:23 to be consecrated to the L"), 3261
2:24 with what is said in the Law of the L: 3261
2:29 **"Sovereign L, as you have promised, you 1305**
2:39 required by the Law of the L, 3261
3:4 'Prepare the way for the L, 3261
4:8 Worship the L your God and serve him only 3261
4:12 'Do not put the L your God to the test.' " 3261
4:18 "The Spirit of the L is on me, 3261
5:8 "Go away from me, L; 3261
5:12 "L, if you are willing, you can make me 3261
5:17 the L was present for him to heal the sick. 3261
6:5 "The Son of Man is L of the Sabbath." 3261
6:46 "Why do you call me, 'L, Lord,' 3261
6:46 "Why do you call me, 'Lord, L,' 3261
7:6 "L, don't trouble yourself, 3261
7:13 When the L saw her, his heart went out to 3261
7:19 he sent them to the L to ask, 3261
9:54 "L, do you want us to call fire down 3261
9:59 But the man replied, "L, first let me go and 3261
9:61 Still another said, "I will follow you, L; 3261
10:1 the L appointed seventy-two others 3261
10:2 Ask the L of the harvest, therefore, 3261
10:17 and said, "L, even the demons submit 3261
10:21 Father, L of heaven and earth, 3261
10:27 " 'Love the L your God with all your heart 3261
10:40 She came to him and asked, "L, 3261
10:41 "Martha, Martha," the L answered, 3261
11:1 one of his disciples said to him, "L, 3261
11:39 Then the L said to him, "Now then, 3261
12:41 "L, are you telling this parable to us, 3261
12:42 The L answered, "Who then is the faithful 3261
13:15 The L answered him, "You hypocrites! 3261
13:23 Someone asked him, "L, are only a few 3261
13:35 he who comes in the name of the L.' " 3261
17:5 The apostles said to the L, "Increase our faith!" 3261
17:37 "Where, L?" they asked. 3261
18:6 And the L said, "Listen to what 3261
18:41 "L, I want to see," he replied. 3261
19:8 But Zacchaeus stood up and said to the L, 3261
19:8 up and said to the Lord, "Look, L! 3261
19:31 tell him, 'The L needs it.' 3261
19:34 They replied, "The L needs it." 3261
19:38 the king who comes in the name of the L!" 3261
20:37 for he calls the L 'the God of Abraham, 3261
20:42 " 'The L said to my Lord: 3261
20:42 " 'The Lord said to my L: 3261
20:44 David calls him 'L.' 3261
22:25 "The kings of the Gentiles l it over them; 3259
22:33 "L, I am ready to go with you to prison 3261
22:38 The disciples said, "See, L, 3261
22:49 "L, should we strike with our swords?" 3261
22:61 The L turned and looked straight at Peter. 3261
22:61 the word the L had spoken to him: 3261
24:3 they did not find the body of the L Jesus. 3261
24:34 L has risen and has appeared to Simon." 3261
Jn 1:23 'Make straight the way for the L.' " 3261
4:3 When the L learned of this, 3261
6:23 the bread after the L had given thanks. 3261
6:68 Simon Peter answered him, "L, 3261
9:38 Then the man said, "L, I believe," 3261
11:2 on the L and wiped his feet with her hair. 3261
11:3 So the sisters sent word to Jesus, "L, 3261
11:12 His disciples replied, "L, if he sleeps, 3261
11:21 "L," Martha said to Jesus, 3261
11:27 "Yes, L," she told him, 3261
11:32 she fell at his feet and said, "L, 3261
11:34 "Come and see, L," they replied. 3261
11:39 "But, L," said Martha, 3261

Jn
12:13 he who comes in the name of the L!" — 3261
12:38 "L, who has believed our message and — 3261
12:38 has the arm of the L been revealed?" — 3261
13: 6 "L, are you going to wash my feet?" — 3261
13: 9 "Then, L," Simon Peter replied, — 3261
13:13 "You call me 'Teacher' and 'L,' — 3261
13:14 Now that I, your L and Teacher, — 3261
13:25 he asked him, "L, who is it?" — 3261
13:36 Simon Peter asked him, "L, — 3261
13:37 "L, why can't I follow you now? — 3261
14: 5 Thomas said to him, "L, — 3261
14: 8 "L, show us the Father and that will — 3261
14:22 Judas (not Judas Iscariot) said, "But, L, — 3261
20: 2 "They have taken the L out of the tomb, — 3261
20:13 "They have taken my L away," she said, — 3261
20:18 "I have seen the L!" — 3261
20:20 when they saw the L. — 3261
20:25 "We have seen the L!" — 3261
20:28 Thomas said to him, "My L and my God!" — 3261
21: 7 "It is the L!" — 3261
21: 7 "It is the L," — 3261
21:12 They knew it was the L. — 3261
21:15 L," he said, "you know that I love you." — 3261
21:16 He answered, "Yes, L, — 3261
21:17 He said, "L, you know all things; — 3261
21:20 "L, who is going to betray you?") — 3261
21:21 When Peter saw him, he asked, "L, — 3261

Ac
1: 6 "L, are you at this time going to restore — 3261
1:21 the whole time the L Jesus went in and out — 3261
1:24 Then they prayed, "L, you know — 3261
2:20 of the great and glorious day of the L. — 3261
2:21 on the name of the L will be saved.' — 3261
2:25 " 'I saw the L always before me. — 3261
2:34 and yet he said, " 'The L said to my Lord: — 3261
2:34 and yet he said, " 'The Lord said to my L: — 3261
2:36 whom you crucified, both L and Christ." — 3261
2:39 for all whom the L our God will call." — 3261
2:47 And the L added to their number daily — 3261
3:19 times of refreshing may come from the L, — 3261
3:22 'The L your God will raise up for you — 3261
4:24 "Sovereign L," they said, "you made the — 1305
4:26 the rulers gather together against the L and — 3261
4:29 Now, L, consider their threats — 3261
4:33 to testify to the resurrection of the L Jesus, — 3261
5: 9 to test the Spirit of the L? — 3261
5:14 in the L and were added to their number. — 3261
5:19 during the night an angel of the L opened — 3261
7:33 the L said to him, 'Take off your sandals; — 3261
7:49 house will you build for me? says the L. — 3261
7:59 "L Jesus, receive my spirit." — 3261
7:60 he fell on his knees and cried out, "L, — 3261
8:16 into the name of the L Jesus. — 3261
8:22 of this wickedness and pray to the L. — 3261
8:24 "Pray to the L for me so — 3261
8:25 and proclaimed the word of the L, — 3261
8:26 Now an angel of the L said to Philip, — 3261
8:39 Spirit of the L suddenly took Philip away, — 3261
9: 5 "Who are you, L?" — 3261
9:10 The L called to him in a vision, — 3261
9:10 "Yes, L," he answered. — 3261
9:11 The L told him, "Go to the house of Judas — 3261
9:13 "L," Ananias answered, — 3261
9:15 But the L said to Ananias, "Go! — 3261
9:17 he said, "Brother Saul, the L— — 3261
9:27 the L and that the Lord had spoken to him, — 3261
9:27 the Lord and that the L had spoken to him, — NIG
9:28 speaking boldly in the name of the L. — 3261
9:31 living in the fear of the L. — 3261
9:35 and Sharon saw him and turned to the L. — 3261
9:42 and many people believed in the L. — 3261
10: 4 "What is it, L?" he asked. — 3261
10:14 "Surely not, L!" Peter replied. — 3261
10:33 to everything the L has commanded you — 3261
10:36 Jesus Christ, who is L of all. — 3261
11: 8 "I replied, 'Surely not, L! — 3261
11:16 Then I remembered what the L had said: — 3261
11:17 who believed in the L Jesus Christ, — 3261
11:20 the good news about the L Jesus. — 3261
11:21 of people believed and turned to the L. — 3261
11:23 remain true to the L with all their hearts. — 3261
11:24 of people were brought to the L. — 3261
12: 7 Suddenly an angel of the L appeared and — 3261
12:11 without a doubt that the L sent his angel — 3261
12:17 how the L had brought him out of prison. — 3261
12:23 an angel of the L struck him down, — 3261
13: 2 While they were worshiping the L — 3261
13:10 perverting the right ways of the L? — 3261
13:11 Now the hand of the L is against you. — 3261
13:12 at the teaching about the L. — 3261
13:44 to hear the word of the L. — 3261
13:47 For this is what the L has commanded us: — 3261
13:48 and honored the word of the L; — 3261
13:49 of the L spread through the whole region. — 3261
14: 3 speaking boldly for the L, — 3261
14:23 committed them to the L, — 3261
15:11 the grace of our L Jesus that we are saved, — 3261
15:17 that the remnant of men may seek the L, — 3261
15:17 Gentiles who bear my name, says the L, — 3261
15:26 for the name of our L Jesus Christ. — 3261
15:35 and preached the word of the L. — 3261
15:36 of the L and see how they are doing. — 3261
15:40 by the brothers to the grace of the L. — 3261
16:14 The L opened her heart to respond — 3261
16:15 "If you consider me a believer in the L," — 3261
16:31 They replied, "Believe in the L Jesus, — 3261
16:32 Then they spoke the word of the L to him, — 3261
17:24 the L of heaven and earth and does not live — 3261

Ac
18: 8 his entire household believed in the L; — 3261
18: 9 One night the L spoke to Paul in a vision: — 3261
18:25 He had been instructed in the way of the L, — 3261
19: 5 baptized into the name of the L Jesus. — 3261
19:10 of Asia heard the word of the L. — 3261
19:13 to invoke the name of the L Jesus — 3261
19:17 name of the L Jesus was held in high honor. — 3261
19:20 of the L spread widely and grew in power. — 3261
20:19 the L with great humility and with tears, — 3261
20:21 and have faith in our L Jesus. — 3261
20:24 the task the L Jesus has given me— — 3261
20:35 the words the L Jesus himself said: — 3261
21:13 in Jerusalem for the name of the L Jesus." — 3261
22: 8 " 'Who are you, L?' — 3261
22:10 " 'What shall I do, L?' — 3261
22:10 " 'Get up,' the L said, — 3261
22:18 and saw the L speaking. — 899S
22:19 " 'L,' I replied, 'these men know — 3261
22:21 "Then the L said to me, 'Go; — NIG
23:11 The following night the L stood near Paul — 3261
26:15 "Then I asked, 'Who are you, L?' — 3261
26:15 whom you are persecuting,' the L replied. — 3261
28:31 and taught about the L Jesus Christ. — 3261

Ro
1: 4 Jesus Christ our L. — 3261
1: 7 and from the L Jesus Christ. — 3261
4: 8 the man whose sin the L will never count — 3261
4:24 in him who raised Jesus our L from — 3261
5: 1 with God through our L Jesus Christ, — 3261
5:11 in God through our L Jesus Christ, — 3261
6:23 eternal life through Jesus Christ our L. — 3261
6:23 of God is eternal life in Christ Jesus our L. — 3261
7:25 through Jesus Christ our L! — 3261
8:39 love of God that is in Christ Jesus our L. — 3261
9:28 the L will carry out his sentence on earth — 3261
9:29 the L Almighty had left us descendants, — 3261
10: 9 with your mouth, "Jesus is L," and believe — 3261
10:12 the same L is Lord of all — 3261
10:12 the same Lord is L of all — NIG
10:13 calls on the name of the L will be saved." — 3261
10:16 "L, who has believed our message?" — 3261
11: 3 "L, they have killed your prophets — 3261
11:34 "Who has known the mind of the L? — 3261
12:11 but keep your spiritual fervor, serving the L. — 3261
12:19 I will repay," says the L. — 3261
13:14 clothe yourselves with the L Jesus Christ, — 3261
14: 4 for he is able to make him stand. — 3261
14: 6 does so to the L. — 3261
14: 6 He who eats meat, eats to the L, — 3261
14: 6 does so to the L and gives thanks to God. — 3261
14: 8 If we live, we live to the L; — 3261
14: 8 and if we die, we die to the L. — 3261
14: 8 live or die, we belong to the L. — 1639+3261
14: 9 returned to life so that he might be the L — 3259
14:11 " 'As surely as I live,' says the L, — 3261
14:14 As one who is in the L Jesus, — 3261
15: 6 the God and Father of our L Jesus Christ, — 3261
15:11 And again, "Praise the L, all you Gentiles; — 3261
15:30 by our L Jesus Christ and by the love of — 3261
16: 2 in the L in a way worthy of the saints and — 3261
16: 8 Greet Ampliatus, whom I love in the L. — 3261
16:11 of Narcissus who are in the L. — 3261
16:12 those women who work hard in the L. — 3261
16:12 woman who has worked very hard in the L. — 3261
16:13 Greet Rufus, chosen in the L, — 3261
16:18 such people are not serving our L Christ, — 3261
16:20 The grace of our L Jesus be with you. — 3261
16:22 greet you in the L. — 3261

1Co
1: 2 call on the name of our L Jesus Christ— — 3261
1: 2 their L and ours: — NIG
1: 3 and the L Jesus Christ. — 3261
1: 7 as you eagerly wait for our L Jesus Christ — 3261
1: 8 on the day of our L Jesus Christ — 3261
1: 9 with his Son Jesus Christ our L, — 3261
1:10 in the name of our L Jesus Christ, — 3261
1:31 "Let him who boasts boast in the L." — 3261
2: 8 they would not have crucified the L — 3261
2:16 "For who has known the mind of the L — 3261
3: 5 as the L has assigned to each his task. — 3261
3:20 "The L knows that the thoughts of the wise — 3261
4: 4 It is the L who judges me. — 3261
4: 5 wait till the L comes. — 3261
4:17 whom I love, who is faithful in the L. — 3261
4:19 come to you very soon, if the L is willing, — 3261
5: 4 the name of our L Jesus and I am with you — 3261
5: 4 and the power of our L Jesus is present, — 3261
5: 5 and his spirit saved on the day of the L. — 3261
6:11 in the name of the L Jesus Christ and by — 3261
6:13 but for the L, and the L for the body. — 3261
6:13 but for the Lord, and the L for the body. — 3261
6:14 By his power God raised the L from — 3261
6:17 with the L is one with him in spirit. — 3261
7:10 I give this command (not I, but the L): — 3261
7:12 To the rest I say this (I, not the L): — 3261
7:17 the place in life that the L assigned to him — 3261
7:22 a slave when he was called by the L is — 3261
7:25 I have no command from the L, — 3261
7:32 how he can please the L. — 3261
7:34 Her aim is to be devoted to the L in — NIG
7:35 in undivided devotion to the L. — 3261
7:39 but he must belong to the L. — 3261
8: 6 and there is but one L, Jesus Christ, — 3261
9: 1 Have I not seen Jesus our L? — 3261
9: 1 not the result of my work in the L? — 3261
9: 2 you are the seal of my apostleship in the L. — 3261
9:14 the L has commanded that those who preach — 3261
10: 9 We should not test the L, — 3261
10:21 You cannot drink the cup of the L and — 3261

1Co
11:11 the L, however, woman is not independent — 3261
11:23 from the L what I also passed on to you: — 3261
11:23 The L Jesus, on the night he was betrayed, — 3261
11:27 the L in an unworthy manner will be guilty — 3261
11:27 against the body and blood of the L. — 3261
11:29 without recognizing the body of the L eats — 3261
11:32 When we are judged by the L, — 3261
12: 3 "Jesus is L," except by the Holy Spirit. — 3261
12: 5 different kinds of service, but the same L. — 3261
14:21 then they will not listen to me," says the L. — 3261
15:31 as I glory over you in Christ Jesus our L. — 3261
15:57 the victory through our L Jesus Christ. — 3261
15:58 give yourselves fully to the work of the L, — 3261
15:58 that your labor in the L is not in vain. — 3261
16: 7 spend some time with you, if the L permits. — 3261
16:10 for he is carrying on the work of the L, — 3261
16:19 and Priscilla greet you warmly in the L, — 3261
16:22 If anyone does not love the L— — 3261
16:22 Come, O L! — 3448
16:23 The grace of the L Jesus be with you. — 3261

2Co
1: 2 and the L Jesus Christ. — 3261
1: 3 the God and Father of our L Jesus Christ, — 3261
1:14 of you in the day of the L Jesus. — 3261
1:24 Not that we l it over your faith, — 3259
2:12 of Christ and found that the L had opened — 3261
3:16 But whenever anyone turns to the L, — 3261
3:17 Now the L is the Spirit, — 3261
3:17 and where the Spirit of the L is, — 3261
3:18 which comes from the L, who is the Spirit. — 3261
4: 5 not preach ourselves, but Jesus Christ as L, — 3261
4:14 the L Jesus from the dead will also raise us — 3261
5: 6 in the body we are away from the L. — 3261
5: 8 from the body and at home with the L. — 3261
5:11 then, we know what it is to fear the L, — 3261
6:17 from them and be separate, says the L. — 3261
6:18 says the L Almighty." — 3261
8: 5 but they gave themselves first to the L and — 3261
8: 9 you know the grace of our L Jesus Christ, — 3261
8:19 the L himself and to show our eagerness — 3261
8:21 not only in the eyes of the L but also in — 3261
10: 8 about the authority the L gave us — 3261
10:17 But, "Let him who boasts boast in the L." — 3261
10:18 but the one whom the L commends. — 3261
11:17 not talking as the L would, — 3261
11:31 The God and Father of the L Jesus, — 3261
12: 1 on to visions and revelations from the L. — 3261
12: 8 with the L to take it away from me. — 3261
13:10 the L gave me for building you up, — 3261
13:14 May the grace of the L Jesus Christ, — 3261

Gal
1: 3 and the L Jesus Christ, — 3261
5:10 in the L that you will take no other view. — 3261
6:14 in the cross of our L Jesus Christ, — 3261
6:18 of our L Jesus Christ be with your spirit, — 3261

Eph
1: 2 and the L Jesus Christ. — 3261
1: 3 the God and Father of our L Jesus Christ, — 3261
1:15 the L Jesus and your love for all the saints, — 3261
1:17 that the God of our L Jesus Christ, — 3261
2:21 and rises to become a holy temple in the L. — 3261
3:11 he accomplished in Christ Jesus our L. — 3261
4: 1 As a prisoner for the L, then, — 3261
4: 5 one L, one faith, one baptism; — 3261
4:17 So I tell you this, and insist on it in the L, — 3261
5: 8 but now you are light in the L. — 3261
5:10 and find out what pleases the L. — 3261
5:19 and make music in your heart to the L, — 3261
5:20 in the name of our L Jesus Christ. — 3261
5:22 submit to your husbands as to the L. — 3261
6: 1 Children, obey your parents in the L, — 3261
6: 4 up in the training and instruction of the L. — 3261
6: 7 as if you were serving the L, not men, — 3261
6: 8 that the L will reward everyone for — 3261
6:10 in the L and in his mighty power. — 3261
6:21 and faithful servant in the L, — 3261
6:23 the Father and the L Jesus Christ. — 3261
6:24 Grace to all who love our L Jesus Christ — 3261

Php
1: 2 and the L Jesus Christ. — 3261
1:14 the brothers in the L have been encouraged — 3261
2:11 every tongue confess that Jesus Christ is L, — 3261
2:19 the L Jesus to send Timothy to you soon, — 3261
2:24 in the L that I myself will come soon. — 3261
2:29 Welcome him in the L with great joy, — 3261
3: 1 Finally, my brothers, rejoice in the L! — 3261
3: 8 greatness of knowing Christ Jesus my L, — 3261
3:20 a Savior from there, the L Jesus Christ, — 3261
4: 1 that is how you should stand firm in the L, — 3261
4: 2 to agree with each other in the L. — 3261
4: 4 Rejoice in the L always. — 3261
4: 5 The L is near. — 3261
4:10 I rejoice greatly in the L that — 3261
4:23 of the L Jesus Christ be with your spirit. — 3261

Col
1: 3 the Father of our L Jesus Christ, — 3261
1:10 of the L and may please him in every way: — 3261
2: 6 just as you received Christ Jesus as L, — 3261
3:13 Forgive as the L forgave you. — 3261
3:17 do it all in the name of the L Jesus, — 3261
3:18 as is fitting in the L. — 3261
3:20 for this pleases the L. — 3261
3:22 of heart and reverence for the L. — 3261
3:23 as working for the L, not for men, — 3261
3:24 an inheritance from the L as a reward. — 3261
3:24 It is the L Christ you are serving. — 3261
4: 7 and fellow servant in the L. — 3261
4:17 the work you have received in the L." — 3261

1Th
1: 1 in God the Father and the L Jesus Christ: — 3261
1: 3 by hope in our L Jesus Christ. — 3261
1: 6 You became imitators of us and of the L; — 3261
2:15 who killed the L Jesus and the prophets — 3261

1Th
2:19 of our L Jesus when he comes? 3261
3: 8 since you are standing firm in the L. 3261
3:11 and Father himself and our L Jesus clear 3261
3:12 May the L make your love increase 3261
3:13 and Father when our L Jesus comes 3261
4: 1 and urge you in the L Jesus to do this more 3261
4: 2 by the authority of the L Jesus. 3261
4: 6 The L will punish men for all such sins, 3261
4:15 who are left till the coming of the L, 3261
4:16 L himself will come down from heaven, 3261
4:17 with them in the clouds to meet the L in 3261
4:17 And so we will be with the L forever. 3261
5: 2 of the L will come like a thief in the night. 3261
5: 9 through our L Jesus Christ. 3261
5:12 over you in the L and who admonish you. 3261
5:23 at the coming of our L Jesus Christ. 3261
5:27 before the L to have this letter read to all 3261
5:28 grace of our L Jesus Christ be with you. 3261

2Th
1: 1 in God our Father and the L Jesus Christ: 3261
1: 2 the Father and the L Jesus Christ. 3261
1: 7 when the L Jesus is revealed from heaven 3261
1: 8 and do not obey the gospel of our L Jesus. 3261
1: 9 the L and from the majesty of his power 3261
1:12 the name of our L Jesus may be glorified 3261
1:12 of our God and the L Jesus Christ. 3261
2: 1 the coming of our L Jesus Christ 3261
2: 2 that the day of the L has already come. 3261
2: 8 the L Jesus will overthrow with the breath 3261
2:13 brothers loved by the L, 3261
2:14 in the glory of our L Jesus Christ. 3261
2:16 May our L Jesus Christ himself 3261
3: 1 the L may spread rapidly and be honored, 3261
3: 3 But the L is faithful, 3261
3: 4 the L that you are doing and will continue 3261
3: 5 the L direct your hearts into God's love 3261
3: 6 In the name of the L Jesus Christ, 3261
3:12 the L Jesus Christ to settle down and earn 3261
3:16 the L of peace himself give you peace 3261
3:16 The L be with all of you. 3261
3:18 of our L Jesus Christ be with you all. 3261

1Ti
1: 2 the Father and Christ Jesus our L. 3261
1:12 I thank Christ Jesus our L, 3261
1:14 The grace of our L was poured out 3261
6: 3 the sound instruction of our L Jesus Christ 3261
6:14 until the appearing of our L Jesus Christ, 3261
6:15 the King of kings and of lords, 3261

2Ti
1: 2 the Father and Christ Jesus our L. 3261
1: 8 do not be ashamed to testify about our L, 3261
1:16 May the L show mercy to the household 3261
1:18 the L grant that he will find mercy from 3261
1:18 that he will find mercy from the L on 3261
2: 7 for the L will give you insight into all this. 3261
2:19 "The L knows those who are his," and, 3261
2:19 the L must turn away from wickedness." 3261
2:22 along with those who call on the L out of 3261
3:11 Yet the L rescued me from all of them. 3261
4: 8 which the L, the righteous Judge, 3261
4:14 L will repay him for what he has done. 3261
4:17 L stood at my side and gave me strength, 3261
4:18 The L will rescue me from every evil attack 3261
4:22 The L be with your spirit. 3261

Phm
1: 3 and the L Jesus Christ. 3261
1: 5 the L Jesus and your love for all the saints. 3261
1:16 both as a man and as a brother in the L. 3261
1:20 some benefit from you in the L; 3261
1:25 of the L Jesus Christ be with your spirit. 3261

Heb
1:10 He also says, "In the beginning, O L, 3261
2: 3 which was first announced by the L, 3261
7:14 For it is clear that our L descended 3261
7:21 L has sworn and will not change his mind: 3261
8: 2 the true tabernacle set up by the L, 3261
8: 8 "The time is coming, declares the L, 3261
8: 9 turned away from them, declares the L. 3261
8:10 of Israel after that time, declares the L. 3261
8:11 saying, 'Know the L,' 3261
10:16 with them after that time, says the L. 3261
10:30 and again, "The L will judge his people." 3261
12: 6 because the L disciplines those he loves, 3261
12:14 without holiness no one will see the L. 3261
13: 6 "The L is my helper; I will not be afraid. 3261
13:20 brought back from the dead our L Jesus, 3261

Jas
1: 1 a servant of God and of the L Jesus Christ, 3261
1: 7 That man should not think he will receive
    anything from the L; 3261
2: 1 as believers in our glorious L Jesus Christ, 3261
3: 9 the tongue we praise our L and Father, 3261
4:10 Humble yourselves before the L, 3261
5: 4 have reached the ears of the L Almighty. 3261
5:10 prophets who spoke in the name of the L. 3261
5:11 have seen what the L finally brought about. 3261
5:11 The L is full of compassion and mercy. 3261
5:14 anoint him with oil in the name of the L, 3261
5:15 the L will raise him up. 3261

1Pe
1: 3 the God and Father of our L Jesus Christ! 3261
1:25 but the word of the L stands forever." 3261
2: 3 that you have tasted that the L is good. 3261
3:12 For the eyes of the L are on the righteous 3261
3:12 of the L is against those who do evil." 3261
3:15 But in your hearts set apart Christ as L. 3261

2Pe
1: 2 the knowledge of God and of Jesus our L. 3261
1: 8 in your knowledge of our L Jesus Christ. 3261
1:11 into the eternal kingdom of our L 3261
1:14 our L Jesus Christ has made clear to me. 3261
1:16 power and coming of our L Jesus Christ, 3261
2: 1 denying the **sovereign** L who bought them 1305
2: 9 then the L knows how to rescue godly men 3261
2:11 against such beings in the presence of the L. 3261

2Pe
2:20 by knowing our L and Savior Jesus Christ 3261
3: 2 by our L and Savior through your apostles. 3261
3: 8 With the L a day is like a thousand years, 3261
3: 9 The L is not slow in keeping his promise. 3261
3:10 But the day of the L will come like a thief. 3261
3:18 in the grace and knowledge of our L 3261

Jude
1: 4 deny Jesus Christ our only Sovereign and L. 3261
1: 5 the L delivered his people out of Egypt, 3261
1: 9 but said, "The L rebuke you!" 3261
1:14 "See, the L is coming with thousands 3261
1:17 the apostles of our L Jesus Christ foretold. 3261
1:21 for the mercy of our L Jesus Christ 3261
1:25 through Jesus Christ our L, 3261

Rev
1: 8 says the L God, "who is, and who was, 3261
4: 8 "Holy, holy, holy is the L God Almighty, 3261
4:11 "You are worthy, our L and God, 3261
6:10 "How long, **Sovereign** L, holy and true, 1305
11: 4 the two lampstands that stand before the L 3261
11: 8 where also their L was crucified. 3261
11:15 the kingdom of our L and of his Christ, 3261
11:17 "We give thanks to you, L God Almighty, 3261
14:13 Blessed are the dead who die in the L from 3261
15: 3 marvelous are your deeds, L God Almighty. 3261
15: 4 Who will not fear you, O L, 3261
16: 7 "Yes, L God Almighty, 3261
17:14 because he is L of lords and King 3261
18: 8 for mighty is the L God who judges her. 3261
19: 6 For our L God Almighty reigns. 3261
19:16 KING OF KINGS AND L OF LORDS. 3261
21:22 because the L God Almighty and 3261
22: 5 for the L God will give them light. 3261
22: 6 The L, the God of the spirits of 3261
22:20 Come, L Jesus. 3261
22:21 grace of the L Jesus be with God's people. 3261

*LORD'S (43) [*LORD]

Ge 44: 9 the rest of us will become my l slaves." 123+4200
44:16 We are now my l slaves— 123+4200
44:33 as my l slave in place of the boy, 123+4200
Nu 14:17 "Now may the L strength be displayed, 151
2Sa 11:11 and my l men are camped in the open fields. 123
1Ki 1:33 "Take your l servants with you 123
3:15 stood before the ark of the L covenant 151
1Ch 21: 3 are they not all my l subjects? 123+4200
Mal 1:12 you profane it by saying of the L table, 151
Lk 1: 6 observing all the L commandments 3261
1:38 "I am the L servant," Mary answered. 3261
1:66 For the L hand was with him. 3261
2:26 not die before he had seen the L Christ. 3261
4:19 to proclaim the year of the L favor." 3261
10:39 at the L feet listening to what he said. 3261
Ac 7:31 he heard the L voice: 3261
9: 1 murderous threats against the L disciples. 3261
11:21 The L hand was with them, 3261
21:14 "The L will be done." 3261
1Co 7:22 by the Lord is the L freedman; 3261
7:25 as one who by the L mercy is trustworthy. 3261
7:32 is concerned about the L affairs— 3261
7:34 or virgin is concerned about the L affairs: 3261
9: 5 as do the other apostles and the L brothers 3261
10:21 you cannot have a part in both the L table 3261
10:22 Are we trying to arouse the L jealousy? 3261
10:26 "The earth is the L, and everything in it." 3261
11:20 it is not the L Supper you eat, 3258
11:26 you proclaim the L death until he comes. 3261
14:37 what I am writing to you is the L command. 3261
2Co 3:18 with unveiled faces all reflect the L glory, 3261
Gal 1:19 only James, the L brother. 3261
Eph 5:17 but understand what the L will is. 3261
1Th 1: 8 The L message rang out from you not only 3261
4:15 According to the L own word, 3261
2Ti 2:24 And the L servant must not quarrel; 3261
Heb 12: 5 do not make light of the L discipline, 3261
Jas 4:15 you ought to say, "If it is the L will, 3261
5: 7 then, brothers, until the L coming. 3261
5: 8 because the L coming is near. 3261
1Pe 2:13 for the L sake to every authority instituted 3261
2Pe 3:15 that our L patience means salvation, 3261
Rev 1:10 On the L Day I was in the Spirit, 3258

†LORD (6551) [†LORD'S]

Ge 2: 4 When the L God made the earth and 3378
2: 5 for the L God had not sent rain on 3378
2: 7 the L God formed the man from the dust 3378
2: 8 Now the L God had planted a garden in 3378
2: 9 And the L God made all kinds 3378
2:15 The L God took the man and put him in 3378
2:16 And the L God commanded the man, 3378
2:18 The L God said, "It is not good for the man 3378
2:19 Now the L God had formed out of 3378
2:21 So the L God caused the man to fall into 3378
2:22 Then the L God made a woman from 3378
3: 1 of the wild animals the L God had made. 3378
3: 8 the sound of the L God as he was walking 3378
3: 8 and they hid from the L God among 3378
3: 9 But the L God called to the man, 3378
3:13 Then the L God said to the woman, 3378
3:14 So the L God said to the serpent, 3378
3:21 The L God made garments of skin 3378
3:22 And the L God said, "The man has now 3378
3:23 So the L God banished him from 3378
4: 1 the help of the L I have brought forth 3378
4: 3 of the soil as an offering to the L. 3378
4: 4 The L looked with favor on Abel 3378
4: 6 the L said to Cain, "Why are you angry? 3378

Ge 4: 9 Then the L said to Cain, "Where is 3378
4:10 The L said, "What have you done? NIH
4:13 Cain said to the L, "My punishment 3378
4:15 But the L said to him, "Not so; 3378
4:15 Then the L put a mark on Cain so 3378
4:26 to call on the name of the L. 3378
5:29 by the ground the L has cursed." 3378
6: 3 Then the L said, "My Spirit will not 3378
6: 5 The L saw how great man's wickedness 3378
6: 6 The L was grieved that he had made man 3378
6: 7 So the L said, "I will wipe mankind, 3378
6: 8 Noah found favor in the eyes of the L. 3378
7: 1 The L then said to Noah, "Go into the ark, 3378
7: 5 Noah did all that the L commanded him. 3378
7:16 Then the L shut him in. 3378
8:20 Then Noah built an altar to the L and, 3378
8:21 The L smelled the pleasing aroma 3378
9:26 He also said, "Blessed be the L, 3378
10: 9 He was a mighty hunter before the L; 3378
10: 9 a mighty hunter before the L." 3378
11: 5 But the L came down to see the city and 3378
11: 6 The L said, "If as one people speaking 3378
11: 8 So the L scattered them from there 3378
11: 9 because there the L confused the language 3378
11: 9 From there the L scattered them over 3378
12: 1 The L had said to Abram, "Leave your 3378
12: 4 So Abram left, as the L had told him; 3378
12: 7 The L appeared to Abram and said, 3378
12: 7 So he built an altar there to the L, 3378
12: 8 There he built an altar to the L and called 3378
12: 8 and called on the name of the L. 3378
12:17 But the L inflicted serious diseases 3378
13: 4 Abram called on the name of the L. 3378
13:10 like the garden of the L, 3378
13:10 (This was before the L destroyed Sodom 3378
13:13 and were sinning greatly against the L. 3378
13:14 The L said to Abram after Lot had parted 3378
13:18 where he built an altar to the L, 3378
14:22 "I have raised my hand to the L, 3378
15: 1 the word of the L came to Abram in 3378
15: 2 But Abram said, "O Sovereign L, 3378
15: 4 Then the word of the L came to him: 3378
15: 6 Abram believed the L, and he credited it 3378
15: 7 He also said to him, "I am the L, 3378
15: 8 But Abram said, "O Sovereign L, 3378
15: 9 So the L said to him, "Bring me a heifer, NIH
15:13 Then the L said to him, NIH
15:18 On that day the L made a covenant 3378
16: 2 "The L has kept me from having children. 3378
16: 5 May the L judge between you and me." 3378
16: 7 of the L found Hagar near a spring in 3378
16: 9 Then the angel of the L told her, 3378
16:11 The angel of the L also said to her: 3378
16:11 for the L has heard of your misery. 3378
16:13 She gave this name to the L who spoke 3378
17: 1 the L appeared to him and said, 3378
18: 1 The L appeared to Abraham near 3378
18:10 Then the L said, "I will surely return NIH
18:13 Then the L said to Abraham, 3378
18:14 Is anything too hard for the L? 3378
18:17 Then the L said, "Shall I hide from
    Abraham what I am about to do? 3378
18:19 of the L by doing what is right and just, 3378
18:19 so that the L will bring about 3378
18:20 Then the L said, 3378
18:22 Abraham remained standing before the L. 3378
18:26 The L said, "If I find fifty righteous people 3378
18:33 When the L had finished speaking 3378
19:13 The outcry to the L against its people is 3378
19:14 the L is about to destroy the city!" 3378
19:16 for the L was merciful to them. 3378
19:24 Then the L rained down burning sulfur 3378
19:24 from the L out of the heavens. 3378
19:27 where he had stood before the L. 3378
20:18 for the L had closed up every womb 3378
21: 1 Now the L was gracious to Sarah 3378
21: 1 and the L did for Sarah what he had 3378
21:33 upon the name of the L, the Eternal God. 3378
22:11 But the angel of the L called out to him 3378
22:14 that place The L Will Provide. 3378
22:14 "On the mountain of the L it will 3378
22:15 of the L called to Abraham from heaven 3378
22:16 "I swear by myself, declares the L, 3378
24: 1 and the L had blessed him in every way. 3378
24: 3 I want you to swear by the L, 3378
24: 7 "The L, the God of heaven, 3378
24:12 Then he prayed, "O L, God of my master 3378
24:21 the L had made his journey successful. 3378
24:26 man bowed down and worshiped the L, 3378
24:27 "Praise be to the L, the God of my master 3378
24:27 the L has led me on the journey to 3378
24:31 "Come, you who are blessed by the L," 3378
24:35 The L has blessed my master abundantly, 3378
24:40 "He replied, 'The L, before whom I 3378
24:42 I came to the spring today, I said, 'O L, 3378
24:44 let her be the one the L has chosen 3378
24:48 and I bowed down and worshiped the L. 3378
24:48 I praised the L, the God of my master 3378
24:50 "This is from the L; 3378
24:51 as the L has directed." 3378
24:52 down to the ground before the L. 3378
24:56 the L has granted success to my journey. 3378
25:21 Isaac prayed to the L on behalf 3378
25:21 The L answered his prayer, 3378
25:22 So she went to inquire of the L. 3378
25:23 The L said to her, "Two nations are in your 3378
26: 2 The L appeared to Isaac and said, 3378

Ref	Text	Strong's
Ge 26:12	because **the L** blessed him.	3378
26:22	"Now **the L** has given us room	3378
26:24	That night **the L** appeared to him	3378
26:25	and called on the name of **the L.**	3378
26:28	"We saw clearly that **the L** was with you;	3378
26:29	And now you are blessed by **the L.**'	3378
27:7	in the presence of **the L** before I die.'	3378
27:20	"**The L** your God gave me success,"	3378
27:27	the smell of a field that **the L** has blessed.	3378
28:13	There above it stood **the L**, and he said:	3378
28:13	"I am **the L**, the God of your father	3378
28:16	he thought, "Surely **the L** is in this place,	3378
28:21	then **the L** will be my God	3378
29:31	When **the L** saw that Leah was not loved,	3378
29:32	"It is because **the L** has seen my misery.	3378
29:33	"Because **the L** heard that I am not loved,	3378
29:35	"This time I will praise **the L.**"	3378
30:24	"May **the L** add to me another son."	3378
30:27	by divination that **the L** has blessed me	3378
30:30	**the L** has blessed you wherever I have been.	3378
31:3	Then **the L** said to Jacob,	3378
31:49	"May **the L** keep watch between you	3378
32:9	God of my father Isaac, O **L**,	3378
38:7	so **the L** put him to death.	3378
39:2	**The L** was with Joseph and he prospered,	3378
39:3	When his master saw that **the L** was with	3378
39:3	with him and that **the L** gave him success	3378
39:5	**the L** blessed the household of the Egyptian	3378
39:5	of **the L** was on everything Potiphar had,	3378
39:21	**the L** was with him;	3378
39:23	because **the L** was with Joseph	3378
49:18	"I look for your deliverance, O **L**,	3378
Ex 3:2	of **the L** appeared to him in flames of fire	3378
3:4	**the L** saw that he had gone over to look,	3378
3:7	**The L** said, "I have indeed seen	3378
3:15	'**The L**, the God of your fathers—	3378
3:16	'**The L**, the God of your fathers—	3378
3:18	'**The L**, the God of the Hebrews,	3378
3:18	to offer sacrifices to **the L** our God.'	3378
4:1	'**The L** did not appear to you'?"	3378
4:2	Then **the L** said to him,	3378
4:3	**The L** said, "Throw it on the ground."	NIH
4:4	Then **the L** said to him,	3378
4:5	said **the L**, "is so that they may believe	NIH
4:5	"is so that they may believe that **the L**,	3378
4:6	Then **the L** said, "Put your hand inside	3378
4:8	Then **the L** said, "If they do not believe	NIH
4:10	Moses said to **the L**, "O Lord,	3378
4:11	**The L** said to him, "Who gave man his	3378
4:11	Is it not I, **the L**?	3378
4:19	Now **the L** had said to Moses in Midian,	3378
4:21	**The L** said to Moses, "When you return	3378
4:22	say to Pharaoh, 'This is what **the L** says:	3378
4:24	**the L** met [Moses] and was about	3378
4:26	So **the L** let him alone.	NIH
4:27	**The L** said to Aaron, "Go into the desert	3378
4:28	Moses told Aaron everything **the L** had sent him to say,	3378
4:30	Aaron told them everything **the L** had said	3378
4:31	that **the L** was concerned about them	3378
5:1	"This is what **the L**, the God of Israel,	3378
5:2	Pharaoh said, "Who is **the L**,	3378
5:2	I do not know **the L** and I will not let	3378
5:3	to offer sacrifices to **the L.**'	3378
5:17	'Let us go and sacrifice to **the L.**'	3378
5:21	"May **the L** look upon you and judge	3378
5:22	Moses returned to **the L** and said,	3378
6:1	Then **the L** said to Moses,	3378
6:2	God also said to Moses, "I am **the L**.	3378
6:3	but by my name **the L** I did not make	3378
6:6	'I am **the L**, and I will bring you out	3378
6:7	you will know that I am **the L** your God,	3378
6:8	I am **the L.**'"	3378
6:10	Then **the L** said to Moses,	3378
6:12	But Moses said to **the L**,	3378
6:13	Now **the L** spoke to Moses and Aaron,	3378
6:26	and Moses to whom **the L** said,	3378
6:28	when **the L** spoke to Moses in Egypt,	3378
6:29	"I am **the L**. Tell Pharaoh king of Egypt	3378
6:30	But Moses said to **the L**,	3378
7:1	Then **the L** said to Moses, "See,	3378
7:5	the Egyptians will know that I am **the L**	3378
7:6	as **the L** commanded them.	3378
7:8	**The L** said to Moses and Aaron,	3378
7:10	and did just as **the L** commanded.	3378
7:13	just as **the L** had said.	3378
7:14	Then **the L** said to Moses,	3378
7:16	Then say to him, '**The L**,	3378
7:17	This is what **the L** says:	3378
7:17	By this you will know that I am **the L**:	3378
7:19	**The L** said to Moses, "Tell Aaron,	3378
7:20	as **the L** had commanded.	3378
7:22	just as **the L** had said.	3378
7:25	Seven days passed after **the L** struck	3378
8:1	Then **the L** said to Moses,	3378
8:1	'This is what **the L** says:	3378
8:5	Then **the L** said to Moses, "Tell Aaron,	3378
8:8	to take the frogs away from me	3378
8:8	to offer sacrifices to **the L.**"	3378
8:10	there is no one like **the L** our God.	3378
8:12	to **the L** about the frogs he had brought	3378
8:13	And **the L** did what Moses asked.	3378
8:15	just as **the L** had said.	3378
8:16	Then **the L** said to Moses, "Tell Aaron,	3378
8:19	just as **the L** had said.	3378
8:20	Then **the L** said to Moses,	3378
8:20	'This is what **the L** says:	3378
Ex 8:22	so that you will know that I, **the L**,	3378
8:24	And **the L** did this.	3378
8:26	The sacrifices we offer **the L** our God	3378
8:28	to offer sacrifices to **the L** our God,	3378
8:28	to offer sacrifices to **the L** your God in	3378
8:29	I will pray to **the L**,	3378
8:29	the people go to offer sacrifices to **the L.**"	3378
8:30	Moses left Pharaoh and prayed to **the L**,	3378
8:31	and **the L** did what Moses asked:	3378
9:1	Then **the L** said to Moses,	3378
9:1	'This is what **the L**, the God of the Hebrews	3378
9:3	hand of **the L** will bring a terrible plague	3378
9:4	But **the L** will make a distinction between	3378
9:5	**The L** set a time and said,	3378
9:5	"Tomorrow **the L** will do this in	3378
9:6	And the next day **the L** did it:	3378
9:8	Then **the L** said to Moses and Aaron,	3378
9:12	But **the L** hardened Pharaoh's heart	3378
9:12	just as **the L** had said to Moses.	3378
9:13	Then **the L** said to Moses,	3378
9:13	'This is what **the L**,	3378
9:20	of **the L** hurried to bring their slaves	3378
9:21	of **the L** left their slaves and livestock in	3378
9:22	Then **the L** said to Moses,	3378
9:23	**the L** sent thunder and hail,	3378
9:23	So **the L** rained hail on the land of Egypt;	3378
9:27	"**The L** is in the right,	3378
9:28	Pray to **the L**, for we have had enough	3378
9:29	spread out my hands in prayer to **the L.**	3378
9:30	still do not fear **the L** God.	3378
9:33	He spread out his hands toward **the L**;	3378
9:35	just as **the L** had said through Moses.	3378
10:1	Then **the L** said to Moses,	3378
10:2	and that you may know that I am **the L.**"	3378
10:3	"This is what **the L**,	3378
10:7	so that they may worship **the L** their God.	3378
10:8	"Go, worship **the L** your God," he said.	3378
10:9	to celebrate a festival to **the L.**"	3378
10:10	Pharaoh said, "**The L** be with you—	3378
10:11	and worship **the L**,	3378
10:12	And **the L** said to Moses,	3378
10:13	and **the L** made an east wind blow across	3378
10:16	against **the L** your God and against you.	3378
10:17	and pray to **the L** your God	3378
10:18	then left Pharaoh and prayed to **the L.**	3378
10:19	And **the L** changed the wind to	3378
10:20	But **the L** hardened Pharaoh's heart,	3378
10:21	Then **the L** said to Moses,	3378
10:24	and said, "Go, worship **the L.**	3378
10:25	to present to **the L** our God.	3378
10:26	of them in worshiping **the L** our God,	3378
10:26	to use to worship **the L.**"	3378
10:27	But **the L** hardened Pharaoh's heart,	3378
11:1	Now **the L** had said to Moses,	3378
11:3	(**The L** made the Egyptians favorably disposed toward the people,	3378
11:4	So Moses said, "This is what **the L** says:	3378
11:7	Then you will know that **the L** makes	3378
11:9	**The L** had said to Moses,	3378
11:10	but **the L** hardened Pharaoh's heart,	3378
12:1	**The L** said to Moses and Aaron in Egypt,	3378
12:12	judgment on all the gods of Egypt. I am **the L.**	3378
12:14	celebrate it as a festival to **the L**—	3378
12:23	When **the L** goes through the land	3378
12:25	that **the L** will give you as he promised,	3378
12:27	'It is the Passover sacrifice to **the L**,	3378
12:28	The Israelites did just what **the L** commanded Moses	3378
12:29	At midnight **the L** struck down all	3378
12:31	Go, worship **the L** as you have requested.	3378
12:36	**The L** had made the Egyptians favorably disposed toward the people,	3378
12:42	Because **the L** kept vigil that night	3378
12:42	to honor **the L** for the generations	3378
12:43	**The L** said to Moses and Aaron,	3378
12:50	Israelites did just what **the L** had commanded Moses	3378
12:51	And on that very day **the L** brought	3378
13:1	**The L** said to Moses,	3378
13:3	because **the L** brought you out of it with	3378
13:5	When **the L** brings you into the land of	3378
13:6	the seventh day hold a festival to **the L.**	3378
13:8	of what **the L** did for me when I came out	3378
13:9	that the law of **the L** is to be on your lips.	3378
13:9	For **the L** brought you out of Egypt	3378
13:11	"After **the L** brings you into the land of	3378
13:12	to give over to **the L** the first offspring	3378
13:12	of your livestock belong to **the L.**	3378
13:14	'With a mighty hand **the L** brought us out	3378
13:15	**the L** killed every firstborn in Egypt,	3378
13:15	to **the L** the first male offspring	3378
13:16	that **the L** brought us out of Egypt	3378
13:21	By day **the L** went ahead of them in	3378
14:1	Then **the L** said to Moses,	3378
14:4	the Egyptians will know that I am **the L.**"	3378
14:8	**The L** hardened the heart of Pharaoh king	3378
14:10	and cried out to **the L.**	3378
14:13	deliverance **the L** will bring you today.	3378
14:14	**The L** will fight for you;	3378
14:15	Then **the L** said to Moses,	3378
14:18	The Egyptians will know that I am **the L**	3378
14:21	and all that night **the L** drove the sea back	3378
14:24	the last watch of the night **the L** looked	3378
14:25	**The L** is fighting for them against Egypt."	3378
14:26	Then **the L** said to Moses,	3378
14:27	and **the L** swept them into the sea.	3378
Ex 14:30	That day **the L** saved Israel from	3378
14:31	the great power **the L** displayed against	3378
14:31	the people feared **the L** and put their trust	3378
15:1	and the Israelites sang this song to **the L**:	3378
15:1	"I will sing to **the L**,	3378
15:2	**The L** is my strength and my song;	3363
15:3	**The L** is a warrior; the LORD is his name.	3378
15:3	LORD is a warrior; **the L** is his name.	3378
15:6	"Your right hand, O **L**, was majestic	3378
15:6	Your right hand, O **L**, shattered the enemy.	3378
15:11	"Who among the gods is like you, O **L**?	3378
15:16	until your people pass by, O **L**,	3378
15:17	O **L**, you made for your dwelling,	3378
15:18	**The L** will reign for ever and ever."	3378
15:19	**the L** brought the waters of the sea back	3378
15:21	"Sing to **the L**, for he is highly exalted.	3378
15:25	Then Moses cried out to **the L**,	3378
15:25	and **the L** showed him a piece of wood.	3378
15:25	**the L** made a decree and a law for them,	NIH
15:26	of **the L** your God and do what is right	3378
15:26	for I am **the L**, who heals you."	3378
16:4	Then **the L** said to Moses,	3378
16:6	that it was **the L** who brought you out	3378
16:7	you will see the glory of **the L**,	3378
16:8	that it was **the L** when he gives you meat	3378
16:8	grumbling against us, but against **the L.**"	3378
16:9	'Come before **the L**,	3378
16:10	the glory of **the L** appearing in the cloud.	3378
16:11	**The L** said to Moses,	3378
16:12	that I am **the L** your God.'"	3378
16:15	"It is the bread **the L** has given you to eat.	3378
16:16	This is what **the L** has commanded:	3378
16:23	"This is what **the L** commanded:	3378
16:23	a holy Sabbath to **the L.**	3378
16:25	"because today is a Sabbath to **the L.**	3378
16:28	Then **the L** said to Moses,	3378
16:29	Bear in mind that **the L** has given you	3378
16:32	"This is what **the L** has commanded:	3378
16:33	Then place it before **the L** to be kept for	3378
16:34	As **the L** commanded Moses,	3378
17:1	from place to place as **the L** commanded.	3378
17:2	Why do you put **the L** to the test?"	3378
17:4	Then Moses cried out to **the L**,	3378
17:5	**The L** answered Moses,	3378
17:7	and because they tested **the L** saying,	3378
17:7	"Is **the L** among us or not?"	3378
17:14	Then **the L** said to Moses,	3378
17:15	an altar and called it **The L** is my Banner.	3378
17:16	hands were lifted up to the throne of **the L.**	3363
17:16	**The L** will be at war against the Amalekites	3378
18:1	**the L** had brought Israel out of Egypt.	3378
18:8	about everything **the L** had done	3378
18:8	the way and how **the L** had saved them.	3378
18:9	the good things **the L** had done for Israel	3378
18:10	He said, "Praise be to **the L**,	3378
18:11	that **the L** is greater than all other gods,	3378
19:3	and **the L** called to him from	3378
19:7	the words **the L** had commanded him	3378
19:8	"We will do everything **the L** has said."	3378
19:8	Moses brought their answer back to **the L.**	3378
19:9	**The L** said to Moses,	3378
19:9	Then Moses told **the L** what the people	3378
19:10	And **the L** said to Moses,	3378
19:11	because on that day **the L** will come	3378
19:18	because **the L** descended on it in fire.	3378
19:20	**The L** descended to the top of Mount Sinai	3378
19:21	and **the L** said to him,	3378
19:21	not force their way through to see **the L**	3378
19:22	Even the priests, who approach **the L**,	3378
19:22	or **the L** will break out against them."	3378
19:23	Moses said to **the L**,	3378
19:24	**The L** replied, "Go down and bring Aaron	3378
19:24	through to come up to **the L**,	3378
20:2	"I am **the L** your God, who brought you	3378
20:5	for I, **the L** your God, am a jealous God,	3378
20:7	not misuse the name of **the L** your God,	3378
20:7	for **the L** will not hold anyone guiltless who	3378
20:10	a Sabbath to **the L** your God.	3378
20:11	in six days **the L** made the heavens and	3378
20:11	Therefore **the L** blessed the Sabbath day	3378
20:12	in the land **the L** your God is giving you.	3378
20:22	Then **the L** said to Moses,	3378
22:11	an oath before **the L** that the neighbor did	3378
22:20	to any god other than **the L** must	3378
23:17	to appear before the Sovereign **L.**	3378
23:19	to the house of **the L** your God.	3378
23:25	Worship **the L** your God,	3378
24:1	he said to Moses, "Come up to **the L**,	3378
24:2	but Moses alone is to approach **the L**;	3378
24:3	"Everything **the L** has said we will do."	3378
24:4	then wrote down everything **the L** had said.	3378
24:5	as fellowship offerings to **the L.**	3378
24:7	"We will do everything **the L** has said;	3378
24:7	of the covenant that **the L** has made	3378
24:12	**The L** said to Moses,	3378
24:16	the glory of **the L** settled on Mount Sinai.	3378
24:16	on the seventh day **the L** called to Moses	NIH
24:17	To the Israelites the glory of **the L** looked	3378
25:1	**The L** said to Moses,	3378
27:21	before **the L** from evening till morning.	3378
28:12	as a memorial before **the L.**	3378
28:29	as a continuing memorial before **the L.**	3378
28:30	whenever he enters the presence of **the L.**	3378
28:30	the Israelites over his heart before **the L.**	3378
28:35	before **the L** and when he comes out,	3378
28:36	as on a seal: HOLY TO **THE L.**	3378
28:38	so that they will be acceptable to **the L.**	3378

†**LORD** distinguishes the proper name of God, *Yahweh*, indicated in the NIV by "LORD," from the words translated "Lord" and "lord," indexed under the heading *LORD, pages 683-86.

Ref	Text	Num
Ex 29:18	It is a burnt offering to **the L**,	3378
29:18	an offering made to **the L** by fire.	3378
29:23	which is before **the L**, take a loaf,	3378
29:24	and his sons and wave them before **the L**	3378
29:25	for a pleasing aroma to **the L**,	3378
29:25	an offering made to **the L** by fire.	3378
29:26	wave it before **the L** as a wave offering,	3378
29:28	to **the L** from their fellowship offerings.	3378
29:41	an offering made to **the L** by fire.	3378
29:42	to the Tent of Meeting before **the L**.	3378
29:46	They will know that I am **the L** their God,	3378
29:46	I am **the L** their God.	3378
30:8	before **the L** for the generations to come.	3378
30:10	It is most holy to **the L**."	3378
30:11	Then **the L** said to Moses,	3378
30:12	each one must pay **the L** a ransom	3378
30:13	This half shekel is an offering to **the L**.	3378
30:14	are to give an offering to **the L**.	3378
30:15	when you make the offering to **the L**	3378
30:16	a memorial for the Israelites before **the L**,	3378
30:17	Then **the L** said to Moses,	3378
30:20	by presenting an offering made to **the L**	3378
30:22	Then **the L** said to Moses,	3378
30:34	Then **the L** said to Moses,	3378
30:37	consider it holy to **the L**.	3378
31:1	Then **the L** said to Moses,	3378
31:12	Then **the L** said to Moses,	3378
31:13	so you may know that I am **the L**,	3378
31:15	a Sabbath of rest, holy to **the L**.	3378
31:17	in six days **the L** made the heavens and	3378
31:18	When **the L** finished speaking to Moses	2257S
32:5	Tomorrow there will be a festival to **the L**.	3378
32:7	Then **the L** said to Moses, "Go down,	3378
32:9	**the L** said to Moses,	3378
32:11	Moses sought the favor of **the L** his God.	3378
32:11	favor of the LORD his God. "O **L**,"	3378
32:14	Then **the L** relented and did not bring	3378
32:26	"Whoever is for **the L**, come to me."	3378
32:27	he said to them, "This is what **the L**,	3378
32:29	"You have been set apart to **the L** today,	3378
32:30	But now I will go up to **the L**;	3378
32:31	So Moses went back to **the L** and said,	3378
32:33	**The L** replied to Moses,	3378
32:35	And **the L** struck the people with a plague	3378
33:1	Then **the L** said to Moses,	3378
33:5	For **the L** had said to Moses,	3378
33:7	Anyone inquiring of **the L** would go to	3378
33:9	while **the L** spoke with Moses.	NIH
33:11	**The L** would speak to Moses face to face,	3378
33:12	Moses said to **the L**,	3378
33:14	**The L** replied, "My Presence will go	NIH
33:17	And **the L** said to Moses,	NIH
33:19	And **the L** said, "I will cause all my	NIH
33:19	and I will proclaim my name, **the L**,	3378
33:21	Then **the L** said, "There is a place near me	3378
34:1	**The L** said to Moses,	3378
34:4	as **the L** had commanded him;	3378
34:5	Then **the L** came down in the cloud	3378
34:5	with him and proclaimed his name, **the L**.	3378
34:6	proclaiming, "**The L**, the LORD,	3378
34:6	proclaiming, "The LORD, **the L**,	3378
34:10	Then **the L** said: "I am making a covenant	NIH
34:10	the work that I, **the L**, will do for you.	3378
34:14	Do not worship any other god, for **the L**,	3378
34:23	to appear before the Sovereign **L**,	3378
34:24	to appear before **the L** your God.	3378
34:26	to the house of **the L** your God.	3378
34:27	Then **the L** said to Moses,	3378
34:28	Moses was there with **the L** forty days	3378
34:29	because he had spoken with **the L**.	2257S
34:32	the commands **the L** had given him	3378
34:35	until he went in to speak with **the L**.	2257S
35:1	the things **the L** has commanded you	3378
35:2	a Sabbath of rest to **the L**.	3378
35:4	"This is what **the L** has commanded:	3378
35:5	take an offering for **the L**.	3378
35:5	to bring to **the L** an offering of gold,	3378
35:10	make everything **the L** has commanded:	3378
35:21	and brought an offering to **the L** for	3378
35:22	as a wave offering to **the L**.	3378
35:24	as an offering to **the L**,	3378
35:29	to **the L** freewill offerings for all the work	3378
35:29	for all the work **the L**	3378
35:30	**the L** has chosen Bezalel son of Uri,	3378
36:1	to whom **the L** has given skill and ability	3378
36:1	the work just as **the L** has commanded."	3378
36:2	to whom **the L** had given ability	3378
36:5	the work **the L** commanded to be done."	3378
38:22	made everything **the L** commanded Moses;	3378
39:1	as **the L** commanded Moses.	3378
39:5	as **the L** commanded Moses.	3378
39:7	as **the L** commanded Moses.	3378
39:21	as **the L** commanded Moses.	3378
39:26	as **the L** commanded Moses.	3378
39:29	as **the L** commanded Moses.	3378
39:30	an inscription on a seal: HOLY TO THE **L**.	3378
39:31	as **the L** commanded Moses.	3378
39:32	as **the L** commanded Moses.	3378
39:42	as **the L** had commanded Moses.	3378
39:43	as **the L** had commanded.	3378
40:1	Then **the L** said to Moses:	3378
40:16	as **the L** commanded him.	3378
40:19	as **the L** commanded him.	3378
40:21	as **the L** commanded him.	3378
40:23	and set out the bread on it before **the L**,	3378
40:23	as **the L** commanded him.	3378
40:25	and set up the lamps before **the L**,	3378
Ex 40:25	as **the L** commanded him.	3378
40:27	as **the L** commanded him.	3378
40:29	as **the L** commanded him.	3378
40:32	as **the L** commanded Moses.	3378
40:34	the glory of **the L** filled the tabernacle.	3378
40:35	the glory of **the L** filled the tabernacle.	3378
40:38	the cloud of **the L** was over the tabernacle	3378
Lev 1:1	**The L** called to Moses and spoke to him	3378
1:2	any of you brings an offering to **the L**,	3378
1:3	so that it will be acceptable to **the L**.	3378
1:5	to slaughter the young bull before **the L**,	3378
1:9	an aroma pleasing to **the L**.	3378
1:11	at the north side of the altar before **the L**,	3378
1:13	an aroma pleasing to **the L**.	3378
1:14	the offering to **the L** is a burnt offering	3378
1:17	an aroma pleasing to **the L**.	3378
2:1	a grain offering to **the L**,	3378
2:2	an aroma pleasing to **the L**.	3378
2:3	of the offerings made to **the L** by fire.	3378
2:8	of these things to **the L**;	3378
2:9	an aroma pleasing to **the L**.	3378
2:10	of the offerings made to **the L** by fire.	3378
2:11	to **the L** must be made without yeast,	3378
2:11	or honey in an offering made to **the L**	3378
2:12	to **the L** as an offering of the firstfruits,	3378
2:14	a grain offering of firstfruits to **the L**,	3378
2:16	as an offering made to **the L** by fire.	3378
3:1	he is to present before **the L** an animal	3378
3:3	to bring a sacrifice made to **the L** by fire:	3378
3:5	an aroma pleasing to **the L**.	3378
3:6	as a fellowship offering to **the L**,	3378
3:7	he is to present it before **the L**.	3378
3:9	to bring a sacrifice made to **the L** by fire:	3378
3:11	an offering made to **the L** by fire.	3378
3:12	he is to present it before **the L**.	3378
3:14	to make this offering to **the L** by fire:	3378
4:1	**The L** said to Moses,	3378
4:3	to **the L** a young bull without defect as	3378
4:4	to the Tent of Meeting before **the L**.	3378
4:4	on its head and slaughter it before **the L**.	3378
4:6	of it seven times before **the L**,	3378
4:7	of fragrant incense that is before **the L** in	3378
4:15	on the bull's head before **the L**,	3378
4:15	the bull shall be slaughtered before **the L**.	3378
4:17	and sprinkle it before **the L** seven times	3378
4:18	of the altar that is before **the L** in the Tent	3378
4:22	in any of the commands of **the L** his God,	3378
4:24	where the burnt offering is slaughtered before **the L**.	3378
4:31	on the altar as an aroma pleasing to **the L**.	3378
4:35	of the offerings made to **the L** by fire.	3378
5:6	he must bring to **the L** a female lamb	3378
5:7	to **the L** as a penalty for his sin—	3378
5:12	of the offerings made to **the L** by fire.	3378
5:14	**The L** said to Moses:	3378
5:15	to **the L** as a penalty a ram from the flock,	3378
5:19	of wrongdoing against the **L**."	3378
6:1	**The L** said to Moses:	3378
6:2	"If anyone sins and is unfaithful to **the L**	3378
6:6	that is, to **the L**, his guilt offering,	3378
6:7	for him before **the L**,	3378
6:8	**The L** said to Moses:	3378
6:14	Aaron's sons are to bring it before **the L**,	3378
6:15	on the altar as an aroma pleasing to **the L**.	3378
6:18	of the offerings made to **the L** by fire for	3378
6:19	**The L** also said to Moses,	3378
6:20	and his sons are to bring to **the L** on	3378
6:21	in pieces as an aroma pleasing to **the L**.	3378
6:24	**The L** said to Moses:	3378
6:25	be slaughtered before **the L** in the place	3378
7:5	on the altar as an offering made to **the L**	3378
7:11	a person may present to **the L**:	3378
7:14	a contribution to **the L**;	3378
7:20	to **the L**, that person must be cut off	3378
7:21	to **the L**, that person must be cut off	3378
7:22	**The L** said to Moses,	3378
7:25	to **the L** must be cut off from his people.	3378
7:28	**The L** said to Moses,	3378
7:29	a fellowship offering to **the L** is	3378
7:29	to bring part of it as his sacrifice to **the L**.	3378
7:30	to bring the offering made to **the L**	3378
7:30	and wave the breast before **the L** as	3378
7:35	the portion of the offerings made to **the L**	3378
7:35	to serve **the L** as priests.	3378
7:36	**the L** commanded that the Israelites	3378
7:38	which **the L** gave Moses on Mount Sinai	3378
7:38	to bring their offerings to **the L**,	3378
8:1	**The L** said to Moses,	3378
8:4	Moses did as **the L** commanded him,	3378
8:5	"This is what **the L** has commanded to	3378
8:9	as **the L** commanded Moses.	3378
8:13	as **the L** commanded Moses.	3378
8:17	as **the L** commanded Moses.	3378
8:21	an offering made to **the L** by fire,	3378
8:21	as **the L** commanded Moses.	3378
8:26	which was before **the L**,	3378
8:27	and waved them before **the L** as	3378
8:28	an offering made to **the L** by fire.	3378
8:29	waved it before **the L** as a wave offering,	3378
8:29	as **the L** commanded Moses.	3378
8:34	by **the L** to make atonement for you.	3378
8:35	and do what **the L** requires, so you will	3378
8:36	his sons did everything **the L** commanded	3378
9:2	and present them before **the L**.	3378
9:4	to sacrifice before **the L**,	3378
9:4	For today **the L** will appear to you."	3378
9:5	near and stood before **the L**.	3378
Lev 9:6	"This is what **the L** has commanded you	3378
9:6	the glory of **the L** may appear to you."	3378
9:7	as **the L** has commanded."	3378
9:10	as **the L** commanded Moses;	3378
9:21	and the right thigh before **the L** as	3378
9:23	glory of **the L** appeared to all the people.	3378
9:24	from the presence of **the L** and consumed	3378
10:1	before **the L**, contrary to his command.	3378
10:2	of **the L** and consumed them,	3378
10:2	and they died before **the L**.	3378
10:3	"This is what **the L** spoke of	3378
10:6	or you will die and **the L** will be angry	NIH
10:6	may mourn for those **the L** has destroyed	3378
10:8	Then **the L** said to Aaron,	3378
10:11	the decrees **the L** has given them	3378
10:12	from the offerings made to **the L** by fire	3378
10:13	of the offerings made to **the L** by fire;	3378
10:15	be waved before **the L** as a wave offering.	3378
10:15	as **the L** has commanded."	3378
10:17	atonement for them before **the L**.	3378
10:19	and their burnt offering before **the L**,	3378
10:19	Would **the L** have been pleased	3378
11:1	**The L** said to Moses and Aaron,	3378
11:44	I am **the L** your God;	3378
11:45	I am **the L** who brought you up out	3378
12:1	**The L** said to Moses,	3378
12:7	before **the L** to make atonement for her,	3378
13:1	**The L** said to Moses and Aaron,	3378
14:1	**The L** said to Moses,	3378
14:11	be cleansed and his offerings before **the L**	3378
14:12	he shall wave them before **the L** as	3378
14:16	of it before **the L** seven times.	3378
14:18	make atonement for him before **the L**.	3378
14:23	to the Tent of Meeting, before **the L**.	3378
14:24	before **the L** as a wave offering.	3378
14:27	from his palm seven times before **the L**.	3378
14:29	to make atonement for him before **the L**.	3378
14:31	before **the L** on behalf of the one to	3378
14:33	**The L** said to Moses and Aaron,	3378
15:1	**The L** said to Moses and Aaron,	3378
15:14	and come before **the L** to the entrance to	3378
15:15	before **the L** for the man because	3378
15:30	for her before **the L** for the uncleanness	3378
16:1	**The L** spoke to Moses after the death of	3378
16:1	when they approached **the L**.	3378
16:2	**The L** said to Moses:	3378
16:7	before **the L** at the entrance to the Tent	3378
16:8	for **the L** and the other for the scapegoat.	3378
16:9	to **the L** and sacrifice it for a sin offering.	3378
16:10	be presented alive before **the L** to be used	3378
16:12	the altar before **the L** and two handfuls	3378
16:13	the incense on the fire before **the L**,	3378
16:18	that is before **the L** and make atonement	3378
16:30	Then, before **the L**, you will be clean	3378
16:34	it was done, as **the L** commanded Moses.	3378
17:1	**The L** said to Moses:	3378
17:2	'This is what **the L** has commanded:	3378
17:4	to **the L** in front of the tabernacle of	3378
17:4	in front of the tabernacle of the **L**—	3378
17:5	This is so the Israelites will bring to **the L**	3378
17:5	bring them to the priest, that is, to **the L**,	3378
17:6	against the altar of **the L** at the entrance	3378
17:6	the fat as an aroma pleasing to **the L**.	3378
17:9	the Tent of Meeting to sacrifice it to **the L**	3378
18:1	**The L** said to Moses,	3378
18:2	'I am **the L** your God.	3378
18:4	I am **the L** your God.	3378
18:5	follow my decrees. I am **the L**.	3378
18:6	obeys them will live by them. I am **the L**.	3378
18:21	relative to have sexual relations. I am **the L**.	3378
18:30	I am **the L** your God.' "	3378
19:1	**The L** said to Moses,	3378
19:2	Be holy because I, **the L** your God, am holy	3378
19:3	I am **the L** your God.	3378
19:4	I am **the L** your God.	3378
19:5	a fellowship offering to **the L**,	3378
19:8	he has desecrated what is holy to **the L**;	3378
19:10	I am **the L** your God.	3378
19:12	profane the name of your God. I am **the L**.	3378
19:14	but fear your God. I am **the L**.	3378
19:16	endangers your neighbor's life. I am **the L**.	3378
19:18	love your neighbor as yourself. I am **the L**.	3378
19:21	Tent of Meeting for a guilt offering to **the L**	3378
19:22	before **the L** for the sin he has committed,	3378
19:24	an offering of praise to **the L**.	3378
19:25	I am **the L** your God.	3378
19:28	put tattoo marks on yourselves. I am **the L**.	3378
19:30	reverence for my sanctuary. I am **the L**.	3378
19:31	I am **the L** your God.	3378
19:32	revere your God. I am **the L**.	3378
19:34	I am **the L** your God.	3378
19:36	I am **the L** your God, who brought you out	3378
19:37	all my laws and follow them. I am **the L**.' "	3378
20:1	**The L** said to Moses,	3378
20:7	because I am **the L** your God.	3378
20:8	I am **the L**, who makes you holy.	3378
20:24	I am **the L** your God,	3378
20:26	be holy to me because I, **the L**, am holy,	3378
21:1	**The L** said to Moses,	3378
21:6	the offerings made to **the L** by fire,	3378
21:8	Consider them holy, because I **the L** am holy—	3378
21:12	anointing oil of his God. I am **the L**.	3378
21:15	I am **the L**, who makes him holy.' "	3378
21:16	**The L** said to Moses,	3378
21:21	to present the offerings made to **the L**	3378
21:23	I am **the L**, who makes them holy.' "	3378

†LORD distinguishes the proper name of God, *Yahweh*, indicated in the NIV by "LORD," from the words translated "Lord" and "lord," indexed under the heading ***LORD**, pages 683-86.

Ref	Text	Num
Lev 22: 1	**The L** said to Moses,	3378
22: 2	not profane my holy name. I am **the L.**	3378
22: 3	that the Israelites consecrate to **the L,**	3378
22: 3	cut off from my presence. I am **the L.**	3378
22: 8	become unclean through it. I am **the L.**	3378
22: 9	I am **the L,** who makes them holy.	3378
22:15	the Israelites present to **the L**	3378
22:16	I am **the L,** who makes them holy.' "	3378
22:17	**The L** said to Moses,	3378
22:18	a gift for a burnt offering to **the L,**	3378
22:21	a fellowship offering to **the L** to fulfill	3378
22:22	Do not offer to **the L** the blind,	3378
22:22	on the altar as an offering made to **the L**	3378
22:24	You must not offer to **the L**	3378
22:26	**The L** said to Moses,	3378
22:27	as an offering made to **the L** by fire.	3378
22:29	a thank offering to **the L,**	3378
22:30	leave none of it till morning. I am **the L.**	3378
22:31	my commands and follow them. I am **the L.**	3378
22:32	I am **the L,** who makes you holy.	3378
22:33	to be your God. I am **the L."**	3378
23: 1	**The L** said to Moses,	3378
23: 2	the appointed feasts of **the L,**	3378
23: 3	it is a Sabbath to **the L.**	3378
23: 8	an offering made to **the L** by fire.	3378
23: 9	**The L** said to Moses,	3378
23:11	to wave the sheaf before **the L** so it will	3378
23:12	a burnt offering to **the L** a lamb a year old	3378
23:13	an offering made to **the L** by fire,	3378
23:16	present an offering of new grain to **the L.**	3378
23:17	as a wave offering of firstfruits to **the L.**	3378
23:18	They will be a burnt offering to **the L,**	3378
23:18	an aroma pleasing to **the L.**	3378
23:20	to wave the two lambs before **the L** as	3378
23:20	a sacred offering to **the L** for the priest.	3378
23:22	I am **the L** your God.' "	3378
23:23	**The L** said to Moses,	3378
23:25	but present an offering made to **the L**	3378
23:26	**The L** said to Moses,	3378
23:27	and present an offering made to **the L**	3378
23:28	for you before **the L** your God.	3378
23:33	**The L** said to Moses,	3378
23:36	an offering made to **the L** by fire,	3378
23:36	and present an offering made to **the L**	3378
23:37	for bringing offerings made to **the L**	3378
23:38	the freewill offerings you give to **the L.)**	3378
23:39	the festival to **the L** for seven days;	3378
23:40	before **the L** your God for seven days.	3378
23:41	Celebrate this as a festival to **the L**	3378
23:43	I am **the L** your God.' "	3378
23:44	the appointed feasts of **the L.**	3378
24: 1	**The L** said to Moses,	3378
24: 3	before **the L** from evening till morning,	3378
24: 4	before **the L** must be tended continually.	3378
24: 6	on the table of pure gold before **the L.**	3378
24: 7	to be an offering made to **the L** by fire.	3378
24: 8	to be set out before **the L** regularly,	3378
24: 9	of the offerings made to **the L** by fire."	3378
24:12	in custody until the will of **the L** should	3378
24:13	Then **the L** said to Moses:	3378
24:16	the name of **the L** must be put to death.	3378
24:22	I am **the L** your God.' "	3378
24:23	as **the L** commanded Moses.	3378
25: 1	**The L** said to Moses on Mount Sinai,	3378
25: 2	a sabbath to **the L.**	3378
25: 4	a sabbath to **the L.**	3378
25:17	but fear your God. I am **the L** your God.	3378
25:38	I am **the L** your God, who brought you out	3378
25:55	I am **the L** your God.	3378
26: 1	I am **the L** your God.	3378
26: 2	reverence for my sanctuary. I am **the L.**	3378
26:13	I am **the L** your God, who brought you out	3378
26:44	I am **the L** their God.	3378
26:45	to be their God. I am **the L.'** "	3378
26:46	and the regulations that **the L** established	3378
27: 1	**The L** said to Moses,	3378
27: 2	a special vow to dedicate persons to **the L**	3378
27: 9	that is acceptable as an offering to **the L,**	3378
27: 9	an animal given to **the L** becomes holy.	3378
27:11	not acceptable as an offering to **the L—**	3378
27:14	as something holy to **the L,**	3378
27:16	" 'If a man dedicates to **the L** part	3378
27:21	like a field devoted to **the L;**	3378
27:22	to **the L** a field he has bought,	3378
27:23	on that day as something holy to **the L.**	3378
27:26	the firstborn already belongs to **the L;**	3378
27:28	that a man owns and devotes to **the L—**	3378
27:28	so devoted is most holy to **the L.**	3378
27:30	or fruit from the trees, belongs to **the L;**	3378
27:30	it is holy to **the L.**	3378
27:32	will be holy to **the L.**	3378
27:34	the commands **the L** gave Moses	3378
Nu 1: 1	**The L** spoke to Moses in the Tent	3378
1:19	as **the L** commanded Moses.	3378
1:48	**The L** had said to Moses:	3378
1:54	as **the L** commanded Moses.	3378
2: 1	**The L** said to Moses and Aaron,	3378
2:33	as **the L** commanded Moses.	3378
2:34	Israelites did everything **the L** commanded Moses;	3378
3: 1	at the time **the L** talked with Moses	3378
3: 4	before **the L** when they made an offering	3378
3: 5	**The L** said to Moses,	3378
3:11	**The L** also said to Moses,	3378
3:13	They are to be mine. I am **the L."**	3378
3:14	**The L** said to Moses in the Desert	3378
3:16	he was commanded by the word of **the L.**	3378

Ref	Text	Num
Nu 3:40	**The L** said to Moses,	3378
3:41	of the livestock of the Israelites. I am **the L.**	3378
3:42	as **the L** commanded him.	3378
3:44	**The L** also said to Moses,	3378
3:45	The Levites are to be mine. I am **the L.**	3378
3:51	he was commanded by the word of **the L.**	3378
4: 1	**The L** said to Moses and Aaron:	3378
4:17	**The L** said to Moses and Aaron,	3378
4:21	**The L** said to Moses,	3378
4:49	as **the L** commanded Moses.	3378
5: 1	**The L** said to Moses,	3378
5: 4	as **the L** had instructed Moses.	3378
5: 5	**The L** said to Moses,	3378
5: 6	in any way and so is unfaithful to **the L,**	3378
5: 8	the restitution belongs to **the L** and must	3378
5:11	Then **the L** said to Moses,	3378
5:16	and have her stand before **the L.**	3378
5:18	the woman stand before **the L,**	3378
5:21	"may **the L** cause your people to curse	3378
5:25	before **the L** and bring it to the altar.	3378
5:30	to have her stand before **the L** and is	3378
6: 1	**The L** said to Moses,	3378
6: 2	a vow of separation to **the L** as a Nazirite,	3378
6: 5	of his separation to **the L** is over;	3378
6: 6	to **the L** he must not go near a dead body.	3378
6: 8	of his separation he is consecrated to **the L.**	3378
6:12	to **the L** for the period of his separation	3378
6:14	to present his offerings to **the L:**	3378
6:16	to present them before **the L** and make	3378
6:17	the ram as a fellowship offering to **the L,**	3378
6:20	before **the L** as a wave offering;	3378
6:21	Nazirite who vows his offering to **the L**	3378
6:22	**The L** said to Moses,	3378
6:24	" " 'The L bless you and keep you;	3378
6:25	**the L** make his face shine upon you and	3378
6:26	**the L** turn his face toward you	3378
7: 3	before **the L** six covered carts	3378
7: 4	**The L** said to Moses,	3378
7:11	For **the L** had said to Moses:	3378
7:89	the Tent of Meeting to speak with **the L,**	2257S
8: 1	**The L** said to Moses,	3378
8: 3	just as **the L** commanded Moses.	3378
8: 4	like the pattern **the L** had shown Moses.	3378
8: 5	**The L** said to Moses:	3378
8:10	You are to bring the Levites before **the L,**	3378
8:11	to present the Levites before **the L** as	3378
8:11	be ready to do the work of **the L.**	3378
8:12	to **the L** and the other for a burnt offering,	3378
8:13	as a wave offering to **the L.**	3378
8:20	as **the L** commanded Moses.	3378
8:21	before **the L** and made atonement	3378
8:22	as **the L** commanded Moses.	3378
8:23	**The L** said to Moses,	3378
9: 1	**The L** spoke to Moses in the Desert	3378
9: 5	as **the L** commanded Moses.	3378
9: 8	until I find out what **the L** commands	3378
9: 9	Then **the L** said to Moses:	3378
10: 1	**The L** said to Moses:	3378
10: 9	be remembered by **the L** your God	3378
10:10	I am **the L** your God."	3378
10:29	for the place about which **the L** said,	3378
10:29	for **the L** has promised good things	3378
10:32	whatever good things **the L** gives us."	3378
10:33	from the mountain of **the L** and traveled	3378
10:33	the covenant of **the L** went before them	3378
10:34	The cloud of **the L** was over them by day	3378
10:35	Moses said, "Rise up, O **L!**	3378
10:36	he said, "Return, O **L!**	3378
11: 1	complained about their hardships in the hearing of **the L,**	3378
11: 1	Then fire from **the L** burned among them	3378
11: 2	he prayed to **the L** and the fire died down.	3378
11: 3	fire from **the L** had burned among them.	3378
11:10	**The L** became exceedingly angry,	3378
11:11	He asked **the L,**	3378
11:16	**The L** said to Moses:	3378
11:18	**The L** heard you when you wailed,	3378
11:18	Now **the L** will give you meat,	3378
11:20	because you have rejected **the L,**	3378
11:23	**The L** answered Moses,	3378
11:24	and told the people what **the L** had said.	3378
11:25	Then **the L** came down in the cloud	3378
11:29	that **the L** would put his Spirit on them!"	3378
11:31	from **the L** and drove quail in from	3378
11:33	of **the L** burned against the people,	3378
12: 2	"Has **the L** spoken only through Moses?"	3378
12: 2	And **the L** heard this.	3378
12: 4	At once **the L** said to Moses,	3378
12: 5	**the L** came down in a pillar of cloud;	3378
12: 6	"When a prophet of **the L** is among you,	3378
12: 8	he sees the form of **the L.**	3378
12: 9	The anger of **the L** burned against them,	3378
12:13	So Moses cried out to **the L,** "O God,	3378
12:14	**The L** replied to Moses,	3378
13: 1	**The L** said to Moses,	3378
14: 3	Why is **the L** bringing us to this land only	3378
14: 8	If **the L** is pleased with us,	3378
14: 9	Only do not rebel against **the L.**	3378
14: 9	but **the L** is with us.	3378
14:10	of **the L** appeared at the Tent of Meeting	3378
14:11	**The L** said to Moses,	3378
14:11	Moses said to **the L,**	3378
14:14	They have already heard that you, O **L,**	3378
14:14	are with these people and that you, O **L,**	3378
14:16	'The L was not able to bring these people	3378
14:18	'The L is slow to anger,	3378
14:20	**The L** replied, "I have forgiven them,	3378

Ref	Text	Num
Nu 14:21	as the glory of **the L** fills the whole earth,	3378
14:26	**The L** said to Moses and Aaron:	3378
14:28	'As surely as I live, declares **the L,**	3378
14:35	I, **the L,** have spoken,	3378
14:37	down and died of a plague before **the L.**	3378
14:40	up to the place **the L** promised."	3378
14:42	because **the L** is not with you.	3378
14:43	you have turned away from **the L,**	3378
15: 1	**The L** said to Moses,	3378
15: 3	and you present to **the L** offerings made	3378
15: 3	as an aroma pleasing to **the L—**	3378
15: 4	to **the L** a grain offering of a tenth of	3378
15: 7	Offer it as an aroma pleasing to **the L.**	3378
15: 8	or a fellowship offering to **the L,**	3378
15:10	an aroma pleasing to **the L.**	3378
15:13	by fire as an aroma pleasing to **the L.**	3378
15:14	by fire as an aroma pleasing to **the L,**	3378
15:15	the alien shall be the same before **the L:**	3378
15:17	**The L** said to Moses,	3378
15:19	present a portion as an offering to **the L.**	3378
15:21	to give this offering to **the L** from the first	3378
15:22	of these commands **the L** gave Moses—	3378
15:23	the day **the L** gave them and continuing	3378
15:24	as an aroma pleasing to **the L,**	3378
15:25	to **the L** for their wrong an offering made	3378
15:28	to make atonement before **the L** for	3378
15:30	blasphemes **the L,** and that person must	3378
15:35	**the L** said to Moses, "The man must die.	3378
15:36	as **the L** commanded Moses.	3378
15:37	**The L** said to Moses,	3378
15:39	remember all the commands of **the L,**	3378
15:41	I am **the L** your God,	3378
15:41	I am **the L** your God.' "	3378
16: 3	and **the L** is with them.	3378
16: 5	the morning **the L** will show who belongs	3378
16: 7	and incense in them before **the L.**	3378
16: 7	The man **the L** chooses will be	3378
16:11	It is against **the L** that you	3378
16:15	and said to **the L,**	3378
16:16	to appear before **the L** tomorrow—	3378
16:17	and present it before **the L.**	3378
16:19	of **the L** appeared to the entire assembly.	3378
16:20	**The L** said to Moses and Aaron,	3378
16:23	Then **the L** said to Moses,	3378
16:28	how you will know that **the L** has sent me	3378
16:29	then **the L** has not sent me.	3378
16:30	**the L** brings about something totally new,	3378
16:30	these men have treated **the L** with contempt	3378
16:35	And fire came out from **the L**	3378
16:36	**The L** said to Moses,	3378
16:38	for they were presented before **the L**	3378
16:40	as **the L** directed him through Moses.	3378
16:40	to burn incense before **the L,**	3378
16:42	and the glory of **the L** appeared.	3378
16:44	and **the L** said to Moses,	3378
16:46	Wrath has come out from **the L;**	3378
17: 1	**The L** said to Moses,	3378
17: 7	before **the L** in the Tent of the Testimony.	3378
17:10	**The L** said to Moses,	3378
17:11	Moses did just as **the L** commanded him.	3378
17:13	near the tabernacle of **the L** will die.	3378
18: 1	**The L** said to Aaron, "You, your sons and	3378
18: 6	dedicated to **the L** to do the work at	3378
18: 8	Then **the L** said to Aaron,	3378
18:12	and grain they give **the L** as the firstfruits	3378
18:13	that they bring to **the L** will be yours.	3378
18:14	in Israel is **devoted** to **the L** is yours.	3051
18:15	that is offered to **the L** is yours.	3378
18:17	an aroma pleasing to **the L.**	3378
18:19	to **the L** I give to you and your sons	3378
18:19	of salt before **the L** for both you	3378
18:20	**The L** said to Aaron,	3378
18:24	as an offering to **the L.**	3378
18:25	**The L** said to Moses,	3378
18:28	to **the L** from all the tithes you receive	3378
19: 1	**The L** said to Moses and Aaron:	3378
19: 2	of the law that **the L** has commanded:	3378
19:20	he has defiled the sanctuary of **the L.**	3378
20: 3	when our brothers fell dead before **the L!**	3378
20: 6	and the glory of **the L** appeared to them.	3378
20: 7	**The L** said to Moses,	3378
20:12	But **the L** said to Moses and Aaron,	3378
20:13	where the Israelites quarreled with **the L**	3378
20:16	but when we cried out to **the L,**	3378
20:23	**the L** said to Moses and Aaron,	3378
20:27	Moses did as **the L** commanded.	3378
21: 2	Then Israel made this vow to **the L:**	3378
21: 3	**The L** listened to Israel's plea and gave	3378
21: 6	**the L** sent venomous snakes among them;	3378
21: 7	"We sinned when we spoke against **the L**	3378
21: 7	Pray that **the L** will take the snakes away	3378
21: 8	**The L** said to Moses,	3378
21:14	the Book of the Wars of **the L** says:	3378
21:16	the well where **the L** said to Moses,	3378
21:34	**The L** said to Moses,	3378
22: 8	the answer **the L** gives me."	3378
22:13	**the L** has refused to let me go with you."	3378
22:18	beyond the command of **the L** my God.	3378
22:19	I will find out what else **the L** will tell me."	3378
22:22	of **the L** stood in the road to oppose him.	3378
22:23	the angel of **the L** standing in the road	3378
22:24	the angel of **the L** stood in a narrow path	3378
22:25	When the donkey saw the angel of **the L,**	3378
22:26	Then the angel of **the L** moved on ahead	3378
22:27	When the donkey saw the angel of **the L,**	3378
22:28	Then **the L** opened the donkey's mouth,	3378
22:31	Then **the L** opened Balaam's eyes,	3378

†**LORD** distinguishes the proper name of God, *Yahweh*, indicated in the NIV by "Lᴏʀᴅ," from the words translated "Lord" and "lord," indexed under the heading *LORD, pages 683-86.

Nu			
22:31	and he saw the angel of **the L** standing in	3378
22:32	The angel of **the L** asked him,	3378
22:34	Balaam said to the angel of **the L,**	3378
22:35	The angel of **the L** said to Balaam,	3378
23: 3	Perhaps **the L** will come to meet with me.	3378
23: 5	**The L** put a message in Balaam's mouth	3378
23: 8	How can I denounce those whom **the L** has	3378
23:12	not speak what **the L** puts in my mouth?"	3378
23:16	**The L** met with Balaam and put	3378
23:17	Balak asked him, "What did **the L** say?"	3378
23:21	**The L** their God is with them;	3378
23:26	tell you I must do whatever **the L** says?"	3378
24: 1	when Balaam saw that it pleased **the L**	3378
24: 6	like aloes planted by **the L,**	3378
24:11	but **the L** has kept you	3378
24:13	to go beyond the command of **the L—**	3378
24:13	and I must say only what **the L** says'?	3378
25: 4	**The L** said to Moses,	3378
25: 4	in broad daylight before **the L,**	3378
25:10	**The L** said to Moses,	3378
25:16	**The L** said to Moses,	3378
26: 1	After the plague **the L** said to Moses	3378
26: 4	as **the L** commanded Moses."	3378
26: 9	when they rebelled against **the L.**	3378
26:52	**The L** said to Moses,	3378
26:61	when they made an offering before **the L**	3378
26:65	**the L** had told those Israelites they would	3378
27: 3	who banded together against **the L,**	3378
27: 5	So Moses brought their case before **the L**	3378
27: 6	and **the L** said to him,	3378
27:11	as **the L** commanded Moses.' "	3378
27:12	Then **the L** said to Moses,	3378
27:15	Moses said to **the L,**	3378
27:16	"May **the L,** the God of the spirits	3378
27:18	So **the L** said to Moses,	3378
27:21	by inquiring of the Urim before **the L.**	3378
27:22	Moses did as **the L** commanded him.	3378
27:23	as **the L** instructed through Moses.	3378
28: 1	**The L** said to Moses,	3378
28: 3	by fire that you are to present to **the L:**	3378
28: 6	an offering made to **the L** by fire.	3378
28: 7	Pour out the drink offering to **the L** at	3378
28: 8	an aroma pleasing to **the L.**	3378
28:11	present to **the L** a burnt offering	3378
28:13	an offering made to **the L** by fire.	3378
28:15	to be presented to **the L** as a sin offering.	3378
28:19	Present to **the L** an offering made by fire,	3378
28:24	as an aroma pleasing to **the L,**	3378
28:26	to **the L** an offering of new grain during	3378
28:27	a year old as an aroma pleasing to **the L.**	3378
29: 2	As an aroma pleasing to **the L,**	3378
29: 6	They are offerings made to **the L**	3378
29: 8	Present as an aroma pleasing to **the L**	3378
29:12	a festival to **the L** for seven days.	3378
29:13	by fire as an aroma pleasing to **the L,**	3378
29:36	by fire as an aroma pleasing to **the L,**	3378
29:39	for **the L** at your appointed feasts.	3378
29:40	that **the L** commanded him.	3378
30: 1	"This is what **the L** commands:	3378
30: 2	a man makes a vow to **the L** or takes	3378
30: 3	to **the L** or obligates herself by a pledge	3378
30: 5	**the L** will release her.	3378
30: 8	and **the L** will release her.	3378
30:12	and **the L** will release her.	3378
30:16	the regulations **the L** gave Moses	3378
31: 1	**The L** said to Moses,	3378
31: 7	as **the L** commanded Moses,	3378
31:16	of turning the Israelites away from **the L**	3378
31:21	of the law that **the L** gave Moses:	3378
31:25	**The L** said to Moses,	3378
31:28	for **the L** one out of every five hundred,	3378
31:31	as **the L** commanded Moses.	3378
31:37	of which the tribute for **the L** was 675;	3378
31:38	of which the tribute for **the L** was 72;	3378
31:39	of which the tribute for **the L** was 61;	3378
31:40	of which the tribute for **the L** was 32.	3378
31:41	as **the L** commanded Moses.	3378
31:47	as **the L** commanded him,	3378
31:50	an offering to **the L** the gold articles each	3378
31:50	for ourselves before **the L."**	3378
31:52	as a gift to **the L** weighed 16,750	3378
31:54	a memorial for the Israelites before **the L.**	3378
32: 4	the land **the L** subdued before the people	3378
32: 7	over into the land **the L** has given them?	3378
32: 9	the land **the L** had given them.	3378
32:12	for they followed **the L** wholeheartedly.'	3378
32:14	and making **the L** even more angry	3378
32:20	if you will arm yourselves before **the L**	3378
32:21	over the Jordan before **the L**	3378
32:22	when the land is subdued before **the L,**	3378
32:22	be free from your obligation to **the L** and	3378
32:22	be your possession before **the L.**	3378
32:23	you will be sinning against **the L;**	3378
32:27	will cross over to fight before **the L,**	3378
32:29	over the Jordan with you before **the L,**	3378
32:31	"Your servants will do what **the L** has said.	3378
32:32	over before **the L** into Canaan armed,	3378
33: 4	whom **the L** had struck down	3378
33: 4	for **the L** had brought judgment	3378
33:50	the Jordan across from Jericho **the L** said	3378
34: 1	**The L** said to Moses,	3378
34:13	**The L** has ordered that it be given to	3378
34:16	**The L** said to Moses,	3378
34:29	These are the men **the L** commanded	3378
35: 1	**the L** said to Moses,	3378
35: 9	Then **the L** said to Moses:	3378
35:34	for I, **the L,** dwell among the Israelites.' "	3378

Nu			
36: 2	"When **the L** commanded my lord to give	3378
36: 6	This is what **the L** commands	3378
36:10	as **the L** commanded Moses.	3378
36:13	the commands and regulations **the L** gave	3378

Dt			
1: 3	that **the L** had commanded him	3378
1: 6	**The L** our God said to us at Horeb,	3378
1: 8	the land that **the L** swore he would give	3378
1:10	**The L** your God has increased your numbers	3378
1:11	May **the L,** the God of your fathers,	3378
1:19	Then, as **the L** our God commanded us,	3378
1:20	which **the L** our God is giving us.	3378
1:21	**the L** your God has given you the land.	3378
1:21	Go up and take possession of it as **the L,**	3378
1:25	that **the L** our God is giving us."	3378
1:26	against the command of **the L** your God.	3378
1:27	and said, "**The L** hates us;	3378
1:30	**The L** your God, who is going before you,	3378
1:31	how **the L** your God carried you,	3378
1:32	you did not trust in **the L** your God,	3378
1:34	When **the L** heard what you said,	3378
1:36	because he followed **the L** wholeheartedly."	3378
1:37	of you **the L** became angry with me also	3378
1:41	"We have sinned against **the L.**	3378
1:41	as **the L** our God commanded us."	3378
1:42	But **the L** said to me, "Tell them,	3378
1:45	You came back and wept before **the L,**	3378
2: 1	as **the L** had directed me.	3378
2: 2	Then **the L** said to me,	3378
2: 7	**The L** your God has blessed you in all	3378
2: 7	These forty years **the L** your God has been	3378
2: 9	Then **the L** said to me,	3378
2:12	as Israel did in the land **the L** gave them	3378
2:13	And **the L** said, "Now get up and cross	NIH
2:14	as **the L** had sworn to them.	3378
2:17	**the L** said to me,	3378
2:21	**The L** destroyed them from before	3378
2:22	**The L** had done the same for	NIH
2:29	into the land **the L** our God is giving us."	3378
2:30	For **the L** your God had made his spirit stubborn	3378
2:31	**The L** said to me, "See, I have begun	3378
2:33	**the L** our God delivered him over to us	3378
2:36	**The L** our God gave us all of them.	3378
2:37	with the command of **the L** our God,	3378
3: 2	**The L** said to me, "Do not be afraid of him,	3378
3: 3	So **the L** our God also gave	3378
3:18	"**The L** your God has given you this land	3378
3:20	until **the L** gives rest to your brothers	3378
3:20	that **the L** your God is giving them,	3378
3:21	that **the L** your God has done	3378
3:21	**The L** will do the same to all	3378
3:22	**the L** your God himself will fight	3378
3:23	At that time I pleaded with **the L:**	3378
3:24	"O Sovereign **L,** you have begun to show	3378
3:26	because of you **the L** was angry with me	3378
3:26	"That is enough," **the L** said.	3378
4: 1	take possession of the land that **the L,**	3378
4: 2	of **the L** your God that I give you.	3378
4: 3	with your own eyes what **the L** did	3378
4: 3	**The L** your God destroyed from	3378
4: 4	to **the L** your God are still alive today.	3378
4: 5	as **the L** my God commanded me,	3378
4:10	the day you stood before **the L** your God	3378
4:12	Then **the L** spoke to you out of the fire.	3378
4:14	And **the L** directed me at that time	3378
4:15	the day **the L** spoke to you at Horeb out	3378
4:19	worshiping things **the L** your God has	3378
4:20	**the L** took you and brought you out of	3378
4:21	**The L** was angry with me because of you,	3378
4:21	good land that **the L** your God is giving you	3378
4:23	of **the L** your God that he made with you;	3378
4:23	of anything **the L** your God has forbidden.	3378
4:24	For **the L** your God is a consuming fire,	3378
4:25	doing evil in the eyes of **the L** your God	3378
4:27	**The L** will scatter you among the peoples,	3378
4:27	the nations to which **the L** will drive you.	3378
4:29	if from there you seek **the L** your God,	3378
4:30	to **the L** your God and obey him.	3378
4:31	For **the L** your God is a merciful God;	3378
4:34	the things **the L** your God did for you	3378
4:35	so that you might know that **the L** is God;	3378
4:39	that **the L** is God in heaven above and on	3378
4:40	in the land **the L** your God gives you	3378
5: 2	**The L** our God made a covenant with us	3378
5: 3	that **the L** made this covenant,	3378
5: 4	**The L** spoke to you face to face out of	3378
5: 5	between **the L** and you to declare to you	3378
5: 5	to declare to you the word of **the L,**	3378
5: 6	"I am **the L** your God,	3378
5: 9	for I, **the L** your God, am a jealous God,	3378
5:11	not misuse the name of **the L** your God,	3378
5:11	for **the L** will not hold anyone guiltless who	3378
5:12	as **the L** your God has commanded you.	3378
5:14	a Sabbath to **the L** your God.	3378
5:15	and that **the L** your God brought you out	3378
5:15	Therefore **the L** your God has commanded	3378
5:16	as **the L** your God has commanded you,	3378
5:16	in the land **the L** your God is giving you.	3378
5:22	the commandments **the L** proclaimed in	3378
5:24	"**The L** our God has shown us his glory	3378
5:25	the voice of **the L** our God any longer.	3378
5:27	and listen to all that **the L** our God says.	3378
5:27	tell us whatever **the L** our God tells us."	3378
5:28	**The L** heard you when you spoke to me	3378
5:28	when you spoke to me and the L said	3378

Dt			
5:32	careful to do what **the L** your God has commanded you;	3378
5:33	that **the L** your God has commanded you,	3378
6: 1	and laws **the L** your God directed me	3378
6: 2	after them may fear **the L** your God	3378
6: 3	just as **the L,** the God of your fathers,	3378
6: 4	**The L** our God, the LORD is one.	3378
6: 4	The LORD our God, **the L** is one.	3378
6: 5	Love **the L** your God with all your heart	3378
6:10	When **the L** your God brings you into	3378
6:12	be careful that you do not forget **the L,**	3378
6:13	Fear **the L** your God,	3378
6:15	for **the L** your God, who is among you,	3378
6:16	Do not test **the L** your God as you did	3378
6:17	to keep the commands of **the L** your God	3378
6:18	the good land that **the L** promised on oath	3378
6:19	your enemies before you, as **the L** said.	3378
6:20	laws **the L** our God has commanded you?"	3378
6:21	but **the L** brought us out of Egypt with	3378
6:22	Before our eyes **the L** sent miraculous signs	3378
6:24	**The L** commanded us to obey all	3378
6:24	and to fear **the L** our God,	3378
6:25	to obey all this law before **the L** our God,	3378
7: 1	When **the L** your God brings you into	3378
7: 2	when **the L** your God has delivered them	3378
7: 6	you are a people holy to **the L** your God.	3378
7: 6	**The L** your God has chosen you out of all	3378
7: 7	**The L** did not set his affection on you	3378
7: 8	But it was because **the L** loved you	3378
7: 9	therefore that **the L** your God is God;	3378
7:12	**the L** your God will keep his covenant	3378
7:15	**The L** will keep you free from every disease.	3378
7:16	the peoples **the L** your God gives over	3378
7:18	remember well what **the L** your God did	3378
7:19	which **the L** your God brought you out.	3378
7:19	**The L** your God will do the same to all	3378
7:20	**the L** your God will send the hornet	3378
7:21	for **the L** your God, who is among you,	3378
7:22	**The L** your God will drive out those nations	3378
7:23	But **the L** your God will deliver them	3378
7:25	for it is detestable to **the L** your God.	3378
8: 1	and possess the land that **the L** promised	3378
8: 2	how **the L** your God led you all the way	3378
8: 3	that comes from the mouth of **the L.**	3378
8: 5	so **the L** your God disciplines you.	3378
8: 6	the commands of **the L** your God,	3378
8: 7	For **the L** your God is bringing you into	3378
8:10	praise **the L** your God for	3378
8:11	that you do not forget **the L** your God,	3378
8:14	and you will forget **the L** your God,	3378
8:18	But remember **the L** your God,	3378
8:19	If you ever forget **the L** your God	3378
8:20	the nations **the L** destroyed before you,	3378
8:20	for not obeying **the L** your God.	3378
9: 3	that **the L** your God is the one who goes	3378
9: 3	as **the L** has promised you.	3378
9: 4	After **the L** your God *has* driven them out	3378
9: 4	"**The L** has brought me here	3378
9: 4	that **the L** is going to drive them out	3378
9: 5	the **the L** your God will drive them out	3378
9: 6	**the L** your God is giving you this good land	3378
9: 7	how you provoked **the L** your God	3378
9: 7	you have been rebellious against **the L.**	3378
9: 9	that **the L** had made with you, I stayed on	3378
9:10	**The L** gave me two stone tablets inscribed	3378
9:10	the commandments **the L** proclaimed	3378
9:11	**the L** gave me the two stone tablets,	3378
9:12	Then **the L** told me, "Go down from here	3378
9:13	And **the L** said to me, "I have seen this	3378
9:16	sinned against **the L** your God;	3378
9:16	the way that **the L** had commanded you.	3378
9:18	before **the L** for forty days	3378
9:19	I feared the anger and wrath of **the L,**	3378
9:19	But again **the L** listened to me.	3378
9:20	And **the L** was angry enough with Aaron	3378
9:22	You also made **the L** angry at Taberah,	3378
9:23	**the L** sent you out from Kadesh Barnea	3378
9:23	against the command of **the L** your God.	3378
9:24	rebellious against **the L** ever since	3378
9:25	before **the L** those forty days	3378
9:25	**the L** had said he would destroy you.	3378
9:26	I prayed to **the L** and said,	3378
9:26	the LORD and said, "O Sovereign **L,** do	3378
9:28	'Because **the L** was not able to take them	3378
10: 1	At that time **the L** said to me,	3378
10: 4	**The L** wrote on these tablets	3378
10: 4	And **the L** gave them to me.	3378
10: 5	as **the L** commanded me,	3378
10: 8	that time **the L** set apart the tribe of Levi	3378
10: 8	to carry the ark of the covenant of **the L,**	3378
10: 8	to stand before **the L** to minister and	3378
10: 9	**the L** is their inheritance,	3378
10: 9	as **the L** your God told them.)	3378
10:10	and **the L** listened to me at this time also.	3378
10:11	"Go," **the L** said to me,	3378
10:12	what does **the L** your God ask of you but	3378
10:12	of you but to fear **the L** your God,	3378
10:12	to serve **the L** your God	3378
10:14	To **the L** your God belong the heavens,	3378
10:15	Yet **the L** set his affection on your	3378
10:17	For **the L** your God is God of gods	3378
10:20	Fear **the L** your God and serve him.	3378
10:22	and now **the L** your God has made you	3378
11: 1	Love **the L** your God and keep his	3378
11: 2	the discipline of **the L** your God:	3378
11: 4	how **the L** brought lasting ruin on them.	3378

†**LORD** distinguishes the proper name of God, *Yahweh*, indicated in the NIV by "LORD," from the words translated "Lord" and "lord," indexed under the heading *LORD, pages 683-86.

Dt	11: 7	saw all these great things **the L** has done.	3378
	11: 9	that **the L** swore to your forefathers	3378
	11:12	It is a land **the L** your God cares for;	3378
	11:12	of **the L** your God are continually on it	3378
	11:13	to love **the L** your God and to serve him	3378
	11:17	from the good land **the L** is giving you.	3378
	11:21	that **the L** swore to give your forefathers,	3378
	11:22	to love **the L** your God, to walk in all his	3378
	11:23	then **the L** will drive out all these nations	3378
	11:25	**The L** your God, as he promised you,	3378
	11:27	the commands of **the L** your God	3378
	11:28	of **the L** your God and turn from the way	3378
	11:29	When **the L** your God has brought you	3378
	11:31	of the land **the L** your God is giving you.	3378
	12: 1	be careful to follow in the land that **the L,**	3378
	12: 4	not worship **the L** your God in their way.	3378
	12: 5	the place **the L** your God will choose	3378
	12: 7	There, in the presence of **the L** your God,	3378
	12: 7	because **the L** your God has blessed you.	3378
	12: 9	inheritance **the L** your God is giving you.	3378
	12:10	the land **the L** your God is giving you as	3378
	12:11	the place **the L** your God will choose as	3378
	12:11	and all the choice possessions you have vowed to **the L.**	3378
	12:12	And there rejoice before **the L** your God,	3378
	12:14	at the place **the L** will choose in one	3378
	12:15	to the blessing **the L** your God gives you.	3378
	12:18	in the presence of **the L** your God at	3378
	12:18	at the place **the L** your God will choose—	3378
	12:18	to rejoice before **the L** your God	3378
	12:20	**the L** your God has enlarged your territory	3378
	12:21	the place where **the L** your God chooses	3378
	12:21	the herds and flocks **the L** has given you,	3378
	12:25	doing what is right in the eyes of **the L.**	3378
	12:26	and go to the place **the L** will choose.	3378
	12:27	on the altar of **the L** your God,	3378
	12:27	beside the altar of **the L** your God,	3378
	12:28	and right in the eyes of **the L** your God.	3378
	12:29	**The L** your God will cut off before you	3378
	12:31	not worship **the L** your God in their way,	3378
	12:31	of detestable things **the L** hates.	3378
	13: 3	**The L** your God is testing you	3378
	13: 4	It is **the L** your God you must follow,	3378
	13: 5	rebellion against **the L** your God,	3378
	13: 5	the way **the L** your God commanded you	3378
	13:10	to turn you away from **the L** your God,	3378
	13:12	of the towns **the L** your God is giving you	3378
	13:16	a whole burnt offering to **the L** your God	3378
	13:17	that **the L** will turn from his fierce anger;	3378
	13:18	because you obey **the L** your God,	3378
	14: 1	You are the children of **the L** your God.	3378
	14: 2	you are a people holy to **the L** your God.	3378
	14: 2	**the L** has chosen you to be his treasured	3378
	14:21	you are a people holy to **the L** your God.	3378
	14:23	in the presence of **the L** your God at	3378
	14:23	to revere **the L** your God always.	3378
	14:24	you have been blessed by **the L** your God	3378
	14:24	the place where **the L** will choose	3378
	14:25	to the place **the L** your God will choose.	3378
	14:26	in the presence of **the L** your God	3378
	14:29	and so that **the L** your God may bless you	3378
	15: 4	in the land **the L** your God is giving you	3378
	15: 5	if only you fully obey **the L** your God	3378
	15: 6	For **the L** your God will bless you	3378
	15: 7	that **the L** your God is giving you,	3378
	15: 9	He may then appeal to **the L** against you,	3378
	15:10	of this **the L** your God will bless you	3378
	15:14	as **the L** your God has blessed you.	3378
	15:15	and **the L** your God redeemed you.	3378
	15:18	And **the L** your God will bless you	3378
	15:19	for **the L** your God every firstborn male	3378
	15:20	in the presence of **the L** your God	3378
	15:21	not sacrifice it to **the L** your God.	3378
	16: 1	the Passover of **the L** your God,	3378
	16: 2	the Passover to **the L** your God an animal	3378
	16: 2	the place **the L** will choose as a dwelling	3378
	16: 5	in any town **the L** your God gives you	3378
	16: 7	at the place **the L** your God will choose.	3378
	16: 8	to **the L** your God and do no work.	3378
	16:10	Feast of Weeks to **the L** your God by giving	3378
	16:10	blessings **the L** your God has given you.	3378
	16:11	And rejoice before **the L** your God at	3378
	16:15	the Feast to **the L** your God at the place	3378
	16:15	at the place **the L** will choose.	3378
	16:15	For **the L** your God will bless you	3378
	16:16	before **the L** your God at	3378
	16:16	before **the L** empty-handed:	3378
	16:17	the way **the L** your God has blessed you.	3378
	16:18	in every town **the L** your God is giving you,	3378
	16:20	the land **the L** your God is giving you.	3378
	16:21	the altar you build to **the L** your God,	3378
	16:22	for these **the L** your God hates.	3378
	17: 1	Do not sacrifice to **the L** your God an ox	3378
	17: 2	towns **the L** gives you is found doing evil	3378
	17: 2	in the eyes of **the L** your God in violation	3378
	17: 8	to the place **the L** your God will choose.	3378
	17:10	at the place **the L** will choose.	3378
	17:12	to **the L** your God must be put to death.	3378
	17:14	the land **the L** your God is giving you	3378
	17:15	the king **the L** your God chooses.	3378
	17:16	for **the L** has told you,	3378
	17:19	that he may learn to revere **the L** his God	3378
	18: 1	on the offerings made to **the L** by fire,	3378
	18: 2	**the L** is their inheritance.	3378
	18: 5	for **the L** your God has chosen them	3378
	18: 6	to the place **the L** will choose,	3378
	18: 7	in the name of **the L** his God	3378
	18: 7	serve there in the presence of **the L.**	3378
	18: 9	the land **the L** your God is giving you,	3378
	18:12	who does these things is detestable to **the L,**	3378
	18:12	of these detestable practices **the L** your God will drive out those nations	3378
	18:13	be blameless before **the L** your God.	3378
	18:14	**the L** your God has not permitted you	3378
	18:15	**The L** your God will raise up for you	3378
	18:16	of **the L** your God at Horeb on the day of	3378
	18:16	not hear the voice of **the L** our God	3378
	18:17	**The L** said to me: "What they say is good.	3378
	18:21	not been spoken by **the L?"**	3378
	18:22	of **the L** does not take place or come true,	3378
	18:22	that is a message **the L** has not spoken.	3378
	19: 1	When **the L** your God has destroyed	3378
	19: 2	in the land **the L** your God is giving you	3378
	19: 3	the land **the L** your God is giving you as	3378
	19: 8	If **the L** your God enlarges your territory	3378
	19: 9	to love **the L** your God and to walk always	3378
	19:10	which **the L** your God is giving you	3378
	19:14	in the land **the L** your God is giving you	3378
	19:17	in the presence of **the L** before the priests	3378
	20: 1	because **the L** your God,	3378
	20: 4	For **the L** your God is the one who goes	3378
	20:13	**the L** your God delivers it into your hand,	3378
	20:14	the plunder **the L** your God gives you	3378
	20:16	the nations **the L** your God is giving you	3378
	20:17	as **the L** your God has commanded you.	3378
	20:18	and you will sin against **the L** your God.	3378
	21: 1	in the land **the L** your God is giving you	3378
	21: 5	for **the L** your God has chosen them	3378
	21: 5	of **the L** and to decide all cases of dispute	3378
	21: 8	whom you have redeemed, O L,	3378
	21: 9	done what is right in the eyes of **the L.**	3378
	21:10	and **the L** your God delivers them	3378
	21:23	the land **the L** your God is giving you as	3378
	22: 5	**the L** your God detests anyone who does this.	3378
	23: 1	the assembly of **the L.**	3378
	23: 2	the assembly of **the L,**	3378
	23: 3	the assembly of **the L,**	3378
	23: 5	**the L** your God would not listen	3378
	23: 5	because **the L** your God loves you.	3378
	23: 8	to them may enter the assembly of **the L.**	3378
	23:14	For **the L** your God moves about	3378
	23:18	of **the L** your God to pay any vow,	3378
	23:18	**the L** your God detests them both.	3378
	23:20	so that **the L** your God may bless you	3378
	23:21	If you make a vow to **the L** your God,	3378
	23:21	**the L** your God will certainly demand it	3378
	23:23	to **the L** your God with your own mouth.	3378
	24: 4	be detestable in the eyes of **the L.**	3378
	24: 4	the land **the L** your God is giving you as	3378
	24: 9	Remember what **the L** your God did	3378
	24:13	in the sight of **the L** your God.	3378
	24:15	Otherwise he may cry to **the L**	3378
	24:18	and **the L** your God redeemed you	3378
	24:19	that **the L** your God may bless you in all	3378
	25:15	in the land **the L** your God is giving you.	3378
	25:16	**the L** your God detests anyone who does these things,	3378
	25:19	When **the L** your God gives you rest	3378
	26: 1	the land **the L** your God is giving you as	3378
	26: 2	of the land **the L** your God is giving you	3378
	26: 2	the place **the L** your God will choose as	3378
	26: 3	to **the L** your God that I have come to	3378
	26: 3	to the land **the L** swore to our forefathers	3378
	26: 4	in front of the altar of **the L** your God.	3378
	26: 5	you shall declare before **the L** your God:	3378
	26: 7	Then we cried out to **the L,**	3378
	26: 7	and **the L** heard our voice	3378
	26: 8	So **the L** brought us out of Egypt with	3378
	26:10	O L, have given me."	3378
	26:10	Place the basket before **the L** your God	3378
	26:11	the good things **the L** your God has given	3378
	26:13	Then say to **the L** your God:	3378
	26:14	I have obeyed **the L** my God;	3378
	26:16	**The L** your God commands you this day	3378
	26:17	that **the L** is your God and	3378
	26:18	And **the L** has declared this day	3378
	26:19	be a people holy to **the L** your God,	3378
	27: 2	the land **the L** your God is giving you,	3378
	27: 3	the land **the L** your God is giving you,	3378
	27: 3	just as **the L,** the God of your fathers,	3378
	27: 5	Build there an altar to **the L** your God,	3378
	27: 5	of **the L** your God with fieldstones	3378
	27: 6	on it to **the L** your God.	3378
	27: 7	in the presence of **the L** your God.	3378
	27: 9	the people of **the L** your God.	3378
	27:10	Obey **the L** your God and follow his	3378
	27:15	a thing detestable to **the L,**	3378
	28: 1	If you fully obey **the L** your God	3378
	28: 1	**the L** your God will set you high	3378
	28: 2	if you obey **the L** your God:	3378
	28: 7	**The L** will grant that the enemies who	3378
	28: 8	**The L** will send a blessing on your barns	3378
	28: 8	**The L** your God will bless you in	3378
	28: 9	**The L** will establish you as his holy people	3378
	28: 9	of **the L** your God and walk in his ways.	3378
	28:10	that you are called by the name of **the L,**	3378
	28:11	**The L** will grant you abundant prosperity—	3378
	28:12	**The L** will open the heavens,	3378
	28:13	**The L** will make you the head,	3378
	28:13	of **the L** your God that I give you this day	3378
	28:15	if you do not obey **the L** your God and do	3378
	28:20	**The L** will send on you curses,	3378
	28:21	**The L** will plague you with diseases	3378
Dt	28:22	**The L** will strike you with wasting disease,	3378
	28:24	**The L** will turn the rain of your country	3378
	28:25	**The L** will cause you to be defeated	3378
	28:27	**The L** will afflict you with the boils	3378
	28:28	**The L** will afflict you with madness,	3378
	28:35	**The L** will afflict your knees and legs	3378
	28:36	**The L** will drive you and the king you set	3378
	28:37	the nations where **the L** will drive you.	3378
	28:45	because you did not obey **the L** your God	3378
	28:47	not serve **the L** your God joyfully	3378
	28:48	you will serve the enemies **the L** sends	3378
	28:49	**The L** will bring a nation against you	3378
	28:52	the land **the L** your God is giving you.	3378
	28:53	daughters **the L** your God has given you.	3378
	28:58	and awesome name—**the L** your God—	3378
	28:59	**the L** will send fearful plagues on you	3378
	28:61	**The L** will also bring on you every kind	3378
	28:62	because you did not obey **the L** your God.	3378
	28:63	as it pleased **the L** to make you prosper	3378
	28:64	**the L** will scatter you among all nations,	3378
	28:65	There **the L** will give you	3378
	28:68	**the L** will send you back in ships	3378
	29: 1	of the covenant **the L** commanded Moses	3378
	29: 2	Your eyes have seen all that **the L** did	3378
	29: 4	But to this day **the L** has not given you	3378
	29: 6	that I am **the L** your God.	3378
	29:10	in the presence of **the L** your God—	3378
	29:12	into a covenant with **the L** your God,	3378
	29:12	a covenant **the L** is making	3378
	29:15	in the presence of **the L** our God but also	3378
	29:18	from **the L** our God to go and worship	3378
	29:20	**The L** will never be willing	3378
	29:20	and **the L** will blot out his name from	3378
	29:21	**The L** will single him out from all	3378
	29:22	with which **the L** has afflicted it.	3378
	29:23	which **the L** overthrew in fierce anger.	3378
	29:24	"Why has **the L** done this to this land?	3378
	29:25	the covenant of **the L,** the God of their	3378
	29:28	and in great wrath **the L** uprooted them	3378
	29:29	secret things belong to **the L** our God,	3378
	30: 1	wherever **the L** your God disperses you	3378
	30: 2	return to **the L** your God and obey him	3378
	30: 3	**the L** your God will restore your fortunes	3378
	30: 4	from there **the L** your God will gather you	3378
	30: 6	**The L** your God will circumcise your hearts	3378
	30: 7	**The L** your God will put all these curses	3378
	30: 8	You will again obey **the L**	3378
	30: 9	**the L** your God will make you most prosperous	3378
	30: 9	**The L** will again delight in you	3378
	30:10	if you obey **the L** your God	3378
	30:10	to **the L** your God with all your heart and	3378
	30:16	to love **the L** your God, to walk	3378
	30:16	and **the L** your God will bless you in	3378
	30:20	and that you may love **the L** your God,	3378
	30:20	For **the L** is your life,	3378
	31: 2	**The L** has said to me,	3378
	31: 3	**The L** your God himself will cross over	3378
	31: 3	cross over ahead of you, as **the L** said.	3378
	31: 4	And **the L** will do to them what he did	3378
	31: 5	**The L** will deliver them to you,	3378
	31: 6	for **the L** your God goes with you;	3378
	31: 7	that **the L** swore to their forefathers	3378
	31: 8	**The L** himself goes before you and will	3378
	31: 9	the ark of the covenant of **the L,**	3378
	31:11	to appear before **the L** your God at	3378
	31:12	and learn to fear **the L** your God	3378
	31:13	to fear **the L** your God as long as you live	3378
	31:14	**The L** said to Moses,	3378
	31:15	Then **the L** appeared at the Tent in	3378
	31:16	And **the L** said to Moses:	3378
	31:23	**The L** gave this command to Joshua son	NIH
	31:25	the ark of the covenant of **the L:**	3378
	31:26	of the covenant of **the L** your God.	3378
	31:27	If you have been rebellious against **the L**	3378
	31:29	in the sight of **the L** and provoke him	3378
	32: 3	I will proclaim the name of **the L.**	3378
	32: 6	Is this the way you repay **the L,**	3378
	32:12	**The L** alone led him;	3378
	32:19	**The L** saw this and rejected them	3378
	32:27	**the L** has not done all this.' "	3378
	32:30	unless **the L** had given them up?	3378
	32:36	**The L** will judge his people	3378
	32:48	On that same day **the L** told Moses,	3378
	33: 2	"**The L** came from Sinai and dawned	3378
	33: 7	"Hear, O L, the cry of Judah;	3378
	33:11	Bless all his skills, O L,	3378
	33:12	the beloved of **the L** rest secure in him,	3378
	33:12	**the L** loves rests between his shoulders."	NIH
	33:13	"May **the L** bless his land with	3378
	33:23	of **the L** and is full of his blessing;	3378
	33:29	a people saved by **the L?**	3378
	34: 1	There **the L** showed him the whole land—	3378
	34: 1	Then **the L** said to him,	3378
	34: 5	Moses the servant of **the L** died there in Moab,	3378
	34: 5	as **the L** had said.	3378
	34: 9	did what **the L** had commanded Moses.	3378
	34:10	whom **the L** knew face to face,	3378
	34:11	and wonders **the L** sent him to do	3378
Jos	1: 1	the death of Moses the servant of **the L,**	3378
	1: 1	**the L** said to Joshua son of Nun,	3378
	1: 9	be discouraged, for **the L** your God will	3378
	1:11	of the land **the L** your God is giving you	3378
	1:13	that Moses the servant of **the L** gave you:	3378
	1:13	'**The L** your God is giving you rest	3378
	1:15	until **the L** gives them rest,	3378

†**LORD** distinguishes the proper name of God, *Yahweh,* indicated in the NIV by "L ORD," from the words translated "Lord" and "lord," indexed under the heading *LORD, pages 683-86.

Jos	1:15	that the L your God is giving them.	3378
	1:15	the servant of the L gave you east of	3378
	1:17	Only may the L your God be with you	3378
	2: 9	that the L has given this land to you and	3378
	2:10	We have heard how the L dried up	3378
	2:11	for the L your God is God in heaven	3378
	2:12	by the L that you will show kindness	3378
	2:14	and faithfully when the L gives us	3378
	2:24	"The L has surely given the whole land	3378
	3: 3	of the covenant of the L your God,	3378
	3: 5	tomorrow the L will do amazing things	3378
	3: 7	And the L said to Joshua,	3378
	3: 9	and listen to the words of the L your God.	3378
	3:13	as the priests who carry the ark of the L—	3378
	3:17	of the L stood firm on dry ground in	3378
	4: 1	the L said to Joshua,	3378
	4: 5	the ark of the L your God into the middle	3378
	4: 7	before the ark of the covenant of the L.	3378
	4: 8	as the L had told Joshua;	3378
	4:10	until everything the L had commanded Joshua was done	3378
	4:11	the ark of the L and the priests came to	3378
	4:13	over before the L to the plains of Jericho	3378
	4:14	That day the L exalted Joshua in the sight	3378
	4:15	Then the L said to Joshua,	3378
	4:18	the ark of the covenant of the L,	3378
	4:23	For the L your God dried up the Jordan	3378
	4:23	The L your God did to the Jordan	3378
	4:24	that the hand of the L is powerful and so	3378
	4:24	you might always fear the L your God."	3378
	5: 1	along the coast heard how the L had dried	3378
	5: 2	At that time the L said to Joshua,	3378
	5: 6	since they had not obeyed the L.	3378
	5: 6	For the L had sworn to them	3378
	5: 9	Then the L said to Joshua,	3378
	5:14	as commander of the army of the L I have	3378
	6: 2	Then the L said to Joshua, "See.	3378
	6: 6	"Take up the ark of the covenant of the L	3378
	6: 7	ahead of the ark of the L."	3378
	6: 8	before the L went forward,	3378
	6:11	So he had the ark of the L carried around	3378
	6:12	and the priests took up the ark of the L.	3378
	6:13	before the ark of the L and blowing	3378
	6:13	the rear guard followed the ark of the L,	3378
	6:16	For the L has given you the city!	3378
	6:17	that is in it are to be devoted to the L.	3378
	6:19	and iron are sacred to the L and must go	3378
	6:21	the city to the L and destroyed with	NIH
	6:26	before the L is the man who undertakes	3378
	6:27	So the L was with Joshua,	3378
	7: 6	to the ground before the ark of the L,	3378
	7: 7	And Joshua said, "Ah, Sovereign L,	3378
	7:10	The L said to Joshua, "Stand up!	3378
	7:13	this is what the L, the God of Israel, says:	3378
	7:14	that the L takes shall come forward clan	3378
	7:14	the L takes shall come forward family	3378
	7:14	that the L takes shall come forward man	3378
	7:15	of the L and has done a disgraceful thing	3378
	7:19	give glory to the L, the God of Israel,	3378
	7:20	I have sinned against the L,	3378
	7:23	and spread them out before the L.	3378
	7:25	The L will bring trouble on you today."	3378
	7:26	Then the L turned from his fierce anger.	3378
	8: 1	the L said to Joshua, "Do not be afraid;	3378
	8: 7	The L your God will give it	3378
	8: 8	Do what the L has commanded.	3378
	8:18	Then the L said to Joshua,	3378
	8:27	as the L had instructed Joshua.	3378
	8:30	on Mount Ebal an altar to the L,	3378
	8:31	of the L had commanded the Israelites.	3378
	8:31	On it they offered to the L burnt offerings	3378
	8:33	of the L, facing those who carried it—	3378
	8:33	of the L had formerly commanded	3378
	9: 9	because of the fame of the L your God.	3378
	9:14	but did not inquire of the L.	3378
	9:18	had sworn an oath to them by the L,	3378
	9:19	"We have given them our oath by the L,	3378
	9:24	the L your God had commanded his servant Moses	3378
	9:27	the community and for the altar of the L	3378
	9:27	at the place the L would choose.	NIH
	10: 8	The L said to Joshua,	3378
	10:10	The L threw them into confusion	3378
	10:11	the L hurled large hailstones down	3378
	10:12	On the day the L gave the Amorites over	3378
	10:12	Joshua said to the L in the presence	3378
	10:14	a day when the L listened to a man.	3378
	10:14	Surely the L was fighting for Israel!	3378
	10:19	for the L your God has given them	3378
	10:25	This is what the L will do to all	3378
	10:30	The L also gave that city and its king	3378
	10:32	The L handed Lachish over to Israel,	3378
	10:40	just as the L, the God of Israel,	3378
	10:42	because the L, the God of Israel,	3378
	11: 6	The L said to Joshua,	3378
	11: 8	the L gave them into the hand of Israel.	3378
	11: 9	Joshua did to them as the L had directed:	3378
	11:12	the servant of the L had commanded.	3378
	11:15	As the L commanded his servant Moses,	3378
	11:15	of all that the L commanded Moses.	3378
	11:20	was the L himself who hardened their hearts	3378
	11:20	as the L had commanded Moses.	3378
	11:23	just as the L had directed Moses,	3378
	12: 6	Moses, the servant of the L,	3378
	12: 6	of the L gave their land to the Reubenites,	3378
	13: 1	the L said to him, "You are very old,	3378
	13: 8	as he, the servant of the L, had assigned	3378
Jos	13:14	since the offerings made by fire to the L,	3378
	13:33	the L, the God of Israel,	3378
	14: 2	as the L had commanded through Moses.	3378
	14: 5	just as the L had commanded Moses.	3378
	14: 6	"You know what the L said to Moses	3378
	14: 7	when Moses the servant of the L sent me	3378
	14: 8	followed the L my God wholeheartedly.	3378
	14: 9	you have followed the L my God wholeheartedly.'	3378
	14:10	"Now then, just as the L promised,	3378
	14:12	that the L promised me that day.	3378
	14:12	but, the L helping me,	3378
	14:14	because he followed the L,	3378
	17: 4	"The L commanded Moses to give us	3378
	17:14	and the L has blessed us abundantly."	3378
	18: 3	to take possession of the land that the L,	3378
	18: 6	for you in the presence of the L our God.	3378
	18: 7	of the L is their inheritance.	3378
	18: 7	the servant of the L gave it to them."	3378
	18: 8	at Shiloh in the presence of the L."	3378
	18:10	in Shiloh in the presence of the L,	3378
	19:50	as the L had commanded.	3378
	19:51	by lot at Shiloh in the presence of the L at	3378
	20: 1	Then the L said to Joshua:	3378
	21: 2	"The L commanded through Moses	3378
	21: 3	So, as the L had commanded,	3378
	21: 8	as the L had commanded through Moses.	3378
	21:43	So the L gave Israel all the land	3378
	21:44	The L gave them rest on every side,	3378
	21:44	the L handed all their enemies over	3378
	22: 2	the servant of the L commanded,	3378
	22: 3	the mission the L your God gave you.	3378
	22: 4	the L your God has given your brothers rest	3378
	22: 4	that Moses the servant of the L gave you	3378
	22: 5	that Moses the servant of the L gave you:	3378
	22: 5	to love the L your God, to walk in all his	3378
	22: 9	in accordance with the command of the L	3378
	22:16	"The whole assembly of the L says:	3378
	22:16	from the L and build yourselves an altar	3378
	22:17	a plague fell on the community of the L!	3378
	22:18	are you now turning away from the L?	3378
	22:18	" 'If you rebel against the L today,	3378
	22:19	against the L or against us by building	3378
	22:19	other than the altar of the L our God.	3378
	22:22	"The Mighty One, God, the L!	3378
	22:22	The Mighty One, God, the L!	3378
	22:22	in rebellion or disobedience to the L,	3378
	22:23	from the L and to offer burnt offerings	3378
	22:23	may the L himself call us to account.	3378
	22:24	'What do you have to do with the L,	3378
	22:25	The L has made the Jordan a boundary	3378
	22:25	You have no share in the L.'	3378
	22:25	to stop fearing the L.	3378
	22:27	that we will worship the L	3378
	22:27	'You have no share in the L.'	3378
	22:29	"Far be it from us to rebel against the L	3378
	22:29	the altar of the L our God that stands	3378
	22:31	"Today we know that the L is with us,	3378
	22:31	not acted unfaithfully toward the L	3378
	22:34	A Witness Between Us that the L is God.	3378
	23: 1	and the L had given Israel rest	3378
	23: 3	You yourselves have seen everything the L your God has done	3378
	23: 3	it was the L your God who fought	3378
	23: 5	The L your God himself will drive them out	3378
	23: 5	as the L your God promised you.	3378
	23: 8	you are to hold fast to the L your God,	3378
	23: 9	"The L has driven out before you great	3378
	23:10	because the L your God fights for you,	3378
	23:11	be very careful to love the L your God.	3378
	23:13	the L your God will no longer drive out these nations	3378
	23:13	which the L your God has given you.	3378
	23:14	not one of all the good promises the L your God gave you has failed.	3378
	23:15	of the L your God has come true,	3378
	23:15	so the L will bring on you all	3378
	23:16	the covenant of the L your God,	3378
	24: 2	"This is what the L, the God of Israel,	3378
	24: 7	But they cried to the L for help,	3378
	24:14	"Now fear the L and serve him	3378
	24:14	and serve the L.	3378
	24:15	if serving the L seems undesirable to you,	3378
	24:15	me and my household, we will serve the L."	3378
	24:16	to forsake the L to serve other gods!	3378
	24:17	was the L our God himself who brought us	3378
	24:18	the L drove out before us all the nations,	3378
	24:18	We too will serve the L,	3378
	24:19	"You are not able to serve the L.	3378
	24:20	you forsake the L and serve foreign gods,	3378
	24:21	We will serve the L."	3378
	24:22	that you have chosen to serve the L."	3378
	24:23	and yield your hearts to the L,	3378
	24:24	"We will serve the L our God	3378
	24:26	the oak near the holy place of the L.	3378
	24:27	It has heard all the words the L has said	3378
	24:29	Joshua son of Nun, the servant of the L,	3378
	24:31	Israel served the L throughout	3378
	24:31	had experienced everything the L had done	3378
Jdg	1: 1	the Israelites asked the L,	3378
	1: 2	The L answered, "Judah is to go;	3378
	1: 4	the L gave the Canaanites and Perizzites	3378
	1:19	The L was with the men of Judah.	3378
	1:22	and the L was with them.	3378
	2: 1	The angel of the L went up from Gilgal	3378
	2: 4	of the L had spoken these things to all	3378
	2: 5	There they offered sacrifices to the L.	3378
Jdg	2: 7	The people served the L throughout	3378
	2: 7	the great things the L had done for Israel.	3378
	2: 8	Joshua son of Nun, the servant of the L,	3378
	2:10	who knew neither the L nor what he had	3378
	2:11	in the eyes of the L and served the Baals.	3378
	2:12	They forsook the L, the God of their fathers	3378
	2:12	They provoked the L to anger	3378
	2:14	against Israel the L handed them over	3378
	2:15	of the L was against them to defeat them,	3378
	2:16	Then the L raised up judges,	3378
	2:18	Whenever the L raised up a judge	3378
	2:18	for the L had compassion on them	3378
	2:20	the L was very angry with Israel and said,	3378
	2:22	the way of the L and walk in it	3378
	2:23	The L had allowed those nations	3378
	3: 1	These are the nations the L left	3378
	3: 7	Israelites did evil in the eyes of the L;	3378
	3: 7	they forgot the L their God and served	3378
	3: 8	The anger of the L burned against Israel	3378
	3: 9	But when they cried out to the L,	3378
	3:10	The Spirit of the L came upon him,	3378
	3:10	The L gave Cushan-Rishathaim king	3378
	3:12	the Israelites did evil in the eyes of the L,	3378
	3:12	they did this evil the L gave Eglon king	3378
	3:15	Again the Israelites cried out to the L,	3378
	3:28	"for the L has given Moab, your enemy,	3378
	4: 1	again did evil in the eyes of the L,	3378
	4: 2	the L sold them into the hands of Jabin	3378
	4: 3	they cried to the L for help.	3378
	4: 6	"The L, the God of Israel,	3378
	4: 9	the L will hand Sisera over to a woman."	3378
	4:14	This is the day the L has given Sisera	3378
	4:14	Has not the L gone ahead of you?"	3378
	4:15	the L routed Sisera and all his chariots	3378
	5: 2	when the people willingly offer themselves—praise the L!	3378
	5: 3	I will sing to the L, I will sing;	3378
	5: 3	I will make music to the L,	3378
	5: 4	"O L, when you went out from Seir,	3378
	5: 5	The mountains quaked before the L,	3378
	5: 5	before the L, the God of Israel.	3378
	5: 9	Praise the L!	3378
	5:11	They recite the righteous acts of the L,	3378
	5:11	"Then the people of the L went down to	3378
	5:13	of the L came to me with the mighty.	3378
	5:23	'Curse Meroz,' said the angel of the L.	3378
	5:23	because they did not come to help the L,	3378
	5:23	to help the L against the mighty.'	3378
	5:31	"So may all your enemies perish, O L!	3378
	6: 1	the Israelites did evil in the eyes of the L,	3378
	6: 6	the Israelites that they cried out to the L	3378
	6: 7	When the Israelites cried to the L because	3378
	6: 8	"This is what the L, the God of Israel,	3378
	6:10	I said to you, 'I am the L your God;	3378
	6:11	of the L came and sat down under the oak	3378
	6:12	the angel of the L appeared to Gideon,	3378
	6:12	"The L is with you, mighty warrior."	3378
	6:13	Gideon replied, "if the L is with us,	3378
	6:13	'Did not the L bring us up out of Egypt?'	3378
	6:13	now the L has abandoned us and put us	3378
	6:14	The L turned to him and said,	3378
	6:16	The L answered, "I will be with you,	3378
	6:18	the L said, "I will wait until you return."	NIH
	6:21	the angel of the L touched the meat and	3378
	6:21	And the angel of the L disappeared.	3378
	6:22	that it was the angel of the L,	3378
	6:22	he exclaimed, "Ah, Sovereign L!	3378
	6:22	I have seen the angel of the L face	3378
	6:23	But the L said to him, "Peace!	3378
	6:24	So Gideon built an altar to the L there	3378
	6:24	and called it The L is Peace.	3378
	6:25	That same night the L said to him,	3378
	6:26	a proper kind of altar to the L your God	3378
	6:27	of his servants and did as the L told him.	3378
	6:34	the Spirit of the L came upon Gideon,	3378
	7: 2	The L said to Gideon, "You have too many	3378
	7: 4	But the L said to Gideon, "There are still	3378
	7: 5	There the L told him, "Separate those who	3378
	7: 7	The L said to Gideon,	3378
	7: 9	During that night the L said to Gideon,	3378
	7:15	The L has given the Midianite camp	3378
	7:18	'For the L and for Gideon.' '	3378
	7:20	"A sword for the L and for Gideon!"	3378
	7:22	the L caused the men throughout	3378
	8: 7	when the L has given Zebah	3378
	8:19	As surely as the L lives,	3378
	8:23	The L will rule over you."	3378
	8:34	and did not remember the L their God,	3378
	10: 6	the Israelites did evil in the eyes of the L.	3378
	10: 6	And because the Israelites forsook the L	3378
	10:10	Then the Israelites cried out to the L,	3378
	10:11	The L replied, "When the Egyptians,	3378
	10:15	Israelites said to the L, "We have sinned.	3378
	10:16	among them and served the L.	3378
	11: 9	the Ammonites and the L gives them	3378
	11:10	"The L is our witness,	3378
	11:11	before the L in Mizpah.	3378
	11:21	"Then the L, the God of Israel,	3378
	11:23	"Now since the L, the God of Israel,	3378
	11:24	whatever the L our God has given us,	3378
	11:27	Let the L, the Judge, decide the dispute	3378
	11:29	the Spirit of the L came upon Jephthah.	3378
	11:30	And Jephthah made a vow to the L:	3378
	11:32	and the L gave them into his hands.	3378
	11:35	because I have made a vow to the L	3378
	11:36	"you have given your word to the L.	3378
	11:36	now that the L has avenged you	3378

Jdg 12: 3	and the L gave me the victory over them.	3378
13: 1	the Israelites did evil in the eyes of the L,	3378
13: 1	so the L delivered them into the hands of	3378
13: 3	The angel of the L appeared to her	3378
13: 8	Then Manoah prayed to the L:	3378
13:13	The angel of the L answered,	3378
13:15	Manoah said to the angel of the L,	3378
13:16	The angel of the L replied,	3378
13:16	a burnt offering, offer it to the L."	3378
13:16	not realize that it was the angel of the L.)	3378
13:17	Manoah inquired of the angel of the L,	3378
13:19	and sacrificed it on a rock to the L.	3378
13:19	And the L did an amazing thing	NIH
13:20	the angel of the L ascended in the flame.	3378
13:21	of the L did not show himself again	3378
13:21	that it was the angel of the L.	3378
13:23	"If the L had meant to kill us,	3378
13:24	He grew and the L blessed him,	3378
13:25	and the Spirit of the L began to stir him	3378
14: 4	from the L, who was seeking an occasion	3378
14: 6	Spirit of the L came upon him in power	3378
14:19	Spirit of the L came upon him in power.	3378
15:14	The Spirit of the L came upon him	3378
15:18	he was very thirsty, he cried out to the L,	3378
16:20	he did not know that the L had left him.	3378
16:28	Then Samson prayed to the L,	3378
16:28	"O Sovereign L, remember me.	3378
17: 2	Then his mother said, "The L bless you,	3378
17: 3	"I solemnly consecrate my silver to the L	3378
17:13	I know that the L will be good to me,	3378
19:18	and now I am going to the house of the L.	3378
20: 1	as one man and assembled before the L	3378
20:18	The L replied, "Judah shall go first."	3378
20:23	up and wept before the L until evening,	3378
20:23	and they inquired of the L.	3378
20:23	The L answered, "Go up against them."	3378
20:26	and there they sat weeping before the L.	3378
20:26	and fellowship offerings to the L.	3378
20:27	And the Israelites inquired of the L.	3378
20:28	The L responded, "Go,	3378
20:35	The L defeated Benjamin before Israel,	3378
21: 3	"O L, the God of Israel," they cried,	3378
21: 5	failed to assemble before the L?"	3378
21: 5	before the L at Mizpah should certainly	3378
21: 7	since we have taken an oath by the L not	3378
21: 8	of Israel failed to assemble before the L	3378
21:15	because the L had made a gap in	3378
21:19	the annual festival of the L in Shiloh,	3378
Ru 1: 6	in Moab that the L had come to the aid	3378
1: 8	May the L show kindness to you,	3378
1: 9	May the L grant that each of you will find	3378
1:17	May the L deal with me,	3378
1:21	but the L has brought me back empty.	3378
1:21	The L has afflicted me; the Almighty	3378
2: 4	"The L be with you!"	3378
2: 4	"The L bless you!"	3378
2:12	May the L repay you for what you have	3378
2:12	May you be richly rewarded by the L,	3378
2:20	"The L bless him!"	3378
3:10	"The L bless you, my daughter,"	3378
3:13	as surely as the L lives I will do it.	3378
4:11	May the L make the woman who	3378
4:12	Through the offspring the L gives you	3378
4:13	and the L enabled her to conceive,	3378
4:14	"Praise be to the L,	3378
1Sa 1: 3	and sacrifice to the L Almighty at Shiloh,	3378
1: 3	the two sons of Eli, were priests of the L.	3378
1: 5	and the L had closed her womb.	3378
1: 6	And because the L had closed her womb,	3378
1: 7	Hannah went up to the house of the L,	3378
1:10	and prayed to the L.	3378
1:11	she made a vow, saying, "O L Almighty,	3378
1:11	then I will give him to the L for all	3378
1:12	As she kept on praying to the L,	3378
1:15	I was pouring out my soul to the L.	3378
1:19	before the L and then went back	3378
1:19	and the L remembered her.	3378
1:20	saying, "Because I asked the L for him."	3378
1:21	to offer the annual sacrifice to the L and	3378
1:22	and present him before the L	3378
1:23	only may the L make good his word."	3378
1:24	and brought him to the house of the L	3378
1:26	beside you praying to the L.	3378
1:27	and the L has granted me what I asked	3378
1:28	So now I give him to the L.	3378
1:28	be given over to the L."	3378
1:28	And he worshiped the L there.	3378
2: 1	"My heart rejoices in the L;	3378
2: 1	in the L my horn is lifted high.	3378
2: 2	"There is no one holy like the L;	3378
2: 3	for the L is a God who knows,	3378
2: 6	"The L brings death and makes alive;	3378
2: 7	The L sends poverty and wealth;	3378
2:10	those who oppose the L will be shattered.	3378
2:10	the L will judge the ends of the earth.	3378
2:11	the boy ministered before the L under Eli	3378
2:12	they had no regard for the L.	3378
2:18	But Samuel was ministering before the L—	3378
2:20	"May the L give you children	3378
2:20	the one she prayed for and gave to the L."	3378
2:21	And the L was gracious to Hannah;	3378
2:21	Samuel grew up in the presence of the L.	3378
2:25	but if a man sins against the L,	3378
2:26	to grow in stature and in favor with the L	3378
2:27	"This is what the L says:	3378
2:30	"Therefore the L, the God of Israel,	3378
2:30	now the L declares: 'Far be it from me!	3378

1Sa 3: 1	The boy Samuel ministered before the L	3378
3: 1	In those days the word of the L was rare;	3378
3: 3	down in the temple of the L,	3378
3: 4	Then the L called Samuel.	3378
3: 6	Again the L called, "Samuel!"	3378
3: 7	Now Samuel did not yet know the L:	3378
3: 7	of the L had not yet been revealed to him.	3378
3: 8	The L called Samuel a third time,	3378
3: 8	Then Eli realized that the L was calling	3378
3: 9	and if he calls you, say, 'Speak, L,	3378
3:10	The L came and stood there,	3378
3:11	And the L said to Samuel:	3378
3:15	the doors of the house of the L.	3378
3:18	Then Eli said, "He is the L;	3378
3:19	The L was with Samuel as he grew up,	3378
3:20	Samuel was attested as a prophet of the L.	3378
3:21	The L continued to appear at Shiloh,	3378
4: 3	"Why did the L bring defeat	3378
4: 4	of the covenant of the L Almighty,	3378
4: 6	the ark of the L had come into the camp,	3378
5: 3	on the ground before the ark of the L!	3378
5: 4	on the ground before the ark of the L!	3378
6: 1	When the ark of the L had been	3378
6: 2	"What shall we do with the ark of the L?	3378
6: 8	the ark of the L and put it on the cart,	3378
6: 9	then the L has brought this great disaster	2085S
6:11	They placed the ark of the L on the cart	3378
6:14	the cows as a burnt offering to the L.	3378
6:15	The Levites took down the ark of the L,	3378
6:15	and made sacrifices to the L.	3378
6:17	as a guilt offering to the L—	3378
6:18	on which they set the ark of the L,	3378
6:19	into the ark of the L.	3378
6:19	of the heavy blow the L had dealt them,	3378
6:20	"Who can stand in the presence of the L,	3378
6:21	Philistines have returned the ark of the L,	3378
7: 1	and took up the ark of the L.	3378
7: 1	to guard the ark of the L.	3378
7: 2	of Israel mourned and sought after the L.	3378
7: 3	"If you are returning to the L	3378
7: 3	and commit yourselves to the L	3378
7: 4	and served the L only.	3378
7: 5	at Mizpah and I will intercede with the L	3378
7: 6	and poured it out before the L.	3378
7: 6	"We have sinned against the L."	3378
7: 8	"Do not stop crying out to the L our God	3378
7: 9	up as a whole burnt offering to the L.	3378
7: 9	He cried out to the L on Israel's behalf,	3378
7: 9	and the L answered him.	3378
7:10	But that day the L thundered	3378
7:12	saying, "Thus far has the L helped us."	3378
7:13	hand of the L was against the Philistines.	3378
7:17	And he built an altar there to the L.	3378
8: 6	so he prayed to the L.	3378
8: 7	And the L told him: "Listen to all that	3378
8:10	Samuel told all the words of the L to	3378
8:18	and the L will not answer you in	3378
8:21	he repeated it before the L.	3378
8:22	The L answered, "Listen to them	3378
9:15	the L had revealed this to Samuel:	3378
9:17	the L said to him, "This is the man	3378
10: 1	"Has not the L anointed you leader	3378
10: 6	The Spirit of the L will come upon you	3378
10:17	the people of Israel to the L at Mizpah	3378
10:18	"This is what the L, the God of Israel,	3378
10:19	So now present yourselves before the L	3378
10:22	So they inquired further of the L,	3378
10:22	And the L said, "Yes,	3378
10:22	"Do you see the man the L has chosen?	3378
10:25	on a scroll and deposited it before the L.	3378
11: 7	the terror of the L fell on the people,	3378
11:13	for this day the L has rescued Israel."	3378
11:15	as king in the presence of the L.	3378
11:15	before the L, and Saul and all	3378
12: 3	in the presence of the L and his anointed.	3378
12: 5	"The L is witness against you,	3378
12: 6	"It is the L who appointed Moses	3378
12: 7	with evidence before the L as to all	3378
12: 7	the righteous acts performed by the L	3378
12: 8	they cried to the L for help,	3378
12: 8	and the L sent Moses and Aaron,	3378
12: 9	"But they forgot the L their God;	3378
12:10	They cried out to the L and said,	3378
12:10	we have forsaken the L and served	3378
12:11	Then the L sent Jerub-Baal, Barak,	3378
12:12	though the L your God was your king.	3378
12:13	see, the L has set a king over you.	3378
12:14	If you fear the L and serve and obey him	3378
12:14	over you follow the L your God—	3378
12:15	But if you do not obey the L,	3378
12:16	stand still and see this great thing the L is	3378
12:17	I will call upon the L to send thunder	3378
12:17	an evil thing you did in the eyes of the L	3378
12:18	Then Samuel called upon the L,	3378
12:18	that same day the L sent thunder and rain.	3378
12:18	So all the people stood in awe of the L	3378
12:19	"Pray to the L your God for your servants	3378
12:20	yet do not turn away from the L,	3378
12:20	but serve the L with all your heart.	3378
12:22	For the sake of his great name the L will	3378
12:22	the L was pleased to make you his own.	3378
12:23	that I should sin against the L by failing	3378
12:24	to fear the L and serve him faithfully	3378
13:13	the command the L your God gave you;	3378
13:14	the L has sought out a man	3378
14: 6	Perhaps the L will act in our behalf.	3378
14: 6	Nothing can hinder the L from saving,	3378

1Sa 14:10	that the L has given them into our hands."	3378
14:12	the L has given them into the hand	3378
14:23	So the L rescued Israel that day,	3378
14:33	the men are sinning against the L	3378
14:34	Do not sin against the L by eating meat	3378
14:35	Then Saul built an altar to the L;	3378
14:39	surely as the L who rescues Israel lives,	3378
14:41	Then Saul prayed to the L,	3378
14:45	As surely as the L lives,	3378
15: 1	the one the L sent to anoint you king	3378
15: 1	so listen now to the message from the L.	3378
15: 2	This is what the L Almighty says:	3378
15:10	Then the word of the L came to Samuel:	3378
15:11	and he cried out to the L all that night.	3378
15:13	Saul said, "The L bless you!	3378
15:15	and cattle to sacrifice to the L your God,	3378
15:16	"Let me tell you what the L said	3378
15:17	The L anointed you king over Israel.	3378
15:19	Why did you not obey the L?	3378
15:19	and do evil in the eyes of the L?"	3378
15:20	"But I did obey the L," Saul said.	3378
15:20	"I went on the mission the L assigned me.	3378
15:21	to sacrifice them to the L your God	3378
15:22	"Does the L delight in burnt offerings	3378
15:22	as in obeying the voice of the L?	3378
15:23	you have rejected the word of the L,	3378
15:25	so that I may worship the L."	3378
15:26	You have rejected the word of the L,	3378
15:26	and the L has rejected you as king	3378
15:28	"The L has torn the kingdom of Israel	3378
15:30	so that I may worship the L your God."	3378
15:31	and Saul worshiped the L.	3378
15:33	put Agag to death before the L at Gilgal.	3378
15:35	the L was grieved that he had made Saul	3378
16: 1	The L said to Samuel,	3378
16: 2	The L said, "Take a heifer with you	3378
16: 2	'I have come to sacrifice to the L.'	3378
16: 4	Samuel did what the L said.	3378
16: 5	I have come to sacrifice to the L.	3378
16: 6	"Surely the LORD's anointed stands here before the L."	3378
16: 7	But the L said to Samuel,	3378
16: 7	The L does not look at the things man looks	NIH
16: 7	but the L looks at the heart."	3378
16: 8	"The L has not chosen this one either."	3378
16: 9	"Nor has the L chosen this one."	3378
16:10	"The L has not chosen these."	3378
16:12	Then the L said, "Rise and anoint him;	3378
16:13	from that day on the Spirit of the L came	3378
16:14	Spirit of the L had departed from Saul,	3378
16:14	an evil spirit from the L tormented him.	3378
16:18	And the L is with him."	3378
17:37	The L who delivered me from the paw of	3378
17:37	"Go, and the L be with you."	3378
17:45	in the name of the L Almighty,	3378
17:46	This day the L will hand you over to me,	3378
17:47	not by sword or spear that the L saves;	3378
18:12	the L was with David but had left Saul.	3378
18:14	because the L was with him.	3378
18:17	and fight the battles of the L."	3378
18:28	When Saul realized that the L was	3378
19: 5	The L won a great victory for all Israel,	3378
19: 6	"As surely as the L lives,	3378
19: 9	an evil spirit from the L came upon Saul	3378
20: 3	as surely as the L lives and as you live,	3378
20: 8	into a covenant with you before the L.	3378
20:13	Then Jonathan said to David: "By the L,	3378
20:13	may the L deal with me,	3378
20:13	May the L be with you as he has been	3378
20:14	like that of the L as long as I live,	3378
20:15	not even when the L has cut off every one	3378
20:16	May the L call David's enemies to account.	3378
20:21	as surely as the L lives, you are safe;	3378
20:22	because the L has sent you away.	3378
20:23	remember, the L is witness between you	3378
20:42	with each other in the name of the L,	3378
20:42	'The L is witness between you and me,	3378
21: 6	before the L and replaced by hot bread on	3378
21: 7	detained before the L;	3378
22:10	Ahimelech inquired of the L for him;	3378
22:17	"Turn and kill the priests of the L,	3378
22:17	a hand to strike the priests of the L.	3378
22:21	that Saul had killed the priests of the L.	3378
23: 2	he inquired of the L, saying,	3378
23: 2	The L answered him, "Go,	3378
23: 4	Once again David inquired of the L,	3378
23: 4	and the L answered him,	3378
23:10	David said, "O L, God of Israel,	3378
23:11	O L, God of Israel, tell your servant."	3378
23:11	And the L said, "He will."	3378
23:12	And the L said, "They will."	3378
23:18	of them made a covenant before the L.	3378
23:21	"The L bless you for your concern for me.	3378
24: 4	the day the L spoke of when he said	3378
24: 6	"The L forbid that I should do such	3378
24: 6	for he is the anointed of the L."	3378
24:10	how the L delivered you into my hands in	3378
24:12	May the L judge between you and me.	3378
24:12	And may the L avenge the wrongs you	3378
24:15	May the L be our judge and decide	3378
24:18	the L delivered me into your hands,	3378
24:19	May the L reward you well for the way	3378
24:21	Now swear to me by the L that you will	3378
25:26	"Now since the L has kept you,	3378
25:26	as surely as the L lives and as you live,	3378
25:28	the L will certainly make a lasting dynasty	3378
25:29	bundle of the living by the L your God.	3378

†**LORD** distinguishes the proper name of God, *Yahweh*, indicated in the NIV by "L<small>ORD</small>," from the words translated "Lord" and "lord," indexed under the heading ***LORD**, pages 683–86.

Ref	Text	Strong
1Sa 25:30	When the L has done for my master	3378
25:31	the L has brought my master success,	3378
25:32	"Praise be to the L, the God of Israel,	3378
25:34	Otherwise, as surely as the L,	3378
25:38	the L struck Nabal and he died.	3378
25:39	he said, "Praise be to the L,	3378
26:10	As surely as the L lives," he said,	3378
26:10	he said, "the L himself will strike him;	3378
26:11	But "As surely as I should lay a hand	3378
26:12	the L had put them into a deep sleep.	3378
26:16	As surely as the L lives,	3378
26:19	If the L has incited you against me,	3378
26:19	may they be cursed before the L!	3378
26:20	the ground far from the presence of the L.	3378
26:23	The L rewards every man for his	3378
26:23	The L delivered you into my hands today,	3378
26:24	so may the L value my life	3378
28:6	He inquired of the L,	3378
28:6	but the L did not answer him by dreams	3378
28:10	Saul swore to her by the L,	3378
28:10	"As surely as the L lives,	3378
28:16	now that the L has turned away from you	3378
28:17	The L has done what he predicted	3378
28:17	The L has torn the kingdom out	3378
28:18	Because you did not obey the L	3378
28:18	the L has done this to you today.	3378
28:19	The L will hand over both Israel and you	3378
28:19	The L will also hand over the army	3378
29:6	"As surely as the L lives,	3378
30:6	David found strength in the L his God.	3378
30:8	and David inquired of the L,	3378
30:23	not do that with what the L has given us.	3378
2Sa 1:12	the army of the L and the house of Israel,	3378
2:1	David inquired of the L.	3378
2:1	The L said, "Go up."	3378
2:1	"To Hebron," the L answered.	NIH
2:5	"The L bless you for showing this kindness	3378
2:6	May the L now show you kindness	3378
3:9	for David what the L promised him	3378
3:18	For the L promised David,	3378
3:28	before the L concerning the blood	3378
3:39	May the L repay the evildoer according	3378
4:8	This day the L has avenged my lord	3378
4:9	"As surely as the L lives,	3378
5:2	And the L said to you,	3378
5:3	with them at Hebron before the L,	3378
5:10	the L God Almighty was with him,	3378
5:12	that the L had established him as king	3378
5:19	so David inquired of the L,	3378
5:19	The L answered him, "Go,	3378
5:20	the L has broken out against my enemies	3378
5:23	so David inquired of the L,	3378
5:24	because that will mean the L has gone out	3378
5:25	So David did as the L commanded him,	3378
6:2	the name of the L Almighty,	3378
6:5	with all their might before the L,	3378
6:9	David was afraid of the L that day	3378
6:9	can the ark of the L ever come to me?"	3378
6:10	the ark of the L to be with him in the City	3378
6:11	The ark of the L remained in the house	3378
6:11	and the L blessed him	3378
6:12	"The L has blessed the household	3378
6:13	those who were carrying the ark of the L	3378
6:14	danced before the L with all his might,	3378
6:15	the ark of the L with shouts and the sound	3378
6:16	As the ark of the L was entering the City	3378
6:16	and dancing before the L,	3378
6:17	They brought the ark of the L and set it	3378
6:17	and fellowship offerings before the L.	3378
6:18	the people in the name of the L Almighty.	3378
6:21	"It was before the L,	3378
6:21	I will celebrate before the L.	3378
7:1	in his palace and the L had given him rest	3378
7:3	go ahead and do it, for the L is with you."	3378
7:4	the word of the L came to Nathan,	3378
7:5	'This is what the L says:	3378
7:8	'This is what the L Almighty says:	3378
7:11	" 'The L declares to you that	3378
7:11	that the L himself will establish a house	3378
7:18	King David went in and sat before the L,	3378
7:18	"Who am I, O Sovereign L,	3378
7:19	not enough in your sight, O Sovereign L,	3378
7:19	of dealing with man, O Sovereign L?	3378
7:20	you know your servant, O Sovereign L.	3378
7:22	"How great you are, O Sovereign L!	3378
7:24	and you, O L, have become their God.	3378
7:25	"And now, L God, keep forever	3378
7:26	'The L Almighty is God over Israel!'	3378
7:27	"O L Almighty, God of Israel,	3378
7:28	O Sovereign L, you are God!	3378
7:29	for you, O Sovereign L, have spoken,	3378
8:6	The L gave David victory wherever he went	3378
8:11	to the L, as he had done with the silver	3378
8:14	The L gave David victory wherever he went	3378
10:12	The L will do what is good in his sight."	3378
11:27	thing David had done displeased the L.	3378
12:1	The L sent Nathan to David.	3378
12:5	"As surely as the L lives,	3378
12:7	This is what the L, the God of Israel,	3378
12:9	of the L by doing what is evil in his eyes?	3378
12:11	"This is what the L says:	3378
12:13	"I have sinned against the L."	3378
12:13	"The L has taken away your sin.	3378
12:14	the enemies of the L show utter contempt,	3378
12:15	the L struck the child that Uriah's wife	3378
12:20	into the house of the L and worshiped.	3378
12:22	The L may be gracious to me and let	3378
2Sa 12:24	named him Solomon. The L loved him;	3378
12:25	and because the L loved him,	3378
14:11	the king invoke the L his God to prevent	3378
14:11	"As surely as the L lives," he said,	3378
14:17	May the L your God be with you.' "	3378
15:7	and fulfill a vow I made to the L.	3378
15:8	'If the L takes me back to Jerusalem,	3378
15:8	I will worship the L in Hebron.' "	3378
15:21	"As surely as the L lives,	3378
15:31	So David prayed, "O L,	3378
16:8	The L has repaid you for all	3378
16:8	The L has handed the kingdom over	3378
16:10	If he is cursing because the L said to him,	3378
16:11	let him curse, for the L has told him to.	3378
16:12	It may be that the L will see my distress	3378
16:18	the one chosen by the L, by these people,	3378
17:14	For the L had determined to frustrate	3378
18:19	to the king that the L has delivered him	3378
18:28	"Praise be to the L your God!	3378
18:31	The L has delivered you today	3378
19:7	I swear by the L that if you don't go out,	3378
21:1	so David sought the face of the L.	3378
21:1	The L said, "It is on account of Saul	3378
21:6	to be killed and exposed before the L	3378
21:7	of the oath before the L between David	3378
21:9	and exposed them on a hill before the L.	3378
22:1	to the L the words of this song when	3378
22:1	when the L delivered him from the hand	3378
22:2	He said: "The L is my rock,	3378
22:4	I call to the L, who is worthy of praise,	3378
22:7	In my distress I called to the L;	3378
22:14	The L thundered from heaven;	3378
22:16	the earth laid bare at the rebuke of the L,	3378
22:19	but the L was my support.	3378
22:21	"The L has dealt with me according	3378
22:22	For I have kept the ways of the L;	3378
22:25	The L has rewarded me according	3378
22:29	You are my lamp, O L;	3378
22:29	the L turns my darkness into light.	3378
22:31	the word of the L is flawless.	3378
22:32	For who is God besides the L?	3378
22:42	to the L, but he did not answer.	3378
22:47	"The L lives! Praise be to my Rock!	3378
22:50	Therefore I will praise you, O L,	3378
23:2	"The Spirit of the L spoke through me;	3378
23:10	The L brought about a great victory.	3378
23:12	and the L brought about a great victory.	3378
23:16	instead, he poured it out before the L.	3378
23:17	"Far be it from me, O L, to do this!"	3378
24:1	the anger of the L burned against Israel,	3378
24:3	"May the L your God multiply the troops	3378
24:10	and he said to the L,	3378
24:10	Now, O L, I beg you,	3378
24:11	of the L had come to Gad the prophet,	3378
24:12	'This is what the L says:	3378
24:14	Let us fall into the hands of the L,	3378
24:15	So the L sent a plague on Israel from	3378
24:16	the L was grieved because of the calamity	3378
24:16	of the L was then at the threshing floor	3378
24:17	said to the L, "I am the one who has sinned	3378
24:18	to the L on the threshing floor of Araunah	3378
24:19	as the L had commanded through Gad.	3378
24:21	"so I can build an altar to the L,	3378
24:23	"May the L your God accept you."	3378
24:24	to the L my God burnt offerings	3378
24:25	David built an altar to the L there	3378
24:25	Then the L answered prayer in behalf of	3378
1Ki 1:17	to me your servant by the L your God:	3378
1:29	"As surely as the L lives,	3378
1:30	to you by the L, the God of Israel:	3378
1:36	May the L, the God of my lord the king,	3378
1:37	As the L was with my lord the king,	3378
1:48	'Praise be to the L, the God of Israel,	3378
2:3	observe what the L your God requires:	3378
2:4	that the L may keep his promise to me:	3378
2:8	I swore to him by the L:	3378
2:15	for it has come to him from the L.	3378
2:23	Then King Solomon swore by the L:	3378
2:24	And now, as surely as the L lives—	3378
2:26	the ark of the Sovereign L	3378
2:27	from the priesthood of the L,	3378
2:27	the word the L had spoken at Shiloh	3378
2:28	he fled to the tent of the L and took hold	3378
2:29	the tent of the L and was beside the altar.	3378
2:30	So Benaiah entered the tent of the L	3378
2:32	The L will repay him for the blood	3378
2:42	"Did I not make you swear by the L	3378
2:43	then did you not keep your oath to the L	3378
2:44	Now the L will repay you for your	3378
2:45	will remain secure before the L forever."	3378
3:1	and the temple of the L,	3378
3:2	not yet been built for the Name of the L.	3378
3:3	Solomon showed his love for the L	3378
3:5	At Gibeon the L appeared to Solomon	3378
3:7	"Now, O L my God,	3378
5:3	a temple for the Name of the L his God	3378
5:3	until the L put his enemies under his feet.	3378
5:4	But now the L my God has given me rest	3378
5:5	a temple for the Name of the L my God,	3378
5:5	as the L told my father David,	3378
5:7	"Praise be to the L,	3378
5:12	The L gave Solomon wisdom,	3378
6:1	he began to build the temple of the L.	3378
6:2	for the L was sixty cubits long,	3378
6:11	The word of the L came to Solomon:	3378
6:19	the ark of the covenant of the L.	3378
6:37	temple of the L was laid in the fourth year,	3378
1Ki 7:12	the inner courtyard of the temple of the L	3378
7:40	for King Solomon in the temple of the L:	3378
7:45	temple of the L were of burnished bronze.	3378
7:51	for the temple of the L was finished.	3378
8:4	and they brought up the ark of the L and	3378
8:9	where the L made a covenant with	3378
8:10	the cloud filled the temple of the L.	3378
8:11	for the glory of the L filled his temple.	3378
8:12	"The L has said that he would dwell in	3378
8:15	"Praise be to the L, the God of Israel,	3378
8:17	to build a temple for the Name of the L,	3378
8:18	But the L said to my father David,	3378
8:20	"The L has kept the promise he made:	3378
8:20	just as the L promised,	3378
8:20	the temple for the Name of the L,	3378
8:21	of the L that he made with our fathers	3378
8:22	of the L in front of the whole assembly	3378
8:23	"O L, God of Israel,	3378
8:25	"Now L, God of Israel,	3378
8:28	O L my God.	3378
8:44	to the L toward the city you have chosen	3378
8:53	O Sovereign L, brought our fathers out	3378
8:54	and supplications to the L,	3378
8:54	he rose from before the altar of the L,	3378
8:56	"Praise be to the L,	3378
8:57	May the L our God be with us as he was	3378
8:59	which I have prayed before the L,	3378
8:59	be near to the L our God day and night,	3378
8:60	the earth may know that the L is God and	3378
8:61	be fully committed to the L our God,	3378
8:62	with him offered sacrifices before the L.	3378
8:63	of fellowship offerings to the L:	3378
8:63	Israelites dedicated the temple of the L.	3378
8:64	in front of the temple of the L,	3378
8:64	before the L was too small to hold	3378
8:65	They celebrated it before the L our God	3378
8:66	for all the good things the L had done	3378
9:1	the temple of the L and the royal palace,	3378
9:2	the L appeared to him a second time,	3378
9:3	The L said to him:	3378
9:8	'Why has the L done such a thing	3378
9:9	they have forsaken the L their God,	3378
9:9	that is why the L brought all this disaster	3378
9:10	of the L and the royal palace—	3378
9:25	on the altar he had built for the L,	3378
9:25	burning incense before the L along	3378
10:1	and his relation to the name of the L,	3378
10:5	offerings he made at the temple of the L,	3378
10:9	Praise be to the L your God,	3378
10:12	to make supports for the temple of the L	3378
11:2	about which the L had told the Israelites,	3378
11:4	not fully devoted to the L his God,	3378
11:6	So Solomon did evil in the eyes of the L;	3378
11:6	he did not follow the L completely,	3378
11:9	The L became angry with Solomon	3378
11:9	from the L, the God of Israel,	3378
11:11	So the L said to Solomon,	3378
11:14	Then the L raised up against Solomon	3378
11:31	for this is what the L, the God of Israel,	3378
12:15	for this turn of events was from the L,	3378
12:15	to fulfill the word the L had spoken	3378
12:24	'This is what the L says:	3378
12:24	the word of the L and went home again,	3378
12:24	as the L had ordered.	3378
12:27	to offer sacrifices at the temple of the L	3378
13:1	By the word of the L a man of God came	3378
13:2	against the altar by the word of the L:	3378
13:2	This is what the L says:	3378
13:3	"This is the sign the L has declared:	3378
13:5	by the man of God by the word of the L.	3378
13:6	"Intercede with the L your God and pray	3378
13:6	So the man of God interceded with the L,	3378
13:9	I was commanded by the word of the L:	3378
13:17	I have been told by the word of the L:	3378
13:18	an angel said to me by the word of the L:	3378
13:20	the word of the L came to the old prophet	3378
13:21	"This is what the L says:	3378
13:21	of the L and have not kept the command	3378
13:21	the command the L your God gave you.	3378
13:26	of God who defied the word of the L.	3378
13:26	The L has given him over to the lion,	3378
13:26	as the word of the L had warned him."	3378
13:32	of the L against the altar in Bethel and	3378
14:5	But the L had told Ahijah,	3378
14:7	Go, tell Jeroboam that this is what the L,	3378
14:11	The L has spoken!'	3378
14:13	in the house of Jeroboam in whom the L,	3378
14:14	"The L will raise up for himself a king	3378
14:15	And the L will strike Israel,	3378
14:15	because they provoked the L to anger	3378
14:18	as the L had said through his servant	3378
14:21	the city the L had chosen out of all	3378
14:22	Judah did evil in the eyes of the L.	3378
14:24	of the nations the L had driven out before	3378
14:26	of the temple of the L and the treasures of	3378
15:3	not fully devoted to the L his God,	3378
15:4	for David's sake the L his God gave him	3378
15:5	of the L and had not failed to keep any of	3378
15:11	did what was right in the eyes of the L,	3378
15:14	fully committed to the L all his life.	3378
15:15	the temple of the L the silver and gold	3378
15:26	He did evil in the eyes of the L,	3378
15:29	of the L given through his servant Ahijah	3378
15:30	and because he provoked the L,	3378
15:34	He did evil in the eyes of the L,	3378
16:1	Then the word of the L came to Jehu son	3378
16:7	the word of the L came through	3378

†LORD distinguishes the proper name of God, *Yahweh*, indicated in the NIV by "Lord," from the words translated "Lord" and "lord," indexed under the heading *LORD, pages 683-86.

Ref	Text	Num
1Ki 16: 7	the eyes of **the L**, provoking him to anger	3378
16:12	the word of **the L** spoken against Baasha	3378
16:13	so that they provoked **the L**,	3378
16:19	the eyes of **the L** and walking in the ways	3378
16:25	of **the L** and sinned more than all those	3378
16:26	so that they provoked **the L**,	3378
16:30	of **the L** than any of those before him.	3378
16:33	and did more to provoke **the L**,	3378
16:34	the word of **the L** spoken by Joshua son	3378
17: 1	"As **the L**, the God of Israel, lives,	3378
17: 2	Then the word of **the L** came to Elijah:	3378
17: 5	So he did what **the L** had told him.	3378
17: 8	Then the word of **the L** came to him:	3378
17:12	"As surely as **the L** your God lives,"	3378
17:14	this is what **the L**, the God of Israel, says:	3378
17:14	not run dry until the day **the L** gives rain	3378
17:16	in keeping with the word of **the L** spoken	3378
17:20	Then he cried out to **the L**,	3378
17:20	"O L my God, you have brought tragedy	3378
17:21	on the boy three times and cried to **the L**,	3378
17:21	"O L my God, let this boy's life return	3378
17:22	**The L** heard Elijah's cry,	3378
17:24	that the word of **the L** from your mouth is	3378
18: 1	the word of **the L** came to Elijah:	3378
18: 3	(Obadiah was a devout believer in **the L**.	3378
18:10	As surely as **the L** your God lives,	3378
18:12	of **the L** may carry you when I leave you.	3378
18:12	Yet I your servant have worshiped **the L**	3378
18:13	Jezebel was killing the prophets of **the L**?	3378
18:15	Elijah said, "As **the L** Almighty lives,	3378
18:21	If **the L** is God, follow him;	3378
18:24	and I will call on the name of **the L**,	3378
18:30	and he repaired the altar of **the L**,	3378
18:31	to whom the word of **the L** had come,	3378
18:32	an altar in the name of **the L**.	3378
18:36	"O L, God of Abraham, Isaac and Israel,	3378
18:37	Answer me, O L, answer me,	3378
18:37	so these people will know that you, O L,	3378
18:38	Then the fire of **the L** fell and burned up	3378
18:39	they fell prostrate and cried, "**The L**—	3378
18:39	**The L**—he is God!"	3378
18:46	The power of **the L** came upon Elijah	3378
19: 4	"I have had enough, **L**," he said.	3378
19: 7	The angel of **the L** came back a second time	3378
19: 9	And the word of **the L** came to him:	3378
19:10	for **the L** God Almighty.	3378
19:11	The L said, "Go out and stand on	NIH
19:11	on the mountain in the presence of **the L**,	3378
19:11	for **the L** is about to pass by."	3378
19:11	and shattered the rocks before **the L**,	3378
19:11	but **the L** was not in the wind.	3378
19:11	but **the L** was not in the earthquake.	3378
19:12	but **the L** was not in the fire.	3378
19:14	very zealous for **the L** God Almighty.	3378
19:15	**The L** said to him,	3378
20:13	"This is what **the L** says:	3378
20:13	and then you will know that I am **the L**.' "	3378
20:14	"This is what **the L** says:	3378
20:28	"This is what **the L** says:	3378
20:28	'Because the Arameans think **the L** is	3378
20:28	and you will know that I am **the L**.' "	3378
20:35	By the word of **the L** one of the sons of	3378
20:36	"Because you have not obeyed **the L**,	3378
20:42	"This is what **the L** says:	3378
21: 3	"**The L** forbid that I should give you	3378
21:17	word of **the L** came to Elijah the Tishbite:	3378
21:19	Say to him, 'This is what **the L** says:	3378
21:19	Then say to him, 'This is what **the L** says:	3378
21:20	to do evil in the eyes of **the L**.	3378
21:23	"And also concerning Jezebel **the L** says:	3378
21:25	to do evil in the eyes of **the L**,	3378
21:26	like the Amorites **the L** drove out	3378
21:28	word of **the L** came to Elijah the Tishbite:	3378
22: 5	"First seek the counsel of **the L**."	3378
22: 7	of **the L** here whom we can inquire of?"	3378
22: 8	through whom we can inquire of **the L**,	3378
22:11	"This is what **the L** says:	3378
22:12	**the L** will give it into the king's hand."	3378
22:14	Micaiah said, "As surely as **the L** lives,	3378
22:14	I can tell him only what **the L** tells me."	3378
22:15	"for **the L** will give it into the king's hand."	3378
22:16	but the truth in the name of **the L**?"	3378
22:17	and **the L** said,	3378
22:19	"Therefore hear the word of **the L**:	3378
22:19	I saw **the L** sitting on his throne with all	3378
22:20	And **the L** said, 'These people have no	3378
22:21	stood before **the L** and said,	3378
22:22	" 'By what means?' **the L** asked.	3378
22:22	succeed in enticing him,' said the L.	NIH
22:23	"So now **the L** has put a lying spirit in	3378
22:23	**The L** has decreed disaster for you."	3378
22:24	"Which way did the spirit from **the L** go	3378
22:28	**the L** has not spoken through me."	3378
22:38	as the word of **the L** had declared.	3378
22:43	he did what was right in the eyes of **the L**.	3378
22:52	he did evil in the eyes of **the L**,	3378
22:53	and worshiped Baal and provoked **the L**,	3378
2Ki 1: 3	angel of **the L** said to Elijah the Tishbite,	3378
1: 4	Therefore this is what **the L** says:	3378
1: 6	"This is what **the L** says:	3378
1:15	The angel of **the L** said to Elijah,	3378
1:16	"This is what **the L** says:	3378
1:17	the word of **the L** that Elijah had spoken.	3378
2: 1	When **the L** was about to take Elijah up	3378
2: 2	**the L** has sent me to Bethel."	3378
2: 2	"As surely as **the L** lives and as you live,	3378
2: 3	that **the L** is going to take your master	3378

Ref	Text	Num
2Ki 2: 4	**the L** has sent me to Jericho."	3378
2: 4	"As surely as **the L** lives and as you live,	3378
2: 5	that **the L** is going to take your master	3378
2: 6	**the L** has sent me to the Jordan."	3378
2: 6	"As surely as **the L** lives and as you live,	3378
2:14	"Where now is **the L**, the God of Elijah?"	3378
2:16	the Spirit of **the L** has picked him up and	3378
2:21	saying, "This is what **the L** says:	3378
2:24	a curse on them in the name of **the L**.	3378
3: 2	He did evil in the eyes of **the L**,	3378
3:10	"Has **the L** called us three kings together	3378
3:11	"Is there no prophet of **the L** here,	3378
3:11	we may inquire of **the L** through him?"	3378
3:12	"The word of **the L** is with him."	3378
3:13	"because it was **the L** who called us three kings together	3378
3:14	"As surely as **the L** Almighty lives,	3378
3:15	the hand of **the L** came upon Elisha	3378
3:16	"This is what **the L** says:	3378
3:17	For this is what **the L** says:	3378
3:18	This is an easy thing in the eyes of **the L**;	3378
4: 1	and you know that he revered **the L**.	3378
4:27	but **the L** has hidden it from me and has	3378
4:30	"As surely as **the L** lives and as you live,	3378
4:33	on the two of them and prayed to **the L**.	3378
4:43	For this is what **the L** says:	3378
4:44	according to the word of **the L**.	3378
5: 1	through him **the L** had given victory	3378
5:11	and call on the name of **the L** his God,	3378
5:16	"As surely as **the L** lives, whom I serve,	3378
5:17	and sacrifices to any other god but **the L**.	3378
5:18	But may **the L** forgive your servant	3378
5:18	may **the L** forgive your servant for this."	3378
5:20	As surely as **the L** lives,	3378
6:17	And Elisha prayed, "O L, open his eyes	3378
6:17	Then **the L** opened the servant's eyes,	3378
6:18	Elisha prayed to **the L**,	3378
6:20	the city, Elisha said, "L, open the eyes	3378
6:20	**the L** opened their eyes and they looked,	3378
6:27	"If **the L** does not help you,	3378
6:33	said, "This disaster is from **the L**.	3378
6:33	Why should I wait for **the L** any longer?"	3378
7: 1	Elisha said, "Hear the word of **the L**.	3378
7: 1	This is what **the L** says:	3378
7: 2	even if **the L** should open the floodgates	3378
7:16	as **the L** had said.	3378
7:19	even if **the L** should open the floodgates	3378
8: 1	because **the L** has decreed a famine in	3378
8: 8	Consult **the L** through him;	3378
8:10	but **the L** has revealed to me that he will	3378
8:13	"**The L** has shown me that you will become	3378
8:18	He did evil in the eyes of **the L**.	3378
8:19	**the L** was not willing to destroy Judah.	3378
8:27	of Ahab and did evil in the eyes of **the L**,	3378
9: 3	'This is what **the L** says:	3378
9: 6	"This is what **the L**, the God of Israel,	3378
9:12	'This is what **the L** says:	3378
9:25	when **the L** made this prophecy	3378
9:26	and the blood of his sons, declares **the L**,	3378
9:26	on this plot of ground, declares **the L**.'	3378
9:26	in accordance with the word of **the L**."	3378
9:36	"This is the word of **the L** that he spoke	3378
10:10	that not a word **the L** has spoken against	3378
10:10	**The L** has done what he promised	3378
10:16	with me and see my zeal for **the L**."	3378
10:17	according to the word of **the L** spoken	3378
10:23	and see that no servants of **the L** are here	3378
10:30	**The L** said to Jehu, "Because you have	3378
10:31	not careful to keep the law of **the L**,	3378
10:32	In those days **the L** began to reduce	3378
11: 3	with his nurse at the temple of **the L**	3378
11: 4	to him at the temple of **the L**.	3378
11: 4	under oath at the temple of **the L**.	3378
11:10	and that were in the temple of **the L**.	3378
11:13	to the people at the temple of **the L**.	3378
11:15	not be put to death in the temple of **the L**."	3378
11:17	then made a covenant between **the L** and	3378
11:18	posted guards at the temple of **the L**.	3378
11:19	down from the temple of **the L** and went	3378
12: 2	in the eyes of **the L** all the years Jehoiada	3378
12: 4	as sacred offerings to the temple of **the L**—	3378
12: 9	as one enters the temple of **the L**.	3378
12: 9	that was brought to the temple of **the L**.	3378
12:10	the temple of **the L** and put it into bags.	3378
12:11	worked on the temple of **the L**—	3378
12:12	for the repair of the temple of **the L**,	3378
12:13	of gold or silver for the temple of **the L**;	3378
12:16	not brought into the temple of **the L**.	3378
12:18	the treasures of the temple of **the L** and	3378
13: 2	in the eyes of **the L** by following the sins	3378
13: 4	and **the L** listened to him,	3378
13: 5	**The L** provided a deliverer for Israel,	3378
13:11	in the eyes of **the L** and did not turn away	3378
13:23	But **the L** was gracious to them	3378
14: 3	He did what was right in the eyes of **the L**,	3378
14: 6	of Moses where **the L** commanded:	3378
14:14	the temple of **the L** and in the treasuries	3378
14:24	in the eyes of **the L** and did not turn away	3378
14:25	in accordance with the word of **the L**,	3378
14:26	**The L** had seen how bitterly everyone	3378
14:27	since **the L** had not said he would blot out	3378
15: 3	He did what was right in the eyes of **the L**,	3378
15: 5	**The L** afflicted the king with leprosy until	3378
15: 9	He did evil in the eyes of **the L**,	3378
15:12	of **the L** spoken to Jehu was fulfilled:	3378
15:18	He did evil in the eyes of **the L**.	3378
15:24	Pekahiah did evil in the eyes of **the L**.	3378

Ref	Text	Num
2Ki 15:28	He did evil in the eyes of **the L**.	3378
15:34	He did what was right in the eyes of **the L**,	3378
15:35	the Upper Gate of the temple of **the L**.	3378
15:37	(In those days **the L** began	3378
16: 2	what was right in the eyes of **the L** his God.	3378
16: 3	of the nations **the L** had driven out before	3378
16: 8	and gold found in the temple of **the L** and	3378
16:14	before **the L** he brought from the front of	3378
16:14	the new altar and the temple of **the L**—	3378
16:18	royal entryway outside the temple of **the L**,	3378
17: 2	He did evil in the eyes of **the L**,	3378
17: 7	sinned against **the L** their God,	3378
17: 8	of the nations **the L** had driven out	3378
17: 9	against **the L** their God that were	3378
17:11	as the nations whom **the L** had driven out	3378
17:11	that provoked **the L** to anger.	3378
17:12	though **the L** had said,	3378
17:13	**The L** warned Israel and Judah	3378
17:14	who did not trust in **the L** their God.	3378
17:15	although **the L** had ordered them,	3378
17:15	the things the L had forbidden them	NIH
17:16	the commands of **the L** their God	3378
17:17	to do evil in the eyes of **the L**,	3378
17:18	So **the L** was very angry with Israel	3378
17:19	the commands of **the L** their God.	3378
17:20	**the L** rejected all the people of Israel;	3378
17:21	from following **the L** and caused them	3378
17:23	until **the L** removed them from his presence	3378
17:25	they did not worship **the L**;	3378
17:28	and taught them how to worship **the L**.	3378
17:32	They worshiped **the L**,	3378
17:33	They worshiped **the L**,	3378
17:34	They neither worship **the L** nor adhere to	3378
17:34	that **the L** gave the descendants of Jacob,	3378
17:35	**the L** made a covenant with the Israelites,	3378
17:36	But **the L**, who brought you up out	3378
17:39	Rather, worship **the L** your God;	3378
17:41	these people were worshiping **the L**,	3378
18: 3	He did what was right in the eyes of **the L**,	3378
18: 5	Hezekiah trusted in **the L**,	3378
18: 6	to **the L** and did not cease to follow him;	3378
18: 6	the commands **the L** had given Moses.	3378
18: 7	And **the L** was with him;	3378
18:12	not obeyed **the L** their God,	3378
18:12	the servant of **the L** commanded.	3378
18:15	that was found in the temple of **the L** and	3378
18:16	and doorposts of the temple of **the L**,	3378
18:22	"We are depending on **the L** our God"—	3378
18:25	without word from **the L**?	3378
18:25	**The L** himself told me to march	3378
18:30	in **the L** when he says, '**the LORD**	3378
18:30	'**The L** will surely deliver us;	3378
18:32	'**The L** will deliver us.'	3378
18:35	How then can **the L** deliver Jerusalem	3378
19: 1	and went into the temple of **the L**.	3378
19: 4	be that **the L** your God will hear all	3378
19: 4	for the words **the L** your God has heard.	3378
19: 6	'This is what **the L** says:	3378
19:14	up to the temple of **the L** and spread it out	3378
19:14	and spread it out before **the L**.	3378
19:15	And Hezekiah prayed to **the L**:	3378
19:15	"O L, God of Israel, enthroned	3378
19:16	Give ear, O L, and hear;	3378
19:16	open your eyes, O L, and see;	3378
19:17	"It is true, O L, that the Assyrian kings	3378
19:19	Now, O L our God, deliver us	3378
19:19	on earth may know that you alone, O L,	3378
19:20	"This is what **the L**, the God of Israel,	3378
19:21	This is the word that **the L** has spoken	3378
19:31	of **the L** Almighty will accomplish this.	3378
19:32	"Therefore this is what **the L** says	3378
19:33	he will not enter this city, declares **the L**.	3378
19:35	That night the angel of **the L** went out	3378
20: 1	"This is what **the L** says:	3378
20: 2	to the wall and prayed to **the L**,	3378
20: 3	O L, how I have walked before you	3378
20: 4	the word of **the L** came to him:	3378
20: 5	'This is what **the L**,	3378
20: 5	you will go up to the temple of **the L**.	3378
20: 8	the sign that **the L** will heal me and	3378
20: 8	that I will go up to the temple of **the L** on	3378
20: 9	that **the L** will do what he has promised:	3378
20:11	the prophet Isaiah called upon **the L**,	3378
20:11	and **the L** made the shadow go back	NIH
20:16	"Hear the word of **the L**:	3378
20:17	Nothing will be left, says **the L**.	3378
20:19	of **the L** you have spoken is good,"	3378
21: 2	He did evil in the eyes of **the L**,	3378
21: 2	of the nations **the L** had driven out before	3378
21: 4	He built altars in the temple of **the L**,	3378
21: 4	of which **the L** had said,	3378
21: 5	In both courts of the temple of **the L**,	3378
21: 6	He did much evil in the eyes of **the L**,	3378
21: 7	of which **the L** had said to David and	3378
21: 9	the nations **the L** had destroyed before	3378
21:10	**The L** said through his servants	3378
21:12	Therefore this is what **the L**,	3378
21:16	so that they did evil in the eyes of **the L**.	3378
21:20	He did evil in the eyes of **the L**,	3378
21:22	He forsook **the L**, the God of his fathers,	3378
21:22	and did not walk in the way of **the L**.	3378
22: 2	He did what was right in the eyes of **the L**	3378
22: 3	to the temple of **the L**.	3378
22: 4	brought into the temple of **the L**,	3378
22: 5	workers who repair the temple of **the L**—	3378
22: 8	of the Law in the temple of **the L**."	3378
22: 9	the money that was in the temple of **the L**	3378

†**LORD** distinguishes the proper name of God, *Yahweh*, indicated in the NIV by "L ORD," from the words translated "Lord" and "lord," indexed under the heading *L ORD, pages 683–86.

2Ki 22:13 "Go and inquire of the L for me and for 3378
22:15 She said to them, "This is what the L, 3378
22:16 'This is what the L says: 3378
22:18 who sent you to inquire of the L, 3378
22:18 'This is what the L, the God of Israel, 3378
22:19 and you humbled yourself before the L 3378
22:19 I have heard you, declares the L. 3378
23: 2 He went up to the temple of the L with 3378
23: 2 found in the temple of the L. 3378
23: 3 the covenant in the presence of the L— 3378
23: 3 to follow the L and keep his commands, 3378
23: 4 the temple of the L all the articles made 3378
23: 6 the Asherah pole from the temple of the L 3378
23: 7 of the L and where women did weaving 3378
23: 9 at the altar of the L in Jerusalem, 3378
23:11 from the entrance to the temple of the L. 3378
23:12 in the two courts of the temple of the L. 3378
23:16 the word of the L proclaimed by the man 3378
23:19 of Samaria that had provoked the L NIH
23:21 the Passover to the L your God, 3378
23:23 this Passover was celebrated to the L 3378
23:24 had discovered in the temple of the L. 3378
23:25 like him who turned to the L as he did— 3378
23:26 the L did not turn away from the heat 3378
23:27 So the L said, "I will remove Judah also 3378
23:32 He did evil in the eyes of the L, 3378
23:37 And he did evil in the eyes of the L, 3378
24: 2 The L sent Babylonian, Aramean, 3378
24: 2 of the L proclaimed by his servants 3378
24: 4 and the L was not willing to forgive. 3378
24: 9 He did evil in the eyes of the L, 3378
24:13 As the L had declared, 3378
24:13 the treasures from the temple of the L and 3378
24:13 for the temple of the L. 3378
24:19 He did evil in the eyes of the L, 3378
25: 9 He set fire to the temple of the L, 3378
25:13 at the temple of the L and they carried 3378
25:16 for the temple of the L, 3378

1Ch 2: 3 so the L put him to death. NIH
6:15 when the L sent Judah and Jerusalem 3378
6:31 of the L after the ark came to rest there. 3378
6:32 until Solomon built the temple of the L. 3378
9:19 the entrance to the dwelling of the L. 3378
9:20 and the L was with him. 3378
9:23 the gates of the house of the L— 3378
10:13 because he was unfaithful to the L; 3378
10:13 of the L and even consulted a medium 3378
10:14 and did not inquire of the L 3378
10:14 So the L put him to death and turned NIH
11: 2 And the L your God said to you, 3378
11: 3 with them at Hebron before the L, 3378
11: 3 as the L had promised through Samuel. 3378
11: 9 because the L Almighty was with him. 3378
11:10 as the L had promised— 3378
11:14 and the L brought about a great victory. 3378
11:18 instead, he poured it out before the L. 3378
12:23 as the L had said: 3378
13: 2 and if it is the will of the L our God, 3378
13: 6 of God the L, who is enthroned between 3378
13:14 and the L blessed his household 3378
14: 2 that the L had established him as king 3378
14:10 The L answered him, "Go, 3378
14:17 and the L made all the nations fear him. 3378
15: 2 because the L chose them to carry the ark 3378
15: 2 to carry the ark of the L and to minister 3378
15: 3 in Jerusalem to bring up the ark of the L 3378
15:12 and bring up the ark of the L, 3378
15:13 the first time that the L our God broke out 3378
15:14 in order to bring up the ark of the L, 3378
15:15 in accordance with the word of the L. 3378
15:25 up the ark of the covenant of the L from 3378
15:26 the ark of the covenant of the L, 3378
15:28 of the covenant of the L with shouts, 3378
15:29 of the L was entering the City of David, 3378
16: 2 the people in the name of the L. 3378
16: 4 of the L, to make petition, to give thanks, 3378
16: 4 and to praise the L, the God of Israel: 3378
16: 7 of thanks to the L: 3378
16: 8 Give thanks to the L, call on his name; 3378
16:10 of those who seek the L rejoice. 3378
16:11 Look to the L and his strength; 3378
16:14 He is the L our God; 3378
16:23 Sing to the L, all the earth; 3378
16:25 great is the L and most worthy of praise; 3378
16:26 but the L made the heavens. 3378
16:28 Ascribe to the L, O families of nations, 3378
16:28 ascribe to the L glory and strength, 3378
16:29 ascribe to the L the glory due his name. 3378
16:29 worship the L in the splendor 3378
16:31 among the nations, "The L reigns!" 3378
16:33 they will sing for joy before the L, 3378
16:34 Give thanks to the L, for he is good; 3378
16:36 Praise be to the L, the God of Israel, 3378
16:36 and "Praise the L." 3378
16:37 before the ark of the covenant of the L 3378
16:39 the tabernacle of the L at the high place 3378
16:40 to present burnt offerings to the L on 3378
16:40 everything written in the Law of the L, 3378
16:41 by name to give thanks to the L, 3378
17: 1 of the covenant of the L is under a tent." 3378
17: 3 'This is what the L says: 3378
17: 7 'This is what the L Almighty says: 3378
17:10 " 'I declare to you that the L will build 3378
17:16 King David went in and sat before the L, 3378
17:16 "Who am I, O L God, 3378
17:17 the most exalted of men, O L God. 3378
17:19 O L, For the sake of your servant 3378

1Ch 17:20 "There is no one like you, O L, 3378
17:22 and you, O L, have become their God. 3378
17:23 now, L, let the promise you have made 3378
17:24 Then men will say, 'The L Almighty, 3378
17:26 O L, you are God! 3378
17:27 for you, O L, have blessed it, 3378
18: 6 The L gave David victory everywhere he went. 3378
18:11 David dedicated these articles to the L, 3378
18:13 The L gave David victory everywhere he went. 3378
19:13 The L will do what is good in his sight." 3378
21: 3 "May the L multiply his troops 3378
21: 9 The L said to Gad, David's seer, 3378
21:10 'This is what the L says: 3378
21:11 "This is what the L says: 3378
21:12 or three days of the sword of the L— 3378
21:12 of the L ravaging every part of Israel.' 3378
21:13 Let me fall into the hands of the L, 3378
21:14 So the L sent a plague on Israel, 3378
21:15 the L saw it and was grieved because of 3378
21:15 The angel of the L was then standing at 3378
21:16 up and saw the angel of the L standing 3378
21:17 O L my God, let your hand fall upon me 3378
21:18 of the L ordered Gad to tell David to go 3378
21:18 to the L on the threshing floor of Araunah 3378
21:19 that Gad had spoken in the name of the L. 3378
21:22 so I can build an altar to the L, 3378
21:24 I will not take for the L what is yours, 3378
21:26 David built an altar to the L there 3378
21:26 He called on the L, 3378
21:26 and he answered him with fire NIH
21:27 Then the L spoke to the angel, 3378
21:28 that the L had answered him on 3378
21:29 The tabernacle of the L, 3378
21:30 of the sword of the angel of the L. 3378
22: 1 "The house of the L God is to be here, 3378
22: 5 for the L should be of great magnificence 3378
22: 6 to build a house for the L, 3378
22: 7 a house for the Name of the L my God. 3378
22: 8 But this word of the L came to me: 3378
22:11 "Now, my son, the L be with you, 3378
22:11 and build the house of the L your God. 3378
22:12 May the L give you discretion 3378
22:12 the law of the L your God. 3378
22:13 and laws that the L gave Moses for Israel. 3378
22:14 temple of the L a hundred thousand talents 3378
22:16 begin the work, and the L be with you. 3378
22:18 "Is not the L your God with you? 3378
22:18 land is subject to the L and to his people. 3378
22:19 and soul to seeking the L your God. 3378
22:19 to build the sanctuary of the L God, 3378
22:19 of the L and the sacred articles belonging 3378
22:19 that will be built for the Name of the L." 3378
23: 4 the temple of the L and six thousand are 3378
23: 5 and four thousand are to praise the L with 3378
23:13 to offer sacrifices before the L, 3378
23:24 who served in the temple of the L. 3378
23:25 For David had said, "Since the L, 3378
23:28 in the service of the temple of the L: 3378
23:30 to thank and praise the L. 3378
23:31 to the L on Sabbaths and 3378
23:31 They were to serve before the L regularly 3378
23:32 for the service of the temple of the L, 3378
24:19 when they entered the temple of the L, 3378
24:19 as the L, the God of Israel. 3378
25: 3 the harp in thanking and praising the L. 3378
25: 6 for the music of the temple of the L, 3378
25: 7 and skilled in music for the L— 3378
26:12 for ministering in the temple of the L, 3378
26:22 of the treasuries of the temple of the L. 3378
26:27 for the repair of the temple of the L. 3378
26:30 of the Jordan for all the work of the L and 3378
27:23 because the L had promised 3378
28: 2 for the ark of the covenant of the L, 3378
28: 4 "Yet the L, the God of Israel, 3378
28: 5 and the L has given me many— 3378
28: 5 on the throne of the kingdom of the L 3378
28: 8 of all Israel and of the assembly of the L, 3378
28: 8 the commands of the L your God, 3378
28: 9 for the L searches every heart 3378
28:10 for the L has chosen you to build 3378
28:12 the courts of the temple of the L and all 3378
28:13 of serving in the temple of the L, 3378
28:18 the ark of the covenant of the L. 3378
28:19 "I have in writing from the hand of the L 3378
28:20 for the L God, my God, is with you. 3378
28:20 of the temple of the L is finished. 3378
29: 1 not for man but for the L God. 3378
29: 5 to consecrate himself today to the L?" 3378
29: 8 to the treasury of the temple of the L in 3378
29: 9 given freely and wholeheartedly to the L. 3378
29:10 David praised the L in the presence of 3378
29:10 saying, "Praise be to you, O L, 3378
29:11 O L, is the greatness and the power and 3378
29:11 Yours, O L, is the kingdom; 3378
29:16 O L our God, as for all this abundance 3378
29:18 O L, God of our fathers Abraham, 3378
29:20 "Praise the L your God." 3378
29:20 So they all praised the L, 3378
29:20 and fell prostrate before the L and 3378
29:21 to the L and presented burnt offerings 3378
29:22 with great joy in the presence of the L 3378
29:22 anointing him before the L to be ruler 3378
29:23 So Solomon sat on the throne of the L 3378
29:25 The L highly exalted Solomon in the sight 3378

2Ch 1: 1 for the L his God was with him 3378

2Ch 1: 5 in front of the tabernacle of the L; 3378
1: 6 the bronze altar before the L in the Tent 3378
1: 9 Now, L God, let your promise 3378
2: 1 for the Name of the L and a royal palace 3378
2: 4 of the L my God and to dedicate it to him 3378
2: 4 at the appointed feasts of the L our God. 3378
2:11 "Because the L loves his people, 3378
2:12 And Hiram added: "Praise be to the L, 3378
2:12 who will build a temple for the L and 3378
3: 1 to build the temple of the L in Jerusalem 3378
3: 1 the L had appeared to his father David. NIH
4:16 temple of the L were of polished bronze. 3378
5: 1 for the temple of the L was finished, 3378
5:10 where the L made a covenant with 3378
5:13 to give praise and thanks to the L. 3378
5:13 they raised their voices in praise to the L 3378
5:13 temple of the L was filled with a cloud, 3378
5:14 glory of the L filled the temple of God. 3378
6: 1 "The L has said that he would dwell in 3378
6: 4 "Praise be to the L, the God of Israel, 3378
6: 7 to build a temple for the Name of the L, 3378
6: 8 But the L said to my father David, 3378
6:10 "The L has kept the promise he made. 3378
6:10 just as the L promised, 3378
6:10 the temple for the Name of the L, 3378
6:11 the covenant of the L that he made with 3378
6:12 of the L in front of the whole assembly 3378
6:14 He said: "O L, God of Israel, 3378
6:16 "Now, L, God of Israel, 3378
6:17 And now, O L, God of Israel, 3378
6:19 his plea for mercy, O L my God. 3378
6:41 "Now arise, O L God, 3378
6:41 May your priests, O L God, 3378
6:42 O L God, do not reject your anointed one. 3378
7: 1 and the glory of the L filled the temple. 3378
7: 2 the temple of the L because the glory of 3378
7: 2 because the glory of the L filled it. 3378
7: 3 and the glory of the L above the temple, 3378
7: 3 they worshiped and gave thanks to the L, 3378
7: 4 the people offered sacrifices before the L. 3378
7: 6 for praising the L and which were used 3378
7: 7 in front of the temple of the L, 3378
7:10 the good things the L had done for David 3378
7:11 the temple of the L and the royal palace, 3378
7:11 the temple of the L and in his own palace, 3378
7:12 the L appeared to him at night and said: 3378
7:21 'Why has the L done such a thing 3378
7:22 'Because they have forsaken the L, 3378
8: 1 the temple of the L and his own palace, 3378
8:11 the ark of the L has entered are holy." 3378
8:12 the altar of the L that he had built in front 3378
8:12 Solomon sacrificed burnt offerings to the L, 3378
8:16 temple of the L was laid until its completion. 3378
8:16 So the temple of the L was finished. 3378
9: 4 offerings he made at the temple of the L, 3378
9: 8 Praise be to the L your God, 3378
9: 8 as king to rule for the L your God. 3378
9:11 to make steps for the temple of the L and 3378
10:15 to fulfill the word the L had spoken 3378
11: 2 But this word of the L came to Shemaiah 3378
11: 4 'This is what the L says: 3378
11: 4 of the L and turned back from marching 3378
11:14 rejected them as priests of the L 3378
11:16 set their hearts on seeking the L, 3378
11:16 to Jerusalem to offer sacrifices to the L, 3378
12: 1 with him abandoned the law of the L. 3378
12: 2 Because they had been unfaithful to the L, 3378
12: 5 "This is what the L says, 3378
12: 6 "The L is just." 3378
12: 7 When the L saw that they humbled 3378
12: 7 this word of the L came to Shemaiah: 3378
12: 9 of the temple of the L and the treasures of 3378
12:13 the city the L had chosen out of all 3378
12:14 not set his heart on seeking the L. 3378
13: 5 Don't you know that the L, 3378
13: 8 you plan to resist the kingdom of the L, 3378
13: 9 you drive out the priests of the L, 3378
13:10 "As for us, the L is our God, 3378
13:10 The priests who serve the L are sons 3378
13:11 and fragrant incense to the L. 3378
13:11 the requirements of the L our God. 3378
13:12 Men of Israel, do not fight against the L, 3378
13:14 Then they cried out to the L. 3378
13:18 because they relied on the L, 3378
13:20 And the L struck him down and he died. 3378
14: 2 and right in the eyes of the L his God. 3378
14: 4 He commanded Judah to seek the L, 3378
14: 6 for the L gave him rest. 3378
14: 7 because we have sought the L our God; 3378
14:11 Asa called to the L his God and said, 3378
14:11 and said, "L, there is no one like you 3378
14:11 Help us, O L our God, 3378
14:11 O L, you are our God; 3378
14:12 The L struck down the Cushites 3378
14:13 they were crushed before the L 3378
14:14 the terror of the L had fallen upon them. 3378
15: 2 The L is with you when you are with him. 3378
15: 4 But in their distress they turned to the L, 3378
15: 8 of the L that was in front of the portico of 3378
15: 9 when they saw that the L his God was 3378
15:11 to the L seven hundred head of cattle 3378
15:12 into a covenant to seek the L, 3378
15:13 All who would not seek the L, 3378
15:14 an oath to the L with loud acclamation, 3378
15:15 So the L gave them rest on every side. 3378
15:17 fully committed [to the L] all his life. NIH

2Ch 16: 7 of Aram and not on the L your God, 3378
16: 8 Yet when you relied on the L, 3378
16: 9 For the eyes of the L range throughout 3378
16:12 not seek help from the L, 3378
17: 3 The L was with Jehoshaphat because 3378
17: 5 The L established the kingdom 3378
17: 6 devoted to the ways of the L; 3378
17: 9 with them the Book of the Law of the L; 3378
17:10 The fear of the L fell on all the kingdoms 3378
17:16 volunteered himself for the service of the L, 3378
18: 4 "First seek the counsel of the L," 3378
18: 6 of the L here whom we can inquire of?" 3378
18: 7 through whom we can inquire of the L, 3378
18:10 and he declared, "This is what the L says: 3378
18:11 the L will give it into the king's hand." 3378
18:13 Micaiah said, "As surely as the L lives, 3378
18:15 but the truth in the name of the L?" 3378
18:16 and he said, 'These people have no 3378
18:18 "Therefore hear the word of the L: 3378
18:18 I saw the L sitting on his throne with all 3378
18:19 And the L said, 'Who will entice Ahab 3378
18:20 stood before the L and said, 3378
18:20 " 'By what means?' the L asked. 3378
18:21 succeed in enticing him,' said the L. NIH
18:22 "So now the L has put a lying spirit in 3378
18:22 The L has decreed disaster for you." 3378
18:23 "Which way did the spirit from the L go 3378
18:27 the L has not spoken through me." 3378
18:31 and the L helped him. 3378
19: 2 and love those who hate the L? 3378
19: 2 the wrath of the L is upon you. 3378
19: 4 and turned them back to the L, 3378
19: 6 you are not judging for man but for the L, 3378
19: 7 Now let the fear of the L be upon you. 3378
19: 7 with the L our God there is no injustice 3378
19: 8 the law of the L and to settle disputes. 3378
19: 9 and wholeheartedly in the fear of the L. 3378
19:10 to warn them not to sin against the L; 3378
19:11 over you in any matter concerning the L, 3378
19:11 may the L be with those who do well." 3378
20: 3 Jehoshaphat resolved to inquire of the L, 3378
20: 4 to seek help from the L; 3378
20: 5 of the L in the front of the new courtyard 3378
20: 6 "O L, God of our fathers, 3378
20:13 stood there before the L. 3378
20:14 of the L came upon Jahaziel son 3378
20:15 This is what the L says to you: 3378
20:17 the deliverance the L will give you, 3378
20:17 and the L will be with you.' " 3378
20:18 down in worship before the L. 3378
20:19 and Korahites stood up and praised the L, 3378
20:20 Have faith in the L your God and you will 3378
20:21 to sing to the L and to praise him for 3378
20:21 "Give thanks to the L, 3378
20:22 the L set ambushes against the men 3378
20:26 where they praised the L. 3378
20:27 for the L had given them cause to rejoice 3378
20:28 the temple of the L with harps and lutes 3378
20:29 how the L had fought against the enemies 3378
20:32 he did what was right in the eyes of the L. 3378
20:37 the L will destroy what you have made." 3378
21: 6 He did evil in the eyes of the L. 3378
21: 7 the covenant the L had made with David, 3378
21: 7 the L was not willing to destroy NIH
21:10 because Jehoram had forsaken the L, 3378
21:12 "This is what the L, the God of your father 3378
21:14 now the L is about to strike your people, 3378
21:16 The L aroused against Jehoram 3378
21:18 the L afflicted Jehoram with 3378
22: 4 He did evil in the eyes of the L, 3378
22: 7 whom the L had anointed to destroy 3378
22: 9 who sought the L with all his heart." 3378
23: 3 as the L promised concerning 3378
23: 5 in the courtyards of the temple of the L. 3378
23: 6 of the L except the priests and Levites 3378
23: 6 to guard what the L has assigned to them. 3378
23:12 she went to them at the temple of the L. 3378
23:14 to death at the temple of the L." 3378
23:18 the oversight of the temple of the L in 3378
23:18 of the L as written in the Law of Moses, 3378
23:20 the king down from the temple of the L. 3378
24: 2 the eyes of the L all the years of Jehoiada 3378
24: 4 to restore the temple of the L. 3378
24: 6 of the L and by the assembly of Israel for 3378
24: 8 at the gate of the temple of the L. 3378
24: 9 to the L the tax that Moses the servant 3378
24:12 the work required for the temple of the L. 3378
24:14 presented continually in the temple of the L 3378
24:18 They abandoned the temple of the L, 3378
24:19 Although the L sent prophets to the people 3378
24:20 Because you have forsaken the L, 3378
24:22 "May the L see this and call you 3378
24:24 the L delivered into their hands 3378
24:24 Because Judah had forsaken the L, 3378
25: 2 He did what was right in the eyes of the L, 3378
25: 4 where the L commanded: 3378
25: 7 for the L is not with Israel— 3378
25: 9 "The L can give you much more than that." 3378
25:15 of the L burned against Amaziah, 3378
25:27 turned away from following the L, 3378
26: 4 He did what was right in the eyes of the L, 3378
26: 5 As long as he sought the L, 3378
26:16 He was unfaithful to the L his God, 3378
26:16 the temple of the L to burn incense on 3378
26:17 priests of the L followed him in. 3378
26:18 Uzziah, to burn incense to the L. 3378
26:18 you will not be honored by the L God." 3378

2Ch 26:20 because the L had afflicted him. 3378
26:21 and excluded from the temple of the L. 3378
27: 2 He did what was right in the eyes of the L, 3378
27: 2 not enter the temple of the L. 3378
27: 3 the Upper Gate of the temple of the L 3378
27: 6 walked steadfastly before the L his God. 3378
28: 1 do what was right in the eyes of the L. 3378
28: 3 of the nations the L had driven out before 3378
28: 5 Therefore the L his God handed him over 3378
28: 6 because Judah had forsaken the L, 3378
28: 9 a prophet of the L named Oded was there, 3378
28: 9 He said to them, "Because the L, 3378
28:10 of sins against the L your God? 3378
28:13 "or we will be guilty before the L. 3378
28:19 The L had humbled Judah because 3378
28:19 and had been most unfaithful to the L. 3378
28:21 of the things from the temple of the L and 3378
28:22 even more unfaithful to the L. 3378
28:25 to other gods and provoked the L, 3378
29: 2 He did what was right in the eyes of the L, 3378
29: 3 of the temple of the L and repaired them. 3378
29: 5 now and consecrate the temple of the L, 3378
29: 6 they did evil in the eyes of the L our God 3378
29: 8 the anger of the L has fallen on Judah 3378
29:10 I intend to make a covenant with the L, 3378
29:11 for the L has chosen you to stand 3378
29:15 in to purify the temple of the L, 3378
29:15 following the word of the L. 3378
29:16 into the sanctuary of the L to purify it. 3378
29:16 that they found in the temple of the L. 3378
29:17 the portico of the L. 3378
29:17 the temple of the L itself, 3378
29:18 the entire temple of the L, 3378
29:20 and went up to the temple of the L. 3378
29:21 to offer these on the altar of the L. 3378
29:25 of the L with cymbals, harps and lyres in 3378
29:25 by the L through his prophets. 3378
29:27 singing to the L began also, 3378
29:30 the Levites to praise the L with the words 3378
29:31 now dedicated yourselves to the L, 3378
29:31 to the temple of the L." 3378
29:32 all of them for burnt offerings to the L, 3378
29:35 of the temple of the L was reestablished. 3378
30: 1 of the L in Jerusalem and celebrate 3378
30: 1 and celebrate the Passover to the L, 3378
30: 5 and celebrate the Passover to the L, 3378
30: 6 "People of Israel, return to the L, 3378
30: 7 who were unfaithful to the L, 3378
30: 8 as you fathers were; submit to the L. 3378
30: 8 Serve the L your God, 3378
30: 9 If you return to the L, 3378
30: 9 for the L your God is gracious and 3378
30:12 following the word of the L. 3378
30:15 burnt offerings to the temple of the L. 3378
30:17 not consecrate [their lambs] to the L. 3378
30:18 saying, "May the L, who is good, 3378
30:19 the L, the God of his fathers— 3378
30:20 And the L heard Hezekiah and healed 3378
30:21 and priests sang to the L every day, 3378
30:22 understanding of the service of the L. 3378
30:22 and praised the L, 3378
31: 3 as written in the Law of the L. 3378
31: 6 devote themselves to the L their God, 3378
31: 6 dedicated to the L their God, 3378
31: 8 they praised the L 3378
31:10 contributions to the temple of the L, 3378
31:10 because the L has blessed his people, 3378
31:11 storerooms in the temple of the L, 3378
31:14 the contributions made to the L and also 3378
31:16 all who would enter the temple of the L 3378
31:20 and faithful before the L his God. 3378
32: 8 with us is the L our God to help us and 3378
32:11 'The L our God will save us from 3378
32:16 spoke further against the L God and 3378
32:17 king also wrote letters insulting the L, 3378
32:21 And the L sent an angel, 3378
32:22 So the L saved Hezekiah and the people 3378
32:23 to Jerusalem for the L and valuable gifts 3378
32:24 He prayed to the L, 3378
33: 2 He did evil in the eyes of the L, 3378
33: 2 of the nations the L had driven out before 3378
33: 4 He built altars in the temple of the L, 3378
33: 4 of which the L had said, 3378
33: 5 In both courts the L built altars 3378
33: 6 He did much evil in the eyes of the L, 3378
33: 9 the nations the L had destroyed before 3378
33:10 The L spoke to Manasseh and his people, 3378
33:11 So the L brought against them 3378
33:12 the favor of the L his God 3378
33:13 the L was moved by his entreaty NIH
33:13 Then Manasseh knew that the L is God. 3378
33:15 from the temple of the L, as well as all 3378
33:16 Then he restored the altar of the L, 3378
33:16 and told Judah to serve the L, 3378
33:17 but only to the L their God. 3378
33:18 to him in the name of the L, 3378
33:22 He did evil in the eyes of the L, 3378
33:23 he did not humble himself before the L; 3378
34: 2 He did what was right in the eyes of the L 3378
34: 8 to repair the temple of the L his God. 3378
34:14 taken into the temple of the L, 3378
34:14 found the Book of the Law of the L 3378
34:15 the Book of the Law in the temple of the L. 3378
34:17 the money that was in the temple of the L 3378
34:21 "Go and inquire of the L for me and for 3378
34:21 our fathers have not kept the word of the L; 3378
34:23 She said to them, "This is what the L, 3378

2Ch 34:24 'This is what the L says: 3378
34:26 who sent you to inquire of the L, 3378
34:26 'This is what the L, the God of Israel, 3378
34:27 I have heard you, declares the L. 3378
34:30 He went up to the temple of the L with 3378
34:30 in the temple of the L. 3378
34:31 the covenant in the presence of the L— 3378
34:31 to follow the L and keep his commands, 3378
34:33 in Israel serve the L their God. 3378
34:33 they did not fail to follow the L, 3378
35: 1 Josiah celebrated the Passover to the L 3378
35: 3 and who had been consecrated to the L: 3378
35: 3 Now serve the L your God 3378
35: 6 doing what the L commanded 3378
35:12 of the people to offer to the L, 3378
35:16 the entire service of the L was carried out 3378
35:16 of burnt offerings on the altar of the L, 3378
35:26 to what is written in the Law of the L— 3378
36: 5 He did evil in the eyes of the L his God. 3378
36: 7 of the L and put them in his temple there. 3378
36: 9 He did evil in the eyes of the L. 3378
36:10 articles of value from the temple of the L, 3378
36:12 He did evil in the eyes of the L his God 3378
36:12 who spoke the word of the L. 3378
36:13 and would not turn to the L, 3378
36:14 and defiling the temple of the L. 3378
36:15 The L, the God of their fathers, 3378
36:16 of the L was aroused against his people 3378
36:21 in fulfillment of the word of the L spoken 3378
36:22 the word of the L spoken by Jeremiah 3378
36:22 the L moved the heart of Cyrus king 3378
36:23 " 'The L, the God of heaven, 3378
36:23 may the L his God be with him, 3378
Ezr 1: 1 the word of the L spoken by Jeremiah, 3378
1: 1 the L moved the heart of Cyrus king 3378
1: 2 " 'The L, the God of heaven, 3378
1: 3 in Judah and build the temple of the L, 3378
1: 5 and build the house of the L in Jerusalem. 3378
1: 7 articles belonging to the temple of the L, 3378
2:68 When they arrived at the house of the L 3378
3: 3 sacrificed burnt offerings on it to the L, 3378
3: 5 the appointed sacred feasts of the L, 3378
3: 5 as freewill offerings to the L. 3378
3: 6 to offer burnt offerings to the L, 3378
3: 6 the building of the house of the L, 3378
3:10 the foundation of the temple of the L, 3378
3:10 took their places to praise the L, 3378
3:11 and thanksgiving they sang to the L: 3378
3:11 a great shout of praise to the L, 3378
3:11 foundation of the house of the L was laid. 3378
4: 1 a temple for the L, the God of Israel, 3378
4: 3 We alone will build it for the L, the God of Israel. 3378
6:21 in order to seek the L, the God of Israel. 3378
6:22 because the L had filled them with joy 3378
7: 6 which the L, the God of Israel, had given. 3378
7: 6 for the hand of the L his God was on him. 3378
7:10 and observance of the Law of the L, 3378
7:11 the commands and decrees of the L, 3378
7:27 Praise be to the L, the God of our fathers, 3378
7:27 to bring honor to the house of the L 3378
7:28 the hand of the L my God was on me, 3378
8:28 as these articles are consecrated to the L. 3378
8:28 and gold are a freewill offering to the L, 3378
8:29 of the house of the L in Jerusalem before 3378
8:35 All this was a burnt offering to the L. 3378
9: 5 my hands spread out to the L my God 3378
9: 8 the L our God has been gracious 3378
9:15 O L, God of Israel, you are righteous! 3378
10:11 Now make confession to the L, 3378
Ne 1: 5 Then I said: "O L, God of heaven, 3378
5:13 "Amen," and praised the L. 3378
8: 1 which the L had commanded for Israel. 3378
8: 6 Ezra praised the L, the great God; 3378
8: 6 and worshiped the L with their faces to 3378
8: 9 "This day is sacred to the L your God. 3378
8:10 for the joy of the L is your strength." 3378
8:14 which the L had commanded 3378
9: 3 the Law of the L their God for a quarter 3378
9: 4 and in worshiping the L their God. 3378
9: 5 "Stand up and praise the L your God, 3378
9: 6 You alone are the L. 3378
9: 7 "You are the L God. 3378
10:29 and decrees of the L our Lord. 3378
10:34 to burn on the altar of the L our God, 3378
10:35 the house of the L each year the firstfruits 3378
Job 1: 6 came to present themselves before the L, 3378
1: 7 The L said to Satan, "Where have you 3378
1: 7 Satan answered the L, "From roaming 3378
1: 8 The L said to Satan, "Have you considered 3378
1:12 The L said to Satan, "Very well, then, 3378
1:12 from the presence of the L. 3378
1:21 The L gave and the LORD has taken away; 3378
1:21 and the L has taken away; 3378
1:21 may the name of the L be praised." 3378
2: 1 came to present themselves before the L, 3378
2: 2 And the L said to Satan, "Where have you 3378
2: 2 Satan answered the L, "From roaming 3378
2: 3 the L said to Satan, "Have you considered 3378
2: 6 The L said to Satan, "Very well, then, 3378
2: 7 the presence of the L and afflicted Job 3378
12: 9 that the hand of the L has done this? 3378
38: 1 The L answered Job out of the storm. 3378
40: 1 The L said to Job: 3378
40: 3 Then Job answered the L: 3378
40: 6 Then the L spoke to Job out of the storm: 3378
42: 1 Then Job replied to the L: 3378

†LORD distinguishes the proper name of God, *Yahweh*, indicated in the NIV by "LORD," from the words translated "Lord" and "lord," indexed under the heading *LORD, pages 683-86.

Job	42: 7	After the L had said these things to Job,	3378
	42: 9	the Naamathite did what the L told them;	3378
	42: 9	and the L accepted Job's prayer.	3378
	42:10	the L made him prosperous again	3378
	42:11	the trouble the L had brought upon him,	3378
	42:12	The L blessed the latter part of Job's life	3378
Ps	1: 2	But his delight is in the law of the L,	3378
	1: 6	For the L watches over the way of	3378
	2: 2	the rulers gather together against the L	3378
	2: 7	I will proclaim the decree of the L:	3378
	2:11	Serve the L with fear and rejoice	3378
	3: 1	O L, how many are my foes!	3378
	3: 3	But you are a shield around me, O L;	3378
	3: 4	To the L I cry aloud,	3378
	3: 5	I wake again, because the L sustains me.	3378
	3: 7	Arise, O L! Deliver me, O my God!	3378
	3: 8	From the L comes deliverance.	3378
	4: 3	Know that the L has set apart the godly	3378
	4: 3	the L will hear when I call to him.	3378
	4: 5	Offer right sacrifices and trust in the L.	3378
	4: 6	the light of your face shine upon us, O L.	3378
	4: 8	O L, make me dwell in safety.	3378
	5: 1	Give ear to my words, O L,	3378
	5: 3	In the morning, O L, you hear my voice;	3378
	5: 6	and deceitful men the L abhors.	3378
	5: 8	O L, in your righteousness because	3378
	5:12	For surely, O L, you bless the righteous;	3378
	6: 1	O L, do not rebuke me in your anger	3378
	6: 2	Be merciful to me, L, for I am faint;	3378
	6: 2	O L, heal me, for my bones are in agony.	3378
	6: 3	How long, O L, how long?	3378
	6: 4	Turn, O L, and deliver me;	3378
	6: 8	for the L has heard my weeping.	3378
	6: 9	The L has heard my cry for mercy;	3378
	6: 9	the L accepts my prayer.	3378
	7: T	which he sang to the L concerning Cush,	3378
	7: 1	O L my God, I take refuge in you;	3378
	7: 3	O L my God, if I have done this	3378
	7: 6	Arise, O L, in your anger;	3378
	7: 8	let the L judge the peoples.	3378
	7: 8	O L, according to my righteousness,	3378
	7:17	to the L because of his righteousness	3378
	7:17	to the name of the L Most High.	3378
	8: 1	O L, our Lord, how majestic is your name	3378
	8: 9	O L, our Lord, how majestic is your name	3378
	9: 1	I will praise you, O L, with all my heart;	3378
	9: 7	The L reigns forever;	3378
	9: 9	The L is a refuge for the oppressed,	3378
	9:10	for you, L, have never forsaken those who	
		seek you.	3378
	9:11	Sing praises to the L, enthroned in Zion;	3378
	9:13	O L, see how my enemies persecute me!	3378
	9:19	Arise, O L, let not man triumph;	3378
	9:20	Strike them with terror, O L;	3378
	10: 1	O L, do you stand far off?	3378
	10: 3	he blesses the greedy and reviles the L.	3378
	10:12	L! Lift up your hand,	3378
	10:16	The L is King for ever and ever;	3378
	10:17	You hear, O L, the desire of the afflicted;	3378
	11: 1	In the L I take refuge.	3378
	11: 4	The L is in his holy temple;	3378
	11: 4	the L is on his heavenly throne.	3378
	11: 5	The L examines the righteous,	3378
	11: 7	For the L is righteous, he loves justice;	3378
	12: 1	Help, L, for the godly are no more;	3378
	12: 3	May the L cut off all flattering lips	3378
	12: 5	I will now arise," says the L.	3378
	12: 6	And the words of the L are flawless,	3378
	12: 7	O L, you will keep us safe and protect us	3378
	13: 1	How long, O L?	3378
	13: 3	Look on me and answer, O L my God.	3378
	13: 6	I will sing to the L,	3378
	14: 2	The L looks down from heaven on	3378
	14: 4	and who do not call on the L?	3378
	14: 6	but the L is their refuge.	3378
	14: 7	the L restores the fortunes of his people,	3378
	15: 1	L, who may dwell in your sanctuary?	3378
	15: 4	but honors those who fear the L,	3378
	16: 2	I said to the L, "You are my Lord;	3378
	16: 5	L, you have assigned me my portion	3378
	16: 7	I will praise the L, who counsels me;	3378
	16: 8	I have set the L always before me.	3378
	17: 1	Hear, O L, my righteous plea;	3378
	17:13	Rise up, O L, confront them,	3378
	17:14	O L, by your hand save me	3378
	18: T	Of David the servant of the L.	3378
	18: T	He sang to the L the words of this song	3378
	18: T	when the L delivered him from the hand	3378
	18: 1	I love you, O L, my strength.	3378
	18: 2	The L is my rock,	3378
	18: 3	I call to the L, who is worthy of praise,	3378
	18: 6	In my distress I called to the L;	3378
	18:13	The L thundered from heaven;	3378
	18:15	at your rebuke, O L, at the blast of breath	3378
	18:18	but the L was my support.	3378
	18:20	The L has dealt with me according	3378
	18:21	For I have kept the ways of the L;	3378
	18:24	The L has rewarded me according	3378
	18:28	You, O L, keep my lamp burning;	3378
	18:30	the word of the L is flawless.	3378
	18:31	For who is God besides the L?	3378
	18:41	to the L, but he did not answer.	3378
	18:46	The L lives! Praise be to my Rock!	3378
	18:49	O L; I will sing praises to your name.	3378
	19: 1	law of the L is perfect, reviving the soul.	3378
	19: 7	The statutes of the L are trustworthy,	3378

Ps	19: 8	The precepts of the L are right,	3378
	19: 8	The commands of the L are radiant,	3378
	19: 9	fear of the L is pure, enduring forever.	3378
	19: 9	of the L are sure and altogether righteous.	3378
	19:14	O L, my Rock and my Redeemer.	3378
	20: 1	May the L answer you when you are	3378
	20: 5	May the L grant all your requests.	3378
	20: 6	I know that the L saves his anointed;	3378
	20: 7	we trust in the name of the L our God.	3378
	20: 9	O L, save the king!	3378
	21: 1	O L, the king rejoices in your strength.	3378
	21: 7	For the king trusts in the L;	3378
	21: 9	In his wrath the L will swallow them up,	3378
	21:13	Be exalted, O L, in your strength;	3378
	22: 8	"He trusts in the L;	3378
	22: 8	let the L rescue him.	NIH
	22:19	But you, O L, be not far off;	3378
	22:23	You who fear the L, praise him!	3378
	22:26	they who seek the L will praise him—	3378
	22:27	and turn to the L,	3378
	22:28	to the L and he rules over the nations.	3378
	23: 1	The L is my shepherd, I shall not be in want	3378
	23: 6	I will dwell in the house of the L forever.	3378
	24: 3	Who may ascend the hill of the L?	3378
	24: 5	He will receive blessing from the L	3378
	24: 8	The L strong and mighty,	3378
	24: 8	the L mighty in battle.	3378
	24:10	of glory? The L Almighty—	3378
	25: 1	To you, O L, I lift up my soul;	3378
	25: 4	Show me your ways, O L,	3378
	25: 6	O L, your great mercy and love,	3378
	25: 7	for you are good, O L.	3378
	25: 8	Good and upright is the L;	3378
	25:10	The ways of the L are loving and faithful	3378
	25:11	For the sake of your name, O L,	3378
	25:12	Who, then, is the man that fears the L?	3378
	25:14	The L confides in those who fear him;	3378
	25:15	My eyes are ever on the L,	3378
	26: 1	for I have led a blameless life;	3378
	26: 1	I have trusted in the L without wavering.	3378
	26: 2	Test me, O L, and try me,	3378
	26: 6	and go about your altar, O L,	3378
	26: 8	I love the house where you live, O L,	3378
	26:12	in the great assembly I will praise the L.	3378
	27: 1	The L is my light and my salvation—	3378
	27: 1	The L is the stronghold of my life—	3378
	27: 4	One thing I ask of the L,	3378
	27: 4	the house of the L all the days of my life,	3378
	27: 4	upon the beauty of the L and to seek him	3378
	27: 6	I will sing and make music to the L.	3378
	27: 7	Hear my voice when I call, O L;	3378
	27: 8	Your face, L, I will seek.	3378
	27:10	the L will receive me.	3378
	27:11	Teach me your way, O L;	3378
	27:13	the goodness of the L in the land of	3378
	27:14	Wait for the L; be strong and take heart	3378
	27:14	and take heart and wait for the L.	3378
	28: 1	To you I call, O L my Rock;	3378
	28: 5	of the L and what his hands have done,	3378
	28: 6	Praise be to the L,	3378
	28: 7	The L is my strength and my shield;	3378
	28: 8	The L is the strength of his people,	3378
	29: 1	Ascribe to the L, O mighty ones,	3378
	29: 1	ascribe to the L glory and strength.	3378
	29: 2	Ascribe to the L the glory due his name;	3378
	29: 2	worship the L in the splendor	3378
	29: 3	The voice of the L is over the waters;	3378
	29: 3	the L thunders over the mighty waters.	3378
	29: 4	The voice of the L is powerful;	3378
	29: 4	the voice of the L is majestic.	3378
	29: 5	The voice of the L breaks the cedars;	3378
	29: 5	the L breaks in pieces the cedars	3378
	29: 7	of the L strikes with flashes of lightning.	3378
	29: 8	The voice of the L shakes the desert;	3378
	29: 8	the L shakes the Desert of Kadesh.	3378
	29: 9	The voice of the L twists the oaks	3378
	29:10	The L sits enthroned over the flood;	3378
	29:10	the L is enthroned as King forever.	3378
	29:11	The L gives strength to his people;	3378
	29:11	the L blesses his people with peace.	3378
	30: 1	I will exalt you, O L,	3378
	30: 2	O L my God, I called to you for help	3378
	30: 3	O L, you brought me up from the grave;	3378
	30: 4	Sing to the L, you saints of his;	3378
	30: 7	O L, when you favored me,	3378
	30: 8	To you, O L, I called;	3378
	30:10	Hear, O L, and be merciful to me;	3378
	30:10	O L, be my help."	3378
	30:12	O L my God, I will give you thanks forever.	3378
	31: 1	In you, O L, I have taken refuge;	3378
	31: 5	redeem me, O L, the God of truth.	3378
	31: 6	I trust in the L.	3378
	31: 9	Be merciful to me, O L,	3378
	31:14	But I trust in you, O L;	3378
	31:17	Let me not be put to shame, O L,	3378
	31:21	Praise be to the L,	3378
	31:23	Love the L, all his saints!	3378
	31:23	The L preserves the faithful,	3378
	31:24	all you who hope in the L.	3378
	32: 2	Blessed is the man whose sin the L does	3378
	32: 5	"I will confess my transgressions to the L"	3378
	32:11	Rejoice in the L and be glad,	3378
	33: 1	Sing joyfully to the L, you righteous;	3378
	33: 2	Praise the L with the harp;	3378
	33: 4	For the word of the L is right and true;	3378
	33: 5	The L loves righteousness and justice;	3378
	33: 6	the word of the L were the heavens made,	3378

Ps	33: 8	Let all the earth fear the L;	3378
	33:10	The L foils the plans of the nations;	3378
	33:11	But the plans of the L stand firm forever,	3378
	33:12	Blessed is the nation whose God is the L,	3378
	33:13	From heaven the L looks down	3378
	33:18	eyes of the L are on those who fear him,	3378
	33:20	We wait in hope for the L;	3378
	33:22	O L, even as we put our hope in you.	3378
	34: 1	I will extol the L at all times;	3378
	34: 2	My soul will boast in the L;	3378
	34: 3	Glorify the L with me;	3378
	34: 4	I sought the L, and he answered me;	3378
	34: 6	and the L heard him;	3378
	34: 7	The angel of the L encamps	3378
	34: 8	Taste and see that the L is good;	3378
	34: 9	Fear the L, you his saints,	3378
	34:10	those who seek the L lack no good thing.	3378
	34:11	I will teach you the fear of the L.	3378
	34:15	The eyes of the L are on the righteous	3378
	34:16	face of the L is against those who do evil,	3378
	34:17	righteous cry out, and the L hears them;	3378
	34:18	The L is close to the brokenhearted	3378
	34:19	but the L delivers him from them all;	3378
	34:22	The L redeems his servants;	3378
	35: 1	O L, with those who contend with me;	3378
	35: 5	the angel of the L driving them away;	3378
	35: 6	with the angel of the L pursuing them.	3378
	35: 9	in the L and delight in his salvation.	3378
	35:10	"Who is like you, O L?	3378
	35:22	O L, you have seen this; be not silent.	3378
	35:24	Vindicate me in your righteousness, O L	3378
	35:27	may they always say, "The L be exalted,	3378
	36: T	Of David the servant of the L.	3378
	36: 5	Your love, O L, reaches to the heavens,	3378
	36: 6	O L, you preserve both man and beast.	3378
	37: 3	Trust in the L and do good;	3378
	37: 4	in the L and he will give you the desires	3378
	37: 5	Commit your way to the L;	3378
	37: 7	before the L and wait patiently for him;	3378
	37: 9	but those who hope in the L will inherit	3378
	37:17	but the L upholds the righteous.	3378
	37:18	days of the blameless are known to the L,	3378
	37:22	those the L blesses will inherit the land,	2257S
	37:23	If the L delights in a man's way,	3378
	37:24	for the L upholds him with his hand.	3378
	37:28	For the L loves the just and will	3378
	37:33	but the L will not leave them	3378
	37:34	Wait for the L and keep his way.	3378
	37:39	of the righteous comes from the L;	3378
	37:40	The L helps them and delivers them;	3378
	38: 1	O L, do not rebuke me in your anger	3378
	38:15	I wait for you, O L;	3378
	38:21	O L, do not forsake me.	3378
	39: 4	O L, my life's end and the number	3378
	39:12	O L, listen to my cry for help;	3378
	40: 1	I waited patiently for the L;	3378
	40: 3	and fear and put their trust in the L.	3378
	40: 4	the man who makes the L his trust,	3378
	40: 5	Many, O L my God, are the wonders	3378
	40: 9	I do not seal my lips, as you know, O L.	3378
	40:11	not withhold your mercy from me, O L;	3378
	40:13	Be pleased, O L, to save me;	3378
	40:13	O L, come quickly to help me.	3378
	40:16	"The L be exalted!"	3378
	41: 1	the L delivers him in times of trouble.	3378
	41: 2	The L will protect him and preserve his life;	3378
	41: 3	The L will sustain him on his sickbed	3378
	41: 4	I said, "O L, have mercy on me;	3378
	41:10	But you, O L, have mercy on me,	3378
	41:13	Praise be to the L, the God of Israel,	3378
	42: 8	By day the L directs his love,	3378
	46: 7	The L Almighty is with us;	3378
	46: 8	Come and see the works of the L,	3378
	46:11	The L Almighty is with us;	3378
	47: 2	How awesome is the L Most High,	3378
	47: 5	the L amid the sounding of trumpets.	3378
	48: 1	Great is the L, and most worthy of praise,	3378
	48: 8	of the L Almighty, in the city of our God:	3378
	50: 1	The Mighty One, God, the L,	3378
	54: 6	I will praise your name, O L,	3378
	55:16	But I call to God, and the L saves me.	3378
	55:22	on the L and he will sustain you;	3378
	56:10	In God, whose word I praise, in the L,	3378
	58: 6	tear out, O L, the fangs of the lions!	3378
	59: 3	for no offense or sin of mine, O L.	3378
	59: 5	O L God Almighty, the God of Israel,	3378
	59: 8	But you, O L, laugh at them;	3378
	64:10	Let the righteous rejoice in the L	3378
	68: 4	his name is the L—and rejoice before him.	3363
	68:16	where the L himself will dwell forever?	3378
	68:18	that you O L God, might dwell there.	3363
	68:20	from the Sovereign L comes escape	3378
	68:26	praise the L in the assembly of Israel.	3378
	69: 6	O Lord, the L Almighty;	3378
	69:13	But I pray to you, O L,	3378
	69:16	O L, out of the goodness of your love;	3378
	69:31	This will please the L more than an ox,	3378
	69:33	The L hears the needy and does	3378
	70: 1	O L, come quickly to help me.	3378
	70: 5	O L, do not delay.	3378
	71: 1	In you, O L, I have taken refuge;	3378
	71: 5	you have been my hope, O Sovereign L,	3378
	71:16	proclaim your mighty acts, O Sovereign L;	3378
	72:18	Praise be to the L God, the God of Israel,	3378
	73:28	I have made the Sovereign L my refuge;	3378
	74:18	how the enemy has mocked you, O L,	3378
	75: 8	In the hand of the L is a cup full	3378

Ps 76:11 Make vows to **the L** your God and fulfill
them; — 3378
77:11 I will remember the deeds of **the L;** — 3363
78: 4 the praiseworthy deeds of **the L,** — 3378
78:21 When **the L** heard them, — 3378
79: 5 How long, O **L?** — 3378
80: 4 O **L** God Almighty, — 3378
80:19 Restore us, O **L** God Almighty; — 3378
81:10 I am **the L** your God, — 3378
81:15 Those who hate **the L** would cringe — 3378
83:16 so that men will seek your name, O **L.** — 3378
83:18 whose name is **the L**— — 3378
84: 1 How lovely is your dwelling place, O **L**
Almighty! — 3378
84: 2 even faints, for the courts of **the L;** — 3378
84: 3 a place near your altar, O **L** Almighty, — 3378
84: 8 Hear my prayer, O **L** God Almighty; — 3378
84:11 For **the L** God is a sun and shield; — 3378
84:11 **the L** bestows favor and honor; — 3378
84:12 O **L** Almighty, blessed is the man who
trusts in you. — 3378
85: 1 You showed favor to your land, O **L;** — 3378
85: 7 Show us your unfailing love, O **L,** — 3378
85: 8 I will listen to what God **the L** will say; — 3378
85:12 **The L** will indeed give what is good, — 3378
86: 1 Hear, O **L,** and answer me, — 3378
86: 6 Hear my prayer, O **L,** — 3378
86:11 Teach me your way, O **L,** — 3378
86:17 O **L,** have helped me and comforted me. — 3378
87: 2 **the L** loves the gates of Zion more than — 3378
87: 6 **The L** will write in the register of the — 3378
88: 1 O **L,** the God who saves me, — 3378
88: 9 I call to you, O **L,** every day; — 3378
88:13 But I cry to you for help, O **L;** — 3378
88:14 O **L,** do you reject me and hide your face — 3378
89: 5 O **L,** your faithfulness too, — 3378
89: 6 the skies above can compare with **the L?** — 3378
89: 6 Who is like **the L** among the heavenly
beings? — 3378
89: 8 O **L** God Almighty, who is like you? — 3378
89: 8 You are mighty, O **L,** — 3363
89:15 in the light of your presence, O **L.** — 3378
89:18 Indeed, our shield belongs to **the L,** — 3378
89:46 How long, O **L?** Will you hide yourself
forever? — 3378
89:51 which your enemies have mocked, O **L,** — 3378
89:52 Praise be to **the L** forever! — 3378
90:13 Relent, O **L!** How long will it be? — 3378
91: 2 I will say of **the L,** — 3378
91: 9 even **the L,** who is my refuge— — 3378
91:14 "Because he loves me," says **the L,** — NIH
92: 1 It is good to praise **the L** and make music — 3378
92: 4 you make me glad by your deeds, O **L;** — 3378
92: 5 How great are your works, O **L,** — 3378
92: 8 But you, O **L,** are exalted forever. — 3378
92: 9 For surely your enemies, O **L,** — 3378
92:13 planted in the house of **the L,** — 3378
92:15 "**The L** is upright; he is my Rock, — 3378
93: 1 **The L** reigns, he is robed in majesty; — 3378
93: 1 **the L** is robed in majesty and is armed — 3378
93: 3 The seas have lifted up, O **L,** — 3378
93: 4 **the L** on high is mighty. — 3378
93: 5 holiness adorns your house for endless
days, O **L.** — 3378
94: 1 O **L,** the God who avenges, — 3378
94: 3 How long will the wicked, O **L,** — 3378
94: 5 They crush your people, O **L;** — 3378
94: 7 They say, "**The L** does not see; — 3363
94:11 **The L** knows the thoughts of man; — 3378
94:12 Blessed is the man you discipline, O **L,** — 3363
94:14 For **the L** will not reject his people; — 3378
94:17 Unless **the L** had given me help, — 3378
94:18 your love, O **L,** supported me. — 3378
94:22 But **the L** has become my fortress, — 3378
94:23 **the L** our God will destroy them. — 3378
95: 1 Come, let us sing for joy to **the L;** — 3378
95: 3 For **the L** is the great God, — 3378
95: 6 let us kneel before **the L** our Maker; — 3378
96: 1 Sing to **the L** a new song, — 3378
96: 1 sing to **the L,** all the earth. — 3378
96: 2 Sing to **the L,** praise his name; — 3378
96: 4 great is **the L** and most worthy of praise; — 3378
96: 5 but **the L** made the heavens. — 3378
96: 7 Ascribe to **the L,** O families of nations, — 3378
96: 7 ascribe to **the L** glory and strength. — 3378
96: 8 Ascribe to **the L** the glory due his name; — 3378
96: 9 Worship **the L** in the splendor — 3378
96:10 Say among the nations, "**The L** reigns." — 3378
96:13 they will sing before **the L,** — 3378
97: 1 **The L** reigns, let the earth be glad; — 3378
97: 5 mountains melt like wax before **the L,** — 3378
97: 8 because of your judgments, O **L.** — 3378
97: 9 O **L,** are the Most High over all the earth; — 3378
97:10 Let those who love **the L** hate evil, — 3378
97:12 Rejoice in **the L,** you who are righteous, — 3378
98: 1 Sing to **the L** a new song, — 3378
98: 2 **The L** has made his salvation known — 3378
98: 4 Shout for joy to **the L,** all the earth, — 3378
98: 5 make music to **the L** with the harp, — 3378
98: 6 shout for joy before **the L,** the King. — 3378
98: 9 let them sing before **the L,** — 3378
99: 1 **The L** reigns, let the nations tremble; — 3378
99: 2 Great is **the L** in Zion; — 3378
99: 5 Exalt **the L** our God and worship — 3378
99: 6 on **the L** and he answered them. — 3378
99: 8 O **L** our God, you answered them; — 3378
99: 9 Exalt **the L** our God and worship — 3378

Ps 99: 9 for **the L** our God is holy. — 3378
100: 1 Shout for joy to **the L,** all the earth. — 3378
100: 2 Worship **the L** with gladness; — 3378
100: 3 Know that **the L** is God. — 3378
100: 5 For **the L** is good and his love endures — 3378
101: 1 to you, O **L,** I will sing praise. — 3378
101: 8 from the city of **the L.** — 3378
102: T and pours out his lament before **the L.** — 3378
102: 1 Hear my prayer, O **L;** — 3378
102:12 But you, O **L,** sit enthroned forever; — 3378
102:15 The nations will fear the name of **the L,** — 3378
102:16 For **the L** will rebuild Zion and appear — 3378
102:18 a people not yet created may praise **the L:** — 3363
102:19 "**The L** looked down from his sanctuary — 3378
102:21 So the name of **the L** will be declared — 3378
102:22 the kingdoms assemble to worship **the L.** — 3378
103: 1 Praise **the L,** O my soul; — 3378
103: 2 Praise **the L,** O my soul, — 3378
103: 6 **The L** works righteousness and justice — 3378
103: 8 **The L** is compassionate and gracious, — 3378
103:13 so **the L** has compassion on those who fear
him; — 3378
103:19 **The L** has established his throne — 3378
103:20 Praise **the L,** you his angels, — 3378
103:21 Praise **the L,** all his heavenly hosts, — 3378
103:22 Praise **the L,** all his works everywhere — 3378
103:22 Praise **the L,** O my soul. — 3378
104: 1 Praise **the L,** O my soul. — 3378
104: 1 O **L** my God, you are very great; — 3378
104:16 The trees of **the L** are well watered, — 3378
104:24 How many are your works, O **L!** — 3378
104:31 May the glory of **the L** endure forever; — 3378
104:31 may **the L** rejoice in his works— — 3378
104:33 I will sing to **the L** all my life; — 3378
104:34 as I rejoice in **the L.** — 3378
104:35 Praise **the L,** O my soul. — 3378
104:35 O my soul. Praise **the L.** — 3363
105: 1 Give thanks to **the L,** call on his name; — 3378
105: 3 of those who seek **the L** rejoice. — 3378
105: 4 Look to **the L** and his strength; — 3378
105: 7 He is **the L** our God; — 3378
105:19 till the word of **the L** proved him true. — 3378
105:24 **The L** made his people very fruitful; — NIH
105:45 Praise **the L.** — 3363
106: 1 Praise **the L.** Give thanks to the LORD, — 3363
106: 1 Give thanks to **the L,** for he is good; — 3378
106: 2 of **the L** or fully declare his praise? — 3378
106: 4 Remember me, O **L,** — 3378
106:16 who was consecrated to **the L.** — 3378
106:25 in their tents and did not obey **the L.** — 3378
106:29 **the L** to anger by their wicked deeds, — NIH
106:32 By the waters of Meribah they angered **the L** — NIH
106:34 as **the L** had commanded them, — 3378
106:40 Therefore **the L** was angry — 3378
106:47 Save us, O **L** our God, — 3378
106:48 Praise be to **the L,** the God of Israel, — 3378
106:48 Praise **the L.** — 3363
107: 1 Give thanks to **the L,** for he is good; — 3378
107: 2 Let the redeemed of **the L** say this— — 3378
107: 6 they cried out to **the L** in their trouble, — 3378
107: 8 Let them give thanks to **the L** — 3378
107:13 Then they cried to **the L** in their trouble, — 3378
107:15 Let them give thanks to **the L** — 3378
107:19 Then they cried to **the L** in their trouble, — 3378
107:21 Let them give thanks to **the L** — 3378
107:24 They saw the works of **the L,** — 3378
107:28 they cried out to **the L** in their trouble, — 3378
107:31 Let them give thanks to **the L** — 3378
107:43 and consider the great love of **the L.** — 3378
108: 3 I will praise you, O **L,** — 3378
109: 14 be remembered before **the L;** — 3378
109:15 before **the L,** that he may cut off — 3378
109:21 But you, O Sovereign **L,** — 3378
109:26 Help me, O **L** my God; — 3378
109:27 that you, O **L,** have done it. — 3378
109:30 With my mouth I will greatly extol **the L;** — 3378
110: 1 **The L** says to my Lord: — 3378
110: 2 **The L** will extend your mighty scepter — 3378
110: 4 **The L** has sworn and will — 3378
111: 1 Praise **the L.** — 3363
111: 1 I will extol **the L** with all my heart in — 3378
111: 2 Great are the works of **the L;** — 3378
111: 4 **the L** is gracious and compassionate. — 3378
111:10 fear of **the L** is the beginning of wisdom; — 3378
112: 1 Praise **the L.** — 3363
112: 1 Blessed is the man who fears **the L,** — 3378
112: 7 his heart is steadfast, trusting in **the L.** — 3378
113: 1 Praise **the L.** — 3363
113: 1 Praise, O servants of **the L,** — 3378
113: 1 praise the name of **the L.** — 3378
113: 2 Let the name of **the L** be praised. — 3378
113: 3 the name of **the L** is to be praised. — 3378
113: 4 **The L** is exalted over all the nations, — 3378
113: 5 Who is like **the L** our God, — 3378
113: 9 Praise **the L.** — 3363
115: 1 Not to us, O **L,** — 3378
115: 9 O house of Israel, trust in **the L**— — 3378
115:10 O house of Aaron, trust in **the L**— — 3378
115:11 You who fear him, trust in **the L**— — 3378
115:12 **The L** remembers us and will bless us: — 3378
115:13 he will bless those who fear **the L**— — 3378
115:14 May **the L** make you increase, — 3378
115:15 May you be blessed by **the L,** — 3378
115:16 The highest heavens belong to **the L,** — 3378
115:17 It is not the dead who praise **the L,** — 3363
115:18 it is we who extol **the L,** — 3363
115:18 Praise **the L.** — 3363

Ps 116: 1 I love **the L,** for he heard my voice; — 3378
116: 4 Then I called on the name of **the L:** — 3378
116: 4 "O **L,** save me!" — 3378
116: 5 **The L** is gracious and righteous; — 3378
116: 6 **The L** protects the simplehearted; — 3378
116: 7 for **the L** has been good to you. — 3378
116: 8 O **L,** have delivered my soul from death, — NIH
116: 9 that I may walk before **the L** in the land — 3378
116:12 How can I repay **the L** — 3378
116:13 and call on the name of **the L.** — 3378
116:14 to **the L** in the presence of all his people. — 3378
116:15 Precious in the sight of **the L** is the death — 3378
116:16 O **L,** truly I am your servant; — 3378
116:17 to you and call on the name of **the L.** — 3378
116:18 to **the L** in the presence of all his people, — 3378
116:19 in the courts of the house of **the L**— — 3378
116:19 Praise **the L.** — 3363
117: 1 Praise **the L,** all you nations; — 3378
117: 2 the faithfulness of **the L** endures forever. — 3378
117: 2 Praise **the L.** — 3363
118: 1 Give thanks to **the L,** for he is good; — 3378
118: 4 Let those who fear **the L** say: — 3378
118: 5 In my anguish I cried to **the L,** — 3363
118: 6 **The L** is with me; I will not be afraid. — 3378
118: 7 **The L** is with me; he is my helper. — 3378
118: 8 It is better to take refuge in **the L** than — 3378
118: 9 It is better to take refuge in **the L** than — 3378
118:10 but in the name of **the L** I cut them off. — 3378
118:11 but in the name of **the L** I cut them off. — 3378
118:12 in the name of **the L** I cut them off. — 3378
118:13 but **the L** helped me. — 3378
118:14 **The L** is my strength and my song; — 3363
118:17 and will proclaim what **the L** has done. — 3363
118:18 **The L** has chastened me severely, — 3363
118:19 I will enter and give thanks to **the L.** — 3363
118:20 This is the gate of **the L** through which — 3378
118:23 **the L** has done this; — 3378
118:24 This is the day **the L** has made; — 3378
118:25 O **L,** save us; — 3378
118:25 O **L,** grant us success. — 3378
118:26 in the name of **the L.** — 3378
118:26 From the house of **the L** we bless you. — 3378
118:27 **The L** is God, he has made his light shine — 3378
118:29 Give thanks to **the L,** for he is good; — 3378
119: 1 who walk according to the law of **the L.** — 3378
119:12 Praise be to you, O **L;** — 3378
119:31 I hold fast to your statutes, O **L;** — 3378
119:33 Teach me, O **L,** to follow your decrees; — 3378
119:41 May your unfailing love come to me, O **L,** — 3378
119:52 I remember your ancient laws, O **L,** — 3378
119:55 In the night I remember your name, O **L,** — 3378
119:57 You are my portion, O **L;** — 3378
119:64 The earth is filled with your love, O **L;** — 3378
119:65 according to your word, O **L.** — 3378
119:75 O **L,** that your laws are righteous, — 3378
119:89 Your word, O **L,** is eternal; — 3378
119:107 preserve my life, O **L,** — 3378
119:108 O **L,** the willing praise of my mouth, — 3378
119:126 It is time for you to act, O **L;** — 3378
119:137 Righteous are you, O **L,** — 3378
119:145 I call with all my heart; answer me, O **L,** — 3378
119:149 preserve my life, O **L,** — 3378
119:151 Yet you are near, O **L,** — 3378
119:156 Your compassion is great, O **L;** — 3378
119:159 preserve my life, O **L,** — 3378
119:166 I wait for your salvation, O **L,** — 3378
119:169 May my cry come before you, O **L;** — 3378
119:174 I long for your salvation, O **L,** — 3378
120: 1 I call on **the L** in my distress, — 3378
120: 2 O **L,** from lying lips and — 3378
121: 2 My help comes from **the L,** — 3378
121: 5 **The L** watches over you— — 3378
121: 5 **the L** is your shade at your right hand; — 3378
121: 7 **The L** will keep you from all harm— — 3378
121: 8 **the L** will watch over your coming — 3378
122: 1 "Let us go to the house of **the L.**" — 3378
122: 4 where the tribes go up, the tribes of **the L,** — 3363
122: 4 to praise the name of **the L** according to — 3378
122: 9 the sake of the house of **the L** our God, — 3378
123: 2 so our eyes look to **the L** our God, — 3378
123: 3 Have mercy on us, O **L,** — 3378
124: 1 If **the L** had not been on our side— — 3378
124: 2 if **the L** had not been on our side — 3378
124: 6 Praise be to **the L,** — 3378
124: 8 Our help is in the name of **the L,** — 3378
125: 1 who trust in **the L** are like Mount Zion, — 3378
125: 2 so **the L** surrounds his people both now — 3378
125: 4 Do good, O **L,** to those who are good, — 3378
125: 5 to crooked ways **the L** will banish with — 3378
126: 1 **the L** brought back the captives to Zion, — 3378
126: 2 "**The L** has done great things for them." — 3378
126: 3 **The L** has done great things for us, — 3378
126: 4 Restore our fortunes, O **L,** — 3378
127: 1 Unless **the L** builds the house, — 3378
127: 1 Unless **the L** watches over the city, — 3378
127: 3 Sons are a heritage from **the L,** — 3378
128: 1 Blessed are all who fear **the L,** — 3378
128: 4 Thus is the man blessed who fears **the L.** — 3378
128: 5 May **the L** bless you from Zion all — 3378
129: 4 But **the L** is righteous; — 3378
129: 8 "The blessing of **the L** be upon you; — 3378
129: 8 we bless you in the name of **the L.**" — 3378
130: 1 Out of the depths I cry to you, O **L;** — 3378
130: 3 If you, O **L,** kept a record of sins, — 3363
130: 5 I wait for **the L,** my soul waits, — 3378
130: 7 O Israel, put your hope in **the L,** — 3378
130: 7 for with **the L** is unfailing love and — 3378

†LORD distinguishes the proper name of God, *Yahweh*, indicated in the NIV by "LORD," from the words translated "Lord" and "lord," indexed under the heading ***LORD,** pages 683-86.

Ref	Text	No.
Ps 131: 1	My heart is not proud, O L,	3378
131: 3	O Israel, put your hope in the L	3378
132: 1	O L, remember David and all	3378
132: 2	He swore an oath to the L and made	3378
132: 5	till I find a place for the L,	3378
132: 8	O L, and come to your resting place,	3378
132:11	The L swore an oath to David,	3378
132:13	For there the L has chosen Zion,	3378
133: 3	For there the L bestows his blessing,	3378
134: 1	Praise the L, all you servants of	3378
134: 1	all you servants of the L who minister	3378
134: 1	by night in the house of the L.	3378
134: 2	in the sanctuary and praise the L.	3378
134: 3	May the L, the Maker of heaven	3378
135: 1	Praise the L.	3363
135: 1	Praise the name of the L;	3378
135: 1	praise him, you servants of the L,	3378
135: 2	you who minister in the house of the L,	3378
135: 3	Praise the L, for the LORD is good;	3363
135: 3	Praise the LORD, for the L is good;	3378
135: 4	For the L has chosen Jacob to be his own,	3363
135: 5	I know that the L is great,	3378
135: 6	The L does whatever pleases him,	3378
135:13	Your name, O L, endures forever,	3378
135:13	endures forever, your renown, O L,	3378
135:14	For the L will vindicate his people	3378
135:19	O house of Israel, praise the L;	3378
135:19	O house of Aaron, praise the L;	3378
135:20	O house of Levi, praise the L;	3378
135:20	you who fear him, praise the L.	3378
135:21	Praise be to the L from Zion,	3378
135:21	Praise the L.	3363
136: 1	Give thanks to the L, for he is good.	3378
137: 4	How can we sing the songs of the L while	3378
137: 7	O L, what the Edomites did on	3378
138: 1	I will praise you, O L, with all my heart;	NIH
138: 4	the earth praise you, O L, when they hear	3378
138: 5	May they sing of the ways of the L,	3378
138: 5	for the glory of the L is great.	3378
138: 6	Though the L is on high,	3378
138: 8	The L will fulfill [his purpose] for me;	3378
138: 8	your love, O L, endures forever—	3378
139: 1	O L, you have searched me	3378
139: 4	on my tongue you know it completely, O L.	3378
139:21	Do I not hate those who hate you, O L,	3378
140: 1	Rescue me, O L, from evil men;	3378
140: 4	O L, from the hands of the wicked;	3378
140: 6	O L, I say to you,	3378
140: 6	Hear, O L, my cry for mercy.	3378
140: 7	O Sovereign L, my strong deliverer,	3378
140: 8	not grant the wicked their desires, O L;	3378
140:12	that the L secures justice for the poor	3378
141: 1	O L, I call to you; come quickly to me.	3378
141: 3	Set a guard over my mouth, O L;	3378
141: 8	my eyes are fixed on you, O Sovereign L;	3378
142: 1	I cry aloud to the L;	3378
142: 1	I lift up my voice to the L for mercy.	3378
142: 5	I cry to you, O L;	3378
143: 1	O L, hear my prayer,	3378
143: 7	Answer me quickly, O L; my spirit fails.	3378
143: 9	Rescue me from my enemies, O L,	3378
143:11	your name's sake, O L, preserve my life;	3378
144: 1	Praise be to the L my Rock,	3378
144: 3	O L, what is man that you care for him,	3378
144: 5	Part your heavens, O L, and come down;	3378
144:15	the people whose God is the L.	3378
145: 3	Great is the L and most worthy of praise;	3378
145: 8	The L is gracious and compassionate,	3378
145: 9	The L is good to all;	3378
145:10	All you have made will praise you, O L;	3378
145:13	The L is faithful to all his promises	3378
145:14	The L upholds all those who fall and lifts	3378
145:17	The L is righteous in all his ways	3378
145:18	The L is near to all who call on him,	3378
145:20	The L watches over all who love him,	3378
145:21	My mouth will speak in praise of the L.	3378
146: 1	Praise the L.	3363
146: 1	Praise the L, O my soul.	3378
146: 2	I will praise the L all my life;	3378
146: 5	whose hope is in the L his God,	3378
146: 6	the L, who remains faithful forever.	NIH
146: 7	The L sets prisoners free,	3378
146: 8	the L gives sight to the blind,	3378
146: 8	the L lifts up those who are bowed down,	3378
146: 8	the L loves the righteous.	3378
146: 9	The L watches over the alien and sustains	3378
146:10	The L reigns forever, your God, O Zion,	3378
146:10	Praise the L.	3363
147: 1	Praise the L.	3363
147: 2	The L builds up Jerusalem;	3378
147: 6	The L sustains the humble but casts	3378
147: 7	Sing to the L with thanksgiving;	3378
147:11	the L delights in those who fear him,	3378
147:12	Extol the L, O Jerusalem;	3378
147:20	Praise the L.	3363
148: 1	Praise the L.	3363
148: 1	Praise the L from the heavens,	3378
148: 5	Let them praise the name of the L,	3378
148: 7	Praise the L from the earth,	3378
148:13	Let them praise the name of the L,	3378
148:14	Praise the L.	3363
149: 1	Praise the L.	3363
149: 1	Sing to the L a new song,	3378
149: 4	For the L takes delight in his people;	3378
149: 9	Praise the L.	3363
150: 1	Praise the L.	3363
150: 6	Let everything that has breath praise the L.	3363
Ps 150: 6	Praise the L.	3363
Pr 1: 7	fear of the L is the beginning of knowledge,	3378
1:29	and did not choose to fear the L,	3378
2: 5	then you will understand the fear of the L	3378
2: 6	For the L gives wisdom,	3378
3: 5	Trust in the L with all your heart and lean	3378
3: 7	fear the L and shun evil.	3378
3: 9	Honor the L with your wealth,	3378
3:12	because the L disciplines those he loves,	3378
3:19	By wisdom the L laid the earth's foundations,	3378
3:26	for the L will be your confidence	3378
3:32	for the L detests a perverse man but takes	3378
5:21	a man's ways are in full view of the L,	3378
6:16	There are six things the L hates,	3378
8:13	To fear the L is to hate evil;	3378
8:22	"The L brought me forth as the first	3378
8:35	and receives favor from the L.	3378
9:10	fear of the L is the beginning of wisdom,	3378
10: 3	The L does not let the righteous go hungry	3378
10:22	The blessing of the L brings wealth,	3378
10:27	The fear of the L adds length to life,	3378
10:29	way of the L is a refuge for the righteous,	3378
11: 1	The L abhors dishonest scales,	3378
11:20	The L detests men of perverse heart	3378
12: 2	A good man obtains favor from the L,	3378
12: 2	but the L condemns a crafty man.	NIH
12:22	The L detests lying lips,	3378
14: 2	He whose walk is upright fears the L,	3378
14:16	A wise man fears the L and shuns evil,	NIH
14:26	He who fears the L has a secure fortress,	3378
14:27	The fear of the L is a fountain of life,	3378
15: 3	The eyes of the L are everywhere,	3378
15: 8	The L detests the sacrifice of the wicked,	3378
15: 9	The L detests the way of the wicked	3378
15:11	and Destruction lie open before the L—	3378
15:16	Better a little with the fear of the L than	3378
15:25	The L tears down the proud man's house	3378
15:26	The L detests the thoughts of the wicked,	3378
15:29	The L is far from the wicked but he hears	3378
15:33	The fear of the L teaches a man wisdom,	3378
16: 1	from the L comes the reply of the tongue.	3378
16: 2	but motives are weighed by the L.	3378
16: 3	Commit to the L whatever you do,	3378
16: 4	The L works out everything for his own ends—	3378
16: 5	The L detests all the proud of heart.	3378
16: 6	the fear of the L a man avoids evil.	3378
16: 7	a man's ways are pleasing to the L,	3378
16: 9	but the L determines his steps.	3378
16:11	and balances are from the L;	3378
16:20	and blessed is he who trusts in the L.	3378
16:33	but its every decision is from the L.	3378
17: 3	but the L tests the heart.	3378
17:15	the L detests them both.	3378
18:10	The name of the L is a strong tower;	3378
18:22	and receives favor from the L.	3378
19: 3	yet his heart rages against the L.	3378
19:14	but a prudent wife is from the L.	3378
19:17	He who is kind to the poor lends to the L,	3378
19:23	The fear of the L leads to life:	3378
20:10	the L detests them both.	3378
20:12	the L has made them both.	3378
20:22	Wait for the L, and he will deliver you.	3378
20:23	The L detests differing weights,	3378
20:24	A man's steps are directed by the L.	3378
20:27	The lamp of the L searches the spirit of	3378
21: 1	The king's heart is in the hand of the L;	3378
21: 2	but the L weighs the heart.	3378
21: 3	to the L than sacrifice.	3378
21:30	no plan that can succeed against the L.	3378
21:31	but victory rests with the L.	3378
22: 2	The L is the Maker of them all.	3378
22: 4	of the L bring wealth and honor and life.	3378
22:12	of the L keep watch over knowledge,	3378
22:19	So that your trust may be in the L,	3378
22:23	for the L will take up their case	3378
23:17	always be zealous for the fear of the L.	3378
24:18	or the L will see and disapprove	3378
24:21	Fear the L and the king, my son,	3378
25:22	and the L will reward you.	3378
28: 5	those who seek the L understand it fully.	3378
28:14	the man who always fears the L,	NIH
28:25	but he who trusts in the L will prosper.	3378
29:13	The L gives sight to the eyes of both.	3378
29:25	but whoever trusts in the L is kept safe.	3378
29:26	but it is from the L that man gets justice.	3378
30: 7	"Two things I ask of you, O L;	NIH
30: 9	and say, 'Who is the L?'	3378
31:30	a woman who fears the L is to be praised.	3378
Isa 1: 2	For the L has spoken:	3378
1: 4	They have forsaken the L;	3378
1: 9	the L Almighty had left us some survivors,	3378
1:10	Hear the word of the L,	3378
1:11	what are they to me?" says the L.	3378
1:18	let us reason together," says the L.	3378
1:20	For the mouth of the L has spoken.	3378
1:24	Therefore the Lord, the L Almighty,	3378
1:28	and those who forsake the L will perish.	3378
2: 3	let us go up to the mountain of the L,	3378
2: 3	the word of the L from Jerusalem.	3378
2: 5	let us walk in the light of the L.	3378
2:10	of the L and the splendor of his majesty!	3378
2:11	the L alone will be exalted in that day.	3378
2:12	The L Almighty has a day in store for all	3378
2:17	the L alone will be exalted in that day,	3378
2:19	to holes in the ground from dread of the L	3378
Isa 2:21	of the L and the splendor of his majesty,	3378
3: 1	See now, the Lord, the L Almighty,	3378
3: 8	their words and deeds are against the L,	3378
3:13	The L takes his place in court;	3378
3:14	The L enters into judgment against	3378
3:15	declares the Lord, the L Almighty.	3378
3:16	The L says, "The women of Zion	3378
3:17	the L will make their scalps bald."	3378
4: 2	of the L will be beautiful and glorious,	3378
4: 5	Then the L will create over all of Mount	3378
5: 7	of the L Almighty is the house of Israel,	3378
5: 9	The L Almighty has declared	3378
5:12	for the deeds of the L,	3378
5:16	But the L Almighty will be exalted	3378
5:24	of the L Almighty and spurned the word	3378
6: 3	"Holy, holy, holy is the L Almighty;	3378
6: 5	the King, the L Almighty."	3378
6:12	until the L has sent everyone far away	3378
7: 3	Then the L said to Isaiah, "Go out,	3378
7: 7	Yet this is what the Sovereign L says:	3378
7:10	Again the L spoke to Ahaz,	3378
7:11	"Ask the L your God for a sign,	3378
7:12	I will not put the L to the test."	3378
7:17	The L will bring on you and	3378
7:18	that day the L will whistle for flies from	3378
8: 1	The L said to me,	3378
8: 3	And the L said to me,	3378
8: 5	The L spoke to me again:	3378
8:11	The L spoke to me with his strong hand	3378
8:13	The L Almighty is the one you are	3378
8:17	I will wait for the L,	3378
8:18	and the children the L has given me.	3378
8:18	in Israel from the L Almighty,	3378
9: 7	of the L Almighty will accomplish this.	3378
9:11	But the L has strengthened Rezin's foes	3378
9:13	nor have they sought the L Almighty.	3378
9:14	So the L will cut off from Israel	3378
9:19	the wrath of the L Almighty the land will	3378
10:16	Therefore, the Lord, the L Almighty,	3378
10:20	down but will truly rely on the L,	3378
10:23	The Lord, the L Almighty,	3378
10:24	this is what the Lord, the L Almighty,	3378
10:26	The L Almighty will lash them with	3378
10:33	See, the Lord, the L Almighty,	3378
11: 2	The Spirit of the L will rest on him—	3378
11: 2	of knowledge and of the fear of the L—	3378
11: 3	and he will delight in the fear of the L.	3378
11: 9	of the L as the waters cover the sea.	3378
11:15	The L will dry up the gulf of the Egyptian	3378
12: 1	"I will praise you, O L.	3378
12: 2	The L, the LORD, is my strength	3363
12: 2	the L, is my strength and my song;	3378
12: 4	"Give thanks to the L, call on his name;	3378
12: 5	to the L, for he has done glorious things;	3378
13: 4	The L Almighty is mustering an army	3378
13: 5	the L and the weapons of his wrath—	3378
13: 6	Wail, for the day of the L is near;	3378
13: 9	See, the day of the L is coming—	3378
13:13	at the wrath of the L Almighty,	3378
14: 1	The L will have compassion on Jacob;	3378
14: 3	On the day the L gives you relief	3378
14: 5	The L has broken the rod of the wicked,	3378
14:22	declares the L Almighty.	3378
14:22	and descendants," declares the L.	3378
14:23	declares the L Almighty.	3378
14:24	The L Almighty has sworn, "Surely,	3378
14:27	For the L Almighty has purposed,	3378
14:32	"The L has established Zion,	3378
16:13	This is the word the L has already spoken	3378
16:14	But now the L says:	3378
17: 3	declares the L Almighty.	3378
17: 6	declares the L, the God of Israel.	3378
18: 4	This is what the L says to me:	3378
18: 7	to the L Almighty from a people tall	3378
18: 7	the place of the Name of the L Almighty.	3378
19: 1	the L rides on a swift cloud and is coming	3378
19: 4	declares the Lord, the L Almighty.	3378
19:12	make known what the L Almighty has planned	3378
19:14	The L has poured into them a spirit	3378
19:16	that the L Almighty raises against them.	3378
19:17	of what the L Almighty is planning	3378
19:18	and swear allegiance to the L Almighty.	3378
19:19	be an altar to the L in the heart of Egypt,	3378
19:19	and a monument to the L at its border.	3378
19:20	and witness to the L Almighty in the land	3378
19:20	to the L because of their oppressors,	3378
19:21	So the L will make himself known to	3378
19:21	in that day they will acknowledge the L.	3378
19:21	they will make vows to the L	3378
19:22	The L will strike Egypt with a plague;	3378
19:22	They will turn to the L,	3378
19:25	The L Almighty will bless them, saying,	3378
20: 2	that time the L spoke through Isaiah son	3378
20: 3	Then the L said,	3378
21:10	from the L Almighty,	3378
21:17	The L, the God of Israel, has spoken.	3378
22: 5	The Lord, the L Almighty,	3378
22:12	The Lord, the L Almighty,	3378
22:14	The L Almighty has revealed this	3378
22:14	says the Lord, the L Almighty.	3378
22:15	This is what the Lord, the L Almighty,	3378
22:17	the L is about to take firm hold of you	3378
22:25	"In that day," declares the L Almighty,	3378
22:25	The L has spoken.	3378
23: 9	The L Almighty planned it,	3378
23:11	The L has stretched out his hand over	3378

Ref	Text	Num
Isa 23:17	**the L** will deal with Tyre.	3378
23:18	her earnings will be set apart for **the L**;	3378
23:18	to those who live before **the L**,	3378
24: 1	**the L** is going to lay waste the earth	3378
24: 3	**The L** has spoken this word.	3378
24:15	Therefore in the east give glory to **the L**;	3378
24:15	exalt the name of **the L**,	3378
24:21	In that day **the L** will punish the powers	3378
24:23	for **the L** Almighty will reign	3378
25: 1	O **L**, you are my God;	3378
25: 6	On this mountain **the L** Almighty will prepare a feast	3378
25: 8	**The Sovereign L** will wipe away the tears	3378
25: 8	**The L** has spoken.	3378
25: 9	This is **the L**, we trusted in him;	3378
25:10	of **the L** will rest on this mountain;	3378
26: 4	Trust in **the L** forever, for **the L**,	3378
26: 4	Trust in the LORD forever, for **the L**,	3363
26: 4	is the Rock eternal.	3378
26: 8	Yes, **L**, walking in the way of your laws,	3378
26:10	and regard not the majesty of **the L**.	3378
26:11	O **L**, your hand is lifted high,	3378
26:12	**L**, you establish peace for us;	3378
26:13	O **L**, our God, other lords besides you have ruled over us,	3378
26:15	You have enlarged the nation, O **L**;	3378
26:16	**L**, they came to you in their distress;	3378
26:17	so were we in your presence, O **L**.	3378
26:21	**the L** is coming out of his dwelling	3378
27: 1	**the L** will punish with his sword,	3378
27: 3	I, **the L**, watch over it;	3378
27: 7	Has [the **L**] struck her as he struck	NIH
27:12	In that day **the L** will thresh from	3378
27:13	in Egypt will come and worship **the L** on	3378
28: 5	In that day **the L** Almighty will be	3378
28:13	the word of **the L** to them will become:	3378
28:14	Therefore hear the word of **the L**,	3378
28:16	So this is what **the Sovereign L** says:	3378
28:21	**The L** will rise up as he did	3378
28:22	the Lord, **the L** Almighty,	3378
28:29	All this also comes from **the L** Almighty,	3378
29: 6	**the L** Almighty will come with thunder	3378
29:10	**The L** has brought over you a deep sleep:	3378
29:15	to hide their plans from **the L**,	3378
29:19	the humble will rejoice in **the L**;	3378
29:22	Therefore this is what **the L**,	3378
30: 1	to the obstinate children," declares **the L**,	3378
30:15	This is what **the Sovereign L**,	3378
30:18	Yet **the L** longs to be gracious to you;	3378
30:18	For **the L** is a God of justice.	3378
30:26	when **the L** binds up the bruises	3378
30:27	See, the Name of **the L** comes from afar,	3378
30:29	up with flutes to the mountain of **the L**,	3378
30:30	**The L** will cause men to hear his	3378
30:31	The voice of **the L** will shatter Assyria;	3378
30:32	Every stroke **the L** lays on them	3378
30:33	the breath of **the L**, like a stream of burning	3378
31: 1	or seek help from **the L**.	3378
31: 3	When **the L** stretches out his hand,	3378
31: 4	This is what **the L** says to me:	3378
31: 4	so **the L** Almighty will come down	3378
31: 5	**the L** Almighty will shield Jerusalem;	3378
31: 9	declares **the L**, whose fire is in Zion,	3378
32: 6	and spreads error concerning **the L**;	3378
33: 2	O **L**, be gracious to us; we long for you.	3378
33: 5	**The L** is exalted, for he dwells on high;	3378
33: 6	fear of **the L** is the key to this treasure.	3378
33:10	"Now I will arise," says **the L**.	3378
33:21	There **the L** will be our Mighty One.	3378
33:22	For **the L** is our judge,	3378
33:22	**the L** is our lawgiver,	3378
33:22	**the L** is our king;	3378
34: 2	**The L** is angry with all nations,	3378
34: 6	The sword of **the L** is bathed in blood,	3378
34: 6	For **the L** has a sacrifice in Bozrah and	3378
34: 8	For **the L** has a day of vengeance,	3378
34:16	Look in the scroll of **the L** and read:	3378
35: 2	they will see the glory of **the L**,	3378
35:10	and the ransomed of **the L** will return.	3378
36: 7	"We are depending on **the L** our God"—	3378
36:10	and destroy this land without **the L**?	3378
36:10	**The L** himself told me to march	3378
36:15	in **the L** when he says, 'The LORD will	3378
36:15	'**The L** will surely deliver us;	3378
36:18	'**The L** will deliver us.'	3378
36:20	How then can **the L** deliver Jerusalem	3378
37: 1	and went into the temple of **the L**.	3378
37: 4	that **the L** your God will hear the words	3378
37: 4	for the words **the L** your God has heard.	3378
37: 6	'This is what **the L** says:	3378
37:14	up to the temple of **the L** and spread it out	3378
37:14	and spread it out before **the L**.	3378
37:15	And Hezekiah prayed to **the L**:	3378
37:16	"O **L** Almighty, God of Israel, enthroned	3378
37:17	Give ear, O **L**, and hear;	3378
37:17	open your eyes, O **L**, and see;	3378
37:18	"It is true, O **L**, that the Assyrian kings	3378
37:20	Now, O **L** our God, deliver us	3378
37:20	on earth may know that you alone, O **L**,	3378
37:21	"This is what **the L**, the God of Israel,	3378
37:22	the word **the L** has spoken against him:	3378
37:32	zeal of **the L** Almighty will accomplish this.	3378
37:33	"Therefore this is what **the L** says	3378
37:34	he will not enter this city," declares **the L**.	3378
37:36	Then the angel of **the L** went out and put	3378
38: 1	"This is what **the L** says:	3378
38: 2	to the wall and prayed to **the L**,	3378

Ref	Text	Num
Isa 38: 3	"Remember, O **L**, how I have walked	3378
38: 4	Then the word of **the L** came to Isaiah:	3378
38: 5	'This is what **the L**,	3378
38: 7	that **the L** will do what he has promised:	3378
38:11	I said, "I will not again see **the L**,	3363
38:11	"I will not again see the LORD, **the L**,	3363
38:20	**The L** will save me,	3378
38:20	of our lives in the temple of **the L**.	3378
38:22	that I will go up to the temple of **the L**?"	3378
39: 5	"Hear the word of **the L** Almighty:	3378
39: 6	Nothing will be left, says **the L**.	3378
39: 8	of **the L** you have spoken is good,"	3378
40: 3	"In the desert prepare the way for **the L**;	3378
40: 5	And the glory of **the L** will be revealed,	3378
40: 5	For the mouth of **the L** has spoken."	3378
40: 7	the breath of **the L** blows on them.	3378
40:10	See, **the Sovereign L** comes with power,	3378
40:13	Who has understood the mind of **the L**,	3378
40:14	**the L** consult to enlighten him,	NIH
40:27	O Israel, "My way is hidden from **the L**;	3378
40:28	**The L** is the everlasting God,	3378
40:31	in **the L** will renew their strength.	3378
41: 4	from the beginning? I, **the L**—	3378
41:13	For I am **the L**, your God,	3378
41:14	declares **the L**, your Redeemer,	3378
41:16	But you will rejoice in **the L** and glory in	3378
41:17	But I **the L** will answer them;	3378
41:20	that the hand of **the L** has done this,	3378
41:21	"Present your case," says **the L**.	3378
42: 5	This is what God **the L** says—	3378
42: 6	**the L**, have called you in righteousness;	3378
42: 8	"I am **the L**; that is my name!	3378
42:10	Sing to **the L** a new song,	3378
42:12	to **the L** and proclaim his praise in	3378
42:13	**The L** will march out like a mighty man,	3378
42:19	blind like the servant of **the L**?	3378
42:21	It pleased **the L** for the sake	3378
42:24	Was it not **the L**,	3378
43: 1	But now, this is what **the L** says—	3378
43: 3	For I am **the L**, your God,	3378
43:10	"You are my witnesses," declares **the L**,	3378
43:11	I, even I, am **the L**,	3378
43:12	You are my witnesses," declares **the L**,	3378
43:14	This is what **the L** says—	3378
43:15	I am **the L**, your Holy One,	3378
43:16	This is what **the L** says—	3378
44: 2	This is what **the L** says—	3378
44: 5	One will say, 'I belong to **the L**';	3378
44: 6	"This is what **the L** says—	3378
44: 6	and Redeemer, **the L** Almighty:	3378
44:23	O heavens, for **the L** has done this;	3378
44:23	for **the L** has redeemed Jacob,	3378
44:24	"This is what **the L** says—	3378
44:24	I am **the L**, who has made all things,	3378
45: 1	"This is what **the L** says to his anointed,	3378
45: 3	so that you may know that I am **the L**,	3378
45: 5	I am **the L**, and there is no other;	3378
45: 6	I am **the L**, and there is no other.	3378
45: 7	I, **the L**, do all these things.	3378
45: 8	I, **the L**, have created it.	3378
45:11	"This is what **the L** says—	3378
45:13	says **the L** Almighty."	3378
45:14	This is what **the L** says:	3378
45:17	by **the L** with an everlasting salvation;	3378
45:18	For this is what **the L** says—	3378
45:18	"I am **the L**, and there is no other.	3378
45:19	I, **the L**, speak the truth;	3378
45:21	Was it not I, **the L**?	3378
45:24	'In **the L** alone are righteousness	3378
45:25	in **the L** all the descendants of Israel will	3378
47: 4	**the L** Almighty is his name—	3378
48: 1	in the name of **the L** and invoke the God	3378
48: 2	**the L** Almighty is his name:	3378
48:16	And now **the Sovereign L** has sent me,	3378
48:17	This is what **the L** says—	3378
48:17	"I am **the L** your God,	3378
48:20	"**The L** has redeemed his servant Jacob."	3378
48:22	"There is no peace," says **the L**, "for the wicked."	3378
49: 1	Before I was born **the L** called me;	3378
49: 5	And now **the L** says—	3378
49: 5	for I am honored in the eyes of **the L**	3378
49: 7	This is what **the L** says—	3378
49: 7	because of **the L**, who is faithful,	3378
49: 8	This is what **the L** says:	3378
49:13	For **the L** comforts his people	NIH
49:14	But Zion said, "**The L** has forsaken me,	3378
49:18	As surely as I live," declares **the L**,	3378
49:22	This is what **the Sovereign L** says:	3378
49:23	Then you will know that I am **the L**;	3378
49:25	But this is what **the L** says:	3378
49:26	Then all mankind will know that I, **the L**,	3378
50: 1	This is what **the L** says:	3378
50: 4	**The Sovereign L** has given me	3378
50: 5	**The Sovereign L** has opened my ears,	3378
50: 7	Because **the Sovereign L** helps me,	3378
50: 9	It is **the Sovereign L** who helps me.	3378
50:10	Who among you fears **the L** and obeys	3378
50:10	in the name of **the L** and rely on his God.	3378
51: 1	and who seek **the L**:	3378
51: 3	**The L** will surely comfort Zion	3378
51: 3	her wastelands like the garden of **the L**.	3378
51: 9	O arm of **the L**;	3378
51:11	The ransomed of **the L** will return.	3378
51:13	that you forget **the L** your Maker,	3378
51:15	For I am **the L** your God,	3378
51:15	**the L** Almighty is his name.	3378

Ref	Text	Num
Isa 51:17	the hand of **the L** the cup of his wrath,	3378
51:20	with the wrath of **the L** and the rebuke	3378
51:22	This is what your Sovereign **L** says.	3378
52: 3	For this is what **the L** says:	3378
52: 4	For this is what **the Sovereign L** says:	3378
52: 5	what do I have here?" declares **the L**.	3378
52: 5	and those who rule them mock," declares **the L**.	3378
52: 8	When **the L** returns to Zion,	3378
52: 9	for **the L** has comforted his people,	3378
52:10	**The L** will lay bare his holy arm in	3378
52:11	you who carry the vessels of **the L**.	3378
52:12	for **the L** will go before you,	3378
53: 1	the arm of **the L** been revealed?	3378
53: 6	and **the L** has laid on him the iniquity	3378
53:10	**the L** makes his life a guilt offering,	NIH
53:10	the will of **the L** will prosper in his hand.	3378
54: 1	of her who has a husband," says **the L**.	3378
54: 5	**the L** Almighty is his name—	3378
54: 6	**The L** will call you back as if you were	3378
54: 8	says **the L** your Redeemer.	3378
54:10	says **the L**, who has compassion on you.	3378
54:13	All your sons will be taught by **the L**,	3378
54:17	the heritage of the servants of **the L**,	3378
54:17	vindication from me," declares **the L**.	3378
55: 5	because of **the L** your God,	3378
55: 6	Seek **the L** while he may be found;	3378
55: 7	Let him turn to **the L**,	3378
55: 8	neither are your ways my ways," declares **the L**.	3378
56: 1	This is what **the L** says:	3378
56: 3	who has bound himself to **the L** say,	3378
56: 3	"**The L** will surely exclude me	3378
56: 4	For this is what **the L** says:	3378
56: 6	to **the L** to serve him, to love the name of	3378
56: 6	to love the name of **the L**,	3378
56: 8	**The Sovereign L** declares—	3378
57:19	peace, to those far and near," says **the L**.	3378
58: 5	a day acceptable to **the L**?	3378
58: 8	the glory of **the L** will be your rear guard.	3378
58: 9	Then you will call, and **the L** will answer;	3378
58:11	**The L** will guide you always;	3378
58:14	then you will find your joy in **the L**,	3378
58:14	The mouth of **the L** has spoken.	3378
59: 1	the arm of **the L** is not too short to save,	3378
59:13	rebellion and treachery against **the L**,	3378
59:15	**The L** looked and was displeased	3378
59:19	men will fear the name of **the L**,	3378
59:19	that the breath of **the L** drives along.	3378
59:20	who repent of their sins," declares **the L**.	3378
59:21	my covenant with them," says **the L**.	3378
59:21	this time on and forever," says **the L**.	3378
60: 1	and the glory of **the L** rises upon you.	3378
60: 2	but **the L** rises upon you	3378
60: 6	and proclaiming the praise of **the L**.	3378
60: 9	to the honor of **the L** your God,	3378
60:14	and will call you the City of **the L**,	3378
60:16	Then you will know that I, **the L**,	3378
60:19	for **the L** will be your everlasting light,	3378
60:19	**the L** will be your everlasting light,	3378
60:22	I am **the L**;	3378
61: 1	The Spirit of **the Sovereign L** is on me,	3378
61: 1	because **the L** has anointed me	3378
61: 3	of **the L** for the display of his splendor.	3378
61: 6	And you will be called priests of **the L**,	3378
61: 8	"For I, **the L**, love justice;	3378
61: 9	that they are a people **the L** has blessed."	3378
61:10	I delight greatly in **the L**;	3378
61:11	so **the Sovereign L** will make righteousness	3378
62: 2	that the mouth of **the L** will bestow.	3378
62: 4	for **the L** will take delight in you.	3378
62: 6	You who call on **the L**,	3378
62: 8	**The L** has sworn by his right hand and	3378
62: 9	will eat it and praise **the L**,	3378
62:11	**The L** has made proclamation to the ends	3378
62:12	the Redeemed of **the L**;	3378
63: 7	I will tell of the kindnesses of **the L**,	3378
63: 7	according to all **the L** has done for us—	3378
63:14	by the Spirit of **the L**.	3378
63:16	you, O **L**, are our Father,	3378
63:17	O **L**, do you make us wander	3378
64: 8	Yet, O **L**, you are our Father.	3378
64: 9	Do not be angry beyond measure, O **L**;	3378
64:12	After all this, O **L**,	3378
65: 7	and the sins of your fathers," says **the L**.	3378
65: 8	This is what **the L** says:	3378
65:11	"But as for you who forsake **the L**	3378
65:13	Therefore this is what **the Sovereign L** says:	3378
65:13	**the Sovereign L** will put you to death,	3378
65:23	they will be a people blessed by **the L**,	3378
65:25	on all my holy mountain," says **the L**.	3378
66: 1	This is what **the L** says:	3378
66: 2	so they came into being?" declares **the L**.	3378
66: 5	Hear the word of **the L**,	3378
66: 5	have said, 'Let **the L** be glorified,	3378
66: 6	**the L** repaying his enemies all they deserve.	3378
66: 9	and not give delivery?" says **the L**.	3378
66:12	For this is what **the L** says:	3378
66:14	the hand of **the L** will be made known	3378
66:15	See, **the L** is coming with fire,	3378
66:16	with his sword **the L** will execute judgment	3378
66:17	meet their end together," declares **the L**.	3378
66:20	in Jerusalem as an offering to **the L**—	3378
66:20	and on mules and camels," says **the L**.	3378
66:20	of **the L** in ceremonially clean vessels.	3378
66:21	to be priests and Levites," says **the L**.	3378

Isa	66:22	declares the L, "so will your name	3378
	66:23	and bow down before me," says the L.	3378
Jer	1: 2	The word of the L came to him in	3378
	1: 4	The word of the L came to me, saying,	3378
	1: 6	"Ah, Sovereign L," I said,	3378
	1: 7	But the L said to me, "Do not say,	3378
	1: 8	and will rescue you," declares the L.	3378
	1: 9	Then the L reached out his hand	3378
	1:11	The word of the L came to me:	3378
	1:12	The L said to me,	3378
	1:13	The word of the L came to me again:	3378
	1:14	The L said to me,	3378
	1:15	the northern kingdoms," declares the L.	3378
	1:19	and will rescue you," declares the L.	3378
	2: 1	The word of the L came to me:	3378
	2: 3	Israel was holy to the L,	3378
	2: 3	disaster overtook them,' " declares the L.	3378
	2: 4	Hear the word of the L,	3378
	2: 5	This is what the L says:	3378
	2: 6	They did not ask, 'Where is the L,	3378
	2: 8	priests did not ask, 'Where is the L?'	3378
	2: 9	against you again," declares the L.	3378
	2:12	with great horror," declares the L.	3378
	2:17	by forsaking the L your God	3378
	2:19	for you when you forsake the L your God	3378
	2:19	declares the Lord, the L Almighty.	3378
	2:22	declares the Sovereign L.	3378
	2:29	against me," declares the L.	3378
	2:31	consider the word of the L:	3378
	2:37	for the L has rejected those you trust;	3378
	3: 1	you now return to me?" declares the L.	3378
	3: 6	the L said to me,	3378
	3:10	but only in pretense," declares the L.	3378
	3:11	The L said to me,	3378
	3:12	" 'Return, faithless Israel,' declares the L,	3378
	3:12	for I am merciful,' declares the L,	3378
	3:13	against the L your God,	3378
	3:13	not obeyed me,' " declares the L.	3378
	3:14	"Return, faithless people," declares the L,	3378
	3:16	declares the L, "men will no longer say,	3378
	3:16	'The ark of the covenant of the L.'	3378
	3:17	will call Jerusalem The Throne of the L,	3378
	3:17	in Jerusalem to honor the name of the L.	3378
	3:20	O house of Israel," declares the L.	3378
	3:21	and have forgotten the L their God.	3378
	3:22	for you are the L our God.	3378
	3:23	in the L our God is the salvation of Israel.	3378
	3:25	We have sinned against the L our God,	3378
	3:25	not obeyed the L our God."	3378
	4: 1	O Israel, return to me," declares the L.	3378
	4: 2	'As surely as the L lives,'	3378
	4: 3	This is what the L says to the men	3378
	4: 4	Circumcise yourselves to the L,	3378
	4: 8	of the L has not turned away from us.	3378
	4: 9	"In that day," declares the L,	3378
	4:10	Then I said, "Ah, Sovereign L,	3378
	4:17	against me,' " declares the L.	3378
	4:26	all its towns lay in ruins before the L,	3378
	4:27	This is what the L says:	3378
	5: 2	'As surely as the L lives,'	3378
	5: 3	O L, do not your eyes look for truth?	3378
	5: 4	for they do not know the way of the L,	3378
	5: 5	surely they know the way of the L,	3378
	5: 9	punish them for this?" declares the L.	3378
	5:10	for these people do not belong to the L.	3378
	5:11	to me," declares the L.	3378
	5:11	They have lied about the L;	3378
	5:14	this is what the L God Almighty says:	3378
	5:15	O house of Israel," declares the L,	3378
	5:18	"Yet even in those days," declares the L,	3378
	5:19	'Why has the L our God done all this	3378
	5:22	Should you not fear me?" declares the L.	3378
	5:24	'Let us fear the L our God,	3378
	5:29	punish them for this?" declares the L.	3378
	6: 6	This is what the L Almighty says:	3378
	6: 9	This is what the L Almighty says:	3378
	6:10	The word of the L is offensive to them;	3378
	6:11	But I am full of the wrath of the L,	3378
	6:12	who live in the land," declares the L.	3378
	6:15	down when I punish them," says the L.	3378
	6:16	This is what the L says:	3378
	6:21	Therefore this is what the L says:	3378
	6:22	This is what the L says:	3378
	6:30	because the L has rejected them."	3378
	7: 1	that came to Jeremiah from the L:	3378
	7: 2	" 'Hear the word of the L,	3378
	7: 2	through these gates to worship the L.	3378
	7: 3	This is what the L Almighty,	3378
	7: 4	"This is the temple of the L,	3378
	7: 4	the temple of the L,	3378
	7: 4	the temple of the L!"	3378
	7:11	I have been watching! declares the L.	3378
	7:13	declares the L, I spoke to you again	3378
	7:19	the one they are provoking? declares the L.	3378
	7:20	Therefore this is what the Sovereign L says:	3378
	7:21	" 'This is what the L Almighty,	3378
	7:28	not obeyed the L its God or responded	3378
	7:29	the barren heights, for the L has rejected	3378
	7:30	in my eyes, declares the L,	3378
	7:32	the days are coming, declares the L,	3378
	8: 1	" 'At that time, declares the L,	3378
	8: 3	declares the L Almighty.'	3378
	8: 4	"Say to them, 'This is what the L says:	3378
	8: 7	not know the requirements of the L.	3378
	8: 8	for we have the law of the L,"	3378
	8: 9	they have rejected the word of the L,	3378
	8:12	down when they are punished, says the L.	3378

Jer	8:13	" 'I will take away their harvest, declares		
		the L.		3378
	8:14	For the L our God has doomed us		3378
	8:17	and they will bite you," declares the L.		3378
	8:19	"Is the L not in Zion?		3378
	9: 3	not acknowledge me," declares the L.		3378
	9: 6	to acknowledge me," declares the L.		3378
	9: 7	Therefore this is what the L Almighty says:		3378
	9: 9	punish them for this?" declares the L.		3378
	9:12	Who has been instructed by the L		3378
	9:13	The L said, "It is because		3378
	9:15	Therefore, this is what the L Almighty,		3378
	9:17	This is what the L Almighty says:		3378
	9:20	Now, O women, hear the word of the L;		3378
	9:22	Say, "This is what the L declares:		3378
	9:23	This is what the L says:		3378
	9:24	that I am the L, who exercises kindness,		3378
	9:24	for in these I delight," declares the L.		3378
	9:25	"The days are coming," declares the L,		3378
	10: 1	Hear what the L says to you,		3378
	10: 2	This is what the L says:		3378
	10: 6	No one is like you, O L;		3378
	10:10	But the L is the true God;		3378
	10:16	the L Almighty is his name.		3378
	10:18	For this is what the L says:		3378
	10:21	and do not inquire of the L;		3378
	10:23	O L, that a man's life is not his own;		3378
	10:24	Correct me, L, but only with justice—		3378
	11: 1	that came to Jeremiah from the L:		3378
	11: 3	Tell them that this is what the L,		3378
	11: 5	I answered, "Amen, L."		3378
	11: 6	The L said to me,		3378
	11: 9	Then the L said to me,		3378
	11:11	Therefore this is what the L says:		3378
	11:16	called you a thriving olive tree		3378
	11:17	The L Almighty, who planted you,		3378
	11:18	Because the L revealed their plot to me,		3378
	11:20	O L Almighty, you who judge righteously		3378
	11:21	"Therefore this is what the L says about		3378
	11:21	of the L or you will die by our hands'—		3378
	11:22	therefore this is what the L Almighty says:		3378
	12: 1	You are always righteous, O L,		3378
	12: 3	Yet you know me, O L;		3378
	12:12	sword of the L will devour from one end of		3378
	12:14	This is what the L says:		3378
	12:16	saying, 'As surely as the L lives'—		3378
	12:17	and destroy it," declares the L.		3378
	13: 1	This is what the L said to me:		3378
	13: 2	So I bought a belt, as the L directed,		3378
	13: 3	word of the L came to me a second time:		3378
	13: 5	as the L told me.		3378
	13: 6	Many days later the L said to me,		3378
	13: 8	Then the word of the L came to me:		3378
	13: 9	"This is what the L says:		3378
	13:11	declares the L, 'to be my people for my		3378
	13:12	'This is what the L, the God of Israel,		3378
	13:13	then tell them, 'This is what the L says:		3378
	13:14	fathers and sons alike, declares the L.		3378
	13:15	do not be arrogant, for the L has spoken.		3378
	13:16	to the L your God before he brings		3378
	13:21	What will you say when [the L] sets		NIH
	13:25	I have decreed for you," declares the L,		3378
	14: 1	the word of the L to Jeremiah concerning		3378
	14: 7	Although our sins testify against us, O L,		3378
	14: 9	You are among us, O L,		3378
	14:10	This is what the L says about this people:		3378
	14:10	So the L does not accept them;		3378
	14:11	Then the L said to me,		3378
	14:13	But I said, "Ah, Sovereign L,		3378
	14:14	Then the L said to me,		3378
	14:15	this is what the L says about		3378
	14:20	O L, we acknowledge our wickedness		3378
	14:22	No, it is you, O L our God.		3378
	15: 1	Then the L said to me:		3378
	15: 2	tell them, 'This is what the L says:		3378
	15: 3	against them," declares the L, "the sword		3378
	15: 6	You have rejected me," declares the L.		3378
	15: 9	before their enemies," declares the L.		3378
	15:11	The L said, "Surely I will deliver you for		3378
	15:15	You understand, O L;		3378
	15:16	for I bear your name, O L God Almighty.		3378
	15:19	Therefore this is what the L says:		3378
	15:20	to rescue and save you," declares the L.		3378
	16: 1	Then the word of the L came to me:		3378
	16: 3	For this is what the L says about the sons		3378
	16: 5	For this is what the L says:		3378
	16: 5	from this people," declares the L.		3378
	16: 9	For this is what the L Almighty,		3378
	16:10	'Why has the L decreed such		3378
	16:10	against the L our God?'		3378
	16:11	declares the L, 'and followed other gods		3378
	16:14	the days are coming," declares the L,		3378
	16:14	'As surely as the L lives,		3378
	16:15	'As surely as the L lives,		3378
	16:16	declares the L, "and they will catch them.		3378
	16:19	O L, my strength and my fortress,		3378
	16:21	that my name is the L.		3378
	17: 5	This is what the L says:		3378
	17: 5	and whose heart turns away from the L.		3378
	17: 7	blessed is the man who trusts in the L,		3378
	17:10	"I the L search the heart and examine		3378
	17:13	O L, the hope of Israel,		3378
	17:13	because they have forsaken the L,		3378
	17:14	Heal me, O L, and I will be healed;		3378
	17:15	"Where is the word of the L?		3378
	17:19	This is what the L said to me:		3378
	17:20	Say to them, 'Hear the word of the L,		3378

Jer	17:21	This is what the L says:	3378
	17:24	declares the L, and bring no load through	3378
	17:26	and thank offerings to the house of the L.	3378
	18: 1	that came to Jeremiah from the L:	3378
	18: 5	Then the word of the L came to me:	3378
	18: 6	as this potter does?" declares the L.	3378
	18:11	'This is what the L says: Look!	3378
	18:13	Therefore this is what the L says:	3378
	18:19	Listen to me, O L;	3378
	18:23	you know, O L, all their plots to kill me.	3378
	19: 1	This is what the L says:	3378
	19: 3	'Hear the word of the L,	3378
	19: 3	This is what the L Almighty,	3378
	19: 6	the days are coming, declares the L,	3378
	19:11	'This is what the L Almighty says:	3378
	19:12	to those who live here, declares the L.	3378
	19:14	where the L had sent him to prophesy,	3378
	19:15	"This is what the L Almighty, the God	3378
	20: 1	the chief officer in the temple of the L,	3378
	20: 4	For this is what the L says:	3378
	20: 7	O L, you deceived me,	3378
	20: 8	the word of the L has brought me insult	3378
	20:11	the L is with me like a mighty warrior;	3378
	20:12	O L Almighty, you who examine	3378
	20:13	Sing to the L!	3378
	20:13	Give praise to the L!	3378
	20:16	the towns the L overthrew without pity.	3378
	21: 1	The word came to Jeremiah from the L	3378
	21: 2	"Inquire now of the L for us	3378
	21: 2	Perhaps the L will perform wonders	3378
	21: 4	'This is what the L, the God	3378
	21: 7	After that, declares the L,	3378
	21: 8	tell the people, 'This is what the L says:	3378
	21:10	and not good, declares the L.	3378
	21:11	'Hear the word of the L;	3378
	21:12	this is what the L says:	3378
	21:13	on the rocky plateau, declares the L—	3378
	21:14	as your deeds deserve, declares the L.	3378
	22: 1	This is what the L says:	3378
	22: 2	of the L, O king of Judah, you who sit	3378
	22: 3	This is what the L says:	3378
	22: 5	not obey these commands, declares the L,	3378
	22: 6	For this is what the L says about	3378
	22: 8	'Why has the L done such a thing	3378
	22: 9	of the L their God and have worshiped	3378
	22:11	For this is what the L says	3378
	22:16	what it means to know me?" declares the L.	3378
	22:18	Therefore this is what the L says	3378
	22:24	"As surely as I live," declares the L,	3378
	22:29	land, land, hear the word of the L!	3378
	22:30	This is what the L says:	3378
	23: 1	the sheep of my pasture!" declares the L.	3378
	23: 2	Therefore this is what the L,	3378
	23: 2	the evil you have done," declares the L.	3378
	23: 4	nor will any be missing," declares the L.	3378
	23: 5	"The days are coming," declares the L,	3378
	23: 6	The L Our Righteousness.	3378
	23: 7	the days are coming," declares the L,	3378
	23: 7	'As surely as the L lives,	3378
	23: 8	'As surely as the L lives,	3378
	23: 9	because of the L and his holy words.	3378
	23:11	in my temple I find their wickedness,"	3378
		declares the L.	3378
	23:12	the year they are punished," declares the L.	3378
	23:15	this is what the L Almighty says	3378
	23:16	This is what the L Almighty says:	3378
	23:16	not from the mouth of the L.	3378
	23:17	'The L says: You will have peace.'	3378
	23:18	of them has stood in the council of the L	3378
	23:19	the storm of the L will burst out in wrath,	3378
	23:20	The anger of the L will not turn back	3378
	23:23	declares the L, "and not a God far away?	3378
	23:24	I fill heaven and earth?" declares the L.	3378
	23:24	I fill heaven and earth?" declares the L.	3378
	23:28	straw to do with grain?" declares the L.	3378
	23:29	"Is not my word like fire," declares the L,	3378
	23:30	"Therefore," declares the L,	3378
	23:31	Yes," declares the L,	3378
	23:31	and yet declare, 'The L declares.'	NIH
	23:32	against those who prophesy false dreams,"	
		declares the L.	3378
	23:32	in the least," declares the L.	3378
	23:33	ask you, 'What is the oracle of the L?'	3378
	23:33	I will forsake you, declares the L.'	3378
	23:34	'This is the oracle of the L,'	3378
	23:35	or 'What has the L spoken?'	3378
	23:36	not mention 'the oracle of the L' again,	3378
	23:36	the L Almighty, our God.	3378
	23:37	or 'What has the L spoken?'	3378
	23:38	'This is the oracle of the L,'	3378
	23:38	this is what the L says:	3378
	23:38	This is the oracle of the L,'	3378
	23:38	This is the oracle of the L,'	3378
	24: 1	the L showed me two baskets	3378
	24: 1	in front of the temple of the L.	3378
	24: 3	Then the L asked me, "What do you see,	3378
	24: 4	Then the word of the L came to me:	3378
	24: 5	"This is what the L, the God	3378
	24: 7	a heart to know me, that I am the L.	3378
	24: 8	so bad they cannot be eaten,' says the L,	3378
	25: 3	the word of the L has come to me	3378
	25: 4	And though the L has sent all his servants	3378
	25: 5	and you can stay in the land the L gave	3378
	25: 7	you did not listen to me," declares the L.	3378
	25: 8	Therefore the L Almighty says this:	3378
	25: 9	declares the L, "and I will bring them	3378
	25:12	for their guilt," declares the L,	3378

†LORD distinguishes the proper name of God, *Yahweh*, indicated in the NIV by "Lord," from the words translated "Lord" and "lord," indexed under the heading *LORD, pages 683–86.

Ref	Text	Num
Jer 25:15	This is what **the L**, the God of Israel,	3378
25:27	tell them, 'This is what **the L** Almighty,	3378
25:28	'This is what **the L** Almighty says:	3378
25:29	who live on earth, declares **the L** Almighty.	3378
25:30	" '**The L** will roar from on high;	3378
25:31	for **the L** will bring charges against	3378
25:31	to the sword,' " declares **the L**.	3378
25:32	This is what **the L** Almighty says: "Look!	3378
25:33	At that time those slain by **the L** will	3378
25:36	for **the L** is destroying their pasture.	3378
25:37	because of the fierce anger of **the L**.	3378
26: 1	this word came from **the L**:	3378
26: 2	"This is what **the L** says:	3378
26: 2	to worship in the house of **the L**.	3378
26: 4	Say to them, 'This is what **the L** says:	3378
26: 7	these words in the house of **the L**.	3378
26: 8	everything **the L** had commanded him	3378
26: 9	around Jeremiah in the house of **the L**.	3378
26:10	to the house of **the L** and took their places	3378
26:12	"**The L** sent me to prophesy	3378
26:13	and obey **the L** your God.	3378
26:13	Then **the L** will relent and not bring	3378
26:15	for in truth **the L** has sent me to you	3378
26:16	to us in the name of **the L** our God."	3378
26:18	'This is what **the L** Almighty says:	3378
26:19	Did not Hezekiah fear **the L**	3378
26:19	And did not **the L** relent,	3378
26:20	prophesied in the name of **the L**;	3378
27: 1	this word came to Jeremiah from **the L**:	3378
27: 2	This is what **the L** said to me:	3378
27: 4	'This is what **the L** Almighty,	3378
27: 8	famine and plague, declares **the L**,	3378
27:11	till it and to live there, declares **the L**." ' "	3378
27:13	with which **the L** has threatened any nation	3378
27:15	'I have not sent them,' declares **the L**.	3378
27:16	"This is what **the L** says:	3378
27:18	and have the word of **the L**,	3378
27:18	let them plead with **the L** Almighty that	3378
27:18	in the house of **the L** and in the palace of	3378
27:19	For this is what **the L** Almighty says	3378
27:21	this is what **the L** Almighty,	3378
27:21	in the house of **the L** and in the palace of	3378
27:22	the day I come for them,' declares **the L**.	3378
28: 1	in the house of **the L** in the presence of	3378
28: 2	"This is what **the L** Almighty, the God	3378
28: 4	declares **the L**, 'for I will break the yoke	3378
28: 5	in the house of **the L**.	3378
28: 6	May **the L** do so!	3378
28: 6	May **the L** fulfill the words	3378
28: 9	as one truly sent by **the L** only	3378
28:11	"This is what **the L** says:	3378
28:12	the word of **the L** came to Jeremiah:	3378
28:13	'This is what **the L** says:	3378
28:14	This is what **the L** Almighty,	3378
28:15	**The L** has not sent you,	3378
28:16	Therefore, this is what **the L** says:	3378
28:16	have preached rebellion against **the L**.' "	3378
29: 4	This is what **the L** Almighty, the God	3378
29: 7	Pray to **the L** for it, because if it prospers,	3378
29: 8	Yes, this is what **the L** Almighty,	3378
29: 9	I have not sent them," declares **the L**.	3378
29:10	This is what **the L** says:	3378
29:11	declares **the L**, "plans to prosper you and	3378
29:14	I will be found by you," declares **the L**,	3378
29:14	declares **the L**, "and will bring you back	3378
29:15	"**The L** has raised up prophets for us	3378
29:16	but this is what **the L** says about	3378
29:17	this is what **the L** Almighty says:	3378
29:19	not listened to my words," declares **the L**,	3378
29:19	not listened either," declares **the L**.	3378
29:20	Therefore, hear the word of **the L**,	3378
29:21	This is what **the L** Almighty,	3378
29:22	'**The L** treat you like Zedekiah and Ahab,	3378
29:23	and am a witness to it," declares **the L**.	3378
29:25	"This is what **the L** Almighty, the God	3378
29:26	'**The L** has appointed you priest in place	3378
29:26	to be in charge of the house of **the L**;	3378
29:30	Then the word of **the L** came to Jeremiah:	3378
29:31	'This is what **the L** says about Shemaiah	3378
29:32	this is what **the L** says:	3378
29:32	for my people, declares **the L**,	3378
30: 1	that came to Jeremiah from **the L**:	3378
30: 2	"This is what **the L**, the God	3378
30: 3	The days are coming,' declares **the L**,	3378
30: 3	to possess,' says **the L**."	3378
30: 4	the words **the L** spoke concerning Israel	3378
30: 5	"This is what **the L** says:	3378
30: 8	" 'In that day,' declares **the L** Almighty,	3378
30: 9	they will serve **the L** their God	3378
30:10	O Israel,' declares **the L**.	3378
30:11	and will save you," declares **the L**.	3378
30:12	"This is what **the L** says:	3378
30:17	and heal your wounds," declares **the L**,	3378
30:18	"This is what **the L** says:	3378
30:21	to be close to me?" declares **the L**.	3378
30:23	the storm of **the L** will burst out in wrath,	3378
30:24	The fierce anger of **the L** will	3378
31: 1	"At that time," declares **the L**,	3378
31: 2	This is what **the L** says:	3378
31: 3	**The L** appeared to us in the past, saying:	3378
31: 6	let us go up to Zion, to **the L** our God.' "	3378
31: 7	This is what **the L** says:	3378
31: 7	Make your praises heard, and say, 'O **L**,	3378
31:10	"Hear the word of **the L**, O nations;	3378
31:11	For **the L** will ransom Jacob	3378
31:12	they will rejoice in the bounty of **the L**—	3378
31:14	be filled with my bounty," declares **the L**.	3378

Ref	Text	Num
Jer 31:15	This is what **the L** says:	3378
31:16	This is what **the L** says:	3378
31:16	work will be rewarded," declares **the L**.	3378
31:17	for your future," declares **the L**.	3378
31:18	because you are **the L** my God.	3378
31:20	great compassion for him," declares **the L**.	3378
31:22	**The L** will create a new thing on earth—	3378
31:23	This is what **the L** Almighty,	3378
31:23	'**The L** bless you, O righteous dwelling,	3378
31:27	"The days are coming," declares **the L**,	3378
31:28	to build and to plant," declares **the L**.	3378
31:31	"The time is coming," declares **the L**,	3378
31:32	a husband to them," declares **the L**.	3378
31:33	of Israel after that time," declares **the L**.	3378
31:34	saying, 'Know **the L**,'	3378
31:34	of them to the greatest," declares **the L**.	3378
31:35	This is what **the L** says,	3378
31:35	**the L** Almighty is his name:	3378
31:36	from my sight," declares **the L**, "will	3378
31:37	This is what **the L** says:	3378
31:37	of all they have done," declares **the L**.	3378
31:38	"The days are coming," declares **the L**,	3378
31:40	will be holy to **the L**.	3378
32: 1	to Jeremiah from **the L** in the tenth year	3378
32: 3	You say, 'This is what **the L** says:	3378
32: 5	until I deal with him, declares **the L**.	3378
32: 6	"The word of **the L** came to me:	3378
32: 8	"Then, just as **the L** had said,	3378
32: 8	"I knew that this was the word of **the L**;	3378
32:14	'This is what **the L** Almighty, the God	3378
32:15	For this is what **the L** Almighty,	3378
32:16	I prayed to **the L**:	3378
32:17	Sovereign **L**, you have made the heavens	3378
32:18	whose name is **the L** Almighty,	3378
32:25	you, O Sovereign **L**, say to me,	3378
32:26	Then the word of **the L** came to Jeremiah:	3378
32:27	"I am **the L**, the God of all mankind.	3378
32:28	Therefore, this is what **the L** says:	3378
32:30	what their hands have made, declares **the L**.	3378
32:36	but this is what **the L**, the God of Israel,	3378
32:42	"This is what **the L** says:	3378
32:44	because I will restore their fortunes,	
	declares **the L**."	3378
33: 1	word of **the L** came to him a second time:	3378
33: 2	"This is what **the L** says, he who made	3378
33: 2	**the L** who formed it and established it—	3378
33: 2	**the L** is his name:	3378
33: 4	For this is what **the L**, the God of Israel,	3378
33:10	"This is what **the L** says:	3378
33:11	the house of **the L**, saying, "Give thanks	3378
33:11	saying, "Give thanks to **the L** Almighty,	3378
33:11	for **the L** is good;	3378
33:11	the land as they were before,' says **the L**.	3378
33:12	"This is what **the L** Almighty says:	3378
33:13	of the one who counts them,' says **the L**.	3378
33:14	" 'The days are coming,' declares **the L**,	3378
33:16	**The L** Our Righteousness.'	3378
33:17	For this is what **the L** says:	3378
33:19	The word of **the L** came to Jeremiah:	3378
33:20	"This is what **the L** says:	3378
33:23	The word of **the L** came to Jeremiah:	3378
33:24	'**The L** has rejected the two kingdoms	3378
33:25	This is what **the L** says:	3378
34: 1	this word came to Jeremiah from **the L**:	3378
34: 2	"This is what **the L**, the God	3378
34: 2	'This is what **the L** says:	3378
34: 4	" 'Yet hear the promise of **L**,	3378
34: 4	This is what **the L** says concerning you:	3378
34: 5	I myself make this promise, declares **the L**.	3378
34: 8	from **the L** after King Zedekiah had made	3378
34:13	Then the word of **the L** came to Jeremiah:	3378
34:13	"This is what **the L**, the God	3378
34:17	"Therefore, this is what **the L** says:	3378
34:17	'freedom' for you, declares **the L**—	3378
34:22	declares **the L**, and I will bring them back	3378
35: 1	that came to Jeremiah from **the L** during	3378
35: 2	of the house of **the L** and give them wine	3378
35: 4	I brought them into the house of **the L**,	3378
35:12	word of **the L** came to Jeremiah, saying:	3378
35:13	"This is what **the L** Almighty, the God	3378
35:13	and obey my words?' declares **the L**.	3378
35:17	this is what **the L** God Almighty,	3378
35:18	"This is what **the L** Almighty,	3378
35:19	Therefore, this is what **the L** Almighty,	3378
36: 1	this word came to Jeremiah from **the L**:	3378
36: 4	the words **the L** had spoken to him,	3378
36: 6	So you go to the house of **the L** on a day	3378
36: 6	of **the L** that you wrote as I dictated.	3378
36: 6	before **the L**, and each will turn	3378
36: 7	against this people by **the L** are great."	3378
36: 8	the words of **the L** from the scroll.	3378
36: 9	of fasting before **the L** was proclaimed	3378
36:11	the words of **the L** from the scroll,	3378
36:26	But **the L** had hidden them.	3378
36:27	the word of **the L** came to Jeremiah:	3378
36:29	'This is what **the L** says:	3378
36:30	this is what **the L** says	3378
37: 2	to the words **the L** had spoken	3378
37: 3	"Please pray to **the L** our God for us."	3378
37: 6	Then the word of **the L** came to Jeremiah	3378
37: 7	"This is what **the L**, the God	3378
37: 9	"This is what **the L** says:	3378
37:17	"Is there any word from **the L**?"	3378
38: 2	"This is what **the L** says:	3378
38: 3	And this is what **the L** says:	3378
38:14	the third entrance to the temple of **the L**.	3378
38:16	"As surely as **the L** lives,	3378

Ref	Text	Num
Jer 38:17	"This is what **the L** God Almighty,	3378
38:20	"Obey **the L** by doing what I tell you.	3378
38:21	this is what **the L** has revealed to me:	3378
39:15	the word of **the L** came to him:	3378
39:16	'This is what **the L** Almighty,	3378
39:17	on that day, declares **the L**;	3378
39:18	because you trust in me, declares **the L**.' "	3378
40: 1	The word came to Jeremiah from **the L**	3378
40: 2	"**The L** your God decreed this disaster	3378
40: 3	And now **the L** has brought it about;	3378
40: 3	because you people sinned against **the L**	3378
41: 5	with them to the house of **the L**.	3378
42: 2	to **the L** your God for this entire remnant.	3378
42: 3	Pray that **the L** your God will tell us	3378
42: 4	to **the L** your God as you have requested;	3378
42: 4	I will tell you everything **the L** says	3378
42: 5	"May **the L** be a true and faithful witness	3378
42: 5	with everything **the L** your God sends you	3378
42: 6	we will obey **the L** our God,	3378
42: 6	for we will obey **the L** our God."	3378
42: 7	Ten days later the word of **the L** came	3378
42: 9	He said to them, "This is what **the L**,	3378
42:11	Do not be afraid of him, declares **the L**,	3378
42:13	and so disobey **the L** your God,	3378
42:15	then hear the word of **the L**.	3378
42:15	This is what **the L** Almighty, the God of	3378
42:18	This is what **the L** Almighty, the God of	3378
42:19	"O remnant of Judah, **the L** has told you,	3378
42:20	when you sent me to **the L** your God	3378
42:20	'Pray to **the L** our God for us;	3378
42:21	not obeyed **the L** your God	3378
43: 1	the words of **the L** their God—	3378
43: 1	everything **the L** had sent him	3378
43: 2	**The L** our God has not sent you to say,	3378
43: 7	in disobedience to **the L** and went as far	3378
43: 8	In Tahpanhes the word of **the L** came	3378
43:10	'This is what **the L** Almighty, the God of	3378
44: 2	"This is what **the L** Almighty, the God of	3378
44: 7	"Now this is what **the L** God Almighty,	3378
44:11	"Therefore, this is what **the L** Almighty,	3378
44:16	spoken to us in the name of **the L**!	3378
44:21	"Did not **the L** remember and think about	3378
44:22	**the L** could no longer endure your wicked	
	actions	3378
44:23	and have sinned against **the L** and have	3378
44:24	"Hear the word of **the L**,	3378
44:25	This is what **the L** Almighty, the God of	3378
44:26	But hear the word of **the L**,	3378
44:26	'I swear by my great name,' says **the L**,	3378
44:26	"As surely as the Sovereign **L** lives."	3378
44:29	declares **the L**, 'so that you will know	3378
44:30	This is what **the L** says:	3378
45: 2	"This is what **the L**, the God	3378
45: 3	**The L** has added sorrow to my pain;	3378
45: 3	[**The L** said,] "Say this to him:	NIH
45: 4	'This is what **the L** says:	3378
45: 5	on all people, declares **the L**,	3378
46: 1	the word of **the L** that came to Jeremiah	3378
46: 5	on every side," declares **the L**.	3378
46:10	to the Lord, **the L** Almighty—	3378
46:10	For the Lord, **the L** Almighty,	3378
46:13	the message **the L** spoke to Jeremiah	3378
46:15	for **the L** will push them down.	3378
46:18	whose name is **the L** Almighty,	3378
46:23	declares **the L**, "dense though it be.	3378
46:25	**The L** Almighty, the God of Israel, says:	3378
46:26	as in times past," declares **the L**.	3378
46:28	for I am with you," declares **the L**.	3378
47: 1	the word of **the L** that came to Jeremiah	3378
47: 2	This is what **the L** says:	3378
47: 4	**The L** is about to destroy the Philistines,	3378
47: 6	" 'Ah, sword of **the L**,'	3378
47: 7	can it rest when **the L** has commanded it,	3378
48: 1	This is what **the L** Almighty,	3378
48: 8	because **the L** has spoken.	3378
48:12	But days are coming," declares **the L**,	3378
48:15	whose name is **the L** Almighty.	3378
48:25	her arm is broken," declares **the L**.	3378
48:26	for she has defied **the L**.	3378
48:30	but it is futile," declares **the L**,	3378
48:35	to their gods," declares **the L**.	3378
48:38	a jar that no one wants," declares **the L**.	3378
48:40	This is what **the L** says: "Look!	3378
48:42	as a nation because she defied **the L**.	3378
48:43	O people of Moab," declares **the L**.	3378
48:44	of her punishment," declares **the L**.	3378
48:47	of Moab in days to come," declares **the L**.	3378
49: 1	This is what **the L** says:	3378
49: 2	But the days are coming," declares **the L**,	3378
49: 2	Then Israel will drive out those who drove	
	her out," says **the L**.	3378
49: 5	declares the Lord, **the L** Almighty.	3378
49: 6	of the Ammonites," declares **the L**.	3378
49: 7	This is what **the L** Almighty says:	3378
49:12	This is what **the L** says:	3378
49:13	I swear by myself," declares **the L**,	3378
49:14	I have heard a message from **the L**:	3378
49:16	I will bring you down," declares **the L**.	3378
49:18	says **the L**, "so no one will live there;	3378
49:20	hear what **the L** has planned	3378
49:26	silenced in that day," declares **the L**	
	Almighty.	3378
49:28	This is what **the L** says:	3378
49:30	you who live in Hazor," declares **the L**.	3378
49:31	declares **the L**, "a nation that has neither	3378
49:32	on them from every side," declares **the L**.	3378
49:34	the word of **the L** that came to Jeremiah	3378

†**LORD** distinguishes the proper name of God, *Yahweh*, indicated in the NIV by "Lord," from the words translated "Lord" and "lord," indexed under the heading ***LORD**, pages 683-86.

Jer	49:35	This is what **the L** Almighty says:	3378
	49:37	even my fierce anger," declares **the L.**	3378
	49:38	her king and officials," declares **the L.**	3378
	49:39	of Elam in days to come," declares **the L.**	3378
	50: 1	the word **the L** spoke through Jeremiah	3378
	50: 4	at that time," declares **the L,**	3378
	50: 4	in tears to seek **the L** their God.	3378
	50: 5	to **the L** in an everlasting covenant	3378
	50: 7	for they sinned against **the L,**	3378
	50: 7	**the L,** the hope of their fathers.'	3378
	50:10	all who plunder her will have their fill," declares **the L.**	3378
	50:14	for she has sinned against **the L.**	3378
	50:15	Since this is the vengeance of **the L,**	3378
	50:18	Therefore this is what **the L** Almighty,	3378
	50:20	at that time," declares **the L,**	3378
	50:21	completely destroy them," declares **the L.**	3378
	50:24	and captured because you opposed **the L.**	3378
	50:25	**The L** has opened his arsenal	3378
	50:25	for the Sovereign **L** Almighty has work	3378
	50:28	how **the L** our God has taken vengeance,	3378
	50:29	For she has defied **the L,**	3378
	50:30	be silenced in that day," declares **the L.**	3378
	50:31	**the L** Almighty, "for your day has come,	3378
	50:33	This is what **the L** Almighty says:	3378
	50:34	**the L** Almighty is his name.	3378
	50:35	against the Babylonians!" declares **the L—**	3378
	50:40	declares **the L,** "so no one will live there;	3378
	50:45	hear what **the L** has planned	3378
	51: 1	This is what **the L** says:	3378
	51: 5	**the L** Almighty, though their land is full	3378
	51:10	" '**The L** has vindicated us;	3378
	51:10	in Zion what **the L** our God has done.'	3378
	51:11	**The L** has stirred up the kings of	3378
	51:11	**The L** will take vengeance,	3378
	51:12	**The L** will carry out his purpose,	3378
	51:14	**The L** Almighty has sworn by himself:	3378
	51:19	**the L** Almighty is his name.	3378
	51:24	in Zion," declares **the L.**	3378
	51:25	the whole earth," declares **the L.**	3378
	51:26	be desolate forever," declares **the L.**	3378
	51:33	This is what **the L** Almighty,	3378
	51:36	Therefore, this is what **the L** says:	3378
	51:39	and not awake," declares **the L.**	3378
	51:45	Run from the fierce anger of **the L.**	3378
	51:48	out of the north destroyers will attack her," declares **the L.**	3378
	51:50	Remember **the L** in a distant land,	3378
	51:52	"But days are coming," declares **the L,**	3378
	51:53	send destroyers against her," declares **the L.**	3378
	51:55	**The L** will destroy Babylon;	3378
	51:56	For **the L** is a God of retribution;	3378
	51:57	whose name is **the L** Almighty.	3378
	51:58	This is what **the L** Almighty says:	3378
	51:62	Then say, 'O **L,** you have said you will destroy this place,	3378
	52: 2	He did evil in the eyes of **the L,**	3378
	52:13	He set fire to the temple of **the L,**	3378
	52:17	at the temple of **the L** and they carried all	3378
	52:20	for the temple of **the L,**	3378
La	1: 5	**The L** has brought her grief because	3378
	1: 9	"Look, O **L,** on my affliction,	3378
	1:11	"Look, O **L,** and consider,	3378
	1:12	that **the L** brought on me in the day	3378
	1:17	**The L** has decreed for Jacob	3378
	1:18	"**The L** is righteous,	3378
	1:20	"See, O **L,** how distressed I am!	3378
	2: 6	**The L** has made Zion forget her appointed feasts	3378
	2: 7	raised a shout in the house of **the L**	3378
	2: 8	**The L** determined to tear down the wall	3378
	2: 9	prophets no longer find visions from **the L.**	3378
	2:17	**The L** has done what he planned;	3378
	2:20	"Look, O **L,** and consider:	3378
	3:18	and all that I had hoped from **the L.**"	3378
	3:24	I say to myself, "**The L** is my portion;	3378
	3:25	**The L** is good to those whose hope is	3378
	3:26	to wait quietly for the salvation of **the L.**	3378
	3:28	for **the L** has laid it on him.	NIH
	3:40	and let us return to **the L.**	3378
	3:50	until **the L** looks down from heaven	3378
	3:55	I called on your name, O **L,**	3378
	3:59	You have seen, O **L,**	3378
	3:61	O **L,** you have heard their insults,	3378
	3:64	Pay them back what they deserve, O **L,**	3378
	3:66	from under the heavens of **the L.**	3378
	4:11	**The L** has given full vent to his wrath;	3378
	4:16	**The L** himself has scattered them;	3378+7156
	5: 1	O **L,** what has happened to us;	3378
	5:19	You, O **L,** reign forever;	3378
	5:21	Restore us to yourself, O **L,**	3378
Eze	1: 3	word of **the L** came to Ezekiel the priest,	3378
	1: 3	There the hand of **the L** was upon him.	3378
	1:28	of the likeness of the glory of **the L.**	3378
	2: 4	'This is what **the Sovereign L** says.'	3378
	3:11	'This is what **the Sovereign L** says.'	3378
	3:12	May the glory of **the L** be praised	3378
	3:14	with the strong hand of **the L** upon me.	3378
	3:16	of seven days the word of **the L** came	3378
	3:22	The hand of **the L** was upon me there,	3378
	3:23	the glory of **the L** was standing there,	3378
	3:27	'This is what **the Sovereign L** says.'	3378
	4:13	**The L** said, "In this way the people	3378
	4:14	Then I said, "Not so, Sovereign **L!**	3378
	5: 5	"This is what **the Sovereign L** says:	3378
	5: 7	Therefore this is what **the Sovereign L** says:	3378
	5: 8	Therefore this is what **the Sovereign L** says:	3378

Eze	5:11	declares **the Sovereign L,**	3378
	5:13	they will know that I **the L** have spoken	3378
	5:15	I **the L** have spoken."	3378
	5:17	I **the L** have spoken."	3378
	6: 1	The word of **the L** came to me:	3378
	6: 3	hear the word of **the Sovereign L.**	3378
	6: 3	This is what **the Sovereign L** says to	3378
	6: 7	and you will know that I am **the L.**	3378
	6:10	And they will know that I am **the L;**	3378
	6:11	" 'This is what **the Sovereign L** says:	3378
	6:13	And they will know that I am **the L,**	3378
	6:14	Then they will know that I am **the L.' "**	3378
	7: 1	The word of **the L** came to me:	3378
	7: 2	this is what **the Sovereign L** says to	3378
	7: 4	Then you will know that I am **the L.**	3378
	7: 5	"This is what **the Sovereign L** says:	3378
	7: 9	that it is I **the L** who strikes the blow.	3378
	7:27	Then they will know that I am **the L.**"	3378
	8: 1	of **the Sovereign L** came upon me there.	3378
	8:12	They say, '**The L** does not see us;	3378
	8:12	**the L** has forsaken the land.' "	3378
	8:14	to the north gate of the house of **the L,**	3378
	8:16	into the inner court of the house of **the L,**	3378
	8:16	the temple of **the L** and their faces toward	3378
	9: 3	Then **the L** called to the man clothed	NIH
	9: 8	crying out, "Ah, Sovereign **L!**	3378
	9: 9	They say, '**The L** has forsaken the land;	3378
	9: 9	**the L** does not see.'	3378
	10: 2	**The L** said to the man clothed in linen,	NIH
	10: 4	Then the glory of **the L** rose from above	3378
	10: 4	of the radiance of the glory of **the L.**	3378
	10: 6	When **the L** commanded the man	2257ˢ
	10:18	of **the L** departed from over the threshold	3378
	11: 1	of the house of **the L** that faces east.	3378
	11: 2	**The L** said to me, "Son of man,	NIH
	11: 5	Then the Spirit of **the L** came upon me,	3378
	11: 5	"This is what **the L** says:	3378
	11: 7	Therefore this is what **the Sovereign L** says:	3378
	11: 8	declares **the Sovereign L.**	3378
	11:10	Then you will know that I am **the L.**	3378
	11:12	And you will know that I am **the L,**	3378
	11:13	in a loud voice, "Ah, Sovereign **L!**	3378
	11:14	The word of **the L** came to me:	3378
	11:15	'They are far away from **the L;**	3378
	11:16	'This is what **the Sovereign L** says:	3378
	11:17	'This is what **the Sovereign L** says:	3378
	11:21	declares **the Sovereign L.**"	3378
	11:23	The glory of **the L** went up from within	3378
	11:25	exiles everything **the L** had shown me.	3378
	12: 1	The word of **the L** came to me:	3378
	12: 8	In the morning the word of **the L** came	3378
	12:10	'This is what **the Sovereign L** says:	3378
	12:15	"They will know that I am **the L,**	3378
	12:16	Then they will know that I am **the L.**"	3378
	12:17	The word of **the L** came to me:	3378
	12:19	'This is what **the Sovereign L** says:	3378
	12:20	Then you will know that I am **the L.'** "	3378
	12:21	The word of **the L** came to me:	3378
	12:23	'This is what **the Sovereign L** says:	3378
	12:25	But I **the L** will speak what I will,	3378
	12:25	declares **the Sovereign L.'** "	3378
	12:26	The word of **the L** came to me:	3378
	12:28	'This is what **the Sovereign L** says:	3378
	12:28	declares **the Sovereign L.'** "	3378
	13: 1	The word of **the L** came to me:	3378
	13: 2	'Hear the word of **the L!**	3378
	13: 3	This is what **the Sovereign L** says:	3378
	13: 5	in the battle on the day of **the L.**	3378
	13: 6	They say, "**The L** declares,"	3378
	13: 6	when **the L** has not sent them;	3378
	13: 7	when you say, "**The L** declares,"	3378
	13: 8	Therefore this is what **the Sovereign L** says:	3378
	13: 8	declares **the Sovereign L.**	3378
	13: 9	you will know that I am **the Sovereign L.**	3378
	13:13	Therefore this is what **the Sovereign L** says:	3378
	13:14	and you will know that I am **the L.**	3378
	13:16	declares **the Sovereign L.**" '	3378
	13:18	'This is what **the Sovereign L** says:	3378
	13:20	Therefore this is what **the Sovereign L** says:	3378
	13:21	Then you will know that I am **the L.**	3378
	13:23	And then you will know that I am **the L.'** "	3378
	14: 2	Then the word of **the L** came to me:	3378
	14: 4	'This is what **the Sovereign L** says:	3378
	14: 4	I **the L** will answer him myself in keeping	3378
	14: 6	'This is what **the Sovereign L** says:	3378
	14: 7	I **the L** will answer him myself.	3378
	14: 8	Then you will know that I am **the L.**	3378
	14: 9	I **the L** have enticed that prophet,	3378
	14:11	declares **the Sovereign L.**" '	3378
	14:12	The word of **the L** came to me:	3378
	14:14	declares **the Sovereign L,**	3378
	14:16	declares **the Sovereign L,**	3378
	14:18	declares **the Sovereign L,**	3378
	14:20	declares **the Sovereign L,** even if Noah,	3378
	14:21	"For this is what **the Sovereign L** says:	3378
	14:23	declares **the Sovereign L.**"	3378
	15: 1	The word of **the L** came to me:	3378
	15: 6	Therefore this is what **the Sovereign L** says:	3378
	15: 7	you will know that I am **the L.**	3378
	15: 8	declares **the Sovereign L.**"	3378
	16: 1	The word of **the L** came to me:	3378
	16: 3	'This is what **the Sovereign L** says	3378
	16: 8	declares **the Sovereign L,**	3378
	16:14	declares **the Sovereign L.**	3378
	16:19	declares **the Sovereign L.**	3378
	16:23	Woe to you, declares **the Sovereign L,**	3378
	16:30	declares **the Sovereign L,**	3378

Eze	16:35	you prostitute, hear the word of **the L!**	3378
	16:36	This is what **the Sovereign L** says:	3378
	16:43	declares **the Sovereign L.**	3378
	16:48	surely as I live, declares **the Sovereign L,**	3378
	16:58	your detestable practices, declares **the L.**	3378
	16:59	" This is what **the Sovereign L** says:	3378
	16:62	and you will know that I am **the L.**	3378
	16:63	declares **the Sovereign L.'** "	3378
	17: 1	The word of **the L** came to me:	3378
	17: 3	'This is what **the Sovereign L** says:	3378
	17: 9	'This is what **the Sovereign L** says:	3378
	17:11	Then the word of **the L** came to me:	3378
	17:16	surely as I live, declares **the Sovereign L,**	3378
	17:19	Therefore this is what **the Sovereign L** says:	3378
	17:21	you will know that I **the L** have spoken.	3378
	17:22	" This is what **the Sovereign L** says:	3378
	17:24	of the field will know that I **the L** bring	3378
	17:24	" I **the L** have spoken, and I will do it. "	3378
	18: 1	The word of **the L** came to me:	3378
	18: 3	surely as I live, declares **the Sovereign L,**	3378
	18: 9	declares **the Sovereign L.**	3378
	18:23	declares **the Sovereign L.**	3378
	18:30	declares **the Sovereign L.**	3378
	18:32	declares **the Sovereign L.**	3378
	20: 1	of Israel came to inquire of **the L,**	3378
	20: 2	Then the word of **the L** came to me:	3378
	20: 3	'This is what **the Sovereign L** says:	3378
	20: 3	declares **the Sovereign L.'**	3378
	20: 5	'This is what **the Sovereign L** says:	3378
	20: 5	"I am **the L** your God."	3378
	20: 7	I am **the L** your God."	3378
	20:12	that I **the L** made them holy.	3378
	20:19	I am **the L** your God;	3378
	20:20	that I am **the L** your God."	3378
	20:26	so they would know that I am **the L.'**	3378
	20:27	'This is what **the Sovereign L** says:	3378
	20:30	'This is what **the Sovereign L** says:	3378
	20:31	surely as I live, declares **the Sovereign L,**	3378
	20:33	surely as I live, declares **the Sovereign L,**	3378
	20:36	declares **the Sovereign L.**	3378
	20:38	Then you will know that I am **the L.**	3378
	20:39	this is what **the Sovereign L** says:	3378
	20:40	declares **the Sovereign L.**	3378
	20:42	Then you will know that I am **the L,**	3378
	20:44	You will know that I am **the L,**	3378
	20:44	declares **the Sovereign L.'** "	3378
	20:45	The word of **the L** came to me:	3378
	20:47	'Hear the word of **the L.**	3378
	20:47	This is what **the Sovereign L** says:	3378
	20:48	that I **the L** have kindled it;	3378
	20:49	Then I said, "Ah, Sovereign **L!**	3378
	21: 1	The word of **the L** came to me:	3378
	21: 3	'This is what **the L** says:	3378
	21: 5	that I **the L** have drawn my sword	3378
	21: 7	declares **the Sovereign L.**"	3378
	21: 8	The word of **the L** came to me:	3378
	21:13	declares **the Sovereign L.'**	3378
	21:17	I **the L** have spoken."	3378
	21:18	The word of **the L** came to me:	3378
	21:24	Therefore this is what **the Sovereign L** says:	3378
	21:26	this is what **the Sovereign L** says:	3378
	21:28	'This is what **the Sovereign L** says about	3378
	21:32	for I **the L** have spoken.' "	3378
	22: 1	The word of **the L** came to me:	3378
	22: 3	'This is what **the Sovereign L** says:	3378
	22:12	declares **the Sovereign L.**	3378
	22:14	I **the L** have spoken, and I will do it.	3378
	22:16	you will know that I am **the L.'** "	3378
	22:17	Then the word of **the L** came to me:	3378
	22:19	Therefore this is what **the Sovereign L** says:	3378
	22:22	that I **the L** have poured out my wrath	3378
	22:23	Again the word of **the L** came to me:	3378
	22:28	'This is what **the Sovereign L** says'—	3378
	22:28	when **the L** has not spoken.	3378
	22:31	declares **the Sovereign L.**"	3378
	23: 1	The word of **the L** came to me:	3378
	23:22	this is what **the Sovereign L** says:	3378
	23:28	"For this is what **the Sovereign L** says:	3378
	23:32	"This is what **the Sovereign L** says:	3378
	23:34	I have spoken, declares **the Sovereign L.**	3378
	23:35	Therefore this is what **the Sovereign L** says:	3378
	23:36	**The L** said to me:	3378
	23:46	"This is what **the Sovereign L** says:	3378
	23:49	you will know that I am **the Sovereign L.**"	3378
	24: 1	the word of **the L** came to me:	3378
	24: 3	'This is what **the Sovereign L** says:	3378
	24: 6	" 'For this is what **the Sovereign L** says:	3378
	24: 9	Therefore this is what **the Sovereign L** says:	3378
	24:14	" 'I **the L** have spoken.	3378
	24:14	declares **the Sovereign L.'** "	3378
	24:15	The word of **the L** came to me:	3378
	24:20	"The word of **the L** came to me:	3378
	24:21	'This is what **the Sovereign L** says:	3378
	24:24	that I am **the Sovereign L.'**	3378
	24:27	and they will know that I am **the L.**"	3378
	25: 1	The word of **the L** came to me:	3378
	25: 3	'Hear the word of **the Sovereign L.**	3378
	25: 3	This is what **the Sovereign L** says:	3378
	25: 5	Then you will know that I am **the L.**	3378
	25: 6	For this is what **the Sovereign L** says:	3378
	25: 7	and you will know that I am **the L.'** "	3378
	25: 8	"This is what **the Sovereign L** says:	3378
	25:11	Then they will know that I am **the L.'** "	3378
	25:12	"This is what **the Sovereign L** says:	3378
	25:13	therefore this is what **the Sovereign L** says:	3378
	25:14	declares **the Sovereign L.'** "	3378
	25:15	"This is what **the Sovereign L** says:	3378

†LORD distinguishes the proper name of God, *Yahweh*, indicated in the NIV by "LORD," from the words translated "Lord" and "lord," indexed under the heading ***LORD**, pages 683-86.

Eze	25:16	therefore this is what **the** Sovereign **L** says:	3378
	25:17	Then they will know that I am **the L,**	3378
	26: 1	the word of **the L** came to me:	3378
	26: 3	therefore this is what **the** Sovereign **L** says:	3378
	26: 5	declares **the** Sovereign **L.**	3378
	26: 6	Then they will know that I am **the L.**	3378
	26: 7	"For this is what **the** Sovereign **L** says:	3378
	26:14	for I **the L** have spoken,	3378
	26:14	declares **the** Sovereign **L.**	3378
	26:15	"This is what **the** Sovereign **L** says	3378
	26:19	"This is what **the** Sovereign **L** says	3378
	26:21	declares **the** Sovereign **L.**"	3378
	27: 1	The word of **the L** came to me:	3378
	27: 3	'This is what **the** Sovereign **L** says:	3378
	28: 1	The word of **the L** came to me:	3378
	28: 2	'This is what **the** Sovereign **L** says:	3378
	28: 6	Therefore this is what **the** Sovereign **L** says:	3378
	28:10	declares **the** Sovereign **L.**' "	3378
	28:11	The word of **the L** came to me:	3378
	28:12	'This is what **the** Sovereign **L** says:	3378
	28:20	The word of **the L** came to me:	3378
	28:22	'This is what **the** Sovereign **L** says:	3378
	28:22	They will know that I am **the L,**	3378
	28:23	Then they will know that I am **the L.**	3378
	28:24	they will know that I am **the** Sovereign **L.**	3378
	28:25	" 'This is what **the** Sovereign **L** says:	3378
	28:26	they will know that I am **the L** their God.' "	3378
	29: 1	the word of **the L** came to me:	3378
	29: 3	'This is what **the** Sovereign **L** says:	3378
	29: 6	in Egypt will know that I am **the L.**	3378
	29: 8	Therefore this is what **the** Sovereign **L** says:	3378
	29: 9	They will know that I am **the L.**	3378
	29:13	" 'Yet this is what **the** Sovereign **L** says:	3378
	29:16	that I am **the** Sovereign **L.**' "	3378
	29:17	the word of **the L** came to me:	3378
	29:19	Therefore this is what **the** Sovereign **L** says:	3378
	29:20	declares **the** Sovereign **L.**	3378
	29:21	declares **the** Sovereign **L.**"	3378
	30: 1	The word of **the L** came to me:	3378
	30: 2	'This is what **the** Sovereign **L** says:	3378
	30: 3	the day is near, the day of **the L** is near—	3378
	30: 6	" 'This is what **the L** says:	3378
	30: 6	declares **the** Sovereign **L.**	3378
	30: 8	Then they will know that I am **the L,**	3378
	30:10	" 'This is what **the** Sovereign **L** says:	3378
	30:12	I **the L** have spoken.	3378
	30:13	" 'This is what **the** Sovereign **L** says:	3378
	30:19	and they will know that I am **the L.**' "	3378
	30:20	the word of **the L** came to me:	3378
	30:22	Therefore this is what **the** Sovereign **L** says:	3378
	30:25	Then they will know that I am **the L,**	3378
	30:26	Then they will know that I am **the L.**"	3378
	31: 1	the word of **the L** came to me:	3378
	31:10	Therefore this is what **the** Sovereign **L** says:	3378
	31:15	" 'This is what **the** Sovereign **L** says:	3378
	31:18	declares **the** Sovereign **L.**' "	3378
	32: 1	the word of **the L** came to me:	3378
	32: 3	" 'This is what **the** Sovereign **L** says:	3378
	32: 8	declares **the** Sovereign **L.**	3378
	32:11	" 'For this is what **the** Sovereign **L** says:	3378
	32:14	declares **the** Sovereign **L.**	3378
	32:15	then they will know that I am **the L.**'	3378
	32:16	declares **the** Sovereign **L.**"	3378
	32:17	the word of **the L** came to me:	3378
	32:31	declares **the** Sovereign **L.**	3378
	32:32	declares **the** Sovereign **L.**"	3378
	33: 1	The word of **the L** came to me:	3378
	33:11	declares **the** Sovereign **L,**	3378
	33:22	the hand of **the L** was upon me,	3378
	33:23	then the word of **the L** came to me:	3378
	33:25	'This is what **the** Sovereign **L** says:	3378
	33:27	'This is what **the** Sovereign **L** says:	3378
	33:29	Then they will know that I am **the L,**	3378
	33:30	the message that has come from **the L.**'	3378
	34: 1	The word of **the L** came to me:	3378
	34: 2	'This is what **the** Sovereign **L** says:	3378
	34: 7	you shepherds, hear the word of **the L:**	3378
	34: 8	declares **the** Sovereign **L,**	3378
	34: 9	O shepherds, hear the word of **the L:**	3378
	34:10	This is what **the** Sovereign **L** says:	3378
	34:11	" 'For this is what **the** Sovereign **L** says:	3378
	34:15	declares **the** Sovereign **L.**	3378
	34:17	this is what **the** Sovereign **L** says:	3378
	34:20	Therefore this is what **the** Sovereign **L** says	3378
	34:24	I **the L** will be their God,	3378
	34:24	I **the L** have spoken.	3378
	34:27	They will know that I am **the L,**	3378
	34:30	they will know that I, **the L** their God,	3378
	34:30	are my people, declares **the** Sovereign **L.**	3378
	34:31	declares **the** Sovereign **L.**' "	3378
	35: 1	The word of **the L** came to me:	3378
	35: 3	'This is what **the** Sovereign **L** says:	3378
	35: 4	Then you will know that I am **the L.**	3378
	35: 6	declares **the** Sovereign **L,**	3378
	35: 9	Then you will know that I am **the L.**	3378
	35:10	even though I **the L** was there,	3378
	35:11	declares **the** Sovereign **L,**	3378
	35:12	that I **the L** have heard all	3378
	35:14	This is what **the** Sovereign **L** says:	3378
	35:15	Then they will know that I am **the L.**' "	3378
	36: 1	hear the word of **the L.**	3378
	36: 2	This is what **the** Sovereign **L** says:	3378
	36: 3	'This is what **the** Sovereign **L** says:	3378
	36: 4	hear the word of **the** Sovereign **L:**	3378
	36: 4	This is what **the** Sovereign **L** says to	3378
	36: 5	this is what **the** Sovereign **L** says:	3378
	36: 6	This is what **the** Sovereign **L** says:	3378

Eze	36: 7	Therefore this is what **the** Sovereign **L** says:	3378
	36:11	Then you will know that I am **the L.**	3378
	36:13	" 'This is what **the** Sovereign **L** says:	3378
	36:14	declares **the** Sovereign **L.**	3378
	36:15	declares **the** Sovereign **L.**' "	3378
	36:16	Again the word of **the L** came to me:	3378
	36:22	'This is what **the** Sovereign **L** says:	3378
	36:23	the nations will know that I am **the L,**	3378
	36:23	declares **the** Sovereign **L,**	3378
	36:32	declares **the** Sovereign **L.**	3378
	36:33	" 'This is what **the** Sovereign **L** says:	3378
	36:36	I **the L** have rebuilt what was destroyed	3378
	36:36	I **the L** have spoken, and I will do it.'	3378
	36:37	"This is what **the** Sovereign **L** says:	3378
	36:38	Then they will know that I am **the L.**"	3378
	37: 1	The hand of **the L** was upon me,	3378
	37: 1	of **the L** and set me in the middle of	3378
	37: 3	I said, "O Sovereign **L,** you alone know."	3378
	37: 4	'Dry bones, hear the word of **the L!**	3378
	37: 5	This is what **the** Sovereign **L** says	3378
	37: 6	Then you will know that I am **the L.**' "	3378
	37: 9	'This is what **the** Sovereign **L** says:	3378
	37:12	'This is what **the** Sovereign **L** says:	3378
	37:13	my people, will know that I am **the L,**	3378
	37:14	you will know that I **the L** have spoken,	3378
	37:14	and I have done it, declares **the L.**' "	3378
	37:15	The word of **the L** came to me:	3378
	37:19	'This is what **the** Sovereign **L** says:	3378
	37:21	'This is what **the** Sovereign **L** says:	3378
	37:28	that I **the L** make Israel holy,	3378
	38: 1	The word of **the L** came to me:	3378
	38: 3	'This is what **the** Sovereign **L** says:	3378
	38:10	" 'This is what **the** Sovereign **L** says:	3378
	38:14	'This is what **the** Sovereign **L** says:	3378
	38:17	" 'This is what **the** Sovereign **L** says:	3378
	38:18	declares **the** Sovereign **L.**	3378
	38:21	declares **the** Sovereign **L.**	3378
	38:23	Then they will know that I am **the L.**'	3378
	39: 1	'This is what **the** Sovereign **L** says:	3378
	39: 5	declares **the** Sovereign **L.**	3378
	39: 6	and they will know that I am **the L.**	3378
	39: 7	and the nations will know that I **the L** am	3378
	39: 8	declares **the** Sovereign **L.**	3378
	39:10	declares **the** Sovereign **L.**	3378
	39:13	declares **the** Sovereign **L.**	3378
	39:17	this is what **the** Sovereign **L** says:	3378
	39:20	declares **the** Sovereign **L.**	3378
	39:22	that I am **the L** their God.	3378
	39:25	Therefore this is what **the** Sovereign **L** says:	3378
	39:28	they will know that I am **the L** their God,	3378
	39:29	declares **the** Sovereign **L.**"	3378
	40: 1	on that very day the hand of **the L** was	3378
	40:46	near to **the L** to minister before him."	3378
	41:22	"This is the table that is before **the L.**"	3378
	42:13	the priests who approach **the L** will eat	3378
	43: 4	The glory of **the L** entered the temple	3378
	43: 5	and the glory of **the L** filled the temple.	3378
	43:18	this is what **the** Sovereign **L** says:	3378
	43:19	declares **the** Sovereign **L.**	3378
	43:24	You are to offer them before **the L,**	3378
	43:24	as a burnt offering to **the L.**	3378
	43:27	declares **the** Sovereign **L.**"	3378
	44: 2	**The L** said to me,	3378
	44: 2	It is to remain shut because **the L,**	3378
	44: 3	to eat in the presence of **the L.**	3378
	44: 4	I looked and saw the glory of **the L** filling	3378
	44: 4	of the **LORD** filling the temple of **the L,**	3378
	44: 5	**The L** said to me, "Son of man,	3378
	44: 5	regulations regarding the temple of **the L.**	3378
	44: 6	'This is what **the** Sovereign **L** says:	3378
	44: 9	This is what **the** Sovereign **L** says:	3378
	44:12	declares **the** Sovereign **L.**	3378
	44:15	declares **the** Sovereign **L.**	3378
	44:27	declares **the** Sovereign **L.**	3378
	44:29	in Israel devoted to **the L** will belong	NIH
	45: 1	to present to **the L** a portion of the land as	3378
	45: 4	near to minister before **the L.**	3378
	45: 9	" 'This is what **the** Sovereign **L** says:	3378
	45: 9	declares **the** Sovereign **L.**	3378
	45:15	declares **the** Sovereign **L.**	3378
	45:18	" 'This is what **the** Sovereign **L** says:	3378
	45:23	as a burnt offering to **the L,**	3378
	46: 1	" 'This is what **the** Sovereign **L** says:	3378
	46: 3	in the presence of **the L** at the entrance to	3378
	46: 4	to **the L** on the Sabbath day is to	3378
	46: 9	the people of the land come before **the L**	3378
	46:12	a freewill offering to **the L**—	3378
	46:13	for a burnt offering to **the L,**	3378
	46:14	of this grain offering to **the L** is	3378
	46:16	" 'This is what **the** Sovereign **L** says:	3378
	47:13	This is what **the** Sovereign **L** says:	3378
	47:23	declares **the** Sovereign **L.**	3378
	48: 9	to offer to **the L** will be 25,000	3378
	48:10	of it will be the sanctuary of **the L.**	3378
	48:14	because it is holy to **the L.**	3378
	48:29	declares **the** Sovereign **L.**	3378
	48:35	THE **L** IS THERE."	3378
Da	9: 2	word of **the L** given to Jeremiah the prophet	3378
	9: 4	I prayed to **the L** my God and confessed:	3378
	9: 8	O **L,** we and our kings,	3378
	9:10	not obeyed **the L** our God	3378
	9:13	of **the L** our God by turning from our sins	3378
	9:14	**The L** did not hesitate to bring	3378
	9:14	for **the L** our God is righteous	3378
	9:20	and making my request to **the L** my God	3378
Hos	1: 1	The word of **the L** that came to Hosea son	3378
	1: 2	**the L** began to speak through Hosea,	3378

Hos	1: 2	**the L** said to him, "Go, take to yourself	3378
	1: 2	adultery in departing from **the L.**"	3378
	1: 4	Then **the L** said to Hosea	3378
	1: 6	Then **the L** said to Hosea,	NIH
	1: 7	but by **the L** their God."	3378
	1: 9	Then **the L** said, "Call him Lo-Ammi,	NIH
	2:13	but me she forgot," declares **the L.**	3378
	2:16	"In that day," declares **the L,**	3378
	2:20	and you will acknowledge **the L.**	3378
	2:21	that day I will respond," declares **the L**—	3378
	3: 1	**The L** said to me, "Go, show your love	3378
	3: 1	Love her as **the L** loves the Israelites,	3378
	3: 5	and seek **the L** their God	3378
	3: 5	They will come trembling to **the L** and	3378
	4: 1	Hear the word of **the L,** you Israelites,	3378
	4: 1	because **the L** has a charge to bring	3378
	4:10	because they have deserted **the L**	3378
	4:15	'As surely as **the L** lives!'	3378
	4:16	then can **the L** pasture them like lambs in	3378
	5: 4	they do not acknowledge **the L.**	3378
	5: 6	with their flocks and herds to seek **the L,**	3378
	5: 7	They are unfaithful to **the L;**	3378
	6: 1	"Come, let us return to **the L.**	3378
	6: 3	Let us acknowledge **the L;**	3378
	7:10	not return to **the L** his God or search	3378
	8: 1	An eagle is over the house of **the L**	3378
	8:13	but **the L** is not pleased with them.	3378
	9: 4	not pour out wine offerings to **the L,**	3378
	9: 4	it will not come into the temple of **the L.**	3378
	9: 5	on the festival days of **the L?**	3378
	9:14	Give them, O **L**—what will you give them?	3378
	10: 2	**The L** will demolish their altars	2085**S**
	10: 3	because we did not revere **the L.**	3378
	10:12	for it is time to seek **the L,**	3378
	11:10	They will follow **the L;**	3378
	11:11	settle them in their homes," declares **the L.**	3378
	12: 2	**The L** has a charge to bring	3378
	12: 5	**the L** God Almighty,	3378
	12: 5	**the L** is his name of renown!	3378
	12: 9	"I am **the L** your God,	3378
	12:13	**The L** used a prophet to bring Israel up	3378
	13: 4	"But I am **the L** your God,	3378
	13:15	An east wind from **the L** will come,	3378
	14: 1	Return, O Israel, to **the L** your God.	3378
	14: 2	Take words with you and return to **the L.**	3378
	14: 9	The ways of **the L** are right;	3378
Joel	1: 1	The word of **the L** that came to Joel son of	3378
	1: 9	from the house of **the L.**	3378
	1: 9	those who minister before **the L.**	3378
	1:14	the land to the house of **the L** your God,	3378
	1:14	and cry out to **the L.**	3378
	1:15	For the day of **the L** is near:	3378
	1:19	To you, O **L,** I call,	3378
	2: 1	for the day of **the L** is coming.	3378
	2:11	**The L** thunders at the head of his army;	3378
	2:11	The day of **the L** is great; it is dreadful.	3378
	2:12	"Even now," declares **the L,**	3378
	2:13	Return to **the L** your God,	3378
	2:14	and drink offerings for **the L** your God.	3378
	2:17	who minister before **the L,**	3378
	2:17	Let them say, "Spare your people, O **L.**	3378
	2:18	Then **the L** will be jealous for his land	3378
	2:19	**The L** will reply to them:	3378
	2:21	Surely **the L** has done great things.	3378
	2:23	rejoice in **the L** your God,	3378
	2:26	the name of **the L** your God,	3378
	2:27	that I am **the L** your God,	3378
	2:31	of the great and dreadful day of **the L.**	3378
	2:32	on the name of **the L** will be saved;	3378
	2:32	as what **the L** has said,	3378
	2:32	among the survivors whom **the L** calls.	3378
	3: 8	**The L** has spoken.	3378
	3:11	Bring down your warriors, O **L!**	3378
	3:14	of **the L** is near in the valley of decision.	3378
	3:16	**The L** will roar from Zion and thunder	3378
	3:16	But **the L** will be a refuge for his people,	3378
	3:17	you will know that I, **the L** your God,	3378
	3:21	**The L** dwells in Zion!	3378
Am	1: 2	"**The L** roars from Zion and thunders	3378
	1: 3	This is what **the L** says:	3378
	1: 5	into exile to Kir," says **the L.**	3378
	1: 6	This is what **the L** says:	3378
	1: 8	says **the** Sovereign **L.**	3378
	1: 9	This is what **the L** says:	3378
	1:11	This is what **the L** says:	3378
	1:13	This is what **the L** says:	3378
	1:15	he and his officials together," says **the L.**	3378
	2: 1	This is what **the L** says:	3378
	2: 3	her officials with him," says **the L.**	3378
	2: 4	This is what **the L** says:	3378
	2: 4	of **the L** and have not kept his decrees,	3378
	2: 6	This is what **the L** says:	3378
	2:11	not true, people of Israel?" declares **the L.**	3378
	2:16	on that day," declares **the L.**	3378
	3: 1	Hear this word **the L** has spoken	3378
	3: 6	has not **the L** caused it?	3378
	3: 7	Surely **the** Sovereign **L** does nothing	3378
	3: 8	**The** Sovereign **L** has spoken—	3378
	3:10	declares **the L,** "who hoard plunder	3378
	3:11	Therefore this is what **the** Sovereign **L** says:	3378
	3:12	This is what **the L** says:	3378
	3:13	declares the Lord, **the L** God Almighty.	3378
	3:15	will be demolished," declares **the L**	3378
	4: 2	**The** Sovereign **L** has sworn by his holiness	3378
	4: 3	cast out toward Harmon," declares **the L.**	3378
	4: 5	declares **the** Sovereign **L.**	3378
	4: 6	not returned to me," declares **the L.**	3378

Am	4: 8	not returned to me," declares **the L.**	3378
	4: 9	not returned to me," declares **the L.**	3378
	4:10	not returned to me," declares **the L.**	3378
	4:11	not returned to me," declares **the L.**	3378
	4:13	**the L** God Almighty is his name.	3378
	5: 3	This is what the Sovereign **L** says:	3378
	5: 4	This is what **the L** says to the house	3378
	5: 6	Seek **the L** and live,	3378
	5: 8	**the L** is his name—	3378
	5:14	**the L** God Almighty will be with you,	3378
	5:15	Perhaps **the L** God Almighty will have mercy	3378
	5:16	**the L** God Almighty, says:	3378
	5:17	pass through your midst," says **the L.**	3378
	5:18	to you who long for the day of **the L!**	3378
	5:18	Why do you long for the day of **the L?**	3378
	5:20	Will not the day of **the L** be darkness,	3378
	5:27	into exile beyond Damascus," says **the L,**	3378
	6: 8	The Sovereign **L** has sworn by himself—	3378
	6: 8	**the L** God Almighty declares:	3378
	6:10	We must not mention the name of **the L.**"	3378
	6:11	For **the L** has given the command,	3378
	6:14	For **the L** God Almighty declares,	3378
	7: 1	This is what the Sovereign **L** showed me:	3378
	7: 2	I cried out, "Sovereign **L,** forgive!	3378
	7: 3	So **the L** relented.	3378
	7: 3	"This will not happen," **the L** said.	3378
	7: 4	This is what the Sovereign **L** showed me:	3378
	7: 4	**The** Sovereign **L** was calling	3378
	7: 5	Then I cried out, "Sovereign **L,** I beg you,	3378
	7: 6	So **the L** relented.	3378
	7: 6	**the** Sovereign **L** said.	3378
	7: 8	And **the L** asked me, "What do you see,	3378
	7:15	But **the L** took me from tending the flock	3378
	7:16	Now then, hear the word of **the L.**	3378
	7:17	"Therefore this is what **the L** says:	3378
	8: 1	This is what the Sovereign **L** showed me:	3378
	8: 2	Then **the L** said to me,	3378
	8: 3	"In that day," declares the Sovereign **L,**	3378
	8: 7	**The L** has sworn by the Pride of Jacob:	3378
	8: 9	"In that day," declares the Sovereign **L,**	3378
	8:11	declares the Sovereign **L,**	3378
	8:11	a famine of hearing the words of **the L.**	3378
	8:12	searching for the word of **the L,**	3378
	9: 5	The Lord, **the L** Almighty,	3378
	9: 6	**the L** is his name.	3378
	9: 7	to me as the Cushites?" declares **the L.**	3378
	9: 8	"Surely the eyes of the Sovereign **L** are	3378
	9: 8	the house of Jacob," declares **the L.**	3378
	9:12	declares **the L,** who will do these things.	3378
	9:13	"The days are coming," declares **the L,**	3378
	9:15	says **the L** your God.	3378
Ob	1: 1	This is what the Sovereign **L** says	3378
	1: 1	We have heard a message from **the L:**	3378
	1: 4	I will bring you down," declares **the L.**	3378
	1: 8	"In that day," declares **the L,**	3378
	1:15	"The day of **the L** is near for all nations.	3378
	1:18	**The L** has spoken.	3378
Jnh	1: 1	word of **the L** came to Jonah son of Amittai	3378
	1: 3	from **the L** and headed for Tarshish	3378
	1: 3	and sailed for Tarshish to flee from **the L.**	3378
	1: 4	Then **the L** sent a great wind on the sea,	3378
	1: 9	"I am a Hebrew and I worship **the L,**	3378
	1:10	knew he was running away from **the L,**	3378
	1:14	Then they cried to **the L,** "O Lᴏʀᴅ,	3378
	1:14	Then they cried to the Lᴏʀᴅ, "O **L,**	3378
	1:14	for you, O **L,** have done as you pleased."	3378
	1:16	At this the men greatly feared **the L,**	3378
	1:16	and they offered a sacrifice to **the L**	3378
	1:17	But **the L** provided a great fish	3378
	2: 1	From inside the fish Jonah prayed to **the L**	3378
	2: 2	He said: "In my distress I called to **the L,**	3378
	2: 6	my life up from the pit, O **L** my God.	3378
	2: 7	**L,** and my prayer rose to you,	3378
	2: 9	Salvation comes from **the L.**"	3378
	2:10	And **the L** commanded the fish,	3378
	3: 1	Then the word of **the L** came to Jonah	3378
	3: 3	Jonah obeyed the word of **the L** and went	3378
	4: 2	He prayed to **the L,** "O Lᴏʀᴅ,	3378
	4: 2	He prayed to the Lᴏʀᴅ, "O **L,**	3378
	4: 3	Now, O **L,** take away my life,	3378
	4: 4	But **the L** replied,	3378
	4: 6	Then **the L** God provided a vine	3378
	4:10	But **the L** said, "You have been concerned	3378
Mic	1: 1	The word of **the L** that came to Micah of	3378
	1: 2	the Sovereign **L** may witness against you,	3378
	1: 3	**The L** is coming from his dwelling place;	3378
	1:12	because disaster has come from **the L,**	3378
	2: 3	Therefore, **the L** says:	3378
	2: 5	the assembly of **the L** to divide the land	3378
	2: 7	"Is the Spirit of **the L** angry?	3378
	2:13	**the L** at their head."	3378
	3: 4	Then they will cry out to **the L,**	3378
	3: 5	This is what **the L** says:	3378
	3: 8	with the Spirit of **the L,**	3378
	3:11	Yet they lean upon the **L** and say,	3378
	3:11	"Is not the **L** among us?	3378
	4: 2	let us go up to the mountain of **the L,**	3378
	4: 2	the word of **the L** from Jerusalem.	3378
	4: 4	for **the L** Almighty has spoken.	3378
	4: 5	in the name of the **L** our God for ever	3378
	4: 6	"In that day," declares **the L,**	3378
	4: 7	**The L** will rule over them in Mount Zion	3378
	4:10	There **the L** will redeem you out of	3378
	4:12	they do not know the thoughts of **the L;**	3378
	4:13	to **the L,** their wealth to the Lord of all	3378
	5: 4	shepherd his flock in the strength of **the L,**	3378
Mic	5: 4	the majesty of the name of **the L** his God.	3378
	5: 7	of many peoples like dew from **the L,**	3378
	5:10	"In that day," declares **the L,**	3378
	6: 1	Listen to what **the L** says:	3378
	6: 2	For **the L** has a case against his people;	3378
	6: 5	the righteous acts of **the L.**"	3378
	6: 6	With what shall I come before **the L**	3378
	6: 7	Will **the L** be pleased with thousands	3378
	6: 8	And what does **the L** require of you?	3378
	6: 9	**The L** is calling to the city—	3378
	7: 7	But as for me, I watch in hope for **the L,**	3378
	7: 8	I sit in darkness, **the L** will be my light.	3378
	7:10	"Where is **the L** your God?"	3378
	7:17	in fear to **the L** our God and will be afraid	3378
Na	1: 2	**The L** is a jealous and avenging God;	3378
	1: 2	**the L** takes vengeance and is filled	3378
	1: 2	**The L** takes vengeance on his foes	3378
	1: 3	**The L** is slow to anger and great	3378
	1: 3	**the L** will not leave the guilty unpunished.	3378
	1: 7	**The L** is good, a refuge in times of trouble.	3378
	1: 9	against **the L** he will bring to an end;	3378
	1:11	against **the L** and counsels wickedness.	3378
	1:12	This is what **the L** says:	3378
	1:14	**The L** has given a command	3378
	2: 2	**The L** will restore the splendor of Jacob	3378
	2:13	declares **the L** Almighty.	3378
	3: 5	declares **the L** Almighty.	3378
Hab	1: 2	How long, O **L,** must I call for help,	3378
	1:12	O **L,** are you not from everlasting?	3378
	1:12	O **L,** you have appointed them	3378
	2: 2	Then **the L** replied:	3378
	2:13	Has not **the L** Almighty determined that	3378
	2:14	with the knowledge of the glory of **the L,**	3378
	2:20	But **the L** is in his holy temple;	3378
	3: 2	**L,** I have heard of your fame;	3378
	3: 2	I stand in awe of your deeds, O **L.**	3378
	3: 8	Were you angry with the rivers, O **L?**	3378
	3:18	yet I will rejoice in **the L,**	3378
	3:19	The Sovereign **L** is my strength;	3378
Zep	1: 1	The word of **the L** that came to Zephaniah	3378
	1: 2	the face of the earth," declares **the L.**	3378
	1: 3	the face of the earth," declares **the L.**	3378
	1: 5	those who bow down and swear by **the L**	3378
	1: 6	those who turn back from following **the L**	3378
	1: 6	and neither seek **the L** nor inquire of him.	3378
	1: 7	Be silent before the Sovereign **L,**	3378
	1: 7	for the day of **the L** is near.	3378
	1: 7	**The L** has prepared a sacrifice;	3378
	1:10	"On that day," declares **the L,**	3378
	1:12	who think, '**The L** will do nothing,	3378
	1:14	"The great day of **the L** is near—	3378
	1:14	The cry on the day of **the L** will be bitter,	3378
	1:17	because they have sinned against **the L.**	3378
	2: 2	the fierce anger of **the L** comes upon you,	3378
	2: 3	Seek **the L,** all you humble of the land,	3378
	2: 5	the word of **the L** is against you,	3378
	2: 7	**The L** their God will care for them;	3378
	2: 9	declares **the L** Almighty,	3378
	2:10	the people of **the L** Almighty.	3378
	2:11	**The L** will be awesome to them	3378
	3: 2	She does not trust in **the L,**	3378
	3: 5	**The L** within her is righteous;	3378
	3: 8	Therefore wait for me," declares **the L,**	3378
	3: 9	call on the name of **the L** and serve him	3378
	3:12	who trust in the name of **the L.**	3378
	3:15	**The L** has taken away your punishment,	3378
	3:15	**The L,** the King of Israel, is with you;	3378
	3:17	**The L** your God is with you,	3378
	3:20	before your very eyes," says **the L.**	3378
Hag	1: 1	the word of **the L** came through the prophet Haggai to Zerubbabel	3378
	1: 2	This is what **the L** Almighty says:	3378
	1: 3	Then the word of **the L** came through	3378
	1: 5	Now this is what **the L** Almighty says:	3378
	1: 7	This is what **the L** Almighty says:	3378
	1: 8	in it and be honored," says **the L.**	3378
	1: 9	declares **the L** Almighty.	3378
	1:12	of **the L** their God and the message of	3378
	1:12	because **the L** their God had sent him.	3378
	1:12	And the people feared **the L.**	3378
	1:13	gave this message of **the L** to the people:	3378
	1:13	"I am with you," declares **the L.**	3378
	1:14	So **the L** stirred up the spirit of Zerubbabel	3378
	1:14	to work on the house of **the L** Almighty,	3378
	2: 1	the word of **the L** came through the prophet	3378
	2: 4	be strong, O Zerubbabel,' declares **the L**	3378
	2: 4	declares **the L,** 'and work.	3378
	2: 4	I am with you,' declares **the L** Almighty.	3378
	2: 6	"This is what **the L** Almighty says:	3378
	2: 7	says **the L** Almighty.	3378
	2: 8	declares **the L** Almighty.	3378
	2: 9	says **the L** Almighty.	3378
	2: 9	declares **the L** Almighty."	3378
	2:10	word of **the L** came to the prophet Haggai:	3378
	2:11	"This is what **the L** Almighty says:	3378
	2:14	in my sight,' declares **the L.**	3378
	2:17	not turn to me,' declares **the L.**	3378
	2:20	The word of **the L** came to Haggai a second time	3378
	2:23	" 'On that day,' declares **the L** Almighty,	3378
	2:23	declares **the L,** 'and I will make you	3378
	2:23	declares **the L** Almighty."	3378
Zec	1: 1	the word of **the L** came to the prophet Zechariah	3378
	1: 2	"**The L** was very angry	3378
	1: 3	This is what **the L** Almighty says:	3378
	1: 3	'Return to me,' declares **the L** Almighty,	3378
Zec	1: 3	says **the L** Almighty.	3378
	1: 4	This is what **the L** Almighty says:	3378
	1: 4	or pay attention to me, declares **the L.**	3378
	1: 6	'**The L** Almighty has done to us what	3378
	1: 7	the word of **the L** came to the prophet Zechariah	3378
	1:10	the ones **the L** has sent to go throughout	3378
	1:11	And they reported to the angel of **the L,**	3378
	1:12	Then the angel of **the L** said,	3378
	1:12	angel of the Lᴏʀᴅ said, "**L** Almighty,	3378
	1:13	So **the L** spoke kind and comforting words	3378
	1:14	This is what **the L** Almighty says:	3378
	1:16	"Therefore, this is what **the L** says:	3378
	1:16	declares **the L** Almighty.	3378
	1:17	This is what **the L** Almighty says:	3378
	1:17	and **the L** will again comfort Zion	3378
	1:20	Then **the L** showed me four craftsmen.	3378
	2: 5	a wall of fire around it,' declares **the L,**	3378
	2: 6	declares **the L,** "for I have scattered you	3378
	2: 6	the four winds of heaven," declares **the L.**	3378
	2: 8	For this is what **the L** Almighty says:	3378
	2: 9	that **the L** Almighty has sent me.	3378
	2:10	among you," declares **the L.**	3378
	2:11	"Many nations will be joined with **the L**	3378
	2:11	that **the L** Almighty has sent me to you.	3378
	2:12	**The L** will inherit Judah as his portion in	3378
	2:13	Be still before **the L,** all mankind,	3378
	3: 1	before the angel of **the L,**	3378
	3: 2	**The L** said to Satan, "The Lᴏʀᴅ rebuke you	3378
	3: 2	"**The L** rebuke you, Satan!	3378
	3: 2	**The L,** who has chosen Jerusalem,	3378
	3: 5	while the angel of **the L** stood by.	3378
	3: 6	of **the L** gave this charge to Joshua:	3378
	3: 7	"This is what **the L** Almighty says:	3378
	3: 9	says **the L** Almighty,	3378
	3:10	declares **the L** Almighty."	3378
	4: 6	"This is the word of **the L** to Zerubbabel:	3378
	4: 6	but by my Spirit,' says **the L** Almighty.	3378
	4: 8	Then the word of **the L** came to me:	3378
	4: 9	that **the L** Almighty has sent me to you.	3378
	4:10	"(These seven are the eyes of **the L,**	3378
	5: 4	**The L** Almighty declares,	3378
	6: 9	The word of **the L** came to me:	3378
	6:12	Tell him this is what **the L** Almighty says:	3378
	6:12	and build the temple of **the L.**	3378
	6:13	he who will build the temple of **the L,**	3378
	6:14	as a memorial in the temple of **the L.**	3378
	6:15	and help to build the temple of **the L,**	3378
	6:15	that **the L** Almighty has sent me to you.	3378
	6:15	if you diligently obey **the L** your God."	3378
	7: 1	the word of **the L** came to Zechariah on	3378
	7: 2	together with their men, to entreat **the L**	3378
	7: 3	the priests of the house of **the L** Almighty	3378
	7: 4	the word of **the L** Almighty came to me:	3378
	7: 7	Are these not the words **the L** proclaimed	3378
	7: 9	word of **the L** came again to Zechariah:	3378
	7: 9	"This is what **the L** Almighty says:	3378
	7:12	to the words that **the L** Almighty had sent	3378
	7:12	So **the L** Almighty was very angry.	3378
	7:13	I would not listen,' says **the L** Almighty.	3378
	8: 1	the word of **the L** Almighty came to me.	3378
	8: 2	This is what **the L** Almighty says:	3378
	8: 3	This is what **the L** says:	3378
	8: 3	mountain of **the L** Almighty will be called	3378
	8: 4	This is what **the L** Almighty says:	3378
	8: 6	This is what **the L** Almighty says:	3378
	8: 6	declares **the L** Almighty.	3378
	8: 7	This is what **the L** Almighty says:	3378
	8: 9	This is what **the L** Almighty says:	3378
	8: 9	for the house of **the L** Almighty,	3378
	8:11	declares **the L** Almighty.	3378
	8:14	This is what **the L** Almighty says:	3378
	8:14	says **the L** Almighty.	3378
	8:17	I hate all this," declares **the L.**	3378
	8:18	the word of **the L** Almighty came to me.	3378
	8:19	This is what **the L** Almighty says:	3378
	8:20	This is what **the L** Almighty says:	3378
	8:21	'Let us go at once to entreat **the L**	3378
	8:21	the Lᴏʀᴅ and seek **the L** Almighty.	3378
	8:22	to Jerusalem to seek **the L** Almighty and	3378
	8:23	This is what **the L** Almighty says:	3378
	9: 1	The word of **the L** is against	3378
	9: 1	and all the tribes of Israel are on **the L—**	3378
	9:14	Then **the L** will appear over them;	3378
	9:14	The Sovereign **L** will sound the trumpet;	3378
	9:15	and **the L** Almighty will shield them.	3378
	9:16	**The L** their God will save them on	3378
	10: 1	Ask **the L** for rain in the springtime;	3378
	10: 1	it is **the L** who makes the storm clouds.	3378
	10: 3	for **the L** Almighty will care for his flock,	3378
	10: 5	Because **the L** is with them,	3378
	10: 6	for I am **the L** their God	3378
	10: 7	their hearts will rejoice in **the L,**	3378
	10:12	in **the L** and in his name they will walk,"	3378
	10:12	in his name they will walk," declares **the L.**	3378
	11: 4	This is what **the L** my God says:	3378
	11: 5	Those who sell them say, 'Praise **the L,**	3378
	11: 6	on the people of the land," declares **the L.**	3378
	11:11	knew it was the word of **the L.**	3378
	11:13	And **the L** said to me,	3378
	11:13	and threw them into the house of **the L** to	3378
	11:15	Then **the L** said to me,	3378
	12: 1	the word of **the L** concerning Israel.	3378
	12: 1	**The L,** who stretches out the heavens,	3378
	12: 4	its rider with madness," declares **the L.**	3378
	12: 5	because **the L** Almighty is their God.'	3378
	12: 7	"**The L** will save the dwellings	3378

†**LORD** distinguishes the proper name of God, *Yahweh,* indicated in the NIV by "Lᴏʀᴅ," from the words translated "Lord" and "lord," indexed under the heading *LORD, pages 683-86.

Zec	12: 8	that day the L will shield those who live	3378
	12: 8	the Angel of the L going before them.	3378
	13: 2	declares the L Almighty.	3378
	13: 7	declares the L Almighty.	3378
	13: 8	In the whole land," declares the L,	3378
	13: 9	and they will say, 'The L is our God.' "	3378
	14: 1	A day of the L is coming	3378
	14: 3	Then the L will go out and fight	3378
	14: 5	Then the L my God will come,	3378
	14: 7	a day known to the L.	3378
	14: 9	The L will be king over the whole earth.	3378
	14: 9	On that day there will be one L,	3378
	14:12	the plague with which the L will strike all	3378
	14:13	On that day men will be stricken by the L	3378
	14:16	to worship the King, the L Almighty, and	3378
	14:17	the L Almighty, they will have no rain.	3378
	14:18	The L will bring on them	3378
	14:20	HOLY TO THE L will be inscribed on	3378
	14:21	and Judah will be holy to the L Almighty,	3378
	14:21	in the house of the L Almighty.	3378
Mal	1: 1	word of the L to Israel through Malachi.	3378
	1: 2	"I have loved you," says the L.	3378
	1: 2	the L says. "Yet I have loved Jacob,	3378
	1: 4	But this is what the L Almighty says:	3378
	1: 4	a people always under the wrath of the L.	3378
	1: 5	'Great is the L—even beyond the borders	3378
	1: 6	the respect due me?" says the L Almighty.	3378
	1: 8	he accept you?" says the L Almighty.	3378
	1: 9	he accept you?"—says the L Almighty.	3378
	1:10	not pleased with you," says the L Almighty,	3378
	1:11	my name will be great among the nations," says the L Almighty.	3378
	1:13	you sniff at it contemptuously, says the L Almighty.	3378
	1:13	accept them from your hands?" says the L.	3378
	1:14	I am a great king," says the L Almighty,	3378
	2: 2	to honor my name," says the L Almighty,	3378
	2: 4	covenant with Levi may continue," says the L Almighty.	3378
	2: 7	he is the messenger of the L Almighty.	3378
	2: 8	covenant with Levi," says the L Almighty.	3378
	2:11	the sanctuary the L loves,	3378
	2:12	may the L cut him off from the tents	3378
	2:12	he brings offerings to the L Almighty.	3378
	2:14	It is because the L is acting as the witness	3378
	2:15	Has not [the L] made them one?	NIH
	2:16	"I hate divorce," says the L God of Israel,	3378
	2:16	as with his garment," says the L Almighty.	3378
	2:17	You have wearied the L with your words.	3378
	2:17	who do evil are good in the eyes of the L,	3378
	3: 1	will come," says the L Almighty.	3378
	3: 3	the L will have men who will bring offerings in righteousness,	3378
	3: 4	will be acceptable to the L,	3378
	3: 5	but do not fear me," says the L Almighty.	3378
	3: 6	"I the L do not change.	3378
	3: 7	I will return to you," says the L Almighty.	3378
	3:10	Test me in this," says the L Almighty,	3378
	3:11	not cast their fruit," says the L Almighty,	3378
	3:12	a delightful land," says the L Almighty.	3378
	3:13	harsh things against me," says the L.	3378
	3:14	like mourners before the L Almighty?	3378
	3:16	Then those who feared the L talked	3378
	3:16	and the L listened and heard.	3378
	3:16	concerning those who feared the L	3378
	3:17	"They will be mine," says the L Almighty,	3378
	4: 1	set them on fire," says the L Almighty.	3378
	4: 3	I do these things," says the L Almighty.	3378
	4: 5	and dreadful day of the L comes.	3378

†LORD'S (278) [†LORD]

Ge	4:16	from the L presence and lived in the land	3378
	38: 7	Judah's firstborn, was wicked in the L sight	3378
	38:10	What he did was wicked in the L sight;	3378
Ex	4:14	Then the L anger burned against Moses	3378
	9:29	you may know that the earth is the L.	3378+4200
	12:11	Eat it in haste; it is the L Passover.	3378+4200
	12:41	all the L divisions left Egypt.	3378
	12:48	to celebrate the L Passover must	3378+4200
	16: 3	only we had died by the L hand in Egypt!	3378
	24: 3	the people all the L words and laws,	3378
	29:11	in the L presence at the entrance to	3378
	34:34	But whenever he entered the L presence	3378
Lev	3:16	All the fat is the L.	3378+4200
	4: 2	forbidden in any of the L commands—	3378
	4:13	forbidden in any of the L commands,	3378
	4:27	forbidden in any of the L commands,	3378
	5:15	in regard to any of the L holy things,	3378
	5:17	forbidden in any of the L commands,	3378
	6:22	It is the L regular share and is to	3378+4200
	10: 7	because the L anointing oil is on you."	3378+4200
	23: 4	" 'These are the L appointed feasts,	3378
	23: 5	The L Passover begins at twilight on	3378+4200
	23: 6	the L Feast of Unleavened Bread	3378+4200
	23:34	the L Feast of Tabernacles begins,	3378+4200
	23:37	(" 'These are the L appointed feasts,	3378
	23:38	in addition to those for the L Sabbaths	3378
	27:26	whether an ox or a sheep, it is the L.	3378+4200
Nu	3:39	at the L command by Moses and Aaron	3378
	4:37	to the L command through Moses.	3378
	4:41	according to the L command.	3378
	4:45	to the L command through Moses.	3378
	4:49	at the L command through Moses,	3378
	9: 7	be kept from presenting the L offering	3378
	9:10	may still celebrate the L Passover.	3378+4200
	9:13	because he did not present the L offering	3378

Nu	9:14	to celebrate the L Passover must do so	3378+4200
	9:18	At the L command the Israelites set out,	3378
	9:19	the Israelites obeyed the L order and did	3378
	9:20	at the L command they would encamp,	3378
	9:23	At the L command they encamped,	3378
	9:23	and at the L command they set out.	3378
	9:23	They obeyed the L order,	3378
	10:13	at the L command through Moses.	3378
	11:23	"Is the L arm too short?	3378
	11:29	I wish that all the L people were prophets	3378
	13: 3	at the L command Moses sent them out	3378
	14:41	"Why are you disobeying the L command?	3378
	14:44	nor the ark of the L covenant moved from	3378
	15:23	of the L commands to you through him,	3378
	15:31	Because he has despised the L word	3378
	16: 3	you set yourselves above the L assembly?"	3378
	16: 9	the work at the L tabernacle and to stand	3378
	16:41	"You have killed the L people,"	3378
	17: 9	from the L presence to all the Israelites.	3378
	18:26	a tenth of that tithe as the L offering.	3378
	18:28	From these tithes you must give the L portion to Aaron	3378
	18:29	as the L portion the best and holiest part	3378
	19:13	to purify himself defiles the L tabernacle.	3378
	20: 4	Why did you bring the L community	3378
	20: 9	Moses took the staff from the L presence,	3378
	25: 3	And the L anger burned against them.	3378
	25: 4	so that the L fierce anger may turn away	3378
	27:17	so the L people will not be like sheep	3378
	28:16	of the first month the L Passover is to	3378+4200
	31: 3	to carry out the L vengeance on them.	3378
	31:16	so that a plague struck the L people.	3378
	31:29	to Eleazar the priest as the L part.	3378
	31:30	for the care of the L tabernacle."	3378
	31:41	to Eleazar the priest as the L part,	3378
	31:47	for the care of the L tabernacle.	3378
	32:10	The L anger was aroused that day	3378
	32:13	The L anger burned against Israel	3378
	33: 2	At the L command Moses recorded	3378
	33:38	At the L command Aaron the priest went	3378
	36: 5	at the L command Moses gave this order	3378
Dt	1:43	You rebelled against the L command and	3378
	2:15	The L hand was against them	3378
	6:18	Do what is right and good in the L sight,	3378
	7: 4	and the L anger will burn against you	3378
	9: 8	At Horeb you aroused the L wrath so	3378
	9:18	doing what was evil in the L sight and	3378
	10:13	to observe the L commands and decrees	3378
	11:17	Then the L anger will burn against you,	3378
	15: 2	because the L time for canceling debts	3378+4200
	18: 5	and minister in the L name always.	3378
	29:27	the L anger burned against this land,	3378
	32: 9	For the L portion is his people,	3378
	33:21	he carried out the L righteous will,	3378
Jos	5:15	The commander of the L army replied,	3378
	6: 8	the ark of the L covenant followed them.	3378
	6:24	and iron into the treasury of the L house.	3378
	7: 1	So the L anger burned against Israel.	3378
	15:13	with the L command to him, Joshua gave	3378
	17: 4	according to the L command.	3378
	21:45	of all the L good promises to the house	3378
	22:19	come over to the L land,	3378
	22:19	where the L tabernacle stands,	3378
	22:28	Look at the replica of the L altar,	3378
	22:31	the Israelites from the L hand."	3378
	23:16	the L anger will burn against you,	3378
Jdg	2:17	the way of obedience to the L commands.	3378
	3: 4	to see whether they would obey the L commands,	3378
	11:31	from the Ammonites will be the L,	3378+4200
	18: 6	Your journey has the L approval."	3378
Ru	1:13	the L hand has gone out against me!"	3378
1Sa	1: 9	a chair by the doorpost of the L temple.	3378
	2: 8	the foundations of the earth are the L;	3378+4200
	2:17	was very great in the L sight,	3378
	2:17	for they were treating the L offering	3378
	2:24	that I hear spreading among the L people.	3378
	2:25	for it was the L will to put them to death.	3378
	4: 3	the ark of the L covenant from Shiloh.	3378
	4: 5	of the L covenant came into the camp,	3378
	5: 6	The L hand was heavy upon the people	3378
	5: 9	the L hand was against that city,	3378
	13:12	and I have not sought the L favor.'	3378
	13:14	you have not kept the L command."	3378
	14: 3	the son of Eli, the L priest in Shiloh.	3378
	15:13	I have carried out the L instructions."	3378
	15:24	I violated the L command	3378
	16: 6	"Surely the L anointed stands here before	2257S
	17:47	for the battle is the L,	3378+4200
	24: 6	the L anointed, or lift my hand against him;	3378
	24:10	because he is the L anointed.'	3378
	25:28	because he fights the L battles.	3378
	26: 9	Who can lay a hand on the L anointed	3378
	26:11	that I should lay a hand on the L anointed.	3378
	26:16	not guard your master, the L anointed.	3378
	26:19	from my share in the L inheritance	3378
	26:23	I would not lay a hand on the L anointed.	3378
	30:26	from the plunder of the L enemies."	3378
2Sa	1:14	to destroy the L anointed?"	3378
	1:16	'I killed the L anointed.' "	3378
	6: 7	The L anger burned against Uzzah	3378
	6: 8	because the L wrath had broken out	3378
	6:21	over the L people Israel—	3378
	15:25	If I find favor in the L eyes,	3378
	19:21	He cursed the L anointed."	3378
	20:19	to swallow up the L inheritance?"	3378
	21: 3	so that you will bless the L inheritance?"	3378

2Sa	21: 6	of Saul—the L chosen one."	3378
1Ki	2:33	there be the L peace forever."	3378+4946+6640
	7:48	the furnishings that were in the L temple:	3378
	7:51	in the treasuries of the L temple.	3378
	8: 1	up the ark of the L covenant from Zion,	3378
	8: 6	the ark of the L covenant to its place in	3378
	9:15	to build the L temple,	3378
	10: 9	Because of the L eternal love for Israel,	3378
	11:10	Solomon did not keep the L command.	3378
	14:28	Whenever the king went to the L temple,	3378
	15: 5	the L commands all the days of his life—	NIH
	15:18	of the L temple and of his own palace.	3378
	18: 4	Jezebel was killing off the L prophets,	3378
	18:13	a hundred of the L prophets in two caves,	3378
	18:18	You have abandoned the L commands	3378
	18:22	"I am the only one of the L prophets left,	3378+4200
2Ki	9: 6	'I anoint you king over the L people Israel.	3378
	9: 7	and the blood of all the L servants shed	3378+4200
	11:17	that they would be the L people.	3378
	13: 3	So the L anger burned against Israel,	3378
	13: 4	Then Jehoahaz sought the L favor,	3378
	13:17	"The L arrow of victory,	3378+4200
	20: 9	"This is the L sign to you that	907+3378+4946
	22:13	Great is the L anger that burns against us	3378
	24: 3	to Judah according to the L command,	3378
	24:20	of the L anger that all this happened	3378
1Ch	2: 3	Judah's firstborn, was wicked in the L sight	3378
	13:10	The L anger burned against Uzzah	3378
	13:11	because the L wrath had broken out	3378
2Ch	1: 3	which Moses the L servant had made in	3378
	5: 2	up the ark of the L covenant from Zion,	3378
	5: 7	the ark of the L covenant to its place in	3378
	7: 6	with the L musical instruments,	3378
	12:11	Whenever the king went to the L temple,	3378
	12:12	the L anger turned from him,	3378
	15: 8	in front of the portico of the L temple.	3378
	16: 2	of the L temple and of his own palace	3378
	23:16	and the king would be the L people.	3378+4200
	23:19	of the L temple so that no one who was	3378
	24:12	and carpenters to restore the L temple,	3378
	24:14	made articles for the L temple:	3378
	24:20	'Why do you disobey the L commands?	3378
	24:21	to death in the courtyard of the L temple.	3378
	26:19	before the incense altar in the L temple,	3378
	28:11	for the L fierce anger rests on you."	3378
	28:24	the doors of the L temple and set up altars	3378
	29: 6	from the L dwelling place	3378
	29:16	of the L temple everything unclean	3378
	29:19	They are now in front of the L altar."	3378
	30:21	accompanied by the L instruments	3378+4200
	31: 2	at the gates of the L dwelling.	3378
	32:25	therefore the L wrath was on him and	NIH
	32:26	therefore the L wrath did not come	3378
	34:10	to supervise the work on the L temple.	3378
	34:21	Great is the L anger that is poured out	3378
	35: 2	in the service of the L temple.	3378
	36:18	and the treasures of the L temple and	3378
Ezr	3: 6	the foundation of the L temple had not	3378
Ps	24: 1	The earth is the L, and everything in it	3378+4200
	32:10	but the L unfailing love surrounds	3378
	37:20	The L enemies will be like the beauty of	3378
	89: 1	I will sing of the L great love forever;	3378
	103:17	the L love is with those who fear him,	3378
	109:20	the L payment to my accusers,	907+3378+4946
	118:15	"The L right hand has done mighty things!	3378
	118:16	The L right hand is lifted high;	3378
	118:16	the L right hand has done mighty things!"	3378
Pr	3:11	do not despise the L discipline and do	3378
	3:33	The L curse is on the house of the wicked,	3378
	19:21	but it is the L purpose that prevails.	3378
	22:14	he who is under the L wrath will fall into it.	3378
Isa	2: 2	the mountain of the L temple will be established	3378
	5:25	Therefore the L anger burns	3378
	24:14	and maidservants in the L land.	3378
	24:14	from the west they acclaim the L majesty.	3378
	30: 9	to listen to the L instruction.	3378
	38: 7	" 'This is the L sign to you that	907+3378+4946
	40: 2	from the L hand double for all her sins.	3378
	44: 5	'The L,' and will take the name Israel.	3378+4200
	48:14	The L chosen ally will carry out his purpose	3378
	49: 4	Yet what is due me is in the L hand,	3378
	53:10	Yet it was the L will to crush him	3378
	55:13	This will be for the L renown,	3378+4200
	58:13	a delight and the L holy day honorable,	3378
	61: 2	to proclaim the year of the L favor	3378+4200
	62: 3	be a crown of splendor in the L hand,	3378
Jer	7: 2	"Stand at the gate of the L house	3378
	12:13	because of the L fierce anger.	3378
	13:17	because the L flock will be taken captive.	3378
	19:14	in the court of the L temple and said to all	3378
	20: 2	of Benjamin at the L temple.	3378
	20: 3	"The L name for you is not Pashhur,	3378
	23:35	'What is the L answer?'	3378
	23:37	'What is the L answer to you?'	3378
	25:17	from the L hand and made all the nations	3378
	25:38	and because of the L fierce anger.	2257S
	26: 2	of the L house and speak to all the people	3378
	26: 9	Why do you prophesy in the L name	3378
	26:10	of the New Gate of the L house.	3378
	27:16	from the L house will be brought back	3378
	28: 3	to this place all the articles of the L house	3378
	28: 6	by bringing the articles of the L house	3378
	36: 5	I cannot go to the L temple.	3378
	36: 8	at the L temple he read the words of	3378
	36:10	at the L temple the words of Jeremiah	3378

Column 1

Jer	43: 4	the people disobeyed **the L** command	3378
	48:10	on him who is lax in doing **the L** work!	3378
	50:13	of **the L** anger she will not be inhabited	3378
	51: 6	It is time for **the L** vengeance;	3378+4200
	51: 7	Babylon was a gold cup in **the L** hand;	3378
	51:29	**the L** purposes against Babylon stand—	3378
	51:51	the holy places of **the L** house."	3378
	52: 3	because of **the L** anger that all this happened to Jerusalem	3378
La	2:22	In the day of **the L** anger no one escaped	3378
	3:22	of **the L** great love we are not consumed,	3378
	4:20	**The L** anointed, our very life breath,	3378
Eze	7:19	to save them in the day of **the L** wrath.	3378
	10:19	to the east gate of **the L** house,	3378
	36:20	'These are **the L** people,	3378
Hos	9: 3	They will not remain in **the L** land;	3378
Joel	3:18	of **the L** house and will water the valley	3378
Ob	1:21	And the kingdom will be **the L**.	3378+4200
Mic	4: 1	the mountain of **the L** temple will be established	3378
	6: 2	Hear, O mountains, **the L** accusation;	3378
	7: 9	I will bear **the L** wrath,	3378
Hab	2:16	The cup from **the L** right hand is coming	3378
Zep	1: 8	On the day of **the L** sacrifice I will punish	3378
	1:18	to save them on the day of **the L** wrath.	3378
	2: 2	the day of **the L** wrath comes upon you.	3378
	2: 3	be sheltered on the day of **the L** anger.	3378
Hag	1: 2	yet come for **the L** house to be built.' "	3378
	1:13	Then Haggai, **the L** messenger,	3378
	2:15	stone was laid on another in **the L** temple.	3378
	2:18	the foundation of **the L** temple was laid.	3378
Zec	13: 3	you have told lies in **the L** name.'	3378
	14:20	cooking pots in **the L** house will be like	3378
Mal	1: 7	saying that **the L** table is contemptible.	3378
	2:13	You flood **the L** altar with tears.	3378

LORDED (1) [*LORD]

Ne	5:15	Their assistants also **l** it over the people.	8948

LORDING (1) [*LORD]

1Pe	5: 3	not **l** it over those entrusted to you,	2894

LORDS (10) [*LORD]

Ge	19: 2	"My **l**," he said, "please turn aside	123
	19:18	But Lot said to them, "No, my **l**, please!	123
Dt	10:17	your God is God of gods and Lord of **l**,	123
Ps	136: 3	Give thanks to the Lord of **l**;	123
Ecc	8: 9	a man **l** it over others to his own hurt.	8948
Isa	26:13	other **l** besides you have ruled over us,	123
1Co	8: 5	(as indeed there are many "gods" and many "**l**"),	3261
1Ti	6:15	the King of kings and Lord of **l**,	3259
Rev	17:14	because he is Lord *of* **l** and King of kings—	3261
	19:16	KING OF KINGS AND LORD OF **L**.	3261

LORDSHIP (KJV) See LORD OVER

LOSE (36) [LOSES, LOSS, LOSSES, LOST]

Ge	26: 9	"Because I thought *I* might **l** my **life**	4637
	27:45	Why **should** I **l** both of you in one day?"	8897
Dt	1:28	Our brothers *have* **made** us **l** heart.	5022
Jdg	18:25	you and your family will **l** your lives."	665
1Sa	17:32	"Let no one **l** heart on account	5877
2Sa	22:46	They all **l heart**; they come trembling	5570
Ps	18:45	They all **l heart**; they come trembling	5570
Pr	25:10	and *you* will never **l** your bad reputation.	8740
Isa	7: 4	*Do* not **l** heart because of these two	8216
	19: 3	The Egyptians *will* **l** heart,	928+1327+7931+8120
	19: 9	the weavers of fine linen will **l** hope.	NIH
Jer	4: 9	"the king and the officials will **l** heart,	6
	17: 4	Through your own fault *you* will **l**	9023
	51:46	*Do* not **l** heart or be afraid	8216
Da	11:30	and *he will* **l heart**.	3874
Zec	9: 5	Gaza *will* **l** her king and Ashkelon will	6
Mt	5:29	better for you to **l** one part of your body than	660
	5:30	better for you to **l** one part of your body than	660
	10:39	Whoever finds his life *will* **l** it,	660
	10:42	*he* will certainly not **l** his reward.	660
	16:25	whoever wants to save his life *will* **l** it,	660
Mk	8:35	whoever wants to save his life *will* **l** it,	660
	9:41	to Christ will certainly not **l** his reward.	660
Lk	9:24	whoever wants to save his life *will* **l** it,	660
	9:25	and yet **l** or forfeit his very self?	660
	16: 4	when *I* **l** my job here,	1666+3496
	17:33	Whoever tries to keep his life *will* **l** it,	660
Jn	6:39	*I* shall **l** none of all that he has given me,	660
	12:25	The man who loves his life *will* **l** it,	660
Ac	19:27	our trade *will* **l** its **good name**,	591+1650+2262
	27:34	of you *will* **l** a single hair from his head."	660
2Co	4: 1	*we do* not **l** heart.	1591
	4:16	Therefore *we do* not **l heart**.	1591
Heb	12: 3	that you will not grow weary and **l** heart.	1725
	12: 5	and *do* not **l heart** when he rebukes you,	1725
2Jn	1: 8	that *you do* not **l** what you have worked	660

LOSES (13) [LOSE]

Dt	22: 3	or his cloak or anything he **l**.	6+8
1Sa	20: 7	But *if he* **l temper**,	3013+3013
Isa	44:12	He gets hungry and **l** his strength;	401
Mt	5:13	But if the salt **l** its **saltiness**,	3701
	10:39	whoever **l** his life for my sake will find it.	660
	16:25	but whoever **l** his life for me will find it.	660
Mk	8:35	but whoever **l** his life for me and for	660

Column 2

Mk	9:50	"Salt is good, but if it **l** its saltiness,	1181
Lk	9:24	but whoever **l** his life for me will save it.	660
	14:34	"Salt is good, but if *it* **l** its saltiness,	3701
	15: 4	of you has a hundred sheep and **l** one	660
	15: 8	a woman has ten silver coins and **l** one.	660
	17:33	and whoever **l** his life will preserve it.	660

LOSS (18) [LOSE]

Ge	31:39	I bore the **l** myself.	2627
Ex	21:19	the injured man for the **l** of his **time**	8700
	21:34	the owner of the pit *must* **pay for the l**;	8966
	22:15	the money paid for the hire covers the **l**.	NIH
Isa	47: 8	be a widow or suffer the **l of children.**'	8890
	47: 9	**l** of children and widowhood.	8890
Jer	22:10	for the dead [king] or **mourn** his **l**;	5653
Da	6: 2	to them so that the king *might* not **suffer l**.	10472
Jn	11:19	to comfort them in the **l** of their brother.	NIG
	13:22	**at a l** to know which of them he meant.	679
Ac	25:20	I *was* **at a l** how to investigate such matters	679
	27:10	and bring great **l** to ship and cargo,	2422
	27:21	have spared yourselves this damage and **l**.	2422
Ro	11:12	and their **l** means riches for the Gentiles,	2488
1Co	3:15	If it is burned up, *he* will **suffer l**;	2423
Php	3: 7	to my profit I now consider **l** for the sake	2422
	3: 8	a **l** compared to the surpassing greatness	2422
Heb	6: 6	because to their **l** they are crucifying	NIG

LOSSES (4) [LOSE]

1Sa	4:17	and the army has suffered heavy **l**.	4487
	23: 5	He inflicted heavy **l** on the Philistines	4804
1Ki	20:21	and inflicted heavy **l** on the Arameans.	4804
2Ch	13:17	and his men inflicted heavy **l** on them,	4804

LOST (45) [LOSE]

Ge	34:19	**l** no **time** in doing what they said,	336
Ex	14: 5	the Israelites go and have **l** their services!"	4946
	22: 9	or any other *l property*	6
Lev	6: 3	or if he finds **l property** and lies about it,	8
	6: 4	or the **l property** he found,	8
	13:40	When a man *has* **l** his **hair** and is bald,	5307+8031
	13:41	If *he has* **l** his **hair** from the front	5307+8031
Nu	11: 6	But now we have **l** our appetite;	3313
	17:12	*We are* **l**, we are all lost!	6
	17:12	We are lost, we *are* all **l**!	6
1Sa	4:10	Israel **l** thirty thousand foot soldiers.	4946+5877
	9: 3	belonging to Saul's father Kish *were* **l**,	6
	9:20	As for the donkeys you **l** three days ago,	6
	25:18	Abigail **l** no **time**.	4554
2Sa	4: 1	had died in Hebron, he **l courage**,	3338+8332
1Ki	20:25	raise an army like the one you **l**	907+4946+5877
Ne	6:16	**l** their **self-confidence**,	928+4394+5877+6524
Ps	73: 2	I *had* nearly **l** my foothold.	9161
	119:176	I have strayed like a sheep.	6
Ecc	5:14	or wealth **l** through some misfortune,	6
Jer	18:18	of the law by the priest *will* not *be* **l**,	6
	50: 6	"My people have been **l** sheep;	6
La	4: 1	How the gold *has* **l** its **luster**,	6670
Eze	7:26	of the law by the priest *will be* **l**,	6
	34: 4	the strays or searched for the **l**.	6
	34:16	I will search for the **l** and bring back	6
Zec	11:16	over the land who will not care for the **l**,	3948
Mt	10: 6	Go rather to the **l** sheep of Israel.	660
	15:24	"I was sent only to the **l** sheep of Israel."	660
	18:14	that any of these little ones *should be* **l**.	660
Lk	15: 4	the open country and go after the **l** sheep	660
	15: 6	I have found my **l** sheep.'	660
	15: 9	I have found my **l** coin.'	660
	15:24	he was **l** and is found.'	660
	15:32	he was **l** and is found.' "	660
	19:10	to seek and to save what was **l**."	660
Jn	17:12	None *has been* **l** except the one doomed	660
	18: 9	"I have not **l** one of those you gave me."	660
Ac	27: 9	Much time *had* been **l**,	1335
	27:22	because not one of you will be **l**;	613
1Co	15:18	also who have fallen asleep in Christ *are* **l**.	660
Eph	4:19	*Having* **l all** sensitivity, they have given	556
Php	3: 8	for whose sake I *have* **l** all things.	2423
Col	2:19	He has **l connection with** the Head,	3195+4024
Rev	12: 8	and they **l** their place in heaven.	NIG

LOT (87) [LOT'S, LOTS, PUR]

Ge	11:27	And Haran became the father of **L**.	4288
	11:31	his grandson **L** son of Haran,	4288
	12: 4	and **L** went with him.	4288
	12: 5	He took his wife Sarai, his nephew **L**,	4288
	13: 1	and **L** went with him.	4288
	13: 5	Now **L**, who was moving about	4288
	13: 7	Abram's herdsmen and the herdsmen of **L**.	4288
	13: 8	So Abram said to **L**,	4288
	13:10	**L** looked up and saw that the whole plain	4288
	13:11	So **L** chose for himself the whole plain of	4288
	13:12	while **L** lived among the cities of the plain	4288
	13:14	to Abram after **L** had parted from him,	4288
	14:12	They also carried off Abram's nephew **L**	4288
	14:16	the goods and brought back his relative **L**	4288
	19: 1	**L** was sitting in the gateway of the city.	4288
	19: 5	They called to **L**, "Where are the men	4288
	19: 6	**L** went outside to meet them and shut	4288
	19: 9	on **L** and moved forward to break down	4288
	19:10	and pulled **L** back into the house and shut	4288
	19:12	The two men said to **L**,	4288
	19:14	**L** went out and spoke to his sons-in-law	4288
	19:15	the angels urged **L**, saying, "Hurry!	4288
	19:18	But **L** said to them, "No, my lords, please!	4288

Column 3

Ge	19:23	By the time **L** reached Zoar,	4288
	19:29	and he brought **L** out of the catastrophe	4288
	19:29	the cities where **L** had lived.	4288
	19:30	**L** and his two daughters left Zoar	4288
Lev	16: 8	one **l** for the LORD and the other for	1598
	16: 9	Aaron shall bring the goat whose **l** falls to	1598
	16:10	the goat chosen by **l** as the scapegoat shall	1598
Nu	26:55	Be sure that the land is distributed by **l**.	1598
	26:56	Each inheritance is to be distributed by **l**."	1598
	33:54	Distribute the land by **l**,	1598
	33:54	Whatever falls to them by **l** will be theirs.	1598
	34:13	"Assign this land by **l** as an inheritance.	1598
	36: 2	as an inheritance to the Israelites by **l**,	1598
Dt	2: 9	I have given Ar to the descendants of **L** as	4288
	2:19	as a possession to the descendants of **L**."	4288
Jos	14: 2	Their inheritances were assigned by **l** to	1598
	18:11	The **l** came up *for* the tribe of Benjamin,	1598
	19: 1	second **l** came out for the tribe of Simeon,	1598
	19:10	The third **l** came up for Zebulun,	1598
	19:17	The fourth **l** came out for Issachar,	1598
	19:24	The fifth **l** came out for the tribe of Asher,	1598
	19:32	The sixth **l** came out for Naphtali,	1598
	19:40	seventh **l** came out for the tribe of Dan,	1598
	19:51	of the tribal clans of Israel assigned by **l**	1598
	21: 4	The first **l** came out for the Kohathites,	1598
	21:10	because the first **l** fell to them):	1598
Jdg	20: 9	We'll go up against it as the **l** directs.	1598
1Sa	14:41	And Jonathan and Saul were taken by **l**,	NIH
	14:42	the **l** between me and Jonathan my son."	NIH
1Ch	6:54	because the first **l** fell for them):	1598
	24: 7	The first **l** fell to Jehoiarib,	1598
	25: 9	The first **l**, which was for Asaph,	1598
	26:14	The **l** for the East Gate fell to Shelemiah,	1598
	26:14	and the **l** for the North Gate fell to him.	1598
	26:15	**l** for the South Gate fell to Obed-Edom,	NIH
	26:15	the **l** for the storehouse fell to his sons.	NIH
Est	3: 7	they cast the pur (that is, the **l**)	1598
	3: 7	And the **l** fell on the twelfth month,	NIH
	9:24	cast the pur (that is, the **l**) for their ruin.	1598
Job	31: 2	For what is man's **l** *from* God above,	2750
Ps	11: 6	a scorching wind will be their **l**.	3926+4987
	16: 5	you have made my **l** secure.	1598
	50:18	you throw in your **l** with adulterers.	2750
	83: 8	to lend strength to the descendants of **L**.	4288
Pr	1:14	throw in your **l** with us, and we will share	1598
	6:33	Blows and disgrace *are* his **l**,	5162
	16:33	The **l** is cast into the lap, but its every	1598
	18:18	Casting the **l** settles disputes	1598
Ecc	3:22	because that is his **l**.	2750
	5:18	life God has given him—for this is his **l**.	2750
	5:19	to accept his **l** and be happy in his work—	2750
	9: 9	For this is your **l** in life and	2750
Isa	17:14	the **l** of those who plunder us.	1598
	57: 6	are your portion; they, they are your **l**.	1598
Jer	13:25	This is your **l**, the portion I have decreed	1598
Eze	21:27	Into his right hand will come the **l**	7877
Jnh	1: 7	They cast lots and the **l** fell on Jonah.	1598
Mic	2: 5	of the LORD to divide the land by **l**.	1598
Lk	1: 9	he *was* **chosen** by **l**, according to	3275
	17:28	"It was the same in the days *of* **L**.	3397
	17:29	But the day **L** left Sodom,	3397
Jn	19:24	"Let's **decide by l** who will get it."	3275
Ac	1:26	they cast lots, and the **l** fell to Matthias;	3102
2Pe	2: 7	and if he rescued **L**, a righteous man,	3397

LOT'S (3) [LOT]

Ge	19:26	But **L** wife looked back,	2257S
	19:36	So both of **L** daughters became pregnant	4288
Lk	17:32	Remember **L** wife!	3397

LOTAN (5) [LOTAN'S]

Ge	36:20	**L**, Shobal, Zibeon, Anah,	4289
	36:22	The sons of **L**: Hori and Homam.	4289
	36:29	These were the Horite chiefs: **L**, Shobal,	4289
1Ch	1:38	The sons of Seir: **L**, Shobal, Zibeon,	4289
	1:39	The sons of **L**: Hori and Homam.	4289

LOTAN'S (2) [LOTAN]

Ge	36:22	Timna was **L** sister.	4289
1Ch	1:39	Timna was **L** sister.	4289

LOTHE (KJV) See LOATHE, NOT ABLE

LOTIONS (4)

2Sa	12:20	**put on l** and changed his clothes,	6057
	14: 2	and don't use any **cosmetic l**.	9043
Da	10: 3	and *I* used no **l** at all	6057+6057
Am	6: 6	by the bowlful and use the finest **l**,	9043

LOTS (26) [LOT]

Lev	16: 8	He is to cast **l** for the two goats—	1598
Jos	18: 6	and I will cast **l** for you in the presence of	1598
	18: 8	and I will cast **l** for you here at Shiloh in	1598
	18:10	Joshua then cast **l** for them in Shiloh in	1598
1Ch	24:31	by **drawing l**, for there were officials of	1598
	24:31	They also cast **l**, just as their brothers	1598
	25: 8	cast **l** for their duties.	1598
	26:13	were cast for each gate,	1598
	26:14	Then **l** were cast for his son Zechariah,	1598
	26:16	The **l** for the West Gate and	NIH
Ne	10:34	have cast **l** to determine when each	1598
	11: 1	of the people cast **l** to bring one out	1598
Job	6:27	You would even cast **l** for the fatherless	NIH

†**LORD'S** distinguishes the proper name of God, *Yahweh's*, indicated in the NIV by "LORD's," from the words translated "Lord's" and "lord's," indexed under the heading *LORD'S, page 686.

Ps 22:18 among them and cast l for my clothing. 1598
Eze 21:21 *He will cast* l with arrows, 7837
24: 6 Empty it piece by piece without casting l 1598
Joel 3: 3 They cast l for my people and traded boys 1598
Ob 1:11 and foreigners entered his gates and cast l 1598
Jnh 1: 7 let us cast l to find out who is responsible 1598
1: 7 They cast l and the lot fell on Jonah. 1598
Na 3:10 L were cast for her nobles. 1598
Mt 27:35 they divided up his clothes by casting l. 3102
Mk 15:24 they cast l to see what each would get. 3102
Lk 23:34 they divided up his clothes by casting l. 3102
Jn 19:24 among them and cast l for my clothing." 3102
Ac 1:26 they cast l, and the lot fell to Matthias; 3102

LOTUS (1) [LOTUSES]
Job 40:21 Under the l **plants** he lies, 7365

LOTUSES (1) [LOTUS]
Job 40:22 The l conceal him in their shadow; 7365

LOUD (61) [ALOUD, LOUDER, LOUDLY]
Ge 27:34 burst out with a l and bitter cry 1524+4394+6330
Ex 11: 6 be l wailing throughout Egypt— 1524
12:30 and there was l wailing in Egypt, 1524
19:16 and a very l trumpet blast. 2617
Dt 5:22 a l voice to your whole assembly there on 1524
27:14 to all the people of Israel in a l voice: 8123
Jos 6: 5 have all the people give a l shout; 1524
6:20 when the people gave a l shout, 1524
1Sa 7:10 the LORD thundered with l thunder 1524
1Ki 8:55 the whole assembly of Israel in a l voice, 1524
2Ch 15:14 an oath to the LORD with l acclamation, 1524
20:19 the God of Israel, with very l voice. 1524
Ezr 10:12 whole assembly responded with a l voice: 1524
Ne 9: 4 with l voices to the LORD their God. 1524
Ps 102: 5 Because of my l groaning I am reduced 7754
Pr 7:11 (She *is* l and defiant, 2159
9:13 The woman Folly *is* l; 2159
Jer 4:19 they have raised a l cry against you. 4849
46:17 'Pharaoh king of Egypt is only a l **noise;** 8623
Eze 3:12 I heard behind me a l rumbling sound— 1524
3:13 a l rumbling sound. 1524
9: 1 Then I heard him call out in a l voice, 1524
11:13 I fell facedown and cried out in a l voice, 1524
Da 4:14 He called in a *l voice:* 10264
Zep 1:10 and a l crash from the hills. 1524
Mt 24:31 with a l trumpet call, 3489
27:46 the ninth hour Jesus cried out *in a* l voice, 3489
27:50 Jesus had cried out again *in a* l voice, 3489
Mk 15:34 the ninth hour Jesus cried out *in a* l voice, 3489
15:37 With a l cry, Jesus breathed his last. 3489
Lk 1:42 *In a* l voice she exclaimed: 3489
17:13 and **called out in a** l voice, 149+5889
17:15 came back, praising God in a l voice. 3489
19:37 to praise God in l voices for all 3489
23:23 *with* l shouts they insistently demanded 3489
23:46 Jesus called out *with* a l voice, "Father, 3489
Jn 7:37 Jesus stood and said in **a l voice,** 3189
11:43 Jesus called *in a* l voice, "Lazarus, 3489
1Th 4:16 down from heaven, with a l **command,** 3026
Heb 5: 7 and petitions with l cries and tears to 2708
Rev 1:10 I heard behind me a l voice like a trumpet, 3489
5: 2 a mighty angel proclaiming in a l voice, 3489
5:12 *In a* l voice they sang: 3489
6:10 They called out in a l voice, "How long, 3489
7: 2 He called out *in a* l voice to the four angels 3489
7:10 And they cried out *in a* l voice: 3489
8:13 in midair call out in a l voice: 3489
10: 3 he gave a l shout like the roar of a lion. 3489
11:12 a l voice from heaven saying to them, 3489
11:15 and there were l voices in heaven, 3489
12:10 Then I heard a l voice in heaven say: 3489
14: 2 the roar of rushing waters and like a l peal 3489
14: 7 He said in a l voice, 3489
14: 9 and said in a l voice: 3489
14:15 in a l voice to him who was sitting on 3489
14:18 came from the altar and called *in a* l voice 3489
16: 1 a l voice from the temple saying to 3489
16:17 the temple came a l voice from the throne, 3489
19: 6 the roar of rushing waters and like l peals 2708
19:17 a l voice to all the birds flying in midair, 3489
21: 3 I heard a l voice from the throne saying, 3489

LOUDER (7) [LOUD]
Ex 19:19 the sound of the trumpet **grew l and louder.** 2143+2256+2618+4394
19:19 the sound of the trumpet **grew louder and l.** 2143+2256+2618+4394
1Ki 18:27 Elijah began to taunt them. "Shout l!" 1524
18:28 So they shouted l and slashed themselves 1524
Mt 20:31 but they shouted **all the l,** "Lord, 3505
27:23 But they shouted **all the l,** "Crucify him!" 4360
Mk 15:14 But they shouted **all the l,** "Crucify him!" 4360

LOUDLY (7) [LOUD]
Ge 45: 2 he **wept so l** that the Egyptians heard him, 906+928+1140+5989+7754
50:10 they lamented l and bitterly; 1524
2Sa 13:36 the king's sons came in, wailing l. 5951+7754
Est 4: 1 wailing l and bitterly. 1524
Pr 27:14 If a man l blesses his neighbor early in the morning, 928+1524+7754
Da 3: 4 Then the herald l proclaimed, 10089+10264
Mk 5:38 with people crying and wailing l. 4498

LOUNGE (1) [LOUNGING]
Am 6: 4 You lie on beds inlaid with ivory and l 6242

LOUNGING (2) [LOUNGE]
Isa 47: 8 l in your security and saying to yourself, 3782
Am 6: 7 your feasting and l will end. 6242

LOVE (551) [BELOVED, LOVED, LOVELY, LOVER, LOVER'S, LOVERS, LOVES, LOVING, LOVING-KINDNESS, LOVINGLY]
Ge 20:13 'This is how you can show your l to me: 2876
22: 2 your only son, Isaac, whom you l, 170
29:18 Jacob *was* in l with Rachel and said, 170
29:20 a few days to him because of his l *for* her. 173
29:32 Surely my husband *will* l me now." 170
Ex 15:13 "In your **unfailing** l you will lead 2876
20: 6 but showing l to a thousand [generations] 2876
20: 6 a thousand [generations] of *those who* l me 170
21: 5 '*I* l my master and my wife and children 170
34: 6 abounding in l and faithfulness, 2876
34: 7 maintaining l to thousands, 2876
Lev 19:18 but l your neighbor as yourself. 170
19:34 L him as yourself, 170
Nu 14:18 in l and forgiving sin and rebellion. 2876
14:19 In accordance with your great l, 2876
Dt 5:10 but showing l to a thousand [generations] 2876
5:10 *those who* l me and keep my commandments 170
6: 5 L the LORD your God with all your heart 170
7: 9 the faithful God, keeping his covenant of l 2876
7: 9 a thousand generations of *those who* l him 170
7:12 will keep his covenant of l with you, 2876
7:13 *He will* l you and bless you 170
10:12 to walk in all his ways, to l him, 170
10:19 And *you are to* l those who are aliens, 170
11: 1 L the LORD your God and keep his 170
11:13 to l the LORD your God and to serve 170
11:22 to l the LORD your God, to walk in all his 170
13: 3 to find out whether you l him with all 170
13: 6 or your son or daughter, or the wife you l, 2668
19: 9 to l the LORD your God and to walk 170
21:15 the son of the wife he does *not* l, 8535
21:16 the son of the wife *he does not* l. 8533
30: 6 that you *may* l him with all your heart and 170
30:16 to l the LORD your God, to walk in his ways 170
30:20 and that you *may* l the LORD your God, 170
33: 3 Surely it is you *who* l the people; 2462
Jos 22: 5 to l the LORD your God, 170
23:11 be very careful to l the LORD your God. 170
Jdg 5:31 But *may they who* l you be like the sun 170
14:16 *You* don't really l me. 170
16: 4 he fell in l with a woman in the Valley 170
16:15 '*I* l you,' when you won't confide in me? 170
1Sa 18:20 Now Saul's daughter Michal *was* in l with 170
20:17 David reaffirm his oath out of l *for* him, 170
2Sa 1:26 Your l for me was wonderful, 173
7:15 my l will never be taken away from him, 2876
13: 1 Amnon son of David fell in l with Tamar. 170
13: 4 Amnon said to him, "I'm in l with Tamar, 170
16:17 "Is this the l you show your friend? 2876
19: 6 You l *those who* hate you 170
19: 6 and hate *those who* l you. 170
1Ki 3: 3 Solomon **showed** *his* l *for* the LORD 170
8:23 you who keep your covenant of l 2876
10: 9 of the LORD's eternal l *for* Israel, 173
11: 2 Solomon held fast to them in l. 173
1Ch 16:34 his l endures forever. 2876
16:41 "for his l endures forever." 2876
17:13 I will never take my l away from him, 2876
2Ch 5:13 his l endures forever." 2876
6:14 you who keep your covenant of l 2876
6:42 Remember the **great** l *promised* 2876
7: 3 his l endures forever." 2876
7: 6 saying, "His l endures forever." 2876
9: 8 the l of your God *for* Israel and his desire 170
19: 2 and *those who* hate the LORD? 170
20:21 for his l endures forever. 2876
Ezr 3:11 his l to Israel endures forever." 2876
Ne 1: 5 his covenant of l *with those who* love him 2876
1: 5 his covenant of love with *those who* l him 170
9:17 slow to anger and abounding in l. 2876
9:32 who keeps his covenant of l, 2876
13:22 to me according to your great l. 2876
Job 15:34 the tents of *those who* l **bribes.** 8816
19:19 those *I* l have turned against me. 170
37:13 or to water his earth and show his l. 2876
Ps 4: 2 How long *will you* l delusions 170
5:11 *those who* l your name may rejoice in you. 170
6: 4 save me because of your **unfailing** l. 2876
11: 5 and *those who* l violence his soul hates. 170
13: 5 But I trust in your **unfailing** l; 2876
17: 7 Show the wonder of your **great** l, 2876
18: 1 *I* l you, O LORD, my strength. 8163
21: 7 through the **unfailing** l *of* the Most High 2876
23: 6 Surely goodness and l will follow me all 2876
25: 6 O LORD, your great mercy and l, 2876
25: 7 according to your l remember me, 2876
26: 3 for your l is ever before me, 2876
26: 8 *I* l the house where you live, O LORD, 170
31: 7 I will be glad and rejoice in your l, 2876
31:16 save me in your **unfailing** l. 2876
31:21 for he showed his wonderful l to me 2876
31:23 L the LORD, all his saints! 170
32:10 but the LORD's **unfailing** l surrounds 2876
33: 5 the earth is full of his **unfailing** l. 2876

Ps 33:18 those who hope in his **unfailing** l, 2876
33:22 May your **unfailing** l rest upon us, 2876
36: 5 Your l, O LORD, reaches to the heavens, 2876
36: 7 How priceless is your **unfailing** l! 2876
36:10 Continue your l to those who know you, 2876
40:10 not conceal your l and your truth from 2876
40:11 your l and your truth always protect 2876
40:16 may *those who* l your salvation always say, 170
42: 8 By day the LORD directs his l, 2876
44:26 redeem us because of your **unfailing** l. 2876
45: 7 *You* l righteousness and hate wickedness; 170
48: 9 O God, we meditate on your **unfailing** l. 2876
51: 1 O God, according to your **unfailing** l; 2876
52: 3 *You* l evil rather than good, 170
52: 4 *You* l every harmful word, 170
52: 8 in God's **unfailing** l for ever and ever. 2876
57: 3 God sends his l and his faithfulness. 2876
57:10 great is your l, reaching to the heavens, 2876
59:16 in the morning I will sing of your l; 2876
60: 5 that *those* you l may be delivered. 3351
61: 7 appoint your l and faithfulness 2876
63: 3 Because your l is better than life, 2876
66:20 not rejected my prayer or withheld his l 2876
69:13 in your great l, O God, 2876
69:16 O LORD, out of the goodness of your l; 2876
69:36 and *those who* l his name will dwell there. 170
70: 4 may *those who* l your salvation always say, 170
77: 8 Has his **unfailing** l vanished forever? 2876
85: 7 Show us your **unfailing** l, O LORD, 2876
85:10 L and faithfulness meet together; 2876
86: 5 abounding in l to all who call to you. 2876
86:13 For great is your l toward me; 2876
86:15 abounding in l and faithfulness. 2876
88:11 Is your l declared in the grave, 2876
89: 1 of the LORD's **great** l forever; 2876
89: 2 that your l stands firm forever, 2876
89:14 l and faithfulness go before you. 2876
89:24 My faithful l will be with him, 2876
89:28 I will maintain my l to him forever, 2876
89:33 but I will not take my l from him, 2876
89:49 where is your former **great** l, 2876
90:14 in the morning with your **unfailing** l, 2876
92: 2 to proclaim your l in the morning 2876
94:18 I said, "My foot is slipping," your l, 2876
97:10 *Let those who* l the LORD hate evil, 170
98: 3 He has remembered his l 2876
100: 5 LORD is good and his l endures forever; 2876
101: 1 I will sing of your l and justice; 2876
103: 4 and crowns you with l and compassion, 2876
103: 8 slow to anger, abounding in l. 2876
103:11 so great is his l for those who fear him; 2876
103:17 the LORD's l is with those who fear him, 2876
106: 1 for he is good; his l endures forever. 2876
106:45 and out of his great l he relented. 2876
107: 1 for he is good; his l endures forever. 2876
107: 8 give thanks to the LORD for his **unfailing** l 2876
107:15 give thanks to the LORD for his **unfailing** l 2876
107:21 give thanks to the LORD for his **unfailing** l 2876
107:31 give thanks to the LORD for his **unfailing** l 2876
107:43 and consider the **great** l *of* the LORD. 2876
108: 4 great is your l, higher than the heavens; 2876
108: 6 that *those* you l may be delivered. 3351
109:21 out of the goodness of your l, deliver me. 2876
109:26 save me in accordance with your l. 2876
115: 1 because of your l and faithfulness. 2876
116: 1 *I* l the LORD, for he heard my voice; 170
117: 2 For great is his l toward us, 2876
118: 1 for he is good; his l endures forever. 2876
118: 2 Let Israel say: "His l endures forever." 2876
118: 3 "His l endures forever." 2876
118: 4 "His l endures forever." 2876
118:29 for he is good; his l endures forever. 2876
119:41 May your **unfailing** l come to me, 2876
119:47 delight in your commands because *I* l them. 170
119:48 my hands to your commands, which *I* l, 170
119:64 The earth is filled with your l, O LORD; 2876
119:76 May your **unfailing** l be my comfort, 2876
119:88 Preserve my life according to your l, 2876
119:97 Oh, how *I* l your law! 170
119:113 but *I* l your law. 170
119:119 therefore *I* l your statutes. 170
119:124 Deal with your servant according to your l 2876
119:127 Because *I* l your commands more than gold, 170
119:132 you always do to *those who* l your name. 170
119:149 Hear my voice in accordance with your l; 2876
119:159 See how *I* l your precepts; 170
119:159 O LORD, according to your l, 2876
119:163 and abhor falsehood but *I* l your law. 170
119:165 Great peace have *they who* l your law, 170
119:167 I obey your statutes, for *I* l them greatly. 170
122: 6 "May *those who* l you be secure. 170
130: 7 for with the LORD is **unfailing** l and 2876
136: 1 His l endures forever. 2876
136: 2 His l endures forever. 2876
136: 3 His l endures forever. 2876
136: 4 His l endures forever. 2876
136: 5 His l endures forever. 2876
136: 6 His l endures forever. 2876
136: 7 His l endures forever. 2876
136: 8 His l endures forever. 2876
136: 9 His l endures forever. 2876
136:10 His l endures forever. 2876
136:11 His l endures forever. 2876
136:12 His l endures forever. 2876
136:13 His l endures forever. 2876
136:14 His l endures forever. 2876
136:15 His l endures forever. 2876

Ps	136:16	His l endures forever.	2876

Ps 136:16 His l endures forever. 2876
136:17 His l endures forever. 2876
136:18 His l endures forever. 2876
136:19 His l endures forever. 2876
136:20 His l endures forever. 2876
136:21 His l endures forever. 2876
136:22 His l endures forever. 2876
136:23 His l endures forever. 2876
136:24 His l endures forever. 2876
136:25 His l endures forever. 2876
136:26 His l endures forever. 2876
138:2 and will praise your name for your l 2876
138:8 your l, O LORD, endures forever— 2876
143:8 bring me word of your unfailing l, 2876
143:12 In your unfailing l, silence my enemies; 2876
145:8 slow to anger and rich in l. 170
145:20 The LORD watches over all who l him, 170
147:11 who put their hope in his unfailing l, 2876
Pr 1:22 "How long will you simple ones l your simple ways? 170
3:3 Let l and faithfulness never leave you; 2876
4:6 l her, and she will watch over you. 170
5:19 may you ever be captivated by her l. 173
7:18 Come, let's drink deep of l till morning; 1856
7:18 let's enjoy ourselves with l! 171
8:17 I l those who love me, 170
8:17 I love those who l me, 170
8:21 bestowing wealth on those who l me 170
8:36 all who hate me l death." 170
9:8 rebuke a wise man and he will l you. 170
10:12 but l covers over all wrongs. 173
14:22 But those who plan what is good find l 2876
15:17 a meal of vegetables where there is l than 173
16:6 Through l and faithfulness sin is atoned for; 2876
17:9 He who covers over an offense promotes l, 173
18:21 and those who l it will eat its fruit. 170
19:22 What a man desires is unfailing l; 2876
20:6 Many a man claims to have unfailing l, 2876
20:13 Do not l sleep or you will grow poor; 170
20:28 L and faithfulness keep a king safe; 2876
20:28 through l his throne is made secure. 2876
21:21 who pursues righteousness and l finds life, 2876
27:5 Better is open rebuke than hidden l. 173
Ecc 3:8 a time to l and a time to hate, 170
9:1 but no man knows whether l or hate awaits 173
9:6 Their l, their hate and their jealousy 173
9:9 Enjoy life with your wife, whom you l, 170
SS 1:2 for your l is more delightful than wine. 1856
1:3 No wonder the maidens l you! 170
1:4 we will praise your l more than wine. 1856
1:7 Tell me, you whom I l, 170
2:4 and his banner over me is l. 173
2:5 for I am faint with l. 173
2:7 not arouse or awaken l until it so desires. 173
3:5 not arouse or awaken l until it so desires. 173
4:10 delightful is your l, my sister, my bride! 1856
4:10 much more pleasing is your l than wine, 1856
5:8 Tell him I am faint with l. 173
7:6 beautiful you are and how pleasing, O l, 173
7:12 there I will give you my l. 1856
8:4 not arouse or awaken l until it so desires. 173
8:6 for l is as strong as death, 173
8:7 Many waters cannot quench l; 173
8:7 to give all the wealth of his house for l, 173
Isa 1:23 they all l bribes and chase after gifts. 170
5:1 for the one I l a song about his vineyard: 3351
16:5 In l a throne will be established; 2876
38:17 In your l you kept me from the pit 3137
43:4 honored in my sight, and because I l you, 170
54:10 yet my unfailing l for you will not 2876
55:3 my faithful l promised to David. 2876
56:6 to l the name of the LORD, 170
56:10 they lie around and dream, they l to sleep. 170
57:8 a pact with those whose beds you l, 170
61:8 "For I, the LORD, l justice; 170
63:9 In his l and mercy he redeemed them; 173
66:10 be glad for her, all you who l her; 170
Jer 2:25 I l foreign gods, and I must go after them.' 170
2:33 How skilled you are at pursuing l! 173
5:31 and my people l it this way. 170
12:7 the one I l into the hands of her enemies. 3342
14:10 "They greatly l to wander; 170
16:5 my l and my pity from this people," 2876
31:3 "I have loved you with an everlasting l; 173
32:18 You show l to thousands but bring 2876
33:11 the LORD is good; his l endures forever." 2876
La 3:22 Because of the LORD's great l we are 2876
3:32 so great is his unfailing l. 2876
Eze 16:8 and saw that you were old enough for l, 1856
23:17 Babylonians came to her, to the bed of l, 1856
33:32 are nothing more than one who sings l songs 6312
Da 9:4 who keeps his covenant of l with all who 2876
9:4 his covenant of love with all who l him 170
Hos 1:6 for I will no longer show l to the house 8163
1:7 Yet I will show l to the house of Judah, 8163
2:4 I will not show my l to her children, 8163
2:19 and justice, in l and compassion. 170
2:23 I will show my l to the one I called 8163
3:1 "Go, show your l to your wife again, 170
3:1 L her as the LORD loves the Israelites, NIH
3:1 though they turn to other gods and l 170
4:1 "There is no faithfulness, no l, 2876
4:18 their rulers dearly l shameful ways. 170
6:4 Your l is like the morning mist, 2876
9:1 you l the wages of a prostitute 170
9:15 I will no longer l them; 170
10:12 reap the fruit of unfailing l, 2876

Hos 11:4 with cords of human kindness, with ties of l; 173
12:6 maintain l and justice, and wait for 2876
14:4 heal their waywardness and l them freely, 170
Joel 2:13 slow to anger and abounding in l, 2876
Am 4:5 for this is what you l to do," 170
5:15 l good; maintain justice in the courts. 170
Jnh 4:2 slow to anger and abounding in l, 2876
Mic 3:2 you who hate good and l evil; 170
6:8 and to l mercy and to walk humbly 170
Zep 3:17 he will quiet you with his l, 173
Zec 8:17 and do not l to swear falsely. 170
8:19 Therefore l truth and peace." 170
Mt 3:17 Son, whom I l; with him I am well pleased." 28
5:43 'L your neighbor and hate your enemy.' 26
5:44 L your enemies and pray for those who 26
5:46 If you l those who love you, 26
5:46 If you l those who l you, 26
6:5 for they l to pray standing in the 5797
6:24 Either he will hate the one and l the other, 26
12:18 the one I l, in whom I delight; 28
17:5 whom I l; with him I am well pleased. 28
19:19 and 'l your neighbor as yourself.' " 26
22:37 " 'L the Lord your God with all your heart 26
22:39 'L your neighbor as yourself.' 26
23:6 they l the place of honor at banquets and 5797
23:7 they l to be greeted in the marketplaces NIG
24:12 the l of most will grow cold, 27
Mk 1:11 "You are my Son, whom I l. 28
9:7 "This is my Son, whom I l. 28
12:30 L the Lord your God with all your heart 26
12:31 'L your neighbor as yourself.' 26
12:33 To l him with all your heart, 26
12:33 and to l your neighbor as yourself.' 26
Lk 3:22 "You are my Son, whom I l; 28
6:27 L your enemies, do good to those who hate 26
6:32 "If you l those who love you, 26
6:32 "If you love those who l you, 26
6:32 Even 'sinners' l those who love them. 26
6:32 Even 'sinners' love those who l them. 26
6:35 But l your enemies, do good to them, 26
7:42 Now which of them will l him more?" 26
10:27 " 'L the Lord your God with all your heart 26
10:27 and, 'L your neighbor as yourself.' " NIG
11:42 but you neglect justice and the l of God. 27
11:43 because you l the most important seats in 26
16:13 Either he will hate the one and l the other, 26
20:13 I will send my son, whom I l; 28
20:46 like to walk around in flowing robes and l 5797
Jn 5:42 I know that you do not have the l of God 27
8:42 "If God were your Father, you would l me, 26
11:3 "Lord, the one you l is sick." 5797
13:1 showed them the full extent of his l. 26
13:34 new command I give you: L one another. 26
13:34 As I have loved you, so you must l one another. 26
13:35 my disciples, if you l one another." 27+2400
14:15 "If you l me, you will obey what I command. 26
14:21 I too will l him and show myself to him." 26
14:23 My Father will l him, and we will come 26
14:24 does not l me will not obey my teaching. 26
14:31 the world must learn that I l the Father 26
15:9 Now remain in my l. 27
15:10 If you obey my commands, you will remain in my l, 27
15:10 my Father's commands and remain in his l. 27
15:12 L each other as I have loved you. 26
15:13 Greater l has no one than this, 27
15:17 This is my command: L each other. 26
15:19 it would l you as its own. 5797
17:26 in order that the l you have for me may be 26+27
21:15 do you truly l me more than these?" 26
21:15 Lord," he said, "you know that I l you." 5797
21:16 "Simon son of John, do you truly l me?" 26
21:16 "Yes, Lord, you know that I l you." 5797
21:17 "Simon son of John, do you l me?" 5797
21:17 asked him the third time, "Do you l me?" 5797
21:17 you know all things; you know that I l you." 5797
Ro 5:5 because God has poured out his l 27
5:8 God demonstrates his own l for us in this: 27
8:28 for the good of those who l him, 26
8:35 Who shall separate us from the l of Christ? 27
8:39 be able to separate us from the l of God 27
12:9 L must be sincere. 27
12:10 Be devoted to one another in brotherly l. 5789
13:8 the continuing debt to l one another, 26
13:9 "L your neighbor as yourself." 26
13:10 L does no harm to its neighbor. 27
13:10 Therefore l is the fulfillment of the law. 27
14:15 you are no longer acting in l. 27
15:30 Lord Jesus Christ and by the l of the Spirit, 27
16:8 Greet Ampliatus, whom I l in the Lord. 28
1Co 2:9 God has prepared for those who l him"— 26
4:17 Timothy, my son whom I l, 28
4:21 or in l and with a gentle spirit? 27
8:1 Knowledge puffs up, but l builds up. 27
13:1 but have not l, I am only a resounding gong 27
13:2 but have not l, I am nothing. 27
13:3 but have not l, I gain nothing. 27
13:4 L is patient, love is kind. 27
13:4 Love is patient, l is kind. 27
13:6 L does not delight in evil but rejoices with NIG
13:8 L never fails. 27
13:13 now these three remain: faith, hope and l. 27
13:13 But the greatest of these is l. 27
14:1 Follow the way of l and 27
16:14 Do everything in l. 27
16:22 If anyone does not l the Lord— 5797

1Co 16:24 My l to all of you in Christ Jesus. Amen. 27
2Co 2:4 to let you know the depth of my l for you. 27
2:8 therefore, to reaffirm your l for him. 27
5:14 For Christ's l compels us, 27
6:6 in the Holy Spirit and in sincere l; 27
8:7 in complete earnestness and in your l 27
8:8 but I want to test the sincerity of your l 27
8:24 of your l and the reason for our pride 27
11:11 Because I do not l you? 26
12:15 If I l you more, will you love me less? 26
12:15 If I love you more, will you l me less? 26
13:11 the God of l and peace will be with you. 27
13:14 and the l of God, and the fellowship of 27
Gal 5:6 counts is faith expressing itself through l. 27
5:13 rather, serve one another in l. 26
5:14 "L your neighbor as yourself." 26
5:22 But the fruit of the Spirit is l, joy, peace, 27
Eph 1:4 holy and blameless in his sight. In l 27
1:15 the Lord Jesus and your l for all the saints, 27
2:4 But because of his great l for us, God, 26+27
3:17 being rooted and established in l, 27
3:18 and high and deep is the l of Christ, 27
3:19 to know this l that surpasses knowledge— NIG
4:2 be patient, bearing with one another in l. 27
4:15 Instead, speaking the truth in l, 27
4:16 grows and builds itself up in l, 27
5:2 and live a life of l, just as Christ loved us 27
5:25 Husbands, l your wives, just as Christ loved 26
5:28 to l their wives as their own bodies. 26
5:33 also must l his wife as he loves himself, 26
6:23 and l with faith from God the Father and 27
6:24 Grace to all who l our Lord Jesus Christ 26
6:24 Lord Jesus Christ with an undying l. NIG
Php 1:9 that your l may abound more and more 27
1:16 The latter do so in l, 27
2:1 if any comfort from his l, 27
2:2 by being like-minded, having the same l, 27
2:2 my brothers, you whom I l and long for, 28
Col 1:4 and of the l you have for all the saints— 27
1:5 the faith and l that spring from the hope NIG
1:8 who also told us of your l in the Spirit. 27
2:2 be encouraged in heart and united in l, 27
3:14 And over all these virtues put on l, 27
3:19 Husbands, l your wives and do not be harsh 26
1Th 1:3 your labor prompted by l, 27
3:6 good news about your faith and l. 27
3:12 May the Lord make your l increase 27
4:9 about brotherly l we do not need to write 5789
4:9 have been taught by God to l each other. 27
4:10 you do l all the brothers 899S
5:8 putting on faith and l as a breastplate, 27
5:13 Hold them in the highest regard in l 27
2Th 1:3 and the l every one of you has for each 27
2:10 because they refused to l the truth and so 27
3:5 the Lord direct your hearts into God's l 27
1Ti 1:5 The goal of this command is l, 27
1:14 the faith and l that are in Christ Jesus. 27
2:15 l and holiness with propriety. 27
4:12 in life, in l, in faith and in purity. 27
6:10 the l of money is a root of all kinds of evil. 5794
6:11 faith, l, endurance and gentleness. 27
2Ti 1:7 a spirit of power, of l and of self-discipline. 27
1:13 with faith and l in Christ Jesus. 27
2:22 and pursue righteousness, faith, l and peace, 27
3:3 without l, unforgiving, slanderous, 845
3:10 my purpose, faith, patience, l, endurance, 27
Tit 2:2 and sound in faith, in l and in endurance. 27
2:4 the younger women to l their husbands 5791
3:4 and l of God our Savior appeared, 5792
3:15 Greet those who l us in the faith. 5797
Phm 1:5 the Lord Jesus and your l for all the saints. 27
1:7 Your l has given me great joy 27
1:9 yet I appeal to you on the basis of l. 27
Heb 6:10 and the l you have shown him 27
10:24 how we may spur one another on toward l 27
13:5 Keep your lives free from the l of money 921
Jas 1:12 that God has promised to those who l him. 26
2:5 kingdom he promised those who l him? 26
2:8 "L your neighbor as yourself," 26
1Pe 1:8 Though you have not seen him, you l him; 26
1:22 that you have sincere l for your brothers, 5789
1:22 l one another deeply, from the heart. 26
2:17 L the brotherhood of believers, fear God, 27
3:8 be sympathetic, l as brothers, 5790
3:10 "Whoever would l life and see good days 26
4:8 Above all, l each other deeply, 27+2400
4:8 because l covers over a multitude of sins. 26
5:14 Greet one another with a kiss of l. 27
2Pe 1:7 and to brotherly kindness, l. 27
1:17 whom I l; with him I am well pleased." 28
1Jn 2:5 God's love is truly made complete in him. 27
2:15 Do not l the world or anything in the world. 26
2:15 the l of the Father is not in him. 27
3:1 How great is the l the Father has lavished 27
3:10 nor is anyone who does not l his brother. 26
3:11 We should l one another. 26
3:14 because we l our brothers. 26
3:14 Anyone who does not l remains in death. 26
3:16 This is how we know what l is: 27
3:17 how can the l of God be in him? 27
3:18 let us not l with words or tongue but 26
3:23 and to l one another as he commanded us. 26
4:7 Dear friends, let us l one another, 26
4:7 for l comes from God. 27
4:8 Whoever does not l does not know God, 26
4:8 because God is l. 27
4:9 This is how God showed his l among us: 27

1Jn	4:10	This is l: not that we loved God, but that	27
	4:11	we also ought to l one another.	26
	4:12	but if we l one another,	26
	4:12	God lives in us and his l is made complete	27
	4:16	we know and rely on the l God has for us.	27
	4:16	God is l.	27
	4:16	Whoever lives in l lives in God,	27
	4:17	In this way, l is made complete among us	27
	4:18	There is no fear in l.	27
	4:18	But perfect l drives out fear,	27
	4:18	The one who fears is not made perfect in l.	27
	4:19	We l because he first loved us.	26
	4:20	If anyone says, "I l God,"	26
	4:20	For anyone who *does* not l his brother,	26
	4:20	cannot l God, whom he has not seen.	26
	4:21	Whoever loves God must also l his brother.	26
	5:2	how we know that *we* l the children	26
	5:3	This is l for God: to obey his commands.	27
2Jn	1:1	whom I l in the truth—	26
	1:3	will be with us in truth and l.	27
	1:5	I ask that *we* l one another.	26
	1:6	And this is l:	27
	1:6	his command is that you walk in l.	899S
3Jn	1:1	and her children, whom I l in the truth.	26
	1:6	They have told the church about your l.	27
Jude	1:2	peace and l be yours in abundance.	27
	1:12	These men are blemishes at your **l feasts,**	27
	1:21	Keep yourselves in God's l as you wait	27
Rev	2:4	You have forsaken your first l.	27
	2:19	I know your deeds, your l and faith,	27
	3:19	Those whom I l I rebuke and discipline.	5797
	12:11	not l their lives so much as to shrink	26

LOVED (94) [LOVE]

Ge	24:67	So she became his wife, and *he* l her;	170
	25:28	who had a taste for wild game, l Esau,	170
	25:28	loved Esau, but Rebekah l Jacob.	170
	29:30	and *he* l Rachel more than Leah.	170
	29:31	the LORD saw that Leah *was* not l,	8533
	29:33	the LORD heard that I am not l,	8533
	34:3	and *he* l the girl and spoke tenderly to her.	170
	37:3	Now Israel l Joseph more than any	170
	37:4	that their father l him more than any	170
Dt	4:37	Because *he* l your forefathers	170
	7:8	But it was because the LORD l you	170
	10:15	on your forefathers and l them,	170
1Sa	1:5	a double portion because *he* l her,	170
	18:1	and *he* l him as himself.	170
	18:3	with David because he l him as himself.	170
	18:16	But all Israel and Judah l David,	170
	18:28	and that his daughter Michal l David,	170
	20:17	because *he* l him as he loved himself.	170
	20:17	because he loved him as he l himself.	173
2Sa	1:23	in life they *were* l and gracious,	170
	12:24	named him Solomon. The LORD l him;	170
	12:25	and because the LORD l him,	NIH
	13:15	In fact, he hated her more than *he had* l her.	170
1Ki	11:1	Solomon l many foreign women besides Pharaoh's daughter—	170
2Ch	11:21	Rehoboam l Maacah daughter	170
	26:10	for he l the soil.	170
Ne	13:26	*He was* l by his God,	170
Ps	44:3	and the light of your face, for *you* l them.	8354
	47:4	the pride of Jacob, whom he l.	170
	78:68	Mount Zion, which he l.	170
	88:18	and l ones from me;	170
	109:17	He l to pronounce a curse—	170
Isa	5:1	My **l one** had a vineyard on	3351
Jer	2:2	how as a bride you l me and followed me	173
	8:2	which *they have* l and served	170
	31:3	"I have l you *with* an everlasting love;	170
Eze	16:37	those you l as well as those you hated.	170
Hos	2:1	and of your sisters, 'My l one.'	8163
	2:23	to the one called 'Not my l one,'	8163
	3:1	she is l by another and is an adulteress.	170
	9:10	and became as vile as the **thing** they l.	171
	11:1	"When Israel was a child, I l him,	170
Mal	1:2	"*I have* l you," says the LORD.	170
	1:2	"But you ask, 'How *have you* l us?'	170
	1:2	"Yet *I have* l Jacob,	170
Mk	10:21	Jesus looked at him and l him.	26
	12:6	He had one left to send, a son, whom he l.	28
Lk	7:47	sins have been forgiven—for *she* l much.	26
	16:14	The Pharisees, *who* l money,	5639+5795
Jn	3:16	"For God so l the world that he gave his one and only Son,	26
	3:19	but men l darkness instead of light	26
	11:5	Jesus l Martha and her sister and Lazarus.	26
	11:36	Then the Jews said, "See how he l him!"	5797
	12:43	for *they* l praise from men more than	26
	13:1	*Having* l his own who were in the world,	26
	13:23	One of them, the disciple whom Jesus l,	26
	13:34	As *I have* l you, so you must love	26
	14:21	He who loves me *will be* l by my Father,	26
	14:28	If *you* l me, you would be glad that I am	26
	15:9	the Father *has* l me, so have I loved you.	26
	15:9	the Father has loved me, so *have I* l you.	26
	15:12	Love each other as *I have* l you.	26
	16:27	because you *have* l me and have believed	5797
	17:23	that you sent me and *have* l them even	26
	17:23	even as you have l me.	26
	17:24	because *you* l me before the creation of	26
	19:26	the disciple whom he l standing nearby,	26
	20:2	other disciple, the one Jesus l, and said,	5797
	21:7	the disciple whom Jesus l said to Peter,	26
	21:20	disciple whom Jesus was l following them.	26

Ro	1:7	in Rome who are l by God and called to	28
	8:37	more than conquerors through him who l us.	26
	9:13	"Jacob *I* l, but Esau I hated."	26
	9:25	and I will call her 'my l one' who is	26
	9:25	who is not my l one,"	26
	11:28	they are l on account of the patriarchs,	28
Gal	2:20	who l me and gave himself for me	26
Eph	5:1	Be imitators of God, therefore, as **dearly l** children	28
	5:2	as Christ l us and gave himself up for us	26
	5:25	as Christ l the church and gave himself up	26
Col	3:12	God's chosen people, holy and dearly l,	26
1Th	1:4	For we know, brothers l by God,	26
	2:8	*We* l you so much that we were delighted	3916
2Th	2:13	thank God for you, brothers l by the Lord,	26
	2:16	God our Father, who l us and	26
2Ti	4:10	for Demas, *because he* l this world,	26
Heb	1:9	*You have* l righteousness and hated	26
2Pe	2:15	who l the wages of wickedness.	26
1Jn	4:10	This is love: not that we l God,	26
	4:10	not that we loved God, but that he l us	26
	4:11	Dear friends, since God so l us,	26
	4:19	We love because he first l us.	26
Jude	1:1	*who are* l by God the Father and kept	26
Rev	3:9	and acknowledge that I *have* l you.	26

LOVELY (11) [LOVE]

Ge	29:17	but Rachel was l in form, and beautiful.	3637
Est	1:11	for she was l to look at.	3202
	2:7	Esther was l in form and features,	3637
Ps	84:1	How l is your dwelling place,	3351
SS	1:5	Dark am I, yet l,	5534
	2:14	for your voice is sweet, and your face is l.	5534
	4:3	your mouth is l.	5534
	5:16	he is altogether l.	4718
	6:4	my darling, as Tirzah, l as Jerusalem,	5534
Am	8:13	"the l young women and strong young men	3637
Php	4:8	whatever is l, whatever is admirable—	4713

LOVER (29) [LOVE]

SS	1:13	My l is to me a sachet of myrrh resting	1856
	1:14	My l is to me a cluster of henna blossoms	1856
	1:16	How handsome you are, my l!	1856
	2:3	is my l among the young men.	1856
	2:8	My l! Look! Here he comes,	1856
	2:9	My l is like a gazelle or a young stag.	1856
	2:10	My l spoke and said to me, "Arise,	1856
	2:16	My l is mine and I am his;	1856
	2:17	the shadows flee, turn, my l, and be like	1856
	4:16	Let my l come into his garden	1856
	5:2	My l is knocking:	1856
	5:4	My l thrust his hand through	1856
	5:5	I arose to open for my l,	1856
	5:6	I opened for my l, but my lover had left;	1856
	5:6	I opened for my lover, but my l had left;	1856
	5:8	if you find my l, what will you tell him?	1856
	5:10	My l is radiant and ruddy,	1856
	5:16	This is my l, this my friend,	1856
	6:1	Where has your l gone,	1856
	6:1	Which way did your l turn,	1856
	6:2	My l has gone down to his garden,	1856
	6:3	I am my lover's and my l is mine;	1856
	7:9	May the wine go straight to my l,	1856
	7:10	I belong to my l, and his desire is for me.	1856
	7:11	Come, my l, let us go to the countryside,	1856
	7:13	that I have stored up for you, my l.	1856
	8:5	up from the desert leaning on her l?	1856
	8:14	Come away, my l, and be like a gazelle	1856
1Ti	3:3	not quarrelsome, **not a l of money.**	921

LOVER'S (1) [LOVE]

SS	6:3	I am my l and my lover is mine;	1856+4200

LOVERS (25) [LOVE]

SS	5:1	drink your fill, O l.	1856
Jer	3:1	as a prostitute with many l—	8276
	3:2	By the roadside you sat waiting for l,	2157S
	4:30	Your l despise you; they seek your life.	6311
La	1:2	Among all her l there is none to comfort her.	170
Eze	16:33	but you give gifts to all your l,	170
	16:36	in your promiscuity with your l,	170
	16:37	therefore I am going to gather all your l,	170
	16:39	Then I will hand you over to your l,	4392S
	16:41	and you will no longer pay your l.	NIH
	23:5	and she lusted after her l, the Assyrians—	170
	23:9	"Therefore I handed her over to her l,	170
	23:20	There she lusted after her l,	7108
	23:22	I will stir up your l against you,	170
Hos	2:5	She said, 'I will go after my l,	170
	2:7	after her l but not catch them;	170
	2:10	before the eyes of her l;	170
	2:12	which she said were her pay from her l;	170
	2:13	and went after her l, but me she forgot,"	170
	8:9	Ephraim has sold herself to l.	172
2Ti	3:2	People will be l of themselves,	5796
	3:2	l of money, boastful, proud, abusive,	5795
	3:3	self-control, brutal, **not l of the good,**	920
	3:4	l of pleasure rather than lovers of God—	5798
	3:4	lovers of pleasure rather than l of God—	5806

LOVES (76) [LOVE]

Ge	44:20	and his father l him.'	170
Dt	10:18	the fatherless and the widow, and l the alien,	170
	15:16	because *he* l you and your family	170
	21:15	and he l one but not the other,	170
	21:16	of the firstborn to the son of the wife he l	170
	23:5	because the LORD your God l you.	170
	28:54	or the wife he l or his surviving children,	2668
	28:56	the husband she l and her own son	2668
	33:12	the LORD l rests between his shoulders."	NIH
Ru	4:15	daughter-in-law, who l you and who is better	170
2Ch	2:11	"Because the LORD l his people,	170
Ps	11:7	For the LORD is righteous, *he* l justice;	170
	33:5	The LORD l righteousness and justice;	170
	34:12	Whoever of you l life and desires	2913
	37:28	For the LORD l the just and will	170
	87:2	the LORD l the gates of Zion more than	170
	91:14	"Because *he* l me," says the LORD,	3137
	99:4	The King is mighty, he l justice—	170
	119:140	and your servant l them.	170
	127:2	for he grants sleep to *those* he l.	3351
	146:8	the LORD l the righteous.	170
Pr	3:12	because the LORD disciplines those he l,	170
	12:1	*Whoever* l discipline loves knowledge,	170
	12:1	Whoever loves discipline l knowledge,	170
	13:24	*he who* l him is careful to discipline him.	170
	15:9	but he l those who pursue righteousness.	170
	17:17	A friend l at all times;	170
	17:19	He who l a quarrel loves sin;	170
	17:19	He who loves a quarrel l sin;	170
	19:8	He who gets wisdom l his own soul;	170
	21:17	He *who* l pleasure will become poor;	170
	21:17	*whoever* l wine and oil will never be rich.	170
	22:11	*He who* l a pure heart	170
	29:3	man *who* l wisdom brings joy to his father,	170
Ecc	5:10	*Whoever* l money never has money enough;	170
	5:10	whoever l wealth is never satisfied	170
SS	3:1	I looked for the one my heart l;	170
	3:2	I will search for the one my heart l.	170
	3:3	"Have you seen the one my heart l?"	170
	3:4	when I found the one my heart l.	170
Hos	3:1	Love her as the LORD l the Israelites,	170
	10:11	Ephraim is a trained heifer *that* l to thresh;	170
	12:7	uses dishonest scales; *he* l to defraud.	170
Mal	2:11	has desecrated the sanctuary the LORD l,	170
Mt	10:37	"Anyone who l his father or mother more	5797
	10:37	anyone who l his son or daughter more	5797
Lk	7:5	because he l our nation and has built our	26
	7:47	he who has been forgiven little l little."	26
Jn	3:35	The Father l the Son and has placed	26
	5:20	For the Father l the Son and shows him all	5797
	10:17	The reason my Father l me is that I lay	26
	12:25	The man who l his life will lose it,	5797
	14:21	he is the one who l me.	26
	14:21	He who l me will be loved by my Father,	26
	14:23	Jesus replied, "If anyone l me,	26
	16:27	the Father himself l you	5797
Ro	13:8	for he who l his fellowman has fulfilled	26
1Co	8:3	But the man who l God is known by God.	26
2Co	9:7	for God l a cheerful giver.	26
Eph	1:6	he has freely given us in the One he l.	26
	5:28	He who l his wife loves himself.	26
	5:28	He who loves his wife l himself.	26
	5:33	also must love his wife as he l himself,	NIG
Col	1:13	into the kingdom of the Son he l,	27
Tit	1:8	be hospitable, **one who l what is good,**	5787
Heb	12:6	because the Lord disciplines those he l,	26
1Jn	2:10	Whoever l his brother lives in the light,	26
	2:15	If anyone l the world, the love of the Father	26
	4:7	Everyone who l has been born of God	26
	4:21	Whoever l God must also love his brother.	26
	5:1	and everyone who l the father loves his	26
	5:1	who loves the father l his child as well.	26
3Jn	1:9	but Diotrephes, who **l to be first,**	5812
Rev	1:5	*To* him who l us and has freed us	26
	20:9	the camp of God's people, the city he l.	26
	22:15	and everyone *who* l and practices falsehood.	5797

LOVING (10) [LOVE]

Ps	25:10	the ways of the LORD are l and faithful	2876
	59:10	my l God. God will go before me	2876
	59:17	you, O God, are my fortress, my l God.	2876
	62:12	and that you, O Lord, are l.	2876
	144:2	He is my l God and my fortress,	2876
	145:13	and l toward all he has made.	2883
	145:17	and l toward all he has made.	2883
Pr	5:19	A l doe, a graceful deer—	172
Heb	13:1	Keep on **l each other as brothers.**	5789
1Jn	5:2	by l God and carrying out his commands.	26

LOVING-KINDNESS (1) [LOVE]

Jer	31:3	I have drawn you with l.	2876

LOVINGKINDNESS (KJV) See LOVE, UNFAILING LOVE

LOVINGLY (1) [LOVE]

SS	3:10	its interior l inlaid by the daughters	173

LOW (45) [BELOW, LOWBORN, LOWER, LOWERED, LOWEST, LOWLIEST, LOWLY]

Ge	18:2	to meet them and bowed l to the ground.	2556
	43:28	And *they* bowed l to pay him honor.	7702
Nu	22:31	So *he* bowed l and fell facedown.	7702
2Sa	22:28	on the haughty to **bring** them l.	9164
1Ki	1:16	Bathsheba bowed l and knelt before	7702
	1:31	Then Bathsheba bowed l with her face to	7702

1Ch 29:20	*they* **bowed** l and fell prostrate before	7702
Job 14:10	But man dies and *is* **laid** l;	2764
14:21	if *they are* **brought** l, he does not see it.	7592
22:29	When *men are* **brought** l and you say,	9164
24:24	*they are* **brought** l and gathered up	4812
40:11	look at every proud man and **bring** him l,	9164
Ps 18:27	but **bring** l those whose eyes are haughty.	9164
36: 7	Both high and l **among men** find refuge in the shadow of your wings.	132+1201
38: 6	I am bowed down and **brought** very l;	8820
49: 2	both l and high, rich and poor alike:	132+1201
119:25	I am **laid** l in the dust;	1815
136:23	in our l **estate** His love endures forever.	9165
Pr 29:23	A man's pride **brings** him l,	9164
Ecc 10: 6	while the rich occupy the l *ones.*	9165
Isa 2: 9	So man *will be* **brought** l	8820
2:11	and the pride of men **brought** l;	8820
2:17	The arrogance of man *will be* **brought** l	8820
5:15	So man *will be* **brought** l	8820
10:33	the tall ones *will be* **brought** l.	9164
14: 8	"Now that *you have been* **laid** l,	8886
14:12	*you who once* **laid** l the nations!	2765
23: 9	to **bring** l the pride of all glory and	2725
25:12	your high fortified walls and **lay** *them* l;	9164
26: 5	*he* **lays** the lofty city l;	9164
28: 1	the pride of *those* **laid** l *by* wine!	2150
29: 4	**Brought** l, you will speak from the ground;	9164
40: 4	every mountain and hill *made* l,	9164
46: 1	Bel bows down, Nebo **stoops** l;	7970
Jer 16: 6	"Both high and l will die in this land.	7783
46:15	Why *will* your warriors **be laid** l?	6085
Eze 17: 6	and became a l, spreading vine.	7757+9166
17:14	so that the kingdom would be **brought** l,	9166
17:24	the tall tree and make the l tree grow tall.	9166
21:26	and the exalted *will be* **brought** l.	9164
Da 8:11	the place of his sanctuary **was brought** l.	8959
Lk 3: 5	every mountain and hill **made** l.	5427
Ac 8:10	both high and l, gave him their attention.	3625
Ro 12:16	to associate *with people* **of** l position.	5424
Jas 1:10	rich should take pride in his l **position**,	5428

LOWBORN (1) [BEAR, LOW]

Ps 62: 9	**L** men are but a breath,	132+1201

LOWER (30) [LOW]

Ge 6:16	the ark and make l, middle and upper decks	9397
Lev 13:45	cover the l **part of** his face	8559
Dt 28:43	but you will sink l and lower.	4752
28:43	but you will sink lower and l.	4752
Jos 15:19	So Caleb gave her the upper and l springs.	9397
16: 3	as far as the region of L Beth Horon and	9396
18:13	on the hill south of L Beth Horon.	9396
Jdg 1:15	Caleb gave her the upper and l springs.	9397
1Ki 9:17	He built up L Beth Horon,	9396
1Ch 7:24	who built L and Upper Beth Horon as well	9396
2Ch 8: 5	and L Beth Horon as fortified cities,	9396
Job 41:24	hard as rock, hard as a l millstone.	9396
Ps 8: 5	**made** him a little l than the heavenly beings	2893
Isa 11:11	from L Egypt, from Upper Egypt,	5213
22: 9	you stored up water in the L Pool.	9166
Jer 44: 1	all the Jews living in L **Egypt**—	824+5213
44:15	people living in L and Upper Egypt,	824+5213
Eze 24:17	do not cover the l **part of** your face	8559
24:22	You will not cover the l **part of** your **face**	8559
40:18	this was the l **pavement.**	9396
40:19	the inside of the l gateway to the outside	9396
42: 5	from the rooms on the l and middle floors	9396
42: 6	in floor space than those on the l	9396
42: 9	The l rooms had an entrance on	4946+9393
43:14	up to the l ledge it is two cubits high and	9396
Ac 27:30	to l some anchors from the bow.	1753
2Co 11: 7	for *me to* l myself in order to elevate you	5427
Eph 4: 9	that he also descended to the l,	3005
Heb 2: 7	*You* **made** him a little l than the angels;	1783
2: 9	who *was* **made** a little l than the angels,	1783

LOWERED (12) [LOW]

Ge 24:18	and quickly l the jar to her hands	3718
24:46	"*She* quickly l her jar from her shoulder	3718
44:11	of them quickly l his sack to the ground	3718
Ex 17:11	but whenever *he* l his hands,	5663
Jer 38: 6	*They* l Jeremiah by ropes into the cistern;	8938
Eze 1:24	When they stood still, *they* l their wings.	8332
1:25	as they stood with l wings.	8332
Mk 2: 4	l the mat the paralyzed man was lying on.	5899
Lk 5:19	and l him on his mat through the tiles into	2768
Ac 9:25	l him in a basket through an opening	2768+5899
27:17	they l the sea anchor and let the ship	5899
2Co 11:33	But *I was* l in a basket from a window in	5899

LOWEST (7) [LOW]

Ge 9:25	l **of slaves** will he be to his brothers."	6269+6269
1Ki 6: 6	The l floor was five cubits wide,	9396
6: 8	to the l floor was on the south side of	9396
Ne 4:13	the people behind the l points of the wall	9397
Ps 88: 6	You have put me in the l pit,	9397
Eze 41: 7	from the l *floor* to the top floor through	9396
Lk 14:10	But when you are invited, take the l place,	2274

LOWING (3)

1Sa 6:12	keeping on the road and l all the way;	1716
15:14	What is this l *of* cattle that I hear?"	7754
Jer 9:10	and the l *of* cattle is not heard.	7754

LOWLIEST (2) [LOW]

Eze 29:15	It will be the l of kingdoms	9166
Da 4:17	and sets over them the l *of* men.'	10738

LOWLY (11) [LOW]

Job 5:11	The l he sets on high,	9166
Ps 119:141	Though I am l and despised,	7582
138: 6	LORD is on high, he looks upon the l,	9166
Pr 16:19	Better to be l *in* spirit and among	9166
29:23	but a *man of* l spirit gains honor.	9166
Isa 57:15	with him who is contrite and l *in* spirit,	9166
57:15	the l and to revive the heart of the contrite.	9166
Eze 21:26	The l will be exalted and the exalted will	9166
29:14	There they will be a l kingdom.	9166
1Co 1:28	He chose the l **things** of this world and	38
Php 3:21	will transform our l **bodies** so	5428

LOWRING (KJV) See OVERCAST

LOYAL (8) [LOYALTY]

1Sa 22:14	"Who of all your servants *is* as l David,	586
2Sa 3: 3	This very day I am l to the house	2876
1Ki 12:20	the tribe of Judah remained l **to the** house	339
1Ch 12:29	had remained l to Saul's house	5466+9068
29:18	and **keep** their hearts l to you.	3922
Ps 78: 8	whose hearts *were* not l to God,	3922
78:37	their hearts *were* not l to him,	3922
Php 4: 3	Yes, and I ask you, l yokefellow,	1188

LOYALTY (1) [LOYAL]

1Ch 12:33	to help David with **undivided** l—50,000;	2256+4202+4213+4213

LUBIM, LUBIMS (KJV) See LIBYA, LIBYANS

LUCAS (KJV) See LUKE

LUCIFER (KJV) See MORNING STAR

LUCIUS (2)

Ac 13: 1	Simeon called Niger, L of Cyrene,	3372
Ro 16:21	as do L, Jason and Sosipater, my relatives.	3372

LUCRE (KJV) See DISHONEST GAIN, MONEY

LUD (2) [LUDITES]

Ge 10:22	Elam, Asshur, Arphaxad, L and Aram.	4276
1Ch 1:17	Elam, Asshur, Arphaxad, L and Aram.	4276

LUDITES (2) [LUD]

Ge 10:13	Mizraim was the father of the L,	4276
1Ch 1:11	Mizraim was the father of the L,	4276

LUHITH (2)

Isa 15: 5	They go up the way to L,	4284
Jer 48: 5	They go up the way to L,	4284

LUKE (3)

Col 4:14	Our dear friend L, the doctor,	3371
2Ti 4:11	Only L is with me.	3371
Phm 1:24	so do Mark, Aristarchus, Demas and L,	3371

LUKEWARM (1) [WARM]

Rev 3:16	So, because you are l—	5950

LUMBER (1)

2Ch 2: 9	to provide me with plenty of l,	6770

LUMP (1)

Ro 9:21	of the same l **of clay** some pottery	5878

LUNATICK (KJV) See HAVING SEIZURES

LUNCHEON (1)

Lk 14:12	"When you give a l or dinner,	756

LURE (2) [LURED]

Jdg 4: 7	*I will* l Sisera, the commander of Jabin's	5432
16: 5	"See *if you can* l him *into* showing you	7331

LURED (2) [LURE]

Jos 8: 6	until *we have* l them **away** from the city,	5998
8:16	and they pursued Joshua and **were l away**	5998

LURK (2) [LURKED, LURKS]

Ps 56: 6	They conspire, they l,	7621
Hos 13: 7	like a leopard *I will* l by the path.	8800

LURKED (1) [LURK]

Job 31: 9	or if *I have* l at my neighbor's door,	741

LURKS (1) [LURK]

Pr 7:12	now in the squares, at every corner *she* l.)	741

LUSH (2)

Am 5:11	though you have planted l vineyards,	2774
Zec 11: 3	the l **thicket** *of* the Jordan is ruined!	1454

LUST (13) [LUSTED, LUSTFUL, LUSTFULLY, LUSTS, LUSTY]

Pr 6:25	*Do not* l in your heart **after** her beauty	2773
Isa 57: 5	You **burn with** l among the oaks and	2801
Eze 20:30	the way your fathers did and l **after**	339+2388
23: 8	and poured out their l upon her.	9373
23:11	yet *in* her l and prostitution she was more	6312
23:17	and in their l they defiled her.	9373
Na 3: 4	all because of the **wanton** l *of* a harlot,	2393
Ro 1:27	and were inflamed with l for one another.	3979
Eph 4:19	with a continual l for more.	4432
Col 3: 5	sexual immorality, impurity, l,	4079
1Th 4: 5	in passionate l like the heathen, who do	4079
1Pe 4: 3	living in debauchery, l, drunkenness,	2123
1Jn 2:16	of sinful man, the l of his eyes and	2123

LUSTED (9) [LUST]

Eze 6: 9	which *have* l after their idols.	2388
20:24	and their eyes [l] after their fathers' idols.	NIH
23: 5	*she* l **after** her lovers, the Assyrians	6311+6584
23: 7	with all the idols of everyone *she* l **after.**	6311
23: 9	the Assyrians, for whom *she* l.	6311
23:12	*She* too l **after** the Assyrians—	448+6311
23:16	*she* l **after** them and sent messengers	6311+6584
23:20	There *she* l **after** her lovers,	6311+6584
23:30	because you l **after** the nations	339+2388

LUSTER (1)

La 4: 1	How the gold *has* **lost** *its* l,	6670

LUSTFUL (3) [LUST]

Jer 13:27	your adulteries and l **neighings,**	5177
Eze 16:26	with the Egyptians, your l **neighbors,**	1414+1541
2Pe 2:18	to the l **desires** of sinful human nature,	816+2123

LUSTFULLY (2) [LUST]

Job 31: 1	a covenant with my eyes not *to* look l at	1067
Mt 5:28	who looks at a woman l has already committed adultery	2121+3836+4639

LUSTS (2) [LUST]

Nu 15:39	after the l of your own hearts and eyes.	NIH
Ro 1:26	of this, God gave them over to shameful l.	4079

LUSTY (1) [LUST]

Jer 5: 8	They are well-fed, l stallions,	3469

LUTES (2) [LUTE]

1Sa 10: 6	and with tambourines and l.	8956
2Ch 20:28	the LORD with harps and l and trumpets.	4036

LUXURIES (1) [LUXURY]

Rev 18: 3	the earth grew rich from her excessive l."	5140

LUXURIOUS (1) [LUXURY]

Isa 13:22	jackals in her l palaces.	6696

LUXURY (7) [LUXURIES, LUXURIOUS]

Pr 19:10	It is not fitting for a fool to **live in** l—	9503
Hab 1:16	for by his net he lives in l and enjoys	9045
Lk 7:25	and indulge in l are in palaces.	5588
16:19	and fine linen and lived in l every day.	3289
Jas 5: 5	*You* have **lived** on earth in l	5587
Rev 18: 7	as the glory and l she gave herself.	5139
18: 9	with her and **shared** her l see the smoke	5139

LUZ (7) [BETHEL]

Ge 28:19	though the city used to be called L.	4281
35: 6	the people with him came to L (that is,	4281
48: 3	"God Almighty appeared to me at L in	4281
Jos 16: 2	It went on from Bethel (that is, L),	4281
18:13	to the south slope of L (that is,	4281
Jdg 1:23	to spy out Bethel (formerly called L),	4281
1:26	where he built a city and called it L,	4281

LYCAONIAN (2)

Ac 14: 6	and fled to the L cities of Lystra and Derbe	3377
14:11	they shouted *in* **the** L **language,**	3378

LYCIA (1)

Ac 27: 5	we landed at Myra *in* L.	3379

LYDDA (4)

Ac 9:32	he went to visit the saints in L.	3375
9:35	in L and Sharon saw him and turned to	3375
9:38	L was near Joppa;	3375
9:38	the disciples heard that Peter was in L,	8998

LYDIA (4) [LYDIA'S, LYDIANS]
Jer	46: 9	men of L who draw the bow.	4276
Eze	27:10	L and Put served as soldiers in your army.	4276
	30: 5	Cush and Put, L and all Arabia,	4276
Ac	16:14	of those listening was a woman named L,	3376

LYDIA'S (1) [LYDIA]
Ac	16:40	they went to L house,	3376

LYDIANS (1) [LYDIA]
Isa	66:19	to the Libyans and L (famous as archers),	4276

LYING (82) [LIE]
Ge	28:13	the land on which you are l.	8886
	29: 2	with three flocks of sheep l near it because	8069
	34: 7	in Israel by l with Jacob's daughter—	907+8886
	49:14	"Issachar is a rawboned donkey l down	8069
Ex	14:30	and Israel saw the Egyptians l dead on	AIT
Dt	21: 1	If a man is found slain, l in a field	5877
	22:13	If a man takes a wife and, after l with her,	448+995
Jos	17: 9	There were towns belonging to Ephraim l	NIH
Jdg	16:13	making a fool of me and l to me.	1819+3942
Ru	3: 4	note the place where he is l.	8886
	3: 8	and he turned and discovered a woman l	8886
1Sa	3: 2	was l down in his usual place.	8886
	3: 3	and Samuel was l down in the temple of	8886
	5: 4	and were l on the threshold;	448
	26: 5	Saul was l inside the camp,	8886
	26: 7	l asleep inside the camp	8886
	26: 7	Abner and the soldiers were l around him.	8886
2Sa	4: 7	while he was l on the bed in his bedroom.	8886
	12:16	into his house and spent the nights l on	8886
	13: 8	her brother Amnon, who was l down.	8886
1Ki	13:18	(But he was l to him.)	3950
	22:22	a l spirit in the mouths of all his prophets,'	9214
	22:23	the LORD has put a l spirit in the mouths	9214
2Ki	1: 4	'You will not leave the bed you are l on.	6590
	1: 6	not leave the bed you are l on.	6590
	1:16	you will never leave the bed you are l on.	6590
	4:32	there was the boy l dead on his couch.	8886
2Ch	18:21	a l spirit in the mouths of all his prophets,'	9214
	18:22	the LORD has put a l spirit in the mouths	9214
	20:24	they saw only dead bodies l on the ground;	5877
Job	3:13	For now I would be l down in peace;	8886
	3:14	places now l in ruins,	2999
Ps	31:18	Let their l lips be silenced,	9214
	78:36	l to him with their tongues;	3941
	109: 2	they have spoken against me with l tongues.	9214
	120: 2	from l lips and from deceitful tongues.	9214
	139: 3	You discern my going out and my l down;	8061
Pr	6:17	haughty eyes, a l tongue, hands	9214
	10:18	He who conceals his hatred has l lips,	9214
	12:19	but a l tongue lasts only a moment.	9214
	12:22	The LORD detests l lips,	9214
	17: 7	how much worse l lips to a ruler!	9214
	21: 6	A fortune made by a l tongue is a fleeting vapor	9214
	23:34	l on top of the rigging.	8886
	26:28	A l tongue hates those it hurts,	9214
Isa	58: 5	for bowing one's head like a reed and for l	3667
Jer	8: 2	but will be like refuse l on the ground.	6584+7156
	8: 8	when actually the l pen of the scribes	9214
	16: 4	but will be like refuse l on the ground.	2118
	23:26	in the hearts of these l prophets,	9214
	25:33	but will be like refuse l on the ground.	6584+7156
	43: 2	said to Jeremiah, "You are l!	1819+9214
La	3:10	Like a bear l in wait, like a lion in hiding,	741
Eze	13: 7	and uttered l divinations when you say,	3942
	13: 8	Because of your false words and l visions,	3942
	13: 9	see false visions and utter l divinations.	3942
	13:19	By l to my people, who listen to lies,	3941
	21:29	concerning you and l divinations	3942
	22:28	by false visions and l divinations	3942
	29: 3	you great monster l among your streams.	8069
	36:34	instead of l desolate in the sight of all who	2118
	36:35	the cities that were l in ruins,	NIH
Da	2:29	"As you were l there,	10542
	4: 5	As I was l in my bed,	10542
	4:10	These are the visions I saw while I in	10542
	4:13	"In the visions I saw while I in my bed,	10542
	7: 1	through his mind as he was l on his bed.	10542
Hos	4: 2	There is only cursing, l and murder,	3950
Mt	8:14	he saw Peter's mother-in-law l in bed with	965
	9: 2	brought to him a paralytic, l on a mat.	965
Mk	2: 4	the mat the paralyzed man was l on.	2879
	7:30	She went home and found her child l on	965
Lk	2:12	a baby wrapped in cloths and l in	3023
	2:16	and the baby, who was l in the manger.	3023
	5:25	took what he had been l on	2879
	24:12	he saw the strips of linen l by themselves,	NIG
Jn	5: 6	When Jesus saw him l there and learned	2879
	20: 5	the strips of linen l there but did not go in.	3023
	20: 6	He saw the strips of linen l there,	3023
Ro	9: 1	I speak the truth in Christ—I am not l,	6017
2Co	11:31	knows that I am not l.	6017
1Ti	2: 7	I am telling the truth, I am not l—	6017

LYRE (12) [LYRES]
Ps	33: 2	make music to him on the ten-stringed l.	5575
	57: 8	Awake, harp and l!	5575
	71:22	I will sing praise to you with the l,	4036
	81: 2	play the melodious harp and l.	5575
	92: 3	to the music of the ten-stringed l and	5575

Ps	108: 2	Awake, harp and l!	5575
	144: 9	on the ten-stringed l I will make music	5575
	150: 3	praise him with the harp and l,	5575
Da	3: 5	l, harp, pipes and all kinds of music,	10676
	3: 7	zither, l, harp and all kinds of music,	10676
	3:10	of the horn, flute, zither, l, harp, pipes	10676
	3:15	l, harp, pipes and all kinds of music,	10676

LYRES (15) [LYRE]
1Sa	10: 5	down from the high place with l,	5575
2Sa	6: 5	with songs and with harps, l, tambourines,	5575
1Ki	10:12	and to make harps and l for the musicians.	5575
1Ch	13: 8	with songs and with harps, l, tambourines,	5575
	15:16	l, harps and cymbals.	5575
	15:20	and Benaiah were to play the l according	5575
	15:28	and the playing of l and harps.	5575
	16: 5	They were to play the l and harps,	5575
	25: 1	accompanied by harps, l and cymbals.	5575
	25: 6	with cymbals, l and harps,	5575
2Ch	5:12	and playing cymbals, harps and l.	5575
	9:11	and to make harps and l for the musicians.	5575
	29:25	and l in the way prescribed by David	5575
Ne	12:27	with the music of cymbals, harps and l.	5575
Isa	5:12	They have harps and l at their banquets,	5575

LYSANIAS (1)
Lk	3: 1	and L tetrarch of Abilene—	3384

LYSIAS (2)
Ac	23:26	Claudius L, To His Excellency,	3385
	24:22	"When L the commander comes," he said,	3385

LYSTRA (6)
Ac	14: 6	the Lycaonian cities of L and Derbe and to	3388
	14: 8	In L there sat a man crippled in his feet,	3388
	14:21	Then they returned to L,	3388
	16: 1	He came to Derbe and then to L,	3388
	16: 2	The brothers at L and Iconium spoke well	3388
2Ti	3:11	Iconium and L, the persecutions I endured.	3388

M

MAACAH (25) [ABEL BETH MAACAH, ARAM MAACAH, MAACATHITE, MAACATHITES]
Ge	22:24	Tebah, Gaham, Tahash and M.	5082
Jos	12: 5	the border of the people of Geshur and M,	5084
	13:11	the territory of the people of Geshur and M,	5084
	13:13	not drive out the people of Geshur and M,	5084
2Sa	3: 3	the third, Absalom the son of M daughter	5082
	10: 6	well as the king of M with a thousand men,	5081
	10: 8	and Rehob and the men of Tob and M were	5081
1Ki	2:39	ran off to Achish son of M, king of Gath.	5082
	15: 2	His mother's name was M daughter	5082
	15:10	His grandmother's name was M daughter	5082
	15:13	He even deposed his grandmother M	5082
1Ch	2:48	Caleb's concubine M was the mother	5082
	3: 2	of M daughter of Talmai king of Geshur;	5082
	7:15	His sister's name was M.	5082
	7:16	Makir's wife M gave birth to a son	5082
	8:29	His wife's name was M,	5082
	9:35	His wife's name was M,	5082
	11:43	Hanan son of M, Joshaphat the Mithnite,	5082
	19: 7	as well as the king of M with his troops,	5081
	27:16	Shephatiah son of M;	5082
2Ch	11:20	Then he married M daughter of Absalom,	5082
	11:21	Rehoboam loved M daughter	5082
	11:22	Rehoboam appointed Abijah son of M to be	5082
	13: 2	His mother's name was M,	5082
	15:16	King Asa also deposed his grandmother M	5082

MAACATHITE (4) [MAACAH]
2Sa	23:34	Eliphelet son of Ahasbai the M,	1201+5084
2Ki	25:23	Jaazaniah the son of the M, and their men.	5084
1Ch	4:19	the Garmite, and Eshtemoa the M.	5084
Jer	40: 8	and Jaazaniah the son of the M,	5084

MAACATHITES (1) [MAACAH]
Dt	3:14	as the border of the Geshurites and the M;	5084

MAACHAH (KJV) See MAACAH

MAACHATHI, MAACHATHITE, MAACHATHITES (KJV) See MAACATHITE, MAACATHITES

MAADAI (1)
Ezr	10:34	From the descendants of Bani: M, Amram,	5049

MAAI (1)
Ne	12:36	Shemaiah, Azarel, Milalai, Gilalai, M,	5076

MAALEH-ACRABBIM (KJV) See SCORPION PASS

MAARATH (1)
Jos	15:59	M, Beth Anoth and Eltekon—	5125

MAASAI (1)
1Ch	9:12	and M son of Adiel, the son of Jahzerah,	5127

MAASEIAH (23)
1Ch	15:18	Jehiel, Unni, Eliab, Benaiah, M, Mattithiah,	5129
	15:20	M and Benaiah were to play the lyres	5129
2Ch	23: 1	Azariah son of Obed, M son of Adaiah,	5129
	26:11	as mustered by Jeiel the secretary and M	5129
	28: 7	killed M the king's son,	5129
	34: 8	he sent Shaphan son of Azaliah and M	5129
Ezr	10:18	M, Eliezer, Jarib and Gedaliah.	5128
	10:21	M, Elijah, Shemaiah, Jehiel and Uzziah.	5128
	10:22	Elioenai, M, Ishmael, Nethanel,	5128
	10:30	Adna, Kelal, Benaiah, M, Mattaniah,	5128
Ne	3:23	and next to them, Azariah son of M,	5128
	8: 4	Shema, Anaiah, Uriah, Hilkiah and M;	5128
	8: 7	Shabbethai, Hodiah, M, Kelita, Azariah,	5128
	10:25	Rehum, Hashabnah, M,	5128
	11: 5	and M son of Baruch,	5128
	11: 7	the son of Kolaiah, the son of M,	5128
	12:41	Eliakim, M, Miniamin, Micaiah, Elioenai,	5128
	12:42	also M, Shemaiah, Eleazar,	5128
Jer	21: 1	and the priest Zephaniah son of M.	5128
	29:21	of M, who are prophesying lies to you	5128
	29:25	to Zephaniah son of M the priest,	5128
	35: 4	which was over that of M son of Shallum	5129
	37: 3	the priest Zephaniah son of M to Jeremiah	5128

MAASIAI (KJV) See MAASAI

MAATH (1)
Lk	3:26	the son of M, the son of Mattathias,	3399

MAAZ (1)
1Ch	2:27	Ram the firstborn of Jerahmeel: M, Jamin	5106

MAAZIAH (2)
1Ch	24:18	to Delaiah and the twenty-fourth to M.	5069
Ne	10: 8	M, Bilgai and Shemaiah.	5068

MACBANNAI (1)
1Ch	12:13	Jeremiah the tenth and M the eleventh.	4801

MACBENAH (1)
1Ch	2:49	and to Sheva the father of M and Gibea.	4800

MACEDONIA (23) [MACEDONIAN, MACEDONIANS]
Ac	16: 9	of a man of M standing and begging him,	3424
	16: 9	"Come over to M and help us."	3423
	16:10	we got ready at once to leave for M,	3423
	16:12	and the leading city of that district of M.	3423
	18: 5	When Silas and Timothy came from M,	3423
	19:21	passing through M and Achaia.	3423
	19:22	Timothy and Erastus, to M,	3423
	19:29	Paul's traveling companions from M,	3424
	20: 1	said good-by and set out for M.	3423
	20: 3	he decided to go back through M.	3423
Ro	15:26	For M and Achaia were pleased to make	3423
1Co	16: 5	After I go through M, I will come to you—	3423
	16: 5	for I will be going through M.	3423
2Co	1:16	I planned to visit you on my way to M and	3423
	1:16	and to come back to you from M,	3423
	2:13	I said good-by to them and went on to M.	3423
	7: 5	For when we came into M,	3423
	11: 9	from M supplied what I needed.	3423
Php	4:15	when I set out from M,	3423
1Th	1: 7	to all the believers in M and Achaia.	3423
	1: 8	from you not only in M and Achaia—	3423
	4:10	you do love all the brothers throughout M.	3423
1Ti	1: 3	As I urged you when I went into M,	3423

MACEDONIAN (2) [MACEDONIA]
Ac	27: 2	Aristarchus, a M from Thessalonica,	3424
2Co	8: 1	that God has given the M churches.	3423

MACEDONIANS (2) [MACEDONIA]
2Co	9: 2	and I have been boasting about it to the M,	3424
	9: 4	For if any M come with me	3424

MACHBANAI (KJV) See MACBANNAI

MACHBENAH (KJV) See MACBENAH

MACHI (KJV) See MAKI

MACHINES (1)

2Ch 26:15   In Jerusalem he made **m** designed by   3115

MACHIR, MACHIRITES (KJV) See MAKIR, MAKIRITE

MACHNADEBAI (KJV) See MACNADEBAI

MACHPELAH (6)

Ge	23: 9	so he will sell me the cave of **M**,	4834
	23:17	So Ephron's field in **M** near Mamre—	4834
	23:19	field of **M** near Mamre (which is at Hebron)	4834
	25: 9	and Ishmael buried him in the cave of **M**	4834
	49:30	the cave in the field of **M**,	4834
	50:13	in the cave in the field of **M**,	4834

MACNADEBAI (1)

Ezr 10:40   **M**, Shashai, Sharai,   4827

MAD (5) [MADDENING, MADMAN, MADMEN, MADNESS]

Dt	28:34	The sights you see will **drive** you **m**.	8713
Jer	25:16	and **go m** because of the sword I will send	2147
	50:38	idols *that will* **go m** with terror.	2147
	51: 7	therefore they *have* now **gone m**.	2147
Jn	10:20	"He is demon-possessed and **raving m**.	*3419*

MADAI (2)

Ge	10: 2	The sons of Japheth: Gomer, Magog, **M**,	4512
1Ch	1: 5	The sons of Japheth: Gomer, Magog, **M**,	4512

MADDENING (2) [MAD]

Rev	14: 8	which made all the nations drink the **m** wine	2596
	18: 3	For all the nations have drunk the **m** wine	2596

MADE (1111) [MAKE]

Ge	1: 7	So God **m** the expanse and separated	6913
	1:16	God **m** two great lights—	6913
	1:16	He also **m** the stars.	NIH
	1:25	God **m** the wild animals according	6913
	1:31	God saw all that *he had* **m**,	6913
	2: 3	God blessed the seventh day and **m** it **holy**,	7727
	2: 4	When the LORD God **m** the earth and	6913
	2: 9	the LORD God **m** all kinds of trees **grow**	7541
	2:22	the LORD God **m** a woman *from* the rib	1215
	3: 1	of the wild animals the LORD God *had* **m**.	6913
	3: 7	and **m** coverings for themselves.	6913
	3:21	The LORD God **m** garments of skin	6913
	5: 1	*he* **m** him in the likeness of God.	6913
	6: 6	The LORD was grieved that *he had* **m** man	6913
	6: 7	for I am grieved that *I have* **m them**."	6913
	7: 4	of the earth every living creature *I have* **m**."	6913
	8: 6	the window *he had* **m** in the ark	6913
	9: 6	for in the image of God *has* God **m** man.	6913
	14:23	'I **m** Abram **rich**.'	6947
	15:18	the LORD **m** a covenant with Abram	4162
	17: 5	for *I have* **m** you a father of many nations.	5989
	21:27	and the two men **m** a treaty.	4162
	21:32	After the treaty *had been* **m** at Beersheba,	4162
	24:10	for Aram Naharaim and **m** *his* **way** to	2143
	24:21	the LORD *had* **m** his journey **successful**.	7503
	24:37	my master **m** me **swear an oath**,	8678
	26:30	Isaac then **m** a feast for them,	6913
	27:17	the tasty food and the bread *she had* **m**.	6913
	27:37	"I have **m** him lord over you	8492
	27:37	and *have* **m** all his relatives his servants,	5989
	28:20	Then Jacob **m** a **vow**, saying,	5623+5624
	30:37	**m** white stripes on them *by* **peeling**	AIT
	30:40	but **m** the rest **face** the streaked	5989+7156
	30:40	Thus *he* **m** separate flocks for himself	8883
	31:13	a pillar and where *you* **m** a **vow** to me.	5623+5624
	33:17	for himself and **m** shelters for his livestock.	6913
	37: 3	and *he* **m** a richly ornamented robe for him.	6913
	39:22	and he was **m responsible** *for* all	AIT
	41:39	"Since God has **m** all this **known** *to* you,	3359
	41:51	God *has* **m** me **forget** all my trouble	5960
	41:52	because God *has* **m** me **fruitful** in the land	7238
	45: 1	when he **m himself known** to his brothers.	3359
	45: 8	*He* **m** me father to Pharaoh,	8492
	45: 9	God *has* **m** me lord of all Egypt.	8492
	46:29	Joseph *had* his chariot **m ready** and went	673
	50: 5	'My father **m** me **swear an oath**	8678
	50: 6	as *he* **m** you **swear** *to* do."	8678
	50:25	Joseph **m** the sons of Israel **swear an oath**	8678
Ex	1:14	*They* **m** their lives **bitter** with hard labor	5352
	2:14	"Who **m** you ruler and judge over us?"	8492
	5:21	*You have* **m** us a **stench** to Pharaoh	944+8194
	7: 1	"See, *I have* **m** you like God to Pharaoh,	5989
	8: 7	also **m** frogs **come up** on the land of Egypt.	6590
	10:13	the LORD **m** an east wind **blow**	5627
	11: 3	(The LORD **m** the Egyptians favorably disposed toward the people,	5989
	12: 8	and **bread m without yeast**.	5174
	12:15	to eat **bread m without yeast**.	5174
	12:18	**bread m without yeast**,	5174
	12:20	Eat nothing **m with yeast**.	4721
	12:36	The LORD *had* **m** the Egyptians favorably disposed toward the people,	5989
	13: 6	For seven days eat **bread m without yeast**	5174
	13:19	**m** the sons of Israel **swear an oath**.	8678+8678
Ex	14: 6	So *he* *had* his chariot **m ready**	673
	14:25	**m** the wheels of their chariots **come off**	6073
	15:17	place, O LORD, *you* **m** for your dwelling,	7188
	15:25	the LORD **m** a decree and a law for them,	8492
	16:31	and tasted like wafers **m with** honey.	928
	18:25	from all Israel and **m** them leaders of	5989
	20:11	in six days the LORD **m** the heavens and	6913
	20:11	the Sabbath day and **m** it **holy**.	7727
	23:15	eat **bread m without yeast**,	5174
	24: 8	the LORD *has* **m** with you in accordance	4162
	24:10	like a pavement **m** *of* sapphire,	5126
	27: 8	*It is to be* **m** just as you were **shown** on	6913
	28: 8	of one piece with the ephod and **m**	2118
	29:18	an **offering m** to the LORD by fire.	852
	29:23	the basket of **bread m without yeast**,	5174
	29:23	and a **cake** *m* **with** oil, and a wafer.	AIT
	29:25	an **offering m** to the LORD by fire.	852
	29:33	by which **atonement was m**	4105
	29:41	an **offering m** to the LORD by fire.	852
	29:42	to be **m** regularly at the entrance to the Tent	NIH
	30:10	This annual **atonement** *must be* **m** with	4105
	30:20	an **offering m** to the LORD by fire,	852
	31:17	in six days the LORD **m** the heavens and	6913
	32: 4	and **m** it *into* an idol cast in the shape of	6913
	32: 8	and *have* **m** themselves an idol cast in	6913
	32:20	the calf *they had* **m** and burned it in the fire;	6913
	32:20	on the water and **m** the Israelites **drink** it.	9197
	32:31	*They have* **m** themselves gods of gold.	6913
	32:35	of what they did with the calf Aaron *had* **m**.	6913
	34:18	eat **bread m without yeast**,	5174
	34:27	in accordance with these words *I have* **m**	4162
	36: 8	All the skilled men among the workmen **m**	6913
	36:11	Then *they* **m** loops of blue material along	6913
	36:12	*They have* **m** fifty loops on one curtain	6913
	36:13	Then *they* **m** fifty gold clasps and used them	6913
	36:14	*They* **m** curtains of goat hair for the tent	6913
	36:17	Then *they* **m** fifty loops along the edge of	6913
	36:18	*They* **m** fifty bronze clasps to fasten	6913
	36:19	Then *they* **m** for the tent a covering	6913
	36:20	*They* **m** upright frames of acacia wood for	6913
	36:22	*They* **m** all the frames of the tabernacle	6913
	36:23	*They* **m** twenty frames for the south side of	6913
	36:24	and **m** forty silver bases to go under them—	6913
	36:25	*they* **m** twenty frames	6913
	36:27	*They* **m** six frames for the far end, that is,	6913
	36:28	and two frames *were* **m** for the corners of	6913
	36:29	both *were* **m** alike.	6913
	36:31	*They* also **m** crossbars of acacia wood:	6913
	36:33	*They* **m** the center crossbar so	6913
	36:34	and **m** gold rings to hold the crossbars.	6913
	36:35	*They* **m** the curtain *of* blue,	6913
	36:36	*They* **m** four posts of acacia wood for it	6913
	36:36	They **m** gold hooks for them	NIH
	36:37	For the entrance to the tent *they* **m** a curtain	6913
	36:38	and they **m** five posts with hooks for them.	NIH
	36:38	with gold and **m** their five bases of bronze.	NIH
	37: 1	Bezalel **m** the ark *of* acacia wood—	6913
	37: 2	and **m** a gold molding around it.	6913
	37: 4	Then *he* **m** poles of acacia wood	6913
	37: 6	*He* **m** the atonement cover *of* pure gold—	6913
	37: 7	Then *he* **m** two cherubim **out**	6913
	37: 8	He **m** one cherub on one end and	NIH
	37: 8	at the two ends *he* **m** them of one piece with	6913
	37:10	*They* **m** the table of acacia wood—	6913
	37:11	Then they overlaid it with pure gold and **m**	6913
	37:12	also **m** around it a rim a handbreadth wide	6913
	37:15	The poles for carrying the table *were* **m**	6913
	37:16	And *they* **m** *from* pure gold the articles for	6913
	37:17	*They* **m** the lampstand *of* pure gold	6913
	37:23	*They* **m** its seven lamps,	6913
	37:24	*They* **m** the lampstand and all its accessories	6913
	37:25	*They* **m** the altar of incense **out**	6913
	37:26	and **m** a gold molding around it.	6913
	37:27	*They* **m** two gold rings below the molding—	6913
	37:28	*They* **m** the poles of acacia wood	6913
	37:29	also **m** the sacred anointing oil and the pure,	6913
	38: 2	*They* **m** a horn at each of the four corners,	6913
	38: 3	*They* **m** all its utensils of bronze—	6913
	38: 4	*They* **m** a grating for the altar,	6913
	38: 6	*They* **m** the poles of acacia wood	6913
	38: 7	*They* **m** it hollow, out of boards.	6913
	38: 8	*They* **m** the bronze basin	6913
	38: 9	Next *they* **m** the courtyard.	6913
	38:22	of Hur, of the tribe of Judah, **m** everything	6913
	39: 1	and scarlet yarn *they* **m** woven garments	6913
	39: 1	*They* also **m** sacred garments for Aaron,	6913
	39: 2	*They* **m** the ephod *of* gold, and of blue,	6913
	39: 4	*They* **m** shoulder pieces for the ephod,	6913
	39: 5	of one piece with the ephod and **m**	NIH
	39: 8	*They* **m** it like the ephod:	5126
	39:15	For the breastpiece *they* **m** braided chains	6913
	39:16	*They* **m** two gold filigree settings	6913
	39:19	*They* **m** two gold rings and attached them to	6913
	39:20	Then *they* **m** two more gold rings	6913
	39:22	*They* **m** the robe of the ephod entirely	6913
	39:24	*They* **m** pomegranates of blue,	6913
	39:25	And *they* **m** bells of pure gold	6913
	39:27	*they* **m** tunics of fine linen—	6913
	39:30	*They* **m** the plate, the sacred diadem,	6913
Lev	1: 9	It is a burnt offering, an **offering m by fire**,	852
	1:13	It is a burnt offering, an **offering m by fire**,	852
	1:17	It is a burnt offering, an **offering m by fire**,	852
	2: 2	on the altar, an **offering m by fire**,	852
	2: 3	of the **offerings m** *to* the LORD by fire.	852
	2: 4	**cakes** *m* without yeast and mixed with oil,	AIT
	2: 4	**wafers** *m* without yeast and spread with oil.	AIT
	2: 5	it is to be **m** of fine flour mixed with oil,	NIH
Lev	2: 7	*it is to* be **m** *of* fine flour and oil.	6913
	2: 8	Bring the grain offering **m** of these things to	6913
	2: 9	on the altar as an **offering m by fire** to	852
	2:10	**offerings m** *to* the LORD by fire.	852
	2:11	to the LORD *must be* **m** without yeast,	6913
	2:11	**offering m** to the LORD by fire.	852
	2:16	**offering m** to the LORD by fire.	852
	3: 3	**sacrifice m** to the LORD by fire:	852
	3: 5	as an **offering m by fire**,	852
	3: 9	**sacrifice m** to the LORD by fire:	852
	3:11	**offering m** to the LORD by fire.	852
	3:16	an **offering m by fire**, a pleasing aroma.	852
	4:23	he is **m** aware *of* the sin he committed,	3359
	4:28	he is **m** aware *of* the sin he committed,	3359
	4:35	**offerings m** *to* the LORD by fire.	852
	5:12	**offerings m** *to* the LORD by fire.	852
	6: 7	of these things he did that **m** him guilty."	928
	6:17	**offerings m** *to* me by fire.	852
	6:18	**offerings m** *to* the LORD by fire	852
	7: 5	**offerings m** to the LORD by fire.	852
	7:12	to offer cakes of **bread m without yeast**	5174
	7:12	wafers **m** without yeast and spread with oil,	5174
	7:13	with cakes of **bread m with yeast**.	2809
	7:25	from which an offering by fire *may be* **m** to	7928
	7:30	**offering m** *to* the LORD by fire;	852
	7:35	**offerings m** *to* the LORD by fire	852
	8: 2	the basket of **bread m without yeast**,	5174
	8:21	**offering m** *to* the LORD by fire,	852
	8:26	the basket of **bread m without yeast**,	5174
	8:26	he took a cake of bread, and one **m** with oil,	NIH
	8:28	**offering m** *to* the LORD by fire.	852
	10:12	**offerings m** *to* the LORD by fire	852
	10:13	**offerings m** *to* the LORD by fire.	852
	10:15	the fat portions of the **offerings m by fire**,	852
	11:32	will be unclean, whether it is **m** of wood,	4946
	11:43	by means of them or **be m unclean**	3237
	13:48	any leather or anything **m** *of* leather—	4856
	15:32	for *anyone* **m** unclean by an emission	AIT
	16:17	having **m atonement** for himself,	4105
	16:30	on this day **atonement** *will be* **m** for you,	4105
	16:34	**Atonement** *is to be* **m** once a year	4105
	21: 6	**offerings m** *to* the LORD by fire,	852
	21:21	**offerings m** *to* the LORD by fire.	852
	22:22	**offering m** *to* the LORD by fire.	852
	22:27	**offering m** *to* the LORD by fire.	852+7933
	23: 6	you must eat **bread m without yeast**.	5174
	23: 8	**offering m** *to* the LORD by fire,	852
	23:13	**offering m** *to* the LORD by fire,	852
	23:17	bring two loaves **m** *of* two-tenths of	2118
	23:18	an **offering m by fire**,	852
	23:25	**offering m** *to* the LORD by fire.' "	852
	23:27	**offering m** *to* the LORD by fire,	852
	23:28	when **atonement** *is* **m** for you before	4105
	23:36	**offerings m** *to* the LORD by fire,	852
	23:36	**offerings m** *to* the LORD by fire,	852
	23:37	**offering m** *to* the LORD by fire—	852
	24: 7	**offering m** *to* the LORD by fire.	852
	24: 9	**offerings m** *to* the LORD by fire."	852
	24:12	of the LORD *should be* **m** clear to them.	7300
	26:41	which **m** me hostile toward them so	NIH
Nu	3: 4	before the LORD when they **m an offering**	7928
	5: 8	to whom **restitution** *can be* **m** *for*	8740
	5: 8	the ram with which **atonement** *is* **m**	4105+4113
	5:27	then when she *is* **m** to **drink** the water	9197
	6: 3	and must not drink **vinegar** *m from* wine or	AIT
	6:15	and a basket of **bread m without yeast**—	5174
	6:15	**cakes** *m* of fine flour mixed with oil,	AIT
	6:19	both **m** without yeast.	5174
	6:21	He must fulfill the **vow** he has **m**,	5623+5624
	7: 2	of those who were counted, **m** offerings.	7928
	8: 4	This is how the lampstand was **m**:	5126
	8: 4	It was **m** of hammered gold—	NIH
	8: 4	The lampstand *was* **m** exactly like	6913
	8:21	and **m atonement** for them to purify them.	4105
	11: 8	They cooked it in a pot or **m** it *into* cakes.	6913
	11: 8	it tasted like something **m** *with* olive oil.	4382
	14:36	**m** the whole community **grumble** against	4296
	15: 3	to the LORD **offerings m by fire**, from	852
	15:10	It will be an **offering m by fire**,	852
	15:13	an **offering m by fire** as an aroma pleasing	852
	15:14	an **offering m by fire** as an aroma pleasing	852
	15:25	for their wrong an offering **m by fire** and	852
	15:28	and when **atonement** *has been* **m** for him,	4105
	16:47	the incense and **m atonement** for them.	4105
	18:17	and burn their fat as an **offering m by fire**,	852
	21: 2	Then Israel **m** this **vow** to the LORD:	5623+5624
	21: 9	So Moses **m** a bronze snake and put it up on	6913
	22:29	"You have **m** a **fool** of me!"	6618
	25:13	the honor of his God and **m atonement** for	4105
	26:61	when they **m an offering** before the LORD	7928
	28: 2	the food for my offerings **m by fire**,	852
	28: 3	'This is the **offering m by fire** that you are	852
	28: 6	**offering m** to the LORD by fire.	852
	28: 8	This is an **offering m by fire**.	852
	28:13	**offering m** to the LORD by fire.	852
	28:14	to be **m** at each new moon during the year.	NIH
	28:17	for seven days eat **bread m without yeast**.	5174
	28:19	to the LORD an **offering m by fire**,	852
	28:24	for the **offering m by fire** every day	852
	29: 6	**offerings m** *to* the LORD by fire—	852
	29:13	an **offering m by fire** as an aroma pleasing	852
	29:36	an **offering m by fire** as an aroma pleasing	852
	31:20	as well as everything **m** *of* leather,	5126
	32:13	against Israel and **m** them **wander** in	5675
	35:33	**atonement** cannot **be m** for the land	4105
Dt	1:28	Our brothers *have* **m** us **lose heart**.	5022
	2: 1	For a long time *we* **m** *our* **way around**	6015

Dt	2: 3	"You *have* **m** your **way around**	6015
	2:30	LORD your God *had* **m** his spirit **stubborn**	7996
	3:11	His **bed** was *m of* iron	AIT
	4:23	of the LORD your God that *he* **m** with you;	4162
	4:36	From heaven *he* **m** you **hear** his voice	9048
	5: 2	The LORD our God **m** a covenant with us	4162
	5: 3	that the LORD **m** this covenant,	4162
	9: 9	the covenant that the LORD *had* **m** with you,	4162
	9:12	from what I commanded them and *have* **m**	6913
	9:16	*you had* **m** for yourselves an idol cast in	6913
	9:21	the calf *you had* **m,** and burned it in the fire.	6913
	9:22	You also **m** the LORD **angry** at Taberah,	2118+7911
	10: 3	So *I* **m** the ark *out of* acacia wood	6913
	10: 5	and put the tablets in the ark *I had* **m,**	6913
	10:22	and now the LORD your God *has* **m** you	8492
	15: 2	*the* **loan** he has **m** to his fellow Israelite.	5957
	16: 3	Do not eat it with **bread m** with yeast,	2809
	18: 1	**offerings m** *to* the LORD **by fire,**	852
	23:23	because *you* **m** *your* **vow** freely to	5623
	26: 6	Egyptians mistreated us and **m** us **suffer,**	6700
	26:19	the nations he has **m** and that you will be	6913
	29: 1	the covenant he had **m** with them at Horeb.	4162
	29:25	the covenant *he* **m** with them	4162
	31:16	and break the covenant *I* **m** with them.	4162
	31:29	to anger by **what** your hands have **m.**"	5126
	32: 6	your **Creator,** who **m** you and formed you?	6913
	32:13	*He* **m** him **ride** on the heights of the land	8206
	32:15	He abandoned the God *who* **m** him	6913
	32:16	*They* **m** him **jealous** with their foreign gods	7861
	32:21	They **m** me **jealous** by what is no god	7861
Jos	2:17	"This oath *you* **m** us **swear.**"	8678
	2:20	be released from the oath *you* **m** us **swear.**"	8678
	5: 3	So Joshua **m** flint knives and circumcised	6913
	7:12	and run because *they have been* **m** liable	2118
	8:28	and **m** it a permanent heap of ruins,	8492
	9:15	Then Joshua **m** a treaty of peace with them	4162
	9:16	after *they* **m** the treaty with the Gibeonites,	4162
	9:27	That day he **m** the Gibeonites woodcutters	5989
	10: 1	Gibeon had **m** a treaty of peace with Israel	8966
	10: 4	"because *it has* **m** peace with Joshua and	8966
	11: 5	and **m camp** together at the Waters	2837
	11:19	**m** a treaty of peace with the Israelites,	8966
	13:14	since the **offerings m** by fire *to* the LORD,	852
	14: 8	**m** the hearts of the people **melt** with fear.	4998
	22:25	The LORD *has* **m** the Jordan a boundary	5989
	24:25	that day Joshua **m** a covenant for the people,	4162
Jdg	3:16	Now Ehud *had* **m** a double-edged sword	6913
	3:30	That day Moab *was* **m subject to** Israel,	3338+4044+9393
	6:19	an ephah of flour he **m** bread without yeast.	NIH
	8: 8	to Peniel and **m** *the* same **request** of them,	1819
	8:27	Gideon **m** the gold into an ephod,	6913
	9:16	in good faith when *you* **m** Abimelech king,	4887
	9:18	**m** Abimelech, the son of his slave girl, **king**	4887
	9:57	the men of Shechem **pay for**	928+8031+8740
	11: 4	when the Ammonites **m war** on Israel,	4309
	11:11	and the people **m** him head and commander	8492
	11:30	And Jephthah **m** a **vow** to the LORD:	5623+5624
	11:35	*have* **m** me **miserable** and wretched,	4156+4156
	11:35	because I *have* **m** a vow to the LORD	7023+7198
	14:10	And Samson **m** a feast there,	6913
	15:16	a donkey's jawbone I have **m** donkeys	NIH
	16: 2	*They* **m** no move during the night, saying,	3087
	16:10	"You have **m** a fool of me; you lied to me.	9438
	16:15	This is the third time *you have* **m a fool of**	9438
	17: 4	who **m** them *into* the image and the idol.	6913
	17: 5	and he **m** an ephod and some idols	6913
	18:24	He replied, "You took the gods *I* **m,**	6913
	18:27	Then they took what Micah *had* **m,**	6913
	18:31	to use the idols Micah *had* **m,**	6913
	20:34	of Israel's finest men **m** a frontal **attack**	995
	20:37	in ambush **m** a sudden **dash** into Gibeah,	7320
	21:15	LORD *had* **m** a gap in the tribes of Israel.	6913
Ru	1:20	the Almighty *has* **m** my life very **bitter.**	5352
1Sa	1:11	And *she* **m** a **vow,** saying,	5623+5624
	2:19	Each year his mother **m** him a little robe	6913
	2:28	the **offerings m** with fire *by* the Israelites,	852
	2:29	of every **offering** *m* by my people Israel?'	AIT
	3:13	**m** themselves **contemptible,**	7837
	6:15	and **m sacrifices** to the LORD.	2284+2285
	14:29	"My father *has* **m trouble** *for* the country.	6579
	15:11	"I am grieved that *I* **have m** Saul **king,**	4887+4889
	15:33	"As your sword *has* **m** women **childless,**	8897
	15:35	that *he had* **m** Saul **king** over Israel.	4887
	18: 3	And Jonathan **m** a covenant with David	4162
	19:10	That night David **m good** *his* **escape.**	2256+4880+5674
	19:18	When David had fled and **m** *his* **escape,**	4880
	20: 6	because an annual sacrifice is being **m** there	NIH
	20:16	So Jonathan **m a covenant** with the house	4162
	23:18	of them **m** a covenant before the LORD.	4162
	26: 3	Saul **m** *his* **camp** beside the road on the hill	2837
	30:25	David **m** this a statute and ordinance	8492
2Sa	2: 9	*He* **m** him **king** over Gilead,	4887
	5: 3	the king **m** a compact with them at Hebron	4162
	7:21	and **m** it **known** *to* your servant.	3359
	7:25	keep forever the promise *you have* **m**	1819
	8: 2	*He* **m** them **lie down** on the ground	8886
	10:19	*they* **m peace** with the Israelites	8966
	11:13	and David **m** him **drunk.**	8910
	12:14	*you have* **m** the enemies of the LORD **show utter contempt,**	5540+5540
	12:31	and he **m** them **work** at brickmaking.	6296
	13: 8	**m** *the* **bread** in his sight and baked it.	4221
	14:15	because the people *have* **m** me **afraid.**	3707
	15: 7	go to Hebron and fulfill a **vow** *I* **m**	5623+5624
2Sa	15: 8	*I* **m** this **vow:**	5623+5624
	16:21	that *you have* **m yourself a stench**	944
	19: 6	*You have* **m** it **clear** today that	5583
	22:12	*He* **m** darkness his canopy around him—	8883
	22:40	*you* **m** my adversaries **bow** at my feet.	4156
	22:41	You **m** my enemies **turn** their backs	5989
	23: 5	not **m** with me an everlasting covenant,	8492
1Ki	1:43	"Our lord King David *has* **m** Solomon **king.**	4887
	3: 1	Solomon **m an alliance** with Pharaoh	3161
	3: 7	you *have* **m** your servant **king** in place	4887
	5:12	and the two of them **m** a treaty.	4162
	6: 4	He **m** narrow clerestory windows in	6913
	6: 6	He **m** offset ledges around the outside of	5989
	6:23	the inner sanctuary he **m** a pair of cherubim	6913
	6:31	of the inner sanctuary he **m** doors	6913
	6:33	In the same way he **m** four-sided jambs	6913
	6:34	He also **m** two pine doors,	NIH
	7: 6	He **m** a colonnade fifty cubits long	6913
	7: 8	Solomon also **m** a palace like this hall	6913
	7: 9	were **m** of blocks of high-grade stone cut	NIH
	7:16	also **m** two capitals of cast bronze to set on	6913
	7:18	He **m** pomegranates in two rows	6913
	7:23	He **m** the Sea of cast metal, circular	6913
	7:27	He also **m** ten movable stands of bronze;	6913
	7:28	This is **how** the stands were **m:**	5126
	7:33	The wheels were **m** like chariot wheels;	5126
	7:37	This is the way he **m** the ten stands.	6913
	7:38	He then **m** ten bronze basins,	6913
	7:40	He also **m** the basins and shovels	6913
	7:45	that Huram **m** for King Solomon for	6913
	7:48	also **m** all the furnishings that were in	6913
	8: 9	where the LORD **m a covenant** with	4162
	8:20	"The LORD has kept the promise he **m:**	1819
	8:21	of the LORD that *he* **m** with our fathers	4162
	8:25	the **promises** *you* **m** to him when you said,	1819
	8:38	or plea *is* **m** by any of your people Israel—	2118
	9: 3	the prayer and plea *you have* **m** before me;	2858S
	10: 5	and the burnt offerings *he* **m** at the temple	6590
	10: 9	*he has* **m** you king, to maintain justice	8492
	10:16	King Solomon **m** two hundred large shields	6913
	10:17	He also **m** three hundred small shields	NIH
	10:18	the king **m** a great throne inlaid with ivory	6913
	10:20	Nothing like it *had ever* **been m**	6913
	10:21	Nothing was **m** of silver,	NIH
	10:27	The king **m** silver as common in Jerusalem	5989
	11:34	*I have* **m** him ruler all the days of his life	8883
	12:14	"My father **m** your yoke **heavy;**	3877
	12:20	assembly and **m** him **king** over all Israel.	4887
	12:28	the king **m** two golden calves.	6913
	12:32	sacrificing to the calves he had **m.**	6913
	12:32	priests at the high places he had **m.**	6913
	14: 7	from among the people and **m** you a leader	5989
	14: 9	*You have* **m** for yourself other gods,	6913
	14: 9	other gods, **idols m of metal;**	5011
	14:26	the gold shields Solomon had **m.**	6913
	14:27	So King Rehoboam **m** bronze shields	6913
	15:12	and got rid of all the idols his fathers had **m.**	6913
	15:13	she had **m** a repulsive Asherah pole.	6913
	16: 2	and **m** you leader of my people Israel,	5989
	16:33	Ahab also **m** an Asherah pole and did more	6913
	18:10	he **m** them **swear** they could not find you.	8678
	18:18	"*I have* not **m trouble** *for* Israel,"	6579
	18:26	they danced around the altar *they* had **m.**	6913
	20:34	So he **m** a treaty with him, and let him go.	4162
	22:11	of Kenaanah had **m** iron horns	6913
2Ki	3: 2	of Baal that his father had **m.**	6913
	6: 6	and the iron **float.**	7429
	9:25	the LORD **m** this prophecy about him:	5951
	11: 4	*He* **m** a covenant with them and put them	4162
	11:13	the **noise** *m* by the guards and the people,	AIT
	11:17	then **m** a covenant between the LORD and	4162
	11:17	He also **m** a covenant between the king and	NIH
	13: 7	of Aram had destroyed the rest and **m** them	8492
	14:21	and **m** him **king** in place of his father	4887
	17:15	the covenant he had **m** with their fathers	4162
	17:16	and **m** for themselves two idols cast in	6913
	17:21	**m** Jeroboam son of Nebat *their* **king.**	4887
	17:29	each national group **m** its own gods in	6913
	17:29	in the shrines the people of Samaria had **m**	6913
	17:30	The men from Babylon **m** Succoth Benoth,	6913
	17:30	the men from Cuthah **m** Nergal,	6913
	17:30	and the men from Hamath **m** Ashima;	6913
	17:31	the Avvites **m** Nibhaz and Tartak,	6913
	17:35	the LORD **m** a covenant with the Israelites,	4162
	17:38	not forget the covenant *I* **m** with you,	4162
	18: 4	into pieces the bronze snake Moses had **m,**	6913
	19:15	You *have* **m** heaven and earth.	6913
	20:11	the LORD **m** the shadow **go back**	8740
	20:20	all his achievements and how he **m** the pool	6913
	21: 3	he also erected altars to Baal and **m**	6913
	21: 7	the carved Asherah pole he had **m** and put it	6913
	21:24	**m** Josiah his son **king** in his place.	4887
	22:17	**idols** their hands have **m,**	5126
	23: 4	the articles **m** for Baal and Asherah and all	6913
	23:15	the high place **m** by Jeroboam son of Nebat,	6913
	23:30	of Josiah and anointed him and **m** him **king**	4887
	23:34	**m** Eliakim son of Josiah **king**	4887
	24:13	of Israel had **m** for the temple of the LORD.	6913
	24:17	**m** Mattaniah, Jehoiachin's uncle, **king**	4887
	25:15	all that were **m** of pure gold or silver.	NIH
	25:16	which Solomon had **m** for the temple of	6913
1Ch	11: 3	he **m** a compact with them at Hebron before	4162
	12:18	So David received them and **m** them leaders	5989
	14:17	and the LORD **m** all the nations fear him.	5989
	16:16	the covenant he **m** with Abraham,	4162
	16:26	but the LORD **m** the heavens.	6913
	17:19	and **m known** all these great promises.	3359
1Ch	17:22	You **m** your people Israel your very own forever,	5989
	17:23	let the promise *you have* **m** concerning	1819
	19:19	*they* **m peace** with David	8966
	21:29	which Moses *had* **m** in the desert,	6913
	22: 5	So David **m** extensive **preparations**	3922
	23: 1	**m** his son Solomon **king** over Israel.	4887
	26:31	of David's reign *a* **search was m** in	2011
	28: 2	and *I* **m plans** to build it.	3922
	29:21	The next day they **m sacrifices** to	2284+2285
2Ch	1: 1	and **m** him exceedingly **great.**	1540
	1: 3	which Moses the LORD's **servant** had **m** in	6913
	1: 5	*had* **m** was in Gibeon in front of	6913
	1: 8	to David my father and *have* **m** me **king**	4887
	1: 9	for you *have* **m** me **king** over a people	4887
	1:11	over whom *I have* **m** you **king,**	4887
	1:15	The king **m** silver and gold as common	5989
	2:11	*he has* **m** you their king.	5989
	2:12	the God of Israel, who **m** heaven and earth!	6913
	3:10	In the Most Holy Place *he* **m** a pair of	6913
	3:14	*He* **m** the curtain of blue,	6913
	3:15	In the front of the temple *he* **m** two pillars,	6913
	3:16	*He* **m** interwoven chains and put them	6913
	3:16	He also **m** a hundred pomegranates	6913
	4: 1	*He* **m** a bronze altar twenty cubits long,	6913
	4: 2	*He* **m** the Sea of cast metal, circular in	6913
	4: 6	He then **m** ten basins for washing	6913
	4: 7	*He* **m** ten gold lampstands according to	6913
	4: 8	*He* **m** ten tables and placed them in	6913
	4: 8	He also **m** a hundred gold sprinkling bowls.	6913
	4: 9	*He* **m** the courtyard of the priests,	6913
	4:11	He also **m** the pots and shovels	6913
	4:16	that Huram-Abi **m** for King Solomon for	6913
	4:18	All these things that Solomon **m** amounted	6913
	4:19	also **m** all the furnishings that were	6913
	5:10	where the LORD **m a covenant** with	4162
	6:10	"The LORD has kept the promise he **m.**	1819
	6:11	the covenant of the LORD that *he* **m** with	4162
	6:13	Now he *had* **m** a bronze platform,	6913
	6:16	*the* **promises** *you* **m** to him when you said,	1819
	6:29	or plea *is* **m** by any of your people Israel—	2118
	7: 6	which King David had **m** for praising	6913
	7: 7	the bronze altar he had **m** could not hold	6913
	9: 4	and the burnt offerings *he* **m** at the temple	6590
	9: 8	*he has* **m** you king over them,	5989
	9:15	King Solomon **m** two hundred large shields	6913
	9:16	He also **m** three hundred small shields	NIH
	9:17	the king **m** a great throne inlaid with ivory	6913
	9:19	Nothing like it *had ever* **been m**	6913
	9:20	Nothing was **m** of silver,	NIH
	9:27	The king **m** silver as common in Jerusalem	5989
	10:14	"My father **m** your yoke **heavy;**	3877
	11:12	and **m** them very **strong.**	2616
	11:15	and for the goat and calf idols *he had* **m.**	6913
	12: 9	including the gold shields Solomon had **m.**	6913
	12:10	So King Rehoboam **m** bronze shields	6913
	13: 8	with you the golden calves that Jeroboam **m**	6913
	15:16	she had **m** a repulsive Asherah pole.	6913
	16:14	and they **m** a huge fire in his honor.	8596
	18:10	Zedekiah son of Kenaanah had **m** iron horns	6913
	20:35	of Judah **m an alliance** with Ahaziah king	2489
	20:37	*you have* **m an alliance** with Ahaziah,	2489
	20:37	the LORD will destroy **what** you have **m.**"	5126
	21: 7	the covenant the LORD *had* **m** with David,	4162
	21:19	His people **m** no fire in his honor,	NIH
	22: 1	**m** Ahaziah, Jehoram's youngest son, **king**	4887
	23: 1	*He* **m** a covenant *with the* **commanders**	928+4374
	23: 3	the whole assembly **m** a covenant with	4162
	23:16	then **m** a covenant that he and the people	4162
	23:18	*to* whom David *had* **m assignments** in	2745
	24: 8	a chest *was* **m** and placed outside,	6913
	24:14	and *with* it *were* **m** articles for	6913
	26: 1	**m** him **king** in place of his father Amaziah.	4887
	26:15	In Jerusalem *he* **m** machines designed	6913
	27: 5	Jotham **m war** on the king of the Ammonites	4309
	28: 2	also **m** cast idols for worshiping the Baals.	6913
	29: 8	*he has* **m** them an object of dread and horror	5989
	30: 7	so that *he* **m** them an object of horror,	5989
	31:14	the **contributions** *m* to the LORD and also	AIT
	32: 5	*He* also **m** large numbers of weapons	6913
	32:27	and *he* **m** treasuries for his silver and gold	6913
	32:28	He also **m** buildings to store the harvest	NIH
	32:28	and **m** stalls for various kinds of cattle,	NIH
	33: 3	to the Baals and **m** Asherah poles.	6913
	33: 7	He took the carved image he had **m** and put	6913
	33:14	*he* also **m** it much **higher.**	1467
	33:22	to all the idols Manasseh had **m.**	6913
	33:25	**m** Josiah his son **king** in his place.	4887
	34:25	to anger by all **that** their hands have **m,**	5126
	35:14	*they* **m preparations** for themselves and for	3922
	35:14	the Levites **m preparations** for themselves	3922
	35:15	their fellow Levites **m** *the* **preparations**	3922
	36: 1	of Josiah and **m** him **king** in Jerusalem	4887
	36: 4	**m** Eliakim, a brother of Jehoahaz, **king**	4887
	36:10	**m** Jehoiachin's uncle, Zedekiah, **king**	4887
	36:13	**m** him **take an oath** in God's name.	8678
Ezr	3:13	because the people **m** so much noise.	8131+9558
	4:15	*a* **search** *may be* **m** in the royal archives	10118
	4:19	I issued an order and *a* **search** *was* **m,**	10118
	5:17	*let a* **search** be **m** in the royal archives	10118
	6:11	for this crime his house *is to* be **m** a pile	10522
Ne	3: 4	the son of Meshezabel, **m repairs,**	2616
	3: 4	to him Zadok son of Baana also **m repairs.**	2616
	3: 7	**repairs** *were* **m** by men from Gibeon	2616
	3: 8	perfume-makers, **m repairs** next to that.	2616
	3:10	of Harumaph **m repairs** opposite his house,	2616
	3:10	of Hashabneiah **m repairs** next to him.	2616

Ne	3:16	*m* repairs up to a point opposite the tombs	2616
	3:17	*the* repairs were *m* by the Levites	2616
	3:18	*the* repairs were *m* by their countrymen	2616
	3:22	repairs next to him *were m*	2616
	3:23	Benjamin and Hasshub *m* repairs in front	2616
	3:23	*m* repairs beside his house.	2616
	3:26	of Ophel *m* repairs up to a point opposite	NIH
	3:28	the Horse Gate, the priests *m* repairs,	2616
	3:29	of Immer *m* repairs opposite his house.	2616
	3:29	the guard at the East Gate, *m* repairs.	2616
	3:30	*m* repairs opposite his living quarters.	2616
	3:31	*m* repairs as far as the house of	2616
	3:32	the goldsmiths and merchants *m* repairs.	2616
	5:12	*m* the nobles and officials take an oath	8678
	8: 2	which was *m* up of men and women	4946
	8:12	the words that *had been* m known to them.	3359
	9: 6	You *m* the heavens,	6913
	9: 8	and you *m* a covenant with him to give	4162
	9:10	*You m* a name for yourself,	
	9:14	*You* m known to them your holy Sabbath	3359
	9:23	*m* their sons as numerous	8049
	13:13	the storerooms and *m* Hanan son of Zaccur,	NIH
	13:13	They were *m* responsible for distributing	NIH
	13:25	*m* them take an oath	8678
	13:26	and God *m* him king over all Israel,	5989
	13:31	I also *m* provision for contributions of wood	NIH
Est	2: 2	a search be *m* for beautiful young virgins	1335
	2:17	on her head and *m* her queen instead	4887
	3:14	and *m* known to the people of every	1655
	7: 9	He had it *m* for Mordecai,	6913
	8:13	and *m* known to the people of every	1655
	9:17	on the fourteenth they rested and *m* it a day	6913
	9:18	on the fifteenth they rested and *m* it a day	6913
Job	4:14	and *m* all my bones shake.	7064
	7:20	Why have you *m* me your target?	8492
	10: 8	"Your hands shaped me and *m* me.	6913
	14:15	the creature your hands have *m.*	5126
	16:12	He has *m* me his target;	7756
	17: 6	"God has *m* me a byword to everyone,	3657
	23:16	God has *m* my heart faint;	8216
	27: 2	who has *m* me taste bitterness of soul,	5352
	27:18	like a hut *m* by a watchman.	6913
	28:26	when he *m* a decree for the rain and a path	6913
	29:13	*I m* the widow's heart sing.	8264
	31: 1	"*I m* a covenant with my eyes not	4162
	31:15	not *he who m* me in the womb make them?	6913
	33: 4	The Spirit of God has *m* me;	6913
	37: 7	that all men he has *m* may know his work,	5126
	38: 9	when I *m* the clouds its garment	8492
	40:15	which *I m* along with you and which feeds	6913
	40:19	the LORD *m* him prosperous again	8654+8740
Ps	7:15	and scoops it out falls into the pit *he has m.*	7188
	8: 5	*You m* him a little lower than the heavenly beings	2893
	8: 6	*You m* him ruler over the works	5440
	16: 5	you have *m* my lot secure.	9461
	16:11	You have *m* known to me the path of life;	3359
	18:11	He *m* darkness his covering,	8883
	18:39	you *m* my adversaries bow at my feet.	4156
	18:40	You *m* my enemies turn their backs	5989
	18:43	you have *m* me the head of nations;	8492
	21: 6	and *m* him glad with the joy	2525
	22: 9	you *m* me trust in you even	1053
	30: 7	you *m* my mountain stand firm;	6641
	33: 6	the word of the LORD were the heavens *m,*	6913
	39: 5	*You have m* my days a mere handbreadth;	5989
	44: 2	*m* our fathers flourish.	8938
	44:10	*You m* us retreat before the enemy,	294+8740
	44:13	You have *m* us a reproach to our neighbors,	8492
	44:14	You have *m* us a byword among the nations;	8492
	44:19	and *m* us a haunt for jackals and covered us	928
	50: 5	who *m* a covenant with me by sacrifice."	4162
	71:20	*I have m* me see troubles,	8011
	73:28	*I have m* the Sovereign LORD my refuge;	8883
	74:17	you *m* both summer and winter.	3670
	78:13	*m* the water stand firm	5893
	78:16	of a rocky crag and *m* water flow down	3718
	78:28	He *m* them come down inside their camp,	5877
	80: 5	you have *m* them drink tears by the bowlful	9197
	80: 6	You have *m* us a source of contention	8492
	86: 9	All the nations you have *m* will come	6913
	88: 8	and have *m* me repulsive to them.	8883
	89: 3	"*I have m* a covenant with my chosen one,	4162
	89:42	*m* all his enemies rejoice.	8523
	95: 5	The sea is his, for he *m* it,	6913
	96: 5	but the LORD *m* the heavens.	6913
	98: 2	The LORD *has m* his salvation known	3359
	100: 3	It is *he who m* us, and we are his;	6913
	103: 7	*He m* known his ways to Moses,	3359
	104:24	In wisdom *you m* them all;	6913
	105: 9	the covenant *he m* with Abraham,	4162
	105:21	*He m* him master of his household,	8492
	105:24	*m* his people very fruitful;	7238
	105:24	*he m* them too numerous for their foes,	6793
	105:28	He sent darkness and *m* the land dark—	3124
	106:19	At Horeb they *m* a calf and worshiped	6913
	107:40	*m* them wander in a trackless waste.	9494
	115: 4	*m* by the hands of men.	5126
	118:24	This is the day the LORD *has m*;	6913
	118:27	and he has *m his* light shine upon us.	239
	119:73	Your hands *m* me and formed me;	6913
	129: 3	and *m* their furrows long.	799
	132: 2	and *m* a vow to the Mighty One of Jacob;	5623
	135:15	*m* by the hands of men.	5126
	136: 5	*who* by his understanding *m* the heavens,	6913
	136: 7	*who m* the great lights—	6913
	138: 3	*you m* me bold and stouthearted.	8104
Ps	139:14	*I am* fearfully and wonderfully *m;*	7098
	139:15	from you when *I was m* in the secret place.	6913
	145: 9	he has compassion on all he has *m.*	5126
	145:10	All you have *m* will praise you, O LORD,	5126
	145:13	and loving toward all he has *m.*	5126
	145:17	and loving toward all he has *m.*	5126
Pr	1:23	to you and *m* my thoughts known *to* you.	3359
	2:17	the covenant she *m before* God.	AIT
	8:26	before he *m* the earth or its fields or any of	6913
	20:12	the LORD *has m* them both.	6913
	20:28	through love his throne is *m* secure.	6184
	21: 6	A fortune *m* by a lying tongue is	7189
	21:31	The horse *is m* ready for the day of battle,	3922
Ecc	2: 5	*I m* gardens and parks and planted all kinds	6913
	2: 6	*I m* reservoirs to water groves	6913
	3:11	He *has m* everything beautiful in its time.	6913
	7:13	Who can straighten what *he has m* crooked?	6430
	7:14	God *has m* the one as well as the other.	6913
	7:29	God *m* mankind upright,	6913
	10:19	A feast *is m* for laughter,	6913
SS	1: 6	and *m* me take care of the vineyards;	8492
	3: 3	as they *m their* rounds in the city.	6015
	3: 6	perfumed with myrrh and incense *m* from	4946
	3: 9	King Solomon *m* for himself the carriage;	6913
	3: 9	he *m* it of wood from Lebanon.	NIH
	3:10	Its posts he *m* of silver, its base of gold.	6913
	5: 7	as they *m their* rounds in the city.	6015
Isa	2: 8	to what their fingers have *m.*	6913
	2:20	which *they m* to worship.	6913
	14:16	the earth and *m* kingdoms tremble,	8321
	14:17	the man who *m* the world a desert,	8492
	17: 8	and the incense altars their fingers *have m.*	6913
	22:11	but you did not look to the *One who m* it,	6913
	23:11	*m* its kingdoms tremble.	8074
	23:13	The Assyrians *have m* it *a place*	3569
	25: 2	*You have m* the city a heap of rubble,	8492
	28:15	with the grave *we have m* an agreement,	6913
	28:15	for *we have m* a lie our refuge	8492
	29:13	of me is *m up only of* rules taught by men.	AIT
	30:33	it *has been m* ready for the king.	3922
	30:33	Its fire pit *has been m* deep and wide,	6676
	31: 7	of silver and gold your sinful hands *have m.*	6913
	37:16	*You have m* heaven and earth.	6913
	38:12	day and night *you m an end of* me.	8966
	38:13	day and night *you m an end of* me.	8966
	40: 4	every mountain and hill *m* low;	AIT
	42:22	they have been *m* loot, with no one to say,	NIH
	43: 7	whom I formed and *m.*"	6913
	43:16	he *who m* a way through the sea,	5989
	44: 2	he *who m* you, who formed you in the womb,	6913
	44:14	or planted a pine, and the rain *m* it grow.	1540
	44:21	*I have m* you, you are my servant;	3670
	44:24	I am the LORD, *who has m* all things,	6913
	45:12	It is *I who m* the earth and created mankind	6913
	45:18	he who fashioned and *m* the earth,	6913
	46: 4	*I have m* you and I will carry you;	6913
	48: 3	and *I m* them known;	9048
	48:21	he *m* water flow for them from the rock;	5688
	49: 1	from my birth he *has m* mention of	2349
	49: 2	*He m* my mouth like a sharpened sword,	8492
	49: 2	he *m* me into a polished arrow	8492
	49:19	"Though you were ruined and *m* desolate	9037
	51: 2	and I blessed him and *m* him many.	8049
	51:10	who *m* a road in the depths of the sea so that	8492
	51:21	*m* drunk, but not with wine.	8912
	51:22	of your hand the cup that *m* you stagger;	9570
	51:23	And *you m* your back like the ground,	8492
	53:12	and *m* intercession for the transgressors.	7003
	55: 4	See, *I have m* him a witness to the peoples,	5989
	57: 7	*You have m* your bed on a high	8492
	57: 8	*you m* a pact with those whose beds you	4162
	62:11	The LORD *has m* proclamation to the ends	9048
	63: 6	in my wrath *I m* them drunk	8910
	64: 7	and *m* us waste away because of our sins.	4570
	66: 2	*Has* not my hand *m* all these things,	6913
	66:14	the hand of the LORD *will be m* known	3359
Jer	1:16	worshiping *what* their hands have *m.*	5126
	1:18	Today *I have m* you a fortified city,	5989
	2: 7	and *m* my inheritance detestable.	8492
	2:28	then are the gods you *m* for yourselves?	6913
	3:16	nor *will* another *one be m.*	6913
	5: 3	*They m* their faces harder than stone	2616
	5:22	*I m* the sand a boundary for the sea,	8492
	6:27	"*I have m* you a tester of metals	5989
	7:12	where *I* first *m a dwelling for* my Name,	8905
	10: 9	*What* the craftsman and goldsmith *have m*	5126
	10: 9	all *m by* skilled workers.	5126
	10:12	But God *m* the earth by his power;	6913
	11:10	the covenant *I m* with their forefathers	4162
	12:11	It *will be m* a wasteland,	8492
	15:17	never *m* merry with them;	6600
	18:15	*which m* them stumble in their ways and in	4173
	18:15	*They m* them walk *in* bypaths and on roads	AIT
	18:21	*Let* their wives *be m* childless and widows;	AIT
	19: 4	*m* this a place of foreign	5796
	20:15	*who m* him very glad,	8523+8523
	25: 6	to anger with *what* your hands have *m.*	5126
	25: 7	provoked me with *what* your hands have *m,*	5126
	25:17	*m* all the nations to whom he sent me drink	9197
	27: 5	and outstretched arm *I m* the earth	6913
	31:32	like the covenant *I m* with their forefathers	4162
	32:17	*you have m* the heavens and the earth	6913
	32:30	provoke me with *what* their hands have *m,*	5126
	33: 2	*he who m* the earth,	6913
	33:14	the gracious promise *I m* to the house	1819
Jer	34: 5	As people *m* a funeral fire in honor	NIH
	34: 8	after King Zedekiah *had m* a covenant	4162
	34:13	*I m* a covenant with your forefathers	4162
	34:15	even a covenant before me in the house	4162
	34:18	the terms of the covenant they *m* before me,	4162
	37: 1	Zedekiah son of Josiah *was m* king of Judah	4887
	37:15	which *they had m* into a prison.	6913
	41: 9	with Gedaliah was the one King Asa *had m*	6913
	41:10	Ishmael *m* captives of all the rest of	8647
	42:20	that *you m* a fatal mistake	928+5883+9494
	44: 6	and the streets of Jerusalem and *m* them	NIH
	44: 8	to anger with *what* your hands have *m,*	5126
	44:25	'We will certainly carry out the vows we *m*	5623+5624
	49:37	the sword until I have *m an end of* them.	3983
	50:20	"search *will be m* for Israel's guilt,	1335
	51: 7	*m* the whole earth drunk.	8910
	51:15	"He *m* the earth by his power;	6913
	51:34	he *has m* us an empty jar.	3657
	52:19	all that were *m* of pure gold or silver.	NIH
	52:20	which King Solomon *had m* for the temple	6913
La	1:13	He *m* me desolate, faint all the day long.	5989
	2: 6	LORD *has m* Zion forget her appointed feasts	8894
	2: 8	*m* ramparts and walls lament;	61
	3: 2	He has driven me away and *m* me walk	2143
	3: 4	*m* my skin and my flesh grow old	1162
	3: 6	He *has m* me dwell in darkness	3782
	3: 9	he *has m* my paths crooked.	6390
	3:12	He drew his bow and *m* me the target	5893
	3:45	*You have m* us scum and refuse among	8492
Eze	1:16	to be *m* like a wheel intersecting a wheel.	5126
	3:17	*I have m* you a watchman for the house	5989
	6: 6	and *what* you have *m* wiped out.	5126
	7:19	for it *has m* them stumble into sin.	2118
	12: 6	*I have m* you a sign to the house of Israel."	5989
	15: 5	how much less *can it be m*	6913
	16: 7	*I m* you grow like a plant of the field.	5989
	16:14	splendor I had given you *m* your beauty perfect,	NIH
	16:17	the jewelry *m of* my gold and silver,	4946
	16:17	and *you m* for yourself male idols	6913
	16:24	and *m* a lofty shrine in every public square.	6913
	16:31	of every street and *m* your lofty shrines	6913
	16:51	*m* your sisters seem righteous	7405
	16:52	*m* your sisters appear righteous.	7405
	16:60	Yet I will remember the covenant *I m*	NIH
	17:13	a member of the royal family and *m* a treaty	4162
	19: 5	she took another of her cubs and *m* him	8492
	19:12	The east wind *m it* shrivel,	3312
	20:11	I gave them my decrees and *m* known	3359
	20:12	that I the LORD *m* them holy.	7727
	20:28	*m* offerings that provoked me to anger,	5989
	21:11	*m* ready for the hand of the slayer.	5989
	21:15	*It is m* to flash like lightning,	6913
	22: 4	by the idols *you have m.*	6913
	22:13	at the unjust gain *you have m* and at	6913
	27: 5	*They m* all your timbers *of* pine trees	1215
	27: 6	*Of* oaks from Bashan *they m* your oars;	6913
	27: 6	the coasts of Cyprus *they m* your deck,	6913
	28:13	Your settings and mountings were *m*	NIH
	28:17	*I m* a spectacle of you before kings.	5989
	28:18	So *I m* a fire come out from you,	3655
	29: 3	*I m* it for myself."	6913
	29: 9	"The Nile is mine; I *m* it,"	6913
	29:18	and every shoulder *m* raw.	5307
	31: 4	deep springs *m it* grow tall;	8123
	31: 9	*I m* it beautiful with abundant branches,	6913
	31:16	*I m* the nations tremble at the sound	8321
	32:25	A bed *is m* for her among the slain,	5989
	33: 7	*I have m* you a watchman for the house	5989
	33:29	when *I have m* the land a desolate waste	5989
	36: 5	*they m* my land their own possession	6913
	44:12	*m* the house of Israel fall	2118+4200+4842
	45:21	during which you shall eat bread *m* without yeast.	5174
Da	2:12	**This m** the king so angry	10180+10353+10619
	2:23	*you have m* known *to* me what we asked	10313
	2:23	*you have m* known *to* us the dream	10313
	2:32	The head of the statue was *m* of pure gold,	NIH
	2:38	*he has m* you ruler over them all.	10715
	2:48	*He m* him ruler over the entire province	10715
	3: 1	King Nebuchadnezzar *m* an image of gold,	10522
	3: 5	to fall down and worship the image *I m,*	10522
	4: 5	I had a dream *that m* me afraid.	10167
	5: 7	*m* the third highest ruler	AIT
	5:16	*m* the third highest ruler	AIT
	6: 2	The satraps were *m* accountable to them so	10314
	6:14	to rescue Daniel and *m every effort*	10700
	9: 1	who *was m* ruler over	4887
	9:15	and *who m* for yourself a name that endures	6913
	9:16	of our fathers have *m* Jerusalem	928
	11:35	and *m* spotless until the time of the end,	4235
	12:10	*m* spotless and refined,	4235
Hos	8: 6	a craftsman *has m* it; it is not God.	6913
	14: 3	*what* our own hands have *m,*	5126
Am	2:12	"But you *m* the Nazirites drink wine	9197
	5: 8	(*he who m* the Pleiades and Orion,	6913
	5:26	which *you m* for yourselves.	6913
Jnh	1: 9	who *m* the sea and the land."	6913
	1:16	a sacrifice to the LORD and *m* vows	5623+5624
	4: 5	There he *m* himself a shelter,	6913
	4: 6	and *m it* grow up over Jonah to give shade	6590
Na	2: 3	on the day they *are m* ready;	3922
Hab	1:14	*You have m* men like fish in the sea,	6913
	3: 6	he looked, and *m* the nations tremble.	6001

Zep	2: 8	who insulted my people and **m** threats	1540
Zec	7:12	*They* **m** their hearts as hard as flint	8492
	7:14	how *they* **m** the pleasant land desolate.' "	8492
	11:10	the covenant *I had* **m** with all the nations.	4162
Mal	2:15	*Has* not [the LORD] **m** them one?	6913
Mt	3: 4	John's clothes *were* **m** of camel's hair,	2400
	5:13	how *can it be* **m** salty again?	245
	5:33	but keep the oaths you have **m** to the Lord.'	NIG
	10:26	or hidden that *will* not *be* **m** known.	1182
	14:22	Immediately Jesus **m** the disciples get into	337
	15:31	the mute speaking, the crippled **m** well,	5618
	19: 4	at the beginning the Creator '**m** them male	
	19:12	others *were* **m** that way by men;	2335S+2336
	20:12	'and *you have* **m** them equal	4472
	27:14	But Jesus **m** no *reply,*	646
	27:64	the tomb *to be* **m** secure until the third day.	856
	27:66	and **m** the tomb secure by putting a seal on	856
Mk	1: 6	John wore clothing *m of* camel's **hair,**	AIT
	2: 4	*they* **m** an opening in the roof above Jesus	689
	2:27	"The Sabbath was **m** for man,	1181
	6:45	Immediately Jesus **m** his disciples get into	337
	10: 6	of creation God '**m** them male and female.'	4472
	11:17	But you *have* **m** it 'a den of robbers.' "	4472
	14: 3	very expensive perfume, *m of* pure nard.	AIT
	14:58	build another, not **m** by man.' "	942
	15: 5	But Jesus still **m** no *reply,*	646
Lk	1:62	Then *they* **m** signs to his father,	1935
	3: 5	every mountain and hill **m** low.	5427
	10:40	**preparations** that had to be **m**.	1355
	11:40	Did not the one who **m** the outside make the	4472
	12: 2	or hidden that *will* not *be* **m** known.	1182
	13:22	teaching as he **m** his way to Jerusalem.	4472
	14:34	how *can it be* **m** salty again?	789
	17:19	your faith *has* **m** you well."	5392
	19:15	"He *was* **m** king, however,	993+3284+3836
	19:46	but you *have* **m** it 'a den of robbers.' "	4472
	23:26	and put the cross on him and **m** him carry it	NIG
Jn	1: 3	Through him all things *were* **m**,	1181
	1: 3	without him nothing *was* **m** that has been	1181
	1: 3	nothing was made that *has been* **m**.	1181
	1:10	and though the world *was* **m** through him,	1181
	1:14	The Word became flesh and **m** his **dwelling**	5012
	1:18	at the Father's side, *has* **m** him **known**.	2007
	2:15	So *he* **m** a whip out of cords,	4472
	4:30	They came out of the town and **m** their **way**	2262
	5:11	"The man who **m** me well said to me,	4472
	5:15	that it was Jesus who *had* **m** him well.	4472
	8: 3	*They* **m** her **stand** before the group	2705
	8:22	**This** **m** the Jews ask, "Will he kill himself?"	4036
	9: 6	**m** some mud with the saliva,	4472
	9:11	"The man they call Jesus **m** some mud	4472
	9:14	Now the day on which Jesus *had* **m** the mud	4472
	12:10	So the chief priests **m** plans to kill Lazarus	1086
	15:15	from my Father *I have* **m** known to you.	1192
	17:26	*I have* **m** you **known** to them,	1192
	18:18	and officials stood around a fire *they had* **m**	4472
Ac	2:13	Some, however, **m** fun of them and said,	1430
	2:28	*You have* **m** known to me the paths of life;	1192
	2:36	God *has* **m** this Jesus, whom you crucified,	4472
	3:12	or godliness we *had* **m** this man walk?	4472
	3:16	and know *was* **m** strong.	AIT
	3:25	prophets of the **covenant** God	1347+1416
	4:24	"you **m** the heaven and the earth and	4472
	5: 4	What **m** you **think** of doing such a thing?	
			1877+2840+3836+5502
	5:27	*they* **m** them **appear** before the Sanhedrin to	AIT
	7:10	so *he* **m** him ruler over Egypt	2770
	7:27	'Who **m** you ruler and judge over us?'	2770
	7:35	'Who **m** you ruler and judge?'	2770
	7:41	**m** an idol **in the form of** a calf.	3674
	7:41	in honor of what their hands had **m**.	2240
	7:43	the idols *you* **m** to worship.	4472
	7:44	It had been **m** as God directed Moses,	4472
	7:48	the Most High does not live in houses **m** by **men.**	5935
	7:50	*Has* not my hand **m** all these things?'	4472
	9:39	that Dorcas *had* **m** while she was still	4472
	10:15	call anything impure that God *has* **m** **clean.**	2751
	10:26	But Peter **m** him **get up.**	1586
	11: 9	call anything impure that God *has* **m** **clean.**	2751
	12:19	Herod *had* a **thorough search** for **m** him	2118
	13:22	After removing Saul, *he* **m** David their king.	1586
	13:47	" '*I have* **m** you a light for the Gentiles,	5502
	14:15	who **m** heaven and earth and sea	4472
	15: 3	*This* news **m** all the brothers very glad.	4472
	15: 7	that some time ago God **m** a choice	1721
	15: 9	*He* **m** no **distinction** between us and them,	1359
	17: 9	Then *they* **m** Jason and the others post bond	3284
	17:24	"The God who **m** the world and everything	4472
	17:26	From one man he **m** every nation of men,	4472
	17:29	an image *m by* **man's** design and skill.	AIT
	18:12	the Jews **m** a united **attack on** Paul	2987
	19:24	who **m** silver shrines of Artemis,	4472
	20: 3	*Because* the Jews **m** a plot against him just	1181
	20:13	*He had* **m** this **arrangement**	1411
	20:28	the Holy Spirit *has* **m** you overseers.	5502
	21:23	There are four men with us *who have* **m**	2400
	21:26	**offering** to be **m** for each of them.	4712+2714
	25: 8	Then Paul **m** *his* **defense.**	664
	25:21	*When* Paul **m** his **appeal** to be held over for	2126
	25:25	but *because* he **m** his **appeal** to	2126
	27: 7	*We* **m** slow **headway** for many days	1095
	27:40	the foresail to the wind and **m** for the beach.	2988
	28:25	*after* Paul *had* **m** this final **statement:**	3306+4839
Ro	1:19	because God *has* **m** it **plain** to them.	5746
	1:20	being understood *from* what *has been* **m**,	4473

Ro	1:23	the glory of the immortal God for images **m**	NIG
	3: 9	*We have* **already m** the **charge** that Jews	4577
	3:21	apart from law, *has been* **m** known,	5746
	4:17	"*I have* **m** you a father of many nations."	5502
	5:19	of the one man the many *were* **m** sinners,	2770
	5:19	the one man the many *will be* **m** righteous.	2770
	15: 8	to confirm the promises *m* to the **patriarchs**	AIT
	15:28	and *have* **m** sure that they have received	5381
	16:26	**m** known through the prophetic writings	1192
1Co	1:20	*Has* not God **m** foolish the wisdom of	3701
	3: 6	Apollos watered it, but God **m** *it* grow.	889
	4: 9	*We have* been **m** a spectacle to the whole	1181
	7:37	and *who has* **m** up his mind not to marry	3212
	12:12	though *it is* **m** up of many parts,	2400
	12:14	Now the body is not **m** up of one part but	NIG
	15:22	so in Christ all *will be* **m** alive.	2443
	15:28	be **m** **subject** to him who put everything	AIT
	16: 2	I come no collections *will* have to *be* **m**.	1181
2Co	1:20	no matter how many promises God has **m**,	NIG
	2: 1	So *I* **m** up my mind that I would	3212
	3: 6	He *has* **m** us **competent** as ministers of	2655
	3:14	But their minds *were* **m** dull,	4800
	4: 6	**m** his light **shine** in our hearts to give us	3290
	5: 5	Now it is God who *has* **m** us	2981
	5:21	God *m* him who had no sin to be sin for us,	4472
	7: 9	not because *you were* **m** sorry,	3382
	8: 6	since he *had* **earlier m** a beginning,	4599
	9:11	*You will be* **m** rich in every way so	4457
	11: 6	*We have* **m** this perfectly **clear** to you	5746
	12: 9	for my power *is m* **perfect** in weakness."	5464
	12:11	*I have* **m** a fool of myself,	1181
Gal	1:11	**something** that **man m** up.	476+2848
	4: 7	you are a son, God has **m** you also an heir.	NIG
Eph	1: 9	And he *m* **known** to us the mystery	AIT
	2: 5	**m** us alive with Christ even	5188
	2:14	who *has* **m** the two one and has destroyed	4472
	3: 3	the mystery *m* **known** to me by revelation,	AIT
	3:10	not **m** known to men in other generations	1192
	3:10	be *m* known to the rulers and authorities in	AIT
	4:23	to be **m** new in the attitude of your minds;	391
Php	2: 7	but **m** himself **nothing,** taking the very	3033
	2: 7	*being* **m** in human likeness.	1181
	3:12	or *have* already *been* **m** perfect,	5457
Col	2:13	God *m* you **alive with** Christ.	5188
	2:15	he *m* a public **spectacle** of them,	1258
1Th	2: 2	of our intense longing *we* **m** every **effort**	5079
1Ti	1: 9	that law *is* **m** not for the righteous but	3023
	1:18	with the prophecies once **m** about you,	4575
	2: 1	and thanksgiving *be* **m** for everyone—	4472
	6:12	**m** *your* good **confession**	3933+3934
	6:13	**m** the good **confession,**	3934
2Ti	2:21	an instrument for noble purposes, **m** holy,	39
Heb	1: 2	and through whom *he* **m** the universe.	4472
	2: 7	*You* **m** him a little **lower** than the angels;	1783
	2: 9	who *was* **m** a little **lower** than the angels,	1783
	2:11	and those who *are* **m** holy are of	39
	2:17	*to be* **m** like his brothers in every way,	3929
	5: 9	and, *once* **m** perfect, he became the source	5457
	6:13	*When* God **m** his **promise** to Abraham,	2040
	7:19	(for the law **m** nothing **perfect**),	5457
	7:28	*who has been* **m** perfect forever.	5457
	8: 9	like the covenant *I* **m** with their forefathers	4472
	8:13	By calling this covenant "new," **m** the first one **obsolete;**	4096
	9:16	to prove the death *of* the one who **m** it,	1416
	9:17	while the one who **m** it is living.	1416
	10: 8	(although the law required them *to be* **m**).	4712S
	10:10	*we have been* **m** holy through the sacrifice of the body of Jesus Christ	39+1639
	10:13	for his enemies *to be* **m** his footstool,	5502
	10:14	by one sacrifice *he has* **m** perfect forever those who are being made holy.	5457
	10:14	by one sacrifice he has **m** perfect forever those who *are being* **m** holy.	39
	11: 3	so that what is seen was not **m** out	NIG
	11: 9	By faith *he* **m** his **home** in the promised land	4228
	11:11	he considered him faithful who *had* **m** the **promise.**	2040
	11:40	with us *would they be* **m** perfect.	5457
	12:23	to the spirits of righteous men **m** perfect,	5457
Jas	2:22	his faith *was* **m** complete by what he did.	5457
	3: 9	who *have been* **m** in God's likeness.	1181
1Pe	2:23	when he suffered, *he* **m** no **threats.**	580
	3:18	in the body but **m** alive by the Spirit,	2443
2Pe	1:14	as our Lord Jesus Christ *has* **m** clear to me.	1317
	1:19	the word of the prophets **m** more certain,	NIG
	2: 3	*with* stories they have **m** up.	4422
	2: 6	and them an example of what is going	5502
1Jn	2: 5	God's love *is* truly **m** complete in him.	5457
	3: 2	what we will be *has* not *been* **m** known.	5746
	4:12	God lives in us and his love is **m** complete	5457
	4:17	love *is* **m** complete among us so	5457
	4:18	The one who fears *is* not **m** perfect in love.	5457
	5:10	God *has* **m** him **out to be** a liar.	4472
Rev	1: 1	*He* **m** it **known** by sending his angel	4955
	1: 6	and *has* **m** us to be a kingdom and priests	4472
	5:10	*You have* **m** them to be a kingdom	4472
	6:12	like sackcloth **m** of goat **hair,**	5570
	7:14	and them white in the blood of the Lamb.	3326
	13:12	and the earth and its inhabitants worship	4472
	14: 7	Worship him who **m** the heavens, the earth,	4472
	14: 8	**m** all the nations **drink** the maddening wine	4540
	18:12	and articles of every kind *m of* ivory,	AIT
	19: 7	and his bride *has* **m** herself **ready.**	2286
	21:18	The wall was **m** of jasper,	NIG
	21:21	each gate **m** of a single pearl.	1639

MADE   (Anglicized) See also HAD

MADIAN   (KJV) See MIDIAN

MADMAN   (5) [MAD]

1Sa	21:13	he was in their hands *he* **acted like a m,**	2147
2Ki	9:11	Why did this **m** come to you?"	8713
	9:20	he drives like a **m**."	8714
Pr	26:18	a **m** shooting firebrands or deadly arrows	4263
Jer	29:26	you should put any **m** who acts like	408+8713

MADMANNAH   (2)

Jos	15:31	Ziklag, **M**, Sansannah,	4526
1Ch	2:49	of **M** and to Sheva the father of Macbenah	4525

MADMEN   (2) [MAD]

1Sa	21:15	short of **m** that you have to bring this fellow	8713
Jer	48: 2	You too, O **M**, will be silenced;	4522

MADMENAH   (1)

Isa	10:31	**M** is in flight; the people of Gebim take	4524

MADNESS   (8) [MAD]

Dt	28:28	The LORD will afflict you with **m**,	8714
Ecc	1:17	and also of **m** and folly,	2099
	2:12	and also **m** and folly.	2099
	7:25	the stupidity of wickedness and the **m**	2099
	9: 3	are full of evil and there is **m** in their hearts	2099
	10:13	at the end they are wicked **m**—	2100
Zec	12: 4	with panic and its rider with **m**,"	8714
2Pe	2:16	and restrained the prophet's **m**.	4197

MADON   (2)

Jos	11: 1	he sent word to Jobab king of **M**,	4507
	12:19	the king of **M** one the king of Hazor one	4507

MAGADAN   (1)

Mt	15:39	into the boat and went to the vicinity *of* **M**.	3400

MAGBISH   (1)

Ezr	2:30	of **M** 156	4455

MAGDALA   (KJV) See MAGADAN

MAGDALENE   (12)

Mt	27:56	Among them were Mary **M**,	3402
	27:61	Mary **M** and the other Mary were sitting there opposite the tomb.	3402
	28: 1	Mary **M** and the other Mary went to look at	3402
Mk	15:40	Among them were Mary **M**,	3402
	15:47	Mary **M** and Mary the mother of Joses saw	3402
	16: 1	When the Sabbath was over, Mary **M**,	3402
	16: 9	he appeared first to Mary **M**,	3402
Lk	8: 2	(called **M**) from whom seven demons had come out;	3402
	24:10	It was Mary **M**, Joanna,	3402
Jn	19:25	Mary the wife of Clopas, and Mary **M**.	3402
	20: 1	Mary **M** went to the tomb and saw that	3402
	20:18	Mary **M** went to the disciples with	3402

MAGDIEL   (2)

Ge	36:43	**M** and Iram. These were the chiefs of Edom	4462
1Ch	1:54	**M** and Iram. These were the chiefs of Edom	4462

MAGGOT   (1) [MAGGOTS]

Job	25: 6	how much less man, who is but a **m**—	8231

MAGGOTS   (3) [MAGGOT]

Ex	16:20	but it was full of **m** and began to smell.	9357
	16:24	and it did not stink or get **m** in it.	8231
Isa	14:11	**m** are spread out beneath you	8231

MAGI   (4)

Mt	2: 1	**M** from the east came to Jerusalem	3407
	2: 7	the **M** secretly and found out from them	3407
	2:16	that he had been outwitted by the **M**,	3407
	2:16	with the time he had learned from the **M**.	3407

MAGIC   (8) [MAGICIAN, MAGICIANS]

Isa	47:12	with your **m** spells and	2490
Eze	13:18	Woe to the women who sew **m** charms	4086
	13:20	I am against your **m** charms	4086
Ac	8:11	for a long time *with* his **m**.	3404
Rev	9:21	their **m** arts, their sexual immorality	5760
	18:23	By your **m** spell all the nations were led	5758
	21: 8	**those who practice m** arts, the idolaters	5761
	22:15	the dogs, those who **practice m** arts,	5761

MAGICIAN   (2) [MAGIC]

Da	2:10	a thing of any **m** or enchanter or astrologer.	10282
	2:27	**m** or diviner can explain to the king	10282

MAGICIANS   (13) [MAGIC]

Ge	41: 8	he sent for all the **m** and wise men of Egypt.	3033
	41:24	I told this to the **m**,	3033

Ex	7:11	and the Egyptian **m** also did the same things	3033
	7:22	But the Egyptian **m** did the same things	3033
	8: 7	**m** did the same things by their secret arts;	3033
	8:18	**m** tried to produce gnats by their secret arts,	3033
	8:19	The **m** said to Pharaoh,	3033
	9:11	The **m** could not stand before Moses	3033
Da	1:20	the **m** and enchanters in his whole kingdom.	3033
	2: 2	So the king summoned the **m**, enchanters,	3033
	4: 7	When the **m**, enchanters,	10282
	4: 9	I said, "Belteshazzar, chief of the **m**,	10282
	5:11	appointed him chief of the **m**, enchanters,	10282

MAGISTRATE (1) [MAGISTRATES]

Lk	12:58	with your adversary to the **m**,	*807*

MAGISTRATES (8) [MAGISTRATE]

Ezr	7:25	appoint **m** and judges to administer justice	10735
Da	3: 2	**m** and all the other provincial officials	10767
	3: 3	treasurers, judges, **m** and all	10767
Ac	16:20	They brought them before the **m** and said,	5130
	16:22	**m** ordered them to be stripped and beaten.	5130
	16:35	the **m** sent their officers to the jailer with	5130
	16:36	"The **m** have ordered that you and Silas	5130
	16:38	The officers reported this *to* the **m**,	5130

MAGNIFICENCE (1) [MAGNIFY]

1Ch	22: 5	for the Lord should be of great **m**	2025+5087

MAGNIFICENT (5) [MAGNIFY]

1Ki	8:13	I have indeed built a **m** temple for you,	2292
2Ch	2: 9	the temple I build *must be* large and **m**.	7098
	6: 2	I have built a **m** temple for you,	2292
Isa	28:29	wonderful in counsel and **m** *in* wisdom.	1540
Mk	13: 1	What **m** buildings!"	*4534*

MAGNIFY (1) [MAGNIFICENCE, MAGNIFICENT]

Da	11:36	and **m** himself above every god	1540

MAGOG (5)

Ge	10: 2	The sons of Japheth: Gomer, **M**, Madai,	4470
1Ch	1: 5	The sons of Japheth: Gomer, **M**, Madai,	4470
Eze	38: 2	set your face against Gog, of the land of **M**,	4470
	39: 6	I will send fire on **M** and on those who live	4470
Rev	20: 8	Gog and **M**—to gather them for battle.	*3408*

MAGOR-MISSABIB (1)

Jer	20: 3	Lord's name for you is not Pashhur, but **M**.	4474

MAGPIASH (1)

Ne	10:20	**M**, Meshullam, Hezir,	4488

MAHALAH (KJV) See MAHLAH

MAHALALEL (8)

Ge	5:12	he became the father of **M**.	4546
	5:13	And after he became the father of **M**,	4546
	5:15	When **M** had lived 65 years,	4546
	5:16	**M** lived 830 years and had other sons	4546
	5:17	Altogether, **M** lived 895 years,	4546
1Ch	1: 2	Kenan, **M**, Jared,	4546
Ne	11: 4	the son of **M**, a descendant of Perez;	4546
Lk	3:37	the son *of* **M**, the son of Kenan,	*3435*

MAHALATH (4)

Ge	28: 9	so he went to Ishmael and married **M**,	4715
2Ch	11:18	Rehoboam married **M**,	4715
Ps	53: T	According to **m**.	4714
	88: T	According to **m** leannoth.	4714

MAHALI (KJV) See MAHLI

MAHANAIM (14)

Ge	32: 2	So he named that place **M**.	4724
Jos	13:26	and from **M** to the territory of Debir,	4724
	13:30	from **M** and including all of Bashan,	4724
	21:38	of refuge for one accused of murder), **M**,	4724
2Sa	2: 8	of Saul and brought him over to **M**.	4724
	2:12	left **M** and went to Gibeon.	4724
	2:29	through the whole Bithron and came to **M**.	4724
	17:24	David went to **M**,	4724
	17:27	When David came to **M**,	4724
	19:32	for the king during his stay in **M**,	4724
1Ki	2: 8	on me the day I went to **M**.	4724
	4:14	Ahinadab son of Iddo—in **M**;	4724
1Ch	6:80	of Gad they received Ramoth in Gilead, **M**,	4724
SS	6:13	on the Shulammite as on the dance of **M**?	4724

MAHANEH DAN (2) [DAN]

Jdg	13:25	the Spirit of the Lord to stir him while he was in **M**,	4723
	18:12	place west of Kiriath Jearim is called **M**	4723

MAHARAI (3)

2Sa	23:28	Zalmon the Ahohite, **M** the Netophathite,	4560
1Ch	11:30	**M** the Netophathite, Heled son of Baanah	4560
	27:13	was **M** the Netophathite, a Zerahite.	4560

MAHATH (3)

1Ch	6:35	the son of Elkanah, the son of **M**,	4744
2Ch	29:12	**M** son of Amasai and Joel son of Azariah;	4744
	31:13	**M** and Benaiah were supervisors	4744

MAHAVITE (1)

1Ch	11:46	Eliel the **M**, Jeribai and Joshaviah the sons	4687

MAHAZIOTH (2)

1Ch	25: 4	Joshbekashah, Mallothi, Hothir and **M**.	4692
	25:30	the twenty-third to **M**,	4692

MAHER-SHALAL-HASH-BAZ (2)

Isa	8: 1	write on it with an ordinary pen: **M**.	4561
	8: 3	And the Lord said to me, "Name him **M**.	4561

MAHLAH (5) [MAHLITE, MAHLITES]

Nu	26:33	whose names were **M**, Noah, Hoglah,	4702
	27: 1	The names of the daughters were **M**, Noah,	4702
	36:11	**M**, Tirzah, Hoglah, Milcah and Noah—	4702
Jos	17: 3	whose names were **M**, Noah, Hoglah,	4702
1Ch	7:18	to Ishhod, Abiezer and **M**.	4702

MAHLI (12)

Ex	6:19	The sons of Merari were **M** and Mushi.	4706
Nu	3:20	The Merarite clans: **M** and Mushi.	4706
1Ch	6:19	The sons of Merari: **M** and Mushi.	4706
	6:29	**M**, Libni his son, Shimei his son,	4706
	6:47	the son of **M**, the son of Mushi,	4706
	23:21	The sons of Merari: **M** and Mushi.	4706
	23:21	The sons of **M**: Eleazar and Kish.	4706
	23:23	**M**, Eder and Jerimoth—three in all.	4706
	24:26	The sons of Merari: **M** and Mushi.	4706
	24:28	From **M**: Eleazar, who had no sons.	4706
	24:30	the sons of Mushi: **M**, Eder and Jerimoth.	4706
Ezr	8:18	from the descendants of **M** son of Levi,	4706

MAHLITE (1) [MAHLAH]

Nu	26:58	Libnite clan, the Hebronite clan, the **M** clan,	4707

MAHLITES (1) [MAHLAH]

Nu	3:33	To Merari belonged the clans of the **M** and	4707

MAHLON (3) [MAHLON'S]

Ru	1: 2	names of his two sons were **M** and Kilion.	4705
	1: 5	both **M** and Kilion also died,	4705
	4: 9	the property of Elimelech, Kilion and **M**.	4705

MAHLON'S (1) [MAHLON]

Ru	4:10	Ruth the Moabitess, **M** widow, as my wife,	4705

MAHOL (1)

1Ki	4:31	Calcol and Darda, the sons of **M**.	4689

MAHSEIAH (2)

Jer	32:12	Baruch son of Neriah, the son of **M**,	4729
	51:59	Seraiah son of Neriah, the son of **M**,	4729

MAID (2) [MAIDEN, MAIDENS, MAIDS]

Ps	123: 2	eyes of a **m** look to the hand of her mistress,	9148
Isa	24: 2	for mistress as for **m**, for seller as for buyer,	9148

MAIDEN (5) [MAID]

Ge	24:43	if a **m** comes out to draw water and I say	6625
Pr	30:19	and the way of a man with a **m**.	6625
Isa	62: 5	As a young man marries a **m**,	1435
Jer	2:32	Does a **m** forget her jewelry,	1435
	51:22	with you I shatter young man and **m**,	1435

MAIDENS (11) [MAID]

Ps	68:25	with them are the **m** playing tambourines.	6625
	78:63	and their **m** had no wedding songs;	1435
	148:12	young men and **m**, old men and children.	1435
SS	1: 3	No wonder the **m** love you!	6625
	2: 2	among thorns is my darling among the **m**.	1426
	6: 9	The **m** saw her and called her blessed;	1426
Jer	31:13	Then **m** will dance and be glad,	1435
La	1: 4	her **m** grieve, and she is in bitter anguish.	1435
	1:18	My young men and **m** have gone into exile.	1435
	2:21	my young men and **m** have fallen by	1435
Eze	9: 6	Slaughter old men, young men and **m**,	1435

MAIDS (7) [MAID]

Ge	24:61	Then Rebekah and her **m** got ready	5855
1Sa	25:42	attended by her five **m**,	5855
Est	2: 9	He assigned to her seven **m** selected from	5855
	2: 9	and moved her and her **m** into the best place	5855
	4: 4	When Esther's **m** and eunuchs came	5855
	4:16	and I and my **m** will fast as you do.	5855
Pr	9: 3	She has sent out her **m**,	5855

MAIDSERVANT (28) [SERVANT]

Ge	16: 1	But she had an Egyptian **m** named Hagar;	9148
	16: 2	Go, sleep with my **m**.	9148
	16: 3	Sarai his wife took her Egyptian **m** Hagar	9148
	21:12	be so distressed about the boy and your **m**.	563

Ge	21:13	I will make the son of the **m** into a nation	563
	25:12	whom Sarah's **m**, Hagar the Egyptian,	9148
	29:24	to his daughter as her **m**.	9148
	29:29	to his daughter Rachel as her **m**.	9148
	30: 3	Then she said, "Here is Bilhah, my **m**.	563
	30: 9	she took her **m** Zilpah and gave her to Jacob	9148
	30:18	"God has rewarded me for giving my **m**	9148
	35:25	The sons of Rachel's **m** Bilhah:	9148
	35:26	The sons of Leah's **m** Zilpah:	9148
Ex	20:10	nor your manservant or **m**,	563
	20:17	or his manservant or **m**, his ox or donkey,	563
	21:26	"If a man hits a manservant or **m** in the eye	563
	21:27	the tooth of a manservant or **m**,	563
Lev	25: 6	for yourself, your manservant and **m**,	563
Dt	5:14	nor your manservant or **m**, nor your ox,	563
	5:14	so that your manservant and **m** may rest,	563
	5:21	his manservant or **m**, his ox or donkey,	563
	15:17	Do the same for your **m**.	563
Jdg	19:19	me, your **m**, and the young man with us.	563
1Sa	25:41	"Here is your **m**, ready to serve you	563
	28:21	she said, "Look, your **m** has obeyed you.	9148
Ps	86:16	to your servant and save the son of your **m**.	563
	116:16	I am your servant, the son of your **m**;	563
Pr	30:23	and a **m** who displaces her mistress.	9148

MAIDSERVANTS (21) [SERVANT]

Ge	12:16	menservants and **m**, and camels.	9148
	24:35	silver and gold, menservants and **m**,	9148
	30:43	and **m** and menservants,	9148
	31:33	and into the tent of the two **m**,	563
	32: 5	sheep and goats, menservants and **m**.	9148
	32:22	his two **m** and his eleven sons and crossed	9148
	33: 1	Rachel and the two **m**.	9148
	33: 2	He put the **m** and their children in front,	9148
	33: 6	Then the **m** and their children approached	9148
Dt	12:12	your menservants and **m**,	563
	12:18	your menservants and **m**,	563
	16:11	your menservants and **m**,	563
	16:14	your menservants and **m**, and the Levites,	563
1Sa	8:16	Your menservants and **m** and the best	9148
2Ki	5:26	flocks, herds, or menservants and **m**?	9148
Ezr	2:65	besides their 7,337 menservants and **m**;	563
Ne	7:67	besides their 7,337 menservants and **m**;	563
Job	19:15	My guests and my **m** count me a stranger;	563
	31:13	to my menservants and **m** when they had	563
Isa	14: 2	as menservants and **m** in the Lord's land.	9148
Lk	12:45	the menservants and **m** and to eat and drink	*4087*

MAIL (KJV) See SCALE ARMOR

MAIM See ABEL MAIM, MISREPHOTH MAIM

MAIMED (3)

Lev	22:22	the injured or the **m**,	3024
Mt	18: 8	for you to enter life **m** or crippled than	*3245*
Mk	9:43	for you to enter life **m** than with two hands	*3245*

MAIN (11)

Nu	20:19	"We will go along the **m road**,	5019
Dt	2:27	We will stay on the **m road**;	2006+2006
1Ki	6: 3	The portico at the front of the **m hall** *of*	2121
	6: 5	of the **m hall** and inner sanctuary he built	2121
	6:17	The **m hall** in front	2121
	6:33	for the entrance to the **m hall**.	2121
	7:50	for the doors of the **m hall** of the temple.	2121
2Ch	3:13	facing the **m hall**.	1524
	4:22	and the doors of the **m hall**.	1074
Eze	19:14	its **m branches** and consumed its fruit.	964+4751

MAINLAND (2) [LAND]

Eze	26: 6	on the **m** will be ravaged by the sword.	8441
	26: 8	He will ravage your settlements on the **m**	8441

MAINSAIL (KJV) See FORESAIL

MAINSTAY (1)

Jer	49:35	the bow of Elam, the **m** *of* their might.	8040

MAINTAIN (16) [MAINTAINED, MAINTAINING, MAINTAINS]

Ru	4: 5	in order to **m** the name of the dead	7756
	4:10	to **m** the name of the dead with his property,	7756
1Ki	10: 9	to **m** justice and righteousness.	6913
2Ki	8:19	He had promised to **m** a lamp for David	5989
2Ch	9: 8	to **m** justice and righteousness."	6913
	21: 7	He had promised to **m** a lamp for him	5989
Job	27: 6	*I will* **m** my righteousness	2616
Ps	82: 3	**m** *the rights of* the poor and oppressed;	7405
	89:28	*I will* **m** my love to him forever;	9068
	106: 3	Blessed are *they who* **m** justice,	9068
Pr	5: 2	that you *may* **m** discretion	9068
Isa	56: 1	"**M** justice and do what is right,	9068
Da	11:20	a tax collector to **m** the royal splendor.	NIH
Hos	12: 6	**m** love and justice,	9068
Am	5:15	Hate evil, love good; **m** justice in the courts.	3657
Ro	3:28	For *we* **m** that a man is justified	*3357*

MAINTAINED (1) [MAINTAIN]

Rev	6: 9	of God and the testimony *they had* **m**.	2400

MAINTAINING (1) [MAINTAIN]
Ex 34: 7   m love to thousands, and forgiving   5915

MAINTAINS (3) [MAINTAIN]
Job 2: 3   And he still m his integrity,   2616
Pr 28: 2   of understanding and knowledge m order.   799
Na 1: 2   and m his wrath against his enemies.   5757

MAJESTIC (14) [MAJESTY]
Ex 15: 6   Your right hand, O LORD, was m in power.   158
    15:11   Who is like you—m in holiness,   158
Job 37: 4   he thunders with his m voice.   1454
Ps 8: 1   how m is your name in all the earth!   129
    8: 9   how m is your name in all the earth!   129
    29: 4   the voice of the LORD is m.   2077
    68:15   The mountains of Bashan are m mountains;   466
    76: 4   more m than mountains rich with game.   129
    111: 3   Glorious and m are his deeds,   2077
SS 6: 4   m as troops with banners.   398
    6:10   m as the stars in procession?   398
Isa 30:30   LORD will cause men to hear his m voice   2086
Eze 31: 7   It was m in beauty,   3636
2Pe 1:17   the voice came to him from the M Glory,   3485

MAJESTY (39) [MAJESTIC]
Ex 15: 7   In the greatness of your m you threw   1454
Dt 5:24   and his m, and we have heard his voice   1542
    11: 2   his m, his mighty hand,   1542
    33:17   In m he is like a firstborn bull;   2077
    33:26   to help you and on the clouds in his m.   1452
1Ch 16:27   Splendor and m are before him;   2077
    29:11   and the power and the glory and the m and   5905
Est 1: 4   and the splendor and glory of his m.   1525
    7: 3   and if it pleases your m, grant me my life—   4889
Job 37:22   God comes in awesome m,   2086
    40:10   and clothe yourself in honor and m.   2077
Ps 21: 5   you have bestowed on him splendor and m.   2077
    45: 3   clothe yourself with splendor and m.   2077
    45: 4   In your m ride forth victoriously in behalf   2077
    68:34   whose m is over Israel,   1452
    93: 1   The LORD reigns, he is robed in m;   1455
    93: 1   the LORD is robed in m and is armed   NIH
    96: 6   Splendor and m are before him;   2077
    104: 1   you are clothed with splendor and m.   2077
    110: 3   Arrayed in holy m,   2077
    145: 5   of the glorious splendor of your m,   2086
Isa 2:10   of the LORD and the splendor of his m!   1454
    2:19   of the LORD and the splendor of his m,   1454
    2:21   of the LORD and the splendor of his m,   1454
    24:14   from the west they acclaim the LORD's m.   1454
    26:10   on doing evil and regard not the m of   1455
    53: 2   He had no beauty or m to attract us to him,   2077
Eze 31: 7   " 'Who can be compared with you in m?   1542
    31:18   be compared with you in splendor and m?   1542
Da 4:30   and for the glory of my m?"   10199
Mic 5: 4   the m of the LORD his God.   1454
Zec 6:13   with m and will sit and rule on his throne.   2086
Ac 19:27   will be robbed of her divine m."   3484
    25:26   I have nothing definite to write to His M   3261
2Th 1: 9   of the Lord and from the m of his power   1518
Heb 1: 3   down at the right hand of the M in heaven.   3488
    8: 1   at the right hand of the throne of the M   3488
2Pe 1:16   but we were eyewitnesses of his m.   3484
Jude 1:25   m, power and authority,   3488

MAJOR (1) [MAJORITY]
2Ki 3:19   every fortified city and every m town.   4435

MAJORITY (2) [MAJOR]
Ac 27:12   the m decided that we should sail on,   4498
2Co 2: 6   on him by the m is sufficient for him.   4498

MAKAZ (1)
1Ki 4: 9   in M, Shaalbim, Beth Shemesh   5242

MAKE (857) [MADE, MAKER, MAKERS, MAKES, MAKING, MAN-MADE]
Ge 1:26   God said, "Let us m man in our image,   6913
    2:18   I will m a helper suitable for him."   6913
    6:14   So m yourself an ark of cypress wood;   6913
    6:14   m rooms in it and coat it with pitch inside   6913
    6:16   M a roof for it and finish the ark to   6913
    6:16   a door in the side of the ark and m lower,   6913
    11: 3   let's m bricks and bake them   4236+4246
    11: 4   that we may m a name for ourselves and not   6913
    12: 2   "I will m you into a great nation   6913
    12: 2   I will m your name great,   1540
    13:16   I will m your offspring like the dust of   8492
    17: 6   I will m you very fruitful;   7238
    17: 6   I will m nations of you,   5989
    17:20   I will m him fruitful   7238
    17:20   and I will m him into a great nation.   5989
    21:13   I will m the son of the maidservant into   8492
    21:18   for I will m him into a great nation."   8492
    22:17   m your descendants as numerous as   8049+8049
    24: 6   "M sure that you do not take my son back   9068
    24:40   m your journey a success,   7503
    26: 4   m your descendants as numerous   8049
    26:28   Let us m a treaty with you   4162
    28: 3   God Almighty bless you and m you fruitful   7238
    31:44   Come now, let's m a covenant, you and I,   4162

Ge 32: 9   and I will m you prosper,'   3512
    32:12   'I will surely m you prosper   3512+3512
    32:12   and will m your descendants like the sand   8492
    34:12   M the price for the bride and the gift I am
         to bring as great as you like,   4394+8049
    39:14   to us to m sport of us!   7464
    39:17   to me to m sport of me.   7464
    41:43   and men shouted before him, "M way!"   91
    46: 3   for I will m you into a great nation there.   8492
    48: 4   'I am going to m you fruitful   7238
    48: 4   I will m you a community of peoples,   5989
    48:20   'May God m you like Ephraim   8492
Ex 3:21   "And I will m the Egyptians favorably   5989
    5: 8   to m the same number of bricks as before;   6913
    5: 9   M the work harder for the men so   AIT
    5:16   yet we are told, 'M bricks!'   6913
    6: 3   the LORD I did not m myself known   3359
    8: 5   and m frogs come up on the land of Egypt.'   6590
    8:23   I will m a distinction between my people   8492
    9: 4   the LORD will m a distinction between   7111
    10:28   M sure you do not appear before me again!   9068
    17: 3   m us and our children and livestock die   4637
    17:14   m sure that Joshua hears   265+928+8492
    18:22   That will m your load lighter,   7837
    20: 4   "You shall not m for yourself an idol in   6913
    20:23   Do not m any gods to be alongside me;   6913
    20:23   not m for yourselves gods of silver or gods   6913
    20:24   " 'M an altar of earth for me and sacrifice   6913
    20:25   If you m an altar of stones for me,   6913
    22: 3   must certainly m restitution,   8966+8966
    22: 5   he must m restitution from the best   8966
    22: 6   one who started the fire must m restitution.   8966+8966
    22:12   he must m restitution to the owner.   8966
    22:14   he must m restitution.   8966+8966
    23:27   all your enemies turn their backs   448+5989
    23:32   Do not m a covenant with them or   4162
    25: 8   "Then have them m a sanctuary for me,   6913
    25: 9   M this tabernacle and all its furnishings   6913
    25:10   "Have them m a chest of acacia wood—   6913
    25:11   and m a gold molding around it.   6913
    25:13   Then m poles of acacia wood   6913
    25:17   "M an atonement cover of pure gold—   6913
    25:18   And m two cherubim out of hammered   6913
    25:19   M one cherub on one end and   6913
    25:19   m the cherubim of one piece with the cover,   6913
    25:23   "M a table of acacia wood—   6913
    25:24   with pure gold and m a gold molding   6913
    25:25   Also m around it a rim a handbreadth wide   6913
    25:26   M four gold rings for the table   6913
    25:28   M the poles of acacia wood,   6913
    25:29   And m its plates and dishes of pure gold,   6913
    25:31   "M a lampstand of pure gold   6913
    25:37   "Then m its seven lamps and set them up   6913
    25:40   See that you m them according to   6913
    26: 1   "M the tabernacle with ten curtains   6913
    26: 4   M loops of blue material along the edge of   6913
    26: 5   M fifty loops on one curtain and fifty loops   6913
    26: 6   Then m fifty gold clasps and use them   6913
    26: 7   "M curtains of goat hair for the tent over   6913
    26:10   M fifty loops along the edge of   6913
    26:11   Then m fifty bronze clasps and put them in   6913
    26:14   M for the tent a covering   6913
    26:15   "M upright frames of acacia wood for   6913
    26:17   M all the frames of the tabernacle   6913
    26:18   M twenty frames for the south side of   6913
    26:19   and m forty silver bases to go under them—   6913
    26:20   of the tabernacle, m twenty frames   NIH
    26:22   M six frames for the far end, that is,   6913
    26:23   m two frames for the corners at the far end.   6913
    26:26   "Also m crossbars of acacia wood: 6913
    26:29   and m gold rings to hold the crossbars.   6913
    26:31   "M a curtain of blue,   6913
    26:36   the entrance to the tent m a curtain of blue,   6913
    26:37   M gold hooks for this curtain and five posts   6913
    27: 2   M a horn at each of the four corners,   6913
    27: 3   M all its utensils of bronze—   6913
    27: 4   M a grating for it, a bronze network,   6913
    27: 4   and m a bronze ring at each of   6913
    27: 6   M poles of acacia wood for the altar   6913
    27: 8   M the altar hollow, out of boards.   6913
    27: 9   "M a courtyard for the tabernacle.   6913
    28: 2   M sacred garments for your brother Aaron,   6913
    28: 3   in such matters that they are to m garments   6913
    28: 4   These are the garments they are to m: 6913
    28: 4   They are to m these sacred garments   6913
    28: 6   "M the ephod of gold, and of blue,   6913
    28:13   M gold filigree settings   6913
    28:15   M it like the ephod: 6913
    28:22   "For the breastpiece m braided chains   6913
    28:23   M two gold rings for it and fasten them   6913
    28:26   M two gold rings and attach them to   6913
    28:27   M two more gold rings and attach them to   6913
    28:31   "M the robe of the ephod entirely   6913
    28:33   M pomegranates of blue,   6913
    28:36   "M a plate of pure gold and engrave on it as   6913
    28:39   of fine linen and m the turban of fine linen.   6913
    28:40   M tunics, sashes and headbands   6913
    28:42   "M linen undergarments as a covering for   6913
    29: 2   m bread, and cakes mixed with oil,   6913
    29:28   It is the contribution the Israelites are to m   2118
    29:36   as a sin offering to m atonement.   NIH
    29:37   For seven days m atonement for the altar   4105
    30: 1   "M an altar of acacia wood   6913
    30: 3   and m a gold molding around it.   6913
    30: 4   M two gold rings for the altar below   6913
    30: 5   M the poles of acacia wood   6913

Ex 30:10   Once a year Aaron shall m atonement   4105
    30:15   not to give less when you m the offering to   5989
    30:18   "M a bronze basin,   6913
    30:25   M these into a sacred anointing oil,   6913
    30:32   and do not m any oil with the same formula.   6913
    30:35   and m a fragrant blend of incense,   6913
    30:37   Do not m any incense with this formula   6913
    31: 4   to m artistic designs for work in gold,   3108
    31: 6   to m everything I have commanded you: 6913
    31:11   to m them just as I commanded you."   6913
    32: 1   "Come, m us gods who will go before us.   6913
    32:10   Then I will m you into a great nation."   6913
    32:13   m your descendants as numerous   8049
    32:23   'M us gods who will go before us.   6913
    32:30   perhaps I can m atonement for your sin."   4105
    34:12   not to m a treaty with those who live in   4162
    34:15   not to m a treaty with those who live in   4162
    34:17   "Do not m cast idols.   6913
    35:10   among you are to come and m everything   6913
    35:32   to m artistic designs for work in gold,   3108
    36: 6   "No man or woman is to m anything else   6913
    38:28   used the 1,775 shekels to m the hooks   6913
    38:28   and to m their bands.   3138
    38:30   They used it to m the bases for the entrance   6913
Lev 1: 4   be accepted on his behalf to m atonement   4105
    3:14   to m this offering to the LORD by fire: 7928
    4:20   In this way the priest will m atonement   4105
    4:26   In this way the priest will m atonement for   4105
    4:31   In this way the priest will m atonement for   4105
    4:35   In this way the priest will m atonement for   4105
    5: 3   anything that would m him unclean—   AIT
    5: 6   and the priest shall m atonement for him   4105
    5:10   in the prescribed way and m atonement   4105
    5:13   the priest will m atonement for him for any   4105
    5:16   He must m restitution for what   8966
    5:16   who will m atonement for him with   4105
    5:18   In this way the priest will m atonement   4105
    6: 5   He must m restitution in full,   8966
    6: 7   the priest will m atonement for him before   4105
    6:30   into the Tent of Meeting to m atonement in   4105
    8:15   So he consecrated it to m atonement for it.   4105
    8:34   by the LORD to m atonement for you.   6913
    9: 7   and your burnt offering and m atonement   4105
    9: 7   for the people and m atonement for them,   4105
    11:24   m yourselves unclean by these: 3237
    11:43   Do not m yourselves unclean by   3237
    11:44   Do not m yourselves unclean by   3237
    12: 7   before the LORD to m atonement for her,   4105
    12: 8   In this way the priest will m atonement   4105
    14:18   be cleansed and m atonement for him   4105
    14:19   and m atonement for the one to be cleansed   4105
    14:20   and m atonement for him,   4105
    14:21   guilt offering to be waved to m atonement   4105
    14:29   to m atonement for him before the LORD.   4105
    14:31   In this way the priest will m atonement   4105
    14:53   In this way he will m atonement for   4105
    15: 3   it will m him unclean.   NIH
    15:15   In this way he will m atonement before   4105
    15:30   In this way he will m atonement for her   4105
    15:31   things that m them unclean,   3240
    16: 6   for his own sin offering to m atonement   4105
    16:11   for his own sin offering to m atonement   4105
    16:16   In this way he will m atonement for   4105
    16:18   the time Aaron goes in to m atonement   4105
    16:18   that is before the LORD and m atonement   4105
    16:24   to m atonement for himself and for   4105
    16:27   the Most Holy Place to m atonement, must   4105
    16:32   as high priest is to m atonement.   4105
    16:33   and m atonement for the Most Holy Place,   4105
    17:11   to m atonement for yourselves on the altar;   4105
    19: 4   not turn to idols or m gods of cast metal   6913
    19:22   the priest is to m atonement for him before   4105
    20:25   therefore m a distinction between clean   976
    21: 1   m himself ceremonially unclean   3237
    21: 3   for her he may m himself unclean.   3237
    21: 4   not m himself unclean for people related   3237
    21: 8   I who m you holy.   7727
    21:11   He must not m himself unclean,   3237
    22:14   he must m restitution to the priest for   5989
    24:18   of someone's animal must m restitution—   8966
    24:21   an animal must m restitution,   8966
    25:39   do not m him work as a slave.   6268
    25:46   and can m them slaves for life,   6268
    26: 1   " 'Do not m idols or set up an image or   6913
    26: 6   down and no one will m you afraid.   3006
    26: 9   on you with favor and m you fruitful   7238
    26:10   to move it out to m room for the new.   4946+7156
    26:19   down your stubborn pride and m the sky   5989
    26:22   m you so few in number   5070
    26:36   I will m their hearts so fearful in the lands   995
    27:33   from the bad or m any substitution.   4614
    27:33   If he does m a substitution,   4614+4614
Nu 3:40   or more and m a list of their names.   5951
    5: 7   He must m full restitution   928+8031+8740
    6: 2   or woman wants to m a special vow,   5623+7098
    6: 7   m himself ceremonially unclean   3237
    6:11   as a burnt offering to m atonement for him   4105
    6:16   before the LORD and m the sin offering   6913
    6:25   the LORD m his face shine upon you and   239
    8: 6   m them ceremonially clean.   3197
    8:12   to m atonement for the Levites.   4105
    8:19   the Israelites and to m atonement for them   4105
    10: 2   "M two trumpets of hammered silver,   6913
    14:12   but I will m you into a nation greater   6913
    14:30   with uplifted hand to m your home,   8905
    15:25   The priest is to m atonement for   4105
    15:28   to m atonement before the LORD for   4105

Nu	15:38	to come *you are to* **m** tassels on the corners	6913
	16:46	and hurry to the assembly *to* **m** atonement	4105
	21: 8	"**M** a snake and put it up on a pole;	6913
	22:28	*to* **m** *you* beat me these three times?"	AIT
	28: 9	**m** an offering of two lambs a year old	NIH
	28:22	as a sin offering to **m** atonement for you.	4105
	28:30	Include one male goat to **m** atonement	4105
	29: 5	as a sin offering to **m** atonement for you.	4105
	31:50	to **m** atonement for ourselves before	4105
	32: 5	*Do not* **m** us cross the Jordan."	6296
Dt	4:16	not become corrupt and **m** for yourselves	6913
	4:23	*do not* **m** for yourselves an idol in the form	6913
	4:25	then become corrupt and **m** any kind of idol,	6913
	5: 8	"*You shall* not **m** for yourself an idol in	6913
	7: 2	**M** no treaty with them,	4162
	9:14	And *I will* **m** you into a nation stronger	6913
	10: 1	Also **m** a wooden chest.	6913
	17:16	or **m** the people **return** to Egypt to get	8740
	19:18	**m** *a* thorough **investigation,**	2011
	20:10	**m** its people **an offer** of peace.	7924
	20:12	to **m** peace and they engage you in battle,	8966
	22: 8	**m** a parapet around your roof so	6913
	22:12	**M** tassels on the four corners of	6913
	23:21	If *you* **m** a vow to the LORD your God,	5623+5624
	24:10	When *you* **m** a loan of any kind	5394+5957
	25: 2	the judge *shall* **m** him lie down	5877
	28:13	The LORD *will* **m** you the head,	5989
	28:63	the LORD to **m** you **prosper** and increase	3512
	28:68	I said you *should* never **m** again.	3578+6388
	29: 1	the LORD commanded Moses to **m** with	4162
	29:18	**M** sure there is no man or woman,	NIH
	29:18	**m** sure there is no root among you	NIH
	30: 5	*He will* **m** you **more prosperous**	3512
	30: 9	LORD your God *will* **m** you **most prosperous**	AIT
	30: 9	delight in you and **m** you prosperous,	NIH
	32:21	I *will* **m** them **envious** by those who are not	7861
	32:21	I *will* **m** them **angry** by a nation	4087
	32:25	the sword *will* **m** them **childless;**	8897
	32:42	I *will* **m** my arrows **drunk** with blood,	8910
	32:43	and **m** atonement *for* his land and people.	4105
Jos	5: 2	"**M** flint knives and circumcise	6913
	6:18	Otherwise *you will* **m** the camp	8492
	9: 2	they came together to **m** war against Joshua	4309
	9: 6	**m** a treaty with us."	4162
	9: 7	How then *can we* **m** a treaty with you?"	4162
	9:11	**m** a treaty with us.' "	4162
	18: 4	*to* **m** a survey of the land and to write	928+2143
	18: 8	"Go and **m** a survey of the land and	928+2143
	24:20	and bring disaster on you and **m** an end	3983
Jdg	2: 2	and *you shall* not **m** a covenant with	4162
	5: 3	I *will* **m** music to the LORD,	2376
	6:39	**m** just one more **request.**	1819
	6:39	This time **m** the fleece dry and	2118
	17: 3	the LORD for my son to **m** a carved image	6913
Ru	4:11	the LORD **m** the woman who is coming	5989
1Sa	1:23	only *may* the LORD **m** good his word."	7756
	3:11	that *will* **m** the ears of everyone who hears	
		of it **tingle.**	AIT
	6: 5	**M** models of the tumors and of the rats	6913
	8:11	will take your sons and daughters **serve**	4200+8492
	8:12	to **m** weapons of war and equipment	6913
	11: 1	"**M** a treaty with us,	4162
	11: 2	"I *will* **m** a treaty with you only on	4162
	12: 3	a bribe *to* **m** *me* **shut** my eyes?	6623
	12: 3	I *will* **m** it **right.**"	8740
	12:22	the LORD was pleased to **m** you his own.	6913
	13:19	"Otherwise the Hebrews *will* **m** swords	6913
	15:18	**m** war on them until you have wiped them	4309
	20:26	to David to **m** him ceremonially unclean—	NIH
	22: 7	*Will he* **m** all of you commanders	8492
	23:22	Go and **m** further **preparation.**	3922
	25:28	for the LORD *will* **certainly m**	6913+6913
	28: 2	I *will* **m** you my bodyguard for life."	8492
2Sa	3:12	**M** an agreement with me,	4162
	3:13	"I *will* **m** an agreement with you.	4162
	3:17	"For some time *you have* **wanted to m**	
		David your king.	1335+4200
	3:21	so that *they may* **m** a compact with you,	4162
	7: 9	Now I *will* **m** your name great,	6913
	7:23	and to **m** a name for himself,	8492
	13: 6	**m** some **special bread** in my sight,	4221+4223
	15:20	today *shall I* **m** you **wander about** with us,	5675
	19:28	to **m** any more **appeals** to the king?"	2410
	21: 3	How shall I **m amends** so	4105
	22:36	you stoop down to **m** me great.	8049
1Ki	1:37	**m** his throne *even* **greater**	1540
	1:47	**m** Solomon's name more **famous**	3512
	2:16	Now *I have* one **request to m**	8626+8629
	2:16	"You may **m** it," she said.	1819
	2:20	"I *have* one small **request to m**	8626+8629
	2:20	The king replied, "**M** it, my mother;	8626ˢ
	2:42	"*Did I* not **m** you **swear** by the LORD	8678
	9:22	But Solomon did not **m** slaves of any of	5989
	10:12	**used** the almugwood to **m** supports	6913
	10:12	and to **m** harps and lyres for the musicians.	NIH
	12: 1	the Israelites had gone there to **m** him **king.**	4887
	12:10	but **m** our yoke **lighter'**—	7837
	12:11	I *will* **m** it **even heavier.**	3578
	12:14	I *will* **m** it **even heavier.**	3578
	12:21	to **m** war against the house of Israel and	4309
	12:33	and went up to the altar to **m offerings.**	7787
	13: 1	by the altar to **m** *an* **offering.**	7787
	13: 2	the high places who now **m offerings** here,	7787
	16: 3	and *I will* **m** your house like that	5989
	17:12	a few sticks to take home and **m** a meal	6913
	17:13	But first **m** a small cake of bread for me	6913
	17:13	then **m** something for yourself and your son.	6913

1Ki	19: 2	*I do not* **m** your life like that of one of	8492
	21:22	I *will* **m** your house like that	5989
	22:16	"How many times *must* I **m** you **swear**	8678
2Ki	2:21	or **m** the land **unproductive.' "**	8897
	3:16	**M** this valley full of ditches.	6913
	4:10	*Let's* **m** a small room on the roof and put	6913
	5:17	your servant *will* never again **m** burnt	
		offerings and sacrifices	6913
	9: 9	I *will* **m** the house of Ahab like the house	5989
	9:26	and I *will* surely **m** you **pay** *for* it	8966
	10:24	in to **m** sacrifices and burnt offerings.	6913
	18:23	" 'Come now, **m** a **bargain** with my master,	6842
	18:31	**M** peace with me and come out to me.	1293
	19:28	and *I will* **m** you **return** by	8740
	21: 8	**m** the feet of the Israelites **wander**	5653
1Ch	12:31	by name to come and **m** David **king**—	4887
	12:38	to Hebron fully determined to **m** David **king**	4887
	12:38	also of one mind to **m** David **king.**	4887
	16: 4	to **m petition,** to give thanks,	2349
	16: 8	**m known** among the nations what he has	
		done.	3359
	17: 8	Now I *will* **m** your name like the names of	6913
	17:21	and to **m** a name for yourself,	8492
	18: 8	which Solomon used *to* **m** the bronze Sea,	6913
	22: 3	to **m** nails for the doors of the gateways and	NIH
	22: 5	Therefore I *will* **m preparations** for it."	3922
	27:23	to **m** Israel as **numerous** as the stars in	8049
	28: 4	to **m** me king over all Israel.	4887
2Ch	7:20	I *will* **m** it a byword and an object	5989
	8: 9	not **m** slaves of the Israelites for his work;	5989
	9:11	**used** the algumwood to **m**	6913
	9:11	and to **m** harps and lyres for the musicians.	NIH
	10:10	the Israelites had gone there to **m** him **king.**	4887
	10:10	but **m** our yoke **lighter'**—	7837
	10:11	I *will* **m** it **even heavier.**	3578
	10:14	I *will* **m** it **even heavier.**	3578
	11: 1	to **m war** against Israel and to regain	4309
	11:22	in order to **m** him **king.**	4887
	13: 9	and **m** priests of your own as the peoples	6913
	17:10	that *they did* not **m war** with Jehoshaphat.	4309
	18:15	"How many times *must* I **m** you **swear**	8678
	20: 1	with some of the Meunites came to **m war**	NIH
	28:10	**m** the **men** and women of Judah and	
		Jerusalem your **slaves.**	3899+6269
	29:10	I intend to **m** a covenant with the LORD,	4162
	32: 2	and that he intended to *m* **war** on Jerusalem,	AIT
	32:18	to terrify them and **m** them **afraid** in order	987
	33: 8	**m** the feet of the Israelites **leave**	6073
	36:22	of Cyrus king of Persia *to* **m** a proclamation	6296
Ezr	1: 1	of Cyrus king of Persia *to* **m** a proclamation	6296
	4: 4	the people of Judah and **m** them **afraid**	987
	10: 3	Now *let us* **m** a covenant before our God	4162
	10:11	Now **m** confession to the LORD,	5989
Ne	2: 8	to **m** beams *for* the gates of the citadel by	7936
	6: 7	to **m** *this* **proclamation** about you	7924
	8:15	palms and shade trees, to **m booths**"—	6913
	10:33	for sin offerings to **m atonement** for Israel;	4105
Job	7:17	"What is man that *you* **m** so much of him,	1540
	11:19	with no one to **m** you **afraid,**	3006
	13:26	and **m** me **inherit** the sins of my youth.	3769
	16: 4	I could **m fine speeches** against you	
			928+2488+4863
	20:10	His children *must* **m amends** *to* the poor;	8355
	20:15	**m** his stomach **vomit** them **up.**	3769
	21:12	*they* **m merry** to the sound of the flute.	8523
	24:17	*they* **m friends with** the terrors of darkness.	5795
	31:15	not he who made me in the womb **m** them?	6913
	36:33	even the cattle **m** known its approach.	NIH
	38:27	a desolate wasteland and **m** it **sprout**	7541
	39:20	*Do you* **m** him **leap** like a locust,	8321
	41: 4	*Will he* **m** an **agreement** with you for you	4162
	41: 5	*Can you* **m** a **pet** of him like a bird	8471
	41:28	Arrows *do not* **m** him **flee;**	1368
Ps	2: 8	and I *will* **m** the nations your inheritance,	5989
	4: 8	O LORD, **m** me **dwell** in safety.	3782
	5: 8	**m** straight your way before me.	3837
	7: 5	to the ground and **m** me **sleep** in the dust.	8905
	7: 9	**m** the righteous **secure.**	3922
	18:35	you stoop down to **m** me great.	8049
	20: 4	**m** all your plans **succeed.**	4848
	21: 9	of your appearing *you will* **m** them like	8883
	21:12	for *you will* **m** them **turn** their backs	8883
	27: 6	I will sing and **m** music to the LORD.	2376
	33: 2	**m** music to him on the ten-stringed lyre.	2376
	37: 6	**m** your righteousness **shine** like the dawn,	3655
	39: 8	*do not* **m** me the scorn of fools.	8492
	44: 8	In God we **m** *our* **boast** all day long,	2146
	45:16	*you will* **m** them princes throughout	8883
	46: 4	There is a river whose streams **m glad**	8523
	51:18	In your good pleasure **m** Zion **prosper;**	3512
	52: 7	the man *who did* not **m** God his stronghold	8492
	57: 7	I will sing and **m** music.	2376
	59:11	In your might **m** them **wander about,**	5675
	66: 2	**m** his praise glorious!	8492
	67: 1	and bless us and **m** his face **shine** upon us,	239
	69:11	people **m sport** of *me.*	2118+4200+5442
	76:11	**M** vows to the LORD your God	5623
	79:10	**m known** among the nations that you	
		avenge	3359
	80: 3	**m** your face **shine** upon us,	239
	80: 7	**m** your face **shine** upon us,	239
	80:19	**m** your face **shine** upon us,	239
	83:11	**M** their nobles like Oreb and Zeeb,	8883
	83:13	**M** them like tumbleweed, O my God,	8883
	84: 6	*they* **m** it a place of springs;	8883
	87: 7	As *they* **m music** they will sing,	2727
	89: 1	I *will* **m** your faithfulness **known**	3359

Ps	89: 4	and **m** your throne **firm**	1215
	90:15	**M** us **glad** for as many days	8523
	91: 9	If you **m** the Most High your dwelling—	8492
	92: 1	It is good to praise the LORD and **m music**	2376
	92: 4	*you* **m** me **glad** by your deeds, O LORD;	8523
	98: 5	**m music** to the LORD with the harp,	2376
	104:15	oil to **m** his face **shine,**	7413
	104:17	There the birds **m** *their* **nests;**	7873
	105: 1	**m known** among the nations what he has	
		done.	3359
	106: 8	**m** his mighty power **known.**	3359
	106:26	that he *would* **m** them **fall** in the desert,	5877
	106:27	**m** their descendants **fall**	5877
	108: 1	I will sing and **m music** *with* all my soul.	2376
	110: 1	at my right hand until I **m** your enemies	8883
	115: 8	*Those who* **m** them will be like them,	6913
	115:14	*May* the LORD **m** you **increase,**	3578
	119:98	Your commands **m** me **wiser** than my	
		enemies,	2681
	119:135	**M** your face **shine** upon your servant	239
	119:165	and nothing can **m** them **stumble.**	4842
	132:17	"Here I *will* **m** a horn **grow** for David	7541
	135:18	*Those who* **m** them will be like them,	6913
	139: 8	if *I* **m** my bed *in* the depths, you are there.	3667
	140: 3	**m** their tongues as **sharp** as a serpent's;	9111
	144: 9	the ten-stringed lyre I *will* **m music** to you,	2376
	147: 7	**m music** to our God on the harp.	2376
	149: 3	and **m music** to him with tambourine	2376
Pr	3: 6	and he *will* **m** your paths **straight.**	3837
	4:16	of slumber till *they* **m** someone **fall.**	4173
	4:26	**M** level paths for your feet	7142
	8:15	By me kings reign and rulers **m** laws	2980
	10: 4	Lazy hands **m** a man poor,	6913
	11:14	but many advisers **m** victory sure.	NIH
	20:18	**M** plans by seeking advice;	3922
	22:24	*Do not* **m friends** with a hot-tempered man,	8287
	30:26	yet *they* **m** their home in the crags;	8492
Ecc	5: 4	When *you* **m** a vow to God,	5623+5624
	5: 5	It is better not to vow than *to* **m** a vow and	5623
SS	1:11	We *will* **m** you earrings of gold,	6913
Isa	1:16	wash and **m yourselves clean.**	2342
	3: 4	I *will* **m** boys their officials;	5989
	3: 7	*do not* **m** me the leader of the people."	8492
	3:17	the LORD *will* **m** their scalps **bald."**	6867
	5: 6	I *will* **m** it a wasteland,	8883
	6:10	**M** the heart of this people **calloused;**	9042
	6:10	**m** their ears **dull** and close their eyes.	3877
	7: 6	**m** the son of Tabeel **king** over it."	4887+4889
	10: 1	Woe to those *who* **m** unjust **laws,**	2976+2980
	12: 4	**m known** among the nations what he has	
		done,	3359
	13: 9	to **m** the land desolate and destroy	8492
	13:12	I *will* **m** man **scarcer** than pure gold,	3700
	13:13	Therefore I *will* **m** the heavens **tremble;**	8074
	14: 2	*They will* **m captives** of their captors	8647
	14:14	I *will* **m** myself **like** the Most High."	1948
	16: 3	**M** your shadow like night—at high noon.	8883
	17: 2	with no one to **m** them **afraid.**	3006
	17:11	*you* **m** them **grow,**	8451
	19:12	Let them show you and **m known** what	3359
	19:14	*they* **m** Egypt **stagger** in all that she does,	9494
	19:21	So the LORD *will* **m** himself **known** to	3359
	19:21	*they will* **m** vows to the LORD	5623+5624
	26: 7	**m** the way of the righteous **smooth.**	7142
	27: 5	*let them* **m** peace with me, yes,	6913
	27: 5	yes, *let them* **m** peace with me."	6913
	27:11	and women come and **m fires** *with* them.	239
	28:17	I *will* **m** justice the measuring line	8492
	28:28	Grain must be ground to **m** bread;	NIH
	29:16	"He did not **m** me"?	6913
	29:21	**m** a man out to be **guilty,**	2627
	30:30	and *will* **m** them **see** his arm coming down	8011
	36: 8	" 'Come now, **m** a **bargain** with my master,	6842
	36:16	**M** peace with me and come out to me.	6913
	37:29	I *will* **m** you **return** by the way you came.	8740
	38: 8	**m** the shadow cast by the sun **go**	8740
	40: 3	**m straight** in the wilderness a highway	3837
	41:15	"See, I *will* **m** you into a threshing sledge,	8492
	41:18	I *will* **m** rivers **flow** on barren heights,	7337
	42: 6	I will keep you and *will* **m** you to be	5989
	42:16	before them and **m** the rough places smooth.	NIH
	42:21	of his righteousness *to* **m** *his* law **great**	1540
	44: 9	All who **m** idols are nothing,	3670
	44:19	*Shall I* **m** a detestable thing	6913
	45:13	**m** all his ways **straight.**	3837
	46: 6	they hire a goldsmith to **m** it *into* a god,	6913
	46:10	I **m known** the end from the beginning,	5583
	47: 13	those stargazers *who* **m** **predictions** month	3359
	49: 6	I *will* also **m** you a light for the Gentiles,	5989
	49: 8	I will keep you and *will* **m** you to be	5989
	49:26	I *will* **m** your oppressors **eat** their own flesh;	430
	50: 3	and sackcloth its covering."	8492
	51: 3	he *will* **m** her deserts like Eden,	8492
	54:12	I *will* **m** your **battlements** of rubies,	8492
	55: 3	I *will* **m** an everlasting **covenant** with you,	4162
	59: 6	cannot cover themselves with **what** they **m.**	5126
	60:15	I *will* **m** the everlasting **pride** and	8492
	60:17	I *will* **m** peace your governor	8492
	61: 8	and **m** an everlasting covenant with them.	4162
	61:11	**m** righteousness and praise **spring up**	7541
	63:14	This is how you guided your people to **m**	6913
	63:17	*do you* **m** us **wander** from your ways	9494
	64: 2	to **m** your name **known** to your enemies	3359
	66:22	and the new earth that I **m** will endure	6913
Jer	5:14	I *will* **m** my words in your mouth a fire	
	6: 8	and **m** your land desolate so no one can live	8492
	7:18	the women knead the dough and **m** cakes	6913

Jer
9: 3 m ready their tongue like a bow, **to shoot** 2005
9:11 "*I will* m Jerusalem a heap of ruins, 5989
9:15 *I will* m this people **eat bitter food** 430
10:11 who *did not* m the heavens and the earth, 10522
10:22 *It will* m the towns of Judah desolate, 8492
15: 4 *I will* m them abhorrent to all 5989
15: 8 *m* their widows more **numerous** AIT
15:11 m your enemies **plead** 7003
15:20 *I will* m a wall to this people, 5989
16:20 *Do men* m their own gods? 6913
18:18 Come, *let's* m **plans** against Jeremiah; 3108+4742
19: 3 that *will* m the ears of everyone who hears of it **tingle.** 7509
19: 7 *I will* m them **fall** by the sword 5877
19: 8 *I will* devastate this city and m it an object 8492
19: 9 *I will* m them **eat** the flesh of their sons 430
19:12 *I will* m this city like Topheth. 5989
20: 4 '*I will* m you a terror to yourself and 5989
22: 6 *I will* surely m you like a desert, 8883
22:15 "*Does it* m *you* a **king** to have more AIT
23:15 "*I will* m them **eat bitter food** 430
23:27 dreams they tell one another *will* m my people **forget** my name, 8894
24: 9 *I will* m them abhorrent and an offense 5989
25: 9 *I will* completely destroy them and m them 8492
25:12 "and *will* m it desolate forever. 8492
25:15 m all the nations to whom I send you **drink** 9197
25:18 to m them a ruin and an object of horror 5989
26: 6 then *I will* m this house like Shiloh 5989
27: 2 "**M** a yoke out of straps and crossbars 6913
27: 6 *I will* m even the wild animals subject 5989
28:14 to *m* them **serve** Nebuchadnezzar king AIT
29:17 and *I will* m them like poor figs that are 5989
29:18 and plague and *will* m them abhorrent 5989
30:10 and no *one will* m them **afraid.** 3006
30:16 all *who* m **spoil** of you I will despoil. 1024
31: 7 **M** your praises **heard,** and say, 'O LORD, 9048
31:31 "when *I will* m a new covenant with 4162
31:33 the covenant *I will* m with the house 4162
32:35 a detestable thing and so m Judah **sin.** 2627
32:40 *I will* m an everlasting covenant 4162
33:15 *I will* m a righteous Branch **sprout** 7541
33:22 m the descendants of David my servant and the Levites who minister before me as **countless** as 889+4202+6218+8049
34: 5 so *they will* m a **fire** in your honor 8596
34: 5 *I* myself m *this* **promise,** 1819+1821
34:17 *I will* m you abhorrent to all the kingdoms 5989
44: 8 and m yourselves an object of cursing 2118
46:27 and no *one will* m him **afraid.** 3006
48:26 "**M** her drunk, for she has defied 8910
48:35 to *those who* m **offerings** *on* the high places 6590
49:15 "Now *I will* m you small among 5989
51:25 and m you a burned-out mountain. 5989
51:36 I will dry up her sea and m her springs **dry.** 3312
51:39 a feast for them and m them **drunk,** so 8910
51:44 and m him **spew out** what he has **swallowed.** 3655+4946+7023
51:57 m her officials and wise men **drunk,** 8910

Eze
3: 8 But *I will* m you as unyielding 5989
3: 9 *I will* m your forehead like the hardest stone 5989
3:26 *I will* m your tongue **stick** to the roof 1815
4: 9 in a storage jar and **use** them to m bread 6913
5:14 "*I will* m you a ruin and a reproach among 5989
6:14 and m the land a desolate waste *from* 5989
7:20 *to* m their detestable idols and vile images. 6913
13:18 and m veils of various lengths 6913
14: 8 against that man and m him an example and 8492
15: 3 from it to m anything useful? 6913
15: 3 *Do they* m **pegs** from it to hang things on? 4374
15: 8 m the land desolate 5989
16: 4 with water to m you **clean,** 5470
16:16 of your garments *to* m gaudy high places, 6913
16:63 when I m **atonement** for you 4105
17:24 and m the low tree **grow tall.** 1467
17:24 and m the dry tree **flourish.** 7255
21:19 **M** a signpost where the road branches off to 1345
21:27 *I will* m it a ruin! 8492
22: 4 Therefore *I will* m you an object of scorn 5989
22:12 and excessive interest and m **unjust gain** 1298
22:25 and precious things and m **many** widows 8049
22:27 and kill people to m **unjust gain.** 1298+1299
26: 4 I will scrape away her rubble and m her 5989
26:14 *I will* m you a bare rock, 5989
26:19 When I m you a desolate city, 5989
26:20 *I will* m you **dwell** in the earth below, 3782
27: 5 they took a cedar from Lebanon to m a mast 6913
28:23 upon her and m blood flow in her streets. NIH
29: 4 m the fish of your streams **stick** 1815
29:10 and *I will* m the land of Egypt a ruin and 5989
29:12 *I will* m the land of Egypt desolate 5989
29:15 *I will* m it *so* **weak** 5070
29:21 "On that day *I will* m a horn **grow** for 7541
30:22 and m the sword **fall** from his hand. 5877
32:14 and m her streams **flow** like oil, 2143
32:15 When I m Egypt desolate and strip the land 5989
33: 2 of their men and m him their watchman, 5989
33:28 *I will* m the land a desolate waste, 5989
34:25 "'*I will* m a covenant of peace with them 4162
34:28 and no *one will* m them **afraid.** 3006
35: 3 against you and m you a desolate waste. 5989
35: 7 *I will* m Mount Seir a desolate waste 5989
35: 9 *I will* m you desolate forever; 5989
35:11 and *I will* m **myself known** among them 3359
35:14 *I will* m you desolate. 6913
36:11 and *will* m you **prosper** more than before. 3201
36:14 m your nation **childless,** 8897

Eze
36:15 No longer *will I* m you **hear** the taunts of 9048
36:29 I will call for the grain and m it **plentiful** 8049
36:37 *I will* m their people as **numerous** as 8049
37: 5 *I will* m breath **enter** you, 928+995
37: 6 and m flesh **come** upon you and cover you 6590
37:22 *I will* m them one nation in the land, 6913
37:26 *I will* m a covenant of peace with them; 4162
37:28 that the LORD m Israel holy, 7727
38:23 and *I will* m **myself known** in the sight 3359
39: 3 your left hand and m your arrows **drop** 5877
39: 7 "'*I will* m **known** my holy name 3359
39:26 in their land with no *one* to m them **afraid.** 3006
43:11 m **known** *to* them the design of the temple 3359
43:20 so purify the altar and m **atonement** *for* it. 4105
43:26 For seven days *they are to* m **atonement** for 4105
45:15 fellowship offerings to m **atonement** for 4105
45:17 fellowship offerings to m **atonement** for 4105
45:20 so *you are to* m **atonement** *for* the temple. 4105
45:25 *to* m the same **provision** *for* sin offerings, 6913

Da
9:18 We *do not* m requests of you 5877
11: 6 to the king of the North to m an alliance, 6913
11:17 the might of his entire kingdom and *will* m 6913
11:39 He *will* m them **rulers** over many people 5440

Hos
2: 3 and m her as **bare** as on 3657
2: 3 *I will* m her like a desert, 8492
2:12 *I will* m them a thicket, 8492
2:15 will m the Valley of Achor a door of hope. NIH
2:18 that day *I will* m a covenant for them with 4162
8: 4 With their silver and gold *they* m idols 6913
10: 4 *They* **m many promises,** take false 1819+1821
10: 4 take false oaths and m **agreements;** 4162
11: 8 How *can I* m you like Zeboiim? 8492
12: 9 *I will* m you **live** in tents again, 3782
13: 2 *they* m idols for themselves 6913

Joel
2:17 not m your inheritance an object of scorn, 5989
2:19 never again *will I* m you an object 5989

Am
8: 9 "*I will* m the sun **go down** 995
8:10 m all of you **wear** sackcloth 5516+6584+6590
8:10 *I will* m that time like mourning for 8492
9:14 *they will* m gardens and eat their fruit. 6913

Ob
1: 2 *I will* m you small among the nations, 5989
1: 3 the clefts of the rocks and m your home on NIH
1: 4 the eagle and m your nest among the stars, 8492

Jnh
1:11 *m* the sea **calm down** for us?" AIT
2: 9 What I have vowed *I will* m **good.** 8966
4:10 though you did not tend it or m it **grow.** 1540

Mic
1: 6 *I will* m Samaria a heap of rubble, 8492
1:16 m yourselves as **bald** as the vulture, 7947+8143
4: 4 and no *one will* m them **afraid,** 3006
4: 7 *I will* m the lame a remnant, 8492

Na
1: 8 but with an overwhelming flood *he will* m 6913
3: 6 I will treat you with contempt and m you 8492

Hab
1: 3 Why *do you* m me **look** *at* injustice? 8011
2: 2 "Write down the revelation and m it **plain** 930
2: 7 Will they not wake up and m you **tremble?** 2316
3: 2 in our time m them **known;** 3359

Zep
1:18 for *he will* m a sudden end of all who live 6913
3:13 down and no *one will* m them **afraid.**" 3006

Hag
2:23 'and *I will* m you like my signet ring, 8492

Zec
6:11 Take the silver and gold and m a crown, 6913
9:13 Greece, and m you like a warrior's sword. 8492
9:17 Grain will m the young men **thrive,** 5649
10: 3 and m them like a proud horse in battle. 8492
12: 2 *to* m Jerusalem a cup that sends all 8492
12: 3 *I will* m Jerusalem an immovable rock 8492
12: 6 "On that day *I will* m the leaders of Judah 8492

Mal
3:17 when I m up my **treasured possession.** 6913

Mt
2: 8 "Go and m a careful **search** for the child. 2004
3: 3 m straight paths for him.'" 4472
4:19 "and *I will* m you fishers of men." 4472
5:36 you cannot m even one hair white or black. 4472
8: 2 if you are willing, you can m me **clean.**" 2751
12:33 "**M** a tree good and its fruit will be good, 4472
12:33 or m a tree bad and its fruit will be bad, 4472
15:11 What goes into a man's mouth *does not* m him '**unclean,**' 3124
15:18 and these m a man '**unclean.**' 3124
15:20 These are what m a man '**unclean**'; 3124
15:20 unwashed hands *does not* m him '**unclean.**' 3124
23: 5 m their phylacteries **wide** 4425
23:15 *you* m him twice as much a son of hell 4472
26:17 "Where do you want *us to* m **preparations** 2286
27:65 m the tomb as **secure** as you know how." 856
28:19 Therefore go and m **disciples** of all nations, 3411

Mk
1: 3 m straight paths for him.'" 4472
1:17 "and *I will* m you fishers of men." 4472
1:40 "If you are willing, you can m me **clean.**" 2751
7:15 a man can m him '**unclean**' by going 3124
7:18 from the outside can m him '**unclean**'? 3124
7:23 from inside and m a man '**unclean.**'" 3124
9:50 how *can you* m it **salty** again? 789
12:40 and for a show m lengthy **prayers.** 4667
14:12 to go and m **preparations** for you to eat 2286
14:15 **M preparations** for us there." 2286

Lk
1:17 *to* m **ready** a people prepared for the Lord." 2286
3: 4 m straight paths for him. 4472
5:12 if you are willing, you can m me **clean.**" 2751
5:34 "Can you m the guests of the bridegroom 4472
11:40 *Did* not the one who made the outside m the 4472
13:24 "**M every effort** to enter through 76
14:18 "But they all alike began *to* m **excuses.** 4148
14:23 and country lanes and m them come in, 337
15:19 m me like one of your hired men." 4472
16: 6 sit down quickly, and m it four hundred.' 1211
16: 7 'Take your bill and m it eight hundred.' 1211
20:43 until *I* m your enemies a footstool 5502
20:47 and for a show m lengthy **prayers.** 4667

Lk
21:14 But *m* up your **mind** not to worry beforehand 1877+2840+3836+5502
22: 8 "Go and m **preparations** for us to eat 2286
22:12 **M preparations** there." 2286

Jn
1:23 '**M straight** the way for the Lord.'" 2316
5:44 m no **effort to obtain** praise that comes 2426
6:15 that they intended to come and m him king 4472
7:24 and m a right **judgment.**" 3212+3213
11:52 bring them together and m them **one.** 1650+1651
14:23 and we will come to him and m our home 4472
16:15 from what is mine and m it **known** to you. 334
17:26 and *will* continue to m you **known** 1192

Ac
2:35 until *I* m your enemies a footstool 5502
5:28 and are determined *to* m us **guilty of** 2042+2093
7:40 '**M** us gods who will go before us. 4472
15:19 that *we should* not m it difficult for 4214
19:33 *in order to* m a defense before the people. 664+2527
24:10 so *I* gladly m my **defense.** 664
26: 2 as *I* m *my* **defense** against all the accusations 664
27:16 we were hardly able *to* m the lifeboat secure 1181

Ro
1:11 to you some spiritual gift to m you **strong** 5114
9:20 'Why *did you* m me like this?'" 4472
9:21 Does not the potter have the right *to* m out 4472
9:22 to show his wrath and m his power **known,** 1192
9:23 m the riches of his glory **known** 1192
10:19 "*I will* m you **envious** by those who are not 4143
10:19 *I will* m you **angry** by a nation 4239
11:11 to the Gentiles to m Israel **envious.** 4143
11:13 *I* m much of my ministry 1519
14: 4 for the Lord is able to m him **stand.** 2705
14:13 m up *your* **mind** not to put any stumbling 3212
14:19 m **every effort** to do what leads 1503
15:26 to m a contribution for the poor among 4472

1Co
4: 4 but that *does not* m *me* **innocent.** 1467
9:18 so not m **use** of my rights in preaching it. 2974
9:19 *I* m myself **a slave** to everyone, 1530
9:27 I beat my body and m it my **slave** so that 1524
14: 7 in the case of lifeless things *that* m sounds, 1443
16: 7 to see you now and m only a passing visit; NIG

2Co
1:17 Or *do I* m *my* **plans** in a worldly manner so 1086
2: 1 m another painful **visit** 2262
2: 2 who is left to m me **glad** 2370
2: 3 by those who ought *to* m me **rejoice.** 5897
5: 9 So *we* m *it* our **goal** to please him, 5818
7: 2 **M room** for us in your hearts. 6003
9: 8 God is able to m *all* grace **abound** to you, 4355
10: 5 to m it obedient to Christ. NIG

Gal
3: 9 in Christ Jesus and to m us **slaves.** 2871
6:12 *to* m a good **impression** outwardly 2349

Eph
3: 9 *to* m **plain** to everyone the administration 5894
4: 3 **M every effort** to keep the unity of 5079
5:19 Sing and m **music** in your heart to the Lord, 6010
5:26 to m her **holy,** cleansing her by the washing 39
6:19 so that I will fearlessly m **known** the 1192

Php
2: 2 m my joy **complete** by being like-minded, 4444
2:30 to m up for the help you could not give me. 405
3:15 that too God *will* m **clear** to you. 636

Col
1:27 To them God has chosen *to* m **known** 1192
4: 5 toward outsiders; m the most of *every* **opportunity.** 1973+2789+3836

1Th
2: 3 the appeal we m does not spring from error NIG
3:12 the Lord m your love **increase** and overflow 4429
4:11 **M it** *your* **ambition** to lead a quiet life, 5818
4:11 **M sure that** nobody pays back wrong 3972

2Th
3: 9 but in order *to* m ourselves a model for you 1443

2Ti
3:15 which are able *to* m you **wise** for salvation 5054

Tit
2:10 *they will* m the teaching about God our Savior **attractive.** 3175

Heb
1:13 at my right hand until *I* m your enemies 5502
2:10 m the author of their salvation **perfect** 5457
2:17 and that *he might* m **atonement for** the sins 2661
4:11 therefore, m **every effort** to enter that rest, 5079
6:11 in order to m your hope sure. NIG
6:17 m the unchanging nature of his purpose very **clear** 2109
8: 5 "See to it that *you* m everything according 4472
8: 8 the Lord, when *I will* m a new covenant 5334
8:10 the **covenant** *I will* m with the house 1347+1416
10: 1 m **perfect** those who draw near to worship. 5457
10:16 the **covenant** *I will* m with them 1347+1416
12: 5 *do not* m **light** of the Lord's discipline, 3902
12:13 "**M** level paths for your feet," 4472
12:14 **M every effort** to live in peace 1503
13:12 the city gate to m the people **holy** 39

Jas
3: 3 the mouths of horses to m them **obey** us, 4275
4:13 carry on business and m **money.**" 3045
5:15 m the sick person **well;** 5392

1Pe
3: 5 m themselves **beautiful.** 3175
5:10 *will* himself restore you and m you **strong,** 5114

2Pe
1: 5 m **every effort** to add to your faith 4210
1:10 be all the more eager *to* m your **calling** 4472
1:15 And *I will* m **every effort** to see that 5079
3:14 m **every effort** to be found spotless, 5079

1Jn
1: 4 We write this to m our joy **complete.** 1639+4444
1:10 *we* m him **out** to be a liar and 4472
2:10 there is nothing in him to m him stumble. NIG

Rev
2:22 and I will m those who commit adultery NIG
3: 9 *I will* m those who are of the synagogue 1443
3: 9 *I will* m them come and fall down 4472
3:12 Him who overcomes *I will* m a pillar in 4472
6: 4 the earth and to m men slay each other. NIH
12:17 at the woman and went off *to* m war against 4472
13: 4 Who can m war against him?" 4482
13: 7 He was given power to m war against 4472
17:14 They *will* m **war** against the Lamb, 4482
19:19 and their armies gathered together *to* m war 4472

MAKE (Anglicized) See also HAVE

MAKER (26) [MAKE]

Job	4:17	Can a man be more pure than his **M**?	6913
	9: 9	*He is* the **M** of the Bear and Orion,	6913
	32:22	my **M** would soon take me away.	6913
	35:10	But no one says, 'Where is God my **M**,	6913
	36: 3	I will ascribe justice to my **M**.	7188
	40:19	yet his **M** can approach him with his sword.	6913
Ps	95: 6	let us kneel before the LORD our **M**;	6913
	115:15	the LORD, the **M** of heaven and earth.	6913
	121: 2	the LORD, the **M** of heaven and earth.	6913
	124: 8	the LORD, the **M** of heaven and earth,	6913
	134: 3	the LORD, the **M** of heaven and earth,	6913
	146: 6	the **M** of heaven and earth, the sea,	6913
	149: 2	Let Israel rejoice in their **M**;	6913
Pr	14:31	the poor shows contempt for their **M**,	6913
	17: 5	the poor shows contempt for their **M**;	6913
	22: 2	The LORD *is* the **M** of them all.	6913
Ecc	11: 5	the work of God, the **M** of all things.	6913
Isa	17: 7	In that day men will look to their **M**	6913
	27:11	so their **M** has no compassion on them,	6913
	45: 9	"Woe to him who quarrels with his **M**,	3670
	45:11	the Holy One of Israel, and its **M**:	3670
	51:13	that you forget the LORD your **M**,	6913
	54: 5	For your **M** is your husband—	6913
Jer	10:16	for he *is* the **M** of all things,	3670
	51:19	for he *is* the **M** of all things,	3670
Hos	8:14	Israel has forgotten his **M** and built palaces;	6913

MAKERS (1) [MAKE]

Isa	45:16	All the **m** of idols will be put to shame	3093

MAKES (118) [MAKE]

Ex	4:11	Who **m** him deaf or mute?	8492
	4:11	Who gives him sight or **m** him blind?	NIH
	11: 7	the LORD **m** a distinction between Egypt	7111
	30:33	Whoever **m** perfume like it	8379
	30:38	Whoever **m** any like it	6913
	31:13	I am the LORD, *who* **m** you holy.	7727
Lev	7: 7	They belong to the priest who **m** atonement	4105
	17:11	the blood *that* **m** atonement for one's life.	4105
	20: 8	I am the LORD, *who* **m** you holy.	7727
	21:15	I am the LORD, *who* **m** him holy.' "	7727
	21:23	I am the LORD, *who* **m** them holy.' "	7727
	22: 5	that *m* him **unclean**,	AIT
	22: 5	or any person who *m* him **unclean**,	AIT
	22: 9	I am the LORD, *who* **m** them holy.	7727
	22:16	I am the LORD, *who* **m** them holy.' "	7727
	22:32	I am the LORD, *who* **m** you holy	7727
	27: 2	'If anyone **m** a special vow	5624+7098
Nu	30: 2	a man **m** a vow or takes	5623+5624
	30: 3	father's house **m** a vow to the LORD	5623+5624
	30: 6	after she **m** a vow or after her lips utter	NIH
	30:10	a woman living with her husband **m** a vow	5623
	30:13	or nullify any vow she **m**	NIH
1Sa	2: 6	"The LORD brings death and **m** alive;	2649
	22: 8	when my son **m** a covenant with the son	4162
2Sa	22:33	with strength and **m** my way perfect.	5989
	22:34	He **m** my feet like the feet of a deer;	8751
Job	6: 7	I refuse to touch it; such food **m** me ill.	NIH
	9: 6	from its place and **m** its pillars tremble.	7145
	12:17	and **m** fools of judges.	2147
	12:23	He **m** nations great, and destroys them;	8434
	12:25	he **m** them stagger like drunkards.	9494
	35:11	and **m** us wiser than the birds of the air?'	2681
	36:10	He **m** them listen to correction	265+1655
	37:15	and **m** his lightning flash?	3649
	41:31	He **m** the depths churn like a boiling caldron	8409
Ps	7:13	he **m** ready his flaming arrows.	7188
	18:32	with strength and **m** my way perfect.	5989
	18:33	He **m** my feet like the feet of a deer;	8751
	19: 6	of the heavens and its circuit to the other;	NIH
	23: 2	He **m** me lie down in green pastures,	8069
	25:14	he **m** his covenant known *to* them.	3359
	29: 6	He **m** Lebanon skip like a calf,	8376
	37:23	he **m** his steps firm;	3922
	40: 4	the man who **m** the LORD his trust,	8492
	45: 8	the music of the strings **m** you glad.	8523
	46: 9	He **m** wars cease to the ends of the earth;	8697
	48: 8	God **m** her secure forever.	3922
	60: 3	you have given us wine that **m** us stagger.	9570
	104: 3	He **m** the clouds his chariot and rides on	8492
	104: 4	He **m** winds his messengers,	6913
	104:10	He **m** springs pour water into the ravines;	8938
	104:14	He **m** grass grow for the cattle,	7541
	135: 7	He **m** clouds rise from the ends of the earth;	6590
	143: 3	he **m** me dwell in darkness	3782
	147: 8	the earth with rain and **m** grass grow *on*	7541
Pr	1:21	in the gateways of the city she **m** her speech;	606+609
	4:19	they do not know what *m* them **stumble**.	AIT
	11: 5	of the blameless **m** a straight way for them,	3837
	13:11	by little **m** it grow.	8049
	13:12	Hope deferred **m** the heart sick,	2703
	15:13	A happy heart **m** the face cheerful,	3512
	16: 7	**m** even his enemies live at peace	8966
	31:22	She **m** coverings for her bed;	6913
	31:24	She **m** linen garments and sells them;	6913
Ecc	7:19	Wisdom **m** one wise man more powerful	6451
	10:19	and wine **m** life merry,	8523
Isa	8:14	to stumble and a rock that **m** them fall.	4842
	14: 9	*it* **m** them rise from their thrones—	7756

Isa	21: 4	My heart falters, fear **m** me tremble;	1286
	26: 1	God **m** salvation its walls and ramparts.	8883
	27: 9	When he **m** all the altar stones to be	8492
	32: 7	he **m** up evil schemes to destroy the poor	3619
	32: 8	But the noble man **m** noble plans,	3619
	44:13	a line and **m** an outline with a marker;	9306
	44:15	he **m** an idol and bows down to it.	6913
	44:17	*From* the rest he **m** a god, his idol;	6913
	44:25	the signs of false prophets and **m** fools of	2147
	51:17	to its dregs the goblet that **m** men stagger.	9570
	53:10	the LORD **m** his life a guilt offering,	8492
	57:13	the *man who* **m** me *his* refuge will inherit	2879
	61:11	the soil **m** the sprout come up	3655
	62: 7	till he establishes Jerusalem and **m** her	8492
	66: 3	*whoever* **m** a grain offering *is*	6590
Jer	10:13	he **m** clouds rise from the ends of the earth.	6590
	22:14	So he **m** large windows in it,	7973
	48:28	Be like a dove *that* **m** its nest at the mouth	7873
	51:16	he **m** clouds rise from the ends of the earth.	6590
Eze	44:18	not wear anything that **m** them perspire.	928
	46:16	If the prince **m** a gift *from* his inheritance	5989
	46:17	he **m** a gift from his inheritance to one	5989
	47: 9	flows there and **m** the salt water **fresh**;	8324
Hos	12: 1	*He* **m** a treaty with Assyria	4162
Na	1: 4	**m** all the rivers run dry.	2990
Hab	2: 6	up stolen goods and **m** himself wealthy	3877
	2:18	For *he who* **m** it trusts in his own creation;	3670
	2:18	he **m** idols that cannot speak.	6913
	3:19	he **m** my feet like the feet of a deer,	8492
Zec	10: 1	it is the LORD *who* **m** the storm clouds.	6913
Mt	15:11	that is what **m** him 'unclean.' "	3124
	23:17	gold, or the temple that **m** the gold sacred?	39
	23:19	the gift, or the altar that **m** the gift sacred?	39
Mk	7:15	comes out of a man that **m** him 'unclean.' "	3124
	7:20	out of a man is what **m** him 'unclean.'	3124
	7:37	even the deaf hear and the mute speak."	4472
Jn	16:30	This **m** us believe that you came from God."	1877+4047
Ro	8:15	a spirit that **m** you a slave again to fear,	1525
	9:33	to stumble and a rock *that* **m** them fall,	4998
1Co	2:15	The spiritual man **m** judgments about	373
	3: 7	but only God, who **m** things grow.	889
	4: 7	For who **m** you different from anyone else?	1359
2Co	1:21	**m** both us and you stand firm	1011
Gal	2: 6	whatever they were **m** no difference to me;	1422
Eph	5:14	for it is light that **m** everything visible.	5746
Heb	1: 7	"He **m** his angels winds,	4472
	2:11	Both the one who **m** men holy	39
Jas	3: 5	but *it* **m** great boasts.	902
1Pe	2: 8	to stumble and a rock *that* **m** them fall."	4998
Rev	19:11	With justice *he* judges and **m** war.	4482

MAKHELOTH (2)

Nu	33:25	They left Haradah and camped at **M**.	5221
	33:26	They left **M** and camped at Tahath.	5221

MAKI (1)

Nu	13:15	from the tribe of Gad, Geuel son of **M**.	4809

MAKING (70) [MAKE]

Ge	9:12	of the covenant I am **m** between me and you	5989
	34:30	on me by **m** me a stench to the Canaanites	944
Ex	5: 7	the people with straw for **m** bricks;	4236+4246
	28:15	"Fashion a breastpiece for **m** decisions—	5477
	28:30	the means of **m** decisions *for* the Israelites	5477
	29:36	Purify the altar by **m** atonement for it,	4105
	30:16	**m** atonement for your lives."	4105
	34:10	LORD said: "I am **m** a covenant with you.	4162
Lev	16:17	of the community by **m** atonement for them	4105
	16:18	be used for **m** atonement by sending it into	4105
	16:20	When Aaron has finished **m** atonement *for*	4105
	17: 5	the LORD the sacrifices they *are* now **m** in	2284
	19:29	by **m** her a prostitute,	2388
	27: 8	If anyone **m** the vow is too poor to pay	NIH
	27: 8	to what the *man* **m** the *vow* can afford.	5623
Nu	25:12	Therefore tell him I *am* **m** my covenant	5989
	32:14	the LORD even more angry with Israel.	3578
Dt	23:22	But if you refrain from **m** a vow,	5623
	24:11	the man to whom you are **m** the loan bring	5957
	29:12	the LORD *is* **m** with you this day	4162
	29:14	I *am* **m** this covenant, with its oath,	4162
Jdg	16:13	*you have been* **m** a fool of me and lying	9438
1Sa	13:10	Just as he finished **m** the offering,	6590
	21:13	madman, **m** marks on the doors of the gate	9344
1Ki	8:33	and **m** supplication to you in this temple,	2858
	14:15	the LORD to anger *by* **m** Asherah poles.	6913
	15: 4	to succeed him and by **m** Jerusalem strong.	6641
2Ki	10:25	as Jehu had finished **m** the burnt offering,	6913
	12:13	was not spent for **m** silver basins,	4946+6913
1Ch	6:49	**m** atonement for Israel,	4105
2Ch	2: 4	and for **m** burnt offerings every morning	NIH
	6:24	praying and **m** supplication before you	2858
Ezr	5: 8	on with diligence and *is* **m** rapid progress	10613
Ne	6: 8	you *are* just **m** it up out of your head."	968
	8: 8	**m** it clear and giving the meaning so that	7300
	9:38	we *are* **m** a binding agreement,	4162
Ps	19: 7	trustworthy, **m** wise the simple.	2681
Pr	8:21	and their treasuries full.	4848
	14: 9	Fools mock at **m** amends for sin,	871
	16:11	all the weights in the bag are of his **m**.	5126
	24: 2	and their lips talk about **m** trouble.	6662
Ecc	12:12	Of **m** many books there is no end,	6913
Isa	10: 2	**m** widows their prey and robbing	2118
	43:19	I *am* **m** a way in the desert and streams in	8492
	45: 9	'What *are* you **m**?'	6913

Isa	55:10	without watering the earth and **m** it bud	3528
Jer	22:13	**m** his countrymen work for nothing,	6268
	44:19	that *we were* **m** cakes like her image	6913
Eze	22: 3	in her midst and defiles herself by **m** idols,	6913
	37:19	**m** them a single stick of wood,	6913
Da	9:20	and **m** my request to the LORD my God	5877
Jnh	1: 8	who is responsible for **m** all this trouble	NIH
Mt	13:22	of wealth choke it, **m** it unfruitful.	1181
	13:22	but *you are* **m** it a 'den of robbers.' "	4472
Mk	2:21	pull away from the old, **m** the tear worse.	1181
	4:19	in and choke the word, **m** it unfruitful.	1181
Lk	1:22	for he *kept* **m** signs to them	1377+1639
Jn	5:18	**m** himself equal with God.	4472
Ac	16:14	taking from what is mine and **m** it known	334
	16:19	that their hope of **m** money was gone,	2238
	18:14	"If you Jews *were* **m** a complaint about	1639S
	24:13	charges they are now **m** against me	2989
Ro	7:23	of my mind and **m** me a prisoner of the law	170
2Co	5:20	though God *were* **m** his appeal through us.	4151
	6:10	poor, yet **m** many rich;	4457
Eph	2:15	one new man out of the two, thus **m** peace,	4472
	5:16	**m** the most of every opportunity,	1973
Col	1:20	by **m** peace through his blood,	1647
Rev	21: 5	"I am **m** everything new!"	4472

MAKIR (21) [MAKIR'S, MAKIRITE, MAKIRITES]

Ge	50:23	of **M** son of Manasseh were placed at birth	4810
Nu	26:29	through **M**, the Makir clan (Makir was	4810
	26:29	Makirite clan (**M** was the father of Gilead);	4810
	27: 1	the son of **M**, the son of Manasseh,	4810
	32:39	of **M** son of Manasseh went to Gilead,	4810
	36: 1	of the clan of Gilead son of **M**,	4810
Dt	3:15	And I gave Gilead to **M**.	4810
Jos	13:31	the descendants of **M** son of Manasseh—	4810
	13:31	for half of the sons of **M**, clan by clan.	4810
	17: 1	that is, for **M**, Manasseh's firstborn.	4810
	17: 1	**M** was the ancestor of the Gileadites,	NIH
	17: 3	the son of **M**, the son of Manasseh,	4810
Jdg	5:14	From **M** captains came down,	4810
2Sa	9: 4	"He is at the house of **M** son of Ammiel	4810
	9: 5	from the house of **M** son of Ammiel.	4810
	17:27	and **M** son of Ammiel from Lo Debar,	4810
1Ch	2:21	Hezron lay with the daughter of **M**	4810
	2:23	All these were descendants of **M** the father	4810
	7:14	She gave birth to **M** the father of Gilead.	4810
	7:15	**M** took a wife from among the Huppites	4810
	7:17	These were the sons of Gilead son of **M**,	4810

MAKIR'S (1) [MAKIR]

1Ch	7:16	**M** wife Maacah gave birth to a son	4810

MAKIRITE (1) [MAKIR]

Nu	26:29	**M** clan (Makir was the father of Gilead);	4811

MAKIRITES (2) [MAKIR]

Nu	32:40	So Moses gave Gilead to the **M**,	4810
Jos	17: 1	because **the M** were great soldiers.	2085S

MAKKEDAH (9)

Jos	10:10	down all the way to Azekah and **M**.	5218
	10:16	and hidden in the cave at **M**.	5218
	10:17	had been found hiding in the cave at **M**,	5218
	10:21	to Joshua in the camp at **M**,	5218
	10:28	That day Joshua took **M**.	5218
	10:28	And he did to the king of **M** as he had done	5218
	10:29	and all Israel with him moved on from **M**	5218
	12:16	the king of **M** one the king of Bethel one	5218
	15:41	Beth Dagon, Naamah and **M**—	5218

MAKTESH (KJV) See MARKET DISTRICT

MALACHI (1)

Mal	1: 1	word of the LORD to Israel through **M**.	4858

MALCAM (1)

1Ch	8: 9	he had Jobab, Zibia, Mesha, **M**,	4903

MALCHI-SHUA (KJV) See MALKI-SHUA

MALCHIAH (KJV) See MALKIJAH

MALCHIEL, MALCHIELITES (KJV) See MALKIEL, MALKIELITE

MALCHIJAH (KJV) See MALKIJAH

MALCHIRAM (KJV) See MALKIRAM

MALCHUS (1)

Jn	18:10	(The servant's name was **M**.)	3438

MALE (184) [MALES]

Ge	1:27	**m** and female he created them.	2351
	5: 2	He created them **m** and female	2351
	6:19	**m** and female, to keep them alive with you.	2351

Ge	7: 2	a **m** and its mate,	408
	7: 2	a **m** and its mate,	408
	7: 3	and also seven of every kind of bird, **m**	2351
	7: 9	**m** and female, came to Noah and entered	2351
	7:16	were **m** and female of every living thing,	2351
	12:16	**m** and female donkeys,	2789
	17:10	Every **m** among you shall be circumcised.	2351
	17:12	For the generations to come every **m**	2351
	17:14	Any uncircumcised **m,**	2351
	17:23	every **m** in his household,	2351
	17:27	And every **m** in Abraham's household,	408
	20:14	and **m** and female **slaves** and gave them	6269
	30:35	That same day he removed all the **m goats**	9411
	31:10	up and saw that the **m goats** mating with	6966
	31:12	up and see that all the **m goats** mating with	6966
	32:14	female goats and twenty **m goats,**	9411
	32:15	twenty female donkeys and ten **m donkeys.**	6555
	34:24	and every **m** in the city was circumcised.	2351
	34:25	the unsuspecting city, killing every **m.**	2351
Ex	12:48	No **uncircumcised** *m* may eat of it.	AIT
	13: 2	"Consecrate to me every **firstborn** *m.*	AIT
	13:15	the first **m** offspring of every womb	2351
	21:20	"If a man beats his **m** or female **slave** with	6269
	21:32	If the bull gores a **m** or female **slave,**	6269
Lev	1: 3	he is to offer a **m** without defect.	2351
	1:10	he is to offer a **m** without defect.	2351
	3: 1	whether **m** or female,	2351
	3: 6	he is to offer a **m** or female without defect.	2351
	4:23	as his offering a **m goat** without defect.	2351
	6:18	Any **m** descendant of Aaron may eat it.	2351
	6:29	Any **m** in a priest's family may eat it;	2351
	7: 6	Any **m** in a priest's family may eat it,	2351
	9: 3	'Take a **m goat** for a sin offering,	6436+8538
	14:10	the eighth day he must bring two **m lambs**	3897
	14:12	the **m lambs** and offer it as a guilt offering.	3897
	14:21	he must take one **m lamb** as a guilt offering	3897
	16: 5	to take two **m goats** for a sin offering	6436+8538
	22:19	you must present a **m** without defect from	2351
	23:18	Present with this bread seven **m lambs,**	3897
	23:19	sacrifice one **m goat** for a sin offering	6436+8538
	25:44	" 'Your **m** and female **slaves** are to come	6269
	27: 3	of a **m** between the ages of twenty and sixty	2351
	27: 5	set the value of a **m** at twenty shekels and of	2351
	27: 6	the value of a **m** at five shekels of silver and	2351
	27: 7	set the value of a **m** at fifteen shekels and of	2351
Nu	3:12	in place of the **first** *m* **offspring** 1147+7081+8167	
	3:15	Count every **m** a month old or more."	2351
	3:39	including every **m** a month old or more,	2351
	5: 3	Send away **m** and female alike;	2351
	6:12	a year-old **m lamb** as a guilt offering.	3897
	6:14	one **m lamb** without defect for	3897
	7:15	one ram and one **m lamb** a year old,	3897
	7:16	one **m goat** for a sin offering	6436+8538
	7:17	five **m lambs** and five male lambs	6966
	7:17	five male goats and five **m lambs**	3897
	7:21	one ram and one **m lamb** a year old,	3897
	7:22	one **m goat** for a sin offering	6436+8538
	7:23	five **m goats** and five male lambs	6966
	7:23	five male goats and five **m lambs**	3897
	7:27	one ram and one **m lamb** a year old,	3897
	7:28	one **m goat** for a sin offering	6436+8538
	7:29	five **m goats** and five male lambs	6966
	7:29	five male goats and five **m lambs**	3897
	7:33	one ram and one **m lamb** a year old,	3897
	7:34	one **m goat** for a sin offering	6436+8538
	7:35	five **m goats** and five male lambs	6966
	7:35	five male goats and five **m lambs**	3897
	7:39	one ram and one **m lamb** a year old,	3897
	7:40	one **m goat** for a sin offering	6436+8538
	7:41	five **m goats** and five male lambs	6966
	7:41	five male goats and five **m lambs**	3897
	7:45	one ram and one **m lamb** a year old,	3897
	7:46	one **m goat** for a sin offering	6436+8538
	7:47	five **m goats** and five male lambs	6966
	7:47	five male goats and five **m lambs**	3897
	7:51	one ram and one **m lamb** a year old,	3897
	7:52	one **m goat** for a sin offering	6436+8538
	7:53	five **m goats** and five male lambs	6966
	7:53	five male goats and five **m lambs**	3897
	7:57	one ram and one **m lamb** a year old,	3897
	7:58	one **m goat** for a sin offering	6436+8538
	7:59	five **m goats** and five male lambs	6966
	7:59	five male goats and five **m lambs**	3897
	7:63	one ram and one **m lamb** a year old,	3897
	7:64	one **m goat** for a sin offering;	6436+8538
	7:65	five **m goats** and five male lambs	6966
	7:65	five male goats and five **m lambs**	3897
	7:69	one ram and one **m lamb** a year old,	3897
	7:70	one **m goat** for a sin offering;	6436+8538
	7:71	five **m goats** and five male lambs	6966
	7:71	five male goats and five **m lambs**	3897
	7:75	one ram and one **m lamb** a year old,	3897
	7:76	one **m goat** for a sin offering;	6436+8538
	7:77	five **m goats** and five male lambs	6966
	7:77	five male goats and five **m lambs**	3897
	7:81	one ram and one **m lamb** a year old,	3897
	7:82	one **m goat** for a sin offering;	6436+8538
	7:83	five **m goats** and five male lambs	6966
	7:83	five male goats and five **m lambs**	3897
	7:87	twelve rams and twelve **m lambs** a year old,	3897
	7:87	Twelve **m goats** were used for	6436+8538
	7:88	sixty **m goats** and sixty male lambs	6966
	7:88	sixty male goats and sixty **m lambs**	3897
	8:16	the **first** *m* **offspring** from every Israelite	1147
	8:17	Every **firstborn m** in Israel,	1147
	15:24	and a **m goat** for a sin offering.	6436+8538
	18:10	something most place; every **m** shall eat it.	2351

Nu	18:15	and every **firstborn m** *of* unclean animals.	1147
	26:62	All the **m** Levites a month old	2351
	28:11	one ram and seven **m lambs** a year old,	3897
	28:15	one **m goat** is to be presented to	6436+8538
	28:19	one ram and seven **m lambs** a year old,	3897
	28:22	Include one **m goat** as a sin offering	8538
	28:27	one ram and seven **m lambs** a year old as	3897
	28:30	Include one **m goat** to make atonement	6436+8538
	29: 2	one ram and seven **m lambs** a year old,	3897
	29: 5	Include one **m goat** as a sin offering	6436+8538
	29: 8	one ram and seven **m lambs** a year old,	3897
	29:11	Include one **m goat** as a sin offering,	6436+8538
	29:13	two rams and fourteen **m lambs** a year old,	3897
	29:16	Include one **m goat** as a sin offering	6436+8538
	29:17	two rams and fourteen **m lambs** a year old,	3897
	29:19	Include one **m goat** as a sin offering,	6436+8538
	29:20	two rams and fourteen **m lambs** a year old,	3897
	29:22	Include one **m goat** as a sin offering,	8538
	29:23	two rams and fourteen **m lambs** a year old,	3897
	29:25	Include one **m goat** as a sin offering	6436+8538
	29:26	two rams and fourteen **m lambs** a year old,	3897
	29:28	Include one **m goat** as a sin offering,	8538
	29:29	two rams and fourteen **m lambs** a year old,	3897
	29:31	Include one **m goat** as a sin offering,	8538
	29:32	two rams and fourteen **m lambs** a year old,	3897
	29:34	Include one **m goat** as a sin offering,	8538
	29:36	one ram and seven **m lambs** a year old,	3897
	29:38	Include one **m goat** as a sin offering.	8538
Dt	15:19	for the LORD your God every firstborn **m**	2351
	23:18	a female prostitute or the income of a **m** prostitute into	3978
	28:68	to your enemies as **m** and female **slaves,**	6269
Jos	17: 2	the other **m** descendants of Manasseh son	2351
Jdg	21:11	"Kill every **m** and every woman who is not	2351
1Sa	25:22	if by morning I leave alive one **m** 928+7815+8874	
	25:34	not *one* **m** belonging to Nabal 928+7815+8874	
2Sa	21: 6	let seven of his **m** descendants be given	408
1Ki	14:10	I will cut off from Jeroboam **every last m**	
			928+7815+8874
	14:24	There were even *m* **shrine prostitutes** in	AIT
	15:12	He expelled the *m* **shrine prostitutes** from	AIT
	16:11	He did not spare a **single m,** 928+7815+8874	
	21:21	cut off from Ahab **every last m** 928+7815+8874	
	22:46	*m* **shrine prostitutes** who remained there	AIT
2Ki	9: 8	I will cut off from Ahab **every last m**	
			928+7815+8874
	23: 7	the quarters of the *m* **shrine prostitutes,**	AIT
1Ch	29:21	a thousand rams and a thousand **m lambs,**	3897
2Ch	29:21	seven **m lambs** and seven male goats as	3897
	29:21	seven male lambs and seven **m goats**	6436+7618
	29:32	a hundred rams and two hundred **m lambs**	3897
Ezr	6: 9	**m lambs** for burnt offerings to the God	10043
	6:17	four hundred **m lambs** and,	10043
	6:17	for all Israel, twelve **m goats,**	10535+10615
	7:17	rams and **m lambs,**	10043
	8:35	seventy-seven **m lambs** and,	3897
	8:35	as a sin offering, twelve **m goats.**	7618
Est	7: 4	as **m** and female **slaves,**	6269
Job	36:14	among *m* **prostitutes of the shrines.**	AIT
Ecc	2: 7	I bought **m** and female **slaves**	6269
Jer	34: 9	to free his Hebrew **slaves,** both **m**	6269
	34:10	they would free their **m** and female **slaves**	6269
	34:16	the **m** and female **slaves** you had set free	6269
Eze	16:17	and you made for yourself **m** idols	2351
	43:22	a **m goat** without defect for a sin offering,	
			6436+8538
	43:25	to provide a **m goat** daily for a sin offering;	8538
	45:23	and a **m goat** for a sin offering.	6436+8538
	46: 4	on the Sabbath day is to be six **m lambs** and	3897
Mal	1:14	an acceptable **m** in his flock and vows	2351
Mt	19: 4	the Creator 'made them **m** and female,'	781
Mk	10: 6	of creation God 'made them **m** and female.'	781
Lk	2:23	"Every firstborn **m** is to be consecrated to	781
1Co	6: 9	nor adulterers nor **m prostitutes**	3434
Gal	3:28	slave nor free, **m** nor female,	781
Rev	12: 5	She gave birth to a son, a **m** child,	781
	12:13	woman who had given birth to the **m** child.	781

MALEFACTOR, MALEFACTORS (KJV)
See CRIMINAL, CRIMINALS

MALELEEL (KJV) See MAHALALEL

MALES (13) [MALE]

Ge	34:15	like us by circumcising all your **m.**	2351
	34:22	on the condition that our **m** be circumcised,	2351
Ex	12: 5	The animals you choose must be year-old **m**	2351
	12:48	the LORD's Passover must have all the **m**	2351
	13:12	All the firstborn **m** of your livestock belong	2351
	34:19	the firstborn **m** of your livestock,	2350
Nu	3:22	The number of all the **m** a month old	2351
	3:28	for all the **m** a month old or more was 8,600.	2351
	3:34	The number of all the **m** a month old	2351
	3:40	"Count all the firstborn Israelite **m** who are	2351
	3:43	The total number of firstborn **m** a month old	2351
2Ch	31:16	they distributed to the **m** three years old	2351
Jer	2:24	Any *m that* pursue her need	AIT

MALICE (21) [MALICIOUS, MALICIOUSLY]

Nu	35:20	with **m aforethought** shoves another	8534
Dt	4:42	without **m aforethought.** 4946+8533+8997+9453	
	19: 4	without **m aforethought.** 4946+8533+8997+9453	
	19: 6	without **m aforethought.** 4946+8533+8997+9453	
Jos	20: 5	without **m aforethought.** 4946+8533+8997+9453	

Job	6:30	Can my mouth not discern **m?**	2095
Ps	28: 3	with their neighbors but harbor **m**	8288
	41: 5	My enemies say of me in **m,**	8273
	55:10	**m** and abuse are within it.	224
	73: 8	They scoff, and speak with **m;**	8273
Pr	26:26	His **m** may be concealed by deception,	8534
Eze	25: 6	with all the **m** of your heart against the land	8624
	25:15	and took revenge with **m** in their hearts,	8624
	36: 5	against all Edom, for with glee and with **m**	8624
Mk	7:22	**m,** deceit, lewdness, envy, slander,	4504
Ro	1:29	murder, strife, deceit and **m.**	2799
1Co	5: 8	the yeast *of* **m** and wickedness,	2798
Eph	4:31	along with every form of **m.**	2798
Col	3: 8	anger, rage, **m,** slander,	2798
Tit	3: 3	We lived in **m** and envy,	2798
1Pe	2: 1	rid yourselves of all **m** and all deceit,	2798

MALICIOUS (9) [MALICE]

Ex	23: 1	help a wicked man by being a **m** witness.	2805
Dt	19:16	a **m** witness takes the stand to accuse a man	2805
Pr	17: 4	a liar pays attention to a **m** tongue.	2095
	26:24	A **m** *man* disguises himself with his lips,	8533
Isa	58: 9	with the pointing finger and **m** talk,	224
Eze	28:24	people of Israel have **m** neighbors who are painful briers	8764
	36: 3	**object of** people's **m** talk 4383+6584+6590+8557	
1Ti	3:11	not **m** talkers but temperate	1333
	6: 4	that result in envy, strife, **m** talk,	1060

MALICIOUSLY (5) [MALICE]

Ps	35:16	Like the ungodly *they* **m** mocked;	4352+4352
	35:19	without reason **m** wink the eye.	7975
Pr	10:10	*He who* **winks m** causes grief,	6524+7975
1Pe	3:16	so that those who **speak m against**	2092
3Jn	1:10	gossiping **m** about us.	3364+4505

MALIGN (2) [MALIGNED]

Ps	12: 5	from *those who* **m** them."	7032
Tit	2: 5	so that no one *will* **m** the word of God.	1059

MALIGNED (2) [MALIGN]

Eze	28:26	on all their neighbors who **m** them.	8764
Ac	19: 9	they refused to believe and publicly **m**	2800

MALIGNITY (KJV) See MALICE

MALKI-SHUA (5)

1Sa	14:49	Saul's sons were Jonathan, Ishvi and **M.**	4902
	31: 2	killed his sons Jonathan, Abinadab and **M.**	4902
1Ch	8:33	and Saul the father of Jonathan, **M,**	4902
	9:39	and Saul the father of Jonathan, **M,**	4902
	10: 2	killed his sons Jonathan, Abinadab and **M.**	4902

MALKIEL (3) [MALKIELITE]

Ge	46:17	The sons of Beriah: Heber and **M.**	4896
Nu	26:45	through **M,** the Malkielite clan.	4896
1Ch	7:31	The sons of Beriah: Heber and **M,**	4896

MALKIELITE (1) [MALKIEL]

Nu	26:45	through Malkiel, the **M** clan.	4897

MALKIJAH (16)

1Ch	6:40	the son of Baaseiah, the son of **M,**	4898
	9:12	the son of Pashhur, the son of **M;**	4898
	24: 9	the fifth to **M,** the sixth to Mijamin,	4898
Ezr	10:25	Ramiah, Izziah, **M,** Mijamin, Eleazar,	4898
	10:25	Mijamin, Eleazar, **M** and Benaiah.	4898
	10:31	Eliezer, Ishijah, **M,** Shemaiah, Shimeon,	4898
Ne	3:11	**M** son of Harim and Hasshub son	4898
	3:14	The Dung Gate was repaired by **M** son	4898
	3:31	Next to him, **M,** one of the goldsmiths,	4898
	8: 4	and on his left were Pedaiah, Mishael, **M,**	4898
	10: 3	Pashhur, Amariah, **M,**	4898
	11:12	the son of Pashhur, the son of **M,**	4898
	12:42	Shemaiah, Eleazar, Uzzi, Jehohanan, **M,**	4898
Jer	21: 1	of **M** and the priest Zephaniah son	4898
	38: 1	of **M** heard what Jeremiah was telling all	4898
	38: 6	and put him into the cistern of **M,**	4899

MALKIRAM (1)

1Ch	3:18	**M,** Pedaiah, Shenazzar,	4901

MALLOTHI (2)

1Ch	25: 4	Joshbekashah, **M,** Hothir and Mahazioth.	4871
	25:26	the nineteenth to **M,**	4871

MALLOWS (KJV) See SALT HERB

MALLUCH (6) [MALLUCH'S]

1Ch	6:44	the son of Abdi, the son of **M,**	4866
Ezr	10:29	Meshullam, **M,** Adaiah, Jashub,	4866
	10:32	Benjamin, **M** and Shemariah.	4866
Ne	10: 4	Hattush, Shebaniah, **M,**	4866
	10:27	**M,** Harim and Baanah.	4866
	12: 2	Amariah, **M,** Hattush,	4866

MALLUCH'S (1) [MALLUCH]

Ne	12:14	of **M,** Jonathan; of Shecaniah's, Joseph;	4868

MALTA (1)
Ac 28: 1 we found out that the island was called **M.** 3514

MAMMON (KJV) See MONEY, WEALTH

MAMRE (10)
Ge 13:18 to live near the great trees of **M** at Hebron, 4934
14:13 near the great trees of **M** the Amorite, 4935
14:24 to Aner, Eshcol and **M.** 4935
18: 1 the great trees of **M** while he was sitting at 4934
23:17 So Ephron's field in Machpelah near **M**— 4934
23:19 in the field of Machpelah near **M** 4934
25: 9 in the cave of Machpelah near **M,** 4934
35:27 Jacob came home to his father Isaac in **M,** 4934
49:30 the field of Machpelah, near **M** in Canaan, 4934
50:13 the cave in the field of Machpelah, near **M,** 4934

MAN (2079) [COUNTRYMAN, COUNTRYMEN, FELLOWMAN, HORSEMAN, HORSEMEN, MAN'S, MAN-MADE, MANHOOD, MANKIND, MANNED, MEN, MEN'S, SPOKESMAN, SPOKESMEN, WOODSMAN, WOODSMEN, WORKMAN, WORKMAN'S, WORKMEN]

Ge 1:26 God said, "Let us make **m** in our image, 132
1:27 So God created **m** in his own image, 132
2: 5 on the earth and there was no **m** to work 132
2: 7 the LORD God formed the **m** from the dust 132
2: 7 and the **m** became a living being. 132
2: 8 and there he put the **m** he had formed. 132
2:15 The LORD God took the **m** and put him in 132
2:16 And the LORD God commanded the **m,** 132
2:18 "It is not good for the **m** to be alone. 132
2:19 to the **m** to see what he would name them; 132
2:19 whatever the **m** called each living creature, 132
2:20 So the **m** gave names to all the livestock, 132
2:21 So the LORD God caused the **m** to fall into 132
2:22 from the rib he had taken out of the **m,** 132
2:22 and he brought her to the **m.** 132
2:23 The **m** said, "This is now bone of my bones 132
2:23 for she was taken out of **m."** 408
2:24 a **m** will leave his father and mother and 408
2:25 The **m** and his wife were both naked, 132
3: 8 Then the **m** and his wife heard the sound of 132
3: 9 But the LORD God called to the **m,** 132
3:12 The **m** said, "The woman you put here 132
3:22 "The **m** has now become like one of us, 132
3:24 After he drove the **m** out, 132
4: 1 of the LORD I have brought forth a **m."** 408
4:23 I have killed a **m** for wounding me, 408
4:23 a young **m** for injuring me. 3529
5: 1 When God created **m,** he made him in 132
5: 2 they were created, he called them "**m.**" 132
6: 3 "My Spirit will not contend with **m** forever, 132
6: 6 that he had made **m** on the earth, 132
6: 9 Noah was a righteous **m,** 408
8:21 will I curse the ground because of **m,** 132
9: 5 And from each **m,** too, 132
9: 5 an accounting for the life of his *fellow* **m.** 132
9: 6 "Whoever sheds the blood of **m,** 132
9: 6 by **m** shall his blood be shed; 132
9: 6 for in the image of God has God made **m.** 132
9:20 Noah, a **m** *of* the soil, 408
15: 4 "This **m** will not be your heir, AIT
16:12 He will be a wild donkey of a **m;** 132
17:17 **m** a hundred years **old?** AIT
19: 8 I have two daughters who have never slept
       with a **m.** 408
19:31 and there is no **m** around here to lie with us, 408
24:16 no **m** had ever lain with her. 408
24:21 the **m** watched her closely to learn whether 408
24:22 the **m** took out a gold nose ring weighing 408
24:26 **m** bowed down and worshiped the LORD, 408
24:29 and he hurried out to the **m** at the spring. 408
24:30 and had heard Rebekah tell what the **m** said 408
24:30 the **m** and found him standing by the camels 408
24:58 So the **m** went to the house, 408
24:58 "Will you go with this **m?"** 408
24:61 and went back with the **m.** 408
24:65 that **m** in the field coming to meet us?" 408
25: 8 an old **m** and full of years; AIT
25:27 a **m** *of* the open country, 408
25:27 while Jacob was a quiet **m,** 408
26:11 "Anyone who molests this **m** 408
26:13 The **m** became rich, 408
27: 2 "*I* am now an old **m** and don't know the day AIT
27:11 "But my brother Esau is a hairy **m,** 408
27:11 and I'm a **m** with smooth skin. 408
29:19 that I give her to you than to some other **m.** 408
30:43 the **m** grew exceedingly prosperous 408
32:24 and a **m** wrestled with him till daybreak. 408
32:25 the **m** saw that he could not overpower him, NIH
32:25 as he wrestled with the **m.** 2257S
32:26 the **m** said, "Let me go, for it is daybreak." NIH
32:27 The **m** asked him, "What is your name?" NIH
32:28 the **m** said, "Your name will no longer be NIH
34:14 we can't give our sister to a **m** who is 408
34:19 The young **m,** who was the most honored 5853
37: 2 Joseph, a **young m** of seventeen. 5853
37:15 a **m** found him wandering around in 408
37:17 they moved on from here," the **m** answered. 408

Ge 38: 1 to stay with a **m** of Adullam named Hirah. 408
38: 2 the daughter of a Canaanite **m** named Shua. 408
38:25 "I am pregnant by the **m** who owns these," 408
41:12 giving *each* **m** the interpretation 408
41:13 and **the other** **m** was hanged." 2257S
41:33 for a discerning and wise **m** and put him 408
41:38 "Can we find anyone like this **m,** 408
42:11 We are all the sons of one **m.** 408
42:13 twelve brothers, the sons of one **m,** 408
42:30 "The **m** who is lord over 408
42:33 the **m** who is lord over the land said to us, 408
43: 3 "The **m** warned us solemnly, 408
43: 5 because the **m** said to us, 408
43: 6 by telling the **m** you had another brother?" 408
43: 7 "The **m** questioned us closely 408
43:11 in your bags and take them down to the **m** 408
43:13 Take your brother also and go back to the **m** 408
43:14 the **m** so that he will let your other brother 408
43:17 The **m** did as Joseph told him and took 408
44:15 that a **m** like me can find things out 408
44:17 Only the **m** who was found to have 408
Ex 2: 1 Now a **m** of the house of Levi married 408
2:14 *The* **m** said, "Who made you ruler and judge AIT
2:21 Moses agreed to stay with the **m,** 408
4:11 "Who gave **m** his mouth? 132
9:19 the hail will fall on every **m** and animal 132
10: 7 "How long will this **m** be a snare to us? AIT
11: 7 the Israelites not a dog will bark at any **m** 408
12: 3 that on the tenth day of this month *each* **m** 408
13: 2 belongs to me, whether **m** or animal. 132
13:15 firstborn in Egypt, both **m** and animal. 132
19:13 Whether **m** or animal, 132
21: 4 and only the **m** shall go free. 2085S
21: 7 "If a **m** sells his daughter as a servant, 408
21:12 "Anyone who strikes a **m** and kills him shall 408
21:14 But if a **m** schemes and kills another man 408
21:14 and kills **another** **m** deliberately, AIT
21:20 "If a **m** beats his male or female slave with 408
21:26 "If a **m** hits a manservant or maidservant in 408
21:28 "If a bull gores a **m** or a woman to death, 408
21:29 but has not kept it penned up and it kills a **m** 408
21:33 "If a **m** uncovers a pit or digs one and fails 408
22: 1 a **m** steals an ox or a sheep and slaughters it 408
22: 5 "If a **m** grazes his livestock in a field 408
22: 7 "If a **m** gives his neighbor silver or goods 408
22:10 "If a **m** gives a donkey, an ox, 408
22:14 a **m** borrows an animal from his neighbor 408
22:16 "If a **m** seduces a virgin who is not pledged 408
23: 1 a **wicked** **m** by being a malicious witness. AIT
23: 3 and do not show favoritism to a **poor** *m* AIT
25: 2 from each **m** whose heart prompts him 408
32:27 '**Each** *m* strap a sword to his side. AIT
33:11 as a **m** speaks with his friend. 408
36: 6 "No **m** or woman is to make anything else 408
Lev 13: 6 The **m** must wash his clothes, NIH
13:29 "If a **m** or woman has a sore on the head or 408
13:38 a **m** or woman has white spots on the skin, 408
13:40 "When a **m** has lost his hair and is bald, 408
13:44 the **m** is diseased and is unclean. 408
15: 2 'When **any** **m** has a bodily discharge, 408+408
15: 4 "'**Any** bed the *m with a* **discharge** lies AIT
15: 6 on anything that the *m with a* **discharge** sat AIT
15: 7 touches the *m who has a* **discharge** AIT
15: 8 "'If the *m with the* **discharge** spits AIT
15: 9 'Everything the **m** sits on when riding will 2307S
15:11 "Anyone the *m with a* **discharge** touches AIT
15:12 "'A clay pot that the **m** touches must 2307S
15:13 'When a **m** is cleansed from his discharge, 2307S
15:15 before the LORD because 2257S
15:16 "'When a **m** has an emission of semen, 408
15:18 When a **m** lies with a woman and there is 408
15:24 "'If a **m** lies with her 408
15:32 the regulations for a *m with a* **discharge,** AIT
15:33 for a **m** or woman with a discharge, 2351
15:33 and for a **m** who lies with 408
16:21 into the desert in the care of a **m** appointed 408
16:22 and the **m** shall release it in the desert. NIH
16:26 "'The *m who* **releases** the goat as AIT
16:28 *m who* **burns** them must wash his clothes AIT
17: 4 that **m** shall be considered guilty 408
17: 9 that **m** must be cut off from his people. 408
18: 5 for the **m** who obeys them will live by them. 132
18:22 not lie with a **m** as one lies with a woman; 2351
19:13 the wages of a **hired** **m** overnight. 8502
19:20 "'If a **m** sleeps with a woman who is 408
19:20 a slave girl promised to another **m** 408
19:21 The **m,** however, must bring a ram to 2257S
20: 3 against that **m** and I will cut him off 408
20: 4 that **m** gives one of his children to Molech 408
20: 5 that **m** and his family and will cut off 408
20:10 "'If a **m** commits adultery 408
20:11 "'If a **m** sleeps with his father's wife, 408
20:11 Both the **m** and the **woman** must be 2157S
20:12 "'If a **m** sleeps with his daughter-in-law, 408
20:13 **m** lies with a man as one lies with a woman, 408
20:13 man lies with a **m** as one lies with a woman, 2351
20:14 a **m** marries both a woman and her mother, 408
20:15 a **m** has sexual relations with an animal, 408
20:17 "'If a **m** marries his sister, 408
20:18 "'If a **m** lies with a woman 408
20:20 "'If a **m** sleeps with his aunt, 408
20:21 "'If a **m** marries his brother's wife, 408
20:27 "'A **m** or woman who is a medium 408
21: 9 No **m** who has any defect may come near: 408
21:18 no **m** who is blind or lame, 408
21:19 no **m** with a crippled foot or hand, 408

Lev 24:21 but whoever kills a **m** must be put to death. 132
25:26 a **m** has no one to redeem it for him 408
25:27 the balance to the **m** to whom he sold it; 408
25:29 "'If a **m** sells a house in a walled city, 408
25:50 the rate paid to a **hired** **m** for that number 8502
25:53 to be treated as a **m** **hired** *from* year to year; 8502
27: 8 to what the *m* **making** *the* vow can afford. AIT
27:14 a **m** dedicates his house as something holy 408
27:15 If the *m who* **dedicates** his house redeems it, AIT
27:16 "'If a **m** dedicates to the LORD part 408
27:19 If the *m who* **dedicates** the field wishes AIT
27:22 "'If a **m** **dedicates** to the LORD AIT
27:23 and the **m** must pay its value on that day NIH
27:28 "'But nothing that a **m** owns and devotes to 408
27:28 whether **m** or animal or family land— 132
27:31 If a **m** redeems any of his tithe, 408
Nu 1: 2 listing every **m** by name, one by one. 2351
1: 4 One **m** from each tribe, 408
1:52 *each* **m** in his own camp 408
2: 2 *each* **m** under his standard with the banners 408
3:13 whether **m** or animal. 132
4:19 the sanctuary and assign to each **m** his work 408
4:32 Assign **to each** **m** the specific things he 928+9005
5: 6 a **m** or woman wrongs another in any way 408
5:13 by sleeping with another **m,** 408
5:19 "If no other **m** has slept with you 408
5:20 with a **m** other than your husband"— 408
5:30 or when feelings of jealousy come over a **m** 408
6: 2 a **m** or woman wants to make a special vow, 408
8:17 whether **m** or animal, is mine. 132
9:13 if a **m** who is ceremonially clean and not on 408
9:13 That **m** will bear the consequences 408
11:27 A **young** **m** ran and told Moses, 5853
12: 3 (Now Moses was a very humble **m,** 408
15:32 a **m** was found gathering wood on 408
15:35 the LORD said to Moses, "The **m** must die. 408
16: 5 The **m** he chooses he will cause to come 2257S
16: 7 The **m** the LORD chooses will be 408
16:17 *Each* **m** is to take his censer and put incense 408
16:18 So *each* **m** took his censer, 408
16:22 the entire assembly when only one **m** sins?" 408
17: 2 Write the name of *each* **m** on his staff. 408
17: 5 to the **m** I choose will sprout, 408
17: 9 and *each* **m** took his own staff. 408
18:15 both **m** and animal, 132
19: 8 The *m who* **burns** it must AIT
19: 9 "A **m** who is clean shall gather up the ashes 408
19:10 The *m who* **gathers up** the ashes of AIT
19:18 Then a **m** who is ceremonially clean is 408
19:19 The **m** who is **clean** is to sprinkle AIT
19:21 "The *m who* **sprinkles** the water AIT
23:19 God is not a **m,** that he should lie, 408
23:19 that he should lie, nor a son of **m,** 132
25: 6 Then an Israelite **m** brought to his family 408
27: 8 'If a **m** dies and leaves no son, 408
27:16 appoint a **m** over this community 408
27:18 a **m** in whom is the spirit, 408
30: 2 a **m** makes a vow to the LORD or takes 408
30:16 concerning relationships between a **m** 408
31: 7 and killed every **m.** 2351
31:17 kill every woman who has slept with a **m,** 2351
31:18 every girl who has never slept with a **m,** 2351
31:35 women who had never slept with a **m.** 5883
32:27 your servants, every *m* **armed** *for* battle, AIT
32:29 every *m* **armed** for battle, AIT
35:16 If *a m* **strikes** someone with an iron object AIT
Dt 1:17 Do not be afraid of any **m,** 408
1:23 one **m** from each tribe. 408
1:35 "Not a **m** of this evil generation shall see 408
4:16 whether formed like a **m** or a woman, 2351
4:32 from the day God created **m** on the earth; 132
5:24 Today we have seen that a **m** can live even 132
5:26 For what **mortal** **m** has ever heard 1414
8: 3 that **m** does not live on bread alone but 132
8: 5 in your heart that as a **m** disciplines his son, 408
11:25 No **m** will be able to stand against you. 408
15: 7 If there is a **poor** *m* among your brothers AIT
15:12 If a fellow **Hebrew,** a *m* or a woman, AIT
16:16 No **m** should appear before NIH
17: 2 If a **m** or woman living among you in one of 408
17: 5 take the **m** or woman who has done this 408
17: 6 or three witnesses a **m** shall be put to death, 4637S
17:12 The **m** who shows contempt for the judge or 408
19: 3 that anyone *who* **kills a m** may flee there. 8357
19: 4 the rule concerning the *m who* **kills another** AIT
19: 5 a **m** may go into the forest with his neighbor 889S
19: 5 **That m** may flee to one of these cities 2085S
19:11 if a **m** hates his neighbor and lies in wait 408
19:15 to convict a **m** accused of any crime 408
19:16 the stand to accuse a **m** of a crime, 408
20: 8 "Is **any** *m* afraid or fainthearted? 408+2021+4769
21: 1 If a *m* **is found** slain, AIT
21: 8 of the blood of an **innocent** *m.*" AIT
21:15 If a **m** has two wives, 408
21:18 If a **m** has a stubborn and rebellious son 408
21:22 If a **m** guilty of a capital offense is put 408
22: 5 nor a **m** wear women's clothing, 1505
22:13 If a **m** takes a wife and, after lying with her, 408
22:18 "I gave my daughter in marriage to this **m,** 408
22:18 the elders shall take the **m** and punish him. 408
22:19 because this **m** has given an Israelite virgin NIH
22:22 If a **m** is found sleeping with another man's 408
22:22 both the **m** who slept with her and 408
22:23 If a **m** happens to meet in a town 408
22:24 and did not scream for help, and the **m** 408
22:25 if out in the country a **m** happens to meet 408
22:25 only the **m** who has done this shall die. 408

Dt
22:27 for the m found the girl out in the country, NIH
22:28 If a m happens to meet a virgin who is 408
22:30 A m is not to marry his father's wife; 408
23:17 No Israelite m or woman is to become 1201
24: 1 If a m marries a woman who becomes 408
24: 2 the wife of another m, 408
24: 5 If a m has recently married, 408
24: 7 If a m is caught kidnapping one 408
24:11 and let the m to whom you are making 408
24:12 If the m is poor, 408
24:14 not take advantage of a hired m who is poor AIT
25: 2 If the guilty m deserves to be beaten, AIT
25: 7 m does not want to marry his brother's wife, 408
25: 9 "This is what is done to the m who will 408
27:15 "Cursed is the m who carves an image 408
27:16 "Cursed is the m who dishonors his father NIH
27:17 "Cursed is the m who moves his neighbor's boundary stone." NIH
27:18 "Cursed is the m who leads the blind astray NIH
27:19 "Cursed is the m who withholds justice from the alien, NIH
27:20 "Cursed is the m who sleeps with his father's wife, NIH
27:21 "Cursed is the m who has sexual relations NIH
27:22 "Cursed is the m who sleeps with his sister, NIH
27:23 "Cursed is the m who sleeps with his mother-in-law." NIH
27:24 "Cursed is the m who kills his neighbor secretly." NIH
27:25 "Cursed is the m who accepts a bribe to kill NIH
27:26 "Cursed is the m who does not uphold NIH
28:29 about like a blind m in the dark. AIT
28:54 Even the most gentle and sensitive m 408
29:18 Make sure there is no m or woman, 408
29:20 his wrath and zeal will burn against that m. 408
32:30 How could one m chase a thousand, AIT
33: 1 the m of God pronounced on the Israelites 408
33: 8 and Urim belong to the m you favored. 408

Jos
5:13 he looked up and saw a m standing in front 408
6: 5 the people will go up, every m straight in." 408
6:20 so every m charged straight in, 6639
6:26 before the LORD is the m who undertakes 408
7:14 that the LORD takes shall come forward m NIH
7:14 LORD takes shall come forward man by m. 1505
7:18 Joshua had his family come forward m NIH
7:18 by m, and Achan son of Carmi, the son 1505
8:17 Not a m remained in Ai or Bethel who did 408
10:14 a day when the LORD listened to a m. 408
10:20 completely—almost to a m— 4392+6330+9462
14: 6 the m of God at Kadesh Barnea about you 408
14:15 the greatest m among the Anakites.) 132
15:16 Acsah in marriage to the m who attacks 2257S

Jdg
1:12 Acsah in marriage to the m who attacks 2257S
1:24 a coming out of the city and they said 408
1:25 but spared the m and his whole family. 408
3:15 Ehud, a left-handed m, the son of Gera 408
3:17 Eglon king of Moab, who was a very fat m. 408
3:29 not a m escaped. 408
4:16 not a m was left. 285S
4:22 "I will show you the m you're looking for." 408
5:30 a girl or two for each m, 1505
7:13 Gideon arrived just as a m was telling 408
7:21 each m held his position around the camp, 408
8:14 a young m of Succoth and questioned him, 408
8:14 the young m wrote down for him the names NIH
8:21 'As is the m, so is his strength.' " 408
8:25 each m threw a ring from his plunder onto 408
9: 2 sons rule over you, or just one m?' 408
10: 1 the time of Abimelech a m of Issachar, 408
13: 2 A certain m of Zorah, named Manoah, 408
13: 6 "A m of God came to me. 408
13: 8 let the m of God you sent to us come again 408
13:10 The m who appeared to me the other day!" 408
13:11 When he came to the m, he said, 408
16: 7 I'll become as weak as any other m." 132
16:11 I'll become as weak as any other m." 132
16:13 I'll become as weak as any other m." 132
16:17 I would become as weak as any other m." 132
16:19 a m to shave off the seven braids of his hair, 408
17: 1 a m named Micah from the hill country 408
17: 5 Now this m Micah had a shrine, 408
17:11 young m was to him like one of his sons. 5853
17:12 the young m became his priest and lived 5853
19: 7 And when the m got up to go, 408
19: 9 Then when the m, with his concubine 408
19:10 the m left and went toward Jebus (that is, 408
19:16 That evening an old m from the hill country 408
19:17 the old m asked, "Where are you going? 408
19:19 your maidservant, and the young m with us. 5853
19:20 welcome at my house," the old m said. 408
19:22 they shouted to the m who owned 408
19:22 "Bring out the m who came to your house 408
19:23 Since this m is my guest, 408
19:24 But to this m, don't do such a disgraceful 408
19:25 So the m took his concubine 408
19:28 the m put her on his donkey and set out 408
20: 1 of Gilead came out as one m and assembled 408
20: 8 All the people rose as one m, saying, 408
20:11 of Israel got together and united as one m 408
21:12 with a m, and they took them to the camp 408
21:23 each m caught one and carried her off to 4392S

Ru
1: 1 and a m from Bethlehem in Judah, 408
2: 1 a m of standing, whose name was Boaz. 408
2:19 Blessed be the m who took notice of you!" AIT
2:19 of the m I worked with today is Boaz," 408
2:20 She added, "That m is our close relative; 408
3: 8 of the night something startled the m, 408
3:18 For the m will not rest until the matter 408

1Sa
1: 1 There was a certain m from Ramathaim, 408
1: 3 after year this m went up from his town 408
1:21 the m Elkanah went up with all his family 408
2:15 and say to the m who was sacrificing, "Give 408
2:16 If the m said to him, 408
2:25 If a m sins against another man, 408
2:25 If a man sins against another m, 408
2:25 but if a m sins against the LORD, 408
2:27 a m of God came to Eli and said to him, 408
2:31 not be an old m in your family line AIT
2:32 there will never be an old m. AIT
4:10 and every m fled to his tent. 408
4:13 When the m entered the town 408
4:14 The m hurried over to Eli, 408
4:17 m who brought the news AIT
4:18 for he was an old m and heavy. 408
9: 1 There was a Benjamite, a m of standing, 1475
9: 2 an impressive young m without equal 1033
9: 6 "Look, in this town there is a m of God; 408
9: 7 "If we go, what can we give the m? 408
9: 7 We have no gift to take to the m of God. 408
9: 8 I will give it to the m of God so 408
9: 9 if a m went to inquire of God, he would say, 408
9:10 So they set out for the town where the m 408
9:16 a m from the land of Benjamin. 408
9:17 "This is the m I spoke to you about; 408
10:12 A m who lived there answered, 408
10:22 "Has the m come here yet?" 408
10:24 "Do you see the m the LORD has chosen? 889S
11: 7 and they turned out as one m. 408
13:14 the LORD has sought out a m 408
14: 1 to the young m bearing his armor, 5853
14:24 "Cursed be any m who eats food 408
14:28 'Cursed be any m who eats food today!' 408
14:52 whenever Saul saw a mighty or brave m, 408
15:29 for he is not a m, that he should change his mind. 132
16: 7 LORD does not look at the things m looks at. 132
16: 7 M looks at the outward appearance, 132
16:18 He is a brave m and a warrior. 1475+2657
16:18 He speaks well and is a fine-looking m. 408
17: 8 Choose a m and have him come down 408
17:10 Give me a m and let us fight each other." 408
17:24 When the Israelites saw the m, 408
17:25 "Do you see how this m keeps coming out? 408
17:25 give great wealth to the m who kills him. 408
17:26 be done for the m who kills this Philistine 408
17:27 be done for the m who kills him." 408
17:33 he has been a fighting m from his youth." 408
17:55 "Abner, whose son is that young m?" 5853
17:56 "Find out whose son this young m is." 6624
17:58 "Whose son are you, young m?" 5853
18:23 I'm only a poor m and little known." 408
19: 5 would you do wrong to an innocent m 1947+5929
21:14 Achish said to his servants, "Look at the m! 408
21:15 Must this m come into my house?" AIT
22:23 the m who is seeking your life is seeking mine also. AIT
24:19 When a m finds his enemy, 408
25: 2 A certain m in Maon, 408
25:17 He is such a wicked m that no one can talk 1201
25:25 to that wicked m Nabal. 408
26:15 David said, "You're a m, aren't you? 408
26:23 The LORD rewards every m 408
27: 3 Each m had his family with him, 408
27: 9 he did not leave a m or woman alive, 408
27:11 not leave a m or woman alive to be brought 408
28:14 "An old m wearing a robe is coming up," 408
29: 4 "Send the m back, 408
30:22 each m may take his wife and children 408
30:24 of the m who stayed with the supplies AIT

2Sa
1: 2 the third day a m arrived from Saul's camp, 408
1: 5 to the young m who brought him the report, 5853
1: 6 the young m said, "and there was Saul, 5853
1:13 David said to the young m who brought 5853
2:16 Then each m grabbed his opponent by 408
2:23 And every m stopped when he came to AIT
3:38 and a great m has fallen in Israel this day? AIT
4:10 when a m told me, 'Saul is dead,' AIT
4:11 an innocent m in his own house and 408
7:19 Is this your usual way of dealing with m, 132
11: 3 The m said, "Isn't this Bathsheba, AIT
12: 2 The rich m had a very large number AIT
12: 3 poor m had nothing except one little ewe AIT
12: 4 "Now a traveler came to the rich m, 408
12: 4 but the rich m refrained from taking one NIH
12: 4 that belonged to the poor m and prepared it 408
12: 5 with anger against the m and said to Nathan, 408
12: 5 the m who did this deserves to die! 408
12: 7 Then Nathan said to David, "You are the m! 408
13: 3 Jonadab was a very shrewd m. 408
13:34 Now the m standing watch looked up 5853
14:16 the hand of the m who is trying to cut off 408
14:21 Go, bring back the young m Absalom." 5853
14:25 In all Israel there was not a m so highly 408
16: 5 a m from the same clan 408
16: 7 get out, you m of blood, you scoundrel! 408
16: 8 You have come to ruin because you are a m 408
17: 3 the m you seek will mean the return of all; 408
17:18 But a young m saw them and told Absalom. 5853
17:18 and went to the house of a m in Bahurim. 408
17:25 Amasa was the son of a m named Jether, 408
18: 5 with the young m Absalom for my sake." 5853
18:11 Joab said to the m who had told him this, 408
18:12 But the m replied, 408
18:12 Protect the young m Absalom for my sake. 5853
18:24 As he looked out, he saw a m running alone. 408
18:25 And the m came closer and closer. NIH
18:26 Then the watchman saw another m running, 408
18:26 "Look, another m running alone!" 408
18:27 "He's a good m," the king said. 408
18:29 "Is the young m Absalom safe?" 5853
18:32 "Is the young m Absalom safe?" 5853
18:32 up to harm you be like that young m." 5853
19: 7 not a m will be left with you by nightfall. 408
19:14 of Judah as though they were one m. 408
19:32 Now Barzillai was a very old m. AIT
19:32 for he was a very wealthy m. 408
20: 1 Every m to his tent, O Israel!" 408
20:12 and the m saw that all the troops came to 408
20:21 A m named Sheba son of Bicri, 408
20:21 Hand over this one m, 2257S
21: 5 "As for the m who destroyed us and plotted 408
21:20 a huge m with six fingers on each hand 408
23: 1 of Jesse, the oracle of the m exalted by 1505
23: 1 the m anointed by the God of Jacob, NIH

1Ki
1:42 A worthy m like you must 408
1:52 "If he shows himself to be a worthy m, 1201
2: 2 "So be strong, show yourself a m, 408
2: 4 you will never fail to have a m on the throne 408
2: 9 You are a m of wisdom; 408
4:25 each m under his own vine and fig tree. 408
4:31 He was wiser than any other m, 132
7:14 a m of Tyre and a craftsman in bronze. 408
8:25 a m to sit before me on the throne of Israel, 408
8:31 a m wrongs his neighbor and is required 408
8:39 deal with each m according to all he does, 408
9: 5 'You shall never fail to have a m on 408
11:28 Now Jeroboam was a m of standing, 408
11:28 how well the young m did his work, 5853
12:22 of God came to Shemaiah the m of God: NIH
13: 1 of the LORD a m of God came from Judah 408
13: 3 That same day the m of God gave a sign: NIH
13: 4 When King Jeroboam heard what the m 408
13: 4 stretched out toward the m shriveled up, 2257S
13: 5 according to the sign given by the m of God 408
13: 6 Then the king said to the m of God, 408
13: 6 the m of God interceded with the LORD. 408
13: 7 The king said to the m of God, 408
13: 8 But the m of God answered the king, 408
13:11 whose sons came and told him all that the m 408
13:12 And his sons showed him which road the m 408
13:14 and rode after the m of God. 408
13:14 the m of God who came from Judah?" 408
13:16 The m of God said, "I cannot turn back NIH
13:19 So the m of God returned with him and ate NIH
13:21 He cried out to the m of God who had come 408
13:23 When the m of God had finished eating NIH
13:26 "It is the m of God who defied the word of 408
13:29 So the prophet picked up the body of the m 408
13:31 in the grave where the m of God is buried; 408
16: 9 the m in charge of the palace at Tirzah. 889S
17:18 "What do you have against me, m of God? 408
17:24 a m of God and that the word of the LORD 408
20: 7 "See how this m is looking for trouble! AIT
20:28 The m of God came up and told the king 408
20:35 but the m refused. 408
20:36 And after the m went away, NIH
20:37 The prophet found another m and said, 408
20:37 So the m struck him and wounded him. 408
20:39 with a captive and said, 'Guard this m. 408
20:40 and there, the m disappeared." 2085S
20:42 a m I had determined should die. 408
21:19 not murdered a m and seized his property?' NIH
21:25 (There was never a m like Ahab, NIH
22: 8 "There is still one m through whom we can 408
22:13 "Look, as one m the other prophets are 7023
22:36 "Every m to his tent; everyone to his land!" 408

2Ki
1: 6 "A m came to meet us," they replied. 408
1: 7 of m was it who came to meet you 408
1: 8 "He was a m with a garment of hair and 408
1: 9 "M of God, the king says, 'Come down!' " 408
1:10 "If I am a m of God, 408
1:11 The captain said to him, "M of God, 408
1:12 "If I am a m of God," Elijah replied, 408
1:13 "M of God," he begged, 408
3:21 so every m, young and old, AIT
3:25 and each m threw a stone 408
4: 1 The wife of a m from the company of NIH
4: 7 She went and told the m of God, 408
4: 9 that this m who often comes our way is 2085S
4: 9 a holy m of God. 408
4:16 "Don't mislead your servant, O m of God!" 408
4:21 up and laid him on the bed of the m of God, 408
4:22 to the m of God quickly and return." 408
4:25 So she set out and came to the m of God 408
4:25 of God said to his servant Gehazi, 408
4:27 she reached the m of God at the mountain, 408
4:27 of God said, "Leave her alone! 408
4:40 "O m of God, there is death in the pot!" 408
4:42 A m came from Baal Shalishah, 408
4:42 bringing the m of God twenty loaves 408
5: 1 He was a great m in the sight of his master 408
5: 8 When Elisha the m of God heard that 408
5: 8 Have the m come to me and he will know NIH
5:14 as the m of God had told him, 408
5:15 and all his attendants went back to the m 408
5:20 the servant of Elisha the m of God, 408
5:26 not my spirit with you when the m got down 408
6: 6 The m of God asked, "Where did it fall?" 408
6: 7 the m reached out his hand and took it. NIH
6: 9 The m of God sent word to the king 408
6:10 on the place indicated by the m of God. 408

Ref	Text	No.
2Ki 6:15	of the m *of* God got up and went out early	408
6:19	to the m you are looking for."	408
7: 2	the king was leaning said to the m *of* God,	408
7: 5	not a m was there,	408
7:10	the Aramean camp and not a m was there—	408
7:17	just as the m *of* God had foretold when	408
7:18	It happened as the m *of* God had said to	408
7:19	The officer had said to the m *of* God,	408
7:19	The m *of* God had replied,	NIH
8: 2	The woman proceeded to do as the m	408
8: 4	the servant of the m *of* God, and had said,	408
8: 7	"The m *of* God has come all the way	408
8: 8	"Take a gift with you and go to meet the m	408
8:11	Then the m *of* God began to weep.	408
9: 1	The prophet Elisha summoned a m from	285S
9: 4	So the young m, the prophet,	5853
9:11	the m and the sort of things he says,"	408
11: 8	*each* m with his weapon in his hand.	408
13:19	The m *of* God was angry with him and said,	408
13:21	a m, suddenly they saw a band of raiders.	408
13:21	the m came to life and stood up on his feet.	408
14:12	and *every* m fled to his home.	408
15:20	Every wealthy m had to contribute	1475
22:15	Tell the m who sent you to me,	408
23:16	by the m *of* God who foretold these things.	408
23:17	of the m *of* God who came from Judah	408
1Ch 12: 4	a **mighty** m among the Thirty,	1475
16: 3	of raisins to each Israelite m and woman.	408
16:21	He allowed no m to oppress them;	408
20: 6	a huge man with six fingers on each hand	408
22: 9	a son who will be a m *of* peace and rest,	408
23:14	the m *of* God were counted as part of	408
27: 6	This was the Benaiah who was a **mighty m**	1475
27:32	a m of insight and a scribe.	408
28:21	and every **willing** m skilled	AIT
29: 1	because this palatial structure is not for m	132
2Ch 2: 7	a m skilled to work in gold and silver,	408
2:13	Huram-Abi, a m of great skill,	408
6:16	a m to sit before me on the throne of Israel,	408
6:22	a m wrongs his neighbor and is required	408
6:30	deal with each m according to all he does,	408
7:18	'You shall never fail to have a m to rule	408
8:14	because this was what David the m *of* God	408
11: 2	of the LORD came to Shemaiah the m	408
14:11	do not let m prevail against you."	632
15:13	whether small or great, m or woman.	408
18: 7	"There is still one m through whom we can	408
18:12	"Look, as one m the other prophets are	7023
19: 6	because you are not judging for m but for	132
23: 7	each m with his weapons in his hand.	408
25: 7	But a m of God came to him and said,	408
25: 9	Amaziah asked the m *of* God,	408
25: 9	The m *of* God replied,	408
25:22	and *every* m fled to his home.	408
30:16	as prescribed in the Law of Moses the m	408
34:23	Tell the m who sent you to me,	408
36:17	spared neither **young** m nor young woman,	1033
36:17	**old** m or aged.	AIT
Ezr 2:61	Hakkoz and Barzillai (a m who had married	NIH
3: 1	the people assembled as one m	408
3: 2	in the Law of Moses the m *of* God.	408
5:14	to a m named Sheshbazzar,	10192S
7:11	a m **learned** *in* matters concerning	6221
8:18	they brought us Sherebiah, a capable m,	408
Ne 1:11	in the presence of this m."	408
4:18	m who **sounded** the trumpet stayed with me.	AIT
4:22	"Have *every* m and his helper stay	408
5:13	and possessions every m who does	408
5:13	a m be shaken out and emptied!"	AIT
6:11	But I said, "Should a m like me run away?	408
7: 2	because he was a m of integrity	408
7:63	Hakkoz and Barzillai (a m who had married	NIH
8: 1	the people assembled as one m in the square	408
9:29	by which a m will live if he obeys them.	132
12:24	as prescribed by David the m *of* God.	408
12:36	David the m *of* God.	408
Est 1: 8	to serve *each* m what he wished.	408+408+2256
1:22	in each people's tongue that every m should	408
4:11	of the royal provinces know that for any m	408
6: 6	for the m the king delights to honor?"	408
6: 7	"For the m the king delights to honor,	408
6: 9	Let them robe the m the king delights	408
6: 9	for the m the king delights to honor!' "	408
6:11	for the m the king delights to honor!"	408
7: 5	Where is **the** m who has dared to do such	2085S
Job 1: 1	Of Uz there lived a m whose name was Job.	408
1: 1	This m was blameless and upright;	408
1: 3	He was the greatest m among all the people	408
1: 8	a m who fears God and shuns evil."	408
1:12	but on **the** m himself do not lay a finger."	2257S
2: 3	the m who fears God and shuns evil.	408
2: 4	"A m will give all he has for his own life.	408
3:23	to a m whose way is hidden,	1505
4:17	Can a m be more pure than his Maker?	1505
5: 7	Yet m is born to trouble as surely	132
5:17	"Blessed is the m whom God corrects;	632
6:14	"A **despairing** m should have the devotion	4988
6:26	treat the words of a **despairing** m as wind?	AIT
7: 1	"Does not m have hard service on earth?	632
7: 1	Are not his days like those of a **hired** m?	8502
7: 2	or a **hired** m waiting eagerly for his wages,	8502
7:17	"What is m that you make so much of him,	632
8:20	"Surely God does not reject a **blameless** m	AIT
9:32	not a m like me that I might answer him,	408
10: 5	of a mortal or your years like those of a m,	1505
11:12	a witless m can no more become wise than	408
11:12	a wild donkey's colt can be born a m.	132
Job 12:14	the m he imprisons cannot be released.	408
13:16	no **godless** m would dare come before him!	AIT
13:28	"So m wastes away like something rotten,	2085S
14: 1	"M born of woman is of few days and full	132
14: 6	till he has put in his time like a **hired** m.	8502
14:10	But m dies and is laid low;	1505
14:12	so m lies down and does not rise;	408
14:14	If a m dies, will he live again?	1505
15: 2	Would a **wise** m answer with empty notions	AIT
15: 7	"Are you the first m ever born?	132
15:14	"What is m, that he could be pure,	632
15:16	how much less m, who is vile and corrupt,	408
15:20	All his days the **wicked** m suffers torment,	AIT
16:21	of a m he pleads with God as a man pleads	1505
16:21	with God as a m pleads for his friend.	132+1201
17: 5	If *a* m **denounces** his friends for reward,	AIT
17: 6	a m in whose face people spit.	NIH
17:10	I will not find a **wise** m among you.	AIT
18:21	Surely such is the dwelling of an **evil** m;	6405
20: 4	ever since m was placed on the earth,	132
21: 4	"Is my complaint directed to m?	132
21:19	Let him repay **the** m himself,	2257S
21:23	One m dies in full vigor,	2296S
21:25	*Another* m dies in bitterness of soul,	2296S
21:30	**evil** m is spared from the day of calamity,	AIT
22: 2	"Can a m be of benefit to God?	1505
22: 2	Can even a **wise** m benefit him?	AIT
22: 8	you were a powerful m, owning land,	408
22: 8	an **honored** m, living on it.	AIT
23: 7	There an **upright** m could present his case	AIT
25: 4	How then can a m be righteous before God?	632
25: 6	how much less m, who is but a maggot—	632
25: 6	a son of m, who is only a worm!"	132
27:13	a **ruthless** m receives from the Almighty:	AIT
28: 3	*M* puts an end to the darkness;	AIT
28: 4	in places forgotten by the foot of m;	NIH
28:13	M does not comprehend its worth;	632
28:28	And he said to m, 'The fear of the Lord—	132
29:13	The *m who was* **dying** blessed me;	AIT
30:24	no one lays a hand on a **broken** m when	6505
31:19	or a **needy** m without a garment,	AIT
32: 8	But it is the spirit in a m,	632
32:13	let God refute him, not m.'	408
32:21	nor will I flatter *any* m;	132
33:12	for God is greater than m.	632
33:14	though m may not **perceive** it,	AIT
33:17	to turn m from wrongdoing and keep him	132
33:19	Or a m may be chastened on a bed of pain	NIH
33:23	to tell a m what is right for him,	132
33:29	"God does all these things to a m—	1505
34: 7	What m is like Job,	1505
34: 9	a m nothing when he tries to please God.'	1505
34:11	He repays a m for what he has done;	132
34:15	and m would return to the dust.	132
34:29	Yet he is over m and nation alike,	132
34:30	to keep a godless m from ruling,	132
34:31	"Suppose a m **says** to God,	AIT
34:36	the utmost for answering like a wicked m!	408
35: 8	Your wickedness affects only a m	408
37: 7	he stops every m from his labor.	132
37:20	Would any m ask to be swallowed up?	408
38: 3	Brace yourself like a m;	1505
38:26	to water a land where no m lives,	408
40: 7	"Brace yourself like a m;	1505
40:11	look at every **proud** m and bring him low,	AIT
40:12	look at every **proud** m and humble him,	AIT
Ps 1: 1	Blessed is the m who does not walk in	408
8: 4	what is m that you are mindful of him,	632
8: 4	the son of m that you care for him?	132
9:19	Arise, O LORD, let not m triumph;	632
10: 2	In his arrogance the **wicked** m hunts down	AIT
10:13	Why does the **wicked** m revile God?	AIT
10:15	Break the arm of the wicked and **evil** m;	AIT
10:18	in order that m, who is of the earth,	632
15: 4	a **vile** m but honors those who fear	AIT
22: 6	But I am a worm and not a m,	408
25:12	Who, then, is the m that fears the LORD?	408
32: 2	Blessed is the m whose sin the LORD does	132
32:10	love surrounds the *m who* **trusts** in him.	AIT
34: 6	This **poor** m called, and the LORD heard	AIT
34: 8	blessed is the m who takes refuge in him.	1505
34:19	A **righteous** m may have many troubles,	AIT
36: 6	O LORD, you preserve both m and beast.	132
37:30	mouth of the **righteous** m utters wisdom,	AIT
37:35	and **ruthless** m flourishing like a green tree	AIT
37:37	there is a future for the m of peace.	408
38:13	I am like a **deaf** m, who cannot hear,	AIT
38:14	I have become like a m who does not hear,	408
39: 6	M is a mere phantom as he goes to and fro:	408
39:11	each m is but a breath.	132
40: 4	the m who makes the LORD his trust,	1505
49: 7	No m can redeem the life of another or give	408
49:12	But m, despite his riches, does not endure;	132
49:16	Do not be overawed when a m grows rich,	408
49:20	A m who has riches without understanding	132
52: 1	Why do you boast of evil, you **mighty m**?	1475
52: 7	the m who did not make God his stronghold	1505
55:13	But it is you, a m like myself,	632
56: 4	What can mortal m do to me?	1414
56:11	What can m do to me?	132
60:11	for the help of m is worthless.	132
62: 3	How long will you assault a m?	408
64: 4	from ambush at the **innocent** m;	AIT
64: 6	Surely the mind and heart of m are cunning.	408
73: 5	from the burdens common to m;	632
75: 6	or the west or from the desert can exalt a m.	NIH
78:65	as a m wakes from the stupor of wine.	1475
Ps 80:17	your hand rest on the m *at* your right hand,	408
80:17	the son of m you have raised up for yourself.	132
84:12	blessed is the m who trusts in you.	132
88: 4	I am like a m without strength.	1505
89:19	I have exalted a **young** m from among	1033
89:22	no wicked m will oppress him.	1201
89:48	What m can live and not see death,	1505
90: T	A prayer of Moses the m of God.	408
92: 6	The senseless m does not know,	408
94:10	Does he who teaches m lack knowledge?	132
94:11	The LORD knows the thoughts of m;	1505
94:12	Blessed is the m you discipline, O LORD,	1505
94:12	O LORD, **the** m you teach from your law;	5647S
102: T	A prayer of an **afflicted** m.	AIT
103:15	As for m, his days are like grass,	632
104:14	and plants for m to cultivate—	132
104:15	wine that gladdens the heart of m,	632
104:23	Then m goes out to his work,	132
105:17	and he sent a m before them—	408
108:12	for the help of m is worthless.	132
109: 4	but I am a m of prayer.	NIH
109: 6	Appoint an **evil** m to oppose him;	AIT
112: 1	Blessed is the m who fears the LORD,	408
112: 4	and compassionate and **righteous** m.	AIT
112: 6	a **righteous** m will be remembered forever.	AIT
112:10	The **wicked** m will see and be vexed,	AIT
115:16	but the earth he has given to m.	132+1201
118: 6	What can m do to me?	132
118: 8	in the LORD than to trust in m.	132
119: 9	How can a **young** m keep his way pure?	5853
120: 7	I am a m of peace;	NIH
127: 5	Blessed is the m whose quiver is full	1505
128: 4	the m blessed who fears the LORD.	1505
141: 5	Let a **righteous** m strike me—	AIT
144: 3	O LORD, what is m that you care for him,	132
144: 3	the son of m that you think of him?	632
144: 4	**M** is like a breath;	132
144: 4	nor his delight in the legs of a m;	408
Pr 3: 4	and a good name in the sight of God and m.	132
3:13	Blessed is the m who finds wisdom,	132
3:13	the m who gains understanding,	132
3:30	Do not accuse a m for no reason—	132
3:31	Do not envy a **violent** m or choose any	408
3:32	the LORD detests a **perverse** m but takes	AIT
5:22	The evil deeds of a **wicked** m ensnare him;	AIT
6:11	like a bandit and scarcity like an armed m.	408
6:19	*a m who* **stirs up** dissension among brothers.	AIT
6:27	Can a m scoop fire into his lap	408
6:28	Can a m walk on hot coals	408
6:32	*m who* **commits adultery** lacks judgment;	AIT
8:34	Blessed is the m who listens to me,	132
9: 7	whoever rebukes a **wicked** m incurs abuse.	AIT
9: 8	rebuke a **wise** m and he will love you.	AIT
9: 9	Instruct a **wise** m and he will be wiser still;	AIT
9: 9	teach a **righteous** m and he will add	AIT
10: 4	Lazy hands make *a* m **poor**,	AIT
10: 9	The m of integrity walks securely,	2143S
10:23	a m of understanding delights in wisdom.	408
11: 7	When a **wicked** m dies, his hope perishes;	132
11: 8	The **righteous** m is rescued from trouble,	AIT
11:12	m who lacks judgment derides his neighbor,	NIH
11:12	but a m of understanding holds his tongue.	408
11:13	but a **trustworthy** m keeps a secret.	AIT
11:17	A **kind** m benefits himself,	408
11:17	but a **cruel** m brings trouble on himself.	AIT
11:18	The **wicked** m earns deceptive wages,	AIT
11:19	The truly **righteous** m attains life,	AIT
11:24	*One* m **gives freely**, yet gains even more;	AIT
11:25	A generous m will prosper;	5883
11:26	People curse the *m who* **hoards** grain,	AIT
12: 2	A **good** m obtains favor from the LORD,	AIT
12: 2	but the LORD condemns a crafty m.	408
12: 3	A m cannot be established through wickedness,	132
12: 8	A m is praised according to his wisdom,	408
12:10	A **righteous** m cares for the needs	AIT
12:13	An **evil** m is trapped by his sinful talk,	AIT
12:13	but a **righteous** m escapes trouble.	AIT
12:14	of his lips a m is filled with good things as	408
12:15	but a **wise** m listens to advice.	AIT
12:16	but a **prudent** m overlooks an insult.	AIT
12:23	prudent m keeps his knowledge to himself,	132
12:25	An anxious heart weighs a m down,	408
12:26	A **righteous** m is cautious in friendship,	AIT
12:27	The **lazy** m does not roast his game,	AIT
12:27	but the diligent m prizes his possessions.	132
13: 2	the fruit of his lips a m enjoys good things,	408
13: 6	Righteousness guards the m of integrity,	2006+9448
13: 7	m pretends to be rich, yet has nothing;	AIT
13: 8	a **poor** m hears no threat.	AIT
13:14	turning a m from the snares of death.	NIH
13:16	Every **prudent** m acts out of knowledge,	AIT
13:22	A **good** m leaves an inheritance for his	AIT
14: 7	Stay away from a foolish m,	408
14:12	There is a way that seems right to a m,	408
14:14	and the good m rewarded for his.	408
14:15	A **simple** m believes anything,	AIT
14:15	but a **prudent** m gives thought to his steps.	AIT
14:16	A **wise** m fears the LORD and shuns evil,	AIT
14:17	A **quick-tempered** m does foolish things,	AIT
14:17	and a crafty m is hated.	AIT
14:27	turning a m from the snares of death.	NIH
14:29	A **patient** m has great understanding,	AIT
14:29	but a **quick-tempered** m displays folly.	AIT
15:18	A hot-tempered m stirs up dissension,	408
15:18	but a **patient** m calms a quarrel.	AIT

Ref		Text	Num
Pr	15:20	but a foolish **m** despises his mother.	132
	15:21	Folly delights a *m who* **lacks** judgment,	AIT
	15:21	**m** *of* understanding keeps a straight course.	408
	15:23	A **m** finds joy in giving an apt reply—	408
	15:27	A **greedy** *m* brings trouble to his family,	AIT
	15:33	The fear of the LORD teaches a **m** wisdom,	NIH
	16: 1	To **m** belong the plans of the heart,	132
	16: 6	through the fear of the LORD *a* **m** **avoids** evil.	AIT
	16: 9	In his heart a **m** plans his course,	132
	16:13	they value a *m who* **speaks** the truth.	AIT
	16:14	but a wise **m** will appease it.	408
	16:25	There is a way that seems right to a **m**,	408
	16:28	A perverse **m** stirs up dissension,	408
	16:29	A violent **m** entices his neighbor	408
	16:32	Better a **patient** *m* than a warrior,	AIT
	16:32	a *m who* **controls** his temper than	AIT
	17: 4	A **wicked** *m* listens to evil lips;	AIT
	17:10	A rebuke impresses a *m of* **discernment**	AIT
	17:11	An **evil** *m* is bent only on rebellion;	AIT
	17:13	If a *m* **pays back** evil for good,	AIT
	17:18	A **m** lacking in judgment strikes hands	132
	17:20	A *m of* **perverse** heart does not prosper;	AIT
	17:23	A **wicked** *m* accepts a bribe in secret	AIT
	17:24	A **discerning** *m* keeps wisdom in view,	AIT
	17:26	It is not good to punish an **innocent** *m*,	AIT
	17:27	A **m of knowledge** uses words with	
		restraint,	1981+3359
	17:27	and a **m** *of* understanding is even-tempered.	408
	18: 1	An **unfriendly** *m* pursues selfish ends;	AIT
	18:23	A **poor** *m* pleads for mercy,	AIT
	18:23	but a **rich** *m* answers harshly.	AIT
	18:24	**m** *of* many companions may come to ruin,	408
	19: 1	a **poor** *m* whose walk is blameless than	AIT
	19: 6	the friend of a *m who* **gives** gifts.	408
	19: 7	A **poor** *m* is shunned by all his relatives—	AIT
	19:15	and the shiftless **m** goes hungry.	5883
	19:19	A **hot-tempered** *m* must pay the penalty;	AIT
	19:22	What a **m** desires is unfailing love;	132
	19:25	rebuke a **discerning** *m*,	AIT
	20: 5	but a **m** *of* understanding draws them out.	408
	20: 6	Many a **m** claims to have unfailing love,	132
	20: 6	but a faithful **m** who can find?	408
	20: 7	The **righteous** *m* leads a blameless life;	AIT
	20:17	Food gained by fraud tastes sweet to a **m**,	408
	20:19	*m who* **talks too much.**	AIT
	20:20	If a **m** **curses** his father or mother,	AIT
	20:25	a trap for a **m** to dedicate something rashly	132
	20:27	lamp of the LORD searches the spirit of a **m**;	132
	21:10	The wicked **m** craves evil;	5883
	21:11	when a **wise** *m* is instructed,	AIT
	21:13	If a *m* **shuts** his ears to the cry of the poor,	AIT
	21:16	A **m** who strays from the path	132
	21:20	but a foolish **m** devours all he has.	132
	21:22	A **wise** *m* attacks the city of the mighty	AIT
	21:24	The proud and **arrogant** *m*—	AIT
	21:29	A wicked **m** puts on a bold front,	408
	21:29	but an **upright** *m* gives thought to his ways.	AIT
	22: 3	A **prudent** *m* sees danger and takes refuge,	AIT
	22: 9	**generous** **m** will himself be blessed,	3202+6524
	22:24	not make friends with a hot-tempered **m**,	1251
	22:26	*m who* **strikes** hands **in pledge**	AIT
	22:29	Do you see a **m** skilled in his work?	408
	23: 6	Do not eat the food of a **stingy m**,	6524+8273
	23: 7	*m who* is always **thinking** about the cost.	AIT
	23:24	The father of a **righteous** *m* has great joy;	AIT
	24: 5	A wise **m** has great power,	1505
	24: 5	and a **m** *of* knowledge increases strength;	408
	24:16	for though a **righteous** *m* falls seven times,	AIT
	24:20	for the **evil** *m* has no future hope,	AIT
	24:29	I'll pay that back for what he did."	408
	24:30	the vineyard of the *m who* **lacks** judgment;	132
	24:34	like a bandit and scarcity like an armed **m**.	408
	25:14	a **m** who boasts of gifts he does not give.	408
	25:18	the **m** who gives false testimony	408
	25:26	a **righteous** *m* who gives way to the wicked.	AIT
	25:28	down is a **m** who lacks self-control.	408
	26:12	Do you see a **m** wise in his own eyes?	408
	26:19	is a **m** who deceives his neighbor and says,	408
	26:21	so is a quarrelsome **m** for kindling strife.	408
	26:24	**malicious** **m** disguises himself with his lips,	AIT
	26:27	If a *m* **digs** a pit, he will fall into it;	AIT
	26:27	if a *m* **rolls** a stone, it will roll back on him.	AIT
	27: 8	that strays from its nest is a **m** who strays	408
	27:14	If a **m** loudly **blesses** his neighbor early in	AIT
	27:17	sharpens iron, so *one* **m** sharpens another.	408
	27:17	so a man's heart **reflects** the **m**.	132+2021+4200
	27:20	and neither are the eyes of **m**.	132
	27:21	but **m** is tested by the praise he receives.	408
	28: 1	The **wicked** *m* flees though no one pursues,	AIT
	28: 2	but a **m** of understanding and knowledge	132
	28: 6	a **poor** *m* whose walk is blameless than	AIT
	28: 6	a **rich** *m* whose ways are perverse.	AIT
	28:11	A rich **m** may be wise in his own eyes,	408
	28:11	but a **poor** *m* who has discernment sees	AIT
	28:14	the **m** who always fears the LORD,	132
	28:15	or a charging bear is a **wicked** *m* ruling over	AIT
	28:17	A **m** tormented by the guilt of murder will	132
	28:20	A faithful **m** will be richly blessed,	408
	28:21	yet a **m** will do wrong for a piece of bread.	1505
	28:22	A stingy **m** is eager to get rich	408
	28:23	He who rebukes a **m** will in the end gain	132
	28:25	A **greedy** *m* stirs up dissension,	5883+8146
	29: 1	A **m** who remains stiff-necked after many	408
	29: 3	A **m** who loves wisdom brings joy	408
	29: 6	An evil **m** is snared by his own sin,	408
	29: 9	If a wise **m** goes to court with a fool,	408
	29:10	Bloodthirsty men hate a *m of* **integrity**	AIT

Ref		Text	Num
Pr	29:11	but a **wise** *m* keeps himself under control.	AIT
	29:13	The **poor** *m* and the oppressor have this	AIT
	29:20	Do you see a **m** who speaks in haste?	408
	29:21	If a *m* **pampers** his servant from youth,	AIT
	29:22	An angry **m** stirs up dissension,	408
	29:23	but a *m of* **lowly** spirit gains honor.	AIT
	29:25	Fear of **m** will prove to be a snare,	132
	29:26	but it is from the LORD that **m** gets justice.	408
	30: 1	This **m** declared to Ithiel,	1505
	30:19	and the way of a **m** with a maiden.	1505
Ecc	1: 3	What does **m** gain from all his labor	132
	2: 8	the delights of the heart of **m**.	132+1201
	2:14	The **wise** *m* has eyes in his head,	AIT
	2:16	For the **wise** *m*, like the fool,	AIT
	2:16	Like the fool, the **wise** *m* too must die!	AIT
	2:19	who knows whether he will be a **wise** *m*	AIT
	2:21	For a **m** may do his work with wisdom,	132
	2:22	a **m** get for all the toil and anxious striving	132
	2:24	A **m** can do nothing better than to eat	132
	2:26	To the **m** who pleases him,	132
	3:19	**m** has no advantage over the animal.	132
	3:21	knows if the spirit of **m** rises upward	132+1201
	3:22	that there is nothing better for a **m** than	132
	4: 8	There was a **m** all alone;	285ˢ
	4:10	But pity the **m** who falls and has no one	285ˢ
	5:12	abundance of a **rich** *m* permits him no sleep.	AIT
	5:15	Naked a **m** **comes** from his mother's womb,	AIT
	5:16	This too is a grievous evil: As a **m** **comes**,	AIT
	5:18	a **m** to eat and drink, and to find satisfaction	NIH
	5:19	God gives any **m** wealth and possessions,	132
	6: 2	God gives a **m** wealth,	408
	6: 3	A **m** may have a hundred children	408
	6: 5	it has more rest than does **that** *m*—	AIT
	6: 8	What advantage has a **wise** *m* over a fool?	AIT
	6: 8	What does a **poor** *m* gain by knowing how	AIT
	6:10	and what **m** is has been known;	132
	6:10	no **m** can contend with one who is stronger	NIH
	6:12	For who knows what is good for a **m** in life,	132
	7: 2	for death is the destiny of every **m**;	132
	7: 7	Extortion turns a **wise** *m* into a fool,	AIT
	7:14	a **m** cannot discover anything	132
	7:15	a **righteous** *m* perishing in his righteousness,	AIT
	7:15	a **wicked** *m* living long in his wickedness.	AIT
	7:18	The *m who* **fears** God will avoid all	AIT
	7:19	Wisdom makes one **wise** *m* more powerful	
		than ten rulers	AIT
	7:20	There is not a righteous **m**	132
	7:26	The *m who* **pleases** God will escape her,	AIT
	7:28	I found one [upright] **m** among a thousand,	132
	8: 1	Who is like the **wise** *m*?	AIT
	8: 7	Since no **m** knows the future,	5647ˢ
	8: 8	No **m** has power over the wind to contain it;	132
	8: 9	a **m** lords it over others to his own hurt.	132
	8:12	a **wicked** *m* commits a hundred crimes	AIT
	8:15	a **m** under the sun than to eat and drink and	132
	8:17	**m** cannot discover its meaning.	132
	8:17	Even if a **wise** *m* claims he knows,	AIT
	9: 1	but no **m** knows whether love or hate awaits	132
	9: 2	As it is with the **good** *m*, so with the sinner;	AIT
	9:12	no **m** knows when his hour will come:	132
	9:15	there lived in that city a **m** poor but wise,	408
	9:15	But nobody remembered that poor **m**.	408
	10:18	If a **m** is lazy, the rafters sag;	NIH
	11: 8	However many years a **m** may live,	132
	11: 9	Be happy, **young m**, while you are young,	1033
	12: 5	Then **m** goes to his eternal home	132
	12:13	for this is the whole [duty] of **m**.	132
Isa	1:31	The **mighty** *m* will become tinder	AIT
	2: 9	So **m** will be brought low	132
	2:11	The eyes of the arrogant **m** will be humbled	132
	2:17	The arrogance of **m** will be brought low and	132
	2:22	Stop trusting in **m**,	132
	3: 3	the captain of fifty and **m** of rank,	5951+7156
	3: 5	**m** against man, neighbor against neighbor.	408
	3: 5	man against **m**, neighbor against neighbor.	408
	3: 6	A **m** will seize one of his brothers	408
	4: 1	seven women will take hold of one **m**	408
	5:15	So **m** will be brought low	132
	6: 5	For I am a **m** *of* unclean lips,	408
	7:21	a **m** will keep alive a young cow	132
	10:18	as when a **sick** *m* wastes away.	AIT
	13:12	I will make **m** scarcer than pure gold,	632
	14:16	"Is this the **m** who shook the earth	408
	14:17	the *m who* **made** the world a desert,	AIT
	16: 5	in faithfulness *a m will* **sit** on it—	AIT
	17: 5	a *m* **gleans** heads of grain in the Valley	AIT
	21: 9	here comes a **m** in a chariot *with* a team	408
	22:17	O you **mighty m**.	1505
	29: 8	when a **hungry** *m* dreams that he is eating,	AIT
	29: 8	when a **thirsty** *m* dreams that he is drinking,	AIT
	29:21	those who with a word make a **m** out to	132
	31: 8	by a sword that is not *of* **m**;	408
	32: 2	*Each* **m** will be like a shelter from the wind	408
	32: 8	But the **noble** *m* makes noble plans,	AIT
	33:16	the *m who will* **dwell** on the heights,	AIT
	40:20	A **m** *too* **poor** *to* present such	AIT
	42:13	The LORD will march out like a **mighty m**,	1475
	44:13	He shapes it in the form of **m**,	408
	44:13	of **m** in all his glory,	132
	46:11	a **m** *to* **fulfill** my purpose.	408
	52:14	disfigured beyond that of *any* **m** and	408
	53: 3	a *m of* **sorrows**, and familiar with suffering.	408
	55: 7	and the evil **m** his thoughts.	408
	56: 2	Blessed is the **m** who does this,	632
	56: 2	the **m** who holds it fast,	132+1201
	57:13	*m who* **makes** me *his* refuge.	AIT
	57:16	spirit of **m** would grow faint before me—	NIH

Ref		Text	Num
Isa	57:16	the breath of **m** that I have created.	NIH
	58: 5	only a day for a **m** to humble himself?	132
	62: 5	As a **young m** marries a maiden,	1033
	65:20	an **old** *m* who does not live out his years;	AIT
	66: 3	like one who kills a **m**, and whoever offers	408
Jer	3: 1	"If a **m** divorces his wife and she leaves him	408
	3: 1	and she leaves him and marries another **m**,	408
	7:20	be poured out on this place, on **m** and beast,	132
	8: 4	When a **m** **turns away**, does he not return?	AIT
	9:12	What **m** is wise enough to understand this?	408
	9:23	"Let not the **wise** *m* boast of his wisdom or	AIT
	9:23	or the **strong** *m* boast of his strength or	1475
	9:23	of his strength or the **rich** *m* boast	AIT
	10:23	it is not for **m** to direct his steps.	408
	11: 3	'Cursed is the **m** who does not obey	408
	14: 9	Why are you like a **m** taken by surprise,	408
	15:10	a **m** with whom the whole land strives	408
	15:12	"Can a *m* **break** iron—	AIT
	17: 5	"Cursed is the one who trusts in **m**,	132
	17: 7	blessed is the **m** who trusts in the LORD,	1505
	17:10	to reward a **m** according to his conduct,	408
	17:11	the *m who* **gains** riches by unjust means.	AIT
	20:15	be the **m** who brought my father the news,	408
	20:16	May that **m** be like the towns	408
	22: 7	*each* **m** with his weapons,	408
	22:28	Is this **m** Jehoiachin a despised, broken pot,	408
	22:30	"Record this **m** as if childless,	408
	22:30	a **m** who will not prosper in his lifetime,	1505
	23: 9	I am like a drunken **m**,	408
	23: 9	like a **m** overcome by wine,	1505
	23:34	I will punish that **m** and his household.	408
	26:11	"This **m** should be sentenced to death	408
	26:16	"This **m** should not be sentenced to death!	408
	26:20	another **m** who prophesied in the name	408
	30: 6	Ask and see: Can a **m** bear children?	2351
	30: 6	Then why do I see every **strong m**	1505
	31:22	a woman will surround a **m**."	1505
	31:34	No longer will a **m** teach his neighbor,	408
	31:34	or a **m** his brother, saying, 'Know the LORD,'	408
	33:17	to have a **m** to sit on the throne of the house	408
	33:18	to have a **m** to stand before me continually	408
	35: 4	of the sons of Hanan son of Igdaliah the **m**	408
	35:19	son of Recab will never fail to have a **m**	408
	38: 4	"This **m** should be put to death.	408
	38: 4	This **m** is not seeking the good	408
	48:19	the *m* **fleeing** and the woman escaping,	AIT
	49:18	no **m** will dwell in it.	132+1201
	49:33	no **m** will dwell in it."	132+1201
	50:40	no **m** will dwell in it.	132+1201
	51:17	"Every **m** is senseless and without	132
	51:22	with you I shatter **m** and woman,	408
	51:22	with you I shatter **old** *m* and youth,	AIT
	51:22	with you I shatter **young m** and maiden,	1033
	51:43	through which no **m** travels.	132+1201
	51:62	so that neither **m** nor animal will live in it;	132
La	3: 1	the **m** who has seen affliction by the rod	1505
	3:27	for a **m** to bear the yoke while he is young.	1505
	3:35	to deny a **m** his rights before the Most High,	1505
	3:36	to deprive a **m** of justice—	132
	3:39	Why should any living **m** complain	132
Eze	1: 5	In appearance their form was that of a **m**,	132
	1: 8	they had the hands of a **m**.	132
	1:10	Each of the four had the face of a **m**,	132
	1:26	on the throne was a figure like that of a **m**.	132
	2: 1	He said to me, "Son of **m**,	132
	2: 3	He said: "Son of **m**,	132
	2: 6	And you, son of **m**,	132
	2: 8	you, son of **m**, listen to what I say to you.	132
	3: 1	And he said to me, "Son of **m**,	132
	3: 3	Then he said to me, "Son of **m**,	132
	3: 4	He then said to me: "Son of **m**,	132
	3:10	And he said to me, "Son of **m**,	132
	3:17	"Son of **m**, I have made you a watchman for	132
	3:18	When I say to a **wicked** *m*,	AIT
	3:18	that **wicked** *m* will die for his sin,	AIT
	3:19	But if you do warn the **wicked** *m* and	AIT
	3:20	a **righteous** *m* turns from his righteousness	AIT
	3:21	if you do warn the **righteous** *m* not to sin	AIT
	3:25	And you, son of **m**, they will tie with ropes;	132
	4: 1	"Now, son of **m**, take a clay tablet,	132
	4:16	He then said to me: "Son of **m**,	132
	5: 1	son of **m**, take a sharp sword and use it as	132
	6: 2	"Son of **m**, set your face against the	132
	7: 2	"Son of **m**, this is what	132
	8: 2	I looked, and I saw a figure like that of a **m**.	408
	8: 5	Then he said to me, "Son of **m**,	132
	8: 6	And he said to me, "Son of **m**,	132
	8: 8	He said to me, "Son of **m**,	132
	8:12	He said to me, "Son of **m**,	132
	8:15	He said to me, "Do you see this, son of **m**?	132
	8:17	"Have you seen this, son of **m**?	132
	9: 2	a **m** clothed in linen who had a writing kit	408
	9: 3	Then the LORD called to the **m** clothed	408
	9:11	Then the **m** in linen with the writing kit	408
	10: 2	The LORD said to the **m** clothed in linen,	408
	10: 3	of the temple when the **m** went in,	408
	10: 6	the LORD commanded the **m** in linen,	408
	10: 6	the **m** went in and stood beside a wheel.	NIH
	10: 7	and put it into the hands of the **m** in linen,	NIH
	10: 8	be seen what looked like the hands of a **m**.)	132
	10:14	the second the face of a **m**,	132
	10:21	like the hands of a **m**.	132
	11: 2	The LORD said to me, "Son of **m**,	132
	11: 4	prophesy, son of **m**."	132
	11:15	"Son of **m**, your brothers—	132
	12: 2	"Son of **m**, you are living among	132
	12: 3	"Therefore, son of **m**, pack your belongings	132

Eze	12: 9	"Son of m, did not that rebellious house	132
	12:18	"Son of m, tremble as you eat your food,	132
	12:22	"Son of m, what is this proverb you have in	132
	12:27	"Son of m, the house of Israel is saying,	132
	13: 2	"Son of m, prophesy against the prophets	132
	13:17	son of m, set your face against the daughters	132
	14: 3	"Son of m, these men have set up idols	132
	14: 8	against that m and make him an example	408
	14:13	"Son of m, if a country sins against me	132
	15: 2	of m, how is the wood of a vine better than	132
	16: 2	"Son of m, confront Jerusalem	132
	17: 2	"Son of m, set forth an allegory and tell	132
	18: 5	a righteous m who does what is just	408
	18: 8	and judges fairly between m and man.	408
	18: 8	and judges fairly between man and m.	408
	18: 9	That m is righteous;	AIT
	18:13	Will such a m live?	AIT
	18:20	of the righteous m will be credited to him,	AIT
	18:21	"But if a wicked m turns away from all	AIT
	18:24	if a righteous m turns from his righteousness	AIT
	18:24	the wicked m does,	AIT
	18:26	If a righteous m turns from his righteousness	AIT
	18:27	But if a wicked m turns away from	AIT
	20: 3	of m, speak to the elders of Israel and say	132
	20: 4	Will you judge them, son of m?	132
	20:11	for the m who obeys them will live by them.	132
	20:13	the m who obeys them will live by them—	132
	20:21	the m who obeys them will live by them—	132
	20:27	of m, speak to the people of Israel and say	132
	20:46	"Son of m, set your face toward the south;	132
	21: 2	"Son of m, set your face against Jerusalem	132
	21: 6	"Therefore groan, son of m!	132
	21: 9	"Son of m, prophesy and say, 'This is what	132
	21:12	Cry out and wail, son of m,	132
	21:14	"So then, son of m,	132
	21:19	"Son of m, mark out two roads for the sword	132
	21:28	"And you, son of m, prophesy and say,	132
	22: 2	"Son of m, will you judge her?	132
	22:11	In you one m commits a detestable offense	408
	22:18	"Son of m, the house of Israel has become	132
	22:24	"Son of m, say to the land, 'You are a land	132
	22:30	for a m among them who would build up	408
	23: 2	"Son of m, there were two women, daughters	132
	23:36	The LORD said to me: "Son of m,	132
	24: 2	"Son of m, record this date, this very date,	132
	24:16	"Son of m, with one blow I am about	132
	24:25	"And you, son of m,	132
	25: 2	of m, set your face against the Ammonites	132
	26: 2	"Son of m, because Tyre has said	132
	27: 2	"Son of m, take up a lament	132
	28: 2	"Son of m, say to the ruler of Tyre, 'This	132
	28: 2	But you are a m and not a god,	132
	28: 9	You will be but a m, not a god,	132
	28:12	"Son of m, take up a lament concerning	132
	28:21	"Son of m, set your face against Sidon;	132
	29: 2	"Son of m, set your face against Pharaoh	132
	29:11	No foot of m or animal will pass through it;	132
	29:18	"Son of m, Nebuchadnezzar king	132
	30: 2	"Son of m, prophesy and say:	132
	30:21	"Son of m, I have broken the arm	132
	30:24	like a mortally wounded m.	2728
	31: 2	"Son of m, say to Pharaoh king of Egypt	132
	32: 2	"Son of m, take up a lament	132
	32:13	to be stirred by the foot of m or muddied by	132
	32:18	"Son of m, wail for the hordes of Egypt	132
	33: 2	"Son of m, speak to your countrymen	132
	33: 6	that m will be taken away because	2085S
	33: 7	"Son of m, I have made you a watchman for	132
	33: 8	When I say to the wicked, 'O wicked m,	AIT
	33: 8	that wicked m will die for his sin,	AIT
	33: 9	But if you do warn the wicked m to turn	AIT
	33:10	"Son of m, say to the house of Israel,	132
	33:12	son of m, say to your countrymen,	132
	33:12	'The righteousness of the righteous m will	AIT
	33:12	of the wicked m will not cause him to fall	AIT
	33:12	The righteous m, if he sins,	AIT
	33:13	I tell the righteous m that he will surely live	AIT
	33:14	And if I say to the wicked m,	AIT
	33:18	If a righteous m turns from his righteousness	AIT
	33:19	a wicked m turns away from his wickedness	AIT
	33:21	a m who had escaped from Jerusalem came	7127
	33:22	Now the evening before the m arrived,	7127S
	33:22	and he opened my mouth before the m came	NIH
	33:24	"Son of m, the people living in those ruins	132
	33:24	'Abraham was only one m,	AIT
	33:30	"As for you, son of m,	132
	34: 2	"Son of m, prophesy against the shepherds	132
	35: 2	of m, set your face against Mount Seir;	132
	36: 1	of m, prophesy to the mountains of Israel	132
	36:17	"Son of m, when the people of Israel were	132
	37: 3	He asked me, "Son of m,	132
	37: 9	prophesy, son of m, and say to it,	132
	37:11	Then he said to me: "Son of m,	132
	37:16	"Son of m, take a stick of wood and write	132
	38: 2	"Son of m, set your face against Gog,	132
	38:14	son of m, prophesy and say to Gog:	132
	39: 1	"Son of m, prophesy against Gog and say:	132
	39:17	"Son of m, this is what	132
	40: 3	a m whose appearance was like bronze;	408
	40: 4	The m said to me, "Son of man,	408
	40: 4	to me, "Son of m,	132
	41: 1	the m brought me to the outer sanctuary	NIH
	41:19	of a m toward the palm tree on one side and	132
	41:22	The m said to me,	NIH
	42: 1	the m led me northward into the outer court	NIH
	43: 1	the m brought me to the gate facing east,	NIH
	43: 6	While the m was standing beside me,	408

Eze	43: 7	He said: "Son of m, this is the place	132
	43:10	of m, describe the temple to the people	132
	43:18	Then he said to me, "Son of m,	132
	44: 1	the m brought me back to the outer gate	NIH
	44: 4	the m brought me by way of the north gate	NIH
	44: 5	The LORD said to me, "Son of m,	132
	46:19	the m brought me through the entrance at	NIH
	47: 1	The m brought me back to the entrance of	NIH
	47: 3	the m went eastward with a measuring line	408
	47: 6	He asked me, "Son of m, do you see this?"	132
Da	2:10	"There is not a m on earth who can do what	10050
	2:25	"I have found a m among the exiles	10131
	2:27	Daniel replied, "No wise m, enchanter,	AIT
	4:16	that of a m and let him be given the mind of	10050
	5:11	a m in your kingdom who has the spirit of	10131
	5:12	This m Daniel, whom the king called Belteshazzar,	NIH
	6: 5	for charges against this m Daniel	AIT
	6: 7	to any god or m during the next thirty days,	10050
	6:12	to any god or m except to you,	10050
	7: 4	so that it stood on two feet like a m,	10050
	7: 4	and the heart of a m was given to it.	10050
	7: 8	This horn had eyes like the eyes of a m	10050
	7:13	before me was one like a son of m,	10050
	8:15	before me stood one who looked like a m.	1505
	8:16	tell this m the meaning of the vision."	AIT
	8:17	"Son of m," he said to me,	132
	9:21	the m I had seen in the earlier vision,	408
	10: 5	up and there before me was a m dressed	408
	10:16	who looked like a m touched my lips,	132+1201
	10:18	like a m touched me and gave me strength.	132
	10:19	"Do not be afraid, O m highly esteemed,"	408
	12: 6	One of them said to the m clothed in linen,	408
	12: 7	The m clothed in linen,	408
Hos	3: 3	be a prostitute or be intimate with any m,	408
	4: 4	"But let no m bring a charge,	408
	4: 4	let no m accuse another,	408
	6: 9	As marauders lie in ambush for a m,	408
	9: 7	the inspired m a maniac.	408
	11: 9	For I am God, and not m—	408
	12: 3	as a m he struggled with God.	226
Am	4:13	and reveals his thoughts to m,	132
	5:13	the prudent m keeps quiet in such times,	AIT
	5:19	as though a m fled from a lion only to meet	408
Jnh	1:14	for killing an innocent m,	AIT
	3: 7	Do not let any m or beast, herd or flock,	132
	3: 8	let m and beast be covered with sackcloth.	132
Mic	2: 2	They defraud a m of his home,	1505
	4: 4	Every m will sit under his own vine and	408
	5: 4	not wait for m or linger for mankind.	408
	6: 8	He has showed you, O m, what is good.	132
	6:11	Shall I acquit a m with dishonest scales,	NIH
	7: 2	not one upright m remains.	132
Hab	2:18	since a m has carved it?	3670
Zep	1: 3	when I cut off m from the face of the earth,"	132
Zec	1: 8	there before me was a m riding a red horse!	408
	1:10	Then the m standing among the myrtle	408
	2: 1	before me was a m with a measuring line	408
	2: 4	"Run, tell that young m,	5853
	3: 2	Is not this m a burning stick snatched from	AIT
	4: 1	as a m is wakened from his sleep.	408
	6:12	'Here is the m whose name is the Branch,	408
	8:10	Before that time there were no wages for m	132
	8:10	I had turned every m against his neighbor.	132
	12: 1	and who forms the spirit of m within him,	132
	13: 7	against the m who is close to me!"	1505
	14:13	Each m will seize the hand of another,	408
Mal	2:12	As for the m who does this,	408
	3: 8	"Will a m rob God?	132
	3: 8	a m spares his son who serves him.	408
Mt	1:19	righteous m and did not want to expose her	AIT
	4: 4	'M does not live on bread alone,	476
	7:24	a wise m who built his house on the rock.	467
	7:26	a foolish m who built his house on sand.	467
	8: 2	A m with leprosy came and knelt	3320
	8: 3	his hand and touched the m.	899S
	8: 9	For I myself am a m under authority,	476
	8:20	the Son of M has no place to lay his head."	476
	8:27	"What kind of m is this?	AIT
	9: 6	that the Son of M has authority on earth	476
	9: 7	And the m got up and went home.	NIG
	9: 9	he saw a m named Matthew sitting at	476
	9:32	a m who was demon-possessed and could	476
	9:33	the m who had been mute spoke.	3273
	10:23	cities of Israel before the Son of M comes.	476
	10:35	to turn " 'a m against his father, a daughter	476
	10:41	and anyone who receives a righteous m	AIT
	10:41	because he is a righteous m will receive	AIT
	11: 6	the m who does not fall away on account	1569
	11: 8	A m dressed in fine clothes?	476
	11:19	The Son of M came eating and drinking,	476
	12: 8	For the Son of M is Lord of the Sabbath."	476
	12:10	and a m with a shriveled hand was there.	476
	12:12	How much more valuable is a m than	476
	12:13	he said to the m, "Stretch out your hand,"	476
	12:22	a demon-possessed m who was blind and	AIT
	12:29	unless he first ties up the strong m?	AIT
	12:32	against the Son of M will be forgiven,	476
	12:35	The good m brings good things out of	476
	12:35	and the evil m brings evil things out of	476
	12:40	Son of M will be three days and three nights	476
	12:43	"When an evil spirit comes out of a m,	476
	12:45	the final condition of that m is worse than	476
	13:20	on rocky places is the m who hears the word	AIT
	13:23	that fell among the thorns is the m who hears	AIT
	13:23	on good soil is the m who hears the word	AIT
	13:24	of heaven is like a m who sowed good seed	476

Mt	13:31	which a m took and planted in his field.	476
	13:37	the good seed is the Son of M.	476
	13:41	The Son of M will send out his angels,	476
	13:44	When a m found it, he hid it again,	476
	13:54	"Where did this m get this wisdom	AIT
	13:56	Where then did this m get all these things?"	AIT
	15: 5	But you say that if a m says to his father	4005S
	15:14	If a blind m leads a blind man, '	AIT
	15:14	If a blind man leads a blind m,	AIT
	15:18	and these make a m 'unclean.'	476
	15:20	These are what make a m 'unclean';	476
	16:13	"Who do people say the Son of M is?"	476
	16:17	was not revealed to you by m,	135+2779+4922
	16:26	What good will it be for a m if he gains	476
	16:26	what can a m give in exchange for his soul?	476
	16:27	the Son of M is going to come in his Father's glory	476
	16:28	the Son of M coming in his kingdom."	476
	17: 9	until the Son of M has been raised from	476
	17:12	In the same way the Son of M is going	476
	17:14	a m approached Jesus and knelt before him.	476
	17:22	"The Son of M is going to be betrayed into	476
	18: 7	but woe to the m through whom they come!	476
	18:12	If a m owns a hundred sheep,	476
	18:24	a m who owed him ten thousand talents	1651
	18:30	he went off and had the m thrown	899S
	19: 3	"Is it lawful for a m to divorce his wife	476
	19: 5	'For this reason a m will leave his father	476
	19: 6	God has joined together, let m not separate.	476
	19: 7	"did Moses command that a m give his wife	NIG
	19:16	Now a m came up to Jesus and asked,	1651
	19:18	"Which ones?" the m inquired.	NIG
	19:20	"All these I have kept," the young m said.	3734
	19:22	When the young m heard this,	3734
	19:23	for a rich m to enter the kingdom of heaven.	AIT
	19:24	for a rich m to enter the kingdom of God."	AIT
	19:26	"With m this is impossible,	476
	19:28	the Son of M sits on his glorious throne,	476
	20:14	to give the m who was hired last the same	AIT
	20:18	the Son of M will be betrayed to the	476
	20:28	as the Son of M did not come to be served,	476
	21:28	There was a m who had two sons.	476
	22:11	he noticed a m there who was	476
	22:12	The m was speechless.	1254+3836S
	22:16	a m of integrity and that you teach the way	AIT
	22:24	that if a m dies without having children,	AIT
	24:27	so will be the coming of the Son of M.	476
	24:30	the sign of the Son of M will appear in	476
	24:30	They will see the Son of M coming on	476
	24:37	so it will be at the coming of the Son of M.	476
	24:39	be at the coming of the Son of M.	476
	24:44	because the Son of M will come at an hour	476
	25:14	it will be like a m going on a journey,	476
	25:16	The m who had received the five talents	AIT
	25:18	But the m who had received the one talent	AIT
	25:20	The m who had received the five talents	AIT
	25:22	"The m with the two talents also came.	3836
	25:24	the m who had received the one talent	AIT
	25:24	he said, 'I knew that you are a hard m,	476
	25:31	"When the Son of M comes in his glory,	476
	26: 2	the Son of M will be handed over to be crucified."	476
	26: 6	the home of a m known as Simon the Leper,	NIG
	26:18	into the city to a certain m and tell him,	AIT
	26:24	Son of M will go just as it is written about	476
	26:24	woe to that m who betrays the Son of Man!	476
	26:24	woe to that man who betrays the Son of M!	476
	26:45	and the Son of M is betrayed into the hands	476
	26:48	"The one I kiss is the m; arrest him."	899S
	26:64	the future you will see the Son of M sitting	476
	26:72	"I don't know the m!"	476
	26:74	"I don't know the m!"	476
	27:19	to do with that innocent m,	AIT
	27:32	they met a m from Cyrene, named Simon,	476
	27:57	there came a rich m from Arimathea,	476
Mk	1:23	a m in their synagogue who was possessed	476
	1:26	The evil spirit shook the m violently	899S
	1:40	A m with leprosy came to him	3320
	1:41	his hand and touched the m.	NIG
	2: 4	the mat the paralyzed m was lying on.	AIT
	2:10	that the Son of M has authority on earth	476
	2:27	"The Sabbath was made for m,	476
	2:27	not m for the Sabbath.	476
	2:28	the Son of M is Lord even of the Sabbath."	476
	3: 1	and a m with a shriveled hand was there.	476
	3: 3	Jesus said to the m with the shriveled hand,	476
	3: 5	said to the m, "Stretch out your hand."	476
	3:27	unless he first ties up the strong m.	AIT
	4:26	A m scatters seed on the ground.	476
	5: 2	a m with an evil spirit came from the tombs	476
	5: 3	This m lived in the tombs,	476
	5: 8	Jesus had said to him, "Come out of this m,	476
	5:15	they saw the m who had been possessed by	AIT
	5:16	happened to the demon-possessed m—	AIT
	5:18	the m who had been demon-possessed	AIT
	5:20	So the m went away and began to tell in	476
	6: 2	"Where did this m get these things?"	AIT
	6:16	he said, "John, the m I beheaded,	AIT
	6:20	knowing him to be a righteous and holy m.	467
	6:27	The m went, beheaded John in the prison,	NIG
	7:11	But you say that if a m says to his father	476
	7:15	Nothing outside a m can make him 'unclean'	476
	7:15	comes out of a m that makes him 'unclean.'	476
	7:18	"Don't you see that nothing that enters a m	476
	7:20	out of a m is what makes him 'unclean.'	476
	7:23	from inside and make a m 'unclean.' "	476
	7:32	a m who was deaf and could hardly talk,	AIT

Mk
7:32 they begged him to place his hand on the **m.** NIG
8:22 a blind *m* and begged Jesus to touch him. AIT
8:23 He took the **blind** *m* by the hand AIT
8:31 that the Son *of* M must suffer many things 476
8:36 for a *m* to gain the whole world, 476
8:37 what can a *m* give in exchange for his soul? 476
8:38 the Son *of* M will be ashamed of him 476
9:9 until the Son *of* M had risen from the dead. 476
9:12 Son *of* M must suffer much and be rejected? 476
9:17 A *m* in the crowd answered, "Teacher, 1651
9:31 "The Son *of* M is going to be betrayed into 476
9:38 "we saw **a** *m* driving out demons AIT
10:2 "Is it lawful *for* a *m* to divorce his wife?" 467
10:4 "Moses permitted a *m* to write a certificate NIG
10:7 'For this reason a *m* will leave his father 476
10:9 God has joined together, let *m* not separate. 476
10:12 and marries **another** *m*, 476
10:17 a *m* ran up to him and fell on his knees 1651
10:25 for a **rich** *m* to enter the kingdom of God." AIT
10:27 "With *m* this is impossible, 476
10:33 the Son *of* M will be betrayed to the chief 476
10:45 the Son *of* M did not come to be served, 476
10:46 were leaving the city, a **blind** *m*, AIT
10:49 So they called to the **blind** *m*, "Cheer up! AIT
10:51 The **blind** *m* said, "Rabbi, I want to see." AIT
12:1 "A *m* planted a vineyard, 476
12:4 they struck **this** *m* on the head AIT
12:14 we know you are a *m* of **integrity**. AIT
12:19 the *m* must marry the widow 81
12:32 "Well said, teacher," the *m* replied. NIG
13:26 Son *of* M coming in clouds with great power 476
13:34 It's like a *m* going away: 476
14:3 the home of a *m* known as Simon the Leper, NIG
14:13 a *m* carrying a jar of water will meet you. 476
14:21 Son *of* M will go just as it is written about 476
14:21 woe *to* that *m* who betrays the Son of Man! 476
14:21 woe to that man who betrays the Son *of* M! 476
14:41 the Son *of* M is betrayed into the hands of sinners. 476
14:44 "The one I kiss is the **m**; 899S
14:51 A **young** *m*, wearing nothing but 3734
14:58 will build another, **not made by m.' "** 942
14:62 "And you will see the Son *of* M sitting at 476
14:71 "I don't know this *m* you're talking about." 476
15:7 A *m* called Barabbas was in prison with AIT
15:21 "A **certain** *m* from Cyrene, Simon, AIT
15:36 One *m* ran, filled a sponge AIT
15:39 "Surely this *m* was the Son of God!" 476
16:5 a **young** *m* dressed in a white robe sitting on 3734

Lk
1:18 I am an **old** *m* and my wife is well along 4566
1:27 to be married to a *m* named Joseph, 467
2:25 there was a *m* in Jerusalem called Simeon, 476
3:11 "The *m* with two tunics should share AIT
4:4 'M does not live on bread alone.' " 476
4:33 the synagogue there was a *m* possessed by 476
4:35 Then the demon threw the **m** down 899S
5:8 I am a sinful **m!"** 467
5:12 a *m* came along who was covered 467
5:13 his hand and touched the **m.** 899S
5:24 that the Son *of* M has authority on earth 476
5:24 He said *to* the **paralyzed** *m*, "I tell you, AIT
6:5 "The Son *of* M is Lord of the Sabbath." 476
6:6 *m* was there whose right hand was shriveled, 476
6:8 said *to* the *m* with the shriveled hand, 476
6:10 and then said *to* the **m,** 899S
6:22 your name as evil, because of the Son *of* M. 476
6:39 "Can a **blind** *m* lead a blind man? AIT
6:39 "Can a blind man lead a **blind** *m?* AIT
6:45 The good *m* brings good things out of 476
6:45 and the evil *m* brings evil things out of AIT
6:48 He is like a *m* building a house, 476
6:49 into practice is like a *m* who built a house 476
7:4 "This *m* **deserves** to have you do this, AIT
7:8 For I myself am a *m* under authority, 476
7:14 he said, **"Young m,** I say to you, get up!" 3734
7:15 The **dead** *m* sat up and began to talk, AIT
7:23 the *m* **who** does not fall away on account 476
7:25 A *m* dressed in fine clothes? 476
7:34 The Son *of* M came eating and drinking, 476
7:39 he said to himself, "If **this** *m* were a prophet, AIT
8:27 he was met by a demon-possessed *m* from 467
8:27 For a long time this *m* had not worn clothes NIG
8:29 the evil spirit to come out of the **m.** 476
8:33 When the demons came out of the **m,** 476
8:35 the *m* from whom the demons had gone out, 476
8:36 how the **demon-possessed** *m* had been cured. AIT
8:38 The *m* from whom the demons had gone out 467
8:39 So the *m* went away and told all over town NIG
8:41 Then a *m* named Jairus, 467
9:22 "The Son *of* M must suffer many things 476
9:25 for a *m* to gain the whole world, 476
9:26 the Son *of* M will be ashamed of him 476
9:38 A *m* in the crowd called out, "Teacher, 467
9:44 The Son *of* M is going to be betrayed into 476
9:49 "we saw **a** *m* driving out demons AIT
9:57 a *m* said to him, "I will follow you AIT
9:58 the Son *of* M has no place to lay his head." 476
9:59 He said to **another** *m*, "Follow me." AIT
9:59 But he replied, "Lord, 3836S
10:6 If a *m* of peace is there, 5626
10:30 "A *m* was going down from Jerusalem 476
10:31 and when he saw the **m,** 899S
10:33 as he traveled, came where the **m** was; 899S
10:34 Then he put the **m** on his own donkey, 899S
10:36 *to* the *m* **who** fell into the hands of robbers?" AIT
11:14 the *m* **who** had been mute spoke, 3273
11:21 "When a **strong** *m*, fully armed, AIT

Lk
11:22 the *m* **trusted** and divides up the spoils. AIT
11:24 "When an evil spirit comes out of a *m*, 476
11:26 the final condition *of* that *m* is worse than 476
11:30 will the Son *of* M be to this generation. 476
12:8 the Son *of* M will also acknowledge him 476
12:10 against the Son *of* M will be forgiven, 476
12:14 "M, who appointed me a judge or an arbiter 476
12:16 "The ground of a certain rich *m* produced 476
12:40 because the Son *of* M will come at an hour 476
13:6 "A *m* had a fig tree, planted in his vineyard, AIT
13:7 to the *m* who took care of the vineyard, AIT
13:8 the *m* replied, 'leave it alone 1254+3836S
13:19 which a *m* took and planted in his garden. 476
14:2 There in front of him was a *m* suffering 476
14:4 So taking hold of the **m,** NIG
14:9 'Give **this** *m* your seat.' AIT
14:15 "Blessed is the *m* **who** will eat at the feast in AIT
14:16 "A certain *m* was preparing a great banquet. 476
15:2 **"This** *m* welcomes sinners and eats 476
15:11 "There was a *m* who had two sons. 476
16:1 a rich *m* whose manager was accused 476
16:18 and the *m* who marries a divorced woman AIT
16:19 "There was a rich *m* who was dressed 476
16:22 The **rich** *m* also died and was buried. AIT
17:22 to see one of the days of the Son *of* M, 476
17:24 Son *of* M in his day will be like the lightning, 476
17:26 also will it be in the days of the Son *of* M. 476
17:30 on the day the Son *of* M is revealed. 476
18:8 However, when the Son *of* M comes, 476
18:14 "I tell you that **this** *m*, rather than the other, AIT
18:23 because he was a *m* of great **wealth.** AIT
18:25 for a **rich** *m* to enter the kingdom of God." AIT
18:31 by the prophets *about* the Son *of* M will 476
18:35 a **blind** *m* was sitting by the roadside AIT
18:40 and ordered the *m* to be brought to him. 899S
19:2 A *m* was there by the name of Zacchaeus; 467
19:3 but being a **short** *m* he could not, AIT
19:9 because **this** *m*, too, is a son of Abraham. AIT
19:10 For the Son *of* M came to seek and 476
19:12 "A *m* of noble birth went to 476
19:14 'We don't want **this** *m* to be our king.' AIT
19:21 because you are a hard **m.** 476
19:22 You knew, did you, that I am a hard **m,** 476
20:9 "A *m* planted a vineyard, 476
20:28 the *m* must marry the widow 81
21:27 the Son *of* M coming in a cloud with power 476
21:36 be able to stand before the Son *of* M." 476
22:10 a *m* carrying a jar of water will meet you. 476
22:22 *of* M will go as it has been decreed, 476
22:22 but woe *to* that *m* who betrays him." AIT
22:47 and the *m* who was called Judas, AIT
22:48 are you betraying the Son *of* M with a kiss? 476
22:56 **"This** *m* was with him." AIT
22:58 **"M,** I am not!" Peter replied. 476
22:60 M, I don't know what you're talking about! 476
22:69 Son *of* M will be seated at the right hand of 476
23:2 "We have found **this** *m* subverting our nation. AIT
23:4 "I find no basis for a charge against this **m."** 476
23:6 Pilate asked if the *m* was a Galilean. 476
23:14 "You brought me this *m* as one who 476
23:18 "Away with **this** *m!* AIT
23:22 What crime has **this** *m* committed? AIT
23:25 He released the *m* who had been thrown AIT
23:41 But **this** *m* has done nothing wrong." 476
23:47 "Surely this was a righteous **m."** 476
23:50 Now there was a *m* named Joseph, 467
23:50 a good and upright **m,** 467
24:7 Son *of* M must be delivered into the hands 476

Jn
1:6 There came a *m* who was sent from God; 476
1:9 that gives light to every *m* was coming into 476
1:30 'A *m* who comes after me has surpassed me 467
1:33 'The *m* on **whom** you see the Spirit come AIT
1:51 and descending on the Son *of* M.' 476
2:25 He did not need man's testimony about *m*, 476
2:25 for he knew what was in a *m*. 476
3:1 a *m* of the Pharisees named Nicodemus, 476
3:4 "How can a *m* be born when he is old?" 476
3:13 who came from heaven—the Son *of* M. 476
3:14 so the Son *of* M must be lifted up, 476
3:26 that *m* who was with you on the other side NIG
3:27 "A *m* can receive only what is given 476
3:33 The *m* who has accepted it has certified 476
4:18 the *m* you now have is not your husband. 4005S
4:29 see a *m* who told me everything I ever did. 476
4:42 this *m* really is the Savior of the world." AIT
4:47 When **this** *m* heard that Jesus had arrived AIT
4:50 The *m* took Jesus at his word and departed. 476
5:9 At once the *m* was cured; 476
5:10 the Jews said *to* the *m* **who** had been healed, AIT
5:11 "The *m* who made me well said to me, AIT
5:13 The *m* who was healed had no idea who it was, AIT
5:15 The *m* went away and told the Jews 476
5:27 authority to judge because he is the Son *of* M 476
6:27 which the Son *of* M will give you. 476
6:50 which a *m* may eat and not die. AIT
6:52 "How can **this** *m* give us his flesh to eat?" AIT
6:53 unless you eat the flesh of the Son *of* M 476
6:62 What if you see the Son *of* M ascend to 476
7:11 "Where is **that** *m?"* AIT
7:12 Some said, "He is a **good** *m."* AIT
7:15 "How did **this** *m* get such learning AIT
7:23 of the one who sent him is a *m of* **truth;** AIT
7:23 for healing the whole *m* on the Sabbath? 476
7:25 "Isn't this the *m* they are trying to kill? 4005S
7:27 But we know where **this** *m* is from; AIT

Jn
7:31 he do more miraculous signs than **this** *m?"* AIT
7:35 "Where does **this** *m* intend to go AIT
7:40 "Surely **this** *m* is the Prophet." AIT
7:46 "No one ever spoke the way this *m* does," 476
8:28 "When you have lifted up the Son *of* M, 476
8:40 a *m* who has told you the truth that I heard 476
9:1 he saw a *m* blind from birth. 476
9:2 "Rabbi, who sinned, **this** *m* or his parents, AIT
9:3 "Neither **this** *m* nor his parents sinned," AIT
9:7 *m* went and washed, and came home seeing. NIG
9:8 "Isn't **this** the same *m* who used to sit AIT
9:9 But he himself insisted, "I am the **m."** NIG
9:11 "The *m* they call Jesus made some mud 476
9:12 "Where is **this** *m?"* AIT
9:13 to the Pharisees the *m* who had been blind. 899S
9:15 put mud on my eyes," the *m* replied, 1254+3836S
9:16 "This *m* is not from God, 476
9:17 Finally they turned again *to* the **blind** *m*, AIT
9:17 The *m* replied, "He is a prophet." 1254+3836S
9:24 the *m* who had been blind. 476
9:24 "We know this *m* is a sinner." 476
9:30 The *m* answered, "Now that is remarkable! 476
9:31 to the **godly** *m* who does his will. 2538
9:32 of opening the eyes of a *m* **born** blind. AIT
9:33 If **this** *m* were not from God, 476
9:35 he said, "Do you believe in the Son *of* M?" 476
9:36 "Who is he, sir?" the *m* asked. 1697S
9:38 Then the *m* said, "Lord, I believe," 3836S
10:1 the *m* **who** does not enter the sheep pen by AIT
10:2 The *m* who enters by the gate is the shepherd AIT
10:13 The *m* runs away because he is a hired hand NIG
10:21 *m* possessed by a demon. AIT
10:33 "but for blasphemy, because you, a mere **m,** AIT
10:41 all that John said about **this** *m* was true." AIT
11:1 Now a *m* named Lazarus was sick. 476
11:9 A *m* who walks by day will not stumble, AIT
11:37 the eyes of the **blind** *m* have kept this man AIT
11:37 the eyes of the blind man have kept **this** *m* AIT
11:39 Lord," said Martha, the sister of the **dead** *m*, AIT
11:44 The **dead** *m* came out, AIT
11:47 Here is this *m* performing many miraculous signs. 476
11:50 for you that one *m* die for the people than 476
12:23 "The hour has come for the Son *of* M to 476
12:25 The *m* **who** loves his life will lose it, AIT
12:25 while the *m* who hates his life AIT
12:34 'The Son *of* M must be lifted up'? 476
12:34 Who is this 'Son *of* M'?" 476
12:35 The *m* **who** walks in the dark does not know AIT
12:44 Jesus cried out, "When a *m* believes in me, AIT
13:31 the Son *of* M glorified and God is glorified 476
15:5 If a *m* remains in me and I in him, 3836S
18:14 the Jews that it would be good if one *m* died 476
18:26 *of* the *m* whose ear Peter had cut off, 4005
18:29 "What charges are you bringing against this **m?"** 476
19:5 Pilate said to them, "Here is the **m!"** 476
19:12 "If you let **this** *m* go, you are no friend of AIT
19:21 that **this** *m* claimed to be king of the Jews." AIT
19:32 of the **first** *m* who had been crucified AIT
19:35 The *m* **who** saw it has given testimony, AIT
19:39 the *m* **who** earlier had visited Jesus at night. AIT

Ac
2:22 a *m* accredited by God to you by miracles, 467
2:23 **This** *m* was handed over to you AIT
3:2 a *m* crippled from birth was being carried to 467
3:5 So the *m* gave them his attention, 3836S
3:10 they recognized him as the **same** *m* who 476
3:12 or godliness we had made **this** *m* walk? 899S
3:16 **this** *m* whom you see and know was made AIT
4:10 that **this** *m* stands before you healed. AIT
4:14 the *m* who had been healed standing there 476
4:22 For the *m* who was miraculously healed was 476
5:1 Now a *m* named Ananias, 467
6:5 a *m* full of faith and of the Holy Spirit; 467
6:5 Stephen, a *m* full of God's grace and power, NIG
7:27 "But the *m* **who** was mistreating AIT
7:56 and the Son *of* M standing at the right hand 476
7:58 at the feet of a **young** *m* named Saul. 3733
8:9 a *m* named Simon had practiced sorcery in 467
8:10 **"This** *m* is the divine power known as AIT
8:27 **This** *m* had gone to Jerusalem to worship, 4005S
8:30 the chariot and heard the *m* reading Isaiah 899S
9:11 and ask for a *m* from Tarsus named Saul, 5432
9:12 a *m* named Ananias come and place his 467
9:13 about this *m* and all the harm he has done 467
9:15 **This** *m* is my chosen instrument AIT
9:21 "Isn't he the *m* **who** raised havoc AIT
9:33 There he found a *m* named Aeneas, 476
10:1 a *m* named Cornelius, 467
10:5 back a *m* named Simon who is called Peter. AIT
10:22 He is a righteous and God-fearing **m,** 467
10:26 he said, "I am only a *m* myself." 476
10:28 that I should not call any *m* impure 476
10:30 a *m* in shining clothes stood before me 467
11:24 He was a good **m,** 467
12:22 "This is the voice of a god, not of a **m."** 476
13:7 The proconsul, an intelligent **m,** 467
13:22 'I have found David son of Jesse a *m* 467
14:8 In Lystra there sat a *m* crippled in his feet, 467
14:10 *m* jumped up and *began to* **walk.** AIT
16:9 During the night Paul had a vision of a *m* 467
17:26 From **one** *m* he made every nation of men, AIT
17:31 with justice by the *m* he has appointed. 467
18:13 **"This** *m*," they charged, "is persuading AIT
18:24 He was a learned **m,** with a thorough 467
19:16 Then the *m* who had the evil spirit jumped 476
19:29 and rushed **as one** *m* into the theater. 3924

Ac	20: 9	a window was a **young m** named Eutychus,	3733
	20:10	on the **young m** and put his arms	899S
	20:12	The people took the **young m** home alive	4090
	21:16	He was a **m** from Cyprus and one of	AIT
	21:28	the **m** who teaches all men everywhere	476
	22:12	"A **m** named Ananias came to see me.	467
	22:26	"This **m** is a Roman citizen."	476
	23: 9	"We find nothing wrong with this **m**,"	476
	23:17	"Take this **young m** to the commander;	3733
	23:18	for me and asked me to bring this **young m**	3734
	23:19	The commander took **the young m** by	899S
	23:22	The commander dismissed the **young m**	3734
	23:27	This **m** was seized by the Jews	467
	23:30	of a plot to be carried out against the **m**,	467
	24: 5	"We have found this **m** to be	476
	24:16	conscience clear before God and **m**.	476
	25: 5	and press charges against the **m** there,	899S
	25:14	a **m** here whom Felix left as a prisoner.	467
	25:16	over any **m** before he has faced his accusers	476
	25:17	the court the next day and ordered the **m** to	467
	25:19	about a **dead** m named Jesus who Paul	AIT
		claimed was alive.	
	25:22	"I would like to hear this **m** myself."	476
	25:24	with us, you see this **m**!	AIT
	26:31	"This **m** is not doing anything that deserves	476
	26:32	"This **m** could have been set free if he had	476
	28: 4	"This **m** must be a murderer;	476
Ro	1:23	to look like mortal **m** and birds and animals	476
	2: 3	So when you, a mere **m**,	476
	2:28	A **m** is not a Jew if he is only one outwardly	476
	2:29	No, a **m** is a Jew if he is one inwardly;	3836S
	3: 4	Let God be true, and every **m** a liar.	476
	3:28	For we maintain that a **m** is justified	476
	4: 4	Now when a **m** works,	3836S
	4: 5	to the **m** who does not work	AIT
	4: 6	when he speaks of the blessedness of the **m**	476
	4: 8	the **m** whose sin the Lord will never count	467
	5: 7	rarely will anyone die for a **righteous** m,	AIT
	5: 7	**good** m someone might possibly dare to die.	AIT
	5:12	just as sin entered the world through one **m**,	476
	5:15	the many died by the trespass of the **one** m,	AIT
	5:15	that came by the grace of the one **m**,	476
	5:17	For if, by the trespass of the **one** m,	476
	5:17	death reigned through that **one** m,	AIT
	5:17	reign in life through the **one** m,	AIT
	5:19	of the one **m** the many were made sinners,	476
	5:19	the **one** m the many will be made righteous.	AIT
	7: 1	the law has authority over a **m** only as long	476
	7: 3	if she marries another **m** while her husband	467
	7: 3	even though she marries another **m**.	467
	7:24	What a wretched **m** I am!	476
	8: 3	the likeness of sinful **m** to be a sin offering.	4922
	8: 3	And so he condemned sin in **sinful m**,	4922
	8: 6	The mind of **sinful m** is death;	4922
	9:20	But who are you, O **m**, to talk back to God?	476
	10: 5	"The **m** who does these things will live	476
	14: 2	but another **m**, whose faith is weak,	3836S
	14: 3	The **m** who eats everything must not look	AIT
	14: 3	and the **m** who does not eat everything must	AIT
	14: 3	not condemn the **m** who does,	AIT
	14: 5	**One** m considers one day more sacred than	
		another;	AIT
	14: 5	another **m** considers every day alike.	1254+4005
	14:20	but it is wrong for a **m** to eat anything	476
	14:22	Blessed is the **m** who does not condemn	AIT
	14:23	But the **m** who has doubts is condemned	AIT
1Co	1:20	Where is the **wise** m?	AIT
	2:11	the thoughts of a **m** except the man's spirit	476
	2:14	The **m** without the Spirit does not accept	476
	2:15	The spiritual **m** makes judgments	NIG
	3: 8	The **m** who plants and the man who waters	AIT
	3: 8	and the **m** who waters have one purpose,	AIT
	3:12	If any **m** builds on this foundation	AIT
	4: 6	not take pride in **one** m over against another.	AIT
	5: 1	A **m** has his father's wife.	AIT
	5: 2	out of your fellowship the **m** who did this?	AIT
	5: 5	hand this **m** over to Satan,	AIT
	5:11	With **such a m** do not even eat.	5525
	5:13	"Expel the **wicked m** from among you."	AIT
	6:18	other sins a **m** commits are outside his body,	476
	7: 1	It is good for a **m** not to marry.	476
	7: 2	**each** m should have his own wife,	AIT
	7: 7	But **each** m has his own gift from God;	AIT
	7:15	A **believing** m or woman is not bound	81
	7:18	Was a **m** already circumcised when he was	AIT
	7:18	Was a **m** uncircumcised when he was called?	AIT
	7:22	similarly, he who was a **free** m	AIT
	7:24	Brothers, **each** m, as responsible to God,	AIT
	7:32	An **unmarried** m is concerned about	AIT
	7:33	a **married** m is concerned about the affairs	AIT
	7:37	But the **m** who has settled the matter	AIT
	7:37	this **m** also does the right thing.	AIT
	8: 2	The **m** who thinks he knows something does	AIT
	8: 3	But the **m** who loves God is known by God.	AIT
	9:19	I am **free and belong to no m**,	1666+1801+4246
	9:26	I do not run like a **m** running aimlessly;	NIG
	9:26	I do not fight like a **m** beating the air.	NIG
	10:13	No temptation has seized you except what	
		is **common to m**.	474
	10:28	both for the sake of the **m** who told you	1697S
	11: 3	to realize that the head of every **m** is Christ,	467
	11: 3	and the head of the woman is **m**,	467
	11: 4	Every **m** who prays or prophesies	467
	11: 7	A **m** ought not to cover his head,	467
	11: 7	but the woman is the glory of **m**.	467
	11: 8	For **m** did not come from woman,	467
	11: 8	from woman, but woman from **m**;	467
1Co	11: 9	neither was **m** created for woman,	467
	11: 9	for woman, but woman for **m**.	467
	11:11	however, woman is not independent of **m**,	467
	11:11	nor is **m** independent of woman.	467
	11:12	For as woman came from **m**,	467
	11:12	so also **m** is born of woman.	467
	11:14	of things teach you that if a **m** has long hair,	467
	11:28	A **m** ought to examine himself	476
	13:11	When I became a **m**,	467
	14:17	but the **other** m is not edified.	AIT
	15:21	For since death came through a **m**,	476
	15:21	of the dead comes also through a **m**.	476
	15:45	"The first **m** Adam became a living being";	476
	15:47	The first **m** was of the dust of the earth,	476
	15:47	the second **m** from heaven.	AIT
	15:48	As was the **earthly** m,	AIT
	15:48	and as is the **m** from heaven,	AIT
	15:49	the likeness of the **earthly** m,	AIT
	15:49	the likeness of the **m** from heaven.	AIT
2Co	9: 7	Each **m** should give what he has decided	476
	12: 2	I know a **m** in Christ who fourteen years ago	476
	12: 3	And I know that this **m**—	476
	12: 4	things that **m** is not permitted to tell.	476
	12: 5	I will boast about a **m** like that,	5525
Gal	1: 1	sent not from men nor by **m**,	476
	1:11	something that **m** made up.	476+2848
	1:12	I did not receive it from any **m**,	476
	1:16	I did not consult any **m**,	135+2779+4922
	1:23	"The **m** who formerly persecuted us is	AIT
	2:16	a **m** is not justified by observing the law,	476
	3: 9	along with Abraham, **the** m of faith.	AIT
	3:12	"The **m** who does these things will live	AIT
	5: 3	Again I declare to every **m** who lets himself	476
	6: 7	A **m** reaps what he sows.	476
Eph	2:15	to create in himself one new **m** out of	476
	5: 5	**such a m** is an idolater—	4005
	5:31	"For this reason a **m** will leave his father	476
Php	1:27	contending as one **m** for the faith of	6034
	2: 8	And being found in appearance as a **m**,	476
1Th	4: 8	does not reject **m** but God,	476
2Th	2: 3	and the **m** of lawlessness is revealed,	476
	2: 3	the **m** doomed to destruction.	5626
	3:10	"If a **m** will not work, he shall not eat."	AIT
1Ti	1:13	and a persecutor and a **violent m**,	5616
	2: 5	between God and men, the **m** Christ Jesus,	476
	2:12	to teach or to have authority over a **m**;	476
	5: 1	Do not rebuke an **older m** harshly,	4565
	6:11	But you, **m** of God, flee from all this,	476
2Ti	2:21	If a **m** cleanses himself from the latter,	AIT
	3:17	the **m** of God may be thoroughly equipped	476
Tit	1: 6	a **m** whose children believe and are not open	AIT
	3:11	be sure that such a **m** is warped and sinful;	5525
Phm	1: 9	an **old m** and now also a prisoner	4566
	1:16	as a **m** and as a brother in the Lord.	1877+4922
Heb	2: 6	"What is **m** that you are mindful of him,	476
	2: 6	the son of **m** that you care for him?	476
	7: 6	**This m**, however, did not trace his descent	3836S
	8: 2	tabernacle set up by the Lord, not by **m**.	476
	8:11	No longer will a **m** teach his neighbor,	1667S
	8:11	a **m** his brother, saying, 'Know the Lord,'	1667S
	9:27	Just as **m** is destined to die once,	476
	10:29	do you think a **m** deserves to be punished	AIT
	11: 4	commended as a **righteous** m,	AIT
	11:12	And so from this **one** m,	476
	13: 6	What can **m** do to me?"	476
Jas	1: 7	That **m** should not think he will receive	476
	1: 8	he is a double-minded **m**,	467
	1:11	the **rich m** will fade away even	AIT
	1:12	Blessed is the **m** who perseveres under trial,	467
	1:23	like a **m** who looks at his face in a mirror	467
	1:25	But the **m** who looks intently into	AIT
	2: 2	a **m** comes into your meeting wearing	467
	2: 2	a **poor** m in shabby clothes also comes in.	AIT
	2: 3	to the **m** wearing fine clothes and say,	AIT
	2: 3	but say to the **poor** m, "You stand there"	AIT
	2:14	a **m** claims to have faith but has no deeds?	AIT
	2:20	You foolish **m**, do you want evidence	476
	3: 2	he is a perfect **m**, able to keep his whole	467
	3: 7	and have been tamed by **m**,	474
	3: 8	but no **m** can tame the tongue.	476
	5:16	of a **righteous** m is powerful and effective.	AIT
	5:17	Elijah was a **m** just like us.	476
1Pe	2:19	For it is commendable if a **m** bears up	
		under the pain of unjust suffering	AIT
2Pe	1:21	For prophecy never had its origin in the will	
		of **m**,	476
	2: 7	a **righteous** m, who was distressed by	AIT
	2: 8	that **righteous** m, living among them day	AIT
	2:19	for a **m** is a slave to whatever has mastered	AIT
1Jn	2: 4	The **m** who says, "I know him,"	AIT
	2:16	the cravings of **sinful m**,	4922
	2:17	the **m** who does the will of God lives	
		forever.	AIT
	2:22	It is the **m** who denies that Jesus is the	
		Christ.	AIT
	2:22	**Such a m** is the antichrist—	AIT
Rev	1:13	was someone "like a son of **m**," dressed in	476
	4: 7	the third had a face like a **m**,	476
	6:15	and every **free m** hid in caves and among	AIT
	9: 5	the sting of a scorpion when it strikes a **m**.	476
	14:14	one "like a son of **m**" with a crown of gold	AIT
	16: 3	it turned into blood like that of a **dead m**,	AIT
	16:18	like it has ever occurred since **m** has been	476

MAN'S (140) [MAN]

Ge	2:21	he took one of the **m** ribs and closed up	2257S

Ge	6: 5	The LORD saw how great **m** wickedness	132
	20: 7	Now return the **m** wife, for he is a prophet,	408
	42:25	to put each **m** silver back in his sack,	2157S
	42:35	in each **m** sack was his pouch of silver!	2257S
	44: 1	put **each m** silver in the mouth of his sack.	408
	44:26	the **m** face unless our youngest brother is	408
Ex	21:35	"If a **m** bull injures the bull of another	408
	22: 5	and they graze in **another** m field,	AIT
	22: 8	on the **other** m property.	AIT
Lev	4:26	priest will make atonement for the **m** sin,	2257S
	20:10	commits adultery with another **m** wife—	408
Nu	5:10	**Each** m sacred gifts are his own,	408
	5:12	**m** wife goes astray and is unfaithful to him	408
	7: 5	to the Levites as **each** m work requires."	408
Dt	22:22	man is found sleeping with another **m** wife,	1251
	22:24	because he violated **another m** wife.	8276
	24: 6	would be taking a **m** livelihood as security.	NIH
	25:10	That **m** line shall be known in Israel as	2257S
Jdg	18:19	as priest rather than just one **m** household?"	408
Ru	1: 2	The **m** name was Elimelech,	AIT
	4: 5	you acquire the **dead** m widow,	AIT
2Sa	10: 4	shaved off half of **each** m beard,	4392S
1Ki	18:44	"A cloud as small as a **m** hand is rising from	408
2Ki	13:21	they threw the **m** body into Elisha's tomb.	408
	18:21	a **m** hand and wounds him if he leans on it!	408
Job	14: 5	**M** days are determined;	2257S
	14:19	so you destroy **m** hope.	632
	21:19	up a **m** punishment for his sons.'	2257S
	21:28	You say, 'Where now is the **great m** house,	5618
	28: 9	**M** hand assaults the flinty rock	2257S
	31: 2	For what is **m** lot from God above,	NIH
	31:10	then may my wife grind **another** m grain,	AIT
	33:13	to him that he answers none of **m** words?	2257S
Ps	37:23	If the LORD delights in a **m** way,	1505
	39: 5	Each **m** life is but a breath.	132
	66: 5	how awesome his works in **m** behalf!	132+1201
Pr	4:22	and health to a **m** whole body.	2257S
	5:10	and your toil enrich **another** m house.	5799
	5:20	the bosom of **another** m wife?	AIT
	5:21	a **m** ways are in full view of the LORD,	408
	6:29	So is he who sleeps with **another m** wife;	8276
	13: 8	A **m** riches may ransom his life,	408
	13:23	A **poor** m field may produce abundant food,	AIT
	15:25	The LORD tears down the **proud** m house	AIT
	16: 2	All a **m** ways seem innocent to him,	408
	16: 7	When a **m** ways are pleasing to the LORD,	408
	16:23	A **wise** m heart guides his mouth,	AIT
	18: 4	The words of a **m** mouth are deep waters,	408
	18: 8	they go down to a **m** inmost parts.	NIH
	18:12	Before his downfall a **m** heart is proud,	408
	18:14	A **m** spirit sustains him in sickness,	408
	18:20	the fruit of his mouth a **m** stomach is filled;	408
	19: 3	A **m** own folly ruins his life,	132
	19: 4	but a **poor** m friend deserts him.	AIT
	19:11	A **m** wisdom gives him patience;	132
	19:21	Many are the plans in a **m** heart,	408
	20: 3	It is to a **m** honor to avoid strife,	408
	20: 5	The purposes of a **m** heart are deep waters,	408
	20:24	A **m** steps are directed by the LORD.	1505
	21: 2	All a **m** ways seem right to him,	408
	24:15	like an outlaw against a **righteous** m house,	AIT
	25: 9	do not betray **another** m confidence,	AIT
	25:12	an ornament of fine gold is a **wise** m rebuke	AIT
	26: 7	a **lame** m legs that hang limp is a proverb in	AIT
	26:22	they go down to a **m** inmost parts.	NIH
	27:19	so a **m** heart reflects the man.	132
	29:23	A **m** pride brings him low,	132
	30: 2	I do not have a **m** understanding.	132
Ecc	3:19	**M** fate is like that of the animals;	132+1201
	4: 4	and all achievement spring from **m** envy	408
	6: 7	All **m** efforts are for his mouth,	132
	7: 5	a **wise** m rebuke than to listen to the song	AIT
	8: 1	a **m** face and changes his hard appearance.	132
	8: 6	a **m** misery weighs heavily upon him.	132
	8:16	to know wisdom and to observe **m** labor	2021S
	9:16	But the **poor** m wisdom is despised,	AIT
	10:12	Words from a **wise** m mouth are gracious,	AIT
Isa	13: 7	every **m** heart will melt.	632
	36: 6	a **m** hand and wounds him if he leans on it!	408
	44:15	It is **m** fuel for burning;	132+4200
Jer	5: 8	each neighing for **another** m wife.	AIT
	10:23	O LORD, that a **m** life is not his own;	132+4200
	13:11	For as a belt is bound around a **m** waist,	408
	23:36	**every** m own word becomes his oracle	408
Eze	38:21	**Every** m sword will be against his brother.	408
	40: 5	rod in the hand was six long cubits,	408
Da	8:16	And I heard a **m** voice from the Ulai calling,	132
Jnh	1:14	not let us die for taking this **m** life.	408
Mic	7: 6	a **m** enemies are the members	408
Hab	2: 8	For you have shed **m** blood;	132
	2:17	For you have shed **m** blood;	132
Mal	2:16	a **m** covering himself with violence as well	AIT
Mt	10:36	a **m** enemies will be the members	476
	10:41	will receive a **righteous** m reward.	AIT
	12:29	how can anyone enter a **strong m** house	AIT
	15:11	a **m** mouth does not make him 'unclean,'	476
	27: 4	"I am innocent of **this m** blood," he said.	AIT
Mk	3:27	no one can enter a **strong m** house	AIT
	6:37	take **eight months of a m** wages!	1324+1357
	7:33	Jesus put his fingers into the **m** ears.	899S
	7:33	Then he spit and touched the **m** tongue.	899S
	7:35	At this, the **m** ears were opened,	899S
	8:23	on the **m** eyes and put his hands on him,	899S
	8:25	Jesus put his hands on the **m** eyes.	899S
	10:22	At this the **m** face fell.	1254+3836S
	12:19	"Moses wrote for us that if a **m** brother dies	AIT
Lk	11: 8	yet because of the **m** boldness he will get up	899S

Lk	12:15	a **m** life does not consist in the abundance	899S
	16:21	to eat what fell from the **rich** *m* table.	AIT
	20:28	"Moses wrote for us that if a *m* brother dies	AIT
	22:51	And he touched the **m** ear and healed him.	NIG
Jn	2:25	He did not need **m** testimony about man,	5516S
	9: 6	and put it on the **m** eyes.	899S
	9:14	and opened the **m** eyes was a Sabbath.	899S
	9:18	until they sent for the **m** parents.	899S
Ac	3: 7	and instantly the **m** feet and ankles became	899S
	5:28	to make us guilty of this **m** blood."	476
	11:12	and we entered the **m** house.	467
	13:23	"From this *m* descendants God has brought	AIT
	17:29	an image made by **m** design and skill.	476
Ro	2:29	Such a *m* praise is not from men,	4005S
	5:16	the gift of God is not like the result of the	
		one *m* sin:	AIT
	9:16	therefore, depend on **m** desire or effort,	3836S
	12: 6	If a *m* gift is prophesying,	NIG
	14: 2	**One** *m* faith allows him to eat everything,	AIT
1Co	1:25	foolishness of God is wiser than **m** wisdom,	476
	1:25	weakness of God is stronger than **m** strength.	476
	2:11	the thoughts of a man except the **m** spirit	476
	2:15	**not** subject to **any** *m* judgment:	476
	3:13	the fire will test the quality of **each** *m* work.	AIT
	10:29	the **other** *m* conscience, I mean, not yours.	AIT
2Co	4: 2	to every **m** conscience in the sight of God.	476
	10:16	work already done in **another** *m* territory.	AIT
Jas	1:20	for **m** anger does not bring about	467
1Pe	1:17	Father who judges **each** *m* work impartially,	AIT
2Pe	2:16	who spoke with a **m** voice and restrained	476
1Jn	5: 9	We accept **m** testimony, but God's	476
Rev	13:18	for it is **m** number. His number is 666.	476
	21:17	144 cubits thick, by **m** measurement,	476

MAN-MADE (5) [MAN, MAKE]

Dt	4:28	There you will worship **m** gods of wood	
			132+3338+5126
Mk	14:58	'I will destroy this **m** temple and	5935
Ac	19:26	He says that **m** gods are no gods at all.	
			1181+1328+5931
Heb	9:11	and more perfect tabernacle that is not **m**,	5935
	9:24	not enter a **m** sanctuary that was only a copy	5935

MANAEN (1)

Ac	13: 1	**M** (who had been brought up with Herod	3441

MANAGE (5) [MANAGED, MANAGEMENT, MANAGER]

Jer	12: 5	how will you **m** in the thickets by	6913
1Ti	3: 4	**m** his own family well **and see that**	4613
	3: 5	not know how to **m** his own family,	4613
	3:12	of but one wife and **must m** his children	4613
	5:14	to have children, to **m** their **homes** and	3866

MANAGED (2) [MANAGE]

1Ki	12:18	**m** to get into his chariot and escape	599
2Ch	10:18	**m** to get into his chariot and escape	599

MANAGEMENT (1) [MANAGE]

Lk	16: 2	Give an account of your **m**,	3873

MANAGER (7) [MANAGE]

Lk	8: 3	the **m** of Herod's household;	2208
	12:42	"Who then is the faithful and wise **m**,	3874
	16: 1	a rich man whose **m** was accused	3874
	16: 2	because you cannot **be m** any longer.'	3872
	16: 3	"The **m** said to himself,	3874
	16: 6	"The **m** told him, 'Take your bill,	1254+3836S
	16: 8	"The master commended the dishonest **m**	3874

MANAHATH (3) [MANAHATHITES]

Ge	36:23	Alvan, **M**, Ebal, Shepho and Onam.	4969
1Ch	1:40	Alvan, **M**, Ebal, Shepho and Onam.	4969
	8: 6	in Geba and were deported to **M**:	4970

MANAHATHITES (2) [MANAHATH]

1Ch	2:52	Haroeh, half the **M**,	4971
	2:54	Atroth Beth Joab, half the **M**, the Zorites,	4971

MANASSEH (144) [MANASSEH'S, MANASSITES]

Ge	41:51	Joseph named his firstborn **M** and said,	4985
	46:20	and Ephraim were born to Joseph	4985
	48: 1	So he took his two sons **M** and Ephraim	4985
	48: 5	Ephraim and **M** will be mine,	4985
	48:13	and **M** on his left toward Israel's right hand,	4985
	48:14	even though **M** was the firstborn.	4985
	48:20	'May God make you like Ephraim and **M**.'	4985
	48:20	So he put Ephraim ahead of **M**.	4985
	50:23	the children of Makir son of **M** were placed	4985
Nu	1:10	from **M**, Gamaliel son of Pedahzur;	4985
	1:34	From the descendants of **M**:	4985
	1:35	number from the tribe of **M** was 32,200.	4985
	2:20	The tribe of **M** will be next to them.	4985
	2:20	of the people of **M** is Gamaliel son	4985
	7:54	the leader of the people of **M**,	4985
	10:23	over the division of the tribe of **M**,	1201+4985
	13:11	the tribe of **M** (a tribe of Joseph), Gaddi son	4985
	26:28	of Joseph by their clans through **M**	4985
	26:29	The descendants of **M**:	4985S
Nu	26:34	These were the clans of **M**;	4985
	27: 1	the son of Makir, the son of **M**,	4985
	27: 1	belonged to the clans of **M** son of Joseph.	4985
	32:33	the Reubenites and the half-tribe of **M** son	4985
	32:39	The descendants of Makir son of **M** went	4985
	32:40	the descendants of **M**,	4985
	32:41	Jair, a descendant of **M**,	4985
	34:14	of **M** have received their inheritance	4985
	34:23	from the tribe of **M** son of Joseph;	1201+4985
	36: 1	Gilead son of Makir, the son of **M**,	4985
	36:12	of the descendants of **M** son of Joseph,	4985
Dt	3:13	I gave to the half tribe of **M**.	4985
	3:14	Jair, a descendant of **M**,	4985
	29: 8	the Gadites and the half-tribe of **M**.	4986
	33:17	such are the thousands of **M**."	4985
	34: 2	the territory of Ephraim and **M**,	4985
Jos	1:12	the Gadites and the half-tribe of **M**,	4985
	4:12	Gad and the half-tribe of **M** crossed over,	4985
	12: 6	the half-tribe of **M** to be their possession.	4985
	13: 7	the nine tribes and half of the tribe of **M**."	4985
	13: 8	**The other half of M**, the Reubenites and	2257S
	13:29	to the half-tribe of **M**, that is, to half	4985
	13:29	to half the family of the descendants of **M**,	4985
	13:31	for the descendants of Makir son of **M**—	4985
	14: 4	Joseph had become two tribes—**M** and Ephraim.	4985
	16: 4	So **M** and Ephraim, the descendants of	4985
	17: 1	This was the allotment for the tribe of **M**	4985
	17: 2	for the rest of the people of **M**—	4985
	17: 2	the other male descendants of **M** son	4985
	17: 3	the son of Makir, the son of **M**,	4985
	17: 6	of the **tribe of M** received an inheritance	4985
	17: 6	to the rest of the descendants of **M**,	4985
	17: 7	The territory of **M** extended from Asher	4985
	17: 8	(**M** had the land of Tappuah,	4985
	17: 8	but Tappuah itself, on the boundary of **M**,	4985
	17: 9	to Ephraim lying among the towns of **M**.	4985
	17: 9	the boundary of **M** was the northern side of	4985
	17:10	on the north to **M**.	4985
	17:10	of **M** reached the sea and bordered Asher on	2257S
	17:11	**M** also had Beth Shan,	4985
	17:17	house of Joseph—to Ephraim and **M**—	4985
	18: 7	of **M** have already received their inheritance	4985
	20: 8	and Golan in Bashan in the tribe of **M**.	4985
	21: 5	Ephraim, Dan and half of **M**.	4985
	21: 6	Naphtali and the half-tribe of **M** in Bashan.	4985
	21:25	the tribe of **M** they received Taanach	4985
	21:27	from the half-tribe of **M**,	4985
	22: 1	the Gadites and the half-tribe of **M**	4985
	22: 7	the half-tribe of **M** Moses had given land	4985
	22: 9	of **M** left the Israelites at Shiloh in Canaan	4985
	22:10	the Gadites and the half-tribe of **M** built	4985
	22:13	to Reuben, Gad and the half-tribe of **M**,	4985
	22:15	to Reuben, Gad and the half-tribe of **M**—	4985
	22:21	and the half-tribe of **M** replied to the heads	4985
	22:30	what Reuben, Gad and the half-tribe say,	1201+4985
	22:31	the priest, said to Reuben, Gad and **M**,	1201+4985
Jdg	1:27	But **M** did not drive out the people	4985
	6:15	My clan is the weakest in **M**,	4985
	6:35	He sent messengers throughout **M**,	4985
	7:23	Asher and all **M** were called out,	4985
	11:29	He crossed Gilead and **M**,	4985
	12: 4	renegades from Ephraim and **M**."	4985
1Ki	4:13	of Jair son of **M** in Gilead were his, as well	4985
2Ki	10:33	and **M**), from Aroer by the Arnon Gorge	4986
	20:21	And **M** his son succeeded him as king.	4985
	21: 1	**M** was twelve years old when he became	4985
	21: 9	**M** led them astray,	4985
	21:11	"**M** king of Judah has committed these detestable sins.	4985
	21:16	**M** also shed so much innocent blood	4985
	21:18	**M** rested with his fathers and was buried	4985
	21:20	as his father **M** had done.	4985
	23:12	and the altars **M** had built in the two courts	4985
	23:26	that **M** had done to provoke him to anger.	4985
	24: 3	from his presence because of the sins of **M**	4985
1Ch	3:13	Ahaz his son, Hezekiah his son, **M** his son,	4985
	5:18	the half-tribe of **M** had 44,760 men ready	4985
	5:23	of the half-tribe of **M** were numerous;	4985
	5:26	the Gadites and the half-tribe of **M**	4985
	6:61	from the clans of half the tribe of **M**.	4985
	6:62	the part of the tribe of **M** that is in Bashan.	4985
	6:70	of **M** the Israelites gave Aner and Bileam,	4985
	6:71	of the half-tribe of **M** they received Golan	4985
	7:14	The descendants of **M**:	4985
	7:17	Gilead son of Makir, the son of **M**.	4985
	7:29	the borders of **M** were Beth Shan,	1201+4985
	9: 3	and **M** who lived in Jerusalem were:	4985
	12:19	of **M** defected to David when he went with	4985
	12:20	these were the men of **M** who defected	4985
	12:20	leaders of units of a thousand in **M**.	4985
	12:31	the tribe of **M**, designated by name to come	4985
	12:37	Reuben, Gad and the half-tribe of **M**,	4985
	26:32	of **M** for every matter pertaining to God and	4986
	27:20	over half the tribe of **M**:	4985
	27:21	over the half-tribe of **M** in Gilead:	4985
2Ch	15: 9	**M** and Simeon who had settled	4985
	30: 1	and also wrote letters to Ephraim and **M**,	4985
	30:10	from town to town in Ephraim and **M**,	4985
	30:11	**M** and Zebulun humbled themselves	4985
	30:18	**M**, Issachar and Zebulun had	4985
	31: 1	and Benjamin and in Ephraim and **M**.	4985
	32:33	And **M** his son succeeded him as king.	4985
	33: 1	**M** was twelve years old when he became	4985
	33: 9	But **M** led Judah and the people of	4985
	33:10	The LORD spoke to **M** and his people,	4985
	33:11	king of Assyria, who took **M** prisoner,	4985

2Ch	33:13	Then **M** knew that the LORD is God.	4985
	33:20	**M** rested with his fathers and was buried	4985
	33:22	as his father **M** had done.	4985
	33:22	to all the idols **M** had made.	4985
	33:23	But unlike his father **M**,	4985
	34: 6	In the towns of **M**, Ephraim and Simeon,	4985
	34: 9	from the people of **M**,	4985
Ezr	10:30	Mattaniah, Bezalel, Binnui and **M**.	4985
	10:33	Zabad, Eliphelet, Jeremai, **M** and Shimei.	4985
Ps	60: 7	Gilead is mine, and **M** is mine;	4985
	80: 2	before Ephraim, Benjamin and **M**.	4985
	108: 8	Gilead is mine, **M** is mine;	4985
Isa	9:21	**M** will feed on Ephraim, and Ephraim	4985
	9:21	and Ephraim on **M**;	4985
Jer	15: 4	because of what **M** son of Hezekiah king	4985
Eze	48: 4	"**M** will have one portion;	4985
	48: 5	it will border the territory of **M** from east	4985
Mt	1:10	Hezekiah the father of **M**,	3442
	1:10	**M** the father of Amon,	3442
Rev	7: 6	from the tribe of **M** 12,000,	3442

MANASSEH'S (6) [MANASSEH]

Ge	48:14	he put his left hand on **M** head,	4985
	48:17	to move it from Ephraim's head to **M** head.	4985
Jos	17: 1	that is, for Makir, **M** firstborn.	4985
	17: 5	**M** share consisted of ten tracts	4985
2Ki	21:17	As for the other events of **M** reign,	4985
2Ch	33:18	The other events of **M** reign,	4985

MANASSES (KJV) See MANASSEH

MANASSITES (3) [MANASSEH]

Dt	4:43	and Golan in Bashan, for the **M**.	4986
Jos	16: 9	within the inheritance of the **M**.	1201+4985
	17:12	the **M** were not able to occupy these towns,	1201+4985

MANDRAKE (1) [MANDRAKES]

Ge	30:14	into the fields and found some **m** plants,	1859

MANDRAKES (5) [MANDRAKE]

Ge	30:14	"Please give me some of your son's **m**."	1859
	30:15	Will you take my son's **m** too?"	1859
	30:15	with you tonight in return for your son's **m**.	1859
	30:16	"I have hired you with my son's **m**."	1859
SS	7:13	The **m** send out their fragrance,	1859

MANE (1)

Job	39:19	or clothe his neck with a **flowing m**?	8310

MANEH (KJV) See MINAH

MANGER (6)

Job	39: 9	Will he stay by your **m** at night?	17
Pr	14: 4	Where there are no oxen, the **m** is empty,	17
Isa	1: 3	the donkey his owner's **m**,	17
Lk	2: 7	in cloths and placed him in a **m**,	5764
	2:12	a baby wrapped in cloths and lying in a **m**."	5764
	2:16	and the baby, who was lying in the **m**.	5764

MANGLED (1) [MANGLES]

La	3:11	the path and **m** me and left me without help.	7318

MANGLES (1) [MANGLED]

Mic	5: 8	which mauls and **m** as it goes,	3271

MANHOOD (2) [MAN]

Ps	78:51	the firstfruits of **m** in the tents of Ham.	226
	105:36	the firstfruits of all their **m**.	226

MANIAC (1)

Hos	9: 7	the inspired man a **m**.	8713

MANIFESTATION (1)

1Co	12: 7	Now to each one the **m** of the Spirit is given	5748

MANIFOLD (1)

Eph	3:10	**m** wisdom of God should be made known	4497

MANKIND (36) [MAN]

Ge	6: 7	So the LORD said, "I will wipe **m**,	132
	7:21	that swarm over the earth, and all **m**.	132
Nu	16:22	"O God, God of the spirits of all **m**,	1414
	27:16	the God of the spirits of all **m**,	1414
Dt	32: 8	when he divided all **m**,	132+1201
	32:26	and blot out their memory from **m**,	632
Job	12:10	every creature and the breath of all **m**.	408+1414
	34:15	all **m** would perish together	1414
	36:25	All **m** has seen it; men gaze on it from afar.	132
	36:28	and abundant showers fall on **m**.	132
Ps	21:10	their posterity from **m**.	132+1201
	33:13	the LORD looks down and sees all **m**;	132+1201
	64: 9	All **m** will fear;	132
Pr	8: 4	I raise my voice to **all m**.	132+1201
	8:31	in his whole world and delighting in **m**.	132+1201
	30:14	the needy from among **m**.	132
Ecc	7:29	God made **m** upright, but men have gone	132

Isa	2: 9	man will be brought low and **m** humbled—	408
	5:15	man will be brought low and **m** humbled,	408
	38:11	no longer will I look on **m**,	132
	40: 5	and all **m** together will see it.	1414
	45:12	It is I who made the earth and created **m**	132
	49:26	Then all **m** will know that I, the LORD,	1414
	66:23	all **m** will come and bow down before me,"	1414
	66:24	and they will be loathsome to all **m**."	1414
Jer	25:31	on all **m** and put the wicked to the sword,' "	1414
	32:20	both in Israel and among all **m**,	132
Da	2:38	I am the LORD, the God of all **m**,	1414
	2:38	in your hands he has placed **m** and	10050+10120
Joel	1:12	Surely the joy of **m** is withered away.	132+1201
Mic	5: 7	do not wait for man or linger for **m**.	132+1201
Zec	2:13	Be still before the LORD, all **m**,	1414
Lk	3: 6	And all **m** will see God's salvation.' "	4922
Rev	9:15	and year were released to kill a third *of* **m**.	476
	9:18	A third *of* **m** was killed by the three plagues	476
	9:20	The rest *of* **m** that were not killed	476

MANNA (20)

Ex	16:31	The people of Israel called the bread **m**.	4942
	16:32	omer of **m** and keep it for the generations	5647S
	16:33	"Take a jar and put an omer of **m** in it.	4942
	16:34	Aaron put the **m** in front of the Testimony,	2084S
	16:35	The Israelites ate **m** forty years,	4942
	16:35	they ate **m** until they reached the border	4942
Nu	11: 6	we never see anything but this **m**!"	4942
	11: 7	The **m** was like coriander seed and looked	4942
	11: 9	the **m** also came down.	4942
Dt	8: 3	to hunger and then feeding you with **m**,	4942
	8:16	He gave you **m** to eat in the desert,	4942
Jos	5:12	The **m** stopped the day after they ate	4942
	5:12	there was no longer any **m** for the Israelites,	4942
Ne	9:20	not withhold your **m** from their mouths,	4942
Ps	78:24	he rained down **m** for the people to eat,	4942
Jn	6:31	Our forefathers ate the **m** in the desert;	3445
	6:49	Your forefathers ate the **m** in the desert,	3445
	6:58	Your forefathers ate **m** and died,	3445
Heb	9: 4	This ark contained the gold jar of **m**,	3445
Rev	2:17	I will give some of the hidden **m**.	3445

MANNED (2) [MAN]

2Ch	9:21	a fleet of trading ships **m** by Hiram's men.	6640
Eze	27:11	Men of Arvad and Helech **m** your walls	6584

MANNER (7)

Nu	15:11	is to be prepared **in this m**.	3970
Jos	6:15	around the city seven times in the same **m**,	5477
1Ki	21:26	**behaved in the vilest m** by going	4394+9493
1Co	11:27	of the Lord in an **unworthy m** will be guilty	397
2Co	1:17	Or do I make my plans in a **worldly m** so	4922
Php	1:27	**conduct yourselves in a m** worthy of	4488
3Jn	1: 6	to send them on their way **in a m** worthy	545

MANOAH (15)

Jdg	13: 2	A certain man of Zorah, named **M**,	4956
	13: 8	Then **M** prayed to the LORD:	4956
	13: 9	God heard **M**, and the angel	4956
	13: 9	but her husband **M** was not with her.	4956
	13:11	**M** got up and followed his wife.	4956
	13:12	So **M** asked him, "When your words	4956
	13:15	**M** said to the angel of the LORD,	4956
	13:16	(**M** did not realize that it was the angel of	4956
	13:17	**M** inquired of the angel of the LORD,	4956
	13:19	Then **M** took a young goat,	4956
	13:19	the LORD did an amazing thing while **M**	4956
	13:20	**M** and his wife fell with their faces to	4956
	13:21	not show himself again to **M** and his wife,	4956
	13:21	**M** realized that it was the angel of	4956
	16:31	and Eshtaol in the tomb of **M** his father.	4956

MANSERVANT (8) [SERVANT]

Ex	20:10	nor your **m** or maidservant,	6269
	20:17	or his **m** or maidservant, his ox or donkey,	6269
	21:26	"If a man hits a **m** or maidservant in the eye	6269
	21:27	And if he knocks out the tooth of a **m**	6269
Lev	25: 6	for yourself, your **m** and maidservant,	6269
Dt	5:14	nor your **m** or maidservant, nor your ox,	6269
	5:14	so that your **m** and maidservant may rest,	6269
	5:21	his **m** or maidservant, his ox or donkey,	6269

MANSIONS (4)

Ps	49:14	far from their **princely m**.	2292
Isa	5: 9	the fine **m** left without occupants.	NIH
Am	3:15	and the **m** will be demolished,"	1074+8041
	5:11	Therefore, though you have built stone **m**,	1074

MANSLAYER, MANSLAYER (KJV) See ACCUSED OF MURDER, WHO HAS KILLED

MANTLE (1) [MANTLED]

Ps	89:45	*you have* **covered** him **with a m** of shame.	6486

MANTLED (1) [MANTLE]

Ps	65:13	with flocks and the valleys *are* **m**	6493

MANURE (3)

Isa	25:10	as straw is trampled down in the **m**.	4523

Eze	4:15	over cow **m** instead of human excrement."	7616
Lk	14:35	for the soil nor for the **m** pile;	3161

MANY (517)

Ge	17: 4	You will be the father of **m** nations.	2162
	17: 5	for I have made you a father of **m** nations.	2162
	26:14	He had **so m** flocks and herds and servants	8041
	37:34	and mourned for his son **m** days.	8041
	50:20	the saving of **m** lives.	8041
Ex	12:38	**M** other people went up with them,	8041
	19:21	to see the LORD and **m** of them perish.	8041
Lev	11:42	or walks on all fours or on **m** feet;	8049
	15:25	a discharge of blood for **m** days at	8041
	25:16	When the years are **m**, you are to increase	8044
	25:51	If **m** years remain, he must pay for his	8041
Nu	13:18	who live here are strong or weak, few or **m**.	8041
	15:12	for as **m** as you prepare.	5031
	20:15	and we lived there **m** years.	8041
	21: 6	they bit the people and **m** Israelites died.	8041
	22: 3	because there were so **m** people.	8041
	35: 8	**Take m** towns from a tribe that has many,	8049
	35: 8	Take many towns from a tribe that has **m**,	8041
Dt	1:10	so that today you are as **m** as the stars in	8044
	1:46	And so you stayed in Kadesh **m** days—	8041
	3: 5	there were also a great **m** unwalled villages.	2221
	7: 1	and drives out before you **m** nations—	8041
	11:21	and the days of your children *may be* **m** in	8049
	11:21	**as m** as the days that the heavens are above	3869
	15: 6	to **m** nations but will borrow from none.	8041
	15: 6	over **m** nations but none will rule over you.	8041
	17:17	*He must* not **take m** wives,	8049
	28:12	You will lend to **m** nations but will borrow	8041
	30:20	he will give you **m** years in the land	802+3427
	31:17	**M** disasters and difficulties will come	8041
	31:21	And when **m** disasters and difficulties come	8041
Jos	24: 3	and **gave** him **m** descendants.	8049
Jdg	7: 2	"You have too **m** men for me	8041
	7: 4	"There are still too **m** men.	8041
	8:30	for he had **m** wives.	8041
	9:40	and **m** fell wounded in the flight—	8041
	15: 8	and slaughtered **m** of them.	1524
	16:30	Thus he killed **m** more when he died than	8041
1Sa	2: 5	but *she who has had* **m** sons pines away.	8041
	3: 1	there were not **m** visions.	7287
	14: 6	whether by **m** or by few."	8041
	25:10	**M** servants are breaking away	8045
	31: 1	and **m** fell slain on Mount Gilboa.	AIT
2Sa	1: 4	**M** of them fell and died.	2221
	13:34	and saw **m** people on the road west of him,	8041
	14: 2	a woman who has spent **m** days grieving for	8041
	19:34	"How **m** more years will I live,	3869+4537
	24: 2	so that I may know how **m** there are."	5031
1Ki	7:47	because there were so **m**;	8044
	8: 5	sacrificing so **m** sheep and cattle	4946+8044
	10:10	Never again were so **m** spices brought	4200+8044
	11: 1	Solomon loved **m** foreign women besides Pharaoh's daughter—	8041
	18:25	since there are so **m** of you.	8041
	22:16	"How **m** times must I make you swear	3869+4537+6330
2Ki	19:23	"With my **m** chariots I have ascended	8044
1Ch	4:27	but his brothers did not have **m** children;	8041
	5:22	and *others* fell slain,	8041
	7: 4	for *they* **had m** wives and children.	8049
	7:22	Ephraim mourned for them **m** days,	8041
	8:40	*They* **had m** sons and grandsons—150 in all	8049
	10: 1	and *m* fell slain on Mount Gilboa.	AIT
	21: 2	to me so that I may know how **m** there are."	5031
	22: 8	and have fought **m** wars.	1524
	22:15	You have **m** workmen:	4200+8044
	23:11	but Jeush and Beriah *did* not **have m** sons;	8049
	28: 5	and the LORD has given me **m**—	8041
2Ch	5: 6	sacrificing so **m** sheep and cattle	4946+8044
	11:23	and took **m** wives for them.	2162
	18: 2	Ahab slaughtered **m** sheep,and cattle	4200+8044
	18:15	"How **m** times must I make you swear	3869+4537+6330
	21: 3	Their father had given them **m** gifts of silver	8041
	24:27	the **m** prophecies about him,	8044
	26:10	in the desert and dug **m** cisterns,	8041
	28: 5	The Arameans defeated him and took **m**	1524
	30:17	Since **m** in the crowd had	8041
	30:18	Although most of the **m** people who came	8041
	32:23	**M** brought offerings to Jerusalem for	8041
Ezr	3:12	But **m** of the older priests and Levites	8041
	3:12	while *others* shouted for joy.	8041
	5:11	the temple that was built **m** years ago,	10678
	10:13	But there are **m** people here and it is	8041
Ne	6:17	of Judah *were* sending **m** letters to Tobiah,	8049
	6:18	For **m** in Judah were under oath to him,	8041
	9:30	For **m** years you were patient with them,	8041
	13:26	the **m** nations there was no king like him.	8041
Est	2: 8	**m** girls were brought to the citadel of Susa	8041
	4: 3	**M** lay in sackcloth and ashes.	8041
	5:11	to them about his vast wealth, his **m** sons,	8044
	8:17	And **m** *people* of other nationalities	8041
	10: 3	held in high esteem by his **m** fellow Jews,	8044
Job	4: 3	Think how you have instructed **m**,	8041
	5:25	You will know that your children will be **m**,	8041
	11:19	and **m** will court your favor.	8041
	13:23	**How m** wrongs and sins have I	3869+4537
	16: 2	"I have heard **m** *things* like these;	8041
	23:14	and **m** such plans he still has in store.	8041
	27:14	**m** his children, their fate is the sword;	8049
	35: 6	your sins are **m**, what does that do to him?	8045
	38:21	You have lived so **m** years!	5031+8041

Ps	3: 1	O LORD, how **m** *are* my foes!	8045
	3: 1	How **m** rise up against me!	8041
	3: 2	**M** are saying of me, "God will not deliver	8041
	4: 6	**M** are asking, "Who can show us any good?"	8045
	5:10	Banish them for their **m** sins.	8044
	22:12	**M** bulls surround me;	8041
	31:13	For I hear the slander of **m**;	8041
	32:10	**M** are the woes of the wicked,	8041
	34:12	and desires to see *m* good days,	AIT
	34:19	A righteous man may have **m** troubles,	8041
	37:16	the wealth of **m** wicked;	8041
	38:19	**M** *are* those who are my vigorous enemies;	6793
	40: 3	**M** will see and fear and put their trust in	8041
	40: 5	**M**, O LORD my God,	8041
	40: 5	*they would be* too **m** to declare.	6793
	55:18	even though **m** oppose me.	8041
	56: 2	**m** are attacking me in their pride.	8041
	61: 6	his years for **m** generations.	1887+1887+2256
	69: 4	*m are* my enemies without cause,	6793
	71: 7	I have become like a portent to **m**,	8041
	71:20	**m** and bitter, you will restore my life again;	8041
	90:15	for **as m** days as you have afflicted us,	3869
	90:15	for **as m** years as we have seen trouble.	NIH
	104:24	How **m** *are* your works, O LORD!	8045
	106: 7	they did not remember your **m** kindnesses,	8044
	106:43	**M** times he delivered them,	8041
	119:157	**M** are the foes who persecute me,	8041
	135:10	down **m** nations and killed mighty kings—	8041
Pr	3: 2	for they will prolong your life **m** years	2256+3427+9102
	4:10	and the years of your life *will be* **m**.	8049
	7:26	**M** are the victims she has brought down;	8041
	9:11	For through me your days will be **m**,	8049
	10:19	When words are **m**, sin is not absent,	8044
	10:21	The lips of the righteous nourish **m**,	8041
	11:14	but **m** advisers make victory sure.	8044
	14:20	but the rich have **m** friends.	8044
	15:22	but with **m** advisers they succeed.	8044
	18:24	A man of *m* **companions** may come to ruin,	AIT
	19: 4	Wealth brings **m** friends,	8041
	19: 6	**M** curry favor with a ruler,	8041
	19:21	**M** are the plans in a man's heart,	8041
	20: 6	**M** a man claims to have unfailing love,	8044
	24: 6	and for victory **m** advisers.	8044
	28: 2	a country is rebellious, it has **m** rulers,	8041
	28:27	to them receives **m** curses.	8041
	29: 1	after **m** rebukes will suddenly	NIH
	29:22	and a hot-tempered one commits **m** sins.	8041
	29:26	**M** seek an audience with a ruler,	8041
	31:29	"M women do noble things,	8041
Ecc	5: 3	As a dream comes when there are **m** cares,	8044
	5: 3	speech of a fool when there are **m** words.	8044
	5: 7	and **m** words are meaningless.	2221
	6: 3	a hundred children and live **m** years;	8041
	7:22	**m** times you yourself have cursed others.	8041
	7:29	men have gone in search of **m** schemes."	8041
	10: 6	Fools are put in **m** high positions,	8041
	11: 1	for after **m** days you will find it again.	8044
	11: 8	However **m** years a man may live,	2221
	11: 8	the days of darkness, for they will be **m**.	2221
	12: 9	and set in order **m** proverbs.	2221
	12:12	Of making **m** books there is no end,	2221
SS	8: 7	**M** waters cannot quench love;	8041
Isa	1:15	if *you* **offer m** prayers, I will not listen.	8049
	2: 3	**M** peoples will come and say, "Come,	8041
	2: 4	and will settle disputes for **m** peoples.	8041
	8:15	**M** of them will stumble;	8041
	10: 7	to put an end to **m** nations.	4202+5071
	16:14	Moab's splendor and all her **m** people will	8041
	17:12	Oh, the raging of **m** nations—	8041
	22: 9	of David *had* **m** breaches in its defenses;	8045
	23:16	play the harp well, sing **m** a song,	8049
	24:22	up in prison and be punished after **m** days.	8044
	29: 5	your **m** enemies will become like fine dust,	2162
	37:24	'With my **m** chariots I have ascended	8044
	41:15	new and sharp, with **m** teeth.	7092
	42:20	You have seen **m** *things*,	8041
	47: 9	in spite of your **m** sorceries	8044
	47:12	and with your **m** sorceries	8044
	51: 2	and I blessed him and **made** him **m**.	8049
	52:14	Just as there were **m** who were appalled	8041
	52:15	so will he sprinkle **m** nations,	8041
	53:11	by his knowledge my righteous servant will justify **m**,	8041
	53:12	For he bore the sin of **m**,	8041
	59:12	For our offenses *are* **m** in your sight,	8045
	63: 7	the **m** good things he has done for the house	8041
	63: 7	to his compassion and **m** kindnesses.	8044
	66:16	and **m** *will be* those slain by the LORD.	8045
Jer	2:28	For you have as **m** gods as you have towns,	5031
	3: 1	as a prostitute with **m** lovers—	8041
	5: 6	and their backslidings **m**.	6793
	11:13	You have as **m** gods as you have towns,	5031
	11:13	to that shameful god Baal as **m** as	5031
	11:15	as she works out her evil schemes with **m**?	8041
	12:10	**M** shepherds will ruin my vineyard	8041
	13: 6	**M** days later the LORD said to me,	8041
	13:22	it is because of your **m** sins	8044
	16:16	"But now I will send for **m** fishermen,	8041
	16:16	After that I will send for **m** hunters,	8041
	20:10	I hear **m** whispering, "Terror on every side!	8041
	22: 8	from **m** nations will pass by this city	8041
	25:14	be enslaved by **m** nations and great kings;	8041
	27: 7	**m** nations and great kings will subjugate	8041
	28: 8	against **m** countries and great kingdoms.	8041
	30:14	your guilt is so great and your sins so **m**.	6793

Jer	30:15	and m sins I have done these things to you.	6793
	36:32	And m similar words were added to them.	8041
	42: 2	as you now see, though we were once m,	2221
	50:41	a great nation and m kings are being stirred	8041
	51:13	You who live by m waters and are rich	8041
La	1: 5	because of her m sins.	8044
	1:22	My groans are m and my heart is faint."	8041
Eze	3: 6	not to m peoples of obscure speech	8041
	11: 6	*You have* killed m people in this city	8049
	12:27	The vision he sees is for m years from now,	8041
	16:41	on you in the sight of m women.	8041
	17: 9	not take a strong arm or m people to pull it	8041
	17:17	and siege works erected to destroy m lives.	8041
	19:11	for its height and for its m branches.	8044
	21:15	So that hearts may melt and the fallen *be* m,	8049
	22:25	and precious things and make m widows	8049
	26: 3	and I will bring m nations against you,	8041
	26:10	be so m that they will cover you with dust.	9180
	27: 3	merchant of peoples on m coasts,	8041
	27:15	and m coastlands were your customers;	8041
	27:16	with you because of your m products;	8044
	27:16	of your m products and great wealth	8044
	27:33	you satisfied m nations;	8041
	28:18	By your m sins and dishonest trade	8044
	32: 9	I will trouble the hearts of m peoples	8041
	32:10	I will cause m peoples to be appalled at you,	8041
	33:24	But we are m; surely the land has been	8044
	37: 2	a great m bones on the floor of the valley,	8041
	38: 6	the m nations with you.	8041
	38: 8	After m days you will be called to arms.	8041
	38: 8	whose people were gathered from m nations	8041
	38: 9	You and all your troops and the m nations	8041
	38:15	you and m nations with you,	8041
	38:22	and on his troops and on the m nations	8041
	38:23	in the sight of m nations.	8041
	39:27	through them in the sight of m nations.	8041
	47:10	The fish will be of m kinds—	4394+8041
Da	2:48	and lavished m gifts on him.	10647+10678
	8:25	he will destroy m and take his stand against	8041
	9:27	He will confirm a covenant with m	8041
	11:12	with pride and will slaughter m **thousands,**	8052
	11:14	"In those times m will rise against the king	8041
	11:18	to the coastlands and will take m of them,	8041
	11:26	and m will fall in battle.	8041
	11:33	"Those who are wise will instruct m,	8041
	11:34	and m who are not sincere will join them.	8041
	11:39	over m *people* and will distribute the land at	8041
	11:40	He will invade *m* **countries** and sweep	AIT
	11:41	M *countries* will fall, but Edom,	8041
	11:42	He will extend his power over *m* **countries;**	AIT
	11:44	in a great rage to destroy and annihilate m.	8041
	12: 3	and those who lead m to righteousness,	8041
	12: 4	M will go here and there	8041
	12:10	M will be purified, made spotless and	8041
Hos	3: 3	I told her, "You are to live with me m days;	8041
	3: 4	the Israelites will live m days without king	8041
	8:11	Ephraim **built** m altars for sin offerings,	8049
	8:12	I wrote for them the m *things of* my law,	8044
	8:14	Judah *has* fortified m towns.	8049
	9: 7	Because your sins are so m	8044
	10: 4	*They* **make** m **promises,** take false	1819+1821
	10:13	and on your m warriors,	8044
	12:10	**gave** them m visions and told parables	8049
Am	4: 9	"M times I struck your gardens	8049
	5:12	For I know how m are your offenses and	8041
	8: 3	M, many bodies—flung everywhere!	8041
	8: 3	Many, m bodies—flung everywhere!	NIH
Jnh	4:11	and m cattle as well.	8041
Mic	2: 2	M nations will come and say, "Come,	8041
	4: 3	between m peoples and will settle disputes	8041
	4:11	now m nations are gathered against you.	8041
	4:13	and you will break to pieces m nations."	8041
	5: 7	be in the midst of m peoples like dew from	8041
	5: 8	in the midst of m peoples,	8041
Na	3: 3	M casualties, piles of dead,	8044
Hab	2: 8	Because you have plundered m nations,	8041
	2:10	You have plotted the ruin of m peoples,	8041
	3: 9	you called for m arrows.	8679
Zec	2:11	"M nations will be joined with the LORD	3869+4537
	7: 3	as I have done for so m years?"	
	8:20	"M peoples and the inhabitants	NIH
	8:20	the inhabitants of m cities will yet come,	8041
	8:22	And m peoples and powerful nations will come to Jerusalem	8041
Mal	2: 6	and turned m from sin.	8041
	2: 8	by your teaching have caused m to stumble;	8041
Mt	3: 7	But when he saw m of the Pharisees	4498
	6: 7	be heard because of their m **words.**	4494
	7:13	leads to destruction, and m enter through it.	4498
	7:22	M will say to me on that day, 'Lord, Lord,	4498
	7:22	and perform m miracles?'	4498
	8:11	that m will come from the east and the west,	4498
	8:16	the who were demon-possessed were brought	4498
	9:10	m tax collectors and "sinners" came and ate	4498
	10:31	you are worth more than m sparrows.	4498
	12:15	M followed him, and he healed all their sick	4498
	13: 3	he told them m *things* in parables, saying:	4498
	13:17	m prophets and righteous men longed	4498
	13:58	And he did not do m miracles there because	4498
	15:30	the crippled, the mute and m others,	4498
	15:34	"How m loaves do you have?"	4531
	16: 9	and how m basketfuls you gathered?	4531
	16:10	and how m basketfuls you gathered?	4531
	16:21	to Jerusalem and suffer m *things* at	4498
	18:21	how m times shall I forgive my brother	4529
	19:30	But m who are first will be last,	4498
	19:30	and m who are last will be first.	NIG

Mt	20:28	and to give his life as a ransom for m."	4498
	22:14	"For m are invited, but few are chosen."	4498
	24: 5	For m will come in my name, claiming,	4498
	24: 5	'I am the Christ,' and will deceive m.	4498
	24:10	At that time m will turn away from the faith	4498
	24:11	and m false prophets will appear	4498
	24:11	and deceive m *people.*	4498
	25:21	I will put you in charge of m *things.*	4498
	25:23	I will put you in charge of m *things.*	4498
	26:28	for m for the forgiveness of sins.	4498
	26:60	though m false witnesses came forward.	4498
	27:52	of m holy people who had died were raised	NIG
	27:53	the holy city and appeared *to* m people.	4498
	27:55	M women were there, watching from a	4498
Mk	1:34	Jesus healed m who had various diseases.	4498
	1:34	He also drove out m demons,	4498
	2: 2	So m gathered that there was no room left,	4498
	2:15	m tax collectors and "sinners" were eating	4498
	2:15	for there were m who followed him.	4498
	3: 8	m people came to him from Judea,	4498
	3:10	For he had healed m,	4498
	4: 2	He taught them m *things* by parables,	4498
	4:33	*With* m similar parables Jesus spoke	4498
	5: 9	Legion," he replied, "for we are m."	4498
	5:26	a great deal under the care *of* m doctors	4498
	6: 2	and m who heard him were amazed.	4498
	6:13	They drove out m demons	4498
	6:13	and anointed m sick people with oil	4498
	6:31	because so m *people* were coming and	4498
	6:33	and m who saw them leaving recognized them	4498
	6:34	So he began teaching them m *things.*	4498
	6:38	"How m loaves do you have?"	4531
	7: 4	And they observe m other traditions,	4498
	7:13	And you do m *things* like that."	4498
	8: 5	"How m loaves do you have?"	4531
	8:19	for the five thousand, how m basketfuls	4531
	8:20	for the four thousand, how m basketfuls	4531
	8:31	that the Son of Man must suffer m *things*	4498
	9:26	so much like a corpse that m said,	4498
	10:31	But m who are first will be last,	4498
	10:45	and to give his life as a ransom for m."	4498
	10:48	M rebuked him and told him to be quiet,	4498
	11: 8	M *people* spread their cloaks on the road,	4498
	12: 5	He sent m others; some of them they beat,	4498
	12:41	M rich people threw in large amounts.	4498
	13: 6	M will come in my name, claiming,	4498
	13: 6	claiming, 'I am he,' and will deceive m.	4498
	14:24	which is poured out for m," he said to them.	4498
	14:56	M testified falsely against him,	4498
	15: 3	The chief priests accused him of m *things.*	4498
	15: 4	See how m *things* they are accusing you of.	4531
	15:41	M other *women* who had come up with him	4498
Lk	1: 1	M have undertaken to draw up an account	4498
	1:14	and m will rejoice because of his birth.	4498
	1:16	M of the people of Israel will he bring back	4498
	2:34	The falling and rising of m in Israel,	4498
	2:35	the thoughts of m hearts will be revealed.	4498
	3:18	And with m other words John exhorted	4498
	4:25	I assure you that there were m widows	4498
	4:27	And there were m in Israel with leprosy in	4498
	4:41	Moreover, demons came out of m *people,*	4498
	7:21	very time Jesus cured m who had diseases,	4498
	7:21	and gave sight *to* m who were blind.	4498
	7:47	I tell you, her m sins have been forgiven—	4498
	8: 3	Susanna; and m others.	4498
	8:29	M times it had seized him,	4498
	8:30	because m demons had gone into him.	4498
	9:22	"The Son of Man must suffer m *things* and	4498
	10:24	that m prophets and kings wanted	4498
	10:41	"you are worried and upset about m *things,*	4498
	12: 1	a crowd *of* m **thousands** had gathered,	3689
	12: 7	you are worth more than m sparrows.	4498
	12:19	of good things laid up for m years.	4498
	12:47	be beaten with m blows.	4498
	13:24	because m, I tell you, will try to enter	4498
	14:16	a great banquet and invited m guests.	4498
	15:17	'How m of my father's hired men have food	4531
	17:25	But first he must suffer m *things* and	4498
	18:30	to receive m **times as much** in this age and,	4491
	21: 8	For m will come in my name, claiming,	4498
	22:65	they said m other insulting *things* to him.	4498
	23: 9	He plied him with m questions,	2653
Jn	2:23	at the Passover Feast, m *people* saw	4498
	4:39	M of the Samaritans from that town	4498
	4:41	of his words m more became believers.	4498
	6: 9	but how far will they go among so m?"	5537
	6:60	On hearing it, m of his disciples said,	4498
	6:66	From this time m of his disciples turned	4498
	7:31	Still, m in the crowd put their faith in him.	4498
	8:30	Even as he spoke, m put their faith in him.	4498
	10:20	M of them said, "He is demon-possessed	4498
	10:32	"I have shown you m great miracles from	4498
	10:41	and m people came to him.	4498
	10:42	And in that place m believed in Jesus.	4498
	11:19	and m Jews had come to Martha and Mary	4498
	11:45	m of the Jews who had come to visit Mary,	4498
	11:47	"Here is this man performing m miraculous signs.	4498
	11:55	m went up from the country to Jerusalem	4498
	12:11	on account of him m of the Jews were going	4498
	12:18	M people, because they had heard	4063
	12:24	But if it dies, it produces m seeds.	4498
	12:42	Yet at the same time m even among	4498
	14: 2	In my Father's house are m rooms;	4498
	19:20	M of the Jews read this sign,	4498
	20:30	Jesus did m other miraculous signs in	4498
	21:11	but even with so m the net was not torn.	5537

Jn	21:25	Jesus did m other things as well.	4498
Ac	1: 3	to these men and gave m convincing proofs	4498
	2:40	With m other words he warned them;	4498
	2:43	and m wonders and miraculous signs	4498
	3:24	as m as have spoken,	4012
	4: 4	But m who heard the message believed,	4498
	5:12	The apostles performed m miraculous signs	4498
	8: 7	With shrieks, evil spirits came out of m,	4498
	8: 7	and m paralytics and cripples were healed.	4498
	8:25	preaching the gospel in m Samaritan	4498
	9:13	"I have heard m reports about this man	4498
	9:23	After m days had gone by,	2653
	9:42	and m *people* believed in the Lord.	4498
	12:12	m people had gathered and were praying,	2653
	13:31	and for m days he was seen	4498
	13:43	m of the Jews and devout converts	4498
	14:22	"We must go through m hardships to enter	4498
	15:35	and m others taught and preached the word	4498
	16:18	She kept this up for m days.	4498
	17:12	M of the Jews believed, as did also	4498
	17:12	Greek women and m Greek men.	3900+4024
	18: 8	and m of the Corinthians who heard him	4498
	18:10	because I have m people in this city."	4498
	20: 2	speaking m words of encouragement to	4498
	20: 8	There were m lamps in the upstairs room	2653
	21:20	**how** m thousands of Jews have believed,	4531
	25: 7	bringing m serious charges against him,	4498
	25:14	Since they were spending m days there,	4498
	26:10	On the authority of the chief priests I put m	4498
	26:11	M **a time** I went from one synagogue	4490
	27: 7	We made slow headway for m days	2653
	27:20	for m days and the storm continued raging,	4498
	28:10	in m ways and when we were ready to sail,	4498
Ro	1:13	that I planned m **times** to come to you	4490
	4:17	"I have made you a father *of* m nations."	4498
	4:18	and so became the father *of* m nations,	4498
	5:15	if the m died by the trespass of the one man,	4498
	5:15	Jesus Christ, overflow to the m!	4498
	5:16	but the gift followed m trespasses	4498
	5:19	of the one man the m were made sinners,	4498
	5:19	the one man the m will be made righteous.	4498
	8:29	be the firstborn among m brothers.	4498
	12: 4	of us has one body with m members,	4498
	12: 5	so in Christ we who are m form one body,	4498
	15:23	I have been longing for m years to see you,	4498
	16: 2	for she has been a great help *to* m people,	4498
1Co	1:26	Not m of you were wise	4498
	1:26	not m were influential;	4498
	1:26	not m were of noble birth.	4498
	4:15	you do not have m fathers,	4498
	7:28	But those who marry will face m troubles	NIG
	8: 5	or on earth (as indeed there are m "gods"	4498
	8: 5	there are many "gods" and m "lords",	4498
	9:19	to win as m as possible.	4498
	10:17	Because there is one loaf, we, who are m,	4498
	10:33	seeking my own good but the good *of* m,	4498
	11:30	That is why m among you are weak	4498
	12:12	though it is made up of m parts;	4498
	12:12	all its parts are m, they form one body.	4498
	12:14	not made up of one part but of m.	4498
	12:20	As it is, there are m parts, but one body.	4498
	16: 9	and there are m who oppose me.	4498
2Co	1:11	Then m will give thanks on our behalf for	4498
	1:11	in answer to the prayers of m.	4498
	1:20	no matter **how** m promises God has made,	4012
	2: 4	and anguish of heart and with m tears,	4498
	2:17	so m, we do not peddle the word of God	4498
	6:10	poor, yet making m rich;	4498
	8:22	to us in m ways that he is zealous,	4498
	9:12	also overflowing in m expressions of thanks	4498
	11:18	m are boasting in the way the world does,	4498
	12:21	be grieved over m who have sinned earlier	4498
Gal	1:14	I was advancing in Judaism beyond m Jews	4498
	3:16	meaning m *people,* but "and to your seed,"	4498
Php	3:18	m live as enemies of the cross of Christ.	4498
1Ti	6: 9	and into m foolish and harmful desires	4498
	6:10	and pierced themselves with m griefs.	4498
	6:12	in the presence of m witnesses.	4498
2Ti	1:18	in **how** m *ways* he helped me in Ephesus.	4012
	2: 2	in the presence of m witnesses entrust	4498
Tit	1:10	For there are m rebellious people,	4498
Heb	1: 1	prophets at m times and in various ways,	4495
	1:10	In bringing m sons to glory,	4498
	6:14	and give you m **descendants."**	4437+4437
	7:23	Now there have been m of those priests,	4498
	9:26	to suffer m times since the creation of	4490
	9:28	to take away the sins of m *people;*	4498
	12:15	up to cause trouble and defile m.	4498
Jas	1: 2	whenever you face trials of m **kinds,**	4476
	3: 1	m of you should presume to be teachers,	4498
	3: 2	We all stumble in m *ways.*	4498
2Pe	2: 2	M will follow their shameful ways	4498
1Jn	2:18	even now m antichrists have come,	4498
	4: 1	because m false prophets have gone out into	4498
2Jn	1: 7	M deceivers, who do not acknowledge	4498
Rev	5:11	I looked and heard the voice of m angels,	4498
	8:11	and m people died from the waters	4498
	9: 9	*of* m horses and chariots rushing into battle.	4498
	10:11	"You must prophesy again about m peoples,	4498
	17: 1	the great prostitute, who sits on m waters.	4498
	19:12	and on his head are m crowns.	4498

MAOCH (1)

1Sa	27: 2	and went over to Achish son of M king of	5059

MAON (8) [MAONITES]
Jos	15:55	M, Carmel, Ziph, Juttah,	5063
1Sa	23:24	David and his men were in the Desert of M,	5063
	23:25	to the rock and stayed in the Desert of M.	5063
	23:25	into the Desert of M in pursuit of David.	5063
	25: 1	David moved down into the Desert of M.	5063
	25: 2	A certain man in M,	5063
1Ch	2:45	The son of Shammai was M,	5062
	2:45	and M was the father of Beth Zur.	5062

MAONITES (1) [MAON]
Jdg	10:12	the M oppressed you and you cried to me	5062

MAP (1)
Jos	18: 8	As the men started on their way to m out	4180

MAR (KJV) See BREAK UP, CLIP OFF, DESTROYING, ENDANGER

MARA (1)
Ru	1:20	call me Naomi," she told them. "Call me M,	5259

MARAH (4)
Ex	15:23	When they came to M,	5288
	15:23	(That is why the place is called M.)	5288
Nu	33: 8	the Desert of Etham, they camped at M.	5288
	33: 9	They left M and went to Elim,	5288

MARALAH (1)
Jos	19:11	Going west it ran to M,	5339

MARANATHA (KJV) See COME O LORD

MARAUDERS (3) [MARAUDING]
Job	12: 6	The tents of m are undisturbed,	8720
	15:21	when all seems well, m attack him.	8720
Hos	6: 9	As m lie in ambush for a man,	1522

MARAUDING (1) [MARAUDERS]
Zec	9: 8	I will defend my house against m forces.	2256+6296+8740

MARBLE (5)
1Ch	29: 2	and all kinds of fine stone and m—	74+8880
Est	1: 6	to silver rings on m pillars.	9253
	1: 6	m, mother-of-pearl and other costly stones.	9253
SS	5:15	His legs are pillars of m set on bases	9253
Rev	18:12	costly wood, bronze, iron and m;	3454

MARCABOTH See BETH MARCABOTH

MARCH (24) [MARCHED, MARCHES, MARCHING]
Nu	10:28	the order of m for the Israelite divisions	5023
	20:18	if you try, we will m out and attack you	3655
Dt	20:10	When you m up to attack a city,	7928
Jos	6: 3	M around the city once with all	5938+6015
	6: 4	m around the city seven times,	6015
	6: 7	"Advance! M around the city,	6015
	10: 9	After an all-night m from Gilgal,	6590
Jdg	5:21	M on, my soul; be strong!	2005
2Sa	15:22	David said to Ittai, "Go ahead, m on."	6296
	18: 2	I myself will surely m out with you."	3655+3655
2Ki	3: 9	After a roundabout m of seven days,	2006
	18:25	to m against this country and destroy it.' "	6590
	24: 7	not m out from his own country again,	3655
2Ch	20:16	Tomorrow m down against them.	3718
	25: 7	not m with you, for the LORD is not	995
Isa	27: 4	I would m against them in battle;	7314
	36:10	to m against this country and destroy it.' "	6590
	42:13	The LORD will m out like a mighty man,	3655
Jer	46: 3	both large and small, and m out for battle!	5602
	46: 9	M on, O warriors—	3655
Da	11:11	of the South will m out in a rage and fight	3655
Joel	2: 7	They all m in line,	2143
Ob	1:13	not m through the gates of my people in	995
Zec	9:14	he will m in the storms of the south,	2143

MARCHED (45) [MARCH]
Ge	14: 8	Zoar) m out and drew up their battle lines	3655
Nu	21:23	He mustered his entire army and m out into	3655
	21:33	and his whole army m out to meet them	3655
	33: 3	They m out boldly in full view of all	3655
Dt	1:43	and in your arrogance you m up into	6590
	3: 1	with his whole army m out to meet us	3655
Jos	6: 9	The armed guard m ahead of	2143
	6:14	the second day they m around the city once	6015
	6:15	they got up at daybreak and m around	6015
	8:10	the leaders of Israel m before them to Ai.	6590
	8:11	The entire force that was with him m up	6590
	10: 7	So Joshua m up from Gilgal	6590
	15:15	From there he m against the people living	6590
Jdg	5: 4	when you m from the land of Edom,	7575
1Sa	29: 2	As the Philistine rulers m with their units	6296
2Sa	2:29	All that night Abner and his men m through	2143
	2:32	and his men m all night and arrived	2143
	5: 6	The king and his men m to Jerusalem.	2143

2Sa	15:18	All his men m past him,	3338+6296+6584
	15:18	from Gath m before the king.	6296
	15:22	So Ittai the Gittite m on with all his men	6296
	18: 4	the gate while all the men m out in units	3655
	18: 6	The army m into the field to fight Israel,	3655
	20: 7	They m out from Jerusalem	3655
1Ki	20:19	of the provincial commanders m out of	3655
	20:27	they m out to meet them.	2143
2Ki	6:24	and m up and laid siege to Samaria.	6590
	16: 5	of Israel m up to fight against Jerusalem	6590
	17: 5	m against Samaria and laid siege to it	6590
	18: 9	of Assyria m against Samaria and laid siege	6590
	23:29	King Josiah m out to meet him in battle,	2143
	25: 1	Nebuchadnezzar king of Babylon m	995
1Ch	11: 4	and all the Israelites m to Jerusalem (that is,	2143
2Ch	14: 9	Zerah the Cushite m out against them with	3655
	24:23	the army of Aram m against Joash;	6590
	35:20	and Josiah m out to meet him in battle.	6590
Job	18:14	of his tent and m off to the king of terrors.	7575
Ps	68: 7	O God, when you m through the wasteland,	7575
Isa	7: 1	of Israel m up to fight against Jerusalem,	6590
Jer	37: 5	Pharaoh's army had m out of Egypt,	3655
	37: 7	which has m out to support you,	3655
	39: 1	Nebuchadnezzar king of Babylon m	995
	52: 4	Nebuchadnezzar king of Babylon m	995
Heb	11:30	people had m around them for seven days.	3240
Rev	20: 9	They m across the breadth of the earth	326

MARCHES (5) [MARCH]
Joel	2: 8	each m straight ahead.	2143
Am	5: 3	"The city that m out a thousand strong	3655
	5: 3	the town that m out a hundred strong	3655
Mic	5: 5	When the Assyrian invades our land and m	2005
	5: 6	when he invades our land and m	2005

MARCHING (9) [MARCH]
Ex	14: 8	who were m out boldly.	3655
	14:10	and there were the Egyptians, m after them.	5825
Jos	6:13	m before the ark of the LORD and blowing	2143
1Sa	29: 2	and his men were m at the rear with Achish.	6296
2Sa	5:24	as you hear the sound of m in the tops of	7577
2Ki	19: 9	was m out to fight against him.	3655
1Ch	14:15	as you hear the sound of m in the tops of	7577
2Ch	11: 4	and turned back from m against Jeroboam.	2143
Isa	37: 9	was m out to fight against him.	3655

MARCUS (KJV) See MARK

MARDUK (1)
Jer	50: 2	be put to shame, M filled with terror.	5281

MARE (1)
SS	1: 9	to a m harnessed to one of the chariots	6063

MARESHAH (8)
Jos	15:44	Aczib and M—nine towns and their villages	5358
1Ch	2:42	who was the father of Ziph, and his son M,	5359
	4:21	the father of Lecah, Laadah the father of M	5359
2Ch	11: 8	Gath, M, Ziph,	5358
	14: 9	and came as far as M.	5358
	14:10	in the Valley of Zephathah near M.	5358
	20:37	Eliezer son of Dodavahu of M prophesied	5358
Mic	1:15	a conqueror against you who live in M.	5358

MARINERS (2) [MARITIME]
Eze	27:27	your m, seamen and shipwrights,	4876
	27:29	the m and all the seamen will stand on	4876

MARISHES (KJV) See MARSHES

MARITAL (4) [MARRY]
Ex	21:10	food, clothing and m rights.	6703
Mt	5:32	except for m unfaithfulness,	4518
	19: 9	except for m unfaithfulness,	4518
1Co	7: 3	The husband should fulfill his m duty	NIG

MARITIME (1) [MARINERS]
Ge	10: 5	(From these the m peoples spread out	362

MARK (30) [MARKED, MARKER, MARKS]
Ge	1:14	as signs to m seasons and days and years,	NIH
	4:15	Then the LORD put a m on Cain so	253
1Ki	22:28	he added, "M my words, all you people!"	9048
2Ch	18:27	he added, "M my words, all you people!"	9048
Job	36:32	and commands it to strike its m.	7003
Isa	59: 7	ruin and destruction mark their ways.	928
Eze	9: 4	and put a m on the foreheads	9338+9344
	9: 6	but do not touch anyone who has the m.	9338
	21:19	two roads for the sword of the king	8492
	21:20	M out one road for the sword to come	8492
Ac	12:12	of Mary the mother of John, also called M,	3453
	12:25	taking with them John, also called M.	3453
	15:37	wanted to take John, also called M,	3453
	15:39	Barnabas took M and sailed for Cyprus,	3453
Ro	3:16	ruin and misery m their ways,	NIG
2Co	12:12	The things that m an apostle—	4956
Gal	5: 2	M my words!	3972
Col	4:10	as does M, the cousin of Barnabas.	3453
2Th	3:17	is the distinguishing m in all my letters.	4956
2Ti	3: 1	But m this: There will be terrible times	1182

2Ti	4:11	Get M and bring him with you,	3453
Phm	1:24	And so do M, Aristarchus,	3453
1Pe	5:13	and so does my son M.	3453
Rev	13:16	a m on his right hand or on his forehead,	5916
	13:17	or sell unless he had the m,	5916
	14: 9	the beast and his image and receives his m	5916
	14:11	anyone who receives the m of his name."	5916
	16: 2	the m of the beast and worshiped his image.	5916
	19:20	the m of the beast and worshiped his image.	5916
	20: 4	or his image and had not received his m	5916

MARKED (10) [MARK]
Jos	18:20	the boundaries that m out the inheritance of	NIH
Job	15:22	he is m for the sword.	7595
	38: 5	Who m off its dimensions?	8492
Pr	8:27	when he m out the horizon on the face of	2980
	8:29	when he m out the foundations of the earth.	2980
Isa	40:12	the breadth of his hand m off the heavens?	9419
Zec	11: 4	"Pasture the flock m for slaughter.	AIT
	11: 7	So I pastured the flock m for slaughter,	AIT
Eph	1:13	you were m in him with a seal,	5381
Heb	12: 1	with perseverance the race m out for us.	4618

MARKER (2) [MARK]
Isa	44:13	with a line and makes an outline with a m;	8574
Eze	39:15	he will set up a m beside it until	7483

MARKET (5) [MARKETPLACE, MARKETPLACES]
1Ki	20:34	"You may set up your own m areas	2575
Am	8: 5	Sabbath be ended that we may m wheat?"—	7337
Zep	1:11	Wail, you who live in the m district;	4847
Jn	2:16	you turn my Father's house into a m!"	1866+3875
1Co	10:25	in the meat m without raising questions	3425

MARKETPLACE (8) [MARKET]
Isa	23: 3	and she became the m of the nations.	6087
Eze	27:24	In your m they traded with you	5326
Mt	20: 3	standing in the m doing nothing.	59
Mk	7: 4	When they come from the m they do not eat	59
Lk	7:32	like children sitting in the m and calling out	59
Ac	16:19	and Silas and dragged them into the m	59
	17: 5	up some bad characters from the m,	61
	17:17	the m day by day with those who happened	59

MARKETPLACES (6) [MARKET]
Mt	11:16	like children sitting in the m and calling out	59
	23: 7	in the m and to have men call them 'Rabbi.'	59
Mk	6:56	they placed the sick in the m.	59
	12:38	in flowing robes and be greeted in the m,	59
Lk	11:43	in the synagogues and greetings in the m.	59
	20:46	and love to be greeted in the m and	59

MARKS (10) [MARK]
Ge	35:20	and to this day that pillar m Rachel's tomb.	NIH
Lev	19:28	for the dead or put tattoo m on yourselves.	4182
1Sa	21:13	like a madman, making m on the doors of	9344
2Ki	23:17	"It m the tomb of the man of God who came	NIH
Job	13:27	on all my paths by putting m on the soles	2977
	26:10	He m out the horizon on the face of	2552
Ps	104:19	The moon m off the seasons,	6913
Isa	44:13	with chisels and m it with compasses.	9306
Jn	20:25	the nail m in his hands and put my finger	5596
Gal	6:17	for I bear on my body the m of Jesus.	5116

MAROTH (1)
Mic	1:12	Those who live in M writhe in pain,	5300

MARRED (2)
Isa	52:14	and his form m beyond human likeness—	NIH
Jer	18: 4	the pot he was shaping from the clay was m	8845

MARRIAGE (43) [MARRY]
Ge	29:26	give the younger daughter in m	5989
Ex	2:21	gave his daughter Zipporah to Moses in m.	5989
Lev	21: 4	related to him by m,	1251
Dt	22:16	gave my daughter in m	851+4200+5989
	23: 2	one born of a forbidden m	4927
Jos	15:16	give my daughter Acsah in m	851+4200+5989
	15:17	gave my daughter Acsah to him in m.	851+4200+5989
Jdg	1:12	give my daughter Acsah in m	851+4200+5989
	1:13	gave his daughter Acsah to him in m.	851+4200+5989
	3: 6	took their daughters in m	851+4200+4374
	12: 9	gave his daughters away in m	8938
	21: 1	give his daughter in m	851+4200+5989
	21: 7	to give them any of our daughters in m?"	851+4200+5989
1Sa	17:25	give him his daughter in m	5989
	18:17	give her to you in m;	851+4200+5989
	18:19	she was given in m to Adriel	851+4200+5989
	18:27	Saul gave him his daughter Michal in m.	851+4200+5989
1Ki	2:21	"Let Abishag the Shunammite be given in m to your brother Adonijah."	851+4200+5989
	11:19	gave him a sister of his own wife, Queen Tahpenes, in m.	851+5989
2Ki	8:27	for he was related by m to Ahab's family.	3163
	14: 9	'Give your daughter to my son in m.'	851+4200+5989

1Ch	2:35	Sheshan **gave** his daughter in m	851+4200+5989
	5: 1	but when he defiled his father's **m** bed,	3661
2Ch	18: 1	**allied himself** with Ahab by m.	3161
	25:18	'Give your daughter to my son in m.'	851+4200+5989
Ezr	9:12	*do not give* your daughters in m	5989
Ne	10:30	not to give our daughters in m	5989
	13:25	*You are* not *to give* your daughters in m	5989
	13:25	nor *are you to* take their daughters in m	5951
Jer	29: 6	give your daughters in m,	408+4200+5989
Da	11:17	give him a daughter in m.	851+2021+5989
Mal	2:14	the wife of your **m covenant**.	1382
Mt	19:12	and others *have* **renounced** m because of the kingdom	1571+2335+2336
	22:30	neither marry nor *be* given in m;	1139
	24:38	marrying and **giving in** m,	1139
Mk	12:25	they will neither marry nor *be* given in m;	1139
Lk	2:36	with her husband seven years after her m,	NIG
	17:27	marrying and *being* **given in** m up to	1139
	20:34	of this age marry and *are* given in m.	1140
	20:35	neither marry nor *be* given in m,	1139
Ro	7: 2	she is released from the law *of* m.	467
Heb	13: 4	**M** should be honored by all,	1141
	13: 4	and the **m** bed kept pure,	3130

MARRIAGES (1) [MARRY]

Ne	13:26	because of **m** like these that Solomon king	NIH

MARRIED (78) [MARRY]

Ge	4:19	Lamech **m** two women,	4374
	6: 2	and *they* **m** any of them they chose.	851+4374
	11:29	Abram and Nahor both **m**.	851+4374
	20: 3	she *is a* **m** woman."	1249+1251
	24:67	of his mother Sarah, and *he* **m** Rebekah	4374
	25:20	when he **m** Rebekah daughter of Bethuel	851+2257+4200+4200+4374
	26:34	he **m** Judith daughter of Beeri the Hittite,	851+4374
	28: 9	so he went to Ishmael and **m** Mahalath,	851+4374
	38: 2	*He* **m** her and lay with her;	4374
Ex	2: 1	of the house of Levi **m** a Levite woman,	4374
	6:20	Amram **m** his father's sister Jochebed,	851+4200+4374
	6:23	Aaron **m** Elisheba, daughter of Amminadab	851+4200+4374
	6:25	Eliezer son of Aaron **m** one of the daughters of Putiel,	851+4200+4374
Nu	22:16	seduces a virgin who *is* not **pledged to be m**	829
	5:19	and become impure **while m** to	9393
	5:20	But if you have gone astray **while m** to	9393
	5:29	and defiles herself **while m** to her husband,	9393
	12: 1	for *he had* **m** a Cushite.	851+4374
	36:11	**m** their cousins on their father's side.	851+2118+4200
	36:12	*They* **m** within the clans of the	851+2118+4200
Dt	20: 7	pledged to a woman and not **m** her?	4374
	22:14	saying, "*I* **m** this woman,	4374
	22:23	to meet in a town a virgin **pledged to be m**	829
	22:25	a girl **pledged to be m** and rapes her,	829
	22:28	a virgin who *is* not **pledged to be m**	829
	24: 5	If a man *has* recently **m**,	851+4374
	24: 5	and bring happiness to the wife *he has* **m**.	4374
	28:30	*You will* be **pledged to be m** *to* a woman,	829
Ru	1: 4	*They* **m** Moabite women,	851+5951
1Sa	25:43	David *had* also **m** Ahinoam of Jezreel,	4374
2Sa	13:13	he will not keep me from being **m** to you."	NIH
	17:25	an Israelite who *had* **m** Abigail,	448+995
1Ki	3: 1	of Egypt and **m** his daughter.	4374
	4:11	(he *was* **m** to Taphath daughter	851+2118+4200
	4:15	(he *had* **m** Basemath daughter of	851+4200+4374
	7: 8	Pharaoh's daughter, whom *he had* **m**.	4374
	16:31	**m** Jezebel daughter of Ethbaal king of	851+4374
2Ki	8:18	for *he* **m** a daughter of Ahab.	851+2118+4200
1Ch	2:19	When Azubah died, Caleb **m** Ephrath,	4374
	2:21	(he *had* **m** her when he was sixty years old)	4374
	4:18	Bithiah, whom Mered *had* **m**.	4374
	23:22	Their cousins, the sons of Kish, **m** them.	5951
2Ch	11:18	Rehoboam **m** Mahalath,	851+4374
	11:20	Then *he* **m** Maacah daughter of Absalom,	4374
	13:21	*He* **m** fourteen wives and had	5951
	21: 6	for *he* **m** a daughter of Ahab.	851+2118
Ezr	2:61	Barzillai (a man who *had* **m** a daughter	851+4374
	10:10	you have **m** foreign women,	3782
	10:14	Then let everyone in our towns who *has* **m**	3782
	10:17	with all the men who *had* **m** foreign women.	3782
	10:18	the following *had* **m** foreign women:	3782
	10:44	All these *had* **m** foreign women,	5951
Ne	6:18	and his son Jehohanan *had* **m** the daughter	4374
	7:63	Barzillai (a man who *had* **m** a daughter	851+4374
	13:23	of Judah *who had* **m** women from Ashdod,	3782
Pr	30:23	an unloved woman who *is* **m**,	1249
Isa	54: 6	a **wife** who *m* young, only to be rejected,"	AIT
	62: 4	and your land *will* be **m**.	1249
Hos	1: 3	So he **m** Gomer daughter of Diblaim,	4374
Mt	1:18	His mother Mary *was* **pledged to be m**	3650
	22:25	The first one **m** and died,	1138
	22:28	since all of them *were* **m** to her?"	2400
Mk	6:17	his brother Philip's wife, whom *he had* **m**.	1138
	12:20	The first one **m** and died	1222+3284
	12:21	The second one **m** the widow,	3284
	12:23	since the seven *were* **m** to her?"	2400
Lk	1:27	to a virgin **pledged to be m** to a man	3650
	2: 5	Mary, who *was* **pledged to be m** to him	3650
	14:20	"Still another said, 'I just **got m**,	1138+1222
	20:29	one **m** a **woman** and died childless.	1222+3284

Lk	20:31	and then the third **m** her,	3284
	20:33	since the seven were **m** to her?"	1222
Ro	7: 2	a **m** woman is bound to her husband as long	5635
1Co	7:10	To the **m** I give this command (not I, but	1222+1313
	7:27	Are you **m**? Do not seek a divorce.	1222+1313
	7:33	But a *man* is concerned about the affairs	1138
	7:34	a **m** *woman* is concerned about the affairs	1138
	7:36	*They should* get **m**.	1138

MARRIES (20) [MARRY]

Ex	21:10	If *he* **m** another woman,	4374
Lev	20:14	a man **m** both a woman and her mother,	4374
	20:17	"'If a man **m** his sister,	4374
	20:21	"'If a man **m** his brother's wife,	4374
	21:13	"'The woman he **m** must be a virgin.	4374
	22:12	If a priest's daughter **m** anyone other than a priest,	408+2118+4200
Nu	30: 6	"If *she* **m** after she makes a vow or	408+2118+2118+4200
Dt	24: 1	If a man **m** a woman who becomes displeasing to him because	1249+2256+4374
Isa	62: 5	As a young man **m** a maiden,	1249
Jer	3: 1	she leaves him and **m** another man,	2118+4200
Mt	5:32	and anyone who **m** the divorced woman	1138
	19: 9	and **m** another woman commits adultery."	1138
Mk	10:11	and **m** another woman commits adultery	1138
	10:12	divorces her husband and **m** another man,	1138
Lk	16:18	and **m** another woman commits adultery	1138
	16:18	and the man who **m** a divorced woman	1138
Ro	7: 3	if *she* **m** another man while her husband is	1181
	7: 3	*even though she* **m** another man.	1181
1Co	7:28	and if a virgin **m**, she has not sinned,	1138
	7:38	So then, he who **m** the virgin does right,	1139

MARROW (2)

Job	21:24	body well nourished, his bones rich with **m**.	4672
Heb	4:12	to dividing soul and spirit, joints and **m**;	3678

MARRY (49) [INTERMARRY, MARITAL, MARRIAGE, MARRIAGES, MARRIED, MARRIES, MARRYING]

Ge	19:14	who were **pledged to m** his daughters.	4374
	28: 1	"Do not **m** a Canaanite woman.	851+4374
	28: 6	"Do not **m** a Canaanite woman,"	851+4374
	34:21	We *can* **m** their daughters	851+4200+4374
	34:21	and they *can* **m** ours.	5989
Lev	21: 7	not **m** women defiled by prostitution	4374
	21:14	He *must* not **m** a widow, a divorced woman,	4374
Nu	36: 3	Now suppose *they* **m** men	851+2118+4200
	36: 3	added to that of the tribe *they* **m** into.	2118+4200
	36: 4	to that of the tribe *into* which *they* **m**,	2118+4200
	36: 6	*They may* **m** anyone they please as long as	851+2118+4200
	36: 6	as long as *they* **m** within the tribal clan	851+2118+4200
	36: 8	*must* **m** someone in her father's tribal clan,	851+2118+4200
Dt	20: 7	die in battle and someone else **m** her."	4374
	22:29	He *must* **m** the girl, for he has violated her.	851+2118+4200
	22:30	A man *is* not *to* **m** his father's wife;	4374
	24: 4	to **m** her again after she has been defiled.	851+4200+4374
	25: 5	his widow *must* not **m** outside the family.	408+2118+4200
	25: 5	and **m** her and fulfill the duty of	851+4200+4374
	25: 7	man does not want to **m** his brother's wife,	4374
	25: 8	"I do not want to **m** her,"	4374
Jdg	11:37	because I will never **m**."	1436
	11:38	and wept because she would never **m**.	1436
	14: 8	when he went back to **m** her,	4374
Isa	62: 5	so *will* your sons **m** you;	1249
Jer	16: 2	"You must not **m** and have sons or	851+4374
	29: 6	**M** and have sons and daughters;	851+4374
Eze	44:22	not **m** widows or divorced women;	851+4200+4374
	44:22	*they may* **m** only virgins of Israelite descent	4374
Mt	19:10	it is better not to **m**."	1138
	22:24	his brother must **m** the widow	2102
	22:30	the resurrection *people will* neither **m** nor	1138
Mk	12:19	the man *must* **m** the widow	3284
	12:25	*they will* neither **m** nor be given	1138
Lk	20:28	the man *must* **m** the widow	3284
	20:34	"The people of this age **m** and are given	1138
	20:35	from the dead *will* neither **m** nor be given	1138
1Co	7: 1	It is good for a man not to **m**.	721+1222
	7: 9	*they should* **m**, for it is better to marry than	1138
	7: 9	it is better to **m** than to burn with passion.	1138
	7:28	But if you *do* **m**, you have not sinned;	1138
	7:28	But **those who** **m** will face many troubles	3836+5525ˢ
	7:36	and he feels he ought **to m**,	1181+4048ˢ
	7:37	and who has made up his mind not to **m**	5498
	7:38	but he who *does* not **m** her does even better.	1139
	7:39	she is free *to* **m** anyone she wishes,	1138
1Ti	4: 3	They forbid people *to* **m** and order them	1138
	5:11	their dedication to Christ, they want *to* **m**.	1138
	5:14	So I counsel younger widows *to* **m**,	1138

MARRYING (5) [MARRY]

Ezr	10: 2	*by* **m** foreign women from the peoples	3782
Ne	13:27	to our God by **m** foreign women?"	3782
Mal	2:11	*by* **m** the daughter of a foreign god.	1249

Mt	24:38	**m** and giving in marriage,	1138
Lk	17:27	**m** and being given in marriage up to	1138

MARS' (KJV) See AREOPAGUS

MARSENA (1)

Est	1:14	Tarshish, Meres, **M** and Memucan,	5333

MARSH (2)

Job	8:11	Can papyrus grow tall where there is no **m**?	1289
	40:21	hidden among the reeds in the **m**.	1289

MARSHAL (2) [MARSHALED]

Mic	5: 1	**M** your **troops**, O city of troops,	1518
Na	2: 1	brace yourselves, **m** all your strength!	599

MARSHALED (4) [MARSHAL]

2Ch	25:11	then **m** his **strength** and led his army to	2616
Job	6: 4	God's terrors *are* **m** against me.	6885
	32:14	But Job *has* not **m** his words against me,	6885
Isa	45:12	*I* **m** their starry hosts.	7422

MARSHES (2)

Jer	51:32	the **m** set on fire, and the soldiers terrified."	106
Eze	47:11	the swamps and **m** will not become fresh;	1465

MARTHA (13)

Lk	10:38	where a woman named **M** opened her home	3450
	10:40	But **M** was distracted by all the preparations	3450
	10:41	"**M**, Martha," the Lord answered,	3450
	10:41	"Martha, **M**," the Lord answered,	3450
Jn	11: 1	the village of Mary and her sister **M**.	3450
	11: 5	Jesus loved **M** and her sister and Lazarus.	3450
	11:19	to **M** and Mary to comfort them in the loss	3450
	11:20	When **M** heard that Jesus was coming,	3450
	11:21	"Lord," **M** said to Jesus,	3450
	11:24	**M** answered, "I know he will rise again in	3450
	11:30	was still at the place where **M** had met him.	3450
	11:39	Lord," said **M**, the sister of the dead man,	3450
	12: 2	**M** served, while Lazarus was	3450

MARTYR (1)

Ac	22:20	the blood *of* your **m** Stephen was shed,	3459

MARVELED (2) [MARVELOUS]

Lk	2:33	mother **m** at what was said about him.	1639+2513
2Th	1:10	*to be* **m** at among all those who have believed.	2513

MARVELING (1) [MARVELOUS]

Lk	9:43	While everyone was **m** at all that Jesus did,	2513

MARVELOUS (15) [MARVELED, MARVELING]

1Ch	16:24	his **m** deeds among all peoples.	7098
Job	37: 5	God's voice thunders *in* **m** ways;	7098
Ps	71:17	and to this day I declare your **m** deeds.	7098
	72:18	the God of Israel, who alone does **m** deeds.	7098
	86:10	For you are great and do **m** deeds;	7098
	96: 3	his **m** deeds among all peoples.	7098
	98: 1	for he has done **m** things;	7098
	118:23	and it *is* **m** in our eyes.	7098
Isa	25: 1	in perfect faithfulness you have done **m** things,	7099
Zec	8: 6	"It *may* seem **m** to the remnant	7098
	8: 6	but *will it* seem **m** to me?"	7098
Mt	21:42	Lord has done this, and it is **m** in our eyes'?	2515
Mk	12:11	Lord has done this, and it is **m** in our eyes'?	2515
Rev	15: 1	I saw in heaven another great and **m** sign:	2515
	15: 3	"Great and **m** are your deeds,	2515

MARY (57) [MARY'S]

Mt	1:16	the husband *of* **M**, of whom was born Jesus,	3451
	1:18	His mother **M** was pledged to be married	3451
	1:20	not be afraid to take **M** home as your wife,	3451
	1:24	and took **M** home as his wife.	NIG
	2:11	they saw the child with his mother **M**,	3451
	13:55	Isn't his mother's name **M**,	3451
	27:56	Among them were **M** Magdalene,	3451
	27:56	**M** the mother of James and Joses,	3451
	27:61	**M** Magdalene and the other Mary were sitting there opposite the tomb.	3451
	27:61	and the other **M** were sitting there opposite	3451
	28: 1	**M** Magdalene and the other Mary went	3451
	28: 1	and the other **M** went to look at the tomb.	3451
Mk	15:40	Among them were **M** Magdalene,	3451
	15:40	**M** the mother of James the younger and	3451
	15:47	**M** Magdalene and Mary the mother	3451
	15:47	Mary Magdalene and **M** the mother	3451
	16: 1	When the Sabbath was over, **M** Magdalene,	3451
	16: 1	Mary Magdalene and **M** the mother of James,	3451
	16: 9	he appeared first to **M** Magdalene,	3451
Lk	1:27	The virgin's name was **M**.	3451
	1:29	**M** was greatly troubled at his words	1254+3836ˢ
	1:30	the angel said to her, "Do not be afraid, **M**,	3451
	1:34	"How will this be," **M** asked the angel,	3451
	1:38	"I am the Lord's servant," **M** answered.	3451
	1:39	that time **M** got ready and hurried to a town	3451
	1:46	And **M** said: "My soul glorifies the Lord	3451

Lk	1:56	**M** stayed with Elizabeth for about three	3451
	2: 5	He went there to register with **M**,	3451
	2:16	they hurried off and found **M** and Joseph,	3451
	2:19	But **M** treasured up all these things	3451
	2:22	and **M** took him to Jerusalem to present him	NIG
	2:34	Then Simeon blessed them and said to **M**,	3451
	2:39	and **M** had done everything required by	NIG
	8: 2	**M** (called Magdalene) from whom seven demons had come out;	3451
	10:39	She had a sister called **M**,	3451
	10:42	**M** has chosen what is better,	3451
	24:10	It was **M** Magdalene, Joanna,	3451
	24:10	Joanna, **M** the mother of James,	3451
Jn	11: 1	the village *of* **M** and her sister Martha.	3451
	11: 2	This **M**, whose brother Lazarus	3451
	11:19	many Jews had come to Martha and **M**	3451
	11:20	but **M** stayed at home.	3451
	11:28	she went back and called her sister **M** aside.	3451
	11:29	When **M** heard this, she got up quickly	1697S
	11:31	Jews who had been with **M** in the house,	899S
	11:32	When **M** reached the place where Jesus was	3451
	11:45	many of the Jews who had come to visit **M**,	3451
	12: 3	Then **M** took about a pint of pure nard,	3451
	19:25	his mother's sister, **M** the wife of Clopas,	3451
	19:25	the wife of Clopas, and **M** Magdalene.	3451
	20: 1	**M** Magdalene went to the tomb and saw	3451
	20:11	but **M** stood outside the tomb crying.	3451
	20:16	Jesus said to her, **"M."**	3451
	20:18	**M** Magdalene went to the disciples with	3451
Ac	1:14	with the women and **M** the mother of Jesus,	3451
	12:12	to the house *of* **M** the mother of John,	3451
Ro	16: 6	Greet **M**, who worked very hard for you.	3451

MARY'S (2) [MARY]

Mk	6: 3	Isn't this **M** son and the brother of James,	3451
Lk	1:41	When Elizabeth heard **M** greeting,	3451

MASH (1)

Isa	30:24	that work the soil will eat fodder and **m**,	2796

MASHAL (1)

1Ch	6:74	from the tribe of Asher they received **M**,	5443

MASK (1)

1Th	2: 5	nor *did we* put on a **m** to cover up greed—	4733

MASKIL (13)

Ps	32: T	Of David. A **m**.	5380
	42: T	A **m** of the Sons of Korah.	5380
	44: T	Of the Sons of Korah. A **m**.	5380
	45: T	Of the Sons of Korah. A **m**.	5380
	52: T	A **m** of David.	5380
	53: T	A **m** of David.	5380
	54: T	A **m** of David.	5380
	55: T	A **m** of David.	5380
	74: T	A **m** of Asaph.	5380
	78: T	A **m** of Asaph.	5380
	88: T	A **m** of Heman the Ezrahite.	5380
	89: T	A **m** of Ethan the Ezrahite.	5380
	142: T	A **m** of David.	5380

MASONS (5)

2Ki	12:12	the **m** and stonecutters.	1553
	22: 6	the builders and the **m**.	1553
1Ch	22:15	stonecutters, **m** and carpenters,	74+3093
2Ch	24:12	They hired **m** and carpenters to restore	2935
Ezr	3: 7	they gave money to the **m** and carpenters,	2935

MASQUERADE (1) [MASQUERADES, MASQUERADING]

2Co	11:15	his servants **m** as servants of righteousness.	3571

MASQUERADES (1) [MASQUERADE]

2Co	11:14	for Satan himself **m** as an angel of light.	3571

MASQUERADING (1) [MASQUERADE]

2Co	11:13	deceitful workmen, **m** as apostles of Christ.	3571

MASREKAH (2)

Ge	36:36	Samlah from **M** succeeded him as king.	5388
1Ch	1:47	Samlah from **M** succeeded him as king.	5388

MASSA (2)

Ge	25:14	Mishma, Dumah, **M**,	5364
1Ch	1:30	Mishma, Dumah, **M**, Hadad, Tema,	5364

MASSACRE (1)

Hos	1: 4	the house of Jehu for the **m** *at* Jezreel,	1947

MASSAH (5)

Ex	17: 7	And he called the place **M** and Meribah	5001
Dt	6:16	the LORD your God as you did at **M**.	5001
	9:22	at **M** and at Kibroth Hattaavah.	5001
	33: 8	You tested him at **M**;	5001
Ps	95: 8	as you did that day at **M** in the desert,	5001

MASSES (2) [MASSING]

Isa	5:13	and their **m** will be parched with thirst.	2162

Isa	5:14	and **m** with all their brawlers and revelers.	2162

MASSING (1) [MASSES]

Isa	13: 4	like nations **m** together!	665

MASSIVE (1)

Mk	13: 1	What **m** stones!	4534

MAST (2)

Isa	33:23	**m** is not held secure, the sail is not spread.	4029+9568
Eze	27: 5	a cedar from Lebanon to make a **m** for you.	9568

MASTER (164) [MASTER'S, MASTERED, MASTERS, MASTERS', MASTERY]

Ge	4: 7	it desires to have you, but you *must* **m** it."	5440
	18:12	"After I am worn out and my **m** is old,	123
	24: 9	of his **m** Abraham and swore an oath to him	123
	24:10	of good things from his **m**.	123
	24:12	"O LORD, God of my **m** Abraham,	123
	24:12	and show kindness to my **m** Abraham.	123
	24:14	that you have shown kindness to my **m**."	123
	24:27	the LORD, the God of my **m** Abraham,	123
	24:27	and faithfulness to my **m**.	123
	24:35	The LORD has blessed my **m** abundantly,	123
	24:37	And my **m** made me swear an oath,	123
	24:39	"Then I asked my **m**,	123
	24:42	I said, 'O LORD, God of my **m** Abraham,	123
	24:48	the LORD, the God of my **m** Abraham,	123
	24:49	and faithfulness to my **m**, tell me;	123
	24:54	he said, "Send me on my way to my **m**."	123
	24:56	Send me on my way so I may go to my **m**."	123
	24:65	"He is my **m**," the servant answered.	123
	32: 4	"This is what you are to say to my **m** Esau:	123
	39: 2	and he lived in the house of his Egyptian **m**.	123
	39: 3	When his **m** saw that the LORD was	123
	39: 8	"my **m** does not concern himself	123
	39: 9	My **m** has withheld nothing	NIH
	39:16	beside her until his **m** came home.	123
	39:19	When his **m** heard the story his wife told	123
	39:20	Joseph's **m** took him and put him in prison,	123
	40: 1	of the king of Egypt offended their **m**,	123
	44: 5	the cup my **m** drinks from and also uses	123
Ex	21: 4	If his **m** gives him a wife	123
	21: 4	and her children shall belong to her **m**,	123
	21: 5	'I love my **m** and my wife and children	123
	21: 6	then his **m** must take him before the judges.	123
	21: 8	the **m** who has selected her for himself,	123
	21:32	shekels of silver to the **m** *of* the slave,	123
	35:35	of them **m** craftsmen and designers.	4856+6913
Dt	23:15	do not hand him over to his **m**.	123
Jdg	19:11	the servant said to his **m**, "Come,	123
	19:12	His **m** replied, "No.	123
	19:26	to the house where her **m** was staying,	123
	19:27	When her **m** got up in the morning	123
1Sa	20:38	up the arrow and returned to his **m**.	123
	24: 6	such a thing to my **m**, the LORD's anointed,	123
	24:10	I said, 'I will not lift my hand against my **m**,	123
	25:14	from the desert to give our **m** his greetings,	123
	25:17	because disaster is hanging over our **m**	123
	25:25	I did not see the men my **m** sent.	123
	25:26	since the LORD has kept you, my **m**,	123
	25:26	and all who intend to harm my **m** be	123
	25:27	which your servant has brought to my **m**,	123
	25:28	a lasting dynasty for my **m**,	123
	25:29	the life of my **m** will be bound securely in	123
	25:30	for my **m** every good thing he promised	123
	25:31	my **m** will not have on his conscience	123
	25:31	the LORD has brought my **m** success,	123
	26:16	because you did not guard your **m**,	123
	30:13	My **m** abandoned me when I became ill	123
	30:15	not kill me or hand me over to my **m**,	123
2Sa	2: 5	for showing this kindness to Saul your **m**	123
	2: 7	for Saul your **m** is dead,	123
	9:10	And Mephibosheth, grandson of your **m**,	123
	11:11	and my **m** Joab and my lord's men	123
1Ki	11:23	who had fled from his **m**,	123
	18: 8	"Go tell your **m**, 'Elijah is here.' "	123
	18:10	where my **m** has not sent someone to look	123
	18:11	But now you tell me to go to my **m** and say,	123
	18:14	now you tell me to go to my **m** and say,	123
	22:17	'These people have no **m**.	123
2Ki	2: 3	that the LORD is going to take your **m**	123
	2: 5	that the LORD is going to take your **m**	123
	2:16	Let them go and look for your **m**.	123
	5: 1	in the sight of his **m** and highly regarded,	123
	5: 3	"If only my **m** would see the prophet who is	123
	5: 4	Naaman went to his **m** and told him what	123
	5:18	When my **m** enters the temple of Rimmon	123
	5:20	"My **m** was too easy on Naaman,	123
	5:22	"My **m** sent me to say,	123
	5:25	he went in and stood before his **m** Elisha.	123
	6:22	and drink and then go back to their **m**."	123
	6:23	and they returned to their **m**.	123
	8:14	Hazael left Elisha and returned to his **m**.	123
	9: 7	to destroy the house of Ahab your **m**,	123
	9:31	Zimri, you murderer of your **m**?"	123
	10: 9	It was I who conspired against my **m**	123
	18:23	" 'Come now, make a bargain with my **m**,	123
	18:27	to your **m** and you that my master sent me	123
	18:27	that my **m** sent me to say these things, and	123
	19: 4	whom his **m**, the king of Assyria,	123
	19: 6	"Tell your **m**, 'This is what	123
1Ch	12:19	our heads if he deserts to his **m** Saul.")	123

2Ch	13: 6	rebelled against his **m**.	123
	18:16	'These people have no **m**.'	123
Job	3:19	and the slave is freed from his **m**.	123
Ps	12: 4	we own our lips—who is our **m**?"	123
	105:21	He made him **m** of his household,	123
	123: 2	of slaves look to the hand of their **m**,	123
Pr	27:18	he who looks after his **m** will be honored.	123
	30:10	"Do not slander a servant to his **m**,	123
Isa	1: 3	The ox knows his **m**,	7864
	19: 4	over to the power of a cruel **m**,	123
	24: 2	for **m** as for servant,	123
	36: 8	" 'Come now, make a bargain with my **m**,	123
	36:12	to your **m** and you that my master sent me	123
	36:12	that my **m** sent me to say these things, and	123
	37: 4	whom his **m**, the king of Assyria,	123
	37: 6	"Tell your **m**, 'This is what	123
Jer	22:18	They will not mourn for him: 'Alas, my **m**!	123
	34: 5	in your honor and lament, "Alas, O **m**!"	123
Da	8:23	a stern-faced king, a **m** *of* intrigue,	1067
Hos	2:16	you will no longer call me 'my **m**.'	1251
Mal	1: 6	son honors his father, and a servant his **m**.	123
	1: 6	If I am a **m**, where is the respect due me?"	123
Mt	10:24	nor a servant above his **m**.	3261
	10:25	and the servant like his **m**.	3261
	18:25	the **m** ordered that he and his wife	3261
	18:27	The servant's **m** took pity on him,	3261
	18:31	and went and told their **m** everything	3261
	18:32	"Then the **m** called the servant in.	3261
	18:34	In anger his **m** turned him over to the jailers	3261
	23: 8	for you have only one **M**	1437
	24:45	the **m** has put in charge of the servants	3261
	24:46	for that servant whose **m** finds him doing so	3261
	24:48	'My **m** is staying away a long time,'	3261
	24:50	The **m** of that servant will come on a day	3261
	25:19	a long time the **m** of those servants returned	3261
	25:20	'**M**,' he said, 'you entrusted me	3261
	25:21	"His **m** replied, 'Well done,	3261
	25:22	'**M**,' he said, 'you entrusted me	3261
	25:23	"His **m** replied, 'Well done,	3261
	25:24	'**M**,' he said, 'I knew that you are	3261
	25:26	"His **m** replied, 'You wicked, lazy servant!	3261
Lk	5: 5	"**M**, we've worked hard all night	2181
	7: 2	whom his **m** valued highly,	899S
	8:24	disciples went and woke him, saying, "**M**,	2181
	8:24	saying, "Master, **M**, we're going to drown!"	2181
	8:45	When they all denied it, Peter said, "**M**,	2181
	9:33	"**M**, it is good for us to be here.	2181
	9:49	"**M**," said John, "we saw a man driving out	2181
	12:36	like men waiting for their **m** to return from	3261
	12:37	servants whose **m** finds them watching	3261
	12:38	those servants whose **m** finds them ready,	NIG
	12:42	whom the **m** puts in charge of his servants	3261
	12:43	for that servant whom the **m** finds doing so	3261
	12:45	'My **m** is taking a long time in coming,'	3261
	12:46	The **m** of that servant will come on a day	3261
	12:47	not do what his **m** wants will be beaten	899S
	14:21	and reported this *to* his **m**.	3261
	14:23	"Then the **m** told his servant,	3261
	16: 3	My **m** is taking away my job.	3261
	16: 5	'How much do you owe my **m**?'	3261
	16: 8	"The **m** commended the dishonest manager	3261
	17:13	"Jesus, **M**, have pity on us!"	2181
	19:17	"Well done, my good servant!" his **m** replied.	NIG
	19:19	"His **m** answered, 'You take charge	4047S
	19:22	"His **m** replied, 'I will judge you	NIG
Jn	2: 8	and take it *to* the **m** of the banquet."	804
	2: 9	and the **m** of the banquet tasted the water	804
	13:16	no servant is greater than his **m**,	3261
	15:20	'No servant is greater than his **m**.'	3261
Ro	6:14	For sin *shall* not *be* your **m**,	3259
	14: 4	*To* his own **m** he stands or falls.	3261
Eph	6: 9	since you know that he who is both their **M**	3261
Col	4: 1	you know that you also have a **M** in heaven.	3261
2Ti	2:21	the **M** and prepared to do any good work.	1305
1Pe	3: 6	who obeyed Abraham and called him her **m**.	3261

MASTER'S (34) [MASTER]

Ge	24:10	servant took ten of his **m** camels and left,	123
	24:27	the journey to the house of my **m** relatives."	123
	24:36	My **m** wife Sarah has borne him a son	123
	24:44	the LORD has chosen for my **m** son.'	123
	24:48	to get the granddaughter of my **m** brother	123
	24:51	and let her become the wife of your **m** son,	123
	39: 7	a while his **m** wife took notice of Joseph	123
	40: 7	in custody with him in his **m** house,	123
	44: 8	or gold from your **m** house?	123
1Sa	25:41	and wash the feet of my **m** servants."	123
	29: 4	How better could he regain his **m** favor than	123
	29:10	along with your **m** servants who have come	123
2Sa	9: 9	"I have given your **m** grandson everything	123
	9:10	that your **m** grandson may be provided for.	123
	11: 9	to the palace with all his **m** servants and did	123
	11:13	to sleep on his mat among his **m** servants;	123
	12: 8	I gave your **m** house to you,	123
	12: 8	and your **m** wives into your arms.	123
	16: 3	"Where is your **m** grandson?"	123
	20: 6	Take your **m** men and pursue him,	123
2Ki	6:32	the sound of his **m** footsteps behind him?"	123
	10: 2	since your **m** sons are with you	123
	10: 3	and most worthy of your **m** sons and set him	123
	10: 3	Then fight for your **m** house."	123
	10: 6	of your **m** sons and come to me in Jezreel	123
	18:24	of the least of my **m** officials,	123
Isa	22:18	you disgrace to your **m** house!	123
	36: 9	of the least of my **m** officials,	123

Mt	25:18	a hole in the ground and hid his **m** money.	*3261*
	25:21	Come and share your **m** happiness!'	*3261*
	25:23	Come and share your **m** happiness!'	*3261*
Lk	12:47	"That servant who knows his **m** will	*3261*
	16: 5	"So he called in each one of his **m** debtors.	*3261*
Jn	15:15	a servant does not know his **m** business.	*3261*

MASTERBUILDER (KJV) See EXPERT
BUILDER

MASTERED (2) [MASTER]
1Co	6:12	but I *will* not *be* **m** by anything.	*2027*
2Pe	2:19	for a man is a slave to whatever *has* **m**.	*2487*

MASTERS (16) [MASTER]
Ex	1:11	So they put slave **m** over them	*8569*
1Sa	25:10	breaking away from their **m** these days.	*123*
Pr	25:13	he refreshes the spirit of his **m**.	*123*
Jer	27: 4	Give them a message for their **m** and say,	*123*
	27: 4	"Tell this to your **m**:	*123*
La	1: 5	Her foes have become her **m**;	*8031*
Mt	6:24	"No one can serve two **m**.	*3261*
Lk	16:13	"No servant can serve two **m**.	*3261*
Eph	6: 5	obey your earthly **m** with respect and fear,	*3261*
	6: 9	And **m**, treat your slaves in the same way.	*3261*
Col	3:22	Slaves, obey your earthly **m** in everything;	*3261*
	4: 1	**M**, provide your slaves with what is right	*3261*
1Ti	6: 1	of slavery should consider their **m** worthy	*1305*
	6: 2	Those who have believing **m** are not	*1305*
Tit	2: 9	to be subject to their **m** in everything,	*1305*
1Pe	2:18	submit yourselves *to* your **m**	*1305*

MASTERS' (1) [MASTER]
Mt	15:27	the crumbs that fall from their **m'** table."	*3261*

MASTERY (1) [MASTER]
Ro	6: 9	death no longer *has* **m** over him.	*3259*

MAT (15) [MATS]
2Sa	11:13	on his **m** among his master's servants,	*5435*
Mt	9: 2	brought to him a paralytic, lying on a **m**.	*3109*
	9: 6	"Get up, take your **m** and go home."	*3109*
Mk	2: 4	the **m** the paralyzed man was lying on.	*3187*
	2: 9	or to say, 'Get up, take your **m** and walk'?	*3187*
	2:11	get up, take your **m** and go home."	*3187*
	2:12	took his **m** and walked out in full view	*3187*
Lk	5:18	Some men came carrying a paralytic on a **m**	*3109*
	5:19	on his **m** through the tiles into the middle of	*3110*
	5:24	get up, take your **m** and go home."	*3110*
Jn	5: 8	Pick up your **m** and walk."	*3187*
	5: 9	he picked up his **m** and walked.	*3187*
	5:10	the law forbids you to carry your **m**."	*3187*
	5:11	'Pick up your **m** and walk.' "	*3187*
Ac	9:34	Get up and **take care of** your **m**."	*4932+5143*

MATCH (3) [MATCHED, MATCHING]
1Ch	12:14	the least was a **m** for a hundred,	*4200*
Eze	31: 8	in the garden of God *could* **m** its beauty.	*1948*
Lk	5:36	the patch from the new *will* not **m** the old.	*5244*

MATCHED (1) [MATCH]
2Co	8:11	willingness to do it may be **m** by your completion of it,	*2749+2779+4048*

MATCHING (1) [MATCH]
Ezr	1:10	gold bowls 30 **m** silver bowls 410	*5467*

MATE (7) [MATED, MATING]
Ge	7: 2	a male and its **m**,	*851*
	7: 2	a male and its **m**,	*851*
	30:41	in front of the animals so they *would* **m** near	*3501*
Lev	19:19	" 'Do not **m** different kinds of animals.	*8061*
Isa	34:15	also the falcons will gather, each with its **m**.	*8295*
	34:16	not one will lack her **m**.	*8295*
Na	2:12	and strangled the prey for his **m**,	*4218*

MATED (1) [MATE]
Ge	30:39	they **m** in front of the branches.	*3501*

MATERIAL (18) [MATERIALS]
Ex	26: 4	of blue **m** along the edge of the end curtain	*9418*
	36:11	of **blue m** along the edge of the end curtain	*9418*
Lev	13:48	or knitted **m** of linen or wool, any leather	*6849*
	13:49	or leather, or woven or **knitted m**,	*6849*
	13:51	the woven or **knitted m**, or the leather,	*6849*
	13:52	or the woven or **knitted m** of wool or linen,	*6849*
	13:53	or the woven or **knitted m**,	*6849*
	13:56	or the leather, or the woven or **knitted m**,	*6849*
	13:57	or in the woven or **knitted m**,	*6849*
	13:58	The clothing, or the woven or **knitted m**,	*6849*
	13:59	woven or **knitted m**, or any leather article,	*6849*
	14:41	inside walls of the house scraped and the **m**	*6760*
	19:19	**woven** of two kinds of **m**.	*9122*
Est	1: 6	of white linen and **purple m** to silver rings	*763*
Pr	25: 4	and out comes **m** for the silversmith;	*3998*
Ro	15:27	to share with them their **m** blessings.	*4920*
1Co	9:11	is it too much if we reap a **m** harvest	*4920*
1Jn	3:17	If anyone has **m** possessions	*3180*

MATERIALS (2) [MATERIAL]
Ex	38:21	These are the amounts of the **m** used for	NIH
Ne	4:17	Those who carried **m** did their work	*6023*

MATHUSALA (KJV) See METHUSELAH

MATING (3) [MATE]
Ge	31:10	and saw that the male goats **m with**	*6584+6590*
	31:12	the male goats **m with** the flock are streaked,	*6584+6590*
Jer	2:24	at **m** time they will find her.	*2544*

MATRED (2)
Ge	36:39	wife's name was Mehetabel daughter of **M**,	*4765*
1Ch	1:50	wife's name was Mehetabel daughter of **M**,	*4765*

MATRI'S (1)
1Sa	10:21	clan by clan, and **M** clan was chosen.	*4767*

MATRIX (KJV) See WOMB

MATS (2) [MAT]
Mk	6:55	that whole region and carried the sick on **m**	*3187*
Ac	5:15	into the streets and laid them on beds and **m**	*3187*

MATTAN (3)
2Ki	11:18	to pieces and killed **M** the priest	*5509*
2Ch	23:17	the altars and idols and killed **M** the priest	*5509*
Jer	38: 1	Shephatiah son of **M**,	*5509*

MATTANAH (2)
Nu	21:18	Then they went from the desert to **M**,	*5511*
	21:19	from **M** to Nahaliel,	*5511*

MATTANIAH (16)
2Ki	24:17	He made **M**, Jehoiachin's uncle, king	*5514*
1Ch	9:15	Galal and **M** son of Mica, the son of Zicri,	*5514*
	25: 4	Bukkiah, **M**, Uzziel, Shubael and Jerimoth;	*5515*
	25:16	the ninth to **M**, his sons and relatives, 12	*5515*
2Ch	20:14	the son of Jeiel, the son of **M**,	*5514*
	29:13	of Asaph, Zechariah and **M**;	*5515*
Ezr	10:26	From the descendants of Elam: **M**,	*5514*
	10:27	Elioenai, Eliashib, **M**, Jeremoth,	*5514*
	10:30	Adna, Kelal, Benaiah, Maaseiah, **M**,	*5514*
	10:37	**M**, Mattenai and Jaasu.	*5514*
Ne	11:17	**M** son of Mica, the son of Zabdi, the son	*5514*
	11:22	the son of Hashabiah, the son of **M**,	*5514*
	12: 8	Kadmiel, Sherebiah, Judah, and also **M**,	*5514*
	12:25	**M**, Bakbukiah, Obadiah, Meshullam,	*5514*
	12:35	the son of Shemaiah, the son of **M**,	*5514*
	13:13	the son of **M**, their assistant,	*5514*

MATTATHA (1)
Lk	3:31	the son *of* **M**, the son of Nathan,	*3477*

MATTATHAH (KJV) See MATTATTAH

MATTATHIAS (2)
Lk	3:25	the son of **M**, the son of Amos,	*3478*
	3:26	the son of **M**, the son of Semein,	*3478*

MATTATTAH (1)
Ezr	10:33	Mattenai, **M**, Zabad, Eliphelet, Jeremai,	*5523*

MATTENAI (3)
Ezr	10:33	**M**, Mattattah, Zabad, Eliphelet, Jeremai,	*5513*
	10:37	Mattaniah, **M** and Jaasu.	*5513*
Ne	12:19	of Joiarib's, **M**; of Jedaiah's, Uzzi;	*5513*

MATTER (69) [MATTERED, MATTERS]
Ge	21:11	The **m** distressed Abraham greatly	*1821*
	21:17	"**What is the m**, Hagar?	*3871+4200+4537*
	24: 9	and swore an oath to him concerning this **m**.	*1821*
	37:11	but his father kept the **m** in mind.	*1821*
	41:32	that the **m** has been firmly decided by God,	*1821*
Lev	4:13	though the community is unaware of the **m**,	*1821*
	5: 4	in any **m** one might carelessly swear about	*889S*
Nu	18:32	of it you will not be guilty in this **m**;	*2257S*
Dt	3:26	"Do not speak to me anymore about this **m**.	*1821*
	19:15	A **m** must be established by the testimony	*1821*
Jos	22:31	unfaithfully toward the LORD in this **m**.	*5086*
Jdg	18:23	"**What's the m** with you	*4537*
	18:24	'**What's the m** with you?' "	*4537*
Ru	3:18	not rest until the **m** is settled today."	*1821*
	4: 4	the **m** to your attention and suggest	NIH
1Sa	17:30	and brought up the same **m**,	*1821*
	18:23	"*Do you think it is a* **small** *m* to become	AIT
	20:23	And about the **m** you and I discussed—	*1821*
	21: 2	"The king charged me with a *certain* **m**	*1821*
2Sa	15:11	knowing nothing about the **m**.	*1821*
2Ki	6:28	Then he asked her, "**What's the m**?"	*4537*
	20:10	"*It is a* **simple** *m* for the shadow	AIT
1Ch	26:32	of Manasseh for every **m** *pertaining to* God	*1821*
2Ch	8:15	to the priests or to the Levites in any **m**	*1821*
	19:11	over you in any **m** *concerning* the LORD,	*1821*
	19:11	be over you in any **m** *concerning* the king,	*1821*
Ezr	4:22	Be careful not to neglect this **m**.	AIT

Ezr	5:17	let the king send us his decision in **this** *m*.	AIT
	10: 4	Rise up; this **m** is in your hands.	*1821*
	10:13	this **m** cannot be taken care of in a day	*4856*
	10:14	of our God in this **m** is turned away	*1821*
Job	9:19	If it is **a m of** strength, he is mighty!	*4200*
	9:19	And if it is **a m of** justice,	*4200*
Pr	17: 9	repeats the **m** separates close friends.	*1821*
	17:14	so drop the **m** before a dispute breaks out.	NIH
	25: 2	It is the glory of God to conceal a **m**;	*1821*
	25: 2	to search out a **m** is the glory of kings.	*1821*
Ecc	6: 3	yet no **m** how long he lives,	NIH
	7: 8	The end of a **m** is better than its beginning,	*1821*
	8: 6	a proper time and procedure for every **m**,	*2914*
	12:13	here is the conclusion of the **m**:	*1821*
Isa	43:26	*let us* **argue** *the* **m** together;	AIT
Eze	8:17	*Is it a* **trivial** *m* for the house of Judah	AIT
Da	1:20	In every **m** of wisdom and understanding	*1821*
	2:15	Arioch then explained the **m** to Daniel.	*10418*
	2:17	returned to his house and explained the **m**	*10418*
	3:16	to defend ourselves before you in **this** *m*.	AIT
	7:28	"This is the end of the **m**.	*10418*
	7:28	but I kept the **m** to myself."	*10418*
Mt	18:16	so that 'every **m** may be established by the	*4839*
Mk	9:10	They kept the **m** to themselves,	*3364*
Lk	19:17	have been trustworthy in a **very small** *m*,	AIT
	20:14	*they* **talked the m** over.	*253+1368+4639*
Jn	3:25	Jew over the **m** of ceremonial washing.	*4309*
Ac	18:15	settle the **m** yourselves.	*3972*
Ro	4: 1	our forefather, discovered in this **m**?	NIG
	14:17	For the kingdom of God is not a **m** of eating	NIG
1Co	4:20	For the kingdom of God is not a **m** of talk	NIG
	7:37	But the man who has **settled the m**	*1612+2705*
2Co	1:20	no **m** how many promises God has made,	NIG
	7:11	to be innocent *in* this **m**.	*4547*
	8:10	about what is best for you in this **m**:	NIG
	9: 3	that our boasting about you in this **m** should	*3538*
	13: 1	"Every **m** must be established by the	*4839*
Gal	2: 4	[This **m** arose] because some false brothers	NIG
Php	1:18	But **what does it m**?	*1142+5515*
	4:15	with me in the **m** of giving and receiving,	*3364*
1Th	4: 6	in this **m** no one should wrong his brother	*4547*
Heb	9:10	They are only a **m** of food and drink	NIG

MATTERED (1) [MATTER]
Jer	3: 9	Israel's immorality **m** so little to her,	*2118*

MATTERS (15) [MATTER]
Ex	28: 3	in such **m** that they are to make garments	NIH
Ezr	7:11	in **m** concerning the commands and decrees	*1821*
Est	1:13	for the king to consult experts in **m** of **law**	AIT
Ps	131: 1	I do not concern myself with **m** too **great**	AIT
Mal	2: 9	but have shown partiality in **m** of the **law**."	*9368*
Mt	5:25	"**Settle m** quickly with your	*1639+2333*
	23:23	the *more* **important m** of the law—	*987*
Ac	25:20	I was at a loss how to investigate **such** *m*;	AIT
Ro	14: 1	without passing judgment *on* **disputable** *m*.	AIT
1Co	6: 4	if you have disputes about **such m**,	*1053S*
	7: 1	Now for the **m** you wrote about:	*4005*
1Ti	4:15	Be diligent in **these** *m*;	AIT
Heb	5: 1	to represent them in **m** related to God,	*3836*
2Pe	2:12	But these men blaspheme in **m** they do	*4005*
	3:16	speaking in them of **these** *m*.	AIT

MATTHAN (2)
Mt	1:15	Eleazar the father of **M**,	*3474*
	1:15	**M** the father of Jacob,	*3474*

MATTHAT (2)
Lk	3:24	the son of **M**, the son of Levi,	*3415*
	3:29	the son of Jorim, the son *of* **M**,	*3415*

MATTHEW (6) [MATTHEW'S]
Mt	9: 9	he saw a man named **M** sitting at the tax	*3414*
	9: 9	and **M** got up and followed him.	NIH
	10: 3	Thomas and **M** the tax collector;	*3414*
Mk	3:18	**M**, Thomas, James son of Alphaeus,	*3414*
Lk	6:15	**M**, Thomas, James son of Alphaeus,	*3414*
Ac	1:13	Philip and Thomas, Bartholomew and **M**;	*3414*

MATTHEW'S (1) [MATTHEW]
Mt	9:10	While Jesus was having dinner at **M** house,	NIG

MATTHIAS (2)
Ac	1:23	Barsabbas (also known as Justus) and **M**.	*3416*
	1:26	Then they cast lots, and the lot fell to **M**;	*3416*

MATTITHIAH (8)
1Ch	9:31	A Levite named **M**,	*5524*
	15:18	Jehiel, Unni, Eliab, Benaiah, Maaseiah, **M**,	*5525*
	15:21	and **M**, Eliphelehu, Mikneiah,	*5525*
	16: 5	then Jeiel, Shemiramoth, Jehiel, **M**, Eliab,	*5524*
	25: 3	Zeri, Jeshaiah, Shimei, Hashabiah and **M**,	*5525*
	25:21	the fourteenth to **M**,	*5525*
Ezr	10:43	From the descendants of Nebo: Jeiel, **M**,	*5524*
Ne	8: 4	Beside him on his right stood **M**, Shema,	*5524*

MATTOCKS (2)
1Sa	13:20	plowshares, **m**, axes and sickles sharpened.	*908*
	13:21	a shekel for sharpening plowshares and **m**,	*908*

MATURE (7) [MATURITY, PREMATURELY]

Lk	8:14	riches and pleasures, and *they do* not m.	5461
1Co	2: 6	speak a message of wisdom among the m,	5455
Eph	4:13	of the Son of God and become m,	467+5455
Php	3:15	All of us who are m should take such a view	5455
Col	4:12	in all the will of God, m and fully assured.	5455
Heb	5:14	But solid food is *for* the m,	5455
Jas	1: 4	so that you may be m and complete,	5455

MATURITY (1) [MATURE]

Heb	6: 1	go on to m, not laying again the foundation	5456

MAULED (3) [MAULS]

1Ki	13:26	*which has* m him and killed him,	8689
	13:28	The lion had neither eaten the body nor m	8689
2Ki	2:24	of the woods and m forty-two of the youths.	1324

MAULS (1) [MAULED]

Mic	5: 8	which m and mangles as it goes,	8252

MAW (KJV) See INNER PARTS

MAXIMS (1)

Job	13:12	Your m are proverbs of ashes;	2355

MAY (1231) See Index of Articles Etc.

MAYBE (3)

1Ki	18: 5	M we can find some grass to keep	218
	18:27	M he is sleeping and must be awakened."	218
Jnh	1: 6	M he will take notice of us,	218

MAZZAROTH (KJV) See CONSTELLATIONS

ME (4015) [I] See Index of Articles Etc.

ME JARKON (1)

Jos	19:46	M and Rakkon, with the area facing Joppa.	4770

ME-ZAHAB (2)

Ge	36:39	daughter of Matred, the daughter of M.	4771
1Ch	1:50	daughter of Matred, the daughter of M.	4771

MEADOW (2) [MEADOWS]

Isa	44: 4	They will spring up like grass in a m,	NIH
Hos	4:16	pasture them like lambs in a m?	5303

MEADOWS (3) [MEADOW]

Ps	65:13	The m are covered with flocks and	4120
Isa	30:23	that day your cattle will graze in broad m.	4120
Jer	25:37	The peaceful m will be laid waste because	5661

MEAH (KJV) See HUNDRED

MEAL (25) [MEALTIME]

Ge	19: 3	He prepared a m for them,	5492
	31:54	and invited his relatives to a m.	430+4312
	37:25	As they sat down to eat their m,	4312
Nu	15:21	the first of your **ground** m and present it as	6881
	15:21	the LORD from the first of your **ground** m.	6881
1Sa	20:27	the son of Jesse come to the m,	4312
2Sa	12: 4	of his own sheep or cattle to prepare a m for	NIH
1Ki	4:22	of fine flour and sixty cors of m,	7854
	17:12	a few sticks to take home and make a m	2084S
2Ki	4: 8	who urged him to **stay for a** m.	430+4312
Ne	10:37	to the priests, the first of our **ground** m,	6881
Job	33:20	and his soul loathes the choicest m.	4407
Pr	15:17	a m *of* vegetables where there is love than	786
Isa	44:16	over it he prepares his m,	1414
Jer	16: 5	a house where there is a **funeral**;	5301
Eze	44:30	your **ground** m so that a blessing may rest	6881
Lk	11:38	that Jesus did not first wash before the m,	756
Jn	13: 2	The **evening** m was being served,	1270
	13: 4	so he got up from the m,	1270
	13:28	no one **at the** m understood why Jesus said this	367+3836
Ac	10:10	and while the m was being prepared,	NIG
	16:34	his house and **set a** m before them;	4192+5544
1Co	10:27	If some unbeliever invites you to a m	NIG
	10:30	If I take part in the m with thankfulness,	NIG
Heb	12:16	for a single m sold his inheritance rights as	1111

MEALTIME (1) [MEAL]

Ru	2:14	At m Boaz said to her, "Come	431+2021+6961

MEAN (33) [MEANING, MEANINGLESS, MEANS, MEANT]

Ge	33: 8	"What do you m by all these droves I met?"	4200
Ex	12:26	'What does this ceremony m to you?'	4200
	13:14	'What does this m?'	4537
Jos	4: 6	'What do these stones m?'	4537
	4:21	'What do these stones m?'	4537
1Sa	1: 8	Don't I m more to you than ten sons?"	3202
	25: 3	a Calebite, was surly and m in his dealings.	8273

2Sa	5:24	because **that will** m the LORD has gone out	255
	17: 3	of the man you seek will m the return of all;	NIH
	19: 6	and their men m nothing **to** you.	4200
1Ch	14:15	**because that will** m God has gone out	3954
Job	6:26	*Do you* m to correct what I say,	3108
Isa	3:15	What do you m by crushing my people	4200
Eze	17:12	what these things m?"	4537
	18: 2	"What do you people m	4013+4200+4537
	37:18	'Won't you tell us what you m by this?'	4200
Da	5:26	"This is what these words m:	10600
Mt	12: 7	If you had known what these words m,	1639
Jn	7:36	What *did* he m when he said,	1639
	7:47	"You m he has deceived you also?"	NIG
	16:17	"What *does* he m by saying,	1639
	16:18	"What *does* he m by 'a little while'?	1639
Ac	2:12	"What *does* this m?"	1639+2527
	17:20	and we want to know what they m."	1639+2527
1Co	1:12	What *I* m is this: One of you says,	3306
	7:29	What *I* m, brothers, is that the time is short.	5774
	10:19	*Do I* m then that a sacrifice offered to	5774
	10:29	the other man's conscience, *I* m, not yours.	3306
	15:31	I m that, brothers—**just as surely**	3755
Gal	2:17	does that m that Christ promotes sin?	727
	3:17	What *I* m is this: The law, introduced	3306
Eph	4: 9	(What *does* "he ascended" m except that he	1639
Php	1:22	this will m fruitful labor for me.	NIG

MEANING (27) [MEAN]

Ge	21:29	"What is the m *of* these seven ewe	2179+4537
	40: 5	and each dream had a m *of* its own.	7355
	41:11	and each dream had a m *of* its own.	7355
Dt	6:20	"What is the m *of* the stipulations, decrees	4537
1Sa	4:14	"What is the m *of* this uproar?"	4537
1Ki	1:41	"What's the m *of* all the noise in the city?"	4508
Ne	8: 8	making it clear and giving the m so that	8507
Job	7:16	Let me alone; my days have no m.	2039
Ecc	6: 4	It comes **without** m, it departs in darkness,	928+2021+2039
	6:11	The more the words, the **less** the m,	2039+8049
	8:17	man cannot **discover** *its* m.	5162
Da	2:45	**This is the** m *of* the vision of the rock cut out of a mountain,	10168+10353+10619
	4:19	do not let the dream or its m alarm you."	10600
	4:19	your enemies and its m to your adversaries!	10600
	7:16	and asked him the **true** m of all this.	10327
	7:19	to **know** the **true** m of the fourth beast,	10326
	8:16	**tell** this man the m of the vision."	1067
Lk	8:11	"This is the m of the parable:	NIG
	18:34	Its m was hidden from them,	4839
	20:17	what is the m *of* that which is written:	5515
Ac	10:17	While Peter was wondering about the m of	1639
1Co	4: 6	you may learn from us the m of the saying,	NIG
	5:10	not at all m the people of this world	NIG
	14:10	yet none of them is **without** m.	936
	14:11	not **grasp the** m of what someone is saying,	1539+3836+3857
Gal	3:16	no say "and to seeds," m many people, but	6055
	3:16	but "and to your seed," m one person,	6055

MEANINGLESS (38) [MEAN]

Job	27:12	Why then this m talk?	2038+2039
Ecc	1: 2	"M! Meaningless!" says the Teacher. "Utterly meaningless!	2039
	1: 2	"Meaningless! M!" says the Teacher.	2039
	1: 2	says the Teacher. "**Utterly** m!	2039+2039
	1: 2	Everything is m."	2039
	1:14	all of them are m, a chasing after the wind.	2039
	2: 1	But that also proved to be m.	2039
	2:11	everything was m, a chasing after the wind;	2039
	2:15	I said in my heart, "This too is m."	2039
	2:17	All of it is m, a chasing after the wind.	2039
	2:19	This too is m.	2039
	2:21	This too is m and a great misfortune.	2039
	2:23	This too is m.	2039
	2:26	This too is m, a chasing after the wind.	2039
	3:19	Everything is m.	2039
	4: 4	This too is m, a chasing after the wind.	2039
	4: 7	Again I saw *something* m under the sun:	2039
	4: 8	This too is m—a miserable business!	2039
	4:16	This too is m, a chasing after the wind.	2039
	5: 7	Much dreaming and many words are m.	2039
	5:10	This too is m.	2039
	6: 2	This is m, a grievous evil.	2039
	6: 9	This too is m, a chasing after the wind.	2039
	6:12	the few and m days he passes through like	2039
	7: 6	This too is m.	2039
	7:15	In this m life of mine I have seen both	2039
	8:10	This too is m.	2039
	8:14	There is something else m that occurs	2039
	8:14	This too, I say, is m.	2039
	9: 9	of this m life that God has given you under	2039
	9: 9	given you under the sun—all your m days.	2039
	11: 8	Everything to come is m.	2039
	11:10	for youth and vigor are m.	2039
	12: 8	"M! Meaningless!" says the Teacher.	2039
	12: 8	"Meaningless! M!" says the Teacher.	2039
	12: 8	says the Teacher. "Everything is m!"	2039
Isa	1:13	Stop bringing m offerings!	8736
1Ti	1: 6	from these and turned to m talk.	3467

MEANS (66) [MEAN]

Ge	40:12	"This is *what* it m," Joseph said to him.	7355
	40:18	"This is *what* it m," Joseph said.	7355
Ex	28:30	the m of making decisions *for* the Israelites	5477
Lev	11:43	not make yourselves unclean **by** m of them	928

Ex	25:26	acquires **sufficient** m *to* redeem it,	1896+3869
	25:28	if he does not acquire the m to repay him,	1896
Nu	31:16	and were **the** m of turning	5034
1Sa	6: 3	but **by all** m send a guilt offering	8740+8740
2Sa	15:21	whether it m life or death,	4200
1Ki	22:15	" **'By what** m?' the LORD asked.	928+4537
2Ki	5: 5	"By all m, go," the king of Aram	995+2143
	5:23	"By all m, take two talents,"	3283
2Ch	18:20	" **'By what** m?' the LORD asked.	928+4537
Pr	16:15	When a king's face brightens, it m life;	NIH
	22:27	if you lack the m to pay,	NIH
Jer	17:11	the man who gains riches **by unjust** m.	928
	22:16	Is that not what it m to know me?"	NIH
Eze	44:19	the people **by** m of their garments.	928
Da	2: 3	and I want to **know** what it m."	3359
	2:25	who can tell the king *what* his dream m."	10600
	4:18	Now, Belteshazzar, tell me *what* it m,	10600
	4:26	with its roots that your kingdom will	NIH
	5: 7	and tells me *what* it m will be clothed	10600
	5:12	and he will tell you *what* the writing m."	10600
	5:15	to read this writing and tell me *what* it m,	10600
	5:16	and tell me *what* it m,	10600
	5:17	for the king and tell him *what* it m.	10600
Hos	11: 7	he will **by no** m exalt them.	3480+4202
Mt	1:23	Immanuel—which m, "God with us."	1639+3493
	2: 6	by no m least among the rulers of Judah;	4027
	5:18	will by any m disappear from the Law	NIG
	9:13	But go and learn what *this* m:	1639
	13:18	then to what the parable of the sower m:	NIG
	23:16	swears by the temple, it m nothing;	1639
	23:18	swears by the altar, *it* m nothing;	1639
	27:33	Golgotha (which m The Place of the Skull).	1639+3306
	27:46	which m, "My God, my God, why have	1639
Mk	3:17	Boanerges, which m Sons of Thunder),	1639
	5:41	(which m, "Little girl, I say to you,	1639+3493
	7:34	(which m, "Be opened!").	1639
	15:22	Golgotha (which m The Place of the Skull).	1639+3493
	15:34	which m, "My God, my God, why	1639+3493
Lk	8: 3	to support them out of their own m.	5639
Jn	1:38	They said, "Rabbi" (which m Teacher),	3493
	8:54	"If I glorify myself, my glory m nothing.	1639
	9: 7	in the Pool of Siloam" (this word m Sent).	2257
	13:24	"Ask him which one he m."	3306
	20:16	in Aramaic, "Rabboni!" (which m Teacher).	3306
Ac	4:36	apostles called Barnabas (which m Son of Encouragement),	1639+3493
	13: 8	(for that is what his name m) opposed them	3493
Ro	6: 2	By no m! We died to sin;	1181+3590
	6:15	but under grace? By no m!	1181+3590
	7:13	become death to me? By no m!	1181+3590
	11: 1	Did God reject his people? By no m!	1181+3590
	11:12	if their transgression m riches for the world,	NIG
	11:12	and their loss m riches for the Gentiles,	NIG
1Co	6: 7	lawsuits among you m you have been completely defeated already.	1639
	9:22	that by all possible m I might save some.	4122
	12: 8	of knowledge **by** m of the same Spirit,	2848
2Co	8:11	according to your m.	1666+2400+3836
Gal	6:15	nor circumcision m anything;	1639
1Ti	6: 5	think that godliness is a m to **financial gain**	4516
Heb	7: 2	First, his name m "king of righteousness";	2257
	7: 2	"king of Salem" m "king of peace."	1639+4005
	9:12	He did not enter **by** m of the blood of goats	1328
2Pe	3:15	that our Lord's patience m salvation,	NIG

MEANT (15) [MEAN]

Jdg	13:23	"If the LORD *had* m to kill us,	2911
Da	5: 8	the writing or tell the king *what* it m.	10600
Mk	4:22	For whatever is hidden is m to be disclosed,	2671
	4:22	whatever is concealed is m to be brought	2671
	9:10	discussing what "rising from the dead" m.	1639
	9:32	not understand what he m and were afraid	NIG
Lk	8: 9	His disciples asked him what this parable m	1639
	9:45	But they did not understand what this m.	4839
Jn	1:30	This is the one I m when I said,	NIG
	6:71	(*He* m Judas, the son of Simon Iscariot,	3306
	7:39	By this *he* m the Spirit,	3306+4309
	11:13	disciples thought *he* m natural sleep.	3306+4309
	13:22	at a loss to know which of them he m.	3306
	16:19	Are you asking one another what I m	4047+4309
1Co	6:13	The body is not m *for* sexual immorality,	AIT

MEANWHILE (32) [WHILE]

Ge	26:26	M, Abimelech had come to him	2256
	37:36	M, the Midianites sold Joseph in Egypt	2256
	38:20	M Judah sent the young goat by his friend	2256
Nu	32:17	M our women and children will live	2256
Jos	10:33	M, Horam king of Gezer had come up	255
Ru	4: 1	M Boaz went up to the town gate	2256
1Sa	2:18	M, the boy Samuel was grin the presence	2256
	17:41	M, the Philistine, with his shield bearer	2256
2Sa	2: 8	M, Abner son of Ner,	2256
	12:26	M Joab fought against Rabbah of	2256
	13:34	M, Absalom had fled.	2256
	16:15	M, Absalom and all the men of Israel came	2256
	18:17	M, all the Israelites fled to their homes.	2256
	19: 8	M, the Israelites had fled to their homes.	2256
1Ki	18:45	M, the sky grew black with clouds,	2256+3907+3907+6330+6330
	20:13	M a prophet came to Ahab king of Israel	2180
	20:23	M, the officials of the king	2256
2Ch	25:13	M the troops that Amaziah had sent back	2256
Ne	4:10	M, the people in Judah said,	2256

Est	9:16	**M**, the remainder of the Jews who were in	2256
Mt	27:11	**M** Jesus stood before the governor,	1254
Lk	1:21	**M**, the people were waiting for Zechariah	2779
	8:52	**M**, all the people were wailing	1254
	12: 1	**M**, when a crowd of many thousands	NIG
	15:25	"**M**, the older son was in the field.	1254
Jn	4:31	**M** his disciples urged him,	1877+3568+3836
	12: 9	**M** a large crowd of Jews found out	4036
	18:19	**M**, the high priest questioned Jesus	4036
Ac	7:58	**M**, the witnesses laid their clothes at	2779
	9: 1	**M**, Saul was still breathing out murderous	1254
		threats against the Lord's disciples.	
	18:24	**M** a Jew named Apollos,	1254
2Co	5: 2	**M** we groan, longing to be clothed	NIG

MEARAH (KJV) See ARAH

MEASURE (36) [IMMEASURABLY, MEASURED, MEASURELESS, MEASUREMENT, MEASUREMENTS, MEASURES, MEASURING]

Ge	15:16	not yet reached its **full m.**"	8969
	41:49	because it was beyond **m.**	5031
Nu	35: 5	**m** three thousand feet on the east side,	4499
Dt	21: 2	and judges shall go out and **m** *the* **distance**	4499
1Ki	7:23	a line of thirty cubits *to* **m around** it.	6015+6017
2Ch	4: 2	a line of thirty cubits *to* **m around** it.	6015+6017
Job	11: 9	Their **m** is longer than the earth	4500
Ps	60: 6	and **m** off the Valley of Succoth.	4499
	71:15	though I know not its **m.**	6228
	108: 7	and **m** off the Valley of Succoth.	4499
Isa	34:17	his hand distributes them by **m.**	7742
	47: 9	They will come upon you in **full m,**	9448
	64: 9	Do not be angry **beyond m,** O Lord;	4394+6330
	64:12	and punish us **beyond m?**	4394+6330
	65: 7	**m** into their laps the **full payment**	4499
La	5:22	and are angry with us **beyond m.**	4394+6330
Eze	4:11	Also **m out** a sixth of a hin of water	5374
	45: 3	**m off** a section 25,000	4499
	45:11	the homer is to be the **standard m** *for* both.	5504
Am	8: 5	the **m,** boosting the price and cheating	406
Zec	2: 2	He answered me, "To **m** Jerusalem,	4499
Mt	7: 2	you will be judged, and with the **m** you use,	3586
	23:32	then, the **m** of the sin of your forefathers!	3586
Mk	4:24	"With the **m** you use,	3586
Lk	6:38	A good **m,** pressed down,	3586
	6:38	For *with* the **m** you use,	3586
Jn	17:13	so that they may have the full **m** of my joy	NIG
Ro	12: 3	with the **m** of faith God has given you.	3586
	15:29	I will come in the **full m** of the blessing	4445
2Co	10:12	*When* they **m** themselves by themselves	3582
Eph	3:19	be filled to the **m** of all the fullness of God.	NIG
	4:13	to the whole of the fullness of Christ.	3586
2Pe	1: 8	you possess these qualities in increasing **m,**	NIG
Rev	11: 1	"Go and **m** the temple of God and the altar,	3582
	11: 2	But exclude the outer court; *do* not **m** it,	3582
	21:15	with me had a measuring rod of gold to **m**	3582

MEASURED (48) [MEASURE]

Ex	16:18	And when *they* **m** it by the omer,	4499
2Sa	8: 2	on the ground and **m** them off with a length	4499
1Ki	6:25	The second cherub also **m** ten cubits,	NIH
	7:31	with its basework it **m** a cubit and a half.	NIH
Job	28:25	and **m out** the waters,	928+4500+9419
Isa	40:12	Who *has* **m** the waters in the hollow	4499
Jer	31:37	"Only if the heavens above *can* be **m** and	4499
Eze	40: 5	*He* **m** the wall.	4499
	40: 6	He climbed its steps and **m** the threshold of	4499
	40: 8	Then he **m** the portico of the gateway;	4499
	40:11	Then *he* **m** the width of the entrance to	4499
	40:13	Then *he* **m** the gateway from the top of	4499
	40:14	*He* **m** *along* the faces of	6913
	40:19	Then *he* **m** the distance from the inside of	4499
	40:20	Then *he* **m** the length and width of	4499
	40:23	*He* **m** from one gate to the opposite one;	4499
	40:24	*He* **m** its jambs and its portico,	4499
	40:27	and *he* **m** from this gate to the outer gate on	4499
	40:28	and **he m** the south gate;	4499
	40:32	and **he m** the gateway;	4499
	40:35	he brought me to the north gate and **m** it.	4499
	40:47	Then *he* **m** the court:	4499
	40:48	the portico of the temple and **m** the jambs of	4499
	41: 1	to the outer sanctuary and **m** the jambs;	4499
	41: 2	*He* also **m** the outer sanctuary;	4499
	41: 3	into the inner sanctuary and **m** the jambs of	4499
	41: 4	And *he* **m** the length of the inner sanctuary;	4499
	41: 5	Then *he* **m** the wall of the temple;	4499
	41:13	Then *he* **m** the temple;	4499
	41:15	Then *he* **m** the length of the building facing	4499
	42:15	by the east gate and **m** the area all around:	4499
	42:16	*He* **m** the east side with the measuring rod;	4499
	42:17	*He* **m** the north side;	4499
	42:18	*He* **m** the south side;	4499
	42:19	Then he turned to the west side and **m;**	4499
	42:20	So *he* **m** the area on all four sides.	4499
	45:14	The prescribed portion of oil, **m** by the bath,	NIH
	47: 3	*he* **m** off a thousand cubits and then led me	4499
	47: 4	*He* **m** off another thousand cubits	4499
	47: 4	*He* **m** off another thousand and led me	4499
	47: 5	*He* **m** off another thousand,	4499
Hos	1:10	which cannot **be m** or counted.	4499
Am	7:17	Your land will be **m** and divided up,	2475
Mt	7: 2	the measure you use, *it will be* **m** to you.	3582
Mk	4:24	*it will be* **m** to you—and even more.	3586

Lk	6:38	the measure you use, *it will be* **m** to you."	520
Rev	21:16	*He* **m** the city with the rod and found it to	3582
	21:17	*He* **m** its wall and it was 144 cubits thick,	3582

MEASURELESS (2) [MEASURE]

1Ki	4:29	a breadth of understanding **as m as** the sand	3869
Jer	33:22	and as **m** as the sand on the seashore.'	4202+4499

MEASUREMENT (2) [MEASURE]

Eze	40:14	The **m** was up to the portico facing	NIH
Rev	21:17	by man's **m,** which the angel was using.	3586

MEASUREMENTS (13) [MEASURE]

1Ch	23:29	and all **m** of **quantity** and size.	5374
Eze	40:10	the three had the same **m,**	4500
	40:10	on each side had the same **m.**	4500
	40:21	and its portico had the same **m** as those of	4500
	40:22	the same **m** as those of the gate facing east.	4500
	40:24	and they had the same **m** as the others.	4500
	40:28	it had the same **m** as the others.	4500
	40:29	and its portico had the same **m** as the others.	4500
	40:32	it had the same **m** as the others.	4500
	40:33	and its portico had the same **m** as the others.	4500
	40:35	It had the same **m** as the others,	4500
	43:13	"These are the **m** *of* the altar in long cubits,	4500
	48:16	and will have these **m:**	4500

MEASURES (9) [MEASURE]

Dt	25:14	not have **two differing m** in your house—	406+406+2256
	25:15	accurate and honest weights and **m,**	406
Ru	3:15	**poured into** it six **m** of barley	4499
	3:17	"He gave me these six **m** of barley, saying,	NIH
Pr	20:10	Differing weights and **differing m**	406+406+2256
Isa	44:13	The carpenter **m** *with* a line and makes	5742
Eze	48:33	"On the south side, which **m** 4,500 cubits,	4500
Hag	2:16	When anyone came to a heap of twenty, **m**	NIH
	2:16	anyone went to a wine vat to draw fifty **m,**	7053

MEASURING (26) [MEASURE]

Lev	19:35	not use dishonest **standards** when **m** length,	5477
1Ki	7:10	some **m** ten cubits and some eight.	NIH
	7:23	**m** ten cubits from rim to rim	NIH
	7:38	each holding forty baths and **m** four cubits	NIH
2Ki	21:13	the **m line** *used against* Samaria and	7742
2Ch	3:15	each with a capital on top **m** five cubits.	NIH
	4: 2	**m** ten cubits from rim to rim	NIH
Job	38: 5	Who stretched a **m line** across it?	7742
Isa	28:17	I will make justice the **m line**	7742
	34:11	God will stretch out over Edom the **m line**	7742
Jer	31:39	The **m line** will stretch from there straight to	4500
La	2: 8	a **m line** and did not withhold his hand	7742
Eze	40: 3	the gateway with a linen cord and a **m rod**	4500
	40: 5	The length of the **m rod** in the man's hand	4500
	40: 5	it was one **m rod** thick and one rod high.	7866
	42:15	When he had finished **m** what was inside	4500
	42:16	He measured the east side with the **m rod;**	4500
	42:17	it was five hundred cubits by the **m rod.**	4500
	42:18	it was five hundred cubits by the **m rod.**	4500
	42:19	it was five hundred cubits by the **m rod.**	4500
	47: 3	As the man went eastward with a **m line**	7742
Zec	1:16	And the **m line** will be stretched out	7742
	2: 1	before me was a man with a **m line**	4500
	5: 6	He replied, "It is a **m basket.**"	406
Rev	11: 1	a reed like a **m rod** and was told,	4811
	21:15	The angel who talked with me had a **m rod**	3586

MEAT (91) [MEATS]

Ge	9: 4	not eat **m** that has its lifeblood still in it.	1414
Ex	12: 8	to eat the **m** roasted over the fire,	1414
	12: 9	Do not eat the **m** raw or cooked in water,	5647S
	12:46	take none of the **m** outside the house.	1414
	16: 3	There we sat around pots of **m** and ate all	1414
	16: 8	that it was the Lord when he gives you **m**	1414
	16:12	Tell them, 'At twilight you will eat **m,**	1414
	21:28	and its **m** must not be eaten.	1414
	22:31	the **m** of an animal torn by wild beasts;	1414
	27: 3	sprinkling bowls, **m forks** and firepans.	4657
	29:31	the ram for the ordination and cook the **m** in	1414
	29:32	and his sons are to eat the **m** *of* the ram and	1414
	29:34	And if any of the **m** of the ordination ram	1414
	38: 3	sprinkling bowls, **m forks** and firepans.	4657
Lev	6:28	The clay pot the **m** is cooked in must	NIH
	7:15	The **m** *of* his fellowship offering,	1414
	7:17	Any **m** *of* the sacrifice left over till	1414
	7:18	If any **m** *of* the fellowship offering is eaten	1414
	7:19	" '**M** that touches anything ceremonially	1414
		unclean must not be eaten;	
	7:19	As for other **m,** anyone ceremonially clean	1414
	7:20	But if anyone who is unclean eats any **m** of	1414
	7:21	the **m** *of* the fellowship offering belonging	1414
	8:31	the **m** at the entrance to the Tent of Meeting	1414
	8:32	burn up the rest of the **m** and the bread.	1414
	11: 8	not eat their **m** or touch their carcasses.	1414
	11:11	you must not eat their **m**	1414
	19:26	" 'Do not eat any **m** with the blood still in it.	NIH
Nu	4:14	**m forks,** shovels and sprinkling bowls.	4657
	11: 4	"If only we had **m** to eat!"	1414
	11:13	Where can I get **m** for all these people?	1414
	11:13	'Give us **m** to eat!'	1414
	11:18	when you will eat **m.**	1414
	11:18	"If only we had **m** to eat!	1414
	11:18	Lord will give you **m,** and you will eat it.	1414

Nu	11:21	'I will give them **m** to eat for a whole month	1414
	11:33	while the **m** was still between their teeth	1414
	18:18	Their **m** is to be yours,	1414
Dt	12:15	of your towns and eat as much of the **m**	1414
	12:20	and you crave **m** and say,	1414
	12:20	"I would like *some* **m,**"	1414
	12:23	and you must not eat the life with the **m.**	1414
	12:27	both the **m** and the blood.	1414
	12:27	but you may eat the **m.**	1414
	14: 8	not to eat their **m** or touch their carcasses.	1414
	16: 4	of the **m** you sacrifice on the evening of	1414
Jdg	6:19	Putting the **m** in a basket and its broth in	1414
	6:20	"Take the **m** and the unleavened bread,	1414
	6:21	the angel of the Lord touched the **m** and	1414
	6:21	consuming the **m** and the bread.	1414
1Sa	1: 4	he would give **portions** of the **m**	4950
	2:13	and while the **m** was being boiled,	1414
	2:15	"Give the priest *some* **m** to roast;	1414
	2:15	he won't accept boiled **m** from you,	1414
	9:23	"Bring the **piece of m** I gave you,	4950
	14:33	the Lord by eating **m** that has blood	NIH
	14:34	Do not sin against the Lord by eating **m**	NIH
	25:11	the **m** I have slaughtered for my shearers,	3186
1Ki	17: 6	and **m** in the morning and bread and meat in	1414
	17: 6	and meat in the morning and bread and **m** in	1414
	19:21	to cook the **m** and gave it to the people,	1414
2Ch	4:16	shovels, **m forks** and all related articles.	4657
Job	31:31	'Who has not had his fill of Job's **m?**'—	1414
Ps	78:20	Can he supply **m** for his people?"	8638
	78:27	He rained **m** down on them like dust,	8638
Pr	9: 2	She has prepared her **m** and mixed her wine	3181
	23:20	or gorge themselves on **m,**	1414
Isa	22:13	eating of **m** and drinking of wine!	1414
	44:16	he roasts his **m** and eats his fill.	7507
	44:19	I roasted an **m** and I ate.	1414
	65: 4	and whose pots hold broth of **unclean m;**	7002
Jer	7:21	and eat the **m** yourselves!	1414
	11:15	Can consecrated **m** avert	1414
Eze	4:14	No unclean **m** has ever entered my mouth."	1414
	11: 3	city is a cooking pot, and we are the **m.**'	1414
	11: 7	The bodies you have thrown there are the **m**	1414
	11:11	nor will you be the **m** in it;	1414
	24: 4	Put into it the **pieces of m,**	5984
	24:10	Cook the **m** well, mixing in the spices;	1414
	33:25	Since you eat **m** with the blood still in it	NIH
Da	10: 3	no **m** or wine touched my lips;	1414
Hos	8:13	sacrifices given to me and they eat the **m,**	1414
Mic	3: 3	who chop them up like **m** for the pan,	NIH
Hag	2:12	If a person carries consecrated **m** in the fold	1414
Zec	11:16	but will eat the **m** *of* the choice sheep,	1414
Ac	15:20	**m of strangled animals** and from blood.	4465
	15:29	blood, *from* the **m of strangled animals**	4465
	21:25	blood, *from* the **m of strangled animals**	4465
Ro	14: 6	He who eats **m,** eats to the Lord,	NIG
	14:21	to eat **m** or drink wine or to do anything else	3200
1Co	8:13	I will never eat **m** again, so that I will not	3200
	10:25	in the **market** without raising questions	3425

MEATS (1) [MEAT]

Isa	25: 6	the best of **m** and the finest of wines.	4683

MEBUNNAI (1)

2Sa	23:27	Abiezer from Anathoth, **M** the Hushathite,	4446

MECHERATHITE (KJV) See MEKERATHITE

MECONAH (1)

Ne	11:28	in Ziklag, in **M** and its settlements,	4828

MEDAD (2)

Nu	11:26	two men, whose names were Eldad and **M,**	4773
	11:27	and **M** are prophesying in the camp."	4773

MEDAN (2)

Ge	25: 2	She bore him Zimran, Jokshan, **M,** Midian,	4527
1Ch	1:32	Zimran, Jokshan, **M,** Midian,	4527

MEDDLER (1) [MEDDLES]

1Pe	4:15	any other kind of criminal, or even as a **m.**	258

MEDDLES (1) [MEDDLER]

Pr	26:17	a passer-by *who* **m** in a quarrel not his own.	6297

MEDE (3) [MEDIA]

Da	5:31	and Darius the **M** took over the kingdom,	10404
	9: 1	(a **M** by descent), who was made ruler over	4512
	11: 1	And in the first year of Darius the **M,**	4513

MEDEBA (5)

Nu	21:30	which extends to **M.**"	4772
Jos	13: 9	and included the whole plateau of **M** as far	4772
	13:16	and the whole plateau past **M**	4772
1Ch	19: 7	who came and camped near **M,**	4772
Isa	15: 2	Moab wails over Nebo and **M.**	4772

MEDES (10) [MEDIA]

2Ki	17: 6	the Habor River and in the towns of the **M.**	4512
	18:11	on the Habor River and in towns of the **M.**	4512

Isa 13:17 See, I will stir up against them the M, 4512
Jer 51:11 LORD has stirred up the kings of the M, 4512
51:28 battle against her—the kings of the M, 4512
Da 5:28 and given to the M and Persians." 10404
6:8 in accordance with the laws of the M 10404
6:12 in accordance with the laws of the M 10404
6:15 to the law of the M and Persians no decree 10404
Ac 2:9 Parthians, M and Elamites; 3597

MEDIA (8) [MEDE, MEDES, MEDIAN]
Ezr 6:2 in the province of M, and this was written 10404
Est 1:3 The military leaders of Persia and M, 4512
1:14 of Persia and M who had special access to 4512
1:19 be written in the laws of Persia and M, 4512
10:2 of the annals of the kings of M and Persia? 4512
Isa 21:2 M, lay siege! 4512
Jer 25:25 all the kings of Zimri, Elam and M; 4512
Da 8:20 that you saw represents the kings of M 4512

MEDIAN (1) [MEDIA]
Est 1:18 This very day the Persian and M women of 4512

MEDIATE (1) [MEDIATOR]
1Sa 2:25 God may m for him; 7136

MEDIATOR (7) [MEDIATE]
Job 33:23 "Yet if there is an angel on his side as a m, 4885
Gal 3:19 The law was put into effect through angels by a m. 3542
3:20 A m, however, does represent just one 3542
1Ti 2:5 there is one God and one m between God 3542
Heb 8:6 as the covenant of which he is m is superior 3542
9:15 Christ is the m of a new covenant, 3542
12:24 to Jesus the m of a new covenant, 3542

MEDICINE (1)
Pr 17:22 A cheerful heart is good m, 1565

MEDITATE (14) [MEDITATED, MEDITATES, MEDITATION]
Ge 24:63 He went out to the field one evening to m, 8452
Jos 1:8 m on it day and night, 2047
Ps 48:9 O God, we m on your unfailing love. 1948
77:12 I will m on all your works 2047
119:15 I m on your precepts. 8488
119:23 your servant will m on your decrees. 8488
119:27 then I will m on your wonders. 8488
119:48 which I love, and I m on your decrees. 8488
119:78 but I will m on your precepts. 8488
119:97 I m on it all day long. 8491
119:99 for I m on your statutes. 8491
119:148 that I may m on your promises. 8488
143:5 I m on all your works 2047
145:5 and I will m on your wonderful works. 8488

MEDITATED (1) [MEDITATE]
Ps 39:3 My heart grew hot within me, and as I m, 2052

MEDITATES (1) [MEDITATE]
Ps 1:2 and on his law he m day and night. 2047

MEDITATION (2) [MEDITATE]
Ps 19:14 the m of my heart be pleasing in your sight, 2053
104:34 May my m be pleasing to him, 8490

MEDIUM (4) [MEDIUMS]
Lev 20:27 "'A man or woman who is a m or spiritist 200
Dt 18:11 who is a m or spiritist or who consults 200+8626
1Sa 28:7 "Find me a woman who is a m, 200+1266
1Ch 10:13 and even consulted a m for guidance, 200

MEDIUMS (10) [MEDIUM]
Lev 19:31 "'Do not turn to m or seek out spiritists, 200
20:6 the person who turns to m and spiritists 200
1Sa 28:3 Saul had expelled the m and spiritists from 200
28:9 He has cut off the m and spiritists from 200
2Ki 21:6 and consulted m and spiritists. 200
23:24 Josiah got rid of the m and spiritists, 200
2Ch 33:6 and consulted m and spiritists. 200
Isa 8:19 When men tell you to consult m 200
19:3 the m and the spiritists. 200
Jer 27:9 your m or your sorcerers who tell you, 6726

MEEK (3) [MEEKLY, MEEKNESS]
Ps 37:11 But the m will inherit the land 6705
Zep 3:12 I will leave within you the m and humble, 6714
Mt 5:5 Blessed are the m, for they will inherit 4558

MEEKLY (1) [MEEK]
1Ki 21:27 He lay in sackcloth and went around m. 351

MEEKNESS (1) [MEEK]
2Co 10:1 By the m and gentleness of Christ, 4559

MEET (145) [MEETING, MEETINGS, MEETS, MET]
Ge 14:17 the king of Sodom came out to m him 7925

Ge 18:2 to m them and bowed low to the ground. 7925
19:1 up to m them and bowed down with his face 7925
19:6 to m them and shut the door behind him NIH
24:17 The servant hurried to m her and said, 7925
24:65 that man in the field coming to m us?" 7925
29:13 his sister's son, he hurried to m him. 7925
30:16 Leah went out to m him. 7925
32:6 and now he is coming to m you, 7925
32:19 the same thing to Esau when you m him. 5162
33:4 But Esau ran to m Jacob and embraced him; 7925
46:29 and went to Goshen to m his father Israel. 7925
Ex 4:14 He is already on his way to m you, 7925
4:27 "Go into the desert to m Moses." 7925
5:14 "Why didn't you m your quota 3983
5:20 and Aaron waiting to m them, 7925
7:15 Wait on the bank of the Nile to m him. 7925
18:7 So Moses went out to m his father-in-law 7925
19:17 the people out of the camp to m with God, 7925
25:22 I will m with you and give you all my 3585
29:42 There I will m you and speak to you; 3585
29:43 there also I will m with the Israelites, 3585
30:6 where I will m with you. 3585
30:36 where I will m with you. 3585
Nu 14:35 They will m their end in this desert; 9462
17:4 where I m with you. 3585
21:33 and his whole army marched out to m them 7925
22:36 he went out to m him at the Moabite town 7925
23:3 the LORD will come to m with me. 7925
23:15 "Stay here beside your offering while I m 7936
23:16 of the community went to m them outside 7925
Dt 2:32 and all his army came out to m us in battle 7925
3:1 with his whole army marched out to m us 7925
22:23 to m in a town a virgin pledged to 5162
22:25 out in the country a man happens to m a girl 5162
22:28 If a man happens to m a virgin who is 5162
23:4 For they did not come to m you with bread 7709
Jos 8:14 in the morning to m Israel in battle at 7925
9:11 go and m them and say to them, 7925
Jdg 4:18 Jael went out to m Sisera and said to him, 7925
4:22 and Jael went out to m him. 7925
6:35 so that they too went up to m them. 7925
11:31 the door of my house to m me when I return 7925
11:34 who should come out to m him 7925
20:31 to m them and were drawn away from 7925
1Sa 4:2 Philistines deployed their forces to m Israel, 7925
10:2 you will m two men near Rachel's tomb, 5162
10:3 up to God at Bethel will m you there. 5162
10:5 you will m a procession of prophets 7003
15:12 Samuel got up and went to m Saul, 7925
17:2 of Elah and drew up their battle line to m 7925
17:48 toward the battle line to m him. 7925
17:55 As Saul watched David going out to m 7925
18:6 from all the towns of Israel to m King Saul 7925
21:2 I have told them to m me at a certain place. NIH
23:28 of David and went to m the Philistines. 7925
25:32 who has sent you today to m me. 7925
25:34 if you had not come quickly to m me, 7925
30:21 They came out to m David and the people 7925
2Sa 6:20 Michal daughter of Saul came out to m him 7925
10:5 he sent messengers to m the men, 7925
10:17 to m David and fought against him. 7925
15:32 Hushai the Arkite was there to m him, 7925
16:1 steward of Mephibosheth, waiting to m him. 7925
18:9 Absalom happened to m David's men. 4200+7156
19:15 to go out and m the king and bring him 7925
19:16 with the men of Judah to m King David. 7925
19:20 to come down and m my lord the king." 7925
19:24 also went down to m the king. 7925
19:25 When he came from Jerusalem to m 7925
20:8 Amasa came to m them. 4200+7156
1Ki 2:8 When he came down to m me at the Jordan, 7925
2:19 the king stood up to m her, 7925
18:16 So Obadiah went to m Ahab and told him, 7925
18:16 and Ahab went to m Elijah. 7925
18:19 the people from all over Israel to m me 7925
20:9 but this demand I cannot m.'" 6913
20:27 they marched out to m them. 7925
21:18 "Go down to m Ahab king of Israel, 7925
2Ki 1:3 "Go up and m the messengers of the king 7925
1:6 "A man came to m us," they replied. 7925
1:7 of man was it who came to m you 7925
2:15 And they went to m him and bowed to 7925
4:26 Run to m her and ask her, 7925
4:29 If you m anyone, do not greet him, 5162
4:31 Gehazi went back to m Elisha and told him, 7925
5:21 he got down from the chariot to m him. 7925
5:26 down from his chariot to m you? 3782
6:1 the place where we m with you is too small 7925
8:8 a gift with you and go to m the man of God. 7925
8:9 Hazael went to m Elisha, 7925
9:17 "Send him to m them and ask, 7925
9:18 The horseman rode off to m Jehu and said, 7925
9:21 each in his own chariot, to m Jehu. 7925
10:15 who was on his way to m him. 7925
14:8 "Come, m me face to face." 8011
16:10 to Damascus to m Tiglath-Pileser king 7925
23:29 Josiah marched out to m him in battle, 7925
1Ch 12:17 David went out to m them and said 4200+7156
14:8 about it and went out to m them. 4200+7156
19:5 he sent messengers to m them, 7925
19:17 David formed his lines to m the Arameans 7925
2Ch 14:10 Asa went out to m him, 4200+7156
15:2 He went out to m Asa and said to him, 4200+7156
19:2 went out to m him and said to him, 448+7156
22:7 he went out with Joram to m Jehu son 448
25:17 "Come, m me face to face." 8011
28:9 to m the army when it returned to 4200+7156

2Ch 35:20 Josiah marched out to m him in battle. 7925
Ne 4:9 a guard day and night to m this threat. 4946+7156
6:2 let us m together in one of the villages on 3585
6:10 He said, "Let us m in the house of God, 3585
Ps 42:2 When can I go and m with God? 7156+8011
79:8 may your mercy come quickly to m us, 7709
85:10 Love and faithfulness m together; 7008
Pr 7:10 Then out came a woman to m him, 7925
7:15 So I came out to m you; 7925
8:2 where the paths m, she takes her stand; 1075
17:12 Better to m a bear robbed of her cubs than 7008
Isa 7:3 to m Ahaz at the end of the aqueduct of 7925
14:9 The grave below is all astir to m you 7925
34:14 Desert creatures will m with hyenas, 7008
41:1 let us m together at the place of judgment. 7928
66:17 they will m their end together," 6066
Jer 41:6 went out from Mizpah to m them, 7925
Am 4:12 prepare to m your God, O Israel." 7125
5:19 as though a man fled from a lion only to m 7003
9:10 'Disaster will not overtake or m us.' 7709
Zec 2:3 and another angel came to m him 7925
Mt 8:34 Then the whole town went out to m Jesus. 5637
25:1 and went out to m the bridegroom. 5637
25:6 Come out to m him!' 561
Mk 5:2 from the tombs to m him. 5636
14:13 a man carrying a jar of water will m you. 560
Lk 22:10 a man carrying a jar of water will m you. 5267
Jn 11:20 she went out to m him, 5636
12:13 and went out to m him, shouting, 5637
12:18 went out to m him. 5636
Ac 2:46 Every day they continued to m together in NIG
5:12 And all the believers used to m together 1639
28:15 of Appius and the Three Taverns to m us. 561
28:23 They arranged to m Paul on a certain day, NIG
1Co 11:34 that when you m together it may not result 5302
Php 4:19 And my God will m all your needs 4444
1Th 4:17 up together with them in the clouds to m 561

MEETING (158) [MEET]
Ex 27:21 In the Tent of M, outside the curtain 4595
28:43 enter the Tent of M or approach the altar 4595
29:4 to the Tent of M and wash them with water. 4595
29:10 the bull to the front of the Tent of M, 4595
29:11 at the entrance to the Tent of M. 4595
29:30 and comes to the Tent of M to minister in 4595
29:32 At the entrance to the Tent of M, 4595
29:42 at the entrance to the Tent of M before 4595
29:44 "So I will consecrate the Tent of M and 4595
30:16 and use it for the service of the Tent of M. 4595
30:18 between the Tent of M and the altar, 4595
30:20 Whenever they enter the Tent of M, 4595
30:26 Then use it to anoint the Tent of M, 4595
30:36 in front of the Testimony in the Tent of M, 4595
31:7 the Tent of M, the ark of the Testimony 4595
33:7 calling it the "tent of m." 4595
33:7 to the tent of m outside the camp. 4595
35:21 the LORD for the work on the Tent of M, 4595
38:8 at the entrance to the Tent of M. 4595
38:30 the bases for the entrance to the Tent of M, 4595
39:32 the Tent of M, was completed. 4595
39:40 for the tabernacle, the Tent of M; 4595
40:2 the tabernacle, the Tent of M, 4595
40:6 the tabernacle, the Tent of M; 4595
40:7 place the basin between the Tent of M and 4595
40:12 to the Tent of M and wash them with water. 4595
40:22 Moses placed the table in the Tent of M on 4595
40:24 of M opposite the table on the south side of 4595
40:26 the gold altar in the Tent of M in front of 4595
40:29 the tabernacle, the Tent of M, 4595
40:30 He placed the basin between the Tent of M 4595
40:32 the Tent of M or approached the altar, 4595
40:34 Then the cloud covered the Tent of M, 4595
40:35 the Tent of M because the cloud had settled 4595
Lev 1:1 and spoke to him from the Tent of M. 4595
1:3 the entrance to the Tent of M so that it will 4595
1:5 on all sides at the entrance to the Tent of M. 4595
3:2 at the entrance to the Tent of M. 4595
3:8 and slaughter it in front of the Tent of M. 4595
3:13 and slaughter it in front of the Tent of M. 4595
4:4 the bull at the entrance to the Tent of M. 4595
4:5 and carry it into the Tent of M. 4595
4:7 that is before the LORD in the Tent of M. 4595
4:14 and present it before the Tent of M. 4595
4:16 of the bull's blood into the Tent of M. 4595
4:18 that is before the LORD in the Tent of M. 4595
4:18 at the entrance to the Tent of M. 4595
6:16 to eat it in the courtyard of the Tent of M. 4595
6:26 in the courtyard of the Tent of M. 4595
6:30 into the Tent of M to make atonement in 4595
8:3 at the entrance to the Tent of M." 4595
8:4 at the entrance to the Tent of M. 4595
8:31 the Tent of M and eat it there with the bread 4595
8:33 Do not leave the entrance to the Tent of M 4595
8:35 the entrance to the Tent of M day and night 4595
9:5 to the front of the Tent of M, 4595
9:23 and Aaron then went into the Tent of M. 4595
10:7 Do not leave the entrance to the Tent of M 4595
10:9 into the Tent of M, or you will die. 4595
12:6 to the priest at the entrance to the Tent of M 4595
14:11 the priest at the entrance to the Tent of M, 4595
14:23 the priest at the entrance to the Tent of M, 4595
15:14 to the Tent of M and give them to the priest. 4595
15:29 the priest at the entrance to the Tent of M, 4595
16:7 at the entrance to the Tent of M. 4595
16:16 He is to do the same for the Tent of M, 4595

Lev	16:17	the Tent of M from the time Aaron goes in	4595
	16:20	the Tent of M and the altar,	4595
	16:23	of M and take off the linen garments he put	4595
	16:33	for the Tent of M and the altar,	4595
	17: 4	the entrance to the Tent of M to present it as	4595
	17: 5	to the Tent of M and sacrifice them	4595
	17: 6	the LORD at the entrance to the Tent of M	4595
	17: 9	not bring it to the entrance to the Tent of M	4595
	19:21	a ram to the entrance to the Tent of M for	4595
	24: 3	of the Testimony in the Tent of M,	4595
Nu	1: 1	of M in the Desert of Sinai on the first day	4595
	2: 2	around the Tent of M some distance from it,	4595
	2:17	Then the Tent of M and the camp of	4595
	3: 7	for the whole community at the Tent of M	4595
	3: 8	of all the furnishings of the Tent of M,	4595
	3:25	of M the Gershonites were responsible for	4595
	3:25	the curtain at the entrance to the Tent of M,	4595
	3:38	in front of the Tent of M.	4595
	4: 3	to serve in the work in the Tent of M.	4595
	4: 4	of the Kohathites in the Tent of M:	4595
	4:15	that are in the Tent of M.	4595
	4:23	to serve in the work at the Tent of M.	4595
	4:25	curtains of the tabernacle, the Tent of M,	4595
	4:25	for the entrance to the Tent of M,	4595
	4:28	of the Gershonite clans at the Tent of M.	4595
	4:30	to serve in the work at the Tent of M.	4595
	4:31	as they perform service at the Tent of M:	4595
	4:33	of M under the direction of Ithamar son	4595
	4:35	to serve in the work in the Tent of M,	4595
	4:37	who served in the Tent of M.	4595
	4:39	to serve in the work at the Tent of M,	4595
	4:41	who served at the Tent of M.	4595
	4:43	to serve in the work at the Tent of M,	4595
	4:47	of serving and carrying the Tent of M	4595
	6:10	the priest at the entrance to the Tent of M.	4595
	6:13	be brought to the entrance to the Tent of M.	4595
	6:18	" 'Then at the entrance to the Tent of M,	4595
	7: 5	be used in the work at the Tent of M.	4595
	7:89	the Tent of M to speak with the LORD,	4595
	8: 9	to the front of the Tent of M and assemble	4595
	8:15	to come to do their work at the Tent of M.	4595
	8:19	and his sons to do the work at the Tent of M	4595
	8:22	to do their work at the Tent of M under	4595
	8:24	to take part in the work at the Tent of M,	4595
	8:26	in performing their duties at the Tent of M,	4595
	10: 3	before you at the entrance to the Tent of M.	4595
	11:16	Have them come to the Tent of M,	4595
	12: 4	"Come out to the Tent of M."	4595
	14:10	the LORD appeared at the Tent of M to all	4595
	16:18	and Aaron at the entrance to the Tent of M.	4595
	16:19	to them at the entrance to the Tent of M,	4595
	16:42	and turned toward the Tent of M,	4595
	16:43	to the front of the Tent of M,	4595
	16:50	to Moses at the entrance to the Tent of M.	4595
	17: 4	in the Tent of M in front of the Testimony,	4595
	18: 4	be responsible for the care of the Tent of M	4595
	18: 6	the LORD to do the work at the Tent of M.	4595
	18:21	while serving at the Tent of M.	4595
	18:22	not go near the Tent of M.	4595
	18:23	at the Tent of M and bear the responsibility	4595
	18:31	for your work at the Tent of M.	4595
	19: 4	toward the front of the Tent of M.	4595
	20: 6	to the Tent of M and fell facedown,	4595
	25: 6	at the entrance to the Tent of M.	4595
	27: 2	to the Tent of M and stood before Moses,	4595
	31:54	Tent of M as a memorial for the Israelites	4595
Dt	31:14	and present yourselves at the Tent of M.	4595
	31:14	and presented themselves at the Tent of M.	4595
Jos	18: 1	at Shiloh and set up the Tent of M there.	4595
	19:51	at the entrance to the Tent of M.	4595
	22:32	to Canaan from their m with the Reubenites	NIH
1Sa	2:22	at the entrance to the Tent of M.	4595
	20:35	to the field for his m with David.	4595
1Ki	8: 4	the Tent of M and all the sacred furnishings	4595
2Ki	4:38	company of the prophets was m with him,	3782
1Ch	6:32	music before the tabernacle, the Tent of M,	4595
	9:21	at the entrance to the Tent of M.	4595
	23:32	for the Tent of M, for the Holy Place and,	4595
2Ch	1: 3	for God's Tent of M was there,	4595
	1: 6	of M and offered a thousand burnt offerings	4595
	1:13	from before the Tent of M.	4595
	5: 5	the Tent of M and all the sacred furnishings	4595
Ne	5: 7	I called together a large m to deal with them	7737
La	2: 6	he has destroyed his place of m.	4595
Jn	11:47	the Pharisees called a m of the Sanhedrin.	5251
Ac	4:31	the place where they were m was shaken.	5251
	17:19	and brought him to a m of the Areopagus,	740
	17:22	then stood up in the m of the Areopagus	740
	20: 8	in the upstairs room where we were m.	5251
Heb	10:25	Let us not give up m together,	2191
Jas	2: 2	Suppose a man comes into your m wearing	5252

MEETINGS (1) [MEET]

1Co	11:17	for your m do more harm than good.	5302

MEETS (7) [MEET]

Ge	32:17	"When my brother Esau m you and asks,	7008
Nu	35:19	when he m him, he shall put him to death.	7003
	35:21	the murderer to death when he m him.	7003
Ro	16: 5	Greet also the church that m at their house.	NIG
1Co	16:19	and so does the church that m at their house.	NIG
Phm	1: 2	and to the church that m in your home:	2848
Heb	7:26	Such a high priest m our need—	4560

MEGIDDO (12)

Jos	12:21	the king of Taanach one the king of M one	4459
	17:11	Endor, Taanach and M,	4459
Jdg	1:27	or M and their surrounding settlements,	4459
	5:19	at Taanach by the waters of M,	4459
1Ki	4:12	and M, and in all of Beth Shan next	4459
	9:15	and Hazor, M and Gezer.	4459
2Ki	9:27	but he escaped to M and died there.	4459
	23:29	but Neco faced him and killed him at M.	4459
	23:30	from M to Jerusalem and buried him	4459
1Ch	7:29	M and Dor, together with their villages.	4459
2Ch	35:22	but went to fight him on the plain of M.	4459
Zec	12:11	of Hadad Rimmon in the plain of M.	4461

MEGIDDON (KJV) See MEGIDDO

MEHETABEL (3)

Ge	36:39	his wife's name was M daughter of Matred,	4541
1Ch	1:50	his wife's name was M daughter of Matred,	4541
Ne	6:10	the son of M, who was shut in at his home.	4541

MEHIDA (2)

Ezr	2:52	Bazluth, M, Harsha,	4694
Ne	7:54	Bazluth, M, Harsha,	4694

MEHIR (1)

1Ch	4:11	Shuhah's brother, was the father of M,	4698

MEHOLAH (1)

1Sa	18:19	she was given in marriage to Adriel of M.	4716

MEHOLATHITE (1)

2Sa	21: 8	to Adriel son of Barzillai the M.	4716

MEHUJAEL (2)

Ge	4:18	and Irad was the father of M,	4686
	4:18	and M was the father of Methushael,	4686

MEHUMAN (1)

Est	1:10	M, Biztha, Harbona, Bigtha, Abagtha,	4540

MEHUNIM (KJV) See MEUNIM

MEHUNIMS (KJV) See MEUNITES

MEKERATHITE (1)

1Ch	11:36	Hepher the M, Ahijah the Pelonite,	4841

MEKONAH (KJV) See MECONAH

MELAH See TEL MELAH

MELATIAH (1)

Ne	3: 7	M of Gibeon and Jadon of Meronoth—	4882

MELCHI (KJV) See MELKI

MELCHI-SHUA (KJV) See MALKI-SHUA

MELCHIAH (KJV) See MALKIJAH

MELCHISEDEC (KJV) See MELCHIZEDEK

MELCHIZEDEK (10)

Ge	14:18	Then M king of Salem brought out bread	4900
Ps	110: 4	You are a priest forever, in the order of M."	4900
Heb	5: 6	You are a priest forever, in the order of M."	3519
	5:10	by God to be high priest in the order of M.	3519
	6:20	a high priest forever, in the order of M.	3519
	7: 1	This M was king of Salem and priest	3519
	7:10	because when M met Abraham,	3519
	7:11	one in the order of M,	3519
	7:15	if another priest like M appears,	3519
	7:17	You are a priest forever, in the order of M."	3519

MELEA (1)

Lk	3:31	the son of M, the son of Menna,	3507

MELECH (2)

1Ch	8:35	Pithon, M, Tarea and Ahaz.	4890
	9:41	Pithon, M, Tahrea and Ahaz.	4890

MELICU (KJV) See MALLUCH

MELITA (KJV) See MALTA

MELKI (2)

Lk	3:24	the son of M, the son of Jannai,	3518
	3:28	the son of M, the son of Addi,	3518

MELODIOUS (1) [MELODY]

Ps	81: 2	play the m harp and lyre.	5834

MELODY (1) [MELODIOUS]

Ps	92: 3	ten-stringed lyre and the m of the harp.	2053

MELON (1) [MELONS]

Jer	10: 5	Like a scarecrow in a m patch,	5252

MELONS (2) [MELON]

Nu	11: 5	the cucumbers, m, leeks, onions and garlic.	19
Isa	1: 8	like a hut in a field of m,	5252

MELT (15) [MELTED, MELTING, MELTS]

Ex	15:15	the people of Canaan will m away;	4570
Jos	14: 8	made the hearts of the people m with fear.	4998
2Sa	17:10	will m with fear, for all Israel knows	5022+5022
Ps	97: 5	mountains m like wax before the LORD,	5022
Isa	13: 7	every man's heart will m.	5022
	14:31	M away, all you Philistines!	4570
	19: 1	the hearts of the Egyptians m within them.	5022
Eze	21: 7	Every heart will m and every hand go limp;	5022
	21:15	that hearts may m and the fallen be many,	4570
	22:20	into a furnace to m it with a fiery blast,	5988
	22:20	and put you inside the city and m you.	5988
Mic	1: 4	The mountains m beneath him and	5022
Na	1: 5	before him and the hills m away.	4570
	2:10	Hearts m, knees give way, bodies tremble,	5022
2Pe	3:12	and the elements will m in the heat.	5494

MELTED (11) [MELT]

Ex	16:21	and when the sun grew hot, it m away.	5022
Jos	2:11	our hearts m and everyone's courage failed	5022
	5: 1	their hearts m and they no longer had	5022
	7: 5	of the people m and became like water.	5022
Job	24:19	heat and drought snatch away the m snow,	4784
Ps	22:14	it has m away within me.	5022
	107:26	in their peril their courage m away.	4570
Eze	22:21	and you will be m inside her.	5988
	22:22	As silver is m in a furnace,	2247
	22:22	so you will be m inside her,	5988
	24:11	so its impurities may be m	5988

MELTING (5) [MELT]

Jos	2: 9	this country are m in fear because of you.	4570
	2:24	all the people are m in fear because of us."	4570
1Sa	14:16	Benjamin saw the army m away	2143+2256+4570
Job	6:16	by thawing ice and swollen with m snow,	NIH
Ps	58: 8	Like a slug m away as it moves along,	9468

MELTS (4) [MELT]

Ps	46: 6	he lifts his voice, the earth m.	4570
	68: 2	as wax m before the fire,	5022
	147:18	He sends his word and m them;	4998
Am	9: 5	he who touches the earth and it m,	4570

MELZAR (KJV) See GUARD

MEMBER (8) [MEMBERS]

Lev	4:27	a m of the community sins unintentionally	5883
	25:47	to the alien living among you or to a m of	6830
Eze	17:13	a m of the royal family and made a treaty	4946
Mk	15:43	a prominent m of the Council,	1085
Lk	23:50	a man named Joseph, a m of the Council,	1085
Jn	3: 1	Nicodemus, a m of the Jewish ruling council.	NIG
Ac	17:34	Dionysius, a m of the Areopagus,	741
Ro	12: 5	each m belongs to all the others.	2848+3517+3836

MEMBERS (25) [MEMBER]

Ge	36: 6	and sons and daughters and all the m	5883
	46:27	the m of Jacob's family,	5883
	50: 8	besides all the m of Joseph's household	AIT
Lev	25:45	and m of their clans born in your country,	1201
Nu	16: 2	who had been appointed m of the council.	AIT
2Sa	9:12	the m of Ziba's household were servants	4632
2Ch	21:13	m of your father's house,	AIT
Mic	7: 6	the m of his own household.	408
Mt	10:25	how much more the m of his household!	3865
	10:36	will be the m of his own household.'	3865
Ac	5:17	who were m of the party of the Sadducees	NIG
	6: 9	from m of the Synagogue of the Freedmen	5516S
	16:15	and the m of her household were baptized,	3875
Ro	7:23	law at work in the m of my body,	3517
	7:23	of the law of sin at work within my m.	3517
	12: 4	as each of us has one body with many m,	3517
	12: 4	these m do not all have the same function,	3517
1Co	6:15	that your bodies are m of Christ himself?	3517
	6:15	then take the m of Christ and unite them	3517
	6:15	But God has combined the m of the body	NIG
Eph	2:19	and m of God's household,	3858
	3: 6	m together of one body, and sharers	5362
	4:25	for we are all m of one body.	3517
	5:30	for we are m of his body.	3517
Col	3:15	as m of one body you were called to peace.	NIG

MEMORABLE (1) [MEMORY]

Eze	39:13	day I am glorified will be a m day for them,	9005

MEMORANDUM (1)

| Ezr | 6: 2 | and this was written on it: **M:** | 10176 |

MEMORIAL (19) [MEMORY]

Ex	28:12	the shoulder pieces of the ephod as **m** stones	2355
	28:12	on his shoulders as a **m** before the LORD.	2355
	28:29	as a continuing **m** before the LORD.	2355
	30:16	be a **m** for the Israelites before the LORD,	2355
	39: 7	the shoulder pieces of the ephod as **m** stones	2355
Lev	2: 2	and burn this as a **m** portion on the altar,	260
	2: 9	the **m** portion from the grain offering	260
	2:16	the **m** portion of the crushed grain and	260
	5:12	a handful of it as a **m** portion and burn it on	260
	6:15	and burn the **m** portion on the altar as	260
	24: 7	a **m** portion to represent the bread and to be	260
Nu	5:26	as a **m** offering and burn it on the altar;	260
	10:10	be a **m** for you before your God.	2355
	31:54	the Tent of Meeting as a **m** for the Israelites	2355
Jos	4: 7	to be a **m** to the people of Israel forever."	2355
Isa	56: 5	within my temple and its walls a **m** and	3338
	66: 3	and *whoever* **burns m** incense,	2349
Zec	6:14	Jedaiah and Hen son of Zephaniah as a **m** in	2355
Ac	10: 4	to the poor have come up as a **m offering**	3649

MEMORIES (1) [MEMORY]

| 1Th | 3: 6 | that you always have pleasant **m** of us and | 3644 |

MEMORY (16) [MEMORABLE, MEMORIAL, MEMORIES]

Ex	17:14	because I will completely blot out the **m**	2352
Dt	25:19	you shall blot out the **m** of Amalek from	2352
	32:26	and blot out their **m** from mankind.	2352
2Sa	18:18	"I have no son to **carry on the m**	2349
Est	9:28	nor should the **m** of them die out	2352
Job	18:17	The **m** of him perishes from the earth;	2352
Ps	9: 6	even the **m** of them has perished.	2352
	34:16	to cut off the **m** of them from the earth.	2352
	45:17	*I will* **perpetuate** your **m**	2349+9005
	109:15	that he may cut off the **m** of them from	2352
Pr	10: 7	The **m** of the righteous will be a blessing,	2352
Ecc	9: 5	and even the **m** of them is forgotten.	2352
Isa	26:14	you wiped out all **m** of them.	2352
Mt	26:13	she has done will also be told, in **m** of her."	3649
Mk	14: 9	she has done will also be told, in **m** of her."	3649
2Pe	1:13	to refresh your **m** as long as I live in the tent	5704

MEMPHIS (8)

Isa	19:13	the leaders of **M** are deceived;	5862
Jer	2:16	of **M** and Tahpanhes have shaved the crown	5862
	44: 1	in Migdol, Tahpanhes and **M—**	5862
	46:14	proclaim it also in **M** and Tahpanhes:	5862
	46:19	for **M** will be laid waste and lie in ruins	5862
Eze	30:13	the idols and put an end to the images in **M.**	5862
	30:16	**M** will be in constant distress.	5862
Hos	9: 6	and **M** will bury them.	5132

MEMUCAN (3)

Est	1:14	Admatha, Tarshish, Meres, Marsena and **M,**	4925
	1:16	Then **M** replied in the presence of the king	4925
	1:21	so the king did as **M** proposed.	4925

MEN (1819) [MAN]

Ge	4:26	At that time *m* began to call on the name of	AIT
	6: 1	When **m** began to increase in number on	132
	6: 2	that the daughters of **m** were beautiful,	132
	6: 4	the sons of God went to the daughters of **m**	132
	6: 4	They were the heroes of old, **m** of renown.	408
	6: 7	**m** and animals, and creatures that move	132
	7:23	**m** and animals and the creatures that move	132
	11: 2	As **m** moved eastward,	4392S
	11: 5	and the tower that the **m** were building.	132+1201
	12:20	Pharaoh gave orders about Abram to his **m,**	408
	13:11	The two **m** parted company.	408
	13:13	Now the **m** of Sodom were wicked	408
	14:10	*of the m* **fell** into them and the rest fled	AIT
	14:14	the 318 **trained m** born in his household	2849
	14:15	During the night Abram divided his **m**	6269
	14:24	but what my **m** have eaten and the share	5853
	14:24	that belongs to the **m** who went with me—	408
	18: 2	up and saw three **m** standing nearby.	408
	18:16	When the **m** got up to leave,	408
	18:22	The **m** turned away and went	408
	19: 4	all the **m** from every part of the city	408
	19: 5	"Where are the **m** who came to you tonight?	408
	19: 8	But don't do anything to these **m,**	408
	19:10	But the **m** inside reached out	408
	19:11	the **m** who were at the door of the house,	408
	19:12	The two **m** said to Lot,	408
	19:16	the **m** grasped his hand and the hands	408
	21:27	and the two **m** made a treaty.	2157S
	21:31	because the two **m** swore an oath there.	2157S
	24:32	water for him and his **m** to wash their feet.	408
	24:54	and the **m** who were with him ate and drank	408
	24:59	and Abraham's servant and his **m**	408
	26: 7	**m** of that place asked him about his wife,	408
	26: 7	"The **m** of this place might kill me	408
	26:10	the **m** might well have slept with your wife,	6639
	26:31	Early the next morning *the m* **swore an oath**	AIT
	32: 6	and four hundred **m** are with him."	408
	32:28	with God and with **m** and have overcome."	408
	33: 1	coming with his four hundred **m;**	408
	33:15	let me leave some of my **m** with you."	6639

Ge	34:21	"These **m** are friendly toward us," they said.	408
	34:22	But the **m** will consent to live with us	408
	34:24	the *m who* **went out** *of* the city gate agreed	AIT
	38:12	to the *m who* were **shearing** his sheep,	AIT
	38:21	He asked the **m** *who lived* there,	408
	38:22	Besides, the *m who lived* there said,	408
	40: 5	each of the two **m—**	2157S
	41: 8	so he sent for all the magicians and **wise** *m*	AIT
	41:43	and *m* **shouted** before him, "Make way!"	AIT
	42:11	Your servants are **honest** *m,* not spies."	AIT
	42:19	If you are **honest** *m,*	AIT
	42:31	But we said to him, 'We are **honest** *m;*	AIT
	42:33	how I will know whether you are **honest** *m:*	AIT
	42:34	that you are not spies but **honest** *m.*	AIT
	43:15	the **m** took the gifts and double the amount	408
	43:16	"Take these **m** to my house,	408
	43:17	as Joseph told him and took the **m**	408
	43:18	the **m** were frightened when they were taken	408
	43:24	The steward took the **m** into Joseph's house,	408
	43:33	The **m** had been seated before him in	NIH
	44: 3	the **m** were sent on their way	408
	44: 4	"Go after those **m** at once,	408
	46:32	The **m** are shepherds;	408
	49: 6	for they have killed **m** in their anger	408
Ex	4:19	all the **m** who wanted to kill you are dead."	408
	5: 9	for the **m** so that they keep working	408
	7:11	then summoned **wise** *m* and sorcerers, and	AIT
	8:17	gnats came upon **m** and animals.	132
	8:18	And the gnats were on **m** and animals.	132
	9: 7	Pharaoh sent **m** to investigate and found that	NIH
	9: 9	on **m** and animals throughout the land."	132
	9:10	festering boils broke out on **m** and animals.	132
	9:22	on **m** and animals and on everything	132
	9:25	both **m** and animals;	132
	10:11	Have only the **m** go;	1505
	11: 2	Tell the people that **m** and women alike are	408
	12:12	both **m** and animals.	132
	12:37	There were about six hundred thousand **m**	1505
	17: 9	*of* our **m** and go out to fight the Amalekites.	408
	18:21	But select capable **m** from all the people—	408
	18:21	*m who* **fear** God, trustworthy men	AIT
	18:21	trustworthy **m** who hate dishonest gain—	408
	18:25	He chose capable **m** from all Israel	408
	21:18	"If **m** quarrel and one hits the other with	408
	21:22	"If **m** who are fighting hit	408
	23:17	"Three times a year all the **m** are to appear	2344
	24: 5	Then he sent **young** Israelite **m,**	5853
	28: 3	Tell all the **skilled** *m* to whom I have given	AIT
	34:23	Three times a year all your **m** are to appear	2344
	35:22	All who were willing, **m** and women alike,	408
	35:29	All the Israelite **m** and women who	408
	36: 8	the **skilled** *m* among the workmen made	AIT
	38:26	a total of 603,550 **m.**	NIH
Nu	1: 3	to number by their divisions all the **m**	NIH
	1: 5	the names of the **m** who are to assist you:	408
	1:16	These **were** the **m** appointed *from*	AIT
	1:17	Aaron took these **m** whose names had been given,	408
	1:18	the **m** twenty years old or more were listed	NIH
	1:20	All the **m** twenty years old or more	2351
	1:22	All the **m** twenty years old or more	2351
	1:24	All the **m** twenty years old or more	NIH
	1:26	All the **m** twenty years old or more	NIH
	1:28	All the **m** twenty years old or more	NIH
	1:30	All the **m** twenty years old or more	NIH
	1:32	All the **m** twenty years old or more	NIH
	1:34	All the **m** twenty years old or more	NIH
	1:36	All the **m** twenty years old or more	NIH
	1:38	All the **m** twenty years old or more	NIH
	1:40	All the **m** twenty years old or more	NIH
	1:42	All the **m** twenty years old or more	NIH
	1:44	the **m** counted by Moses and Aaron and	AIT
	2: 9	All the *m* **assigned** to the camp of Judah,	AIT
	2:16	All the *m* **assigned** to the camp of Reuben,	AIT
	2:24	All the *m* **assigned** to the camp of Ephraim,	AIT
	2:31	All the *m* **assigned** to the camp	AIT
	4: 3	Count all the **m** from thirty to fifty years	NIH
	4:23	Count all the **m** from thirty to fifty years	NIH
	4:30	Count all the **m** from thirty to fifty years	NIH
	4:35	All the **m** from thirty to fifty years	NIH
	4:39	All the **m** from thirty to fifty years	NIH
	4:43	All the **m** from thirty to fifty years	NIH
	4:47	All the **m** from thirty to fifty years	NIH
	8:24	**M** twenty-five years or more shall come	NIH
	11:21	"Here I am among six hundred thousand **m**	6639
	11:26	However, two **m,** whose names were Eldad	408
	13: 2	"Send some **m** to explore the land	408
	13:16	the names of the **m** Moses sent to explore	408
	13:31	But the **m** who had gone up with him said,	408
	14:22	not one of the **m** who saw my glory and	408
	14:36	the **m** Moses had sent to explore the land,	408
	14:37	these **m** responsible for spreading	408
	14:38	Of the **m** who went to explore the land,	408
	16: 2	With them were 250 Israelite **m,**	408
	16:14	Will you gouge out the eyes of these **m?**	408
	16:26	from the tents of these wicked **m!**	408
	16:29	If **these** *m* die a natural death	AIT
	16:29	happens to **m,** then the LORD has not sent me.	132
	16:30	that these **m** have treated the LORD	408
	16:32	and all Korah's **m** and all their possessions.	132
	16:35	and consumed the 250 **m** who were offering	408
	16:38	the censers of the **m** who sinned at the cost	465S
	22: 9	"Who are these **m** with you?"	408
	22:20	"Since these **m** have come to summon you,	408
	22:35	"Go with the **m,**	408
	25: 1	the **m** began to indulge in sexual immorality	6639
	25: 5	to death those of your **m** who have joined	408

Ex	26: 4	"Take a census of the **m** twenty years **old**	AIT
	26:10	when the fire devoured the 250 **m.**	408
	26:14	clans of Simeon; there were 22,200 **m.**	NIH
	26:51	of the **m** of Israel was 601,730.	1201
	31: 3	"Arm some of your **m** to go to war against	408
	31: 4	Send into battle a **thousand** *m* from each of	AIT
	31: 5	So twelve thousand *m* **armed** *for* battle,	AIT
	31:42	from that of the fighting **m—**	408
	32:11	the **m** twenty years old or more who came	408
	34:17	the **m** who are to assign the land for you as	408
	34:29	These are the **m** the LORD commanded	889S
	36: 3	Now suppose they marry **m**	1201
Dt	1:13	understanding and respected **m** from each	408
	1:15	So I took the **leading** *m* of your tribes,	AIT
	1:15	wise and respected **m,** and appointed them	408
	1:22	"Let us send **m** ahead to spy out the land	408
	2:14	of fighting **m** had perished from the camp,	408
	2:16	when the last of these fighting **m** among	408
	2:34	**m,** women and children.	5493
	3: 6	**m,** women and children.	5493
	3:18	But all your **able-bodied m,**	1201
	5:23	all the **leading m** of your tribes	8031
	7:14	*m* or women will be childless, nor any of your livestock **without young.**	AIT
	13:13	that wicked **m** have arisen among you	408
	16:16	Three times a year all your **m** must appear	2344
	19:17	the two **m** involved in	408
	20:13	put to the sword all the **m** *in* it.	2344
	21:21	the **m** of his town shall stone him to death.	408
	22:21	and there the **m** *of* her town shall stone her	408
	23:10	If one of your **m** is unclean because of	408
	25: 1	When **m** have a dispute,	408
	25:11	If **two** *m* are fighting and the wife of one of them comes to rescue	278+408+2256+3481
	29:10	your leaders and **chief m,**	8657
	29:10	and all the other **m** of Israel,	408
	31:12	Assemble the people—**m,** women and	408
	32:25	**Young m** and young women will perish,	1033
	32:25	infants and gray-haired **m.**	408
	33: 6	nor his **m** be few."	5493
Jos	1:14	but all your **fighting m,** fully armed,	1475+2657
	2: 3	"Bring out the **m** who came to you	408
	2: 4	But the woman had taken the two **m**	408
	2: 4	She said, "Yes, the **m** came to me,	408
	2: 5	to close the city gate, the **m** left.	408
	2: 7	So the **m** set out in pursuit of the spies on	408
	2:14	the **m** assured her.	408
	2:17	The **m** said to her, "This oath you made us	408
	2:23	Then the two **m** started back.	408
	3:12	choose twelve **m** from the tribes of Israel,	408
	4: 2	"Choose twelve **m** from among the people,	408
	4: 4	the twelve **m** he had appointed from	408
	4:12	The **m** of Reuben, Gad and the half-tribe	1201
	5: 4	all the **m** of military age—	2351
	5: 6	until all the **m** who were *of* military age	408
	6: 2	along with its king and its **fighting m.**	1475+2657
	6: 3	around the city once with all the armed **m.**	408
	6:13	The **armed** *m* went ahead of them and	AIT
	6:21	**m** and women, young and old, cattle,	408
	6:22	Joshua said to the two **m** who had spied out	408
	6:23	the **young m** who had done the spying went	5853
	6:25	the **m** Joshua had sent as spies to Jericho—	4855S
	7: 2	Now Joshua sent **m** from Jericho to Ai,	408
	7: 2	So the **m** went up and spied out Ai.	408
	7: 3	Send two or three thousand **m** to take it	408
	7: 3	for only a few **m** are there."	2156S
	7: 4	So about three thousand **m** went up;	408
	7: 4	but they were routed by the **m** *of* Ai,	408
	8: 3	his **best fighting m** and sent them out	1475+2657
	8: 5	and when the **m** come out against us,	NIH
	8:10	the next morning Joshua mustered his **m,**	6639
	8:12	Joshua had taken about five thousand **m**	408
	8:14	he and all the **m** *of* the city hurried out early	408
	8:16	All the **m** of Ai were called to pursue them,	6639
	8:19	the **m** in *the* **ambush** rose quickly	AIT
	8:20	The **m** of Ai looked back and saw	408
	8:21	they turned around and attacked the **m**	408
	8:22	The **m** of the ambush also came out	465S
	8:24	When Israel had finished killing all the **m**	3782
	8:25	Twelve thousand **m** and women fell	408
	9: 5	The **m** put worn and patched sandals	NIH
	9: 6	to him and the **m** of Israel, "We have come	408
	9: 7	The **m** of Israel said to the Hivites,	408
	9:14	The **m** of Israel sampled their provisions	408
	10: 2	and all its **m** were good fighters.	408
	10: 7	including all the **best fighting m.**	1475+2657
	10:18	and post *some* **m** there to guard it.	408
	10:24	he summoned all the **m** *of* Israel and said to	408
	14: 6	**m** of Judah approached Joshua at Gilgal,	1201
	18: 4	Appoint three **m** from each tribe.	408
	18: 8	As the **m** started on their way to map out	408
	18: 9	So the **m** left and went through the land.	408
	22:14	With him they sent ten of the **chief** *m,*	AIT
Jdg	1: 3	Then the **m** of Judah said to	NIH
	1: 4	and they struck down ten thousand **m**	408
	1: 8	The **m** *of* Judah attacked Jerusalem also	1201
	1: 9	the **m** *of* Judah went down to fight against	1201
	1:16	of Palms with the **m** *of* Judah to live among	1201
	1:17	Then the **m** *of* Judah went with	NIH
	1:18	The **m** *of* Judah also took Gaza,	NIH
	1:19	The LORD was with the **m** of Judah.	NIH
	1:23	sent **m** to spy out Bethel	AIT
	3:18	on their way the **m** who had carried it.	6639
	4:10	take with you ten thousand **m** of Naphtali.	408
	4:10	Ten thousand **m** followed him,	408
	4:13	and all the **m** with him,	6639
	4:14	followed by ten thousand **m.**	408

Ref	Text	Num
Jdg 5:13	**m** who were left came down to the nobles;	8586
6: 5	It was impossible to count the **m**	2157ˢ
6:27	of his family and the **m** of the town,	408
6:28	the morning when the **m** of the town got up,	408
6:30	The **m** of the town demanded of Joash,	408
7: 1	and all his **m** camped at the spring of Harod.	6639
7: 2	"You have too many **m** for me	6639
7: 3	So twenty-two thousand **m** left,	6639
7: 4	"There are still too many **m.**	6639
7: 5	So Gideon took the **m** down to the water.	6639
7: 6	Three hundred **m** lapped with their hands	408
7: 7	"With the three hundred **m**	408
7: 7	Let all the other **m** go,	6639
7:16	the three hundred **m** into three companies,	408
7:19	the hundred **m** with him reached the edge of	408
7:22	the LORD caused the **m** throughout	408
7:24	So all the **m** of Ephraim were called out	408
8: 4	Gideon and his three hundred **m,**	408
8: 5	He said to the **m** of Succoth,	408
8: 8	but they answered as the **m** of Succoth had.	408
8: 9	So he said to the **m** of Peniel,	408
8:10	with a force of about fifteen thousand **m,** all	NIH
8:15	Gideon came and said to the **m** of Succoth,	408
8:15	to your exhausted **m?**" "	408
8:16	of the town and taught the **m** of Succoth	408
8:17	down the tower of Peniel and killed the **m**	408
8:18	"What kind of **m** did you kill at Tabor?"	408
8:18	"**M** like you," they answered,	2157ˢ
9: 9	by which both gods and **m** are honored,	408
9:13	which cheers both gods and **m,**	408
9:25	of Shechem set **m** on the hilltops to ambush	NIH
9:28	Serve the **m** of Hamor, Shechem's father!	408
9:32	and your **m** should come and lie in wait in	6639
9:33	When Gaal and his **m** come out against you,	6639
9:36	the shadows of the mountains for **m.**"	408
9:38	Aren't these the **m** you ridiculed?	6639
9:43	So he took his **m,**	6639
9:48	he and all his **m** went up Mount Zalmon.	6639
9:48	He ordered the **m** with him, "Quick!	6639
9:49	So all the **m** cut branches	6639
9:49	about a thousand **m** and women, also died.	408
9:51	to which all the **m** and women—	408
9:57	God also made the **m** of Shechem pay	408
11:20	He mustered all his **m** and encamped	6639
11:21	gave Sihon and all his **m** into Israel's hands,	6639
12: 1	The **m** of Ephraim called out their forces,	408
12: 4	then called together the **m** of Gilead	408
12: 5	the **m** of Gilead asked him,	408
14:18	Before sunset on the seventh day the **m** of	408
14:19	struck down thirty of their **m,**	408
15:10	The **m** of Judah asked,	408
15:11	Then three thousand **m** from Judah went	408
15:15	and struck down a thousand **m.**	408
15:16	With a donkey's jawbone I have killed a thousand **m.**"	408
16: 9	With **m** hidden in the room,	2021ˢ
16:12	Then, with **m** hidden in the room,	2021ˢ
16:27	temple was crowded with **m** and women;	408
16:27	on the roof were about three thousand **m**	408
18: 2	These **m** represented all their clans.	408
18: 2	The **m** entered the hill country of Ephraim	NIH
18: 7	So the five **m** left and came to Laish,	408
18:11	six hundred **m** from the clan of the Danites,	408
18:14	Then the five **m** who had spied out the land	408
18:17	The five **m** who had spied out the land went	408
18:17	and the six hundred armed **m** stood at	408
18:18	When these **m** went into Micah's house	AIT
18:22	the **m** who lived near Micah	408
18:23	that you called out your **m** to fight?"	NIH
18:25	or some hot-tempered **m** will attack you,	408
19:16	(the **m** of the place were Benjamites,	408
19:22	of the wicked **m** of the city surrounded	408
19:25	But the **m** would not listen to him.	408
20: 5	the night the **m** of Gibeah came after me	1251
20:10	We'll take ten **m** out of every hundred	408
20:11	of Israel got together and united	408
20:12	The tribes of Israel sent **m** throughout	408
20:13	Now surrender those wicked **m** of Gibeah	408
20:15	in addition to seven hundred chosen **m**	408
20:16	Among all these soldiers there were seven hundred chosen **m** who were left-handed,	408
20:17	all of them fighting **m.**	408
20:20	The **m** of Israel went out to fight	408
20:22	But the **m** of Israel encouraged one another	408
20:31	that about thirty **m** fell in the open field and	408
20:33	All the **m** of Israel moved from their places	408
20:34	Then ten thousand of Israel's finest made	408
20:36	**m** of Israel had given way before Benjamin,	408
20:37	**m** who had been in **ambush**	AIT
20:38	The **m** of Israel had arranged with	408
20:39	then the **m** of Israel would turn in the battle.	408
20:39	to inflict casualties on the **m** of Israel	408
20:41	Then the **m** of Israel turned on them,	408
20:41	and the **m** of Benjamin were terrified,	408
20:42	And the **m** of Israel who came out of	NIH
20:45	the Israelites cut down five thousand **m**	408
20:47	But six hundred **m** turned and fled into	408
20:48	The **m** of Israel went back to Benjamin	408
21: 1	The **m** of Israel had taken an oath	408
21:10	assembly sent twelve thousand fighting **m**	408
21:16	for the **m** who are **left?**	AIT
Ru 2: 9	Watch the field where the **m** are **harvesting,**	AIT
2: 9	I have told the **m** not to touch you.	5853
2: 9	from the water jars the **m** have filled."	5853
2:15	Boaz gave orders to his **m,**	5853
3:10	You have not run after the **younger m,**	1033
1Sa 2:12	Eli's sons were wicked **m;**	1201

Ref	Text	Num
1Sa 2:17	This sin of the **young m** was very great in	5853
2:26	and in favor with the LORD and with **m.**	408
4: 4	So the people sent **m** to Shiloh,	NIH
4: 9	Be **m,** or you will be subject to	408
4: 9	Be **m,** and fight!"	408
5: 7	the **m** of Ashdod saw what was happening,	408
6:19	down some of the **m** of Beth Shemesh,	408
6:20	and the **m** of Beth Shemesh asked,	408
7: 1	So the **m** of Kiriath Jearim came and took	408
7:11	The **m** of Israel rushed out of Mizpah	408
8:22	Then Samuel said to the **m** of Israel,	408
10: 2	you will meet two **m** near Rachel's tomb,	408
10: 3	Three **m** going up to God	408
10:26	**valiant** m whose hearts God had touched.	AIT
11: 1	And all the **m** of Jabesh said to him,	408
11: 5	to him what the **m** of Jabesh had said.	408
11: 8	When Saul mustered them at Bezek, the **m**	1201
11: 8	and the **m** of Judah thirty thousand.	408
11: 9	"Say to the **m** of Jabesh Gilead,	408
11: 9	and reported this to the **m** of Jabesh,	408
11:11	The next day Saul separated his **m**	6639
11:12	Bring these **m** to us and we will put them	408
13: 2	Saul chose three **thousand** m from Israel;	AIT
13: 2	of the **m** he sent back to their homes.	6639
13: 6	When the **m** of Israel saw that their situation	408
13: 8	and Saul's **m** began to scatter.	6639
13:11	"When I saw that the **m** were scattering,	6639
13:15	and Saul counted the **m** who were with him.	6639
13:16	and the **m** with them were staying in Gibeah	6639
14: 2	With him were about six hundred **m,**	408
14: 8	over toward the **m** and let them see us.	408
14:12	The **m** of the outpost shouted to Jonathan	408
14:14	and his armor-bearer killed some twenty **m**	408
14:17	Then Saul said to the **m** who were with him,	6639
14:20	Then Saul and all his **m** assembled and went	6639
14:24	the **m** of Israel were in distress that day,	408
14:28	That is why the **m** are faint."	6639
14:30	if the **m** had eaten today some of	6639
14:33	the **m** are sinning against the LORD	6639
14:34	he said, "Go out among the **m** and tell them,	6639
14:39	But not one of the **m** said a word.	6639
14:40	"Do what seems best to you," the **m** replied.	6639
14:41	and the **m** were cleared.	6639
14:45	the **m** said to Saul, "Should Jonathan die—	6639
14:45	So the **m** rescued Jonathan,	6639
15: 3	put to death **m** and women,	408
15: 4	the **m** and mustered them at Telaim;	6639
15: 4	and ten thousand **m** from Judah.	408
17:19	They are with Saul and all the **m** of Israel in	408
17:26	David asked the **m** standing near him,	408
17:28	heard him speaking with the **m,**	408
17:30	and the **m** answered him as before.	6639
17:52	the **m** of Israel and Judah surged forward	408
18: 6	When the **m** were returning home	4392ˢ
18:13	and gave him command over a **thousand** m,	AIT
18:27	David and his **m** went out	408
19:11	Saul sent **m** to David's house to watch it	4855
19:14	When Saul sent the **m** to capture David,	4855
19:15	Then Saul sent the **m** back to see David	4855
19:16	But when the **m** entered,	4855
19:20	so he sent **m** to capture him.	4855
19:20	upon Saul's **m** and they also prophesied.	4855
19:21	Saul was told about it, and he sent more **m,**	4855
19:21	Saul sent **m** a third time,	4855
21: 2	As for my **m,** I have told them	5853
21: 4	the **m** have kept themselves from women."	5853
22: 2	About four hundred **m** were with him.	408
22: 6	that David and his **m** had been discovered.	408
22: 7	Saul said to them, "Listen, **m of Benjamin!**	1229
22:18	That day he killed eighty-five **m** who wore	408
22:19	with its **m** and women, its children and	408
23: 3	But David's **m** said to him,	408
23: 5	So David and his **m** went to Keilah,	408
23: 8	down to Keilah to besiege David and his **m.**	408
23:12	of Keilah surrender me and my **m** to Saul?"	408
23:13	So David and his **m,** about six hundred	408
23:24	Now David and his **m** were in the Desert	408
23:25	Saul and his **m** began the search,	408
23:26	and David and his **m** were on the other side,	408
23:26	in on David and his **m** to capture them.	408
24: 2	So Saul took three thousand chosen **m**	408
24: 2	and set out to look for David and his **m** near	408
24: 3	David and his **m** were far back in the cave.	408
24: 4	The **m** said, "This is the day	408
24: 6	He said to his **m,**	408
24: 7	With these words David rebuked his **m**	408
24: 9	"Why do you listen when **m** say,	132
24:22	and his **m** went up to the stronghold.	408
25: 5	So he sent ten **young m** and said to them,	5853
25: 8	be favorable toward my **young m,**	5853
25: 9	When David's **m** arrived,	5853
25:11	to **m** coming from who knows where?"	408
25:12	David's **m** turned around and went back.	5853
25:13	David said to his **m,** "Put on your swords!"	408
25:13	About four hundred **m** went up with David,	408
25:15	Yet these **m** were very good to us.	408
25:20	there were David and his **m** descending	408
25:25	I did not see the **m** my master sent.	5853
25:27	be given to the **m** who follow you.	5853
26: 2	with his three thousand chosen **m** of Israel,	408
26:16	**you and your m** deserve to die,	408
26:19	If, however, **m** have done it,	132+1201+2021
26:22	of your **young m** come over and get it.	5853
27: 2	the six hundred **m** with him left and went	408
27: 3	and his **m** settled in Gath with Achish.	408
27: 8	Now David and his **m** went up and raided	408
28: 1	that you and your **m** will accompany me in	408

Ref	Text	Num
1Sa 28: 8	at night he and two **m** went to the woman.	408
28:23	But his **m** joined the woman in urging him,	6269
28:25	Then she set it before Saul and his **m,**	6269
29: 2	David and his **m** were marching at the rear	408
29: 4	by taking the heads of our own **m?**	408
29:11	and his **m** got up early in the morning	408
30: 1	and his **m** reached Ziklag on the third day.	408
30: 3	When David and his **m** came to Ziklag,	408
30: 4	So David and his **m** wept aloud	6639
30: 6	because the **m** were talking of stoning him;	6639
30: 9	David and the six hundred **m** with him came	408
30:10	for two hundred **m** were too exhausted	408
30:10	and four hundred **m** continued the pursuit.	408
30:17	except four hundred young **m** who rode off	408
30:20	and his **m** drove them ahead of	NIH
30:21	two hundred **m** who had been too exhausted	408
30:21	As David and his **m** approached,	6639
30:22	But all the evil **m** and troublemakers	408
30:31	where David and his **m** had roamed.	408
31: 6	and all his **m** died together that same day.	408
31:12	all their valiant **m** journeyed through	408
2Sa 1: 4	He said, "The **m** fled from the battle.	6639
1:11	the **m** with him took hold of their clothes	408
1:15	Then David called one of his **m** and said,	5853
1:18	that the **m** of Judah be taught this lament of	1201
2: 3	David also took the **m** who were with him,	408
2: 4	Then the **m** of Judah came to Hebron	408
2: 4	When David was told that it was the **m** of	408
2: 5	to the **m** of Jabesh Gilead to say to them,	408
2:12	together with the **m** of Ish-Bosheth went	408
2:13	Joab son of Zeruiah and David's **m** went out	6269
2:14	the **young m** get up and fight hand to hand	5853
2:15	twelve **m** for Benjamin and Ish-Bosheth son	NIH
2:17	and the **m** of Israel were defeated	408
2:17	of Israel were defeated by David's **m.**	6269
2:21	the **young m** and strip him of his weapons."	5853
2:25	the **m** of Benjamin rallied behind Abner.	1201
2:26	How long before you order your **m**	6639
2:27	the **m** would have continued the pursuit	6639
2:28	and all the **m** came to a halt;	6639
2:29	that night Abner and his **m** marched through	408
2:30	and assembled all his **m.**	6639
2:30	nineteen of David's **m** were found missing.	6269
2:31	But David's **m** had killed three hundred	6269
2:32	and his **m** marched all night and arrived	408
3:20	When Abner, who had twenty **m** with him,	408
3:20	David prepared a feast for him and his **m.**	408
3:22	Just then David's **m** and Joab returned from	6269
3:34	You fell as one falls before wicked **m.**"	1201
3:38	Then the king said to his **m,**	6269
4: 2	Saul's son had two **m** who were leaders	408
4:11	when wicked **m** have killed	408
4:12	So David gave an order to his **m,**	5853
5: 6	The king and his **m** marched to Jerusalem	408
5:21	and David and his **m** carried them off.	408
6: 1	brought together out of Israel **chosen** m.	AIT
6: 2	and all his **m** set out from Baalah of Judah	6639
6:19	both **m** and women.	408
7: 9	the names of the **greatest** m of the earth.	AIT
7:14	I will punish him with the rod of **m,**	408
7:14	with floggings inflicted by **m.**	132+1201
7:26	Then **m** will say, 'The LORD Almighty	NIH
10: 2	When David's **m** came to the land of	6269
10: 3	by sending **m** to you to express sympathy?	6269
10: 4	So Hanun seized David's **m,**	6269
10: 5	he sent messengers to meet the **m,**	408
10: 6	as the king of Maacah with a thousand **m,**	408
10: 6	and also twelve thousand **m** from Tob.	408
10: 7	with the entire army of **fighting m.**	1475
10: 8	of Zobah and Rehob and the **m** of Tob	408
10:10	He put the rest of the **m** under the command	6639
11: 1	David sent Joab out with the king's **m** and	6269
11:11	and my lord's **m** are camped in	6269
11:17	When the **m** of the city came out and fought	408
11:17	some of the **m** in David's army fell;	6269
11:23	"The **m** overpowered us and came out	408
11:24	and some of the king's **m** died.	6269
12: 1	"There were two **m** in a certain town,	408
13:28	Absalom ordered his **m,** "Listen!	5853
13:29	So Absalom's **m** did to Amnon	5853
13:34	"I see **m** in the direction of Horonaim,	408
15: 1	a chariot and horses and with fifty **m** to run	408
15: 6	and so he stole the hearts of the **m** of Israel.	408
15:11	Two hundred **m** from Jerusalem	408
15:13	hearts of the **m** of Israel are with Absalom."	408
15:18	All his **m** marched past him,	6269
15:22	on with all his **m** and the families that were	408
16: 2	the bread and fruit are for the **m** to eat,	5853
16:13	So David and his **m** continued along	408
16:15	and all the **m** of Israel came to Jerusalem,	6639
16:18	and by all the **m** of Israel—	408
17: 1	"I would choose twelve thousand **m**	408
17: 8	You know your father and his **m;**	408
17:12	nor any of his **m** will be left alive.	408
17:14	Absalom and all the **m** of Israel said,	408
17:20	When Absalom's **m** came to the woman at	6269
17:20	The **m** searched but found no one,	NIH
17:21	After the **m** had gone,	4392ˢ
17:24	the Jordan with all the **m** of Israel.	408
18: 1	David mustered the **m** who were with him	6639
18: 3	But the said, "You must not go;	408
18: 4	the gate while all the **m** marched out in units	6639
18: 7	of Israel was defeated by David's **m,** and	6269
18: 7	that day were great—twenty thousand **m.**	NIH
18: 9	Absalom happened to meet David's **m.**	6269
18:10	When one of the **m** saw this, he told Joab,	408
18:28	the **m** who lifted their hands against my lord	408

2Sa	19: 3	The **m** stole into the city that day	6639
	19: 3	that day as **m** steal in who are ashamed	6639
	19: 5	"Today you have humiliated all your **m**,	6269
	19: 6	the commanders and their **m** mean nothing	6269
	19: 7	Now go out and encourage your **m**.	6269
	19: 8	When the **m** were told,	6639
	19:14	over the hearts of all the **m** *of* Judah as	408
	19:14	"Return, you and all your **m**."	6269
	19:15	the **m** of Judah had come to Gilgal to go out	NIH
	19:16	with the **m** *of* Judah to meet King David.	408
	19:35	**m** and women **singers**?	AIT
	19:41	Soon all the **m** of Israel were coming to	408
	19:41	"Why did our brothers, the **m** of Judah,	408
	19:41	together with all his **m**?"	408
	19:42	the **m** *of* Judah answered the men of Israel,	408
	19:42	the men of Judah answered the **m** of Israel,	408
	19:43	the **m** *of* Israel answered the men of Judah,	408
	19:43	the men of Israel answered the **m** of Judah,	408
	19:43	But the **m** *of* Judah responded	408
	19:43	even more harshly than the **m** of Israel.	408
	20: 2	So all the **m** *of* Israel deserted David	408
	20: 2	But the **m** *of* Judah stayed by their king all	408
	20: 4	"Summon the **m** *of* Judah to come to me	408
	20: 6	Take your master's **m** and pursue him,	6269
	20: 7	So Joab's **m** and the Kerethites	408
	20:11	of Joab's **m** stood beside Amasa and said,	5853
	20:13	all the **m** went on with Joab	408
	20:22	and his **m** dispersed from the city,	NIH
	21:15	with his **m** to fight against the Philistines,	6269
	21:17	Then David's **m** swore to him, saying,	408
	21:22	they fell at the hands of David and his **m**,	6269
	22: 3	from **violent** *m* you save me.	AIT
	22:49	from violent **m** you rescued me.	408
	23: 3	'When one rules over **m** in righteousness,	132
	23: 6	**evil m** are all to be cast aside like thorns,	1175
	23: 8	These are the names of David's **mighty m**:	1475
	23: 8	he raised his spear against eight hundred **m**,	NIH
	23: 9	As one of the three **mighty m**,	1475
	23: 9	Then the **m** *of* Israel retreated,	408
	23:13	of the thirty **chief** *m* came down to David at	AIT
	23:16	So the three **mighty m** broke through	1475
	23:17	of **m** who went at the risk of their lives?"	408
	23:17	the exploits of the three **mighty m**.	1475
	23:18	He raised his spear against three hundred **m**,	NIH
	23:20	He struck down two of Moab's **best m**.	738
	23:22	too was as famous as the three **mighty m**.	1475
	24: 2	to Beersheba and enroll the **fighting m**,	6639
	24: 4	the king to enroll the **fighting m** *of* Israel.	6639
	24: 9	Joab reported the number of the **fighting m**	6639
	24: 9	In Israel there were eight hundred thousand	
		able-bodied **m** who could handle a sword,	408
	24:10	after he had counted the **fighting m**,	6639
	24:14	but do not let me fall into the hands of **m**."	132
	24:20	the king and his **m** coming toward him,	6269
1Ki	1: 5	with fifty **m** to run ahead of him.	408
	1: 9	all the **m** of Judah who were royal officials,	408
	1:53	Then King Solomon sent **m**,	NIH
	2:32	of my father David he attacked two **m**	408
	2:32	were **better** *m* and more upright than he.	AIT
	4:30	the wisdom of all the **m** of the East,	1201
	4:34	**M** of all nations **came** to listen to	AIT
	5: 6	My **m** will work with yours,	6269
	5: 6	for your **m** whatever wages you set.	6269
	5: 9	My **m** will haul them down from Lebanon	6269
	5:13	from all Israel—thirty thousand **m**.	408
	5:18	the **m** of **Gebal** cut and prepared the timber	1490
	8: 2	All the **m** *of* Israel came together	408
	8:39	(for you alone know the hearts of all **m**)	132+1201
	8:42	for *m* will **hear** *of* your great name	AIT
	9:22	they were his fighting **m**,	408
	9:23	550 officials supervising the **m** who did	6639
	9:27	And Hiram sent his **m**—	6269
	9:27	to serve in the fleet with Solomon's **m**.	6269
	10: 8	How happy your **m** must be!	408
	11:15	had struck down all the **m** in Edom.	2351
	11:16	until they had destroyed all the **m** in Edom.	2351
	11:18	Then taking **m** from Paran with them,	408
	11:24	He gathered **m** around him and became	408
	12: 8	and consulted the **young m** who had grown	3529
	12:10	The **young m** who had grown up	3529
	12:14	he followed the advice of the **young m**	3529
	12:21	a hundred and eighty thousand fighting **m**—	1033
	20:10	in Samaria to give each of my **m** a handful."	6639
	20:12	and he ordered his **m**: "Prepare to attack."	6269
	20:15	of the provincial commanders, 232 **m**.	NIH
	20:17	"**M** are advancing from Samaria."	408
	20:33	The **m** took this as a good sign	408
	22: 6	about four hundred **m**—	408
	22:49	"Let my **m** sail with your men,"	6269
	22:49	"Let my men sail with your **m**,"	6269
2Ki	1: 6	in Israel that you are sending **m**	NIH
	1: 9	a captain with his *company of* **fifty m**.	AIT
	1:10	and consume you and your **fifty m**!'	AIT
	1:10	and consumed the captain and his **m**.	2822S
	1:11	to Elijah another captain with his **fifty m**.	AIT
	1:12	and consume you and your **fifty m**!'	AIT
	1:12	and consumed him and his **fifty m**.	AIT
	1:13	king sent a third captain with his **fifty m**.	AIT
	1:13	for my life and the lives of these **fifty m**,	AIT
	1:14	the first two captains and *all* their **m**.	2822S
	2: 7	Fifty **m** of the company of	408
	2:16	"we your servants have fifty able **m**.	408
	2:17	And they sent fifty **m**,	408
	2:19	The **m** of the city said to Elisha, "Look,	408
	3:25	but **m** **armed with slings** surrounded it	7847
	4:38	cook some stew for these **m**."	1201+2021+5566S
	4:40	The stew was poured out for the **m**,	408

2Ki	4:43	"How can I set this before a hundred **m**?"	408
	5:22	'Two **young m** from the company of	5853
	5:24	He sent the **m** away and they left.	408
	6:13	"so I can send **m** and capture him."	408
	6:20	open the eyes of **these** *m* so they can see."	AIT
	6:22	"Would you kill **m** you have captured	889S
	7: 3	Now there were four **m** with leprosy at	AIT
	7: 8	The *m who* had leprosy reached the edge of	AIT
	7:13	"*Have some* **m** *take* five of the horses	AIT
	8:12	kill their young **m** with the sword,	1033
	10: 6	were with the **leading** *m* of the city,	AIT
	10: 7	**these m** took the princes	2157S
	10:11	as well as all his **chief** *m*,	AIT
	10:11	of Beth Eked—forty-two **m**.	408
	10:24	Now Jehu had posted eighty **m** outside	408
	10:24	"If one of you lets any of the **m** I am placing	408
	11: 9	Each one took his **m**—	408
	12:11	to the **m appointed** to supervise the work on	AIT
	14:19	but they sent **m** after him to Lachish	NIH
	15:25	Taking fifty **m** of Gilead with him,	408
	16: 6	for Aram by driving out the **m of Judah**.	3374
	17:30	The **m** *from* Babylon made Succoth Benoth,	408
	17:30	the **m** *from* Cuthah made Nergal,	408
	17:30	and the **m** *from* Hamath made Ashima;	408
	18:27	and not to the **m** sitting on the wall—	408
	19:35	a hundred and eighty-five thousand **m** in	NIH
	20:14	"What did those **m** say,	408
	22: 5	to the **m appointed** to supervise the work on	AIT
	22: 5	And *have* **these** *m* **pay** the workers	AIT
	23: 2	the LORD with the **m** *of* Judah, the people	408
	23:17	The **m** *of* the city said,	408
	24:14	all the officers and **fighting m**,	1475+2657
	24:15	his officials and the **leading** *m* of the land.	380
	24:16	of seven thousand fighting **m**,	408
	25:19	of the fighting **m** and five royal advisers.	408
	25:19	the land and sixty of his **m** who were found	6639
	25:23	the army officers and their **m** heard that	408
	25:23	the son of the Maacathite, and their **m**,	408
	25:24	an oath to reassure them and their **m**.	408
	25:25	came with ten **m** and assassinated Gedaliah	408
	25:25	and also the **m** *of* Judah and	3374
1Ch	4:12	These were the **m** *of* Recah.	408
	4:22	the **m** *of* Cozeba, and Joash and Saraph,	408
	4:38	The **m** listed above by name were leaders	465S
	4:41	**The m** whose names were listed came in	465S
	5:18	**m** for military service—	NIH
	5:18	able-bodied **m** who could handle shield	408
	5:24	They were brave warriors, famous **m**,	408
	6:31	These are the **m** David put in charge of	889S
	6:33	Here are the *m who* **served**,	AIT
	7: 2	of Tola listed as **fighting m**	1475+2657
	7: 4	had 36,000 **m** ready for battle,	1522+4878+7372
	7: 5	The relatives who were **fighting m**	1475+2657
	7: 7	Their genealogical record listed 22,034	
		fighting m.	1475+2657
	7: 9	of families and 20,200 **fighting m**.	1475+2657
	7:11	**fighting m** ready to go out to war.	1475+2657
	7:21	and Elead were killed by the native-born **m**	408
	7:40	heads of families, **choice** *m*,	AIT
	7:40	The number of **m** ready for battle,	408
	9: 9	All these **m** were heads of their families.	408
	9:13	They were **able m**, responsible for	1475+2657
	10:12	all their valiant **m** went and took the bodies	408
	11:10	These were the chiefs of David's **mighty m**	1475
	11:11	this is the list of David's **mighty m**—	1475
	11:11	against three hundred *m*, whom he **killed**	AIT
	11:12	one of the three **mighty m**.	1475
	11:19	the blood of these **m** who went at the risk	408
	11:19	the exploits of the three **mighty m**.	1475
	11:20	against three hundred *m*, whom he **killed**,	AIT
	11:22	He struck down two of Moab's **best m**.	738
	11:24	too was as famous as the three **mighty m**.	1475
	11:26	The **mighty m** were:	1475+2657
	12: 1	These were the *m who* **came** to David	AIT
	12:16	*m* from Judah also came	AIT
	12:19	**m** of Manasseh **defected**	AIT
	12:19	(*He and his m did* not **help** the Philistines	AIT
	12:20	of Manasseh *who* **defected**	AIT
	12:22	Day after day *m* came to help David,	AIT
	12:23	the **m** armed for battle who came to David	8031
	12:24	**m** of Judah, carrying shield and spear—	1201
	12:25	**m** of Simeon, warriors ready for battle—	1201
	12:26	**m** of Levi—4,600,	1201
	12:27	leader of the family of Aaron, with 3,700 **m**,	NIH
	12:29	**m** of Benjamin, Saul's kinsmen—	1201
	12:30	**m** of Ephraim, brave warriors, famous	1201
	12:31	**m** of half the tribe of Manasseh, designated	NIH
	12:32	**m** of Issachar, who understood the times	1201
	12:33	**m** of Zebulun, experienced soldiers	NIH
	12:34	**m** of Naphtali—1,000	NIH
	12:34	**m** carrying shields and spears;	NIH
	12:35	**m** of **Dan**, ready for battle—28,600;	1974
	12:36	**m** of Asher, experienced soldiers prepared	NIH
	12:37	**m** of **Reuben**, Gad and the half-tribe	8018
	12:38	All these were fighting **m** who volunteered	408
	12:39	The *m* **spent** three days there with David,	AIT
	14:11	David and *his* **m** went up to Baal Perazim,	AIT
	17: 8	the names of the **greatest** *m* of the earth.	AIT
	17:17	as though I were the most exalted of **m**,	132
	17:24	Then **m** will say, 'The LORD Almighty,	NIH
	19: 2	When David's **m** came to Hanun in the land	6269
	19: 3	by sending **m** to you to express sympathy?	NIH
	19: 3	Haven't his **m** come to you to explore	6269
	19: 4	So Hanun seized David's **m**, shaved them,	6269
	19: 5	someone came and told David about the **m**,	408
	19: 8	with the entire army of **fighting m**.	1475
	19:11	He put the rest of the **m** under the command	6639

1Ch	20: 8	they fell at the hands of David and his **m**.	6269
	21: 5	Joab reported the number of the **fighting m**	6639
	21: 5	In all Israel there were one million one	
		hundred thousand **m** who could handle	408
	21:13	but do not let me fall into the hands of **m**."	132
	21:14	and seventy thousand **m** of Israel fell dead.	408
	21:17	"Was it not I who ordered the **fighting m** to	6639
	22:15	as well as **m** skilled in every kind of work	3972S
	23: 3	number of **m** was thirty-eight thousand.	1505
	25: 1	the list of the **m** who performed this service:	408
	25: 6	All **these** *m* were under the supervision	AIT
	26: 6	because they were **very capable m**.	1475+2657
	26: 7	and Semakiah were also **able m**.	1201+2657
	26: 8	and their relatives were capable **m** with	408
	26: 9	who were **able m**—18 in all.	1201+2657
	26:12	through their chief **m**,	1505
	26:30	seventeen hundred **able m**—	1201+2657
	26:31	**capable m** among the Hebronites	1475+2657
	26:32	were **able m** and heads of families,	1201+2657
	27: 1	Each division consisted of 24,000 **m**.	NIH
	27: 2	There were 24,000 **m** in his division.	NIH
	27: 4	There were 24,000 **m** in his division.	NIH
	27: 5	and there were 24,000 **m** in his division.	NIH
	27: 7	There were 24,000 **m** in his division.	NIH
	27: 8	There were 24,000 **m** in his division.	NIH
	27: 9	There were 24,000 **m** in his division.	NIH
	27:10	There were 24,000 **m** in his division.	NIH
	27:11	There were 24,000 **m** in his division.	NIH
	27:12	There were 24,000 **m** in his division.	NIH
	27:13	There were 24,000 **m** in his division.	NIH
	27:14	There were 24,000 **m** in his division.	NIH
	27:15	There were 24,000 **m** in his division.	NIH
	27:23	the number of the **m** twenty years old	NIH
	27:24	Joab son of Zeruiah began to count the **m**	NIH
	28: 1	the **mighty m** and all the brave warriors.	1475
	29:24	All the officers and **mighty m**,	1475
2Ch	2: 2	He conscripted seventy thousand **m**	408
	2: 8	for I know that your **m** are skilled	6269
	2: 8	My **m** will work with yours	6269
	5: 3	the **m** *of* Israel came together to the king at	408
	6:18	will God really dwell on earth with **m**?	132
	6:30	(for you alone know the hearts of **m**),	132+1201
	8: 9	they were his fighting **m**,	408
	8:10	and fifty officials supervising the **m**.	6639
	8:18	**m** who knew the sea.	6269
	8:18	These, with Solomon's **m**,	6269
	9: 7	How happy your **m** must be!	408
	9:10	(The **m** of Hiram and the men	6269
	9:10	the **m** of Solomon brought gold from Ophir;	6269
	9:21	of trading ships manned by Hiram's **m**.	6269
	10: 8	and consulted the **young m** who had grown	3529
	10:10	The **young m** who had grown up	3529
	10:14	he followed the advice of the **young m**	3529
	11: 1	a hundred and eighty thousand fighting **m**—	1033
	13: 3	of four hundred thousand able fighting **m**,	1475
	13:12	**M** of Israel, do not fight against	1201
	13:15	and the **m** *of* Judah raised the battle cry.	408
	13:17	and his **m** inflicted heavy losses on them,	6639
	13:17	among Israel's able **m**.	408
	13:18	The **m** *of* Israel were subdued on	1201
	13:18	and the **m** *of* Judah were victorious	1201
	14: 8	of three hundred thousand **m** from Judah,	1475+2657
	14: 8	All these were **brave fighting m**.	1475+2657
	14:13	The **m** of Judah carried off a large amount	NIH
	16: 6	Then King Asa brought all the **m** of Judah,	NIH
	17:13	**experienced fighting m**	408+1475+2657+4878
	17:14	with 300,000 **fighting m**;	1475+2657
	17:17	*m* armed *with* bows and shields;	AIT
	17:18	with 180,000 *m* armed for battle.	AIT
	17:19	These were the **m** *who* **served** the king,	AIT
	18: 5	together the prophets—four hundred **m**—	408
	20: 2	*Some* **m** came and told Jehoshaphat,	AIT
	20:10	"But now here are **m** *from* Ammon,	1201
	20:13	All the **m** of Judah,	NIH
	20:21	Jehoshaphat appointed *m* to sing to	AIT
	20:22	the LORD set ambushes against the **m**	1201
	20:23	The **m** of Ammon and Moab rose up	1201
	20:23	up against the **m** *from* Mount Seir to destroy	3782
	20:23	After they finished slaughtering the **m**	3782
	20:24	When the **m** of Judah came to the place	NIH
	20:25	and his **m** went to carry off their plunder,	6639
	20:27	all the **m** of Judah	408
	21:13	**m** who were better than you.	2021S
	22: 9	and *his* **m** captured him	AIT
	23: 5	the other **m** are to be in the courtyards of	6639
	23: 6	but all the other **m** are to guard what	6639
	23: 8	The Levites and all the **m** of Judah did just	NIH
	23: 8	Each one took his **m**—	408
	23:10	He stationed all the **m**,	6639
	24:12	the *m who* **carried out** the work required for	AIT
	24:13	The **m** in charge of the work were diligent,	AIT
	24:24	Aramean army had come with only a few **m**,	408
	25: 5	there were three hundred thousand **m** ready	1033
	25: 6	a hundred thousand **fighting m** from	1475+2657
	25:11	where he killed ten thousand **m** of Seir.	1201
	25:12	also captured ten thousand *m* **alive**,	AIT
	25:27	but they sent **m** after him to Lachish	NIH
	26:12	over the **fighting m** was 2,600.	1475+2657
	26:13	an army of 307,500 **m trained** for war,	AIT
	26:15	by **skilful m** for use on the towers and	3110
	28:10	**make** the **m** and women of Judah and	
		Jerusalem your **slaves**.	3899+6269
	28:15	The **m** designated by name took	408
	30:11	Nevertheless, *some* **m** of Asher,	408
	31: 6	The **m** of Israel and Judah who lived in	1201
	31:19	**m** were designated by name	408
	32: 4	A large **force** of **m** assembled,	6639

2Ch	32:21	the fighting m and the leaders and	1475+2657
	34:10	to the m appointed to supervise the work on	AIT
	34:10	These m paid the workers who	2021+4856+6913S
	34:12	The m did the work faithfully.	408
	34:30	the LORD with the m of Judah, the people	408
	35:25	m and women singers commemorate Josiah	AIT
	36:17	who killed their young m with the sword in	1033
Ezr	2:2	The list of the m of the people of Israel:	408
	2:21	the m of Bethlehem 123	1201
	2:65	they also had 200 m and women singers.	AIT
	4:9	and officials over the m from Tripolis,	10305
	4:11	the m of Trans-Euphrates:	10050
	4:21	Now issue an order to these m to stop work,	10131
	5:4	of the m constructing this building?"	10131
	6:8	of these m are to be fully paid out of	10131
	7:28	and gathered leading m from Israel to go	AIT
	8:3	and with him were registered 150 m;	2351
	8:4	and with him 200 m;	2351
	8:5	and with him 300 m;	2351
	8:6	Ebed son of Jonathan, and with him 50 m;	2351
	8:7	and with him 70 m;	2351
	8:8	and with him 80 m;	2351
	8:9	Obadiah son of Jehiel, and with him 218 m;	2351
	8:10	and with him 160 m;	2351
	8:11	and with him 28 m;	2351
	8:12	and with him 110 m;	2351
	8:13	Jeuel and Shemaiah, and with them 60 m;	2351
	8:14	Uthai and Zaccur, and with them 70 m.	2351
	8:16	who were m of learning,	AIT
	8:18	and Sherebiah's sons and brothers, 18 m;	AIT
	8:19	his brothers and nephews, 20 m.	AIT
	10:1	m, women and children—	408
	10:9	the m of Judah and Benjamin had gathered	408
	10:16	priest selected m who were family heads,	408
	10:17	the m who had married foreign women.	408
Ne	1:2	came from Judah with some other m,	408
	2:12	I set out during the night with a few m.	408
	3:2	The m of Jericho built the adjoining	408
	3:5	repaired by the m of Tekoa,	9542
	3:7	repairs were made by m from Gibeon	408
	3:27	the m of Tekoa repaired another section,	9542
	4:7	the Ammonites and the m of Ashdod heard	847
	4:16	half of my m did the work,	5853
	4:21	the work with half the m holding spears,	4392S
	4:23	nor my brothers nor my m nor the guards	5853
	5:1	the m and their wives raised a great outcry	6639
	5:10	and my brothers and my m are also lending	5853
	5:16	All my m were assembled there for	5853
	6:10	because m are coming to kill you—	AIT
	7:2	and feared God more than most m do.	AIT
	7:7	The list of the m of Israel:	408
	7:26	the m of Bethlehem and Netophah 188	408
	7:67	they also had 245 m and women singers.	AIT
	8:3	up of m and women and all who were able	408
	8:3	the Water Gate in the presence of the m,	408
	11:2	the m who volunteered to live in Jerusalem	408
	11:6	in Jerusalem totaled 468 able m.	408
	11:8	Gabbai and Sallai—928 m.	NIH
	11:12	for the temple—822 m;	NIH
	11:13	who were heads of families—242 m;	NIH
	11:14	who were able m—128.	1475+2657
	11:19	at the gates—172 m.	NIH
	12:44	that time m were appointed to be in charge	408
	13:13	these m were considered trustworthy.	AIT
	13:15	In those days I saw m in Judah treading winepresses on the Sabbath	AIT
	13:16	M from Tyre who lived in Jerusalem	7660
	13:19	I stationed some of my own m at the gates	5853
	13:23	I saw m of Judah who had married women	3374
	13:25	beat some of the m and pulled out their hair.	408
Est	1:13	with the wise m who understood the times	AIT
	3:9	for the m who carry out this business."	AIT
	9:6	Jews killed and destroyed five hundred m.	408
	9:12	and destroyed five hundred m and	408
	9:15	they put to death in Susa three hundred m,	408
Job	4:13	when deep sleep falls on m,	AIT
	7:20	what have I done to you, O watcher of m?	132
	11:3	Will your idle talk reduce m to silence?	5493
	11:11	Surely he recognizes deceitful m;	5493
	12:5	M at ease have contempt for misfortune as	AIT
	12:19	and overthrows m long established.	AIT
	13:9	as you might deceive m?	632
	14:12	the heavens are no more, m will not wake	NIH
	15:10	m even older than your father.	AIT
	15:18	what wise m have declared,	AIT
	16:10	M open their mouths to jeer at me;	AIT
	16:11	to evil m and thrown me into the clutches	6397
	17:8	Upright m are appalled at this;	AIT
	17:12	These m turn night into day;	NIH
	18:20	M of the west are appalled at his fate;	AIT
	18:20	m of the east are seized with horror.	AIT
	21:28	the tents where wicked m lived?'	AIT
	21:33	all m follow after him,	132
	22:6	you stripped m of their clothing,	NIH
	22:15	to the old path that evil m have trod?	5493
	22:29	When m are brought low and you say,	AIT
	24:2	M move boundary stones;	AIT
	24:16	In the dark, m break into houses,	AIT
	24:20	evil m are no longer remembered	AIT
	28:4	far from m he dangles and sways.	632
	29:8	the young m saw me and stepped aside and	5853
	29:8	and stepped aside and the old m rose	3813
	29:9	the chief m refrained from speaking	8569
	29:21	"M listened to me expectantly,	AIT
	30:1	"But now they mock me, m younger than I,	AIT
	30:5	They were banished from their fellow m,	1569
	31:10	and may other m sleep with her.	AIT

Job	31:31	if the m of my household have never said,	5493
	31:33	if I have concealed my sin as m do,	132
	32:1	So these three m stopped answering Job,	408
	32:5	that the three m had nothing more to say,	408
	33:15	when deep sleep falls on m as they slumber	AIT
	33:27	Then he comes to m and says, 'I sinned,	408
	34:2	"Hear my words, you wise m;	AIT
	34:2	listen to me, you m of learning.	AIT
	34:8	he associates with wicked m.	408
	34:10	"So listen to me, you m of understanding.	AIT
	34:21	"His eyes are on the ways of m;	408
	34:23	God has no need to examine m further,	408
	34:34	"M of understanding declare,	408
	34:34	wise m who hear me say to me,	1505
	35:8	and your righteousness only the sons of m.	132
	35:9	"M cry out under a load of oppression;	AIT
	35:12	when m cry out because of the arrogance of	AIT
	36:5	"God is mighty, but does not despise m;	NIH
	36:8	But if m are bound in chains,	AIT
	36:24	which m have praised in song.	408
	36:25	m gaze on it from afar.	632
	37:7	that all m he has made may know his work,	408
	37:13	He brings the clouds to punish m,	NIH
	37:24	Therefore, m revere him,	408
Ps	4:2	m, will you turn my glory into shame?	408+1201
	5:6	and deceitful m the LORD abhors.	408
	9:20	let the nations know they are but m.	632
	11:4	He observes the sons of m;	132
	11:7	upright m will see his face.	AIT
	12:1	faithful have vanished from among m.	132+1201
	12:8	when what is vile is honored among m.	132+1201
	14:2	of m to see if there are any who understand,	132
	14:4	those who devour my people as m eat bread	AIT
	17:4	As for the deeds of m—	132
	17:14	by your hand save me from such m,	5493
	17:14	from m of this world whose reward is	5493
	18:48	from violent m you rescued me.	408
	22:6	scorned by m and despised by the people.	132
	24:16	a band of evil m has encircled me,	AIT
	26:4	I do not sit with deceitful m,	5493
	26:9	my life with bloodthirsty m,	408
	27:2	When evil m advance against me	AIT
	31:19	you bestow in the sight of m on those	132+1201
	31:20	from the intrigues of m;	408
	36:7	high and low among m find refuge in the shadow of your wings.	132+1201
	37:1	not fret because of evil m or be envious	AIT
	37:1	do not fret when m succeed in their ways,	408
	37:9	For evil m will be cut off,	AIT
	39:11	You rebuke and discipline m for their sin;	408
	42:3	while m say to me all day long,	NIH
	43:1	rescue me from deceitful and wicked m.	408
	45:2	You are the most excellent of m	132+1201
	45:12	m of wealth will seek your favor.	6639
	49:10	For all can see that wise m die;	AIT
	49:18	and m praise you when you prosper—	AIT
	53:2	of m to see if there are any who understand,	132
	53:4	those who devour my people as m eat bread	AIT
	54:3	ruthless m seek my life—	AIT
	54:3	m without regard for God.	4392S
	55:19	m who never change their ways	AIT
	55:23	bloodthirsty and deceitful m will not live	408
	56:1	O God, for m hotly pursue me;	632
	57:4	m whose teeth are spears and arrows,	132+1201
	58:1	Do you judge uprightly among m?	132+1201
	58:11	Then m will say, "Surely the righteous	132
	59:T	When Saul had sent m to watch David's	NIH
	59:2	and save me from bloodthirsty m.	408
	59:3	Fierce m conspire against me for no offense	AIT
	62:9	Lowborn m are but a breath,	132+1201
	65:2	to you all m will come.	1414
	66:12	You let m ride over our heads;	632
	68:12	in the camps m divide the plunder.	AIT
	68:18	you received gifts from m,	132
	71:7	from the grasp of evil and cruel m.	AIT
	74:5	They behaved like m wielding axes to cut	AIT
	75:1	m tell of your wonderful deeds.	AIT
	76:5	Valiant m lie plundered,	52+4213
	76:10	your wrath against m brings you praise,	132
	78:9	The m of Ephraim, though armed	1201
	78:25	M ate the bread of angels;	408
	78:31	cutting down the young m of Israel.	1033
	78:60	the tent he had set up among m.	132
	78:63	Fire consumed their young m,	1033
	82:7	But you will die like mere m;	132
	83:16	with shame so that m will seek your name,	AIT
	86:14	a band of ruthless m seeks my life—	AIT
	86:14	m without regard for you.	4392S
	89:47	For what futility you have created all m!	132+1201
	90:3	You turn m back to dust, saying,	632
	90:3	saying, "Return to dust, O sons of m."	132
	90:5	You sweep m away in the sleep of death;	4392S
	101:3	The deeds of faithless m I hate;	AIT
	101:4	M of perverse heart shall be far from me;	AIT
	107:8	and his wonderful deeds for m,	132+1201
	107:15	and his wonderful deeds for m,	132+1201
	107:21	and his wonderful deeds for m,	132+1201
	107:27	They reeled and staggered like drunken m;	8893
	107:31	and his wonderful deeds for m.	132+1201
	109:2	and deceitful m have opened their mouths	AIT
	115:4	silver and gold, made by the hands of m.	132
	116:11	And in my dismay I said, "All m are liars."	132
	119:86	help me, for m persecute me without cause.	AIT
	119:113	I hate double-minded m, but I love your law.	AIT
	119:134	Redeem me from the oppression of m,	132
	124:2	not been on our side when m attacked us,	132

Ps	126:1	we were like m who dreamed.	AIT
	135:8	the firstborn of m and animals.	132
	135:15	silver and gold, made by the hands of m.	132
	139:19	Away from me, you bloodthirsty m!	408
	140:1	Rescue me, O LORD, from evil m;	132
	140:1	protect me from m of violence,	408
	140:4	protect me from m of violence who plan	408
	140:5	Proud m have hidden a snare for me;	AIT
	140:11	may disaster hunt down m of violence.	408
	141:4	in wicked deeds with m who are evildoers;	AIT
	142:3	where I walk m have hidden a snare.	AIT
	145:12	that all m may know of your mighty acts	132+1201+2021
	146:3	in mortal m, who cannot save.	132+1201
	148:12	young m and maidens,	1033
	148:12	old m and children.	408
Pr	1:18	These m lie in wait for their own blood;	AIT
	2:12	save you from the ways of wicked m,	AIT
	2:12	from m whose words are perverse,	408
	2:20	the ways of good m and keep to the paths of	AIT
	4:14	the wicked or walk in the way of evil m.	AIT
	6:30	M do not despise a thief if he steals	AIT
	7:7	I noticed among the young m,	1201
	8:4	"To you, O m, I call out;	408
	10:14	Wise m store up knowledge,	AIT
	11:16	but ruthless m gain only wealth.	AIT
	11:20	The LORD detests m of perverse heart	AIT
	12:7	Wicked m are overthrown and are no more,	AIT
	12:8	but m with warped minds are despised.	AIT
	12:12	The wicked desire the plunder of evil m,	AIT
	12:22	but he delights in m who are truthful.	AIT
	14:19	Evil m will bow down in the presence of	AIT
	15:11	how much more the hearts of m!	132+1201
	20:29	The glory of young m is their strength,	1033
	22:29	he will not serve before obscure m.	AIT
	23:28	and multiplies the unfaithful among m.	132
	24:1	Do not envy wicked m,	408
	24:9	and m detest a mocker.	132
	24:19	not fret because of evil m or be envious of	AIT
	25:1	copied by the m of Hezekiah king of Judah:	408
	25:6	and do not claim a place among great m;	AIT
	26:16	than seven m who answer discreetly.	AIT
	28:5	Evil m do not understand justice,	408
	28:12	the wicked rise to power, m go into hiding.	132
	29:8	but wise m turn away anger.	AIT
	29:10	Bloodthirsty m hate a man of integrity	408
	30:2	"I am the most ignorant of m;	408
Ecc	1:11	There is no remembrance of m of old,	AIT
	1:13	a heavy burden God has laid on m!	132+1201
	2:3	to see what was worthwhile for m	132+1201
	2:8	I acquired m and women singers,	AIT
	3:10	seen the burden God has laid on m.	132+1201
	3:11	He has also set eternity in the hearts of m;	4392S
	3:12	that there is nothing better for m than to	4392
	3:14	God does it so that m will revere him.	408
	3:18	I also thought, "As for m,	132+1201
	6:1	and it weighs heavily on m:	132
	7:29	m have gone in search of many schemes."	2156S
	8:12	that it will go better with God-fearing m,	AIT
	8:14	righteous m who get what the wicked	AIT
	8:14	and wicked m who get what the righteous	AIT
	9:3	The hearts of m, moreover,	132+1201
	9:12	a snare, so m are trapped by evil times	132+1201
	12:3	and the strong m stoop,	408
	12:4	when m rise up at the sound of birds,	AIT
	12:5	when m are afraid of heights and	AIT
SS	2:3	the forest is my lover among the young m.	1201
Isa	2:11	be humbled and the pride of m brought low;	408
	2:17	be brought low and the pride of m humbled;	408
	2:19	M will flee to caves in the rocks and	AIT
	2:20	In that day m will throw away to the rodents	132
	3:25	Your m will fall by the sword,	5493
	5:3	"Now you dwellers in Jerusalem and m	408
	5:7	the m of Judah are the garden of his delight.	408
	5:13	their m of rank will die of hunger	3883
	7:13	Is it not enough to try the patience of m?	408
	7:24	M will go there with bow and arrow,	AIT
	8:14	a stone that causes m to stumble and a rock	NIH
	8:19	When m tell you to consult mediums	AIT
	9:3	as m rejoice when dividing the plunder.	AIT
	9:15	the elders and prominent m are the head,	AIT
	9:17	will take not pleasure in the young m,	1033
	10:14	as m gather abandoned eggs,	NIH
	11:15	into seven streams so that m can cross over	AIT
	13:18	Their bows will strike down the young m;	5853
	15:4	Therefore the armed m of Moab cry out,	AIT
	16:7	and grieve for the m of Kir Hareseth.	861
	17:7	In that day m will look to their Maker	132
	19:11	"I am one of the wise m,	AIT
	19:12	Where are your wise m now?	AIT
	29:13	of me is made up only of rules taught by m.	408
	30:30	The LORD will cause m to hear	NIH
	31:3	But the Egyptians are m and not God;	132
	31:8	before the sword and their young m will	1033
	33:3	like a swarm of locusts m pounce on it.	AIT
	33:7	Look, their brave m cry aloud in the streets;	737
	36:12	and not to the m sitting on the wall—	408
	37:36	a hundred and eighty-five thousand m in	NIH
	38:16	Lord, by such things m live;	AIT
	39:3	"What did those m say,	408
	40:6	"All m are like grass,	1414
	40:30	and my dismay I said, "All m stumble and fall;	1033
	43:4	I will give m in exchange for you,	132
	44:11	craftsmen are nothing but m.	132
	45:6	m may know there is none besides me.	132
	51:7	Do not fear the reproach of m or be terrified	632
	51:12	Who are you that you fear mortal m,	632

Isa	51:12	the sons of **m**, who are but grass,	132
	51:17	to its dregs the goblet that makes **m** stagger.	NIH
	53: 3	He was despised and rejected by **m**,	408
	53: 3	from whom **m** hide their faces he was despised,	NIH
	57: 1	devout **m** are taken away,	408
	59:10	feeling our way like **m** without eyes.	NIH
	59:19	**m** will **fear** the name of the LORD,	AIT
	60:11	so that **m** may bring you the wealth of	NIH
	65: 8	and **m** say, 'Don't destroy it, there is	AIT
	66:16	upon all **m**, and many will be those slain by	1414
Jer	2:16	the **m** of Memphis and Tahpanhes	1201
	2:34	On your clothes you **m** the lifeblood of	AIT
	3:16	"**m** will no longer say,	AIT
	4: 3	the LORD says to the **m** of Judah and	408
	4: 4	you **m** of Judah and people of Jerusalem,	408
	4:17	They surround her like **m** guarding a field,	AIT
	5:26	"Among my people are **wicked m** who lie	AIT
	5:26	in wait like **m** who snare birds and	3687
	5:26	and like those who set traps to catch **m**.	408
	6:11	and on the **young m** gathered together;	1033
	6:23	like **m** in battle formation to attack you,	408
	8: 4	" 'When **m** fall down, do they not get up?	AIT
	8:10	Therefore I will give their wives to **other m**	AIT
	9:21	and the **young m** from the public squares.	1033
	9:22	" 'The dead bodies of **m** will lie like refuse	132
	10: 7	Among all the **wise m** of the nations and	AIT
	11:21	the LORD says about the **m**	408
	11:22	Their **young m** will die by the sword,	1033
	11:23	because I will bring disaster on the **m**	408
	12: 5	with **m** on foot and they have worn you out,	NIH
	15: 8	against the mothers of their **young m**;	1033
	16: 3	and the **m** who are their fathers:	3528S
	16:14	**m** will no longer say,	AIT
	16:20	Do **m** make their own gods?	132
	17:25	by the **m** of Judah and those living	408
	18:21	let their **m** be put to death,	408
	18:21	their **young m** slain by the sword in battle.	1033
	21: 6	both **m** and animals—	132
	26:22	along with some other **m**.	408
	31:13	**young m** and old as well.	1033
	31:27	the house of Judah with the offspring of **m**	132
	32:19	Your eyes are open to all the ways of **m**	132+1201
	32:32	the **m** of Judah and the people of Jerusalem.	408
	32:43	without **m** or animals.	132
	33: 5	of the **m** I will slay in my anger and wrath.	132
	33:10	without **m** or animals."	132
	33:10	inhabited by neither **m** nor animals,	132
	33:12	desolate and without **m** or animals—	132
	34:18	The **m** who have violated my covenant	408
	35: 5	of wine and some cups before the **m** of	1201
	35:13	the **m** of Judah and the people of Jerusalem,	408
	36:29	and cut off both **m** and animals from it?"	132
	37:10	and only wounded **m** were left in their tents,	408
	38: 9	these **m** have acted wickedly	408
	38:10	"Take thirty **m** from here with you	408
	38:11	the **m** with him and went to a room under	408
	40: 7	the army officers and their **m** who were still	408
	40: 7	the land and had put him in charge of the **m**,	408
	40: 8	the son of the Maacathite, and their **m**.	408
	40: 9	took an oath to reassure them and their **m**.	408
	41: 1	came with ten **m** to Gedaliah son of Ahikam	408
	41: 2	and the ten **m** who were with him got up	408
	41: 5	eighty **m** who had shaved off their beards,	408
	41: 7	the **m** who were with him slaughtered them	408
	41: 9	the bodies of the **m** he had killed along	408
	41:12	they took all their **m** and went	408
	41:15	of his **m** escaped from Johanan and fled to	408
	43: 2	and all the arrogant **m** said to Jeremiah,	408
	43: 6	They also led away all the **m**,	1505
	44: 7	by cutting off from Judah the **m**	408
	44:15	Then all the **m** who knew	408
	44:20	both **m** and women,	1505
	46: 9	**m** of Cush and Put who carry shields,	NIH
	46: 9	**m** of Lydia who draw the bow.	4276
	46:22	like **m** who cut down trees.	AIT
	48: 2	in Heshbon **m** will plot her downfall:	AIT
	48:12	"when I will send **m** who pour from jars,	AIT
	48:14	'We are warriors, **m** valiant in battle'?	408
	48:15	her finest **young m** will go down in	1033
	48:31	I moan for the **m** of Kir Hareseth.	408
	48:36	like a flute for the **m** of Kir Hareseth.	408
	49:15	among the nations, despised among **m**.	132
	49:26	Surely, her **young m** will fall in the streets;	1033
	49:29	**M** will shout to them,	AIT
	50: 3	both **m** and animals will flee away.	132
	50:30	her **young m** will fall in the streets;	1033
	50:35	and against her officials and **wise m**!	AIT
	50:42	like **m** in battle formation to attack you,	408
	51: 3	Do not spare her **young m**;	1033
	51:14	I will surely fill you with **m**,	132
	51:57	I will make her officials and **wise m** drunk,	AIT
	52:25	the officer in charge of the fighting **m**,	408
	52:25	the land and sixty of his **m** who were found	6639
La	1:15	an army against me to crush my **young m**.	1033
	1:18	My **young m** and maidens have gone	1033
	2:12	as they faint like **wounded m** in the streets	AIT
	2:21	my **young m** and maidens have fallen by	1033
	3:31	For **m** are not cast off by the Lord forever.	AIT
	3:33	or grief to the children of **m**.	408
	4:14	through the streets like **m** who are blind.	AIT
	4:15	You are unclean!" **m** cry to them.	AIT
	4:18	**M** stalked us at every step,	AIT
	5:13	**Young m** toil at the millstones;	1033
	5:14	**young m** have stopped their music.	1033
Eze	8:16	were about twenty-five **m**.	408
	9: 2	And I saw six **m** coming from the direction	408

Eze	9: 6	Slaughter old **m**, young men and maidens,	AIT
	9: 6	Slaughter old men, **young m** and maidens,	1033
	11: 1	the entrance to the gate were twenty-five **m**,	408
	11: 2	these are the **m** who are plotting evil	408
	14: 3	these **m** have set up idols in their hearts	408
	14:13	upon it and kill its **m** and their animals,	132
	14:14	if these three **m**—Noah, Daniel and Job	408
	14:16	even if these three **m** were in it,	408
	14:17	and I kill its **m** and their animals,	132
	14:18	even if these three **m** were in it,	408
	14:19	killing its **m** and their animals,	132
	14:21	to kill its **m** and their animals!	132
	17:13	He also carried away the **leading m** of	380
	19: 3	to tear the prey and he devoured **m**.	132
	19: 6	to tear the prey and he devoured **m**.	132
	21:31	I will hand you over to brutal **m**,	408
	21:31	**m** skilled in destruction.	AIT
	22:12	In you are slanderous **m** bent	408
	22:12	In you **m** accept bribes to shed blood;	AIT
	22:20	As **m** gather silver, copper, iron,	NIH
	23: 6	all of them handsome **young m**,	1033
	23: 8	when during her youth **m** slept with her,	AIT
	23:12	mounted horsemen, all handsome **young m**.	1033
	23:14	She saw **m** portrayed on a wall,	408
	23:23	the **m** of Pekod and Shoa and Koa,	NIH
	23:23	handsome **young m**, all of them governors	1033
	23:23	chariot officers and **m** of high rank,	7924
	23:40	even sent messengers for **m** who came	408
	23:42	the desert along with **m** from the rabble,	408
	23:44	As **m** sleep with a prostitute,	AIT
	23:45	But righteous **m** will sentence them to	408
	25:13	and kill its **m** and their animals.	132
	26:10	when he enters your gates as **m** enter	AIT
	26:17	O city of renown, peopled by **m** of the sea!	AIT
	27: 8	**M** of Sidon and Arvad were your oarsmen;	3782
	27: 8	your skilled **m**, O Tyre,	AIT
	27:10	" '**M** of Persia, Lydia and Put served	NIH
	27:11	**M** of Arvad and Helech manned your walls	1201
	27:11	**m** of Gammad were in your towers.	1689
	27:14	" '**M** of Beth Togarmah exchanged work horses,	NIH
	27:15	" 'The **m** of Rhodes traded with you,	1201
	29: 8	a sword against you and kill your **m**	132
	30:12	of the Nile and sell the land to **evil m**;	AIT
	30:17	The **young m** of Heliopolis	1033
	31:14	for the earth below, among **mortal m**,	132+1201
	32:12	to fall by the swords of **mighty m**—	1475
	33: 2	the people of the land choose one of their **m**	408
	36:11	I will increase the number of **m** and animals	132
	36:13	Because people say to you, "You devour **m**	132
	36:14	therefore you will no longer devour **m**	132
	39:14	" '**M** will be regularly employed to cleanse	408
	39:18	You will eat the flesh of **mighty m** and	1475
	39:20	**mighty m** and soldiers of every kind,'	1475
Da	1: 4	**young m** without any physical defect,	3529
	1:10	the other **young m** your age?	3529
	1:13	that of the **young m** who eat the royal food,	3529
	1:15	of the **young m** who ate the royal food.	3529
	1:17	these four **young m** God gave knowledge	3529
	2:11	and they do not live among **m**."	10125
	2:12	the execution of all the **wise m** of Babylon.	AIT
	2:13	decree was issued to put the **wise m** to death	AIT
	2:13	**m** were sent to look for Daniel	AIT
	2:14	had gone out to put to death the **wise m**	AIT
	2:18	not be executed with the rest of the **wise m**	AIT
	2:24	king had appointed to execute the **wise m**	AIT
	2:24	"Do not execute the **wise m** of Babylon.	AIT
	2:30	I have greater wisdom than other **living m**,	AIT
	2:48	and placed him in charge of all its **wise m**,	AIT
	3: 4	**m** of every language:	10392
	3: 7	nations and **m** of every language fell down	10392
	3:13	So these **m** were brought before the king,	10131
	3:21	So these **m**, wearing their robes, trousers,	10131
	3:23	and these three **m**, firmly tied, fell into	10131
	3:24	"Weren't there three **m** that we tied up	10131
	3:25	I see four **m** walking around in the fire,	10131
	4: 1	**m** of every language,	10392
	4: 6	the **wise m** of Babylon be brought before me	AIT
	4:17	of **m** and gives them to anyone he wishes	10050
	4:17	and sets over them the lowliest of **m**.'	AIT
	4:18	of the **wise m** in my kingdom can interpret it	AIT
	4:25	of **m** and gives them to anyone he wishes.	10050
	4:32	of **m** and gives them to anyone he wishes."	10050
	5: 7	to be brought and said to these **wise m**	AIT
	5: 8	Then all the king's **wise m** came in,	AIT
	5:15	The **wise m** and enchanters were brought	AIT
	5:19	and **m** of every language dreaded	10392
	5:21	of **m** and sets over them anyone he wishes.	10050
	6: 5	Finally these **m** said,	10131
	6:11	Then these **m** went as a group	10131
	6:15	the **m** went as a group to the king and said	10131
	6:24	the **m** who had falsely accused Daniel were brought in and thrown into the lions'	10131
	6:25	and **m** of every language throughout	10392
	7:14	and **m** of every language worshiped him.	10392
	8:24	the **mighty m** and the holy people.	AIT
	9: 7	the **m** of Judah and people of Jerusalem,	408
	10: 7	the **m** with me did not see it,	408
	11:14	The violent **m** among your own people	1201
Hos	4:14	the **m** themselves consort with harlots	AIT
	6: 8	Gilead is a city of **wicked m**,	224+7188
	13: 1	When Ephraim spoke, **m** trembled;	NIH
	14: 7	**M** will dwell again in his shade.	AIT
Joel	2:28	your old **m** will dream dreams,	AIT
	2:28	your **young m** will see visions.	1033
	2:29	Even on my **servants**, both **m** and women,	6269
	3: 9	Let all the fighting **m** draw near and attack.	408

Am	2:11	and Nazirites from among your **young m**.	1033
	4:10	I killed your **young m** with the sword,	1033
	6: 1	you **notable m** of the foremost nation,	AIT
	6: 9	If ten **m** are left in one house,	408
	8:12	**M** will stagger from sea to sea and wander	AIT
	8:13	and strong **young m** will faint because	1033
Ob	1: 8	"will I not destroy the **wise m** of Edom,	AIT
	1: 8	**m** of understanding in the mountains	AIT
Jnh	1:13	the **m** did their best to row back to land.	408
	1:16	At this the **m** greatly feared the LORD,	408
Mic	2: 4	In that day **m** will ridicule you;	AIT
	2: 8	like **m** returning from battle.	AIT
	5: 5	even eight leaders of **m**.	132
	6:12	Her rich **m** are violent;	AIT
	7: 2	All **m** lie in wait to shed blood;	4392S
Na	2: 3	and all her great **m** were put in chains.	AIT
Hab	1:11	**guilty m**, whose own strength is their god."	AIT
	1:14	You have made **m** like fish in the sea,	132
Zep	1: 3	"I will sweep away both **m** and animals;	132
	1:17	the people and they will walk like **blind m**,	AIT
	3: 4	they are treacherous **m**.	408
Hag	1:11	on **m** and cattle, and on the labor	132
Zec	2: 4	of the great number of **m** and livestock in it.	132
	3: 8	who are symbolic of things to come:	408
	4:10	"**M** will rejoice when they see	AIT
	7: 2	together with their **m**, to entreat the LORD	408
	8: 4	**m** and women of ripe old age	AIT
	8:23	"In those days ten **m** from all languages	408
	9: 1	the eyes of **m** and all the tribes of Israel are	132
	9:17	Grain will make the **young m** thrive,	1033
	10: 1	He gives showers of rain to **m**,	2157S
	10: 5	like **mighty m** trampling the muddy streets	1475
	10: 7	Ephraimites will become like **mighty m**,	1475
	14:13	that day **m** will be stricken by the LORD	2157S
Mal	2: 7	from his mouth **m** should seek instruction—	AIT
	3: 3	LORD will have **m** who will bring offerings	AIT
Mt	4:19	"and I will make you **fishers of m**."	476
	5:13	except to be thrown out and trampled by **m**.	476
	5:16	let your light shine before **m**,	476
	6: 1	to do your 'acts of righteousness' before **m**,	476
	6: 2	to be honored by **m**.	476
	6: 5	and on the street corners to be seen by **m**.	476
	6:14	if you forgive **m** when they sin against you,	476
	6:15	But if you do not forgive **m** their sins,	476
	6:16	to show **m** they are fasting,	476
	6:18	not be obvious to **m** that you are fasting,	476
	8:27	The **m** were amazed and asked,	AIT
	8:28	two **demon-possessed m** coming from	AIT
	8:33	to the **demon-possessed m**.	AIT
	9: 2	Some **m** brought to him a paralytic,	AIT
	9: 8	who had given such authority to **m**.	476
	9:17	Neither do **m** pour new wine	AIT
	9:27	two **blind m** followed him, calling out,	AIT
	9:28	the **blind m** came to him,	AIT
	10:17	"Be on your guard against **m**;	AIT
	10:22	All **m** will hate you because of me,	AIT
	10:32	"Whoever acknowledges me before **m**,	476
	10:33	But whoever disowns me before **m**,	476
	11:12	and **forceful m** lay hold of it.	AIT
	12:31	and blasphemy will be forgiven **m**,	476
	12:36	that **m** will have to give account on the day	476
	12:41	The **m** of Nineveh will stand up at	467
	13:17	and **righteous m** longed to see what you see	467
	14:21	about five thousand **m**,	467
	14:35	when the **m** of that place recognized Jesus,	467
	15: 9	their teachings are but rules taught by **m**.' "	476
	16:23	but the things of **m**."	476
	17:22	to be betrayed into the hands of **m**,	476
	19:12	others were made that way by **m**;	476
	20: 1	to hire **m** to work in his vineyard.	2239
	20:12	'These **m** who were hired last worked only one hour,'	AIT
	20:30	Two **blind m** were sitting by the roadside,	AIT
	21:25	Was it from heaven, or from **m**?"	476
	21:26	But if we say, 'From **m**'—	476
	22:16	You aren't swayed by **m**,	4029
	23: 5	"Everything they do is done for **m** to see:	476
	23: 7	and to have **m** call them 'Rabbi.'	476
	23:19	You **blind m**! Which is greater:	AIT
	23:34	and **wise m** and teachers.	AIT
	24:40	Two **m** will be in the field;	AIT
	26:40	"Could you **m** not keep watch with me	NIG
	26:50	Then the **m** stepped forward,	AIT
	26:62	that these **m** are bringing against you?"	AIT
	28: 4	that they shook and became like **dead m**.	AIT
Mk	1:17	"and I will make you **fishers of m**."	476
	1:20	the boat with the **hired m** and followed him.	3638
	2: 3	Some **m** came, bringing to him a paralytic,	AIT
	3:28	all the sins and blasphemies of **m** will be forgiven them.	476+3836+3836+5626
	5:35	some **m** came from the house of Jairus,	AIT
	6:21	and the **leading m** of Galilee.	AIT
	6:44	of the **m** who had eaten was five thousand.	467
	7: 7	their teachings are but rules taught by **m**.'	476
	7: 8	and are holding on to the traditions of **m**."	476
	8: 9	About **four thousand m** were present.	AIT
	8:33	the things of God, but the things of **m**."	476
	9:31	to be betrayed into the hands of **m**.	476
	11:30	was it from heaven, or from **m**?	476
	11:32	But if we say, 'From **m**'.—	476
	12:14	You aren't swayed by **m**,	4029S
	12:40	Such **m** will be punished most severely."	AIT
	13:13	All **m** will hate you because of me,	AIT
	13:26	that time **m** will see the Son of Man coming	AIT
	14:46	The **m** seized Jesus and arrested him.	1254+3836
	14:60	that these **m** are bringing against you?"	AIT
Lk	2:14	peace to **m** on whom his favor rests."	476

Lk		
2:52	and in favor with God and **m**.	476
5:10	from now on you will catch **m**."	476
5:18	Some **m** came carrying a paralytic on a mat	467
6:22	Blessed are you when **m** hate you,	476
6:26	Woe to you when all **m** speak well of you,	476
7:10	Then the **m** who had been sent returned to	AIT
7:20	When the **m** came to Jesus, they said,	467
7:41	"Two **m** owed money to a certain	NIG
9:14	(About five thousand **m** were there.)	467
9:30	Two **m**, Moses and Elijah,	467
9:32	they saw his glory and the two **m** standing	467
9:33	As the **m** were leaving Jesus,	899S
9:44	to be betrayed into the hands of **m**."	476
11:31	the **m** of this generation and condemn them;	476
11:32	The **m** of Nineveh will stand up at	467
11:44	which **m** walk over without knowing it."	476
12: 8	whoever acknowledges me before **m**,	476
12: 9	before **m** will be disowned before the angels	476
12:36	like **m** waiting for their master to return	476
14:24	of those **m** who were invited will get a taste	467
14:31	with ten **thousand** m to oppose	AIT
15:17	of my father's **hired** m have food to spare,	3634
15:19	make me like one of your **hired m**.'	3634
16:15	who justify yourselves in the eyes of **m**,	476
16:15	among **m** is detestable in God's sight.	476
17:12	ten **m** who had leprosy met him.	467
17:23	**M** will tell you, 'There he is!'	AIT
18: 2	neither feared God nor cared about **m**.	476
18: 4	though I don't fear God or care about **m**,	476
18:10	"Two **m** went up to the temple to pray,	467
18:11	'God, I thank you that I am not like other **m**	476
18:27	"What is impossible with **m** is possible	476
20: 4	was it from heaven, or from **m?**"	476
20:47	Such **m** will be punished most severely."	AIT
21:17	**All** m will hate you because of me.	AIT
21:26	**M** will faint from terror,	476
22:63	The **m** who were guarding Jesus began mocking and beating him.	467
23:31	if **m** do these things when the tree is green,	AIT
23:32	Two **other** m, both criminals,	AIT
24: 4	suddenly two **m** in clothes that gleamed	467
24: 5	but the **m** said to them,	AIT
24: 7	be delivered into the hands of sinful **m**,	476
Jn		
1: 4	and that life was the light of **m**.	476
1: 7	so that through him all **m** might believe.	AIT
2:14	the temple courts he found **m** selling cattle,	3836S
2:24	for he knew all **m**.	AIT
3:19	into the world, but **m** loved darkness instead	476
5:41	"I do not accept praise from **m**,	476
6:10	and the **m** sat down, about five thousand	467
8:17	that the testimony of two **m** is valid.	476
12:32	will draw all **m** to myself."	AIT
12:43	from **m** more than praise from God.	AIT
13:35	By this all **m** will know	AIT
16: 9	because **m** do not believe in me;	AIT
18: 8	you are looking for me, then let these **m** go.	AIT
Ac		
1: 3	showed himself to these **m** and gave	4005S
1:10	when suddenly two **m** dressed in white	467
1:11	"**M** of Galilee," they said,	467
1:21	to choose one of the **m** who have been	467
1:23	So they proposed two **m**:	AIT
2: 7	not all these **m** who are speaking Galileans?	AIT
2:15	These **m** are not drunk, as you suppose.	AIT
2:17	your **young** m will see visions,	3734
2:17	your old **m** will dream **dreams**.	AIT
2:18	Even on my servants, both **m** and women,	NIG
2:22	"**M** of Israel, listen to this:	467
2:23	and you, with the help of **wicked** m,	AIT
3:12	"**M** of Israel, why does this surprise you?	467
4: 4	number of **m** grew to about five thousand.	467
4: 6	and the **other** m of the high priest's family.	476
4:12	under heaven given to **m** by which we must	476
4:13	that they were unschooled, ordinary **m**,	476
4:13	and they took note that these **m** had been	NIG
4:16	"What are we going to do with these **m?**"	476
4:17	we must warn these **m** to speak no longer	AIT
5: 4	You have not lied to **m** but to God."	476
5: 6	Then the **young** m came forward,	AIT
5: 9	of the **m** who buried your husband are at	AIT
5:10	Then the **young** m came in and,	3734
5:14	more and more **m** and women believed in	467
5:25	The **m** you put in jail are standing in	476
5:29	"We must obey God rather than **m!**	476
5:34	up in the Sanhedrin and ordered that the **m**	476
5:35	Then he addressed them: "**M** of Israel,	467
5:35	what you intend to do to these **m**.	476
5:36	and about four hundred **m** rallied to him.	467
5:38	Leave these **m** alone!	476
5:39	you will not be able to stop these **m**;	899S
6: 3	choose seven **m** from among you	476
6: 6	They presented these **m** to the apostles,	AIT
6: 9	**m** began to **argue** with Stephen,	AIT
6:11	they secretly persuaded some **m** to say,	467
7:26	He tried to reconcile them by saying, '**M**,	467
7:48	the Most High does not live in houses made by **m**.	5935
8: 2	Godly **m** buried Stephen	467
8: 3	he dragged off **m** and women and put them	467
8:12	they were baptized, both **m** and women.	467
9: 2	whether **m** or women,	467
9: 7	The **m** traveling with Saul	467
9:38	they sent two **m** to him and urged him,	467
10: 5	Now send **m** to Joppa to bring back	476
10:17	the **m** sent by Cornelius found out	467
10:19	"Simon, three **m** are looking for you.	476
10:21	Peter went down and said to the **m**,	467

Ac		
10:22	The **m** replied, "We have come	1254+3836S
10:23	Then Peter invited the **m** into the house to	899S
10:35	but accepts **m** from every nation	NIG
11: 3	into the house of uncircumcised **m** and ate	467
11:11	"Right then three **m** who had been sent	467
11:20	however, **m** from Cyprus and Cyrene,	467
13:16	"**M** of Israel and you Gentiles who worship	467
13:50	of high standing and the **leading** m of	AIT
14:15	"**M**, why are you doing this?	467
14:15	We too are only **m**, human like you.	476
15: 1	Some **m** came down from Judea to Antioch	AIT
15:17	that the remnant of **m** may seek the Lord,	476
15:22	of their own **m** and send them to Antioch	467
15:22	two **m** who were leaders among	467
15:25	to choose some **m** and send them to you	467
15:26	**m** who have risked their lives for the name	476
15:30	The **m** were sent off and went down	3525+3836S
16:17	"These **m** are servants of the Most High God	476
16:20	"These **m** are Jews,	476
16:35	with the order: "Release those **m**."	476
17: 6	"These **m** who have caused trouble all over	AIT
17:12	Greek women and many Greek **m**.	467
17:15	The **m** who escorted Paul brought him	AIT
17:22	and said: "**M** of Athens!	467
17:25	because he himself gives all **m** life	AIT
17:26	From one man he made every nation of **m**,	476
17:27	God did this so that **m** would seek him	NIG
17:31	to all **m** by raising him from the dead."	AIT
17:34	A few **m** became followers of Paul	467
19: 7	There were about twelve **m** in all.	467
19:25	"**M**, you know we receive a good income	467
19:35	"**M** of Ephesus, doesn't all the world know	467
19:37	You have brought these **m** here,	467
20: 5	These **m** went on ahead and waited for us	AIT
20:26	that I am innocent of the blood of all **m**.	AIT
20:30	Even from your own number **m** will arise	467
21:23	There are four **m** with us who have made	467
21:24	Take these **m**, join in their purification rites	AIT
21:26	the **m** and purified himself along with them.	467
21:28	"**M** of Israel, help us!	467
21:28	the man who teaches all **m** everywhere	AIT
22: 4	both **m** and women and throwing them	467
22:15	to all **m** of what you have seen and heard.	476
22:19	'these **m** know that I went	AIT
23:13	More than **forty** m were involved	AIT
24:15	and I have the same hope in God as these **m**,	AIT
25:23	the high ranking officers and the leading **m**	467
27:10	"**M**, I can see that our voyage is going to	467
27:17	When the **m** had hoisted it aboard,	NIG
27:21	the **m** had gone a long time without food,	NIG
27:21	"**M**, you should have taken my advice not	467
27:25	So keep up your courage, **m**,	467
27:31	"Unless these **m** stay with the ship,	AIT
28:15	At the sight of these **m** Paul thanked God	AIT
Ro		
1:18	and wickedness of **m** who suppress	476
1:20	so that **m** are without excuse.	899S
1:27	the **m** also abandoned natural relations	781
1:27	**M** committed indecent acts with other men,	781
1:27	Men committed indecent acts with other **m**,	781
2:29	Such a man's praise is not from **m**,	476
5:12	and in this way death came to all **m**,	476
5:18	of one trespass was condemnation for all **m**,	476
5:18	that brings life for all **m**.	476
7: 1	for I am speaking to **m** who **know** the law—	AIT
9:33	a stone that **causes m to stumble**	4682
11:32	For God has bound all **m** over	AIT
14:18	to God and approved by **m**.	476
1Co		
2:11	For who **among** m knows the thoughts of	476
3: 3	Are you not acting like mere **m**?	476
3: 4	"I follow Apollos," are you not mere **m?**	476
3:21	So then, no more boasting about **m!**	476
4: 1	**m** ought to regard us as servants of Christ	476
4: 9	like **m condemned to die** in the arena.	AIT
4: 9	to angels as well as to **m**.	476
6: 4	appoint as judges even **m** of little account	4047S
7: 7	I wish that all **m** were as I am.	476
7:23	do not become slaves of **m**.	476
9:22	I have become all things to all **m** so that	AIT
12: 6	the same God works all of them in all **m**.	AIT
13: 1	If I speak in the tongues of **m** and of angels,	476
14: 2	in a tongue does not speak to **m** but to God.	476
14: 3	But everyone who prophesies speaks to **m**	AIT
14:21	"Through **m** of **strange tongues** and	AIT
15:19	we are to be pitied more than all **m**.	476
15:39	**M** have one kind of flesh,	476
16: 3	of introduction to the **m** you approve	4005S
16:13	be **m of courage**; be strong.	437
16:18	Such **m** deserve recognition.	AIT
2Co		
2:17	like **m** sent from God.	NIG
3: 9	If the ministry that condemns **m** is glorious,	NIG
5:11	we try to persuade **m**.	476
8:21	of the Lord but also in the eyes of **m**.	476
8:24	Therefore show these **m** the proof	AIT
9:13	**m** will **praise** God for the obedience	AIT
11:13	For such **m** are false apostles,	AIT
12:17	through any of the **m** I sent you?	4005S
Gal		
1: 1	sent not from **m** nor by man,	476
1:10	Am I now trying to win the approval of **m**,	476
1:10	Or am I trying to please **m?**	476
1:10	If I were still trying to please **m**,	476
2: 6	those **m** added nothing to my message.	1506S
2:12	Before **certain** m came from James,	AIT
Eph		
2:11	(that done in the body by the hands of **m**)—	NIG
3: 5	not made known to **m** in other generations	476+3836+3836+5626
4: 8	in his train and gave gifts to **m**."	476
4:14	and by the cunning and craftiness of **m**	476

Eph		
6: 7	as if you were serving the Lord, not **m**,	476
Php		
2:29	and honor **m** like him,	5525
3: 2	those **m** who do evil,	AIT
Col		
2:11	not with a circumcision **done by the hands of m**	942
3:23	as working for the Lord, not **for** m,	476
1Th		
3:23	as **m** approved by God to be entrusted with	NIG
2: 4	We are not trying to please **m** but God,	476
2: 6	We were not looking for praise from **m**,	476
2:13	you accepted it not as the word of **m**,	476
2:15	They displease God and are hostile to all **m**	476
4: 6	The Lord will punish **m** for all such sins,	NIG
4:13	or to grieve like the **rest** of m,	AIT
2Th		
3: 2	be delivered from wicked and evil **m**,	AIT
1Ti		
1: 3	so that you may command **certain** m not	AIT
2: 4	who wants all **m** to be saved and to come to	476
2: 5	and one mediator between God and **m**,	476
2: 6	who gave himself as a ransom for **all m**—	AIT
2: 8	I want **m** everywhere to lift up holy hands	467
3: 8	likewise, are to be **m** worthy of respect,	NIG
4:10	who is the Savior of all **m**,	476
5: 1	Treat **younger** m as brothers,	AIT
5:24	The sins of some **m** are obvious,	476
6: 5	and constant friction between **m**	476
6: 9	and harmful desires that plunge **m** into ruin	476
2Ti		
2: 2	to reliable **m** who will also be qualified	476
3: 8	so also these **m** oppose the truth—	476
3: 8	**m** of depraved minds, who,	476
3: 9	as in the case of **those** m,	AIT
3:13	while evil **m** and impostors will go	476
4: 3	**m** will not **put up with** sound doctrine.	AIT
Tit		
2: 2	Teach the **older** m to be temperate,	AIT
2: 6	the **young** m to be self-controlled.	AIT
2:11	that brings salvation has appeared to all **m**.	476
3: 2	and to show true humility toward all **m**.	AIT
Heb		
2:11	Both the one who makes **m** holy	NIG
5: 1	among **m** and is appointed to represent them	476
6:16	**M** swear by someone greater than themselves,	476
7: 8	the tenth is collected by **m** who die;	476
7:28	as high priests **m** who are weak;	476
8: 4	for there are already **m who** offer	3836S
12: 3	from **sinful** m, so that you will	AIT
12:14	to live in peace with all **m** and to be holy;	AIT
12:23	You have come to God, the judge of all **m**,	AIT
12:23	to the spirits of **righteous** m made perfect,	AIT
13:17	over you as **m** who must give an account.	NIG
Jas		
3: 9	and with it we curse **m**,	476
5: 6	and murdered **innocent** m,	AIT
1Pe		
1:24	For, "All **m** are like grass,	4922
2: 4	by **m** but chosen by God and precious	476
2: 8	"A stone that **causes m to stumble** and	4682
2:13	to every authority instituted **among m:**	474
2:15	the ignorant talk of foolish **m**.	476
2:16	Live as **free** m, but do not use your freedom	AIT
4: 6	so that they might be judged according to **m**	AIT
5: 5	Young **m**, in the same way be submissive	AIT
2Pe		
1:21	but **m** spoke from God as they were carried	476
2: 9	to rescue godly **m** from trials and to hold	AIT
2:10	these **m** are not afraid to slander celestial	NIG
2:12	But these **m** blaspheme in matters they do	AIT
2:17	These **m** are springs without water	AIT
3: 7	of judgment and destruction of ungodly **m**.	476
3:17	be carried away by the error of lawless **m**	AIT
1Jn		
2:13	I write to you, **young m**,	3734
2:14	I write to you, **young m**,	3734
3Jn		
1: 8	to such **m** so that we may work together for	AIT
Jude		
1: 4	certain **m** whose condemnation was written	476
1: 4	They are **godless** m,	AIT
1:10	Yet these **m** speak abusively	AIT
1:12	These **m** are blemishes at your love feasts,	AIT
1:14	prophesied **about these** m:	AIT
1:16	These **m** are grumblers and faultfinders;	AIT
1:19	These are the **m** who divide you,	AIT
Rev		
2: 2	I know that you cannot tolerate **wicked** m,	AIT
5: 9	with your blood you purchased **m** for God	NIG
6: 4	the earth and to make **m** slay each other.	NIG
9: 6	During those days **m** will seek death,	476
9: 6	These **m** have power to shut up the sky so	AIT
11: 9	**m** from every people, tribe, language and nation **will gaze on**	AIT
13: 4	**M worshiped** the dragon	AIT
13:13	from heaven to earth in full view of **m**.	476
14: 4	among **m** and offered as firstfruits to God	AIT
16:10	**M gnawed** their tongues in agony	AIT
16:21	about a hundred pounds each fell upon **m**.	476
18:13	and bodies and souls of **m**.	AIT
18:23	Your merchants were the world's **great** m.	AIT
19:18	and **mighty** m, of horses and their riders,	AIT
21: 3	"Now the dwelling of God is with **m**,	476

MEN'S (14) [MAN]

Ge	44: 1	"Fill the **m** sacks with as much food	408
Ex	30:32	on **m** bodies and do not make any oil with	132
Dt	22: 5	A woman must not wear **m** clothing,	1505
1Sa	19:18	The **m** things are holy even on missions	5853
2Ki	19:18	wood and stone, fashioned by **m** hands.	132
2Ch	32:19	the work of **m** hands.	132
Mt	23: 4	and put them on **m** shoulders,	476
	23:13	You shut the kingdom of heaven in **m** faces.	476
	23:27	but on the inside are full of **dead** m bones	AIT
Mk	7:21	For from within, out of **m** hearts,	476
Ro	2:16	on the day when God will judge **m** secrets	476
1Co	2: 5	that your faith might not rest on **m** wisdom,	476
	4: 5	and will expose the motives of **m** hearts.	NIG

2Co 5:19 not counting **m** sins against them.   899ˢ

MENAHEM (7) [MENAHEM'S]
2Ki 15:14 Then **M** son of Gadi went from Tirzah up   4968
15:16 At that time **M**, starting out from Tirzah   4968
15:17 **M** son of Gadi became king of Israel,   4968
15:19 and **M** gave him a thousand talents of silver   4968
15:20 **M** exacted this money from Israel.   4968
15:22 **M** rested with his fathers.   4968
15:23 Pekahiah son of **M** became king of Israel   4968

MENAHEM'S (1) [MENAHEM]
2Ki 15:21 As for the other events of **M** reign,   4968

MENAN (KJV) See MENNA

MENCHILDREN (KJV) See MEN

MEND (2) [MENDED]
Ps 60: 2 **m** its fractures, for it is quaking.   8324
Ecc 3: 7 a time to tear and a time to **m**,   9529

MENDED (1) [MEND]
Jos 9: 4 and old wineskins, cracked and **m**.   7674

MENE (3)
Da 5:25 **M**, MENE, TEKEL, PARSIN   10428
5:25 MENE, **M**, TEKEL, PARSIN   10428
5:26 "This is what these words mean: **M**:   10428

MENPLEASERS (KJV) See WIN FAVOR

MENSTEALERS (KJV) See SLAVE TRADERS

MENNA (1)
Lk 3:31 the son of **M**, the son of Mattatha,   3527

MENSERVANTS (16) [SERVANT]
Ge 12:16 **m** and maidservants, and camels.   6269
24:35 silver and gold, **m** and maidservants,   6269
30:43 and maidservants and **m**,   6269
32: 5 sheep and goats, **m** and maidservants.   6269
Ex 21: 7 she is not to go free as **m** do.   6269
Dt 12:12 your **m** and maidservants,   6269
12:18 your **m** and maidservants,   6269
16:11 your **m** and maidservants,   6269
16:14 your **m** and maidservants, and the Levites.   6269
1Sa 8:16 Your **m** and maidservants and the best   6269
2Ki 5:26 flocks, herds, or **m** and maidservants?   6269
Ezr 2:65 besides their 7,337 **m** and maidservants;   6269
Ne 7:67 besides their 7,337 **m** and maidservants;   6269
Job 31:13 to my **m** and maidservants when they had   6269
Isa 14: 2 of Israel will possess the nations as **m**   6269
Lk 12:45 the **m** and maidservants and to eat and drink   4090

MENSTRUAL (1)
Isa 30:22 you will throw them away like a **m cloth**   1865

MENTION (11) [MENTIONED, MENTIONING]
Ge 40:14 **m** me to Pharaoh and get me out   2349
Job 28:18 Coral and jasper *are* not **worthy of m**;   2349
Isa 49: 1 from my birth *he* has **made m** of my name.   2349
Jer 19: 5 something I did not command or **m**,   1819
20: 9 not **m** him or speak any more in his name,"   2349
23:36 not **m** 'the oracle of the LORD' again,   2349
Eze 16:56 You would not even **m** your sister Sodom in   928+7023+9019
Am 6:10 *We must* not **m** the name of the LORD."   2349
Jn 5:34 but *I* **m** it that you may be saved.   3306
Eph 5:12 even *to* **m** what the disobedient do in secret.   3306
Phm 1:19 not *to* **m** that you owe me your very self.   3306

MENTIONED (4) [MENTION]
Ru 4: 1 kinsman-redeemer *he* had **m** came along,   1819
1Sa 4:18 When he **m** the ark of God,   2349
Isa 14:20 of the wicked *will* never be **m** again.   7924
19:17 to whom Judah *is* **m** will be terrified,   2349

MENTIONING (1) [MENTION]
1Th 1: 2 for all of you, **m** you in our prayers.   3644+4472

MEON See BAAL MEON, BETH MEON

MEONENIM (KJV) See SOOTHSAYER'S

MEONOTHAI (2)
1Ch 4:13 The sons of Othniel: Hathath and **M**.   5065
4:14 **M** was the father of Ophrah.   5065

MEPHAATH (4)
Jos 13:18 Jahaz, Kedemoth, **M**,   4789
21:37 and **M**, together with their pasturelands—   4789

1Ch 6:79 and **M**, together with their pasturelands;   4789
Jer 48:21 to Holon, Jahzah and **M**,   4789

MEPHIBOSHETH (16) [MERIB-BAAL]
2Sa 4: 4 His name was **M**.)   5136
9: 6 When **M** son of Jonathan, the son of Saul,   5136
9: 6 David said, "**M!**"   5136
9: 8 **M** bowed down and said,   NIH
9:10 And **M**, grandson of your master,   5136
9:11 So **M** ate at David's table like one of   5136
9:12 **M** had a young son named Mica.   5136
9:12 of Ziba's household were servants of **M**.   5136
9:13 And **M** lived in Jerusalem.   5136
16: 1 the steward of **M**, waiting to meet him.   5136
16: 4 "All that belonged to **M** is now yours."   5136
19:24 **M**, Saul's grandson, also went down   5136
19:25 "Why didn't you go with me, **M?**"   5136
19:30 **M** said to the king,   5136
21: 7 The king spared **M** son of Jonathan,   5136
21: 8 But the king took Armoni and **M**,   5136

MERAB (4)
1Sa 14:49 The name of his older daughter was **M**,   5266
18:17 "Here is my older daughter **M**.   5266
18:19 So when the time came for **M**,   5266
2Sa 21: 8 with the five sons of Saul's daughter **M**,   5266

MERAIAH (1)
Ne 12:12 of Seraiah's family, **M**;   5316

MERAIOTH (6)
1Ch 6: 6 Zerahiah the father of **M**,   5318
6: 7 **M** the father of Amariah,   5318
6:52 **M** his son, Amariah his son, Ahitub his son,   5318
9:11 the son of **M**, the son of Ahitub,   5318
Ezr 7: 3 the son of Azariah, the son of **M**,   5318
Ne 11:11 the son of **M**, the son of Ahitub,   5318

MERARI (21) [MERARITE, MERARITES]
Ge 46:11 The sons of Levi: Gershon, Kohath and **M**.   5356
Ex 6:16 Gershon, Kohath and **M**.   5356
6:19 The sons of **M** were Mahli and Mushi.   5356
Nu 3:17 Gershon, Kohath and **M**.   5356
3:33 To **M** belonged the clans of the Mahlites   5356
26:57 through **M**, the Merarite clan.   5356
Jos 21: 7 The descendants of **M**, clan by clan,   5356
1Ch 6: 1 The sons of Levi: Gershon, Kohath and **M**.   5356
6:16 The sons of Levi: Gershon, Kohath and **M**.   5356
6:19 The sons of **M**: Mahli and Mushi.   5356
6:29 The descendants of **M**:   5356
6:47 the son of Mushi, the son of **M**,   5356
6:63 The descendants of **M**, clan by clan,   5356
15: 6 of **M**, Asaiah the leader and 220 relatives;   5356
23: 6 Gershon, Kohath and **M**.   5356
23:21 The sons of **M**: Mahli and Mushi.   5356
24:26 The sons of **M**: Mahli and Mushi.   5356
24:27 The sons of **M**: from Jaaziah: 5356
26:19 descendants of Korah and **M**.   5356
2Ch 34:12 Levites descended from **M**,   5356
Ezr 8:19 with Jeshaiah from the descendants of **M**,   5356

MERARITE (10) [MERARI]
Nu 3:20 The **M** clans: Mahli and Mushi.   1201+5356
3:33 these were the **M** clans.   5356
3:35 the families of the **M** clans was Zuriel son   5356
4:33 service of the **M** clans as they work at   1201+5356
4:45 This was the total of those in the **M**   1201+5356
26:57 through Merari, the **M** clan.   5357
Jos 21:34 The **M** clans (the rest of the Levites)   1201+5356
21:40 All the towns allotted to the **M** clans,   1201+5356
1Ch 6:44 the son of Hashabiah, a **M**;   1201+5356
26:10 Hosah the **M** had sons: 1201+5356

MERARITES (9) [MERARI]
Nu 3:36 The **M** were appointed to take care of   1201+5356
4:29 "Count the **M** by their clans and   1201+5356
4:42 The **M** were counted by their clans   1201+5356
7: 8 four carts and eight oxen to the **M**,   1201+5356
10:17 the Gershonites and **M**, who carried it,   1201+5356
1Ch 6:44 the **M**, at his left hand: 1201+5356
6:77 The **M** (the rest of the Levites)   1201+5356
15:17 and from their brothers the **M**,   1201+5356
2Ch 29:12 the **M**, Kish son of Abdi and Azariah   1201+5356

MERATHAIM (1)
Jer 50:21 the land of **M** and those who live in Pekod.   5361

MERCENARIES (1)
Jer 46:21 The **m** in her ranks are like fattened calves.   8502

MERCHANDISE (12)
Ne 10:31 the neighboring peoples bring **m** or grain   5229
13:16 in fish and all kinds of **m** and selling them   4836
Isa 45:14 "The products of Egypt and the **m** of Cush,   6087
Eze 26:12 and loot your **m**;   8219
27:12 iron, tin and lead for your **m**.   6442
27:14 war horses and mules for your **m**.   6442
27:16 fine linen, coral and rubies for your **m**.   6442
27:19 and Greeks from Uzal bought your **m**;   6442
27:22 for your **m** they exchanged the finest   6442

Eze 27:27 Your wealth, **m** and wares, your mariners,   6442
27:33 When your **m** went out on the seas,   6442
Mk 11:16 and would not allow anyone to carry **m**   5007

MERCHANT (5) [MERCHANTS]
Pr 31:14 She is like the **m** ships,   6086
SS 3: 6 from all the spices of the **m**?   8217
Eze 27: 3 **m** of peoples on many coasts,   8217
Hos 12: 7 The **m** uses dishonest scales;   4047
Mt 13:45 kingdom of heaven is like a **m** looking   476+1867

MERCHANTMEN (KJV) See MERCHANTS

MERCHANTS (28) [MERCHANT]
Ge 23:16 to the weight current among the **m**.   6086
37:28 So when the Midianite **m** came by,   6086
1Ki 10:15 the revenues from **m** and traders and   408+9365
10:28 the royal **m** purchased them from Kue.   6086
2Ch 1:16 the royal **m** purchased them from Kue.   6086
9:14 the revenues brought in by **m**   408+9365
Ne 3:31 the house of the temple servants and the **m**,   8217
3:32 the goldsmiths and **m** made repairs.   8217
13:20 the **m** and sellers of all kinds of goods spent   8217
Job 6:19 the **traveling m** of Sheba look in hope.   2142
41: 6 Will they divide him up among the **m**?   4051
Ps 107:23 *they were* **m** on the mighty waters.   4856+6913
Pr 31:24 and supplies the **m** with sashes.   4051
Isa 23: 2 you people of the island and you **m**   6086
23: 8 whose **m** are princes,   6086
Eze 16:29 Babylonia, a land of **m**,   4047
17: 4 and carried it away to a land of **m**,   4047
27:22 **m** of Sheba and Raamah traded with you;   8217
27:23 Canneh and Eden and **m** of Sheba,   8217
27:27 your **m** and all your soldiers,   5114+6842
27:36 The **m** among the nations hiss at you;   6086
38:13 Sheba and Dedan and the **m** of Tarshish   8217
Na 3:16 the number of your **m** till they are more than   8217
Zep 1:11 all your **m** will be wiped out,   4047+6639
Rev 18: 3 and the **m** of the earth grew rich   1867
18:11 "The **m** of the earth will weep and mourn   1867
18:15 The **m** who sold these things   1867
18:23 Your **m** were the world's great men.   1867

MERCIFUL (22) [MERCY]
Ge 19:16 for the LORD was **m** to them.   2799
Dt 4:31 For the LORD your God is a **m** God;   8157
1Ki 20:31 that the kings of the house of Israel are **m**.   2876
Ne 9:31 for you are a gracious and **m** God.   8157
Ps 4: 1 be **m** *to* me and hear my prayer.   2858
6: 2 *Be* **m** *to* me, LORD, for I am faint;   2858
26:11 redeem me and be **m** *to* me.   2858
27: 7 be **m** *to* me and answer me.   2858
30:10 Hear, O LORD, and be **m** *to* me;   2858
31: 9 *Be* **m** *to* me, O LORD, for I am in distress;   2858
56: 1 *Be* **m** *to* me, O God,   2858
77: 9 Has God forgotten *to be* **m**?   2858
78:38 Yet he was **m**; he forgave their iniquities   8157
Jer 3:12 'I will frown on you no longer, for I am **m**,'   2883
Da 9: 9 The Lord our God is **m** and forgiving,   8171
Mt 5: 7 Blessed are the **m**, for they will be shown mercy.   1798
Lk 1:54 remembering to be **m**   1799
6:36 Be **m**, just as your Father is merciful.   3881
6:36 Be merciful, just as your Father is **m**.   3881
Heb 2:17 a **m** and faithful high priest in service   1798
Jas 2:13 be shown to anyone who has not been **m**.   1799
Jude 1:22 Be **m** to those who doubt;   1796

MERCILESS (1) [MERCY]
Pr 17:11 a **m** official will be sent against him.   426

MERCILESSLY (1) [MERCY]
Isa 30:14 shattered *so* **m** that among its pieces   2798+4202

MERCURIUS (KJV) See HERMES

MERCY (129) [MERCIFUL, MERCILESS, MERCILESSLY]
Ge 43:14 And may God Almighty grant you **m** before   8171
Ex 33:19 *I will* have **m** on whom I will have mercy,   2858
33:19 I will have mercy on whom *I will* have **m**,   2858
Dt 7: 2 and **show** them no **m**.   2858
13:17 he will show you **m**,   8171
Jos 11:20 exterminating them without **m**,   9382
2Sa 24:14 for his **m** is great;   8171
1Ki 8:28 and his **plea for m**,   9382
8:50 and cause their conquerors *to* **show** them **m**;   8163
1Ch 21:13 for his **m** is very great;   8171
2Ch 6:19 and his **plea for m**,   9382
Ne 9:31 But in your great **m** you did not put an end   8171
13:22 **show m** to me according to your great love.   2571
Est 4: 8 the king's presence to **beg for m** and plead   2858
Job 9:15 **plead** with my Judge for **m**.   2858
27:22 against him without **m** as he flees headlong   2798
41: 3 Will he keep **begging** you **for m**?   9384
Ps 5: 7 But I, by your great **m**,   2876
6: 9 The LORD has heard my **cry for m**;   9382
9:13 **Have m** and lift me up from the gates   2858
25: 6 O LORD, your **great m** and love,   8171
28: 2 Hear my **cry for m** as I call to you   7754+9384
28: 6 for he has heard my **cry for m**.   7754+9384

Ps	30: 8	to the Lord I **cried for m:**	2858
	31:22	you heard my **cry for m** when I called	7754+9384
	40:11	Do not withhold your **m** from me,	8171
	41: 4	I said, "O LORD, **have m** on me;	2858
	41:10	But you, O LORD, **have m** on me;	2858
	51: 1	**Have m** on me, O God,	2858
	57: 1	**Have m** on me, O God, have mercy on me,	2858
	57: 1	Have mercy on me, O God, **have m** on me,	2858
	59: 5	**show** no **m** to wicked traitors.	2858
	69:16	in your great **m** turn to me.	8171
	79: 8	may your **m** come quickly to meet us,	8171
	86: 3	**Have m** on me, O Lord,	2858
	86: 6	listen to my **cry for m.**	7754+9384
	86:16	Turn to me and **have m** on me,	2858
	116: 1	he heard my **cry for m.**	9384
	119:132	Turn to me and **have m** on me,	2858
	123: 2	till **he shows** us **his m.**	2858
	123: 3	**Have m** on us, O LORD, have mercy on us,	2858
	123: 3	Have mercy on us, O LORD, **have m** on us,	2858
	130: 2	your ears be attentive to my **cry for m.**	7754+9384
	140: 6	Hear, O LORD, my **cry for m.**	7754+9384
	142: 1	**lift up** my voice to the LORD **for m.**	2858
	143: 1	hear my prayer, listen to my **cry for m;**	9384
Pr	6:34	he will **show** no **m** when he takes revenge.	2798
	18:23	A poor man pleads for **m,**	9384
	21:10	his neighbor **gets** no **m** from him.	2858
	28:13	and renounces them **finds m.**	8163
Isa	13:18	they will **have** no **m** on infants	8163
	47: 6	and you showed them no **m.**	8171
	55: 7	and he will **have m** on him, and to our God,	8163
	63: 9	In his love and **m** he redeemed them;	2799
Jer	6:23	they are cruel and **show** no **m.**	8163
	13:14	I will allow no pity or **m** or compassion	2571
	21: 7	he will **show** them no **m** or pity	2571
	50:42	they are cruel and without **m.**	8163
Da	2:18	He urged them to plead for **m** from the God	10664
	9:18	but because of your great **m.**	8171
Hos	6: 6	For I desire **m,** not sacrifice,	2876
Am	5:15	the LORD God Almighty will **have m** on	2858
Mic	6: 8	and to love **m** and to walk humbly	2876
	7:18	but delight to show **m.**	2876
	7:20	and show **m** to Abraham,	2876
Hab	1:17	destroying nations without **m?**	2798
	3: 2	in wrath remember **m.**	8163
Zec	1:12	how long will you withhold **m**	8163
	1:16	'I will return to Jerusalem with **m,**	8171
	7: 9	show **m** and compassion to one another.	2876
Mt	5: 7	for they will be **shown m.**	1796
	9:13	'I desire **m,** not sacrifice.'	1796
	9:27	calling out, **"Have m** on us, Son of David!"	1796
	12: 7	'I desire **m,** not sacrifice,'	1799
	15:22	"Lord, Son of David, **have m** on me!	1796
	17:15	"Lord, **have m** on my son," he said.	1799
	18:33	Shouldn't you **have had m** on your fellow	1796
	20:30	"Lord, Son of David, **have m** on us!"	1796
	20:31	"Lord, **have m** on us!"	1796
	23:23	justice, **m** and faithfulness.	1799
Mk	5:19	and how he has **had m** on you."	1796
	10:47	"Jesus, Son of David, **have m** on me!"	1796
	10:48	"Son of David, **have m** on me!"	1796
Lk	1:50	His **m** extends to those who fear him,	1799
	1:58	that the Lord had shown her great **m,**	1799
	1:72	to show **m** to our fathers and	1799
	1:78	because of the **tender m** of our God,	1799+5073
	10:37	"The one who had **m** on him."	1799
	18:13	'God, **have m** on me, a sinner.'	2661
	18:38	"Jesus, Son of David, **have m** on me!"	1796
	18:39	"Son of David, **have m** on me!"	1796
Ro	9:15	"I will **have m** on whom I have mercy,	1796
	9:15	"I will have mercy on whom I **have m,**	1796
	9:16	not, therefore, depend on man's desire or effort, but on God's **m.**	1796
	9:18	Therefore God **has m** on whom he wants	1796
	9:18	on whom he wants to have **m,**	NIG
	9:23	of his glory known to the objects of his **m,**	1799
	11:30	to God **have** now **received m** as a result	1796
	11:31	in order that they too may now **receive m** as	1796
	11:31	now receive mercy as a result of God's **m**	1799
	11:32	to disobedience so that he may **have m** on	1796
	12: 1	I urge you, brothers, in view of God's **m,**	3880
	12: 8	if it is **showing m,** let him do it cheerfully.	1796
	15: 9	that the Gentiles may glorify God for his **m,**	1799
1Co		as one who by the Lord's **m** is trustworthy.	1796
2Co	4: 1	through God's **m** we have this ministry,	1796
Gal	6:16	Peace and **m** to all who follow this rule,	1799
Eph	2: 4	God, who is rich in **m,**	1799
Php	2:27	But God **had m** on him,	1796
1Ti	1: 2	Grace, **m** and peace from God the Father	1799
	1:13	I was **shown m** because I acted in ignorance	1796
	1:16	for that very reason I was **shown m** so that	1796
2Ti	1: 2	Grace, **m** and peace from God the Father	1799
	1:16	May the Lord show **m** to the household	1799
	1:18	May the Lord grant that he will find **m** from	1799
Tit	3: 5	but because of his **m.**	1799
Heb	4:16	so that we may receive **m** and find grace	1799
	10:28	rejected the law of Moses died without **m**	3880
Jas	2:13	because judgment **without m** will be shown	447
	2:13	**M** triumphs over judgment!	1799
	3:17	submissive, full of **m** and good fruit,	1799
	5:11	The Lord is full of compassion and **m.**	3881
1Pe	1: 3	In his great **m** he has given us new birth into	1799
	2:10	once you had not **received m,**	1796
	2:10	but now you **have received m.**	1796
2Jn	1: 3	**m** and peace from God the Father and	1799
Jude	1: 2	**M,** peace and love be yours in abundance.	1799
	1:21	the **m** of our Lord Jesus Christ to bring you	1799
	1:23	**to** others **show m,** mixed with fear.	1796

MERCYSEAT (KJV) See PLACE OF ATONEMENT

MERE (20) [MERELY]

2Ki	8:13	"How could your servant, a **m** dog,	NIH
Job	12: 4	a **m** laughingstock, though righteous	NIH
	41: 9	the **m** sight of him is overpowering.	1685
Ps	39: 5	You have made my days a **m** handbreadth;	NIH
	39: 6	Man is a **m** phantom as he goes to and fro:	421
	82: 7	But you will die like **m** men;	NIH
Pr	14:23	but **m** talk leads only to poverty.	1821+8557
	29:19	A servant cannot be corrected by **m** words;	NIH
Isa	3: 4	**m children** will govern them.	9500
	50: 2	By a **m** rebuke I dry up the sea,	NIH
	57:13	a **m** breath will blow them away.	2039
	65:20	at a hundred will be thought a **m** youth;	AIT
Jn	7:24	Stop judging by **m** appearances,	NIG
	10:33	"but for blasphemy, because you, a **m** man,	NIG
Ro	2: 3	So when you, a **m** man,	NIG
1Co	3: 1	but as worldly—**m** infants in Christ.	NIG
	3: 3	Are you not acting like **m** men?	NIG
	3: 4	"I follow Apollos," are you not **m** men?	NIG
Tit	1:10	**m talkers** and deceivers,	3468
Jude	1:19	who **follow m natural instincts** and	6035

MERED (2) [MERED'S]

1Ch	4:17	Jether, **M,** Epher and Jalon.	5279
	4:18	whom **M** had married.	5279

MERED'S (1) [MERED]

1Ch	4:17	One of **M** wives gave birth to Miriam,	NIH

MERELY (8) [MERE]

Jdg	15:11	"I **m** did to them what they did to me."	NIH
1Sa	14:43	"I **m** tasted a little honey with the end	3247+3247
Est	7: 4	If we had **m** been sold as male	NIH
Job	30:20	I stand up, but you **m** look at me.	AIT
Ro	2:28	nor is circumcision **m** outward and physical.	NIG
1Co	9: 8	Do I say this **m** from a human point	NIG
	15:32	in Ephesus for **m** human reasons,	NIG
Jas	1:22	Do not **m** listen to the word,	3667

MEREMOTH (6) [MEREMOTH'S]

Ezr	8:33	the sacred articles into the hands of **M** son	5329
	10:36	Vaniah, **M,** Eliashib,	5329
Ne	3: 4	**M** son of Uriah, the son of Hakkoz,	5329
	3:21	Next to him, **M** son of Uriah,	5329
	10: 5	Harim, **M,** Obadiah,	5329
	12: 3	Shecaniah, Rehum, **M,**	5329

MEREMOTH'S (1) [MEREMOTH]

Ne	12:15	of Harim's, Adna; of **M,** Helkai;	5329

MERES (1)

Est	1:14	Carshena, Shethar, Admatha, Tarshish, **M,**	5332

MERIB-BAAL (2) [MEPHIBOSHETH]

1Ch	8:34	**M,** who was the father of Micah.	5311
	9:40	**M,** who was the father of Micah.	5311

MERIBAH (7) [MERIBAH KADESH]

Ex	17: 7	and **M** because the Israelites quarreled and	5313
Nu	20:13	These were the waters of **M,**	5313
	20:24	against my command at the waters of **M.**	5313
Dt	33: 8	you contended with him at the waters of **M.**	5313
Ps	81: 7	I tested you at the waters of **M.**	5313
	95: 8	do not harden your hearts as you did at **M,**	5313
	106:32	the waters of **M** they angered the LORD,	5313

MERIBAH KADESH (4) [MERIBAH]

Nu	27:14	(These were the waters of **M,**	5315
Dt	32:51	the Israelites at the waters of **M** in	5315
Eze	47:19	as far as the waters of **M,**	5315
	48:28	from Tamar to the waters of **M,**	5315

MERODACH (KJV) See MARDUK

MERODACH-BALADAN (2)

2Ki	20:12	At that time **M** son of Baladan king	5282
Isa	39: 1	At that time **M** son of Baladan king	5282

MEROM (2)

Jos	11: 5	at the Waters of **M,**	5295
	11: 7	against them suddenly at the Waters of **M**	5295

MERON See SHIMRON MERON

MERONOTH (1) [MERONOTHITE]

Ne	3: 7	Melatiah of Gibeon and Jadon of **M**—	5331

MERONOTHITE (1) [MERONOTH]

1Ch	27:30	the **M** was in charge of the donkeys.	5331

MEROZ (1)

Jdg	5:23	'Curse **M,**' said the angel of the LORD.	5292

MERRIMENT (1) [MERRY]

Isa	32:13	mourn for all houses of **m** and for this city	5375

MERRY (4) [MERRIMENT, MERRYMAKERS]

Job	21:12	they **make m** to the sound of the flute.	8523
Ecc	10:19	and wine **makes** life **m,**	8523
Jer	15:17	never **made m** with them;	6600
Lk	12:19	Take life easy; eat, drink and be **m.**'	2370

MERRYMAKERS (1) [MERRY]

Isa	24: 7	the vine withers; all the **m** groan.	4213+8524

MESECH (KJV) See MESHECH

MESH (1)

Job	18: 8	into a net and he wanders into its **m.**	8422

MESHA (4)

Ge	10:30	where they lived stretched from **M**	5392
2Ki	3: 4	Now **M** king of Moab raised sheep,	4795
1Ch	2:42	**M** his firstborn, who was the father of Ziph,	4796
	8: 9	By his wife Hodesh he had Jobab, Zibia, **M,**	4791

MESHACH (14)

Da	1: 7	to Mishael, **M;** and to Azariah, Abednego.	4794
	2:49	**M** and Abednego administrators over	10415
	3:12	Shadrach, **M** and Abednego—	10415
	3:13	Nebuchadnezzar summoned Shadrach, **M** and Abednego.	10415
	3:14	"Is it true, Shadrach, **M** and Abednego,	10415
	3:16	**M** and Abednego replied to the king,	10415
	3:19	**M** and Abednego, and his attitude	10415
	3:20	**M** and Abednego and throw them into	10415
	3:22	the soldiers who took up Shadrach, **M**	10415
	3:26	"Shadrach, **M** and Abednego,	10415
	3:26	**M** and Abednego came out of the fire,	10415
	3:28	to the God of Shadrach, **M** and Abednego,	10415
	3:29	**M** and Abednego be cut into pieces	10415
	3:30	**M** and Abednego in the province	10415

MESHECH (10)

Ge	10: 2	Magog, Madai, Javan, Tubal, **M** and Tiras.	5434
	10:23	The sons of Aram: Uz, Hul, Gether and **M.**	5434
1Ch	1: 5	Magog, Madai, Javan, Tubal, **M** and Tiras.	5434
	1:17	The sons of Aram: Uz, Hul, Gether and **M.**	5434
Ps	120: 5	Woe to me that I dwell in **M,**	5434
Eze	27:13	" 'Greece, Tubal and **M** traded with you;	5434
	32:26	"**M** and Tubal are there,	5434
	38: 2	the chief prince of **M** and Tubal.	5434
	38: 3	O Gog, chief prince of **M** and Tubal.	5434
	39: 1	O Gog, chief prince of **M** and Tubal.	5434

MESHELEMIAH (4)

1Ch	9:21	of **M** was the gatekeeper at the entrance to	5452
	26: 1	**M** son of Kore, one of the sons of Asaph.	5453
	26: 2	**M** had sons: Zechariah the firstborn,	5453
	26: 9	**M** had sons and relatives,	5453

MESHEZABEL (3)

Ne	3: 4	the son of **M,** made repairs,	5430
	10:21	Zadok, Jaddua,	5430
	11:24	Pethahiah son of **M,**	5430

MESHILLEMITH (1)

1Ch	9:12	the son of Meshullam, the son of	5454

MESHILLEMOTH (2)

2Ch	28:12	of Jehohanan, Berekiah son of **M,**	5451
Ne	11:13	the son of **M,** the son of Immer,	5451

MESHOBAB (1)

1Ch	4:34	**M,** Jamlech, Joshah son of Amaziah,	5411

MESHULLAM (25)

2Ki	22: 3	the son of **M,** to the temple of the LORD.	5450
1Ch	3:19	The sons of Zerubbabel: **M** and Hananiah.	5450
	5:13	Michael, **M,** Sheba, Jorai, Jacan,	5450
	8:17	Zebadiah, **M,** Hizki, Heber,	5450
	9: 7	Sallu son of **M,** the son of Hodaviah,	5450
	9: 8	and **M** son of Shephatiah, the son of Reuel,	5450
	9:11	the son of **M,** the son of Zadok,	5450
	9:12	the son of **M,** the son of Meshillemith,	5450
2Ch	34:12	and Zechariah and **M,**	5450
Ezr	8:16	Jarib, Elnathan, Nathan, Zechariah and **M,**	5450
	10:15	supported by **M** and Shabbethai the Levite,	5450
	10:29	From the descendants of Bani: **M,** Malluch,	5450
Ne	3: 4	Next to him **M** son of Berekiah,	5450
	3: 6	of Paseah and **M** son of Besodeiah.	5450
	3:30	Next to them, **M** son	5450
	6:18	the daughter of **M** son of Berekiah.	5450
	8: 4	Hashum, Hashbaddanah, Zechariah and **M.**	5450
	10: 7	**M,** Abijah, Mijamin,	5450
	10:20	Magpiash, **M,** Hezir,	5450
	11: 7	Sallu son of **M,** the son of Joed,	5450
	11:11	the son of **M,** the son of Zadok,	5450
	12:13	of Ezra's, **M;** of Amariah's, Jehohanan;	5450
	12:16	of Iddo's, Zechariah; of Ginnethon's, **M;**	5450

Ne	12:25	Mattaniah, Bakbukiah, Obadiah, **M**,	5450
	12:33	along with Azariah, Ezra, **M**,	5450

MESHULLEMETH (1)

2Ki	21:19	His mother's name was **M** daughter	5455

MESOBAITE (KJV) See MEZOBAITE

MESOPOTAMIA (2)

Ac	2: 9	residents of **M**, Judea and Cappadocia,	3544
	7: 2	Abraham while he was still in **M**,	3544

MESS (KJV) See GIFT, PORTION

MESSAGE (118) [MESSENGER, MESSENGERS]

Ge	32: 5	Now I am sending *this* **m** to my lord,	5583
	38:25	she **sent a m** to her father-in-law.	8938
	50:17	When their **m** came to him, Joseph wept.	1819
Nu	22:10	king of Moab, **sent me** *this* **m**:	8938
	23: 5	The LORD put a **m** in Balaam's mouth	1821
	23: 5	"Go back to Balak and **give** him this **m**."	1819
	23:16	The LORD met with Balaam and put a **m**	1821
	23:16	"Go back to Balak and **give** him this **m**."	1819
Dt	18:21	a **m** has not been spoken by the LORD?"	1821
	18:22	that is a **m** the LORD has not spoken.	1821
Jos	2: 3	So the king of Jericho **sent** *this* **m** to Rahab:	8938
	5:14	"What **m** *does* my Lord have	1819
Jdg	3:19	"I have a secret **m** for you, O king."	1821
	3:20	"I have a **m** *from* God for you."	1821
	11:28	to the **m** Jephthah sent him.	1821
1Sa	9:27	so that I may give you a **m** *from* God."	1821
	15: 1	so listen now to the **m** *from* the LORD.	1821
	25: 9	they gave Nabal this **m** in David's name.	1821
2Sa	17:16	Now **send a m** immediately and tell David,	8938
	19:11	King David sent this **m** to Zadok	606
1Ki	5: 2	Solomon sent back this **m** to Hiram:	606
	5: 7	When Hiram heard Solomon's **m**,	1821
	5: 8	"*I have* **received** the **m** you sent me	9048
	13:32	For the **m** he declared by the word of	1821
	20:10	Then Ben-Hadad sent another **m** to Ahab:	606
	20:12	Ben-Hadad heard this **m** while he and	1821
2Ki	3: 7	He also sent this **m** to Jehoshaphat king	606
	5: 8	he sent him *this* **m**:	606
	9: 5	"I have a **m** for you, commander," he said.	1821
	10: 5	the elders and the guardians sent this **m**	606
	14: 9	in Lebanon sent a **m** to a cedar in Lebanon,	606
	18:14	of Judah sent this **m** to the king of Assyria	606
	19:20	Isaiah son of Amoz sent a **m** to Hezekiah:	606
2Ch	2: 3	Solomon sent this **m** to Hiram king of Tyre:	606
	25:18	in Lebanon sent a **m** to a cedar in Lebanon,	606
	32: 9	with *this* **m** for Hezekiah king of Judah and	606
Ezr	4:14	*we are sending* this **m** to inform the king,	10714
Ne	6: 2	Sanballat and Geshem sent me this **m**:	606
	6: 4	Four times they sent me the same **m**,	1821
	6: 5	to me with the same **m**,	1821
Pr	26: 6	or drinking violence is the sending of a **m**	1821
Isa	9: 8	The Lord has sent a **m** against Jacob;	1821
	28: 9	To whom is he explaining his **m**?	9019
	28:19	of this **m** will bring sheer terror.	9019
	30:12	"Because you have rejected this **m**,	1821
	37:21	Isaiah son of Amoz sent a **m** to Hezekiah:	606
	53: 1	Who has believed our **m** and to whom has	9019
Jer	3:12	Go, proclaim this **m** toward the north:	1821
	7: 2	and there proclaim this **m**:	1821
	18: 2	and there I will give you my **m**."	1821
	22: 1	the king of Judah and proclaim this **m** there:	1821
	23:21	yet they have run with their **m**;	NIH
	27: 4	**Give** them a **m** for their masters and say,	7422
	27:12	*I* gave the same **m** to Zedekiah king of	
		Judah.	465+1819+1821+2021+2021+3972
	29:28	He has sent this **m** to us in Babylon:	606
	29:31	"Send this **m** to all the exiles:	606
	37: 3	to Jeremiah the prophet with *this* **m**:	606
	44:16	not listen to the **m** you have spoken to us in	1821
	46: 2	This is the **m** against the army	NIH
	46:13	This is the **m** the LORD spoke to Jeremiah	1821
	49:14	I have heard a **m** from the LORD:	9019
	51:59	This is the **m** Jeremiah gave to	1821
Eze	33:30	'Come and hear the **m** that has come from	1821
Da	9:23	consider the **m** and understand the vision:	1821
	10: 1	Its **m** was true and it concerned a great war.	1821
	10: 1	The understanding of the **m** came to him in	1821
Am	7:10	Then Amaziah the priest of Bethel sent a **m**	606
Ob	1: 1	We have heard a **m** from the LORD:	9019
Jnh	3: 2	and proclaim to it the **m** I give you."	7952
Hag	1:12	the voice of the LORD their God and the **m**	1821
	1:13	gave this **m** *of* the LORD to the people:	4857
Mt	10: 7	As you go, preach this **m**:	4022
	13:19	the **m** about the kingdom and does	3364
	27:19	his wife **sent** him this **m**:	690
Mk	1: 7	And this *was his* **m**:	3062
Lk	4:32	because his **m** had authority.	3364
Jn	12:38	who has believed our **m** and to whom has	198
	17:20	in me through their **m**,	3364
Ac	2:41	Those who accepted his **m** were baptized,	3364
	4: 4	But many who heard the **m** believed,	3364
	5:20	tell the people the full **m** of this new life."	4839
	10:36	You know the **m** God sent to the people	3364
	10:44	Holy Spirit came on all who heard the **m**.	3364
	11:14	He *will* **bring** you a **m** through which	3281+4839
	11:19	telling the **m** only to Jews.	3364
	13:15	if you have a **m** of encouragement for	3364

Ac	13:26	to us that this **m** of salvation has been sent.	3364
	14: 3	the **m** of his grace by enabling them	3364
	15: 7	the Gentiles might hear from my lips the **m**	3364
	15:31	and were glad for its **encouraging m**.	4155
	16:14	to respond to Paul's **m**.	3281
	17:11	for they received the **m** with great eagerness	3364
	19:31	sent him a **m** begging him not to venture	NIG
Ro	10:16	"Lord, who has believed our **m**?"	198
	10:17	faith comes from hearing the **m**,	198
	10:17	the **m** is heard through the word of Christ.	198
1Co	1:18	For the **m** of the cross is foolishness	3364
	2: 4	My **m** and my preaching were not with wise	3364
	2: 6	speak a **m** of wisdom among the mature,	NIG
	12: 8	through the Spirit the **m** of wisdom,	3364
	12: 8	to another the **m** of knowledge by means of	3364
2Co	1:18	our **m** to you is not "Yes" and "No."	3364
	5:19	And he has committed to us the **m**	NIG
Gal	2: 6	those men added nothing to my **m**.	NIG
Col	4: 3	too, that God may open a door for our **m**,	3364
1Th	1: 6	the **m** with the joy given by the Holy Spirit.	3364
	1: 8	The Lord's **m** rang out from you not only	3364
2Th	3: 1	that the **m** of the Lord may spread rapidly	3364
1Ti	4:14	was given you through a **prophetic m**	4735
2Ti	4:15	because he strongly opposed our **m**.	3364
	4:17	through me the **m** might be fully proclaimed	3060
Tit	1: 9	to the trustworthy **m** as it has been taught,	3364
Heb	2: 2	For if the **m** spoken by angels was binding,	3364
	4: 2	the **m** they heard was of no value to them,	3364
1Pe	2: 8	They stumble because they disobey the **m**—	3364
1Jn	1: 5	the **m** we have heard from him and declare	32
	2: 7	This old command is the **m** you have heard.	3364
	3:11	This is the **m** you heard from the beginning:	32

MESSENGER (39) [MESSAGE]

1Sa	23:27	a **m** came to Saul, saying, "Come quickly!	4855
2Sa	11:19	He instructed the **m**:	4855
	11:22	The **m** set out, and when he arrived	4855
	11:23	**m** said to David, "The men overpowered	4855
	11:25	David told the **m**, "Say this to Joab:	4855
	15:13	A **m** came and told David,	5583
1Ki	19: 2	So Jezebel sent a **m** to Elijah to say,	4855
	22:13	The **m** who had gone to summon Micaiah	4855
2Ki	5:10	Elisha sent a **m** to say to him, "Go,	4855
	6:32	The king sent a **m** ahead,	4855
	6:32	Look, when the **m** comes,	4855
	6:33	the **m** came down to him.	4855
	9:18	"The **m** has reached them,	4855
	10: 8	When the **m** arrived, he told Jehu,	4855
2Ch	18:12	The **m** who had gone to summon Micaiah	4855
Job	1:14	a **m** came to Job and said,	4855
	1:16	**another m** came and said,	2296S
	1:17	**another m** came and said,	2296
	1:18	yet **another m** came and said,	2296S
Pr	13:17	A wicked **m** falls into trouble,	4855
	16:14	A king's wrath is a **m** of death,	4855
	25:13	is a trustworthy **m** to those who send him;	7495
Ecc	5: 6	And do not protest to the [temple] **m**,	4855
Isa	41:27	I gave to Jerusalem a **m** of good tidings.	1413
	42:19	and deaf like the **m** I send?	4855
Jer	51:31	and **m** follows messenger to announce to	5583
	51:31	and messenger follows **m** to announce to	5583S
Da	4:13	and there before me was a **m**, a holy one,	10541
	4:23	"You, O king, saw a **m**, a holy one,	10541
Hag	1:13	Then Haggai, the LORD's **m**,	4855
Mal	2: 7	he is the **m** *of* the LORD Almighty.	4855
	3: 1	"See, I will send my **m**, who will prepare	4855
	3: 1	the **m** *of* the covenant, whom you desire,	4855
Mt	11:10	" 'I will send my **m** ahead of you,	34
Mk	1: 2	"I will send my **m** ahead of you,	34
Lk	7:27	" 'I will send my **m** ahead of you,	34
Jn	13:16	nor is a **m** greater than the one who sent him.	693
2Co	12: 7	thorn in my flesh, a **m** of Satan, to torment	
		me.	34
Php	2:25	who is also your **m**,	693

MESSENGERS (72) [MESSAGE]

Ge	32: 3	Jacob sent **m** ahead of him	4855
	32: 6	When the **m** returned to Jacob, they said,	4855
Nu	20:14	Moses sent **m** from Kadesh to the king	4855
	21:21	Israel sent **m** to say to Sihon king of	4855
	22: 5	sent **m** to summon Balaam son of Beor,	4855
	24:12	"Did I not tell the **m** you sent me,	4855
Dt	2:26	From the desert of Kedemoth I sent **m**	4855
Jos	7:22	So Joshua sent **m**, and they ran to the tent,	4855
Jdg	6:35	He sent **m** throughout Manasseh,	4855
	7:24	Gideon sent **m** throughout the hill country	4855
	9:31	Under cover he sent **m** to Abimelech,	4855
	11:12	Then Jephthah sent **m** to the Ammonite king	4855
	11:13	of the Ammonites answered Jephthah's **m**,	4855
	11:14	Jephthah sent back to the Ammonite king	4855
	11:17	Then Israel sent **m** to the king of Edom,	4855
	11:19	Israel sent **m** to Sihon king of the Amorites,	4855
1Sa	6:21	they sent **m** to the people of Kiriath Jearim,	4855
	11: 3	"Give us seven days so we can send **m**	4855
	11: 4	When the **m** came to Gibeah of Saul	4855
	11: 7	and sent the pieces by **m** throughout Israel,	4855
	11: 9	They told the **m** who had come,	4855
	11: 9	the **m** went and reported this to the men	4855
	19:11	Then Saul sent **m** to Jesse and said,	4855
	25:14	"David sent **m** from the desert	4855
	25:42	went with David's **m** and became his wife.	4855
	31: 9	sent **m** throughout the land of	NIH
2Sa	2: 5	he sent **m** to the men of Jabesh Gilead	4855
	3:12	Abner sent **m** on his behalf to say to David,	4855
	3:14	David sent **m** to Ish-Bosheth son of Saul,	4855

2Sa	3:26	Joab then left David and sent **m** after Abner,	4855
	5:11	Now Hiram king of Tyre sent **m** to David,	4855
	10: 5	he sent **m** to meet the men,	NIH
	11: 4	Then David sent **m** to get her.	4855
	12:27	Joab then sent **m** to David, saying,	4855
	15:10	Then Absalom sent **secret m** throughout	8078
1Ki	20: 2	He sent **m** into the city to Ahab king	4855
	20: 5	The **m** came again and said,	4855
	20: 9	So he replied to Ben-Hadad's **m**,	4855
2Ki	1: 2	So he sent **m**, saying to them,	4855
	1: 3	the **m** *of* the king of Samaria and ask them,	4855
	1: 5	When the **m** returned to the king,	4855
	1:16	that you have sent **m** to consult Baal-Zebub,	4855
	7:15	So the **m** returned and reported to the king.	4855
	14: 8	Then Amaziah sent **m** to Jehoash son	4855
	16: 7	Ahaz sent **m** to say to Tiglath-Pileser king	4855
	19: 9	he again sent **m** to Hezekiah with this word:	4855
	19:14	Hezekiah received the letter from the **m**	4855
	19:23	By your **m** you have heaped insults on	4855
	20:13	Hezekiah received the **m** and showed	2157S
1Ch	10: 9	and **sent m** throughout the land of	8938
	14: 1	Now Hiram king of Tyre sent **m** to David,	4855
	19: 5	he sent **m** to meet them,	NIH
	19:16	they sent **m** and had Arameans brought	4855
2Ch	35:21	But Neco sent **m** to him, saying,	4855
	36:15	to them through his **m** again and again,	4855
	36:16	But they mocked God's **m**,	4855
Ne	6: 3	so I sent **m** to them with this reply:	4855
Job	33:22	and his life to the **m** of death.	4637
Ps	104: 4	He makes winds his **m**,	4855
Isa	18: 2	Go, swift **m**, to a people tall and	4855
	37: 9	he sent **m** to Hezekiah with this word:	4855
	37:14	Hezekiah received the letter from the **m**	4855
	37:24	By your **m** you have heaped insults on	6269
	44:26	and fulfills the predictions of his **m**,	4855
Eze	23:16	after them and sent **m** to them in Chaldea.	4855
	23:40	"They even sent **m** for men who came	4855
	30: 9	that day I will go out from me in ships	4855
Da	4:17	" 'The decision is announced by **m**,	10541
Na	2:13	voices of your **m** will no longer be heard."	4855
Lk	7:22	So he replied to the **m**,	899S
	7:24	After John's **m** left, Jesus began to speak to	34
	9:52	And he sent **m** on ahead,	34

MESSIAH (2) [CHRIST]

Jn	1:41	"We have found the **M**" (that is, the Christ).	3549
	4:25	"I know that **M**" (called Christ) "is coming.	3549

MESSIAS (KJV) See MESSIAH

MET (55) [MEET]

Ge	32: 1	and the angels of God **m** him.	7003
	33: 8	by all these droves *I* **m**?"	7008
	38: 2	There Judah **m** the daughter of	8011
Ex	3:18	the God of the Hebrews, *has* **m** with us.	7936
	4:24	the LORD **m** [Moses] and was about	7008
	4:27	So **he m** Moses at the mountain of God	7008
	5: 3	"The God of the Hebrews *has* **m** with us.	7925
	18: 8	about all the hardships they *had* **m** along	5162
Nu	23: 4	God **m** with him, and Balaam said,	7936
	23:16	The LORD **m** with Balaam and put	7936
Dt	25:18	they **m** you on your journey	7936
1Sa	9:11	they **m** some girls coming out	5162
	10:10	a procession of prophets **m** him;	7925
	16: 4	of the town trembled when *they* **m** him.	7125
	18:30	David **m with** more **success** than the rest	8505
	21: 1	Ahimelech trembled when *he* **m** him,	7925
2Sa	2:13	descending toward her and *she* **m** them.	7008
		and David's men went out and **m** them at	7008
1Ki	11:29	and Ahijah the prophet of Shiloh **m** him on	5162
	13:24	a lion **m** him on the road and killed him,	5162
	18: 7	Obadiah was walking along, Elijah **m** him.	7925
2Ki	9:21	*They* **m** him at the plot of ground	5162
	10:13	he **m** some relatives of Ahaziah king	5162
	12:12	**m** all *the other* **expenses**	3655
Ne	13: 2	not **m** the Israelites with food and water	7709
Job	2:11	**m** together **by agreement**	3585
Ps	74: 4	Your foes roared in the **place where** you **m**	4595
Jer	41: 6	When he **m** them, he said,	7008
Mt	8:28	men coming from the tombs **m** him.	5636
	27:32	they **m** a man from Cyrene, named Simon,	2351
	28: 9	Suddenly Jesus **m** them.	5636
	28:12	*When* the chief priests *had* **m** with the elders	5251
Lk	8:27	he was **m** by a demon-possessed man from	5636
	9:37	a large crowd **m** him.	5267
	17:12	ten men who had leprosy **m** him.	560
	22:66	**m together**, and Jesus was led before them.	5251
Jn	4:51	his servants **m** him with the news	5636
	11:30	at the place where Martha *had* **m** him.	5636
	18: 2	Jesus *had* often **m** there with his disciples.	5251
Ac	1: 6	So *when* they **m together**, they asked him,	5302
	4: 5	and teachers of the law **m** in Jerusalem.	5251
	4:27	Indeed Herod and Pontius Pilate **m together**	5251
	8:27	and on his way he **m** an Ethiopian eunuch,	NIG
	10:25	Cornelius **m** him and fell at his feet.	5267
	11:26	for a whole year Barnabas and Saul **m** with	5251
	13: 6	There *they* **m** a Jewish sorcerer	2351
	15: 6	and elders **m** to consider this question.	5251
	16:16	we *were* **m** by a slave girl who had a spirit	5636
	16:40	where *they* **m with** the brothers	3972
	18: 2	There *he* **m** a Jew named Aquila,	2351
	20:14	When *he* **m** us at Assos,	5202
Ro	8: 4	of the law *might be* **fully m** in us,	4444
Col	2: 1	and for all who *have* not **m** me **personally**.	

1877+3836+3972+4725+4922

Heb 7: 1 He **m** Abraham returning from the defeat of 5267
7:10 because when Melchizedek **m** Abraham, 5267

METAL (12) [METALS, METALWORKER]
Lev 19: 4 not turn to idols or make gods of **cast m** 5011
1Ki 7:23 He made the Sea of **cast m**, 4607
7:33 rims, spokes and hubs were all of **cast m.** 4607
14: 9 other gods, **idols made of m**; 5011
2Ch 4: 2 He made the Sea of **cast m**, 4607
Ps 106:19 a calf and worshiped an **idol cast from m.** 5011
Isa 48: 5 and **m god** ordained them.' 5822
Eze 1: 4 of the fire looked like **glowing m**, 3133
1:27 his waist up he looked like **glowing m**, 3133
8: 2 as bright as **glowing m.** 3133
Da 11: 8 their **m images** and their valuable articles 5816
Na 2: 3 The **m** on the chariots flashes on 7110

METALS (1) [METAL]
Jer 6:27 a **tester of m** and my people the ore, 1031

METALWORKER (1) [METAL, WORK]
2Ti 4:14 Alexander the **m** did me a great deal 5906

METE (1)
Ps 58: 2 and your hands **m out** violence on the earth. 7142

METEYARD (KJV) See MEASURING LENGTH

METHEG AMMAH (1)
2Sa 8: 1 and he took **M** from the control of 5497

METHOD (1) [METHODS]
Ru 4: 7 This was the **m of legalizing transactions** 9496

METHODS (1) [METHOD]
Isa 32: 7 The scoundrel's **m** are wicked, 3998

METHUSAEL (KJV) See METHUSHAEL

METHUSELAH (7)
Ge 5:21 he became the father of **M.** 5500
5:22 And after he became the father of **M**, 5500
5:25 When **M** had lived 187 years, 5500
5:26 **M** lived 782 years and had other sons 5500
5:27 Altogether, **M** lived 969 years, 5500
1Ch 1: 3 Enoch, **M**, Lamech, Noah. 5500
Lk 3:37 the son of **M**, son of Enoch, 3417

METHUSHAEL (2)
Ge 4:18 and Mehujael was the father of **M**, 5499
4:18 and **M** was the father of Lamech. 5499

MEUNIM (2)
Ezr 2:50 Asnah, **M**, Nephussim, 5064
Ne 7:52 Besai, **M**, Nephussim, 5064

MEUNITES (3)
1Ch 4:41 and also the **M** who were there 5064
2Ch 20: 1 of the **M** came to make war on Jehoshaphat. 5064
26: 7 in Gur Baal and against the **M.** 5064

MEZAHAB (KJV) See ME-ZAHAB

MEZOBAITE (1)
1Ch 11:47 Eliel, Obed and Jaasiel the **M.** 5168

MIAMIN (KJV) See MIJAMIN

MIBHAR (1)
1Ch 11:38 Joel the brother of Nathan, **M** son of Hagri, 4437

MIBSAM (3)
Ge 25:13 the firstborn of Ishmael, Kedar, Adbeel, **M**, 4452
1Ch 1:29 the firstborn of Ishmael, Kedar, Adbeel, **M**, 4452
4:25 **M** his son and Mishma his son. 4452

MIBZAR (2)
Ge 36:42 Kenaz, Teman, **M**, 4449
1Ch 1:53 Kenaz, Teman, **M**, 4449

MICA (5)
2Sa 9:12 Mephibosheth had a young son named **M**, 4775
1Ch 9:15 Heresh, Galal and Mattaniah son of **M**, 4775
Ne 10:11 **M**, Rehob, Hashabiah, 4775
11:17 of **M**, the son of Zabdi, the son of Asaph, 4777
11:22 the son of Mattaniah, the son of **M.** 4775

MICAH (25) [MICAH'S]
Jdg 17: 1 Now a man named **M** from the hill country 4781
17: 5 Now this man **M** had a shrine, 4777
17: 9 **M** asked him, "Where are you from?" 4777
17:10 Then **M** said to him, "Live with me 4777

Jdg 17:12 Then **M** installed the Levite, 4777
17:13 And **M** said, "Now I know that 4777
18: 2 of Ephraim and came to the house of **M**, 4777
18: 4 He told them what **M** had done for him, 4777
18:22 near **M** were called together and overtook 4777
18:23 the Danites turned and said to **M**, 4777
18:26 So the Danites went their way, and **M**, 4777
18:27 Then they took what **M** had made, 4777
18:31 to use the idols **M** had made, 4777
1Ch 5: 5 **M** his son, Reaiah his son, Baal his son, 4777
8:34 Merib-Baal, who was the father of **M.** 4777
8:35 The sons of **M**: Pithon, Melech, 4777
9:40 Merib-Baal, who was the father of **M.** 4777
9:41 The sons of **M**: Pithon, Melech, 4777
23:20 **M** the first and Isshiah the second. 4777
24:24 **M**; from the sons of Micah: Shamir. 4777
24:24 from the sons of **M**: Shamir. 4777
24:25 The brother of **M**: Isshiah; 4777
2Ch 34:20 Ahikam son of Shaphan, Abdon son of **M**, 4777
Jer 26:18 "**M** of Moresheth prophesied in the days 4777
Mic 1: 1 The word of the LORD that came to **M** of Moresheth 4777

MICAH'S (7) [MICAH]
Jdg 17: 4 And they were put in **M** house. 4781
17: 8 to **M** house in the hill country of Ephraim. 4777
18: 3 When they were near **M** house, 4777
18:13 of Ephraim and came to **M** house. 4777
18:15 to the house of the young Levite at **M** place 4777
18:18 into **M** house and took the carved image, 4777
18:22 they had gone some distance from **M** house, 4777

MICAIAH (28)
1Ki 22: 8 He is **M** son of Imlah." 4781
22: 9 "Bring **M** son of Imlah at once." 4781
22:13 to summon **M** said to him, 4781
22:14 But **M** said, "As surely as the LORD lives, 4781
22:15 When he arrived, the king asked him, "**M**, 4781
22:17 **M** answered, "I saw all Israel scattered NIH
22:19 **M** continued, "Therefore hear the word of NIH
22:24 of Kenaanah went up and slapped **M** in 4781
22:25 **M** replied, "You will find out on 4781
22:26 "Take **M** and send him back to Amon 4781
22:28 **M** declared, "If you ever return safely, 4781
2Ki 22:12 Ahikam son of Shaphan, Acbor son of **M**, 4779
2Ch 17: 7 and **M** to teach in the towns of Judah. 4780
18: 7 He is **M** son of Imlah." 4781
18: 8 "Bring **M** son of Imlah at once." 4781
18:12 to summon **M** said to him, 4781
18:13 But **M** said, "As surely as the LORD lives, 4781
18:14 When he arrived, the king asked him, "**M**, 4777
18:16 **M** answered, "I saw all Israel scattered NIH
18:18 **M** continued, "Therefore hear the word of NIH
18:23 of Kenaanah went up and slapped **M** in 4781
18:24 **M** replied, "You will find out on 4781
18:25 "Take **M** and send him back to Amon 4781
18:27 **M** declared, "If you ever return safely, 4781
Ne 12:35 the son of Mattaniah, the son of **M**, 4779
12:41 Eliakim, Maaseiah, Miniamin, **M**, Elioenai, 4779
Jer 36:11 When **M** son of Gemariah, 4781
36:13 **M** told them everything he had heard Baruch read to the people 4781

MICE (KJV) See RATS

MICHA (KJV) See MICA

MICHAEL (15)
Nu 13:13 from the tribe of Asher, Sethur son of **M**; 4776
1Ch 5:13 Their relatives, by families, were: **M**, 4776
5:14 the son of **M**, the son of Jeshishai, 4776
6:40 the son of **M**, the son of Baaseiah, 4776
7: 3 **M**, Obadiah, Joel and Isshiah. 4776
8:16 **M**, Ishpah and Joha were the sons 4776
12:20 Adnah, Jozabad, Jediael, **M**, Jozabad, 4776
27:18 Omri son of **M**; 4776
2Ch 21: 2 Zechariah, Azariahu, **M** and Shephatiah. 4776
Ezr 8: 8 Zebadiah son of **M**, and with him 80 men; 4776
Da 10:13 Then **M**, one of the chief princes, 4776
10:21 No one supports me against them except **M**, 4776
12: 1 "At that time **M**, the great prince 4776
Jude 1: 9 But even the archangel **M**, 3640
Rev 12: 7 **M** and his angels fought against the dragon, 3640

MICHAH (KJV) See MICAH

MICHAIAH (KJV) See MICAIAH

MICHAL (18)
1Sa 14:49 and that of the younger was **M.** 4783
18:20 Saul's daughter **M** was in love with David, 4783
18:27 Saul gave him his daughter **M** in marriage, 4783
18:28 and that his daughter **M** loved David, 4783
19:11 But **M**, David's wife, warned him, 4783
19:12 So **M** let David down through a window, 4783
19:13 Then **M** took an idol and laid it on the bed, 4783
19:14 Saul sent the men to capture David, **M** said, NIH
19:17 Saul said to **M**, "Why did you deceive me 4783
19:17 **M** told him, "He said to me, 4783
25:44 But Saul had given his daughter **M**, 4783
2Sa 3:13 unless you bring **M** daughter of Saul 4783
3:14 demanding, "Give me my wife **M**, 4783

2Sa 6:16 **M** daughter of Saul watched from 4783
6:20 **M** daughter of Saul came out to meet him 4783
6:21 David said to **M**, "It was before 4783
6:23 And **M** daughter of Saul had no children to 4783
1Ch 15:29 **M** daughter of Saul watched from 4783

MICHMAS, MICHMASH (Anglicized, KJV) See MICMASH

MICHMETHAH (KJV) See MICMETHATH

MICHRI (KJV) See MICRI

MICMASH (11)
1Sa 13: 2 two thousand were with him at **M** and in 4825
13: 5 They went up and camped at **M**, 4825
13:11 that the Philistines were assembling at **M**, 4825
13:16 while the Philistines camped at **M.** 4825
13:23 of Philistines had gone out to the pass at **M.** 4825
14: 5 One cliff stood to the north toward **M**, 4825
14:31 down the Philistines from **M** to Aijalon, 4825
Ezr 2:27 of **M** 122 4820
Ne 7:31 of **M** 122 4820
11:31 of the Benjamites from Geba lived in **M**, 4825
Isa 10:28 they store supplies at **M.** 4825

MICMETHATH (2)
Jos 16: 6 From **M** on the north it curved eastward 4826
17: 7 from Asher to **M** east of Shechem. 4826

MICRI (1)
1Ch 9: 8 Elah son of Uzzi, the son of **M**; 4840

MIDAIR (4) [AIR]
2Sa 18: 9 He was left hanging in **m**, 824+1068+1068+2021+2021+2256+9028
Rev 8:13 heard an eagle that was flying in **m** call out 3547
14: 6 Then I saw another angel flying in **m**, 3547
19:17 in a loud voice to all the birds flying in **m**, 3547

MIDDAY (7) [DAY]
Dt 28:29 At **m** you will grope about like a blind man 7416
1Ki 18:29 **M** passed, and they continued their frantic prophesying until 7416
Ps 91: 6 nor the plague that destroys at **m.** 7416
SS 1: 7 and where you rest your sheep at **m.** 7416
Isa 59:10 At **m** we stumble as if it were twilight; 7416
Jer 15: 8 At **m** I will bring a destroyer against 7416
Zep 2: 4 At **m** Ashdod will be emptied 7416

MIDDIN (1)
Jos 15:61 In the desert: Beth Arabah, **M**, Secacah, 4516

MIDDLE (49) [AMID, MIDST]
Ge 2: 9 the **m** of the garden were the tree of life and 9348
3: 3 not eat fruit from the tree that is in the **m of** 9348
6:16 and make lower, **m** and upper decks. 9108
Ex 26:28 from end to end at the **m of** the frames. 9348
36:33 that it extended from end to end at the **m of** 9348
Nu 2:17 the camp of the Levites will set out in the **m** 9348
Dt 3:16 the Arnon Gorge (the **m of** the gorge being 9348
11: 6 the **m of** all Israel and swallowed them up 7931
13:16 of the town into the **m of** the public square 9348
Jos 3:17 on dry ground in the **m of** the Jordan, 9348
4: 3 from the **m of** the Jordan from right where 9348
4: 5 the ark of the LORD your God into the **m** 9348
4: 8 They took twelve stones from the **m of** 9348
4: 9 the twelve stones that had been in the **m of** 9348
4:10 in the **m of** the Jordan until everything 9348
8:22 so that they were caught in the **m**, 9348
10:13 in the **m of** the sky and delayed going down 2942
12: 2 from the **m of** the gorge— 9348
13: 9 and from the town in the **m of** the gorge, 9348
13:16 and from the town in the **m of** the gorge, 9348
Jdg 7:19 the camp at the beginning of the **m** watch, 9399
16: 3 But Samson lay there only until the **m** 2942
Ru 3: 8 In the **m of** the night something startled 2942
2Sa 10: 4 cut off their garments in the **m** at 9348
20:12 Amasa lay wallowing in his blood in the **m** 9348
23:12 But Shammah took his stand in the **m of** 9348
1Ki 3:20 up in the **m of** the night and took my son 9348
6: 6 the **m** floor six cubits and 9399
6: 8 to the **m** level and from there to the third. 9399
6:27 and their wings touched each other in the **m** 9348
8:64 the **m** part of the courtyard in front of 9348
2Ki 20: 4 Before Isaiah had left the **m** court, 9399
1Ch 11:14 they took their stand in the **m of** the field, 9348
19: 4 cut off their garments in the **m** at 2942
2Ch 7: 7 the **m** part of the courtyard in front of 9348
Job 34:20 They die in an instant, in the **m of** the night; 2940
Jer 39: 3 and took seats in the **M Gate.** 9348
Eze 15: 4 the fire burns both ends and chars the **m**, 9348
37: 1 the Spirit of the LORD and set me in the **m** 9348
41: 7 to the top floor through the **m** floor. 9399
42: 5 on the lower and **m** floors of the building. 9399
42: 6 on the lower and **m** floors. 9399
Da 4:10 there before me stood a tree in the **m of** 10135
9:27 In the **m of** the 'seven' he will put an end 2942
Mk 6:47 the boat was in the **m of** the lake, 3545
Lk 5:19 through the tiles into the **m of** the crowd, 3545

Lk 22:55 But when they had kindled a fire in the **m** of 3545
Jn 19:18 one on each side and Jesus in the **m**. 3545
Rev 22: 2 down the **m** of the great street of the city. 3545

MIDIAN (35) [MIDIAN'S, MIDIANITE, MIDIANITES]

Ge 25: 2 She bore him Zimran, Jokshan, Medan, **M**, 4518
25: 4 The sons of **M** were Ephah, Epher, Hanoch, 4518
36:35 who defeated **M** in the country of Moab, 4518
Ex 2:15 from Pharaoh and went to live in **M**, 824+4518
2:16 Now a priest of **M** had seven daughters, 4518
3: 1 Jethro his father-in-law, the priest of **M**, 4518
4:19 Now the LORD had said to Moses in **M**, 4518
18: 1 the priest of **M** and father-in-law of Moses, 4518
Nu 22: 4 The Moabites said to the elders of **M**, 4518
22: 7 The elders of Moab and **M** left, 4518
31: 7 They fought against **M**, 4518
31: 8 the five kings of **M**. 4518
Jdg 6: 2 Because the power of **M** was so oppressive, 4518
6: 6 **M** so impoverished the Israelites 4518
6: 7 cried to the LORD because of **M**, 4518
6:13 and put us into the hand of **M**." 4518
7: 1 of **M** was north of them in the valley near 4518
7: 2 for me to deliver **M** into their hands. 4518
7: 8 the camp of **M** lay below him in the valley. 4518
8: 1 when you went to fight **M**?" 4518
8: 5 Zebah and Zalmunna, the kings of **M**." 4518
8:12 Zebah and Zalmunna, the two kings of **M**. 4518
8:22 you have saved us out of the hand of **M**." 4518
8:26 the purple garments worn by the kings of **M** 4518
8:28 Thus **M** was subdued before the Israelites 4518
9:17 to rescue you from the hand of **M** 4518
1Ki 11:18 They set out from **M** and went to Paran. 4518
1Ch 1:32 Zimran, Jokshan, Medan, **M**, 4518
1:33 The sons of **M**: Ephah, Epher, Hanoch, 4518
1:46 who defeated **M** in the country of Moab, 4518
Ps 83: 9 Do to them as you did to **M**, 4518
Isa 10:26 he struck down **M** at the rock of Oreb; 4518
60: 6 young camels of **M** and Ephah. 4518
Hab 3: 7 the dwellings of **M** in anguish. 824+4518
Ac 7:29 When Moses heard this, he fled to **M**, 1178+3409

MIDIAN'S (2) [MIDIAN]

Jdg 6:14 and save Israel out of **M** hand. 4518
Isa 9: 4 For as in the day of **M** defeat, 4518

MIDIANITE (14) [MIDIAN]

Ge 37:28 So when the **M** merchants came by, 4520
Nu 10:29 Moses said to Hobab son of Reuel the **M**, 4520
25: 6 a **M** *woman* right before the eyes of Moses 4520
25:14 with the **M** *woman* was Zimri son of Salu, 4520
25:15 the name of the **M** *woman* who was put 4520
25:15 a tribal chief of a **M** family. 4518
25:18 the daughter of a **M** leader, 4518
31: 9 the **M** women and children and took all 4518
31: 9 and children and took all the **M** herds, 4392S
Jos 13:21 Moses had defeated him and the **M** chiefs, 4518
Jdg 7:13 bread came tumbling into the **M** camp. 4518
7:15 The LORD has given the **M** camp 4518
7:25 They also captured two of the **M** leaders, 4518
8: 3 God gave Oreb and Zeeb, the **M** leaders, 4518

MIDIANITES (17) [MIDIAN]

Ge 37:36 the **M** sold Joseph in Egypt to Potiphar, 4520
Nu 25:17 "Treat the **M** as enemies and kill them, 4520
31: 2 "Take vengeance on the **M** for 4520
31: 3 of your men to go to war against the **M** and 4518
31:10 the towns where the **M** had settled, 4392S
Jdg 6: 1 into the hands of the **M**. 4518
6: 3 the Israelites planted their crops, the **M**, 4518
6:11 in a winepress to keep it from the **M**. 4518
6:16 you will strike down all the **M** together." 4518
6:33 Now all the **M**, Amalekites and other 4518
7: 7 that lapped I will save you and give the **M** 4518
7:12 The **M**, the Amalekites and all 4518
7:14 the **M** and the whole camp into his hands." 4518
7:21 all the **M**, crying out as they fled, 4722S
7:23 and they pursued the **M** 4518
7:24 down against the **M** and seize the waters of 4518
7:25 They pursued the **M** and brought the heads 4518

MIDIANITISH (KJV) See MIDIANITES

MIDNIGHT (9) [NIGHT]

Ex 11: 4 'About **m** I will go throughout Egypt. 2940+4326
12:29 At **m** the LORD struck down all 2021+2942+4326
Ps 119:62 At **m** I rise to give you thanks 2940+4326
Mt 25: 6 'At **m** the cry rang out: 3545+3816
Mk 13:35 whether in the evening, or at **m**, 3543
Lk 11: 5 and he goes to him at **m** and says, 'Friend, 3543
Ac 16:25 About **m** Paul and Silas were praying 3543
20: 7 kept on talking until **m**. 3543
27:27 when about **m** the sailors sensed 3545+3816+3836

MIDST (23) [MIDDLE]

Lev 16:16 among them in the **m** of their uncleanness. 9348
Nu 16:47 and ran into the **m** of the assembly. 9348
Job 20:22 In the **m** of his plenty, 4848
Ps 57: 4 I am in the **m** of lions; 9348
102:24 O my God, in the **m** of my days; 2942
110: 2 you will rule in the **m** of your enemies. 7931
116:19 in your **m**, O Jerusalem. 9348

Ps 135: 9 He sent his signs and wonders into your **m**, 9348
136:14 and brought Israel through the **m** of it, 9348
138: 7 Though I walk in the **m** of trouble, 7931
Pr 5:14 to the brink of utter ruin in the **m** of 9348
Isa 66:17 following the one in the **m** of those who eat 9348
Jer 9: 6 You live in the **m** of deception; 9348
48:45 a blaze from the **m** of Sihon; 1068
La 1: 3 overtaken her **in the m** of her distress. 1068
1:15 Lord has rejected all the warriors in my **m**; 7931
Eze 5:10 in your **m** fathers will eat their children, 9348
22: 3 on herself doom by shedding blood in her **m** 9348
22:13 and at the blood you have shed in your **m**. 9348
24: 7 "'For the blood she shed is in her **m**: 9348
Am 5:17 for I will pass through your **m**," 7931
Mic 5: 7 be in the **m** of many peoples like dew from 7931
5: 8 in the **m** of many peoples, 7931

MIDWIFE (2) [MIDWIVES]

Ge 35:17 the **m** said to her, "Don't be afraid, 3528
38:28 so the **m** took a scarlet thread and tied it 3528

MIDWIVES (7) [MIDWIFE]

Ex 1:15 The king of Egypt said to the Hebrew **m**, 3528
1:17 The **m**, however, feared God and did 3528
1:18 of Egypt summoned the **m** and asked them, 3528
1:19 The **m** answered Pharaoh, 3528
1:19 and give birth before the **m** arrive." 3528
1:20 the **m** and the people increased and became 3528
1:21 And because the **m** feared God, 3528

MIGDAL EDER (1) [EDER]

Ge 35:21 and pitched his tent beyond **M**. 4468

MIGDAL EL (1)

Jos 19:38 **M**, Horem, Beth Anath 4466

MIGDAL GAD (1) [GAD]

Jos 15:37 Zenan, Hadashah, **M**, 4467

MIGDOL (6)

Ex 14: 2 between **M** and the sea. 4465
Nu 33: 7 and camped near **M**. 4465
Jer 44: 1 in **M**, Tahpanhes and Memphis— 4465
46:14 and proclaim it in **M**; 4465
Eze 29:10 and a desolate waste from **M** to Aswan, 4465
30: 6 From **M** to Aswan they will fall by 4465

MIGHT (190) [ALMIGHTY, MIGHTIER, MIGHTIEST, MIGHTILY, MIGHTY]

Ge 17:18 only Ishmael **m** live under your blessing!" AIT
26: 7 "The men of this place **m** kill me on account 7153
26: 9 "Because I thought I **m** lose my life 7153
26:10 men **m** well have slept with your wife, 3869+5071
42: 4 he was afraid that harm **m** come to him. AIT
49: 3 "Reuben, you are my firstborn, my **m**, 3946
Ex 9:16 that I **m** show you my power and AIT
9:16 and that my name **m** be proclaimed in all AIT
13:17 they **m** change their minds and return 7153
16:34 that it **m** be kept. NIH
29:46 of Egypt so that I **m** dwell among them. AIT
33: 3 a stiff-necked people and I **m** destroy you AIT
33: 5 even for a moment, I **m** destroy you. AIT
Lev 5: 4 in any matter one **m** carelessly swear about AIT
Dt 4:35 so that *you* **m** know that the LORD is God; AIT
5:29 so that *it* **m** go well with them AIT
6:24 that we **m** always prosper and be kept alive, NIH
8:16 to test you so that in the end *it* **m** go well AIT
19: 6 avenger of blood **m** pursue him in a rage, AIT
29: 6 I did this so that *you* **m** know that I am AIT
Jos 4:24 the peoples of the earth **m** know that the AIT
4:24 hand of the LORD is powerful AIT
4:24 and so that *you* **m** always fear AIT
11:20 **m** destroy them totally, AIT
22:24 that some day your descendants **m** say AIT
22:25 **m** cause ours to stop fearing the LORD. AIT
Jdg 9:24 **m** be avenged on their brother Abimelech AIT
14: 6 with his bare hands as *he* **m** have torn AIT
16:30 Then he pushed with all his **m**, 3946
18: 1 a place of their own where they **m** settle, AIT
Ru 2:22 in someone else's field you **m** be harmed." AIT
2:23 because I **m** endanger my own estate. AIT
1Sa 18:27 **m** become the king's son-in-law. AIT
27:11 "They **m** inform on us and say, 7153
2Sa 6: 5 of Israel were celebrating with all their **m** 6437
6:14 danced before the LORD with all his **m**, 6437
1Ki 2:22 You **m** as well request the kingdom AIT
19: 4 sat down under it and prayed that he **m** die. AIT
2Ki 23:33 in the land of Hamath so that he **m** not reign AIT
1Ch 13: 8 with all their **m** before God, 6437
2Ch 6:41 you and the ark of your **m**. 6437
20: 6 Power and **m** are in your hand, 1476
23:19 in any way unclean **m** enter. AIT
25:20 that he **m** hand them over to [Jehoash], AIT
Ezr 8:17 so that they **m** bring attendants to us for AIT
8:21 that we **m** humble ourselves before our God AIT
Est 9: 1 that **m** attack them and their women AIT
10: 2 And all his acts of power and **m**, 1476
Job 3:12 and breasts that I **m** be nursed? AIT
6: 8 "Oh, that I **m** have my request, AIT
9:32 not a man like me that I **m** answer him, AIT
9:32 that *we* **m** confront each other in court. AIT
13: 9 as you **m** deceive men? AIT

Job 30:21 with the **m** of your hand you attack me. 6797
34:36 that Job **m** be tested to the utmost AIT
38:13 that *it m* take the earth by the edges AIT
Ps 21:13 we will sing and praise your **m**. 1476
54: 1 vindicate me by your **m**. 1476
59:11 In your **m** make them wander about, 2657
68:18 that you, O LORD God, **m** dwell there. AIT
71:18 your **m** to all who are to come. 1476
78:61 He sent [the ark of] his **m** into captivity, 6437
80: 2 Awaken your **m**; come and save us. 1476
105:45 that *they* **m** keep his precepts AIT
119:11 in my heart that I **m** not sin against you. AIT
119:71 be afflicted so that I **m** learn your decrees. AIT
119:101 so that I **m** obey your word. AIT
125: 3 the righteous **m** use their hands to do evil. AIT
132: 8 you and the ark of your **m**. 6437
145:11 of your kingdom and speak of your **m**, 1476
Ecc 9:10 do it with all your **m**, for in the grave, 3946
Isa 6:10 Otherwise *they* **m** see with their eyes, AIT
44:12 he forges it with the **m** of his arm. 3946
47: 7 or reflect on what **m** happen. 344
51:10 the sea so that the redeemed **m** cross over? 1476
63:15 Where are your zeal and your **m**? 1476
Jer 9: 2 so that I **m** leave my people and go away AIT
16:21 this time I will teach them my power and **m**. 1476
49:35 the mainstay of their **m**. 1476
Eze 20:26 **m** fill them with horror AIT
36: 5 so that they **m** plunder its pastureland.' NIH
Da 2:16 so that he **m** interpret the dream for him. AIT
2:18 so that he and his friends **m** not be executed AIT
2:37 and power and **m** and glory; 10773
5: 2 and his concubines **m** drink from them. AIT
6: 2 to them so that the king **m** not suffer loss. AIT
6:17 so that Daniel's situation **m** not be changed. AIT
11:17 the **m** of his entire kingdom and will make 9549
Joel 3: 3 they sold girls for wine that *they* **m** drink. AIT
3: 6 *you* **m** send them far from their homeland. AIT
Mic 3: 8 and with justice and **m**, 1476
Zec 4: 6 'Not by **m** nor by power, but by my Spirit,' 2657
Mt 12:14 and plotted how *they* **m** kill Jesus. *AIT*
13:15 Otherwise *they* **m** see with their eyes, *AIT*
15: 5 'Whatever help you **m** otherwise have
received from me *NIG*
26:56 writings of the prophets **m** be fulfilled." *AIT*
Mk 3: 6 with the Herodians how *they* **m** kill Jesus. *AIT*
3:14 that *they* **m** be with him *AIT*
3:14 be with him and that *he* **m** send them out *AIT*
4:12 otherwise they **m** turn and be forgiven!' " *AIT*
7:11 help *you* **m** otherwise have received *AIT*
14:35 and prayed that if possible the hour **m** pass *AIT*
16: 1 so that *they* **m** go to anoint Jesus' body. *AIT*
Lk 1:29 what kind of greeting this **m** be. *AIT*
3:15 if John **m** *possibly* be the Christ. *AIT*
6:11 to discuss with one another what they **m** do 323
11:54 waiting to catch him in something he **m** say.
1666+3836+5125
20:20 so that *they* **m** hand him over to the power *AIT*
22: 4 with them how *he* **m** betray Jesus. *AIT*
22:23 among themselves which of them *it* **m** be *AIT*
Jn 1: 7 so that through him all men **m** believe. *AIT*
1:31 with water was that *he* **m** be revealed *AIT*
9: 3 the work of God **m** be displayed in his life. *AIT*
11:57 so that *they* **m** arrest him. *AIT*
17: 2 over all people that he **m** give eternal life *AIT*
19:24 the scripture **m** be fulfilled which said, *AIT*
Ac 5:15 so that at least Peter's shadow **m** fall on *AIT*
5:31 *that* he **m** give repentance and forgiveness *AIT*
7:46 that he **m** provide a dwelling place for *AIT*
8:15 for them that *they* **m** receive the Holy Spirit, *AIT*
9: 2 he **m** take them as prisoners to Jerusalem. *AIT*
15: 7 that the Gentiles **m** hear from my lips *AIT*
27: 3 to go to his friends *so* they **m** provide *AIT*
28:27 Otherwise *they* **m** see with their eyes, *AIT*
Ro 1:13 in order that I **m** have a harvest among you, *AIT*
3: 7 Someone **m** argue, "If my falsehood
enhances God's truthfulness *NIG*
4:11 that righteousness **m** be credited to them. *AIT*
5: 7 for a good man someone **m** possibly dare
to die. *AIT*
5:20 so that the trespass **m** increase. *AIT*
5:21 so also grace **m** reign through righteousness *AIT*
6: 6 so that the body of sin **m** be done away with, *AIT*
7: 4 that you **m** belong to another, *AIT*
7: 4 in order that we **m** bear fruit to God. *AIT*
7:13 But in order that sin **m** be recognized as sin, *AIT*
7:13 commandment sin **m** become utterly sinful. *AIT*
8: 4 requirements of the law **m** be fully met in us, *AIT*
8:29 that he **m** be the firstborn among many *AIT*
9:11 that God's purpose in election **m** stand: *AIT*
9:17 that I **m** display my power in you and *AIT*
9:17 in you and that my name **m** be proclaimed *AIT*
14: 9 and returned to life so that *he* **m** be the Lord *AIT*
15: 4 of the Scriptures we **m** have hope. *AIT*
15:16 Gentiles **m** become an offering acceptable *AIT*
16:26 that all nations **m** believe and obey him— *NIG*
1Co 2: 5 that your faith **m** not rest on men's wisdom, *AIT*
4: 8 so that we **m** be kings with you! *AIT*
9:22 that by all possible means I **m** save some. *AIT*
2Co 1: 9 that *we* **m** not rely on ourselves but on God, *AIT*
1:15 so that *you* **m** benefit twice. *AIT*
2:11 in order that Satan **m** not outwit *us*. *AIT*
5:21 that in him we **m** become the righteousness *AIT*
8: 9 you through his poverty **m** become rich. *AIT*
8:13 Our desire is not that others **m** be relieved *NIG*
8:13 but that there **m** be equality. *NIG*
11: 2 I **m** present you as a pure virgin to him. *AIT*
Gal 1:16 so that I **m** preach him among the Gentiles, *AIT*

Gal 2: 5 the truth of the gospel *m* **remain** with you.   AIT
2:19 the law I died to the law so that *I m* **live**   AIT
3:14 that the blessing given to Abraham *m* **come**   AIT
3:14 so that by faith *we m* **receive** the promise of   AIT
3:22 *m* **be given** to those who believe.   AIT
3:24 to lead us to Christ that *we m* **justified**   AIT
4: 5 that *we m* **receive** the full rights of sons.   AIT
Eph 1:12 *m* **be** for the praise of his glory.   AIT
2: 7 in order that in the coming ages *he m* **show**   AIT
Col 1:11 with all power according to his glorious *m*   3197
1:18 that in everything *he m* **have** the supremacy.   AIT
1Th 3: 5 the tempter *m* **have** tempted you   NIG
3: 5 and our efforts *m* **have been** useless.   AIT
2Th 2:14 that you *m* **share** in the glory   NIG
1Ti 1:16 Christ Jesus *m* **display** his unlimited
    patience as an example   AIT
6:16 To him be honor and *m* **forever.**   3197
2Ti 4:17 the message *m* **be fully** proclaimed   AIT
4:17 and all the Gentiles *m* **hear** it.   AIT
Tit 1: 5 that *you m* **straighten out** what was left
    unfinished   AIT
3: 7 *we m* **become** heirs having the hope   AIT
Phm 1:15 a little while was that *you m* **have** him **back**   AIT
Heb 2: 9 so that by the grace of God *he m* **taste** death   AIT
2:14 by his death *he m* **destroy** him who holds   AIT
2:17 in order that *he m* **become** a merciful   AIT
2:17 that *he m* **make atonement for** the sins of   AIT
7: 9 One *m* even **say** that Levi,   2229+3306+6055
11:35 so that *they m* **gain** a better resurrection.   AIT
Jas 1:18 that *we m* **be** a kind of firstfruits of all   AIT
1Pe 2:24 *m* **die** to sins and **live** for righteousness   AIT
4: 6 so that *they m* **be judged** according to men   AIT
1Jn 3: 5 so that *he m* **take away** our sins.   AIT
4: 9 and only Son into the world that *we m* **live**   AIT
Rev 12: 4 so that *he m* **devour** her child   AIT
12: 6 *she m* **be taken care of** for 1,260 days.   AIT
12:14 that *she m* **fly** to the place prepared for her   AIT

MIGHTIER (2) [MIGHT]

Ps 93: 4 **M** than the thunder of the great waters,   NIH
93: 4 **m** than the breakers of the sea—   129

MIGHTIEST (1) [MIGHT]

Da 11:39 He will attack the **m fortresses** with   4448+5057

MIGHTILY (1) [MIGHT]

Jer 25:30 from his holy dwelling and **roar m**   8613+8613

MIGHTY (187) [MIGHT]

Ge 10: 8 who grew to be a **m warrior** on the earth.   1475
10: 9 He was a **m** hunter before the LORD;   1475
10: 9 Like Nimrod, a **m** hunter before the LORD."   1475
23: 6 You are a **m** prince among us.   466
49:24 because of the hand of the **M One** of Jacob.   51
Ex 3:19 unless a **m** hand compels him.   2617
6: 1 Because of my **m** hand he will let them go;   2617
6: 1 of my **m** hand he will drive them out   2617
6: 6 with an outstretched arm and with **m** acts   1524
7: 4 on Egypt and with **m** acts of judgment   1524
13: 3 LORD brought you out of it with a **m** hand.   2620
13: 9 out of Egypt with his **m** hand.   2617
13:14 'With a **m** hand the LORD brought us out   2620
13:16 of Egypt with his **m** hand.'"   2620
15:10 They sank like lead in the **m** waters.   129
32:11 of Egypt with great power and a **m** hand?   2617
Dt 3:24 the deeds and **m works** you do?   1476
4:34 by a **m** hand and an outstretched arm,   2617
5:15 with a **m** hand and an outstretched arm.   2617
6:21 out of Egypt with a **m** hand.   2617
7: 8 a **m** hand and redeemed you from the land   2617
7:19 the **m** hand and outstretched arm,   2617
9:26 and brought out of Egypt with a **m** hand.   2617
10:17 the great God, **m** and awesome,   1475
11: 2 his majesty, his **m** hand, his outstretched   2617
26: 8 with a **m** hand and an outstretched arm,   2617
34:12 For no one has ever shown the **m** power   2617
Jos 22:22 "The **M One,** God, the LORD!   446
22:22 The **M One,** God, the LORD!   446
Jdg 5:13 of the LORD came to me with the **m.**   1475
5:22 galloping, galloping go his **m** steeds.   52
5:23 to help the LORD against the **m.'**   1475
6:12 "The LORD is with you, **m** warrior."   2657
11: 1 Jephthah the Gileadite was a **m warrior.**
  1475+2657
1Sa 4: 8 from the hand of these **m** gods?   129
14:52 and whenever Saul saw a **m** or brave man,   1475
2Sa 1:19 How the **m** have fallen!   1475
1:21 For there the shield of the **m** was defiled,   1475
1:22 from the flesh of the **m,**   1475
1:25 "How the **m** have fallen in battle!   1475
1:27 "How the **m** have fallen!   1475
20: 7 the **m** warriors went out under the
    command of Abishai.   1475
23: 8 These are the names of David's **m men:**   1475
23: 9 As one of the three **m men,**   1475
23:16 So the three **m men** broke through   1475
23:17 Such were the exploits of the three **m men.**   1475
23:22 he too was as famous as the three **m men.**   1475
1Ki 8:42 of your great name and your **m** hand   2617
2Ki 17:36 with power and outstretched arm,   1524
1Ch 1:10 who grew to be a **m** warrior on earth.   1475
11:10 These were the chiefs of David's **m men**—   1475
11:11 this is the list of David's **m men.**   1475
11:12 the Ahohite, one of the three **m men.**   1475

1Ch 11:19 Such were the exploits of the three **m men.**   1475
11:24 he too was as famous as the three **m men.**   1475
11:26 The **m men** were: 1475+2657
12: 4 a **m man** among the Thirty,   1475
27: 6 This was the Benaiah who was a **m man**   1475
28: 1 the **m men** and all the brave warriors.   1475
29:24 All the officers and **m men,**   1475
2Ch 6:32 of your great name and your **m** hand   2617
14:11 to help the powerless against the **m.**   8041
16: 8 Libyans a **m** army with great numbers   4200+8044
Ne 1:10 by your great strength and your **m** hand.   2617
9:11 like a stone into **m** waters.   6434
9:32 O our God, the great, **m** and awesome God,   1475
Job 1:19 when suddenly a **m** wind swept in from   1524
9:19 If it is a matter of strength, he is **m!**   579
12:21 on nobles and disarms the **m.**   693
24:22 But God drags away the **m** by his power;   52
34:17 Will you condemn the just and **m One?**   3888
34:20 the **m** are removed without human hand.   52
34:24 Without inquiry he shatters the **m** and sets   3888
36: 5 "God is **m,** but does not despise men;   3888
36: 5 he is **m,** and firm in his purpose.   3888
36:19 or even all your **m** efforts sustain you   3946
37: 6 and to the rain shower, 'Be a **m** downpour.'   6437
41:25 When he rises up, the **m** are terrified;   446
Ps 24: 8 The LORD strong and **m,**   1475
24: 8 the LORD **m** in battle.   1475
29: 1 Ascribe to the LORD, O **m ones,**   446+1201
29: 3 the LORD thunders over the **m** waters.   8041
32: 6 the **m** waters rise, they will not reach him.   8041
36: 6 Your righteousness is like the **m** mountains,   446
45: 3 Gird your sword upon your side, O **m** one;   1475
50: 1 The **M One,** God, the LORD,   446
52: 1 Why do you boast of evil, you **m man?**   1475
62: 7 he is my **m** rock, my refuge.   6437
68:33 who thunders with **m** voice.   6437
71:16 I will come and proclaim your **m** acts,   1476
77:12 and consider all your **m deeds.**   6613
77:15 With your **m** arm you redeemed your people,   NIH
77:19 your way through the **m** waters,   8041
80:10 the **m** cedars with its branches.   446
89: 8 You are **m,** O LORD,   2886
93: 4 the LORD on high is **m.**   129
99: 4 The King is **m,** he loves justice—   6437
103:20 you **m ones** who do his bidding,   1475+3946
106: 2 Who can proclaim the **m** acts of   1476
106: 8 to make his **m** power known.   1476
107:23 they were merchants on the **m** waters.   8041
110: 2 The LORD will extend your **m** scepter   6437
112: 2 His children will be **m** in the land;   1475
118:15 The LORD's right hand has done **m things!**   2657
118:16 the LORD's right hand has done **m things!"**   2657
132: 2 and made a vow to the **M One** of Jacob.   51
132: 5 a dwelling for the **M One** of Jacob."   51
135:10 down many nations and killed **m** kings—   6786
136:12 with a **m** hand and outstretched arm;   2617
136:18 killed **m** kings—His love endures forever.   129
144: 7 and rescue me from the **m** waters,   8041
145: 4 they will tell of your **m** acts.   1476
145:12 that all men may know of your **m** acts and   1476
147: 5 Great is our Lord and **m** in power;   8041
150: 1 praise him in his **m** heavens.   6437
Pr 7:26 her slain are a **m** throng.   6786
21:22 of the **m** and pulls down the stronghold   1475
30:30 **m** among beasts, who retreats   1475
SS 8: 6 It burns like blazing fire, like a **m flame.**   8928
Isa 1:24 the LORD Almighty, the **M One** of Israel,   51
1:31 The **m man** will become tinder and his work   2891
8: 7 to bring against them the **m** floodwaters of   6786
9: 6 **M** God, Everlasting Father, Prince of Peace.   1475
10:13 like a **m** one I subdued their kings.   52
10:21 remnant of Jacob will return to the **M** God.   1475
10:34 Lebanon will fall before the **M One.**   129
22:17 O you **m** man.   1505
33:21 There the LORD will be our **M One.**   129
33:21 no **m** ship will sail them.   129
40:26 Because of his great power and **m** strength,   579
42:13 The LORD will march out like a **m man,**   1475
43:16 a path through the **m** waters,   6434
49:26 your Redeemer, the **M One** of Jacob."   51
56:11 They are dogs with **m** appetites;   6434
60:16 your Redeemer, the **M One** of Jacob.   51
60:22 the smallest a **m** nation.   6786
62: 8 by his right hand and by his **m** arm: 6437
63: 1 speaking in righteousness, **m** to save.   8041
Jer 5:16 all of them are **m** warriors.   1475
10: 6 you are great, and your name is **m** in power.   1524
11:16 But with the roar of a **m** storm he will set it   1524
20:11 But the LORD is with me like a **m** warrior;   1475
21: 5 a **m** arm in anger and fury and great wrath.   2617
25:32 a **m** storm is rising from the ends of   1524
32:19 and **m** are your deeds.   8041
32:21 by a **m** hand and an outstretched arm and   2617
48:17 say, 'How broken is the **m** scepter,   6437
Eze 7:24 I will put an end to the pride of the **m,**   6434
17:17 with his **m** army and great horde will be   1524
20:33 with a **m** hand and an outstretched arm and   2617
20:34 with a **m** hand and an outstretched arm and   2617
32:12 to fall by the swords of **m men**—   1475
32:18 both her and the daughters of **m** nations,   129
32:21 the grave the **m** leaders will say of Egypt   446
38:15 a great horde, a **m** army.   8041
39:18 of **m** men and drink the blood of the princes   1475
39:20 **m** men and soldiers of every kind,'   1475
Da 2:10 No king, however great and **m,**   10718
3: 3 how **m** his wonders!   10768
4: 30 by my **m** power and for the glory   10278

Da 8:24 the **m** *men* and the holy people.   6786
9:15 a **m** hand and who made for yourself a name   2617
11: 3 Then a **m** king will appear,   1475
Hos 8:10 under the oppression of the **m** king.   8569
Joel 2: 2 the mountains a large and **m** army comes,   6786
2: 5 like a **m** army drawn up for battle.   6786
2:11 and **m** are those who obey his command.   6786
Zep 3:17 your God is with you, he is **m** to save.   1475
Zec 4: 7 "What are you, O **m** mountain?   1524
10: 5 Together they will be like **m** men trampling   1475
10: 7 The Ephraimites will become like **m** men,   1475
Mt 26:64 the right hand *of* the **M** One and coming on   1539
Mk 14:62 the right hand *of* the **M** One and coming on   1539
Lk 1:49 the **M** One has done great things for me—   1543
1:51 He has performed **m** deeds with his arm;   3197
22:69 be seated at the right hand *of* the **M** One.   1539
Ac 13:17 in Egypt, with **m** power he led them out of   5734
Eph 1:19 power is like the working *of* his **m** strength,   2709
6:10 be strong in the Lord and in his **m** power.   2709
1Pe 5: 6 therefore, under God's **m** hand,   3193
Rev 5: 2 I saw a **m** angel proclaiming in a loud voice,   2708
6:15 the princes, the generals, the rich, the **m,**   2708
10: 1 Then I saw another **m** angel coming down   2708
18: 2 With a **m** voice he shouted: "Fallen!   2708
18: 8 for **m** is the Lord God who judges her.   2708
18:21 Then a **m** angel picked up a boulder the size   2708
19:18 and **m** men, of horses and their riders,   2708

MIGRATION (1)

Jer 8: 7 and the thrush observe the time of their **m.**   995

MIGRON (2)

1Sa 14: 2 of Gibeah under a pomegranate tree in **M.**   4491
Isa 10:28 They enter Aiath; they pass through **M;**   4491

MIJAMIN (4)

1Ch 24: 9 the fifth to Malkijah, the sixth to **M,**   4785
Ezr 10:25 Ramiah, Izziah, Malkijah, **M,** Eleazar,   4785
Ne 10: 7 Meshullam, Abijah, **M,**   4785
12: 5 **M,** Moadiah, Bilgah,   4785

MIKLOTH (4)

1Ch 8:32 and **M,** who was the father of Shimeah.   5235
9:37 Gedor, Ahio, Zechariah and **M.**   5235
9:38 **M** was the father of Shimeam.   5235
27: 4 **M** was the leader of his division.   5235

MIKNEIAH (2)

1Ch 15:18 **M,** Obed-Edom and Jeiel, the gatekeepers.   5240
15:21 Eliphelehu, **M,** Obed-Edom,   5240

MIKTAM (6)

Ps 16: T A **m** of David.   4846
56: T "A Dove on Distant Oaks." Of David. A **m.**   4846
57: T "Do Not Destroy." Of David. A **m.**   4846
58: T "Do Not Destroy." Of David. A **m.**   4846
59: T "Do Not Destroy." Of David. A **m.**   4846
60: T "The Lily of the Covenant." A **m** of David.   4846

MILALAI (1)

Ne 12:36 Shemaiah, Azarel, **M,** Gilalai, Maai,   4912

MILCAH (11)

Ge 11:29 and the name of Nahor's wife was **M;**   4894
11:29 the father of both **M** and Iscah.   4894
22:20 "**M** is also a mother;   4894
22:23 **M** bore these eight sons   4894
24:15 She was the daughter of Bethuel son of **M,**   4894
24:24 Bethuel, the son that **M** bore to Nahor."   4894
24:47 whom **M** bore to him.'   4894
Nu 26:33 Noah, Hoglah, **M** and Tirzah.)   4894
27: 1 Noah, Hoglah, **M** and Tirzah.   4894
36:11 Mahlah, Tirzah, Hoglah, **M** and Noah—   4894
Jos 17: 3 Noah, Hoglah, **M** and Tirzah.   4894

MILCH (KJV) See COWS THAT HAVE CALVED, FEMALE

MILDEW (30)

Lev 13:47 "If any clothing is contaminated with **m**—   7669
13:49 it is a **spreading m** and must be shown to   7669
13:50 The priest is to examine the **m** and isolate   5596
13:51 and if the **m** has spread in the clothing,   5596
13:51 it is a destructive **m;** the article is unclean.   7669
13:52 because the **m** is destructive;   7669
13:53 the **m** has not spread in the clothing,   5596
13:55 and if the **m** has not changed its appearance,   5596
13:55 has affected one side or the other.   7076
13:56 the **m** has faded after the article has been   5596
13:57 and whatever has the **m** must be burned   5596
13:58 that has been washed and is rid of the **m,**   5596
13:59 concerning contamination by **m** in woolen   7669
14:34 I put a **spreading m** in a house in that land,   5596+7669
14:35 'I have seen something that looks like **m**   5596
14:36 before he goes in to examine the **m.**   5596
14:37 He is to examine the **m** on the walls,   5596
14:39 If the **m** has spread on the walls,   5596
14:43 "If the **m** reappears in the house after   5596
14:44 if the **m** has spread in the house,   5596

Lev	14:44	it is a destructive **m**; the house is unclean.	7669
	14:48	the priest comes to examine it and the **m** has	5596
	14:48	because the **m** is gone.	5596
	14:55	for **m** *in* clothing or in a house,	7669
	14:57	**infectious skin diseases and m.**	7669
Dt	28:22	with blight and **m**,	3766
1Ki	8:37	or blight or **m**, locusts or grasshoppers,	3766
2Ch	6:28	or blight or **m**, locusts or grasshoppers,	3766
Am	4: 9	I struck them with blight and **m.**	3766
Hag	2:17	**m** and hail, yet you did not turn to me,'	3766

MILE (1) [MILES]

Mt	5:41	If someone forces you to go one **m**,	*3627*

MILES (4) [MILE]

Mt	5:41	to go one mile, go with him two **m.**	NIG
Lk	24:13	about **seven m** from Jerusalem.	*2008+5084*
Jn	6:19	they had rowed **three or three and**	
		a half m,	*1633+2445+4297+5084+5558*
	11:18	Bethany was less than **two m** from	*1278+5084*

MILETUS (3)

Ac	20:15	and on the following day arrived at **M.**	*3626*
	20:17	From **M**, Paul sent to Ephesus for the elders	*3626*
2Ti	4:20	and I left Trophimus sick in **M.**	*3626*

MILITARY (16)

Jos	5: 4	all the men of **m age**—	4878
	5: 6	of **m age** when they left Egypt had died,	4878
2Sa	2: 8	**led** Israel **on** their **m campaigns.**	995+2256+3655
	20: 8	Joab was wearing his **m tunic**,	4230+4496
1Ki	22:45	the things he achieved and *his* **m exploits**,	4309
2Ki	14:28	all he did, and his **m achievements**,	4309
	18:20	You say you have strategy and **m strength**—	4878
1Ch	5:18	men **ready for m service**—	3655+7372
	11: 2	**led** Israel **on** their **m campaigns.**	995+2256+3655
2Ch	25: 5	there were three hundred thousand men	
		ready for m service,	3655+7372
	32: 3	he consulted with his officials and **m staff**	1475
	32: 6	He appointed **m** officers over the people	4878
	33:14	He stationed **m** commanders in all	2657
Est	1: 3	The **m leaders** *of* Persia and Media,	2657
Isa	36: 5	You say you have strategy and **m strength**—	4878
Mk	6:21	*for* his high officials and **m commanders**	5941

MILK (48)

Ge	18: 8	then brought some curds and **m** and the calf	2692
	49:12	his teeth whiter than **m.**	2692
Ex	3: 8	a land flowing with **m** and honey—	2692
	3:17	a land flowing with **m** and honey.'	2692
	13: 5	a land flowing with **m** and honey—	2692
	23:19	Do not cook a young goat in its mother's **m.**	2692
	33: 3	up to the land flowing with **m** and honey.	2692
	34:26	Do not cook a young goat in its mother's **m.**	2692
Lev	20:24	a land flowing with **m** and honey.'	2692
Nu	13:27	and it does flow with **m** and honey!	2692
	14: 8	a land flowing with **m** and honey,	2692
	16:13	up out of a land flowing with **m** and honey	2692
	16:14	with and honey or given us an inheritance	2692
Dt	6: 3	in a land flowing with **m** and honey,	2692
	11: 9	a land flowing with **m** and honey,	2692
	14:21	Do not cook a young goat in its mother's **m.**	2692
	26: 9	a land flowing with **m** and honey;	2692
	26:15	a land flowing with **m** and honey."	2692
	27: 3	a land flowing with **m** and honey,	2692
	31:20	into the land flowing with **m** and honey,	2692
	32:14	with curds and **m** *from* herd and flock and	2692
Jos	5: 6	a land flowing with **m** and honey.	2692
Jdg	4:19	She opened a skin of **m**, gave him a drink,	2692
	5:25	He asked for water, and she gave him **m**;	2692
	5:25	for nobles she brought him **curdled m.**	2772
2Sa	17:29	from cows' **m** for David and his people	NIH
Job	10:10	not pour me out like **m** and curdle me	2692
Pr	27:27	of goats' **m** to feed you and your family and	2692
	30:33	For as churning the **m** produces butter,	2692
SS	4:11	**m** and honey are under your tongue.	2692
	5: 1	I have drunk my wine and my **m.**	2692
	5:12	washed in **m**, mounted like jewels.	2692
Isa	7:22	of the abundance of the **m** they give,	2692
	28: 9	To children weaned from their **m**,	2692
	55: 1	and **m** without money and without cost.	2692
	60:16	You will drink the **m** *of* nations and	2692
Jer	11: 5	a land flowing with **m** and honey'—	2692
	32:22	a land flowing with **m** and honey.	2692
La	4: 7	and whiter than **m**,	2692
Eze	20: 6	a land flowing with **m** and honey,	2692
	20:15	a land flowing with **m** and honey,	2692
	25: 4	they will eat your fruit and drink your **m.**	2692
Joel	3:18	and the hills will flow with **m**;	2692
1Co	3: 2	I gave you **m**, not solid food,	1128
	9: 7	a flock and does not drink of the **m?**	1128
Heb	5:12	You need **m**, not solid food!	1128
	5:13	Anyone who lives on **m**, being still an infant	1128
1Pe	2: 2	Like newborn babies, crave pure spiritual **m**	1128

MILL (3) [HANDMILL]

Ex	11: 5	who is at her **hand m**,	8160
Joel	1:18	The herds **m about** because they have no	1003
Mt	24:41	women will be grinding with a **hand m**;	3685

MILLET (1)

Eze	4: 9	beans and lentils, **m** and spelt;	1893

MILLION (3)

1Ch	21: 5	In all Israel there were *one* **m** one hundred	
		thousand men who could handle	547+547
	22:14	talents of gold, a **m** talents of silver,	547+547
Rev	9:16	mounted troops was **two hundred m.**	*1490+3689*

MILLO   See BETH MILLO

MILLSTONE (8) [STONE]

Jdg	9:53	a woman dropped an upper **m** on his head	7115
2Sa	11:21	Didn't a woman throw an upper **m** on him	7115
Job	41:24	His chest is hard as rock, hard as a lower **m.**	7115
Mt	18: 6	better for him to have a **large m** hung	3685+3948
Mk	9:42	to be thrown into the sea with a large **m** tied	3685
Lk	17: 2	to be thrown into the sea with a **m** tied	3345+3683
Rev	18:21	A large **m** and threw it into the sea, and said:	3684
	18:22	of a **m** will never be heard in you again.	3685

MILLSTONES (4) [STONE]

Dt	24: 6	Do not take a **pair of m**—	8160
Isa	47: 2	Take **m** and grind flour; take off your veil.	8160
Jer	25:10	the sound of **m** and the light of the lamp.	8160
La	5:13	Young men toil at the **m**;	3218

MINA (5) [MINAS]

Eze	45:12	Twenty shekels plus twenty-five shekels	
		plus fifteen shekels equal one **m.**	4949
Lk	19:16	'Sir, your **m** has earned ten more.'	3641
	19:18	'Sir, your **m** has earned five more.'	3641
	19:20	'Sir, here is your **m**;	3641
	19:24	'Take his **m** away from him and give it to	3641

MINAS (6) [MINA]

1Ki	10:17	with three **m** of gold in each shield.	4949
Ezr	2:69	5,000 **m** of gold and 100 priestly garments.	4949
Ne	7:71	drachmas of gold and 2,200 **m** of silver.	4949
	7:72	2,000 **m** of silver and 67 garments for	4949
Lk	19:13	of his servants and gave them ten **m.**	3641
	19:24	and give it to the one who has ten **m.'**	3641

MINCING (1)

Isa	3:16	**tripping along with m** steps,	2143+2256+3262

MIND (121) [DOUBLE-MINDED, LIKE-MINDED, MINDED, MINDFUL, MINDS]

Ge	37:11	his father **kept** the matter **in m.**	9068
	41: 8	In the morning his **m** was troubled,	8120
	45:20	Never *m* about your belongings,	2571
Ex	16:29	**Bear in m** that the LORD has given you	8011
Nu	23:19	that *he should* **change** *his* **m.**	5714
Dt	28:28	blindness and confusion of **m.**	4222
	28:65	the LORD will give you an anxious **m**,	4213
	29: 4	a **m** that understands or eyes that see or ears	4213
1Sa	2:35	according to what is in my heart and **m.**	5883
	14: 7	"Do all that you have in **m**,"	4222
	15:29	of Israel does not lie or **change** *his* **m**;	5714
	15:29	that *he should* **change** *his* **m.**"	5714
2Sa	7: 3	"Whatever you have in **m**,	4222
	19:19	May the king put it out of his **m.**	4213
1Ki	10: 2	with him about all that she had on her **m.**	4222
2Ki	10:30	to the house of Ahab all I had in **m** to do,	4222
	24: 1	But then *he* **changed** *his* **m** and rebelled	8740
1Ch	12:38	the rest of the Israelites were also of one **m**	4213
	17: 2	"Whatever you have in **m**, do it,	4222
	28: 9	and with a willing **m**,	5883
	28:12	that the Spirit had put in his **m** for the courts	NIH
2Ch	7:11	in **m** to do in the temple of the LORD and	4213
	9: 1	with him about all she had on her **m**,	4222
	30:12	to give them unity of **m** to carry out what	4213
Ne	5: 7	I pondered them in my **m** and then accused	4213
Job	10:13	and I know that this was **in** your **m**:	6640
	12: 3	But I have a **m** as well as you;	4222
	38:36	or gave understanding to the **m?**	8498
Ps	26: 2	and try me, examine my heart and my **m**;	4213
	64: 6	Surely the heart and **m** of man are cunning.	7931
	83: 5	*With one* **m** they plot together;	4213
	110: 4	LORD has sworn and *will* not **change** *his* **m**:	5714
Pr	23:33	and your **imagine** confusing things.	4213
Ecc	2: 3	my **m** still guiding me with wisdom.	4213
	2:23	even at night his **m** does not rest.	4213
	7:25	So I turned my **m** to understand,	4213
	8: 9	as I applied my **m** to everything done under	4213
	8:16	When I applied my **m** to know wisdom and	4213
Isa	10: 7	this is not what he **has in m**;	3108+4222
	26: 3	in perfect peace him whose **m** is steadfast,	3671
	32: 4	The **m** of the rash will know	4222
	32: 6	fool speaks folly, his **m** is busy with evil:	4213
	40:13	Who has understood the **m** of the LORD,	8120
	46: 8	"Remember this, **fix it in m**, take it to heart,	899
	65:17	nor will they come to **m.**	4213
Jer	7:31	nor did it enter my **m.**	4213
	11:20	and test the heart and **m**,	4000
	17:10	the heart and examine the **m**,	4000
	19: 5	nor did it enter my **m.**	4213
	20:12	the righteous and probe the heart and **m**,	4000
	32:35	nor did it enter my **m**,	4213
La	3:21	Yet this I **call to m** and	448+4213+8740
Eze	11: 5	but I know what is going through your **m.**	8120
	20:32	But what you have in **m** will never happen.	8120
	21:24	you people *have* **brought to m** your guilt	2349

Eze	38:10	On that day thoughts will come into your **m**	4222
Da	2: 1	his **m** was troubled and he could not sleep.	8120
	2:28	and the visions that passed through your **m**	10646
	2:29	O king, your **m** turned to things to come,	10669
	2:30	that you may understand what went through	
		your **m.**	10381+10669
	4: 5	that passed through my **m** terrified me.	10646
	4:16	Let his **m** be changed from that of a man	10381
	4:16	let him be given the **m** *of* an animal,	10381
	5:12	keen **m** and knowledge and understanding,	10658
	5:21	from people and given the **m** of an animal;	10381
	7: 1	through his **m** as he was lying on his bed.	10646
	7:15	that passed through my **m** disturbed me.	10646
	10:12	that you set your **m** to gain understanding	4213
Mt	1:19	he **had** in **m** to divorce her quietly.	1089
	16:23	you **do** not **have** in **m** the things of God,	5858
	21:29	but later **he changed** *his* **m** and went.	3564
	22:37	and with all your soul and with all your **m.'**	1379
Mk	3:21	they said, "He is **out of** *his* **m.**"	2014
	5:15	sitting there, dressed and in *his* **right m**;	5404
	8:33	"You **do** not **have** in **m** the things of God,	5858
	12:30	with all your **m** and with all your strength.'	1379
Lk	8:35	dressed and in *his* **right m**;	5404
	10:27	with all your strength and with all your **m'**;	1379
	21:14	But **make up** your **m** not to worry	
		beforehand	1877+2840+3836+5502
Jn	6: 6	*already had* in **m** what he was going to do.	3857
	15:18	**keep** in **m** that it hated me first.	1182
Ac	4:32	All the believers were one in heart and **m.**	6034
	12:15	"You're **out of** *your* **m**," they told her.	3419
	26:24	"You **are out of** *your* **m**, Paul!"	3419
Ro	1:28	he gave them over to a depraved **m**,	3808
	7:23	the law of my **m** and making me a prisoner	3808
	7:25	I myself *in* my **m** am a slave to God's law,	3808
	8: 6	The **m** of sinful man is death,	5859
	8: 6	**m** controlled by the Spirit is life and peace;	5859
	8: 7	the sinful **m** is hostile to God.	5859
	8:27	knows the **m** of the Spirit,	5859
	11:34	"Who has known the **m** of the Lord?	3808
	12: 2	be transformed by the renewing *of* your **m.**	3808
	14: 5	be fully convinced in his own **m.**	3808
	14:13	**make up** *your* **m** not to put any stumbling	3212
1Co	1:10	and that you may be perfectly united in **m**	3808
	2: 9	no **m** has conceived what God has prepared	2840
	2:16	"For who has known the **m** of the Lord	3808
	2:16	But we have the **m** of Christ.	3808
	7:37	in his own **m**, who is under no compulsion	2840
	7:37	and who has made up his **m** not to marry	2840
	14:14	my spirit prays, but my **m** is unfruitful.	3808
	14:15	but I will also pray *with* my **m**;	3808
	14:15	but I will also sing *with* my **m.**	3808
	14:23	not say that *you are* **out of** *your* **m?**	3419
2Co	2: 1	So I **made up** my **m** that I would not make	3212
	2:13	I still had no peace *of* **m**,	4460
	5:13	If *we are* **out of** our **m**, it is for the sake of	
		God;	2014
	5:13	if *we are* **in** our **right m**, it is for you.	5404
	11:23	(I am **out of** *my* **m** to talk like this.)	4196
	13:11	listen to my appeal, *be of* one **m**,	5858
Eph	6:18	With this in **m**, be alert and always keep on	NIG
Php	3:19	Their **m** is on earthly things.	5858
Col	2:18	and his unspiritual **m** puffs him up	3808
1Th	4:11	*to* **m** your own **business** and to work	4556
2Th	1:11	With this in **m**, we constantly pray for you,	NIG
1Ti	6: 5	constant friction between men of corrupt **m**,	3808
Heb	7:21	Lord has sworn and *will* not **change** *his* **m.**	3564
	12:17	He could bring about no **change of m**,	3567
2Pe	3:15	**Bear in m** that our Lord's patience means	
		salvation,	2451
Rev	17: 9	"This calls for a **m** with wisdom.	3808

MINDED (1) [MIND]

1Pe	4: 7	Therefore *be* **clear m** and self-controlled	5404

MINDFUL (3) [MIND]

Ps	8: 4	what is man that *you are* **m** of him,	2349
Lk	1:48	for *he* has been **m** of the humble state	2098
Heb	2: 6	"What is man that *you* **are m** of him,	3630

MINDS (35) [MIND]

Ex	13:17	they might **change** *their* **m** and return	5714
	14: 5	and his officials changed their **m** about them	4222
Dt	11:18	these words of mine in your hearts and **m**;	5883
Job	17: 4	You have closed their **m** to understanding.	4213
Ps	7: 9	who searches **m** and hearts,	4000
	73: 7	the evil conceits of their **m** know no limits.	4222
Pr	12: 8	but men with warped **m** are despised.	4213
Isa	44:18	their **m** closed so they cannot understand.	4213
Jer	3:16	It will never enter their **m** or be remembered	4213
	14:14	idolatries and the delusions of their own **m.**	4213
	23:16	They speak visions from their own **m**,	4213
	23:26	the delusions of their own **m?**	4213
	31:33	"I will put my law in their **m** and write it	7931
	34:11	But afterward *they* **changed** *their* **m**	8740
Lk	24:38	and why do doubts rise in your **m?**	2840
	24:45	Then he opened their **m** so they could	3808
Ac	14: 2	and poisoned their **m** against the brothers.	6034
	15:24	troubling your **m** by what they said.	6034
	28: 6	**changed** *their* **m** and said he was a god.	3554
Ro	8: 5	to the sinful nature *have* their **m set on** what	5858
	8: 5	with the Spirit have their **m set on** what	NIG
	16:18	and flattery they deceive the **m** of naive	2840
2Co	3:14	But their **m** were made dull,	3784
	4: 4	of this age has blinded the **m** of unbelievers,	3784
	11: 3	your **m** may somehow be led astray	3784

Eph	4:23	to be made new in the attitude *of* your **m**;	3808
Php	4: 7	will guard your hearts and your **m**	3784
Col	1:21	*in* your **m** because of your evil behavior.	1379
	3: 2	**Set** *your* **m** on things above, not on	5858
2Ti	3: 8	men of depraved **m**, who,	3808
Tit	1:15	both their **m** and consciences are corrupted.	3808
Heb	8:10	I will put my laws in their **m** and write them	1379
	10:16	and I will write them on their **m**."	1379
1Pe	1:13	Therefore, prepare your **m** for action;	1379
Rev	2:23	that I am he who searches hearts and **m**,	3752

MINE (77) [l]

Ge	13: 8	or between your herdsmen and **m**,	3276
	24: 8	you will be released from this oath of **m**.	3276
	29:15	"Just because you are a relative of **m**,	3276
	31:37	Put it here in front of your relatives and **m**,	3276
	31:43	All you see is **m**.	3276+4200
	31:43	about these daughters of **m**,	3276
	37: 7	while your sheaves gathered around **m**	3276
	48: 5	to you here will be reckoned as **m**;	3276+4200
	48: 5	Ephraim and Manasseh will be **m**,	3276+4200
	48: 5	just as Reuben and Simeon are **m**.	NIH
Ex	10: 1	these miraculous signs of **m** among them	3276
	19: 5	Although the whole earth is **m**,	3276
	22: 9	about which somebody says, 'This is **m**,'	2085
Lev	25:23	the land is **m** and you are but aliens	3276
Nu	3:12	The Levites are **m**,	3276+4200
	3:13	for all the firstborn are **m**.	3276+4200
	3:13	They are to be **m**.	3276+4200
	3:45	The Levites are to be **m**.	3276+4200
	8:14	and the Levites will be **m**.	3276+4200
	8:17	whether man or animal, is **m**.	3276+4200
Dt	11:18	Fix these words of **m** in your hearts	3276
	32:35	It is **m** to avenge; I will repay.	3276+4200
1Sa	22:23	the man who is seeking your life is seeking **m** also.	3276
2Sa	14:30	"Look, Joab's field is next to **m**,	3276
1Ki	2:15	he said, "the kingdom was **m**.	3276+4200
	3:22	The dead one is yours; the living one is **m**."	3276
	3:23	"Your son is dead and **m** is alive." "	3276
	8:59	And may these words of **m**,	3276
	20: 3	'Your silver and gold are **m**,	3276+4200
	20: 3	best of your wives and children are **m**.	3276+4200
Job	7:15	rather than this body of **m**.	3276
	15: 6	Your own mouth condemns you, not **m**;	638
	28: 1	"There is a **m** for silver and a place	4604
Ps	50:10	for every animal of the forest is **m**,	3276+4200
	50:11	and the creatures of the field are **m**.	3276+6643
	50:12	for the world is **m**, and all that is in it.	3276+4200
	59: 3	against me for no offense or sin of **m**,	3276
	60: 7	Gilead is **m**, and Manasseh is mine;	3276+4200
	60: 7	Gilead is mine, and Manasseh is **m**;	3276+4200
	108: 8	Gilead is **m**, Manasseh is mine;	3276+4200
	108: 8	Gilead is mine, Manasseh is **m**;	3276+4200
Pr	8:14	Counsel and sound judgment are **m**;	3276+4200
Ecc	7:15	In this meaningless life of **m** I have seen	3276
SS	2:16	My lover is **m** and I am his;	3276+4200
	6: 3	I am my lover's and my lover is **m**;	3276+4200
	8:12	my own vineyard is **m** to give;	3276+4200+8611
Isa	30: 1	who carry out plans that are not **m**,	4946+5761
	43: 1	by name; you are **m**.	3276+4200
Jer	44:28	in Egypt will know whose word will stand—**m** or theirs.	4946+5761
Eze	16: 8	and you became **m**.	3276+4200
	23: 4	They were **m** and gave birth to sons	3276+4200
	23: 5	in prostitution while she was still **m**;	3276+9393
	29: 3	You say, "The Nile is **m**;	3276+4200
	29: 9	" 'Because you said, "The Nile is **m**;	3276+4200
Mic	7: 1	What misery is **m**!	3276+4200
Hag	2: 8	'The silver is **m** and the gold is mine,'	3276+4200
	2: 8	'The silver is mine and the gold is **m**,'	3276+4200
Mal	3:17	"They will be **m**,"	3276+4200
Mt	7:24	everyone who hears these words *of* **m**	1609
	7:26	But everyone who hears these words *of* **m**	1609
	20:21	of these two sons *of* **m** may sit at your right	1609
	25:40	for one of the least of these brothers *of* **m**,	1609
Lk	11: 6	a friend *of* **m** on a journey has come to me,	1609
	15:24	this son *of* **m** was dead and is alive again;	1609
	19:27	*of* **m** who did not want me to be king	1609
	22:21	of him who is going to betray me is with **m**	1609
Jn	3:29	That joy is **m**, and it is now complete.	1847
	12:30	"This voice was for your benefit, not **m**.	1609
	16:14	from what is **m** and making it known	1847
	16:15	All that belongs to the Father is **m**.	1847
	16:15	from what is **m** and make it known to you.	1847
	17:10	All I have is yours, and all you have is **m**.	1847
Ac	20:34	hands of **m** have supplied my own needs	NIG
Ro	12:19	"It is **m** to avenge; I will repay,"	1609
1Co	5:12	**What business is it of m** to judge	1609+5515
2Co	11:10	of Achaia will stop this boasting of **m**.	1609+1650
Heb	10:30	we know him who said, "It is **m** to avenge;	1609

MINGLE (1) [MINGLED]

Ps	102: 9	For I eat ashes as my food and **m** my drink	5007

MINGLED (2) [MINGLE]

Ezr	9: 2	and *have* **m** the holy race with the peoples	6843
Ps	106:35	but *they* **m** with the nations	6843

MINIAMIN (2) [MINIAMIN'S]

2Ch	31:15	Eden, **M**, Jeshua, Shemaiah,	4975
Ne	12:41	Eliakim, Maaseiah, **M**, Micaiah, Elioenai,	4975

MINIAMIN'S (1) [MINIAMIN]

Ne	12:17	of **M** and of Moadiah's, Piltai;	4975

MINISH, MINISHED (KJV) See
DECREASED, REDUCE

MINISTER (40) [MINISTERED, MINISTERING, MINISTERS, MINISTRY]

Ex	28:43	or approach the altar to **m** in the Holy Place,	9250
	29:30	and comes to the Tent of Meeting to **m** in	9250
	30:20	to **m** by presenting an offering made to	9250
Nu	16: 9	and to stand before the community and **m**	9250
	16:37	when you and your sons **m** before the Tent	NIH
Dt	10: 8	the LORD to **m** and to pronounce blessings	9250
	18: 5	and **m** in the LORD's name always.	9250
	18: 7	*he may* **m** in the name of the LORD his God	9250
	21: 5	the LORD your God has chosen them to **m**	9250
1Sa	2:30	and your father's house would **m**	2143
	2:35	*he will* **m** before my anointed one always.	2143
1Ch	15: 2	the LORD and to **m** *before* him forever."	9250
	16: 4	He appointed some of the Levites *to* **m**	9250
	16:37	of the LORD to **m** there regularly,	9250
	16:38	and his sixty-eight associates to **m**	NIH
	23:13	to **m** *before* him and to pronounce blessings	9250
2Ch	29:11	to **m** before him and to burn incense."	9250
	31: 2	and fellowship offerings, to **m**,	9250
Ps	101: 6	he whose walk is blameless *will* **m** *to* me.	9250
	134: 1	the LORD who **m** by night in the house of	6641
	135: 2	you who **m** in the house of the LORD,	6641
Jer	33:22	the Levites *who* **m** before me as countless as	9250
Eze	40:46	near to the LORD to **m** *before* him."	9250
	42:14	behind the garments in which *they* **m**,	9250
	43:19	who come near to **m** *before* me,	9250
	44:15	are to come near to **m** *before* me;	9250
	44:16	they alone are to come near my table to **m**	9250
	44:27	into the inner court of the sanctuary to **m** in	9250
	45: 4	*who* **m** in the sanctuary and who draw near	9250
	45: 4	and who draw near to **m** *before* the LORD.	9250
	46:24	where *those who* **m** at the temple will cook	9250
Joel	1: 9	*those who* **m** *before* the LORD.	9250
	1:13	wail, *you who* **m** *before* the altar.	9250
	1:13	*you who* **m** *before* my God;	9250
	2:17	Let the priests, *who* **m** *before* the LORD,	9250
Ro	15:16	be a **m** of Christ Jesus to the Gentiles with	3313
Col	1: 7	who is a faithful **m** of Christ on our behalf,	1356
	4: 7	a faithful **m** and fellow servant in the Lord.	1356
1Ti	4: 6	you will be a good **m** of Christ Jesus,	1356
Heb	13:10	We have an altar from which those who **m**	3302

MINISTERED (3) [MINISTER]

1Sa	2:11	but the boy **m** before the LORD under Eli	9250
	3: 1	The boy Samuel **m** before the LORD	9250
1Ch	6:32	*They* **m** with music before the tabernacle,	9250

MINISTERING (23) [MINISTER]

Ex	35:19	the woven garments worn for **m** in	9250
	39: 1	woven garments for **m** in the sanctuary.	9250
	39:26	the hem of the robe to be worn for **m**,	9250
	39:41	and the woven garments worn for **m** in	9250
Nu	3:31	the articles of the sanctuary used in **m**,	9250
	4:12	are to take all the articles used for **m**	9250+9251
	4:14	on it all the utensils used *for* **m** at the altar,	9250
Dt	17:12	or for the priest who stands there to **m**	9250
Jdg	20:28	the son of Aaron, **m** before it.)	6641
1Sa	2:18	But Samuel *was* **m** before the LORD—	9250
1Ch	9:13	responsible for **m** *in* the house of God.	6275
	24: 3	for their appointed order of **m**.	6275
	24:19	of **m** when they entered the temple of	6275
	26:12	for **m** in the temple of the LORD,	9250
Ezr	2:63	a priest **m** with the Urim and Thummim.	6641
Ne	7:65	a priest **m** with the Urim and Thummim.	6641
	10:36	to the priests **m** there.	9250
	10:39	and where the **m** priests,	9250
	12:44	for Judah was pleased with the **m** priests	6641
Jer	33:21	the Levites who are priests **m** *before* me—	9250
Eze	44:17	not wear any woolen garment while **m** at	9250
	44:19	to take off the clothes they *have* been in **m**	9250
Heb	1:14	Are not all angels **m** spirits sent	3312

MINISTERS (9) [MINISTER]

Ex	28:35	Aaron must wear it when *he* **m**.	9250
2Ki	10:19	Baal, all his **m** and all his priests.	6268
	10:19	in order to destroy the **m** *of* Baal.	6268
	10:21	and all the **m** *of* Baal came;	6268
	10:22	"Bring robes for all the **m** *of* Baal."	6268
	10:23	Jehu said to the **m** of Baal,	6268
	10:23	only **m** of Baal."	6268
Isa	61: 6	you will be named **m** *of* our God.	9250
2Co	3: 6	He has made us competent as **m** of a new covenant—	1356

MINISTRATION (KJV) See
DISTRIBUTION, MINISTRY, SERVICE

MINISTRY (24) [MINISTER]

1Ch	25: 1	and Jeduthun for the **m** of prophesying,	6275
	25: 6	for the **m** *at* the house of God.	6275
Lk	3:23	about thirty years old when he began his **m**.	NIG
Ac	1:17	of our number and shared *in* this **m**."	1355
	1:25	to take over this apostolic **m**,	1355
	6: 2	to neglect the **m** of the word of God in order	NIG
	6: 4	to prayer and the **m** of the word."	1355
	8:21	You have no part or share in this **m**,	3364
	21:19	among the Gentiles through his **m**.	1355
Ro	11:13	to the Gentiles, I make much of my **m**	1355
2Co	3: 3	the result of our **m**, written not with ink	1354
	3: 7	Now if the **m** that brought death,	1355
	3: 8	the **m** of the Spirit be even more glorious?	1355
	3: 9	If the **m** that condemns men is glorious,	1355
	3: 9	how much more glorious is the **m**	1355
	4: 1	since through God's mercy we have this **m**,	1355
	5:18	to himself through Christ and gave us the **m**	1355
	6: 3	so that our **m** will not be discredited.	1355
Gal	2: 8	in the **m** of Peter as **an apostle** to the Jews	692
	2: 8	at work in my **m** as an apostle to the Gentiles	NIG
2Ti	4: 5	discharge all the duties of your **m**.	1355
	4:11	because he is helpful to me in my **m**.	1355
Heb	4: 5	But the **m** Jesus has received is as superior	3311
	9: 6	into the outer room to carry on their **m**.	3301

MINNI (1)

Jer	51:27	Ararat, **M** and Ashkenaz.	4973

MINNITH (2)

Jdg	11:33	from Aroer to the vicinity of **M**,	4976
Eze	27:17	they exchanged wheat from **M**	4976

MINSTREL (KJV) See HARPIST

MINT (2)

Mt	23:23	You give a tenth of your **spices—m**,	2455
Lk	11:42	because you give God a tenth of your **m**,	2455

MINUS (1)

2Co	11:24	from the Jews the forty lashes **m** one.	4123

MIPHKAD (KJV) See INSPECTION GATE

MIRACLE (5) [MIRACLES, MIRACULOUS, MIRACULOUSLY]

Ex	7: 9	'Perform a **m**,' then say to Aaron,	4603
Mk	9:39	"No one who does a **m** in my name can in	1539
Lk	23: 8	he hoped to see him perform some **m**.	4956
Jn	7:21	Jesus said to them, "I did one **m**,	2240
Ac	4:16	knows they have done an outstanding **m**,	4956

MIRACLES (37) [MIRACLE]

1Ch	16:12	Remember the wonders he has done, his **m**,	4603
Ne	9:17	the **m** you performed among them.	7098
Job	5: 9	**m** that cannot be counted.	7098
	9:10	**m** that cannot be counted.	7098
Ps	77:11	yes, I will remember your **m** of long ago.	7099
	77:14	You are the God who performs **m**;	7099
	78:12	He did **m** in the sight of their fathers in	7099
	105: 5	Remember the wonders he has done, his **m**,	4603
	106: 7	they gave no thought to your **m**;	7098
	106:22	**m** in the land of Ham and awesome deeds	7098
Mt	7:22	and perform many **m?'**	1539
	11:20	*of* his **m** had been performed,	1539
	11:21	If the **m** that were performed	1539
	11:23	If the **m** that were performed	1539
	13:58	not do many **m** there because of their lack	1539
	24:24	and perform great signs and **m** to deceive	5469
Mk	6: 2	that he even does **m!**	1539
	6: 5	He could not do any **m** there,	1539
	13:22	and perform signs and **m** to deceive	5469
Lk	10:13	For if the **m** that were performed	1539
	19:37	in loud voices for all the **m** they had seen:	1539
Jn	7: 3	so that your disciples may see the **m** you do.	2240
	10:25	**m** I do in my Father's name speak for me,	2240
	10:32	"I have shown you many great **m** from	2240
	10:38	believe the **m**, that you may know	2240
	14:11	on the evidence of the **m** themselves.	2240
	15:24	But now they have seen these **m**,	2240
Ac	2:22	a man accredited by God to you *by* **m**,	1539
	8:13	astonished by the great signs and **m** he saw.	1539
	19:11	God did extraordinary **m** through Paul,	1539
Ro	15:19	by the power *of* signs and **m**,	5469
1Co	12:28	third teachers, then **workers of m**,	1539
	12:29	Do all **work m?**	1539
2Co	12:12	that mark an apostle—signs, wonders and **m**	1539
Gal	3: 5	Does God give you his Spirit and work **m**	1539
2Th	2: 9	displayed in all kinds of counterfeit **m**,	1539
Heb	2: 4	by signs, wonders and various **m**,	1539

MIRACULOUS (61) [MIRACLE]

Ex	4: 8	or pay attention to the first **m sign**,	253
	4:17	in your hand so you can perform **m signs**	253
	4:28	the **m signs** he had commanded him	253
	7: 3	though I multiply my **m signs** and wonders	253
	8:23	This **m sign** will occur tomorrow.' "	253
	10: 1	so that I may perform these **m signs** *of* mine	253
Nu	14:11	the **m signs** I have performed among them?	253
	14:22	and the **m signs** I performed in Egypt and in	253
Dt	4:34	by testings, by **m signs** and wonders, by war,	253
	6:22	Before our eyes the LORD sent **m signs**	253
	7:19	the **m signs** and wonders,	253
	13: 1	among you and announces to you a **m sign**	253
	26: 8	with great terror and **m signs**	253
	29: 3	those **m signs** and great wonders.	253
	34:11	who did all those **m signs** and wonders	253
2Ch	32:24	who answered him and gave him a **m sign**.	4603

2Ch	32:31	the **m** sign that had occurred in the land,	4603
Ne	9:10	You sent **m** signs and wonders	253
Ps	74: 9	We are given no **m** signs;	253
	78:43	the day he displayed his **m** signs in Egypt,	253
	105:27	They performed his **m** signs among them,	253
Jer	32:20	You performed **m** signs and wonders	253
Da	4: 2	to tell you about the **m** signs and wonders	10084
Mt	12:38	we want to see a **m** sign from you."	4956
	12:39	and adulterous generation asks for a **m** sign!	4956
	13:54	get this wisdom and these **m** powers?"	1539
	14: 2	That is why **m** powers are at work in him."	1539
	16: 4	adulterous generation looks for a **m** sign,	4956
Mk	6:14	that is why **m** powers are at work in him."	1539
	8:12	Why does this generation ask for a **m** sign?	4956
Lk	11:29	It asks for a **m** sign, but none will be given	4956
Jn	2:11	This, the first of his **m** signs,	4956
	2:18	"What **m** sign can you show us	4956
	2:23	many people saw the **m** signs he was doing	4956
	3: 2	the **m** signs you are doing if God were not	4956
	4:48	"Unless you people see **m** signs	4956
	4:54	the second **m** sign that Jesus performed,	4956
	6: 2	the **m** signs he had performed on the sick.	4956
	6:14	the people saw the **m** sign that Jesus did,	4956
	6:26	not because you saw **m** signs but	4956
	6:30	"What **m** sign then will you give	4956
	7:31	will he do more **m** signs than this man?"	4956
	9:16	"How can a sinner do such **m** signs?"	4956
	10:41	"Though John never performed a **m** sign,	4956
	11:47	Here is this man performing many **m** signs.	4956
	12:18	that he had given this **m** sign,	4956
	12:37	Even after Jesus had done all these **m** signs	4956
Ac	2:43	Jesus did many other **m** signs in the	4956
	4:30	and many wonders and **m** signs were done	4956
	5:12	and perform **m** signs and wonders through	4956
	6: 8	The apostles performed many **m** signs	4956
	7:36	did great wonders and **m** signs among	4956
	8: 6	and did wonders and **m** signs in Egypt,	4956
	14: 3	and saw the **m** signs he did,	4956
1Co	1:22	of his grace by enabling them to do **m** signs	4956
	2:10	the **m** signs and wonders God had done	4956
Rev	13:13	Jews demand **m** signs and Greeks look	4956
	16:14	to another **m** powers,	1539+1920
	19:20	And he performed great and **m** signs,	4956
		of demons performing **m** signs,	4956
		the **m** signs on his behalf.	4956

MIRACULOUSLY (1) [MIRACLE]

Ac	4:22	For the man who was **m** healed was	4956

MIRE (4) [MIRY]

Ps	40: 2	out of the mud and **m**;	3431
	69:14	Rescue me from the **m**, do not let me sink;	3226
Isa	57:20	whose waves cast up **m** and mud.	8347
Mic	7:10	be trampled underfoot like **m** in the streets.	3226

MIRIAM (13)

Ex	15:20	Then **M** the prophetess, Aaron's sister,	5319
	15:21	**M** sang to them: "Sing to the LORD,	5319
Nu	12: 1	**M** and Aaron began to talk against Moses	5319
	12: 4	the LORD said to Moses, Aaron and **M**,	5319
	12: 5	to the Tent and summoned Aaron and **M**.	5319
	12:10	there stood **M**—leprous, like snow.	5319
	12:15	So **M** was confined outside the camp	5319
	20: 1	There **M** died and was buried.	5319
	26:59	Moses and their sister **M**.	5319
Dt	24: 9	to **M** along the way after you came out	5319
1Ch	4:17	One of Mered's wives gave birth to **M**,	5319
	6: 3	of Amram: Aaron, Moses and **M**.	5319
Mic	6: 4	sent Moses to lead you, also Aaron and **M**.	5319

MIRMAH (1)

1Ch	8:10	Jeuz, Sakia and **M**. These were his sons,	5328

MIRROR (3) [MIRRORS]

Job	37:18	hard as a **m** of cast bronze?	8023
1Co	13:12	we see but a poor **reflection** as in a **m**;	2269
Jas	1:23	like a man who looks at his face in a **m**	2269

MIRRORS (2) [MIRROR]

Ex	38: 8	from the **m** of the women who served at	5262
Isa	3:23	and **m**, and the linen garments and tiaras	1663

MIRTH (1)

Job	20: 5	that the **m** of the wicked is brief,	8265

MIRY (2) [MIRE]

Ps	69: 2	I sink in the **m** depths,	3431
	140:10	into **m** pits, never to rise.	4549

MISCARRIED (1) [MISCARRY]

Ge	31:38	Your sheep and goats have not **m**,	8897

MISCARRY (3) [MISCARRIED]

Ex	23:26	and none will **m** or be barren in your land.	8897
Job	21:10	their cows calve and do not **m**.	8897
Hos	9:14	Give them wombs that **m** and breasts	8897

MISCHIEF, MISCHIEFS (KJV) See
ASSAULT, CALAMITY, EVIL, HARM,

MALICE, MISERY, PUNISHMENT, RUIN,
SCHEMES, SERIOUS INJURY, TROUBLE

MISDEEDS (2)

Ps	99: 8	though you punished their **m**.	6613
Ro	8:13	but if by the Spirit you put to death the **m** of	4552

MISDEMEANOR (1)

Ac	18:14	a complaint about some **m** or serious crime,	93

MISERABLE (5) [MISERY]

Nu	21: 5	And we detest this **m** food!"	7848
Jdg	11:35	You have made me **m** and wretched,	4156+4156
Job	16: 2	**m** comforters are you all!	6662
Ecc	4: 8	This too is meaningless—a **m** business!	8273
Gal	4: 9	to those weak and **m** principles?	4777

MISERY (24) [MISERABLE]

Ge	16:11	for the LORD has heard of your **m**.	6715
	29:32	"It is because the LORD has seen my **m**.	6715
	44:29	bring my gray head down to the grave in **m**	8288
	44:34	Do not let me see the **m** that would come	8273
Ex	3: 7	"I have indeed seen the **m** of my people	6715
	3:17	to bring you up out of your **m** in Egypt into	6715
	4:31	about them and had seen their **m**,	6715
Nu	23:21	no **m** observed in Israel.	6662
Dt	26: 7	the LORD heard our voice and saw our **m**,	6715
Jdg	10:16	And he could bear Israel's **m** no longer.	6662
1Sa	1:11	if you will only look upon your servant's **m**	6715
Job	3:20	"Why is light given to those in **m**,	6664
	6: 2	and all my **m** be placed on the scales!	2095
	7: 3	and nights of **m** have been assigned to me.	6662
	9:18	but would overwhelm me with **m**.	4936
	20:22	the full force of **m** will come upon him.	6664
Ps	44:24	and forget our **m** and oppression?	6715
	94:20	one that brings on **m** by its decrees?	6662
Pr	31: 7	and remember their **m** no more.	6662
Ecc	8: 6	though a man's **m** weighs heavily upon him.	8288
Hos	5:15	in their **m** they will earnestly seek me."	7639
Mic	7: 1	What **m** is mine!	518
Ro	3:16	ruin and **m** mark their ways,	5416
Jas	5: 1	because of the **m** that is coming upon you.	5416

MISFORTUNE (10)

Nu	23:21	"No **m** is seen in Jacob,	224
Ru	1:21	the Almighty has **brought m** upon me."	8317
1Ch	7:23	because there had been **m** in his family.	8288
Job	12: 5	Men at ease have contempt for **m** as the fate	7085
	31:29	"If I have rejoiced at my enemy's **m** or	7085
Pr	13:21	**M** pursues the sinner.	8288
Ecc	2:21	This too is meaningless and a great **m**.	8288
	5:14	or wealth lost through some **m**,	6721+8273
Isa	65:23	in vain or bear children doomed to **m**;	988
Ob	1:12	down on your brother in the day of his **m**,	5798

MISHAEL (8)

Ex	6:22	The sons of Uzziel were **M**,	4792
Lev	10: 4	Moses summoned **M** and Elzaphan,	4792
Ne	8: 4	and on his left were Pedaiah, **M**, Malkijah,	4792
Da	1: 6	Daniel, Hananiah, **M** and Azariah.	4792
	1: 7	to **M**, Meshach; and to Azariah, Abednego.	4792
	1:11	Hananiah, **M** and Azariah,	4792
	1:19	Hananiah, **M** and Azariah;	4792
	2:17	to his friends Hananiah, **M** and Azariah.	10414

MISHAL (2)

Jos	19:26	Allammelech, Amad and **M**.	5398
	21:30	from the tribe of Asher, **M**, Abdon,	5398

MISHAM (1)

1Ch	8:12	The sons of Elpaal: Eber, **M**,	5471

MISHEAL (KJV) See MISHAL

MISHMA (4)

Ge	25:14	**M**, Dumah, Massa,	5462
1Ch	1:30	**M**, Dumah, Massa, Hadad, Tema,	5462
	4:25	Mibsam his son and **M** his son.	5462
	4:26	The descendants of **M**:	5462

MISHMANNAH (1)

1Ch	12:10	**M** the fourth, Jeremiah the fifth,	5459

MISHPAT See EN MISHPAT

MISHRAITES (1)

1Ch	2:53	the Ithrites, Puthites, Shumathites and **M**.	5490

MISLEAD (5) [MISLEADING, MISLEADS, MISLED]

2Ki	4:16	"Don't **m** your servant, O man of God!"	3941
2Ch	32:15	not let Hezekiah deceive you and **m** you	6077
Isa	9:16	Those who guide this people **m** them,	9494
	36:18	"Do not let Hezekiah **m** you when he says,	6077
	47:10	and knowledge **m** you when you say	8740

MISLEADING (4) [MISLEAD]

2Ki	18:32	for he is **m** you when he says,	6077
2Ch	32:11	he is **m** you, to let you die of hunger and	6077
La	2:14	The oracles they gave you were false and **m**.	4505
Da	2: 9	You have conspired to tell me **m** and	10343

MISLEADS (2) [MISLEAD]

Isa	44:20	He feeds on ashes, a deluded heart **m** him;	5742
Rev	2:20	By her teaching she **m** my servants	4414

MISLED (2) [MISLEAD]

Jer	38:22	" 'They **m** you and overcame you—	6077
1Co	15:33	Do not be **m**: "Bad company corrupts—	4414

MISPAR (1)

Ezr	2: 2	Bilshan, **M**, Bigvai, Rehum and Baanah):	5032

MISPERETH (1)

Ne	7: 7	Nahamani, Mordecai, Bilshan, **M**, Bigvai,	5033

MISREPHOTH MAIM (2)

Jos	11: 8	the way to Greater Sidon, to **M**, and	5387
	13: 6	from Lebanon to **M**,	5387

MISS (2) [MISSED, MISSES, MISSING]

Jdg	20:16	could sling a stone at a hair and not **m**.	2627
Pr	19: 2	nor to be hasty and **m** the way.	2627

MISSED (3) [MISS]

1Sa	20:18	You will be **m**, because your seat will be	7212
Jer	3:16	it will not be **m**, nor will another one be	7212
	46:17	he has **m** his opportunity.'	6296

MISSES (2) [MISS]

1Sa	20: 6	If your father **m** me at all, tell him,	7212+7212
Heb	12:15	See to it that no one **m** the grace of God and	5728

MISSING (13) [MISS]

Nu	31:49	and not one is **m**.	7212
Jdg	21: 3	Why should one tribe be **m**	7212
1Sa	25: 7	at Carmel nothing of theirs was **m**.	7212
	25:15	in the fields near them nothing was **m**.	7212
	25:21	in the desert so that nothing of his was **m**.	7212
	30:19	Nothing was **m**: young or old,	6372
2Sa	2:30	of David's men were found **m**.	7212
1Ki	20:39	If he is **m**, it will be your life for his	7212+7212
2Ki	10:19	See that no one is **m**,	7212
Job	5:24	of your property and **find** nothing **m**.	2627
Isa	34:16	None of these will be **m**,	6372
	40:26	not one of them is **m**.	6372
Jer	23: 4	nor will any be **m**," declares the LORD.	7212

MISSION (6) [MISSIONS]

Jos	22: 3	the **m** the LORD your God gave you.	5466
1Sa	15:18	And he sent you on a **m**, saying,	2006
	15:20	"I went on the **m** the LORD assigned me.	2006
	21: 2	'No one is to know anything about your **m**	889+1821+8938
Isa	48:15	and he will succeed in his **m**.	2006
Ac	12:25	Barnabas and Saul had finished their **m**,	1355

MISSIONS (1) [MISSION]

1Sa	21: 5	The men's things are holy even on **m**	2006

MIST (5) [MISTS]

Isa	44:22	your sins like the **morning m**.	6727
Hos	6: 4	Your love is like the morning **m**,	6727
	13: 3	Therefore they will be like the morning **m**,	6727
Ac	13:11	Immediately **m** and darkness came	944
Jas	4:14	You are a **m** that appears for a little while	874

MISTAKE (5) [MISTAKEN]

Ge	43:12	Perhaps it was a **m**.	5405
Lev	22:14	"If anyone eats a sacred offering by **m**,	8705
Jdg	9:36	**m** the shadows of the mountains for	3869+8011
Ecc	5: 6	"My vow was a **m**."	8705
Jer	42:20	that you made a fatal **m** when	928+5883+9494

MISTAKEN (1) [MISTAKE]

Mk	12:27	You are badly **m**!"	4414

MISTREAT (9) [MISTREATED, MISTREATING]

Ge	31:50	If you **m** my daughters or if you take any	6700
Ex	22:21	"Do not **m** an alien or oppress him,	3561
Lev	19:33	lives with you in your land, do not **m** him.	3561
1Sa	25: 7	we did not **m** them,	4007
	25:15	They did not **m** us,	4007
Jer	38:19	over to them and they will **m** me.	6618
Eze	22:29	and **m** the alien, denying the justice,	6943
Lk	6:28	pray for those who **m** you.	2092
Ac	14: 5	to **m** them and stone them.	5614

MISTREATED (12) [MISTREAT]

Ge	15:13	be enslaved and **m** four hundred years.	6700
	16: 6	Then Sarai **m** Hagar; so she fled from her.	6700

Nu	20:15	The Egyptians **m** us and our fathers,	8317
Dt	26: 6	But the Egyptians **m** us and made us suffer,	8317
Jer	13:22	torn off and your body **m**.	2803
Eze	22: 7	in you they have oppressed the alien and **m**	3561
Mt	22: 6	**m** them and killed them.	5614
Ac	7: 6	be enslaved and **m** four hundred years.	2808
	7:24	of them *being* **m** by an Egyptian,	92
Heb	11:25	He chose *to be* **m** along with the people	5156
	11:37	destitute, persecuted and **m**—	2807
	13: 3	and those who *are* **m** as if you yourselves	2807

MISTREATING (1) [MISTREAT]
Ac	7:27	"But the man who *was* **m** the other	92

MISTRESS (8)
Ge	16: 4	she began to despise her **m**.	1485
	16: 8	"I'm running away from my **m** Sarai,"	1485
	16: 9	"Go back to your **m** and submit to her."	1485
2Ki	5: 3	She said to her **m**, "If only my master	1485
Ps	123: 2	eyes of a maid look to the hand of her **m**,	1485
Pr	30:23	and a maidservant who displaces her **m**.	1485
Isa	24: 2	for master as for servant, for **m** as for maid,	1485
Na	3: 4	alluring, the **m** *of* sorceries,	1266

MISTS (1) [MIST]
2Pe	2:17	without water and **m** driven by a storm.	3920

MISUNDERSTAND (1)
Dt	32:27	lest the adversary **m** and say,	5795

MISUSE (3) [MISUSES]
Ex	20: 7	"You shall not **m** the name of the LORD your God,	2021+4200+5951+8736
Dt	5:11	"You shall not **m** the name of the LORD your God,	2021+4200+5951+8736
Ps	139:20	adversaries **m** your name.	2021+4200+5951+8736

MISUSES (2) [MISUSE]
Ex	20: 7	the LORD will not hold anyone guiltless who **m** his name.	2021+4200+5951+8736
Dt	5:11	the LORD will not hold anyone guiltless *who* **m** his name.	2021+4200+5951+8736

MITE, MITES (KJV) See PENNY, SMALL COPPER COINS

MITHCAH (2)
Nu	33:28	They left Terah and camped at **M**.	5520
	33:29	They left **M** and camped at Hashmonah.	5520

MITHNITE (1)
1Ch	11:43	Hanan son of Maacah, Joshaphat the **M**,	5512

MITHREDATH (2)
Ezr	1: 8	of Persia had them brought by **M**	5521
	4: 7	of Persia, Bishlam, **M**, Tabeel and the rest	5521

MITRE (KJV) See TURBAN

MITYLENE (1)
Ac	20:14	we took him aboard and went on to **M**.	3639

MIX (1) [MIXED, MIXES, MIXING, MIXTURE, WELL-MIXED]
Rev	18: 6	**M** her a double portion from her own cup.	3042

MIXED (53) [MIX]
Ex	29: 2	make bread, and cakes **m** with oil,	1176
	29:40	of an ephah of fine flour **m** with a quarter of	1176
Lev	2: 4	cakes made without yeast and **m** with oil,	1176
	2: 5	it is to be made of fine flour **m** with oil,	1176
	7:10	whether **m** with oil or dry,	1176
	7:12	of bread made without yeast and **m** with oil,	1176
	7:12	and cakes of fine flour well-kneaded and **m**	1176
	9: 4	together with a grain offering **m** with oil.	1176
	14:10	with three-tenths of an ephah of fine flour **m**	1176
	14:21	of fine flour **m** with oil for a grain offering,	1176
	23:13	of two-tenths of an ephah of fine flour **m**	1176
Nu	6:15	cakes made of fine flour **m** with oil as	1176
	7:13	each filled with fine flour **m** with oil as	1176
	7:19	each filled with fine flour **m** with oil as	1176
	7:25	each filled with fine flour **m** with oil as	1176
	7:31	each filled with fine flour **m** with oil as	1176
	7:37	each filled with fine flour **m** with oil as	1176
	7:43	each filled with fine flour **m** with oil as	1176
	7:49	each filled with fine flour **m** with oil as	1176
	7:55	each filled with fine flour **m** with oil as	1176
	7:61	each filled with fine flour **m** with oil as	1176
	7:67	each filled with fine flour **m** with oil as	1176
	7:73	each filled with fine flour **m** with oil as	1176
	7:79	each filled with fine flour **m** with oil as	1176
	8: 8	with its grain offering of fine flour **m**	1176
	15: 4	of an ephah of fine flour **m** with a quarter of	1176
	15: 6	of an ephah of fine flour **m** with a third of	1176
	15: 9	of an ephah of fine flour **m** with half a hin	1176
	28: 5	of an ephah of fine flour **m** with a quarter of	1176
	28: 9	of two-tenths of an ephah of fine flour **m**	1176

Nu	28:12	of three-tenths of an ephah of fine flour **m**	1176
	28:12	of two-tenths of an ephah of fine flour **m**	1176
	28:13	a tenth of an ephah of fine flour **m** with oil.	1176
	28:20	of three-tenths of an ephah of fine flour **m**	1176
	28:28	of three-tenths of an ephah of fine flour **m**	1176
	29: 3	of three-tenths of an ephah of fine flour **m**	1176
	29: 9	of three-tenths of an ephah of fine flour **m**	1176
	29:14	of three-tenths of an ephah of fine flour **m**	1176
Ps	75: 8	a cup full of foaming wine **m** with spices;	5008
Pr	9: 2	She has prepared her meat and **m** her wine;	5007
	9: 5	eat my food and drink the wine *I have* **m**.	5007
	23:30	who go to sample bowls of **m** wine.	4932
Isa	65:11	a table for Fortune and fill bowls of **m** wine	4932
Da	2:41	even as you saw iron **m** with clay.	10569
	2:43	just as you saw the iron **m** with baked clay,	10569
Mt	13:33	a woman took and **m** into a large amount	1606
	27:34	offered Jesus wine to drink, **m** with gall;	3502
Mk	15:23	Then they offered him wine **m** with myrrh,	5046
Lk	3:17	the Galileans whose blood Pilate had **m**	3502
	13:21	It is like yeast that a woman took and **m** into	1606
Jude	1:23	to others show mercy, **m** with fear—	NIG
Rev	8: 7	and there came hail and fire **m** with blood,	3502
	15: 2	And I saw what looked like a sea of glass **m**	3502

MIXES (2) [MIX]
Da	2:43	any more than iron **m** with clay.	10569
Hos	7: 8	"Ephraim **m** with the nations;	1176

MIXING (4) [MIX]
1Ch	9:30	the priests **took care of m** the spices.	5351+8379
	23:29	the baking and the **m**,	8057
Isa	5:22	and champions at **m** drinks,	5007
Eze	24:10	Cook the meat well, **m** in the spices;	8379

MIXTURE (2) [MIX]
Da	2:43	will be a **m** and will not remain united,	10569
Jn	19:39	Nicodemus brought a **m** of myrrh and aloes,	3623

MIZAR (1)
Ps	42: 6	the heights of Hermon—from Mount **M**.	5204

MIZPAH (43) [RAMATH MIZPAH]
Ge	31:49	It was also called **M**, because he said,	5207
Jos	11: 3	below Hermon in the region of **M**.	5207
	11: 8	and to the Valley of **M** on the east,	5207
	15:38	Dilean, **M**, Joktheel,	5206
	18:26	**M**, Kephirah, Mozah,	5206
Jdg	10:17	the Israelites assembled and camped at **M**.	5207
	11:11	all his words before the LORD in **M**.	5207
	11:29	passed through **M** *of* Gilead,	5206
	11:34	When Jephthah returned to his home in **M**,	5207
	20: 1	and assembled before the LORD in **M**.	5207
	20: 3	that the Israelites had gone up to **M**.)	5207
	21: 1	The men of Israel had taken an oath at **M**:	5207
	21: 5	before the LORD at **M** should certainly	5207
	21: 8	to assemble before the LORD at **M**?"	5207
1Sa	7: 5	at **M** and I will intercede with the LORD	5207
	7: 6	When they had assembled at **M**,	5207
	7: 6	And Samuel was leader of Israel at **M**.	5207
	7: 7	that Israel had assembled at **M**,	5207
	7:11	of Israel rushed out of **M** and pursued	5207
	7:12	a stone and set it up between **M** and Shen.	5207
	7:16	on a circuit from Bethel to Gilgal to **M**,	5207
	10:17	the people of Israel to the LORD at **M**	5207
	22: 3	From there David went to **M** *in* Moab	5206
1Ki	15:22	up Geba in Benjamin, and also **M**.	5207
2Ki	25:23	they came to Gedaliah at **M**—	5207
	25:25	the Babylonians who were with him at **M**.	5207
2Ch	16: 6	With them he built up Geba and **M**.	5207
Ne	3: 7	by men from Gibeon and **M**—	5207
	3:15	ruler of the district of **M**.	5207
	3:19	Next to him, Ezer son of Jeshua, ruler of **M**,	5207
Jer	40: 6	to Gedaliah son of Ahikam at **M** and stayed	5207
	40: 8	they came to Gedaliah at **M**—	5207
	40:10	I myself will stay at **M** to represent you	5207
	40:12	to Gedaliah at **M**,	5207
	40:13	in the open country came to Gedaliah at **M**	5207
	40:15	of Kareah said privately to Gedaliah in **M**,	5207
	41: 1	to Gedaliah son of Ahikam at **M**.	5207
	41: 3	the Jews who were with Gedaliah at **M**,	5207
	41: 6	Ishmael son of Nethaniah went out from **M**	5207
	41:10	all the rest of the people who were in **M**—	5207
	41:14	at **M** turned and went over to Johanan son	5207
	41:16	from **M** whom he had recovered	5207
Hos	5: 1	You have been a snare at **M**,	5207

MIZPAR (KJV) See MISPAR

MIZPEH (KJV) See MIZPAH

MIZRAIM (4) [ABEL MIZRAIM]
Ge	10: 6	Cush, **M**, Put and Canaan.	5213
	10:13	**M** was the father of the Ludites, Anamites,	5213
1Ch	1: 8	sons of Ham: Cush, **M**, Put and Canaan.	5213
	1:11	**M** was the father of the Ludites, Anamites,	5213

MIZZAH (3)
Ge	36:13	Nahath, Zerah, Shammah and **M**.	4645
	36:17	Chiefs Nahath, Zerah, Shammah and **M**.	4645
1Ch	1:37	Nahath, Zerah, Shammah and **M**.	4645

MNASON (1)
Ac	21:16	and brought us to the home of **M**,	3643

MOAB (152) [MOAB'S, MOABITE, MOABITES, MOABITESS]
Ge	19:37	and she named him **M**;	4565
	36:35	who defeated Midian in the country of **M**,	4565
Ex	15:15	leaders of **M** will be seized with trembling,	4566
Nu	21:11	the desert that faces **M** toward the sunrise.	4566
	21:13	The Arnon is the border of **M**,	4566
	21:13	between **M** and the Amorites.	4566
	21:15	the site of Ar and lie along the border of **M**.	4566
	21:20	and from Bamoth to the valley in **M**	4566+8441
	21:26	against the former king of **M** and had taken	4566
	21:28	It consumed Ar of **M**,	4566
	21:29	Woe to you, O **M**!	4566
	22: 1	of **M** and camped along the Jordan across	4566
	22: 3	and **M** was terrified because there were	4566
	22: 3	**M** was filled with dread because of	4566
	22: 4	who was king of **M** at that time,	4566
	22: 7	The elders of **M** and Midian left,	4566
	22:10	"Balak son of Zippor, king of **M**,	4566
	22:21	and went with the princes of **M**.	4566
	23: 6	with all the princes of **M**.	4566
	23: 7	the king of **M** from the eastern mountains.	4566
	23:17	with the princes of **M**.	4566
	24:17	He will crush the foreheads of **M**,	4566
	26: 3	So on the plains of **M** by the Jordan across	4566
	26:63	of **M** by the Jordan across from Jericho.	4566
	31:12	at their camp on the plains of **M**,	4566
	33:44	Iye Abarim on the border of **M**.	4566
	33:48	of Abarim and camped on the plains of **M**	4566
	33:49	There on the plains of **M** they camped	4566
	33:50	On the plains of **M** by the Jordan across	4566
	35: 1	On the plains of **M** by the Jordan across	4566
	36:13	by the Jordan across from Jericho.	4566
Dt	1: 5	East of the Jordan in the territory of **M**,	4566
	2: 8	and traveled along the desert road of **M**.	4566
	2:18	"Today you are to pass by the region of **M**	4566
	29: 1	to make with the Israelites in **M**,	824+4566
	32:49	the Abarim Range to Mount Nebo in **M**,	824+4566
	34: 1	from the plains of **M** to the top of Pisgah,	4566
	34: 5	the servant of the LORD died there in **M**,	824+4566
	34: 6	He buried him in **M**,	824+4566
	34: 8	for Moses in the plains of **M** thirty days,	4566
Jos	13:32	in the plains of **M** across the Jordan east	4566
	24: 9	When Balak son of Zippor, the king of **M**,	4566
Jdg	3:12	the LORD gave Eglon king of **M** power	4566
	3:14	to Eglon king of **M** for eighteen years.	4566
	3:15	with tribute to Eglon king of **M**.	4566
	3:17	the tribute to Eglon king of **M**,	4566
	3:28	"for the LORD has given **M**, your enemy,	4566
	3:28	of the fords of the Jordan that led to **M**,	4566
	3:30	That day **M** was made subject to Israel,	4566
	10: 6	the gods of Sidon, the gods of **M**,	4566
	11:15	the land of **M** or the land of the Ammonites.	4566
	11:17	They sent also to the king of **M**,	4566
	11:18	skirted the lands of Edom and **M**,	4566
	11:18	along the eastern side of the country of **M**,	4566
	11:18	They did not enter the territory of **M**,	4566
	11:25	Balak son of Zippor, king of **M**?	4566
Ru	1: 1	went to live for a while in the country of **M**.	4566
	1: 2	And they went to **M** and lived there.	4566+8441
	1: 6	**M** that the LORD had come to the aid	4566+8441
	1:22	So Naomi returned from **M**	4566+8441
	2: 6	the Moabitess who came back from **M**	4566+8441
	4: 3	"Naomi, who has come back from **M**,	4566+8441
1Sa	12: 9	of the Philistines and the king of **M**,	4566
	14:47	**M**, the Ammonites, Edom,	4566
	22: 3	From there David went to Mizpah in **M**	4566
	22: 3	in Moab and said to the king of **M**,	4566
	22: 4	So he left them with the king of **M**,	4566
2Sa	8:12	and **M**, the Ammonites and the Philistines,	4566
1Ki	11: 7	for Chemosh the detestable god of **M**,	4566
2Ki	1: 1	Ahab's death, **M** rebelled against Israel.	4566
	3: 4	Now Mesha king of **M** raised sheep,	4566
	3: 5	of **M** rebelled against the king of Israel.	4566
	3: 7	"The king of **M** has rebelled against me.	4566
	3: 7	Will you go with me to fight against **M**?"	4566
	3:10	to hand us over to **M**?"	4566
	3:13	to hand us over to **M**."	4566
	3:18	he will also hand **M** over to you.	4566
	3:23	Now to the plunder, **M**!"	4566
	3:26	the king of **M** saw that the battle had gone	4566
	23:13	for Chemosh the vile god of **M**,	4566
1Ch	1:46	who defeated Midian in the country of **M**,	4566
	4:22	who ruled in **M** and Jashubi Lehem.	4566
	8: 8	Sons were born to Shaharaim in **M**	4566+8441
	18:11	and **M**, the Ammonites and the Philistines,	4566
2Ch	20:10	men from Ammon, **M** and Mount Seir,	4566
	20:22	against the men of Ammon and **M**	4566
	20:23	The men of Ammon and **M** rose up against	4566
Ne	13:23	from Ashdod, Ammon and **M**.	4567
Ps	60: 8	**M** is my washbasin,	4566
	83: 6	of **M** and the Hagrites,	4566
	108: 9	**M** is my washbasin,	4566
Isa	11:14	They will lay hands on Edom and **M**,	4566
	15: 1	An oracle concerning **M**:	4566
	15: 1	Ar in **M** is ruined, destroyed in a night!	4566
	15: 1	Kir in **M** is ruined, destroyed in a night!	4566
	15: 2	**M** wails over Nebo and Medeba.	4566
	15: 4	Therefore the armed men of **M** cry out,	4566
	15: 5	My heart cries out over **M**;	4566
	15: 8	Their outcry echoes along the border of **M**;	4566
	15: 9	fugitives of **M** and upon those who remain	4566

Isa	16: 2	the women of **M** at the fords of the Arnon.	4566
	16: 7	they wail together for **M.**	4566
	16:11	My heart laments for **M** like a harp,	4566
	16:12	When **M** appears at her high place,	4566
	16:13	LORD has already spoken concerning **M.**	4566
	25:10	but **M** will be trampled under him	4566
Jer	9:26	**M** and all who live in the desert	4566
	25:21	Edom, **M** and Ammon;	4566
	27: 3	Then send word to the kings of Edom, **M,**	4566
	40:11	When all the Jews in **M,** Ammon,	4566
	48: 1	Concerning **M:** This is what the LORD Almighty,	4566
	48: 2	**M** will be praised no more;	4566
	48: 4	**M** will be broken;	4566
	48: 9	Put salt on **M,** for she will be laid waste;	4566
	48:11	**M** has been at rest from youth,	4566
	48:13	Then **M** will be ashamed of Chemosh,	4566
	48:15	**M** will be destroyed and her towns invaded;	4566
	48:16	"The fall of **M** is at hand;	4566
	48:18	for he who destroys **M** will come up	4566
	48:20	**M** is disgraced, for she is shattered.	4566
	48:20	by the Arnon that **M** is destroyed.	4566
	48:24	to all the towns of **M,** far and near.	824+4566
	48:26	Let **M** wallow in her vomit;	4566
	48:28	you who live in **M.**	4566
	48:31	Therefore I wail over **M,**	4566
	48:31	for all **M** I cry out,	4566
	48:33	from the orchards and fields of **M.**	4566
	48:35	In **M** I will put an end	4566
	48:36	"So my heart laments for **M** like a flute;	4566
	48:38	On all the roofs in **M** and in	4566
	48:38	for I have broken **M** like a jar	4566
	48:39	How **M** turns her back in shame!	4566
	48:39	**M** has become an object of ridicule,	4566
	48:40	spreading its wings over **M.**	4566
	48:42	**M** will be destroyed as a nation	4566
	48:43	O people of **M,**" declares the LORD.	4566
	48:44	bring upon **M** the year of her punishment,"	4566
	48:45	it burns the foreheads of **M,**	4566
	48:46	Woe to you, O **M!**	4566
	48:47	"Yet I will restore the fortunes of **M** in days	4566
	48:47	Here ends the judgment on **M.**	4566
Eze	25: 8	'Because **M** and Seir said, "Look,	4566
	25: 9	flank of **M,** beginning at its frontier towns	4566
	25:10	I will give **M** along with the Ammonites to	2023ˢ
	25:11	and I will inflict punishment on **M.**	4566
Da	11:41	**M** and the leaders of Ammon will	4566
Am	2: 1	"For three sins of **M,** even for four,	4566
	2: 2	I will send fire upon **M** that will consume	4566
	2: 2	**M** will go down in great tumult	4566
Mic	6: 5	remember what Balak king of **M** counseled	4566
Zep	2: 8	of **M** and the taunts of the Ammonites,	4566
	2: 9	"surely **M** will become like Sodom,	4566

MOAB'S (7) [MOAB]

2Sa	23:20	He struck down two of **M** best men.	4566
1Ch	11:22	He struck down two of **M** best men.	4566
Isa	16: 6	We have heard of **M** pride—	4566
	16:14	by contract would count them, **M** splendor	4566
Jer	48:25	**M** horn is cut off;	4566
	48:29	"We have heard of **M** pride—	4566
	48:41	In that day the hearts of **M** warriors will be	4566

MOABITE (12) [MOAB]

Nu	22: 8	So the **M** princes stayed with him.	4566
	22:14	the **M** princes returned to Balak and said,	4566
	22:36	he went out to meet him at the **M** town on	4566
	25: 1	in sexual immorality with **M** women,	4566
Dt	23: 3	or **M** or any of his descendants may enter	4567
Ru	1: 4	They married **M** *women,*	4567
2Ki	13:20	Now **M** raiders used to enter	4566
	24: 2	**M** and Ammonite raiders against him.	4566
1Ch	11:46	the sons of Elnaam, Ithmah the **M,**	4567
2Ch	24:26	and Jehozabad, son of Shimrith a **M** *woman.*	4567
Ne	13: 1	that no Ammonite or **M** should ever	4567
Isa	16: 4	Let the **M** fugitives stay with you;	4566

MOABITES (18) [MOAB]

Ge	19:37	he is the father of the **M** of today.	4566
Nu	22: 4	The **M** said to the elders of Midian,	4566
Dt	2: 9	not harass the **M** or provoke them to war,	4566
	2:11	but the **M** called them Emites.	4567
	2:29	who live in Seir, and the **M,** who live in Ar,	4567
Jdg	3:29	struck down about ten thousand **M,**	408+4566
2Sa	8: 2	David also defeated the **M.**	4566
	8: 2	So the **M** became subject to David	4566
1Ki	11: 1	**M,** Ammonites, Edomites,	4567
	11:33	Chemosh the god of the **M,**	4566
2Ki	3:21	the **M** had heard that the kings had come	4566
	3:22	To the **M** across the way,	4566
	3:24	But when the **M** came to the camp of Israel,	4566
	3:24	the land and slaughtered the **M.**	4566
1Ch	18: 2	David also defeated the **M,**	4566
2Ch	20: 1	the **M** and Ammonites with some of	1201+4566
Ezr	9: 1	Ammonites, **M,** Egyptians and Amorites.	4567
Isa	16: 7	Therefore the **M** wail,	4566

MOABITESS (6) [MOAB]

Ru	1:22	from Moab accompanied by Ruth the **M,**	4567
	2: 2	And Ruth the **M** said to Naomi,	4567
	2: 6	"She is the **M** who came back from Moab	4567
	2:21	Then Ruth the **M** said, "He even said to me,	4567
	4: 5	the land from Naomi and from Ruth the **M,**	4567
	4:10	I have also acquired Ruth the **M,**	4567

MOABITISH (KJV) See MOABITESS

MOADIAH (1) [MOADIAH'S]

Ne	12: 5	Mijamin, **M,** Bilgah,	5050

MOADIAH'S (1) [MOADIAH]

Ne	12:17	of Miniamin's and of **M,** Piltai;	4598

MOAN (6) [MOANED, MOANING]

Ps	90: 9	we finish our years with a **m.**	2049
Isa	59:11	we **m** mournfully like doves.	2047+2047
Jer	48:31	I **m** for the men of Kir Hareseth.	2047
Joel	1:18	How the cattle **m!**	634
Mic	1: 8	I will howl like a jackal and **m** like an owl.	65
Na	2: 7	Its slave girls **m** like doves and beat	5628

MOANED (1) [MOAN]

Isa	38:14	I **m** like a mourning dove.	2047

MOANING (2) [MOAN]

Jer	31:18	"I have surely heard Ephraim's **m:**	5653
Eze	7:16	**m** like doves of the valleys,	2159

MOB (6)

Eze	16:40	They will bring a **m** against you,	7736
	23:46	Bring a **m** against them and give them over	7736
	23:47	The **m** will stone them and cut them down	7736
Jn	7:49	But this **m** that knows nothing of the law—	4063
Ac	17: 5	formed a **m** and started a riot in the city.	4062
	21:35	the violence *of* the **m** was so great he had to	4063

MOBILIZED (3)

Jdg	20:15	the Benjamites **m** twenty-six thousand	7212
2Ki	3: 6	from Samaria and **m** all Israel.	7212
	6:24	Ben-Hadad king of Aram **m** his entire army	7695

MOCK (19) [MOCKED, MOCKER, MOCKERS, MOCKERY, MOCKING, MOCKS]

Job	11: 3	Will no one rebuke you when *you* **m?**	4352
	21: 3	and after I have spoken, **m** *on.*	4352
	22:19	the innocent **m** them, saying,	4352
	30: 1	"But now *they* **m** me, men younger than I,	8471
	30: 9	"And now their sons **m** me **in song;**	5593
Ps	22: 7	All who see me **m** me;	4352
	69:12	Those who sit at the gate **m** me,	8488
	74:10	How long *will* the enemy **m** you, O God?	3070
	74:22	remember how fools **m** you all day long.	3075
	80: 6	and our enemies **m** us.	4352
	119:51	The arrogant **m** me without restraint,	4329
Pr	1:26	I *will* **m** when calamity overtakes you—	4352
	14: 9	Fools **m** *at* making amends for sin,	4329
Isa	52: 5	and those who rule them **m,**"	2147
La	3:14	they **m** me **in song** all day long.	5593
	3:63	**m** me in their songs.	4947
Eze	22: 5	and those who are far away *will* **m** you,	7840
Mk	10:34	who *will* **m** him and spit on him,	1850
Lk	18:32	They *will* **m** *him,* insult him, spit on him,	1850

MOCKED (16) [MOCK]

2Ch	36:16	But *they* **m** God's messengers,	4351
Ne	2:19	*they* **m** and ridiculed us.	4352
Ps	35:16	Like the ungodly *they* **maliciously m;**	4352+4352
	74:18	Remember how the enemy *has* **m** you,	3070
	89:50	Lord, how your servant has been **m,**	3075
	89:51	the taunts with which your enemies *have,* **m,**	3070
	89:51	with which *they have* **m** every step	3070
Mt	20:19	over to the Gentiles to *be* **m** and flogged	1850
	27:29	and knelt in front of him and **m** him.	1850
	27:31	After *they* had **m** him,	1850
	27:41	of the law and the elders **m** him.	1850
Mk	15:20	And when *they* had **m** him,	1850
	15:31	of the law **m** him among themselves.	1850
Lk	23:11	Herod and his soldiers ridiculed and **m** him.	1850
	23:36	The soldiers also came up and **m** him,	1850
Gal	6: 7	Do not be deceived: God cannot *be* **m.**	3682

MOCKER (12) [MOCK]

Pr	9: 7	"Whoever corrects a **m** invites insult;	4370
	9: 8	Do not rebuke a **m** or he will hate you;	4370
	9:12	if *you are* a **m,** you alone will suffer."	4329
	13: 1	but a **m** does not listen to rebuke.	4370
	14: 6	The **m** seeks wisdom and finds none,	4370
	15:12	A **m** resents correction;	4370
	19:25	a **m,** and the simple will learn prudence;	4370
	20: 1	Wine is a **m** and beer a brawler;	4370
	21:11	When a **m** is punished, the simple gain wisdom;	4370
	21:24	proud and arrogant man—"**M**" is his name;	4370
	22:10	Drive out the **m,** and out goes strife;	4370
	24: 9	and men detest a **m.**	4370

MOCKERS (8) [MOCK]

Job	17: 2	Surely **m** surround me;	2253
Ps	1: 1	in the way of sinners or sit in the seat of **m.**	4370
Pr	1:22	How long will **m** delight in mockery	4370
	3:34	He mocks **proud m** but gives grace to	4370
	19:29	Penalties are prepared for **m,**	4370
	29: 8	**M** stir up a city,	408+4371

Isa	29:20	the **m** will disappear, and all who have	4370
Hos	7: 5	and he joins hands with the **m.**	4372

MOCKERY (3) [MOCK]

Pr	1:22	How long will mockers delight in **m**	4371
Jer	10:15	They are worthless, the objects of **m;**	9511
	51:18	They are worthless, the objects of **m;**	9511

MOCKING (6) [MOCK]

Ge	21: 9	the Egyptian had borne to Abraham *was* **m,**	7464
Isa	28:22	Now stop *your* **m,** or your chains will	4372
	50: 6	I did not hide my face from **m** and spitting.	4009
	57: 4	Whom *are you* **m?**	6695
Zep	2:10	and **m** the people of the LORD Almighty.	1540
Lk	22:63	The men who were guarding Jesus **began m**	1850

MOCKS (8) [MOCK]

2Ki	19:21	of Zion despises you and **m** you.	4352
Job	9:23	*he* **m** the despair of the innocent.	4352
Pr	3:34	He **m** proud mockers but gives grace to	4329
	17: 5	*He who* **m** the poor shows contempt	4352
	19:28	A corrupt witness **m** *at* justice,	4329
	30:17	"The eye *that* **m** a father,	4352
Isa	37:22	Daughter of Zion despises and **m** you.	4352
Jer	20: 7	I am ridiculed all day long; everyone **m** me.	4352

MODEL (3) [MODELS]

Eze	28:12	" 'You were the **m** *of* perfection,	3159
1Th	1: 7	And so you became a **m** to all the believers	5596
2Th	3: 9	but in order to make ourselves a **m** for you	5596

MODELS (2) [MODEL]

1Sa	6: 5	Make **m** *of* the tumors and of the rats	7512
	6:11	the chest containing the gold rats and the **m**	7512

MODERATION (KJV) See GENTLENESS

MODESTLY (1) [MODESTY]

1Ti	2: 9	I also want women to dress **m,**	2950+3177

MODESTY (1) [MODESTLY]

1Co	12:23	parts that are unpresentable are treated with special **m,**	2362

MOISTEN (1) [MOISTURE]

Eze	46:14	of an ephah with a third of a hin of oil to **m**	8272

MOISTURE (3) [MOISTEN]

Job	36:28	the clouds **pour down** *their* **m**	5688
	37:11	He loads the clouds with **m;**	8188
Lk	8: 6	the plants withered because they had no **m.**	2657

MOLADAH (4)

Jos	15:26	Amam, Shema, **M,**	4579
	19: 2	It included: Beersheba (or Sheba), **M,**	4579
1Ch	4:28	They lived in Beersheba, **M,** Hazar Shual,	4579
Ne	11:26	in Jeshua, in **M,** in Beth Pelet,	4579

MOLDED (1) [MOLDS]

Job	10: 9	Remember that *you* **m** me like clay.	6913

MOLDING (10) [MOLDS]

Ex	25:11	and make a gold **m** around it.	2425
	25:24	with pure gold and make a gold **m** around it.	2425
	25:25	a rim a handbreadth wide and put a gold **m**	2425
	30: 3	and make a gold **m** around it.	2425
	30: 4	for the altar below the **m**—	2425
	37: 2	and made a gold **m** around it.	2425
	37:11	with pure gold and made a gold **m** around it.	2425
	37:12	a rim a handbreadth wide and put a gold **m**	2425
	37:26	and made a gold **m** around it.	2425
	37:27	They made two gold rings below the **m**—	2425

MOLDS (3) [MOLDED, MOLDING, MOLDY]

1Ki	7:37	They were all **cast in** the same **m**	4607
	7:46	The king had them cast in clay **m** in	5043
2Ch	4:17	The king had them cast in clay **m** in	6295

MOLDY (2) [MOLDS]

Jos	9: 5	of their food supply was dry and **m.**	5926
	9:12	But now see how dry and **m** it is.	5926

MOLE, MOLES (KJV) See CHAMELEON, RODENTS

MOLECH (16)

Lev	18:21	of your children to be sacrificed to **M,**	4891
	20: 2	of his children to **M** must be put to death.	4891
	20: 3	for by giving his children to **M,**	4891
	20: 4	of his children to **M** and they fail to put him	4891
	20: 5	in prostituting themselves to **M.**	4891
1Ki	11: 5	**M** the detestable god of the Ammonites.	4904
	11: 7	for **M** the detestable god of the Ammonites,	4891
	11:33	and **M** the god of the Ammonites,	4904
2Ki	23:10	or daughter in the fire to **M.**	4891
	23:13	and for **M** the detestable god of the people	4904

Isa	57: 9	You went to **M** with olive oil	4891
Jer	32:35	to sacrifice their sons and daughters to **M**,	4891
	49: 1	Why then has **M** taken possession of Gad?	4903
	49: 3	for **M** will go into exile,	4903
Zep	1: 5	by the LORD and who also swear by **M**,	4903
Ac	7:43	You have lifted up the shrine *of* **M** and	3661

MOLEST (2) [MOLESTS]

Ge	26:29	not **m** you but always treated you well	5595
Est	7: 8	even **m** the queen while she is with me in	3899

MOLESTS (1) [MOLEST]

Ge	26:11	"Anyone *who* **m** this man or his wife shall	5595

MOLID (1)

1Ch	2:29	who bore him Ahban and **M**.	4582

MOLLIFIED (KJV) See SOOTHED

MOLOCH (KJV) See MOLECH

MOLTEN (KJV) See IDOL CAST IN THE SHAPE

MOMENT (31) [MOMENT'S, MOMENTARY]

Ex	33: 5	If I were to go with you even for a **m**,	8092
Nu	4:20	even for a **m**, or they will die."	1180
Ezr	9: 8	"But now, for a brief **m**,	8092
Job	7:18	and test him every **m**?	8092
	20: 5	the joy of the godless lasts but a **m**.	8092
Ps	2:12	for his wrath can flare up **in a m**,	3869+5071
	30: 5	For his anger lasts only a **m**,	8092
Pr	12:19	but a lying tongue lasts *only a* **m**.	8088
Isa	47: 9	Both of these will overtake you **in a m**,	8092
	54: 7	"For a brief **m** I abandoned you,	8092
	54: 8	of anger I hid my face from you *for a* **m**,	8092
	66: 8	a day or a nation be brought forth in a **m**?	7193
	66: 9	*Do I* bring to the **m** of birth	8689
Jer	4:20	tents are destroyed, my shelter **in a m**.	8092
La	4: 6	which was overthrown **in a m** without	4017+8092
Eze	26:16	trembling every **m**, appalled at you.	8092
	32:10	of them will tremble every **m** for his life.	8092
Mt	3:16	At that **m** heaven was opened,	NIG
	9:22	And the woman was healed from that **m**.	6052
	17:18	and he was healed from that **m**.	6052
	27:51	At that **m** the curtain of the temple was torn	NIG
Mk	9:39	**in the next m** say anything bad about me	5444
Lk	2:38	Coming up to them *at* that very **m**,	6052
	6:49	**The m** the torrent struck that house,	2317
Jn	18:27	and **at that m** a rooster began to crow.	2311
Ac	5:10	**At that m** she fell down at his feet	4202
	16:18	*At* that **m** the spirit left her.	6052
	22:13	And *at* that very **m** I was able to see him.	6052
1Co	4: 5	Up to **this m** we have become the scum of	785
Gal	2: 5	We did not give in to them for a **m**,	6052
Rev	12: 4	might devour her child **the m** it was born.	4020

MOMENT'S (1) [MOMENT]

Job	10:20	Turn away from me so I can have a **m** joy	5071

MOMENTARY (1) [MOMENT]

2Co	4:17	For our light and **m** troubles are achieving	4194

MONEY (123)

Ge	17:12	in your household or bought with **m** from	4084
	17:13	in your household or bought with your **m**,	4084
	17:23	in his household or bought with his **m**,	4084
	42:35	they and their father saw the **m** pouches,	4084
	47:14	Joseph collected all the **m** that was to	4084
	47:15	When the **m** of the people of Egypt and	4084
	47:15	Our **m** is used up."	4084
	47:16	for your livestock, since your **m** is gone."	4084
	47:18	the fact that since our **m** is gone	4084
Ex	21:11	without any payment *of* **m**.	4084
	21:35	to sell the live one and divide both the **m**	4084
	22:15	**m paid for the hire** covers the loss.	8510
	22:25	"If you lend **m** to one of my people	4084
	30:16	Receive the atonement **m** from the Israelites	4084
Lev	22:11	But if a priest buys a slave with **m**,	4084
	25:37	not lend him **m** at interest or sell him food	4084
Nu	3:48	Give the **m** for the redemption of	4084
	3:49	the redemption **m** from those who exceeded	4084
	3:51	the redemption **m** to Aaron and his sons,	4084
Dt	18: 8	though he has received **m** from the sale	4928
	23:19	whether on **m** or food or anything else	4084
2Ki	12: 4	Is this the time to take **m**,	4084
	12: 4	the **m** that is brought as sacred offerings to	4084
	12: 4	the **m** *collected* in the census,	4084
	12: 4	the **m** *received from* personal vows and	4084
	12: 4	and the **m** brought voluntarily to the temple.	4084
	12: 5	Let every priest receive the **m** from one of	NIH
	12: 7	Take no more **m** from your treasurers,	4084
	12: 8	not collect any more **m** from the people and	4084
	12: 9	into the chest all the **m** that was brought to	4084
	12:10	that there was a large amount of **m** in	4084
	12:10	the **m** that had been brought into the temple	4084
	12:11	the **m** to the men appointed to supervise	4084
	12:13	The **m** brought into the temple was	4084
	12:15	from those to whom they gave the **m** to pay	4084
	12:16	The **m** *from* the guilt offerings	4084

2Ki	15:20	Menahem exacted this **m** from Israel.	4084
	22: 4	the high priest and have him get ready the **m**	4084
	22: 7	not account for the **m** entrusted to them,	4084
	22: 9	"Your officials have paid out the **m** that was	4084
2Ch	24: 5	of Judah and collect the **m** due annually	4084
	24:11	that there was a large amount of **m**,	4084
	24:11	and collected a great amount of **m**,	4084
	24:14	the rest of the **m** to the king and Jehoiada,	4084
	34: 9	the **m** that had been brought into the temple	4084
	34:11	also gave **m** to the carpenters and builders	NIH
	34:14	the **m** that had been taken into the temple of	4084
	34:17	the **m** that was in the temple of the LORD	4084
Ezr	3: 7	they gave **m** to the masons and carpenters,	4084
	7:17	With this **m** be sure to buy bulls,	10362
Ne	5: 4	"We have had to borrow **m** to pay	4084
	5:10	and my men are also lending the people **m**	4084
	5:11	the hundredth part of the **m**, the grain,	4084
Est	3:11	"Keep the **m**," the king said to Haman,	4084
	4: 7	the exact amount of **m** Haman had promised	4084
Ps	15: 5	who lends his **m** without usury and does	4084
Pr	7:20	with **m** and will not be home till full moon."	4084
	13:11	Dishonest **m** dwindles away,	2104
	13:11	but he who gathers **m** little by little	NIH
	17:16	Of what use is **m** in the hand of a fool,	4697
Ecc	5:10	Whoever loves **m** never has money enough;	4084
	5:10	Whoever loves money never has **m** enough;	4084
	7:12	Wisdom is a shelter as **m** is a shelter,	4084
	10:19	but **m** is the answer for everything.	4084
Isa	52: 3	and without **m** you will be redeemed."	4084
	55: 1	and you who have no **m**, come, buy and eat!	4084
	55: 1	and milk without **m** and without cost.	4084
	55: 2	Why spend **m** on what is not bread,	4084
Mic	3:11	and her prophets tell fortunes for **m**.	4084
Mt	6:24	You cannot serve both God and **M**.	3440
	20:15	to do what I want with my own **m**?	3836
	21:12	He overturned the tables of the **m** changers	3142
	25:15	To one he gave five **talents of m**,	5419
	25:16	and put his **m** to work and gained five more.	899S
	25:18	a hole in the ground and hid his master's **m**.	736
	25:27	you should have put my **m** on deposit with	736
	26: 9	at a high price and the **m** given to the poor."	NIG
	27: 5	Judas threw the **m** into the temple and left.	736
	27: 6	into the treasury, since it is **blood m**."	135+5507
	27: 7	to use the **m** to buy the potter's field as	899S
	28:12	they gave the soldiers a large sum of **m**,	736
	28:15	the **m** and did as they were instructed.	736
Mk	6: 8	no bread, no bag, no **m** in your belts.	5910
	11:15	He overturned the tables of the **m** changers	3142
	12:41	and watched the crowd putting their **m** into	5910
	14: 5	a year's wages and the **m** given to the poor.	NIG
	14:11	to hear this and promised to give him **m**.	736
Lk	3:14	He replied, "Don't **extort m** and	1398
	7:41	"Two men **owed m** to a certain	1639+5971
	7:42	Neither of them had the **m** to pay him back,	NIG
	9: 3	no staff, no bag, no bread, no **m**,	736
	14:28	to see if he has enough **m** to complete it?	NIG
	16:13	You cannot serve both God and **M**."	3440
	16:14	The Pharisees, *who* **loved m**,	5639+5795
	19:13	'Put this **m** to work,' he said,	736
	19:15	the servants to whom he had given the **m**,	736
	19:23	Why then didn't you put my **m** on deposit,	736
	22: 5	and agreed to give him **m**.	736
Jn	2:14	and others sitting at tables **exchanging m**.	3048
	2:15	the **m** changers and overturned their tables.	3142
	12: 5	the **m** given to the poor? It was **worth a year's wages**."	1324+5559
	12: 6	was a thief; as **keeper** of the **m** bag,	1186+2400
	13:29	Since Judas had charge of the **m**,	1186
Ac	3: 3	he asked them for **m**.	1797+3284
	4:34	brought the **m** from the sales	5507
	4:37	sold a field he owned and brought the **m**	5975
	5: 2	he kept back part of the **m** for himself,	5507
	5: 3	for yourself some *of* the **m** you received for	5507
	5: 4	it was sold, wasn't the **m** at your disposal?	NIG
	7:16	at Shechem for a certain sum of **m**.	736
	8:18	he offered them **m**	5975
	8:20	"May your **m** perish with you,	736
	8:20	you could buy the gift of God with **m**!	5975
	16:16	She earned a great deal of **m** for her owners	2238
	16:19	that their hope of **making m** was gone,	2238
1Co	16: 2	each one of you should set aside a **sum of m**	2564
1Ti	3: 3	not quarrelsome, **not a lover of m**.	921
	6:10	the **love of m** is a root of all kinds of evil.	5794
	6:10	Some people, eager for **m**, have wandered	NIG
2Ti	3: 2	**lovers of m**, boastful, proud, abusive,	5795
Heb	13: 5	Keep your lives **free from the love of m**	921
Jas	4:13	carry on business and **make m**."	3045
1Pe	5: 2	not **greedy for m**, but eager to serve;	154

MONEYLENDER (2) [LEND]

Ex	22:25	do not be like a **m**; charge him no interest.	5957
Lk	7:41	"Two men owed money to a certain **m**.	1250

MONITOR (1)

Lev	11:30	the **m lizard**, the wall lizard,	3947

MONSTER (6)

Job	7:12	Am I the sea, or the **m of the deep**,	9490
Ps	74:13	you broke the heads of the **m** in the waters.	9490
Isa	27: 1	he will slay the **m** of the sea.	9490
	51: 9	who pierced that **m** through?	9490
Eze	29: 3	you great **m** lying among your streams.	9490
	32: 2	you are like a **m** in the seas thrashing about	9490

[SEA] MONSTERS (KJV) See JACKALS

MONTH (211) [MONTHLY, MONTHS, MONTHS']

Ge	7:11	on the seventeenth day of the second **m**—	2544
	8: 4	and on the seventeenth day of the seventh **m**	2544
	8: 5	to recede until the tenth **m**,	2544
	8: 5	and on the first day of the tenth **m** the tops	2544
	8:13	of the first **m** of Noah's six hundred	2544
	8:14	the second **m** the earth was completely dry.	2544
	29:14	stayed with him for a **whole m**,	2544+3427
Ex	12: 2	"This **m** is to be for you the first month,	2544
	12: 2	"This month is to be for you the first **m**,	2544
	12: 2	the first **m** *of* your year.	2544
	12: 3	that on the tenth day of this **m** each man is	2544
	12: 6	of them until the fourteenth day of the **m**,	2544
	12:18	In the first **m** you are to eat bread made	2544
	13: 4	Today, in the **m** of Abib, you are leaving.	2544
	13: 5	you are to observe this ceremony in this **m**:	2544
	16: 1	of the second **m** after they had come out	2544
	19: 1	the third **m** after the Israelites left Egypt—	2544
	23:15	at the appointed time in the **m** *of* Abib,	2544
	23:15	for in **that m** you came out of Egypt.	2257S
	34:18	at the appointed time in the **m** *of* Abib,	2544
	34:18	for in that **m** you came out of Egypt.	2544
	40: 2	on the first day of the first **m**.	2544
	40:17	up on the first day of the first **m** in	2544
Lev	16:29	of the seventh **m** you must deny yourselves	2544
	23: 5	on the fourteenth day of the first **m**.	2544
	23: 6	On the fifteenth day of that **m**	2544
	23:24	the seventh **m** you are to have a day of rest,	2544
	23:27	"The tenth day of this seventh **m** is the Day	2544
	23:32	of the **m** until the following evening you are	2544
	23:34	'On the fifteenth day of the seventh **m**	2544
	23:39	of the seventh **m**, after you have gathered	2544
	23:41	celebrate it in the seventh **m**.	2544
	25: 9	on the tenth day of the seventh **m**;	2544
	27: 6	a person between *one* **m** and five years,	2544
Nu	1: 1	of Sinai on the first day of the second **m** of	2544
	1:18	on the first day of the second **m**.	2544
	3:15	Count every male a **m** old or more."	2544
	3:22	The number of all the males a **m** old	2544
	3:28	of all the males a **m** old or more was 8,600.	2544
	3:34	The number of all the males a **m** old	2544
	3:39	including every male a **m** old or more,	2544
	3:40	the firstborn Israelite males who are a **m** old	2544
	3:43	The total number of firstborn males a **m** old	2544
	9: 1	to Moses in the Desert of Sinai in the first **m**	2544
	9: 3	at twilight on the fourteenth day of this **m**,	2544
	9: 5	on the fourteenth day of the first **m**.	2544
	9:11	on the fourteenth day of the second **m**	2544
	9:22	or a **m** or a year, the Israelites would remain	2544
	10:11	On the twentieth day of the second **m** of	2544
	11:20	but *for* a whole **m**—until it comes out of	2544
	11:21	give them meat to eat *for* a whole **m**!'	2544
	18:16	When they are a **m** old,	2544
	20: 1	In the first **m** the whole Israelite community	2544
	26:62	a **m** old or more numbered 23,000.	2544
	28:11	" 'On the first of every **m**,	2544
	28:16	of the first **m** the LORD's Passover is to	2544
	28:17	On the fifteenth day of this **m** there is to be	2544
	29: 1	" 'On the first day of the seventh **m** hold	2544
	29: 7	" 'On the tenth day of this seventh **m** hold	2544
	29:12	" 'On the fifteenth day of the seventh **m**,	2544
	33: 3	on the fifteenth day of the first **m**,	2544
	33:38	where he died on the first day of the fifth **m**	2544
Dt	1: 3	on the first day of the eleventh **m**,	2544
	16: 1	the **m** *of* Abib and celebrate the Passover of	2544
	16: 1	the **m** *of* Abib he brought you out of Egypt	2544
	21:13	her father and mother *for* a full **m**,	3732
Jos	4:19	the tenth day of the first **m** the people went	2544
	5:10	the evening of the fourteenth day of the **m**,	2544
1Sa	20:27	But the next day, the second day of the **m**,	2544
	20:34	on that second day of the **m** he did not eat,	2544
1Ki	4: 7	Each one had to provide supplies for one **m**	2544
	4:27	The district officers, each in his **m**,	2544
	5:14	to Lebanon in shifts of ten thousand a **m**,	2544
	5:14	so that they spent one **m** in Lebanon	2544
	6: 1	in the **m** *of* Ziv, the second month,	2544
	6: 1	in the month of Ziv, the second **m**,	2544
	6:37	in the fourth year, in the **m** *of* Ziv.	3732
	6:38	In the eleventh year in the **m** *of* Bul,	3732
	6:38	the eighth **m**, the temple was finished	2544
	8: 2	the time of the festival in the **m** *of* Ethanim,	3732
	8: 2	in the month of Ethanim, the seventh **m**.	2544
	12:32	on the fifteenth day of the eighth **m**,	2544
	12:33	On the fifteenth day of the eighth **m**,	2544
	12:33	a **m** of his own choosing,	2544
2Ki	15:13	and he reigned in Samaria one **m**.	3427+3732
	25: 1	on the tenth day of the tenth **m**,	2544
	25: 3	the ninth day of the [fourth] **m** the famine in	2544
	25: 8	On the seventh day of the fifth **m**,	2544
	25:25	In the seventh **m**, however,	2544
	25:27	on the twenty-seventh day of the twelfth **m**,	2544
1Ch	12:15	who crossed the Jordan in the first **m**	2544
	27: 1	that were on duty **m** by month throughout	2544
	27: 1	that were on duty month by **m** throughout	2544
	27: 2	the first division, for the first **m**,	2544
	27: 3	of all the army officers for the first **m**.	2544
	27: 4	of the division for the second **m** was Dodai	2544
	27: 5	The third army commander, for the third **m**,	2544
	27: 7	The fourth, for the fourth **m**,	2544
	27: 8	The fifth, for the fifth **m**,	2544
	27: 9	The sixth, for the sixth **m**,	2544
	27:10	The seventh, for the seventh **m**,	2544

1Ch	27:11	The eighth, for the eighth **m**,	2544
	27:12	The ninth, for the ninth **m**,	2544
	27:13	The tenth, for the tenth **m**,	2544
	27:14	The eleventh, for the eleventh **m**,	2544
	27:15	The twelfth, for the twelfth **m**,	2544
2Ch	3: 2	the second **m** in the fourth year of his reign.	2544
	5: 3	at the time of the festival in the seventh **m**.	2544
	7:10	of the seventh **m** he sent the people	2544
	15:10	They assembled at Jerusalem in the third **m**	2544
	29: 3	In the first **m** of the first year of his reign,	2544
	29:17	on the first day of the first **m**,	2544
	29:17	and by the eighth day of the **m** they reached	2544
	29:17	finishing on the sixteenth day of the first **m**.	2544
	30: 2	to celebrate the Passover in the second **m**.	2544
	30:13	of Unleavened Bread in the second **m**,	2544
	30:15	on the fourteenth day of the second **m**.	2544
	31: 7	They began doing this in the third **m**	2544
	31: 7	and finished in the seventh **m**.	2544
	35: 1	on the fourteenth day of the first **m**.	2544
Ezr	3: 1	When the seventh **m** came and	2544
	3: 6	On the first day of the seventh **m** they began	2544
	3: 8	In the second **m** of the second year	2544
	6:15	on the third day of the **m** Adar,	10333
	6:19	On the fourteenth day of the first **m**,	2544
	7: 8	the fifth **m** of the seventh year of the king.	2544
	7: 9	from Babylon on the first day of the first **m**,	2544
	7: 9	in Jerusalem on the first day of the fifth **m**,	2544
	8:31	the first **m** we set out from the Ahava Canal	2544
	10: 9	And on the twentieth day of the ninth **m**,	2544
	10:16	of the tenth **m** they sat down to investigate	2544
	10:17	of the first **m** they finished dealing with all	2544
Ne	1: 1	In the **m** of Kislev in the twentieth year,	2544
	2: 1	In the **m** of Nisan in the twentieth year	2544
	7:73	When the seventh **m** came and	2544
	8: 2	So on the first day of the seventh **m** Ezra	2544
	8:13	On the second day of the **m**,	NIH
	8:14	in booths during the feast of the seventh **m**	2544
	9: 1	On the twenty-fourth day of the same **m**,	2544
Est	2:16	in the royal residence in the tenth **m**,	2544
	2:16	the **m** of Tebeth, in the seventh year	2544
	3: 7	in the first **m**, the month of Nisan,	2544
	3: 7	the **m** of Nisan, they cast the pur	2544
	3: 7	of Haman to select a day and **m**.	2544
	3: 7	lot fell on the twelfth **m**, the month of Adar.	2544
	3: 7	lot fell on the twelfth month, the **m** of Adar.	2544
	3:12	Then on the thirteenth day of the first **m**	2544
	3:13	the thirteenth day of the twelfth **m**,	2544
	3:13	the **m** of Adar, and to plunder their goods.	2544
	8: 9	on the twenty-third day of the third **m**,	2544
	8: 9	of the third month, the **m** of Sivan,	2544
	8:12	the thirteenth day of the twelfth **m**,	2544
	8:12	the twelfth month, the **m** of Adar.	2544
	9: 1	On the thirteenth day of the twelfth **m**,	2544
	9: 1	the twelfth month, the **m** of Adar,	2544
	9:15	on the fourteenth day of the **m** of Adar,	2544
	9:17	on the thirteenth day of the **m** of Adar,	2544
	9:19	the **m** of Adar as a day of joy and feasting,	2544
	9:21	the fourteenth and fifteenth days of the **m**	2544
	9:22	the **m** when their sorrow was turned into joy	2544
Isa	47:13	those stargazers who make predictions **m**	NIH
	47:13	by **m**, let them save you	2544
Jer	1: 3	down to the fifth **m** of the eleventh year	2544
	28: 1	In the fifth **m** of that same year,	2544
	28:17	In the seventh **m** of that same year,	2544
	36: 9	In the ninth **m** of the fifth year	2544
	36:22	It was the ninth **m** and the king was sitting	2544
	39: 1	in the tenth **m**, Nebuchadnezzar king of	2544
	39: 2	of the fourth **m** of Zedekiah's eleventh year,	2544
	41: 1	In the seventh **m** Ishmael son of Nethaniah,	2544
	52: 4	on the tenth day of the tenth **m**,	2544
	52: 6	By the ninth day of the fourth **m** the famine	2544
	52:12	On the tenth day of the fifth **m**,	2544
	52:31	on the twenty-fifth day of the twelfth **m**.	2544
Eze	1: 1	in the fourth **m** on the fifth day,	2544
	1: 2	On the fifth of the **m**—	2544
	8: 1	in the sixth **m** on the fifth day,	2544
	20: 1	in the fifth **m** on the tenth day,	2544
	24: 1	in the tenth **m** on the tenth day,	2544
	26: 1	on the first day of the **m**,	2544
	29: 1	in the tenth **m** on the twelfth day,	2544
	29:17	the first **m** on the first day,	2544
	30:20	in the first **m** on the seventh day,	2544
	31: 1	in the third **m** on the first day,	2544
	32: 1	in the twelfth **m** on the first day,	2544
	32:17	on the fifteenth day of the **m**,	2544
	33:21	in the tenth **m** on the fifth day,	2544
	40: 1	on the tenth of the **m**, in the fourteenth	2544
	45:18	In the first **m** on the first day you are to take	2544
	45:20	to do the same on the seventh day of the **m**	2544
	45:21	the first **m** on the fourteenth day you are	2544
	45:25	in the seventh **m** on the fifteenth day,	2544
	47:12	Every **m** they will bear,	2544
Da	10: 4	On the twenty-fourth day of the first **m**,	2544
Hag	1: 1	on the first day of the sixth **m**,	2544
	1:15	on the twenty-fourth day of the sixth **m** in	2544
	2: 1	On the twenty-first day of the seventh **m**,	2544
	2:10	On the twenty-fourth day of the ninth **m**,	NIH
	2:18	from this twenty-fourth day of the ninth **m**,	NIH
	2:20	on the twenty-fourth day of the **m**:	2544
Zec	1: 1	the eighth **m** of the second year of Darius,	2544
	1: 7	On the twenty-fourth day of the eleventh **m**,	2544
	1: 7	the eleventh month, the **m** of Shebat,	2544
	7: 1	on the fourth day of the ninth **m**,	2544
	7: 1	the ninth month, the **m** of Kislev.	NIH
	7: 3	"Should I mourn and fast in the fifth **m**,	2544
	11: 8	In one **m** I got rid of the three shepherds.	3732
Lk	1:26	In the sixth **m**, God sent the angel Gabriel	3604

Lk	1:36	who was said to be barren is in her sixth **m**.	3604
Rev	9:15	and **m** and year were released to kill a third	3604
	22: 2	yielding its fruit every **m**.	3604

MONTHLY (11) [MONTH]

Lev	12: 2	she is unclean during her **m** period.	1864+5614
	15:19	impurity of her **m** period	5614
	15:24	with her and her **m** flow touches him,	5614
	15:25	at a time other than her **m** period or has	5614
	15:26	as is her bed during her **m** period,	5614
	15:33	for a woman in her **m** period,	1865+5614
	18:19	during the uncleanness of her **m** period.	5614
	20:18	lies with a woman during her **m** period	1865
Nu	28:14	This is the **m** burnt offering to	928+2544+2544
	29: 6	to the **m** and daily burnt offerings	2544
Eze	36:17	like a woman's **m** uncleanness	2021+3240+5614

MONTHS (52) [MONTH]

Ge	38:24	About three **m** later Judah was told,	2544
Ex	2: 2	she hid him for three **m**.	3732
Jdg	11:37	"Give me two **m** to roam the hills and weep	2544
	11:38	And he let her go for two **m**.	2544
	11:39	After the two **m**, she returned to her father	2544
	19: 2	After she had been there four **m**,	2544
	20:47	where they stayed four **m**.	2544
1Sa	6: 1	in Philistine territory seven **m**,	2544
	27: 7	in Philistine territory a year and four **m**.	2544
2Sa	2:11	of Judah was seven years and six **m**.	2544
	5: 5	over Judah seven years and six **m**,	2544
	6:11	of Obed-Edom the Gittite for three **m**,	2544
	24: 8	at the end of nine **m** and twenty days.	2544
	24:13	Or three **m** of fleeing from your enemies	2544
1Ki	5:14	in Lebanon and two **m** at home.	2544
	11:16	and all the Israelites stayed there for six **m**,	2544
2Ki	15: 8	and he reigned six **m**.	2544
	23:31	and he reigned in Jerusalem three **m**.	2544
	24: 8	and he reigned in Jerusalem three **m**.	2544
1Ch	3: 4	where he reigned seven years and six **m**.	2544
	13:14	of Obed-Edom in his house for three **m**,	2544
	21:12	three **m** of being swept away	2544
2Ch	36: 2	and he reigned in Jerusalem three **m**.	2544
	36: 9	and he reigned in Jerusalem three **m**.	2544
Est	2:12	she had to complete twelve **m**	2544
	2:12	six **m** with oil of myrrh and six	2544
Job	3: 6	of the year nor be entered in any of the **m**.	3732
	7: 3	so I have been allotted **m** of futility,	3732
	14: 5	you have decreed the number of his **m**	2544
	21:21	behind when his allotted **m** come to an end?	2544
	29: 2	"How I long for the **m** gone by,	3732
	39: 2	Do you count the **m** till they bear?	3732
Eze	39:12	" 'For seven **m** the house of Israel will	2544
	39:14	of the seven **m** they will begin their search.	2544
Da	4:29	Twelve **m** later, as the king was walking on	10333
Am	4: 7	when the harvest was still three **m** away.	2544
Zec	7: 5	and mourned in the fifth and seventh **m** for	NIH
	8:19	seventh and tenth **m** will become joyful	NIH
Mk	6:37	take eight **m** of a man's wages!	1324+1357
Lk	1:24	and for five **m** remained in seclusion.	3604
	1:56	for about three **m** and then returned home.	3604
Jn	4:35	'Four **m** more and then the harvest'?	5485
Ac	7:20	For three **m** he was cared for	3604
	19: 8	and spoke boldly there for three **m**,	3604
	20: 3	where he stayed three **m**.	3604
	28:11	After three **m** we put out to sea in a ship	3604
Gal	4:10	You are observing special days and **m**	3604
Heb	11:23	By faith Moses' parents hid him for three	
		m after he was born,	5564
Rev	9: 5	but only to torture them for five **m**.	3604
	9:10	to torment people for five **m**.	3604
	11: 2	They will trample on the holy city for 42 **m**.	3604
	13: 5	to exercise his authority for forty-two **m**.	3604

MONTHS' (1) [MONTH]

Jn	6: 7	Eight **m** wages would not buy enough	1324+1357

MONUMENT (4)

1Sa	15:12	There he has set up a **m** in his own honor	3338
2Sa	18:18	erected it in the King's Valley as a **m**	5893
	18:18	and it is called Absalom's **M** to this day.	3338
Isa	19:19	and a **m** to the LORD at its border.	5167

MOON (61) [MOONS]

Ge	37: 9	the sun and **m** and eleven stars were bowing	3734
Nu	10:10	your appointed feasts and New M	
		festivals—	2544+8031
	28:14	to be made at each new **m** during the year.	2544
Dt	4:19	the sun, the **m** and the stars—	3734
	17: 3	or to the sun or the **m** or the stars of the sky,	3734
	33:14	and the finest the **m** can yield;	3732
Jos	10:12	"O sun, stand still over Gibeon, O **m**,	3734
	10:13	So the sun stood still, and the **m** stopped,	3734
1Sa	20: 5	"Look, tomorrow is the New M festival,	2544
	20:18	"Tomorrow is the New M festival.	2544
	20:24	and when the New M festival came,	2544
2Ki	23: 5	"It's not the New M or the Sabbath."	2544
	23: 5	burned incense to Baal, to the sun and **m**,	3734
1Ch	23:31	on Sabbaths and at New M festivals and	2544
Ezr	3: 5	New M sacrifices and the sacrifices	2544
Ne	10:33	New M festivals and appointed feasts;	2544
Job	25: 5	the **m** is not bright and the stars are not pure	3734
	26: 9	He covers the face of the full **m**,	4057
	31:26	in its radiance or the **m** moving in splendor,	3734
Ps	8: 3	the **m** and the stars, which you have set in	3734
	72: 5	as long as the **m**, through all generations.	3734

Ps	72: 7	prosperity will abound till the **m** is no more.	3734
	74:16	you established the sun and **m**.	4401
	81: 3	Sound the ram's horn at the New M,	2544
	81: 3	and when the **m** is full,	4057
	89:37	it will be established forever like the **m**,	3734
	104:19	The **m** marks off the seasons,	3734
	121: 6	nor the **m** by night.	3734
	136: 9	the **m** and stars to govern the night;	3734
	148: 3	Praise him, sun and **m**, praise him,	3734
Pr	7:20	and will not be home till full **m**."	3427+4057
Ecc	12: 2	the light and the **m** and the stars grow dark,	3734
SS	6:10	fair as the **m**, bright as the sun,	4244
Isa	1:14	Your New M festivals and your appointed	2544
	13:10	and the **m** will not give its light.	3734
	24:23	The **m** will be abashed, the sun ashamed;	4244
	30:26	The **m** will shine like the sun,	4244
	60:19	nor will the brightness of the **m** shine	3734
	60:20	and your **m** will wane no more;	3734
	66:23	From one New M to another and	2544
Jer	8: 2	They will be exposed to the sun and the **m**	3734
	31:35	the **m** and stars to shine by night, who stirs	3734
Eze	32: 7	and the **m** will not give its light.	3734
	46: 1	on the day of the New M it is to be opened.	2544
	46: 6	of the New M he is to offer a young bull,	2544
Hos	5: 7	their New M festivals will devour them	2544
Joel	2:10	the sun and **m** are darkened,	3734
	2:31	be turned to darkness and the **m** to blood	3734
	3:15	The sun and **m** will be darkened,	3734
Am	8: 5	the New M be over that we may sell grain,	2544
Hab	3:11	and **m** stood still in the heavens at the glint	3734
Mt	24:29	and the **m** will not give its light;	4943
Mk	13:24	and the **m** will not give its light;	4943
Lk	21:25	"There will be signs in the sun, **m** and stars.	4943
Ac	2:20	be turned to darkness and the **m** to blood	4943
1Co	15:41	the **m** another and the stars another;	4943
Col	2:16	a New M celebration or a Sabbath day.	3741
Rev	6:12	the whole **m** turned blood red,	4943
	8:12	a third of the **m**, and a third of the stars,	4943
	12: 1	with the sun, with the **m** under her feet and	4943
	21:23	not need the sun or the **m** to shine on it,	4943

MOONS (7) [MOON]

2Ch	2: 4	and New M and at the appointed feasts of	2544
	8:13	New M and the three annual feasts—	2544
	31: 3	New M and appointed feasts as written in	2544
Isa	1:13	New M, Sabbaths and convocations—	2544
Eze	45:17	the New M and the Sabbaths—	2544
	46: 3	On the Sabbaths and New M the people of	2544
Hos	2:11	her yearly festivals, her New M,	2544

MORAL (1)

Jas	1:21	get rid of all **m** filth and the evil that is	4864

MORASTHITE (KJV) See MORESHETH

MORDECAI (53) [MORDECAI'S]

Ezr	2: 2	Nehemiah, Seraiah, Reelaiah, **M**, Bilshan,	5283
Ne	7: 7	Nahamani, **M**, Bilshan, Mispereth, Bigvai,	5283
Est	2: 5	named **M** son of Jair, the son of Shimei,	5283
	2: 7	**M** had a cousin named Hadassah,	NIH
	2: 7	and **M** had taken her as his own daughter	5283
	2:10	because **M** had forbidden her to do so.	5283
	2:15	for Esther (the girl **M** had adopted,	5283
	2:19	**M** was sitting at the king's gate.	5283
	2:20	and nationality just as **M** had told her to do,	5283
	2:21	the time **M** was sitting at the king's gate,	5283
	2:22	But **M** found out about the plot	5283
	2:22	reported it to the king, giving credit to **M**.	5283
	3: 2	**M** would not kneel down or pay him honor.	5283
	3: 3	royal officials at the king's gate asked **M**,	5283
	3: 5	When Haman saw that **M** would not kneel	5283
	3: 6	he scorned the idea of killing only **M**.	5283
	4: 1	When **M** learned of all that had been done,	5283
	4: 4	and eunuchs came and told her about **M**,	NIH
	4: 5	to find out what was troubling **M** and why.	5283
	4: 6	to **M** in the open square of the city in front	5283
	4: 7	**M** told him everything that had happened	5283
	4: 9	and reported to Esther what **M** had said.	5283
	4:10	Then she instructed him to say to **M**,	5283
	4:12	When Esther's words were reported to **M**,	5283
	4:15	Then Esther sent this reply to **M**:	5283
	4:17	So **M** went away and carried out all	5283
	5: 9	But when he saw **M** at the king's gate	5283
	5: 9	he was filled with rage against **M**.	5283
	5:13	that Jew **M** sitting at the king's gate."	5283
	5:14	the king in the morning to have **M** hanged	5283
	6: 2	that **M** had exposed Bigthana and Teresh,	5283
	6: 3	and recognition has **M** received for this?"	5283
	6: 4	to speak to the king about hanging **M** on	5283
	6:10	and do just as you have suggested for **M**	5283
	6:11	He robed **M**, and led him on horseback	5283
	6:12	Afterward **M** returned to the king's gate.	5283
	6:13	and his wife Zeresh said to him, "Since **M**,	5283
	7: 9	He had it made for **M**,	5283
	7:10	on the gallows he had prepared for **M**.	5283
	8: 1	And **M** came into the presence of the king,	5283
	8: 2	and presented it to **M**.	5283
	8: 7	to Queen Esther and to **M** the Jew,	5283
	8:10	**M** wrote in the name of King Xerxes,	NIH
	8:15	**M** left the king's presence wearing royal	5283
	9: 3	because fear of **M** had seized them.	5283
	9: 4	**M** was prominent in the palace;	5283
	9:20	**M** recorded these events,	5283
	9:23	doing what **M** had written to them.	5283

Est	9:29	daughter of Abihail, along with **M** the Jew,	5283
	9:30	And **M** sent letters to all the Jews in	NIH
	9:31	as **M** the Jew and Queen Esther had decreed	5283
	10: 2	with a full account of the greatness of **M**	5283
	10: 3	**M** the Jew was second in rank	5283

MORDECAI'S (5) [MORDECAI]

Est	2:20	for she continued to follow **M** instructions	5283
	3: 4	about it to see whether **M** behavior would	5283
	3: 6	Yet having learned who **M** people were,	5283
	3: 6	for a way to destroy all **M** people,	5283
	8: 9	They wrote out all **M** orders to the Jews,	5283

MORE (584)

Ge	3: 1	Now the serpent was **m** crafty **than** any of	4946
	4:13	"My punishment is **m** than I can bear.	1524
	5:24	he was no **m**, because God took him away.	401
	7:20	to a depth of **m** than twenty feet.	4946
	8:10	He waited seven **m** days and again sent	337+6388
	8:12	He waited seven **m** days and sent	337+6388
	18:32	but let me speak just **once m.**	7193
	24:20	ran back to the well to draw **m** water,	AIT
	29:30	and he loved Rachel **m** than Leah.	4946
	37: 3	Now Israel loved Joseph **m** than any	4946
	37: 4	that their father loved him **m** than any	4946
	37: 5	they hated him **all the m.**	3578+6388
	37: 8	And they hated him **all the m** because	3578+6388
	38:26	"She is **m** righteous **than** I,	4946
	42:13	and one **is no m.**"	401
	42:32	One **is no m**, and the youngest is now	401
	42:36	Joseph **is no m** and Simeon is no more,	401
	42:36	Joseph is no more and Simeon **is no m,**	401
	43: 2	"Go back and buy us a little **m** food.	NIH
	44:25	'Go back and buy a **little m** food.'	5071
Ex	1:10	or **they will become even m numerous** and,	AIT
	1:12	But the **m** they were oppressed,	889+3869
	1:12	the **m** they multiplied and spread;	4027
	1:20	and became **even m** numerous.	4394
	5:10	'I will not give you any **m** straw.	NIH
	9:29	and there will be no **m** hail,	4946
	10:17	Now forgive my sin **once m** and	421+2021+7193
	11: 1	"I will bring one **m** plague on Pharaoh and	6388
	28:27	Make two **m** gold rings and attach them to	NIH
	30:14	those twenty years old or **m,**	2025+5087
	30:15	not to **give m** than a half shekel and	8049
	36: 5	"The people are bringing **m** than enough	4946
	36: 6	the people were restrained from bringing **m,**	NIH
	36: 7	what they already had **was m** than enough	3855
	38:26	twenty years old or **m,** a total of 603,550	2025+5087
		men.	
	39:20	Then they made two **m** gold rings	NIH
Lev	13: 3	the sore appears to be **m** than skin deep,	4946
	13: 4	to be **m** than skin deep and the hair in it has	4946
	13:20	and if it appears to be **m** than skin deep and	4946
	13:21	it is not **m** than skin deep and has faded,	4946
	13:25	and it appears to be **m** than skin deep,	4946
	13:26	in the spot and if it is not **m** than skin deep	4946
	13:30	and if it appears to be **m** than skin deep and	4946
	13:31	it does not seem to be **m** than skin deep	4946
	13:32	not appear to be **m** than skin deep,	4946
	13:34	and appears to be no **m** than skin deep,	4946
	27: 7	If it is a person sixty years old or **m,**	2025+5087
Nu	1: 3	in Israel twenty years old or **m** who	2025+5087
	1:18	men twenty years old or **m** were listed	2025+5087
	1:20	men twenty years old or **m** who were	2025+5087
	1:22	men twenty years old or **m** who were	2025+5087
	1:24	men twenty years old or **m** who were	2025+5087
	1:26	men twenty years old or **m** who were	2025+5087
	1:28	men twenty years old or **m** who were	2025+5087
	1:30	men twenty years old or **m** who were	2025+5087
	1:32	men twenty years old or **m** who were	2025+5087
	1:34	men twenty years old or **m** who were	2025+5087
	1:36	men twenty years old or **m** who were	2025+5087
	1:38	men twenty years old or **m** who were	2025+5087
	1:40	men twenty years old or **m** who were	2025+5087
	1:42	men twenty years old or **m** who were	2025+5087
	1:45	twenty years old or **m** who were able	2025+5087
	3:15	Count every male a month old or **m.**"	2025+5087
	3:22	or **m** who were counted was 7,500.	2025+5087
	3:28	males a month old or **m** was 8,600.	2025+5087
	3:34	or **m** who were counted was 6,200.	2025+5087
	3:39	every male a month old or **m,**	2025+5087
	3:40	or **m** and make a list of their names.	2025+5087
	3:43	of firstborn males a month old or **m,**	2025+5087
	8:24	Men twenty-five years old or **m** shall	2025+5087
	12: 3	**m** humble **than** anyone else	4946
	14:29	or **m** who was counted in the census	2025+5087
	22:15	**m** numerous and more distinguished than	NIH
	22:15	more numerous and **m** distinguished **than**	4946
	26: 2	all those twenty years old or **m** who	2025+5087
	26: 4	of the men twenty years old or **m**	2025+5087
	26:62	a month old or **m** numbered 23,000.	2025+5087
	32:11	men twenty years old or **m** who came	2025+5087
	32:14	**making** the LORD even **m** angry with	3578
Dt	3:11	and was **m** than thirteen feet long	564+9596
	5:22	and he added **nothing m.**	AIT
	7: 7	you were **m** numerous **than** other peoples,	4946
	7:14	be blessed **m** than any other people;	4946
	9:14	and **m** numerous **than** they."	4946
	17:16	or make the people return to Egypt to **get m**	8049
	19: 9	then you are to set aside three **m** cities.	3578+6388
	25: 3	he must not give him **m** than forty lashes.	3578
	25: 3	If he is flogged **m** than that,	3578+8041
	30: 5	He will **make** you **m prosperous** and	
		numerous than your fathers.	3512

Dt	31:27	how much **m** will you rebel after I die!	
			677+2256+3954
	33:11	strike his foes **till they rise no m.**"	4946
Jos	10:11	and **m** of them died from the hailstorm	8041
	19: 9	Judah's portion was **m** than they needed.	8041
	22:33	And they talked **no m** about going to war	AIT
Jdg	2:19	to ways **even m** corrupt **than** those	4946
	6:39	Let me make just **one m** request.	7193
	6:39	Allow me **one m** test with the fleece.	7193
	7:12	Their camels could no **m** be counted than	NIH
	15: 2	Isn't her younger sister **m** attractive?	4946
	16:18	"Come back **once m;**	7193
	16:28	O God, please strengthen me just **once m,**	7193
	16:30	he killed **m** when he died **than** while	4946
	20:45	as Gidom and struck down two thousand **m.**	408S
Ru	1:11	Am I going to have **any m** sons,	6388
	1:13	It is **m** bitter for me than for you,"	4394
1Sa	1: 8	Don't I **mean m** to you than ten sons?	3202
	2: 5	but those who were hungry hunger **no m.**	2532
	2:29	Why do you honor your sons **m** than me	4946
	14:19	tumult in the Philistine camp **increased m**	
		and more.	2143+2143+2256+8041
	14:19	tumult in the Philistine camp **increased**	
		more and m.	2143+2143+2256+8041
	18: 8	What **m** can he get but the kingdom?"	6388
	18:29	Saul **became** still **m** afraid of him,	3578
	18:30	David met with **m** success **than** the rest	4946
	19: 8	**Once m** war broke out,	3578
	19:21	Saul was told about it, and he sent **m** men,	337
	21: 5	**How much m** so today!"	677+3954
	23: 3	**How much m,** then, if we go to Keilah	677
	24:17	"You are **m** righteous **than** I," he said.	4946
2Sa	1:26	**m** wonderful **than** that of women.	4946
	4:11	**How much m**—when wicked men have	
		killed an innocent man in his	677
	5:10	And he **became m and more powerful,**	
			1524+2143+2143+2256
	5:10	And he **became more and m powerful,**	
			1524+2143+2143+2256
	5:13	David took **m** concubines and wives	6388
	5:13	and **m** sons and daughters were born to him.	6388
	5:22	**Once m** the Philistines came up	3578+6388
	6:22	I will become even **m** undignified **than** this,	4946
	7:20	"What **m** can David say to you?	3578+6388
	11:12	David said to him, "Stay here one **m** day,	1685
	12: 8	I would have **given** you **even m.**	
			2179+2179+2256+3578+3869+3869
	13:15	he hated her **m** than he had loved her.	1524
	16:11	**How much m,** then, this Benjamite!	677+3954
	18: 8	and the forest claimed **m** lives that day than	8049
	19:28	to make **any m** appeals to the king?"	6388
	19:29	The king said to him, "Why say **m?**	6388
	19:34	"**How many m** years will I live,	3869+4537
	19:43	of Judah responded **even m** harshly **than**	4946
	20: 6	son of Bicri will do us **m** harm **than**	
		Absalom did.	4946
1Ki	1:47	'May your God make Solomon's name **m**	
		famous **than** yours	4946
	2:32	were better men and **m** upright **than** he.	4946
	8:65	for seven days and seven days **m,**	NIH
	13:33	but **once m** appointed priests for	8740
	14: 9	You have done **m** evil **than** all who lived	4946
	14:22	stirred up his jealous anger **m than** their	
		fathers had done.	4946
	16:25	of the LORD and sinned **m than** all those	4946
	16:30	**m** evil in the eyes of the LORD **than**	4946
	16:33	Ahab also made an Asherah pole and did **m**	3578
2Ki	2:12	And Elisha saw him no **m.**	6388
	3: 9	the army had **no m** water for themselves or	AIT
	4:35	the bed and stretched out upon him once **m.**	NIH
	5:13	**How much m,** then, when he tells you,	677
	6:16	with us are **m** than those who are	8041
	12: 7	Take **no m** money from your treasurers,	AIT
	12: 8	not collect any **m** money from the people	NIH
	19:30	**Once m** a remnant of the house	3578
	21: 9	so that they did **m** evil **than** the nations	4946
	21:11	He has done **m** evil than	3972
	25:16	was **m** than could be weighed.	4202
1Ch	4: 9	Jabez was **m** honorable **than** his brothers.	4946
	11: 9	And David **became m and more powerful,**	
			1524+2143+2143+2256
	11: 9	And David **became more and m powerful,**	
			1524+2143+2143+2256
	14: 3	In Jerusalem David took **m** wives	6388
	14: 3	the father of **m** sons and daughters.	6388
	14:13	**Once m** the Philistines raided the valley;	
			3578+6388
	17:18	"What **m** can David say to you	3578+6388
	22: 3	and **m** bronze than could be weighed.	4200+8044
	22: 4	He also provided **m** cedar logs **than**	401+4200
	23: 3	thirty years old or **m** were counted,	2025+5087
	23:24	twenty years old or **m** who served	2025+5087
	23:27	those twenty years old or **m.**	2025+4200+5087
2Ch	7: 9	and the festival for seven days **m.**	NIH
	9:12	he gave her **m** than she had brought to him.	
			963+4200+4946
	11:21	of Absalom **m than** any of his other wives	4946
	15:19	There was **no m** war until	AIT
	17:12	became **m and more powerful;**	
			1541+2025+2143+2256+4200+5087+6330
	17:12	became **more and m powerful;**	
			1541+2025+2143+2256+4200+5087+6330
	20:25	**m** than they could take away.	401+4200
	25: 5	mustered those twenty years old or **m**	2025+5087
	25: 9	The LORD can give you much **m** than that.	4946
	28:22	even **m** unfaithful to the LORD.	3578
	29:17	For eight **m** days they consecrated	NIH

2Ch	29:34	**m** conscientious in consecrating themselves	
		than the priests	4946
	30:23	to celebrate the festival seven **m** days;	4946
	31:16	or **m** whose names were in	2025+5087
	31:17	to the Levites twenty years old or **m,**	2025+5087
	33: 9	so that they did **m** evil **than** the nations	4946
	36:14	**m and more unfaithful,**	5085+5086+8049
	36:14	**more and m unfaithful,**	5085+5086+8049
Ezr	4:13	**no m** taxes, tribute or duty will be paid,	AIT
Ne	5:12	we will not demand anything **m** from them.	NIH
	7: 2	and feared God **m** than most men do.	4946
	13:18	Now you are **stirring up m** wrath	3578
Est	2:17	Esther **m** than to any of the other women,	4946
	2:17	his favor and approval **m** than any of	4946
	9: 4	became **m and more powerful.** 1524+2143+2256
	9: 4	became **more and m powerful.** 1524+2143+2256
Job	3: 5	and deep shadow claim it once **m;**	NIH
	3:21	for it **m** than for hidden treasure,	4946
	4:17	'Can a mortal be righteous **than** God?	4946
	4:17	Can a man be **m** pure **than** his Maker?	4946
	4:19	how much **m** those who live in houses of	
		clay,	677
	4:19	are crushed **m readily than** a moth!	4200+7156
	7: 8	you will look for me, but I will **be no m.**	401
	7:10	his place will know him no **m.**	6388
	7:21	you will search for me, but I will **be no m.**"	401
	8:12	they wither **m quickly than** grass.	4200+7156
	8:22	and the tents of the wicked will **be no m.**"	401
	9:34	so that his terror would frighten me **no m.**	AIT
	11:12	a witless man can **no m** become wise **than**	2256
	14:10	he breathes his last and is **no m.**	361
	14:12	till the heavens are **no m,**	1194
	20: 8	**no m** to be found,	AIT
	20: 9	his place will see him no **m.**	6388
	23:12	of his mouth **m** than my daily bread.	4946
	27:19	He lies down wealthy, but will do so no **m;**	665
	29:22	After I had spoken, they spoke no **m,**	9101
	32: 5	that the three men had **nothing m** to say,	AIT
	32:15	"They are dismayed and have **no m** to say;	6388
	34:31	'I am guilty but will offend **no m.**	AIT
	35:11	who teaches **m** to us **than** to the beasts of	4946
	36: 2	that there is **m** to be said in God's behalf.	6388
	40: 5	twice, but I will say no **m.**"	3578
	42:12	the latter part of Job's life **m** than the first.	4946
Ps	10:18	who is of the earth, may terrify no **m.** 3578+6388
	12: 1	Help, LORD, for the godly are **no m;**	1698
	19:10	They are **m** precious **than** gold,	4946
	37:10	A little while, and the wicked will **be no m;**	401
	37:36	but he soon passed away and was **no m;**	401
	39:13	before I depart and am **no m.**"	401
	40:12	They are **m** than the hairs of my head,	6793
	55:21	his words are **m** soothing **than** oil,	4946
	59:13	consume them till they are **no m.**	401
	69:31	This will please the LORD **m** than an ox,	4946
	69:31	**m** than a bull with its horns and hoofs.	NIH
	71:14	I will praise you **m and more.** 3578+3972+6584
	71:14	I will praise you **more and m.** 3578+3972+6584
	72: 7	till the moon is **no m.**	1172
	75: 4	'Boast no **m,**' and to the wicked,	AIT
	76: 4	**m** majestic **than** mountains rich with game.	4946
	78:29	They ate till they had **m** than enough,	4394
	83: 4	the name of Israel be remembered no **m.**"	6388
	87: 2	of Zion **m** than all the dwellings of Jacob.	4946
	88: 5	whom you remember no **m,**	6388
	89: 7	is **m** awesome **than** all who surround him.	6584
	103:16	and its place remembers it no **m.**	6388
	104:35	from the earth and the wicked be no **m.**	6388
	116: 7	Be at rest **once m,** O my soul,	8740
	119:72	**m** precious to me than thousands of pieces	4946
	119:99	I have **m** insight **than** all my teachers,	4946
	119:100	I have **m** understanding **than** the elders,	4946
	119:127	I love your commands **m than** gold,	4946
	119:127	**m than** pure gold,	4946
	120: 3	What will he do to you, and what **m besides**	3578
	130: 6	My soul waits for the Lord **m than**	4946
	130: 6	**m** than watchmen wait for the morning.	NIH
Pr	3:14	for she is **m** profitable **than** silver	4946
	3:15	She is **m** precious **than** rubies;	4946
	8:11	for wisdom is **m** precious **than** rubies,	4946
	11:24	One man gives freely, yet gains **even m;**	6388
	11:31	how much **m** the ungodly and the sinner!	
			677+3954
	12: 7	Wicked men are overthrown and **are no m,**	401
	15:11	how much **m** the hearts of men!	677+3954
	17:10	of discernment **m than** a hundred lashes	4946
	18:19	An offended brother is **m** unyielding **than**	4946
	19: 7	how much **m** do his friends avoid him!	677+3954
	21: 3	**m** acceptable to the LORD **than**	4946
	21:26	All day long he **craves for m,**	203+9294
	21:27	how much **m** so when brought with evil	
		intent!	677+3954
	22: 1	good name is **m** desirable **than** great riches;	4946
	25: 1	These are **m** proverbs of Solomon,	1685
	26:12	There is **m** hope for a fool **than**	4946
	28:23	in the end gain **m** favor **than** he who has	4946
	29:20	There is **m** hope for a fool than for him.	4200
	31: 7	and remember their misery no **m.**	6388
	31:10	She is worth far **m** than rubies.	4946
Ecc	1: 8	things are wearisome, **m** than one can say.	4202
	1:16	in wisdom **m than** anyone who has ruled	6584
	1:18	the **m** knowledge, the more grief.	3578
	1:18	the more knowledge, the **m** grief.	3578
	2: 7	also owned **m** herds and flocks than anyone	2221
	2:12	**What m** can the king's successor do than	
		what has already been done?	3954+4537
	6: 5	it has **m** rest **than** does that man—	4946
	6:11	The **m** the words, the less the meaning,	2221

Ecc 7:19 Wisdom makes one wise man **m** powerful than ten rulers — 4946
   7:26 I find **m** bitter than death the woman who is — 4946
   9:17 words of the wise are **m** to be heeded than — 4946
  10:10 **m** strength is needed but skill will bring — AIT
SS 1: 2 for your love is **m** delightful than wine. — 4946
   1: 4 we will praise your love **m** than wine. — 4946
  4:10 much **m** pleasing is your love than — 4946
Isa 1:11 "I have **m** than enough of burnt offerings. — 8425
   5: 4 What **m** could have been done — 6388
   9: 1 be no **m** gloom for those who were — AIT
  13:12 **m** rare than the gold of Ophir. — 4946
  15: 9 but I will bring **still m** upon Dimon— — 3578
  19: 7 will blow away and be no **m.** — 401
  23:12 He said, "No **m** of your reveling, — 3578+6388
  25: 2 the foreigners' stronghold a city **no m;** — 4946
  26:14 They are now dead, they live no **m;** — AIT
  29:14 once **m** I will astound these people — 3578
  29:19 Once **m** the humble will rejoice in — 3578
  30:10 They say to the seers, "See no **m** visions!" — AIT
  30:10 "Give us no **m** visions — AIT
  30:19 you will weep no **m.** — AIT
  30:20 your teachers will be hidden no **m;** — 6388
  32:10 In little **m** than a year you who feel — 3427+6584
  33:19 You will see those arrogant people no **m,** — AIT
  33:31 Once **m** a remnant of the house — 3578
  43:25 and remembers your sins no **m.** — AIT
  47: 1 No **m** will you be called tender or delicate. — 3578
  47: 5 no **m** will you be called queen of kingdoms. — 3578
  49:20 give us **m** space to live in.' — 5602
  54: 1 because **m** are the children of the desolate — 8041
  54: 4 remember no **m** the reproach of your — 6388
  60:19 The sun will no **m** be your light by day, — 6388
  60:20 and your moon will wane no **m,** — AIT
  65:19 and of crying will be heard in it no **m.** — 6388
Jer 2:31 we will come to you no **m**'? — 6388
  3:11 "Faithless Israel is **m** righteous than unfaithful Judah. — 4946
  7:26 and did **m** evil than their forefathers.' — 4946
  7:32 in Topheth until there is no **m** room. — AIT
  10:20 My sons are gone from me and are no **m;** — 401
  11:19 that his name be remembered no **m."** — 6388
  15: 8 I will make their widows **m** numerous than — 4946
  16:12 you have behaved **m** wickedly than your fathers. — 4946
  19:11 in Topheth until there is no **m** room. — AIT
  20: 9 "I will not mention his name or speak any **m** — 6388
  22:15 a king to have **m** and more cedar? — 3013
  22:15 a king to have **more** and **m** cedar? — 3013
  25:27 and fall to rise no **m** because of the sword — 6388
  31:12 and they will sorrow no **m.** — 3578+6388
  31:15 because her children are no **m."** — 401
  31:34 and will remember their sins no **m."** — 6388
  32:43 Once **m** fields will be bought in this land — 2256
  33:10 there will be heard once **m** — 6388
  38:27 So they said no **m** to him, — 3087
  46:23 They are **m** numerous than locusts, — 4946
  48: 2 Moab will be praised no **m;** — 6388
  49:10 and he will be no **m.** — 401
  51:64 'So will Babylon sink to rise no **m** because — AIT
  52:20 was **m** than could be weighed. — 4202
La 2: 9 the law is no **m,** and her prophets no longer — 401
  4: 7 their bodies **m** ruddy than rubies, — 4946
  5: 7 Our fathers sinned and are no **m,** — 401
Eze 5: 6 against my laws and decrees **m** than — 4946
  5: 7 You have been **m** unruly than the nations — 4946
  5:16 I will bring **m** and more famine upon you — 3578
  5:16 I will bring **more** and **m** famine upon you — 3578
  8: 6 that are even **m** detestable." — 1524
  8:13 that are even **m** detestable." — 1524
  8:13 that are **m** detestable than this." — 1524
  12:24 For there will be no **m** false visions — 6388
  16:47 in all your ways you soon became **m** depraved than they. — 4946
  16:51 You have done **m** detestable things than they, — 8049
  16:52 Because your sins were **m** vile than theirs, — 4946
  16:52 they appear **m** righteous than you. — 4946
  21:32 you will be remembered no **m;** — AIT
  23:11 she was **m** depraved than her sister. — 4946
  23:19 Yet she became **m** and more promiscuous — 8049
  23:19 Yet she became **more** and **m** promiscuous — 8049
  26:13 the music of your harps will be heard no **m.** — 6388
  26:21 to a horrible end and you will be no **m.** — 401
  27:36 to a horrible end and will be no **m.'** — 6330+6409
  28:19 to a horrible end and will be no **m.'** — 6330+6409
  32:19 'Are you **m** favored than others? — 5838
  33:32 to them you are **nothing m** than one who sings love songs — 3869
  36:11 and will make you prosper **m** than before. — 4946
  42: 5 **m** space from them than — 4946
Da 2: 7 Once **m** they replied, — 10766
  2:43 any **m** than iron mixes with clay. — 10168+10195+10341
  5: 9 King Belshazzar became **even m** terrified — 10678
  5: 9 and his face grew **m** pale. — NIH
  7:20 that looked **m** imposing than the others — 10427
  11: 2 Three **m** kings will appear in Persia, — 6388
  11:19 will stumble and fall, to be seen no **m.** — AIT
Hos 4: 7 The **m** the priests increased, — 3869
  4: 7 the **m** they sinned against me; — 4027
  10: 1 As his fruit increased, he built **m** altars; — 8049
  11: 2 But the **m** I called Israel, the further they — NIH
  13: 2 Now they sin **m** and more; — 3578
  13: 2 Now they sin **more** and **m;** — 3578
  14: 8 O Ephraim, what **m** have I to do with idols? — 6388
Am 4: 4 go to Gilgal and sin **yet m.** — 8049

Jnh 3: 4 "Forty **m** days and Nineveh will — 6388
  4:11 But Nineveh has **m** than a hundred and twenty thousand people who cannot — 2221
Na 1:12 I will afflict you no **m.** — 6388
  1:15 No **m** will the wicked invade you; — 3578+6388
  3:16 till they are **m** than the stars of the sky, — 4946
Hab 1:13 up those **m** righteous than themselves? — 4946
Hag 2: 6 while I will once **m** shake the heavens and — 6388
Zec 13: 2 and they will be remembered no **m,"** — 6388
Mt 2:18 because they are no **m.** — 4024
  3:11 will come one who is **m** powerful than I, — 2708
  5:47 what are you doing **m** than others? — 4356
  6:25 Is not life **m** important than food, — 4498
  6:25 and the body **m** important than clothes? — NIG
  6:26 Are you not much **m** valuable than they? — 1422
  6:30 will he not much **m** clothe you, — 3437
  7:11 how much **m** will your Father — 3437
  10:15 be **m** bearable for Sodom and Gomorrah on — 445
  10:25 how much **m** the members of his household! — 3437
  10:31 you are worth **m** than many sparrows. — 1422
  10:37 or mother **m** than me is not worthy of me; — 5642
  10:37 or daughter **m** than me is not worthy of me; — 5642
  11: 9 Yes, I tell you, and **m** than a prophet. — 4358
  11:22 it will be **m** bearable for Tyre and Sidon on — 445
  11:24 that it will be **m** bearable for Sodom on — 445
  12:12 How much **m** valuable is a man than a sheep! — 4531
  12:45 seven other spirits **m** wicked than itself, — 4505
  13:12 Whoever has will be given **m,** — NIG
  20:10 they expected to receive **m.** — 4498
  21:36 **m** than the first time, — 4498
  22: 4 "Then he sent some **m** servants and said, — 257
  22:46 to ask him any **m** questions. — 4033
  23:23 the **m** important matters of the law— — AIT
  25:16 to work and gained five **m.** — 257
  25:17 the one with the two talents gained two **m.** — 257
  25:20 See, I have gained five **m.'** — 257
  25:22 see, I have gained two **m.'** — 257
  25:29 For everyone who has will be given **m,** — NIG
  26:44 So he left them and went away **once m** — 4099
  26:53 at my disposal **m** than twelve legions — 4498
  26:65 Why do we need any **m** witnesses? — 2285
Mk 1: 7 After me will come one **m** powerful than I, — 2708
  4:24 measured to you—and even **m.** — 2779+4707+5148
  4:25 Whoever has will be given **m;** — NIG
  5: 3 and no one could bind him any **m,** — 4033
  5:35 "Why bother the teacher any **m?"** — 2285
  7:36 But the **m** he did so, — 4012
  7:36 the **m** they kept talking about it. — 3437+4358
  8:25 Once **m** Jesus put his hands on — 1663+4099
  10:26 The disciples were **even m** amazed, — 4360
  10:48 but he shouted all the **m,** "Son of David, — 3189+3437+4498
  12:33 is **m** important than all burnt offerings — 4358
  12:34 on no one dared ask him any **m** questions. — NIG
  12:43 this poor widow has put **m** into — 4498
  14: 5 It could have been sold for **m** than — 2062
  14:39 Once **m** he went away and prayed — 4099
  14:63 "Why do we need any **m** witnesses? — 2285
Lk 3:13 "Don't collect any **m** than you are required — 4123+4498
  3:16 But one **m** powerful than I will come, — 2708
  5:15 Yet the news about him spread **all the m,** — 3437
  7:26 Yes, I tell you, and **m** than a prophet. — 4358
  7:42 Now which of them will love him **m?"** — 4498
  8: 8 a hundred times **m** than was sown." — NIG
  8:18 Whoever has will be given **m;** — NIG
  8:49 "Don't bother the teacher any **m."** — 3600
  10:12 be **m** bearable on that day for Sodom than — 445
  10:14 be **m** bearable for Tyre and Sidon at — 445
  11:13 how much **m** will your Father — 3437
  11:26 seven other spirits **m** wicked than itself, — 4505
  12: 4 the body and after that can do no **m.** — 4358
  12: 7 you are worth **m** than many sparrows. — 1422
  12:23 Life is **m** than food, — 4498
  12:23 and the body **m** than clothes. — NIG
  12:24 how much **m** valuable you are than birds! — 3437
  12:28 how much **m** will he clothe you, — 3437
  12:48 how much **m** will be asked. — 4358
  13: 4 do you think they were **m** guilty than all — NIG
  13: 8 'leave it alone for one **m** year, — NIG
  14: 8 a person **m** distinguished than you — 1952
  15: 7 there will be **m** rejoicing in heaven over one sinner who repents than — 2445
  16: 8 For the people of this world are **m** shrewd — AIT
  18:39 but he shouted all the **m,** "Son of David, have mercy on me!" — 3437+4498
  19:16 'Sir, your mina has earned ten **m.'** — 4664
  19:18 'Sir, your mina has earned five **m.'** — 3641ˢ
  19:26 to everyone who has, **m** will be given, — NIG
  20:40 no one dared to ask him any **m** questions. — 4033
  21: 3 "this poor widow has put in **m** than all — 4498
  22:44 being in anguish, he prayed **m** earnestly, — AIT
  22:51 But Jesus answered, "No **m** of this!" — 1572
  22:71 "Why do we need any **m** testimony? — 2285
  24:21 And what is **m,** it is the third day since — 247+1145+2779+4047+4246+5250
Jn 2: 3 "They have no **m** wine." — NIG
  4: 1 and baptizing **m** disciples than John, — 4498
  4: 3 he left Judea and went back once **m** — 4099
  4:35 "Four months **m** and then the harvest'? — 2285
  4:41 of his words many **m** became believers. — 4498
  4:46 Once **m** he visited Cana in Galilee, — 4099
  7:31 he do **m** miraculous signs than this man?" — 4498
  8: 2 Once **m** Jesus said to them, — 4099
  11: 6 he stayed where he was two **m** days. — NIG
  11:38 Jesus, once **m** deeply moved, — 4099

Jn 12:43 praise from men **m** than praise from God. — 3437
  15: 2 so that it will be even **m** fruitful. — 4498
  16:12 "I have much **m** to say to you, — 2285
  16:12 **m** than you can now bear. — NIG
  16:16 "In a little while you will see me no **m,** — 4033
  16:17 'In a little while you will see me no **m,** — 4024
  16:19 'In a little while you will see me no **m,** — 4024
  17:14 world any **m** than I am of the world. — 2777+4024
  19: 4 Once **m** Pilate came out and said to — 2779+4099
  19: 8 he was even **m** afraid, — NIG
  21:15 do you truly love me **m** than these?" — 4498
Ac 5:14 **m** and more men and women believed in — 3437
  5:14 **more** and **m** men and women believed in — 3437
  7:31 As he went over to look **m** closely, — 2917
  9:22 Yet Saul grew **m** and more powerful — 3437
  9:22 and **m** powerful and baffled the Jews living — NIG
  17:11 Bereans were of **m** noble character than — 2302
  18:20 When they asked him to spend **m** time — 4498
  18:26 to him the way of God **m** adequately. — 209
  20:35 'It is **m** blessed to give than to receive.'" — 3437
  23:13 **M** than forty men were involved — 4498
  23:15 pretext of wanting **m** accurate information — AIT
  23:20 pretext of wanting **m** accurate information — AIT
  23:21 because **m** than forty of them are waiting — 4498
  24:11 that no **m** than twelve days ago I went up — 4498
Ro 3: 5 brings out God's righteousness **m** clearly, — 5319
  5: 9 how much **m** shall we be saved — 3437
  5:10 how much **m,** having been reconciled, — 3437
  5:15 how much **m** did God's grace and the gift — 3437
  5:17 much **m** will those who receive God's abundant provision of grace — 3437
  5:20 sin increased, grace increased all the **m,** — 5668
  8:34 **m** than that, who was raised to life— — 3437
  8:37 in all these things we are **m** than conquerors through him — 5664
  11:24 how much **m** readily will these, — 3437
  12: 3 of yourself **m** highly than you ought, — 4123
  14: 5 One man considers one day **m** sacred than another; — 4123
  15:23 now that there is no **m** place for me to work — 3600
1Co 3:21 So then, no **m** boasting about men! — NIG
  6: 3 How much **m** the things of this life! — 3615
  9:12 shouldn't we have it **all the m?** — 3437
  11:17 for your meetings do **m** harm than good. — NIG
  14:18 that I speak in tongues **m** than all of you. — 3437
  15: 6 to **m** than five hundred of the brothers at — 2062
  15:15 **M than that,** we are then found to — 2779
  15:19 we are to be pitied **m** than all men. — 1795
2Co 3: 8 of the Spirit be even **m** glorious? — 3437
  3: 9 how much **m** glorious is the ministry — 3437
  4:15 grace that is reaching **m** and more people may cause thanksgiving — 1328+3836+4429+4498
  4:15 grace that is reaching **more** and **m** people may cause thanksgiving — 1328+3836+4429+4498
  8:19 What is **m,** he was chosen by the churches — 247+1254+2779+3667+4024
  8:22 zealous, and now **even m** so because — 4498+5080ˢ
  11:23 I am, I have worked much harder, — 5642
  11:23 been in prison **m** frequently, — 4359
  11:23 been flogged **m** severely, — 5649
  12: 6 no one will think **m** of me than is warranted — 5642
  12: 9 Therefore I will boast **all the m** gladly — 3437
  12:15 If I love you **m,** will you love me less? — 4359
Gal 4:27 because **m** are the children of the desolate — 4498
Eph 3:20 to do immeasurably **m** than all we ask — 5642
  4: 1 with a continual lust for **m.** — NIE
Php 1: 9 that your love may abound **m** and more — 3437
  1: 9 in knowledge and depth of insight, — 3437
  1:14 to speak the word of God **m** courageously — 4359
  1:24 but it is **m** necessary for you that I remain — 338
  2:12 but now much **m** in my absence— — 3437
  2:28 I am all the **m** eager to send him, — 5081
  3: 4 to put confidence in the flesh, I have **m:** — 3437
  3: 8 What is **m,** I consider everything — 247+3529
  4:18 I have received full payment and even **m;** — 4355
1Th 4: 1 to do this and **more.** — 3437+4355
  4: 1 to do this **more** and **m.** — 3437+4355
  4:10 to do so **m** and more. — 3437+4355
  4:10 to do so **more** and **m.** — 3437+4355
2Th 1: 3 because your faith is growing **m** and more, — 5647
  1: 3 because your faith is growing **more** and **m,** — 5647
2Ti 2:16 it will become **m** and more ungodly. — 2093+4498
  2:16 it will become **more** and **m** ungodly. — 2093+4498
Phm 1:21 knowing that you will do even **m** than I ask — 5642
  1:22 And one thing **m:** Prepare a guest room — 275
Heb 2: 1 We must pay **m** careful attention, — 4359
  7:15 And what we have said is even **m** clear — 4358
  8:12 and will remember their sins no **m."** — 2285
  9:11 the greater and **m** perfect tabernacle that is — AIT
  9:14 how much **m,** then, will the blood — 3437
  10:17 and lawless acts I will remember no **m."** — 2285
  10:25 all the **m** as you see the Day approaching. — 3437+5537
  10:29 How much **m** severely do you think — 5937
  11:32 And what shall I say? — 2285
  12: 9 How much **m** should we submit to — 3437
  12:26 "Once **m** I will shake not only the earth but — 2285
  12:27 The words "once **m**" indicate the removing — 2285
Jas 3: 1 that we who teach will be judged **m** strictly. — 3505
  4: 6 But he gives us **m** grace. — 3505
2Pe 1:10 be all the **m** eager to make your calling — 3437
  1:19 the word of the prophets made **m** certain, — AIT
  2:19 although they are stronger and **m** powerful, — 3505
Rev 2:19 and that you are now doing **m** than you did — 4498
  10: 6 and said, "There will be no **m** delay! — 4033
  10: 8 from heaven spoke to me once **m:** — 4099
  18:11 because no one buys their cargoes any **m**— — 4033

Rev 21: 4 There will be no **m** death or mourning 2285
    22: 5 There will be no **m** night. 2285

MOREH (3)

Ge 12: 6 the site of the great tree of **M** at Shechem. 4622
Dt 11:30 near the great trees of **M**, 4622
Jdg 7: 1 of them in the valley near the hill of **M**. 4622

MOREOVER (33)

Ge 31:20 **M**, Jacob deceived Laban the Aramean by 2256
Ex 6: 5 **M**, I have heard the groaning of 1685+2256
    31: 6 **M**, I have appointed Oholiab son 2256
Nu 16:14 **M**, you haven't brought us into 677
Dt 2: 7 **M**, the LORD your God will send 1685+2256
    17:16 **m**, must not acquire great numbers 8370
2Sa 8: 3 **M**, David fought Hadadezer son of Rehob, 2256
    11:17 **m**, Uriah the Hittite died. 1685+2256
    11:24 **M**, your servant Uriah the Hittite is dead." 1685+2256
1Ki 1:46 **M**, Solomon has taken his seat on 1685+2256
    3:13 **M**, I will give you what you have 1685+2256
    16: 7 **M**, the word of the LORD came 1685+2256
2Ki 21:16 **M**, Manasseh also shed so much innocent 1685
1Ch 18: 3 **M**, David fought Hadadezer king of Zobah, 2256
Ezr 1: 7 **M**, King Cyrus brought out the articles 2256
    6: 8 **M**, I hereby decree what you are to do 10221
    7:15 **M**, you are to take with you the silver 10221
Ne 5:14 **M**, from the twentieth year 1685
    6: 6 **M**, according to these reports you are about 2256
    6:19 **M**, they kept reporting to me 1685
    10:37 "**M**, we will bring to the storerooms of 2256
    13:23 **M**, in those days I saw men 1685
Ecc 5:19 **M**, when God gives any man wealth 1685
    9: 3 The hearts of men, **m**, 1685+2256
    9:12 **M**, no man knows when his hour 1685+3954
Jer 12: 1 **M**, the people are saying, 3954
    21:11 "**M**, say to the royal house of Judah, 2256
La 4:17 **M**, our eyes failed, looking in vain for help; 6388
Da 2:49 **M**, at Daniel's request the king 10221
Lk 4:41 **M**, demons came out of many people, 1254
Jn 5:22 **M**, the Father judges no one, 1142
Php 4:15 **M**, as you Philippians know, 1254
Heb 12: 9 **M**, we have all had human fathers who
           disciplined us 1663

MORESHETH (2) [MORESHETH GATH]

Jer 26:18 "Micah **of M** prophesied in the days 4629
Mic 1: 1 to Micah **of M** during the reigns of Jotham, 4629

MORESHETH GATH (1) [MORESHETH]

Mic 1:14 Therefore you will give parting gifts to **M**. 4628

MORIAH (2)

Ge 22: 2 whom you love, and go to the region of **M**. 5317
2Ch 3: 1 of the LORD in Jerusalem on Mount **M**, 5317

MORNING (218) [MORNING'S, MORNINGS]

Ge 1: 5 And there was evening, and there was **m**— 1332
    1: 8 And there was evening, and there was **m**— 1332
    1:13 And there was evening, and there was **m**— 1332
    1:19 And there was evening, and there was **m**— 1332
    1:23 And there was evening, and there was **m**— 1332
    1:31 And there was evening, and there was **m**— 1332
    19: 2 and then go on your way **early in the m**." 8899
    19:27 the next **m** Abraham got up and returned to 1332
    20: 8 the next **m** Abimelech summoned all his
           officials, 1332
    21:14 Early the next **m** Abraham took some food 1332
    22: 3 Early the next **m** Abraham got up 1332
    24:54 When they got up the next **m**, he said, 1332
    26:31 Early the next **m** the men swore an oath 1332
    28:18 Early the next **m** Jacob took 1332
    29:25 When **m** came, there was Leah! 1332
    31:55 the next **m** Laban kissed his grandchildren 1332
    40: 6 When Joseph came to them the next **m**, 1332
    41: 8 In the **m** his mind was troubled, 1332
    44: 3 As **m** dawned, the men were sent 1332
    49:27 in the **m** he devours the prey, 1332
Ex 7:15 Go to Pharaoh in the **m** as he goes out to 1332
    8:20 "Get up early in the **m** and confront Pharaoh 1332
    9:13 "Get up early in the **m**, 1332
    10:13 *By* **m** the wind had brought the locusts; 1332
    12:10 Do not leave any of it till **m**; 1332
    12:10 if some is left till **m**, you must burn it. 1332
    12:22 the door of his house until **m**. 1332
    16: 7 the **m** you will see the glory of the LORD, 1332
    16: 8 and all the bread you want in the **m**, 1332
    16:12 and in the **m** you will be filled with bread. 1332
    16:13 in the **m** there was a layer of dew around 1332
    16:19 "No one is to keep any of it until **m**." 1332
    16:20 they kept part of it until **m**, 1332
    16:21 **Each m** everyone gathered as much as he
           needed, 928+928+1332+1332+2021+2021
    16:23 Save whatever is left and keep it until **m**.' " 1332
    16:24 So they saved it until **m**, 1332
    18:13 they stood around him from **m** till evening. 1332
    18:14 around you from **m** till evening?" 1332
    19:16 On the **m** of the third day there was thunder 1332
    23:18 not be kept until **m**. 1332
    24: 4 He got up early the next **m** and built an altar 1332
    27:21 before the LORD from evening till **m**. 1332
    29:34 or any bread is left over till **m**, 1332

Ex 29:39 Offer one in the **m** and the other at twilight. 1332
    29:41 and its drink offering as in the **m**— 1332
    30: 7 Aaron must burn fragrant incense on the
           altar **every m** 928+928+1332+1332+2021+2021
    34: 2 Be ready in the **m**, and then come up 1332
    34: 4 the **m**, as the LORD had commanded him; 1332
    34:25 from the Passover Feast remain until **m**. 1332
    36: 3 to bring freewill offerings **m** after morning. 1332
    36: 3 to bring freewill offerings morning after **m**. 1332
Lev 6: 9 the altar hearth throughout the night, till **m**, 1332
    6:12 **Every m** the priest is to add firewood
           928+928+1332+1332+2021+2021
    6:20 half of it in the **m** and half in the evening. 1332
    7:15 he must leave none of it till **m**. 1332
    22:30 leave none of it till **m**. 1332
    24: 3 before the LORD from evening till **m**. 1332
Nu 9:12 not leave any of it till **m** or break any 1332
    9:15 till **m** the cloud above the tabernacle looked 1332
    9:21 the cloud stayed only from evening till **m**, 1332
    9:21 and when it lifted in the **m**, they set out. 1332
    14:40 Early the next **m** they went up toward 1332
    16: 5 the **m** the LORD will show who belongs 1332
    22:13 The next **m** Balaam got up and said 1332
    22:21 Balaam got up in the **m**, 1332
    22:41 The next **m** Balak took Balaam up 1332
    28: 4 Prepare one lamb in the **m** and the other 1332
    28: 8 that you prepare in the **m**. 1332
    28:23 in addition to the regular **m** burnt offering. 1332
Dt 16: 4 the evening of the first day remain until **m**. 1332
    16: 7 Then in the **m** return to your tents. 1332
    28:67 In the **m** you will say, 1332
    28:67 and in the evening, "If only it were **m**!"— 1332
Jos 3: 1 in the Joshua and all the Israelites set out 1332
    6:12 the next **m** and the priests took up the ark of 1332
    7:14 " 'In the **m**, present yourselves tribe 1332
    7:16 the next **m** Joshua had Israel come forward 1332
    8:10 Early the next **m** Joshua mustered his men, 1332
    8:14 of the city hurried out **early in the m** 8899
Jdg 6:28 In the **m** when the men of the town got up, 1332
    6:31 for him shall be put to death by **m**! 1332
    7: 1 **Early in the m**, Jerub-Baal (that is, 8899
    9:33 In the **m** at sunrise, advance against the city. 1332
    19: 8 On the **m** of the fifth day, 1332
    19: 9 **Early** tomorrow **m** *you can* **get up** 8899
    19:27 in the **m** and opened the door of the house 1332
    20:19 The next **m** the Israelites got up 1332
Ru 2: 7 the field and has worked steadily from **m** till 1332
    3:13 and in the **m** if he wants to redeem, good; 1332
    3:13 Lie here until **m**." 1332
    3:14 So she lay at his feet until **m**, 1332
1Sa 1:19 the next **m** they arose and worshiped before 1332
    3:15 down until **m** and then opened the doors of 1332
    5: 4 But the following **m** when they rose, 1332
    9:19 the **m** I will let you go and will tell you all 1332
    15:12 the **m** Samuel got up and went to meet Saul, 1332
    17:16 The Philistine came forward *every* **m** 8899
    17:20 the **m** David left the flock with a shepherd, 1332
    19: 2 Be on your guard tomorrow **m**; 1332
    19:11 to watch it and to kill him in the **m**. 1332
    20:35 In the **m** Jonathan went out to the field 1332
    25:22 if by **m** I leave alive one male 1332
    25:37 Then in the **m**, when Nabal was sober, 1332
    29:10 and leave in the **m** as soon as it is light." 1332
    29:11 and his men got up early in the **m** to go back 1332
2Sa 2:27 the pursuit of their brothers until **m**." 1332
    11:14 In the **m** David wrote a letter to Joab 1332
    13: 4 look so haggard **m** after morning? 1332
    13: 4 look so haggard morning after **m**? 1332
    23: 4 of **m** at sunrise on a cloudless morning, 1332
    23: 4 of morning at sunrise on a cloudless **m**, 1332
    24:11 Before David got up the next **m**, 1332
    24:15 a plague on Israel from that **m** until the end 1332
1Ki 3:21 The next **m**, I got up to nurse my son— 1332
    3:21 I looked at him closely in the **m** light, 1332
    17: 6 in the **m** and bread and meat in the evening, 1332
    18:26 on the name of Baal from **m** till noon. 1332
2Ki 3:20 The next **m**, about the time for offering 1332
    3:22 When they got up early in the **m**, 1332
    6:15 up and went out **early the next m**, 8899
    10: 8 at the entrance of the city gate until **m**." 1332
    10: 9 The next **m** Jehu went out. 1332
    16:15 offer the **m** burnt offering and 1332
    19:35 When the people got up the next **m**— 1332
1Ch 9:27 had charge of the key for opening it **each m**.
           1332+1332+2021+2021+4200+4200
    16:40 of burnt offering regularly, in the **m** and evening, 1332
    23:30 They were also to stand **every m** to thank
           and praise 928+1332+1332+2021+2021
2Ch 2: 4 and for making burnt offerings every **m** 1332
    13:11 **Every m** and evening they present burnt
           offerings 928+928+1332+1332+2021+2021
    20:20 in the **m** they left for the Desert of Tekoa. 1332
    29:20 **Early the next m** King Hezekiah gathered 8899
    31: 3 the **m** and evening burnt offerings and for 1332
Ezr 3: 3 both the **m** and evening sacrifices. 1332
Est 2:14 the **m** return to another part of the harem to 1332
    5:14 the king in the **m** to have Mordecai hanged 1332
Job 1: 5 in the **m** he would sacrifice a burnt offering 1332
    3: 9 May its **m** stars become dark; 5974
    7:18 that you examine him every **m** 1332
    11:17 and darkness will become like **m**. 1332
    24:17 For all of them, deep darkness is their **m**; 1332
    38: 7 while the **m** stars sang together and all 1332
    38:12 "Have you ever given orders to the **m**, 1332
Ps 5: 3 In the **m**, O LORD, you hear my voice; 1332
    5: 3 the **m** I lay my requests before you and wait 1332
    22: T To [the tune of] "The Doe of the **M**." 8840

Ps 30: 5 but rejoicing comes in the **m**. 1332
    49:14 The upright will rule over them in the **m**; 1332
    55:17 Evening, **m** and noon I cry out in distress, 1332
    59:16 in the **m** I will sing of your love; 1332
    65: 8 where **m** dawns and evening fades you call 1332
    73:14 I have been punished every **m**. 1332
    88:13 in the **m** my prayer comes before you. 1332
    90: 5 they are like the new grass of the **m**— 1332
    90: 6 though in the **m** it springs up new, 1332
    90:14 Satisfy us in the **m** with your unfailing love, 1332
    92: 2 in the **m** and your faithfulness at night, 1332
    101: 8 Every **m** I will put to silence all the wicked 1332
    130: 6 for the **m**, more than watchmen wait for 1332
    130: 6 more than watchmen wait for the **m**, 1332
    143:8 the **m** bring me word of your unfailing love, 1332
Pr 7:18 Come, let's drink deep of love till **m**; 1332
    27:14 a man loudly blesses his neighbor in the **m**, 1332
Ecc 10:16 a servant and whose princes feast in the **m**. 1332
    11: 6 Sow your seed in the **m**, 1332
Isa 5:11 Woe to those who rise early in the **m** to run 1332
    14:12 you have fallen from heaven, O **m** star, 2122
    17:11 and on the **m** when you plant them, 1332
    17:14 Before the **m**, they are gone! 1332
    21:12 The watchman replies, "**M** is coming, 1332
    26: 9 in the **m** my spirit longs for you. 1332
    26:19 Your dew is like the dew of the **m**; 245
    28:19 **m** after morning, by day and by night, 1332
    28:19 morning after **m**, by day and by night, 1332
    33: 2 Be our strength every **m**, 1332
    37:36 When the people got up the next **m**— 1332
    44:22 your sins like the **m** mist. 6727
    50: 4 He wakens me **m** by morning, 1332
    50: 4 He wakens me morning by **m**, 1332
Jer 20:16 May he hear wailing in the **m**, 1332
    21:12 " 'Administer justice every **m**; 1332
La 3:23 They are new every **m**; 1332
Eze 12: 8 the **m** the word of the LORD came to me: 1332
    24:18 So I spoke to the people in the **m**, 1332
    24:18 The next **m** I did as I had been commanded. 1332
    33:22 before the man came to me in the **m**. 1332
    46:13 **m** by morning you shall provide it. 1332
    46:13 morning by **m** you shall provide it. 1332
    46:14 with it by morning a grain offering, 1332
    46:14 with it morning by **m** a grain offering, 1332
    46:15 and the oil shall be provided **m** by morning 1332
    46:15 and the oil shall be provided morning by **m** 1332
Hos 6: 4 Your love is like the **m** mist, 1332
    7: 6 in the **m** it blazes like a flaming fire. 1332
    13: 3 Therefore they will be like the **m** mist, 1332
Am 4: 4 Bring your sacrifices every **m**, 1332
Zep 3: 3 who leave nothing for the **m**. 1332
    3: 5 **M** by morning he dispenses his justice, 1332
    3: 5 Morning by **m** he dispenses his justice, 1332
Mt 16: 3 and in the **m**, 'Today it will be stormy, 4745
    20: 1 landowner who went out **early in the m** 275+4745
    21:18 **Early in the m**, as he was on his way 4745
    27: 1 **Early in the m**, all the chief priests and 4746
Mk 1:35 Very **early in the m**, while it was still dark, 4745
    11:20 **In the m**, as they went along, 4745
    15: 1 Very **early in the m**, the chief priests 2317+4745
Lk 6:13 When **m** came, he called his disciples 2465
    21:38 all the people came **early in the m** 4745
    24: 1 **very early in the m**, the women took 960+3986
    24:22 They went to the tomb **early this m** 3984
Jn 18:28 By now it was **early m**, 4745
    21: 4 **Early in the m**, Jesus stood on the shore,
           1181+4746
Ac 2:15 It's only **nine in the m**! 2465+3836+5569+6052
    12:18 **In the m**, there was no small commotion
           among the soldiers 1181+2465
    23:12 **The next m** the Jews formed a conspiracy
           1181+2465
    28:23 From **m** till evening he explained 4745
2Pe 1:19 until the day dawns and the **m** star rises 5892
Rev 2:28 I will also give him the **m** star. 4748
    22:16 and the bright **M** Star." 4748

MORNING'S (2) [MORNING]

Lev 9:17 the altar in addition to the **m** burnt offering. 1332
Mic 2: 1 At **m** light they carry it out because it is 1332

MORNINGS (2) [MORNING]

Da 8:14 "It will take 2,300 evenings and **m**; 1332
    8:26 and **m** that has been given you is true, 1332

MORROW (KJV) See FOLLOWING DAY, MORNING, NEXT DAY, TOMORROW

MORSELS (2)

Pr 18: 8 The words of a gossip are like **choice m**; 4269
    26:22 The words of a gossip are like **choice m**; 4269

MORTAL (19) [MORTALLY, MORTALS]

Ge 6: 3 not contend with man forever, for he is **m**; 1414
Dt 5:26 For what **m** man has ever heard the voice of 1414
Job 4:17 'Can a **m** be more righteous than God? 632
    4:17 But how can a **m** be righteous before God? 632
    10: 4 Do you see as a **m** sees? 632
    10: 5 like those of a **m** or your years like those of 632
Ps 42:10 My bones suffer **m** agony 8358
    56: 4 What can **m** man do to me? 1414
    56: 4 from my enemies who surround me. 928+5883
    146: 3 not put your trust in princes, in **m** men, 132+1201

Isa	51:12	Who are you that you fear **m** men,	4637
Eze	31:14	for the earth below, among **m** men,	132+1201
Ro	1:23	to look like **m** man and birds and animals	5778
	6:12	not let sin reign in your **m** body so	2570
	8:11	the dead will also give life *to* your **m** bodies	2570
1Co	15:53	and the **m** with immortality.	2570
	15:54	and the **m** with immortality.	2570
2Co	4:11	that his life may be revealed in our **m** body.	2570
	5: 4	what *is* **m** may be swallowed up by life.	2570

MORTALITY (KJV) See MORTAL

MORTALLY (1) [MORTAL]

Eze	30:24	before him like a **m** wounded man.	2728

MORTALS (1) [MORTAL]

Isa	31: 8	a sword, not *of* **m**, will devour them.	132

MORTAR (6)

Ge	11: 3	used brick instead of stone, and tar for **m**.	2817
Ex	1:14	in brick and **m** and with all kinds of work in	2817
Nu	11: 8	ground it in a handmill or crushed it in a **m**.	4521
Pr	27:22	Though you grind a fool in a **m**,	4847
Isa	41:25	He treads on rulers as if they were **m**,	2817
Na	3:14	Work the clay, tread the **m**,	2817

MORTER (KJV) See CLAY, MORTAR, PLASTER, WHITEWASH

MORTGAGING (1)

Ne	5: 3	Others were saying, "We *are* **m** our fields,	6842

MORTIFY (KJV) See PUT TO DEATH

MOSAIC (1)

Est	1: 6	and silver on a **m** pavement *of* porphyry,	8367

MOSERAH (1)

Dt	10: 6	from the wells of the Jaakanites to **M**.	4594

MOSEROTH (2)

Nu	33:30	They left Hashmonah and camped at **M**.	5035
	33:31	They left **M** and camped at Bene Jaakan.	5035

MOSES (828) [MOSES']

Ex	2:10	She named him **M**, saying, "I drew him out	5407
	2:11	One day, after **M** had grown up,	5407
	2:14	Then **M** was afraid and thought,	5407
	2:15	Pharaoh heard of this, he tried to kill **M**,	5407
	2:15	but **M** fled from Pharaoh and went to live	5407
	2:17	but **M** got up and came to their rescue	5407
	2:21	**M** agreed to stay with the man,	5407
	2:21	who gave his daughter Zipporah to **M**	5407
	2:22	and **M** named him Gershom, saying,	NIH
	3: 1	Now **M** was tending the flock	5407
	3: 2	**M** saw that though the bush was	NIH
	3: 3	So **M** thought, "I will go over	5407
	3: 4	called to him from within the bush, "**M**!	5407
	3: 4	from within the bush, **M**!"	5407
	3: 4	And **M** said, "Here I am."	NIH
	3: 6	At this, **M** hid his face,	5407
	3:11	But **M** said to God, "Who am I,	5407
	3:13	**M** said to God, "Suppose I go	5407
	3:14	God said to **M**, "I AM WHO I AM.	5407
	3:15	God also said to **M**, "Say to the Israelites,	5407
	4: 1	**M** answered, "What if they do not believe	5407
	4: 3	**M** threw it on the ground and it became	5407
	4: 4	So **M** reached out and took hold of	5407
	4: 6	So **M** put his hand into his cloak,	NIH
	4: 7	So **M** put his hand back into his cloak,	NIH
	4:10	**M** said to the LORD, "O Lord,	5407
	4:13	But **M** said, "O Lord, please send someone	NIH
	4:14	Then the LORD's anger burned against **M**	5407
	4:18	Then **M** went back to Jethro	5407
	4:19	Now the LORD had said to **M** in Midian,	5407
	4:20	So **M** took his wife and sons,	5407
	4:21	The LORD said to **M**, "When you return	5407
	4:24	the LORD met **M** and was about to kill	2084ˢ
	4:27	"Go into the desert to meet **M**."	5407
	4:27	So he met **M** at the mountain of God	2084ˢ
	4:28	Then **M** told Aaron everything	5407
	4:29	**M** and Aaron brought together all the elders	5407
	4:30	the LORD had said to **M**.	5407
	5: 1	Afterward **M** and Aaron went to Pharaoh	5407
	5: 4	But the king of Egypt said, "**M** and Aaron,	5407
	5:20	they found **M** and Aaron waiting	5407
	5:22	**M** returned to the LORD and said,	5407
	6: 1	the LORD said to **M**, "Now you will see	5407
	6: 2	God also said to **M**, "I am the LORD.	5407
	6: 9	**M** reported this to the Israelites,	5407
	6:10	Then the LORD said to **M**,	5407
	6:12	But **M** said to the LORD,	5407
	6:13	the LORD spoke to **M** and Aaron about	5407
	6:20	Jochebed, who bore him Aaron and **M**.	5407
	6:26	It was this same Aaron and **M** to whom	5407
	6:27	It was the same **M** and Aaron.	5407
	6:28	when the LORD spoke to **M** in Egypt,	5407
	6:30	But **M** said to the LORD, "Since I speak	5407
	7: 1	Then the LORD said to **M**, "See,	5407

Ex	7: 6	**M** and Aaron did just as the LORD	5407
	7: 7	**M** was eighty years old and Aaron	5407
	7: 8	The LORD said to **M** and Aaron,	5407
	7:10	So **M** and Aaron went to Pharaoh	5407
	7:14	Then the LORD said to **M**,	5407
	7:19	The LORD said to **M**, "Tell Aaron,	5407
	7:20	**M** and Aaron did just as the LORD	5407
	7:22	he would not listen to **M and Aaron**,	2157ˢ
	8: 1	Then the LORD said to **M**, "Go to Pharaoh	5407
	8: 5	Then the LORD said to **M**, "Tell Aaron,	5407
	8: 8	Pharaoh summoned **M** and Aaron and said,	5407
	8: 9	**M** said to Pharaoh, "I leave to you	5407
	8:10	**M** replied, "It will be as you say,	NIH
	8:12	After **M** and Aaron left Pharaoh,	5407
	8:12	**M** cried out to the LORD about the frogs	5407
	8:13	And the LORD did what **M** asked.	5407
	8:15	and would not listen to **M and Aaron**,	2157ˢ
	8:16	Then the LORD said to **M**, "Tell Aaron,	5407
	8:20	Then the LORD said to **M**, "Get up early	5407
	8:25	Pharaoh summoned **M** and Aaron and said,	5407
	8:26	But **M** said, "That would not be right.	5407
	8:29	**M** answered, "As soon as I leave you,	5407
	8:30	**M** left Pharaoh and prayed to the LORD,	5407
	8:31	and the LORD did what **M** asked:	5407
	9: 1	Then the LORD said to **M**, "Go to Pharaoh	5407
	9: 8	Then the LORD said to **M** and Aaron,	5407
	9: 8	a furnace and have **M** toss it into the air in	5407
	9:10	**M** tossed it into the air,	5407
	9:11	The magicians could not stand before **M**	5407
	9:12	and he would not listen to **M and Aaron**,	2157ˢ
	9:12	just as the LORD had said to **M**.	5407
	9:13	Then the LORD said to **M**, "Get up early	5407
	9:22	Then the LORD said to **M**, "Stretch out	5407
	9:23	**M** stretched out his staff toward the sky,	5407
	9:27	Then Pharaoh summoned **M** and Aaron.	5407
	9:29	**M** replied, "When I have gone out of	5407
	9:33	**M** left Pharaoh and went out of the city.	5407
	9:35	just as the LORD had said through **M**.	5407
	10: 1	Then the LORD said to **M**, "Go to Pharaoh	5407
	10: 3	So **M** and Aaron went to Pharaoh and said	5407
	10: 6	Then **M** turned and left Pharaoh.	NIH
	10: 8	Then **M** and Aaron were brought back	5407
	10: 9	**M** answered, "We will go with our young	5407
	10:11	Then **M and Aaron** were driven out	4392ˢ
	10:12	And the LORD said to **M**, "Stretch out	5407
	10:13	So **M** stretched out his staff over Egypt,	5407
	10:16	Pharaoh quickly summoned **M** and Aaron	5407
	10:18	**M** then left Pharaoh and prayed to the LORD	NIH
	10:21	Then the LORD said to **M**, "Stretch out	5407
	10:22	So **M** stretched out his hand toward the sky,	5407
	10:24	Then Pharaoh summoned **M** and said, "Go,	5407
	10:25	But **M** said, "You must allow us	5407
	10:28	Pharaoh said to **M**, "Get out of my sight!	2257ˢ
	10:29	"Just as you say," **M** replied,	5407
	11: 1	Now the LORD had said to **M**,	5407
	11: 3	and **M** himself was highly regarded	5407
	11: 4	So **M** said, "This is what the LORD says:	5407
	11: 8	Then **M**, hot with anger, left Pharaoh.	NIH
	11: 9	The LORD had said to **M**, "Pharaoh will	5407
	11:10	**M** and Aaron performed all these wonders	5407
	12: 1	The LORD said to **M** and Aaron in Egypt,	5407
	12:21	Then **M** summoned all the elders of Israel	5407
	12:28	the LORD commanded **M** and Aaron.	5407
	12:31	the night Pharaoh summoned **M** and Aaron	5407
	12:35	The Israelites did as **M** instructed and asked	5407
	12:43	The LORD said to **M** and Aaron,	5407
	12:50	the LORD had commanded **M** and Aaron.	5407
	13: 1	The LORD said to **M**,	5407
	13: 3	Then **M** said to the people, "Commemorate	5407
	13:19	**M** took the bones of Joseph with him	5407
	14: 1	Then the LORD said to **M**,	5407
	14:11	They said to **M**, "Was it because	5407
	14:13	**M** answered the people, "Do not be afraid.	5407
	14:15	Then the LORD said to **M**, "Why are you	5407
	14:21	Then **M** stretched out his hand over the sea,	5407
	14:26	Then the LORD said to **M**, "Stretch out	5407
	14:27	**M** stretched out his hand over the sea,	5407
	14:31	put their trust in him and in **M** his servant.	5407
	15: 1	Then **M** and the Israelites sang this song to	5407
	15:22	Then **M** led Israel from the Red Sea	5407
	15:24	So the people grumbled against **M**, saying,	5407
	15:25	Then **M** cried out to the LORD,	NIH
	16: 2	the whole community grumbled against **M**	5407
	16: 4	Then the LORD said to **M**, "I will rain down	5407
	16: 6	So **M** and Aaron said to all the Israelites,	5407
	16: 8	**M** also said, "You will know that it was	5407
	16: 9	Then **M** told Aaron, "Say to the entire	5407
	16:11	The LORD said to **M**,	5407
	16:15	**M** said to them, "It is the bread the LORD	5407
	16:19	Then **M** said to them, "No one is to keep	5407
	16:20	some of them paid no attention to **M**;	5407
	16:20	So **M** was angry with them.	5407
	16:22	and reported this to **M**.	5407
	16:24	until morning, as **M** commanded, and it did	5407
	16:25	"Eat it today," **M** said,	5407
	16:28	Then the LORD said to **M**,	5407
	16:32	**M** said, "This is what the LORD	5407
	16:33	So **M** said to Aaron, "Take a jar	5407
	16:34	As the LORD commanded **M**,	5407
	17: 2	So they quarreled with **M** and said,	5407
	17: 2	**M** replied, "Why do you quarrel with me?	5407
	17: 3	and they grumbled against **M**.	5407
	17: 4	Then **M** cried out to the LORD,	5407
	17: 5	The LORD answered **M**, "Walk on ahead	5407
	17: 6	So **M** did this in the sight of the elders	5407
	17: 9	**M** said to Joshua, "Choose some of our men	5407
	17:10	fought the Amalekites as **M** had ordered,	5407

Ex	17:10	and **M**, Aaron and Hur went to the top of	5407
	17:11	As long as **M** held up his hands,	5407
	17:14	Then the LORD said to **M**, "Write this	5407
	17:15	**M** built an altar and called it The LORD is my Banner.	5407
	18: 1	the priest of Midian and father-in-law of **M**,	5407
	18: 1	heard of everything God had done for **M**	5407
	18: 2	After **M** had sent away his wife Zipporah,	5407
	18: 3	One son was named Gershom, for **M** said,	NIH
	18: 7	So **M** went out to meet his father-in-law	5407
	18: 8	**M** told his father-in-law about everything	5407
	18:13	The next day **M** took his seat to serve	5407
	18:14	that **M** was doing for the people,	5407
	18:15	**M** answered him, "Because	5407
	18:24	**M** listened to his father-in-law	5407
	18:26	The difficult cases they brought to **M**,	5407
	18:27	Then **M** sent his father-in-law on his way,	5407
	19: 3	Then **M** went up to God,	5407
	19: 7	So **M** went back and summoned the elders	5407
	19: 8	**M** brought their answer back to the LORD.	5407
	19: 9	The LORD said to **M**, "I am going to come	5407
	19: 9	Then **M** told the LORD what the people	5407
	19:10	And the LORD said to **M**, "Go to the people	5407
	19:14	After **M** had gone down the mountain to	5407
	19:17	Then **M** led the people out of the camp	5407
	19:19	Then **M** spoke and the voice of God	5407
	19:20	of Mount Sinai and called **M** to the top of	5407
	19:20	So **M** went up	5407
	19:23	**M** said to the LORD, "The people cannot	5407
	19:25	**M** went down to the people and told them.	5407
	20:19	and said to **M**, "Speak to us yourself	5407
	20:20	**M** said to the people, "Do not be afraid.	5407
	20:21	while **M** approached the thick darkness	5407
	20:22	LORD said to **M**, "Tell the Israelites this:	5407
	24: 1	Then he said to **M**, "Come up to the LORD,	5407
	24: 2	but **M** alone is to approach the LORD;	5407
	24: 3	When **M** went and told the people all	5407
	24: 4	**M** then wrote down everything	5407
	24: 6	**M** took half of the blood and put it	5407
	24: 8	**M** then took the blood,	5407
	24: 9	**M** and Aaron, Nadab and Abihu,	5407
	24:12	The LORD said to **M**, "Come up to me	5407
	24:13	Then **M** set out with Joshua his aide,	5407
	24:13	and **M** went up on the mountain of God.	5407
	24:15	When **M** went up on the mountain,	5407
	24:16	on the seventh day the LORD called to **M**	5407
	24:18	Then **M** entered the cloud as he went on up	5407
	25: 1	The LORD said to **M**,	5407
	30:11	Then the LORD said to **M**,	5407
	30:17	Then the LORD said to **M**,	5407
	30:22	Then the LORD said to **M**,	5407
	30:34	LORD said to **M**, "Take fragrant spices—	5407
	31: 1	Then the LORD said to **M**,	5407
	31:12	Then the LORD said to **M**,	5407
	31:18	When the LORD finished speaking to **M**	5407
	32: 1	that **M** was so long in coming down from	5407
	32: 1	As for this fellow **M** who brought us up out	5407
	32: 7	Then the LORD said to **M**, "Go down,	5407
	32: 9	the LORD said to **M**,	5407
	32:11	**M** sought the favor of the LORD his God.	5407
	32:15	**M** turned and went down the mountain with	5407
	32:17	noise of the people shouting, he said to **M**,	5407
	32:18	**M** replied: "It is not the sound of victory,	NIH
	32:19	When **M** approached the camp and saw	5407
	32:23	As for this fellow **M** who brought us up out	5407
	32:25	**M** saw that the people were running wild	5407
	32:28	The Levites did as **M** commanded,	5407
	32:29	Then **M** said, "You have been set apart to	5407
	32:30	The next day **M** said to the people,	5407
	32:31	So **M** went back to the LORD and said,	5407
	32:33	LORD replied to **M**, "Whoever has sinned	5407
	33: 1	Then the LORD said to **M**, "Leave this	5407
	33: 5	For the LORD had said to **M**,	5407
	33: 7	Now **M** used to take a tent	5407
	33: 8	And whenever **M** went out to the tent,	5407
	33: 8	watching **M** until he entered the tent.	5407
	33: 9	As **M** went into the tent,	5407
	33: 9	while the LORD spoke with **M**.	5407
	33:11	The LORD would speak to **M** face to face,	5407
	33:11	Then **M** would return to the camp,	NIH
	33:12	**M** said to the LORD, "You have been telling	5407
	33:15	Then **M** said to him, "If your Presence	NIH
	33:17	And the LORD said to **M**, "I will do	5407
	33:18	Then **M** said, "Now show me your glory."	NIH
	34: 1	The LORD said to **M**, "Chisel out two	5407
	34: 4	So **M** chiseled out two stone tablets like	5407
	34: 6	And he passed in front of **M**, proclaiming,	2257ˢ
	34: 8	**M** bowed to the ground at once	5407
	34:27	Then the LORD said to **M**, "Write down	5407
	34:28	**M** was there with the LORD forty days	NIH
	34:29	When **M** came down from Mount Sinai	5407
	34:30	When Aaron and all the Israelites saw **M**,	5407
	34:31	But **M** called to them;	5407
	34:33	When **M** finished speaking to them,	5407
	34:35	Then **M** would put the veil back	5407
	35: 1	**M** assembled the whole Israelite community	5407
	35: 4	**M** said to the whole Israelite community,	5407
	35:29	through **M** had commanded them to do.	5407
	35:30	Then **M** said to the Israelites, "See,	5407
	36: 2	Then **M** summoned Bezalel and Oholiab	5407
	36: 3	They received from **M** all the offerings	5407
	36: 5	and said to **M**, "The people are bringing	5407
	36: 6	Then **M** gave an order and they sent	5407
	38:22	made everything the LORD commanded **M**;	5407
	39: 1	as the LORD commanded **M**.	5407
	39: 5	as the LORD commanded **M**.	5407
	39: 7	as the LORD commanded **M**.	5407

Ref	Text	Strong
Ex 39:21	as the LORD commanded M.	5407
39:26	as the LORD commanded M.	5407
39:29	as the LORD commanded M.	5407
39:31	as the LORD commanded M.	5407
39:32	as the LORD commanded M.	5407
39:33	Then they brought the tabernacle to M:	5407
39:42	as the LORD had commanded M.	5407
39:43	M inspected the work and saw	5407
39:43	So M blessed them.	5407
40: 1	Then the LORD said to M:	5407
40:16	M did everything just as the LORD	5407
40:18	When M set up the tabernacle,	5407
40:22	M placed the table in the Tent of Meeting	NIH
40:26	M placed the gold altar in the Tent	NIH
40:31	and M and Aaron and his sons used it	5407
40:32	as the LORD commanded M.	5407
40:33	Then M set up the courtyard around	NIH
40:33	And so M finished the work.	5407
40:35	M could not enter the Tent of Meeting	5407
Lev 1: 1	The LORD called to M and spoke to him	5407
4: 1	The LORD said to M,	5407
5:14	The LORD said to M:	5407
6: 1	The LORD said to M:	5407
6: 8	The LORD said to M,	5407
6:19	The LORD also said to M,	5407
6:24	The LORD said to M,	5407
7:22	The LORD said to M,	5407
7:28	The LORD said to M,	5407
7:38	which the LORD gave M on Mount Sinai	5407
8: 1	The LORD said to M,	5407
8: 4	M did as the LORD commanded him,	5407
8: 5	M said to the assembly, "This is what	5407
8: 6	Then M brought Aaron and his sons	5407
8: 9	as the LORD commanded M.	5407
8:10	Then M took the anointing oil and anointed	5407
8:13	as the LORD commanded M.	5407
8:15	M slaughtered the bull and took some of	5407
8:16	M also took all the fat around	5407
8:17	as the LORD commanded M.	5407
8:19	Then M slaughtered the ram and sprinkled	5407
8:21	as the LORD commanded M.	5407
8:23	M slaughtered the ram and took some	5407
8:24	M also brought Aaron's sons forward	5407
8:28	Then M took them from their hands	5407
8:29	as the LORD commanded M.	5407
8:30	Then M took some of the anointing oil	5407
8:31	M then said to Aaron and his sons,	5407
8:36	the LORD commanded through M.	5407
9: 1	On the eighth day M summoned Aaron	5407
9: 5	the things M commanded to the front of	5407
9: 6	Then M said, "This is what	5407
9: 7	M said to Aaron, "Come to the altar	5407
9:10	as the LORD commanded M;	5407
9:21	as a wave offering, as M commanded.	5407
9:23	M and Aaron then went into the Tent	5407
10: 3	M then said to Aaron, "This is what	5407
10: 4	M summoned Mishael and Elzaphan,	5407
10: 5	outside the camp, as M ordered.	5407
10: 6	Then M said to Aaron and his sons Eleazar	5407
10: 7	So they did as M said.	5407
10:11	the LORD has given them through M."	5407
10:12	M said to Aaron and his remaining sons,	5407
10:16	When M inquired about the goat of	5407
10:19	Aaron replied to M, "Today they sacrificed	5407
10:20	When M heard this, he was satisfied.	5407
11: 1	The LORD said to M and Aaron,	5407
12: 1	The LORD said to M,	5407
13: 1	The LORD said to M and Aaron,	5407
14: 1	The LORD said to M,	5407
14:33	The LORD said to M and Aaron,	5407
15: 1	The LORD said to M and Aaron,	5407
16: 1	The LORD spoke to M after the death of	5407
16: 2	The LORD said to M:	5407
16:34	it was done, as the LORD commanded M.	5407
17: 1	The LORD said to M,	5407
18: 1	The LORD said to M,	5407
19: 1	The LORD said to M,	5407
20: 1	The LORD said to M,	5407
21: 1	The LORD said to M, "Speak to the priests,	5407
21:16	The LORD said to M,	5407
21:24	So M told this to Aaron and his sons and	5407
22: 1	The LORD said to M,	5407
22:17	The LORD said to M,	5407
22:26	The LORD said to M,	5407
23: 1	The LORD said to M,	5407
23: 9	The LORD said to M,	5407
23:23	The LORD said to M,	5407
23:26	The LORD said to M,	5407
23:33	The LORD said to M,	5407
23:44	So M announced to the Israelites	5407
24: 1	The LORD said to M,	5407
24:11	so they brought him to M.	5407
24:13	Then the LORD said to M:	5407
24:23	Then M spoke to the Israelites,	5407
24:23	as the LORD commanded M.	5407
25: 1	The LORD said to M on Mount Sinai,	5407
26:46	and the Israelites through M.	5407
27: 1	The LORD said to M,	5407
27:34	These are the commands the LORD gave M on Mount Sinai	5407
Nu 1: 1	to M in the Tent of Meeting in the Desert	
1:17	M and Aaron took these men whose names had been given,	5407
1:19	as the LORD commanded M.	5407
1:44	by M and Aaron and the twelve leaders	5407
1:48	The LORD had said to M:	5407
1:54	as the LORD commanded M.	5407

Ref	Text	Strong
Nu 2: 1	The LORD said to M and Aaron:	5407
2:33	as the LORD commanded M.	5407
2:34	the LORD commanded M;	5407
3: 1	the account of the family of Aaron and M at	5407
3: 1	the LORD talked with M on Mount Sinai.	5407
3: 5	The LORD said to M,	5407
3:11	The LORD also said to M,	5407
3:14	The LORD said to M in the Desert	5407
3:16	So M counted them,	5407
3:38	M and Aaron and his sons were to camp to	5407
3:39	at the LORD's command by M and Aaron	5407
3:40	The LORD said to M, "Count all the	5407
3:42	M counted all the firstborn of the Israelites,	5407
3:44	The LORD also said to M,	5407
3:49	So M collected the redemption money	5407
3:51	M gave the redemption money to Aaron	5407
4: 1	The LORD said to M and Aaron:	5407
4:17	The LORD said to M and Aaron,	5407
4:21	The LORD said to M,	5407
4:34	M, Aaron and the leaders of the community	5407
4:37	M and Aaron counted them according to	5407
4:37	to the LORD's command through M.	5407
4:41	M and Aaron counted them according to	5407
4:45	M and Aaron counted them according to	5407
4:45	to the LORD's command through M.	5407
4:46	So M, Aaron and the leaders	5407
4:49	At the LORD's command through M	5407
4:49	as the LORD commanded M.	5407
5: 1	The LORD said to M,	5407
5: 4	as the LORD had instructed M.	5407
5: 5	The LORD said to M,	5407
5:11	Then the LORD said to M,	5407
6: 1	The LORD said to M,	5407
6:22	The LORD said to M,	5407
7: 1	When M finished setting up the tabernacle,	5407
7: 4	The LORD said to M,	5407
7: 6	So M took the carts and oxen	5407
7: 9	But M did not give any to the Kohathites,	NIH
7:11	For the LORD had said to M,	5407
7:89	When M entered the Tent of Meeting	5407
8: 1	The LORD said to M,	5407
8: 3	just as the LORD commanded M.	5407
8: 4	like the pattern the LORD had shown M.	5407
8: 5	The LORD said to M:	5407
8:20	M, Aaron and the whole Israelite community did with the	5407
8:20	as the LORD commanded M.	5407
8:22	as the LORD commanded M.	5407
8:23	The LORD said to M,	5407
9: 1	The LORD spoke to M in the Desert	5407
9: 4	So M told the Israelites to celebrate	5407
9: 5	as the LORD commanded M.	5407
9: 6	they came to M and Aaron that same day	5407
9: 7	and said to M, "We have become unclean	2257S
9: 8	M answered them, "Wait until I find out	5407
9: 9	Then the LORD said to M,	5407
9:23	with his command through M.	5407
10: 1	The LORD said to M:	5407
10:13	at the LORD's command through M.	5407
10:29	Now M said to Hobab son of Reuel	5407
10:31	But M said, "Please do not leave us.	NIH
10:35	Whenever the ark set out, M said, "Rise up,	5407
11: 2	When the people cried out to M,	5407
11:10	M heard the people of every family wailing,	5407
11:10	and M was troubled.	5407
11:16	The LORD said to M: "Bring me seventy	5407
11:21	But M said, "Here I am among	5407
11:23	The LORD answered M, "Is the LORD's arm	5407
11:24	So M went out and told the people what	5407
11:27	A young man ran and told M,	5407
11:28	spoke up and said, "M, my lord,	5407
11:29	M replied, "Are you jealous for my sake?	5407
11:30	Then M and the elders of Israel returned to	5407
12: 1	and Aaron began to talk against M because	5407
12: 2	"Has the LORD spoken only through M?"	5407
12: 3	(Now M was a very humble man,	5407
12: 4	At once the LORD said to M,	5407
12: 7	But this is not true of my servant M;	5407
12: 8	not afraid to speak against my servant M?"	5407
12:11	and he said to M, "Please, my lord,	5407
12:13	So M cried out to the LORD, "O God,	5407
12:14	The LORD replied to M, "If her father	5407
13: 1	The LORD said to M,	5407
13: 3	at the LORD's command M sent them out	5407
13:16	the names of the men M sent to explore	5407
13:16	(M gave Hoshea son of Nun the name Joshua.)	5407
13:17	When M sent them to explore Canaan,	5407
13:26	They came back to M and Aaron and	5407
13:27	They gave M this account:	2257S
13:30	Then Caleb silenced the people before M	5407
14: 2	All the Israelites grumbled against M	5407
14: 5	Then M and Aaron fell facedown in front of	5407
14:11	The LORD said to M, "How long will these	5407
14:13	M said to the LORD, "Then the Egyptians	5407
14:26	The LORD said to M and Aaron:	5407
14:36	So the men M had sent to explore the land,	5407
14:39	When M reported this to all the Israelites,	5407
14:41	But M said, "Why are you disobeying	5407
14:44	though neither M nor the ark of the LORD's	5407
15: 1	The LORD said to M,	5407
15:17	The LORD said to M,	5407
15:22	of these commands the LORD gave M—	5407
15:33	to M and Aaron and the whole assembly,	5407
15:35	the LORD said to M, "The man must die.	5407
15:36	as the LORD commanded M.	5407
15:37	The LORD said to M,	5407

Ref	Text	Strong
Nu 16: 2	and rose up against M.	5407
16: 3	as a group to oppose M and Aaron and said	5407
16: 4	When M heard this, he fell facedown.	5407
16: 8	M also said to Korah, "Now listen,	5407
16:12	Then M summoned Dathan and Abiram,	5407
16:15	Then M became very angry and said to	5407
16:16	M said to Korah, "You and all your	5407
16:18	and stood with M and Aaron at the entrance	5407
16:20	The LORD said to M and Aaron,	5407
16:22	M and Aaron fell facedown and cried out,	NIH
16:23	Then the LORD said to M,	5407
16:25	M got up and went to Dathan and Abiram,	5407
16:28	Then M said, "This is how you will know	5407
16:36	The LORD said to M,	5407
16:40	as the LORD directed him through M.	5407
16:41	community grumbled against M and Aaron.	5407
16:42	to M and Aaron and turned toward the Tent	5407
16:43	Then M and Aaron went to the front of	5407
16:44	and the LORD said to M,	5407
16:46	Then M said to Aaron, "Take your censer	5407
16:47	So Aaron did as M said,	5407
16:50	Then Aaron returned to M at the entrance to	5407
17: 1	The LORD said to M,	5407
17: 6	So M spoke to the Israelites,	5407
17: 7	M placed the staffs before the LORD in	5407
17: 8	The next day M entered the Tent of	5407
17: 9	Then M brought out all the staffs from	5407
17:10	The LORD said to M, "Put back Aaron's	5407
17:11	M did just as the LORD commanded him.	5407
17:12	The Israelites said to M, "We will die!	5407
18:25	The LORD said to M,	5407
19: 1	The LORD said to M and Aaron:	5407
20: 2	and the people gathered in opposition to M	5407
20: 3	They quarreled with M and said,	5407
20: 6	M and Aaron went from the assembly to	5407
20: 7	The LORD said to M,	5407
20: 9	So M took the staff from the LORD's	5407
20:10	in front of the rock and M said to them,	NIH
20:11	Then M raised his arm and struck	5407
20:12	But the LORD said to M and Aaron,	5407
20:14	M sent messengers from Kadesh to the king	5407
20:23	the LORD said to M and Aaron,	5407
20:27	M did as the LORD commanded:	5407
20:28	M removed Aaron's garments and put them	5407
20:28	Then M and Eleazar came down from	5407
21: 5	they spoke against God and against M,	5407
21: 7	The people came to M and said,	5407
21: 7	So M prayed for the people.	5407
21: 8	The LORD said to M, "Make a snake	5407
21: 9	So M made a bronze snake and put it up on	5407
21:16	the well where the LORD said to M,	5407
21:32	After M had sent spies to Jazer,	5407
21:34	The LORD said to M, "Do not be afraid	5407
25: 4	The LORD said to M, "Take all the leaders	5407
25: 5	So M said to Israel's judges,	5407
25: 6	of M and the whole assembly of Israel	5407
25:10	The LORD said to M,	5407
25:16	The LORD said to M,	5407
26: 1	After the plague the LORD said to M	5407
26: 3	M and Eleazar the priest spoke with them	5407
26: 4	as the LORD commanded M."	5407
26: 9	against M and Aaron and were	5407
26:52	The LORD said to M,	5407
26:59	M and their sister Miriam.	5407
26:63	the ones counted by M and Eleazar	5407
26:64	of them was among those counted by M	5407
27: 2	to the Tent of Meeting and stood before M,	5407
27: 5	So M brought their case before the LORD	5407
27:11	as the LORD commanded M.' "	5407
27:12	the LORD said to M, "Go up this mountain	5407
27:15	M said to the LORD,	5407
27:18	So the LORD said to M, "Take Joshua	5407
27:22	M did as the LORD commanded him.	5407
27:23	as the LORD instructed through M.	5407
28: 1	The LORD said to M,	5407
29:40	M told the Israelites all that the LORD	5407
30: 1	M said to the heads of the tribes of Israel:	5407
30:16	the regulations the LORD gave M:	5407
31: 1	The LORD said to M,	5407
31: 3	So M said to the people, "Arm some of your	5407
31: 6	M sent them into battle,	5407
31: 7	as the LORD commanded M,	5407
31:12	and plunder to M and Eleazar the priest and	5407
31:13	M, Eleazar the priest and all the leaders of	5407
31:14	M was angry with the officers of the army	5407
31:21	of the law that the LORD gave M:	5407
31:25	The LORD said to M,	5407
31:31	M and Eleazar the priest did as	5407
31:31	the priest did as the LORD commanded M.	5407
31:41	M gave the tribute to Eleazar the priest as	5407
31:41	as the LORD commanded M.	5407
31:42	which M set apart from that of	5407
31:47	M selected one out of every fifty persons	5407
31:48	commanders of hundreds—went to M	5407
31:51	M and Eleazar the priest accepted	5407
31:52	of hundreds that M and Eleazar presented	NIH
31:54	M and Eleazar the priest accepted the gold	5407
32: 2	So they came to M and Eleazar the priest	5407
32: 6	M said to the Gadites and Reubenites,	5407
32:20	Then M said to them, "If you will do this—	5407
32:25	The Gadites and Reubenites said to M,	5407
32:28	Then M gave orders about them to Eleazar	5407
32:33	Then M gave to the Gadites,	5407
32:40	So M gave Gilead to the Makirites	5407
33: 1	by divisions under the leadership of M	5407
33: 2	At the LORD's command M recorded	5407
33:50	across from Jericho the LORD said to M,	5407

Nu	34: 1	The LORD said to M,	5407
	34:13	M commanded the Israelites:	5407
	34:16	The LORD said to M,	5407
	35: 1	the LORD said to M,	5407
	35: 9	Then the LORD said to M:	5407
	36: 1	came and spoke before M and the leaders,	5407
	36: 5	the LORD's command M gave this order	5407
	36:10	as the LORD commanded M.	5407
	36:13	and regulations the LORD gave through M	5407
Dt	1: 1	These are the words M spoke to all Israel in	5407
	1: 3	M proclaimed to the Israelites all that	5407
	1: 5	M began to expound this law, saying:	5407
	4:41	M set aside three cities east of the Jordan,	5407
	4:44	This is the law M set before the Israelites.	5407
	4:45	and laws M gave them when they came out	5407
	4:46	and was defeated by M and the Israelites	5407
	5: 1	M summoned all Israel and said:	5407
	27: 1	M and the elders of Israel commanded	5407
	27: 9	Then M and the priests, who are Levites,	5407
	27:11	On the same day M commanded the people:	5407
	29: 1	of the covenant the LORD commanded M	5407
	29: 2	M summoned all the Israelites and said	5407
	31: 1	Then M went out and spoke these words	5407
	31: 7	Then M summoned Joshua and said to him	5407
	31: 9	So M wrote down this law and gave it to	5407
	31:10	Then M commanded them:	5407
	31:14	The LORD said to M, "Now the day of your	5407
	31:14	So M and Joshua came and presented	5407
	31:16	And the LORD said to M:	5407
	31:22	So M wrote down this song that day	5407
	31:24	After M finished writing in a book	5407
	31:30	And M recited the words of this song	5407
	32:44	M came with Joshua son of Nun	5407
	32:45	When M finished reciting all these words	5407
	32:48	On that same day the LORD told M,	5407
	33: 1	that M the man of God pronounced on	5407
	33: 4	the law that M gave us,	5407
	34: 1	Then M climbed Mount Nebo from	5407
	34: 5	And M the servant of the LORD died there	5407
	34: 7	M was a hundred and twenty years old	5407
	34: 8	The Israelites grieved for M in the plains	5407
	34: 9	of wisdom because M had laid his hands	5407
	34: 9	the LORD had commanded M.	5407
	34:10	no prophet has risen in Israel like M,	5407
	34:12	or performed the awesome deeds that M did	5407
Jos	1: 1	the death of M the servant of the LORD,	5407
	1: 2	"M my servant is dead.	5407
	1: 3	as I promised M.	5407
	1: 5	As I was with M, so I will be with you;	5407
	1: 7	to obey all the law my servant M gave you;	5407
	1:13	that M the servant of the LORD gave you:	5407
	1:14	the land that M gave you east of the Jordan,	5407
	1:15	which M the servant of the LORD gave you	5407
	1:17	Just as we fully obeyed M,	5407
	1:17	be with you as he was with M.	5407
	3: 7	that I am with you as I was with M.	5407
	4:10	just as M had directed Joshua.	5407
	4:12	as M had directed them.	5407
	4:14	just as they had revered M.	5407
	8:31	as M the servant of the LORD had	5407
	8:31	written in the Book of the Law of M—	5407
	8:32	Joshua copied on stones the law of M	5407
	8:33	as M the servant of the LORD	5407
	8:35	not a word of all that M had commanded	5407
	9:24	LORD your God had commanded his	
		servant M to give you	5407
	11:12	as M the servant of the LORD	5407
	11:15	As the LORD commanded his servant M,	5407
	11:15	so M commanded Joshua, and Joshua did it;	5407
	11:15	of all that the LORD commanded M.	5407
	11:20	as the LORD had commanded M.	5407
	11:23	just as the LORD had directed M,	5407
	12: 6	M, the servant of the LORD,	5407
	12: 6	And M the servant of the LORD gave	5407
	13: 8	the inheritance that M had given them east	5407
	13:12	M had defeated them and taken	5407
	13:15	This is what M had given to the tribe	5407
	13:21	M had defeated him and the Midianite	5407
	13:24	This is what M had given to the tribe	5407
	13:29	This is what M had given to the half-tribe	5407
	13:32	the inheritance M had given when he was in	5407
	13:33	tribe of Levi, M had given no inheritance;	5407
	14: 2	as the LORD had commanded through M.	5407
	14: 3	M had granted the two-and-a-half tribes	
		their inheritance east of the Jordan	5407
	14: 5	just as the LORD had commanded M.	5407
	14: 6	to M the man of God at Kadesh Barnea	5407
	14: 7	I was forty years old when M the servant of	5407
	14: 9	So on that day M swore to me,	5407
	14:10	since the time he said this to M,	5407
	14:11	as strong today as the day M sent me out;	5407
	17: 4	"The LORD commanded M to give us	5407
	18: 7	M the servant of the LORD gave it	5407
	20: 2	as I instructed you through M,	5407
	21: 2	through M that you give us towns to live in,	5407
	21: 8	as the LORD commanded through M.	5407
	22: 2	"You have done all that M the servant of	5407
	22: 4	to your homes in the land that M the servant	5407
	22: 5	that M the servant of the LORD gave you:	5407
	22: 7	of Manasseh M had given land in Bashan,	5407
	22: 9	the command of the LORD through M.	5407
	23: 6	that is written in the Book of the Law of M,	5407
	24: 5	"Then I sent M and Aaron,	5407
Jdg	1:20	As M had promised, Hebron was given	5407
	3: 4	he had given their forefathers through M.	5407
	18:30	Gershom, the son of M, and his sons	5407
1Sa	12: 6	the LORD who appointed M and Aaron	5407

1Sa	12: 8	and the LORD sent M and Aaron,	5407
1Ki	2: 3	as written in the Law of M,	5407
	8: 9	the two stone tablets that M had placed in it	5407
	8:53	just as you declared through your servant M	5407
	8:56	promises he gave through his servant M.	5407
2Ki	14: 6	of M where the LORD commanded:	5407
	18: 4	into pieces the bronze snake M had made,	5407
	18: 6	the commands the LORD had given M.	5407
	18:12	all that M the servant of the LORD	5407
	21: 8	that my servant M gave them."	5407
	23:25	in accordance with all the Law of M.	5407
1Ch	6: 3	of Amram: Aaron, M and Miriam.	5407
	6:49	that M the servant of God had commanded.	5407
	15:15	as M had commanded in accordance with	5407
	21:29	which M had made in the desert,	5407
	22:13	and laws that the LORD gave M for Israel.	5407
	23:13	The sons of Amram: Aaron and M.	5407
	23:14	of the man of God were counted as part	5407
	23:15	The sons of M: Gershom and Eliezer.	5407
	26:24	a descendant of Gershom son of M,	5407
2Ch	1: 3	which M the LORD's servant had made in	5407
	5:10	the two tablets that M had placed in it	5407
	8:13	by M for Sabbaths, New Moons and	5407
	23:18	of the LORD as written in the Law of M,	5407
	24: 6	by M the servant of the LORD and by	5407
	24: 9	to the LORD the tax that M the servant	5407
	25: 4	written in the Law, in the Book of M,	5407
	30:16	as prescribed in the Law of M the man	5407
	33: 8	decrees and ordinances given through M."	5407
	34:14	the LORD that had been given through M.	5407
	35: 6	the LORD commanded through M."	5407
	35:12	as is written in the Book of M.	5407
Ezr	3: 2	with what is written in the Law of M	5407
	6:18	to what is written in the Book of M.	10441
	7: 6	a teacher well versed in the Law of M,	5407
Ne	1: 7	decrees and laws you gave your servant M.	5407
	1: 8	the instruction you gave your servant M,	5407
	8: 1	to bring out the Book of the Law of M,	5407
	8:14	the LORD had commanded through M,	5407
	9:14	decrees and laws through your servant M.	5407
	10:29	of God given through M the servant of God	5407
	13: 1	On that day the Book of M was read aloud	5407
Ps	77:20	like a flock by the hand of M and Aaron.	5407
	90: T	A prayer of M the man of God.	5407
	99: 6	M and Aaron were among his priests,	5407
	103: 7	He made known his ways to M,	5407
	105:26	He sent M his servant, and Aaron,	5407
	106:16	In the camp they grew envious of M and	5407
	106:23	had not M, his chosen one, stood in	5407
	106:32	and trouble came to M because of them;	5407
Isa	63:11	the days of M and his people—	5407
Jer	15: 1	if M and Samuel were to stand before me,	5407
Da	9:11	sworn judgments written in the Law of M,	5407
	9:13	Just as it is written in the Law of M,	5407
Mic	6: 4	I sent M to lead you,	5407
Mal	4: 4	"Remember the law of my servant M,	5407
Mt	8: 4	the priest and offer the gift M commanded,	3707
	17: 3	Just then there appeared before them M	3707
	17: 4	one for you, one for M and one for Elijah."	3707
	19: 7	"did M command that a man give his wife	3707
	19: 8	"M permitted you to divorce your wives	3707
	22:24	"M told us that if a man dies	3707
Mk	1:44	and offer the sacrifices that M commanded	3707
	7:10	For M said, 'Honor your father	3707
	9: 4	there appeared before them Elijah and M,	3707
	9: 5	one for you, one for M and one for Elijah."	3707
	10: 3	"What did M command you?" he replied.	3707
	10: 4	"M permitted a man to write a certificate	3707
	10: 5	that M wrote you this law,"	NIG
	12:19	"M wrote for us that if a man's brother dies	3707
	12:26	have you not read in the book of M,	3707
Lk	2:22	to the Law of M had been completed,	3707
	5:14	and offer the sacrifices that M commanded	3707
	9:30	Two men, M and Elijah,	3707
	9:33	one for you, one for M and one for Elijah."	3707
	16:29	'They have M and the Prophets;	3707
	16:31	'If they do not listen to M and the Prophets,	3707
	20:28	"M wrote for us that if a man's brother	3707
	20:37	even M showed that the dead rise,	3707
	24:27	And beginning with M and all the Prophets,	3707
	24:44	that is written about me in the Law of M,	3707
Jn	1:17	For the law was given through M;	3707
	1:45	"We have found the one M wrote about in	3707
	3:14	Just as M lifted up the snake in the desert,	3707
	5:45	Your accuser is M, on whom your hopes are	3707
	5:46	If you believed M, you would believe me,	3707
	6:32	it is not M who has given you the bread	3707
	7:19	Has not M given you the law?	3707
	7:22	because M gave you circumcision	3707
	7:22	(though actually it did not come from M,	3707
	7:23	the Sabbath so that the law of M may not	3707
	8: 5	In the Law M commanded us to stone such	3707
	9:28	We are disciples of M!	3707
	9:29	We know that God spoke to M,	3707
Ac	3:22	For M said, 'The Lord your God will raise	3707
	6:11	of blasphemy against M and against God."	3707
	6:14	and change the customs M handed down	3707
	7:20	"At that time M was born,	3707
	7:22	M was educated in all the wisdom of	3707
	7:23	"When M was forty years old,	899S
	7:25	M thought that his own people would realize	NIG
	7:26	The next day M came upon two Israelites	NIG
	7:27	the other pushed M aside and said,	899S
	7:29	When M heard this, he fled to Midian,	899S
	7:30	an angel appeared to M in the flames of	899S
	7:32	M trembled with fear and did not dare	3707
	7:35	the same M whom they had rejected with	3707

Ac	7:37	"This is that M who told the Israelites,	3707
	7:40	for this fellow M who led us out of Egypt—	3707
	7:44	It had been made as God directed M,	3707
	13:39	not be justified from by the law of M.	3707
	15: 1	according to the custom taught by M,	3707
	15: 5	and required to obey the law of M."	3707
	15:21	For M has been preached in every city from	3707
	21:21	among the Gentiles to turn away from M,	3707
	26:22	the prophets and M said would happen—	3707
	28:23	from the Law of M and from the Prophets.	3707
Ro	5:14	from the time of Adam to the time of M,	3707
	9:15	For he says to M, "I will have mercy on	3707
	10: 5	M describes in this way the righteousness	3707
	10:19	M says, "I will make you envious	3707
1Co	9: 9	For it is written in the Law of M:	3707
	10: 2	They were all baptized into M in the cloud	3707
2Co	3: 7	not look steadily at the face of M because	3707
	3:13	We are not like M, who would put a veil	3707
	3:15	Even to this day when M is read,	3707
2Ti	3: 8	Just as Jannes and Jambres opposed M,	3707
Heb	3: 2	just as M was faithful in all God's house.	3707
	3: 3	found worthy of greater honor than M,	3707
	3: 5	M was faithful as a servant in all God's	3707
	3:16	Were they not all those M led out of Egypt?	3707
	7:14	to that tribe M said nothing about priests.	3707
	8: 5	This is why M was warned when he was	3707
	9:19	M had proclaimed every commandment	3707
	10:28	rejected the law of M died without mercy	3707
	11:24	By faith M, when he had grown up,	3707
	12:21	The sight was so terrifying that M said,	3707
Jude	1: 9	with the devil about the body of M,	3707
Rev	15: 3	and sang the song of M the servant of God	3707

MOSES' (19) [MOSES]

Ex	4:25	and touched [M'] feet with it.	2257S
	17:12	When M' hands grew tired,	5407
	18: 5	Jethro, M' father-in-law, together with	5407
	18: 5	together with M' sons and wife,	2257S
	18:12	Then Jethro, M' father-in-law,	5407
	18:12	of Israel to eat bread with M' father-in-law	5407
	18:17	M' father-in-law replied, "What you are	5407
	35:20	Then the whole Israelite community	
		withdrew from M' presence,	5407
	38:21	recorded at M' command by the Levites	5407
Lev	8:29	M' share of the ordination ram—	4200+5407
Nu	10:29	of Reuel the Midianite, M' father-in-law,	5407
	11:28	who had been M' aide since youth,	5407
Jos	1: 1	to Joshua son of Nun, M' aide:	5407
Jdg	1:16	The descendants of M' father-in-law,	5407
	4:11	M' brother-in-law, and pitched his tent by	5407
Ps	106:33	and rash words came from M' lips.	2257S
Isa	63:12	arm of power to be at M' right hand,	5407
Mt	23: 2	of the law and the Pharisees sit in M' seat.	3707
Heb	11:23	By faith M' parents hid him	3707

MOST (187) [FOREMOST, INMOST, INNERMOST, SOUTHERNMOST, TOPMOST]

Ge	14:18	He was priest of God M High,	6610
	14:19	"Blessed be Abram by God M High,	6610
	14:20	And blessed be God M High,	6610
	14:22	God M High, Creator of heaven and earth,	6610
	34:19	the m honored of all his father's household.	4946
Ex	26:33	Holy Place from the M Holy Place.	7731+7731
	26:34	the Testimony in the M Holy Place.	7731+7731
	29:37	Then the altar will be m holy,	7731+7731
	30:10	It is m holy to the LORD."	7731+7731
	30:29	so they will be m holy,	7731+7731
	30:36	It shall be m holy to you.	7731+7731
	40:10	the altar, and it will be m holy.	7731+7731
Lev	2: 3	it is a m holy part of the offerings	7731+7731
	2:10	it is a m holy part of the offerings	7731+7731
	6:17	the guilt offering, it is m holy.	7731+7731
	6:25	offering is slaughtered; it is m holy.	7731+7731
	6:29	priest's family may eat it; it is m holy.	7731+7731
	7: 1	guilt offering, which is m holy:	7731+7731
	7: 6	in a holy place; it is m holy.	7731+7731
	10:12	beside the altar, for it is m holy.	7731+7731
	10:17	It is m holy; it was given to you	7731+7731
	14:13	belongs to the priest; it is m holy.	7731+7731
	16: 2	into the M Holy Place behind the curtain	7731
	16:16	for the M Holy Place because of	7731
	16:17	in to make atonement in the M Holy Place	7731
	16:20	making atonement at the face of M holy,	7731
	16:23	on before he entered the M Holy Place,	7731
	16:27	into the M Holy Place to make atonement,	7731
	16:33	make atonement for the M Holy Place	5219+7731
	21:22	may eat the m holy food of his God,	7731+7731
	24: 9	a m holy part of their regular share of	7731+7731
	27:28	so devoted is m holy to the LORD.	7731+7731
Nu	4: 4	the care of the m holy things.	7731+7731
	4:19	they come near the m holy things,	7731+7731
	18: 9	of the m holy offerings that is kept	7731+7731
	18: 9	they bring me as m holy offerings,	7731+7731
	18:10	Eat it as something m holy;	7731+7731
	24:16	who has knowledge from the M High,	6610
Dt	28:54	Even the m gentle and sensitive man	4394
	28:56	The m gentle and sensitive woman	NIH
	30: 4	to the m distant land under the heavens,	7895
	30: 9	Then the LORD your God will make you m	
		prosperous	3855
	32: 8	M High gave the nations their inheritance,	6610
	33:24	"M blessed of sons is Asher;	AIT
Jdg	5:24	"M blessed of women be Jael,	4946
	5:24	m blessed of tent-dwelling women.	4946

Ref	Text	Num
1Sa 20:41	but David wept the **m**.	1540
2Sa 22:14	the voice of the **M High** resounded.	6610
23: 1	oracle of the man exalted by the **M High**,	6583
1Ki 3: 4	for that was the **m important** high place,	1524
6:16	inner sanctuary, the **M Holy Place**,	7731+7731
7:50	innermost room, the **M Holy Place**,	7731+7731
8: 6	of the temple, the **M Holy Place**,	7731+7731
11:11	**m certainly tear** the kingdom **away**	7973+7973
2Ki 10: 3	and **m** worthy of your master's sons	4946
1Ch 6:49	that was done in the **M Holy Place**,	7731+7731
12:29	3,000, **m** *of* whom had remained loyal	5270
16:25	great is the LORD and **m** worthy of praise;	4394
17:17	though I were the **m exalted** *of* men,	5092+9366
23:13	to consecrate the **m holy things**,	7731+7731
2Ch 3: 8	He built the **M Holy Place**,	7731+7731
3:10	In the **M Holy Place** he made a pair	7731+7731
4:22	the inner doors to the **M Holy Place**,	7731+7731
5: 7	of the temple, the **M Holy Place**,	7731+7731
28:19	had been **m unfaithful** to the LORD.	5085+5086
30:18	Although **m** of the many people who came	5270
Ezr 2:63	of the **m sacred** *food* until there was	7731+7731
Ne 7: 2	and feared God more than **m** men do.	8041
7:65	not to eat any of the **m sacred food**	7731+7731
Est 6: 9	to one of the king's **m noble** princes.	7312
Ps 7: 8	according to my integrity, O **M High**.	6604
7:10	My shield is God **M High**.	6583
7:17	to the name of the LORD **M High**.	6610
9: 2	I will sing praise to your name, O **M High**.	6610
18:13	the voice of the **M High** resounded.	6610
21: 7	the unfailing love of the **M High** he will not be shaken.	6610
28: 2	my hands toward your **M High** place.	1808+7731
45: 2	*You are the* **m excellent** of men	3636
46: 4	the holy place where the **M High** dwells.	6610
47: 2	How awesome is the LORD **M High**,	6610
48: 1	Great is the LORD, and **m** worthy of praise,	4394
50:14	fulfill your vows to the **M High**,	6610
57: 2	I cry out to God **M High**, to God,	6610
73:11	Does the **M High** have knowledge?"	6610
77:10	the years of the right hand of the **M High**."	6610
78:17	rebelling in the desert against the **M High**.	6610
78:35	that God **M High** was their Redeemer.	6610
78:56	to the test and rebelled against the **M High**;	6610
82: 6	you are all sons of the **M High**.'	6610
83:18	you alone are the **M High** over all the earth.	6610
87: 5	and the **M High** himself will establish her.	6610
89:27	the **m exalted** of the kings of the earth.	6609
91: 1	of the **M High** will rest in the shadow of the	6610
91: 9	If you make the **M High** your dwelling—	6610
92: 1	and make music to your name, O **M High**,	6610
96: 4	great is the LORD and **m** worthy of praise;	4394
97: 9	O LORD, are the **M High** over all the earth;	6610
107:11	and despised the counsel of the **M High**.	6610
145: 3	Great is the LORD and **m** worthy of praise;	4394
Pr 30: 2	"I am the **m ignorant of** men;	4946
Ecc 7:24	it is far off and **m profound**—	6678+6678
SS 1: 8	you do not know, *m* **beautiful** of women,	AIT
5: 9	*m* **beautiful** of women?	AIT
6: 1	*m* **beautiful** of women?	AIT
Isa 14:14	I will make myself like the **M High**."	6610
Jer 3:19	**m beautiful** inheritance of any nation.	7382+7382
9:17	send for the *m* **skillful** of them.	AIT
18:13	A **m** horrible thing has been done	4394
La 1:20	for *I have been* **m rebellious**.	5286+5286
3:35	to deny a man his rights before the **M High**,	6610
3:38	the **M High** that both calamities and good	6610
Eze 7:24	I will bring the **m wicked** of the nations	AIT
16: 7	became the **m beautiful** of jewels.	6344+6344
20: 6	the **m beautiful** of all lands.	7382
20:15	**m beautiful** of all lands;	7382
28: 7	the *m* **ruthless** *of* nations;	AIT
30:11	the *m* **ruthless** *of* nations—	AIT
31:12	and the *m* **ruthless** *of* foreign nations cut it	AIT
32:12	the *m* **ruthless** *of* all nations.	AIT
41: 4	"This is the **M Holy Place**."	7731+7731
41:21	the front of the **M Holy Place** was similar.	7731
41:23	and the **M Holy Place** had double doors.	7731
42:13	will eat the **m holy offerings**.	7731+7731
42:13	they will put the **m holy offerings**—	7731+7731
43:12	on top of the mountain will be **m holy**.	7731+7731
44:13	holy things or my **m holy offerings**;	7731+7731
45: 3	the sanctuary, the **M Holy Place**.	7731+7731
48:12	portion of the land, a **m holy** portion,	7731+7731
Da 3:26	servants of the **M High** God, come out!	10546
4: 2	that the **M High** God has performed for me.	10546
4:17	**M High** is sovereign over the kingdoms	10546
4:24	this is the decree the **M High** has issued	10546
4:25	**M High** is sovereign over the kingdoms	10546
4:32	**M High** is sovereign over the kingdoms	10546
4:34	Then I praised the **M High**;	10546
5:18	the **M High** God gave your father Nebuchadnezzar sovereignty	10546
5:21	that the **M High** God is sovereign over	10546
7:18	But the saints of the **M High** will receive	10548
7:19	from all the others and **m** terrifying,	10339
7:22	in favor of the saints of the **M High**,	10548
7:25	against the **M High** and oppress his saints	10546
7:27	the people of the **M High**.	10548
9:24	prophecy and to anoint the **m holy**.	7731+7731
Hos 7:16	They do not turn to the **M High**;	6583
11: 7	Even if they call to the **M High**,	6583
Mic 7: 4	the **m upright** worse than a thorn hedge.	NIH
Mt 11:20	to denounce the cities in which **m** of his	4498
23: 6	the **m important seats** in the synagogues;	4751
24:12	the love *of* **m** will grow cold,	4498
Mk 5: 7	Jesus, Son of the **M High God**?	5736
12:28	which is the **m important**?"	4755

Ref	Text	Num
Mk 12:29	"The **m important** *one*," answered Jesus,	4755
12:39	the **m important seats** in the synagogues	4751
12:40	Such men will be punished **m severely**."	4358
Lk 1: 3	account for you, **m excellent** Theophilus,	3196
1:32	and will be called the Son of the **M High**.	5736
1:35	power of the **M High** will overshadow you.	5736
1:76	will be called a prophet of the **M High**;	5736
6:35	and you will be sons of the **M High**,	5736
8:28	Jesus, Son of the **M High God**?	5736
11:43	because you love the **m important seats** in	4751
20:46	the **m important seats** in the synagogues	4751
20:47	Such men will be punished **m severely**."	4358
Ac 7:48	the **M High** does not live in houses made	5736
16:17	These men are servants of the **M High God**,	5736
19:32	**M** of the *people* did not even know	3836+4498
20:38	What grieved them **m** was his statement	3436
24: 3	**m excellent** Felix, we acknowledge this	3196
26:25	"I am not insane, **m excellent** Festus,"	3196
1Co 10: 5	God was not pleased with **m** of them;	4498
12:31	I will show you the **m excellent** way.	2848+5651
14:27	two—or at the **m** three—should speak,	4498
15: 6	**m** of whom are still living,	4498
2Co 8: 2	Out of the **m** severe trial,	4498
9: 2	and your enthusiasm has stirred **m** *of* them	4498
Eph 5:16	**making the m of** every opportunity,	1973
Php 1:14	Because of my chains, **m** of the brothers	4498
Col 4: 5	toward outsiders; **make the m of** every opportunity.	1973+2789+3836
1Th 3:10	Night and day we pray **m earnestly**	5655
Heb 7: 1	of Salem and priest of God **M High**.	5736
9: 3	a room called the **M Holy Place**,	41+41
9: 8	that the way into the **M Holy Place** had not	NIG
9:12	but he entered the **M Holy Place** once	NIG
9:25	the **M Holy Place** every year with blood	NIG
10:19	the **M Holy Place** by the blood of Jesus,	NIG
13:11	the blood of animals into the **M Holy Place**	NIG
Jude 1:20	build yourselves up *in* your **m holy** faith	AIT

MOTE (KJV) See SPECK OF SAWDUST

MOTH (7)

Ref	Text	Num
Job 4:19	who are crushed more readily than a **m**!	6931
Ps 39:11	you consume their wealth like a **m**—	6931
Isa 51: 8	For the **m** will eat them up like a garment;	6931
Hos 5:12	I am like a **m** to Ephraim,	6931
Mt 6:19	where **m** and rust destroy,	4962
6:20	where **m** and rust do not destroy,	4962
Lk 12:33	no thief comes near and no **m** destroys.	4962

MOTH'S (1) [MOTHS]

Ref	Text	Num
Job 27:18	The house he builds is like a **m cocoon**,	6931

MOTHEATEN (KJV) See MOTHS

MOTHER (237) [GRANDMOTHER, GRANDMOTHER'S, MOTHER-IN-LAW, MOTHER'S, MOTHERS, MOTHERS']

Ref	Text	Num
Ge 2:24	a man will leave his father and and	562
3:20	she would become the **m** *of* all the living.	562
17:16	I will bless her so that she will be the **m**	NIH
20:12	daughter of my father though not of my **m**;	562
21:21	his **m** got a wife for him from Egypt.	562
22:20	"Milcah is also a **m**;	NIH
24:53	gave costly gifts to her brother and to her **m**.	562
24:55	But her brother and her **m** replied,	562
24:67	brought her into the tent of his **m** Sarah,	562
27:11	Jacob said to Rebekah his **m**,	562
27:13	His **m** said to him, "My son,	562
27:14	and got them and brought them to his **m**,	562
27:29	may the sons of your **m** bow down to you.	562
28: 5	who was the **m** *of* Jacob and Esau.	562
28: 7	and that Jacob had obeyed his father and **m**	562
30:14	which he brought to his **m** Leah.	562
37:10	Will your **m** and I and your brothers	562
Ex 2: 8	And the girl went and got the baby's **m**.	562
20:12	"Honor your father and your **m**,	562
21:15	"Anyone who attacks his father or his **m** must be put to death.	562
21:17	"Anyone who curses his father or **m** must be put to death.	562
Lev 18: 7	by having sexual relations with your **m**.	562
18: 7	She is your **m**; do not have relations with	562
19: 3	Each of you must respect his **m** and father,	562
20: 9	" 'If anyone curses his father or **m**,	562
20: 9	He has cursed his father or his **m**,	562
20:14	a man marries both a woman and her **m**,	562
20:17	the daughter of either his father or his **m**,	562
20:19	the sister of either your **m** or your father, for	562
21: 2	such as his **m** or father, his son or daughter,	562
21:11	even for his father or **m**,	562
22:27	it is to remain with its **m** for seven days.	562
24:10	Now the son of an Israelite **m** and	851
Nu 6: 7	his own father or **m** or brother or sister dies,	562
Dt 5:16	"Honor your father and your **m**,	562
21:13	in your house and mourned her father and **m**	562
21:18	not obey his father and **m** and will not listen	562
21:19	and **m** shall take hold of him and bring him	562
22: 6	the **m** is sitting on the young or on the eggs,	562
22: 6	do not take the **m** with the young.	562
22: 7	but be sure to let the **m** go,	562
22:15	then the girl's father and **m** shall bring proof	562
27:16	the man who dishonors his father or his **m**."	562
27:22	of his father or the daughter of his **m**."	562

Ref	Text	Num
Dt 33: 9	He said of his father and **m**,	562
Jos 2:13	you will spare the lives of my father and **m**,	562
2:18	unless you have brought your father and **m**,	562
6:23	and **m** and brothers and all who belonged	562
Jdg 5: 7	Deborah, arose, arose a **m** in Israel.	562
5:28	"Through the window peered Sisera's **m**;	562
8:19	my brothers, the sons of my own **m**.	562
11: 1	his **m** was a prostitute.	851
14: 2	he returned, he said to his father and **m**,	562
14: 3	His father and **m** replied,	562
14: 5	to Timnah together with his father and **m**.	562
14: 6	his father nor his **m** what he had done.	562
14:16	even explained it to my father or **m**,"	562
17: 2	said to his **m**, "The eleven hundred shekels	562
17: 2	Then his **m** said, "The LORD bless you,	562
17: 3	eleven hundred shekels of silver to his **m**,	562
17: 4	So he returned the silver to his **m**,	562
Ru 2:11	and **m** and your homeland and came to live	562
1Sa 2:19	Each year his **m** made him a little robe	562
15:33	so will your **m** be childless among women."	562
20:30	and to the shame of the **m** *who bore* you?	562
22: 3	"Would you let my father and **m** come	562
2Sa 17:25	of Nahash and sister of Zeruiah the **m**	562
19:37	near the tomb of my father and **m**.	562
20:19	You are trying to destroy a city that is a **m**	562
1Ki 1: 5	Now Adonijah, whose **m** was Haggith,	NIH
1:11	Nathan asked Bathsheba, Solomon's **m**,	562
2:13	went to Bathsheba, Solomon's **m**.	562
2:19	He had a throne brought for the king's **m**,	562
2:20	The king replied, "Make it, my **m**;	562
2:22	King Solomon answered his **m**,	562
3:27	Do not kill him; she is his **m**."	562
7:14	whose **m** was a widow from the tribe	851
11:26	and his **m** was a widow named Zeruah.	562
15:13	Maacah from her **position as queen m**,	1485
17:23	He gave him to his **m** and said, "Look,	562
19:20	"Let me kiss my father and **m** good-by,"	562
22:52	and **m** and in the ways of Jeroboam son	562
2Ki 3: 2	but not as his father and **m** had done.	562
3:13	of your father and the prophets of your **m**."	562
4:19	"Carry him to his **m**."	562
4:20	lifted him up and carried him to his **m**,	562
4:30	But the child's **m** said,	562
9:22	and witchcraft of your **m** Jezebel abound?"	562
10:13	the families of the king and of the **queen m**.	1485
11: 1	When Athaliah the **m** of Ahaziah saw	562
24:12	Jehoiachin king of Judah, his **m**,	562
24:15	from Jerusalem to Babylon the king's **m**,	562
1Ch 2:17	Abigail *was the* **m** *of* Amasa,	3528
2:26	she was the **m** *of* Onam.	562
2:46	Caleb's concubine Ephah *was the* **m**	3528
2:48	Caleb's concubine Maacah *was the* **m**	3528
4: 9	His **m** had named him Jabez, saying,	562
2Ch 2:14	whose **m** was from Dan	851
15:16	Maacah from her **position as queen m**,	1485
22: 3	for his **m** encouraged him in doing wrong.	562
22:10	When Athaliah the **m** of Ahaziah saw	562
Est 2: 7	up because she had neither father nor **m**.	562
2: 7	when her father and **m** died.	562
Job 17:14	and to the worm, 'My **m**' or 'My sister,'	562
Ps 27:10	Though my father and **m** forsake me,	562
35:14	in grief as though weeping for my **m**,	562
51: 5	sinful from the time my **m** conceived me.	562
109:14	may the sin of his **m** never be blotted out.	562
113: 9	the barren woman in her home as a happy **m**	562
131: 2	like a weaned child with its **m**,	562
Pr 4: 3	still tender, and an only child of my **m**,	562
10: 1	but a foolish son grief to his **m**.	562
15:20	but a foolish man despises his **m**.	562
19:26	drives out his **m** is a son who brings shame	562
20:20	If a man curses his father or **m**,	562
23:22	and do not despise your **m** when she is old.	562
23:25	May your father and **m** be glad;	562
28:24	He who robs his father or **m** and says,	562
29:15	but a child left to himself disgraces his **m**.	562
30:17	that scorns obedience to a **m**,	562
31: 1	an oracle his **m** taught him:	562
SS 3:11	with which his **m** crowned him on the day	562
6: 9	is unique, the only daughter of her **m**,	562
8: 5	there your **m** conceived you,	562
Isa 8: 4	how to say 'My father' or 'My **m**,'	562
45:10	to his **m**, 'What have you brought to birth?'	851
49:15	"Can a **m** forget the baby at her breast	851
50: 1	your transgressions your **m** was sent away.	562
66:13	**m** comforts her child, so will I comfort you;	562
Jer 13:18	to the king and to the **queen m**,	1485
15: 9	The **m** *of* seven will grow faint	3528
15:10	Alas, my **m**, that you gave me birth,	562
16: 7	even for a father or a **m**—	562
20:14	May the day my **m** bore me not be blessed!	562
20:17	with my **m** as my grave,	562
22:26	and the **m** who gave you birth	562
29: 2	after King Jehoiachin and the **queen m**,	1485
50:12	your **m** will be greatly ashamed;	562
Eze 16: 3	your father was an Amorite and your **m**	562
16:44	"Like **m**, like daughter."	562
16:45	You are a true daughter of your **m**,	562
16:45	Your **m** was a Hittite and your father	562
19: 2	a lioness was your **m** among the lions!	562
19:10	" 'Your **m** was like a vine	562
22: 7	In you they have treated father and **m**	562
23: 2	daughters of the same **m**.	562
44:25	if the dead person was his father or **m**,	562
Hos 2: 2	"Rebuke your **m**, rebuke her,	562
2: 5	Their **m** has been unfaithful and	562
4: 5	So I will destroy your **m**—	562
Mic 7: 6	a daughter rises up against her **m**,	562

Zec	13: 3	if anyone still prophesies, his father and m,	562
Mt	1: 3	Perez and Zerah, whose m was Tamar,	1666
	1: 5	Boaz, whose m was Rahab,	1666
	1: 5	Obed, whose m was Ruth,	1666
	1: 6	Solomon, whose m had been Uriah's wife,	1666
	1:18	His m Mary was pledged to be married	3613
	2:11	they saw the child with his m Mary,	3613
	2:13	the child and his m and escape to Egypt.	3613
	2:14	the child and his m during the night and left	3613
	2:20	take the child and his m and go to the land	3613
	2:21	and his m and went to the land of Israel.	3613
	10:35	a daughter against her m,	3613
	10:37	or m more than me is not worthy of me;	3613
	12:46	his m and brothers stood outside.	3613
	12:47	"Your m and brothers are standing outside,	3613
	12:48	He replied to him, "Who is my m,	3613
	12:49	he said, "Here are my m and my brothers.	3613
	12:50	in heaven is my brother and sister and m."	3613
	14: 8	Prompted by her m, she said,	3613
	14:11	who carried it to her m.	3613
	15: 4	God said, 'Honor your father and m'	3613
	15: 4	curses his father or m must be put to death.'	3613
	15: 5	that if a man says to his father or m,	3613
	19: 5	a man will leave his father and m and	3613
	19:19	honor your father and m,'	3613
	19:29	or sisters or father or m or children or fields	3613
	20:20	Then the m of Zebedee's sons came to Jesus	3613
	27:56	Mary the m of James and Joses,	3613
	27:56	and the m of Zebedee's sons.	3613
Mk	3:31	Then Jesus' m and brothers arrived.	3613
	3:32	"Your m and brothers are outside looking	3613
	3:33	"Who are my m and my brothers?"	3613
	3:34	"Here are my m and my brothers!	3613
	3:35	God's will is my brother and sister and m."	3613
	5:40	and m and the disciples who were with him,	3613
	6:24	She went out and said to her m,	3613
	6:28	and she gave it to her m.	3613
	7:10	'Honor your father and your m,' and,	3613
	7:10	'Anyone who curses his father or m must	3613
	7:11	you say that if a man says to his father or m:	3613
	7:12	let him do anything for his father or m,	3613
	10: 7	a man will leave his father and m and	3613
	10:19	do not defraud, honor your father and m.' "	3613
	10:29	or sisters or m or father or children or fields	3613
	15:40	the m of James the younger and of Joses,	3613
	15:47	the m of Joses saw where he was laid.	3836
	16: 1	Mary Magdalene, Mary the m of James,	3836
Lk	1:43	that the m of my Lord should come to me?	3613
	1:60	but his m spoke up and said,	3613
	2:33	and m marveled at what was said about him.	3613
	2:34	blessed them and said to Mary, his m:	3613
	2:48	His m said to him, "Son, why have you	3613
	2:51	His m treasured all these things in her heart.	3613
	7:12	only son of his m, and she was a widow.	3613
	7:15	and Jesus gave him back to his m.	3613
	8:19	Jesus' m and brothers came to see him,	3613
	8:20	"Your m and brothers are standing outside,	3613
	8:21	He replied, "My m and brothers are	3613
	8:51	and the child's father and m.	3613
	11:27	the m who gave you birth and nursed you."	3120
	12:53	m against daughter and daughter	3613
	12:53	against daughter and daughter against m,	3613
	14:26	and does not hate his father and m, his wife	3613
	18:20	honor your father and m.' "	3613
	24:10	Joanna, Mary the m of James,	3836
Jn	2: 1	Jesus' m was there,	3613
	2: 3	Jesus' m said to him, "They have no more	3613
	2: 5	His m said to the servants,	3613
	2:12	down to Capernaum with his m and brothers	3613
	6:42	whose father and m we know?	3613
	19:25	Near the cross of Jesus stood his m,	3613
	19:26	When Jesus saw his m there,	3613
	19:26	he said to his m, "Dear woman, here is your son,"	3613
	19:27	"Here is your m."	3613
Ac	1:14	with the women and Mary the m of Jesus,	3613
	12:12	he went to the house of Mary the m of John,	3613
	16: 1	whose m was a Jewess and a believer,	1222
Ro	16:13	Greet Rufus, chosen in the Lord, and his m,	3613
	16:13	his mother, who has been a mother to me,	NIG
Gal	4:26	that is above is free, and she is our m.	3613
Eph	5:31	a man will leave his father and m and	3613
	6: 2	"Honor your father and m"—	3613
1Th	2: 7	like a m caring for her little children.	5577
2Ti	1: 5	Lois and in your m Eunice and,	3613
Heb	7: 3	Without father or m, without genealogy,	298
Rev	17: 5	BABYLON THE GREAT THE M OF PROSTITUTES	3613

MOTHER'S (64) [MOTHER]

Ge	24:28	The girl ran and told her m household	562
	24:67	and Isaac was comforted after his m death.	562
	28: 2	to the house of your m father Bethuel.	562
	28: 2	the daughters of Laban, your m brother.	562
	29:10	his m brother, and Laban's sheep,	562
	43:29	brother Benjamin, his own m son, he asked,	562
	44:20	and he is the only one of his m sons left,	562
Ex	23:19	"Do not cook a young goat in its m milk.	562
	34:26	"Do not cook a young goat in its m milk.'	562
Lev	18: 9	your father's daughter or your m daughter,	562
	18:13	not have sexual relations with your m sister,	562
	18:13	because she is your m close relative.	562
	24:11	(His m name was Shelomith,	562
Nu	12:12	a stillborn infant coming from its m womb	562
Dt	14:21	Do not cook a young goat in its m milk.	562
Jdg	9: 1	to his m brothers in Shechem and said	562
	9: 1	and said to them and to all his m clan,	562

Ru	1: 8	"Go back, each of you, to your m home.	562
1Ki	14:21	His m name was Naamah;	562
	14:31	His m name was Naamah;	562
	15: 2	His m name was Maacah daughter	562
	22:42	His m name was Azubah daughter of Shilhi.	562
2Ki	8:26	His m name was Athaliah,	562
	12: 1	His m name was Zibiah;	562
	14: 2	His m name was Jehoaddin;	562
	15: 2	His m name was Jecoliah;	562
	15:33	His m name was Jerusha daughter of Zadok.	562
	18: 2	His m name was Abijah daughter	562
	21: 1	His m name was Hephzibah.	562
	21:19	His m name was Meshullemeth daughter	562
	22: 1	His m name was Jedidah daughter	562
	23:31	His m name was Hamutal daughter	562
	23:36	His m name was Zebidah daughter	562
	24: 8	His m name was Nehushta daughter	562
	24:18	His m name was Hamutal daughter	562
2Ch	12:13	His m name was Naamah;	562
	13: 2	His m name was Maacah,	562
	20:31	His m name was Azubah daughter of Shilhi.	562
	22: 2	His m name was Athaliah,	562
	24: 1	His m name was Zibiah;	562
	25: 1	His m name was Jehoaddin;	562
	26: 3	His m name was Jecoliah;	562
	27: 1	His m name was Jerusha daughter of Zadok.	562
	29: 1	His m name was Abijah daughter	562
Job	1:21	"Naked I came from my m womb,	562
Ps	22: 9	in you even at my m breast.	562
	22:10	from my m womb you have been my God.	562
	50:20	and slander your own m son.	562
	69: 8	an alien to my own m sons;	562
	71: 6	you brought me forth from my m womb.	562
	139:13	you knit me together in my m womb.	562
Pr	1: 8	and do not forsake your m teaching.	562
	6:20	and do not forsake your m teaching.	562
Ecc	5:15	Naked a man comes from his m womb,	562
	11: 5	or how the body is formed in a m womb,	4849S
SS	1: 6	My m sons were angry with me	562
	3: 4	till I had brought him to my m house,	562
	8: 1	who was nursed at my m breasts!	562
	8: 2	and bring you to my m house—	562
Isa	50: 1	"Where is your m certificate of divorce	562
Jer	52: 1	His m name was Hamutal daughter	562
Mt	13:55	Isn't his m name Mary,	3613
Jn	3: 4	a second time into his m womb to be born!"	3613
	19:25	his m sister, Mary the wife of Clopas,	3613

MOTHER-IN-LAW (18) [MOTHER]

Dt	27:23	"Cursed is the man who sleeps with his m."	3165
Ru	1:14	Then Orpah kissed her m good-by,	2792
	2:11	about what you have done for your m since	2792
	2:18	and her m saw how much she had gathered.	2792
	2:19	Her m asked her, "Where did you glean	2792
	2:19	Then Ruth told her m about the one	2792
	2:23	And she lived with her m.	2792
	3: 1	One day Naomi her m said to her,	2792
	3: 6	and did everything her m told her to do.	2792
	3:16	When Ruth came to her m, Naomi asked,	2792
	3:17	'Don't go back to your m empty-handed.' "	2792
Mic	7: 6	a daughter-in-law against her m—	2792
Mt	8:14	he saw Peter's m lying in bed with a fever.	4289
	10:35	a daughter-in-law against her m—	4289
Mk	1:30	Simon's m was in bed with a fever,	4289
Lk	4:38	Simon's m was suffering from a high fever,	4289
	12:53	m against daughter-in-law	4289
	12:53	and daughter-in-law against m."	4289

MOTHER-OF-PEARL (1) [PEARL]

Est	1: 6	marble, m and other costly stones.	1993

MOTHERS (17) [MOTHER]

Ge	32:11	and also the m with their children.	562
Ex	22:30	Let them stay with their m for seven days,	562
Job	31:15	the same one form us both within our m?	8167
Pr	30:11	and do not bless their m;	562
Isa	49:23	and their queens your nursing m.	4787
Jer	15: 8	against the m of their young men;	562
	16: 3	and about the women who are their m and	562
	31: 8	expectant m and women in labor;	2226
La	2:12	They say to their m, "Where is bread	562
	5: 3	and fatherless, our m like widows.	562
Hos	10:14	of battle, when m were dashed to the ground	562
Mt	24:19	for pregnant women and nursing m!	2558
Mk	10:30	brothers, sisters, m, children and fields—	3613
	13:17	for pregnant women and nursing m!	2558
Lk	21:23	for pregnant women and nursing m!	2558
1Ti	1: 9	for those who kill their fathers or m,	3618
	5: 2	older women as m, and younger women as	3613

MOTHERS' (1) [MOTHER]

La	2:12	as their lives ebb away in their m' arms.	562

MOTHS (3) [MOTH'S]

Job	13:28	like a garment eaten by m.	6931
Isa	50: 9	the m will eat them up.	6931
Jas	5: 2	and m have eaten your clothes.	1181+4963

MOTIONED (7) [MOTIONS]

Jn	13:24	Simon Peter m to this disciple and said,	3748
Ac	12:17	Peter m with his hand for them to be quiet	2939
	13:16	Standing up, Paul m with his hand and said:	2939
	19:33	He m for silence in order to make a defense	2939

Ac	21:40	Paul stood on the steps and m to the crowd.	2939+3836+5931
	24:10	When the governor m for him to speak,	3748
	26: 1	Paul m with his hand and began his defense	1753

MOTIONS (1) [MOTIONED]

Pr	6:13	signals with his feet and m with his fingers,	3721

MOTIVE (1) [MOTIVES]

1Ch	28: 9	understands every m behind the thoughts.	3671

MOTIVES (5) [MOTIVE]

Pr	16: 2	but m are weighed by the LORD.	8120
1Co	4: 5	and will expose the m of men's hearts.	1087
Php	1:18	whether from false or true,	4733
1Th	2: 3	not spring from error or impure m,	NIG
Jas	4: 3	because you ask with wrong m,	NIG

MOUND (5) [MOUNDS]

SS	7: 2	Your waist is a m of wheat encircled	6894
Jer	26:18	the temple hill a m overgrown with thickets.	1195
	49: 2	it will become a m of ruins,	9424
Eze	16:24	a m for yourself and made a lofty shrine	1461
Mic	3:12	the temple hill a m overgrown with thickets.	1195

MOUNDS (3) [MOUND]

Jos	11:13	not burn any of the cities built on their m—	9424
Eze	16:31	When you built your m at the head	1461
	16:39	down your m and destroy your lofty shrines.	1461

MOUNT (146) [MOUNTAIN, MOUNTAINS, MOUNTAINSIDE, MOUNTAINTOP, MOUNTAINTOPS, MOUNTED, MOUNTINGS, MOUNTS]

Ex	19:11	the LORD will come down on M Sinai in	2215
	19:18	M Sinai was covered with smoke,	2215
	19:20	of M Sinai and called Moses to the top of	2215
	19:23	"The people cannot come up M Sinai,	2215
	24:16	the glory of the LORD settled on M Sinai.	2215
	28:11	Then m the stones in gold filigree settings	6913
	28:17	Then m four rows of precious stones	4848+4853
	28:20	M them in gold filigree settings.	2118+4853
	31:18	finished speaking to Moses on M Sinai,	2215
	33: 6	So the Israelites stripped off their ornaments at M Horeb.	2215
	34: 2	and then come up on M Sinai.	2215
	34: 4	the first ones and went up M Sinai early in	2215
	34:29	down from M Sinai with the two tablets of	2215
	34:32	the LORD had given him on M Sinai.	2215
Lev	7:38	which the LORD gave Moses on M Sinai	2215
	25: 1	The LORD said to Moses on M Sinai,	2215
	26:46	that the LORD established on M Sinai	2215
	27:34	the LORD gave Moses on M Sinai for	2215
Nu	3: 1	the LORD talked with Moses on M Sinai.	2215
	20:22	from Kadesh and came to M Hor.	2215
	20:23	At M Hor, near the border of Edom,	2215
	20:25	and take them up M Hor.	2215
	20:27	They went up M Hor in the sight of	2215
	21: 4	from M Hor along the route to the Red Sea,	2215
	28: 6	at M Sinai as a pleasing aroma,	2215
	33:23	and camped at M Shepher.	2215
	33:24	They left M Shepher and camped	2215
	33:37	They left Kadesh and camped at M Hor,	2215
	33:38	the priest went up M Hor,	2215
	33:39	when he died on M Hor.	2215
	33:41	They left M Hor and camped at Zalmonah.	2215
	34: 7	run a line from the Great Sea to M Hor	2215
	34: 8	and from M Hor to Lebo Hamath.	2215
Dt	1: 2	to Kadesh Barnea by the M Seir road.)	2215
	3: 8	from the Arnon Gorge as far as M Hermon.	2215
	4:48	on the rim of the Arnon Gorge to M Siyon	2215
	11:29	to proclaim on M Gerizim the blessings,	2215
	11:29	and on M Ebal the curses.	2215
	27: 4	set up these stones on M Ebal,	2215
	27:12	these tribes shall stand on M Gerizim	2215
	27:13	And these tribes shall stand on M Ebal	2215
	32:49	into the Abarim Range to M Nebo in Moab,	2215
	32:50	on M Hor and was gathered to his people.	2215
	33: 2	he shone forth from M Paran.	2215
	34: 1	Then Moses climbed M Nebo from	2215
Jos	8:30	Then Joshua built on M Ebal an altar to	2215
	8:33	of the people stood in front of M Gerizim	2215
	8:33	and half of them in front of M Ebal.	2215
	11:17	from Halak, which rises toward Seir,	2215
	11:17	in the Valley of Lebanon below M Hermon.	2215
	12: 1	from the Arnon Gorge to M Hermon,	2215
	12: 5	He ruled over M Hermon, Salecah,	2215
	12: 7	in the Valley of Lebanon to M Halak,	2215
	13: 5	the east, from Baal Gad below M Hermon	2215
	13:11	all of M Hermon and all Bashan as far	2215
	15: 9	of M Ephron and went down toward Baalah	2215
	15:10	it curved westward from Baalah to M Seir,	2215
	15:10	ran along the northern slope of M Jearim	2215
	15:11	along to M Baalah and reached Jabneel.	2215
	24:30	hill country of Ephraim, north of M Gaash.	2215
Jdg	1:35	also to hold out in M Heres,	2215
	2: 9	hill country of Ephraim, north of M Gaash.	2215
	3: 3	from M Baal Hermon to Lebo Hamath.	2215
	4: 6	and Zebulun and lead the way to M Tabor.	2215
	4:12	of Abinoam had gone up to M Tabor,	2215
	4:14	So Barak went down M Tabor,	2215
	7: 3	may turn back and leave M Gilead.' "	2215

Jdg	9: 7	the top of **M** Gerizim and shouted to them,	2215
	9:48	he and all his men went up **M** Zalmon.	2215
1Sa	31: 1	and many fell slain on **M** Gilboa.	2215
	31: 8	and his three sons fallen on **M** Gilboa.	2215
2Sa	1: 6	"I happened to be on **M** Gilboa,"	2215
	15:30	But David continued up the **M** of Olives,	5090
1Ki	18:19	over Israel to meet me on **M** Carmel.	2215
	18:20	and assembled the prophets on **M** Carmel.	2215
2Ki	2:25	on to **M** Carmel and from there returned	2215
	4:25	and came to the man of God at **M** Carmel.	2215
	19:31	and out of **M** Zion a band of survivors.	2215
1Ch	5:23	that is, to Senir (**M** Hermon).	2215
	10: 1	and many fell slain on **M** Gilboa.	2215
	10: 8	and his sons fallen on **M** Gilboa.	2215
2Ch	3: 1	of the LORD in Jerusalem on **M** Moriah,	2215
	13: 4	Abijah stood on **M** Zemaraim,	2215
	20:10	and **M** Seir, whose territory you would	2215
	20:22	and **M** Seir who were invading Judah,	2215
	20:23	from **M** Seir to destroy and annihilate them.	2215
Ne	2:14	not enough room for my **m** to get through;	989
	9:13	"You came down on **M** Sinai;	2215
Ps	42: 6	of Hermon—from **M** Mizar.	2215
	48: 2	the utmost heights of Zaphon is **M** Zion,	2215
	48:11	**M** Zion rejoices, the villages	2215
	74: 2	**M** Zion, where you dwelt.	2215
	78:68	**M** Zion, which he loved.	2215
	89: 9	when its waves **m up**, you still them.	5951
	125: 1	who trust in the LORD are like **M** Zion,	2215
	133: 3	the dew of Hermon were falling on **M** Zion.	2215
SS	4: 1	a flock of goats descending from **M** Gilead.	2215
	7: 5	Your head crowns you like **M** Carmel.	NIH
Isa	4: 5	the LORD will create over all of **M** Zion	2215
	8:18	the LORD Almighty, who dwells on **M** Zion.	2215
	10:12	against **M** Zion and Jerusalem,	2215
	10:32	they will shake their fist at the **m** of	2215
	14:13	I will sit enthroned on the **m** of assembly,	2215
	16: 1	to the **m** of the Daughter of Zion.	2215
	18: 7	the gifts will be brought to **M** Zion,	2215
	24:23	the LORD Almighty will reign on **M** Zion	2215
	28:21	at **M** Perazim, he will rouse himself as in	2215
	29: 8	of all the nations that fight against **M** Zion.	2215
	31: 4	to do battle on **M** Zion and on its heights.	2215
	37:32	and out of **M** Zion a band of survivors.	2215
Jer	46: 4	Harness the horses, **m** the steeds!	6590
La	5:18	for **M** Zion, which lies desolate,	2215
Eze	28:14	You were on the holy **m** of God;	2215
	28:16	I drove you in disgrace from the **m** of God,	2215
	35: 2	set your face against **M** Seir;	2215
	35: 3	I am against you, **M** Seir,	2215
	35: 7	I will make **M** Seir a desolate waste	2215
	35:15	You will be desolate, O **M** Seir,	2215
Hos	14: 3	we will not **m** war-horses.	8206
Joel	2:32	for on **M** Zion and in Jerusalem there will	2215
Am	4: 1	you cows of Bashan on **M** Samaria,	2215
	6: 1	and to you who feel secure on **M** Samaria,	2215
Ob	1:17	But on **M** Zion will be deliverance;	2215
	1:21	Deliverers will go up on **M** Zion to govern	2215
Mic	4: 7	The LORD will rule over them in **M** Zion	2215
Hab	3: 3	the Holy One from **M** Paran.	2215
Zec	14: 4	On that day his feet will stand on the **M**	2215
	14: 4	and the **M** of Olives will be split in two	2215
Mt	21: 1	and came to Bethphage on the **M** of Olives,	4001
	24: 3	As Jesus was sitting on the **M** of Olives,	4001
	26:30	they went out to the **M** of Olives.	4001
Mk	11: 1	to Bethphage and Bethany at the **M**	4001
	13: 3	on the **M** of Olives opposite the temple,	4001
	14:26	they went out to the **M** of Olives.	4001
Lk	19:29	at the hill called the **M of Olives,**	1777
	19:37	where the road goes down the **M** of Olives,	4001
	21:37	on the hill called the **M of Olives,**	1777
	22:39	Jesus went out as usual to the **M** of Olives,	4001
Jn	8: 1	But Jesus went to the **M** of Olives.	4001
Ac	1:12	from the hill called the **M of Olives,**	1779
	7:30	a burning bush in the desert near **M** Sinai.	4001
	7:38	the angel who spoke to him on **M** Sinai, and	4001
Gal	4:24	from **M** Sinai and bears children who are to	4001
	4:25	Hagar stands for **M** Sinai in Arabia and	4001
Heb	12:22	But you have come to **M** Zion,	4001
Rev	14: 1	standing on **M** Zion, and with him 144,000	4001

MOUNTAIN (154) [MOUNT]

Ge	22:14	the **m** of the LORD it will be provided."	2215
Ex	3: 1	and came to Horeb, the **m** of God.	2215
	3:12	you will worship God on this **m**."	2215
	4:27	So he met Moses at the **m** of God	2215
	15:17	on the **m** of your inheritance—	2215
	18: 5	where he was camped near the **m** of God.	2215
	19: 2	in the desert in front of the **m**.	2215
	19: 3	LORD called to him from the **m** and said,	2215
	19:12	for the people around the **m** and tell them,	NIH
	19:12	'Be careful that you do not go up the **m**	2215
	19:12	Whoever touches the **m** shall surely be put	2215
	19:13	a long blast may they go up to the **m**."	2215
	19:14	Moses had gone down the **m** to the people,	2215
	19:16	with a thick cloud over the **m**,	2215
	19:17	and they stood at the foot of the **m**.	2215
	19:18	the whole **m** trembled violently,	2215
	19:20	and called Moses to the top of the **m**.	2215
	19:23	'Put limits around the **m** and set it apart	2215
	20:18	and heard the trumpet and saw the **m**	2215
	24: 4	and built an altar at the foot of the **m** and set	2215
	24:12	"Come up to me on the **m** and stay here,	2215
	24:13	and Moses went up on the **m** of God.	2215
	24:15	When Moses went up on the **m**,	2215
	24:16	For six days the cloud covered the **m**,	2084S
	24:17	like a consuming fire on top of the **m**.	2215

Ex	24:18	the cloud as he went on up the **m**.	2215
	24:18	on the **m** forty days and forty nights.	2215
	25:40	to the pattern shown you on the **m**.	2215
	26:30	according to the plan shown you on the **m**.	2215
	27: 8	be made just as you were shown on the **m**.	2215
	32: 1	so long in coming down from the **m**,	2215
	32:15	and went down the **m** with the two tablets	2215
	32:19	breaking them to pieces at the foot of the **m**.	2215
	34: 2	to me there on top of the **m**.	2215
	34: 3	with you or be seen anywhere on the **m**;	2215
	34: 3	and herds may graze in front of the **m**."	2215
Nu	10:33	So they set out from the **m** of the LORD	2215
	20:28	And Aaron died there on top of the **m**.	2215
	20:28	Moses and Eleazar came down from the **m**,	2215
	27:12	"Go up this **m** in the Abarim range and see	2215
Dt	1: 6	"You have stayed long enough at this **m**.	2215
	4:11	the foot of the **m** while it blazed with fire to	2215
	5: 4	to you face to face out of the fire on the **m**.	2215
	5: 5	of the fire and shall not go up the **m**.)	2215
	5:22	on the **m** from out of the fire, the cloud and	2215
	5:23	while the **m** was ablaze with fire,	2215
	9: 9	up on the **m** to receive the tablets of stone,	2215
	9: 9	on the **m** forty days and forty nights;	2215
	9:10	the LORD proclaimed to you on the **m** out	2215
	9:15	from the **m** while it was ablaze with fire.	2215
	9:21	into a stream that flowed down the **m**.	2215
	10: 1	the first ones and come up to me on the **m**,	2215
	10: 3	and I went up on the **m** with the two tablets	2215
	10: 4	he had proclaimed to you on the **m**,	2215
	10: 5	Then I came back down the **m** and put	2215
	10:10	I had stayed on the **m** forty days and nights,	2215
	14: 5	the ibex, the antelope and the **m** sheep.	2378
	32:50	on the **m** that you have climbed you will die	2215
	33: 2	from the south, from his **m** slopes.	850
	33: 3	They will summon peoples to the **m**	2215
Jos	10:40	the western foothills and the **m** slopes,	844
	12: 8	the **m** slopes, the desert and the Negev—	844
	13: 6	"As for all the inhabitants of the **m** regions	2215
Jdg	6: 2	shelters for themselves in **m** clefts,	2215
1Sa	23:26	Saul was going along one side of the **m**,	2215
	25:20	she came riding her donkey into a **m** ravine,	2215
1Ki	19: 8	until he reached Horeb, the **m** of God.	2215
	19:11	"Go out and stand on the **m** in the presence	2215
2Ki	2:16	down on some **m** or in some valley."	2215
	4:27	When she reached the man of God at the **m**,	2215
Job	14:18	"But as a **m** erodes and crumbles and as	2215
	24: 8	They are drenched by **m** rains and hug	2215
	39: 1	"Do you know when the **m** goats give birth?	6152
Ps	11: 1	"Flee like a bird to your **m**.	2215
	30: 7	you made my **m** stand firm;	2215
	43: 3	let them bring me to your holy **m**,	2215
	48: 1	in the city of our God, his holy **m**.	2215
	68:16	at the **m** where God chooses to reign,	2215
	87: 1	He has set his foundation on the holy **m**;	2215
	95: 4	and the **m** peaks belong to him.	2215
	99: 9	and worship at his holy **m**,	2215
SS	4: 6	to the **m** of myrrh and to the hill of incense.	2215
	4: 8	and the **m** haunts of the leopards.	2215
Isa	2: 2	the **m** of the LORD's temple will be established	2215
	2: 3	"Come, let us go up to the **m** of the LORD,	2215
	11: 9	harm nor destroy on all my holy **m**,	2215
	14:13	on the utmost heights of the **sacred m**.	7600
	18: 6	the birds of prey and to the wild animals;	2215
	25: 6	On this **m** the LORD Almighty will prepare	2215
	25: 7	On this **m** he will destroy the shroud	2215
	25:10	The hand of the LORD will rest on this **m**;	2215
	27:13	the LORD on the holy **m** in Jerusalem.	2215
	30:25	streams of water will flow on every high **m**	2215
	30:29	go up with flutes to the **m** of the LORD.	2215
	33:16	whose refuge will be the **m** fortress.	6152
	40: 4	every **m** and hill made low;	2215
	40: 9	good tidings to Zion, go up on a high **m**.	2215
	56: 7	to my holy **m** and give them joy	2215
	57:13	the land and possess my holy **m**."	2215
	65:11	the LORD and forget my holy **m**,	2215
	65:25	nor destroy on all my holy **m**,"	2215
	66:20	to my holy **m** in Jerusalem as an offering to	2215
Jer	16:16	on every **m** and hill and from the crevices of	2215
	17: 3	My **m** in the land and your wealth	2215
	31:23	O righteous dwelling, O sacred **m**.'	2215
	50: 6	They wandered over **m** and hill	2215
	51:25	"I am against you, O destroying **m**,	2215
	51:25	and make you a burned-out **m**.	2215
Eze	17:22	within the city and stopped above the **m** east	2215
	17:22	and plant it on a high and lofty **m**.	2215
	17:23	On the **m** heights of Israel I will plant it;	2215
	18: 6	the **m** shrines or look to the idols of the	2215
	18:11	"He eats at the **m** shrines.	2215
	18:15	the **m** shrines or look to the idols of the	2215
	20:40	For on my holy **m**, the high mountain of	2215
	20:40	on my holy mountain, the high **m** of Israel,	2215
	22: 9	in you are those who eat at the **m** shrines	2215
	34:14	and the **m** heights of Israel will	2215
	40: 2	of Israel and set me on a very high **m**,	2215
	43:12	the surrounding area on top of the **m** will	2215
Da	2:35	that struck the statue became a huge **m**	10296
	2:45	vision of the rock cut out of a **m**, but not	10296
	11:45	between the seas at the beautiful holy **m**.	2215
Mic	4: 1	the **m** of the LORD's temple will be established	2215
	4: 2	"Come, let us go up to the **m** of the LORD,	2215
	7:12	from sea to sea and from **m** to mountain.	2215
	7:12	from sea to sea and from mountain to **m**.	2215
Zec	4: 7	"What are you, O mighty **m**?	2215
	8: 3	and the **m** of the LORD Almighty will	2215
	8: 3	will be called the Holy **M**."	2215

Zec	14: 4	the **m** moving north and half moving south.	2215
	14: 5	You will flee by my **m** valley,	2215
Mt	4: 8	to a very high **m** and showed him all	4001
	17: 1	and led them up a high **m** by themselves.	4001
	17: 9	As they were coming down the **m**,	4001
	17:20	you can say to this **m**, 'Move from here	4001
	21:21	but also you can say to this **m**, 'Go,	4001
	28:16	to the **m** where Jesus had told them to go.	4001
Mk	9: 2	with him and led them up a high **m**,	4001
	9: 9	As they were coming down the **m**,	4001
	11:23	if anyone says to this **m**, 'Go,	4001
Lk	3: 5	every **m** and hill made low.	4001
	9:28	and James with him and went up onto a **m**	4001
	9:37	when they came down from the **m**,	4001
Jn	4:20	Our fathers worshiped on this **m**,	4001
	4:21	the Father neither on this **m** nor	4001
	6:15	withdrew again to a **m** by himself.	4001
Heb	8: 5	to the pattern shown you on the **m**."	4001
	12:18	a **m** that can be touched and that is burning	4001
	12:20	"If even an animal touches the **m**,	4001
2Pe	1:18	when we were with him on the sacred **m**.	4001
Rev	6:14	and every **m** and island was removed	4001
	8: 8	and something like a huge **m**, all ablaze,	4001
	21:10	in the Spirit to a **m** great and high,	4001

MOUNTAINS (154) [MOUNT]

Ge	7:19	and all the high **m** under the entire heavens	2215
	7:20	the **m** to a depth of more than twenty feet.	2215
	8: 4	the ark came to rest on the **m** of Ararat.	2215
	8: 5	the tops of the **m** became visible.	2215
	19:17	Flee to the **m** or you will be swept away!"	2215
	19:19	But I can't flee to the **m**;	2215
	19:30	and settled in the **m**,	2215
	22: 2	on one of the **m** I will tell you about."	2215
	49:26	the blessings of the ancient **m**,	2215
Ex	32:12	to kill them in the **m** and to wipe them off	2215
Nu	23: 7	the king of Moab from the eastern **m**.	2215
	33:47	and camped in the **m** of Abarim,	2215
	33:48	the **m** of Abarim and camped on the plains	2215
Dt	1: 7	in the **m**, in the western foothills,	2215
	11:11	of is a land of **m** and valleys that drinks rain	2215
	11:30	As you know, these **m** are across the Jordan,	NIH
	12: 2	the places on the high **m** and on the hills	2215
	32:22	and set afire the foundations of the **m**.	2215
	33:15	with the choicest gifts of the ancient **m** and	2215
Jos	11: 2	to the northern kings who were in the **m**, in	2215
	11:16	the western foothills, the Arabah and the **m**	2215
Jdg	3: 3	in the Lebanon **m** from Mount Baal Hermon	2215
	5: 5	The **m** quaked before the LORD,	2215
	9:36	coming down from the tops of the **m**!"	2215
	9:36	"You mistake the shadows of the **m**.	2215
1Sa	26:20	as one hunts a partridge in the **m**."	2215
2Sa	1:21	"O m of Gilboa, may you have neither	2215
1Ki	19:11	a great and powerful wind tore the **m** apart	2215
2Ki	19:23	I have ascended the heights of the **m**,	2215
1Ch	12: 8	and they were as swift as gazelles in the **m**.	2215
Job	9: 5	He moves **m** without their knowing it	2215
	28: 9	and lays bare the roots of the **m**,	2215
Ps	18: 7	and the foundations of the **m** shook;	2215
	36: 6	Your righteousness is like the mighty **m**,	2215
	46: 2	though the earth give way and the **m** fall	2215
	46: 3	and the **m** quake with their surging.	2215
	50:11	I know every bird in the **m**,	2215
	65: 6	who formed the **m** by your power,	2215
	68:15	The **m** of Bashan are majestic mountains;	2215
	68:15	The mountains of Bashan are majestic **m**;	2215
	68:15	rugged are the **m** of Bashan.	2215
	68:16	Why gaze in envy, O rugged **m**,	2215
	72: 3	The **m** will bring prosperity to the people,	2215
	76: 4	more majestic than **m** rich with game.	2215
	80:10	The **m** were covered with its shade,	2215
	83:14	the forest or a flame sets the **m** ablaze,	2215
	90: 2	the **m** were born or you brought forth	2215
	97: 5	The **m** melt like wax before the LORD,	2215
	98: 8	let the **m** sing together for joy;	2215
	104: 6	the waters stood above the **m**.	2215
	104: 8	they flowed over the **m**,	2215
	104:10	it flows between the **m**.	2215
	104:13	He waters the **m** from his upper chambers;	2215
	104:18	The high **m** belong to the wild goats,	2215
	104:32	who touches the **m**, and they smoke.	2215
	114: 4	the **m** skipped like rams,	2215
	114: 6	you **m**, that you skipped	2215
	125: 2	As the **m** surround Jerusalem,	2215
	144: 5	touch the **m**, so that they smoke.	2215
	148: 9	you **m** and all hills, fruit trees and all cedars,	2215
Pr	8:25	before the **m** were settled in place,	2215
SS	2: 8	Here he comes, leaping across the **m**,	2215
	8:14	or like a young stag on the spice-laden **m**.	2215
Isa	2: 2	be established as chief among the **m**;	2215
	2:14	for all the towering **m** and all the high hills,	2215
	5:25	The **m** shake, and the dead bodies are	2215
	13: 4	Listen, a noise on the **m**,	2215
	14:25	on my **m** I will trample him down.	2215
	18: 3	when a banner is raised on the **m**,	2215
	22: 5	down walls and of crying out to the **m**.	2215
	34: 3	the **m** will be soaked with their blood.	2215
	37:24	I have ascended the heights of the **m**,	2215
	40:12	or weighed the **m** on the scales and the hills	2215
	41:15	You will thresh the **m** and crush them,	2215
	42:15	I will lay waste the **m** and hills and dry	2215
	44:23	Burst into song, you **m**,	2215
	45: 2	I will level the **m**;	2065
	49:11	I will turn all my **m** into roads,	2215
	49:13	burst into song, O **m**!	2215
	52: 7	How beautiful on the **m** are the feet	2215

Isa 54:10 the **m** be shaken and the hills be removed, 2215
55:12 **m** and hills will burst into song before you, 2215
64: 1 that the **m** would tremble before you! 2215
64: 3 and the **m** trembled before you. 2215
65: 7 "Because they burned sacrifices on the **m** 2215
65: 9 from Judah those who will possess my **m**; 2215
Jer 3:23 on the hills and **m** is a deception; 2215
4:24 I looked at the **m**, and they were quaking; 2215
9:10 I will weep and wail for the **m** and take up 2215
46:18 who is like Tabor among the **m**, 2215
50: 6 and caused them to roam on the **m**. 2215
La 4:19 they chased us over the **m** and lay in wait 2215
Eze 6: 2 set your face against the **m** of Israel; 2215
6: 3 'O **m** of Israel, hear the word 2215
6: 3 the **m** and hills, to the ravines and valleys; 2215
7: 7 there is panic, not joy, upon the **m**. 2215
7:16 and escape will be in the **m**, 2215
19: 9 so his roar was heard no longer on the **m** 2215
31:12 Its boughs fell on the **m** and in all 2215
32: 5 the **m** and fill the valleys with your remains. 2215
32: 6 your flowing blood all the way to the **m**, 2215
33:28 and the **m** of Israel will become desolate so 2215
34: 6 My sheep wandered over all the **m** and 2215
34:13 I will pasture them on the **m** of Israel, 2215
34:14 in a rich pasture on the **m** of Israel. 2215
35: 8 I will fill your **m** with the slain; 2215
35:12 you have said against the **m** of Israel, 2215
36: 1 prophesy to the **m** of Israel and say, 2215
36: 1 'O **m** of Israel, hear the word of 2215
36: 4 O **m** of Israel, hear the word of 2215
36: 4 the **m** and hills, to the ravines and valleys, 2215
36: 6 the land of Israel and say to the **m** and hills, 2215
36: 8 " 'But you, O **m** of Israel, will produce 2215
37:22 in the land, on the **m** of Israel. 2215
38: 8 from many nations to the **m** of Israel. 2215
38:20 The **m** will be overturned, 2215
38:21 a sword against Gog on all my **m**, 2215
39: 2 the far north and send you against the **m** 2215
39: 4 On the **m** of Israel you will fall, 2215
39:17 the great sacrifice on the **m** of Israel. 2215
Hos 10: 8 Then they will say to the **m**, "Cover us!" 2215
Joel 2: 2 Like dawn spreading across the **m** a large 2215
3:18 "In that day the **m** will drip new wine, 2215
Am 3: 9 "Assemble yourselves on the **m** of Samaria; 2215
4:13 He who forms the **m**, creates the wind, 2215
9:13 New wine will drip from the **m** and flow 2215
Ob 1: 8 men of understanding in the **m** of Esau? 2215
1: 9 and everyone in Esau's **m** will be cut down 2215
1:19 from the Negev will occupy the **m** of Esau, 2215
1:21 up on Mount Zion to govern the **m** of Esau. 2215
Jnh 2: 6 To the roots of the **m** I sank down; 2215
Mic 1: 4 The **m** melt beneath him and 2215
4: 1 be established as chief among the **m**; 2215
6: 1 "Stand up, plead your case before the **m**; 2215
6: 2 Hear, O **m**, the LORD's accusation; 2215
Na 1: 5 **m** quake before him and the hills melt away. 2215
1:15 Look, there on the **m**, the feet of one who 2215
3:18 on the **m** with no one to gather them. 2215
Hab 3: 6 The ancient **m** crumbled and 2215
3:10 the **m** saw you and writhed. 2215
Hag 1: 8 into the **m** and bring down timber and build 2215
1:11 for a drought on the fields and the **m**, 2215
Zec 6: 1 between two **m**—mountains of bronze! 2215
6: 1 between two mountains—of **m** of bronze! 2215
Mal 1: 3 and I have turned his **m** into a wasteland 2215
Mt 24:16 let those who are in Judea flee to the **m**. 4001
Mk 13:14 let those who are in Judea flee to the **m**. 4001
Lk 21:21 let those who are in Judea flee to the **m**, 4001
23:30 " 'they will say to the **m**, "Fall on us!" 4001
1Co 13: 2 and if I have a faith that can move **m**, 4001
Heb 11:38 They wandered in deserts and **m**, 4001
Rev 6:15 in caves and among the rocks of the **m**. 4001
6:16 They called to the **m** and the rocks, 4001
16:20 Every island fled away and the **m** could not 4001

MOUNTAINSIDE (9) [MOUNT]

SS 2:14 in the hiding places on the **m**, 4533
Mt 5: 1 he went up on a **m** and sat down. 4001
8: 1 When he came down from the **m**, 4001
14:23 he went up on a **m** by himself to pray. 4001
15:29 Then he went up on a **m** and sat down. 4001
Mk 3:13 on a **m** and called to him those he wanted, 4001
6:46 he went up on a **m** to pray. 4001
Lk 6:12 of those days Jesus went out to a **m** to pray, 4001
Jn 6: 3 up on a **m** and sat down with his disciples. 4001

MOUNTAINTOP (1) [MOUNT]

Isa 30:17 till you are left like a flagstaff on a **m**, 2215+8031

MOUNTAINTOPS (4) [MOUNT]

Isa 42:11 let them shout from the **m**. 2215+8031
Eze 6:13 on every high hill and on all the **m**, 2215+8031
Hos 4:13 They sacrifice on the **m** and burn 2215+8031
Joel 2: 5 that of chariots they leap over the **m**, 2215+8031

MOUNTED (18) [MOUNT]

Ge 24:61 and her maids got ready and **m** their camels 8206
Ex 25: 7 and onyx stones and other gems to be **m** on 4853
35: 9 and onyx stones and other gems to be **m** on 4854
35:27 to be **m** on the ephod and breastpiece. 4854
39: 6 They **m** the onyx stones 6913
39:10 they **m** four rows of precious stones on it. 4848
39:13 They were **m** in gold filigree settings. 6015
2Sa 13:29 **m** their mules and fled. 8206

2Sa 22:11 He **m** the cherubim and flew; 8206
1Ki 13:13 the donkey for him, he **m** it 8206
Est 8:10 and sent them by **m** couriers, 928+2021+6061
Ps 18:10 He **m** the cherubim and flew; 8206
107:26 They **m** up to the heavens and went down 6590
SS 5:12 washed in milk, **m** like jewels. 3782+4859+6584
Eze 23: 6 young men, and **m** horsemen; 6061+8206
23:12 **m** horsemen, all handsome young 6061+8206
23:23 men of high rank, all **m** on horses. 8206
Rev 9:16 of the **m** troops was two hundred million. 2690

MOUNTINGS (1) [MOUNT]

Eze 28:13 Your settings and **m** were made of gold; 5920

MOUNTS (2) [MOUNT]

Ne 2:12 There were no **m** with me except 989
Ac 23:24 Provide **m** for Paul so that he may 3229

MOURN (56) [MOURNED, MOURNERS, MOURNFUL, MOURNFULLY, MOURNING, MOURNS]

Ge 23: 2 and Abraham went to **m** for Sarah and 6199
Ex 33: 4 to **m** and no one put on any ornaments. 61
Lev 10: 6 may **m** for those the LORD has destroyed 1134
1Sa 16: 1 "How long will you **m** for Saul, 61
1Ki 13:29 to his own city to **m** for him and bury him. 6199
14:13 All Israel will **m** for him and bury him. 6199
Ezr 10: 6 to **m** over the unfaithfulness of the exiles. 61
Ne 8: 9 Do not **m** or weep." 61
Job 5:11 and those who **m** are lifted to safety. 7722
Ecc 3: 4 a time to **m** and a time to dance, 6199
Isa 3:26 The gates of Zion will lament and **m**; 61
29: 2 she will **m** and lament, 9302
32:13 yes, **m** for all houses of merriment and NIH
61: 2 to comfort all who **m**, 63
66:10 all you who **m** over her. 61
Jer 4:28 Therefore the earth will **m** and the heavens 61
6:26 **m** with bitter wailing as for an only son, 65+6913
8:21 I **m**, and horror grips me. 7722
15: 5 Who will **m** for you? 5653
16: 5 do not go to **m** or show sympathy, 6199
16: 7 to comfort those who **m** for the dead— 65
22:10 not weep for the dead [king] or **m** his loss; 5653
22:18 "They will not **m** for him: 6199
22:18 They will not **m** for him: 'Alas, my master!' 6199
48:17 **M** for him, all who live around her, 5653
49: 3 Put on sackcloth and **m**; 6199
La 1: 4 The roads to Zion **m**, for no one comes 63
Eze 7:27 The king will **m**, the prince will be clothed 61
24:17 Groan quietly; do not **m** for the dead. 65
24:23 not **m** or weep but will waste away because 61
27:32 As they wail and **m** over you, 5951+7806
Hos 10: 5 Its people will **m** over it, 61
Joel 1: 8 **M** like a virgin in sackcloth grieving for 458
1:13 Put on sackcloth, O priests, and **m**; 6199
Am 8: 8 and all who live in it **m**? 61
9: 5 and all who live in it **m**— 61
Na 3: 7 who will **m** for her?' 5653
Zec 7: 3 "Should I **m** and fast in the fifth month, 1134
12:10 and they will **m** for him as one mourns for 6199
12:12 The land will **m**, each clan by itself, 6199
Mt 5: 4 Blessed are those who **m**, 4291
9:15 of the bridegroom **m** while he is with them? 4291
11:17 we sang a dirge, and you did not **m**.' 3164
24:30 and all the nations of the earth will **m**. 3164
Lk 6:25 for you will **m** and weep. 4291
Jn 11: 8 to the tomb to there. 3081
16:20 and **m** while the world rejoices. 2577
Ro 12:15 **m** with those who mourn. 3081
12:15 mourn with those who **m**. 3081
1Co 7:30 those who **m**, as if they did not; 3081
Jas 4: 9 Grieve, **m** and wail. 4291
Rev 1: 7 the peoples of the earth will **m** because 3164
18: 7 I am not a widow, and I will never **m**. 3972+4292
18: 9 they will weep and **m** over her. 3164
18:11 of the earth will weep and **m** over her 4291
18:15 They will weep and **m** 4291

MOURNED (25) [MOURN]

Ge 37:34 on sackcloth and **m** for his son many days. 61
50: 3 And the Egyptians **m** for him seventy days. 1134
Nu 14:39 to all the Israelites, they **m** bitterly. 61
20:29 of Israel **m** for him thirty days. 1134
Dt 21:13 in your house and **m** her father and mother 1134
1Sa 6:19 The people because of the heavy blow 61
7: 2 and all the people of Israel **m** and sought 5629
15:35 though Samuel **m** for him. 61
25: 1 and all Israel assembled and **m** for him; 6199
28: 3 and all Israel had **m** for him and buried him 6199
2Sa 1:12 They **m** and wept and fasted till evening 6199
11:26 that her husband was dead, she **m** for him. 6199
13:37 But King David **m** for his son every day. 61
1Ki 13:30 and they **m** over him and said, "Oh, 6199
14:18 They buried him, and all Israel **m** for him, 6199
1Ch 7:22 Their father Ephraim **m** for them many 61
2Ch 35:24 and all Judah and Jerusalem **m** for him. 61
Ne 1: 4 For some days I **m** and fasted and prayed 61
Jer 16: 4 They will not be **m** or buried but will be 6199
16: 6 They will not be buried or **m**, 6199
25:33 They will not be **m** or gathered up 6199
Da 10: 2 At that time I, Daniel, **m** for three weeks. 61
Zec 7: 5 and **m** in the fifth and seventh months for 6199
Lk 23:27 including women who **m** and wailed 3164

Ac 8: 2 Godly men buried Stephen and **m** deeply for him. 3157+3489+4472

MOURNERS (8) [MOURN]

Job 29:25 I was like one who comforts **m**. 63
Ecc 12: 5 to his eternal home and **m** go about 6199
Isa 57:19 creating praise on the lips of the **m** in Israel. 63
Eze 24:17 or eat the customary food [of **m**]." 408S
24:22 or eat the customary food [of **m**]. 408S
Hos 9: 4 be to them like the bread of **m**; 230
Am 5:16 summoned to weep and the **m** to wail. 3359+5631
Mal 3:14 about like **m** before the LORD Almighty? 7726

MOURNFUL (1) [MOURN]

Mic 2: 4 they will taunt you with this **m** song: 5631

MOURNFULLY (1) [MOURN]

Isa 59:11 we moan **m** like doves. 2047+2047

MOURNING (48) [MOURN]

Ge 27:41 "The days of **m** for my father are near; 65
37:35 "in **m** will I go down to the grave 63
50: 4 When the days of **m** had passed, 1143
50:10 a seven-day period of **m** for his father. 65
50:11 the Canaanites who lived there saw the **m** at 65
50:11 a solemn ceremony of **m**." 65
Dt 26:14 of the sacred portion while I was in **m**, 627
34: 8 until the time of weeping and **m** was over. 65
2Sa 3:31 and put on sackcloth and walk in **m** in front 6199
11:27 After the time of **m** was over, 65
14: 2 "Pretend you are in **m**. 61
14: 2 Dress in **m** clothes, 65
19: 1 "The king is weeping and **m** for Absalom." 61
19: 2 the victory that day was turned into **m**, 65
Est 4: 3 there was great **m** among the Jews, 65
9:22 and their **m** into a day of celebration. 65
Job 30:31 My harp is tuned to **m**, 65
Ps 35:14 about **m** as though for my friend or brother. NIH
38: 6 all day long I go about **m**. 7722
42: 9 Why must I go about **m**, 7722
43: 2 Why must I go about **m**, 7722
Ecc 7: 2 to go to a house of **m** than to go to a house 65
7: 4 The heart of the wise is in the house of **m**, 65
Isa 38:14 I moaned like a **m** dove. NIH
61: 3 the oil of gladness instead of **m**, 65
Jer 31:13 I will turn their **m** into gladness; 65
31:15 in Ramah, **m** and great weeping, 5631
47: 5 Gaza will shave her head in **m**; 995+7947
48:38 in the public squares there is nothing but **m**, 5027
La 2: 5 He has multiplied **m** and lamentation for 9302
5:15 our dancing has turned to **m**. 65
Eze 2:10 of it were written words of lament and **m** 2049
8:14 and I saw women sitting there, **m** 1134
27:31 with anguish of soul and with bitter **m**. 5027
31:15 the grave I covered the deep springs with **m** 61
Joel 1: 8 The priests are in **m**, 61
2:12 with fasting and weeping and **m**." 5027
Am 8:10 into **m** and all your singing into weeping. 65
8:10 that time like **m** for an only son and the end 65
Mic 1:11 Beth Ezel is in **m**; 5027
1:16 in **m** for the children in whom you delight; NIH
Mt 2:18 weeping and great **m**, Rachel weeping for 3851
Mk 16:10 with him who were **m** and weeping. 4291
Lk 8:52 all the people were wailing and **m** for her. 3164
Jas 4: 9 Change your laughter to **m** and your joy 4292
Rev 18: 8 death, and famine. 4292
18:19 and with weeping and **m** cry out: " 'Woe! 4291
21: 4 There will be no more death or **m** or crying 4292

MOURNS (5) [MOURN]

Job 14:22 of his own body and **m** only for himself." 61
Isa 33: 9 The land **m** and wastes away, 61
Jer 14: 2 "Judah **m**, her cities languish; 61
Hos 4: 3 Because of this the land **m**, 61
Zec 12:10 mourn for him as one **m** for an only child, 5027

MOUSE (KJV) See RAT

MOUTH (270) [MOUTHS]

Ge 4:11 opened its **m** to receive your brother's blood 7023
29: 2 The stone over the **m** of the well was large. 7023
29: 3 the stone away from the well's **m** and water 7023
29: 3 the stone to its place over the **m** of the well. 7023
29: 8 the stone has been rolled away from the **m** 7023
29:10 over and rolled the stone away from the **m** 7023
42:27 and he saw his silver in the **m** of his sack. 7023
43:21 in the **m** of his sack. 7023
44: 1 put each man's silver in the **m** of his sack. 7023
44: 2 in the **m** of the youngest one's sack, 7023
Ex 4:11 "Who gave man his **m**? 7023
4:15 to him and put words in his **m**; 7023
4:16 as if he were your **m** and as if you were God 7023
Nu 16:30 the earth opens its **m** and swallows them, 7023
16:32 the earth opened its **m** and swallowed them, 7023
22:28 Then the LORD opened the donkey's **m**, 7023
22:38 I must speak only what God puts in my **m**." 7023
23: 5 The LORD put a message in Balaam's **m** 7023
23:12 not speak what the LORD puts in my **m**?" 7023
23:16 with Balaam and put a message in his **m** 7023
26:10 The earth opened its **m** and swallowed them 7023
Dt 8: 3 but on every word that comes from the **m** of the LORD. 7023

Dt	11: 6	the earth opened its **m** right in the middle	7023
	18:18	I will put my words in his **m**,	7023
	23:23	to the LORD your God with your own **m**.	7023
	30:14	it is in your **m** and in your heart	7023
	32: 1	hear, O earth, the words of my **m**.	7023
Jos	1: 8	of the Law depart from your **m**;	7023
	10:18	"Roll large rocks up to the **m** of the cave,	7023
	10:22	"Open the **m** of the cave	7023
	10:27	the **m** of the cave they placed large rocks,	7023
	15: 5	the Salt Sea as far as the **m** of the Jordan.	7895
	15: 5	the bay of the sea at the **m** of the Jordan.	7895
	18:19	at the **m** of the Jordan in the south.	7895
1Sa	1:12	Eli observed her **m**.	7023
	2: 1	My **m** boasts over my enemies,	7023
	2: 3	or let your **m** speak such arrogance,	7023
	14:26	yet no one put his hand to his **m**,	7023
	14:27	He raised his hand to his **m**,	7023
	17:35	struck it and rescued the sheep from its **m**.	7023
2Sa	1:16	Your own **m** testified against you	7023
	14: 3	And Joab put the words in her **m**.	7023
	14:19	and who put all these words into the **m**	7023
	22: 9	consuming fire came from his **m**,	7023
1Ki	8:15	promised with his own **m** to my father David.	7023
	8:24	with your **m** you have promised and	7023
	17:24	that the word of the LORD from your **m** is	7023
	19:13	and went out and stood at the **m** of the cave.	7339
2Ki	4:34	**m** to mouth, eyes to eyes, hands to hands.	7023
	4:34	mouth to **m**, eyes to eyes, hands to hands.	7023
	19:28	hook in your nose and my bit in your **m**,	8557
2Ch	6: 4	promised with his **m** to my father David.	7023
	6:15	with your **m** you have promised and	7023
Est	7: 8	As soon as the word left the king's **m**,	7023
Job	3: 1	Job opened his **m** and cursed the day	7023
	5:15	the needy from the sword in their **m**;	7023
	5:16	poor have hope, and injustice shuts its **m**.	7023
	6:30	Can my **m** not discern malice?	2674
	8:21	yet fill your **m** with laughter and your lips	7023
	9:20	I were innocent, my **m** would condemn me;	7023
	15: 5	Your sin prompts your **m**;	7023
	15: 6	Your own **m** condemns you, not mine;	7023
	15:13	and pour out such words from your **m**?	7023
	15:30	the breath of God's **m** will carry him away.	7023
	16: 5	But my **m** would encourage you;	7023
	19:16	though I beg him with my own **m**.	7023
	20:12	in his **m** and he hides it under his tongue,	7023
	20:13	to let it go and keeps it in his **m**,	2674
	21: 5	clap your hand over your **m**.	7023
	22:22	Accept instruction from his **m** and lay	7023
	23: 4	before him and fill my **m** with arguments.	7023
	23:12	of his **m** more than my daily bread.	7023
	26: 4	And whose spirit spoke from your **m**?	NIH
	31:30	not allowed my **m** to sin by invoking a curse	2674
	33: 2	I am about to open my **m**;	7023
	35:16	So Job opens his **m** with empty talk;	7023
	37: 2	to the rumbling that comes from his **m**.	7023
	40: 4	I put my hand over my **m**.	7023
	40:23	the Jordan should surge against his **m**.	7023
	41:14	Who dares open the doors of his **m**,	7156
	41:19	Firebrands stream from his **m**;	7023
	41:21	and flames dart from his **m**.	7023
Ps	5: 9	Not a word from their **m** can be trusted;	7023
	10: 7	His **m** is full of curses and lies and threats;	7023
	17: 3	I have resolved that my **m** will not sin.	7023
	18: 8	consuming fire came from his **m**,	7023
	19:14	May the words of my **m** and the meditation	7023
	22:15	and my tongue sticks to the **roof of** my **m**;	4918
	22:21	Rescue me from the **m** of the lions;	7023
	33: 6	their starry host by the breath of his **m**.	7023
	36: 3	words of his **m** are wicked and deceitful;	7023
	37:30	The **m** of the righteous man utters wisdom,	7023
	38:13	like a mute, who cannot open his **m**;	7023
	38:14	whose **m** can offer no reply.	7023
	39: 1	I will put a muzzle on my **m** as long as	7023
	39: 9	I was silent; I would not open my **m**,	7023
	40: 3	He put a new song in my **m**,	7023
	49: 3	My **m** will speak words of wisdom;	7023
	50:19	You use your **m** for evil	7023
	51:15	and my **m** will declare your praise.	7023
	54: 2	listen to the words of my **m**.	7023
	63: 5	with singing lips my **m** will praise you.	7023
	66:14	vows my lips promised and my **m** spoke	7023
	66:17	I cried out to him with my **m**;	7023
	69:15	up or the pit close its **m** over me.	7023
	71: 8	My **m** is filled with your praise,	7023
	71:15	My **m** will tell of your righteousness,	7023
	78: 1	listen to the words of my **m**.	7023
	78: 2	I will open my **m** in parables,	7023
	81:10	Open wide your **m** and I will fill it.	7023
	89: 1	with my **m** I will make your faithfulness known through all generations.	7023
	109:30	With my **m** I will greatly extol the LORD;	7023
	119:13	the laws that come from your **m**.	7023
	119:43	Do not snatch the word of truth from my **m**,	7023
	119:72	The law from your **m** is more precious	7023
	119:88	and I will obey the statutes of your **m**.	7023
	119:103	sweeter than honey to my **m**!	7023
	119:108	O LORD, the willing praise of my **m**,	7023
	119:131	I open my **m** and pant,	7023
	137: 6	the **roof of** my **m** if I do not remember you,	2674
	138: 4	when they hear the words of your **m**.	7023
	141: 3	Set a guard over my **m**, O LORD;	7023
	141: 7	so our bones have been scattered at the **m**	7023
	145:21	My **m** will speak in praise of the LORD.	7023
Pr	2: 6	and from his **m** come knowledge	7023
	4:24	Put away perversity from your **m**;	7023
	6: 2	ensnared by the words of your **m**,	7023

Pr	6:12	who goes about with a corrupt **m**,	7023
	8: 7	My **m** speaks what is true,	2674
	8: 8	All the words of my **m** are just;	7023
	10: 6	violence overwhelms the **m** of the wicked.	7023
	10:11	The **m** of the righteous is a fountain of life,	7023
	10:11	violence overwhelms the **m** of the wicked.	7023
	10:14	but the **m** of a fool invites ruin.	7023
	10:31	**m** of the righteous brings forth wisdom,	7023
	10:32	the **m** of the wicked only what is perverse.	7023
	11: 9	With his **m** the godless destroys his neighbor,	7023
	11:11	but by the **m** of the wicked it is destroyed.	7023
	15: 2	but the **m** of the fool gushes folly.	7023
	15:14	but the **m** of a fool feeds on folly.	7023
	15:28	but the **m** of the wicked gushes evil.	7023
	16:10	and his **m** should not betray justice.	7023
	16:23	A wise man's heart guides his **m**,	7023
	18: 4	The words of a man's **m** are deep waters,	7023
	18: 6	and his **m** invites a beating.	7023
	18: 7	A fool's **m** is his undoing,	7023
	18:20	the fruit of his **m** a man's stomach is filled;	7023
	19:24	he will not even bring it back to his **m**!	7023
	19:28	and the **m** of the wicked gulps down evil.	7023
	20:17	but he ends up with a **m** full of gravel.	7023
	21:23	He who guards his **m** and tongue	7023
	22:14	The **m** of an adulteress is a deep pit;	7023
	26: 7	hang limp is a proverb in the **m** of a fool.	7023
	26: 9	a drunkard's hand is a proverb in the **m** of	7023
	26:15	he is too lazy to bring it back to his **m**.	7023
	26:28	and a flattering **m** works ruin.	7023
	27: 2	and not your own **m**;	7023
	30:20	She eats and wipes her **m** and says,	7023
	30:32	clap your hand over your **m**!	7023
Ecc	5: 2	Do not be quick with your **m**,	7023
	5: 6	Do not let your **m** lead you into sin.	7023
	6: 7	All man's efforts are for his **m**,	7023
SS	1: 2	Let him kiss me with the kisses of his **m**—	7023
	4: 3	your **m** is lovely.	4498
	5:16	His **m** is sweetness itself;	2674
	7: 9	and your **m** like the best wine.	2674
Isa	1:20	For the **m** of the LORD has spoken.	7023
	5:14	and opens its **m** without limit;	7023
	6: 7	With it he touched my **m** and said, "See,	7023
	9:12	the west have devoured Israel with open **m**.	7023
	9:17	every **m** speaks vileness.	7023
	10:14	or opened its **m** to chirp."	7023
	11: 4	the earth with the rod of his **m**;	7023
	19: 7	at the **m** of the river.	7023
	29:13	"These people come near to me with their **m**	7023
	34:16	For it is his **m** that has given the order,	7023
	37:29	hook in your nose and my bit in your **m**,	8557
	40: 5	For the **m** of the LORD has spoken.	7023
	45:23	my **m** has uttered in all integrity a word	7023
	48: 3	my **m** announced them	7023
	49: 2	He made my **m** like a sharpened sword,	7023
	51:16	in your **m** and covered you with the shadow	7023
	53: 7	and afflicted; yet he did not open his **m**;	7023
	53: 7	so he did not open his **m**.	7023
	53: 9	nor was any deceit in his **m**.	7023
	55:11	so is my word that goes out from my **m**:	7023
	58:14	The **m** of the LORD has spoken.	7023
	59:21	and my words that I have put in your **m** will	7023
	59:21	in your mouth will not depart from your **m**,	7023
	62: 2	you will be called by a new name that the **m**	7023
Jer	1: 9	and touched my **m** and said to me,	7023
	1: 9	"Now, I have put my words in your **m**.	7023
	5:14	I will make my words in your **m** a fire	7023
	9: 8	With his **m** each speaks cordially	7023
	9:20	open your ears to the words of his **m**.	7023
	23:16	not from the **m** of the LORD.	7023
	48:28	Be like a dove that makes its nest at the **m**	7023
La	3:38	the **m** of the Most High that both calamities	7023
	4: 4	infant's tongue sticks to the **roof of** its **m**;	2674
Eze	2: 8	open your **m** and eat what I give you."	7023
	3: 2	I opened my **m**, and he gave me the scroll	7023
	3: 3	and it tasted as sweet as honey in my **m**.	7023
	3:26	the **roof of** your **m** so that you will be silent	2674
	3:27	I will open your **m** and you shall say	7023
	4:14	No unclean meat has ever entered my **m**."	7023
	16:63	be ashamed and never again open your **m**	7023
	24:27	At that time your **m** will be opened;	7023
	29:21	and I will open your **m** among them.	7023
	33:22	and he opened my **m** before the man came	7023
	33:22	So my **m** was opened and I was no longer	7023
Da	6:17	A stone was brought and placed over the **m**	10588
	7: 5	it had three ribs in its **m** between its teeth.	10588
	7: 8	of a man and a **m** that spoke boastfully.	10588
	7:20	that had eyes and a **m** that spoke boastfully.	10588
	10:16	and I opened my **m** and began to speak.	7023
Hos	6: 5	I killed you with the words of my **m**;	7023
Am	3:12	the lion's **m** only two leg bones or a piece	7023
Na	3:12	the figs fall into the **m** of the eater.	7023
Zec	5: 8	and pushed the lead cover down over its **m**.	7023
Mal	2: 6	in his **m** and nothing false was found	7023
	2: 7	from his **m** men should seek instruction—	7023
Mt	4: 4	but on every word that comes from the **m**	5125
	12:34	of the overflow of the heart the **m** speaks.	5125
	13:35	"I will open my **m** in parables,	5125
	15:11	a man's **m** does not make him 'unclean,'	5125
	15:11	but what comes out of his **m**,	5125
	15:17	the **m** goes into the stomach and then out of	5125
	15:18	the things that come out of the **m** come from	5125
	17:27	open its **m** and you will find	5125
Mk	9:18	He **foams at the m**, gnashes his teeth and	930
	9:20	and rolled around, **foaming at the m**.	930
Lk	1:64	Immediately his **m** was opened	5125

Lk	6:45	of the overflow of his heart his **m** speaks.	5125
	9:39	into convulsions so that he **foams at the m**.	931
Ac	1:16	through the **m** of David concerning Judas,	5125
	4:25	You spoke by the Holy Spirit *through* the **m**	5125
	8:32	so he did not open his **m**.	5125
	11: 8	or unclean has ever entered my **m**.'	5125
	15:27	by word of **m** what we are writing.	NIG
	22:14	and to hear words from his **m**.	5125
	23: 2	near Paul to strike him on the **m**.	5125
Ro	3:19	so that every **m** may be silenced and	5125
	10: 8	it is in your **m** and in your heart," that is,	5125
	10: 9	That if you confess with your **m**,	5125
	10:10	*with* your **m** that you confess and are saved.	5125
	15: 6	and **m** you may glorify the God and Father	5125
Eph	6:19	that whenever I open my **m**,	5125
2Th	2: 8	with the breath of his **m** and destroy by	5125
	2:15	whether by **word of m** or by letter.	3364
2Ti	4:17	I was delivered from the lion's **m**.	5125
Jas	3:10	Out of the same **m** come praise and cursing.	5125
1Pe	2:22	and no deceit was found in his **m**."	5125
2Pe	2:18	**m** empty, boastful **words**	5779
Rev	1:16	of his **m** came a sharp double-edged sword.	5125
	2:16	against them with the sword *of* my **m**.	5125
	3:16	I am about to spit you out of my **m**.	5125
	10: 9	but in your **m** it will be as sweet as honey."	5125
	10:10	It tasted as sweet as honey in my **m**,	5125
	12:15	Then from his **m** the serpent spewed water	5125
	12:16	by opening its **m** and swallowing the river	5125
	12:16	that the dragon had spewed out of his **m**.	5125
	13: 2	but had feet like those of a bear and a **m** like	5125
	13: 5	a **m** to utter proud words and blasphemies	5125
	13: 6	He opened his **m** to blaspheme God,	5125
	16:13	they came out of the **m** of the dragon,	5125
	16:13	the dragon, out of the **m** of the beast and out	5125
	16:13	the mouth of the beast and out of the **m** of	5125
	19:15	of his **m** comes a sharp sword with which	5125
	19:21	sword that came out of the **m** of the rider	5125

MOUTHS (52) [MOUTH]

Ge	43:12	that was put back into the **m** of your sacks.	7023
	44: 8	of Canaan the silver we found inside the **m**	7023
Jdg	7: 6	with their hands to their **m**.	7023
1Ki	19:18	and all whose **m** have not kissed him."	7023
	22:22	" 'I will go out and be a lying spirit in the **m**	7023
	22:23	a lying spirit in the **m** of all these prophets	7023
2Ch	18:21	a lying spirit in the **m** of all his prophets,'	7023
	18:22	the LORD has put a lying spirit in the **m**	7023
Ne	9:20	not withhold your manna from their **m**,	7023
Job	16:10	Men open their **m** to jeer at me;	7023
	29: 9	and covered their **m** with their hands;	7023
	29:10	their tongues stuck to the **roof of** their **m**.	2674
Ps	17:10	and their **m** speak with arrogance.	7023
	22:13	lions tearing their prey open their **m** wide	7023
	58: 6	Break the teeth in their **m**, O God;	7023
	59: 7	See what they spew from their **m**—	7023
	59:12	For the sins of their **m**,	7023
	62: 4	With their **m** they bless,	7023
	63:11	while the **m** of liars will be silenced.	7023
	73: 9	Their **m** lay claim to heaven,	7023
	78:30	even while it was still in their **m**,	7023
	78:36	then they would flatter him with their **m**,	7023
	107:42	but all the wicked shut their **m**.	7023
	109: 2	and deceitful men have opened their **m**	7023
	115: 5	They have **m**, but cannot speak, eyes,	7023
	126: 2	Our **m** were filled with laughter,	7023
	135:16	They have **m**, but cannot speak, eyes,	7023
	135:17	nor is there breath in their **m**.	7023
	144: 8	whose **m** are full of lies,	7023
	144:11	the hands of foreigners whose **m** are full	7023
	149: 6	May the praise of God be in their **m** and	1744
Isa	52:15	and kings will shut their **m** because of him.	7023
	59:21	or from the **m** of your children,	7023
	59:21	the **m** of their descendants from this time	7023
La	2:16	All your enemies open their **m** wide	7023
	3:46	"All our enemies have opened their **m** wide	7023
Eze	33:31	With their **m** they express devotion,	7023
	34:10	I will rescue my flock from their **m**,	7023
Da	6:22	and he shut the **m** of the lions.	10588
Mic	7:16	on their **m** and their ears will become deaf.	7023
Zep	3:13	nor will deceit be found in their **m**.	7023
Zec	9: 7	I will take the blood from their **m**,	7023
	14:12	and their tongues will rot in their **m**.	7023
Ro	3:14	"Their **m** are full of cursing and bitterness."	5125
Eph	4:29	of your **m**, but only what is helpful	5125
Heb	11:33	who shut the **m** of lions,	5125
Jas	3: 3	of horses to make them obey us,	5125
Rev	9:17	and out of their **m** came fire,	5125
	9:18	smoke and sulfur that came out of their **m**.	5125
	9:19	The power of the horses was in their **m** and	5125
	11: 5	from their **m** and devours their enemies.	5125
	14: 5	No lie was found in their **m**;	5125

MOVABLE (7) [MOVE]

1Ki	7:27	He also made ten **m** stands of bronze;	4807
2Ki	16:17	and removed the basins from the **m stands**.	4807
	25:13	the **m stands** and the bronze Sea	4807
	25:16	the Sea and the **m stands**,	4807
Jer	27:19	the **m stands** and the other furnishings	4807
	52:17	the **m stands** and the bronze Sea	4807
	52:20	and the **m stands**, which King Solomon	4807

MOVE (50) [MOVABLE, MOVED, MOVEMENTS, MOVES, MOVING]

Ge	1:24	**creatures that m** along the ground,	8254

Ge	1:25	the **creatures that m** along the ground	8254
	1:26	the **creatures that m** along the ground."	8253
	1:30	of the air and all the **creatures that m** on	8253
	6: 7	**creatures that m** along the ground,	8254
	7: 8	of birds and of all creatures *that* **m** along	8253
	7:23	and animals and the **creatures that m** along	8254
	8:17	all the creatures that **m** along the ground—	8253
	8:19	All the animals and all the **creatures that m**	8254
	26:16	Abimelech said to Isaac, "**M** away from us;	2143
	33:14	while I **m** along slowly at the pace of	5633
	48:17	so he took hold of his father's hand to **m** it	6073
Ex	14:15	Tell the Israelites *to* **m** on.	5825
Lev	5: 2	**creatures that m** along the ground—	9238
	11:29	the animals that **m** about on the ground,	9237
	11:31	Of all those *that* **m** along the ground,	9238
	26:10	*to* **m** it out to make room for the new.	3655
Nu	1:51	Whenever the tabernacle *is to* **m**,	5825
	4: 5	When the camp *is to* **m**,	5825
	4:15	and when the camp *is ready to* **m**,	5825
	12:15	not **m** on till she was brought back.	5825
	16:24	'**M** away from the tents of Korah,	6590
	16:26	"**M** back from the tents of these wicked	6073
Dt	19:14	not **m** your neighbor's boundary stone set	6047
Jos	3: 3	*to* **m** out from your positions and follow it.	5825
Jdg	16: 2	*They* **made no m** during the night, saying,	3087
2Sa	5:24	in the tops of the balsam trees, **m quickly**,	3077
	15:14	or he will **m quickly** to overtake us	4554
1Ch	14:15	**m** out to battle, because that will mean	3655
Job	24: 2	Men **m** boundary stones;	5952
Ps	69:34	the seas and all *that* **m** in them,	8253
Pr	22:28	*Do not* **m** an ancient boundary stone set up	6047
	23:10	*Do not* **m** an ancient boundary stone	6047
	30:29	four *that* **m** with stately bearing:	2143
Isa	46: 7	From that spot it cannot **m**.	4631
Jer	31:24	and *those who* **m** about with their flocks.	5825
Eze	36:27	in you and **m** you to follow my decrees and	6913
Hos	2:18	the birds of the air and the **creatures that m**	8254
	5:10	like *those who* **m** boundary stones.	6047
Zec	1:21	All *who try to* **m** it will injure themselves.	6673
Mt	17:20	'**M** from here to there' and it will move.	3553
	17:20	'Move from here to there' and *it will* **m**.	3553
	23:4	not willing to lift a finger *to* **m** them.	3075
Lk	10: 7	*Do not* **m** around from house to house.	3553
	14:10	'Friend, **m** up to a better place.'	4646
Ac	17:28	in him *we* live and **m** and have our being.'	3075
	27:41	The bow stuck fast and **would not m**,	810+3551
1Co	13: 2	and if I have a faith that can **m** mountains,	3496
	15:58	brothers, stand firm. Let **nothing m** you.	293
2Co	11:26	I have been constantly **on the m**.	3845

MOVEABLE (KJV) See CROOKED

MOVED (77) [MOVE]

Ge	7:21	living thing that **m** on the earth perished—	8253
	11: 2	As men **m** eastward, they found a plain	5825
	13:18	So Abram **m** *his* **tents** and went to live near	182
	19: 9	and **m forward** to break down the door.	5602
	20: 1	Now Abraham **m** from there into	5825
	26:17	So Isaac **m** away from there and encamped	2143
	26:22	*He* **m** on from there and dug another well,	6980
	35:16	Then *they* **m** on from Bethel.	5825
	35:21	Israel **m** on again and pitched his tent	5825
	36: 6	and **m** to a land some distance	2143
	37:17	"*They* have **m** on from here,"	5825
	43:30	**Deeply m** at the sight of his brother,	4023+8171
Ex	14:19	also **m** from in front and stood behind them,	5825
	35:21	and whose heart **m** him came and brought	5951
Nu	14:44	of the LORD's covenant **m** from the camp.	4631
	16:27	So *they* **m** away from the tents of Korah,	6590
	21:10	The Israelites **m** on and camped at Oboth,	5825
	21:12	From there *they* **m** on and camped in	5825
	22:26	Then the angel of the LORD **m** on ahead	6296
Jos	5: 6	The Israelites *had* **m** about in	2143
	8: 3	and the whole army **m** out to attack Ai.	7756
	10: 5	They **m** up with all their troops and took	6590
	10:29	with him **m** on from Makkedah to Libnah	6296
	10:31	Then Joshua and all Israel with him **m** on	6296
	10:34	and all Israel with him **m** on from Lachish	6296
	14:10	while Israel **m** about in the desert.	2143
Jdg	9:26	of Ebed **m** with his brothers into Shechem,	995
	20:33	All the men of Israel **m** from their places	7756
1Sa	5: 8	the ark of the god of Israel **m** *to* Gath."	6015
	5: 8	So *they* **m** the ark of the God of Israel.	6015
	5: 9	But after *they* had **m** it,	6015
	14:23	and the battle **m** on beyond Beth Aven.	6296
	15: 6	the Kenites **m** away from the Amalekites.	6073
	17:48	As the Philistine **m** closer to attack him,	2143
	25: 1	David **m down** into the Desert of Maon.	3718
2Sa	7: 7	Wherever *I have* **m** with all the Israelites,	2143
	7: 7	and all the people **m** on toward the desert.	6296
2Ki	16: 6	then **m into** Elath and have lived there	995
1Ch	13: 7	*They* **m** the ark of God from	8206
	16:30	firmly established; *it cannot* **be m**.	4572
	17: 5	*I have* **m** from one tent site to another,	2118
	17: 7	Wherever *I have* **m** with all the Israelites,	2143
	19: 7	from their towns and **m** out for battle.	995
2Ch	33:13	the LORD **was m** by his entreaty	6983
	33:19	how God **was m** by his entreaty,	6983
	36:22	the LORD **m** the heart of Cyrus king	6424
Ezr	1: 1	the LORD **m** the heart of Cyrus king	6424
	1: 5	everyone whose heart God had **m**—	6424
Ne	2:14	Then *I* **m** on toward the Fountain Gate and	6296
Est	2: 9	and **m** her and her maids into the best place	9101
Job	14:18	and as a rock *is* **m** from its place,	6980
	18: 4	Or *must* the rocks *be* **m** from their place?	6980

Ps	93: 1	world is firmly established; *it cannot* **be m**.	4572
	96:10	world is firmly established; *it cannot* **be m**;	4572
	104: 5	on its foundations; *it can never* **be m**.	4572
Isa	33:20	a tent *that will* not **be m**;	7585
Eze	1: 9	they did not turn as they **m**.	2143
	1:13	Fire **m back and forth** among the creatures;	2143
	1:17	As they **m**, they would go in any one of	2143
	1:19	When the living creatures **m**,	2143
	1:19	the wheels beside them **m**;	2143
	1:21	When the creatures **m**, they also moved;	2143
	1:21	When the creatures moved, *they* also **m**;	2143
	1:24	When the creatures **m**,	2143
	9: 3	and **m** to the threshold of the temple.	NIH
	10: 4	above the cherubim and **m** to the threshold	NIH
	10:11	As they **m**, they would go in any one of	2143
	10:16	When the cherubim **m**,	2143
	10:16	the wheels beside them **m**;	2143
Mt	13:53	*he* **m** on from there.	3558
Lk	2:27	**M** by the Spirit, he went into the temple	NIG
Jn	11:33	*he* was **deeply m** in spirit and troubled.	1839
	11:38	Jesus, once more **deeply m**,	1839
	11:54	Therefore Jesus no longer **m** about publicly	4344
Ac	9:28	and **moved freely** in Jerusalem,	1660+1744+2779
	27: 8	We **m** along the coast with difficulty	4162
Col	1:23	not **m** from the hope held out in the gospel.	3560

MOVEMENTS (1) [MOVE]

2Sa	3:25	he came to deceive you and observe your **m**	2256+4569+4604

MOVER (KJV) See STIRRING UP

MOVES (22) [MOVE]

Ge	1:28	the air and over every living creature that **m**	8253
	6:20	and of every kind of **creature that m** *along*	8254
	7:14	every creature that **m** along the ground	8253
	8:19	everything *that* **m** on the earth—	8253
	9: 2	*that* **m** along the ground, and upon all	8253
	9: 3	Everything that lives and **m** will be food	8254
Lev	11:41	that **m** about on the ground is detestable;	9237
	11:42	You are not to eat any creature that **m** about	9237
	11:42	whether *it* **m** on its belly or walks	2143
	11:44	by any creature that **m** about on the ground.	8253
	11:46	that **m** in the water and every creature	8253
	11:46	every creature that **m** about on the ground.	9237
	20:25	or anything that **m** along the ground—	8253
Dt	4:18	like any **creature that m** along the ground	8253
	18: 6	If a Levite **m** from *one of your towns*	995
	23:14	the LORD your God **m** about in your camp	2143
	27:17	man *who* **m** his neighbor's boundary stone."	6047
Job	9: 5	He **m** mountains without their knowing it	6980
Ps	58: 8	Like a slug melting away *as it* **m** along,	2143
	102:14	her very dust *m* **them to pity**.	2858
Isa	41: 3	He pursues them and **m** on unscathed,	6296
Eze	38:20	every creature that **m** along the ground,	8253

MOVING (9) [MOVE]

Ge	1:21	and **m** thing with which the water teems,	8253
	13: 5	Now Lot, *who* was **m** about with Abram,	2143
1Sa	1:13	her lips *were* **m** but her voice was not heard.	5675
	12:12	the Ammonites *was* **m** against you, you said	995
	23:13	**m** from place to place.	889+928+2143+2143
2Sa	7: 6	*I have been* **m from place to place**	2143
Job	31:26	in its radiance or the moon **m** in splendor,	2143
Zec	14: 4	with half of the mountain **m** north	4631
	14: 4	and half **m** south.	NIH

MOWED (1) [MOWN]

Jas	5: 4	workmen who **m** your fields are crying out	286

MOWN (1) [MOWED]

Ps	72: 6	He will be like rain falling on a **m field**,	1600

MOZA (5)

1Ch	2:46	the mother of Haran, **M** and Gazez.	4605
	8:36	and Zimri was the father of **M**.	4605
	8:37	**M** was the father of Binea;	4605
	9:42	and Zimri was the father of **M**.	4605
	9:43	**M** was the father of Binea;	4605

MOZAH (1)

Jos	18:26	Mizpah, Kephirah, **M**,	5173

MUCH (196)

Ge	20: 8	they were **very m** afraid.	4394
	30:26	You know **how m** work I've done for you."	889
	41:49	it was so **m** that he stopped keeping records	6330
	43:34	Benjamin's portion *was* five times **as m as**	4946+8049
	44: 1	"Fill the men's sacks with **as m** food **as**	889+3869
Ex	1: 9	"the Israelites have become **too m**	2256
		numerous for us.	2256+6786+8041
	16: 5	and that is to be **twice as m** as they gather	5467
	16:16	Each one is to gather **as m as** he needs	4200+7023
	16:17	some gathered **m**, some little.	8049
	16:18	he *who* **gathered m** did not have too much,	8049
	16:18	he who gathered much *did not* **have too m**,	6369
	16:18	Each one gathered **as m as** he needed.	4200+7023
	16:21	Each morning everyone gathered **as m as**	
		he needed,	3869+7023
	16:22	On the sixth day, they gathered **twice as m**	5467

Ex	30:23	half as **m** (that is, 250 shekels)	4734
Nu	16:15	not taken so **m** as a donkey from them,	NIH
Dt	3:19	livestock (I know you have **m** livestock)	8041
	12:15	of your towns and eat as **m** *of the* meat	3972
	12:20	then you may eat as **m** *of* it as you want.	3972
	12:21	and in your own towns you may eat as **m**	3972
	15:18	these six years has been worth **twice as m**	5467
	28:38	You will sow **m** seed in the field	8041
	31:27	**how m** more will you rebel after I die!	8041
			677+2256+3954
Jos	10: 2	and his people were **very m** alarmed at this,	4394
Jdg	5:15	of Reuben there was **m** searching of heart.	1524
	5:16	of Reuben there was **m** searching of heart.	1524
Ru	2:18	mother-in-law saw **how m** she had gathered.	889
1Sa	1:10	Hannah **wept m** and prayed to	1134+1134
	14:30	**How m** better it would have been if	677+3954
	15:22	and sacrifices **as m as** in obeying the voice	3869
	16:21	Saul liked him **very m**,	4394
	21: 5	**How m** more so today!"	677+3954
	21:12	and was **very m** afraid of Achish king	4394
	23: 3	**How m** more, then, if we go to Keilah	677
2Sa	4:11	**How m** more—when wicked men have	677
		killed an innocent man	677
	16:11	**How m** more, then, this Benjamite!	677+3954
1Ki	8:27	**How m** less this temple I have built!	677+3954
	10:12	So **m** almugwood has never been imported	4027
	12:28	"It is too **m** for you to go up to Jerusalem.	8041
	19: 7	for the journey is too **m** for you."	8041
2Ki	5:13	**How m** more, then, when he tells you,	677
	5:17	as **m** earth as a pair of mules can carry,	NIH
	10:18	Jehu will serve him **m**.	2221
	21: 6	He did **m** evil in the eyes of the LORD,	8049
	21:16	so **m** innocent blood that he filled Jerusalem	2221
1Ch	22: 8	'You have shed **m** blood	4200+8044
	22: 8	because you have shed **m** blood on the earth	8041
2Ch	4:18	that Solomon made amounted to so **m**	4200+8044
	6:18	**How m** less this temple I have built!	677+3954
	14:14	since there was **m** booty there.	8041
	20:25	There was so **m** plunder that it took	8041
	24:24	into their hands a **m** larger army.	4394
	25: 9	"The LORD can give you **m** more than that."	2221
	26:10	because he had **m** livestock in the foothills	8041
	32:15	**How m** less will your god deliver you	
			677+3954+4202
	33: 6	He did **m** evil in the eyes of the LORD,	8049
	33:14	he also made it **m** higher.	4394
Ezr	3:13	because the people made so **m** noise.	1524
Ne	2: 2	I was **very m** afraid.	2221
	2:10	they were **very m** disturbed	1524
	4:10	there is so **m** rubble that we cannot rebuild	2221
Job	4:19	**how m** more those who live in houses of	
		clay,	677
	7:17	"What is man that *you* **make so m** of him,	1540
	7:17	that you give him so **m** attention,	NIH
	15:16	**how m** less man, who is vile and	677+3954
	25: 6	**how m** less man, who is but a maggot—	677+3954
	35:14	**How m** less, then, will he listen	677+3954
	42:10	and gave him twice as **m** as he had before.	3972
Ps	19:10	more precious than gold, than **m** pure gold;	8041
	36: 2	in his own eyes he **flatters** himself *too* **m**	AIT
	119:107	I have suffered **m**;	4394+6330
	123: 3	for we have endured **m** contempt,	8041
	123: 4	We have endured **m** ridicule from the proud	8041
	123: 4	**m** contempt from the arrogant.	NIH
Pr	11:31	**how m** more the ungodly and the sinner!	
			677+3954
	15:11	**how m** more the hearts of men!	677+3954
	16: 8	a little with righteousness than **m** gain	8044
	16:16	**How m** better to get wisdom than gold,	4537
	17: 7	**how m** worse lying lips to a ruler!	677+3954
	19: 7	**how m** more do his friends avoid him!	677+3954
	19:10	**how m** worse for a slave to rule over	
		princes!	677+3954
	20:19	so avoid a **man who talks too m**.	7331+8557
	21:27	**how m** more so when brought with evil	
		intent!	677+3954
	23:20	Do not join *those who* **drink too m** wine	6010
	25:16	**too m** of it, and you will vomit.	8425
	25:17	**too m** of you, and he will hate you.	8425
	25:27	It is not good to eat **too m** honey,	8049
	30: 9	*I may* **have too m** and disown you and say,	8425
Ecc	1:16	I have experienced **m** of wisdom	2221
	1:18	For with **m** wisdom comes much sorrow;	8044
	1:18	For with much wisdom comes **m** sorrow;	8044
	5: 7	**M** dreaming and many words are	
		meaningless.	8044
	5:12	whether he eats little or **m**,	2221
	9:18	but one sinner destroys **m** good.	2221
	12:12	and **m** study wearies the body.	2221
SS	4:10	**m** more pleasing is your love **than** wine,	4946
Jer	2:36	Why do you go about so **m**,	4394
	49: 9	steal only **as m as** they **wanted**?	1896
Eze	14:21	**How m** worse will it be when I send	677+3954
	15: 5	**how m** less can it be made	677+3954
	23:32	for it holds so **m**.	5268
	38:13	and goods and to seize **m** plunder?" '	1524
	46: 5	is to be **as m as** he **pleases**,	3338+5522
	46: 7	and with the lambs **as m as** he wants to	
		give,	889+3869
	46:11	with the lambs **as m as** one **pleases**,	3338+5522
Ob	1: 5	**as m as** they **wanted**?	1896
	1:12	nor **boast so m** in the day of their trouble.	
			1540+3870+7023
Hag	1: 6	You have planted **m**, but have harvested	2221
	1: 9	"You expected **m**, but see, it turned out	2221
Zec	9:12	that I will restore **twice as m** to you.	5467
Mal	3:10	and pour out so **m** blessing *that* you	6330

Mt	6:26	Are you not **m** more valuable than they?	3437
	6:30	will he not **m** more clothe you,	4498
	7:11	**how m** more will your Father in heaven	4531
	10:25	**how m** more the members of his household!	4531
	12:12	**How m** more valuable is a man than a sheep!	4531
	13: 5	where it did not have **m** soil.	4498
	14: 6	danced for them and pleased Herod so **m**	NIG
	19:29	a hundred times as **m** and will inherit eternal life.	NIG
	23:15	you make him **twice as m** a son of hell	1486
Mk	4: 5	where it did not have **m** soil.	4498
	4:33	**as m as** they could understand.	2777
	5:19	and tell them **how m** the Lord has done	4012
	5:20	how **m** Jesus had done for him.	4012
	6:37	that **m** on bread and give it to them to eat?"	NIG
	9:12	of Man must suffer **m** and be rejected?	NIG
	9:26	The boy **looked so m** like a corpse	1181+6059
	10:30	will fail to receive a hundred times as **m**	NIG
Lk	7:47	have been forgiven—for she loved **m**.	4498
	8:39	"Return home and tell **how m** God has done	4012
	8:39	told all over town **how m** Jesus had done	4012
	11: 8	up and give him **as m as** he needs.	4012
	11:13	**how m** more will your Father in heaven give the Holy Spirit	4531
	12:24	**how m** more valuable you are than birds!	4531
	12:28	**how m** more will he clothe you,	4531
	12:48	From everyone who has been given **m**,	4498
	12:48	given much, **m** will be demanded;	4498
	12:48	the one who has been entrusted with **m**,	4498
	12:48	**m** more will be asked.	4358
	16: 5	'How **m** do you owe my master?'	4531
	16: 7	'And **how m** do you owe?'	4531
	16:10	with very little can also be trusted with **m**,	4498
	16:10	also be dishonest with **m**.	4498
	18:30	to receive **many times as m** in this age and,	4498
Jn	2:10	after the guests have **had too m to** drink;	3499
	6:11	to those who were seated **as m as**	4012
	8:26	"I have **m** to say in judgment of you.	4498
	14:30	I will not speak with you **m** longer,	4498
	15: 5	and I in him, he will bear **m** fruit;	4498
	15: 8	my Father's glory, that you bear **m** fruit,	4498
	16:12	"I have **m** more to say to you,	4498
Ac	2:13	'They have **had too m** wine.'	1639+3551
	4:33	and **m** grace was upon them all.	3489
	9:16	I will show him **how m** he must suffer	4012
	15: 7	After **m** discussion, Peter got up	4498
	15:32	said **m** to encourage and strengthen	4498
	27: 9	**M** time had been lost,	2653
	27:38	**eaten as m as** they **wanted,**	3170
Ro	3: 2	**M** in every way!	4498
	5: 9	**how m** more shall we be saved	4498
	5:10	**how m** more, having been reconciled,	4498
	5:15	**how m** more did God's grace and the gift	4498
	5:17	**how m** more will those who receive God's abundant provision	4498
	11:12	**how m** greater riches will their fullness bring!	4531
	11:13	I **make m of** my ministry	1519
	11:24	**how m** more readily will these,	4531
1Co	2: 3	weakness and fear, and with **m** trembling.	4498
	6: 3	**How m** more the things of this life!	3615
	7: 2	But since there is so **m** immorality,	NIG
	9:11	is it too **m** if we reap a material harvest	3489
2Co	2: 5	not so **m** grieved me as he has grieved all	NIG
	3: 9	how **m** more glorious is the ministry	4498
	3:11	**m** greater is the glory of that which lasts!	4498
	8: 3	they gave **as m as** they **were able,**	1539+2848
	8:15	"He who gathered **m** did not have too much,	4498
	8:15	He who gathered much **did not have too m,**	4429
	8:17	with **m enthusiasm** and on his own initiative.	AIT
	10: 7	that we belong to Christ just as **m** as he.	NIG
	11:23	I have worked **m harder,**	4359
Gal	3: 4	Have you suffered **so m** for nothing—	5537
Php	2:12	but now **m** more in my absence—	4498
Col	2: 1	to know **how m** I am struggling for you and	2462
1Th	2: 8	We loved you **so m** that we were delighted	4048
1Ti	3: 8	sincere, not indulging **in m** wine,	4498
Tit	2: 3	not to be slanderers or addicted to **m** wine,	4498
Heb	1: 4	So he became **as m** superior to the angels as	5537
	5:11	We have **m** to say about this,	4498
	9:14	**How m** more, then, will the blood of Christ,	4531
	10:29	**How m** more severely do you think	4531
	12: 9	How **m** more should we submit to	4498
	12:25	how **m** less will we, if we turn away	4498
2Jn	1:12	I have **m** to write to you,	4498
3Jn	1:13	I have **m** to write you,	4498
Rev	8: 3	He was given **m** incense to offer,	4498
	2:11	not love their lives **so m as** to shrink	948
	18: 7	Give her **as m** torture and grief as the glory	5537

MUD (15) [MUDDIED, MUDDY, MUDDYING]

2Sa	22:43	and trampled them like **m** in the streets.	3226
Job	30:19	He throws me into the **m**,	2817
	41:30	a trail in the **m** like a threshing sledge.	3226
Ps	18:42	I poured them out like **m** in the streets.	3226
	40: 2	out of the **m** and mire;	3226
Isa	10: 6	to trample them down like **m** in the streets.	2817
	57:20	whose waves cast up mire and **m**.	3226
Jer	38: 6	it had no water in it, only **m**,	3226
	38: 6	and Jeremiah sank down into the **m**.	3226
	38:22	Your feet are sunk in the **m**;	1288
Jn	9: 6	made some **m** with the saliva,	4384
	9:11	"The man they call Jesus made some **m**	4384
	9:14	on which Jesus had made the **m** and opened	4384
	9:15	"He put **m** on my eyes," the man replied,	4384

2Pe	2:22	goes back to her wallowing **in** the **m**."	1079

MUDDIED (3) [MUD]

Pr	25:26	Like a **m** spring or a polluted well is	8346
Eze	32:13	the foot of man or **m** by the hoofs of cattle.	1931
	34:19	and drink **what** you have **m** with your feet?	5343

MUDDY (2) [MUD]

Eze	34:18	**Must you** also **m** the rest with your feet?	8346
Zec	10: 5	be like mighty men trampling the **m** streets	3226

MUDDYING (1) [MUD]

Eze	32: 2	the water with your feet and **m** the streams.	8346

MUFFLERS (KJV) See VEILS

MULBERRY (1)

Lk	17: 6	you can say to this **m tree,** 'Be uprooted	5189

MULE (7) [MULES]

2Sa	18: 9	He was riding his **m**,	7234
	18: 9	and as the **m** went under the thick branches	7234
	18: 9	while the **m** he was riding kept on going.	7234
1Ki	1:33	on my own **m** and take him down to Gihon.	7235
	1:38	down and put Solomon on King David's **m**	7235
	1:44	and they have put him on the king's **m**,	7235
Ps	32: 9	Do not be like the horse or the **m**,	7234

MULES (11) [MULE]

2Sa	13:29	mounted their **m** and fled.	7234
1Ki	10:25	weapons and spices, and horses and **m**.	7234
	18: 5	and **m** alive so we will not have to kill any	7234
2Ki	5:17	as much earth as a pair of **m** can carry,	7234
1Ch	12:40	on donkeys, camels, **m** and oxen.	7234
2Ch	9:24	weapons and spices, and horses and **m**.	7234
Ezr	2:66	They had 736 horses, 245 **m**,	7234
Ne	7:68	There were 736 horses, 245 **m**,	NIH
Isa	66:20	and on **m** and camels," says the LORD.	7234
Eze	27:14	war horses and **m** for your merchandise.	7234
Zec	14:15	similar plague will strike the horses and **m**,	7234

MULTICOLORED (1) [COLORED]

Eze	27:24	embroidered work and **m** rugs	1394

MULTIPLIED (7) [MULTIPLY]

Ex	1: 7	but the Israelites were fruitful and **m** greatly	9237
	1:12	the more they **m** and spread;	8049
	11: 9	so that my wonders **may be m** in Egypt."	8049
Dt	8:13	and gold increase and all you have is **m**,	8049
Jdg	16:24	who laid waste our land and **m** our slain."	8049
Ps	25:17	The troubles of my heart have **m**;	8143
La	2: 5	He has **m** mourning and lamentation for	8049

MULTIPLIES (6) [MULTIPLY]

Job	34:37	among us and **m** his words against God."	8049
	35:16	without knowledge he **m** words."	3892
Pr	23:28	and **m** the unfaithful among men.	3578
	27: 6	but an enemy **m** kisses.	6984
Ecc	10:14	and the fool **m** words.	8049
Hos	12: 1	he pursues the east wind all day and **m** lies	8049

MULTIPLY (12) [MULTIPLIED, MULTIPLIES, MULTIPLYING]

Ge	8:17	so they can **m** on the earth and be fruitful	9237
	9: 7	**m** on the earth and increase upon it."	9237
Ex	7: 3	and though I **m** my miraculous signs	8049
Lev	26:21	I will **m** your afflictions seven times over,	3578
Dt	7:22	or the wild animals will **m** around you.	8049
2Sa	24: 3	"May the LORD your God **m** the troops	3578
1Ch	21: 3	"May the LORD **m** his troops	3578
Job	9:17	a storm and **m** my wounds for no reason.	8049
Jer	46:11	But you **m** remedies in vain;	8049
Eze	36:10	I will **m the number** of people upon you,	8049
Na	3:15	**M** like grasshoppers, multiply like locusts!	3877
	3:15	Multiply like grasshoppers, **m** like locusts!	3877

MULTIPLYING (1) [MULTIPLY]

Mk	4: 8	grew and produced a crop, **m** thirty, sixty,	5770

MULTITUDE (10) [MULTITUDES]

Ps	42: 4	how I used to go with the **m**,	6107
Isa	1:11	"The **m** of your sacrifices—	8044
	13: 4	like that of a great **m**!	6639
	31: 1	who trust in the **m** of their chariots and in	8041
Da	10: 6	and his voice like the sound of a **m**.	2162
Jas	5:20	from death and cover over a **m** of sins.	4436
1Pe	4: 8	because love covers over a **m** of sins.	4436
Rev	7: 9	and there before me was a great **m**	4063
	19: 1	the roar of a great **m** in heaven shouting:	4063
	19: 6	Then I heard what sounded like a great **m**,	4063

MULTITUDES (5) [MULTITUDE]

Ne	9: 6	the **m** of heaven worship you.	7372
Da	12: 2	**M** who sleep in the dust of the earth will awake;	8041
Joel	3:14	**M**, multitudes in the valley of decision!	2162
	3:14	Multitudes, **m** in the valley of decision!	2162
Rev	17:15	where the prostitute sits, are peoples, **m**,	4063

MUMBLE (1)

Isa	29: 4	your speech will **m** out of the dust.	8820

MUNITION (KJV) See FORTRESS

MUPPIM (1)

Ge	46:21	Naaman, Ehi, Rosh, **M**, Huppim and Ard.	5137

MURDER (32) [MURDERED, MURDERER, MURDERERS, MURDERING, MURDEROUS, MURDERS]

Ex	20:13	"You shall not **m**.	8357
Nu	35:12	so that a **person accused of m** may not die	8357
	35:25	the **one accused of m** from the avenger	8357
	35:27	the accused without being **guilty of m**.	1947
Dt	5:17	"You shall not **m**.	8357
Jos	21:13	(a city of refuge for **one accused of m**),	8357
	21:21	(a city of refuge for **one accused of m**),	8357
	21:27	(a city of refuge for **one accused of m**) and	8357
	21:32	(a city of refuge for **one accused of m**),	8357
	21:38	(a city of refuge for **one accused of m**),	8357
Jdg	9:24	who had helped him **m** his brothers.	2222
2Sa	3:37	the king had no part in the **m** of Abner son	4637
Ps	94: 6	they **m** the fatherless.	8357
Pr	28:17	A man tormented by the **guilt of m**	1947+5883
Isa	1:15	who stops his ears against plots of **m**	1947
Jer	7: 9	" 'Will you steal and **m**,	8357
Hos	4: 2	There is only cursing, lying and **m**,	8357
	6: 9	they **m** on the road to Shechem.	8357
Mt	5:21	'Do not **m**, and anyone who murders will	5839
	15:19	For out of the heart come evil thoughts, **m**,	5840
	19:18	Jesus replied, " 'Do not **m**,	5839
Mk	7:21	sexual immorality, theft, **m**, adultery,	5840
	10:19	You know the commandments: 'Do not **m**,	5839
	15: 7	the insurrectionists who had committed **m**	5840
Lk	18:20	'Do not commit adultery, do not **m**,	5839
	23:19	for an insurrection in the city, and for **m**.)	5840
	23:25	into prison for insurrection and **m**,	5840
Ro	1:29	They are full of envy, **m**, strife,	5840
	13: 9	"Do not **m**," "Do not steal,"	5839
Jas	2:11	also said, "Do not **m**."	5839
	2:11	not commit adultery but do **commit m**,	5839
1Jn	3:12	And why did he **m** him?	5377

MURDERED (18) [MURDER]

Jdg	9: 5	and on one stone he **m** his seventy brothers,	2222
	9:18	**m** his seventy sons on a single stone,	2222
	20: 4	So the Levite, the husband of the **m** woman,	8357
2Sa	3:30	(Joab and his brother Abishai **m** Abner	2222
1Ki	16:16	against the king and **m** him,	5782
	21:19	not **m** a man and seized his property?'	8357
2Ki	11: 2	who were about to be **m**.	4637
	12:21	The officials who **m** him were Jozabad son	5782
	14: 5	the officials who had **m** his father the king.	5782
2Ch	21:13	You have also **m** your own brothers,	2222
	22:11	about to be **m** and put him and his nurse in	4637
	25: 3	the officials who had **m** his father the king.	5782
Pr	22:13	or, "I will be **m** in the streets!"	8357
Mt	23:31	descendants of those who **m** the prophets.	5839
	23:35	whom you **m** between the temple and	5839
Ac	7:52	And now you have betrayed and **m** him—	5838
Jas	5: 6	You have condemned and **m** innocent men,	5839
1Jn	3:12	to the evil one and **m** his brother.	5377

MURDERER (20) [MURDER]

Nu	35:16	an iron object so that he dies, he is a **m**;	8357
	35:16	the **m** shall be put to death.	8357
	35:17	strikes someone so that he dies, he is a **m**;	8357
	35:17	the **m** shall be put to death.	8357
	35:18	hits someone so that he dies, he is a **m**;	8357
	35:18	the **m** shall be put to death.	8357
	35:19	avenger of blood shall put the **m** to death;	8357
	35:21	shall be put to death; he is a **m**.	8357
	35:21	avenger of blood shall put the **m** to death	8357
	35:30	be put to death as a **m** only on the testimony	8357
	35:31	not accept a ransom for the life of a **m**,	8357
2Ki	6:32	how this **m** is sending someone	1201+8357
	9:31	Zimri, you **m** of your master?"	2222
Job	24:14	the **m** rises up and kills the poor and needy;	8357
Jn	8:44	He was a **m** from the beginning,	475
Ac	3:14	and asked that a **m** be released to you.	467+5838
	28: 4	"This man must be a **m**;	5838
1Pe	4:15	as a **m** or thief or any other kind of criminal,	5838
1Jn	3:15	Anyone who hates his brother is a **m**,	475
	3:15	you know that no **m** has eternal life in him.	475

MURDERERS (6) [MURDER]

Isa	1:21	used to dwell in her—but now **m**!	8357
Jer	4:31	I am fainting; my life is given over to **m**."	2222
Mt	22: 7	and destroyed those **m** and burned their city.	5838
1Ti	1: 9	who kill their fathers or mothers, for **m**,	439
Rev	21: 8	cowardly, the unbelieving, the vile, the **m**,	5838
	22:15	the sexually immoral, the **m**,	5838

MURDERING (2) [MURDER]

Jdg	9:56	to his father by **m** his seventy brothers.	2222
2Ch	24:25	His officials conspired against him for **m**	1947

MURDEROUS (1) [MURDER]

Ac	9: 1	Saul was still breathing out **m** threats	5840

MURDERS (4) [MURDER]

Dt	22:26	who attacks and **m** his neighbor,	5883+8357
Ps	10: 8	from ambush *he* **m** the innocent,	2222
Mt	5:21	anyone who **m** will be subject to judgment.'	5839
Rev	9:21	Nor did they repent of their **m**,	5840

MURMUR, MURMURED, MURMURERS, MURMURING, MURMURINGS (KJV) See COMPLAIN, COMPLAINED, GRUMBLE, GRUMBLED, GRUMBLERS, GRUMBLING, MUTTER, MUTTERED, WHISPERING

MURRAIN (KJV) See PLAGUE

MUSCLES (1)

Job	40:16	what power in the **m** *of* his belly!	9235

MUSED (2)

Ps	77: 3	*I* **m**, and my spirit grew faint.	8488
	77: 6	My heart **m** and my spirit inquired:	8488

MUSHI (8) [MUSHITE, MUSHITES]

Ex	6:19	The sons of Merari were Mahli and **M**.	4633
Nu	3:20	The Merarite clans: Mahli and **M**.	4633
1Ch	6:19	The sons of Merari: Mahli and **M**.	4633
	6:47	the son of **M**, the son of Merari,	4633
	23:21	The sons of Merari: Mahli and **M**.	4633
	23:23	The sons of **M**: Mahli, Eder and Jerimoth—	4633
	24:26	The sons of Merari: Mahli and **M**.	4633
	24:30	the sons of **M**: Mahli, Eder and Jerimoth.	4633

MUSHITE (1) [MUSHI]

Nu	26:58	the **M** clan, the Korahite clan.	4634

MUSHITES (1) [MUSHI]

Nu	3:33	the clans of the Mahlites and the **M**;	4634

MUSIC (90) [MUSICAL, MUSICIAN, MUSICIANS]

Ge	31:27	and singing to the **m** of tambourines	9512
Jdg	5: 3	*I* will **make m** to the LORD,	2376
1Ch	6:31	of the **m** *in* the house of the LORD after	8877
	6:32	They ministered with **m** before the	8877
	25: 6	the supervision of their fathers for the **m** of	8877
	25: 7	all of them trained and skilled in **m** for	8877
Ne	12:27	of thanksgiving and with the **m** of cymbals,	8877
Job	21:12	They sing to the **m** of tambourine and harp	9512
Ps	4: T	For the **director of m**. With stringed	5904
	5: T	For the **director of m**. For flutes.	5904
	6: T	For the **director of m**. With stringed	5904
	8: T	For the **director of m**. According to gittith.	5904
	9: T	For the **director of m**.	5904
	11: T	For the **director of m**. Of David.	5904
	12: T	For the **director of m**. According to	5904
	13: T	For the **director of m**. A psalm of David.	5904
	14: T	For the **director of m**. Of David.	5904
	18: T	For the **director of m**. Of David the servant	5904
	19: T	For the **director of m**. A psalm of David.	5904
	20: T	For the **director of m**. A psalm of David.	5904
	21: T	For the **director of m**. A psalm of David.	5904
	22: T	For the **director of m**.	5904
	27: 6	I will sing and **make m** to the LORD.	2376
	31: T	For the **director of m**. A psalm of David.	5904
	33: 2	**make m** to him on the ten-stringed lyre.	2376
	36: T	For the **director of m**. Of David the servant	5904
	39: T	For the **director of m**. For Jeduthun.	5904
	40: T	For the **director of m**. Of David. A psalm.	5904
	41: T	For the **director of m**. A psalm of David.	5904
	42: T	For the **director of m**. A maskil of	5904
	44: T	For the **director of m**. Of the Sons of Korah	5904
	45: T	For the **director of m**.	5904
	45: 8	the **m** of the **strings** makes you glad.	4944
	46: T	For the **director of m**. Of the Sons of Korah	5904
	47: T	For the **director of m**. Of the Sons of Korah	5904
	49: T	For the **director of m**. Of the Sons of Korah	5904
	51: T	For the **director of m**. A psalm of David.	5904
	52: T	For the **director of m**. A maskil of David.	5904
	53: T	For the **director of m**. According to	5904
	54: T	For the **director of m**. With stringed	5904
	55: T	For the **director of m**. With stringed	5904
	56: T	For the **director of m**.	5904
	57: T	For the **director of m**.	5904
	57: 7	I will sing and **make m**.	2376
	58: T	For the **director of m**.	5904
	59: T	For the **director of m**.	5904
	60: T	For the **director of m**.	5904
	61: T	For the **director of m**. With stringed	5904
	62: T	For the **director of m**. For Jeduthun.	5904
	64: T	For the **director of m**. A psalm of David.	5904
	65: T	For the **director of m**. A psalm of David.	5904
	66: T	For the **director of m**. A song. A psalm.	5904
	67: T	For the **director of m**. With stringed	5904
	68: T	For the **director of m**. Of David. A psalm.	5904
	69: T	For the **director of m**.	5904
	70: T	For the **director of m**. Of David. A petition.	5904
	75: T	For the **director of m**.	5904
	76: T	For the **director of m**. With stringed	5904
	77: T	For the **director of m**. For Jeduthun.	5904
	80: T	For the **director of m**.	5904
	81: T	For the **director of m**. According to gittith.	5904
	81: 2	Begin the **m**, strike the tambourine,	2379
	84: T	For the **director of m**. According to gittith.	5904
	85: T	For the **director of m**. Of the Sons of Korah	5904
	87: 7	As *they* **make m** they will sing,	2727
	88: T	of the Sons of Korah. For the **director of m**.	5904
	92: 1	It is good to praise the LORD and **make m**	2376
	92: 3	to the **m** of the ten-stringed lyre and	NIH
	95: 2	and extol him with **m** and song.	2369
	98: 4	burst into jubilant song with **m**;	2376
	98: 5	**make m** to the LORD with the harp,	2376
	108: 1	I will sing and **make m** *with* all my soul.	2376
	109: T	For the **director of m**. Of David. A psalm.	5904
	139: T	For the **director of m**. Of David. A psalm.	5904
	140: T	For the **director of m**. A psalm of David.	5904
	144: 9	the ten-stringed lyre *I* will **make m** to you,	2376
	147: 7	**make m** to our God on the harp.	2376
	149: 3	and **make m** to him with tambourine	2376
Isa	30:32	be to the **m** of tambourines and harps,	9512
La	5:14	the young men have stopped their **m**.	5593
Eze	26:13	the **m** of your harps will be heard no more.	7754
Da	3: 5	zither, lyre, harp, pipes and all kinds of **m**,	10233
	3: 7	flute, zither, lyre, harp and all kinds of **m**,	10233
	3:10	of **m** must fall down and worship the image	10233
	3:15	zither, lyre, harp, pipes and all kinds of **m**,	10233
Am	5:23	I will not listen to the **m** *of* your harps.	2379
Hab	3:19	For the **director of m**. On my stringed	5904
Lk	15:25	he heard **m** and dancing.	5246
Eph	5:19	Sing and **make m** in your heart to the Lord,	6010
Rev	18:22	The **m** of harpists and musicians,	5889

MUSICAL (7) [MUSIC]

1Ch	15:16	accompanied by **m** instruments:	8877
	23: 5	with the **m instruments** I have provided for	AIT
2Ch	7: 6	with the LORD's **m** instruments,	8877
	23:13	with **m** instruments were leading	8877
	34:12	in playing **m** instruments—	8877
Ne	12:36	with **m** instruments [prescribed by] David	8877
Am	6: 5	like David and improvise on **m** instruments.	8877

MUSICIAN (1) [MUSIC]

1Ch	6:33	Heman, the **m**, the son of Joel,	8876

MUSICIANS (8) [MUSIC]

1Ki	10:12	and to make harps and lyres for the **m**.	8876
1Ch	9:33	Those who were **m**, heads of Levite families	8876
	15:19	The **m** Heman, Asaph and Ethan were	8876
2Ch	5:12	All the Levites who were **m**—	8876
	9:11	and to make harps and lyres for the **m**,	8876
	35:15	The **m**, the descendants of Asaph,	8876
Ps	68:25	In front are the singers, after them the **m**;	5594
Rev	18:22	The music of harpists and **m**,	3676

MUSICK (KJV) See MUSICAL

MUST (786)

Ge	2:17	but *you* **m** not **eat** from the tree of	AIT
	3: 1	'*You* **m** not **eat** from any tree in	AIT
	3: 3	'*You* **m** not **eat** fruit from the tree that is in	AIT
	3: 3	and *you* **m** not **touch** it, or you will die.' "	AIT
	3:17	'*You* **m** not **eat** of it,'	AIT
	3:22	**m** not be allowed *to* **reach** out	AIT
	4: 7	it desires to have you, but *you* **m master** it."	AIT
	9: 4	"But *you* **m** not **eat** meat that has its lifeblood still in it.	AIT
	17: 9	"As for you, *you* **m keep** my covenant,	AIT
	17:12	who is eight days old **m be circumcised**,	AIT
	17:13	they **m** be **circumcised**.	4576+4576
	24:37	'*You* **m** not **get** a wife for my son from	AIT
	30:16	*You* **m sleep with me**," she said.	AIT
	33:13	that the children are tender and that I **m** care	NIH
	42:20	*you* **m bring** your youngest brother to me,	AIT
	42:22	**m give an accounting** for his blood."	AIT
	43:11	their father Israel said to them, "If it **m** be,	4027
	43:12	for *you* **m return** the silver	AIT
	50:25	**m carry** my bones **up** from this place."	AIT
Ex	1:10	we **m deal shrewdly** with them	AIT
	1:22	"Every boy that is born *you* **m throw** into	AIT
	2:14	"What I did **m** have **become known**."	AIT
	5:18	*you* **m produce** your full quota of bricks."	AIT
	8:27	*We* **m take** a three-day journey into	AIT
	8:28	but *you* **m** not go **very far**.	8178+8178
	10:25	"You **m allow** us to have sacrifices	AIT
	10:26	Our livestock too **m go** with us;	AIT
	12: 4	they **m share** one with their nearest neighbor,	AIT
	12: 5	The animals you choose **m** be year-old	AIT
	12: 6	the community of Israel **m slaughter** them	AIT
	12:10	if some is left till morning, *you* **m burn** it.	AIT
	12:15	the seventh **m** be **cut off** from Israel.	AIT
	12:19	in it **m** be **cut off** from the community	AIT
	12:20	*you* **m eat** unleavened bread."	AIT
	12:46	"*It* **m** be **eaten** inside one house;	AIT
	12:47	whole community of Israel **m celebrate** it.	AIT
	12:48	**m** have all the males in his household **circumcised**;	AIT
	13:10	*You* **m keep** this ordinance at the appointed	AIT
	13:19	**m carry** my bones **up** with you	AIT
	18:19	*You* **m** be the people's representative	AIT
	19:22	**m consecrate** themselves,	AIT
	19:24	**m** not **force** *their* **way through**	AIT
	21: 6	his master **m take** him before the judges.	AIT
	21: 8	**m** let her be **redeemed**.	AIT
	21: 9	he **m grant** her the rights of a daughter.	AIT
	21:10	he **m** not **deprive** the first one *of* her food,	AIT
	21:15	or his mother **m** be **put to death**.	4637+4637
	21:16	when he is caught **m** be **put to death**.	4637+4637
	21:17	or mother **m** be **put to death**.	4637+4637
	21:19	however, *he* **m pay** the injured man *for*	AIT
	21:20	he **m** be **punished**,	5933+5933
	21:22	the offender **m** be **fined** whatever	6740+6740
	21:26	**m** let the servant **go free**	AIT
	21:27	**m** let the servant **go free**	AIT
	21:28	**m** be **stoned to death**,	6232+6232
	21:28	and its meat **m** not be **eaten**.	AIT
	21:29	the bull **m** be **stoned** and the owner	AIT
	21:29	**m** be **put to death**.	AIT
	21:32	the owner **m pay** thirty shekels of silver to	AIT
	21:32	and the bull **m** be **stoned**.	AIT
	21:34	**m pay for the loss**;	AIT
	21:34	he **m pay** its owner,	AIT
	21:36	the owner **m pay**, animal for animal,	8966+8966
	22: 1	he **m pay back** five head of cattle for the ox	AIT
	22: 3	**m certainly make restitution**,	8966+8966
	22: 3	he **m** be **sold** to pay for his theft.	AIT
	22: 4	he **m pay back** double.	AIT
	22: 5	he **m make restitution** *from* the best	AIT
	22: 6	one who started the fire **m make restitution**.	8966+8966
	22: 7	the thief, if he is caught, **m pay back** double.	AIT
	22: 8	of the house **m appear** before the judges	AIT
	22: 9	the judges declare guilty **m pay back** double	AIT
	22:12	he **m make restitution** to the owner.	AIT
	22:14	he **m make restitution**.	8966+8966
	22:16	he **m pay** the **bride-price**,	4555+4555
	22:17	he **m** *still* **pay** the bride-price for virgins.	AIT
	22:19	with an animal **m** be **put to death**.	4637+4637
	22:20	god other than the LORD **m** be **destroyed**.	AIT
	22:29	"*You* **m give** me the firstborn of your sons.	AIT
	23:18	of my festival offerings **m** not be **kept**	AIT
	23:24	*You* **m demolish** them	2238+2238
	24: 2	the others **m** not **come near**.	AIT
	26:24	At these two corners they **m** be double from	AIT
	28:35	Aaron **m wear** *it* when he ministers.	AIT
	28:43	his sons **m wear** them whenever they enter	AIT
	29:34	It **m** not be **eaten**, because it is sacred.	AIT
	30: 7	"Aaron **m burn** fragrant incense on	AIT
	30: 8	He **m burn** incense again when he lights	AIT
	30:10	This annual **atonement m** be **made** with	AIT
	30:12	each one **m pay** the LORD a ransom	AIT
	30:33	on anyone other than a priest **m** be **cut off**	AIT
	30:38	like it to enjoy its fragrance **m** be **cut off**	AIT
	31:13	'*You* **m observe** my Sabbaths.	AIT
	31:14	work on that day **m** be **put to death**;	4637+4637
	31:14	on that day **m** be **cut off** from his people.	AIT
	31:15	Sabbath day **m** be **put to death**.	4637+4637
	33:23	but my face **m** not be **seen**."	AIT
	34:21	the plowing season and harvest *you* **m rest**.	AIT
	35: 2	any work on it **m** be **put to death**.	AIT
Lev	1: 3	He **m present** it at the entrance to the Tent	AIT
	2:11	to the LORD **m** be **made** without yeast,	AIT
	3:17	*You* **m** not **eat** any fat or any blood.' "	AIT
	4: 3	he **m bring** to the LORD a young bull	AIT
	4:12	he **m take** outside the camp to	AIT
	4:14	the assembly **m bring** a young bull as	AIT
	4:23	he **m bring** as his offering a male goat	AIT
	4:28	he **m bring** as his offering for	AIT
	5: 5	he **m confess** in what way he has sinned	AIT
	5: 6	he **m bring** to the LORD a female lamb	AIT
	5: 9	of the blood **m** be **drained** out at the base of	AIT
	5:11	He **m** not **put** oil or incense on it,	AIT
	5:16	He **m make restitution** *for* what he has failed to do	AIT
	6: 4	he **m return** what he has stolen or taken	AIT
	6: 5	He **m make restitution** in full,	AIT
	6: 6	And as a penalty *he* **m bring** to the priest,	AIT
	6: 9	and the fire **m** be **kept burning** on the altar.	AIT
	6:12	The fire on the altar **m** be **kept burning**;	AIT
	6:12	it **m** not **go out**.	AIT
	6:13	The fire **m** be **kept burning** on the altar	AIT
	6:13	it **m** not **go out**.	AIT
	6:17	It **m** not be **baked** *with* yeast;	AIT
	6:23	it **m** not be **eaten**."	AIT
	6:27	*you* **m wash** it in a holy place.	AIT
	6:28	the meat is cooked in **m** be **broken**;	AIT
	6:30	in the Holy Place **m** not be **eaten**;	AIT
	6:30	it **m** be **burned**.	AIT
	7: 6	but it **m** be **eaten** in a holy place;	AIT
	7:15	of thanksgiving **m** be **eaten** on	AIT
	7:15	he **m leave** none of it till morning.	AIT
	7:17	over till the third day **m** be **burned up**.	AIT
	7:19	touches anything ceremonially unclean **m** not be **eaten**;	AIT
	7:19	it **m** be **burned up**.	AIT
	7:20	that person **m** be **cut off** from his people.	AIT
	7:21	that person **m** be **cut off** from his people.' "	AIT
	7:24	but *you* **m** not **eat** it.	430+430
	7:25	**m** be **cut off** from his people.	AIT
	7:26	*you* **m** not **eat** the blood of any bird	AIT
	7:27	that person **m** be **cut off** from his people.' "	AIT
	8:35	*You* **m stay** at the entrance to the Tent	AIT
	10:10	You **m distinguish** between the holy and	AIT
	10:11	and you **m teach** the Israelites all	AIT
	10:15	and the breast that was waved **m** be **brought**	AIT
	11: 4	but *you* **m** not **eat** them.	AIT
	11: 8	*You* **m** not **eat** their meat or touch	AIT
	11:11	*you* **m** not **eat** their meat	AIT
	11:11	you **m detest** their carcasses.	AIT
	11:25	**m wash** his clothes,	AIT
	11:28	picks up their carcasses **m wash** his clothes,	AIT

Lev 11:33	and *you m* **break** the pot.	AIT
11:35	an oven or cooking pot *m* **be broken up.**	AIT
11:40	of the carcass *m* **wash** his clothes,	AIT
11:40	up the carcass *m* **wash** his clothes,	AIT
11:47	You *m* **distinguish** between the unclean and	AIT
12: 4	Then the woman *m* **wait** thirty-three days to	AIT
12: 4	*She m* not **touch** anything sacred or go to	AIT
12: 5	Then *she m* **wait** sixty-six days to	AIT
13: 2	*he m* **be brought** to Aaron the priest or to	AIT
13: 6	The man *m* **wash** his clothes,	AIT
13: 7	*he m* **appear** before the priest again.	AIT
13: 9	*he m* **be brought** to the priest.	AIT
13:16	*he m* **go** to the priest.	AIT
13:19	*he m* **present himself** to the priest.	AIT
13:33	*he m* **be shaved** except for the diseased area	AIT
13:34	*He m* **wash** his clothes, and he will be clean.	AIT
13:45	*m* **wear** torn clothes, let his hair be unkempt,	AIT
13:46	*He m* **live** alone;	AIT
13:46	he *m* **live** outside the camp.	NIH
13:49	it is a spreading mildew and *m* **be shown** *to*	AIT
13:52	*He m* **burn up** the clothing,	AIT
13:52	the article *m* **be burned up.**	AIT
13:57	and whatever has the mildew *m* **be burned**	AIT
13:58	*m* **be washed** again, and it will be clean."	AIT
14: 8	to be cleansed *m* **wash** his clothes,	AIT
14: 8	*he m* **stay** outside his tent for seven days.	AIT
14: 9	the seventh day *he m* **shave off** all his hair;	AIT
14: 9	*he m* **shave** his head, his beard,	AIT
14: 9	*He m* **wash** his clothes and bathe himself	AIT
14:10	the eighth day *he m* **bring** two male lambs	AIT
14:21	*he m* **take** one male lamb as a guilt offering	AIT
14:23	"On the eighth day *he m* **bring** them	AIT
14:35	the owner of the house *m* **go** and tell	AIT
14:41	*m* **have** all the inside walls of the house **scraped**	AIT
14:45	It *m* **be torn down**—	AIT
14:47	or eats in the house *m* **wash** his clothes.	AIT
15: 5	who touches his bed *m* **wash** his clothes	AIT
15: 6	on *m* **wash** his clothes and bathe with water,	AIT
15: 7	*m* **wash** his clothes and bathe with water,	AIT
15: 8	that person *m* **wash** his clothes and bathe	AIT
15:10	*m* **wash** his clothes and bathe with water,	AIT
15:11	with water *m* **wash** his clothes and bathe	AIT
15:12	that the man touches *m* **be broken,**	AIT
15:13	*he m* **wash** his clothes and bathe himself	AIT
15:14	On the eighth day *he m* **take** two doves	AIT
15:16	*he m* **bathe** his whole body with water,	AIT
15:17	has semen on it *m* **be washed** with water,	AIT
15:18	*both m* **bathe** with water,	AIT
15:21	touches her bed *m* **wash** his clothes	AIT
15:22	on *m* **wash** his clothes and bathe with water	AIT
15:27	*he m* **wash** his clothes and bathe with water,	AIT
15:28	*she m* **count off** seven days,	AIT
15:29	On the eighth day *she m* **take** two doves	AIT
15:31	*m* **keep** the Israelites **separate**	AIT
16: 4	so *he m* **bathe** himself with water	AIT
16:26	the goat as a scapegoat *m* **wash** his clothes	AIT
16:27	*m* **be taken** outside the camp;	AIT
16:28	man who burns them *m* **wash** his clothes	AIT
16:29	the seventh month *you m* **deny** yourselves	AIT
16:31	and *you m* **deny** yourselves;	AIT
17: 4	he has shed blood and *m* **be cut off**	AIT
17: 5	*They m* **bring** them to the priest, that is,	AIT
17: 7	*They m* no longer **offer** any	AIT
17: 9	that man *m* **be cut off** from his people.	AIT
17:13	be eaten *m* **drain out** the blood and cover it	AIT
17:14	"*You m* not **eat** the blood of any creature,	AIT
17:14	anyone who eats it *m* **be cut off.**"	AIT
17:15	or torn by wild animals *m* **wash** his clothes	AIT
18: 3	*You m* not **do** as they do in Egypt,	AIT
18: 3	and *you m* not **do** as they do in the land	AIT
18: 4	*You m* **obey** my laws and be careful	AIT
18:21	*you m* not **profane** the name of your God.	AIT
18:23	A woman *m* not **present** *herself* to	AIT
18:26	But *you m* **keep** my decrees and my laws.	AIT
18:26	the aliens living among you *m* not **do** any	AIT
18:29	such persons *m* **be cut off**	AIT
19: 3	of you *m* **respect** his mother and father,	AIT
19: 3	and *you m* **observe** my Sabbaths.	AIT
19: 6	over until the third day *m* **be burned up.**	AIT
19: 8	that person *m* **be cut off** from his people.	AIT
19:20	*there m* **be** due punishment.	AIT
19:21	*m* **bring** a ram to the entrance to the Tent	AIT
19:23	it *m* not **be eaten.**	AIT
19:34	The alien living with you *m* **be treated**	AIT
20: 2	children to Molech *m* **be put to death.**	4637+4637
20: 9	or mother, *m* **be put to death.**	4637+4637
20:10	and the adulteress *m* **be put to death.**	4637+4637
20:11	and the woman *m* **be put to death;**	4637+4637
20:12	both of them *m* **be put to death.**	4637+4637
20:13	*They m* **be put to death;**	AIT
20:14	Both he and they *m* **be burned** in the fire,	4637+4637
20:15	with an animal, *he m* **be put to death,**	4637+4637
20:15	and *you m* **kill** the animal.	AIT
20:16	*They m* **be put to death;**	4637+4637
20:17	*They m* **be cut off** before the eyes	AIT
20:18	of them *m* **be cut off** from their people.	AIT
20:23	*You m* not **live** according to the customs of	AIT
20:25	*m* therefore **make a distinction**	AIT
20:27	among you *m* **be put to death.**	4637+4637
21: 1	*m* not **make himself ceremonially unclean**	AIT
21: 4	*m* not **make himself unclean**	AIT
21: 5	" 'Priests *m* not **shave** their heads	7942+7947
21: 6	*They m* **be** holy to their God and must	AIT
21: 6	and *m* not **profane** the name of their God.	AIT
21: 7	" *They m* not **marry** women defiled	AIT
21: 9	*she m* **be burned** in the fire.	AIT

Lev 21:10	*m* not *let* his hair *become* **unkempt**	AIT
21:11	*He m* not **enter** a place where there is	AIT
21:11	*m* not **make** himself unclean,	AIT
21:13	" 'The woman he marries *m* **be** a virgin.	NIH
21:14	*He m* not **marry** a widow, a divorced woman,	AIT
21:21	*he m* not **come near** to offer the food	AIT
21:23	*he m* not **go** near the curtain or approach	AIT
22: 3	that person *m* **be cut off** from my presence.	AIT
22: 6	*He m* not **eat** any of the sacred offerings	AIT
22: 8	*He m* not **eat** anything found dead or torn	AIT
22:14	*he m* **make** restitution to the priest *for*	AIT
22:15	The priests *m* not **desecrate**	AIT
22:19	you *m* **present** a male without defect from	NIH
22:21	*it m* **be** without defect or blemish to	AIT
22:24	*You m* not **offer** to the LORD	AIT
22:24	*You m* not **do** this in your own land,	AIT
22:25	and you *m* not **accept** such animals from	NIH
22:30	*It m* **be eaten** that same day;	AIT
22:32	*I m* **be acknowledged as** holy	AIT
23: 6	for seven days *you m* **eat** bread made	AIT
23:12	you *m* **sacrifice** as a burnt offering to	AIT
23:14	*You m* not **eat** any bread,	AIT
23:29	not deny himself on that day *m* **be cut off**	AIT
23:32	and *you m* **deny** yourselves.	AIT
24: 4	before the LORD *m* **be** tended continually.	AIT
24:16	*m* **be put to death.**	4637+4637
24:16	The entire assembly *m* **stone** him.	8083+8083
24:16	he *m* **be put to death.**	4637
24:17	*he m* **be put to death.**	4637+4637
24:18	of someone's animal *m* **make restitution**—	AIT
24:19	whatever he has done *m* **be done** to him:	AIT
24:21	an animal *m* **make restitution,**	AIT
24:21	*m* **be put to death.**	AIT
25: 2	the land itself *m* **observe** a sabbath to	8697+8701
25:23	" 'The land *m* not **be sold** permanently,	AIT
25:24	*you m* **provide** *for* the redemption of	AIT
25:34	to their towns *m* not **be sold;**	AIT
25:37	*You m* not **lend** him money at interest	AIT
25:42	*they m* not **be sold** as slaves.	4835+4929
25:46	but *you m* not **rule** over your fellow	AIT
25:51	*he m* **pay** *for* his redemption a larger share	AIT
25:53	you *m* **see** to it that his owner does not rule	NIH
27:10	*He m* not **exchange** it or substitute a good	AIT
27:11	the animal *m be* **presented** to the priest,	AIT
27:13	*he m* **add** a fifth to its value.	AIT
27:15	*he m* **add** a fifth to its value,	AIT
27:19	*he m* **add** a fifth to its value,	AIT
27:23	and the man *m* **pay** its value on that day	AIT
27:29	*he m* **be put to death.**	4637+4637
27:31	*he m* **add** a fifth of the value to it.	AIT
27:33	*He m* not **pick out** the good from the bad	AIT
Nu 1:49	"*You m* not **count** the tribe of Levi	AIT
3:10	*m* **be put to death.**"	AIT
4:15	But *they m* not **touch** the holy things	AIT
4:20	But the Kohathites *m* not **go in** to look at	AIT
5: 7	*m* **confess** the sin he has committed.	AIT
5: 7	*m* **make** full restitution	AIT
5: 8	the restitution belongs to the LORD and *m*	NIH
5:15	*He m* also **take** an offering of a tenth of	AIT
5:15	*He m* not **pour** oil on it or put incense on it,	AIT
6: 3	*he m* **abstain** from wine	AIT
6: 3	and *m* not **drink** vinegar made from wine or	AIT
6: 3	*He m* not **drink** grape juice or eat grapes	AIT
6: 4	*he m* not **eat** anything that comes from	AIT
6: 5	*He m* **be** holy until the period	AIT
6: 5	*m* let the hair of his head **grow long.**	AIT
6: 6	to the LORD *he m* not **go** near a dead body.	AIT
6: 7	*m* not **make himself ceremonially unclean**	AIT
6: 9	*he m* **shave** his head on the day	AIT
6:10	on the eighth day *he m* **bring** two doves	AIT
6:12	*He m* **dedicate** *himself* to the LORD for	AIT
6:12	for the period of his separation and *m* **bring**	AIT
6:18	the Nazirite *m* **shave off** the hair	AIT
6:21	*He m* **fulfill** the vow he has made,	AIT
8:25	*they m* **retire** from their regular service	AIT
8:26	but *they themselves m* not **do** the work.	AIT
9:12	*They m* not **leave** any of it till morning	AIT
9:12	they *m* **follow** all the regulations.	NIH
9:13	that person *m* **be cut off** from his people	AIT
9:14	to celebrate the LORD's Passover *m* **do** so	AIT
9:14	You *m* **have** the same regulations for	AIT
15:13	Everyone who is native-born *m* **do** these	AIT
15:14	*he m* **do** exactly as you do.	AIT
15:27	*he m* **bring** a year-old female goat for	AIT
15:30	that person *m* **be cut off** from his people.	AIT
15:31	*m* surely **be cut off;** his guilt remains	4162+4162
15:35	said to Moses, "The man *m* **die.**	4637+4637
15:35	the whole assembly *m* **stone** him outside	AIT
17: 3	for there *m* **be** one staff for the head	NIH
18: 3	but *they m* not **go** near the furnishings of	AIT
18: 7	*m* **be put to death.**"	AIT
18:10	You *m* **regard** it *as* holy.	AIT
18:15	But *you m* **redeem** every firstborn son	7009+7009
18:16	*you m* **redeem** them at the redemption price	AIT
18:17	*you m* not **redeem** the firstborn of an ox,	AIT
18:22	now on the Israelites *m* not **go** near the Tent	AIT
18:26	as your inheritance, *you m* **present** a tenth	AIT
18:28	From these tithes *you m* **give**	AIT
18:29	*You m* **present** as the LORD's portion	AIT
19: 7	the priest *m* **wash** his clothes	AIT
19: 8	man who burns it *m* also **wash** his clothes	AIT
19:10	of the heifer *m* also **wash** his clothes,	AIT
19:12	*He m* **purify** himself with the water on	AIT
19:13	That person *m* **be cut off** from Israel.	AIT
19:18	*He m* also **sprinkle** anyone who has touched	NIH
19:19	person being cleansed *m* **wash** his clothes	AIT

Nu 19:20	he *m* **be cut off** from the community,	AIT
19:21	of cleansing *m* also **wash** his clothes,	AIT
20:10	*m* we **bring** you water out of this rock?	AIT
22:12	*m* not **put** a curse on those people,	AIT
22:38	*I m* **speak** only what God puts	AIT
23:12	"*M I* not **speak** what the LORD puts	9068
23:26	"Did I not tell you *I m* **do** whatever	AIT
24:13	and *I m* **say** only what the LORD says'?	AIT
25: 5	"Each of *you m* **put to death** those	AIT
27: 7	*You m* **certainly give** them property	5989+5989
29: 7	*You m* **deny** yourselves and do no work.	AIT
30: 2	*he m* not **break** his word	AIT
30: 2	but *m* **do** everything he said.	AIT
31:19	touched anyone who was killed *m* **stay** outside the camp	AIT
31:19	and seventh days you *m* **purify yourselves**	AIT
31:23	that can withstand fire *m be* **put** through	AIT
31:23	But *it m* also **be purified** with the water	AIT
31:23	whatever cannot withstand fire *m* **be put**	AIT
32:30	*m* **accept** *their* **possession**	AIT
35: 7	In all *you m* **give** the Levites forty-eight	AIT
35:24	the assembly *m* **judge** between him and	AIT
35:25	The assembly *m* **protect** the one accused	AIT
35:25	*He m* **stay** there until the death of	AIT
35:28	The accused *m* **stay** in his city of refuge	AIT
35:31	*He m* surely **be put to death.**	4637+4637
36: 8	in any Israelite tribe *m* **marry** someone	AIT
Dt 3:18	*m* **cross over** ahead of your brother	AIT
7: 2	then *you m* **destroy** them **totally.**	3049+3049
7:16	*You m* **destroy** all the peoples	AIT
12: 1	and laws *you m* **be** careful to follow in	AIT
12: 4	*You m* not **worship** the LORD your God	AIT
12: 5	To that place *you m* **go;**	AIT
12:16	But *you m* not **eat** the blood;	AIT
12:17	*You m* not **eat** in your own towns the tithe	3523
12:23	and *you m* not **eat** the life with the meat.	AIT
12:24	*You m* not **eat** the blood;	AIT
12:27	The blood of your sacrifices *m* **be poured**	AIT
12:31	*You m* not **worship** the LORD your God	AIT
13: 3	*you m* not **listen** to the words of	AIT
13: 4	It is the LORD your God *you m* **follow,**	AIT
13: 4	and him *you m* **revere.**	AIT
13: 5	prophet or dreamer *m* **be put to death,**	AIT
13: 5	*You m* **purge** the evil from among you.	AIT
13: 9	*You m* **certainly put** him **to death.**	2222+2222
13: 9	Your hand *m* **be** the first in putting him	AIT
13:14	then *you m* **inquire,**	AIT
13:15	*you m* **certainly put** to the sword	5782+5782
15: 1	of every seven years *you m* **cancel debts.**	AIT
15: 3	*you m* **cancel** *any* **debt** your brother owes	AIT
15:12	in the seventh year *you m* **let** him **go** free.	AIT
15:21	*you m* not **sacrifice** it to the LORD	AIT
15:23	But *you m* not **eat** the blood;	AIT
16: 5	*You m* not **sacrifice** the Passover	3523
16: 6	There *you m* **sacrifice** the Passover in	AIT
16:16	Three times a year all your men *m* **appear**	AIT
16:17	Each of you *m* **bring** a gift in proportion to	NIH
17: 4	then *you m* **investigate** it thoroughly.	AIT
17: 7	of the witnesses *m* **be** the first in putting him	AIT
17: 7	*You m* **purge** the evil from among you.	AIT
17:10	*You m* **act** according to the decisions	AIT
17:12	*m* **be put to death.**	AIT
17:12	*You m* **purge** the evil from Israel.	AIT
17:15	He *m* **be** from among your own brothers.	NIH
17:16	*m* not **acquire** great numbers	AIT
17:17	*He m* not **take** many wives,	AIT
17:17	*m* not **accumulate large amounts**	AIT
18:13	*You m* **be** blameless before the LORD	AIT
18:15	*You m* **listen** to him.	AIT
18:20	name of other gods, *m* **be put to death.**"	AIT
19:13	*You m* **purge** from Israel the guilt	AIT
19:15	A matter *m* **be established** by the testimony	AIT
19:17	in the dispute *m* **stand** in the presence of	AIT
19:18	*m* **make** *a* thorough **investigation,**	AIT
19:19	*You m* **purge** the evil from among you.	AIT
21:14	*You m* not **sell** her or treat her as a slave,	928+2021+4084+4835+4835
21:16	he *m* not **give** the rights of the firstborn to	3523
21:17	*He m* **acknowledge** the son	AIT
21:21	*You m* **purge** the evil from among you.	AIT
21:23	*m* not **leave** his body on the tree **overnight.**	AIT
21:23	*You m* not **desecrate** the land	AIT
22: 5	A woman *m* not **wear** men's clothing,	AIT
22:19	he *m* not **divorce** her as long as he lives.	3523
22:21	*You m* **purge** the evil from among you.	AIT
22:22	with her and the woman *m* **die.**	AIT
22:22	*You m* **purge** the evil from Israel.	AIT
22:24	*You m* **purge** the evil from among you.	AIT
22:29	He *m* **marry** the girl, for he has violated her.	AIT
22:30	*m* not **dishonor** his father's **bed.**	AIT
23:14	Your camp *m* **be** holy,	AIT
23:18	*You m* not **bring** the earnings of	AIT
23:23	Whatever your lips utter *you m* **be sure**	AIT
23:25	but *you m* not **put** a sickle to his	AIT
24: 5	he *m* not **be sent** to war	AIT
24: 7	the kidnapper *m* **die.**	AIT
24: 7	*You m* **purge** the evil from among you.	AIT
24: 8	You *m* **follow** carefully what I have commanded them.	AIT
25: 3	*m* not **give** him more than forty **lashes.**	AIT
25: 5	his widow *m* not **marry** outside the family.	AIT
25:15	You *m* **have** accurate and honest weights	AIT
31: 5	and *you m* **do** to them all that I have	AIT
31: 7	for you *m* **go** with this people into the land	AIT
31: 7	*you m* **divide** it *among* them as their **inheritance.**	AIT
31:13	*m* **hear** it and learn to fear the LORD	AIT

Jos	1:14	*m* **cross over** ahead of your brothers."	AIT
	6:19	to the LORD and *m* **go into** his treasury."	AIT
	20: 5	*they m* not **surrender** the one accused,	AIT
	23: 7	*You m* not **serve** them or bow down to them.	AIT
Jdg	3:24	"He *m* be **relieving** himself	AIT
	6:30	He *m* **die**, because he has broken	AIT
	13:13	"Your wife *m* **do** all that I have told her.	AIT
	13:14	She *m* not **eat** anything that comes from	AIT
	13:14	She *m* **do** everything I have commanded her.	AIT
	14: 3	*M* you **go** to the uncircumcised Philistines	AIT
	14:13	you *m* **give** me thirty linen garments	AIT
	15:18	*M* I now **die** of thirst and fall into the hands	AIT
	21:17	The Benjamite survivors *m* have heirs,"	NIH
1Sa	5: 7	of the god of Israel *m* not **stay** here with us,	AIT
	9:13	because he *m* **bless** the sacrifice;	AIT
	10: 8	but you *m* **wait** seven days until I come	AIT
	14:39	if it lies with my son Jonathan, *he m* **die**."	4637+4637
	14:43	And now I *m* **die**?'"	AIT
	20: 3	'Jonathan *m* not **know** this or he will	AIT
	20:22	the arrows are beyond you,' then *you m* **go**,	AIT
	20:26	"Something *m* have happened to David	NIH
	20:31	bring him to me, for he *m* **die**!"	1201+4638
	21:15	*M* this man **come** into my house?"	AIT
	28: 1	"You *m* **understand** that you	3359+3359
	29: 4	He *m* not **go** with us into battle,	AIT
	29: 9	'He *m* not **go up** with us into battle.'	AIT
	30:23	*you m* not **do** that with what	AIT
2Sa	2:26	"M the sword **devour** forever?	AIT
	12: 6	He *m* **pay** *for* that lamb four times over,	AIT
	14:14	cannot be recovered, so *we m* **die**.	4637+4637
	14:24	the king said, "He *m* **go** to his own house;	AIT
	14:24	he *m* not **see** my face.	AIT
	15:14	We *m* **flee**, or none of us will escape	AIT
	15:14	We *m* **leave immediately**,	AIT
	18: 3	But the men said, "You *m* not **go out**;	AIT
	18:20	but *you m* not **do** so today,	AIT
	18:25	"If he is alone, he *m* have **good news**."	NIH
	18:26	*m* be **bringing good news**,	AIT
1Ki	1:42	*m* be **bringing good news**."	AIT
	8:61	But your hearts *m* be fully committed to	AIT
	10: 8	How happy your men *m* be!	NIH
	11: 2	"You *m* not **intermarry** with them,	AIT
	13: 9	'You *m* not **eat** bread or drink water	AIT
	13:17	'You *m* not **eat** bread or drink there	AIT
	18:27	Maybe he is sleeping and *m* be **awakened**."	AIT
	20:22	and see what *m* be **done**,	AIT
	20:25	You *m* also **raise** an army like the one	AIT
	20:39	or you *m* **pay** a talent of silver.'	AIT
	22:16	How many times *m* I **make** you **swear**	AIT
2Ki	3:23	"Those kings *m* have **fought**	2991+2991
	11: 8	approaches your ranks *m* be **put to death**.	AIT
	11:15	*m* not be **put to death** in the temple	AIT
	17:36	is the one *you m* **worship**.	AIT
	17:37	You *m* always be **careful** to keep	AIT
	18:22	"You *m* **worship** before this altar	AIT
2Ch	2: 9	*m* be large and **magnificent**.	AIT
	8:11	"My wife *m* not **live** in the palace	NIH
	9: 7	How happy your men *m* be!	AIT
	18:15	How many times *m* I **make** you **swear**	AIT
	19: 9	"You *m* **serve** faithfully and wholeheartedly	AIT
	23: 7	who enters the temple *m* be **put to death**.	AIT
	25: 7	from Israel *m* not **march** with you, for	AIT
	28:13	"You *m* not **bring** those prisoners here,"	AIT
	32:12	'You *m* **worship** before one altar	AIT
Ezr	6: 9	*m* be given them daily without fail,	AIT
	7:26	the law of the king *m* surely be **punished**	AIT
	10:12	We *m* **do** as you say.	AIT
Ne	5: 2	for us to eat and stay alive, we *m* **get** grain."	AIT
	13:27	*M* we **hear** now that you too are doing	AIT
Est	1:15	what *m* be **done** to Queen Vashti?"	AIT
Job	2: 6	but you *m* **spare** his life."	AIT
	10: 6	that *you m* **search out** my faults and probe	AIT
	17: 2	my eyes *m* **dwell** *on* their hostility.	AIT
	18: 4	*m* the rocks be **moved** from their place?	AIT
	20:10	His children *m* **make amends** *to* the poor;	AIT
	20:10	his own hands *m* **give back** his wealth.	AIT
	20:18	What he toiled for *he m* **give back** uneaten;	AIT
	24: 1	Why *m* those who know him **look** in vain	AIT
	32:16	*M* I **wait**, now that they are silent,	AIT
	32:20	*I m* **speak** and find relief;	AIT
	32:20	*I m* **open** my lips and reply.	AIT
	34:33	You *m* **decide**, not I;	AIT
	35:14	that your case is before him and *you m* **wait**	AIT
	41:11	Who has a claim against me that *I m* **pay**?	AIT
Ps	13: 2	How long *m* I **wrestle** *with* my thoughts	AIT
	32: 9	but *m* be **controlled** by bit and bridle	AIT
	42: 9	Why *m* I **go about** mourning,	AIT
	43: 2	Why *m* I **go about** mourning,	AIT
	69:10	When I weep and fast, I *m* **endure** scorn;	AIT
	119:84	How long *m* your servant **wait**?	3427+3869+4537
Pr	6:31	Yet if he is caught, *he m* **pay** sevenfold,	AIT
	19:19	A hot-tempered man *m* **pay** the penalty;	AIT
Ecc	2:16	Like the fool, the wise man too *m* **die**!	AIT
	2:18	because *I m* **leave** them to the one who	AIT
	2:21	and then he *m* **leave** all he owns to someone	AIT
SS	5: 3	*m* I **put** it **on** again?	AIT
	5: 3	*m* I **soil** them again?	AIT
Isa	24: 6	its people *m* **bear** *their* guilt.	AIT
	28:28	Grain *m* be **ground** to make bread;	AIT
	36: 7	"You *m* **worship** before this altar"?	AIT
	38:10	"In the prime of my life *m* I **go** through	AIT
Jer	1: 7	*You m* **go** to everyone I send you to	AIT
	2:25	I love foreign gods, and *I m* **go** after them.'	AIT
	4:21	How long *m* I **see** the battle standard	AIT
	6: 6	This city *m* be **punished**;	AIT

Jer	9:19	*We m* **leave** our land because our houses	AIT
	10: 5	*they m* be **carried** because they cannot walk.	5951+5951
	10:19	"This is my sickness, and *I m* **endure** it."	AIT
	15:19	but you *m* not **turn** to them.	AIT
	16: 2	"You *m* not **marry** and have sons or daughters	AIT
	23:36	But *you m* not **mention** 'the oracle of	AIT
	23:38	though I told you that *you m* not **claim**,	AIT
	25:28	*You m* **drink** it!	9272+9272
	26: 8	seized him and said, "You *m* **die**!"	4637+4637
	32:31	and wrath that *I m* **remove** it from my sight.	AIT
	34:14	*you m* **free** any fellow Hebrew who has sold himself	AIT
	34:14	*you m* **let** him **go** free.'	AIT
	35: 6	nor your descendants *m* ever **drink** wine.	AIT
	35: 7	Also you *m* never **build** houses,	AIT
	35: 7	you *m* never **have** any of these things,	AIT
	35: 7	but *m* always **live** in tents.	AIT
	35:11	*we m* **go** to Jerusalem to escape	AIT
	35:15	of *you m* **turn** from your wicked ways	AIT
	36:16	"We *m* **report** all these words to the king."	5583+5583
	43: 2	'You *m* not **go** *to* Egypt to settle there.'	AIT
	49:12	who do not deserve to drink the cup *m* **drink** it,	9272+9272
	49:12	You will not go unpunished, but *m* **drink** it.	9272+9272
	51:49	"Babylon *m* **fall** because of Israel's slain,	AIT
La	5: 4	We *m* **buy** the water we drink;	NIH
Eze	2: 7	*You m* **speak** my words to them,	AIT
	8:17	*M* they also **fill** the land *with* violence	AIT
	23:35	and thrust me behind your back, you *m* **bear**	AIT
	34:18	*M* you also **trample** the rest of your pasture	AIT
	34:18	*M* you also **muddy** the rest with your feet?	AIT
	34:19	*M* my flock **feed on** what you have trampled	AIT
	44: 2	*It m* not be **opened**,	AIT
	44:10	after their idols *m* **bear** the consequences	AIT
	44:12	with uplifted hand that *they m* **bear**	AIT
	44:13	*they m* **bear** the shame	AIT
	44:17	they *m* not **wear** any woolen garment	AIT
	44:18	They *m* not **wear** anything that makes	AIT
	44:20	" 'They *m* not **shave** their heads	AIT
	44:22	They *m* not **marry** widows	AIT
	44:25	" 'A priest *m* not **defile** *himself* by going	AIT
	44:25	After he is cleansed, *he m* **wait** seven days.	AIT
	44:31	The priests *m* not **eat** anything,	AIT
	46:18	The prince *m* not **take** any of the inheritance	AIT
	48:14	They *m* not **sell** or exchange any of it.	AIT
	48:14	*m* not **pass** into other hands,	AIT
Da	3: 5	*you m* **fall down** and worship the image	AIT
	3:10	pipes and all kinds of music *m* **fall down**	AIT
	6:26	*people* m **fear** and reverence the God of	10201
	11:36	what has been determined *m* **take place**.	AIT
Hos	3: 3	*you m* not be a **prostitute**	AIT
	10: 2	and now *they m* **bear** *their* guilt.	AIT
	10:11	I will drive Ephraim, Judah *m* **plow**,	AIT
	10:11	and Jacob *m* **break up the ground**.	AIT
	12: 6	But you *m* **return** to your God.	AIT
	13:16	The people of Samaria *m* **bear** *their* guilt,	AIT
Am	6:10	*We m* not **mention** the name of the LORD."	AIT
Mic	4:10	for now you *m* **leave** the city to camp in	AIT
Hab	1: 2	How long, O LORD, *m I* **call for help**,	AIT
	2: 6	How long *m* this go on?'	NIH
Zec	13: 3	will say to him, 'You *m* **die**,	AIT
Mt	5:31	'Anyone who divorces his wife *m* **give** her	AIT
	15: 4	or mother *m* be **put to death**.'	AIT
	16:21	to his disciples that he *m* **go** to Jerusalem	1256
	16:21	and that he *m* be **killed** and on the third day	NIG
	16:24	he *m* **deny** himself and take up his cross	AIT
	17:10	of the law say that Elijah *m* **come** first?"	1256
	18: 7	Such things *m* **come**, but woe to the man	340
	19:16	what good thing *m I* **do** to get eternal life?"	AIT
	20:26	great among you *m* be your servant,	AIT
	20:27	whoever wants to be first *m* be your slave—	AIT
	22:24	his brother *m* **marry** the widow	NIG
	23: 3	So *you m* **obey** them and do everything	AIT
	24: 6	Such things *m* **happen**, but the end	1256
	24:44	So you also *m* be **ready**,	AIT
	26:54	that say *it m* **happen** in this way?"	1256
Mk	7:10	or mother *m* be **put to death**.'	AIT
	8:31	that the Son of Man *m* **suffer** many things	1256
	8:31	and that he *m* be **killed** and	NIG
	8:34	he *m* **deny** himself and take up his cross	AIT
	9:11	of the law say that Elijah *m* **come** first?"	1256
	9:12	of Man *m* **suffer** much and be rejected?	NIG
	9:35	he *m* be the very last, and the servant of all."	AIT
	10:17	"what *m I* **do** to inherit eternal life?"	AIT
	10:43	to become great among you *m* be	AIT
	10:44	whoever wants to be first *m* be slave of all.	AIT
	12:19	the man *m* **marry** the widow	AIT
	13: 7	Such things *m* **happen**, but the end	1256
	13: 9	"You *m* be **on** your **guard**.	AIT
	13:10	the gospel *m* be **preached** to all nations.	1256
	14:49	But the Scriptures *m* be **fulfilled**."	AIT
Lk	4:43	"I *m* **preach** the good news of the kingdom	1256
	5:38	new wine *m* be **poured** into new wineskins.	1064
	9:22	"The Son of Man *m* **suffer** many things and	1256
	9:22	and he *m* be **killed** and on the third day	NIG
	9:23	after me, *he m* **deny** himself and take	AIT
	10:25	"what *m I* **do** to inherit eternal life?"	AIT
	12:40	You also *m* be **ready**,	AIT
	13:33	I *m* **keep** going today and tomorrow and	1256
	14:18	and I *m* **go** and see it.	340+2400
	17:25	But first he *m* **suffer** many things and	1256
	18:18	what *m I* **do** to inherit eternal life?"	AIT
	19: 5	I *m* **stay** at your house today."	1256

Lk	20:28	the man *m* **marry** the widow	AIT
	21: 9	These things *m* **happen** first, but the end	1256
	22:37	and I tell you that this *m* be **fulfilled** in me.	1256
	24: 7	Son of Man *m* be **delivered** into the hands	1256
	24:44	Everything *m* be **fulfilled** that is written	1256
Jn	3: 7	'You *m* be **born again**.'	1256
	3:14	so the Son of Man *m* be **lifted up**,	1256
	3:30	He *m* become greater; I must become less.	1256
	3:30	He must become greater; I *m* become less.	NIG
	4:20	where we *m* **worship** is in Jerusalem."	1256
	4:24	and his worshipers *m* **worship** in spirit and	1256
	6:28	"What *m* we **do** to do the works God	AIT
	9: 4	we *m* **do** the work of him who sent me.	1256
	10:16	I *m* **bring** them also.	1256
	12:26	Whoever serves me *m* **follow** me;	AIT
	12:34	'The Son of Man *m* be **lifted up**'?	1256
	13:34	so you *m* **love** one another.	AIT
	14:31	but the world *m* **learn** that I love the Father	AIT
	15: 4	*it m* **remain** in the vine.	AIT
	15:27	And you also *m* **testify**,	AIT
	19: 7	and according to that law *he m* **die**,	4053
	21:22	You *m* **follow** me."	AIT
Ac	1:22	one of these *m* **become** a witness with us	AIT
	3:21	He *m* **remain** in heaven until the time comes	1256
	3:22	*you m* **listen** to everything he tells you.	AIT
	4:12	under heaven given to men by which we *m*	1256
	4:17	we *m* **warn** these men to speak no longer	AIT
	5:29	"We *m* **obey** God rather than men!	1256
	9: 6	and you will be told what you *m* **do**."	1256
	9:16	I will show him how much he *m* **suffer**	1256
	12:15	they said, "It *m* be his angel."	AIT
	14:22	"We *m* **go** through many hardships to enter	1256
	15: 5	"The Gentiles *m* be **circumcised**	1256
	16:30	"Sirs, what *m I* **do** to be saved?"	1256
	19:21	he said, "I *m* **visit** Rome also."	1256
	19:39	*it m* be **settled** in a legal assembly.	2147
	20:21	to both Jews and Greeks that they *m* **turn**	NIG
	20:35	that by this kind of hard work we *m* **help**	1256
	23:11	so you *m* also **testify** in Rome."	1256
	27:24	You *m* **stand** trial before Caesar;	1256
	27:26	we *m* **run aground** on some island."	1256
	28: 4	"This man *m* be a murderer;	4122
Ro	12: 9	Love *m* be sincere.	NIG
	13: 1	Everyone *m* **submit** *himself* to the governing	AIT
	14: 3	*m* not **look down on** him who does not,	AIT
	14: 3	*m* not **condemn** the man who does,	AIT
1Co	4: 2	have been given a trust *m* **prove** faithful.	AIT
	5:11	that *you m* not **associate with** anyone who	AIT
	7:10	A wife *m* not **separate** from her husband.	AIT
	7:11	she *m* **remain** unmarried or else	AIT
	7:11	And a husband *m* not **divorce** his wife.	AIT
	7:12	*he m* not **divorce** her.	AIT
	7:13	*she m* not **divorce** him.	AIT
	7:39	but he *m* **belong** to the Lord.	NIG
	9: 6	only I and Barnabas who *m* **work** for	2026+2400
	14:26	All of these *m* be **done** for the strengthening	AIT
	14:27	one at a time, and someone *m* **interpret**.	AIT
	14:34	but *m* be **in submission**, as the Law says.	AIT
	15:25	For he *m* **reign** until he has put all his	1256
	15:53	For the perishable *m* **clothe** itself with	1256
2Co	5:10	For we *m* all **appear** before the judgment	1256
	11:30	If *I m* **boast**, I will boast of the things that	1256
	12: 1	*I m* **go on** boasting.	1256
	13: 1	"Every matter *m* be **established** by	AIT
Gal	6: 6	in the word *m* **share** all good things with	AIT
Eph	4:17	you *m* no longer **live** as the Gentiles do,	AIT
	4:25	Therefore each of you *m* **put off** falsehood	AIT
	4:28	He who has been stealing *m* **steal** no longer,	AIT
	4:28	but *m* **work**, doing something useful	AIT
	5: 3	*m* not be even a hint of sexual immorality,	AIT
	5:33	also *m* **love** his wife as he loves himself,	AIT
	5:33	and the wife *m* **respect** her husband.	AIT
Col	3: 8	But now you *m* **rid** *yourselves* of all such	AIT
1Ti	2:12	authority over a man; *she m* be **silent**.	AIT
	3: 2	Now the overseer *m* be above reproach,	1256
	3: 4	*m* **manage** his own family well **and see that** his children obey him	AIT
	3: 6	He *m* not be a recent convert,	NIG
	3: 7	He *m* also have a good reputation	1256
	3: 9	They *m* **keep** hold of the deep truths of	NIG
	3:10	They *m* first be **tested**;	AIT
	3:12	A deacon *m* be the husband of but one wife	AIT
	3:12	of but one wife and *m* **manage** his children	AIT
2Ti	2:19	*m* **turn away from** wickedness."	AIT
	2:24	And the Lord's servant *m* not **quarrel**;	1256
	2:24	instead, *he m* be kind to everyone,	AIT
	2:25	Those who oppose him *he m* gently **instruct**	AIT
Tit	1: 6	An elder *m* be **blameless**,	NIG
	1: 7	*he m* be **blameless**—	1256
	1: 8	Rather he *m* be **hospitable**,	NIG
	1: 9	He *m* hold firmly to the trustworthy message	NIG
	1:11	They *m* be **silenced**, because they are	1256
	2: 1	You *m* **teach** what is in accord with sound	AIT
Heb	2: 1	We *m* **pay** more careful attention, therefore,	1256
	4:13	of him to whom we *m* **give** account.	NIG
	5: 4	he *m* be called by God, just as Aaron was.	NIG
	7:12	there *m* also be a change of the law.	340
	11: 6	to him *m* **believe** that he exists and	1256
	12:20	touches the mountain, *it m* be **stoned**."	AIT
	13:17	over you as men who *m* **give** an account.	AIT
Jas	1: 4	Perseverance *m* **finish** its work so	AIT
	1: 6	when he asks, *he m* **believe** and not doubt,	AIT
1Pe	3:10	and see good days *m* **keep** his tongue	AIT
	3:11	*He m* **turn** from evil and do good;	AIT
	3:11	*he m* **seek** peace and pursue it.	AIT
	5: 2	not *because* you *m*, but because you are	339

2Pe	1:20	you **m** understand that no prophecy	NIG
	3: 3	*you m* **understand** that in the last days	AIT
1Jn	2: 6	Whoever claims to live in him **m** walk	4053
	4:21	Whoever loves God *m* also **love** his brother.	AIT
Rev	1: 1	show his servants what **m** soon take place.	1256
	4: 1	and I will show you what **m** take place	1256
	10:11	"You **m** prophesy again	1256
	11: 5	how anyone who wants to harm them **m** die.	1256
	17:10	he **m** remain for a little while.	1256
	20: 3	After that, he **m** be set free for a short time.	1256
	22: 6	the things that **m** soon take place."	1256

MUSTACHE (1)
2Sa	19:24	not taken care of his feet or trimmed his **m**	8559

MUSTARD (5)
Mt	13:31	The kingdom of heaven is like a **m** seed,	4983
	17:20	if you have faith as small as a **m** seed,	4983
Mk	4:31	It is like a **m** seed, which is the smallest	4983
Lk	13:19	It is like a **m** seed, which a man took	4983
	17: 6	"If you have faith as small as a **m** seed,	4983

MUSTER (4) [MUSTERED, MUSTERING]
1Sa	14:17	"**M** the forces and see who has left us."	7212
2Sa	12:28	Now **m** the rest of the troops and besiege	665
Da	11:13	the king of the North *will* **m** another army,	6641
Am	2:14	the strong *will* not **m** their strength,	599

MUSTERED (16) [MUSTER]
Nu	21:23	He **m** his entire army and marched out into	665
Jos	8:10	Early the next morning Joshua **m** his men,	7212
Jdg	11:20	He **m** all his men and encamped at Jahaz	665
	20:17	**m** four hundred thousand swordsmen,	7212
1Sa	11: 8	When Saul **m** them at Bezek,	7212
	15: 4	So Saul summoned the men and **m** them	7212
2Sa	12:29	So David **m** the entire army and went	665
	18: 1	David **m** the men who were with him	7212
1Ki	12:21	he **m** the whole house of Judah and the tribe	7735
	20: 1	Ben-Hadad king of Aram **m** his entire army.	7695
	20:26	next spring Ben-Hadad **m** the Arameans	7212
	20:27	Israelites *were* also **m** and given provisions,	7212
1Ch	19: 7	the Ammonites *were* **m** from their towns	665
2Ch	11: 1	he **m** the house of Judah and Benjamin—	7735
	25: 5	He then **m** those twenty years old or more	7212
	26:11	to their numbers as **m** by Jeiel the secretary	7213

MUSTERING (1) [MUSTER]
Isa	13: 4	LORD Almighty *is* **m** an army for war.	7212

MUTE (13)
Ex	4:11	Who makes him deaf or **m**?	522
Ps	38:13	like a **m**, who cannot open his mouth;	522
Isa	35: 6	and the **m** tongue shout for joy.	522
	56:10	they are all **m** dogs, they cannot bark;	522
Mt	9:33	the **man who had been m** spoke.	3273
	12:22	blind and **m**, and Jesus healed him,	3273
	15:30	the crippled, the **m** and many others,	3273
	15:31	when they saw the **m** speaking,	3273
Mk	7:37	even makes the deaf hear and the **m** speak."	228
	9:25	"*You* deaf and **m** spirit," he said,	228
Lk	11:14	Jesus was driving out a demon that was **m**.	3273
	11:14	the **man who had been m** spoke,	3273
1Co	12: 2	and led astray to **m** idols.	936

MUTILATORS (1)
Php	3: 2	those men who do evil, those **m** of the flesh.	2961

MUTTER (3) [MUTTERED, MUTTERS]
Isa	8:19	who whisper and **m**,	2047
La	3:62	what my enemies whisper and **m**	2053
Lk	19: 7	All the people saw this and *began to* **m**,	1339

MUTTERED (1) [MUTTER]
Lk	15: 2	the Pharisees and the teachers of the law **m**,	1339

MUTTERS (1) [MUTTER]
Isa	59: 3	and your tongue **m** wicked things.	2047

MUTUAL (2) [MUTUALLY]
Ro	14:19	do what leads to peace and to **m** edification.	253
1Co	7: 5	not deprive each other except by **m consent**	5247

MUTUALLY (1) [MUTUAL]
Ro	1:12	*be* **m encouraged** by each other's faith.	5220

MUZZLE (4)
Dt	25: 4	*Do* not **m** an ox while it is treading out	2888
Ps	39: 1	I will put a **m** on my mouth as long as	4727
1Co	9: 9	"*Do* not **m** an ox while it is treading out"	3055
1Ti	5:18	"*Do* not **m** the ox while it is treading out"	5821

MY (4597) [I] See Index of Articles Etc.

MYRA (1)
Ac	27: 5	we landed at **M** in Lycia.	3688

MYRIADS (1)
Dt	33: 2	with **M** of holy ones from the south,	8047

MYRRH (18)
Ge	37:25	balm and **m**, and they were on their way	4320
	43:11	and a little honey, some spices and **m**,	4320
Ex	30:23	500 shekels of liquid **m**,	5255
Est	2:12	of **m** and six with perfumes and cosmetics.	5255
Ps	45: 8	All your robes are fragrant with **m** and aloes	5255
Pr	7:17	I have perfumed my bed with **m**,	5255
SS	1:13	a sachet of **m** resting between my breasts.	5255
	3: 6	with **m** and incense made from all the spices	5255
	4: 6	I will go to the mountain of **m** and to the hill	5255
	4:14	with **m** and aloes and all the finest spices.	5255
	5: 1	I have gathered my **m** with my spice.	5255
	5: 5	and my hands dripped with **m**,	5255
	5: 5	my fingers with flowing **m**,	5255
	5:13	His lips are like lilies dripping with **m**.	5255
Mt	2:11	with gifts of gold and of incense and of **m**.	5043
Mk	15:23	Then they offered him wine **mixed with m**,	5046
Jn	19:39	Nicodemus brought a mixture *of* **m**	5043
Rev	18:13	**m** and frankincense, of wine and olive oil,	3693

MYRTLE (5) [MYRTLES]
Isa	41:19	and the acacia, the **m** and the olive.	2072
	55:13	and instead of briers the **m** will grow.	2072
Zec	1: 8	He was standing among the **m trees** in	2072
	1:10	man standing among the **m trees** explained,	2072
	1:11	who was standing among the **m trees**,	2072

MYRTLES (1) [MYRTLE]
Ne	8:15	and from **m**, palms and shade trees,	2072

MYSELF (153) [I, SELF] See Index of Articles Etc.

MYSIA (2)
Ac	16: 7	When they came to the border of **M**,	3695
	16: 8	they passed by **M** and went down to Troas.	3695

MYSTERIES (6) [MYSTERY]
Job	11: 7	"Can you fathom the **m** *of* God?	2984
Da	2:28	but there is a God in heaven who reveals **m**.	10661
	2:29	the revealer of **m** showed you what is going	10661
	2:47	and the Lord of kings and a revealer of **m**,	10661
1Co	13: 2	the gift of prophecy and can fathom all **m**	3696
	14: 2	he utters **m** with his spirit.	3696

MYSTERY (25) [MYSTERIES]
Da	2:18	from the God of heaven concerning this **m**,	10661
	2:19	the night the **m** was revealed to Daniel in	10661
	2:27	to the king the **m** he has asked about,	10661
	2:30	As for me, this **m** has been revealed to me,	10661
	2:47	for you were able to reveal this **m**."	10661
	4: 9	and no **m** is too difficult for you.	10661
Ro	11:25	I do not want you to be ignorant of this **m**,	3696
	16:25	the revelation *of* the **m** hidden for long ages	3696
1Co	15:51	Listen, I tell you a **m**:	3696
Eph	1: 9	And he made known to us the **m** of his will	3696
	3: 3	the **m** made known to me by revelation,	3696
	3: 4	be able to understand my insight into the **m**	3696
	3: 6	This **m** is that through the gospel	NIG
	3: 9	to everyone the administration *of* this **m**,	3696
	5:32	This is a profound **m**—	3696
	6:19	so that I will fearlessly make known the **m**	3696
Col	1:26	the **m** that has been kept hidden for ages	3696
	1:27	the Gentiles the glorious riches *of* this **m**,	3696
	2: 2	in order that they may know the **m** of God,	3696
	4: 3	so that we may proclaim the **m** of Christ,	3696
1Ti	3:16	the **m** of godliness is great:	3696
Rev	1:20	The **m** of the seven stars that you saw	3696
	10: 7	the **m** of God will be accomplished,	3696
	17: 5	**M** BABYLON THE GREAT THE MOTHER OF PROSTITUTES	3696
	17: 7	I will explain to you the **m** of the woman	3696

MYTHS (4)
1Ti	1: 4	nor to devote themselves *to* **m**	3680
	4: 7	to do with godless **m** and old wives' tales;	3680
2Ti	4: 4	from the truth and turn aside to **m**.	3680
Tit	1:14	and will pay no attention *to* Jewish **m** or to	3680

N

NAAM (1)
1Ch	4:15	Iru, Elah and **N**.	5839

NAAMAH (5)
Ge	4:22	Tubal-Cain's sister was **N**.	5841
Jos	15:41	Beth Dagon, **N** and Makkedah—	5842
1Ki	14:21	His mother's name was **N**;	5841
	14:31	His mother's name was **N**;	5841
2Ch	12:13	His mother's name was **N**;	5841

NAAMAN (20) [NAAMAN'S, NAAMITE]
Ge	46:21	Bela, Beker, Ashbel, Gera, **N**, Ehi, Rosh,	5845
Nu	26:40	of Bela through Ard and **N** were:	5845
	26:40	through **N**, the Naamite clan.	5845
2Ki	5: 1	Now **N** was commander of the army of	5845
	5: 4	**N** went to his master and told him what	NIH
	5: 5	So **N** left, taking with him ten talents	NIH
	5: 6	"With this letter I am sending my servant **N**	5845
	5: 9	So **N** went with his horses and chariots	5845
	5:11	But **N** went away angry and said,	5845
	5:15	Then **N** and all his attendants went back to	2085S
	5:16	And even though **N** urged him, he refused.	NIH
	5:17	"If you will not," said **N**, "please let me,	5845
	5:19	After **N** had traveled some distance,	NIH
	5:20	"My master was too easy on **N**,	5845
	5:21	So Gehazi hurried after **N**.	5845
	5:21	When **N** saw him running toward him,	5845
	5:23	"By all means, take two talents," said **N**.	5845
1Ch	8: 4	Abishua, **N**, Ahoah,	5845
	8: 7	**N**, Ahijah, and Gera, who deported them	5845
Lk	4:27	was cleansed—only **N** the Syrian."	3722

NAAMAN'S (3) [NAAMAN]
2Ki	5: 2	and she served **N** wife.	5845S
	5:13	**N** servants went to him and said,	2257S
	5:27	**N** leprosy will cling to you and	5845

NAAMATHITE (4)
Job	2:11	Bildad the Shuhite and Zophar the **N**,	5847
	11: 1	Then Zophar the **N** replied:	5847
	20: 1	Then Zophar the **N** replied:	5847
	42: 9	the Shuhite and Zophar the **N** did what	5847

NAAMITE (1) [NAAMAN]
Nu	26:40	through Naaman, the **N** clan.	5844

NAARAH (4)
Jos	16: 7	down from Janoah to Ataroth and **N**,	5857
1Ch	4: 5	of Tekoa had two wives, Helah and **N**.	5856
	4: 6	**N** bore him Ahuzzam, Hepher,	5856
	4: 6	These were the descendants of **N**.	5856

NAARAI (1)
1Ch	11:37	Hezro the Carmelite, **N** son of Ezbai,	5858

NAARAN (1)
1Ch	7:28	**N** to the east,	5860

NAARATH (KJV) See NAARAH

NAASHON, NAASSON (KJV) See NAHSHON

NABAL (18) [NABAL'S]
1Sa	25: 3	His name was **N** and his wife's name	5573
	25: 4	he heard that **N** was shearing sheep.	5573
	25: 5	to **N** at Carmel and greet him in my name.	5573
	25: 9	they gave **N** this message in David's name.	5573
	25:10	**N** answered David's servants,	5573
	25:19	But she did not tell her husband **N**.	5573
	25:25	pay no attention to that wicked man **N**.	5573
	25:26	to harm my master be like **N**.	5573
	25:34	belonging to **N** would have been left alive	5573
	25:36	When Abigail went to **N**,	5573
	25:37	Then in the morning, when **N** was sober,	5573
	25:38	the LORD struck **N** and he died.	5573
	25:39	When David heard that **N** was dead,	5573
	25:39	against **N** for treating me with contempt.	5573
	27: 3	and Abigail of Carmel, the widow of **N**.	5573
	30: 5	Abigail, the widow of **N** of Carmel.	5573
2Sa	2: 2	Abigail, the widow of **N** of Carmel.	5573
	3: 3	Kileab the son of Abigail the widow of **N**	5573

NABAL'S (2) [NABAL]
1Sa	25:14	One of the servants told **N** wife Abigail:	5573
	25:39	and has brought **N** wrongdoing down	5573

NABOTH (17) [NABOTH'S]
1Ki	21: 1	a vineyard belonging to **N** the Jezreelite.	5559
	21: 2	Ahab said to **N**, "Let me have your vineyard	5559
	21: 3	But **N** replied, "The LORD forbid	5559
	21: 4	because **N** the Jezreelite had said,	5559
	21: 6	"Because I said to **N** the Jezreelite,	5559
	21: 7	the vineyard of **N** the Jezreelite."	5559
	21: 9	of fasting and seat **N** in a prominent place	5559
	21:12	and seated **N** in a prominent place among	5559
	21:13	and brought charges against **N** before	5559
	21:13	"**N** has cursed both God and the king."	5559
	21:14	"**N** has been stoned and is dead."	5559
	21:15	as Jezebel heard that **N** had been stoned	5559
	21:15	up and take possession of the vineyard of **N**	5559
	21:16	When Ahab heard that **N** was dead,	5559
2Ki	9:21	at the plot of ground that had belonged to **N**	5559
	9:25	the field that belonged to **N** the Jezreelite.	5559
	9:26	the blood of **N** and the blood of his sons,	5559

NABOTH'S (5) [NABOTH]
1Ki	21: 8	to the elders and nobles who lived in N city	5559
	21:11	and nobles who lived in N city did	2257S
	21:16	down to take possession of N vineyard.	5559
	21:18	He is now in N vineyard,	5559
	21:19	In the place where dogs licked up N blood,	5559

NACHON'S (KJV) See NACON

NACHOR (KJV) See NAHOR

NACON (1)
2Sa	6: 6	they came to the threshing floor of N,	5789

NADAB (20) [NADAB'S]
Ex	6:23	and she bore him N and Abihu,	5606
	24: 1	you and Aaron, N and Abihu,	5606
	24: 9	Moses and Aaron, N and Abihu,	5606
	28: 1	along with his sons N and Abihu,	5606
Lev	10: 1	Aaron's sons N and Abihu took their censers,	5606
Nu	3: 2	of Aaron were N the firstborn and Abihu,	5606
	3: 4	N and Abihu, however, fell dead	5606
	26:60	Aaron was the father of N and Abihu,	5606
	26:61	But N and Abihu died when they made	5606
1Ki	14:20	And N his son succeeded him as king.	5606
	15:25	N son of Jeroboam became king of Israel in	5606
	15:27	while N and all Israel were besieging it.	5606
	15:28	Baasha killed N in the third year	2084S
1Ch	2:28	The sons of Shammai: N and Abishur.	5606
	2:30	The sons of N: Seled and Appaim.	5606
	6: 3	N, Abihu, Eleazar and Ithamar.	5606
	8:30	followed by Zur, Kish, Baal, Ner, N,	5606
	9:36	followed by Zur, Kish, Baal, Ner, N,	5606
	24: 1	The sons of Aaron were N, Abihu,	5606
	24: 2	N and Abihu died before their father did,	5606

NADAB'S (1) [NADAB]
1Ki	15:31	As for the other events of N reign,	5606

NAGGAI (1)
Lk	3:25	the son of Esli, the son of N,	3710

NAGGING (1)
Jdg	16:16	With such n she prodded him day after day	7439

NAHALAL (2)
Jos	19:15	Included were Kattath, N, Shimron,	5634
	21:35	and N, together with their pasturelands—	5634

NAHALIEL (2)
Nu	21:19	from Mattanah to N,	5712
	21:19	from N to Bamoth,	5712

NAHALOL (1)
Jdg	1:30	in Kitron or N, who remained among them;	5636

NAHAM (1)
1Ch	4:19	The sons of Hodiah's wife, the sister of N:	5715

NAHAMANI (1)
Ne	7: 7	Raamiah, N, Mordecai, Bilshan, Mispereth,	5720

NAHARAI (2)
2Sa	23:37	N the Beerothite, the armor-bearer	5726
1Ch	11:39	N the Berothite, the armor-bearer	5726

NAHARAIM   See ARAM NAHARAIM

NAHASH (8) [IR NAHASH]
1Sa	11: 1	N the Ammonite went up	5731
	11: 2	But N the Ammonite replied,	5731
	12:12	that N king of the Ammonites was moving	5731
2Sa	10: 2	"I will show kindness to Hanun son of N,	5731
	17:25	the daughter of N and sister of Zeruiah	5731
	17:27	of N from Rabbah of the Ammonites,	5731
1Ch	19: 1	N king of the Ammonites died,	5731
	19: 2	"I will show kindness to Hanun son of N,	5731

NAHATH (5)
Ge	36:13	N, Zerah, Shammah and Mizzah.	5740
	36:17	Chiefs N, Zerah, Shammah and Mizzah.	5740
1Ch	1:37	N, Zerah, Shammah and Mizzah.	5740
	6:26	Elkanah his son, Zophai his son, N his son,	5740
2Ch	31:13	Jehiel, Azaziah, N, Asahel, Jerimoth,	5740

NAHBI (1)
Nu	13:14	N son of Vophsi;	5696

NAHOR (17) [NAHOR'S]
Ge	11:22	he became the father of N.	5701
	11:23	And after he became the father of N,	5701
	11:24	When N had lived 29 years,	5701
	11:25	N lived 119 years and had other sons	5701
	11:26	the father of Abram, N and Haran.	5701
	11:27	the father of Abram, N and Haran.	5701
	11:29	Abram and N both married.	5701
	22:20	she has borne sons to your brother N:	5701
	22:23	to Abraham's brother N.	5701
	24:10	and made his way to the town of N.	5701
	24:15	who was the wife of Abraham's brother N.	5701
	24:24	the son that Milcah bore to N."	5701
	24:47	'The daughter of Bethuel son of N,	5701
	31:53	the God of Abraham and the God of N,	5701
Jos	24: 2	the father of Abraham and N,	5701
1Ch	1:26	Serug, N, Terah	5701
Lk	3:34	the son of Terah, the son of N,	3732

NAHOR'S (2) [NAHOR]
Ge	11:29	and the name of N wife was Milcah;	5701
	29: 5	"Do you know Laban, N grandson?"	5701

NAHSHON (13)
Ex	6:23	daughter of Amminadab and sister of N,	5732
Nu	1: 7	from Judah, N son of Amminadab;	5732
	2: 3	The leader of the people of Judah is N son	5732
	7:12	on the first day was N son of Amminadab	5732
	7:17	the offering of N son of Amminadab.	5732
	10:14	N son of Amminadab was in command.	5732
Ru	4:20	Amminadab the father of N,	5732
	4:20	N the father of Salmon,	5732
1Ch	2:10	and Amminadab the father of N,	5732
	2:10	N was the father of Salmon,	5732
Mt	1: 4	Amminadab the father of N,	3709
	1: 4	N the father of Salmon,	3709
Lk	3:32	the son of Salmon, the son of N,	3709

NAHUM (2)
Na	1: 1	The book of the vision of N the Elkoshite.	5699
Lk	3:25	the son of Amos, the son of N,	3725

NAIL (1) [NAILING, NAILS]
Jn	20:25	the n marks in his hands and put my finger	2464

NAILING (2) [NAIL]
Ac	2:23	put him to death by n him to the cross.	4699
Col	2:14	he took it away, n it to the cross.	4669

NAILS (8) [NAIL]
Dt	21:12	and have her shave her head, trim her n	7632
1Ch	22: 3	to make n for the doors of the gateways and	5021
2Ch	3: 9	The gold n weighed fifty shekels.	5021
Ecc	12:11	collected sayings like firmly embedded n	5383
Isa	41: 7	He n down the idol so it will not topple.	928+2616+5021
Jer	10: 4	they fasten it with hammer and n so it will	5021
Da	4:33	an eagle and his n like the claws of a bird.	10303
Jn	20:25	and put my finger where the n were,	2464

NAIN (1)
Lk	7:11	Jesus went to a town called N,	3723

NAIOTH (6)
1Sa	19:18	he and Samuel went to N and stayed there.	5766
	19:19	"David is in N at Ramah";	5766
	19:22	"Over in N at Ramah," they said.	5766
	19:23	So Saul went to N at Ramah.	5766
	19:23	along prophesying until he came to N.	5766
	20: 1	from N at Ramah and went to Jonathan	5766

NAIVE (1)
Ro	16:18	they deceive the minds of n people.	179

NAKED (32) [NAKEDNESS]
Ge	2:25	The man and his wife were both n,	6873
	3: 7	and they realized they were n;	6567
	3:10	and I was afraid because I was n; so I hid."	6567
	3:11	he said, "Who told you that you were n?	6567
2Ch	28:15	the plunder they clothed all who were n.	5122
Job	1:21	"N I came from my mother's womb,	6873
	1:21	and n I will depart.	6873
	22: 6	of their clothing, leaving them n.	6873
	24: 7	Lacking clothes, they spend the night n;	6873
	24:10	Lacking clothes, they go about n;	6873
	26: 6	Death is n before God;	6873
Ecc	5:15	N a man comes from his mother's womb,	6873
Isa	58: 7	when you see the n, to clothe him,	6873
La	4:21	you will be drunk and stripped n.	6867
Eze	16: 7	you who were n and bare.	6567
	16:22	when you were n and bare,	6567
	16:39	and take your fine jewelry and leave you n	6567
	18: 7	the hungry and provides clothing for the n.	6567
	18:16	the hungry and provides clothing for the n.	6567
	23:10	They stripped her n, took away her sons	6872
	23:29	They will leave you n and bare,	6567
Hos	2: 3	Otherwise I will strip her n and make her	6873
Am	2:16	bravest warriors will flee n on that day,"	6873
Mic	1: 8	I will go about barefoot and n.	6873
Hab	2:15	so that he can gaze on their n bodies.	5067
Mk	14:52	he fled n, leaving his garment behind.	1218
Ac	19:16	a beating that they ran out of the house	1218
2Co	5: 3	when we are clothed, we will not be found n	1218
	5: 3	I have been cold and n.	1218
Rev	3:17	pitiful, poor, blind and n.	1218
	16:15	not go n and be shamefully exposed."	1218
	17:16	They will bring her to ruin and leave her n;	1218

NAKEDNESS (17) [NAKED]
Ge	9:22	the father of Canaan, saw his father's n	6872
	9:23	in backward and covered their father's n.	6872
	9:23	so that they would not see their father's n.	6872
Ex	20:26	lest your n be exposed on it.'	6567
Dt	28:48	in n and dire poverty,	6567
Isa	47: 3	Your n will be exposed and your shame	6872
	57: 8	and you looked on their n.	3338
La	1: 8	for they have seen her n;	6872
Eze	16:36	over you and covered your n.	6872
	16:36	and exposed your n in your promiscuity	6872
	16:37	and they will see all your n.	6872
	23:18	and exposed her n,	6872
Hos	2: 9	intended to cover her n.	6872
Mic	1:11	Pass on in n and shame,	6880
Na	3: 5	I will show the nations your n and	5113
Ro	8:35	or hardship or persecution or famine or n	1219
Rev	3:18	so you can cover your shameful n;	1219

NAME (764) [NAME'S, NAMED, NAMELESS, NAMELY, NAMES]
Ge	2:11	The n of the first is the Pishon;	9005
	2:13	The n of the second river is the Gihon;	9005
	2:14	The n of the third river is the Tigris;	9005
	2:19	to the man to see what he would n them;	7924
	2:19	called each living creature, that was its n.	9005
	4:21	His brother's n was Jubal;	9005
	4:26	men began to call on the n of the LORD.	9005
	11: 4	that we may make a n for ourselves and not	9005
	11:29	the n of Abram's wife was Sarai,	9005
	11:29	and the n of Nahor's wife was Milcah;	9005
	12: 2	I will make your n great,	9005
	12: 8	and called on the n of the LORD.	9005
	13: 4	There Abram called on the n of the LORD	9005
	16:11	You shall n him Ishmael,	7924+9005
	16:13	She gave this n to the LORD who spoke	9005
	16:15	the n Ishmael to the son she had borne.	9005
	17: 5	your n will be Abraham,	9005
	17:15	her n will be Sarah.	9005
	21: 3	the n Isaac to the son Sarah bore him.	9005
	21:33	and there he called upon the n	9005
	22:24	His concubine, whose n was Reumah,	9005
	25: 1	whose n was Keturah.	9005
	26:25	Isaac built an altar there and called on the n	9005
	26:33	the n of the town has been Beersheba.	9005
	29:16	the n of the older was Leah,	9005
	29:16	and the n of the younger was Rachel.	9005
	30:28	He added, "N your wages,	5918
	31:53	So Jacob took an oath in the n of the Fear	928
	32:27	The man asked him, "What is your n?"	9005
	32:28	man said, "Your n will no longer be Jacob,	9005
	32:29	Jacob said, "Please tell me your n."	9005
	32:29	But he replied, "Why do you ask my n?"	9005
	35:10	God said to him, "Your n is Jacob,	9005
	35:10	your n will be Israel."	9005
	36:39	and his wife's n was Mehetabel daughter	9005
	36:40	by n, according to their clans and regions:	9005
	38: 6	his firstborn, and her n was Tamar.	9005
	38:30	came out and he was given the n Zerah.	9005
	41:45	gave Joseph the n Zaphenath-Paneah	9005
	48:16	May they be called by my n and the names	9005
	48:20	"In your n will Israel pronounce this blessing:	NIH
Ex	3:13	and they ask me, 'What is his n?'	9005
	3:15	This is my n forever,	9005
	3:15	n by which I am to be remembered	2352
	5:23	since I went to Pharaoh to speak in your n,	9005
	6: 3	but by my n the LORD I did not make	9005
	9:16	and that my n might be proclaimed in all	9005
	15: 3	LORD is a warrior; the LORD is his n.	9005
	20: 7	not misuse the n of the LORD your God,	9005
	20: 7	hold anyone guiltless who misuses his n.	9005
	20:24	Wherever I cause my n to be honored,	9005
	23:21	since my N is in him.	9005
	28:21	each engraved like a seal with the n of one	9005
	33:12	'I know you by n and you have found favor	9005
	33:17	with you and I know you by n."	9005
	33:19	and I will proclaim my n, the LORD,	9005
	34: 5	with him and proclaimed his n,	9005
	34:14	whose n is Jealous, is a jealous God.	9005
	39:14	a seal with the n of one of the twelve tribes.	9005
Lev	18:21	you must not profane the n of your God.	9005
	19:12	not swear falsely by my n and so profane	9005
	19:12	and so profane the n of your God.	9005
	20: 3	and profaned my holy n.	9005
	21: 6	and must not profane the n of their God.	9005
	22: 2	so they will not profane my holy n.	9005
	22:32	Do not profane my holy n.	9005
	24:11	the Israelite woman blasphemed the N with	9005
	24:11	(His mother's n was Shelomith,	9005
	24:16	anyone who blasphemes the n of the LORD	9005
	24:16	when he blasphemes the N,	9005
Nu	1: 2	listing every man by n, one by one.	9005
	1:18	or more were listed by n,	9005
	1:20	to serve in the army were listed by n,	9005
	1:22	in the army were counted and listed by n,	9005
	1:24	to serve in the army were listed by n,	9005
	1:26	to serve in the army were listed by n,	9005
	1:28	to serve in the army were listed by n,	9005
	1:30	to serve in the army were listed by n,	9005
	1:32	to serve in the army were listed by n,	9005
	1:34	to serve in the army were listed by n,	9005
	1:36	to serve in the army were listed by n,	9005

Nu		
1:38	to serve in the army were listed by **n**,	9005
1:40	to serve in the army were listed by **n**,	9005
1:42	to serve in the army were listed by **n**,	9005
3:43	listed by **n**, was 22,273.	9005
6:27	"So they will put my **n** on the Israelites,	9005
13:16	**gave** Hoshea son of Nun *the* **n** Joshua.)	7924
17: 2	Write the **n** of each man on his staff.	9005
17: 3	On the staff of Levi write Aaron's **n**,	9005
25:14	The **n** of the Israelite who was killed with	9005
25:15	the **n** of the Midianite woman who was put	9005
26:59	the **n** of Amram's wife was Jochebed,	9005
27: 4	Why should our father's **n** disappear	9005

Dt		
5:11	not misuse the **n** of the LORD your God,	9005
5:11	hold anyone guiltless who misuses his **n**.	9005
6:13	serve him only and take your oaths in his **n**.	9005
9:14	that I may destroy them and blot out their **n**	9005
10: 8	and to pronounce blessings in his **n**,	9005
10:20	to him and take your oaths in his **n**.	9005
12: 5	among all your tribes to put his **N** there	9005
12:11	as a dwelling for his **N**—	9005
12:21	to put his **N** is too far away from you,	9005
14:23	as a dwelling for his **N**,	9005
14:24	the LORD will choose to put his **N** is	9005
16: 2	as a dwelling for his **N**.	9005
16: 6	as a dwelling for his **N**.	9005
16:11	as a dwelling for his **N**—	9005
18: 5	and minister in the LORD's **n** always.	9005
18: 7	in the **n** of the LORD his God	9005
18:19	that the prophet speaks in my **n**,	9005
18:20	to speak in my **n** anything I have	9005
18:20	prophet who speaks in the **n** of other gods,	9005
18:22	in the **n** of the LORD does not take place	9005
21: 5	the **n** of the LORD and to decide all cases	9005
22:14	and slanders her and gives her a bad **n**,	9005
22:19	has given an Israelite virgin a bad **n**.	9005
25: 6	The first son she bears shall carry on the **n**	9005
25: 6	of the dead brother so that his **n** will not	9005
25: 7	to carry on his brother's **n** in Israel.	9005
26: 2	as a dwelling for his **N**	9005
28:10	that you are called by the **n** of the LORD,	9005
28:58	do not revere this glorious and awesome **n**	9005
29:20	and the LORD will blot out his **n** from	9005
32: 3	I will proclaim the **n** of the LORD.	9005

Jos		
7: 9	and wipe out our **n** from the earth.	9005
7: 9	then will you do for your own great **n**?"	9005
21: 9	they allotted the following towns by **n**	9005
22:34	**gave** the altar *this* **n**: A Witness Between Us	7924

Jdg		
1:26	which is its **n** to this day.	9005
13: 6	and he didn't tell me his **n**.	9005
13:17	"What is your **n**,	9005
13:18	He replied, "Why do you ask my **n**?	9005
16: 4	in the Valley of Sorek whose **n** was Delilah.	9005

Ru		
1: 2	The man's **n** was Elimelech,	9005
1: 2	his wife's **n** Naomi,	9005
2: 1	a man of standing, whose **n** was Boaz.	9005
2:19	"The **n** of the man I worked	9005
4: 5	in order to maintain the **n** of the dead	9005
4:10	in order to maintain the **n** of the dead	9005
4:10	so that his **n** will not disappear from	9005

1Sa		
1: 1	whose **n** was Elkanah son of Jeroham,	9005
8: 2	The **n** of his firstborn was Joel and	9005
8: 2	and the **n** of his second was Abijah,	9005
9: 1	whose **n** was Kish son of Abiel,	9005
12:22	For the sake of his great **n** the LORD will	9005
14:49	The **n** of his older daughter was Merab,	9005
14:50	His wife's **n** was Ahinoam daughter	9005
14:50	The **n** of the commander of Saul's army	9005
17:45	but I come against you in the **n** of the LORD	9005
18:30	and his **n** became well known.	9005
20:42	with each other in the **n** of the LORD,	9005
24:21	or wipe out my **n** from my father's family."	9005
25: 3	His **n** was Nabal	9005
25: 3	and his wife's **n** was Abigail.	9005
25: 5	to Nabal at Carmel and greet him in my **n**.	9005
25: 9	they gave Nabal this message in David's **n**.	9005
25:25	He is just like his **n**—	9005
25:25	his **n** is Fool, and folly goes with him.	9005
28: 8	he said, "and bring up for me the one *I* **n**."	606

2Sa		
4: 4	His **n** was Mephibosheth.)	9005
6: 2	which is called by the **N**,	9005
6: 2	the **n** of the LORD Almighty,	9005
6:18	in the **n** of the LORD Almighty.	9005
7: 9	Now I will make your **n** great,	9005
7:13	the one who will build a house for my **N**,	9005
7:23	and to make a **n** for himself,	9005
7:26	so that your **n** will be great forever.	9005
12:25	the prophet *to* **n** him Jedidiah.	7924+9005
14: 7	leaving my husband neither **n** nor	9005
14:27	The daughter's **n** was Tamar,	9005
16: 5	His **n** was Shimei son of Gera,	9005
18:18	to carry on the memory of my **n**."	9005
22:50	I will sing praises to your **n**.	9005

1Ki		
1:47	'May your God make Solomon's **n** more famous than yours	9005
3: 2	a temple had not yet been built for the **N** *of*	9005
5: 3	a temple for the **N** of the LORD his God	9005
5: 5	a temple for the **N** of the LORD my God,	9005
5: 5	the temple for my **N**.'	9005
8:16	to have a temple built for my **N** to be there,	9005
8:17	to build a temple for the **N** of the LORD.	9005
8:18	in your heart to build a temple for my **N**,	9005
8:19	the temple for my **N**.'	9005
8:20	I have built the temple for the **N** of the LORD	9005
8:29	'My **N** shall be there,'	9005
8:33	they turn back to you and confess your **n**,	9005
8:35	and confess your **n** and turn from their sin	9005
8:41	from a distant land because of your **n**—	9005

1Ki		
8:42	of your great **n** and your mighty hand	9005
8:43	of the earth may know your **n** and fear you,	9005
8:43	that this house I have built bears your **N**.	9005
8:44	and the temple I have built for your **N**,	9005
8:48	and the temple I have built for your **N**;	9005
9: 3	by putting my **N** there forever.	9005
9: 7	and will reject this temple I have consecrated for my **N**.	9005
9:13	a **n** they have to this day.	NIH
10: 1	and his relation to the **n** *of* the LORD,	9005
11:36	the city where I chose to put my **N**.	9005
14:21	the tribes of Israel in which to put his **N**.	9005
14:21	His mother's **n** was Naamah;	9005
14:31	His mother's **n** was Naamah;	9005
15: 2	His mother's **n** was Maacah daughter	9005
15:10	His grandmother's **n** was Maacah daughter	9005
16:24	the **n** of the former owner of the hill.	9005
18:24	Then you call on the **n** of your god,	9005
18:24	and I will call on the **n** of the LORD.	9005
18:25	Call on the **n** of your god,	9005
18:26	on the **n** of Baal from morning till noon.	9005
18:31	saying, "Your **n** shall be Israel."	9005
18:32	With the stones he built an altar in the **n** of	9005
21: 8	So she wrote letters in Ahab's **n**,	9005
22:16	to tell me nothing but the truth in the **n** of	9005
22:42	His mother's **n** was Azubah daughter	9005

2Ki		
2:24	and called down a curse on them in the **n**	9005
5:11	and call on the **n** of the LORD his God,	9005
8:26	His mother's **n** was Athaliah;	9005
12: 1	His mother's **n** was Zibiah;	9005
14: 2	His mother's **n** was Jehoaddin;	9005
14: 7	calling it Joktheel, the **n** it has to this day.	9005
14:27	not said he would blot out the **n** of Israel	9005
15: 2	His mother's **n** was Jecoliah;	9005
15:33	His mother's **n** was Jerusha daughter	9005
18: 2	His mother's **n** was Abijah daughter	9005
21: 1	His mother's **n** was Hephzibah.	9005
21: 4	"In Jerusalem I will put my **N**."	9005
21: 7	I will put my **N** forever.	9005
21:19	His mother's **n** was Meshullemeth daughter	9005
22: 1	His mother's **n** was Jedidah daughter	9005
23:27	'There shall my **N** be.' "	9005
23:31	His mother's **n** was Hamutal daughter	9005
23:34	and changed Eliakim's **n** to Jehoiakim.	9005
23:36	His mother's **n** was Zebidah daughter	9005
24: 8	His mother's **n** was Nehushta daughter	9005
24:17	in his place and changed his **n** to Zedekiah.	9005
24:18	His mother's **n** was Hamutal daughter	9005

1Ch		
1:50	and his wife's **n** was Mehetabel daughter	9005
2:26	whose **n** was Atarah;	9005
4:38	The men listed above by **n** were leaders	9005
7:15	His sister's **n** was Maacah.	9005
8:29	His wife's **n** was Maacah,	9005
9:35	His wife's **n** was Maacah,	9005
12:31	by **n** to come and make David king—	9005
13: 6	the ark that is called by the **N**.	9005
16: 2	the people in the **n** of the LORD.	9005
16: 8	Give thanks to the LORD; call on his **n**;	9005
16:10	Glory in his holy **n**;	9005
16:29	ascribe to the LORD the glory due his **n**.	9005
16:35	that we may give thanks to your holy **n**,	9005
16:41	and designated by **n** to give thanks to	9005
17: 8	Now I will make your **n** like the names of	9005
17:21	and to make a **n** for yourself,	9005
17:24	and that your **n** will be great forever.	9005
21:19	to the word that Gad had spoken in the **n** of	9005
22: 7	a house for the **N** of the LORD my God.	9005
22: 8	You are not to build a house for my **N**,	9005
22: 9	His **n** will be Solomon,	9005
22:10	the one who will build a house for my **N**.	9005
22:19	that will be built for the **N** of the LORD."	9005
28: 3	'You are not to build a house for my **N**,	9005
29:13	and praise your glorious **n**.	9005
29:16	for building you a temple for your Holy **N**,	9005

2Ch		
2: 1	for the **N** of the LORD and a royal palace	9005
2: 4	Now I am about to build a temple for the **N**	9005
6: 5	to have a temple built for my **N** to be there,	9005
6: 6	But now I have chosen Jerusalem for my **N**	9005
6: 7	to build a temple for the **N** of the LORD,	9005
6: 8	in your heart to build a temple for my **N**,	9005
6: 9	who will build the temple for my **N**.'	9005
6:10	and I have built the temple for the **N** of	9005
6:20	which you said you would put your **N** there	9005
6:24	when they turn back and confess your **n**,	9005
6:26	and confess your **n** and turn from their sin	9005
6:32	from a distant land because of your great **n**	9005
6:33	of the earth may know your **n** and fear you,	9005
6:33	that this house I have built bears your **N**.	9005
6:34	and the temple I have built for your **N**,	9005
6:38	toward the temple I have built for your **N**;	9005
7:14	if my people, who are called by my **n**,	9005
7:16	so that my **N** may be there forever.	9005
7:20	and will reject this temple I have consecrated for my **N**.	9005
12:13	the tribes of Israel in which to put his **N**.	9005
12:13	His mother's **n** was Naamah;	9005
13: 2	His mother's **n** was Maacah,	9005
14:11	and in your **n** we have come	9005
18:15	to tell me nothing but the truth in the **n** of	9005
20: 8	and have built in it a sanctuary for your **N**,	9005
20: 9	that bears your **N** and will cry out to you	9005
20:31	His mother's **n** was Azubah daughter	9005
22: 2	His mother's **n** was Athaliah,	9005
24: 1	His mother's **n** was Zibiah;	9005
25: 1	His mother's **n** was Jehoaddin;	9005
26: 3	His mother's **n** was Jecoliah;	9005

2Ch		
27: 1	His mother's **n** was Jerusha daughter	9005
28:15	The men designated by **n** took	9005
29: 1	His mother's **n** was Abijah daughter	9005
31:19	by **n** to distribute portions to every male	9005
33: 4	"My **N** will remain in Jerusalem forever."	9005
33: 7	I will put my **N** forever.	9005
33:18	the words the seers spoke to him in the **n**	9005
36: 4	and Jerusalem and changed Eliakim's **n**	9005
36:13	who had made him take an oath in God's **n**.	NIH

Ezr		
2:61	the Gileadite and was called by that **n**).	9005
5: 1	the Jews in Judah and Jerusalem in the **n** *of*	10721
6:12	who has caused his **N** to dwell there,	10721
8:20	All were registered by **n**.	9005
10:16	and all of them designated by **n**.	9005

Ne		
1: 9	chosen as a dwelling for my **N**.'	9005
1:11	who delight in revering your **n**.	9005
6:13	they would give me a bad **n** to discredit me.	9005
7:63	the Gileadite and was called by that **n**).	9005
9: 5	"Blessed be your glorious **n**,	9005
9:10	You made a **n** for yourself,	9005
13:25	I made them take an oath in God's **n**	NIH

Est		
2:14	with her and summoned her by **n**.	9005
3:12	in the **n** of King Xerxes himself and sealed	9005
8: 8	Now write another decree in the king's **n**	9005
8: 8	in the king's **n** and sealed with his ring can	9005
8:10	Mordecai wrote in the **n** of King Xerxes,	9005

Job		
1: 1	of Uz there lived a man whose **n** was Job.	9005
1:21	may the **n** of the LORD be praised."	9005
18:17	he has no **n** in the land.	9005

Ps		
5:11	those who love your **n** may rejoice in you.	9005
7:17	to the **n** of the LORD Most High.	9005
8: 1	how majestic is your **n** in all the earth!	9005
8: 9	how majestic is your **n** in all the earth!	9005
9: 2	I will sing praise to your **n**, O Most High.	9005
9: 5	you have blotted out their **n** for ever	9005
9:10	Those who know your **n** will trust in you,	9005
18:49	I will sing praises to your **n**.	9005
20: 1	may the **n** *of* the God of Jacob protect you.	9005
20: 5	up our banners in the **n** of our God.	9005
20: 7	we trust in the **n** of the LORD our God.	9005
22:22	I will declare your **n** to my brothers;	9005
25:11	For the sake of your **n**, O LORD,	9005
29: 2	Ascribe to the LORD the glory due his **n**;	9005
30: 4	praise his holy **n**.	2352
31: 3	for the sake of your **n** lead and guide me.	9005
33:21	for we trust in his holy **n**.	9005
34: 3	let us exalt his **n** together.	9005
41: 5	"When will he die and his **n** perish?"	9005
44: 5	through your **n** we trample our foes.	9005
44: 8	and we will praise your **n** forever.	9005
44:20	the **n** of our God or spread out our hands to	9005
48:10	Like your **n**, O God, your praise reaches	9005
52: 9	in your **n** I will hope,	9005
52: 9	for your **n** is good.	NIH
54: 1	Save me, O God, by your **n**;	9005
54: 6	I will praise your **n**, O LORD,	9005
61: 5	the heritage of those who fear your **n**.	9005
61: 8	to your **n** and fulfill my vows day after day.	9005
63: 4	and in your **n** I will lift up my hands.	9005
63:11	all who swear by **God's n** will praise him,	2257S
66: 2	Sing the glory of his **n**;	9005
66: 4	they sing praise to your **n**."	9005
68: 4	Sing to God, sing praise to his **n**,	9005
68: 4	his **n** is the LORD—	9005
69:30	I will praise God's **n** in song	9005
69:36	and those who love his **n** will dwell there.	9005
72:17	May his **n** endure forever;	9005
72:19	Praise be to his glorious **n** forever;	9005
74: 7	they defiled the dwelling place of your **N**.	9005
74:10	Will the foe revile your **n** forever?	9005
74:18	how foolish people have reviled your **n**.	9005
74:21	may the poor and needy praise your **n**.	9005
75: 1	O God, we give thanks, for your **N** is near;	9005
76: 1	his **n** is great in Israel.	9005
79: 6	on the kingdoms that do not call on your **n**;	9005
79: 9	O God our Savior, for the glory of your **n**;	9005
80:18	revive us, and we will call on your **n**.	9005
83: 4	the **n** of Israel be remembered no more."	9005
83:16	with shame so that men will seek your **n**,	9005
83:18	whose **n** is the LORD—	9005
86: 9	they will bring glory to your **n**.	9005
86:11	that I may fear your **n**.	9005
86:12	I will glorify your **n** forever.	9005
89:12	Tabor and Hermon sing for joy at your **n**.	9005
89:16	They rejoice in your **n** all day long;	9005
89:24	and through my **n** his horn will be exalted.	9005
91:14	for he acknowledges my **n**.	9005
92: 1	the LORD and make music to your **n**,	9005
96: 2	Sing to the LORD, praise his **n**;	9005
96: 8	Ascribe to the LORD the glory due his **n**;	9005
97:12	and praise his holy **n**.	2352
99: 3	Let them praise your great and awesome **n**	9005
99: 6	among those who called on his **n**;	9005
100: 4	give thanks to him and praise his **n**.	9005
102: 8	against me **use** my **n** as a curse.	928+8678
102:15	The nations will fear the **n** of the LORD,	9005
102:21	So the **n** of the LORD will be declared	9005
103: 1	all my inmost being, praise his holy **n**.	9005
105: 1	Give thanks to the LORD, call on his **n**;	9005
105: 3	Glory in his holy **n**;	9005
106:47	to your holy **n** and glory in your praise.	9005
111: 9	holy and awesome is his **n**.	9005
113: 1	praise the **n** of the LORD.	9005
113: 2	Let the **n** of the LORD be praised.	9005
113: 3	the **n** of the LORD is to be praised.	9005
115: 1	not to us but to your **n** be the glory,	9005
116: 4	Then I called on the **n** of the LORD:	9005

Ps 116:13 up of salvation and call on the n of the LORD 9005
116:17 and call on the n of the LORD. 9005
118:10 but in the n of the LORD I cut them off. 9005
118:11 but in the n of the LORD I cut them off. 9005
118:12 in the n of the LORD I cut them off. 9005
118:26 Blessed is he who comes in the n of 9005
119:55 In the night I remember your n, O LORD, 9005
119:132 as you always do to those who love your n. 9005
122: 4 to praise the n of the LORD according to 9005
124: 8 Our help is in the n of the LORD, 9005
129: 8 we bless you in the n of the LORD." 9005
135: 1 Praise the n of the LORD; 9005
135: 3 sing praise to his n, for that is pleasant. 9005
135:13 Your n, O LORD, endures forever, 9005
138: 2 and will praise your n for your love 9005
138: 2 above all things your n and your word. 9005
139:20 your adversaries misuse your n. NIH
140:13 Surely the righteous will praise your n and 9005
142: 7 that I may praise your n. 9005
145: 1 I will praise your n for ever and ever. 9005
145: 2 and extol your n for ever and ever. 9005
145:21 Let every creature praise his holy n for ever 9005
147: 4 of the stars and calls them each by n. 9005
148: 5 Let them praise the n of the LORD, 9005
— 148:13 Let them praise the n of the LORD 9005
148:13 for his n alone is exalted; 9005
149: 3 Let them praise his n with dancing 9005
Pr 3: 4 and a good n in the sight of God and man. 8507
10: 7 but the n of the wicked will rot. 9005
18:10 The n of the LORD is a strong tower; 9005
21:24 "Mocker" is his n; 9005
22: 1 good n is more desirable than great riches; 9005
30: 4 What is his n, and the name of his son? 9005
30: 4 What is his name, and the n of his son? 9005
30: 9 and so dishonor the n of my God. 9005
Ecc 6: 4 and in darkness its n is shrouded. 9005
7: 1 A good n is better than fine perfume, 9005
SS 1: 3 your n is like perfume poured out. 9005
Isa 4: 1 only let us be called by your n. 9005
8: 3 "N him Maher-Shalal-Hash-Baz. 7924+9005
12: 4 "Give thanks to the LORD, call on his n; 9005
12: 4 and proclaim that his n is exalted. 9005
14:22 from Babylon her n and survivors, 9005
18: 7 the place of the N of the LORD Almighty. 9005
24:15 exalt the n of the LORD, 9005
25: 1 I will exalt you and praise your n, 9005
26: 8 your n and renown are the desire 9005
26:13 but your n alone do we honor. 9005
29:23 they will keep my n holy; 9005
30:27 See, the N of the LORD comes from afar, 9005
40:26 and calls them each by n. 9005
41:25 one from the rising sun who calls on my n. 9005
42: 8 "I am the LORD; that is my n! 9005
43: 1 I have summoned you by n; you are mine. 9005
43: 7 everyone who is called by my n, 9005
44: 5 another will call himself by the n of Jacob; 9005
44: 5 'The LORD's,' and will take the n Israel. 9005
45: 3 the God of Israel, who summons you by n. 9005
45: 4 by n and bestow on you a title of honor, 9005
47: 4 the LORD Almighty is his n— 9005
48: 1 by the n of Israel and come from the line 9005
48: 1 in the n of the LORD and invoke the God 9005
48: 2 the LORD Almighty is his n: 9005
48:19 their n would never be cut off 9005
49: 1 from my birth he has made mention of my n 9005
50:10 in the n of the LORD and rely on his God. 9005
51:15 the LORD Almighty is his n. 9005
52: 5 all day long my n is constantly blasphemed. 9005
52: 6 Therefore my people will know my n; 9005
54: 5 the LORD Almighty is his n— 9005
56: 5 and a n better than sons and daughters; 9005
56: 5 I will give them an everlasting n that will 9005
56: 6 to love the n of the LORD, 9005
57:15 he who lives forever, whose n is holy: 9005
59:19 men will fear the n of the LORD, 9005
62: 2 be called by a new n that the mouth of 9005
62: 4 or n your land Desolate. 606
63:14 to make for yourself a glorious n. 9005
63:16 our Redeemer from of old is your n. 9005
63:19 they have not been called by your n. 9005
64: 2 to make your n known to your enemies 9005
64: 7 on your n or strives to lay hold of you; 9005
65: 1 To a nation that did not call on my n, 9005
65:15 You will leave your n to my chosen ones as 9005
65:15 but to his servants he will give another n. 9005
66: 5 and exclude you because of my n, 9005
66:22 "so will your n and descendants endure. 9005
Jer 3:17 in Jerusalem to honor the n of the LORD. 9005
7:10 which bears my N, and say, 9005
7:11 Has this house, which bears my N, 9005
7:12 where I first made a dwelling for my N, 9005
7:14 now do to the house that bears my N, 9005
7:30 that bears my N and have defiled it. 9005
10: 6 and your n is mighty in power. 9005
10:16 the LORD Almighty is his n. 9005
10:25 on the peoples who do not call on your n. 9005
11:19 that his n be remembered no more." 9005
11:21 'Do not prophesy in the n of the LORD 9005
12:16 the ways of my people and swear by my n, 9005
14: 7 do something for the sake of your n. 9005
14: 9 and we bear your n; do not forsake us! 9005
14:14 prophets are prophesying lies in my n. 9005
14:15 the prophets who are prophesying in my n: 9005
14:21 For the sake of your n do not despise us; 9005
15:16 for I bear your n, O LORD God Almighty. 9005
16:21 Then they will know that my n is the LORD. 9005
20: 3 "The LORD's n for you is not Pashhur, 7924+9005

Jer 20: 9 or speak any more in his n," 9005
23: 6 This is the n by which he will be called: 9005
23:25 "I have heard what the prophets say who prophesy lies in my n. 9005
23:27 dreams they tell one another will make my people forget my n, 9005
23:27 just as their fathers forgot my n 9005
25:29 on the city that bears my N, 9005
26: 9 Why do you prophesy in the LORD's n 9005
26:16 to us in the n of the LORD our God." 9005
26:20 prophesied in the n of the LORD; 9005
27:15 'They are prophesying lies in my n. 9005
29: 9 They are prophesying lies to you in my n. 9005
29:21 who are prophesying lies to you in my n: 9005
29:23 and in my n have spoken lies, 9005
29:25 You sent letters in your own n to all 9005
31:35 the LORD Almighty is his n: 9005
32:18 whose n is the LORD Almighty, 9005
32:34 in the house that bears my N and defiled it. 9005
33: 2 the LORD is his n: 9005
33:16 This is the n by which it will be called: 889S
34:15 before me in the house that bears my N. 9005
34:16 around and profaned my n; 9005
37:13 whose n was Irijah son of Shelemiah, 9005
44:16 the message you have spoken to us in the n 9005
44:26 'I swear by my great n,' says the LORD, 9005
44:26 in Egypt will ever again invoke my n 9005
46:18 whose n is the LORD Almighty, 9005
48:15 whose n is the LORD Almighty. 9005
50:34 the LORD Almighty is his n. 9005
51:19 the LORD Almighty is his n. 9005
51:57 whose n is the LORD Almighty. 9005
52: 1 His mother's n was Hamutal daughter 9005
La 3:55 I called on your n, O LORD, 9005
Eze 20: 9 the sake of my n I did what would keep it 9005
20:14 the sake of my n I did what would keep it 9005
20:22 the sake of my n I did what would keep it 9005
20:39 to me and no longer profane my holy n, 9005
36:20 the nations they profaned my holy n, 9005
36:21 I had concern for my holy n, 9005
36:22 but for the sake of my holy n, 9005
36:23 I will show the holiness of my great n, 9005
36:23 the n you have profaned among them. 889S
39: 7 " 'I will make known my holy n 9005
39: 7 I will no longer let my holy n be profaned, 9005
39:25 and I will be zealous for my holy n. 9005
43: 7 Israel will never again defile my holy n— 9005
43: 8 they defiled my holy n 9005
48: 1 "These are the tribes, listed by n: 9005
48:35 the n of the city from that time on will be: 9005
Da 1: 7 to Daniel, the n Belteshazzar; NIH
2:20 be to the n of God for ever and ever; 10721
4: 8 after the n of my god, 10721
9: 6 who spoke in your n to our kings, 9005
9:15 and who made for yourself a n that endures 9005
9:18 the desolation of the city that bears your N. 9005
9:19 your city and your people bear your N." 9005
12: 1 everyone whose n is found written in NIH
Hos 12: 5 the LORD is his n of renown! 2352
Joel 2:26 the n of the LORD your God, 9005
2:32 on the n of the LORD will be saved; 9005
Am 2: 7 the same girl and so profane my holy n. 9005
4:13 the LORD God Almighty is his n. 9005
5: 8 the LORD is his n— 9005
5:27 whose n is God Almighty. 9005
6:10 not mention the n of the LORD." 9005
9: 6 the LORD is his n. 9005
9:12 of Edom and all the nations that bear my n," 9005
Mic 4: 5 the nations may walk in the n of their gods; 9005
4: 5 in the n of the LORD our God for ever 9005
5: 4 of the n of the LORD his God. 9005
5: 4 and to fear your n is wisdom— 9005
Na 1:14 no descendants to bear your n. 9005
Zep 3: 9 all of them may call on the n of the LORD 9005
3:12 who trust in the n of the LORD. 9005
Zec 5: 4 of him who swears falsely by my n. 9005
6:12 'Here is the man whose n is the Branch, 9005
10:12 in the LORD and in his n they will walk," 9005
13: 3 you have told lies in the LORD's n.' 9005
13: 9 call on my n and I will answer them; 9005
14: 9 and his n the only name. 9005
14: 9 and his name the only n. NIH
Mal 1: 6 O priests, who show contempt for my n. 9005
1: 6 'How have we shown contempt for your n?' 9005
1:11 My n will be great among the nations, 9005
1:11 and pure offerings will be brought to my n, 9005
1:11 my n will be great among the nations," 9005
1:14 my n is to be feared among the nations. 9005
2: 2 if you do not set your heart to honor my n," 9005
2: 5 and stood in awe of my n. 9005
3:16 the LORD and honored his n. 9005
4: 2 But for you who revere my n, 9005
Mt 1:21 and you are to give him the n Jesus, 3950
1:25 And he gave him the n Jesus. 3950
6: 9 in heaven, hallowed be your n, 3950
7:22 Lord, did we not prophesy in your n, 3950
7:22 and in your n drive out demons 3950
12:21 In his n the nations will put their hope." 3950
13:55 Isn't his mother's n Mary, 3306
18: 5 a little child like this in my n welcomes me. 3950
18:20 where two or three come together in my n, 3950
21: 9 "Blessed is he who comes in the n of 3950
23:39 'Blessed is he who comes in the n of 3950
24: 5 For many will come in my n, claiming, 3950
26: 3 high priest, whose n was Caiaphas, 3306
28:19 baptizing them in the n of the Father and of 3950
Mk 3:16 Simon (to whom he gave the n Peter); 3950

Mk 3:17 n Boanerges, which means Sons of Thunder 3950
5: 9 Then Jesus asked him, "What is your n?" 3950
5: 9 "My n is Legion," he replied, 3950
6:14 for Jesus' n had become well known. 3950
9:37 in my n welcomes me; 3950
9:38 a man driving out demons in your n 3950
9:39 "No one who does a miracle in my n can in 3950
9:41 a cup of water in my n because you belong 3950
11: 9 "Blessed is he who comes in the n of 3950
13: 6 Many will come in my n, claiming, 3950
16:17 In my n they will drive out demons; 3950
Lk 1:13 and you are to give him the n John. 3950
1:27 The virgin's n was Mary. 3950
1:31 and you are to give him the n Jesus. 3950
1:49 done great things for me—holy is his n. 3950
1:59 to n him after his father Zechariah, 2813+3836+3950
1:61 among your relatives who has that n." 3950
1:62 to find out what he would like to n 2813
1:63 "His n is John." 3950
2:21 Jesus, the n the angel had given him NIG
5:27 by the n of Levi sitting at his tax booth. 3950
6:22 and insult you and reject your n as evil, 3950
8:30 Jesus asked him, "What is your n?" 3950
9:48 in my n welcomes me; 3950
9:49 a man driving out demons in your n 3950
10:17 even the demons submit to us in your n." 3950
11: 2 " 'Father, hallowed be your n, 3950
13:35 'Blessed is he who comes in the n of 3950
19: 2 A man was there by the n of Zacchaeus; 3950
19:38 "Blessed is the king who comes in the n of 3950
21: 8 For many will come in my n, claiming, 3950
21:12 and all on account of my n. 3950
24:47 be preached in his n to all nations, 3950
Jn 1: 6 who was sent from God; his n was John. 3950
1:12 to those who believed in his n, 3950
2:23 and believed in his n. 3950
3:18 because he has not believed in the n 3950
5:43 I have come in my Father's n, 3950
5:43 but if someone else comes in his own n, 3950
10: 3 He calls his own sheep by n 3950
10:25 The miracles I do in my Father's n speak 3950
12:13 "Blessed is he who comes in the n of 3950
12:28 Father, glorify your n!" 3950
14:13 And I will do whatever you ask in my n, 3950
14:14 You may ask me for anything in my n, 3950
14:26 whom the Father will send in my n, 3950
15:21 will treat you this way because of my n, 3950
16:23 my Father will give you whatever you ask in my n. 3950
16:24 not asked for anything in my n. 3950
16:26 In that day you will ask in my n. 3950
17:11 protect them by the power of your n— 3950
17:11 the n you gave me. 4005S
17:12 and kept them safe by that n you gave me. 3950
18:10 (The servant's n was Malchus.) 3950
20:31 by believing you may have life in his n. 3950
Ac 2:21 everyone who calls on the n of the Lord 3950
2:38 in the n of Jesus Christ for the forgiveness 3950
3: 6 In the n of Jesus Christ of Nazareth, walk." 3950
3:16 By faith in the n of Jesus, 3950
3:16 It is Jesus' n and the faith that comes 3950
4: 7 or what n did you do this?" 3950
4:10 It is by the n of Jesus Christ of Nazareth, 3950
4:12 for there is no other n under heaven given 3950
4:17 to speak no longer to anyone in this n." 3950
4:18 not to speak or teach at all in the n of Jesus. 3950
4:30 through the n of your holy servant Jesus. 3950
5:28 not to teach in this n," 3950
5:40 not to speak in the n of Jesus, 3950
5:41 of suffering disgrace for the N. 3950
8:12 of God and the n of Jesus Christ, 3950
8:16 they had simply been baptized into the n of 3950
9:14 to arrest all who call on your n." 3950
9:15 to carry my n before the Gentiles 3950
9:16 how much he must suffer for my n." 3950
9:21 among those who call on this n? 3950
9:27 preached fearlessly in the n of Jesus. 3950
9:28 speaking boldly in the n of the Lord. 3950
10:43 forgiveness of sins through his n." 3950
10:48 So he ordered that they be baptized in the n 3950
13: 8 (for that is what his n means) opposed them 3950
15:17 and all the Gentiles who bear my n, 3950
15:26 men who have risked their lives for the n 3950
16:18 "In the n of Jesus Christ I command you 3950
19: 5 they were baptized into the n of the Lord 3950
19:13 to **invoke** the n of the Lord Jesus 3950+3951
19:13 They would say, "In the n of Jesus, NIG
19:17 n of the Lord Jesus was held in high honor. 3950
19:27 that our trade will lose its good n, 591+1650+2262
21:13 in Jerusalem for the n of the Lord Jesus." 3950
22:16 wash your sins away, calling on his n.' 3950
26: 9 to do all that was possible to oppose the n 3950
Ro 2:24 "God's n is blasphemed among 3950
9:17 in you and that my n might be proclaimed 3950
10:13 on the n of the Lord will be saved." 3950
15: 9 I will sing hymns to your n." 3950
1Co 1: 2 with all those everywhere who call on the n 3950
1:10 brothers, in the n of our Lord Jesus Christ, 3950
1:13 Were you baptized into the n of Paul? 3950
1:15 that you were baptized into my n. 3950
5: 4 the n of our Lord Jesus and I am with you 3950
6:11 in the n of the Lord Jesus Christ and by 3950
Eph 3:15 in heaven and on earth **derives** its n. 3951
5:20 in the n of our Lord Jesus Christ. 3950

Php	2: 9	gave him the **n** that is above every name,	3950
	2: 9	the name that is above every **n**,	3950
	2:10	at the **n** of Jesus every knee should bow,	3950
Col	3:17	do it all in the **n** of the Lord Jesus,	3950
2Th	1:12	the **n** of our Lord Jesus may be glorified	3950
	3: 6	In the **n** of the Lord Jesus Christ,	3950
1Ti	6: 1	so that God's **n** and our teaching may not	3950
2Ti	2:19	"Everyone who confesses the **n** of the Lord	3950
Heb	1: 4	the **n** he has inherited is superior to theirs.	3950
	2:12	"I will declare your **n** to my brothers;	3950
	7: 2	First, his **n** means "king of righteousness";	NIG
	13:15	the fruit of lips that confess his **n**.	3950
Jas	2: 7	not the ones who are slandering the noble **n**	3950
	5:10	take the prophets who spoke in the **n** of	3950
	5:14	over him and anoint him with oil in the **n** of	3950
1Pe	4:14	you are insulted because of the **n** of Christ,	3950
	4:16	but praise God that you bear that **n**.	3950
1Jn	2:12	have been forgiven on account of his **n**.	3950
	3:23	to believe in the **n** of his Son, Jesus Christ,	3950
	5:13	to you who believe in the **n** of the Son	3950
3Jn	1: 7	for the sake of the **N** that they went out,	3950
	1:14	Greet the friends there by **n**.	3950
Rev	2: 3	and have endured hardships for my **n**,	3950
	2:13	Yet you remain true to my **n**.	3950
	2:17	a white stone with a new **n** written on it,	3950
	3: 5	I will never blot out his **n** from the book	3950
	3: 5	will acknowledge his **n** before my Father	3950
	3: 8	and have not denied my **n**.	3950
	3:12	the **n** of my God and the name of the city	3950
	3:12	of my God and the **n** of the city of my God,	3950
	3:12	and I will also write on him my new **n**.	3950
	8:11	the **n** of the star is Wormwood.	3950
	9:11	whose **n** in Hebrew is Abaddon,	3950
	11:18	and those who reverence your **n**, both small	3950
	13: 1	and on each head a blasphemous **n**.	3950
	13: 6	and to slander his **n** and his dwelling place	3950
	13:17	which is the **n** of the beast or the number	3950
	13:17	of the beast or the number *of* his **n**.	3950
	14: 1	who had his **n** and his Father's name written	3950
	14: 1	and his Father's **n** written on their foreheads	3950
	14:11	for anyone who receives the mark *of* his **n**."	3950
	15: 2	and over the number of his **n**.	3950
	15: 4	O Lord, and bring glory to your **n**?	3950
	16: 9	by the intense heat and they cursed the **n**	3950
	19:12	a **n** written on him that no one knows	3950
	19:13	and his **n** is the Word of God.	3950
	19:16	and on his thigh he has this **n** written:	3950
	20:15	If anyone's **n** was not found written in	NIG
	22: 4	and his **n** will be on their foreheads.	3950

NAME'S (8) [NAME]

Ps	23: 3	in paths of righteousness for his **n** sake.	9005
	79: 9	and forgive our sins for your **n** sake.	9005
	106: 8	Yet he saved them for his **n** sake,	9005
	109:21	deal well with me for your **n** sake;	9005
	143:11	your **n** sake, O LORD, preserve my life;	9005
Isa	48: 9	For my own **n** sake I delay my wrath;	9005
Eze	20:44	when I deal with you for my **n** sake and not	9005
Ro	1: 5	Through him and for his **n** sake,	3950

NAMED (161) [NAME]

Ge	3:20	Adam **n** his wife Eve,	7924+9005
	4:17	and he **n** it after his son Enoch.	7924+9005
	4:19	one **n** Adah and the other Zillah.	9005
	4:25	she gave birth to a son and **n** him Seth,	7924+9005
	4:26	Seth also had a son, and *he* **n** him Enosh.	7924+9005
	5: 3	and *he* **n** him Seth.	7924+9005
	5:29	*He* **n** him Noah and said,	7924+9005
	10:25	One was **n** Peleg, because in his time	9005
	10:25	his brother was **n** Joktan.	9005
	16: 1	she had an Egyptian maidservant **n** Hagar,	9005
	19:37	and *she* **n** him Moab;	7924+9005
	19:38	and *she* **n** him Ben-Ammi;	7924+9005
	23:16	and weighed out for him the price *he had* **n**	1819
	24:29	Now Rebekah had a brother **n** Laban,	9005
	25:25	so *they* **n** him Esau.	7924+9005
	25:26	so *he was* **n** Jacob.	7924+9005
	26:20	So *he* **n** the well Esek,	7924+9005
	26:21	so *he* **n** it Sitnah.	7924+9005
	26:22	*He* **n** it Rehoboth, saying,	7924+9005
	27:36	Esau said, *"Isn't he* rightly **n** Jacob?	3951
	29:32	*She* **n** him Reuben, for she said,	7924+9005
	29:33	So *she* **n** him Simeon.	7924+9005
	29:34	So he *was* **n** Levi.	7924+9005
	29:35	So *she* **n** him Judah.	7924+9005
	30: 6	Because of this *she* **n** him Dan.	7924+9005
	30: 8	So *she* **n** him Naphtali.	7924+9005
	30:11	So *she* **n** him Gad.	7924+9005
	30:13	So *she* **n** him Asher.	7924+9005
	30:18	So *she* **n** him Issachar.	7924+9005
	30:20	So *she* **n** him Zebulun.	7924+9005
	30:21	birth to a daughter and **n** her Dinah.	7924+9005
	30:24	*She* **n** him Joseph, and said,	7924+9005
	32: 2	So *he* **n** that place Mahanaim.	7924+9005
	35: 8	So it *was* **n** Allon Bacuth.	7924+9005
	35:10	So *he* **n** him Israel.	7924+9005
	35:18	*she* **n** her son Ben-Oni.	7924+9005
	35:18	But his father **n** him Benjamin.	7924
	36:12	also had a concubine **n** Timna.	NIH
	36:32	His city was **n** Dinhabah.	9005
	36:35	His city was **n** Avith.	9005
	36:39	His city was **n** Pau.	9005
	38: 1	to stay with a man of Adullam **n** Hirah.	9005
	38: 2	the daughter of a Canaanite man **n** Shua.	9005
Ge	38: 3	who *was* **n** Er.	7924+9005
	38: 4	gave birth to a son and **n** him Onan.	7924+9005
	38: 5	to still another son and **n** him Shelah.	7924+9005
	38:29	And he *was* **n** Perez.	7924+9005
	41:51	Joseph **n** his firstborn Manasseh and	7924+9005
	41:52	The second son he **n** Ephraim and	7924+9005
Ex	2:10	*She* **n** him Moses, saying,	7924+9005
	2:22	and Moses **n** him Gershom, saying,	7924+9005
	18: 3	One son was **n** Gershom, for Moses said,	9005
	18: 4	and the other was **n** Eliezer,	9005
Nu	11:34	the place *was* **n** Kibroth Hattaavah,	7924+9005
	21: 3	so the place *was* **n** Hormah.	7924+9005
	26:46	(Asher had a daughter **n** Serah.)	9005
Dt	3:14	it *was* **n** after him,	7924+9005
Jos	2: 1	of a prostitute **n** Rahab and stayed there.	9005
	19:47	They settled in Leshem and **n** it Dan.	7924
Jdg	8:31	a son, whom *he* **n** Abimelech.	8492+9005
	13: 2	A certain man of Zorah, **n** Manoah,	9005
	13:24	to a boy and **n** him Samson.	7924+9005
	17: 1	Now a man **n** Micah from the hill country	9005
	18:29	*They* **n** it Dan after their forefather Dan,	7924+9005
Ru	1: 4	one **n** Orpah and the other Ruth.	9005
	4:17	And *they* **n** him Obed.	7924+9005
1Sa	1:20	*She* **n** him Samuel, saying,	7924+9005
	4:21	*She* **n** the boy Ichabod, saying,	7924
	7:12	*He* **n** it Ebenezer, saying,	7924+9005
	9: 2	He had a son **n** Saul,	9005
	17: 4	A champion **n** Goliath,	9005
	17:12	David was the son of an Ephrathite **n** Jesse,	9005
2Sa	3: 7	a concubine **n** Rizpah daughter of Aiah.	9005
	4: 2	One was **n** Baanah and the other Recab;	9005
	9: 2	a servant of Saul's household **n** Ziba.	9005
	9:12	Mephibosheth had a young son **n** Mica,	9005
	12:24	and *they* **n** him Solomon.	7924+9005
	12:28	and it *will be* **n** after me."	7924+9005
	13: 3	Now Amnon had a friend **n** Jonadab son	9005
	17:25	Amasa was the son of a man **n** Jether,	9005
	18:18	*He* **n** the pillar after himself,	7924+9005
	20: 1	Now a troublemaker **n** Sheba son of Bicri,	9005
	20:21	A man **n** Sheba son of Bicri,	9005
1Ki	7:21	to the south *he* **n** Jakin and the one to	7924+9005
	11:20	of Tahpenes bore him a son **n** Genubath,	NIH
	11:26	and his mother was a widow **n** Zeruah.	9005
	13: 2	'A son **n** Josiah will be born to the house	9005
2Ki	17:34	whom *he* **n** Israel.	8492+9005
	23:11	the room of an official **n** Nathan-Melech.	NIH
1Ch	1:19	One was **n** Peleg, because in his time	9005
	1:19	his brother was **n** Joktan.	9005
	1:43	whose city was **n** Dinhabah.	9005
	1:46	His city was **n** Avith.	9005
	1:50	His city was **n** Pau.	9005
	2:29	Abishur's wife was **n** Abihail,	9005
	2:34	He had an Egyptian servant **n** Jarha.	9005
	4: 3	Their sister was **n** Hazzelelponi.	9005
	4: 9	His mother *had* **n** him Jabez, saying,	7924+9005
	6:65	the *previously* **n** towns.	928+7924+9005
	7:15	Another descendant was **n** Zelophehad,	9005
	7:16	to a son and **n** him Peresh.	7924+9005
	7:16	His brother was **n** Sheresh.	9005
	7:23	*He* **n** him Beriah.	7924+9005
	9:31	A Levite **n** Mattithiah.	NIH
2Ch	3:17	The one to the south *he* **n** Jakin and	7924+9005
	28: 9	a prophet of the LORD **n** Oded was there,	9005
Ezr	5: 14	to a man **n** Sheshbazzar,	10721
Ne	9: 7	of the Chaldeans and **n** him Abraham.	8492+9005
	13:13	and a Levite **n** Pedaiah in charge of	NIH
Est	2: 5	**n** Mordecai son of Jair, the son of Shimei,	9005
	2: 7	Mordecai had a cousin **n** Hadassah,	NIH
Job	42:14	The first daughter he **n** Jemimah,	7924+9005
Ps	49:11	*they had* **n** lands after themselves,	7924+9005
Ecc	6:10	Whatever exists *has* already **been, n,**	7924+9005
Isa	61: 6	you *will be* **n** ministers of our God.	606
Eze	23: 4	The older was **n** Oholah,	9005
	48:31	the city will be **n** after the tribes of Israel.	9005
Mt	9: 9	he saw a man **n** Matthew sitting at	3306
	27:32	they met a man from Cyrene, **n** Simon,	3950
	27:57	a rich man from Arimathea, **n** Joseph,	3950
Mk	5:22	Then one of the synagogue rulers, **n** Jairus,	3950
Lk	1: 5	of Judea there was a priest **n** Zechariah,	3950
	1:27	to be married to a man **n** Joseph,	3950
	2:21	he *was* **n** Jesus, the name the angel	2813+3950
	6:14	Simon (whom he **n** Peter),	3951
	8:41	Then a man **n** Jairus,	3950
	10:38	where a woman **n** Martha opened her home	3950
	16:20	At his gate was laid a beggar **n** Lazarus,	3950
	23:50	Now there was a man **n** Joseph,	3950
	24:18	One of them, **n** Cleopas, asked him,	3950
Jn	3: 1	a man of the Pharisees **n** Nicodemus,	899+3950
	11: 1	Now a man **n** Lazarus was sick.	NIG
	11:49	Then one of them, **n** Caiaphas,	NIG
Ac	5: 1	Now a man **n** Ananias,	3950
	5:34	But a Pharisee **n** Gamaliel,	3950
	7:58	at the feet of a young man **n** Saul,	2813
	8: 9	a man **n** Simon had practiced sorcery in	3950
	9:10	a disciple **n** Ananias.	3950
	9:11	and ask for a man from Tarsus **n** Saul,	3950
	9:12	a vision he has seen a man **n** Ananias come	3950
	9:33	There he found a man **n** Aeneas,	3950
	9:36	a disciple **n** Tabitha.	3950
	9:43	for some time with a tanner **n** Simon.	5516
	10: 1	At Caesarea there was a man **n** Cornelius,	3950
	10: 5	a man **n** Simon who is called Peter.	NIG
	11:28	One of them, **n** Agabus,	3950
	12:13	and a servant girl **n** Rhoda came to answer	3950
	13: 6	and false prophet **n** Bar-Jesus,	3950
	16: 1	where a disciple **n** Timothy lived,	3950
Ac	16:14	of those listening was a woman **n** Lydia,	3950
	17:34	also a woman **n** Damaris,	3950
	18: 2	There he met a Jew **n** Aquila,	3950
	18:24	Meanwhile a Jew **n** Apollos,	3950
	19:24	A silversmith **n** Demetrius,	3950
	20: 9	in a window was a young man **n** Eutychus,	3950
	21:10	prophet **n** Agabus came down from Judea.	3950
	22:12	"A man **n** Ananias came to see me.	NIG
	24: 1	of the elders and a lawyer **n** Tertullus,	NIG
	25:19	about a dead man **n** Jesus who Paul claimed was alive.	NIG
	27: 1	over *to* a centurion **n** Julius,	3950
Rev	6: 8	Its rider was **n** Death,	899+3950

NAMELESS (1) [NAME]

Job	30: 8	A base and **n** brood,	1172+9005

NAMELY (1) [NAME]

Col	2: 2	that they may know the mystery of God, **n**,	NIG

NAMES (79) [NAME]

Ge	2:20	So the man gave **n** to all the livestock,	9005
	25:13	These are the **n** of the sons of Ishmael,	9005
	25:16	the **n** of the twelve tribal rulers according	9005
	26:18	the same **n** his father had given them.	9005
	36:10	These are the **n** of Esau's sons:	9005
	46: 8	These are the **n** of the sons of Israel (Jacob	9005
	48: 6	be reckoned under the **n** *of* their brothers.	9005
	48:16	May they be called by my name and the **n**	9005
Ex	1: 1	the **n** *of* the sons of Israel who went	9005
	1:15	whose **n** were Shiphrah and Puah,	9005
	6:16	These were the **n** of the sons of Levi	9005
	23:13	Do not invoke the **n** *of* other gods;	9005
	28: 9	and engrave on them the **n** of the sons	9005
	28:10	six **n** on one stone and the remaining six on	9005
	28:11	the **n** of the sons of Israel on the two stones	9005
	28:12	the **n** on his shoulders as a memorial before	9005
	28:21	one for each of the **n** of the sons of Israel,	9005
	28:29	the **n** of the sons of Israel over his heart on	9005
	39: 6	and engraved them like a seal with the **n** *of*	9005
	39:14	one for each of the **n** *of* the sons of Israel,	9005
Nu	1: 5	the **n** *of* the men who are to assist you:	9005
	1:17	Aaron took these men whose **n** had been given,	9005
	3: 2	The **n** *of* the sons of Aaron were Nadab	9005
	3: 3	Those were the **n** *of* Aaron's sons,	9005
	3:17	These were the **n** of the sons of Levi:	9005
	3:18	These were the **n** of the Gershonite clans:	9005
	3:40	or more and make a list of their **n**.	9005
	11:26	two men, whose **n** were Eldad and Medad,	9005
	13: 4	These are their **n**:	9005
	13:16	the **n** of the men Moses sent to explore	9005
	26:33	whose **n** were Mahlah, Noah, Hoglah,	9005
	26:53	as an inheritance based on the number of **n**.	9005
	26:55	be according to the **n** *for* its ancestral tribe.	9005
	27: 1	The **n** of the daughters were Mahlah,	9005
	32:38	and Baal Meon (these **n** were changed)	9005
	32:38	They gave **n** to the cities they rebuilt.	9005
	34:17	the **n** *of* the men who are to assign the land	9005
	34:19	These are their **n**:	9005
Dt	7:24	and you will wipe out their **n** from	9005
	12: 3	the idols of their gods and wipe out their **n**	9005
Jos	17: 3	whose **n** were Mahlah, Noah, Hoglah,	9005
	23: 7	do not invoke the **n** of their gods or swear	9005
Jdg	8:14	the young man wrote down for him the **n** of	NIH
Ru	1: 2	**n** *of* his two sons were Mahlon and Kilion.	9005
2Sa	5:14	the **n** of the children born to him there:	9005
	7: 9	like the **n** of the greatest men of the earth.	9005
	23: 8	These are the **n** of David's mighty men:	9005
1Ki	4: 8	These are their **n**:	9005
1Ch	4:41	The men whose **n** were listed came in	9005
	6:17	These are the **n** of the sons of Gershon;	9005
	8:38	Azel had six sons, and these were their **n**:	9005
	9:44	Azel had six sons, and these were their **n**:	9005
	14: 4	the **n** of the children born to him there:	9005
	17: 8	like the **n** of the greatest men of the earth.	9005
	23:24	under their **n** and counted individually,	9005
	24: 6	recorded their **n** in the presence of the king	NIH
2Ch	31:16	**n** were in the genealogical records—	3509
Ezr	5: 4	"What are the **n** of the men constructing	10721
	5:10	We also asked them their **n**,	10721
	5:10	the **n** of their leaders for your information.	10721
Ps	16: 4	of blood or take up their **n** on my lips.	9005
	109:13	their **n** blotted out from the next generation.	9005
Da	1: 7	The chief official gave them new **n**:	9005
Hos	2:17	the **n** of the Baals from her lips;	9005
	2:17	no longer will their **n** be invoked.	9005
Zep	1: 4	the **n** of the pagan and and the idolatrous	9005
Zec	13: 2	I will banish the **n** *of* the idols from	9005
Mt	10: 2	These are the **n** of the twelve apostles:	3950
Lk	10:20	rejoice that your **n** are written in heaven."	3950
Ac	18:15	about words and **n** and your own law—	3950
Php	4: 3	whose **n** are in the book of life.	3950
Heb	12:23	whose **n** are written in heaven.	NIG
Rev	13: 8	all whose **n** have not been written in	3950
	17: 3	with blasphemous **n** and had seven heads	3950
	17: 8	of the earth whose **n** have not been written	3950
	21:12	the **n** of the twelve tribes of Israel.	3950
	21:14	on them were the **n** of the twelve apostles	3950
	21:27	but only those whose **n** are written in	NIG

NAOMI (26) [NAOMI'S]

Ru	1: 2	Elimelech, his wife's name **N**,	5843

Ru 1: 5 and N was left without her two sons   851+2021S
   1: 6 N and her daughters-in-law prepared   2085S
   1: 8 Then N said to her two daughters-in-law,   5843
   1:11 But N said, "Return home, my daughters.   5843
   1:15 said N, "your sister-in-law is going back   NIH
   1:18 When N realized that Ruth was determined   NIH
   1:19 "Can this be N?"   5843
   1:20 "Don't call me N," she told them.   5843
   1:21 Why call me N? The LORD has afflicted me   5843
   1:22 So N returned from Moab accompanied   5843
   2: 1 N had a relative on her husband's side,   5843
   2: 2 And Ruth the Moabitess said to N,   5843
   2: 2 N said to her, "Go ahead, my daughter."   NIH
   2: 6 who came back from Moab with N.   5843
   2:20 N said to her daughter-in-law.   5843
   2:22 N said to Ruth her daughter-in-law,   5843
   3: 1 One day N her mother-in-law said to her,   5843
   3:16 Ruth came to her mother-in-law, N asked,   NIH
   3:18 Then N said, "Wait, my daughter,   NIH
   4: 3 Then he said to the kinsman-redeemer, "N,   5843
   4: 5 "On the day you buy the land from N and   5843
   4: 9 that I have bought from N all the property   5843
   4:14 The women said to N: 5843
   4:16 Then N took the child,   5843
   4:17 women living there said, "N has a son."   5843

NAOMI'S (1) [NAOMI]

Ru 1: 3 Now Elimelech, N husband, died,   5843

NAPHISH (3)

Ge 25:15 Hadad, Tema, Jetur, N and Kedemah.   5874
1Ch 1:31 N and Kedemah. These were the sons of Ishmael.   5874
   5:19 against the Hagrites, Jetur, N and Nodab.   5874

NAPHOTH (1) [NAPHOTH DOR]

Jos 17:11 (the third in the list is N).   5868

NAPHOTH DOR (3) [NAPHOTH]

Jos 11: 2 in the western foothills and in N on   5869
   12:23 the king of Dor (in N) one   5869
1Ki 4:11 Ben-Abinadab—in N (he was married   5869

NAPHTALI (53) [NAPHTALITES]

Ge 30: 8 So she named him N.   5889
   35:25 of Rachel's maidservant Bilhah: Dan and N.   5889
   46:24 The sons of N: 5889
   49:21 "N is a doe set free   5889
Ex 1: 4 Dan and N; Gad and Asher.   5889
Nu 1:15 from N, Ahira son of Enan."   5889
   1:42 From the descendants of N: 5889
   1:43 number from the tribe of N was 53,400.   5889
   2:29 The tribe of N will be next.   5889
   2:29 The leader of the people of N is Ahira son   5889
   7:78 the leader of the people of N,   5889
   10:27 over the division of the tribe of N.   1201+5889
   13:14 from the tribe of N, Nahbi son of Vophsi;   5889
   26:48 The descendants of N by their clans were: 5889
   26:50 These were the clans of N;   5889
   34:28 the leader from the tribe of N."   1201+5889
Dt 27:13 Reuben, Gad, Asher, Zebulun, Dan and N.   5889
   33:23 About N he said: 5889
   33:23 "N is abounding with the favor of   5889
   34: 2 all of N, the territory of Ephraim   5889
Jos 19:32 The sixth lot came out for N, clan by   1201+5889
   19:39 the inheritance of the tribe of N,   1201+5889
   20: 7 in Galilee in the hill country of N,   5889
   21: 6 N and the half-tribe of Manasseh   5889
   21:32 of N, Kedesh in Galilee (a city of refuge   5889
Jdg 1:33 Neither did N drive out those living   5889
   4: 6 of Abinoam from Kedesh in N and said   5889
   4: 6 take with you ten thousand men of N   1201+5889
   4:10 where he summoned Zebulun and N.   5889
   5:18 so did N on the heights of the field.   5889
   6:35 and also into Asher, Zebulun and N,   5889
   7:23 Israelites from N, Asher   5889
1Ki 4:15 in N (he had married Basemath daughter   5889
   7:14 the tribe of N and whose father was a man   5889
   15:20 and all Kinnereth in addition to N.   824+5889
2Ki 15:29 including all the land of N,   5889
1Ch 2: 2 Dan, Joseph, Benjamin, N, Gad and Asher.   5889
   6:62 of Issachar, Asher and N, and from the part   5889
   6:76 from the tribe of N they received Kedesh   5889
   7:13 The sons of N: 5889
   12:34 men of N—1,000 officers,   5889
   12:40 and N came bringing food on donkeys,   5889
   27:19 Ishmaiah son of Obadiah; over N: 5889
2Ch 16: 4 Abel Maim and all the store cities of N.   5889
   34: 6 as far as N, and in the ruins around them,   5889
Ps 68:27 and there the princes of Zebulun and of N.   5889
Isa 9: 1 of N, but in the future he will honor Galilee   5889
Eze 48: 3 "N will have one portion;   5889
   48: 4 it will border the territory of N from east   5889
   48:34 the gate of Asher and the gate of N.   5889
Mt 4:13 by the lake in the area of Zebulun and N—   3750
   4:15 "Land of Zebulun and land of N, the way   3750
Rev 7: 6 from the tribe of N 12,000,   3750

NAPHTALITES (1) [NAPHTALI]

Jdg 1:33 but the N too lived among the Canaanite   NIH

NAPHTUHITES (2)

Ge 10:13 Anamites, Lehabites, N,   5888
1Ch 1:11 Anamites, Lehabites, N,   5888

NAPKIN (KJV) See BURIAL CLOTH, CLOTH

NARCISSUS (1)

Ro 16:11 in the household of N who are in the Lord.   3727

NARD (4)

SS 4:13 with henna and n,   5948
   4:14 n and saffron, calamus and cinnamon,   5948
Mk 14: 3 very expensive perfume, made of pure n.   3726
Jn 12: 3 Then Mary took about a pint of pure n,   3726

NARROW (12) [NARROWER]

Nu 22:24 the angel of the LORD stood in a n path   5469
   22:26 a place where there was no room to turn,   7639
1Ki 6: 4 He made n clerestory windows in   357
Pr 23:27 a deep pit and a wayward wife is a n well.   7639
Isa 28:20 the blanket too n to wrap around you.   7639
Eze 40:16 by n parapet openings all around, as was   357
   40:25 and its portico had n openings all around,   NIH
   41:16 as well as the thresholds and the n windows   357
   41:26 of the portico were n windows   357
Mt 7:13 "Enter through the n gate.   5101
   7:14 the gate and n the road that leads to life,   2567
Lk 13:24 to enter through the n door,   5101

NARROWER (1) [NARROW]

Eze 42: 5 Now the upper rooms were n,   7900

NATHAN (43)

2Sa 5:14 Shammua, Shobab, N, Solomon,   5990
   7: 2 he said to N the prophet, "Here I am,   5990
   7: 3 N replied to the king, "Whatever you have   5990
   7: 4 the word of the LORD came to N, saying: 5990
   7:17 N reported to David all the words   5990
   12: 1 The LORD sent N to David.   5990
   12: 5 with anger against the man and said to N,   5990
   12: 7 Then N said to David, "You are the man!   5990
   12:13 Then David said to N, "I have sinned   5990
   12:13 sinned against the LORD." N replied,   5990
   12:15 After N had gone home,   5990
   12:25 he sent word through N the prophet   5990
   23:36 Igal son of N from Zobah, the son of Hagri,   5990
1Ki 1: 8 Benaiah son of Jehoiada, N the prophet,   5990
   1:10 not invite N the prophet or Benaiah or   5990
   1:11 Then N asked Bathsheba, Solomon's   5990
   1:22 N the prophet arrived.   5990
   1:23 they told the king, "N the prophet is here."   5990
   1:24 N said, "Have you, my lord the king,   5990
   1:32 N the prophet and Benaiah son   5990
   1:34 There have Zadok the priest and N   5990
   1:38 So Zadok the priest, N the prophet,   5990
   1:44 N the prophet, Benaiah son of Jehoiada,   5990
   1:45 and N the prophet have anointed him king   5990
   4: 5 Azariah son of N—   5990
   4: 5 Zabud son of N—   5990
1Ch 2:36 Attai was the father of N,   5990
   2:36 N the father of Zabad,   5990
   3: 5 Shammua, Shobab, N and Solomon.   5990
   11:38 Joel the brother of N, Mibhar son of Hagri,   5990
   14: 4 Shammua, Shobab, N, Solomon,   5990
   17: 1 he said to N the prophet, "Here I am,   5990
   17: 2 N replied to David, "Whatever you have   5990
   17: 3 That night the word of God came to N,   5990
   17:15 N reported to David all the words   5990
   29:29 of N the prophet and the records of Gad   5990
2Ch 9:29 not written in the records of N the prophet,   5990
   29:25 and Gad the king's seer and N the prophet;   5990
Ezr 8:16 Shemaiah, Elnathan, Jarib, Elnathan, N,   5990
   10:39 Shelemiah, N, Adaiah,   5990
Ps 51: T When the prophet N came to him   5990
Zec 12:12 the clan of the house of N and their wives,   5990
Lk 3:31 the son of Mattatha, the son of N,   3718

NATHAN-MELECH (1)

2Ki 23:11 near the room of an official named N.   5994

NATHANAEL (6)

Jn 1:45 Philip found N and told him,   3720
   1:46 anything good come from there?" N asked.   3720
   1:47 When Jesus saw N approaching,   3720
   1:48 "How do you know me?" N asked.   3720
   1:49 Then N declared, "Rabbi, you are the Son   3720
   21: 2 N from Cana in Galilee.   3720

NATION (155) [NATIONAL, NATIONALITIES, NATIONALITY, NATIONS, NATIONS']

Ge 12: 2 into a great n and I will bless you;   1580
   15:14 But I will punish the n they serve as slaves,   1580
   17:20 and I will make him into a great n.   1580
   18:18 surely become a great and powerful n,   1580
   20: 4 "Lord, will you destroy an innocent n?   1580
   21:13 the son of the maidservant into a n also,   1580
   21:18 for I will make him into a great n."   1580

Ge 35:11 A n and a community of nations will come   1580
   46: 3 for I will make you into a great n there.   1580
Ex 9:24 the land of Egypt since it had become a n.   1580
   19: 6 for me a kingdom of priests and a holy n.'   1580
   23:27 into confusion every n you encounter.   6639
   32:10 Then I will make you into a great n."   1580
   33:13 Remember that this n is your people."   1580
   34:10 before done in any n in all the world.   1580
Nu 14:12 into a n greater and stronger than they."   1580
Dt 4: 6 "Surely this great n is a wise   1580
   4: 7 What other n is so great as   1580
   4: 8 And what other n is so great as   1580
   4:34 for himself one n out of another nation,   1580
   4:34 for himself one nation out of another, n,   1580
   9:14 And I will make you into a n stronger   1580
   26: 5 and lived there and became a great n,   1580
   28:32 and daughters will be given to another n,   6639
   28:36 the king you set over you to a n unknown   1580
   28:49 The LORD will bring a n against you   1580
   28:49 in whose language you will not understand,   1580
   28:50 a fierce-looking n without respect for   1580
   32:21 by a n that has no understanding.   1580
   32:28 They are a n without sense,   1580
Jos 3:17 the whole n had completed the crossing   1580
   4: 1 When the whole n had finished crossing   1580
   5: 8 after the whole n had been circumcised,   1580
   10:13 till the n avenged itself on its enemies,   1580
Jdg 2:20 "Because this n has violated the covenant   1580
2Sa 7:23 the one n on earth that God went out   1580
1Ki 5: 7 a wise son to rule over this great n."   6639
   18:10 not a n or kingdom where my master has   1580
   18:10 a n or kingdom claimed you were not there,   1580
   18:33 the god of any n ever delivered his land   1580
1Ch 16:20 they wandered from n to nation,   1580
   16:20 they wandered from nation to n,   1580
   17:21 the one n on earth whose God went out   1580
2Ch 15: 6 One n was being crushed by another   1580
   32:15 of any n or kingdom has been able   1580
Job 34:29 Yet he is over man and n alike,   1580
Ps 33:12 Blessed is the n whose God is the LORD,   1580
   43: 1 and plead my cause against an ungodly n;   1580
   83: 4 they say, "let us destroy them as a n,   1580
   105:13 they wandered from n to nation,   1580
   105:13 they wandered from nation to n,   1580
   106: 5 the joy of your n and join your inheritance   1580
   147:20 He has done this for no other n;   1580
Pr 11:14 For lack of guidance a n falls,   6639
   14:34 Righteousness exalts a n,   1580
Isa 1: 4 Ah, sinful n, a people loaded with guilt,   1580
   2: 4 N will not take up sword against nation,   1580
   2: 4 Nation will not take up sword against n,   1580
   9: 3 the n and increased their joy;   1580
   10: 6 I send him against a godless n,   1580
   14:32 be given to the envoys of that n?   1580
   18: 2 an aggressive n of strange speech,   1580
   18: 7 an aggressive n of strange speech,   1580
   26: 2 the gates that the righteous n may enter,   1580
   26: 2 the n that keeps faith.   NIH
   26:15 You have enlarged the n, O LORD;   1580
   26:15 you have enlarged the n.   1580
   30: 6 the humps of camels, to that unprofitable n,   6639
   36:18 the god of any n ever delivered his land   1580
   49: 7 and abhorred by the n, to the servant   1580
   51: 4 "Listen to me, my people; hear me, my n: 4211
   58: 2 as if they were a n that does what is right   1580
   60:12 For the n or kingdom that will   1580
   60:22 the smallest a mighty n.   1580
   65: 1 To a n that did not call on my name, I said,   1580
   66: 8 a day or a n be brought forth in a moment?   1580
Jer 2:11 Has a n ever changed its gods?   1580
   3:19 the most beautiful inheritance of any n.'   1580
   5: 9 "Should I not avenge myself on such a n   1580
   5:15 "I am bringing a distant n against you—   1580
   5:15 an ancient and enduring n,   1580
   5:29 "Should I not avenge myself on such a n   1580
   6:22 a great n is being stirred up from the ends   1580
   7:28 'This is the n that has not obeyed   1580
   8: 3 the survivors of this evil n will prefer death   5476
   9: 9 "Should I not avenge myself on such a n?   1580
   12:17 But if any n does not listen,   1580
   18: 7 that a n or kingdom is to be uprooted,   1580
   18: 8 and if that n I warned repents of its evil,   1580
   18: 9 And if at another time I announce that a n   1580
   19:11 I will smash this n and this city just   6639
   25:12 I will punish the king of Babylon and his n,   1580
   25:32 Disaster is spreading from n to nation;   1580
   25:32 Disaster is spreading from nation to n;   1580
   27: 8 any n or kingdom will not serve   1580
   27: 8 I will punish that n with the sword,   1580
   27:11 if any n will bow its neck under the yoke of   1580
   27:11 I will let that n remain in its own land to   2257S
   27:13 the LORD has threatened any n that will   1580
   28:15 you have persuaded this n to trust in lies.   6639
   31:36 'Israel ever cease to be a n before me."   1580
   33:24 and no longer regard them as a n.   1580
   48: 2 'Come, let us put an end to that n.'   1580
   48:42 be destroyed as a n because she defied   6639
   49:31 "Arise and attack a n at ease,   1580
   49:31 "a n that has neither gates nor bars;   NIH
   49:36 to the four winds, and there will not be a n   1580
   50: 3 A n from the north will attack her   1580
   50:41 a great n and many kings are being stirred   1580
La 4:17 from our towers we watched for a n   1580
Eze 2: 3 a rebellious n that has rebelled against me;   1580
   36:13 "You devour men and deprive your n   1580
   36:14 or make your n childless,   1580
   36:15 the scorn of the peoples or cause your n   1580

Eze	37:22	I will make them one **n** in the land,	1580
Da	3:29	Therefore I decree that the people of any **n**	10040
	8:22	that will emerge from his **n** but will	1580
Joel	1: 6	A **n** has invaded my land,	1580
	3: 8	sell them to the Sabeans, a **n** far away."	1580
Am	6: 1	you notable men of the foremost **n**,	1580
	6:14	"I will stir up a **n** against you,	1580
Mic	4: 3	**N** will not take up sword against nation,	1580
	4: 3	Nation will not take up sword against **n**,	1580
	4: 7	those driven away a strong **n**.	1580
Hab	3:16	of calamity to come on the **n** invading us.	6639
Zep	2: 1	gather together, O shameful **n**,	1580
	2: 9	of my **n** will inherit their land."	1580
Hag	2:14	with this people and this **n** in my sight,'	1580
Mal	1: 4	under a curse—the whole **n** of you—	1580
Mt	24: 7	**N** will rise against nation,	1620
	24: 7	Nation will rise against **n**,	1620
Mk	13: 8	**N** will rise against nation,	1620
	13: 8	Nation will rise against **n**,	1620
Lk	7: 5	because he loves our **n**	1620
	21:10	"**N** will rise against nation,	1620
	21:10	"Nation will rise against **n**,	1620
	23: 2	"We have found this man subverting our **n**.	1620
Jn	11:48	and take away both our place and our **n**."	1620
	11:50	the people than that the whole **n** perish."	1620
	11:51	that Jesus would die for the Jewish **n**,	1620
	11:52	for that **n** but also for the scattered children	1620
Ac	2: 5	from every **n** under heaven.	1620
	7: 7	I will punish the **n** they serve as slaves,'	1620
	10:35	but accepts men from every **n** who fear him	1620
	17:26	From one man he made every **n** of men,	1620
	24: 2	has brought about reforms *in* this **n**.	1620
	24:10	of years you have been a judge *over* this **n**;	1620
Ro	10:19	envious by those who are not a **n**,	1620
	10:19	angry by a **n** that has no understanding."	1620
1Pe	2: 9	a holy **n**, a people belonging to God,	1620
Rev	5: 9	and language and people and **n**.	1620
	7: 9	from every **n**, tribe, people and language,	1620
	11: 9	language and **n** will gaze on their bodies	1620
	13: 7	people, language and **n**.	1620
	14: 6	to every **n**, tribe, language and people.	1620

NATIONAL (1) [NATION]

2Ki	17:29	**each n group** made its own gods in	1580+1580

NATIONALITIES (2) [NATION]

Est	8:17	And many people of **other n** became Jews	824+2021+6639
	9: 2	the people of all the other **n** were afraid	6639

NATIONALITY (5) [NATION]

Est	2:10	not revealed her **n** and family background,	6639
	2:20	and **n** just as Mordecai had told her to do,	6639
	3:14	and made known to the people of every **n**	NIH
	8:11	kill and annihilate any armed force of any **n**	6639
	8:13	of every **n** so that the Jews would be ready	6639

NATIONS (559) [NATION]

Ge	10: 5	by their clans within their **n**,	1580
	10:20	in their territories and **n**.	1580
	10:31	in their territories and **n**.	1580
	10:32	to their lines of descent, within their **n**.	1580
	10:32	From these the **n** spread out over the earth	1580
	17: 4	You will be the father of many **n**.	1580
	17: 5	for I have made you a father of many **n**.	1580
	17: 6	I will make **n** of you,	1580
	17:16	so that she will be the mother of **n**;	1580
	18:18	all **n** on earth will be blessed through him.	1580
	22:18	through your offspring all **n** *on* earth will	1580
	25:23	"Two **n** are in your womb,	1580
	26: 4	through your offspring all **n** *on* earth will	1580
	27:29	May **n** serve you and peoples bow down	6639
	35:11	and a community of **n** will come from you,	1580
	48:19	his descendants will become a group of **n**."	1580
	49:10	and the obedience of the **n** is his.	6639
Ex	15:14	The **n** will hear and tremble;	6639
	19: 5	then out of all **n** you will be my treasured	6639
	34:24	I will drive out **n** before you	1580
Lev	18:24	because this is how the **n** that I am going	1580
	18:28	it will vomit you out as it vomited out the **n**	1580
	20:23	the customs of the **n** I am going to drive out	1580
	20:24	who has set you apart from the **n**.	6639
	20:26	and I have set you apart from the **n** to	6639
	25:44	and female slaves are to come from the **n**	1580
	26:33	among the **n** and will draw out my sword	1580
	26:38	You will perish among the **n**;	1580
	26:45	in the sight of the **n** to be their God.	1580
Nu	14:15	the **n** who have heard this report	1580
	23: 9	not consider themselves one of the **n**.	1580
	24: 8	They devour hostile **n**	1580
	24:20	"Amalek was first among the **n**,	1580
Dt	2:25	to put the terror and fear of you on all the **n**	6639
	4: 6	and understanding to the **n**,	6639
	4:19	to all the **n** under heaven.	6639
	4:27	the **n** to which the LORD will drive you.	1580
	4:38	before you greater and stronger than you	1580
	7: 1	and drives out before you many **n**—	1580
	7: 1	seven **n** larger and stronger than you—	1580
	7:17	"These **n** are stronger than we are.	1580
	7:22	The LORD your God will drive out those **n**	1580
	8:20	the **n** the LORD destroyed before you,	1580
	9: 1	the Jordan to go in and dispossess **n** greater	1580
	9: 4	on account of the wickedness of these **n**	1580
	9: 5	on account of the wickedness of these **n**,	1580

Dt	10:15	their descendants, above all the **n**,	6639
	11:23	then the LORD will drive out all these **n**	1580
	11:23	and you will dispossess **n** larger	1580
	12: 2	**n** you are dispossessing worship their gods.	1580
	12:29	before you the **n** you are about to invade	1580
	12:30	saying, "How do these **n** serve their gods?	1580
	15: 6	lend to many **n** but will borrow from none.	1580
	15: 6	over many **n** but none will rule over you.	1580
	17:14	a king over us like all the **n** around us,"	1580
	18: 9	the detestable ways of the **n** there.	1580
	18:12	the LORD your God will drive out *those* **n**	4392S
	18:14	The **n** you will dispossess listen	1580
	19: 1	the **n** whose land he is giving you,	1580
	20:15	and do not belong to the **n** nearby.	1580
	20:16	the **n** the LORD your God is giving you as	6639
	26:19	and honor high above all the **n** he has made	1580
	28: 1	above all the **n** *on* earth.	1580
	28:12	You will lend to many **n** but will borrow	1580
	28:37	an object of scorn and ridicule to all the **n**	6639
	28:64	the LORD will scatter you among all **n**,	6639
	28:65	Among those **n** you will find no repose,	1580
	29:18	to go and worship the gods of those **n**;	1580
	29:24	All the **n** will ask:	1580
	30: 1	LORD your God disperses you among the **n**,	1580
	30: 3	on you and gather you again from all the **n**	6639
	31: 3	He will destroy these **n** before you,	1580
	32: 8	the Most High gave the **n** their inheritance,	1580
	32:43	Rejoice, O **n**, with his people,	1580
	33:17	With them he will gore the **n**,	6639
Jos	23: 3	to all these **n** for your sake;	1580
	23: 4	for your tribes all the land of the **n**	1580
	23: 4	the **n** I conquered—	1580
	23: 7	Do not associate with these **n** that remain	1580
	23: 9	before you great and powerful **n**;	1580
	23:12	with the survivors of these **n** that remain	1580
	23:13	LORD your God will no longer drive out these **n** before you.	1580
	24:17	among all the **n** through which we traveled.	6639
	24:18	the LORD drove out before us all the **n**,	6639
Jdg	2:21	before them any of the **n** Joshua left	1580
	2:23	The LORD had allowed those **n** to remain;	1580
	3: 1	These are the **n** the LORD left	1580
1Sa	8: 5	such as all the other **n** have."	1580
	8:20	Then we will be like all the other **n**,	1580
2Sa	7:23	and awesome wonders by driving out **n**	1580
	8:11	and gold from all the **n** he had subdued:	1580
	22:44	you have preserved me as the head of **n**.	1580
	22:48	who puts the **n** under me,	6639
	22:50	I will praise you, O LORD, among the **n**;	1580
1Ki	4:31	his fame spread to all the surrounding **n**.	1580
	4:34	Men of all **n** came to listen	6639
	8:53	For you singled them out from all the **n** of	6639
	11: 2	from **n** about which the LORD had told	1580
	14:24	of the **n** the LORD had driven out before	1580
2Ki	16: 3	of the **n** the LORD had driven out before	1580
	17: 8	of the **n** the LORD had driven out	1580
	17:11	as the **n** whom the LORD had driven out	1580
	17:15	They imitated the **n** around them although	1580
	17:33	of the **n** from which they had been brought.	1580
	19:12	Did the gods of the **n** that were destroyed	1580
	19:17	the Assyrian kings have laid waste these **n**	1580
	21: 2	following the detestable practices of the **n**	1580
	21: 9	than the **n** the LORD had destroyed before	1580
1Ch	14:17	and the LORD made all the **n** fear him	1580
	16: 8	among the **n** what he has done.	6639
	16:24	Declare his glory among the **n**,	6639
	16:26	For all the gods of the **n** are idols,	6639
	16:28	Ascribe to the LORD, O families of **n**,	6639
	16:31	let them say among the **n**,	1580
	16:35	gather us and deliver us from the **n**,	1580
	17:21	by driving out **n** from before your people,	1580
	18:11	and gold he had taken from all these **n**:	824
2Ch	20: 6	You rule over all the kingdoms of the **n**.	1580
	28: 3	of the **n** the LORD had driven out before	1580
	32:13	of those **n** ever able to deliver their land	824+1580
	32:14	Who of all the gods of these **n**	1580
	32:23	then on he was highly regarded by all the **n**.	1580
	33: 2	following the detestable practices of the **n**	1580
	33: 9	the **n** the LORD had destroyed before	1580
	36:14	practices of the **n** and defiling the temple of	1580
Ne	1: 8	I will scatter you among the **n**,	1580
	5:17	to us from the surrounding **n**.	1580
	6: 6	"It is reported among the **n**—	1580
	6:16	all the surrounding **n** were afraid	1580
	9:22	"You gave them kingdoms and **n**,	6639
	13:26	the many **n** there was no king like him.	1580
Job	12:23	He makes **n** great, and destroys them;	1580
	12:23	he enlarges **n**, and disperses them.	1580
	36:31	the way he governs the **n** and provides food	6639
Ps	2: 1	Why do the **n** conspire and the peoples plot	1580
	2: 8	and I will make the **n** your inheritance,	1580
	9: 5	You have rebuked the **n** and destroyed	1580
	9:11	proclaim among the **n** what he has done.	6639
	9:15	**n** have fallen into the pit they have dug;	1580
	9:17	all the **n** that forget God.	1580
	9:19	let the **n** be judged in your presence.	1580
	9:20	let the **n** know they are but men.	1580
	10:16	the **n** will perish from his land.	1580
	18:43	you have made me the head of **n**;	1580
	18:47	who subdues **n** under me,	6639
	18:49	Therefore I will praise you among the **n**;	1580
	22:27	and all the families of the **n** will bow down	1580
	22:28	to the LORD and he rules over the **n**.	1580
	33:10	The LORD foils the plans of the **n**;	1580
	44: 2	With your hand you drove out the **n**	1580
	44:11	and have scattered us among the **n**.	1580

Ps	44:14	You have made us a byword among the **n**;	1580
	45: 5	let the **n** fall beneath your feet.	6639
	45:17	the **n** will praise you for ever and ever.	6639
	46: 6	**N** are in uproar, kingdoms fall;	1580
	46:10	I will be exalted among the **n**,	1580
	47: 1	Clap your hands, all you **n**;	6639
	47: 3	He subdued **n** under us,	6639
	47: 8	God reigns over the **n**;	1580
	47: 9	The nobles of the **n** assemble as the people	6639
	56: 7	in your anger, O God, bring down the **n**.	6639
	57: 9	I will praise you, O Lord, among the **n**;	6639
	59: 5	rouse yourself to punish all the **n**;	1580
	59: 8	you scoff at all those **n**.	1580
	65: 7	and the turmoil of the **n**.	4211
	66: 7	his eyes watch the **n**—	1580
	67: 2	your salvation among all **n**.	1580
	67: 4	May the **n** be glad and sing for joy,	4211
	67: 4	the peoples justly and guide the **n** of	4211
	68:30	the herd of bulls among the calves of the **n**.	6639
	68:30	Scatter the **n** who delight in war.	6639
	72:11	down to him and all **n** will serve him.	1580
	72:17	All **n** will be blessed through him,	1580
	78:55	He drove out **n** before them	1580
	79: 1	the **n** have invaded your inheritance;	1580
	79: 6	on the **n** that do not acknowledge you,	1580
	79:10	Why should the **n** say,	1580
	79:10	make known among the **n** that you avenge	1580
	80: 8	you drove out the **n** and planted it.	1580
	82: 8	for all the **n** are your inheritance.	1580
	86: 9	All the **n** you have made will come	1580
	89:50	I bear in my heart the taunts of all the **n**,	6639
	94:10	Does he who disciplines **n** not punish?	1580
	96: 3	Declare his glory among the **n**,	1580
	96: 5	For all the gods of the **n** are idols,	6639
	96: 7	Ascribe to the LORD, O families of **n**,	6639
	96:10	Say among the **n**, "The LORD reigns."	1580
	98: 2	and revealed his righteousness to the **n**.	1580
	99: 1	The LORD reigns, let the **n** tremble;	1580
	99: 2	he is exalted over all the **n**.	1580
	102:15	The **n** will fear the name of the LORD,	1580
	105: 1	among the **n** what he has done.	6639
	105:44	the lands of the **n**, and they fell heir	1580
	106:27	the **n** and scatter them throughout the lands.	1580
	106:35	with the **n** and adopted their customs.	1580
	106:41	He handed them over to the **n**,	1580
	106:47	and gather us from the **n**,	1580
	108: 3	I will praise you, O LORD, among the **n**;	6639
	110: 6	He will judge the **n**,	1580
	111: 6	giving them the lands of other **n**.	1580
	113: 4	The LORD is exalted over all the **n**,	1580
	115: 2	Why do the **n** say, "Where is their God?"	1580
	117: 1	Praise the LORD, all you **n**;	1580
	118:10	All the **n** surrounded me,	1580
	126: 2	Then it was said among the **n**,	1580
	135:10	down many **n** and killed mighty kings—	1580
	135:15	The idols of the **n** are silver and gold,	1580
	148:11	kings of the earth and all **n**,	4211
	149: 7	on the **n** and punishment on the peoples,	1580
Pr	24:24	and **n** denounce him.	4211
Isa	2: 2	All the **n** will stream to it.	1580
	2: 4	He will judge between the **n**	1580
	5:26	He lifts up a banner for the distant **n**,	1580
	8: 9	Raise the war cry, you **n**, and be shattered!	6639
	10: 7	to put an end to many **n**.	1580
	10:13	I removed the boundaries of **n**,	6639
	10:14	my hand reached for the wealth of the **n**;	6639
	11:10	the **n** will rally to him,	1580
	11:12	He will raise a banner for the **n** and gather	1580
	12: 4	among the **n** what he has done,	6639
	13: 4	like **n** massing together!	1580
	14: 2	**N** will take them and bring them	6639
	14: 2	of Israel will possess **the n** as menservants	4392S
	14: 6	in fury subdued **n** with relentless aggression	1580
	14: 9	all those who were kings over the **n**.	1580
	14:12	you who once laid low the **n**!	1580
	14:18	All the kings of the **n** lie in state,	1580
	14:26	this is the hand stretched out over all **n**.	1580
	16: 8	The rulers of the **n** have trampled down	1580
	17:12	Oh, the raging of many **n**—	6639
	23: 3	and she became the marketplace of the **n**.	1580
	24:13	So will it be on the earth and among the **n**,	6639
	25: 3	cities of ruthless **n** will revere you.	1580
	25: 7	the sheet that covers all **n**;	1580
	29: 7	hordes of all the **n** that fight against Ariel,	1580
	29: 8	of all the **n** that fight against Mount Zion.	1580
	30:28	He shakes the **n** in the sieve of destruction;	1580
	33: 3	when you rise up, the **n** scatter.	1580
	33: 4	O **n**, is harvested as by young locusts;	NIH
	34: 1	Come near, you **n**, and listen;	1580
	34: 2	The LORD is angry with all **n**;	1580
	37:12	Did the gods of the **n** that were destroyed	1580
	40:15	Surely the **n** are like a drop in a bucket;	1580
	40:17	Before him all the **n** are as nothing;	1580
	41: 1	Let the **n** renew their strength!	4211
	41: 2	He hands **n** over to him and subdues kings	1580
	42: 1	on him and he will bring justice to the **n**.	1580
	43: 9	All the **n** gather together and	1580
	45: 1	of to subdue **n** before him and to strip kings	1580
	45:20	assemble, you fugitives from the **n**.	1580
	49: 1	hear this, you distant **n**:	4211
	51: 4	my justice will become a light to the **n**.	6639
	51: 5	and my arm will bring justice to the **n**.	6639
	52:10	bare his holy arm in the sight of all the **n**,	1580
	52:15	so will he sprinkle many **n**,	1580
	54: 3	your descendants will dispossess **n**	1580
	55: 5	Surely you will summon **n** you know not,	1580
	55: 5	**n** that do not know you will hasten to you,	1580

Isa	56: 7	be called a house of prayer for all **n**."	6639
	60: 3	**N** will come to your light,	1580
	60: 5	to you the riches of the **n** will come.	1580
	60:11	that men may bring you the wealth of the **n**	1580
	60:16	the milk of **n** and be nursed at royal breasts.	1580
	61: 6	You will feed on the wealth of **n**,	1580
	61: 9	be known among the **n** and their offspring	1580
	61:11	and praise spring up before all **n**.	1580
	62: 2	The **n** will see your righteousness.	1580
	62:10	Raise a banner for the **n**.	6639
	63: 3	from the **n** no one was with me.	6639
	63: 6	I trampled the **n** in my anger;	6639
	64: 2	to your enemies and cause the **n** to quake	1580
	66:12	and the wealth of **n** like a flooding stream;	1580
	66:18	about to come and gather in all **n** and tongues,	1580
	66:19	of those who survive to the **n**—	1580
	66:19	They will proclaim my glory among the **n**.	1580
	66:20	**n**, to my holy mountain in Jerusalem as	1580
Jer	1: 5	I appointed you as a prophet to the **n**."	1580
	1:10	today I appoint you over **n** and kingdoms	1580
	3:17	and all **n** will gather in Jerusalem to honor	1580
	4: 2	then the **n** will be blessed by him and	1580
	4: 7	a destroyer of **n** has set out.	1580
	4:16	"Tell this to the **n**, proclaim it to Jerusalem:	1580
	6:18	Therefore hear, O **n**; observe,	1580
	9:16	I will scatter them among **n**	1580
	9:26	For all these **n** are really uncircumcised,	1580
	10: 2	the ways of the **n** or be terrified by signs in	1580
	10: 2	though the **n** are terrified by them.	1580
	10: 7	O King of the **n**?	1580
	10: 7	Among all the wise men of the **n** and	1580
	10:10	the **n** cannot endure his wrath.	1580
	10:25	on the **n** that do not acknowledge you,	1580
	14:22	of the worthless idols of the **n** bring rain?	1580
	16:19	the **n** will come from the ends of the earth	1580
	18:13	Inquire among the **n**:	1580
	22: 8	"People from many **n** will pass by this city	1580
	25: 9	and against all the surrounding **n**.	1580
	25:11	and these **n** will serve the king	1580
	25:13	by Jeremiah against all the **n**.	1580
	25:14	be enslaved by many **n** and great kings;	1580
	25:15	the wine of my wrath and make all the **n**	1580
	25:17	from the LORD's hand and made all the **n**	1580
	25:31	the LORD will bring charges against the **n**;	1580
	26: 6	of cursing among all the **n** of the earth.'"	1580
	27: 7	All **n** will serve him and his son	1580
	27: 7	then many **n** and great kings will subjugate	1580
	28:11	the neck of all the **n** within two years.'"	1580
	28:14	an iron yoke on the necks of all these **n**	1580
	29:14	I will gather you from all the **n** and places	1580
	29:18	among all the **n** where I drive them.	1580
	30:11	'Though I completely destroy all the **n**	1580
	31: 7	shout for the foremost of the **n**.	1580
	31:10	"Hear the word of the LORD, O **n**;	1580
	33: 9	and honor before all **n** on earth that hear	1580
	36: 2	the other **n** from the time I began speaking	1580
	43: 5	to live in the land of Judah from all the **n**	1580
	44: 8	of cursing and reproach among all the **n**	1580
	46: 1	to Jeremiah the prophet concerning the **n**:	1580
	46:12	The **n** will hear of your shame;	1580
	46:28	"Though I completely destroy all the **n**	1580
	49:14	An envoy was sent to the **n** to say,	1580
	49:15	"Now I will make you small among the **n**,	1580
	50: 2	and proclaim among the **n**, lift up a banner	1580
	50: 9	against Babylon an alliance of great **n** from	1580
	50:12	She will be the least of the **n**—	1580
	50:23	How desolate is Babylon among the **n**!	1580
	50:46	its cry will resound among the **n**.	1580
	51: 7	The **n** drank her wine;	1580
	51:20	with you I shatter **n**,	1580
	51:27	Blow the trumpet among the **n**!	1580
	51:27	Prepare the **n** for battle against her;	1580
	51:28	Prepare the **n** for battle against her—	1580
	51:41	a horror Babylon will be among the **n**!	1580
	51:44	The **n** will no longer stream to him.	1580
La	1: 1	who once was great among the **n**!	1580
	1: 3	She dwells among the **n**;	1580
	1:10	she saw **pagan n** enter her sanctuary—	1580
	2: 9	and her princes are exiled among the **n**,	1580
	3:45	and refuse among the **n**.	6639
	4:15	people among the **n** say,	1580
	4:20	under his shadow we would live among the **n**.	1580
Eze	4:13	of Israel will eat defiled food among the **n**	1580
	5: 5	which I have set in the center of the **n**,	1580
	5: 6	and decrees more than the **n** and countries	1580
	5: 7	You have been more unruly than the **n**	1580
	5: 7	even conformed to the standards of the **n**.	1580
	5: 8	punishment on you in the sight of the **n**.	1580
	5:14	and a reproach among the **n** around you,	1580
	5:15	the **n** around you when I inflict punishment	1580
	6: 8	among the lands and **n**.	1580
	6: 9	the **n** where they have been carried captive,	1580
	7:24	the most wicked of the **n** to take possession	1580
	11:12	to the standards of the **n** around you."	1580
	11:16	Although I sent them far away among the **n**	1580
	11:17	the **n** and bring you back from the countries	6639
	12:15	among the **n** and scatter them through	1580
	12:16	so that in the **n** where they go	1580
	16:14	among the **n** on account of your beauty,	1580
	19: 4	The **n** heard about him,	1580
	19: 8	Then the **n** came against him,	1580
	20: 9	in the eyes of the **n** they lived among and	1580
	20:14	from being profaned in the eyes of the **n**	1580
	20:22	from being profaned in the eyes of the **n**	1580
	20:23	that I would disperse them among the **n**	1580
	20:32	" 'You say, "We want to be like the **n**,	1580
Eze	20:34	I will bring you from the **n** and gather you	6639
	20:35	I will bring you into the desert of the **n**	6639
	20:41	the **n** and gather you from the countries	6639
	20:41	among you in the sight of the **n**.	1580
	22: 4	of scorn to the **n** and a laughingstock to all	1580
	22:15	the **n** and scatter you through the countries;	1580
	22:16	you have been defiled in the eyes of the **n**,	1580
	23:30	the **n** and be defiled yourself with their idols.	1580
	25: 7	and give you as plunder to the **n**.	1580
	25: 7	from the **n** and exterminate you from	1580
	25: 8	of Judah has become like all the other **n**,"	1580
	25:10	not be remembered among the **n**;	1580
	26: 2	The gate to the **n** is broken,	1580
	26: 3	and I will bring many **n** against you,	1580
	26: 5	She will become plunder for the **n**,	1580
	27:33	you satisfied many **n**;	6639
	27:36	The merchants among the **n** hiss at you;	6639
	28:19	the most ruthless of **n**;	1580
	28:19	the **n** who knew you are appalled at you;	6639
	28:25	from the **n** where they have been scattered,	6639
	28:25	among them in the sight of the **n**.	1580
	29:12	the Egyptians among the **n** and scatter them	1580
	29:13	from the **n** where they were scattered.	6639
	29:15	never again exalt itself above the other **n**.	1580
	29:15	that it will never again rule over the **n**.	1580
	30: 3	a day of clouds, a time of doom for the **n**.	1580
	30:11	He and his army—the most ruthless of **n**—	1580
	30:23	the Egyptians among the **n** and scatter them	1580
	30:26	the Egyptians among the **n** and scatter them	1580
	31: 6	all the great **n** lived in its shade.	1580
	31:11	I handed it over to the ruler of the **n**,	1580
	31:12	the most ruthless of foreign **n** cut it down	1580
	31:12	All the **n** of the earth came out from	6639
	31:16	I made the **n** tremble at the sound of its fall	1580
	31:17	its allies among the **n**,	1580
	32: 2	" 'You are like a lion among the **n**;	1580
	32: 9	about your destruction among the **n**,	1580
	32:12	the most ruthless of all **n**.	1580
	32:16	The daughters of the **n** will chant it;	1580
	32:18	both her and the daughters of mighty **n**,	1580
	34:13	the **n** and gather them from the countries,	6639
	34:28	They will no longer be plundered by the **n**,	1580
	34:29	in the land or bear the scorn of the **n**.	1580
	35:10	"These two **n** and countries will be ours	1580
	36: 3	the possession of the rest of the **n** and	1580
	36: 4	by the rest of the **n** around you—	1580
	36: 5	against the rest of the **n**,	1580
	36: 6	you have suffered the scorn of the **n**.	1580
	36: 7	that the **n** around you will also suffer scorn.	1580
	36:15	will I make you hear the taunts of the **n**,	1580
	36:19	I dispersed them among the **n**,	1580
	36:20	among the **n** they profaned my holy name,	1580
	36:21	the house of Israel profaned among the **n**	1580
	36:22	which you have profaned among the **n**	1580
	36:23	which has been profaned among the **n**	1580
	36:23	Then the **n** will know that I am the LORD,	1580
	36:24	" 'For I will take you out of the **n**;	1580
	36:30	among the **n** because of famine.	1580
	36:36	the **n** around you that remain will know	1580
	37:21	I will take the Israelites out of the **n**	1580
	37:22	and they will never again be two **n**	1580
	37:28	Then the **n** will know that I the LORD	1580
	38: 6	the many **n** with you.	6639
	38: 8	whose people were gathered from many **n**	6639
	38: 8	They had been brought out from the **n**,	6639
	38: 9	the many **n** with you will go up, advancing	1580
	38:12	and the people gathered from the **n**,	1580
	38:15	you and many **n** with you,	6639
	38:16	so that the **n** may know me	1580
	38:22	on his troops and on the many **n** with him.	6639
	38:23	make myself known in the sight of many **n**.	1580
	39: 4	you and all your troops and the **n** with you.	6639
	39: 7	and the **n** will know that I the LORD am	1580
	39:21	"I will display my glory among the **n**,	1580
	39:21	the **n** will see the punishment I inflict and	1580
	39:23	and the **n** will know that the people	1580
	39:27	When I have brought them back from the **n**	6639
	39:27	through them in the sight of many **n**.	1580
	39:28	though I sent them into exile among the **n**,	1580
Da	3: 4	O peoples, **n** and men of every language:	10040
	3: 7	**n** and men of every language fell down	10040
	4: 1	**n** and men of every language,	10040
	5:19	and **n** and men of every language dreaded	10040
	6:25	**n** and men of every language throughout	10040
	7:14	all peoples, **n** and men of every language	10040
	12: 1	not happened from the beginning of **n**	1580
Hos	7: 8	"Ephraim mixes with the **n**;	6639
	8: 8	she is among the **n** like a worthless thing.	1580
	8:10	they have sold themselves among the **n**,	1580
	9: 1	do not be jubilant like the other **n**.	6639
	9:17	they will be wanderers among the **n**.	1580
	10:10	**n** will be gathered against them to put them	6639
Joel	2: 6	At the sight of them, **n** are in anguish;	6639
	2:17	a byword among the **n**.	1580
	2:19	an object of scorn to the **n**.	1580
	3: 2	I will gather all **n** and bring them down to	1580
	3: 2	for they scattered my people among the **n**	1580
	3: 9	Proclaim this among the **n**:	1580
	3:11	Come quickly, all you **n** from every side,	1580
	3:12	"Let the **n** be roused;	1580
	3:12	for there I will sit to judge all the **n**	1580
Am	9: 9	of Israel among all the **n** as grain is shaken	1580
	9:12	of Edom and all the **n** that bear my name,"	1580
Ob	1: 1	An envoy was sent to the **n** to say, "Rise,	1580
	1: 2	I will make you small among the **n**,	1580
	1:15	"The day of the LORD is near for all **n**.	1580
	1:16	so all the **n** will drink continually;	1580
Mic	4: 2	Many **n** will come and say, "Come,	1580
	4: 3	and will settle disputes for strong **n** far	1580
	4: 5	the **n** may walk in the name of their gods;	6639
	4:11	But now many **n** are gathered against you.	1580
	4:13	and you will break to pieces many **n**."	6639
	5: 8	The remnant of Jacob will be among the **n**,	1580
	5:15	in anger and wrath upon the **n** that have	1580
	6:16	you will bear the scorn of the **n**."	6639
	7:16	**N** will see and be ashamed,	1580
Na	3: 4	who enslaved **n** by her prostitution	1580
	3: 5	I will show the **n** your nakedness and	1580
Hab	1: 5	"Look at the **n** and watch—	1580
	1:17	destroying **n** without mercy?	1580
	2: 5	to himself all the **n** and takes captive all	1580
	2: 8	Because you have plundered many **n**,	1580
	2:13	that the **n** exhaust themselves for nothing?	4211
	3: 6	he looked, and made the **n** tremble.	1580
	3:12	the earth and in anger you threshed the **n**.	1580
Zep	2:11	The **n** on every shore will worship him,	1580
	3: 6	"I have cut off **n**; their strongholds	1580
	3: 8	I have decided to assemble the **n**,	1580
Hag	2: 7	I will shake all **n**,	1580
	2: 7	and the desired of all **n** will come,	1580
Zec	1:15	I am very angry with the **n** that feel secure.	1580
	1:21	of the **n** who lifted up their horns against	1580
	2: 8	against the **n** that have plundered you—	1580
	2:11	"Many **n** will be joined with the LORD in	1580
	7:14	with a whirlwind among all the **n**,	1580
	8:13	an object of cursing among the **n**,	1580
	8:22	and powerful **n** will come to Jerusalem	1580
	8:23	and **n** will take firm hold of one Jew by	1580
	9:10	He will proclaim peace to the **n**.	1580
	11:10	the covenant I had made with all the **n**.	6639
	12: 3	the **n** of the earth are gathered against her,	1580
	12: 3	an immovable rock for all the **n**.	6639
	12: 4	but I will blind all the horses of the **n**.	6639
	12: 9	to destroy all the **n** that attack Jerusalem.	1580
	14: 2	I will gather all the **n** to Jerusalem to fight	1580
	14: 3	and fight against those **n**,	1580
	14:12	with which the LORD will strike all the **n**	6639
	14:14	of all the surrounding **n** will be collected—	1580
	14:16	the **n** that have attacked Jerusalem will go	1580
	14:18	on them the plague he inflicts on the **n**	1580
	14:19	the punishment of all the **n** that do not go	1580
Mal	1:11	My name will be great among the **n**,	1580
	1:11	my name will be great among the **n**,"	1580
	1:14	"and my name is to be feared among the **n**.	1580
	3:12	"Then all the **n** will call you blessed,	1580
Mt	12:18	and he will proclaim justice to the **n**.	*1620*
	12:21	In his name the **n** will put their hope."	*1620*
	24: 9	you will be hated by all **n** because of me.	*1620*
	24:14	in the whole world as a testimony to all **n**,	*1620*
	24:30	and all the **n** of the earth will mourn.	*5876*
	25:32	All the **n** will be gathered before him,	*1620*
	28:19	Therefore go and make disciples of all **n**,	*1620*
Mk	11:17	be called a house of prayer *for* all **n**'?	*1620*
	13:10	the gospel must first be preached to all **n**.	*1620*
Lk	21:24	and will be taken as prisoners to all the **n**.	*1620*
	21:25	**n** will be in anguish and perplexity at	*1620*
	24:47	be preached in his name to all **n**,	*1620*
Ac	4:25	" 'Why do the **n** rage and the peoples plot	*1620*
	7:45	*from* the **n** God drove out before them.	*1620*
	13:19	he overthrew seven **n** in Canaan	*1620*
	14:16	In the past, he let all **n** go their own way.	*1620*
Ro	4:17	"I have made you a father of many **n**."	*1620*
	4:18	and so became the father *of* many **n**,	*1620*
	15:12	one who will arise to rule over the **n**;	*1620*
	16:26	so that all **n** might believe and obey him—	*1620*
Gal	3: 8	"All **n** will be blessed through you."	*1620*
1Ti	3:16	was preached among the **n**,	*1620*
Jas	1: 1	To the twelve tribes scattered among the **n**:	*NIG*
Rev	2:26	I will give authority over the **n**—	*1620*
	10:11	many peoples, **n**, languages and kings."	*1620*
	11:18	The **n** were angry;	*1620*
	12: 5	who will rule all the **n** with an iron scepter.	*1620*
	14: 8	the **n** drink the maddening wine	*1620*
	15: 4	All **n** will come and worship before you,	*1620*
	16:19	and the cities *of* the **n** collapsed.	*1620*
	17:15	are peoples, multitudes, **n** and languages.	*1620*
	18: 3	the **n** have drunk the maddening wine	*1620*
	18:23	your magic spell all the **n** were led astray.	*1620*
	19:15	with which to strike down the **n**.	*1620*
	20: 3	to keep him from deceiving the **n** anymore	*1620*
	20: 8	the **n** in the four corners of the earth—	*1620*
	21:24	The **n** will walk by its light,	*1620*
	21:26	and honor *of* the **n** will be brought into it.	*1620*
	22: 2	of the tree are for the healing *of* the **n**.	*1620*

NATIONS' (1) [NATION]

Jer	51:58	the **n'** labor is only fuel for the flames."	4211

NATIVE (13) [NATIVES]

Ge	24: 7	of my father's household and my **n** land	4580
	31:13	at once and go back to your **n** land.'"	4580
Nu		near the River, in his **n** land.	1201+6639
Ps	37:35	like a green tree in its **n** soil,	275
Isa	13:14	each will flee to his **n** land.	824
Jer	22:10	nor see his **n** land again	4580
	46:16	to our own people and our **n** lands,	4580
Am	7:11	away from their **n** land.'"	141
	7:17	away from their **n** land.'"	141
Jn	8:44	When he lies, he speaks **his n language**, *1666+2625+3836*
Ac	2: 8	each of us hears them in his own language? *1164+1877+4005*

Ac 18: 2 a Jew named Aquila, a **n** of Pontus,   *1169*
18:24 a Jew named Apollos, a **n** of Alexandria,   *1169*

NATIVE-BORN (15) [BEAR]

Ex 12:19 whether he is an alien or **n**.   275+824+2021
12:49 to the **n** and to the alien living among you."   275
Lev 16:29 whether **n** or an alien living among you—   275
17:15 " 'Anyone, whether **n** or alien,   275
18:26 The **n** and the aliens living   275
19:34 with you must be treated as one of your **n**.   275
23:42 All **n** Israelites are to live in booths   275
24:16 Whether an alien or **n**,   275
24:22 the same law for the alien and the **n**.   275
Nu 9:14 for the alien and the **n**.' "   275+824
15:13 " 'Everyone who is **n** must do these things   275
15:29 whether he is a **n** Israelite or an alien.   275
15:30 whether **n** or alien, blasphemes the LORD,   275
1Ch 7:21 Ezer and Elead were killed by the **n** men   824+928+2021+3528
Eze 47:22 You are to consider them as **n** Israelites;   275

NATIVES (1) [NATIVE]

Eze 23:15 Babylonian chariot officers, **n** of Chaldea.   4580

NATIVITY (KJV) See ANCESTRY, BIRTH, HOMELAND, NATIVE

NATURAL (15) [NATURE]

Nu 16:29 If these men die a **n** death   132+2021+3869+3972
19:16 or *someone who has* died a **n** death,   4637
19:18 or *someone who has* died a **n** death.   4637
Jn 1:13 children born not of **n** descent,   135
11:13 but his disciples thought he meant **n** sleep.   3122+3836+3836+5678
Ro 1:26 Even their women exchanged **n** relations   5879
1:27 also abandoned **n** relations with women   5879
6:19 because you are weak in your **n** selves.   4922
9: 8 not the **n** children who are God's children,   4922
11:21 if God did not spare the **n** branches,   2848+5882
11:24 the **n** branches, be grafted into their   2848+5882
1Co 15:44 it is sown a **n** body, it is raised a spiritual   6035
15:44 If there is a **n** body, there is also a spiritual   6035
15:46 The spiritual did not come first, but the **n**,   6035
Jude 1:19 who follow mere **n** instincts   6035

NATURE (39) [NATURAL]

Ro 1: 3 to his human **n** was a descendant of David,   4922
1:20 his eternal power and divine **n**—   2522
2:14 do by **n** things required by the law,   5882
7: 5 when we were controlled by the sinful **n**,   4922
7:18 that is, in my sinful **n**.   4922
7:25 *in* the sinful **n** a slave to the law of sin.   4922
8: 3 in that it was weakened by the sinful **n**,   4922
8: 4 to the sinful **n** but according to the Spirit.   4922
8: 5 the sinful **n** have their minds set on what   4922
8: 5 minds set on what that **n** desires;   4922
8: 8 controlled by the sinful **n** cannot please God   4922
8: 9 are controlled not by the sinful **n** but by   4922
8:12 but it is not *to* the sinful **n**,   4922
8:13 For if you live according to the sinful **n**,   4922
11:24 of an olive tree that is wild by **n**,   5882
11:24 and contrary to **n** grafted into   5882
13:14 how to gratify the desires of the sinful **n**.   4922
1Co 5: 5 so that the sinful **n** may be destroyed   4922
11:14 Does not the very **n** of things teach you that   5882
Gal 4: 8 you were slaves to those who by **n** are   5882
5:13 to indulge the sinful **n**;   4922
5:16 not gratify the desires of the sinful **n**.   4922
5:17 For the sinful **n** desires what is contrary to   4922
5:17 the Spirit what is contrary to the sinful **n**.   4922
5:19 The acts *of* the sinful **n** are obvious: 4922
5:24 to Christ Jesus have crucified the sinful **n**   4922
6: 8 The one who sows to please his sinful **n**,   4922
6: 8 from that **n** will reap destruction;   4922
Eph 2: 3 of our sinful **n** and following its desires   4922
2: 3 we were *by* **n** objects of wrath.   5882
Php 2: 6 being in very **n** God,   3671
2: 7 taking the very **n** of a servant,   3671
Col 2:11 in the putting off of the sinful **n**,   4922
2:13 in the uncircumcision *of* your sinful **n**,   4922
3: 5 whatever belongs to your earthly **n**:   3517
Heb 6:17 the unchanging **n** of his purpose very clear   NIG
2Pe 1: 4 in the divine **n** and escape the corruption in   5882
2:10 *of* the sinful **n** and despise authority.   4922
2:18 to the lustful desires *of* sinful human **n**,   4922

NAUGHT (1)

Isa 40:23 He brings princes to **n** and reduces   401

NAUGHTINESS, NAUGHTY (KJV) See EVIL, MALICIOUS, POOR, SCOUNDREL, WICKED

NAUM (KJV) See NAHUM

NAVEL (1)

SS 7: 2 Your **n** is a rounded goblet   9219

NAVES (KJV) See HUB

NAVY (KJV) See FLEET, SHIPS

NAY (KJV) See NO

NAZARENE (4) [NAZARETH]

Mt 2:23 "He will be called a **N**."   *3717*
Mk 14:67 "You also were with that **N**, Jesus,"   *3716*
16: 6 "You are looking for Jesus the **N**,   *3716*
Ac 24: 5 He is a ringleader of the **N** sect   *3717*

NAZARETH (27) [NAZARETH]

Mt 2:23 and he went and lived in a town called **N**.   *3714*
4:13 Leaving **N**, he went and lived   *3714*
21:11 the prophet from **N** in Galilee."   *3714*
26:71 "This fellow was with Jesus of **N**."   *3717*
Mk 1: 9 At that time Jesus came from **N** in Galilee   *3714*
1:24 "What do you want with us, Jesus of **N**?   *3716*
10:47 When he heard that it was Jesus of **N**,   *3716*
Lk 1:26 God sent the angel Gabriel to **N**,   *3714*
2: 4 So Joseph also went up from the town of **N**   *3714*
2:39 to Galilee to their own town *of* **N**.   *3714*
2:51 to **N** with them and was obedient to them.   *3714*
4:16 He went to **N**, where he had been   *3714*
4:34 What do you want with us, Jesus *of* **N**?   *3716*
18:37 told him, "Jesus *of* **N** is passing by."   *3717*
24:19 "About Jesus of **N**," they replied.   *3716*
Jn 1:45 Jesus of **N**, the son of Joseph."   *3714*
1:46 "**N**! Can anything good come from there?"   *3714*
18: 5 "Jesus *of* **N**," they replied.   *3717*
18: 7 And they said, "Jesus *of* **N**."   *3717*
19:19 JESUS *OF* **N**, THE KING OF THE JEWS.   *3717*
Ac 2:22 Jesus of **N** was a man accredited by God   *3717*
3: 6 In the name of Jesus Christ of **N**, walk."   *3717*
4:10 It is by the name of Jesus Christ of **N**   *3717*
6:14 that this Jesus of **N** will destroy this place   *3717*
10:38 Jesus of **N** with the Holy Spirit and power,   *3714*
22: 8 I am Jesus *of* **N**, whom you are persecuting,   *3717*
26: 9 to oppose the name of Jesus *of* **N**.   *3717*

NAZARITE (KJV) See NAZIRITE

NAZIRITE (11) [NAZIRITES]

Nu 6: 2 a vow of separation to the LORD as a **N**,   5693
6: 4 As long as he is a **N**,   5694
6:13 " 'Now this is the law for the **N** when   5687
6:18 **N** must shave off the hair that he dedicated.   5687
6:19 **N** has shaved off the hair of his dedication.   5687
6:20 After that, the **N** may drink wine.   5687
6:21 the **N** who vows his offering to the LORD   5687
6:21 according to the law of the **N**.' "   5694
Jdg 13: 5 because the boy is to be a **N**,   5687
13: 7 the boy will be a **N** *of* God from birth until   5687
16:17 "because I have been a **N** *set apart to* God   5687

NAZIRITES (2) [NAZIRITE]

Am 2:11 up prophets from among your sons and **N**   5687
2:12 "But you made the **N** drink wine and   5687

NEAH (1)

Jos 19:13 at Rimmon and turned toward **N**.   5828

NEAPOLIS (1)

Ac 16:11 and the next day on to **N**.   *3735*

NEAR (300) [NEARBY, NEARED, NEARER, NEAREST, NEARLY, NEARSIGHTED]

Ge 13:12 of the plain and pitched his tents **n** Sodom.   6330
13:18 and went to live **n** the great trees of Mamre   928
14: 6 as far as El Paran **n** the desert.   6584
14:13 Now Abram was living **n** the great trees   928
16: 7 angel of the LORD found Hagar **n** a spring   6584
18: 1 to Abraham **n** the great trees of Mamre   928
18: 8 he stood **n** them under a tree.   6584
19:20 Look, here is a town **n** *enough* to run to,   7940
20: 4 Now Abimelech *had* not gone **n** her,   7928
23:17 Ephron's field in Machpelah **n** Mamre   4200+7156
23:19 the field of Machpelah **n** Mamre   6584+7156
24:11 the camels kneel down **n** the well outside   448
24:30 and found him standing by the camels **n**   6584
25: 9 in the cave of Machpelah **n** Mamre,   6584+7156
25:11 who then lived **n** Beer Lahai Roi.   6640
25:18 to Shur, **n** the border of Egypt,   6584
27:21 "Come **n** so I can touch you, my son,   5602
27:41 of mourning for my father *are* **n**;   7928
29: 2 with three flocks of sheep lying **n** it   6584
30:41 of the animals so they would mate **n**   928
32:32 of Jacob's hip was touched **n** the tendon.   928
35:27 **n** Kiriath Arba (that is, Hebron),   NIH
37:12 to graze their father's flocks **n** Shechem   928
37:13 your brothers are grazing the flocks **n**   928
37:17 after his brothers and found them **n** Dothan.   928
45:10 in the region of Goshen and be **n** me—   7940
47:29 When the time drew **n** for Israel to die,   7928
49:22 a fruitful vine **n** a spring,   6584
49:30 **n** Mamre in Canaan,   6584+7156
50:10 **n** the Jordan, they lamented loudly   928+6298
50:11 That is why that place **n** the Jordan   928+6298
50:13 field of Machpelah **n** Mamre,   6584+7156
Ex 14: 2 and encamp **n** Pi Hahiroth,   4200+7156
14: 9 as they camped by the sea **n** Pi Hahiroth,   6584

Ex 14:20 so neither went **n** the other all night long.   7928
15:27 and they camped there **n** the water.   6584
18: 5 where he was camped **n** the mountain   NIH
24: 2 the others *must* not come **n**.   5602
33:21 a place **n** me where you may stand on   907
34:30 and they were afraid *to* come **n** him.   5602
34:32 Afterward all the Israelites came **n** him,   5602
40:29 the altar of burnt offering **n** the entrance to   NIH
Lev 3: 4 kidneys with the fat on them **n** the loins,   6584
3:10 kidneys with the fat on them **n** the loins,   6584
3:15 kidneys with the fat on them **n** the loins,   6584
4: 9 kidneys with the fat on them **n** the loins,   6584
7: 4 kidneys with the fat on them **n** the loins,   6584
9: 5 the entire assembly came **n** and stood   7928
21:17 a defect *may* come **n** to offer the food   7928
21:18 No man who has any defect *may* come **n**:   7928
21:21 the priest who has any defect *is to* come **n**   5602
21:21 not come **n** to offer the food of his God.   5602
21:23 not go **n** the curtain or approach the altar,   448
22: 3 and yet comes **n** the sacred offerings that   7928
Nu 1:51 Anyone else who goes **n** it shall be put   7929
4:19 when they come **n** the most holy things,   5602
6: 6 the LORD he must not go **n** a dead body.   6584
8:19 when they go **n** the sanctuary."   5602
13:29 and the Canaanites live **n** the sea and along   6584
16: 5 *he will* have that person come **n**   7928
16: 5 man he chooses *he will* cause to come **n**   7928
16: 9 the Israelite community and brought you **n**   7928
16:10 brought you and all your fellow Levites **n**   7928
17:13 Anyone who *even* comes **n** the tabernacle of the LORD will die.   7929+7929
18: 3 not go **n** the furnishings of the sanctuary or   7928
18: 4 and no *one* else *may* come **n** where you are.   7928
18: 7 Anyone else who comes **n** the sanctuary   7929
18:22 From now on the Israelites *must* not go **n**   7928
20:23 At Mount Hor, **n** the border of Edom,   6584
22: 5 who was at Pethor, **n** the River,   6584
24:17 I behold him, but not **n**.   7940
33: 7 and camped **n** Migdol.   4200+7156
33:47 in the mountains of Abarim, **n** Nebo.   4200+7156
Dt 3:29 So we stayed in the valley **n** Beth Peor.   4578
4: 7 as to have their gods **n** them the way   7940
4: 7 the way the LORD our God is **n** us   NIH
4:11 *You came* **n** and stood at the foot of   7928
4:46 in the valley **n** Beth Peor east of the Jordan,   4578
5:27 Go **n** and listen to all that   7928
11:30 **n** the great trees of Moreh,   725
13: 7 whether **n** or far,   7940
15: 9 the year for canceling debts, *is* **n**,"   7928
22: 2 the brother does not live **n** you or if you do   7940
30:14 No, the word is very **n** you;   7940
31:14 "Now the day of your death *is* **n**.   7928
32:35 of disaster is **n** and their doom rushes   7940
Jos 3: 4 between you and the ark; *do* not go **n** it."   7928
5:13 Now when Joshua was **n** Jericho,   928
7: 2 which is **n** Beth Aven to the east of Bethel,   6640
9: 7 "But perhaps you live **n** us.   928+7931
9:16 that they were neighbors, living **n** them.   928+7931
9:22 while actually you live **n** us?   928+7931
10: 1 of peace with Israel and were living **n**   928+7931
12: 9 the king of Ai (**n** Bethel) one   4946+7396
13:25 as far as Aroer, **n** Rabbah;   6584+7156
19:11 and extended to the ravine **n** Jokneam.   6584+7156
22:10 When they came to Geliloth **n** *the* Jordan   AIT
22:11 of Canaan at Geliloth **n** the Jordan on   AIT
24:26 up there under the oak **n** the holy place of   928
Jdg 1:16 of the Desert of Judah in the Negev **n** Arad.   AIT
3:19 the idols **n** Gilgal he himself turned back   907
4:11 by the great tree in Zaanannim **n** Kedesh.   907
7: 1 of Midian was north of them in the valley **n**   4946
7:22 as the border of Abel Meholah **n** Tabbath.   6584
9:34 and took up concealed positions **n** Shechem   6584
15: 9 spreading out **n** Lehi.   928
18: 3 When they were **n** Micah's house,   6640
18:12 up camp **n** Kiriath Jearim in Judah.   928
18:22 the men who lived **n** Micah   6640
18:28 The city was in a valley **n** Beth Rehob.   4200
19:11 When they were **n** Jebus   6640
20:19 the Israelites got up and pitched camp **n**   6584
20:24 Then the Israelites drew **n** to Benjamin   7928
20:34 that the Benjamites did not realize how **n**   5595
20:36 on the ambush they had set **n** Gibeah.   448
Ru 3:12 Although it is true that I *am* **n** of kin,   1457
1Sa 4:19 pregnant and **n** the time of delivery.   3528
7:10 the Philistines drew **n** to engage Israel   5602
10: 2 you will meet two men **n** Rachel's tomb,   6640
10:20 brought all the tribes of Israel **n**,   7928
17:26 David asked the men standing **n** him,   6640
24: 2 for David and his men **n** the Crags   6584+7156
25:15 time we were out in the fields **n** them   907+2143
25:16 the time we were herding our sheep **n** them.   6640
26: 7 in the ground **n** his head.   5265
26:11 the spear and water jug that are **n** his head,   5265
26:12 the spear and water jug **n** Saul's head,   5265
26:12 and water jug that were **n** his head?"   5265
2Sa 2:24 **n** Giah on the way to the wasteland   6584+7156
13:23 at Baal Hazor **n** the border of Ephraim,   6640
19:37 that I may die in my own town **n** the tomb   6640
23:15 a drink of water from the well **n** the gate   928
23:16 from the well **n** the gate of Bethlehem   928
24: 5 crossing the Jordan, they camped **n** Aroer,   928
1Ki 1: 9 at the Stone of Zoheleth **n** En Rogel.   725
2: 1 When the time drew **n** for David to die,   7928
8:46 to his own land, far away or **n**;   7940
8:59 be **n** to the LORD our God day and night,   7940
9:26 which is **n** Elath in Edom,   907
16:15 The army was encamped **n** Gibbethon,   6584

2Ki 9:27	in his chariot on the way up to Gur n	907
11:11	n the altar and the temple,	4200
15: 7	with his fathers and was buried n them in	6640
23:11	They were in the court n the room of	448
23:12	on the **roof** n the upper room of Ahaz,	AIT
25: 4	between the two walls n the king's garden,	6584
1Ch 8:32	They too lived n their relatives	5584
9:38	They too lived n their relatives	5584
11:17	a drink of water from the well n the gate	928
11:18	from the well n the gate of Bethlehem	928
19: 7	who came and camped n Medeba,	4200+7156
2Ch 6:36	to a land far away or n;	7940
14:10	in the Valley of Zephathah n Mareshah.	4200
21:16	of the Arabs who lived n the Cushites.	3338+6584
23:10	n the altar and the temple,	4200
26: 6	then rebuilt towns n Ashdod and elsewhere	928
26:23	and was buried n them in a field for burial	6640
Ne 3:25	the upper palace n the court of the guard.	4200
4:12	Then the Jews who lived n them came	725
7: 3	some at their posts and some n their own	5584
Est 2:11	and forth n the courtyard of the harem	4200+7156
9:20	the provinces of King Xerxes, n and far,	7940
Job 17:12	the face of darkness they say, 'Light is n.'	7940
33:22	His soul draws n to the pit,	7928
Ps 10: 8	He lies in **wait** n the villages;	AIT
22:11	for trouble is n and there is no one to help.	7940
65: 4	Blessed are those you choose and **bring** n	7928
69:18	**Come** n and rescue me;	7928
73:28	But as for me, it is good to be n God.	7932
75: 1	we give thanks, for your Name is n;	7940
84: 3	a place n your altar, O LORD Almighty,	907
85: 9	his salvation is n those who fear him,	7940
88: 3	of trouble and my life **draws** n the grave.	5595
91: 7	but *it* will not **come** n you.	5602
91:10	no disaster *will* **come** n your tent.	7928
107:18	They loathed all food and **drew** n the gates	5595
119:150	Those who devise wicked schemes *are* n,	7928
119:151	Yet you are n, O LORD,	7940
145:18	The LORD is n to all who call on him,	7940
	who lives trustfully n you.	907
Pr 3:29		
5: 8	*do* not **go** n the door of her house,	7928
7: 8	He was going down the street n her corner,	725
Ecc 5: 1	**Go** n to listen rather than to offer	7928
Isa 11: 8	The infant will play n the hole of the cobra,	6584
29:13	"These people **come** n to me	5602
33:13	you *who* are n, acknowledge my power!	7940
34: 1	**Come** n, you nations, and listen;	7928
46:13	**bringing** my righteousness n,	7928
48:16	"**Come** n me and listen to this:	7928
50: 8	He who vindicates me is n.	7940
51: 5	My righteousness *draws* n speedily,	7940
54:14	*it will not* **come** n you.	7928
55: 6	call on him while he is n.	7940
57:19	Peace, peace, to those far and n,"	7940
58: 2	and seem eager for God to **come** n them.	7932
65: 5	don't **come** n me,	5602
Jer 5: 6	a leopard that will lie in wait n their towns	6584
19: 2	n the entrance of the Potsherd Gate.	NIH
25:26	n and far, one after the other—	7940
30:21	*I will* **bring** him n and he will come close	7928
41:12	They caught up with him n the great pool	448
41:17	stopping at Geruth Kimham n Bethlehem	725
48:24	to all the towns of Moab, far and n,	7940
52: 7	between the two walls n the king's garden,	6584
La 1:16	No one is n to comfort me,	8178
3:57	*You* came n when I called you,	7928
4:18	Our end *was* n, our days were numbered,	7928
Eze 3:15	to the exiles who lived at Tel Abib n	448
6:12	and he *that* is n will fall by the sword,	7940
7: 7	The time has come, the day is n;	7940
12:23	'The days *are* n when every vision will	7928
22: 5	Those who are n and those who are far	7940
30: 3	day is n, the day of the LORD is near	7940
30: 3	the day is near, the day of the LORD is n—	7940
40:40	n the steps at the entrance to	4200
40:46	are the only Levites who may **draw** n	7929
42:14	on other clothes before *they* **go** n the places	7928
43:19	who **come** n to minister before me,	7940
44:13	*to* **come** n to serve me as priests or come	5602
44:13	as priests or **come** n any of my holy things	5602
44:15	or **come** n to minister before me;	7928
44:16	*to* **come** n my table to minister before me	7928
44:25	not defile himself by going n a dead	448
45: 4	in the sanctuary and who **draw** n to minister	7929
Da 5: 5	n the lampstand in the royal palace.	10378+10619
6:20	When he came n the den,	10638
8:17	he came n the place where I was standing,	725
9: 7	of Jerusalem and all Israel, both n and far,	7940
Joel 1:15	For the day of the LORD is n;	7940
3: 9	*Let* all the fighting men **draw** n and attack.	5602
3:14	of the LORD is n in the valley of decision.	7940
Am 6: 3	You put off the evil day and **bring** n a reign	5602
Ob 1:15	"The day of the LORD is n for all nations.	7940
Zep 1: 7	for the day of the LORD is n.	7940
1:14	"The great day of the LORD is n—	7940
1:14	n and coming quickly.	7940
3: 2	*she* does not **draw** n to her God.	7928
Mal 3: 5	"So I will **come** n to you for judgment.	7928
Mt 3: 2	"Repent, for the kingdom of heaven is n."	1581
4:17	"Repent, for the kingdom of heaven is n."	1581
10: 7	'The kingdom of heaven is n.'	1581
24:32	you know that summer is n.	1584
24:33	you know that it is n, right at the door.	1584
26:18	My appointed time is n.	1584
26:45	Look, the hour is n,	1581
Mk 1:15	"The kingdom of God is n.	1581

Mk 13:28	you know that summer is n.	1584
13:29	you know that it is n, right at the door.	1584
14:47	*of* those **standing** n drew his sword	4225
14:70	those **standing** n said to Peter,	4225
15:35	When some of those **standing** n heard this,	4225
Lk 8:19	but they were not able *to* **get** n him	5344
10: 9	'The kingdom of God is n you.'	1581
10:11	be sure of this: The kingdom of God is n.'	1581
12:33	no thief **comes** n and no moth destroys.	1581
15:25	When *he* came n the house,	1581
18:40	When *he* came n, Jesus asked him,	1584
19:11	because he was n Jerusalem and	1584
19:37	When *he* came n the place where	1584
21: 8	claiming, 'I am he,' and, 'The time is n.'	1581
21:20	you will know that its desolation is n.	1581
21:28	because your redemption is **drawing** n."	1581
21:30	for yourselves and know that summer is n.	1584
21:31	you know that the kingdom of God is n.	1584
Jn 3:23	John also was baptizing at Aenon n Salim,	1584
4: 5	n the plot of ground Jacob had given	4446
5: 2	Now there is in Jerusalem n the Sheep Gate	2093
6: 4	The Jewish Passover Feast was n.	1584
6:23	Then some boats from Tiberias landed n	1584
7: 2	the Jewish Feast of Tabernacles was n,	1584
8:20	in the temple area n the place where	1877
11:54	Instead he withdrew to a region n	1584
19:20	the place where Jesus was crucified was n	1584
19:25	N the cross of Jesus stood his mother,	4123
Ac 2:10	Egypt and the parts of Libya n Cyrene;	2848
7:17	"As the time **drew** n for God	1581
7:30	a burning bush in the desert n Mount Sinai.	NIG
8:29	"Go to that chariot and **stay** n it."	3140
9:38	Lydda was n Joppa;	1584
22: 6	"About noon *as* I came n Damascus,	1581
23: 2	Ananias ordered those **standing** n Paul	4225
23: 4	Those who *were* **standing** n Paul said,	4225
23:11	The following night the Lord **stood** n Paul	2392
27: 8	n the town of Lasea.	1584
Ro 10: 8	"The word is n you;	1584
1Co 8: 8	But food *does* not **bring** us n to God;	4225
Eph 2:13	in Christ Jesus you who once were far away have been brought n	1584
2:17	and peace to those who were n.	1584
Php 4: 5	The Lord is n.	1584
Heb 7:19	by which *we* **draw** n to God.	1581
10: 1	make perfect those who **draw** n to worship.	4665
10:22	*let us* **draw** n to God with a sincere heart	4665
11:22	By faith Joseph, *when his* end was n,	5462
Jas 4: 8	**Come** n to God and he will come near	1581
4: 8	near to God and *he will* **come** n to you.	1581
5: 8	because the Lord's coming *is* n.	1581
1Pe 4: 7	The end of all things *is* n.	1581
Rev 1: 3	because the time is n.	1584
22:10	because the time is n.	1584

NEARBY (16) [NEAR]

Ge 18: 2	up and saw three men standing n.	6584
21:16	Then she went off and sat down n,	4946+5584
21:16	as she sat there, n, she began to sob.	4946+5584
Dt 20:15	and do not belong to the nations n	2178
Job 1:14	and the donkeys were grazing n,	3338+6584
4:20	and all the wild animals gone,	9004
Pr 27:10	better a neighbor n than a brother far away.	7940
Jer 23:23	"Am I only a God n," declares the LORD,	4946+7940
Mk 1:38	go somewhere else—to the n villages—	2400
5:11	herd of pigs was feeding on the n hillside.	1695
Lk 2: 8	shepherds living out in the fields n,	899+3836
Jn 2: 6	N stood six stone water jars,	1695
18:22	one of the officials n struck him in the face.	4225
19:26	and the disciple whom he loved **standing** n,	4225
19:42	of Preparation and since the tomb was n,	1584
Ac 28: 7	There was an estate that belonged to Publius,	3836+4309+5536

NEARED (2) [NEAR]

Jdg 19:14	sun set as *they* n Gibeah in Benjamin.	725+2143
Ac 9: 3	As he n Damascus on his journey,	1181+1581

NEARER (2) [NEAR]

Ru 3:12	there is a kinsman-redeemer n than I.	7940
Ro 13:11	because our salvation is n now than	1584

NEAREST (7) [NEAR]

Ex 12: 4	they must share one with their n neighbor,	7940
Lev 25:25	his n relative is to come	7940
Nu 27:11	give his inheritance to the n relative	7940
Dt 21: 3	the elders of the town n the body shall take	7940
21: 6	the town n the body shall wash their hands	7940
Jer 32: 7	as n relative it is your right and **duty**	1460
Eze 42: 8	the row on the side n the sanctuary	6584+7156

NEARIAH (3)

1Ch 3:22	Hattush, Igal, Bariah, N and Shaphat—	5859
3:23	The sons of N:	5859
4:42	N, Rephaiah and Uzziel, the sons of Ishi,	5859

NEARLY (7) [NEAR]

Jdg 19: 9	Spend the night here; the day *is* n over.	2837
Ps 73: 2	I had n lost my foothold.	401+3869
Mk 4:37	so that it was n swamped.	2453
Lk 24:29	for it is evening; the day is almost over."	4639
Ac 21:27	When the seven days were n over,	3516

Ro 13:12	night *is* n over; the day is almost here.	4621
Heb 9:22	that n everything be cleansed with blood,	5385

NEARSIGHTED (1) [NEAR, SEE]

2Pe 1: 9	does not have them, he is n and blind,	3697

NEBAI (1)

Ne 10:19	Hariph, Anathoth, N,	5763

NEBAIOTH (5)

Ge 25:13	N the firstborn of Ishmael, Kedar, Adbeel,	5568
28: 9	the sister of N and daughter of Ishmael son	5568
36: 3	of Ishmael and sister of N.	5568
1Ch 1:29	N the firstborn of Ishmael, Kedar, Adbeel,	5568
Isa 60: 7	the rams of N will serve you;	5568

NEBAJOTH (KJV) See NEBAIOTH

NEBALLAT (1)

Ne 11:34	in Hadid, Zeboim and N,	5579

NEBAT (25)

1Ki 11:26	Jeroboam son of N rebelled against	5565
12: 2	son of N heard this (he was still in Egypt,	5565
12:15	to Jeroboam son of N through Ahijah	5565
15: 1	of the reign of Jeroboam son of N,	5565
16: 3	like that of Jeroboam son of N.	5565
16:26	in all the ways of Jeroboam son of N and	5565
16:31	to commit the sins of Jeroboam son of N,	5565
21:22	like that of Jeroboam son of N and that	5565
22:52	and in the ways of Jeroboam son of N,	5565
2Ki 3: 3	he clung to the sins of Jeroboam son of N,	5565
9: 9	of Jeroboam son of N and like the house	5565
10:29	from the sins of Jeroboam son of N,	5565
13: 2	the sins of Jeroboam son of N,	5565
13:11	from any of the sins of Jeroboam son of N,	5565
14:24	from any of the sins of Jeroboam son of N,	5565
15: 9	from the sins of Jeroboam son of N,	5565
15:18	from the sins of Jeroboam son of N,	5565
15:24	from the sins of Jeroboam son of N,	5565
15:28	from the sins of Jeroboam son of N,	5565
17:21	they made Jeroboam son of N their king.	5565
23:15	the high place made by Jeroboam son of N,	5565
2Ch 9:29	the seer concerning Jeroboam son of N?	5565
10: 2	son of N heard this (he was in Egypt,	5565
10:15	to Jeroboam son of N through Ahijah	5565
13: 6	Yet Jeroboam son of N,	5565

NEBO (13) [NEBO-SARSEKIM]

Nu 32: 3	Heshbon, Elealeh, Sebam, N and Beon—	5549
32:38	as well as N and Baal Meon	5549
33:47	in the mountains of Abarim, near N.	5549
Dt 32:49	"Go up into the Abarim Range to Mount N	5549
34: 1	Then Moses climbed Mount N from	5549
1Ch 5: 8	in the area from Aroer to N and Baal Meon.	5549
Ezr 2:29	of N 52	5551
10:43	From the descendants of N:	5549
Ne 7:33	of the other N 52	5549
Isa 15: 2	Moab wails over N and Medeba.	5549
46: 1	Bel bows down, N stoops low;	5550
Jer 48: 1	"Woe to N, for it will be ruined.	5549
48:22	to Dibon, N and Beth Diblathaim,	5549

NEBO-SARSEKIM (1) [NEBO]

Jer 39: 3	Nergal-Sharezer of Samgar, N	5552

NEBUCHADNEZZAR (89)
[NEBUCHADNEZZAR'S]

2Ki 24: 1	N king of Babylon invaded the land,	5556
24: 1	and rebelled against N.	2257S
24:10	the officers of N king of Babylon advanced	5556
24:11	and N himself came up to the city	5556
24:13	N removed all the treasures from	NIH
24:15	N took Jehoiachin captive to Babylon.	NIH
25: 1	N king of Babylon marched	5556
25: 8	the nineteenth year of N king of Babylon,	5556
25:22	N king of Babylon appointed Gedaliah son	5556
1Ch 6:15	and Jerusalem into exile by the hand of N.	5556
2Ch 36: 6	N king of Babylon attacked him	5556
36: 7	N also took to Babylon articles from	5556
36:10	King N sent for him and brought him	5556
36:13	He also rebelled against King N,	5556
36:17	God handed all of them over to N.	2257S
Ezr 2: 1	which N had carried away from Jerusalem	5556
2: 1	whom N king of Babylon had taken captive	5556
5:12	he handed them over to N the Chaldean,	10453
5:14	which N had taken from the temple	10453
6: 5	which N took from the temple in Jerusalem	10453
Ne 7: 6	the captivity of the exiles whom N king	5556
Est 2: 6	from Jerusalem by N king of Babylon.	5556
Jer 21: 2	because N king of Babylon is attacking us.	5557
21: 7	to N king of Babylon and to	5557
22:25	to N king of Babylon and to	5557
24: 1	from Jerusalem to Babylon by N king	5557
25: 1	the first year of N king of Babylon.	5557
25: 9	and my servant N king of Babylon,"	5557
27: 6	over to my servant N king of Babylon,	5556
27: 8	or kingdom will not serve N king	5556
27:20	which N king of Babylon did not take away	5556
28: 3	that N king of Babylon removed from here	5556
28:11	the yoke of N king of Babylon off the neck	5556

Jer	28:14	to make them serve **N** king of Babylon,	5556
	29: 1	the other people **N** had carried into exile	5556
	29: 3	of Judah sent to King **N** in Babylon.	5556
	29:21	"I will hand them over to **N** king	5557
	32: 1	which was the eighteenth year of **N**.	5557
	32:28	the Babylonians and to **N** king of Babylon,	5557
	34: 1	While **N** king of Babylon and all his army	5557
	35:11	when **N** king of Babylon invaded this land,	5557
	37: 1	of Judah by **N** king of Babylon;	5557
	39: 1	**N** king of Babylon marched	5557
	39: 5	They captured him and took him to **N** king	5557
	39:11	Now **N** king of Babylon	5557
	43:10	for my servant **N** king of Babylon,	5557
	44:30	of Judah over to **N** king of Babylon,	5557
	46: 2	the Euphrates River by **N** king of Babylon	5557
	46:13	the prophet about the coming of **N** king	5557
	46:26	to **N** king of Babylon and his officers.	5557
	49:28	which **N** king of Babylon attacked:	5557
	49:30	"**N** king of Babylon has plotted	5557
	50:17	to crush his bones was **N** king of Babylon."	5557
	51:34	"**N** king of Babylon has devoured us,	5557
	52: 4	**N** king of Babylon marched	5557
	52:12	the nineteenth year of **N** king of Babylon,	5557
	52:28	This is the number of the people **N** carried	5557
Eze	26: 7	to bring against Tyre **N** king of Babylon	5557
	29:18	**N** king of Babylon drove his army in	5557
	29:19	to give Egypt to **N** king of Babylon,	5557
	30:10	of Egypt by the hand of **N** king of Babylon.	5557
Da	1: 1	**N** king of Babylon came to Jerusalem	5556
	1:18	the chief official presented them to **N**.	5556
	2: 1	the second year of his reign, **N** had dreams;	5556
	2:28	He has shown King **N** what will happen	10453
	2:46	Then King **N** fell prostrate before Daniel	10453
	3: 1	King **N** made an image of gold,	10453
	3: 3	of the image that King **N** had set up,	10453
	3: 5	the image of gold that King **N** has set up.	10453
	3: 7	the image of gold that King **N** had set up.	10453
	3: 9	They said to King **N**, "O king, live forever!	10453
	3:13	Furious with rage, **N** summoned Shadrach,	10453
	3:14	and **N** said to them,	10453
	3:16	"O **N**, we do not need to defend ourselves	10453
	3:19	Then **N** was furious with Shadrach,	10453
	3:24	Then King **N** leaped to his feet	10453
	3:26	**N** then approached the opening of	10453
	3:28	Then **N** said, "Praise be to the God	10453
	4: 1	King **N**, To the peoples,	10453
	4: 4	I, **N**, was at home in my palace,	10453
	4:18	"This is the dream that I, King **N**, had.	10453
	4:28	All this happened to King **N**.	10453
	4:31	"This is what is decreed for you, King **N**:	10453
	4:33	about **N** was fulfilled.	10453
	4:34	At the end of that time, I, **N**,	10453
	4:37	**N**, praise and exalt and glorify the King	10453
	5: 2	that **N** his father had taken from the temple	10453
	5:11	King **N** your father—	10453
	5:18	the Most High God gave your father **N** sovereignty	10453

NEBUCHADNEZZAR'S (1)
[NEBUCHADNEZZAR]

Jer	52:29	in **N** eighteenth year, 832 people	4200+5557

NEBUSHAZBAN (1)

Jer	39:13	**N** a chief officer,	5558

NEBUZARADAN (16)

2Ki	25: 8	**N** commander of the imperial guard,	5555
	25:11	**N** the commander of the guard carried	5555
	25:20	**N** the commander took them all	5555
Jer	39: 9	**N** commander of the imperial guard carried	5555
	39:10	but **N** the commander of the guard left	5555
	39:11	about Jeremiah through **N** commander of	5555
	39:13	So **N** the commander of the guard,	5555
	40: 1	from the LORD after **N** commander of	5555
	40: 5	before Jeremiah turned to go, **N** added,	NIH
	41:10	over whom **N** commander of the imperial	5555
	43: 6	the king's daughters whom **N** commander	5555
	52:12	**N** commander of the imperial guard,	5555
	52:15	**N** the commander of the guard carried	5555
	52:16	But **N** left behind the rest of	5555
	52:26	**N** the commander took them all	5555
	52:30	by **N** the commander of the imperial guard.	5555

NECESSARY (8) [NECESSITIES]

Ac	1:21	Therefore *it is* **n** to choose one of	1256
Ro	13: 5	it is **n** to submit to the authorities,	340
2Co	9: 5	So I thought it **n** to urge the brothers	338
Php	1:24	but it is **more n** for you that I remain in	338
	2:25	But I think it is **n** to send back	338
Heb	8: 3	and so *it was* **n** for this one also	338
	9:16	it is **n** to prove the death of the one who	340
	9:23	It was **n**, then, for the copies of	340

NECESSITIES (1) [NECESSARY]

Tit	3:14	they may provide for **daily n** and not live unproductive lives.	338+5970

NECHO (KJV) See NECO

NECK (51) [NECKS, STIFF-NECKED]

Ge	27:16	the smooth part of his **n** with the goatskins.	7418
	27:40	you will throw his yoke from off your **n**."	7418

Ge	33: 4	he threw his arms around his **n**	7418
	41:42	and put a gold chain around his **n**.	7418
	49: 8	be on the **n** *of* your enemies;	6902
Ex	13:13	but if you do not redeem it, **break** its **n**.	6904
	34:20	but if you do not redeem it, **break** its **n**.	6904
Lev	5: 8	He is to wring its head from its **n**,	6902
Dt	21: 4	the valley *they are* to **break** the heifer's **n**.	6904
	21: 6	the heifer whose **n** **was broken** in the valley,	6904
	28:48	on your **n** until he has destroyed you.	7418
Jdg	5:30	highly embroidered garments for my **n**—	7418
1Sa	4:18	His **n** was broken and he died,	5154
Job	16:12	he seized me by the **n** and crushed me.	6902
	30:18	he binds me like the **n** *of* my garment.	7023
	39:19	the horse his strength or clothe his **n** with	7418
	41:22	Strength resides in his **n**;	7418
Ps	69: 1	for the waters have come up to my **n**.	5883
	75: 5	do not speak with outstretched **n**.' "	7418
	105:18	his **n** was put in irons,	5883
Pr	1: 9	and a chain to adorn your **n**.	1738
	3: 3	bind them around your **n**,	1738
	3:22	an ornament to grace your **n**.	1738
	6:21	fasten them around your **n**.	1738
SS	1:10	your **n** with strings of jewels.	7418
	4: 4	Your **n** is like the tower of David,	7418
	7: 4	Your **n** is like an ivory tower.	7418
Isa	8: 8	passing through it and reaching up to the **n**.	7418
	10:27	their yoke from your **n**;	7418
	30:28	rising up to the **n**.	7418
	48: 4	the sinews of your **n** were iron,	6902
	52: 2	Free yourself from the chains on your **n**,	7418
	66: 3	like *one who* **breaks** a dog's **n**;	6904
Jer	27: 2	of straps and crossbars and put it on your **n**.	7418
	27: 8	of Babylon or bow its **n** under his yoke,	7418
	27:11	if any nation will bow its **n** under the yoke	7418
	27:12	"Bow your **n** under the yoke of the king	7418
	28:10	the **n** of the prophet Jeremiah and broke it,	7418
	28:11	the **n** of all the nations within two years.' "	7418
	28:12	the yoke off the **n** *of* the prophet Jeremiah.	7418
La	1:14	They have come upon my **n** and	7418
Eze	16:11	and a necklace around your **n**,	1744
Da	5: 7	and have a gold chain placed around his **n**,	10611
	5:16	a gold chain placed around your **n**,	10611
	5:29	a gold chain was placed around his **n**,	10611
Hos	10:11	so I will put a yoke on her fair **n**.	7418
	11: 4	I lifted the yoke from their **n** and bent down	4305
Na	1:13	from your **n** and tear your shackles away."	NIH
Mt	18: 6	to have a large millstone hung around his **n**	5549
Mk	9:42	with a large millstone tied around his **n**.	5549
Lk	17: 2	a millstone tied around his **n** than for him	5549

NECK-IRONS (1) [IRON]

Jer	29:26	like a prophet into the stocks and **n**.	7485

NECKLACE (3) [NECKLACES]

Ps	73: 6	Therefore pride is their **n**;	6735
SS	4: 9	with one jewel of your **n**.	7454
Eze	16:11	on your arms and a **n** around your neck,	8054

NECKLACES (2) [NECKLACE]

Nu	31:50	bracelets, signet rings, earrings and **n**—	3921
Isa	3:18	the bangles and headbands and **crescent n**,	8448

NECKS (9) [NECK]

Jos	10:24	and put your feet on the **n** *of* these kings."	7418
	10:24	and placed their feet on their **n**.	7418
Jdg	8:21	and took the ornaments off their camels' **n**.	7418
	8:26	or the chains that were on their camels' **n**.	7418
Isa	3:16	walking along with outstretched **n**,	1744
Jer	28:14	an iron yoke on the **n** *of* all these nations	7418
	30: 8	'I will break the yoke off their **n**	7418
Eze	21:29	on the **n** of the wicked who are to be slain,	7418
Ac	15:10	the **n** of the disciples a yoke that neither we	5549

NECO (10)

2Ki	23:29	Pharaoh **N** king of Egypt went up to	5785
	23:29	**N** faced him and killed him at Megiddo.	2257^S
	23:33	Pharaoh **N** put him in chains at Riblah in	5785
	23:34	Pharaoh **N** made Eliakim son of Josiah king	5785
	23:35	Jehoiakim paid Pharaoh **N** the silver	NIH
2Ch	35:20	**N** king of Egypt went up to fight	5786
	35:21	But **N** sent messengers to him, saying,	NIH
	35:22	He would not listen to what **N** had said	5786
	36: 4	But **N** took Eliakim's brother Jehoahaz	5786
Jer	46: 2	the army of Pharaoh **N** king of Egypt,	5786

NECROMANCER (KJV) See CONSULTS THE DEAD

NECTAR (1)

SS	8: 2	the **n** of my pomegranates.	6747

NEDABIAH (1)

1Ch	3:18	Shenazzar, Jekamiah, Hoshama and **N**.	5608

NEED (77) [NEEDED, NEEDING, NEEDLESS, NEEDS, NEEDY]

Ge	33:11	has been gracious to me and I have **all** I **n**."	AIT
Ex	14:14	the LORD will fight for you; *you* **n** only to be **still**.	AIT

Lev	13:36	priest *does* not **n** to **look** for yellow hair;	AIT
Jdg	19:19	We don't **n** anything."	4728
	19:20	"Let me supply whatever you **n**.	4728
1Ki	8:59	according to each day's **n**,	1821
2Ki	22: 7	But they *n* not **account for** the money	AIT
1Ch	23:26	the Levites no *longer* **n** to **carry**	AIT
2Ch	2: 8	for I know that your men **n** skill to cut timber in rafts	7664
	35:15	at each gate *did* not **n** to **leave** their posts,	AIT
Job	5:21	and **n** not **fear** when destruction comes,	AIT
	5:22	and **n** not **fear** the beasts of the earth.	AIT
	34:23	God has no **n** to **examine** men further,	AIT
Ps	50: 9	I have no **n** of a bull from your stall or	4374
	79: 8	for we are in desperate **n**.	1937
	116: 6	when I was in great **n**, he saved me.	1937
	142: 6	Listen to my cry, for *I am* in desperate **n**;	1937
Pr	24: 6	for waging war you **n** guidance,	NIH
Jer	2:24	that pursue her *n* not **tire** *themselves*;	AIT
Eze	39:10	They will not **n** to **gather** wood from	AIT
Da	3:16	we *do* not **n** to defend ourselves before you	10287
Hos	7: 4	like an oven whose fire the baker **n** not stir	8697
Mt	3:14	saying, "I **n** to be baptized by you,	2400+5970
	6: 8	for your Father knows what *you* **n**	5974
	6:32	your heavenly Father that *you* **n** them.	5974
	9:12	"It is not the healthy **who n** a doctor,	2400+5970
	14:16	Jesus replied, "They *do* not **n** to go away.	2400+5970
	26:65	Why *do we* **n** any more witnesses?	2400+5970
Mk	2:17	"It is not the healthy who **n** a doctor,	2400+5970
	2:25	his companions were hungry and in **n**?	2400+5970
	14:63	"Why *do we* **n** any more witnesses?"	2400+5970
Lk	5:31	"It is not the healthy who **n** a doctor,	2400+5970
	12:30	and your Father knows that *you* **n** them.	5974
	15: 7	persons who *do* not **n** to repent.	2400+5970
	15:14	and he began to be in **n**.	5728
	22:71	"Why *do we* **n** any more testimony?"	2400+5970
Jn	2:25	He did not **n** man's testimony about man,	2400+5970
	16:30	*you do* not even **n** to have anyone ask you questions.	2400+5970
Ac	2:45	they gave to anyone as he had **n**.	5970
	4:35	it was distributed to anyone as he had **n**.	5970
	10: 2	**gave** generously to those in **n**	1797+4472
	27:34	You **n** it to survive.	NIG
Ro	12:13	Share with God's people who are in **n**.	5970
	16: 2	to give her any help *she may* **n** from you,	5974
1Co	12:21	say to the hand, "I don't **n** you!"	2400+5970
	12:21	say to the feet, "I don't **n** you!"	2400+5970
	12:24	our presentable parts **n** no special treatment.	2400+5970
2Co	3: 1	Or *do we* **n**, like some people,	5974
	8:14	your plenty will supply what they **n**,	5729
	8:14	in turn their plenty will supply what you **n**.	5729
	9: 1	There is **no n** for me to write to you	4356
	9: 8	having all that you **n**,	894
Eph	4:28	to share with those in **n**.	2400+5970
Php	4:11	I am not saying this because I am in **n**,	5730
	4:12	I know what it is *to be in* **n**,	5427
	4:16	and again when I was in **n**.	5970
1Th	1: 8	*we do* not **n** to say anything about it,	2400+5970
	4: 9	brotherly love *we do* not **n** to write	2400+5970
	5: 1	times and dates *we do* not **n** to write	2400+5970
1Ti	5: 3	to those widows who are really in **n**.	NIG
	5: 5	in **n** and left all alone puts her hope in God	NIG
	5:16	that the church can help those widows who are really in **n**.	NIG
2Ti	2:15	workman who **does** not **n** to be ashamed	454
Tit	3:13	see that they **have everything** they **n**.	3309+3594
Heb	4:16	and find grace to help us in our **time of n**.	2322
	5:12	*you* **n** someone to teach you	2400+5970
	5:12	You **n** milk, not solid food!	1181+2400+5970
	7:11	why was there still **n** for another priest	5970
	7:26	Such a high priest **meets** our **n**—	4560
	7:27	not **n** to offer sacrifices day after day,	340+2400
	10:36	You **n** to persevere so that	2400+5970
2Pe	1: 3	His divine power has given us everything we **n** for life and godliness	NIG
1Jn	2:27	and *you do* not **n** anyone to teach you.	2400+5970
	3:17	sees his brother in **n** but has no pity	2400+5970
Rev	3:17	I have acquired wealth and *do* not **n**	2400+5970
	21:23	The city *does* not **n** the sun or the moon to shine on it,	2400+5970
	22: 5	not **n** the light of a lamp or the light of	2400+5970

NEEDED (16) [NEED]

Ex	12: 4	**determine** the **amount** *of* lamb **n**	4082
	16:18	Each one gathered as much as he **n**	430
	16:21	everyone gathered as much as he **n**,	430
Jos	19: 9	Judah's portion was more than they **n**,	NIH
Ezr	6: 9	Whatever is **n**—young bulls,	10288
	6:20	And anything else **n** for the temple	10289
Ecc	10:10	more strength *is* **n** but skill will bring success.	1504
Mt	25:36	I **n** **clothes** and you clothed me,	1218
	25:43	I **n** **clothes** and you did not clothe me,	1218
Lk	9:11	and healed those who **n** healing.	2400+5970
	10:42	but only one thing is **n**.	5970
Jn	13:29	to buy what *was* **n** for the Feast,	2400+5970
Ac	17:25	*as if he* **n** anything,	4656
	28:10	they furnished us with the supplies we **n**.	5970
2Co	11: 9	And when I was with you and **n** something,	5728
	11: 9	from Macedonia supplied what I **n**.	5729

NEEDING (2) [NEED]

Mt	25:38	or **n** **clothes** and clothe you?	1218
	25:44	a stranger or **n** **clothes** or sick or in prison,	1218

NEEDLE (3)

Mt	19:24	through the eye of a **n** than for a rich man	4827
Mk	10:25	through the eye of a **n** than for a rich man	4827
Lk	18:25	through the eye of a **n** than for a rich man	1017

NEEDLESS (2) [NEED]

1Sa	25:31	the staggering burden of **n** bloodshed or	2855
Pr	23:29	Who has **n** bruises?	2855

NEEDS (25) [NEED]

Ex	16:16	'Each one is to gather as much as he **n**.	430
Nu	4:26	to do all that **n** to be done with these things.	AIT
Dt	15: 8	and freely lend him whatever he **n**.	2893+4728
Pr	12:10	righteous man cares for the **n** of his animal,	5883
Isa	58:10	and satisfy the **n** of the oppressed,	5883
	58:11	he will satisfy your **n** in a sun-scorched land	5883
Jer	5: 7	*I* supplied all their **n**,	8425
Mt	21: 3	tell him that the Lord **n** them,	2400+5970
	27:55	from Galilee to care for his **n**.	NIG
Mk	11: 3	'The Lord **n** it and will send it back	2400+5970
	15:41	followed him and **cared for** his **n**.	1354
Lk	11: 8	up and give him as much as he **n**.	5974
	19:31	tell him, 'The Lord **n** it.'	2400+5970
	19:34	They replied, "The Lord **n** it."	2400+5970
Jn	13:10	"A person who has had a bath **n** only	2400+5970
Ac	20:34	hands of mine have supplied my own **n** and	5970
	20:34	and the **n** of my companions.	NIG
	24:23	permit his friends to **take care of** his **n**.	5676
	27: 3	so they might provide for his **n**.	2149
Ro	12: 8	if it is contributing to the **n** of others,	NIG
2Co	9:12	not only supplying the **n** of God's people	5729
Eph	4:29	for building others up according to their **n**,	5970
Php	2:25	whom you sent to take care of my **n**.	5970
	4:19	And my God will meet all your **n** according	5970
Jas	2:16	but does nothing about his physical **n**,	2201

NEEDY (55) [NEED]

Ex	22:25	of my people among you who is **n**, do not	6714
Dt	15: 9	not show ill will toward your **n** brother	36
	15:11	and toward the poor and **n** in your land.	36
	24:14	of a hired man who is poor and **n**,	36
1Sa	2: 8	the poor from the dust and lifts the **n** from	36
Job	5:15	the **n** from the sword in their mouth;	36
	24: 4	the **n** from the path and force all the poor of	36
	24:14	murderer rises up and kills the poor and **n**;	36
	29:16	I was a father to the **n**;	36
	31:19	or a **n** *man* without a garment,	36
	34:28	so that he heard the cry of the **n**,	6714
Ps	9:18	But the **n** will not always be forgotten,	36
	12: 5	of the weak and the groaning of the **n**,	36
	35:10	the poor and **n** from those who rob them."	36
	37:14	the bow to bring down the poor and **n**,	36
	40:17	Yet I am poor and **n**;	36
	69:33	The Lord hears the **n** and does	36
	70: 5	Yet I am poor and **n**;	36
	72: 4	the people and save the children of the **n**;	36
	72:12	For he will deliver the **n** who cry out,	36
	72:13	on the weak and the **n** and save the needy	36
	72:13	on the weak and the needy and save the **n**	36
	74:21	may the poor and **n** praise your name.	36
	82: 4	Rescue the weak and **n**;	36
	86: 1	and answer me, for I am poor and **n**.	36
	107:41	But he lifted the **n** out of their affliction	36
	109:16	the poor and the **n** and the brokenhearted.	36
	109:22	For I am poor and **n**,	36
	109:31	For he stands at the right hand of the **n** *one*,	36
	113: 7	the poor from the dust and lifts the **n** from	36
	140:12	for the poor and upholds the cause of the **n**.	36
Pr	14:21	but blessed is he who is kind to the **n**.	6705
	14:31	but whoever is kind to the **n** honors God.	36
	22:22	and do not crush the **n** in court,	6714
	30:14	the **n** from among mankind.	36
	31: 9	defend the rights of the poor and **n**."	36
	31:20	to the poor and extends her hands to the **n**.	36
Isa	11: 4	but with righteousness he will judge the **n**,	1924
	14:30	and the **n** will lie down in safety.	36
	25: 4	a refuge for the **n** in his distress,	36
	29:19	**n** will rejoice in the Holy One of Israel.	36+132
	32: 7	even when the plea of the **n** is just.	36
	41:17	"The poor and **n** search for water,	36
Jer	20:13	He rescues the life of the **n** from the hands	36
	22:16	He defended the cause of the poor and **n**,	36
Eze	16:49	they did not help the poor and **n**.	36
	18:12	He oppresses the poor and **n**.	36
	22:29	they oppress the poor and **n** and mistreat	36
Am	2: 6	and the **n** for a pair of sandals.	36
	4: 1	and crush the **n** and say to your husbands,	36
	8: 4	you who trample the **n** and do away with	36
	8: 6	with silver and the **n** for a pair of sandals,	36
Mt	6: 2	"So when *you* give to the **n**,	1797+4472
	6: 3	But *when you* give to the **n**,	1797+4472
Ac	4:34	There were no **n** persons among them.	1890

NEESINGS (KJV) See SNORTING

NEGEV (38) [RAMOTH NEGEV]

Ge	12: 9	Abram set out and continued toward the **N**.	5582
	13: 1	So Abram went up from Egypt to the **N**,	5582
	13: 3	From the **N** he went from place to place	5582
	20: 1	He lived between Kadesh and Shur.	5582
	24:62	for he was living in the **N**.	824+5582
Nu	13:17	through the **N** and on into the hill country.	5582
	13:22	up through the **N** and came to Hebron,	5582
	13:29	The Amalekites live in the **N**;	824+5582
	21: 1	who lived in the **N**,	5582
	33:40	who lived in the **N** of Canaan,	5582
Dt	1: 7	in the **N** and along the coast,	5582
	34: 3	the **N** and the whole region from the Valley	5582
Jos	10:40	including the hill country, the **N**,	5582
	11:16	the hill country, all the **N**,	5582
	12: 8	the mountain slopes, the desert and the **N**—	5582
	15:19	Since you have given me land in the **N**,	5582
	15:21	the **N** toward the boundary of Edom were:	5582
	19: 8	as far as Baalath Beer (Ramah in the **N**).	5582
Jdg	1: 9	the **N** and the western foothills.	5582
	1:15	Since you have given me land in the **N**,	5582
	1:16	of the Desert of Judah in the **N** near Arad.	5582
1Sa	27:10	the **N** *of* Judah" or "Against the Negev	5582
	27:10	the **N** of Jerahmeel" or "Against the Negev	5582
	27:10	the Negev of Jerahmeel" or "Against the **N**	5582
	30: 1	Amalekites had raided the **N** and Ziklag.	5582
	30:14	We raided the **N** of the Kerethites and	5582
	30:14	the territory belonging to Judah and the **N**	5582
2Sa	24: 7	they went on to Beersheba in the **N**	5582
2Ch	28:18	in the foothills and in the **N** of Judah.	5582
Ps	126: 4	O Lord, like streams in the **N**.	5582
Isa	30: 6	An oracle concerning the animals of the **N**:	5582
Jer	13:19	The cities in the **N** will be shut up,	5582
	17:26	from the hill country and the **N**,	5582
	32:44	of the western foothills and of the **N**,	5582
	33:13	of the western foothills and of the **N**,	5582
Ob	1:19	the **N** will occupy the mountains of Esau,	5582
	1:20	the towns of the **N**.	5582
Zec	7: 7	**N** and the western foothills were settled?' "	5582

NEGLECT (9) [NEGLECTED, NEGLECTING, NEGLIGENT]

Dt	12:19	not *to* **n** the Levites as long as you live	6440
	14:27	*do* not **n** the Levites living in your towns,	6440
Ezr	4:22	Be careful not to **n** this matter.	10522+10712
Ne	10:39	*"We will* not **n** the house of our God."	6440
Est	6:10	not **n** anything you have recommended."	5877
Ps	119:16	I will not **n** your word.	8894
Lk	11:42	but *you* **n** justice and the love of God.	4216
Ac	6: 2	for us *to* **n** the ministry of the word of God	2901
1Ti	4:14	*Do* not **n** your gift,	288

NEGLECTED (3) [NEGLECT]

Ne	13:11	is the house of God **n**?"	6440
SS	1: 6	my own vineyard *I have* **n**.	4202+5757
Mt	23:23	But *you* **have** **n** the more important matters	918

NEGLECTING (1) [NEGLECT]

Mt	23:23	without **n** the former.	918

NEGLIGENT (2) [NEGLECT]

2Ch	29:11	My sons, *do not be* **n** now,	8922
Da	6: 4	and neither corrupt nor **n**.	10712

NEHELAMITE (3)

Jer	29:24	Tell Shemaiah the **N**,	5713
	29:31	the Lord says about Shemaiah the **N**:	5713
	29:32	I will surely punish Shemaiah the **N**	5713

NEHEMIAH (9)

Ezr	2: 2	**N**, Seraiah, Reelaiah, Mordecai, Bilshan,	5718
Ne	1: 1	The words of **N** son of Hacaliah:	5718
	3:16	Beyond him, **N** son of Azbuk,	5718
	7: 7	Jeshua, **N**, Azariah, Raamiah, Nahamani,	5718
	8: 9	Then **N** the governor,	5718
	8:10	**N** said, "Go and enjoy choice food	NIH
	10: 1	**N** the governor, the son of Hacaliah.	5718
	12:26	in the days of **N** the governor and of Ezra	5718
	12:47	So in the days of Zerubbabel and of **N**,	5718

NEHUM (1)

Ne	7: 7	Mispereth, Bigvai, **N** and Baanah):	5700

NEHUSHTA (1)

2Ki	24: 8	His mother's name was **N** daughter	5735

NEHUSHTAN (1)

2Ki	18: 4	(It was called **N**.)	5736

NEIEL (1)

Jos	19:27	and went north to Beth Emek and **N**,	5832

NEIGH (1) [NEIGHING, NEIGHINGS]

Jer	50:11	a heifer threshing grain and **n** like stallions,	7412

NEIGHBOR (81) [NEIGHBOR'S, NEIGHBORING, NEIGHBORS, NEIGHBORS']

Ex	3:22	to ask her **n** and any woman living	8907
	12: 4	they must share one with their nearest **n**,	8907
	20:16	not give false testimony against your **n**.	8276
	20:17	or anything that belongs to your **n**."	8276
	22: 7	If a man gives his **n** silver or goods	8276
	22: 9	guilty must pay back double to his **n**.	8276
	22:10	or any other animal to his **n** for safekeeping	8276
	22:11	of an oath before the Lord that the **n** did	2257S
Ex	22:12	But if the animal was stolen from **the n**,	2257S
	22:14	from his **n** and it is injured or dies while	8276
	32:27	each killing his brother and friend and **n**.' "	7940
Lev	6: 2	unfaithful to the Lord by deceiving his **n**	6660
	19:13	" 'Do not defraud your **n** or rob him.	8276
	19:15	but judge your **n** fairly.	6660
	19:17	Rebuke your **n** frankly so you will	6660
	19:18	but love your **n** as yourself.	8276
	20:10	with the wife of his **n**—	8276
	24:19	If anyone injures his **n**,	6660
Dt	4:42	if he had unintentionally killed his **n**	8276
	5:20	not give false testimony against your **n**.	8276
	5:21	or anything that belongs to your **n**,"	8276
	19: 4	one who kills his **n** unintentionally,	8276
	19: 5	a man may go into the forest with his **n**	8276
	19: 5	the head may fly off and hit his **n**	8276
	19: 6	to **his n** without malice aforethought.	2257S
	19:11	a man hates his **n** and lies in wait for him,	8276
	22:26	of someone who attacks and murders his **n**,	8276
	24:10	you make a loan of any kind to your **n**,	8276
	27:24	the man who kills his **n** secretly."	8276
Jos	20: 5	because he killed his **n** unintentionally and	8276
1Ki	8:31	"When a man wrongs his **n** and is required	8276
2Ch	6:22	"When a man wrongs his **n** and is required	8276
Ps	12: 2	Everyone lies to his **n**;	8276
	15: 3	who does his **n** no wrong and casts no slur	8276
	101: 5	Whoever slanders his **n** in secret,	8276
Pr	3:28	Do not say to your **n**, "Come back later;	8276
	3:29	Do not plot harm against your **n**,	8276
	6: 1	if you have put up security for your **n**,	8276
	6: 3	press your plea with your **n**!	8276
	11: 9	With his mouth the godless destroys his **n**,	8276
	11:12	A man who lacks judgment derides his **n**,	8276
	14:21	He who despises his **n** sins,	8276
	16:29	A violent man entices his **n** and leads him	8276
	17:18	in pledge and puts up security for his **n**.	8276
	21:10	his **n** gets no mercy from him.	8276
	24:28	Do not testify against your **n** without cause,	8276
	25: 8	in the end if your **n** puts you to shame?	8276
	25: 9	If you argue your case with a **n**,	8276
	25:18	who gives false testimony against his **n**.	8276
	26:19	is a man who deceives his **n** and says,	8276
	27:10	better a nearby than a brother far away.	8907
	27:14	If a man loudly blesses his **n** early in	8276
	29: 5	Whoever flatters his **n** is spreading a net	8276
Ecc	4: 4	from man's envy of his **n**.	8276
Isa	3: 5	man against man, **n** against neighbor.	408S
	3: 5	man against man, neighbor against **n**.	8276
	19: 2	**n** against neighbor, city against city,	408S
	19: 2	neighbor against **n**, city against city,	8276
Jer	9: 8	to his **n**, but in his heart he sets a trap	8276
	31:34	No longer will a man teach his **n**,	8276
Mic	7: 5	Do not trust a **n**;	8276
Zec	3:10	of you will invite his **n** to sit under his vine	8276
	8:10	for I had turned every man against his **n**.	8276
	8:17	do not plot evil against your **n**,	8276
	11: 6	"I will hand everyone over to his **n**	8276
Mt	5:43	'Love your **n** and hate your enemy.'	4446
	19:19	and 'love your **n** as yourself.'	4446
	22:39	second is like it: 'Love your **n** as yourself.'	4446
Mk	12:31	second is this: 'Love your **n** as yourself.'	4446
	12:33	and to love your **n** as yourself is more	4446
Lk	10:27	and, 'Love your **n** as yourself.' "	4446
	10:29	he asked Jesus, "And who is my **n**?"	4446
	10:36	"Which of these three do you think was a **n**	4446
Ro	13: 9	"Love your **n** as yourself."	4446
	13:10	Love does no harm to its **n**.	4446
	15: 2	Each of us should please his **n** for his good,	4446
Gal	5:14	"Love your **n** as yourself."	4446
Eph	4:25	and speak truthfully to his **n**,	4446
Heb	8:11	No longer will a man teach his **n**,	4489
Jas	2: 8	"Love your **n** as yourself,"	4446
	4:12	But you—who are you to judge your **n**?	4446

NEIGHBOR'S (20) [NEIGHBOR]

Ex	20:17	"You shall not covet your **n** house.	8276
	20:17	You shall not covet your **n** wife,	8276
	22: 7	and they are stolen from the **n** house,	408
	22:26	If you take your **n** cloak as a pledge,	8276
Lev	18:20	not have sexual relations with your **n** wife	6660
	19:16	not do anything that endangers your **n** life.	8276
Dt	5:21	"You shall not covet your **n** wife.	8276
	5:21	not set your desire on your **n** house or land,	8276
	19:14	Do not move your **n** boundary stone set up	8276
	23:24	If you enter your **n** vineyard,	8276
	23:25	If you enter your **n** grainfield,	8276
	27:17	the man who moves his **n** boundary stone."	8276
Job	31: 9	or if I have lurked at my **n** door,	8276
Pr	6: 3	since you have fallen into your **n** hands:	8276
	25:17	Seldom set foot in your **n** house—	8276
Eze	18: 6	not defile his **n** wife or lie with a woman	8276
	18:11	He defiles his **n** wife.	8276
	18:15	He does not defile his **n** wife.	8276
	22:11	a detestable offense with his **n** wife,	8276
	33:26	and each of you defiles his **n** wife.	8276

NEIGHBORING (10) [NEIGHBOR]

Dt	1: 7	go to all the **n** peoples in the Arabah,	8907
	21: 2	the distance from the body to the **n** towns.	6017
1Sa	7:14	and Israel delivered the **n** territory from	1473
Ezr	9: 1	themselves separate from the **n** peoples	824
Ne	10:28	so you handed them over to the **n** peoples.	824
	10:31	from the **n** peoples for the sake of the Law	824
	10:31	the **n** peoples bring merchandise or grain	824
Ps	76:11	let all the **n** *lands* bring gifts to the One to	6017

Jer 49:18 along with their **n** towns," says the LORD, 8907
    50:40 with their **n** towns," declares the LORD, 8907

NEIGHBORS (33) [NEIGHBOR]

Ex 11: 2 that men and women alike are to ask their **n** 8276
Jos 9:16 the Israelites heard that they were **n,** 7940
1Sa 15:28 and has given it to one of your **n**— 8276
    28:17 and given it to one of your **n**— 8276
2Ki 4: 3 around and ask all your **n** for empty jars. 8907
1Ch 12:40 Also, their **n** from as far away as Issachar, 7940
Ezr 1: 6 All their **n** assisted them with articles 6017
    6:21 the unclean practices of their Gentile **n** 824
Ps 28: 3 who speak cordially with their **n** 8276
    31:11 I am the utter contempt of my **n;** 8907
    38:11 my **n** stay far away. 7940
    44:13 You have made us a reproach to our **n,** 8907
    79: 4 We are objects of reproach to our **n,** 8907
    79:12 Pay back into the laps of our **n** seven times 8907
    80: 6 a source of contention to our **n,** 8907
    89:41 he has become the scorn of his **n.** 8907
Pr 14:20 The poor are shunned even by their **n,** 8276
Jer 6:21 **n** and friends will perish." 8907
    12:14 "As for all my wicked **n** who seize 8907
    49:10 His children, relatives and **n** will perish, 8907
La 1:17 for Jacob that his **n** become his foes; 6017
Eze 16:26 your lustful **n,** and provoked me to anger 8907
    16:57 by the daughters of Edom and all her **n** and 6017
    22:12 and make unjust gain from your **n** 8276
    28:24 people of Israel have malicious **n** who are
         painful briers 6017
    28:26 on all their **n** who maligned them. 6017
Hab 2:15 "Woe to him who gives drink to his **n,** 8276
Lk 1:58 Her **n** and relatives heard that 4341
    1:65 The **n** were all filled with awe, 4340
    14:12 your brothers or relatives, or your rich **n;** 1150
    15: 6 he calls his friends and **n** together and says, 1150
    15: 9 and **n** together and says, 'Rejoice with me; 1150
Jn 9: 8 His **n** and those who had formerly seen him
         begging asked, 1150

NEIGHBORS' (1) [NEIGHBOR]

Jer 29:23 committed adultery with their **n'** wives and 8276

NEIGHING (2) [NEIGH]

Jer 5: 8 each **n** for another man's wife. 7412
    8:16 at the **n** *of* their stallions 5177+7754

NEIGHINGS (1) [NEIGH]

Jer 13:27 your adulteries and **lustful n,** 5177

NEITHER (117) [NOR]

Ex 4:10 **n** in the past nor since you have spoken 1685
    10: 6 something **n** your fathers 4202
    13:22 N the pillar of cloud by day nor the pillar 4202
    14:20 so **n** went near the other all night long. 2296+4202
    20:10 On it you shall not do any work, **n** you, NIH
Nu 14:44 though **n** Moses nor the ark of the LORD's 4202
    23:25 "N curse them at all nor bless them at all!" 1685+4202
Dt 2:37 **n** the land along the course of the Jabbok NIH
    5:14 On it you shall not do any work, **n** you, NIH
    8: 3 which **n** you nor your fathers had known, 4202
    13: 6 and worship other gods" (gods that **n** you 4202
    28:64 which **n** you nor your fathers have known. 4202
Jos 5:14 "N," he replied, "but as commander of 4202
    8:22 leaving them **n** survivors nor fugitives. 1194
Jdg 1:30 N did Zebulun drive out the Canaanites 4202
    1:33 N did Naphtali drive out those living 4202
    2:10 who knew **n** the LORD nor what he had done 4202
    6: 4 **n** sheep nor cattle nor donkeys. 2256
    11:34 Except for her he had **n** son nor daughter. 401
    14: 6 But he told **n** his father 4202
1Sa 5: 5 That is why to this day **n** the priests 4202
    20:31 **n** you nor your kingdom will 4202
2Sa 1:21 may you have **n** dew nor rain, 440
    2:19 turning **n** to the right nor to the left 4202
    14: 7 leaving my husband **n** name nor descendant 1194
    17:12 N he nor any of his men will be left alive. 4202
1Ki 3:26 said, "N I nor you shall have him. 1685+4202
    13:28 The lion had **n** eaten the body nor mauled 4202
    17: 1 there will be **n** dew nor rain in 561
2Ki 3:17 You will see **n** wind nor rain, 4202
    17:34 They **n** worship the LORD nor adhere to 401
    18:12 They **n** listened to the commands 4202
    23:25 N before nor after Josiah was there a king
         like him 2256+4202
2Ch 36:17 spared **n** young man nor young woman, 4202
Ne 4:23 N I nor my brothers nor my men nor 401
    5:14 **n** I nor my brothers ate the food allotted to 4202
Est 2: 7 up because she had **n** father nor mother. 401
    5: 9 the king's gate and observed that he **n** rose 401
Job 28:17 N gold nor crystal can compare with it, 4202
Ps 121: 4 he who watches over Israel will **n** slumber 4202
Pr 27:20 and **n** are the eyes of man. 4202
    30: 8 give me **n** poverty nor riches, 440
Ecc 4: 8 he had **n** son nor brother. 401
    7:16 Do not be overrighteous, **n** be overwise 440+2256
    9:10 there is **n** working nor planning 401
Isa 5: 6 **n** pruned nor cultivated. 4202
    11: 9 They will **n** harm nor destroy 4202
    23: 4 "I have **n** been in labor nor given birth; 4202
    23: 4 I have **n** reared sons nor brought 2256
    30: 5 who bring **n** help nor advantage, 4202
    48: 8 You have **n** heard nor understood; 1685+4202

Isa 49:10 They will **n** hunger nor thirst, 4202
    55: 8 **n** are your ways my ways," 2256+4202
    57:11 and have **n** remembered me 4202
    65:25 They will **n** harm nor destroy 4202
Jer 9:16 that **n** they nor their fathers have known, 4202
    13:23 N can you do good who are accustomed 1685
    15:10 I have **n** lent nor borrowed, 4202
    16:13 a land **n** you nor your fathers have known, 4202
    19: 4 in it to gods that **n** they nor their fathers nor 4202
    22:26 where **n** of you was born, 4202
    33:10 inhabited by **n** men nor animals, 401+4946
    35: 6 N you nor your descendants must ever drink 4202
    35: 8 N we nor our wives nor our sons 1194
    37: 2 N he nor his attendants nor the people 2256+4202
    38:16 I will **n** kill you nor hand you over 561
    44: 3 and by worshiping other gods that **n** they 4202
    49:31 "a nation that has **n** gates nor bars; 4202
    51:62 so that **n** man nor animal will live in it; 1194
Eze 14:20 they could save **n** son nor daughter. 561
Da 3: 7 **n** they nor their kings— NIH
    3:12 They **n** serve your gods nor worship 10379
    6: 4 because he was trustworthy and **n** corrupt NIH
    11:24 and will achieve what **n** his fathers 4202
Am 7:14 "I was **n** a prophet nor a prophet's son, 4202
Zep 1: 6 and **n** seek the LORD nor inquire of him. 4202
    1:18 N their silver nor their gold will be 1685+4202
Mt 5:15 N do people light a lamp and put it under 4028
    9:17 N do men pour new wine 4028
    11:18 For John came **n** eating nor drinking, 3612
    21:27 "N will I tell you by what authority 4028
    22:30 At the resurrection people will **n** marry nor 4046
Mk 11:33 "N will I tell you by what authority 4028
    12:25 they will **n** marry nor be given in marriage; 4046
Lk 7:33 For John the Baptist came **n** eating bread 3590
    7:42 N of them had the money to pay him back, 3590
    14:35 It is fit **n** for the soil nor for 4046
    18: 2 a judge who **n** feared God nor cared 3590
    20: 8 "N will I tell you by what authority 4028
    20:35 the resurrection from the dead will **n** marry 4046
    23:15 N has Herod, for he sent him back to us; 4028
Jn 4:21 when you will worship the Father **n** 4046
    6:24 that **n** Jesus nor his disciples were there, 4024
    8:11 so do I condemn you," Jesus declared. 4028
    9: 3 "N this man nor his parents sinned," 4046
    12:40 so they can **n** see with their eyes, 3590
    14:17 because it **n** sees him nor knows him 4024
    15: 4 N can you bear fruit unless you remain 4028
Ac 15:10 the necks of the disciples a yoke that **n** we 4046
    19:37 though they have **n** robbed temples 4046
    23: 8 and that there are **n** angels nor spirits, 3612
    27:20 When **n** sun nor stars appeared 3612
Ro 1:21 they **n** glorified him as God 4024
    8:38 For I am convinced that **n** death nor life, 4046
    8:38 **n** angels nor demons, 4046
    8:38 **n** the present nor the future, 4046
    8:39 **n** height nor depth, nor anything else 4046
1Co 3: 7 So he who plants nor he who waters 4046
    6: 9 N the sexually immoral nor idolaters 4046
    11: 9 **n** was man created for woman, 2779+4024
2Co 10:15 N do we go beyond our limits by boasting 4024
Gal 3:28 There is **n** Jew nor Greek, slave nor free, 4024
    5: 6 For in Christ Jesus **n** circumcision 4046
    6:15 N circumcision nor uncircumcision means
         anything; 4046
Jas 3:12 N can a salt spring produce fresh water. 4046
Rev 3:15 that you are **n** cold nor hot. 4046
    3:16 you are lukewarm—**n** hot nor cold— 4046

NEKEB See ADAMI NEKEB

NEKODA (4)

Ezr 2:48 Rezin, N, Gazzam, 5928
    2:60 Tobiah and N 652 5928
Ne 7:50 Reaiah, Rezin, N, 5928
    7:62 Tobiah and N 642 5928

NEMUEL (3) [NEMUELITE]

Nu 26: 9 and the sons of Eliab were N, 5803
    26:12 through N, the Nemuelite clan; 5803
1Ch 4:24 N, Jamin, Jarib, Zerah and Shaul; 5803

NEMUELITE (1) [NEMUEL]

Nu 26:12 through Nemuel, the N clan; 5804

NEPHEG (4)

Ex 6:21 The sons of Izhar were Korah, N and Zicri. 5863
2Sa 5:15 Ibhar, Elishua, N, Japhia, 5863
1Ch 3: 7 Nogah, N, Japhia, 5863
    14: 6 Nogah, N, Japhia, 5863

NEPHEW (2) [NEPHEWS]

Ge 12: 5 He took his wife Sarai, his **n** Lot, 278+1201
    14:12 They also carried off Abram's **n** Lot 278+1201

NEPHEWS (1) [NEPHEW]

Ezr 8:19 and his brothers and **n,** 20 men. 1201+2157

NEPHILIM (3)

Ge 6: 4 The N were on the earth in those days— 5872
Nu 13:33 the N there (the descendants of Anak come 5872
    13:33 descendants of Anak come from the N). 5872

NEPHISH (KJV) See NAPHISH

NEPHISHESIM (KJV) See NEPHUSSIM

NEPHTHALIM, NEPTHALIM (KJV) See NAPHTALI

NEPHTOAH (2)

Jos 15: 9 toward the spring of the waters of N, 5886
    18:15 at the spring of the waters of N. 5886

NEPHUSSIM (2)

Ezr 2:50 Asnah, Meunim, N, 5866
Ne 7:52 Besai, Meunim, N, 5867

NER (18)

1Sa 14:50 of Saul's army was Abner son of N, 5945
    14:50 and N was Saul's uncle. NIH
    14:51 and Abner's father N were sons of Abiel. 5945
    26: 5 He saw where Saul and Abner son of N, 5945
    26:14 to the army and to Abner son of N, 5945
2Sa 2: 8 Meanwhile, Abner son of N, 5945
    2:12 Abner son of N, together with the men 5945
    3:23 he was told that Abner son of N had come 5945
    3:25 You know Abner son of N; 5945
    3:28 concerning the blood of Abner son of N. 5945
    3:37 in the murder of Abner son of N. 5945
1Ki 2: 5 Abner son of N and Amasa son of Jether. 5945
    2:32 Both of them—Abner son of N, 5945
1Ch 8:30 followed by Zur, Kish, Baal, N, Nadab, 5945
    8:33 N was the father of Kish, 5945
    9:36 followed by Zur, Kish, Baal, N, Nadab, 5945
    9:39 N was the father of Kish, 5945
    26:28 Abner son of N and Joab son of Zeruiah, 5945

NEREUS (1)

Ro 16:15 Greet Philologus, Julia, N and his sister, 3759

NERGAL (1)

2Ki 17:30 the men from Cuthah made N, 5946

NERGAL-SHAREZER (3)

Jer 39: 3 N *of* Samgar, Nebo-Sarsekim 5947
    39: 3 N a high official and all the other officials 5947
    39:13 N a high official and all the other officers 5947

NERI (1)

Lk 3:27 the son of Shealtiel, the son *of* N, 3760

NERIAH (10)

Jer 32:12 and I gave this deed to Baruch son of N, 5949
    32:16 of purchase to Baruch son of N, I prayed to 5949
    36: 4 So Jeremiah called Baruch son of N, 5949
    36: 8 Baruch son of N did everything Jeremiah 5949
    36:14 So Baruch son of N went to them with 5950
    36:32 and gave it to the scribe Baruch son of N, 5950
    43: 3 of N is inciting you against us to hand us 5949
    43: 6 Jeremiah the prophet and Baruch son of N. 5950
    45: 1 of N in the fourth year of Jehoiakim son 5949
    51:59 to the staff officer Seraiah son of N, 5949

NEST (17) [NESTED, NESTING, NESTS]

Nu 24:21 your **n** is set in a rock; 7860
Dt 22: 6 you come across a bird's **n** beside the road, 7860
    32:11 that stirs up its **n** and hovers over its young, 7860
Job 39:27 at your command and build his **n** on high? 7860
Ps 84: 3 and the swallow a **n** for herself, 7860
    104:12 The birds of the air **n** by the waters; 8905
Pr 27: 8 that strays from its **n** is a man who strays 7860
Isa 10:14 As one reaches into a **n,** 7860
    11: 8 young child put his hand into the viper's **n.** 4402
    16: 2 Like fluttering birds pushed from the **n,** 7860
    34:11 the great owl and the raven will **n** there. 8905
    34:15 The owl will **n** there and lay eggs, 7873
Jer 48:28 like a dove *that* **makes** *its* **n** at the mouth of 7873
    49:16 you build your **n** as high as the eagle's, 7860
Eze 17:23 Birds of every kind will **n** in it; 8905
Ob 1: 4 the eagle and make your **n** among the stars, 7860
Hab 2: 9 by unjust gain to set his **n** on high, 7860

NESTED (1) [NEST]

Eze 31: 6 All the birds of the air **n** in its boughs, 7873

NESTING (1) [NEST]

Da 4:21 and *having* **n** places in its branches for 10709

NESTLED (1)

Jer 22:23 who are **n** in cedar buildings, 7873

NESTS (4) [NEST]

Ps 104:17 There the birds **make** *their* **n;** 7873
Isa 60: 8 like doves to their **n?** 748
Mt 8:20 birds of the air have **n,** but the Son of Man 2943
Lk 9:58 birds of the air have **n,** but the Son of Man 2943

NET (33) [DRAGNET, FISHNETS, NETS]

Job	18: 8	His feet thrust him into a **n** and he wanders	8407
	19: 6	that God has wronged me and drawn his **n**	5178
Ps	9:15	in the **n** they have hidden.	8407
	10: 9	the helpless and drags them off in his **n**.	8407
	35: 7	Since they hid their **n** for me without cause	8407
	35: 8	may the **n** they hid entangle them,	8407
	57: 6	They spread a **n** for my feet;	8407
	140: 5	they have spread out the cords of their **n**	8407
Pr	1:17	to spread a **n** in full view of all the birds!	8407
	29: 5	is spreading a **n** for his feet.	8407
Ecc	9:12	As fish are caught in a cruel **n**,	5182
Isa	51:20	like antelope caught in a **n**.	4821
La	1:13	a **n** for my feet and turned me back.	8407
Eze	12:13	I will spread my **n** for him,	8407
	17:20	I will spread my **n** for him,	8407
	19: 8	They spread their **n** for him,	8407
	32: 3	a great throng of people I will cast my **n**	8407
	32: 3	and they will haul you up in my **n**.	3052
Hos	5: 1	a **n** spread out on Tabor.	8407
	7:12	they go, I will throw my **n** over them;	8407
Mic	7: 2	each hunts his brother with a **n**.	3052
Hab	1:15	he catches them in his **n**,	3052
	1:16	to his **n** and burns incense to his dragnet,	3052
	1:16	for by **his n** he lives in luxury and enjoys	2156S
	1:17	Is he to keep on emptying his **n**,	3052
Mt	4:18	They were casting a **n** into the lake,	312
	13:47	of heaven is like a **n** that was let down into	4880
Mk	1:16	and his brother Andrew **casting a n** into	311
Jn	21: 6	"Throw your **n** on the right side of the boat	1473
	21: 6	they were unable to haul **the n** in because of	899S
	21: 8	towing the **n** full of fish,	1473
	21:11	aboard and dragged the **n** ashore.	1473
	21:11	but even with so many the **n** was not torn.	1473

NETAIM (1)

1Ch	4:23	the potters who lived at **N** and Gederah;	5751

NETHANEL (14)

Nu	1: 8	from Issachar, **N** son of Zuar;	5991
	2: 5	of the people of Issachar is **N** son of Zuar.	5991
	7:18	On the second day **N** son of Zuar,	5991
	7:23	This was the offering of **N** son of Zuar.	5991
	10:15	**N** son of Zuar was over the division of	5991
1Ch	2:14	the fourth **N**, the fifth Raddai,	5991
	15:24	Shebaniah, Joshaphat, **N**, Amasai,	5991
	24: 6	The scribe Shemaiah son of **N**, a Levite,	5991
	26: 4	Joah the third, Sacar the fourth, **N** the fifth,	5991
2Ch	17: 7	and Micaiah to teach in the towns	5991
	35: 9	Conaniah along with Shemaiah and **N**,	5991
Ezr	10:22	Elioenai, Maaseiah, Ishmael, **N**,	5991
Ne	12:21	of Hilkiah's, Hashabiah; of Jedaiah's, **N**.	5991
	12:36	Gilalai, Maai, **N**, Judah and Hanani—	5991

NETHANIAH (20)

2Ki	25:23	Ishmael son of **N**, Johanan son of Kareah,	5992
	25:25	Ishmael son of **N**, the son of Elishama,	5992
1Ch	25: 2	Zaccur, Joseph, **N** and Asarelah.	5992
	25:12	the fifth to **N**, his sons and relatives, 12	5993
2Ch	17: 8	Shemaiah, **N**, Zebadiah, Asahel,	5993
Jer	36:14	all the officials sent Jehudi son of **N**,	5993
	40: 8	Ishmael son of **N**,	5993
	40:14	the Ammonites has sent Ishmael son of **N**	5992
	40:15	"Let me go and kill Ishmael son of **N**,	5992
	41: 1	In the seventh month Ishmael son of **N**,	5992
	41: 2	of **N** and the ten men who were	5992
	41: 6	of **N** went out from Mizpah to meet them,	5992
	41: 7	Ishmael son of **N** and the men who were	5992
	41: 9	Ishmael son of **N** filled it with the dead.	5993
	41:10	Ishmael son of **N** took them captive	5992
	41:11	crimes Ishmael son of **N** had committed,	5992
	41:12	and went to fight Ishmael son of **N**.	5992
	41:15	Ishmael son of **N** and eight of his men	5992
	41:16	of **N** after he had assassinated Gedaliah son	5992
	41:18	of **N** had killed Gedaliah son of Ahikam,	5992

NETHER, NETHERMOST (KJV) See BELOW, FOOT, LOWER, LOWEST

NETHINIMS (KJV) See TEMPLE SERVANTS

NETOPHAH (2)

Ezr	2:22	of **N** 56	5756
Ne	7:26	the men of Bethlehem and **N** 188	5756

NETOPHATHITE (8) [NETOPHATHITES]

2Sa	23:28	Zalmon the Ahohite, Maharai the **N**,	5743
	23:29	Heled son of Baanah the **N**,	5743
2Ki	25:23	Seraiah son of Tanhumeth the **N**,	5743
1Ch	11:30	Maharai the **N**, Heled son of Baanah	5743
	11:30	Heled son of Baanah the **N**,	5743
	27:13	for the tenth month, was Maharai the **N**,	5743
	27:15	for the twelfth month, was Heldai the **N**,	5743
Jer	40: 8	the sons of Ephai the **N**,	5743

NETOPHATHITES (3) [NETOPHATHITE]

1Ch	2:54	Bethlehem, the **N**, Atroth Beth Joab,	5743
	9:16	who lived in the villages of the **N**.	5743
Ne	12:28	from the villages of the **N**,	5743

NETS (11) [NET]

Ps	141:10	Let the wicked fall into their own **n**,	4821
Isa	19: 8	those who throw **n** on the water will pine	4823
Eze	47:10	will be places for spreading **n**.	3052
Mt	4:20	At once they left their **n** and followed him.	1473
	4:21	with their father Zebedee, preparing their **n**.	1473
Mk	1:18	At once they left their **n** and followed him.	1473
	1:19	in a boat, preparing their **n**.	1473
Lk	5: 2	who were washing their **n**.	1473
	5: 4	and let down the **n** for a catch."	1473
	5: 5	because you say so, I will let down the **n**."	1473
	5: 6	a large number of fish that their **n** began	1473

NETTLES (1)

Isa	34:13	**n** and brambles her strongholds.	7853

NETWORK (16)

Ex	27: 4	Make a grating for it, a bronze **n**,	5126+8407
	27: 4	at each of the four corners of the **n**.	8407
	38: 4	a bronze **n**, to be under its ledge,	5126+8407
1Ki	7:17	A **n** of interwoven chains	5126+8422+8422
	7:18	in two rows encircling each **n** to decorate	8422
	7:20	above the bowl-shaped part next to the **n**,	8422
	7:41	the two sets of **n** decorating	8422
	7:42	two sets of **n** (two rows of pomegranates	8422
	7:42	of pomegranates for each **n**, decorating	8422
2Ki	25:17	a **n** and pomegranates of bronze all around.	8422
	25:17	The other pillar, with its **n**, was similar.	8422
2Ch	4:12	the two sets of **n** decorating	8422
	4:13	two sets of **n** (two rows of pomegranates	8422
	4:13	of pomegranates for each **n**, decorating	8422
Jer	52:22	a **n** and pomegranates of bronze all around.	8422
	52:23	above the surrounding **n** was a hundred.	8422

NETWORKS (KJV) See GRATING

NEVER (343)

Ge	8:21	"**N** again will I curse the ground because	4202
	8:21	**n** again will I destroy all living creatures,	4202
	8:22	day and night will **n** cease."	4202
	9:11	**N** again will all life be cut off by the waters	4202
	9:11	**n** again will there be a flood to destroy	4202
	9:15	**N** again will the waters become a flood	4202
	14:23	so that you will **n** be able to say,	4202
	19: 8	I have two daughters who have **n** slept with	4202
	21:10	for that slave woman's son will **n** share in	4202
	41:19	I had **n** seen such ugly cows in all the land	4202
	45:20	**N** mind about your belongings,	440+6524
	48:11	"I **n** expected to see your face again,	4202
Ex	4:10	"O Lord, I have **n** been eloquent,	4202
	10:14	**N** before had there been such a plague	4202
	10:29	"I will **n** appear before you again."	4202
	14:13	The Egyptians you see today you will **n** see again.	4202+6330+6409
	34:10	Before all your people I will do wonders **n**	4202
Lev	27:20	it can be redeemed.	4202+6388
Nu	11: 6	we **n** see anything but this manna!"	401
	19: 2	or blemish and that has **n** been under	4202
	31:18	for yourselves every girl who has **n** slept	4202
	31:35	women who had **n** slept with a man.	4202
Dt	8:16	something your fathers had **n** known,	4202
	9: 7	and **n** forget how you provoked	440
	13:16	a ruin forever, **n** to be rebuilt.	4202+6388
	19:20	and **n** again will such an evil thing be done	4202
	21: 3	that has **n** been worked and has never worn	4202
	21: 3	that has never been worked and has **n** worn	4202
	22:29	He can **n** divorce her as long as he lives.	4202
	28:13	always be at the top, **n** at the bottom.	4202
	28:66	**n** sure of your life.	4202
	28:68	a journey I said you should **n** make again.	4202
	29:20	Lord will **n** be willing to forgive him;	4202
	31: 6	he will **n** leave you nor forsake you."	4202
	31: 8	he will **n** leave you nor forsake you.	4202
Jos	1: 5	I will **n** leave you nor forsake you.	4202
	3: 4	since you have **n** been this way before.	4202
	9:23	You will **n** cease to serve as woodcutters	4202
	10:14	There has **n** been a day like it before or	4202
Jdg	1:28	but **n** drove them out completely.	4202
	2: 1	'I will **n** break my covenant with you,	4200+4202+6409
	11:37	because I will **n** marry."	1436
	11:38	and wept because she would **n** marry.	1436
	16:11	with new ropes that have **n** been used,	4202
	19:30	"Such a thing has **n** been seen or done,	4202
	21:12	young women who had **n** slept with a man,	4202
1Sa	2:32	in your family line there will **n** be an old man.	2021+3427+3972+4202
	3:14	'The guilt of Eli's house will **n** be atoned for	561+6330+6409
	6: 7	that have calved and have **n** been yoked.	4202
	14:45	about this great deliverance in Israel? **N**!	2721
	20: 2	"**N**!" Jonathan replied. "You are not	2721
	20: 9	"**N**!" Jonathan said. "If I had the least	2721
2Sa	3:29	May Joab's house **n** be without someone	440
	7:15	my love will **n** be taken away from him,	4202
	12:10	the sword will **n** depart from your house,	4202+6330+6409
	13:22	Absalom **n** said a word to Amnon.	4202
	21:17	"**N** again will you go out with us to battle,	4202
1Ki	1: 6	(His father had **n** interfered with him by asking,	3427+4202+4946
	2: 4	with all their heart and soul, you will **n** fail	4202
	3:12	that there will **n** have been anyone like you,	4200+4202+7156
1Ki	8:25	'You shall **n** fail to have a man to sit before	4202
	8:57	may he **n** leave us nor forsake us.	440
	9: 5	'You shall **n** fail to have a man on	4202
	10:10	**N** again were so many spices brought in	4202
	10:12	So much almugwood has **n** been imported	4202
	21:25	(There was **n** a man like Ahab,	4202
	22: 8	because he **n** prophesies anything good	4202
	22:18	that he **n** prophesies anything good	4202
	22:48	but they **n** set sail—	4202
2Ki	1:16	you will **n** leave the bed you are lying on.	4202
	2:21	**N** again will it cause death or make	4202
	5:17	servant will **n** again make burnt offerings	4202
1Ch	17:13	I will **n** take my love away from him,	4202
2Ch	6:16	'You shall **n** fail to have a man to sit	4202
	7:18	'You shall **n** fail to have a man to rule	4202
	9: 9	There had **n** been such spices as those	4202
	18: 7	because he **n** prophesies anything good	401
	18:17	that he **n** prophesies anything good	4202
Ne	5:18	I demanded the food allotted to	4202
Est	1:19	that Vashti is **n** again to enter the presence	4202
	9:28	of Purim should **n** cease to be celebrated by	4202
Job	3:16	like an infant who **n** saw the light of day?	4202
	7: 7	my eyes will **n** see happiness again.	4202
	7:10	He will **n** come to his house again;	4202
	7:19	Will you **n** look away from me,	4202
	8:18	'I **n** saw you.'	4202
	10:19	If only I had **n** come into being,	4202
	16: 3	Will your long-winded speeches **n** end?	NIH
	16:18	may my cry **n** be laid to rest!	440
	19:22	Will you **n** get enough of my flesh?	4202
	21:10	Their bulls **n** fail to breed;	4202
	21:25	**n** having enjoyed anything good.	4202
	21:29	Have you **n** questioned those who travel?	4202
	27: 5	I will **n** admit you are in the right;	561+2721
	27: 6	my righteousness and **n** let go of it;	4202
	27:14	his offspring will **n** have enough to eat.	4202
	30:17	my gnawing pains **n** rest.	4202
	31:31	if the men of my household have **n** said,	4202
	35:15	that his anger **n** punishes and he does	401
	41: 8	the struggle and **n** do it again!	440
Ps	9:10	have **n** forsaken those who seek you.	4202
	10: 6	I'll always be happy and **n** have trouble."	4202
	10:11	he covers his face and **n** sees."	1153+4200+5905
	14: 4	Will evildoers **n** learn—	4202
	15: 5	He who does these things will **n** be shaken.	4200+4202+6409
	28: 5	he will tear them down and **n** build them	4202
	30: 6	I felt secure, I said, "I will **n** be shaken."	1153+4200+6409
	31: 1	let me **n** be put to shame;	440+4200+6409
	34: 5	their faces are **n** covered with shame.	440
	37:25	yet I have **n** seen the righteous forsaken	4202
	41: 8	he will **n** get up from the place	3578+4202
	49:19	who will **n** see the light [of life].	4202+5905+6330
	53: 4	Will the evildoers **n** learn—	4202
	55:11	threats and lies **n** leave its streets.	4202
	55:19	men who **n** change their ways	401
	55:22	he will **n** let the righteous fall.	4200+4202+6409
	62: 2	he is my fortress, I will **n** be shaken.	4202+8041
	71: 1	let me **n** be put to shame.	440+4200+6409
	77: 7	"Will he **n** show his favor again?	4202
	89:28	and my covenant with him *will* **n** fail.	586
	94: 14	he will **n** forsake his inheritance.	4202
	95:11	"They shall **n** enter my rest."	561
	102:27	and your years will **n** end.	4202
	104: 5	it can be moved.	1153+2256+6329+6409
	104: 9	**n** again will they cover the earth.	1153
	109:14	may the sin of his mother be **n** blotted out.	440
	109:16	For he **n** thought of doing a kindness,	4202
	112: 6	Surely he will **n** be shaken;	4200+4202+6409
	119:93	I will **n** forget your precepts,	4200+4202+6409
	140:10	into miry pits, **n** to rise.	1153
	148: 6	he gave a decree that will **n** pass away.	4202
Pr	3: 3	Let love and faithfulness **n** leave you;	440
	5:17	**n** to be shared with strangers.	401
	6:33	and his shame will **n** be wiped away;	4202
	7:11	her feet **n** stay at home;	4202
	10:30	righteous will **n** be uprooted.	1153+4200+6409
	17:13	evil will **n** leave his house.	4202
	21:17	whoever loves wine and oil will **n** be rich.	4202
	25:10	and you will **n** lose your bad reputation.	4202
	27:20	Death and Destruction **n** satisfied,	4202
	30:15	"There are three things that are **n** satisfied,	4202
	30:15	four that **n** say, 'Enough!':	4202
	30:16	which is **n** satisfied with water, and fire,	4202
	30:16	and fire, which **n** says, 'Enough!'	4202
Ecc	1: 7	flow into the sea, yet the sea is **n** full.	401
	1: 8	The eye **n** has enough of seeing,	4202
	5:10	Whoever loves money **n** has money enough;	4202
	5:10	whoever loves wealth is **n** satisfied	4202
	6: 5	Though it **n** saw the sun or knew anything,	4202
	6: 7	yet his appetite is **n** satisfied.	4202
	7:20	on earth who does what is right and **n** sins.	4202
	9: 6	**n** again will they have a part in anything that happens	401+4200+6409
SS	7: 2	a rounded goblet that **n** lacks blended wine.	440
Isa	6: 9	' 'Be ever hearing, but **n** understanding;	440
	6: 9	be ever seeing, but **n** perceiving.'	440
	13:20	She will **n** be inhabited or lived	4200+4202+5905
	14:20	of the wicked will **n** be mentioned again.	4202
	24:20	that it falls—**n** to rise again.	4202
	25: 2	it will **n** be rebuilt.	4200+4202+6409
	28:16	the one who trusts will **n** be dismayed.	4202
	33:20	its stakes will **n** be pulled up,	1153+4200+5905
	43:17	and they lay there, **n** to rise again,	1153
	45:17	you will **n** be put to shame or disgraced,	4202

Isa	47: 8	I will **n** be a widow or suffer the loss	4202
	48:19	their name would **n** be cut off	4202
	51: 6	my righteousness will **n** fail.	4202
	51:22	you will **n** drink again.	3578+4202
	54: 1	O barren woman, you who **n** bore a child;	4202
	54: 1	shout for joy, you who were in **n** labor;	4202
	54: 9	the waters of Noah would **n** again cover	4946
	54: 9	**n** to rebuke you again.	4946
	56:11	they **n** have enough.	4202
	58:11	like a spring whose waters **n** fail.	4202
	60:11	they will **n** be shut, day or night,	4202
	60:20	Your sun will **n** set again,	4202
	62: 6	they will **n** be silent day or night.	4202+9458
	62: 8	"**N** again will I give your grain as food	561
	62: 8	and **n** again will foreigners drink	561
	65:20	"**N** again will there be in it	4202
Jer	3:16	It will **n** enter their minds or	4202
	5:12	we will **n** see sword or famine.	4202
	15:17	I **n** sat in the company of revelers,	4202
	15:17	**n** made merry with them;	NIH
	17: 8	a year of drought and **n** fails to bear fruit."	4202
	20:11	their dishonor will **n** be forgotten.	4202+6400
	22:10	because he will **n** return	4202+6388
	22:11	"He will **n** return.	4202+6388
	22:27	You will **n** come back to the land you long	4202
	31:40	city will **n** again be uprooted	4200+4202+6409
	32:35	though I **n** commanded,	4202
	32:40	I will **n** stop doing good to them,	4202
	32:40	so that they will **n** turn away from me.	1194
	33:17	'David will **n** fail to have a man to sit on	4202
	35: 7	Also you must **n** build houses,	4202
	35: 7	you must **n** have any of these things,	4202
	35:19	'Jonadab son of Recab will **n** fail to have a man to serve me.'	2021+3427+3972+4202
	42:18	you will **n** see this place again.'	4202
	50:39	It will **n** again be inhabited or	4200+4202+5905
La	3:22	for his compassions **n** fail.	4202
Eze	4:14	I have **n** defiled myself.	4202
	4:14	now I have **n** eaten anything found dead	4202
	5: 9	I will do to you what I have **n** done before	4202
	5: 9	before and will **n** do again.	4202
	16:48	and her daughters **n** did what you	561
	16:63	be ashamed and **n** again open your mouth	4202
	20:32	But what you have in mind will **n** happen.	4202
	26:14	You will **n** be rebuilt,	4202+6388
	26:21	and **n** again be found,	4200+4202+6409
	29:15	of kingdoms and will **n** again exalt itself	4202
	29:15	that it will **n** again rule over the nations.	1194
	36:12	you will **n** again deprive them	4202
	37:22	and they will **n** again be two nations or	4202
	43: 7	of Israel will **n** again defile my holy name—	4202
Da	2:44	God of heaven will set up a kingdom that will **n** be destroyed,	10378+10379+10550
	6: 5	"We will **n** find any basis for charges	10379
	6:26	his dominion will **n** end.	10002+10509+10527
	6:26	his kingdom is one that will **n** be destroyed.	10379
Hos	14: 3	We will **n** again say 'Our gods'	4202
Joel	2: 2	as **n** was of old nor ever will be in ages	4202
	2:19	**n** again will I make you an object of scorn	4202
	2:26	**n** again will my people be shamed.	4200+4202+6409
	2:27	**n** again will my people be shamed.	4200+4202+6409
	3:17	**n** again will foreigners invade her.	4202
Am	5: 2	**n** to rise again, deserted in her own land,	4202
	8: 7	"I will **n** forget anything they have done.	561+4200+5905
	8:14	they will fall, **n** to rise again."	4202
	9:15	**n** again to be uprooted from	4202
Ob	1:16	and drink and be as if they had **n** been.	4202
Na	3: 1	full of plunder, **n** without victims!	4202
Hab	2: 5	and justice **n** prevails.	4200+4202+5905
	2: 5	he is arrogant and **n** at rest.	4202
	2: 5	as the grave and like death is **n** satisfied,	4202
Zep	3:11	**N** again will you be haughty	4202
	3:15	**n** again will you fear any harm.	4202
Hag	1: 6	You eat, but **n** have enough.	401
	1: 6	You drink, but **n** have your fill.	401
Zec	9: 8	**N** again will an oppressor overrun my people,	4202
	14:11	**n** again will it be destroyed.	4202
Mt	7:23	'I **n** knew you. Away from me,	4030
	13:14	be ever hearing but **n** understanding;	3590+4024
	13:14	will be ever seeing but **n** perceiving.	3590+4024
	16:22	and began to rebuke him. "**N**, Lord!"	2664
	16:22	"This shall **n** happen to you!"	3590+4024
	18: 3	will **n** enter the kingdom of heaven.	3590+4024
	21:16	"Yes," replied Jesus, "have you **n** read,	4030
	21:19	"May you **n** bear fruit again!"	3600
	21:42	"Have you **n** read in the Scriptures:	4030
	24:21	**n** to be equaled **again**.	3590+4024
	24:35	but my words will **n** pass away.	3590+4024
	26:33	if all fall away on account of you, I **n** will."	4030
	26:35	I will **n** disown you."	3590+4024
Mk	2:12	"We have **n** seen anything like this!"	4030
	2:25	"Have you **n** read what David did when he	4030
	3:29	whoever blasphemes against the Holy Spirit will **n** be forgiven;	172+1650+3836+4024
	4:12	but **n** perceiving, and ever hearing	3590
	4:12	and ever hearing but **n** understanding;	3590
	9:25	come out of him and **n** enter him **again**."	3600
	9:43	where the fire **n** goes out.	812
	10:15	like a little child will **n** enter it.	3590+4024
	13:19	and to be equaled **again**.	3590+4024
	13:31	but my words will **n** pass away.	3590+4024
	14:31	I will **n** disown you."	3590+4024
Lk	1:15	He is **n** to take wine or other	3590+4024

Lk	1:33	his kingdom will **n** end."	4024
	2:37	She **n** left the temple but worshiped night	4024
	6: 3	"Have you **n** read what David did when he	4028
	15:29	for you and **n** disobeyed your orders.	4030
	15:29	Yet you **n** gave me even a young goat	4030
	18:17	like a little child will **n** enter it."	3590+4024
	20:16	they said, "May this **n** be!"	3590
	21:33	but my words will **n** pass away.	3590+4024
	23:29	the wombs that **n** bore and the breasts	4024
	23:29	and the breasts that **n** nursed!'	4024
Jn	4:14	whoever drinks the water I give him will **n** thirst.	172+1650+3590+3836+4024
	4:48	Jesus told him, "you will **n** believe."	3590+4024
	5:37	You have **n** heard his voice	4046+4799
	6:35	He who comes to me will **n** go hungry,	3590+4024
	6:35	and he who believes in me will **n** be thirsty.	3590+4024+4799
	6:37	comes to me I will **n** drive away.	3590+4024
	8:12	Whoever follows me will **n** walk	3590+4024
	8:33	and have **n** been slaves of anyone.	4799
	8:51	he will **n** see death."	172+1650+3590+3836+4024
	8:52	he will **n** taste death.	172+1650+3590+3836+4024
	10: 5	But they will **n** follow a stranger;	3590+4024
	10:28	they shall **n** perish;	173+1650+3590+3836+4024
	10:41	"Though John **n** performed a miraculous	4029
	11:26	whoever lives and believes in me will **n** die.	172+1650+3590+3836+4024
	13: 8	said Peter, "you shall **n** wash my feet."	172+1650+3836+4024
Ac	5:42	they **n** stopped teaching and proclaiming	4024
	6:13	"This fellow **n** stops speaking	4024
	10:14	"I have **n** eaten anything impure	4030
	13:10	Will you **n** stop perverting the right ways	4024
	13:34	**n** to decay, is stated in these words:	3516+3600
	13:41	in your days that you would **n** believe,	3590+4024
	14: 8	lame from birth and had **n** walked.	4030
	20:31	for three years I **n** stopped warning each	4024
	20:38	they would **n** see his face again.	4033
	28:26	be ever hearing but **n** understanding;	3590+4024
	28:26	be ever seeing but **n** perceiving."	3590+4024
Ro	4: 8	man whose sin the Lord will **n** count	3590+4024
	9:33	and the one who trusts in him will **n** be put	4024
	10:11	"Anyone who trusts in him will **n** be put	4024
	12:11	**N** be lacking in zeal,	3590
1Co	6:15	and unite them with a prostitute? **N**!	1181+3590
	8:13	causes my brother to fall into sin, I will **n** eat meat **again**,	172+1650+3590+3836+4024
	13: 8	Love **n** fails.	4030
2Co	12:13	except that I was **n** a burden to you?	4030
Gal	4:30	the slave woman's son will **n** share in	3590+4024
	6:14	May I **n** boast except in the cross	1181+3590
1Th	2: 5	You know we **n** used flattery,	4046+4537
2Th	3:13	you, brothers, **n** tire of doing what is right.	3590
2Ti	3: 7	always learning but **n** able to acknowledge	3595
Heb	1:12	and your years will **n** end."	4024
	3:11	'They shall **n** enter my rest.'"	1623
	3:18	that they would **n** enter his rest if not	3590
	4: 3	'They shall **n** enter my rest.'"	1623
	4: 5	"They shall **n** enter my rest."	1623
	9: 7	only once a year and **n** without blood,	4024
	9:17	it **n** takes effect while the one who made it	3607
	10: 1	for this reason it can **n**,	4030
	10:11	which can **n** take away sins.	4030
	13: 5	God has said, "**N** will I leave you,"	3590+4024
	13: 5	**n** will I forsake you."	3590+4024
Jas	3: 2	If anyone is **n** at fault in what he says,	4024
1Pe	1: 4	into an inheritance that can **n** perish, spoil	915
	2: 6	trusts in him will **n** be put to shame."	3590+4024
	5: 4	the crown of glory that will **n** fade away.	277
2Pe	1:10	For if you do these things, you will **n** fall,	3590+4024+4537
	1:21	For prophecy **n** had its origin in the will of man,	4024+4537
	2:14	eyes full of adultery, they **n** stop sinning;	188
Rev	3: 5	I will **n** blot out his name from the book of life,	3590+4024
	3:12	**N** again will he leave it.	3590+4024
	4: 8	Day and night they **n** stop saying:	4024
	7:16	**N** again will they hunger;	2285+4024
	7:16	**n** again will they thirst.	2285+4028
	18: 7	I am not a widow, and I will **n** mourn.	3590+4024
	18:14	**n** to be recovered.'	3590+4024+4033
	18:21	**n** to be found again.	3590+4024
	18:22	will **n** be heard in you again.	3590+4024
	18:22	millstone will **n** be heard in you.	3590+4024
	18:23	of a lamp will **n** shine in you again.	3590+4024
	18:23	voice of bridegroom and bride will **n**	3590+4024

NEVER-FAILING (1)

Am	5:24	righteousness like a **n** stream!	419

NEVERTHELESS (34)

Ge	48:19	**N**, his younger brother will	219+2256
Ex	16:27	**N**, some of the people went out on	2256
Nu	14:21	**N**, as surely as I live and as surely as	219+2256
	14:44	**N**, in their presumption they went up	2256
Dt	12:15	**N**, you may slaughter your animals in any	8370
Jdg	11: 8	The elders of Gilead said to him, "**N**,	4027+4200
1Sa	29: 9	**n**, the Philistine commanders have said,	421
2Sa	5: 7	**N**, David captured the fortress of Zion,	2256
1Ki	8:19	**N**, you are not the one to build the temple,	8370
	11: 9	**N**, Solomon held fast to them in love.	NIH
	11:12	**N**, for the sake of David your father,	421
	15: 4	**N**, for David's sake the LORD his God gave him a lamp in Jerusalem	3954

2Ki	3: 3	**N** he clung to the sins of Jeroboam son	8370
	8:19	**N**, for the sake of his servant David,	2256
	17:29	**N**, each national group made its own gods	2256
	23:26	**N**, the LORD did not turn away from	421
1Ch	11: 5	**N**, David captured the fortress of Zion,	2256
2Ch	6: 9	**N**, you are not the one to build the temple,	8370
	21: 7	**N**, because of the covenant the LORD	2256
	30:11	**N**, some men of Asher,	421
Est	5:10	**N**, Haman restrained himself	2256
Job	17: 9	**N**, the righteous will hold to their ways,	2256
Isa	9: 1	**N**, there will be no more gloom	3954
Jer	28: 7	**N**, listen to what I have to say	2256
	33: 6	" '**N**, I will bring health and healing to it;	2180
Da	5:17	**N**, I will read the writing for the king	10124
Ac	5:14	**N**, more and more men and women believed	1254
	27:26	**N**, we must run aground on some island."	1254
Ro	5:14	**N**, death reigned from the time of Adam to	247
1Co	7:17	**N**, each one should retain the place	1623+3590
	10: 5	**N**, God was not pleased with most of them;	247
2Ti	2:19	**N**, God's solid foundation stands firm,	3530
Rev	2:14	**N**, I have a few things against you:	247
	2:20	**N**, I have this against you:	247

NEW (192) [ANEW, NEWLY]

Ge	27:28	an abundance of grain and **n** wine.	9408
	27:37	I have sustained him with grain and **n** wine.	9408
	45:22	To each of them he gave **n** clothing,	2722
Ex	1: 8	Then a **n** king, who did not know about	2543
Lev	2:14	offer crushed heads of **n** grain roasted in	4152
	14:42	to replace these and take **n** clay and plaster	337
	23:14	or roasted or **n** grain,	4152
	23:16	and then present an offering of **n** grain to	2543
	26:10	to move it out to make room for the **n**.	2543
Nu	10:10	feasts and **N** Moon festivals—	2544+8031
	16:30	LORD brings about **something totally n**,	1375
	18:12	and all the finest **n** wine and grain they give	9408
	28:14	to be made at each **n** moon *during the year*.	2544
	28:26	to the LORD an offering of **n** grain during	2543
Dt	7:13	your grain, **n** wine and oil.	9408
	11:14	gather in your grain, **n** wine and oil.	9408
	12:17	the tithe of your grain or **n** wine and oil,	9408
	14:23	Eat the tithe of your grain, **n** wine and oil,	9408
	18: 4	firstfruits of your grain, **n** wine and oil,	9408
	20: 5	"Has anyone built a **n** house and	2543
	22: 8	When you build a **n** house,	2543
	28:51	They will leave you no grain, **n** wine or oil,	9408
	32: 2	like showers on **n** grass,	2013
	33:28	in a land of grain and **n** wine,	9408
Jos	9:13	And these wineskins that we filled were **n**,	2543
Jdg	5: 8	When they chose **n** gods,	2543
	15:13	with two **n** ropes and led him up from	2543
	16:11	"If anyone ties me securely with **n** ropes	2543
	16:12	So Delilah took **n** ropes and tied him	2543
1Sa	6: 7	"Now then, get a **n** cart ready,	2543
	20: 5	"Look, tomorrow is the **N** Moon festival,	2544
	20:18	"Tomorrow is the **N** Moon festival.	2544
	20:24	and when the **N** Moon festival came,	2544
2Sa	6: 3	on a **n** cart and brought it from the house	2543
	6: 3	were guiding the **n** cart	2543
	21:16	and who was armed with a **n** [sword],	2543
1Ki	11:29	wearing a **n** cloak.	2543
	11:30	of the **n** cloak he was wearing and tore it	2543
2Ki	2:20	"Bring me a **n** bowl," he said,	2543
	4:23	"It's not the **N** Moon or the Sabbath."	2544
	4:42	along with *some* heads of **n** grain.	4152
	16:14	the **n** altar and the temple of the LORD—	NIH
	16:14	and put it on the north side of the **n** altar.	NIH
	16:15	"On the large **n** altar,	NIH
1Ch	13: 7	of God from Abinadab's house on a **n** cart,	2543
	23:31	on Sabbaths and at **N** Moon festivals and	2544
2Ch	2: 4	and **N** Moons and at the appointed feasts of	2544
	8:13	**N** Moons and the three annual feasts—	2544
	20: 5	the LORD in the front of the **n** courtyard	2543
	31: 3	**N** Moons and appointed feasts as written in	2544
	31: 5	of their grain, **n** wine, oil and honey and all	9408
Ezr	3: 5	the harvest of grain, **n** wine and oil;	9408
	9: 9	He has granted us **n** life to rebuild	4695
Ne	5:11	grain, **n** wine and oil.	9408
	10:33	**N** Moon festivals and appointed feasts;	2544
	10:37	of the fruit of all our trees and of our **n** wine	9408
	10:39	**n** wine and oil to the storerooms where	9408
	13: 5	**n** wine and oil prescribed for the Levites,	9408
	13:12	**n** wine and oil into the storerooms.	9408
Job	10:17	*You* bring **n** witnesses against me	2542
	14: 7	and its **n** shoots will not fail.	3438
	29:20	the bow *ever* **n** in my hand."	2736
	32:19	like **n** wineskins ready to burst.	2543
Ps	4: 7	when their grain and **n** wine abound.	9408
	33: 3	Sing to him a **n** song;	2543
	40: 3	He put a **n** song in my mouth,	2543
	81: 3	Sound the ram's horn at the **N** Moon,	2544
	90: 5	they are like the **n** grass of the morning—	2736
	90: 6	though in the morning it springs up **n**,	2736
	96: 1	Sing to the LORD a **n** song;	2543
	98: 1	Sing to the LORD a **n** song,	2543
	144: 9	I will sing a **n** song to you, O God;	2543
	149: 1	Sing to the LORD a **n** song,	2543
Pr	3:10	and your vats will brim over with **n** wine.	9408
	27:25	the hay is removed and **n** growth appears	2013
Ecc	1: 9	there is nothing **n** under the sun.	2543
	1:10	This is something **n**"?	2543
SS	6:11	of nut trees to look at the **n** growth *in*	4
	7:13	at our door is every delicacy, both **n** and old	2543
Isa	1:13	**N** Moons, Sabbaths and convocations—	2544

Isa	1:14	Your **N Moon festivals** and your appointed	2544
	24: 7	The **n wine** dries up and the vine withers;	9408
	36:17	a land of grain and **n wine,**	9408
	41:15	**n** and sharp, with many teeth.	2543
	42: 9	and **n things** I declare;	2543
	42:10	Sing to the LORD a **n** song,	2543
	43:19	See, I am doing a **n thing!**	2543
	48: 6	"From now on I will tell you of **n things,**	2543
	62: 2	be called by a **n** name that the mouth of	2543
	62: 8	the **n wine** for which you have toiled;	9408
	65:17	I will create **new** heavens and a **n** earth.	2543
	65:17	I will create new heavens and a **n** earth.	2543
	66:22	"As the **n** heavens and the new earth	2543
	66:22	and the **n** earth that I make will endure	2543
	66:23	From one **N Moon** to another and	2544
Jer	8:10	to other men and their fields to **n owners.**	3769
	26:10	of the **N Gate** of the LORD's house.	2543
	31:12	the grain, the **n wine** and the oil,	9408
	31:22	The LORD will create a **n thing**	2543
	31:31	a **n** covenant with the house of Israel and	2543
	36:10	at the entrance of the **N Gate** of the temple,	2543
La	3:23	They are **n** every morning;	2543
Eze	11:19	an undivided heart and put a **n** spirit	2543
	17: 9	All its **n** growth will wither.	3273
	18:31	and get a **n** heart and a new spirit.	2543
	18:31	and get a new heart and a **n** spirit.	2543
	36:26	a **n** heart and put a new spirit in you;	2543
	36:26	a new heart and put a **n** spirit in you;	2543
	45:17	the **N Moons** and the Sabbaths—	2544
	46: 1	on the day of the **N Moon** it is to be opened.	2544
	46: 3	On the Sabbaths and **N Moons** the people of	2544
	46: 6	of the **N Moon** he is to offer a young bull,	2544
Da	1: 7	The chief official gave them **n** names:	NIH
Hos	2: 8	the grain, the **n wine** and oil,	9408
	2: 9	and my **n wine** when it is ready.	9408
	2:11	her yearly festivals, her **N Moons,**	2544
	2:22	to the grain, the **n wine** and oil,	9408
	4:11	to prostitution, to old wine and **n,**	9408
	5: 7	their **N Moon** festivals will devour them	2544
	7:14	grain and **n wine** but turn away from me.	9408
	9: 2	the **n wine** will fail them.	9408
Joel	1: 5	wail because of the **n wine,**	6747
	1:10	the **n wine** is dried up, the oil fails.	9408
	2:19	"I am sending you grain, **n wine** and oil,	9408
	2:24	the vats will overflow with **n wine** and oil.	9408
	3:18	"In that day the mountains will drip **n wine,**	6747
Am	8: 5	the **N Moon** be over that we may sell grain,	2544
	9:13	**N wine** will drip from the mountains	6747
Zep	1:10	wailing from the **N Quarter,**	5467
	3: 5	and every **n** day he does not fail,	240
Hag	1:11	on the grain, the **n wine,**	9408
Zec	9:17	and **n wine** the young women.	9408
Mt	9:17	Neither do men pour **n wine**	3742
	9:17	No, they pour **n** wine into new wineskins,	3742
	9:17	No, they pour new wine into **n** wineskins,	2785
	13:52	of his storeroom **n** treasures as well as old."	2785
	27:60	in his own **n** tomb that he had cut out of	2785
Mk	1:27	A **n** teaching—and with authority!	2785
	2:21	the **n** piece will pull away from the old,	2785
	2:22	no one pours **n** wine into old wineskins.	3742
	2:22	No, he pours **n** wine into new wineskins."	3742
	2:22	No, he pours new wine into **n** wineskins."	2785
	16:17	they will speak in **n** tongues;	2785
Lk	5:36	from a **n** garment and sews it on an old one.	2785
	5:36	If he does, he will have torn the **n** garment,	2785
	5:36	the patch from the **n** will not match the old.	2785
	5:37	no one pours a **n** wine into old wineskins.	3742
	5:37	If he does, the **n** wine will burst the skins,	3742
	5:38	**n** wine must be poured into new wineskins,	3742
	5:38	new wine must be poured into **n** wineskins,	2785
	5:39	no one after drinking old wine wants the **n,**	3742
	22:20	"This cup is the **n** covenant in my blood,	2785
Jn	13:34	a command I give you: Love one another.	2785
	19:41	and in the garden a **n** tomb,	2785
Ac	17: 6	the people the full message of this **n** life."	NIG
	17:19	"May we know what this **n** teaching is	2785
Ro	6: 4	we too may live a **n** life.	2786
	7: 6	from the law so that we serve in the **n** way	2786
1Co	5: 7	that you may be a **n** batch without yeast—	3742
	11:25	"This cup is the **n** covenant in my blood;	2785
2Co	3: 6	competent as ministers of a **n** covenant—	2785
	5:17	if anyone is in Christ, he is a **n** creation;	2785
	5:17	the old has gone, the **n** has come!	2785
Gal	6:15	what counts is a **n** creation.	2785
Eph	2:15	to create in himself one **n** man out of	2785
	4:23	to be **made** in the attitude of your minds;	391
	4:24	and to put on the **n** self,	2785
Col	2:16	a **N Moon** celebration or a Sabbath day.	3741
	3:10	and have put on the **n** self,	3742
Heb	8: 8	a **n** covenant with the house of Israel and	2785
	8:13	By calling this covenant **"n,"**	2785
	9:10	until the time of the **n** order.	1481
	9:15	the mediator of a **n** covenant,	2785
	10:20	a **n** and living way opened for us through	4710
	12:24	to Jesus the mediator of a **n** covenant,	3742
1Pe	1: 3	In his great mercy he has **given** us **n birth**	335
2Pe	3:13	to a **n** heaven and a new earth,	2785
	3:13	to a new heaven and a **n** earth,	2785
1Jn	2: 7	I am not writing you a **n** command but	2785
	2: 8	Yet I am writing you a **n** command;	2785
2Jn	1: 5	a **n** command but one we have had from	2785
Rev	2:17	a white stone with a **n** name written on it,	2785
	3:12	the **n** Jerusalem, which is coming down out of	2785
	3:12	and will also write on him my **n** name.	2785
	5: 9	And they sang a **n** song:	2785
	14: 3	And they sang a **n** song before the throne	2785
	21: 1	Then I saw a **n** heaven and a new earth,	2785

Rev	21: 1	Then I saw a new heaven and a **n** earth,	2785
	21: 2	I saw the Holy City, the **n** Jerusalem,	2785
	21: 5	"I am making everything **n!"**	2785

NEWBORN (3) [BEAR]

Jer	14: 5	Even the doe in the field deserts her **n** fawn	3528
Ac	7:19	by forcing them to throw out their **n babies**	1100
1Pe	2: 2	Like **n** babies, crave pure spiritual milk,	786

NEWLY (1) [NEW]

Jdg	6:28	second bull sacrificed on the **n** built altar!	1215

NEWS (79)

Ge	29:13	As soon as Laban heard the **n** about Jacob,	9051
	45:16	When the **n** reached Pharaoh's palace	7754
1Sa	4:17	The man who **brought** the **n** replied,	1413
	4:19	the **n** that the ark of God had been captured	9019
	13: 4	So all Israel heard the **n:**	606
	31: 9	to **proclaim** the **n** in the temple of their	1413
2Sa	4: 4	when the **n** about Saul and Jonathan came	9019
	4:10	and thought he was **bringing good n,**	1413
	4:10	**reward** I gave him for his **n!**	1415
	18:19	"Let me run and **take the n** to the king that	1413
	18:20	"You are not the one to take the **n** today,"	1415
	18:20	"You may **take the n** another time,	1415
	18:22	You don't have any **n** that will bring you	1415
	18:25	"If he is alone, he must have **good n.**"	1415
	18:26	"He must be **bringing good n,** too."	1413
	18:27	"He comes with **good n.**"	1415
	18:31	"My lord the king, **hear** the good **n!**	1413
1Ki	1:42	like you must be **bringing** good **n.**"	1413
	2:28	When the **n** reached Joab,	9019
	14: 6	I have been sent to you with **bad n.**	7997
2Ki	7: 9	a day of **good n** and we are keeping it	1415
	7:11	The gatekeepers **shouted** the **n,**	7924
	9:15	of the city to go and **tell the n** in Jezreel."	5583
1Ch	10: 9	to **proclaim** the **n** among their idols	1413
Ps	112: 7	He will have no fear of bad **n;**	9019
Pr	15:30	and good **n** gives health to the bones.	9019
	25:25	a weary soul is good **n** from a distant land.	9019
Isa	52: 7	the feet of those who **bring good n,**	1413
	61: 1	to **preach good n** to the poor.	1413
Jer	20:15	who **brought** my father **the n,**	1413
	49:23	for they have heard bad **n.**	9019
Eze	21: 7	'Because of the **n** that is coming.	9019
	24:26	a fugitive will come to tell you the **n.**	265+2245
Jnh	3: 6	When the **n** reached the king of Nineveh,	1821
Na	1:15	the feet of one who **brings good n,**	1413
	3:19	who hears the **n** about you claps his hands	9051
Mt	4:23	preaching the **good n** of the kingdom,	2295
	4:24	**N** about him spread all over Syria,	198
	9:26	**N** of this spread through all that region.	5773
	9:31	But they went out and **spread the n** about	1424
	9:35	preaching the **good n** of the kingdom	2295
	11: 5	the **good n is preached** to the poor.	2294
Mk	1:14	proclaiming the **good n** of God.	2295
	1:15	Repent and believe the **good n!**"	2295
	1:28	**N** about him spread quickly over	198
	1:45	and began to talk freely, spreading the **n.**	3364
	16:15	into all the world and preach the **good n**	2295
Lk	1:19	and to **tell** you this **good n.**	2294
	2:10	I **bring** you **good n** of great joy that will be	2294
	3:18	and **preached the good n** to them.	2294
	4:14	and **n** about him spread through	5773
	4:18	to **preach good n** to the poor.	2294
	4:37	And the **n** about him spread throughout	2491
	4:43	"I must **preach the good n** of the kingdom	2294
	5:15	Yet the **n** about him spread all the more,	3364
	7:17	This **n** about Jesus spread throughout Judea	3364
	7:22	the **good n is preached** to the poor.	2294
	8: 1	**proclaiming the good n** of the kingdom	2294
	16:16	the **good n** of the kingdom of God is being	2294
		preached,	2294
Jn	4:51	his servants met him **with the n**	3306
	20:18	went to the disciples with the **n:**	33
Ac	5:42	**proclaiming the good n** that Jesus is the	2294
	8:12	as he **preached the good n** of the kingdom	2294
	8:35	**told** him **the good n** about about Jesus.	2294
	10:36	**telling the good n** of peace	2294
	11:20	**telling** them **the good n about**	2294
	11:22	**N** of this reached the ears of the church	3364
	13:32	"We **tell** you the good **n:**	2294
	14: 7	where they continued to **preach the good n.**	2294
	14:15	We are **bringing** you **good n,**	2294
	14:21	They **preached the good n** in that city	2294
	15: 3	This **n** made all the brothers very glad.	NIG
	17:18	because Paul was **preaching the good n**	2294
	21:31	**n** reached the commander of the Roman	5762
Ro	10:15	the feet of those who **bring good n!**"	2294
	10:16	not all the Israelites accepted the **good n.**	2295
Php	2:19	that I also may be cheered when I **receive n**	1182
Col	4: 7	Tychicus will tell you all the **n** about me.	NIG
1Th	3: 6	and has **brought good n about** your faith	2294

NEXT (187)

Ge	17:21	to you by this time **n** year."	337
	18:10	surely return to you about this time **n year,**	2645
	18:14	to you at the appointed time **n year**	2645
	19:27	Early the **n** morning Abraham got up	NIH
	19:34	The **n** day the older daughter said to	4740
	20: 8	morning Abimelech summoned all his	
		officials,	NIH
	21:14	the **n** morning Abraham took some food	NIH
	22: 3	Early the **n** morning Abraham got up	NIH

Ge	24:54	When they got up the **n** morning, he said,	NIH
	26:31	Early the **n** morning the men swore an oath	NIH
	28:18	Early the **n** morning Jacob took	NIH
	31:55	**n** morning Laban kissed his grandchildren	340
	33: 2	Leah and her children **n,**	
	33: 7	**N,** Leah and her children came	1685
	40: 6	When Joseph came to them the **n** morning,	NIH
	45: 6	the **n** five years there will not be plowing	6388
Ex	2:13	The **n** day he went out and saw	9108
	9: 6	And the **n** day the LORD did it:	4740
	18:13	The **n** day Moses took his seat to serve	4740
	24: 4	up early the **n** morning and built an altar at	NIH
	25:33	three on the **n** branch,	285
	28:26	the breastpiece on the inside edge **n** to	448+6298
	32: 6	So the **n** day the people rose early	4740
	32:30	The **n** day Moses said to the people,	4740
	37:19	three on the **n** branch and the same	285
	38: 9	**N** they made the courtyard.	2256
	39:19	the breastpiece on the inside edge **n** to	448+6298
Lev	6:10	with linen undergarments **n** to his body,	6584
	7:16	over may be eaten on the **n** day.	4740
	16: 4	with linen undergarments **n** to his body;	6584
	19: 6	on the day you sacrifice it or on the **n** day;	4740
	27:18	that remain until the **n** Year of Jubilee.	NIH
Nu	2: 5	The tribe of Issachar will camp **n** to them.	6584
	2: 7	The tribe of Zebulun will be **n.**	NIH
	2:12	The tribe of Simeon will camp **n** to them.	6584
	2:14	The tribe of Gad will be **n.**	2256
	2:20	The tribe of Manasseh will be **n** to them.	6584
	2:22	The tribe of Benjamin will be **n.**	2256
	2:27	The tribe of Asher will camp **n** to them.	6584
	2:29	The tribe of Naphtali will be **n.**	2256
	10:18	divisions of the camp of Reuben went **n,**	2256
	10:22	divisions of the camp of Ephraim went **n,**	2256
	11:32	All that day and night and all the **n** day	4740
	14:40	Early the **n** morning they went up toward	NIH
	16:41	The **n** day the whole Israelite community	
		grumbled against Moses	4740
	17: 8	The **n** day Moses entered the Tent of	4740
	22: 5	and have settled **n** to me.	4578+4946
	22:13	The **n** morning Balaam got up and said	NIH
	22:41	The **n** morning Balak took Balaam up	NIH
Dt	3: 1	**N** we turned and went up along the road	2256
Jos	6:12	up early the **n** morning and the priests took	NIH
	7:16	**n** morning Joshua had Israel come forward	NIH
	8:10	**n** morning Joshua mustered his men,	NIH
Jdg	6:38	Gideon rose early the **n** day;	4740
	9:10	"**N,** the trees said to the fig tree,	2256
	9:42	The **n** day the people of Shechem went out	4740
	9:50	**N** Abimelech went to Thebez	2256
	11:18	"**N** they traveled through the desert,	2256
	20:19	The **n** morning the Israelites got up	NIH
	21: 4	Early the **n** day the people built an altar	4740
Ru	4: 4	and I am **n** in line."	339
1Sa	1:19	the **n** morning they arose and worshiped	NIH
	5: 3	the people of Ashdod rose early the **n** day,	4740
	11:11	The **n** day Saul separated his men	4740
	18:10	The **n** day an evil spirit from God	4740
	20:25	and Abner sat **n** to Saul,	4946+7396
	20:27	But the **n** day, the second day of the month,	4740
	30:17	from dusk until the evening of the **n** day,	4740
	31: 8	The **n** day, when the Philistines came	4740
2Sa	11:12	in Jerusalem that day and the **n.**	4740
	14:30	"Look, Joab's field is **n** to mine,	448+3338
	23: 9	**N** to him was Eleazar son of Dodai	339
	23:11	**N** to him was Shammah son of Agee	339
	24:11	Before David got up the **n** morning,	NIH
1Ki	1: 6	also very handsome and was born **n after**	339
	3:21	The **n** morning, I got up to nurse my son—	NIH
	4:12	and Megiddo, and in all of Beth Shan **n** to	725
	7:20	the bowl-shaped part **n** to the network,	4200+6298
	17: 1	in the **n** few years except at my word."	465S
	20:22	because **n** spring the king of Aram	NIH
	20:26	The **n** spring Ben-Hadad mustered	NIH
2Ki	3:20	**n** morning, about the time for offering	NIH
	4:16	"About this time **n year,**" Elisha said,	2645+6961
	4:17	and the **n** year about that same time	2645+6961
	6:15	up and went out **early the n morning,**	8899
	6:29	The **n** day I said to her,	337
	8:15	But the **n** day he took a thick cloth,	4740
	10: 9	The **n** morning Jehu went out.	NIH
	19:35	When the people got up the **n** morning—	NIH
	23: 4	the priests **n** in rank and the doorkeepers	5467
	25:18	Zephaniah the priest **n** in rank and	5467
1Ch	5:11	The Gadites lived **n** to them in Bashan,	4200+5584
	10: 8	The **n** day, when the Philistines came	4740
	11:12	**N** to him was Eleazar son of Dodai	339
	15:18	and with them their brothers **n** in rank:	5467
	29:21	The **n** day they made sacrifices to the LORD	4740
2Ch	17:15	**n,** Jehohanan the commander,	3338+6584
	17:16	**n,** Amasiah son of Zicri,	3338+6584
	17:18	**n,** Jehozabad, with 180,000 men	3338+6584
	29:20	**Early the n morning** King Hezekiah	
		gathered the city officials	8899
	29:22	**n** they slaughtered the rams	2256
	31:12	and his brother Shimei was **n** in rank.	5467
Ne	3: 2	Zaccur son of Imri built **n** to them.	3338+6584
	3: 4	son of Hakkoz, repaired the **n** section.	3338+6584
	3: 4	**N** to him Meshullam son of Berekiah,	3338+6584
	3: 4	and **n** to him Zadok son of Baana	3338+6584
	3: 5	The **n** section was repaired by the men	3338+6584
	3: 7	**N** to them, repairs were made by men	3338+6584
	3: 8	repaired the **n** section;	3338+6584
	3: 8	made repairs **n** to that.	3338+6584
	3: 8	repaired the **n** section.	3338+6584
	3:10	of Hashabneiah made repairs **n** to him.	3338+6584
	3:12	the **n** section with the help of his	3338+6584

Ne	3:17	**N** to him, the repairs were made by	339
	3:18	**N** to him, the repairs were made	339
	3:19	**N** to him, Ezer son of Jeshua,	3338+6584
	3:20	**N** to him, Baruch son	339
	3:21	**N** to him, Meremoth son of Uriah,	339
	3:22	The repairs **n** to him were made by	339
	3:23	and **n** to them, Azariah son of Maaseiah,	339
	3:24	and **n** to them, Binnui son	339
	3:25	**N** to him, Pedaiah son	339
	3:27	**N** to them, the men	339
	3:29	**N** to them, Zadok son	339
	3:29	**N** to him, Shemaiah son of Shecaniah,	339
	3:30	**N** to him, Hananiah son of Shelemiah,	339
	3:30	**N** to him, Meshullam son	339
	3:31	**N** to him, Malkijah, one of the goldsmiths,	339
Job	41:16	to the **n** that no air can pass between.	285
Ps	48:13	you may tell of them to the **n** generation.	340
	71:18	your power to the **n** generation,	NIH
	78: 4	the **n** generation the praiseworthy deeds of	340
	78: 6	so the **n** generation would know them,	340
	109:13	names blotted out from the **n** generation.	337
Isa	37:36	When the people got up the **n** morning—	NIH
Jer	20: 3	The **n** day, when Pashhur released him	4740
	35: 4	It was **n** to the room of the officials,	725
	51:46	one rumor comes this year, another the **n**,	339
	52:24	Zephaniah the priest **n** in rank and	5467
Eze	24:18	The **n** morning I did as I had been	NIH
	40: 7	And the threshold of the gate **n** to	725+4946
	42: 8	While the row of rooms on the side **n** to	4200
	43: 8	When they placed their threshold **n** to	907
	48: 1	the northern border of Damascus **n** to	448+3338
Da	2:39	**N**, a third kingdom, one of bronze,	10221
	6: 7	to any god or man during the **n** thirty days,	NIH
	6:12	during the **n** thirty days anyone who prays	NIH
Joel	1: 3	and their children to the **n** generation.	337
Jnh	4: 7	at dawn the **n** day God provided a worm,	4740
Mt	27:62	The **n** day, the one after Preparation Day,	2069
Mk	9:39	in my name can in the **n** moment say	
		anything bad about me,	5444
	11:12	The **n** day as they were leaving Bethany,	2069
Lk	9:37	The **n** day, when they came down from	2009
	10:35	The **n** day he took out two silver coins	892
	13: 9	If it bears fruit **n** year, fine!	1650+3516+3836
	13:33	and tomorrow and the **n** day—	2400
Jn	1:29	The **n** day John saw Jesus coming	2069
	1:35	The **n** day John was there again with two	2069
	1:43	**n** day Jesus decided to leave for Galilee.	2069
	6:22	The **n** day the crowd that had stayed on	2069
	12:12	The **n** day the great crowd that had come	2069
	13:23	was reclining **n** to him.	1877
	19:31	and the **n** day was to be a special Sabbath.	1697
Ac	4: 3	they put them in jail until the **n** day.	892
	4: 5	The **n** day the rulers, elders and	892
	7:26	The **n** day Moses came upon two	2079
	10:23	The **n** day Peter started out with them,	2069
	13:42	about these things on the **n** Sabbath.	3568
	13:44	*On* the **n** Sabbath almost the whole city	2262
	14:20	The **n** day he and Barnabas left for Derbe.	2069
	16:11	and the **n** day on to Neapolis.	2079
	18: 7	the synagogue and went **n** door to	5327
	20: 7	because he intended to leave the **n** day,	2069
	20:15	The **n** day we set sail from there	2079
	21: 1	The **n** day we went to Rhodes and	2009
	21: 8	Leaving the **n** day,	2069
	21:18	The **n** day Paul and the rest of us went	2079
	21:26	The **n** day Paul took the men	2400
	22:30	The **n** day, since the commander wanted	2069
	23:12	**The n morning** the Jews formed	1181+2465
	23:32	The **n** day they let the cavalry go on	2069
	25: 6	and the **n** day he convened the court	2069
	25:17	the court the **n** day and ordered the man to	2009
	25:23	The **n** day Agrippa and Bernice came	2069
	27: 3	The **n** day we landed at Sidon;	2283
	27:18	from the storm that the **n** day they began	2009
	28:13	**The n day** the south wind came	1651+2465+3552

NEZIAH (2)

Ezr	2:54	**N** and Hatipha	5909
Ne	7:56	**N** and Hatipha	5909

NEZIB (1)

Jos	15:43	Iphtah, Ashnah, **N**,	5908

NIBHAZ (1)

2Ki	17:31	the Avvites made **N** and Tartak,	5563

NIBSHAN (1)

Jos	15:62	**N**, the City of Salt and En Gedi—	5581

NICANOR (1)

Ac	6: 5	also Philip, Procorus, **N**, Timon, Parmenas,	3770

NICODEMUS (6)

Jn	3: 1	there was a man of the Pharisees named **N**,	3773
	3: 4	man be born when he is old?" **N** asked.	3773
	3: 9	"How can this be?" **N** asked.	3773
	7:50	**N**, who had gone to Jesus earlier	3773
	19:39	He was accompanied by **N**,	3773
	19:39	**N** brought a mixture of myrrh and aloes,	NIG

NICOLAITANS (2)

Rev	2: 6	You hate the practices *of* the **N**,	3774

Rev	2:15	to the teaching *of* the **N**.	3774

NICOLAS (1)

Ac	6: 5	and **N** from Antioch, a convert to Judaism.	3775

NICOPOLIS (1)

Tit	3:12	do your best to come to me at **N**,	3776

NIGER (1)

Ac	13: 1	Barnabas, Simeon called **N**,	3769

NIGH (KJV) See NEAR

NIGHT (314) [ALL-NIGHT, MIDNIGHT, NIGHTFALL, NIGHTS, NIGHTTIME, OVERNIGHT]

Ge	1: 5	and the darkness he called "**n**."	4326
	1:14	of the sky to separate the day from the **n**,	4326
	1:16	the day and the lesser light to govern the **n**.	4326
	1:18	to govern the day and the **n**,	4326
	8:22	day and **n** will never cease."	4326
	14:15	*During the* **n** Abram divided his men	4326
	19: 2	You can wash your feet and **spend the n**	4328
	19: 2	"*we will* **spend the n** in the square."	4328
	19:33	That **n** they got their father to drink wine,	4326
	19:34	"**Last n** I lay with my father.	621
	19:35	So they got their father to drink wine that **n**	4326
	20: 3	in a dream one **n** and said to him, "You are	4326
	24:23	for us to **spend the n**?"	4328
	24:25	as well as room for you to **spend the n**."	4328
	24:54	and drank and **spent the n** there.	4328
	26:24	That **n** the LORD appeared to him	4326
	28:11	he **stopped for the n** because	4328
	30:16	So he slept with her that **n**.	4326
	31:24	to Laban the Aramean in a dream at **n**	4326
	31:29	**last n** the God of your father said to me,	621
	31:39	for whatever was stolen by day or **n**.	4326
	31:40	in the daytime and the cold at **n**,	4326
	31:42	and **last n** he rebuked you."	621
	31:54	After they had eaten, *they* **spent the n** there.	4328
	32:13	He spent the **n** there,	4326
	32:21	but he himself spent the **n** in the camp.	4326
	32:22	That **n** Jacob got up	4326
	40: 5	had a dream the same **n**,	4326
	41:11	Each of us had a dream the same **n**,	4326
	42:27	**place where they stopped for the n**	4869
	43:21	**place where we stopped for the n**	4869
	46: 2	And God spoke to Israel in a vision at **n**	4326
Ex	10:13	across the land all that day and all that **n**.	4326
	12: 8	That same **n** they are to eat	4326
	12:12	"On that same **n** I will pass through Egypt	4326
	12:30	and all the Egyptians got up *during* the **n**,	4326
	12:31	the **n** Pharaoh summoned Moses and Aaron	4326
	12:42	Because the LORD kept vigil that **n**	4325
	12:42	on this **n** all the Israelites are to keep vigil	4326
	13:21	*by* **n** in a pillar of fire to give them light,	4326
	13:21	so that they could travel by day or **n**.	4326
	13:22	the pillar of fire *by* **n** left its place in front	4326
	14:20	the **n** the cloud brought darkness to	4326
	14:20	so neither went near the other all **n** long.	4326
	14:21	that **n** the LORD drove the sea back with	4326
	14:24	During the **last watch of the n**	874+1332
	40:38	and fire was in the cloud *by* **n**,	4326
Lev	6: 9	on the altar hearth throughout the **n**,	4326
	8:35	of Meeting day and **n** for seven days	4326
Nu	9:16	and *at* **n** it looked like fire.	4326
	9:21	Whether by day or *by* **n**,	4326
	11: 9	When the dew settled on the camp *at* **n**,	4326
	11:32	All that day and **n** and all the next day	4326
	14: 1	That **n** all the people of the community	4326
	14:14	of cloud by day and a pillar of fire *by* **n**.	4326
	22: 8	"Spend the **n** here," Balaam said to them,	4326
	22:20	That **n** God came to Balaam and said,	4326
Dt	1:33	in fire *by* **n** and in a cloud by day,	4326
	16: 1	of Abib he brought you out of Egypt *by* **n**.	4326
	28:66	filled with dread both **n** and day,	4326
Jos	1: 8	meditate on it day and **n**,	4326
	2: 8	Before the spies lay down for the **n**,	NIH
	6:11	to camp and **spend the n** there.	4328
	8: 3	and sent them out *at* **n**	4326
	8: 9	but Joshua spent that **n** with the people.	4326
	8:13	That **n** Joshua went into the valley.	4326
Jdg	6:25	That same **n** the LORD said to him,	4326
	6:27	he did it *at* **n** rather than in the daytime.	4326
	6:40	That **n** God did so.	4326
	7: 9	During that **n** the LORD said to Gideon,	4326
	9:32	the **n** you and your men should come	4326
	9:34	and all his troops set out *by* **n** and took	4326
	16: 1	**went in** to **spend the n** with her.	448+995
	16: 2	and lay in wait for him all **n** at the city gate.	4326
	16: 2	They made no move during the **n**, saying,	4326
	16: 3	until the middle of the **n**.	4326
	18: 2	where *they* **spent the n**.	4328
	19: 7	so he **stayed** there *that* **n**.	2256+3782+4328
	19: 9	**Spend the n** here; the day is nearly over.	4328
	19:10	But, unwilling to **stay** another **n**,	4328
	19:11	at this city of the Jebusites and **spend the n**	4328
	19:13	to reach Gibeah or Ramah and **spend the n**	4328
	19:15	There they stopped to **spend the n**.	4328
	19:15	no one took them into his home for the **n**.	4328
	19:20	Only don't **spend the n** in the square."	4328
	19:25	and abused her throughout the **n**,	4326
	20: 4	to Gibeah in Benjamin to **spend the n**.	4328

Jdg	20: 5	the **n** the men of Gibeah came after me	4326
Ru	3: 8	In the middle of the **n** something startled	4326
	3:13	Stay here *for* the **n**,	4326
1Sa	3: 2	One **n** Eli, whose eyes were becoming	3427
	11:11	during the **last watch of the n**	874+1332+2021
	14:34	So everyone brought his ox that **n**	4326
	14:36	after the Philistines *by* **n** and plunder them	4326
	15:11	and he cried out to the LORD all that **n**.	4326
	15:16	the LORD said to me **last n**."	2021+4326
	19:10	That **n** David made good his escape.	4326
	19:24	He lay that way all that day and **n**.	4326
	25:16	**N** and day they were a wall around us all	4326
	26: 7	David and Abishai went to the army *by* **n**,	4326
	28: 8	*at* **n** he and two men went to the woman.	4326
	28:20	for he had eaten nothing all that day and **n**.	4326
	28:25	That same **n** they got up and left.	4326
	31:12	through the **n** to Beth Shan.	4326
2Sa	2:29	that **n** Abner and his men marched through	4326
	2:32	and his men marched all **n** and arrived	4326
	4: 7	they traveled all **n** by way of the Arabah.	4326
	7: 4	That **n** the word of the LORD came	4326
	17: 8	he will not **spend the n** with the troops.	4328
	17:16	not spend the **n** at the fords in the desert;	4326
	21:10	by day or the wild animals *by* **n**.	4326
1Ki	3: 5	to Solomon *during* the **n** in a dream,	4326
	3:19	"During the **n** this woman's son died	4326
	3:20	up in the middle of the **n** and took my son	4326
	8:29	be open toward this temple day and **n**,	4326
	8:59	be near to the LORD our God day and **n**,	4326
	19: 9	There he went into a cave and **spent the n**.	4328
2Ki	6:14	They went *by* **n** and surrounded the city.	4326
	7:12	up *in* the **n** and said to his officers,	4326
	8:21	but he rose up and broke through *by* **n**;	4326
	19:35	That **n** the angel of the LORD went out	4326
	25: 4	the whole army fled *at* **n** through the gate	4326
1Ch	9:27	*They* would **spend** the **n** stationed around	4328
	9:33	for the work day and **n**.	4326
	17: 3	That **n** the word of God came to Nathan,	4326
2Ch	1: 7	That **n** God appeared to Solomon and said	4326
	6:20	be open toward this temple day and **n**,	4326
	7:12	the LORD appeared to him at **n** and said:	4326
	21: 9	but he rose up and broke through *by* **n**.	4326
Ne	1: 6	before you day and **n** for your servants,	4326
	2:12	I set out *during* the **n** with a few men.	4326
	2:13	*By* **n** I went out through the Valley Gate	4326
	2:15	so I went up the valley *by* **n**,	4326
	4: 9	to our God and posted a guard day and **n**	4326
	4:22	**stay** inside Jerusalem *at* **n**,	4328
	4:22	as guards *by* **n** and workmen by day."	4326
	6:10	*by* **n** they are coming to kill you."	4326
	9:12	*by* **n** with a pillar of fire to give them light	4326
	9:19	*by* **n** to shine on the way they were to take.	4326
	13:20	of goods **spent the n** outside Jerusalem.	4328
	13:21	"Why *do you* **spend the n** by the wall?	4328
Est	4:16	Do not eat or drink for three days, **n** or day.	4326
	6: 1	That **n** the king could not sleep;	4326
Job	3: 3	and the **n** it was said, 'A boy is born!'	4326
	3: 6	That **n**—may thick darkness seize it;	4326
	3: 7	May that **n** be barren;	4326
	4:13	Amid disquieting dreams in the **n**,	4326
	5:14	at noon they grope as *in* the **n**.	4326
	7: 4	The **n** drags on, and I toss till dawn.	6847
	10:22	to the land of **deepest n**,	694+4017+6547
	17:12	These men turn **n** into day;	4326
	20: 8	banished like a vision of the **n**.	4326
	24: 7	Lacking clothes, *they* **spend the n** naked;	4328
	24:14	in the **n** he steals forth like a thief.	4326
	27:20	a tempest snatches him away *in* the **n**.	4326
	29:19	the dew *will* **lie** all **n** on my branches.	4328
	30: 3	in desolate wastelands *at* **n**.	621
	30:17	**N** pierces my bones;	4326
	31:32	but no stranger *had to* **spend the n** in	4328
	33:15	In a dream, in a vision of the **n**,	4326
	34:20	in the middle of the **n**;	4326
	34:25	*in* the **n** and they are crushed.	4326
	35:10	who gives songs in the **n**,	4326
	36:20	Do not long for the **n**,	4326
	39: 9	**stay** by your manger at **n**?	4328
	39:28	He dwells on a cliff and **stays** there **at n**;	4328
Ps	1: 2	and on his law he meditates day and **n**.	4326
	6: 6	all **n** long I flood my bed with weeping	4326
	16: 7	even *at* **n** my heart instructs me.	4326
	17: 3	you probe my heart and examine me *at* **n**,	4326
	19: 2	**n** after night they display knowledge.	4326
	19: 2	night after **n** they display knowledge.	4326
	22: 2	but you do not answer, *by* **n**,	4326
	30: 5	weeping may remain for a **n**,	6847
	32: 4	day and **n** your hand was heavy upon me;	4326
	42: 3	My tears have been my food day and **n**,	4326
	42: 8	at **n** his song is with me—	4326
	55:10	Day and **n** they prowl about on its walls;	4326
	63: 6	I think of you through the **watches of the n**.	874
	74:16	The day is yours, and yours also the **n**;	4326
	77: 2	*at* **n** I stretched out untiring hands	4326
	77: 6	I remembered my songs in the **n**.	4326
	78:14	by day and with light from the fire all **n**.	4326
	88: 1	day and **n** I cry out before you.	4326
	90: 4	or like a watch in the **n**.	4326
	91: 5	You will not fear the terror of **n**,	4326
	92: 2	in the morning and your faithfulness at **n**,	4326
	104:20	You bring darkness, it becomes **n**,	4326
	105:39	and a fire to give light at **n**.	4326
	119:55	In the **n** I remember your name, O LORD,	4326
	119:148	through the **watches of the n**,	874
	121: 6	nor the moon by **n**.	4326
	134: 1	the LORD who minister by **n** in the house	4326
	136: 9	the moon and stars to govern the **n**;	4326

Ps	139:11	and the light become **n** around me,"	4326
	139:12	the **n** will shine like the day,	4326
Pr	7: 9	as the dark of **n** set in.	4326
	31:18	and her lamp does not go out at **n**.	4326
Ecc	2:23	even at **n** his mind does not rest.	4326
	8:16	his eyes not seeing sleep day or **n**—	4326
SS	3: 1	**All n long** on my bed I looked	928+2021+4326
	3: 8	prepared for the terrors of the **n**.	4326
	5: 2	my hair with the dampness of the **n**."	4326
	7:11	*let us* **spend the n** in the villages.	4328
Isa	4: 5	by day and a glow of flaming fire *by* **n**;	4326
	5:11	up late at **n** till they are inflamed with wine.	5974
	15: 1	Ar in Moab is ruined, destroyed in a **n**!	4325
	15: 1	Kir in Moab is ruined, destroyed in a **n**!	4325
	16: 3	Make your shadow like **n**—at high noon.	4325
	21: 8	every **n** I stay at my post.	4326
	21:11	"Watchman, what is left of the **n**?	4326
	21:11	Watchman, what is left of the **n**?"	4326
	21:12	"Morning is coming, but also the **n**.	4326
	26: 9	My soul yearns for you in the **n**;	4326
	27: 3	and **n** so that no one may harm it.	4326
	28:19	morning after morning, by day and by **n**,	4326
	29: 7	with a vision in the **n**—	4326
	30:29	And you will sing as on the **n** you celebrate	4325
	34:10	It will not be quenched **n** and day;	4326
	34:14	the **n creatures** will also repose and find	4327
	38:12	day and **n** you made an end of me.	4326
	38:13	day and **n** you made an end of me.	4326
	58:10	and your **n** will become like the noonday.	696
	60:11	they will never be shut, day or **n**,	4326
	62: 6	they will never be silent day or **n**.	4326
Jer	6: 5	at **n** and destroy her fortresses!"	4326
	9: 1	I would weep day and **n** for the slain	4326
	14: 8	like a traveler *who* **stays only a n?**	4328+5742
	14:17	with tears night and day without ceasing;	4326
	16:13	there you will serve other gods day and **n**,	4326
	31:35	and stars to shine *by* **n**, who stirs up the sea	4326
	33:20	with the day and my covenant with the **n**,	4326
	33:20	the night, so that day and **n** no longer come	4326
	33:25	not established my covenant with day and **n**	4326
	36:30	to the heat by day and the frost by **n**.	4326
	39: 4	the city *at* **n** by way of the king's garden,	4326
	49: 9	If thieves came during the **n**,	4326
	52: 7	They left the city *at* **n** through the gate	4326
La	1: 2	Bitterly she weeps at **n**,	4326
	2:18	let your tears flow like a river day and **n**;	4326
	2:19	Arise, cry out in the **n**,	4326
	2:19	as the **watches of the n** begin;	874
Da	2:19	the **n** the mystery was revealed to Daniel in	10391
	5:30	That very **n** Belshazzar,	10391
	6:18	to his palace and **spent the n** without eating	10102
	7: 2	Daniel said: "In my vision at **n** I looked,	10391
	7: 7	"After that, in my vision at **n** I looked,	10391
	7:13	"In my vision at **n** I looked,	10391
Hos	4: 5	You stumble day and **n**,	4326
	7: 6	Their passion smolders all **n**;	4326
Joel	1:13	Come, **spend the n** in sackcloth,	4328
Am	5: 8	into **n**, who calls for the waters of the sea	4326
Ob	1: 5	"If thieves came to you, if robbers in the **n**	4326
Mic	3: 6	Therefore **n** will come over you,	4326
Zec	1: 8	During the **n** I had a vision—	4326
Mt	2:14	took the child and his mother *during the* **n**	3816
	14:25	the fourth watch of the **n** Jesus went out	3816
	21:17	where *he* **spent the n**.	887
	24:43	of the house had known *at* what **time of n**	5871
	26:31	"This very **n** you will all fall away	3816
	26:34	"this very **n**, before the rooster crows,	3816
	28:13	'His disciples came *during the* **n**	3816
Mk	4:27	**N** and day, whether he sleeps or gets up,	3816
	5: 5	**N** and day among the tombs	1328+3816+4246
	6:48	the fourth watch *of the* **n** he went out	3816
Lk	2: 8	keeping watch over their flocks *at* **n**.	3816
	2:37	She never left the temple but worshiped **n**	3816
	5: 5	we've worked hard all **n**	3816
	6:12	and **spent the n** praying to God.	1381+1639
	12:20	This very **n** your life will be demanded	3816
	12:38	in the second or third **watch of the n**.	5871
	17:34	*on that* **n** two people will be in one bed;	3816
	18: 7	who cry out to him day and **n**?	3816
	21:37	each evening *he* went out to **spend the n**	887
Jn	3: 2	He came to Jesus *at* **n** and said, "Rabbi,	3816
	9: 4	**N** is coming, when no one can work.	3816
	11:10	It is when he walks by **n** that he stumbles,	3816
	13:30	he went out. And it was **n**.	3816
	19:39	the man who earlier had visited Jesus *at* **n**.	3816
	21: 3	but that **n** they caught nothing.	3816
Ac	5:19	the **n** an angel of the Lord opened the doors	3816
	9:24	Day and **n** they kept close watch on	3816
	9:25	by **n** and lowered him in a basket through	3816
	12: 6	The **n** before Herod was to bring him	3816
	16: 9	During the **n** Paul had a vision of a man	3816
	16:33	At that hour *of the* **n** the jailer took them	3816
	17:10	As soon as it was **n**,	3816
	18: 9	One **n** the Lord spoke to Paul in a vision:	3816
	20:31	of you **n** and day with tears.	3816
	23:11	The following **n** the Lord stood near Paul	3816
	23:31	the **n** and brought him as far as Antipatris.	3816
	26: 7	as they earnestly serve God day and **n**.	3816
	27:23	**Last n** an angel of the God	3816+3836+4047
	27:27	the fourteenth **n** we were still being driven	3816
Ro	13:12	The **n** is nearly over; the day is almost here.	3816
1Co	11:23	The Lord Jesus, on the **n** he was betrayed,	3816
2Co	11:25	I spent **a n and a day** in the open sea,	3819
1Th	2: 9	We worked **n** and day in order not to be	3816
	3:10	**N** and day we pray most earnestly	3816
	5: 2	of the Lord will come like a thief in the **n**.	3816
	5: 5	not belong to the **n** or to the darkness.	3816
1Th	5: 7	For those who sleep, sleep *at* **n**,	3816
	5: 7	and those who get drunk, get drunk *at* **n**.	3816
2Th	3: 8	On the contrary, we worked **n** and day,	3816
1Ti	5: 5	in God and continues **n** and day to pray and	3816
2Ti	1: 3	as **n** and day I constantly remember you	3816
Rev	4: 8	Day and **n** they never stop saying:	3816
	7:15	the throne of God and serve him day and **n**	3816
	8:12	and also a third of the **n**.	3816
	12:10	before our God day and **n**,	3816
	14:11	or **n** for those who worship the beast	3816
	20:10	They will be tormented day and **n** for ever	3816
	21:25	for there will be no **n**.	3816
	22: 5	There will be no more **n**.	3816

NIGHTFALL (2) [NIGHT]

2Sa	19: 7	not a man will be left with you *by* **n**.	2021+4326
2Ch	35:14	and the fat portions until **n**.	4326

NIGHTS (20) [NIGHT]

Ge	7: 4	on the earth for forty days and forty **n**,	4326
	7:12	rain fell on the earth forty days and forty **n**.	4326
Ex	24:18	on the mountain forty days and forty **n**.	4326
	34:28	with the LORD forty days and forty **n**.	4326
Dt	9: 9	on the mountain forty days and forty **n**;	4326
	9:11	At the end of the forty days and forty **n**,	4326
	9:18	the LORD for forty days and forty **n**;	4326
	9:25	the LORD those forty days and forty **n**	4326
	10:10	on the mountain forty days and forty **n**,	4326
1Sa	30:12	for three days and three **n**.	4326
2Sa	12:16	into his house and **spent the n** lying on	4328
1Ki	19: 8	and forty **n** until he reached Horeb,	4326
Job	2:13	with him for seven days and seven **n**.	4326
	7: 3	and **n** *of* misery have been assigned to me.	4326
Isa	65: 4	and **spend** *their* **n** keeping secret vigil;	4328
Jnh	1:17	inside the fish three days and three **n**.	4326
Mt	4: 2	After fasting forty days and forty **n**,	3816
	12:40	For as Jonah was three days and three **n** in	3816
	12:40	of Man will be three days and three **n** in	3816
2Co	6: 5	in hard work, **sleepless n** and hunger;	71

NIGHTTIME (1) [NIGHT]

Zec	14: 7	a unique day, without daytime or **n**—	4326

NILE (32)

Ge	41: 1	He was standing by the **N**,	3284
	41: 3	up out of the **N** and stood beside those on	3284
	41:17	I was standing on the bank of the **N**,	3284
Ex	1:22	that is born you must throw into the **N**,	3284
	2: 3	among the reeds along the bank of the **N**.	3284
	2: 5	went down to the **N** to bathe,	3284
	4: 9	take some water from the **N** and pour it on	3284
	7:15	Wait on the bank of the **N** to meet him,	3284
	7:17	in my hand I will strike the water of the **N**,	3284
	7:18	The fish in the **N** will die,	3284
	7:20	and struck the water of the **N**,	3284
	7:21	The fish in the **N** died,	3284
	7:24	And all the Egyptians dug along the **N**	3284
	7:25	after the LORD struck the **N**.	3284
	8: 3	The **N** will teem with frogs.	3284
	8: 9	except for those that remain in the **N**."	3284
	8:11	they will remain only in the **N**."	3284
	17: 5	the staff with which you struck the **N**,	3284
Isa	19: 7	also the plants along the **N**,	3284
	19: 7	along the **N** will become parched,	3284
	19: 8	all who cast hooks into the **N**;	3284
	23: 3	harvest of the **N** was the revenue of Tyre,	3284
	23:10	Till your land as along the **N**,	3284
Jer	46: 7	"Who is this that rises like the **N**,	3284
	46: 8	Egypt rises like the **N**,	3284
Eze	29: 3	You say, "The **N** is mine;	3284
	29: 9	" 'Because you said, "The **N** is mine;	3284
	30:12	I will dry up the **streams of the N** and sell	3284
Am	8: 8	The whole land will rise like the **N**;	3284
	9: 5	the whole land rises like the **N**,	3284
Na	3: 8	situated on the **N**, with water around her?	3284
Zec	10:11	and all the depths of the **N** will dry up.	3284

NIMRAH (1) [BETH NIMRAH]

Nu	32: 3	Dibon, Jazer, **N**, Heshbon, Elealeh, Sebam,	5809

NIMRIM (2)

Isa	15: 6	of **N** are dried up and the grass is withered;	5810
Jer	48:34	for even the waters of **N** are dried up.	5810

NIMROD (4)

Ge	10: 8	Cush was the father of **N**,	5808
	10: 9	"Like **N**, a mighty hunter before the LORD."	5808
1Ch	1:10	Cush was the father of **N**,	5808
Mic	5: 6	the land of **N** with drawn sword.	5808

NIMSHI (5)

1Ki	19:16	Also, anoint Jehu son of **N** king over Israel,	5811
2Ki	9: 2	Jehu son of Jehoshaphat, the son of **N**.	5811
	9:14	So Jehu son of Jehoshaphat, the son of **N**,	5811
	9:20	The driving is like that of Jehu son of **N**—	5811
2Ch	22: 7	with Joram to meet Jehu son of **N**,	5811

NINE (17) [NINTH]

Nu	29:26	" 'On the fifth day prepare **n** bulls,	9596
	34:13	that it be given to the **n** and a half tribes,	9596
Jos	13: 7	an inheritance among the **n** tribes and half	9596

Jos	15:44	**n** towns and their villages.	9596
	15:54	**n** towns and their villages.	9596
	21:16	**n** towns from these two tribes.	9596
Jdg	4: 3	Because he had **n** hundred iron chariots	9596
	4:13	Sisera gathered together his **n** hundred iron chariots	9596
1Sa	17: 4	He was **over n feet** tall.	564+2256+2455+9252
2Sa	24: 8	at the end of **n** months and twenty days.	9596
2Ki	17: 1	and he reigned **n** years.	9596
1Ch	3: 8	Elishama, Eliada and Eliphelet—**n** in all.	9596
Ne	11: 1	while the remaining **n** were to stay	9596
Da	3: 1	ninety feet high and **n feet** wide,	10039+10747
Lk	17:17	Where are the other **n**?	1933
Ac	2:15	only **n in the morning!**	2465+3836+5569+6052
	23:23	to go to Caesarea at **n** tonight.	5569+6052

NINE-AND-A-HALF (1)

Jos	14: 2	by lot to the **n** tribes,	2256+2942+9596

NINETEEN (2) [NINETEENTH]

Jos	19:38	There were **n** towns and their villages.	6926+9596
2Sa	2:30	**n** of David's men were found missing.	6925+9596

NINETEENTH (4) [NINETEEN]

2Ki	25: 8	in the **n** year of Nebuchadnezzar king	6926+9596
1Ch	24:16	the **n** to Pethahiah,	6925+9596
	25:26	the **n** to Mallothi, his sons and	6925+9596
Jer	52:12	in the **n** year of Nebuchadnezzar king	6926+9596

NINETY (6) [90]

Ge	17:17	Will Sarah bear a child at the age of **n**?"	9596
Ezr	6: 3	be **n feet** high and ninety feet wide,	10039+10749
	6: 3	be ninety feet high and **n feet** wide,	10039+10749
Eze	41:12	and its length was **n** cubits.	9596
Da	3: 1	**n feet** high and nine feet wide,	10039+10749
Ac	27:28	and found it was **n feet deep.**	1278+3976

NINETY-EIGHT (1) [98]

1Sa	4:15	who was **n** years old	2256+9046+9596

NINETY-NINE (6)

Ge	17: 1	When Abram was **n** years old,	2256+9596+9596
	17:24	Abraham was **n** years old	2256+9596+9596
Mt	18:12	leave the **n** on the hills and go to look for the one that wandered off?	1916+1933
	18:13	than about the **n** that did not wander	1916+1933
Lk	15: 4	Does he not leave the **n** in the open	1916+1933
	15: 7	than over **n** righteous persons who do not need to repent.	1916+1933

NINETY-SIX (2)

Ezr	8:35	bulls for all Israel, **n** rams,	2256+9252+9596
Jer	52:23	**n** pomegranates on the sides;	2256+9252+9596

NINEVEH (22) [NINEVITES]

Ge	10:11	where he built **N**, Rehoboth Ir,	5770
	10:12	which is between **N** and Calah;	5770
2Ki	19:36	He returned to **N** and stayed there.	5770
Isa	37:37	He returned to **N** and stayed there.	5770
Jnh	1: 2	to the great city of **N** and preach against it,	5770
	3: 2	"Go to the great city of **N** and proclaim	5770
	3: 3	the word of the LORD and went to **N**.	5770
	3: 3	Now **N** was a very important city—	5770
	3: 4	Forty more days and **N** will be overturned.	5770
	3: 6	When the news reached the king of **N**,	5770
	3: 7	Then he issued a proclamation in **N**:	5770
	4:11	But **N** has more than a hundred	5770
Na	1: 1	An oracle concerning **N**.	5770
	1: 8	he will make an end of [**N**];	2023+5226S
	1:11	[O **N**,] has one come forth who plots evil	NIH
	1:14	a command concerning you, [**N**]:	NIH
	2: 1	An attacker advances against you, [**N**].	NIH
	2: 8	**N** is like a pool, and its water is draining	5770
	3: 7	'**N** is in ruins—who will mourn for her?'	5770
Zep	2:13	leaving **N** utterly desolate and dry as	5770
Mt	12:41	The men of **N** will stand up at the judgment	3780
Lk	11:32	The men of **N** will stand up at the judgment	3780

NINEVITES (2) [NINEVEH]

Jnh	3: 5	The **N** believed God.	408+5770
Lk	11:30	For as Jonah was a sign *to* the **N**,	3780

NINTH (30) [NINE]

Lev	23:32	From the evening of the **n** day of the month	9596
	25:22	until the harvest of the **n** year comes in.	9595
Nu	7:60	On the **n** day Abidan son of Gideoni,	9595
2Ki	17: 6	In the **n** year of Hoshea,	9595
	18:10	which was the **n** year of Hoshea king	9596
	25: 1	So in the **n** year of Zedekiah's reign,	9595
	25: 3	**n** day of the [fourth] month the famine	9596
1Ch	12:12	Johanan the eighth, Elzabad the **n**,	9595
	24:11	the **n** to Jeshua, the tenth to Shecaniah,	9595
	25:16	the **n** to Mattaniah,	9595
	27:12	The **n**, for the ninth month,	9595
	27:12	The ninth, for the **n** month,	9595
Ezr	10: 9	And on the twentieth day of the **n** month,	9595
Jer	36: 9	In the **n** month of the fifth year	9595
	36:22	It was the **n** month and the king was sitting	9595
	39: 1	In the **n** year of Zedekiah king of Judah,	9595
	39: 2	And on the **n** day of the fourth month	9596

Jer 52: 4 So in the **n** year of Zedekiah's reign, 9595
  52: 6 the **n** day of the fourth month the famine in 9596
Eze 24: 1 In the **n** year, in the tenth month on 9595
Hag 2:10 On the twenty-fourth day of the **n** month, 9595
  2:18 from this twenty-fourth day of the **n** month, 9595
Zec 7: 1 on the fourth day of the **n** month, 9595
Mt 20: 5 about the sixth hour and the **n** hour and did *1888*
  27:45 the **n** hour darkness came over all the land. *1888*
  27:46 the **n** hour Jesus cried out in a loud voice, *1888*
Mk 15:33 over the whole land until the **n** hour. *1888*
  15:34 the **n** hour Jesus cried out in a loud voice, *1888*
Lk 23:44 over the whole land until the **n** hour, *1888*
Rev 21:20 the **n** topaz, the tenth chrysoprase, *1888*

NISAN (2)
Ne 2: 1 In the month of **N** in the twentieth year 5772
Est 3: 7 the month of **N**, they cast the pur 5772

NISROCH (2)
2Ki 19:37 in the temple of his god **N**, 5827
Isa 37:38 in the temple of his god **N**, 5827

NITRE (KJV) See SODA

NO (1735) [NAUGHT, NONE, NOR, NOT, NOTHING]
Ge 2: 5 **n** shrub of the field had **yet** appeared 3270
  2: 5 **n** plant of the field had **yet** appeared 3270+3972
  2: 5 on the earth and **there was n** man to work 401
  2:20 But for Adam **n** suitable helper was found. 4202
  2:25 and they felt **n** shame. 4202
  4:12 it will **n** longer yield its crops for you. 4202
  4:15 that **n** one who found him would kill him. 1194
  5:24 he **was n more,** because God took him away. 401
  8: 9 the dove could find **n** place to set its feet 4202
  11:30 Now Sarai was barren; she had **n** children. 401
  15: 3 "You have given me **n** children; 4202
  16: 1 Abram's wife, had borne him **n** children. 4202
  17: 5 **N** longer will you be called Abram; 4202
  17:15 you are **n** *longer* to call her Sarai; 4202
  19: 2 "**N**," they answered, "we will spend 4202
  19: 7 and said, "**N**, my friends. NIH
  19:18 But Lot said to them, "**N**, my lords, please! 440
  19:31 **there is n** man around here to lie with us, 401
  20:11 'There is surely **n** fear of God in this place, 401
  23:11 "**N**, my lord," he said. 4202
  24:16 **n** man had ever lain with her. 4202
  26:22 and **n** one quarreled over it. 4202
  26:29 that we did you **n** harm, 561
  27: 1 so weak *that* he could **n** *longer* see, 4946
  27:45 When your brother *is* **n longer** angry 8740
  31:50 even though **n** one is with us, 401
  32:28 "Your name will **n** longer be Jacob, 4202
  33:10 "**N**, please!" said Jacob. 440
  34:19 lost **n** time in doing what they said, 4202
  35: 5 around them so that **n** one pursued them. 4202
  35:10 but you will **n** longer be called Jacob; 4202
  37:24 cistern was empty; **there was n** water in it. 401
  37:35 "**N**," he said, "in mourning will I go down 3954
  39: 9 **N** one is greater in this house than I am. 401
  39:23 The warden paid **n** attention to anything 401
  40: 8 "but **there is n** one to interpret them," 401
  41: 8 but **n** one could interpret them for him. 401
  41:15 "I had a dream, and **n** one can interpret it. 401
  41:21 **n** one could tell that they had done so; 4202
  41:39 **there is n** one so discerning and wise as you 401
  41:44 but without your word **n** one will lift hand 4202
  42:10 "**N**, my lord," they answered. 4202
  42:12 "**N!**" he said to them. 4202
  42:13 and one is **n more.**" 401
  42:32 One **is n more,** 401
  42:36 Joseph **is n more** and Simeon is no more, 401
  42:36 Joseph is no more and Simeon **is n more,** 401
  44:34 if the boy is not with me? **N!** NIH
  45: 1 Then Joseph could **n** *longer* control himself 4202
  45: 1 So there was **n** one with Joseph 4202
  47: 4 and your servants' flocks have **n** pasture. 401
  47:13 **There was n** food, however, 401
  48:18 Joseph said to him, "**N**, my father, 4027+4202
  49: 4 you will **n** *longer* excel, 440
Ex 2: 3 But when she could hide him **n** longer, 4202
  2:12 and that and seeing **n** one, 401
  5: 7 "You are **n** longer to supply the people 4202
  5: 9 that they keep working and pay **n** attention 440
  5:16 Your servants are given **n** straw, 401
  8:10 so that you may know **there is n** *one* like 401
  8:22 **n** swarms of flies will be there, 1194
  9: 4 so that **n** animal belonging to 3972+4202+4946
  9:14 you may know that **there is n** *one* like me 401
  9:29 and there will be **n** more hail, 4202
  9:33 the rain **n** longer poured down on the land. 4202
  10:11 **N!** Have only the men go; 4027+4202
  10:23 **N** one could see anyone else 4202
  12:13 **N** destructive plague will touch you 4202
  12:16 Do **n** work at all on these days, 4202
  12:19 For seven days **n** yeast is to be found 4202
  12:43 "**N** foreigner is to eat of it. 3972+4202
  12:48 **N** uncircumcised male may eat of it. 3972+4202
  14:11 because **there were n** graves in Egypt 401+1172
  16:19 "**N** one is to keep any of it until morning." 440
  16:20 some of them paid **n** attention to Moses; 4202
  16:29 **n** one is to go out." 440
  17: 1 **there was n** water for the people to drink. 401

Ex 20: 3 "You shall have **n** other gods before me. 4202
  21: 8 He has **n** right to sell her to foreigners, 4202
  21:22 but there is **n** serious injury, 4202
  22:10 or is taken away while **n** one is looking, 401
  22:11 and **n** restitution is required. 4202
  22:25 charge him **n** interest. 4202
  23:15 **N** one is to appear before me empty-handed 4202
  29:33 But **n** one may eat them, 4202
  30:12 Then **n** plague will come on them 4202
  33: 4 to mourn and **n** one put on any ornaments. 4202
  33:20 for **n** one may see me and live." 4202
  34: 3 **N** one is to come with you or 4202
  34:20 **N** one is to appear before me empty-handed 4202
  34:24 and **n** one will covet your land 4202
  36: 6 "**N** man or woman is to make anything else 440
Lev 13:21 **there is n** white hair in it and it is 401
  13:26 and **there is n** white hair in the spot and 401
  13:31 and **there is n** black hair in it, 401
  13:32 and there is **n** yellow hair in it and it does 4202
  13:34 and appears to **be n** more than skin deep, 401
  16:17 **N** one is to be in the Tent of Meeting 3972+4202
  17: 7 They must **n** longer offer any 4202
  18: 6 " '**N** one is to approach any close relative 4202
  20:14 so that **n** wickedness will be among you. 4202
  21: 3 on him since she has **n** husband— 4202
  21:18 **N** man who has any defect may come 3972+4202
  21:18 **n** man who is blind or lame, NIH
  21:19 **n** man with a crippled foot or hand, NIH
  21:21 **N** descendant of Aaron the priest who 3972+4202
  22:10 " '**N** one outside a priest's family may eat 4202
  22:13 yet has **n** children, 401
  22:13 **N** unauthorized person, however, 3972+4202
  23: 7 assembly and do **n** regular work. 3972+4202
  23: 8 and do **n** regular work.' " 3972+4202
  23:21 assembly and do **n** regular work. 3972+4202
  23:25 Do **n** regular work, 3972+4202
  23:28 Do **n** work on that day, 4202
  23:31 You shall do **n** work at all. 4202
  23:35 do **n** regular work. 3972+4202
  23:36 do **n** regular work. 3972+4202
  25:26 a man has **n** one to redeem it for him 4202
  26: 6 down and **n** one will make you afraid. 401
  26:13 **so that** you would **n** longer be slaves 4946
  26:17 even when **n** one is pursuing you. 401
  26:31 and I will take **n** delight in 4202
  26:36 even though **n** one is pursuing them. 401
  26:37 even though **n** one is pursuing them. 401
  27:26 " '**N** one, however, may dedicate 4202
  27:29 " '**N** person devoted to destruction 3972+4202
Nu 3: 4 They had **n** sons; 4202
  5: 8 But if that person has **n** close relative 401
  5:13 (since **there is n** witness against her 401
  5:19 "If **n** other man has slept with you 4202
  6: 5 of his vow of separation **n** razor may 4202
  8:19 so that **n** plague will strike the Israelites 4202
  8:25 and work **n** longer. 4202
  10:30 He answered, "**N**, I will not go; 4202
  11: 5 the fish we ate in Egypt **at n cost**— 2855
  11:32 **N** one gathered **less than** 5070
  14:23 **N** one who has treated me 5070
  16:14 **N**, we will not come!" 4202
  16:40 the Israelites that **n** one except a descendant 4202
  18: 4 **n** one else may come near where you are. 4202
  18:20 "You will have **n** inheritance in their land, 4202
  18:23 They will receive **n** inheritance among 4202
  18:24 'They will have **n** inheritance among 4202
  20: 2 Now there was **n** water for the community, 4202
  20: 5 It has **n** grain or figs, 4202
  20: 5 And **there is n** water to drink!" 401
  21: 5 **There is n** bread! 401
  21: 5 **There is n** water! 401
  21:35 leaving them **n** survivors. 1194
  22:26 in a narrow place where **there was n** room 401
  22:30 "**N**," he said. 4202
  23:21 "**N** misfortune is seen in Jacob, 4202
  23:21 **n** misery observed in Israel. 4202
  23:23 There is **n** sorcery against Jacob, 4202
  23:23 **n** divination against Israel. 4202
  26:33 (Zelophehad son of Hepher had **n** sons; 4202
  26:62 because they received **n** inheritance 4202
  27: 3 but he died for his own sin and left **n** sons. 4202
  27: 4 from his clan because he had **n** son? 401
  27: 8 'If a man dies and leaves **n** son, 401
  27: 9 If he has **n** daughter, 401
  27:10 If he has **n** brothers, 401
  27:11 If his father had **n** brothers, 401
  28:18 assembly and do **n** regular work. 3972+4202
  28:25 assembly and do **n** regular work. 3972+4202
  28:26 assembly and do **n** regular work. 3972+4202
  29: 1 assembly and do **n** regular work. 3972+4202
  29: 7 must deny yourselves and do **n** work. 4202
  29:12 assembly and do **n** regular work. 3972+4202
  29:35 an assembly and do **n** regular work. 3972+4202
  33:14 where there was **n** water for the people 4202
  35:30 But **n** one is to be put to death on 4202
  36: 7 **N** inheritance in Israel is to pass from tribe 4202
  36: 9 **N** inheritance may pass from tribe to tribe, 4202
Dt 1:45 but he paid **n** attention to your weeping 4202
  2:34 We left **n** survivors. 4202
  3: 3 We struck them down, leaving **n** survivors. 1194
  4:12 the sound of words but saw **n** form; 401
  4:15 You saw **n** form of any kind the day 4202
  4:35 besides him **there is n** other. 401
  4:39 **There is n** other. 401
  5: 7 "You shall have **n** other gods before me. 4202
  7: 2 Make **n** treaty with them, 4202
  7: 2 and show them **n** mercy. 4202

Dt 7:24 **N** one will be able to stand up against you; 4202
  9: 4 **N**, it is on account of the wickedness NIH
  9: 9 I ate **n** bread and drank **n** water. 4202
  9: 9 I ate no bread and drank **n** water. 4202
  9:18 I ate **n** bread and drank no water, 4202
  9:18 I ate no bread and drank **n** water, 4202
  10: 9 the Levites have **n** share or inheritance 4202
  10:17 who shows **n** partiality 4202
  10:17 and accepts **n** bribes. 4202
  11:17 and the ground will yield **n** produce, 4202
  11:25 **N** man will be able to stand against you. 4202
  12:12 who have **n** allotment or inheritance 401
  13: 8 Show him **n** pity. 4202
  13:11 and **n** *one* among you will do such 4202
  14:27 for they have **n** allotment or inheritance 401
  14:29 so that the Levites (who have **n** allotment 401
  15: 4 there should be **n** poor among you, 4202
  16: 4 Let **n** yeast be found in your possession 4202
  16: 8 to the LORD your God and do **n** work. 4202
  16:16 **N** man should appear before 4202
  17: 6 but **n** one shall be put to death on 4202
  18: 1 are to have **n** allotment or inheritance 4202
  18: 2 They shall have **n** inheritance 4202
  18:10 Let **n** one be found among you who 4202
  19:13 Show him **n** pity. 4202
  19:21 Show **n** pity: life for life, 4202
  22:20 and **n** proof of the girl's virginity can 4202
  22:26 she has committed **n** sin deserving death. 401
  22:27 **there was n** one to rescue her. 401
  23: 1 **N** one who has been emasculated 4202
  23: 2 **N** one born of a forbidden marriage nor any 4202
  23: 3 **N** Ammonite or Moabite or any 4202
  23:17 **N** Israelite man or woman is to become 4202
  25:12 you shall cut off her hand. Show her **n** pity. 4202
  25:18 they had **n** fear of God. 4202
  28:26 **there will be n** one to frighten them away. 401
  28:29 with **n** one to rescue you 401
  28:31 and **n** one will rescue them. 401
  28:51 They will leave you **n** grain, 4202
  28:54 among you *will* **have n** compassion 6524+8317
  28:65 Among those nations you will find **n** repose, 4202
  28:65 **n** resting place for the sole of your foot. 4202
  28:68 but **n** one will buy you. 401
  29: 6 You ate **n** bread and drank no wine 4202
  29: 6 and drank **n** wine or other fermented drink. 4202
  29:18 Make sure there is **n** man or woman, 7153
  29:18 make sure there is **n** root among you 7153
  29:23 **n** vegetation growing on it. 3972+4202
  30:14 **N**, the word is very near you; 3954
  31: 2 and twenty years old and I am **n** longer able 4202
  32: 4 A faithful God who does **n** wrong, 401
  32: 5 their shame they are **n** *longer* his children, 4202
  32:12 **n** foreign god was with him. 401
  32:21 They made me jealous by what is **n** god 4202
  32:21 by a nation that has **n** understanding. 5572
  32:28 there is **n** discernment in them. 401
  32:36 and **n** one is left, 700
  32:39 **There is n** god besides me. 401
  32:39 and **n** one can deliver out of my hand. 401
  33: 9 'I have **n** regard for them.' 4202
  33:11 **till** they rise **n more.**" 4946
  33:26 "There is **n** *one* like the God of Jeshurun, 401
  34: 6 to this day **n** one knows where his grave is. 4202
  34:10 **n** prophet has risen in Israel like Moses, 4202
  34:12 For **n** one has ever shown NIH
Jos 1: 5 **N** one will be able to stand up 4202
  4:18 **N sooner** had they set their feet on the dry ground **than** 3869
  5: 1 and they **n** longer had the courage to face 4202
  5:12 there was **n** longer any manna for 4202
  6: 1 **N** one went out and no one came in. 401
  6: 1 No one went out and **n** one came in. 401
  8:20 but they had **n** chance to escape 4202
  8:31 on which **n** iron tool had been used. 4202
  10:21 **n** one uttered a word against the Israelites. 4202
  10:28 He left **n** survivors. 4202
  10:30 He left **n** survivors there. 4202
  10:33 until **n** survivors were left. 1194
  10:37 They left **n** survivors. 4202
  10:39 They left **n** survivors. 4202
  10:40 He left **n** survivors. 4202
  11: 8 until **n** survivors were left. 1194
  11:22 **N** Anakites were left in Israelite territory; 4202
  13:14 to the tribe of Levi he gave **n** inheritance, 4202
  13:33 Moses had given **n** inheritance: 4202
  14: 4 The Levites received **n** share of the land 4202
  17: 3 had **n** sons but only daughters, 4202
  22:24 "**N!** We did it for fear that some day 4202
  22:25 You have **n** share in the LORD.' 401
  22:27 'You have **n** share in the LORD.' 401
  22:33 And they talked **n** *more* about going to war 4202
  23: 9 to this day **n** one has been able 4202
  23:13 LORD your God will **n** longer drive out these nations before you. 4202
  24:21 But the people said to Joshua, "**N!** 4202
Jdg 2:14 whom they were **n** longer able to resist. 4202
  2:21 I will **n** longer drive out before them any of 4202
  3:28 they allowed **n** one to cross over. 4202
  4:20 'Is anyone here?' say '**N**.' " 401
  5:19 but they carried off **n** silver, no plunder. 4202
  5:19 but they carried off no silver, **n** plunder. NIH
  7:12 Their camels could **n** more be counted than 401
  8:33 **N sooner** had Gideon died **than** 889+3869
  10: 6 the LORD and **n** longer served him, 4202
  10:13 so I will **n** longer save you. 4202
  10:16 bear Israel's misery **n longer.** 7918
  11:28 paid **n** attention to the message Jephthah 4202

Jdg	12: 5	you an Ephraimite?" If he replied, **"N,"**	4202
	13: 4	Now see to it that you drink **n** wine	440
	13: 5	**N** razor may be used on his head,	4202
	13: 7	drink **n** wine or other fermented drink	440
	16: 2	*They* **made n move** during the night, saying,	3087
	16:17	**"N** razor has ever been used on my head,"	4202
	17: 6	In those days Israel had **n** king.	401
	18: 1	In those days Israel had **n** king.	401
	18: 7	from the Sidonians and had **n** relationship	401
	18:28	**There was n** one to rescue them	401
	18:28	and had **n** relationship with anyone else.	401
	19: 1	In those days Israel had **n** king.	401
	19:12	His master replied, **"N.**	NIH
	19:15	but **n** one took them into his home for	401
	19:18	**N** one has taken me into his house.	401
	19:23	**"N,** my friends, don't be so vile.	440
	19:28	But **there was n** answer.	401
	20: 8	**N,** not one of us will return to his house.	NIH
	21: 8	that **n** one from Jabesh Gilead had come to	4202
	21:25	In those days Israel had **n** king;	401
Ru	1:13	**N,** my daughters,	440
	4: 4	For **n** one has the right to do it except you,	401
1Sa	1:11	and **n** razor will ever be used on his head."	4202
	1:18	and her face was **n** longer downcast.	4202
	2: 2	**"There is n** one holy like the LORD;	401
	2: 2	there is **n** *one* besides you;	401
	2: 2	**there is n** Rock like our God.	401
	2: 5	but those who were hungry hunger **n more.**	2532
	2:12	they had **n** regard for the LORD.	4202
	2:16	the servant would then answer, **"N,**	4202
	2:24	**N,** my sons; it is not a good report	440
	8:19	refused to listen to Samuel. **"N!"**	4202
	9: 7	We have **n** gift to take to the man of God.	401
	10:19	And you have said, '**N,** set a king over us.'	4202
	10:24	**There is n** *one* like him among all	401
	10:27	They despised him and brought him **n** gifts.	4202
	11: 3	if **n** one comes to rescue us,	401
	11:11	so that **n** two of them were left together.	4202
	11:13	**"N** one shall be put to death today,	4202
	12:12	**'N,** we want a king to rule over us'—	4202
	12:21	They can do you **n** good,	4202
	14: 3	**N** one was aware that Jonathan had left.	4202
	14:26	yet **n** one put his hand to his mouth,	401
	17:32	"Let **n** one lose heart on account	440
	18:25	'The king wants **n** other price for	401
	19: 5	like David by killing him **for n reason?"**	2855
	20:21	you are safe; **there is n** danger.	401
	21: 1	Why is **n** one with you?"	401
	21: 2	'**N** one is to know anything	440
	21: 6	since there was **n** bread there except	4202
	21: 9	**there is n** sword here but that one."	401
	22: 8	**N** one tells me when my son makes	401
	25:17	a wicked man that **n** one can talk to him."	4946
	25:18	Abigail **lost n** time.	4554
	25:25	May my lord pay **n** attention to	440
	25:28	Let **n** wrongdoing be found in you as long	4202
	26:12	**N** one saw or knew about it,	401
	27: 4	he **n** longer searched for him.	4202
	28:15	he **n** longer answers me,	4202
	29: 3	I have found **n** fault in him."	4202
	29: 6	I have found **n** fault in you,	4202
	30: 4	until they had **n** strength left to weep.	401
	30:23	David replied, **"N,** my brothers,	4202
2Sa	1:21	**n** longer rubbed with oil.	1172
	2:28	they **n** longer pursued Israel,	4202
	3:22	Abner **was n** *longer* with David in Hebron,	401
	3:37	and all Israel knew that the king had **n** part	4202
	6:23	of Saul had **n** children to the day	4202
	7:10	of their own and **n** longer be disturbed.	4202
	7:22	**There is n** *one* like you,	401
	7:22	and **there is n** God but you,	401
	9: 3	"Is there **n** one still left of the house of Saul	700
	12: 6	he did such a thing and had **n** pity."	4202
	13:16	**"N!"** she said to him.	440
	13:25	**"N,** my son," the king replied.	440
	14: 6	and **n** one was there to separate them.	401
	14:19	**n** one can turn to the right or to the left	561
	14:25	to the sole of his foot there was **n** blemish	4202
	15: 3	but **there is n** representative of the king	401
	16:18	Hushai said to Absalom, **"N,**	4202
	17:19	**N** one knew anything about it.	4202
	17:20	The men searched but found **n** *one,*	4202
	17:22	**n** one was left who had not crossed	4202
	18:18	"I have **n** son to carry on the memory	401
	20: 1	"We have **n** share in David,	401
	20: 1	**n** part in Jesse's son!"	4202
	21: 4	"We have **n** right to demand silver or gold	401
	21: 5	and have **n** place anywhere in Israel,	4946
	22:42	but **there was n** one to save them—	401
	24:24	But the king replied to Araunah, **"N,**	4202
1Ki	1: 4	the king had **n** intimate relations with her.	4202
	2:30	But he answered, **"N,** I will die here."	4202
	3:13	that in your lifetime you will have **n** equal	4202
	3:18	**there was n** one in the house but the two	401
	3:22	The other woman said, **"N!**	4202
	3:22	But the first one insisted, **"N!**	4202
	3:23	while that one says, '**N!**	4202
	5: 4	and **there is n** adversary or disaster.	401
	5: 6	You know that we have **n** one so skilled	401
	6: 7	the quarry were used, and **n** hammer, chisel	4202
	6:18	**n** stone was to be seen.	401
	8:23	of Israel, **there is n** God like you in heaven	401
	8:35	the heavens are shut up and there is **n** rain	4202
	8:46	for **there is n** one who does not sin—	401
	8:60	the LORD is God and that **there is n** other.	401
	15:22	**n** *one* was exempt—	401
	17: 7	because there had been **n** rain in the land.	4202

1Ki	18:26	But **there was n** response; no one answered.	401
	18:26	But there was no response; **n** one answered.	401
	18:29	But **there was n** response, no one answered,	401
	18:29	But there was no response, **n** one answered,	401
	18:29	no one answered, **n** *one* paid attention.	401
	19: 4	I am **n** better than my ancestors."	4202
	21:15	He is **n** *longer* alive, but dead."	401
	22: 1	For three years **there was n** war	401
	22:17	'These people have **n** master.	4202
	22:47	**There was** then **n** king in Edom;	401
2Ki	1: 3	'Is it because **there is n** God in Israel	401+1172
	1: 6	Is it because **there is n** God in Israel	401+1172
	1:16	Is it because **there is n** God in Israel	401+1172
	1:17	Because Ahaziah had **n** son,	4202
	2:12	And Elisha saw him **n** more.	4202
	2:16	**"N,"** Elisha replied, "do not send them."	NIH
	3: 9	the army had **n** *more* water for themselves	4202
	3:11	**"Is there n** prophet of the LORD here,	401
	3:13	**"N,"** the king of Israel answered,	440
	4:14	she has **n** son and her husband is old."	401
	4:16	**"N,** my lord," she objected.	440
	4:31	but **there was n** sound or response.	401
	4:39	though **n** one knew what they were.	4202
	5:15	that **there is n** God in all the world except	401
	9:10	and **n** one will bury her.' "	401
	9:37	so that **n** one will be able to say,	4202
	10:11	leaving him **n** survivor.	1194
	10:14	He left **n** survivor.	4202
	10:19	See that **n** one is missing,	440
	10:19	to come will **n** longer live."	4202
	10:23	"Look around and see **that n** servants of	7153
	10:25	let **n** one escape."	440
	12: 7	Take **n** *more* money from your treasurers,	440
	14:26	**there was n** one to help them.	401
	15:20	and stayed in the land **n** longer.	4202
	17: 4	and he **n** longer paid tribute to the king	4202
	18: 5	**There was n** one like him among all	4202
	19: 3	to the point of birth and **there is n** strength	401
	23:10	so **n** one could use it to sacrifice his son	1194
	25: 3	that **there was n** food for the people to eat.	4202
1Ch	2:34	Sheshan had **n** sons—only daughters.	4202
	15: 2	**"N** *one* but the Levites may carry the ark	4202
	16:21	He allowed **n** man to oppress them;	4202
	16:22	do my prophets **n** harm."	440
	17: 9	of their own and **n** longer be disturbed.	4202
	17:20	**"There is n** *one* like you, O LORD,	401
	17:20	O LORD, and **there is n** God but you,	401
	21:24	But King David replied to Araunah, **"N,**	4202
	23:17	Eliezer had **n** other sons,	4202
	23:26	the Levites **n** longer need to carry	401
	24: 2	and they had **n** sons,	4202
	24:28	From Mahli: Eleazar, who had **n** sons.	4202
	29:25	as **n** king over Israel ever had before.	4202
2Ch	1:12	as **n** king who was before you ever had	4202
	6:14	of Israel, **there is n** God like you in heaven	401
	6:26	the heavens are shut up and there is **n** rain	4202
	6:36	for **there is n** one who does not sin—	401
	7:13	I shut up the heavens so that there is **n** rain,	4202
	14: 6	**N** one was at war with him	401
	14:11	**there is n** *one* like you to help the powerless	401
	15:19	There was **n** *more* war until	4202
	18:16	'These people have **n** master.	4202
	19: 7	with the LORD our God **there is n** injustice	401
	20: 6	and **n** *one* can withstand you.	401
	20:12	For we have **n** power to face this vast army	401
	20:24	**n** *one* had escaped.	401
	21:19	His people made **n** fire in his honor,	4202
	21:20	He passed away, to **n** *one's* regret,	4202
	22: 9	So there was **n** one in the house	401
	23: 6	**N** one is to enter the temple of	440
	23:19	the LORD's temple so that **n** one who was	4202
	32:15	**n** god of any nation	3972+4202
	33:10	but they paid **n** attention.	4202
	36:16	against his people and **there was n** remedy.	401
Ezr	3:13	**N** one could distinguish the sound of	401
	4: 3	"You have **n** part with us in building	4202
	4:13	**n** *more* taxes, tribute or duty will be paid,	10379
	7:24	that you have **n** authority to impose taxes,	10379
	8:15	I found **n** Levites there.	4202
	9:14	leaving us **n** remnant or survivor?	401
	10: 6	he ate **n** food and drank no water,	4202
	10: 6	he ate no food and drank **n** water,	4202
Ne	2:12	**There were n** mounts with me except	401
	2:17	and we will **n** longer be in disgrace."	4202
	2:20	you have **n** share in Jerusalem or any claim	401
	9:30	Yet they paid **n** attention.	4202
	13: 1	that **n** Ammonite or Moabite should ever	4202
	13:19	the gates so that **n** load could be brought in	4202
	13:21	From that time on they **n** *longer* came on	4202
	13:26	the many nations there was **n** king like him.	4202
Est	1:18	be **n** *end of* disrespect and discord.	1896+3869
	4: 2	because **n** one clothed in sackcloth	401
	5:13	But all this gives me **n** satisfaction as long	401
	7: 4	in such distress would justify disturbing	401
	8: 8	for **n** document written in the king's name	401
	8: 8	**N** one could stand against them,	4202
Job	1: 8	**There is n** one on earth like him;	401
	2: 3	**There is n** one on earth like him;	401
	2:13	**N** one said a word to him,	4202
	3: 4	may **n** light shine upon it.	440
	3: 7	may **n** shout of joy be heard in it.	440
	3:18	they **n** *longer* hear the slave driver's shout.	4202
	3:26	I have **n** peace, no quietness;	4202
	3:26	I have no peace, **n** quietness;	4202
	3:26	I have **n** rest, but only turmoil."	4202
	4:18	If God places **n** trust in his servants,	4202
	5:12	so that their hands achieve **n** success.	4202

Job	5:19	in seven **n** harm will befall you.	4202
	6: 3	**n wonder** my words have been impetuous.	4027+6584
	6:21	Now you too have proved to be of **n** help;	4202
	7: 8	eye that now sees me will see me **n** *longer;*	4202
	7: 8	you will look for me, but I will **be n more.**	401
	7:10	his place will know him **n** more.	4202
	7:16	Let me alone; my days have **n** **meaning.**	2039
	7:21	you will search for me, but I will **be n more."**	401
	8:11	where there is **n** marsh?	4202
	8:22	and the tents of the wicked will **be n more."**	401
	9:17	and multiply my wounds **for n reason.**	2855
	9:21	I have **n** concern for myself;	4202
	9:34	so that his terror would frighten me **n** *more.*	440
	10: 7	that **n** one can rescue me from your hand?	401
	10:21	before I go to the place of **n** return,	4202
	11: 3	Will **n** one rebuke you when you mock?	401
	11:12	witless man can **n more** become wise than	2256
	11:14	the sin that is in your hand and allow **n** evil	440
	11:19	with **n** one to make you afraid,	401
	12:25	They grope in darkness with **n** light;	4202
	13:16	for **n** godless man would dare come	4202
	14: 4	bring what is pure from the impure? **N** one!	4202
	14:10	he breathes his last and is **n** more.	361
	14:12	till the heavens are **n** more,	1194
	15: 3	with speeches that have **n** value?	4202
	15:15	If God places **n** trust in his holy ones,	4202
	15:19	the land was given when **n** alien passed	4202
	15:28	and houses where **n** one lives,	4202
	15:29	He will **n** *longer* be rich and his wealth will	4202
	16:22	before I go on the journey of **n** return.	4202
	18:17	he has **n** name in the land.	4202
	18:19	He has **n** offspring or descendants	4202
	18:19	**n** survivor where once he lived.	401
	19: 7	I get **n** response;	4202
	19: 7	though I call for help, **there is n** justice.	401
	20: 8	**n** *more* to be found,	4202
	20: 9	his place will look on him **n** more.	4202
	20:20	he will have **n** respite from his craving;	4202
	21:14	We have **n** desire to know your ways.	4202
	21:29	Have you paid **n** regard to their accounts—	4202
	22: 6	from your brothers **for n reason;**	2855
	22: 7	You gave **n** water to the weary	4202
	23: 6	he would not press charges against me.	4202
	23: 9	I catch **n** glimpse of him.	4202
	24:12	But God charges **n** one with wrongdoing.	4202
	24:15	he thinks, '**N** eye will see me,'	4202
	24:18	so that **n** one goes to the vineyards.	4202
	24:20	evil men are **n** longer remembered	4202
	24:21	and to the widow show **n** kindness.	4202
	24:22	they have **n** assurance of life.	4202
	27: 4	and my tongue will utter **n** deceit.	561
	27:19	but will do so **n** more;	4202
	28: 7	**N** bird of prey knows that hidden path,	4202
	28: 7	**n** falcon's eye has seen it.	4202
	28: 8	and **n** lion prowls there.	4202
	29:22	After I had spoken, they spoke **n** more;	4202
	30:24	"Surely **n** one lays a hand on a broken man	4202
	31:32	but **n** stranger had to spend the night in	4202
	32: 3	they had found **n** way to refute Job,	4202
	32:15	"They are dismayed and have **n** more	4202
	32:16	now that they stand there with **n** reply?	4202
	32:21	I will show partiality to **n** one,	440
	33: 7	**N** fear of me should alarm you,	4202
	34:19	who shows **n** partiality to princes and does	4202
	34:22	**There is n** dark place, no deep shadow,	401
	34:22	There is no dark place, **n** deep shadow,	401
	34:23	God has **n** need to examine men further,	4202
	34:27	and had **n** regard for any of his ways.	4202
	34:31	'I am guilty but will offend **n** *more.*	4202
	35:10	But **n** one says, 'Where is God my Maker,	4202
	35:13	the Almighty pays **n** attention to it.	4202
	36:18	Be careful **that n** one entices you by riches;	7153
	37:21	Now **n** one can look at the sun,	4202
	38:11	'This far you may come and **n** farther;	4202
	38:26	to water a land where **n** man lives,	4202
	38:26	a desert with **n** one in it,	4202
	40: 5	I spoke once, but I have **n** answer—	4202
	40: 5	twice, but I will say **n** more."	4202
	41:10	**N** one is fierce enough to rouse him.	4202
	41:16	to the next that **n** air can pass between.	4202
	41:26	The sword that reaches him has **n** effect,	1172
	42: 2	**n** plan of yours can be thwarted.	4202
Ps	6: 5	**N** one remembers you when he is dead.	401
	7: 2	rip me to pieces with **n** one to rescue me.	401
	10: 4	in all his thoughts **there is n** room for God.	401
	10:18	**in order that** man, who is of the earth, may terrify **n** more.	1153
	12: 1	Help, LORD, for the godly *are* **n more;**	1698
	14: 1	The fool says in his heart, **"There is n** God."	401
	14: 1	**there is n** one who does good.	401
	14: 3	**there is n** one who does good, not even one.	401
	15: 3	and has **n** slander on his tongue,	4202
	15: 3	who does his neighbor **n** wrong	4202
	15: 3	and casts **n** slur on his fellowman,	4202
	16: 2	apart from you I have **n** good thing."	1153
	18:41	but **there was n** one to save them—	401
	19: 3	**There is n** speech or language	401
	22:11	for trouble is near and **there is n** one to help.	401
	23: 4	I will fear **n** evil, for you are with me;	4202
	25: 3	**N** one whose hope is in you will ever	4202
	28: 5	Since they show **n** regard for the works of	4202
	32: 2	against him and in whose spirit is **n** deceit.	401
	32: 9	which have **n** understanding but must	401
	33:16	**N** king is saved by the size of his army;	401
	33:16	**n** warrior escapes by his great strength.	4202

Ps	34:10	who seek the LORD lack **n** good thing. 3972+4202
	34:22	**n** one will be condemned who takes refuge 4202
	36: 1	**There is n** fear of God before his eyes. 401
	37:10	and the wicked will **be n more;** 401
	37:36	but he soon passed away and **was n more;** 401
	38: 3	of your wrath **there is n** health in my body; 401
	38: 3	my bones have **n** soundness because 401
	38: 7	**there is n** health in my body. 401
	38:14	whose mouth can offer **n** reply. 401
	39:13	before I depart and **am n more."** 401
	40: 5	for us **n** one can recount to you; 401
	44: 9	you **n** longer go out with our armies. 4202
	49: 7	**N** man can redeem the life of another 4202
	49: 8	**n** payment **is** ever **enough—** 2532
	50: 9	I have **n** need of a bull from your stall or 4202
	53: 1	The fool says in his heart, **"There is n** God." 401
	53: 1	**there is n** one who does good. 401
	53: 3	**there is n** one who does good, not even one. 401
	55:19	and have **n** fear of God. 401
	56: 7	**On n** account let them escape; 224+6584
	58: 2	**N,** in your heart you devise injustice, 677
	59: 3	against me for **n** offense or sin of mine, 4202
	59: 4	I have done **n** wrong, 1172
	59: 5	show **n** mercy to wicked traitors. 440
	59:13	consume them till they **are n more.** 401
	60:10	and **n** longer go out with our armies? 4202
	63: 1	and weary land where there is **n** water. 1172
	69: 2	where **there is n** foothold. 401
	69:25	let there be **n** one to dwell in their tents. 440
	71:11	for **n** one will rescue him." 401
	72: 7	till the moon is **n more.** 1172
	72:12	the afflicted who have **n** one to help. 401
	73: 4	They have **n** struggles; 401
	73: 7	of their minds **know n** limits. 6296
	74: 9	We are given **n** miraculous signs; 4202
	74: 9	**n** prophets are left, 401
	75: 4	'Boast **n** more,' and to the wicked, 440
	75: 6	**N** one from the east or the west or from 4202
	78:63	and their maidens had **n** wedding songs; 4202
	79: 3	and **there is n** one to bury the dead. 401
	81: 9	You shall have **n** foreign god among you; 4202
	83: 4	the name of Israel be remembered **n** more." 4202
	84:11	**n** good thing does he withhold 4202
	86: 8	**n** deeds can compare with yours. 401
	88: 5	whom you remember **n** more, 4202
	89:22	**N** enemy will subject him to tribute; 4202
	89:22	**n** wicked man will oppress him. 4202
	91:10	then **n** harm will befall you, 4202
	91:10	**n** disaster will come near your tent. 4202
	92:15	and there is **n** wickedness in him." 4202
	94: 7	the God of Jacob pays **n** heed." 4202
	101: 3	I will set before my eyes **n** vile thing. 4202
	101: 7	**N** one who practices deceit will dwell 4202
	101: 7	**n** one who speaks falsely will stand 4202
	103:16	and its place remembers it **n** more. 4202
	104:35	from the earth and the wicked be **n** more. 401
	105:14	He allowed **n** one to oppress them; 4202
	105:15	do my prophets **n** harm." 440
	105:37	and from among their tribes **n** one faltered. 401
	106: 7	they gave **n** thought to your miracles. 4202
	107: 4	finding **n** way to a city 4202
	107:12	they stumbled, and **there was n** one to help. 401
	108:11	and **n** longer go out with our armies? 4202
	109:12	May **n** one extend kindness to him 440
	109:17	he found **n** pleasure in blessing— 4202
	112: 7	He will have **n** fear of bad news; 4202
	112: 8	His heart is secure, he will have **n** fear; 4202
	119:133	let **n** sin rule over me. 440
	132: 4	I will allow **n** sleep to my eyes, 561
	132: 4	**n** slumber to my eyelids, NIH
	142: 4	**n** one is concerned for me. 401
	142: 4	I have **n** refuge; no one cares for my life. 6+4996
	142: 4	I have no refuge; **n** one cares for my life. 401
	143: 2	for **n** one living is righteous before you. 4202
	144:14	**There will be n** breaching of walls, 401
	144:14	**n** going into captivity, 401
	144:14	**n** cry of distress in our streets. 401
	145: 3	his greatness **n** one can fathom. 401
	147: 5	his understanding has **n** limit. 401
	147:20	He has done this for **n** other nation; 4202
Pr	1:24	when I called and **n** one gave heed 401
	3:25	Have **n** fear of sudden disaster or of 440
	3:30	Do not accuse a man **for n** reason— 2855
	3:30	when he has done you **n** harm. 4202
	5: 6	She gives **n** thought to the way of life; 7153
	6: 4	Allow **n** sleep to your eyes, 440
	6: 4	**n** slumber to your eyelids. NIH
	6: 7	It has **n** commander, no overseer or ruler, 401
	6: 7	It has no commander, **n** overseer or ruler, NIH
	6:29	**n** one who touches her will go unpunished. 4202
	6:34	and he will show **n** mercy 4202
	8:24	When **there were n** oceans, I was given birth 401
	8:24	when **there were n** springs abounding 401
	10: 2	Ill-gotten treasures are of **n** value, 4202
	10:22	and he adds **n** trouble to it. 4202
	11:22	a beautiful woman **who shows n** discretion. 6073
	12: 7	are overthrown and **are n more,** 401
	12: 9	to be somebody and **have n** food. 2894
	12:21	**N** harm befalls the righteous, 3972+4202
	13: 8	but a poor man hears **n** threat. 4202
	14: 4	Where **there are n** oxen, 401
	14:10	and **n** one else can share its joy. 4202
	17:16	since he has **n** desire to get wisdom? 401
	17:21	there is **n** joy for the father of a fool. 4202
	18: 2	A fool finds **n** pleasure in understanding 4202
	20:14	"It's **n good,** it's no good!" 8273
	20:14	"It's no good, it's **n good!"** 8273

Pr	21:10	his neighbor gets **n** mercy from him. 4202
	21:30	**There is n** wisdom, no insight, 401
	21:30	There is no wisdom, **n** insight, 401
	21:30	**n** plan that can succeed against the LORD. 401
	24:20	for the evil man has **n** future hope, 4202
	28: 1	wicked man flees though **n** one pursues, 401
	28: 3	like a driving rain that leaves **n** crops. 401
	28:17	let **n** one support him. 440
	29: 7	but the wicked have **n** such concern. 4202
	29: 9	and **there is n** peace. 401
	29:18	Where **there is n** revelation, 401
	30:27	locusts have **n** king, 401
	31: 7	and remember their misery **n** more. 4202
	31:21	it snows, she has **n** fear for her household; 4202
Ecc	1:11	**There is n** remembrance of men of old, 401
	2:10	I refused my heart **n** pleasure. 3972+4202+4946
	3:19	man has **n** advantage over the animal. 401
	4: 1	and they have **n** comforter; 401
	4: 1	and they have **n** comforter. 401
	4: 8	**There was n** end to his toil, 401
	4:10	But pity the man who falls and has **n** one 401
	4:13	an old but foolish king who **n** longer knows 4202
	4:16	**There was n** end to all the people who were 401
	5: 4	He has **n** pleasure in fools; fulfill your vow. 401
	5:12	of a rich man permits him **n** sleep. 401
	6: 3	yet **n** matter how long he lives, NIH
	6:10	**n** man can contend with one who is stronger 4202
	8: 5	to **n** harm, and the wise heart will know 4202
	8: 7	Since **n** man knows the future, 401
	8: 8	**N** man has power over the wind 401
	8: 8	**n** one has power over the day of his death. 401
	8: 8	As **n** one is discharged in time of war, 401
	8:17	**N** one can comprehend what goes on under 4202
	9: 1	but **n** man knows whether love or hate awaits 401
	9: 5	they have **n** further reward, 401
	9:12	**n** man knows when his hour will come: 4202
	9:16	and his words are **n** longer heeded. 401
	10:11	there is **n** profit for the charmer. 401
	10:14	**N** one knows what is coming— 4202
	12: 1	"I find **n** pleasure in them"— 2654
	12: 5	along and desire **n** longer **is** stirred. 7296
	12:12	Of making many books **there is n** end, 401
SS	1: 7	**I wonder** the maidens love you! 4027+6584
	4: 7	**there is n** flaw in you. 401
	8: 1	and **n** one would despise me. 4202
Isa	1: 6	to the top of your head **there is n** soundness— 401
	1:11	I have **n** pleasure in the blood of bulls 4202
	1:31	with **n** one to quench the fire. 401
	2: 7	**there is n** end to their treasures. 401
	2: 7	**there is n** end to their chariots. 401
	3: 7	"I have **n** remedy. 4202
	3: 7	I have **n** food or clothing in my house; 401
	5: 8	and join field to field till **n** space is left 700
	5:12	but they have **n** regard for the deeds of 4202
	5:12	**n** respect for the work of his hands. 4202
	5:29	and carry it off with **n** one to rescue. 4202
	7:25	you will **n** longer go there for fear of 4202
	8:20	they have **n** light of dawn. 401
	9: 1	be **n** more gloom for those who were 4202
	9: 7	and peace **there will be n** end. 401
	9:17	Therefore the Lord will take **n** pleasure in 4202
	9:19	**n** one will spare his brother. 401
	10:20	will **n** longer rely on him who struck them 4202
	13:17	not care for silver and have **n** delight 4202
	13:18	they will have **n** mercy on infants 4202
	13:20	**n** Arab will pitch his tent there, 4202
	13:20	**n** shepherd will rest his flocks there. 4202
	14: 8	**n** woodsman comes to cut us down." 4202
	16:10	**n** one sings or shouts in the vineyards; 4202
	16:10	**n** one treads out wine at the presses, 4202
	16:12	it is to **n** avail. 4202
	17: 1	Damascus **will n longer be** a city 4946+6073
	17: 2	with **n** one to make them afraid. 401
	17: 8	and they will have **n** regard for 4202
	19: 7	will blow away and **be n more.** 401
	22:22	what he opens **n** one can shut, 401
	22:22	and what he shuts **n** one can open. 401
	23:10	for you **n** longer have a harbor. 401
	23:12	He said, **"N** more of your reveling, 4202
	23:12	even there you will find **n** rest." 4202
	23:13	this people that is now **of n account!** 4202
	24: 9	**N** longer do they drink wine with a song; 4202
	25: 2	the foreigners' stronghold a city **n** more; 4946
	26:14	They are now dead, they live **n** more; 1153
	26:21	will conceal her slain **n** longer. 4202
	27: 3	and night **so that n** one may harm it. 7153
	27: 9	**n** Asherah poles or incense altars will 4202
	27:11	so their Maker has **n** compassion on them, 4202
	27:11	and their Creator shows them **n** favor. 4202
	29:22	**"N** longer will Jacob be ashamed; 4202
	29:22	**n** longer will their faces grow pale. 4202
	30:10	"See **n** more visions!" 4202
	30:10	"Give us **n** more visions of what is right! 4202
	30:16	You said, **'N,** we will flee on horses.' 4202
	30:19	you will weep **n** more. 4202
	30:20	your teachers will be hidden **n** more; 4202
	32: 3	of those who see will **n** longer be closed, 4202
	32: 5	**N** longer will the fool be called noble nor 4202
	33: 8	**n** travelers **are** on the roads. 8697
	33: 8	**n** one is respected. 4202
	33:19	You will see those arrogant people **n** more, 4202
	33:21	**N** galley with oars will ride them, 1153
	33:21	**n** mighty ship will sail them. 4202
	33:24	**N** one living in Zion will say, "I am ill"; 1153
	34:10	**N** one will ever pass through it again. 401
	35: 9	**N** lion will be there, 401
	37: 3	to the point of birth and **there is n** strength 401

Isa	38:11	**n** longer will I look on mankind, 4202
	40:24	**N sooner** are they planted, 677+1153
	40:24	**n sooner** are they sown, 677+1153
	40:24	**n sooner** do they take root in the ground, 677+1153
	40:28	and his understanding **n** one can fathom. 401
	41:26	**N** one told of this, no one foretold it, 401
	41:26	No one told of this, **n** one foretold it, 401
	41:26	**n** one heard any words from you. 401
	41:28	I look but **there is n** one— 401
	41:28	**n** one among them to give counsel, 401
	41:28	**n** one to give answer when I ask them. NIH
	42:20	but have paid **n** attention; 4202
	42:22	with **n** one to rescue them; 401
	42:22	with **n** one to say, "Send them back." 401
	43:10	Before me **n** god was formed, 4202
	43:11	and apart from me **there is n** savior. 401
	43:13	**N** one can deliver out of my hand. 401
	43:25	and remembers your sins **n** more. 4202
	44: 6	apart from me **there is n** God. 401
	44: 8	**N,** there is no other Rock; I know not one." NIH
	44: 8	No, **there is n** other Rock; I know not one." 401
	44:12	he drinks **n** water and grows faint. 4202
	44:19	**N** one stops to think, 4202
	44:19	**n** one has the knowledge or understanding 4202
	45: 5	I am the LORD, and **there is n** other; 401
	45: 5	apart from me **there is n** God. 401
	45: 6	I am the LORD, and **there is n** other. 401
	45: 9	Does your work say, 'He has **n** hands'? 401
	45:14	and **there is n** other; there is no other god.' 401
	45:14	there is **n** other god.' " 700
	45:18	"I am the LORD, and **there is n** other. 401
	45:21	And **there is n** God apart from me, 401
	45:22	for I am God, and **there is n** other. 401
	46: 9	I am God, and **there is n** other; 401
	47: 1	**N** more will you be called tender 4202
	47: 3	I will take vengeance; I will spare **n** one." 4202
	47: 5	**n** more will you be called queen 4202
	47: 6	and you showed them **n** mercy. 4202
	47:10	**'N** one sees me.' 401
	47:14	**Here are n** coals to warm anyone; 401
	47:14	here is **n** fire to sit by. NIH
	48:22	**"There is n** peace," says the LORD, 401
	49: 4	But I said, "I have labored to **n purpose;** 8198
	49:15	at her breast and have **n** compassion on 4946
	50: 2	When I came, why **was there n** one? 401
	50: 2	I called, why **was there n** one to answer? 401
	50:10	who has **n** light, 401
	52:11	Touch **n** unclean thing! 440
	53: 2	He had **n** beauty or majesty to attract us 4202
	53: 9	though he had done **n** violence, 4202
	54: 4	of your youth and remember **n** more 4202
	54:17	**n** weapon forged against you will prevail, 3972+4202
	55: 1	you who have **n** money, come, buy and eat! 401
	56: 3	Let **n** foreigner who has bound himself to 440
	57: 1	and **n** one ponders it in his heart; 401
	57: 1	and **n** one understands that 401
	57:21	**"There is n** peace," says my God, 401
	59: 4	**N** one calls for justice; 401
	59: 4	**n** one pleads his case with integrity. 401
	59: 8	**there is n** justice in their paths; 401
	59: 8	**n** one who walks in them will know peace. 4202
	59:15	and was displeased that **there was n** justice. 401
	59:16	He saw that **there was n** one, 401
	59:16	he was appalled that **there was n** one 401
	60:15	with **n** one traveling through, 401
	60:18	**N** longer will violence be heard 4202
	60:19	The sun will **n** more be your light by day, 4202
	60:20	and your moon will wane **n** more; 4202
	62: 4	**N** longer will they call you Deserted, 4202
	62: 6	give yourselves **n** rest, 440
	62: 7	and give him **n** rest 440
	62:12	the City **N** Longer Deserted. 4202
	63: 3	from the nations **n** one was with me. 401
	63: 5	I looked, but **there was n** one to help, 401
	63: 5	I was appalled that **n** one gave support; 401
	64: 4	Since ancient times **n** one has heard, 4202
	64: 4	**n** ear has perceived, 4202
	64: 4	**n** eye has seen any God besides you, 4202
	64: 7	**N** one calls on your name or strives 401
	65:19	and of crying will be heard in it **n** more. 4202
	65:22	**N** longer will they build houses 4202
	66: 4	For when I called, **n** one answered, 401
	66: 4	when I spoke, **n** one listened. 4202
	66: 8	**n sooner** is Zion in labor **than** 1685
Jer	2: 6	where **n** one travels and no one lives?' 4202
	2: 6	where no one travels and **n** one lives?' 4202
	2:19	the LORD your God and have **n** awe 4202
	2:25	But you said, 'It's **n** use! 4202
	2:31	we will come to you **n** more'? 4202
	3: 3	and **n** spring rains have fallen. 4202
	3: 8	that her unfaithful sister Judah had **n** fear; 4202
	3:12	'I will frown on you **n** longer, 4202
	3:16	"men will **n** longer say, 4202
	3:17	**N** longer will they follow the stubbornness 4202
	4: 1	of my sight and **n** longer go astray, 4202
	4: 4	burn with **n** one to quench it. 401
	4:22	they have **n** understanding. 4202
	4:25	I looked, and **there were n** people; 401
	4:29	**n** one lives in them. 401
	5: 3	You struck them, but they felt **n** pain; 4202
	5:12	**N** harm will come to us; 4202
	5:28	Their evil deeds **have n** limit; 6296
	6: 8	so **n** one can live in it." 4202
	6:10	they find **n** pleasure in it. 4202
	6:14	peace,' they say, when **there is n** peace. 401

Jer	6:15	N, they have no shame at all;	1685
	6:15	No, they have n shame at all;	4202
	6:23	they are cruel and show n mercy;	4202
	7:32	when people will n longer call it Topheth	4202
	7:32	in Topheth until there is n *more* room.	401
	7:33	there will be n one to frighten them away.	401
	8:6	N one repents of his wickedness, saying,	401
	8:11	peace," they say, when there is n peace.	401
	8:12	N, they have no shame at all;	1685
	8:12	No, they have n shame at all;	4202
	8:13	There will be n grapes on the vine.	401
	8:13	There will be n figs on the tree,	401
	8:15	We hoped for peace but n good has come,	401
	8:19	Is her King n *longer* there?"	401
	8:22	Is there n balm in Gilead?	401
	8:22	Is there n physician there?	401
	8:22	Why then is there n healing for the wound	4202
	9:5	and n one speaks the truth.	4202
	9:11	the towns of Judah so n one can live there."	1172
	9:12	like a desert that n one can cross?	1172+4946
	9:22	with n one to gather them.' "	401
	10:5	they can do n harm	4202
	10:6	N one is like you, O LORD;	401+4946
	10:7	there is n one like you.	401+4946
	10:14	they have n breath in them.	4202
	10:20	My sons are gone from me and are n more;	401
	10:20	n one is left now to pitch my tent or to set	401
	11:19	that his name be remembered n more."	4202
	12:11	because there is n one who cares.	401
	12:12	n one will be safe.	401
	13:14	I will allow n pity or mercy or compassion	4202
	13:19	and there will be n one to open them.	401
	14:3	they go to the cisterns but find n water.	4202
	14:4	because there is n rain in the land;	4202
	14:5	because there is n grass.	4202
	14:15	'N sword or famine will touch this land.'	4202
	14:16	There will be n one to bury them	401
	14:19	We hoped for peace but n good has come,	401
	14:22	N, it is you, O LORD our God.	4202
	15:6	*I* can n longer show compassion.	4206
	16:6	and n one will cut himself	4202
	16:7	N one will offer food	4202
	16:13	for I will show you n favor.'	4202
	16:14	"when men will n longer say,	4202
	16:19	worthless idols that did them n good.	401
	17:6	in a salt land where n one lives.	4202
	17:8	It has n worries in a year of drought	4202
	17:24	and bring n load through the gates	1194
	18:12	But they will reply, '*It's* n use.	3286
	18:18	and pay n attention to anything he says."	440
	19:6	people will n longer call this place Topheth	4202
	19:11	in Topheth until there is n *more* room.	401
	21:7	he will show them n mercy or pity	4202
	21:12	burn with n one to quench it.	401
	22:3	Do n wrong or violence to the alien,	440
	22:28	broken pot, an object n *one* wants?	401
	23:4	and they will n longer be afraid or terrified,	4202
	23:7	"when people will n longer say,	4202
	23:14	so that n one turns from his wickedness,	1194
	23:17	'N harm will come to you.'	4202
	25:27	and vomit, and fall to rise n *more* because	4202
	25:35	the leaders of the flock n place to escape.	4946
	29:32	He will have n one left among this people,	4202
	30:8	n longer will foreigners enslave them.	4202
	30:10	and n one will make him afraid.	401
	30:13	There is n one to plead your cause,	401
	30:13	n remedy for your sore, no healing for you.	NIH
	30:13	no remedy for your sore, n healing for you.	401
	30:15	your pain that has n cure?	631
	30:17	Zion for whom n one cares.'	401
	31:12	and they will sorrow n more."	4202
	31:15	because their children are n more."	401
	31:29	"In those days people will n longer say,	4202
	31:34	N longer will a man teach his neighbor,	4202
	31:34	and will remember their sins n more."	4202
	33:20	so that day and night n longer come	1194
	33:21	can be broken and David will n *longer* have	4946
	33:24	and n longer regard them as a nation.	4946
	34:9	n one was to hold a fellow Jew in bondage.	1194
	34:10	and female slaves and n longer hold them	1194
	34:22	the towns of Judah so n one can live there."	401
	36:24	who heard all these words showed n fear,	4202
	36:30	He will have n one to sit on the throne	4202
	38:6	it had n water in it, only mud,	401
	38:9	to death when there is n longer any bread in	401
	38:27	So *they* said n more to him,	3087
	38:27	for n one had heard his conversation with	4202
	40:15	and n one will know it.	4202
	42:14	'N, we will go and live in Egypt,	4202
	44:17	and were well off and suffered n harm.	4202
	44:22	LORD could n longer endure your wicked	4202
	44:26	'that n one from Judah living anywhere	561
	45:3	with groaning and find n rest.' "	4202
	46:11	there is n healing for you.	401
	46:27	and n one will make him afraid.	401
	48:2	Moab will be praised n more;	401
	48:9	with n one to live in them.	401+4946
	48:33	n one treads them with shouts of joy.	4202
	48:38	like a jar that n *one* wants,"	401
	49:1	"Has Israel n sons?	401
	49:1	Has she n heirs?	401
	49:5	and n one will gather the fugitives.	401
	49:7	"Is there n longer wisdom in Teman?	401
	49:10	he *will* be n more.	401
	49:18	says the LORD, "so n one will live there;	4202
	49:18	n man will dwell in it.	4202
	49:33	N one will live there;	4202
Jer	49:33	n man will dwell in it."	4202
	50:3	N one will live in it;	4202
	50:14	Spare n arrows, for she has sinned against	440
	50:26	and leave her n remnant.	440
	50:29	Encamp all around her; let n one escape.	440
	50:32	and fall and n one will help her up;	401
	50:40	"so n one will live there;	4202
	50:40	n man will dwell in it.	4202
	51:17	they have n breath in them.	4202
	51:26	N rock will be taken from you for	4202
	51:29	of Babylon so that n one will live there.	4202
	51:37	a place where n one lives,	401+4946
	51:43	a land where n one lives,	3972+4202
	51:43	through which n man travels.	4202
	51:44	The nations will n longer stream to him.	4202
	51:64	'So will Babylon sink to rise n *more*	4202
	52:6	that there was n food for the people to eat.	4202
La	1:3	she finds n resting place.	4202
	1:4	for n one comes to her appointed feasts,	1172
	1:6	like deer that find n pasture;	4202
	1:7	there was n one to help her.	401
	1:16	N *one* is *near* to comfort me,	8178
	1:16	n one to restore my spirit.	NIH
	1:17	but there is n one to comfort her.	401
	1:21	but there is n one to comfort me.	401
	2:9	the law is n more,	401
	2:9	and her prophets n *longer* find visions from	4202
	2:18	give yourself n relief, your eyes no rest.	440
	2:18	give yourself no relief, your eyes n rest.	440
	2:22	of the LORD's anger n *one* escaped	401
	3:44	a cloud so that n prayer can get through.	4946
	4:4	but n one gives it to them.	401
	4:14	that n one dares to touch their garments.	4202
	4:15	"They can stay here n longer."	4202
	4:15	he n longer watches over them.	4202
	4:16	The priests are shown n honor,	4202
	4:16	the elders n favor.	4202
	5:5	we are weary and find n rest.	4202
	5:7	Our fathers sinned and are n more,	401
	5:12	elders are shown n respect.	4202
Eze	4:14	N unclean meat has ever entered my mouth.	4202
	7:11	n wealth, nothing of value.	4202
	7:14	n one will go into battle,	401
	12:23	and they will n longer quote it in Israel.'	4202
	12:24	For there will be n more false visions	4202
	13:10	saying, "Peace," when there is n peace,	401
	13:16	of peace for her when there was n peace,	401
	13:21	they will n longer fall prey to your power.	4202
	13:22	when I had brought them n grief,	4202
	13:23	therefore you will n longer see false visions	4202
	14:11	Then the people of Israel will n longer stray	4202
	14:15	so that n one can pass through it because of	1172
	16:5	N one looked on you with pity	4202
	16:34	n one runs after you for your favors.	4202
	16:41	and you will n longer pay your lovers.	4202
	16:42	I will be calm and n longer angry.	4202
	17:17	and great horde will be of n help to him	4202
	18:3	you will n longer quote this proverb	561
	18:17	and takes n usury or excessive interest.	4202
	18:32	I take n pleasure in the death of anyone,	4202
	19:9	so his roar was heard n longer on	4202
	19:14	N strong branch is left on it fit for	4202
	20:39	to me and n longer profane my holy name	4202
	21:32	you will be remembered n *more*;	4202
	22:24	that has had n rain or showers in the day	4202
	22:26	they teach that there is n difference	4202
	24:27	you will speak with him and will n longer	4202
	26:13	music of your harps will be heard n more.	4202
	26:19	like cities *longer* inhabited,	4202
	26:21	to a horrible end and you *will* be n more.	401
	27:36	to a horrible end and *will* be n more.' "	401
	28:3	Is n secret hidden from you?	4202
	28:19	to a horrible end and *will* be n more.' "	401
	28:24	" 'N longer will the people	4202
	29:11	N foot of man or animal will pass	4202
	29:11	n one will live there for forty years.	4202
	29:16	Egypt will n longer be a source	4202
	29:16	Yet he and his army got n reward from	4202
	30:13	N longer will there be a prince in Egypt,	4202
	31:8	n tree in the garden of God	3972+4202
	31:14	Therefore n other trees by	4202
	31:14	N other trees so well-watered are ever	4202
	32:13	from beside abundant waters n longer to	4202
	33:11	I take n pleasure in the death of the wicked,	561
	33:15	and does n evil, he will surely live;	1194
	33:22	and I was n longer silent.	4202
	33:28	so that n one will cross them.	401
	34:5	because there was n shepherd,	1172
	34:6	and n one searched or looked for them.	401
	34:10	shepherds can n longer feed themselves.	4202
	34:10	and it will n *longer* be food for them.	4202
	34:22	and they will n longer be plundered.	4202
	34:28	They will n longer be plundered by	4202
	34:28	and n one will make them afraid.	401
	34:29	and they will n longer be victims of famine	4202
	36:14	therefore you will n longer devour men	4202
	36:15	N longer will I make you hear the taunts of	4202
	36:15	and n longer will you suffer the scorn of	4202
	36:30	so that you will n longer suffer disgrace	4202
	37:8	but there was n breath in them.	401
	37:23	They will n longer defile themselves	4202
	39:7	I will n longer let my holy name	4202
	39:26	in safety in their land with n one	401
	39:29	I will n longer hide my face from them,	4202
	42:6	The rooms on the third floor had n pillars,	401
	44:2	n one may enter through it.	401
	44:9	N foreigner uncircumcised in heart	3972+4202
Eze	44:21	N priest is to drink wine when he	3972+4202
	44:28	You are to give them n possession in Israel;	4202
	45:8	my princes will n longer oppress my people	4202
	46:9	N one is to return through the gate	4202
	47:5	a river that n one could cross.	4202
Da	2:10	N king, however great and mighty,	10353+10379
	2:11	N one can reveal it to the king except	10379
	2:27	Daniel replied, "N wise man, enchanter,	10379
	3:12	who pay n attention to you, O king.	10379
	3:27	and there was n smell of fire on them.	10379
	3:29	for n other god can save in this way."	10379
	4:9	n mystery is too difficult for you.	10353+10379
	4:35	N one can hold back his hand or say	10379
	6:4	They could find n corruption in him,	10379
	6:13	pays n attention to you, O king,	10379
	6:15	Medes and Persians n decree or	10353+10379
	6:23	n wound was found on him,	10353+10379
	8:4	N animal could stand against him,	3972+4202
	10:3	I ate n choice food;	4202
	10:3	n meat or wine touched my lips;	4202
	10:3	and I used n lotions at all until	4202
	10:8	I had n strength left,	4202
	10:21	(N one supports me	401
	11:16	n one will be able to stand against him,	401
	11:19	to be seen n *more.*	4202
	11:27	but to n avail,	4202
	11:37	He will show n regard for the gods	4202
	11:45	and n one will help him.	401
Hos	1:6	for I will n longer show love to the house	4202
	2:10	n one will take her out of my hands.	4202
	2:16	you will n longer call me 'my master.'	4202
	2:17	n longer will their names be invoked.	4202
	4:1	"There is n faithfulness, no love,	401
	4:1	"There is no faithfulness, n love,	401
	4:1	n acknowledgment of God in the land.	401
	4:4	"But let n man bring a charge,	440
	4:4	let n man accuse another,	440
	5:14	with n one to rescue them.	401
	8:7	stalk has n head; it will produce no flour.	401
	8:7	stalk has no head; it will produce n flour.	1172
	9:11	n birth, no pregnancy, no conception.	4946
	9:11	no birth, n pregnancy, no conception.	4946
	9:11	no birth, no pregnancy, n conception.	4946
	9:15	I will n longer love them;	4202
	9:16	their root is withered, they yield n fruit.	1153
	10:3	"We have n king because we did not revere	401
	11:7	he will by n means exalt them.	3480+4202
	13:4	You shall acknowledge n God but me,	4202
	13:4	a Savior except me.	401
	13:14	"I *will* have n compassion,	4946+6259+6524
Joel	1:18	about because they have n pasture;	401
	2:10	and the stars n longer shine.	665+5586
	2:27	and that there is n other;	401
	3:15	and the stars n longer shine.	665+5586
Am	3:4	in the thicket when he has n prey?	401
	3:5	on the ground where n snare has been set?	401
	5:2	with n one to lift her up."	401
	5:6	and Bethel will have n one to quench it.	401
	5:22	I will have n regard for them.	4202
	6:10	and he says, "N," then he will say, "Hush!	700
	7:8	I will spare them n longer.	4202
	8:2	I will spare them n longer.	4202
Ob	1:18	There will be n survivors from the house	4202
Mic	2:3	You will n *longer* walk proudly,	4202
	2:5	Therefore you will have n one in	4202
	3:7	because there is n answer from God."	401
	3:11	N disaster will come upon us."	4202
	4:4	and n one will make them afraid,	401
	4:9	have you n king?	401
	5:8	and n one can rescue.	401
	5:12	and you will n longer cast spells.	4202
	5:13	you will n longer bow down to the work	4202
	7:1	there is n cluster of grapes to eat,	401
	7:5	put n confidence in a friend.	440
Na	1:12	I will afflict you n more.	4202
	1:14	"You will have n descendants	4202
	1:15	N more will the wicked invade you;	4202
	2:8	they cry, but n one turns back.	401
	2:13	*I will* **leave** you n prey on the earth.	4162
	2:13	of your messengers will n longer be heard."	4202
	3:17	and n one knows where.	4202
	3:18	the mountains with n one to gather them.	401
Hab	1:14	like sea creatures that have n ruler.	401+3972
	2:19	there is n breath in it.	401+3972
	3:17	not bud and there are n grapes on the vines,	401
	3:17	and the fields produce n food,	401
	3:17	though there are n sheep in the pen	1615
	3:17	in the pen and n cattle in the stalls,	401
Zep	3:2	She obeys n one, she accepts no correction.	4202
	3:2	She obeys no one, she accepts n correction.	4202
	3:5	he does n wrong.	4202
	3:5	yet the unrighteous know n shame.	4202
	3:6	with n one passing through.	1172
	3:6	n one will be left—no one at all.	401+4946
	3:6	n one at all.	1172+4946
	3:13	The remnant of Israel will do n wrong;	4202
	3:13	they will speak n lies,	4202
	3:13	down and n one will make them afraid."	401
Hag	2:12	The priests answered, "N."	4202
Zec	1:21	so that n one could raise his head,	4202
	4:5	"N, my lord," I replied.	4202
	4:13	"N, my lord," I said.	4202
	7:14	behind them that n one could come or go.	4946
	8:10	that time there were n wages for man	4202
	8:10	N one could go about his business safely	401
	8:14	upon you and showed n pity	4202
	11:6	For I will n longer have pity on the people	4202

Ref		Text	Strong's
Zec	13: 2	and they will be remembered n more,"	4202
	14: 6	On that day there will be n light,	4202
	14: 6	n cold or frost.	NIH
	14:17	they will have n rain.	4202
	14:18	they will have n rain.	4202
	14:21	that day there will n longer be a Canaanite	4202
Mal	1:10	I will accept n offering from your hands.	4202
	2:13	and wail because he n longer pays attention	401
Mt	1:25	But he had n union with her	4024
	2: 6	are by n means least among the rulers	4027
	2:18	because they are n more."	4024
	5:13	n longer good for anything,	4029
	5:37	be 'Yes,' and your 'N,' 'No';	4024
	5:37	be 'Yes,' and your 'No,' 'N';	4024
	6: 1	you will have n reward from your Father	4024
	6:24	"N one can serve two masters.	4029
	7: 3	in your brother's eye and pay n attention to	4024
	8:20	Son of Man has n place to lay his head."	4024
	8:28	They were so violent that n one could pass	3590
	9:16	"N one sews a patch of unshrunk cloth on	4029
	9:17	N, they pour new wine into new wineskins,	247
	9:30	"See that n one knows about this."	3594
	10:10	take n bag for the journey, or extra tunic,	3590
	11: 8	N, those who wear fine clothes	NIG
	11:23	N, you will go down to the depths.	3590
	11:27	N one knows the Son except the Father,	4029
	11:27	and n one knows the Father except the Son	4028
	12:19	n one will hear his voice in the streets.	4028
	13: 6	and they withered because they had n root.	3590
	13:21	he has n root, he lasts only a short time.	4024
	13:29	"'N,' he answered, 'because	4024
	16: 8	among yourselves about having n bread?	4024
	17: 8	they saw n one except Jesus.	4029
	19: 6	So they are n longer two, but one.	4033
	20: 7	n one has hired us,' they answered.	4029
	22: 5	"But they paid n attention and went off—	288
	22:16	you pay n attention to who they are.	4024
	22:23	who say there is n resurrection,	3590
	22:25	and since he had n children,	3590
	22:46	N one could say a word in reply,	4029
	22:46	and from that day on n one dared	4028
	24: 4	"Watch out that n one deceives you.	3590
	24:17	Let n one on the roof of his house go down	3590
	24:18	Let n one in the field go back	3590
	24:22	n one would survive.	4024
	24:36	"N one knows about that day or hour,	4029
	25: 9	"'N,' they replied, 'there may not	3607
	27:12	he gave n answer.	4029
	27:14	But Jesus made n reply,	4024
Mk	1:45	Jesus could n longer enter a town openly	3600
	2: 2	that there was n room left,	3600
	2:21	"N one sews a patch of unshrunk cloth on	4029
	2:22	n one pours new wine into old wineskins.	4029
	2:22	N, he pours new wine into new wineskins."	247
	3:27	n one can enter a strong man's house	4029
	4: 6	and they withered because they had n root.	3590
	4:17	But since they have n root,	4024
	4:40	Do you still have n faith?"	4037
	5: 3	and n one could bind him any more,	4029
	5: 4	N one was strong enough to subdue him.	4029
	6: 8	n bread, no bag, no money in your belts.	3590
	6: 8	no bread, no bag, no money in your belts.	3590
	6: 8	no bread, no bag, n money in your belts.	3590
	7:12	then you n longer let him do anything	4033
	8:12	n sign will be given to it."	1623
	8:16	"It is because we have n bread."	4024
	8:17	about having n bread?	4024
	9: 8	they n longer saw anyone	4033
	9:39	"N one who does a miracle in my name can	4029
	10: 8	So they are n longer two, but one.	4033
	10:18	"N one is good—except God alone.	4029
	10:29	"n one who has left home or brothers	4024
	11: 2	which n one has ever ridden.	476+4029
	11:14	"May n one ever eat fruit from you again."	3594
	12:14	you pay n attention to who they are;	4024
	12:18	Sadducees, who say there is n resurrection,	3590
	12:19	and leaves a wife but n children,	3590
	12:21	but he also died, leaving n child.	3590
	12:31	There is n commandment greater than these.	4024
	12:32	that God is one and there is n other	4024
	12:34	on n one dared ask him any more questions.	4029
	13: 5	"Watch out that n one deceives you.	3590
	13:15	Let n one on the roof of his house go down	3590
	13:16	Let n one in the field go back	3590
	13:20	n one would survive.	4024
	13:32	"N one knows about that day or hour,	4029
	14:61	and gave n answer.	4024
	15: 5	But Jesus still made n reply,	4033
Lk	1: 7	But they had n children,	4024
	1:60	but his mother spoke up and said, "N!	4049
	1:61	"There is n one among your relatives who	4029
	2: 7	there was n room for them in the inn.	4024
	4:24	"n prophet is accepted in his hometown.	4029
	5:36	"N one tears a patch from a new garment	4029
	5:37	n one pours new wine into old wineskins.	4029
	5:38	N, new wine must be poured	247
	5:39	And n one after drinking old wine wants	4029
	6:41	in your brother's eye and pay n attention to	4024
	6:43	"N good tree bears bad fruit,	4024
	7:25	N, those who wear expensive clothes	NIG
	7:28	of women there is n one greater than John;	4024
	8: 6	because they had n moisture.	3590
	8:13	but they have n root.	4024
	8:16	"N one lights a lamp and hides it in a jar	4029
	8:43	but n one could heal her.	4024+4029
	9: 3	n staff, no bag, no bread, no money,	3612
	9: 3	no staff, n bag, no bread, no money,	3612
	9: 3	no staff, no bag, n bread, no money,	3612
	9: 3	no staff, no bag, no bread, n money,	3612
	9: 3	no bag, no bread, no money, n extra tunic.	3612
	9:36	told n one at that time what they had seen.	4024
	9:58	Son of Man has n place to lay his head."	4024
	9:62	"N one who puts his hand to the plow	4029
	10:15	N, you will go down to the depths.	3590
	10:22	N one knows who the Son is except	4029
	10:22	and n one knows who the Father is except	NIG
	11:33	"N one lights a lamp and puts it in a place	4029
	11:36	full of light, and n part of it dark,	3590
	12: 4	the body and after that can do n more.	3590
	12:17	I have n place to store my crops.'	4024+4544
	12:24	they have n storeroom or barn;	4024
	12:33	n thief comes near and no moth destroys.	4024
	12:33	no thief comes near and n moth destroys.	4028
	12:51	N, I tell you, but division.	4049
	13: 3	I tell you, n!	4049
	13: 5	I tell you, n!	4049
	13:33	surely n prophet can die outside Jerusalem!	4024
	15:16	but n one gave him anything.	4029
	15:19	I am n longer worthy to	4033
	15:21	I am n longer worthy to	4033
	16:13	"N servant can serve two masters.	4029
	16:30	"'N, father Abraham,' he said,	4049
	17:18	Was n one found to return and give praise	4024
	17:31	On that day n one who is on the roof	3590
	17:31	n one in the field should go back	3590
	18:19	"N one is good—except God alone.	4029
	18:29	"n one who has left home or wife	4024
	19:30	which n one has ever ridden.	4029
	20:27	who say there is n resurrection,	3590
	20:28	and leaves a wife but n children,	866
	20:31	the seven died, leaving n children.	4024
	20:36	and they can n longer die;	4028
	20:40	n one dared to ask him any more	4033
	22: 6	when n crowd was present.	868
	22:51	But Jesus answered, "N more of this!"	1572
	23: 4	"I find n basis for a charge	4029
	23: 9	but Jesus gave him n answer.	4024
	23:14	in your presence and have found n basis	4029
	23:22	in him n grounds for the death penalty.	4029
	23:53	one in which n one had yet been laid.	4029
Jn	1:18	N one has ever seen God,	4029
	1:21	He answered, "N."	4024
	2: 3	"They have n more wine."	4024
	3: 2	For n one could perform	4029
	3: 3	n one can see the kingdom of God unless	4024
	3: 5	n one can enter the kingdom of God unless	4024
	3:13	N one has ever gone into heaven except	4029
	3:32	but n one accepts his testimony.	4029
	4:17	"I have n husband," she replied.	4024
	4:17	when you say you have n husband.	4024
	4:27	But n one asked, "What do you want?"	4029
	4:42	"We n longer believe just because	4033
	4:44	a prophet has n honor in his own country.)	4024
	5: 7	"I have n one to help me into the pool	4024
	5:13	The man who was healed had n idea who it was,	4024
	5:22	Moreover, the Father judges n one,	4029
	5:44	yet make n effort to obtain the praise	4024
	6:44	"N one can come to me unless	4024
	6:46	N one has seen the Father except	4024
	6:53	you have n life in you.	4024
	6:65	"This is why I told you that n one can come	4029
	6:66	and n longer followed him.	4033
	7: 4	N one who wants to become	4029
	7:12	"N, he deceives the people."	4024
	7:13	But n one would say anything publicly	4029
	7:27	n one will know where he is from."	4029
	7:30	but n one laid a hand on him,	4029
	7:44	but n one laid a hand on him.	4029
	7:46	"N one ever spoke the way this man does,"	4030
	7:49	N! But this mob	NIG
	8:10	"Has n one condemned you?"	4029
	8:11	"N one, sir," she said.	4029
	8:14	But you have n idea where I come from or	4024
	8:15	I pass judgment on n one.	4024+4029
	8:20	Yet n one seized him,	4029
	8:35	a slave has n permanent place in the family,	4024
	8:37	because you have n room for my word.	4024
	8:44	for there is n truth in him.	4024
	9: 4	Night is coming, when n one can work.	4024
	9: 9	Others said, "N, he only looks like him."	4049
	10:18	N one takes it from me,	4029
	10:28	n one can snatch them out of my hand.	4024
	10:29	n one can snatch them out	4029
	11: 4	N, it is for God's glory so	247
	11:10	for he has n light.	4024
	11:54	Therefore Jesus n longer moved	4033
	12:27	N, it was for this very reason I came	247
	12:46	that n one who believes in me should stay	3590
	13: 8	"N," said Peter, "you shall never wash my feet."	3590
	13: 8	you have n part with me."	4024
	13:16	n servant is greater than his master,	4024
	13:28	but n one at the meal understood why	4029
	14: 6	No one comes to the Father except	4029
	14:30	He has n hold on me,	4024+4029
	15: 2	cuts off every branch in me that bears n fruit	3590
	15: 4	N branch can bear fruit by itself,	4024
	15:13	Greater love has n one than this,	4029
	15:15	I n longer call you servants,	4033
	15:15	'N servant is greater than his master.'	4024
	15:22	however, they have n excuse for their sin.	4024
	15:24	not done among them what n one else did,	4029
	16:10	where you can see me n longer;	4033
Jn	16:16	"In a little while you will see me n more,	4033
	16:17	'In a little while you will see me n more,	4024
	16:19	'In a little while you will see me n more,	4024
	16:22	and n one will take away your joy.	4029
	16:23	that day you will n longer ask me anything.	4024
	16:25	when I will n longer use this kind	4033
	16:27	N, the Father himself loves you	1142
	17:11	I will remain in the world n longer,	4033
	18:31	"But we have n right to execute anyone,"	4024
	18:38	"I find n basis for a charge against him.	4029
	18:40	They shouted back, "N, not him!	NIG
	19: 4	that I find n basis for a charge against him."	4029
	19: 6	I find n basis for a charge against him."	4024
	19: 9	but Jesus gave him n answer.	4024
	19:11	"You would have n power over me	4024+4029
	19:12	you are n friend of Caesar.	4024
	19:15	"We have n king but Caesar,"	4024
	19:41	in which n one had ever been laid.	4029
	21: 5	"N," they answered.	4024
Ac	1:20	let there be n one to dwell in it,' and,	3590
	2:16	N, this is what was spoken by	247
	4:12	Salvation is found in n one else,	4024+4029
	4:12	for there is n other name under heaven	4028
	4:17	we must warn these men to speak n longer	3600
	4:32	N one claimed that any of his possessions	4028
	4:34	There were n needy persons among them.	4028
	5:13	N one else dared join them,	4029
	5:23	we opened them, we found n one inside."	4029
	7: 5	He gave him n inheritance here,	4024
	7: 5	though at that time Abraham had n child.	4024
	7:20	and he was n ordinary child.	842
	8:21	You have n part or share in this ministry,	4024
	11:12	to have n hesitation about going with them.	3594
	11:18	*they had* n further **objections**	2483
	12: 9	but he had n idea that what	4024
	12:18	there was n small commotion among	4024
	13:25	N, but he is coming after me,	NIG
	13:28	Though they found n proper ground for	3594
	15: 9	He made n distinction between us	4029
	15:11	N! We believe it is through the grace	247
	16:37	to get rid of us quietly? N!	4024
	18:10	and n one is going to attack and harm you,	4029
	18:17	But Gallio showed n concern whatever.	4029
	19: 2	"N, we have not even heard that there is	247
	19:24	in n little business for the craftsmen.	4024
	19:26	that man-made gods are n gods at all.	4024
	19:40	since there is n reason for it."	3594
	21:24	Then everybody will know there is n truth	4029
	21:39	a citizen of n ordinary city.	4024
	23: 8	that there is n resurrection,	3590
	23:29	but there was n charge against him	3594
	24:11	that n more than twelve days ago I went up	4024
	24:18	There was n crowd with me;	4024
	25:11	n one has the right to hand me over to them.	4029
	28: 5	into the fire and suffered n ill effects.	4029
Ro	2: 1	You, therefore, have n **excuse**,	406
	2:29	N, a man is a Jew if he is one inwardly;	247
	3:10	"There is n one righteous, not even one;	4024
	3:11	there is n one who understands,	4024
	3:11	n one who seeks God.	4024
	3:12	there is n one who does good,	4024
	3:18	"There is n fear of God before their eyes."	4024
	3:20	n one will be declared righteous	4024+4246
	3:22	There is n difference,	4024
	3:27	N, but on that of faith.	4049
	4:14	faith *has* n **value** and the promise is	3033
	4:15	there is n law there is n transgression.	4024
	4:15	there is no law there is n transgression.	4028
	5:13	not taken into account when there is n law.	3590
	6: 2	By n means! We died to sin;	1181+3590
	6: 6	that we should n longer be slaves to sin—	3600
	6: 9	death n longer has mastery over him.	4033
	6:15	but under grace? By n means!	1181+3590
	7:13	become death to me? By n means!	1181+3590
	7:17	As it is, it is n longer I myself who do it,	4033
	7:19	n, the evil I do not want to do—	247
	7:20	it is n longer I who do it,	4033
	8: 1	now n condemnation for those who are	4024
	8:24	But hope that is seen is n hope at all.	4024
	8:37	N, in all these things we are more than conquerors through him	247
	10:12	For there is n difference between Jew	4024
	10:19	by a nation that has n **understanding**."	852
	11: 1	God reject his people? By n means!	1181+3590
	11: 6	if by grace, then it is n longer by works;	4033
	11: 6	if it were, grace would n longer be grace.	4033
	13: 1	for there is n authority except	4024
	13: 3	rulers hold n terror for those who do right,	4024
	13: 8	Let n debt remain outstanding,	3594
	13:10	Love does n harm to its neighbor.	4024
	14:14	I am fully convinced that n food is unclean	4029
	14:15	you are n longer acting in love.	4033
	15:23	But now that there is n **more** place for me	3600
1Co	1:10	be n divisions among you and that you may	3590
	1:15	so n one can say that you were baptized	3590
	1:29	so that n one may boast before him.	3590
	2: 7	N, we speak of God's secret wisdom,	247
	2: 9	However, as it is written: "N eye has seen,	4024
	2: 9	"No eye has seen, n ear has heard,	4024
	2: 9	n mind has conceived what God has prepared for those who love him"—	4024
	2:11	In the same way n one knows the thoughts	4029
	3:11	For n one can lay any foundation other than	4029
	3:21	So then, n more boasting about men!	3594
	7:25	I have n command from the Lord,	4024
	7:37	who is under n compulsion but has control	3590
	8: 4	the world and that there is n God but one.	4029

1Co	8: 8	we are **n** worse if we do not eat,	4046
	8: 8	and **n** better if we do.	4046
	9:19	I am **free and belong to n** man,	1666+1801+4246
	9:27	**N**, I beat my body and make it my slave so	247
	10:13	**N** temptation has seized you except what is common to man.	4024
	10:20	**N**, but the sacrifices of pagans are offered	NIG
	11:16	we have **n** other practice—	4024
	11:17	In the following directives I have **n** praise	4024
	11:19	**N** doubt there have to be differences	NIG
	12: 3	that **n** one who is speaking by the Spirit	4029
	12: 3	"Jesus be cursed," and **n** one can say,	4029
	12:24	presentable parts need **n** special treatment.	4024
	12:25	that there should be **n** division in the body,	3590
	13: 5	it keeps **n** record of wrongs.	4029
	14: 2	Indeed, **n** one understands him;	4029
	14:28	If there is **n** interpreter,	3590
	15:10	**N**, I worked harder than all of them—	247
	15:12	of you say that there is **n** resurrection of	4024
	15:13	If there is **n** resurrection of the dead,	4024
	15:29	Now if there is **n** resurrection,	NIG
	16: 2	I come **n** collections will have to be made.	3590
	16:11	**N** one, then, should refuse to accept him.	3590
2Co	1:17	"Yes, yes" and "**N**, no"?	4024
	1:17	"Yes, yes" and "No, **n**,"?	4024
	1:18	our message to you is not "Yes" and "**N**."	4024
	1:19	was not "Yes" and "**N**,"	4024
	1:20	**n** matter how many promises God has made,	NIG
	2:13	I still had **n** peace of mind,	4024
	3:10	For what was glorious has **n** glory now	4024
	5:15	that those who live should **n longer** live	3600
	5:16	on we regard **n** one from a worldly point	4029
	5:16	we do so **n longer**.	4033
	5:21	God made him who had **n** sin to be sin	3590
	6: 3	We put **n** stumbling block in anyone's path,	3594
	6:17	Touch **n** unclean thing,	3590
	7: 2	We have wronged **n** one,	4029
	7: 2	We have corrupted **n** one,	4029
	7: 2	we have exploited **n** one.	4029
	7: 4	in all our troubles my joy **knows n** bounds.	5668
	7: 5	this body of ours had **n** rest,	4024
	7:10	that leads to salvation and leaves **n regret,**	294
	9: 1	There is **n need** for me to write to you	4356
	11:14	**n** wonder, for Satan himself masquerades	4024
	11:16	I repeat: Let **n** one take me for a fool.	3590
	12: 6	so **n** one will think more	3590
Gal	1: 7	which is really **n** gospel **at all.**	4024
	1:20	that what I am writing you is **n** lie.	4024
	2: 6	whatever they were makes **n** difference	4029
	2:16	because by observing the law **n** one will	4024
	2:20	with Christ and I **n longer** live,	4033
	3:11	Clearly **n** one is justified before God by	4029
	3:15	Just as **n** one can set aside or add to	4029
	3:18	then it **n longer** depends on a promise;	4033
	3:25	we are **n longer** under the supervision of	4033
	4: 1	he is **n** different from a slave,	4029
	4: 7	So you are **n longer** a slave, but a son;	4033
	4:12	You have done me **n** wrong.	4024
	4:17	but for **n** good.	4024
	4:27	O barren woman, who bears **n** children;	4024
	4:27	you who have **n** labor pains;	4024
	5: 2	**n** value to you **at all.**	4024
	5:10	in the Lord that you will take **n** other view.	4029
	5:23	Against such things there is **n** law.	4024
	6:17	Finally, let **n one** cause me trouble,	3594
Eph	2: 9	not by works, so that **n** one can boast.	3590
	2:19	you are **n longer** foreigners and aliens,	4033
	4:14	Then we will **n longer** be infants,	3600
	4:17	you must **n longer** live as the Gentiles do,	3600
	4:28	He who has been stealing must steal **n longer,**	3600
	5: 5	**N** immoral, impure or greedy person	4024+4246
	5: 6	Let **n one** deceive you with empty words,	3594
	5:29	After all, **n one** ever hated his own body,	4029
	6: 9	and there is **n** favoritism with him.	4024
Php	1:20	and hope that I will in **n way** be ashamed,	4029
	2:20	I have **n** one else like him,	4029
	3: 1	It is **n** trouble for me to write	4024
	3: 3	and who put **n** confidence in the flesh—	4024
	4:10	but *you* **had n opportunity** to show it.	177
Col	2: 4	so that **n** one may deceive you	3594
	2: 8	that **n** one takes you captive through hollow	3590
	3:11	Here there is **n** Greek or Jew,	4024
	3:25	and there is **n** favoritism.	4024
1Th	3: 1	So when we could stand it **n longer,**	3600
	3: 3	**n** one would be unsettled by these trials.	3594
	3: 5	when I could stand it **n longer,**	3600
	4: 6	this matter **n** one should wrong his brother	3590
	4:13	who have **n** hope.	3590
1Ti	5: 7	**n** one may be **open to blame.**	455
	5: 9	**N** widow may be put on the list of widows	3590
	5:14	the enemy **n** opportunity for slander.	3594
	6:16	whom **n** one has seen or can see.	4029
2Ti	2: 4	**N** one serving as a soldier gets involved	4029
	2:14	it is of **n** value,	4029
	4:16	one came to my support,	4029
Tit	1:14	and will pay **n** attention to Jewish myths or	3590
	2: 5	so that **n** one will malign the word of God.	3590
	2:12	It teaches us to **say "N"** to ungodliness	766
	3: 2	to slander **n** one,	3594
Phm	1:16	**n longer** as a slave,	4033
Heb	2: 8	message they heard was of **n** value to them,	3590
	4:11	so that **n** one will fall	3590
	5: 4	**N** one takes this honor upon himself;	4024
	6:13	there was **n** one greater for him to swear by,	4029
	7:13	and **n** one from that tribe has ever served at	4029
	8: 7	**n** place would have been sought	4024
Heb	8:11	**N longer** will a man teach his neighbor,	3590+4024
	8:12	and will remember their sins **n** more."	3590+4024
	9:22	of blood there is **n** forgiveness.	4024
	10: 2	and would **n longer** have felt guilty	3594
	10:17	lawless acts I will remember **n** more."	3590+4024
	10:18	there is **n longer** any sacrifice for sin.	4033
	10:26	**n** sacrifice for sins is left,	4033
	11:23	because they saw *he was* **n ordinary** child,	842
	12:11	**N** discipline seems pleasant at the time,	4024
	12:14	without holiness **n** one will see the Lord.	4029
	12:15	to it that **n** one misses the grace of God and	3590
	12:15	that **n** bitter root grows up to cause trouble	3590
	12:16	See that **n** one is sexually immoral,	3590
	12:17	He could bring about **n** change of mind,	4024
	12:19	that **n** further word be spoken to them,	3590
	13:10	which are of **n** value to those who eat them.	4024
	13:10	at the tabernacle have **n** right to eat.	4024
	13:17	for that would be of **n advantage** to you.	269
Jas	1:13	When tempted, **n** one should say,	3594
	2:14	a man claims to have faith but has **n** deeds?	3590
	3: 8	but **n** man can tame the tongue.	4029
	5:12	Let your "Yes" be yes, and your "**N**," no,	4024
	5:12	Let your "Yes" be yes, and your "No," **n**,	4024
1Pe	2:22	"He committed **n** sin,	4024
	2:22	**and n** deceit was found in his mouth."	4028
	2:23	when he suffered, he made **n** threats.	4024
2Pe	1:20	that **n** prophecy of Scripture came about by	4024
1Jn	1: 5	in him there is **n** darkness at all.	4024
	1:10	a liar and his word has **n** place in our lives.	4024
	2:21	because **n** lie comes from the truth.	4024+4246
	2:23	**N** one who denies the Son has the Father;	4028+4246
	3: 5	And in him is **n** sin.	4024
	3: 6	**N** one who lives in him keeps on sinning.	4024+4246
	3: 6	**N** one who continues to sin has	4024+4246
	3: 9	**N** one who is born of God will continue to sin,	4024+4246
	3:15	that **n** murderer has eternal life in him.	4024+4246
	3:17	sees his brother in need but **has n pity**	3091+3836+5073
	4:12	**N** one has ever seen God;	4029
	4:18	There is **n** fear in love.	4024
3Jn	1: 4	I have **n** greater joy than to hear	4024
	1: 7	receiving **n** help from the pagans.	3594
Rev	3: 7	What he opens **n** one can shut,	4029
	3: 7	and what he shuts **n** one can open.	4029
	3: 8	an open door that **n** one can shut.	4029
	3:11	so that **n** one will take your crown.	3594
	5: 3	But **n** one in heaven or on earth or under	4029
	5: 4	because **n** one was found who was worthy	4029
	7: 9	a great multitude that **n** one could count,	4029
	10: 6	and said, "There will be **n more** delay!	4033
	13:17	that **n** one could buy or sell unless he had	3590
	14: 3	**N** one could learn the song except	4029
	14: 5	**N** lie was found in their mouths;	4024
	14:11	There is **n** rest day or night	4024
	15: 8	and **n** one could enter the temple until	4029
	16:18	**N** earthquake like it has ever occurred	4024
	18:11	**n** one buys their cargoes any more—	4029
	18:22	**N** workman of any trade will ever be found	4024
	19:12	on him that **n** one knows but he himself.	4029
	20: 6	The second death has **n** power over them,	4024
	20:11	and there was **n** place for them.	4024
	21: 1	and there was **n longer** any sea.	4024
	21: 4	There will be **n** more death or mourning	4024
	21:25	On **n** day will its gates ever be shut,	4024
	21:25	**ever** be shut, for there will be **n**	3590+4024
	22: 3	**N longer** will there be any curse.	4024
	22: 5	There will be **n** more night.	4024

NO [THE CITY] (KJV) See THEBES

NOADIAH (2)

Ezr	8:33	of Jeshua and **N** son of Binnui.	5676
Ne	6:14	remember also the prophetess **N** and	5676

NOAH (54) [NOAH'S]

Ge	5:29	He named him **N** and said,	5695
	5:30	After **N** was born, Lamech lived 595 years	5695
	5:32	After **N** was 500 years old,	5695
	6: 8	**N** found favor in the eyes of the LORD.	5695
	6: 9	This is the account of **N**.	5695
	6: 9	**N** was a righteous man,	5695
	6:10	**N** had three sons: Shem, Ham and Japheth.	5695
	6:13	So God said to **N**, "I am going to put an end	5695
	6:22	**N** did everything just as God commanded	5695
	7: 1	The LORD then said to **N**,	5695
	7: 5	**N** did all that the LORD commanded him.	5695
	7: 6	**N** was six hundred years old when	5695
	7: 7	And **N** and his sons and his wife	5695
	7: 9	came to **N** and entered the ark,	5695
	7: 9	as God had commanded **N**.	5695
	7:13	On that very day **N** and his sons, Shem,	5695
	7:15	in them came to **N** and entered the ark.	5695
	7:16	as God had commanded **N**.	2257S
	7:23	Only **N** was left, and those with him	5695
	8: 1	But God remembered **N** and all the wild	5695
	8: 6	After forty days **N** opened the window	5695
	8: 9	so it returned to **N** in the ark.	2257S
	8:11	**N** knew that the water had receded	5695
	8:13	**N** then removed the covering from the ark	5695
	8:15	Then God said to **N**,	5695
	8:18	So **N** came out, together with his sons	5695
Ge	8:20	Then **N** built an altar to the LORD and,	5695
	9: 1	Then God blessed **N** and his sons,	5695
	9: 8	God said to **N** and to his sons with him:	5695
	9:17	So God said to **N**, "This is the sign	5695
	9:18	of **N** who came out of the ark were Shem,	5695
	9:19	These were the three sons of **N**,	5695
	9:20	**N**, a man of the soil,	5695
	9:24	When **N** awoke from his wine	5695
	9:28	After the flood **N** lived 350 years.	5695
	9:29	Altogether, **N** lived 950 years,	5695
Nu	26:33	whose names were Mahlah, **N**, Hoglah,	5829
	27: 1	**N**, Hoglah, Milcah and Tirzah.	5829
	36:11	Mahlah, Tirzah, Hoglah, Milcah and **N**—	5829
Jos	17: 3	whose names were Mahlah, **N**, Hoglah,	5829
1Ch	1: 3	Enoch, Methuselah, Lamech, **N**.	5695
	1: 4	The sons of **N**: Shem, Ham and Japheth.	5695
Isa	54: 9	"To me this is like the days of **N**,	5695
	54: 9	the waters of **N** would never again cover	5695
Eze	14:14	these three men—**N**, Daniel and Job—	5695
	14:20	declares the Sovereign LORD, even if **N**,	5695
Mt	24:37	As it was in the days *of* **N**,	3820
	24:38	up to the day **N** entered the ark;	3820
Lk	3:36	the son *of* **N**, the son of Lamech,	3820
	17:26	"Just as it was in the days *of* **N**,	3820
	17:27	in marriage up to the day **N** entered the ark.	3820
Heb	11: 7	By faith **N**, when warned about things not	3820
1Pe	3:20	the days *of* **N** while the ark was being built.	3820
2Pe	2: 5	but protected **N**, a preacher of righteousness	3820

NOAH'S (4) [NOAH]

Ge	7:11	In the six hundredth year of **N** life,	5695
	8:13	first month of **N** six hundred and first year,	NIH
	10: 1	Ham and Japheth, **N** sons,	5695
	10:32	These are the clans of **N** sons,	5695

NOB (6)

1Sa	21: 1	David went to **N**, to Ahimelech the priest.	5546
	22: 9	to Ahimelech son of Ahitub at **N**.	5546
	22:11	who were the priests at **N**,	5546
	22:19	He also put to the sword **N**,	5546
Ne	11:32	in Anathoth, **N** and Ananiah,	5546
Isa	10:32	This day they will halt at **N**;	5546

NOBAH (3)

Nu	32:42	And **N** captured Kenath	5561
	32:42	and called it **N** after himself.	5562
Jdg	8:11	the nomads east of **N** and Jogbehah and fell	5562

NOBILITY (2) [NOBLE]

Est	1:18	Median **women of** the **n** who have heard	8576
Da	1: 3	from the royal family and the **n**—	7312

NOBLE (21) [NOBILITY, NOBLEMAN, NOBLES, NOBLEST]

Ru	3:11	that you are a woman of **n character.**	2657
Est	6: 9	to one of the king's **most n** princes.	7312
Ps	45: 1	a theme as I recite my verses for the king;	3202
Pr	12: 4	wife of **n character** is her husband's crown,	2657
	31:10	A wife of **n character** who can find?	2657
	31:29	"Many women do **n** *things*,	2657
Ecc	10:17	of **n** birth and whose princes eat at	2985
Isa	32: 5	No longer will the fool be called **n** nor	5618
	32: 8	But the *man* makes noble plans,	5618
	32: 8	But the noble man makes **n** plans,	5619
	32: 8	and by **n** *deeds* he stands.	5619
Lk	8:15	on good soil stands for those with a **n**	2819
	19:12	"A man *of* **n birth** went to a distant country	2302
Ac	17:11	Bereans were **of more n** character than	2302
Ro	9:21	for **n** purposes and some for common use?	5507
1Co	1:26	not many were **of n birth.**	2302
Php	4: 8	brothers, whatever is true, whatever is **n,**	4948
1Ti	3: 1	being an overseer, he desires a **n** task.	2819
2Ti	2:20	for **n purposes** and some for ignoble.	5507
	2:21	he will be an instrument for **n purposes,**	5507
Jas	2: 7	not the ones who are slandering the **n** name	2819

NOBLEMAN (1) [NOBLE]

Pr	25: 7	than for him to humiliate you before a **n.**	5618

NOBLES (60) [NOBLE]

Nu	21:18	that the **n** of the people sank—	5618
	21:18	the **n** with scepters and staffs."	NIH
Jdg	5:13	men who were left came down to the **n;**	129
	5:25	for **n** she brought him curdled milk.	129
2Sa	10: 3	the Ammonite **n** said to Hanun their lord,	8569
1Ki	21: 8	and sent them to the elders and **n** who lived	2985
	21:11	and **n** who lived in Naboth's city did	2985
2Ki	24:12	his **n** and his officials all surrendered	8569
1Ch	19: 3	the Ammonite **n** said to Hanun,	8569
2Ch	23:20	of hundreds, the **n**, the rulers of the people	129
Ne	2:16	or **n** or officials or any others who would	2985
	3: 5	but their **n** would not put their shoulders to	129
	4:14	I stood up and said to the **n,**	2985
	4:19	Then I said to the **n,**	2985
	5: 7	and then accused the **n** and officials.	2985
	5:12	and made **the n and officials** take an oath	4392S
	6:17	the **n** of Judah were sending many letters	2985
	7: 5	into my heart to assemble the **n,**	129
	10:29	all these now join their brothers the **n,**	129
	13:17	I rebuked the **n** *of* Judah and said to them,	2985
Est	1: 3	of his reign he gave a banquet for all his **n**	8569
	1: 3	and the **n** *of* the provinces were present.	8569

Est	1:11	to display her beauty to the people and **n**,	8569
	1:14	and Memucan, the seven **n** *of* Persia	8569
	1:16	in the presence of the king and the **n,**	8569
	1:16	also against all the **n** and the peoples of all	8569
	1:18	to all the king's **n** in the same way.	8569
	1:21	and his **n** were pleased with this advice,	8569
	2:18	Esther's banquet, for all his **n** and officials.	8569
	3:1	of honor higher than that of all the other **n.**	8569
	3:12	of the various provinces and the **n** of	8569
	5:11	how he had elevated him above the other **n**	8569
	8:9	and **n** of the 127 provinces stretching	8569
	9:3	And all the **n** of the provinces, the satraps,	8569
Job	12:21	He pours contempt on **n** and disarms	5618
	29:10	the voices of the **n** were hushed,	5592
	34:18	and to **n**, 'You are wicked,'	5618
Ps	47:9	The **n** of the nations assemble as	5618
	83:11	Make their **n** like Oreb and Zeeb,	5618
	107:40	who pours contempt on **n** made them	5618
	149:8	their **n** with shackles of iron,	3877
Pr	8:16	and all **n** who rule on earth.	5618
Isa	5:14	into it will descend their **n** and masses	2077
	13:2	beckon to them to enter the gates of the **n.**	5618
	34:12	Her **n** will have nothing there to be called	2985
Jer	14:3	The **n** send their servants for water;	129
	27:20	with all the **n** of Judah and Jerusalem—	2985
	39:6	before his eyes and also killed all the **n**	2985
Eze	17:12	and carried off her king and her **n,**	8569
Da	4:36	My advisers and **n** sought me out,	10652
	5:1	for a thousand of his **n** and drank wine	10652
	5:2	so that the king and his **n,**	10652
	5:3	and the king and his **n,**	10652
	5:9	His **n** were baffled.	10652
	5:10	hearing the voices of the king and his **n,**	10652
	5:23	and you and your **n,**	10652
	6:17	and with the rings of his **n,**	10652
Jnh	3:7	"By the decree of the king and his **n:**	1524
Na	3:10	Lots were cast for her **n,**	3877
	3:18	your **n** lie down to rest.	129

NOBLEST (1) [NOBLE]
SS	3:7	by sixty warriors, the **n** of Israel,	1475+4946

NOBODY (7)
Pr	12:9	Better *to* be a **n** and yet have a servant	7829
Ecc	9:15	But **n** remembered that poor man.	132+4202
Jn	9:32	**N** has ever heard of opening the eyes	4024+5516
1Co	6:5	that there is **n** among you wise enough	4029
	10:24	**N** should seek his own good,	3594
2Co	11:10	**n** in the regions of Achaia will stop this	4024
1Th	5:15	that **n** pays back wrong for wrong,	3590+5516

NOCTURNAL (1)
Dt	23:10	unclean because of a **n** emission,	4326

NOD (1)
Ge	4:16	and lived in the land of **N,**	5655

NODAB (1)
1Ch	5:19	against the Hagrites, Jetur, Naphish and **N.**	5656

NOE (KJV) See NOAH

NOGAH (2)
1Ch	3:7	**N**, Nepheg, Japhia,	5587
	14:6	**N**, Nepheg, Japhia,	5587

NOHAH (1)
1Ch	8:2	**N** the fourth and Rapha the fifth.	5666

NOISE (20) [NOISY]
Ex	32:17	Joshua heard the **n** of the people shouting,	7754
1Ki	1:41	the meaning of all the **n** *in* the city?"	2159+7754
	1:45	That's the **n** you hear.	7754
2Ki	11:13	the **n** made by the guards and the people,	7754
2Ch	23:12	the **n** of the people running and cheering	7754
Ezr	3:13	because the people made so much **n.**	8131+9558
Isa	13:4	Listen, a **n** on the mountains,	2162
	14:11	along with the **n** of your harps;	2166
	24:8	the **n** of the revelers has stopped,	8623
	29:6	with thunder and earthquake and great **n,**	7754
	66:6	hear that **n** from the temple!	7754
Jer	46:17	'Pharaoh king of Egypt is only a **loud n;**	8623
	47:3	at the **n** of enemy chariots and the rumble	8323
	50:22	The **n** of battle is in the land,	7754
	50:22	the **n** of great destruction!	NIH
Eze	23:42	"The **n** of a carefree crowd was around her;	7754
	26:10	Your walls will tremble at the **n** of	7754
	37:7	And as I was prophesying, there was a **n,**	7754
Joel	2:5	With a **n** like that of chariots they leap over	7754
Am	5:23	Away with the **n** of your songs!	2162

NOISED (KJV) See HEARD, SPREAD, TALKING

NOISOME (KJV) See DEADLY, UGLY, WILD

NOISY (7) [NOISE]
Ps	64:2	from that **n crowd** of evildoers.	8095
Pr	1:21	at the head of the **n** streets she cries out,	2159
Isa	32:14	the **n** city deserted;	2162
Jer	48:45	the skulls of the **n boasters.**	1201+8623
Eze	26:13	I will put an end to your **n** songs,	2162
Mt	9:23	and saw the flute players and the **n** crowd,	2572

NOMAD (1) [NOMADS]
Jer	3:2	sat like a **n** in the desert.	6862

NOMADS (2) [NOMAD]
Jdg	8:11	the **n** east of Nobah and Jogbehah	185+928+8905
Jer	35:7	a long time in the land where you *are* **n.'**	1591

NON (KJV) See NUN

NON-GREEKS (1)
Ro	1:14	I am obligated both to Greeks and **n,**	975

NONE (111) [NO]
Ge	23:6	**N** of us will refuse you his tomb	408+4202
	28:17	This is **none** other than the house of God;	401
	39:11	**n** of the household servants was inside.	401+408
	41:24	but **n** could explain it to me."	401
Ex	12:46	take **n** of the meat outside the house.	4202
	16:27	but they found **n.**	4202
	23:26	**n** will miscarry or be barren in your land.	4202
Lev	7:15	he must leave **n** of it till morning.	4202
	17:12	"**N** of you may eat blood,	3972+4202+5883
	21:17	**n** of your descendants who has a defect	408+4202
	22:30	leave **n** of it till morning.	4202
Nu	30:5	**n** of her vows or the pledges	3972+4202
	30:12	then **n** of the vows or pledges that	3972+4202
Dt	7:14	**n** of your men or women will be childless,	4202
	13:17	**N** of those condemned things shall	4202+4399
	15:6	to many nations but will borrow from **n.**	4202
	15:6	over many nations but **n** will rule over you.	4202
	28:12	to many nations but will borrow from **n.**	4202
	28:31	but you will eat **n** of it.	4202
Jdg	20:8	saying, "**N** of us will go home.	408+4202
	21:9	they found that **n** of the people	401+408
1Sa	1:2	Peninnah had children, but Hannah had **n.**	401
	3:19	he let **n** of his words fall to the ground.	3972+4202
	14:24	So **n** of the troops tasted food.	3972+4202
	21:9	David said, "There is **n** like it;	401
	22:8	**N** of you is concerned about me or tells me	401
	30:2	They killed **n** of them,	4202
	30:17	and **n** of them got away,	408+4202
2Sa	15:14	or **n** of us will escape from Absalom.	4202
2Ki	6:12	"**N** of us, my lord the king,"	4202
2Ch	1:12	and **n** after you will have."	4202
	35:18	and **n** of the kings of Israel had ever	3972+4202
Job	29:12	and the fatherless who had **n** to assist him.	4202
	32:12	**n** of you has answered his arguments.	NIH
	33:13	that he answers **n** *of* man's words?	3972+4202
Ps	50:22	with **n** to rescue:	401
	69:20	I looked for sympathy, but **there was n,**	401
	69:20	for comforters, but I found **n.**	4202
	74:9	and **n** of us knows how long this will be.	4202
	86:8	Among the gods **there is n** like you, O Lord;	401
Pr	2:19	**N** who go to her return or	3972+4202
	8:8	**n** of them is crooked or perverse.	401
	14:6	The mocker seeks wisdom and *finds* **n,**	401
Isa	30:15	but you would have **n** of it.	4202
	34:16	**N** of these will be missing,	285+4202
	41:17	but **there is n;**	401
	45:6	men may know there is **n** besides me.	700
	45:21	**there is n** but me.	401
	46:9	I am God, and there is **n** like me.	401
	47:8	'I am, and there is **n** besides me.	700
	47:10	'I am, and there is **n** besides me.'	700
	51:18	the sons she bore **there was n** to guide her;	401
	51:18	the sons she reared **there was n** to take her	401
	59:11	We look for justice, but find **n;**	401
Jer	22:30	for **n** of his offspring will prosper,	4202
	22:30	of his offspring will prosper, **n** will sit on	408S
	30:7	**N** will be like it.	401+4946
	44:14	**N** of the remnant of Judah who have gone	4202
	44:14	**n** will return except a few fugitives."	4202
	50:20	but **there will be n,**	401
	50:20	but **n** will be found,	4202
La	1:2	Among all her lovers **there is n**	401
	1:9	**there was n** to comfort her.	401
	5:8	and **there is n** to free us from their hands.	401
Eze	7:11	**n** of the people will be left,	4202
	7:11	of the people will be left, **n** of that crowd—	4202
	7:25	they will seek peace, but **there will be n.**	401
	12:28	**N** of my words will be delayed any	3972+4202
	16:34	for you give payment and **n** is given to you.	4202
	18:11	(though the father has done **n** of them)	3972+4202
	18:22	**N** of the offenses he has committed	3972+4202
	18:24	**N** of the righteous things he has done	3972+4202
	22:30	but I found **n.**	4202
	33:13	of the righteous things he has done	3972+4202
	33:16	**N** *of* the sins he has committed will	3972+4202
	46:18	that **n** of my people will be separated	408+4202
Da	1:19	and he found **n** equal to Daniel,	3972+4202+4946
	4:18	for **n** of the wise men in my	10353+10379
	8:4	and **n** could rescue from his power.	4202
	8:7	and **n** could rescue the ram from his power.	4202
	9:7	of the wicked will understand,	3972+4202
Hos	7:7	and **n** of them calls on me.	401
Am	4:7	another had **n** and dried up.	4202
	9:1	Not one will get away, **n** will escape.	4202
Mic	7:1	**n** of the early figs that I crave.	NIH
Zep	2:5	"I will destroy you, and **n** will be left."	401+4946
	2:15	"I am, and there is **n** besides me."	700
Mt	12:39	But **n** will be given it except the sign of the prophet Jonah.	4024+4956S
	16:4	**n** will be given it except the sign of Jonah."	4024+4956S
Mk	12:22	In fact, **n** of the seven left any children.	4024
Lk	3:11	with him who has **n,**	3590
	11:29	**n** will be given it except the sign of Jonah.	4024+4956S
	21:15	that **n** of your adversaries will be able	570+4024
Jn	6:39	I shall lose **n** of all that he has given me,	3590
	16:5	yet **n** of you asks me,	4029
	17:12	**N** has been lost except the one doomed	4029
	21:12	**N** of the disciples dared ask him,	4029
Ac	20:25	that **n** of you among whom I have gone	4246
	26:26	that **n** of this has escaped his notice,	4024+4029
	28:21	and **n** of the brothers who have come	4046+5516
Ro	14:7	For **n** of us lives to himself alone and none	4029
	14:7	of us lives to himself alone and **n** of us dies	4029
1Co	2:8	**N** of the rulers of this age understood it,	4029
	7:29	who have wives should live as if they had **n;**	3590
	14:10	yet **n** of them is without meaning.	4029
Gal	1:19	I saw **n** of the other apostles—	4024
Heb	3:12	brothers, **that n** of you has a sinful,	3607+5516
	3:13	so that **n** of you may be hardened	3590+5516
	4:1	let us be careful that **n** of you be found to have fallen short	3607+5516
	11:39	yet **n** of them received what had been	4024
1Jn	2:19	that **n** *of* them belonged to us.	4024+4246

NONSENSE (3)
Job	21:34	"So how can you console me with your **n?**	2039
Isa	44:25	the learning of the wise and **turns it into n,**	6118
Lk	24:11	because their words seemed to them like **n.**	3333

NOON (16) [AFTERNOON, NOONDAY]
Ge	43:16	they are to eat with me at **n."**	7416
	43:25	gifts for Joseph's arrival at **n,**	7416
1Ki	18:26	on the name of Baal from morning till **n.**	7416
	18:27	At **n** Elijah began to taunt them.	7416
	20:16	They set out at **n** while Ben-Hadad and	7416
2Ki	4:20	the boy sat on her lap until **n,**	7416
Ne	8:3	from daybreak till **n** as he faced the square	2021+3427+4734
Job	5:14	at **n** they grope as in the night.	7416
Ps	55:17	morning and **n** I cry out in distress,	7416
Isa	16:3	Make your shadow like night—at **high n.**	7416
Jer	6:4	Arise, let us attack at **n!**	7416
	20:16	a battle cry at **n.**	7416
Am	8:9	at **n** and darken the earth in broad daylight.	7416
Ac	10:9	About **n** the following day as they	1761+6052
	22:6	"About **n** as I came near Damascus,	3540
	26:13	About **n,** O king, as I was on the road,	2465+3545

NOONDAY (4) [NOON]
2Sa	4:5	of the day while he was taking his **n** rest.	7416
Job	11:17	Life will be brighter than **n,**	7416
Ps	37:6	the justice of your cause like the **n sun.**	7416
Isa	58:10	and your night will become like the **n.**	7416

NOOSE (2)
Job	18:10	A **n** is hidden *for* him on the ground;	2475
Pr	7:22	like a deer stepping into a **n**	4591+6577

NOPHAH (1)
Nu	21:30	We have demolished them as far as **N,**	5871

NOR (328) [NEITHER, NO]
Ge	31:38	**n** have I eaten rams from your flocks.	2256+4202
	49:10	**n** the ruler's staff from between his feet,	2256
Ex	4:10	neither in the past **n** since you have spoken	1685
	10:6	something neither your fathers **n**	2256
	10:14	**n** will there ever be again.	2256+4202
	13:7	**n** shall any yeast be seen anywhere	2256+4202
	13:22	the pillar of cloud by day **n** the pillar of fire	2256
	20:10	neither you, **n** your son or daughter,	2256
	20:10	**n** your manservant or maidservant,	NIH
	20:10	nor your manservant or maidservant, **n**	2256
	20:10	**n** the alien within your gates.	2256
Lev	17:12	**n** may an alien living	2256+4202
	21:12	**n** leave the sanctuary of his God	2256+4202
	22:10	**n** may the guest of a priest	4202
	26:20	**n** will the trees of the land yield their	2256+4202
Nu	14:44	though neither Moses **n** the ark of	2256
	16:15	**n** have I wronged one of them.	2256+4202
	18:20	**n** will you have any share among them	2256+4202
	23:19	that he should lie, **n** a son of man,	2256
	23:25	**n** curse them at all **n** bless them	1685+4202
Dt	2:37	the land along the course of the Jabbok **n**	2256
	5:14	neither you, **n** your son or daughter,	2256
	5:14	**n** your manservant or maidservant,	2256
	5:14	or maidservant, **n** your ox, your donkey	2256
	5:14	**n** the alien within your gates,	2256
	7:14	**n** any of your livestock without young.	2256
	8:3	which neither you **n** your fathers	2256+4202
	13:6	that neither you **n** your fathers have known,	2256
	18:16	the LORD our God **n** see this great fire	2256+4202
	21:7	**n** did our eyes see it done.	2256+4202
	22:5	**n** a man wear women's clothing,	2256+4202
	23:2	No one born of a forbidden marriage **n** any	4202
	24:16	**n** children put to death for their fathers	2256+4202

Dt	26:13	n have I forgotten any of them.	2256+4202
	26:14	n have I removed any of it	2256+4202
	26:14	n have I offered any of it to the dead.	2256+4202
	28:51	n any calves of your herds or lambs	NIH
	28:64	neither you n your fathers have known.	2256
	29: 5	n did the sandals on your feet.	2256+4202
	30:13	N is it beyond the sea,	2256+4202
	31: 6	he will never leave you n forsake you.	2256+4202
	31: 8	he will never leave you n forsake you.	2256+4202
	33: 6	n his men be few."	2256
	34: 7	were not weak n his strength gone.	2256+4202
Jos	1: 5	I will never leave you n forsake you.	2256+4202
	8:22	leaving them neither survivors n fugitives.	2256
Jdg	1:29	N did Ephraim drive out	4202
	1:31	N did Asher drive out those living in Acco	4202
	2:10	LORD n what he had done for Israel.	1685+2256
	6: 4	neither sheep n cattle nor donkeys.	2256
	6: 4	neither sheep nor cattle n donkeys.	2256
	8:23	n will my son rule over you.	2256+4202
	11:34	for her he had neither son n daughter.	196
	13:14	n drink any wine or other fermented	440+2256
	13:14	or other fermented drink n eat	440+2256
	13:23	n shown us all these things or	2256+4202
	14: 6	But he told neither his father n	2256
1Sa	5: 5	to this day neither the priests of Dagon n	2256
	12:21	n can they rescue you,	2256+4202
	16: 9	"N has the LORD chosen this one."	1685+4202
	20:31	neither you n your kingdom will	2256
	26:12	n did anyone wake up.	401+2256
2Sa	1:21	may you have neither dew n rain,	440+2256
	1:21	n fields that yield offerings	2256
	2:19	to the right n to the left as he pursued him.	2256
	2:28	n did they fight anymore.	2256+4202
	14: 7	leaving my husband neither name n	2256
	17:12	Neither he n any of his men will	2256
	21: 4	n do we have the right to put anyone	401+2256
1Ki	3:11	n have asked for the death of your enemies	2256+4202
	3:12	n will there ever be.	2256+4202
	3:26	other said, "Neither I n you shall have him.	1685
	8:57	may he never leave us n forsake us.	440+2256
	11:33	n done what is right in my eyes,	NIH
	11:33	n kept my statutes and laws as David,	2256
	13: 8	n would I eat bread or drink water	2256+4202
	13:16	n can I eat bread or drink water with	2256+4202
	13:28	The lion had neither eaten the body n	2256+4202
	17: 1	there will be neither dew n rain in	2256
2Ki	3:17	You will see neither wind n rain,	2256+4202
	14: 6	n children put to death for their fathers	2256+4202
	17:34	neither worship the LORD n adhere	401+2256
	18:12	neither listened to the commands n	2256+4202
	23:22	n throughout the days of the kings of Israel	2256
	23:25	Neither before n after Josiah was there	2256+4202
2Ch	1:11	n for the death of your enemies,	2256
	6: 5	n have I chosen anyone to be the leader over my people	2256+4202
	25: 4	n children put to death for their fathers	2256+4202
	36:17	spared neither young man n young woman,	2256
Ne	4:23	Neither I n my brothers nor my men nor	2256
	4:23	nor my brothers n my men nor the guards	2256
	4:23	nor my brothers nor my men n the guards	2256
	5:14	neither I n my brothers ate the food allotted	2256
	9:19	n the pillar of fire by night to shine on	2256
	9:21	their clothes did not wear out n	2256+4202
	13:25	in marriage to their sons, n are you	561
Est	2: 7	up because she had neither father n mother.	2256
	5: 9	and observed that he neither rose n	2256+4202
	9:28	n should the memory of them die out	2256+4202
Job	3: 6	the year n be entered in any of the months.	440
	5: 6	n does trouble sprout from the ground.	2256+4202
	15:29	n will his possessions spread over the land.	2256+4202
	28:15	n can its price be weighed in silver.	2256+4202
	28:17	Neither gold n crystal can compare with it,	2256
	28:17	n can it be had for jewels of gold,	2256
	32:21	n will I flatter any man;	2256+4202
	33: 7	n should my hand be heavy upon you.	2256+4202
	41:26	n does the spear or the dart or the javelin.	NIH
Ps	1: 5	n sinners in the assembly of the righteous.	2256
	9:18	n the hope of the afflicted ever perish.	NIH
	16:10	n will you let your Holy One see decay.	4202
	25: 2	n let my enemies triumph over me.	440
	26: 4	n do I consort with hypocrites;	2256+4202
	36:11	n the hand of the wicked drive me	440+2256
	44: 3	n did their arm bring them victory;	2256+4202
	89:33	n will I ever betray my faithfulness.	2256+4202
	91: 5	n the arrow that flies by day,	NIH
	91: 6	n the pestilence that stalks in the darkness,	NIH
	91: 6	n the plague that destroys at midday.	NIH
	103: 9	n will he harbor his anger forever;	2256+4202
	115: 7	n can they utter a sound with their throats.	4202
	121: 4	who watches over Israel will neither slumber n sleep.	2256+4202
	121: 6	n the moon by night.	2256
	129: 7	n the one who gathers fill his arms.	2256
	135:17	n is there breath in their mouths.	401+677
	147:10	n his delight in the legs of a man;	4202
Pr	19: 2	n to be hasty and miss the way.	2256
	25:27	n is it honorable to seek one's own honor.	2256
	30: 3	n have I knowledge of the Holy One.	2256
	30: 8	give me neither poverty n riches,	2256
Ecc	1: 8	n the ear its fill of hearing.	2256+4202
	4: 8	he had neither son n brother.	2256
	9: 7	there is neither working n planning	2256
	9:10	nor planning n knowledge nor wisdom,	2256
	9:10	nor planning nor knowledge n wisdom.	2256
	9:11	n does food come to the wise	1685+2256+4202

Isa	2: 4	n will they train for war anymore.	2256+4202
	5: 6	neither pruned n cultivated,	2256+4202
	9:13	n have they sought the LORD	2256+4202
	9:17	n will he pity the fatherless and	2256+4202
	11: 9	They will neither harm n destroy	2256+4202
	11:13	n Judah hostile toward Ephraim.	2256+4202
	13:18	on infants n will they look with compassion	4202
	22: 2	n did they die in battle.	2256+4202
	23: 4	neither been in labor n given birth;	2256+4202
	23: 4	I have neither reared sons n brought	4202
	28:27	n is a cartwheel rolled over cummin;	2256
	30: 5	who bring neither help n advantage,	2256+4202
	32: 5	fool be called noble n the scoundrel	2256+4202
	33:20	n any of its ropes broken.	2256
	35: 9	n will any ferocious beast get up on it;	1153+2256
	40:16	n its animals enough for burnt offerings	401+2256
	43:10	n will there be one after me.	2256+4202
	43:23	n honored me with your sacrifices.	2256+4202
	43:23	n wearied you with demands for	2256+4202
	48: 8	You have neither heard n understood;	1685+4202
	48:19	cut off n destroyed from before me."	2256+4202
	49:10	They will neither hunger n thirst,	2256+4202
	49:10	n will the desert heat or the sun beat	2256+4202
	51:14	n will they lack bread.	2256+4202
	53: 9	n was any deceit in his mouth.	2256+4202
	54:10	you will not be shaken n my covenant	2256+4202
	57:11	have neither remembered me n pondered	4202
	57:16	n will I always be angry,	2256+4202
	59: 1	n his ear too dull to hear.	2256+4202
	60:18	n ruin or destruction within your borders,	NIH
	60:19	n will the brightness of the moon	2256+4202
	65:17	n will they come to mind.	2256+4202
	65:25	They will neither harm n destroy	2256+4202
	66:24	n will their fire be quenched,	2256+4202
Jer	3:16	n will another one be made.	2256+4202
	7:16	this people n offer any plea or petition	440+2256
	7:31	n did it enter my mind.	2256+4202
	9:16	among nations that neither they n	2256+4202
	10: 5	they can do no harm	401+1685+2256
	11:14	this people n offer any plea or petition	440+2256
	15:10	I have neither lent n borrowed,	2256+4202
	16: 7	n will anyone give them a drink	NIH
	16:13	of this land into a land neither you n	2256
	16:17	n is their sin concealed from my eyes.	2256+4202
	18:18	n will counsel from the wise,	2256
	18:18	n the word from the prophets.	2256
	19: 4	in it to gods that neither they n their fathers	2256
	19: 4	to gods that neither they nor their fathers n	2256
	19: 5	n did it enter my mind.	2256+4202
	22:10	because he will never return n	2256
	23: 4	n will any be missing,"	2256+4202
	29:32	n will he see the good things I will do	2256+4202
	32:35	n did it enter my mind,	2256+4202
	33:10	by neither men n animals,	401+2256+4946
	33:18	n will the priests,	2256+4202
	35: 6	'Neither you n your descendants must ever drink wine.	2256
	35: 8	Neither we n our wives nor our sons	NIH
	35: 8	Neither we nor our wives n our sons	NIH
	36:24	n did they tear their clothes.	2256+4202
	37: 2	Neither he n his attendants nor the people	2256
	37: 2	Neither he nor his attendants n the people	2256
	38:16	I will neither kill you n hand you over	561+2256
	44: 3	that neither they n you	NIH
	44: 3	nor you n your fathers ever knew.	2256
	44:10	n have they followed my law and	2256+4202
	46: 6	swift cannot flee n the strong escape.	440+2256
	49:31	a nation that has neither gates n bars;	2256+4202
	51: 3	n let him put on his armor.	440+2256
	51:26	n any stone for a foundation,	2256
	51:62	so that neither man n animal will live in it;	2256
La	4:12	n did any of the world's people,	2256
Eze	7:12	not the buyer rejoice n the seller grieve,	440+2256
	11:11	n will you be the meat in it;	2256
	13: 9	n will they enter the land of Israel.	2256
	14:11	n will they defile themselves anymore	2256+4202
	14:20	they could save neither son n daughter.	561
	16: 4	n were you washed with water	2256+4202
	16: 4	n were you rubbed with salt or	2256+4202
	16:16	n should they ever occur.	2256+4202
	18:20	n will the father share the guilt of the son.	2256+4202
	20: 8	n did they forsake the idols of Egypt.	2256+4202
	24:14	I will not have pity, n will I relent.	2256+4202
	31: 8	n could the pine trees equal its boughs,	4202
	31: 8	n could the plane trees compare	4202
	34:28	n will wild animals devour them.	2256+4202
	43: 7	neither they n their kings—	2256
	47:12	n will their fruit fail.	2256+4202
Da	2:44	n will it be left to another people.	10221+10379
	3:12	neither serve your gods n worship	10221+10379
	3:27	n was a hair of their heads singed;	10221+10379
	6: 4	and neither corrupt n negligent.	10221
	6:22	N have I ever done any wrong before you,	10059+10221+10379
	11: 4	n will it have the power he exercised,	2256+4202
	11:24	and will achieve what neither his fathers n	2256
	11:37	n will he regard any god,	2256
Hos	4:14	n your daughters-in-law	2256
	9: 4	n will their sacrifices please him.	2256
	11: 9	n will I turn and devastate Ephraim.	4202
Joel	2: 2	never was of old n ever will be in ages	2256+4202
Am	7:14	neither a prophet n a prophet's son,	2256+4202
Ob	1:12	n rejoice over the people of Judah in	440+2256
	1:12	n boast so much in the day of their trouble.	440+2256
	1:13	n look down on them in their calamity in	440

Ob	1:13	n seize their wealth in the day	440+2256
	1:14	n hand over their survivors in the day	440+2256
Mic	4: 3	n will they train for war anymore.	2256+4202
Zep	1: 6	the LORD and neither seek the LORD n	1685
	1:18	Neither their silver n their gold will be able	1685
	3: 7	n all my punishments come upon her.	NIH
	3:13	n will deceit be found in their mouths.	2256+4202
Zec	4: 6	'Not by might n by power,	2256+4202
Mt	10:24	n a servant above his master.	4028
	11:18	For John came neither eating n drinking,	3612
	22:30	the resurrection people will neither marry n	4046
	23:10	N are you to be called 'teacher,'	3593
	23:13	n will you let those enter who are trying to.	4028
	24:36	not even the angels in heaven, n the Son,	4028
Mk	12:25	they will neither marry n be given	4046
	13:32	not even the angels in heaven, n the Son,	4028
Lk	6:43	n does a bad tree bear good fruit.	4028
	7:33	the Baptist came neither eating bread n	3612
	14:35	for the soil n for the manure pile;	4028
	16:26	n can anyone cross over from there to us.'	3593
	17:21	n will people say,	4028
	18: 2	judge who neither feared God n cared	2779+3590
	20:35	from the dead will neither marry n be given	4046
Jn	1:13	n of human decision or a husband's will,	4028
	1:25	n Elijah, nor the Prophet?"	4028
	1:25	nor Elijah, n the Prophet?"	4028
	4:21	the Father neither on this mountain n	4046
	5:37	You have never heard his voice n	4046
	5:38	n does his word dwell in you,	2779+4024
	6:24	that neither Jesus n his disciples were there,	4028
	9: 3	"Neither this man n his parents sinned,"	4046
	12:40	n understand with their hearts, nor turn—	2779
	12:40	nor understand with their hearts, n turn—	2779
	13:16	n is a messenger greater than	4028
	14:17	because it neither sees him n knows him.	4028
Ac	2:27	n will you let your Holy One see decay.	4028
	2:31	n did his body see decay.	4046
	15:10	that neither we n our fathers have been able	4046
	19:37	though they have neither robbed temples n	4046
	23: 8	and that there are neither angels n spirits,	3612
	24:18	n was I involved in any disturbance.	4028
	27:20	When neither sun n stars appeared	3612
Ro	1:21	they neither glorified him as God n	2445
	2:28	n is circumcision merely outward	4028
	8: 7	not submit to God's law, n can it do so.	4028
	8:38	I am convinced that neither death n life,	4046
	8:38	neither angels n demons,	4046
	8:38	neither the present n the future,	4046
	8:38	the present nor the future, n any powers,	4046
	8:39	neither height n depth,	4046
	8:39	n anything else in all creation,	4046
	9: 7	N because they are his descendants are they all Abraham's children.	4028
1Co	3: 7	So neither he who plants n he who waters	4046
	6: 9	Neither the sexually immoral n idolaters	4046
	6: 9	the sexually immoral nor idolaters n	4046
	6: 9	nor adulterers n male prostitutes	4046
	6: 9	nor adulterers nor male prostitutes n	4046
	6:10	n thieves nor the greedy nor drunkards	4046
	6:10	nor thieves n the greedy nor drunkards	4046
	6:10	nor the greedy n drunkards nor slanderers	4024
	6:10	nor the greedy nor drunkards n slanderers	4024
	6:10	nor drunkards nor slanderers n swindlers	4024
	11:11	n is man independent of woman.	4046
	11:16	n do the churches of God.	4028
	15:50	n does the perishable inherit	4028
2Co	4: 2	n do we distort the word of God.	3593
Gal	1: 1	sent not from men n by man,	4028
	1:12	n was I taught it;	4046
	1:17	n did I go up to Jerusalem	4028
	3:28	There is neither Jew n Greek,	4028
	3:28	slave n free, male nor female,	4028
	3:28	slave nor free, male n female,	2779
	5: 6	For in Christ Jesus neither circumcision n	4046
	6:15	Neither circumcision n	4046
Eph	5: 4	N should there be obscenity,	2779
1Th	2: 3	n are we trying to trick you.	4028
	2: 5	n did we put on a mask to cover up greed—	4046
2Th	3: 8	n did we eat anyone's food without paying	4028
1Ti	1: 4	n to devote themselves to myths	3593
	6:17	to be arrogant n to put their hope in wealth,	3593
Heb	9:25	N did he enter heaven to offer himself	4028
	10: 8	n were you pleased with them"	4028
Jas	1:13	n does he tempt anyone;	1254+4029
1Jn	3:10	n is anyone who does not love his brother.	2779
Rev	3:15	that you are neither cold n hot.	4046
	3:16	you are lukewarm—neither hot n cold—	4046
	7:16	n any scorching heat.	4028
	9:21	N did they repent of their murders,	2779+4024
	21:27	n will anyone who does what is shameful	2779+4024

NORMALLY (1) [ABNORMALLY]

2Ki	11: 7	that n go off Sabbath duty are all to guard	NIH

NORTH (150) [NORTHERN, NORTHWARD]

Ge	13:14	where you are and look n and south,	2025+7600
	14:15	as far as Hobah, n of Damascus.	4946+8520
	28:14	to the n and to the south.	7600
Ex	26:20	the n side of the tabernacle,	7600
	26:35	the table outside the curtain on the n side of	7600
	27:11	The n side shall also be	7600
	36:25	the n side of the tabernacle,	7600
	38:11	The n side was also a hundred cubits long	7600
	40:22	the Tent of Meeting on the n side of	2025+7600

Lev	1:11	to slaughter it at the **n** side of the altar	2025+7600
Nu	2:25	On the **n** will be the divisions of the camp	7600
	3:35	camp on the **n** side of the tabernacle,	2025+7600
	34: 9	This will be your boundary on the **n**.	7600
	35: 5	on the west and three thousand on the **n**,	7600
Dt	2: 3	hill country long enough; now turn **n**.	2025+7600
	3:12	and the Gadites the territory **n** of Aroer by	NIH
	3:27	the top of Pisgah and look west and **n**	2025+7600
Jos	8:11	They set up camp **n** of Ai,	7600
	8:13	all those in the camp to the **n** of the city and	7600
	13: 3	of Egypt to the territory of Ekron on the **n**,	7600
	15: 6	up to Beth Hoglah and continued **n**	4946+7600
	15: 7	of Achor and turned **n** to Gilgal,	2025+7600
	16: 6	the **n** it curved eastward to Taanath Shiloh,	7600
	17:10	on the **n** to Manasseh.	7600
	17:10	and bordered Asher on the **n** and Issachar	7600
	18: 5	the house of Joseph in its territory on the **n**.	7600
	18:12	On the **n** side their boundary began at	2025+7600
	18:16	**n** of the Valley of Rephaim.	7600
	18:17	It then curved **n**, went to En Shemesh,	4946+7600
	19:14	the **n** to Hannathon and ended at the Valley	7600
	19:27	and went to Beth Emek and Neiel,	2025+7600
	24:30	of Ephraim, **n** of Mount Gaash.	4946+7600
Jdg	2: 9	of Ephraim, **n** of Mount Gaash.	4946+7600
	7: 1	Midian was **n** of them in the valley	4946+7600
	21:19	to the **n** of Bethel,	4946+7600
1Sa	14: 5	One cliff stood to the **n** toward Micmash,	7600
1Ki	7:21	and the one to the **n** Boaz.	8522
	7:25	stood on twelve bulls, three facing **n**,	2025+7600
	7:39	of the temple and five on the **n**.	4946+8520
2Ki	11:11	the temple, from the south side to the **n** side	8522
	16:14	put it on the **n** side of the new altar.	2025+7600
1Ch	9:24	east, west, **n** and south.	2025+7600
	26:14	and the lot for the N Gate fell to him.	7600
	26:17	four a day on the **n**,	2025+7600
2Ch	3:17	one to the south and one to the **n**.	8520
	3:17	and the *one to the* **n** Boaz.	8522
	4: 4	stood on twelve bulls, three facing **n**,	2025+7600
	4: 6	on the south side and five on the **n**.	8520
	4: 7	five on the south side and five on the **n**.	8520
	4: 8	five on the south side and five on the **n**.	8520
	23:10	the temple, from the south side to the **n** side	8522
Job	23: 9	he is at work in the **n**, I do not see him;	8520
	37:22	Out of the **n** he comes in golden splendor;	6828
Ps	89:12	You created the **n** and the south;	7600
	107: 3	from east and west, from **n** and south.	7600
Pr	25:23	As a **n** wind brings rain,	7600
Ecc	1: 6	wind blows to the south and turns to the **n**;	7600
	11: 3	Whether a tree falls to the south or to the **n**,	7600
SS	4:16	Awake, **n** wind, and come, south wind!	7600
Isa	14:31	A cloud of smoke comes from the **n**,	7600
	41:25	"I have stirred up one from the **n**,	7600
	43: 6	I will say to the **n**, 'Give them up!'	7600
	49:12	some from the **n**, some from the west,	7600
Jer	1:13	tilting away from the **n**," I answered.	2025+7600
	1:14	"From the **n** disaster will be poured out	7600
	3:12	Go, proclaim this message toward the **n**:	7600
	4: 6	For I am bringing disaster from the **n**,	7600
	6: 1	For disaster looms out of the **n**,	7600
	6:22	an army is coming from the land of the **n**;	7600
	10:22	a great commotion from the land of the **n**!	7600
	13:20	and see those who are coming from the **n**.	7600
	15:12	"Can a man break iron—iron from the **n**—	7600
	16:15	the land of the **n** and out of all the countries	7600
	23: 8	the land of the **n** and out of all the	2025+7600
	25: 9	the **n** and my servant Nebuchadnezzar king	7600
	25:26	of the **n**, near and far, one after the other—	7600
	31: 8	of the **n** and gather them from the ends of	7600
	46: 6	the **n** by the River Euphrates they stumble	7600
	46:10	in the land of the **n** by the River Euphrates.	7600
	46:20	a gadfly is coming against her from the **n**.	7600
	46:24	handed over to the people of the **n**."	7600
	47: 2	"See how the waters are rising in the **n**;	7600
	50: 3	the **n** will attack her and lay waste her land.	7600
	50: 9	of great nations from the land of the **n**.	7600
	50: 9	and from **the** **n** she will be captured.	9004S
	50:41	An army is coming from the **n**;	7600
	51:48	for out of the **n** destroyers will attack her,"	7600
Eze	1: 4	and I saw a windstorm coming out of the **n**	7600
	8: 3	to the **n** gate of the inner court,	2025+7600
	8: 5	"Son of man, look toward the **n**."	2025+7600
	8: 5	and in the entrance **n** of the gate of	4946+7600
	8:14	entrance to the **n** gate of the house of	2025+7600
	9: 2	of the upper gate, which faces **n**,	2025+7600
	16:46	to the **n** *of* you with her daughters;	8520
	20:47	from south to **n** will be scorched by it.	7600
	21: 4	against everyone from south to **n**.	7600
	26: 7	From the **n** I am going to bring	7600
	32:30	of the **n** and all the Sidonians are there;	7600
	38: 6	from the far **n** with all its troops—	7600
	38:15	You will come from your place in the far **n**,	7600
	39: 2	from the far **n** and send you against	7600
	40:19	on the east side as well as on the **n**.	7600
	40:20	the length and width of the gate facing **n**,	7600
	40:23	a gate to the inner court facing the **n** gate,	7600
	40:35	Then he brought me to the **n** gate	7600
	40:40	to the **n** gateway were two tables,	2025+7600
	40:44	at the side of the **n** gate and facing south,	7600
	40:44	at the side of the south gate and facing **n**.	7600
	40:46	and the room facing **n** is for	7600
	41:11	one on the **n** and another on the south;	7600
	42: 1	and opposite the outer wall on the **n** *side*.	7600
	42: 2	The building whose door faced **n** was	7600
	42: 4	Their doors were on the **n**.	7600
	42:11	These were like the rooms on the **n**;	7600
	42:11	Similar to the doorways on the **n**	NIH
	42:13	"The **n** and south rooms facing	7600

Eze	42:17	He measured the **n** side;	7600
	44: 4	the man brought me by way of the **n** gate to	7600
	46: 9	whoever enters by the **n** gate to worship is	7600
	46: 9	the south gate is to go out the **n** gate.	2025+7600
	46:19	the gate to the sacred rooms facing **n**,	2025+7600
	47: 2	**n** gate and led me around the outside	2025+7600
	47:15	**n** side it will run from the Great Sea	2025+7600
	47:17	with the border of Hamath to the **n**.	7600
	47:17	This will be the **n** boundary.	7600
	48:10	It will be 25,000 cubits long on the **n** *side*,	7600
	48:16	the **n** side 4,500 cubits, the south side 4,500	7600
	48:17	for the city will be 250 cubits on the **n**,	7600
	48:30	Beginning on the **n** side, which is 4,500	7600
	48:31	on the **n** *side* will be the gate of Reuben,	7600
Da	8: 4	toward the west and the **n** and the south.	7600
	11: 6	to the king of the N to make an alliance,	7600
	11: 7	of the king of the N and enter his fortress;	7600
	11: 8	he will leave the king of the N alone.	7600
	11: 9	the N will invade the realm of the king of	NIH
	11:11	a rage and fight against the king of the N,	7600
	11:13	the king of the N will muster another army,	7600
	11:15	Then the king of the N will come and build	7600
	11:28	of the N will return to his own country	NIH
	11:40	the king of the N will storm out against him	7600
	11:44	from the east and the **n** will alarm him,	7600
Am	8:12	from sea to sea and wander from **n** to east,	7600
Zep	2:13	he will stretch out his hand against the **n**	7600
Zec	2: 6	Flee from the land of the **n**,"	7600
	6: 6	is going toward the **n** country,	7600
	6: 8	the **n** country have given my Spirit rest in	7600
	6: 8	in the land of the **n**."	7600
Lk	13:29	People will come from east and west and **n**	1080
Rev	21:13	three gates on the east, three on the **n**,	1080

NORTHEASTER (1) [EAST]

| Ac | 27:14 | called the "**n**," swept down from the island. | 2350 |

NORTHERN (18) [NORTH]

Nu	34: 7	" 'For your **n** boundary,	7600
Jos	11: 3	**n** kings who were in the mountains,	4946+7600
	15: 5	The **n** boundary started from the bay	2025+7600
	15: 8	at the **n** end of the Valley of Rephaim.	2025+7600
	15:10	the **n** slope of Mount Jearim	2025+4946+7600
	15:11	It went to the **n** slope of Ekron,	2025+7600
	17: 9	boundary of Manasseh was the **n** *side*	4946+7600
	18:12	the **n** slope of Jericho and headed west	4946+7600
	18:18	to the **n** slope of Beth Arabah and	2025+7600
	18:19	to the **n** slope of Beth Hoglah and	2025+7600
	18:19	and came out at the **n** bay	2025+7600
Job	26: 7	spreads out the **n** [skies] over empty space;	7600
Jer	1:15	the peoples of the **n** kingdoms,"	2025+7600
	3:18	a land to the land I gave your forefathers	7600
Eze	47:17	along the **n** border of Damascus.	7600
	48: 1	**n** frontier, Dan will have one portion;	2025+7600
	48: 1	on the **n** border of Damascus next	2025+7600
Joel	2:20	"I will drive the **n** *army* far from you,	7603

NORTHWARD (1) [NORTH]

| Eze | 42: 1 | Then the man led me **n** into the outer court | 2006+2021+7600 |

NORTHWEST (1) [WEST]

| Ac | 27:12 | facing both southwest and **n**. | 6008 |

NOSE (13) [NOSES]

Ge	24:22	the man took out a gold **n** ring weighing	5690
	24:30	As soon as he had seen the **n** ring,	5690
	24:47	in her **n** and the bracelets on her arms,	678
2Ki	19:28	I will put my hook in your **n** and my bit	678
2Ch	33:11	put a hook in his **n**,	NIH
Job	40:24	or trap him and pierce his **n**?	678
	41: 2	a cord through his **n** or pierce his jaw with	678
Pr	30:33	and as twisting the **n** produces blood,	639
SS	7: 4	Your **n** is like the tower	639
Isa	3:21	the signet rings and rings,	639
	37:29	I will put my hook in your **n** and my bit	639
Eze	8:17	Look at them putting the branch to their **n**!	639
	16:12	and I put a ring on your **n**,	639

NOSES (2) [NOSE]

| Ps | 115: 6 | but cannot hear, **n**, but they cannot smell; | 678 |
| Eze | 23:25 | They will cut off your **n** and your ears, | 639 |

NOSTRILS (16)

Ge	2: 7	and breathed into his **n** the breath of life,	678
	7:22	that had the breath of life in its **n** died.	678
Ex	15: 8	By the blast of your **n** the waters piled up.	678
Nu	11:20	comes out of your **n** and you loathe it—	678
2Sa	10: 6	they had become a stench in David's,	NIH
	16:21	made yourself a stench in your father's **n**,	NIH
	22: 9	Smoke rose from his **n**;	678
	22:16	at the blast of breath from his **n**.	678
1Ch	19: 6	they had become a stench in David's **n**,	NIH
Job	27: 3	the breath of God in my **n**,	639
	41:20	from his **n** as from a boiling pot over a fire	5705
Ps	18: 8	Smoke rose from his **n**;	639
	18:15	at the blast of breath from your **n**.	639
Isa	2:22	who has but a breath in his **n**.	639
	65: 5	Such people are smoke in my **n**,	639
Am	4:10	I filled your **n** with the stench	639

NOT (5888) [AREN'T, CAN'T, COULDN'T, DIDN'T, DOESN'T, DON'T, HASN'T, HAVEN'T, ISN'T, NO, SHOULDN'T, WASN'T, WEREN'T, WON'T, WOULDN'T] See Index of Articles Etc.

NOTABLE (1) [NOTE]

| Am | 6: 1 | *you* **n** men of the foremost nation, | 5918 |

NOTE (13) [ANNOTATIONS, NOTABLE, NOTES]

Ru	3: 4	**n** the place where he is lying.	3359
2Sa	3:36	All the people **took n** and were pleased;	5795
Job	11:11	and when he sees evil, *does he* not **take n**?	1067
	34:25	Because *he* **takes n** of their deeds,	5795
Ps	106:44	But *he* **took n** of their distress	8011
Pr	21:12	The Righteous One **takes n** of the house of	8505
	23: 1	**n** well what is before you,	1067+1067
Jer	31:21	**Take n** of the highway,	4213+8883
Eze	20:37	**take n** *of* you **as you pass**	6296
Ac	4:13	and *they* **took n** that these men had been	2105
Php	3:17	and **take n** of those who live according to	5023
2Th	3:14	**take special n** of him.	4957
Jas	1:19	My dear brothers, **take n** of this:	3857

NOTES (1) [NOTE]

| 1Co | 14: 7 | unless there is a distinction *in the* **n**? | 5782 |

NOTHING (342) [NO, THING]

Ge	11: 6	then **n** they plan to do will be impossible for them.	3972+4202
	14:23	I will accept **n** belonging to you,	561+3972+4946
	14:24	I will accept **n** but what my men have eaten	1187
	18:27	though I am **n** but dust and ashes,	NIH
	24:50	we can say **n** to you one way or the other.	4202
	29:15	should you work for me for **n**?	2855
	31:33	but he found **n**.	4202
	31:34	through everything in the tent but found **n**.	4202
	39: 9	My master has withheld **n**	4202+4399
	40:15	and even here I have done **n**	4202+4399
	47:18	there is **n** left for our lord except our bodies	4202
Ex	10:15	N green remained on tree or plant in	3972+4202
	12:20	Eat **n** made with yeast.	3972+4202
	13: 3	Eat **n** containing yeast.	4202
	13: 7	**n** with yeast in it is to be seen among you,	4202
	22: 3	but if he has **n**, he must be sold to pay	401
	23: 7	**Have n to do** with a false charge and do	8178
Lev	14:36	**n** in the house will be pronounced unclean.	3972+4202
	27:28	But **n** that a man owns and devotes to	3972+4202
Nu	20:19	to pass through on foot—**n** else."	401
	23:11	but *you have* **done n but bless** them!"	1385+1385
	30: 4	about her vow or pledge but **says n** to her,	3087
	30: 7	her husband hears about it but **says n** to her,	3087
	30:11	and her husband hears about it but **says n**	3087
	30:14	if her husband **says n** to her *about* it	3087+3087
	30:14	He confirms them by **saying n** to her	3087
Dt	5:22	and he added **n** *more*.	4202
	8: 9	not be scarce and you will lack **n**;	3972+4202
	15: 9	toward your needy brother and give him **n**.	4202
	22:26	Do to the girl;	1821+4202
	28:33	and you will have **n** but cruel oppression	8370
	29:23	**n** planted, nothing sprouting,	4202
	29:23	nothing planted, **n** sprouting,	4202
Jos	11:15	he left **n** undone of all that	1821+4202
Jdg	7:14	"This can be **n** other than the sword	401+1194
	18: 7	land lacked **n**, they were prosperous.	401+1821
	18:10	a land that lacks **n whatever**."	401+1821+3972
1Sa	3:18	hiding **n** from him.	4202
	4: 7	N like this has happened before.	4202
	14: 6	N can hinder the Lord from saving,	401
	20:26	Saul said **n** that day, for he thought,	4202+4399
	20:39	(The boy knew **n** of all this;	4202
	22:15	for your servant knows **n** at all	4202
	25: 7	the whole time they were at Carmel **n**	4202+4399
	25:15	in the fields near them **n** was missing.	4202+4399
	25:21	the desert so that **n** of his was missing.	4202+4399
	25:36	So she told him **n** until daybreak.	1524+1821+2256+4202+7785
	28:20	he had eaten **n** all that day and night.	4202+4312
	29: 7	do **n** to displease the Philistine rulers."	4202
	30:19	N was missing: young or old,	4202
2Sa	12: 3	poor man had **n** except one little ewe lamb he had bought.	401+3972
	15:11	knowing **n** about the matter.	3972+4202
	18:13	and **n** is hidden from the king—	1821+3972+4202
	19: 6	commanders and their men mean **n** to you.	401
	19:10	So why *do you* **say n** *about* bringing	3087
	19:28	my grandfather's descendants deserved **n**	4202
	24:24	burnt offerings that **cost** me **n**."	2855
1Ki	4:27	They saw to it that **n** was lacking.	1821+4202
	6: 6	the temple so that **n** would be inserted into	1194
	8: 9	There was **n** in the ark except	401
	10: 3	**n** was too hard for the king to explain	1821+4202
	10:20	N like it had ever been made	4202
	10:21	N was made of silver,	401
	11:22	"N," Hadad replied, "but do let me go!"	4202
	18:21	But the people said **n**.	1821+4202
	18:43	"There is **n** there," he said.	401+4399
	22: 3	and yet we *are* **doing n** to retake it from	3120
	22:16	to tell me **n** but the truth in the name of	4202
	22:27	Put this fellow in prison and give him **n but**	4316

2Ki	4: 2	"Your servant has **n** there at all," she said,	401
	4:41	And there was **n** harmful in the pot.	1821+4202
	9:35	they found **n** except her skull,	4202
	13: 7	**N** had been left of the army	4202
	18:36	remained silent and said **n** in reply,	1821+4202
	20:13	There was **n** in his palace or	1821+4202
	20:15	"There is **n** among my treasures that	1821+4202
	20:17	**N** will be left, says the LORD.	1821+4202
1Ch	21:24	sacrifice a burnt offering that **costs** me **n**."	2855
2Ch	5:10	**There was n** in the ark except	401
	9: 2	**n** was too hard for him to explain	1821+4202
	9:11	**N** like them had ever been seen in Judah.)	4202
	9:19	**N** like it had ever been made	4202
	9:20	**N** was made of silver,	401
	18:15	to tell me **n** but the truth in the name of	4202
	18:26	Put this fellow in prison and give him **n but**	4316
	30:26	of David king of Israel there had been **n**	4202
Ezr	4:16	be left with **n** in Trans-Euphrates.	10269+10379
Ne	2: 2	This can be **n** except sadness of heart."	401
	2:16	as yet I had said **n** to the Jews or the priests	4202
	5: 8	because they could find **n** to say.	4202
	6: 8	"**N** like what you are saying is happening;	4202
	8:10	send some to those who have **n** prepared.	401
	9:21	they lacked **n**, their clothes did	4202
Est	2:15	she asked for **n** other than what Hegai,	1821+4202
	6: 3	"**N** has been done for him,"	1821+4202
Job	1: 9	"Does Job fear God **for n**?" Satan replied.	2855
	5:24	of your property and find **n** missing.	4202
	8: 9	we were born only yesterday and know **n**,	4202
	15:18	hiding **n** received from their fathers	4202
	15:31	for he will get **n** in return.	8736
	19:20	I am **n but skin** and bones;	1414+2256+6425
	20:21	**N** is left for him to devour;	401
	21:34	**N** is left of your answers but falsehood!"	NIH
	24: 7	they have **n** to cover themselves in the cold.	401
	24:16	they want **n** to do with the light.	4202
	24:25	and reduce my words to **n**?"	440
	26: 7	he suspends the earth over **n**.	1172+4537
	32: 5	he saw that the three men had **n more** to say,	401
	33:21	His flesh wastes away to **n**,	4946+8024
	34: 9	a man **n** when he tries to please God.'	4202
	37: 4	When his voice resounds, he holds **n** back.	4202
	39:22	He laughs at fear, afraid of **n**;	4202
	41:33	**N** on earth is his equal—	401
Ps	10: 6	He says to himself, "**N** will shake me;	1153
	17: 3	though you test me, you will find **n**;	1153
	19: 6	**n** is hidden from its heat.	401
	34: 9	for those who fear him lack **n**.	401
	35:11	they question me on things I know **n** about.	4202
	39: 5	the span of my years is **as n** before you.	401
	44:12	gaining **n** from their sale.	4202
	49:17	for he will take **n** with him when he dies,	2021+3972+4202
	53: 5	where there was **n** to dread.	4202
	62: 9	if weighed on a balance, they are **n**;	NIH
	73:25	And earth has **n** I desire besides you.	4202
	82: 5	"They know **n**, they understand nothing.	4202
	82: 5	"They know nothing, they understand **n**.	4202
	101: 4	I will have **n** to do with evil.	4202
	112:10	the longings of the wicked **will come to n**.	6
	119: 3	They do **n** wrong; they walk in his ways.	4202
	119:165	and **n** can make them stumble.	401
	139:22	I have **n but** hatred for them;	9417
	146: 4	on that very day their plans **come to n**.	6
Pr	3:15	**n** you desire can compare with her.	3972+4202
	8:11	**n** you desire can compare with her.	3972+4202
	10:28	but the hopes of the wicked **come to n**.	6
	11: 7	all he expected from his power **comes to n**.	6
	13: 4	The sluggard craves and **gets n**,	401
	13: 7	One man pretends to be rich, yet **has n**;	401+3972
	20: 4	so at harvest time he looks but finds **n**.	401
	24: 7	in the assembly at the gate he has **n** to say.	4202
	24:12	If you say, "But we knew **n** about this,"	4202
	28:27	He who gives to the poor will lack **n**,	401
	30:20	and says, 'I've done **n** wrong.'	4202
	30:30	who retreats before **n**;	3972+4202
	31:11	in her and lacks **n** of value.	4202
Ecc	1: 9	**there is n** new under the sun.	401+3972
	2:10	I denied myself **n** my eyes desired;	3972+4202
	2:11	**n** was gained under the sun.	401
	2:24	A man can do **n** better than to eat and drink	401
	3:12	I know that **there is n** better for men than to	401
	3:14	**n** can be added to it and nothing taken	401
	3:14	nothing can be added to it and **n** taken	401
	3:22	So I saw that **there is n** better for a man	401
	5:14	he has a son **there is n** left for him.	401+4399
	5:15	He takes **n** from his labor that he can carry	
		in his hand.	4202+4399
	6: 2	so that he lacks **n** his heart desires,	401+3972
	8:15	because **n** is better for a man under	401
	9: 5	but the dead know **n**;	401+4399
Isa	10: 4	**N** will remain but to cringe among	1194
	15: 6	the vegetation is gone and **n** green is left.	401
	17:11	yet the harvest **will be as n** in the day	5610
	19: 3	**bring** their plans **to n**;	1182
	19: 3	The officials of Zoan are **n but** fools;	421
	19:15	There is **n** Egypt can do—	4202+5126
	29:11	For you this whole vision is **n but**	3869
	29:16	the pot say of the potter, "He knows **n**"?	4202
	34:12	Her nobles will have **n** there to be called	401
	36:21	remained silent and said **n** in reply,	1821+4202
	39: 2	There was **n** in his palace or	1821+4202
	39: 4	"There is **n** among my treasures that	1821+4202
	39: 6	**N** will be left, says the LORD.	1821+4202
	40:17	Before him all the nations are as **n**;	401
	40:17	by him as worthless and less than **n**.	700
	40:23	and reduces the rulers of this world to **n**.	9332

Isa	41:11	those who oppose you will be as **n**	401
	41:12	against you will be as **n at all**.	401+700+2256
	41:24	But you are less than **n**	401
	41:29	Their deeds **amount to n**;	700
	42:20	your ears are open, but you hear **n**."	4202
	44: 9	All who make idols are **n**,	9332
	44:10	which can profit him **n**?	1194
	44:11	craftsmen are **n** but men.	4946
	44:18	They know **n**, they understand nothing;	4202
	44:18	They know nothing, they understand **n**;	4202
	49: 4	I have spent my strength in vain and for **n**.	9332
	52: 3	"You were sold **for n**,	2855
	52: 5	my people have been taken away **for n**,	2855
	53: 2	**n** in his appearance	4202
	54:14	you will have **n** to fear.	4202
Jer	5:12	they said, "He will do **n**!	4202
	10:24	not in your anger, lest *you* **reduce** me to **n**.	5070
	12:13	they will wear themselves out but gain **n**.	4202
	16:19	"Our fathers possessed **n** but false gods,	421
	22:13	making his countrymen work **for n**,	2855
	30:14	they care **n** for you.	4202
	32:17	**N** is too hard for you.	1821+3972+4202
	32:30	and Judah have done **n but** evil in my sight	421
	32:30	of Israel have done **n but** provoke me	421
	38: 5	"The king can do **n** to oppose you."	401+1821
	39:10	of the poor people, who owned **n**;	401+4399
	42: 4	the LORD says and will keep **n** back	1821+4202
	44:18	*have* **had n** and have been perishing	2893+3972
	48:30	"and her boasts accomplish **n**,	4027+4202
	48:38	the public squares there is **n but** mourning,	3972
	50: 2	keep **n** back, but say,	440
	51:58	exhaust themselves **for n**,	928+1896+8198
La	1:12	"Is it **n** to you, all you who pass by?	4202
Eze	7:11	no wealth, **n** of value.	4202
	12:22	days go by and every vision **comes to n**'?	6
	13: 3	and have seen **n**!	1194
	14:23	know that I have done **n** in it without cause,	889+3972+4202
	33:32	to them you are **n more than** one who	
		sings love songs	3869
Da	1:12	Give us **n but** vegetables to eat and water	4946
	4:35	the peoples of the earth are regarded as **n**.	10379
	9:12	the whole heaven **n** has ever been done	4202
	9:26	be cut off and will have **n**.	401
Joel	2: 3	a desert waste—**n** escapes them.	4202
Am	3: 4	in his den when he has caught **n**?	1194
	3: 5	up from the earth when there is **n** to catch?	4202
	3: 7	Surely the Sovereign LORD does **n**	1821+4202
	5: 5	and Bethel will be reduced to **n**."	224
Mic	6:14	You will store up but save **n**,	4202
Na	2:11	and the cubs, with **n** to fear?	401
	3:19	**N** can heal your wound; your injury is fatal.	401
Hab	2:13	exhaust themselves **for n**?	928+1896+8198
Zep	1:12	'The LORD will do **n**, either good or bad.'	4202
	3: 3	who leave **n** for the morning.	4202
Hag	2: 3	Does it not seem to you like **n**?	401
Mal	2: 6	in his mouth and **n** false was found	4202
Mt	9:33	"**N** like this has **ever** been seen	4030
	10:26	There is **n** concealed that will not	4029
	15:32	with me three days and have **n** to eat.	4024+5515
	17:20	**N** will be impossible for you."	4029
	20: 3	in the marketplace **doing n**.	734
	20: 6	standing here all day long **doing n?**'	734
	21:19	up to it but found **n** on it except leaves.	4029
	23:16	anyone swears by the temple, it means **n**;	4029
	23:18	'If anyone swears by the altar, it means **n**;	4029
	24:39	and they knew **n** about what would happen	4024
	25:42	For I was hungry and you gave me **n** to eat,	4024
	25:42	I was thirsty and you gave me **n** to drink,	4024
Mk	6: 8	"Take **n** for the journey except a staff—	3594
	7:15	**N** outside a man can make him 'unclean'	4029
	7:18	Don't you see that **n** that enters a man	4024+4246
	8: 1	Since they had **n** to eat,	3590+5515
	8: 2	with me three days and have **n** to eat.	4024+5515
	11:13	When he reached it, he found **n** but leaves.	4029
	14:51	**wearing n** but a linen garment,	1218+2093+4314
	16: 8	They said to anyone,	4029
Lk	1:37	For **n** is impossible with God."	4024+4246+4839
	4: 2	He ate **n** during those days,	4029
	8:17	there is **n** hidden that will not be disclosed,	4024
	8:17	**and n** concealed that will not be known	4028
	9: 3	He told them: "Take **n** for the journey—	3594
	10:19	**n** will harm you.	3590+4024+4029
	11: 6	and I have **n** to set before him.'	4024
	12: 2	There is **n** concealed that will not be	4029
	14: 6	And they had **n** to say.	4024
	19:26	but as for the one who has **n**,	3590
	22:35	"**N**," they answered.	4029
	23:15	he has done **n** to deserve death.	4029
	23:41	But this man has done **n** wrong."	4029
Jn	1: 3	without him **n** was made	1651+4028
	1:47	in whom there is **n** false."	4024
	4:11	"you have **n** to draw with and the well	4046
	4:32	"I have food to eat that you know **n** about."	4024
	5:19	the Son can do **n** by himself;	4024+4029
	5:30	By myself I can do **n**;	4024+4029
	6:12	Let **n** be wasted."	3590+5516
	6:63	The Spirit gives life; the flesh counts for **n**.	4024+4029
	7:18	there is **n** false about him.	94+4024
	7:49	But this mob that knows **n** of the law—	3590
	8:28	that I do **n** on my own but speak just what	4029
	8:54	If I glorify myself, my glory means **n**.	4029
	9:33	If this man were not from God, he could	
		do **n**."	4024+4029
	10:13	because he is a hired hand and cares for **n**	4024
	11:49	spoke up, "You know **n at all**!	4024+4029

Jn	15: 5	apart from me you can do **n**.	4024+4029
	18:20	I said **n** in secret.	4029
	21: 3	but that night they caught **n**.	4029
Ac	4:14	there was **n** they could say.	4029
	5:36	and it all came to **n**.	4029
	7:18	another king, who knew **n** about Joseph,	4024
	8:24	so that **n** you have said may happen to me."	3594
	9: 8	when he opened his eyes he could see **n**.	4029
	11: 8	**N** impure or unclean has **ever**	4030
	17:21	who lived there spent their time doing **n**	4029
	20:24	I consider my life worth **n** to me,	3364+4029
	23: 9	"We find **n** wrong with this man,"	4029
	25: 8	"I have done **n** wrong against the law	4046+5516
	25:25	I found he had done **n** deserving of death,	3594
	25:26	But I have **n** definite to write	4024+5516
	26:22	I am saying **n** beyond what the prophets	4029
	28: 6	a long time and seeing **n** unusual happen	3594
	28:17	although I have done **n** against our people	4029
Ro	3: 3	I know that **n** good lives in me, that is,	4024
	13: 4	for he does not bear the sword **for n**.	1632
1Co	2: 2	For I resolved to know **n** while I was	4024+5516
	2: 6	rulers of this age, who *are* **coming to n**.	2934
	4: 5	judge **n** before the appointed time;	3590+5516
	7:19	Circumcision is **n** and uncircumcision is	4029
	7:19	and uncircumcision is **n**.	4029
	8: 4	that an idol is **n** at all in the world and	4029
	11:22	of God and humiliate those who have **n**?	3590
	13: 2	but have not love, I am **n**.	4029
	13: 3	but have not love, I gain **n**.	4029
	15:58	Let **n** move you.	293
	16:10	that he has **n to fear** while he is with you,	925
2Co	6:10	having **n**, and yet possessing everything.	3594
	10:10	and his speaking **amounts to n**."	2024
	12: 1	Although there is **n** to be gained,	4024
	12:11	even though I am **n**.	4029
Gal	2: 6	those men added **n** to my message.	4029
	2:21	gained through the law, Christ died **for n**!"	1562
	3: 4	Have you suffered so much **for n**—	1632
	3: 4	if it really was **for n**?	1632
	6: 3	anyone thinks he is something when he is **n**,	3594
Eph	5:11	Have **n** to do with the fruitless deeds	3590
Php	2: 3	Do **n** out of selfish ambition	3594
	2: 7	but **made** himself **n**, taking the very nature	3033
	2:16	of Christ that I did not run or labor for **n**.	3031
1Ti	3:10	and then if there is **n against them**,	441
	4: 4	and **n** is to be rejected if it is received	4029
	4: 7	*Have* **n to do with** godless myths	4148
	5:21	and to do **n** out of favoritism.	3594
	6: 4	he is conceited and understands **n**.	3594
	6: 7	For we brought **n** into the world,	4029
	6: 7	**and** we can take **n** out of it.	4028+5516
2Ti	3: 5	**Have n to do with** them.	706
Tit	1:15	and do not believe, **n** is pure.	4029
	2: 8	be ashamed because they have **n** bad to say	3594
	3:10	After that, *have* **n to do with** him.	4148
Heb	2: 8	God left **n** that is not subject to him.	4029
	4:13	**N** in all creation is hidden	4024
	7:14	to that tribe Moses said **n** about priests.	4029
	7:19	(for the law made **n** perfect),	4029
	8: 7	For if there had been **n wrong with**	289
Jas	1: 4	but does **n** about his physical needs,	3590
1Pe	3: 7	so that **n** will hinder your prayers.	3590
1Jn	2:10	and there is **n** in him to make him stumble.	4024
3Jn	1: 9	will have **n** to do with us.	4024
Rev	21:27	**N** impure will **ever** enter it,	3590

NOTICE (15) [NOTICED, NOTICING]

Ge	39: 7	his master's wife **took n** of Joseph	5951+6524
Dt	21:11	if *you* **n** among the captives a beautiful	8011
Ru	2:10	such favor in your eyes that you **n** me—	5795
	2:19	Blessed be the *man* who **took n** *of* you!"	5795
2Sa	9: 8	that *you should* **n** a dead dog like me?"	7155
2Ki	3:14	I would not look at you or even **n** you.	8011
Job	35:15	not **take** the least **n** of wickedness,	3359
Eze	38:14	*will you* not **take n** *of* it?	3359
Hos	7: 9	but he *does* not **n**.	3359
Jnh	1: 6	Maybe he *will* **take n** of us,	6951
Mk	15:26	The **written n** of the charge against him	2107
Lk	23:38	There was a **written n** above him,	2107
Jn	19:19	Pilate **had a n** prepared and fastened	1211+5518
Ac	21:24	to the temple to **give n** of the date when	1334
	26:26	that none of this *has* **escaped** his **n**,	3291

NOTICED (9) [NOTICE]

Ge	31: 2	And Jacob **n** *that* Laban's attitude	8011
2Sa	12:19	David **n** that his servants were whispering	8011
1Ki	21:29	*Have you* **n** how Ahab has humbled himself	8011
Pr	7: 7	*I* **n** among the young men,	1067
Isa	58: 3	and *you have* not **n**?'	3359
Jer	33:24	not **n** that these people are saying,	8011
Mt	22:11	he **n** a man there who was not wearing	3972
Lk	14: 7	*When* he **n** how the guests picked the places	2091
Jn	11:31	**n** how quickly she got up and went out,	3972

NOTICING (2) [NOTICE]

Mk	12:28	**N** that Jesus had given them a good answer,	3972
Lk	11:38	**n** that Jesus did not first wash before	3972

NOTIONS (2)

Job	15: 2	"Would a wise man answer with empty **n**	1981
Col	2:18	unspiritual mind puffs him up *with* idle **n**.	1632

NOTORIOUS (1)

Mt	27:16	At that time they had a **n** prisoner,	2168

NOTWITHSTANDING (KJV) See BUT, HOWEVER, NEVERTHELESS, YET

NOUGHT (KJV) See CRUMBLES, FAILS, FOILS, FRUSTRATED, IDOLATRIES, IGNORED, LO DEBAR, NO REASON, NONE, NOTHING, NULLIFY, PITTANCE, REJECTED, RIDICULED, RUIN, THWARTED, USELESS, VANISHED, WORTHLESS

NOURISH (2) [NOURISHED, NOURISHING, NOURISHMENT, WELL-NOURISHED]
Pr	10:21	The lips of the righteous n many,	8286
	27:27	and your family and to n your servant girls.	2644

NOURISHED (4) [NOURISH]
Dt	32:13	*He* n him *with* honey from the rock,	3567
Job	21:24	his body **well** n, his bones rich with	2692+4848
Eze	31:4	waters n it, deep springs made it grow tall;	1540
Da	1:15	looked healthier and better n than any	1374+1414

NOURISHING (1) [NOURISH]
Ro	11:17	the others and now share in the n sap from	*4404*

NOURISHMENT (1) [NOURISH]
Pr	3:8	This will bring health to your body and n	9198

NOVICE (KJV) See RECENT CONVERT

NOW (1208)
Ge	1:2	N the earth was formless and empty,	2256
	2:8	N the LORD God had planted a garden in	2256
	2:19	N the LORD God had formed out of	2256
	2:23	"This is n bone of my bones and flesh	7193
	3:1	N the serpent was more crafty than any of	2256
	3:22	"The man has n become like one of us,	6964
	4:2	N Abel kept flocks,	2256
	4:8	N Cain said to his brother Abel,	2256
	4:11	N you are under a curse and driven from	6964
	6:11	N the earth was corrupt in God's sight	2256
	7:4	Seven days from n I will send rain on	6388
	8:2	N the springs of the deep and	2256
	9:3	I n give you everything.	NIH
	9:9	"I n establish my covenant with you and	2180
	11:1	N the whole world had one language and	2256
	11:30	N Sarai was barren; she had no children.	2256
	12:10	N there was a famine in the land,	2256
	12:19	N then, here is your wife.	6964
	13:5	N Lot, who was moving about with Abram,	2256
	13:13	N the men of Sodom were wicked	2256
	14:10	N the Valley of Siddim was full of tar pits,	2256
	14:13	N Abram was living near the great trees	2256
	16:1	N Sarai, Abram's wife,	2256
	16:5	and n that she knows she is pregnant,	2256
	16:11	"You are n with child and you will have	2180
	16:13	"I have n seen the One who sees me."	2151
	17:8	where you are n an alien,	NIH
	18:5	n that you have come to your servant."	3954
	18:10	N Sarah was listening at the entrance to	2256
	18:12	*will I* n *have this pleasure?"*	AIT
	18:13	n that I am old?'	2256
	18:27	"N that I have been so bold as to speak to	2180
	18:31	"N that I have been so bold as to speak to	2180
	19:9	and n he wants to play the judge!	6964
	20:1	N Abraham moved on from there into	2256
	20:4	N Abimelech had not gone near her,	2256
	20:7	N return the man's wife,	6964
	21:1	N the LORD was gracious to Sarah	2256
	21:23	N swear to me here before God	6964
	22:12	N I know that you fear God,	6964
	24:1	Abraham was n old and well advanced	2256
	24:29	N Rebekah had a brother named Laban,	2256
	24:49	N if you will show kindness	6964
	24:56	n that the LORD has granted success	2256
	24:62	N Isaac had come from Beer Lahai Roi,	2256
	26:1	N there was a famine in the land—	2256
	26:22	"N the LORD has given us room	6964
	26:29	And n you are blessed by the LORD."	6964
	27:2	"I am n an old man and don't know the day	2180
	27:3	N then, get your weapons—	6964
	27:6	N Rebekah was listening as Isaac spoke	2256
	27:8	N, my son, listen carefully	6964
	27:36	and n he's taken my blessing!"	6964
	27:43	N then, my son, do what I say:	6964
	28:4	of the land where you n live as an alien,	NIH
	28:6	N Esau learned that Isaac had blessed Jacob	2256
	29:16	N Laban had two daughters;	2256
	29:32	Surely my husband will love me n."	6964
	29:34	when she gave birth to a son she said, "N	6964
	30:30	But n, when may I do something	6964
	31:13	N leave this land at once and go back	6964
	31:30	N you have gone off because you longed	6964
	31:32	N Jacob did not know	2256
	31:34	N Rachel had taken the household gods	2256
	31:37	N that you have searched	3954
	31:38	"I have been with you for twenty years n.	2296
Ge	31:44	Come n, let's make a covenant, you and I,	6964
	32:4	with Laban and have remained there till n.	2256
	32:5	N I am sending this message to my lord,	2256
	32:6	and n he is coming to meet you,	1685
	32:10	but n I have become two groups.	6964
	33:10	n that you have received me favorably.	2256
	34:1	N Dinah, the daughter Leah had borne	2256
	34:7	N Jacob's sons had come in from the fields	2256
	35:8	N Deborah, Rebekah's nurse,	2256
	37:3	N Israel loved Joseph more than any	2256
	37:12	N his brothers had gone	2256
	37:20	"Come n, let's kill him and throw him	6964
	37:24	N the cistern was empty;	2256
	37:30	Where *can* I **turn** n?"	AIT
	38:14	though Shelah had n grown up,	2256
	38:16	"Come n, let me sleep with you."	5528
	38:24	and as a result she is n pregnant."	2180
	39:1	N Joseph had been taken down to Egypt.	2256
	39:6	N Joseph was well-built and handsome,	2256
	40:20	N the third day was Pharaoh's birthday,	2256
	41:12	N a young Hebrew was there with us,	2256
	41:33	"And n let Pharaoh look for a discerning	6964
	42:6	N Joseph was the governor of the land,	2256
	42:13	The youngest is n with our father,	2021+3427
	42:22	We must give an accounting	2180
	42:32	and the youngest is n with our father	2021+3427
	42:36	and n you want to take Benjamin.	2256
	43:1	N the famine was still severe in the land.	2256
	43:18	N the men were frightened	2256
	44:1	N Joseph gave these instructions to	2256
	44:16	We are n my lord's slaves—	2180
	44:30	"So n, if the boy is not with us	6964
	44:33	"N then, please let your servant remain here	6964
	45:5	And n, do not be distressed and do not	6964
	45:6	For two years n there has been famine	2296+3954
	45:9	N hurry back to my father and say to him,	6964
	46:28	N Jacob sent Judah ahead of him to Joseph	2256
	46:30	Israel said to Joseph, "N I am ready to die,	2021+7193
	47:1	the land of Canaan and are n in Goshen."	2180
	47:4	So n, please let your servants settle	6964
	47:23	"N *that* I have bought you	2176
	47:27	N the Israelites settled in Egypt in	2256
	48:5	"N then, your two sons born to you	6964
	48:10	N Israel's eyes were failing because	2256
	48:11	and n God has allowed me	2180
	50:5	N let me go up and bury my father;	6964
	50:17	N please forgive the sins of the servants of	6964
	50:20	to accomplish what is n being done,	2021+2021+2296+3427
Ex	1:6	N Joseph and all his brothers and all	2256
	2:1	N a man of the house of Levi married	2256
	2:16	N a priest of Midian had seven daughters,	2256
	3:1	N Moses was tending the flock	2256
	3:9	n the cry of the Israelites has reached me,	6964
	3:10	So n, go.	6964
	4:7	"N put it back into your cloak," he said.	2256
	4:12	N go; I will help you speak	6964
	4:19	the LORD had said to Moses in Midian,	2256
	5:3	N let us take a three-day journey into	5528
	5:5	the people of the land are n numerous,	6964
	5:18	N get to work.	6964
	6:1	"N you will see what I will do to Pharaoh:	6964
	6:13	N the LORD spoke to Moses and Aaron	2256
	6:28	N when the LORD spoke to Moses	2256
	7:16	But until n you have not listened.	3907
	8:28	N pray for me."	NIH
	9:15	*by* n I could have stretched out my hand	6964
	9:18	from the day it was founded till	6964
	9:19	Give an order n to bring your livestock	6964
	10:6	the day they settled in this land till n.' "	2021+2021+2296+3427
	10:17	N forgive my sin once more and pray to	6964
	11:1	N the LORD had said to Moses,	2256
	12:40	N the length of time the Israelite people	2256
	18:1	N Jethro, the priest of Midian	2256
	18:11	N I know that the LORD is greater than all	6964
	18:19	Listen n to me and I will give you some	6964
	19:5	N if you obey me fully and keep my	6964
	32:10	N leave me alone so that my anger may	6964
	32:30	But n I will go up to the LORD;	6964
	32:32	But n, please forgive their sin—	6964
	32:34	N go, lead the people to the place I spoke	6964
	33:5	N take off your ornaments	6964
	33:7	N Moses used to take a tent	2256
	33:18	Then Moses said, "N show me your glory."	5528
Lev	17:5	the LORD the sacrifices they *are* n making	AIT
	24:10	N the son of an Israelite mother and	2256
Nu	6:13	" 'N this is the law for the Nazirite when	2256
	10:29	N Moses said to Hobab son of Reuel	2256
	11:1	N the people complained	2256
	11:6	But n we have lost our appetite;	6964
	11:15	put me to death **right** n—	5528
	11:18	N the LORD will give you meat,	2256
	11:23	You will n see whether or	6964
	11:31	N a wind went out from the LORD	2256
	12:3	(N Moses was a very humble man,	2256
	14:17	"N may the Lord's strength be displayed,	2256+6964
	14:19	from the time they left Egypt until n."	2178
	15:22	" 'N if you unintentionally fail to keep any	6964
	16:8	Moses also said to Korah, "N listen,	5528
	16:10	**but** n you are trying to get	2256
	16:13	And n you also want to lord it over us?	3954
	18:22	**From** n **on** the Israelites must not go near	6388
	20:2	N there was no water for the community,	2256
	20:16	"N we are here at Kadesh,	2180
Nu	22:2	N Balak son of Zippor saw all	2256
	22:6	N come and put a curse on these people,	6964
	22:11	N come and put a curse on them for me.	6964
	22:19	N stay here tonight as the others did,	6964
	22:29	I would kill you **right** n."	6964
	22:33	I would certainly have killed you by n,	6964
	22:34	N if you are displeased, I will go back."	6964
	22:38	"Well, I have come to you n,"	6964
	23:23	It will n be said of Jacob and of Israel,	2021+3869+6961
	24:1	N when Balaam saw that it pleased	2256
	24:11	N leave at once and go home!	6964
	24:14	N I am going back to my people, but come,	6964
	24:17	but not n; I behold him, but not near.	6964
	31:17	N kill all the boys.	6964
	36:3	N suppose they marry men	2256
Dt	2:3	this hill country long enough; n turn north.	NIH
	2:13	"N get up and cross the Zered Valley."	6964
	2:16	N when the last of these fighting men	2256
	2:24	"Set out n and cross the Arnon Gorge.	7756
	2:30	as he has n done.	2021+2021+2296+3427
	2:31	N begin to conquer and possess his land."	NIH
	4:1	Hear n, O Israel, the decrees and laws I am	6964
	4:20	as you n are.	2021+2021+2296+3427
	4:32	Ask n about the former days,	5528
	5:25	But n, why should we die?	6964
	7:19	the same to all the peoples you n fear.	NIH
	9:1	You are n about to cross the Jordan	2021+3427
	10:5	and they are there n.	NIH
	10:10	N I had stayed on the mountain forty days	2256
	10:12	And n, O Israel, what does	6964
	10:22	and the LORD your God has made you	6964
	22:17	N he has slandered her and said,	2180
	26:10	n I bring the firstfruits of the soil that you,	6964
	27:9	You have n become the people of the LORD your God.	2021+2021+2296+3427
	29:28	another land, as it is n."	2021+2021+2296+3427
	30:11	N what I am commanding you today is	3954
	30:19	N choose life, so that you	2256
	31:2	I am n a hundred and twenty years old	2021+3427
	31:14	"N the day of your death is near.	2176
	31:19	"N write down for yourselves this song	6964
	32:37	He will say: "N where are their gods,	NIH
	32:39	"See n that I myself am He!	6964
	34:9	N Joshua son of Nun was filled with	2256
Jos	1:2	N then, you and all these people,	2256
	1:11	Three days **from** n you will cross	928+6388
	2:12	N then, please swear to me by the LORD	6964
	2:16	N she had said to them,	2256
	3:12	N then, choose twelve men from the tribes	6964
	3:15	N the Jordan is at flood stage all	2256
	4:10	N the priests who carried	2256
	5:1	N when all the Amorite kings west of	2256
	5:4	N this is why he did so:	2256
	5:13	N when Joshua was near Jericho,	2256
	5:14	of the army of the LORD I have n come."	6964
	6:1	N Jericho was tightly shut up because of	2256
	7:2	N Joshua sent men from Jericho to Ai,	2256
	7:8	n that Israel has been routed	339
	9:1	N when all the kings west of	2256
	9:12	But n see how dry and moldy it is.	6964
	9:19	and we cannot touch them n.	6964
	9:23	You are n under a curse:	6964
	9:25	We are n in your hands.	6964
	10:1	N Adoni-Zedek king of Jerusalem heard	2256
	10:16	N the five kings had fled and hidden in	2256
	14:1	N these are the areas the Israelites received	2256
	14:6	N the men of Judah approached Joshua	2256
	14:10	"N then, just as the LORD promised,	6964
	14:11	I'm just as vigorous to go out to battle n	6964
	14:12	N give me this hill country that	6964
	17:3	N Zelophehad son of Hepher,	2256
	21:1	N the family heads of	2256
	22:3	For a long time n—	2296
	22:4	N that the LORD your God has given your brothers rest	6964
	22:16	an altar in rebellion against him n?	2021+3427
	22:18	you n turning away from the LORD?	2021+3427
	22:31	N you have rescued the Israelites from	255
	23:8	as you have until n.	2021+2021+2296+3427
	23:14	"N I am about to go the way of all	2021+3427
	24:14	"N fear the LORD and serve him	6964
	24:23	N then," said Joshua,	6964
Jdg	1:7	N God has paid me back for what I did	NIH
	1:22	N the house of Joseph attacked Bethel,	2256
	2:3	N therefore I tell you that I will	1685
	3:16	N Ehud had made a double-edged sword	2256
	4:11	N Heber the Kenite had left	2256
	6:13	But n the LORD has abandoned us	6964
	6:17	"If n I have found favor in your eyes,	5528
	6:33	N all the Midianites,	2256
	7:3	announce n to the people,	6964
	7:8	N the camp of Midian lay below him in	2256
	8:1	N the Ephraimites asked Gideon,	2256
	8:10	N Zebah and Zalmunna were in Karkor	2256
	9:16	"N if you have acted honorably and	6964
	9:26	N Gaal son of Ebed moved	2256
	9:32	N then, during the night you	6964
	9:35	N Gaal son of Ebed had gone out	2256
	9:38	"Where is your big talk n, you who said,	686
	10:15	but please rescue us n."	2021+2021+2296+3427
	11:7	Why do you come to me n,	6964
	11:8	"Nevertheless, we are turning to you n;	6964
	11:13	give it back peaceably."	6964
	11:23	"N since the LORD, the God of Israel,	6964
	11:36	n that the LORD has avenged you	339
	12:3	N why have you come up today	2256

Ref	Text	Strong
Jdg 13: 4	N see to it that you drink no wine	6964
13: 7	N then, drink no wine	6964
13:23	or n told us this."	2021+3869+6961
14: 2	n get her for me as my wife."	6964
14:10	N his father went down to see the woman.	2256
15:18	Must I n die of thirst and fall into the hands	6964
16:10	**Come n,** tell me how you can be tied."	5528+6964
16:13	Delilah then said to Samson, "Until n,	2178
16:23	N the rulers of the Philistines assembled	2256
16:27	N the temple was crowded with men	2256
17: 1	N a man named Micah from	2256
17: 5	N this man Micah had a shrine,	2256
17:13	"N I know that the LORD will be good	6964
18:14	N you know what to do."	6964
19: 1	N a Levite who lived in a remote area in	2256
19: 9	said, "N look, it's almost evening.	5528
19:18	to Bethlehem in Judah and n I am going to	2256
19:24	I will bring them out to you n,	5528
20: 7	N, all you Israelites, speak up	2180
20: 9	But n this is what we'll do to Gibeah:	6964
20:13	N surrender those wicked men of Gibeah	6964
20:36	N the men of Israel had given way	2256
21: 6	N the Israelites grieved for their brothers,	2256
Ru 1: 2	N Elimelech, Naomi's husband, died,	2256
2: 1	N Naomi had a relative	2256
2: 7	from morning till n,	6964
3:11	And n, my daughter, don't be afraid.	6964
4: 7	(N in earlier times in Israel,	2256
1Sa 1: 9	N Eli the priest was sitting on a chair by	2256
1:28	So I give him to the LORD.	1685
2:13	N it was the practice of the priests with	2256
2:16	"No, hand it over n;	6964
2:22	N Eli, who was very old,	2256
2:27	N a man of God came to Eli and said	2256
2:30	n the LORD declares: 'Far be it from me!	6964
3: 7	N Samuel did not yet know the LORD;	2256
4: 1	N the Israelites went out to fight against	2256
6: 7	"N then, get a new cart ready,	2256
6:13	N the people of Beth	2256
8: 5	n appoint a king to lead us,	6964
8: 9	N listen to them;	6964
9: 3	N the donkeys belonging	2256
9: 6	Let's go there n.	6964
9:12	"He's ahead of you. Hurry n;	6964
9:13	those who are invited will eat. Go up n;	6964
9:15	N the day before Saul came,	2256
10: 2	And n your father has stopped thinking	2180
10:14	N Saul's uncle asked him and his servant,	2256
10:19	But you have n rejected your God,	2021+3427
10:19	So n present yourselves before the LORD	6964
12: 2	N you have a king as your leader.	6964
12: 7	N then, stand here, because I am going	6964
12:10	n deliver us from the hands of our enemies,	6964
12:13	N here is the king you have chosen,	6964
12:16	"N then, stand still and see this great thing	6964
12:17	Is it not wheat harvest n?	2021+3427
13: 4	and n Israel has become a stench to	1685
13:12	'N the Philistines will come down	6964
13:14	But n your kingdom will not endure;	6964
13:23	N a detachment of Philistines had gone out	2256
14:24	N the men of Israel were in distress	2256
14:43	And n must I die?"	2180
15: 1	so listen n to the message from the LORD.	6964
15: 3	N go, attack the Amalekites	6964
15:25	N I beg you,	6964
16:14	N the Spirit of the LORD had departed	2256
17: 1	N the Philistines gathered their forces	2256
17:12	N David was the son of	2256
17:17	N Jesse said to his son David,	2256
17:25	N the Israelites had been saying,	2256
17:29	"N what have I done?"	6964
18:20	N Saul's daughter Michal was in love	2256
18:21	"N you have a second opportunity	2021+3427
18:22	n become his son-in-law.' "	6964
20:31	N send and bring him to me,	6964
21: 3	N then, what do you have on hand?	6964
21: 7	N one of Saul's servants was there that day,	2256
22: 6	N Saul heard that David	2256
22:12	Saul said, "Listen n, son of Ahitub."	5528
23: 6	(N Abiathar son of Ahimelech had brought	2256
23:20	N, O king, come down	6964
23:24	N David and his men were in the Desert	2256
24:11	N understand and recognize that I am	NIH
24:18	You have **just n** told me of	2021+3427
24:21	N swear to me by the LORD that you will	6964
25: 1	N Samuel died, and all Israel assembled	2256
25: 7	" "N I hear that it is sheep-shearing time.	6964
25:17	N think it over and see what you can do,	6964
25:26	"N since the LORD has kept you,	6964
26: 8	N let me pin him to the ground	6964
26:11	N get the spear and water jug that are	6964
26:19	N let my lord the king listen	6964
26:19	They have n driven me from my share	2021+3427
26:20	N do not let my blood fall to the ground far	6964
27: 8	N David and his men went up and raided	2256
28: 3	N Samuel was dead,	2256
28:16	n that the LORD has turned away	2256
28:22	N please listen to your servant	6964
29: 3	and from the day he left Saul until n,	2021+2021+2296+3427
29: 6	From the day you came to me until n,	2021+2021+2296+3427
29: 8	from the day I came to you until n?	2021+2021+2296+3427
29:10	N get up early,	6964
30: 1	N the Amalekites had raided the Negev	2256
31: 1	N the Philistines fought against Israel;	2256
2Sa 2: 6	May the LORD n show you kindness	6964
2: 7	N then, be strong and brave,	6964
2:18	N Asahel was as fleet-footed as	2256
3: 7	N Saul had had a concubine	2256
3: 8	Yet n you accuse me of	2021+3427
3:18	N do it!	6964
3:24	N he is gone!	2256
3:27	N when Abner returned to Hebron,	2256
4: 2	N Saul's son had two men who were leaders	2256
4: 5	N Recab and Baanah,	2256
4:11	not n demand his blood from your hand	6964
5:11	N Hiram king of Tyre sent messengers	2256
5:18	N the Philistines had come and spread out	2256
6:12	N King David was told,	2256
7: 8	"N then, tell my servant David,	6964
7: 9	N I will make your name great,	2256
7:25	"And n, LORD God,	6964
7:29	N be pleased to bless the house	6964
9: 2	N there was a servant	2256
9:10	(N Ziba had fifteen sons	2256
12: 4	"N a traveler came to the rich man,	2256
12:10	N, therefore, the sword will never depart	6964
12:21	but n that the child is dead,	889+3869
12:23	But n that he is dead, why should I fast?	6964
12:28	N muster the rest of the troops and besiege	6964
13: 3	N Amnon had a friend named Jonadab son	2256
13:20	Be quiet n, my sister; he is your brother.	6964
13:34	N the man standing watch looked up	2256
14: 7	N the whole clan has risen up	2180
14:15	"And n I have come to say this to my lord	6964
14:17	"And n your servant says,	6964
14:32	N then, I want to see the king's face,	6964
15:31	N David had been told,	2256
15:34	but n I will be your servant,'	6964
16:23	that belonged to Mephibosheth is n yours."	2180
16:23	N in those days	2256
17: 9	Even n, he is hidden in a cave	6964
17:16	N send a message immediately	6964
18: 3	be better n for you to give us support from	6964
18: 9	N Absalom happened to meet David's men.	2256
18:19	N Ahimaaz son of Zadok said,	2256
19: 7	N go out and encourage your men.	6964
19: 7	upon you from your youth till n."	6964
19: 9	But n he has fled the country because	6964
19:13	if from n on you are not the commander	2021+3427+3972
19:15	N the men of Judah had come to Gilgal	2256
19:30	n that my lord the king has arrived	339
19:32	N Barzillai was a very old man,	2256
19:35	I am n eighty years old.	2021+3427
20: 1	N a troublemaker named Sheba son	2256
20: 6	to Abishai, "N Sheba son of Bicri	6964
21: 2	(N the Gibeonites were not a part of Israel	2256
24:10	N, O LORD, I beg you,	6964
24:13	N then, think it over and decide	6964
1Ki 1: 5	N Adonijah, whose mother was Haggith,	2256
1:12	N then, let me advise you	6964
1:18	But n Adonijah has become king, and you,	6964
1:25	Right n they are eating and drinking	2180
2: 5	"N you yourself know what Joab son	1685+2256
2: 9	But n, do not consider him innocent.	6964
2:13	N Adonijah, the son of Haggith,	2256
2:16	N I have one request to make of you.	6964
2:24	And n, as surely as the LORD lives—	6964
2:26	but I will not put you to death n,	2021+2021+2296+3427
2:44	N the LORD will repay you	2256
2:46	The kingdom was n firmly established	2256
3: 7	"N, O LORD my God,	6964
3: 7	N two prostitutes came to the king	255
5: 4	But n the LORD my God has given me rest	6964
8:20	I have succeeded David my father and n	2256
8:25	"N LORD, God of Israel,	6964
8:26	And n, O God of Israel,	6964
9: 8	And though this temple is n imposing,	AIT
9:14	N Hiram had sent to the king 120 talents	2256
11:28	N Jeroboam was a man of standing,	2256
12: 4	but n lighten the harsh labor and	6964
12:26	"The kingdom will n likely revert to	6964
13: 2	the high places who n make offerings here,	NIH
13:11	N there was a certain old prophet living	2256
14: 4	N Ahijah could not see;	2256
14:14	Yes, even n.	6964
15:19	N break your treaty with Baasha king	NIH
17: 1	N Elijah the Tishbite,	2256
17:24	"N I know that you are a man of God	2296+6964
18: 2	N the famine was severe in Samaria,	2256
18:11	n you tell me to go to my master and say,	6964
18:14	n you tell me to go to my master and say,	6964
18:19	N summon the people from all over Israel	6964
19: 1	N Ahab told Jezebel everything Elijah had done	2256
19:10	and n they are trying to kill me too."	2256
19:14	and n they are trying to kill me too."	2256
20: 1	N Ben-Hadad king of Aram	2256
20:17	N Ben-Hadad had dispatched scouts,	2256
21:18	He is n in Naboth's vineyard,	2180
22:11	N Zedekiah son of Kenaanah	2256
22:23	"So n the LORD has put a lying spirit in	6964
22:31	N the king of Aram	2256
22:48	N Jehoshaphat built a fleet of trading ships	NIH
2Ki 1: 2	N Ahaziah had fallen through the lattice	2256
1:14	But n have respect for my life!"	6964
2:14	"Where n is the LORD,	677
3: 4	N Mesha king of Moab raised sheep,	2256
3:15	But n bring me a harpist."	6964
3:21	N all the Moabites had heard that	2256
2Ki 3:23	N to the plunder, Moab!"	6964
4: 1	But n his creditor is coming	2256
4:13	N what can be done for you?	NIH
5: 1	N Naaman was commander of the army of	2256
5: 2	N bands from Aram had gone out	2256
5:15	"N I know that there is no God in all	2180
5:15	Please accept n a gift from your servant.	6964
6: 8	N the king of Aram was at war with Israel.	2256
6:32	N Elisha was sitting in his house,	2256
7: 3	N there were four men with leprosy at	2256
7:17	N the king had put the officer	2256
8: 1	N Elisha had said to the woman	2256
8: 6	from the day she left the country until n."	6964
9:14	(N Joram and all Israel had been defending	2256
9:26	N then, pick him up and throw him on	6964
10: 1	N there were in Samaria seventy sons of	2256
10: 6	N the royal princes, seventy of them,	2256
10:19	N summon all the prophets of Baal,	6964
10:24	N Jehu had posted eighty men outside	2256
13:14	N Elisha was suffering from the illness	2256
13:19	But n you will defeat it only three times."	6964
13:20	N Moabite raiders used to enter	2256
14:10	You have indeed defeated Edom and n	2256
18:21	Look n, you are depending on Egypt,	6964
18:23	" 'Come n, make a bargain with my master,	5528+6964
19: 9	N Sennacherib received a report	2256
19:19	N, O LORD our God,	6964
19:25	n I have brought it to pass,	6964
20: 5	On the third day from n you will go up to	NIH
20: 8	of the LORD on the third day from n?"	NIH
24:20	N Zedekiah rebelled against the king	2256
1Ch 9: 2	N the first to resettle on their own property	2256
10: 1	N the Philistines fought against Israel;	2256
14: 1	N Hiram king of Tyre sent messengers	2256
14: 9	N the Philistines had come and raided	2256
15:27	N David was clothed in a robe of fine linen,	2256
17: 7	"N then, tell my servant David,	6964
17: 8	N I will make your name like the names of	2256
17:23	"And n, LORD, let the promise you have made concerning your servant	6964
17:27	N you have been pleased to bless the house	6964
21: 8	N, I beg you, take away the guilt	6964
21:12	N then, decide how I should answer	6964
22:11	"N, my son, the LORD be with you,	6964
22:16	N begin the work,	NIH
22:19	N devote your heart and soul to seeking	6964
28: 8	"So n I charge you in the sight of all Israel	6964
28:10	Consider n, for the LORD has chosen you	6964
29: 3	of my God I n give my personal treasures	AIT
29: 5	N, who is willing to consecrate	2256
29:13	N, our God, we give you thanks,	6964
29:17	And n I have seen with joy	6964
2Ch 1: 4	N David had brought up the ark of God	66
1: 9	N, LORD God, let your promise	6964
2: 4	N I am about to build a temple for	2180
2:15	"N let my lord send his servants the wheat	6964
6: 6	But n I have chosen Jerusalem	2256
6:10	I have succeeded David my father and n	2256
6:13	N he had made a bronze platform,	3954
6:16	"N LORD, God of Israel,	6964
6:17	And n, O LORD, God of Israel,	6964
6:40	"N, my God, may your eyes be open	6964
6:41	"N arise, O LORD God,	6964
7:15	N my eyes will be open	6964
7:21	And though this temple is n so imposing,	NIH
10: 4	but n lighten the harsh labor and	6964
12: 5	therefore, I n abandon you to Shishak.' "	677
13: 8	"And n you plan to resist the kingdom of	6964
13:13	N Jeroboam had sent troops around to	2256
16: 3	N break your treaty with Baasha king	NIH
16: 9	and from n on you will be at war."	6964
18: 1	N Jehoshaphat had great wealth and honor,	2256
18:10	N Zedekiah son of Kenaanah	2256
18:22	"So n the LORD has put a lying spirit in	6964
18:30	N the king of Aram	2256
19: 7	N let the fear of the LORD be upon you.	6964
20:10	"But n here are men from Ammon,	6964
21:14	n the LORD is about to strike your people,	2180
23: 4	N this is what you are to do:	NIH
24: 5	Do it n."	4554
24: 7	N the sons of that wicked woman Athaliah	3954
24:15	N Jehoiada was old and full of years,	2256
25:19	and n you are arrogant and proud.	6964
28:10	And n you intend to make the men	6964
28:11	N listen to me!	6964
29: 5	Consecrate yourselves n and consecrate	6964
29:10	N I intend to make a covenant with	6964
29:11	My sons, do not be negligent n,	6964
29:19	They are n in front of the LORD's altar."	2180
29:31	"You have n dedicated yourselves to	6964
32:15	N do not let Hezekiah deceive you	6964
34:28	N I will gather you to your fathers,	2180
35: 3	N serve the LORD your God	6964
Ezr 1: 4	where survivors may n be **living** are	AIT
2: 1	N these are the people of	2256
4:14	N since we are under obligation to	10363
4:21	N issue an order to these men to stop work,	10363
5: 1	N Haggai the prophet and Zechariah	10221
5:17	N if it pleases the king,	10363
6: 6	N then, Tattenai, governor	10363
7:13	N I decree that any of the Israelites	10221
7:21	N I, King Artaxerxes, order all	10221
9: 7	From the days of our forefathers until n,	2021+2021+2296+3427
9: 8	"But n, for a brief moment,	6964
9:10	n, O our God, what can we say after this?	6964

Ref		Text	Strong's
Ezr	10: 3	N let us make a covenant before our God	6964
	10:11	N make confession to the LORD,	6964
Ne	5: 1	N the men and their wives raised	2256
	5: 8	N you are selling your brothers,	1685+2256
	6: 7	N this report will get back to the king;	6964
	6: 9	"N strengthen my hands."	6964
	7: 4	N the city was large and spacious,	2256
	8:12	because they n understood the words	NIH
	9:32	"N therefore, O our God, the great,	6964
	10:29	all these n join their brothers the nobles,	NIH
	11: 1	N the leaders of the people settled	2256
	11: 3	in Jerusalem (n some Israelites,	2256
	13:18	N you are stirring up more wrath	2256
	13:27	Must we hear n that you too are doing	NIH
Est	2: 5	N there was in the citadel of Susa a Jew of	NIH
	2:17	N the king was attracted	2256
	5: 6	"N what is your petition?	NIH
	6: 4	N Haman had just entered the outer court	2256
	6: 6	N Haman thought to himself,	2256
	8: 8	N write another decree in the king's name	2256
	9: 1	but n the tables were turned and	2256
	9:12	N what is your petition?	2256
Job	3:13	For n I would be lying down in peace;	6964
	3:14	who built for themselves places n lying	NIH
	4: 5	But n trouble comes to you,	6964
	4: 7	"Consider n: Who, being innocent,	5528
	6:13	n that success has been driven from me?	NIH
	6:21	N you too have proved to be of no help;	6964
	6:28	"But n be so kind as to look at me.	2256
	7: 8	eye that n sees me will see me no longer;	AIT
	8: 6	even n he will rouse himself on your behalf	6964
	9:35	but as it n stands with me, I cannot.	NIH
	10: 8	Will you n turn and destroy me?	3480
	10: 9	Will you n turn me to dust again?	2256
	13: 6	Hear n my argument;	5528
	13:18	N that I have prepared my case,	2180
	16:19	Even n my witness is in heaven;	6964
	19: 3	Ten times n you have reproached me;	2296
	21:28	'Where n is the great man's house,	NIH
	30: 1	"But n they mock me, men younger than I,	6964
	30: 9	"And n their sons mock me in song;	6964
	30:11	N that God has unstrung my bow	3954
	30:16	"And n my life ebbs away;	6964
	31:35	I sign n my defense—	2176
	32: 4	N Elihu had waited before speaking to Job	2256
	32:16	Must I wait, n that they are silent,	3954
	32:16	in that they stand there with no reply?	3954
	33: 1	"But n, Job, listen to my words;	5528
	33:14	n one way, now another—	NIH
	33:14	now one way, n another—	2256
	33:21	and his bones, once hidden, n stick out.	NIH
	36:17	But n you are laden with the judgment due	2256
	37:21	N no one can look at the sun,	6964
	42: 4	'Listen n, and I will speak;	5528
	42: 5	of you but n my eyes have seen you.	6964
	42: 8	So n take seven bulls and seven rams	6964
Ps	12: 5	I will n arise," says the LORD.	6964
	17:11	they n surround me, with eyes alert,	6964
	20: 6	N I know that the LORD saves his anointed;	6964
	37:25	I was young and n I am old,	1685
	39: 7	"But n, Lord, what do I look for?	6964
	44: 9	But n you have rejected and humbled us;	677
	52: 7	"Here n is the man who did	2180
	60: 1	you have been angry—n restore us!	NIH
	113: 2	both n and forevermore.	6964
	115:18	both n and forevermore.	6964
	119:67	but n I obey your word.	6964
	121: 8	over your coming and going both n	6964
	125: 2	so the LORD surrounds his people both n	6964
	131: 3	in the LORD both n and forevermore.	6964
Pr	3:28	when you n have it with you.	AIT
	5: 7	N then, my sons, listen to me;	6964
	7:12	n in the street,	7193
	7:12	n in the squares, at every corner she lurks.)	7193
	7:24	N then, my sons, listen to me;	6964
	8:32	"N then, my sons, listen to me;	6964
Ecc	2: 1	I thought in my heart, "Come n,	5528
	9: 7	for it is n that God favors what you do.	3893
	9:15	N there lived in that city a man poor	2256
	12:13	N all has been heard;	NIH
SS	3: 2	I will get up n and go about the city,	5528
Isa	1:18	"Come n, let us reason together,"	5528
	1:21	in her—but n murderers!	AIT
	3: 1	See n, the Lord, the LORD Almighty,	3954
	5: 3	"N you dwellers in Jerusalem and men	6964
	5: 5	N I will tell you what I am going to do	6964
	7: 2	N the house of David was told,	2256
	7:13	Isaiah said, "Hear n, you house of David!	5528
	14: 8	"N that you have been laid low,	255+4946
	16:14	But n the LORD says:	6964
	19:12	Where are your wise men n?	686
	22: 1	What troubles you n,	686
	23:12	O Virgin Daughter of Sidon, n crushed!	AIT
	23:13	this people that is n of no account!	AIT
	26:14	They are n dead, they live no more;	AIT
	28:22	N stop your mocking,	6964
	30: 8	Go n, write it on a tablet for them,	6964
	33:10	"N will I arise," says the LORD.	6964
	33:10	"N will I be exalted;	6964
	33:10	will I be exalted; n will I be lifted up.	6964
	36: 6	Look n, you are depending on Egypt,	NIH
	36: 8	" 'Come n, make a bargain with my master,	5528+6964
	37: 9	N Sennacherib received a report	2256
	37:20	N, O LORD our God,	6964
	37:26	n I have brought it to pass,	6964
	38:11	or be with those who n dwell in this world.	AIT
Isa	42:14	But n, like a woman in childbirth, I cry out,	NIH
	43: 1	But n, this is what the LORD says—	6964
	43:19	N it springs up; do you not perceive it?	6964
	44: 1	"But n listen, O Jacob, my servant, Israel,	6964
	47: 8	"N then, listen, you wanton creature,	6964
	48: 6	"From n on I will tell you of new things,	6964
	48: 7	They are created n, and not long ago;	6964
	48:16	And n the Sovereign LORD has sent me,	6964
	49: 5	And n the LORD says—	6964
	49:19	n you will be too small for your people,	6964
	50:11	But n, all you who light fires	2176
	52: 5	"And n what do I have here?"	6964
	54: 9	So n I have sworn not to be angry with you,	NIH
	63:18	but n our enemies have trampled	NIH
Jer	1: 9	"N, I have put my words in your mouth.	2180
	2:18	N why go to Egypt to drink water from	6964
	3: 1	would you n return to me?"	2256
	4:12	N I pronounce my judgments	6964
	5:19	so n you will serve foreigners in a land	NIH
	7:12	" 'Go n to the place in Shiloh	5528
	7:14	what I did to Shiloh I will n do to	AIT
	7:25	the time your forefathers left Egypt until n,	2021+2021+2296+3427
	9:17	the LORD Almighty says: "Consider n!	2256
	9:20	N, O women, hear the word of the LORD!	3954
	10:20	no one is left n to pitch my tent or to set	6388
	13: 4	and go n to Perath and hide it there in	7756
	13: 6	"Go n to Perath and get the belt I told you	7756
	13: 7	but n it was ruined and completely useless.	2180
	14:10	he will n remember their wickedness	6964
	16:16	"But n I will send for many fishermen,"	2180
	17:15	Let it n be fulfilled!"	5528
	18:11	N therefore say to the people of Judah	6964
	21: 2	"Inquire n of the LORD for us	5528
	25: 5	They said, "Turn n, each of you,	5528
	25:30	"N prophesy all these words against them	2256
	26:13	N reform your ways and your actions	6964
	26:20	(N Uriah son of Shemaiah	2256
	27: 6	N I will hand all your countries over	6964
	27:16	to the prophets who say, 'Very soon n	6964
	32: 3	N Zedekiah king of Judah	NIH
	32:24	What you said has happened, as you n see.	2180
	32:31	From the day it was built until n,	2021+2021+2296+3427
	34:16	But n you have turned around	2256
	34:17	So I n proclaim 'freedom' for you,	2180
	36: 2	the reign of Josiah till n.	2021+2021+2296+3427
	37: 4	N Jeremiah was free to come and go among	2256
	37:20	But n, my lord the king, please listen.	6964
	39:11	N Nebuchadnezzar king of Babylon	2256
	40: 3	And n the LORD has brought it about;	2256
	41: 9	N the cistern where he threw all the bodies	2256
	42: 2	For as you n see,	NIH
	42: 2	n only a few are left.	NIH
	42:11	whom you n fear.	NIH
	42:22	So n, be sure of this:	6964
	44: 7	"N this is what the LORD God Almighty,	6964
	44:23	as you n see."	2021+2021+2296+3427
	49:15	"N I will make you small among	2180
	51: 7	therefore they have n gone mad.	AIT
	52: 3	N Zedekiah rebelled against the king	2256
La	1: 1	among the provinces has n become a slave.	AIT
	4: 2	are n considered as pots of clay,	NIH
	4: 5	Those nurtured in purple n lie on ash heaps.	NIH
	4: 8	But n they are blacker than soot;	NIH
	4:14	N they grope through the streets	NIH
Eze	3: 4	Son of man, go n to the house of Israel	995+2143
	3:11	Go n to your countrymen in exile	995+2143
	4: 1	"N, son of man, take a clay tablet,	2256
	4:14	From my youth until n	6964
	5: 1	"N, son of man, take a sharp sword	2256
	7: 3	The end is n upon you	6964
	8: 8	"Son of man, n dig into the wall."	5528
	9: 3	N the glory of the God of Israel went up	2256
	10: 3	N the cherubim were standing on	2256
	11:13	N as I was prophesying,	2256
	12:27	for many years from n,	AIT
	13: 2	of Israel who are n prophesying.	AIT
	13:17	"N, son of man, set your face against	2256
	16:49	" 'N this was the sin of your sister Sodom:	2180
	16:57	you are n scorned by the daughters	6961
	17: 7	The vine n sent out its roots toward him	2180
	19: 6	for he was n a strong lion.	NIH
	19:13	N it is planted in the desert,	6964
	23:43	'N let them use her as a prostitute,	6964
	24: 6	to the pot n encrusted,	NIH
	24:13	" 'N your impurity is lewdness.	928
	26: 2	n that she lies in ruins I will prosper,'	NIH
	26:18	N the coastlands tremble on the day	6964
	27:34	N you are shattered by the sea in the depths	6961
	33:22	The evening before the man arrived,	2256
	36:35	n fortified and inhabited."	AIT
	38: 8	and n all of them live in safety.	2256
	39:25	I will n bring Jacob back from captivity	6964
	42: 5	N the upper rooms were narrower,	2256
	43: 9	N let them put away from me	6964
	47: 5	but n it was a river that I could not cross,	NIH
Da	1: 9	N God had caused the official	2256
	2:36	and n we will interpret it to the king.	10221
	3:15	N when you hear the sound of the horn,	10363
	4:18	N, Belteshazzar, tell me what it means,	10221
	4:37	N I, Nebuchadnezzar, praise and exalt	10363
	5:16	N I have heard that you are able	10221
	6: 3	N Daniel so distinguished himself among	10008
	6: 8	N, O king, issue the decree and put it	10363
	6:10	N when Daniel learned that	10221
	9:15	"N, O Lord our God,	6964
Da	9:17	"N, our God, hear the prayers and petitions	6964
	9:22	I have n come to give you insight	6964
	10:11	for I have n been sent to you."	6964
	10:14	N I have come to explain	2256
	10:19	Be strong n; be strong."	2256
	11: 2	"N then, I tell you the truth:	6964
Hos	2: 7	for then I was better off than n.'	6964
	2:10	So n I will expose her lewdness before	6964
	2:14	"Therefore I am n going to allure her;	2180
	5: 3	Ephraim, you have n turned to prostitution;	6964
	5: 7	N their New Moon festivals will devour	6964
	7:11	n calling to Egypt, now turning to Assyria.	NIH
	7:11	now calling to Egypt, n turning to Assyria.	NIH
	8: 8	n she is among the nations like	6964
	8:10	I will n gather them together.	6964
	8:13	N he will remember their wickedness	6964
	10: 2	and n they must bear their guilt.	6964
	13: 2	N they sin more and more;	6964
Joel	2:12	"Even n," declares the LORD,	6964
	3: 4	N what have you against me,	1685+2256
Am	2:13	"N then, I will crush you as a cart crushes	2180
	2:16	N then, hear the word of the LORD.	6964
Jnh	3: 3	N Nineveh was a very important city—	2256
	4: 3	N, O LORD, take away my life,	6964
Mic	4: 9	Why do you n cry aloud—	6964
	4:10	for n you must leave the city to camp in	6964
	4:11	n many nations are gathered against you.	6964
	7: 4	N is the time of their confusion.	6964
	7:10	even n she will be trampled underfoot	6964
Na	1:13	N I will break their yoke from your neck	6964
	2:11	Where n is the lions' den,	NIH
Hab	2:16	N it is your turn!	1685
Hag	1: 5	N this is what the LORD Almighty says:	6964
	2: 3	How does it look to you n?	6964
	2: 4	But n be strong, O Zerubbabel,'	6964
	2:15	" 'N give careful thought to this	6964
	2:19	Until n, the vine and the fig tree,	NIH
Zec	1: 5	Where are your forefathers n?	NIH
	3: 3	N Joshua was dressed in filthy clothes	2256
	8: 9	"You who n hear these words spoken	465+928+2021+2021+3427
	8:11	But n I will not deal with the remnant	6964
	8:15	"so n I have determined to do good again to Jerusalem	465+928+2021+2021+3427
	9: 8	for n I am keeping watch.	6964
	9:12	n I announce that I will restore twice	2021+3427
Mal	1: 9	"N implore God to be gracious to us.	6964
	2: 1	n this admonition is for you, O priests.	6964
	3:15	But n we call the arrogant blessed.	6964
Mt	3:15	Jesus replied, "Let it be so n;	785
	5: 1	N when he saw the crowds,	1254
	11:12	From the days of John the Baptist until n,	785
	12:41	and n one greater than Jonah is here.	2627
	12:42	and n one greater than Solomon is here.	2627
	14: 3	N Herod had arrested John and bound him	1142
	19:16	N a man came up to Jesus and asked,	2779
	20:17	N as Jesus was going up to Jerusalem,	2779
	22:25	N there were seven brothers among us.	1254
	22:28	N then, at the resurrection,	4036
	24:21	from the beginning of the world until n—	3814
	24:32	"N learn this lesson from the fig tree:	1254
	26:29	not drink of this fruit of the vine from n on	785
	26:48	N the betrayer had arranged a signal	1254
	26:65	Look, n you have heard the blasphemy.	3814
	26:69	N Peter was sitting out in the courtyard,	1254
	27:15	N it was the governor's custom at the Feast	1254
	27:42	Let him come down n from the cross,	3814
	27:43	Let God rescue him n if he wants him,	3814
	27:49	The rest said, "N leave him alone.	NIG
	28: 7	N I have told you."	2627
Mk	2: 6	N some teachers of the law were sitting	1254
	2:18	N John's disciples and the Pharisees	2779
	6:25	"I want you to give me right n the head	1994
	12:20	N there were seven brothers.	NIG
	12:26	N about the dead rising—	1254
	13:19	until n—and never to be equaled again.	3814
	13:28	"N learn this lesson from the fig tree:	1254
	14: 1	N the Passover and the Feast	1254
	14:44	N the betrayer had arranged a signal	1254
	15: 6	N it was the custom at the Feast to release	1254
	15:32	come down n from the cross,	3814
	15:36	"N leave him alone.	NIG
Lk	1:20	And n you will be silent and not able	2627
	1:48	From n on all generations will call me blessed,	3814
	2:25	N there was a man in Jerusalem	2779
	2:29	you n dismiss your servant in peace.	3814
	3:23	N Jesus himself was about thirty years old	2779
	4:38	N Simon's mother-in-law was suffering	1254
	5:10	from n on you will catch men."	3814+3836
	6:21	Blessed are you who hunger n,	3814
	6:21	Blessed are you who weep n,	3814
	6:25	Woe to you who are well fed n,	3814
	6:25	Woe to you who laugh n,	3814
	7:36	N one of the Pharisees invited Jesus	1254
	7:42	N which of them will love him more?"	4036
	8:19	N Jesus' mother and brothers came	1254
	8:40	N when Jesus returned,	1254
	9: 7	N Herod the tetrarch heard about all	1254
	11:19	N if I drive out demons by Beelzebub,	1254
	11:31	and n one greater than Solomon is here.	2627
	11:32	and n one greater than Jonah is here.	2627
	11:39	Then the Lord said to him, "N then,	3814
	12:52	From n on there will be five	3814+3836
	13: 1	N there were some present at	1254
	13: 7	three years n I've been coming to look	608+4005
	14:17	'Come, for everything is n ready.'	2453

Ref		Text	Strong's
Lk	15: 1	N the tax collectors and "sinners"	1254
	16: 3	'What shall I do n?	NIG
	16:25	but n he is comforted here and you are	3814
	17: 7	'Come along n and sit down to eat'?	2311
	17:11	N on his way to Jerusalem,	1181+2779
	19: 8	Here and n I give half of my possessions	AIT
	19:42	but n it is hidden from your eyes.	3814
	20:29	N there were seven brothers.	4036
	20:33	N then, at the resurrection whose wife will she be,	4036
	22: 1	N the Feast of Unleavened Bread,	1254
	22:36	"But n if you have a purse, take it,	3814
	22:69	But from n on,	3814+3836
	23:44	It was n about the sixth hour,	2453
	23:50	N there was a man named Joseph,	2779
	24:13	N that same day two of them were going to	2779
Jn	1:19	N this is John's testimony when the Jews	2779
	1:24	N some Pharisees who had been sent	2779
	2: 8	"N draw some out and take it to the master	3814
	2:10	but you have saved the best till n."	785
	2:23	N while he was in Jerusalem at	1254
	3: 1	N there was a man of the Pharisees	1254
	3:23	N John also was baptizing at Aenon	1254
	3:29	That joy is mine, and it is n complete.	AIT
	4: 4	N he had to go through Samaria.	3814
	4:18	the man you n have is not your husband.	3814
	4:23	Yet a time is coming and has n come when	3814
	4:36	Even n the reaper draws his wages,	2453
	4:36	even n he harvests the crop for eternal life,	NIG
	4:42	n we have heard for ourselves,	1142
	4:44	(N Jesus himself had pointed out that	1142
	5: 2	N there is in Jerusalem near the Sheep Gate	1254
	5:25	N a come when the dead will hear	3814
	6:17	By n it was dark,	2453
	6:34	they said, "from n on give us this bread."	4121
	6:42	can he n say, 'I came down from heaven'?"	3814
	7:11	N at the Feast the Jews were watching	4036
	7:23	N if a child can be circumcised on	NIG
	8: 5	N what do you say?"	4036
	8:11	"Go n and leave your life of sin."	608+3814+3836
	8:35	N a slave has no permanent place in	1254
	8:42	for I came from God and n am here.	AIT
	8:52	At this the Jews exclaimed, "N we know	3814
	9:14	N the day on which Jesus had made	1254
	9:15	"and I washed, and n I see."	AIT
	9:19	How is it that he can see?"	785
	9:21	But how he can see n,	3814
	9:25	I was blind but n I see!"	785
	9:30	The man answered, "N that is remarkable!	1142
	9:37	Jesus said, "You have n seen him;	2779
	9:41	but n that you claim you can see,	3814
	11: 1	N a man named Lazarus was sick.	1254
	11: 2	whose brother Lazarus n lay sick,	NIG
	11:22	But I know that even n	3814
	11:30	N Jesus had not yet entered the village,	1254
	12:17	N the crowd that was with him	4036
	12:20	N there were some Greeks	1254
	12:27	"N my heart is troubled,	3814
	12:31	N is the time for judgment on this world;	3814
	12:31	n the prince of this world will	3814
	13: 1	he n showed them the full extent	NIG
	13: 7	"You do not realize n what I am doing,	785
	13:14	N that I, your Lord and Teacher,	4036
	13:17	N that you know these things,	NIG
	13:19	"I am telling you n before it happens,	608+785
	13:31	"N is the Son of Man glorified	3814
	13:33	and just as I told the Jews, so I tell you:	785
	13:36	"Where I am going, you cannot follow n,	3814
	13:37	"Lord, why can't I follow you n?	785
	14: 7	From n on, you do know him	785
	14:29	I have told you n before it happens,	3814
	14:31	"Come n; let us leave.	1586
	15: 9	N remain in my love.	NIG
	15:22	N, however, they have no excuse	3814
	15:24	but they have seen these miracles,	3814
	16: 5	"N I am going to him who sent me,	3814
	16:11	prince of this world n stands condemned.	AIT
	16:12	more than you can n bear.	785
	16:22	So with you: N is your time of grief,	3814
	16:24	Until n you have not asked for anything	785
	16:28	I am leaving the world and going back to	4099
	16:29	"N you are speaking clearly and	3814
	16:30	we can see that you know all things and	3814
	17: 3	N this is eternal life:	1254
	17: 5	And n, Father, glorify me in your presence	3814
	17: 7	N they know that everything you have given me comes from you.	3814
	17:13	"I am coming to you n,	3814
	18: 2	N Judas, who betrayed him,	1254
	18:28	By n it was early morning,	1254
	18:36	But n my kingdom is from another place."	3814
	18:40	N Barabbas had taken part in a rebellion.	1254
	19:28	Later, knowing that all was n completed,	2453
	19:31	N it was the day of Preparation,	4036
	19:38	N Joseph was a disciple of Jesus,	NIG
	20:24	N Thomas (called Didymus),	1254
	21:14	This was n the third time Jesus appeared	2453
Ac	2: 5	N there were staying in Jerusalem	1254
	2:33	and has poured out what you n see	NIG
	3: 2	N a man crippled from birth	2779
	3:17	"N, brothers, I know that you acted	3814
	4:29	N, Lord, consider their threats	3814
	5: 1	N a man named Ananias,	1254
	6: 8	N Stephen, a man full of God's grace	1254
	7: 4	God sent him to this land where you are n	3814
	7:34	N come, I will send you back to Egypt.'	3814
	7:52	n you have betrayed and murdered him—	3814
Ac	8: 9	N for some time a man named Simon	1254
	8:26	N an angel of the Lord said to Philip,	1254
	9: 6	"N get up and go into the city,	247
	10: 5	N send men to Joppa to bring back	3814
	10:33	N we are all here in the presence of God	3814
	10:34	"I n realize how true it is that God does	AIT
	11:19	N those who had been scattered by	4036
	12:11	"N I know without a doubt that	3814
	12:20	they n joined together and sought	NIG
	13:11	N the hand of the Lord is against you.	3814
	13:31	They are n his witnesses to our people.	3814
	13:46	we n turn to the Gentiles.	2627
	14:26	to the grace of God for the work they had n	NIG
	15:10	N then, why do you try to test God	3814
	16:36	N you can leave.	3814
	16:37	And n do they want to get rid of us quietly?	3814
	17: 6	over the world have n come here,	2779
	17:11	N the Bereans were of more noble character	1254
	17:23	N what you worship as something unknown	4036
	17:30	n he commands all people everywhere to repent.	3814+3836
	18: 6	From n on I will go to the Gentiles."	3814
	19:18	Many of those who believed n came	NIG
	20:22	"And n, compelled by the Spirit,	3814
	20:25	"N I know that none of you	3814
	20:32	"N I commit you to God and to the word of his grace,	3814+3836
	22: 1	listen n to my defense."	3815
	22:16	And n what are you waiting for?	3814
	23:15	N then, you and the Sanhedrin petition	3814
	23:21	They are ready n,	3814
	24:13	the charges they are n making against me.	3815
	24:25	"That's enough for n!	2400+3814+3836
	25:10	"I am n standing before Caesar's court,	NIG
	26: 6	And n it is because of my hope	3814
	26:16	"N get up and stand on your feet.	247
	27: 9	because by n it was after the Fast,	2453
	27:22	But n I urge you to keep up your courage,	3814+3836
	27:34	"N I urge you to take some food.	1475
Ro	1:10	that n at last by God's will the way may be opened	2453+4537
	1:13	been prevented from doing so until n)	1306
	2: 2	N we know that God's judgment	1254
	2:15	and their thoughts n accusing,	NIG
	2:15	n even defending them.)	NIG
	2:17	N you, if you call yourself a Jew;	1254
	3:19	N we know that whatever the law says,	1254
	3:21	But n a righteousness from God,	3815
	4: 4	N when a man works,	1254
	5: 2	by faith into this grace in which we n stand.	AIT
	5: 9	Since we have n been justified	3814
	5:11	whom we have n received reconciliation.	3814
	6: 8	N if we died with Christ,	1254
	6:19	so n offer them in slavery	3814
	6:21	from the things you are n ashamed of?	3814
	6:22	But n that you have been set free from sin	3815
	7: 6	But n, by dying to what once bound us,	3815
	7:20	N if I do what I do not want to do,	1254
	8: 1	there is n no condemnation for those	3814
	8:17	N if we are children, then we are heirs—	1254
	11:17	the others and n share in the nourishing sap	NIG
	11:30	to God have n received mercy as a result	3814
	11:31	so they too have n become disobedient	3814
	11:31	in order that they too may n receive mercy	3814
	13:11	because our salvation is nearer n than	3814
	15:23	But n that there is no more place for me	3815
	15:25	N, however, I am on my way to Jerusalem	3815
	16:25	N to him who is able to establish you	1254
	16:26	but n revealed and made known through	3814
1Co	4: 2	N it is required that those who have been	3370
	4: 6	N, brothers, I have applied these things	1254
	5:11	But n I am writing that you must	3814
	7: 1	N for the matters you wrote about:	1254
	7: 8	N to the unmarried and the widows I say:	1254
	7:25	N about virgins: I have no command from	1254
	7:29	n on those who have wives should live as if they have none;	3370+3836
	8: 1	N about food sacrificed to idols:	1254
	10: 6	N these things occurred as examples	1254
	11: 3	N I want you to realize that the head	1254
	12: 1	N about spiritual gifts, brothers,	1254
	12: 7	N to each one the manifestation of	1254
	12:14	N the body is not made up of one part but	2779
	12:27	N you are the body of Christ,	1254
	12:31	n I will show you the most excellent way.	2285
	13:12	N we see but a poor reflection as in	785
	13:12	N I know in part;	785
	13:13	n these three remain: faith, hope and love.	3815
	14: 6	N, brothers, if I come to you and speak	3814
	15: 1	N, brothers, I want to remind you of	1254
	15:27	N when it says that "everything" has been	1254
	15:29	N if there is no resurrection,	2075
	16: 1	N about the collection for God's people:	1254
	16: 7	to see you n and make only a passing visit;	785
	16:12	N about our brother Apollos:	1254
	16:12	He was quite unwilling to go n,	3814
2Co	1:12	N this is our boast:	1142
	1:21	N it is God who makes both us	1254
	2: 7	N instead, you ought to forgive	6063
	2:12	N when I went to Troas to preach	1254
	3: 7	N if the ministry that brought death,	1254
	3:10	For what was glorious has no glory n	AIT
	3:17	N the Lord is the Spirit,	1254
	5: 1	N we know that if the earthly tent we live	1142
	5: 5	N it is God who has made us	1254
	5:16	So from n on we regard no one from	3814+3836
2Co	6: 2	I tell you, n is the time of God's favor,	3814
	6: 2	n is the day of salvation.	3814
	7: 9	yet n I am happy,	3814
	8: 1	And n, brothers, we want you to know	1254
	8:11	N finish the work,	3815
	8:22	and n even more so because	3815
	9:10	N he who supplies seed to the sower	1254
	12:14	N I am ready to visit you for the third time,	2627
	13: 2	I n repeat it while absent:	3814
	13: 7	N we pray to God that you will	1254
Gal	1: 9	As we have already said, so I n say again:	785
	1:10	Am I n trying to win the approval of men,	785
	1:23	"The man who formerly persecuted us is n	3814
	3: 3	are you n trying to attain your goal	3814
	3:25	N that faith has come,	1254
	4: 9	But n that you know God—	3814
	4:16	Have I n become your enemy	NIG
	4:20	be with you n and change my tone,	785
	4:25	N Hagar stands for Mount Sinai in Arabia	1254
	4:28	N you, brothers, like Isaac,	1254
	4:29	It is the same n.	3814
Eph	2: 2	the spirit who is n at work in those who	3814
	2:13	But n in Christ Jesus you who once were far away have been brought near	3815
	3: 5	to men in other generations as it has n	3814
	3:10	His intent was that n, through the church,	3814
	3:20	N to him who is able to do immeasurably	1254
	5: 8	but n you are light in the Lord.	3814
	5:24	N as the church submits to Christ,	247
Php	1: 5	in the gospel from the first day until n,	3814
	1:12	N I want you to know, brothers,	1254
	1:20	so that n as always Christ will be exalted	3814
	1:30	and hear that I still have.	3814
	2:12	but n much more in my absence—	3814
	3: 7	to my profit I n consider loss for the sake	AIT
	3:18	before and n say again even with tears,	3814
	4:18	I am amply supplied, n that I have received	NIG
Col	1:22	But n he has reconciled you	3815
	1:24	N I rejoice in what was suffered for you,	3814
	1:26	but is n disclosed to the saints.	3814
	3: 3	your life is n hidden with Christ in God.	AIT
	3: 8	But n you must rid yourselves	3815
1Th	3: 6	But Timothy has just n come to us	785
	3: 8	For n we really live,	3814
	3:11	N may our God and Father himself	1254
	4: 1	N we ask you and urge you in	NIG
	4: 9	N about brotherly love we do not need	1254
	5: 1	N, brothers, about times and dates we do	1254
	5:12	N we ask you, brothers,	1254
2Th	2: 6	And n you know what is holding him back,	3814
	2: 7	the one who n holds it back will continue	785
	3:16	N may the Lord of peace himself give you	1254
1Ti	1:17	N to the King eternal, immortal, invisible,	1254
	3: 2	N the overseer must be above reproach,	4036
2Ti	1: 5	I am persuaded, n lives in you also.	NIG
	1:10	but it has n been revealed through	3814
	4: 8	N there is in store for me the crown	3370
Phm	1: 9	and n also a prisoner of Christ Jesus—	3815
	1:11	but n he has become useful both to you and	3815
Heb	2: 9	n crowned with glory and honor	NIG
	4: 3	N we who have believed enter that rest,	1142
	7: 5	N the law requires the descendants	2779
	7:23	N there have been many of those priests,	3525
	9: 1	N the first covenant had regulations	4036
	9: 5	we cannot discuss these things in detail n.	3814
	9:15	n that he has died as a ransom	AIT
	9:24	n to appear for us in God's presence.	3814
	9:26	But n he has appeared once for all at	3815
	11: 1	N faith is being sure of what we hope for	1254
	12:26	but n he has promised,	3814
Jas	4:13	N listen, you who say,	3814
	5: 1	N listen, you rich people,	3814
1Pe	1: 6	though n for a little while you may have	785
	1: 8	and even though you do not see him n,	785
	1:12	when they spoke of the things that have n	3814
	1:22	N that you have purified yourselves	AIT
	2: 3	n that you have tasted that	1623
	2:10	N to you who believe,	4036
	2:10	but n you are the people of God;	3814
	2:10	but n you have received mercy.	3814
	2:25	but n you have returned to the Shepherd	3814
	3:21	and this water symbolizes baptism that n	3814
	4: 6	even to those who are n dead,	NIG
2Pe	1:12	firmly established in the truth you n have.	4205
	3: 1	this is n my second letter to you.	2453
	3:18	To him be glory both n and forever!	3814
1Jn	2:18	even n many antichrists have come.	3814
	2:28	And n, dear children, continue in him,	3814
	3: 2	Dear friends, n we are children of God,	3814
	4: 3	and even n is already in the world.	3814
2Jn	1: 5	And n, dear lady, I am not writing you	3814
Jude	1:25	before all ages, n and forevermore!	3814
Rev	1:19	what is n and what will take place later.	1639
	2:19	and that you are n doing more than you did	2274
	2:24	N I say to the rest of you in Thyatira,	1254
	11: 7	N when they have finished their testimony,	2779
	12:10	"N have come the salvation and the power	785
	14:13	the dead who die in the Lord from n on."	785
	17: 8	beast, which you saw, once was, n is not,	AIT
	17: 8	because he once was, n is not,	AIT
	17:11	The beast who once was, and n is not,	AIT
	21: 3	"N the dwelling of God is with men,	2627

NOWHERE (6)

Ref		Text	Strong's
Job	42:15	N in all the land were there found women	4202
Pr	19: 7	they are n to be found.	4202

Isa	59:15	Truth is **n** to be found,	6372
Jer	25:35	The shepherds *will* **have n** to flee,	6+4946
Mt	27:24	Pilate saw that *he* **was getting n**,	4029+6067
Jn	12:19	"See, *this is* **getting** us **n**.	4024+4029+6067

NOWHERE (Anglicized) See also NO PLACE

NUBIANS (1)
Da	11:43	with the Libyans and **N** in submission.	3934

NUGGETS (2)
Job	22:24	and assign your **n** to the dust,	1309
	28:6	and its dust contains **n of** gold.	2298

NULLIFIED (1) [ANNULLED, NULLIFY]
Nu	30:12	Her husband *has* **n** them,	7296

NULLIFIES (3) [NULLIFY]
Nu	30:8	*he* **n** the vow that obligates her or	7296
	30:12	But if her husband **n** them when	7296+7296
	30:15	*he* **n** them some time after he hears	7296+7296

NULLIFY (6) [NULLIFIED, NULLIFIES]
Nu	30:13	Her husband may confirm or **n** any vow she makes	7296
Mt	15:6	Thus *you* **n** the word of God for the sake	218
Mk	7:13	Thus *you* **n** the word of God	218
Ro	3:3	of faith **n** God's faithfulness?	2934
	3:31	*Do we*, then, **n** the law by this faith?	2934
1Co	1:28	to **n** the things that are,	2934

NUMBER (164) [NUMBERED, NUMBERING, NUMBERLESS, NUMBERS, NUMEROUS]
Ge	1:22	and **increase in n** and fill the water in	8049
	1:28	"Be fruitful and **increase in n**;	8049
	6:1	When men began to **increase in n** on	8045
	8:17	and be fruitful and **increase in n** upon it."	8049
	9:1	"Be fruitful and **increase in n** and fill	8049
	9:7	As for you, be fruitful and **increase in n**;	8049
	18:28	**n** of the righteous is five **less than**	2893
	26:24	I will bless you and *will* **increase the n**	8049
	34:30	We are few in **n**,	5031
	35:11	be fruitful and **increase in n**.	8049
	42:16	Send one of **your** *n* to get your brother;	AIT
	47:12	according to the **n** of their children.	7023
	47:27	were fruitful and **increased** greatly **in n**.	8049
Ex	5:8	to make the same *n* of bricks as before;	5504
	5:19	*to* **reduce the** *n* of bricks required of you	1757
	12:4	into account the **n** of people there are.	4831
	30:12	on them when *you* **n** them,	7212
Lev	25:15	the basis of the **n** of years since the Jubilee.	5031
	25:15	of the **n** of years left for harvesting crops.	5031
	25:16	really selling you is the **n** of crops.	5031
	25:50	on the rate paid to a hired man for that **n**	5031
	26:22	**make** you *so* **few in n** that your roads	5070
	27:18	according to the **n** of years that remain	7023
Nu	1:3	and Aaron *are to* **n** by their divisions all	7212
	1:21	The **n** from the tribe of Reuben was 46,500.	7212
	1:23	The **n** from the tribe of Simeon was 59,300.	7212
	1:25	The **n** from the tribe of Gad was 45,650.	7212
	1:27	The **n** from the tribe of Judah was 74,600.	7212
	1:29	**n** from the tribe of Issachar was 54,400.	7212
	1:31	**n** from the tribe of Zebulun was 57,400.	7212
	1:33	**n** from the tribe of Ephraim was 40,500.	7212
	1:35	**n** from the tribe of Manasseh was 32,200.	7212
	1:37	**n** from the tribe of Benjamin was 35,400.	7212
	1:39	**n** from the tribe of Dan was 62,700.	7212
	1:41	**n** from the tribe of Asher was 41,500.	7212
	1:43	**n** from the tribe of Naphtali was 53,400.	7212
	1:46	The total **n** was 603,550.	7212
	2:9	according to their divisions, **n** 186,400.	NIH
	2:16	according to their divisions **n** 151,450.	NIH
	2:24	according to their divisions, **n** 108,100.	NIH
	2:31	to the camp of Dan **n** 157,600.	NIH
	2:32	by their divisions, **n** 603,550.	7212
	3:22	The **n** of all the males a month old	5031
	3:28	The **n** of all the males a month old	5031
	3:34	The **n** of all the males a month old	5031
	3:39	The total **n** of Levites counted at	7212
	3:43	The total **n** of firstborn males a month old	7212
	3:46	the 273 firstborn Israelites who **exceed the n**	6369
	3:49	from those who **exceeded the n** redeemed	6369
	7:87	The **total** *n* of animals for the burnt offering	AIT
	7:88	The **total** *n* of animals for the sacrifice of	AIT
	23:10	of Jacob or the fourth part of Israel?	5031
	26:51	total **n** of the men of Israel was 601,730.	7212
	26:53	as an inheritance based on the **n** of names.	5031
	26:54	to receive its inheritance according to the **n**	7023
	29:18	according to the **n** specified.	5031
	29:21	according to the **n** specified.	5031
	29:24	according to the **n** specified.	5031
	29:27	according to the **n** specified.	5031
	29:30	according to the **n** specified.	5031
	29:33	according to the **n** specified.	5031
Dt	25:2	with the **n** of lashes his crime deserves,	5031
	28:62	will be left but **few in n**,	5071+5493
	28:63	to make you prosper and **increase in n**,	8049
	32:8	the peoples according to the **n** of the sons	5031

Jos	4:5	to the **n** of the tribes of the Israelites,	5031
	4:8	to the **n** of the tribes of the Israelites, as	5031
	11:4	with all their troops and a large **n** of horses	8041
1Sa	6:4	according to the **n** of the Philistine rulers,	5031
	6:18	And the **n** of the gold rats was according to	5031
	6:18	to the **n** of Philistine towns belonging to	NIH
	9:22	who were invited—about thirty in **n**.	NIH
	18:27	and **presented the full n** to the king so	4848
	23:13	David and his men, about six hundred in **n**,	NIH
2Sa	12:2	The rich man had a very **large n** of sheep	2221
	24:9	Joab reported the **n** of the fighting men	5031+5152
1Ki	3:8	a great people, too numerous to count or **n**.	4948
1Ch	7:40	The **n** of men ready for battle,	5031
	16:19	When they were but few in **n**, few indeed,	5031
	21:5	Joab reported the **n** of the fighting men	5031+5152
	22:16	and iron—craftsmen beyond **n**.	5031
	23:3	the total **n** of men was thirty-eight thousand.	5031
	23:31	before the LORD regularly in the *proper* **n**	5031
	24:4	A **larger** *n* of leaders were found	8041
	27:23	not take the **n** of the men twenty years old	5031
	27:24	and the **n** was not entered in the book of	5031
2Ch	14:13	a great **n** of Cushites fell that they could	NIH
	26:12	The total *n* of family leaders over	5031
	29:32	The *n* of burnt offerings	5031
	30:24	A **great n** of priests consecrated	4200+8044
Ezr	3:4	the required **n** of burnt offerings prescribed	5031
	8:34	Everything was accounted for by **n**	5031
Est	9:11	The **n** of those slain in the citadel	5031
Job	1:3	and had a large **n** of servants.	8041
	1:5	you have decreed the **n** of his months	5031
	36:26	The **n** of his years is past finding out.	5031
Ps	39:4	my life's end and the **n** of my days;	4500
	40:12	For troubles without **n** surround me;	5031
	90:12	Teach us to **n** our days aright,	4948
	104:25	teeming with creatures beyond **n**—	5031
	105:12	When they were but few in **n**, few indeed,	5031
	105:34	grasshoppers without **n**;	5031
	147:4	the **n** of the stars and calls them each	5031
SS	6:8	and virgins beyond **n**;	5031
Jer	2:32	Yet my people have forgotten me, days without **n**.	5031
	23:3	they will be fruitful and **increase in n**.	8049
	29:6	**Increase in n** there; do not decrease.	8049
	52:23	the **total** *n* of pomegranates above	AIT
	52:28	the **n** of the people Nebuchadnezzar carried	NIH
Eze	4:4	to bear their sin for the **n** of days you lie	5031
	4:5	the same **n** of days as the years of their sin.	5031
	36:10	and I *will* **multiply the n** of people	8049
	36:11	I *will* **increase the n** of men and animals	8049
	47:7	a great **n** of trees on each side of the river.	8041
Joel	1:6	powerful and without **n**;	5031
	2:11	his forces are **beyond n**,	4394+8041
Na	3:3	piles of dead, bodies without **n**,	7897
	3:16	*You have* **increased** *the* **n** of your merchants	8049
Zec	2:4	a city without walls because of the **great n**	8044
Mt	14:21	of those who ate was about five thousand,	NIG
	15:38	The **n** of those who ate was four thousand,	NIG
Mk	5:13	The herd, about two thousand in **n**,	NIG
	6:44	The **n** of the men who had eaten was five thousand.	NIG
Lk	5:6	a large **n** of fish that their nets began	4436
	6:17	and a great **n** of people from all over Judea,	4436
	23:27	A large **n** of people followed him,	4436
Jn	5:3	a great **n** of disabled people used to lie—	4436
	7:50	and who was one of **their own n**,	899
	21:6	the net in because of the **large n** of fish.	4436
Ac	1:17	of our **n** and shared in this ministry."	2935
	2:41	about three thousand were added to their **n**	NIG
	2:47	Lord added **to their n** daily those who were being saved.	899+2093+3836
	4:4	the **n** of men grew to about five thousand.	750
	5:14	in the Lord and were added to their **n**.	4436
	6:1	when the **n** of disciples was increasing,	NIG
	6:7	The **n** of disciples in Jerusalem increased	750
	6:7	and a large **n** of priests became obedient to	4063
	7:17	**n** of our people in Egypt greatly increased.	NIG
	11:21	and a great **n** of people believed and turned	750
	11:24	and a **great n** of people were brought to	2653
	14:1	a great **n** of Jews and Gentiles believed.	4436
	14:21	in that city and won a **large n** of disciples.	2653
	17:4	as did a large **n** of God-fearing Greeks and	4436
	17:12	as did also a **n** of prominent Greek women	NIG
	17:34	a woman named Damaris, and a **n** of others.	NIG
	19:19	A **n** who had practiced sorcery brought	2653
	20:30	from your own **n** men will arise and distort	NIG
	21:10	After we had been there a **n** of days,	4498
	24:10	"I know that for a **n** of years you have been	4498
Ro	9:27	the **n** of the Israelites be like the sand by	750
	11:25	the **full n** of the Gentiles has come in.	4445
1Co	11:30	and **n** of you have fallen asleep.	2653
2Ti	4:3	they will gather around them a great **n**	NIG
Rev	6:11	until the **n** of their fellow servants	NIG
	7:4	I heard the **n** of those who were sealed:	750
	9:16	The **n** of the mounted troops was two hundred million.	750
	9:16	I heard their **n**.	750
	13:17	the name of the beast or the **n** of his name.	750
	13:18	let him calculate the **n** of the beast,	750
	13:18	the number of the beast, for it is man's **n**.	750
	13:18	His **n** is 666.	750
	15:2	and his image and over the **n** of his name.	750
	20:8	**In n** they are like the sand on the seashore.	750+3836+4005

NUMBERED (34) [NUMBER]
Ge	46:26	**n** sixty-six persons.	3972

Ex	1:5	The descendants of Jacob **n** seventy in all;	2118
Nu	4:48	**n** 8,580.	7212
	25:9	but those who died in the plague **n** 24,000.	2118
	26:7	Reuben; those **n** were 43,730.	7212
	26:18	Gad; those **n** were 40,500.	7212
	26:22	Judah; those **n** were 76,500.	7212
	26:25	Issachar; those **n** were 64,300.	7212
	26:27	Zebulun; those **n** were 60,500.	7212
	26:34	Manasseh; those **n** were 52,700.	7212
	26:37	Ephraim; those **n** were 32,500.	7212
	26:41	Benjamin; those **n** were 45,600.	7212
	26:43	Shuhamite clans; and those **n** were 64,400.	7212
	26:47	Asher; those **n** were 53,400.	7212
	26:50	Naphtali; those **n** were 45,400.	7212
	26:62	Levites a month old or more **n** 23,000.	7212
1Sa	11:8	the men of Israel three hundred thousand	2118
	13:15	They **n** about six hundred.	NIH
1Ki	4:32	and his songs **n** a thousand and five.	2118
1Ch	7:2	in their genealogy **n** 22,600.	7212
	9:6	The people from Judah **n** 690.	NIH
	9:9	as listed in their genealogy, **n** 956.	NIH
	9:13	who were heads of families, **n** 1,760.	NIH
	9:22	to be gatekeepers at the thresholds **n** 212.	NIH
	25:7	skilled in music for the LORD—they **n** 288.	5031
Ezr	2:64	The whole company **n** 42,360,	285+3869
Ne	7:66	The whole company **n** 42,360,	285+3869
Job	25:3	Can his forces be **n**?	5031
Isa	53:12	and *was* **n** with the transgressors.	4948
La	4:18	Our end was near, our days *were* **n**,	4848
Da	5:26	God *has* **n** the days of your reign	10431
Mt	10:30	even the very hairs of your head are all **n**.	749
Lk	12:7	the very hairs of your head *are* all **n**.	749
	22:37	'And *he was* **n** with the transgressors';	3357

NUMBERING (4) [NUMBER]
1Ch	21:6	not include Levi and Benjamin *in the* **n**,	7212
	27:24	Wrath came on Israel on account of this **n**,	NIH
Ac	1:15	the believers (a group **n about** a hundred and twenty)	6059
Rev	5:11	angels, **n** thousands upon thousands,	750+1639

NUMBERLESS (1) [NUMBER]
Isa	48:19	your children like its **n** grains;	5054

NUMBERS (43) [NUMBER]
Ge	17:2	and you and *will* **greatly increase your n**."	8049
	17:20	and *will* **greatly increase his n**.	8049
	28:3	and make you fruitful and **increase your n**	8049
	48:4	and *will* **increase your n**.	8049
Ex	10:14	in every area of the country *in* great **n**.	3878+4394
Lev	26:9	and make you fruitful and **increase your n**,	8049
Nu	2:4	His division **n** 74,600.	7212
	2:6	His division **n** 54,400.	7212
	2:8	His division **n** 57,400.	7212
	2:11	His division **n** 46,500.	7212
	2:13	His division **n** 59,300.	7212
	2:15	His division **n** 45,650.	7212
	2:19	His division **n** 40,500.	7212
	2:21	His division **n** 32,200.	7212
	2:23	His division **n** 35,400.	7212
	2:26	His division **n** 62,700.	7212
	2:28	His division **n** 41,500.	7212
	2:30	His division **n** 53,400.	7212
Dt	1:10	The LORD your God *has* **increased** your **n**	8049
	7:13	and bless you and **increase your n**.	8049
	13:17	on you, and **increase your n**,	8049
	17:16	not **acquire great n** of horses for himself	8049
1Ki	1:19	He has sacrificed **great n** of cattle,	8044
	1:25	down and sacrificed **great n** of cattle,	8044
1Ch		These are the **n** of the men armed	5031
	22:4	Tyrians had brought **large n** of them	4200+8044
2Ch	15:9	for **large n** had come over to him	4200+8044
	16:8	Libyans a mighty army with **great n**	2221+4394
	26:11	to their **n** as mustered by Jeiel the secretary	5031
	30:5	It had not been celebrated in **large n**	4200+8044
	32:5	made **large n** of weapons and shields,	4200+8044
	32:29	acquired **great n** of flocks and herds,	4200+8044
Ps	107:38	and *their* **n** greatly **increased**,	8049
	107:39	Then *their* **n decreased**,	5070
Jer	3:16	your **n** have **increased greatly**	2256+7238+8049
	30:19	I *will* **add** to their **n**,	8049
Eze	37:26	I will establish them and **increase** their **n**,	8049
	47:9	There will be **large n** of fish,	8041
Ac	9:31	*it* grew in **n**, living in the fear of the Lord.	4437
	11:26	the church and taught great **n of people**.	4063
	16:5	in the faith and grew daily in **n**.	750
	19:26	and led astray **large n** of people here	2653
	28:23	and came in even **larger** *n* to the place	AIT

NUMEROUS (45) [NUMBER]
Ge	16:10	that they will be too **n** to count."	8044
	22:17	and **make** your descendants as **n** as	8049+8049
	26:4	I *will* **make** your descendants as **n** as	8049
Ex	1:7	and *became* exceedingly **n**,	6793
	1:9	Israelites have become **much too n** for us.	2256+6786+8041
	1:10	or they will become even more **n** and,	8049
	1:20	and *became* even more **n**.	6793
	5:5	"Look, the people of the land are now **n**,	8041
	23:29	and the wild animals too **n** for you.	8041
	32:13	'*I will* **make** your descendants as **n** as	8049
Nu	22:15	more **n** and more distinguished than	8041
Dt	2:10	a people strong and **n**,	8041
	2:21	They were a people strong and **n**,	8041

Dt	7: 7	you *were* more **n** than other peoples,	8045
	9:14	a nation stronger and more **n** than they."	8041
	10:22	the LORD your God has made you as **n** as	8044
	26: 5	and became a great nation, powerful and **n.**	8041
	28:62	as **n** as the stars in the sky will be left	4200+8044
	30: 5	more prosperous and **n** than your fathers.	8049
Jos	11: 4	as **n** as the sand on the seashore.	8044
	17:14	We are a **n** people and	8041
	17:15	"If you are so **n,**" Joshua answered,	8041
	17:17	"You are **n** and very powerful.	8041
1Sa	13: 5	soldiers as **n** as the sand on the seashore.	8044
2Sa	17:11	as **n** as the sand on the seashore—	8044
1Ki	3: 8	a great people, too **n** to count or number.	8044
	4:20	of Judah and Israel were as **n** as the sand on	8041
1Ch	4:27	so their entire clan *did* not *become* as **n** as	8049
	5:23	of the half-tribe of Manasseh *were* **n.**	8049
	23:17	but the sons of Rehabiah *were* very **n.**	8049
	27:23	the LORD had promised to **make** Israel as **n**	8049
2Ch	1: 9	over a people who are as **n** as the dust of	8041
Ne	5: 2	"We and our sons and daughters are **n;**	8041
	9:23	**made** their sons as **n** as the stars in the sky,	8049
Job	29:18	my days as **n** as the grains of sand.	8049
Ps	38:19	those who hate me without reason *are* **n.**	8045
	105:24	he **made** them too **n** for their foes,	6793
Jer	15: 8	I *will* make their widows more **n** than	6793
	46:23	*They are* more **n** than locusts,	8045
Eze	36:11	and they will be fruitful and **become n.**	8049
	36:37	I *will* **make** their people as **n** as sheep,	8049
	36:38	as the flocks for offerings at Jerusalem	NIH
Na	1:12	"Although they have allies and are **n,**	8041
Zec	10: 8	*they will* be as **n** as before.	8049
Heb	11:12	as **n** as the stars in the sky and as countless	4436

NUN (30)

Ex	33:11	but his young aide Joshua son of **N** did	5673
Nu	11:28	Joshua son of **N,**	5673
	13: 8	Hoshea son of **N;**	5673
	13:16	(Moses gave Hoshea son of **N** the name Joshua.)	5673
	14: 6	Joshua son of **N** and Caleb son of	5673
	14:30	son of Jephunneh and Joshua son of **N.**	5673
	14:38	of **N** and Caleb son of Jephunneh survived.	5673
	26:65	son of Jephunneh and Joshua son of **N.**	5673
	27:18	"Take Joshua son of **N,**	5673
	32:12	the Kenizzite and Joshua son of **N,**	5673
	32:28	to Eleazar the priest and Joshua son of **N**	5673
	34:17	Eleazar the priest and Joshua son of **N.**	5673
Dt	1:38	But your assistant, Joshua son of **N,**	5673
	31:23	gave this command to Joshua son of **N:**	5673
	32:44	of **N** and spoke all the words of this song	5673
	34: 9	of **N** was filled with the spirit of wisdom	5673
Jos	1: 1	the LORD said to Joshua son of **N,**	5673
	2: 1	of **N** secretly sent two spies from Shittim.	5673
	2:23	to Joshua son of **N** and told him everything	5673
	6: 6	of **N** called the priests and said to them,	5673
	14: 1	of **N** and the heads of the tribal clans	5673
	17: 4	Joshua son of **N,** and the leaders and said,	5673
	19:49	the Israelites gave Joshua son of **N**	5673
	19:51	Joshua son of **N** and the heads of	5673
	21: 1	Joshua son of **N,**	5673
	24:29	After these things, Joshua son of **N,**	5673
Jdg	2: 8	Joshua son of **N,** the servant of the LORD,	5673
1Ki	16:34	of the LORD spoken by Joshua son of **N.**	5673
1Ch	7:27	**N** his son and Joshua his son.	5673
Ne	8:17	the days of Joshua son of **N** until that day,	5673

NURSE (14) [NURSED, NURSING]

Ge	21: 7	to Abraham that Sarah *would* **n** children?	3567
	24:59	along with her **n** and Abraham's servant	4787
	35: 8	Now Deborah, Rebekah's **n,**	4787
Ex	2: 7	the Hebrew women to **n** the baby for you?"	3567
	2: 9	"Take this baby and **n** him for me,	3567
Nu	11:12	as a **n** carries an infant,	587
2Sa	4: 4	His **n** picked him up and fled,	587
1Ki	1:21	The next morning, I got up to **n** my son—	3567
2Ki	11: 2	She put him and his **n** in a bedroom	4787
	11: 3	remained hidden with his **n** at the temple	2023S
2Ch	22:11	about to be murdered and put him and his **n**	4787
Isa	66:11	For *you will* **n** and be satisfied	3567
	66:12	*you will* **n** and be carried on her arm	3567
La	4: 3	jackals offer their breasts *to* **n** their young,	3567

NURSED (8) [NURSE]

Ex	2: 9	So the woman took the baby and **n** him.	3567
1Sa	1:23	the woman stayed at home and **n** her son	3567
Job	3:12	and breasts that *I might be* **n?**	3567
SS	8: 1	who was **n** at my mother's breasts!	3437
Isa	60:16	and be **n** at royal breasts.	3567
Mk	6:19	So Herodias **n** a grudge against John	1923
Lk	11:27	the mother who gave you birth and **n** you."	2558
	23:29	and the breasts that never **n!'**	5555

NURSING (6) [NURSE]

Ge	33:13	the ewes and cows *that are* **n** their **young.**	6402
Isa	49:23	and their queens your **n** mothers.	4787
Joel	2:16	gather the children, *those* **n** at the breast.	3437
Mt	24:19	for pregnant women and **n** mothers!	2558
Mk	13:17	for pregnant women and **n** mothers!	2558
Lk	21:23	for pregnant women and **n** mothers!	2558

NURTURED (1) [WELL-NURTURED]

La	4: 5	Those **n** in purple now lie on ash heaps.	587

NUT (1) [NUTS]

SS	6:11	I went down to the grove of **n** trees to look	100

NUTS (1) [NUT]

Ge	43:11	*some* pistachio **n** and almonds.	1063

NYMPHA (1)

Col	4:15	and to **N** and the church in her house.	3809

O

O (978) [OH] See Index of Articles Etc.

OAK (14) [OAKS]

Ge	35: 4	Jacob buried them under the **o** at Shechem.	461
	35: 8	and was buried under the **o** below Bethel.	473
Jos	24:26	a large stone and set it up there under the **o**	464
Jdg	6:11	the LORD came and sat down under the **o**	461
	6:19	and offered them to him under the **o.**	461
2Sa	18: 9	under the thick branches of a large **o,**	461
	18:10	"I just saw Absalom hanging in an **o** tree."	461
	18:14	while Absalom was still alive in the **o** tree.	461
1Ki	13:14	He found him sitting under an **o** tree	461
Isa	1:30	You will be like an **o** with fading leaves,	461
	6:13	But as the terebinth **o** leave stumps	473
	44:14	or perhaps took a cypress or an **o.**	473
Eze	6:13	and every leafy **o**—	461
Hos	4:13	under **o,** poplar and terebinth,	473

OAKS (9) [OAK]

Ps	29: 9	The voice of the LORD twists the **o**	381
	56: T	To [the tune of] "A Dove on Distant **O.**"	381
Isa	1:29	the **sacred o** in which you have delighted;	381
	2:13	tall and lofty, and all the **o** *of* Bashan,	473
	57: 5	the **o** and under every spreading tree;	381
	61: 3	They will be called **o** *of* righteousness,	381
Eze	27: 6	Of **o** from Bashan they made your oars;	473
Am	2: 9	as the cedars and strong as the **o.**	473
Zec	11: 2	Wail, **o** *of* Bashan;	473

OARS (4) [OARSMEN]

Isa	33:21	No galley with **o** will ride them,	8868
Eze	27: 6	Of oaks from Bashan they made your **o;**	5415
	27:29	the **o** will abandon their ships;	5414
Mk	6:48	He saw the disciples straining at the **o,**	1785

OARSMEN (2) [OARS]

Eze	27: 8	Men of Sidon and Arvad were your **o;**	8763
	27:26	Your **o** take you out to the high seas.	8763

OATH (128) [OATHS]

Ge	14:22	I have **raised** my hand to the LORD, God Most High, Creator of heaven and earth, **and** *have* **taken an o**	8123
	21:31	because the two men **swore an o** there.	8678
	24: 7	who spoke to me and **promised** me on **o,**	8678
	24: 8	you will be released from this **o** *of* mine.	8652
	24: 9	of his master Abraham and **swore an o**	8678
	24:37	my master **made** me **swear an o,**	8678
	24:41	be released from my **o** even if they refuse	460
	24:41	you will be released from my **o.'**	460
	25:33	So he **swore an o** to him,	8678
	26: 3	the **o** I swore to your father Abraham.	8652
	26:31	Early the next morning *the men* **swore an o**	8678
	31:53	So Jacob **took an o** in the name of the Fear	8678
	50: 5	'My father **made** me **swear an o**	8678
	50:24	to the land he **promised on o** to Abraham,	8678
	50:25	Joseph **made** the sons of Israel **swear an o**	8678
Ex	13:11	as he **promised on o** to you	8678
	13:19	**made** the sons of Israel **swear an o.**	8678+8678
	22:11	the taking of an **o** *before* the LORD that	8652
	33: 1	up to the land I **promised on o** to Abraham,	8678
Lev	5: 4	'Or if a person thoughtlessly **takes an o**	8678
Nu	5:19	priest *shall* put the woman **under o**	8678
	5:21	priest *is to* put the woman under this curse of the **o**—	8652+8678
	11:12	to the land *you* **promised on o**	8678
	14:16	into the land *he* **promised** them **on o;**	8678
	14:23	the land I **promised on o**	8678
	30: 2	or **takes an o** to obligate himself	8652+8678
	30:10	or obligates herself by a pledge under **o**	8652
	32:10	that day and he **swore** *this* **o:**	8678
	32:11	the land I **promised on o** to Abraham, Isaac	8678
Dt	4:31	**confirmed** to them by **o.**	8678
	6:18	the good land that the LORD **promised on o**	8678
	6:23	give us the land that he **promised on o**	8678
	7: 8	and kept the **o** he swore to your forefathers	8652
	8: 1	the land that the LORD **promised on o**	8678
	13:17	as *he* **promised on o** to your forefathers,	8678
	19: 8	as *he* **promised on o** to your forefathers,	8678
	26:15	as *you* **promised** us **on o** to our fathers,	8678
	28: 9	as *he* **promised** you **on o,**	8678

Dt	29:12	with you this day and sealing with an **o,**	460
	29:14	I am making this covenant, with its **o,**	460
	29:19	a person hears the words of this **o,**	460
	31:20	land I **promised on o** to their forefathers,	8678
	31:21	into the land I **promised** them **on o."**	8678
	31:23	into the land I **promised** them **on o,**	8678
	34: 4	the land I **promised on o** to Abraham,	8678
Jos	2:17	"This **o** you made us swear will not	8652
	2:20	be released from the **o** you made us swear."	8652
	6:22	in accordance with *your* **o** to her."	8678
	6:26	Joshua **pronounced** *this* **solemn o:**	8678
	9:15	the leaders of the assembly **ratified** it by **o.**	8652
	9:18	the leaders of the assembly *had* **sworn an o**	8678
	9:19	"We **have given** them *our* **o** by the LORD,	8678
	9:20	not fall on us for breaking the **o** we swore	8652
Jdg	21: 1	men of Israel *had* **taken an o** at Mizpah:	8678
	21: 5	a solemn **o** that anyone who failed	8652
	21: 7	since we **have taken an o** by the LORD not	8678
	21:18	since *we* Israelites **have taken** *this* **o:**	8678
1Sa	14:24	**bound** the people **under an o,**	457
	14:26	because they feared the **o.**	8652
	14:27	**bound** the people **with the o,**	8678
	14:28	**bound** the army **under a strict o,**	8678+8678
	19: 6	Saul listened to Jonathan and **took** *this* **o:**	8678
	20: 3	But David **took an o** and said,	8678
	20:17	And Jonathan had David reaffirm his **o** out	8678
	24:22	So David **gave** *his* **o** to Saul.	8678
2Sa	3: 9	the LORD **promised** him on **o**	8678
	3:35	but David **took an o,** saying,	8678
	19:23	And the king **promised** him on **o.**	8678
	21: 7	of the **o** *before* the LORD between David	8652
1Ki	1:29	The king then **took an o:**	8678
	2:43	not keep your **o** *to* the LORD and obey	8652
	8:31	and is required to **take an o** and he comes	457
	8:31	an oath and he comes and **swears the o**	457
2Ki	11: 4	a covenant with them and **put** them **under o**	8678
	25:24	Gedaliah **took an o** to reassure them	8678
1Ch	16:16	the **o** he **swore** to Isaac.	8652
2Ch	6:22	and is required to **take an o** and he comes	457
	6:22	an oath and he comes and **swears the o**	457
	15:14	*They* **took an o** to the LORD	8678
	15:15	All Judah rejoiced about the **o**	8652
	36:13	**made** him **take an o**	8678
Ezr	10: 5	**put** the leading priests and Levites and all Israel **under o**	8678
	10: 5	And *they* **took the o.**	8678
Ne	5:12	**made** the nobles and officials **take an o**	8678
	6:18	many in Judah were **under** o to him,	1251+8652
	10:29	and bind themselves with a curse and an **o**	8652
	13:25	**made** them **take an o**	8678
Ps	15: 4	who keeps *his* **o** even when it hurts,	8678
	95:11	So I **declared** on **o** in my anger,	8678
	105: 9	the **o** he swore to Isaac.	8652
	119:106	I **have taken an o** and confirmed it,	8678
	132: 2	He **swore an o** to the LORD and made	8678
	132:11	The LORD **swore an o** to David,	8678
	132:11	a sure **o** that he will not revoke:	NIH
Pr	29:24	*he is* **put under** o and dare not testify.	460+9048
Ecc	8: 2	because you took an **o** *before* God.	8652
Isa	65:16	he *who* **takes an o** in the land will swear by	8678
Jer	11: 5	the **o** I swore to your forefathers,	8652
	38:16	But King Zedekiah **swore** *this* **o** secretly	8678
	40: 9	**took an o** to reassure them and their men.	8678
Eze	16:59	I **gave** you my **solemn o**	8678
	16:59	because you have despised my **o**	460
	17:13	putting him under **o.**	460
	17:16	whose **o** he despised	460
	17:18	the **o** by breaking the covenant.	460
	17:19	down on his head my **o** that he despised	460
Mic	7:20	as *you* **pledged** on **o** to our fathers	8678
Mt	5:33	'Do not **break** *your* **o,**	2155
	14: 7	with an **o** to give her whatever she asked.	3992
	23:16	*he is* **bound** by his **o.'**	4053
	23:18	*he is* **bound** by his **o.'**	4053
	26:63	"I **charge** you **under o** by the living God:	2019
	26:72	He denied it again, with an **o:**	3992
Mk	6:23	**promised** her **with** an **o,**	3923
Lk	1:73	the **o** he **swore** to our father Abraham:	3992
Ac	2:30	and knew that God had **promised** him *on* **o**	3992
	23:12	**bound** themselves with an **o**	354
	23:14	"We **have taken a solemn o** not	353+354
	23:21	They **have taken an o** not to eat or drink	354
Heb	3:11	So I **declared** on **o** in my anger,	3923
	4: 3	"So I **declared** on **o** in my anger,	3923
	6:16	the **o** confirms what is said and puts an end	3992
	6:17	he confirmed it *with* an **o.**	3992
	7:20	And it was not without an **o!**	3993
	7:20	Others became priests without any **o,**	3993
	7:21	a priest with an **o** when God said to him:	3993
	7:22	Because of this **o,** Jesus has become	NIG
	7:28	but the **o,** which came after the law,	3993

OATHS (8) [OATH]

Dt	6:13	serve him only and **take** *your* **o** in his name.	8678
	10:20	to him and **take** *your* **o** in his name.	8678
Ecc	9: 2	as it is with those *who* **take o,**	8678
Isa	48: 1	you who **take o** in the name of the LORD	8678
Hos	10: 4	**take** false **o** and make agreements;	457
Mt	5:33	but keep the **o** you have made to the Lord.'	3992
	14: 9	but because of his **o** and his dinner guests,	3992
Mk	6:26	but because of his **o** and his dinner guests,	3992

OBADIAH (22)

1Ki	18: 3	and Ahab had summoned **O,**	6282
	18: 3	(**O** was a devout believer in the LORD.	6282

1Ki	18: 4	O had taken a hundred prophets	6282
	18: 5	Ahab had said to O,	6282
	18: 6	Ahab going in one direction and O	6282
	18: 7	As O was walking along, Elijah met him.	6282
	18: 7	O recognized him, bowed down to	NIH
	18: 9	"What have I done wrong," asked O,	NIH
	18:16	So O went to meet Ahab and told him,	6282
1Ch	3:21	of Arnan, of O and of Shecaniah.	6281
	7: 3	Michael, O, Joel and Isshiah.	6281
	8:38	Bokeru, Ishmael, Sheariah, O and Hanan.	6281
	9:16	O son of Shemaiah, the son of Galal,	6281
	9:44	Bokeru, Ishmael, Sheariah, O and Hanan.	6281
	12: 9	O the second in command, Eliab the third,	6281
	27:19	Ishmaiah son of O;	6281
2Ch	17: 7	O, Zechariah, Nethanel and Micaiah	6281
	34:12	to direct them were Jahath and O,	6282
Ezr	8: 9	O son of Jehiel, and with him 218 men;	6281
Ne	10: 5	Harim, Meremoth, O,	6281
	12:25	Mattaniah, Bakbukiah, O, Meshullam,	6281
Ob	1: 1	The vision of O.	6281

OBAL (2)

Ge	10:28	O, Abimael, Sheba,	6382
1Ch	1:22	O, Abimael, Sheba,	6382

OBED (13)

Ru	4:17	And they named him O.	6381
	4:21	Boaz the father of O,	6381
	4:22	O the father of Jesse.	6381
1Ch	2:12	the father of O and Obed the father of Jesse.	6381
	2:12	the father of Obed and O the father of Jesse.	6381
	2:37	Ephlal the father of O,	6381
	2:38	O the father of Jehu,	6381
	11:47	Eliel, O and Jaasiel the Mezobaite.	6381
	26: 7	Othni, Rephael, O and Elzabad;	6381
2Ch	23: 1	Azariah son of O, Maaseiah son of Adaiah,	6381
Mt	1: 5	Boaz the father of O,	2725
	1: 5	O the father of Jesse,	2725
Lk	3:32	the son of O, the son of Boaz,	2725

OBED-EDOM (19)

2Sa	6:10	he took it aside to the house of O	6273
	6:11	the house of O the Gittite for three months,	6273
	6:12	the household of O and everything he has,	6273
	6:12	up the ark of God from the house of O to	6273
1Ch	13:13	he took it aside to the house of O	6273
	13:14	of God remained with the family of O	6273
	15:18	Mikneiah, O and Jeiel, the gatekeepers.	6273
	15:21	O, Jeiel and Azaziah were to play the harps,	6273
	15:24	O and Jehiah were also to be doorkeepers	6273
	15:25	of the LORD from the house of O	6273
	16: 5	Mattithiah, Eliab, Benaiah, O and Jeiel.	6273
	16:38	He also left O and his sixty-eight associates	6273
	16:38	O son of Jeduthun, and also Hosah,	6273
	26: 4	O also had sons:	6273
	26: 5	(For God had blessed O.)	2257S
	26: 8	All these were descendants of O;	6273
	26: 8	descendants of O, 62 in all.	6273
	26:15	The lot for the South Gate fell to O,	6273
2Ch	25:24	of God that had been in the care of O,	6273

OBEDIENCE (17) [OBEY]

Ge	49:10	and the o of the nations is his.	3682
Jdg	2:17	the way of o to the LORD's commands.	9048
1Ch	21:19	up in o to the word that Gad had spoken in	928
2Ch	31:21	in the service of God's temple and in o to	928
Pr	30:17	that scorns o to a mother,	3682
Lk	23:56	on the Sabbath in o to the commandment.	2848
Ac	21:24	that you yourself are living in o to the law.	5875
Ro	1: 5	the Gentiles to the o that comes from faith.	5633
	5:19	through the o of the one man the many will	5633
	6:16	or to o, which leads to righteousness?	5633
	16:19	Everyone has heard about your o,	5633
2Co	9:13	for the o that accompanies your confession	5717
	10: 6	once your o is complete.	5633
Phm	1:21	Confident of your o, I write to you,	5633
Heb	5: 8	he learned o from what he suffered	5633
1Pe	1: 2	for o to Jesus Christ and sprinkling	5633
2Jn	1: 6	that we walk in o to his commands.	2848

OBEDIENT (10) [OBEY]

Dt	30:17	if your heart turns away and you are not o,	9048
Isa	1:19	If you are willing and o,	9048
Lk	2:51	to Nazareth with them and was o to them.	5718
Ac	6: 7	and a large number of priests became o to	5634
2Co	2: 9	to see if you would stand the test and be	5675
	7:15	when he remembers that you were all o,	5633
	10: 5	every thought to make it o to Christ.	5633
Php	2: 8	he humbled himself and became o	5675
Tit	3: 1	and authorities, to be o, to be ready	4272
1Pe	1:14	As o children, do not conform to	5633

OBEY (165) [OBEDIENCE, OBEDIENT, OBEYED, OBEYING, OBEYS]

Ex	5: 2	the LORD, that I should o him and let Israel go?	928+7754+9048
	12:24	"O these instructions as a lasting ordinance	9068
	19: 5	if you o me fully and keep my covenant,	928+7754+9048+9048
	24: 7	"We will do everything the LORD has said; we will o."	9048
	34:11	O what I command you today.	9068
Lev	18: 4	You must o my laws and be careful	6913
Lev	25:18	and be careful to o my laws,	6913
	26: 3	and are careful to o my commands,	6913
Nu	15:39	that you may o them and	6913
	15:40	to o all my commands and will	6913
	27:20	the whole Israelite community will o him.	9048
Dt	4:30	to the LORD your God and o him.	928+7754+9048
	5:27	We will listen and o."	6913
	6: 3	and be careful to o so that it may go well	6913
	6:24	to o all these decrees and to fear the LORD	6913
	6:25	if we are careful to o all this law before	6913
	9:23	You did not trust him or o him.	928+7754+9048
	11:13	So if you faithfully o all	9048+9048
	11:27	the blessing if you o the commands of	9048
	11:32	be sure that you o all the decrees	6913
	12:28	to o all these regulations I am giving you,	6913
	13: 4	Keep his commands and o him;	928+7754+9048
	13:18	you o the LORD your God	928+7754+9048
	15: 5	if only you fully o the LORD your God	928+7754+9048+9048
	21:18	does not o his father and mother	928+7754+9048
	21:20	He will not o us.	928+7754+9048
	26:17	and that you will o him.	928+7754+9048
	27:10	O the LORD your God	928+7754+9048
	28: 1	If you fully o the LORD your God	928+7754+9048+9048
	28: 2	and accompany you if you o	928+7754+9048
	28:15	you do not o the LORD your God	928+7754+9048
	28:45	not o the LORD your God and	928+7754+9048
	28:62	not o the LORD your God.	928+7754+9048
	30: 2	to the LORD your God and o him	928+7754+9048
	30: 8	You will again o the LORD	928+7754+9048
	30:10	if you o the LORD your God	928+7754+9048
	30:12	and proclaim it to us so we may o it?"	6913
	30:13	and proclaim it to us so we may o it?"	6913
	30:14	and in your heart so you may o it.	6913
	32:46	to o carefully all the words of this law.	6913
Jos	1: 7	Be careful to o all the words of this	6913
	1:17	we fully obeyed Moses, so we will o you.	9048
	1:18	and does not o your words,	9048
	22: 5	to walk in all his ways, to o his commands,	9068
	23: 6	to o all that is written in the Book of	6913
	24:24	the LORD our God and o him."	928+7754+9048
Jdg	3: 4	the Israelites to see whether they would o	9048
1Sa	12:14	If you fear the LORD and serve and o him	928+7754+9048
	12:15	But if you do not o the LORD,	928+7754+9048
	15:19	Why did you not o the LORD?	928+7754+9048
	15:20	"But I did o the LORD," Saul said	928+7754+9048
	15:22	To o is better than sacrifice,	9048
	28:18	Because you did not o the LORD	928+7754+9048
2Sa	22:45	as soon as they hear me, they o me.	9048
1Ki	2:42	'What you say is good. I will o.'	9048
	2:43	not keep your oath to the LORD and o	NIH
	3:14	if you walk in my ways and o my statutes	9048
	6:12	and keep all my commands and o them,	928+2143
	8:61	to live by his decrees and o his commands,	9068
2Ki	10: 6	"If you are on my side and will o me,	4200+7754+9048
	17:13	that I commanded your fathers to o and	NIH
1Ch	28:21	the people will o your every command."	4200
2Ch	14: 4	and to o his laws and commands.	6913
	34:31	and to o the words of the covenant written	6913
Ezr	7:26	Whoever does not o the law of your written	10522
Ne	1: 5	who love him and o his commands,	9068
	1: 9	if you return to me and o my commands,	2256+6913+9048
	9:16	and did not o your commands.	9048
	10:29	the servant of God and to o carefully all	6913
Est	3: 8	of all other people and who do not o	6913
Job	36:11	If they o and serve him,	9048
Ps	18:44	As soon as they hear me, they o me;	9048
	103:18	and remember to o his precepts.	6913
	103:20	who o his word.	928+7754+9048
	106:25	They grumbled in their tents and did not o	928+7754+9048
	119: 8	I will o your decrees;	9068
	119:17	I will o your word.	9068
	119:34	and I will keep your law and o it	9068
	119:44	I will always o your law,	9068
	119:56	I o your precepts.	5915
	119:57	I have promised to o your words.	9068
	119:60	and not delay to o your commands.	9068
	119:67	but now I o your word.	9068
	119:88	and I will o the statutes of your mouth.	9068
	119:100	for I o your precepts.	5915
	119:101	so that I might o your word.	9068
	119:129	therefore I o them.	5915
	119:134	that I may o your precepts.	5915
	119:145	O LORD, and I will o your decrees.	5915
	119:158	for they do not o your word.	9068
	119:167	I o your statutes, for I love them greatly.	9068
	119:168	I o your precepts and your statutes,	9068
Pr	5:13	I would not o my teachers or	928+7754+9048
Ecc	8: 2	O the king's command, I say,	9068
Isa	42:24	they did not o his law.	9048
Jer	7:23	O me, and I will be your God	928+7754+9048
	11: 3	'Cursed is the man who does not o	9048
	11: 4	'O me and do everything I command you,	928+7754+9048
	11: 7	again and again, saying, "O me."	928+7754+9048
	17:24	But if you are careful to o me,	9048+9048
	17:27	But if you do not o me to keep the Sabbath day holy by	9048
	18:10	in my sight and does not o me,	9048
	26:13	and o the LORD your God.	928+7754+9048
	32:23	but they did not o you or follow your law;	928+7754+9048
Jer	35:13	not learn a lesson and o my words?'	9048
	35:14	because they o their forefather's command.	9048
	38:20	"O the LORD by doing what I tell you.	9048
	40: 3	sinned against the LORD and did not o him.	928+7754+9048
	42: 6	we will o the LORD our God,	928+7754+9048
	42: 6	for we will o the LORD our God."	10725
Da	7:21	and all rulers will worship and o him.'	10725
	9: 4	with all who love him and o his commands,	9068
	9:11	turned away, refusing to o you.	928+7754+9048
Joel	2:11	and mighty are those who o his command.	6913
Zec	6:15	This will happen if you diligently o the LORD your God."	928+7754+9048+9048
Mt	8:27	Even the winds and the waves o him!"	5634
	19:17	want to enter life, o the commandments."	5498
	23: 3	So you must o them	5498
	28:20	to o everything I have commanded you.	5498
Mk	1:27	to evil spirits and they o him."	5634
	4:41	Even the wind and the waves o him!"	5634
Lk	8:25	the winds and the water, and they o him."	5634
	11:28	who hear the word of God and o it."	5875
	17: 6	and it will o you.	5634
Jn	14:15	you love me, you will o what I command.	5498
	14:23	he will o my teaching.	5498
	14:24	not love me will not o my teaching.	5498
	15:10	If you o my commands,	5498
	15:20	they will o yours also.	5498
Ac	4:19	in God's sight to o you rather than God.	201
	5:29	"We must o God rather than men!	4272
	5:32	whom God has given to those who o him."	4272
	7:39	"But our fathers refused to o him.	1181+5675
	15: 5	be circumcised and required to o the law	5498
	16: 4	and elders in Jerusalem for the people to o.	5875
Ro	2:13	but it is those who o the law who will	4475
	6:12	so that you o its evil desires.	5634
	6:16	to o him as slaves, you are slaves to the one	5633
	6:16	you are slaves to the one whom you o—	5634
	15:18	the Gentiles to o God by what I have said	5633
	16:26	that all nations might believe and o him—	5633
Gal	5: 3	be circumcised that he is obligated to o	4472
	6:13	even those who are circumcised o the law,	5875
Eph	6: 1	Children, o your parents in the Lord,	5634
	6: 5	o your earthly masters with respect	5634
	6: 5	just as you would o Christ.	NIG
	6: 6	O them not only to win their favor	NIG
Col	3:20	Children, o your parents in everything,	5634
	3:22	o your earthly masters in everything;	5634
2Th	1: 8	and do not o the gospel of our Lord Jesus.	5634
	3:14	If anyone does not o our instruction	5634
1Ti	3: 4	his children o him with proper respect.	2400+5717
Heb	5: 9	source of eternal salvation for all who o him	5219
	13:17	O your leaders and submit to their	4275
	13:17	O them so that their work will be a joy,	NIG
Jas	3: 3	the mouths of horses to make them o us,	4275
1Pe	4:17	for those who do not o the gospel of God?	578
1Jn	2: 3	to know him if we o his commands.	5498
	3:22	because we o his commands	5498
	3:24	Those who o his commands live in him,	5498
	5: 3	This is love for God: to o his commands.	5498
Rev	3: 3	what you have received and heard; o it,	5498
	12:17	those who o God's commandments	5498
	14:12	of the saints who o God's commandments	5498

OBEYED (48) [OBEY]

Ge	22:18	because you have o me."	928+7754+9048
	26: 5	Abraham o me and kept my requirements,	928+7754+9048
	28: 7	and that Jacob had o his father and mother	9048
Nu	9:19	the Israelites o the LORD's order and did	9068
	9:23	They o the LORD's order,	9068
Dt	26:14	I have o the LORD my God;	928+7754+9048
Jos	1:17	Just as we fully o Moses, so we will obey	9048
	5: 6	since they had not o the LORD.	928+7754+9048
	22: 2	and you have o me	928+7754+9048
1Sa	28:21	your maidservant has o you.	928+7754+9048
1Ki	12:24	So they o the word of the LORD	9048
	20:36	Because you have not o the LORD	928+7754+9048
2Ki	18:12	because they had not o the LORD	928+7754+9048
	22:13	against us because our fathers have not o	9048
1Ch	29:23	He prospered and all Israel o him.	9048
2Ch	11: 4	So they o the words of the LORD	9048
Ne	9:16	We have not o the commands,	9068
Est	1:15	She has not o the command of King Xerxes	6913
Ps	119: 4	laid down precepts that are to be fully o.	9068
	119:136	for your law is not o.	9068
Jer	3:13	and have not o me,'" declares the LORD.	928+7754+9048
	3:25	from our youth till this day we have not o the LORD our God.	928+7754+9048
	7:28	the nation that has not o the LORD its God	928+7754+9048
	9:13	they have not o me or followed	928+7754+9048
	22:21	you have not o me.	928+7754+9048
	34:17	You have not o me;	9048
	35: 8	We have o everything our forefather Jonadab son of Recab	928+7754+9048
	35:10	have fully o everything our forefather Jonadab commanded us.	2256+6913+9048
	35:14	yet you have not o me.	9048
	35:16	but these people have not o me.'	9048
	35:18	'You have o the command	9048
	42:21	not o the LORD your God	928+7754+9048
	44:23	and have not o him or followed	928+7754+9048
Eze	20:24	not o my laws but had rejected my decrees	6913
Da	9:10	we have not o the LORD our God	928+7754+9048

Da	9:14	yet *we* have not o him.	928+7754+9048
Hos	9:17	because *they* have not o him;	9048
Jnh	3: 3	Jonah o the word of the LORD and	3869+7756
Mic	5:15	upon the nations that *have* not o me."	9048
Hag	1:12	and the whole remnant of the people o	9048
Jn	15:10	just as I *have* o my Father's commands	5498
	15:20	If *they* o my teaching,	5498
	17: 6	to me and *they* have o your word.	5498
Ac	7:53	into effect through angels but *have* not o it."	5875
Ro	6:17	*you* wholeheartedly o the form of teaching	5634
Php	2:12	my dear friends, as *you have* always o—	5634
Heb	11: 8	o and went, even though he did not know	5634
1Pe	3: 6	who o Abraham and called him her master.	5634

OBEYING (6) [OBEY]

Dt	8:20	so you will be destroyed for not o	928+7754+9048
1Sa	15:22	and sacrifices as much as *in* o the voice of	9048
Ps	119: 5	my ways were steadfast *in* o your decrees!	9068
Jer	16:12	of his evil heart instead of o me.	9048
Gal	5: 7	in on you and kept you from o the truth?	4275
1Pe	1:22	Now that you have purified yourselves by o	5633

OBEYS (12) [OBEY]

Lev	18: 5	for the man who o them will live by them.	6913
Ne	9:29	by which a man will live if he o them.	6913
Pr	19:16	*He who* o instructions guards his life,	9068
Ecc	8: 5	*Whoever* o his command will come	9068
Isa	50:10	the LORD and o the word of his servant?	9048
Eze	20:11	for the man *who* o them will live by them.	6913
	20:13	the man who o them will live by them.	6913
	20:21	the man who o them will live by them—	6913
Zep	3: 2	*She* o no one, she accepts no correction.	928+7754+9048
Jn	14:21	Whoever has my commands and o them,	5498
Ro	2: 27	and yet o the law will condemn you who,	5464
1Jn	2: 5	But if anyone o his word,	5498

OBIL (1)

1Ch	27:30	O the Ishmaelite was in charge of the camels	201

OBEISANCE (KJV) See BOWED

OBJECT (35) [OBJECTED, OBJECTION, OBJECTIONS, OBJECTS]

Nu	35:16	" 'If a man strikes someone with an iron o	3998
	35:18	Or if anyone has a wooden o *in* his hand	3998
Dt	28:37	an o of scorn and ridicule to all the nations	5442
1Ki	9: 7	and an o of ridicule among all peoples.	9110
2Ch	7:20	and an o of ridicule among all peoples.	9110
	29: 8	he has made them an o of dread and horror	2317
	30: 7	so that he made them an o of horror,	9014
Ps	109:25	I am an o of scorn to my accusers;	3075
Jer	18:16	an o of lasting scorn;	9241
	19: 8	and make it an o of scorn;	9240
	22:28	broken pot, an o no one wants?	3998
	24: 9	an o of ridicule and cursing;	9110
	25: 9	and make them an o of horror and scorn,	9014
	25:18	and an o of horror and scorn and cursing;	9014
	26: 6	an o of cursing among all the nations of	7839
	29:18	of the earth and an o of cursing and horror,	460
	42:18	You will be an o of cursing and horror,	460
	44: 8	an o of cursing and reproach among all	7839
	44:12	They will become an o of cursing	460
	44:22	your land became an o of cursing and	7839
	48:26	let her be an o of ridicule.	8468
	48:27	Was not Israel the o of your ridicule?	8468
	48:39	Moab has become an o of ridicule.	8468
	48:39	an o of horror to all those around her."	4745
	49:13	an o of horror, of reproach and cursing;	2997
	49:17	"Edom will become an o of horror;	9014
	51:37	a haunt of jackals, an o of horror and scorn,	9014
Eze	5:15	a warning and an o of horror to the nations	5457
	22: 4	Therefore I will make you an o of scorn to	3075
	24:21	the o of your affection.	4720
	36: 3	and an o of people's malicious talk	4383+6584+6590+8557
Da	9:16	and your people an o of scorn to all those	3075
Joel	2:17	not make your inheritance an o of scorn,	3075
	2:19	never again will I make you an o of scorn	3075
Zec	8:13	As you have been an o of cursing among	7839

OBJECTED (4) [OBJECT]

2Ki	4:16	"No, my lord," *she* o.	606
Jn	12: 4	Judas Iscariot, who was later to betray him, o,	3306
	18:31	no right to execute anyone," the Jews o.	3306
Ac	28:19	But *when* the Jews o,	515

OBJECTION (1) [OBJECT]

Ac	10:29	I came without raising any o.	395

OBJECTIONS (1) [OBJECT]

Ac	11:18	*they had* no further o and praised God,	2483

OBJECTS (14) [OBJECT]

1Sa	6: 8	the gold o you are sending back to him as	3998
	6:15	with the chest containing the gold o,	3998
1Ki	7:45	All these o that Huram made	3998
2Ki	12:18	of Judah took all the sacred o dedicated	7731
2Ch	4:16	All the o that Huram-Abi made	NIH
	24: 7	of God and had used even its sacred o for	7731

2Ch	24:14	also dishes and other o *of* gold and silver.	3998
Ps	79: 4	We are o of reproach to our neighbors,	3075
Jer	10:15	They are worthless, the o of mockery;	5126
	51:18	They are worthless, the o of mockery;	5126
Ac	17:23	and looked carefully at your o of worship,	4934
Ro	9:22	with great patience the o of his wrath—	5007
	9:23	of his glory known to the o of his mercy,	5007
Eph	2: 3	Like the rest, we were by nature o of wrath.	5451

OBLATION, OBLATIONS (KJV) See GIFTS, OFFERING, OFFERINGS, PORTION, SACRIFICE

OBLIGATE (1) [OBLIGATED, OBLIGATES, OBLIGATION, OBLIGATIONS]

Nu	30: 2	or takes an oath to o himself by a pledge,	673

OBLIGATED (6) [OBLIGATE]

Nu	30: 4	by which *she* o herself will stand.	673
	30: 5	by which *she* o herself will stand;	673
	30: 7	by which *she* o herself will stand;	673
	30:11	by which *she* o herself will stand.	673
Ro	1:14	I am o both to Greeks and non-Greeks,	4050
Gal	5: 3	circumcised that he is o to obey the whole	4050

OBLIGATES (5) [OBLIGATE]

Nu	30: 3	to the LORD or o *herself* by a pledge	673
	30: 6	a rash promise by which *she* o herself	673
	30: 8	the vow that o her or the rash promise	6584
	30: 8	or the rash promise by which *she* o herself,	673
	30:10	with her husband makes a vow or o herself	673

OBLIGATION (5) [OBLIGATE]

Nu	30: 9	"Any vow or o taken by a widow	673
	32:22	and be free from your o to the LORD and	5929
Ezr	4:14	since *we are* under o to the palace	10419+10420
Ro	4: 4	not credited to him as a gift, but as an o.	4052
	8:12	Therefore, brothers, *we* have an o—	1639+4050

OBLIGATIONS (2) [OBLIGATE]

Nu	3: 8	the o of the Israelites by doing the work of	5466
1Ki	9:25	fulfilled the temple o.	8966

OBLIVION (1)

Ps	88:12	or your righteous deeds in the land of o?	5964

OBOTH (4)

Nu	21:10	The Israelites moved on and camped at O.	95
	21:11	Then they set out from O and camped	95
	33:43	They left Punon and camped at O.	95
	33:44	They left O and camped at Iye Abarim,	95

OBSCENITY (1)

Eph	5: 4	Nor should there be o,	157

OBSCURE (4) [OBSCURES]

Pr	22:29	he will not serve before o *men*.	3126
Isa	33:19	those people of an o speech,	4946+6680+9048
Eze	3: 5	a people of o speech and difficult language,	6680
	3: 6	of o speech and difficult language,	6680

OBSCURES (1) [OBSCURE]

Job	42: 3	*that* o my counsel without knowledge?'	6623

OBSERVANCE (2) [OBSERVE]

Ex	13: 9	This o will be for you like a sign	NIH
Ezr	7:10	the study and o *of* the Law of the LORD,	6913

OBSERVATION (1) [OBSERVE]

Lk	17:20	not come with your careful o,	4191

OBSERVE (47) [OBSERVANCE, OBSERVATION, OBSERVED, OBSERVER, OBSERVES, OBSERVING]

Ex	1:16	and o them on the delivery stool,	8011
	12:25	as he promised, o this ceremony.	9068
	13: 5	*you are to* o this ceremony in this month:	6268
	31:13	'You must o my Sabbaths.	9068
	31:14	" 'O the Sabbath, because it is holy to you.	9068
	31:16	The Israelites *are to* o the Sabbath.	9068
Lev	19: 3	and *you must* o my Sabbaths.	9068
	19:30	" 'O my Sabbaths and have reverence	9068
	23:32	to o your sabbath."	8697+8701
	25: 2	the land itself *must* o a sabbath	8697+8701
	26: 2	" 'O my Sabbaths and have reverence	9068
Dt	4: 6	O them carefully, for this will show your wisdom	6913
	5:12	"O the Sabbath day by keeping it holy,	9068
	5:15	commanded you to o the Sabbath day.	6913
	6: 1	to teach you to o in the land	6913
	8: 6	O the commands of the LORD your God,	9068
	8:11	failing *to* o his commands,	9068
	10:13	to o the LORD's commands and decrees	9068
	11: 8	to o everything I command you today and	9068
	11:22	If *you* carefully o all these commands	9068+9068
	12:14	and there o everything I command you.	6913

Dt	16: 1	O the month of Abib and celebrate	9068
	26:16	carefully o them with all your heart and	6913
	28:45	the LORD your God and o the commands	9068
2Sa	3:25	to deceive you and o your movements	3359
1Ki	2: 3	and o what the LORD your God requires:	9068
	9: 4	and do all I command and o my decrees	9068
	9: 6	from me and *do* not o the commands	9068
2Ki	17:13	O my commands and decrees,	9068
1Ch	22:13	if you are careful to o the decrees and laws	6913
2Ch	7:17	and o my decrees and laws,	9068
Est	9:19	o the fourteenth of the month of Adar as	6913
	9:22	to o the days as days of feasting and joy	6913
	9:27	without fail o these two days every year,	6913
Ps	37:37	Consider the blameless, o the upright;	8011
	91: 8	*You will* only o with your eyes and see	5564
	105:45	keep his precepts and o his laws.	5915
Ecc	8:16	to know wisdom and to o man's labor	8011
Jer	2:10	send to Kedar and o closely;	1067
	6:18	o, O witnesses, what will happen to them.	3359
	6:27	that *you may* o and test their ways.	3359
	8: 7	and the thrush o the time of their migration.	9068
Eze	45:21	on the fourteenth day you *are to* o	2118
Mk	7: 4	And *they* o many other traditions,	3195
	7: 9	of God in order to o your own traditions!	5498
Ro	2:25	Circumcision has value if *you* o the law,	4556
Gal	3: 5	among you because you o the law,	2240

OBSERVED (14) [OBSERVE]

Ge	50:10	and there Joseph o a seven-day period	6213
Nu	23:21	no misery in Israel.	8011
1Sa	1:12	Eli o her mouth.	9068
1Ki	8:65	So Solomon o the festival at that time,	6213
	11:34	whom I chose and who o my commands	9068
2Ki	23:22	*had* any such Passover been o.	6213
2Ch	7: 8	So Solomon o the festival at that time	6213
	35:17	the Passover at that time and o the Feast	NIH
	35:18	not been o like this in Israel since the days	6213
Est	5: 9	at the king's gate and o that he neither rose	NIH
	9:28	and o in every generation by every family,	6213
Job	4: 8	As *I have* o, those who plow evil	8011
Pr	24:32	I applied my heart to what *I* o and learned	2600
Mic	6:16	*You have* o the statutes of Omri and all	9068

OBSERVER (1) [OBSERVE]

Ac	22:12	He was a devout o of the law and	2848+3795

OBSERVES (1) [OBSERVE]

Ps	11: 4	He o the sons of men;	2600

OBSERVING (12) [OBSERVE]

1Sa	20:29	because our family is o a sacrifice in	NIH
2Ch	13:11	We *are* o the requirements of the LORD	9068
Lk	1: 6	o all the Lord's commandments	1877+4513
Ro	3:20	be declared righteous in his sight by o	2240
	3:27	On that *of* o the law?	2240
	3:28	that a man is justified by faith apart from o	2240
Gal	2:16	that a man is not justified by o the law,	2240
	2:16	be justified by faith in Christ and not by o	2240
	2:16	by o the law no one will be justified.	2240
	3: 2	Did you receive the Spirit by o the law,	2240
	3:10	All who rely on o the law are under a curse,	2240
	4:10	*You are* o special days and months	4190

OBSESSION (1)

Ac	26:11	*In my* o against them,	1841+4360

OBSOLETE (2)

Heb	8:13	he has made the first one o;	4096
	8:13	what is o and aging will soon disappear.	4096

OBSTACLE (1) [OBSTACLES]

Ro	14:13	not to put any stumbling block or o	4998

OBSTACLES (3) [OBSTACLE]

Isa	57:14	the o out of the way of my people."	4842
Jer	6:21	"I will put o before this people.	4842
Ro	16:17	and put o in your way that are contrary to	4998

OBSTINATE (7)

Dt	2:30	and his heart o in order to give him	599
Isa	30: 1	"Woe to the o children,"	6253
	65: 2	to an o people, who walk in ways	6253
Eze	2: 4	to whom I am sending you are	7156+7997
	3: 7	house of Israel is hardened and o.	4213+7997
Ac	19: 9	But some of them *became* o;	5020
Ro	10:21	to a disobedient and o people."	515

OBTAIN (6) [OBTAINED, OBTAINS]

Nu	27:21	who will o decisions for him by inquiring of	8626
Ezr	7:16	with all the silver and gold *you may* o from	10708
Pr	20:18	if you wage war, o guidance.	NIH
Jn	5:44	make no effort to o the praise that comes	2426
Ro	11: 7	so earnestly *it* did not o,	2209
2Ti	2:10	that they too *may* o the salvation that is	5593

OBTAINED (6) [OBTAIN]

Ex	38:25	The silver o *from* those of the community	AIT
Ac	2: 5	*I* even *in* letters from them to their brothers	1312
	27:13	they thought they had o what they wanted;	3195
Ro	9:30	who did not pursue righteousness, *have* o it,	2898

Php	3:12	Not that *I have* already o all this,	3284
Heb	9:12	*having* o eternal redemption.	2351

OBTAINS (1) [OBTAIN]
Pr	12: 2	A good man o favor from the LORD,	7049

OBVIOUS (4)
Mt	6:18	*be* o to men that you are fasting, but only	5743
Gal	5:19	The acts of the sinful nature are o:	5745
1Ti	5:24	The sins of some men are o,	4593
	5:25	In the same way, good deeds are o,	4593

OCCASION (9) [OCCASIONS]
Jdg	14: 4	who was seeking an o to confront	9301
1Sa	9:24	because it was set aside for you for this o,	4595
2Ch	13:18	The men of Israel were subdued on that o,	6961
Ezr	7:20	that you *may* have o to supply,	10484
	10: 9	greatly distressed by the o and because of	1821
Ne	8: 4	on a high wooden platform built for the o.	1821
Lk	10:25	**On one** o an expert in the law stood	2627+2779
Ac	1: 4	**On one** o, while he was eating with them,	2779
2Co	9:11	so that you can be generous on **every** o,	AIT

OCCASIONED (KJV) See RESPONSIBLE

OCCASIONS (2) [OCCASION]
Zec	8:19	and glad o and happy festivals for Judah.	8525
Eph	6:18	the Spirit on all o with all kinds of prayers	2789

OCCUPANTS (1) [OCCUPY]
Isa	5: 9	the fine mansions left without o.	3782

OCCUPATION (2)
Ge	46:33	'What is your o?'	5126
	47: 3	"What is your o?"	5126

OCCUPIED (12) [OCCUPY]
Ge	36:43	to their settlements in the land they o.	299
Nu	21:25	the cities of the Amorites and o them,	3782
Jos	19:47	took it, put it to the sword and o it.	3769
Jdg	11:26	For three hundred years Israel o Heshbon,	3782
1Sa	17: 3	The Philistines o one hill and	448+6641
	31: 7	And the Philistines came and o them.	3782
1Ch	5: 9	To the east *they* o the land up to the edge	3782
	5:10	*they* o the dwellings of the Hagrites	3782
	5:22	And *they* o the land until the exile.	3782
	10: 7	And the Philistines came and o them.	3782
2Ch	28:18	They captured and o Beth Shemesh,	3782
Ecc	5:20	God keeps him o with gladness of heart.	6701

OCCUPY (8) [OCCUPANTS, OCCUPIED]
Jos	1:15	you may go back and o your own land,	3769
	17:12	Manassites were not able to o these towns,	3769
Ne	2: 8	and for the residence *I will* o?"	448+995
Ecc	10: 6	while the rich o the low ones.	3782
Jer	49:16	*who* o the heights of the hill.	9530
Ob	1:19	The Negev *will* o the mountains of Esau,	3769
	1:19	*They will* o the fields of Ephraim	3769
Zec	9: 6	Foreigners *will* o Ashdod,	3782

OCCUR (3) [OCCURRED, OCCURS]
Ex	8:23	This miraculous sign *will* o tomorrow.' "	2118
Eze	16:16	nor *should they ever* o.	2118
1Co	5: 1	a kind that does not o even among pagans:	NIG

OCCURRED (3) [OCCUR]
2Ch	32:31	the miraculous sign that *had* o in the land,	2118
1Co	10: 6	Now these things o as examples to keep us	1181
Rev	16:18	like it *has* ever o since man has been	1181

OCCURS (2) [OCCUR]
Ecc	8:14	There is something else meaningless that o	6913
2Th	2: 3	until the rebellion o and the man of	2262

OCEAN (2) [OCEANS]
Ps	148: 7	you great sea creatures and all o **depths,**	9333
Eze	26:19	and when I bring the o **depths** over you	9333

OCEANS (1) [OCEAN]
Pr	8:24	When there were no o, I was given birth,	9333

OCRAN (5)
Nu	1:13	from Asher, Pagiel son of O;	6581
	2:27	of the people of Asher is Pagiel son of O.	6581
	7:72	On the eleventh day Pagiel son of O,	6581
	7:77	This was the offering of Pagiel son of O.	6581
	10:26	Pagiel son of O was over the division of	6581

ODD (KJV) See ADDITIONAL

ODED (3)
2Ch	15: 1	of God came upon Azariah son of O.	6389
	15: 8	and the prophecy of Azariah son of O	6389
	28: 9	prophet of the LORD named O was there,	6389

ODIOUS (1)
1Sa	27:12	"He has become so o to his people,	944+944

ODOR (1)
Jn	11:39	"by this time *there is* **a bad** o,	3853

ODOUR (KJV) See AROMA

OF (25210) See Index of Articles Etc.

OFF (437) [OFFSET, OFFSHOOTS, OFFSPRING]
Ge	9:11	Never again *will* all life be cut o by	4162
	14:12	They also carried o Abram's nephew Lot	2143
	17:14	*will* be cut o from his people;	4162
	21:14	on her shoulders and then sent her o with	8938
	21:16	Then *she* went o and sat down nearby,	2143
	22:19	and *they* set o together for Beersheba.	2143
	27:40	throw his yoke from o	7293
	31:26	and *you've* carried o my daughters	5627
	31:27	Why *did you* run o secretly	1368
	31:30	Now *you have* gone o because	2143+2143
	34:29	*They* carried o all their wealth	8647
	37:14	he sent him o from the Valley of Hebron.	8938
	38:14	*she* took o her widow's clothes,	6073
	38:19	*she* took o her veil and put	6073
	40:15	was forcibly carried o	1704+1704
	40:19	Pharaoh will lift o your head	4946+6584
Ex	3: 5	"Take o your sandals,	5970
	4:25	cut o her son's foreskin	4162
	9:15	with a plague that would have wiped you o	4946
	12:15	the seventh must be cut o from Israel.	4162
	12:19	in it *must* be cut o from the community	4162
	14:25	made the wheels of their chariots come o	6073
	23: 4	or donkey wandering o,	9494
	30:33	a priest *must* be cut o from his people.' "	4162
	30:38	like it to enjoy its fragrance *must* be cut o	4162
	31:14	on that day *must* be cut o from his people.	4162
	32: 2	"Take o the gold earrings that your wives,	7293
	32: 3	So all the people took o their earrings	7293
	32:12	and to wipe them o the face	4946+6584
	32:24	'Whoever has any gold jewelry, take it o.'	7293
	33: 5	Now take o your ornaments	3718+4946+6584
	33: 6	So the Israelites stripped o their ornaments	5911
Lev	1:15	wring o the head and burn it on the altar;	4916
	3: 9	entire fat tail cut o close to the backbone,	6073
	6:11	Then *he is to* take o these clothes and put	7320
	7:20	that person *must* be cut o from his people.	4162
	7:21	to the LORD, that person *must* be cut o	4162
	7:25	the LORD *must* be cut o from his people.	4162
	7:27	that person *must* be cut o	4162
	14: 8	shave o all his hair and bathe with water;	1662
	14: 9	seventh day *he* must shave o all his hair;	1662
	14:41	the material that *is* scraped o dumped into	7894
	15:13	*he is to* count o seven days	6218
	15:28	*she* must count o seven days,	6218
	16:23	to go into the Tent of Meeting and take o	7320
	17: 4	he has shed blood and *must* be cut o	4162
	17: 9	that man *must* be cut o from his people.	4162
	17:10	and *will* cut him o from his people.	4162
	17:14	anyone who eats it *must* be cut o."	4162
	18:29	such persons *must* be cut o	4162
	19: 8	that person *must* be cut o from his people.	4162
	19:27	the hair at the sides of your head or clip o	8845
	20: 3	and *I will* cut him o from his people;	4162
	20: 5	and *will* cut o from their people both him	4162
	20: 6	and *I will* cut him o from his people.	4162
	20:17	*They* must be cut o before the eyes	4162
	20:18	of them *must* be cut o from their people.	4162
	21: 5	not shave their heads or shave o the edges	1662
	22: 3	to the LORD, that person *must* be cut o	4162
	23:15	count o seven full weeks.	6218
	23:16	Count o fifty days up to the day after	6218
	23:29	not deny himself on that day *must* be cut o	4162
	25: 8	" 'Count o seven sabbaths of years—	6218
	26:26	When I cut o your supply of bread,	8689
Nu	4:18	the Kohathite tribal clans *are not* cut o	4162
	5:23	and then **wash** them o into the bitter water.	4681
	6:18	the Nazirite *must* shave o the hair	1662
	6:19	" 'After the Nazirite *has* shaved o the hair	1662
	9:13	that person *must* be cut o from his people	4162
	11:18	We were better o in Egypt!"	3202
	13:23	*they* cut o a branch bearing a single cluster	4162
	13:24	of grapes the Israelites cut o there.	4162
	15:30	that person *must* be cut o from his people.	4162
	15:31	must surely be cut o;	4162+4162
	19:13	That person *must* be cut o from Israel.	4162
	19:20	he *must* be cut o from the community,	4162
	22:23	she turned o the road into a field.	4946
	23: 3	Then *he* went o to a barren height.	2143
Dt	2:35	the towns we had captured *we* carried o	1024
	3: 7	from their cities *we* carried o for ourselves.	1024
	12:29	The LORD your God *will* cut o	4162
	15:16	and your family and *is* **well** o with you,	3201
	16: 9	Count o seven weeks from	6218
	19: 5	the head *may* fly o and hit his neighbor	5970
	25: 9	take o one of his sandals,	2740
	25:12	you shall cut o her hand.	7915
	25:18	and cut o all who were lagging behind;	2386
	28:40	because the olives *will* drop o.	5970
	29:26	*They* went o and worshiped other gods	2143
Jos	3:13	its waters flowing downstream *will* be cut o	4162
	3:16	(the Salt Sea) was completely cut o.	4162

Jos	4: 7	that the flow of the Jordan *was* cut o before	4162
	4: 7	the waters of the Jordan *were* cut o.	4162
	5:15	"Take o your sandals,	5970
	8: 2	except that *you may* carry o their plunder	1024
	8: 9	Then Joshua sent them o,	8938
	8:27	But Israel *did* carry o for themselves	1024
	11:14	The Israelites carried o for themselves all	1024
	15:18	When *she* got o her donkey,	4946+6584+7563
Jdg	1: 6	and cut o his thumbs and big toes.	7915
	1: 7	and big toes cut o have picked up scraps	7915
	1:14	When *she* got o her donkey,	4946+6584+7563
	5:19	but *they* carried o no silver, no plunder.	4374
	8:21	the ornaments o their camels' necks.	928
	9:48	He took an ax and cut o some branches,	4162
	16:12	he snapped the ropes o his arms	4946+6584
	16:19	*to* shave o the seven braids of his hair,	1662
	21: 6	"Today one tribe *is* cut o from Israel,"	1548
	21:23	each man caught one and **carried** her o to	5951
Ru	4: 7	one party took o his sandal and gave it to	8990
1Sa	2:33	not cut o from my altar will be spared only	4162
	4:18	Eli fell backward o his chair by the	4946+6584
	5: 4	and hands *had* been broken o and	4162
	17:34	a lion or a bear came and carried o a sheep	5951
	17:39	So he took them o.	6073
	17:46	I'll strike you down and cut o your head.	6073
	17:51	he cut o his head with the sword.	4162
	18: 4	Jonathan took o the robe he was wearing	7320
	19:24	He stripped o his robes and also prophesied	7320
	20:15	and *do* not ever cut o your kindness	4162
	20:15	even when the LORD *has* cut o every one	4162
	23: 5	the Philistines and carried o their livestock.	5627
	23:28	Saul broke o his pursuit of David	4946+8740
	24: 4	Then David crept up unnoticed and cut o	4162
	24: 5	for *having* cut o a corner of his robe.	4162
	24:11	I cut o the corner of your robe but did	4162
	24:21	that *you will* not cut o my descendants	4162
	25:23	she quickly got o her donkey	3718+4946+6584
	28: 9	He has cut o the mediums and spiritists	4162
	30: 2	carried them o as they went on their way.	5627
	30:17	except four hundred young men who rode o	8206
	31: 9	*They* cut o his head	7320
	31: 9	and stripped o his armor,	7320
2Sa	2:15	stood up and *were* counted o—	928+5031+6296
	4: 7	*they* cut o his head.	6073
	4:12	*They* cut o their hands and feet and hung	7915
	5: 6	the blind and the lame *can* ward you o."	6073
	5:21	and David and his men carried them o.	5951
	7: 9	and *I have* cut o all your enemies from	4162
	8: 2	and measured them o with a length of cord.	4499
	10: 4	shaved o half of each man's beard,	1662
	10: 4	cut o their garments in the middle at	4162
	11: 1	at the time when kings go o to war,	3655
	14:16	the hand of the man *who is trying to* cut o	9012
	16: 9	Let me go over and cut o his head."	6073
	18:21	down before Joab and ran o.	8132
	20:22	and *they* cut o the head of Sheba son	4162
1Ki	2:39	two of Shimei's slaves ran o to Achish son	1368
	5:14	He sent them o to Lebanon in shifts	8938
	6:16	He partitioned o twenty cubits at the rear	1215
	9: 6	and decrees I have given you and go o	2143
	9: 7	then *I will* cut o Israel from	4162
	14:10	*I will* cut o from Jeroboam	4162
	14:14	over Israel who *will* cut o the family	4162
	14:26	He carried o the treasures of the temple of	4374
	16:11	he killed o Baasha's whole family.	5782
	18: 4	While Jezebel *was* killing o the LORD's	4162
	18:42	So Ahab went o to eat and drink,	6590
	18:45	a heavy rain came on and Ahab rode o	8206
	20:11	not boast like *one who* takes *it* o.' "	7337
	21:21	I will consume your descendants and cut o	4162
2Ki	1: 3	that you *are going* o to consult Baal-Zebub,	2143
	5:12	So he turned and went o in a rage.	2143
	6:32	to cut o my head?	6073
	7: 8	gold and clothes, and went o and hid them.	2143
	9: 8	*I will* cut o from Ahab every last male	4162
	9:18	The horseman rode o to meet Jehu and said,	2143
	11: 7	*that* normally go o Sabbath duty are all	3655
	11: 9	and *those who were* going o duty—	3655
	17:26	which *are* killing them o,	4637
	18:16	stripped o the gold	7915
	20:17	*will* be carried o to Babylon.	5951
	23:34	But he took Jehoahaz and carried him o	995
1Ch	17: 8	and *I have* cut o all your enemies from	4162
	19: 4	cut o their garments in the middle at	4162
	20: 1	at the time when kings go o to war,	3655
2Ch	7:19	and commands I have given you and go o	2143
	12: 9	he carried o the treasures of the temple of	4374
	14:13	The men of Judah carried o a large amount	5951
	14:15	the herdsmen and carried o droves of sheep	8647
	20:25	and his men went to **carry** o their plunder,	1024
	21:17	invaded it and carried o all the goods found	8647
	23: 8	and *those who were* going o duty—	3655
	25:13	and carried o great quantities of plunder.	1024
	32: 3	and military staff about blocking o	6258
	36: 4	and carried him o to Egypt.	995
Ne	4:23	nor the guards with me took o our clothes;	7320
Est	8: 2	The king took o his signet ring,	6073
Job	1:15	the Sabeans attacked and carried them o.	4374
	1:17	down on your camels and carried them o.	4374
	6: 9	to let loose his hand and cut me o!	1298
	9: 7	he seals o the light of the stars.	1237+3159
	12:18	He takes o the shackles put on by kings	7337
	18:14	from the security of his tent and marched o	7575
	20:28	A flood *will* carry o his house,	1655
	22:16	They *were* carried o before their time,	7855
	24:24	*they are* cut o like heads of grain.	4909
	27: 8	the godless when *he is* cut o,	1298

Job	27:21	east wind **carries** him o, and he is gone;	5951
	30:11	*they* **throw** o restraint in my presence.	8938
	31:22	*let* it **be broken** o at the joint.	8689
	36: 7	He does not take his eyes o the righteous;	4946
	38: 5	Who **marked** o its dimensions?	8492
	41:13	Who *can* **strip** o his outer coat?	1655
Ps	2: 3	they say, "and **throw** o their fetters."	8959
	10: 1	O LORD, do you stand **far** o?	928+8158
	10: 9	he catches the helpless and **drags** them o	5432
	12: 3	*May* the LORD **cut** o all flattering lips	4162
	22:19	But you, O LORD, *be* not **far** o;	8178
	31:22	"I am **cut** o from your sight!"	1746
	34:16	to **cut** o the memory of them from	4162
	37: 9	For evil men *will* **be cut** o,	4162
	37:22	but those he curses *will* **be cut** o.	4162
	37:28	the offspring of the wicked *will* **be cut** o;	4162
	37:34	when the wicked **are cut** o, you will see it.	4162
	37:38	the future of the wicked *will* **be cut** o.	4162
	60: 6	and **measure** o the Valley of Succoth.	4499
	75:10	*I will* **cut** o the horns of all the wicked,	1548
	88: 5	who **are cut** o from your care.	1615
	101: 8	I *will* **cut** o every evildoer from the city	4162
	104:19	The moon **marks** o the seasons,	6913
	108: 7	and **measure** o the Valley of Succoth.	4499
	109:13	May his descendants be **cut** o,	4162
	109:15	that *he may* **cut** o the memory of them from	4162
	109:23	I am **shaken** o like a locust.	5850
	118:10	in the name of the LORD I **cut** them o.	4577
	118:11	in the name of the LORD I **cut** them o.	4577
	118:12	in the name of the LORD I **cut** them o.	4577
Pr	2:22	the wicked *will* **be cut** o from the land,	4162
	20:14	o *he* **goes** and boasts about his purchase.	261
	23: 5	for they will surely sprout wings and **fly** o	6414
	23:18	and your hope *will* not **be cut** o.	4162
	24:14	and your hope *will* not **be cut** o.	4162
	26: 6	Like **cutting** o one's feet	7894
	29:18	the people **cast** o restraint;	7277
Ecc	6: 3	that a stillborn child is **better** o than he.	3202
	7:24	it is **far** o and most profound—	8158
	9: 4	even a live dog is **better** o than a dead lion!	3202
	11:10	banish anxiety from your heart and **cast** o	6296
SS	5: 3	I have **taken** o my robe—	7320
Isa	5:29	as they seize their prey and **carry** it o	7117
	7:20	and to **take** o your beards also.	6200
	8: 4	the plunder of Samaria *will* **be carried** o by	5951
	9:14	So the LORD *will* **cut** o from Israel	4162
	10:33	*will* **lop** o the boughs with great power.	6188
	11:13	Judah's enemies *will* **be cut** o;	4162
	14:22	"I will **cut** o from Babylon her name	4162
	15: 2	and every beard **cut** o.	1757
	18: 5	he *will* **cut** o the shoots	4162
	20: 2	"**Take** o the sackcloth from your body and	7337
	22:25	*it will* **be sheared** o and will fall,	1548
	27:11	*they* **are broken** o and women come	8689
	30:11	Leave this way, **get** o this path,	5742
	30:16	You said, '*We will* **ride** o on swift horses.'	8206
	32:11	**Strip** o your clothes,	2256+6910+7320
	33:23	and even the lame *will* **carry** o plunder.	1024
	38:12	and *he has* **cut** me o from the loom;	1298
	39: 6	*will* **be carried** o to Babylon.	5951
	40:12	or with the breadth of his hand **marked** o	9419
	45:16	*they will* **go** o into disgrace together.	2143
	46: 2	*they* themselves **go** o into captivity.	2143
	47: 2	**take** o your veil.	1655
	47:11	**ward** o with a ransom;	4105
	48: 9	so as not to **cut** you o.	4162
	48:19	their name would never **be cut** o	4162
	52: 2	**Shake** o your dust;	5850
	53: 8	For *he* was **cut** o from the land of the living;	1615
	56: 5	an everlasting name that *will* not **be cut** o.	4162
	57:13	**carry** all of them o,	5951
Jer	2:20	"Long ago *you* **broke** o your yoke	8689
	2:20	and **tore** o your bonds;	5998
	5: 5	But with one accord they too *had* **broken** o	8689
	5: 5	the yoke and **torn** o the bonds.	5998
	5:10	**Strip** o her branches,	6073
	7:29	**Cut** o your hair and throw it away;	1605
	9:21	it has **cut** o the children from the streets	4162
	11:19	*let us* **cut** him o from the land of	4162
	12: 3	**Drag** them o like sheep to be butchered!	5998
	13:22	that your skirts *have* **been torn** o,	1655
	20: 5	as plunder and **carry** it o to Babylon.	995
	22:24	I *would* still **pull** you o.	5998
	28:10	the yoke o the neck of the prophet	4946+6584
	28:11	Babylon o the neck of all the nations	4946+6584
	28:12	the yoke o the neck of the prophet	4946+6584
	30: 8	'I will break the yoke o their necks	4946+6584
	30: 8	and *will* **tear** o their bonds;	5998
	36:23	the king **cut** them o with a scribe's knife	7973
	36:29	and **cut** o both man and animals from it?"	8697
	41: 5	eighty men *who had* **shaved** o their beards,	1662
	44: 7	on yourselves by **cutting** o from Judah	4162
	44:17	and were **well** o and suffered no harm.	3202
	47: 4	to **cut** o all survivors who could help Tyre	4162
	48:25	Moab's horn *is* **cut** o;	1548
	48:37	and every beard **cut** o;	1757
	49:29	*be* **carried** o with all their goods	5951
	50:16	**Cut** o from Babylon the sower,	4162
	51:13	the time for you to **be cut** o.	1299
	51:25	roll you o the cliffs,	4946
La	2: 3	In fierce anger *he has* **cut** o every horn	1548
	2:14	to **ward** o your captivity.	8740
	3:31	For *men* are not **cast** o by the Lord forever.	2396
	3:54	and I thought *I was* **about** to **be cut** o.	1615
	4: 9	the sword are **better** o than those who die	3202
Eze	4:16	"Son of man, I *will* **cut** o the supply of food	8689
	5:16	upon you and **cut** o your supply of food.	8689

Eze	13:21	*I will* **tear** o your veils	7973
	14: 8	I *will* **cut** him o from my people.	4162
	14:13	to **cut** o its food supply and send famine	8689
	17: 4	*he* **broke** o its topmost shoot	7786
	17:12	and **carried** o her king and her nobles,	4374
	17:22	I *will* **break** o a tender sprig	7786
	21: 3	from its scabbard and **cut** o from you both	4162
	21: 4	Because *I am going* to **cut** o the righteous	4162
	21:19	Make a signpost where the road **branches** o	8031
	21:26	**Take** o the turban, remove the crown.	6073
	23:25	*They will* **cut** o your noses and your ears,	6073
	25: 7	I *will* **cut** you o from the nations	4162
	25:16	against the Philistines, and I *will* **cut** o	4162
	26:16	and **take** o their embroidered garments.	7320
	29:19	and *he will* **carry** o its wealth.	5951
	30:15	and **cut** o the hordes of Thebes.	4162
	32:20	*let her* **be dragged** o with all her hordes.	5432
	35: 7	and **cut** o from it all who come and go.	4162
	37:11	we **are cut** o.'	1615
	38:13	to **carry** o silver and gold,	5951
	44:19	*they are* to **take** o	7320
	45: 3	**measure** o a section 25,000	4499
	46:18	driving them o their property.	4946
	47: 3	*he* **measured** o a thousand cubits	4499
	47: 4	He **measured** o another thousand cubits	4499
	47: 4	He **measured** o another thousand and	4499
	47: 5	He **measured** o another thousand	4499
Da	1: 2	These *he* **carried** o to the temple of his god	995
	4:14	'Cut down the tree and **trim** o its branches;	10635
	4:14	**strip** o its leaves and scatter its fruit.	10499
	7: 4	until its wings **were torn** o and it was lifted	10440
	8: 8	of his power his large horn was **broken** o,	8689
	8:22	*that* was **broken** o represent four kingdoms	8689
	9:26	the Anointed One *will* **be cut** o	4162
	11: 8	and **carry** them o to Egypt.	928+995+2021+8660
	11:12	When the army is **carried** o,	5951
Hos	2: 7	for then I was **better** o than now.'	3202
	5:14	I *will* **carry** them o,	5951
Joel	1: 7	It has **stripped** o their **bark**	3106+3106
	1: 9	and drink offerings *are* **cut** o from	4162
	1:16	the food been **cut** o before our very eyes—	4162
	3: 5	and **carried** o my finest treasures	995
Am	3:14	the horns of the altar *will* **be cut** o and fall	1548
	6: 2	Are *they* **better** o than your two kingdoms?	3202
	6: 3	*You* **put** o the evil day and bring near	5612
Ob	1:11	while strangers **carried** o his wealth	8647
Jnh	3: 6	took o his royal robes,	6296
Mic	2: 8	You **strip** o the rich robe	4578+4496
	3: 3	**strip** o their skin and break their bones	7320
Na	1:12	*they* will **be cut** o and pass away.	1605
Zep	1: 3	of rubble when I *will* **cut** o man from the face	4162
	1: 4	I *will* **cut** o from this place every remnant	4162
	3: 6	"I have **cut** o nations;	4162
	3: 7	Then her dwelling *would* not **be cut** o,	4162
Zec	3: 4	"**Take** o his filthy clothes."	6073
	9: 6	I *will* **cut** o the pride of the Philistines.	4162
	11:16	tearing o their hoofs.	7293
Mal	2: 3	and you *will* **be carried** o with it.	5951
	2:12	*may* the LORD **cut** him o from the tents	4162
Mt	5:30	**cut** it o and throw it away.	1716
	8:33	Those tending the pigs **ran** o,	5771
	10:14	**shake** the dust o your feet when you leave	1759
	12:29	and **carry** o his possessions	773
	18: 8	**cut** it o and throw it away.	1716
	18:12	and go to look for the one that **wandered** o?	4414
	18:13	about the ninety-nine that *did* not **wander** o.	4414
	18:30	he **went** o and had the man thrown	599
	22: 5	"But *they* paid no attention and **went** o—	599
	25:18	the one talent **went** o,	599
	26:51	**cutting** o his ear.	904
	27:31	*they* **took** o the robe	1694
Mk	1:35	left the house and **went** o to a solitary place,	599
	3:27	and **carry** o his possessions	1395
	5:14	**ran** o and reported this in the town	5771
	6:11	**shake** the dust o your feet when you leave,	1759
	9:43	If your hand causes you to sin, **cut** it o.	644
	9:45	And if your foot causes you to sin, **cut** it o.	644
	14:47	**cutting** o his ear.	904
	15:20	*they* **took** o the purple robe	1694
Lk	2:16	*they* **hurried** o and found Mary and	2262+5067
	8:34	*they* **ran** o and reported this in the town	5771
	9: 5	**shake** the dust o your feet	701
	10:11	that sticks to our feet *we* **wipe** o against	669
	12:58	or *he may* **drag** you o to the judge,	2955
	14:32	the other is still a **long way** o and will ask	4522
	15:13	**set** o for a distant country	623
	15:20	"But while he was still a **long way** o,	3426
	17:23	*Do* not **go** running o after them.	599+1503+3593
	18: 7	*Will* he keep **putting** them o?	3428
	22:50	**cutting** o his right ear.	904
	23: 1	the whole assembly rose and led him o	NIG
Jn	6:17	where they got into a boat and **set** o across	2262
	11:44	"**Take** o the grave clothes and let him go."	3395
	13: 4	**took** o his outer clothing,	5502
	15: 2	He **cuts** o every branch in me	149
	18:10	**cutting** o his right ear.	644
	18:26	of the man whose ear Peter *had* **cut** o,	644
	21: 7	(for he had **taken** it o) and jumped into	1218
Ac	2:39	and for all who are **far** o—	1650+3426
	3:23	*will* be **completely cut** o from among	2017
	7:33	the Lord said to him, '**Take** o your sandals;	3395
	8: 3	he **dragged** o men and women and put them	5359
	9:30	down to Caesarea and **sent** him o to Tarsus.	1990
	12: 7	and the chains **fell** o Peter's wrists.	1738
	13: 3	on them and **sent** them o.	668
	15:30	The men *were* **sent** o and went down	668
	15:33	*they were* **sent** o by the brothers with	668

Ac	18:18	he had his hair **cut** o at Cenchrea because of	3025
	20:15	from there and arrived o Kios,	513
	22:23	and **throwing** o their cloaks	4849
	27: 5	When we had sailed across the open sea o	2848
	27: 7	and had difficulty arriving o Cnidus.	2848
	28: 5	But Paul **shook** the snake o into the fire	701
Ro	9: 3	that I myself were cursed and **cut** o from	608
	11:17	some of the branches *have* **been broken** o,	1709
	11:19	"Branches **were broken** o so that I could	1709
	11:20	they were **broken** o because of unbelief,	1709
	11:22	Otherwise, you also *will* **be cut** o.	1716
1Co	11: 6	she should *have* her hair **cut** o;	3025
	11: 6	a woman *to have* her hair cut or **shaved** o,	3834
Eph	4:22	to **put** o your old self,	700
	4:25	of you *must* **put** o falsehood	700
Col	2:11	in the **putting** o of the sinful nature,	589
	3: 9	since you *have* **taken** o your old self	588
Heb	12: 1	*let us* **throw** o everything that hinders and	700
Jas	2:25	and **sent** them o in a different direction?	1675
2Pe	2:15	the straight way and **wandered** o to follow	4414
	2:20	**worse** o at the end **than** they were	5937
Rev	12: 7	the woman and **went** o to make war against	599
	18:10	they will stand **far** o and cry: "'Woe!	608+3427
	18:15	from her will stand **far** o,	608+3427
	18:17	will stand **far** o.	608+3427

OFFAL (6)

Ex	29:14	and its hide and its o outside the camp.	7302
Lev	4:11	the inner parts and o—	7302
	8:17	and its flesh and its o he burned up outside	7302
	16:27	their hides, flesh and o are to be burned up.	7302
Nu	19: 5	its hide, flesh, blood and o.	7302
Mal	2: 3	the o *from* your festival sacrifices,	7302

OFFEND (3) [OFFENDED, OFFENDER, OFFENDERS, OFFENSE, OFFENSES, OFFENSIVE]

Job	34:31	'I am guilty but *will* o no more.	2472
Mt	17:27	"But so that *we may* not o them,	4997
Jn	6:61	Jesus said to them, "*Does* this o you?	4997

OFFENDED (3) [OFFEND]

Ge	40: 1	of the king of Egypt o their master,	2627
Pr	18:19	An o brother is more unyielding than	7321
Mt	15:12	the Pharisees *were* o when they heard this?"	4997

OFFENDER (1) [OFFEND]

Ex	21:22	the o must be fined whatever	2257S

OFFENDERS (1) [OFFEND]

1Co	6: 9	nor male prostitutes nor **homosexual** o	780

OFFENSE (15) [OFFEND]

Ge	20:16	This is to **cover** o against you	4064+6524
Dt	19:15	of any crime or o he may have committed.	2633
	21:22	guilty of a **capital** o is put to death	4638+5477
1Sa	25:28	Please forgive your servant's o,	7322
2Sa	3: 8	of an o *involving* this woman!	6411
Job	10:14	and would not let my o go unpunished.	6411
	13:23	Show me my o and my sin.	7322
Ps	59: 3	Fierce men conspire against me *for* no o	7322
Pr	17: 9	He who covers over an o promotes love,	7322
	19:11	it is to his glory to overlook an o.	7322
Jer	24: 9	I will make them abhorrent and an o to all	8288
Eze	16:27	a **detestable** o with her neighbor's wife,	9359
Mt	13:57	And *they* **took** o at him.	4997
Mk	6: 3	And *they* **took** o at him.	4997
Gal	5:11	the o of the cross has been abolished.	4998

OFFENSE (Anglicized) See also STENCH

OFFENSES (18) [OFFEND]

Nu	18: 1	to bear the **responsibility for** o *against*	6411
	18: 1	to bear the **responsibility for** o *against*	6411
	18:23	the **responsibility for** o *against* it.	6411
1Ki	8:50	the o they have committed against you,	7322
Job	7:21	not pardon my o and forgive my sins?	7322
	14:17	My o *will* be sealed up in a bag;	7322
Isa	43:24	with your sins and wearied me with your o.	6411
	44:22	I have swept away your o like a cloud,	7322
	59:12	For o are many in your sight,	7322
	59:12	Our o are ever with us,	7322
Eze	18:22	the o he has committed *will* be remembered	7322
	18:28	the o he has committed and turns away	7322
	18:30	Turn away from all your o;	7322
	18:31	of all the o you have committed,	7322
	33:10	"Our o and sins weigh us down,	7322
	37:23	and vile images or with any of their o,	7322
	39:24	according to their uncleanness and their o,	7322
Am	5:12	For I know how many are your o and	7322

OFFENSIVE (3) [OFFEND]

Job	19:17	My breath *is* o to my wife;	2320
Ps	139:24	See if there is any o way in me,	6778
Jer	6:10	The word of the LORD is o to them;	3075

OFFER (126) [OFFERED, OFFERING, OFFERINGS, OFFERS]

Ex	3:18	*to* o **sacrifices** to the LORD our God.'	2284

Ex	5: 3	*to* o **sacrifices** to the LORD our God,	2284
	8: 8	and I will let your people go *to* o **sacrifices**	2284
	8:26	*The* **sacrifices** we o the LORD	2284
	8:26	And if *we* o **sacrifices** that are detestable	2284
	8:27	*to* o **sacrifices** to the LORD our God,	2284
	8:28	*to* o **sacrifices** to the LORD your God in	2284
	8:29	by not letting the people go to o **sacrifices**	2284
	23:18	not o the blood of a sacrifice to me along	2284
	29:38	*to* o on the altar regularly each day:	6913
	29:39	O one in the morning and the other	6913
	29:40	With the first lamb o a tenth of an ephah	NIH
	30: 9	*Do* not o on this altar any other incense	6590
	34:25	not o the blood of a sacrifice to me along	8821
Lev	1: 3	he is *to* o a male without defect.	7928
	1:10	he is *to* o a male without defect.	7928
	1:14	he is *to* o a dove or a young pigeon.	7928
	2:14	crushed heads of new grain roasted in a	7928
	3: 6	he is *to* o a male or female without defect.	7928
	5: 8	who *shall* first o the one for	7928
	5:10	then o the other as a burnt offering in	6913
	7:12	with this thank offering he is *to* o cakes	7928
	12: 7	*He shall* o before the LORD	7928
	14:12	the male lambs and o it as a guilt offering,	7928
	14:20	and o it on the altar,	6590
	16: 6	*to* o the bull for his own sin offering	7928
	17: 7	*They* must no longer o any of their	2284
	21: 8	because they o up the food of your God.	7928
	21:17	a o of your God may come near to o the food	7928
	21:21	not come near to o the food of his God.	7928
	22:22	*Do* not o to the LORD the blind,	7928
	22:24	*You* must not o to the LORD an animal	7928
	22:25	from the hand of a foreigner and o them as	7928
Nu	6:11	The priest is *to* o one as a sin offering and	6913
	15: 7	O it as an aroma pleasing to the LORD.	7928
	15:24	the whole community is *to* o a young bull	6913
Dt	12:14	O them only at the place the LORD	6590
	20:10	**make** its people **an** o of peace.	7924
	27: 6	with fieldstones and o burnt offerings on it	6590
	28:68	There *you will* o **yourselves for sale**	4835
	33:19	and there o sacrifices of righteousness;	2284
Jos	22:23	from the LORD and *to* o burnt offerings	6590
Jdg	5: 2	the people **willingly** o **themselves**—	5605
	6:26	o the second bull as a burnt offering."	6590
	13:16	o it to the LORD."	6590
	16:23	the rulers of the Philistines assembled to o	2284
	21:13	an o *of* peace to the Benjamites at the rock	7924
1Sa	1:21	with all his family *to* o the annual sacrifice	2284
	2:19	with her husband *to* o the annual sacrifice	2284
	10: 4	*They* will greet you and o you two loaves	5989
	13:12	*to* o the burnt offering."	6590
2Sa	7:27	found courage *to* o you this **prayer.**	7137+9525
	24:22	take whatever pleases him and o it **up.**	6590
1Ki	3: 4	The king went to Gibeon *to* o **sacrifices,**	2284
	12:27	*to* o sacrifices at the temple of the LORD	6913
	22:43	and the people continued *to* o **sacrifices**	2284
2Ki	12: 3	*to* o **sacrifices** and burn incense there.	2284
	14: 4	*to* o **sacrifices** and burn incense there.	2284
	15: 4	*to* o **sacrifices** and burn incense there.	2284
	15:35	o **sacrifices** and burn incense there.	2284
	16:15	o the morning burnt offering and	7787
	17:36	down and to him o **sacrifices.**	2284
1Ch	23:13	to o **sacrifices** before the LORD,	7787
2Ch	11:16	to Jerusalem *to* o **sacrifices** to the LORD.	2284
	29:21	to o these on the altar of the LORD.	6590
	31: 2	*to* o burnt offerings	NIH
	35:12	of the families of the people to o to	7928
Ezr	3: 6	to o burnt offerings to the LORD,	6590
	6:10	so that *they may* o **sacrifices** pleasing to	10638
Ne	4: 2	*Will they* o **sacrifices?**	2284
Ps	4: 5	O right sacrifices and trust in the LORD.	2284
	38:14	whose mouth can o no reply.	928
	66:15	*I will* o bulls and goats.	6913
Ecc	5: 1	near to listen rather than *to* o the sacrifice	5989
	9: 2	*who* o **sacrifices** and those who do not.	2284
Isa	1:15	if *you* o **many** prayers, I will not listen.	8049
	57: 7	there you went up *to* o your sacrifices.	2284
Jer	7:16	for this people nor o any plea or petition	5951
	11:14	*Do* not pray for this people nor o any plea	5951
	14:12	though *they* o burnt offerings	6590
	16: 7	No *one* will o **food** to comfort	7271
	33:18	before me continually *to* o burnt offerings,	6590
	46:10	will o sacrifice in the land of the north by	NIH
La	3:30	*Let him* o his cheek	5989
	4: 3	jackals o their breasts to nurse their young,	2740
Eze	20:31	When you o your **gifts**—	5951
	43:22	the second day *you are to* o a male goat	7928
	43:23	*to* o a young bull and a ram from the flock,	7928
	43:24	*You are to* o them before the LORD,	7928
	44:15	before me *to* o **sacrifices** *of* fat and blood,	7928
	44:27	he is *to* o a sin offering *for* himself,	7928
	45:13	" 'This is the special gift *you are to* o:	8123
	46: 6	of the New Moon he is *to* o a young bull,	NIH
	46:12	*He shall* o his burnt offering	6913
	48: 9	"The special portion *you are to* o	8123
Hos	8:13	*They* o **sacrifices** given to me and they eat	2284
	13: 2	"They o **human sacrifice** and kiss	2284
	14: 2	that *we may* o the fruit of our lips.	8966
Mic	6: 7	*Shall I* o my firstborn for my transgression,	5989
Hag	2:14	and whatever *they* o there is defiled.	7928
Mal	1:13	crippled or diseased animals and o them	995
Mt	5:24	then come and o your gift.	4712
	8: 4	the priest and o the **gift** that Moses commanded	4712
Mk	1:44	and o the **sacrifices** that Moses commanded	4712
Lk	2:24	*to* o a sacrifice in keeping with what is said	1443
	5:14	and o the **sacrifices** that Moses commanded	4712
Ac	14:13	the crowd wanted *to* o **sacrifices** to them.	2604
	24:26	that Paul *would* o him a bribe,	1443

Ro	6:13	*Do* not o the parts of your body to sin,	4225
	6:13	but rather o yourselves to God,	4225
	6:13	and o the parts of your body to him	NIG
	6:16	that when *you* o yourselves to someone	4225
	6:19	as *you* used *to* o the parts of your body	4225
	6:19	so now o them in slavery	4225
1Co	9:18	*I to* o your bodies as living sacrifices,	4225
	9:18	that in preaching the gospel *I may* o it free	5502
Heb	5: 1	*to* o gifts and sacrifices for sins.	4712
	5: 3	This is why he has *to* o **sacrifices**	4712
	7:27	not need *to* o sacrifices day after day,	429
	8: 3	Every high priest is appointed to o	4712
	8: 3	for this one also to have something *to* o.	4712
	8: 4	for there are already men who o	4712
	9:25	Nor did he enter heaven to o himself again	4712
	13:15	*let us* continually o to God a sacrifice	429
1Pe	4: 9	O hospitality to one another	NIG
Rev	8: 3	He was given much incense to o,	1443

OFFERED (90) [OFFER]

Ge	31:54	He o a sacrifice there in the hill country	2284
	46: 1	he o sacrifices to the God	2284
Ex	24: 5	and *they* o burnt offerings	6590
	40:29	o on it burnt offerings and grain offerings,	6590
Lev	2:12	*to be* o on the altar as a pleasing aroma.	6590
	7: 3	All its fat *shall be* o:	7928
	7:15	be eaten on the day it is o;	7933
	7:18	It will not be credited to the *one who* o it,	7928
	9:15	o it **for a sin offering**	2627
	9:16	He brought the burnt offering and o it in	6913
	10: 1	*they* o unauthorized fire before the LORD,	7928
Nu	16:47	but Aaron o the incense	5989
	18:15	that *is* o to the LORD is yours.	7928
	23: 2	of them o a bull and a ram on each altar."	6590
	23: 4	on each altar *I have* o a bull and a ram."	6590
	23:14	and there he built seven altars and o a bull	6590
	23:30	o a bull and a ram on each altar.	6590
Dt	26:14	nor *have I* o any of it to the dead.	5989
Jos	8:31	On it *they* o to the LORD burnt offerings	6590
Jdg	2: 5	There *they* o **sacrifices** to the LORD.	2284
	6:19	he brought them out and o them *to* him	5602
Ru	2:14	he o her some roasted grain.	7381
1Sa	2:13	with the people that whenever anyone o	2284
	6:15	of Beth Shemesh o burnt offerings	6590
	7: 9	and o it **up** as a whole burnt offering to	6590
	13: 9	And Saul o up the burnt offering.	6590
2Sa	15:24	and Abiathar o **sacrifices** until all	6590
1Ki	3: 3	that he o **sacrifices** and burned incense on	2284
	3: 4	and Solomon o a thousand burnt offerings	6590
	8:62	the king and all Israel with him o sacrifices	2284
	8:63	Solomon o a sacrifice	2284
	8:64	and there *he* o burnt offerings,	6913
	11: 8	who burned incense and o **sacrifices**	2284
	12:32	and o **sacrifices** on the altar.	6590
	12:33	he o **sacrifices** on the altar he had built	6590
2Ki	3:27	and o him as a sacrifice on the city wall.	6590
	16: 4	*He* o **sacrifices** and burned incense at	2284
	16:13	He o **up** his burnt offering	7787
1Ch	21:28	he o **sacrifices** there.	2284
2Ch	1: 6	and o a thousand burnt offerings on it.	6590
	6:40	and your ears attentive to the **prayers** o	AIT
	7: 4	the people o sacrifices before the LORD.	2284
	7: 5	And King Solomon o a sacrifice	2284
	7: 7	and there *he* o burnt offerings and the fat of	6913
	7:15	and my ears attentive to the **prayers** o	AIT
	28: 4	*He* o **sacrifices** and burned incense at	2284
	28:23	*He* o **sacrifices** to the gods of Damascus,	2284
	30:22	and o fellowship offerings and praised	2284
	33:22	Amon worshiped and o **sacrifices** to all	2284
Ezr	6:17	the dedication of this house of God *they* o	10638
Ne	12:43	And on that day *they* o great sacrifices,	2284
Job	26: 3	What **advice** *you have* o to one	3619
	31:27	o them a **kiss of homage,**	4200+5975+7023
Ps	51:19	then bulls *will be* o on your altar.	6590
	106:28	and ate **sacrifices** o to lifeless gods;	AIT
Isa	50: 6	*I* o my back to those who beat me,	5989
	57: 6	and o grain offerings.	6590
Eze	6:13	places where *they* o fragrant incense	5989
	16:18	and o my oil and incense before them.	5989
	16:19	*you* o o as fragrant incense before them.	5989
	20:28	there *they* o their sacrifices,	2284
	44: 7	while you o me food,	7928
Jnh	1:16	and *they* o a sacrifice to the LORD	2284
Mt	26:27	gave thanks and o it to them, saying,	1443
	27:34	There *they* o Jesus wine to drink,	1443
	27:48	o it to Jesus **to drink.**	4540
Mk	14:23	gave thanks and o it to them,	1443
	15:23	Then *they* o him wine mixed with myrrh,	1443
	15:36	o it to Jesus **to drink.**	4540
Lk	23:36	*They* o him wine vinegar	4712
Ac	8:18	*he* o them money	4712
Ro	11:16	the part of the dough o as firstfruits is holy,	NIG
1Co	9:13	at the altar share in what is o on the altar?	NIG
	10:19	**sacrifice** o **to an idol** is anything,	1628
	10:20	**sacrifices** of pagans *are* o to demons,	2604
	10:28	"This has been o **in sacrifice,"**	2638
Heb	5: 7	he o **up** prayers and petitions	4712
	6:18	to take hold *of* the hope o to us may	4618
	7:27	for their sins once for all *when he* o himself.	429
	9: 7	which *he* o for himself and for the sins	4712
	9: 9	that the gifts and sacrifices *being* o were	4712
	9:14	the eternal Spirit o himself unblemished	4712
	10: 2	would they not have stopped *being* o?	4712
	10:12	But *when* this priest had o	4712
	11: 4	By faith Abel o God a better sacrifice	4712

Heb	11:17	when God tested him, o Isaac **as a sacrifice.**	4712
Jas	2:21	for what he did *when he* o his son Isaac on	429
	5:15	And the prayer o in faith will make	NIG
Rev	14: 4	from among men and o as firstfruits to God	NIG

OFFERING (689) [OFFER]

Ge	4: 3	the fruits of the soil as an o to the LORD.	4966
	4: 4	LORD looked with favor on Abel and his o,	4966
	4: 5	but on Cain and his o he did not look	4966
	22: 2	Sacrifice him there as a **burnt** o on one of	6592
	22: 3	he had cut enough wood for the **burnt** o,	6592
	22: 6	the **burnt** o and placed it on his son Isaac,	6592
	22: 7	"but where is the lamb for the **burnt** o?"	6592
	22: 8	the lamb for the **burnt** o,	6592
	22:13	and sacrificed it as a **burnt** o instead	6592
	35:14	and he poured out a **drink** o on it.	5821
Ex	18:12	brought a **burnt** o and other sacrifices	6592
	25: 2	"Tell the Israelites to bring me an o.	9556
	25: 2	You are to receive the o *for* me	9556
	29:14	It is a **sin** o.	2633
	29:18	It is a **burnt** o to the LORD,	6592
	29:18	o **made** to the LORD **by fire.**	852
	29:24	before the LORD as a **wave** o.	9485
	29:25	along with the **burnt** o for a pleasing aroma	6592
	29:25	o **made** to the LORD **by fire.**	852
	29:26	wave it before the LORD as a **wave** o,	9485
	29:36	Sacrifice a bull each day as a **sin** o	2633
	29:40	and a quarter of a hin of wine as a **drink** o.	5821
	29:41	the same **grain** o and its drink offering as in	4966
	29:41	the same grain offering and its **drink** o as in	5821
	29:41	o **made** to the LORD **by fire.**	852
	29:42	the generations to come this **burnt** o is to	6592
	30: 9	or any **burnt** o or grain offering,	6592
	30: 9	or any burnt offering or **grain** o,	4966
	30: 9	and do not pour a **drink** o on it.	5821
	30:10	be made with the blood of the atoning **sin** o	2633
	30:13	This half shekel is an o to the LORD.	9556
	30:14	are to give an o *to* the LORD.	9556
	30:15	the o *to* the LORD to atone for your lives.	9556
	30:20	o **made** to the LORD **by fire,**	852
	30:28	the altar of **burnt** o and all its utensils,	6592
	31: 9	the altar of **burnt** o and all its utensils,	6592
	35: 5	take an o for the LORD.	9556
	35: 5	the LORD an o *of* gold, silver and bronze;	9556
	35:16	the altar of **burnt** o with its bronze grating,	6592
	35:21	and brought an o *to* the LORD for	9556
	35:22	They all presented their gold as a **wave** o to	9485
	35:24	an o *of* silver or bronze brought it as	9556
	35:24	or bronze brought it as an o *to* the LORD,	9556
	36: 6	or woman is to make anything else as an o	9556
	38: 1	the altar of **burnt** o of acacia wood,	6592
	38:24	from the **wave** o used for all the work on	9485
	38:29	The bronze from the **wave** o was 70 talents	9485
	40: 6	the altar of **burnt** o in front of the entrance	6592
	40:10	the altar of **burnt** o and all its utensils;	6592
	40:29	He set the altar of **burnt** o near the entrance	6592
Lev	1: 2	any of you brings an o to the LORD,	7933
	1: 2	the LORD, bring as your o an animal from	7933
	1: 3	" 'If the o is a burnt offering from the herd,	7933
	1: 3	" 'If the offering is a **burnt** o from the herd,	6592
	1: 4	to lay his hand on the head of the **burnt** o,	6592
	1: 6	to skin the **burnt** o and cut it into pieces.	6592
	1: 9	It is a **burnt** o, an offering made by fire,	6592
	1: 9	It is a burnt offering, an o **made by fire,**	852
	1:10	the o is a burnt offering from the flock,	7933
	1:10	the offering is a **burnt** o from the flock,	6592
	1:13	It is a **burnt** o, an offering made by fire,	6592
	1:13	It is a burnt offering, an o **made by fire,**	852
	1:14	" 'If the o to the LORD is a burnt offering	7933
	1:14	" 'If the offering to the LORD is a **burnt** o	6592
	1:17	It is a **burnt** o, an offering made by fire,	6592
	1:17	It is a burnt offering, an o **made by fire,**	852
	2: 1	" 'When someone brings a **grain** o to	4966
	2: 1	his o is to be of fine flour.	7933
	2: 2	an o **made by fire,**	852
	2: 3	the grain o belongs to Aaron and his sons;	4966
	2: 4	" 'If you bring a **grain** o baked in an oven,	4966
	2: 5	If your **grain** o is prepared on a griddle,	4966
	2: 6	it is a **grain** o.	4966
	2: 7	If your **grain** o is cooked in a pan,	4966
	2: 8	Bring the **grain** o made of these things to	4966
	2: 9	from the **grain** o and burn it on the altar as	4966
	2: 9	burn it on the altar as an o **made by fire,**	852
	2:10	the grain o belongs to Aaron and his sons;	4966
	2:11	" 'Every **grain** o you bring to the LORD	4966
	2:11	o **made** to the LORD **by fire.**	852
	2:12	You may bring them to the LORD as an o	7933
	2:14	" 'If you bring a **grain** o *of* firstfruits to	4966
	2:15	Put oil and incense on it; it is a **grain** o.	4966
	2:16	o **made** to the LORD **by fire.**	852
	3: 1	" 'If someone's o is a fellowship offering,	7933
	3: 1	" 'If someone's offering is a fellowship o,	2285
	3: 2	of his o and slaughter it at the entrance to	7933
	3: 3	From the fellowship o he is to bring	2285
	3: 5	of the **burnt** o that is on the burning wood,	6592
	3: 5	as an o **made by fire,**	852
	3: 6	an animal from the flock as a fellowship o	2285
	3: 8	on the head of his o and slaughter it in front	7933
	3: 8	From the fellowship o he is to bring	2285
	3:11	o **made** to the LORD **by fire.**	852
	3:12	" 'If his o is a goat,	7933
	3:14	o to the LORD **by fire:**	852
	3:16	an o **made by fire,** a pleasing aroma.	852
	4: 3	a young bull without defect as a **sin** o for	2633
	4: 7	of the altar of **burnt** o at the entrance to	6592
	4: 8	the fat from the bull of the **sin** o—	2633

Lev 4:10 from the ox sacrificed as a **fellowship o**. 8968
4:10 burn them on the altar of **burnt o**. 6592
4:14 a young bull as a **sin o** and present it before 2633
4:18 of the altar of **burnt o** at the entrance to 6592
4:20 as he did with the bull for the **sin o**. 2633
4:21 This is the **sin o** for the community. 2633
4:23 as his **o** a male goat without defect. 7933
4:24 the place where the **burnt o** is slaughtered 6592
4:24 It is a **sin o**. 2633
4:25 of the **sin o** with his finger and put it on 2633
4:25 the altar of **burnt o** and pour out the rest of 6592
4:26 he burned the fat of the **fellowship o**. 2285
4:28 as his **o** for the sin he committed 7933
4:29 of the **sin o** and slaughter it at the place of 2633
4:29 and slaughter it at the place of the **burnt o**. 6592
4:30 the altar of **burnt o** and pour out the rest of 6592
4:31 as the fat is removed from the fellowship **o**, 2285
4:32 " 'If he brings a lamb as his **sin o**, 7933
4:33 on its head and slaughter it for a **sin o** at 2633
4:33 the place where the **burnt o** is slaughtered. 6592
4:34 of the **sin o** with his finger and put it on 2633
4:34 the altar of **burnt o** and pour out the rest of 6592
4:35 from the lamb of the **fellowship o**, 2285
5: 6 or goat from the flock as a **sin o**; 2633
5: 7 a **sin o** and the other for a burnt offering. 2633
5: 7 a sin offering and the other for a **burnt o**. 6592
5: 8 who shall first offer the one for the **sin o**. 2633
5: 9 of the blood of the **sin o** against the side of 2633
5: 9 It is a **sin o**. 2633
5:10 the other as a **burnt o** in the prescribed way 6592
5:11 he is to bring as an **o** for his sin a tenth of 7933
5:11 a tenth of an ephah of fine flour for a **sin o**. 2633
5:11 because it is a **sin o**. 2633
5:12 It is a **sin o**. 2633
5:13 The rest of the **o** will belong to the priest, NIH
5:13 as in the case of the **grain o**.' " 4966
5:15 It is a **guilt o**. 871
5:16 for him with the ram as a **guilt o**, 871
5:18 to bring to the priest as a **guilt o** a ram 871
5:19 It is a **guilt o**; 871
6: 5 on the day he presents his **guilt o**. 873
6: 6 that is, to the LORD, his **guilt o**, 871
6: 9 'These are the regulations for the **burnt o**: 6592
6: 9 The **burnt o** is to remain on the altar hearth 6592
6:10 and shall remove the ashes of the **burnt o** 6592
6:12 to add firewood and arrange the **burnt o** on 6592
6:14 " 'These are the regulations for the **grain o**, 4966
6:15 together with all the incense on the **grain o**, 4966
6:17 Like the **sin o** and the guilt offering, 2633
6:17 Like the sin offering and the **guilt o**, 871
6:20 the **o** Aaron and his sons are to bring to 7933
6:20 an ephah of fine flour as a regular **grain o**, 4966
6:21 and present the **grain o** broken in pieces as 4966
6:23 Every **grain o** of a priest shall 4966
6:25 'These are the regulations for the **sin o**: 2633
6:25 The **sin o** is to be slaughtered before 2633
6:25 in the place the **burnt o** is slaughtered; 6592
6:30 But any **sin o** whose blood is brought into 2633
7: 1 for the **guilt o**, which is most holy: 871
7: 2 The **guilt o** is to be slaughtered in 871
7: 2 the place where the **burnt o** is slaughtered, 6592
7: 5 **o made** to the LORD by fire. 852
7: 5 It is a **guilt o**. 871
7: 7 " 'The same law applies to both the **sin o** 2633
7: 7 to both the sin offering and the **guilt o**: 871
7: 8 a **burnt o** for anyone may keep its hide 6592
7: 9 Every **grain o** baked in an oven or cooked 4966
7:10 and every **grain o**, 4966
7:11 for the **fellowship o** a person may present 2285
7:12 along with this thank **o** he is to offer cakes 2285
7:13 with his **fellowship o** of thanksgiving he is 2285
7:13 an **o** with cakes of bread made with yeast. 7933
7:14 He is to bring one of each kind as an **o**, 7933
7:15 of his **fellowship o** of thanksgiving must 2285
7:16 his **o** is the result of a vow or is 7933
7:16 the result of a vow or is a freewill **o**, 2285
7:18 If any meat of the **fellowship o** is eaten on 2285
7:20 the **fellowship o** belonging to the LORD, 2285
7:21 the **fellowship o** belonging to the LORD, 2285
7:25 of an animal from which an **o** by fire may 852
7:29 'Anyone who brings a **fellowship o** to 2285
7:30 **o made** to the LORD by fire; 852
7:30 the breast before the LORD as a **wave o**. 9485
7:33 the **fellowship o** shall have the right thigh 8968
7:37 then, are the regulations for the **burnt o**, 6592
7:37 the **grain o**, the sin offering, 4966
7:37 the grain offering, the **sin o**, 2633
7:37 the sin offering, the **guilt o**, 871
7:37 the **ordination o** and the fellowship 4854
7:37 and the **fellowship o**, 2285
8: 2 the anointing oil, the bull for the **sin o**, 2633
8:14 He then presented the bull for the **sin o**, 2633
8:18 He then presented the ram for the **burnt o**, AIT
8:21 the whole ram on the altar as a **burnt o**. 6592
8:21 **o made** to the LORD by fire, 852
8:27 before the LORD as a **wave o**. 9485
8:28 of the **burnt o** as an ordination offering, 6592
8:28 of the burnt offering as an **ordination o**, 4854
8:28 **o made** to the LORD by fire. 852
8:29 waved it before the LORD as a **wave o**, 9485
9: 2 "Take a bull calf for your **sin o** and a ram 2633
9: 2 and a ram for your **burnt o**, 6592
9: 3 'Take a male goat for a **sin o**, 2633
9: 3 and without defect—for a **burnt o**, 6592
9: 4 a ram for a **fellowship o** to sacrifice before 8968
9: 4 together with a **grain o** mixed with oil. 4966
9: 7 "Come to the altar and sacrifice your **sin o** 2633

Lev 9: 7 and your **burnt o** and make atonement 6592
9: 7 sacrifice the **o** that is for the people 7933
9: 8 the altar and slaughtered the calf as a **sin o** 2633
9:10 and the covering of the liver from the **sin o**, 2633
9:12 Then he slaughtered the **burnt o**. 6592
9:13 They handed him the **burnt o** piece 6592
9:14 and burned them on top of the **burnt o** on 6592
9:15 then brought the **o** that was for the people. 7933
9:15 for the people's **sin o** and slaughtered it 2633
9:15 **offered** it for a **sin o** as he did 2627
9:16 He brought the **burnt o** and offered it in 6592
9:17 He also brought the **grain o**, 4966
9:17 in addition to the morning's **burnt o**. 6592
9:18 the ram as the **fellowship o** for the people. 2285
9:21 before the LORD as a **wave o**, 9485
9:22 And having sacrificed the **sin o**, 2633
9:22 the **burnt o** and the fellowship offering, 6592
9:22 the burnt offering and the **fellowship o**, 8968
9:24 the LORD and consumed the **burnt o** and 6592
10:12 "Take the **grain o** left over from 4966
10:15 be waved before the LORD as a **wave o**. 9485
10:16 the **sin o** and found that it had been burned 2633
10:17 "Why didn't you eat the **sin o** in 2633
10:19 "Today they sacrificed their **sin o** 2633
10:19 and their **burnt o** before the LORD, 6592
10:19 if I had eaten the **sin o** today?" 2633
12: 6 a **burnt o** and a young pigeon or a dove for 6592
12: 6 and a young pigeon or a dove for a **sin o**. 2633
12: 8 a **burnt o** and the other for a sin offering. 6592
12: 8 a burnt offering and the other for a **sin o**. 2633
14:10 of fine flour mixed with oil for a **grain o**, 4966
14:12 of the male lambs and offer it as a **guilt o**, 871
14:12 before the LORD as a **wave o**. 9485
14:13 the lamb in the holy place where the **sin o** 2633
14:13 and the **burnt o** are slaughtered. 6592
14:13 Like the **sin o**, the guilt offering belongs to 2633
14:13 the **guilt o** belongs to the priest; 871
14:14 to take some of the blood of the **guilt o** 871
14:17 on top of the blood of the **guilt o**. 871
14:19 the **sin o** and make atonement for the one to 2633
14:19 the priest shall slaughter the **burnt o** 6592
14:20 together with the **grain o**, 4966
14:21 a **guilt o** to be waved to make atonement 871
14:21 of fine flour mixed with oil for a **grain o**, 4966
14:22 a **sin o** and the other for a burnt offering. 2633
14:22 a sin offering and the other for a **burnt o**. 6592
14:24 to take the lamb for the **guilt o**, 871
14:24 wave them before the LORD as a **wave o**. 9485
14:25 He shall slaughter the lamb for the **guilt o** 871
14:28 the blood of the **guilt o**— 871
14:31 as a **sin o** and the other as a burnt offering, 2633
14:31 as a sin offering and the other as a **burnt o** 6592
14:31 together with the **grain o**. 4966
15:15 a **sin o** and the other for a burnt offering. 2633
15:15 a sin offering and the other for a **burnt o**. 6592
15:30 The priest is to sacrifice one for a **sin o** and 2633
15:30 a sin offering and the other for a **burnt o**. 6592
16: 3 with a young bull for a **sin o** and a ram for 2633
16: 3 for a **sin offering** and a ram for a **burnt o**. 6592
16: 5 to take two male goats for a **sin o** and a ram 2633
16: 5 for a sin offering and a ram for a **burnt o**. 6592
16: 6 "Aaron is to offer the bull for his own **sin o** 2633
16: 9 to the LORD and sacrifice it for a **sin o**. 2633
16:11 for his own **sin o** to make atonement 2633
16:11 he is to slaughter the bull for his own **sin o**. 2633
16:15 the **sin o** for the people and take its blood 2633
16:24 and sacrifice the **burnt o** for himself and 6592
16:24 for himself and the **burnt o** for the people, 6592
16:25 also burn the fat of the **sin o** on the altar. 2633
17: 4 the Tent of Meeting to present it as an **o** to 7933
17: 8 among them who offers a **burnt o** or 6592
19: 5 " 'When you sacrifice a **fellowship o** to 2285
19:21 Tent of Meeting for a **guilt o** to the LORD. 871
19:22 the **guilt o** the priest is to make atonement 871
19:24 an **o** of **praise** to the LORD. 2136
22:10 a priest's family may eat the **sacred o**, 7731
22:14 " 'If anyone eats a **sacred o** by mistake, 7731
22:14 for the **o** and add a fifth of the value to it. 7731
22:18 presents a gift for a **burnt o** to the LORD, 6592
22:18 either to fulfill a vow or as a **freewill o**, 5607
22:21 from the herd or flock as a **fellowship o** 2285
22:21 to fulfill a special vow or as a **freewill o**, 5607
22:22 **o made** to the LORD by fire. 852
22:23 present as a **freewill o** an ox or a sheep 5607
22:27 **o made** to the LORD by fire. 852+7933
22:29 "When you sacrifice a thank **o** to 2285
23: 8 **o made** to the LORD by fire. 852
23:12 a **burnt o** to the LORD a lamb a year old 6592
23:13 with its **grain o** of two-tenths of an ephah 4966
23:13 **o made** to the LORD by fire, 852
23:13 and its **drink o** of a quarter of a hin of wine 5821
23:14 the very day you bring this **o** to your God. 7933
23:15 the sheaf of the **wave o**, 9485
23:16 present an **o** of new **grain** to the LORD. 4966
23:17 as a **wave o** of firstfruits to the LORD. 9485
23:18 They will be a **burnt o** to the LORD, 6592
23:18 an **o** made **by fire**, 852
23:19 Then sacrifice one male goat for a **sin o** 2633
23:19 each a year old, for a **fellowship o**. 2285
23:20 before the LORD as a **wave o**, 9485
23:20 a **sacred o** to the LORD for the priest. 7731
23:25 **o made** to the LORD by fire.' " 852
23:27 **o made** to the LORD by fire. 852
23:36 **o made** to the LORD by fire. 852
24: 7 **o made** to the LORD by fire. 852
27: 9 that is acceptable as an **o** to the LORD, 7933
27:11 not acceptable as an **o** to the LORD— 7933

Nu 3: 4 when they **made an o** with unauthorized fire 7928
4:16 the regular **grain o** and the anointing oil. 4966
5:15 an **o** of a tenth of an ephah of barley flour 7933
5:15 because it is a **grain o** for jealousy, 4966
5:15 a reminder **o** to draw attention to guilt. 4966
5:18 and place in her hands the reminder **o**, 4966
5:18 the **grain o** for jealousy, 4966
5:25 from her hands the **grain o** for jealousy, 4966
5:26 then to take a handful of the **grain o** as 4966
5:26 as a **memorial o** and burn it on the altar; 260
6:11 as a **sin o** and the other as a burnt offering 2633
6:11 as a sin offering and the other as a **burnt o** 6592
6:12 a year-old male lamb as a **guilt o**. 871
6:14 without defect for a **burnt o**, 6592
6:14 without defect for a **sin o**, 2633
6:14 a ram without defect for a **fellowship o**, 8968
6:16 before the LORD and make the **sin o** and 2633
6:16 and make the sin offering and the **burnt o**. 6592
6:17 and is to sacrifice the ram as a **fellowship o** 2285
6:17 together with its **grain o** and drink offering. 4966
6:17 together with its grain offering and **drink o**. 5821
6:18 under the sacrifice of the **fellowship o**. 8968
6:20 before the LORD as a **wave o**; 9485
6:21 the Nazirite who vows his **o** to the LORD 7933
7:11 "Each day one leader is to bring his **o** for 7933
7:12 The one who brought his **o** on 7933
7:13 His **o** was one silver plate weighing 7933
7:13 with fine flour mixed with oil as a **grain o**; 4966
7:15 one male lamb a year old, for a **burnt o**; 6592
7:16 one male goat for a **sin o**; 2633
7:17 to be sacrificed as a **fellowship o**. 8968
7:17 the **o** of Nahshon son of Amminadab. 7933
7:18 the leader of Issachar, **brought** his **o**. 7928
7:19 **o** he brought was one silver plate weighing 7933
7:19 with fine flour mixed with oil as a **grain o**; 4966
7:21 one male lamb a year old, for a **burnt o**; 6592
7:22 one male goat for a **sin o**; 2633
7:23 to be sacrificed as a **fellowship o**. 8968
7:23 This was the **o** of Nethanel son of Zuar. 7933
7:24 of the people of Zebulun, brought his **o**. NIH
7:25 His **o** was one silver plate weighing 7933
7:25 with fine flour mixed with oil as a **grain o**; 4966
7:27 one male lamb a year old, for a **burnt o**; 6592
7:28 one male goat for a **sin o**; 2633
7:29 to be sacrificed as a **fellowship o**. 8968
7:29 This was the **o** of Eliab son of Helon. 7933
7:30 of the people of Reuben, brought his **o**. NIH
7:31 His **o** was one silver plate weighing 7933
7:31 with fine flour mixed with oil as a **grain o**; 4966
7:33 one male lamb a year old, for a **burnt o**; 6592
7:34 one male goat for a **sin o**; 2633
7:35 to be sacrificed as a **fellowship o**. 8968
7:35 This was the **o** of Elizur son of Shedeur. 7933
7:36 of the people of Simeon, brought his **o**. NIH
7:37 His **o** was one silver plate weighing 7933
7:37 with fine flour mixed with oil as a **grain o**; 4966
7:39 one male lamb a year old, for a **burnt o**; 6592
7:40 one male goat for a **sin o**; 2633
7:41 to be sacrificed as a **fellowship o**. 8968
7:41 the **o** of Shelumiel son of Zurishaddai. 7933
7:42 of the people of Gad, brought his **o**. NIH
7:43 His **o** was one silver plate weighing 7933
7:43 with fine flour mixed with oil as a **grain o**; 4966
7:45 one male lamb a year old, for a **burnt o**; 6592
7:46 one male goat for a **sin o**; 2633
7:47 to be sacrificed as a **fellowship o**. 8968
7:47 This was the **o** of Eliasaph son of Deuel. 7933
7:48 of the people of Ephraim, brought his **o**. NIH
7:49 His **o** was one silver plate weighing 7933
7:49 with fine flour mixed with oil as a **grain o**; 4966
7:51 one male lamb a year old, for a **burnt o**; 6592
7:52 one male goat for a **sin o**; 2633
7:53 to be sacrificed as a **fellowship o**. 8968
7:53 the **o** of Elishama son of Ammihud. 7933
7:54 of the people of Manasseh, brought his **o**. NIH
7:55 His **o** was one silver plate weighing 7933
7:55 with fine flour mixed with oil as a **grain o**; 4966
7:57 one male lamb a year old, for a **burnt o**; 6592
7:58 one male goat for a **sin o**; 2633
7:59 to be sacrificed as a **fellowship o**. 8968
7:59 the **o** of Gamaliel son of Pedahzur. 7933
7:60 of the people of Benjamin, brought his **o**. NIH
7:61 His **o** was one silver plate weighing 7933
7:61 with fine flour mixed with oil as a **grain o**; 4966
7:63 one male lamb a year old, for a **burnt o**; 6592
7:64 one male goat for a **sin o**; 2633
7:65 to be sacrificed as a **fellowship o**. 8968
7:65 This was the **o** of Abidan son of Gideoni. 7933
7:66 of the people of Dan, brought his **o**. NIH
7:67 His **o** was one silver plate weighing 7933
7:67 with fine flour mixed with oil as a **grain o**; 4966
7:69 one male lamb a year old, for a **burnt o**; 6592
7:70 one male goat for a **sin o**; 2633
7:71 to be sacrificed as a **fellowship o**. 8968
7:71 the **o** of Ahiezer son of Ammishaddai. 7933
7:72 of the people of Asher, brought his **o**. NIH
7:73 His **o** was one silver plate weighing 7933
7:73 with fine flour mixed with oil as a **grain o**; 4966
7:75 one male lamb a year old, for a **burnt o**; 6592
7:76 one male goat for a **sin o**; 2633
7:77 to be sacrificed as a **fellowship o**. 8968
7:77 This was the **o** of Pagiel son of Ocran. 7933
7:78 of the people of Naphtali, brought his **o**. NIH
7:79 His **o** was one silver plate weighing 7933
7:79 with fine flour mixed with oil as a **grain o**; 4966
7:81 one male lamb a year old, for a **burnt o**; 6592
7:82 one male goat for a **sin o**; 2633

Nu	7:83	to be sacrificed as a **fellowship o.**	8968
	7:83	This was the o of Ahira son of Enan.	7933
	7:87	for the **burnt o** came to twelve young bulls,	6592
	7:87	together with their **grain o.**	4966
	7:87	Twelve male goats were used for the **sin o.**	2633
	7:88	for the sacrifice of the **fellowship o** came	8968
	8: 8	with its **grain o** of fine flour mixed	4966
	8: 8	to take a second young bull for a **sin o.**	2633
	8:11	the LORD as a **wave o** from the Israelites,	9485
	8:12	for a **sin o** to the LORD and the other for	2633
	8:12	to the LORD and the other for a **burnt o,**	6592
	8:13	and then present them as a **wave o**	9485
	8:15	and presented them as a **wave o,**	9485
	8:21	Then Aaron presented them as a **wave o**	9485
	9: 7	the LORD's **o** with the other Israelites at	7933
	9:13	because he did not present the LORD's **o**	7933
	15: 4	then the one who brings his **o** shall present	7933
	15: 4	the LORD a **grain o** of a tenth of an ephah	4966
	15: 5	With each lamb for the **burnt o** or	6592
	15: 5	a quarter of a hin of wine as a **drink o.**	5821
	15: 6	a ram prepare a **grain o** of two-tenths of	4966
	15: 7	and a third of a hin of wine as a **drink o.**	5821
	15: 8	a young bull as a **burnt o** or sacrifice,	6592
	15: 8	for a special vow or **fellowship o**	8968
	15: 9	bring with the bull a **grain o** of three-tenths	4966
	15:10	Also bring half a hin of wine as a **drink o.**	5821
	15:10	It will be an **o made by fire,**	852
	15:13	an **o made by fire** as an aroma pleasing to	852
	15:14	an **o made by fire** as an aroma pleasing to	852
	15:19	present a portion as an **o** to the LORD.	9556
	15:20	of your ground meal and present it as an **o**	9556
	15:21	to give this **o** to the LORD from the first	9556
	15:21	for a **burnt o** as an aroma pleasing to	6592
	15:24	along with its prescribed **grain o**	4966
	15:24	and **drink o,** and a male goat for	5821
	15:24	and a male goat for a **sin o.**	2633
	15:25	to the LORD for their wrong an **o** made	7933
	15:25	an offering made by fire for a **sin o.**	2633
	15:27	a year-old female goat for a **sin o.**	2633
	16:15	"Do not accept their **o.**	4966
	16:35	and consumed the 250 men who were **o**	7928
	18:17	and burn their fat as an **o made by fire,**	852
	18:18	of the **wave o** and the right thigh are yours.	9485
	18:24	the Israelites present as an **o** to the LORD.	9556
	18:26	a tenth of that tithe as the LORD's **o.**	9556
	18:27	Your **o** will be reckoned to you as grain	9556
	18:28	In this way you also will present an **o** to	9556
	19:17	from the burned **purification** o for a **sin o**	2633
	23: 3	"Stay here beside your **o** while I go aside.	6592
	23: 6	and found him standing beside his **o,**	6592
	23:15	"Stay here beside your **o** while I meet	6592
	23:17	and found him standing beside his **o,**	6592
	26:61	and Abihu died when they **made an o**	7928
	28: 3	the **o made by fire** that you are to present to	852
	28: 3	as a regular **burnt o** each day.	6592
	28: 5	with a **grain o** of a tenth of an ephah	4966
	28: 6	This is the regular **burnt o** instituted	6592
	28: 6	**o made** to the LORD **by fire.**	852
	28: 7	The accompanying **drink o** is to be a	5821
	28: 7	the **drink o** to the LORD at the sanctuary.	5821
	28: 8	the same kind of **grain o** and drink offering	4966
	28: 8	**drink o** that you prepare in the morning.	5821
	28: 8	This is an **o made by fire,**	852
	28: 9	make an o of two lambs a year old	NIH
	28: 9	with its **drink o** and a grain offering	5821
	28: 9	and a **grain o** of two-tenths of an ephah	4966
	28:10	This is the **burnt o** for every Sabbath,	6592
	28:10	the regular burnt offering and its **drink o.**	5821
	28:10	to the regular burnt offering and its **drink o.**	5821
	28:11	the LORD a **burnt o** of two young bulls,	6592
	28:12	to be a **grain o** of three-tenths of an ephah	4966
	28:12	with the ram, a **grain o** of two-tenths of	4966
	28:13	a **grain o** of a tenth of an ephah	4966
	28:13	This is for a **burnt o,** a pleasing aroma,	6592
	28:13	**o made** to the LORD **by fire.**	852
	28:14	With each bull there is to be a **drink o**	5821
	28:14	This is the monthly **burnt o** to be made	6592
	28:15	the regular **burnt o** with its drink offering,	6592
	28:15	the regular burnt offering with its **drink o,**	5821
	28:15	to be presented to the LORD as a **sin o.**	2633
	28:19	Present to the LORD an **o made by fire,**	852
	28:19	a **burnt o** of two young bulls,	6592
	28:20	a **grain o** of three-tenths of an ephah	4966
	28:22	as a **sin o** to make atonement for you.	2633
	28:23	in addition to the regular morning **burnt o.**	6592
	28:24	the **o made by fire** every day for seven days	852
	28:24	the regular **burnt o** and its drink offering.	6592
	28:24	to the regular burnt offering and its **drink o.**	5821
	28:26	to the LORD an **o** of new **grain** during	4966
	28:27	Present a **burnt o** of two young bulls,	6592
	28:28	to be a **grain o** of three-tenths of an ephah	4966
	28:31	the regular **burnt o** and its grain offering.	6592
	28:31	to the regular burnt offering and its **grain o.**	6592
	29: 2	prepare a **burnt o** of one young bull,	6592
	29: 3	the bull prepare a **grain o** of three-tenths of	4966
	29: 5	as a **sin o** to make atonement for you.	2633
	29: 8	to the LORD a **burnt o** of one young bull,	6592
	29: 9	the bull prepare a **grain o** of three-tenths of	4966
	29:11	Include one male goat as a **sin o,**	2633
	29:11	in addition to the **sin o** for atonement and	2633
	29:11	the regular **burnt o** with its grain offering,	6592
	29:11	the regular burnt offering with its **grain o,**	4966
	29:13	an **o made by fire** as an aroma pleasing to	852
	29:13	a **burnt o** of thirteen young bulls,	6592
	29:14	of the thirteen bulls prepare a **grain o**	4966
	29:16	Include one male goat as a **sin o,**	2633
	29:16	the regular **burnt o** with its grain offering	6592

Nu	29:16	the regular burnt offering with its **grain o**	4966
	29:16	with its grain offering and **drink o.**	5821
	29:19	Include one male goat as a **sin o,**	2633
	29:19	the regular **burnt o** with its grain offering,	6592
	29:19	the regular burnt offering with its **grain o,**	4966
	29:22	Include one male goat as a **sin o,**	2633
	29:22	the regular **burnt o** with its grain offering	6592
	29:22	the regular burnt offering with its **grain o**	4966
	29:22	with its grain offering and **drink o.**	5821
	29:25	Include one male goat as a **sin o,**	2633
	29:25	the regular **burnt o** with its grain offering	6592
	29:25	the regular burnt offering with its **grain o**	4966
	29:25	with its grain offering and **drink o.**	5821
	29:28	Include one male goat as a **sin o,**	2633
	29:28	the regular **burnt o** with its grain offering	6592
	29:28	the regular burnt offering with its **grain o**	4966
	29:28	with its grain offering and **drink o.**	5821
	29:31	Include one male goat as a **sin o,**	2633
	29:31	the regular **burnt o** with its grain offering	6592
	29:31	the regular burnt offering with its **grain o**	4966
	29:31	with its grain offering and **drink o.**	5821
	29:34	Include one male goat as a **sin o,**	2633
	29:34	the regular **burnt o** with its grain offering	6592
	29:34	the regular burnt offering with its **grain o**	4966
	29:34	with its grain offering and **drink o.**	5821
	29:36	an **o made by fire** as an aroma pleasing to	852
	29:36	a **burnt o** of one bull,	6592
	29:38	Include one male goat as a **sin o,**	2633
	29:38	the regular **burnt o** with its grain offering	6592
	29:38	the regular burnt offering with its **grain o**	4966
	29:38	with its grain offering and **drink o.**	5821
	31:50	So we have brought as an **o** to the LORD	7933
Dt	2:26	to Sihon king of Heshbon **o** peace	1821
	13:16	a **whole burnt o** to the LORD your God.	4003
	16:10	a **freewill o** in proportion to the blessings	5607
	24:10	to get what he is **o** as a pledge.	6287
Jdg	6:18	until I come back and bring my **o** and set it	4966
	6:26	the second bull as a **burnt o.**"	6592
	11:31	and I will sacrifice it as a **burnt o.**"	6592
	13:16	But if you prepare a **burnt o,**	6592
	13:19	together with the **grain o,**	4966
	13:23	he would not have accepted a **burnt o**	6592
	13:23	and **grain o** from our hands,	4966
1Sa	2:17	for they were treating the LORD's **o**	4966
	2:29	and o that I prescribed for my dwelling?	4966
	2:29	of every **o** made by my people Israel?'	4966
	3:14	be atoned for by sacrifice or **o.**'"	4966
	6: 3	but by all means send a **guilt o** to him.	871
	6: 4	"What **guilt o** should we send to him?"	871
	6: 8	to him as a **guilt o.**	871
	6:14	and sacrificed the cows as a **burnt o** to	6592
	6:17	the Philistines sent as a **guilt o** to the LORD	871
	7: 9	and offered it up as a whole **burnt o** to	6592
	7:10	While Samuel was sacrificing the **burnt o,**	6592
	13: 9	the **burnt o** and the fellowship offerings."	6592
	13: 9	And Saul offered up the **burnt o.**	6592
	13:10	Just as he finished making the **o,**	6592
	13:12	So I felt compelled to offer the **burnt o.**"	6592
	26:19	then may he accept an **o.**	4966
2Sa	15:12	While Absalom was **o** sacrifices,	2284
	24:22	Here are oxen for the **burnt o,**	6592
1Ki	13: 1	by the altar to **make an o.**	7787
	18:33	and pour it on the **o** and on the wood."	6592
2Ki	3:20	about the time for the **o** the sacrifice,	6590
	10:25	as Jehu had finished making the **burnt o,**	6592
	16:13	up his **burnt o** and grain offering,	6592
	16:13	up his burnt offering and **grain o,**	4966
	16:13	poured out his **drink o,**	5821
	16:15	offer the morning **burnt o** and	6592
	16:15	and the evening **grain o,**	4966
	16:15	the king's **burnt o** and his grain offering,	6592
	16:15	the king's burnt offering and his **grain o,**	4966
	16:15	the **burnt o** of all the people of the land,	6592
	16:15	and their **grain o** and their drink offering.	4966
	16:15	and their grain offering and their **drink o.**	5821
1Ch	6:49	on the altar of **burnt o** and on the altar	6592
	9:31	the responsibility for baking the **o bread.**	2503
	16:29	Bring an **o** and come before him;	4966
	16:40	on the altar of **burnt o** regularly,	6592
	21:23	and the wheat for the **grain o.**	4966
	21:24	sacrifice a **burnt o** that costs me nothing."	6592
	21:26	from heaven on the altar of **burnt o.**	6592
	21:29	and the altar of **burnt o** were at that time on	6592
	22: 1	and also the altar of **burnt o** for Israel."	6592
2Ch	7: 1	from heaven and consumed the **burnt o** and	6592
	29:18	the altar of **burnt o** with all its utensils,	6592
	29:21	and seven male goats as a **sin o** for	2633
	29:23	The goats for the **sin o** were brought before	2633
	29:24	**presented** their blood on the altar **for a sin**	
		o to atone for all Israel,	2627
	29:24	because the king had ordered the **burnt o**	6592
	29:24	the burnt offering and the **sin o**	2633
	29:27	the order to sacrifice the **burnt o** on	6592
	29:27	As the **o** began, singing to the LORD began	6592
	29:28	the sacrifice of the **burnt o** was completed.	6592
	35:16	of the Passover and the **o** of burnt offerings	6590
Ezr	6:17	as a **sin o** for all Israel, twelve male goats,	10260
	8:25	the **o** of silver and gold and the articles that	9556
	8:28	and gold are a **freewill o** to the LORD,	5607
	8:35	seventy-seven male lambs and, as a **sin o,**	2633
	8:35	All this was a **burnt o** to the LORD,	6592
	10:19	a ram from the flock as a **guilt o.**)	871
Job	1: 5	in the morning he would sacrifice a **burnt o**	6592
	42: 8	to my servant Job and sacrifice a **burnt o**	6592
Ps	40: 6	Sacrifice and **o** you did not desire,	4966
	54: 6	I will sacrifice a **freewill o** to you;	5607
	66:15	I will sacrifice fat animals to you and an **o**	7792

Ps	96: 8	bring an **o** and come into his courts.	4966
	116:17	I will sacrifice a thank **o** to you and call on	2285
Isa	40:20	to **present** such an **o** selects wood that will	9556
	53:10	the LORD makes his life a **guilt o,**	871
	65: 3	**o sacrifices** in gardens and burning incense	2284
	66: 3	whoever **makes** a grain **o** is	6590
	66:20	to my holy mountain in Jerusalem as an **o**	4966
Eze	16:25	**o** your body with increasing promiscuity	
			906+7316+8079
	43:19	to give a young bull as a **sin o** to the priests,	2633
	43:21	the **sin o** and burn it in the designated part	2633
	43:22	a male goat without defect for a **sin o,**	2633
	43:24	on them and sacrifice them as a **burnt o** to	6592
	43:25	to provide a male goat daily for a **sin o;**	2633
	44:27	he is to offer a **sin o** for himself,	2633
	45:19	of the **sin o** and put it on the doorposts of	2633
	45:22	a **sin o** for himself and for all the people of	2633
	45:23	and seven rams without defect as a **burnt o**	6592
	45:23	and a male goat for a **sin o.**	2633
	45:24	as a **grain o** an ephah for each bull and	4966
	46: 2	The priests are to sacrifice his **burnt o**	6592
	46: 4	The **burnt o** the prince brings to	6592
	46: 5	The **grain o** given with the ram is to be	4966
	46: 5	the **grain o** with the lambs is to be as much	4966
	46: 7	He is to provide as a **grain o** one ephah	4966
	46:11	the **grain o** is to be an ephah with a bull,	4966
	46:12	When the prince provides a **freewill o**	5607
	46:12	a **burnt o** or fellowship offerings—	6592
	46:12	He shall offer his **burnt o**	6592
	46:13	without defect for a **burnt o** to the LORD;	6592
	46:14	with it morning by morning a **grain o,**	4966
	46:14	The presenting of this **grain o**	4966
	46:15	the lamb and the **grain o** and the oil shall	4966
	46:15	by morning for a regular **burnt o.**	6592
	46:20	where the priests will cook the **guilt o** and	871
	46:20	and the **sin o** and bake the grain offering,	2633
	46:20	and the sin offering and bake the **grain o,**	4966
Da	2:46	that an **o** and incense be presented to him.	10432
	9:27	he will put an end to sacrifice and **o.**	4966
Am	4: 5	Burn leavened bread as a **thank o** and brag	9343
Mal	1: 8	**Try o** them to your governor!	7928
	1:10	"and I will accept no **o** from your hands.	4966
Mt	5:23	if you are **o** your gift at the altar	4712
Jn	16: 2	anyone who kills you will think he is **o**	4712
Ac	10: 4	to the poor have come up as a **memorial o**	3649
	21:26	the **o** would be **made** for each of them. 4712+4714
Ro	8: 3	in the likeness of sinful man to be a **sin o,**	281
	8: 3	the Gentiles might become an **o** acceptable	4714
2Co	8:19	to accompany us as we carry the **o,**	5921
Eph	5: 2	for us as a fragrant **o** and sacrifice to God.	4714
Php	2:17	I am being **poured out like a drink o**	5064
	4:18	They are a fragrant **o,** an acceptable	2602
2Ti	4: 6	I am already being **poured out like a**	
		drink o,	5064
Heb	10: 5	"Sacrifice and **o** you did not desire,	4714
	13:11	into the Most Holy Place as a **sin o,**	281
1Pe	2: 5	**o** spiritual sacrifices acceptable to God	429

OFFERINGS (377) [OFFER]

Ge	8:20	he sacrificed **burnt o** on it.	6592
Ex	10:25	to have sacrifices and **burnt o** to present to	6592
	20:24	on it your **burnt o** and fellowship offerings,	6592
	20:24	and fellowship **o,** your sheep and goats	8968
	22:29	"Do not hold back **o** from your granaries	NIH
	23:18	"The fat of my **festival o** must not	2504
	24: 5	and they offered **burnt o**	6592
	24: 5	and sacrificed young bulls as fellowship **o**	2285
	25: 3	the **o** you are to receive from them:	9556
	25:29	and bowls for the **pouring out of o.**	5818
	29:28	to the LORD from their fellowship **o.**	2285
	29:33	eat **these o** by which atonement was made	4392S
	32: 6	the people rose early and sacrificed **burnt o**	6592
	32: 6	and presented **fellowship o.**	8968
	35:29	to the LORD **freewill o** for all the work	5607
	36: 3	the **o** the Israelites had brought to carry out	9556
	36: 3	to bring **freewill o** morning	5607
	37:16	pitchers for the **pouring out of drink o.**	5818
	40:29	offered on it **burnt o** and grain offerings,	6592
	40:29	offered on it burnt offerings and **grain o,**	4966
Lev	2: 3	**o made** to the LORD **by fire.**	852
	2:10	**o made** to the LORD **by fire.**	852
	2:13	Season all your **grain o** with salt.	4966
	2:13	of your God out of your **grain o;**	4966
	2:13	add salt to all your **o.**	7933
	4:35	**o made** to the LORD **by fire.**	852
	5:12	**o made** to the LORD **by fire.**	852
	6:12	and burn the fat of the **fellowship o** on it.	8968
	6:17	**o made** to me **by fire.**	852
	6:18	**o made** to the LORD **by fire.**	852
	7:14	the blood of the **fellowship o.**	8968
	7:32	to give the right thigh of your fellowship **o**	2285
	7:34	From the fellowship **o** of the Israelites,	2285
	7:35	**o made** to the LORD **by fire**	852
	7:38	the Israelites to bring their **o** to the LORD,	7933
	8:31	the bread from the basket of **ordination o,**	4854
	10:12	**o made** to the LORD **by fire**	852
	10:13	**o made** to the LORD **by fire**	852
	10:14	as your share of the Israelites' fellowship **o.**	2285
	10:15	with the fat portions of the **o made by fire,**	852
	14:11	both the one to be cleansed and **his o** before	4392S
	14:32	and who cannot afford the regular **o,**	NIH
	16:27	The bull and the goat for the **sin o,**	2633
	17: 5	and sacrifice them as fellowship **o.**	2285
	21: 6	**o made** to the LORD **by fire,**	852
	21:21	**o made** to the LORD **by fire.**	852
	22: 2	the **sacred o** the Israelites consecrate to me,	7731

Lev	22: 3	the **sacred** o that the Israelites consecrate to	7731
	22: 4	not eat the **sacred** o until he is cleansed.	7731
	22: 6	of the **sacred** o unless he has bathed himself	7731
	22: 7	and after that he may eat the **sacred** o,	7731
	22:15	The priests must not desecrate the **sacred** o	7731
	22:16	by allowing them to eat the **sacred** o	7731
	23:18	with their **grain** o and drink offerings—	4966
	23:18	with their grain offerings and **drink** o—	5821
	23:36	o made the LORD **by fire**,	852
	23:37	o made to the LORD **by fire**—	852
	23:37	the **burnt** and grain offerings,	6592
	23:37	the burnt offerings and **grain** o,	4966
	23:37	and **drink** o required for each day.	5821
	23:38	These o are in addition to those for	NIH
	23:38	the **freewill** o you give to the LORD.)	5607
	24: 9	o made *to* the LORD **by fire**."	852
	26:31	in the pleasing aroma of your o.	NIH
Nu	4: 7	dishes and bowls, and the jars for **drink** o;	5821
	6:14	There he is to present his o to the LORD:	7933
	6:15	with their **grain** and drink offerings, and	4966
	6:15	with their grain offerings and **drink** o, and	5821
	7: 2	of those who were counted, **made** o.	7928
	7:10	the leaders brought their o	7933
	7:84	o of the Israelite leaders **for the dedication**	2853
	7:88	These were the o **for the dedication** *of*	2853
	10:10	over your **burnt** o and fellowship offerings,	6592
	10:10	over your burnt o and fellowship o,	2285
	15: 3	the LORD o **made by fire**, from the herd or	852
	15: 3	whether **burnt** o or sacrifices,	6592
	15: 3	or **freewill** o or festival offerings—	5607
	15: 3	or freewill offerings or **festival** o—	4595
	18: 8	in charge of the o *presented to* me;	9556
	18: 8	all the **holy** o the Israelites give me I give	7731
	18: 9	**most holy** o that is kept from the fire.	7731+7731
	18: 9	the gifts they present me as **most holy** o,	7731+7731
	18: 9	whether grain or sin or **guilt** o,	871
	18:11	the gifts of all the **wave** o of the Israelites.	9485
	18:19	from the **holy** o the Israelites present to	7731
	18:32	not defile the **holy** o *of* the Israelites,	7731
	28: 2	the appointed time the food for my o **made**	7933
	28:31	Prepare these together with their **drink** o,	5821
	29: 6	and daily **burnt** o with their grain offerings	6592
	29: 6	and daily burnt offerings with their **grain** o	4966
	29: 6	with their grain offerings and **drink** o	5821
	29: 6	o made the LORD **by fire**—	852
	29:11	and their **drink** o.	5821
	29:18	prepare their **grain** o and drink offerings	4966
	29:18	prepare their grain offerings and **drink** o	5821
	29:19	and their **drink** o.	5821
	29:21	prepare their **grain** o and drink offerings	4966
	29:21	prepare their grain offerings and **drink** o	5821
	29:24	prepare their **grain** o and drink offerings	4966
	29:24	prepare their grain offerings and **drink** o	5821
	29:27	prepare their **grain** o and drink offerings	4966
	29:27	prepare their grain offerings and **drink** o	5821
	29:30	prepare their **grain** o and drink offerings	4966
	29:30	prepare their grain offerings and **drink** o	5821
	29:33	prepare their **grain** o and drink offerings	4966
	29:33	prepare their grain offerings and **drink** o	5821
	29:37	prepare their **grain** o and drink offerings	4966
	29:37	prepare their grain offerings and **drink** o	5821
	29:39	and your **freewill** o, prepare these for	5607
	29:39	your **burnt** o, grain offerings,	6592
	29:39	your burnt offerings, **grain** o,	4966
	29:39	**drink** o and fellowship offerings.' "	5821
	29:39	drink offerings and **fellowship** o.' "	8968
Dt	12: 6	there bring your **burnt** o and sacrifices,	6592
	12: 6	vowed to give and your **freewill** o,	5607
	12:11	your **burnt** o and sacrifices,	6592
	12:13	not to sacrifice your **burnt** o anywhere you please.	6592
	12:17	or your **freewill** o or special gifts.	5607
	12:27	Present your **burnt** o on the altar of	6592
	18: 1	o made *to* the LORD **by fire**,	852
	27: 6	with fieldstones and offer **burnt** o on it to	6592
	27: 7	Sacrifice **fellowship** o there,	8968
	32:38	and drank the wine of their **drink** o?	5816
	33:10	and **whole burnt** o on your altar.	4003
Jos	8:31	On it they offered to the LORD **burnt** o	6592
	8:31	and sacrificed **fellowship** o.	8968
	13:14	since the o **made by fire** *to* the LORD,	852
	22:23	and to offer **burnt** o and grain offerings,	6592
	22:23	and to offer burnt offerings and **grain** o,	4966
	22:23	or to sacrifice fellowship o on it,	2285
	22:26	but not for **burnt** o or sacrifices.'	6592
	22:27	at his sanctuary with our **burnt** o,	6592
	22:27	sacrifices and **fellowship** o.	8968
	22:28	not for **burnt** o and sacrifices,	6592
	22:29	by building an altar for **burnt** o,	6592
	22:29	**grain** o and sacrifices,	4966
Jdg	20:26	until evening and presented **burnt** o	6592
	20:26	and **fellowship** o to the LORD.	8968
	21: 4	an altar and presented **burnt** o and	6592
	21: 4	burnt offerings and **fellowship** o.	8968
1Sa	2:28	the o **made with fire** *by* the Israelites.	852
	6:15	people of Beth Shemesh offered **burnt** o	6592
	10: 8	down to you to sacrifice **burnt** o	6592
	10: 8	to sacrifice burnt offerings and fellowship o,	2285
	11:15	There they sacrificed fellowship o before	2285
	13: 9	the burnt offering and the **fellowship** o."	8968
	13: 9	"Does the LORD delight in **burnt** o	6592
2Sa	1:21	neither dew nor rain, nor fields that yield o	9556
	6:17	and David sacrificed **burnt** o	6592
	6:17	and **fellowship** o before the LORD.	8968
	6:18	the **burnt** o and fellowship offerings,	6592
	6:18	the burnt offerings and **fellowship** o,	8968
	24:24	**burnt** o that cost me nothing."	6592

2Sa	24:25	to the LORD there and sacrificed **burnt** o	6592
	24:25	sacrificed burnt offerings and **fellowship** o.	8968
1Ki	3: 4	and Solomon offered a thousand **burnt** o	6592
	3:15	the Lord's covenant and sacrificed **burnt** o	6592
	3:15	sacrificed burnt offerings and **fellowship** o.	8968
	8:63	Solomon offered a sacrifice of fellowship o	2285
	8:64	and there he offered **burnt** o,	6592
	8:64	**grain** o and the fat of	4966
	8:64	and the fat of the **fellowship** o,	8968
	8:64	to hold the **burnt** o,	6592
	8:64	the **grain** o and the fat of	4966
	8:64	and the fat of the **fellowship** o.	8968
	9:25	a year Solomon sacrificed **burnt** o	6592
	9:25	and **fellowship** o on the altar he had built	8968
	10: 5	and the **burnt** o he made at the temple of	6592
	12:33	and went up to the altar to **make** o.	7787
	13: 2	of the high places who now **make** o here,	7787
2Ki	5:17	your servant will never again make **burnt** o	6592
	10:24	in to make sacrifices and **burnt** o.	6592
	12: 4	that is brought as **sacred** o to the temple of	7731
	12:16	from the **guilt** and sin offerings was	871
	12:16	and **sin** o was not brought into the temple of	2633
	16:12	he approached it and **presented** o on it.	6590
	16:13	the blood of his **fellowship** o on the altar.	8968
	16:15	on the altar all the blood of the **burnt** o	6592
1Ch	6:49	the *ones who* **presented** o on the altar	7787
	16: 1	and they presented **burnt** o and	6592
	16: 1	and **fellowship** o before God.	8968
	16: 2	the **burnt** o and fellowship offerings,	6592
	16: 2	the burnt offerings and **fellowship** o,	8968
	16:40	to present **burnt** o to the LORD on	6592
	21:23	Look, I will give the oxen for the **burnt** o,	6592
	21:26	to the LORD there and sacrificed **burnt** o	6592
	21:26	sacrificed burnt offerings and **fellowship** o.	8968
	23:29	the flour for the **grain** o,	4966
	23:31	and whenever **burnt** o were presented to	6592
	29:21	the LORD and presented **burnt** o to him:	6592
	29:21	together with their **drink** o,	5821
2Ch	1: 6	of Meeting and offered a thousand **burnt** o	6592
	2: 4	and for making **burnt** o every morning	6592
	4: 6	to be used for the **burnt** o were rinsed,	6592
	7: 7	and there he offered **burnt** o and the fat of	6592
	7: 7	and the fat of the **fellowship** o,	8968
	7: 7	could not hold the **burnt** o,	6592
	7: 7	the **grain** o and the fat portions.	4966
	8:12	Solomon sacrificed **burnt** o to the LORD,	6592
	8:13	to the daily requirement for o commanded	6590
	9: 4	and the **burnt** o he made at the temple of	6592
	13:11	and evening they present **burnt** o	6592
	23:18	the **burnt** o *of* the LORD as written in	6592
	24:14	articles for the service and for the **burnt** o,	6592
	24:14	**burnt** o were presented continually in	6592
	29: 7	not burn incense or present any **burnt** o at	6592
	29:29	When the o were finished,	6590
	29:31	and **thank** o to the temple of the LORD."	9343
	29:31	assembly brought sacrifices and **thank** o,	9343
	29:31	all whose hearts were willing brought **burnt** o.	6592
	29:32	The number of **burnt** o the assembly	6592
	29:32	all of them for **burnt** o to the LORD.	6592
	29:34	were too few to skin all the **burnt** o;	6592
	29:35	There were **burnt** o in abundance,	6592
	29:35	of the **fellowship** o and the drink offerings	8968
	29:35	of the fellowship offerings and the **drink** o	5821
	29:35	that accompanied the **burnt** o.	6592
	30:15	and brought **burnt** o to the temple of	6592
	30:22	and offered fellowship o and praised	2285
	31: 2	to offer **burnt** o and fellowship offerings,	6592
	31: 2	to offer burnt offerings and **fellowship** o,	8968
	31: 3	the morning and evening **burnt** o and for	6592
	31: 3	and for the **burnt** o on the Sabbaths,	6592
	31:14	in charge of the **freewill** o *given to* God,	5607
	32:23	Many brought o to Jerusalem for	4966
	33:16	of the LORD and sacrificed fellowship o	2285
	33:16	fellowship offerings and **thank** o on it,	9343
	35: 7	and goats for the **Passover** o, and	7175
	35: 8	the priests twenty-six hundred **Passover** o	7175
	35: 9	provided five thousand **Passover** o	7175
	35:12	They set aside the **burnt** o to give them to	6592
	35:13	and boiled the **holy** o in pots,	7731
	35:14	were sacrificing the **burnt** o and	6592
	35:16	the Passover and the offering of **burnt** o on	6592
Ezr	1: 4	and with **freewill** o for the temple of God	5607
	1: 6	in addition to all the **freewill** o.	5605
	2:68	the heads of the families gave **freewill** o	5605
	3: 2	the God of Israel to sacrifice **burnt** o on it,	6592
	3: 3	and sacrificed **burnt** o on it to the LORD,	6592
	3: 4	the required number of **burnt** o prescribed	6592
	3: 5	they presented the regular **burnt** o,	6592
	3: 5	those **brought as freewill** o	5605+5607
	3: 6	to offer **burnt** o to the LORD,	6592
	6: 9	young bulls, rams, male lambs for **burnt** o	10545
	7:16	as the **freewill** o *of* the people and priests	10461
	7:17	with their **grain** and drink offerings,	10432
	7:17	with their grain offerings and **drink** o,	10483
	8:35	from captivity sacrificed **burnt** o to	6592
Ne	10:33	for the regular **grain** o and burnt offerings;	4966
	10:33	for the regular grain offerings and **burnt** o;	6592
	10:33	for the o on the Sabbaths,	NIH
	10:33	for the **holy** o; for the sin offerings	7731
	10:33	for **sin** o to make atonement for Israel;	2633
	10:37	first of our ground meal, of our [grain] o,	9556
	13: 5	the **grain** o and incense and temple articles,	4966
	13: 9	with the **grain** o and the incense.	4966
Ps	20: 3	and accept your **burnt** o.	6592
	40: 6	**burnt** o and sin offerings you did not	6592
	40: 6	burnt offerings and **sin** o you did not require	2631

Ps	50: 8	for your sacrifices or your **burnt** o,	6592
	50:14	Sacrifice **thank** o to God,	9343
	50:23	He who sacrifices **thank** o honors me,	9343
	51:16	you do not take pleasure in **burnt** o.	6592
	51:19	whole **burnt** o to delight you;	6592
	56:12	I will present my **thank** o to you.	9343
	66:13	with **burnt** o and fulfill my vows to you—	6592
	107:22	Let them sacrifice thank o and tell	2285
Pr	7:14	"I have **fellowship** o at home;	2285
Isa	1:11	"I have more than enough of **burnt** o,	6592
	1:13	Stop bringing meaningless o!	4966
	19:21	with sacrifices and **grain** o;	4966
	40:16	nor its animals enough for **burnt** o.	6592
	43:23	not brought me sheep for **burnt** o,	6592
	43:23	with **grain** o nor wearied you with demands	4966
	56: 7	Their **burnt** o and sacrifices will	6592
	57: 6	to them you have poured out **drink** o	5821
	57: 6	and offered **grain** o.	4966
	60: 7	*they will be* accepted *as* o on my altar,	6590
	66:20	as the Israelites bring their **grain** o,	4966
Jer	6:20	Your **burnt** o are not acceptable;	6592
	7:18	They pour out **drink** o to other gods	5821
	7:21	add your **burnt** o to your other sacrifices	6592
	7:22	about **burnt** o and sacrifices,	6592
	14:12	though they offer **burnt** o	6592
	14:12	and **grain** o, I will not accept them.	4966
	17:26	bringing **burnt** o and sacrifices,	6592
	17:26	**grain** o, incense and thank offerings to	4966
	17:26	and **thank** o to the house of the LORD.	9343
	19: 5	to burn their sons in the fire as o to Baal—	6592
	19:13	and poured out **drink** o to other gods."	5821
	29: 9	and by pouring out **drink** o to other gods.	5821
	33:11	of those who bring **thank** o to the house of	9343
	33:18	before me continually to offer **burnt** o,	6592
	33:18	to burn **grain** o and present offerings.' "	4966
	41: 5	bringing **grain** o and incense with them to	4966
	44:17	and will pour out **drink** o to her just as we	5821
	44:18	of Heaven and pouring out **drink** o to her,	5821
	44:19	of Heaven and poured out **drink** o to her,	5821
	44:19	like her image and pouring out **drink** o	5821
	44:25	to burn incense and pour out **drink** o to	5821
	48:35	to *those who* **make** o on the high places	6590
	52:19	bowls used for **drink** o—	4984
Eze	20:28	made o that provoked me to anger,	7933
	20:28	and poured out their **drink** o.	5821
	20:40	There I will require your o	9556
	36:38	as numerous as the flocks for o	7731
	40:38	where the **burnt** o were washed.	6592
	40:39	on which the **burnt** o,	6592
	40:39	**sin** o and guilt offerings were slaughtered.	2633
	40:39	and **guilt** o were slaughtered.	871
	40:42	of dressed stone for the **burnt** o,	6592
	40:42	the utensils for slaughtering the **burnt** o	7933
	40:43	The tables were for the flesh of the o.	6592
	42:13	the LORD will eat the **most holy** o.	7731+7731
	42:13	There they will put the **most holy** o—	7731+7731
	42:13	the **grain** o, the sin offerings and	4966
	42:13	the **sin** o and the guilt offerings—	2633
	42:13	the sin offerings and the **guilt** o—	871
	43:18	for sacrificing **burnt** o and sprinkling blood	6592
	43:27	the priests are to present your **burnt** o	6592
	43:27	and **fellowship** o on the altar.	8968
	44:11	the **burnt** o and sacrifices for the people	6592
	44:13	of my holy things or my **most holy** o;	7731+7731
	44:29	They will eat the **grain** o,	4966
	44:29	the **sin** o and the guilt offerings;	2633
	44:29	the sin offerings and the **guilt** o;	871
	45:15	These will be used for the **grain** o,	4966
	45:15	**burnt** o and fellowship offerings	6592
	45:15	and **fellowship** o to make atonement for	8968
	45:17	to provide the **burnt** o, grain offerings	6592
	45:17	**grain** o and drink offerings at the festivals,	4966
	45:17	grain offerings and **drink** o at the festivals,	5821
	45:17	He will provide the **sin** o, grain offerings,	2633
	45:17	He will provide the sin offerings, **grain** o,	4966
	45:17	**burnt** o and fellowship offerings	6592
	45:17	and **fellowship** o to make atonement for	8968
	45:25	he is to make the same provision for **sin** o,	2633
	45:25	**burnt** o, grain offerings and oil.	6592
	45:25	burnt offerings, **grain** o and oil.	4966
	46: 2	and his **fellowship** o.	8968
	46:12	whether a burnt offering or **fellowship** o—	8968
	46:12	or his **fellowship** o as he does on	8968
Hos	4:13	the mountaintops and **burn** o on the hills,	7787
	6: 6	and acknowledgment of God rather than **burnt** o.	6592
	8:11	Ephraim built many altars for **sin** o,	2627
	9: 4	not pour out **wine** o to the LORD.	3516
Joel	1: 9	**Grain** o and drink offerings are cut off	4966
	1: 9	Grain offerings and **drink** o are cut off from	5821
	1:13	the **grain** o and drink offerings are withheld	4966
	1:13	the grain offerings and **drink** o are withheld	5821
	2:14	**grain** o and drink offerings for	4966
	2:14	and **drink** o for the LORD your God.	5821
Am	4: 5	and brag about your **freewill** o—	5607
	5:22	you bring me **burnt** o and grain offerings,	6592
	5:22	you bring me burnt offerings and **grain** o,	4966
	5:22	Though you bring choice **fellowship** o,	8968
	5:25	and forty years in the desert,	4966
Mic	6: 6	Shall I come before him with **burnt** o,	6592
Zep	3:10	my scattered people, will bring me o.	4966
Mal	1:10	With **such** o from your hands,	2296ˢ
	1:11	and pure o will be brought to my name,	4966
	2:12	he brings to the LORD Almighty.	4966
	2:13	to your o or accepts them with pleasure	4966
	3: 3	the LORD will have men who will bring o	4966
	3: 4	and the o of Judah and Jerusalem will	4966

Mal	3: 8	"In tithes and o.	9556
Mk	12:33	yourself is more important than all **burnt o**	3906
	12:41	the **place where the o** were put	1126
Jn	8:20	the **place where the o** were put.	1126
Ac	7:42	and o forty years in the desert,	5376
	24:17	for the poor and to present o.	4714
Heb	10: 6	with **burnt o** and sin offerings you were	3906
	10: 6	burnt offerings and **sin** o you were	281+4309
	10: 8	First he said, "Sacrifices and o,	4714
	10: 8	**burnt o** and sin offerings you did	3906
	10: 8	offerings and **sin** o you did not desire,	281+4309
	11: 4	when God spoke well of his o.	1565

OFFERS (14) [OFFER]

Lev	3: 1	and he o an animal from the herd,	7928
	3: 6	" 'If he o an animal from the flock as	7933
	3: 7	If he o a lamb,	7928
	3:14	From what he o he is to make this offering	7933
	6:26	The priest who o it shall eat it;	2627
	7: 8	The priest who o a burnt offering	7928
	7: 9	on a griddle belongs to the priest who o it,	7928
	7:12	he o it as an expression of thankfulness,	7928
	7:16	sacrifice shall be eaten on the day he o it,	7928
	7:33	of Aaron who o the blood and the fat of	7928
	17: 8	or any alien living among them who o	6590
Dt	33:10	He o incense before you	8492
Isa	66: 3	and whoever o a lamb,	2284
Heb	10:11	again and again he o the same sacrifices,	4712

OFFICE (7) [OFFICER, OFFICERS, OFFICIAL, OFFICIALS, OFFICIATE]

Dt	17: 9	and to the **judge** who is **in** o	9149
	19:17	and the **judges** who are **in** o	9149
	24: 5	go to the priest **in** o at the time,	2118
1Sa	2:36	to some **priestly** o so I can have food	3914
Ne	13:29	because they defiled the **priestly** o and	3914
Isa	22:19	I will depose you from your o,	5163
Heb	7:23	death prevented them from continuing in o;	NIG

OFFICER (34) [OFFICE]

1Sa	29: 3	who was an o of Saul king of Israel?	6269
2Ki	3:11	An o of the king of Israel answered,	6269
	7: 2	The o on whose arm the king was leaning	8957
	7:17	the o on whose arm he leaned in charge of	8957
	7:19	The o had said to the man of God, "Look,	8957
	9:25	Jehu said to Bidkar, his **chariot** o,	8957
	18:17	his chief o and his field commander with	6247
	18:24	How can you repulse one o of the least	7068
	25:19	he took the o in charge of the fighting men	6247
	25:19	the secretary who was **chief** o	2021+7372+8569
1Ch	26:24	was the o in charge of the treasuries.	5592
2Ch	24:11	and the o of the chief priest would come	7224
	26:11	by Jeiel the secretary and Maaseiah the o	8853
	28: 7	Azrikam the o **in charge** of the palace,	5592
Ezr	4: 8	Rehum the **commanding** o and	10116+10302
	4: 9	Rehum the **commanding** o and	10116+10302
	4:17	To Rehum the **commanding** o,	10116+10302
Ne	11: 9	Joel son of Zicri was their **chief,** o	7224
	11:14	Their **chief** o was Zabdiel son	7224
	11:22	The **chief** o of the Levites	7224
Isa	33:18	"Where is that **chief** o?	6221
	33:18	Where is the o in charge of the towers?"	6221
	36: 9	then can you repulse one o of the least	7068
Jer	20: 1	the chief o in the temple of the LORD,	7224
	39: 3	Nebo-Sarsekim a chief o,	6247
	39:13	Nebushazban a chief o,	6247
	51:59	to the staff o Seraiah son of Neriah,	8569
	52:25	he took the o in charge of the fighting men,	6247
	52:25	the secretary who was **chief** o	2021+7372+8569
Da	2:15	He asked the king's o,	10718
Mt	5:25	and the judge may hand you over to the o,	5677
Lk	12:58	and the judge turn you over to the o,	4551
	12:58	and the o throw you into prison.	4551
2Ti	2: 4	he wants to please his **commanding** o.	5133

OFFICERS (88) [OFFICE]

Ex	14: 7	with o over all of them.	8957
	15: 4	of Pharaoh's o are drowned in the Red Sea.	8957
Nu	31:14	Moses was angry with the o of the army—	7212
	31:48	o who were over the units of the army—	7212
Dt	20: 5	The o shall say to the army:	8853
	20: 8	Then the o shall add, "Is any man afraid	8853
	20: 9	the o have finished speaking to the army,	8853
Jos	1:10	So Joshua ordered the o of the people:	8853
	3: 2	After three days the o went throughout	8853
1Sa	8:12	and Saul's o as well.	6269
	18: 5	with more success than the rest of Saul's o,	6269
	18:30	with more success than the rest of Saul's o,	6269
2Sa	8: 7	to the o of Hadadezer and brought them	6269
1Ki	4: 5	in charge of the **district** o;	5893
	4:27	The **district** o, each in his month,	5893
	9:22	his government officials, his o,	8569
	20:14	'The **young** o of the provincial commanders	5853
	20:15	the **young** o of the provincial commanders	5853
	20:17	The **young** o of the provincial commanders	5853
	20:19	The **young** o of the provincial commanders	5853
	20:24	and replace them with other o.	7068
2Ki	6: 8	After conferring with his o, he said,	6269
	6:11	He summoned his o and demanded	6269
	6:12	my lord the king," said one of his o,	6269
	7:12	up in the night and said to his o,	6269
	7:13	One of his o answered,	6269
	9: 5	he found the army o sitting together.	6269
	9:11	When Jehu went out to his **fellow** o,	123+6269
	10:25	he ordered the guards and o;	8957

2Ki	10:25	and o threw the bodies out and then entered	8957
	11:14	The o and the trumpeters were beside	8569
	15:25	One of his **chief** o, Pekah son of Remaliah,	8957
	24:10	At that time the o of Nebuchadnezzar king	6269
	24:11	up to the city while his o were besieging it.	6269
	24:14	all the o and fighting men.	8569
	25:23	When all the army o and their men heard	8569
	25:26	together with the army o,	8569
1Ch	11:11	a Hacmonite, was chief of the o;	8957
	12:28	with 22 o from his family;	8569
	12:34	1,000 o, together with 37,000	8569
	13: 1	David conferred with each of his o,	5592
	18: 7	David took the gold shields carried by the o	5592
	27: 1	and commanders of hundreds, and their o,	8853
	27: 3	of Perez and chief of all the army o for	8853
	27:16	The o over the tribes of Israel:	5592
	27:22	These were the o over the tribes of Israel.	8569
	28: 1	the o over the tribes,	8569
	29: 6	the o of the tribes of Israel,	8569
	29:24	All the o and mighty men,	8569
2Ch	8:18	ships commanded by his own o,	6269
	21: 9	So Jehoram went there with his o	8569
	23:13	The o and the trumpeters were beside	8569
	32: 6	He appointed military o over the people	8569
	32: 9	he sent his o to Jerusalem	6269
	32:16	Sennacherib's o spoke further against	8569
	32:21	the fighting men and the leaders and o in	8569
	35:23	Archers shot King Josiah, and he told his o,	6269
Ne	4:16	The king had also sent army o and cavalry	8569
	4:16	The o posted themselves behind all	8569
Est	2:21	of the king's o who guarded the doorway,	6247
	6: 2	of the king's o who guarded the doorway,	6247
Isa	21: 5	Get up, you o, oil the shields!	8569
Jer	26:21	and all his o and officials heard his words,	1475
	38:17	the o of the king of Babylon, your life will	8569
	38:18	the o of the king of Babylon, this city will	8569
	39:13	and all the other o of the king of Babylon	8042
	40: 7	the army o and their men who were still in	8569
	40:13	the army o still in the open country came	8569
	41: 1	and had been one of the king's o,	8042
	41:11	of Kareah and all the army o who were	8569
	41:13	of Kareah and the army o who were	8569
	41:16	the army o who were with him led away all	8569
	42: 1	Then all the army o,	8569
	42: 8	of Kareah and all the army o who were	8569
	43: 4	the army o and all the people disobeyed	8569
	43: 5	o and led away all the remnant	8569
	46:26	of Babylon and his o.	6269
	51:57	her governors, o and warriors as well;	6036
Eze	23:15	them looked like Babylonian **chariot** o,	8957
	23:23	**chariot** o and men of high rank,	8957
Lk	22: 4	and the o of the **temple guard**	5130
	22:52	the o of the temple **guard,**	5130
Ac	5:22	the o did not find them there.	5677
	5:26	the captain went with his o and brought	5677
	16:35	the magistrates sent their o to the jailer	4812
	16:37	But Paul said to the o:	899S
	16:38	The o reported this to the magistrates,	4812
	21:32	at once took some o and soldiers and ran	1672
	25:23	the **high ranking** o and the leading men	5941

OFFICIAL (23) [OFFICE]

2Ki	8: 6	Then he assigned an o to her case and said	6247
	23:11	the room of an o named Nathan-Melech,	6247
	25: 8	an o of the king of Babylon,	6269
1Ch	9:11	the o **in charge** of the house of God;	5592
2Ch	13: 6	an o of Solomon son of David,	6269
	31:13	and Azariah the o **in charge** of the temple	5592
Ne	2:10	and Tobiah the Ammonite o heard	6269
	2:19	Tobiah the Ammonite o and Geshem	6269
Pr	17:11	a merciless o will be sent against him	4855
Ecc	5: 8	for one o is eyed by a higher one,	1469
Jer	38: 7	a Cushite, an o in the royal palace,	6247
	39: 3	a chief officer, Nergal-Sharezer a high o	4454
	39:13	a high o and all the other official o	4454
Da	1: 7	The chief o gave them new names:	6247
	1: 8	and he asked the chief o for permission not	6247
	1: 9	Now God had caused the o to show favor	6247
	1:10	but the o told Daniel, "I am afraid of	6247
	1:11	the guard whom the chief o had appointed	6247
	1:18	the chief o presented them to	6247
Jn	4:46	a certain **royal** o whose son lay sick	997
	4:49	The **royal** o said, "Sir, come down before	997
Ac	8:27	an **important** o in charge of all the treasury	1541
	28: 7	Publius, the **chief** o of the island.	4755

OFFICIALS (226) [OFFICE]

Ge	12:15	And when Pharaoh's o saw her,	8569
	20: 8	Abimelech summoned all his o,	8569
	37:36	Potiphar, one of Pharaoh's o,	6247
	39: 1	an Egyptian who was one of Pharaoh's o,	6247
	40: 2	Pharaoh was angry with his two o,	6247
	40: 7	So he asked Pharaoh's o who were	6247
	40:20	and he gave a feast for all his o.	6269
	40:20	and the chief baker in the presence of his o:	6269
	41:37	to Pharaoh and to all his o.	6269
	45:16	Pharaoh and all his o were pleased.	6269
	50: 7	All Pharaoh's o accompanied him—	6269
Ex	5:21	a stench to Pharaoh and his o and have put	6269
	7:10	down in front of Pharaoh and his o,	6269
	7:20	and his o and struck the water of the Nile,	6269
	8: 3	the houses of your o and on your people,	6269
	8: 4	up on you and your o and your people.' "	6269
	8: 9	to pray for you and your o and your people	6269
	8:11	your o and your people;	6269

Ex	8:21	of flies on you and your o,	6269
	8:24	and into the houses of his o,	6269
	8:29	the flies will leave Pharaoh and his o	6269
	8:31	The flies left Pharaoh and his o	6269
	9:14	and against your o and your people,	6269
	9:20	Those o of Pharaoh who feared the word of	6269
	9:30	But I know that you and your o still do	6269
	9:34	He and his o hardened their hearts.	6269
	10: 1	and the hearts of his o so	6269
	10: 6	of all your o and all the Egyptians—	6269
	10: 7	Pharaoh's o said to him,	6269
	11: 3	by Pharaoh's o and by the people.)	6269
	11: 8	All these o of yours will come to me,	6269
	12:30	and all his o and all the Egyptians got up	6269
	14: 5	and his o changed their minds about them	6269
	18:21	and appoint them as o over thousands,	8569
	18:25	o over thousands, hundreds,	8569
Nu	11:16	to you as leaders and o among the people.	8853
	26: 9	the community o who rebelled	7951
Dt	1:15	of fifties and of tens and as tribal o.	8853
	16:18	and o for each of your tribes in every town	8853
	29: 2	to all his o and to all his land.	6269
	29:10	and chief men, your elders and o,	8853
	31:28	the elders of your tribes and all your o,	8853
	34:11	and to all his o and to his whole land.	6269
Jos	8:33	with their elders, o and judges,	8853
	23: 2	their elders, leaders, judges and o—	8853
	23: 2	leaders, judges and o of Israel,	8853
Jdg	8: 6	But the o of Succoth said,	8569
	8:14	for him the names of the seventy-seven o	8569
1Sa	22: 6	and of your vintage and give it to his o	6247
	22: 6	with all his o standing around him.	6269
	22: 9	who was standing with Saul's o, said,	6269
	22:17	But the king's o were not willing to raise	6269
2Sa	13:24	Will the king and his o please join me?"	6269
	15:14	Then David said to all his o who were	6269
	15:15	The king's o answered him,	6269
	16: 6	He pelted David and all the king's o	6269
1Ki	1: 9	and all the men of Judah who were royal o,	6269
	1:47	the royal o have come to congratulate	6269
	4: 2	And these were his **chief** o:	8569
	9:22	his **government** o, his officers, his captains,	6269
	9:23	They were also the chief o in charge	5893
	9:23	550 o supervising the men who did	8097
	10: 5	the seating of his o,	6269
	10: 8	How happy your o,	6269
	11:17	some Edomite o who had served his father.	408
	11:26	He was one of Solomon's o,	6269
	15:18	to his o and sent them to Ben-Hadad son	6269
	16: 9	Zimri, one of his o,	6269
	20: 6	to send my o to search your palace and	6269
	20: 6	and the houses of your o.	6269
	20:23	the o of the king of Aram advised him,	6269
	20:31	His o said to him, "Look,	6269
	22: 3	The king of Israel had said to his o,	6269
	22: 9	king of Israel called one of his o and said,	6247
2Ki	10: 1	to the o of Jezreel, to the elders	8569
	12:20	His o conspired against him	6269
	12:21	The o who murdered him were Jozabad son	6269
	14: 5	the o who had murdered his father the king.	6269
	18:24	of the least of my master's o,	6269
	19: 5	When King Hezekiah's o came to Isaiah,	6269
	21:23	Amon's o conspired against him	6269
	22: 9	"Your o have paid out the money that was	6269
	24:12	his nobles and his o all surrendered to him.	6247
	24:15	his o and the leading men of the land.	6247
	25:24	"Do not be afraid of the Babylonian o,"	6269
1Ch	18:17	and David's sons were **chief** o at	8037
	23: 4	of the LORD and six thousand are to be o	8853
	24: 5	for there were o of the sanctuary	8269
	24: 5	and o of God among the descendants of	8569
	24: 6	in the presence of the king and of the o:	8569
	26:29	as o and judges over Israel.	8853
	27:31	the o **in charge** of King David's property.	8569
	28: 1	the o of Israel to assemble at Jerusalem:	8569
	28: 1	of hundreds, and the o **in charge** of all	8569
	28: 1	together with the **palace** o,	6247
	28:21	The o and all the people will obey	8569
	29: 6	and the o **in charge** of the king's work	8569
2Ch	8:10	They were also King Solomon's chief o—	5893
	8:10	two hundred and fifty o supervising	8097
	9: 4	the seating of his o,	6269
	9: 7	How happy your o,	6269
	17: 7	of his reign he sent his o Ben-Hail,	8569
	18: 8	king of Israel called one of his o and said,	6247
	19:11	and the Levites will **serve as** o before you.	8853
	24:10	All the o and all the people brought	8569
	24:11	by the Levites to the king's o and they saw	7213
	24:17	the o of Judah came and paid homage to	8569
	24:25	His o conspired against him for murdering	6269
	25: 3	the o who had murdered his father the king.	6269
	26:11	Hananiah, one of the royal o.	8569
	28:14	and plunder in the presence of the o and all	8569
	29:20	the city o together and went up to	8569
	29:30	and his o ordered the Levites to praise	8569
	30: 2	The king and his o and the whole assembly	8569
	30: 6	from the king and from his o, which read:	8569
	30:12	the king and his o had ordered,	8569
	30:24	the o provided them with a thousand bulls	8569
	31: 8	When Hezekiah and his o came and saw	8569
	32: 3	he consulted with his o and military staff	8569
	33:24	Amon's o conspired against him	6269
	34:16	"Your o are doing everything	6269
	35: 8	His o also contributed voluntarily to	8569
	36:18	and the treasures of the king and his o.	8569
Ezr	4: 9	judges and o over the men from Tripolis,	10062

Ezr	5: 6	the o of Trans-Euphrates,	10061
	6: 6	their fellow o of that province,	10061
	7:28	and all the king's powerful o.	8569
	8:20	a body that David and the o had established	8569
	8:25	the articles that the king, his advisers, his o	8569
	9: 2	And the leaders and o have led the way	6036
	10: 8	in accordance with the decision of the o	8569
	10:14	Let our o act for the whole assembly.	8569
Ne	2:16	The o did not know where I had gone	6036
	2:16	or nobles or o or any others who would	6036
	4:14	the o and the rest of the people,	6036
	4:19	the o and the rest of the people,	6036
	5: 7	and then accused the nobles and o.	6036
	5:12	the priests and made **the nobles and** o take	4392S
	5:17	and fifty Jews and o ate at my table,	6036
	7: 5	the o and the common people	6036
	9:10	against all his o and all the people	6269
	12:40	so did I, together with half the o,	6036
	13:11	So I rebuked the o and asked them,	6036
Est	1: 3	a banquet for all his nobles and o.	6269
	2:18	Esther's banquet, for all his nobles and o.	6269
	2:23	the two o were hanged on a gallows.	2157S
	3: 2	the royal o at the king's gate knelt down	6269
	3: 3	royal o at the king's gate asked Mordecai,	6269
	4:11	"All the king's o and the people of	6269
	5:11	above the other nobles and o.	6269
Pr	17:26	or to flog o for their integrity.	5618
	29:12	all his o become wicked.	9250
Isa	3: 4	I will make boys their o;	8569
	19:11	The o of Zoan are nothing but fools;	8569
	19:13	The o of Zoan have become fools,	8569
	30: 4	Though *they* have o in Zoan	8569
	36: 9	of the least of my master's o,	6269
	37: 5	When King Hezekiah's o came to Isaiah,	6269
Jer	1:18	against the kings of Judah, its o,	8569
	2:26	they, their kings and their o,	8569
	4: 9	"the king and the o will lose heart,	8569
	8: 1	the bones of the kings and o *of* Judah,	8569
	17:25	through the gates of this city with their o,	8569
	17:25	and their o will come riding in chariots and	8569
	21: 7	his o and the people	6269
	22: 2	you, your o and your people who come	6269
	22: 4	accompanied by their o and their people.	6269
	24: 1	of Jehoiakim king of Judah and the o,	8569
	24: 8	his o and the survivors from Jerusalem.	8569
	25:18	and o, to make them a ruin and an object	8569
	25:19	his attendants, his o and all his people,	8569
	26:10	the o *of* Judah heard about these things,	8569
	26:11	the priests and the prophets said to the o	8569
	26:12	Then Jeremiah said to all the o and all	8569
	26:16	the o and all the people said to the priests	8569
	26:21	and his officers and o heard his words,	8569
	29: 2	the **court** and the leaders of Judah	6247
	32:32	they, their kings and o,	8569
	34:10	So all the o and people who entered	8569
	34:19	the **court** o, the priests and all the people	6247
	34:21	of Judah and his o over	8569
	35: 4	It was next to the room of the o,	8569
	36:12	where all the o were sitting:	8569
	36:12	and all the other o.	8569
	36:14	all the o sent Jehudi son of Nethaniah,	8569
	36:19	Then the o said to Baruch,	8569
	36:21	the king and all the o standing beside him.	8569
	37:14	and brought him to the o.	8569
	37:18	against you or your o or this people,	6269
	38: 4	Then the o said to the king,	8569
	38:22	king of Judah will be brought out to the o *of*	8569
	38:25	If the o hear that I talked with you,	8569
	38:27	All the o did come to Jeremiah	8569
	39: 3	Then all the o *of* the king of Babylon came	8569
	39: 3	and all the other o *of* the king of Babylon.	8569
	41:16	and **court** o he had brought from Gibeon	6247
	44:17	and our o did in the towns of Judah and in	8569
	44:21	your kings and your o and the people of	8569
	48: 7	together with his priests and o.	8569
	49: 3	together with his priests and o.	8569
	49:38	in Elam and destroy her king and o,"	8569
	50:35	and against her o and wise men!	8569
	51:23	with you I shatter governors and o.	6036
	51:28	their governors and all their o,	6036
	51:57	I will make her o and wise men drunk,	8569
	52:10	he also killed all the o of Judah.	8569
Eze	22:27	Her o within her are like wolves	8569
Da	1: 3	Ashpenaz, chief of his **court** o,	6247
	3: 2	magistrates and all the other provincial o	10716
	3: 3	and all the other provincial o assembled for	10716
Am	1:15	he and his o together," says the LORD.	8569
	2: 3	I will destroy her ruler and kill all her o	8569
Na	3:17	your o are like swarms of locusts that settle in	3261
Zep	3: 3	Her o are roaring lions,	8569
Mt	20:25	their **high** o exercise authority over them.	3489
Mk	6:21	*for* his **high** o and military commanders and	3491
	10:42	their **high** o exercise authority over them.	3489
Jn	18: 3	a detachment of soldiers and some o from	5677
	18:12	and his o arrested Jesus.	5677
	18:18	and o stood around a fire they had made	5677
	18:22	one *of* the o nearby struck him in the face.	5677
	19: 6	as the chief priests and their o saw him,	5677
Ac	17: 6	and some other brothers before the **city** o,	4485
	17: 8	and the **city** o were thrown into turmoil.	4485
	19:31	Even some *of* the o of the province,	825

OFFICIATE (1) [OFFICE]

2Ki	17:32	of their own people *to* o for them *as* priests	6913

OFFSCOURING (KJV) See SCUM

OFFSET (1) [OFF]

1Ki	6: 6	He made o **ledges** around the outside of	4492

OFFSHOOTS (1) [OFF, SHOOT]

Isa	22:24	its offspring and o—all its lesser vessels,	7617

OFFSPRING (61) [OFF]

Ge	3:15	and between your o and hers;	2446
	12: 7	"To your o I will give this land."	2446
	13:15	I will give to you and your o forever.	2446
	13:16	I will make your o like the dust of	2446
	13:16	then your o could be counted.	2446
	15: 5	Then he said to him, "So shall your o be."	2446
	17:12	those who are not your o.	2446
	21:12	through Isaac that your o will be reckoned.	2446
	21:13	because he is your o."	2446
	22:18	your o all nations on earth will be blessed,	2446
	24: 7	saying, 'To your o I will give this land'—	2446
	24:60	may your o possess the gates	2446
	26: 4	your o all nations on earth will be blessed,	2446
	28:14	be blessed through you and your o.	2446
	38: 8	to her as a brother-in-law to produce o	2446
	38: 9	But Onan knew that the o would not be his;	2446
	38: 9	to keep from producing o for his brother.	2446
	46: 6	and Jacob and all his o went to Egypt.	2446
	46: 7	and granddaughters—all his o.	2446
Ex	13: 2	The **first** o *of* every womb among	7081
	13:12	to the LORD the **first** o *of* every womb.	7081
	13:15	the **first** male o *of* every womb	7081
	34:19	"The **first** o *of* every womb belongs to me,	7081
Lev	21:15	he will not defile his o among his people.	2446
Nu	3:12	the **first** male o of every Israelite woman.	
		1147+7081+8167	
	8:16	**first** male o from every Israelite woman.	1147
	18:15	The **first** o *of* every womb,	7081
	18:19	before the LORD for both you and your o."	2446
Ru	4:12	Through the o the LORD gives you	2446
2Sa	4: 8	the king against Saul and his o."	2446
	7:12	I will raise up your o to succeed you,	2446
1Ch	17:11	I will raise up your o to succeed you,	2446
Job	18:19	He has no o or descendants	5769
	21: 8	their o before their eyes.	7368
	27:14	his o will never have enough to eat.	7368
Ps	37:28	but the o of the wicked will be cut off;	2446
Isa	9:20	Each will feed on the flesh of his own o:	2446
	14:20	The o *of* the wicked will never	2446
	14:22	her o and descendants,"	5769
	22:24	its o and offshoots—all its lesser vessels,	7368
	44: 3	I will pour out my Spirit on your o,	2446
	53:10	he will see his o and prolong his days,	2446
	57: 3	you o *of* adulterers and prostitutes!	2446
	57: 4	a brood of rebels, the o *of* liars?	2446
	61: 9	the nations and their o among the peoples.	7368
Jer	22:30	for none of his o will prosper,	2446
	31:27	of Judah with the o *of* men and of animals.	2446
La	2:20	Should women eat their o,	7262
Hos	9:16	I will slay their cherished o."	1061
Mal	2:15	Because he was seeking godly o.	2446
Ac	3:25	'Through your o all peoples on earth will	5065
	17:28	'We are his o.'	1169
	17:29	"Therefore since we are God's o,	1169
Ro	4:13	that Abraham and his o received	5065
	4:16	may be guaranteed *to* all Abraham's o—	5065
	4:18	"So shall your o be."	5065
	9: 7	"It is through Isaac that your o will	5065
	9: 8	children of the promise who are regarded as	
		Abraham's o.	5065
Heb	11:18	"It is through Isaac that your o will	5065
Rev	12:17	to make war against the rest *of* her o—	5065
	22:16	I am the Root and the O of David,	1169

OFTEN (24)

1Sa	18:30	and **as** o **as** they did,	1896+4946
2Ki	4: 9	that this man who o comes our way is	9458
Job	21:17	"Yet **how** o is the lamp of the wicked	3869+4537
	21:17	How o does calamity come upon them,	NIH
	21:18	How o are they like straw before the wind,	NIH
Ps	78:40	**How** o they rebelled against him in	3869+4537
Isa	28:19	**As** o **as** it comes it will carry you away;	
		1896+4946	
Jer	31:20	I o speak against him, I still remember	1896+4946
Mt	17:15	He o falls into the fire or into the water.	4490
	23:37	**how** o I have longed to gather your children	4529
Mk	5: 4	For he had o been chained hand and foot,	4490
	9:22	"It has o thrown him into fire or water	4490
Lk	5:16	But Jesus o **withdrew** to lonely places	AIT
	5:33	"John's disciples o fast and pray,	4781
	13:34	**how** o I have longed to gather your children	4529
Jn	18: 2	Jesus had o met there with his disciples.	4490
Ro	15:22	This is why I have o been hindered	4498
2Co	8:22	with them our brother who has o proved	4490
	11:27	I have labored and toiled and have o gone	4490
	11:27	and thirst and have o gone without food;	4490
Php	3:18	as I have o told you before and	4490
2Ti	1:16	because he o refreshed me and was	4490
Heb	6: 7	in the rain o falling on it and that produces	4490
Rev	11: 6	with every kind of plague **as** o **as** they want.	4006

OG (20) [OG'S]

Nu	21:33	and O king of Bashan and his whole army	6384
	32:33	of the Amorites and the kingdom of O king	6384

Dt	1: 4	and at Edrei had defeated O king of Bashan,	6384
	3: 1	and O king of Bashan with his whole army	6384
	3: 3	also gave into our hands O king of Bashan	6384
	3:11	(Only O king of Bashan was left of	6384
	3:13	all of Bashan, the kingdom of O,	6384
	4:47	and the land of O king of Bashan.	6384
	29: 7	of Heshbon and O king of Bashan came out	6384
	31: 4	to them what he did to Sihon and O,	6384
Jos	2:10	and what you did to Sihon and O,	6384
	9:10	and O king of Bashan.	6384
	12: 4	And the territory of O king of Bashan,	6384
	13:12	the whole kingdom of O in Bashan,	6384
	13:30	the entire realm of O king of Bashan—	6384
	13:31	and Edrei (the royal cities of O in Bashan).	6384
1Ki	4:19	of the Amorites and the country of O king	6384
Ne	9:22	of Heshbon and the country of O king.	6384
Ps	135:11	O king of Bashan and all the kings	6384
	136:20	and O king of Bashan—	6384

OG'S (2) [OG]

Dt	3: 4	O kingdom in Bashan.	6384
	3:10	towns of O kingdom in Bashan.	6384

OH (37) [O] See Index of Articles Etc.

OHAD (2)

Ge	46:10	The sons of Simeon: Jemuel, Jamin, O,	176
Ex	6:15	The sons of Simeon were Jemuel, Jamin, O,	176

OHEL (1)

1Ch	3:20	There were also five others: Hashubah, O,	186

OHOLAH (5)

Eze	23: 4	The older was named O,	188
	23: 4	O is Samaria, and Oholibah is Jerusalem.	188
	23: 5	"O engaged in prostitution	188
	23:36	will you judge O and Oholibah?	188
	23:44	with those lewd women, O and Oholibah.	188

OHOLIAB (5)

Ex	31: 6	I have appointed O son of Ahisamach,	190
	35:34	And he has given both him and O son	190
	36: 1	O and every skilled person to whom	190
	36: 2	and O and every skilled person to whom	190
	38:23	with him was O son of Ahisamach, of	190

OHOLIBAH (6)

Eze	23: 4	and her sister was O.	191
	23: 4	Oholah is Samaria, and O is Jerusalem.	191
	23:11	"Her sister O saw this,	191
	23:22	O, this is what the Sovereign LORD says:	191
	23:36	will you judge Oholah and O?	191
	23:44	with those lewd women, Oholah and O.	191

OHOLIBAMAH (8)

Ge	36: 2	of Elon the Hittite, and O daughter of Anah	192
	36: 5	and O bore Jeush,	192
	36:14	The sons of Esau's wife O daughter	192
	36:18	The sons of Esau's wife O:	192
	36:18	from Esau's wife O daughter of Anah.	192
	36:25	Dishon and O daughter of Anah.	192
	36:41	O, Elah, Pinon,	192
1Ch	1:52	O, Elah, Pinon,	192

OIL (211) [OILS]

Ge	28:18	and set it up as a pillar and poured o on top	9043
	35:14	he also poured o on it.	9043
Ex	25: 6	**olive** o for the light;	9043
	25: 6	the anointing o and for the fragrant incense;	9043
	27:20	to bring you clear o *of* pressed olives for	9043
	29: 2	make bread, and cakes mixed with o,	9043
	29: 2	and wafers spread with o.	9043
	29: 7	Take the anointing o and anoint him	9043
	29:21	and some of the anointing o and sprinkle it	9043
	29:23	and a cake made with o, and a wafer.	9043
	29:40	a quarter of a hin of o *from* pressed olives,	9043
	30:24	and a hin of olive o.	9043
	30:25	Make these into a sacred anointing o,	9043
	30:25	It will be the sacred anointing o.	9043
	30:31	'This is to be my sacred anointing o for	9043
	30:32	on men's bodies and do not make any o	NIH
	31:11	and the anointing o and fragrant incense for	9043
	35: 8	**olive** o for the light;	9043
	35: 8	the anointing o and for the fragrant incense;	9043
	35:14	lamps and o *for* the light;	9043
	35:15	the anointing o and the fragrant incense;	9043
	35:28	They also brought spices and **olive** o for	9043
	35:28	the anointing o and for the fragrant incense.	9043
	37:29	They also made the sacred anointing o and	9043
	39:37	and the o *for* the light;	9043
	39:38	the anointing o, the fragrant incense,	9043
	40: 9	the anointing o and anoint the tabernacle	9043
Lev	2: 1	He is to pour o on it,	9043
	2: 4	a handful of the fine flour and with o,	9043
	2: 4	without yeast and mixed with o,	9043
	2: 4	without yeast and spread with o.	9043
	2: 5	it is to be made of fine flour mixed with o,	9043
	2: 6	Crumble it and pour o on it;	9043
	2: 7	it is to be made of fine flour and o.	9043
	2:15	Put o and incense on it;	9043
	2:16	of the crushed grain and the o,	9043

Lev	5:11	He must not put **o** or incense on it,	9043
	6:15	to take a handful of fine flour and **o**,	9043
	6:21	Prepare it with **o** on a griddle;	9043
	7:10	whether mixed with **o** or dry,	9043
	7:12	without yeast and mixed with **o**,	9043
	7:12	without yeast and spread with **o**,	9043
	7:12	and mixed with **o**.	9043
	8: 2	their garments, the anointing **o**,	9043
	8:10	the anointing **o** and anointed the tabernacle	9043
	8:11	of the **o** on the altar seven times,	5647ˢ
	8:12	of the anointing **o** on Aaron's head	9043
	8:26	and one made with **o**, and a wafer;	9043
	8:30	the anointing **o** and some of the blood from	9043
	9: 4	with a grain offering mixed with **o**.	9043
	10: 7	the LORD's anointing **o** is on you."	9043
	14:10	of an ephah of fine flour mixed with **o** for	9043
	14:10	and one log of **o**.	9043
	14:12	along with the log of **o**;	9043
	14:15	priest shall then take some of the log of **o**,	9043
	14:16	dip his right forefinger into the **o**	9043
	14:17	The priest is to put some of the **o** remaining	9043
	14:18	of the **o** in his palm the priest shall put on	9043
	14:21	of an ephah of fine flour mixed with **o** for	9043
	14:21	a log of **o**,	9043
	14:24	together with the log of **o**,	9043
	14:26	of the **o** into the palm of his own left hand,	9043
	14:27	of the **o** from his palm seven times before	9043
	14:28	Some of the **o** in his palm he is to put on	9043
	14:29	in his palm the priest shall put on	9043
	21:10	the anointing **o** poured on his head	9043
	21:12	by the anointing **o** *of* his God.	9043
	23:13	of an ephah of fine flour mixed with **o**—	9043
	24: 2	to bring you clear **o** *of* pressed olives for	9043
Nu	4: 9	and all its jars for the **o** used to supply it.	9043
	4:16	is to have charge of the **o** *for* the light,	9043
	4:16	and the anointing **o**.	9043
	5:15	He must not pour **o** on it or put incense	9043
	6:15	cakes made of fine flour mixed with **o**,	9043
	6:15	and wafers spread with **o**.	9043
	7:13	each filled with fine flour mixed with **o** as	9043
	7:19	each filled with fine flour mixed with **o** as	9043
	7:25	each filled with fine flour mixed with **o** as	9043
	7:31	each filled with fine flour mixed with **o** as	9043
	7:37	each filled with fine flour mixed with **o** as	9043
	7:43	each filled with fine flour mixed with **o** as	9043
	7:49	each filled with fine flour mixed with **o** as	9043
	7:55	each filled with fine flour mixed with **o** as	9043
	7:61	each filled with fine flour mixed with **o** as	9043
	7:67	each filled with fine flour mixed with **o** as	9043
	7:73	each filled with fine flour mixed with **o** as	9043
	7:79	each filled with fine flour mixed with **o** as	9043
	8: 8	of fine flour mixed with **o**;	9043
	11: 8	like something made with **olive o**.	8992
	15: 4	with a quarter of a hin of **o**.	9043
	15: 6	with a third of a hin of **o**,	9043
	15: 9	of fine flour mixed with half a hin of **o**.	9043
	18:12	"I give you all the finest **olive o** and all	3658
	28: 5	a quarter of a hin of **o** *from* pressed olives.	9043
	28: 9	of an ephah of fine flour mixed with **o**.	9043
	28:12	of an ephah of fine flour mixed with **o**;	9043
	28:12	of an ephah of fine flour mixed with **o** as	9043
	28:13	of an ephah of fine flour mixed with **o**;	9043
	28:20	of an ephah of fine flour mixed with **o**;	9043
	28:28	of an ephah of fine flour mixed with **o**;	9043
	29: 3	of an ephah of fine flour mixed with **o**;	9043
	29: 9	of an ephah of fine flour mixed with **o**;	9043
	29:14	of an ephah of fine flour mixed with **o**;	9043
	35:25	who was anointed with the holy **o**.	9043
Dt	7:13	your grain, new wine and **o**—	3658
	8: 8	pomegranates, olive **o** and honey;	9043
	11:14	gather in your grain, new wine and **o**,	3658
	12:17	the tithe of your grain and new wine and **o**,	3658
	14:23	Eat the tithe of your grain, new wine and **o**,	3658
	18: 4	new wine and **o**,	3658
	28:40	but you will not use the **o**,	3658
	28:51	firstfruits of your grain, new wine or **o**,	3658
	32:13	and with **o** from the flinty crag,	9043
	33:24	and let him bathe his feet in **o**.	9043
Jdg	9: 9	'Should I give up my **o**,	2016
1Sa	10: 1	a flask of **o** and poured it on Saul's head	9043
	16: 1	Fill your horn with **o** and be on your way;	9043
	16:13	of **o** and anointed him in the presence	9043
2Sa	1:21	no longer rubbed with **o**.	9043
1Ki	1:39	Zadok the priest took the horn of **o** from	9043
	5:11	twenty thousand baths of pressed olive **o**.	9043
	17:12	only a handful of flour in a jar and a little **o**	9043
	17:14	be used up and the jug of **o** will not run dry	9043
	17:16	up and the jug of **o** did not run dry,	9043
2Ki	4: 2	she said, "except a little **o**."	9043
	4: 4	Pour **o** into all the jars, and as each is filled,	NIH
	4: 6	Then the **o** stopped flowing.	9043
	4: 7	"Go, sell the **o** and pay your debts.	9043
	9: 1	of **o** with you and go to Ramoth Gilead.	9043
	9: 3	the **o** on his head and declare, 'This is what	9043
	9: 6	the prophet poured the **o** on Jehu's head	9043
	20:13	silver, the gold, the spices and the fine **o**—	9043
1Ch	9:29	as well as the flour and wine, and the **o**,	9043
	12:40	raisin cakes, wine, **o**, cattle and sheep,	9043
	27:28	in charge of the supplies of **olive o**.	9043
2Ch	2:10	and twenty thousand baths of **olive o**."	9043
	2:15	and the **olive o** and wine he promised,	9043
	11:11	with supplies of food, **olive o** and wine.	9043
	31: 5	grain, new wine and **o** and honey and all that	3658
	32:28	harvest of grain, new wine and **o**;	3658
Ezr	3: 7	and **o** to the people of Sidon and Tyre,	9043
	6: 9	and wheat, salt, wine and **o**,	10442
	7:22	a hundred baths of **olive o**,	10442

Ne	5:11	grain, new wine and **o**."	3658
	10:37	of all our trees and of our new wine and **o**.	3658
	10:39	and **o** to the storerooms where the articles	3658
	13: 5	new wine and **o** prescribed for the Levites,	3658
	13:12	new wine and **o** into the storerooms.	3658
Est	2:12	with **o** *of* myrrh and six with perfumes	9043
Job	29: 6	poured out for me streams of **olive o**.	9043
Ps	23: 5	You anoint my head with **o**;	9043
	45: 7	by anointing you with the **o** *of* joy.	9043
	55:21	his words are more soothing than **o**,	9043
	89:20	with my sacred **o** I have anointed him.	9043
	104:15	**o** to make his face shine,	9043
	109:18	into his bones like **o**.	9043
	133: 2	It is like precious **o** poured on the head,	9043
	141: 5	it is **o** *on* my head.	9043
Pr	5: 3	and her speech is smoother than **o**;	9043
	21:17	whoever loves wine and **o** will never	9043
	21:20	of the wise are stores of choice food and **o**,	9043
	27:16	like restraining the wind or grasping **o** with	9043
Ecc	9: 8	and always anoint your head with **o**.	9043
Isa	1: 6	cleansed or bandaged or soothed with **o**.	9043
	21: 5	Get up, you officers, **o** the shields!	5417
	39: 2	the silver, the gold, the spices, the fine **o**,	9043
	57: 9	with **olive o** and increased your perfumes.	9043
	61: 3	the **o** *of* gladness instead of mourning,	9043
Jer	31:12	the grain, the new wine and the **o**,	3658
	40:10	the wine, summer fruit and **o**,	9043
	41: 8	We have wheat and barley, **o** and honey,	9043
Eze	16:13	fine flour, honey and **olive o**.	9043
	16:18	you offered my **o** and incense before them.	9043
	16:19	**olive o** and honey I gave you to eat—	9043
	23:41	on which you had placed the incense and **o**	9043
	27:17	honey, **o** and balm for your wares.	9043
	32:14	and make her streams flow like **o**,	9043
	45:14	The prescribed portion of **o**,	9043
	45:24	along with a hin of **o** for each ephah.	9043
	45:25	burnt offerings, grain offerings and **o**.	9043
	46: 5	along with a hin of **o** for each ephah.	9043
	46: 7	along with a hin of **o** with each ephah.	9043
	46:11	along with a hin of **o** for each ephah.	9043
	46:14	a third of a hin of **o** to moisten the flour.	9043
	46:15	and the grain offering and the **o** shall	9043
Hos	2: 5	my **o** and my drink.'	9043
	2: 8	the new wine and **o**,	3658
	2:22	the new wine and **o**,	3658
	12: 1	with Assyria and sends **olive o** to Egypt.	9043
Joel	1:10	the new wine is dried up, the **o** fails.	3658
	2:19	"I am sending you grain, new wine and **o**,	3658
	2:24	with new wine and **o**.	3658
Mic	6: 7	with ten thousand rivers of **o**?	9043
	6:15	you will press olives but not use the **o**	9043
Hag	1:11	the **o** and whatever the ground produces,	3658
	2:12	some wine, **o** or other food,	9043
Zec	4:12	the two gold pipes that pour out **golden** *o*?"	AIT
Mt	6:17	put **o** on your head and wash your face,	230
	25: 3	but did not take any **o** with them.	1778
	25: 4	took **o** in jars along with their lamps.	1778
	25: 8	'Give us some of your **o**;	1778
	25: 9	go to those who sell **o** and buy some	NIG
	25:10	while they were on their way to buy the **o**,	NIG
Mk	6:13	and anointed many sick people with **o**	1778
Lk	7:46	You did not put **o** on my head,	1778
	10:34	pouring on **o** and wine.	1778
	16: 6	" 'Eight hundred gallons *of* **olive o**,'	1778
Heb	1: 9	by anointing you with the **o** of joy."	1778
Jas	5:14	over him and anoint him *with* **o** in the name	1778
Rev	6: 6	and do not damage the **o** and the wine!"	1778
	18:13	of wine and **olive o**, of fine flour and wheat;	1778

OILS (1) [OIL]

Ps	92:10	fine **o** have been poured upon me.	9043

OINTMENT (1) [OINTMENTS]

Job	41:31	and stirs up the sea like a **pot of o**.	5350

OINTMENTS (1) [OINTMENT]

Eze	16: 9	and washed the blood from you and put **o**	9043

OLD (325) [OLDER, OLDEST]

Ge	5:32	After Noah was 500 years **o**,	1201
	6: 4	They were the heroes of **o**, men of renown.	6409
	7: 6	Noah was six hundred years **o** when	1201
	11:10	when Shem was 100 years **o**,	1201
	12: 4	Abram was seventy-five years **o**	1201
	15: 9	a goat and a ram, each **three** years **o**,	8992
	15:15	in peace and be buried at a good **o** age.	8484
	16:16	Abram was eighty-six years **o**	1201
	17: 1	When Abram was ninety-nine years **o**,	1201
	17:12	among you who is eight days **o** must	1201
	17:17	a son be born to a *man* a hundred years **o**?	1201
	17:24	Abraham was ninety-nine years **o**	1201
	18:11	Abraham and Sarah were already **o**	2418
	18:12	"After I am worn out and my master *is* **o**,	2416
	18:13	I really have a child, now that I *am* **o**?'	2416
	19: 4	both young and **o**—surrounded the house.	2418
	19:11	the house, young and **o**, with blindness so	1524
	19:31	"Our father *is* **o**,	2416
	21: 2	and bore a son to Abraham in his **o** age,	2421
	21: 4	When his son Isaac was eight days **o**,	1201
	21: 5	Abraham was a hundred years **o**	1201
	21: 7	Yet I have borne him a son in his **o** age."	2421
	23: 1	to be a hundred and twenty-seven **years** *o*.	AIT
	24: 1	Abraham *was* now **o** and well advanced	2416
	24:36	Sarah had borne him a son in her **o** age,	2420

Ge	25: 8	a good **o** age, an old man and full of years;	8484
	25: 8	an **o** *man* and full of years;	2418
	25:20	and Isaac was forty years **o**	1201
	25:26	Isaac was sixty years **o**	1201
	26:34	When Esau was forty years **o**,	1201
	27: 1	When Isaac *was* **o** and his eyes were	2416
	27: 2	*I am* now *an* **o** *man* and don't know the day	2416
	35:29	gathered to his people, **o** and full of years.	2418
	37: 3	he had been born to him in his **o** age;	2421
	41:46	Joseph was thirty years **o** when he entered	1201
	44:20	a young son born to him in his **o** age.	2421
	47: 8	Pharaoh asked him, "How **o** are you?"	
			2644+3427+9102
	48:10	Israel's eyes were failing because of **o** age,	2419
Ex	7: 7	Moses was eighty years **o** and Aaron	1201
	10: 9	"We will go with our young and **o**,	2418
	29:38	two lambs a year **o**.	1201
	30:14	those twenty years **o** or more,	1201
	38:26	twenty years **o** or more, a total of 603,550	1201
Lev	9: 3	*both* a year **o** and without defect—	1201
	14:10	and one ewe lamb a year **o**,	1426
	23:12	the LORD a lamb a year **o** without defect,	1201
	23:18	each a year **o** and without defect,	1201
	23:19	each a year **o**, for a fellowship offering.	1201
	25:22	the **o** crop and will continue to eat from it	3824
	27: 7	If it is a person sixty years **o** or more,	1201
Nu	1: 3	the men in Israel twenty years **o** or more	1201
	1:18	the men twenty years **o** or more were listed	1201
	1:20	All the men twenty years **o** or more	1201
	1:22	All the men twenty years **o** or more	1201
	1:24	All the men twenty years **o** or more	1201
	1:26	All the men twenty years **o** or more	1201
	1:28	All the men twenty years **o** or more	1201
	1:30	All the men twenty years **o** or more	1201
	1:32	All the men twenty years **o** or more	1201
	1:34	All the men twenty years **o** or more	1201
	1:36	All the men twenty years **o** or more	1201
	1:38	All the men twenty years **o** or more	1201
	1:40	All the men twenty years **o** or more	1201
	1:42	All the men twenty years **o** or more	1201
	1:45	All the Israelites twenty years **o** or more	1201
	3:15	Count every male a month **o** or more."	1201
	3:22	The number of all the males a month **o**	1201
	3:28	the males a month **o** or more was 8,600.	1201
	3:34	The number of all the males a month **o**	1201
	3:39	including every male a month **o** or more,	1201
	3:40	a month **o** or more and make a list	1201
	3:43	of firstborn males a month **o** or more,	1201
	7:15	one ram and one male lamb a year **o**,	1201
	7:17	and five male lambs a year **o**,	1201
	7:21	one ram and one male lamb a year **o**,	1201
	7:23	and five male lambs a year **o**,	1201
	7:27	one ram and one male lamb a year **o**,	1201
	7:29	and five male lambs a year **o**,	1201
	7:33	one ram and one male lamb a year **o**,	1201
	7:35	and five male lambs a year **o**,	1201
	7:39	one ram and one male lamb a year **o**,	1201
	7:41	and five male lambs a year **o**,	1201
	7:45	one ram and one male lamb a year **o**,	1201
	7:47	and five male lambs a year **o**,	1201
	7:51	one ram and one male lamb a year **o**,	1201
	7:53	and five male lambs a year **o**,	1201
	7:57	one ram and one male lamb a year **o**,	1201
	7:59	and five male lambs a year **o**,	1201
	7:63	one ram and one male lamb a year **o**,	1201
	7:65	and five male lambs a year **o**,	1201
	7:69	one ram and one male lamb a year **o**,	1201
	7:71	and five male lambs a year **o**,	1201
	7:75	one ram and one male lamb a year **o**,	1201
	7:77	and five male lambs a year **o**,	1201
	7:81	one ram and one male lamb a year **o**,	1201
	7:83	and five male lambs a year **o**,	1201
	7:87	and twelve male lambs a year **o**,	1201
	7:88	and sixty male lambs a year **o**.	1201
	8:24	Men twenty-five years **o** or more	1201
	14:29	every one of you twenty years **o** or more	1201
	18:16	When they are a month **o**,	1201
	26: 2	all those twenty years **o** or more	1201
	26: 4	a census of the *men* twenty years **o** or more,	1201
	26:62	a month **o** or more numbered 23,000.	1201
	28: 3	two lambs a year **o** without defect,	1201
	28: 9	make an offering of two lambs a year **o**	1201
	28:11	one ram and seven male lambs a year **o**,	1201
	28:19	one ram and seven male lambs a year **o**,	1201
	28:27	one ram and seven male lambs a year **o** as	1201
	29: 2	one ram and seven male lambs a year **o**,	1201
	29: 8	one ram and seven male lambs a year **o**,	1201
	29:13	two rams and fourteen male lambs a year **o**,	1201
	29:17	two rams and fourteen male lambs a year **o**,	1201
	29:20	two rams and fourteen male lambs a year **o**,	1201
	29:23	two rams and fourteen male lambs a year **o**,	1201
	29:26	two rams and fourteen male lambs a year **o**,	1201
	29:29	two rams and fourteen male lambs a year **o**,	1201
	29:32	two rams and fourteen male lambs a year **o**,	1201
	29:36	one ram and seven male lambs a year **o**,	1201
	32:11	the men twenty years **o** or more who came	1201
	33:39	and twenty-three years **o** when he died	1201
Dt	28:50	without respect for the **o** or pity for	2418
	31: 2	and twenty years **o** and I am no longer able	1201
	32: 7	Remember the days of **o**;	6409
	34: 7	Moses was a hundred and twenty years **o**	1201
Jos	6:21	men and women, young and **o**, cattle,	2418
	9: 4	with worn-out sacks and wineskins,	1165
	9: 5	on their feet and wore **o** clothes.	1165
	13: 1	Joshua *was* **o** and well advanced in years,	2416
	13: 1	the LORD said to him, "You *are* very **o**,	
			928+995+2021+2416+3427

Dt	14: 7	I was forty years o when Moses the servant	1201
	14:10	So here I am today, eighty-five years o!	1201
	23: 1	by then o and well advanced in years,	2416
	23: 2	"I am o and well advanced in years.	2416
Jdg	6:25	the one seven years o.	NIH
	8:32	at a good o age and was buried in the tomb	8484
	19:16	an o man from the hill country of Ephraim,	2418
	19:17	the o man asked, "Where are you going?	2418
	19:20	welcome at my house," the o man said.	2418
	19:22	they shouted to the o man who owned	2418
Ru	1:12	*I am* too o to have another husband.	2418
	4:15	and sustain you in your o age.	8484
1Sa	2:22	Now Eli, *who was* very o,	2416
	2:31	not be an o *man* in your family line	2418
	2:32	family line there will never be an o *man.*	2418
	4:15	who was ninety-eight years o	1201
	4:18	for he was an o man and heavy.	2418
	5: 9	both young and o,	1524
	8: 1	When Samuel grew o,	2416
	8: 5	They said to him, "You *are* o,	2416
	12: 2	As for me, *I am* o and gray,	2416
	13: 1	Saul was [thirty] years o when he became	1201
	17:12	in Saul's time he *was* o and well advanced	2416
	24:13	As the o saying goes, 'From evildoers come	7719
	28:14	"An o man wearing a robe is coming up,"	2418
	30: 2	both young and o,	1524
	30:19	Nothing was missing: young or o,	1524
2Sa	2:10	Ish-Bosheth son of Saul was forty years o	1201
	4: 4	He was five years o when the news	1201
	5: 4	David was thirty years o when he became	1201
	19:32	Now Barzillai *was* a very o *man,*	2416
	19:35	I am now eighty years o.	1201
1Ki	1: 1	When King David *was* o and well advanced	2416
	11: 4	As Solomon grew o, his wives turned his	2420
	13:11	Now there was a certain o prophet living	2418
	13:18	The o prophet answered,	NIH
	13:20	to the o prophet who had brought him back.	NIH
	13:25	in the city where the o prophet lived.	2418
	14:21	He was forty-one years o when he became	1201
	15:23	In his o age, however, his feet became	2420
	22:42	Jehoshaphat was thirty-five years o	1201
2Ki	3:21	so every man, **young and o,**	2025+2256+5087
	4:14	she has no son and her husband *is* o."	2416
	8:17	He was thirty-two years o when he became	1201
	8:26	Ahaziah was twenty-two years o	1201
	11:21	Joash was seven years o when he began	1201
	14: 2	He was twenty-five years o when he became	1201
	14:21	Azariah, who was sixteen years o,	1201
	15: 2	He was sixteen years o when he became	1201
	15:33	He was twenty-five years o when he became	1201
	16: 2	Ahaz was twenty years o when he became	1201
	18: 2	He was twenty-five years o when he became	1201
	19:25	In days of o I planned it;	7710
	21: 1	Manasseh was twelve years o	1201
	21:19	Amon was twenty-two years o	1201
	22: 1	Josiah was eight years o when he became	1201
	23:31	Jehoahaz was twenty-three years o	1201
	23:36	Jehoiakim was twenty-five years o	1201
	24: 8	Jehoiachin was eighteen years o	1201
	24:18	Zedekiah was twenty-one years o	1201
1Ch	2:21	married her when he was sixty years o),	1201
	23: 1	When David *was* o and full of years,	2416
	23: 3	The Levites thirty years o or more	1201
	23:24	that is, the workers twenty years o	1201
	23:27	from *those* twenty years o or more.	1201
	25: 8	Young and o alike,	1524
	26:13	young and o alike.	1524
	27:23	the number of the men twenty years o	1201
	29:28	He died at a good o age,	8484
2Ch	3: 3	the cubit of the o standard).	8037
	12:13	He was forty-one years o when he became	1201
	20:31	He was thirty-five years o when he became	1201
	21: 5	Jehoram was thirty-two years o	1201
	21:20	Jehoram was thirty-two years o	1201
	22: 2	Ahaziah was twenty-two years o	1201
	24: 1	Joash was seven years o when he became	1201
	24:15	Now Jehoiada *was* o and full of years,	2416
	25: 1	Amaziah was twenty-five years o	1201
	25: 5	then mustered those twenty years o or more	1201
	26: 1	Uzziah, who was sixteen years o,	1201
	26: 3	Uzziah was sixteen years o when he became	1201
	27: 1	Jotham was twenty-five years o	1201
	27: 8	He was twenty-five years o when he became	1201
	28: 1	Ahaz was twenty years o when he became	1201
	29: 1	Hezekiah was twenty-five years o	1201
	31:15	o and young alike.	1524
	31:16	they distributed to the males three years o	1201
	31:17	and likewise to the Levites twenty years o	1201
	33: 1	Manasseh was twelve years o	1201
	33:21	Amon was twenty years o	1201
	34: 1	Josiah was eight years o when he became	1201
	36: 2	Jehoahaz was twenty-three years o	1201
	36: 5	Jehoiakim was twenty-five years o	1201
	36: 9	Jehoiachin was eighteen years o	1201
	36:11	Zedekiah was twenty-one years o	1201
	36:17	o man or aged.	2418
Est	3:13	young and o, women and little children—	2418
Job	8: 8	Its roots *may* grow o in the ground	2416
	20: 4	you know how it has been from of o,	6329
	21: 7	growing o and increasing in power?	6980
	22:15	to the o path that evil men have trod?	6409
	29: 8	and stepped aside and the o **men** rose	3813
	32: 6	"I am young in years, and you are o;	3813
	32: 9	It is not only the o who are wise,	8041
	42:17	And so he died, o and full of years.	2418
Ps	25: 6	for they are from of o.	6409
	37:25	I was young and now *I am* o,	2416

Ps	71: 9	Do not cast me away when I am o;	2420
	71:18	Even when I am o and gray,	2420
	74: 2	Remember the people you purchased of o,	7710
	74:12	But you, O God, are my king from of o;	7710
	78: 2	I will utter hidden things, things from of o—	7710
	92:14	They will still bear fruit in o age,	8484
	148:12	o men and children.	2418
Pr	8:22	before his deeds of o;	255
	20:29	gray hair the splendor of the o.	2418
	22: 6	and when *he is* o he will not turn from it.	2416
	23:22	do not despise your mother when *she is* o.	2416
Ecc	1:11	There is no remembrance of *men* of o;	8037
	4:13	an o but foolish king who no longer knows	2418
	7:10	"Why were the o days better than these?"	8037
SS	7:13	every delicacy, both new and o,	3824
Isa	1:26	I will restore your judges as in days of o,	8037
	3: 5	The young will rise up against the o,	2418
	20: 4	young and o, with buttocks bared—	2418
	22:11	the two walls for the water of the O Pool,	2418
	23: 7	city of revelry, the o, old city,	3427+4946+7710
	23: 7	Is this your city of revelry, the old, o city,	7712
	37:26	In days of o I planned it;	7710
	46: 4	Even to your o age and gray hairs I am he,	2420
	48: 8	from of o your ear has not been open.	255
	51: 9	as in days gone by, as in generations of o.	6409
	63: 9	up and carried them all the days of o.	6409
	63:11	Then his people recalled the days of o,	6409
	63:16	our Redeemer from of o is your name.	6409
	63:19	We are yours from of o;	6409
	65:20	or an o man who does not live out his years;	2418
Jer	6:11	and the o, those weighed down with years.	2418
	30:20	Their children will be as in days of o,	7710
	31:13	young men and o as well.	2418
	38:11	He took some o rags and worn-out clothes	1170
	38:12	"Put these o rags and worn-out clothes	1170
	51:22	with you I shatter o man and youth,	2418
	52: 1	Zedekiah was twenty-one years o	1201
La	1: 7	the treasures that were hers in days of o.	7710
	2:21	and o lie together in the dust of the streets;	2418
	3: 4	**made** my skin and my flesh grow o	1162
	5:21	renew our days as of o	7710
Eze	9: 6	Slaughter o *men,* young men and maidens,	2418
	16: 8	and saw that you were o *enough for* love,	6961
Hos	4:11	to o *wine* and new,	3516
Joel	2: 2	as never was o nor ever will be in ages	6409
	2:28	your o *men* will dream dreams,	2418
Mic	5: 2	whose origins are from of o,	7710
	6: 6	with calves a year o?	1201
Zec	8: 4	and women of ripe o age will sit in	2418
Mt	2:16	and its vicinity who were **two years** o and	1453
	9:16	a patch of unshrunk cloth on an o garment,	4094
	9:17	Neither do men pour new wine into o wineskins.	4094
	13:52	his storeroom new treasures as well as o."	4094
Mk	2:21	a patch of unshrunk cloth on an o garment.	4094
	2:21	the new piece will pull away from the o,	4094
	2:22	no one pours new wine into o wineskins.	4094
	5:42	around (she was twelve years o).	NIG
Lk	1:18	I am an o **man** and my wife is well along	4566
	1:36	to have a child in her o age,	1179
	2:36	She *was* very o;	1877+2465+4581
	2:42	When he was twelve **years** o,	2291
	3:23	Now Jesus himself was about thirty **years** o	2291
	5:36	a new garment and sews it on an o one.	4094
	5:36	patch from the new will not match the o.	4094
	5:37	no one pours new wine into o wineskins.	4094
	5:39	And no one after drinking o wine wants	4094
	5:39	for he says, 'The o is better.' "	4094
Jn	3: 4	"How can a man be born when he is o?"	1173
	8:57	"You are not yet fifty **years** o,"	2291
	21:18	*you are* o you will stretch out your hands,	1180
Ac	2:17	your o men will dream dreams.	4565
	4:22	miraculously healed was over forty years o.	NIG
	7:23	"When Moses was forty **years** o,	5989
Ro	4:19	since he was about a **hundred years** o—	1670
	6: 6	For we know that our o self was crucified	4094
	7: 6	and not in the o **way** of the written code.	4095
1Co	5: 7	of the o yeast that you may be a new batch	4094
	5: 8	not with the o yeast,	4094
2Co	3:14	when the o **covenant** is read.	4094
	5:17	the o has gone, the new has come!	792
Eph	4:22	to put off your o self,	4094
Col	3: 9	since you have taken off your o self	4094
1Ti	4: 7	with godless myths and o **wives' tales;**	1212
Phm	1: 9	an o **man** and now also a prisoner	4566
Heb	8: 6	he is mediator is superior to the o one,	NIG
1Jn	2: 7	a new command but an o one,	4094
	2: 7	This o command is the message you have	4094
Rev	21: 4	for the o order of things has passed away."	4755

OLDER (32) [OLD]

Ge	10:21	whose o brother was Japheth;	1524
	19:31	One day the o *daughter* said to the younger,	1142
	19:33	the o *daughter* went in and lay with him.	1142
	19:34	The next day the o *daughter* said to	1142
	19:37	The o *daughter* had a son,	1142
	25:23	and the o will serve the younger."	8041
	27: 1	he called for Esau his o son and said	1524
	27:15	the best clothes of Esau her o son,	1524
	27:42	Rebekah was told what her o son Esau had said,	1524
	29:16	the name of the o was Leah,	1524
	29:26	in marriage before the o *one.*	1142
Ex	2:10	When the child **grew** o,	1540
1Sa	14:49	The name of his o daughter was Merab.	1142
	18:17	"Here is my o daughter Merab.	1524

1Ki	2:22	after all, he is my o brother—	1524+4946
2Ch	22: 1	had killed all the o sons.	8037
Ezr	3: 8	of age and to supervise the building	2025+5087
	3:12	the o priests and Levites and family heads,	2418
Job	15:10	*men even* o than your father.	3427+3888
	32: 4	because they were o than he.	2418+3427+4200
Eze	16:46	Your o sister was Samaria.	1524
	16:61	both those *who* are o than you	1524
	23: 4	The o was named Oholah,	1524
Lk	15:25	"Meanwhile, the o son was in the field.	4565
	15:28	"The o brother became angry and refused	NIG
Jn	8: 9	the o ones first, until only Jesus was left,	4565
Ro	9:12	"The o will serve the younger."	3505
1Ti	5: 1	Do not rebuke an o man harshly,	4565
	5: 2	o *women* as mothers, and younger women	4565
Tit	2: 2	Teach the o *men* to be temperate,	4566
	2: 3	teach the o *women* to be reverent in	4567
1Pe	5: 5	be submissive *to* those who are o.	4565

OLDEST (9) [OLD]

Ge	44:12	with the o and ending with the youngest.	1524
Jdg	8:20	Turning to Jether, his o *son,* he said,	1147
1Sa	17:13	Jesse's three o sons had followed Saul to	1524
	17:14	The three o followed Saul,	1524
	17:28	When Eliab, David's o brother,	1524
1Ch	24:31	the o brother were treated the same as those	8031
Job	1:13	and drinking wine at the o brother's house,	1147
	1:18	and drinking wine at the o brother's house,	1147
Heb	12:16	**inheritance rights as the o son.**	4757

OLDNESS (KJV) See OLD WAY

OLIVE (62) [OLIVES]

Ge	8:11	in its beak was a freshly plucked o leaf!	2339
Ex	23:11	with your vineyard and your o grove.	2339
	25: 6	o oil for the light;	9043
	30:24	and a hin of o oil.	2339
	35: 8	o oil for the light;	9043
	35:28	also brought spices and o oil for the light	9043
Nu	11: 8	it tasted like something made with o oil.	9043
	18:12	the finest o oil and all the finest new wine	3658
Dt	6:11	vineyards and o groves you did not plant—	2339
	8: 8	pomegranates, o oil and honey;	2339
	28:40	You will have o trees throughout	2339
Jos	24:13	from vineyards and o groves that you did	2339
Jdg	9: 8	They said to the o tree, 'Be our king.'	2339
	9: 9	"But the o tree answered,	2339
	15: 5	together with the vineyards and o groves.	2339
1Sa	8:14	and vineyards and o groves and give them	2339
1Ki	5:11	to twenty thousand baths of **pressed** o oil.	4184
	6:23	a pair of cherubim of o wood,	9043
	6:31	of o wood with five-sided jambs.	9043
	6:32	the two o wood doors he carved cherubim,	9043
	6:33	of o wood for the entrance to the main hall.	9043
2Ki	5:26	or to accept clothes, o groves, vineyards,	2339
	18:32	a land of o trees and honey.	2339+3658
1Ch	27:28	in charge of the o and sycamore-fig trees in	2339
	27:28	in charge of the supplies of o oil.	9043
2Ch	2:10	and twenty thousand baths of o oil."	9043
	2:15	and the o oil and wine he promised,	9043
	11:11	with supplies of food, o oil and wine.	9043
Ezr	7:22	a hundred baths of o oil,	10442
Ne	5:11	vineyards, o groves and houses,	2339
	8:15	from o and wild olive trees, and	2339
	8:15	and **wild** o trees, and from myrtles, palms	9043
	9:25	o groves and fruit trees in abundance.	2339
Job	15:33	like an o tree shedding its blossoms.	2339
	29: 6	poured out for me streams of oil.	9043
Ps	52: 8	an o tree flourishing in the house of God;	2339
	128: 3	be like o shoots around your table.	2339
Isa	17: 6	as when an o **tree** is beaten,	2339
	24:13	as when an o **tree** is beaten,	2339
	41:19	the myrtle and the o.	6770+9043
	57: 9	with o oil and increased your perfumes.	9043
Jer	11:16	The LORD called you a thriving o tree	2339
Eze	16:13	Your food was fine flour, honey and oil.	9043
	16:19	o oil and honey I gave you to eat—	9043
Hos	2:22	with Assyria and sends o oil to Egypt.	9043
	14: 6	His splendor will be like an o **tree,**	2339
Am	4: 9	Locusts devoured your fig and o trees,	2339
Hab	3:17	o crop fails and the fields produce no food,	2339
Hag	2:19	the pomegranate and the o tree have	2339
Zec	4: 3	Also there are two o trees by it,	2339
	4:11	"What are these two o trees on the right and	2339
	4:12	"What are these two o branches beside	2339
Lk	16: 6	" 'Eight hundred gallons of o oil,'	1778
Jn	18: 1	On the other side there was an o grove,	NIG
	18:26	"Didn't I see you with him in the o grove?"	NIG
Ro	11: 17	and you, *though* a **wild** o shoot,	66
	11:17	in the nourishing sap *from* the o root,	1777
	11:24	cut out of an o **tree that is** wild	66
	11:24	grafted into a **cultivated** o tree,	2814
	11:24	be grafted into their own o tree!	1777
Rev	11: 4	the two o trees and the two lampstands	1777
	18:13	of wine and o oil, of fine flour and wheat;	1778

OLIVES (25) [OLIVE]

Ex	27:20	to bring you clear oil of pressed o for	2339
	29:40	a quarter of a hin of oil from **pressed** o,	4184
Lev	24: 2	to bring you clear oil of pressed o for	2339
Nu	28: 5	a quarter of a hin of oil from **pressed** o,	4184
Dt	24:20	When you beat the o **from** your trees,	2339
	28:40	because the o will drop off.	2339
2Sa	15:30	But David continued up the Mount of O,	2339

Job	24:11	*They* **crush** o among the terraces;	7414
Isa	17: 6	or three o on the topmost branches,	1737
Mic	6:15	you will press o but not use the oil	2339
Zec	14: 4	his feet will stand on the Mount of O,	2339
	14: 4	of O will be split in two from east to west,	2339
Mt	21: 1	and came to Bethphage on the Mount *of* O,	1777
	24: 3	As Jesus was sitting on the Mount *of* O,	1777
	26:30	they went out to the Mount of O.	1777
Mk	11: 1	and Bethany at the Mount *of* O,	1777
	13: 3	on the Mount *of* O opposite the temple,	1777
	14:26	they went out to the Mount of O.	1777
Lk	19:29	at the hill called the **Mount** *of* O,	1777
	19:37	where the road goes down the Mount of O,	1777
	21:37	the night on the hill called the **Mount** *of* O,	1777
	22:39	Jesus went out as usual to the Mount *of* O,	1777
Jn	8: 1	But Jesus went to the Mount *of* O.	1777
Ac	1:12	from the hill called the **Mount** *of* O,	1779
Jas	3:12	My brothers, can a fig tree bear o,	1777

OLIVET   (KJV) See OLIVES

OLYMPAS (1)

Ro	16:15	and O and all the saints with him.	3912

OMAR (3)

Ge	36:11	Teman, O, Zepho, Gatam and Kenaz.	223
	36:15	Chiefs Teman, O, Zepho, Kenaz,	223
1Ch	1:36	Teman, O, Zepho, Gatam and Kenaz;	223

OMEGA (3)

Rev	1: 8	"I am the Alpha and the O,"	6042
	21: 6	I am the Alpha and the O,	6042
	22:13	I am the Alpha and the O,	6042

OMEN (2) [OMENS]

Eze	21:21	to **seek an o:** he will cast lots	7876+7877
	21:23	It will seem like a false o	7876

OMENS (1) [OMEN]

Dt	18:10	**interprets** o, engages in witchcraft,	5727

OMER (5) [OMERS]

Ex	16:16	Take an o for each person you have	6685
	16:18	And when they measured it by the o,	6685
	16:32	'Take an o of manna and keep it for	6685
	16:33	'Take a jar and put an o *of* manna in it.	6685
	16:36	(An o is one tenth of an ephah.)	6685

OMERS (1) [OMER]

Ex	16:22	two o for each person—	6685

OMIT (1)

Jer	26: 2	everything I command you, *do not* o a word.	1757

OMNIPOTENT   (KJV) See ALMIGHTY

OMRI (15) [OMRI'S]

1Ki	16:16	and murdered him, they proclaimed O,	6687
	16:17	Then O and all the Israelites	6687
	16:21	and the other half supported O.	6687
	16:22	So Tibni died and O became king.	6687
	16:23	O became king of Israel,	6687
	16:25	But O did evil in the eyes of the LORD	6687
	16:28	O rested with his fathers and was buried	6687
	16:29	Ahab son of O became king of Israel,	6687
	16:30	Ahab son of O did more evil in the eyes of	6687
2Ki	8:26	a granddaughter of O king of Israel.	6687
1Ch	7: 8	Zemirah, Joash, Eliezer, Elioenai, O,	6687
	9: 4	the son of O, the son of Imri,	6687
	27:18	O son of Michael,	6687
2Ch	22: 2	a granddaughter of O.	6687
Mic	6:16	You have observed the statutes of O and all	6687

OMRI'S (2) [OMRI]

1Ki	16:22	But O followers proved stronger than those	6687
	16:27	As for the other events of O reign,	6687

ON (4 of 4658) For ON as a Preposition, See Index of Articles Etc. (See Introduction, p. xi)

Ge	41:45	Asenath daughter of Potiphera, priest of O.	228
	41:50	Asenath daughter of Potiphera, priest of O.	228
	46:20	Asenath daughter of Potiphera, priest of O.	228
Nu	16: 1	and O son of Peleth—became insolent	227

ONAM (4)

Ge	36:23	Alvan, Manahath, Ebal, Shepho and O.	231
1Ch	1:40	Alvan, Manahath, Ebal, Shepho and O.	231
	2:26	she was the mother of O.	231
	2:28	The sons of O: Shammai and Jada.	231

ONAN (7)

Ge	38: 4	and gave birth to a son and named him O.	232
	38: 8	Then Judah said to O,	232
	38: 9	O knew that the offspring would not be his;	232
	46:12	The sons of Judah: Er, O, Shelah.	232
	46:12	Perez and Zerah (but Er and O had died in	232
Nu	26:19	Er and O were sons of Judah,	232

1Ch	2: 3	The sons of Judah: Er, O and Shelah.	232

ONCE (179) [ONE]

Ge	18:29	O again he spoke to him,	3578+6388
	18:32	but let me speak just o more.	7193
	25:29	O when Jacob was cooking some stew,	NIH
	27:43	Flee at o to my brother Laban in Haran.	7756
	28: 2	Go at o to Paddan Aram,	7756
	31:10	"In breeding season *I* o *had* a dream	AIT
	31:13	Now leave this land at o and go back	7756
	40:21	he o again **put** the cup into Pharaoh's hand,	AIT
	41:10	Pharaoh *was* o **angry** with his servants,	AIT
	43: 8	the boy along with me and we will go at o,	7756
	43:13	also and go back to the man at o.	7756
	44: 4	"Go after those men at o,	7756
Ex	10:17	Now forgive my sin o more and	421+2021+7193
	12:21	**Go at** o and select the animals	5432
	30:10	O a year Aaron shall make atonement	285
	34: 8	to the ground at o and worshiped.	4554
Lev	16:34	Atonement is to be made o a year for all	285
Nu	12: 4	**At** o the LORD said to Moses,	7328
	16:21	so I can put an end to them **at** o."	3869+8092
	16:45	so I can put an end to them **at** o."	3869+8092
	24:11	Now **leave** at o and go home!	1368
Dt	7:22	be allowed to eliminate them **all at** o,	4554
	9:12	LORD told me, "Go down from here **at** o,	4554
	9:18	Then o **again** I fell prostrate	2021+3869+8037
Jos	6: 3	the city o with all the armed men.	285+7193
	6:11	around the city, circling it o.	285+7193
	6:14	the city o and returned to the camp.	285+7193
Jdg	2:23	not drive them out **at** o by giving them into	4554
	3:12	O **again** the Israelites did evil in the eyes of	3578
	4: 1	the Israelites o **again** did evil in the eyes of	3578
	16:18	"Come back o **more;**	7193
	16:28	O God, please strengthen me just o **more,**	7193
	20:15	**At** o the Benjamites mobilized twenty-six	
		thousand swordsmen	928+2021+2021+2085+3427
1Sa	1: 9	O when they had finished eating	NIH
	10: 7	O these signs are fulfilled,	3954
	14:33	"Roll a large stone over here **at** o."	2021+3427
	15:17	you were o small in your own eyes,	NIH
	19: 8	O **more** war broke out,	3578
	23: 4	O **again** David inquired of the LORD,	3578+6388
	28:24	which she butchered **at** o.	4554
2Sa	3:21	"Let me go **at** o and assemble all Israel	7756
	5:22	O **more** the Philistines came up	3578+6388
	17:21	"Set out and cross the river **at** o;	4559
	21:15	O **again** there was a battle between	6388
1Ki	10:22	O every three years it returned,	285
	13:33	but o **more** appointed priests for	8740
	17: 9	"Go **at** o to Zarephath of Sidon	7756
	19: 5	**All at** o an angel touched him and	2180+2296
	22: 9	"**Bring** Micaiah son of Imlah **at** o."	4554
2Ki	1:11	'Come down **at** o!' "	4559
	4:35	the bed and stretched out upon him o more.	NIH
	7: 9	*Let's* **go at** o and report this to	995+2143+2256
	13:21	O while some Israelites were burying	2118
	19:30	O **more** a remnant of the house	3578
1Ch	14:13	O **more** the Philistines raided the	3578+6388
2Ch	9:21	O every three years it returned,	285
	18: 8	"**Bring** Micaiah son of Imlah **at** o."	4554
	24: 5	But the Levites *did not* **act at** o.	4554
Ne	13:20	O or twice the merchants and sellers	7193
Est	5: 5	"**Bring** Haman **at** o," the king said,	4554
	6:10	"**Go at** o," the king commanded Haman.	4554
	8: 9	**At** o the royal secretaries were	
		summoned—	928+2021+2021+2085+6961
Job	3: 5	and deep shadow claim it o more;	NIH
	14:20	You overpower him o **for all,**	4200+5905
	18:19	no survivor where o he lived.	NIH
	33:21	and his bones, *o* **hidden,** now stick out.	AIT
	40: 5	I spoke o, but I have no answer—	285
Ps	55:14	with whom *I* o **enjoyed sweet** fellowship	AIT
	71:21	and comfort me o **again.**	6015
	89:19	O you spoke in a vision,	255
	89:35	O **for all,** I have sworn	285
	116: 7	*Be* at rest o **more,** O my soul,	8740
Pr	7:22	**All at** o he followed her like an ox going	7328
	12:16	A fool shows his annoyance **at** o,	928+2021+3427
Ecc	9:14	There was o a small city with only	NIH
Isa	1:21	She o was full of justice;	NIH
	7:25	for all the hills o **cultivated** by the hoe,	AIT
	14: 1	o **again** he will choose Israel	6388
	14:12	*you who* o **laid low** the nations!	AIT
	16: 8	*which* o **reached** Jazer and spread toward	AIT
	29:14	o **more** I will astound these people	3578
	29:19	O **more** the humble will rejoice in	3578
	35: 7	In the haunts where jackals o lay,	NIH
	37:31	O **more** a remnant of the house	3578
Jer	12:16	even as *they* o **taught** my people to swear	AIT
	31:23	in its towns will o again use these words:	6388
	32:43	O **more** fields will be bought in this land	2256
	33:10	there will be heard o **more**	6388
	42: 2	as you now see, though we were o many,	4946
La	1: 1	deserted lies the city, o so full of people!	NIH
	1: 1	who o was great among the nations!	NIH
	4: 2	o worth their weight in gold,	NIH
	4: 5	Those *who* o ate delicacies are destitute in	AIT
Eze	31: 3	Consider Assyria, o a cedar in Lebanon,	NIH
	36:37	O **again** I will yield to the plea of the house	2296
	42:14	O the priests enter the holy precincts,	928
Da	2: 7	O **more** they replied,	10766
	2:25	Arioch took Daniel to the king **at** o	10097
Hag	2: 6	while I will o **more** shake the heavens and	285
Zec	8: 4	"O **again** men and women of ripe old age	6388
	8:21	*Let us* **go at** o to entreat the LORD	2143+2143

Mt	4:20	At o they left their nets and followed him.	2311
	13:20	the word and **at** o receives it with joy.	2317
	13:47	"O **again,** the kingdom of heaven is like	4099
	21: 2	and **at** o you will find a donkey tied there,	2311
	25:16	went **at** o and put his money to work	2311
	26:44	So he left them and went away o **more**	4099
	26:49	Going **at** o to Jesus, Judas said,	2311
	26:53	and he will **at** o put at my disposal	785
Mk	1:12	**At** o the Spirit sent him out into the desert,	2317
	1:18	**At** o they left their nets and followed him.	2317
	1:43	Jesus sent him away at o with	2317
	2:13	O **again** Jesus went out beside the lake.	2779
	4:16	the word and **at** o receive it with joy.	2317+4020
	5:30	**At** o Jesus realized that power had gone out	2317
	6:25	**At** o the girl hurried in to the king with	2317
	8:25	O **more** Jesus put his hands on	1663+4099
	14:39	O **more** he went away and prayed	4099
	14:45	Going **at** o to Jesus, Judas said, "Rabbi!"	4099
Lk	1: 8	O when Zechariah's division was on	1181+1254
	4:39	She got up **at** o and began to wait on them.	4202
	8:55	Her spirit returned, and **at** o she stood up.	4202
	9:18	O when Jesus was praying in private	1181+2779
	13:25	O the owner of the house gets up	323+608+4005
	17:20	O, having been asked by the Pharisees	1254
	19: 6	down **at** o and welcomed him gladly.	5067
	19:11	of God was going to appear **at** o.	4202
	24:33	and returned **at** o to Jerusalem.	899+3836+6052
Jn	4: 3	he left Judea and went back o **more**	4099
	4:46	O **more** he visited Cana in Galilee.	4099
	5: 9	**At** o the man was cured;	2311
	6:24	O the crowd realized that neither Jesus	4021
	8:21	O **more** Jesus said to them,	4099
	11:38	Jesus, o **more** deeply moved,	4099
	13:32	and will glorify him **at** o.	2317
	19: 4	O **more** Pilate came out and said	2779+4099
Ac	4:18	O **at** o he began to preach in the synagogues	4202
	9:38	and urged him, "Please come **at** o!"	3590+3890
	16:10	we got ready **at** o to leave for Macedonia,	2311
	16:16	O when we were going to the place	1181+1254
	16:26	**At** o all the prison doors flew open,	4202
	21:32	He **at** o took some officers and soldiers	1994
	23:30	I sent him to you **at** o.	1994
	28: 1	O safely on shore,	5538
Ro	6:10	he died to sin o **for all;**	2384
	7: 6	But now, by dying to what o bound us,	NIG
	7: 9	O I was alive apart from law;	4537
2Co	5:16	Though *we* o **regarded** Christ in this way,	AIT
	10: 6	o your obedience is complete.	4020
	11:25	o I was stoned, three times I was	562
Gal	1:23	now preaching the faith he o **tried**	4537
Eph	2:13	in Christ Jesus you who o were far away	
		have been brought near	4537
	5: 8	For you were o darkness,	4537
Col	1:21	O you were alienated from God	4537
	3: 7	in the life you o lived.	4021
1Ti	1:13	Even though I was o a blasphemer and	4728
	1:18	with the prophecies o **made** about you,	4575
Tit	3:10	Warn a divisive person o,	1651
Heb	5: 9	and, o **made perfect,** he became the source	AIT
	6: 4	for those who have o been enlightened,	562
	7:27	He sacrificed for their sins o **for all**	2384
	9: 7	the inner room, and that only o a year,	562
	9:12	the Most Holy Place o **for all**	2384
	9:26	now he has appeared o **for all** at the end	562
	9:27	Just as man is destined to die o,	562
	9:28	so Christ was sacrificed o to take away	562
	10: 2	would have been cleansed o **for all,**	562
	10:10	sacrifice of the body of Jesus Christ o **for**	
		all.	2384
	12:26	"O **more** I will shake not only the earth but	562
	12:27	The words "o **more**" indicate the removing	562
1Pe	2:10	O you were not a people,	4537
	2:10	o you had not received mercy,	NIG
	3:18	For Christ died for sins o **for all,**	562
Jude	1: 3	that was o **for all** entrusted to the saints.	562
Rev	1:10	**At** o I was in the Spirit,	2311
	10: 8	from heaven spoke to me o **more:**	4099
	17: 8	The beast, which you saw, o **was,**	AIT
	17: 8	because *he* o **was,** now is not,	AIT
	17:11	The beast who *o* **was,** and now is not,	AIT

ONE (2485) [ONCE, ONE'S, ONE-TENTH, ONE-THIRD, ONES, ONESELF]

Ge	1: 9	under the sky be gathered to o place,	285
	2:21	he took o of the man's ribs and closed up	285
	2:24	and they will become o flesh.	285
	3:22	"The man has now become like o of us,	285
	4:15	so that no o who found him would kill him.	3972
	4:19	o named Adah and the other Zillah.	285
	8:19	the ark, o **kind after another.**	2157+4200+5476
	10:25	O was named Peleg, because in his time	285
	11: 1	Now the whole world had o language and	285
	11: 6	"If as o people speaking	285
	14:13	O who had escaped **came** and reported	AIT
	15: 2	the o **who will inherit** my estate is Eliezer	
			1201+5479
	16:13	"I have now seen the O **who sees** me."	AIT
	19:17	*o* of them **said,** "Flee for your lives!"	AIT
	19:31	O **day** the older daughter said to	2256
	20: 3	a dream o night and said to him, "You are	2021
	21:15	she put the boy under o of the bushes.	285
	22: 2	Sacrifice him there as a burnt offering on o	285
	24: 2	the o **in charge** of all that he had,	AIT
	24:14	let her be the o you have chosen	NIH
	24:44	let her be the o the LORD has chosen	851
	24:50	we can say nothing to you o **way** or	8273S

Ref	Text	No.
Ge 24:63	He went out to the field o evening	NIH
25:23	o people will be stronger than the other,	AIT
26:10	O of the men might well have slept	285
26:21	but they quarreled over that o also;	2023
26:22	and no o quarreled over it.	AIT
27:38	"Do you have only o blessing, my father?	285
27:45	Why should I lose both of you in o day?"	285
28:11	Taking o of the stones there,	4946
29:26	in marriage before the older o.	AIT
29:27	then we will give you the younger o also,	2296S
29:33	he gave me this o too."	AIT
30:31	"But if you will do this o thing for me,	AIT
31:50	even though no o is with us,	408
32: 8	"If Esau comes and attacks o group,	285
32:17	He instructed the o in the lead:	8037
33:13	If they are driven hard just o day,	285
34:15	to you on o condition only:	2296S
34:16	among you and become o people with you.	285
34:22	with us as o people only on the condition	285
35: 5	around them so that no o pursued them.	AIT
37:20	and throw him into o of these cisterns	285
37:36	o of Pharaoh's officials,	AIT
38:28	o of them put out his hand;	AIT
38:28	"This o came out first."	AIT
39: 1	Egyptian who was o of Pharaoh's officials,	4946
39: 9	No o is greater in this house than I am.	5647
39:11	O day he went into the house to attend	2296
40: 8	"but there is no o to interpret them."	AIT
41: 8	but no o could interpret them for him.	AIT
41:15	"I had a dream, and no o can interpret it.	AIT
41:21	no o could tell that they had done so;	AIT
41:25	"The dreams of Pharaoh are o and the same.	285
41:26	it is o and the same dream.	285
41:38	o in whom is the spirit of God?"	2257
41:39	there is no o so discerning and wise as you.	AIT
41:44	but without your word no o will lift hand	408
42: 6	the o who sold grain to all its people.	AIT
42:11	We are all the sons of o man.	285
42:13	the sons of o man,	285
42:13	and o is no more."	285
42:16	Send o of your number to get your brother;	285
42:19	let o of your brothers stay here in prison,	285
42:21	They said to o another,	408
42:27	for the night o of them opened his sack	285
42:32	We were twelve brothers, sons of o father.	5646
42:32	O is no more,	285
42:33	Leave o of your brothers here with me,	285
42:38	and he is the only o left.	963+2257+4200
43:29	the o you told me about?"	889
44: 2	Then put my cup, the silver o,	1483S
44:16	and the o who was found to have the cup."	2257
44:20	he is the only o of his mother's sons left,	2257
44:28	O of them went away from me, and I said,	285
44:29	If you take this o from me too	AIT
45: 1	So there was no o with Joseph	408
45: 4	the o you sold into Egypt!	889S
47:20	The Egyptians, o and all,	408
47:21	from o end of Egypt to the other.	AIT
48:18	"No, my father, this o is the firstborn;	AIT
48:22	And to you, as o who is over your brothers,	285
49:16	for his people as o of the tribes of Israel.	285
49:24	of the hand of the Mighty O of Jacob,	51
Ex 2: 6	"This is o of the Hebrew babies," she said.	4946
2: 7	and get o of the Hebrew women to nurse	4946
2:11	O day, after Moses had grown up,	2021
2:11	a Hebrew, o of his own people.	4946
2:12	this way and that and seeing no o,	408
2:13	He asked the o in the wrong,	8401
6:25	son of Aaron married o of the daughters	4946
7:12	Each o threw down his staff and it became	AIT
8:10	so that you may know there is no o like	AIT
9: 6	not o animal belonging to the Israelites died.	285
9: 7	and found that not even o of the animals of	285
9:14	so you may know that there is no o like me	AIT
10:23	No o could see anyone else	408
11: 1	"I will bring o more plague on Pharaoh and	285
12: 3	o for each household.	8445S
12: 4	they must share o with their nearest	NIH
12:16	and another o on the seventh day.	AIT
12:22	Not o of you shall go out the door	408
12:46	"It must be eaten inside o house;	285
12:48	then he may take part like o born in	AIT
14:20	the cloud brought darkness to o side	NIH
14:28	Not o of them survived.	285
16:16	'Each o is to gather as much as he needs.	AIT
16:18	Each o gathered as much as he needed.	AIT
16:19	"No o is to keep any of it until morning."	408
16:29	no o is to go out."	408
16:36	(An omer is o tenth of an ephah.)	NIH
17:12	o on one side, one on the other—	285
17:12	one on o side, one on the other—	AIT
17:12	one on one side, o on the other—	285
18: 3	O son was named Gershom, for Moses said,	285
21:10	he must not deprive the first o of her food,	NIH
21:18	"If men quarrel and o hits the other with	408
21:19	o who struck the blow	AIT
21:33	"If a man uncovers a pit or digs o and fails	1014S
21:35	to sell the live o and divide both the money	8802S
22: 6	o who started the fire must make restitution.	AIT
22: 9	o whom the judges declare guilty must pay back double to his neighbor.	AIT
22:10	is taken away while no o is looking,	AIT
22:25	"If you lend money to o of my people	NIH
23:15	"No o is to appear before me empty-handed	AIT
24: 3	they responded with o voice,	285

Ref	Text	No.
Ex 25:12	with two rings on o side and two rings on	285
25:19	Make o cherub on one end and	285
25:19	on o end and the second cherub on	2296
25:19	the cherubim of o piece with the cover,	4946
25:31	buds and blossoms shall be of o piece with	4946
25:32	three on o side and three on the other.	285
25:33	and blossoms are to be on o branch,	285
25:35	O bud shall be under the first pair	NIH
25:36	and branches shall all be of o piece with	285
26: 4	along the edge of the end curtain in o set,	285
26: 5	on o curtain and fifty loops on	285
26: 9	five of the curtains together into o set	963+4200
26:10	the edge of the end curtain in o set and also	285
26:19	o under each projection.	NIH
26:26	for the frames on o side of the tabernacle,	285
27: 2	that the horns and the altar are of o piece,	4946
27:14	to be of o piece of the entrance,	2021
28: 8	of o piece with the ephod and made	4946
28:10	six names on o stone and the remaining six	285
28:21	for each of the names of the sons	NIH
28:21	with the name of o of the twelve tribes.	NIH
29:15	"Take o of the rams,	285
29:33	But no o else may eat them,	AIT
29:39	Offer o in the morning and the other	285
30: 2	its horns of o piece with it.	4946
30:12	each o must pay the LORD a ransom	AIT
30:13	Each o who crosses over	AIT
32:27	through the camp from o end to the other,	AIT
33: 4	to mourn and no o put on any ornaments.	408
33:20	for no o may see me and live."	132
34: 3	No o is to come with you or	408
34:20	"No o is to appear before me empty-handed	AIT
34:24	and no o will covet your land when you go	408
36:11	along the edge of the end curtain in o set,	285
36:12	They also made fifty loops on o curtain	285
36:16	into o set and the other six into another set.	AIT
36:17	the edge of the end curtain in o set and also	2021
36:24	o under each projection.	NIH
36:31	for the frames on o side of the tabernacle,	285
37: 3	with two rings on o side and two rings on	285
37: 8	He made o cherub on one end and	285
37: 8	on o end and the second cherub on	2296
37: 8	the two ends he made them of o piece with	4946
37:17	buds and blossoms were of o piece with it.	4946
37:18	three on o side and three on the other.	285
37:19	buds and blossoms were on o branch,	285
37:21	O bud was under the first pair	NIH
37:22	and the branches were all of o piece with	4946
37:24	and all its accessories from o talent	AIT
37:25	its horns of o piece with it.	4946
38: 2	that the horns and the altar were of o piece,	4946
38:14	Curtains fifteen cubits long were on o side	2021
38:26	o beka per person,	AIT
38:27	o talent for each base.	NIH
39:14	of o piece with the ephod and made	4946
39:14	o for each of the names of the sons	NIH
39:14	with the name of o of the twelve tribes.	NIH
Lev 5: 4	in any matter o might carelessly swear about	132
5: 7	o for a sin offering and the other for	285
5: 8	who shall first offer the o for	889S
5:15	o without defect and of the proper value.	NIH
5:18	o without defect and of the proper value.	NIH
6: 6	o without defect and of the proper value.	NIH
7:14	He is to bring o of each kind as an offering,	285
7:18	o who offered it, for it is impure;	AIT
8:26	and o made with oil, and a wafer;	285
9:15	for a sin offering as he did with the first o.	AIT
11:25	Whoever picks up o of their carcasses	4946
11:32	When o of them dies and falls	3972
11:33	If o of them falls into a clay pot,	4946
11:35	Anything that o of their carcasses falls	4946
11:36	but anyone who touches o	NIH
12: 8	o for a burnt offering and the other for	285
13: 2	the priest or to o of his sons who is a priest.	285
13:55	the mildew has affected o side or the other.	2257S
14: 4	be brought for the o to be cleansed	AIT
14: 5	that o of the birds be killed over fresh water	285
14: 7	the o to be cleansed of the infections	AIT
14:10	and o ewe lamb a year old,	285
14:10	and o log of oil.	285
14:11	both the o to be cleansed and his offerings	408
14:12	to take o of the male lambs and offer it as	285
14:14	of the right ear of the o to be cleansed,	AIT
14:17	of the right ear of the o to be cleansed,	AIT
14:18	the o to be cleansed and make atonement	AIT
14:19	the o to be cleansed from his uncleanness.	AIT
14:21	he must take o male lamb as	285
14:22	o for a sin offering and the other for	285
14:25	of the right ear of the o to be cleansed,	AIT
14:28	of the right ear of the o to be cleansed,	AIT
14:29	on the head of the o to be cleansed,	AIT
14:31	as a sin offering and the other as	285
14:31	on behalf of the o to be cleansed."	AIT
14:50	He shall kill o of the birds over fresh water	285
15:15	the o for a sin offering and the other for	285
15:30	The priest is to sacrifice o for a sin offering	285
16: 8	o lot for the LORD and the other for	285
16:17	No o is to be in the Tent of Meeting from	132
18: 6	" 'No o is to approach any close relative	408
18:22	not lie with a man as o lies with a woman;	NIH
19:11	" 'Do not deceive o another.	408
19:18	not seek revenge or bear a grudge against o	1201S
19:34	be treated as o of your native-born.	4946
20: 4	that gives o of his children to Molech	4946
20:13	" If a man lies with a man as o lies with	NIH
21:10	the o among his brothers who has had	NIH
22: 6	The o who touches any such thing will	5883

Ref	Text	No.
Lev 22:10	" 'No o outside a priest's family may eat	3972
23:18	o young bull and two rams.	285
23:19	Then sacrifice o male goat for	285
25:10	each o of you is to return to his family	AIT
25:14	" 'If you sell land to o of your countrymen	NIH
25:25	" 'If o of your countrymen becomes poor	NIH
25:26	a man has no o to redeem it for him	AIT
25:35	" 'If o of your countrymen becomes poor	NIH
25:39	" 'If o of your countrymen becomes poor	NIH
25:47	and o of your countrymen becomes poor	NIH
25:48	O of his relatives may redeem him:	285
26: 6	o will make you afraid.	AIT
26:17	even when no o is pursuing you.	AIT
26:26	be able to bake your bread in o oven,	285
26:36	even though no o is pursuing	AIT
26:37	over o another as though fleeing from	408
26:37	even though no o is pursuing them.	AIT
27: 6	a person between o month and five years,	AIT
27:10	not exchange it or substitute a good o for	2257
27:10	for a bad o, or a bad one for a good one;	AIT
27:10	or a bad o for a good one;	AIT
27:10	or a bad one for a good o;	AIT
27:10	if he should substitute o animal	AIT
27:11	o that is not acceptable as an offering to	5626
27:24	the o whose land it was.	2257
27:26	" 'No o, however, may dedicate	AIT
27:27	If it is o of the unclean animals,	928S
Nu 1: 2	every man by name, o by one.	1653+4200+4392
1: 2	every man by name, one by o.	1653+4200+4392
1: 4	O man from each tribe,	408
1:18	were listed by name, o by one,	1653+4200+4392
1:18	were listed by name, one by o,	1653+4200+4392
1:20	were listed by name, o by one,	1653+4200+4392
1:20	were listed by name, one by o,	1653+4200+4392
1:22	and listed by name, o by one,	1653+4200+4392
1:22	and listed by name, one by o,	1653+4200+4392
1:44	each o representing his family.	285
3:47	collect five shekels for each o,	1653
5: 7	add a fifth to it and give it all to	2797
6:11	The priest is to offer o as a sin offering and	285
7:11	"Each day o leader is to bring his offering	285
7:12	The o who brought his offering on	AIT
7:13	His offering was o silver plate weighing	285
7:13	o silver sprinkling bowl weighing seventy	285
7:14	o gold dish weighing ten shekels, filled	285
7:15	o young bull, one ram and one male lamb	285
7:15	o ram and one male lamb a year old,	285
7:15	one ram and o male lamb a year old,	285
7:16	o male goat for a sin offering;	285
7:19	o silver plate weighing weighing	285
7:19	o silver sprinkling bowl weighing seventy	285
7:20	o gold dish weighing ten shekels, filled	285
7:21	o young bull, one ram and one male lamb	285
7:21	o ram and one male lamb a year old,	285
7:21	one ram and o male lamb a year old,	285
7:22	o male goat for a sin offering;	285
7:25	His offering was o silver plate weighing	285
7:25	o silver sprinkling bowl weighing seventy	285
7:26	o gold dish weighing ten shekels, filled	285
7:27	o young bull, one ram and one male lamb	285
7:27	o ram and one male lamb a year old,	285
7:27	one ram and o male lamb a year old,	285
7:28	o male goat for a sin offering;	285
7:31	His offering was o silver plate weighing	285
7:31	o silver sprinkling bowl weighing seventy	285
7:32	o gold dish weighing ten shekels, filled	285
7:33	o young bull, one ram and one male lamb	285
7:33	o ram and one male lamb a year old,	285
7:33	one ram and o male lamb a year old,	285
7:34	o male goat for a sin offering;	285
7:37	His offering was o silver plate weighing	285
7:37	o silver sprinkling bowl weighing seventy	285
7:38	o gold dish weighing ten shekels, filled	285
7:39	o young bull, one ram and one male lamb	285
7:39	o ram and one male lamb a year old,	285
7:39	one ram and o male lamb a year old,	285
7:40	o male goat for a sin offering;	285
7:43	His offering was o silver plate weighing	285
7:43	o silver sprinkling bowl weighing seventy	285
7:44	o gold dish weighing ten shekels, filled	285
7:45	o young bull, one ram and one male lamb	285
7:45	o ram and one male lamb a year old,	285
7:45	one ram and o male lamb a year old,	285
7:46	o male goat for a sin offering;	285
7:49	His offering was o silver plate weighing	285
7:49	o silver sprinkling bowl weighing seventy	285
7:50	o gold dish weighing ten shekels, filled	285
7:51	o young bull, one ram and one male lamb	285
7:51	o ram and one male lamb a year old,	285
7:51	one ram and o male lamb a year old,	285
7:52	o male goat for a sin offering;	285
7:55	His offering was o silver plate weighing	285
7:55	o silver sprinkling bowl weighing seventy	285
7:56	o gold dish weighing ten shekels, filled	285
7:57	o young bull, one ram and one male lamb	285
7:57	o ram and one male lamb a year old,	285
7:57	one ram and o male lamb a year old,	285
7:58	o male goat for a sin offering;	285
7:61	His offering was o silver plate weighing	285
7:61	o silver sprinkling bowl weighing seventy	285
7:62	o gold dish weighing ten shekels, filled	285
7:63	o young bull, one ram and one male lamb	285
7:63	o ram and one male lamb a year old,	285
7:63	one ram and o male lamb a year old,	285
7:64	o male goat for a sin offering;	285
7:67	His offering was o silver plate weighing	285
7:67	o silver sprinkling bowl weighing seventy	285

Nu	7:68	o gold dish weighing ten shekels, filled	285
	7:69	o young bull, one ram and one male lamb	285
	7:69	o ram and one male lamb a year old,	285
	7:69	one ram and o male lamb a year old,	285
	7:70	o male goat for a sin offering;	285
	7:73	His offering was o silver plate weighing	285
	7:73	o silver sprinkling bowl weighing seventy	285
	7:74	o gold dish weighing ten shekels, filled	285
	7:75	o young bull, one ram and one male lamb	285
	7:75	o ram and one male lamb a year old,	285
	7:75	one ram and o male lamb a year old,	285
	7:76	o male goat for a sin offering;	285
	7:79	His offering was o silver plate weighing	285
	7:79	o silver sprinkling bowl weighing seventy	285
	7:80	o gold dish weighing ten shekels, filled	285
	7:81	o young bull, one ram and one male lamb	285
	7:81	o ram and one male lamb a year old,	285
	7:81	one ram and o male lamb a year old,	285
	7:82	o male goat for a sin offering;	285
	8:12	the o for a sin offering to the LORD and	285
	10: 4	If only o is sounded, the leaders—	285
	11:19	You will not eat it for just o day,	285
	11:32	No o gathered less than ten homers.	2021
	13: 2	From each ancestral tribe send o	285
	14:15	you put these people to death all at o time,	285
	14:22	not o of the men who saw my glory and	3972
	14:23	not o of them will ever see the land	AIT
	14:23	No o who has treated me with contempt	3972
	14:29	every o of you twenty years old	AIT
	14:30	Not o of you will enter the land I swore	NIH
	14:34	o year for each of the forty days	2021
	15: 4	the o who brings his offering shall present	AIT
	15:12	Do this for each o,	285
	15:27	" 'But if just o person sins unintentionally,	285
	15:28	the o who erred by sinning unintentionally,	5883
	15:29	O and the same law applies	285
	16: 3	whole community is holy, every o of them,	AIT
	16: 7	be the o who is holy.	2085
	16:22	when only o man sins?"	285
	16:40	no o except a descendant of Aaron	408+2424S
	17: 2	o from the leader of each	4751S
	17: 3	for there must be o staff for the head	285
	17: 6	o for the leader of each	285
	18: 4	and no o else may come near	AIT
	22:32	because your path is a reckless o	AIT
	23: 9	not consider themselves o of the nations.	AIT
	24: 3	the oracle of o whose eye sees clearly,	1505
	24: 4	the oracle of o who hears the words of God,	AIT
	24:15	the oracle of o whose eye sees clearly,	1505
	24:16	the oracle of o who hears the words of God,	AIT
	26:54	and to a smaller group a smaller o;	5709S
	26:64	Not o of them was among those counted	408
	26:65	and not o of them was left except Caleb son	408
	27:17	o who will lead them out	AIT
	28: 4	Prepare o lamb in the morning and	285
	28:11	o ram and seven male lambs a year old,	285
	28:15	o male goat is to be presented to	285
	28:19	o ram and seven male lambs a year old,	285
	28:22	Include o male goat as a sin offering	285
	28:27	o ram and seven male lambs a year old as	285
	28:30	Include o male goat to make atonement	285
	29: 2	prepare a burnt offering of o young bull,	285
	29: 2	o ram and seven male lambs a year old,	285
	29: 5	Include o male goat as a sin offering	285
	29: 8	a burnt offering of o young bull,	285
	29: 8	o ram and seven male lambs a year old,	285
	29:11	Include o male goat as a sin offering,	285
	29:16	Include o male goat as a sin offering,	285
	29:19	Include o male goat as a sin offering,	285
	29:22	Include o male goat as a sin offering,	285
	29:25	Include o male goat as a sin offering,	285
	29:28	Include o male goat as a sin offering,	285
	29:31	Include o male goat as a sin offering,	285
	29:34	Include o male goat as a sin offering,	285
	29:36	a burnt offering of o bull,	285
	29:36	o ram and seven male lambs a year old,	285
	29:38	Include o male goat as a sin offering,	285
	31:28	for the LORD o out of every five hundred,	285
	31:30	select o out of every fifty, whether persons,	285
	31:47	Moses selected o out of every fifty persons	285
	31:49	and not o is missing.	408
	32:11	not o of the men twenty years old	561
	32:12	not o except Caleb son of Jephunneh	NIH
	33:54	and to a smaller group a smaller o.	5709S
	34:18	And appoint o leader from each tribe	285
	35: 8	but few from o that has few."	2021
	35:25	the o accused of murder from the avenger	AIT
	35:30	But no o is to be put to death on	5883
	35:30	to death on the testimony of only o witness.	285
	35:33	except by the blood of the o who shed it.	AIT
Dt	1:16	between brother Israelites or between o	408
	1:23	o man from each tribe.	285
	1:41	So every o of you put on his weapons,	AIT
	2:36	not o town was too strong for us.	NIH
	3: 4	not o of the sixty cities that we did not take	7953S
	4:32	ask from o end of the heavens to the other.	AIT
	4:34	for himself o nation out of another nation,	NIH
	4:42	into o of these cities and save his life.	285
	6: 4	The LORD our God, the LORD is o.	285
	7:24	No o will be able to stand up against you;	408
	9: 3	the o who goes across ahead of you like	AIT
	12:14	the LORD will choose in o of your tribes.	285
	13: 1	o who foretells by dreams,	AIT
	13: 7	from o end of the land to the other),	NIH
	13:11	and no o among you will do such	AIT
	13:12	If you hear it said about o of the towns	285
	17: 2	a man or woman living among you in o of	285

Dt	17: 6	no o shall be put to death on the testimony	AIT
	17: 6	to death on the testimony of only o witness.	285
	17:15	o who is not a brother Israelite.	408
	18: 6	from o of your towns anywhere in Israel	285
	18:10	Let no o be found among you who	AIT
	19: 4	o who kills his neighbor unintentionally,	AIT
	19: 5	That man may flee to o of these cities	285
	19:11	and then flees to o of these cities,	285
	19:15	O witness is not enough to convict	285
	20: 4	For the LORD your God is the o who goes	AIT
	21:15	and he loves o but not the other,	285
	22:27	there was no o to rescue her.	AIT
	23: 1	o who has been emasculated	AIT
	23: 2	o born of a forbidden marriage	4927
	23:10	If o of your men is unclean because of	285
	24: 5	For o year he is to be free to stay at home	285
	24: 6	not even the upper o—	8207
	24: 7	If a man is caught kidnapping o	4946
	24:14	a brother Israelite or an alien living in o	NIH
	25: 5	If brothers are living together and o	285
	25: 9	take off o of his sandals,	NIH
	25:11	of o of them comes to rescue her husband	AIT
	25:13	differing weights in your bag—o heavy,	NIH
	25:13	one heavy, o light.	NIH
	25:14	differing measures in your house—o large,	NIH
	25:14	one large, o small.	NIH
	28: 7	from o direction but flee from you in seven.	285
	28:25	at them from o direction but flee from them	285
	28:26	no o to frighten them away.	AIT
	28:29	with no o to rescue you.	AIT
	28:31	and no o will rescue them.	AIT
	28:55	to o of them any of the flesh of his children	285
	28:64	from o end of the earth to the other.	NIH
	28:68	but no o will buy you.	AIT
	32:22	o that burns to the realm of death below.	285
	32:30	How could o man chase a thousand,	285
	32:36	and no o is left, slave or free.	NIH
	32:39	and no o can deliver out of my hand.	AIT
	33:12	and the o the LORD loves rests	AIT
	33:26	"There is no o like the God of Jeshurun,	AIT
	34: 6	to this day no o knows where his grave is.	408
	34:12	For no o has ever shown the mighty power	NIH
Jos	1: 5	No o will be able to stand up	408
	3:12	o from each tribe.	285
	4: 2	o from each tribe,	285
	4: 4	o from each tribe,	285
	6: 1	No o went out and no one came in.	AIT
	6: 1	No one went out and no o came in.	AIT
	8:24	and when every o of them had been put to	AIT
	10: 2	like o of the royal cities;	285
	10: 8	o of them will be able to withstand you."	AIT
	10:21	no o uttered a word against the Israelites.	408
	10:42	in o campaign, because the LORD,	285
	11:19	nor o city made a treaty of peace with	NIH
	12: 4	o of the last of the Rephaites.	4946
	12: 9	the king of Jericho o the king of Ai	285
	12: 9	the king of Ai (near Bethel) o	285
	12:10	king of Jerusalem o the king of Hebron one	285
	12:10	king of Jerusalem one the king of Hebron o	285
	12:11	king of Jarmuth o the king of Lachish one	285
	12:11	king of Jarmuth one the king of Lachish o	285
	12:12	the king of Eglon o the king of Gezer one	285
	12:12	the king of Eglon one the king of Gezer o	285
	12:13	the king of Debir o the king of Geder one	285
	12:13	the king of Debir one the king of Geder o	285
	12:14	the king of Hormah o the king of Arad one	285
	12:14	the king of Hormah one the king of Arad o	285
	12:15	king of Libnah o the king of Adullam one	285
	12:15	king of Libnah one the king of Adullam o	285
	12:16	king of Makkedah o the king of Bethel one	285
	12:16	king of Makkedah one the king of Bethel o	285
	12:17	king of Tappuah o the king of Hepher one	285
	12:17	king of Tappuah one the king of Hepher o	285
	12:18	king of Aphek o the king of Lasharon one	285
	12:18	king of Aphek one the king of Lasharon o	285
	12:19	the king of Madon o the king of Hazor one	285
	12:19	the king of Madon one the king of Hazor o	285
	12:20	the king of Shimron Meron o	285
	12:20	the king of Acshaph o	285
	12:21	king of Taanach o the king of Megiddo one	285
	12:21	king of Taanach one the king of Megiddo o	285
	12:22	the king of Kedesh o the king of Jokneam	285
	12:22	the king of Jokneam in Carmel o	285
	12:23	the king of Dor (in Naphoth Dor) o	285
	12:23	the king of Goyim in Gilgal o	285
	12:24	the king of Tirzah o thirty-one kings in all.	285
	13:12	and Edrei and had survived as o of the last	4946
	15:18	O day when she came to Othniel,	2118+2256
	17:14	"Why have you given us only o allotment	285
	17:14	and o portion for an inheritance?	285
	17:17	You will have not only o allotment	AIT
	20: 4	"When he flees to o of these cities,	285
	20: 5	They must not surrender the o accused,	AIT
	21:13	(a city of refuge for o accused of murder),	AIT
	21:21	(a city of refuge for o accused of murder)	AIT
	21:27	for o accused of murder) and Be Eshtarah,	AIT
	21:32	(a city of refuge for o accused of murder),	AIT
	21:38	(a city of refuge for o accused of murder),	AIT
	21:44	Not o of their enemies withstood them;	408
	21:45	Not o of all the LORD's good promises to	1821S
	21:45	every o was fulfilled.	AIT
	22:14	o for each of the tribes of Israel,	285
	22:20	not the only o who died for his sin.' "	408
	22:22	"The Mighty O, God, the LORD!	446
	22:22	The Mighty O, God, the LORD!	446
	23: 9	to this day no o has been able	408
	23:10	O of you routs a thousand,	285

Jos	23:14	with all your heart and soul that not o of all	285
	23:14	not o has failed.	285
Jdg	1:14	O day when she came to Othniel,	2118+2256
	3:28	they allowed no o to cross over.	408
	5: 5	the O of Sinai, before the LORD,	2296
	6:25	the o seven years old.	7228S
	6:39	Let me make just o more request.	7193
	6:39	Allow me o more test with the fleece.	7193
	7: 4	If I say, 'This o shall go with you,'	AIT
	7: 4	but if I say, 'This o shall not go with you,'	AIT
	8:18	"each o with the bearing of a prince."	285
	8:24	And he said, "I do have o request,	AIT
	9: 2	over you, or just o man?'	285
	9: 5	on o stone murdered his seventy brothers,	285
	9: 8	O day the trees went out to anoint a king	NIH
	11:37	But grant me this o request," she said.	AIT
	13:11	"Are you the o who talked to my wife?"	408
	14: 3	She's the right o for me."	AIT
	16: 1	O day Samson went to Gaza,	2256
	16: 5	Each o of us will give you eleven hundred shekels of silver."	AIT
	16:24	the o who laid waste our land	AIT
	16:28	with o blow get revenge on the Philistines	285
	16:29	his right hand on the o and his left hand on	285
	17: 5	and some idols and installed o of his sons	285
	17:11	young man was to him like o of his sons.	285
	18:14	"Do you know that o of these houses has	NIH
	18:19	priest rather than just o man's household?"	285
	18:28	There was no o to rescue them	AIT
	19:13	and spend the night in o of those places."	285
	19:15	no o took them into his home for the night.	408
	19:18	No o has taken me into his house.	408
	20: 1	as o man and assembled before the LORD	285
	20: 6	into pieces and sent o piece to each region	AIT
	20: 8	All the people rose as o man, saying,	285
	20: 8	No, not o of us will return to his house.	408
	20:11	of Israel got together and united as o man	285
	20:22	men of Israel encouraged o another	2021+6639
	20:31	the o leading to Bethel and the other	285
	21: 1	"Not o of us will give his daughter	408
	21: 3	Why should o tribe be missing	285
	21: 6	"Today o tribe is cut off from Israel,"	AIT
	21: 8	"Which o of the tribes of Israel failed	285
	21: 8	that no o from Jabesh Gilead had come to	408
	21:23	each man caught o and carried her off to	889S
Ru	1: 4	o named Orpah and the other Ruth.	285
	2:13	the standing of o of your servant girls."	285
	2:19	the o at whose place she had been working.	2257
	2:20	he is o of our kinsman-redeemers."	4946
	3: 1	O day Naomi her mother-in-law said to her,	2256
	4: 4	For no o has the right to do it except you,	AIT
	4: 7	o party took off his sandal and gave it to	408S
1Sa	1: 2	o was called Hannah and	285
	2: 2	"There is no o holy like the LORD;	AIT
	2: 2	there is no o besides you;	AIT
	2: 9	"It is not by strength that o prevails;	408
	2:20	the place of the o she prayed for and gave	AIT
	2:33	Every o of you that I do not cut off	AIT
	2:35	before my anointed o always.	AIT
	3: 2	O night Eli, whose eyes were becoming	2085
	6:17	o each for Ashdod, Gaza, Ashkelon,	285
	9: 3	"Take o of the servants with you and go	285
	9:23	the o I told you to lay aside."	889S
	10: 3	O will be carrying three young goats,	285
	10:24	There is no o like him among all	AIT
	11: 2	that I gouge out the right eye of every o	AIT
	11: 3	if no o comes to rescue us,	AIT
	11: 7	and they turned out as o man.	285
	11:13	"No o shall be put to death today,	408
	12:13	the o you asked for;	889S
	13:17	O turned toward Ophrah in the vicinity	285
	14: 1	O day Jonathan son of Saul said to	2021
	14: 3	No o was aware that Jonathan had left.	2021+6639
	14: 4	o was called Bozez, and the other Seneh.	285
	14: 5	O cliff stood to the north toward Micmash,	285
	14:26	yet no o put his hand to his mouth,	AIT
	14:28	Then o of the soldiers told him,	408
	14:36	and let us not leave o of them alive."	408
	14:39	But not o of the men said a word.	3972
	15: 1	the o the LORD sent to anoint you king	NIH
	15:28	and has given it to o of your neighbors—	NIH
	15:28	one of your neighbors—to o better than you.	2021
	16: 1	I have chosen o of his sons to be king."	928
	16: 3	You are to anoint for me the o I indicate."	889S
	16: 8	"The LORD has not chosen this o either."	AIT
	16: 9	"Nor has the LORD chosen this o."	AIT
	16:12	"Rise and anoint him; he is the o."	2296
	16:18	O of the servants answered,	285
	16:21	and David became o of his armor-bearers.	NIH
	17: 3	The Philistines occupied o hill and	2296
	17:32	"Let no o lose heart on account	132
	17:36	this uncircumcised Philistine will be like o	285
	18: 1	Jonathan became o in spirit with David,	8003
	20:15	even when the LORD has cut off every o	AIT
	21: 1	Why is no o with you?"	408
	21: 2	'No o is to know anything	408
	21: 7	o of Saul's servants was there that day,	408
	21: 9	there is no sword here but that o."	2023
	21:11	the o they sing about in their dances:	NIH
	22: 8	No o tells me when my son makes	AIT
	23:26	Saul was going along o side of	2296
	25:14	O of the servants told Nabal's wife Abigail:	285
	25:17	a wicked man that no o can talk to him."	AIT
	25:22	if by morning I leave alive o male	AIT
	25:34	not o male belonging to Nabal	AIT
	26: 8	to the ground with o thrust of my spear;	285

1Sa 26:12	No *o* saw or knew about it,	AIT
26:20	as *o* hunts a partridge in the mountains."	AIT
26:22	"Let *o* of your young men come over	285
27: 1	"O of these days I will be destroyed by	285
27: 5	let a place be assigned to me in *o of*	285
28: 7	"There is *o* in Endor," they said.	200+1266S
28: 8	he said, "and bring up for me the *o* I name."	889S
28:17	and given it to *o* of your neighbors—	NIH
30: 6	each *o* was bitter in spirit because	408
2Sa 1:15	Then David called *o* of his men and said,	285
2: 1	"Shall I go up to *o of* the towns of Judah?"	285
2:13	O group sat down on one side of the pool	465S
2:13	down on *o* side of the pool and one group	AIT
2:13	down on one side of the pool and *o* group	465S
2:21	take on *o* of the young men and strip him	285
3:13	But I demand *o* thing of you:	285
3:34	You fell as *o* falls before wicked men."	AIT
4: 2	O was named Baanah and the other Recab;	285
5: 2	*o who* led Israel on their **military campaigns.**	AIT
7: 5	the *o* to build me a house to dwell in?	NIH
7:13	the *o* who will build a house for my Name,	NIH
7:22	**There is no** *o* like you,	AIT
7:23	the *o* nation on earth that God went out	285
9: 3	"Is there no *o* still left of the house of Saul	408
9:11	So Mephibosheth ate at David's table like *o*	285
11: 2	O evening David got up from his bed	2021
11:12	David said to him, "Stay here *o* more day,	2021
11:25	the sword devours *o* as well as another.	2297
12: 1	*o* rich and the other poor.	285
12: 3	poor man had nothing except *o* little ewe	285
12: 4	from taking *o of* his own sheep or cattle	4946
12: 4	and prepared it for the *o* who had come	408
12:11	and give them to *o* **who is close** *to* you,	8276
13:13	You would be like *o of* the wicked fools	285
13:30	not *o* of them is left."	285
14: 6	and no *o* was there to **separate**	AIT
14: 6	O struck the other and killed him.	285
14: 7	the *o* who **struck** his brother **down,**	AIT
14:11	"not *o* hair of your son's head will fall to	4946
14:19	no *o* can turn to the right or to the left	838
15: 2	"Your servant is from *o of* the tribes	285
16:18	"No, **the** *o* chosen by the LORD,	889S
16:23	like that of *o* who inquires of God.	408
17:19	No *o* knew anything **about** it.	AIT
17:20	The men searched but found no *o,*	AIT
17:22	no *o* was left who had not crossed	285
18:10	When *o* of the men saw this, he told Joab,	285
18:20	"You are not the *o* to take the news today,"	408
18:27	that the **first** *o* runs like Ahimaaz son	AIT
19: 9	he is the *o* who **rescued** us from the hand of	AIT
19:14	of Judah as though they were *o* man.	285
20:11	O of Joab's men stood beside Amasa	408
20:21	Hand over **this** *o* man,	963+4200
21: 6	the LORD's **chosen** *o.*	AIT
21:16	*o* of the descendants of Rapha.	NIH
21:18	*o* of the descendants of Rapha.	NIH
22:42	but there was no *o to* **save** them—	AIT
23: 3	'*When* *o* **rules** over men in righteousness,	AIT
23: 8	whom he killed in *o* encounter.	285
23: 9	As *o* of the three mighty men,	NIH
24:12	Choose *o* of them for me to carry out	285
24:13	how I should answer the *o who* **sent** me."	AIT
24:17	I am the *o* **who** has **sinned** and done wrong.	AIT
1Ki 2:16	Now I have *o* request to make of you.	285
2:20	"I have *o* small request to make of you,"	285
3:17	O of them said, "My lord,	285
3:18	there was no *o* in the house but the two	2424S
3:22	The **living** *o* is my son;	AIT
3:22	the **dead** *o* is yours."	AIT
3:22	But the **first** *o* insisted, "No!	2296S
3:22	dead *o* is yours; the **living** one is mine."	AIT
3:22	dead one is yours; the **living** *o* is mine."	AIT
3:23	The king said, "**This** *o* says,	AIT
3:23	while **that** *o* says, 'No!	AIT
3:25	Cut the living child in two and give half to *o*	285
4: 7	Each *o* had to provide supplies	285
4: 7	to provide supplies for *o* month in the year.	NIH
5: 6	You know that we have no *o* so skilled	408
5:14	so that they spent *o* month in Lebanon	NIH
6:24	O wing of the first cherub was five cubits long,	NIH
6:27	The wing of *o* cherub touched one wall,	285
6:27	The wing of one cherub touched *o* wall,	2021
6:36	and *o* course of trimmed cedar beams.	NIH
6:36	and *o* course of trimmed cedar beams.	NIH
7:21	to the south he named Jakin and the *o* to	6647S
7:24	in two rows in *o* **piece with** the Sea.	3669
7:31	that had a circular frame *o* cubit deep.	NIH
7:34	*o* on each corner, projecting from the stand.	4190S
7:38	*o* basin to go on each of the ten stands.	285
8:19	you *are* not the *o* to **build** the temple,	AIT
8:19	he is the *o who* will **build** the temple	AIT
8:38	**each** *o* aware of the afflictions	AIT
8:46	for there is no *o* who does not sin—	132
8:56	Not *o* word has failed of all	285
10:20	*o* at either end of each step.	NIH
11:11	and give it to *o* of your subordinates.	NIH
11:13	but will give him *o* tribe for the sake	285
11:26	He was *o* of Solomon's officials,	NIH
11:32	he will have *o* tribe.	285
11:36	I will give *o* tribe to his son so	285
11:38	the *o* I built for David and will give Israel	NIH
12:24	Go home, **every** *o* of you,	285
12:29	O he set up in Bethel, and the other in Dan.	285
12:30	even as far as Dan to worship the *o* there.	285
14: 2	the *o* who told me I would be king	2085

1Ki 14:10	up the house of Jeroboam as *o* **burns** dung,	AIT
14:13	the only *o* belonging to Jeroboam who will	2296
14:13	because he is the only *o* in the house	NIH
15:22	no *o* was exempt—	AIT
16: 9	Zimri, *o* of his officials,	NIH
18: 6	Ahab going in *o* direction and Obadiah	285
18:22	the **only** *o* of the LORD's prophets left,	963+4200
18:23	Let them choose *o* for themselves,	285
18:25	"Choose *o* of the bulls and prepare it first,	285
18:26	But there was no response; no *o* **answered.**	AIT
18:29	But there was no response, no *o* **answered,**	AIT
18:29	no one answered, no *o* paid attention.	AIT
18:31	*o* for **each** of the tribes descended	3869+5031
19: 2	not make your life like that of *o* of them."	285
19:10	I am the **only** *o* left,	963+4200
19:14	I am the **only** *o* left,	963+4200
20:11	'*O who* **puts on** *his* armor should not	AIT
20:11	not boast like *o who* **takes** it **off.**' "	AIT
20:20	and **each** *o* struck down his opponent.	AIT
20:25	also raise an army like the *o* you lost—	2657S
20:29	on the Aramean foot soldiers in *o* day.	285
20:35	By the word of the LORD *o* of the sons of	285
20:41	and the king of Israel recognized him as *o*	4946
22: 8	"There is still *o* man through whom	285
22: 9	So the king of Israel called *o* of his officials	285
22:13	to him, "Look, *as* *o* man the other prophets	285
22:17	Let **each** *o* go home in peace.' "	AIT
22:20	"O suggested this, and another that.	2296
2Ki 4: 4	as each is filled, **put it to** *o* side."	5825
4: 6	she said to her son, "Bring me another *o*."	3998S
4: 8	O day Elisha went to Shunem.	2021
4:11	O day when Elisha came,	2021
4:18	and *o* day he went out to his father,	2021
4:22	"Please send me *o* of the servants and	285
4:39	O of them went out into the fields	285
4:39	though no *o* **knew** what they were.	AIT
5:18	forgive your servant for **this** *o* thing:	AIT
6: 3	Then *o* of them said,	285
6: 5	As *o* of them was cutting down a tree,	285
6:12	my lord the king," said *o* of his officers,	285
7: 6	so that they said to *o* another, "Look,	408
7: 8	of the camp and entered *o* of the tents.	285
7:13	O of his officers answered,	285
8:26	and he reigned in Jerusalem *o* year.	285
9:10	and no *o* will **bury** her.' "	AIT
9:11	*o* of them **asked** him,	AIT
9:37	so that no *o* will be able to **say,**	AIT
10:19	See that no *o* is missing,	408
10:21	not *o* stayed away.	408
10:21	until it was full from *o* **end** to the other.	AIT
10:24	"If *o* of you lets any of the men	NIH
10:25	let no *o* escape.	408
11: 9	**Each** *o* took his men—	AIT
12: 5	Let every priest receive the money from *o*	NIH
12: 9	on the right side as *o* enters the temple of	408
14: 7	the *o* who **defeated** ten thousand Edomites	285
14:22	the *o* who **rebuilt** Elath and restored it	AIT
14:25	the *o* who **restored** the boundaries of Israel	AIT
14:26	there was no *o* to **help** them.	285
15:13	and he reigned in Samaria *o* **month.**	3427+3732
15:25	O of his chief officers,	NIH
17:27	"Have *o* of the priests you took captive	285
17:28	So *o* of the priests who had been exiled	285
17:36	is the *o* you must worship.	2257
18: 5	*There* **was** no *o* like him among all the kings	AIT
18:22	isn't he **the** *o* whose high places	889S
18:24	How can you repulse *o* officer of the least	285
18:31	Then **every** *o* of you will eat	AIT
19:22	Against the **Holy** *O* of Israel!	AIT
19:37	O day, while he was worshiping in	2118+2256
21:13	I will wipe out Jerusalem as *o* **wipes** a dish,	AIT
23:10	so no *o* could use it to sacrifice his son	408
25:17	of *o* pillar was four and a half feet high	NIH
1Ch 1:19	O was named Peleg, because in his time	285
4:17	O of Mered's wives gave birth to Miriam,	NIH
5:21	took *o* **hundred** thousand people captive,	AIT
11: 2	*o who* **led** Israel on their **military campaigns.**	AIT
11:11	whom he killed in *o* encounter.	285
11:12	*o* of the three mighty men.	2085
12:38	the rest of the Israelites were also of *o* mind	285
15: 2	"No *o* but the Levites may carry the ark	AIT
16:20	from *o* kingdom to another.	NIH
17: 4	not the *o* to build me a house to dwell in.	NIH
17: 5	I have moved from *o* tent site to another,	NIH
17: 5	from *o* dwelling place to another.	NIH
17:11	*o* of your own sons,	4946
17:12	the *o* who will **build** a house for me,	AIT
17:20	"There is no *o* like you, O LORD,	AIT
17:21	the *o* nation on earth whose God went out	285
20: 4	*o* of the descendants of the Rephaites,	4946
21: 5	In all Israel there were *o* **million** one hundred thousand men who could handle	AIT
21: 5	one million *o* **hundred** thousand men who	AIT
21:10	Choose *o* of them for me to carry out	285
21:12	how I should answer the *o* who **sent** me".	285
21:17	I am the *o* who has sinned and done wrong.	2085
22:10	He *is* the *o* who will **build** a house	AIT
23:11	as *o* family with one assignment.	NIH
23:11	as one family with *o* assignment.	285
24: 6	*o* family being taken from Eleazar and	285
24: 6	from Eleazar and then *o* from Ithamar.	285
26: 1	*o* of the sons of Asaph.	4946
29: 1	the *o* whom God has chosen,	285
2Ch 3:11	O wing of the first cherub was five cubits	285
3:12	Similarly *o* wing of the second cherub	NIH

2Ch 3:17	*o* to the south and one to the north.	285
3:17	one to the south and *o* to the north.	285
3:17	The *o to the* **south** he named Jakin and	AIT
3:17	and the *o to the* **north** Boaz.	AIT
4: 3	in two rows in *o* **piece with** the Sea.	4609
5:13	joined in unison, as with *o* voice,	285
6: 9	you are not the *o* to **build** the temple,	AIT
6: 9	he is the *o* who will **build** the temple	AIT
6:29	**each** *o* aware of his afflictions and pains,	AIT
6:36	for there is no *o* who does not sin—	132
6:42	do not reject your **anointed** *o.*	AIT
9:19	*o* at either end of each step.	NIH
11: 4	Go home, **every** *o* of you,	AIT
14: 6	No *o* was at war with him	AIT
14:11	**there is no** *o* like you to help the powerless	AIT
15: 6	O **nation** was being crushed by another	AIT
15: 6	by another and *o* **city** by another,	AIT
18: 7	"There is still *o* man through whom	285
18: 8	So the king of Israel called *o* of his officials	285
18:12	to him, "Look, as *o* man the other prophets	285
18:16	Let **each** *o* go home in peace.' "	AIT
18:19	"O suggested this, and another that.	2296
20: 6	and no *o* can withstand you.	AIT
20:23	they helped to destroy *o* another.	408
20:24	no *o* had escaped.	AIT
22: 2	and he reigned in Jerusalem *o* year.	285
22: 9	So **there was no** *o* in the house	AIT
23: 6	No *o is to* **enter** the temple of	AIT
23: 8	**Each** *o* took his men—	AIT
23:19	*o* who was in any way **unclean**	AIT
26: 2	the *o* who rebuilt Elath and restored it	NIH
26:11	*o* of the royal officials.	4946
28: 6	In *o* day Pekah son of Remaliah killed	285
32: 5	He built another wall outside that *o*	NIH
32:12	before *o* altar and burn sacrifices on it'?	285
Ezr 3: 1	the people assembled as *o* man	285
3:13	No *o* could distinguish the sound of	2021+6639S
5:11	the temple that was built many years ago, *o*	10204
6: 4	with three courses of large stones and *o*	10248
6:17	*o* for **each** of the tribes of Israel.	NIH
9:11	with their impurity from *o* **end** to the other.	AIT
9:15	though because of it **not** *o* of us can stand	AIT
10: 2	*o* of the descendants of Elam, said to Ezra,	4946
10:16	*o* from each family division,	NIH
Ne 1: 2	Hanani, *o* of my brothers,	285
2:12	with me except the *o* I was riding on.	989S
3: 8	*o* of the goldsmiths, repaired the next	NIH
3: 8	and Hananiah, *o* of the perfume-makers,	1201S
3:31	Next to him, Malkijah, *o* of the goldsmiths,	1201S
4:17	with *o* hand and held a weapon in the other,	285
5:18	Each day *o* ox, six choice sheep	285
6: 2	let us meet together in *o* of the villages on	NIH
6:10	O day I went to the house of Shemaiah son	2256
6:11	Or should *o* like me go into the temple	4769
8: 1	all the people assembled as *o* man in	285
8:16	the square by the Water Gate and the *o by*	8148S
11: 1	of the people cast lots to bring *o* out	285
11:22	Uzzi was *o* of Asaph's descendants,	4946
11:24	*o* of the descendants of Zerah son of Judah,	4946
12:24	*o* **section** responding to the other,	AIT
12:31	O was to proceed on top of the wall to	NIH
13:24	*o* **of the other peoples,**	2256+6639+6639
13:28	O *of* the sons of Joiada son of Eliashib	4946
Est 1: 7	**each** *o* different from the other.	3998S
4: 2	because no *o* **clothed** in sackcloth	AIT
4: 5	*o* of the king's eunuchs assigned	4946
4:11	the king has but *o* law:	285
6: 8	*o* with a royal crest placed on its head.	889S
6: 9	the robe and horse be entrusted to *o* of	408
7: 9	*o* of the eunuchs attending the king, said,	285
9: 2	No *o* could stand against them,	408
9:22	of food to another and gifts to the poor.	408
Job 1: 6	O day the angels came to present	2021
1: 8	There is no *o* on earth like him;	NIH
1:13	O day when Job's sons	2021
1:15	the **only** *o* who has escaped to tell you!	963+4200
1:16	the **only** *o* who has escaped to tell you!	963+4200
1:17	the **only** *o* who has escaped to tell you!	963+4200
1:19	the **only** *o* who has escaped to tell you!	963+4200
2: 3	There is no *o* on earth like him;	NIH
2:13	No *o* said a word to him,	AIT
6:10	I had not denied the words of the **Holy O.**	7705
9: 3	Though *o* **wished** to dispute with him,	AIT
9: 3	not answer him *o* time out of a thousand.	285
10: 7	that no *o* can **rescue** me from your hand?	AIT
11: 3	Will no *o* **rebuke** you when you mock?	AIT
11:19	with no *o* to **make** you **afraid,**	AIT
14: 3	Do you fix your eye on such *o*?	AIT
14: 4	bring what is pure from the impure? No *o*!	285
15:14	that he could be pure, or *o* **born** of woman,	AIT
15:28	and houses where no *o* lives,	AIT
18:21	such is the place of *o* who **knows** not God."	AIT
21:23	O **man** dies in full vigor,	AIT
22:30	*o* who is not **innocent,**	AIT
24:12	But God charges no *o* with wrongdoing.	NIH
24:18	so that no *o* goes to the vineyards.	AIT
25: 4	How can *o* **born** of woman be pure?	AIT
26: 3	What advice you have offered to *o*	NIH
29:25	I was like *o* who **comforts** mourners.	AIT
30:24	"Surely no *o* lays a hand on a broken man	AIT
31:15	Did not the **same** *o* form us both within our mothers?	285
32:12	But not *o* of you *has* **proved** Job **wrong;**	AIT
32:21	I will show partiality to no *o,*	408
33:14	now *o* **way,** now another—	285+928
33:23	*o* out of a thousand,	285
34:17	Will you condemn the just and **mighty** *O?*	AIT

Ref	Text	Code
Job 34:18	Is he not the *O who* **says** to kings,	AIT
35:10	But no *o* **says**, 'Where is God my Maker,	AIT
36: 4	*o* **perfect** *in* knowledge is with you.	AIT
36:18	Be careful that no *o* **entices** you by riches;	AIT
37:21	Now no *o can* **look** *at* the sun,	AIT
38:26	a desert with no *o* in it,	132
40: 2	*"Will the o who* **contends** with	AIT
41:10	No *o* is **fierce** *enough* to rouse him.	AIT
41:17	They are joined fast to *o* another;	408
41:32	*o would* **think** the deep had white hair.	AIT
42:11	and **each** *o* gave him a piece of silver and	AIT
Ps 2: 2	the LORD and against his **Anointed** *O.*	AIT
2: 4	The *O* **enthroned** in heaven laughs;	AIT
6: 5	**No** *o* remembers you when he is dead.	AIT
7: 2	to pieces with no *o to* **rescue** me.	AIT
14: 1	there is no *o who* **does** good.	AIT
14: 3	there is no *o who* **does** good, not even one.	AIT
14: 3	there is no one who does good, not even **o.**	285
16:10	nor will you let your **Holy** *O* see decay.	AIT
18:41	but there was no *o to* **save** them—	AIT
19: 6	It rises at *o* **end** of the heavens	AIT
22: 3	Yet you are enthroned as the **Holy** *O;*	7705
22:11	trouble is near and there is no *o to* **help.**	AIT
22:24	the suffering of the **afflicted** *o;*	AIT
25: 3	No *o* whose hope is in you will ever be put	3972
27: 4	*O* **thing** I ask of the LORD,	285
28: 8	a fortress of salvation for his **anointed** *o.*	AIT
34:20	not *o* of them will be broken.	285
34:22	no *o* will be condemned who takes refuge	3972
39: 9	for you are the *o who has* **done** this.	AIT
40: 5	for us no *o can* **recount** to you;	AIT
41: 6	Whenever *o* **comes** to see me,	AIT
45: 3	upon your side, O **mighty** *o;*	AIT
50: 1	The **Mighty** *O,* God, the LORD,	446
53: 1	there is no *o who* **does** good.	AIT
53: 3	there is no *o who* **does** good, not even one.	AIT
53: 3	there is no one who does good, not even *o.*	285
54: 4	the Lord is the *o who* **sustains** me.	AIT
62:11	*O* **thing** God has spoken,	285
68: 8	before God, the **O** of Sinai, before God,	2296
69:25	let there be no *o to* **dwell** in their tents.	AIT
71:11	for no *o will* **rescue** him."	AIT
71:22	**O Holy** *O* of Israel.	7705
72:12	the afflicted who have no *o to* **help.**	AIT
73:20	As a dream when *o* **awakes,**	AIT
75: 6	**No** *o* from the east or the west or from	AIT
75: 7	He brings *o* down, he exalts another.	2296
76: 5	not *o* of the warriors can lift his hands.	3972
76:11	bring gifts to the *O* to be **feared.**	AIT
78:41	they vexed the **Holy** *O* of Israel.	7705
79: 3	and there is no *o to* **bury** the dead.	AIT
83: 5	*With o* **mind** they plot together;	AIT
84: 9	look with favor on your **anointed** *o.*	AIT
84:10	Better is *o* **day** in your courts than	AIT
87: 4	and will say, 'This *o* was born in Zion.' "	AIT
87: 5	"This *o* and that one were born in her,	408
87: 5	"This one and *that* **o** were born in her,	408
87: 6	"This *o* was born in Zion."	AIT
89: 3	"I have made a covenant with my **chosen** *o,*	AIT
89:10	You crushed Rahab like *o* of the **slain;**	AIT
89:18	our king to the **Holy** *O* of Israel.	7705
89:38	very angry with your **anointed** *o.*	AIT
89:51	mocked every step of your **anointed** *o.*	AIT
94:20	*o that* **brings on** misery by its decrees?	AIT
101: 7	No *o who* **practices** deceit will dwell	AIT
101: 7	no *o who* **speaks** falsely will stand	AIT
105:13	from *o* **kingdom** to another.	AIT
105:14	He allowed no *o* to oppress them;	132
105:37	and from among their tribes no *o* **faltered.**	AIT
106:11	not *o* of them survived.	285
106:23	had not Moses, his **chosen** *o,*	AIT
107: 1	they stumbled, and there was no *o to* **help.**	AIT
109:12	*May* no *o* **extend** kindness to him	AIT
109:31	he stands at the right hand of the **needy** *o,*	AIT
113: 5	*O who* **sits** enthroned *on* **high,**	AIT
119:14	in following your statutes as *o* rejoices	NIH
119:42	then I will answer the *o who* **taunts** me,	AIT
119:162	in your promise like *o who* **finds** great spoil.	AIT
129: 7	nor the *o who* **gathers** fill his arms.	AIT
132: 2	and made a vow to the **Mighty O** of Jacob:	51
132: 5	a dwelling for the **Mighty O** of Jacob."	51
132:10	do not reject your **anointed** *o.*	AIT
132:11	**"O** of your own descendants I will place	4946
132:17	and set up a lamp for my **anointed** *o.*	AIT
136:23	to the **O** who **remembered** us	AIT
137: 3	they said, "Sing us *o* of the songs of Zion!"	4946
139:16	in your book before *o* of them came to be.	285
141: 7	"As *o* **plows** and breaks up the earth,	AIT
142: 4	no *o* is **concerned** for me.	AIT
142: 4	I have no refuge; no *o* **cares for** my life.	AIT
143: 2	for no *o* living is righteous before you.	3972
144:10	to the *O who* **gives** victory to kings,	AIT
145: 3	his greatness **no** *o* can fathom.	AIT
145: 4	*O* **generation** will commend your works	AIT
Pr 1:24	when I called and no *o* **gave heed**	AIT
5: 9	to others and your years to *o who* is **cruel,**	AIT
6:29	no *o* who touches her will go unpunished.	3972
9:10	knowledge of the **Holy** *O* is understanding.	7705
11:24	*O man* gives freely, yet gains even more;	AIT
13: 7	*O man* pretends to be rich,	AIT
14: 1	the **foolish** *o* tears hers down.	AIT
14:10	and no *o* else can share its joy.	AIT
16:32	controls his temper than *o who* **takes** a city.	AIT
17: 2	the inheritance **as** *o* of the brothers.	928+9348
17: 8	A bribe is a charm to the *o who* **gives** it;	1251
17:25	and bitterness to the *o who* **bore** him.	AIT
18: 9	*O who is* **slack** in his work is brother	AIT

Ref	Text	Code
Pr 18: 9	is brother to *o who* **destroys.**	1251+5422
19:23	Then *o* **rests** content, untouched by trouble.	AIT
20:16	*o who* **puts up security** for a stranger.	AIT
21:12	The **Righteous O** takes note of the house of	7404
22:24	do not associate with *o* easily angered,	408
23:34	be like *o* **sleeping** on the high seas,	AIT
25:20	Like *o who* **takes away** a garment on	AIT
25:20	is *o who* **sings** songs to a heavy heart.	AIT
26:17	Like *o who* **seizes** a dog by the ears is	AIT
27:13	Take the garment of *o* who puts up security	2257
27:17	so *o* **man** sharpens another.	AIT
28: 1	The wicked man flees though no *o* **pursues,**	AIT
28:17	*let no* *o* **support** him.	AIT
28:19	the *o who* **chases** fantasies will have his fill	AIT
28:20	*o* **eager** to get rich will not go unpunished.	AIT
29: 4	but *o* who is **greedy** for bribes tears it down.	408
29: 5	but a **righteous** *o* can sing and be glad.	AIT
29:22	and a **hot-tempered** *o* commits many sins.	AIT
30: 3	nor have I knowledge of the **Holy O.**	7705
Ecc 1: 8	things are wearisome, more than *o* can say.	408
1:10	Is there anything of which *o can* **say,**	AIT
2:18	to the *o who* **comes** after me.	132
2:26	to hand it over to the *o who* **pleases** God.	AIT
3:19	As *o* dies, so dies the other.	2296
4: 6	Better *o* **handful** with tranquillity	AIT
4: 9	Two are better than *o,*	285
4:10	If *o* falls down, his friend can help him up!	285
4:10	But pity the man who falls and has no *o*	9108
4:11	But how can *o* keep warm *alone?*	285
4:12	Though *o* may be overpowered,	285
5: 8	for *o* **official** is eyed by a higher one,	AIT
5: 8	for one official is eyed by a higher *o,*	1469S
6:10	with *o who* is stronger than he.	AIT
7:14	God has made the *o* as well as the other.	2296
7:18	It is good to grasp the *o* and not let go of	2296
7:19	Wisdom makes *o* wise man more powerful	
	than ten rulers	2021
7:27	"Adding *o* **thing** to another to discover	285
7:28	I found *o* [upright] man among a thousand,	285
7:28	but not *o* [upright] woman among them all.	NIH
8: 8	**no** *o* has power over the day of his death.	AIT
8: 8	As **no** *o* is discharged in time of war,	AIT
8:17	No *o* can comprehend what goes on under	132
9:18	but *o* sinner destroys much good.	285
10:14	No *o* knows what is coming—	132
12:11	given by *o* Shepherd.	285
SS 1: 9	to a mare harnessed to *o* of the chariots	NIH
2:10	"Arise, my darling, my **beautiful** *o,*	AIT
2:13	my **beautiful** *o,* come with me."	AIT
3: 1	for the **o** my heart loves.	8611S
3: 2	I will search for **the o** my heart loves.	8611S
3: 3	"Have you seen **the o** my heart loves?"	8611S
3: 4	when I found **the o** my heart loves.	8611S
3: 4	to the room of the *o who* **conceived** me.	AIT
4: 2	Each has its twin; not *o* of them is alone.	NIH
4: 9	you have stolen my heart with *o* glance	285
4: 9	with *o* jewel of your necklace.	285
5: 2	my darling, my dove, my **flawless** *o.*	AIT
6: 6	Each has its twin, not *o* of them is alone.	AIT
6: 9	my **perfect** *o,* is unique,	AIT
6: 9	the favorite of the *o who* **bore** her.	AIT
8: 1	and no *o would* **despise** me.	AIT
8: 7	If *o* were to give all the wealth of his house	408
8:10	in his eyes like *o* **bringing** contentment.	AIT
Isa 1: 4	the **Holy O** of Israel and turned their backs	7705
1:24	the **Mighty O** of Israel, declares:	51
1:31	with no *o to* **quench** *the* **fire."**	AIT
3: 6	A man will seize *o* of his **brothers**	AIT
4: 1	seven women will take hold of *o* man and	285
5: 1	for the *o* I **love** a song about his vineyard:	AIT
5: 1	My **loved** *o* had a vineyard on	3351
5:19	let the plan of the **Holy O** of Israel come,	7705
5:24	and spurned the word of the **Holy O**	7705
5:27	Not *o* of them grows **tired** or stumbles,	AIT
5:27	not *o* **slumbers** or sleeps;	AIT
5:29	and carry it off with no *o to* **rescue.**	AIT
5:30	And if *o* **looks** at the land,	AIT
6: 3	And they were calling to *o* another:	2296
6: 6	Then *o* of the seraphs flew to me with	285
8:13	The LORD Almighty is the **o** you are	2257
8:13	he is the *o* you are to fear,	NIH
8:13	he is the *o* you are to **dread,**	AIT
9:19	no *o* will spare his brother.	408
10:13	like a **mighty** *o* I subdued their kings.	AIT
10:14	As *o* **reaches** into a nest,	AIT
10:14	not *o* **flapped** a wing,	AIT
10:17	their **Holy** *O* a flame;	7705
10:20	rely on the LORD, the **Holy O** of Israel.	7705
10:34	Lebanon will fall before the **Mighty O.**	129
12: 6	great is the **Holy O** of Israel among you."	7705
16: 5	*o* from the house of David—	NIH
16: 5	*o who* in **judging** seeks justice and speeds	AIT
16:10	no *o* **sings** or shouts in the vineyards;	AIT
16:10	no *o* **treads** out wine at the presses,	AIT
17: 2	with no *o to* **make** them **afraid.**	AIT
17: 7	and turn their eyes to the **Holy O** of Israel.	7705
19:11	"I am *o* of the wise men,	1201
19:18	**O** of them will be called the City	285
21:16	"Within *o* **year,** as a servant bound	AIT
22:11	but you did not look to the *O who* **made** it,	AIT
22:11	for the *O who* **planned** it long ago.	AIT
22:22	what he opens no *o can* **shut,**	AIT
22:22	and what he shuts no *o can* **open.**	AIT
24:16	"Glory to the **Righteous O."**	7404
26: 7	**O** upright *O,* you make the way of	AIT
27: 3	and night so that no *o may* **harm** it.	AIT
27:12	O Israelites, will be gathered up by one.	285

Ref	Text	Code
Isa 27:12	O Israelites, will be gathered up one by **o.**	285
28: 2	the Lord has *o who* is **powerful** and strong.	AIT
28:16	the *o who* **trusts** will never be dismayed.	AIT
28:28	*o* does not **go on** threshing	AIT
29:19	the needy will rejoice in the **Holy O**	7705
29:23	the holiness of the **Holy O** of Jacob,	7705
30:11	and stop confronting us with the **Holy O**	7705
30:12	this is what the **Holy O** of Israel says:	7705
30:15	the **Holy O** of Israel, says:	7705
30:17	A thousand will flee at the threat of *o;*	285
31: 1	but do not look to the **Holy O** of Israel,	AIT
31: 7	that day **every** *o* of you will reject the idols	AIT
33: 8	no *o* is respected.	632
33:18	Where is the *o who* **took** *the* **revenue?**	AIT
33:21	There the LORD will be our **Mighty O.**	129
33:24	No *o* living in Zion will say, "I am ill"	8907
34:10	no *o will* ever **pass** through it again.	AIT
34:16	not *o* will lack her mate.	851
36: 7	isn't he **the** *o* whose high places	889S
36: 9	then can you repulse *o* officer of the least	285
36:16	Then **every** *o* of you will eat	AIT
37:23	Against the **Holy O** of Israel!	7705
37:38	**O day,** while he was worshiping in	2118+2256
40: 3	A voice of *o* **calling:**	AIT
40:25	says the **Holy O.**	7705
40:26	who brings out the starry host **o** by one,	928+5031
40:26	who brings out the starry host one by **o,**	928+5031
40:26	not *o* of them is missing.	408
40:28	and his understanding no *o* can fathom.	NIH
41: 2	"Who has stirred up *o* from the east,	NIH
41:14	your Redeemer, the **Holy O** of Israel.	7705
41:16	in the LORD and glory in the **Holy O**	7705
41:20	that the **Holy O** of Israel has created it.	7705
41:25	"I have stirred up *o* from the north,	NIH
41:25	*o* from the rising sun who calls	NIH
41:26	No *o* **told** *of* this, no one foretold it,	AIT
41:26	No one told of this, no *o* **foretold** it,	AIT
41:26	no *o* **heard** any words from you.	AIT
41:28	I look but there is no *o*—	408
41:28	no *o* among them **to give** counsel,	3446
41:28	no *o to* **give** answer when I ask them.	AIT
42: 1	my **chosen** *o* in whom I delight;	AIT
42:19	Who is blind like the *o* **committed** to me,	AIT
42:22	with no *o to* **rescue** them;	AIT
42:22	with no *o to* **say,** "Send them back."	AIT
43: 3	the **Holy O** of Israel, your Savior;	7705
43:10	nor *will there* be *o* after me.	AIT
43:13	No *o can* **deliver** out of my hand.	AIT
43:14	your Redeemer, the **Holy O** of Israel:	7705
43:15	I am the LORD, your **Holy O,**	7705
44: 5	**O** will say, 'I belong to the LORD';	2296
44: 8	No, there is no other Rock; I know not **o."**	NIH
44:19	No *o* stops to think,	2257
44:19	no *o* has the knowledge or understanding	NIH
45:11	the **Holy O** of Israel, and its Maker:	7705
46: 7	Though *o* **cries out** to it, it does not answer;	AIT
47: 3	I will take vengeance; I will spare no **o."**	132
47: 4	is the **Holy O** of Israel.	7705
47:10	'No *o* **sees** me.'	AIT
47:15	there is not *o that can* **save** you.	AIT
48:17	your Redeemer, the **Holy O** of Israel:	7705
49: 7	the Redeemer and **Holy O** of Israel—	7705
49: 7	the **Holy O** of Israel, who has chosen you,"	7731
49:26	your Redeemer, the **Mighty O** of Jacob."	51
50: 2	When I came, why was there no **o?**	408
50: 2	I called, why was there no *o to* **answer?**	AIT
50: 4	to listen like *o* being **taught.**	4341
51: 2	When I called him he was but *o,*	285
51:21	Therefore hear this, you **afflicted** *o,*	AIT
53: 3	Like *o* from whom men **hide** their faces	AIT
54: 5	the **Holy O** of Israel is your Redeemer;	7705
55: 5	the **Holy O** of Israel,	7705
56:12	"Come," each *o* cries, "let me get wine!	NIH
57: 1	and no *o* ponders it in his heart;	408
57: 1	and no *o* **understands** that	AIT
57:15	For this is what the high and lofty **O** says—	AIT
59: 4	No *o* **calls** for justice;	AIT
59: 4	no *o* **pleads** *his* case with integrity.	AIT
59: 5	and when *o* is broken, an adder is hatched.	2021
59: 8	no *o* who walks in them will know peace.	3972
59:16	He saw that there was no *o,*	408
59:16	that there was no *o to* **intervene;**	AIT
60: 9	the **Holy O** of Israel,	7705
60:14	Zion of the **Holy O** of Israel.	7705
60:15	with no *o* **traveling through,**	AIT
60:16	your Redeemer, the **Mighty O** of Jacob.	51
63: 2	like those of *o* **treading** the winepress?	AIT
63: 3	from the nations no *o* was with me.	408
63: 5	I looked, but there was no *o to* **help,**	AIT
63: 5	I was appalled that no *o* **gave support;**	AIT
64: 4	Since ancient times no *o* has **heard,**	AIT
64: 6	of us have become like *o* who is unclean,	2021
64: 7	No *o* **calls** on your name or strives	AIT
66: 2	"This is the *o* I esteem:	AIT
66: 3	like *o who* **kills** a man, and whoever offers	AIT
66: 3	like *o who* **breaks** a dog's **neck;**	AIT
66: 3	like *o who* presents pig's blood,	NIH
66: 3	like *o who* **worships** an idol.	AIT
66: 4	For when I called, no *o* **answered,**	AIT
66: 4	when I spoke, no *o* **listened.**	AIT
66:17	the *o* in the midst of those who eat the flesh	285
66:23	From *o* **New Moon** to another and from	AIT
66:23	to another and from *o* **Sabbath** to another,	AIT
Jer 1: 1	*o* of the priests at Anathoth in the territory	4946
2: 6	where no *o* travels and no one lives?'	408
2: 6	where no one travels and no *o* lives?'	132
3:14	*o* from a town and two from a clan—	285

Jer	3:16	nor *will* another *o* be **made.**	AIT
	4:4	burn with no *o* to **quench** it.	AIT
	4:29	no *o* lives in them.	408
	4:30	What are you doing, O **devastated** *o?*	AIT
	4:31	*o* **bearing** her **first child—**	AIT
	5:1	but *o* **person** who deals honestly and seeks	AIT
	5:5	But **with** *o* **accord** they too had broken off	3481
	6:8	so no *o* can **live** in it."	AIT
	6:9	like *o* **gathering grapes."**	AIT
	7:19	But am I the *o* they are provoking?	NIH
	7:33	be no *o* to **frighten** them **away.**	AIT
	8:6	No *o* repents of his wickedness, saying,	408
	9:3	They go from *o* **sin** to another;	AIT
	9:5	and no *o* **speaks** the truth.	AIT
	9:11	of Judah so no *o* can **live** there.	AIT
	9:12	like a desert that no *o* can **cross."**	AIT
	9:20	teach *o* another a lament.	851
	9:22	with no *o* to **gather** them.'	AIT
	10:6	**No** *o* is like you, O **LORD;**	AIT
	10:7	**there is no** *o* like you.	AIT
	10:20	**no** *o* is left now to pitch my tent or to set	AIT
	12:7	the *o* I **love** into the hands of her enemies.	AIT
	12:11	because there is **no** *o* who cares.	408
	12:12	of the LORD will devour from *o* **end of**	AIT
	12:12	no *o* will be safe.	1414+3972S
	13:14	I will smash them *o* against the other,	408
	13:19	and there will be no *o* to **open** them.	AIT
	14:16	be no *o* to **bury** them or their wives,	AIT
	14:22	for you are the *o* **who does** all this.	AIT
	16:6	and no *o* will **cut himself**	AIT
	16:7	No *o* will **offer food**	AIT
	17:5	"Cursed is the *o* who trusts in man,	1505
	17:6	in a salt land where no *o* **lives.**	AIT
	17:14	for you are the *o* I **praise.**	AIT
	18:11	So turn from your evil ways, **each** *o* of you,	AIT
	19:9	and they will eat *o* another's flesh during	408
	21:12	*o* **who has been robbed,**	AIT
	21:12	burn with no *o* to **quench** it.	AIT
	22:3	*o* **who has been robbed**	AIT
	22:8	by this city and will ask *o* another,	408
	22:28	broken pot, an object **no** *o* wants?	AIT
	23:14	so that no *o* turns from his wickedness.	408
	23:27	dreams they tell *o* another will make my people forget my name,	408
	23:28	the *o* who has my word speak it faithfully.	2257
	23:30	from *o* another words supposedly from me.	408
	24:2	O basket had very good figs,	285
	25:26	near and far, *o* after the other—	408
	25:33	from *o* **end** of the earth to the other.	AIT
	28:9	as *o* truly sent by the LORD only	2021+5566S
	29:32	He will have no *o* left among this people,	408
	30:10	and no *o* will **make** him **afraid.**	AIT
	30:13	There is no *o* to **plead** your cause,	AIT
	30:17	Zion for whom no *o* **cares.'**	AIT
	30:21	Their leader will be *o* of their own;	4946
	33:13	under the hand of the *o* **who counts** them,'	AIT
	33:26	and will not choose *o* of his sons to rule	4946
	34:9	no *o* was to hold a fellow Jew in bondage.	408
	34:22	of Judah so no *o* can **live** there."	AIT
	35:2	to come to *o* of the side rooms of the house	285
	36:30	He will have no *o* to **sit** on the throne	AIT
	38:27	for no *o* had **heard** his conversation with	AIT
	40:15	and no *o* will know it.	408
	41:1	who was of royal blood and had been *o* of	NIH
	41:2	killing the *o* whom the king	2257
	41:9	the *o* King Asa had made as part	2085
	42:17	not *o* of them **will** survive or escape	AIT
	44:26	'that no *o* **from** Judah living anywhere	408
	46:12	O **warrior** will stumble over another;	AIT
	46:18	"*o* **will come** who is like Tabor among	AIT
	46:27	and no *o* will **make** him **afraid.**	AIT
	48:9	with no *o* to **live** in them.	AIT
	48:11	not poured from *o* **jar** to another—	AIT
	48:33	no *o* **treads** them with shouts of joy.	AIT
	48:38	like a jar that **no** *o* wants,"	AIT
	49:5	**"Every** *o* of you will be driven away,	AIT
	49:5	and no *o* will **gather** the fugitives.	AIT
	49:18	says the LORD, "so no *o* will live there;	408
	49:19	Who is the **chosen** *o* I will appoint for this?	AIT
	49:33	No *o* will live there;	408
	50:3	No *o* will live in it;	AIT
	50:29	Encamp all around her; let no *o* **escape.**	AIT
	50:29	the **Holy O** of Israel.	7705
	50:31	"See, I am against you, O **arrogant** *o,*"	AIT
	50:32	The **arrogant** *o* will stumble and fall	AIT
	50:32	and no *o* will **help** her **up;**	AIT
	50:40	"so no *o* will live there;	AIT
	50:44	Who is the **chosen** *o* I will appoint for this?	AIT
	51:5	of guilt before the **Holy O** of Israel.	7705
	51:29	of Babylon so that no *o* **will** live there.	AIT
	51:31	O **courier** follows another	AIT
	51:37	a place where no *o* **lives.**	AIT
	51:43	a land where no *o* lives,	408
	51:46	*o* **rumor** comes this year, another the next,	AIT
	52:22	on top of the *o* pillar was five cubits high	NIH
La	1:4	for no *o* **comes** to her appointed feasts.	AIT
	1:7	there was no *o* to **help** her.	AIT
	1:16	**No** *o* is **near** to comfort me,	AIT
	1:16	no *o* to **restore** my spirit.	AIT
	1:17	but there is no *o* to **comfort** her.	AIT
	1:21	but there is no *o* to **comfort** me.	AIT
	2:22	the day of the LORD's anger **no** *o* escaped	AIT
	3:25	to the *o* who seeks him;	5883
	3:30	to *o* **who would strike** him,	AIT
	4:4	but no *o* **gives** it to them.	AIT
	4:14	that no *o* **dares** to touch their garments.	AIT
Eze	1:9	and their wings touched *o* another.	851

Eze	1:9	**Each** *o* went straight ahead;	AIT
	1:11	*o* **touching** the wing of another creature on	AIT
	1:12	**Each** *o* went straight ahead.	AIT
	1:17	in any *o* of the four directions	NIH
	1:23	expanse their wings were stretched out *o*	851
	1:28	and I heard the voice of *o* **speaking.**	AIT
	4:8	so that you cannot turn from *o* side to	3870S
	7:13	no *o* will preserve his life.	408
	7:14	no *o* will **go** into battle,	AIT
	10:7	Then *o* of the cherubim reached out	2021+4131S
	10:9	*o* beside each of the cherubim;	285
	10:11	in any *o* of the four directions	NIH
	10:14	O face was that of a cherub,	285
	10:22	**Each** *o* went straight ahead.	AIT
	14:10	be as guilty as the *o* **who consults** him.	AIT
	14:15	so that no *o* can **pass through** it because of	AIT
	16:5	*o* **looked** on you **with pity**	AIT
	16:34	*o* **runs after** you **for your favors.**	AIT
	18:4	The soul who sins is the *o* who will die.	2085
	18:20	The soul who sins is the *o* who will die.	2085
	18:30	**each** *o* according to his ways,	AIT
	19:3	She brought up *o* of her cubs,	285
	19:14	Fire spread **from** *o* of its main branches	285
	20:39	Go and serve your idols, **every** *o* of you!	AIT
	21:20	Mark out *o* road for the sword to come	AIT
	22:11	In you *o* **man** commits a detestable offense	AIT
	23:43	I said about the *o* **worn out** by adultery,	AIT
	24:16	with *o* **blow** I am about to take away	AIT
	29:11	no *o* **will** live there for forty years.	AIT
	30:22	the good arm as well as the **broken** *o,*	AIT
	33:2	a land, and the people of the land choose *o*	AIT
	33:6	and the sword comes and takes the life of *o*	NIH
	33:24	'Abraham was only *o* **man,**	285
	33:28	so that no *o* will **cross** them.	AIT
	33:32	nothing more than *o* who sings love songs	NIH
	34:6	and no *o* **searched** or looked for them.	AIT
	34:17	I will judge between *o* **sheep** and another,	AIT
	34:22	I will judge between *o* **sheep** and another.	AIT
	34:23	I will place over them *o* shepherd,	285
	34:28	and not *o* **will make** them **afraid.**	AIT
	37:17	into *o* stick so that they will become one	285
	37:17	into one stick so that they will become *o*	285
	37:19	and they will become *o* in my hand.'	285
	37:22	I will make them *o* nation in the land,	285
	37:22	There will be *o* king over all of them	285
	37:24	and they will all have *o* shepherd.	285
	38:17	Are you not the *o* I spoke of in former days	2085
	39:7	that I the LORD am the **Holy O** in Israel.	7705
	39:15	the land and *o* **of them** sees a human bone,	AIT
	39:26	with no *o* to **make** them **afraid.**	AIT
	40:5	it was *o* measuring rod thick	285
	40:8	and *o* rod high.	285
	40:6	it was *o* rod deep.	285
	40:7	The alcoves for the guards were *o* rod long	285
	40:7	and *o* rod wide,	AIT
	40:7	the temple was *o* rod deep.	285
	40:12	of each alcove was a wall *o* cubit high,	285
	40:13	from the top of the rear wall of *o* alcove to	2021
	40:13	of one alcove to the top of the **opposite** *o;*	AIT
	40:13	from *o* **parapet opening** to	AIT
	40:13	from one parapet opening to the opposite *o.*	7339S
	40:23	from *o* gate to the opposite one;	NIH
	40:23	from one gate to the **opposite** *o;*	AIT
	40:41	So there were four tables on *o* **side** of	AIT
	40:44	*o* at the side of the north gate	285
	41:6	*o* above another, thirty on each level.	7521S
	41:7	that the rooms widened as *o* went upward.	NIH
	41:7	*o* on the north and another on the south;	285
	41:19	toward the palm tree on *o* side and the face	NIH
	41:21	and the *o* at the front of	NIH
	41:24	on the east side as *o* enters them from	2257
	42:12	by which *o* **enters** the rooms.	AIT
	43:13	with a rim of *o* span around the edge.	285
	44:1	the *o* **facing** east, and it was shut.	AIT
	44:2	no *o* may enter through it.	408
	44:3	the **only** *o* who may sit inside the gateway	2085
	45:7	to the eastern border parallel to *o* of	285
	45:12	Twenty shekels plus twenty-five shekels plus fifteen shekels equal *o* mina.	2021
	45:14	of ten baths or *o* homer,	NIH
	45:15	Also *o* sheep is to be taken	285
	46:5	He is to provide as a grain offering *o* **ephah**	AIT
	46:7	*o* **ephah** with the ram,	AIT
	46:9	No *o* is to **return** through the gate	AIT
	46:11	and with the lambs as much as *o* pleases,	2257
	46:16	from his inheritance to *o* of his sons, it will	408
	46:17	to *o* of his servants, the servant may keep it	285
	47:5	a river that no *o* could **cross.**	AIT
	48:1	Dan will have *o* **portion;**	285
	48:2	"Asher will have *o portion;*	285
	48:3	"Naphtali will have *o portion;*	285
	48:4	"Manasseh will have *o portion;*	285
	48:5	"Ephraim will have *o portion;*	285
	48:6	"Reuben will have *o portion;*	285
	48:7	"Judah will have *o portion;*	285
	48:8	and its length from east to west will equal *o*	285
	48:23	Benjamin will have *o portion;*	285
	48:24	"Simeon will have *o portion;*	285
	48:25	"Issachar will have *o portion;*	285
	48:26	"Zebulun will have *o portion;*	285
	48:27	"Gad will have *o portion;*	285
Da	2:9	there is *o* penalty for you.	10248
	2:11	No *o* can reveal it to the king except	10025
	2:39	Next, a third kingdom, *o* of bronze,	10023
	4:13	a **holy** *o,* coming down from heaven.	AIT
	4:23	"You, O king, saw a messenger, a **holy** *o,*	AIT
	4:35	No *o* can hold back his hand or say to him:	10168

Da	5:13	*o* of the exiles my father the king brought	10427
	6:2	*o* of whom was Daniel.	10248
	6:13	"Daniel, who is *o* of the exiles from Judah,	10427
	7:5	It was raised up on *o* of its sides,	10248
	7:6	*o* that looked like a leopard.	NIH
	7:8	a **little** *o,* which came up among them;	AIT
	7:13	and there before me was *o* like a son	NIH
	7:14	and his kingdom is *o* **that** will never	AIT
	7:16	I approached *o* of those standing there	10248
	8:1	*o* **that had already appeared**	AIT
	8:3	O of the horns was longer than the other	285
	8:9	Out of *o* of them came another horn,	285
	8:13	Then I heard a **holy** *o* speaking,	AIT
	8:13	and another **holy** *o* said to him,	AIT
	8:15	before me stood *o* who looked like a man.	NIH
	8:22	*o* **that was broken off**	AIT
	9:25	and rebuild Jerusalem until the **Anointed** *O,*	AIT
	9:26	the **Anointed** *O* will be cut off	AIT
	9:27	a covenant with many for *o* 'seven.'	285
	10:7	was the **only** *o* who saw the vision;	963+4200
	10:13	Then Michael, *o* of the chief princes,	285
	10:16	*o* who looked like a man **touched**	AIT
	10:16	I said to the *o* **standing** before me,	AIT
	10:18	*o* who looked like a man **touched**	AIT
	10:21	(No *o* supports me against them except	285
	11:5	but *o* of his commanders will become	4946
	11:6	and her father and the *o* **who supported** her.	AIT
	11:7	"O from her family line **will arise**	AIT
	11:16	no *o* will be able to **stand** against	AIT
	11:37	or for the *o* **desired** by women,	AIT
	11:45	and no *o* will **help** him.	AIT
	12:5	*o* on this bank of the river and one on	285
	12:5	of the river and *o* on the opposite bank.	285
	12:6	O of them **said** to the man clothed in linen,	285
	12:12	Blessed is the *o* who **waits for** and reaches	AIT
Hos	1:11	and they will appoint *o* leader	285
	2:1	and of your sisters, 'My **loved** *o.*'	AIT
	2:8	the *o* who **gave** her the grain, the new wine	AIT
	2:10	no *o* will take her out of my hands.	408
	2:23	to the *o* I called 'Not my loved one.'	NIH
	2:23	to the one I called 'Not my **loved** *o.*'	AIT
	5:14	with no *o* to **rescue** them.	AIT
	9:12	I will bereave them of **every** *o.*	AIT
	11:9	the **Holy O** among you.	7705
	11:12	even against the faithful **Holy O.**	7705
Am	1:1	*o* of the shepherds of Tekoa—	NIH
	1:5	in the Valley of Aven and the *o* who **holds**	AIT
	1:8	of Ashdod and the *o* who **holds** the scepter	AIT
	4:7	I sent rain on *o* town,	285
	4:7	O field had rain;	285
	5:2	with no *o* to **lift** her **up.**"	AIT
	5:6	and Bethel will have no *o* to **quench** it.	AIT
	5:10	you hate the *o* **who reproves** in court	AIT
	6:9	If ten men are left in *o* house,	285
	6:12	Does *o* **plow** there with oxen?	AIT
	9:1	Not *o* will get away, none will	2157+4200S
	9:13	and the planter by the *o* **treading** grapes.	AIT
Ob	1:11	you were like *o* of them.	285
Mic	2:5	no *o* in the assembly of the LORD **to divide**	AIT
	2:13	O who breaks open the way will go up	2021
	3:5	if *o* feeds them, they proclaim 'peace';	2021
	4:4	and no *o* will **make** them **afraid,**	AIT
	5:2	of you will come for me *o* who will be ruler	AIT
	5:8	and no *o* can **rescue.**	AIT
	6:9	"Heed the rod and the **O** who appointed it.	AIT
	7:1	I am like *o* who **gathers** summer fruit at	AIT
	7:2	not *o* upright man remains.	NIH
Na	1:11	has *o* **come forth** who plots evil against	AIT
	1:15	*o* who **brings good news,**	AIT
	2:8	they cry, but no *o* **turns back.**	AIT
	3:17	and no *o* **knows** where.	AIT
	3:18	on the mountains with no *o* to **gather** them.	AIT
Hab	1:12	My God, my **Holy O,** we will not die.	7705
	3:3	the **Holy O** from Mount Paran.	7705
	3:13	to save your **anointed** *o.*	AIT
Zep	2:11	**every** *o* in its own land.	AIT
	3:2	She obeys no *o,* she accepts no correction.	NIH
	3:6	with no *o* **passing through.**	AIT
	3:6	no *o* **will be left**—no one at all.	AIT
	3:6	no *o* at all.	408
	3:6	and no *o* will **make** them **afraid.**	AIT
Hag	2:13	with a dead body touches *o* of these things,	3972
	2:15	how things were before *o* stone was laid	NIH
Zec	1:21	so that no *o* could raise his head.	408
	3:9	There are seven eyes on that stone,	285
	4:3	*o* on the right of the bowl and the other	285
	4:3	for according to what it says on *o* **side,**	AIT
	6:6	The *o* with the black horses is going toward	2023
	6:6	the *o* with the white horses toward	NIH
	6:6	and the *o* with the dappled horses toward	NIH
	7:9	show mercy and compassion to *o* another.	408
	7:14	behind them that no *o* could **come** or go.	AIT
	8:10	No *o* could go about his business safely	2021
	8:21	the inhabitants of *o* city will go to another	285
	8:23	and nations will take firm hold of *o* Jew by	408
	11:7	Then I took two staffs and called *o* Favor	285
	11:9	In *o* month I got rid of the three shepherds.	AIT
	11:9	Let those who are left eat *o* another's flesh."	851
	12:10	the *o* they have pierced,	889S
	12:10	and they will mourn for him as *o* mourns	NIH
	12:10	and grieve bitterly for him as *o* **grieves** for	AIT
	14:9	On that day there will be *o* LORD,	285
Mal	1:10	that *o* of you would shut the temple doors,	4769
	2:10	Have we not all *o* Father?	285
	2:10	Did not *o* God create us?	285
	2:10	by breaking faith with *o* another?	408
	2:15	Has not [the LORD] made them *o?*	285

Mal	2:15	And why o? Because he was seeking godly	285
Mt	2: 2	"Where is the o who has been born king of the Jews?	AIT
	3: 3	"A voice of o calling in the desert,	AIT
	3:11	will come o who is more powerful than I,	3836
	5:19	Anyone who breaks o of the least	1651
	5:29	for you to lose o part of your body than	1651
	5:30	for you to lose o part of your body than	1651
	5:36	for you cannot make even o hair white	1651
	5:37	beyond this comes from the evil o.	AIT
	5:41	If someone forces you to go o mile,	1651
	5:42	Give to the o who asks you,	AIT
	5:42	and do not turn away from the o who wants	AIT
	6:13	but deliver us from the evil o.'	AIT
	6:24	"No o can serve two masters.	4029
	6:24	Either he will hate the o and love the other,	1651
	6:24	or he will be devoted to the o and despise	1651
	6:29	in all his splendor was dressed like o	1651
	7:29	because he taught as o who had authority,	2400
	8: 9	I tell this o, 'Go,' and he goes;	4047
	8: 9	and that o, 'Come,' and he comes.	257
	8:28	They were so violent that no o could pass	5516
	9:16	"No o sews a patch of unshrunk cloth on	4029
	9:30	"See that no o knows about this."	3594
	10:23	When you are persecuted in o place,	NIG
	10:28	the O who can destroy both soul and body	AIT
	10:29	not o of them will fall to the ground apart	1651
	10:40	he who receives me receives the o who sent me.	AIT
	10:42	a cup of cold water to o of these little ones	1651
	11: 3	"Are you the o who was to come,	AIT
	11:10	This is the o about whom it is written:	NIG
	11:27	No o knows the Son except the Father,	4029
	11:27	and no o knows the Father except the Son	5516
	12: 6	that o greater than the temple is here.	3505
	12:18	the o I love, in whom I delight;	3836
	12:19	no o will hear his voice in the streets.	5516
	12:41	and now o greater than Jonah is here.	AIT
	12:42	and now o greater than Solomon is here.	AIT
	13:19	the evil o comes and snatches away	AIT
	13:20	The o who received the seed that fell	AIT
	13:22	The o who received the seed that fell	AIT
	13:23	But the o who received the seed that fell	AIT
	13:37	"The o who sowed the good seed is the Son	AIT
	13:38	The weeds are the sons of the evil o,	AIT
	13:46	When he found o of great value,	1651
	16:14	still others, Jeremiah or o of the prophets."	1651
	17: 4	o for you, one for Moses and one	1651
	17: 4	o for Moses and one for Elijah."	1651
	17: 4	one for Moses and o for Elijah."	1651
	17: 8	they saw no o except Jesus.	4029
	18: 6	But if anyone causes o of these little ones	1651
	18: 9	with o eye than to have two eyes and	3669
	18:10	not look down on o of these little ones.	1651
	18:12	and if o of them wanders away,	1651
	18:12	and go to look for the o that wandered off?	AIT
	18:13	he is happier about that o sheep than about	899S
	18:16	take o or two others along,	1651
	18:28	when that servant went out, he found o	1651
	19: 5	and the two will become o flesh'?	1651
	19: 6	So they are no longer two, but o.	1651
	19:12	The o who can accept this should accept it."	AIT
	19:17	"There is only O who is good.	4029
	20: 7	no o has hired us,' they answered.	4029
	20:10	each of them also received a denarius.	324+3836
	20:12	who were hired last worked only o hour,'	1651
	20:13	"But he answered o of them, 'Friend,	1651
	20:21	that o of these two sons of mine may sit	NIG
	21:24	"I will also ask you o question.	1651
	21:35	they beat o, killed another,	4005
	22: 5	o to his field, another to his business.	4005
	22:25	The first o married and died,	AIT
	22:35	O of them, an expert in the law,	1651
	22:46	No o could say a word in reply,	4029
	22:46	and from that day on no o dared	5516
	23: 8	for you have only o Master	1651
	23: 9	for you have a Father, and he is in heaven.	1651
	23:10	for you have o Teacher, the Christ.	1651
	23:15	and when he becomes o,	NIG
	23:21	by it and by the o who dwells in it.	AIT
	23:22	by God's throne and by the o who sits on it.	AIT
	24: 2	not o stone here will be left on another;	AIT
	24: 2	every o will be thrown down."	NIG
	24: 4	"Watch out that no o deceives you.	5516
	24:17	Let no o on the roof of his house go down	3836
	24:18	Let no o in the field go back	3836
	24:22	no o would survive,	4246+4922
	24:31	from o end of the heavens to the other.	NIG
	24:36	"No o knows about that day or hour,	4029
	24:40	o will be taken and the other left.	1651
	24:41	o will be taken and the other left.	1651
	25:15	To o he gave five talents of money,	4005
	25:15	and to another o talent,	1651
	25:17	the o with the two talents gained two more.	AIT
	25:18	the o talent went off,	1651
	25:24	man who had received the o talent came.	1651
	25:28	and give it to the o who has the ten talents.	AIT
	25:32	the people o from another as	253
	25:40	for o of the least of these brothers of mine,	1651
	25:45	whatever you did not do for o of the least	1651
	26:14	Then o of the Twelve,	1651
	26:14	o called Judas Iscariot—	AIT
	26:21	o of you will betray me."	1651
	26:22	began to say to him o after the other,	1651+1667
	26:23	"The o who has dipped his hand into	AIT
	26:25	Then Judas, the o who would betray him,	AIT
	26:40	not keep watch with me for o hour?"	1651
Mt	26:47	Judas, o of the Twelve, arrived.	1651
	26:48	"The o I kiss is the man; arrest him."	4005
	26:51	o of Jesus' companions reached	1651
	26:64	the right hand of the Mighty O and coming	AIT
	26:73	"Surely you are o of them,	NIG
	27:17	"Which o do you want me to release to you:	AIT
	27:38	o on his right and one on his left.	1651
	27:38	one on his right and o on his left.	1651
	27:48	Immediately o of them ran and got	1651
	27:62	The next day, the o after Preparation Day,	4015
Mk	1: 3	"a voice of o calling in the desert,	AIT
	1: 7	After me will come o more powerful than I,	3836
	1:22	he taught them as o who had authority,	AIT
	1:24	the Holy O of God!"	AIT
	2:21	"No o sews a patch of unshrunk cloth on	4029
	2:22	no o pours new wine into old wineskins.	4029
	2:23	O Sabbath Jesus was going	1877+3836+4879
	3:27	no o can enter a strong man's house	4029
	5: 3	and no o could bind him any more,	4029
	5: 4	No o was strong enough to subdue him.	4029
	5:22	Then o of the synagogue rulers,	1651
	6:15	like o of the prophets of long ago."	1651
	8:14	for o loaf they had with them in the boat.	1651
	8:16	They discussed this with o another	253
	8:28	and still others, o of the prophets."	1651
	9: 5	Let us put up three shelters—o for you,	1651
	9: 5	o for Moses and one for Elijah."	1651
	9: 5	one for Moses and o for Elijah."	1651
	9:37	Whoever welcomes o of these little children	1651
	9:37	not welcome me but the o who sent me."	AIT
	9:38	because he was not o of us."	NIG
	9:39	"No o who does a miracle in my name can	4029
	9:42	"And if anyone causes o of these little ones	1651
	9:47	to enter the kingdom of God with o eye than	3669
	10: 8	and the two will become o flesh.'	1651
	10: 8	So they are no longer two, but o.	1651
	10:18	"No o is good—except God alone.	4029
	10:21	"O thing you lack," he said.	1651
	10:29	"no o who has left home or brothers	4029
	10:37	"Let o of us sit at your right and the other	1651
	11: 2	which no o has ever ridden.	476+4029
	11:14	"May no o ever eat fruit from you again."	3594
	11:29	Jesus replied, "I will ask you o question.	1651
	12: 5	He sent still another, and that o they killed.	AIT
	12: 6	"He had o left to send, a son,	1651
	12: 7	"But the tenants said to o another,	1571
	12:20	The first o married and died	AIT
	12:21	The second o married the widow,	NIG
	12:28	O of the teachers of the law came	1651
	12:29	"The most important o," answered Jesus,	AIT
	12:29	O Israel, the Lord our God, the Lord is o.	1651
	12:32	in saying that God is o and there is no other	1651
	12:34	on no o dared ask him any more questions.	4029
	13: 1	o of his disciples said to him, "Look,	1651
	13: 2	"Not o stone here will be left on another;	3590+4024
	13: 2	every o will be thrown down."	NIG
	13: 5	"Watch out that no o deceives you.	5516
	13:15	Let no o on the roof of his house go down	3836
	13:16	Let no o in the field go back	3836
	13:20	no o would survive,	4246+4922
	13:32	"No o knows about that day or hour,	4029
	13:34	and tells the o at the door to keep watch.	2601
	14: 4	to o another, "Why this waste	1571
	14:10	Then Judas Iscariot, o of the Twelve,	1651
	14:18	of you will betray me—	1651
	14:18	o who is eating with me."	NIG
	14:19	and o by one they said to him,	1651
	14:19	and one by o they said to him,	1651
	14:20	"It is o of the Twelve," he replied,	1651
	14:20	"o who dips bread into the bowl with me.	NIG
	14:37	Could you not keep watch for o hour?	1651
	14:43	Judas, o of the Twelve, appeared.	1651
	14:44	"The o I kiss is the man;	323+4005
	14:47	Then o of those standing	1651+5516
	14:61	the Christ, the Son of the Blessed O?"	AIT
	14:62	the right hand of the Mighty O and coming	1539
	14:66	o of the servant girls of the high priest	1651
	14:69	"This fellow is o of them."	NIG
	14:70	"Surely you are o of them,	NIG
	15:12	with the o you call the king of the Jews?"	4005
	15:27	o on his right and one on his left.	1651
	15:27	one on his right and o on his left.	1651
	15:36	O man ran, filled a sponge	5516
Lk	1:35	the holy o to be born will be called the Son	AIT
	1:49	Mighty O has done great things for me—	AIT
	1:61	"There is no o among your relatives	4029
	2:15	the shepherds said to o another,	253
	3: 4	"A voice of o calling in the desert,	AIT
	3:11	the o who has food should do the same."	AIT
	3:16	But o more powerful than I will come,	3836
	4:27	yet not o of them was cleansed—	4029
	4:34	the Holy O of God!"	AIT
	4:40	and laying his hands on each o,	1651
	5: 1	O day as Jesus was standing by the	1181+1254
	5: 3	He got into o of the boats,	1651
	5: 3	the o belonging to Simon,	4005
	5:12	While Jesus was in o of the towns,	1651
	5:17	O day as he was teaching,	1651
	5:36	"No o tears a patch from a new garment	4029
	5:36	a new garment and sews it on an old o.	2668S
	5:37	no o pours new wine into old wineskins.	4029
	5:39	no o after drinking old wine wants the new,	4029
	6: 1	O Sabbath Jesus was going through	1877+4879
	6:11	with o another what they might do to Jesus.	253
	6:12	O of those days Jesus went out to	NIG
	6:29	If someone strikes you on o cheek,	NIG
Lk	6:49	But the o who hears my words and does	AIT
	7: 8	I tell this o, 'Go,' and he goes;	AIT
	7: 8	and that o, 'Come,' and he comes.	257
	7:19	"Are you the o who was to come,	AIT
	7:20	'Are you the o who was to come,	AIT
	7:27	This is the o about whom it is written:	4047
	7:28	of women there is no o greater than John;	4029
	7:28	yet the o who is least in the kingdom	AIT
	7:36	Now o of the Pharisees invited Jesus	5516
	7:41	O owed him five hundred denarii,	1651
	7:43	the o who had the bigger debt canceled."	AIT
	8: 1	from o town and village to another,	2848
	8:16	"No o lights a lamp and hides it in a jar	4029
	8:22	O day Jesus said to his disciples,	1651
	8:25	and amazement they asked o another,	253
	8:43	but no o could heal her.	4024+4029
	9: 8	and still others that o of the prophets	5516
	9:19	and still others, that o of the prophets	5516
	9:33	Let us put up three shelters—o for you,	1651
	9:33	o for Moses and one for Elijah."	1651
	9:33	one for Moses and o for Elijah."	1651
	9:36	told no o at that time what they had seen.	4029
	9:48	whoever welcomes me welcomes the o who sent me.	AIT
	9:49	because he is not o of us."	199+1609+3552
	9:62	"No o who puts his hand to the plow	4029
	10:22	No o knows who the Son is except	4029
	10:22	and no o knows who the Father is except	NIG
	10:25	On o occasion an expert in the law	2627+2779
	10:37	"The o who had mercy on him."	AIT
	10:42	but only o thing is needed.	AIT
	11: 1	O day Jesus was praying in a certain	1181+2779
	11: 1	he finished, o of his disciples said to him,	5516
	11: 5	"Suppose o of you has a friend,	5515
	11: 7	"Then the o inside answers,	1697
	11:31	and now o greater than Solomon is here.	AIT
	11:32	and now o greater than Jonah is here.	AIT
	11:33	"No o lights a lamp and puts it in a place	4029
	11:40	Did not the o who made the outside make	AIT
	11:45	O of the experts in the law answered him,	5516
	11:46	and you yourselves will not lift o finger	1651
	12: 1	so that they were trampling on o another,	253
	12: 6	Yet not o of them is forgotten by God.	1651
	12:27	in all his splendor was dressed like o	1651
	12:48	But the o who does not know	AIT
	12:48	the o who has been entrusted with much,	AIT
	12:52	on there will be five in o family divided	1651
	13: 8	'leave it alone for o more year,	NIG
	13:10	On a Sabbath Jesus was teaching in o of	1651
	14: 1	O Sabbath, when Jesus went to eat in	NIG
	14: 5	"If o of you has a son or an ox that falls	5515
	14:15	When o of those at the table	5516
	14:24	I tell you, not o of those men	4029
	14:28	"Suppose o of you wants to build a tower.	5515
	14:31	to oppose the o coming against him	AIT
	15: 4	"Suppose o of you has a hundred sheep	476+5515
	15: 4	of you has a hundred sheep and loses o	1651
	15: 7	in heaven over o sinner who repents than	1651
	15: 8	a woman has ten silver coins and loses o.	1651
	15:10	of God over o sinner who repents."	1651
	15:12	The younger o said to his father, 'Father,	AIT
	15:16	but no o gave him anything.	4029
	15:19	make me like o of your hired men.'	1651
	15:26	So he called o of the servants	1651
	16: 5	he called in each o of his master's debtors.	1651
	16:13	Either he will hate the o and love the other,	1651
	16:13	or he will be devoted to the o and despise	1651
	17: 2	for him to cause o of these little ones to sin.	1651
	17: 7	"Suppose o of you had a servant plowing	5515
	17:15	O of them, when he saw he was healed,	1651
	17:18	Was no o found to return and give praise	1651
	17:22	when you will long to see o of the days of	1651
	17:24	and lights up the sky from o end to	NIG
	17:31	On that day no o who is on the roof	AIT
	17:31	no o in the field should go back	3836
	17:34	on that night two people will be in o bed;	1651
	17:34	o will be taken and the other left.	1651
	17:35	o will be taken and the other left."	1651
	18:10	o a Pharisee and the other a tax collector.	1651
	18:19	"No o is good—except God alone.	4029
	18:22	he said to him, "You still lack o thing.	1651
	18:29	"no o who has left home or wife or brothers	4029
	19:16	"The first o came and said, 'Sir,	AIT
	19:24	and give it to the o who has ten minas.'	AIT
	19:26	but as for the o who has nothing,	AIT
	19:30	which no o has ever ridden.	4029
	19:44	They will not leave o stone on another,	NIG
	20: 1	O day as he was teaching the people in	1651
	20:11	but that o also they beat	AIT
	20:29	The first o married a woman	AIT
	20:40	no o dared to ask him any more questions.	AIT
	21: 6	the time will come when not o stone will	NIG
	21: 6	every o of them will be thrown down."	NIG
	22: 3	called Iscariot, o of the Twelve.	1639
	22:26	the o who rules like the one who serves.	AIT
	22:26	the one who rules like the o who serves.	AIT
	22:27	the o who is at the table or	AIT
	22:27	one who is at the table or the o who serves?	AIT
	22:27	Is it not the o who is at the table?	AIT
	22:27	But I am among you as o who serves.	3836
	22:29	just as my Father conferred on me,	NIG
	22:36	sell your cloak and buy o.	NIG
	22:47	o of the Twelve, was leading them.	1651
	22:50	And o of them struck the servant of	1651+5516
	22:58	"You also are o of them."	NIG
	23:14	o who was inciting the people to rebellion.	AIT
	23:18	With o voice they cried out,	4101

Lk	23:25	the *o* they asked for,	*AIT*
	23:33	*o* on his right, the other on his left.	3525+4005
	23:35	if he is the Christ of God, the **Chosen** *O.*"	*AIT*
	23:39	*O* of the criminals who hung there hurled
		insults at him:	*1651*
	23:53	*o* in which no one had yet been laid.	4023
	23:53	one in which no *o* had yet been laid.	4029
	24:18	*O* of them, named Cleopas, asked him,	1651
	24:21	that he was the *o* who was going	*AIT*
Jn	1:14	the glory of the **O and Only**,	3666
	1:16	of his grace we have all received *o* blessing	*NIG*
	1:18	**No** *o* has ever seen God,	4029
	1:18	but God the **O and Only**,	3666
	1:23	the voice *of o* calling in the desert,	*AIT*
	1:26	"but among you stands *o* you do not know.	4005
	1:27	He is the *o* who comes after me,	*AIT*
	1:30	This is the *o* I meant when I said,	4005
	1:33	except that the *o* who sent me to baptize	*AIT*
	1:40	Simon Peter's brother, was *o* of	1651
	1:45	"We have found the *o* Moses wrote about	4005
	3: 2	For **no** *o* could perform	4029
	3: 3	no *o* can see the kingdom of God	*AIT*
	3: 5	no *o* can enter the kingdom of God	*AIT*
	3:13	**No** *o* has ever gone into heaven except	4029
	3:13	into heaven except the *o* who came	*AIT*
	3:16	the world that he gave his *o* **and only** Son,	3666
	3:18	in the name of God's *o* **and only** Son.	3666
	3:26	the *o* you testified about—	4005
	3:31	"**The** *o* who comes from above is above all;	*AIT*
	3:31	the *o* who is from the earth belongs to	*AIT*
	3:31	and speaks as *o* from the earth.	*NIG*
	3:31	**The** *o* who comes from heaven is above all.	*AIT*
	3:32	but no *o* accepts his testimony.	4029
	3:34	the *o* whom God has sent speaks the words	*AIT*
	4:27	But **no** *o* asked, "What do you want?"	4029
	4:37	Thus the saying '**O** sows and another reaps'	257
	5: 5	**O** who was there had been an invalid	5516
	5: 7	"I have no *o* to help me into the pool when	476ˢ
	5:22	Moreover, the Father judges **no o,**	4029
	5:38	for you do not believe the *o* he sent.	4005
	5:44	if you accept praise from *o* **another,**	253
	6: 7	not buy enough bread for **each** *o* to have	1667
	6:22	that only *o* boat had been there,	257+1651+4024
	6:29	to believe in the *o* he has sent."	4005
	6:44	"**No** *o* can come to me unless	4029
	6:46	No *o* has seen the Father except	5516
	6:46	the Father except the *o* who is from God;	*AIT*
	6:57	so the *o* who feeds on me will live because	*AIT*
	6:65	"This is why I told you that no *o* can come	4029
	6:69	and know that you are the **Holy** *O* of God."	*AIT*
	6:70	Yet *o* of you is a devil!"	1651
	6:71	who, though *o* of the Twelve,	1651
	7: 4	**No** *o* who wants to become	4029
	7:13	But **no** *o* would say anything publicly	4029
	7:18	for the honor *of* the *o* who sent him is a man	*AIT*
	7:19	Yet **not** *o* of you keeps the law.	4029
	7:21	Jesus said to them, "I did *o* miracle,	1651
	7:27	**no** *o* will know where he is from."	4029
	7:30	but no *o* laid a hand on him,	4029
	7:33	and then I go to the *o* who sent me.	*AIT*
	7:35	The Jews said to *o* **another,**	1571
	7:44	but no *o* laid a hand on him.	4029
	7:46	"**No** *o* ever spoke the way this man does,"	4030
	7:50	and who was *o* of their own number,	1651
	8: 7	"If any *o* of you is without sin,	3836
	8: 9	to go away *o* **at a time,**	1651+1651+2848
	8:10	Has **no** *o* condemned you?"	4029
	8:11	"**No** *o,*" she said.	4029
	8:15	I pass judgment on **no** *o.*	4024+4029
	8:18	I am *o* who testifies for myself;	3836
	8:20	Yet **no** *o* seized him,	4029
	8:24	not believe that I am [the *o* I claim to be]	*NIG*
	8:28	you will know that I am [the *o* I claim to be]	*NIG*
	8:29	**The** *o* who sent me is with me;	*AIT*
	8:50	there is *o* who seeks it, and he is the judge.	3836
	8:54	is the *o* who glorifies me.	*AIT*
	9: 4	Night is coming, when no *o* can work.	4029
	9:19	"Is this the *o* you say was born blind?	4005
	9:25	**O** thing I do know.	1651
	9:37	in fact, he is the *o* speaking with you."	*AIT*
	10:16	there shall be *o* flock and one shepherd.	1651
	10:16	there shall be one flock and *o* shepherd.	1651
	10:18	**No** *o* takes it from me,	4029
	10:28	no *o* can snatch them out of my hand.	5516
	10:29	no *o* can snatch them out	4029
	10:30	I and the Father are **o.**"	1651
	10:36	what about the *o* whom the Father set apart	*AIT*
	11: 2	was **the** same *o* who poured perfume on	*AIT*
	11: 3	"Lord, the *o* you love is sick."	4005
	11:49	Then *o* of them, named Caiaphas,	1651+5516
	11:50	for you that *o* man die for the people than	1651
	11:52	bring them together and **make** them **o.**	1650+1651
	11:56	in the temple area they asked *o* **another,**	253
	12: 4	But *o* of his disciples, Judas Iscariot,	
	12:19	So the Pharisees said to *o* **another,** "See,	1571
	12:26	My Father will honor the *o* who serves me.	899ˢ
	12:44	but in the *o* who sent me.	*AIT*
	12:45	he looks at me, he sees the *o* who sent me.	*AIT*
	12:46	so that no *o* who believes in me should stay	4246
	12:48	a judge for the *o* who rejects me and does	*AIT*
	13:10	you are clean, though not **every** *o* of you."	*AIT*
	13:11	That was why he said not **every** *o* was clean.	*AIT*
	13:14	you also should wash *o* **another's** feet.	253
	13:16	messenger greater than the *o* who sent him.	*AIT*
	13:20	accepts me accepts the *o* who sent me."	*AIT*
	13:21	*o* of you is going to betray me."	1651
	13:22	His disciples stared at *o* **another,**	253

Jn	13:23	*O* of them, the disciple whom Jesus loved,	1651
	13:24	"Ask him which *o* he means."	4005
	13:26	"It is the *o* to whom I will give this piece	1697
	13:28	but **no** *o* at the meal understood	4029
	13:34	new command I give you: Love *o* **another.**	253
	13:34	so you must love *o* **another.**	253
	13:35	if you love *o* **another.**"	253
	14: 6	**No** *o* comes to the Father except through me	4029
	14:21	he is the *o* who loves me.	*AIT*
	15:13	Greater love has **no** *o* than this,	4029
	15:21	for they do not know **the** *O* who sent me.	*AIT*
	15:24	not done among them what **no** *o* else did,	4029
	16:17	Some of his disciples said to *o* **another,**	253
	16:19	"Are you asking *o* **another** what I meant	253
	16:22	and no *o* will take away your joy.	4029
	17:11	so that they may be *o* as we are one.	1651
	17:11	so that they may be one as we are **o.**	*NIG*
	17:12	except the *o* doomed to destruction	5626ˢ
	17:15	but that you protect them from the **evil** *o.*	*AIT*
	17:21	that all of them may be **o,**	1651
	17:22	that they may be *o* as we are one:	1651
	17:22	that they may be one as we are **o:**	1651
	18: 9	"I have not lost *o* of those you gave me."	4029
	18:14	Caiaphas was the *o* who had advised	*AIT*
	18:14	that it would be good if *o* man died for	1651
	18:17	"You are not *o* of his disciples, are you?"	*NIG*
	18:22	*o* of the officials nearby struck him in	1651
	18:25	"You are not *o* of his disciples, are you?"	*NIG*
	18:26	**O** of the high priest's servants,	1651
	18:39	to release to you *o* prisoner at the time of	1651
	19:11	Therefore the *o* who handed me over	*AIT*
	19:18	*o* **on each side** and Jesus in the middle.	1949+1949+2779
	19:23	*o* for each of them,	3538ˢ
	19:23	woven in *o* piece from top to bottom.	*NIG*
	19:24	"Let's not tear it," they said to *o* **another.**	253
	19:34	*o* of the soldiers pierced Jesus' side with	1651
	19:36	"Not *o* of his bones will be broken,"	*NIG*
	19:37	on the *o* they have pierced."	4005
	19:41	in which no *o* had ever been laid.	4029
	20: 2	the *o* Jesus loved, and said,	4005
	20:12	*o* at the head and the other at the foot.	1651
	20:24	Thomas (called Didymus), *o* of the Twelve,	1651
	21:20	the *o* who had leaned back against Jesus at	*AIT*
	21:25	If every *o* of them were written down,	1651
Ac	1: 4	**On** *o* **occasion,** while he was eating	2779
	1:17	he was *o* of our **number** and shared	*AIT*
	1:20	let there be no *o* to dwell in it,' and,	3836
	1:21	Therefore it is necessary to choose *o* of	*NIG*
	1:22	For *o* of these must become a witness	1651
	2: 1	they were all together **in** *o* **place.**	899+2093+3836
	2: 6	because each *o* heard them speaking	1651
	2:12	they asked *o* **another,**	257+257+4639
	2:27	nor will you let your **Holy** *O* see decay.	*AIT*
	2:30	that he would place *o* of his descendants	*NIG*
	2:38	"Repent and be baptized, **every** *o* of you,	1667
	3: 1	**O** day Peter and John were going up to	*NIG*
	3:14	You disowned the **Holy** and **Righteous** *O*	*AIT*
	4:12	Salvation is found in **no** *o* else,	4024+4029
	4:26	the Lord and against his **Anointed** *O.*"	5986
	4:32	All the believers were *o* in heart and mind.	1651
	4:32	No *o* claimed that any of their possessions	1651
	5:13	No *o* else dared join them,	4029
	5:23	we opened them, we found **no** *o* inside."	4029
	7:24	He saw *o* of them being mistreated by	5516
	7:52	the coming of the **Righteous** *O.*	*AIT*
	10: 3	**O** day at about three in the afternoon he had	*NIG*
	10: 7	devout soldier who *was o* of his **attendants.**	*AIT*
	10:21	"I'm the *o* you're looking for.	4005
	10:42	he is the *o* whom God appointed as judge	*AIT*
	11:28	**O** of them, named Agabus,	1651
	12:10	they had walked *the length of o* street,	1651
	13:25	I am not that *o.*	*NIG*
	13:35	"'You will not let your **Holy** *O* see decay.'	*AIT*
	13:37	But the *o* whom God raised from the dead	4005
	16:14	**O** of those listening was	5516
	17: 7	that there is another king, *o* called Jesus."	*NIG*
	17:26	From *o* **man** he made every nation of men,	1651
	17:27	though he is not far from each *o* of us.	1651
	18: 9	**O** night the Lord spoke to Paul in a vision:	*NIG*
	18:10	and **no** *o* is going to attack and harm you,	4029
	19: 4	the people to believe in the *o* coming	*AIT*
	19:15	[**O** day] the evil spirit answered them,	*NIG*
	19:29	and rushed **as** *o* **man** into the theater.	3924
	19:32	Some were shouting *o* **thing,** some another.	*AIT*
	21: 8	*o* of the Seven.	1639+1666
	21:16	from Cyprus and *o* of the early disciples.	*NIG*
	21:34	Some in the crowd shouted *o* *thing*	5516
	22:14	to know his will as the **Righteous** *O*	*NIG*
	22:19	**from** *o* synagogue **to another**	2848
	23:17	Paul called *o* of the centurions and said,	1651
	24:21	unless it was this *o thing* I shouted	1651
	25:11	no *o* has the right to hand me over to them.	4029
	26:11	**from** *o* **synagogue to another**	2848+4246+5252
	26:12	"On *o* of these journeys I was going	4005ˢ
	26:31	and while talking with *o* **another,** they said,	253
	27:22	because **not** *o* of you will be lost;	4029
	27:34	**Not** *o* of you will lose a single hair	4029
Ro	1:24	of their bodies with *o* **another.**	899
	1:27	and were inflamed with lust for *o* **another.**	253
	2:27	**The** *o* who is not circumcised physically	*AIT*
	2:28	not a Jew if he is only *o* outwardly,	*NIG*
	2:29	No, a man is a Jew if he is *o* inwardly;	*NIG*
	3:10	"There is no *o* righteous, not even one;	*AIT*
	3:10	"There is no one righteous, not even *o;*	1651
	3:11	there is no *o* who understands,	3836
	3:11	no *o* who seeks God.	3836

Ro	3:12	there is no *o* who does good, not even one."	3836
	3:12	there is no one who does good, not even **o.**"	1651
	3:20	Therefore **no** *o* will be declared righteous	4024+4246
	3:26	and the *o* who **justifies** those who have faith	*AIT*
	3:30	since there is only *o* God,	1651
	5:12	just as sin entered the world through *o* man,	1651
	5:14	who was a pattern *of* the *o* to come.	1651
	5:15	the many died by the trespass *of* the *o* man,	1651
	5:15	that came by the grace *of* the *o* man,	1651
	5:16	not like the result of the *o* man's sin:	1651
	5:16	The judgment followed *o* sin	1651
	5:17	For if, by the trespass *of* the *o* man,	1651
	5:17	death reigned through that *o* man,	1651
	5:17	in life through the *o* man,	1651
	5:18	the result of *o* trespass was condemnation	1651
	5:18	of *o* act of righteousness was justification	1651
	5:19	*of* the *o* man the many were made sinners,	1651
	5:19	the *o* man the many will be made righteous.	1651
	6:16	you are slaves *to* the *o* whom you obey—	4005
	8:20	but by the will of the *o* who subjected it,	*AIT*
	9:10	but Rebekah's children had *o* and the same
		father,	1651+1666
	9:19	**O** of you will say to me:	*NIG*
	9:25	and I will call her 'my **loved** *o*' who is	*AIT*
	9:25	not my **loved** *o,*"	*AIT*
	9:33	and the *o* who trusts in him will never be
		put to shame."	*AIT*
	10:14	on the *o* they have not believed in?	4005
	10:14	in the *o* of whom they have not heard?	*NIG*
	11: 3	I am the **only** *o* left,	1651
	11:30	Just as you who were **at** *o* **time** disobedient	4537
	12: 3	the grace given me I say *to* **every** *o* of you:	*AIT*
	12: 4	of us has *o* body with many members,	1651
	12: 5	so in Christ we who are many form *o* body,	1651
	12:10	Be devoted to *o* **another** in brotherly love.	253
	12:10	Honor *o* **another** above yourselves.	253
	12:16	Live in harmony with *o* **another.**	253
	13: 3	Do you want to be free from fear of the *o*	*AIT*
	13: 8	the continuing debt to love *o* **another,**	253
	13: 9	are summed up in this *o* rule:	3836
	14: 2	**O** *man's* faith allows him to eat everything,	4005
	14: 5	**O** **man** considers one day more sacred than	4005
	14: 5	One man considers *o* day more sacred than	*NIG*
	14: 5	**Each** *o* should be fully convinced	*AIT*
	14: 6	He who regards *o* day as special,	3836
	14:13	let us stop passing judgment on *o* **another.**	253
	14:14	As *o* who is in the Lord Jesus,	*NIG*
	15: 6	with *o* heart and mouth you may glorify	1651
	15: 7	Accept *o* **another,** then,	253
	15:12	*o* who will arise to rule over the nations;	3836
	15:14	and competent to instruct *o* **another.**	253
	16:16	Greet *o* **another** with a holy kiss.	253
1Co	1:10	that all of you agree with *o* another so	*NIG*
	1:12	*O* of you says, "I follow Paul";	1667
	1:15	so no *o* can say that you were baptized	5516
	1:29	so that no *o* may boast before him.	4246+4922
	2:11	In the same way no *o* knows the thoughts	4029
	3: 4	For when *o* says, "I follow Paul,"	5516
	3: 8	and the man who waters have *o* purpose,	1651
	3:10	But **each** *o* should be careful how he builds.	*AIT*
	3:11	For no *o* can lay any foundation other than	4029
	3:11	any foundation other than the *o* already laid,	*AIT*
	3:15	but only as *o* escaping through the flames.	*NIG*
	3:18	If **any** *o* of you thinks he is wise by	5516
	4: 6	you will not take pride in *o* **man** over	1651+3836
	5: 3	on the *o* who did this,	*AIT*
	6: 6	*o* brother goes to law against another—	*NIG*
	6:16	with a prostitute is *o* with her in body?	1651
	6:16	it is said, "The two will become *o* flesh."	1651
	6:17	with the Lord is *o* with him in spirit.	1651
	7: 7	*o* has this gift, another has that.	3525+3836
	7:17	**each** *o* should retain the place in life that	*AIT*
	7:20	**Each** *o* should remain in the situation	*AIT*
	7:25	the Lord, but I give a judgment as *o* who by	*NIG*
	8: 4	in the world and that there is but *o* God.	1651
	8: 6	yet for us there is but *o* God, the Father,	1651
	8: 6	and there is but *o* Lord, Jesus Christ,	1651
	9:20	under the law I became like *o* under the law	
	9:21	To those not having the law I became like *o*	*NIG*
	9:24	but only *o* gets the prize?	1651
	10: 8	and *in o* day twenty-three thousand	1651
	10:17	Because there is *o* loaf, we, who are many,	1651
	10:17	we, who are many, form *o* body,	1651
	10:17	for we all partake of the *o* loaf.	1651
	11:21	**O** remains hungry, another gets drunk.	3525+4005
	12: 3	that no *o* who is speaking by the Spirit	4029
	12: 3	and no *o* can say, "Jesus is Lord," except	4029
	12: 7	Now to **each** *o* the manifestation of	*AIT*
	12: 8	*To o* there is given through the Spirit	4005
	12: 9	to another gifts of healing by that *o* Spirit,	1651
	12:11	the work of *o* and the same Spirit,	1651
	12:11	and he gives them *to* **each** *o,*	*AIT*
	12:12	all its parts are many, they form *o* body.	1651
	12:13	For we were all baptized by *o* Spirit	1651
	12:13	by one Spirit into *o* body—	1651
	12:13	and we were all given the *o* Spirit to drink.	1651
	12:14	Now the body is not made up of *o* part but	1651
	12:18	every *o* of them,	1651
	12:19	If they were all *o* part,	1651
	12:20	As it is, there are many parts, but *o* body.	1651
	12:26	If *o* part suffers, every part suffers with it;	1651
	12:26	if *o* part is honored,	1651
	12:27	and **each** *o* of you is a part of it.	3517ˢ
	14: 2	Indeed, **no** *o* understands him;	4029
	14: 5	like **every** *o* of you to speak in tongues,	*AIT*
	14: 5	who prophesies is greater than *o* who speaks	3836

1Co	14:16	how can o who finds himself	3836
	14:27	should speak, o at a time,	324+3538
	15: 8	as to o abnormally born.	3836
	15:39	Men have o kind of flesh,	NIG
	15:40	of the heavenly bodies is o kind,	NIG
	15:41	The sun has o kind of splendor,	NIG
	16: 2	each o of you should set aside a sum	AIT
	16:11	No o, then, should refuse to accept him.	5516
	16:20	Greet o another with a holy kiss.	253
2Co	2:16	To the o we are the smell of death;	3525+4005
	4:14	that the o who raised the Lord Jesus from	AIT
	5:10	that each o may receive what is due him for	AIT
	5:14	we are convinced that o died for all,	1651
	5:16	on we regard no o from a worldly point	4029
	7: 2	We have wronged no o,	4029
	7: 2	we have corrupted no o,	4029
	7: 2	we have exploited no o.	4029
	7:12	not on account of the o who did the wrong	AIT
	8:12	gift is acceptable according to what o has,	AIT
	9: 5	not as o grudgingly given.	4432
	10:18	the o who commends himself who is approved,	AIT
	10:18	but the o whom the Lord commends.	AIT
	11: 2	I promised you to o husband, to Christ,	1651
	11: 4	a different spirit from the o you received,	4005
	11: 4	a different gospel from the o you accepted,	4005
	11:16	I repeat: let no o take me for a fool.	5515
	11:24	from the Jews the forty lashes minus o.	1651
	12: 6	so no o will think more of me than is	5516
	13:11	listen to my appeal, be of o mind,	899+3836
	13:12	Greet o another with a holy kiss.	253
Gal	1: 6	so quickly deserting the o who called you	AIT
	1: 8	a gospel other than the o we preached	AIT
	2:16	by observing the law no o will be justified.	4246+4922
	3: 2	I would like to learn just o thing from	3668+4047
	3:11	Clearly no o is justified before God by	4029
	3:15	Just as no o can set aside or add to	4029
	3:16	but "and to your seed," meaning o person,	1651
	3:20	however, does not represent just o party;	1651
	3:20	but God is o.	1651
	3:28	for you are all o in Christ Jesus.	1651
	4:22	o by the slave woman and the other by	1651
	4:24	O covenant is from Mount Sinai	1651
	5: 8	not come from the o who calls you.	AIT
	5:10	The o who is throwing you	AIT
	5:13	rather, serve o another in love.	253
	6: 4	Each o should test his own actions.	AIT
	6: 5	for each o should carry his own load.	AIT
	6: 8	The o who sows to please his sinful nature,	AIT
	6: 8	the o who sows to please the Spirit,	AIT
	6:17	Finally, let no o cause me trouble,	3594
Eph	1: 6	in the O he loves.	3836
	1:10	bring all things in heaven and on earth together under o head,	368
	1:21	in the present age but also in the o to come.	4537
	2: 3	All of us also lived among them at o time,	4537
	2: 9	not by works, so that no o can boast.	5516
	2:14	who has made the two and has destroyed	1651
	2:15	to create in himself o new man out of	1651
	2:16	and in this o body to reconcile both of them	1651
	2:18	both have access to the Father by o Spirit.	1651
	3: 6	members together of o body,	5362
	4: 2	be patient, bearing with o another in love.	253
	4: 4	There is o body and one Spirit—	1651
	4: 4	There is one body and o Spirit—	1651
	4: 4	to o hope when you were called—	1651
	4: 5	o Lord, one faith, one baptism;	1651
	4: 5	one Lord, o faith, one baptism;	1651
	4: 5	one Lord, one faith, o baptism;	1651
	4: 6	o God and Father of all,	1651
	4: 7	But to each o of us grace has been given	1651
	4:10	He who descended is the very o who ascended higher than all	899
	4:25	for we are all members of o body.	253
	4:32	Be kind and compassionate to o another,	253
	5: 6	Let no o deceive you with empty words,	3594
	5:19	Speak to o another with psalms,	4932
	5:21	to o another out of reverence for Christ.	253
	5:29	After all, no o ever hated his own body,	1651
	5:31	and the two will become o flesh."	1651
	5:33	each o of you also must love his wife	1651
	6:16	the flaming arrows of the evil o.	4505
Php	1:27	I will know that you stand firm in o spirit,	1651
	1:27	contending as o man for the faith of	1651
	2: 2	being o in spirit and purpose.	4029
	2:20	I have no o else like him,	4029
	3:13	But o thing I do:	1651
	4:15	not o church shared with me in the matter	4029
Col	2: 4	I tell you this so that no o may deceive you	3594
	2: 8	that no o takes you captive through hollow	5516
	3:13	and forgive whatever grievances you may have against o another,	5516
	3:15	as members of o body you were called	1651
	3:16	and admonish o another with all wisdom,	4932
	4: 9	who is o of you.	NIG
	4:12	who is o of you and a servant	1666
1Th	3: 3	that no o would be unsettled by these trials.	3594
	4: 6	in this matter no o should wrong his brother	NIG
	5:11	Therefore encourage o another	253
	5:24	The o who calls you is faithful	AIT
2Th	1: 3	and the love every o of you has	1651
	2: 7	but the o who now holds it back	AIT
	2: 8	And then the lawless o will be revealed,	AIT
	2: 9	of the lawless o will be in accordance	4005S
	3: 3	and protect you from the evil o.	AIT
1Ti	1: 8	that the law is good if o uses it properly.	5516

1Ti	2: 5	For there is o God and one mediator	1651
	2: 5	and o mediator between God and men,	1651
	2:14	And Adam was not the o deceived;	NIG
	3: 2	the husband of but o wife, temperate,	1651
	3:12	of but o wife and must manage his children	1651
	5: 7	too, so that no o may be open to blame.	NIG
	6:16	whom no o has seen or can see.	4029
2Ti	2: 4	No o serving as a soldier gets involved	4029
	2:15	to present yourself to God as o approved,	NIG
	4:16	no o came to my support,	4029
Tit	1: 6	the husband of but o wife,	1651
	1: 8	o who loves what is good,	5787
	1:12	Even o of their own prophets has said,	5516
	2: 5	so that no o will malign the word of God.	NIG
	3: 2	to slander no o, to be peaceable	3594
	3: 3	At o time we too were foolish, disobedient,	4537
	3: 3	being hated and hating o another.	253
Phm	1:22	And o thing more:	275
Heb	2:11	o who makes men holy	AIT
	3: 2	He was faithful to the o who appointed him,	AIT
	3:13	But encourage o another daily,	4932
	4:11	so that no o will fall	5516
	4:15	o who has been tempted	AIT
	5: 4	No o takes this honor upon himself;	5516
	5: 7	to the o who could save him from death,	AIT
	6:13	there was no o greater for him to swear by,	4029
	7: 8	In the o case, the tenth is collected	3525+6045
	7: 9	O might even say that Levi,	2229+3306+6055
	7:11	in the order of Melchizedek,	NIG
	7:13	and no o from that tribe has ever served at	4029
	7:16	o who has become a priest not on the basis	AIT
	7:26	o who is holy, blameless, pure,	AIT
	8: 3	for this o also to have something to offer.	AIT
	8: 6	is superior to the old o,	NIG
	8:13	he has made the first o obsolete;	AIT
	9:16	to prove the death of the o who made it,	AIT
	9:17	while the o who made it is living.	AIT
	9:24	that was only a copy of the true o,	AIT
	10:12	for all time o sacrifice for sins,	1651
	10:14	by o sacrifice he has made perfect forever those who are being made holy.	1651
	10:24	how we may spur o another on toward love	253
	10:25	but let us encourage o another—	NIG
	10:38	But my righteous o will live by faith.	AIT
	11: 5	he was commended as o who pleased God.	NIG
	11:12	And so from this o man,	1651
	11:16	for a better country—a heavenly o.	AIT
	11:17	about to sacrifice his o and only son,	3666
	12:14	without holiness no o will see the Lord.	4029
	12:15	to it that no o misses the grace of God and	5516
	12:15	See that no o is sexually immoral,	5516
Jas	1:10	But the o who is rich should take pride	AIT
	1:13	When tempted, no o should say,	3594
	1:14	but each o is tempted when,	AIT
	2:10	at just o point is guilty of breaking all of it.	1651
	2:16	If o of you says to him, "Go,	5516
	2:19	You believe that there is o God.	1651
	4:11	Brothers, do not slander o another.	253
	4:12	There is only o Lawgiver and Judge,	1651
	4:12	the o who is able to save and destroy.	AIT
	5:13	Is any o of you in trouble?	AIT
	5:14	Is any o of you sick?	5516
	5:19	if o of you should wander from the truth	5516
1Pe	1:22	love o another deeply, from the heart.	253
	2: 6	and the o who trusts in him will never be put to shame."	AIT
	3: 8	all of you, live in harmony with o another;	NIG
	4: 9	to o another without grumbling.	253
	4:10	Each o should use whatever gift he has received	AIT
	4:11	as o speaking the very words of God.	NIG
	5: 1	a witness of Christ's sufferings and o who	3836
	5: 5	with humility toward o another,	253
	5:14	Greet o another with a kiss of love.	253
2Pe	3: 8	But do not forget this o thing, dear friends:	1651
1Jn	1: 7	we have fellowship with o another,	253
	2: 1	o who speaks to the Father in our defense	4156
	2: 1	Jesus Christ, the Righteous O.	AIT
	2: 7	a new command but an old o,	1953S
	2:13	because you have overcome the evil o.	AIT
	2:14	and you have overcome the evil o.	AIT
	2:20	you have an anointing from the Holy O,	AIT
	2:23	No o who denies the Son has the Father;	3836
	3: 6	No o who lives in him keeps on sinning.	4024+4246
	3: 6	No o who continues to sin has	4024+4246
	3: 9	No o who is born of God will continue to sin,	4024+4246
	3:11	We should love o another.	253
	3:12	to the evil o and murdered his brother.	AIT
	3:23	and to love o another as he commanded us.	253
	4: 4	because the o who is in you is greater than	AIT
	4: 4	in you is greater than the o who is in	AIT
	4: 7	Dear friends, let us love o another,	253
	4: 9	He sent his o and only Son into the world	3666
	4:11	we also ought to love o another.	253
	4:12	No o has ever seen God;	4029
	4:12	but if we love o another,	253
	4:18	The o who fears is not made perfect in love.	AIT
	5: 6	This is the o who came by water and blood	AIT
	5:18	the o who was born of God keeps him safe,	AIT
	5:18	and the evil o cannot harm him.	AIT
	5:19	under the control of the evil o.	AIT
2Jn	1: 5	a new command but o we have had from	4005
	1: 5	I ask that we love o another.	253
Rev	1: 3	Blessed is the o who reads the words	AIT
	1:18	I am the Living O; I was dead, and behold	AIT

Rev	3: 7	What he opens no o can shut,	4029
	3: 7	and what he shuts no o can open.	4029
	3: 8	before you an open door that no o can shut.	4029
	3:11	so that no o will take your crown.	3594
	3:15	I wish you were either o or the other!	6037S
	5: 2	But the o who sat there had the appearance	AIT
	5: 3	But no o in heaven or on earth or under	4029
	5: 4	because no o was found who was worthy	4029
	5: 5	of the elders said to me, "Do not weep!	1651
	5: 8	Each o had a harp	AIT
	6: 1	Then I heard o of the four living creatures	1651
	6: 4	Then another horse came out, a fiery red o.	AIT
	7: 9	a great multitude that no o could count,	4029
	7:13	Then o of the elders asked me,	1651
	11:17	the O who is and who was,	AIT
	13: 3	O of the heads of the beast seemed	1651
	13:17	so that no o could buy or sell unless he had	5516
	14: 3	No o could learn the song except	4029
	14:14	seated on the cloud was o	AIT
	15: 7	Then o of the four living creatures gave to	1651
	15: 8	and no o could enter the temple until	4029
	16: 9	the Holy O, because you have so judged;	AIT
	17: 1	O of the seven angels who had	1651
	17:10	Five have fallen, o is, the other has not yet	1651
	17:12	but who for o hour will receive authority	1651
	17:13	They have o purpose and will give their	1651
	18: 8	in o day her plagues will overtake her:	1651
	18:10	In o hour your doom has come!'	1651
	18:11	no o buys their cargoes any more—	4029
	18:17	In o hour such great wealth has been brought to ruin!'	1651
	18:19	In o hour she has been brought to ruin!	1651
	19:12	on him that no o knows but he himself.	4029
	21: 9	O of the seven angels who had the	1651
	22: 8	am the o who heard and saw these things.	AIT

ONE'S (8) [ONE]

Ge	44: 2	in the mouth of the youngest o sack,	AIT
Lev	17:11	the blood that makes atonement for o life.	2021
2Ch	21:20	He passed away, to no o regret,	AIT
Ps	127: 4	of a warrior are sons born in o youth.	2021
Pr	25:27	nor is it honorable to seek o own honor.	4392
	26: 6	Like cutting off o feet	NIH
	27: 9	and the pleasantness of o friend springs	2084
Isa	58: 5	Is it only for bowing o head like a reed and	2257

ONE-TENTH (5) [ONE, TEN]

Nu	28:21	and with each of the seven lambs, o.	6928
	28:29	and with each of the seven lambs, o.	6928
	29: 4	and with each of the seven lambs, o.	285+6928
	29:10	and with each of the seven lambs, o.	6928
	29:15	and with each of the fourteen lambs, o.	6928

ONE-THIRD (1) [ONE, THREE]

Zec	13: 8	yet o will be left in it.	8958

ONES (83) [ONE]

Ge	30:42	to Laban and the strong o to Jacob.	AIT
	31: 8	'The speckled o will be your wages,'	AIT
	31: 8	'The streaked o will be your wages,'	AIT
Ex	6:27	They were the o who spoke to Pharaoh king	AIT
	18:26	but the simple o they decided themselves.	1821S
	34: 1	two stone tablets like the first o,	AIT
	34: 4	and the first o and went up Mount Sinai early	AIT
Lev	11: 2	these are the o you may eat:	2651S
Nu	26:63	the o counted by Moses and Eleazar	AIT
	31:16	the o who followed Balaam's advice	NIH
Dt	1:31	and the little o that you said would	3251
	10: 1	like the first o and come up to me on	AIT
	10: 3	two stone tablets like the first o,	AIT
	11: 2	that your children were not the o who saw	AIT
	33: 2	with myriads of holy o from the south,	7731
	33: 3	all the holy o are in your hand.	AIT
Jos	5: 7	and these were the o Joshua circumcised.	NIH
2Ki	23:13	the o Solomon king of Israel had built	889S
1Ch	6:49	o who presented offerings	AIT
	16:13	O sons of Jacob, his chosen o.	AIT
	16:22	"Do not touch my anointed o;	AIT
2Ch	20:13	and children and little o,	3251
	31:18	They included all the little o, the wives,	3251
Ezr		the last o, whose names were Eliphelet,	AIT
Job	5: 1	To which of the holy o will you turn?	AIT
	15:15	If God places no trust in his holy o,	AIT
	21:11	their little o dance about.	3529
	39:30	His young o feast on blood,	711
Ps	16: 3	the glorious o in whom is all my delight.	AIT
	29: 1	Ascribe to the LORD, O mighty o,	AIT
	37:28	and will not forsake his faithful o.	AIT
	50: 5	"Gather to me my consecrated o,	AIT
	72:	your afflicted o with justice.	AIT
	88:18	taken my companions and loved o from me;	AIT
	89: 5	in the assembly of the holy o.	AIT
	89: 7	of the holy o God is greatly feared;	AIT
	94: 8	you senseless o among the people;	AIT
	97:10	of his faithful o and delivers them from	AIT
	103:20	you mighty o who do his bidding,	AIT
	105: 6	O sons of Jacob, his chosen o.	AIT
	105:15	his chosen o with shouts of joy;	AIT
	106: 5	I may enjoy the prosperity of your chosen o,	AIT
Pr	1:22	"How long will you simple o love your simple ways?	AIT
	2: 8	and protects the way of his faithful o.	AIT

Ecc	10: 6	while the rich occupy the **low** o.	AIT
Isa	1:27	her **penitent** o with righteousness.	AIT
	10:33	the **tall** o will be brought low.	AIT
	13: 3	I have commanded my **holy** o;	AIT
	49:13	have compassion on his **afflicted** o.	AIT
	65:15	You will leave your name to my **chosen** o	AIT
	65:22	my **chosen** o will long enjoy the works	AIT
Jer	24: 3	"The good o are very good,	9300S
	24: 3	but so bad they cannot be eaten."	AIT
	48: 4	her **little** o will cry out.	AIT
Da	4:17	the **holy** o declare the verdict,	AIT
	7:24	different from the **earlier** o.	AIT
Hos	13:16	their **little** o will be dashed to	6407
Zec	1:10	"They are the o the LORD has sent to go	889S
	13: 7	I will turn my hand against the **little** o.	7592
	14: 5	and all the **holy** o with him.	AIT
Mt	10:42	of cold water to one of **these little** o	AIT
	18: 6	of these **little** o who believe in me	AIT
	18:10	not look down on one of **these little** o	AIT
	18:14	that any of these **little** o should be lost.	AIT
	19:18	"**Which** o?" the man inquired.	AIT
	20: 8	beginning with the **last** o hired and going	AIT
	25: 3	The **foolish** o took their lamps but did	AIT
	25: 8	The **foolish** o said to the wise,	AIT
Mk	9:42	of these **little** o who believe in me	AIT
Lk	8:12	Those along the path are **the** o **who** hear,	AIT
	8:13	on the rock are **the** o **who** receive the word	AIT
	12:18	down my barns and build **bigger** o,	AIT
	16:15	"You are **the** o who justify yourselves in	AIT
	17: 2	for him to cause one of these **little** o	AIT
	18: 7	God bring about justice *for* his **chosen** o,	AIT
Jn	8: 9	the **older** o first, until only Jesus was left,	AIT
Ro	1:26	Even their women exchanged natural	
		relations for **unnatural** o.	3836+4123+5882
1Th	3:13	with all his **holy** o.	AIT
Jas	2: 6	not the o who are dragging you into court?	NIG
	2: 7	the o who are slandering the noble name	NIG
Jude	1:14	thousands upon thousands of his **holy** o	41

ONESELF (1) [ONE, SELF]

Jas	1:27	to keep o from being polluted by the world.	1571

ONESIMUS (2)

Col	4: 9	He is coming with O,	3946
Phm	1:10	I appeal to you for my son O,	3946

ONESIPHORUS (2)

2Ti	1:16	the Lord show mercy to the household *of* O,	3947
	4:19	and Aquila and the household *of* O.	3947

ONIONS (1)

Nu	11: 5	the cucumbers, melons, leeks, o and garlic.	1294

ONLY (496)

Ge	6: 5	thoughts of his heart was o evil all the time.	8370
	7:23	O Noah was left, and those with him	421
	17:18	If o Ishmael might live under your blessing!	4273
	18:29	"What if o forty are found there?"	NIH
	18:30	What if o thirty can be found there?"	NIH
	18:31	what if o twenty can be found there?"	NIH
	18:32	what if o ten can be found there?"	NIH
	21:26	and I heard about it o today."	1194+4202
	22: 2	Then God said, "Take your son, your o **son**,	3495
	22:12	not withheld from me your son, your o	
		son."	3495
	22:16	and have not withheld your son, your o **son**,	3495
	24: 8	O do not take my son back there."	8370
	27:38	"Do you have o one blessing, my father?	2085S
	29:20	like o **a few** days to him because of his love	285
	31:15	**Not** o has he sold us,	3954
	32:10	I had o my staff when I crossed this Jordan,	3954
	34:12	O give me the girl as my wife."	2256
	34:15	to you on one condition o:	421
	34:22	**But** the men will consent to live with us as	
		one people o the condition	421
	41:40	O with respect to the throne will I	8370
	42:38	is dead and he is the o **one** left.	963+2257+4200
	44:17	O the man who was found to have	2085S
	44:20	he is the o one of his mother's sons left,	963+4200
	44:26	O if our youngest brother is	561
	47:26	It was o the land of the priests that did	8370
	50: 8	O their children and their flocks	8370
Ex	8:11	they will remain o in the Nile.	8370
	8:29	O be sure that Pharaoh does	8370
	9:26	The o place it did not hail was the land	8370
	10:11	Have o the men go;	NIH
	10:24	o leave your flocks and herds behind."	8370
	14:14	you *need* o **be still.**"	AIT
	16: 3	"If o we had died by the LORD's hand	4769+5989
	18:18	o wear *yourselves* out.	5570+5570
	19:13	O when the ram's horn sounds	NIH
	21: 4	and o the man shall go free.	928+1727+2257
	22:27	his cloak is the o covering he has	963+4200
Lev	11: 4	" 'There are some that o chew the cud	NIH
	11: 4	that only chew the cud or o have	NIH
	13: 6	it is o a rash.	NIH
	13:23	it is o a scar from the boil,	NIH
	13:28	it is o a scar from the burn.	3954
	21:14	**but** o a virgin from his own people,	561+3954
	25:12	eat o what is taken directly from the fields.	NIH
	25:52	If o **a few** years remain until the Year	5071
Nu	3: 4	so o Eleazar and Ithamar served as priests	NIH
	9:20	over the tabernacle o **a few** days;	5031
	9:21	the cloud stayed o from evening	NIH

Nu	10: 4	If o one is sounded, the leaders—	NIH
	11: 4	"**If** o we had meat to eat!	4769
	11:18	"**If** o we had meat to eat!	4769
	12: 2	the LORD spoken o through Moses?"	421+8370
	14: 2	"**If** o we had died in Egypt!	4273
	14: 3	to this land o to let us fall by the sword?"	NIH
	14: 9	O do not rebel against the LORD.	421
	14:38	o Joshua son of Nun and Caleb son	2256
	16:22	the entire assembly when o one man sins?"	NIH
	16:29	and experience o what usually happens	NIH
	17: 8	had not o sprouted but had budded,	NIH
	18: 7	But o you and your sons may serve	NIH
	20: 3	"**If** o we had died when our brothers	4273
	20:19	We o want to pass through on foot—	8370
	21:24	but o as far as the Ammonites,	NIH
	22:20	go with them, but do o what I tell you."	421
	22:35	but speak o what I tell you."	700
	22:38	I must speak o what God puts	NIH
	23:13	you will see o a part but not all of them.	700
	24:13	and I must say o what the LORD says'?	NIH
	26:33	he had o daughters,	561+3954
	35:28	o after the death of the high priest	2256
	35:30	a murderer o on the testimony of witnesses.	NIH
	35:30	to death on the testimony of o one witness.	NIH
Dt	2:28	O let us pass through on foot—	8370
	3:11	(O Og king of Bashan was left of	8370
	4: 9	O be careful, and watch yourselves closely	8370
	4:12	but saw no form; there was o a voice.	2314
	4:27	and o **a few** *of* you will survive among	5031+5493
	6:13	serve him o and take your oaths	NIH
	12:14	Offer them o at the place	561+3954
	15: 5	if o you fully obey the LORD your God	8370
	17: 6	to death on the testimony of o one witness.	NIH
	22: 9	if you do, not o the crops you plant but also	NIH
	22:25	o the man who has done this shall die.	963+4200
	28:67	"**If** o it were evening!"	4769+5989
	28:67	in the evening, "**If** o it were morning!"	4769+5989
	29:14	covenant, *with* its oath, not o with you	963+4200
	32:29	**If** o they were wise,	4273
	32:52	you will see the land o from a distance;	NIH
Jos	1:17	O may the LORD your God be with you	8370
	1:18	O be strong and courageous!"	8370
	6:17	O Rahab the prostitute and all who are	8370
	7: 3	for o **a few** men are there."	5071
	7: 7	**If** o we had been content to stay on	4273
	11:22	o in Gaza, Gath and Ashdod did any	
		survive.	8370
	14: 4	of the land o towns to live in,	561
	17: 3	had no sons but o daughters.	561
	17:14	"Why have you given us o one allotment	NIH
	17:17	You will have not o one allotment	NIH
	22:20	not the o one who died for his sin.' "	285
Jdg	3: 2	(he did this o to teach warfare to	8370
	6:37	If there is dew o on the fleece and all	963+4200
	6:40	O the fleece was dry;	963+4200
	8:20	because he was o a boy and was afraid.	6388
	9:29	**If** o this people were under my command!	
			4769+5989
	11:34	She was an o **child.**	3495
	15:13	"We will o tie you up and hand you over	3954
	16: 3	But Samson lay there o until the middle of	NIH
	19:20	O don't spend the night in the square."	8370
1Sa	1:11	if *you* will o **look** upon your servant's	8011+8011
	1:23	o may the LORD make good his word."	421
	2:15	accept boiled meat from you, but o raw."	561
	2:33	not cut off from my altar will be spared o	NIH
	5: 4	o his body remained.	8370
	7: 3	to the LORD and serve him o,	963+4200
	7: 4	and served the LORD o.	963+4200
	11: 2	a treaty with you o on the condition	NIH
	13:22	o Saul and his son Jonathan had them.	2256
	17:28	you came down o to watch the battle."	3954
	17:33	you are o a boy, and he has been a fighting	3954
	17:42	David over and saw that he was o a boy,	NIH
	18: 8	he thought, "but me with o thousands.	NIH
	18:17	o serve me bravely and fight the battles of	421
	18:23	I'm o a poor man and little known."	NIH
	20: 3	there is o a step between me and death."	3954
	20:39	o Jonathan and David knew.)	421
2Sa	1:24	we would o be a burden to you,"	4202S
	13:32	o Amnon is dead.	963+4200
	13:33	O Amnon is dead."	963+4200
	14: 7	the o burning coal I have left,	NIH
	15: 4	"**If** o I were appointed judge in the land!	4769
	15:20	You came o yesterday.	NIH
	17: 2	I would strike down o the king	963+4200
	18:33	**If** o I had died instead of you—	4769+5989
	22:31	**but** o to strip the dead.	421
1Ki	3: 7	But I am o a little child and do not know	NIH
	4:19	He was the o governor over the district.	285
	6: 7	o blocks dressed at the quarry were used,	NIH
	8:25	if o your sons are careful in all they do	8370
	11:17	But Hadad, still o a boy,	NIH
	12:20	O the tribe of Judah remained loyal to the	
		house of David.	963+2314+4200
	14: 8	doing o what was right in my eyes.	8370
	14:13	the o one belonging to Jeroboam who	963+4200
	14:13	because he is the o one in the house	NIH
	16:31	He **not** o considered it trivial to commit	2022
	17:12	o a handful of flour in a jar and a little	561+3954
	18:22	the o one of the LORD's prophets left,	963+4200
	19:10	I am the o one left,	963+4200
	19:14	I am the o one left,	963+4200
	22:14	I can tell him o what the LORD tells me."	3954
	22:18	anything good about me, but o bad?"	561+3954
2Ki	3:10	the LORD called us three kings together o	NIH
	3:25	O Kir Hareseth was left with its stones	6330

2Ki	5: 3	"**If** o my master would see	332
	7:10	o tethered horses and donkeys,	561+3954
	7:13	yes, they will o be like all these	NIH
	10:23	o ministers of Baal."	561+3954
	13:19	But now you will defeat it o three times."	NIH
	17:18	O the tribe of Judah was left,	4202+8370
	18:20	**but** you speak o empty words.	421
	18:27	"Was it o to your master and you	NIH
	19:18	they were not gods but o wood and stone,	561
	21: 8	if o they will be careful to do everything	8370
	24:14	O the poorest people of the land were	2314+4202
1Ch	2:34	Sheshan had no sons—o daughters.	561+3954
	7:15	who had o daughters.	NIH
	23:22	he had o daughters.	561+3954
	29:14	and we have given you o what comes	NIH
2Ch	6:16	if o your sons are careful in all they do	8370
	16:12	**but** o from the physicians.	3954
	18:13	I can tell him o what my God says."	3954
	18:17	about me, but o bad?"	561
	20:24	they saw o dead bodies lying on	2256
	24:24	Aramean army had come with o a few men,	5203
	32: 8	With him is o the arm of flesh,	NIH
	33: 8	if o they will be careful to do everything	8370
	33:17	**but** o to the LORD their God.	8370
Ezr	10:15	O Jonathan son of Asahel and Jahzeiah son	421
Ne	5: 8	o for them to be sold back to us!"	2256
Est	1:16	not o against the king but also against	963+4200
	3: 6	scorned the idea of killing o Mordecai.	963+4200
	4: 2	But he went o as far as the king's gate,	NIH
	4:11	The o **exception** to this is for the king	963+4200
	5:12	"I'm the o person Queen Esther invited	561+3954
Job	1:15	the o **one** who has escaped to tell you!"	963+4200
	1:16	the o **one** who has escaped to tell you!"	963+4200
	1:17	the o **one** who has escaped to tell you!"	963+4200
	1:19	the o **one** who has escaped to tell you!"	963+4200
	3:26	I have no rest, but o turmoil."	NIH
	6: 2	"**If** o my anguish could be weighed	4273
	6:20	they arrive there, o to be disappointed.	2256
	8: 9	for we were born o yesterday	NIH
	9:15	I could o plead with my Judge for mercy.	NIH
	9:33	**If** o there were someone to arbitrate	4273
	10:19	**If** o I had never come into being,	889+3869
	11:16	recalling it o as waters gone by.	NIH
	13: 5	**If** o you would be altogether silent!	4769+5989
	13:20	"O grant me these two things, O God,	421
	14:13	"**If** o you would hide me in the grave	4769+5989
	14:13	If o you would set me a time and	NIH
	14:22	of his own body and mourns o for himself."	NIH
	16:22	"O a few years will pass before I go on	3954
	17:13	If the o home I hope for is the grave,	NIH
	19:20	I have escaped with o the skin of my teeth.	NIH
	23: 3	**If** o I knew where to find him;	4769+5989
	23: 3	if o I could go to his dwelling!	NIH
	25: 6	a son of man, who is o a worm!"	NIH
	28:22	'O a rumor of it has reached our ears.'	NIH
	32: 9	It is not o the old who are wise,	NIH
	32: 9	not only the old who are wise, not o	NIH
	35: 8	Your wickedness affects o a man	NIH
	35: 8	and your righteousness o the sons of men.	NIH
Ps	25:15	for o he will release my feet from the snare.	NIH
	30: 5	For his anger lasts o a moment,	NIH
	37: 8	it leads o to evil.	421
	39: 6	He bustles about, **but** o in vain;	421
	51: 4	Against you, and you o, have I sinned	963+4200
	62: 9	together they are o a breath.	4946
	91: 8	You will o observe with your eyes and see	8370
	139:19	**If** o you would slay the wicked, O God!	561
Pr	1:18	they waylay o themselves!	NIH
	4: 3	still tender, and an o child of my mother,	3495
	4:26	for your feet and take o ways that are firm.	3972
	10:32	the mouth of the wicked o what is perverse.	NIH
	11:16	but ruthless men gain o wealth.	NIH
	11:23	The desire of the righteous ends o in good,	421
	11:23	but the hope of the wicked o in wrath.	NIH
	11:29	on his family will inherit o wind,	NIH
	12:19	but a lying tongue lasts o a **moment.**	AIT
	13:10	Pride o breeds quarrels,	8370
	14:23	but mere talk leads o to poverty.	421
	17:11	An evil man is bent o on rebellion;	421
	20:25	to dedicate something rashly **and** o later	AIT
	26:19	"I was o joking!"	2022+4202
	30: 8	but give me o my daily bread.	NIH
Ecc	7:29	This o have I found:	963+4200
	9:14	a small city with o **a few** people in it.	5071
	12: 9	**Not** o was the Teacher wise,	3463
SS	6: 9	is unique, the o daughter of her mother;	285
	8: 1	**If** o you were to me like a brother,	4769+5989
Isa	4: 1	o wounds and welts and open sores,	NIH
	4: 1	o let us be called by your name.	8370
	5: 2	but it yielded o bad fruit.	NIH
	5: 4	why did it yield o bad?	NIH
	5:10	A ten-acre vineyard will produce o a bath	NIH
	5:10	a homer of seed o an ephah of grain."	NIH
	7: 8	and the head of Damascus is o Rezin.	NIH
	7: 9	the head of Samaria is o Remaliah's son.	NIH
	7:23	there will be o briers and thorns.	NIH
	8:22	the earth and see o distress and darkness	NIH
	10:22	o a remnant will return.	NIH
	16:12	she o wears herself out;	3954
	27: 4	**If** o there were briers	4769+5989
	29:13	of me **is** *made up o o* of rules taught by men.	AIT
	30: 5	**but** o shame and disgrace."	3954
	35: 9	But o the redeemed will walk there,	NIH
	36: 5	but you speak o empty words.	NIH
	36:12	"Was it o to your master and you	NIH
	37:19	they were not gods but o wood and stone,	561
	47:13	you have received *has* o **worn** *you* out!	AIT

Ref	Text	Num
Isa	48:18	**If** o you had paid attention	4273
	54: 6	wife who married young, **o** to be rejected,"	3954
	56: 3	"I am o a dry tree."	2176
	58: 5	o a day for a man to humble himself?	NIH
	58: 5	Is it o for bowing one's head like a reed	NIH
Jer	1: 6	I am o a child."	3954
	1: 7	"Do not say, 'I am o a child.'	NIH
	3:10	but o in pretense," declares the LORD.	561
	3:13	O acknowledge your guilt—	421
	5: 4	I thought, "These are o the poor;	421
	6:26	mourn with bitter wailing as for an o son,	3495
	8:15	for a time of healing but there was o terror.	NIH
	9:25	I will punish all who are circumcised o	NIH
	10:24	Correct me, LORD, **but** o with justice—	421
	14: 8	like a traveler *who* **stays** o a night?	4328+5742
	14:19	for a time of healing but there is o terror.	NIH
	22:17	your heart are set o on dishonest gain,	561+3954
	23:23	"Am I o a God nearby,"	NIH
	27:10	o serve to **remove** you **far**	AIT
	28: 9	the LORD o if his prediction comes true."	928
	30:11	I will discipline you but o with justice;	NIH
	31:36	"O if these decrees vanish from my sight,"	561
	31:37	"O if the heavens above can be measured	561
	34: 7	These were the o fortified cities left	NIH
	37:10	and o wounded men were left in their tents,	NIH
	38: 6	it had no water in it, o mud,	561+3954
	42: 2	now o a few are left.	5071
	46:17	'Pharaoh king of Egypt is o a loud noise;	NIH
	46:28	I will discipline you but o with justice;	NIH
	49: 9	not steal o as much as they wanted?	NIH
	51:58	the nations' labor is o fuel for the flames."	NIH
La	1:20	inside, there is o death.	3869
	5: 4	our wood can be had o at a price.	NIH
Eze	14:14	were in it, they could save o themselves	NIH
	14:20	They would save o themselves	NIH
	16:47	You not o walked in their ways	2256
	17:14	surviving o by keeping his treaty.	NIH
	33:24	'Abraham was o one man,'	NIH
	34: 2	the shepherds of Israel who o **take care of**	AIT
	40:46	who are the o Levites who may draw near	4946
	43: 8	with o a wall between me and them,	NIH
	44: 3	The prince himself is the o one who may sit	AIT
	44:22	they may marry o virgins	561+3954
	44:28	to be the o inheritance the priests have.	NIH
	46:17	His inheritance belongs to his sons o;	421
Da	4:19	if o the dream applied to your enemies	NIH
	10: 7	Daniel, was the o one who saw the vision;	963+4200
	11:23	with o a few people he will rise to power.	5071
	11:24	overthrow of fortresses—but o for a time.	NIH
Hos	4: 2	There is o cursing, lying and murder,	NIH
Am	3: 2	"You o have I chosen of all the families of	8370
	3:12	the lion's mouth o two leg bones or a piece	NIH
	5: 3	a thousand strong for Israel will have o	NIH
	5: 3	a hundred strong will have o ten left."	NIH
	5:19	as though a man fled from a lion o to meet	2256
	5:19	and rested his hand on the wall o to have	2256
	8:10	like mourning for an o son and the end of it	3495
Ob	1: 5	not steal o as much as they wanted?	NIH
Hab	2:13	that the people's labor is o fuel for the fire,	NIH
Zep	1: 3	The wicked will have o heaps of rubble	NIH
Hag	1: 6	o to put them in a purse with holes in it."	NIH
	2:16	there were o ten.	NIH
	2:16	there were o twenty.	NIH
Zec	1:15	I was o a little angry,	5071
	12:10	for him as one mourns for an o child,	3495
	14: 9	and his name be o the name.	285
Mt	4:10	the Lord your God, and serve him o.' "	3668
	5:47	And if you greet o your brothers,	3668
	6:18	but o to your Father, who is unseen;	NIG
	7:14	and o a few find it.	NIG
	7:21	but o he who does the will	NIG
	9:21	She said to herself, "If I o touch his cloak,	3668
	12: 4	but o for the priests.	3668
	12:24	they said, "It is o by Beelzebub,	1623+3590
	13:21	since he has no root, he lasts o **a short time.**	4672
	13:57	"O in his hometown and in his own house is a prophet without honor."	1623+3590
	14:17	"We have here o five loaves of bread and two fish.	3590+4024
	15:24	"I was sent o to the lost sheep of Israel."	1623+3590+4024
	19:11	but o those to whom it has been given.	NIG
	19:17	"There is o One who is good.	NIG
	20:12	who were hired last worked o one hour,'	NIG
	21:21	o can you do what was done to the fig tree,	3668
	23: 8	for you have o one Master	NIG
	24:36	nor the Son, **but** o the Father.	1623+3590
Mk	2:26	which is lawful o for priests to eat.	1623+3590
	4:17	they have no root, they last o **a short time.**	4672
	6: 4	to them, "O in his hometown,	1623+3590+4024
	9:29	"This kind can come out o by prayer."	1623+3590
	12:42	worth a fraction of a penny.	NIG
	13:32	nor the Son, but o the Father.	1623+3590
	14: 1	Unleavened Bread were o two days away,	NIG
Lk	4: 8	Worship the Lord your God and serve him o	3668
	4:27	o Naaman the Syrian."	1623+3590+4024
	6: 4	he ate what is lawful o for priests to eat.	1623+3590+3668
	7:12	o son of his mother, and she was a widow.	3666
	8:42	Because his o daughter,	1639+3666
	9:13	"We have o five loaves of bread	2445+4024+4498
	9:38	for he is my o **child.**	3666
	10:42	but o one thing is needed.	NIG
	13:23	are o a few people going to be saved?"	NIG
	17:10	we have o done our duty.' "	NIG
	19:42	and said, "If you, even you, had o known	NIG

Ref	Text	Num
Lk	24:18	"Are you o a visitor to Jerusalem and do	3668
Jn	1: 8	he came o as a witness to the light.	247
	1:14	the glory of the **One and O,**	3666
	1:18	but God the **One and O,**	3666
	3:16	the world that he gave his **one and** o Son,	3666
	3:18	in the name of God's **one and** o Son.	3666
	3:27	A man can receive o what is given him	1651+4028
	5:18	not o was he breaking the Sabbath,	3668
	5:19	he can do o what he sees his Father doing,	1569+3590
	5:30	I judge o as I hear,	NIG
	5:44	the praise that comes from the o God?	3668
	6: 6	He asked this o to test him,	NIG
	6:22	that o one boat had been there,	1623+3590
	6:46	o he has seen the Father.	3668
	7:33	"I am with you for o a short time,	2285
	8: 9	the older ones first, until o Jesus was left,	3668
	8:41	**"The** o Father we have is God himself."	1651
	9: 9	Others said, "No, he o looks like him."	247
	10:10	thief comes o to steal and kill	1623+3590+4024
	10:17	lay down my life—o to take it up again.	2671
	11:52	and not o for that nation but also for	3667
	12: 9	o because of him but also to see Lazarus,	3667
	12:16	O after Jesus was glorified did they realize	247
	12:24	it remains o a single seed.	3668
	12:44	he does not believe in me o,	NIG
	13:10	"A person who has had a bath needs o to wash his feet;	1623+3590+4024
	13:33	I will be with you o a little longer.	NIG
	16:13	he will speak o what he hears,	247
	17: 3	that they may know you, the o true God,	3668
	21:23	he o said, "If I want him to remain alive	247
Ac	2:15	It's o nine in the morning!	NIG
	5:39	you will o find yourselves fighting	3607
	10:26	he said, "I am o a man myself."	NIG
	11:19	telling the message o to Jews.	3668
	14:15	We too are o men, human like you.	NIG
	18:25	though he knew o the baptism of John.	3668
	19:27	not o that our trade will lose its good name,	3667
	20:23	I o know that in every city	4440
	20:24	**if** o I may finish the race and complete	6055
	21:13	I am ready not o to be bound,	3667
	26:29	that not o you but all who are listening	3667
	27:22	o the ship will be destroyed.	4440
Ro	1:32	they not o continue to do these very things	3667
	2:28	a Jew if he is o one outwardly,	NIG
	3:29	Is God the God of Jews o?	3668
	3:30	since there is o one God,	NIG
	4: 9	Is this blessedness o for the circumcised,	NIG
	4:12	not o are circumcised but who also walk in	3667
	4:16	not o to those who are of the law but also	3668
	5: 3	Not o so, but we also rejoice	3668
	5:11	Not o is this so, but we also rejoice	3668
	7: 1	a man o **as long as** he lives?	2093+4012+5989
	8:23	Not o so, but we ourselves,	3668
	9:10	Not o that, but Rebekah's children had one	3667
	9:24	o from the Jews but also from the Gentiles?	3668
	9:27	o the remnant will be saved.	NIG
	11: 3	I am the o one left,	3668
	13: 5	not o because of possible punishment but	3667
	14: 2	whose faith is weak, eats o vegetables.	NIG
	16: 4	but o I but all the churches of the Gentiles	3668
	16:27	*to* the o wise God be glory forever	3668
1Co	3: 5	O servants, through whom you came	NIG
	3: 7	**but** o God, who makes things grow.	247
	3:15	but o as one escaping through the flames.	NIG
	4:19	and then I will find out not o how these	NIG
	9: 6	Or is it o I and Barnabas who must work	3668
	9:24	but o one gets the prize?	NIG
	13: 1	I am o a resounding gong or	NIG
	14:36	Or are you the o *people* it has reached?	3668
	15:19	If o for this life we have hope in Christ,	3667
	16: 7	to see you now and make o a passing visit;	NIG
2Co	3:14	because o in Christ is it taken away.	NIG
	7: 7	and not o by his coming but also by	3667
	7: 8	but o for a little while—	NIG
	8:10	Last year you were the first not o to give	3667
	8:17	For Titus not o welcomed our appeal,	NIG
	8:21	not o in the eyes of the Lord but also in	3667
	9:12	not o supplying the needs of God's people	3667
	10: 7	You are looking o on the surface of things.	NIG
	13: 8	**but** o for the truth.	247
Gal	1:19	o James, the Lord's brother.	1623+3590
	1:23	They o heard the report:	3667
	5: 6	The o thing that counts is faith expressing itself through love.	247
	6:12	The o reason they do this is to avoid	3667
Eph	1:21	not o in the present age but also in the one	3668
	4:29	but o what is helpful for building others up	1623
	6: 6	not o to win their favor when their eye is	NIG
Php	1:27	whether I come and see you o or hear	NIG
	1:29	on behalf of Christ not o to believe on him,	3668
	2: 4	Each of you should look **not** o to your own	3590
	2:12	**not** o in my presence,	3590
	2:27	and not on him o but also on me,	3668
	3:16	O let us live up to what we have already	4440
	4:15	of giving and receiving, except you o;	3668
Col	3:22	and do it, not o when their eye is on you	NIG
	4:11	o Jews among my fellow workers for	3668
1Th	1: 8	from you not o in Macedonia and Achaia—	3667
	2: 8	to share with you not o the gospel of God	3667
1Ti	1:17	immortal, invisible, the o God,	3668
	5:13	And not o do they become idlers,	3667
	5:23	Stop **drinking** o **water,**	5621
	6:15	God, the blessed and o Ruler,	3668
2Ti	2:14	and o ruins those who listen.	NIG
	2:20	a large house there are articles not o of gold	3667

Ref	Text	Num
2Ti	4: 8	and not o to me,	3667
	4:11	O Luke is with me.	3668
Heb	9: 7	o the high priest entered the inner room,	3668
	9: 7	and that o once a year,	NIG
	9:10	They are o a matter of food and drink	3667
	9:17	will is in force o when somebody has died;	NIG
	9:24	a man-made sanctuary that was o a copy of	NIG
	10: 1	The law is o a shadow of the good things	NIG
	10:27	but o a fearful expectation of judgment and	NIG
	11:13	they o saw them and welcomed them from	247
	11:17	about to sacrifice his **one and** o **son,**	3666
	11:40	for us so that o together with us would they	NIG
	12:26	"Once more I will shake not o the earth but	3668
	13:22	for I have written you o a short letter.	NIG
Jas	4:12	There is o one Lawgiver and Judge,	NIG
1Pe	2:18	o to those who are good and considerate,	3667
	3:20	In it o a few people, eight in all,	NIG
2Pe	2:12	born o to be caught and destroyed,	NIG
1Jn	2: 2	and not o for ours but also for the sins of	3667
	4: 9	He sent his **one and** o Son into the world	3666
	5: 5	O he who believes that Jesus is the Son of God.	1623+3590
	5: 6	He did not come by water o,	NIG
2Jn	1: 1	not I o, but also all who know the truth—	3668
Jude	1: 4	and deny Jesus Christ our o Sovereign	3668
	1:12	shepherds who feed o themselves.	NIG
	1:25	*to* the o God our Savior be glory,	3668
Rev	2:17	known o to him who receives it.	1623+3590+4029
	2:25	O hold on to what you have until I come.	4440
	9: 4	but o those people who did not have	1623+3590
	9: 5	**but** o to torture them for five months.	247
	21:27	**but** o those whose names are written	1623+3590

ONO (5)

Ref	Text	Num
1Ch	8:12	Misham, Shemed (who built O and Lod	229
Ezr	2:33	of Lod, Hadid and O 725	229
Ne	6: 2	in one of the villages on the plain of O."	229
	7:37	of Lod, Hadid and O 721	229
	11:35	in Lod and O, and in the Valley of the	229

ONTO (9) [ON]

Ref	Text	Num
Ge	49: 4	for *you* went up o your father's bed,	AIT
	49: 4	o my couch and defiled it.	NIH
Ex	8: 3	and your bedroom and o your bed,	6584
Nu	19: 6	and scarlet wool and throw them o	448+9348
Jdg	9: 5	a ring from his plunder o	2025
1Ki	22:35	The blood from his wound ran o the floor	448
Est	9:25	the Jews should come back o his own head,	6584
Jnh	2:10	and it vomited Jonah o dry land.	448
Lk	9:28	with him and went up o a mountain to pray.	1650

ONWARD   (KJV) See SET OUT

ONYCHA (1)

Ref	Text	Num
Ex	30:34	gum resin, o and galbanum—	8829

ONYX (11)

Ref	Text	Num
Ge	2:12	aromatic resin and o are also there.)	74+8732
Ex	25: 7	and o stones and other gems to be mounted	8732
	28: 9	"Take two o stones and engrave on them	8732
	28:20	an o and a jasper.	8732
	35: 9	and o stones and other gems to be mounted	8732
	35:27	The leaders brought o stones	8732
	39: 6	the o stones in gold filigree settings	8732
	39:13	an o and a jasper.	8732
1Ch	29: 2	as well as o for the settings, turquoise,	74+8732
Job	28:16	with precious o or sapphires.	8732
Eze	28:13	topaz and emerald, chrysolite, o and jasper,	8732

OOZING (1)

Ref	Text	Num
1Sa	14:26	they saw the honey o out,	2144

OPEN (164) [OPENED, OPENHANDED, OPENING, OPENINGS, OPENLY, OPENS]

Ref	Text	Num
Ge	25:27	a man of the o country,	8441
	25:29	Esau came in from the o country,	8441
	27: 3	to the o **country** to hunt some wild game	8441
	27: 5	When Esau left for the o **country**	8441
	34:10	the land is o *to* you.	4200+7156
Lev	1:17	*He shall* **tear** it o by the wings,	9117
	14: 7	he is to release the live bird in the o fields.	7156
	14:53	the live bird in the o fields outside	7156
	17: 5	now making in the o fields.	7156
	25:31	to be considered as o country.	8441
Nu	19:15	and every o container without a lid fastened	7337
	19:16	o who touches someone who has been killed	8441
Dt	20:11	If they accept o and their gates,	7337
	28:12	The LORD *will* o the heavens,	7337
Jos	8: 1	They left the city o and went in pursuit	7337
	10:22	"O the mouth of the cave,	7337
Jdg	3:25	when he *did* not o the doors of the room,	7337
	20:31	that about thirty men fell in the o **field**	8441
2Sa	10: 8	by themselves in the o **country.**	8441
	11:11	my lord's men are camped in the o fields.	7156
	11:23	and came out against us in the o,	8441
1Ki	6:18	carved with gourds and o flowers.	7080
	6:29	palm trees and o flowers,	7080
	6:32	palm trees and o flowers.	7080
	6:35	and o flowers on them and overlaid them	7080
	8:29	be o toward this temple night and day,	7337
	8:52	"May your eyes be o to your servant's plea	7337
2Ki	6:17	"O LORD, o his eyes so he may see."	7337

2Ki	6:20	o the eyes of these men so they can see."	7219
	7: 2	if the LORD should o the floodgates of	6913
	7:19	if the LORD should o the floodgates of	6913
	8:12	and rip o their pregnant women."	1324
	9: 3	Then o the door and run; don't delay!"	7337
	13:17	"O the east window," he said,	7337
	15:16	because they refused to o their gates.	7337
	15:16	and ripped o all the pregnant women.	1324
	19:16	o your eyes, O LORD, and see;	7219
1Ch	19: 9	by themselves in the o country.	8441
2Ch	6:20	May your eyes be o toward this temple day	7337
	6:40	may your eyes be o and your ears attentive	7337
	7:15	be o and my ears attentive to	7337
Ne	1: 6	let your ear be attentive and your eyes o	7337
Est	4: 6	to Mordecai in the o square of the city	8148
Job	11: 5	that he would o his lips against you	7337
	16:10	Men o their mouths to jeer at me;	7196
	31:32	for my door was always o to the traveler—	7337
	32:20	I must o my lips and reply.	7337
	33: 2	I am about to o my mouth;	7337
	41:14	Who dares o the doors of his mouth,	7337
Ps	5: 9	Their throat is an o grave;	7337
	22:13	Roaring lions tearing their prey o their	
		mouths wide against me.	7198
	38: 9	All my longings lie o before you, O Lord;	NIH
	38:13	like a mute, who cannot o his mouth;	7337
	39: 9	I was silent; I would not o my mouth,	7337
	51:15	O Lord, o my lips,	7337
	60: 2	You have shaken the land and torn it o;	7204
	74:13	It was you who split o the sea	7297
	78: 2	I will o my mouth in parables,	7337
	81:10	O wide your mouth and I will fill it.	8143
	104:28	when you o your hand,	7337
	118:19	O for me the gates of righteousness;	7337
	119:18	O my eyes that I may see wonderful things	1655
	119:131	I o my mouth and pant,	7196
	119:148	My eyes stay o through the watches of	7709
	145:16	You o your hand and satisfy the desires	7337
Pr	8: 6	I o my lips to speak what is right.	5157
	15:11	and Destruction lie o before the LORD—	NIH
	27: 5	Better is o rebuke than hidden love.	1655
SS	5: 2	My lover is knocking: "O to me, my sister,	7337
	5: 5	I arose to o for my lover,	7337
Isa	1: 6	only wounds and welts and o sores,	3269
	9:12	west have devoured Israel with o mouth.	3972
	22:22	and what he shuts no one can o.	7337
	26: 2	O the gates that the righteous nation may	7337
	37:17	o your eyes, O LORD, and see;	7219
	42: 7	to o eyes that are blind,	7219
	42:20	your ears are o, but you hear nothing."	7219
	45: 1	to o doors before him so that gates will not	7337
	45: 8	Let the earth o wide,	7337
	48: 8	from of old your ear has not been o.	7337
	53: 7	and afflicted, yet he did not o his mouth;	7337
	53: 7	is silent, so he did not o his mouth.	7337
	60:11	Your gates will always stand o,	7337
	63:13	Like a horse in o country,	4497
Jer	5:16	Their quivers are like an o grave;	7337
	9:20	o your ears to the words of his mouth.	4374
	9:22	of men will lie like refuse on the o field,	7156
	13:19	and there will be no one to o them.	7337
	17:16	What passes my lips is o before you.	5790+7156
	32:19	Your eyes are o to all the ways of men;	7219
	40: 7	in the o country heard that the king	8441
	40:13	the o country came to Gedaliah at Mizpah	8441
	50:26	Break o her granaries;	7337
La	2:16	All your enemies o their mouths wide	7198
Eze	2: 8	o your mouth and eat what I give you."	7198
	3:27	I will o your mouth and you shall say	7337
	16: 5	you were thrown out into the o field,	7156
	16:63	be ashamed and never again o your mouth	7341
	21:24	by your rebellion, revealing your sins	1655
	26: 2	and its doors have swung o to me;	6015
	29: 5	You will fall on the o field and not	7156
	29: 7	and you tore o their shoulders;	1324
	29:21	and I will o your mouth among them.	5989+7341
	32: 4	on the land and hurl you on the o field.	7156
	37:12	I am going to o your graves and bring you	7337
	37:13	when I o your graves and bring you up	7337
	39: 5	You will fall in the o field,	8441
	41: 9	The o area between the side rooms of	4965
	41:11	the o area, one on the north and another on	4965
	41:11	the o area was five cubits wide all around.	4965
	45: 2	with 50 cubits around it for o land.	4494
Da	9:18	o your eyes and see the desolation of	7219
Hos	13: 8	will attack them and rip them o.	4213+6033+7973
	13:16	their pregnant women ripped o."	1324
Joel	1:19	the o pastures and flames have burned	4497
	1:20	up and fire has devoured the o pastures.	4497
	2:22	for the o pastures are becoming green.	4497
Am	1:13	Because he ripped o the pregnant women	1324
Mic	2:13	One who breaks o the way will go up	7287
	4:10	the city to camp in the o field.	8441
Na	2: 6	The river gates are thrown o and	7337
	3:13	your land are wide o to your enemies;	7337+7337
Zec	11: 1	O your doors, O Lebanon,	7337
Mal	3:10	not throw o the floodgates of heaven	7337
Mt	13:35	"I will o my mouth in parables,	487
	17:27	o its mouth and you will find a four-drachma	
		coin.	487
	25:11	'O the door for us!'	487
	27:52	The tombs broke o and the bodies	487
Mk	1:10	he saw heaven being torn o and	5387
	4:22	to be brought out into the o.	5745
Lk	8:17	not be known or brought out into the o.	5745
	12:36	and knocks they can immediately o	487
	13:25	'Sir, o the door for us.'	487

Lk	15: 4	in the o country and go after the lost sheep	2245
Jn	1:51	"I tell you the truth, you shall see heaven o,	487
	4:35	o your eyes and look at the fields!"	2048+4057
	9:26	How did he o your eyes?"	487
	10:21	Can a demon o the eyes of the blind?"	487
Ac	1:18	there he fell headlong, his body burst o.	3545
	7:56	"I see heaven o and the Son	1380
	8:32	so he did not o his mouth.	487
	16:26	At once all the prison doors flew o,	487
	16:27	and when he saw the prison doors o,	487
	19:38	the courts are o and there are proconsuls.	61+72
	26:18	to o their eyes and turn them	487
	27: 5	When we had sailed across the o sea off	4283
Ro	3:13	"Their throats are o graves;	487
2Co	6:13	o wide your hearts also.	4425
	11:25	I spent a night and a day in the o sea,	1113
Eph	6:19	that whenever I o my mouth,	489
Col	4: 3	too, that God may o a door for our message,	487
1Ti	5: 7	no one may be o to blame.	455
Tit	1: 6	a man whose children believe and are not o	NIG
Rev	3: 7	and what he shuts no one can o.	487
	3: 8	before you an o door that no one can shut.	487
	4: 1	before me was a door standing o in heaven.	487
	5: 2	"Who is worthy to break the seals and o	487
	5: 3	the earth could o the scroll or even look	487
	5: 4	to o the scroll or look inside.	487
	5: 5	to o the scroll and its seven seals."	487
	5: 9	to take the scroll and to o its seals,	487
	10: 2	which lay o in his hand.	487
	10: 8	"Go, take the scroll that lies o in the hand	487
	19:11	I saw heaven standing o and there	487

OPENED (109) [OPEN]

Ge	3: 5	that when you eat of it your eyes will be o,	7219
	3: 7	Then the eyes of both of them were o,	7219
	4:11	which o its mouth to receive your brother's	7198
	7:11	and the floodgates of the heavens were o.	7337
	8: 6	After forty days Noah o the window	7337
	21:19	Then God o her eyes and she saw a well	7219
	29:31	o her womb, but Rachel was barren.	7337
	30:22	he listened to her and o her womb.	7337
	41:56	Joseph o the storehouses and sold grain to	7337
	42:27	the night one of them o his sack to get feed	7337
	43:21	for the night we o our sacks and each	7337
	44:11	his sack to the ground and o it.	7337
Ex	2: 6	She o it and saw the baby.	7337
Nu	16:32	the earth o its mouth and swallowed them,	7337
	22:28	Then the LORD o the donkey's mouth,	7337
	22:31	Then the LORD o Balaam's eyes,	1655
	24: 4	who falls prostrate, and whose eyes are o:	1655
	24:16	who falls prostrate, and whose eyes are o:	1655
	26:10	The earth o its mouth and swallowed them	7198
Dt	11: 6	the earth o its mouth right in the middle	7198
Jdg	4:19	She o a skin of milk, gave him a drink,	7337
	15:19	Then God o up the hollow place in Lehi,	1324
	19:27	and o the door of the house and stepped out	7337
1Sa	3:15	down until morning and then o the doors of	7337
2Ki	4:35	boy sneezed seven times and o his eyes.	7219
	6:17	Then the LORD o the servant's eyes,	7219
	6:20	the LORD o their eyes and they looked,	7219
	9:10	Then he o the door and ran.	7337
	13:17	he said, and he o it.	7337
2Ch	29: 3	he o the doors of the temple of the LORD	7337
Ne	7: 3	"The gates of Jerusalem are not to be o	7337
	8: 5	Ezra o the book.	7337
	8: 5	and as he o it, the people all stood up.	7337
	13:19	I ordered the doors to be shut and not o	7337
Job	3: 1	Job o his mouth and cursed the day	7337
Ps	74:15	It was you who o up springs and streams;	1324
	78:23	above and o the doors of the heavens;	7337
	105:41	He o the rock, and water gushed out;	7337
	106:17	The earth o up and swallowed Dathan;	7337
	109: 2	and deceitful men have o their mouths	7337
SS	5: 6	I o for my lover, but my lover had left;	7337
	7:12	if their blossoms have o,	7337
Isa	10:14	or o its mouth to chirp.' "	7198
	24:18	The floodgates of the heavens are o,	7337
	35: 5	Then will the eyes of the blind be o and	7219
	50: 5	The Sovereign LORD has o my ears,	7337
	57: 8	you climbed into an o and o it wide;	8143
Jer	50:25	The LORD has o his arsenal	7337
La	3:46	"All our enemies have o their mouths wide	7198
Eze	1: 1	heavens were o and I saw visions of God.	7337
	3: 2	So I o my mouth, and he gave me the scroll	7337
	24:27	At that time your mouth will be o;	7337
	33:22	and he o my mouth before the man came	7337
	33:22	my mouth was o and I was no longer silent.	7337
	44: 2	It must not be o;	7337
	46: 1	on the day of the New Moon it is to be o.	7337
	46:12	the gate facing east is to be o for him.	7337
Da	6:10	to his upstairs room where the windows o	10602
	7:10	court was seated, and the books were o.	10602
	10:16	and I o my mouth and began to speak.	7337
Zec	13: 1	a fountain will be o to the house of David	7337
Mt	2:11	Then they o their treasures	487
	3:16	At that moment heaven was o,	487
	7: 7	knock and the door will be o to you.	487
	7: 8	to him who knocks, the door will be o.	487
Mk	7:34	(which means, "Be o!").	1380
	7:35	At this, the man's ears were o,	487
	8:25	Then his eyes were o, his sight was restored,	1332
Lk	1:64	Immediately his mouth was o	487
	3:21	And as he was praying, heaven was o	487
	10:38	a woman named Martha o her home to him.	5685
	11: 9	knock and the door will be o to you.	487
	11:10	to him who knocks, the door will be o.	487

Lk	24:31	their eyes were o and they recognized him,	1380
	24:32	while he talked with us on the road and o	1380
	24:45	Then he o their minds so they could	1380
Jn	9:10	"How then were your eyes o?"	487
	9:14	and the man's eyes was a Sabbath.	487
	9:17	It was your eyes he o."	487
	9:21	But how he can see now, or who o his eyes,	487
	9:30	yet he o my eyes.	487
	11:37	"Could not he who o the eyes of the blind	487
Ac	5:19	the night an angel of the Lord o the doors	487
	5:23	when we o them, we found no one inside."	487
	9: 8	but when he o his eyes he could see nothing.	487
	9:40	She o her eyes, and seeing Peter she sat up.	487
	10:11	He saw heaven o and something like	487
	12:10	It o for them by itself, and they went through	487
	12:16	and when they o the door and saw him,	487
	14:27	through them and how he had o the door	487
	16:14	The Lord o her heart to respond	1380
Ro	1:10	way may be o for me to come to you.	2338
1Co	16: 9	a great door for effective work has o to me,	487
2Co	2:12	and found that the Lord had o a door for me,	487
	6:11	Corinthians, and o wide our hearts to you.	4425
Heb	10:20	and living way o for us through the curtain,	1590
Rev	6: 1	as the Lamb o the first of the seven seals.	487
	6: 3	When the Lamb o the second seal,	487
	6: 5	When the Lamb o the third seal,	487
	6: 7	When the Lamb o the fourth seal,	487
	6: 9	When he o the fifth seal,	487
	6:12	I watched as he o the sixth seal.	487
	8: 1	When he o the seventh seal,	487
	9: 2	When he o the Abyss,	487
	11:19	Then God's temple in heaven was o,	487
	13: 6	He o his mouth to blaspheme God,	487
	15: 5	the tabernacle of the Testimony, was o.	487
	20:12	before the throne, and books were o.	487
	20:12	Another book was o, which is the book of	
		life.	487

OPENHANDED (2) [OPEN, HAND]

Dt	15: 8	Rather be o and freely lend him whatever	
		he needs.	906+3338+7337+7337
	15:11	be o toward your brothers 906+3338+7337+7337	

OPENING (18) [OPEN]

Ex	28:32	with an o for the head in its center.	7023
	28:32	be a woven edge like a collar around this o,	7023
	39:23	with an o in the center of the robe like	7023
	39:23	the center of the robe like the o of a collar,	7023
	39:23	and a band around this o,	7023
2Sa	17:19	o of the well and scattered grain over it.	7156
1Ki	7:31	inside of the stand there was an o that had	7023
	7:31	This o was round,	7023
	7:31	Around its o there was engraving.	7023
1Ch	9:27	of the key for o it each morning.	5158
Eze	40:13	from one parapet o to the opposite one.	7023
Da	3:26	Nebuchadnezzar then approached the o of	10776
Hos	13:13	does not come to the o of the womb.	1201+5402
Mk	2: 4	they made an o in the roof above Jesus and,	689
Jn	9:32	Nobody has ever heard of o the eyes of the	487
Ac	9:25	and lowered him in a basket through an o	NIG
	12:14	so overjoyed she ran back without o it	487
Rev	12:16	the earth helped the woman by o its mouth	487

OPENINGS (8) [OPEN]

Eze	40:16	by narrow parapet o all around, as was	2707
	40:16	the o all around faced inward.	2707
	40:22	Its o, its portico and its palm tree	2707
	40:25	and its portico had narrow o all around,	2707
	40:25	like the o of the others.	2707
	40:29	and its portico had o all around.	2707
	40:33	and its portico had o all around.	2707
	40:36	and it had o all around.	2707

OPENLY (4) [OPEN]

Eze	23:18	she carried on her prostitution o	1655
Mk	1:45	Jesus could no longer enter a town o	5747
Jn	18:20	"I have spoken o to the world,"	4244
Ac	19:18	came and o confessed their evil deeds.	334+2018

OPENS (10) [OPEN]

Nu	16:30	the earth o its mouth and swallows them,	7198
Job	27:19	when he o his eyes, all is gone.	7219
	35:16	So Job o his mouth with empty talk;	7198
Pr	18:16	A gift o the way for the giver	8143
	31:20	She o her arms to the poor	7298
Isa	5:14	and o its mouth without limit;	7196
	22:22	what he o no one can shut,	7337
Jn	10: 3	The watchman o the gate for him,	487
Rev	3: 7	What he o no one can shut,	487
	3:20	If anyone hears my voice and o the door,	487

OPERATION (KJV) See DONE, POWER, WORK

OPHEL (5)

2Ch	27: 3	on the wall at the hill of O.	6755
	33:14	and encircling the hill of O.	6755
Ne	3:26	living on the hill of O made repairs up to	6755
	3:27	the great projecting tower to the wall of O.	6755
	11:21	The temple servants live on the hill of O,	6755

OPHIR (12)

Ge	10:29	**O**, Havilah and Jobab.	234
1Ki	9:28	to **O** and brought back 420 talents of gold,	234
	10:11	(Hiram's ships brought gold from **O**;	234
	22:48	to go to **O** for gold, but they never set sail—	234
1Ch	1:23	**O**, Havilah and Jobab.	234
	29: 4	three thousand talents of gold (gold of **O**)	234
2Ch	8:18	sailed to **O** and brought back four hundred	234
	9:10	the men of Solomon brought gold from **O**;	234
Job	22:24	your **gold of O** to the rocks in the ravines,	234
	28:16	It cannot be bought with the gold of **O**,	234
Ps	45: 9	the royal bride in gold of **O**.	234
Isa	13:12	more rare than the gold of **O**.	234

OPHNI (1)

Jos	18:24	Kephar Ammoni, **O** and Geba—	6756

OPHRAH (8) [BETH OPHRAH]

Jos	18:23	Avvim, Parah, **O**,	6764
Jdg	6:11	under the oak in **O** that belonged to Joash	6764
	6:24	To this day it stands in **O** of the Abiezrites.	6764
	8:27	which he placed in **O**, his town.	6764
	8:32	of his father Joash in **O** of the Abiezrites.	6764
	9: 5	He went to his father's home in **O** and	6764
1Sa	13:17	One turned toward **O** in the vicinity	6764
1Ch	4:14	Meonothai was the father of **O**.	6763

OPINION (2) [OPINIONS]

2Sa	17: 6	If not, **give** us your **o**."	1819
Mt	22:17	Tell us then, what *is* your **o**?	1506

OPINIONS (2) [OPINION]

1Ki	18:21	"How long will you waver between two **o**?	6191
Pr	18: 2	but delights in airing his own **o**.	4213

OPPONENT (3) [OPPOSE]

2Sa	2:16	Then each man grabbed his **o** by the head	8276
1Ki	20:20	and each one struck down his **o**.	408
Job	16: 9	my **o** fastens on me his piercing eyes.	7640

OPPONENT'S (1) [OPPOSE]

2Sa	2:16	and thrust his dagger into his **o** side,	8276

OPPONENTS (2) [OPPOSE]

Pr	18:18	and keeps **strong o** apart.	AIT
Lk	13:17	all his **o** were humiliated,	512

OPPORTUNE (2) [OPPORTUNITY]

Mk	6:21	Finally the **o** time came.	2322
Lk	4:13	he left him until an **o time**.	2789

OPPORTUNITY (17) [OPPORTUNE]

1Sa	18:21	a **second** *o* to become my son-in-law."	AIT
Jer	46:17	he has missed his **o**.'	4595
Mt	26:16	From then on Judas watched for an **o**	2321
Mk	14:11	So he watched for an **o** to hand him over.	2323
Lk	22: 6	and watched for an **o** to hand Jesus over	2321
Ac	25:16	and has had an **o** to defend himself	5536
Ro	7: 8	the **o** afforded by the commandment,	929
	7:11	the **o** afforded by the commandment,	929
1Co	16:12	but he will go when *he* **has the o**.	2320
2Co	5:12	but are giving you an **o** to take pride in us,	929
	11:12	the ground from under those who want an **o**	929
Gal	6:10	Therefore, as we have **o**, let us do good	2789
Eph	5:16	making the most of every **o**,	2789
Php	4:10	but *you* **had no o** to show it.	177
Col	4: 5	**make the most of** every **o**.	1973+2789+3836
1Ti	5:14	and to give the enemy no **o** for slander.	929
Heb	11:15	they would have had **o** to return.	2789

OPPOSE (28) [OPPONENT, OPPONENT'S, OPPONENTS, OPPOSED, OPPOSES, OPPOSING, OPPOSITE, OPPOSITION]

Ex	23:22	and *will* **o** those who oppose you.	7444
	23:22	and will oppose *those who* **o** you.	7675
Nu	16: 3	as a group to **o** Moses and Aaron and said	6584
	22:22	of the LORD stood in the road to **o** him.	8477
	22:32	to **o** you because your path is a reckless one	8477
	22:34	you were standing in the road to **o** me.	7925
Jdg	20:25	came out from Gibeah to **o** them,	7925
1Sa	2:10	*those who* **o** the LORD will be shattered.	8189
Job	11:10	who *can* **o** him?	8740
	23: 6	Would he **o** me with great power?	6643+8189
	23:13	"But he stands alone, and who *can* **o** him?	8740
Ps	55:18	even though many **o** me.	6643
	109: 6	Appoint an evil man to **o** him;	6584
Isa	41:11	those who **o** you will be as nothing	8190
Jer	38: 5	"The king can do nothing to **o** you."	907
	51: 2	they will **o** her on every side in the day	6584
Da	11:30	of the western coastlands *will* **o** him,	928+995
Lk	11:53	teachers of the law began to **o** him fiercely	1923
	14:31	with ten thousand men *to* **o** the one coming	5636
Ac	11:17	who was I to think that I could **o** God?"	3266
	26: 9	that I ought to do all that was possible to **o**	1885
1Co	16: 9	and there are many who **o** me.	512
Php	1:28	in any way by those who **o** you.	512
2Th	2: 4	He will **o** and will exalt himself	512
2Ti	2:25	Those who **o** him he must gently instruct,	507
	3: 8	so also these men **o** the truth—	468

Tit	1: 9	and refute those who **o** it.	515
	2: 8	that those who **o** you may be ashamed	1666+1885

OPPOSED (11) [OPPOSE]

Ex	15: 7	down *those who* **o** you.	7756
2Ch	13: 7	and **o** Rehoboam son of Solomon	599+6584
Ezr	10:15	and Shabbethai the Levite, **o** this.	6584+6641
Jer	50:24	and captured because *you* **o** the LORD.	1741
Ac	13: 8	(for that is what his name means) **o** them	468
	18: 6	when the Jews **o** Paul and became abusive,	530
Gal	2:11	I **o** him to his face,	468
	3:21	therefore, **o** to the promises of God?	2848
Col	2:14	was against us and that **stood o** to us;	1639+5641
2Ti	3: 8	Just as Jannes and Jambres **o** Moses,	468
	4:15	because *he* strongly **o** our message.	468

OPPOSES (5) [OPPOSE]

Mk	3:26	And if Satan **o** himself and is divided,	482+2093
Lk	23: 2	*He* **o** payment of taxes to Caesar and claims	3266
Jn	19:12	Anyone who claims to be a king **o** Caesar."	515
Jas	4: 6	"God **o** the proud but gives grace to the humble."	530
1Pe	5: 5	"God **o** the proud but gives grace to the humble."	530

OPPOSING (3) [OPPOSE]

2Ch	35:21	God has told me to hurry; so stop **o** God,	4946
1Ti	6:20	from godless chatter and the **o** ideas	509
Jas	5: 6	innocent man, *who were* not **o** you.	530

OPPOSITE (49) [OPPOSE]

Ge	15:10	and arranged the halves **o** each other;	7925
Ex	14: 2	**directly o** Baal Zephon.	4200+5790+7156
	14: 9	near Pi Hahiroth, **o** Baal Zephon.	4200+7156
	26: 5	with the loops **o** each other.	7691
	26:35	the tabernacle and put the lampstand **o** it on	5790
	30: 4	two on **o sides**—	7396+7521
	36:12	with the loops **o** each other.	7691
	37:27	two on **o sides**—	7396+7521
	40:24	of Meeting **o** the table on the south side of	5790
Dt	1: 1	**o** Suph, between Paran and Tophel, Laban,	4578
	34: 6	in the valley **o** Beth Peor,	4578
Jos	3:16	So the people crossed over **o** Jericho.	5584
1Sa	20:25	**o** Jonathan, and Abner sat next to Saul,	7756
2Sa	16:13	along the hillside **o** him,	4200+6645
1Ki	20:27	The Israelites camped **o** them	5584
	20:29	For seven days they camped **o** each other,	5790
	21:10	But seat two scoundrels **o** him	5584
	21:13	Then two scoundrels came and sat **o** him	5584
1Ch	19:17	and formed his battle lines **o** them.	448
2Ch	7: 6	**O** the Levites, the priests blew their trumpets	5584
Ne	3:10	of Harumaph made repairs **o** his house,	5584
	3:16	made repairs up to a point **o** the tombs	5584
	3:25	Palal son of Uzai worked **o** the angle	4946+5584
	3:26	to a point **o** the Water Gate toward the east	5584
	3:29	of Immer made repairs **o** his house.	5584
	3:30	made repairs **o** his living quarters.	5584
	3:31	and the merchants, **o** the Inspection Gate,	5584
	12: 9	stood **o** them in the services.	4200+5584
	12:24	who stood **o** them to give praise	4200+5584
	12:38	proceeded in the **o direction**.	4578
Eze	16:34	in your prostitution you are the **o** of others;	2201
	16:34	You are the **very o**, for you give payment	2201
	40:13	of one alcove to the top of the **o**,	2257S
	40:13	from one parapet opening to the **o** one.	5584
	40:22	with its portico **o** them,	4200+7156
	40:23	He measured from one gate to the **o** one;	9133S
	40:26	with its portico **o** them;	4200+7156
	42: 1	to the rooms **o** the temple courtyard	5584
	42: 1	the temple courtyard and **o** the outer wall	5584
	42: 3	from the inner court and in the section **o**	5584
	42:10	temple courtyard and **o** the outer wall,	448+7156
	46: 9	but each is to go out the **o** gate.	5790
	47:20	be the boundary to a point **o** Lebo Hamath.	5790
Da	12: 5	this bank of the river and one on the **o** bank.	2178
Mt	27:61	and the other Mary were sitting there **o**	595
Mk	12:41	Jesus sat down **o** the place where	2978
	13: 3	on the Mount of Olives **o** the temple,	2978
Jn	6:22	the crowd that had stayed **on the o shore** of	4305
Ac	27: 7	we sailed to the lee of Crete, **o** Salmone.	2848

OPPOSITION (7) [OPPOSE]

Nu	16:19	Korah had gathered all his followers **in o** to	6584
	16:42	when the assembly gathered **in o** to Moses	6584
	20: 2	people gathered **in o** to Moses and Aaron.	6584
Jdg	9:25	**In o** to him these citizens of Shechem	4200
Ac	6: 9	**O** arose, however, from members of	482
1Th	2: 2	to tell you his gospel in spite of strong **o**.	74
Heb	12: 3	Consider him who endured such **o**	517

OPPRESS (28) [OPPRESSED, OPPRESSES, OPPRESSING, OPPRESSION, OPPRESSIVE, OPPRESSOR, OPPRESSORS]

Ex	1:11	over them to **o** them with forced labor.	6700
	22:21	"Do not mistreat an alien or **o** him,	4315
	23: 9	"Do not **o** an alien;	4315
Dt	23:16	Do not **o** him.	3561
2Sa	7:10	Wicked people *will* not **o** them anymore,	6700
1Ch	16:21	He allowed no man to **o** them;	6943
	17: 9	Wicked people *will* not **o** them anymore,	1162
Job	10: 3	Does it please you *to* **o** me,	6943

Job	37:23	and great righteousness, *he does* not **o**.	6700
Ps	89:22	no wicked man *will* **o** him.	6700
	94: 5	*they* **o** your inheritance.	6700
	105:14	He allowed no one to **o** them;	6943
	119:122	*let* not the arrogant **o** me.	6943
Isa	3: 5	People *will* **o** each other—	5601
	3:12	Youths who **o** my people,	5601
Jer	7: 6	if *you do* not **o** the alien,	6943
	30:20	I will punish all *who* **o** them.	4315
Eze	18: 7	*He does* not **o** anyone,	3561
	18:16	not **o** anyone or require a pledge for a loan.	3561
	22:29	they **o** the poor and needy and mistreat	3561
	45: 8	my princes *will* no longer **o** my people	3561
Da	7:25	against the Most High and **o** his saints	10106
Am	4: 1	you women who **o** the poor and crush	6943
	5:12	*You* **o** the righteous and take bribes	7674
	6:14	*that will* **o** you all the way	4315
Zec	7:10	*Do* not **o** the widow or the fatherless,	6943
	11: 6	*They will* **o** the land,	4198
Mal	3: 5	who **o** the widows and the fatherless,	NIH

OPPRESSED (47) [OPPRESS]

Ex	1:12	But the more they *were* **o**,	6700
Dt	28:29	day after day you will be **o** and robbed,	6943
Jdg	2:18	on them as they groaned under *those who* **o**	4315
	4: 3	and *had* cruelly **o** the Israelites	4315
	10: 8	For eighteen years they **o** all the Israelites	NIH
	10:12	the Maonites **o** you and you cried to me	4315
1Sa	10:18	of Egypt and all the kingdoms that **o** you.'	4315
	12: 3	Whom *have* I **o**?	8368
	12: 4	"You have not cheated or **o** us,"	8368
2Ki	13:22	Hazael king of Aram **o** Israel throughout	4315
2Ch	16:10	At the same time Asa **brutally o** some of	8368
Ne	9:27	over to their enemies, *who* **o** them.	7674
	9:27	when they were **o** they cried out to you.	7650
Job	20:19	*he has* **o** the poor and left them destitute;	8368
Ps	9: 9	The LORD is a refuge for the **o**,	1916
	10:18	defending the fatherless and the **o**,	1916
	42: 9	go about mourning, **o** by the enemy?"	4316
	43: 2	go about mourning, **o** by the enemy?	4316
	74:21	Do not let the **o** retreat in disgrace;	1916
	82: 3	maintain the rights of the poor and **o**.	8133
	103: 6	and justice for all the **o**.	6943
	106:42	Their enemies **o** them and subjected them	4315
	129: 1	*They have* greatly **o** me from my youth—	7675
	129: 2	*they have* greatly **o** me from my youth,	7675
	146: 7	of the **o** and gives food to the hungry.	6943
Pr	15:15	All the days of the **o** are wretched,	6714
	16:19	and among the **o** than to share plunder with	6705
	31: 5	and deprive all the **o** of their rights.	1201+6715
Ecc	4: 1	I saw the tears of the **o**—	6943
	5: 8	If you see the poor **o** in a district,	6945
Isa	1:17	Seek justice, encourage the **o**.	2787
	10: 2	and withhold justice from the **o**	6714
	26: 6	the feet of the **o**, the footsteps of the poor.	6714
	52: 4	lately, Assyria *has* **o** them.	6943
	53: 7	He *was* **o** and afflicted,	5601
	58: 6	to set the **o** free and break every yoke?	8368
	58:10	the hungry and satisfy the needs of the **o**,	6700
Jer	50:33	"The people of Israel *are* **o**,	6943
Eze	22: 7	*they have* **o** the alien and	928+2021+6913+6945
Da	4:27	your wickedness by being kind to the **o**.	10559
Hos	5:11	Ephraim *is* **o**, trampled in judgment,	6943
Am	2: 7	of the ground and deny justice to the **o**.	6705
Zep	3:19	At that time I will deal with all *who* **o** you;	6700
Zec	10: 2	the people wander like sheep **o** for lack of	6700
	10:14	particularly the **o** of the flock.	6714
Lk	4:18	sight for the blind, to release the **o**,	2575
Ac	7:19	and **o** our forefathers by forcing them	2808

OPPRESSES (4) [OPPRESS]

Pr	14:31	*He who* **o** the poor shows contempt	6943
	22:16	*He who* **o** the poor to increase his wealth	6943
	28: 3	A ruler *who* **o** the poor is like a driving rain	6943
Eze	18:12	*He* **o** the poor and needy.	3561

OPPRESSING (3) [OPPRESS]

Ex	3: 9	the way the Egyptians *are* **o** them.	4315
Nu	10: 9	against an enemy who *is* **o** you,	7675
2Ki	13: 4	how **severely** the king of Aram *was* **o**	4315+4316

OPPRESSION (20) [OPPRESS]

Dt	26: 7	and saw our misery, toil and **o**.	4316
	28:33	but cruel **o** all your days.	6943
Job	35: 9	"Men cry out under a load of **o**;	6935
Ps	12: 5	Because of the **o** *of* the weak and	8719
	44:24	and forget our misery and **o**?	4316
	72:14	He will rescue them from **o** and violence,	9412
	73: 8	in their arrogance they threaten **o**.	6945
	107:39	and they were humbled by **o**,	6808
	119:134	Redeem me from the **o** *of* men,	6945
Ecc	4: 1	the **o** that was taking place under the sun:	6935
Isa	30:12	relied on **o** and depended on deceit,	6945
	53: 8	By **o** and judgment he was taken away.	6808
	58: 9	"If you do away with the yoke of **o**,	NIH
	59:13	fomenting **o** and revolt,	6945
Jer	6: 6	it is filled with **o**.	6945
	22:17	on shedding innocent blood and on **o**	6945
Eze	22:29	up your violence and evil and do what is just	6945
Hos	8:10	They will begin to waste away under the **o**	5362
Am	3: 9	within her and the **o** among her people."	6935
Ac	7:34	I have indeed seen the **o** of my people	2810

OPPRESSIVE (3) [OPPRESS]
Jdg 6: 2 Because the power of Midian *was so* o, 6451
Ps 73:16 I tried to understand all this, it was o to me 6662
Isa 10: 1 to those who issue o decrees, 6662

OPPRESSOR (14) [OPPRESS]
Ps 72: 4 he will crush the o. 6943
  78:42 the day he redeemed them from the o, 7640
Pr 29:13 and the o have this in common: 408+9412
Isa 9: 4 the rod of their o. 5601
  14: 4 How the o has come to an end! 5601
  16: 4 The o will come to an end, 5160
  51:13 because of the wrath of the o, 7439
  51:13 For where is the wrath of the o? 7439
Jer 21:12 of his o the one who has been robbed, 6943
  22: 3 of his o the one who has been robbed, 6934
  25:38 because of the sword of the o and because 3561
  46:16 away from the sword of the o.' 3561
  50:16 let everyone return to his own people, 3561
Zec 9: 8 Never again will an o overrun my people, 5601

OPPRESSORS (9) [OPPRESS]
Jdg 6: 9 of Egypt and from the hand of all your o. 4315
Ps 27:11 lead me in a straight path because of my o. 8806
  119:121 do not leave me to my o. 6943
Ecc 4: 1 power was on the side of their o— 6943
Isa 14: 2 of their captors and rule over their o. 5601
  19:20 to the LORD because of them o, 4315
  49:26 I will make your o eat their own flesh; 3561
  60:14 sons of your o will come bowing before you 6700
Zep 3: 1 Woe to the city of o, rebellious and defiled! 3561

OPTIONS (2)
2Sa 24:12 I am giving you three o. AIT
1Ch 21:10 I am giving you three o. AIT

OR (1970)
Ge 3: 3 and you must not touch it, o you will die.' " 7153
  13: 8 o between your herdsmen and mine, 2256
  14:23 not even a thread o the thong of a sandal, 2256
  17:12 including those born in your household o 2256
  17:13 *Whether* born in your household o bought 2256
  17:23 in his household o bought with his money, 2256
  17:27 in his household o bought from a foreigner, 2256
  19:12 sons-in-law, sons o daughters, 2256
  19:12 o anyone else in the city who belongs 2256
  19:15 o you will be swept away when 7153
  19:17 the mountains o you will be swept away!" 7153
  19:33 of it when she lay down o when she got up. 2256
  19:35 of it when she lay down o when she got up. 2256
  21:23 with me o my children or my descendants. 2256
  21:23 with me or my children o my descendants. 2256
  24:21 to learn whether o not 561
  24:50 we can say nothing to you one way o 196
  24:55 "Let the girl remain with us ten days o so; 196
  26:11 "Anyone who molests this man o his wife 2256
  27:21 whether you really are my son Esau o 561
  30: 1 "Give me children, o I'll die!" 401+561+2256
  30:32 from them every speckled o spotted sheep, 2256
  30:32 and every spotted o speckled goat. 2256
  30:33 in my possession that is not speckled o 2256
  30:33 o any lamb that is not dark-colored, 2256
  30:35 the male goats that were streaked o spotted, 2256
  30:35 the speckled o spotted female goats 2256
  30:39 And they bore young that were streaked o NIH
  30:39 that were streaked or speckled o spotted. 2256
  31:10 the flock were streaked, speckled o spotted. 2256
  31:12 the flock are streaked, speckled o spotted, 2256
  31:24 to say anything to Jacob, either good o bad. 6330
  31:29 to say anything to Jacob, either good o bad. 6330
  31:39 from me for whatever was stolen by day o 2256
  31:43 about the children they have borne? 196
  31:50 If you mistreat my daughters o if 2256
  38:23 o we will become a laughingstock. 7153
  39:10 he refused to go to bed with her o even be NIH
  41:44 without your word no one will lift hand o 2256
  44: 8 So why would we steal silver o gold 196
  44:19 'Do you have a father o a brother?' 196
Ex 1:10 we must deal shrewdly with them o 7153
  4: 1 "What if they do not believe me o listen 2256
  4: 8 "If they do not believe you o pay attention 2256
  4: 9 But if they do not believe these two signs o 2256
  4:11 Who makes him deaf o mute? 196
  4:11 Who gives him sight o makes him blind? 196
  5: 3 o he may strike us with plagues or with 7153
  5: 3 or he may strike us with plagues o with 196
  5:14 of bricks yesterday o today, 1685
  9:14 o this time I will send the full force 3954
  10:15 Nothing green remained on tree o plant 2256
  10:23 No one could see anyone else o 2256
  11: 6 worse than there has ever been o ever will 2256
  11: 7 not a dog will bark at any man o animal.' 2256
  12: 5 and you may take them from the sheep o 2256
  12: 9 Do not eat the meat raw o cooked in water, 2256
  12:19 whether he is an alien o native-born. 2256
  13: 2 whether man o animal." 2256
  13:21 so that they could travel by day o night. 2256
  16:24 and it did not stink o get maggots in it. 2256
  17: 7 "Is the LORD among us o not?" 561
  19:12 that you do not go up the mountain o touch 2256
  19:13 surely be stoned o shot with arrows; 196
  19:13 Whether man o animal, 561
  19:22 o the LORD will break out against them." 7153
  19:24 o he will break out against them." 7153

Ex 20: 4 the form of anything in heaven above o on 2256
  20: 4 on the earth beneath o in the waters below. 2256
  20: 5 not bow down to them o worship them; 2256
  20:10 neither you, nor your son o daughter, 2256
  20:10 nor your manservant o maidservant, 2256
  20:17 o his manservant or maidservant, 2256
  20:17 or his manservant o maidservant, 2256
  20:17 his ox o donkey, 2256
  20:17 o anything that belongs to your neighbor." 2256
  20:19 do not have God speak to us o we will die." 7153
  20:23 do not make for yourselves gods of silver o 2256
  21: 4 a wife and she bears him sons o daughters, 196
  21: 6 the door o the doorpost and pierce his ear 196
  21:15 "Anyone who attacks his father o his mother 2256
  21:16 and either sells him o still has him 196
  21:17 "Anyone who curses his father o his mother 2256
  21:18 a stone o with his fist and he does not die 196
  21:20 a man beats his male o female slave with 196
  21:21 if the slave gets up after a day o two, 196
  21:26 "If a man hits a manservant o maidservant, 196
  21:27 the tooth of a manservant o maidservant, 196
  21:28 "If a bull gores a man o a woman to death, 196
  21:29 not kept it penned up and it kills a man o 196
  21:31 also applies if the bull gores a son o 196
  21:32 If the bull gores a male o female slave, 196
  21:33 a man uncovers a pit o digs one and fails 196
  21:33 or digs one and fails to cover it and an ox o 196
  22: 1 an ox o a sheep and slaughters it or sells it, 196
  22: 1 an ox or a sheep and slaughters it o sells it, 196
  22: 4 whether ox o donkey or sheep— 6330
  22: 4 whether ox or donkey o sheep— 6330
  22: 5 "If a man grazes his livestock in a field o 196
  22: 5 from the best of his own field o vineyard. 2256
  22: 6 of grain o standing grain or the whole field, 196
  22: 6 of grain or standing grain o the whole field, 196
  22: 7 "If a man gives his neighbor silver o goods 196
  22: 9 o any other lost property NIH
  22:10 o any other animal to his neighbor 2256
  22:10 and it dies o is injured or is taken away 196
  22:10 for safekeeping and it dies or is injured o 196
  22:14 and it is injured o dies while the owner is 196
  22:21 "Do not mistreat an alien o oppress him, 2256
  22:22 not take advantage of a widow o an orphan. 196
  22:28 "Do not blaspheme God o curse the ruler 2256
  22:29 from your granaries o your vats. 2256
  23: 4 "If you come across your enemy's ox o 196
  23: 7 and do not put an innocent o honest person 2256
  23:24 down before their gods o worship them 2256
  23:24 or worship them o follow their practices. 2256
  23:26 and none will miscarry o be barren 2256
  23:32 a covenant with them o with their gods. 2256
  23:33 o they will cause you to sin against me, 7153
  28:43 of Meeting o approach the altar to minister 196
  29:34 the ordination ram o any bread is left over 2256
  30: 9 not offer on this altar any other incense o 2256
  30: 9 or any burnt offering o grain offering, 2256
  30:14 those twenty years old o more, 2256
  34: 3 come with you o be seen anywhere on 1685+2256
  34:12 o they will be a snare among you. 7153
  34:19 whether from herd o flock. 2256
  34:28 and forty nights without eating bread o 2256
  35:23 purple o scarlet yarn or fine linen, 2256
  35:23 purple or scarlet yarn o fine linen, 2256
  35:23 or scarlet yarn or fine linen, o goat hair, 2256
  35:23 ram skins dyed red o hides 2256
  35:24 of silver o bronze brought it as an offering 2256
  35:25 blue, purple o scarlet yarn or fine linen. NIH
  35:25 blue, purple or scarlet yarn o fine linen. 2256
  36: 6 "No man o woman is to make anything else 2256
  38:26 twenty years old o more, a total of 603,550 2256
  40:32 the Tent of Meeting o approached the altar, 2256
Lev 1: 2 an animal from **either** the herd o the flock. 2256
  1:10 from **either** the sheep o the goats, 196
  1:14 he is to offer a dove o a young pigeon. 196
  2: 4 o wafers made without yeast and spread 2256
  2:11 for you are not to burn any yeast o honey in 2256
  3: 1 whether male o female, 561
  3: 3 that covers the inner parts o is connected 2256
  3: 6 to offer a male o female without defect. 196
  3: 9 that covers the inner parts o is connected 2256
  3:14 that covers the inner parts o is connected 2256
  3:17 You must not eat any fat o any blood.' " 2256
  4: 8 that covers the inner parts o is connected 2256
  5: 1 to testify regarding something he has seen o 196
  5: 2 " 'O if a person touches anything ceremonially unclean— 196
  5: 2 the carcasses of unclean wild animals o 196
  5: 3 of unclean livestock o of unclean creatures 196
  5: 3 " 'O if he touches human uncleanness— 196
  5: 4 " 'O if a person thoughtlessly takes an oath 196
  5: 4 whether good o evil— 196
  5: 6 to the LORD a female lamb o goat from 196
  5: 7 to bring two doves o two young pigeons to 196
  5:11 cannot afford two doves o two young 196
  5:11 He must not put oil o incense on it, 2256
  6: 2 about something entrusted to him o left 196
  6: 2 to him or left in his care o stolen, 196
  6: 2 o if he cheats him, 196
  6: 3 o if he finds lost property and lies about it, 196
  6: 3 o if he swears falsely, 2256
  6: 4 o if he commits any such sin NIH
  6: 4 he must return what he has stolen o taken 196
  6: 4 o what was entrusted to him, 196
  6: 5 o whatever it was he swore falsely about. 196
  7: 9 Every grain offering baked in an oven o 2256
  7: 9 or cooked in a pan o on a griddle belongs 2256

Lev 7:10 whether mixed with oil o 2256
  7:16 the result of a vow o is a freewill offering, 196
  7:21 whether human uncleanness o 196
  7:21 or an unclean animal o any unclean, 196
  7:23 'Do not eat any of the fat of cattle, sheep o 2256
  7:24 The fat of an animal found dead o torn 2256
  7:26 you must not eat the blood of any bird o 2256
  10: 6 o you will die and the LORD will 2256+4202
  10: 7 to the Tent of Meeting o you will 7153
  10: 9 "You and your sons are not to drink wine o 2256
  10: 9 the Tent of Meeting, o you will die. 2256+4202
  11: 4 "There are some that only chew the cud o 2256
  11: 8 not eat their meat o touch their carcasses; 2256
  11:10 in the seas o streams that do not have fins 2256
  11:10 whether among all the swarming things o 2256
  11:22 katydid, cricket o grasshopper. 2256
  11:26 a split hoof not completely divided o 2256
  11:32 whether it is made of wood, cloth, hide o 196
  11:35 an oven o cooking pot must be broken up. 2256
  11:36 A spring, however, o a cistern 2256
  11:42 whether it moves on its belly o 2256
  11:42 or walks on all fours o on many feet; 6330
  11:43 by means of them o be made unclean 2256
  12: 4 She must not touch anything sacred o go to 2256
  12: 6 of her purification for a son o daughter she 196
  12: 6 a young pigeon o a dove for a sin offering. 196
  12: 7 for the woman who gives birth to a boy o 196
  12: 8 to bring two doves o two young pigeons, 196
  13: 2 "When anyone has a swelling o a rash or 196
  13: 2 "When anyone has a swelling o a rash 196
  13: 2 he must be brought to Aaron the priest o 196
  13:19 a white swelling o reddish-white spot 196
  13:24 and a reddish-white o white spot appears in 196
  13:29 "If a man o woman has a sore on the head 196
  13:29 a man or woman has a sore on the head o 196
  13:30 an infectious disease of the head o chin. 196
  13:38 "When a man o woman has white spots on 196
  13:42 a reddish-white sore on his bald head o 196
  13:42 on his head o forehead. 196
  13:43 on his head o forehead is reddish-white like 196
  13:47 any woolen o linen clothing, 196
  13:48 any woven o knitted material of linen 196
  13:48 any woven or knitted material of linen o 2256
  13:48 any leather o anything made of leather— 196
  13:49 o leather, or woven or knitted material, 196
  13:49 or leather, o woven or knitted material, 196
  13:49 or leather, or woven o knitted material, 196
  13:49 o any leather article, is greenish o reddish, 196
  13:49 or any leather article, is greenish o reddish, 196
  13:51 o the woven or knitted material, 196
  13:51 or the woven o knitted material, 196
  13:51 o the leather, whatever its use, 196
  13:52 o the woven or knitted material of wool 196
  13:52 or the woven o knitted material of wool 196
  13:52 or the woven or knitted material of wool o 196
  13:52 o any leather article that has 196
  13:53 o the woven or knitted material, 196
  13:53 or the woven o knitted material, 196
  13:53 o the leather article, 196
  13:55 whether the mildew has affected one side o 196
  13:56 the contaminated part out of the clothing, o 196
  13:56 o the woven or knitted material, 196
  13:56 or the woven o knitted material. 196
  13:57 in the woven o knitted material, 196
  13:57 or in the woven o knitted material, 196
  13:57 o in the leather article, it is spreading, 196
  13:58 o the woven or knitted material, 196
  13:58 or the woven o knitted material, 196
  13:58 o any leather article that has been washed 196
  13:59 by mildew in woolen o linen clothing, 196
  13:59 woven o knitted material, 196
  13:59 o any leather article, 196
  13:59 for pronouncing them clean o unclean. 196
  14:22 and two doves o two young pigeons, 196
  14:30 Then he shall sacrifice the doves o 196
  14:37 and if it has greenish o reddish depressions 196
  14:47 Anyone who sleeps o eats in 2256
  14:55 for mildew in clothing o in a house, 2256
  14:56 and for a swelling, a rash o a bright spot, 2256
  14:57 to determine when something is clean o 2256
  15: 3 Whether it continues flowing from his body o is blocked, 196
  15:14 On the eighth day he must take two doves o 196
  15:17 Any clothing o leather that has semen 2256
  15:23 the bed o anything she was sitting on, 2256
  15:25 a time other than her monthly period o has 196
  15:29 the eighth day she must take two doves o 196
  15:33 for a man o a woman with a discharge, 2256
  16: 2 on the ark, o else he will die, 2256
  16:29 whether native-born o an alien living 2256
  17: 3 a lamb o a goat in the camp or outside of it 196
  17: 3 a lamb or a goat in the camp o outside of it 196
  17: 8 'Any Israelite o any alien living 2256
  17: 8 among them who offers a burnt offering o 196
  17:10 " 'Any Israelite o any alien living 2256
  17:13 " 'Any Israelite o any alien living 2256
  17:13 among you who hunts any animal o bird 196
  17:15 " 'Anyone, whether native-born o alien, 2256
  17:15 who eats anything found dead o torn 196
  18: 9 **either** your father's daughter o 196
  18: 9 whether she was born in the same home o 196
  18:10 with your son's daughter o 2256
  18:17 **either** her son's daughter o 2256
  19: 4 not turn to idols o make gods of cast metal 2256
  19: 6 the day you sacrifice it o on the next day; 2256
  19: 9 not reap to the very edges of your field o 2256
  19: 9 not reap to the very edges of your field o 2256
  19:10 over your vineyard a second time o pick up 2256

Ref	Text	No.
Lev 19:13	" 'Do not defraud your neighbor o rob him.	2256
19:14	the deaf o put a stumbling block in front of	2256
19:15	not show partiality to the poor o favoritism	2256
19:18	" 'Do not seek revenge o bear a grudge	2256
19:20	not been ransomed o given her freedom,	196
19:26	" 'Do not practice divination o sorcery.	2256
19:27	the hair at the sides of your head o clip off	2256
19:28	the dead o put tattoo marks on yourselves.	2256
19:29	o the land will turn to prostitution and	2256+4202
19:31	not turn to mediums o seek out spiritists,	2256
19:35	when measuring length, weight o quantity.	2256
20: 2	'Any Israelite o any alien living	2256
20: 9	" 'If anyone curses his father o mother,	2256
20: 9	He has cursed his father o his mother,	2256
20:17	daughter of **either** his father o his mother,	196
20:19	of **either** your mother o your father, for	2256
20:25	not defile yourselves by any animal o bird	2256
20:25	or bird o anything that moves along	2256
20:27	" 'A man o woman who is a medium	196
20:27	" 'A man or woman who is a medium o	196
21: 2	such as his mother o father,	2256
21: 2	his son o daughter, his brother,	2256
21: 3	o an unmarried sister who is dependent	2256
21: 5	not shave their heads o shave off the edges	2256
21: 5	the edges of their beards o cut their bodies.	2256
21: 7	not marry women defiled by prostitution o	2256
21:10	must not let his hair become unkempt o	2256
21:11	even for his father o mother,	2256
21:12	the sanctuary of his God o desecrate it,	2256
21:14	o a woman defiled by prostitution,	2256
21:18	no man who is blind o lame,	196
21:18	disfigured o deformed;	196
21:19	no man with a crippled foot o hand,	196
21:20	o who is hunchbacked or dwarfed,	196
21:20	or who is hunchbacked o dwarfed,	196
21:20	o who has any eye defect,	196
21:20	o who has festering or running sores	196
21:20	or who has festering o running sores	196
21:20	or who has festering or running sores o	196
21:23	not go near the curtain o approach the altar,	2256
22: 4	of Aaron has an infectious skin disease o	196
22: 4	a corpse o anyone who has an emission	196
22: 5	o if he touches any crawling thing	196
22: 5	o any person who makes him unclean,	196
22: 8	He must not eat anything found dead o torn	2256
22:10	of a priest o his hired worker eat it.	2256
22:11	o if a slave is born in his household,	2256
22:13	if a priest's daughter becomes a widow o	2256
22:18	**either** an Israelite o an alien living	2256
22:18	**either** to fulfill a vow o as a freewill	2256
22:19	sheep o goats in order that it may	2256
22:21	from the herd o flock a fellowship offering	196
22:21	to the LORD to fulfill a special vow o as	2256
22:21	without defect o blemish to be acceptable.	4202
22:22	the injured o the maimed,	196
22:22	o anything with warts or festering	196
22:22	with warts o festering or running sores.	196
22:22	with warts or festering o running sores.	196
22:23	an ox o a sheep that is deformed or stunted,	2256
22:23	an ox or a sheep that is deformed o stunted,	2256
22:24	are bruised, crushed, torn o cut.	2256
22:27	a lamb o a goat is born,	196
22:28	not slaughter a cow o a sheep and its young	196
23:14	o roasted or new grain,	2256
23:14	or roasted o new grain,	2256
23:22	not reap to the very edges of your field o	2256
24:16	Whether an alien o native-born,	3869
25: 4	not sow your fields o prune your vineyards.	2256
25: 5	Do not reap what grows of itself o harvest	2256
25:11	not reap what grows of itself o harvest	2256
25:14	of your countrymen o buy any from him,	196
25:20	if we do not plant o harvest our crops?"	2256
25:35	help him as you would an alien o	2256
25:37	You must not lend him money at interest o	2256
25:40	as a hired worker o a temporary resident	NIH
25:47	" 'If an alien o a temporary resident	2256
25:47	the alien living among you o to a member	196
25:49	An uncle o a cousin or any blood relative	196
25:49	An uncle or a cousin o any blood relative	196
25:49	O if he prospers, he may redeem himself.	196
26: 1	" 'Do not make idols o set up an image or	2256
26: 1	or set up an image o a sacred stone	2256
26:44	I will not reject them o abhor them so as	2256
27: 7	If it is a person sixty years old o more,	2256
27:10	not exchange it o substitute a good one for	2256
27:10	o a bad one for a good one;	196
27:12	who will judge its quality as good o	2256
27:14	the priest will judge its quality as good o	2256
27:20	o if he has sold it to someone else,	2256
27:26	whether an ox o a sheep, it is the LORD's.	561
27:28	whether man o animal or family land—	2256
27:28	whether man or animal o family land—	2256
27:28	may be sold o redeemed;	2256
27:30	from the soil o fruit from the trees, belongs	4946
27:33	from the bad o make any substitution.	2256
Nu 1: 3	the men in Israel twenty years old o more	2256
1:18	and the men twenty years old o more	2256
1:20	All the men twenty years old o more	2256
1:22	All the men twenty years old o more	2256
1:24	All the men twenty years old o more	2256
1:26	All the men twenty years old o more	2256
1:28	All the men twenty years old o more	2256
1:30	All the men twenty years old o more	2256
1:32	All the men twenty years old o more	2256
1:34	All the men twenty years old o more	2256
1:36	All the men twenty years old o more	2256
1:38	All the men twenty years old o more	2256
Nu 1:40	All the men twenty years old o more	2256
1:42	All the men twenty years old o more	2256
1:45	All the Israelites twenty years old o more	2256
1:49	not count the tribe of Levi o include them	2256
3:13	whether man o animal.	6330
3:15	Count every male a month old o more."	2256
3:22	number of all the males a month old o more	2256
3:28	number of all the males a month old o more	2256
3:34	number of all the males a month old o more	2256
3:39	including every male a month old o more,	2256
3:40	a month old o more and make a list	2256
3:43	of firstborn males a month old o more,	2256
4:15	But they must not touch the holy things o	2256
4:20	even for a moment, o they will die.	2256
4:27	whether carrying o doing other work,	2256
5: 2	an infectious skin disease o a discharge	2256
5: 2	o who is ceremonially unclean because of	2256
5: 6	a man o woman wrongs another in any way	196
5:14	o if he is jealous and suspects her even	196
5:15	He must not pour oil on it o put incense	2256
5:30	o when feelings of jealousy come over	196
6: 2	'If a man o woman wants to make	196
6: 3	from wine o from other fermented drink.	2256
6: 3	not drink grape juice o eat grapes or raisins.	2256
6: 3	not drink grape juice or eat grapes o raisins.	2256+3313+4300+6694
6: 4	not even the seeds o skins.	2256
6: 7	Even if his own father o mother or brother	2256
6: 7	Even if his own father or mother o brother	NIH
6: 7	or mother or brother o sister dies,	2256
6:10	the eighth day he must bring two doves o	196
8:17	whether man o animal, is mine.	2256
8:24	Men twenty-five years old o more	2256
9:10	of you o your descendants are unclean	196
9:10	of a dead body o are away on a journey,	196
9:12	They must not leave any of it till morning o	2256
9:21	Whether by day o by night,	2256
9:22	over the tabernacle for two days o a month	196
9:22	the tabernacle for two days or a month o	196
11: 8	then ground it in a handmill o crushed it in	196
11: 8	They cooked it in a pot o made it	2256
11:19	o two days, or five, ten or twenty days,	2256
11:19	or two days, or five, ten or twenty days,	2256
11:19	or two days, or five, ten o twenty days,	2256
11:23	You will now see whether o not	561
13:18	the people who live there are strong o weak,	2022
13:18	or weak, few o many.	561
13:19	Is it good o bad?	561
13:19	Are they unwalled o fortified?	561
13:20	Is it fertile o poor?	561
13:20	Are there trees on it o not?	561
14: 2	O in this desert!	196
14:29	every one of you twenty years old o more	2256
15: 3	from the herd o the flock,	196
15: 3	**whether** burnt offerings o sacrifices,	196
15: 3	for special vows o freewill offerings	196
15: 3	or freewill offerings o festival offerings—	196
15: 5	With each lamb for the burnt offering o	196
15: 8	a young bull as a burnt offering o sacrifice,	196
15: 8	for a special vow o a fellowship offering to	196
15:11	Each bull o ram, each lamb or young goat,	196
15:11	Each bull or ram, each lamb o young goat,	196
15:14	whenever an alien o anyone else living	196
15:29	**whether** he is a native-born Israelite o	2256
15:30	**whether** native-born o alien,	2256
16:14	into a land flowing with milk and honey o	2256
16:26	o you will be swept away because	7153
16:40	o he would become like Korah	2256+4202
18: 3	the furnishings of the sanctuary o the altar,	2256
18: 3	o both they and you will die.	2256+4202
18: 9	**whether** grain o sin or guilt offerings,	2256
18: 9	whether grain or sin o guilt offerings,	2256
18:17	a sheep o a goat; they are holy.	196
18:22	o they will bear the consequences	NIH
18:27	as grain from the threshing floor o juice	2256
18:30	of the threshing floor o the winepress.	2256
19: 2	to bring you a red heifer without defect o	401
19:16	with a sword o someone who has died	196
19:16	o anyone who touches a human bone or	196
19:16	who touches a human bone o a grave,	196
19:18	a human bone o a grave	196
19:18	or a grave o someone who has been killed	196
19:18	someone who has been killed o someone	196
20: 5	It has no grain o figs,	2256
20: 5	grapevines o pomegranates.	2256
20:17	not go through any field o vineyard,	2256
20:17	o drink water from any well.	2256
20:17	the right o to the left until we have passed	2256
20:19	we o our livestock drink any of your water,	2256
21:22	not turn aside into any field o vineyard,	2256
21:22	o drink water from any well.	4202
22:18	not do anything great o small to go beyond	196
22:26	the right o to the left.	2256
23:10	of Jacob o number the fourth part of Israel?	2256
24:13	good o bad, to go beyond the command of	196
26: 2	all those twenty years old o more	2256
26: 4	a census of the men twenty years old o more	2256
26:62	a month old o more numbered 23,000.	2256
30: 2	When a man makes a vow to the LORD o	196
30: 3	a vow to the LORD o obligates herself by	2256
30: 4	and her father hears about her vow o pledge	2256
30: 5	none of her vows o the pledges	2256
30: 6	after she makes a vow o after her lips utter	196
30: 7	then her vows o the pledges	2256
30: 8	he nullifies the vow that obligates her o	2256
30: 9	"Any vow o obligation taken by a widow	NIH
30: 9	a widow o divorced woman will be binding	2256
Nu 30:10	a vow o obligates herself by a pledge	196
30:11	then all her vows o the pledges	2256
30:12	then none of the vows o pledges that came	2256
30:13	Her husband may confirm o nullify	2256
30:13	or nullify any vow she makes o any sworn	2256
30:14	then he confirms all her vows o the pledges	196
31:19	"All of you who have killed anyone o	2256
31:20	goat hair o wood.	2256
31:28	cattle, donkeys, **sheep** o **goats**.	7366
31:30	donkeys, **sheep**, **goats** o other animals.	7366
32:11	the men twenty years old o more who came	2256
35:17	O if anyone has a stone in his hand	2256
35:18	O if anyone has a wooden object	196
35:20	with malice aforethought shoves another o	196
35:21	o if in hostility he hits him with his fist so	196
35:22	without hostility someone suddenly shoves another o throws something	196
35:23	o, without seeing him, drops a stone	196
Dt 1:16	**whether** the case is between brother Israelites o between	2256
2: 9	not harass the Moabites o provoke them	2256
2:19	do not harass them o provoke them to war,	2256
2:27	not turn aside to the right o to the left.	2256
3:24	in heaven o on earth who can do the deeds	2256
4:16	not forget the things your eyes have seen o	2256
4:16	**whether** formed like a man o a woman,	196
4:17	o like any animal on earth or any bird	NIH
4:17	on earth o any bird that flies in the air,	NIH
4:18	o like any creature that moves along	NIH
4:18	the ground o any fish in the waters below.	NIH
4:28	which cannot see o hear or eat or smell.	2256
4:28	which cannot see or hear o eat or smell.	2256
4:28	which cannot see or hear or eat o smell.	2256
4:31	he will not abandon o destroy you or forget	2256
4:31	he will not abandon or destroy o you or forget	2256
4:32	o has anything like it ever been heard of?	196
4:34	o by great and awesome deeds,	2256
5: 8	the form of anything in heaven above o on	2256
5: 8	on the earth beneath o in the waters below.	2256
5: 9	not bow down to them o worship them;	2256
5:14	neither you, nor your son o daughter,	2256
5:14	nor your manservant o maidservant,	2256
5:14	your donkey o any of your animals,	2256
5:21	on your neighbor's house o land,	NIH
5:21	his manservant o maidservant,	2256
5:21	his ox o donkey,	2256
5:21	o anything that belongs to your neighbor."	2256
7: 3	do not turn aside to the right o to the left.	2256
7: 3	Do not give your daughters to their sons o	2256
7:14	of your men o women will be childless,	2256
7:22	o the wild animals will multiply	7153
7:25	o you will be ensnared by it,	7153
7:26	a detestable thing into your house o you,	2256
7:26	to know what was in your heart, whether o	561
9: 5	It is not because of your righteousness o	2256
9:23	You did not trust him o obey him.	2256
10: 9	That is why the Levites have no share o	2256
11:16	o you will be enticed to turn away	7153
12:12	who have no allotment o inheritance	2256
12:15	as if it were gazelle o deer,	2256
12:17	o the firstborn of your herds and flocks,	2256
12:17	o whatever you have vowed to give,	2256
12:17	o your freewill offerings or special gifts.	2256
12:17	o your freewill offerings o special gifts.	2256
12:22	Eat them as you would gazelle o deer.	2256
12:32	do not add to it o take away from it.	2256
13: 1	If a prophet, o one who foretells by dreams,	196
13: 1	and announces to you a miraculous sign o	196
13: 2	and if the sign o wonder	2256
13: 3	not listen to the words of that prophet o	196
13: 5	That prophet o dreamer must be put	196
13: 6	o your son or daughter,	196
13: 6	or your son o daughter,	196
13: 6	o the wife you love,	196
13: 6	o your closest friend secretly entices you,	196
13: 7	**whether** near o far,	196
13: 8	do not yield to him o listen to him.	2256
13: 8	Do not spare him o shield him.	2256
14: 1	Do not cut yourselves o shave the front	2256
14: 7	of those that chew the cud o that have	2256
14: 7	the rabbit o the coney.	2256
14: 8	not to eat their meat o touch their carcasses.	2256
14:21	o you may sell it to a foreigner.	196
14:26	cattle, sheep, wine o other fermented drink,	2256
14:26	fermented drink, o anything you wish.	2256
14:27	for they have no allotment o inheritance	2256
14:29	that the Levites (who have no allotment o	2256
15: 2	from his fellow Israelite o brother,	2256
15: 7	do not be hardhearted o tightfisted	2256
15:12	If a fellow Hebrew, a man o a woman,	196
15:21	If an animal has a defect, is lame o blind,	196
15:21	is lame or blind, o has any serious flaw,	NIH
15:22	as if it were gazelle o deer.	2256
16: 2	an animal from your flock o herd at	2256
16:19	Do not pervert justice o show partiality.	4202
17: 1	an ox o a sheep that has any defect or flaw	2256
17: 1	an ox or a sheep that has any defect o flaw	NIH
17: 2	a man o woman living among you in one of	196
17: 3	down to them o to the sun or the moon or	2256
17: 3	the sun o the moon or the stars of the sky,	196
17: 3	the sun or the moon o the stars of the sky,	196
17: 5	take the man o woman who has done this	196
17: 6	of two o three witnesses a man shall be put	196
17: 8	whether bloodshed, lawsuits o assaults—	1068
17:11	to the right o to the left.	2256
17:12	for the judge o for the priest	196
17:16	for himself o make the people return	2256

```
Dt 17:17  o his heart will be led astray.                 2256+4202
   17:20  turn from the law to the right o to the left.        2256
   18: 1  are to have no allotment o inheritance               2256
   18: 3  the people who sacrifice a bull o a sheep:            561
   18:10  among you who sacrifices his son o                   2256
   18:10  who practices divination o sorcery,                 2256
   18:11  o casts spells, or who is a medium                  2256
   18:11  o who is a medium or spiritist                      2256
   18:11  a medium o spiritist or who consults                2256
   18:11  a medium or spiritist o who consults                2256
   18:14  to those who practice sorcery o divination.          2256
   18:16  great fire anymore, o we will die."             2256+4202
   18:20  o a prophet who speaks in the name                  2256
   18:22  does not take place o come true,                    2256
   19:15  to convict a man accused of any crime o              2256
   19:15  by the testimony of two o three witnesses.           196
   20: 3  Do not be fainthearted o afraid;                    2256
   20: 3  do not be terrified o give way to panic             2256
   20: 5  Let him go home, o he may die in battle             7153
   20: 6  Let him go home, o he may die in battle             7153
   20: 7  Let him go home, o he may die in battle             7153
   20: 8  "Is any man afraid o fainthearted?                  2256
   21: 4  a valley that has not been plowed o planted          2256
   21:14  You must not sell her o treat her as a slave,        4202
   22: 1  you see your brother's ox o sheep straying,          196
   22: 3  near you o if you do not know who he is,             2256
   22: 3  if you find your brother's donkey o his             2256
   22: 3  or his cloak o anything he loses.                   2256
   22: 4  If you see your brother's donkey o his ox            196
   22: 6  either in a tree o on the ground,                   196
   22: 6  and the mother is sitting on the young o on          196
   23: 1  emasculated by crushing o cutting may               2256
   23: 3  No Ammonite o Moabite or any of his                 2256
   23: 3  No Ammonite or Moabite o any of his                 NIH
   23:17  No Israelite man o woman is to become               2256
   23:17  of a female prostitute o of a male prostitute        2256
   23:19  whether on money o food or anything else            NIH
   23:19  whether on money or food o anything else            NIH
   24: 3  o if he dies,                                       196
   24: 5  to war a have any other duty laid on him.           2256
   24: 7  and treats him as a slave o sells him,              2256
   24:14  whether he is a brother Israelite o                 196
   24:17  Do not deprive the alien o the fatherless           NIH
   24:17  o take the cloak of the widow as a pledge.           2256
   27:15  "Cursed is the man who carves an image o            2256
   27:16  the man who dishonors his father o                  2256
   27:19  the fatherless o the widow."                        2256
   27:22  of his father o the daughter of his mother."         196
   28:14  to the right o to the left,                         2256
   28:36  to a nation unknown to you o your fathers.           2256
   28:39  but you will not drink the wine o gather            2256
   28:50  without respect for the old o pity for              2256
   28:51  leave you no grain, new wine o oil,                 2256
   28:51  nor any calves of your herds o lambs                2256
   28:54  on his own brother o the wife he loves              2256
   28:54  the wife he loves o his surviving children,          2256
   28:56  the husband she loves and her own son o             2256
   29: 4  not given you a mind that understands o             2256
   29: 4  a mind that understands o eyes that see o           2256
   29: 6  and drank no wine o other fermented drink.           2256
   29:18  Make sure there is no man o woman,                  196
   29:18  or woman, clan o tribe among you today              196
   30:11  difficult for you o beyond your reach.              2256
   31: 6  not be afraid o terrified because of them,           2256
   32:30  o two put ten thousand to flight,                   2256
   32:36  and no one is left, slave o free.                   2256
   33: 9  He did not recognize his brothers o                 2256
   33:20  tearing at arm o head.                              677
   34:12  shown the mighty power o performed                  2256
Jos 1: 7  do not turn from it to the right o to the left,      2256
   5:13  "Are you for us o for our enemies?"                 561
   7: 3  Send two o three thousand men to take               196
   8:17  Not a man remained in Ai o Bethel who did           2256
   10:14  There has never been a day like it before o         2256
   15:36  Adithaim and Gederah (o Gederothaim)—               2256
   19: 2  It included: Beersheba (o Sheba), Moladah,          2256
   20: 9  Any of the Israelites o any alien living            2256
   22:19  against the LORD o against us by building           2256
   22:22  If this has been in rebellion o disobedience         2256
   22:23  o to sacrifice fellowship offerings on it,           2256
   22:26  but not for burnt offerings o sacrifices.'           2256
   22:28  o to our descendants, we will answer:               2256
   23: 6  without turning aside to the right o to             2256
   23: 7  not invoke the names of their gods o swear           2256
   23: 7  You must not serve them o bow down                  2256
   24:15  o the gods of the Amorites,                         561
Jdg 1:27  the people of Beth Shan o Taanach or Dor            2256
   1:27  the people of Beth Shan o Taanach or Dor            2256
   1:27  of Beth Shan or Taanach or Dor o Ibleam              2256
   1:27  or Taanach or Dor o Ibleam o Megiddo                2256
   1:30  the Canaanites living in Kitron o Nahalol,          2256
   1:31  in Acco o Sidon or Ahlab or Aczib                   2256
   1:31  or Sidon o Ahlab or Aczib or Helbah                 2256
   1:31  or Ahlab o Aczib or Helbah or Aphek                 2256
   1:31  or Aczib o Helbah or Aphek or Rehob,                2256
   1:31  or Sidon or Ahlab o Aczib or Helbah                 2256
   1:31  or Ahlab or Aczib or Helbah or Aphek o              2256
   1:33  in Beth Shemesh o Beth Anath;                       2256
   5: 8  and not a shield o spear was seen                   2256
   5:30  a girl o two for each man,                          NIH
   8:26  the kings of Midian o the chains that were           2256
   9: 2  of Jerub-Baal's sons rule over you, o               561
   11:15  not take the land of Moab o the land of             2256
   11:25  Did he ever quarrel with Israel o fight             561
   13: 4  Now see to it that you drink no wine o other        2256
   13: 7  drink no wine o other fermented drink               2256
   13:14  nor drink any wine o other fermented drink          2256
```

```
Jdg 13:23  nor shown us all these things o now told            2256
   14: 3  among your relatives o among all your               2256
   14:15  o we will burn you                                  7153
   14:16  "I haven't even explained it to my father o         2256
   18:25  o some hot-tempered men will attack you,            7153
   19:13  to reach Gibeah o Ramah and spend                  196
   19:30  "Such a thing has never been seen o done,           2256
   20:28  to battle with Benjamin our brother, o              561
   21:22  When their fathers o brothers complain              196
Ru 1:16  "Don't urge me to leave you o to turn back          NIH
   3:10  the younger men, whether rich o poor.           561+2256
   4:10  among his family o from the town records.           2256
1Sa 1:15  I have not been drinking wine o beer;               2256
   2: 3  "Do not keep talking so proudly o let              NIH
   2:14  He would plunge it into the pan o kettle            196
   2:14  into the pan or kettle o caldron or pot,            196
   2:14  into the pan or kettle o caldron or pot,            196
   3:14  be atoned for by sacrifice o offering.' "           2256
   4: 9  o you will be subject to the Hebrews,               7153
   4:20  she did not respond o pay any attention.            2256
   5:11  o it will kill us and our people."              2256+4202
   6:12  they did not turn to the right o to the left.        2256
   9: 5  o my father will stop thinking about               7153
   12: 4  "You have not cheated o oppressed us,"              2256
   13:19  the Hebrews will make swords o spears!"             196
   13:22  with Saul and Jonathan had a sword o spear          2256
   14: 6  whether by many o by few.                          2256
   14:52  whenever Saul saw a mighty o brave man,             2256
   15:29  He who is the Glory of Israel does not lie o         2256
   16: 7  not consider his appearance o his height,          2256
   17:34  a lion o a bear came and carried off a sheep         2256
   17:47  by sword o spear that the LORD saves;              2256
   18:18  and what is my family o my father's clan            NIH
   20: 2  great o small, without confiding in me.            196
   20: 3  'Jonathan must not know this o he will             7153
   20:27  either yesterday o today?"                         1685
   21: 3  o whatever you can find."                          196
   21: 8  "Don't you have a spear o a sword here?            196
   21: 8  I haven't brought my sword o any               1685+2256
   22: 2  All those who were in distress o in debt            2256
   22: 2  in distress or in debt o discontented               2256
   22: 8  of you is concerned about me o tells me             2256
   22:15  Let not the king accuse your servant o any          NIH
   24: 6  o lift my hand against him;                        NIH
   24:11  not guilty of wrongdoing o rebellion.              2256
   24:21  that you will not cut off my descendants o          561
   25:31  of needless bloodshed o of having avenged           2256
   26:10  o he will go into battle and perish.               196
   26:12  No one saw o knew about it,                        2256
   27: 9  he did not leave a man o woman alive,               2256
   27:10  the Negev of Judah" o "Against the Negev            2256
   27:10  of Jerahmeel" o "Against the Negev of              2256
   27:11  He did not leave a man o woman alive to             2256
   28: 6  not answer him by dreams o Urim                    1685
   28: 6  by dreams or Urim o prophets.                      1685
   28:15  either by prophets o by dreams.                    1685
   28:18  Because you did not obey the LORD o                2256
   29: 4  o he will turn against us during               2256+4202
   30:12  not eaten any food o drunk any water                2256
   30:15  not kill me o hand me over to my master,           2256
   30:19  Nothing was missing: young o old,                  2256
   30:19  young or old, boy o girl,                          2256
   30:19  plunder o anything else they had taken.             2256
   31: 4  o these uncircumcised fellows will come             7153
2Sa 2:21  "Turn aside to the right o to the left;            196
   3:29  without someone who has a running sore o            2256
   3:29  a running sore or leprosy o who leans on             2256
   3:29  leans on a crutch o who falls by the sword           2256
   3:29  or who falls by the sword o who lacks food.          2256
   3:35  so severely, if I taste bread o anything else        196
   6:21  who chose me rather than your father o              2256
   12: 4  of his own sheep o cattle to prepare a meal          2256
   13:22  either good o bad;                                 2256
   14:19  the right o to the left from anything my lord        2256
   15: 4  Then everyone who has a complaint o                2256
   15:14  o none of us will escape from Absalom.              3954
   15:14  o he will move quickly to overtake us              7153
   15:21  whether it means life o death,                     561
   17: 9  he is hidden in a cave o some other place.          196
   17:16  o the king and all the people with him will         7153
   19:24  of his feet o trimmed his mustache                 2256
   19:24  trimmed his mustache o washed his clothes           2256
   20: 6  o he will find fortified cities and escape          7153
   20:20  be it from me to swallow up o destroy!          561+2256
   21: 4  "We have no right to demand silver o gold           2256
   21: 4  silver or gold from Saul o his family,             2256
   21:10  the birds of the air touch them by day o            2256
   23: 7  a tool of iron o the shaft of a spear,             2256
   24:13  O three months of fleeing                          561
   24:13  O three days of plague in your land?               561
1Ki 1:10  not invite Nathan the prophet o Benaiah or          2256
   1:10  Nathan the prophet or Benaiah o the special          2256
   1:10  or the special guard o his brother Solomon.          2256
   3: 8  too numerous to count o number.                    2256
   3:11  and not for long life o wealth for yourself,         2256
   5: 4  and there is no adversary o disaster.               2256
   6: 7  chisel o any other iron tool was heard at           NIH
   8: 5  and cattle that they could not be recorded o         2256
   8:23  there is no God like you in heaven above o          2256
   8:37  "When famine o plague comes to the land,           NIH
   8:37  o blight or mildew, locusts or grasshoppers,        NIH
   8:37  or blight or mildew, locusts or grasshoppers,       NIH
   8:37  or blight or mildew, locusts or grasshoppers,       NIH
   8:37  o when an enemy besieges them in any               NIH
   8:37  whatever disaster o disease may come,              NIH
   8:38  and when a prayer o plea is made by any             NIH
   8:46  to his own land, far away o near;                  196
```

```
1Ki 9: 6  "But if you o your sons turn away from me           2256
   10:12  never been imported o seen since that day.)         2256
   13: 8  nor would I eat bread o drink water here.            2256
   13: 9  not eat bread o drink water or return by            2256
   13: 9  'You must not eat bread or drink water o            2256
   13:16  nor can I eat bread o drink water with you           2256
   13:17  'You must not eat bread or drink water there         2256
   13:17  not eat bread or drink water there o return          4202
   13:22  in the place where he told you not to eat o          2256
   14:10  in Israel—slave o free.                            2256
   15:17  to prevent anyone from leaving o entering           2256
   16:11  whether relative o friend.                         2256
   18:10  a nation o kingdom where my master has              2256
   18:10  a nation o kingdom claimed you were                2256
   18:27  Perhaps he is deep in thought, o busy,         2256+3954
   18:27  in thought, or busy, o traveling.              2256+3954
   20: 8  to him o agree to his demands."                    2256
   20:39  o you must pay a talent of silver.'                 196
   21: 2  a better vineyard o, if you prefer, I will pay      NIH
   21: 6  o if you prefer, I will give you another            196
   21:21  in Israel—slave o free.                            2256
   22: 6  against Ramoth Gilead, o shall I refrain?"          561
   22:15  against Ramoth Gilead, o shall I refrain?"          561
   22:31  "Do not fight with anyone, small o great,          2256
2Ki 2:16  down on some mountain o in some valley."           196
   2:21  Never again will it cause death o make             2256
   3: 9  for themselves o for the animals with them.         2256
   3:14  I would not look at you o even notice you.          2256
   4:13  Can we speak on your behalf to the king o           196
   4:23  "It's not the New Moon o the Sabbath."             2256
   4:31  but there was no sound o response.                 2256
   5:26  o to accept clothes, olive groves, vineyards,        2256
   5:26  herds, o menservants and maidservants?             2256
   6:22  with your own sword o bow?                         2256
   9: 8  in Israel—slave o free.                            2256
   9:32  Two o three eunuchs looked down at him.             NIH
   12:13  trumpets o any other articles of gold              NIH
   12:13  or any other articles of gold o silver for          2256
   13:19  "You should have struck the ground five o          196
   13:23  to destroy them o banish them                      2256
   14:26  whether slave o free, was suffering;           700+2256
   17:35  not worship any other gods o bow down              2256
   17:35  serve them o sacrifice to them.                    2256
   18: 5  either before him o after him.                    2256
   19:13  o of Hena or Ivvah?"                               NIH
   19:13  or of Hena or Ivvah?"                              2256
   19:32  not enter this city o shoot an arrow here.          2256
   19:32  with shield o build a siege ramp against it.         2256
   20: 9  o shall it go back ten steps?"                     561
   20:13  There was nothing in his palace o                  2256
   22: 2  not turning aside to the right o to the left.        2256
   23:10  so no one could use it to sacrifice his son o        2256
   25:15  all that were made of pure gold o silver.           2256
1Ch 10: 4  o these uncircumcised fellows will come            7153
   12: 2  with bows and were able to shoot arrows o          2256
   12: 2  to sling stones right-handed o left-handed;         2256
   21:12  o three days of the sword of the LORD—         561+2256
   21:24  o sacrifice a burnt offering                       2256
   22:13  Do not be afraid o discouraged.                    2256
   23: 3  The Levites thirty years old o more                2256
   23:24  the workers twenty years old o more                2256
   23:26  the tabernacle o any of the articles used           2256
   23:27  from those twenty years old o more.                2256
   27:23  the number of the men twenty years old o            2256
   28:20  Do not be afraid o discouraged,                    2256
   28:20  not fail you o forsake you until all the work       2256
2Ch 1:11  for wealth, riches o honor, nor for the death       2256
   5: 6  and cattle that they could not be recorded o         2256
   6:14  there is no God like you in heaven o               2256
   6:28  "When famine o plague comes to the land,           NIH
   6:28  o blight or mildew, locusts or grasshoppers,        NIH
   6:28  or blight or mildew, locusts or grasshoppers,       NIH
   6:28  or blight or mildew, locusts or grasshoppers,       2256
   6:28  o when enemies besiege them in any                 NIH
   6:28  whatever disaster o disease may come,              2256
   6:29  and when a prayer o plea is made by any             NIH
   6:36  to a land far away o near;                         196
   7:13  o command locusts to devour the land               2256
   7:13  the land o send a plague among my people,          2256
   8:15  to the priests o to the Levites in any matter,       2256
   15:13  whether small o great, man o woman                6330
   15:13  whether small or great, man o woman.               6330
   16: 1  to prevent anyone from leaving o entering           2256
   18: 5  against Ramoth Gilead, o shall I refrain?"          561
   18:14  against Ramoth Gilead, o shall I refrain?"          561
   18:30  "Do not fight with anyone, small o great,          NIH
   19: 7  the LORD our God there is no injustice o           2256
   19: 7  or partiality o bribery."                         2256
   19:10  whether bloodshed o other concerns of              1068
   19:10  commands, decrees o ordinances—                    2256
   20: 9  whether the sword of judgment, o                   2256
   20: 9  or plague o famine,                               2256
   20:15  'Do not be afraid o discouraged because            2256
   21:12  of your father Jehoshaphat o of Asa king            2256
   25: 5  He then mustered those twenty years old o           2256
   25: 8  God has the power to help o to overthrow."          2256
   28:13  "o we will be guilty before the LORD.              3954
   29: 7  They did not burn incense o present any            2256
   31: 2  to their duties as priests o Levites—              2256
   31:16  to the males three years old o more                2256
   31:17  to the Levites twenty years old o more,            2256
   31:19  around their towns o in any other towns,           NIH
   32: 7  be afraid o discouraged because of the king         2256
   32:15  of any nation o kingdom has been able              2256
   32:15  from my hand o the hand of my fathers.             2256
   34: 2  not turning aside to the right o to the left.        2256
   35:21  who is with me, o he will destroy you."        440+2256
```

2Ch 36:17	nor young woman, old man o aged.	2256
Ezr 4:13	no more taxes, tribute o duty will be paid,	10221
6:12	overthrow any king o people who lifts	10221
6:12	a hand to change this decree o to destroy	NIH
7:24	tribute o duty on any of the priests, Levites,	10221
7:24	temple servants o other workers	10221
7:26	confiscation of property, o imprisonment.	10221
9:12	to their sons o take their daughters	2256
9:14	leaving us no remnant o survivor?	2256
10:13	be taken care of in a day o two,	2256
Ne 2:16	where I had gone o what I was doing,	2256
2:16	the Jews o the priests or nobles or officials	2256
2:16	the Jews or the priests or nobles or officials	2256
2:16	the Jews or the priests or nobles o officials	2256
2:16	or nobles or officials o any others	2256
2:20	you have no share in Jerusalem o any claim	2256
2:20	in Jerusalem or any claim o historic right	2256
4:5	not cover up their guilt o blot out their sins	2256
4:11	"Before they know it o see us,	2256
6:11	O should one like me go into the temple	2256
8:9	Do not mourn o weep."	2256
9:18	o when they committed awful blasphemies.	2256
9:31	not put an end to them o abandon them,	2256
9:34	not pay attention to your commands o	2256
9:35	not serve you o turn from their evil ways.	2256
10:30	in marriage to the peoples around us o	2256
10:31	neighboring peoples bring merchandise o	2256
10:31	not buy from them on the Sabbath o	2256
13:1	that no Ammonite o Moabite should ever	2256
13:20	Once o twice the merchants and sellers	2256
13:24	the language of Ashdod o the language	2256
13:25	in marriage for your sons o for yourselves.	2256
Est 3:2	But Mordecai would not kneel down o	2256
3:5	that Mordecai would not kneel down o	2256
4:11	that for any man o woman who approaches	2256
4:16	Do not eat o drink for three days,	2256
4:16	not eat or drink for three days, night o day.	2256
4:17	of any nationality o province	2256
Job 3:16	O why was I not hidden in the ground like	196
6:5	o an ox bellow when it has fodder?	561
6:6	o is there flavor in the white of an egg?	561
7:2	o a hired man waiting eagerly	2256
7:12	Am I the sea, o the monster of the deep,	561
7:19	o let me alone even for an instant?	4202
8:20	a blameless man o strengthen the hands	2256
10:5	a mortal o your years like those of a man,	561
10:19	o had been carried straight from the womb	NIH
12:7	o the birds of the air, and they will tell you;	2256
12:8	o speak to the earth,	196
12:8	o let the fish of the sea inform you.	2256
13:22	o let me speak, and you reply.	196
14:11	from the sea o a riverbed becomes parched	2256
14:12	not awake o be roused from their sleep.	2256
15:2	o fill his belly with the hot east wind?	2256
15:14	o one born of woman,	2256
17:14	'My mother' o 'My sister,'	2256
18:4	O must the rocks be moved from their place	2256
18:19	He has no offspring o descendants	2256
19:24	o engraved in rock forever!	NIH
24:13	not know its ways o stay in its paths.	2256
28:16	with precious onyx o sapphires.	2256
31:5	in falsehood o my foot has hurried	2256
31:7	o if my hands have been defiled,	2256
31:9	o if I have lurked at my neighbor's door,	2256
31:16	"If I have denied the desires of the poor o	2256
31:19	o a needy man without a garment,	2256
31:24	"If I have put my trust in gold o said	2256
31:26	if I have regarded the sun in its radiance o	2256
31:29	at my enemy's misfortune o gloated over	2256
31:39	without payment o broken the spirit	2256
33:19	O a man may be chastened on a bed of pain	2256
35:7	o what does he receive from your hand?	196
36:19	Would your wealth o even all your mighty	2256
36:23	o said to him, 'You have done wrong'?	2256
37:13	o to water his earth and show his love.	561
38:6	o who laid its cornerstone—	196
38:12	o shown the dawn its place,	NIH
38:16	of the sea o walked in the recesses of	2256
38:22	the snow o seen the storehouses of the hail,	2256
38:24	o the place where the east winds are	NIH
38:32	o lead out the Bear with its cubs?	2256
38:36	o gave understanding to the mind?	196
38:40	when they crouch in their dens o lie in wait	NIH
39:17	God did not endow her with wisdom o	2256+4202
39:19	the horse his strength o clothe his neck	2022
40:24	o trap him and pierce his nose?	NIH
41:1	with a fishhook o tie down his tongue with	2256
41:2	a cord through his nose o pierce his jaw	2256
41:5	a pet of him like a bird o put him on a leash	2256
41:7	Can you fill his hide with harpoons o	2256
41:26	nor does the spear o the dart or the javelin.	NIH
41:26	nor does the spear or the dart o the javelin.	2256
Ps 1:1	of the wicked o stand in the way of sinners	2256
1:1	way of sinners o sit in the seat of mockers.	2256
6:1	o discipline me in your wrath.	2256
7:2	o they will tear me like a lion and rip me	7153
7:4	o without cause have robbed my foe—	2256
13:3	o I will sleep in death;	7153
16:4	I will not pour out their libations of blood o	2256
19:3	There is no speech o language	2256
22:24	not despised o disdained the suffering o	2256
24:4	who does not lift up his soul to an idol o	2256
27:9	Do not reject me o forsake me,	2256
32:9	Do not be like the horse o the mule,	NIH
32:9	be controlled by bit and bridle o they will	NIH
35:14	about mourning as though for my friend o	NIH
35:25	o say, "We have swallowed him up."	440
Ps 36:2	to detect o hate his sin.	NIH
37:1	not fret because of evil men o be envious	440
37:25	the righteous forsaken o their children	2256
37:33	not leave them in their power o let them	2256
38:1	o discipline me in your wrath.	2256
38:16	"Do not let them gloat o exalt themselves	NIH
44:17	though we had not forgotten you o been	2256
44:20	If we had forgotten the name of our God o	2256
49:7	the life of another o give to God a ransom	4202
50:8	for your sacrifices o your burnt offerings,	2256
50:9	from your stall o of goats from your pens,	NIH
50:13	Do I eat the flesh of bulls o drink the blood	2256
50:16	"What right have you to recite my laws o	2256
50:22	o I will tear you to pieces,	7153
51:11	from your presence o take your Holy Spirit	2256
51:16	o I would bring it;	2256
58:9	whether they be green o dry—	4017
59:3	against me for no offense o sin of mine,	2256
59:11	O Lord our shield, o my people will forget.	7153
62:10	in extortion o take pride in stolen goods;	2256
66:20	not rejected my prayer o withheld his love	2256
69:15	Do not let the floodwaters engulf me o	2256
69:15	o the pit close its mouth over me.	2256
75:6	No one from the east o the west or from	2256
75:6	the west o from the desert can exalt a man.	2256
78:22	for they did not believe in God o trust	2256
83:14	As fire consumes the forest o a flame sets	2256
88:12	o your righteous deeds in the land	2256
89:34	I will not violate my covenant o alter	2256
89:48	o save himself from the power of the grave?	NIH
90:2	Before the mountains were born o you	2256
90:4	o like a watch in the night.	2256
90:10	o eighty, if we have the strength;	2256
103:10	not treat us as our sins deserve o repay us	2256
106:2	of the LORD o fully declare his praise?	NIH
109:12	May no one extend kindness to him o	2256
131:1	with great matters o things too wonderful	2256
132:3	not enter my house o go to my bed—	561
140:8	o they will become proud.	NIH
143:7	Do not hide your face from me o I will be	2256
Pr 2:19	to her return o attain the paths of life.	2256
3:25	Have no fear of sudden disaster o the ruin	2256
3:31	Do not envy a violent man o choose any	2256
4:5	not forget my words o swerve from them.	2256
4:14	on the path of the wicked o walk in the way	2256
4:27	Do not swerve to the right o the left;	2256
5:13	I would not obey my teachers o listen	2256
6:7	It has no commander, no overseer o ruler,	2256
6:25	Do not lust in your heart after her beauty o	2256
7:25	not let your heart turn to her ways o stray	NIH
8:8	none of them is crooked o perverse.	2256
8:26	before he made the earth o its fields or any	2256
8:26	before he made the earth or its fields o any	2256
9:8	Do not rebuke a mocker or he will hate you;	7153
17:26	o to flog officials for their integrity.	NIH
18:5	It is not good to be partial to the wicked o	NIH
20:13	Do not love sleep o you will grow poor;	7153
20:20	If a man curses his father o mother,	2256
22:1	to be esteemed is better than silver o gold.	2256
22:13	o, "I will be murdered in the streets!"	2256
22:25	o you may learn his ways	7153
22:26	not be a man who strikes hands in pledge o	NIH
23:10	Do not move an ancient boundary stone o	2256
23:20	not join those who drink too much wine o	NIH
24:18	the LORD will see and disapprove	7153
24:19	not fret because of evil men o be envious of	440
24:28	o use your lips to deceive.	2256
25:10	o he who hears it may shame you	7153
25:12	Like an earring of gold o an ornament	2256
25:18	Like a club o a sword or a sharp arrow is	2256
25:18	Like a club or a sword o a sharp arrow is	2256
25:19	Like a bad tooth o a lame foot is reliance	2256
25:20	o like vinegar poured on soda,	NIH
25:26	Like a muddied spring o a polluted well is	2256
26:1	Like snow in summer o rain in harvest,	2256
26:2	a fluttering sparrow o a darting swallow,	NIH
26:4	o you will be like him yourself.	7153
26:5	o he will be wise in his own eyes.	7153
26:6	Like cutting off one's feet o drinking	NIH
26:10	is he who hires a fool o any passer-by.	2256
26:18	Like a madman shooting firebrands o	2256
27:16	like restraining the wind o grasping oil with	2256
28:15	Like a roaring lion o a charging bear is	2256
28:24	He who robs his father o mother and says,	2256
30:6	o he will rebuke you and prove you a liar.	7153
30:9	O I may become poor and steal,	7153
30:10	o he will curse you, and you will pay for it.	7153
30:32	o if you have planned evil,	2256
Ecc 2:19	be a wise man o a fool?	196
2:25	who can eat o find enjoyment?	2256
4:14	o he may have been born in poverty	1685+3954
5:12	whether he eats little o much,	2256
5:14	o wealth lost through some misfortune,	2256
6:5	it never saw the sun o knew anything,	2256
7:21	o you may hear your servant cursing you—	889+4202
8:16	his eyes not seeing sleep day o night—	2256
9:1	but no man knows whether love o	1685
9:11	The race is not to the swift o the battle to	1685
9:11	to the wise o wealth to the brilliant	1685+2256
9:11	brilliant o favor to the learned;	1685+2256
9:12	o birds are taken in a snare,	2256
10:20	o curse the rich in your bedroom,	2256
11:3	a tree falls to the south o to the north,	561
11:5	o how the body is formed in	NIH
11:6	which will succeed, whether this o that,	196
11:6	o whether both will do equally well.	2256
Ecc 12:6	o the golden bowl is broken;	2256
12:6	o the wheel broken at the well,	2256
12:14	whether it is good o evil.	2256
SS 2:7	not arouse o awaken love until it so desires.	2256
2:9	My lover is like a gazelle o a young stag.	196
2:17	and be like a gazelle o like a young stag on	196
3:5	not arouse o awaken love until it so desires.	2256
6:11	to see if the vines had budded o	NIH
8:4	not arouse o awaken love until it so desires.	2256
8:14	and be like a gazelle o like a young stag on	196
Isa 1:6	cleansed o bandaged or soothed with oil.	2256
1:6	cleansed or bandaged o soothed with oil.	2256
3:7	I have no food o clothing in my house;	2256
5:27	Not one of them grows tired o stumbles,	2256
5:27	not one slumbers o sleeps;	2256
7:11	**whether** in the deepest depths o in the	196
8:4	Before the boy knows how to say 'My	
	father' o 'My mother'	2256
10:4	among the captives o fall among the slain.	2256
10:14	o opened its mouth to chirp.'	2256
10:15	o the saw boast against him who uses it?	561
10:15	o a club brandish him who is not wood!	NIH
11:3	o decide by what he hears with his ears;	2256
13:20	She will never be inhabited o lived in	2256
16:10	no one sings o shouts in the vineyards;	4202
17:6	leaving two o three olives on	NIH
17:6	four o five on the fruitful boughs,"	NIH
19:15	head o tail, palm branch or reed.	2256
19:15	head or tail, palm branch o reed.	2256
21:7	riders on donkeys o riders on camels,	NIH
22:11	o have regard for the One who planned it	2256
23:1	and left without house o harbor.	NIH
23:18	they will not be stored up o hoarded.	2256
24:13	o as when gleanings are left after	NIH
27:5	O else let them come to me for refuge;	196
27:9	no Asherah poles o incense altars will	2256
28:22	o your chains will become heavier;	7153
29:12	O if you give the scroll	2256
30:14	a hearth o scooping water out of a cistern."	2256
30:21	Whether you turn to the right o to the left,	2256
31:1	o seek help from the LORD.	2256
31:4	not frightened by their shouts o disturbed	2256
37:13	o of Hena or Ivvah?"	NIH
37:13	or of Hena o Ivvah?"	2256
37:33	not enter this city o shoot an arrow here.	2256
37:33	with shield o build a siege ramp against it.	2256
38:11	no longer will I look on mankind, o be	NIH
38:14	I cried like a swift o thrush,	NIH
39:2	There was nothing in his palace o	2256
40:12	o with the breadth of his hand marked off	2256
40:12	o weighed the mountains on the scales and	2256
40:13	o instructed him as his counselor?	2256
40:14	that taught him knowledge o showed him	2256
40:25	O who is my equal?"	2256
40:28	He will not grow tired o weary,	2256
41:22	O declare to us the things to come,	196
41:23	Do something, whether good o bad,	2256
41:26	so we could know, o beforehand,	2256
42:2	He will not shout o cry out,	2256
42:2	o raise his voice in the streets.	2256
42:4	he will not falter o be discouraged	2256
42:8	not give my glory to another o my praise	2256
42:22	all of them trapped in pits o hidden away	2256
42:23	to this o pay close attention in time	NIH
43:24	o lavished on me the fat of your sacrifices.	2256
44:14	o perhaps took a cypress or oak.	2256
44:14	or perhaps took a cypress o oak.	2256
44:14	o planted a pine, and the rain made it grow.	NIH
44:19	no one has the knowledge o understanding	2256
44:20	he cannot save himself, o say,	2256
45:10	o to his mother,	2256
45:11	about my children, o give me orders about	2256
45:13	not for a price o reward,	2256
45:17	you will never be put to shame o disgraced,	2256
46:5	"To whom will you compare me o	2256
47:1	No more will you be called tender o	2256
47:7	But you did not consider these things o	4202
47:8	be a widow o suffer the loss of children.'	2256
48:1	but not in truth o righteousness—	2256
49:10	the desert heat o the sun beat upon them.	2256
49:24	o captives rescued from the fierce?	2256
50:1	O to which of my creditors did I sell you?	196
51:7	not fear the reproach of men o be terrified	2256
52:12	you will not leave in haste o go in flight;	2256
53:2	He had no beauty o majesty to attract us	2256
56:12	like today, o even far better."	NIH
58:13	as you please o speaking idle words,	2256
59:21	o from the mouths of your children,	2256
59:21	o from the mouths of their descendants	2256
60:11	they will never be shut, day o night,	2256
60:12	For the nation o kingdom that will	2256
60:18	nor ruin o destruction within your borders,	2256
62:4	o name your land Desolate.	2256
62:6	they will never be silent day o night.	2256
63:16	not know us o Israel acknowledge us;	2256
64:7	on your name o strives to lay hold of you;	NIH
65:20	o an old man who does not live out	2256
65:22	o plant and others eat.	4202
65:23	not toil in vain o bear children doomed	2256
66:8	be born in a day o a nation be brought forth	561
66:19	not heard of my fame o seen my glory.	2256
Jer 1:17	o I will terrify you before them.	7153
2:31	a desert to Israel o a land of great darkness?	561
3:16	never enter their minds o be remembered;	2256
4:4	o my wrath will break out and burn like fire	7153
4:11	but not to winnow o cleanse;	2256
5:12	we will never see sword o famine.	2256

Isa	6: 8	o I will turn away from you	7153
	6:20	What do I care about incense from Sheba o	2256
	6:25	not go out to the fields o walk on the roads,	2256
	7: 6	the fatherless o the widow and do	2256
	7:16	not pray for this people nor offer any plea o	2256
	7:24	But they did not listen o pay attention;	2256
	7:26	they did not listen to me o pay attention.	2256
	7:28	not obeyed the LORD its God o responded	2256
	7:32	people will no longer call it Topheth o	2256
	8: 2	They will not be gathered up o buried,	2256
	9:13	not obeyed me o followed my law.	2256
	9:23	o the strong man boast of his strength	2256
	9:23	o the rich man boast of his riches,	440
	10: 2	"Do not learn the ways of the nations o	2256
	10:20	now to pitch my tent o to set up my shelter.	2256
	11: 8	But they did not listen o pay attention.	2256
	11:14	not pray for this people nor offer any plea o	2256
	11:21	the LORD o you will die by our hands'	2256+4202
	13:14	I will allow no pity o mercy or compassion	2256
	13:14	I will allow no pity o mercy or compassion	2256
	13:23	Can the Ethiopian change his skin o	2256
	14:13	not see the sword o suffer famine.	2256
	14:14	not sent them o appointed them or spoken	2256
	14:14	not sent them or appointed them o spoken	2256
	14:15	'No sword o famine will touch this land.'	2256
	14:16	be no one to bury them o their wives,	2256
	14:16	their sons o their daughters.	2256
	15:12	from the north—o bronze?	2256
	16: 2	and have sons o daughters in this place."	2256
	16: 4	They will not be mourned o buried but will	2256
	16: 5	do not go to mourn o show sympathy,	2256
	16: 6	They will not be buried o mourned,	2256
	16: 6	and no one will cut himself o	2256
	16: 7	not even for a father o a mother—	2256
	17:21	the Sabbath day o bring it through the gates	2256
	17:22	a load out of your houses o do any work on	2256
	17:23	Yet they did not listen o pay attention;	2256
	17:23	not listen o respond to discipline.	2256
	18: 7	that a nation o kingdom is to be uprooted,	2256
	18: 9	if at another time I announce that a nation o	2256
	18:23	not forgive their crimes o blot out their sins	2256
	19: 5	something I did not command o mention,	2256
	19: 6	Topheth o the Valley of Ben Hinnom,	2256
	20: 4	who will carry them away to Babylon o	2256
	20: 9	"I will not mention him o speak any more	2256
	21: 7	he will show them no mercy o pity	2256
	21: 7	no mercy or pity o compassion.'	2256
	21: 9	will die by the sword, famine o plague.	2256
	21:12	o my wrath will break out and burn like fire	7153
	22: 3	Do no wrong o violence to the alien,	440
	22: 3	the fatherless o the widow,	2256
	22:10	for the dead [king] o mourn his loss;	2256
	22:30	on the throne of David o rule anymore	2256
	23: 4	and they will no longer be afraid o terrified,	2256
	23:18	of the LORD to see o to hear his word?	2256
	23:32	yet I did not send o appoint them.	2256
	23:33	"When these people, o a prophet or a priest,	196
	23:33	"When these people, or a prophet o a priest,	196
	23:34	a prophet or a priest or anyone else claims,	2256
	23:34	a prophet or a priest o anyone else claims,	2256
	23:35	of you keeps on saying to his friend o	2256
	23:35	o 'What has the LORD spoken?'	2256
	23:37	o 'What has the LORD spoken?'	2256
	24: 8	**whether** they remain in this land o	2256
	25: 4	you have not listened o paid any attention.	2256
	25:33	not be mourned o gathered up or buried,	2256
	25:33	not be mourned or gathered up o	2256
	26:19	"Did Hezekiah king of Judah o anyone else	2256
	27: 8	any nation o kingdom will	2256
	27: 8	of Babylon o bow its neck under his yoke,	2256
	27: 9	of dreams, your mediums o your sorcerers	2256
	31:34	o a man his brother, saying,	2256
	31:40	The city will never again be uprooted o	2256
	32:23	they did not obey you o follow your law;	2256
	32:33	and again, they would not listen o respond	NIH
	32:43	without men o animals.	2256
	33:10	without men o animals."	2256
	33:12	desolate and without men o animals—	2256
	34:14	did not listen to me o pay attention to me.	2256
	35: 7	sow seed o plant vineyards;	2256
	35: 9	o built houses to live in or had vineyards,	2256
	35: 9	or built houses to live in o had vineyards,	2256
	35: 9	to live in or had vineyards, fields o crops.	2256
	35:15	But you have not paid attention o listened	2256
	36:23	Whenever Jehudi had read three o	2256
	37:18	against you o your officials or this people,	2256
	37:18	against you or your officials o this people,	2256
	37:19	of Babylon will not attack you o this land'?	2256
	37:20	o I will die there."	2256+4202
	38: 2	will die by the sword, famine o plague,	2256
	38:24	you may die.	2256+4202
	38:25	not hide it from us o we will kill you,'	2256+4202
	40: 5	o go anywhere else you please."	196
	42: 6	Whether it is favorable o unfavorable,	561+2256
	42:14	not see war o hear the trumpet or be hungry	2256
	42:14	not see war or hear the trumpet o be hungry	2256
	42:17	not one of them will survive o escape	2256
	43: 3	so they may kill us o carry us into exile	2256
	44: 5	But they did not listen o pay attention;	2256
	44: 5	they did not turn from their wickedness o	NIH
	44:10	not humbled themselves o shown reverence,	2256
	44:12	by the sword o die from famine.	NIH
	44:12	they will die by sword o famine.	2256
	44:14	in Egypt will escape o survive to return to	2256
	44:23	the LORD and have not obeyed him o	2256
	44:23	not obeyed him or followed his law o	2256
	44:23	or followed his law or his decrees o	2256

Jer	44:26	will ever again invoke my name o swear,	NIH
	44:28	whose word will stand—mine o theirs.	2256
	50:39	It will never again be inhabited o lived in	2256
	51:46	Do not lose heart o be afraid	2256
	52:19	all that were made of pure gold o silver.	2256
La	2:22	of the LORD's anger no one escaped o	2256
	3: 8	Even when I call out o cry for help,	2256
	3:33	For he does not willingly bring affliction o	2256
	3:63	Sitting o standing, they mock me	2256
Eze	1:13	like burning coals of fire o like torches.	NIH
	2: 5	And whether they listen o fail to listen—	2256
	2: 6	do not be afraid of them o their words.	2256
	2: 6	not be afraid of what they say o terrified	2256
	2: 7	whether they listen o fail to listen.	2256
	3: 9	not be afraid of them o terrified by them,	2256
	3:11	whether they listen o fail to listen."	2256
	3:18	not warn him o speak out to dissuade him	2256
	3:19	and he does not turn from his wickedness o	2256
	4:14	I have never eaten anything found dead o	2256
	5: 7	not followed my decrees o kept my laws.	2256
	5:11	not look on you with pity o spare you.	2256
	5:12	the plague o perish by famine inside you;	2256
	7: 4	not look on you with pity o spare you	2256
	7: 9	not look on you with pity o spare you;	2256
	7:19	not satisfy their hunger o fill their stomachs	2256
	8:18	not look on them with pity o spare them.	2256
	9: 5	without showing pity o compassion.	2256
	9:10	not look on them with pity o spare them,	2256
	11:12	not followed my decrees o kept my laws	2256
	12:24	For there will be no more false visions o	2256
	13: 9	of my people o be listed in the records of	2256
	13:23	see false visions o practice divination,	2256
	14: 7	" 'When any Israelite o any alien living	2256
	14:15	"O if I send wild beasts through	NIH
	14:16	they could not save their own sons o	2256
	14:17	"O if I bring a sword against that country	196
	14:18	they could not save their own sons o	2256
	14:19	"O if I send a plague into that land	196
	16: 4	nor were you rubbed with salt o wrapped	2256
	16: 5	on you with pity o had compassion enough	NIH
	17: 9	a strong arm o many people to pull it up by	2256
	18: 6	the mountain shrines o look to the idols of	2256
	18: 6	He does not defile his neighbor's wife o lie	2256
	18: 8	not lend at usury o take excessive interest.	2256
	18:10	who sheds blood o does any of these other	2256
	18:15	"He does not eat at the mountain shrines o	2256
	18:16	not oppress anyone o require a pledge for	4202
	18:17	and takes no usury o excessive interest.	2256
	20:17	not destroy them o put an end to them in	2256
	20:18	not follow the statutes of your fathers o	2256
	20:18	or keep their laws o defile yourselves	2256
	20:28	and they saw any high hill o any leafy tree,	2256
	22:14	Will your courage endure o your hands	561
	22:24	that has had no rain o showers in the day	4202
	23:27	with longing o remember Egypt anymore.	2256
	24:16	do not lament o weep or shed any tears.	2256
	24:16	do not lament or weep o shed any tears.	2256
	24:17	not cover the lower part of your face o eat	2256
	24:22	not cover the lower part of your face o eat	2256
	24:23	not mourn o weep but will waste away	2256
	26:20	and you will not return o take your place in	2256
	29: 5	and not be gathered o picked up.	2256
	29:11	of man o animal will pass through it;	2256
	30:21	It has not been bound up for healing o put	NIH
	32:13	be stirred by the foot of man o muddied by	2256
	34: 4	not strengthened the weak o healed the sick	2256
	34: 4	or healed the sick o bound up the injured.	2256
	34: 4	not brought back the strays o searched for	2256
	34: 6	and no one searched o looked for them.	2256
	34:29	in the land o bear the scorn of the nations.	2256
	36:14	therefore you will no longer devour men o	2256
	36:15	of the peoples o cause your nation to fall,	2256
	37:22	and they will never again be two nations o	2256
	37:23	with their idols and vile images o with any	2256
	39:10	to gather wood from the fields o cut it from	2256
	44:13	near to serve me as priests o come near any	2256
	44:13	or come near any of my holy things o	NIH
	44:17	at the gates of the inner court o inside	2256
	44:20	" 'They must not shave their heads o	2256
	44:22	not marry widows o divorced women;	2256
	44:22	of Israelite descent o widows of priests.	2256
	44:25	if the dead person was his father o mother,	2256
	44:25	son o daughter, brother or unmarried sister,	2256
	44:25	son or daughter, brother o unmarried sister,	2256
	44:31	not eat anything, bird o animal, found dead	2256
	44:31	found dead o torn by wild animals.	2256
	45:14	of ten baths o one homer,	NIH
	45:20	for anyone who sins unintentionally o	2256
	46:12	**whether** a burnt offering o fellowship	196
	46:12	He shall offer his burnt offering o his	2256
	46:14	They must not sell o exchange any of it.	2256
Da	2:10	of any magician o enchanter or astrologer.	10221
	2:10	of any magician or enchanter o astrologer.	10221
	2:27	magician o diviner can explain to the king	NIH
	3:14	that you do not serve my gods o worship	10221
	3:18	that we will not serve your gods o worship	10221
	3:28	to give up their lives rather than serve o	10221
	3:29	of any nation o language who say anything	10221
	4:19	not let the dream o its meaning alarm you."	10221
	4:35	No one can hold back his hand o say	10221
	5: 8	but they could not read the writing o tell	10221
	5:23	which cannot see o hear or understand.	10221
	5:23	which cannot see or hear o understand.	10221
	6: 7	that anyone who prays to any god o man	10221
	6:12	to any god o man except to you,	10221
	6:13	O king, o to the decree you put in writing.	10221
	6:15	of the Medes and Persians no decree o edict	10221

Da	9:10	we have not obeyed the LORD our God o	NIH
	10: 3	no meat o wine touched my lips;	2256
	11:17	but his plans will not succeed o help him.	2256
	11:20	yet not in anger o in battle.	2256
	11:33	they will fall by the sword o be burned or	2256
	11:33	or be burned o captured or plundered.	NIH
	11:33	or be burned or captured o plundered.	2256
	11:37	the gods of his fathers o for the one desired	2256
Hos	1: 7	not by bow, sword o battle,	2256
	1: 7	sword or battle, o by horses and horsemen,	NIH
	1:10	which cannot be measured o counted.	2256
	3: 3	be a prostitute o be intimate with any man,	2256
	3: 4	without king o prince,	2256
	3: 4	without sacrifice o sacred stones,	2256
	3: 4	without ephod o idol.	2256
	7:10	not return to the LORD his God o search	2256
	12: 8	not find in me any iniquity o sin."	889
Joel	1: 2	ever happened in your days o in	561+2256
Am	3:12	from the lion's mouth only two leg bones o	196
	5: 6	o he will sweep through the house	7153
	8:11	not a famine of food o a thirst for water,	2256
	8:14	o say, 'As surely as your god lives, O Dan,'	2256
	8:14	o, 'As surely as the god of Beersheba'	2256
	9:10	'Disaster will not overtake o meet us.'	2256
Jnh	3: 7	Do not let any man o beast, herd or flock,	2256
	3: 7	Do not let any man or beast, herd o flock,	2256
	3: 7	do not let them eat o drink.	2256
	4:10	though you did not tend it o make it grow.	2256
Mic	5: 7	not wait for man o linger for mankind.	2256
Hab	1: 2	O cry out to you, "Violence!"	NIH
	2:18	O an image that teaches lies?	2256
	2:19	O to lifeless stone, 'Wake up!'	NIH
Zep	1:12	either good o bad.'	2256
Hag	2:12	and that fold touches some bread o stew,	2256
	2:12	some wine, oil o other food,	2256
Zec	1: 4	But they would not listen o pay attention	2256
	7:10	Do not oppress the widow o the fatherless,	2256
	7:10	the alien o the poor.	2256
	7:12	as flint and would not listen to the law o to	2256
	7:14	behind them that no one could come o go.	2256
	8:10	that time there were no wages for man o	2256
	11:16	o seek the young, or heal the injured,	4202
	11:16	o heal the injured, or feed the healthy,	2256
	11:16	or heal the injured, o feed the healthy,	4202
	14: 6	no cold o frost.	2256
	14: 6	a unique day, without daytime o nighttime	2256
Mal	1: 8	When you sacrifice crippled o diseased	2256
	1:13	crippled o diseased animals and offer them	2256
	2:13	to your offerings o accepts them	2256
	2:17	o "Where is the God of justice?"	196
	3: 2	be like a refiner's fire o a launderer's soap.	2256
	4: 1	"Not a root o a branch will be left to them.	2256
	4: 6	o else I will come and strike the land with	7153
Mt	5:17	that I have come to abolish the Law o	2445
	5:25	he may hand you over to the judge,	3607
	5:35	o by the earth, for it is his footstool;	3612
	5:35	o by Jerusalem, for it is the city of	3612
	5:36	for you cannot make even one hair white o	2445
	6:24	o he will be devoted to the one and despise	2445
	6:25	what you will eat o drink;	2445
	6:25	o about your body, what you will wear.	3593
	6:26	not sow o reap or store away in barns,	4028
	6:26	not sow or reap o store away in barns,	4028
	6:28	They do not labor o spin.	4028
	6:31	o 'What shall we drink?'	2445
	6:31	o 'What shall we wear?'	2445
	7: 1	Do not judge, o you too will be judged	2671+3590
	7:10	O if he asks for a fish, will give him a snake	2445
	7:16	o figs from thistles?	2445
	9: 5	to say, 'Your sins are forgiven,' o to say,	2445
	10: 5	not go among the Gentiles o enter any town	2779
	10: 9	not take along any gold o silver or copper	3593
	10: 9	not take along any gold or silver o copper	3593
	10:10	o extra tunic, or sandals or a staff;	3593
	10:10	or extra tunic, o sandals or a staff;	3593
	10:10	or extra tunic, or sandals o a staff;	3593
	10:11	"Whatever town o village you enter,	2445
	10:14	not welcome you o listen to your words,	3593
	10:14	when you leave that home o town.	2445
	10:19	do not worry about what to say o how	2445
	10:26	o hidden that will not be made known.	2779
	10:37	"Anyone who loves his father o mother	2445
	10:37	anyone who loves his son o daughter	2445
	11: 3	o should we expect someone else?"	2445
	12: 5	O haven't you read in the Law that on	2445
	12:19	He will not quarrel o cry out;	4028
	12:25	and every city o household divided	2445
	12:29	"O again, how can anyone enter	2445
	12:32	either in this age o in the age to come.	4046
	12:33	o make a tree bad and its fruit will be bad,	2445
	13: 8	sixty o thirty times what was sown.	NIG
	13:13	they do not hear o understand.	4028
	13:21	When trouble o persecution comes because	2445
	13:23	sixty o thirty times what was sown.	1254+4005
	15: 4	and 'Anyone who curses his father o	2445
	15: 5	that if a man says to his father o mother,	2445
	15:32	o they may collapse on the way."	3607
	16:10	O the seven loaves for the four thousand,	4028
	16:14	O one of the prophets.	2445
	16:26	O what can a man give in exchange	2445
	17:15	He often falls into the fire o into the water.	2779
	17:25	from their own sons o from others?"	2445
	18: 8	If your hand o your foot causes you to sin,	2445
	18: 8	to have two hands o two feet and be thrown	2445
	18:16	take one o two others along,	2445
	18:16	by the testimony of two o three witnesses.'	2445

Mt	18:17	as you would a pagan o a tax collector.	2779
	18:20	two o three come together in my name,	2445
	19:29	And everyone who has left houses o	2445
	19:29	or brothers o sisters or father or mother	2445
	19:29	or sisters or father or mother or children	2445
	19:29	or sisters or father o mother or children	2445
	19:29	or sisters or father or mother o children	2445
	19:29	or children o fields for my sake will receive	2445
	20:15	O are you envious because I am generous?'	2445
	20:23	but to sit at my right o left is not for me	2779
	21:25	Was it from heaven, o from men?"	2445
	22:17	Is it right to pay taxes to Caesar o not?"	2445
	22:29	because you do not know the Scriptures o	3593
	23:17	o the temple that makes the gold sacred?	2445
	23:19	gift, o the altar that makes the gift sacred?	2445
	24:20	not take place in winter o on the Sabbath.	3593
	24:23	o, 'There he is!'	2445
	24:26	o, 'Here he is, in the inner rooms,'	NIG
	24:36	"No one knows about that day o hour,	2779
	25:13	you do not know the day o the hour.	4028
	25:37	o thirsty and give you something to drink?	2445
	25:38	o needing clothes and clothe you?	2445
	25:39	When did we see you sick o in prison	2445
	25:44	when did we see you hungry o thirsty or	2445
	25:44	or thirsty o a stranger or needing clothes	2445
	25:44	or a stranger o needing clothes or sick or	2445
	25:44	or a stranger or needing clothes or sick or	2445
	25:44	or needing clothes or sick o in prison,	2445
	26: 5	"o there may be a riot among the people."	
			2671+3590
	27:17	Barabbas, o Jesus who is called Christ?"	2445
Mk	2: 9	o to say, 'Get up, take your mat and walk"	2445
	3: 4	to do good o to do evil,	2445
	3: 4	to save life o to kill?"	2445
	4: 8	sixty, o even a hundred times."	NIG
	4:17	When trouble o persecution comes because	2445
	4:19	thirty, sixty o even a hundred times	2779
	4:21	in a lamp to put it under a bowl o a bed?	2445
	4:27	Night and day, whether he sleeps o gets up,	2779
	4:30	o what parable shall we use to describe it?	2445
	6:11	if any place will not welcome you o listen	3593
	6:56	into villages, towns o countryside—	2445
	7:10	'Anyone who curses his father o mother	2445
	7:11	that if a man says to his father o mother:	2445
	7:12	for his father o mother.	4028
	8:17	Do you still not see o understand?	4028
	8:37	O what can a man give in exchange	NIG
	9:22	"It has often thrown him into fire o water	2779
	10:29	"no one who has left home o brothers	2445
	10:29	who has left home or brothers o sisters	2445
	10:29	or sisters or mother or father o children	2445
	10:29	or sisters or mother o father or children	2445
	10:29	or sisters or mother or father o children	2445
	10:29	mother or father or children o fields for me	2445
	10:38	the cup I drink o be baptized with	2445
	10:40	but to sit at my right o left is not for me	2445
	11:30	was it from heaven, o from men?	2445
	12:14	Is it right to pay taxes to Caesar o not?	2445
	12:15	Should we pay o shouldn't we?"	2445
	12:24	because you do not know the Scriptures o	3593
	13:15	on the roof of his house go down o enter	3593
	13:21	o, 'Look, there he is!'	NIG
	13:32	"No one knows about that day o hour,	2445
	13:35	whether in the evening, o at midnight,	2445
	13:35	or at midnight, o when the rooster crows,	2445
	13:35	or when the rooster crows, o at dawn.	2445
	14: 2	they said, "o the people may riot."	3607
	14:68	"I don't know o understand	4046
Lk	1:15	to take wine o other fermented drink,	2779
	2:24	"a pair of doves o two young pigeons."	2445
	5:23	to say, 'Your sins are forgiven,' o to say,	2445
	6: 9	to do good o to do evil,	2445
	6: 9	to save life o to destroy it?"	2445
	6:44	o grapes from briers.	4028
	7:19	o should we expect someone else?"	2445
	7:20	o should we expect someone else?' " a	2445
	8:16	"No one lights a lamp and hides it in a jar o	2445
	8:17	not be known o brought out into the open.	2779
	8:27	not worn clothes o lived in a house,	2779+4024
	9:25	and yet lose o forfeit his very self?	2445
	10: 4	Do not take a purse o bag or sandals;	3590
	10: 4	Do not take a purse or bag o sandals;	3590
	11:12	O if he asks for an egg,	2445
	11:33	o under a bowl.	4028
	12: 2	o hidden that will not be made known.	2779
	12:11	about how you will defend yourselves o	2445
	12:14	who appointed me a judge o an arbiter	2445
	12:22	o about your body, what you will wear.	3593
	12:24	They do not sow o reap,	4028
	12:24	they have no storeroom o barn;	4028
	12:27	They do not labor o spin.	4028
	12:29	not set your heart on what you will eat o	2779
	12:38	if he comes in the second o third watch of	2779
	12:41	to us, o to everyone?"	2445
	12:47	and does not get ready o does	2445
	12:58	o he may drag you off to the judge,	3607
	13: 4	O those eighteen who died when the tower	2445
	13:15	on the Sabbath untie his ox o donkey from	2445
	13:25	'I don't know you o where you come from.'	NIG
	13:27	'I don't know you o where you come from.	NIG
	14: 3	"Is it lawful to heal on the Sabbath o not?"	2445
	14: 5	"If one of you has a son o an ox that falls	2445
	14:12	"When you give a luncheon o dinner,	2445
	14:12	your brothers o relatives,	3593
	14:12	o your rich neighbors;	3593
	14:31	"O suppose a king is about to go to war	2445
	15: 8	"O suppose a woman has ten silver coins	2445

Lk	16:13	o he will be devoted to the one and despise	2445
	17: 7	a servant plowing o looking after the sheep.	2445
	17:21	'Here it is,' o 'There it is,'	2445
	17:23	o 'Here he is!'	2445
	18: 4	though I don't fear God o care about men,	4028
	18:11	o even like this tax collector.	2445
	18:29	"no one who has left home o wife	2445
	18:29	or wife o brothers or parents or children for	2445
	18:29	or wife or brothers o parents or children for	2445
	18:29	or wife or brothers or parents o children for	2445
	20: 4	was it from heaven, o from men?"	2445
	20:22	Is it right for us to pay taxes to Caesar o	2445
	21:15	of your adversaries will be able to resist o	2445
	21:34	o your hearts will be weighed down	3607
	22:27	at the table o the one who serves?	2445
	22:35	bag o sandals, did you lack anything?"	2779
Jn	1:13	nor of human decision o a husband's will,	4028
	3: 8	but you cannot tell where it comes from o	2779
	4:27	o "Why are you talking with her?"	2445
	5:14	Stop sinning o something worse may happen to you."	2671+3590
	6:19	they had rowed **three o three and a half miles,**	1633+2445+4297+5084+5558
	7:17	from God o whether I speak on my own.	2445
	7:48	of the rulers o of the Pharisees believed	2445
	8:14	But you have no idea where I come from o	2445
	8:19	"You do not know me o my Father,"	4046
	9: 2	"Rabbi, who sinned, this man o his parents,	2445
	9:21	he can see now, o who opened his eyes,	2445
	13:29	o to give something to the poor.	2445
	14:11	o **at least** believe on the evidence of the miracles	1254+1623+3590
	16: 3	because they have not known the Father o	4028
	18:20	"I always taught in synagogues o at	2779
	18:34	"o did others talk to you about me?"	2445
	19:10	either to free you o to crucify you?"	2779
Ac	1: 7	to know the times o dates the Father has set	2445
	3: 6	Peter said, "Silver o gold I do not have,	2779
	3:12	at us as if by our own power o godliness	2445
	4: 7	By what power o what name did you do this	2445
	4:18	to speak o teach at all in the name of Jesus.	3593
	4:34	from time to time those who owned lands o	2445
	5:38	their purpose o activity is of human origin,	2445
	6:10	not stand up against his wisdom o the Spirit	2779
	7:49	O where will my resting place be?	2445
	8:21	You have no part o share in this ministry,	4028
	8:34	himself o someone else?"	2445
	9: 2	whether men o women,	2779
	9: 9	and did not eat o drink anything.	4028
	10:14	"I have never eaten anything impure o	2779
	10:28	to associate with a Gentile o visit him.	2445
	10:28	that I should not call any man impure o	2445
	11: 8	Nothing impure o unclean has ever entered my mouth.'	2445
	16:21	for us Romans to accept o practice."	4028
	17:29	not think that the divine being is like gold o	2445
	17:29	is like gold or silver o stone—	2445
	18:14	about some misdemeanor o serious crime,	2445
	20:33	I have not coveted anyone's silver o gold	2445
	20:33	anyone's silver or gold o clothing.	2445
	21:21	not to circumcise their children o live	3593
	23: 9	if a spirit o an angel has spoken to him?"	2445
	23:12	not to eat o drink until they had killed Paul.	3612
	23:21	They have taken an oath not to eat o drink	3612
	23:29	that deserved death o imprisonment.	2445
	24:12	stirring up a crowd in the synagogues	2445
	24:12	the synagogues o anywhere else in the city.	4046
	24:20	O these who are here should state what crime they found in me	2445
	25: 6	After spending eight o ten days with them,	2445
	25: 8	the law of the Jews or against the temple or	4046
	25: 8	the law of the Jews or against the temple o	4046
	26:29	Paul replied, "Short time o long—	2779
	26:31	not doing anything that deserves death o	2445
	27:44	The rest were to get there on planks o	1254
	28: 6	The people expected him to swell up o	2445
	28:17	against our people o against the customs	2445
	28:21	from there has reported o said anything bad	2445
Ro	2: 4	O do you show contempt for the riches	2445
	3: 1	o what value is there in circumcision?	2445
	4: 9	o upon the uncircumcised?	2445
	4:10	Was it after he was circumcised, o before?	2445
	6: 3	O don't you know that all	2445
	6:16	which leads to death, o to obedience,	2445
	8:35	Shall trouble o hardship or persecution	2445
	8:35	Shall trouble or hardship o persecution	2445
	8:35	or hardship or persecution o famine or	2445
	8:35	or famine o nakedness or danger or sword?	2445
	8:35	or famine or nakedness o danger or sword?	2445
	8:35	or famine or nakedness or danger o sword?	2445
	9:11	before the twins were born o had done	3593
	9:11	or had done anything good o bad—	2445
	9:16	therefore, depend on man's desire o effort,	4028
	10: 7	"o 'Who will descend into the deep?' "	2445
	11:34	O who has been his counselor?"	2445
	14: 4	To his own master he stands o falls.	2445
	14: 8	So, whether we live o die,	5445
	14:10	O why do you look down on your brother?	2445
	14:13	not to put any stumbling block o obstacle	2445
	14:21	not to eat meat o drink wine or	3593
	14:21	It is better not to eat meat o drink wine o	2445
	14:21	not to eat meat or drink wine o to do	3593
1Co	1:20	with eloquence o superior wisdom	2445
	2: 6	not the wisdom of this age o of the rulers	4028
	3:12	silver, costly stones, wood, hay o straw,	NIG
	3:22	whether Paul o Apollos or Cephas or	1664
	3:22	or Apollos o Cephas or the world or life	1664

1Co	3:22	or Cephas o the world or life or death or	1664
	3:22	or the world o life or death or the present or	1664
	3:22	or the world or life o death or the present or	1664
	3:22	or the world or life or death o the present or	1664
	3:22	or life or death or the present o the future—	1664
	4: 3	I care very little if I am judged by you o	2445
	4:21	o in love and with a gentle spirit?	2445
	5:10	o the greedy and swindlers, or idolaters.	2445
	5:10	or the greedy and swindlers, o idolaters.	2445
	5:11	a brother but is sexually immoral o greedy,	2445
	5:11	an idolater o a slanderer,	2445
	5:11	a drunkard o a swindler.	2445
	7:11	she must remain unmarried o else	2445
	7:15	A believing man o woman is not bound	2445
	7:16	O, how do you know, husband,	2445
	7:34	An unmarried woman o virgin is concerned	2779
	8: 5	whether in heaven o on earth	1664
	9: 6	O is it only I and Barnabas who must work	2445
	10:19	o that an idol is anything?	2445
	10:31	So whether you eat o drink or whatever	1664
	10:31	you eat or drink o whatever you do,	1664
	10:32	Greeks o the church of God—	2779
	11: 4	Every man who prays o prophesies	2445
	11: 5	And every woman who prays o prophesies	2445
	11: 6	a woman to have her hair cut o shaved off,	2445
	11:22	O do you despise the church of God	2445
	11:27	whoever eats the bread o drinks the cup of	2445
	12: 2	**somehow o other** you were influenced	323+6055
	12:13	whether Jews o Greeks, slave or free—	1664
	12:13	whether Jews or Greeks, slave o free—	1664
	13: 1	a resounding gong o a clanging cymbal.	2445
	14: 6	unless I bring you some revelation o	2445
	14: 6	or knowledge o prophecy or word	2445
	14: 6	or prophecy o word of instruction?	2445
	14: 7	such as the flute o harp,	1664
	14:23	not understand o some unbelievers come	2445
	14:24	But if an unbeliever o someone who does	2445
	14:26	o a word of instruction, a revelation,	NIG
	14:26	a revelation, a tongue o an interpretation.	NIG
	14:27	o at the most three—should speak,	2445
	14:29	Two o three prophets should speak,	2445
	14:36	O are you the only people it has reached?	2445
	14:37	If anybody thinks he is a prophet o	2445
	15:11	Whether, then, it was I o they,	1664
	15:37	perhaps of wheat o of something else.	2445
	16: 6	o even spend the winter,	2445
2Co	1:13	not write you anything you cannot read o	2445
	1:17	O do I make my plans in a worldly manner	2445
	3: 1	O do we need, like some people,	2445
	3: 1	of recommendation to you o from you?	2445
	5: 9	whether we are at home in the body o away	1664
	5:10	whether good o bad.	1664
	6:14	O what fellowship can light have	2445
	7: 3	a place in our hearts that we would live o	2779
	7:12	on account of the one who did the wrong o	4028
	9: 7	not reluctantly o under compulsion,	2445
	10:12	not dare to classify o compare ourselves	2445
	11: 4	o if you receive a different spirit from	2445
	11: 4	o a different gospel from the one	2445
	11:20	you put up with anyone who enslaves you o	NIG
	11:20	or exploits you o takes advantage of you	NIG
	11:20	advantage of you o pushes himself forward	NIG
	11:20	forward o slaps you in the face.	NIG
	12: 2	the body out of the body I do not know—	1664
	12: 3	in the body o apart from the body I do	1664
	12: 6	of me than is warranted by what I do o say.	2445
	13: 1	by the testimony of two o three witnesses."	2779
	13: 2	not spare those who sinned earlier o any of	2779
Gal	1: 8	if we o an angel from heaven should preach	2445
	1:10	to win the approval of men, o of God?	2445
	1:10	O am I trying to please men?	2445
	2: 2	that I was running o had run my race	2445
	3: 2	o by believing what you heard?	2445
	3: 5	o because you believe what you heard?	2445
	3:15	Just as no one can set aside o add to	1254
	4: 9	o rather are known by God—	1254
	4:14	you did not treat me with contempt o scorn.	4028
	5:15	watch out o you will be destroyed	3590
	6: 1	watch yourself, o you also may be tempted.	3590
Eph	3:20	to do immeasurably more than all we ask o	2445
	5: 3	of any kind of impurity, or of greed,	2445
	5: 3	or of any kind of impurity, o of greed,	NIG
	5: 4	foolish talk o coarse joking,	2445
	5: 5	No immoral, impure o greedy person—	2445
	5:27	without stain o wrinkle	2445
	5:27	or wrinkle o any other blemish,	2445
	6: 8	whether he is slave o free.	NIG
Php	1: 7	for whether I am in chains o defending	2779
	1:18	whether from false motives o true,	1664
	1:20	whether by life o by death.	1664
	1:27	whether I come and see you o only hear	1664
	2: 3	Do nothing out of selfish ambition o	3593
	2:14	Do everything without complaining o	2779
	2:16	the day of Christ that I did not run o labor	4028
	3:12	o have already been made perfect,	2445
	4: 8	if anything is excellent o praiseworthy—	2779
	4: 9	Whatever you have learned o received	2779
	4: 9	learned or received o heard from me, or	2779
	4: 9	or seen in me—put it into practice.	2779
	4:12	whether well fed o hungry,	2779
	4:12	whether living in plenty o in want.	2779
Col	1:16	and invisible, whether thrones o powers	1664
	1:16	whether thrones or powers o rulers	1664
	1:16	thrones or powers or rulers o authorities;	1664
	1:20	whether things on earth o things in heaven,	1664
	2:16	not let anyone judge you by what you eat o	2779
	2:16	o with regard to a religious festival,	2445

Col	2:16	a New Moon celebration o a Sabbath day.	2445
	3:11	Here there is no Greek o Jew,	2779
	3:11	circumcised o uncircumcised, barbarian,	2779
	3:11	slave o free, but Christ is all, and is in all.	NIG
	3:17	whatever you do, whether in word o deed,	2445
	3:21	o they will become discouraged.	2671+3590
1Th	2: 3	not spring from error o impure motives,	4028
	2: 6	not from you o anyone else.	4046
	2:19	o the crown in which we will glory in	2445
	4: 6	no one should wrong his brother o take	2779
	4:13	o to grieve like the rest of men,	NIG
	5: 5	not belong to the night o to the darkness.	4028
	5:10	whether we are awake o asleep,	1664
2Th	2: 2	not to become easily unsettled o alarmed	3593
	2: 2	report o letter supposed to have come	3612
	2: 4	over everything that is called God o	2445
	2:15	whether by word of mouth o by letter.	1664
1Ti	1: 7	about o what they so confidently affirm.	3612
	1: 9	for those who kill their fathers o mothers,	2779
	2: 8	without anger o disputing.	2779
	2: 9	not with braided hair o gold or pearls	2779
	2: 9	or gold o pearls or expensive clothes,	2445
	2: 9	not with braided hair or gold or pearls o	2445
	2:12	a woman to teach o to have authority over	4028
	3: 6	o he may become conceited and	2671+3590
	5: 4	if a widow has children o grandchildren,	2445
	5:19	an elder unless it is brought by two o	2445
	6:14	to keep this command without spot o blame	NIG
	6:16	whom no one has seen o can see.	4028
2Ti	1: 8	ashamed of me his prisoner.	3593
Tit	1:14	pay no attention to Jewish myths o to the	2779
	2: 3	to be slanderers o addicted to much wine,	3593
	3:12	soon as I send Artemas o Tychicus to you,	2445
Phm	1:18	If he has done you any wrong o owes you	2445
Heb	1: 5	O again, "I will be his Father,	2779
	7: 3	Without father o mother,	NIG
	7: 3	without beginning of days o end of life,	3612
	8:11	o a man his brother, saying,	2779
	10:28	on the testimony of two o three witnesses.	2445
	12:16	o is godless like Esau,	2445
	12:19	to a trumpet blast o to such	2779
Jas	2: 3	"You stand there" o "Sit on the floor	2445
	2:15	a brother o sister is without clothes	2445
	3: 4	O take ships as an example.	2779
	3:12	o a grapevine bear figs?	2445
	3:14	do not boast about it o deny the truth.	2779
	4: 5	O do you think Scripture says	2445
	4:11	Anyone who speaks against his brother o	2445
	4:13	"Today o tomorrow we will go to this or	2445
	4:13	we will go to this o that city,	3836+3840
	4:15	we will live and do this o that."	2445
	5: 9	brothers, o you will be judged.	2671+3590
	5:12	by heaven o by earth or by anything else.	3612
	5:12	by heaven or by earth or by anything else.	3612
	5:12	no, o you will be condemned.	2671+3590
1Pe	1: 4	an inheritance that can never perish, spoil o	2779
	1:18	with perishable things such as silver o gold	2445
	1:19	a lamb without blemish o defect.	2779
	2:14	o to governors, who are sent by him	1664
	3: 9	not repay evil with evil o insult with insult,	2445
	4:15	be as a murderer o thief or any other kind	2445
	4:15	be as a murderer or thief o any other kind	2445
	4:15	o even as a meddler.	2445
1Jn	2:15	Do not love the world o anything in the	
		world.	3593+3836
	3: 6	to sin has either seen him o known him.	4028
	3:18	with words o tongue but with actions and	3593
2Jn	1:10	do not take him into your house o	2779
Rev	3:15	I wish you were either one o the other!	2445
	5: 3	But no one in heaven o on earth or under	4028
	5: 3	But no one in heaven or on earth o under	4028
	5: 3	under the earth could open the scroll o even	4046
	5: 4	to open the scroll o look inside.	4046
	7: 1	from blowing on the land o on the sea or	3612
	7: 1	on the land or on the sea o on any tree.	3612
	7: 3	"Do not harm the land o the sea or the trees	3612
	7: 3	"Do not harm the land or the sea o the trees	3612
	9: 4	to harm the grass of the earth o any plant	4028
	9: 4	grass of the earth or any plant o tree,	4028
	9:20	idols that cannot see o hear or walk.	4046
	9:20	idols that cannot see or hear o walk.	4046
	9:21	their sexual immorality o their thefts.	4046
	12: 9	ancient serpent called the devil, o Satan,	2779
	13:16	a mark on his right hand o on his forehead,	2445
	13:17	that no one could buy o sell unless he had	2445
	13:17	of the beast o the number of his name.	2445
	14: 9	and receives his mark on the forehead o on	2445
	14:11	There is no rest day o night	2779
	14:11	o for anyone who receives the mark	2779
	20: 2	who is the devil, o Satan,	2779
	20: 4	not worshiped the beast o his image	4028
	20: 4	not received his mark on their foreheads o	2779
	21: 4	There will be no more death o mourning	4046
	21: 4	no more death or mourning o crying	4046
	21: 4	no more death or mourning or crying o pain,	4046
	21:23	not need the sun o the moon to shine on it,	4028
	21:27	will anyone who does what is shameful o	2779
	22: 5	not need the light of a lamp o the light of	2779

ORACLE (44) [ORACLES]

Nu	23: 7	Then Balaam uttered his o:	5442
	23:18	Then he uttered his o:	5442
	24: 3	and he uttered his o:	5442
	24: 3	"The o of Balaam son of Beor,	5536
	24: 3	the o of one whose eye sees clearly,	5536
	24: 4	the o of one who hears the words of God,	5536

Nu	24:15	Then he uttered his o:	5442
	24:15	"The o of Balaam son of Beor,	5536
	24:15	the o of one whose eye sees clearly,	5536
	24:16	the o of one who hears the words of God,	5536
	24:20	Balaam saw Amalek and uttered his o:	5442
	24:21	Then he saw the Kenites and uttered his o:	5442
	24:23	Then he uttered his o:	5442
2Sa	23: 1	"The o of David son of Jesse,	5536
	23: 1	the o of the man exalted by the Most High,	5536
Ps	36: 1	An o is within my heart concerning	5536
Pr	16:10	The lips of a king speak as an o,	7877
	30: 1	The sayings of Agur son of Jakeh—an o:	5363
	31: 1	an o his mother taught him:	5363
Isa	13: 1	An o concerning Babylon that Isaiah son	5363
	14:28	This o came in the year King Ahaz died:	5363
	15: 1	An o concerning Moab:	5363
	17: 1	An o concerning Damascus:	5363
	19: 1	An o concerning Egypt:	5363
	21: 1	An o concerning the Desert by the Sea:	5363
	21:11	An o concerning Dumah:	5363
	21:13	An o concerning Arabia:	5363
	22: 1	An o concerning the Valley of Vision:	5363
	23: 1	An o concerning Tyre:	5363
	30: 6	An o concerning the animals of the Negev:	5363
Jer	23:33	ask you, 'What is the o of the LORD?'	5363
	23:33	say to them, 'What o?	5363
	23:34	'This is the o of the LORD,'	5363
	23:36	not mention 'the o of the LORD' again,	5363
	23:36	every man's own word becomes his o	5363
	23:38	'This is the o of the LORD,'	5363
	23:38	'This is the o of the LORD,'	5363
	23:38	'This is the o of the LORD,'	5363
Eze	12:10	This o concerns the prince in Jerusalem	5363
Na	1: 1	An o concerning Nineveh.	5363
Hab	1: 1	The o that Habakkuk the prophet received.	5363
Zec	9: 1	An O The word of the LORD is against	5363
	12: 1	An O This is the word of the LORD	5363
Mal	1: 1	An o: The word of the	5363

ORACLES (1) [ORACLE]

La	2:14	The o they gave you were false	5363

ORCHARD (1) [ORCHARDS]

SS	4:13	an o of pomegranates with choice fruits,	7236

ORCHARDS (2) [ORCHARD]

Isa	16:10	and gladness are taken away from the o;	4149
Jer	48:33	and gladness are gone from the o and fields	4149

ORDAIN (3) [ORDAINED, ORDINATION]

Ex	28:41	and his sons, anoint and o them.	906+3338+4848
	29: 9	In this way you shall o Aaron and his	3338+4848
	29:35	taking seven days to o them.	3338+4848

ORDAINED (14) [ORDAIN]

Ex	29:29	so that they can be anointed and o in them.	
			906+3338+4848
Lev	16:32	and o to succeed his father as high priest	
			906+3338+4848
	21:10	and who has been o to wear	906+3338+4848
Nu	3: 3	who were o to serve as priests.	3338+4848
2Ki	19:25	Long ago I o it.	6913
Ps	8: 2	of children and infants you have o praise	3569
	65: 9	for so you have o it.	3922
	111: 9	he o his covenant forever—	7422
	139:16	All the days o for me were written	3670
Isa	37:26	Long ago I o it.	6913
	48: 5	my wooden image and metal god o them.'	7422
Eze	28:14	guardian cherub, for so I o you.	5989
Hab	1:12	O Rock, you have o them to punish.	3569
Mt	21:16	and infants you have o praise'?"	2936

ORDER (148) [ORDERED, ORDERLY, ORDERS]

Ge	25:13	listed in the o of their birth:	9352
	38:20	the Adullamite in o to get his pledge back	4200
	43:33	before him in the o of their ages, from	3869
Ex	1:22	Pharaoh gave this o to all his people:	7422
	5: 6	That same day Pharaoh gave this o to	7422
	9:19	Give an o now to bring your livestock	8938
	28:10	in the o of their birth—	3869
	36: 6	Then Moses gave an o and	7422
Lev	13:54	he shall o that the contaminated article	7422
	14: 4	the priest shall o that two live clean birds	7422
	14: 5	The priest shall o that one of the birds	7422
	14:36	The priest is to o the house to be emptied	7422
	14:40	he is to o that the contaminated stones	7422
	22:19	sheep or goats in o that it may be accepted	4200
Nu	2:17	They will set out in the same o	4027
	9:19	the Israelites obeyed the LORD's o	5466
	9:23	They obeyed the LORD's o,	5466
	10:28	the o of march for the Israelite divisions	5023
	36: 5	LORD's command Moses gave this o	7422
Dt	2:30	and his heart obstinate in o to give him	5100
	8: 2	and to test you in o to know what was	4200
	29:12	You are standing here in o to enter into	4200
Jos	10:27	At sunset Joshua gave the o	7422
Jdg	10: 2	In o that Israel may not boast against me	7153
	9:24	God did this in o that the crime	4200
Ru	4: 5	in o to maintain the name of the dead	4200
	4:10	in o to maintain the name of the dead	4200
1Sa	1: 6	her rival kept provoking her in o to	6288
	15:21	in o to sacrifice them to the LORD	4200

2Sa	2:26	How long before you o your men	606
	4:12	So David gave an o to his men,	7422
	13:28	Have not I given you this o?	7422
	14: 8	and I will issue an o in your behalf."	7422
	14:29	for Joab in o to send him to the king,	4200
	17:14	the good advice of Ahithophel in o to	6288
	17:23	put his house in o and then hanged himself.	7422
	19:29	I o you and Ziba to divide the fields."	606
1Ki	2:46	Then the king gave the o to Benaiah son	7422
	3:25	He then gave an o:	606
		Then King Asa issued an o to all Judah—	9048
2Ki	10:19	But Jehu was acting deceptively in o to	5100
	17:27	Then the king of Assyria gave this o:	7422
	20: 1	Put your house in o,	7422
	23:21	The king gave this o to all the people:	7422
	23:35	In o to do so,	4200
	24: 3	in o to remove them from his presence	4200
1Ch	15:14	Levites consecrated themselves in o to	4200
	24: 3	for their appointed o of ministering.	7213
	24:19	This was their appointed o of ministering	7213
2Ch	11:22	in o to make him king.	3954
	24:21	by o of the king they stoned him to death	5184
	29:27	Hezekiah gave the o to sacrifice	606
	31: 5	As soon as the o went out,	1821
	32:18	and make them afraid in o to capture	5100
	35:20	set the temple in o,	3922
	36:22	in o to fulfill the word of the LORD	4200
Ezr	1: 1	in o to fulfill the word of the LORD	4200
	4:19	I issued an o and a search was made,	10302
	4:21	Now issue an o to these men to stop work,	10302
	4:21	that this city will not be rebuilt until I so o.	
			10002+10302+10682
	6: 1	King Darius then issued an o,	10302
	6:21	of their Gentile neighbors in o to seek	4200
	7:21	o all the treasurers of Trans-Euphrates to	
		provide	10302+10682
Ne	5: 2	in o for us to eat and stay alive,	2256
	9:17	in their rebellion appointed a leader in o to	4200
	9:26	who had admonished them in o to	4200
	13:22	and go and guard the gates in o to keep	4200
Est	1:11	in o to display her beauty to the people	4200
	2: 8	the king's o and edict had been proclaimed,	1821
	3:13	with the o to destroy, kill and annihilate all	NIH
	4: 3	to which the edict and o of the king came,	2017
	8: 5	an o be written overruling the dispatches	4180
Job	25: 2	he establishes o in the heights of heaven.	8934
Ps	10:18	in o that man, who is of the earth, may	
		terrify no more.	1153
	59: T	to watch David's house in o to kill him.	4200
	110: 4	a priest forever, in the o of Melchizedek."	1826
Pr	28: 2	and knowledge maintains o.	4026
Ecc	12: 9	and set in o many proverbs.	9545
Isa	23:11	He has given an o concerning Phoenicia	7422
	34:16	For it is his mouth that has given the o,	7422
	38: 1	Put your house in o,	7422
Jer	34:22	I am going to give the o,	7422
Eze	3:18	to dissuade him from his evil ways in o to	4200
	13:18	of various lengths for their heads in o to	4200
	13:18	be burying them in o to cleanse the land.	5100
Da	6:16	So the king gave the o,	10042
	11:17	in marriage in o to overthrow the kingdom,	4200
Am	1:13	the pregnant women of Gilead in o to	5100
Zec	13: 4	a prophet's garment of hair in o to deceive.	5100
Mt	12:44	swept clean and put in o.	3175
	27:64	So give the o for the tomb	3027
Mk	7: 9	setting aside the commands of God in o to	2671
Lk	4:29	in o to throw him down the cliff.	6063
	8:31	not to o them to go into the Abyss.	2199
	11:25	it finds the house swept clean and put in o.	3175
	19:15	in o to find out what they had gained	2671
Jn	8: 6	in o to have a basis for accusing him.	2671
	17:26	to make you known in o that	2671
Ac	6: 2	of the word of God in o to wait on tables.	AIT
	9:24	on the city gates in o to kill him.	3968
	16:35	the jailer with the o: "Release those men."	3306
	17: 5	in o to bring them out	AIT
	19:33	in o to make a defense	AIT
	20:30	the truth in o to draw away disciples	3836
	24: 4	But in o not to weary you further,	2671
Ro	1:13	until now) in o that I might have a harvest	2671
	4:11	in o that righteousness might be credited	
			1650+3836
	6: 4	through baptism into death in o that,	2671
	7: 4	in o that we might bear fruit to God.	2671
	7:13	But in o that sin might be recognized	2671
	8: 4	in o that the righteous requirements of	2671
	8:17	we share in his sufferings in o that we may	2671
	9:11	in o that God's purpose in election might	2671
	11:31	now become disobedient in o that	2671
	15: 7	in o to bring praise to God.	1650
2Co	1:23	as my witness that it was in o to spare you	AIT
	2:11	in o that Satan might not outwit us.	2671
	8:19	which we administer in o to honor	4639
	9: 3	But I am sending the brothers in o that	2671
	11: 7	Was it a sin for me to lower myself in o to	2671
	11:12	on doing what I am doing in o to cut	2671
	11:32	guarded in o to arrest me.	AIT
Gal	3:14	He redeemed us in o that the blessing	2671
Eph	1:12	in o that we, who were the first	1650+3836
	1:18	heart may be enlightened in o that you	1650+3836
	2: 7	in o that in the coming ages he might show	2671
	4:10	in o to fill the whole universe.)	2671
Php	2:16	in o that I may boast on the day of Christ	AIT
Col	1:10	o that you may live a life worthy	AIT
	2: 2	in o that they may know the mystery	1650
1Th	2: 9	and in o not to be a burden to anyone	4639

1Th	4: 1	we instructed you how to live **in o** to	2671
2Th	3: 9	but **in o** to make ourselves a model for you	2671
	3:14	**in o that** he may feel ashamed.	2671
1Ti	4: 3	and **o** them to abstain from certain foods,	NIG
Tit	3:14	**in o** that they may provide	2671
Phm	1: 8	be bold and **o** you to do what you ought	2199
Heb	2:17	**in o** that he might become a merciful	2671
	5: 6	a priest forever, in the **o** of Melchizedek."	5423
	5:10	to be high priest in the **o** of Melchizedek.	5423
	6:11	**in o** to make your hope sure.	4639
	6:20	high priest forever, in the **o** of Melchizedek.	5423
	7:11	one in the **o** of Melchizedek?	5423
	7:11	not in the **o** of Aaron?	5423
	7:17	a priest forever, in the **o** of Melchizedek."	5423
	9:10	until the time *of* **the new o.**	1481
Rev	21: 4	for the old **o** of things has passed away."	NIG

ORDERED (94) [ORDER]

Ex	17:10	the Amalekites as Moses *had* **o,**	606
Lev	10: 5	outside the camp, as Moses **o.**	1819
Nu	34:13	The LORD *has* **o** that it be given to	7422
	36: 2	he **o** you to give the inheritance	7422
Jos	1:10	So Joshua **o** the officers of the people:	7422
	6: 7	And *he* **o** the people, "Advance!	606
	8:29	Joshua **o** them to take his body from	7422
Jdg	3:28	*he* **o,** "for the LORD has given Moab,	606
	9:48	*He* **o** the men with him, "Quick!	606
1Sa	18:22	Then Saul **o** his attendants:	7422
	20:29	in the town and my brother *has* **o** me to	7422
	22:17	Then the king **o** the guards at his side:	606
	22:18	The king then **o** Doeg,	606
2Sa	1:18	and **o** that the men of Judah	606
	13:28	Absalom **o** his men, "Listen!	7422
	13:29	to Amnon what Absalom *had* **o.**	7422
1Ki	2:29	Then Solomon **o** Benaiah son of Jehoiada,	8938
	12:24	as the LORD had **o.**	1821
	17: 4	and *I have* **o** the ravens to feed you there."	7422
	18:34	"Do it a third time," *he* **o,**	606
	20:12	and *he* **o** his men: "Prepare to attack."	606
	22:26	The king of Israel then **o,**	606
	22:31	*had* **o** his thirty-two chariot commanders,	7422
2Ki	1: 3	"Go, find out where he is," the king **o,**	606
	9:17	"Get a horseman," Joram **o.**	606
	9:21	"Hitch up my chariot," Joram **o.**	606
	10: 8	Then Jehu **o,** "Put them in two piles at	606
	10:14	"Take them alive!" *he* **o.**	606
	10:25	he **o** the guards and officers:	606
	11: 9	a hundred did just as Jehoiada the priest **o.**	7422
	11:15	the priest **o** the commanders of units of	7422
	16:16	Uriah the priest did just as King Ahaz had **o.**	7422
	17:15	although the LORD *had* **o** them,	7422
	23: 4	The king **o** Hilkiah the high priest,	7422
1Ch	21:17	not I *who* **o** the fighting men to be counted?	606
	21:18	the angel of the LORD **o** Gad to tell David	606
	22:17	Then David **o** all the leaders of Israel	7422
2Ch	8:14	the man of God had **o.**	5184
	18:25	The king of Israel then **o,**	606
	18:30	king of Aram *had* **o** his chariot commanders	7422
	23: 8	of Judah did just as Jehoiada the priest **o.**	7422
	23:18	with rejoicing and singing, as David had **o.**	3338
	29:15	as the king had **o,**	5184
	29:24	because the king *had* **o** the burnt offering	606
	29:30	and his officials the Levites to praise	606
	30:12	**what** the king and his officials had **o,**	5184
	31: 4	*He* **o** the people living in Jerusalem to give	606
	35:10	in their divisions as the king had **o.**	5184
	35:16	as King Josiah had **o.**	5184
Ezr	2:63	The governor **o** them not to eat any of	606
Ne	7:65	**o** them not to eat any of the most sacred	606
	13:19	*I* **o** the doors to be shut and not opened	606
Est	4: 5	to attend her, and **o** him to find out	7422
	6: 1	so he **o** the book of the chronicles,	606
	6: 5	"Bring him in," the king **o.**	606
Jer	35:14	son of Recab **o** his sons not to drink wine	7422
	35:18	and have done everything he **o.'**	7422
	38:27	the king *had* **o** him to say.	7422
	47: 7	when *he has* **o** it to attack Ashkelon and	3585
Da	1: 3	Then the king **o** Ashpenaz,	606
	2:12	so angry and furious that *he* **o** the execution	10042
	2:46	and paid him honor and **o** that an offering	10042
	3:19	*He* **o** the furnace heated seven times	10558
Mt	14: 9	he **o** that her request be granted	3027
	18:25	the master **o** that he and his wife	3027
	27:58	and Pilate **o** that it be given to him.	3027
Lk	5:14	Then Jesus **o** him, "Don't tell anyone,	4133
	8:56	but he **o** them not to tell anyone	4133
	14:21	the house became angry and **o** his servant,	3306
	14:22	'what *you* **o** has been done,	2199
	18:40	Jesus stopped and **o** the man to be brought	3027
Ac	4:15	So *they* **o** them to withdraw from	3027
	5:34	up in the Sanhedrin and **o** that the men	3027
	5:40	Then *they* **o** them not to speak in the name	4133
	10:48	So he **o** that they be baptized in the name	4705
	12:19	he cross-examined the guards and **o** that	3027
	16:22	and the magistrates **o** them to be stripped	3027
	16:36	"The magistrates *have* **o** that you and Silas	690
	18: 2	Claudius *had* **o** all the Jews to leave Rome.	1411
	21:33	up and arrested him and **o** him to be bound	3027
	21:34	*he* **o** that Paul be taken into the barracks.	3027
	22:24	the commander **o** Paul to be taken into	3027
	22:30	and **o** the chief priests and all the Sanhedrin	3027
	23: 2	the high priest Ananias **o** those standing	2199
	23:10	*He* **o** the troops to go down	3027
	23:23	he called two of his centurions and **o** them,	3306
	23:30	*I* also **o** his accusers to present	4133
	23:35	then *he* **o** that Paul be kept under guard	3027
Ac	24:23	*He* **o** the centurion to keep Paul under guard	1411
	25: 6	and **o** that Paul be brought before him.	3027
	25:17	but convened the court the next day and **o**	3027
	25:21	*I* **o** him held until I could send him	3027
	27:43	*He* **o** those who could swim	3027
Rev	13:14	*He* **o** them to set up an image in honor of	3306

ORDERLY (3) [ORDER]

Lk	1: 3	also to me to write an **o** account for you,	2759
1Co	14:40	be done in a fitting and **o way.**	2848+5423
Col	2: 5	in spirit and delight to see how **o** you are	5423

ORDERS (50) [ORDER]

Ge	12:20	Pharaoh gave **o** about Abram *to* his men,	7422
	26:11	So Abimelech gave **o** *to* all the people:	7422
	41:40	and all my people are to submit to your **o.**	7023
	42:25	Joseph gave **o** to fill their bags with grain,	7422
Nu	32:28	Then Moses gave **o** about them *to* Eleazar	7422
Dt	2: 4	**Give** the people *these* **o:**	7422
Jos	3: 3	giving **o** to the people:	7422
	8: 4	with these **o:** "Listen carefully,	7422
	8: 8	See to it; you *have* my **o."**	7422
Ru	2:15	Boaz gave **o** *to* his men,	6680
2Sa	3:15	So Ish-Bosheth gave **o**	8938
	18: 5	And all the troops heard the king *giving* **o**	7422
1Ki	2:25	So King Solomon gave **o** *to* Benaiah son	8938
	5: 6	"So give **o** that cedars of Lebanon be cut	7422
2Ki	16:15	King Ahaz then gave *these* **o** *to* Uriah	7422
	22:12	He gave *these* **o** *to* Hilkiah the priest,	7422
1Ch	14:12	and David gave **o** to burn them in the fire.	606
	22: 2	So David gave **o** to assemble	606
2Ch	2: 1	Solomon gave **o** to build a temple for	606
	19: 9	He gave them *these* **o:**	7422
	31:11	Hezekiah gave **o** to prepare storerooms in	606
	34:20	He gave *these* **o** *to* Hilkiah,	7422
Ezr	8:36	the king's **o** to the royal satraps and	2017
Ne	11:23	The singers were under the king's **o,**	5184
	13: 9	*I* gave **o** to purify the rooms,	606
Est	3:12	the language of each people all Haman's **o**	7422
	8: 9	They wrote out all Mordecai's **o** to	7422
	8: 9	These were written in the script	NIH
	9:25	he **issued** written **o** that	606
Job	38:12	*"Have you* ever given **o** *to* the morning,	7422
Isa	45: 1	or give me **o** about the work of my hands?	7422
Jer	37:21	King Zedekiah then gave **o** *for* Jeremiah to	7422
	39:11	of Babylon *had* given *these* **o**	7422
Da	5: 2	he gave **o** to bring in the gold	10042
	6:23	and gave **o** to lift Daniel out of the den.	10042
Mt	2:16	and he gave **o** to kill all the boys	690
	8:18	*he* gave **o** to cross to the other side of	3027
Mk	1:27	*He* even gives **o** to evil spirits	2199
	3:12	But *he* gave them strict **o** not	2203
	5:43	*He* gave strict **o** not to let anyone know	1403
	6:17	For Herod himself *had* given **o**	690
	6:27	an executioner with **o** to bring John's head.	2199
	9: 9	Jesus gave them **o** not to tell	1403
Lk	4:36	With authority and power he gives **o**	2199
	15:29	for you and never disobeyed your **o.**	1953
Jn	11:57	the chief priests and Pharisees had given **o**	1953
Ac	8:28	*"We gave* you **strict o** not to teach	4132+4133
	8:38	And *he* gave **o** to stop the chariot.	3027
	16:24	Upon receiving such **o,**	4132
	23:31	So the soldiers, carrying out their **o,**	1411

ORDINANCE (29) [ORDINANCES]

Ex	12:14	to the LORD—a lasting **o.**	2978
	12:17	as a lasting **o** for the generations to come.	2978
	12:24	as a lasting **o** for you and your descendants.	2976
	13:10	You must keep this **o** at the appointed time	2978
	27:21	to be a lasting **o** among the Israelites for	2978
	28:43	a lasting **o** for Aaron and his descendants.	2978
	29: 9	The priesthood is theirs by a lasting **o.**	2978
	30:21	a lasting **o** for Aaron and his descendants	2976
Lev	3:17	" 'This is a lasting **o** for the generations	2978
	10: 9	a lasting **o** for the generations to come.	2978
	16:29	"This is to be a lasting **o** for you:	2978
	16:31	it is a lasting **o.**	2978
	16:34	"This is to be a lasting **o** for you:	2978
	17: 7	a lasting **o** for them and for the generations	2978
	23:14	This is to be a lasting **o** for the generations	2978
	23:21	This is to be a lasting **o** for the generations	2978
	23:31	This is to be a lasting **o** for the generations	2978
	23:41	This is to be a lasting **o** for the generations	2978
	24: 3	This is to be a lasting **o** for the generations	2978
Nu	10: 8	to be a lasting **o** for you and the generations	2978
	15:15	a lasting **o** for the generations to come.	2978
	18:23	a lasting **o** for the generations to come.	2978
	19:10	be a lasting **o** both for the Israelites and for	2978
	19:21	This is a lasting **o** for them.	2978
1Sa	30:25	David made this a statute and **o** for Israel	5477
2Ch	2:14	This is a lasting **o** for Israel.	NIH
	8:14	In keeping with the **o** *of* his father David,	5477
Ps	81: 4	an **o** of the God of Jacob.	5477
Eze	46:14	grain offering to the LORD is a lasting **o.**	2978

ORDINANCES (7) [ORDINANCE]

2Ki	17:34	nor adhere to the decrees and **o,**	5477
	17:37	be careful to keep the decrees and **o,**	5477
2Ch	19:10	commands, decrees or **o—**	5477
	33: 8	decrees and **o** given through Moses."	5477
Ne	9:29	They sinned against your **o,**	5477
Ps	19: 9	The **o** of the LORD are sure	5477
Eze	44:24	as judges and decide it according to my **o.**	5477

ORDINARY (8)

1Sa	21: 4	"I don't have any **o** bread on hand;	2687
Isa	8: 1	a large scroll and write on it with an **o** pen:	632
Ac	4:13	that they were unschooled, **o** men,	2626
	7:20	and he was no **o** child.	842
	21:39	a citizen of no **o** city.	817
Gal	4:23	His son by the slave woman was born in the **o way;**	2848+4922
	4:29	the son born **in the o way** persecuted	2848+4922
Heb	11:23	because they saw *he was* no **o** child,	842

ORDINATION (13) [ORDAIN]

Ex	29:22	(This is the ram for the **o.**)	4854
	29:26	the breast of the ram for Aaron's **o,**	4854
	29:27	"Consecrate those parts of the **o** ram	4854
	29:31	"Take the ram for the **o** and cook the meat	4854
	29:33	by which atonement was made for their **o**	906+3338+4848
	29:34	of the meat of the **o ram** or any bread is left	4854
Lev	7:37	the **o** offering and the fellowship offering,	4854
	8:22	the ram for the **o,**	4854
	8:28	of the burnt offering as an **o** offering,	4854
	8:29	Moses' share of the **o** ram—	4854
	8:31	the bread from the basket of **o offerings,**	4854
	8:33	until the days of your **o** are completed,	4854
	8:33	for your **o** will last seven days.	906+3338+4848

ORE (3)

Job	28: 2	and copper is smelted from **o.**	74
	28: 3	he searches the farthest recesses for **o** in	74
Jer	6:27	a tester of metals and my people the **o,**	4450

OREB (7)

Jdg	7:25	of the Midianite leaders, **O** and Zeeb.	6855
	7:25	They killed **O** at the rock of Oreb,	6855
	7:25	They killed Oreb at the rock of	6855
	7:25	the Midianites and brought the heads of **O**	6855
	8: 3	God gave **O** and Zeeb,	6855
Ps	83:11	Make their nobles like **O** and Zeeb,	6855
Isa	10:26	he struck down Midian at the rock of **O;**	6855

OREN (1)

1Ch	2:25	Ram his firstborn, Bunah, **O,**	816

ORGAN (KJV) See FLUTE

ORGIES (3)

Ro	13:13	not *in* **o** and drunkenness,	3269
Gal	5:21	drunkenness, **o,** and the like.	3269
1Pe	4: 3	living in debauchery, lust, drunkenness, **o,**	3269

ORIGIN (3) [ORIGINAL, ORIGINATE, ORIGINS]

Est	6:13	is of Jewish **o,** you cannot stand	2446
Ac	5:38	if their purpose or activity is of human **o,**	NIG
2Pe	1:21	For prophecy never *had its* **o** in the will	5770

ORIGINAL (1) [ORIGIN]

2Ch	24:13	the temple of God according to its **o design**	5504

ORIGINATE (1) [ORIGIN]

1Co	14:36	*Did* the word of God **o** with you?	2002

ORIGINS (1) [ORIGIN]

Mic	5: 2	whose **o** are from of old,	4606

ORION (3)

Job	9: 9	He is the Maker of the Bear and **O,**	4068
	38:31	Can you loose the cords of **O?**	4068
Am	5: 8	the Pleiades and **O,** who turns blackness	4068

ORNAMENT (2) [ORNAMENTED, ORNAMENTS]

Pr	3:22	an **o to grace** your neck.	2834
	25:12	or an **o** *of* fine gold is a wise man's rebuke	2717

ORNAMENTED (5) [ORNAMENT]

Ge	37: 3	and he made a **richly o** robe for him.	7168
	37:23	the **richly o** robe he was wearing—	7168
	37:32	They took the **o** robe back to their father	7168
2Sa	13:18	She was wearing a **richly o** robe,	7168
	13:19	and tore the **o** robe she was wearing.	7168

ORNAMENTS (10) [ORNAMENT]

Ex	33: 4	to mourn and no one put on any **o.**	6344
	33: 5	Now take off your **o** and I will decide what	6344
	33: 6	So the Israelites stripped off their **o**	6344
	35:22	brooches, earrings, rings and **o.**	3921
Jdg	8:21	and took the **o** off their camels' necks.	8448
	8:26	not counting the **o,**	8448
2Sa	1:24	who adorned your garments with **o** *of* gold.	6344
Isa	3:16	with **o jingling** on their ankles.	6576
	49:18	"you will wear them all as **o;**	6344
Jer	2:32	a bride her **wedding o?**	8005

ORPAH (2)
Ru 1:4 one named O and the other Ruth. 6905
1:14 Then O kissed her mother-in-law good-by, 6905

ORPHAN (1) [ORPHAN'S, ORPHANS]
Ex 22:22 "Do not take advantage of a widow or an o. 3846

ORPHAN'S (1) [ORPHAN]
Job 24:3 They drive away the o donkey and take 3846

ORPHANS (4) [ORPHAN]
Jer 49:11 Leave your o; I will protect their lives. 3846
La 5:3 We have become o and fatherless, 3846
Jn 14:18 I will not leave you as o; 4003
Jas 1:27 to look after o and widows in their distress 4003

OSEE (KJV) See HOSEA

OSHEA (KJV) See JOSHUA

OSPRAY (KJV) See BLACK VULTURE

OSPREY (2)
Lev 11:18 the white owl, the desert owl, the o, 8164
Dt 14:17 the desert owl, the o, the cormorant, 8168

OSSIFRAGE (KJV) See VULTURE

OSTRICH (1) [OSTRICHES]
Job 39:13 "The wings of the o flap joyfully, 8266

OSTRICHES (1) [OSTRICH]
La 4:3 but my people have become heartless like o 3612

OTHER (730) [OTHER'S, OTHERS, OTHERWISE]
Ge 4:19 one named Adah and the o Zillah. 9108
5:4 Adam lived 800 years and had o sons NIH
5:7 Seth lived 807 years and had o sons NIH
5:10 Enosh lived 815 years and had o sons NIH
5:13 Kenan lived 840 years and had o sons NIH
5:16 Mahalalel lived 830 years and had o sons NIH
5:19 Jared lived 800 years and had o sons NIH
5:22 walked with God 300 years and had o sons NIH
5:26 Methuselah lived 782 years and had o sons NIH
5:30 Lamech lived 595 years and had o sons NIH
9:23 Their faces were turned the o way so 345
11:3 They said to each o, "Come, 8276S
11:7 so they will not understand each o." 8276S
11:11 Shem lived 500 years and had o sons NIH
11:13 Arphaxad lived 403 years and had o sons NIH
11:15 Shelah lived 403 years and had o sons NIH
11:17 Eber lived 430 years and had o sons NIH
11:19 Peleg lived 209 years and had o sons NIH
11:21 Reu lived 207 years and had o sons NIH
11:23 Serug lived 200 years and had o sons NIH
11:25 Nahor lived 119 years and had o sons NIH
14:16 together with the women and the o people. NIH
15:10 and arranged the halves opposite each o; 8276S
24:50 to you one way or the o. 3202S
25:22 The babies jostled each o within her, 8368
25:23 one people will be stronger than the o, 4211S
26:31 the men swore an oath to each o. 278S
28:17 This is none o than the house of God; 561+3954
29:19 that I give her to you than to some o man. 337
31:49 and me when we are away from each o. 8276S
34:23 and all their o animals become ours? AIT
36:6 as his livestock and all his o animals AIT
37:3 of his o sons, because he had been born AIT
37:19 they said to each o. 278S
41:3 After them, seven o cows, ugly and gaunt, 337
41:6 seven o heads of grain sprouted— NIH
41:13 and the o man was hanged." 2257S
41:19 After them, seven o cows came up— 337
41:23 After them, seven o heads sprouted— NIH
41:54 There was famine in all the o lands, NIH
42:1 "Why do you just keep looking at each o?" 8011
42:28 and they turned to each o trembling 278S
43:14 the man so that he will let your o brother 337
43:33 and they looked at each o in astonishment. 8276S
45:23 and bread and o provisions for his journey. AIT
47:21 from one end of Egypt to the o. 7895S
47:24 The o four-fifths you may keep as seed for AIT
Ex 12:38 Many o people went up with them, 6850
14:7 along with all the o chariots of Egypt, NIH
14:20 to the one side and light to the o side; NIH
14:20 so neither went near the o all night long. 2296S
16:5 as much as they gather on the o days." 3427+3427
16:15 the Israelites saw it, they said to each o, 278S
17:12 one on one side, one on the o— 2296S
18:4 and the o was named Eliezer, 285S
18:7 They greeted each o and then went into 8276S
18:11 that the LORD is greater than all o gods, 2021S
18:12 brought a burnt offering and o sacrifices NIH
20:3 "You shall have no o gods before me. 337
21:18 "If men quarrel and one hits the o with 8276S
21:19 if he gets up and walks around outside NIH
22:8 on the o man's property. 8276S
22:9 or any o lost property AIT

Ex 22:10 a sheep or any o animal to his neighbor AIT
22:11 not lay hands on the o person's property. 8276S
22:20 "Whoever sacrifices to any god o than the 963+1194+4200
LORD
23:13 Do not invoke the names of o gods; 337
24:6 and the o half he sprinkled on the altar. 1947S
25:7 and onyx stones and o gems to be mounted AIT
25:12 on one side and two rings on the o. 9108
25:19 and the second cherub on the o. 7896S
25:20 The cherubim are to face each o, 278S
25:32 three on one side and three on the o. 9108
26:3 and do the same with the o five. 3749S
26:4 the same with the end curtain in the o set. 9108
26:5 on the end curtain of the o set, 9108
26:5 with the loops opposite each o. 295S
26:9 into one set and the o six into another set. 3749S
26:10 the edge of the end curtain in the o set. 9108
26:17 with two projections set parallel to each o. 295S
26:20 For the o side, 9108
26:27 five for those on the o side, 9108
27:15 to be on the o side, 9108
28:10 All the o articles used in the service of NIH
28:10 and the remaining six on the o. 9108
28:25 the o ends of the chains to the two settings, 9109S
28:26 the o two corners of the breastpiece on the NIH
29:17 putting them with the head and the o pieces. AIT
29:19 "Take the o ram, 9108
29:39 in the morning and the o at twilight. 9108
29:41 Sacrifice the o lamb at twilight with 9108
30:9 Do not offer on this altar any o incense 2424
30:33 anyone o than a priest must be cut off 2424
31:7 and all the o furnishings of the tent—, 9133S
32:27 through the camp from one end to the o, 9133S
33:16 and your people from all the o people on NIH
34:14 Do not worship any o god, for the LORD, 337
35:9 and onyx stones and o gems to be mounted NIH
35:27 and o gems to be mounted on the ephod NIH
36:10 and did the same with the o five. 3749S
36:11 with the end curtain in the o set. 9108
36:12 on the end curtain of the o set, 9108
36:12 with the loops opposite each o, 285S
36:16 into one set and the o six into another set. 3749S
36:17 the edge of the end curtain in the o set. 9108
36:22 with two projections set parallel to each o. 285S
36:25 For the o side, 9108
36:32 five for those on the o side, 9108
37:3 on one side and two rings on the o. 9108
37:8 and the second cherub on the o; 2296S
37:9 The cherubim faced each o, 278S
37:18 three on one side and three on the o. 9108
38:15 the o side of the entrance to the courtyard, 9108
39:18 the o ends of the chains to the two settings, 9109S
39:19 the o two corners of the breastpiece on the NIH
Lev 5:7 a sin offering and the o for a burnt offering. 285S
5:10 then offer the o as a burnt offering in 9108
7:19 As for o meat, anyone ceremonially clean 2021S
7:24 be used for any o purpose, NIH
8:22 He then presented the ram, 9108
10:9 or o fermented drink whenever you go into NIH
11:10 or among all the o living creatures in NIH
11:23 But all o winged creatures NIH
12:8 a burnt offering and the o for a sin offering. 285S
13:55 the mildew has affected one side or the o. 1478S
14:22 a sin offering and the o for a burnt offering. 285S
14:31 a sin offering and the o as a burnt offering, 285S
14:42 to take o stones to replace these 337
15:15 a sin offering and the o for a burnt offering. 285S
15:25 at a time o than her monthly period or has 4202
15:30 a sin offering and the o for a burnt offering. 285S
16:8 for the LORD and the o for the scapegoat. 285S
22:12 daughter marries anyone o than a priest, 2424
24:20 he has injured the o, so he is to be injured. 132S
25:14 do not take advantage of each o. 278S
25:17 Do not take advantage of each o, 6660S
Nu 1:49 in the census of the o Israelites. NIH
2:33 not counted along with the o Israelites. NIH
4:27 whether carrying or doing o work, 3972S
5:19 "If no o man has slept with you NIH
5:20 with a man o than your husband"— 1187+4946
6:3 from wine and o fermented drink and must NIH
6:3 from wine or from o fermented drink. NIH
6:11 the o as a burnt offering to make atonement 285S
8:6 the Levites from among the o Israelites NIH
8:12 the LORD and the o for a burnt offering, 285S
8:14 the Levites apart from the o Israelites, NIH
9:7 with the o Israelites at the appointed time?" NIH
11:4 with them began to crave o food, 203+9294
11:34 the people who had craved o food. 203
14:2 And they said to each o, 278S
22:15 Then Balak sent o princes, 6388
24:1 he did not resort to sorcery as at o times, 928+7193+7193
26:62 not counted along with the o Israelites NIH
28:4 Prepare one lamb in the morning and the o 9108
31:30 cattle, donkeys, sheep, goats or o animals. 3972S
32:19 inheritance with them on the o side of the 2134+2256+4946+6298
Jordan.
35:3 flocks and all their o livestock. AIT
35:6 In addition, give them forty-two o towns. NIH
35:15 and any o people living among them, AIT
36:3 from o Israelite tribes; 285S
Dt 4:7 What o nation is so great as NIH
4:8 And what o nation is so great NIH
4:32 from one end of the heavens to the o. 7895+9028S
4:33 Has any o people heard the voice NIH
4:35 besides him there is no o. 6388
4:39 There is no o. 6388

Dt 5:7 "You shall have no o gods before me. 337
6:14 Do not follow o gods, 337
7:4 from following me to serve o gods, 337
7:7 you were more numerous than o peoples, 3972S
7:14 be blessed more than any o people; 2021S
8:19 the LORD your God and follow o gods 337
11:16 and worship o gods and bow down to them. 337
11:28 by following o gods, 337
13:2 "Let us follow o gods" (gods you have 337
13:6 and worship o gods" (gods that neither you 337
13:7 one end of the land to the o), 824+2021+7895S
13:13 and worship o gods" (gods you have 337
14:26 cattle, sheep, wine or o fermented drink, 2021S
17:3 to my command has worshiped o gods, 337
18:20 prophet who speaks in the name of o gods, 337
21:15 and he loves one but not the o, 285S
24:5 not be sent to war or have any o duty laid NIH
28:14 following o gods and serving them. 337
28:36 There you will worship o gods, 337
28:64 from one end of the earth to the o. 7895S
28:64 There you will worship o gods— 337
29:6 and drank no wine or o fermented drink. NIH
29:10 and all the o men of Israel, NIH
29:26 and worshiped o gods and bowed down 337
30:17 to bow down to o gods and worship them, 337
31:18 of all their wickedness in turning to o gods. 337
31:20 they will turn to o gods and worship them, 337
Jos 4:11 and the priests came to the o side 6296
7:7 to stay on the o side of the Jordan! 6298
7:9 and the o people of the country will hear 3972S
13:8 The o half of Manasseh, the Reubenites 2257S
17:2 the o male descendants of Manasseh son NIH
21:1 the heads of the o tribal families of Israel NIH
22:4 of the LORD gave you on the o side of 6298
22:7 the o half of the tribe Joshua gave land on NIH
22:19 o than the altar of the LORD our God. 1187+4946
22:29 o than the altar of the LORD our God 963+4200+4946
23:16 and serve o gods and bow down to them, 337
24:2 beyond the River and worshiped o gods. 337
24:16 to forsake the LORD to serve o gods! 337
Jdg 2:17 but prostituted themselves to o gods 337
2:19 following o gods and serving 337
4:11 Heber the Kenite had left the o Kenites, NIH
6:3 and o eastern peoples invaded the country. NIH
6:29 They asked each o, "Who did this?" 8276S
6:33 and o eastern peoples joined forces NIH
7:7 Let all the o men go, NIH
7:12 and all the o eastern peoples had settled in NIH
7:14 be nothing o than the sword of Gideon son 561
7:22 throughout the camp to turn on each o 8276S
10:13 you have forsaken me and served o gods, 337
10:18 of the people of Gilead said to each o, 8276S
11:18 and camped on the o side of the Arnon. 6298
13:4 or o fermented drink and that you do NIH
13:7 drink no wine or o fermented drink and do NIH
13:10 The man who appeared to me the o day!" NIH
13:14 nor drink any wine or o fermented drink NIH
16:7 I'll become as weak as any o man. 2021S
16:11 I'll become as weak as any o man." 2021S
16:13 I'll become as weak as any o man. 2021S
16:17 I would become as weak as any o man." 2021S
16:29 on the one and his left hand on the o, 285S
17:8 that town in search of some o place to stay. 889S
18:14 o household gods, a carved image and NIH
18:17 the o household gods and the cast idol NIH
18:18 the o household gods and the cast idol, NIH
18:20 the o household gods and the carved image NIH
18:20 the one leading to Bethel and the o 285S
Ru 1:4 one named Orpah and the o Ruth. 9108
4:7 and gave it to the o. 8276S
1Sa 1:2 one was called Hannah and the o Peninnah. 9108
3:10 calling as at the o times, "Samuel! 7193S
8:5 such as all the o nations have." NIH
8:8 forsaking me and serving o gods, 337
8:20 Then we will be like all the o nations, NIH
10:11 they asked each o, "What is this 8276S
12:19 for we have added to all our o sins the evil NIH
14:1 over to the Philistine outpost on the o side." 6298
14:4 one was called Bozez, and the o Seneh. 285S
14:5 the o to the south toward Geba. 285S
14:20 striking each o with their swords. 8276S
17:10 Give me a man and let us fight each o." 3480
17:21 up their lines facing each o. 5120+7925
18:25 king wants no o price for the bride than 3954
20:41 they kissed each o and wept together— 8276S
20:42 we have sworn friendship with each o 5646+9109
21:8 haven't brought my sword or any o weapon, AIT
23:26 and David and his men were on the o side, 2296S
26:13 Then David crossed over to the o side 6298
26:19 and have said, 'Go, serve o gods.' 337
28:8 Saul disguised himself, putting on o clothes, 337
30:20 ahead of the o livestock, 2085S
30:31 to those in all the o places where David AIT
2Sa 2:13 of the pool and one group on the o side. AIT
4:2 One was named Baanah and the o Recab; 9108
12:1 one rich and the o poor. 285S
14:6 They got into a fight with each o 2157+9109S
14:6 One struck the o and killed him. 285S
17:9 now, he is hidden in a cave or some o place. 285S
19:9 the people were all arguing with each o, 1906
1Ki 3:22 The o woman said, "No! 337
3:25 and give half to one and half to the o. 337
3:26 o said, "Neither I nor you shall have him. 2296S
4:28 for the chariot horses and the o horses. NIH
4:31 He was wiser than any o man, 2021S
6:7 chisel or any o iron tool was heard at NIH

1Ki
6:24 and the o wing five cubits— 9108
6:27 the wing of the o touched the other wall, 9108
6:27 the wing of the other touched the o wall, 9108
6:27 and their wings touched each o in 4053S
7: 4 in sets of three, **facing each o.** 448+4691+4691
7: 5 in sets of three, **facing each o.** 448+4691+4691
8:60 the LORD is God and that there is no o. 6388
9: 6 to serve o gods and worship them, 337
9: 9 and have embraced o gods, 337
10:20 ever been made for any o kingdom. NIH
10:23 in riches and wisdom than all the o kings of NIH
11: 4 his wives turned his heart after o gods, 337
11:10 forbidden Solomon to follow o gods, 337
11:41 As for the o events of Solomon's reign, 3856
12:29 One he set up in Bethel, and the o in Dan. 285S
14: 9 You have made for yourself o gods, 337
14:19 The o events of Jeroboam's reign, 3856
14:29 As for the o events of Rehoboam's reign, 3856
15: 7 As for the o events of Abijah's reign, 3856
15:23 As for all the o events of Asa's reign, 3856
15:31 As for the o events of Nadab's reign, 3856
16: 5 As for the o events of Baasha's reign, 3856
16:14 As for the o events of Elah's reign, 3856
16:20 As for the o events of Zimri's reign, 3856
16:21 and the o half supported Omri. NIH
16:27 As for the o events of Omri's reign, 3856
18:23 I will prepare the o bull and put it on 285S
20:24 and replace them with o **officers.** AIT
20:29 seven days they camped opposite **each o,** 465
22:12 All the o prophets were prophesying NIH
22:13 the o prophets are predicting success for NIH
22:39 As for the o events of Ahab's reign, 3856
22:45 As for the o events of Jehoshaphat's reign, 3856

2Ki
1:18 As for *all* the o events of Ahaziah's reign, 3856
3:13 "What do we have to do with **each o?** 3870S
3:17 your cattle and your o animals will drink. NIH
3:23 and slaughtered each o. 8276S
5:17 and sacrifices to *any* o god but the LORD. 337
7: 3 They said to each o, "Why stay here 8276S
7: 9 they said to each o, "We're not doing right. 8276S
8:23 As for the o events of Jehoram's reign, 3856
10:21 until it was full from one end to the o. 7023S
10:34 As for the o events of Jehu's reign, 3856
11: 7 and you who are in the o two companies NIH
12: 7 the priest and the o priests and asked them, NIH
12:12 met all *the* o **expenses** of restoring AIT
12:13 trumpets or any o articles of gold or silver NIH
12:19 As for the o events of the reign of Joash, 3856
13: 8 for the o events of the reign of Jehoahaz, 3856
13:12 As for the o events of the reign of Jehoash, 3856
14:11 Amaziah king of Judah **faced o** 7156+8011
14:15 As for the o events of the reign of Jehoash, 3856
14:18 As for the o events of Amaziah's reign, 3856
14:28 As for the o events of Jeroboam's reign, 3856
15: 6 As for the o events of Azariah's reign, 3856
15:11 The o events of Zechariah's reign 3856
15:15 The o events of Shallum's reign, 3856
15:21 As for the o events of Menahem's reign, 3856
15:26 The o events of Pekahiah's reign, 3856
15:31 As for the o events of Pekah's reign, 3856
15:36 As for the o events of Jotham's reign, 3856
16:19 As for the o events of the reign of Ahaz, 3856
17: 7 They worshiped o gods 337
17:35 "Do not worship *any* o gods or bow down 337
17:37 Do not worship o gods. 337
17:38 and do not worship o gods. 337
20:20 As for the o events of Hezekiah's reign, 3856
21:17 As for the o events of Manasseh's reign, 3856
21:25 As for the o events of Amon's reign, 3856
22:17 to o gods and provoked me to anger by all 337
23:24 and all the o detestable things seen in Judah NIH
23:28 As for the o events of Josiah's reign, 3856
24: 5 As for the o events of Jehoiakim's reign, 3856
25:17 The o pillar, with its network, was similar. 9108
25:28 the o kings who were with him in Babylon. NIH

1Ch
6:48 to all the o duties of the tabernacle. NIH
9:29 of the furnishings and all the o articles of NIH
9:33 and were **exempt from** o **duties** because AIT
12:16 O Benjamites and some men from Judah NIH
16:42 and for the playing of the o instruments NIH
23:17 Eliezer had no o sons, 337
23:28 the performance of o **duties** *at* the house AIT
26:26 and by the o army commanders. NIH
26:28 the o dedicated things were in the care NIH
29:21 and o sacrifices in abundance for all Israel. NIH
29:30 and the kingdoms of all the o lands. NIH

2Ch
2: 5 because our God is greater than all o gods. 2021S
3:11 while its o wing, also five cubits long, 337
3:11 touched the wing of the o cherub. 337
3:12 and touched the o temple wall, NIH
3:12 and its o wing, also five cubits long, 337
5:13 cymbals and o instruments, NIH
7:19 to serve o gods and worship them, 337
7:22 and have embraced o gods, 337
9:19 ever been made for any o kingdom. NIH
9:22 in riches and wisdom than all the o kings of NIH
9:28 from Egypt and from all o countries. 2021S
9:29 As for the o events of Solomon's reign, 8637
11:21 of Absalom more than any of his o wives NIH
12: 8 and serving the kings of o lands." 2021S
13: 9 of your own as the peoples of o lands do? 2021S
13:22 The o events of Abijah's reign, 3856
18:11 All the o prophets were prophesying NIH
18:12 the o prophets are predicting success for NIH
19:10 whether bloodshed or o concerns of NIH
20: 2 from the o side of the Sea. 6298
20:34 The o events of Jehoshaphat's reign, 3856

2Ch
23: 5 the o men are to be in the courtyards of NIH
23: 6 but all the o men are to guard what NIH
24:14 also dishes and o objects of gold and silver. NIH
25:21 Amaziah king of Judah **faced each o** 7156+8011
25:26 As for the o events of Amaziah's reign, 3856
26:17 the priest with eighty o courageous priests NIH
26:20 the chief priest and all the o priests looked NIH
26:22 The o events of Uzziah's reign, 3856
27: 7 The o events in Jotham's reign, 3856
27: 7 and the o things he did, NIH
28:25 to burn sacrifices to o gods and provoked 337
28:26 The o events of his reign and all his ways, 3856
29:34 and until o priests had been consecrated, 2021S
31:19 around their towns or in *any* o towns, AIT
32:13 to all the peoples of the o lands? NIH
32:17 as the gods of the peoples of the o lands did NIH
32:19 as they did about the gods of the o peoples NIH
32:32 The o events of Hezekiah's reign 3856
33:18 The o events of Manasseh's reign. 3856
34:25 to o gods and provoked me to anger by all 337
35:24 in the o chariot he had and brought him 5467
35:26 The o events of Josiah's reign and his acts 3856
36: 8 The o events of Jehoiakim's reign, 3856

Ezr
1:10 matching silver bowls 410 o articles 1,000 337
2:31 of the o Elam 1,254 337
2:70 along with some of the o people, NIH
4:10 and the o people whom the great 10692
7:24 temple servants or o workers at this house NIH
9:11 with their impurity from one end to the o. 7023S
10:25 And among the o Israelites: NIH

Ne
1: 2 came from Judah with *some* o men, AIT
3:18 ruler of the o half-district of Keilah, NIH
4:16 while the o half were equipped with spears, NIH
4:17 with one hand and held a weapon in the o, 285S
4:19 and we are widely separated from each o 278S
7:33 of the o Nebo 52 337
7:34 of the o Elam 1,254 337
9:36 and the o good things it produces. NIH
11: 4 while o people from both Judah NIH
12:24 one section responding to the o, 5464S
12:47 also set aside the portion for the o Levites, NIH
13:15 grapes, figs and **all** o **kinds** *of* loads. AIT
13:24 one of the o peoples, 2256+6639+6639

Est
1: 6 mother-of-pearl and o costly stones. NIH
1: 7 each one different from the o, 3998S
2:15 she asked for nothing o than what 561+3954
2:17 to Esther more than to any of the o women, NIH
2:17 approval more than any of the o virgins. NIH
3: 1 higher than that of all the o nobles. 889+907S
3: 8 from those of all o people and who do NIH
5:11 above the o nobles and officials. NIH
8:17 of o nationalities became Jews 824+2021+6639
9: 2 the o nationalities were afraid of them. NIH
9:19 a day for giving presents to each o. 8276S

Job
8:19 and from the soil o plants grow. 337
9:32 that we might confront **each o** in court. 3481
31:10 and may o *men* sleep with her. 337

Ps
16: 4 of those will increase who run after o gods. 337
19: 6 the heavens and makes its circuit to the o; 7895S
64: 5 They encourage **each o** in evil plans, 4564S
82: 7 you will fall like *every* o ruler." 285S
85:10 righteousness and peace **kiss** *each o.* AIT
111: 6 giving them the lands of o nations. NIH
147:20 He has done this for no o nation; 3972S

Ecc
2: 7 and had o slaves who were born NIH
3:19 As one dies, so dies **the o.** 2296S
7:14 God has made the one as well as **the o.** 2296S
7:18 to grasp the one and not let go of **the o.** 2296S

Isa
3: 5 People *will* **oppress each o**— 5601
13: 8 They will look aghast at **each o,** 8276S
26:13 o lords besides you have ruled over us, NIH
34:14 and wild goats will bleat to **each o;** 8276S
41: 6 each helps the o and says to his brother, 8276S
44: 8 No, there is no o Rock; I know not one." NIH
45: 5 I am the LORD, and there is no o; 6388
45: 6 I am the LORD, and there is no o. 6388
45:14 'Surely God is with you, and there is no o; 6388
45:14 there is no o god.' " NIH
45:18 "I am the LORD, and there is no o. 6388
45:22 for I am God, and there is no o. 6388
46: 9 I am God, and there is no o; 6388
50: 8 Let us face **each o!** 3480
58: 4 and in **striking** *each o* with wicked fists. AIT
66:17 of pigs and rats and o abominable things— 2021S

Jer
1:16 in burning incense to o gods and 337
7: 5 and deal with each o justly, 8276S
7: 6 not follow o gods to your own harm, 337
7: 9 and follow o gods you have not known, 337
7:18 They pour out drink offerings to o gods 337
7:21 to your o sacrifices and eat NIH
8:10 Therefore I will give their wives to o *men* 337
11:10 They have followed o gods to serve them. 337
12: 9 that o birds of prey surround and attack? 2021S
12:12 from one end of the land to the o; 7895S
13:10 of their hearts and go after o gods to serve 337
13:14 I will smash them one against the o, 278S
16:11 'and followed o gods and served 337
16:13 there you will serve o gods day and night, 337
17:19 stand also at all the o gates of Jerusalem. NIH
19:13 and poured out drink offerings to o gods.' " 337
22: 9 and have worshiped and served o gods.' " 337
24: 2 the o basket had very poor figs, 285S
25: 6 Do not follow o gods to serve 337
25:26 near and far, one after the o— 278S
25:33 one end of the earth to **the o.** 824+2021+7895S
26:22 along with some o men. NIH
27:19 the movable stands and the o furnishings 3856

Jer
28: 4 and all the o exiles from Judah who went NIH
29: 1 the o people Nebuchadnezzar had carried NIH
29:25 and to all the o priests. NIH
32:29 by pouring out drink offerings to o gods. 337
34: 7 against Jerusalem and the o cities of Judah 3972S
35:15 do not follow o gods to serve them. 337
36: 2 Judah and all the o nations from NIH
36:12 and all the o officials. NIH
36:16 they looked at each o in fear and said 8276S
39: 3 a high official and all the o officials of 8642
39:13 and all the o officers of the king of Babylon NIH
40:11 and all the o countries heard that the king NIH
44: 3 and by worshiping o gods that neither they 337
44: 5 or stop burning incense to o gods. 337
44: 8 burning incense to o gods in Egypt, 337
44:15 burning incense to o gods, along with all 337
46:16 they will fall over each o. 8276S
52:22 The o pillar, with its pomegranates, 9108
52:32 the o kings who were with him in Babylon. NIH

Eze
1:23 wings were stretched out one toward the o, 295S
3:13 the living creatures brushing against each o 295S
4: 8 that you cannot turn from one side to the o 7396S
4:17 They will be appalled at the sight of each o 278S
16:23 In addition to all your o wickedness, NIH
16:43 to all your o detestable practices? NIH
18:10 or does any of these o things 278S
25: 8 of Judah has become like all the o nations," NIH
29:15 exalt itself above the o nations. NIH
31:14 Therefore no o trees by the waters are ever 3972S
31:14 No o trees so well-watered are ever 3972S
32:27 o uncircumcised warriors who have fallen, NIH
33:30 saying to each o, 'Come and hear 285S
40:40 on the o side of the steps were two tables. NIH
40:41 of the gateway and four on the o— 7024S
40:42 the burnt offerings and the o sacrifices. NIH
41:19 of a lion toward the palm tree on the o. 7024S
42:14 They are to put on o clothes before they go 337
44: 7 to all your o detestable practices, NIH
44:19 and put on o clothes, 337
48:14 of the land and *must* not **pass into** o hands, 6296

Da
1:10 the o young men your age? NIH
2:30 I have greater wisdom than o living men, 10353S
3: 2 and all the o provincial officials to come to NIH
3: 3 and all the o provincial officials assembled NIH
3:21 trousers, turbans and o clothes, NIH
3:29 for no o god can save in this way." 10025
7:12 (The o beasts had been stripped NIH
7:20 the o horn that came up, before which three 10023
7:23 It will be different from all the o kingdoms NIH
8: 3 of the horns was longer than the o but grew 9108
11:27 will sit at the same table and **lie** *to each o,* AIT

Hos
3: 1 though they turn to o gods and 337
9: 1 do not be jubilant like the o nations. NIH

Joel
1: 4 young locusts have left o locusts have eaten. 2021S
2: 8 They do not jostle each o; 278S
2:25 the o locusts and the locust swarm— NIH
2:27 the LORD your God, and that there is no o. 6388

Jnh
1: 7 Then the sailors said to each o, "Come, 8276S

Hag
2:12 some wine, oil or o food, 3972S

Zec
4: 3 the right of the bowl and **the** o on its left." 285S
5: 3 and according to what it says on **the o,** 2296S
7:10 In your hearts do not think evil of each o.' 278S
8:16 Speak the truth to each o, 8276S
11: 7 and called one Favor and **the** o Union, 285S
14:13 and they will attack each o. 8276S

Mal
3:16 the LORD talked with each o, 8276S

Mt
4:21 he saw two o brothers, 257
5:39 turn to him the o also. 257
6:24 Either he will hate the one and love the o, 2283
6:24 be devoted to the one and despise the o. 2283
8:18 he gave orders to cross to the o **side** of 4305
8:28 at the o side in the region of the Gadarenes, 4305
12:13 completely restored, just as sound as the o. 257
12:45 seven o spirits more wicked than itself, 2283
13: 7 **O** seed fell among thorns, 257+1254
13: 8 Still o seed fell on good soil, 257
14:22 and go on ahead of him to the o **side,** 4305
18:31 the o servants saw what had happened, NIG
19: 1 into the region of Judea to **the** o **side** of 4305
20:21 and **the** o at your left in your kingdom." 1651S
21:30 "Then the father went to the o son and said 2283
21:36 Then he sent o servants to them, 257
21:38 the tenants saw the son, they said to each o, 1571
21:41 "and he will rent the vineyard *to* o tenants, 257
24:10 the faith and will betray and hate **each o,** 253
24:31 from one end of the heavens to the o. 216S
24:40 one will be taken and the o left. 1651S
24:41 one will be taken and **the** o left. 1651S
25:20 the five talents brought the o five. 257
26:22 began to say to him **one after the o,** 1651+1667
26:35 And all the o disciples said the same. NIG
27:61 and the o Mary were sitting there opposite 257
28: 1 and the o Mary went to look at the tomb. 257

Mk
1:27 so amazed that they asked **each o,** 1571
4: 7 **O** seed fell among thorns, 257
4: 8 Still o seed fell on good soil. 257
4:19 of wealth and the desires for o *things* come 3370
4:35 "Let us go over to the o **side.**" 4305
4:36 There were also o boats with him. 257
4:41 They were terrified and asked **each o,** 253
5:21 over by boat to the o **side** of the lake, 4305
7: 4 And they observe many o traditions, 257
8:13 into the boat and crossed to the o **side.** 4305
9:14 When they came to the o disciples, NIG
9:50 and be at peace with **each o.**" 253
10:26 even more amazed, and said to **each o,** 1571
10:37 of us sit at your right and **the** o at your left 1651S

Mk	12:32	in saying that God is one and there is no **o**	257
	15:41	Many **o** women who had come up with him	257
	16: 3	they asked **each o**, "Who will roll away	1571
Lk	1:15	to take wine or **o** fermented drink,	NIG
	3:18	And with many **o** words John exhorted	2283
	3:19	and all the **o** evil things he had done,	NIG
	4:36	the people were amazed and said to **each o**,	253
	4:43	of the kingdom of God to the **o** towns also,	2283
	5: 7	So they signaled their partners in the **o** boat	2283
	6:29	on one cheek, turn to him the **o** also,	257
	7:32	the marketplace and calling out to **each o:**	253
	7:41	five hundred denarii, and the **o** fifty.	2283
	7:49	The **o** guests began to say	NIG
	8: 7	**O** seed fell among thorns,	2283
	8: 8	Still **o** seed fell on good soil.	2283
	8:22	"Let's go over to the **o** side of the lake."	4305
	10:31	he passed by on the **o** side.	524
	10:32	passed by on the **o** side.	524
	11:26	seven **o** spirits more wicked than itself,	2283
	11:42	rue and all **o** kinds of garden herbs,	NIG
	12:52	in one family divided against each **o**,	NIG
	13: 2	were worse sinners than all the **o** Galileans	2283
	14:32	he will send a delegation while **the o** is still	899S
	16:13	Either he will hate the one and love the **o**,	2283
	16:13	be devoted to the one and despise the **o**.	2283
	17:17	Where are the **o** nine?	NIG
	17:24	and lights up the sky from one end to the **o**.	NIG
	17:34	one will be taken and the **o** left.	2283
	17:35	one will be taken and the **o** left."	2283
	18:10	one a Pharisee and the **o** a tax collector.	2283
	18:11	I thank you that I am not like **o** men—	3370
	18:14	"I tell you that this man, rather than **the o**,	1697
	22:65	they said many **o** insulting things to him.	2283
	23:32	Two **o** men, both criminals,	2283
	23:33	one on his right, **the o** on his left.	1254+4005
	23:40	But the **o** criminal rebuked him.	2283
	24:14	They were talking with **each o**	253
	24:15	and discussed these things with each **o**,	NIG
	24:32	They asked **each o**, "Were not our hearts	253
Jn	1:28	This all happened at Bethany **on the o side**	4305
	3:26	that man who was with you **on the o side** of	4305
	4:33	Then his disciples said to **each o**,	253
	6:25	When they found him **on the o side** of	4305
	8:18	my **o** witness is the Father, who sent me."	NIG
	10: 1	but climbs in by some **o way**,	249
	10:16	I have **o** sheep that are not of this sheep pen.	257
	15:12	Love **each o** as I have loved you.	253
	15:17	This is my command: Love **each o**.	253
	18: 1	**On the o side** there was an olive grove,	3963S
	18:16	The **o** disciple, who was known to	257
	19:32	and then those of the **o**.	257
	20: 2	to Simon Peter and the **o** disciple,	257
	20: 3	and the **o** disciple started for the tomb.	257
	20: 4	but the **o** disciple outran Peter and reached	257
	20: 8	Finally the **o** disciple,	257
	20:12	one at the head and **the o** at the foot.	1651S
	20:25	So the **o** disciples told him,	257
	20:30	Jesus did many **o** miraculous signs in	257
	21: 2	and two **o** disciples were together.	257
	21: 8	The **o** disciples followed in the boat,	257
	21:25	Jesus did many **o** things as well.	257
Ac	2: 4	in **o** tongues as the Spirit enabled them.	2283
	2:37	and said to Peter and the **o** apostles,	3370
	2:40	With many **o** words he warned them;	2283
	4: 6	and the **o** men of the high priest's family.	4012
	4:12	for there is no **o** name under heaven given	2283
	5:29	Peter and the **o** apostles replied:	NIG
	7:26	why do you want to hurt **each o?'**	253
	7:27	the **o** pushed Moses aside and said,	4446
	9:39	and showing him the robes and **o** clothing	NIG
	15: 2	along with some **o** believers,	257
	16:25	and the **o** prisoners were listening to them.	NIG
	17: 6	they dragged Jason and some **o** brothers	NIG
	21: 6	After saying good-by to **each o**,	253
	27: 1	and some **o** prisoners were handed over to	2283
	28: 4	they said to **each o**,	253
Ro	1:13	just as I have had among the **o** Gentiles.	3370
	1:27	Men committed indecent acts with **o** men,	2283
	2: 1	for at whatever point you judge the **o**,	2283
	9: 8	In **o** words, it is not the natural	1639+4047
	13: 9	whatever **o** commandment there may be,	2283
1Co	3:11	For no one can lay any foundation **o** than	257
	6:18	**o** sins a man commits are outside his body;	NIG
	7: 5	Do not deprive **each o** except by mutual	253
	9: 5	as do the **o** apostles and the Lord's brothers	3370
	10:29	the **o** man's conscience, I mean, not yours.	2283
	11:16	we have no **o** practice—nor do the churches	NIG
	11:33	come together to eat, wait for **each o**.	253
	12: 2	somehow or **o** you were influenced	323+6055
	12:25	parts should have equal concern for **each o**.	253
	14:17	but the **o** man is not edified.	2283
2Co	2:16	to the **o**, the fragrance of life.	1254+4005
	11: 4	a Jesus **o** than the Jesus we preached,	257
	11: 8	I robbed **o** churches by receiving support	2283
	12:13	How were you inferior to the **o** churches,	3370
Gal	1: 8	from heaven should preach a gospel **o** than	4123
	1: 9	to you a gospel **o** than what you accepted,	4123
	1:19	I saw none of the **o** apostles—	2283
	2:13	The **o** Jews joined him in his hypocrisy,	3370
	4:22	one by the slave woman and the **o** by	1651S
	5:10	in the Lord that you will take no **o** view.	257
	5:15	If you keep on biting and devouring **each o**,	253
	5:15	or you will be destroyed by **each o**.	253
	5:17	They are in conflict with **each o**,	253
	5:26	provoking and envying **each o**.	253
Eph	3: 5	not made known to men in **o** generations	2283
	4:32	to one another, forgiving **each o**, just as	4932

Eph	5:27	without stain or wrinkle or **any o** blemish,	5516
Php	4: 2	with Syntyche to agree with each **o** in	NIG
Col	3: 9	Do not lie to **each o**,	253
	3:13	Bear with **each o** and forgive whatever	253
1Th	3:12	for **each o** and for everyone else,	253
	4: 9	taught by God to love **each o**.	253
	4:18	encourage **each o** with these words.	253
	5:11	and build **each o** up,	1651+1651+3836
	5:13	Live in peace with **each o**.	4932
	5:15	to be kind to **each o** and to everyone else.	253
2Th	1: 3	of you has for **each o** is increasing.	253
Heb	7: 8	but in the **o** case,	1254+1695
	7:27	Unlike the **o** high priests,	NIG
	10:33	at **o** times you stood side by side	1254+4047
	13: 1	Keep on loving **each o** as brothers.	5789
Jas	5: 9	Don't grumble against **each o**, brothers,	253
	5:16	Therefore confess your sins to **each o**	253
	5:16	for **each o** so that you may be healed.	253
1Pe	4: 8	Above all, love **each o** deeply,	4932
	4:15	not be as a murderer or thief or any **o** kind	NIG
2Pe	3:16	as they do the **o** Scriptures.	3370
Rev	2:24	not impose any **o** burden on you:	257
	3:15	I wish you were either one or **the o!**	2412S
	4: 4	the throne were twenty-four **o** thrones,	NIG
	6: 4	from the earth and to make men slay **each o**.	253
	8:13	about to be sounded by the **o** three angels!"	3370
	9:12	two **o** woes are yet to come.	2285
	11:10	and will celebrate by sending **each o** gifts,	253
	17:10	one is, the **o** has not yet come;	257

OTHER'S (2) [OTHER]

Ro	1:12	be mutually encouraged by **each o** faith.	253
Gal	6: 2	Carry **each o** burdens,	253

OTHERS (177) [OTHER]

Ge	32:19	and all the **o** who followed the herds:	AIT
	42: 4	Joseph's brother, with the **o**,	278S
	50:14	with his brothers and all the **o** who had gone	AIT
Ex	24: 2	the **o** must not come near.	2156S
	35:34	of the tribe of Dan, the ability to teach **o**.	NIH
Lev	6:11	he is to take off these clothes and put on **o**,	337
Nu	1:47	not counted along with the **o**.	4392S
	22:19	Now stay here tonight as the **o** did,	NIH
Jdg	7: 8	over the provisions and trumpets of the **o**.	6639S
1Sa	5: 5	nor any **o** who enter Dagon's temple	AIT
	8:12	**o** to plow his ground and reap his harvest,	NIH
	8:12	and still **o** to make weapons of war	NIH
	9: 2	a head taller than any of the **o**.	6639S
	10:23	a head taller than any of the **o**.	6639S
1Ch	3:20	There were also five **o:**	NIH
	5:22	and many **o** fell slain,	AIT
	9:29	**O** were assigned to take care of	2157+4946S
2Ch	32:22	of Assyria and from the hand of all **o**.	NIH
Ezr	3:12	while many **o** shouted for joy.	AIT
Ne	2:16	or nobles or officials or any **o** who would	3856
	5: 3	**O** were saying, "We are mortgaging	889S
	5: 4	Still **o** were saying, "We have had to borrow	889S
	5: 5	and our vineyards belong to **o**."	337
	8: 3	women and **o** who could understand.	2021S
Job	24:24	and gathered up like all **o;**	AIT
	31: 8	then may **o** eat what I have sown,	337
	34:24	the mighty and sets up **o** in their place.	337
Ps	49:10	and leave their wealth to **o**.	337
	52: 7	and grew strong by destroying **o!**"	2257S
	105:44	and they fell heir to what **o** had toiled for—	4211S
	107:23	**O** went out on the sea in ships;	AIT
Pr	5: 9	to **o** and your years to one who is cruel,	337
	10:17	whoever ignores correction leads **o** astray.	NIH
	11:25	he who refreshes **o** will himself	NIH
Ecc	5: 8	and over them both are **o** higher still.	1469S
	6: 8	how to conduct himself before **o?**	2645S
	7:22	many times you yourself have cursed **o**.	337
	8: 9	when a man lords it over **o** to his own hurt.	132S
SS	5: 9	How is your beloved better than **o**,	1856S
	5: 9	How is your beloved better than **o**,	1856S
Isa	43: 9	so that **o** may hear and say, "It is true."	AIT
	56: 8	"I will gather still **o** to them	6388
	65:22	No longer will they build houses and **o** live	337
	65:22	or plant and **o** eat.	337
Jer	6:12	Their houses will be turned over to **o**,	337
	41: 8	and did not kill them with the **o**.	278S
	41:10	along with all the **o** who were left there,	6639S
	50:15	do to her as she has done to **o**.	NIH
Eze	7: 5	I listened, he said to the **o**,	AIT
	16:34	you are the opposite of **o;**	851+2021S
	32:19	'Are you more favored than **o?**	4769S
	39:14	**o** will bury those that remain on	AIT
	40:24	the same measurements as the **o**.	NIH
	40:25	like the openings of the **o**.	465S
	40:28	it had the same measurements as the **o**.	465S
	40:29	the same measurements as the **o**.	465S
	40:32	it had the same measurements as the **o**.	465S
	40:33	the same measurements as the **o**.	465S
	40:35	It had the same measurements as the **o**,	465S
	44: 8	you put **o** in charge of my sanctuary.	AIT
Da	2:40	so it will crush and break all **the o**.	10036S
	7: 3	each different from the **o**,	10154S
	7:19	which was different from all **the o**	10214S
	7:20	that looked more imposing than the **o** and	10246
	11: 2	who will be far richer than **all the o**.	AIT
	11: 4	his empire will be uprooted and given to **o**.	337
	12: 2	**o** to shame and everlasting contempt.	465S
	12: 5	looked, and there before me stood two **o**,	337
Mt	5:19	commandments and teaches **o** to do the same	476
	5:47	what are you doing more than **o?**	NIG

Mt	7: 2	For in the same way you judge **o**,	NIG
	7:12	to **o** what you would have them do to you,	899
	11:16	in the marketplaces and calling out to **o:**	2283
	15:30	the crippled, the mute and many **o**,	2283
	16:14	"Some say John the Baptist; **o** say Elijah;	257
	16:14	still **o**, Jeremiah or one of the prophets."	2283
	17:25	from their own sons or from **o?**	259
	17:26	"From **o**," Peter answered.	259
	18:16	he will not listen, take one or two **o** along,	NIG
	19:12	**o** were made that way by men;	4015
	19:12	and **o** have renounced marriage because of	4015
	20: 3	and saw **o** standing in the marketplace	257
	20: 6	and found still **o** standing around.	257
	21: 8	while **o** cut branches from the trees	257
	23:34	**o** you will flog in your synagogues	NIG
	25:11	"Later the **o** also came.	3370
	26:67	**O** slapped him	1254+3836
	27:42	"He saved **o**," they said, "but he can't save	257
Mk	4:10	the Twelve and the **o** around him asked him	AIT
	4:16	**O**, like seed sown on rocky places,	4047
	4:18	Still **o**, like seed sown among thorns,	257
	4:20	**O**, like seed sown on good soil,	1697
	6:15	**O** said, "He is Elijah."	257
	6:15	And still **o** claimed, "He is a prophet,	257
	8:28	"Some say John the Baptist; **o** say Elijah;	257
	8:28	and still **o**, one of the prophets."	257
	11: 8	**o** spread branches they had cut in the fields.	257
	12: 5	He sent many **o;**	257
	12: 5	some of them they beat, **o** they killed.	1254+4005
	12: 9	and give the vineyard to **o**.	257
	12:43	into the treasury than all the **o**.	NIG
	14:31	And all the **o** said the same.	NIG
	15:31	"He saved **o**," they said, "but he can't save	257
Lk	5:29	of tax collectors and **o** were eating	257
	6:31	Do to **o** as you would have them do to you.	899
	8: 3	Susanna; and many **o**.	2283
	8:10	but to **o** I speak in parables, so that,	3370
	9: 8	**o** that Elijah had appeared,	5516
	9: 8	and still **o** that one of the prophets	257
	9:19	"Some say John the Baptist; **o** say Elijah;	257
	9:19	and still **o**, that one of the prophets	257
	10: 1	the Lord appointed seventy-two **o**	2283
	11:16	**O** tested him by asking for a sign	2283
	11:49	they will kill **and o** they will persecute.'	2779
	13: 4	the **o** living in Jerusalem?	476
	20:16	and give the vineyard to **o**."	257
	21: 3	poor widow has put in more than all the **o**.	NIG
	23:35	said, "He saved **o;** let him save himself	257
	24: 9	to the Eleven and to all the **o**.	3370
	24:10	**o** with them who told this to the apostles.	3370
Jn	2:14	and **o** sitting at tables exchanging money.	3836
	4:38	**O** have done the hard work,	257
	7:12	**O** replied, "No, he deceives the people."	257+1254
	7:41	**O** said, "He is the Christ."	257
	7:41	Still **o** asked, "How can the Christ	1254+3836
	9: 9	**O** said, "No, he only looks like him."	257
	9:16	But **o** asked, "How can a sinner do such	257
	10:21	But **o** said, "These are not the sayings of	257
	12:29	**o** said an angel had spoken to him.	257
	18:34	"or did **o** talk to you about me?"	257
	19:18	they crucified him, and with him two **o**—	257
Ac	14: 4	with the Jews, **o** with the apostles.	1254+3836
	15:35	and many **o** taught and preached the word	2283
	16:32	the word of the Lord to him and to all the **o**	NIG
	17: 9	Then they made Jason and the **o** post bond	3370
	17:18	**O** remarked, "He seems to be	1254+3836
	17:32	some of them sneered, but **o** said,	3836
	17:34	woman named Damaris, and a number of **o**.	2283
	20: 6	and five days later joined **the o** at Troas,	899
	23: 6	Sadducees and the **o** Pharisees,	2283
	28:24	but **o** would not believe.	3836
Ro	2:21	who teach **o**, do you not teach yourself?	2283
	11: 7	The **o** were hardened,	3370
	11:17	the **o** and now share in the nourishing sap	899
	12: 5	and each member belongs to **all the o**.	253
	12: 8	if it is contributing to the needs of **o**,	NIG
1Co	9: 2	Even though I may not be an apostle to **o**,	257
	9:12	If **o** have this right of support from you,	257
	9:27	so that after I have preached to **o**,	257
	10:24	seek his own good, but the good of **o**.	2283
	12:28	those able to help **o**,	NIG
	14:19	to instruct **o** than ten thousand words in	257
	14:29	the **o** should weigh carefully what is said.	257
2Co	8: 8	by comparing it with the earnestness of **o**.	2283
	8:13	Our desire is not that **o** might be relieved	257
	10:15	by boasting of work done by **o**.	259
	13: 2	who sinned earlier or any of the **o**,	3370
Eph	4:29	for building **o** up according to their needs,	NIG
Php	1:15	but **o** out of goodwill.	5516
	2: 3	in humility consider **o** better than yourselves.	253
	2: 4	but also to the interests of **o**.	2283
	3:17	**Join with o** in following my example,	1181+5213
1Th	5: 6	So then, let us not be like **o**,	3370
1Ti	5:20	so that the **o** may take warning.	3370
	5:22	and do not share in the sins of **o**.	259
	5:24	The sins of **o** trail behind them.	5516
2Ti	2: 2	also be qualified to teach **o**.	2283
Tit	1: 9	that he can encourage **o** by sound doctrine	NIG
Heb	7:20	**O** became priests without any oath,	3525+3836
	11:35	**O** were tortured and refused to be released,	257
	11:36	while still **o** were chained and put in prison.	NIG
	13:16	not forget to do good and to share with **o**,	NIG
1Pe	4:10	Each one should use whatever gift he has received to serve **o**,	1571
2Pe	2: 5	a preacher of righteousness, and seven **o;**	NIG
Jude	1:16	they boast about themselves and flatter **o**	NIG
	1:23	snatch **o** from the fire and save them;	1254+4005

Jude 1:23 to **o** show mercy, mixed with fear—   4005

OTHERWISE (27) [OTHER]

Ge	45:11	**O** you and your household	7153
Ex	12:33	"For **o**," they said, "we will all die!"	3954
Dt	8:12	**O**, when you eat and are satisfied,	7153
	9:28	**O**, the country from which you brought us will say,	7153
	19: 6	**O**, the avenger of blood might pursue him	7153
	20:18	**O**, they will teach you to follow	889+4202+5100
	24:15	**O** he may cry to the LORD against you,	2256+4202
Jos	6:18	**O** you will make the camp of Israel liable	2256
1Sa	13:19	"**O** the Hebrews will make swords	7153
	25:34	**O**, as surely as the LORD,	219
2Sa	12:28	**O** I will take the city,	7153
1Ki	1:21	**O**, as soon as my lord the king is laid to rest	2256
2Ki	2:10	it will be yours—**o** not."	401+561
2Ch	19:10	**o** his wrath will come on you	2256
Pr	30: 9	**O**, I may have too much and disown you	7153
Isa	6:10	**O** they might see with their eyes,	7153
Hos	2: 3	**O** I will strip her naked and make her	7153
Mt	13:15	**O** they might see with their eyes,	3607
	15: 5	'Whatever help you might **o** have received	NIG
	27:64	**O**, his disciples may come and steal	3607
Mk	4:12	**O** they might turn and be forgiven!' "	3607
	7:11	'Whatever help you might **o** have received	NIG
Ac	28:27	**O** they might see with their eyes,	3607
Ro	11:22	**O**, you also will be cut off.	2075
1Co	7:14	**O** your children would be unclean,	726+2075
	15: 2	**O**, you have believed in vain.	1623+1760+3590
Rev	2:16	**O**, I will soon come to you	1254+1623+3590

OTHNI (1)

1Ch 26: 7 **O**, Rephael, Obed and Elzabad;   6978

OTHNIEL (10)

Jos	15:17	**O** son of Kenaz, Caleb's brother, took it;	6979
	15:18	One day when she came to **O**,	NIH
Jdg	1:13	**O** son of Kenaz, Caleb's younger brother,	6979
	1:14	One day when she came to **O**,	NIH
	3: 9	**O** son of Kenaz, Caleb's younger brother,	6979
	3:10	of Aram into the hands of **O**,	2257S
	3:11	until **O** son of Kenaz died.	6979
1Ch	4:13	The sons of Kenaz: **O** and Seraiah,	6979
	4:13	The sons of **O**: Hathath and Meonothai.	6979
	27:15	from the family of **O**.	6979

OUCHES (KJV) See FILIGREE

OUGHT (40)

Ge	26:28	'There **o** to be a sworn agreement	AIT
Mal	2: 7	lips of a priest **o** to preserve knowledge,	AIT
Jn	7: 3	"You **o** to leave here and go to Judea,	AIT
Ac	19:36	you **o** to be quiet and not do anything rash.	1256
	24:19	who **o** to be here before you	1256
	25:10	where I **o** to be tried.	1256
	25:24	shouting that he **o** not to live any longer.	1256
	26: 9	"I too was convinced that I **o** to do all	1256
Ro	1:28	to do what **o** not to be done.	2763
	8:26	We do not know what we **o** to pray for,	1256
	12: 3	of yourself more highly than you **o**,	1256
	15: 1	We who are strong **o** to bear with	4053
1Co	4: 1	men **o** to regard us as servants of Christ	AIT
	7:36	along in years and he feels he **o** to marry,	4053
	8: 2	not yet know as he **o** to know.	1256
	9:10	they **o** to do so in the hope of sharing in	4053
	11: 7	A man **o** not to cover his head,	4053
	11:10	the woman **o** to have a sign of authority	4053
	11:28	A man **o** to examine himself before he eats	AIT
	15:34	Come back to your senses as you **o**,	1469
2Co	2: 3	by those who **o** to make me rejoice.	1256
	2: 7	**o** to forgive and comfort	AIT
	12:11	I **o** to have been commended by you,	4053
Eph	5:28	husbands **o** to love their wives	4053
2Th	1: 3	We **o** always to thank God for you,	4053
	2:13	But we **o** always to thank God for you,	4053
	3: 7	For you yourselves know how you **o**	1256
1Ti	3:15	how people **o** to conduct themselves	1256
	5:13	saying things they **o** not to.	1256
Tit	1:11	by teaching things they **o** not to teach—	1256
Phm	1: 8	you to do what you **o** to do,	465+3836
Heb	5:12	though by this time you **o** to be teachers,	4053
Jas	1: 9	in humble circumstances **o** to take pride	AIT
	4:15	Instead, you **o** to say,	AIT
	4:17	the good he **o** to do and doesn't do it,	AIT
2Pe	3:11	what kind of people **o** you to be?	1256
	3:11	You **o** to live holy and godly lives	NIG
1Jn	3:16	we **o** to lay down our lives for our brothers.	4053
	4:11	we also **o** to love one another.	4053
3Jn	1: 8	We **o** therefore to show hospitality	4053

OUR (1200) [WE] See Index of Articles Etc.

OURS (20) [WE] See Index of Articles Etc.

OURSELVES (45) [SELF, WE] See Index of Articles Etc.

OUSTED (1)

Isa 22:19 and you will be **o** from your position.   2238

OUT (2407) [OUTER] See Index of Articles Etc.

OUTBREAK (1)

1Sa 5: 9 both young and old, with an **o** of tumors.   8609

OUTBURSTS (1)

2Co 12:20 jealousy, **o** of anger, factions, slander,   2596

OUTCAST (1) [CAST]

Jer 30:17 'because you are called an **o**,   5615

OUTCOME (6)

Isa	22:	and know their final **o**.	344
Da	11:29	but this time the **o** will be different	3869+4202
	12: 8	"My lord, what will the **o** of all this be?"	344
Mt	26:58	and sat down with the guards to see the **o**.	5465
Heb	13: 7	Consider the **o** of their way of life	1676
1Pe	4:17	and if it begins with us, what will the **o** be	5465

OUTCRY (8)

Ge	18:20	"The **o** against Sodom and Gomorrah is	2411
	18:21	if what they have done is as bad as the **o**	7591
	19:13	The **o** to the LORD against its people is	7591
1Sa	4:14	Eli heard the **o** and asked,	7591+7754
	5:12	and the **o** of the city went up to heaven.	8784
Ne	5: 1	the men and their wives raised a great **o**	7591
	5: 6	When I heard their **o** and these charges,	2411
Isa	15: 8	Their **o** echoes along the border of Moab;	2411

OUTDOOR (1)

Pr 24:27 Finish your **o** work   928+2021+2575

OUTGOINGS (KJV) See CAME OUT, DAWNS, ENDED, ENDING, FADES, FARTHEST LIMITS

OUTER (49) [OUT]

Nu	4:25	the **o** covering of hides of	2025+4200+4946+5087
2Sa	18:24	between the inner and **o** gates,	9109S
	20:15	and it stood against the **o** fortifications.	2658
1Ki	6:29	in both the inner and **o** rooms,	2667
	6:30	both the inner and **o** rooms	2667
	7: 9	with a saw on their inner and **o** faces.	2575
2Ch	6:13	in the center of the **o** court.	6478
	33:14	Afterward he rebuilt the **o** wall of the City	2667
Est	6: 4	Now Haman had just entered the **o** court of	2667
Job	26:14	these are but the **o** fringe of his works;	7896
	41:13	Who can strip off his **o** coat?	7156
Eze	10: 5	be heard as far away as the **o** court,	2667
	40:17	Then he brought me into the **o** court.	2667
	40:20	leading into the **o** court.	2667
	40:27	to the **o** gate on the south side;	NIH
	40:31	Its portico faced the **o** court;	2667
	40:34	Its portico faced the **o** court;	2667
	40:37	Its portico faced the **o** court;	2667
	41: 1	to the **o** sanctuary and measured the jambs;	2121
	41: 2	He also measured the **o** sanctuary;	NIH
	41: 4	across the end of the **o** sanctuary.	2121
	41: 9	The **o** wall of the side rooms	2575
	41:15	The **o** sanctuary, the inner sanctuary and	2121
	41:17	around the inner and **o** sanctuary	2667
	41:20	on the wall of the **o** sanctuary.	2121
	41:21	**o** sanctuary had a rectangular doorframe,	2121
	41:23	Both the **o** sanctuary and	2121
	41:25	of the **o** sanctuary were carved cherubim	2121
	42: 1	the man led me northward into the **o** court	2667
	42: 1	and opposite the **o** wall on the north side.	1230
	42: 3	the pavement of the **o** court,	2575
	42: 7	an **o** wall parallel to the rooms	2021+2575+4200
	42: 7	to the rooms and the **o** court;	2667
	42: 8	to the court was fifty cubits long,	2667
	42: 9	as one enters them from the **o** court.	2667
	42:10	along the length of the wall of the **o** court,	NIH
	42:10	and opposite the **o** wall,	1230
	42:14	not to go into the **o** court until they leave	2667
	44: 1	the man brought me back to the **o** gate of	2667
	44:19	When they go out into the **o** court where	2667
	46:20	the **o** court and consecrating the people."	2667
	46:21	then brought me to the **o** court and led me	2667
	46:22	the **o** court were enclosed courts,	NIH
	47: 2	around the outside to the **o** gate facing east,	2575
Jn	13: 4	took off his **o** clothing,	2668
	21: 7	he wrapped his **o** garment around him	2087
Ac	12:13	Peter knocked at the **o** entrance,	2598+4784
Heb	9: 6	the priests entered regularly into the **o** room	4755
Rev	11: 2	But exclude the **o** court;	2033

OUTLANDISH (KJV) See FOREIGN

OUTLAW (1)

Pr 24:15 like an **o** against a righteous man's house,   8401

OUTLET (1)

2Ch 32:30 It was Hezekiah who blocked the upper **o**   4604

OUTLINE (1)

Isa 44:13 with a line and makes an **o** with a marker;   9306

OUTLIVED (2) [LIVE]

Jos	24:31	lifetime of Joshua and of the elders who **o** him	339+799+3427
Jdg	2: 7	lifetime of Joshua and of the elders who **o** him	339+799+3427

OUTLYING (2)

1Ch	5:16	in Bashan and its **o** villages,	1426
	27:25	of the storehouses in the **o** districts,	8441

OUTMOST (KJV) See DISTANT, END, TOPMOST

OUTNUMBER (2) [NUMBER]

Ps	69: 4	**o** the hairs of my head;	4946+8045
	139:18	they would **o** the grains of sand.	4946+8049

OUTPOST (8) [OUTPOSTS]

1Sa	10: 5	where there is a Philistine **o**.	5907
	13: 3	Jonathan attacked the Philistine **o** at Geba,	5907
	13: 4	"Saul has attacked the Philistine **o**,	5907
	14: 1	over to the Philistine **o** on the other side."	5163
	14: 4	to cross to reach the Philistine **o** was a cliff;	5163
	14: 6	to the **o** of those uncircumcised fellows.	5163
	14:11	showed themselves to the Philistine **o**.	5163
	14:12	The men of the **o** shouted to Jonathan	5165

OUTPOSTS (2) [OUTPOST]

Jdg	7:11	Purah his servant went down to the **o**	2821+7895
1Sa	14:15	and those in the **o** and raiding parties—	5163

OUTPOURED (3) [POUR]

Ps	79:10	the nations that you avenge the **o** blood	9161
Eze	20:33	and an outstretched arm and with **o** wrath.	9161
	20:34	and an outstretched arm and with **o** wrath.	9161

OUTPOURING (1) [POUR]

Eze 9: 8 in this **o** of your wrath on Jerusalem?"   9161

OUTRAGEOUS (1) [RAGE]

Jer 29:23 For they have done **o** things in Israel;   5576

OUTRAN (2) [RUN]

2Sa	18:23	by way of the plain and **o** the Cushite.	6296
Jn	20: 4	the other disciple **o** Peter and reached	4708+5441

OUTSIDE (130) [OUTSIDERS]

Ge	9:22	and told his two brothers **o**.	928+2021+2575
	15: 5	He took him **o** and said,	2025+2575
	19: 6	Lot went **o** to meet them and	2025+7339
	24:11	the camels kneel down near the well **o**	2575+4946
Ex	12:46	take none of the meat **o** the house.	2025+2575
	21:19	gets up and walks around **o**	928+2021+2575
	26:35	the table **o** the curtain on the north	2575+4946
	27:21	of the curtain that is in front of	2575+4946
	29:14	bull's flesh and its hide and its offal **o**	2575+4946
	33: 7	to take a tent and pitch it **o**	2575+4946
	33: 7	to the tent of meeting **o** the camp.	2575+4946
	40:22	on the north side of the tabernacle **o**	2575+4946
Lev	4:12	he must take **o** the camp to	2575+4946
	4:21	Then he shall take the bull **o** the camp	2575+4946
	6:11	carry the ashes **o** the camp to a place	2575+4946
	8:17	its flesh and its offal he burned up **o**	2575+4946
	9:11	and the hide he burned up **o** the camp.	2575+4946
	10: 4	carry your cousins **o** the camp,	2575+4946
	10: 5	still in their tunics, **o** the camp,	2575+4946
	13:46	he must live **o** the camp.	2575+4946
	14: 3	to go **o** the camp and examine him.	2575+4946
	14: 8	he must stay **o** his tent for seven days.	2575+4946
	14:40	and thrown into an unclean place **o**	2575+4946
	14:41	into an unclean place **o** the town.	2575+4946
	14:53	the live bird in the open fields **o**	2575+4946
	16:27	must be taken **o** the camp;	2575+4946
	17: 3	a lamb or a goat in the camp or **o** of it	2575+4946
	22:10	" 'No one **o** a priest's family may eat	2424
	24: 3	**O** the curtain of the Testimony in the	2575+4946
	24:14	"Take the blasphemer **o** the camp.	2575+4946
	24:23	the blasphemer **o** the camp and stoned	2575+4946
Nu	5: 3	send them **o** the camp so they will	2575+4946
	5: 4	they sent them **o** the camp.	2575+4946
	12:14	Confine her **o** the camp for seven days	2575+4946
	12:15	So Miriam was confined **o** the camp	2575+4946
	15:35	The whole assembly must stone him **o**	2575+4946
	15:36	So the assembly took him **o** the camp	2575+4946
	19: 3	be taken **o** the camp and slaughtered	2575+4946
	19: 9	a ceremonially clean place **o** the camp.	2575+4946
	31:13	the community went to meet them **o**	2575+4946
	31:19	anyone who was killed must stay **o**	2575+4946
	35: 5	**O** the town, measure three thousand	2575+4946
	35:26	" 'But if the accused ever goes **o** the	3655+3655
	35:27	avenger of blood finds him **o** the city,	2575+4946
Dt	23:10	he is to go **o** the camp and stay there.	2575+4946
	23:12	a place **o** the camp where you can go	2575+4946
	24:11	Stay **o** and let the man	2575
	25: 5	his widow must not marry **o** the family.	2021+2025+2424+2575
Jos	2:19	If anyone goes **o** your house into the	1946+4946
	6:23	and put them in a place **o** the camp	2575+4946
Jdg	12: 9	in marriage to those **o** his clan,	2575
	12: 9	as wives from **o** his clan.	2575

Jdg	19:23	The owner of the house **went** o and said	3655
	19:25	the man took his concubine and sent her o	2575
1Sa	9:26	he and Samuel went o together.	2025+2575
1Ki	6: 6	the o of the temple so that nothing	2025+2575
	7: 9	from the o to the great courtyard and	2575
	8: 8	but not from o the Holy Place;	2025+2575
	21:13	took him o the city and stoned him	2575+4946
2Ki	10:24	Jehu had posted eighty men o	928+2021+2575
	16:18	the royal entryway of the temple of	2025+2667
	23: 4	burned them o Jerusalem in the fields	2575+4946
	23: 6	to the Kidron Valley o Jerusalem	2575+4946
	25: 1	He encamped o the city	6584
2Ch	5: 9	but not from o the Holy Place;	2025+2575
	24: 8	a chest was made and placed o,	2025+2575
	32: 3	the water from the springs o the city,	2575+4946
	32: 5	He built another wall o that one	2025+2575
Ezr	10:13	so we cannot stand o.	928+2021+2575
Ne	11:16	who had charge of the o work of the house	2667
	13:20	of goods spent the night o Jerusalem.	2575+4946
Job	31:34	that I kept silent and would not go o	7339
Pr	22:13	sluggard says, "There is a lion o!	928+2021+2575
SS	8: 1	Then, if I found you o, I would kiss you,	928+2021+2575
Jer	21: 4	and the Babylonians who are o	2575+4946
	22:19	and thrown at the gates of Jerusalem	2134+4946
	52: 4	They camped o the city	6584
La	1:20	**O**, the sword bereaves;	2575+4946
Eze	5:12	by the sword o your **walls**;	6017
	7:15	**O** is the sword, inside are plague	928+2021+2575
	40:19	inside of the lower gateway to the o of	2575+4946
	40:40	By the o wall of the portico of	2025+2575+4946
	40:44	**O** the inner gate, within the	2025+2575+4946
	41:17	the o of the entrance to the inner sanctuary	2575
	43:21	designated part of the temple area o	2575+4946
	46: 2	to enter from the o through the portico of	2575
	47: 2	around the o to the outer gate facing east,	2575
Mt	8:12	subjects of the kingdom will be thrown o,	2035
	9:25	After the crowd **had** been **put o**,	1675
	12:46	his mother and brothers stood o,	2032
	12:47	"Your mother and brothers are standing o,	2032
	22:13	'Tie him hand and foot, and **throw** him o,	1675
	23:25	You clean the o of the cup and dish,	2033
	23:26	and then the o also will be clean.	1760
	23:27	which look beautiful **on the** o but on the	2033
	23:28	**on the** o you appear to people as righteous	2033
	25:30	And throw that worthless servant o,	2035
	26:75	And he went o and wept bitterly.	2032
Mk	1:45	a town openly but stayed o in lonely places.	2032
	2: 2	not even o the door,	4639
	3:31	Standing o, they sent someone in	2032
	3:32	"Your mother and brothers are o looking	2032
	4:11	But to those on the o everything is said	2032
	7:15	Nothing o a man can make him 'unclean'	2032
	7:18	a man **from the** o can make him 'unclean'?	2033
	8:23	the blind man by the hand and led him o	2032
	11: 4	They went and found a colt o in the street,	2032
Lk	1:10	the assembled worshipers were praying o.	2032
	8:20	"Your mother and brothers are standing o,	2032
	11:39	you Pharisees clean the o of the cup	2033
	11:40	Did not the one who made the o make the	2033
	13:25	you will stand o knocking and pleading,	2032
	13:33	for surely no prophet can die o Jerusalem!	2032
	22:62	And he went o and wept bitterly.	2032
Jn	18:16	but Peter had to wait o at the door.	2032
	20:11	but Mary stood o the tomb crying.	2032
Ac	5:34	that the men be put o for a little while.	2032
	7:21	When he was **placed o,**	1758
	14:13	whose temple was **just** o the city,	4574
	14:19	They stoned Paul and dragged him o	2032
	16:13	On the Sabbath we went o the city gate to	2032
1Co	5:12	What business is it of mine to judge those o	2032
	5:13	God will judge those o.	
	6:18	other sins a man commits are o his body,	1760
2Co	7: 5	conflicts on the o, fears within.	2033
Heb	13:11	but the bodies are burned o the camp.	2032
	13:12	And so Jesus also suffered o the city gate	2032
	13:13	Let us, then, go to him o the camp,	2032
Rev	14:20	They were trampled in the winepress o	2033
	22:15	**O** are the dogs, those who practice magic	2032

OUTSIDERS (3) [OUTSIDE]

Col	4: 5	Be wise in the way you act toward o;	2032+3836
1Th	4:12	daily life may win the respect of o	2032+3836
1Ti	3: 7	also have a good reputation with o,	2033

OUTSKIRTS (4)

Nu	11: 1	and consumed some of the o of the camp.	7895
Jos	18:15	at the o of Kiriath Jearim on the west,	7895
1Sa	14: 2	Saul was staying on the o of Gibeah under	7895
1Ch	4:39	and they went to the o of Gedor to the east	4427

OUTSPREAD (1) [SPREAD]

Isa	8: 8	Its o wings will cover the breadth	5742

OUTSTANDING (6)

1Ch	7:40	choice men, brave warriors and o leaders.	8031
SS	5:10	o among ten thousand.	1838
Da	5:14	insight, intelligence and o wisdom.	10339
Ac	4:16	Everybody living in Jerusalem knows they have done an o miracle,	1196
Ro	13: 8	**Let** no **debt remain o**, except	4053
	16: 7	They are o among the apostles,	2168

OUTSTRETCHED (19) [STRETCH]

Ex	6: 6	an o arm and with mighty acts of judgment.	5742
Dt	4:34	by war, by a mighty hand and an o arm,	5742
	5:15	of there with a mighty hand and an o arm.	5742
	7:19	the mighty hand and o arm,	5742
	9:29	by your great power and your o arm."	5742
	11: 2	his majesty, his mighty hand, his o arm;	5742
	26: 8	of Egypt with a mighty hand and an o arm,	5742
1Ki	8:42	and your mighty hand and your o arm—	5742
2Ki	17:36	of Egypt with mighty power and o arm,	5742
2Ch	6:32	and your mighty hand and your o arm—	5742
Ps	75: 5	do not speak with o neck.'	6981
	136:12	with a mighty hand and o arm;	5742
Isa	3:16	walking along with o necks,	5742
Jer	21: 5	with an o hand and a mighty arm in anger	5742
	27: 5	and o arm I made the earth and its people	5742
	32:17	the earth by your great power and o arm.	5742
	32:21	by a mighty hand and an o arm and	5742
Eze	20:33	over you with a mighty hand and an o arm	5742
	20:34	and an o arm and with outpoured wrath.	5742

OUTWARD (3) [OUTWARDLY]

1Sa	16: 7	Man looks at the o **appearance**,	6524
Ro	2:28	nor is circumcision merely o and physical.	1877+3836+5745
1Pe	3: 3	beauty should not come **from** o adornment,	2033

OUTWARDLY (4) [OUTWARD]

Ro	2:28	is not a Jew if he is only one o,	1877+3836+5745
2Co	4:16	Though o we are wasting away,	476+2032+3836
Gal	6:12	make a good impression o are trying	1877+4922
Heb	9:13	sanctify them so that they are o clean.	4922

OUTWEIGH (1) [WEIGH]

Job	6: 3	It would surely o the sand of the seas	3877+4946

OUTWEIGHS (2) [WEIGH]

Ecc	10: 1	so a little folly o wisdom and honor.	3701+4946
2Co	4:17	an eternal weight of glory **that far** o **them all.**	983+1650+2848+5651+5651

OUTWENT (KJV) See AHEAD

OUTWIT (1) [OUTWITTED]

2Co	2:11	in order that Satan *might* not o *us*.	4430

OUTWITTED (1) [OUTWIT]

Mt	2:16	When Herod realized that *he had been* o by	1850

OVEN (8) [OVENS]

Lev	2: 4	in an o, it is to consist of fine flour:	9486
	7: 9	Every grain offering baked in an o	9486
	11:35	an o or cooking pot must be broken up.	9486
	26:26	be able to bake your bread in one o,	9486
La	5:10	Our skin is hot as an o,	9486
Hos	7: 4	an o whose fire the baker need not stir from	9486
	7: 6	Their hearts are like an o;	9486
	7: 7	All of them are hot as an o;	9486

OVENS (3) [OVEN]

Ex	8: 3	and into your o and kneading troughs.	9486
Ne	3:11	another section and the Tower of the **O**.	9486
	12:38	past the Tower of the **O** to the Broad Wall,	9486

OVER (1169)

Ge	1: 2	darkness was o the surface of the deep,	6584
	1: 2	the Spirit of God was hovering o the waters.	6584+7156
	1:26	and let them rule o the fish of the sea and	928
	1:26	o the livestock, over all the earth,	928
	1:26	over the livestock, o all the earth,	928
	1:26	and o all the creatures that move along	928
	1:28	Rule o the fish of the sea and the birds of	928
	1:28	and o every living creature that moves on	928
	3:16	and he will rule o you."	4200
	4:15	he will suffer vengeance **seven** *times* o."	AIT
	7:21	all the creatures that swarm o the earth,	6584
	8: 1	and he sent a wind o the earth,	6584
	8: 9	because there was water o all the surface of	6584
	9:14	Whenever I bring clouds o the earth and	6584
	9:19	*the people who were* scattered o the earth.	AIT
	10:32	the nations spread out o the earth after	928
	11: 4	for ourselves and not be scattered o the face	6584
	11: 8	the LORD scattered them from there o	6584+7156
	11: 9	From there the LORD scattered them o	6584
	15:12	a thick and dreadful darkness came o him.	6584
	19:23	the sun had risen o the land.	6584
	19:31	as is the custom **all** o the earth.	AIT
	22: 5	the donkey while I and the boy go o there.	6330
	22:13	He **went** o and took the ram	2143
	23: 2	to mourn for Sarah and to **weep** o her.	AIT
	26:21	but they quarreled o that one also;	6584
	26:22	and no one quarreled o it.	6584
	27:29	Be lord o your brothers,	4200
	27:37	"I have made him lord o you	4200
	28:15	and *will* **watch** o you wherever you go,	9068
	28:20	"If God will be with me and *will* **watch** o	9068
	29: 2	The stone o the mouth of the well	6584
	29: 3	the stone to its place o the mouth of	6584
	29:10	he **went** o and rolled the stone away from	5602

Ge	30:31	on tending your flocks and **watching** o	9068
	32:23	*he* **sent** o all his possessions.	6296
	35:20	**O** her tomb Jacob set up a pillar,	6584
	37: 8	"Do you intend to reign o us?	6584
	38:16	*he* **went** o to her by the roadside and said,	5742
	41:34	Let Pharaoh appoint commissioners o	6584
	41:56	famine had spread o the whole country	6584+7156
	42:30	"The man who is **lord** o the whole	AIT
	42:33	the man who is **lord** o the land said to us,	AIT
	45:15	he kissed all his brothers and wept o them.	6584
	47:18	When that year was o,	9462
	48:22	And to you, as one who is o your brothers,	6584
	49:22	whose branches climb o a wall.	6584
	50: 1	and wept o him and kissed him.	6584
Ex	1:11	So they put slave masters o them	6584
	2:14	"Who made you ruler and judge o us?	6584
	3: 3	"*I will* **go** o and see this strange sight—	6073
	3: 4	the LORD saw that *he had* **gone** o to look,	6073
	3:16	**watched** o you and *have* **seen**	7212+7212
	5:12	So the people scattered all o Egypt	928
	7:19	and stretch out your hand o the waters	6584
	7:19	o the streams and canals,	6584
	7:19	o the ponds and all the reservoirs'—	6584
	8: 5	'Stretch out your hand o the whole	6584
	8: 6	So Aaron stretched out his hand o	6584
	9: 9	It will become fine dust o the whole land	6584
	9:22	the sky so that hail will fall all o Egypt—	928
	10:12	"Stretch out your hand o Egypt so	6584
	10:12	over Egypt so that locusts will swarm o	6584
	10:13	So Moses stretched out his staff o Egypt,	6584
	10:21	so that darkness will spread o Egypt—	6584
	12: 8	to eat the meat **roasted** o the fire,	AIT
	12: 9	but **roast** it o the fire—	AIT
	12:13	*I will* **pass** o you.	7173
	12:23	and sides of the doorframe and *will* **pass** o	7173
	12:27	who **passed** o the houses of the Israelites	7173
	13:12	*to* **give** o to the LORD the first offspring	6296
	14: 7	with officers o all of them.	6584
	14:16	Raise your staff and stretch out your hand o	6584
	14:21	Moses stretched out his hand o the sea,	6584
	14:26	"Stretch out your hand o the sea so that	6584
	14:26	the sea so that the waters may flow back o	6584
	14:27	Moses stretched out his hand o the sea,	6584
	15:19	the waters of the sea back o them,	6584
	18:21	and appoint them as officials o thousands,	6584
	18:25	**officials** o thousands, hundreds,	AIT
	19:16	with a thick cloud o the mountain,	6584
	23:31	*I will* **hand** o to you the people	928+3338+5989
	25:22	between the two cherubim that are o the ark	6584
	26: 7	of goat hair for the tent o the tabernacle—	6584
	26:12	that is **left** o is to hang down at the rear	6369
	26:13	what is left will hang o the sides of	6584
	26:14	and o that a covering of hides of sea cows.	2025+4200+4946+5087
	28:29	the names of the sons of Israel o his heart	6584
	28:30	be o Aaron's heart whenever he enters	6584
	28:30	the Israelites o his heart before the LORD.	6584
	29:34	the ordination ram or any bread *is* **left** o	3855
	30: 6	before the atonement cover that is o	6584
	30:13	Each *one* who **crosses** o	6296
	30:14	All who **cross** o,	6296
	34:33	he put a veil o his face.	6584
	34:35	the veil back o his face until he went in	6584
	36:14	of goat hair for the tent o the tabernacle—	6584
	36:19	and o that a covering of hides of sea cows.	2025+4200+4946+5087
	38:26	from everyone who *had* **crossed** o	6296
	40:19	Then he spread the tent o the tabernacle	6584
	40:19	over the tabernacle and put the covering o	6584
	40:20	to the ark and put the atonement cover o it.	6584
	40:38	of the LORD was o the tabernacle by day,	6584
Lev	7:16	but anything **left** o may be eaten on	3855
	7:17	the sacrifice **left** o till the third day must	3855
	10:12	"Take the grain offering **left** o from	3855
	12: 4	until the days of her purification *are* o.	4848
	12: 6	purification for a son or daughter *are* o,	4848
	13:12	the disease **breaks out all** o his skin	7255+7255
	14: 5	that one of the birds be killed o fresh water	6584
	14: 6	of the bird that was killed o the fresh water.	6584
	14:50	He shall kill one of the birds o fresh water	6584
	16: 2	in the cloud o the atonement cover.	6584
	16:21	the head of the live goat and confess o it all	6584
	19: 6	anything **left** o until the third day must	3855
	19:10	**go** o your vineyard a **second time**	6618
	25:43	Do not rule o them ruthlessly,	928
	25:46	not rule o your fellow Israelites ruthlessly.	928
	25:53	to it that his owner *does* not **rule** o	8097
	26:17	those who hate you will rule o you,	928
	26:18	for your sins seven times o.	3578
	26:21	I will multiply your afflictions **seven** *times* o	AIT
	26:24	afflict you for your sins **seven** *times* o.	AIT
	26:28	punish you for your sins **seven** *times* o.	AIT
	26:37	They will stumble o one another as	AIT
Nu	1:50	o all its furnishings	6584
	3:32	He was **appointed** o those who were	AIT
	4: 6	cloth of solid blue o that	2025+4200+4946+5087
	4: 7	"**O** the table of the Presence they are	6584
	4: 8	**O** these they are to spread a scarlet cloth,	6584
	4:11	"**O** the gold altar they are to spread	6584
	4:13	the bronze altar and spread a purple cloth o	6584
	4:14	**O** it they are to spread a covering of hides	6584
	5:14	if feelings of jealousy come o her husband	6584
	5:30	or when feelings of jealousy come o a man	6584
	6: 5	of his separation to the LORD *is* o;	4848
	6:13	when the period of his separation *is* o.	4848
	9:18	long as the cloud stayed o the tabernacle.	6584
	9:19	When the cloud remained o the tabernacle	6584

Ref		Text	Strong
Nu	9:20	the cloud was o the tabernacle only	6584
	9:22	Whether the cloud stayed o the tabernacle	6584
	10:10	the trumpets o your burnt offerings	6584
	10:15	Nethanel son of Zuar was o the division	6584
	10:16	and Eliab son of Helon was o the division	6584
	10:19	of Zurishaddai was o the division of the	6584
	10:20	of Deuel was o the division of the tribe	6584
	10:23	of Pedahzur was o the division of the tribe	6584
	10:24	of Gideoni was o the division of the tribe	6584
	10:26	Pagiel son of Ocran was o the division of	6584
	10:27	and Ahira son of Enan was o the division	6584
	10:34	The cloud of the LORD was o them	6584
	14:14	that your cloud stays o them,	6584
	16:13	And now you also want to lord it o us?	6584
	16:33	the earth closed o them,	6584
	19:17	into a jar and pour fresh water o them.	6584
	21: 3	gave the Canaanites o them.	5989
	21:24	put him to the sword and took o his land	3769
	21:34	for I have handed him o to you,	928+3338+5989
	23:15	while I meet with him o there."	3907
	27: 7	turn their father's inheritance o	6296
	27: 8	turn his inheritance o to his daughter.	6296
	27:16	appoint a man o this community	6584
	31:48	officers who were o the units of the army—	4200
	32: 7	the Israelites from going o into the land	6296
	32: 8	from Kadesh Barnea to look o the land.	8011
	32:21	of you will go armed o the Jordan before	6296
	32:27	will cross o to fight before the LORD,	6296
	32:29	cross o the Jordan with you before	6296
	32:30	But if they do not cross o with you armed,	6296
	32:32	We will cross o before the LORD	6296
	34: 4	Then it will go to Hazar Addar and o	6296
Dt	1:13	and I will set them o you."	928+8031
	1:15	appointed them to have authority o you—	6584
	2: 7	*He has watched* o your journey	3359
	2:31	**deliver** Sihon and his country o	5989
	2:33	the LORD our God **delivered** him o to us	5989
	3: 2	for I have **handed** him o to you	928+3338+5989
	3:12	Of the land that *we* took o at that time,	3769
	3:18	*must* cross o ahead of your brother	6296
	3:20	and they too have taken the land that	3769
	3:21	o there where you are going.	6296
	3:25	Let me go o and see the good land beyond	6296
	4:22	*about to* cross o and take possession of	6296
	6:18	and you may go in and take o the good land	3769
	7: 2	the LORD your God has **delivered** them o	5989
	7:16	the peoples the LORD your God **gives** o	5989
	7:23	the LORD your God will **deliver** them o	5989
	11: 8	in and take o the land that you are crossing	3769
	11:10	The land you are entering to take o is not	3769
	11:31	you have taken o it and are living there,	3769
	15: 6	You will rule o many nations	928
	15: 6	over many nations but none will rule o you.	928
	17:14	a king o us like all the nations around us,"	6584
	17:15	be sure to appoint o you the king	6584
	17:15	Do not place a foreigner o you,	6584
	17:20	**reign** a long time o his kingdom	6584
	19:12	**hand** him o *to* the avenger of blood to die.	928+3338+5989
	20: 9	they shall appoint commanders o it.	928+8031
	21: 6	the body shall wash their hands o	6584
	23:15	*do* not **hand** him o to his master.	6037
	24:20	not **go** o **the branches a second time.**	339+6994
	24:21	not **go** o **the vines again.**	339+6618
	27: 3	of this law when you *have* **crossed** o to	6296
	28:23	The sky o your head will be bronze,	6584
	28:36	the king you set o you to a nation unknown	6584
	28:42	of locusts *will* **take** o all your trees and	3769
	31: 3	The LORD your God himself *will* **cross** o	6296
	31: 3	Joshua also *will* **cross** o ahead of you,	6296
	31:15	the cloud stood o the entrance to the Tent.	6584
	32:11	that stirs up its nest and hovers o its young,	6584
	33: 2	from Sinai and dawned o them from Seir;	4200
	33: 5	He was king o Jeshurun when the leaders	928
	33: 9	but he **watched** o your word	9068
	34: 4	but *you* will not **cross** o into it."	6296
	34: 8	the time of weeping and mourning *was* o.	9462
Jos	1:14	*must* **cross** o ahead of your brothers.	6296
	2: 1	"Go, **look** o the land," he said,	8011
	3: 1	where they camped before **crossing** o.	6296
	3:16	So the people **crossed** o opposite Jericho.	6296
	4: 3	and to **carry** them o with you and put them	6296
	4: 5	"**Go** o before the ark of the LORD	6296
	4: 8	and *they* **carried** them o with them	6296
	4:10	The people hurried o,	6296
	4:12	and the half-tribe of Manasseh **crossed** o,	6296
	4:13	for battle **crossed** o before the LORD to	6296
	4:23	before you until you *had* **crossed** o.	6296
	4:23	up before us until we *had* **crossed** o.	6296
	5: 1	before the Israelites until we *had* **crossed** o,	6296
	7:26	O Achan they heaped up a large pile	
	8:29	And they raised a large pile of rocks o it,	6584
	10:12	the LORD **gave** the Amorites o to Israel,	5989
	10:12	"O sun, stand still o Gibeon, O moon,	928
	10:12	O moon, o the Valley of Aijalon."	928
	10:32	The LORD **handed** Lachish o to Israel,	928+3338+5989
	11: 6	*I will* **hand** all of them o to Israel,	5989
	12: 1	and whose territory *they* **took** o east of	3769
	12: 3	He also ruled o the eastern Arabah from	NIH
	12: 5	He ruled o Mount Hermon, Salecah	928
	13: 1	still very large areas of land to *be* **taken** o.	3769
	13:12	Moses had defeated them and **taken** o	3769
	15: 3	continued on to Zin and **went** o to the south	6590
	16: 2	**crossed** o to the territory of the Arkites	6296
	21:44	**handed** all their enemies o	928+3338+5989
	22:19	**come** o to the LORD's land,	6296
Jos	24: 7	the sea o them and covered them.	6584
Jdg	2:14	In his anger against Israel the LORD **handed** them o	928+3338+5989
	3:12	gave Eglon king of Moab power o Israel.	6584
	3:22	and the fat closed in o it.	1237
	3:28	they allowed no one to **cross** o.	6296
	4: 9	the LORD *will* **hand** Sisera o *to* a woman."	928+3338+4835
	4:18	and *she* **put** a covering on,	4059
	6:33	and **crossed** o the Jordan and camped in	6296
	7: 8	*who* **took** o the provisions and trumpets of	4374
	8:22	The Israelites said to Gideon, "Rule o us—	928
	8:23	Gideon told them, "I will not rule o you,	928
	8:23	nor will my son rule o you,	928
	8:23	The LORD will rule o you."	928
	9: 2	of Jerub-Baal's sons rule o you,	928
	9: 9	to hold sway o the trees?'	6584
	9:11	to hold sway o the trees?'	6584
	9:13	to hold sway o the trees?'	6584
	9:15	'If you really want to anoint me king o you,	6584
	9:18	king o the citizens of Shechem	6584
	9:45	he destroyed the city and **scattered** salt o it.	AIT
	9:49	against the stronghold and set it on fire o	6584
	11: 8	the Ammonites, and you will be our head o	4200
	11:11	head and commander o them.	4200
	11:21	Israel **took** o all the land of	3769
	11:23	what right have you *to* **take** it o.	3769
	11:32	Jephthah went o to fight the Ammonites,	448
	12: 1	**crossed** o to Zaphon and said to Jephthah,	6296
	12: 1	We're going to burn down your house o	6584
	12: 3	I took my life in my hands and crossed o	448
	12: 3	the LORD **gave** me the **victory** o them.	AIT
	12: 5	*"Let me* **cross** o,"	6296
	14: 4	for at that time they were ruling o Israel.)	928
	15:11	that the Philistines are rulers o us?	928
	15:12	to tie you up and **hand** you o	928+3338+5989
	15:13	only tie you up and **hand** you o	928+3338+5989
	18: 9	Don't hesitate to go there and take o	3769
	19: 9	Spend the night here; the day *is* nearly o.	2837
Ru	2:14	Boaz said to her, "Come o here.	2151
	2:14	She ate all she wanted and had some left o.	3855
	2:18	and gave her what *she* had left o.	3855
	3: 7	*he* **went** o to lie down at the far end of	995
	3: 9	"Spread the corner of your garment o me,	6584
	4: 1	"**Come** o here, my friend, and sit down."	6073
	4: 1	So he **went** o and sat down.	6073
1Sa	1:28	For his whole life he *will* **be given** o to	8626
	2: 1	My mouth boasts o my enemies,	6584
	2:16	"No, **hand** it o now;	5989
	4:14	The man hurried o to Eli,	995
	7:15	Samuel *continued as* **judge** o Israel all	AIT
	8: 9	the king who will reign o them will do."	6584
	8:11	"This is what the king who will reign o	6584
	8:19	"We want a king o us.	6584
	9:16	Anoint him leader o my people Israel;	6584
	10: 1	"Has not the LORD anointed you leader o	6584
	10:19	And you have said, 'No, set a king o us.'	6584
	11:12	'Shall Saul reign o us?'	6584
	12: 1	to me and have set a king o you.	6584
	12:12	'No, we want a king to rule o us'—	6584
	12:13	see, the LORD has set a king o you.	6584
	12:14	and if both you and the king who reigns o	6584
	13: 1	and he reigned o Israel [forty-]two years.	6584
	13:13	he would have established your kingdom o	448
	14: 1	*let's* **go** o to the Philistine outpost on	6296
	14: 6	*let's* **go** o to the outpost	6296
	14: 8	we will **cross** o toward the men	6296
	14:21	up with them to their camp **went** o to	2118+6017
	14:33	"Roll a large stone o here at once."	448
	14:40	"You **stand** o **there;**	285+4200+6298
	14:40	I and Jonathan my son will stand o here."	285+4200+6298
	14:47	After Saul had assumed rule o Israel,	6584
	15: 1	to anoint you king o his people Israel;	6584
	15:17	The LORD anointed you king o Israel.	6584
	15:26	LORD has rejected you as king o Israel!"	6584
	15:35	that he had made Saul king o Israel.	6584
	16: 1	since I have rejected him as king o Israel?	6584
	17: 4	He was o nine feet tall.	564+2256+2455+9252
	17:39	fastened on his sword o the tunic and	4946+6584
	17:42	He **looked** David o and saw	5564
	17:46	day the LORD *will* **hand** you o	928+3338+6037
	17:50	So David triumphed o the Philistine with	4946
	17:51	David ran and stood o him.	448
	18:13	and gave him **command** o *a* thousand men,	AIT
	19:22	"O in Naioth at Ramah," they said.	NIH
	20: 8	Why **hand** me o to your father?"	995
	23: 7	"God has **handed** him o to me,	928+3338+5796
	23:17	You will be king o Israel,	6584
	23:20	responsible for **handing** him o *to*	928+3338+6037
	25:17	Now **think** it o and see what you can do,	3359
	25:17	because disaster is hanging o our master	448
	25:21	all *my* **watching** o this fellow's property in	9068
	25:30	and has appointed him leader o Israel,	6584
	26:13	Then David **crossed** o *to* the other side	6296
	26:22	of your young men **come** o and get it.	6584
	27: 2	and **went** o to Achish son of Maoch king	6296
	28:19	The LORD *will* **hand** o both Israel	928+3338+5989
	28:19	LORD *will* **also hand** o the army	928+3338+5989
	29: 3	He has already been with me for o a year,	196+2296+2296+3427+9102
	30:15	or **hand** me o *to* my master,	928+3338+6037
	30:16	scattered o the countryside, eating,	6584+7156
	30:23	and **handed** o to us the forces	928+3338+5989
2Sa	1: 9	he said to me, 'Stand o me and kill me!	6584
	1:10	"So I stood o him and killed him,	6584
	2: 4	anointed David king o the house of Judah.	6584
2Sa	2: 7	the house of Judah has anointed me king o	6584
	2: 8	of Saul and **brought** him o *to* Mahanaim.	6296
	2: 9	He made him king o Gilead,	448
	2: 9	Ashuri and Jezreel, and also o Ephraim,	6584
	2:10	when he became king o Israel,	6584
	2:11	David was king in Hebron o the house of	6584
	3: 8	*I haven't* **handed** you o *to* David.	928+3338+5162
	3:10	establish David's throne o Israel and Judah	6584
	3:12	I will help you **bring** all Israel o to you."	6015
	3:21	you may rule o all that your heart desires."	928
	3:34	And all the people wept o him again.	6584
	5: 3	In the past, while Saul was king o us,	6584
	5: 3	and they anointed David king o Israel.	6584
	5: 5	In Hebron he reigned o Judah seven years	6584
	5: 5	and in Jerusalem he reigned o all Israel	6584
	5:12	the LORD had established him as king o	6584
	5:17	that David had been anointed king o Israel,	6584
	5:19	*Will you* **hand** them o *to* me?"	928+3338+5989
	5:19	**surely hand** the Philistines o *to* you."	928+3338+5989+5989
	6:21	when he appointed me ruler o	6584
	7: 8	and from following the flock to be ruler o	6584
	7:11	since the time I appointed leaders o	6584
	7:12	When your days *are* o and you rest	4848
	7:26	'The LORD Almighty is God o Israel!'	6584
	8:10	on his victory in battle o Hadadezer,	928
	8:15	David reigned o all Israel,	6584
	8:16	Joab son of Zeruiah was o the army;	6584
	8:18	of Jehoiada was o the Kerethites	NIH
	11:27	After the time of mourning *was* o,	6296
	12: 6	He must pay for that lamb **four** *times* o,	AIT
	12: 7	'I anointed you king o Israel,	6584
	14: 7	'**Hand** o the one who struck his brother	5989
	16: 8	LORD *has* **handed** the kingdom o	928+3338+5989
	16: 9	*Let me* **go** o and cut off his head."	6296
	17:16	**cross** o **without fail,** or the king	6296+6296
	17:19	His wife took a covering and spread it out o	6584
	17:19	of the well and scattered grain o it.	6584
	17:20	"They **crossed** o the brook."	6296
	17:25	Absalom had appointed Amasa o the army	6584
	18: 1	and appointed o them commanders	6584
	18: 8	The battle spread out over the whole	6584+7156
	18:17	and piled up a large heap of rocks o him.	6584
	18:33	up to the **room** o the gateway and wept.	6608
	19:10	whom we anointed to **rule** o us,	6584
	19:14	He **won** the hearts of all the men of Judah	5742
	19:18	**take** the king's household o	6296
	19:22	not know that today I am king o Israel?"	6584
	19:33	"**Cross** o with me and stay with me	6296
	19:36	Your servant *will* **cross** o the Jordan with	6296
	19:37	*Let him* **cross** o with my lord the king.	6296
	19:38	"Kimham *shall* **cross** o with me,	6296
	19:39	and then the king **crossed** o.	6296
	19:40	When the king **crossed** o to Gilgal,	6296
	19:40	the troops of Israel *had* **taken** the king o.	6296
	20: 8	and strapped o it at his waist was a belt	6584
	20:12	the road into a field and threw a garment o	6584
	20:21	**Hand** o this one man,	5989
	20:23	Joab was o Israel's entire army;	448
	20:23	of Jehoiada was o the Kerethites	6584
	21: 9	*He* **handed** them o *to* the Gibeonites,	928+3338+5989
	23: 3	'When one rules o men in righteousness,	928
	24: 3	the troops a hundred **times** o,	AIT
	24:13	**think** *it* o and decide how I should answer	3359
1Ki	1: 1	even when *they* **put** covers o him.	4059
	1:34	and Nathan the prophet anoint him king o	6584
	1:35	I have appointed him ruler o Israel	6584
	2:11	He had reigned forty years o Israel—	6584
	2:35	of Jehoiada o the army in Joab's position	6584
	4: 1	So King Solomon ruled o all Israel.	6584
	4: 7	also had twelve district governors o	6584
	4:19	He was the only governor o the district.	928
	4:21	And Solomon ruled o all the kingdoms	928
	4:24	For he ruled o all the kingdoms west of	928
	5: 7	a wise son to **rule** o this great nation."	6584
	6: 1	the fourth year of Solomon's reign o Israel,	6584
	6:35	with gold hammered evenly o the carvings.	6584
	8: 7	The cherubim spread their wings o	448
	8:46	with them and **give** them o to the enemy,	5989
	9: 5	I will establish your royal throne o	6584
	11:37	you will rule o all that your heart desires;	928
	11:37	you will be king o Israel.	6584
	11:42	in Jerusalem o all Israel forty years.	6584
	12:17	Rehoboam still ruled o them.	6584
	12:20	to the assembly and made him king o	6584
	13:26	The LORD *has* **given** him o to the lion,	5989
	13:30	and they mourned o him and said, "Oh,	6584
	14: 2	the one who told me I would be king o	6584
	14: 7	among the people and made you a leader o	6584
	14:14	for himself a king o Israel who will cut off	6584
	14:17	as she stepped o the threshold of the house,	928
	15:25	and he reigned o Israel two years.	6584
	16:16	king o Israel that very day three in	6584
	16:29	in Samaria o Israel twenty-two years.	6584
	18: 9	**handing** your servant o	928+3338+5989
	18:19	the people from **all** o Israel to meet me	3972
	19: 6	a cake of bread **baked** o hot coals,	8363
	19:13	*he* **pulled** his cloak o his face	4286
	19:15	you get there, anoint Hazael king o Aram.	6584
	19:16	anoint Jehu son of Nimshi king o Israel,	6584
	20:38	with his headband drawn o his eyes.	6584
	21: 7	"Is this how you act as king o Israel?	6584
	21:18	and he reigned o Israel two years.	6584
2Ki	2: 8	the two of them **crossed** o on dry ground.	6296
	2:14	and he **crossed** o.	6296
	3:10	to **hand** us o *to* Moab?"	928+3338+5989

2Ki 3:13	to **hand** us o *to* Moab."	928+3338+5989
3:18	*he will* also **hand** Moab o *to* you.	928+3338+5989
4:27	Gehazi **came** o to push her away,	5602
4:43	'They will eat and **have** *some* **left** o.' "	3855
4:44	and they ate and **had** *some* **left** o,	3855
5:11	wave his hand o the spot and cure me	448
7: 4	So *let's* **go** o to the camp of the Arameans	2143
8:15	in water and spread it o the king's face,	6584
9: 3	I anoint you king o Israel.'	448
9: 6	'I anoint you king o the LORD's people	448
9:12	I anoint you king o Israel.' "	448
10:36	The time that Jehu reigned o Israel	6584
12: 7	but **hand** it o for repairing the temple."	5989
13:14	went down to see him and wept o	6584+7156
13:17	the arrow of victory o Aram!"	928
17:24	*They* **took** o Samaria and lived in its towns.	3769
19:10	'Jerusalem *will* not **be handed** o *to* the king	
	of Assyria.'	928+3338+5989
19:15	you alone are God o all the kingdoms	4200
21: 3	I will stretch out o Jerusalem	6584
21:14	**hand** them o *to* their enemies.	928+3338+5989
23: 6	and scattered the dust o the graves of	6584
25:11	and those who *had* **gone** o to the king	5877
25:22	be o the people he had left behind in Judah.	6584
1Ch 5:20	**handed** the Hagrites and all their allies o	
	them,	928+3338+5989
10:14	and **turned** the kingdom o to David son	6015
11: 3	and they anointed David king o Israel,	6584
11:10	to extend it o the whole land, as	6584
12:23	**turn** Saul's kingdom o to him,	6015
12:38	to make David king o all Israel.	6584
14: 2	the LORD had established him as king o	6584
14: 8	that David had been anointed king o	6584
14:10	*Will you* **hand** them o *to* me?"	928+3338+5989
14:10	"Go, *I will* **hand** them o *to* you."	928+3338+5989
17: 7	to be ruler o my people Israel.	6584
17:10	since the time I appointed leaders o	6584
17:11	When your days *are* o and you go to be	4848
17:14	I will set him o my house	928
17:24	'The LORD Almighty, the **God** o Israel,	AIT
18:10	on his victory in battle o Hadadezer,	928
18:14	David reigned o all Israel,	6584
18:15	Joab son of Zeruiah was o the army;	6584
18:17	of Jehoiada was o the Kerethites	6584
21: 3	multiply his troops a hundred **times** o.	AIT
21:16	with a drawn sword in his hand extended o	6584
22:10	the throne of his kingdom o Israel forever.'	6584
22:12	when he puts you in command o Israel,	6584
22:18	**handed** the inhabitants of the land o *to* me,	
		928+3338+5989
23: 1	he made his son Solomon king o Israel.	6584
26:29	as officials and judges o Israel.	6584
27: 6	a mighty man among the Thirty and was o	6584
27:16	The officers o the tribes of Israel:	6584
27:16	of Israel: o the Reubenites:	4200
27:16	of Zicri; o the Simeonites:	4200
27:17	o Levi: Hashabiah son of Kemuel;	4200
27:17	Hashabiah son of Kemuel; o Aaron:	4200
27:18	o Judah: Elihu, a brother of David;	4200
27:18	a brother of David; o Issachar:	4200
27:19	o Zebulun: Ishmaiah son of Obadiah;	4200
27:19	of Obadiah; o Naphtali:	4200
27:20	o the Ephraimites: Hoshea son of Azaziah;	4200
27:20	o half the tribe of Manasseh:	4200
27:21	o the half-tribe of Manasseh in Gilead:	4200
27:21	of Zechariah; o Benjamin:	4200
27:22	o Dan: Azarel son of Jeroham.	4200
27:22	These were the **officers** o the tribes	AIT
28: 1	the **officers** o the tribes,	AIT
28: 4	from my whole family to be king o	6584
28: 4	to make me king o all Israel.	6584
28: 5	the throne of the kingdom of the LORD o	6584
29: 3	o and above everything I have provided	
		2025+4200+5087
29:11	you are exalted as head o all.	4200
29:25	on him royal splendor such as no king o	6584
29:26	David son of Jesse was king o all Israel.	6584
29:27	He ruled o Israel forty years—	6584
2Ch 1: 1	son of David established himself firmly o	6584
1: 9	for you have made me king o a people	6584
1:11	and knowledge to govern my people o	6584
1:13	And he reigned o Israel.	6584
2: 2	and thirty-six hundred as foremen o them.	6584
2:18	3,600 foremen o them to keep	NIH
5: 8	The cherubim spread their wings o	6584
6: 5	nor have I chosen anyone to be the leader o	6584
6:36	with them and **give** them o to the enemy,	5989
7:18	to have a man to rule o Israel.'	928
9: 8	he has made you king o them,	6584
9:26	He ruled o all the kings from the River to	928
9:30	in Jerusalem o all Israel forty years.	6584
10:17	Rehoboam still ruled o them.	6584
15: 9	for large numbers *had* **come** o to him	5877
19:11	the chief priest will be o you in any matter	6584
19:11	be o you in any matter concerning the king,	NIH
20: 6	You rule o all the kingdoms of the nations.	928
20:27	to rejoice o their enemies.	4946
20:31	So Jehoshaphat reigned o Judah.	6584
21: 4	When Jehoram established himself firmly o	6584
25:20	that he *might* **hand** them o to	928+3338+5989
26:12	The total number of family leaders o	4200
28: 5	Therefore the LORD his God **handed** him o	
		928+3338+5989
31:10	and this great amount *is* **left** o."	3855
32: 6	He appointed military officers o the people	6584
34: 4	he broke to pieces and scattered o	6584+7156
34:12	O them to direct them were Jahath	6584

2Ch 35:13	They roasted the Passover animals o	928
36: 4	king o Judah and Jerusalem	6584
36:10	Zedekiah, king o Judah and Jerusalem.	6584
36:17	**handed** all of them o	928+3338+5989
Ezr 4: 9	and officials o the men from Tripolis,	NIH
4:20	Jerusalem has had powerful kings ruling o	10089
5: 1	God of Israel, who was o them.	10542
5: 5	of their God was watching o the elders of	10542
5:12	*he* **handed** them o *to* Nebuchadnezzar	
		10089+10311+10314
10: 6	to mourn o the unfaithfulness of the exiles.	6584
Ne 3:15	**roofing** it o and putting its doors and bolts	3233
4: 2	**Give** them o as plunder in a land	5989
4:12	near them came and told us ten **times** o,	AIT
4:14	After *I* **looked** things o,	8011
5:15	Their assistants also **lorded** it o	8948
9:22	*They* **took** o the country of Sihon king	3769
9:24	**handed** the Canaanites o to them.	928+3338+5989
9:27	So *you* **handed** them o *to* their enemies,	
		928+3338+5989
9:28	of their enemies so that they ruled o them.	928
9:30	so *you* **handed** them o *to*	928+3338+5989
9:37	to the kings you have placed o us.	6584
9:37	They rule o our bodies and our cattle	6584
11: 9	of Hassenuah was o the Second District of	6584
12:39	o the Gate of Ephraim,	4946+6584
13:19	and not opened until the Sabbath was o.	339
13:26	and God made him king o all Israel,	6584
Est 1: 1	the Xerxes who **ruled** o 127 provinces	4887
1: 5	When these days *were* o,	4848
1:22	that every man should be ruler o	928
8: 2	Esther appointed him o Haman's estate.	6584
9: 1	the upper hand o those who hated them.	928
Job 3: 5	may a cloud settle o it;	6584
8: 4	*he* **gave** them o to the penalty of their sin.	8938
8:16	spreading its shoots o the garden;	6584
10:12	in your providence **watched** o my spirit.	9068
10:20	*Are* not my few days *almost* o?	2532
14:17	you will cover o my sin.	6584
15:29	nor will his possessions spread o the land.	4200
16:11	God *has* **turned** me o to evil men	6037
16:15	"I have sewed sackcloth o my skin	6584
18:15	burning sulfur is scattered o his dwelling.	6584
20:25	Terrors will come o him;	6584
21: 5	clap your hand o your mouth.	6584
21:32	and watch is kept o his tomb.	6584
26: 7	He spreads out the northern [skies] o empty	6584
26: 7	he suspends the earth o nothing.	6584
26: 9	spreading his clouds o it.	6584
29: 2	for the days when God **watched** o me,	9068
31:25	if *I have* **rejoiced** o my great wealth,	AIT
31:29	or **gloated** o the trouble that came to him—	AIT
34:13	Who appointed him o the earth?	2025
34:19	does not favor the rich o the poor,	4200+7156
34:29	Yet he is o man and nation alike,	6584
37:12	around o the face of the whole earth	6584
38:24	the east winds are scattered o the earth?	6584
38:33	Can you set up [God's] dominion o the earth	928
38:37	Who *can* **tip** o the water jars of the heavens	8886
40: 4	I put my hand o my mouth.	4344
41:20	from his nostrils as from a boiling pot o	NIH
41:34	he is king o all that are proud."	6584
42:11	They comforted and consoled him o all	6584
Ps 1: 6	LORD **watches** o the way of the righteous,	3359
5:11	Spread your protection o them,	6584
7: 7	Rule o them from on high;	6584
8: 6	You made him ruler o the works	928
13: 2	How long will my enemy triumph o me?	6584
19:13	may they not rule o me.	928
22:17	people stare and gloat o me.	928
22:28	to the LORD and he rules o the nations.	928
25: 2	nor let my enemies triumph o me.	4200
27:12	*Do* not **turn** me o to the desire of my foes,	5989
29: 3	The voice of the LORD is o the waters;	6584
29: 3	the LORD thunders o the mighty waters.	6584
29:10	The LORD sits enthroned o the flood;	4200
30: 1	and did not let my enemies gloat o me.	4200
31: 8	*You have* not **handed** me o *to* the enemy	
		928+3338+6037
32: 8	I will counsel you and watch o you.	6584
35:19	not those gloat o me who are my enemies	4200
35:24	do not let them gloat o me.	4200
35:26	May all *who* **gloat** o my distress be put	AIT
35:26	may all who exalt themselves o me	6584
38:16	not let them gloat or exalt themselves o me	6584
41:11	for my enemy does not triumph o me.	6584
42: 7	all your waves and breakers have swept o	6584
44: 7	but you give us victory o our enemies,	4946
44:19	and covered us o with deep darkness.	6584
47: 2	the great King o all the earth!	6584
47: 8	God reigns o the nations;	6584
49:14	The upright will rule o them in	928
57: 5	let your glory be o all the earth.	6584
57:11	let your glory be o all the earth.	6584
59:10	before me and will let me gloat o	928
59:13	to the ends of the earth that God rules o	928
60: 8	o Philistia I shout in triumph."	6584
63:10	*be* given o *to* the sword and	3338+5599+6584
66:12	You let men ride o our heads;	4200
68:34	whose majesty is o Israel,	6584
69:15	up or the pit close its mouth o me.	6584
74: 7	*Do* not **hand** o the life of your dove	5989
78:48	*He* **gave** o their cattle to the hail,	6037
78:50	not spare them from death but **gave** them o	6037
78:62	*He* **gave** his people o to the sword;	6037
80:14	**Watch** o this vine,	7212
81:12	So *I* **gave** them o to their stubborn hearts	8938

Ps 83:18	you alone are the Most High o all the earth.	6584
88:16	Your wrath has swept o me;	6584
89: 9	You rule o the surging sea;	928
89:25	I will set his hand o the sea,	928
89:25	his right hand o the rivers.	928
97: 9	are the Most High o all the earth;	6584
99: 2	he is exalted o all the nations.	6584
103:16	the wind blows o it and it is gone,	928
103:19	and his kingdom rules o all.	4910
104: 8	*they* **flowed** o the mountains,	6590
105:21	ruler o all he possessed,	928
106:41	**handed** them o to the nations,	928+3338+5989
106:41	and their foes ruled o them.	928
108: 5	and let your glory be o all the earth.	6584
108: 9	o Philistia I shout in triumph."	6584
113: 4	The LORD is exalted o all the nations,	6584
118:18	but *he has* not **given** me o to death.	5989
119:133	let no sin rule o me.	928
121: 3	*he who* **watches** o you will not slumber;	9068
121: 4	*he who* **watches** o Israel will neither	
	slumber nor sleep.	9068
121: 5	The LORD **watches** o you—	9068
121: 7	*he will* **watch** o your life;	9068
121: 8	the LORD *will* **watch** o your coming	9068
124: 4	the torrent would have swept o us,	6584
125: 3	The scepter of the wicked will not remain o	6584
127: 1	Unless the LORD **watches** o the city,	9068
129: 2	but they have not gained the victory o me.	4200
141: 3	Set a guard o my mouth, O LORD;	4200
141: 3	keep watch o the door of my lips.	6584
141: 8	*do* not **give** me o to death.	6867
145:20	The LORD **watches** o all who love him,	9068
146: 9	The LORD **watches** o the alien	9068
Pr 1:27	disaster **sweeps** o you like a whirlwind,	910
3:10	and your vats *will* **brim** o with new wine.	7287
4: 6	love her, and *she will* **watch** o you;	5915
6:22	when you sleep, they will watch o you;	6584
10:12	but love covers o all wrongs.	6584
17: 2	wise servant will rule o a disgraceful son,	928
17: 5	whoever gloats o disaster will	4200
17: 9	*He who* **covers** o an offense promotes love,	4059
19:10	much worse for a slave to rule o princes!	928
20:26	he drives the threshing wheel o them.	6584
22: 7	The rich rule o the poor,	928
22:12	eyes of the LORD **keep watch** o knowledge,	5915
23:30	Those who linger o wine,	6584
26:23	of glaze o earthenware are fervent lips with	6584
28:15	or a charging bear is a wicked man ruling o	6584
30:32	clap your hand o your mouth!	4200
31:27	She **watches** o the affairs of her household	7595
Ecc 1:12	the Teacher, was king o Israel in Jerusalem.	6584
1:16	in wisdom more than anyone who has	
	ruled o Jerusalem before me:	6584
2:19	Yet he will have control o all the work	928
2:20	to despair o all my toilsome labor under	6584
2:26	to **hand** it o to the one who pleases God.	5989
3:19	man has no advantage o the animal.	4946
5: 8	o them both are others **higher**	6584
6: 6	if he lives a thousand years **twice** o but fails	7193
6: 8	What advantage has a wise man o a fool?	4946
8: 8	No man has power o the wind to contain it;	928
8: 8	so no one has power o the day of his death.	6584
8: 9	a man **lords** it o others to his own hurt.	8948
SS 2: 4	and his banner o me is love.	6584
2: 8	bounding o the hills.	6584
2:11	The winter is past; the rains *are* o and gone.	2736
7: 9	**flowing gently** o lips and teeth.	AIT
8: 6	Place me like a seal o your heart,	6584
Isa 3:12	women rule o them.	928
4: 5	the LORD will create o all of Mount Zion	6584
4: 5	and o those who assemble there a cloud	6584
4: 5	o all the glory will be a canopy.	6584
5:30	that day they will roar o it like the roaring	6584
7: 6	and make the son of Tabeel king o it."	928+9348
8: 6	of Shiloah and rejoices o Rezin and the son	907
8: 7	overflow all its channels, run o all its banks	6584
8: 8	into Judah, **swirling** o it, passing through it	8851
9: 7	He will reign on David's throne and o	6584
10:26	and he will raise his staff o the waters,	6584
10:29	*They* **go** o the pass, and say,	6296
11:15	a scorching wind he will sweep his hand o	6584
11:15	into seven streams so that *men can* **cross** o	2005
14: 2	of their captors and rule o their oppressors.	928
14: 8	the cedars of Lebanon exult o you and say,	4200
14: 9	all *those who* were **kings** o the nations.	AIT
14:26	this is the hand stretched out o all nations.	6584
15: 2	Moab wails o Nebo and Medeba.	6584
15: 5	My heart cries out o Moab;	4200
15: 7	and stored up they carry away o the Ravine	6584
16: 9	The shouts of joy o your ripened fruit and	6584
16: 9	and o your harvests have been stilled.	6584
18: 2	by sea in papyrus boats o the water.	6584+7156
19: 4	*I will* **hand** the Egyptians o to the power	6127
19: 4	and a fierce king will rule o them,"	928
22: 4	Do not try to console me o the destruction	6584
22:21	and **hand** your authority o	928+3338+5989
23: 6	**Cross** o to Tarshish;	6296
23:11	The LORD has stretched out his hand o	6584
23:12	"Up, **cross** o to Cyprus;	6296
26:13	other lords besides you *have* **ruled** o us,	1249
27: 3	**watch** o it; I water it continually.	5915
28:27	nor is a cartwheel rolled o cummin;	6584
28:28	**drives** the wheels of his threshing cart o	2169
29:10	The LORD has brought o you	6584
31: 4	"As a lion growls, a great lion o his prey—	6584
31: 5	*he will* **'pass** o' it and will rescue it."	7173
34: 2	*he will* **give** them o to slaughter.	5989

Isa 34:11	God will stretch out o Edom	6584
37:10	'Jerusalem will not be handed o to the king of Assyria.'	928+3338+5989
37:16	you alone are God o all the kingdoms of	4200
41: 2	*He* hands nations o *to* him	5989
42:13	and will triumph o his enemies.	6584
42:24	Who handed Jacob o to become loot,	5989
43: 2	*they will not* sweep o you.	8851
44:16	o it he prepares his meal,	6584
44:18	their eyes *are* plastered o so they cannot	3220
44:19	I even baked bread o its coals,	6584
45:14	*they will* come o to you and will be yours;	6296
45:14	coming o to you in chains.	6296
51:10	the sea so that the redeemed *might* cross o?	6296
51:23	'Fall prostrate that *we may* walk o you.'	6296
51:23	like a street to *be* walked o."	6296
60: 2	and thick darkness is o the peoples,	NIH
60: 2	upon you and his glory appears o you.	6584
62: 5	as a bridegroom rejoices o his bride,	6584
62: 5	so will your God rejoice o you.	6584
63:19	but you have not ruled o them,	928
65:19	I will rejoice o Jerusalem and take delight	928
66:10	all who mourn o her.	6584
66:13	and you will be comforted o Jerusalem."	928
Jer 1:10	today I appoint you o nations	6584
2:10	Cross o to the coasts of Kittim and look,	6296
4:31	my life is *given o to* murderers."	4200
6: 1	Raise the signal o Beth Hakkerem!	6584
6: 9	pass your hand o the branches again,	6584
6:12	Their houses *will be turned* o to others,	6015
6:17	I appointed watchmen o you and said,	6584
6:21	Fathers and sons alike will stumble o them;	928
9:18	Let them come quickly and wail o us	6584
12:12	O all the barren heights in	6584
13:21	sets o you those you cultivated as your	6584
13:26	I will pull up your skirts o your face	6584
18:21	So **give** their children o to famine;	5989
18:21	**hand** them o to the power of the sword.	5599
20: 4	*I will* **hand** all Judah o *to* the king	928+3338+5989
20: 5	*I will* **hand** o *to* their enemies all	928+3338+5989
20:10	then we will prevail o him	4200
21: 7	*I will* **hand** o Zedekiah king of	928+3338+5989
22:25	*I will* **hand** you o *to* those who	928+3338+5989
23: 4	I will place shepherds o	6584
24: 6	My eyes will **watch** o them for their good,	6584+8492
26:24	so he *was* not **handed** o *to* the people to be put to death.	928+3338+5989
27: 6	**hand** all your countries o	928+3338+5989
28:14	I will even give him control o the wild animals.' "	NIH
29:21	*I will* **hand** o *to* those who	928+3338+5989
30:15	Why do you cry out o your wound,	6584
31:10	and *will* **watch** o his flock like	9068
31:28	Just as I watched o them to uproot and tear	6584
31:28	I will watch o them to build and to plant,"	6584
32: 3	*to* **hand** this city o *to* the king of Babylon,	928+3338+5989
32: 4	but *will* **certainly be handed** o *to* the king of Babylon,	928+3338+5989
32:24	the city *will* **be handed** o *to*	928+3338+5989
32:25	the city *will* **be handed** o *to*	928+3338+5989
32:28	*to* **hand** this city o *to* the Babylonians and	928+3338+5989
32:36	*it will* **be handed** o *to* the king	928+3338+5989
32:43	*it has* **been handed** o *to* the Babylonians.'	928+3338+5989
33:26	to rule o the descendants of Abraham,	448
34: 2	*to* **hand** this city o *to* the king of Babylon,	928+3338+5989
34: 3	surely be captured and **handed** o	928+3338+5989
34:20	*I will* **hand** o *to* their enemies	928+3338+5989
34:21	**hand** Zedekiah king of Judah and his officials o *to* their enemies	928+3338+5989
35: 4	which was o that of Maaseiah son	4946+5087
37:17	*you will* **be handed** o *to* the king	928+3338+5989
38: 2	or plague, but whoever **goes** o *to*	3655
38: 3	'This city *will* **certainly be handed** o *to* the army	928+3338+5989+5989
38:16	neither kill you nor **hand** you o	928+3338+5989
38:18	this city *will* **be handed** o *to*	928+3338+5989
38:19	"I am afraid of the Jews who *have* **gone** o *to*	5877
38:19	for the Babylonians *may* **hand** me o *to* them	928+3338+5989
38:20	*"They will* not **hand** you o,"	5989
39: 9	along with those who *had* **gone** o *to* him,	5877
39:14	*They* **turned** him o *to* Gedaliah son	5989
39:17	*you will* not **be handed** o *to* those you fear.	928+3338+5989
40: 5	whom the king of Babylon has appointed o	928
40: 7	as governor o the land and had put him	928
40:10	and live in the towns you have **taken o.**"	9530
40:11	the son of Shaphan, as governor o them,	6584
41: 2	of Babylon had appointed as governor o	928
41:10	o whom Nebuzaradan commander of the imperial guard *had* **appointed**	AIT
41:10	and set out to **cross** o to the Ammonites.	6296
41:14	and **went** o to Johanan son of Kareah.	2143
41:18	of Babylon had appointed as governor o	928
42:10	and not uproot you, for I am grieved o	448
43: 3	to **hand** us o *to* the Babylonians,	928+3338+5989
43:10	and I will set his throne o these stones	4946+5087
44:27	For I am watching o them for harm,	6584
44:30	**hand** Pharaoh Hophra king of Egypt o *to* his enemies	928+3338+5989
44:30	**handed** Zedekiah king of Judah o *to* Nebuchadnezzar	928+3338+5989

Jer 46:12	One warrior will stumble o another;	928
46:16	they will fall o each other."	448
46:24	**handed** o *to* the people of the north."	928+3338+5989
46:26	*I will* **hand** them o *to* those who	928+3338+5989
48: 5	anguished **cries** o the destruction	AIT
48:31	Therefore I wail o Moab,	6584
48:40	spreading its wings o Moab.	448
49:22	spreading its wings o Bozrah.	6584
50: 6	They wandered o mountain and hill	4946
51: 8	Wail o her!	6584
51:14	and they will shout in triumph o you.	6584
51:42	The sea will rise o Babylon;	6584
51:48	that is in them will shout for joy o Babylon,	6584
52:15	of the craftsmen and those who *had* **gone** o	5877
La 1:14	*He has* **handed** me o *to* those	928+3338+5989
2: 7	*He has* **handed** o *to* the enemy	928+3338+6037
2:17	he has let the enemy gloat o you,	6584
3:54	the waters closed o my head,	6584
3:65	Put a **veil** o their hearts,	AIT
4:16	he no longer **watches** o them.	5564
4:19	they chased us o the mountains and lay	6584
5: 2	Our inheritance *has been* **turned** o to aliens	2200
5: 8	Slaves rule o us,	928
5:18	with jackals prowling o it.	928
Eze 1:25	the expanse o their heads as they stood	6584
1:26	the expanse o their heads was what looked	6584
4:15	"I will let you bake your bread o	6584
7:21	*I will* **hand** it all o as plunder	928+3338+5989
8:10	and I saw portrayed **all** o	6017+6017+6584
9: 4	and lament o all the detestable things	6584
10: 1	above the expanse that was o the heads of	6584
10: 2	the cherubim and scatter them o the city."	6584
10:18	the LORD departed from o the threshold	6584
11: 9	and **hand** you o *to* foreigners	928+3338+5989
16: 8	I spread the corner of my garment o you	6584
16:27	I **gave** you o *to* the greed of your enemies	5989
16:39	*I will* **hand** you o *to* your lovers,	928+3338+5989
20:25	I also **gave** them o statutes that were	5989
20:33	I will rule o you with a mighty hand and	6584
21:31	*I will* **hand** you o *to* brutal men,	928+3338+5989
23: 9	I **handed** her o *to* her lovers,	928+3338+5989
23:24	I will **turn** you o *to* them for punishment,	5989
23:28	*about to* **hand** you o *to* those you hate,	928+3338+5989
23:46	Bring a mob against them and **give** them o	5989
25: 3	o my sanctuary when it was desecrated and	448
25: 3	when it was desecrated and o the land	448
25: 3	and o the people of Judah when they went	448
26:19	and when I bring the ocean depths o you	6584
27:30	and cry bitterly o you;	6584
27:31	They will weep o you with anguish of soul	448
27:32	As they wail and mourn o you,	448
29:15	that it will never again rule o the nations.	928
31:11	I **handed** it o *to* the ruler of the nations,	5989
32: 3	a great throng of people I will cast my net o	6584
32: 8	in the heavens I will darken o you;	6584
32: 8	I will bring darkness o your land,	6584
34: 6	My sheep wandered o all the mountains	928
34: 6	They were scattered o the whole earth,	6584+7156
34:23	I will place o them one shepherd,	6584
35: 5	**delivered** the Israelites o	5599
35: 6	I will **give** you o *to* bloodshed	6913
35:12	and *have been* **given** o *to* us to devour."	5989
37:22	There will be one king o all of them	4200
37:24	" 'My servant David will be king o them,	6584
39:23	**handed** them o *to* their enemies,	928+3338+5989
Da 1:11	the chief official that appointed o Daniel,	6584
2:38	he has made you ruler o them all.	10089
2:39	one of bronze, will rule o the whole earth.	10089
2:48	he made him ruler o the entire province	10542
2:49	Meshach and Abednego administrators o	10168
3:12	there are some Jews whom you have set o	10542
4:17	the Most High is sovereign o the kingdoms	10089
4:17	and sets o them the lowliest of men.'	10542
4:25	the Most High is sovereign o the kingdoms	10089
4:32	the Most High is sovereign o the kingdoms	10089
5:21	that the Most High God is sovereign o	10089
5:21	of men and sets o them anyone he wishes.	10542
5:31	and Darius the Mede **took** o the kingdom,	10618
6: 2	with three administrators o,	10427+10543
6: 3	that the king planned to set him o	10542
6:17	and placed o the mouth of the den,	10542
7:25	The saints *will* **be handed** o *to* him for a time,	10089+10311+10314
7:27	*will* **be handed** o *to* the saints,	10314
8:12	and the daily sacrifice **were given** o to it.	5989
9: 1	who was made ruler o the Babylonian	6584
10: 3	at all until the three weeks **were** o.	4848
11: 8	In those days she *will* **be handed** o,	5989
11:39	He will make them rulers o many people	928
11:42	He will extend his power o many countries;	6584
Hos 7: 8	Ephraim is a flat cake not **turned** o.	2200
7:12	When they go, I will throw my net o them;	6584
8: 1	An eagle is o the house of the LORD	6584
9: 6	Their treasures of silver will be **taken** o	3769
9: 8	*is* the **watchman** o Ephraim,	AIT
10: 5	Its people will mourn o it,	6584
10: 5	those who had rejoiced o its splendor,	6584
11: 5	to Egypt and will not Assyria **rule** o them	4889
11: 8	How *can I* **hand** you o, Israel?	4481
Joel 2: 5	of chariots they leap o the mountaintops,	6584
Am 6: 6	and pours them out o the face of the land—	6584
6: 6	but you do not grieve o the ruin of Joseph.	6584
8: 5	the New Moon be o that we may sell grain,	6296
9: 6	and pours them out o the face of the land—	6584
Ob 1:12	nor rejoice o the people of Judah in the day	4200

Ob 1:14	nor **hand** o their survivors in the day	6037
Jnh 2: 3	all your waves and breakers swept o me.	6584
4: 6	grow up o Jonah to give shade	4200+4946+6584
Mic 3: 6	Therefore night will come o you,	4200
4: 7	The LORD will rule o them	6584
4:11	let our eyes gloat o Zion!"	928
5: 2	for me one who will be ruler o Israel,	928
5: 9	Your hand will be lifted up in triumph o	5989
6:16	Therefore I *will* **give** you o *to* ruin	5989
7: 8	Do not gloat o me, my enemy!	4200
7: 8	people stumbling o the corpses—	928
Na 3: 5	"I will lift your skirts o your face.	6584
Zep 3:17	he will rejoice o you with singing."	6584
Zec 1:16	the measuring line will be stretched out o	6584
5: 3	the curse that is going out o the whole land;	6584+7156
5: 8	and pushed the lead cover down o	448
9:14	Then the LORD will appear o them;	6584
11: 6	"I *will* **hand** everyone o *to* his neighbor	928+3338+5162
11:16	a shepherd o the land who will not care for	928
12: 4	"I will keep a watchful eye o the house	6584
14: 9	The LORD will be king o the whole earth.	6584
Mt 4:24	News about him spread **all** o Syria,	1650+3910
5:25	or he *may* **hand** you o *to* the judge,	4140
5:25	the judge may hand you o *to* the officer,	NIG
8:24	so that the waves **swept** o the boat.	2821
9: 1	**crossed** o and came to his own town.	1385
9:31	the news about him **all** o that region.	3910
10:17	*they will* **hand** you o *to* the local councils	4140
14:20	of broken pieces that *were* **left** o.	4355
14:34	*When they had* **crossed** o,	1385
15:37	of broken pieces that *were* **left** o.	4355
18:15	*you have* **won** your brother o.	3045
18:34	In anger his master **turned** him o to	4140
20:19	and *will* **turn** him o to the Gentiles to	4140
20:25	the rulers of the Gentiles **lord** it o them,	2894
20:25	and their high officials **exercise authority** o	2980
23:15	You **travel** o land and sea to win	4310
24: 9	*be* **handed** o to be persecuted and put	4140
26: 2	of Man *will be* **handed** o to be crucified."	4140
26:15	to give me if I **hand** him o to you?"	4140
26:16	for an opportunity to **hand** him o.	4140
26:36	"Sit here while I **go** o there and pray."	599
27: 2	led him away and **handed** him o to Pilate,	4140
27:18	envy that *they had* **handed** Jesus o to him.	4140
27:26	and **handed** him o to be crucified.	4140
27:36	sitting down, *they* **kept watch** o him there.	5498
27:45	the ninth hour darkness came o all the land.	2093
Mk 1:28	News about him spread quickly o the whole	1650
4:35	"Let us **go** o to the other side."	1451
4:37	and the waves broke o the boat,	1650
5:21	*When* Jesus *had* again **crossed** o by boat to	1385
6: 7	and gave them **authority** o evil spirits.	2026
6:53	*When they had* **crossed** o,	1385
8: 8	of broken pieces that *were* **left** o.	4354
10:33	and *will* **hand** him o to the Gentiles,	4140
10:42	as rulers of the Gentiles **lord** it o them,	2894
10:42	and their high officials **exercise authority** o	2980
11: 7	the colt to Jesus and **threw** their cloaks o it,	2095
13: 9	You *will be* **handed** o to the local councils	4140
14:11	for an opportunity *to* **hand** him o.	4140
15: 1	led him away and **handed** him o to Pilate.	4140
15:10	the chief priests *had* **handed** Jesus o to him.	4140
15:15	and **handed** him o to be crucified.	4140
15:33	At the sixth hour darkness came o	2093
16: 1	*When* the Sabbath *was* o, Mary Magdalene,	1335
Lk 1:33	he will reign o the house of Jacob forever;	2093
2: 8	keeping watch o their flocks at night.	2093
2:43	*After* the Feast *was* o,	5457
4:39	So he bent o her and rebuked the fever,	2062
6:17	and a great number of people from **all** o	4246
6:38	shaken together and **running** o,	5658
8:22	"Let's **go** o to the other side of the lake."	1451
8:39	the man went away and told **all** o town	2848+3910
9:17	of broken pieces that *were* **left** o.	4355
11:44	which men walk o without knowing it."	2062
12:58	and the judge **turn** you o to the officer,	4140
13:11	She was **bent** o and could not straighten up	5174
15: 7	in heaven o one sinner who repents than	2093
15: 7	over one sinner who repents than	2093
15:10	in the presence of the angels of God o	2093
16:26	nor can anyone **cross** o from there to us.'	1385
18:32	*He will be* **handed** o to the Gentiles.	4140
19:27	who did not want me to be king o them—	2093
19:41	and saw the city, he wept o it	2093
20:14	*they* **talked the matter** o.	253+1368+4639
20:20	so that *they might* **hand** him o to the power	4140
22: 4	for an opportunity *to* **hand** Jesus o to	4140
22:25	"The kings of the Gentiles **lord** it o them;	3259
22:25	and those who **exercise authority** o	2027
23: 5	up the people all o Judea by his teaching.	2848
23:44	and darkness came o the whole land until	2093
24:12	**Bending** o, he saw the strips of linen lying	4160
24:20	our rulers **handed** him o to be sentenced	4140
24:29	the day is almost o."	3111
Jn 3:25	and a certain Jew o the matter of	4309
5:24	he has **crossed** o from death to life.	3553
6:12	"Gather the pieces that are **left** o.	4355
6:13	the pieces of the five barley loaves **left** o	4355
12:11	of him many of the Jews were going o	5632
17: 2	For you granted him **authority** o all people	2026
18:30	"we would not *have* **handed** him o to you."	4140
18:35	and your chief priests who **handed** you o	4140
19:11	"You would have no power o me if it were	2848
19:11	one who **handed** me o to you is guilty of	4140

Jn	19:16	Finally Pilate **handed** him o to them to	4140
	20: 5	He **bent** o and looked in at the strips	4160
	20:11	she **bent** o to **look** into the tomb	4160
Ac	1: 3	to them o **a period** of forty days and spoke	1328
	1:25	to **take** o this apostolic ministry,	3284
	2:23	This man was **handed** o to you	1692
	3:13	You **handed** him o to be killed,	4140
	4:22	man who was miraculously healed was o	4498
	6: 3	**turn** this responsibility o to	2770
	7:10	so he made him ruler o Egypt	2093
	7:27	'Who made you ruler and judge o us?'	2093
	7:31	As he **went** o to look more closely,	4665
	7:42	But God turned away and **gave** them o to	4140
	9:42	This became known all o Joppa,	2848
	11:28	that a severe famine would spread o	2093
	12: 4	**handing** him o to be guarded by four	4140
	13:11	Immediately mist and darkness came o	2093
	14:19	and Iconium and **won** the crowd o.	4275
	16: 9	"**Come** o to Macedonia and help us."	1329
	17: 6	"These men have caused trouble all o	
		the world have now come	AIT
	19:13	to invoke the name of the Lord Jesus o	2093
	20:15	The day after that we **crossed** o to Samos,	4125
	20:28	**Keep watch** o yourselves and all the flock	4668
	21: 2	We found a ship **crossing** o to Phoenicia,	1385
	21:11	Coming o to us, he took Paul's belt,	NIG
	21:11	will **hand** him o to the Gentiles.	1650+4140+5931
	21:27	When the seven days were nearly o,	5334
	23:33	the letter to the governor and **handed** Paul o	4225
	24: 5	up riots among the Jews all o the world.	2848
	24:10	a judge o **this nation**;	AIT
	25:11	no one has the right to **hand** me o to them.	5919
	25:16	not the Roman custom to **hand** o any man	5919
	25:21	When Paul made his appeal to be **held** o	5498
	27: 1	and some other prisoners were **handed** o to	4140
	28:17	I was arrested in Jerusalem and **handed** o to	4140
Ro	1: 8	your faith is being reported all o the world.	1877
	1:24	Therefore God **gave** them o in the sinful	4140
	1:26	of this, God **gave** them o to shameful lusts.	4140
	1:28	he **gave** them o to a depraved mind,	4140
	4:25	He was **delivered** o to death for our sins	4140
	5:14	even o those who did not sin by breaking	2093
	6: 9	death no longer **has mastery** o him.	3259
	7: 1	the law **has authority** o a man only as long	3259
	9: 5	who is God o all, forever praised!	2093
	9:32	They **stumbled** o the "stumbling stone."	4684
	11:18	do not **boast** o those branches.	2878
	11:32	God has **bound** all men o to disobedience	5168
	13:12	night is **nearly o**; the day is almost here.	4621
	15:12	one who will arise to **rule** o the nations;	806
	16:19	so I am full of joy o you;	2093
1Co	4: 6	not take pride in one man o **against**	2848
	5: 5	**hand** this man o to Satan,	4140
	7:37	under no compulsion but has control o	4309
	10: 5	their bodies were scattered o the desert.	1877
	15:24	when he **hands** o the kingdom to God	4140
	15:31	I **glory** o you in Christ Jesus our Lord.	2400+3018
2Co	1: 5	For just as the sufferings of Christ **flow** o	4355
	1:24	Not that we **lord** it o your faith,	3259
	3:13	who would put a veil o his face to keep	2093
	4:11	we who are alive are always being **given** o	4140
	12:21	be **grieved** o many who have sinned earlier	4291
Gal	4: 9	to be enslaved by them **all o again**?	540+4099
	4:17	Those people are zealous to win you o,	NIG
Eph	1:22	and appointed him to be head o everything	5642
	4: 6	who is o all and through all and in all.	2093
	4:19	they have **given** themselves o to sensuality	4140
Col	1: 6	**All** o the world this gospel is bearing fruit	4246
	1:15	the firstborn o **all** creation.	AIT
	2:10	the head o **every** power and authority.	AIT
	2:15	**triumphing** o them by the cross.	2581
	3:14	And o all these virtues put on love,	2093
	5:12	who are o you in the Lord	4613
1Th	2: 4	He will oppose and will exalt himself o	2093
2Th	1:20	whom I have **handed** o to Satan to be taught	4140
1Ti	2:12	a woman to teach or to **have authority** o	883
	5: 9	be put on the list of widows unless she is o	NIG
2Ti	3: 6	and **gain control** o weak-willed women,	170
Heb	3: 6	Christ is faithful as a son o God's house.	2093
	5:12	the elementary truths of God's word all o	NIG
	6: 6	**crucifying** the Son of God **all** o **again**	416
	10:21	we have a great priest o the house of God,	2093
	13:17	They keep watch o you	5642
Jas	2:13	Mercy **triumphs** o judgment!	2878
	5:14	of the church to pray o him and anoint him	2093
	5:20	from death and **cover** o a multitude of sins.	2821
1Pe	3: 1	be **won** o without words by the behavior	3045
	4: 8	because love **covers** o a multitude of sins.	2821
	5: 3	not **lording** it o those entrusted to you,	2894
2Pe	2: 3	condemnation has long been hanging o	NIG
Rev	2:26	I will give authority o the nations—	2093
	6: 8	They were given power o a fourth of	2093
	7:15	on the throne will spread his tent o them.	2093
	9:11	as king o them the angel of the Abyss,	2093
	11:10	The inhabitants of the earth will gloat o	2093
	13: 7	And he was given authority o every tribe,	2093
	14:16	on the cloud swung his sickle o the earth,	2093
	15: 2	those who had been victorious o the beast	1666
	15: 2	the beast and his image and o the number	1666
	16: 9	who had control o these plagues,	2093
	17:18	the great city that rules o the kings of	2093
	18: 9	they will weep and mourn o her.	2093
	18:11	of the earth will weep and mourn o her	2093
	18:20	Rejoice o her, O heaven!	2093
	20: 3	and locked and sealed it o him,	2062
	20: 6	The second death has no power o them,	2093
	20: 7	When the thousand years are o,	5464

OVERAWED (1) [AWE]

Ps	49:16	Do not be o when a man grows rich, when	3707

OVERBEARING (1)

Tit	1: 7	not o, not quick-tempered,	881

OVERBOARD (4)

Jnh	1:15	they took Jonah and threw him o,	448+2021+3542
Ac	27:18	began to **throw the cargo** o.	1678
	27:19	they **threw** the ship's tackle o	4849
	27:43	to **jump** o first and get to land.	681

OVERCAME (5) [OVERCOME]

Ex	17:13	So Joshua o the Amalekite army with	2765
Jer	38:22	" 'They misled you and o you—	3523
Hos	12: 4	He struggled with the angel and o him;	3523
Rev	3:21	just as I o and sat down with my Father	3771
	12:11	They o him by the blood of the Lamb and	3771

OVERCAST (1)

Mt	16: 3	for the sky is red and o.'	5145

OVERCHARGE (KJV) See PUT IT TOO SEVERELY

OVERCOME (25) [OVERCAME, OVERCOMES]

Ge	32:28	with God and with men and **have** o."	3523
1Sa	4:19	but was o by her labor pains.	2200
	17: 9	but if I o him and kill him,	3523
Ps	13: 4	"I have o him,"	3523
	39:10	I am o by the blow of your hand.	3983
	116: 3	I was o by trouble and sorrow.	5162
Jer	1:19	against you but will not o you,	3523
	15:20	against you but will not o you,	3523
	23: 9	like a man o by wine,	6296
Da	10:16	"I am o with anguish because of the vision,	2200
Zec	9:15	They will destroy and o with slingstones.	3899
Mt	16:18	and the gates of Hades will not o it.	2996
Mk	9:24	help me o my unbelief!"	NIG
Lk	8:37	because they were o with fear.	5309
	10:19	and scorpions and **to** o all the power of	2093
Jn	16:33	I **have** o the world."	3771
Ro	12:21	Do not **be** o by evil,	3771
	12:21	but o evil with good.	3771
1Ti	5:11	**sensual desires** o their dedication to	2952
2Pe	2:20	and are again entangled in it and o,	2487
1Jn	2:13	because you have o the evil one.	3771
	2:14	and you have o the evil one.	3771
	4: 4	are from God and **have** o them,	3771
	5: 4	This is the victory that **has** o the world,	3771
Rev	17:14	the Lamb will o them because he is Lord	3771

OVERCOMES (10) [OVERCOME]

1Jn	5: 4	for everyone born of God o the world.	3771
	5: 5	Who is it that o the world?	3771
Rev	2: 7	To him who o, I will give the right to eat	3771
	2:11	He who o will not be hurt at all by	3771
	2:17	To him who o, I will give some of	3771
	2:26	To him who o and does my will to the end,	3771
	3: 5	He who o will, like them, be dressed in	3771
	3:12	Him who o I will make a pillar in	3771
	3:21	To him who o, I will give the right to sit	3771
	21: 7	He who o will inherit all this,	3771

OVERDRIVE (KJV) See DRIVEN HARD

OVERFED (1) [FEED]

Eze	16:49	her daughters were arrogant, o and	4312+8430

OVERFLOW (21) [OVERFLOWING, OVERFLOWS]

Job	6:15	as the streams that o	6296
Ps	65:11	and your carts o with abundance.	8319
	65:12	The grasslands of the desert o;	8319
	119:171	May my lips o with praise,	5580
Pr	5:16	Should your springs o in the streets,	7046
Isa	8: 7	It will o all its channels,	6584+6590
	28:17	the lie, and water will o your hiding place.	8851
Jer	9:18	till our eyes o with tears and water streams	3718
	14:17	" 'Let my eyes o with tears night and day	3718
	47: 2	They will o the land and everything in it,	8851
La	1:16	"This is why I weep and my eyes o	3718
Joel	2:24	the vats will o with new wine and oil.	8796
	3:13	for the winepress is full and the vats o—	8796
Zec	1:17	'My towns will again o with prosperity,	7046
Mt	12:34	out of the o of the heart the mouth speaks.	4354
Lk	6:45	out of the o of his heart his mouth speaks.	4354
Ro	5:15	of the one man, Jesus Christ, o to the many!	4355
	15:13	so that you may o with hope by the power	4355
2Co	4:15	thanksgiving to o to the glory of God.	4355
Php	1:26	in Christ Jesus will o on account of me.	4355
1Th	3:12	and o for each other and for everyone else,	4355

OVERFLOWING (8) [OVERFLOW]

1Ch	12:15	the first month when it was o all its banks,	4848
Pr	3:10	then your barns will be filled to o,	8426
Isa	66:11	and delight in her o abundance."	2329

Jer	13:17	my eyes will weep bitterly, o **with** tears,	3718
	47: 2	they will become an o torrent.	8851
2Co	8: 2	of the most severe trial, their o joy	4353
	9:12	but is also o in many expressions of thanks	4355
Col	2: 7	and o with thankfulness.	4355

OVERFLOWS (2) [OVERFLOW]

Ps	23: 5	You anoint my head with oil; my cup o.	8122
2Co	1: 5	so also through Christ our comfort o.	4355

OVERGROWN (3) [GROW]

Isa	32:13	a land o with thorns and briers—	6590
Jer	26:18	the temple hill a **mound** o with thickets.'	AIT
Mic	3:12	the temple hill a mound o with thickets.	NIH

OVERHANG (1) [HANG]

Eze	41:25	and there was a wooden o on the front of	6264

OVERHANGING (3) [HANG]

1Ki	7: 6	in front of that were pillars and an o. **roof.**	6264
Isa	2:21	the rocks and to the o crags from dread of	6186
	57: 5	in the ravines and under the o crags.	6186

OVERHANGS (1) [HANG]

Eze	41:26	The side rooms of the temple also had o.	6264

OVERHEAD (1)

Isa	31: 5	Like birds **hovering** o,	6414

OVERHEARD (2) [HEAR]

Ge	27: 6	I o your father say to your brother Esau,	9048
1Sa	17:31	What David said was o and reported	9048

OVERJOYED (5) [JOY]

Da	6:23	The king was o and gave orders	10293+10678
Mt	2:10	When they saw the star, they were o.	
			3489+5379+5897+5915
Jn	20:20	The disciples were o when they saw	5897
Ac	12:14	so o she ran back without opening it	5915
1Pe	4:13	you may be o when his glory is revealed.	22+5897

OVERLAID (33) [OVERLAY]

Ex	26:32	on four posts of acacia wood o **with** gold	7596
	26:37	and five posts of acacia wood o **with** gold.	7596
	36:34	They o the frames with gold	7596
	36:34	They also o the crossbars **with** gold.	7596
	36:36	of acacia wood for it and o them **with** gold.	7596
	36:38	They o the tops of the posts and their bands	7596
	37: 2	He o it with pure gold, both inside and out,	7596
	37: 4	of acacia wood and o them **with** gold.	7596
	37:11	Then they o it **with** pure gold and made	7596
	37:15	of acacia wood and were o **with** gold.	7596
	37:26	They o the top and all the sides and	7596
	37:28	of acacia wood and o them **with** gold.	7596
	38: 2	and they o the altar **with** bronze.	7596
	38: 6	of acacia wood and o them **with** bronze.	7596
	38:17	and their tops were o **with** silver;	7599
	38:19	and their tops were o **with** silver.	7599
1Ki	6:20	He o the inside with pure gold,	7596
	6:20	and he also o the altar of cedar.	7596
	6:21	which was o with gold.	7596
	6:22	So he o the whole interior **with** gold.	7596
	6:22	He also o **with** gold the altar that belonged	7596
	6:28	He o the cherubim **with** gold.	7596
	6:32	and o the cherubim and palm trees	7596
	6:35	and o them with gold hammered evenly	7596
	10:18	a great throne inlaid with ivory and o	7596
2Ch	3: 4	He o the inside **with** pure gold.	7596
	3: 7	He o the ceiling beams, doorframes,	2902
	3: 8	He o the inside with six hundred talents	2902
	3: 9	He also o the upper parts **with** gold.	2902
	3:10	a pair of sculptured cherubim and o them	7596
	4: 9	and o the doors **with** bronze.	7596
	9:17	a great throne inlaid with ivory and o	7596
Isa	30:22	Then you will defile your idols o	7599

OVERLAY (13) [OVERLAID, OVERLAYING, OVERLAYS]

Ex	25:11	O it with pure gold, both inside and out,	7596
	25:13	of acacia wood and o them **with** gold.	7596
	25:24	O it with pure gold and make	7596
	25:28	o them with gold and carry the table.	7596
	26:29	O the frames **with** gold and make gold rings	7596
	26:29	Also o the crossbars **with** gold.	7596
	27: 2	and o the altar **with** bronze.	7596
	27: 6	of acacia wood for the altar and o them	7596
	30: 3	O the top and all the sides and the horns	7596
	30: 5	Make the poles of acacia wood and o them	7596
	38:28	to o the tops of the posts,	7596
Nu	16:38	Hammer the censers into sheets to o	7599
	16:39	he had them hammered out to o the altar,	7599

OVERLAYING (1) [OVERLAY]

1Ch	29: 4	for the o of the walls of the buildings,	3212

OVERLAYS (1) [OVERLAY]

Isa	40:19	and a goldsmith o it with gold	8392

OVERLIVED (KJV) See OUTLIVED

OVERLOOK (3) [OVERLOOKED, OVERLOOKING, OVERLOOKS]
Dt	9:27	**O** the stubbornness of this people,	440+7155
	24:19	in your field and *you* **o** a sheaf,	8894
Pr	19:11	it is to his glory *to* **o** an offense.	6296

OVERLOOKED (2) [OVERLOOK]
Ac	6: 1	because their widows *were being* **o** in	4145
	17:30	In the past God **o** such ignorance,	5666

OVERLOOKING (3) [OVERLOOK]
Nu	23:28	to the top of Peor, **o** the wasteland.	9207
Jos	8:14	Israel in battle at a certain place **o**	4200+7156
1Sa	13:18	and the third toward the borderland **o**	9207

OVERLOOKS (3) [OVERLOOK]
Nu	21:20	where the top of Pisgah **o** the wasteland.	9207
2Ch	20:24	the men of Judah came to the **place that o**	5205
Pr	12:16	but a prudent man **o** an insult.	4059

OVERMUCH (KJV) See EXCESSIVE

OVERNIGHT (5) [NIGHT]
Lev	19:13	*Do* not **hold back** the wages of a hired man **o**.	1332+4328+6330
Dt	21:23	*you* must not **leave** his body on the tree **o**.	4328
Isa	10:29	and say, "We will **camp o** at Geba."	4869
Jnh	4:10	It sprang up **o** and died overnight.	1201+4326
	4:10	It sprang up overnight and died **o**.	1201+4326

OVERPASS (KJV) See NO LIMIT

OVERPAST (KJV) See PASSED BY

OVERPLUS (KJV) See BALANCE

OVERPOWER (9) [POWER]
Ge	32:25	When the man saw that *he* could not **o** him,	3523
	43:18	He wants to attack us and **o** us and seize us	5877
Jdg	16: 5	of his great strength and how *we can* **o** him	3523
2Ki	16: 5	but they could not **o** him.	4309
Est	9: 1	of the Jews had hoped to **o** them,	8948
Job	14:20	You **o** him once for all, and he is gone;	9548
Isa	7: 1	but they could not **o** it.	4309+6584
Ob	1: 7	your friends will deceive and **o** you;	3523
Rev	11: 7	and **o** and kill them.	3771

OVERPOWERED (8) [POWER]
Jdg	3:10	hands of Othniel, who **o** him.	3338+6451+6584
2Sa	11:23	"The men **o** us and came out against us in	1504
1Ki	20:21	king of Israel advanced and **o** the horses	5782
2Ki	10:32	Hazael **o** the Israelites throughout	5782
Ecc	4:12	Though one *may be* **o**, two can defend	9548
Jer	20: 7	*you* **o** me and prevailed.	2616
Da	6:24	the lions **o** them and crushed all their bones	10715
Ac	19:16	jumped on them and **o** them all.	2894

OVERPOWERING (1) [POWER]
Job	41: 9	the mere sight of him *is* **o**.	3214

OVERPOWERS (1) [POWER]
Lk	11:22	when someone stronger attacks and **o** him,	3771

OVERRAN (1) [RUN]
Jdg	20:43	and easily **o** them in the vicinity of Gibeah	2005

OVERRIGHTEOUS (1) [RIGHTEOUS]
Ecc	7:16	Do not be **o**, neither be overwise—	2221+7404

OVERRULED (2) [OVERRULING]
2Sa	24: 4	**o** Joab and the army commanders;	448+2616
1Ch	21: 4	The king's word, however, **o** Joab;	2616+6584

OVERRULING (1) [OVERRULED]
Est	8: 5	be written the dispatches that Haman son	8740

OVERRUN (4) [RUN]
Isa	34:13	Thorns *will* **o** her citadels,	6590
Hos	9: 6	and thorns will **o** their tents.	928
Am	3:11	"An enemy will **o** the land,	6017
Zec	9: 8	an oppressor **o** my people,	6296

OVERSEER (5) [OVERSEERS, OVERSIGHT]
Pr	6: 7	It has no commander, no **o** or ruler,	8853
1Ti	3: 1	If anyone sets his heart on being an **o**,	2175
	3: 2	Now the **o** must be above reproach,	2176
Tit	1: 7	Since an **o** is entrusted with God's work,	2176
1Pe	2:25	to the Shepherd and **O** of your souls.	2176

OVERSEERS (3) [OVERSEER]
Ac	20:28	of which the Holy Spirit has made you **o**.	2176
Php	1: 1	together with the **o** and deacons:	2176
1Pe	5: 2	that is under your care, **serving as o**—	2174

OVERSHADOW (1) [OVERSHADOWED, OVERSHADOWING]
Lk	1:35	the power of the Most High will **o** you.	2173

OVERSHADOWED (1) [OVERSHADOW]
1Ki	8: 7	the ark and **o** the ark and its carrying poles.	6114

OVERSHADOWING (4) [OVERSHADOW]
Ex	25:20	**o** the cover with them.	6114
	37: 9	**o** the cover with them.	6114
Eze	31: 3	with beautiful branches **o** the forest;	7511
Heb	9: 5	**o** the atonement cover.	2944

OVERSIGHT (1) [OVERSEER]
2Ch	23:18	Then Jehoiada placed the **o** *of* the temple	7213

OVERSPREAD (KJV) See SCATTERED

OVERSTEP (1) [STEP]
Pr	8:29	so the waters *would* not **o** his command,	6296

OVERTAKE (27) [OVERTAKEN, OVERTAKES, OVERTAKING, OVERTOOK]
Ge	19:19	this disaster *will* **o** me, and I'll die.	1815
Ex	15: 9	'I will pursue, *I will* **o** them.	5952
Dt	19: 6	**o** him if the distance is too great,	5952
	28:15	upon you and **o** you:	5952
	28:45	and **o** you until you are destroyed,	5952
1Sa	30: 8	Will I **o** them?"	5952
	30: 8	"You will **certainly o** them and	5952+5952
2Sa	15:14	*to* **o** us and bring ruin upon us and	5952
2Ki	7: 9	punishment will **o** us.	5162
Job	20:22	distress will **o** him;	4200
	27:20	Terrors **o** him like a flood;	5952
Ps	7: 5	then let my enemy pursue and **o** me;	5952
	35: 8	*may* ruin **o** them by surprise—	995
	69:24	*let* your fierce anger **o** them.	5952
Pr	6:15	Therefore disaster *will* **o** him in an instant;	995
	10:24	What the wicked dreads *will* **o** him;	995
Ecc	2:15	"The fate of the fool *will* **o** me also.	7936
Isa	35:10	Gladness and joy *will* **o** them,	5952
	47: 9	Both of these *will* **o** you in a moment,	995
	51:11	Gladness and joy *will* **o** them,	5952
Jer	42:16	then the sword you fear *will* **o** you there,	5952
Hos	10: 9	*Did* not war **o** the evildoers in Gibeah?	5952
Am	9:10	'Disaster *will* not **o** or meet us.'	5602
Mic	2: 6	disgrace *will* not **o** us."	6047
Zec	1: 6	the prophets, **o** your forefathers?	5952
Rev	12:15	to **o** the woman and sweep her away with	3958
	18: 8	in one day her plagues *will* **o** her;	2457

OVERTAKEN (4) [OVERTAKE]
Ps	9: 6	Endless ruin has **o** the enemy,	9462
	40:12	my sins have **o** me, and I cannot see.	5952
La	1: 3	All who pursue her have **o** her in the midst	5952
Am	9:13	"when the reaper *will* **be o** by the plowman	5602

OVERTAKES (6) [OVERTAKE]
Pr	1:26	I will mock when calamity **o** you—	995
	1:27	when calamity **o** you like a storm,	995
	3:25	or of the ruin that **o** the wicked,	995
Ecc	2:14	to realize that the same fate **o** them both.	7936
	9: 3	The same destiny **o** all.	4200
Jn	12:35	before darkness **o** you.	2898

OVERTAKING (1) [OVERTAKE]
1Ch	21:12	with their swords **o** you,	5952

OVERTHREW (9) [OVERTHROW]
Ge	19:25	Thus *he* **o** those cities and the entire plain,	2200
	19:29	that **o** the cities where Lot had lived.	2200
Dt	29:23	which the LORD **o** in fierce anger.	2200
Isa	14:17	*who* **o** its cities and	2238
Jer	20:16	like the towns the LORD **o** without pity.	2200
	50:40	As God **o** Sodom and Gomorrah along	4550
Am	4:11	"*I* **o** some of you as I overthrew Sodom	2200
	4:11	"I overthrew some of you as I **o** Sodom	4550
Ac	13:19	*he* **o** seven nations in Canaan	2747

OVERTHROW (15) [OVERTHREW, OVERTHROWN, OVERTHROWS]
Ge	19:21	I will not **o** the town you speak of.	2200
2Sa	10: 3	to explore the city and spy it out and **o** it?"	2200
2Ki	3:19	You *will* **o** every fortified city	5782
1Ch	19: 3	and spy out the country and **o** it?"	2200
2Ch	25: 8	God *will* **o** you before the enemy,	4173
	25: 8	for God has the power to help or to **o**."	4173
Ezr	6:12	**o** any king or people who lifts a hand	10400
Jer	1:10	to destroy and **o**, to build and to plant."	2238
	31:28	and to **o**, destroy and bring disaster,	2238
	45: 4	I *will* **o** what I have built	2238
Da	11:17	in marriage in order to **o** the kingdom,	8845
	11:24	He will plot the **o** *of* fortresses—	4742

OVERTHROWN (9) [OVERTHROW]
Nu	21:30	"But *we have* **o** them;	3721
Pr	12: 7	Wicked men *are* **o** and are no more,	2200
Isa	1: 7	laid waste as when **o** *by* strangers.	4550
	13:19	be **o** *by* God like Sodom and Gomorrah.	4550
Jer	18:23	Let them be **o** before you;	4173
	49:18	As Sodom and Gomorrah were **o**,	4550
La	2:17	*He has* **o** you without pity,	2238
	4: 6	which *was* **o** in a moment without	2200
Eze	32:12	and all her hordes *will* be **o**.	9012

OVERTHROWS (4) [OVERTHROW]
Job	12:19	and **o** men long established.	6156
	34:25	*he* **o** them in the night and they are crushed.	2200
Pr	13: 6	but wickedness **o** the sinner.	6156
Isa	44:25	*who* **o** the learning of the wise and	294+8740

OVERTOOK (10) [OVERTAKE]
Ge	31:25	hill country of Gilead when Laban **o** him,	5952
Ex	14: 9	the Israelites and **o** them as they camped by	5952
Jdg	18:22	near Micah were called together and **o**	1815
1Sa	31: 3	and when the archers **o** him,	5162
2Ki	25: 5	the king and **o** him in the plains of Jericho.	5952
1Ch	10: 3	and when the archers **o** him,	5162
Ps	18:37	I pursued my enemies and **o** them;	5952
Jer	2: 3	and disaster **o** them.' "	448+995
	39: 5	and **o** Zedekiah in the plains of Jericho.	5952
	52: 8	and **o** him in the plains of Jericho.	5952

OVERTURN (1) [OVERTURNED, OVERTURNS]
Hag	2:22	I *will* **o** royal thrones and shatter	2200

OVERTURNED (6) [OVERTURN]
Jdg	7:13	struck the tent with such force that the tent **o**	2025+2200+4200+5087
Eze	38:20	The mountains *will* be **o**,	2238
Jnh	3: 4	"Forty more days and Nineveh *will* be **o**."	2200
Mt	21:12	*He* **o** the tables of the money changers and	2951
Mk	11:15	*He* **o** the tables of the money changers and	2951
Jn	2:15	of the money changers and **o** their tables.	418

OVERTURNS (1) [OVERTURN]
Job	9: 5	without their knowing it and **o** them	2200

OVERWEENING (3)
Pr	21:24	he behaves with **o pride**.	2295+6301
Isa	16: 6	her **o** pride and conceit,	4394
Jer	48:29	her **o** pride and conceit,	4394

OVERWHELM (7) [OVERWHELMED, OVERWHELMING, OVERWHELMS]
Job	3: 5	*may* blackness **o** its light.	1286
	9:18	but *would* **o** me with misery.	8425
	15:24	*they* **o** him, like a king poised to attack,	9548
	30:15	Terrors **o** me; my dignity is driven away	4059
Pr	1:27	when distress and trouble **o** you.	995+6584
SS	6: 5	Turn your eyes from me; they **o** me.	8104
Hab	2:17	to Lebanon *will* **o** you,	4059

OVERWHELMED (18) [OVERWHELM]
Dt	11: 4	how *he* **o** them *with* the waters of	7429
2Sa	22: 5	the torrents of destruction **o** me.	1286
1Ki	10: 5	she was **o**.	928+2118+4202+6388+8120
2Ch	9: 4	she was **o**.	928+2118+4202+6388+8120
Ps	14: 5	There they are, **o with dread**,	7064+7065
	18: 4	the torrents of destruction **o** me.	1286
	38: 4	My guilt *has* **o** me like a burden	6296+8031
	53: 5	There they were, **o with dread**,	7064+7065
	55: 5	horror *has* **o** me.	4059
	65: 3	*When* we were **o** *by* sins,	1504
	88: 7	*you* have **o** me *with* all your waves.	6700
Eze	3:15	among them for seven days—**o**.	9037
Da	10: 7	but such terror **o** them that they fled	5877+6584
Mt	26:38	"My soul is **o with sorrow** to the point	4337
Mk	7:37	*People were* **o with amazement**.	1742+5669
	9:15	*they* were **o with wonder** and ran	1701
	14:34	"My soul is **o with sorrow** to the point	4337
2Co	2: 7	that he *will* not *be* **o** by excessive sorrow.	2927

OVERWHELMING (6) [OVERWHELM]
Pr	27: 4	Anger is cruel and fury **o**,	8852
Isa	10:22	Destruction has been decreed, **o** and righteous.	8851
	28:15	When an **o** scourge sweeps by,	8851
	28:18	When the **o** scourge sweeps by,	8851
Da	11:22	an **o** army will be swept away before him;	8852
Na	1: 8	but with an **o** flood he will make an end	6296

OVERWHELMS (2) [OVERWHELM]
Pr	10: 6	but violence **o** the mouth of the wicked.	4059
	10:11	but violence **o** the mouth of the wicked.	4059

OVERWICKED (1) [WICKED]
Ecc	7:17	*Do* not *be* **o**, and do not be a fool—	2221+8399

OVERWISE (1) [WISE]

Ecc 7:16 Do not be overrighteous, neither *be* o—2681+3463

OWE (8) [OWED, OWES]

Mt	18:28	'Pay back what *you* o me!'	4053
Lk	16:5	'How much *do you* o my master?'	4053
	16:7	'And how much *do you* o?'	4053
Ro	13:7	Give everyone what *you* o him:	4051
	13:7	If you o taxes, pay taxes;	NIG
	15:27	and indeed *they* o it to them.	1639+4050
	15:27	*they* o it to the Jews to share	4053
Phm	1:19	to mention that *you* o me your very self.	4695

OWED (5) [OWE]

Mt	18:24	*who* o him ten thousand talents was brought	4050
	18:28	one of his fellow servants who o him	4053
	18:34	until he should pay back all he o.	4053
Lk	7:41	"Two men o money to a certain	1639+5971
	7:41	One o him five hundred denarii,	4053

OWES (2) [OWE]

Dt	15:3	must cancel any debt your brother o you.	2118
Phm	1:18	has done you any wrong or o you anything,	4053

OWL (22) [OWLS]

Lev	11:16	the horned o, the screech owl,	1426+3613
	11:16	the screech o, the gull, any kind of hawk,	9379
	11:17	the little o, the cormorant, the great owl,	3927
	11:17	the little owl, the cormorant, the great o,	3568
	11:18	the white o, the desert owl, the osprey,	9492
	11:18	the white owl, the desert o, the osprey,	7684
Dt	14:15	the horned o, the screech owl,	1426+3613
	14:15	the screech o, the gull, any kind of hawk,	9379
	14:16	the little o, the great owl, the white owl,	3927
	14:16	the little owl, the great o, the white owl,	3568
	14:16	the little owl, the great owl, the white o,	9492
	14:17	the desert o, the osprey, the cormorant,	7684
Ps	102:6	I am like a desert o,	7684
	102:6	like an o *among* the ruins.	3927
Isa	34:11	desert o and screech owl will possess it;	7684
	34:11	The desert owl and screech o will possess it	7887
	34:11	the great o and the raven will nest there.	3568
	34:15	The o will nest there and lay eggs,	7889
Jer	50:39	and there the o will dwell.	1426+3613
Mic	1:8	like a jackal and moan like an o.	1426+3613
Zep	2:14	The desert o and the screech owl will roost	7684
	2:14	and the screech o will roost on her columns.	7887

OWLS (5) [OWL]

Job	30:29	brother of jackals, a companion of o.	1426+3613
Isa	13:21	there the o will dwell,	1426+3613
	14:23	into a place for o and into swampland;	7887
	34:13	a haunt for jackals, a home for o.	1426+3613
	43:20	the jackals and the o,	1426+3613

OWN (653) [OWNED, OWNER, OWNER'S, OWNERS, OWNERSHIP, OWNING, OWNS]

Ge	1:27	So God created man in his o image,	2257
	5:3	he had a son in his o likeness,	2257
	5:3	in his o image; and he named him Seth.	2257
	10:5	each with its o language.)	2257
	15:4	but a son coming from your o body will	3870
	15:13	be strangers in a country not their o,	2157+4200
	24:4	but will go to my country and my o relatives	3276
	24:38	go to my father's family and to my o clan,	3276
	24:40	a wife for my son from my o clan and	3276
	29:14	"You are my o flesh and blood."	3276
	30:25	so I can go back to my o homeland.	3276
	30:30	may I do something for my o household?"	3276
	30:43	and *came* to o large flocks,	2118+4200
	37:27	he is our brother, our o flesh and blood."	5646
	40:5	and each dream had a meaning of its o.	2257
	41:11	and each dream had a meaning of its o.	2257
	43:29	his o mother's son, he asked,	2257
	46:4	And Joseph's o hand will close your eyes."	2257
	46:32	and herds and everything they o.'	4200
	47:1	and herds and everything they o,	4200
	47:6	put them in charge of my o livestock."	3276+4200
Ex	1:21	he gave them families of their o.	NIH
	2:11	where his o people were and watched them	2257
	2:11	one of his o people.	2257
	4:18	"Let me go back to my o people in Egypt	3276
	5:7	let them go and gather their o straw.	2157+4200
	5:11	get your o straw wherever you can find it,	4013+4200
	5:16	but the fault is with your o people."	3870
	6:7	I will take you as my o people,	3276+4200
	18:27	and Jethro returned to his o country.	2257
	22:5	from the best of his o field or vineyard.	2084
	32:13	to whom you swore by your o self:	3870
	32:29	you were against your o sons and brothers,	2257
Lev	7:30	With his o hands he is to bring	2257
	14:15	pour it in the palm of his o left hand,	2021+3913[S]
	14:26	oil into the palm of his o left hand,	2021+3913[S]
	16:6	for his o sin offering to make atonement	2257
	16:11	for his o sin offering to make atonement	2257
	16:11	to slaughter the bull for his o sin offering.	2257
	20:9	and his blood will be on his o head.	2257
	20:11	their blood will be on their o heads.	4392
	20:12	their blood will be on their o heads.	4392
	20:13	their blood will be on their o heads.	4392

Lev	20:16	their blood will be on their o heads.	4392
	20:26	from the nations to be my o.	3276+4200
	20:27	their blood will be on their o heads.' "	4392
	21:14	but only a virgin from his o people,	2257
	22:24	You must not do this in your o land,	4013
	25:10	his family property and each to his o clan.	2257
	25:13	to return to his o property.	2257
	25:27	he can then go back to his o property.	2257
	25:41	and he will go back to his o clan and to	2257
Nu	1:52	in his o camp under his own standard.	2084
	1:52	in his own camp under his o standard.	2257
	2:17	each in his o place under his standard.	2257
	5:10	Each man's sacred gifts are his o,	2257+4200
	6:7	Even if his o father or mother or brother	2257
	8:16	I have taken them as my o in place of	3276
	10:9	When you go into battle in your o land	4013
	10:30	to my o land and my own people."	3276
	10:30	to my own land and my o people."	3276
	11:15	and do not let me face my o ruin."	3276
	13:33	like grasshoppers in our o eyes,	5646
	15:39	after the lusts of your o hearts and eyes.	4013
	17:9	and each man took his o staff.	2084
	22:13	"Go back to your o country,	4013
	22:30	"Am I not your o donkey,	3870
	24:13	I could not do anything of my o accord,	3276
	24:25	and Balak went his o way.	2257
	27:3	but he died for his o sin and left no sons.	2257
	35:28	may he return to his o property.	2257
	35:32	and live on his o land before the death of	2021[S]
Dt	2:5	the hill country of Seir as his o.	3772
	3:21	"You have seen with your o eyes all that	3870
	3:27	Look at the land with your o eyes,	3870
	4:3	with your o eyes what the LORD did	4013
	7:19	You saw with your o eyes the great trials,	3870
	9:26	your o inheritance that you redeemed	3870
	10:13	giving you today for your o good?	3870+4200
	10:21	wonders you saw with your o eyes.	3870
	11:7	But it was your o eyes	4013
	12:12	or inheritance of their o.	2257
	12:17	You must not eat in your o towns the tithe	3870
	12:21	and in your o towns you may eat as much	3870
	13:6	If your very o brother,	278+562+1201+3870
	14:27	or inheritance of their o.	NIH
	14:29	or inheritance of their o) and the aliens,	NIH
	15:22	You are to eat it in your o towns.	3870
	17:15	He must be from among your o brothers.	3870
	18:15	like me from among your o brothers.	3870
	23:23	the LORD your God with your o mouth.	3870
	24:16	each is to die for his o sin.	2257
	28:54	on his o brother or the wife he loves	2257
	28:56	the husband she loves and her o son	2023
	29:3	With your o eyes you saw those great trials,	3870
	29:19	persist in going my o way."	4213+9244
	32:49	the Israelites as their o possession.	NIH
	33:7	With his o hands he defends his cause.	2257
	33:9	or acknowledge his o children,	2257
Jos	1:11	the land the LORD your God is giving you for your o.' "	3769
	1:15	you may go back and occupy your o land,	3772
	2:19	his blood will be on his o head;	2257
	6:18	bring about *your* o destruction	AIT
	7:9	then will you do for your o great name?"	3870
	7:11	with their o possessions.	2157
	20:6	Then he may go back to his o home in	2257
	21:3	and pasturelands out of their o inheritance:	4392
	22:9	in Canaan to return to Gilead, their o land,	4392
	22:23	If we have built our o altar to turn away	5646
	24:7	You saw with your o eyes what I did to	4013
	24:12	not do it with your o sword and bow.	3870
	24:28	each to his o inheritance.	2257
Jdg	2:6	each to his o inheritance.	2257
	3:6	and gave their o daughters to their sons,	2157
	7:2	against me that her o strength has saved her,	3276
	7:7	each to his o place."	2257
	8:19	the sons of my o mother.	3276
	8:30	He had seventy sons of his o,	2257+3655+3751
	11:19	through your country to our o place.'	3276
	18:1	the Danites was seeking a place of their o	2257
	21:24	each to his o inheritance.	2257
Ru	4:6	because I might endanger my o estate.	3276
1Sa	5:11	let it go back to its o place,	2257
	6:9	If it goes up to its o territory,	2257
	8:16	and donkeys he will take for his o use.	2257
	10:25	each to his o home.	2257
	12:22	LORD was pleased to make you his o.	2257+4200
	13:14	after his o heart and appointed him leader	2257
	14:46	and they withdrew to their o land.	4392
	15:12	a monument in his o honor and has turned	2257
	15:17	you were once small in your o eyes,	3870
	17:38	Then Saul dressed David in his o tunic.	2257
	17:54	he put the Philistine's weapons in his o tent.	2257
	20:30	of Jesse to your o shame and to the shame	3870
	24:10	This day you have seen with your o eyes	3870
	25:8	Ask your o servants and they will tell you.	3870
	25:26	from avenging yourself with your o hands,	3870
	25:33	and from avenging myself with my o hands.	3276
	25:39	Nabal's wrongdoing down on his o head."	2257
	28:3	and buried him in his o town of Ramah.	2257
	29:4	by taking the heads of our o men?	2156[S]
	31:4	so Saul took his o sword and fell on it.	2021[S]
2Sa	1:16	"Your blood be on your o head.	3870
	1:16	Your o mouth testified against you	3870
	3:6	strengthening his o position in the house	2616
	4:11	in his o house and on his own bed—	2257
	4:11	in his own house and on his o bed—	2257
	5:1	"We are your o flesh and blood.	3870
	6:22	and I will be humiliated in my o eyes.	3276

2Sa	7:10	so that they can have a home of their o	2257
	7:12	who will come from your o body,	3870
	7:22	as we have heard with our o ears.	5646
	7:24	as your very o forever,	3870+4200
	12:4	of his o sheep or cattle to prepare a meal for	2257
	12:9	the sword and took his wife to be your o.	3870
	12:10	wife of Uriah the Hittite to be your o.'	3870+4200
	12:11	'Out of your o household I am going	3870
	12:20	Then he went to his o house,	2257
	14:24	the king said, "He must go to his o house;	2257
	14:24	to his o house and did not see the face of	2257
	16:11	"My son, who is of my o flesh,	3276
	19:12	You are my brothers, my o flesh and blood.	3276
	19:13	'Are you not my o flesh and blood?	3276
	19:37	that I may die in my o town near the tomb	3276
	23:21	and killed him with his o spear.	2257
1Ki	1:12	how you can save your o life and the life	3871
	1:33	set Solomon my son on my o mule	3276+4200
	2:34	he was buried on his o land in the desert.	2257
	2:37	your blood will be on your o head."	3870
	4:25	each man under his o vine and fig tree.	2257
	8:15	his o hand has fulfilled what he promised	2257
	8:15	with his o mouth to my father David.	2257
	8:19	who is your o flesh and blood—	3870
	8:32	down on his o head what he has done.	2257
	8:38	of his o heart, and spreading out his hands	2257
	8:43	as do your o people Israel,	3870
	8:46	who takes them captive to his o land,	367+2021[S]
	8:53	of the world to be your o inheritance,	3870+4200
	9:15	his o palace, the supporting terraces,	2257
	10:6	in my o country about your achievements	3276
	10:7	until I came and saw with my o eyes.	3276
	10:13	with her retinue to her o country.	2023
	11:19	that he gave him a sister of his o wife,	2257
	11:20	with Pharaoh's o children.	AIT
	11:21	that I may return to my o country."	3276
	11:22	to go back to your o country?"	3870
	12:16	Look after your o house, O David!"	3870
	12:33	a month of his o choosing,	2257+4213+4946
	13:29	to his o city to mourn for him and bury him.	2021+2021+2418+5566[S]
	13:30	Then he laid the body in his o tomb,	2257
	15:18	LORD's temple and of his o palace.	2021+4889[S]
	20:34	"You may set up your o market areas	3870+4200
2Ki	2:12	of his o clothes and tore them apart.	2257
	3:27	they withdrew and returned to their o land.	2021[S]
	4:13	"I have a home among my o people."	3276
	6:22	with your o sword or bow?	3870
	7:2	"You will see it with your o eyes,"	3870
	7:19	"You will see it with your o eyes,	3870
	8:20	against Judah and set up its o king.	2157
	9:21	each in his o chariot, to meet Jehu.	2257
	13:5	So the Israelites lived in their o homes.	2157
	14:6	each is to die for his o sins."	2257
	14:10	for trouble and cause your o downfall and	911
	15:19	to gain his support and strengthen his o hold	2257
	17:29	each national group made its o gods in	2257
	17:32	also appointed all sorts of their o people	4392
	17:33	also served their o gods in accordance with	2157
	18:27	who, like you, will have to eat their o filth	2157
	18:27	and drink their o urine?"	2157
	18:31	from his o vine and fig tree and drink water	2257
	18:31	and drink water from his o cistern,	2257
	18:32	and take you to a land like your o,	4013
	19:7	he will return to his o country,	2257
	20:18	your o flesh and blood,	3655+3870+4946
	21:6	He sacrificed his o son in the fire,	2257
	23:30	to Jerusalem and buried him in his o tomb.	2257
	24:7	not march out from his o country again.	2257
1Ch	9:2	Now the first to resettle on their o property	4392
	9:2	in their o towns were some Israelites,	2157
	10:4	so Saul took his o sword and fell on it.	2021[S]
	11:1	"We are your o flesh and blood.	3870
	11:23	and killed him with his o spear.	2257
	12:30	brave warriors, famous in their o clans—	4392
	16:43	all the people left, each for his o home,	2257
	17:9	that *they* can have a home of their o	AIT
	17:11	one of your o sons,	3870
	17:20	as we have heard with our o ears.	5646
	17:22	You made your people Israel your very o forever,	3870+4200
2Ch	6:9	who is your o flesh and blood—	3870
	6:23	down on his o head what he has done.	2257
	6:33	as do your o people Israel,	3870
	7:11	of the LORD and in his o palace,	2257
	8:1	the temple of the LORD and his o palace,	2257
	8:18	ships commanded by his o officers,	2257
	9:5	in my o country about your achievements	3276
	9:6	until I came and saw with my o eyes.	3276
	9:12	with her retinue to her o country.	2023
	10:16	Look after your o house, O David!"	3870
	11:15	And he appointed his o priests for	2257+4200
	16:2	of your o as the peoples of other lands do?	4013
	16:2	LORD's temple and of his o palace	2021+4889[S]
	21:8	against Judah and set up its o king.	2157
	21:13	You have also murdered your o brothers,	3870
	25:4	each is to die for his o sins."	2257
	25:14	He set them up as his o gods,	2257+4200
	25:15	not save their o people from your hand?"	4392
	25:19	for trouble and cause your o downfall and	911
	29:8	as you can see with your o eyes.	4013
	31:1	to their o towns and to their own property.	2157
	31:1	to their own towns and to their o property.	2257
	31:3	The king contributed from his o possessions	2257
	32:21	So he withdrew to his o land in disgrace.	2257
	35:7	all from the king's o possessions.	AIT
Ezr	2:1	each to his o town,	2257

Ezr	2:70	the temple servants settled in **their** o towns,	2157
Ne	3:28	each in front of **his** o house.	2257
	4: 4	Turn their insults back on **their** o heads.	4392
	4:15	each to **his** o work.	2257
	5: 7	from **your** o countrymen!"	2257
	7: 3	and some near **their** o houses."	2257
	7: 6	each to **his** o town,	2257
	7:73	settled in **their** o towns.	2157
	8:16	on **their** o roofs,	2257
	11: 1	to stay in **their** o towns.	2021S
	11: 3	each on **his** o property in the various towns,	2257
	13:10	the service had gone back to **their** o fields.	2084
	13:19	I stationed some of **my** o men at the gates so	3276
	13:30	and assigned them duties, each to **his** o task.	2257
Est	1: 8	was allowed to **drink** in his o way,	9276
	1:22	to each province in **its** o script and	2023
	1:22	and to each people in **its** o language,	2257
	1:22	be ruler over **his** o household.	2257
	2: 7	as **his** o daughter when her father	2257+4200
	3:12	and sealed with **his** o ring.	2021+4889S
	8: 9	to the Jews in **their** o script and language.	4392
	9:25	the Jews should come back onto **his** o head,	2257
Job	2: 4	"A man will give all he has for **his** o life.	2257
	9:21	I despise **my** o life.	3276
	14:22	of **his** o body and mourns only for himself."	2257
	15: 6	**Your** o mouth condemns you, not mine;	3870
	15: 6	**your** o lips testify against you.	3870
	18: 7	**his** o schemes throw him down.	2257
	19:16	though I beg him with **my** o mouth.	3276
	19:17	I am loathsome to **my** o brothers.	3276
	19:27	I myself will see him with **my** o eyes—	3276
	20: 7	he will perish forever, like **his** o dung;	2257
	20:10	**his** o hands must give back his wealth.	2257
	21:16	But their prosperity is not in **their** o hands,	4392
	21:20	Let **his** o eyes see his destruction;	2257
	29:18	"I thought, 'I will die in **my** o house,	3276
	32: 1	because he was righteous in **his** o eyes.	2257
	40:14	to you that **your** o right hand can save you.	3870
Ps	7:16	his violence comes down on **his** o head.	2257
	12: 4	we o our lips—who is our master?"	907
	35:21	With **our** o eyes we have seen it."	5646
	36: 2	in **his** o eyes he flatters himself too much	2257
	37:15	But their swords will pierce **their** o hearts,	4392
	40:15	be appalled at **their** o shame.	4392
	50:20	and slander **your** o mother's son.	3870
	64: 8	He will turn **their** o tongues against them	4392
	69: 8	an alien to **my** o mother's sons;	3276
	81:12	to follow **their** o devices.	2157
	132:11	"One of **your** o descendants I will place	2157
	135: 4	the LORD has chosen Jacob to be **his** o	2257+4200
	141:10	Let the wicked fall into **their** o nets,	2257
Pr	1:18	These men lie in wait for **their** o blood;	4392
	3: 5	and lean not on **your** o understanding;	3870
	3: 7	Do not be wise in **your** o eyes;	3870
	5:15	Drink water from **your** o cistern,	3870
	5:15	running water from **your** o well.	3870
	5:23	led astray by **his** o great folly.	2257
	11: 5	down by **their** o wickedness.	2257
	14: 1	but with **her** o hands the foolish one tears	2023
	14:10	Each heart knows **its** o bitterness,	2257+5883
	16: 4	LORD works out everything for **his** o ends	2084
	18: 2	but delights in airing **his** o opinions.	2257
	19: 3	A **man's** o folly ruins his life,	AIT
	19: 8	He who gets wisdom loves **his** o soul;	2257
	20:24	How then can anyone understand **his** o way?	2257
	25:27	nor is it honorable to seek **one's** o honor.	4392
	26: 5	or he will be wise in **his** o eyes.	2257
	26:12	Do you see a man wise in **his** o eyes?	2257
	26:16	The sluggard is wiser in **his** o eyes than	2257
	26:17	who meddles in a quarrel not **his** o.	2257+4200
	27: 2	and not **your** o mouth;	3870
	27: 2	someone else, and not **your** o lips.	3870
	28:10	along an evil path will fall into **his** o trap,	2257
	28:11	A rich man may be wise in **his** o eyes,	2257
	29: 6	An evil man is snared by **his** o,	NIH
	29:24	accomplice of a thief is **his** o enemy;	2257+5883
	30:12	in **their** o eyes and yet are not cleansed	2257
Ecc	8: 9	man lords it over others to **his** o hurt.	2257+4200
	10:12	but a fool is consumed by **his** o lips.	5647
SS	1: 6	**my** o vineyard I have neglected.	3276+4200+8611
	8:12	But **my** o vineyard is mine to give;	3276
Isa	4: 1	"We will eat **our** o food	5646
	4: 1	and provide **our** o clothes,	5646
	5:17	Then sheep will graze as in **their** o pasture;	4392
	5:21	in **their** o eyes and clever in their own sight.	2157
	5:21	in their own eyes and clever in **their** o sight.	2157
	9:20	on the flesh of **his** o offspring:	2257
	13:14	each will return to **his** o people,	2257
	14: 1	and will settle them in **their** o land.	4392
	14: 2	and bring them to **their** o place.	4392
	14: 2	each in **his** o tomb.	2257
	30:20	with **your** o eyes you will see them.	3870
	36:12	who, like you, will have to eat **their** o filth	2157
	36:12	and drink **their** o urine?"	2157
	36:16	from **his** o vine and fig tree and drink water	2257
	36:16	and drink water from **his** o cistern,	2257
	36:17	and take you to a land like **your** o—	4013
	37: 7	he will return to **his** o country,	2257
	39: 7	**your** o flesh and blood	3655+3870+4946
	43:25	for **my** o sake,	3276
	44: 9	they are ignorant, to *their* o shame.	AIT
	45:12	**My** o hands stretched out the heavens;	3276
	48: 9	For **my** o name's sake I delay my wrath;	3276
	48: 9	For **my** o sake, for my own sake, I do this.	3276
	48:11	For my own sake, for **my** o sake, I do this.	3276
	48:13	**My** o hand laid the foundations of the earth,	3276

Isa	49:26	I will make your oppressors eat **their** o flesh	4392
	49:26	they will be drunk on **their** o blood,	4392
	52: 8	they will see it with **their** o eyes.	NIH
	53: 6	each of us has turned to **his** o way;	2257
	56:11	they all turn to **their** o way,	4392
	56:11	each seeks **his** o gain.	2257
	58: 7	to turn away from **your** o flesh and blood?	3870
	58:13	and if you honor it by not going **your** o way	3870
	59:16	so **his** o arm worked salvation for him,	2257
	59:16	and **his** o righteousness sustained him.	2257
	63: 5	so **my** o arm worked salvation for me,	3276
	63: 5	and **my** o wrath sustained me.	3276
	65: 2	pursuing **their** o imaginations—	2157
	66: 3	They have chosen **their** o ways,	2157
Jer	2:13	and have dug **their** o cisterns,	2157+4200
	3:15	I will give you shepherds after **my** o heart,	3276
	4:18	"**Your** o conduct and actions have brought this upon you.	3871
	5:19	and served foreign gods in **your** o land,	4013
	5:19	in a land not **your** o.'	4013+4200
	5:31	the priests rule by **their** o authority,	2157
	6: 3	each tending **his** o portion."	2257
	7: 6	not follow other gods to **your** o harm,	4013+4200
	7:19	harming themselves, to **their** o shame?	2157+7156
	8: 6	Each pursues **his** o course like	4392
	10:23	O LORD, that a man's life is not **his** o;	2257
	12: 9	Your brothers, **your** o family—	3870
	12:15	to **his** o inheritance and his own country.	2257
	12:15	to his own inheritance and **his** o country.	2257
	14:14	and the delusions of **their** o minds.	4392
	16:20	Do men make **their** o gods?	2257+4200
	17: 4	Through **your** o fault you will lose	3870
	18:12	We will continue with **our** o plans;	5646
	20: 4	with **your** o eyes you will see them fall by	3870
	23: 8	Then they will live in **their** o land."	4392
	23:16	They speak visions from **their** o minds,	4392
	23:26	the delusions of **their** o minds?	4392
	23:31	the prophets who wag **their** o tongues and	4392
	23:36	*every man's* o word becomes his oracle	AIT
	26:11	You have heard it with **your** o ears!"	4013
	27:11	that nation remain in **its** o land to till it and	2257
	29:25	You sent letters in **your** o name to all	3870
	30:21	Their leader will be one of **their** o;	5647
	31:17	"Your children will return to **their** o land.	4392
	31:30	Instead, everyone will die for **his** o sin;	2257
	31:30	**his** o teeth will be set on edge.	2257
	32: 4	to face and see him with **his** o eyes.	2257
	32:39	for **their** o good and the good	2157+4200
	34: 3	the king of Babylon with **your** o eyes,	3870
	37: 7	will go back to **its** o land, to Egypt.	2257
	39:14	So he remained among **his** o people.	2021S
	46:16	to **our** o people and our native lands,	5646
	50: 6	and hill and forgot **their** o resting place.	4392
	50:16	to **his** o people,	2257
	50:16	let everyone flee to **his** o land.	2257
	50:19	to **his** o pasture and he will graze on Carmel	2084
	52: 9	let us leave her and each go to **his** o land,	2257
La	4:10	With **their** o hands compassionate women	NIH
	4:10	With their own hands compassionate women have cooked **their** o children,	2177
Eze	7:27	and by **their** o standards I will judge them.	2157
	8:12	each at the shrine of **his** o idol?"	2257
	9:10	on **their** o heads what they have done."	4392
	11:21	down on **their** o heads what they have done,	4392
	13: 2	of **their** o imagination?	4392
	13: 3	foolish prophets who follow **their** o spirit	4392
	13:17	prophesy out of **their** o imagination.	2177
	13:18	of my people but preserve **your** o?	4032
	14:16	not save **their** o sons or daughters.	NIH
	14:18	not save **their** o sons or daughters.	NIH
	16:32	You prefer strangers to **your** o husband!	2023
	18:13	to death and his blood will be on **his** o head.	2257
	18:18	But his father will die for **his** o sin,	2257
	22:11	violates his sister, **his** o father's daughter.	2257
	22:31	down on **their** o heads all they have done,	4392
	28:25	Then they will live in **their** o land,	4392
	33: 4	his blood will be on **his** o head.	2257
	33: 5	his blood will be on **his** o head.	2257
	33:20	of you according to **his** o ways."	2257
	34:13	and I will bring them into **their** o land.	4392
	36: 5	in their hearts they made my land **their** o possession	2157+4200
	36:17	people of Israel were living in **their** o land,	4392
	36:24	and bring you back into **your** o land.	4013
	37:14	and I will settle you in **your** o land.	4013
	37:21	and bring them back into **their** o land.	4392
	39:28	I will gather them to **their** o land,	4392
	46:18	inheritance out of **his** o property,	2257
Da	3:28	or worship any god except **their** o God.	10203
	6:17	and the king sealed it with **his** o signet ring	10192
	8:24	but not by **his** o power.	2257
	11: 5	and will rule **his** o kingdom	2257
	11: 9	of the South but will retreat to **his** o country.	2257
	11:14	among **your** o people will rebel	3870
	11:19	of **his** o country but will stumble and fall,	2257
	11:28	of the North will return to **his** o country	2257
	11:28	against it and then return to **his** o country.	2257
Hos	8: 4	for themselves, to *their* o **destruction.**	AIT
	10:13	you have depended on **your** o strength	3870
	14: 3	to what **our** o hands have made,	5646
Joel	3: 4	on **your** o heads what you have done.	4013
	3: 7	on **your** o heads what you have done.	4013
Am	5: 2	never to rise again, deserted in **her** o land,	2023
	6:13	not take Karnaim by **our** o strength?"	5646
	9:15	I will plant Israel in **their** o land,	4392
Ob	1:15	your deeds will return upon **your** o head.	3870
Jnh	1: 5	and each cried out to **his** o god.	2257

Mic	4: 4	under **his** o vine and under his own fig tree,	AIT
	4: 4	under his own vine and under **his** o fig tree,	AIT
	7: 6	the members of **his** o household.	AIT
Hab	1: 6	to seize dwelling places not **their** o.	2257+4200
	1: 7	to themselves and promote **their** o honor.	2257
	1:11	guilty men, whose o strength is their god."	2257
	2:10	shaming **your** o house	3870
	2:18	For he who makes it trusts in **his** o creation;	2257
	3:14	With **his** o spear you pierced his head	2257
Zep	2:11	every one in **its** o land.	2257
Hag	1: 9	while each of you is busy with **his** o house.	2257
Zec	11: 5	**Their** o shepherds do not spare them.	2157
	13: 3	**his** o parents will stab him.	2084
Mal	1: 5	You will see it with **your** o eyes and say,	4013
Mt	6:34	Each day has enough trouble *of* its o.	899
	7: 3	to the plank in **your** o eye?	5050
	7: 4	the time there is a plank in **your** o eye?	5148
	7: 5	first take the plank out of **your** o eye,	5148
	8:22	and let the dead bury **their** o dead."	1571
	9: 1	crossed over and came to **his** o town.	2625
	10:36	members of **his** o household.'	899
	13:57	in his o house is a prophet without honor."	NIG
	17:25	from **their** o sons or from others?"	899
	20:15	to do what I want with **my** o money?	1847
	27:31	they took off the robe and put **his** o clothes	899
	27:60	in his o new tomb that he had cut out of	899
Mk	4:34	But when he was alone *with* **his** o disciples,	2625
	6: 4	in **his** o house is a prophet without honor."	899
	7: 9	in order to observe **your** o traditions!	5148
	15:20	purple robe and put **his** o clothes on him.	899
Lk	2: 3	And everyone went to **his** o town to register.	1571
	2:35	And a sword will pierce **your** o soul too."	899
	2:39	they returned to Galilee to **their** o town	1571
	6:41	to the plank in **your** o eye?	2625
	6:42	to see the plank in **your** o eye?	NIG
	6:44	Each tree is recognized by **its** o fruit.	2625
	8: 3	to support them out of **their** o means.	899
	9:60	"Let the dead bury **their** o dead,	1571
	10:34	Then he put the man on **his** o donkey,	2625
	11:21	fully armed, guards his o house,	1571
	14:26	yes, even **his** o life—	1571
	16: 8	with **their** o kind than are the people of	1571
	16:12	who will give you property of **your** o?	5629
	18: 9	of **their** o righteousness and looked down	1571
	19:22	'I will judge you by **your** o words,	5148
	22:71	We have heard it from **his** o lips."	899
Jn	1:11	He came to that which was **his** o,	2625
	1:11	but **his** o did not receive him.	2625
	4:44	a prophet has no honor in **his** o country.)	2625
	5:18	but he was even calling God **his** o Father,	2625
	5:43	but if someone else comes in **his** o name,	2625
	7: 5	even his o brothers did not believe in him.	899
	7:17	Jesus answered, "My teaching is not **my** o.	1847
	7:17	from God or whether I speak on **my** o.	1831
	7:18	on **his** o does so to gain honor for himself,	1571
	7:28	I am not here on **my** o,	1831
	7:50	and who was one of **their** o number,	899
	7:53	Then each went to **his** o home.	899
	8:13	"Here you are, appearing as **your** o witness;	4932
	8:14	"Even if I testify on **my** o behalf,	1831
	8:17	In **your** o Law it is written that	5629
	8:28	to be] and that I do nothing on **my** o	1831
	8:41	the things **your** o father does."	5148
	8:42	I have not come on **my** o; but he sent me.	1831
	10: 3	He calls **his** o sheep by name	2625
	10: 4	When he has brought out all **his** o,	2625
	10:18	but I lay it down of **my** o accord.	1831
	10:36	the Father set apart as his very o and sent	NIG
	11:51	He did not say this on **his** o,	1571
	12:49	For I did not speak of **my** o accord,	1831
	13: 1	Having loved **his** o who were in the world,	2625
	14:10	The words I say to you are not just **my** o.	1831
	14:24	These words you hear are not **my** o;	1847
	15:19	it would love you as **its** o.	2625
	16:13	He will not speak on **his** o;	1571
	16:32	each to **his** o home.	2625+3836
	18:31	and judge him by **your** o law."	5148
	18:34	"Is that **your** o idea," Jesus asked,	4932
	19:17	Carrying **his** o cross,	1571
Ac	1: 7	the Father has set by **his** o authority.	2625
	2: 6	in **his** o language.	2625
	2: 8	of us hears them *in* **his** o native language?	2625
	2:11	the wonders of God *in* **our** o tongues!"	2466
	3:12	Why do you stare at us as if by **our** o power	2625
	3:22	like me from among **your** o people;	5148
	4:23	Peter and John went back to **their** o people	2625
	4:32	that any of his possessions was **his** o,	2625
	5:31	to **his** o right hand as Prince and Savior	899
	7: 6	be strangers in a country not **their** o,	259
	7:21	and brought him up as **her** o son.	1571
	7:25	that his o people would realize	81
	7:37	a prophet like me from your o people.'	81
	13:22	of Jesse a man after **my** o heart;	1609
	13:36	*in* **his** o generation, he fell asleep;	2625
	14:16	In the past, he let all nations go **their** o way.	899
	15:22	of **their** o men and send them to Antioch	899
	17:28	As some of **your** o poets have said,	2848+5148
	18: 6	"Your blood be on **your** o heads!	5148
	18:15	words and names and **your** o law—	2848+5148
	20:28	which he bought with **his** o blood.	2625
	20:30	Even from **your** o number men will arise	899
	20:34	of mine have supplied **my** o needs and	1609
	21:11	tied **his** o hands and feet with it and said,	1571
	25:19	of dispute with him about **their** o religion	2625
	26: 4	the beginning of my life in **my** o country,	1609
	26:17	from **your** o people and from the Gentiles.	3836
	26:23	would proclaim light *to* **his** o people and to	3836

Ac	27:10	and to **our** o lives also."	1609
	27:19	ship's tackle overboard with *their* o hands.	901
	28:19	to bring against my o people.	3836
	28:30	Paul stayed there in **his** o rented house	2625
Ro	5: 8	God demonstrates **his** o love for us in this:	1571
	8: 3	God did by sending **his** o Son in the likeness	1571
	8:20	not **by** its o choice,	1776
	8:32	He who did not spare **his** o Son,	2625
	9: 3	my brothers, those *of* **my** o race,	1609
	10: 3	from God and sought to establish **their** o,	2625
	11:14	that I may somehow arouse **my** o people	1609
	11:24	be grafted into *their* o olive tree!	2625
	14: 4	*To* **his** o master he stands or falls.	2625
	14: 5	be fully convinced in **his** o mind.	2625
	16:18	our Lord Christ, but **their** o appetites.	1571
1Co	3: 8	be rewarded according to **his** o labor.	2625
	4:12	We work hard *with* **our** o hands.	2625
	6:18	who sins sexually sins against **his** o body.	2625
	6:19	You are not **your** o;	4932
	7: 2	each man should have **his** o wife,	1571
	7: 2	and each woman **her** o husband.	2625
	7: 7	But each man has **his** o gift from God;	2625
	7:35	I am saying this for **your** o good,	899
	7:37	in **his** o mind, who is under no compulsion	899
	7:37	over **his** o will, and who has made	2625
	9: 7	Who serves as a soldier *at* **his** o expense?	2625
	10:24	Nobody should seek **his** o good,	1571
	10:33	not seeking **my** o good but the good	1831
	14:35	they should ask **their** o husbands at home;	2625
	15:23	But each in **his** o turn:	2625
	15:38	to each kind of seed he gives **its** o body.	2625
	16:21	I, Paul, write this greeting *in* **my** o hand.	1847
2Co	7:13	In addition to **our** o encouragement,	1609
	8: 3	**Entirely** on **their** o,	882
	8:17	and on **his** o initiative.	882
	11:26	in danger from my o countrymen,	NIG
Gal	1:14	in Judaism beyond many Jews **of** my o age	5312
	6: 4	Each one should test **his** o actions.	1571
	6: 5	for each one should carry **his** o load.	2625
	6:11	as I write to you *with* **my** o hand!	1847
Eph	4:28	doing something useful *with* **his** o hands,	2625
	5:28	love **their** wives as their o bodies.	1571
	5:29	After all, no one ever hated **his** o body,	1571
Php	2: 4	not only to **your** o interests,	4932
	2:21	For everyone looks out for **his** o interests,	1571
	3: 9	a righteousness of **my** o that comes from	1847
Col	4:18	I, Paul, write this greeting *in* **my** o hand.	1847
1Th	2:11	of you as a father deals with **his** o children,	1571
	2:14	You suffered from **your** o countrymen	2625
	4: 4	of you should learn to control **his** o body in	1571
	4:11	to mind **your** o business and to work	2625+3836
	4:15	According to the Lord's o word,	NIG
2Th	3:17	I, Paul, write this greeting *in* **my** o hand,	1847
1Ti	3: 4	He must manage **his** o family well and see	2625
	3: 5	not know how to manage **his** o family,	2625
	5: 4	into practice by caring for **their** o family	2625
	6:15	which God will bring about *in* **his** o time—	2625
2Ti	1: 9	but because of **his** o purpose and grace,	2625
	4: 3	Instead, to suit **their** o desires,	2625
Tit	1:12	Even one of **their** o prophets has said,	2625
	2:14	for himself a people that are **his** very o,	4342
Phm	1:19	I, Paul, am writing this *with* **my** o hand.	1847
Heb	4:10	also rests from **his** o work,	899
	5: 3	to offer sacrifices for **his** o sins,	899
	7:27	first for **his** o sins,	2625
	9:12	Most Holy Place once for all by **his** o blood,	2625
	9:25	every year with blood that is **not** his o.	259
	11:14	looking for a **country** of their o.	4258
	13:12	the people holy through **his** o blood.	2625
Jas	1:14	by **his** o evil desire, he is dragged away	2625
1Pe	3: 5	They were submissive to **their** o husbands,	2625
2Pe	1: 3	of him who called us *by* **his** o glory	2625
	1:20	about by the prophet's o interpretation.	2625
	3: 3	scoffing and following **their** o evil desires.	2625
	3:16	to **their** o destruction.	2625
1Jn	3:12	Because **his** o actions were evil	899
Jude	1: 6	of authority but abandoned **their** o home—	2625
	1: 8	these dreamers pollute their o bodies,	NIG
	1:16	they follow **their** o evil desires;	1571
	1:16	and flatter others for their o advantage.	NIG
	1:18	scoffers who will follow **their** o ungodly desires."	1571
Rev	18: 6	Mix her a double portion from **her** o cup.	3836

OWNED (12) [OWN]

Ge	25: 5	Abraham left everything he o to Isaac.	4200
	31: 1	"Jacob has taken everything our father o	4200
	39: 4	entrusted to his care everything he o.	3780+4200
	39: 5	of his household and of all that he o,	3780+4200
Nu	16:33	with everything they o;	4200
Jdg	19:22	they shouted to the old man who o	1251
1Ki	17:17	of the woman who o the house became ill.	1266
Job	1: 3	and he o seven thousand sheep,	2118+5238
Ecc	2: 7	I also o more herds and flocks than	2118+5238
Jer	39:10	of the poor people, who o nothing;	4200
Ac	4:34	from time to time those who o lands	3230+5639
	4:37	sold a field he o and brought the money	5639

OWNER (36) [OWN]

Ex	21:28	But the o *of* the bull will not be held	1251
	21:29	habit of goring and the o has been warned	1251
	21:29	the bull must be stoned and the o also must	1251
	21:32	the o must pay thirty shekels of silver to	NIH
	21:34	the o *of* the pit must pay for the loss;	1251
	21:34	he must pay its o,	1251

Ex	21:36	yet the o did not keep it penned up,	1251
	21:36	the o must pay, animal for animal,	NIH
	22: 8	the o *of* the house must appear before	1251
	22:11	The o is to accept this,	1251
	22:12	he must make restitution to the o.	1251
	22:14	and it is injured or dies while the o is	1251
	22:15	But if the o is with the animal,	1251
Lev	6: 5	and give it all to the o on the day	2257+4200
	14:35	the o *of* the house must go and tell	2257+4200
	25:53	that his o does not rule over him ruthlessly.	NIH
	27:13	If the o wishes to redeem the animal,	NIH
Jdg	19:23	The o *of* the house went outside and said	1251
1Ki	16:24	the name of the former o *of* the hill.	123
Ecc	5:11	And what benefit are they to the o except	1251
	5:13	wealth hoarded to the harm of its o,	1251
Mt	13:52	like the o *of* a house who brings out	476+3867
	20: 8	the o *of* the vineyard said to his foreman,	3261
	21:40	when the o *of* the vineyard comes,	3261
	24:43	the o *of the house* had known at what time	3867
Mk	12: 9	"What then will the o *of* the vineyard do?	3261
	13:35	when the o *of the house* will come back—	3867
	14:14	Say *to* the o *of the house* he enters,	3867
Lk	12:39	the o *of the house* had known at what hour	3867
	13:25	Once the o *of the house* gets up and closes	3867
	14:21	Then the o *of the house* became angry	3867
	20:13	o *of* the vineyard said, 'What shall I do?	3261
	20:15	then will the o *of* the vineyard do to them?	3261
	22:11	*to* the o *of the house*, 'The Teacher asks:	3867
Ac	21:11	the o *of* this belt and will hand him over	467+4005
	27:11	of the pilot and of the o *of the ship.*	3729

OWNER'S (2) [OWN]

Isa	1: 3	the donkey his o manger,	1251
Mt	13:27	"The o servants came to him and said, 'Sir,	3867

OWNERS (4) [OWN]

Jer	8:10	to other men and their fields to **new** o.	3769
Lk	19:33	its o asked them, "Why are you untying	3261
Ac	16:16	She earned a great deal of money *for* her o	3261
	16:19	When the o *of* the slave girl realized	3261

OWNERSHIP (1) [OWN]

2Co	1:22	set his **seal** of o on us, and put his Spirit in	5381

OWNING (1) [OWN]

Job	22: 8	o land—an honored man, living on it.	4200

OWNS (9) [OWN]

Ge	24:36	and he has given him everything he o.	4200
	32:17	who o all these animals in front of you?'	4200
	38:25	"I am pregnant by the man who o these,"	4200
	39: 8	everything he o he has entrusted	3780+4200
Lev	27:28	" 'But nothing that a man o and devotes to	4200
Ecc	2:21	and then he must leave *all* he o	2750
Mt	18:12	If a man o a hundred sheep,	1181
Jn	10:12	hired hand is not the shepherd who o	1639+2625
Gal	4: 1	*although he* o the whole estate,	1639+3261

OX (53) [OXEN]

Ex	20:17	his o or donkey, or anything that belongs to	8802
	21:33	to cover it and an o or a donkey falls into it,	8802
	22: 1	an o or a sheep and slaughters it or sells it,	8802
	22: 1	for the o and four sheep for the sheep.	8802
	22: 4	whether o or donkey or sheep—	8802
	22: 9	In all cases of illegal possession of an o,	8802
	22:10	"If a man gives a donkey, an o,	8802
	23: 4	"If you come across your enemy's o	8802
	23:12	that your o and your donkey may rest and	8802
Lev	4:10	the fat is removed from the o sacrificed as	8802
	9: 4	an o and a ram for a fellowship offering	8802
	9:18	the o and the ram as the fellowship offering	8802
	9:19	But the fat portions of the o and the ram—	8802
	17: 3	Any Israelite who sacrifices an o,	8802
	22:23	an o or a sheep that is deformed or stunted,	8802
	27:26	whether an o or a sheep, it is the LORD's.	8802
Nu	7: 3	an o from each leader and a cart	8802
	18:17	you must not redeem the firstborn of an o,	8802
	22: 4	as an o licks up the grass of the field."	8802
	23:22	they have the strength of a **wild** o.	8028
	24: 8	they have the strength of a **wild** o.	8028
Dt	5:14	or maidservant, nor your o, your donkey	8802
	5:21	his o or donkey, or anything that belongs to	8802
	14: 4	These are the animals you may eat: the o,	8802
	17: 1	an o or a sheep that has any defect or flaw	8802
	22: 1	you see your brother's o or sheep straying,	8802
	22: 4	or his o fallen on the road,	8802
	22:10	with an o and a donkey yoked together.	8802
	25: 4	Do not muzzle an o while it is treading out	8802
	28:31	Your o will be slaughtered	8802
	33:17	his horns are the horns of a **wild** o.	8028
1Sa	12: 3	Whose o have I taken?	8802
	14:34	So everyone brought his o that night	8802
2Sa	24:22	and here are threshing sledges and o yokes	1330
Ne	5:18	Each day one o, six choice sheep	8802
Job	6: 5	or an o bellow when it has fodder?	8802
	24: 3	and take the widow's o in pledge.	8802
	39: 9	"Will the **wild** o consent to serve you?	8028
	40:15	and which feeds on grass like an o.	1330
Ps	29: 6	Sirion like a young **wild** o.	8028
	69:31	This will please the LORD more than an o,	8802
	92:10	like that of a **wild** o;	8028
Pr	7:22	All at once he followed her like an o going	8802
	14: 4	but from the strength of an o comes	8802

Isa	1: 3	The o knows his master,	8802
	11: 7	and the lion will eat straw like the o,	1330
	65:25	and the lion will eat straw like the o,	1330
Eze	1:10	and on the left the face of an o;	8802
Lk	13:15	of you on the Sabbath untie his o or donkey	1091
	14: 5	"If one of you has a son or an o that falls	1091
1Co	9: 9	"Do not muzzle an o while it is treading out	1091
1Ti	5:18	"Do not muzzle an o while it is treading out	1091
Rev	4: 7	the second was like an o,	3675

OXEN (44) [OX]

Ge	49: 6	and hamstrung o as they pleased.	8802
Nu	7: 3	the LORD six covered carts and twelve o—	1330
	7: 6	and o and gave them to the Levites.	1330
	7: 7	He gave two carts and four o to	1330
	7: 8	and he gave four carts and eight o to	1330
	7:17	and two o, five rams, five male goats	1330
	7:23	and two o, five rams, five male goats	1330
	7:29	and two o, five rams, five male goats	1330
	7:35	and two o, five rams, five male goats	1330
	7:41	and two o, five rams, five male goats	1330
	7:47	and two o, five rams, five male goats	1330
	7:53	and two o, five rams, five male goats	1330
	7:59	and two o, five rams, five male goats	1330
	7:65	and two o, five rams, five male goats	1330
	7:71	and two o, five rams, five male goats	1330
	7:77	and two o, five rams, five male goats	1330
	7:83	and two o, five rams, five male goats	1330
		fellowship offering came to twenty-four o,	7228
Dt	15:19	Do not put the firstborn of your o to work,	8802
1Sa	11: 5	behind his o, and he asked,	1330
	11: 7	He took a pair of o, cut them into pieces,	1330
	11: 7	the o *of* anyone who does not follow Saul	1330
2Sa	6: 6	because the o stumbled.	1330
	24:22	Here are o for the burnt offering,	1330
	24:24	and the o and paid fifty shekels of silver	1330
1Ki	19:19	He was plowing with twelve **yoke** of o,	7538
	19:20	Elisha then left his o and ran after Elijah.	1330
	19:21	took his yoke of o and slaughtered them.	1330
1Ch	12:40	on donkeys, camels, mules and o.	1330
	13: 9	because the o stumbled.	1330
	21:23	I will give the o for the burnt offerings,	1330
Job	1: 3	of o and five hundred donkeys,	1330
	1:14	"The o were plowing and	1330
	42:12	a thousand yoke of o and a thousand	1330
Ps	22:21	save me from the horns of the **wild** o.	8028
	144:14	our o will draw heavy loads,	476
Pr	14: 4	Where there are no o, the manger is empty,	546
Isa	30:24	The o and donkeys that work	546
	34: 7	And the **wild** o will fall with them,	8028
Jer	51:23	with you I shatter farmer and o,	7538
Am	6:12	Does one plow there with o?	1330
Mt	22: 4	o and fattened cattle have been	5436
Lk	14:19	"I have just bought five yoke of o,	1091
1Co	9: 9	Is it *about* o that God is concerned?	1091

OXGOAD (1)

Jdg	3:31	six hundred Philistines with an o.	1330+4913

OZEM (2)

1Ch	2:15	the sixth O and the seventh David.	730
	2:25	Bunah, Oren, O and Ahijah.	730

OZIAS (KJV) See UZZIAH

OZNI (1) [OZNITE]

Nu	26:16	through O, the Oznite clan;	269

OZNITE (1) [OZNI]

Nu	26:16	through Ozni, the O clan;	270

P

PAARAI (1)

2Sa	23:35	Hezro the Carmelite, P the Arbite,	7197

PACE (1)

Ge	33:14	at the p *of* the droves before me and that of	8079

PACES (KJV) See STEPS

PACIFIES (1) [PEACE]

Pr	21:14	bribe concealed in the cloak p great wrath.	NIH

PACIFY (1) [PEACE]

Ge	32:20	"*I will* p him with these gifts	4105+7156

PACK (2) [PACKED]

Jer	46:19	P your belongings for exile,	6913
Eze	12: 3	p your belongings for exile and in	6913

PACKED (3) [PACK]
Jos 9:12 of ours was warm *when we* p it at home on 7472
Eze 12: 4 bring out your belongings p *for* exile. 3998
     12: 7 the day I brought out my things p *for* exile. 3998

PACT (1)
Isa 57: 8 *you* made a p with those whose beds you love, 4162

PAD (1)
Jer 38:12 worn-out clothes under your arms to p 4946+9393

PADAN (KJV) See PADDAN

PADANARAM (KJV) See PADDAN ARAM

PADDAN (1) [PADDAN ARAM]
Ge 48: 7 As I was returning from P, 7019

PADDAN ARAM (10) [ARAM, PADDAN]
Ge 25:20 of Bethuel the Aramean from P 7020
     28: 2 Go at once to P, 7020
     28: 5 and he went to P, 7020
     28: 6 and had sent him to P to take a wife 7020
     28: 7 and mother and had gone to P. 7020
     31:18 the goods he had accumulated in P, 7020
     33:18 After Jacob came from P, 7020
     35: 9 After Jacob returned from P, 7020
     35:26 who were born to him in P, 7020
     46:15 the sons Leah bore to Jacob in P, 7020

PADON (2)
Ezr 2:44 Keros, Siaha, P, 7013
Ne   7:47 Keros, Sia, P, 7013

PAGAN (8) [PAGANS]
2Ki 23: 5 He did away with the p priests appointed 4024
Isa 57: 8 doorposts you have put your p symbols. 2355
La   1:10 she saw **pagan** nations enter her sanctuary— 1580
Am 7:17 and you yourself will die in a p country. 3238
Zep 1: 4 of the p and the idolatrous priests— 4024
Mt 18:17 to the church, treat him as you would a p or 1618
Lk 12:30 For the p world runs after all such things, 1620
1Co 10: 7 and got up to **indulge in** p **revelry."** 4089

PAGANS (10) [PAGAN]
Isa 2: 6 the Philistines and clasp hands with p. 3529+5799
Mt 5:47 Do not even p do that? 1618
      6: 7 you pray, do not keep on babbling like p, 1618
      6:32 For the p run after all these things, 1620
1Co 5: 1 of a kind that does not occur even among p: 1620
    10:20 the sacrifices of p are offered to demons, 1620
    12: 2 You know that when you were p, 1620
1Pe 2:12 Live such good lives among the p that, 1620
      4: 3 in the past doing what p choose to do— 1620
3Jn 1: 7 receiving no help from the p. 1618

PAGIEL (5)
Nu 1:13 from Asher, P son of Ocran; 7005
      2:27 The leader of the people of Asher is P son 7005
      7:72 On the eleventh day P son of Ocran, 7005
      7:77 This was the offering of P son of Ocran. 7005
   10:26 P son of Ocran was over the division of 7005

PAHATH-MOAB (6)
Ezr 2: 6 of P (through the line of Jeshua 7075
      8: 4 of the descendants of P, Eliehoenai son 7075
   10:30 From the descendants of P: 7075
Ne   3:11 of P repaired another section and 7075
      7:11 of P (through the line of Jeshua 7075
   10:14 The leaders of the people: Parosh, P, Elam, 7075

PAID (51) [PAY]
Ge 30:33 check on the **wages** you have p me. AIT
    31:15 but he has used up **what** was p for us. 4084
    39:23 The warden p no **attention** *to* anything 8011
Ex 16:20 some of them p no **attention** to Moses; 9048
    22:15 money p **for** *the* hire covers the loss. 8510
Lev 25:50 **based on the rate** p to a hired man 3427+3869
    25:51 a larger share of the price p for him. 5239
Dt   1:45 but he p no **attention** to your weeping 9048
Jdg 1:45 God has p me **back** *for* what I did to them." 8966
   11:28 p no **attention** to the message Jephthah 9048
1Sa 25:21 *He has* p me **back** evil for good. 8740
2Sa 24:24 and the oxen and p fifty shekels of silver 928
1Ki 18:29 no one answered, no one p **attention.** 7993
2Ki 12:11 *With it they* p those who worked on 3655
    12:14 *it was* p to the workmen, 5989
    17: 3 and *had* p him tribute. 8740
    17: 4 and *he no longer* p tribute to the king 6590
    22: 9 "Your officials *have* p **out** the money 5988
    23:35 Jehoiakim p Pharaoh Neco the silver 5989
1Ch 21:25 David p Araunah six hundred shekels 5486+5989
2Ch 24:17 officials of Judah came and p homage to 2556
    25: 9 "But what about the hundred talents *I* p 5989
    27: 5 the Ammonites p him a hundred talents 5989
    33:10 but *they* p no **attention.** 7992
    34:10 These men p the workers who repaired 5989
    34:17 *They have* p **out** the money that was in 5988

Ezr 4:13 no more taxes, tribute or duty *will be* p, 10498
     4:20 and taxes, tribute and duty *were* p to them. 10314
     6: 4 The costs *are to* be p by the royal treasury. 10314
     6: 8 to be fully p out of the royal treasury. 10314
Ne   9:30 Yet *they* p no **attention,** 263
Est 3: 2 at the king's gate knelt down and p honor 2556
Job 15:32 Before his time *he will* be p in full, 4848
    21:29 *Have you* p no **regard** *to* their accounts— 5795
Isa 3:11 They *will* be p **back** for what their hands 6913
    40: 2 that her sin *has* been p for, 8355
    42:20 but *have* p no **attention;** 9068
    48:18 only *you had* p **attention** to my commands, 7992
Jer 25: 4 you have not listened or p any **attention.** 265+4200+5742+9048
    35:15 *you have* not p **attention** or listened to 265+5742
    37: 2 nor the people of the land p any **attention** 9048
Eze 27:15 *they* p you **with** ivory tusks and ebony. 868+8740
Da 2:46 before Daniel and p him **honor** and ordered 10504
Zec 11:12 So *they* p me thirty pieces of silver. 8510+9202
Mt 5:26 not get out until *you have* p the last penny. 625
   22: 5 "But they p no **attention** and went off— 288
Mk 15:19 *they* p **homage** to him. 4686
Lk 12:59 not get out until *you have* p the last penny." 625
Ac 8: 6 *they* all p **close attention** to what he said. 4668
Heb 7: 9 p **the tenth** through Abraham, 1282
2Pe 2:13 They will be p back with harm for the harm 3635

PAIN (40) [PAINFUL, PAINS]
Ge 3:16 with p you will give birth to children. 6776
      6: 6 and his heart was filled with p. 6772
    34:25 while all of them were *still* in p, 3872
1Ch 4: 9 saying, "I gave birth to him in p." 6778
     4:10 from harm so that I will be free from **p."** 6778
2Ch 21:19 and he died in great p. 9377
Job 6:10 my joy in unrelenting p— 2660
    14:22 *He feels* but the p of his own body 3872
    16: 6 "Yet if I speak, my p is not relieved; 3873
    33:19 Or a man may be chastened on a bed of p 4799
Ps 38: 7 My back is filled with **searing** p; 7828
    38:17 and my p is ever with me. 4799
    48: 6 p like that of a woman in labor. 2659
    69:26 and talk about the p *of* those you hurt. 4799
    69:29 *I am* in p and distress; 3872
Ecc 2:23 All his days his work is p and grief; 4799
Isa 13: 8 p and anguish will grip them; 7496
    17:11 in the day of disease and incurable p. 3873
    21: 3 At this my body is racked with p, 2714
    26:17 to give birth writhes and cries out in her p, 2477
    26:18 We were with child, *we* **writhed** in p, 2655
Jer 4:19 *I* writhe in p. 2655
     5: 3 You struck them, but *they* **felt** no p; 2655
     6:24 p like that of a woman in labor. 2659
    13:21 Will not p grip you like that of a woman 2477
    15:18 Why is my p unending and my wound 3873
    22:23 p like that of a woman in labor! 2659
    30:15 your p that has no cure? 4799
    45: 3 The LORD has added sorrow to my p; 4799
    49:24 anguish and p have seized her, 2477
    49:24 p like that of a woman in labor. NIH
    50:43 p like that of a woman in labor. 2659
    51: 8 Get balm for her p; 4799
Mic 1:12 Those who live in Maroth **writhe** in p, 2655
     4: 9 seizes you like that of a woman in labor? 2659
Mt 4:24 those suffering **severe** p, 992
Jn 16:21 to a child has p because her time has come; 3383
1Pe 2:19 up under the p of unjust suffering 3383
Rev 12: 2 She was pregnant and cried out *in* p 989
    21: 4 no more death or mourning or crying or p, 4506

PAINFUL (10) [PAIN]
Ge 3:17 through p **toil** you will eat of it all 6779
     5:29 "He will comfort us in the labor and p **toil** 6779
Dt 28:35 and legs with p boils that cannot be cured, 8273
Job 2: 7 the LORD and afflicted Job with p sores 8273
     6:25 How p *are* honest words! 5344
Eze 28:24 have malicious neighbors *who are* p briers 4421
2Co 2: 1 that I would not make another p visit 1877+3383
Heb 12:11 discipline seems pleasant at the time, but p. 3383
1Pe 4:12 be surprised *at* the p trial you are suffering, 4796
Rev 16: 2 and ugly and p sores broke out on 4505

PAINS (16) [PAIN]
Ge 3:16 I will greatly increase your p in childbearing 6779
1Sa 4:19 but was overcome by her **labor** p. 7496
1Ch 22:14 "I have **taken great** p to provide for 928+6715
2Ch 6:29 each one aware of his afflictions and p, 4799
Job 30:17 my **gnawing** p never rest. 6908
    39: 3 their **labor** p are ended. 2477
Isa 66: 7 before the p come upon her, 2477
Hos 13:13 P *as of* a woman in childbirth come 2477
Mt 24: 8 All these are the beginning of **birth** p. 6047
Mk 13: 8 These are the beginning *of* **birth** p. 6047
Ro 8:22 has been groaning as **in the** p **of childbirth** 5349
2Co 8:21 For *we are* **taking** p to do what is right, 4629
Gal 4:19 *I am* again **in the** p **of childbirth** 6048
     4:27 you who have **no labor** p; 6048
1Th 5: 3 as **labor** p on a pregnant woman, 6047
Rev 16:11 cursed the God of heaven because of their p 4506

PAINT (1) [PAINTED]
Jer 4:30 Why shade your eyes with p? 7037

PAINTED (2) [PAINT]
2Ki 9:30 *she* p her eyes, 928+2021+7037+8531
Eze 23:40 p your eyes and put on your jewelry. 3949

PAIR (17) [PAIRS]
Ex 25:35 be under the first p *of* branches extending 9109
    25:35 a second bud under the second p, 9109
    25:35 and a third bud under the third p— 9109
    37:21 under the first p *of* branches extending 9109
    37:21 a second bud under the second p, 9109
    37:21 and a third bud under the third p— 9109
Dt 24: 6 Do not take a p *of* millstones— 8160
Jdg 15: 4 He then fastened a torch to every p *of* tails, 9109
1Sa 11: 7 He took a p *of* oxen, cut them into pieces, 7538
1Ki 6:23 In the inner sanctuary he made a p 9109
    19:19 and he himself was driving the twelfth p. NIH
2Ki 5:17 as much earth as a p *of* mules can carry, 7538
2Ch 3:10 In the Most Holy Place he made a p 9109
Am 2: 6 and the needy for a p *of* **sandals.** AIT
     2: 6 and the needy for a p *of* **sandals,** AIT
Lk 2:24 "a p *of* doves or two young pigeons." 2414
Rev 6: 5 Its rider was holding a p *of* scales 2433

PAIRS (3) [PAIR]
Ge 7: 8 P of clean and unclean animals, 9109+9109
     7:15 P of all creatures that have the breath 9109+9109
Jdg 15: 4 and tied them tail to tail in p. NIH

PALACE (166) [PALACES, PALATIAL]
Ge 12:15 and she was taken into his p. 1074
    41:40 You shall be in charge of my p, 1074
    45:16 When the news reached Pharaoh's p 1074
    47:14 and he brought it to Pharaoh's p. 1074
Ex 7:23 Instead, he turned and went into his p, 1074
     8: 3 up into your p and your bedroom 1074
     8:24 of flies poured into Pharaoh's p and into 1074
Nu 22:18 if Balak gave me his p filled with silver 1074
    24:13 if Balak gave me his p filled with silver 1074
Jdg 3:20 in the upper room of his **summer** p and 5249
2Sa 5: 8 "The 'blind and lame' will not enter the **p."** 1074
     5:11 and they built a p for David. 1074
     7: 1 in his p and the LORD had given him rest 1074
     7: 2 "Here I am, living in a p *of* cedar, 1074
    11: 2 walked around on the roof of the p. 1074+4889
    11: 8 So Uriah left the p, 1074+4889
    11: 9 the p with all his master's servants 1074+4889
    13: 7 David sent word to Tamar at the p: 1074
    15:16 he left ten concubines to take care of the p. 1074
    15:35 anything you hear in the king's p 1074
    16:21 whom he left to take care of the p. 1074
    19:11 be the last to bring the king back to his p, 1074
    20: 3 When David returned to his p in Jerusalem, 1074
    20: 3 the p and put them in a house under guard. 1074
1Ki 3: 1 of David until he finished building his p 1074
     4: 6 Ahishar—in charge of the p; 1074
     7: 1 to complete the construction of his p. 1074
     7: 2 He built the P of the Forest of Lebanon 1074
     7: 8 And the p in which he was to live, 1074
     7: 8 a p like this hall for Pharaoh's daughter, 1074
     9: 1 the temple of the LORD and the royal p, 1074
     9:10 the temple of the LORD and the royal p— 1074
     9:15 his own p, the supporting terraces, 1074
     9:24 of David to the p Solomon had built 1074
    10: 4 of Solomon and the p he had built, 1074
    10:12 of the LORD and for the royal p, 1074
    10:17 The king put them in the P of the Forest 1074
    10:21 household articles in the P of the Forest 1074
    11:20 whom Tahpenes brought up in the royal p. 1074
    14:26 the LORD and the treasures of the royal p. 1074
    14:27 on duty at the entrance to the royal p. 1074
    15:18 of the LORD's temple and of his own p. 1074
    16: 9 the man in charge of the p at Tirzah. 1074
    16:18 the citadel of the royal p and set the palace 1074
    16:18 the citadel of the royal palace and set the p 1074
    18: 3 who was in charge of his p. 1074
    20: 6 to send my officials to search your p and 1074
    20:43 the king of Israel went to his p in Samaria. 1074
    21: 1 close to the p of Ahab king of Samaria. 2121
    21: 2 since it is close to my p. 1074
    22:39 the p he built and inlaid with ivory, 1074
2Ki 7: 9 at once and report this to the royal **p."** 1074
     7:11 and it was reported within the p. 1074+4889
    10: 5 So the p administrator, the city governor, 1074
    11: 5 a third of you guarding the royal p, 1074
    11:16 where the horses enter the p **grounds,** 1074+4889
    11:19 of the LORD and went into the p, 1074+4889
    11:20 with the sword at the p. 1074+4889
    12:18 of the LORD and of the royal p, 1074
    14:14 and in the treasuries of the royal p 1074
    15: 5 the p and governed the people of the land. 1074
    15:25 in the citadel of the royal p at Samaria. 1074
    16: 8 in the treasuries of the royal p and sent it as 1074
    18:15 and in the treasuries of the royal p. 1074
    18:18 Eliakim son of Hilkiah the p administrator, 1074
    18:37 Eliakim son of Hilkiah the p administrator, 1074
    19: 2 He sent Eliakim the p administrator, 1074
    20:13 There was nothing in his p or 1074
    20:15 "What did they see in your p?" 1074
    20:15 "They saw everything in my p," 1074
    20:17 surely come when everything in your p, 1074
    20:18 and they will become eunuchs in the p of 2121
    21:18 and was buried in his p garden, 1074
    21:23 and assassinated the king in his p. 1074
    24:13 of the LORD and from the royal p, 1074
    25: 9 the royal p and all the houses of Jerusalem. 1074
1Ch 14: 1 stonemasons and carpenters to build a p 1074
    17: 1 After David was settled in his p, 1074

2Ki	17: 1	"Here I am, living in a **p** of cedar,	1074
	28: 1	together with the **p officials,**	6247
2Ch	2: 1	for the Name of the LORD and a royal **p**	1074
	2: 3	when you sent him cedar to build a **p**	1074
	2:12	for the LORD and a **p** for himself.	1074+4895
	7:11	the temple of the LORD and the royal **p,**	1074
	7:11	the temple of the LORD and in his own **p,**	1074
	8: 1	the temple of the LORD and his own **p,**	1074
	8:11	from the City of David to the **p** he had built	1074
	8:11	not live in the **p** of David king of Israel,	1074
	9: 3	as well as the **p** he had built,	1074
	9:11	of the LORD and for the royal **p,**	1074
	9:16	The king put them in the **P** of the Forest	1074
	9:20	household articles in the **P** of the Forest	1074
	12: 9	the LORD and the treasures of the royal **p**	1074
	12:10	on duty at the entrance to the royal **p.**	1074
	16: 2	of his own **p** and sent it to Ben-Hadad king	1074
	19: 1	of Judah returned safely to his **p**	1074
	21:17	the goods found in the king's **p,**	1074
	23: 5	a third of you at the royal **p** and a third at	1074
	23:15	of the Horse Gate on the **p grounds,**	1074+4889
	23:20	the **p** through the Upper Gate and	1074+4889
	25:24	with the **p** treasures and the hostages,	1074+4889
	26:21	**p** and governed the people of the land.	1074+4889
	28: 7	Azrikam the officer in charge of the **p,**	1074
	28:21	the LORD and from the royal **p** and from	1074
	33:20	with his fathers and was buried in his **p.**	1074
	33:24	against him and assassinated him in his **p.**	1074
Ezr	4:14	Now since we are under obligation to the **p**	10206
Ne	3:25	the tower projecting from the upper **p**	1074+4889
Est	1: 5	in the enclosed garden of the king's **p,**	1131
	1: 9	the women in the royal **p** of King Xerxes.	1074
	2: 8	also was taken to the king's **p** and entrusted	1074
	2: 9	the king's **p** and moved her and her maids	1074
	2:13	with her from the harem to the king's **p.**	1074
	5: 1	and stood in the inner court of the **p,**	1074+4889
	6: 4	court of the **p** to speak to the king	1074+4889
	7: 7	and went out into the **p** garden.	1131
	7: 8	Just as the king returned from the **p** garden	1131
	9: 4	Mordecai was prominent in the **p;**	1074+4889
Ps	45:15	they enter the **p** of the king.	2121
	144:12	be like pillars carved to adorn a **p.**	2121
Isa	22: 8	to the weapons in the **P** of the Forest;	1074
	22:15	to Shebna, who is in charge of the **p:**	1074
	36: 3	Eliakim son of Hilkiah the **p** administrator,	1074
	36:22	Eliakim son of Hilkiah the **p** administrator,	1074
	37: 2	He sent Eliakim the **p** administrator,	1074
	39: 2	There was nothing in his **p** or	1074
	39: 4	"What did they see in your **p?"**	1074
	39: 4	"They saw everything in my **p,"**	1074
	39: 6	surely come when everything in your **p,**	1074
	39: 7	and they will become eunuchs in the **p** of	2121
Jer	22: 1	"Go down to the **p** of the king of Judah	1074
	22: 4	through the gates of this **p,**	1074
	22: 5	by myself that this **p** will become a ruin.' "	1074
	22: 6	the LORD says about the **p** of the king	1074
	22:13	"Woe to him who builds his **p**	1074
	22:14	a great **p** with spacious upper rooms.	1074
	26:10	from the royal **p** to the house of the LORD	1074
	27:18	the **p** of the king of Judah and in Jerusalem	1074
	27:21	in the house of the LORD and in the **p** of	1074
	30:18	and the **p** will stand in its proper place.	810
	32: 2	in the courtyard of the guard in the royal **p**	1074
	36:12	down to the secretary's room in the royal **p,**	1074
	37:17	for him and had him brought to the **p,**	1074
	38: 7	a Cushite, an official in the royal **p,**	1074
	38: 8	Ebed-Melech went out of the **p** and	1074+4889
	38:11	to a room under the treasury in the **p.**	1074+4889
	38:22	All the women left in the **p** of the king	1074
	39: 8	The Babylonians set fire to the royal **p** and	1074
	43: 9	the entrance to Pharaoh's **p** in Tahpanhes.	1074
	52:13	the royal **p** and all the houses of Jerusalem.	1074
Da	1: 4	and qualified to serve in the king's **p.**	2121
	4: 4	I, Nebuchadnezzar, was at home in my **p,**	10206
	4:29	on the roof of the royal **p** of Babylon,	10206
	5: 5	near the lampstand in the royal **p.**	10206
	6:18	to his **p** and spent the night without eating	10206
Am	9: 6	he who builds his **lofty p** in the heavens	5092
Na	2: 6	and the **p** collapses.	2121
Mt	26: 3	the elders of the people assembled in the **p**	885
Mk	15:16	The soldiers led Jesus away into the **p**	885
Jn	18:28	from Caiaphas to **p** the Roman **governor**	4550
	18:28	the Jews did not enter the **p;**	4550
	18:33	Pilate then went back inside the **p,**	4550
	19: 9	and he went back inside the **p.**	4550
Ac	7:10	he made him ruler over Egypt and all his **p.**	3875
	23:35	that Paul be kept under guard in Herod's **p.**	4550
Php	1:13	the whole **p guard** and to everyone else	4550

PALACES (10) [PALACE]

2Ch	36:19	the **p** and destroyed everything	810
Ps	45: 8	from **p** adorned with ivory the music of	2121
Pr	30:28	yet it is found in kings' **p.**	2121
Isa	13:22	jackals in her luxurious **p.**	2121
Jer	33: 4	about the houses in this city and the royal **p**	1074
La	2: 5	up all her **p** and destroyed her strongholds.	810
	2: 7	over to the enemy the walls of her **p;**	810
Hos	8:14	Israel has forgotten his Maker and built **p;**	2121
Mt	11: 8	those who wear fine clothes are in kings' **p.**	3875
Lk	7:25	and indulge in luxury are in **p.**	994

PALAL (1)

Ne	3:25	and **P** son of Uzai worked opposite	7138

PALATIAL (2) [PALACE]

1Ch	29: 1	because this **p structure** is not for man but	1072
	29:19	the **p structure** for which I have provided."	1072

PALE (10)

Isa	29:22	no longer will their faces grow **p.**	2578
Jer	30: 6	every face turned **deathly p?**	3766
Da	5: 6	His face turned **p** and he was so frightened	10228
	5: 9	and his face grew more **p.**	10228
	5:10	Don't look so **p!**	10228+10731
	7:28	and my face turned **p,**	10228
	10: 8	my face turned **deathly p**	5422
Joel	2: 6	every face **turns p.**	6999+7695
Na	2:10	bodies tremble, every face **grows p.**	6999+7695
Rev	6: 8	and there before me was a **p** horse!	5952

PALESTINA, PALESTINE (KJV) See PHILISTIA, PHILISTINE

PALLU (5) [PALLUITE]

Ge	46: 9	Hanoch, **P,** Hezron and Carmi.	7112
Ex	6:14	of Israel were Hanoch and **P,**	7112
Nu	26: 5	through **P,** the Palluite clan;	7112
	26: 8	The son of **P** was Eliab,	7112
1Ch	5: 3	Hanoch, **P,** Hezron and Carmi.	7112

PALLUITE (1) [PALLU]

Nu	26: 5	through Pallu, the **P** clan;	7101

PALM (39) [PALMS]

Ex	15:27	twelve springs and seventy **p trees,**	9469
Lev	14:15	**p** of his own left **hand,**	4090
	14:16	dip his right forefinger into the oil in his **p,**	4090
	14:17	to put some of the oil remaining in his **p** on	4090
	14:18	in his **p** the priest shall put on the head of	4090
	14:26	**p** of his own left **hand,**	4090
	14:27	from his **p** seven times before the LORD.	4090
	14:28	Some of the oil in his **p** he is to put on	4090
	14:29	in his **p** the priest shall put on the head of	4090
	23:40	and **p** fronds, leafy branches and poplars,	9469
Nu	33: 9	twelve springs and seventy **p trees,**	9469
Jdg	4: 5	under the **P** of Deborah between Ramah	9472
1Ki	6:29	**p trees** and open flowers,	9474
	6:32	**p trees** and open flowers,	9474
	6:32	the cherubim and **p trees** with beaten gold.	9474
	6:35	**p trees** and open flowers on them	9474
	7:36	and **p trees** on the surfaces of the supports	9474
2Ch	3: 5	**p tree** and chain **designs.**	9474
Ps	92:12	The righteous will flourish like a **p tree,**	9469
SS	7: 7	Your stature is like that of the,	9469
	7: 8	I said, "I will climb the **p tree;**	9469
Isa	9:14	both **p branch** and reed in a single day;	4093
	19:15	head or tail, **p branch** or reed.	4093
Eze	40:16	walls were decorated with **p trees.**	9474
	40:22	its portico and its **p tree decorations** had	9474
	40:26	it had **p tree** decorations on the faces of	9474
	40:31	**p trees** decorated its jambs,	9474
	40:34	**p trees** decorated the jambs on either side,	9474
	40:37	**p trees** decorated the jambs on either side,	9474
	41:18	were carved cherubim and **p trees.**	9474
	41:18	**P trees** alternated with cherubim.	9474
	41:19	the **p tree** on one side and the face of a lion	9474
	41:19	and the face of a lion toward the **p tree** on	9474
	41:20	and **p trees** were carved on the wall of	9474
	41:25	and **p trees** like those carved on the walls,	9474
	41:26	with **p trees** carved on each side.	9474
Joel	1:12	the pomegranate, the **p** and the apple tree—	9469
Jn	12:13	They took **p branches** and went out	5836
Rev	7: 9	and were holding **p branches** in their hands.	5836

PALMERWORM (KJV) See LOCUST SWARM

PALMS (6) [PALM]

Dt	34: 3	the City of **P,** as far as Zoar.	9469
Jdg	1:16	the City of **P** with the men of Judah to live	9469
	3:13	and they took possession of the City of **P.**	9469
2Ch	28:15	the City of **P,** and returned to Samaria.	9469
Ne	8:15	**p** and shade trees, to make booths"—	9469
Isa	49:16	I have engraved you on the **p of** my **hands;**	4090

PALSY (KJV) See PARALYZED, PARALYTIC

PALTI (1)

Nu	13: 9	**P** son of Raphu;	7120

PALTIEL (3)

Nu	34:26	**P** son of Azzan, the leader from the tribe	7123
1Sa	25:44	to **P** son of Laish, who was from Gallim.	7120
2Sa	3:15	from her husband **P** son of Laish.	7123

PALTITE (1)

2Sa	23:26	Helez the **P,** Ira son of Ikkesh from Tekoa,	7121

PAMPERS (1)

Pr	29:21	If a man **p** his servant from youth,	7167

PAMPHYLIA (5)

Ac	2:10	and **P,** Egypt and the parts of Libya	4103
	13:13	and his companions sailed to Perga in **P,**	4103
	14:24	going through Pisidia, they came into **P,**	4103
	15:38	because he had deserted them in **P** and had	4103
	27: 5	the open sea off the coast of Cilicia and **P,**	4103

PAN (6) [PANS]

Lev	2: 7	If your grain offering is cooked in a **p,**	5306
	7: 9	or cooked in a **p** or on a griddle belongs to	5306
1Sa	2:14	He would plunge it into the **p** or kettle	3963
2Sa	13: 9	she took the **p** and served him the bread,	5389
Eze	4: 3	Then take an iron **p,**	4679
Mic	3: 3	who chop them up like meat for the **p,**	6105

PANELED (2) [PANELING, PANELS]

2Ch	3: 5	He **p** the main hall with pine and covered it	2902
Hag	1: 4	to be living in your **p** houses,	6211

PANELING (2) [PANELED]

1Ki	6:15	**p** them from the floor of the temple to	6770+7596
Ps	74: 6	the **carved p** with their axes and hatchets.	7334

PANELS (9) [PANELED]

1Ki	7:28	They had **side p** attached to uprights.	4995
	7:29	On the **p** between the uprights were lions,	4995
	7:31	The **p** of the stands were square, not round.	4995
	7:32	The four wheels were under the **p,**	4995
	7:35	The supports and **p** were attached to the top	4995
	7:36	the surfaces of the supports and on the **p,**	4995
2Ki	16:17	the **side p** and removed the basins from	4995
SS	8: 9	we will enclose her with **p** of cedar.	4283
Jer	22:14	**p** it with cedar and decorates it in red.	6211

PANGS (2)

Isa	21: 3	**p** seize me, like those of a woman in labor;	7496
Jer	22:23	you will groan when **p** come upon you,	2477

PANIC (11)

Dt	20: 3	be terrified or **give way to p** before them.	6907
1Sa	5: 9	throwing it into a great **p.**	4539
	5:11	For death had filled the city with **p;**	4539
	7:10	**threw** them **into** such a **p**	2169
	14:15	Then **p** struck the whole army—	3010
	14:15	It was a **p** sent by God.	3010
Isa	31: 9	battle standard their commanders will **p,"**	3169
Jer	49:24	to flee and **p** has gripped her;	8185
Eze	7: 7	there is **p,** not joy, upon the mountains.	4539
Zec	12: 4	On that day I will strike every horse with **p**	9451
	14:13	be stricken by the LORD with great **p.**	4539

PANNAG (KJV) See CONFECTIONS

PANS (2) [PAN]

2Ch	35:13	caldrons and **p** served them quickly	7505
Ezr	1: 9	silver dishes 1,000 silver **p** 29	4709

PANT (5) [PANTS]

Job	5: 5	and the thirsty **p** after his wealth.	8634
Ps	119:131	I open my mouth and **p,**	8634
Isa	42:14	I cry out, I gasp and **p.**	8634
Jer	14: 6	the barren heights and **p** like jackals;	8120+8634
Joel	1:20	Even the wild animals **p** for you;	6864

PANTED, PANTETH (KJV) See FALTERS, PANT, PANTS, POUNDS

PANTS (2) [PANT]

Ps	42: 1	As the deer **p** for streams of water,	6864
	42: 1	so my soul **p** for you, O God.	6864

PAPER (1)

2Jn	1:12	but I do not want to use **p** and ink.	5925

PAPHOS (2)

Ac	13: 6	the whole island until they came to **P.**	4265
	13:13	From **P,** Paul and his companions sailed	4265

PARAMOURS (KJV) See LOVERS

PAPYRUS (5)

Ex	2: 3	a **p** basket for him and coated it with tar	1687
Job	8:11	Can **p** grow tall where there is no marsh?	1687
	9:26	They skim past like boats of **p,**	15
Isa	18: 2	which sends envoys by sea in **p** boats over	1687
	35: 7	grass and reeds and **p** will grow.	1687

PARABLE (32) [PARABLES]

Eze	17: 2	an allegory and tell the house of Israel a **p.**	5442
	24: 3	Tell this rebellious house a **p** and say	5442
Mt	13:18	then to what the **p** of the sower means:	4130
	13:24	Jesus told them another **p:**	4130
	13:31	He told them another **p:**	4130
	13:33	He told them still another **p:**	4130
	13:34	not say anything to them without using a **p.**	4130
	13:36	to us the **p** of the weeds in the field."	4130

Mt	15:15	Peter said, "Explain the **p** to us."	4130
	21:33	"Listen to another **p:**	4130
Mk	4:13	"Don't you understand this **p?**	4130
	4:13	How then will you understand any **p?**	4130
	4:30	or what **p** shall we use to describe it?	4130
	4:34	not say anything to them without using a **p.**	4130
	7:17	his disciples asked him about this **p.**	4130
	12:12	because they knew he had spoken the **p**	4130
Lk	5:36	He told them this **p:**	4130
	6:39	He also told them this **p:**	4130
	8: 4	he told this **p:**	4130
	8: 9	His disciples asked him what this **p** meant.	4130
	8:11	"This is the meaning of the **p:**	4130
	12:16	And he told them this **p:**	4130
	12:41	"Lord, are you telling this **p** to us,	4130
	13: 6	Then he told this **p:**	4130
	14: 7	he told them this **p:**	4130
	15: 3	Then Jesus told them this **p:**	4130
	18: 1	Then Jesus told his disciples a **p**	4130
	18: 9	Jesus told this **p:**	4130
	19:11	he went on to tell them a **p,**	4130
	20: 9	He went on to tell the people this **p:**	4130
	20:19	because they knew he had spoken this **p**	4130
	21:29	He told them this **p:**	4130

PARABLES (19) [PARABLE]

Ps	78: 2	I will open my mouth in **p,**	5442
Pr	1: 6	for understanding proverbs and **p,**	4886
Eze	20:49	'Isn't he just telling **p?**"	5442
Hos	12:10	gave them many visions and **told p**	1948
Mt	13: 3	he told them many things in **p,** saying:	4130
	13:10	"Why do you speak to the people in **p?**"	4130
	13:13	This is why I speak to them in **p:**	4130
	13:34	spoke all these things to the crowd in **p;**	4130
	13:35	"I will open my mouth in **p,**	4130
	13:53	When Jesus had finished these **p,**	4130
	21:45	and the Pharisees heard Jesus' **p,**	4130
	22: 1	Jesus spoke to them again in **p,** saying:	4130
Mk	3:23	Jesus called them and spoke to them in **p:**	4130
	4: 2	He taught them many things by **p,**	4130
	4:10	around him asked him *about* the **p.**	4130
	4:11	on the outside everything is said in **p**	4130
	4:33	*With* many similar **p** Jesus spoke the word	4130
	12: 1	He then began to speak to them in **p:**	4130
Lk	8:10	but to others I speak in **p,** so that,	4130

PARADE (1)

Isa	3: 9	*they* **p** their sin like Sodom;	5583

PARADISE (3)

Lk	23:43	today you will be with me in **p.**"	4137
2Co	12: 4	was caught up to **p.**	4137
Rev	2: 7	the tree of life, which is in the **p** of God.	4137

PARAH (1)

Jos	18:23	Avvim, **P,** Ophrah,	7240

PARALLEL (5)

Ex	26:17	with two projections **set p** to each other.	8917
	36:22	with two projections **set p** to each other.	8917
Eze	42: 7	an outer wall **p to** the rooms and	4200+6645
	42:12	beginning of the passageway that was **p**	928+7156
	45: 7	the western to the eastern border **p to**	4200+6645

PARALYTIC (9) [PARALYZED]

Mt	9: 2	Some men brought to him a **p,**	4166
	9: 2	he said *to* the **p,** "Take heart, son;	4166
	9: 6	Then he said *to* the **p,** "Get up,	4166
Mk	2: 3	Some men came, bringing to him a **p,**	4166
	2: 5	said *to* the **p,** "Son, your sins are forgiven."	4166
	2: 9	to say *to* the **p,** 'Your sins are forgiven,'	4166
	2:10	He said *to* the **p,**	4166
Lk	5:18	Some men came carrying a **p** on a mat	4168
Ac	9:33	a **p** who had been bedridden for eight years.	4168

PARALYTICS (1) [PARALYZED]

Ac	8: 7	and many **p** and cripples were healed.	4168

PARALYZED (6) [PARALYTIC, PARALYTICS]

Hab	1: 4	Therefore the law *is* **p,**	7028
Mt	4:24	those having seizures, and the **p,**	4166
	8: 6	at home and in terrible suffering."	4166
Mk	2: 4	lowered the mat the **p** *man* was lying on.	4166
Lk	5:24	He said *to* the **p** *man,* "I tell you, get up,	4168
Jn	5: 3	the blind, the lame, the **p.**	3831

PARAN (10)

Ge	21:21	While he was living in the Desert of **P,**	7000
Nu	10:12	the cloud came to rest in the Desert of **P.**	7000
	12:16	and encamped in the Desert of **P.**	7000
	13: 3	sent them out from the Desert of **P.**	7000
	13:26	at Kadesh in the Desert of **P.**	7000
Dt	1: 1	opposite Suph, between **P** and Tophel,	7000
	33: 2	he shone forth from Mount **P.**	7000
1Ki	11:18	They set out from Midian and went to **P.**	7000
	11:18	Then taking men from **P** with them,	7000
Hab	3: 3	the Holy One from Mount **P.**	7000

PARAPET (3)

Dt	22: 8	make a **p** around your roof so that you may	5111
Eze	40:13	from *one* **p** opening to the opposite one.	7339
	40:16	by narrow **p openings** all around, as was	2707

PARBAR (KJV) See COURT

PARCEL (2) [PARCELED]

Ps	60: 6	"In triumph *I will* **p out** Shechem	2745
	108: 7	"In triumph *I will* **p out** Shechem	2745

PARCELED (1) [PARCEL]

Da	11: 4	and **p out** toward the four winds of heaven.	2936

PARCHED (18)

Job	14:11	the sea or a riverbed *becomes* **p** and dry,	2990
	30: 3	the **p** land in desolate wastelands at night.	7480
Ps	69: 3	calling for help; my throat *is* **p.**	3081
	107:35	and the **p** ground into flowing springs;	7480
	143: 6	my soul thirsts for you like a **p** land.	6546
Isa	5:13	and their masses will be **p** with thirst.	7457
	19: 5	and the riverbed *will be* **p** and dry.	2990
	19: 7	sown field along the Nile *will become* **p,**	3312
	35: 1	The desert and the **p** land will be glad;	7480
	41:17	their tongues *are* **p** with thirst.	5980
	41:18	and the **p** ground into springs.	7480
Jer	12: 4	How long *will* the land **lie p**	62
	12:11	a wasteland, **p** and desolate before me;	62
	17: 6	He will dwell in the **p places** of the desert,	3083
	23:10	the curse the land *lies* **p** and the pastures	62
	48:18	from your glory and sit on the **p ground,**	7533
Hos	2: 3	turn her into a **p** land,	7480
Joel	2:20	pushing it into a **p** and barren land,	7480

PARCHMENTS (1)

2Ti	4:13	and my scrolls, especially the **p.**	3521

PARDON (4) [PARDONED, PARDONS]

2Ch	30:18	the LORD, who is good, **p** everyone	4105
Job	7:21	not **p** my offenses and forgive my sins?	5951
Isa	55: 7	and to our God, for he will freely **p.**	6142
Joel	3:21	which I have not pardoned, *I will* **p.**"	5927

PARDONED (2) [PARDON]

Nu	14:19	as *you have* **p** them from the time they left	5951
Joel	3:21	Their bloodguilt, which *I have* not **p,**	5927

PARDONS (1) [PARDON]

Mic	7:18	*who* **p** sin and forgives the transgression of	5951

PARENTS (29) [GRANDPARENTS]

Dt	22:17	Then her **p** shall display the cloth before	NIH
Jdg	14: 4	(His **p** did not know that this was	3+562+2256
	14: 9	When he rejoined his **p,**	3+562+2256
Pr	17: 6	and **p** are the pride of their children.	3
	19:14	Houses and wealth are inherited from **p,**	3
Zec	13: 3	his own **p** will stab him.	3+562+2256
Mt	10:21	against their **p** and have them put to death.	1204
Mk	13:12	against their **p** and have them put to death.	1204
Lk	2:27	When the **p** brought in the child Jesus to do	1204
	2:41	Every year his **p** went to Jerusalem for	1204
	2:43	while **his p** were returning home,	899S
	2:48	When his **p** saw him, they were astonished.	NIG
	8:56	Her **p** were astonished,	1204
	18:29	or **p** or children for the sake of the kingdom	1204
	21:16	You will be betrayed even by **p,** brothers,	1204
Jn	9: 2	this man or his **p,** that he was born blind?"	1204
	9: 3	"Neither this man nor his **p** sinned,"	1204
	9:18	until they sent for the man's **p.**	1204
	9:20	"We know he is our son," the **p** answered,	1204
	9:22	His **p** said this because they were afraid of	1204
	9:23	That was why his **p** said, "He is of age;	1204
Ro	1:30	ways of doing evil; they disobey their **p;**	1204
2Co	12:14	not have to save *up for* their **p,**	1204
	12:14	but **p** for their children.	1204
Eph	6: 1	Children, obey your **p** in the Lord,	1204
Col	3:20	Children, obey your **p** in everything,	1204
1Ti	5: 4	and so repaying their **p and grandparents,**	4591
2Ti	3: 2	abusive, disobedient to their **p,** ungrateful,	1204
Heb	11:23	By faith Moses' **p** hid him for three months	4252

PARKS (1)

Ecc	2: 5	I made gardens and **p** and planted all kinds	7236

PARMASHTA (1)

Est	9: 9	**P,** Arisai, Aridai and Vaizatha,	7269

PARMENAS (1)

Ac	6: 5	also Philip, Procorus, Nicanor, Timon, **P,**	4226

PARNACH (1)

Nu	34:25	of **P,** the leader from the tribe of Zebulun;	7270

PAROSH (6)

Ezr	2: 3	the descendants of **P** 2,172	7283
	8: 3	of the descendants of **P,** Zechariah,	7283
	10:25	From the descendants of **P:**	7283
Ne	3:25	Pedaiah son of **P**	7283

Ne	7: 8	the descendants of **P** 2,172	7283
	10:14	**P,** Pahath-Moab, Elam, Zattu, Bani,	7283

PARSHANDATHA (1)

Est	9: 7	They also killed **P,** Dalphon, Aspatha,	7309

PARSIN (1)

Da	5:25	that was written: MENE, MENE, TEKEL, **P**	10593

PART (97) [APART, PARTED, PARTING, PARTITIONED, PARTLY, PARTS]

Ge	13: 9	*Let's* **p** company.	7233
	19: 4	from **every p** of the city of Sodom—	7895
	27:16	also covered his hands and the **smooth p**	AIT
	47: 6	and your brothers in the **best** *p* of the land.	AIT
	47:11	gave them property in the **best** *p* of the land,	AIT
Ex	12:48	*may* take **p** like one born in the land.	6913+7928
	16:20	they kept **p** *of* it until morning,	4946
	35:24	for any **p** of the work brought it.	4856
Lev	2: 3	it is a **most holy** *p* of the offerings made to	AIT
	2:10	it is a **most holy** *p* of the offerings made to	AIT
	7:29	to bring **p** *of* it as his sacrifice to	4946
	13:45	cover the **lower p** of his **face**	8559
	13:56	he is to tear the **contaminated p** out of	2257S
	24: 9	a most holy *p* of their regular share of	4946
	27:16	" 'If a man dedicates to the LORD **p**	4946
	27:22	which is not *p* of his family land,	4946
Nu	8:24	shall come to **take p** in the work at	7371+7372
	18: 9	the **p** of the most holy offerings that is kept	4946
	18: 9	**that p** belongs to you and your sons.	2085S
	18:29	the LORD's portion the best and holiest **p**	4946
	18:30	'When you present the best **p,**	4946
	18:32	By presenting the best **p** *of* it you will not	4946
	22:41	and from there he saw **p** of the people.	7895
	23:10	of Jacob or number the **fourth p** of Israel?	8065
	23:13	you will see only a **p** but not all of them.	7895
	31:27	the soldiers who **took p** in the battle	3655+4200
	31:29	to Eleazar the priest as the LORD's **p.**	9556
	31:41	to Eleazar the priest as the LORD's **p,**	9556
	36: 3	so *p* of the inheritance allotted to us will	4946
Dt	4:21	for I will not give you any *p* of their land.	3772
	23:13	As *p* of your equipment have something	6584
Jos	2:15	house she lived in was *p* of the city wall.	928
1Sa	30:12	**p** of a cake of pressed figs and two cakes	7115
2Sa	3: 37	Israel knew that the king **had no p** in	2118+4946
	4: 2	Beeroth is considered *p* of Benjamin,	6584
	4: 6	They went into the **inner p** of the house as	9348
	20: 1	no share in David, no **p** in Jesse's son!	5709
	21: 2	(Now the Gibeonites were not a *p* of Israel	4946
	23: 5	arranged and secured in **every** *p*?	AIT
1Ki	7: 5	they were **in the front p** in sets of three,	4578
	7:20	the **bowl-shaped p** next to the network,	1061
	8:64	the **middle** *p* of the courtyard in front of	AIT
	12:16	what **p** in Jesse's son?	5709
1Ch	6:62	from the **p** of the tribe of Manasseh that is	NIH
	21:12	of the LORD ravaging every *p* of Israel.	1473
	23:14	of God were counted **as p** of the tribe	6584
2Ch	7: 7	the **middle** *p* of the courtyard in front of	AIT
	10:16	what **p** in Jesse's son?	5709
	25:13	*to* take **p** in the war raided Judean	2143+6640
Ezr	4:20	"You **have no p** with us in building	4200
Ne	5:11	the **hundredth** *p* of the money, grain,	AIT
Est	2:14	and in the morning return to **another p** *of*	9108
Job	42:12	The LORD blessed the **latter p** of Job's **life**	344
Ps	141: 4	to take **p** in wicked deeds	6618
	144: 5	**P** your heavens, O LORD,	5742
Ecc	9: 6	a **p** in anything that happens under the sun.	2750
Jer	41: 9	as *p* of his defense against Baasha king	NIH
Eze	24:22	not cover the **lower p** of your **face**	8559
	43:21	the **designated p** *of* the temple area outside	5152
	48: 1	of Damascus next to Hamath will be **p**	AIT
Da	6:26	in every *p* of my kingdom people must fear	10717
	8:23	"In the **latter p** of their reign,	344
Zec	14:18	not go up and **take p,**	995
Mt	5:29	for you to lose one **p** of your **body** than	3517
	5:30	for you to lose one **p** of your **body** than	3517
	23:30	not *have* taken **p** with them in shedding the blood of the prophets.'	1639+3128
Lk	11:36	full of light, and no *p* of it dark,	3538
	20:35	worthy of **taking p** in that age and in	5593
Jn	13: 8	you have no **p** with me."	3538
	18:40	Barabbas **had taken p** in a rebellion.	1639+3334
Ac	5: 2	he kept back **p** of the money for himself,	608
	8:21	You **have no p** or share in this ministry,	3535
Ro	11:16	If the **p** of the dough offered	NIG
	11:16	a hardening **in p** until the full number	608+3538
1Co	10:21	you cannot **have a p** in both the Lord's	3576
	10:30	If I **take p** in the meal with thankfulness,	3576
	12:14	Now the body is not made up of one **p** but	3517
	12:15	it would not for that reason cease to be **p** of	1666
	12:16	it would not for that reason cease to be **p** of	1666
	12:19	If they were all one **p,**	3517
	12:26	If one **p** suffers, every part suffers with it;	3517
	12:26	If one **p** suffers, every part suffers with it;	3517
	12:26	if one **p** is honored, every part rejoices	3517
	12:26	every **p** rejoices with it.	3517
	12:27	and each one of you is a **p** of it.	3538
	13: 9	For we know in **p** and we prophesy in part,	3538
	13: 9	we know in **part** and we prophesy in **p,**	3538
	13:12	Now I know in **p;** then I shall know fully,	3538
2Co	1:14	as you have understood us in **p,**	608+3538
	8: 6	to completion this act of grace on your **p.**	NIG
Eph	4:16	as each **p** does its work.	3538

Heb	9:11	that is to say, not a *p* of this **creation**.	AIT
Jas	3: 5	the tongue is a small **p** of the body,	3517
Rev	13:10	and faithfulness *on the p of* **the saints**.	AIT
	14:12	endurance *on the p of* **the saints** who obey God's commandments	AIT
	20: 6	Blessed and holy are those who have **p** in	3538

PARTAKE (1)

1Co	10:17	are one body, for *we* all **p** of the one loaf.	3576

PARTED (7) [PART]

Ge	13:11	The two men **p company**:	7233
	13:14	The LORD said to Abram after Lot *had* **p**	7233
2Sa	1:23	and in death they **were** not **p**.	7233
	22:10	He **p** the heavens and came down;	5742
Job	41:17	they cling together and cannot **be p**.	7233
Ps	18: 9	He **p** the heavens and came down;	5742
Ac	15:39	such a sharp disagreement that they **p company**.	253+608+714

PARTHIANS (1)

Ac	2: 9	**P**, Medes and Elamites;	4222

PARTIAL (1) [PARTIALITY]

Pr	18: 5	It is not good *to be* **p** to the wicked or	5951+7156

PARTIALITY (15) [PARTIAL]

Lev	19:15	*do not* **show p** to the poor or favoritism to the great,	5951+7156
Dt	1:17	*Do not* **show p** in judging;	5795+7156
	10:17	**shows** no **p** and accepts no bribes.	5951+7156
	16:19	Do not pervert justice or **show p.**	5795+7156
2Ch	19: 7	no injustice or **p** or bribery."	5365+7156
Job	13: 8	*Will you* **show** him **p**?	5951+7156
	13:10	rebuke you if *you* secretly **showed p.**	5951+7156
	32:21	*I will* **show p** to no one,	5951+7156
	34:19	who **shows** no **p** *to* princes and does	5951+7156
Ps	82: 2	the unjust and **show p** *to* the wicked?	5951+7156
Pr	24:23	*To* **show p** in judging is not good:	5795+7156
	28:21	*To* **show p** is not good—	5795+7156
Mal	2: 9	not followed my ways but *have* **shown p** in matters of the law."	5951+7156
Lk	20:21	and that *you do* not **show p** but teach	3284+4725
1Ti	5:21	to keep these instructions without **p,**	4622

PARTICIPANTS (1) [PARTICIPATE]

1Co	10:20	and I do not want you to be **p** with demons.	3128

PARTICIPATE (4) [PARTICIPANTS, PARTICIPATION]

Eze	45:16	of the land *will* **p** in this special gift	448+2118
1Co	10:18	*Do not* those who eat the sacrifices **p** in the altar?	1639+3128
1Pe	4:13	rejoice that *you* **p** in the sufferings of Christ,	3125
2Pe	1: 4	*you may* **p** in the divine nature	1181+3128

PARTICIPATION (2) [PARTICIPATE]

1Co	10:16	for which we give thanks a **p** in the blood	3126
	10:16	not the bread that we break a **p** in the body	3126

PARTICULARLY (2)

Zec	11: 7	**p** the oppressed of the flock.	4027+4200
Heb	13:19	I **p** urge you to pray so that I may	4359

PARTIES (5) [PARTY]

Ex	18:16	I decide between **the p** and	408+2084+2256+8276
	22: 9	**both** *p* are to bring their cases before	AIT
1Sa	13:17	**Raiding p** went out from	8845
	14:15	and those in the outposts and **raiding p**—	8845
Job	1:17	"The Chaldeans formed three **raiding p**	8031

PARTING (1) [PART]

Mic	1:14	Therefore you will give **p** gifts	8933

PARTITIONED (1) [PART]

1Ki	6:16	He **p** off twenty cubits at the rear of the	1215

PARTLY (8) [PART]

Da	2:33	its feet **p** of iron and partly of baked clay.	10427
	2:33	its feet partly of iron and **p** of baked clay.	10427
	2:41	that the feet and toes were **p** *of* baked clay	10427
	2:41	of baked clay and **p** *of* iron, so this will be	10427
	2:42	As the toes were **p** iron and partly clay,	10427
	2:42	As the toes were partly iron and **p** clay,	10427
	2:42	so this kingdom will be **p** strong	10427+10636
	2:42	be partly strong and **p** brittle.	10427

PARTNER (6) [PARTNERS, PARTNERSHIP]

Pr	2:17	who has left the **p** *of* her youth and ignored	476
	28:24	he is **p** to him who destroys.	2492
Mal	2:14	though she is your **p,**	2500
2Co	8:23	he is my **p** and fellow worker among you;	3128
Phm	1:17	So if you consider me a **p,**	3128
1Pe	3: 7	and treat them with respect as the weaker **p**	5007

PARTNERS (3) [PARTNER]

Lk	5: 7	So they signaled their **p** in the other boat	3581
	5:10	the sons of Zebedee, Simon's **p.**	3128
Eph	5: 7	Therefore do not be **p** with them.	5212

PARTNERSHIP (1) [PARTNER]

Php	1: 5	of your **p** in the gospel from the first day	3126

PARTRIDGE (2)

1Sa	26:20	as one hunts a **p** in the mountains."	7926
Jer	17:11	Like a **p** that hatches eggs it did not lay is	7926

PARTS (50) [PART]

Ex	12: 9	head, legs and **inner p.**	7931
	29:13	Then take all the fat around the **inner p,**	7931
	29:17	the ram into pieces and wash the **inner p**	7931
	29:22	the fat tail, the fat around the **inner p,**	7931
	29:27	"Consecrate those **p** of the ordination ram	NIH
Lev	1: 9	to wash the **inner p** and the legs with water,	7931
	1:13	to wash the **inner p** and the legs with water,	7931
	3: 3	that covers the **inner p** or is connected	7931
	3: 9	that covers the **inner p** or is connected	7931
	3:14	that covers the **inner p** or is connected	7931
	4: 8	that covers the **inner p** or is connected	7931
	4:11	the **inner p** and offal—	7931
	7: 3	and the fat that covers the **inner p,**	7931
	8:16	also took all the fat around the **inner p,**	7931
	8:21	He washed the **inner p** and the legs	7931
	8:25	the fat tail, all the fat around the **inner p**	7931
	9:14	the **inner p** and the legs and burned them	7931
Dt	18: 3	the shoulder, the jowls and the **inner p.**	7687
	19: 3	Build roads to them and divide into three **p**	1473
	25:11	and seizes him by his **private p,**	4434
Jos	18: 5	You are to divide the land into seven **p.**	2750
	18: 6	of the seven **p** of the land,	2750
	18: 9	town by town, in seven **p,**	2750
Jdg	19:29	into twelve **p** and sent them into all	5984
1Sa	2:29	on the **choice p** *of* every offering made	8040
2Ki	19:23	I have reached its remotest **p,**	4869
1Ch	28:11	its buildings, its storerooms, its **upper p,**	6608
2Ch	3: 9	He also overlaid the **upper p** with gold.	6608
Est	1:22	her dispatches to all **p** *of* the kingdom,	4519
Job	18:13	It eats away **p** *of* his skin;	963
Ps	51: 6	Surely you desire truth in the **inner p;**	3219
Pr	18: 8	they go down to a man's **inmost p.**	1061+2540
	26:22	they go down to a man's **inmost p.**	1061+2540
Da	4:22	and your dominion extends to **distant p** *of*	10509
Ac	2:10	Egypt and the **p** of Libya near Cyrene;	3538
Ro	6:13	Do not offer the **p** of your body to sin,	3517
	6:13	the **p** of your body to him as instruments	3517
	6:19	Just as you used to offer the **p** of your body	3517
1Co	12:12	though it is made up of many **p,**	3517
	12:12	all its **p** are many, they form one body,	3517
	12:18	in fact God has arranged the **p** in the body,	3517
	12:20	As it is, there are many **p,** but one body.	3517
	12:22	those **p** of the body that seem to	3517
	12:23	and the **p** that we think are less honorable we treat with special honor.	3836+4047+5393
	12:23	And the **p** that are unpresentable are treated	NIG
	12:24	our presentable **p** need no special treatment.	NIG
	12:24	and has given greater honor to the **p**	NIG
	12:25	but that its **p** should have equal concern	3517
Jas	3: 6	a world of evil among the **p** of the body.	3517
Rev	16:19	The great city split into three **p,**	3538

PARTY (8) [PARTIES]

Ru	4: 7	one **p** took off his sandal and gave it to	408
1Sa	30: 8	"Shall I pursue this **raiding p?**	1522
	30:15	"Can you lead me down to this **raiding p?**"	1522
Pr	19:18	*do not* **be a** willing **p** to his death.	5883+5951
Ac	5:17	members of the **p** of the Pharisees	146
	15: 5	to the **p** of the Pharisees stood up and said,	146
2Co	7:12	who did the wrong or of **the** injured **p,**	AIT
Gal	3:20	however, does not represent just **one p;**	AIT

PARUAH (1)

1Ki	4:17	Jehoshaphat son of **P**—in Issachar;	7245

PARVAIM (1)

2Ch	3: 6	And the gold he used was gold of **P.**	7246

PAS DAMMIM (2)

2Sa	23: 9	the Philistines gathered [at **P**]	9004
1Ch	11:13	He was with David at **P** when	7169

PASACH (1)

1Ch	7:33	**P,** Bimhal and Ashvath.	7179

PASEAH (4)

1Ch	4:12	**P** and Tehinnah the father of Ir Nahash.	7176
Ezr	2:49	Uzza, **P,** Besai,	7176
Ne	3: 6	of **P** and Meshullam son of Besodeiah;	7176
	7:51	Gazzam, Uzza, **P,**	7176

PASHHUR (13)

1Ch	9:12	the son of **P,** the son of Malkijah;	7319
Ezr	2:38	of **P** 1,247	7319
	10:22	From the descendants of **P:**	7319
Ne	7:41	of **P** 1,247	7319
	10: 3	**P,** Amariah, Malkijah,	7319
Ne	11:12	the son of Zechariah, the son of **P,**	7319
Jer	20: 1	When the priest **P** son of Immer,	7319
	20: 3	when **P** released him from the stocks,	7319
	20: 3	"The LORD's name for you is not **P,**	7319
	20: 6	**P,** and all who live in your house will go	7319
	21: 1	when King Zedekiah sent to him **P** son	7319
	38: 1	Gedaliah son of **P,**	7319
	38: 1	and **P** son of Malkijah heard what Jeremiah	7319

PASS (115) [PASSED, PASSER-BY, PASSES, PASSING]

Ge	18: 3	my lord, *do not* **p** your servant by.	6296
Ex	12:12	that same night *I will* **p** through Egypt	6296
	12:13	*I will* **p over** you.	7173
	12:23	of the doorframe and *will* **p over**	7173
	15:16	until your people **p by,** O LORD,	6296
	15:16	until the people you bought **p by.**	6296
	33:19	**cause** all my goodness to **p** in front of you,	6296
Lev	26: 6	the sword *will* not **p** through your country.	6296
Nu	20:17	Please *let us* **p** through your country.	6296
	20:18	"*You may* not **p** through here;	6296
	20:19	*We only want to* **p** through on foot—	6296
	20:20	"*You may* not **p** through."	6296
	21:22	"*Let us* **p** through your country.	6296
	21:23	not let Israel **p** through his territory.	6296
	34: 4	cross south of Scorpion **P,**	5090
	36: 7	No inheritance in Israel *is to* **p** from tribe	6015
	36: 9	No inheritance *may* **p** from tribe to tribe,	6015
Dt	2:13	'*You are about to* **p** through the territory	6296
	2:18	"Today you are to **p** by the region of Moab	6296
	2:27	"*Let us* **p** through your country.	6296
	2:28	Only *let us* **p** through on foot—	6296
	2:30	of Heshbon refused *to* let us **p** through.	6296
Jos	3: 6	the covenant and **p** on ahead of the people."	6296
	15: 3	crossed south of Scorpion **P,**	5090
	15: 7	which faces the **P** of Adummim south of	5090
	18:17	which faces the **P** of Adummim,	5090
Jdg	1:36	the Amorites was from Scorpion **P** to Sela	5090
	8:13	then returned from the battle by the **P**	5090
	11:19	'*Let us* **p** through your country	6296
	11:20	not trust Israel *to* **p** through his territory.	6296
1Sa	9: 8	of Philistines had gone out to the **p**	5044
	14: 4	of the **p** that Jonathan intended to cross	5045
	16: 8	Then Jesse called Abinadab and had him **p**	6296
	16: 9	Jesse then had Shammah **p,**	6296
	16:10	had seven of his sons **p** before Samuel,	6296
1Ki	9: 8	all who **p** by will be appalled and will scoff	6296
	19:11	for the LORD *is about to* **p** by."	6296
2Ki	19:25	now *I have* **brought** it *to* **p,**	995
1Ch	28: 8	**p** *it* on as an **inheritance**	5706
2Ch	7:21	all who **p** by will be appalled and say,	6296
	20:16	They will be climbing up by the **P** of Ziz,	5090
Job	16:22	"Only a few years *will* **p** before I go on	910
	19: 8	He has blocked my way so *I* cannot **p;**	6296
	34:20	the people are shaken and *they* **p away.**	6296
	41:16	to the next that no air *can* **p** between.	995
Ps	80:12	so that all *who* **p** by pick its grapes?	2006+6296
	84: 6	*As they* **p** through the Valley of Baca,	6296
	89:41	All *who* **p** by have plundered him;	2006+6296
	90: 9	All our days **p away** under your wrath;	7155
	90:10	for they quickly **p,** and we fly away.	1577
	105:19	till what he foretold **came to p,**	995
	129: 8	May those *who* **p** by not say,	6296
	141:10	while I **p** by in safety.	6296
	148: 6	he gave a decree *that will* never **p away.**	6296
Pr	9:15	calling out *to* those *who* **p** by,	2006+6296
Isa	10:28	They enter Aiath; *they* **p** through Migron;	6296
	10:29	They go over the **p,** and say,	5045
	31: 5	he will '**p over**' it and will rescue it."	7173
	34:10	no one will ever **p** through it again.	6296
	37:26	now *I have* **brought** it *to* **p,**	995
	43: 2	When *you* **p** through the waters,	6296
	43: 2	and when you **p** through the rivers,	NIH
	48: 3	then suddenly I acted, and *they* **came** to **p.**	995
	62:10	**P through,** pass through the gates!	6296
	62:10	Pass through, **p** through the gates!	6296
Jer	2:35	*I will* **p** judgment *on* you because you say,	9149
	6: 9	**p** your hand over the branches **again,**	8740
	18:16	all *who* **p** by will be appalled	6296
	19: 8	all *who* **p** by will be appalled and will scoff	6296
	22: 8	from many nations *will* **p** by this city	6296
	33:13	flocks *will* again **p** under the hand of	6296
	49:17	all *who* **p** by will be appalled and will scoff	6296
	50:13	All *who* **p** Babylon will be horrified.	6296
La	1:12	Is it nothing to you, all *you who* **p** by?	2006+6296
	2:15	All *who* **p** your way clap their hands at you;	6296
Eze	5:14	in the sight of all *who* **p** by.	6296
	14:15	so that no *one can* **p** through it because of	6296
	14:17	'*Let the* sword **p** throughout the land,'	6296
	20:37	**take note** *of* you as you **p**	6296
	29:11	of man or animal *will* **p** through it;	6296
	36:34	in the sight of all *who* **p** through it.	6296
	48:14	the land and *must* not **p** into other hands,	10528
Da	4:16	till seven times **p** by for him.	10268
	4:23	until seven times **p** by for him.'	10268
	4:25	Seven times *will* **p** by for you	10268
	4:32	Seven times *will* **p** by for you	10268
	7:14	everlasting dominion *that will* not **p away.**	10528
Am	5:17	for *I will* **p** through your midst,"	6296
Mic	1:11	**P** on in nakedness and shame,	6296
	2: 8	the rich robe *from those who* **p** by without	6296
	2:13	Their king *will* **p through** before them,	6296
Na	1:12	they will be cut off and **p** away.	6296
Zep	2:15	All *who* **p** by her scoff and shake their fists.	6296
Zec	10:11	*They will* **p** through the sea of trouble;	6296
	10:11	and Egypt's scepter *will* **p away.**	6073

Mt	8:28	They were so violent that no one could **p**	4216
	24:34	this generation *will* certainly not **p away**	4216
	24:35	Heaven and earth *will* **p away**,	4216
	24:35	but my words *will* never **p away**.	4216
Mk	6:48	He was about to **p** by them,	4216
	13:30	this generation *will* certainly not **p away**	4216
	13:31	Heaven and earth *will* **p away**,	4216
	13:31	but my words *will* never **p away**.	4216
	14:35	and prayed that if possible the hour *might* **p**	4216
Lk	21:32	this generation *will* certainly not **p away**	4216
	21:33	Heaven and earth *will* **p away**,	4216
	21:33	but my words *will* never **p away**.	4216
Jn	8:15	I **p** judgment on no one.	3212
Ac	7:38	and he received living words *to* **p on** to us.	1443
Ro	2: 1	you who **p judgment on** someone else,	3212
	2: 1	you who **p judgment** do the same things.	3212
	2: 3	**p judgment on** them and yet do	3212
1Co	13: 8	where there is knowledge, *it will* **p away**.	2934
Jas	1:10	because *he will* **p away** like a wild flower.	4216
1Jn	2:17	The world and its desires **p away**,	4135

PASSAGE (4) [PASSAGEWAY]

Ac	8:32	The eunuch was reading this **p** of Scripture:	4343
	8:35	with that very **p** of Scripture and told him	NIG
Ro	11: 2	the Scripture says in the **p** about Elijah—	NIG
Heb	4: 5	And again in **the p above** he says,	4047

PASSAGEWAY (3) [PASSAGE]

Eze	42: 4	of the rooms was an inner **p** ten cubits wide	4544
	42:11	with a **p** in front of them.	2006
	42:12	the beginning of the **p** that was parallel to	2006

PASSED (78) [PASS]

Ge	15:17	a blazing torch appeared and **p** between	6296
	32:31	The sun rose above him as *he* **p** Peniel,	6296
	41: 1	When two full years had **p**,	7891
	50: 4	When the days of mourning *had* **p**,	6296
Ex	7:25	Seven days **p** after the LORD struck	4848
	12:27	who **p over** the houses of the Israelites	7173
	33:22	with my hand until I have **p by**.	6296
	34: 6	And he **p** in front of Moses, proclaiming,	6296
Lev	25:30	not redeemed before a full year *has* **p**,	4848
Nu	14: 7	"The land *we* **p** through	6296
	20:17	until *we have* **p through** your territory."	6296
	21:22	the king's highway until *we have* **p through**	6296
	33: 8	They left Pi Hahiroth and **p** through the sea	6296
Dt	2:14	Thirty-eight years **p** from the time	NIH
	29:16	and how *we* **p** through the countries on	6296
Jos	3:17	while all Israel **p by** until the whole nation	6296
	15: 4	*It* then **p along** to Azmon and joined	6296
	15:11	**p along** to Mount Baalah	6296
	18:12	**p** the northern slope of Jericho	6590
	23: 1	After a long time *had* **p** and	2118
Jdg	3:26	He **p** by the idols and escaped to Seirah.	6296
	9:25	to ambush and rob everyone who **p** by,	6296
	11:18	**p** along the eastern side of the country	995
	11:29	**p through** Mizpah of Gilead,	6296
1Sa	9: 4	So *he* **p** through the hill country of Ephraim	6296
	9: 4	*he* **p** through the territory of Benjamin,	6296
2Sa	15:23	wept aloud as all the people **p by**.	6296
	20:14	Sheba **p** through all the tribes of Israel	6296
1Ki	13:25	Some people *who* **p** by saw the body thrown	6296
	18:29	Midday **p**, and they continued their frantic	6296
	20:39	As the king **p** by, the prophet called out	6296
2Ch	21:20	He **p away**, to no one's regret,	2143
Ne	9:11	so that their **p** through it on dry ground,	6296
	12:37	and **p** above the house of David to	NIH
Est	4:11	But thirty days have **p** since I was called	NIH
Job	14:13	and conceal me till your anger *has* **p**!	8740
	15:19	the land was given when no alien **p**	6296
	17:11	My days have **p**, my plans are shattered,	6296
Ps	37:36	but he soon **p away** and was no more;	6296
	57: 1	of your wings until the disaster *has* **p**.	6296
	66: 6	*they* **p** through the waters on foot—	6296
SS	3: 4	Scarcely had *I* **p** them when I found	6296
Isa	26:20	for a little while until his wrath *has* **p by**.	6296
La	4:21	But to you also the cup will be **p**;	6296
Eze	16: 6	"'Then *I* **p** by and saw you kicking about	6296
	16: 8	"'Later *I* **p** by, and when I looked at you	6296
	16:15	lavished your favors on anyone who **p by**	6296
	16:25	promiscuity to anyone *who* **p** by.	6296
Da	2:28	and the *visions that* **p** through your mind	AIT
	4: 5	images and *visions that* **p** through my mind	AIT
	7: 1	and *visions* **p** through his mind	AIT
	7:15	and the *visions that* **p** through my mind	AIT
Mt	27:39	Those who **p** by hurled insults at him,	4182
Mk	9:30	*They* left that place and **p** through Galilee.	4182
	15:29	Those who **p** by hurled insults at him,	4182
Lk	10:31	**p** by on the other side.	524
	10:32	**p** by on the other side.	524
Ac	5:15	on some of them *as he* **p** by.	2262
	7:30	"After forty years had **p**,	4444
	12:10	*They* **p** the first and second guards	1451
	16: 8	*they* **p** by Mysia and went down to Troas.	4216
	17: 1	*When they had* **p through** Amphipolis	1476
	24:27	*When* two years had **p**,	4444
	27: 4	and **p to the lee** of Cyprus	5709
	27:16	**p to the lee** of a small island called Cauda,	5720
	27:17	**p** ropes **under** the ship itself **to hold** it **together**.	5690
1Co	5: 3	*I have* already **p judgment on** the one	3212
	10: 1	under the cloud and that *they* all **p through**	1451
	11: 2	just as *I* **p** them on to you.	4140
	11:23	from the Lord what *I* also **p on** to you:	4140
	15: 3	For what I received *I* **p on** to you as	4140

2Th	2:15	and hold to the teachings we **p on** to you,	4142
Heb	11:29	By faith the people **p through** the Red Sea	1329
2Pe	2:21	the sacred command *that was* **p on** to them.	4140
1Jn	3:14	We know that *we have* **p** from death to life,	3553
Rev	11:14	The second woe *has* **p**;	599
	21: 1	first heaven and the first earth *had* **p away**,	599
	21: 4	for the old order of things *has* **p away**."	599

PASSER-BY (2) [PASS]

Pr	26:10	at random is he who hires a fool or any **p**.	6296
	26:17	by the ears is a **p** who meddles in a quarrel	6296

PASSES (5) [PASS]

Ex	33:22	When my glory **p** by,	6296
Lev	27:32	that **p** under the shepherd's rod—	6296
Job	9:11	When *he* **p** me, I cannot see him;	6296
Ecc	6:12	the few and meaningless days *he* **p through**	6913
Jer	17:16	What **p** my lips is open before you.	4604

PASSING (20) [PASS]

Jos	16: 6	**p** by it to Janoah on the east.	6296
	19:27	**p** Cabul on the left.	3655
	19:33	**p** Adami Nekeb and Jabneel to Lakkum	NIH
2Ki	6: 9	"Beware of **p** that place,	6296
	6:26	As the king of Israel was **p** by on the wall,	6296
Ps	78:39	a **p** breeze that does not return.	2143
Isa	8: 8	**p through** it and reaching up to the neck.	6296
Zep	3: 6	with no *one* **p through**.	6296
Mk	15:21	was **p** by on his way in from the country,	4135
Lk	18:37	They told him, "Jesus of Nazareth *is* **p** by."	4216
	19: 1	Jesus entered Jericho and *was* **p through**.	1451
Jn	1:36	When he saw Jesus **p** by, he said, "Look,	4344
Ac	19:21	**p through** Macedonia and Achaia.	1451
	21: 3	After sighting Cyprus and **p** to the south	2901
Ro	14: 1	without **p** *judgment* on disputable matters.	1360
	14:13	*let us* stop **p judgment** on one another.	3212
	15:24	*while* **p through** and to have you assist me	1388
1Co	7:31	this world in its present form *is* **p away**.	4135
	16: 7	to see you now and make only a **p** visit;	4227
1Jn	2: 8	because the darkness *is* **p** and the true light	4135

PASSION (2) [PASSIONATE, PASSIONS]

Hos	7: 6	Their **p** smolders all night;	678
1Co	7: 9	for it is better to marry than *to* **burn with p**.	4792

PASSIONATE (1) [PASSION]

1Th	4: 5	not in **p** lust like the heathen, who do	2123

PASSIONS (4) [PASSION]

Ro	7: 5	the sinful **p** aroused by the law were	4077
Gal	5:24	the sinful nature with its **p** and desires.	4077
Tit	2:12	to say "No" to ungodliness and worldly **p**,	2123
	3: 3	deceived and enslaved by all kinds of **p**	2123

PASSOVER (77)

Ex	12:11	Eat it in haste; it is the LORD's **P**.	7175
	12:21	for your families and slaughter the **P lamb**.	7175
	12:27	'It is the **P** sacrifice to the LORD,	7175
	12:43	"These are the regulations for the **P**:	7175
	12:48	to celebrate the LORD's **P** must have all	7175
	34:25	of the sacrifice from the **P** Feast remain	7175
Lev	23: 5	The LORD's **P** begins at twilight on	7175
Nu	9: 2	"Have the Israelites celebrate the **P** at	7175
	9: 4	Moses told the Israelites to celebrate the **P**,	7175
	9: 6	But some of them could not celebrate the **P**	7175
	9:10	they may still celebrate the LORD's **P**.	7175
	9:12	When they celebrate the **P**,	7175
	9:13	not on a journey fails to celebrate the **P**,	7175
	9:14	the LORD's **P** must do so in accordance	7175
	28:16	of the first month the LORD's **P** is to	7175
	33: 3	the day after the **P**.	7175
Dt	16: 1	the month of Abib and celebrate the **P** of	7175
	16: 2	as the **P** to the LORD your God an animal	7175
	16: 5	You must not sacrifice the **P** in any town	7175
	16: 6	There you must sacrifice the **P** in	7175
Jos	5:10	the Israelites celebrated the **P**.	7175
	5:11	The day after the **P**, that very day,	7175
2Ki	23:21	"Celebrate the **P** to the LORD your God,	7175
	23:22	had any such **P** been observed.	7175
	23:23	this **P** was celebrated to the LORD	7175
2Ch	30: 1	in Jerusalem and celebrate the **P** to	7175
	30: 2	in Jerusalem and celebrate the **P** in	7175
	30: 5	to come to Jerusalem and celebrate the **P** to	7175
	30:15	the **P** lamb on the fourteenth day of	7175
	30:17	to kill the **P** lambs for all those who were	7175
	30:18	not purified themselves, yet they ate the **P**,	7175
	35: 1	Josiah celebrated the **P** to the LORD	7175
	35: 1	and the **P** lamb was slaughtered on	7175
	35: 6	Slaughter the **P** lambs,	7175
	35: 7	and goats for the **P offerings**, and	7175
	35: 8	the priests twenty-six hundred **P offerings**	7175
	35: 9	provided five thousand **P offerings**	7175
	35:11	The **P** lambs were slaughtered.	7175
	35:13	the **P** animals over the fire as prescribed,	7175
	35:16	for the celebration of the **P** and the offering	7175
	35:17	the **P** at that time and observed the Feast	7175
	35:18	The **P** had not been observed like this	7175
	35:18	of Israel had ever celebrated such a **P**	7175
	35:19	This **P** was celebrated in	7175
Ezr	6:19	the exiles celebrated the **P**.	7175
	6:20	The Levites slaughtered the **P** lamb for all	7175
Eze	45:21	to observe the **P**, a feast lasting seven days,	7175

Mt	26: 2	the **P** is two days away—	4247
	26:17	to make preparations for you to eat the **P?"**	4247
	26:18	the **P** with my disciples at your house.' "	4247
	26:19	and prepared the **P**.	4247
Mk	14: 1	the **P** and the Feast of Unleavened Bread	4247
	14:12	it was customary to sacrifice the **P lamb**,	4247
	14:12	make preparations for you to eat the **P?"**	4247
	14:14	where I may eat the **P** with my disciples?'	4247
	14:16	So they prepared the **P**.	4247
Lk	2:41	to Jerusalem for the Feast *of* the **P**.	4247
	22: 1	Feast of Unleavened Bread, called the **P**,	4247
	22: 7	on which the **P** lamb had to be sacrificed,	4247
	22: 8	and make preparations for us to eat the **P**."	4247
	22:11	where I may eat the **P** with my disciples?'	4247
	22:13	So they prepared the **P**.	4247
	22:15	desired to eat this **P** with you before I suffer	4247
Jn	2:13	When it was almost time for the Jewish **P**,	4247
	2:23	while he was in Jerusalem at the **P** Feast,	4247
	4:45	in Jerusalem at the **P Feast**,	2038
	6: 4	The Jewish **P** Feast was near.	4247
	11:55	When it was almost time for the Jewish **P**,	4247
	11:55	for their ceremonial cleansing before the **P**.	4247
	12: 1	Six days before the **P**,	4247
	13: 1	It was just before the **P** Feast.	4247
	18:28	they wanted to be able to eat the **P**.	4247
	18:39	to you one prisoner at the time of the **P**.	4247
	19:14	It was the day of Preparation *of* **P** Week,	4247
Ac	12: 4	to bring him out for public trial after the **P**.	4247
1Co	5: 7	Christ, our **P lamb**, has been sacrificed.	4247
Heb	11:28	By faith he kept the **P** and the sprinkling	4247

PAST (48)

Ge	18:11	and Sarah was **p** the age of childbearing.	2532
	31:52	not go **p** this heap to your side to harm you	6296
	31:52	that you *will* not go **p** this heap and pillar	6296
Ex	4:10	neither in the **p** nor since you have	8997+9453
Dt	2: 8	**p** our brothers the descendants of Esau,	907+4946
	32: 7	consider the **generations long p**.	
			1887+1887+2256+9102
Jos	13:16	and the whole plateau **p** Medeba	6584
	15: 3	Then *it ran* **p** Hezron up to Addar	6296
1Sa	15:32	"Surely the bitterness of death is **p**."	6073
2Sa	5: 2	**In the p**, while Saul was king over us,	
			919+1685+1685+8997
	15:18	All his men **marched p** him,	3338+6296+6584
	15:34	I was your father's servant in the **p**,	255
1Ch	11: 2	**In the p**, even while Saul was king,	8997+9453
Ne	12:38	the Tower of the Ovens to	4946+6584
Job	4:15	A spirit **glided p** my face,	2736
	9:26	*They* skim **p** like boats of papyrus,	2736
	36:26	The number of his years is **p** finding out.	4202
Pr	24:30	*I* went **p** the field of the sluggard,	6584
	24:30	**p** the vineyard of the man who lacks	6584
Ecc	3:15	and God will call the **p** to account.	8103
SS	2:11	winter *is* **p**; the rains are over and gone.	6296
Isa	9: 1	the **p** he humbled the land of Zebulun	6961+8037
	43:18	do not dwell on the **p**.	7719
	43:26	**Review the p** *for* me,	2349
	45:21	who declared it from the **distant p**?	255
	65:16	the **p** troubles will be forgotten and hidden	8037
Jer	8:20	"The harvest is **p**, the summer has ended,	6296
	21: 2	perform wonders for us **as in times p**	3869+3972
	31: 3	the LORD appeared to us in the **p**, saying:	8158
	46:26	Egypt will be inhabited as in times **p**,"	7710
Eze	36:11	I will settle people on you as in the **p**	7712
	47:15	the Hethlon road **p** Lebo Hamath to Zedad,	NIH
Hab	1:11	*they* sweep **p** like the wind and go on—	2736
Zec	7: 5	and seventh months for the **p** seventy years,	NIH
	7: 7	of this people as I did in the **p**,"	3427+8037
Ac	14:16	In the **p**, he let all nations go their own way.	
			1155+4233
	17:30	*In the* **p** God overlooked such ignorance,	5989
	20:16	*to* sail **p** Ephesus to avoid spending time	4179
Ro	15: 4	For everything that *was* **written in the p**	4592
	16:25	of the mystery hidden for long ages **p**,	NIG
Eph	3: 9	which *for* **ages p** was kept hidden in God,	172
Heb	1: 1	**In the p** God spoke to our forefathers	4093
	11:11	even though he was **p** age—	4123
1Pe	3: 5	For this is the way the holy women **of the p**	4537
	4: 3	in the **p** doing what pagans choose to do—	4216
2Pe	1: 9	that he has been cleansed from his **p** sins.	4093
	3: 2	to recall the words **spoken in the p** by	4625
Rev	9:12	The first woe *is* **p**;	599

PASTOR (KJV) See SHEPHERD

PASTORS (1)

Eph	4:11	and some to be **p** and teachers,	4478

PASTURE (41) [PASTURED, PASTURELAND, PASTURELANDS, PASTURES]

Ge	29: 7	Water the sheep and take them back to **p**."	8286
	47: 4	and your servants' flocks have no **p**.	5337
2Sa	7: 8	from the **p** and from following the flock to	5659
1Ch	4:39	of the valley in search of **p** for their flocks.	5337
	4:40	They found rich, good **p**,	5337
	4:41	because there was **p** for their flocks.	5337
	17: 7	I took you from the **p** and from following	5659
Job	24: 2	*they* **p** flocks they have stolen.	8286
	39: 8	for his **p** and searches for any green thing.	5337
Ps	37: 3	dwell in the land and **enjoy** safe **p**.	8286
	74: 1	against the sheep of your **p**?	5338

Ps	79:13	Then we your people, the sheep of your p,	5338
	95: 7	and we are the people of his p,	5338
	100: 3	we are his people, the sheep of his p.	5338
Isa	5:17	Then sheep will graze as in their own p;	1824
	14:30	The poorest of the poor will find p,	8286
	32:14	the delight of donkeys, a p for flocks,	5337
	49: 9	"They will feed beside the roads and find p	5338
	65:10	Sharon will become a p for flocks,	5659
Jer	14: 6	their eyesight fails for lack of p."	6912
	23: 1	and scattering the sheep of my p!"	5338
	23: 3	and will bring them back to their p,	5659
	25:36	for the LORD is destroying their p.	5338
	49:20	he will completely destroy their p because	5659
	50: 7	sinned against the LORD, their true p,	5659
	50:19	to his own p and he will graze on Carmel	5659
	50:45	he will completely destroy their p because	5659
La	1: 6	Her princes are like deer that find no p;	5337
Eze	25: 5	I will turn Rabbah into a p for camels	5659
	34:13	I will tend them on the mountains of Israel,	8286
	34:14	I will tend them in a good p,	5337
	34:14	in a rich p on the mountains of Israel.	5337
	34:18	not enough for you to feed on the good p?	5337
	34:18	Must you also trample the rest of your p	5337
	34:31	You my sheep, the sheep of my p,	5338
Hos	4:16	then can the LORD p them like lambs in	8286
Joel	1:18	herds mill about because they have no p;	5337
Mic	2:12	like a flock in its p;	1824
Zep	2: 7	there they will find p.	8286
Zec	11: 4	"P the flock marked for slaughter.	8286
Jn	10: 9	He will come in and go out, and find p.	3786

PASTURE-FED (1) [FEED]

1Ki	4:23	of p cattle and a hundred sheep and goats,	8297

PASTURED (2) [PASTURE]

Zec	11: 7	So I p the flock marked for slaughter,	8286
	11: 7	and I p the flock.	8286

PASTURELAND (8) [PASTURE]

Lev	25:34	But the p belonging to their towns	4494+8441
Nu	35: 5	They will have this area as p for the towns.	4494
Jos	21:11	Hebron), with its surrounding p,	4494
Jer	49:19	up from Jordan's thickets to a rich p,	5659
	50:44	up from Jordan's thickets to a rich p,	5659
Eze	36: 5	so that they might plunder its p.'	4494
	48:15	use of the city, for houses and for p.	4494
	48:17	The p for the city will be 250 cubits on	4494

PASTURELANDS (43) [PASTURE]

Nu	35: 2	And give them p around the towns.	4494
	35: 3	Then they will have towns to live in and p	4494
	35: 4	"The p around the towns that you give	4494
	35: 7	together with their p.	4494
Jos	14: 4	with p for their flocks and herds.	4494
	21: 2	with p for our livestock."	4494
	21: 3	the Levites the following towns and p out	4494
	21: 8	to the Levites these towns and their p,	4494
	21:16	together with their p—nine towns.	4494
	21:18	together with their p—four towns.	4494
	21:19	were thirteen, together with their p.	4494
	21:22	together with their p—four towns.	4494
	21:24	together with their p—four towns.	4494
	21:25	together with their p—two towns.	4494
	21:26	All these ten towns and their p were given	4494
	21:27	and Be Eshtarah, together with their p—	4494
	21:29	together with their p—four towns;	4494
	21:31	together with their p—four towns;	4494
	21:32	together with their p—three towns.	4494
	21:33	together with their p.	4494
	21:35	together with their p—four towns;	4494
	21:37	together with their p—four towns;	4494
	21:39	together with their p—four towns in all.	4494
	21:41	together with their p.	4494
	21:42	Each of these towns had p surrounding it;	4494
1Ch	5:16	the p of Sharon as far as they extended.	4494
	6:55	in Judah with its surrounding p,	4494
	6:59	together with their p.	4494
	6:60	together with their p.	4494
	6:64	the Levites these towns and their p.	4494
	6:69	together with their p.	4494
	6:70	together with their p,	4494
	6:71	and also Ashtaroth, together with their p;	4494
	6:73	Ramoth and Anem, together with their p;	4494
	6:75	Hukok and Rehob, together with their p;	4494
	6:76	together with their p.	4494
	6:77	Rimmono and Tabor, together with their p;	4494
	6:79	together with their p;	4494
	6:81	Heshbon and Jazer, together with their p.	4494
	13: 2	with them in their towns and p,	4494
2Ch	11:14	even abandoned their p and property,	4494
Ps	83:12	"Let us take possession of the p of God."	5661
Mic	7:14	by itself in a forest, in fertile p.	4149

PASTURES (10) [PASTURE]

Ps	23: 2	He makes me lie down in green p,	5661
Jer	9:10	up a lament concerning the desert p.	5661
	23:10	the curse the land lies parched and the p in	5661
	33:12	be p for shepherds to rest their flocks.	5659
Eze	45:15	of two hundred from the well-watered p	NIH
Joel	1:19	the open p and flames have burned up all	5661
	1:20	up and fire has devoured the open p.	5661
	2:22	for the open p are becoming green.	5661
Am	1: 2	the p of the shepherds dry up,	5661
Zec	11: 3	their rich p are destroyed!	168

PATARA (1)

Ac	21: 1	to Rhodes and from there to P.	4249

PATCH (6) [PATCHED]

Jer	10: 5	Like a scarecrow in a melon p,	5252
Mt	9:16	a p of unshrunk cloth on an old garment,	2099
	9:16	for the p will pull away from the garment,	NIG
Mk	2:21	a p of unshrunk cloth on an old garment.	2099
Lk	5:36	a p from a new garment and sews it on	2099
	5:36	the p from the new will not match the old.	2099

PATCHED (1) [PATCH]

Jos	9: 5	The men put worn and p sandals	3229

PATH (61) [BYPATHS, PATHS]

Ge	49:17	a viper along the p,	784
Nu	22:24	the angel of the LORD stood in a narrow p	5469
	22:32	because your p is a reckless one before me.	2006
2Sa	22:37	You broaden the p beneath me,	7576
Ne	9:19	not cease to guide them on their p,	2006
Job	18:10	a trap lies in his p.	5985
	22:15	to the old p that evil men have trod?	784
	24: 4	from the p and force all the poor of the land	2006
	28: 7	No bird of prey knows that hidden p,	5985
	28:26	when he made a decree for the rain and a p	2006
	29: 6	when my p was drenched with cream and	2141
	31: 7	if my steps have turned from the p,	2006
	38:25	and a p for the thunderstorm,	2006
Ps	16:11	You have made known to me the p of life;	784
	18:36	You broaden the p beneath me,	7576
	27:11	in a straight p because of my oppressors.	784
	35: 6	may their p be dark and slippery,	2006
	44:18	our feet had not strayed from your p.	784
	57: 6	They dug a pit in my p—	4200+7156
	77:19	Your p led through the sea,	2006
	78:50	He prepared a p for his anger;	5985
	119:32	I run in the p of your commands,	2006
	119:35	Direct me in the p of your commands,	5985
	119:101	I have kept my feet from every evil p so	784
	119:104	therefore I hate every wrong p.	784
	119:105	a lamp to my feet and a light for my p.	5986
	119:128	I hate every wrong p.	784
	140: 5	and have set traps for me along my p.	5047
	142: 3	In the p where I walk men have hidden	784
Pr	2: 9	right and just and fair—every good p.	5047
	4:14	not set foot on the p of the wicked or walk	784
	4:18	The p of the righteous is like	784
	5: 8	Keep to a p far from her,	2006
	12:28	along that p is immortality.	5986
	15:10	discipline awaits him who leaves the p;	784
	15:19	but the p of the upright is a highway.	784
	15:24	The p of life leads upward for the wise	784
	16:29	and leads him down a p that is not good.	2006
	21:16	from the p of understanding comes to rest	2006
	23:19	and keep your heart on the right p.	784
	28:10	along an evil p will fall into his own trap,	2006
Ecc	11: 5	As you do not know the p of the wind,	2006
Isa	3:12	they turn you from the p.	784+2006
	26: 7	The p of the righteous is level;	784
	30:11	Leave this way, get off this p,	784
	40:14	or showed him the p of understanding?	2006
	41: 3	by a p his feet have not traveled before.	784
	43:16	a p through the mighty waters,	5986
Jer	23:12	"Therefore their p will become slippery;	2006
	31: 9	on a level p where they will not stumble,	2006
La	3:11	he dragged me from the p and mangled me	2006
Hos	2: 6	Therefore I will block her p	2006
	13: 7	like a leopard I will lurk by the p.	2006
Mt	13: 4	some fell along the p,	3847
	13:19	This is the seed sown along the p.	3847
Mk	4: 4	some fell along the p.	3847
	4:15	Some people are like seed along the p,	3847
Lk	1:79	to guide our feet into the p of peace."	3847
	8: 5	some fell along the p;	3847
	8:12	Those along the p are the ones who hear,	3847
2Co	6: 3	We put no stumbling block in anyone's p,	NIG

PATHRUSITES (2)

Ge	10:14	P, Casluhites (from whom the Philistines	7357
1Ch	1:12	P, Casluhites (from whom the Philistines	7357

PATHS (41) [PATH]

Jdg	5: 6	travelers took to winding p.	784
Job	13:27	on all my p by putting marks on the soles	784
	19: 8	he has shrouded my p in darkness.	5986
	24:13	who do not know its ways or stay in its p.	5986
	33:11	he keeps close watch on all my p.'	784
	38:20	Do you know the p to their dwellings?	5986
Ps	8: 8	all that swim the p of the seas.	784
	17: 5	My steps have held to your p;	5047
	23: 3	in p of righteousness for his name's sake.	5047
	25: 4	O LORD, teach me your p;	2006
Pr	1:15	do not set foot on their p;	5986
	2:13	the straight p to walk in dark ways,	784
	2:15	whose p are crooked and who are devious	5047
	2:18	to death and her p to the spirits of the dead.	5047
	2:19	return or attain the p of life.	784
	2:20	and keep to the p of the righteous.	784
	3: 6	and he will make your p straight.	784
	3:17	and all her p are peace.	5986
	4:11	of wisdom and lead you along straight p.	5047
	4:26	Make level p for your feet	5047
	5: 6	her p are crooked, but she knows it not.	5047

Pr	5:21	and he examines all his p.	5047
	7:25	to her ways or stray into her p.	5986
	8: 2	where the p meet, she takes her stand;	5986
	8:20	along the p of justice,	5986
	10: 9	he who takes crooked p will be found out.	2006
	22: 5	the p of the wicked lie thorns and snares,	2006
Isa	2: 3	so that we may walk in his p."	784
	42:16	along unfamiliar p I will guide them;	5986
	59: 8	there is no justice in their p.	5047
Jer	6:16	ask for the ancient p,	5986
	18:15	in their ways and in the ancient p,	8666
La	3: 9	he has made my p crooked.	5986
Hos	5: 9	yet snares await him on all his p,	2006
Mic	4: 2	so that we may walk in his p."	784
Mt	3: 3	make straight p for him.' "	5561
Mk	1: 3	make straight p for him.' "	5561
Lk	3: 4	make straight p for him.	5561
Ac	2:28	You have made known to me the p of life;	3847
Ro	11:33	and his p beyond tracing out!	3847
Heb	12:13	"Make level p for your feet,"	5579

PATIENCE (17) [PATIENT]

Pr	19:11	A man's wisdom gives him p;	678+799
	25:15	Through a ruler can be persuaded,	678+802
Ecc	7: 8	and p is better than pride.	800+8120
Isa	7:13	Is it not enough to try the p of men?	4206
	7:13	Will you try the p of my God also?	4206
Ro	2: 4	the riches of his kindness, tolerance and p,	3429
	9:22	bore with great p the objects of his wrath—	3429
2Co	6: 6	understanding, p and kindness;	3429
Gal	5:22	the fruit of the Spirit is love, joy, peace, p,	3429
Col	1:11	that you may have great endurance and p,	3429
	3:12	kindness, humility, gentleness and p.	3429
1Ti	1:16	Christ Jesus might display his unlimited p	3429
2Ti	3:10	my way of life, my purpose, faith, p, love,	3429
	4: 2	with great p and careful instruction.	3429+4246
Heb	6:12	and p inherit what has been promised.	3429
Jas	5:10	as an example of p in the face of suffering,	3429
2Pe	3:15	in mind that our Lord's p means salvation,	3429

PATIENT (19) [PATIENCE, PATIENTLY]

Ne	9:30	For many years you were p with them.	5432
Job	6:11	What prospects, that I should be p?	799
Pr	14:29	A p man has great understanding,	678+800
	15:18	but a p man calms a quarrel.	678+800
	16:32	Better a p man than a warrior,	678+800
Mt	18:26	'Be p with me,' he begged,	3428
	18:29	'Be p with me, and I will pay you back.'	3428
Ro	12:12	Be joyful in hope, p in affliction,	5702
1Co	13: 4	Love is p, love is kind.	3428
2Co	1: 6	which produces in you p endurance of	5705
Eph	4: 2	be p, bearing with one another in love.	3429
1Th	5:14	help the weak, be p with everyone.	3428
Jas	5: 7	Be p, then, brothers, until	3428
	5: 7	to yield its valuable crop and how p he is	3428
	5: 8	You too, be p and stand firm,	3428
2Pe	3: 9	He is p with you,	3428
Rev	1: 9	the suffering and kingdom and p endurance	5705
	13:10	for p endurance and faithfulness on the part	5705
	14:12	This calls for p endurance on the part of	5705

PATIENTLY (9) [PATIENT]

Ps	37: 7	before the LORD and wait p for him;	2565
	40: 1	I waited p for the LORD;	7747+7747
Isa	38:13	I waited p till dawn,	8750
Hab	3:16	Yet I will wait p for the day of calamity	5663
Ac	26: 3	Therefore, I beg you to listen to me p.	3428
Ro	8:25	we wait for it p.	1328+5705
Heb	6:15	And so after waiting p,	3428
1Pe	3:20	when God waited p in the days of Noah	3429
Rev	3:10	you have kept my command to endure p,	5705

PATMOS (1)

Rev	1: 9	was on the island of P because of the word	4253

PATRIARCH (2) [PATRIARCHS]

Ac	2:29	that the p David died and was buried,	4256
Heb	7: 4	Even the p Abraham gave him a tenth of	4256

PATRIARCHS (6) [PATRIARCH]

Jn	7:22	did not come from Moses, but from the p),	4252
Ac	7: 8	Jacob became the father of the twelve p.	4256
	7: 9	"Because the p were jealous of Joseph,	4256
Ro	9: 5	Theirs are the p, from them is traced	4252
	11:28	they are loved on account of the p,	4252
	15: 8	to confirm the promises made to the p	4252

PATROBAS (1)

Ro	16:14	Greet Asyncritus, Phlegon, Hermes, P,	4259

PATTERN (9)

Ex	25: 9	like the p I will show you.	9322
	25:40	to the p shown you on the mountain.	9322
Nu	8: 4	The lampstand was made exactly like the p	5260
Ac	7:44	according to the p he had seen.	5596
Ro	5:14	who was a p of the one to come.	5596
	12: 2	Do not conform any longer to the p of	5372
Php	3:17	according to the p we gave you.	5596
2Ti	1:13	keep as the p of sound teaching,	5721
Heb	8: 5	to the p shown you on the mountain."	5596

PAU (2)

Ge	36:39	His city was named **P,**	7185
1Ch	1:50	His city was named **P,**	7185

PAUL (202) [PAUL'S, SAUL]

Ac	13: 9	Then Saul, who was also called **P,**	4263
	13:13	**P** and his companions sailed to Perga	4263
	13:16	**P** motioned with his hand and said:	4263
	13:42	As **P and Barnabas** were leaving	899S
	13:43	and devout converts to Judaism followed **P**	4263
	13:45	abusively against what **P** was saying.	4263
	13:46	and Barnabas answered them boldly:	4263
	13:50	persecution against **P** and Barnabas,	4263
	14: 1	At Iconium **P and Barnabas** went as usual	899S
	14: 3	So **P** and Barnabas spent considerable time there,	NIG
	14: 9	He listened to **P** as he was speaking.	4263
	14: 9	**P** looked directly at him,	4005S
	14:11	When the crowd saw what **P** had done,	4263
	14:12	and they called Hermes because he was	4263
	14:14	the apostles Barnabas and **P** heard of this,	4263
	14:19	They stoned **P** and dragged him outside	4263
	14:23	**P** and Barnabas appointed elders for them	NIG
	15: 2	This brought **P** and Barnabas into sharp	4263
	15: 2	So **P** and Barnabas were appointed,	4263
	15:12	as they listened to Barnabas and **P** telling	4263
	15:22	send them to Antioch with **P** and Barnabas.	4263
	15:25	with our dear friends Barnabas and **P**—	4263
	15:35	But **P** and Barnabas remained in Antioch,	4263
	15:36	Some time later **P** said to Barnabas,	4263
	15:38	but **P** did not think it wise to take him,	4263
	15:40	but **P** chose Silas and left,	4263
	16: 3	**P** wanted to take him along on the journey,	4263
	16: 6	**P** and his companions traveled throughout	NIG
	16: 9	During the night **P** had a vision of a man	4263
	16:10	After **P** had seen the vision,	NIG
	16:17	This girl followed **P** and the rest of us,	4263
	16:18	Finally **P** became so troubled	4263
	16:19	they seized **P** and Silas and dragged them	4263
	16:22	in the attack against **P and Silas,**	899S
	16:25	About midnight **P** and Silas were praying	4263
	16:28	But **P** shouted, "Don't harm yourself!	4263
	16:29	in and fell trembling before **P** and Silas.	4263
	16:36	The jailer told **P,** "The magistrates	4263
	16:37	But **P** said to the officers:	4263
	16:38	that **P** and Silas were Roman citizens,	NIG
	16:40	After **P** and Silas came out of the prison,	NIG
	17: 2	**P** went into the synagogue,	4263
	17: 4	of the Jews were persuaded and joined **P**	4263
	17: 5	to Jason's house in search of **P and Silas**	899S
	17:10	brothers sent **P** and Silas away to Berea.	4263
	17:11	to see if what **P** said was true.	4047S
	17:13	that **P** was preaching the word of God	4263
	17:14	The brothers immediately sent **P** to	4263
	17:15	The men who escorted **P** brought him	4263
	17:16	While **P** was waiting for them in Athens,	4263
	17:16	because **P** was preaching the good news	NIG
	17:22	**P** then stood up in the meeting of	4263
	17:33	At that, **P** left the Council.	4263
	17:34	A few became followers of **P**	899S
	18: 1	this, **P** left Athens and went to Corinth.	NIG
	18: 2	**P** went to see them,	NIG
	18: 5	**P** devoted himself exclusively	4263
	18: 6	the Jews opposed **P** and became abusive,	NIG
	18: 7	Then **P** left the synagogue	NIG
	18: 9	One night the Lord spoke *to* **P** in a vision:	4263
	18:11	So **P** stayed for a year and a half,	NIG
	18:12	a united attack on **P** and brought him	4263
	18:14	Just as **P** was about to speak,	4263
	18:18	**P** stayed on in Corinth for some time.	4263
	18:19	where **P** left Priscilla and Aquila.	NIG
	18:23	**P** set out from there and traveled	NIG
	19: 1	**P** took the road through the interior	4263
	19: 3	So **P** asked, "Then what baptism did you receive?"	NIG
	19: 4	**P** said, "John's baptism was a baptism	4263
	19: 6	When **P** placed his hands on them,	4263
	19: 8	**P** entered the synagogue and spoke	NIG
	19: 9	So **P** left them.	NIG
	19:11	God did extraordinary miracles through **P,**	4263
	19:13	"In the name of Jesus, whom **P** preaches,	4263
	19:15	and I know about **P,** but who are you?"	4263
	19:21	**P** decided to go to Jerusalem,	4263
	19:26	and hear how this fellow **P** has convinced	4263
	19:30	**P** wanted to appear before the crowd,	4263
	19:31	*of* **P,** sent him a message begging him not	899S
	20: 1	**P** sent for the disciples and,	4263
	20: 7	**P** spoke to the people and,	4263
	20: 9	into a deep sleep as **P** talked on and on.	4263
	20:10	**P** went down, threw himself on	4263
	20:13	where we were going to take **P** aboard.	4263
	20:16	**P** had decided to sail past Ephesus	4263
	20:17	**P** sent to Ephesus for the elders of	NIG
	21: 4	Through the Spirit they urged **P** not to go	4263
	21:12	we and the people there pleaded with **P** not	899S
	21:13	Then **P** answered, "Why are you weeping	4263
	21:18	The next day **P** and the rest of us went	4263
	21:19	**P** greeted them and reported	NIG
	21:20	Then they said *to* **P:**	899S
	21:26	The next day **P** took the men	4263
	21:27	the province of Asia saw **P** at the temple.	899S
	21:29	in the city with **P** and assumed	899S
	21:29	and assumed that **P** had brought him into	4263
	21:30	Seizing **P,** they dragged him from the	4263
	21:32	and his soldiers, they stopped beating **P.**	4263
	21:34	that **P** be taken into the barracks.	899S
	21:35	When **P** reached the steps,	NIG
	21:37	As the soldiers were about to take **P** into	4263
	21:39	**P** answered, "I am a Jew,	4263
	21:40	**P** stood on the steps and motioned to	4263
	22: 2	they became very quiet. Then **P** said:	NIG
	22:22	The crowd listened to **P** until he said this.	899S
	22:24	the commander ordered **P** to be taken into	4263
	22:25	**P** said to the centurion standing there,	4263
	22:27	The commander went to **P** and asked,	NIG
	22:28	"But I was born a citizen," **P** replied.	4263
	22:29	when he realized that he had put **P,**	899S
	22:30	to find out exactly why **P** was being accused	NIG
	22:30	Then he brought **P** and had him stand	4263
	23: 1	**P** looked straight at the Sanhedrin and said,	4263
	23: 2	near **P** to strike him on the mouth.	899S
	23: 3	Then **P** said to him, "God will strike you,	4263
	23: 4	Those who were standing near **P** said,	NIG
	23: 5	**P** replied, "Brothers, I did not realize	4263
	23: 6	Then **P,** knowing that some of them	4263
	23:10	the commander was afraid **P** would be torn	4263
	23:11	The following night the Lord stood near **P**	899S
	23:12	not to eat or drink until they had killed **P.**	4263
	23:14	not to eat anything until we have killed **P.**	4263
	23:16	he went into the barracks and told **P.**	4263
	23:17	**P** called one of the centurions and said,	4263
	23:18	The centurion said, "**P,** the prisoner,	4263
	23:20	to bring **P** before the Sanhedrin tomorrow	4263
	23:24	Provide mounts for **P** so that he may	4263
	23:31	took **P** with them during the night	4263
	23:33	to the governor and handed **P** over to him.	4263
	23:35	Then he ordered that **P** be kept under guard	899S
	24: 1	and they brought their charges against **P**	4263
	24: 2	When **P** was called in,	899S
	24:10	for him to speak, **P** replied:	4263
	24:23	the centurion to keep **P** under guard but	899S
	24:24	for **P** and listened to him as he spoke	4263
	24:25	As **P** discoursed on righteousness,	899S
	24:26	that **P** would offer him a bribe,	4263
	24:27	he left **P** in prison.	4263
	25: 2	and presented the charges against **P.**	4263
	25: 3	to have **P** transferred to Jerusalem,	899S
	25: 4	"**P** is being held at Caesarea,	4263
	25: 6	and ordered that **P** be brought before him.	4263
	25: 7	When **P** appeared, the Jews who had come	899S
	25: 8	Then **P** made his defense:	4263
	25: 9	wishing to do the Jews a favor, said *to* **P,**	4263
	25:10	**P** answered: "I am now standing before	4263
	25:19	about a dead man named Jesus who **P** claimed was alive.	4263
	25:21	When **P** made his appeal to be held over	4263
	25:23	**P** was brought in.	4263
	26: 1	Then Agrippa said to **P,**	4263
	26: 1	So **P** motioned with his hand	4263
	26:24	"You are out of your mind, **P!**"	4263
	26:25	most excellent Festus," **P** replied.	4263
	26:28	Then Agrippa said to **P,** "Do you think	4263
	26:29	**P** replied, "Short time or long—	4263
	27: 1	and some other prisoners were handed	4263
	27: 3	and Julius, in kindness *to* **P,**	4263
	27: 9	So **P** warned them,	4263
	27:11	instead of listening to what **P** said,	4263
	27:21	**P** stood up before them and said:	4263
	27:24	and said, 'Do not be afraid, **P.**	4263
	27:31	**P** said to the centurion and the soldiers,	4263
	27:33	Just before dawn **P** urged them all to eat.	4263
	28: 3	**P** gathered a pile of brushwood and,	4263
	28: 5	**P** shook the snake off into the fire	3525+3836S
	28: 8	**P** went in to see him and, after prayer,	4263
	28:15	At the sight of these men **P** thanked God	4263
	28:16	**P** was allowed to live by himself,	4263
	28:17	When they had assembled, **P** said to them:	NIG
	28:23	They arranged to meet **P** on a certain day,	899S
	28:25	after **P** had made this final statement:	4263
	28:30	For two whole years **P** stayed there	NIG
Ro	1: 1	**P,** a servant of Christ Jesus,	4263
1Co	1: 1	**P,** called to be an apostle of Christ Jesus	4263
	1:12	One of you says, "I follow **P**";	4263
	1:13	Was **P** crucified for you?	4263
	1:13	Were you baptized into the name *of* **P?**	4263
	3: 4	For when one says, "I follow **P,**"	4263
	3: 5	And what is **P?** Only servants,	4263
	3:22	whether **P** or Apollos or Cephas or	4263
	16:21	I, **P,** write this greeting in my own hand.	4263
2Co	1: 1	**P,** an apostle of Christ Jesus by the will	4263
	10: 1	I, **P,** who am "timid" when face to face	4263
Gal	1: 1	**P,** an apostle—sent not from men nor by man, but by Jesus Christ	4263
	5: 2	**P,** tell you that if you let yourselves	4263
Eph	1: 1	**P,** an apostle of Christ Jesus by the will	4263
	3: 1	For this reason I, **P,** the prisoner of Christ	4263
Php	1: 1	**P** and Timothy, servants of Christ Jesus,	4263
Col	1: 1	**P,** an apostle of Christ Jesus by the will	4263
	1:23	and of which I, **P,** have become a servant.	4263
	4:18	I, **P,** write this greeting in my own hand.	4263
1Th	1: 1	**P,** Silas and Timothy,	4263
	2:18	certainly I, **P,** did, again and again—	4263
2Th	1: 1	**P,** Silas and Timothy,	4263
	3:17	I, **P,** write this greeting in my own hand,	4263
1Ti	1: 1	**P,** an apostle of Christ Jesus by the command of God our Savior	4263
2Ti	1: 1	**P,** an apostle of Christ Jesus by the will of	4263
Tit	1: 1	**P,** a servant of God and an apostle of Jesus	4263
Phm	1: 1	**P,** a prisoner of Christ Jesus	4263
	1: 9	I then, as **P**—an old man and now also a	4263
	1:19	I, **P,** am writing this with my own hand.	4263
2Pe	3:15	as our dear brother **P** also wrote you with	4263

PAUL'S (7) [PAUL]

Ac	16:14	opened her heart to respond to **P** message.	4263
	19:29	**P** traveling companions from Macedonia,	4263
	21:11	Coming over to us, he took **P** belt,	4263
	23:16	when the son of **P** sister heard of this plot,	4263
	25:14	Festus discussed **P** case with the king.	4263
	26:24	At this point Festus interrupted **P** defense.	899S
	27:43	But the centurion wanted to spare **P** life	4263

PAULUS (1) [SERGIUS]

Ac	13: 7	an attendant of the proconsul, Sergius **P.**	4263

PAVEMENT (9)

Ex	24:10	Under his feet was something like a **p** made	4246
2Ch	7: 3	on the **p** with their faces to the ground,	8367
Est	1: 6	and silver on a **mosaic p** of porphyry,	8367
Jer	43: 9	and bury them in clay in the **brick p** at	4861
Eze	40:17	a **p** that had been constructed all around	8367
	40:17	there were thirty rooms along the **p.**	8367
	40:18	this was the lower **p.**	8367
	42: 3	and in the section opposite the **p** of	8367
Jn	19:13	at a place known as the **Stone P**	3346

PAVILION (2)

Job	36:29	how he thunders from his **p?**	6109
Ps	19: 5	like a bridegroom coming forth from his **p,**	2903

PAW (2) [PAWS]

1Sa	17:37	The LORD who delivered me from the **p**	3338
	17:37	and the **p** of the bear will deliver me from	3338

PAWS (2) [PAW]

Lev	11:27	that walk on their **p** are unclean for you;	4090
Job	39:21	He **p** fiercely, rejoicing in his strength,	2916

PAY (140) [PAID, PAYING, PAYMENT, PAYS, REPAID, REPAY, REPAYING, REPAYMENT, REPAYS]

Ge	23:13	I will **p** the price of the field.	5989
	30:28	"Name your wages, and I will **p** them."	5989
	34:12	and I'll **p** whatever you ask me.	5989
	43:28	And they bowed low to **p** him **honor.**	2556
Ex	2: 9	nurse him for me, and I will **p** you."	5989+8510
	4: 8	or **p attention** to the first miraculous sign,	9048
	5: 9	that they keep working and **p** no **attention**	9120
	15:26	if you **p attention** to his commands	263
	21:19	however, he must **p** the injured man for	5989
	21:32	the owner *must* **p** thirty shekels of silver to	5989
	21:34	the owner of the pit *must* **p for the loss;**	8966
	21:34	he must **p** its owner,	4084+8740
	21:36	the owner **must p,** animal for animal,	8966+8966
	22: 1	he must **p back** five head of cattle for	8966
	22: 3	he must be sold to **p** for his theft.	NIH
	22: 4	he must **p back** double.	8966
	22: 7	if he is caught, *must* **p** back double.	8966
	22: 9	judges declare guilty *must* **p** back double	8966
	22:13	not be required to **p** for the torn animal.	8966
	22:15	the borrower *will not have to* **p.**	8966
	22:16	he **must p** the **bride-price,**	4555+4555
	22:17	he must still **p** the bride-price	4084+9202
	23:21	**P attention** to him and listen	9068
	30:12	each one *must* **p** the LORD a ransom	5989
Lev	25:51	he must **p** for his redemption a larger share	8740
	25:52	that and **p** for his redemption accordingly.	8740
	26:41	and they **p** for their sin,	8355
	26:43	They *will* **p** for their sins	8355
	27: 8	If anyone making the vow *is* too **poor to p**	4575
	27:23	and the man *must* **p** its value on that day,	5989
Nu	20:19	any of your water, *we will* **p** for it.	4836+5989
Dt	2: 6	**p** them in silver for the food you eat	8690
	7:12	If you **p attention** to these laws	9048
	22:29	he *shall* **p** the girl's father fifty shekels	5989
	23:18	of the LORD your God to **p** any vow,	NIH
	23:21	do not be slow to **p** it,	8966
	24:15	**P** him his wages each day before sunset,	5989
	28:13	If you **p attention** to the commands of	9048
Jdg	9:57	made the men of Shechem **p** for	928+8031+8740
1Sa	4:20	But she did not respond or **p** any attention.	8883
	6: 5	and **p** honor to Israel's god.	5989
	25:25	*May* my lord **p** no attention to	8492
2Sa	1: 2	he fell to the ground to **p** him **honor.**	2556
	9: 6	he bowed down *to* **p** him **honor.**	2556
	12: 6	He *must* **p** for that lamb four times over,	8966
	14: 4	with her face to the ground *to* **p** him **honor,**	2556
	14:22	with his face to the ground *to* **p** him **honor,**	2556
1Ki	1: 2	so severely, if Adonijah does not **p with**	928
	5: 6	and I will **p** you for your men whatever	5989
	20:39	or *you must* **p** a talent of silver.'	9202
	21: 2	*I will* **p** you whatever it is worth.	4084+5989
2Ki	4: 7	"Go, sell the oil and **p** your debts.	8966
	9:26	and I will surely **make** you **p** for it	8966
	12:15	to whom they gave the money to **p**	5989
	18:14	*I will* **p** whatever you demand of me."	5951
	22: 5	And *have these men* **p** the workers	5989
Ne	5: 4	"We have had to borrow money to **p**	4200
	9:34	*they did* not **p attention** to your commands	7992
Est	3: 2	not kneel down or **p** him **honor.**	2556
	3: 5	not kneel down or **p** him **honor,**	2556
	4: 7	of money Haman had promised to **p** into	9202
Job	6:22	**p** a ransom for me from your wealth,	8815
	33: 1	**p attention** *to* everything I say.	263
	33:31	"**P attention,** Job, and listen to me;	7992

Job	41:11	a claim against me that *I* must p?	8966
Ps	79:12	**P** back into the laps of our neighbors	8740
	94: 2	p back to the proud what they deserve.	8740
Pr	4: 1	p **attention** and gain understanding.	7992
	4:20	My son, p **attention** to what I say;	7992
	5: 1	My son, p **attention** to my wisdom,	7992
	6:31	Yet if he is caught, *he must* p sevenfold,	8966
	7:24	p **attention** to what I say.	7992
	13:13	He who scorns instruction *will* p for it,	2472
	19:19	A hot-tempered man *must* p the penalty;	5951
	20:22	"I'll p you **back** for this wrong!"	8966
	22:17	**P** attention and listen to the sayings of	265+5742
	22:27	if you lack the means to p,	8966
	24:29	*I'll* p that man **back** for what he did."	8740
	30:10	and *you will* p for it.	870
Ecc	7:21	not p attention to every word people say,	5989
Isa	28:23	p **attention** and hear what I say.	7992
	34: 1	p **attention**, *you* peoples!	7992
	42:23	or p **close** attention in time	2256+7992+9048
	65: 6	not keep silent but *will* p back in full;	8966
	65: 6	*I will* p it **back** into their laps—	8966
Jer	7:24	But they did not listen or p **attention**;	265+5742
	7:26	they did not listen to me or p **attention.**	265+5742
	11: 8	But they did not listen or p **attention**	265+5742
	13:15	Hear and p **attention**, do not be arrogant;	263
	17:23	Yet they did not listen or p **attention**;	265+5742
	18:18	and p no **attention** to anything he says."	7992
	34:14	not listen to me or p **attention** to me.	265+5742
	44: 5	But they did not listen or p **attention**;	265+5742
	51: 6	he *will* p her what she deserves.	8966
La	3:64	**P** them **back** what they deserve, O Lord.	8740
Eze	16:41	and *you will* no longer p your lovers.	924+5989
	29:19	and plunder the land as p for his army.	8510
	40: 4	and p **attention** to everything I am going	8492
Da	3:12	who p no attention to you, O king.	10682
Hos	2:12	which she said were her p from her lovers;	921
	5: 1	**P attention**, *you* Israelites!	7992
	12:12	and to p for her he tended sheep.	NIH
Zec	1: 4	But they would not listen or p **attention**	7992
	7:11	"But they refused to p **attention**;	7992
	11:12	"If you think it best, give me my p;	8510
Mt	7: 3	and p no **attention** to the plank	2917
	17:24	"Doesn't your teacher p the temple tax?"	5464
	18:25	Since he was not able *to* p,	625
	18:26	he begged, 'and *I will* p back everything.'	625
	18:28	**'P back** what you owe me!'	625
	18:29	and *I will* p you **back**.'	625
	18:30	the man thrown into prison until *he could* p	625
	18:34	until *he should* p back all he owed.	625
	20: 2	He agreed to p them a denarius for the day	NIG
	20: 4	and *I will* p you whatever is right.'	1443
	20: 8	'Call the workers and p them their wages,	625
	20:14	Take your p and go.	NIG
	22:16	p no **attention** to who they are.	476+1063+4725
	22:17	Is it right *to* p taxes to Caesar or not?"	1443
Mk	12:14	p no **attention** to who they are;	476+1063+4725
	12:14	Is it right *to* p taxes to Caesar or not?	1443
	12:15	*Should we* p or shouldn't we?"	1443
Lk	3:14	be content with your p."	4072
	6:41	and p no **attention** to the plank	2917
	7:42	of them had the money *to* p him **back**,	625
	19: 8	*I will* p back four times the amount."	625
	20:22	Is it right for us *to* p taxes to Caesar	1443
Ac	21:24	their purification rites and p their **expenses**,	1251
	22:28	p a big price **for** my citizenship."	3227
	25:13	at Caesarea *to* p *their* **respects** to Festus.	832
Ro	13: 6	This is also why *you* p taxes,	5464
	13: 7	If you owe taxes, p taxes;	NIG
Gal	5:10	you into confusion *will* p the penalty,	1002
2Th	1: 6	He *will* p trouble on those who	500
Tit	1:14	and *will* p no **attention** to Jewish myths	4668
Phm	1:19	I *will* p it **back**—not to mention that you owe	702
Heb	2: 1	p more careful **attention**, therefore, to	4668
Jas	5: 4	The wages *you* **failed to** p	691
2Pe	1:19	and you will do well to p **attention** to it,	4668
Rev	18: 6	p her **back** double for what she has done.	1486+1488

PAYING (9) [PAY]

Ex	21: 2	he shall go free, **without** p anything.	2855
	21:30	*by* p whatever is demanded.	5989
2Sa	24:24	*I* **insist on** p you for it.	928+4697+7864+7864
1Ch	21:24	"No, *I* insist on p the full price.	7864+7864
Jer	22:13	not p them *for* their labor.	5989
Joel	3: 4	If you *are* p me **back**,	1694
Jnh	1: 3	After p the fare, he went aboard	5989
Mt	22:19	Show me the coin used for p the tax."	NIG
2Th	3: 8	did we eat anyone's food **without** p for it.	1562

PAYMENT (15) [PAY]

Ge	31:39	And *you* **demanded** p from me	1335
	47:14	Egypt and Canaan **in** p for the grain	928
Ex	21:11	is to go free, **without any** p of money.	401+2855
	21:30	However, *if* p is demanded of him,	4111
Lev	22:16	and so bring upon them guilt **requiring** p.	873
Dt	15: 2	not **require** p *from* his fellow Israelite	5601
	15: 3	*You may* **require** p *from* a foreigner,	5601
Job	31:39	without p or broken the spirit of its tenants,	4084
Ps	49: 8	the ransom for a life is costly, no p is ever enough—	NIH
	109:20	May this be the Lord's p *to* my accusers,	7190
Isa	65: 7	*I will* **measure** into their laps **the full** p	4499
Eze	16:31	because you scorned p.	924
	16:34	for you give p and none is given to you.	924
Lk	23: 2	He opposes p of taxes to Caesar and claims	1443

Php	4:18	*I have* **received** full p and even more;	600

PAYS (9) [PAY]

Ge	50:15	and p us **back** *for* all the wrongs	8740+8740
Job	35:13	the Almighty p no **attention** *to* it.	8800
Ps	31:23	but the proud *he* p **back** in full.	8966
	94: 7	the God of Jacob p no **heed**."	1067
Pr	17: 4	a liar p **attention** to a malicious tongue.	263
	17:13	If a *man* p **back** evil for good,	8740
Da	6:13	p no attention to you, O king,	10682
Mal	2:13	and wail because *he* no longer p **attention**	7155
1Th	5:15	that nobody p **back** wrong for wrong,	625

PAZZEZ See BETH PAZZEZ

PEACE (250) [PACIFIES, PACIFY, PEACE-LOVING, PEACEABLE, PEACEABLY, PEACEFUL, PEACEFULLY, PEACEMAKERS, PEACETIME]

Ge	15:15	will go to your fathers in p and be buried at	8934
	26:29	and sent you away in p.	8934
	26:31	and they left him in p.	8934
	44:17	The rest of you, go back to your father in p.	8934
Lev	26: 6	" 'I will grant p in the land,	8934
Nu	6:26	turn his face toward you and give you p." '	8934
	25:12	I am making my covenant of p with him.	8934
Dt	2:26	to Sihon king of Heshbon offering p	8934
	20:10	make its people an offer of p.	8934
	20:12	If they refuse *to* **make** p and they engage	8966
Jos	9:15	Then Joshua made a treaty of p with them	8934
	10: 1	**made a treaty of** p with Israel	8966
	10: 4	"because *it has* **made** p with Joshua and	8966
	11:19	**made a treaty of** p with the Israelites.	8966
Jdg	3:11	So the land **had** p for forty years,	9200
	3:30	and the land **had** p for eighty years.	9200
	5:31	Then the land **had** p forty years.	9200
	6:23	But the Lord said to him, "**P!**	8934
	6:24	and called it The Lord is **P**.	8934
	8:28	the land **enjoyed** p forty years.	9200
	18: 6	The priest answered them, "Go in p.	8934
	21:13	Then the whole assembly sent an offer of p	8934
1Sa	1:17	Eli answered, "Go in p,	8934
	7:14	And there was p between Israel and	8934
	16: 4	They asked, "Do you come **in** p?"	8934
	16: 5	Samuel replied, "Yes, **in** p;	8934
	20:42	Jonathan said to David, "Go in p,	8934
	25:35	"Go home in p;	8934
	29: 7	Turn back and go in p;	8934
2Sa	3:21	David sent Abner away, and he went in p.	8934
	3:22	and he had gone in p.	8934
	3:23	and that he had gone in p.	8934
	10:19	*they* **made** p with the Israelites	8966
	15: 9	The king said to him, "Go in p."	8934
1Sa	15:27	Go back to the city in p,	8934
1Ki	2: 6	his gray head go down to the grave in p.	8934
	2:33	may there be the Lord's p forever."	8934
	4:24	and had p on all sides.	8934
	20:18	He said, "If they have come out for p,	8934
	22:17	Let each one go home in p.' "	8934
	22:44	Jehoshaphat *was* also **at** p with the king	8966
2Ki	5:19	"Go in p," Elisha said.	8934
	9:17	'Do you **come in** p?' "	8934
	9:18	'Do you **come in** p?' "	8934
	9:18	"What do you have to do with **p**?"	8934
	9:19	'Do you **come in** p?' "	8934
	9:19	"What do you have to do with p?	8934
	9:22	"Have you **come in** p, Jehu?"	8934
	9:22	"How can there be p," Jehu replied,	8934
	9:31	she asked, "Have you **come in** p, Zimri,	8934
	18:31	Make p with me and come out to me.	1388
	20:19	not be p and security in my lifetime?"	8934
	22:20	and you will be buried in p.	8934
1Ch	12:17	"If you have come to me in p, to help me,	8934
	19:19	*they* **made** p with David and became subject	8966
	22: 9	a son who will be a man of p **and rest**,	4957
	22: 9	and I will grant Israel p and quiet	8934
2Ch	14: 1	and in his days the country *was* **at** p	9200
	14: 5	and the kingdom *was* **at** p under him.	9200
	14: 6	since the land *was* **at** p.	9200
	18:16	Let each one go home in p.' "	8934
	20:30	And the kingdom of Jehoshaphat *was* at p,	9200
	34:28	and you will be buried in p.	8934
Job	3:13	For now I would be lying down **in** p;	9200
	3:26	*I* **have** no p, no quietness;	8922
	5:23	the wild animals *will* be **at** p with you.	8966
	21:13	in prosperity and go down to the grave in p.	8092
	22:21	"Submit to God and *be* **at** p with him;	8966
Ps	4: 8	I will lie down and sleep in p,	8934
	7: 4	if I have done evil to *him who is* **at** p	8966
	29:11	the Lord blesses his people with **p**.	8934
	34:14	seek p and pursue it.	8934
	37:11	the land and enjoy great p.	8934
	37:37	there is a future for the man of p.	8934
	85: 8	he promises p to his people, his saints—	8934
	85:10	righteousness and p kiss each other.	8934
	119:165	Great p have they who love your law,	8934
	120: 6	among those who hate p.	8934
	120: 7	I am a man of p;	8934
	122: 6	Pray for the p of Jerusalem:	8934
	122: 7	May there be p within your walls and	8934
	122: 8	I will say, "**P** be within you."	8934
	125: 5	**P** be upon Israel.	8934
	128: 6	**P** be upon Israel.	8934
	147:14	He grants p to your borders	8934

Pr	3:17	and all her paths are p.	8934
	12:20	but joy for those who promote p.	8934
	14:30	A heart **at** p gives life to the body,	5341
	16: 7	**makes** even his enemies **live at** p with him.	8966
	17: 1	Better a dry crust with p **and quiet** than	8932
	29: 9	the fool rages and scoffs, and there is no p.	5739
	29:17	and *he will* **give** you p;	5663
Ecc	3: 8	a time for war and a time for p.	8934
Isa	9: 6	Everlasting Father, Prince of **P**.	8934
	9: 7	of his government and p there will	8934
	14: 7	All the lands are at rest and **at** p;	9200
	26: 3	You will keep in **perfect** p him whose mind is steadfast,	8934+8934
	26:12	Lord, you establish p for us;	8934
	27: 5	let them make p with me, yes,	8934
	27: 5	yes, let them make p with me."	8934
	32:17	The fruit of righteousness will be p;	8934
	33: 7	the envoys of p weep bitterly.	8934
	36:16	Make p with me and come out to me.	1388
	39: 8	be p and security in my lifetime."	8934
	48:18	your p would have been like a river,	8934
	48:22	"There is no p," says the Lord.	8934
	52: 7	who proclaim p, who bring good tidings,	8934
	53: 5	the punishment that brought us p was	8934
	54:10	not be shaken nor my covenant of p	8934
	54:13	and great will be your children's p.	8934
	55:12	in joy and be led forth in p;	8934
	57: 2	Those who walk uprightly enter into p;	8934
	57:19	**P**, peace, to those far and near,"	8934
	57:19	Peace, p, to those far and near,"	8934
	57:21	"There is no p," says my God,	8934
	59: 8	The way of p they do not know;	8934
	59: 8	no one who walks in them will know p.	8934
	60:17	I will make p your governor	8934
	66:12	"I will extend p to her like a river,	8934
Jer	4:10	'You will have p,'	8934
	6:14	'P, peace,' they say, when there is no peace.	8934
	6:14	p,' they say, when there is no peace.	8934
	6:14	peace,' they say, when there is no p.	8934
	8:11	"P, peace," they say, when there is no peace	8934
	8:11	"Peace, p," they say, when there is no peace	8934
	8:11	peace," they say, when there is no p.	8934
	8:15	We hoped for p but no good has come,	8934
	14:13	I will give you lasting p in this place.' "	8934
	14:19	We hoped for p but no good has come,	8934
	23:17	You will have p.'	8934
	28: 9	But the prophet who prophesies p will	8934
	29: 7	seek the p **and prosperity** of the city	8934
	30: 5	of fear are heard—terror, not p.	8934
	30:10	Jacob will again **have** p and security,	9200
	33: 6	and will let them enjoy abundant p	8934
	33: 9	at the abundant prosperity and p I provide	8934
	46:27	Jacob will again **have** p and security,	9200
La	3:17	I have been deprived of p;	8934
Eze	7:25	When terror comes, they will seek p,	8934
	13:10	they lead my people astray, saying, "**P**,"	8934
	13:10	"Peace," when there is no p, and because,	8934
	13:16	to Jerusalem and saw visions of p for her	8934
	13:16	of peace for her when there was no p,	8934
	34:25	a covenant of p with them and rid the land	8934
	37:26	I will make a covenant of p with them;	8934
Da	10:19	O man highly esteemed," he said. "**P!**	8934
Mic	3: 5	if one feeds them, they proclaim '**p**';	8934
	5: 5	And he will be their p.	8934
Na	1:15	brings good news, who proclaims p!	8934
Hag	2: 9	'And in this place I will grant p,'	8934
Zec	1:11	and found the whole world at rest and **in** p.	9200
	8:19	Therefore love truth and p."	8934
	9:10	He will proclaim p to the nations.	8934
Mal	2: 5	a covenant of life and p,	8934
	2: 6	He walked with me in p and uprightness,	8934
Mt	10:13	let your p rest on it;	1645
	10:13	if it is not, let your p return to you.	1645
	10:34	not suppose that I have come to bring p to	1645
	10:34	I did not come to bring p, but a sword.	1645
Mk	5:34	Go in p and be freed from your suffering."	1645
	9:50	and **be at** p with each other."	1644
Lk	1:79	to guide our feet into the path of p."	1645
	2:14	on earth p to men on whom his favor rests."	1645
	2:29	you now dismiss your servant in p.	1645
	7:50	"Your faith has saved you; go in p."	1645
	8:48	your faith has healed you. Go in p."	1645
	10: 5	first say, 'P to this house.'	1645
	10: 6	If a man *of* p is there,	1645
	10: 6	your p will rest on him;	1645
	12:51	Do you think I came to bring p on earth?	1645
	14:32	a long way off and will ask for terms of p.	1645
	19:38	"P in heaven and glory in the highest!"	1645
	19:42	on this day what would bring you p—	1645
	24:36	"P be with you."	1645
Jn	14:27	P I leave with you; my peace I give you.	1645
	14:27	Peace I leave with you; my p I give you.	1645
	16:33	so that in me you may have p.	1645
	20:19	"P be with you!"	1645
	20:21	Again Jesus said, "P be with you!	1645
	20:26	"P be with you!"	1645
Ac	9:31	Galilee and Samaria enjoyed a time of p.	1645
	10:36	the good news of p through Jesus Christ,	1645
	12:20	they asked for p,	1645
	15:33	the brothers with **the blessing of** p to return	1645
	16:36	Now you can leave. Go in p."	1645
	24: 2	"We have enjoyed a long period of p	1645
Ro	1: 7	and p to you from God our Father and from	1645
	2:10	honor and p for everyone who does good:	1645
	3:17	and the way *of* p they do not know."	1645
	5: 1	we have p with God through our Lord	1645
	8: 6	mind controlled by the Spirit is life and p;	1645

Ro	12:18	**live at p** with everyone.	1644
	14:17	righteousness, **p** and joy in the Holy Spirit,	1645
	14:19	to **p** and to mutual edification.	1645
	15:13	the God of hope fill you with all joy and **p**	1645
	15:33	The God *of* **p** be with you all. Amen.	1645
	16:20	The God *of* **p** will soon crush Satan under your feet.	1645
1Co	1:3	Grace and **p** to you from God our Father	1645
	7:15	God has called us to live in **p.**	1645
	14:33	For God is not a God of disorder but *of* **p.**	1645
	16:11	on his way in **p** so that he may return	1645
2Co	1:2	Grace and **p** to you from God our Father	1645
	2:13	I still had no **p** of mind,	457
	13:11	be of one mind, **live in p.**	1644
	13:11	the God *of* love and **p** will be with you.	1645
Gal	1:3	Grace and **p** to you from God our Father	1645
	5:22	But the fruit of the Spirit is love, joy, **p,**	1645
	6:16	**P** and mercy to all who follow this rule,	1645
Eph	1:2	Grace and **p** to you from God our Father	1645
	2:14	For he himself is our **p,**	1645
	2:15	of the two, thus making **p,**	1645
	2:17	and preached **p** to you who were far away	1645
	2:17	to you who were far away and **p**	1645
	4:3	of the Spirit through the bond *of* **p.**	1645
	6:15	that comes from the gospel *of* **p.**	1645
	6:23	**P** to the brothers,	1645
Php	1:2	Grace and **p** to you from God our Father	1645
	4:7	And the **p** of God, which transcends all	1645
	4:9	And the God *of* **p** will be with you.	1645
Col	1:2	Grace and **p** to you from God our Father.	1645
	1:20	*by* **making p** through his blood,	1647
	3:15	Let the **p** of Christ rule in your hearts,	1645
	3:15	members of one body you were called to **p.**	4005S
1Th	1:1	Grace and **p** to you.	1645
	5:3	While people are saying, "**P** and safety,"	1645
	5:13	**Live in p** with each other.	1644
	5:23	May God himself, the God *of* **p,**	1645
2Th	1:2	Grace and **p** to you from God the Father	1645
	3:16	the Lord *of* **p** himself give you peace	1645
	3:16	of peace himself give you **p** at all times and	1645
1Ti	1:2	Grace, mercy and **p** from God the Father	1645
2Ti	1:2	Grace, mercy and **p** from God the Father	1645
	2:22	and pursue righteousness, faith, love and **p,**	1645
Tit	1:4	Grace and **p** from God the Father	1645
Phm	1:3	Grace to you and **p** from God our Father	1645
Heb	7:2	"king of Salem" means "king *of* **p.**"	1645
	12:11	it produces a harvest of righteousness and **p**	1646
	12:14	Make every effort to live in **p** with all men	1645
	13:20	May the God *of* **p,**	1645
Jas	3:18	Peacemakers who sow in **p** raise a harvest	1645
1Pe	1:2	Grace and **p** be yours in abundance.	1645
	3:11	he must seek **p** and pursue it.	1645
	5:14	**P** to all of you who are in Christ.	1645
2Pe	1:2	Grace and **p** be yours in abundance through	1645
	3:14	blameless and at **p** with him.	1645
2Jn	1:3	mercy and **p** from God the Father and	1645
3Jn	1:14	**P** to you.	1645
Jude	1:2	Mercy, **p** and love be yours in abundance.	1645
Rev	1:4	Grace and **p** to you from him who is,	1645
	6:4	Its rider was given power to take **p** from	1645

PEACE-LOVING (1) [PEACE, LOVE]

Jas	3:17	then **p**, considerate, submissive,	1646

PEACEABLE (1) [PEACE]

Tit	3:2	to be **p** and considerate,	285

PEACEABLY (2) [PEACE]

Jdg	11:13	Now give it back **p.**"	928+8934
Ps	35:20	They do not speak **p,**	8934

PEACEFUL (9) [PEACE]

Jdg	18:27	against a **p** and unsuspecting people.	9200
2Sa	20:19	We are the **p** and faithful in Israel.	8966
1Ki	5:12	There were **p** relations between Hiram	8934
1Ch	4:40	and the land was spacious, **p** and quiet.	9200
Isa	32:18	My people will live in **p** dwelling places,	8934
	33:20	your eyes will see Jerusalem, a **p** abode,	8633
Jer	25:37	The **p** meadows will be laid waste because	8934
Eze	38:11	I will attack a **p** and unsuspecting people—	9200
1Ti	2:2	that we may live **p** and quiet lives	2475

PEACEFULLY (3) [PEACE]

1Ki	2:13	Bathsheba asked him, "Do you come **p?**"	8934
	2:13	He answered, "Yes, **p.**"	8934
Jer	34:5	you will die **p.**	928+8934

PEACEMAKERS (2) [PEACE]

Mt	5:9	Blessed are the **p,** for they will be called sons of God.	1648
Jas	3:18	**P** who sow in peace raise a harvest	1645+4472

PEACETIME (1) [PEACE]

1Ki	2:5	shedding their blood in **p** as if in battle,	8934

PEACOCKS (KJV) See BABOON, OSTRICH

PEAKS (2)

Nu	23:9	From the rocky **p** I see them,	8031
Ps	95:4	and the mountain **p** belong to him.	9361

PEAL (1) [PEALS]

Rev	14:2	and like a loud **p of thunder.**	1103

PEALS (5) [PEAL]

Rev	4:5	rumblings and **p of thunder.**	1103
	8:5	and there came **p of thunder**, rumblings,	1103
	11:19	rumblings, **p of thunder**,	1103
	16:18	**p of thunder** and a severe earthquake.	1103
	19:6	the roar of rushing waters and like loud **p**	5889

PEARL (1) [MOTHER-OF-PEARL, PEARLS]

Rev	21:21	each gate made of a single **p.**	3449

PEARLS (7) [PEARL]

Mt	7:6	do not throw your **p** to pigs.	3449
	13:45	like a merchant looking for fine **p.**	3449
1Ti	2:9	or gold or **p** or expensive clothes,	3449
Rev	17:4	precious stones and **p.**	3449
	18:12	silver, precious stones and **p;**	3449
	18:16	precious stones and **p!**	3449
	21:21	The twelve gates were twelve **p,**	3449

PEBBLE (1) [PEBBLES]

Am	9:9	and not a **p** will reach the ground.	7656

PEBBLES (1) [PEBBLE]

Ps	147:17	He hurls down his hail like **p.**	7326

PECKED (1)

Pr	30:17	*will be* **p out** *by* the ravens of the valley,	5941

PEDAHEL (1)

Nu	34:28	**P** son of Ammihud,	7010

PEDAHZUR (5)

Nu	1:10	from Manasseh, Gamaliel son of **P;**	7011
	2:20	of Manasseh is Gamaliel son of **P.**	7011
	7:54	On the eighth day Gamaliel son of **P,**	7011
	7:59	This was the offering of Gamaliel son of **P.**	7011
	10:23	Gamaliel son of **P** was over the division of	7011

PEDAIAH (8)

2Ki	23:36	mother's name was Zebidah daughter of **P;**	7015
1Ch	3:18	**P,** Shenazzar, Jekamiah,	7015
	3:19	The sons of **P:** Zerubbabel and Shimei.	7015
	27:20	of Manasseh: Joel son of **P;**	7016
Ne	3:25	**P** son of Parosh	7015
	8:4	and on his left were **P,** Mishael, Malkijah,	7015
	11:7	the son of **P,** the son of Kolaiah,	7015
	13:13	Levite named **P** in charge of the storerooms	7015

PEDDLE (1)

2Co	2:17	we do not **p** the word of God **for profit.**	2836

PEDESTAL (1)

Am	5:26	the **p** of your idols, the star of your god—	3962

PEELED (1) [PEELING, PEELS]

Ge	30:38	the **p** branches in all the watering troughs,	7202

PEELING (1) [PEELED]

Ge	30:37	on them *by* **p** *the* bark and exposing	7202

PEELS (1) [PEELED]

Job	30:30	My skin grows black and **p;**	4946+6584

PEERED (1) [PEERING]

Jdg	5:28	"Through the window **p** Sisera's mother;	9207

PEERING (1) [PEERED]

SS	2:9	**p** through the lattice.	7438

PEG (7) [PEGS]

Jdg	4:21	up a tent **p** and a hammer and went quietly	3845
	4:21	the **p** through his temple into the ground,	3845
	4:22	with the **tent p** through his temple—	3845
	5:26	Her hand reached for the **tent p,**	3845
Isa	22:23	I will drive him like a **p** into a firm place;	3845
	22:25	**p** driven into the firm place will give way;	3845
Zec	10:4	the cornerstone, from him the **tent p,**	3845

PEGS (8) [PEG]

Ex	27:19	including all the **tent p** *for* it and those for	3845
	35:18	the **tent p** *for* the tabernacle and for	3845
	38:20	All the **tent p** of the tabernacle and of	3845
	38:31	and those for its entrance and all the **tent p**	3845
	39:40	the ropes and **tent p** *for* the courtyard;	3845
Nu	3:37	**tent p** and ropes.	3845
	4:32	**tent p,** ropes, all their equipment	3845
Eze	15:3	Do they make **p** from it to hang things on?	3845

PEKAH (11) [PEKAH'S]

2Ki	15:25	**P** son of Remaliah, conspired against him.	7220
	15:25	So **P** killed Pekahiah and succeeded him	NIH
	15:27	**P** son of Remaliah became king of Israel	7220
	15:29	In the time of **P** king of Israel,	7220
	15:30	of Elah conspired against **P** son	7220
	15:32	the second year of **P** son of Remaliah king	7220
	15:37	and **P** son of Remaliah against Judah.)	7220
	16:1	the seventeenth year of **P** son of Remaliah,	7220
	16:5	of Aram and **P** son of Remaliah king	7220
2Ch	28:6	In one day **P** son of Remaliah killed	7220
Isa	7:1	of Aram and **P** son of Remaliah king	7220

PEKAH'S (1) [PEKAH]

2Ki	15:31	As for the other events of **P** reign,	7220

PEKAHIAH (5) [PEKAHIAH'S]

2Ki	15:22	and **P** his son succeeded him as king.	7222
	15:23	**P** son of Menahem became king of Israel	7222
	15:24	**P** did evil in the eyes of the LORD.	NIH
	15:25	of Gilead with him, he assassinated **P,**	2084S
	15:25	Pekah killed **P** and succeeded him as king.	2084S

PEKAHIAH'S (1) [PEKAHIAH]

2Ki	15:26	The other events of **P** reign, and all he did,	7222

PEKOD (2)

Jer	50:21	of Merathaim and those who live in **P.**	7216
Eze	23:23	the men of **P** and Shoa and Koa,	7216

PELAIAH (3)

1Ch	3:24	Hodaviah, Eliashib, **P,** Akkub, Johanan,	7126
Ne	8:7	Kelita, Azariah, Jozabad, Hanan and **P—**	7102
	10:10	Shebaniah, Hodiah, Kelita, **P,** Hanan,	7102

PELALIAH (1)

Ne	11:12	Adaiah son of Jeroham, the son of **P,**	7139

PELATIAH (5)

1Ch	3:21	**P** and Jeshaiah, and the sons of Rephaiah,	7124
	4:42	five hundred of these Simeonites, led by **P,**	7124
Ne	10:22	**P,** Hanan, Anaiah,	7124
Eze	11:1	son of Azzur and **P** son of Benaiah,	7125
	11:13	**P** son of Benaiah died.	7125

PELEG (8)

Ge	10:25	One was named **P,** because in his time	7105
	11:16	he became the father of **P.**	7105
	11:17	And after he became the father of **P,**	7105
	11:18	When **P** had lived 30 years,	7105
	11:19	**P** lived 209 years and had other sons	7105
1Ch	1:19	One was named **P,** because in his time	7105
	1:25	Eber, **P,** Reu,	7105
Lk	3:35	the son *of* **P,** the son of Eber,	5744

PELET (2) [BETH PELET]

1Ch	2:47	Regem, Jotham, Geshan, **P,**	7118
	12:3	Jeziel and **P** the sons of Azmaveth;	7118

PELETH (2) [PELETHITES]

Nu	16:1	sons of Eliab, and On son of **P—**	7150
1Ch	2:33	The sons of Jonathan: **P** and Zaza.	7150

PELETHITES (7) [PELETH]

2Sa	8:18	of Jehoiada was over the Kerethites and **P;**	7152
	15:18	along with all the Kerethites and **P;**	7152
	20:7	and **P** and all the mighty warriors went out	7152
	20:23	of Jehoiada was over the Kerethites and **P;**	7152
1Ki	1:38	and the **P** went down and put Solomon	7152
	1:44	the Kerethites and the **P,**	7152
1Ch	18:17	of Jehoiada was over the Kerethites and **P;**	7152

PELICAN (KJV) See DESERT OWL

PELONITE (3)

1Ch	11:27	Shammoth the Harorite, Helez the **P,**	7113
	11:36	Hepher the Mekerathite, Ahijah the **P,**	7113
	27:10	for the seventh month, was Helez the **P,**	7113

PELT (1) [PELTED]

Na	3:6	*I will* **p** you *with* filth,	8959

PELTED (1) [PELT]

2Sa	16:6	He **p** David and all the king's officials	6232

PELUSIUM (2)

Eze	30:15	I will pour out my wrath on **P,**	6096
	30:16	**P** will writhe in agony.	6096

PEN (11) [PENNED, PENS, PENT-UP]

1Sa	6:7	take their calves away and **p** them **up.**	1074+2025
Ps	45:1	my tongue is the **p** of a skillful writer.	6485
Isa	8:1	and write on it with an ordinary **p:**	3032
Jer	8:8	when actually the lying **p** of	6485
Mic	2:12	I will bring them together like sheep in a **p,**	1312
Hab	3:17	though there are no sheep in the **p**	4813
Mt	5:18	not the **least stroke of a p,**	3037
Lk	16:17	**least stroke of a p** to drop out of the Law.	3037
Jn	10:1	who does not enter the sheep **p** by the gate,	885

Jn 10:16 other sheep that are not of this **sheep** p. 885
3Jn 1:13 but I do not want to do so with p and ink. 2812

PENALTIES (1) [PENALTY]
Pr 19:29 **P** are prepared for mockers, 9150

PENALTY (11) [PENALTIES]
Lev 5: 6 as a p for the sin he has committed, 871
    5: 7 or two young pigeons to the LORD as a p 871
    5:15 to the LORD as a p a ram from the flock, 871
    6: 6 And as a p he must bring to the priest, 871
Job 8: 4 he gave them over to the **p** of their **sin**. 7322
Pr 19:19 A hot-tempered man must pay the **p**; 6741
Eze 23:49 You will suffer the **p for** your **lewdness** 2365
Da 2: 9 there is just one p for you. 10186
Lk 23:22 no **grounds for the death p**. 165+2505
Ro 1:27 and received in themselves the due p 521
Gal 5:10 into confusion will pay the **p**, 3210

PENCE (KJV) See DENARII, A YEAR'S WAGES, COINS

PENDANTS (1)
Jdg 8:26 the p and the purple garments worn by 5755

PENETRATES (1)
Heb 4:12 it p even to dividing soul and spirit, 1459

PENIEL (6)
Ge 32:30 So Jacob called the place **P**, saying, 7161
    32:31 The sun rose above him as he passed **P**, 7159
Jdg 8: 8 to **P** and made the same request of them, 7159
    8: 9 So he said to the men of **P**, 7159
    8:17 also pulled down the tower of **P** and killed 7159
1Ki 12:25 From there he went out and built up **P**. 7159

PENINNAH (3)
1Sa 1: 2 one was called Hannah and the other **P**. 7166
    1: 2 **P** had children, but Hannah had none. 7166
    1: 4 his wife **P** and to all her sons and daughters. 7166

PENITENT (1) [REPENT]
Isa 1:27 her p ones with righteousness. 8740

PENNED (3) [PEN]
Ex 21:29 but has not **kept** it **p up** and it kills a man 9068
    21:36 yet the owner did not **keep** it **p up**, 9068
1Sa 6:10 and **p up** their calves. 928+1074+2021+3973

PENNIES (1) [PENNY]
Lk 12: 6 Are not five sparrows sold for two **p**? 837

PENNY (4) [PENNIES]
Mt 5:26 not get out until you have paid the last **p**. 3119
    10:29 Are not two sparrows sold for a **p**? 837
Mk 12:42 worth only **a fraction of a** p. 3119
Lk 12:59 not get out until you have paid the last **p**." 3321

PENNYWORTH (KJV) See EIGHT MONTHS' WAGES

PENS (8) [PEN]
Nu 32:16 to build p here for our livestock and 1556+7366
    32:24 and p for your flocks, 1556
    32:36 and built p for their flocks. 1556
1Sa 24: 3 He came to the sheep p along the way; 1556
2Ch 32:28 and p for the flocks. 774
Ps 50: 9 from your stall or of goats from your p, 4813
    78:70 and took him from the sheep p; 4813
Zep 2: 6 will be a place for shepherds and sheep **p**. 1556

PENT-UP (1) [PEN]
Isa 59:19 For he will come like a p flood that 7639

PENTECOST (3)
Ac 2: 1 When the day of **P** came, 4300
    20:16 if possible, by the day of **P**. 4300
1Co 16: 8 But I will stay on at Ephesus until **P**, 4300

PENUEL (2)
1Ch 4: 4 **P** was the father of Gedor, 7158
    8:25 Iphdeiah and **P** were the sons of Shashak. 7158

PEOPLE (2213) [PEOPLE'S, PEOPLED, PEOPLES]
Ge 6: 9 blameless among the **p of** his **time**, 1887
    6:12 the p on earth had corrupted their ways. 1414
    6:13 "I am going to put an end to all **p**, 1414
    9:19 from them came the p who were **scattered** AIT
    11: 6 "If as one p speaking the same language 6639
    12: 1 your p and your father's household and go 4580
    12: 5 and the p they had acquired in Haran, 5883
    14:16 together with the women and the other **p**. 5883
    14:21 the **p** and keep the goods for yourself." 5883
    17:14 will be cut off from his p; 6638

Ge 18:24 if there are fifty **righteous** p in the city? AIT
    18:24 for the sake of the fifty **righteous** p AIT
    18:26 I find fifty **righteous** p in the city of Sodom, AIT
    18:28 the whole city because of **five** p?" AIT
    19:13 against **its** p is so great that he has sent us 4392S
    23: 7 and bowed down before the p of the land, 6639
    23:10 the Hittite was sitting among **his** p 1201+3147S
    23:11 give it to you in the presence of my p. 1201+6639
    23:12 Again Abraham bowed down before the p 6639
    25: 8 and he was gathered to his p. 6638
    25:17 and he was gathered to his **p**. 6638
    25:23 one p will be stronger than the other, 4211
    26:11 So Abimelech gave orders to all the p: 6639
    29:22 So Laban brought together all the p of 408
    32: 7 and distress Jacob divided the p who were 6639
    34:16 We'll settle among you and become one p 6639
    34:22 with us as one p only on the condition 6639
    34:30 the **p living** in this land. AIT
    35: 6 and all the p with him came to Luz 6639
    35:29 and died and was gathered to his **p**, 6638
    41:40 and all my p are to submit to your orders, 6639
    41:55 the p cried to Pharaoh for food. 6639
    42: 6 the one who sold grain to all its p. 6639
    47:15 of the p of Egypt and Canaan was gone, NIH
    47:21 and Joseph reduced the p to servitude, 6639
    47:23 Joseph said to the p, 6639
    48:19 He too will become a p, 6639
    49:16 "Dan will provide justice for his p as one of 6639
    49:29 "I am about to be gathered to my p. 6638
    49:33 breathed his last and was gathered to his **p**. 6638
Ex 1: 9 "Look," he said to his **p**, 6639
    1:20 to the midwives and the p increased 6639
    1:22 Then Pharaoh gave this order to all his **p**: 6639
    2:11 to where his own p were and watched them 278
    2:11 a Hebrew, one of his own **p**. 278
    3: 7 "I have indeed seen the misery of my p 6639
    3:10 I am sending you to Pharaoh to bring my p 6639
    3:12 When you have brought the p out of Egypt, 6639
    3:21 Egyptians favorably disposed toward this p, 6639
    4:16 He will speak to the p for you, 6639
    4:18 "Let me go back to my own p in Egypt 278
    4:21 so that he will not let the p go. 6639
    4:30 He also performed the signs before the p, 6639
    5: 1 'Let my p go, so that they may hold a 6639
    5: 4 why are you taking the p away 6639
    5: 5 the p of the land are now numerous, 6639
    5: 6 and foremen in charge of the p: 6639
    5: 7 the p with straw for making bricks; 6639
    5:10 and the foremen went out and said to the p, 6639
    5:12 So the p scattered all over Egypt 6639
    5:16 but the fault is with your own **p**." 6639
    5:22 why have you brought trouble upon this p? 6639
    5:23 he has brought trouble upon this p, 6639
    5:23 and you have not rescued your p at all." 6639
    6: 7 I will take you as my own p, 6639
    7: 4 bring out my divisions, my p the Israelites. 6639
    7:14 he refuses to let the p go. 6639
    7:16 Let my p go, so that they may worship me 6639
    8: 1 Let my p go, so that they may worship me. 6639
    8: 3 The houses of your officials and on your p, 6639
    8: 4 on you and your p and all your officials.' " 6639
    8: 8 to take the frogs away from me and my p, 6639
    8: 8 and I will let your p go to offer sacrifices to 6639
    8: 9 and your p that you and your houses may 6639
    8:11 your officials and your p; 6639
    8:20 Let my p go, so that they may worship me. 6639
    8:21 If you do not let my p go, 6639
    8:21 on your p and into your houses. 6639
    8:22 land of Goshen, where my p live; 6639
    8:23 I will make a distinction between my p 6639
    8:23 between my people and your p. 6639
    8:29 and his officials and his **p**. 6639
    8:29 by not letting the p go to offer sacrifices to 6639
    8:31 and his officials and his p; 6639
    8:32 and would not let the p go. 6639
    9: 1 Let my p go, so that they may worship me. 6639
    9: 7 and he would not let the p go. 6639
    9:13 Let my p go, so that they may worship me, 6639
    9:14 against you and your officials and your p, 6639
    9:15 and struck you and your p with a plague 6639
    9:17 You still set yourself against my p and will 6639
    9:27 and I and my p are in the wrong. 6639
    10: 3 Let my p go, so that they may worship me. 6639
    10: 7 Let the p go, so that they may worship me. 408
    11: 2 Tell the p that men and women alike are 6639
    11: 3 (The LORD made the Egyptians favorably
          disposed toward the p, 6639
    11: 3 by Pharaoh's officials and by the **p**.) 6639
    11: 8 'Go, you and all the p who follow you!' 6639
    12: 4 into account the number of p there are. 5883
    12: 6 when all the **p of** the community 7736
    12:27 Then the p bowed down and worshiped. 6639
    12:31 Leave my p, you and the Israelites! 6639
    12:33 the p to hurry and leave the country. 6639
    12:34 So the p took their dough before 6639
    12:36 The LORD had made the Egyptians
          favorably disposed toward the p, 6639
    12:38 Many **other** p went up with them, 6850
    12:40 the length of time the **Israelite** p lived AIT
    13: 3 Then Moses said to the p, 6639
    13:17 When Pharaoh let the p go, 6639
    13:18 So God led the p around by the desert road 6639
    13:22 by night left its place in front of the p. 6639
    14: 5 king of Egypt was told that the p had fled, 6639
    14:13 Moses answered the p, "Do not be afraid. 6639
    14:31 the p feared the LORD and put their trust 6639
    15:13 you will lead the p you have redeemed. 6639

Ex 15:14 anguish will grip the p of Philistia. 3782
    15:15 the p of Canaan will melt away; 3782
    15:16 until your p pass by, O LORD, 6639
    15:16 O LORD, until the p you bought pass by. 6639
    15:24 So the p grumbled against Moses, saying, 6639
    16: 4 The p are to go out each day 6639
    16:27 some of the p went out on the seventh day 6639
    16:30 So the p rested on the seventh day. 6639
    16:31 The p of Israel called the bread manna. 1074
    17: 1 but there was no water for the p to drink. 6639
    17: 3 But the p were thirsty for water there, 6639
    17: 4 "What am I to do with these p? 6639
    17: 5 "Walk on ahead of the p. 6639
    17: 6 and water will come out of it for the p to 6639
    18: 1 for Moses and for his p Israel, 6639
    18:10 and who rescued the p from the hand of 6639
    18:13 to serve as judge for the p, 6639
    18:14 that Moses was doing for the p, 6639
    18:14 "What is this you are doing for the p? 6639
    18:14 while all these p stand around you 6639
    18:15 the p come to me to seek God's will. 6639
    18:18 You and these p who come to you 6639
    18:21 But select capable men from all the p— 6639
    18:22 Have them serve as judges for the p 6639
    18:23 and all these p will go home satisfied." 6639
    18:25 and made them leaders of the p, 6639
    18:26 They served as judges for the p at all times. 6639
    19: 3 and what you are to tell the p of Israel: 1201
    19: 7 of the p and set before them all the words 6639
    19: 8 The p all responded together, 6639
    19: 9 that the p will hear me speaking with you 6639
    19: 9 Moses told the LORD what the p had said. 6639
    19:10 "Go to the p and consecrate them today 6639
    19:11 on Mount Sinai in the sight of all the p. 6639
    19:12 the p around the mountain and tell them, 6639
    19:14 down the mountain to the p, 6639
    19:15 Then he said to the p, 6639
    19:17 the p out of the camp to meet with God, 6639
    19:21 the p so they do not force their way through 6639
    19:23 "The p cannot come up Mount Sinai, 6639
    19:24 and the p must not force their way through 6639
    19:25 Moses went down to the p and told them. 6639
    20:18 When the p saw the thunder and lightning 6639
    20:20 Moses said to the p, "Do not be afraid. 6639
    20:21 The p remained at a distance, 6639
    22:25 of my p among you who is needy, do not 6639
    22:28 or curse the ruler of your p. 6639
    22:31 "You are to be my holy p, 408
    23: 6 "Do not deny justice to your **poor** p AIT
    23:11 Then the poor among your p may get food 6639
    23:31 I will hand over to you the p who **live in** AIT
    24: 2 And the p may not come up with him." 6639
    24: 3 the p all the LORD's words and laws, 6639
    24: 7 of the Covenant and read it to the p. 6639
    24: 8 sprinkled it on the p and said, 6639
    30:33 a priest must be cut off from his p.' " 6638
    30:38 be cut off from his **p**." 6638
    31:14 on that day must be cut off from his p. 6638
    32: 1 When the p saw that Moses was so long 6639
    32: 3 So all the p took off their earrings 6639
    32: 6 So the next day the p rose early 6639
    32: 7 "Go down, because your p, 6639
    32: 9 "I have seen these p," 6639
    32: 9 "and they are a stiff-necked p. 6639
    32:11 against your p, whom you brought out 6639
    32:12 relent and do not bring disaster on your p. 6639
    32:14 on his p the disaster he had threatened. 6639
    32:17 Joshua heard the noise of the p shouting, 6639
    32:21 "What did these p do to you, 6639
    32:22 "You know how prone these p are to evil. 6639
    32:25 Moses saw that the p were running wild 6639
    32:28 that day about three thousand of the p died. 6639
    32:30 The next day Moses said to the p, 6639
    32:31 what a great sin these p have committed! 6639
    32:34 Now go, lead the p to the place I spoke of, 6639
    32:35 And the LORD struck the p with a plague 6639
    33: 1 you and the p you brought up out of Egypt, 6639
    33: 3 a stiff-necked p and I might destroy you on 6639
    33: 4 When the p heard these distressing words, 6639
    33: 5 'You are a stiff-necked p. 6639
    33: 8 all the p rose and stood at the entrances 6639
    33:10 the p saw the pillar of cloud standing at 6639
    33:12 "You have been telling me, 'Lead these p,' 6639
    33:13 Remember that this nation is your p." 6639
    33:16 and with your p unless you go with us? 6639
    33:16 What else will distinguish me and your p 6639
    33:16 and your people from all the other p on 6639
    34: 9 Although this is a stiff-necked p, 6639
    34:10 Before all your p I will do wonders never 6639
    34:10 The p you live among will see 6639
    36: 3 And **the** p continued to bring freewill 2156S
    36: 5 "The p are bringing more than enough 6639
    36: 6 the p were restrained from bringing more, 6639
Lev 4: 3 bringing guilt on the p, 6639
    6: 3 if he commits any such sin that may do— 132
    7:20 that person must be cut off from his p. 6638
    7:21 that person must be cut off from his p.' " 6638
    7:25 to the LORD must be cut off from his p. 6638
    7:27 that person must be cut off from his p.' " 6638
    9: 7 make atonement for yourself and the p; 6639
    9: 7 for the p and make atonement for them, 6639
    9:15 then brought the offering that was for the p. 6639
    9:18 the ram as the fellowship offering for the p. 6639
    9:22 Then Aaron lifted his hands toward the p 6639
    9:23 When they came out, they blessed the p; 6639
    9:23 glory of the LORD appeared to all the p. 6639
    9:24 And when all the p saw it, 6639

Lev	10: 3	in the sight of all the **p** I will be honored.' "	6639
	16:15	the sin offering for the **p** and take its blood	6639
	16:24	for himself and the burnt offering for the **p**,	6639
	16:24	make atonement for himself and for the **p**.	6639
	16:33	the priests and all the **p** *of* the community.	6639
	17: 4	and must be cut off from his **p**.	6638
	17: 9	that man must be cut off from his **p**.	6638
	17:10	and will cut him off from his **p**.	6638
	18:27	by the **p** who lived *in* the land before you,	408
	18:29	such persons must be cut off from their **p**.	6638
	19: 8	that person must be cut off from his **p**.	6638
	19:16	about spreading slander among your **p**.	6638
	19:18	or bear a grudge against one of your **p**,	6639
	20: 2	The **p** of the community are to stone him.	6639
	20: 3	that man and I will cut him off from his **p**;	6639
	20: 4	If the **p** *of* the community close their eyes	6639
	20: 5	and his family and will cut off from their **p**	6639
	20: 6	and I will cut him off from his **p**.	6639
	20:17	be cut off before the eyes of their **p**.	1201+6639
	20:18	Both of them must be cut off from their **p**.	6639
	21: 1	for any of his **p** who die,	6638
	21: 4	not make himself unclean for **p** related	6638
	21:14	but only a virgin from his own **p**,	6638
	21:15	his offspring among his **p**.	6638
	23:29	on that day must be cut off from his **p**.	6638
	23:30	among his **p** anyone who does any work on	6639
	26:12	be your God, and you will be my **p**.	6639
Nu	1:18	The **p** indicated their ancestry by their clans	NIH
	2: 3	of the **p** *of* Judah is Nahshon son	1201
	2: 5	the **p** *of* Issachar is Nethanel son of Zuar.	1201
	2: 7	The leader of the **p** *of* Zebulun is Eliab son	1201
	2:10	The leader of the **p** *of* Reuben is Elizur son	1201
	2:12	of the **p** *of* Simeon is Shelumiel son	1201
	2:14	The leader of the **p** *of* Gad is Eliasaph son	1201
	2:18	of the **p** *of* Ephraim is Elishama son	1201
	2:20	of the **p** *of* Manasseh is Gamaliel son	1201
	2:22	of the **p** *of* Benjamin is Abidan son	1201
	2:25	The leader of the **p** *of* Dan is Ahiezer son	1201
	2:27	The leader of the **p** *of* Asher is Pagiel son	1201
	2:29	of the **p** *of* Naphtali is Ahira son of Enan.	1201
	5:21	"may the Lord cause your **p** to curse	6639
	5:27	and she will become accursed among her **p**.	6639
	7:24	the leader of the **p** *of* Zebulun,	1201
	7:30	the leader of the **p** *of* Reuben,	1201
	7:36	the leader of the **p** *of* Simeon,	1201
	7:42	the leader of the **p** *of* Gad,	1201
	7:48	the leader of the **p** *of* Ephraim,	1201
	7:54	the leader of the **p** *of* Manasseh,	1201
	7:60	the leader of the **p** *of* Benjamin,	1201
	7:66	the leader of the **p** *of* Dan,	1201
	7:72	the leader of the **p** *of* Asher,	1201
	7:78	the leader of the **p** *of* Naphtali,	1201
	9:13	that person must be cut off from his **p**	6638
	10:30	to my own land and my own **p**."	4580
	11: 1	the **p** complained about their hardships in	6639
	11: 2	When the **p** cried out to Moses,	6639
	11: 8	The **p** went around gathering it,	6639
	11:10	Moses heard the **p** of every family wailing,	6639
	11:11	that you put the burden of all these **p**	6639
	11:12	Did I conceive all these **p**?	6639
	11:13	Where can I get meat for all these **p**?	6639
	11:14	I cannot carry all these **p** by myself;	6639
	11:16	to you as leaders and officials among the **p**.	6639
	11:17	the burden of the **p** so that you will	6639
	11:18	"Tell the **p**: 'Consecrate yourselves	6639
	11:24	and told the **p** what the Lord had said. "	6639
	11:29	that all the Lord's **p** were prophets and	6639
	11:32	and all the next day the **p** went out	6639
	11:33	of the Lord burned against the **p**,	6639
	11:34	the **p** who had craved other food.	6639
	11:35	the **p** traveled to Hazeroth and stayed there.	6639
	12:15	and the **p** did not move on	6639
	12:16	the **p** left Hazeroth and encamped in	6639
	13:18	and whether the **p** who live there are strong	6639
	13:28	But the **p** who live there are powerful,	6639
	13:30	Caleb silenced the **p** before Moses and said,	6639
	13:31	"We can't attack those **p**;	6639
	13:32	All the **p** we saw there are of great size.	6639
	14: 1	the **p** of the community raised their voices	6639
	14: 9	And do not be afraid of the **p** of the land,	6639
	14:11	"How long will these **p** treat me	6639
	14:13	By your power you brought these **p** up	6639
	14:14	are with these **p** and that you, O Lord,	6639
	14:15	If you put these **p** to death all at one time,	6639
	14:16	'The Lord was not able to bring these **p**	6639
	14:19	forgive the sin of these **p**,	6639
	15:26	because all the **p** were involved in	6639
	15:30	and that person must be cut off from his **p**.	6639
	16:41	"You have killed the Lord's **p**,"	6639
	16:47	among the **p**, but Aaron offered the incense	6639
	16:49	But 14,700 **p** *died* from the plague,	AIT
	19:18	the furnishings and the **p** who were there.	5883
	20: 2	and **p** gathered in opposition to Moses	NIH
	20:24	"Aaron will be gathered to his **p**.	6638
	20:26	for Aaron will be gathered to his **p**;	NIH
	21: 2	"If you will deliver these **p** into our hands,	6639
	21: 4	But the **p** grew impatient on the way;	6639
	21: 6	they bit the **p** and many Israelites died.	6639
	21: 7	The **p** came to Moses and said,	6639
	21: 7	So Moses prayed for the **p**.	6639
	21:16	the **p** together and I will give them water."	6639
	21:18	that the nobles of the **p** sank—	6639
	21:29	You are destroyed, O **p** of Chemosh!	6639
	22: 3	because there were so many **p**.	6639
	22: 5	Balak said: "A **p** has come out of Egypt;	6639
	22: 6	Now come and put a curse on these **p**,	6639
	22:11	'A **p** that has come out of Egypt covers	6639

Nu	22:12	You must not put a curse on those **p**,	6639
	22:17	Come and put a curse on these **p** for me."	6639
	22:41	and from there he saw part of the **p**.	6639
	23: 9	I see a **p** who live apart and do	6639
	23:24	The **p** rise like a lioness;	6639
	24:14	Now I am going back to my **p**, but come,	6639
	24:14	let me warn you of what this **p** will do	6639
	24:14	of what this people will do to your **p**	6639
	25: 2	**p** ate and bowed down before these gods.	6639
	25: 4	"Take all the leaders of these **p**,	6639
	27:13	you too will be gathered to your **p**,	6638
	27:17	so the Lord's **p** will not be like sheep	6337
	31: 2	After that, you will be gathered to your **p**."	6638
	31: 3	So Moses said to the **p**,	6639
	31:11	including the **p** and animals,	132
	31:16	so that a plague struck the Lord's **p**	6337
	31:26	of the community are to count all the **p**	132
	31:40	16,000 **p**, of which the tribute for the Lord	132
	31:46	and 16,000 **p**.	132
	32: 4	the land the Lord subdued before the **p**	6337
	32:15	he will again leave all this **p** in the desert,	6639
	33:14	where there was no water for the **p** to drink.	6639
	35:15	and any *other* **p** **living** among them,	9369
Dt	1:28	'The **p** are stronger and taller than we are;	6639
	2: 4	Give the **p** these orders:	6639
	2:10	a **p** strong and numerous,	6639
	2:16	these fighting men among the **p** had died,	6639
	2:21	They were a **p** strong and numerous,	6639
	3:28	for he will lead this **p** across	6639
	4: 6	a wise and understanding **p**."	6639
	4:10	the **p** before me to hear my words so	6639
	4:20	out of Egypt, to be the **p** of his inheritance,	6639
	4:33	Has any other **p** heard the voice	6639
	5:28	"I have heard what this **p** said to you.	6639
	7: 6	you are a **p** holy to the Lord your God.	6639
	7: 6	on the face of the earth to be his **p**,	6639
	7:14	You will be blessed more than any other **p**;	6639
	9: 2	The **p** are strong and tall—Anakites!	6639
	9: 6	for you are a stiff-necked **p**.	6639
	9:12	because your **p** whom you brought out	6639
	9:13	the Lord said to me, "I have seen this **p**,	6639
	9:13	and they are a stiff-necked **p** indeed!	6639
	9:26	do not destroy your **p**,	6639
	9:27	Overlook the stubbornness of this **p**,	6639
	9:29	But they are your **p**,	6639
	10:11	"and lead the **p** on their way,	6639
	13: 9	and then the hands of all the **p**.	6639
	13:13	and have led the **p** of their town astray,	3782
	13:15	both its **p** and its livestock.	889+928+3972S
	14: 2	you are a **p** holy to the Lord your God.	6639
	14:21	you are a **p** holy to the Lord your God.	6639
	15:11	There will always be **poor** **p** in the land.	AIT
	16:18	and they shall judge the **p** fairly.	6639
	17: 7	and then the hands of all the **p**.	6639
	17:13	All the **p** will hear and be afraid,	6639
	17:16	the **p** return to Egypt to get more of them,	6639
	18: 3	from the **p** who sacrifice a bull or a sheep:	6639
	19:20	The **rest** *of the* **p** will hear of this and	AIT
	20:10	make its **p** an offer of peace.	NIH
	20:11	the **p** in it shall be subject to forced labor	6639
	20:19	Are the trees of the field a **p**,	132
	21: 8	Accept this atonement for your **p** Israel,	6639
	21: 8	and do not hold your **p** guilty of the blood	6639
	26: 5	and he went down into Egypt with a few **p**	5493
	26:15	and bless your **p** Israel and	6639
	26:18	declared this day that you are his **p**,	6639
	26:19	be a **p** holy to the Lord your God,	6639
	27: 1	and the elders of Israel commanded the **p**:	6639
	27: 9	now become the **p** of the Lord your God.	6639
	27:11	On the same day Moses commanded the **p**:	6639
	27:12	on Mount Gerizim to bless the **p**:	6639
	27:14	to all the **p** *of* Israel in a loud voice:	408
	27:15	Then all the **p** shall say, "Amen!"	6639
	27:16	Then all the **p** shall say, "Amen!"	6639
	27:17	Then all the **p** shall say, "Amen!"	6639
	27:18	Then all the **p** shall say, "Amen!"	6639
	27:19	Then all the **p** shall say, "Amen!"	6639
	27:20	Then all the **p** shall say, "Amen!"	6639
	27:21	Then all the **p** shall say, "Amen!"	6639
	27:22	Then all the **p** shall say, "Amen!"	6639
	27:23	Then all the **p** shall say, "Amen!"	6639
	27:24	Then all the **p** shall say, "Amen!"	6639
	27:25	Then all the **p** shall say, "Amen!"	6639
	27:26	Then all the **p** shall say, "Amen!"	6639
	28: 9	Lord will establish you as his holy **p**,	6639
	28:33	A **p** that you do not know will eat what	6639
	29:13	to confirm you this day as his **p**,	6639
	29:25	because they **p** abandoned the covenant of	NIH
	31: 7	for you must go with this **p** into the land	6639
	31:12	Assemble the **p**—men, women	6639
	31:16	and these **p** will soon prostitute themselves	6639
	32: 6	O foolish and unwise **p**?	6639
	32: 9	For the Lord's portion is his **p**,	6639
	32:21	by those who are not a **p**;	6639
	32:36	The Lord will judge his **p**	6639
	32:43	Rejoice, O nations, with his **p**,	6639
	32:43	and make atonement for his land and **p**.	6639
	32:44	of this song in the hearing of the **p**.	6639
	32:50	and be gathered to your **p**,	6638
	32:50	on Mount Hor and was gathered to his **p**.	6639
	32:52	the land I am giving to the **p** *of* Israel."	1201
	33: 3	Surely it is you who love the **p**;	6639
	33: 5	when the leaders of the **p** assembled,	6639
	33: 7	the cry of Judah; bring him to his **p**.	6639
	33:21	When the heads of the **p** assembled,	6639
	33:29	Who is like you, a **p** saved by the Lord?	6639
Jos	1: 2	Now then, you and all these **p**,	6639

Jos	1: 6	because you will lead these **p** to inherit	6639
	1:10	So Joshua ordered the officers of the **p**:	6639
	1:11	"Go through the camp and tell the **p**,	6639
	2:24	all the **p** are melting in fear because of us."	3782
	3: 3	giving orders to the **p**:	6639
	3: 5	Joshua told the **p**, "Consecrate yourselves,	6639
	3: 6	of the covenant and pass on ahead of the **p**."	6639
	3:14	when the **p** broke camp to cross the Jordan,	6639
	3:16	So the **p** crossed over opposite Jericho.	6639
	4: 2	"Choose twelve men from among the **p**,	6639
	4: 7	to be a memorial to the **p** *of* Israel forever."	1201
	4:10	until everything the Lord had commanded Joshua was done by the **p**,	6639
	4:10	The **p** hurried over,	6639
	4:11	to the other side while the **p** watched.	6639
	4:19	the **p** went up from the Jordan and camped	6639
	5: 5	the **p** that came out had been circumcised,	6639
	5: 5	the **p** born in the desert during the journey	6639
	6: 5	have all the **p** give a loud shout;	6639
	6: 5	the city will collapse and the **p** will go up,	6639
	6: 7	And he ordered the **p**, "Advance!	6639
	6: 8	When Joshua had spoken to the **p**,	6639
	6:10	But Joshua had commanded the **p**,	6639
	6:11	Then he returned to camp and spent	NIH
	6:16	Joshua commanded the **p**, "Shout!	6639
	6:20	When the trumpets sounded, the **p** shouted,	6639
	6:20	when the **p** gave a loud shout,	6639
	7: 3	"Not all the **p** will have to go up against Ai.	6639
	7: 3	to take it and do not weary all the **p**,	6639
	7: 5	the hearts of the **p** melted and	6639
	7: 7	why did you ever bring this **p** across	6639
	7: 9	and the other **p** of the country will hear	3782
	7:13	"Go, consecrate the **p**.	6639
	8: 1	his **p**, his city and his land.	6639
	8: 9	but Joshua spent that night with the **p**.	6639
	8:25	all the **p** of Ai.	408
	8:33	of **the p** stood in front of Mount Gerizim	2257S
	8:33	when he gave instructions to bless the **p**	6639
	9: 3	when the **p** *of* Gibeon	3782
	10: 1	the **p** of Gibeon had made a treaty of peace	3782
	10: 2	**p** were very much **alarmed**	AIT
	11:14	but all the **p** they put to the sword	132
	12: 5	the border of the **p** of Geshur and Maacah,	1771
	13:11	territory of the **p** of Geshur and Maacah,	1771
	13:13	not drive out the **p** of Geshur and Maacah,	1771
	14: 8	up with me made the hearts of the **p** melt	6639
	15:12	These are the boundaries around the **p**	1201
	15:15	against the **p** living in Debir	AIT
	15:63	the Jebusites live there with the **p** *of* Judah.	1201
	16:10	to this day the Canaanites live among the **p**	NIH
	17: 2	So this allotment was for the rest of the **p**	1201
	17: 7	to include the **p** *living at* En Tappuah.	AIT
	17:11	Ibleam and the **p** *of* Dor, Endor,	3782
	17:14	The **p** *of* Joseph said to Joshua,	1201
	17:14	We are a numerous **p** and	6639
	17:16	The **p** *of* Joseph replied,	1201
	18:14	Kiriath Jearim), a town of the **p** *of* Judah.	1201
	24: 2	Joshua said to all the **p**,	6639
	24:16	Then the **p** answered,	6639
	24:19	Joshua said to the **p**,	6639
	24:21	But the **p** said to Joshua, "No!	6639
	24:24	And the **p** said to Joshua,	6639
	24:25	that day Joshua made a covenant for the **p**,	6639
	24:27	he said to all the **p**.	6639
	24:28	Then Joshua sent the **p** away,	6639
Jdg	1:11	against the **p** *living in* Debir	AIT
	1:16	with the men of Judah to live among the **p**	6639
	1:19	but they were unable to drive the **p** from	3782
	1:27	*the* **p** *of* Beth Shan or Taanach or Dor	3782
	1:32	because of this the **p** *of* **Asher** lived among	896
	2: 2	a covenant with the **p** *of* this land,	3782
	2: 4	the **p** wept aloud,	6639
	2: 7	The **p** served the Lord throughout	6639
	2:19	*the* **p** *returned to* ways	AIT
	5: 2	when the **p** willingly offer themselves—	6639
	5: 9	with the willing volunteers among the **p**.	6639
	5:11	"Then the **p** *of* the Lord went down to	6639
	5:13	the **p** of the Lord came to me with	6639
	5:14	with the **p** who followed you.	6639
	5:18	The **p** of Zebulun risked their very lives;	6639
	5:23	'Curse its **p** bitterly,	3782
	7: 3	announce now to the **p**,	6639
	9:29	If only this **p** were under my command!	6639
	9:36	**p** are coming down from the tops of	6639
	9:37	"Look, **p** are coming down from the center	6639
	9:42	The next day the **p** of Shechem went out to	6639
	9:43	When he saw the **p** coming out of the city,	6639
	9:45	until he had captured it and killed its **p**.	6639
	9:49	and set it on fire over **the p** inside.	2157S
	9:49	So all the **p** *in* the tower of Shechem,	408
	9:51	all the **p** *of* the city—fled.	1251
	10:18	of the **p** *of* Gilead said to each other,	6639
	11:11	the **p** made him head and commander	6639
	11:23	the Amorites out before his **p** Israel,	6639
	12: 2	and my **p** were engaged in a great struggle	6639
	14: 3	among your relatives or among all our **p**?	6638
	14:16	You've given my **p** a riddle,	1201+6639
	14:17	in turn explained the riddle to her **p**.	1201+6639
	16: 2	The **p** *of* Gaza were told, "Samson is here!"	6484
	16:24	When the **p** saw him, they praised their god,	6639
	16:30	the temple on the rulers and all the **p** in it.	6639
	18: 7	where they saw that the **p** were living	6639
	18:10	an unsuspecting **p** and a spacious land	6639
	18:20	and went along with the **p**.	6639
	18:27	against a peaceful and unsuspecting **p**.	6639
	19:12	whose **p** are not Israelites.	2179S
	20: 2	The leaders of all the **p** *of* the tribes	6639

Jos	20: 2	in the assembly of the **p** *of* God,	6639
	20: 8	All the **p** rose as one man, saying,	6639
	20:26	Then the Israelites, all the **p,**	6639
	21: 2	The **p** went to Bethel,	6639
	21: 4	Early the next day the **p** built an altar	6639
	21: 9	For when they counted the **p,**	6639
	21: 9	of the **p** *of* Jabesh Gilead were there.	3782
	21:12	They found among the **p** living in Jabesh	AIT
	21:15	The **p** grieved for Benjamin,	6639
Ru	1: 6	the aid of his **p** by providing food for them,	6639
	1:10	"We will go back with you to your **p.**"	6639
	1:15	"your sister-in-law is going back to her **p**	6639
	1:16	Your **p** will be my people	6639
	1:16	be my **p** and your God my God.	6639
	2:11	to live with a **p** you did not know before.	6639
	4: 4	and in the presence of the elders of my **p.**	6639
	4: 9	Boaz announced to the elders and all the **p,**	6639
1Sa	2:13	with the **p** that whenever anyone offered	6639
	2:23	the **p** about these wicked deeds of yours.	6639
	2:24	that I hear spreading among the LORD's **p.**	6639
	2:29	of every offering made by my **p** Israel?'	6639
	4: 4	So he sent men to Shiloh,	6639
	5: 3	the **p** *of* Ashdod rose early the next day,	847
	5: 6	upon the **p** *of* Ashdod and its vicinity;	847
	5: 9	He afflicted the **p** *of* the city,	408
	5:10	the **p** *of* Ekron cried out,	6834
	5:10	of Israel around to us to kill us and our **p.**"	6639
	5:11	or it will kill us and our **p.**"	6639
	6:13	Now the **p** *of* Beth Shemesh were	NIH
	6:14	The **p** chopped the wood of the cart	NIH
	6:15	On that day the **p** *of* Beth Shemesh	408
	6:19	The **p** mourned because of the heavy blow	6639
	6:21	Then they sent messengers to the **p**	3782
	7: 2	and all the **p** *of* Israel mourned and sought	1074
	8: 7	"Listen to all that the **p** are saying to you;	6639
	8:10	the LORD to the **p** who were asking him	6639
	8:19	But the **p** refused to listen to Samuel.	6639
	8:21	When Samuel heard all that the **p** said,	6639
	9:12	for the **p** have a sacrifice at the high place.	6639
	9:13	The **p** will not begin eating until he comes,	6639
	9:16	Anoint him leader over my **p** Israel;	6639
	9:16	he will deliver my **p** from the hand of	6639
	9:16	I have looked upon my **p,**	6639
	9:17	he will govern my **p.**"	6639
	10:17	the **p** *of* Israel to the LORD at Mizpah	6639
	10:23	among the **p** he was a head taller than any	6639
	10:24	Samuel said to all the **p,**	6639
	10:24	There is no one like him among all the **p.**"	6639
	10:24	Then the **p** shouted, "Long live the king!"	6639
	10:25	Samuel explained to the **p** the regulations	6639
	10:25	Then Samuel dismissed the **p,**	6639
	11: 4	of Saul and reported these terms to the **p,**	6639
	11: 5	and he asked, "What is wrong with the **p?**	6639
	11: 7	Then the terror of the LORD fell on the **p,**	6639
	11:12	The **p** then said to Samuel,	6639
	11:14	Then Samuel said to the **p,** "Come,	6639
	11:15	the **p** went to Gilgal and confirmed Saul	6639
	12: 6	Then Samuel said to the **p,**	6639
	12:18	So all the **p** stood in awe of the LORD and	6639
	12:19	The **p** all said to Samuel,	6639
	12:22	The LORD will not reject his **p,**	6639
	13: 4	**p** were summoned to join Saul at Gilgal.	6639
	13:14	and appointed him leader of his **p,**	6639
	14:24	Saul had bound the **p** under an oath,	6639
	14:27	not heard that his father had bound the **p**	6639
	15: 1	to anoint you king over his **p** Israel;	6639
	15: 8	and all his **p** he totally destroyed with	6639
	15:18	'Go and completely destroy those wicked **p,**	2629
	15:24	I was afraid of the **p** and so I gave in	6639
	15:30	before the elders of my **p** and before Israel;	6639
	18: 5	This pleased all the **p,** and Saul's officers	6639
	19:24	This is why **p** say, "Is Saul also among	AIT
	23: 5	the Philistines and saved the **p** *of* Keilah.	3782
	27:12	"He has become so odious to his **p,**	6639
	30:21	They came out to meet David and the **p**	6639
	31: 9	the temple of their idols and among their **p.**	6639
	31:11	When the **p** *of* Jabesh Gilead heard of what	3782
2Sa	3:18	'By my servant David I will rescue my **p** Israel	6639
	3:31	David said to Joab and all the **p** with him,	6639
	3:32	All the **p** wept also.	6639
	3:34	And all the **p** wept over him again.	6639
	3:36	All the **p** took note and were pleased;	6639
	3:37	on that day all the **p** and all Israel knew that	6639
	4: 3	because the **p** *of* Beeroth fled to Gittaim	943
	5: 2	'You will shepherd my **p** Israel,	6639
	5:12	for the sake of his **p** Israel.	6639
	6:18	the **p** in the name of the LORD Almighty.	6639
	6:19	And all the **p** went to their homes.	6639
	6:21	appointed me ruler over the LORD's **p** Israel	6639
	7: 7	I commanded to shepherd my **p** Israel,	6639
	7: 8	the flock to be ruler over my **p** Israel.	6639
	7:10	a place for my **p** Israel and will plant them	6639
	7:10	Wicked **p** will not oppress them anymore,	1201
	7:11	I appointed leaders over my **p** Israel.	6639
	7:23	And who is like your **p** Israel—	6639
	7:23	on earth that God went out to redeem as a **p**	6639
	7:23	and their gods from before your **p,**	6639
	7:24	You have established your **p** Israel	6639
	8:15	doing what was just and right for all his **p.**	6639
	10:12	Be strong and let us fight bravely for our **p**	6639
	12:31	and brought out the **p** who were there,	6639
	13:34	and saw many **p** on the road west of him,	6639
	14:13	a thing like this against the **p** *of* God?	6639
	14:15	because the **p** have made me afraid.	6639
	15:17	king set out, with all the **p** following him,	6639
	15:23	wept aloud as all the **p** passed by.	6639

2Sa	15:23	and all the **p** moved on toward the desert.	6639
	15:24	until all the **p** had finished leaving the city.	6639
	15:30	All the **p** with him covered their heads too	6639
	15:32	where **p** used to worship God,	AIT
	16:14	The king and all the **p** with him arrived	6639
	16:18	the one chosen by the LORD, by these **p,**	6639
	17: 2	and then all the **p** with him will flee.	6639
	17: 3	and bring all the **p** back to you.	6639
	17: 3	all the **p** will be unharmed."	6639
	17:16	over without fail, or the king and all the **p**	6639
	17:22	and all the **p** with him set out and crossed	6639
	17:29	from cows' milk for David and his **p** to eat.	6639
	17:29	"The **p** have become hungry and tired	6639
	19: 9	the **p** were all arguing with each other,	6639
	19:39	So all the **p** crossed the Jordan,	6639
	20:22	Then the woman went to all the **p**	6639
	22:44	from the attacks of my **p;**	6639
	22:44	**P** I did not know are subject to me,	6639
	24:15	and seventy thousand of the **p** from Dan	6639
	24:16	to the angel who was afflicting the **p,**	6639
	24:17	the angel who was striking down the **p,**	6639
	24:21	that the plague on the **p** may be stopped."	6639
1Ki	1:39	the trumpet and all the **p** shouted,	6639
	1:40	And all the **p** went up after him,	6639
	3: 2	The **p,** however, were still sacrificing at	6639
	3: 8	among the **p** you have chosen,	6639
	3: 8	the people you have chosen, a great **p,**	6639
	3: 9	a discerning heart to govern your **p** and	6639
	3: 9	For who is able to govern this great **p**	6639
	4:20	The **p** *of* Judah and Israel were	NIH
	6:13	and will not abandon my **p** Israel."	6639
	8:16	the day I brought my **p** Israel out of Egypt,	6639
	8:16	I have chosen David to rule my **p** Israel.'	6639
	8:30	and of your **p** Israel when they pray	6639
	8:33	"When your **p** Israel have been defeated by	6639
	8:34	the sin of your **p** Israel and bring them back	6639
	8:35	because your **p** have sinned against you,	NIH
	8:36	the sin of your servants, your **p;**	6639
	8:36	the land you gave your **p** for an inheritance,	6639
	8:38	or plea is made by any of your **p** Israel—	6639
	8:41	not belong to your **p** Israel but has come	6639
	8:43	as do your own **p** Israel,	6639
	8:44	your **p** go to war against their enemies,	6639
	8:50	And forgive your **p,** who have sinned	6639
	8:51	for they are your **p** and your inheritance,	6639
	8:52	and to the plea of your **p** Israel,	6639
	8:56	who has given rest to his **p** Israel just	6639
	8:59	of his servant and the cause of his **p** Israel	6639
	8:65	**p** from Lebo Hamath to the Wadi of Egypt.	NIH
	8:66	On the following day he sent the **p** away.	6639
	8:66	for his servant David and his **p** Israel.	6639
	9: 9	**P** will answer, 'Because they have forsaken	AIT
	9:20	All the **p** left from the Amorites, Hittites,	6639
	12: 5	So the **p** went away.	6639
	12: 6	would you advise me to answer these **p?**"	6639
	12: 7	"If today you will be a servant to these **p**	6639
	12: 9	How should we answer these **p** who say	6639
	12:10	"Tell these **p** who have said to you,	6639
	12:12	and all the **p** returned to Rehoboam,	6639
	12:13	The king answered the **p** harshly.	6639
	12:15	So the king did not listen to the **p,**	6639
	12:23	and to the rest of the **p,**	6639
	12:27	If these **p** go up to offer sacrifices at	6639
	12:28	He said to the **p,**	2157S
	12:30	the **p** went even as far as Dan to worship	6639
	12:31	and appointed priests from all sorts of **p,**	6639
	13:25	Some **p** who passed by saw the body	408
	13:33	for the high places from all sorts of **p.**	6639
	14: 2	told me I would be king over this **p.**	6639
	14: 7	from among the **p** and made you a leader	6639
	14: 7	and made you a leader over my **p** Israel.	6639
	14:24	the **p** engaged in all the detestable practices	NIH
	16: 2	and made you leader of my **p** Israel,	6639
	16: 2	of Jeroboam and caused my **p** Israel to sin	6639
	16:21	the **p** *of* Israel were split into two factions;	6639
	18:19	Now summon the **p** from all over Israel	NIH
	18:21	Elijah went before the **p** and said,	6639
	18:21	But the **p** said nothing.	6639
	18:24	all the **p** said, "What you say is good."	6639
	18:30	Elijah said to all the **p,** "Come here to me."	6639
	18:37	answer me, so these **p** will know that you,	6639
	18:39	When all the **p** saw this,	6639
	19:21	to cook the meat and gave it to the **p,**	6639
	20: 8	The elders and the **p** all answered,	6639
	20:42	your **p** for his people.' "	6639
	20:42	your people for his **p.**' "	6639
	21: 9	in a prominent place among the **p.**	6639
	21:12	in a prominent place among the **p.**	6639
	21:13	against Naboth before the **p,**	6639
	22: 4	"I am as you are, my **p** as your people,	6639
	22: 4	"I am as you are, my people as your **p,**	6639
	22:17	'**These** **p** have no master.	AIT
	22:28	he added, "Mark my words, all you **p!**"	6639
	22:43	and the **p** continued to offer sacrifices	6639
2Ki	3: 7	"I am as you are, my **p** as your people,	6639
	3: 7	"I am as you are, my people as your **p,**	6639
	4:13	"I have a home among my own **p.**"	6638
	4:41	"Serve it to the **p** to eat."	6639
	4:42	"Give it to the **p** to eat," Elisha said.	6639
	4:43	Elisha answered, "Give it to the **p** to eat.	6639
	6:18	"Strike these **p** with blindness."	1580
	6:30	As he went along the wall, the **p** looked,	6639
	7:16	the **p** went out and plundered the camp of	6639
	7:17	and the **p** trampled him in the gateway,	6639
	7:20	for the **p** trampled him in the gateway,	6639
	9: 6	I anoint you king over the LORD's **p** Israel.	6639
	10: 9	He stood before all the **p** and said,	6639

2Ki	10:18	Then Jehu brought all the **p** together	6639
	10:27	and **p** have used it for a latrine to this day.	AIT
	11:12	and the **p** clapped their hands and shouted,	NIH
	11:13	the noise made by the guards and the **p,**	6639
	11:13	to the **p** at the temple of the LORD.	6639
	11:14	and all the **p** *of* the land were rejoicing	6639
	11:17	between the LORD and the king and **p**	6639
	11:17	that they would be the LORD's **p.**	6639
	11:17	a covenant between the king and the **p**	6639
	11:18	the **p** *of* the land went to the temple of Baal	6639
	11:19	the guards and all the **p** *of* the land,	6639
	11:20	and all the **p** *of* the land rejoiced.	6639
	12: 3	the **p** continued to offer sacrifices	6639
	12: 8	not collect any more money from the **p** and	6639
	14: 4	the **p** continued to offer sacrifices	6639
	14:21	Then all the **p** *of* Judah took Azariah,	6639
	15: 4	the **p** continued to offer sacrifices	6639
	15: 5	the palace and governed the **p** *of* the land.	6639
	15:10	He attacked him in front of the **p,**	6639
	15:29	and deported the **p** to Assyria.	4392S
	15:35	the **p** continued to offer sacrifices	6639
	16:15	the burnt offering of all the **p** *of* the land,	6639
	17:20	the LORD rejected all the **p** *of* Israel;	2446
	17:23	So the **p** *of* Israel were taken	NIH
	17:24	of Assyria brought **p** from Babylon,	NIH
	17:25	among them and they killed some of the **p.**	2157S
	17:26	"The **p** you deported and resettled in	1580
	17:26	the **p** do not know what he requires."	4392S
	17:27	and teach the **p** what the god of the land	4392S
	17:29	in the shrines the **p** *of* Samaria had made at	9085
	17:32	**all sorts** *of* their own **p** to officiate	AIT
	17:41	while these **p** were worshiping the LORD,	1580
	18:26	to us in Hebrew in the hearing of the **p** on	6639
	18:36	**p** remained silent and said nothing in reply,	6639
	19:12	and the **p** *of* Eden who were in Tel Assar?	1201
	19:26	Their **p,** drained of power,	3782
	19:35	When the **p** got up the next morning—	AIT
	20: 5	tell Hezekiah, the leader of my **p,**	6639
	21: 9	But the **p** did not listen.	AIT
	21:24	the **p** *of* the land killed all who had plotted	6639
	22: 4	the doorkeepers have collected from the **p.**	6639
	22:13	of the LORD for me and for the **p** and	6639
	22:16	to bring disaster on this place and its **p,**	3782
	22:19	against this place and its **p,**	3782
	23: 2	the **p** *of* Jerusalem, the priests and	3782
	23: 2	all the **p** from the least to the greatest.	6639
	23: 3	the **p** pledged themselves to the covenant.	6639
	23: 6	over the graves of the **common p.**	1201+6639
	23:10	and for Molech the detestable god of the **p**	1201
	23:21	The king gave this order to all the **p:**	6639
	23:30	And the **p** *of* the land took Jehoahaz son	6639
	23:35	and exacted the silver and gold from the **p**	6639
	24:14	Only the poorest **p** *of* the land were left.	6639
	25: 3	so severe that there was no food for the **p**	6639
	25:11	into exile the **p** who remained in the city,	6639
	25:12	behind some of the **poorest** *of* the land	AIT
	25:19	in charge of conscripting the **p** *of* the land	6639
	25:22	to be over the **p** he had left behind in Judah.	6639
	25:26	all the **p** from the least to the greatest,	6639
1Ch	2:10	the leader of the **p** *of* Judah.	1201
	4:14	because *its* **p** were craftsmen.	AIT
	4:27	not become as numerous as the **p** *of* Judah.	1201
	5:21	took one hundred thousand **p** captive,	132+5883
	5:23	The **p** *of* the half-tribe of Manasseh	1201
	9: 1	The **p** *of* Judah were taken captive	NIH
	9: 6	The **p** from Judah numbered 690.	278+2157
	9: 9	The **p** from Benjamin,	278+2157
	10: 9	the news among their idols and their **p.**	6639
	11: 2	'You will shepherd my **p** Israel,	6639
	11: 3	because it seemed right to all the **p.**	6639
	14: 2	for the sake of his **p** Israel.	6639
	16: 2	he blessed the **p** in the name of the LORD.	6639
	16:36	Then all the **p** said "Amen" and "Praise	6639
	16:43	Then all the **p** left, each for his own home,	6639
	17: 6	whom I commanded to shepherd my **p,**	6639
	17: 7	to be ruler over my **p** Israel.	6639
	17: 9	a place for my **p** Israel and will plant them	6639
	17: 9	Wicked **p** will not oppress them anymore,	1201
	17:10	I appointed leaders over my **p** Israel.	6639
	17:21	And who is like your **p** Israel—	6639
	17:21	on earth whose God went out to redeem a **p**	6639
	17:21	by driving out nations from before your **p,**	6639
	17:22	You made your **p** Israel your very own forever,	6639
	18:14	doing what was just and right for all his **p.**	6639
	19:13	Be strong and let us fight bravely for our **p**	6639
	20: 3	and brought out the **p** who were there,	6639
	21:15	to the angel who was destroying the **p,**	NIH
	21:17	but do not let this plague remain on your **p.**"	6639
	21:22	that the plague on the **p** may be stopped.	6639
	22:18	land is subject to the LORD and to his **p.**	6639
	23:25	has granted rest to his **p** and has come	6639
	28: 2	"Listen to me, my brothers and my **p.**	6639
	28:21	the **p** will obey your every command.	6639
	29: 9	The **p** rejoiced at the willing response	6639
	29:14	"But who am I, and who are my **p,**	6639
	29:17	willingly your **p** who are here have given	6639
	29:18	in the hearts of your **p** forever,	6639
2Ch	1: 9	over a **p** who are as numerous as the dust of	6639
	1:10	and knowledge, that I may lead this **p,**	6639
	1:10	for who is able to govern this great **p**	6639
	1:11	for wisdom and knowledge to govern my **p**	6639
	2:11	"Because the LORD loves his **p,**	6639
	2:18	foremen over them to keep the **p** working.	6639
	6: 5	'Since the day I brought my **p** out of Egypt,	6639
	6: 5	to be the leader over my **p** Israel.	6639
	6: 6	I have chosen David to rule my **p** Israel.'	6639

2Ch	6:11	that he made with the **p** of Israel."	1201
	6:21	and of your **p** Israel when they pray	6639
	6:24	"When your **p** Israel have been defeated by	6639
	6:25	the sin of your **p** Israel and bring them back	6639
	6:26	because your **p** have sinned against you,	NIH
	6:27	the sin of your servants, your **p** Israel.	6639
	6:27	the land you gave your **p** for an inheritance.	6639
	6:29	or plea is made by any of your Israel—	6639
	6:32	not belong to your **p** Israel but has come	6639
	6:33	as do your own **p** Israel,	6639
	6:34	your **p** go to war against their enemies,	6639
	6:39	the sin of your **p**, who have sinned	6639
	7: 4	the **p** offered sacrifices before the LORD.	6639
	7: 5	the king and all the **p** dedicated the temple	6639
	7: 8	**p** from Lebo Hamath to the Wadi of Egypt.	NIH
	7:10	of the seventh month he sent the **p**	6639
	7:10	for David and Solomon and for his **p** Israel.	6639
	7:13	the land or send a plague among my **p**,	6639
	7:14	if my **p**, who are called by my name,	6639
	7:22	**P** will **answer**, 'Because they have forsaken	AIT
	8: 7	All the **p** left from the Hittites, Amorites,	6639
	10: 5	So the **p** went away.	6639
	10: 6	advise me to answer these **p**?"	6639
	10: 7	to these **p** and please them and give them	6639
	10: 9	How should we answer these **p** who say	6639
	10:10	"Tell the **p** who have said to you,	6639
	10:12	and all the **p** returned to Rehoboam,	6639
	10:15	So the king did not listen to the **p**,	6639
	15: 9	**p** from Ephraim, Manasseh and Simeon	
		who had **settled**	AIT
	16:10	Asa brutally oppressed some of the **p**.	6639
	17: 9	to all the towns of Judah and taught the **p**.	6639
	18: 2	for him and the **p** with him and urged him	6639
	18: 3	"I am as you are, and my **p** as your people;	6639
	18: 3	"I am as you are, and my people as your **p**;	6639
	18:16	'These **p** have no master.	AIT
	18:27	he added, "Mark my words, all you **p**!"	6639
	19: 4	the **p** from Beersheba to the hill country	6639
	20: 4	The **p** of Judah came together to seek help	NIH
	20: 7	before your **p** Israel and give it forever to	6639
	20:18	and all the **p** of Judah and Jerusalem fell	3782
	20:20	"Listen to me, Judah and **p** of Jerusalem!	3782
	20:21	After consulting the **p**,	6639
	20:33	and the **p** still had not set their hearts on	6639
	21:11	of Judah and had caused the **p** of Jerusalem	3782
	21:13	of Jerusalem to prostitute themselves,	3782
	21:14	now the LORD is about to strike your **p**,	6639
	21:19	His **p** made no fire in his honor,	6639
	22: 1	The **p** of Jerusalem made Ahaziah,	3782
	23:12	the noise of the **p** running and cheering	6639
	23:13	and all the **p** of the land were rejoicing	6639
	23:16	then made a covenant that he and the **p** and	6639
	23:16	and the king would be the LORD's **p**.	6639
	23:17	All the **p** went to the temple of Baal	6639
	23:20	the rulers of the **p** and all the people of	6639
	23:20	the rulers of the people and all the **p** of	6639
	23:21	and all the **p** of the land rejoiced.	6639
	24:10	the **p** brought their contributions gladly,	6639
	24:19	Although the LORD sent prophets to **the p**	2157S
	24:20	He stood before the **p** and said,	6639
	24:23	and killed all the leaders of the **p**.	6639
	25: 5	the **p** of Judah together and assigned them	NIH
	25: 7	not with any of the **p** of Ephraim.	1201
	25:13	They killed three thousand **p**	2157S
	25:14	he brought back the gods of the **p** of Seir.	1201
	25:15	not save their own **p** from your hand?"	6639
	26: 1	Then all the **p** of Judah took Uzziah,	6639
	26:10	He had **p** working his fields and vineyards	438
	26:21	the palace and governed the **p** of the land.	6639
	26:23	for **p** said, "He had leprosy."	AIT
	27: 2	The **p**, however, continued their corrupt	6639
	28: 5	and took **many** of his **p** as prisoners	AIT
	29:36	the **p** rejoiced at what God had brought	6639
	29:36	at what God had brought about for his **p**,	6639
	30: 3	and the **p** had not assembled in Jerusalem.	6639
	30: 5	the **p** to come to Jerusalem and celebrate	NIH
	30: 6	"**P** of Israel, return to the LORD,	1201
	30:10	but the **p** scorned and ridiculed them.	NIH
	30:12	Also in Judah the hand of God was on the **p**	NIH
	30:13	of **p** assembled in Jerusalem to celebrate	6639
	30:18	Although most of the many **p** who came	6639
	30:20	LORD heard Hezekiah and healed the **p**.	6639
	30:27	and the Levites stood to bless the **p**,	6639
	31: 4	He ordered the **p** living in Jerusalem	6639
	31: 8	the LORD and blessed his **p** Israel.	6639
	31:10	the **p** began to bring their contributions to	NIH
	31:10	because the LORD has blessed his **p**,	6639
	32: 6	over the **p** and assembled them before him	6639
	32: 8	And the **p** gained confidence	6639
	32: 9	for Hezekiah king of Judah and for all the **p**	NIH
	32:14	to save his **p** from me?	6639
	32:15	to deliver his **p** from my hand or the hand	6639
	32:17	of the other lands did not rescue their **p**	6639
	32:17	so the god of Hezekiah will not rescue his **p**	6639
	32:18	in Hebrew to the **p** of Jerusalem who were	6639
	32:22	So the LORD saved Hezekiah and the **p**	3782
	32:26	as did the **p** of Jerusalem;	3782
	32:33	and the **p** of Jerusalem honored him	3782
	33: 9	But Manasseh led Judah and the **p**	3782
	33:10	The LORD spoke to Manasseh and his **p**,	6639
	33:17	The **p**, however, continued to sacrifice at	6639
	33:25	the **p** of the land killed all who had plotted	6639
	34: 9	the doorkeepers had collected from the **p**	NIH
	34:24	from all the **p** of Judah and Benjamin and	NIH
	34:24	to bring disaster on this place and its **p**—	3782
	34:27	against this place and its **p**,	3782
	34:30	the **p** of Jerusalem, the priests and	3782

2Ch	34:30	all the **p** from the least to the greatest.	6639
	34:32	the **p** of Jerusalem did this in accordance	3782
	35: 3	the LORD your God and his **p** Israel.	6639
	35: 5	of your fellow countrymen, the **lay p.**	1201+6639
	35: 7	for all the **lay p** who were there	1201+6639
	35: 8	also contributed voluntarily to the **p** and	6639
	35:12	families of the **p** to offer to the LORD,	1201+6639
	35:13	and served them quickly to all the **p**.	1201+6639
	35:18	and Israel who were there with the **p**	3782
	36: 1	And the **p** of the land took Jehoahaz son	6639
	36:14	the **p** became more and more unfaithful,	6639
	36:15	on his **p** and on his dwelling place.	6639
	36:16	of the LORD was aroused against his **p**	6639
	36:23	Anyone of his **p** among you—	6639
Ezr	1: 3	Anyone of his **p** among you—	6639
	1: 4	the **p** of any place where survivors may	408
	2: 1	the **p** of the province who came up from	1201
	2: 2	The list of the men of the **p** of Israel:	6639
	2:70	along with some of the other **p**,	6639
	3: 1	And the **p** assembled as one man in Jerusalem.	6639
	3: 7	and oil to the **p** of Sidon and Tyre,	7479
	3:11	And all the **p** gave a great shout of praise to	6639
	3:13	because the **p** made so much noise.	6639
	4: 4	the **p** of Judah and make them afraid to go	6639
	4: 6	they lodged an accusation against the **p**	3782
	4:10	and the other **p** whom the great and	10040
	5: 8	The **p** are building it with large stones	NIH
	5:12	and deported the **p** to Babylon.	10553
	6:12	or **p** who lifts a hand to change this decree	10553
	6:16	Then the **p** of Israel—	10120
	7:16	the **p** and priests for the temple of their God	10553
	7:25	and judges to administer justice to all the **p**	10553
	8:15	I checked among the **p** and the priests,	6639
	8:36	who then gave assistance to the **p** and to	6639
	9: 1	"The **p** of Israel, including the priests	6639
	10: 9	all the **p** were sitting in the square before	6639
	10:13	But there are many **p** here and it is	6639
Ne	1: 6	for your servants, the **p** Israel.	1201
	1: 9	if your **exiled p** are at the farthest horizon,	AIT
	1:10	"They are your servants and your **p**,	6639
	4: 6	for the **p** worked with all their heart.	6639
	4:10	Meanwhile, the **p** in Judah said,	NIH
	4:13	the **p** behind the lowest points of the wall at	6639
	4:14	the officials and the rest of the **p**,	6639
	4:16	behind all the **p** of Judah	1074
	4:19	the officials and the rest of the **p**,	6639
	4:22	At that time I also said to the **p**,	6639
	5:10	and my men are also lending **the p** money	2157S
	5:13	And the **p** did as they had promised.	6639
	5:15	on the **p** and took forty shekels of silver	6639
	5:15	Their assistants also lorded it over the **p**.	6639
	5:18	the demands were heavy on these **p**.	6639
	5:19	O my God, for all I have done for these **p**.	6639
	7: 4	but there were few **p** in it,	6639
	7: 5	the **common p** for registration by families.	6639
	7: 6	These are the **p** of the province who came	1201
	7:72	by the rest of the **p** was 20,000	6639
	7:73	along with certain of the **p** and the rest of	6639
	8: 1	the **p** assembled as one man in the square	6639
	8: 3	the **p** listened attentively to the Book of	6639
	8: 5	All the **p** could see him	6639
	8: 5	and as he opened it, the **p** all stood up.	6639
	8: 6	all the **p** lifted their hands and responded,	6639
	8: 7	instructed the **p** in the Law while	6639
	8: 7	in the Law while the **p** were standing there.	6639
	8: 8	**p** could understand what was being read.	NIH
	8: 9	the Levites who were instructing the **p** said	6639
	8: 9	the **p** had been weeping as they listened to	6639
	8:11	The Levites calmed all the **p**, saying,	6639
	8:12	Then all the **p** went away to eat and drink,	6639
	8:16	the **p** went out and brought back branches	6639
	9:10	against all his officials and all the **p**	6639
	9:32	upon our fathers and all your **p**,	6639
	10:14	The leaders of the **p**:	6639
	10:28	"The rest of the **p**—priests, Levites,	6639
	10:34	"We—the priests, the Levites and the **p**—	6639
	10:39	The **p** of Israel, including the Levites,	1201
	11: 1	the leaders of the **p** settled in Jerusalem,	6639
	11: 1	the **p** cast lots to bring one out of every ten	6639
	11: 2	The **p** commended all the men	6639
	11: 4	while other **p** from both Judah	1201
	11:24	in all affairs relating to the **p**.	6639
	11:25	of the **p** of Judah lived in Kiriath Arba	1201
	12:30	they purified the **p**, the gates and the wall.	6639
	12:38	together with half the **p**—	6639
	13: 1	was read aloud in the hearing of the **p**	6639
	13: 3	When **the p** heard this law,	4392S
	13:16	in Jerusalem on the Sabbath to the **p**	1201
Est	1: 5	for all the **p** from the least to the greatest,	6639
	1:11	to display her beauty to the **p** and nobles,	6639
	1:22	to **each p** in its own language,	2256+6639+6639
	3: 6	having learned who Mordecai's **p** were,	6639
	3: 6	for a way to destroy all Mordecai's **p**,	6639
	3: 8	a certain **p** dispersed and scattered among	6639
	3: 8	from those of all other **p** and who do	6639
	3:11	"and do with the **p** as you please."	6639
	3:12	and in the language of **each p**	2256+6639+6639
	3:14	in every province and made known to the **p**	6639
	4: 8	for mercy and plead with him for her **p**.	6639
	4:11	and the **p** of the royal provinces know that	6639
	7: 3	And spare my **p**—this is my request.	6639
	7: 4	and my **p** have been sold for destruction	6639
	8: 6	can I bear to see disaster fall on my **p**?	6639
	8: 9	and the language of **each p**	2256+6639+6639
	8:13	in every province and made known to the **p**	NIH
	8:17	and celebrating. And **many p**	AIT
	9: 2	because the **p** of all the other nationalities	NIH

Est	10: 3	because he worked for the good of his **p**	6639
Job	1: 3	He was the greatest man among all the **p** of	1201
	12: 2	"Doubtless you are the **p**,	6639
	17: 6	a man in whose face **p** spit.	NIH
	18:19	or descendants among his **p**,	6639
	28: 4	Far from where **p** **dwell** he cuts a shaft,	AIT
	34:20	the **p** are shaken and they pass away;	6639
	34:30	from laying snares for the **p**.	6639
	36:20	to drag **p** away from their homes.	6639
Ps	3: 8	May your blessing be on your **p**.	6639
	12: 7	and protect us from such **p** forever.	1887
	14: 4	those who devour my **p** as men eat bread	6639
	14: 7	the LORD restores the fortunes of his **p**,	6639
	18:43	delivered me from the attacks of the **p**;	6639
	18:43	**p** I did not know are subject to me.	6639
	22: 6	scorned by men and despised by the **p**.	6639
	22:17	**p** stare and gloat over me.	2156S
	22:31	They will proclaim his righteousness to a **p**	6639
	28: 8	The LORD is the strength of **his p**,	4564S
	28: 9	Save your **p** and bless your inheritance;	6639
	29:11	The LORD gives strength to his **p**;	6639
	29:11	the LORD blesses his **p** with peace.	6639
	33: 8	let all the **p** of the world revere him.	3782
	33:12	the **p** he chose for his inheritance.	6639
	35:18	among throngs of **p** I will praise you.	6639
	44:12	You sold your **p** for a pittance,	6639
	45:10	Forget your **p** and your father's house.	6639
	47: 9	of the nations assemble as the **p** of the God	6639
	50: 4	and the earth, that he may judge his **p**:	6639
	50: 7	O my **p**, and I will speak, O Israel,	6639
	53: 4	those who devour my **p** as men eat bread	6639
	53: 6	When God restores the fortunes of his **p**,	6639
	59:11	O Lord our shield, or my **p** will forget.	6639
	60: 3	You have shown your **p** desperate times;	6639
	62: 8	Trust in him at all times, O **p**;	6639
	65: 9	with water to provide the **p** with grain,	4392S
	68: 7	When you went out before your **p**, O God,	6639
	68:10	Your **p** settled in it, and from your bounty,	2653
	68:35	of Israel gives power and strength to his **p**.	6639
	69:11	**p** make sport of me.	2157S
	69:33	and does not despise his **captive p**.	AIT
	69:35	Then **p** **will settle** there and possess it;	AIT
	72: 2	He will judge your **p** in righteousness,	6639
	72: 3	mountains will bring prosperity to the **p**,	6639
	72: 4	He will defend the afflicted among the **p**	6639
	72:15	*May* **p** ever **pray** for him and bless him	AIT
	73:10	Therefore their **p** turn to them and drink	6639
	74: 2	Remember the **p** you purchased of old,	6337
	74:18	how foolish **p** have reviled your name.	6639
	74:19	the lives of your **afflicted p** forever.	AIT
	75: 3	When the earth and all its **p** quake,	3782
	77:15	With your mighty arm you redeemed your **p**	6639
	77:20	You led your **p** like a flock by the hand	6639
	78: 1	O my **p**, hear my teaching;	6639
	78:20	Can he supply meat for his **p**?"	6639
	78:24	he rained down manna for **the p** to eat,	2157S
	78:52	But he brought his **p** out like a flock;	6639
	78:62	He gave his **p** over to the sword;	6639
	78:71	to be the shepherd of his **p** Jacob,	6639
	79:13	Then we your **p**, the sheep of your pasture,	6639
	80: 4	against the prayers of your **p**?	6639
	80:16	at your rebuke your **p** perish.	AIT
	81: 8	O my **p**, and I will warn you—	6639
	81:11	"But my **p** would not listen to me;	6639
	81:13	"If my **p** would but listen to me,	6639
	83: 3	With cunning they conspire against your **p**;	6639
	83: 7	Philistia, with the **p** of Tyre.	3782
	85: 2	of your **p** and covered all their sins.	6639
	85: 6	that your **p** may rejoice in you?	6639
	85: 8	he promises peace to his **p**, his saints—	6639
	89:19	to your **faithful p** you said:	AIT
	89:19	a young man from among the **p**.	6639
	94: 5	They crush your **p**, O LORD;	6639
	94: 8	you senseless ones among the **p**;	6639
	94:14	For the LORD will not reject his **p**;	6639
	95: 7	for he is our God and we are the **p**	6639
	95:10	I said, "They are a **p** *whose* hearts go astray,	6639
	100: 3	we are his **p**, the sheep of his pasture.	6639
	102:18	a **p** not yet created may praise the LORD:	6639
	103: 7	his deeds to the **p** of Israel:	1201
	105:24	The LORD made his **p** very fruitful;	6639
	105:25	whose hearts he turned to hate his **p**,	6639
	105:43	He brought out his **p** with rejoicing,	6639
	106: 1	O LORD, when you show favor to your **p**,	6639
	106:40	Therefore the LORD was angry with his **p**	6639
	106:48	Let all the **p** say, "Amen!"	6639
	107:32	Let them exalt him in the assembly of the **p**	6639
	111: 6	He has shown his **p** the power of his works,	6639
	111: 9	He provided redemption for his **p**;	6639
	113: 8	with the princes of their **p**.	6639
	114: 1	house of Jacob from a **p** of foreign tongue,	6639
	116:14	to the LORD in the presence of all his **p**.	6639
	116:18	to the LORD in the presence of all his **p**,	6639
	125: 2	so the LORD surrounds his **p** both now	6639
	135:12	an inheritance to his **p** Israel.	6639
	135:14	For the LORD will vindicate his **p**	6639
	136:16	to him who led his **p** through the desert,	6639
	144:15	Blessed are the **p** of whom this is true;	6639
	144:15	blessed are the **p** whose God is the LORD.	6639
	147:13	the bars of your gates and blesses your **p**	1201
	148:14	He has raised up for his **p** a horn,	6639
	148:14	of Israel, the **p** close to his heart.	6639
	149: 2	let the **p** of Zion be glad in their King.	1201
	149: 4	For the LORD takes delight in his **p**;	6639
Pr	11:26	**P** curse the man who hoards grain,	4211
	14:34	but sin is a disgrace to any **p**.	4211
	28:15	a wicked man ruling over a helpless **p**.	6639

Pr	28:28	the wicked rise to power, **p** go into hiding;	132
	29: 2	When the righteous thrive, the **p** rejoice;	6639
	29: 2	when the wicked rule, the **p** groan.	6639
	29:18	the **p** cast off restraint;	6639
Ecc	4:16	There was no end to all the **p** who were	6639
	7:21	Do not pay attention to every word *p* say,	AIT
	8:11	**p** are filled with schemes to do wrong.	132+1201
	9:14	a small city with only a few **p** in it.	408
	12: 9	but also he imparted knowledge to the **p**.	6639
SS	6:12	among the royal chariots of my **p**.	6639
Isa	1: 3	my **p** do not understand."	6639
	1: 4	Ah, sinful nation, a **p** loaded with guilt,	6639
	1:10	to the law of our God, you **p** *of* Gomorrah!	6639
	2: 6	You have abandoned your **p**,	6639
	3: 5	**P** will oppress each other—	6639
	3: 7	do not make me the leader of the **p**."	6639
	3:12	Youths oppress my **p**,	6639
	3:12	O my **p**, your guides lead you astray;	6639
	3:13	he rises to judge the **p**.	6639
	3:14	against the elders and leaders of his **p**:	6639
	3:15	by crushing my **p** and grinding the faces of	6639
	5:13	Therefore my **p** will go into exile for lack	6639
	5:25	the LORD's anger burns against his **p**;	6639
	6: 5	and I live among a **p** of unclean lips,	6639
	6: 9	He said, "Go and tell this **p**:	6639
	6:10	Make the heart of this **p** calloused;	6639
	7: 2	the hearts of Ahaz and his **p** were shaken,	6639
	7: 8	be too shattered to be a **p**.	6639
	7:17	on your **p** and on the house of your father	6639
	8: 6	"Because this **p** has rejected the gently	6639
	8:11	warning me not to follow the way of this **p**.	6639
	8:12	that these **p** call conspiracy;	6639
	8:14	And for the **p** of Jerusalem he will be a trap	3782
	8:19	should not a **p** inquire of their God?	6639
	9: 2	The **p** walking in darkness have seen	6639
	9: 3	they rejoice before you as **p** rejoice at	NIH
	9: 9	All the **p** will know it—	6639
	9:13	But the **p** have not returned	6639
	9:16	Those who guide this **p** mislead them,	6639
	9:19	the land will be scorched and the **p** will	6639
	10: 2	from the oppressed of my **p**,	6639
	10: 6	I dispatch him against a **p** who anger me,	6639
	10:22	Though your **p**, O Israel,	6639
	10:24	"O my **p** who live in Zion,	6639
	10:31	the **p** of Gebim take cover.	3782
	11:11	to reclaim the remnant that is left of his **p**	6639
	11:12	he will assemble the **scattered** *p* of Judah	AIT
	11:14	together they will plunder the **p** *to* the east.	1201
	11:16	be a highway for the remnant of his **p**	6639
	12: 6	Shout aloud and sing for joy, **p** *of* Zion,	3782
	13:14	each will return to his own **p**,	6639
	14:20	destroyed your land and killed your **p**.	6639
	14:25	His yoke will be taken from **my p**,	2157S
	14:32	and in her his afflicted **p** will find refuge."	6639
	16:14	Moab's splendor and all her many **p** will	2162
	18: 2	to a **p** tall and smooth-skinned,	1580
	18: 2	to a **p** feared far and wide,	6639
	18: 3	All you **p** *of* the world,	3782
	18: 7	from a **p** tall and smooth-skinned, from	6639
	18: 7	from a **p** feared far and wide,	6639
	19:25	saying, "Blessed be Egypt my **p**,	6639
	20: 6	the **p** who live *on* this coast will say,	AIT
	21:10	O my **p**, crushed on the threshing floor,	1201
	22: 4	to console me over the destruction	
		of my **p**."	1426+6639
	23: 2	you **p** of the island and you merchants	3782
	23: 6	wail, you **p** *of* the island.	3782
	23:13	this **p** that is now of no account!	6639
	24: 2	it will be the same for priest as for **p**,	6639
	24: 5	The earth is defiled by its **p**;	3782
	24: 6	its **p** must bear their guilt.	3782
	24:17	O **p** of the earth.	3782
	25: 8	the disgrace of his **p** from all the earth.	6639
	26: 9	the **p** of the world learn righteousness.	3782
	26:11	Let them see your zeal for your **p** and	6639
	26:18	we have not given birth to **p** *of* the world.	3782
	26:20	my **p**, enter your rooms and shut the doors	6639
	26:21	of his dwelling to punish the **p** *of* the earth	3782
	27:11	For this is a **p** without understanding;	6639
	28: 5	a beautiful wreath for the remnant of his **p**.	6639
	28:11	strange tongues God will speak to this **p**,	6639
	28:14	you scoffers who rule this **p** in Jerusalem,	6639
	29:13	"These **p** come near to me with their mouth	6639
	29:14	Therefore once more I will astound these **p**	6639
	30: 5	to shame because of a **p** useless to them,	6639
	30: 9	These are rebellious **p**, deceitful children,	6639
	30:19	O **p** of Zion, who live in Jerusalem,	6639
	30:26	of his **p** and heals the wounds he inflicted.	6639
	30:29	when **p** go up with flutes to the mountain	2021S
	32:13	and for the land of my **p**, a land overgrown	6639
	32:18	My **p** will live in peaceful dwelling places,	6639
	33:19	You will see those arrogant **p** no more,	6639
	33:19	those **p** *of* an obscure speech,	6639
	34: 5	the **p** I have totally destroyed.	6639
	36:11	to us in Hebrew in the hearing of the **p** on	6639
	36:21	*p* remained **silent** and said nothing in reply,	AIT
	37:12	and the **p** *of* Eden who were in Tel Assar?"	1201
	37:27	Their **p**, drained of power,	3782
	37:36	When *the p* get up the next morning—	AIT
	40: 1	Comfort, comfort my **p**, says your God.	6639
	40: 7	Surely the **p** are grass.	6639
	40:22	and its **p** are like grasshoppers.	3782
	41:20	so that **p** may see and know,	3481S
	42: 5	who gives breath to its **p**,	6639
	42: 6	to be a covenant for the **p** and a light for	6639
	42:11	Let the **p** *of* Sela sing for joy;	3782
	42:22	But this is a **p** plundered and looted,	6639

Isa	43: 4	and **p** in exchange for your life.	4211
	43:20	to give drink to my **p**, my chosen,	6639
	43:21	the **p** I formed for myself	6639
	44: 7	since I established my ancient **p**,	6639
	47: 6	with my **p** and desecrated my inheritance;	6639
	49: 8	to be a covenant for the **p**,	6639
	49:13	For the LORD comforts his **p**	6639
	49:19	now you will be too small for your **p**,	3782
	51: 4	"Listen to me, my **p**;	6639
	51: 7	you **p** who have my law in your hearts:	6639
	51:16	and who say to Zion, 'You are my **p**.'"	6639
	51:22	your God, who defends his **p**:	6639
	52: 4	"At first my **p** went down to Egypt to live;	6639
	52: 5	my **p** have been taken away for nothing,	6639
	52: 6	Therefore my **p** will know my name;	6639
	52: 9	for the LORD has comforted his **p**,	6639
	53: 8	the transgression of my **p** he was stricken.	6639
	56: 3	surely exclude me from his **p**."	6639
	57:14	the obstacles out of the way of my **p**."	6639
	58: 1	to my **p** their rebellion and to the house	6639
	58:12	Your **p** will **rebuild** the ancient ruins	AIT
	60:21	Then will all your **p** be righteous,	6639
	61: 7	Instead of their shame my **p** will receive	NIH
	61: 9	that they are a **p** the LORD has blessed."	2446
	62:10	Prepare the way for the **p**.	6639
	62:12	They will be called the Holy **P**,	6639
	63: 8	He said, "Surely they are my **p**,	6639
	63:11	Then *his p* **recalled** the days of old,	AIT
	63:11	the days of Moses and his **p**—	6639
	63:14	This is how you guided your **p** to make	6639
	63:18	while your **p** possessed your holy place,	6639
	64: 9	we pray, for we are all your **p**.	6639
	65: 2	to an obstinate **p**, who walk in ways	6639
	65: 3	a **p** who continually provoke me	6639
	65: 5	**Such** *p* are smoke in my nostrils,	AIT
	65: 9	my **chosen** *p* will inherit them,	AIT
	65:10	for my **p** who seek me.	6639
	65:18	to be a delight and its **p** a joy.	6639
	65:19	over Jerusalem and take delight in my **p**;	6639
	65:22	days of a tree, so will be the days of my **p**;	6639
	65:23	for they will be a **p** blessed by the LORD,	2446
Jer	1: 3	when the **p** of Jerusalem went into exile.	NIH
	1:16	I will pronounce my judgments on **my p**	4392S
	1:18	its priests and the **p** *of* the land.	6639
	2:11	But my **p** have exchanged their Glory	6639
	2:13	"My **p** have committed two sins:	6639
	2:30	"In vain I punished your **p**;	1201
	2:31	Why do my **p** say, 'We are free to roam;	6639
	2:32	Yet my **p** have forgotten me,	6639
	3:14	"Return, faithless **p**," declares the LORD,	1201
	3:21	the weeping and pleading of the **p** *of* Israel,	1201
	3:22	faithless **p**; I will cure you of backsliding."	1201
	4: 4	you men of Judah and **p** *of* Jerusalem,	3782
	4:10	how completely you have deceived this **p**	6639
	4:11	that time this **p** and Jerusalem will be told,	6639
	4:11	in the desert blows toward my **p**,	1426+6639
	4:22	"My **p** are fools; they do not know me.	6639
	4:25	I looked, and there were no **p**;	132
	5:10	for **these** *p* do not belong to the LORD.	AIT
	5:14	"Because the **p** have spoken these words,	4013S
	5:14	a fire and these **p** the wood it consumes.	6639
	5:15	a **p** whose language you do not know,	1580
	5:19	And when *the p* **ask**, 'Why has the LORD	AIT
	5:21	you foolish and senseless **p**,	6639
	5:23	these **p** have stubborn and rebellious hearts;	6639
	5:26	"Among my **p** are wicked men who lie	6639
	5:31	and my **p** love it this way.	6639
	6: 1	"Flee for safety, **p** *of* Benjamin!	1201
	6:14	of my **p** as though it were not serious.	6639
	6:19	I am bringing disaster on this **p**,	6639
	6:21	"I will put obstacles before this **p**.	6639
	6:26	**p**, put on sackcloth and roll in ashes;	1426+6639
	6:27	a tester of metals and my **p** the ore,	6639
	7: 2	"'Hear the word of the LORD, all you **p**	NIH
	7:12	because of the wickedness of my **p** Israel.	6639
	7:15	all your brothers, the **p** *of* Ephraim.'	2446
	7:16	for this **p** nor offer any plea or petition	6639
	7:23	I will be your God and you will be my **p**.	6639
	7:30	"'The **p** *of* Judah have done evil	1201
	7:32	when **p** will no longer call it Topheth or	NIH
	7:33	the carcasses of this **p** will become food for	6639
	8: 1	and the bones of the **p** *of* Jerusalem will	3782
	8: 5	Why then have these **p** turned away?	6639
	8: 7	But my **p** do not know the requirements of	6639
	8:11	of my **p** as though it were not serious.	1426+6639
	8:19	the cry of my **p** from a land far away:	1426+6639
	8:21	Since my **p** are crushed, I am crushed;	1426+6639
	8:22	no healing for the wound of my **p**?	1426+6639
	9: 1	and night for the slain of my **p**.	1426+6639
	9: 2	so that I might leave my **p** and go away	6639
	9: 2	a crowd of **unfaithful** *p*.	AIT
	9: 7	because of the sin of my **p**?	1426+6639
	9:15	"See, I will make this **p** eat bitter food	6639
	11: 4	to the **p** *of* Judah and to those who live	408
	11: 4	you will be my **p**, and I will be your God.	6639
	11: 9	among the **p** *of* Judah and those who live	408
	11:12	and the **p** *of* Jerusalem will go and cry out	3782
	11:14	"Do not pray for this **p** nor offer any plea	6639
	12: 4	Moreover, *the p are* **saying**,	AIT
	12:14	the inheritance I gave my **p** Israel,	6639
	12:16	the ways of my **p** and swear by my name,	6639
	12:16	they once taught my **p** to swear by Baal—	6639
	12:16	then they will be established among my **p**.	6639
	13:10	These wicked **p**, who refuse to listen	6639
	13:11	'to be my **p** for my renown and praise	6639
	14:10	This is what the LORD says about this **p**:	6639
	14:11	"Do not pray for the well-being of this **p**.	6639

Jer	14:16	And the **p** they are prophesying to will	6639
	14:17	for my virgin daughter—my **p**—	6639
	15: 1	my heart would not go out to this **p**.	6639
	15: 7	and destruction on my **p**,	6639
	15:19	Let **this** *p* turn to you,	AIT
	15:20	I will make you a wall to this **p**,	6639
	16: 5	my love and my pity from this **p**,"	6639
	16:10	"When you tell these **p** all this	6639
	17:19	"Go and stand at the gate of the **p**,	1201+6639
	17:20	and all **p** of Judah and everyone living	NIH
	17:26	**P** will **come** from the towns of Judah and	AIT
	18:11	"Now therefore say to the **p** *of* Judah	408
	18:15	Yet my **p** have forgotten me;	6639
	19: 1	Take along some of the elders of the **p** and	6639
	19: 3	O kings of Judah and **p** *of* Jerusalem,	3782
	19: 6	**p** will no longer **call** this place Topheth	AIT
	19:14	the LORD's temple and said to all the **p**,	6639
	21: 7	the **p** in this city who survive the plague,	6639
	21: 8	"Furthermore, tell the **p**,	6639
	22: 2	and your **p** who come through these gates.	6639
	22: 4	accompanied by their officials and their **p**.	6639
	22: 8	"**P** from many nations will pass by this city	NIH
	23: 2	says to the shepherds who tend my **p**:	6639
	23: 7	**p** will no longer **say**,	AIT
	23:13	by Baal and led my **p** Israel astray.	6639
	23:14	the **p** *of* Jerusalem are like Gomorrah."	3782
	23:22	to my **p** and would have turned them	6639
	23:27	will make my **p** forget my name,	6639
	23:32	"They tell them and lead my **p** astray	6639
	23:32	They do not benefit these **p** in the least,"	6639
	23:33	"When these **p**, or a prophet or a priest,	6639
	24: 7	They will be my **p**, and I will be their God,	6639
	25: 1	to Jeremiah concerning all the **p** *of* Judah	6639
	25: 2	to all the **p** *of* Judah and to all those living	6639
	25:19	his attendants, his officials and all his **p**,	6639
	25:20	and all the **foreign p** there;	6850
	25:20	Gaza, Ekron, and the **p** *left* at Ashdod);	AIT
	25:24	and all the kings of the **foreign p** who live	6850
	26: 2	to all the **p** of the towns of Judah who come	NIH
	26: 7	the **p** heard Jeremiah speak these words in	6639
	26: 8	as Jeremiah finished telling all the **p**	6639
	26: 8	the prophets and all the **p** seized him	6639
	26: 9	And all the **p** crowded around Jeremiah in	6639
	26:11	to the officials and all the **p**,	6639
	26:12	to all the officials and all the **p**:	6639
	26:16	the officials and all the **p** said to the priests	6639
	26:17	and said to the entire assembly of **p**,	6639
	26:18	He told all the **p** *of* Judah,	6639
	26:23	the burial place of the **common p**.)	1201+6639
	26:24	not handed over to the **p** to be put to death.	6639
	27: 5	the earth and its **p** and the animals that are	132
	27:12	serve him and his **p**, and you will live.	6639
	27:13	Why will you and your **p** die by the sword,	6639
	27:16	Then I said to the priests and all these **p**,	6639
	28: 1	in the presence of the priests and all the **p**:	6639
	28: 5	the priests and all the **p** who were standing	6639
	28: 7	and in the hearing of all the **p**:	6639
	28:11	and he said before all the **p**, "This is what	6639
	29: 1	the other **p** Nebuchadnezzar had carried	6639
	29:16	on David's throne and all the **p** who remain	6639
	29:25	in your own name to all the **p** in Jerusalem,	6639
	29:32	He will have no one left among this **p**,	6639
	29:32	the good things I will do for my **p**,	6639
	30: 3	'when I will bring my **p** Israel	6639
	30:22	you will be my **p**, and I will be your God.	6639
	31: 1	and they will be my **p**."	6639
	31: 2	"The **p** who survive the sword	6639
	31: 7	save your **p**, the remnant of Israel.'	6639
	31:14	and my **p** will be filled with my bounty,"	6639
	31:23	*p* in the land of Judah and in its towns *will*	
		once again **use** these words:	AIT
	31:24	**P** will **live** together in Judah	AIT
	31:29	*p* will no longer **say**, 'The fathers have eaten	AIT
	31:33	I will be their God, and they will be my **p**.	6639
	32:21	You brought your **p** Israel out of Egypt	6639
	32:29	*p* **provoked** me to anger by burning	AIT
	32:30	"The **p** *of* Israel have done nothing but	1201
	32:30	indeed, the **p** *of* Israel have done nothing	1201
	32:32	The **p** *of* Israel and Judah has provoked	1201
	32:32	the men of Judah and the **p** *of* Jerusalem.	3782
	32:38	They will be my **p**, and I will be their God.	6639
	32:42	all this great calamity on this **p**,	6639
	33: 6	I will heal **my p** and will let them enjoy	4392S
	33:24	not noticed that these **p** are saying,	6639
	33:24	So they despise my **p** and no longer regard	6639
	34: 5	As **p** made a funeral fire in honor	NIH
	34: 8	the **p** in Jerusalem to proclaim freedom for	6639
	34:10	So all the officials and **p** who entered	6639
	34:19	the **p** *of* the land who walked between	6639
	35:13	the men of Judah and the **p** *of* Jerusalem,	3782
	35:16	but these **p** have not obeyed me.'	6639
	36: 3	Perhaps when the **p** *of* Judah hear	1074
	36: 6	and read to the **p** from the scroll the words	6639
	36: 6	to **all** *the p* of Judah who come in	AIT
	36: 7	against this **p** by the LORD are great."	6639
	36: 9	the **p** in Jerusalem and those who had come	6639
	36:10	the **p** at the LORD's temple the words	6639
	36:13	Baruch read to the **p** from the scroll,	6639
	36:14	from which you have read to the **p**	6639
	36:31	the **p** *of* Judah every disaster I pronounced	408
	37: 2	nor the **p** *of* the land paid any attention to	6639
	37: 4	to come and go among the **p**,	6639
	37:12	of the property among the **p** there.	6639
	37:18	against you or your officials or this **p**,	6639
	38: 1	Jeremiah was telling all the **p** when he said,	6639
	38: 4	as well as all the **p**,	6639
	38: 4	This man is not seeking the good of these **p**	6639

```
Jer 39: 8  to the royal palace and the houses of the p       6639
    39: 9  to Babylon the p who remained in the city,          6639
    39: 9  gone over to him, and the rest of the p.            6639
    39:10  in the land of Judah some of the poor p,            6639
    39:14  So he remained among his own p.                     6639
    40: 3  because you p sinned against the LORD               AIT
    40: 5  and live with him among the p,                      6639
    40: 6  with him among the p who were left behind           6639
    41:10  the rest of the p who were in Mizpah—               6639
    41:13  When all the p Ishmael had with him                 6639
    41:14  All the p Ishmael had taken captive                 6639
    42: 1  and all the p from the least to the greatest        6639
    42: 8  and all the p from the least to the greatest.       6639
    43: 1  When Jeremiah finished telling the p all            6639
    43: 4  the army officers and all the p disobeyed           6639
    44:15  all the p living in Lower and Upper Egypt,          6639
    44:20  Then Jeremiah said to all the p,                    6639
    44:21  your kings and your officials and the p of          6639
    44:24  Then Jeremiah said to all the p,                    6639
    44:24  "Hear the word of the LORD, all you p               AIT
    45: 5  For I will bring disaster on all p,                 1414
    46: 8  I will destroy cities and their p.'                 3782
    46:16  to our own p and our native lands,                  6639
    46:24  handed over to the p of the north."                 6639
    47: 2  The p will cry out;                                 132
    48:43  O p of Moab," declares the LORD.                    3782
    48:46  the p of Chemosh are destroyed;                     6639
    49: 1  Why do his p live in its towns?                     6639
    49:28  attack Kedar and destroy the p of the East.         1201
    49:31  neither gates nor bars; its p live alone.           AIT
    50: 4  "the p of Israel and the people of Judah            1201
    50: 4  and the p of Judah together will go in tears        1201
    50: 6  "My p have been lost sheep;                         6639
    50:16  let everyone return to his own p,                   6639
    50:33  "The p of Israel are oppressed,                     1201
    50:33  and the p of Judah as well.                         1201
    51: 1  against Babylon and the p of Leb Kamai.             3782
    51:12  his decree against the p of Babylon.                3782
    51:38  Her p all roar like young lions,                    AIT
    51:45  "Come out of her, my p!                             6639
    51:64  And her p will fall.'"                              AIT
    52: 6  so severe that there was no food for the p          6639
    52:15  of the poorest p and those who remained in          6639
    52:16  the rest of the poorest p of the land to work       AIT
    52:25  in charge of conscripting the p of the land         6639
    52:28  of the p Nebuchadnezzar carried into exile:         6639
    52:29  832 p from Jerusalem;                               5883
    52:30  There were 4,600 p in all.                          5883
La   1: 1  deserted lies the city, once so full of p!          6639
     1: 7  When her p fell into enemy hands,                   6639
     1:11  All her p groan as they search for bread;           6639
     1:21  "P have heard my groaning.                          AIT
     2:11  because my p are destroyed,               1426+6639
     2:18  The hearts of the p cry out to the Lord.           4392S
     3:14  I became the laughingstock of all my p;             6639
     3:48  because my p are destroyed.               1426+6639
     4: 3  but my p have become heartless            1426+6639
     4: 6  The punishment of my p is greater         1426+6639
     4:10  when my p were destroyed.                 1426+6639
     4:12  nor did any of the world's p,                       3782
     4:15  p among the nations say,                            AIT
Eze  2: 4  p to whom I am sending you are obstinate            1201
     3: 5  not being sent to a p of obscure speech            6639
     3:25  so that you cannot go out among the p.             4392S
     4:12  bake it in the sight of the p,                     2157S
     4:13  the p of Israel will eat defiled food among        1201
     4:16  The p will eat rationed food in anxiety             AIT
     5:12  A third of your p will die of the plague            AIT
     6: 4  and I will slay your p in front of your idols.     2728
     6: 7  Your p will fall slain among you,                  AIT
     6:13  when their p lie slain among their idols            AIT
     7:11  none of the p will be left,                        2157S
     7:27  the hands of the p of the land will tremble.        6639
    11: 1  leaders of the p.                                   6639
    11: 6  You have killed many p in this city                AIT
    11:15  of whom the p of Jerusalem have said,              3782
    11:20  They will be my p, and I will be their God.         6639
    12: 2  you are living among a rebellious p.               1074
    12: 2  for they are a rebellious p.                       1074
    12:19  Say to the p of the land:                          6639
    12:24  or flattering divinations among the p              1074
    13: 9  They will not belong to the council of my p         6639
    13:10  " 'Because they lead my p astray, saying,          6639
    13:10  the wall collapses, will p not ask you,             NIH
    13:17  the daughters of your p who prophesy out           6639
    13:18  for their heads in order to ensnare p.             5883
    13:18  the lives of my p but preserve your own?           6639
    13:19  among my p for a few handfuls of barley            6639
    13:19  By lying to my p, who listen to lies,              6639
    13:20  with which you ensnare p like birds                5883
    13:20  I will set free the p that you ensnare             5883
    13:21  I will tear off your veils and save my p           6639
    13:23  I will save my p from your hands.                  6639
    14: 5  I will do this to recapture the hearts of the p    1074
    14: 8  I will cut him off from my p.                      6639
    14: 9  and destroy him from among my p Israel.            6639
    14:11  p of Israel will no longer stray from me,          1074
    14:11  They will be my p, and I will be their God.        6639
    15: 6  so will I treat the p living in Jerusalem.          AIT
    17: 9  not take a strong arm or many p to pull it         6639
    18: 2  "What do you p mean by quoting this                917S
    18:18  and did what was wrong among his p.                6638
    20:13  " 'Yet the p of Israel rebelled against me in      1074
    20:27  speak to the p of Israel and say to them,          1074
    21: 5  Then all p will know that I the LORD               1414
    21:12  son of man, for it is against my p;                6639
    21:12  to the sword along with my p.                      6639

Eze 21:24  'Because you p have brought to mind                 AIT
    22:25  they devour p, take treasures                      5883
    22:27  and kill p to make unjust gain.                    5883
    22:29  The p of the land practice extortion               6639
    23:24  and wagons and with a throng of p;                 6639
    24:18  So I spoke to the p in the morning,                6639
    24:19  Then the p asked me,                               6639
    25: 3  the p of Judah when they went into exile,          1074
    25: 4  therefore I am going to give you to the p of       1201
    25:10  with the Ammonites to the p of the East as         1201
    25:14  the hand of my p Israel, and they will deal        6639
    26:11  he will kill your p with the sword,                6639
    26:20  to the p of long ago.                              6639
    28:24  " 'No longer will the p                            1074
    28:25  When I gather the p of Israel from                 1074
    29:16  of confidence for the p of Israel but will be      1074
    30: 5  and the p of the covenant land will fall by        1201
    32: 3  a great throng of p I will cast my net             6639
    33: 2  the p of the land choose one of their men          6639
    33: 3  and blows the trumpet to warn the p,               6639
    33: 6  not blow the trumpet to warn the p and             6639
    33:24  the p living in those ruins in the land             AIT
    33:31  My p come to you, as they usually do,              6639
    34:27  the p will be secure in their land.                 AIT
    34:30  are my p, declares the Sovereign LORD.             6639
    34:31  the sheep of my pasture, are p,                    132
    36: 8  and fruit for my p Israel,                         6639
    36:10  I will multiply the number of p upon you,          132
    36:11  I will settle p on you as in the past               AIT
    36:12  I will cause p, my people Israel,                  132
    36:12  I will cause people, my p Israel,                  6639
    36:13  Because p say to you,                               AIT
    36:17  p of Israel were living in their own land,         1074
    36:20  'These are the LORD's p,                           6639
    36:28  you will be my p, and I will be your God.          6639
    36:37  I will make their p as numerous as sheep,          132
    36:38  the ruined cities be filled with flocks of p.      132
    37:12  O my p, I am going to open your graves             6639
    37:13  my p, will know that I am the LORD,                6639
    37:23  They will be my p, and I will be their God.        6639
    37:27  I will be their God, and they will be my p.        6639
    38: 8  whose p were gathered from many nations             AIT
    38:11  I will attack a peaceful and unsuspecting p        3782
    38:12  the resettled ruins and the p gathered from        6639
    38:14  when my p Israel are living in safety,             6639
    38:16  against my p like a cloud that covers              6639
    38:20  the p on the face of the earth will tremble        132
    39: 7  my holy name among my p Israel.                    6639
    39:13  All the p of the land will bury them,              6639
    39:23  the p of Israel went into exile for their sin,     1074
    39:25  and will have compassion on all the                1074
    42:14  near the places that are for the p."               6639
    43:10  describe the temple to the p of Israel,            1074
    44:11  the burnt offerings and sacrifices for the p       6639
    44:11  and stand before the p and serve them.            2157S
    44:19  into the outer court where the p are,              6639
    44:19  that they do not consecrate the p by means         6639
    44:23  They are to teach my p the difference              6639
    45: 8  my princes will no longer oppress my p             6639
    45: 9  Stop dispossessing my p,                           6639
    45:15  to make atonement for the p,                      2157S
    45:16  All the p of the land will participate             6639
    45:22  a sin offering for himself and for all the p       6639
    46: 3  On the Sabbaths and New Moons the p of             6639
    46: 9  the p of the land come before the LORD             6639
    46:18  not take any of the inheritance of the p,          6639
    46:18  so that none of my p will be separated             6639
    46:20  into the outer court and consecrating the p."      6639
    46:24  will cook the sacrifices of the p."                6639
Da   2:43  so the p will be a mixture and will     10050+10240
     2:44  nor will it be left to another p.                 10553
     3:29  Therefore I decree that the p of any nation       10553
     4:25  from p and will live with the wild animals;       10050
     4:32  from p and will live with the wild animals;       10050
     4:33  He was driven away from p and ate grass           10050
     5:21  driven away from p and given the mind of 10050+10120
            an animal;
     6:26  of my kingdom p must fear and reverence             AIT
     7:27  the p of the Most High.                           10553
     8:24  the mighty men and the holy p.                     6639
     9: 6  and to all the p of the land.                     6639
     9: 7  of Judah and p of Jerusalem and all Israel,       3782
     9:15  who brought your p out of Egypt with              6639
     9:16  and your p an object of scorn to all those        6639
     9:19  your city and your p bear your Name."             6639
     9:20  of my p Israel and making my request to           6639
     9:24  "Seventy 'sevens' are decreed for your p          6639
     9:26  The p of the ruler who will come will             6639
    10:14  to you what will happen to your p in              6639
    11:14  among your own p will rebel in fulfillment        6639
    11:21  the kingdom when its p feel secure,                NIH
    11:23  and with only a few p he will rise to power.      1580
    11:32  the p who know their God will firmly resist       6639
            him.
    11:39  over many p and will distribute the land at         AIT
    12: 1  the great prince who protects your p,      1201+6639
    12: 1  But at that time your p—                          6639
    12: 7  of the holy p has been finally broken,            6639
Hos  1: 9  "Call him Lo-Ammi, for you are not my p,          6639
     1:10  'You are not my p,' they will be called           6639
     1:11  The p of Judah and the people of Israel           1201
     1:11  and the p of Israel will be reunited.             1201
     2: 1  "Say of your brothers, 'My p,'                    6639
     2:23  I will say to those called 'Not my p,'            6639
     2:23  'You are my p'; and they will say,                6639
     4: 4  for your p are like those who bring charges       6639
     4: 6  my p are destroyed from lack of knowledge         6639

Hos  4: 8  of my p and relish their wickedness.              6639
     4: 9  And it will be: Like p, like priests.             6639
     4:12  of my p. They consult a wooden idol               6639
     4:14  a p without understanding will come               6639
     5:12  like rot to the p of Judah.                       1074
     6:11  I would restore the fortunes of my p,             6639
     8: 1  because the p have broken my covenant              NIH
     9: 2  and winepresses will not feed the p;             4392S
    10: 5  "The p who live in Samaria fear for               8907
    10: 5  Its p will mourn over it,                         6639
    10:14  the roar of battle will rise against your p, so   6639
    11: 7  My p are determined to turn from me.              6639
    12:11  Its p are worthless!                               AIT
    13: 2  It is said of these p,                             AIT
    13:16  The p of Samaria must bear their guilt,            NIH
Joel 2:16  Gather the p, consecrate the assembly;            6639
     2:17  Let them say, "Spare your p, O LORD.              6639
     2:18  for his land and take pity on his p.              6639
     2:23  Be glad, O p of Zion,                             1201
     2:26  never again will my p be shamed.                  6639
     2:27  never again will my p be shamed.                  6639
     2:28  I will pour out my Spirit on all p.               1414
     3: 2  my p Israel, for they scattered my people         6639
     3: 2  for they scattered my p among the nations         889S
     3: 3  for my p and traded boys for prostitutes;         6639
     3: 6  You sold the p of Judah and Jerusalem to          1201
     3: 8  I will sell your sons and daughters to the p      1201
     3:16  But the LORD will be a refuge for his p,          6639
     3:16  a stronghold for the p of Israel.                 1201
     3:19  because of violence done to the p of Judah,       1201
Am   1: 5  The p of Aram will go into exile to Kir,"         6639
     2:11  Is this not true, p of Israel?"                   1201
     3: 1  spoken against you, O p of Israel—                1201
     3: 6  do not the p tremble?                             6639
     3: 9  and the oppression among her p."                   NIH
     4: 8  P staggered from town to town for water
                                              8993+9109S
     6: 1  to whom the p of Israel come!                     1074
     7: 8  a plumb line among my p Israel;                   6639
     7:15  'Go, prophesy to my p Israel.'                    6639
     8: 2  "The time is ripe for my p Israel;                6639
     9: 1  Bring them down on the heads of all the p;       4392S
     9:10  All the sinners among my p will die by            6639
     9:14  I will bring back my exiled p Israel;             6639
Ob   1:12  nor rejoice over the p of Judah in the day        1201
     1:13  not march through the gates of my p in            6639
     1:19  P from the Negev will occupy                       NIH
     1:19  and p from the foothills will possess              NIH
Jnh  1: 8  From what p are you?"                             6639
     4:11  hundred and twenty thousand p who cannot          132
            tell their right hand from their left,
Mic  1: 9  It has reached the very gate of my p,             6639
     2: 3  "I am planning disaster against this p,           5476
     2: 8  Lately my p have risen up like an enemy.          6639
     2: 9  women of my p from their pleasant homes.          6639
     2:11  he would be just the prophet for this p!          6639
     2:12  the place will throng with p.                     132
     3: 2  from my p and the flesh from their bones;        2157S
     3: 5  "As for the prophets who lead my p astray,        6639
     6: 2  For the LORD has a case against his p;            6639
     6: 3  "My p, what have I done to you?                   6639
     6: 5  My p, remember what Balak king                    6639
     6:12  her p are liars and their tongues speak           3782
     6:16  over to ruin and your p to derision;              3782
     7:12  In that day p will come to you from Assyria        AIT
     7:14  Shepherd your p with your staff,                  6639
Na   3: 3  p stumbling over the corpses—                      AIT
     3:18  Your p are scattered on the mountains             1580
Hab  1: 7  They are a feared and dreaded p;                   AIT
     3:13  You came out to deliver your p,                   6639
Zep  1:17  on the p and they will walk like blind men,       132
     2: 5  to you who live by the sea, O Kerethite p;        1580
     2: 8  who insulted my p and made threats                6639
     2: 9  The remnant of my p will plunder them;            6639
     2:10  insulting and mocking the p of the LORD           6639
     2:10  my scattered p, will bring me offerings.          1426
Hag  1: 2  "These p say, 'The time has not yet come          6639
     1:12  and the whole remnant of the p obeyed             6639
     1:12  And the p feared the LORD.                        6639
     1:13  gave this message of the LORD to the p:           6639
     1:14  the spirit of the whole remnant of the p.         6639
     2: 2  the high priest, and to the remnant of the p.     6639
     2: 4  Be strong, all you p of the land,'                6639
     2:14  with this p and this nation in my sight,'         6639
Zec  1: 3  Therefore tell the p:                            2157S
     1:21  against the land of Judah to scatter its p."     2023S
     2:11  in that day will become my p,                     6639
     5: 6  the iniquity of the p throughout the land."      4392
     7: 2  The p of Bethel had sent Sharezer                 NIH
     7: 5  "Ask all the p of the land and the priests,       6639
     8: 6  to the remnant of this p at that time,            6639
     8: 7  "I will save my p from the countries of           6639
     8: 8  they will be my p, and I will be faithful         6639
     8:11  not deal with the remnant of this p as I did      6639
     8:12  an inheritance to the remnant of this p.          6639
     9: 8  an oppressor overrun my p,                       2157S
     9:16  on that day as the flock of his p.                6639
    10: 2  Therefore the p wander like sheep oppressed        AIT
    11: 6  For I will no longer have pity on the p of        3782
    12: 5  'The p of Jerusalem are strong,                   3782
    13: 9  I will say, 'They are my p,'                      6639
    14: 2  rest of the p will not be taken from the city.    6639
    14:18  the Egyptian p do not go up and take part,        5476
Mal  1: 4  a p always under the wrath of the LORD.           6639
     2: 9  be despised and humiliated before all the p,      6639
Mt   1:21  because he will save his p from their sins."      3295
```

Mt	2:6	be the shepherd of my p Israel.' "	3295
	3:5	P went out to him from Jerusalem	NIG
	4:16	p living in darkness have seen a great light;	3295
	4:23	and sickness among the p.	3295
	4:24	and p brought to him all who were ill	NIG
	5:11	"Blessed are you when p insult you,	AIT
	5:15	Neither do p light a lamp and put it under	AIT
	5:21	that it was said to the p long ago,	792
	5:33	that it was said to the p long ago,	792
	7:16	Do p pick grapes from thornbushes,	AIT
	12:23	All the p were astonished and said,	4063
	12:27	by whom do your p drive them out?	3836+5626
	13:2	while all the p stood on the shore.	4063
	13:10	"Why do you speak to the p in parables?"	899S
	13:54	he began teaching the p in their synagogue,	899S
	14:5	but he was afraid of the p,	4063
	14:19	he directed the p to sit down on the grass.	4063
	14:19	and the disciples gave them to the p.	4063
	14:35	P brought all their sick to him	AIT
	15:8	" 'These p honor me with their lips,	3295
	15:31	The p were amazed when they saw	4063
	15:32	"I have compassion for these p;	4063
	15:36	and they in turn to the p.	4063
	16:13	"Who do p say the Son of Man is?"	476
	18:7	the world because of the things that cause p	NIG
	21:23	and the elders of the p came to him.	3295
	21:26	we are afraid of the p,	4063
	21:43	and given to a p who will produce its fruit.	1620
	21:46	of the crowd because the p held that he was	NIG
	22:10	and gathered all the p they could find,	NIG
	22:30	p will neither marry nor be given in marriage;	AIT
	23:28	on the outside you appear to p as righteous	476
	24:11	and deceive many p.	AIT
	24:38	p were eating and drinking,	AIT
	25:32	and he will separate the p one from another	899S
	26:3	the elders of the p assembled in the palace	3295
	26:5	"or there may be a riot among the p."	3295
	26:47	the chief priests and the elders of the p.	3295
	26:71	another girl saw him and said to the p there,	AIT
	27:1	and the elders of the p came to the decision	3295
	27:9	the price set on him by the p of Israel,	2702+5626
	27:25	All the p answered,	3295
	27:52	of many holy p who had died were raised	41
	27:53	into the holy city and appeared to many p.	AIT
	27:64	the p that he has been raised from the dead.	3295
Mk	1:5	the p of Jerusalem went out to him.	2643
	1:22	The p were amazed at his teaching,	AIT
	1:27	The p were all so amazed that they asked	AIT
	1:32	That evening after sunset the p brought	AIT
	1:45	Yet he still came to him from everywhere.	AIT
	2:1	the p heard that he had come home.	AIT
	2:18	Some p came and asked Jesus,	AIT
	3:9	many p came to him from Judea,	4436
	3:9	to keep the p from crowding him.	AIT
	4:1	while all the p were along the shore at	4063
	4:15	Some p are like seed along the path,	AIT
	5:14	the p went out to see what had happened.	AIT
	5:16	had seen it told the p what had happened	899S
	5:17	Then the p began to plead with Jesus	AIT
	5:20	And all the p were amazed.	AIT
	5:31	"You see the p crowding against you,"	4063
	5:38	with p crying and wailing loudly.	NIG
	6:5	except lay his hands on a few sick p	AIT
	6:12	and preached that p should repent.	AIT
	6:13	and anointed many sick p with oil	AIT
	6:31	because so many p were coming and going	AIT
	6:36	Send the p away so they can go to	899S
	6:39	to have all the p sit down in groups on	AIT
	6:41	to his disciples to set before the p.	899S
	6:54	of the boat, p recognized Jesus.	AIT
	7:6	" 'These p honor me with their lips,	3295
	7:32	There some p brought to him a man	AIT
	7:37	P were overwhelmed with amazement.	AIT
	8:2	"I have compassion for these p;	4063
	8:6	to his disciples to set before the p,	4063
	8:8	The p ate and were satisfied.	AIT
	8:22	and some p brought to him a blind man	AIT
	8:24	He looked up and said, "I see p;	476
	8:27	"Who do p say I am?"	476
	9:15	As soon as all the p saw Jesus,	4063
	10:1	Again crowds of p came to him,	NIG
	10:13	P were bringing little children to Jesus	AIT
	11:5	some p standing there asked,	AIT
	11:6	and the p let them go.	AIT
	11:8	Many p spread their cloaks on the road,	AIT
	11:32	(They feared the p,	4063
	12:41	Many rich p threw in large amounts.	AIT
	12:12	they said, "or the p may riot.	3295
	15:6	to release a prisoner whom the p requested.	AIT
	16:18	they will place their hands on sick p,	AIT
Lk	1:16	Many of the p of Israel he will bring back	5626
	1:17	to make ready a p prepared for the Lord."	3295
	1:21	the p were waiting for Zechariah	3295
	1:25	and taken away my disgrace among the p."	476
	1:65	of Judea p were talking about	AIT
	1:68	he has come and has redeemed his p.	3295
	1:77	to give his p the knowledge of salvation	3295
	2:10	of great joy that will be for all the p.	3295
	2:31	you have prepared in the sight of all p,	3295
	2:32	the Gentiles and for glory to your p Israel."	3295
	3:14	and don't accuse p falsely—	NIG
	3:15	The p were waiting expectantly	3295
	3:18	with many other words John exhorted the p	3295
	3:21	When all the p were being baptized,	3295
	4:28	All the p in the synagogue were furious	AIT
	4:31	and on the Sabbath began to teach the p.	899S

Lk	4:36	All the p were amazed and said	AIT
	4:40	When the sun was setting, the p brought	899S
	4:41	Moreover, demons came out of many p,	AIT
	4:42	The p were looking for him and	4063
	5:1	the p crowding around him and listening to	4063
	5:3	he sat down and taught the p from the boat.	4063
	5:15	so that crowds of p came to hear him and	4063
	6:17	a great number of p from all over Judea,	3295
	6:19	and the p all tried to touch him,	4063
	6:44	P do not pick figs from thornbushes,	AIT
	7:1	saying all this in the hearing of the p,	3295
	7:16	"God has come to help his p."	3295
	7:29	(All the p, even the tax collectors,	3295
	7:31	can I compare the p of this generation?	476
	8:4	and p were coming to Jesus from town	3836
	8:35	the p went out to see what had happened.	AIT
	8:36	Those who had seen it told the p how	899S
	8:37	all the p of the region of the Gerasenes	4436
	8:45	p are crowding and pressing against you."	4063
	8:47	In the presence of all the p,	3295
	8:52	all the p were wailing and mourning	AIT
	9:5	If p do not welcome you,	4012
	9:6	the gospel and healing p everywhere.	NIG
	9:16	to the disciples to set before the p.	4063
	9:53	p there did not welcome	AIT
	11:40	You foolish p!	AIT
	11:46	because you load p down	476
	13:14	the synagogue ruler said to the p,	4063
	13:17	but the p were delighted with all	4063
	13:23	"Lord, are only a few p going to be saved?"	3836
	13:29	P will come from east and west and north	AIT
	13:32	'I will drive out demons and heal p	699+2617
	16:4	p will welcome me into their houses.'	AIT
	16:8	For the p of this world are more shrewd	5626
	16:8	with their own kind than are the p of	5626
	17:1	that cause p to sin are bound to come,	4998
	17:21	nor will p say,	AIT
	17:27	P were eating, drinking, marrying and	AIT
	17:28	P were eating and drinking,	AIT
	17:34	on that night two p will be in one bed;	AIT
	18:15	P were also bringing babies to Jesus	AIT
	18:43	all the p saw it, they also praised God.	3295
	19:7	All the p saw this and began to mutter,	AIT
	19:11	near Jerusalem and the p thought that	899S
	19:36	p spread their cloaks on the road.	AIT
	19:48	because all the p hung on his words.	3295
	20:1	the p in the temple courts and preaching	3295
	20:6	we say, 'From men,' all the p will stone us,	3295
	20:9	He went on to tell the p this parable:	3295
	20:16	When the p heard this, they said,	AIT
	20:19	But they were afraid of the p.	3295
	20:34	"The p of this age marry and are given	5626
	20:45	While all the p were listening,	3295
	21:4	All these p gave their gifts out	AIT
	21:23	in the land and wrath against this p.	3295
	21:38	the p came early in the morning to hear him	3295
	22:2	for they were afraid of the p.	3295
	22:66	the council of the elders of the p,	3295
	23:5	up the p all over Judea by his teaching.	3295
	23:13	the rulers and the p,	3295
	23:14	as one who was inciting the p to rebellion.	3295
	23:27	A large number of p followed him,	3295
	23:35	The p stood watching.	3295
	23:48	When all the p who had gathered	4063
	24:19	in word and deed before God and all the p.	3295
Jn	2:23	at the Passover Feast, many p saw	AIT
	3:11	but still you p do not accept our testimony.	AIT
	3:23	p were constantly coming	AIT
	4:28	to the town and said to the p,	476
	4:48	"Unless you p see miraculous signs	AIT
	5:3	a great number of disabled p used to lie—	AIT
	6:2	and a great crowd of p followed him	4063
	6:5	shall we buy bread for these p to eat?"	AIT
	6:10	Jesus said, "Have the p sit down."	476
	6:14	After the p saw the miraculous sign	476
	6:23	the place where the p had eaten the bread	NIG
	7:12	Others replied, "No, he deceives the p."	4063
	7:25	of the p of Jerusalem began to ask,	2643
	7:35	p live scattered among the Greeks,	1402+3836
	7:40	On hearing his words, some of the p said,	4063
	7:43	Thus the p were divided because of Jesus.	4063
	8:2	where all the p gathered around him,	3295
	8:12	When Jesus spoke again to the p, he said,	899S
	10:41	and many p came to him.	AIT
	11:42	for the benefit of the p standing here,	AIT
	11:50	for the p than that the whole nation perish."	3295
	12:18	Many p, because they had heard	4063
	17:2	For you granted him authority over all p	4922
	18:14	be good if one man died for the p.	3295
	18:35	"It was your p and your chief priests	1620
Ac	2:17	God says, I will pour out my Spirit on all p.	4922
	2:37	When the p heard this,	AIT
	2:47	and enjoying the favor of all the p.	3295
	3:9	the p saw him walking and praising God,	3295
	3:11	all the p astonished and came running	3295
	3:22	a prophet like me from among your own p;	81
	3:23	be completely cut off from among his p.'	3295
	4:1	while they were speaking to the p.	3295
	4:2	because the apostles were teaching the p	3295
	4:8	"Rulers and elders of the p!	AIT
	4:10	you and all the p of Israel:	3295
	4:17	from spreading any further among the p,	3295
	4:21	because all the p were praising God	3295
	4:23	Peter and John went back to their own p	AIT
	4:27	the Gentiles and the p of Israel in this city	3295
	5:12	miraculous signs and wonders among the p.	3295

Ac	5:13	though they were highly regarded by the p.	3295
	5:15	p brought the sick into the streets	NIG
	5:20	tell the p the full message of this new life."	3295
	5:21	and began to teach the p.	NIG
	5:25	in the temple courts teaching the p."	3295
	5:26	they feared that the p would stone them.	3295
	5:34	who was honored by all the p,	3295
	5:37	of the census and led a band of p in revolt.	3295
	6:8	and miraculous signs among the p.	3295
	6:12	So they stirred up the p and the elders and	3295
	7:3	'Leave your country and your p,' God said,	5149
	7:17	number of our p in Egypt greatly increased.	3295
	7:19	with our p and oppressed our forefathers	1169
	7:25	Moses thought that his own p would realize	81
	7:34	I have indeed seen the oppression of my p	3295
	7:37	a prophet like me from your own p.'	81
	7:51	"You stiff-necked p, with uncircumcised	AIT
	8:9	in the city and amazed all the p of Samaria.	1620
	8:10	and all the p, both high and low,	AIT
	9:15	and their kings and before the p of Israel.	5626
	9:42	and many p believed in the Lord.	AIT
	10:22	who is respected by all the Jewish p.	1620
	10:27	inside and found a large gathering of p.	NIG
	10:36	You know the message God sent to the p	5626
	10:41	He was not seen by all the p,	3295
	10:42	He commanded us to preach to the p and	3295
	10:47	"Can anyone keep these p from	AIT
	11:21	a great number of p believed and turned to	NIG
	11:24	and a great number of p were brought to	4063
	11:26	the church and taught great numbers of p.	4063
	12:11	the Jewish p were anticipating."	3295
	12:12	many p had gathered and were praying.	AIT
	12:20	He had been quarreling with the p of Tyre	5601
	12:21	and delivered a public address to the p.	899S
	13:15	a message of encouragement for the p,	3295
	13:17	God of the p of Israel chose our fathers;	3295
	13:17	the p prosper during their stay in Egypt,	3295
	13:19	in Canaan and gave their land to his p	NIG
	13:21	Then the p asked for a king,	AIT
	13:24	and baptism to all the p of Israel.	3295
	13:27	The p of Jerusalem and their rulers did	3836
	13:31	They are now his witnesses to our p.	3295
	13:42	the p invited them to speak further	AIT
	14:4	The p of the city were divided;	4436
	15:14	by taking from the Gentiles a p for himself.	3295
	15:31	The p read it and were glad	899S
	16:4	and elders in Jerusalem for the p to obey.	899S
	17:30	but now he commands all p everywhere	476
	18:10	because I have many p in this city."	3295
	18:13	the p to worship God in ways contrary to	476
	19:4	He told the p to believe in the one coming	3295
	19:26	and led astray large numbers of p here	4063
	19:29	p seized Gaius and Aristarchus, Paul's traveling companions from Macedonia, and rushed as one man	AIT
	19:32	Most of the p did not even know why	AIT
	19:33	in order to make a defense before the p,	1322
	20:2	many words of encouragement to the p,	899S
	20:7	Paul spoke to the p and,	899S
	20:12	The p took the young man home alive	AIT
	21:12	and the p there pleaded with Paul not to go	1954
	21:28	against our p and our law and this place.	3295
	21:30	and the p came running from all directions.	3295
	21:39	Please let me speak to the p."	3295
	22:5	to bring these p as prisoners to Jerusalem to	AIT
	22:24	to find out why the p were shouting at him	AIT
	23:5	not speak evil about the ruler of your p.' "	3295
	24:17	I came to Jerusalem to bring my p gifts for	1620
	26:17	from your own p and from the Gentiles.	3295
	26:23	would proclaim light to his own p and to	3295
	28:6	The p expected him to swell up	1254+3836S
	28:17	although I have done nothing against our p	3295
	28:19	to bring against my own p.	1620
	28:22	for we know that p everywhere are talking	NIG
	28:26	to this p and say, "You will be ever hearing	3295
Ro	1:5	we received grace and apostleship to call p	NIG
	2:22	that p should not commit adultery,	NIG
	9:4	the p of Israel. Theirs is the adoption as	4015S
	9:25	"I will call them 'my p' who are not	3295
	9:25	'my people' who are not my p;	3295
	9:26	'You are not my p,'	3295
	10:21	to a disobedient and obstinate p."	3295
	11:1	I ask then: Did God reject his p?	3295
	11:2	God did not reject his p,	3295
	11:14	that I may somehow arouse my own p	4922
	12:13	Share with God's p who are in need.	41
	12:16	to associate with p of low position.	AIT
	15:10	it says, "Rejoice, O Gentiles, with his p."	3295
	16:2	for she has been a great help to many p,	41
	16:18	For such p are not serving our Lord Christ,	AIT
	16:18	they deceive the minds of naive p.	AIT
1Co	4:19	not only how these arrogant p are talking,	AIT
	5:9	not to associate with sexually immoral p—	AIT
	5:10	the p of this world who are immoral,	AIT
	8:7	Some p are still so accustomed to idols that	AIT
	10:7	"The p sat down to eat and drink and got	3295
	10:15	I speak to sensible p;	AIT
	10:18	Consider the p of Israel:	NIG
	14:21	the lips of foreigners I will speak to this p,	3295
	14:36	Or are you the only p it has reached?	AIT
	15:29	why are p baptized for them?	AIT
	16:1	Now about the collection for God's p:	41
2Co	3:1	Or do we need, like some p,	AIT
	4:15	and more p may cause thanksgiving	NIG
	6:16	and they will be my p."	3295
	9:12	not only supplying the needs of God's p	41
	10:2	be toward some p who think that we live by	AIT

2Co	10:11	**Such** *p* should realize that what we are	AIT
	13: 7	that **p** will see that we have stood the test	NIG
Gal	1: 7	Evidently **some** *p* are throwing you	AIT
	3:16	meaning **many** *p*, but "and to your seed,"	AIT
	4:17	*Those p are* **zealous** to win you over,	AIT
	6:10	let us do good to **all** *p*,	AIT
Eph	2:19	but fellow citizens with **God's p**	41
	3: 8	I am less than the least of all **God's p**,	41
	4:12	to prepare **God's p** for works of service,	41
	5: 3	these are improper *for* **God's holy p**.	41
Php	3: 5	*of* the people of Israel, of the tribe of Benjamin,	1169
Col	3:12	Therefore, as God's **chosen** *p*,	AIT
1Th	5: 3	While *p are* **saying**, "Peace and safety,"	AIT
2Th	1:10	he comes to be glorified in his **holy p** and	41
	3:12	**Such** *p* we command and urge in	AIT
1Ti	3:15	how **p** ought to conduct themselves	NIG
	4: 3	They forbid *p* to marry and order them	NIG
	5: 7	Give the **p** these instructions, too,	NIG
	6: 9	**P** who want to get rich fall into temptation	3836
	6:10	**Some** *p*, eager for money,	AIT
2Ti	3: 2	**P** will be lovers of themselves,	476
Tit	1:10	For there are many **rebellious** *p*,	AIT
	2:14	for himself a *p* that are his very own,	3295
	3: 1	Remind **the p** to be subject to rulers	899S
	3:14	**Our** *p* must learn to devote themselves	AIT
Heb	2:17	make atonement for the sins *of* the **p**,	3295
	4: 9	then, a Sabbath-rest *for* the **p** of God;	3295
	5: 3	as well as for the sins *of* the **p**.	3295
	6:10	as you have helped his **p** and continue	41
	7: 5	to collect a tenth from the **p**—	3295
	7:11	the basis of it the law was given to the **p**),	3295
	7:27	and then for the sins *of* the **p**.	3295
	8: 8	But God found fault with **the p** and said:	899S
	8:10	I will be their God, and they will be my **p**.	3295
	9: 7	the sins **p** had committed in ignorance.	3295
	9:19	every commandment of the law *to* all the **p**,	3295
	9:19	and sprinkled the scroll and all the **p**.	3295
	9:28	to take away the sins of **many** *p*;	AIT
	10:30	and again, "The Lord will judge his **p**."	3295
	11:13	All **these** *p* were still living by faith	AIT
	11:14	**P** who say such things show	3836
	11:25	He chose to be mistreated along with the **p**	3295
	11:29	By faith the **p** passed through the Red Sea	NIG
	11:30	**p** had marched around them for seven days.	NIG
	13: 2	by so doing **some** *p* have entertained angels	AIT
	13:12	to make the **p** holy through his own blood.	3295
	13:24	Greet all your leaders and **God's p**.	41
Jas	4: 4	*You* **adulterous** *p*, don't you know	AIT
	5: 1	Now listen, *you* **rich** *p*, weep and wail	AIT
1Pe	2: 9	But you are a chosen **p**, a royal priesthood,	1169
	2: 9	a holy nation, a **p** belonging to God,	3295
	2:10	Once you were not a **p**, but now	3295
	2:10	but now you are the **p** of God;	3295
	3:20	In it only a few **p**, eight in all,	6034
2Pe	2: 1	there were also false prophets among the **p**,	3295
	2: 5	on its ungodly **p**, but protected Noah,	3180
	2:18	they entice **p** who are just escaping	3836
	3:11	**what kind** *of p* ought you to be?	AIT
	3:16	which ignorant and **unstable** *p* distort,	AIT
Jude	1: 5	the Lord delivered his **p** out of Egypt,	3295
Rev	2:14	*p* there *who* **hold** to the teaching of Balaam,	AIT
	3: 4	Yet you have a few **p** in Sardis who have	3950
	5: 9	from every tribe and language and **p**	3295
	7: 9	from every nation, tribe, **p** and language,	3295
	8:11	and many **p** died from the waters	476
	9: 4	but only those **p** who did not have the seal	476
	9:10	in their tails they had power to torment **p**	476
	11: 9	and a half days men from every **p**,	3295
	11:13	Seven **thousand** *p* were killed in	AIT
	13: 7	he was given authority over every tribe, **p**,	3295
	14: 6	to every nation, tribe, language and **p**.	3295
	16: 2	on the **p** who had the mark of the beast	476
	16: 8	sun was given power to scorch **p** with fire.	476
	18: 4	"Come out of her, my **p**,	3295
	19:18	and the flesh *of* all **p**, free and slave,	AIT
	20: 9	and surrounded the camp of **God's p**,	41
	21: 3	They will be his **p**, and God himself	3295
	22:21	grace of the Lord Jesus be with **God's p**.	41

PEOPLE'S (11) [PEOPLE]

Ex	18:19	be the **p** representative before God	4200+6639
Lev	9:15	for the **p** sin offering and slaughtered it	6639
2Ch	25:15	who said, "Why do you consult this **p** gods,	6639
Est	1:22	in each **p** tongue that every man should	6639
Eze	36: 3	the object of **p** malicious talk and slander,	6639
Mic	2: 4	my **p** possession is divided up.	6639
	3: 3	who eat my **p** flesh, strip off their skin	6639
Hab	2:13	that the **p** labor is only fuel for the fire,	6639
Mt	2: 4	the **p** chief priests and teachers of the law,	3295
	13:15	For this **p** heart has become calloused;	3295
Ac	28:27	For this **p** heart has become calloused;	3295

PEOPLED (1) [PEOPLE]

Eze	26:17	O city of renown, **p** *by men* of the sea!	3782

PEOPLES (156) [PEOPLE]

Ge	10: 5	(From these the maritime **p** spread out	1580
	12: 3	all *p on* earth will be blessed through you."	5476
	17:16	kings of **p** will come from her."	6639
	25:23	two *p* from within you will be separated;	4211
	27:29	May nations serve you and **p** bow down	4211
	28: 3	until you become a community of **p**.	6639
	28:14	*p on* earth will be blessed through you	5476
	29: 1	and came to the land of the eastern **p**.	1201
	48: 4	I will make you a community of **p**,	6639

Dt	1: 7	go to all the **neighboring p** in the Arabah,	8907
	4:27	The LORD will scatter you among the **p**,	6639
	6:14	the gods of the **p** around you;	6639
	7: 6	of all the **p** on the face of the earth to	6639
	7: 7	you were more numerous than other **p**,	6639
	7: 7	for you were the fewest of all **p**.	6639
	7:16	the **p** the LORD your God gives over to you.	6639
	7:19	the same to all the **p** you now fear.	6639
	13: 7	gods of the **p** around you,	6639
	14: 2	Out of all the **p** on the face of the earth,	6639
	28:10	the **p** *on* earth will see that you are called	6639
	32: 8	he set up boundaries for the **p** according to	6639
	33:19	They will summon **p** to the mountain	6639
Jos	4:24	the **p** of the earth might know that the hand	6639
Jdg	2:12	and worshiped various gods of the **p**	6639
	6: 3	and other eastern **p** invaded the country.	1201
	6:33	and other eastern **p** joined forces	1201
	7:12	the other eastern **p** had settled in the valley,	1201
	8:10	of the armies of the eastern **p**;	1201
1Sa	27: 8	(From ancient times **these** *p* had lived in	AIT
1Ki	8:43	the **p** of the earth may know your name	6639
	8:60	so that all the **p** of the earth may know that	6639
	9: 7	and an object of ridicule among all **p**.	6639
	9:20	and Jebusites (these **p** were not Israelites),	889S
1Ch	5:25	to the gods of the **p** of the land,	6639
	16:24	his marvelous deeds among all **p**.	6639
2Ch	6:33	the **p** of the earth may know your name	6639
	7:20	and an object of ridicule among all **p**.	6639
	8: 7	and Jebusites (these **p** were not Israelites),	889S
	13: 9	of your own as the **p** *of* other lands do?	6639
	32:13	and my fathers have done to all the **p** *of*	6639
	32:17	as the gods of the **p** of the other lands did	1580
	32:19	as they did about the gods of the other **p** *of*	6639
Ezr	3: 3	Despite their fear of the **p** around them,	6639
	4: 4	the **p** around them set out to discourage	6639
	9: 1	separate from the **neighboring p**	6639
	9: 2	and have mingled the holy race with the **p**	6639
	9:11	a land polluted by the corruption of its **p**.	6639
	9:14	the **p** *who commit* such detestable practices?	6639
	10: 2	by marrying foreign women from the **p**	6639
	10:11	Separate yourselves from the **p** around you	6639
Ne	9:24	to them, along with their kings and the **p** *of*	6639
	9:30	you handed them over to the neighboring **p**.	6639
	10:28	the neighboring **p** for the sake of the Law	6639
	10:30	to give our daughters in marriage to the **p**	6639
	10:31	the neighboring **p** bring merchandise	6639
	13:24	language of **one of the other p**,	2256+6639+6639
Est	1:16	the **p** of all the provinces of King Xerxes,	6639
	3: 8	among the **p** in all the provinces	6639
	3:12	and the nobles of the **various p**,	2256+6639+6639
Ps	2: 1	Why do the nations conspire and the **p** plot	4211
	7: 7	Let the assembled **p** gather around you.	6639
	7: 8	let the LORD judge the **p**.	6639
	9: 8	he will govern the **p** with justice.	4211
	33:10	he thwarts the purposes of the **p**.	6639
	44: 2	the **p** and made our fathers flourish	4211
	44:14	the **p** shake their heads at us.	4211
	47: 3	**p** under our feet.	6639
	49: 1	Hear this, all you **p**;	6639
	57: 9	I will sing of you among the **p**.	4211
	66: 8	O **p**, let the sound of his praise be heard;	6639
	67: 3	May the **p** praise you, O God;	6639
	67: 3	may all the **p** praise you.	6639
	67: 4	the **p** justly and guide the nations of	6639
	67: 5	May the **p** praise you, O God;	6639
	67: 5	may all the **p** praise you.	6639
	77:14	you display your power among the **p**.	6639
	87: 6	LORD will write in the register of the **p**:	6639
	96: 3	his marvelous deeds among all **p**.	6639
	96:10	he will judge the **p** with equity.	6639
	96:13	in righteousness and the **p** in his truth.	6639
	97: 6	and all the **p** see his glory.	6639
	98: 9	in righteousness and the **p** with equity.	6639
	102:22	when the **p** and the kingdoms assemble	6639
	105:20	the ruler of **p** set him free.	6639
	106:34	the **p** as the LORD had commanded them,	6639
	108: 3	I will sing of you among the **p**.	4211
	117: 1	extol him, all you **p**.	569
	144: 2	who subdues **p** under me.	6639
	149: 7	on the nations and punishment on the **p**,	4211
Pr	24:24	**p** will curse him and nations denounce him.	6639
Isa	2: 3	Many **p** will come and say, "Come,	6639
	2: 4	and will settle disputes for many **p**.	6639
	11:10	of Jesse will stand as a banner for the **p**;	6639
	14: 6	struck down **p** with unceasing blows,	6639
	17:12	Oh, the uproar of the **p**—	4211
	17:13	the **p** roar like the roar of surging waters,	4211
	19:13	cornerstones of her **p** have led Egypt astray.	8657
	25: 3	Therefore strong **p** will honor you;	6639
	25: 6	a feast of rich food for all **p**, a banquet	6639
	25: 7	the shroud that enfolds all **p**, the sheet	6639
	30:28	of the **p** a bit that leads them astray.	6639
	33: 3	At the thunder of your voice, the **p** flee;	6639
	33:12	The **p** will be burned as if to lime;	6639
	34: 1	pay attention, you **p**!	4211
	37:18	Assyrian kings have laid waste all these **p**	824
	43: 9	nations gather together and the **p** assemble.	4211
	49:22	I will lift up my banner to the **p**;	6639
	55: 4	See, I have made him a witness to the **p**,	4211
	55: 4	a leader and commander of the **p**.	4211
	60: 2	the earth and thick darkness is over the **p**,	4211
	61: 9	the nations and their offspring among the **p**.	6639
Jer	1:15	I am about to summon all the **p** *of*	5476
	10: 3	For the customs of the **p** are worthless;	6639
	10:25	on the **p** who do not call on your name.	5476
	25: 9	I will summon all the **p** of the north	5476
	34: 1	and all his army and all the kingdoms and **p**	6639

Jer	51:58	the **p** exhaust themselves for nothing,	6639
La	1:18	Listen, all you **p**; look upon my suffering.	6639
Eze	3: 6	not to many **p** of obscure speech	6639
	20:32	like the **p** of the world,	5476
	27: 3	merchant of **p** on many coasts,	6639
	32: 9	I will trouble the hearts of many **p**	6639
	32:10	I will cause many **p** to be appalled at you,	6639
	36:15	the scorn of the **p** or cause your nation	6639
Da	3: 4	O **p**, nations and men of every language:	10553
	3: 7	lyre, harp and all kinds of music, all the **p**,	10553
	4: 1	King Nebuchadnezzar, To the **p**,	10553
	4:35	the **p** of the earth are regarded as nothing.	10163
	4:35	with the powers of heaven and the **p** *of*	10163
	5:19	all the **p** and nations and men	10553
	6:25	then King Darius wrote to all the **p**,	10553
	7:14	all **p**, nations and men of every language	10553
Joel	2:17	Why should they say among the **p**,	6639
Mic	1: 2	Hear, O **p**, all of you, listen,	6639
	4: 1	and **p** will stream to it.	6639
	4: 3	between many **p** and will settle disputes	6639
	5: 7	be in the midst of many **p** like dew from	6639
	5: 8	in the midst of many **p**,	6639
Na	3: 4	by her prostitution and **p** by her witchcraft.	5476
Hab	2: 5	the nations and takes captive all the **p**.	6639
	2: 8	the **p** who are left will plunder you.	6639
	2:10	You have plotted the ruin of many **p**,	6639
Zep	3: 9	"Then will I purify the lips of the **p**,	6639
	3: 9	and praise among all the **p** *of* the earth	6639
Zec	8:20	"Many **p** and the inhabitants	6639
	8:22	And many **p** and powerful nations will come to Jerusalem	6639
	10: 9	Though I scatter them among the **p**,	6639
	12: 2	that sends all the surrounding **p** reeling.	6639
	12: 6	and left all the surrounding **p**,	6639
	14:17	the **p** *of* the earth do not go up to Jerusalem	5476
Ac	3:25	'Through your offspring all **p** on earth will	4255
	4:25	" 'Why do the nations rage and the **p** plot	3295
Ro	15:11	and sing praises to him, all you **p**."	3295
Rev	1: 7	the **p** of the earth will mourn because	5876
	10:11	"You must prophesy again about many **p**,	3295
	17:15	where the prostitute sits, are **p**, multitudes,	3295

PEOR (9) [BAAL PEOR, BETH PEOR]

Nu	23:28	And Balak took Balaam to the top of **P**,	7186
	25: 3	Israel joined in worshiping the Baal of **P**.	7186
	25: 5	in worshiping the Baal of **P**."	7186
	25:18	when they deceived you in the affair of **P**	7186
	25:18	when the plague came as a result of **P**."	7186
	31:16	from the LORD in what happened at **P**,	7186
Dt	4: 3	everyone who followed the Baal of **P**,	7186
Jos	22:17	Was not the sin of **P** enough for us?	7186
Ps	106:28	to the Baal of **P** and ate sacrifices offered	7186

PER (1)

Ex	38:26	one beka **p** person,	4200

PERATH (4)

Jer	13: 4	now to **P** and hide it there in a crevice in	7310
	13: 5	So I went and hid it at **P**,	7310
	13: 6	"Go now to **P** and get the belt I told you	7310
	13: 7	to **P** and dug up the belt and took it from	7310

PERAZIM (1) [BAAL PERAZIM]

Isa	28:21	as he did at Mount **P**, he will rouse himself	7292

PERCEIVE (5) [PERCEIVED, PERCEIVING]

Job	9:11	when he goes by, *I* cannot **p** him.	1067
	33:14	though *man may* not **p** it.	8800
Ps	139: 2	*you* **p** my thoughts from afar.	1067
Pr	24:12	*does* not he who weighs the heart **p** it?	1067
Isa	43:19	Now it springs up; *do you* not **p** it?	3359

PERCEIVED (1) [PERCEIVE]

Isa	64: 4	no one has heard, no **ear** *has* **p**,	263

PERCEIVING (4) [PERCEIVE]

Isa	6: 9	be ever seeing, but never **p**.'	3359
Mt	13:14	you will be ever seeing but never **p**.	3972
Mk	4:12	" 'they may be ever seeing but never **p**,	3972
Ac	28:26	you will be ever seeing but never **p**."	3972

PERCH (2) [PERCHED]

Mt	13:32	birds of the air come and **p** in its branches."	2942
Mk	4:32	that the birds of the air can **p** in its shade."	2942

PERCHED (1) [PERCH]

Lk	13:19	and the birds of the air **p** in its branches."	2942

PERES (1)

Da	5:28	**P**: Your kingdom is divided and given to	10593

PERESH (1)

1Ch	7:16	gave birth to a son and named him **P**.	7303

PEREZ (18) [PEREZ UZZAH, PEREZITE, RIMMON PEREZ]

Ge	38:29	And he was named **P**.	7289
	46:12	**P** and Zerah (but Er and Onan had died in	7289
	46:12	The sons of **P**: Hezron and Hamul.	7289

Nu	26:20	through P, the Perizite clan;	7289
	26:21	The descendants of P were:	7289
Ru	4:12	may your family be like that of P,	7289
	4:18	This, then, is the family line of P:	7289
	4:18	P was the father of Hezron,	7289
1Ch	2: 4	bore him P and Zerah.	7289
	2: 5	The sons of P: Hezron and Hamul.	7289
	4: 1	P, Hezron, Carmi, Hur and Shobal.	7289
	9: 4	a descendant of P son of Judah.	7289
	27: 3	He was a descendant of P and chief of all	7289
Ne	11: 4	the son of Mahalalel, a descendant of P;	7289
	11: 6	The descendants of P who lived	7289
Mt	1: 3	Judah the father of P and Zerah,	5756
	1: 3	P the father of Hezron,	5756
Lk	3:33	the son of Hezron, the son of P,	5756

PEREZ UZZAH (2) [PEREZ]

2Sa	6: 8	to this day that place is called P.	7290
1Ch	13:11	to this day that place is called P.	7290

PEREZITE (1) [PEREZ]

Nu	26:20	through Perez, the P clan;	7291

PERFECT (38) [PERFECTER, PERFECTING, PERFECTION, PERFECTLY]

Dt	32: 4	He is the Rock, his works are p,	9459
2Sa	22:31	"As for God, his way is p;	9459
	22:33	with strength and makes my way p.	9459
Job	36: 4	in knowledge is with you.	9459
	37:16	wonders of him who is p in knowledge?	9459
Ps	18:30	As for God, his way is p;	9459
	18:32	with strength and makes my way p.	9459
	19: 7	law of the LORD is p, reviving the soul.	9459
	50: 2	From Zion, p in beauty, God shines forth.	4817
	64: 6	"We have devised a p plan!"	9462
SS	6: 9	but my dove, my p one, is unique,	9447
Isa	25: 1	in p faithfulness you have done marvelous things,	590
	26: 3	You will keep in p peace him whose mind is steadfast,	8934+8934
Eze	16:14	the splendor I had given you made your beauty p,	4003
	27: 3	" 'You say, O Tyre, "I am p in beauty."	4003
	28:12	full of wisdom and p in beauty.	4003
Mt	5:48	Be p, therefore, as your heavenly Father is perfect.	5455
	5:48	therefore, as your heavenly Father is p.	5455
	19:21	Jesus answered, "If you want to be p, go,	5455
Ro	12: 2	his good, pleasing and p will.	5455
2Co	12: 9	for my power is made p in weakness."	5464
Php	3:12	or have already been made p,	5457
Col	1:28	that we may present everyone p in Christ.	5455
	3:14	which binds them all together in p unity.	5456
Heb	2:10	make the author of their salvation p	5457
	5: 9	and, once made p, he became the source	5457
	7:19	(for the law made nothing p),	5457
	7:28	who has been made p forever.	5457
	9:11	and more p tabernacle that is not man-made,	5455
	10: 1	make those who draw near to worship.	5457
	10:14	by one sacrifice he has made p forever those who are being made holy.	5457
	11:40	with us would they be made p.	5457
	12:23	to the spirits of righteous men made p,	5457
Jas	1:17	Every good and p gift is from above,	5455
	1:25	the p law that gives freedom, and continues	5455
	3: 2	he is a p man, able to keep his whole body	5455
1Jn	4:18	But p love drives out fear,	5455
	4:18	The one who fears is not made p in love.	5457

PERFECTER (1) [PERFECT]

Heb	12: 2	Jesus, the author and p of our faith,	5460

PERFECTING (1) [PERFECT]

2Co	7: 1	p holiness out of reverence for God.	2200

PERFECTION (9) [PERFECT]

Ps	119:96	To all p I see a limit;	9416
La	2:15	the city that was called the p of beauty,	4003
Eze	27: 3	your builders brought your beauty to p.	4005
	27:11	they brought your beauty to p.	4005
	28:12	" 'You were the model of p, full of wisdom	9422
1Co	13:10	but when p comes, the imperfect disappears.	5455
2Co	13: 9	and our prayer is for your p.	2937
	13:11	Aim for p, listen to my appeal,	2936
Heb	7:11	If p could have been attained through	5459

PERFECTLY (2) [PERFECT]

1Co	1:10	and that you may be p united	899+2936+3836
2Co	11: 6	We have made this p clear to you	1877+4246

PERFORM (26) [PERFORMANCE, PERFORMED, PERFORMING, PERFORMS]

Ex	3:20	the wonders that I will p among them.	6913
	4:17	in your hand so you can p miraculous signs	6913
	4:21	that you p before Pharaoh all the wonders	6913
	4:28	miraculous signs he had commanded him to p.	NIH
	7: 9	'P a miracle,' then say to Aaron,	5989

Ex	10: 1	that I may p these miraculous signs of mine	8883
	18:20	the way to live and the duties they are to p.	8883
Nu	3: 7	They are to p duties for him and for	9068
	4:31	as they p service at the Tent of Meeting:	NIH
	18: 3	to be responsible to you and are to p all	NIH
Jdg	16:27	men and women watching Samson p.	8471
2Sa	7:23	to make a name for himself, and to p great	6913
1Ki	8:11	the priests could not p their service because	6641
1Ch	17:21	to make a name for yourself, and to p great	NIH
2Ch	5:14	the priests could not p their service because	6641
	31:16	to p the daily duties of their various tasks,	NIH
Isa	28:21	his strange work, and p his task,	6268
Jer	21: 2	Perhaps the LORD will p wonders for us	6913
Eze	44:16	to minister before me and p my service.	9068
Mt	7:22	drive out demons and p many miracles?'	4472
	24:24	and p great signs and miracles to deceive	1443
Mk	13:22	and false prophets will appear and p signs	1443
Lk	23: 8	he hoped to see him p some miracle.	1181
Jn	3: 2	For no one could p the miraculous signs	4472
Ac	4:30	to heal and p miraculous signs and wonders	1181
2Co	9:12	This service that you p is	1355+3311+3836+4047

PERFORMANCE (1) [PERFORM]

1Ch	23:28	the p of other duties at the house of God.	5126

PERFORMED (35) [PERFORM]

Ex	4:30	He also p the signs before the people,	6913
	10: 2	with the Egyptians and how I p my signs	8492
	11:10	Moses and Aaron p all these wonders	6913
Nu	14:11	in spite of all the miraculous signs I have p	6913
	14:22	and the miraculous signs I p in Egypt and	6913
Dt	10:21	he is your God, who p for you those great	6913
	11: 3	the signs he p and the things he did in	6913
	34:12	the mighty power or p the awesome deeds	NIH
Jos	24:17	and p those great signs before our eyes.	6913
Jdg	16:25	and he p for them.	7464
1Sa	12: 7	as to all the righteous acts p by the LORD	6913
2Sa	23:20	who p great exploits.	NIH
1Ch	6:32	They p their duties according to	6641
	11:22	who p great exploits.	7189
	25: 1	the list of the men who p this service:	4856
Ne	9:17	and failed to remember the miracles you p	6913
	12:45	They p the service of their God and	9068
Ps	105:27	They p his miraculous signs among them,	8492
Jer	32:20	You p miraculous signs and wonders	8492
Da	4: 2	and wonders that the Most High God has p	10522
Mt	11:20	in which most of his miracles had been p,	1181
	11:21	that were p in you had been performed	1181
	11:21	that were performed in you had been p	1181
	11:23	that were p in you had been performed	1181
	11:23	that were performed in you had been p	1181
Lk	1:51	He has p mighty deeds with his arm;	4472
	10:13	that were p in you had been performed	1181
	10:13	that were performed in you had been p	1181
Jn	2:11	Jesus p at Cana in Galilee.	4472
	4:54	the second miraculous sign that Jesus p,	4472
	6: 2	the miraculous signs he had p on the sick.	4472
	10:41	"Though John never p a miraculous sign,	4472
Ac	5:12	The apostles p many miraculous signs	1181
Rev	13:13	And he p great and miraculous signs,	4472
	19:20	and with him the false prophet who had p	4472

PERFORMING (3) [PERFORM]

Nu	8:26	in p their duties at the Tent of Meeting,	9068
Jn	11:47	"Here is this man p many miraculous signs.	4472
Rev	16:14	spirits of demons p miraculous signs,	4472

PERFORMS (5) [PERFORM]

Job	5: 9	He p wonders that cannot be fathomed,	6913
	9:10	He p wonders that cannot be fathomed,	6913
Ps	77:14	You are the God who p miracles;	6913
Da	6:27	he p signs and wonders in the heavens and	10522
Heb	10:11	priest stands and p his religious duties;	3310

PERFUME (25) [PERFUME-MAKERS, PERFUMED, PERFUMER, PERFUMERS, PERFUMES]

Ex	30:33	Whoever makes p like it and whoever puts	8379
Ru	3: 3	Wash and p yourself, and put on	6057
Pr	27: 9	P and incense bring joy to the heart,	9043
Ecc	7: 1	A good name is better than fine p,	9043
	10: 1	As dead flies give p a bad smell,	8379+9043
SS	1: 3	your name is like p poured out.	9043
	1:12	my p spread its fragrance.	5948
	4:10	and the fragrance of your p than any spice!	9043
	5:13	like beds of spice yielding p.	5349
Isa	3:20	the p bottles and charms,	5883
Mt	26: 7	with an alabaster jar of very expensive p,	3693
	26: 9	"This p could have been sold at a high price	3693
	26:12	When she poured this p on my body,	3693
Mk	14: 3	with an alabaster jar of very expensive p,	3693
	14: 3	the jar and poured the p on his head.	899S
	14: 4	"Why this waste of p?	3693
	14: 8	She poured p on my body beforehand to prepare for my burial.	3693
Lk	7:37	she brought an alabaster jar of p,	3693
	7:38	kissed them and poured p on them.	3693
	7:46	but she has poured p on my feet.	3693
Jn	11: 2	the same one who poured p on the Lord	3693
	12: 3	about a pint of pure nard, an expensive p;	3693
	12: 3	with the fragrance of p.	3693
	12: 5	"Why wasn't this p sold and the money	3693
	12: 7	save this p for the day of my burial."	899S

PERFUME-MAKERS (1) [PERFUME]

Ne	3: 8	and Hananiah, one of the p,	8382

PERFUMED (2) [PERFUME]

Pr	7:17	I have p my bed with myrrh,	5678
SS	3: 6	p with myrrh and incense made from all	7787

PERFUMER (3) [PERFUME]

Ex	30:25	a fragrant blend, the work of a p.	8379
	30:35	fragrant blend of incense, the work of a p.	8379
	37:29	fragrant incense—the work of a p.	8379

PERFUMERS (1) [PERFUME]

1Sa	8:13	He will take your daughters to be p	8384

PERFUMES (5) [PERFUME]

2Ch	16:14	with spices and various blended p,	5126+5351
Est	2:12	six months with oil of myrrh and six with p	1411
SS	1: 3	Pleasing is the fragrance of your p;	9043
Isa	57: 9	with olive oil and increased your p.	8383
Lk	23:56	they went home and prepared spices and p.	3693

PERGA (3)

Ac	13:13	Paul and his companions sailed to P	4308
	13:14	From P they went on to Pisidian Antioch.	4308
	14:25	and when they had preached the word in P,	4308

PERGAMOS (KJV) See PERGAMUM

PERGAMUM (2)

Rev	1:11	to Ephesus, Smyrna, P, Thyatira, Sardis,	4307
	2:12	"To the angel of the church in P write:	4307

PERHAPS (36)

Ge	16: 2	p I can build a family through her."	218
	32:20	when I see him, p he will receive me."	218
	43:12	P it was a mistake.	218
Ex	32:30	p I can make atonement for your sin."	218
Nu	22: 6	P then I will be able to defeat them	218
	22:11	P then I will be able to fight them	218
	23: 3	P the LORD will come to meet with me.	218
	23:27	P it will please God to let you curse them	218
Jos	9: 7	"But p you live near us.	218
1Sa	6: 5	P he will lift his hand from you	218
	9: 6	P he will tell us what way to take."	218
	14: 6	P the LORD will act in our behalf.	218
2Sa	14:15	p he will do what his servant asks.	218
	14:16	P the king will agree to deliver his servant	3954
1Ki	18:27	P he is deep in thought, or busy,	3954
	20:31	P he will spare your life."	218
2Ki	2:16	P the Spirit of the LORD has picked him	7153
Job	1: 5	"P my children have sinned	218
Isa	44:14	or p took a cypress or oak.	NIH
	47:12	P you will succeed,	218
	47:12	p you will cause terror.	218
Jer	20:10	saying, "P he will be deceived;	218
	21: 2	P the LORD will perform wonders for us	218
	26: 3	P they will listen and each will turn	218
	36: 3	P when the people of Judah hear	218
	36: 7	P they will bring their petition before	218
	51: 8	Get balm for her pain; p she can be healed.	218
Eze	12: 3	P they will understand.	218
Am	5:15	P the LORD God Almighty will have mercy on the remnant of Joseph.	218
Zep	2: 3	p you will be sheltered on the day of	218
Lk	20:13	p they will respect him.'	2711
Ac	8:22	P he will forgive you for having such	726+1623
	17:27	and p reach out for him and	726+1145+1623
1Co	15:37	p of wheat or of something else.	1623+5593
	16: 6	P I will stay with you awhile,	5593
Phm	1:15	P the reason he was separated from you for	5440

PERIDA (1)

Ne	7:57	the descendants of Sotai, Sophereth, P,	7263

PERIL (3)

Job	22:10	why sudden p terrifies you,	7065
Ps	78:53	in their p their courage melted away.	8288
2Co	1:10	He has delivered us from such a deadly p,	NIG

PERIOD (28) [PERIODS]

Ge	31:35	I'm having my p."	851+2006
	50:10	a seven-day p of mourning for his father.	65
Ex	2:23	During that long p, the king of Egypt died.	3427
Lev	12: 2	she is unclean during her monthly p.	1864+5614
	12: 5	the woman will be unclean, as during her p.	5614
	15:19	the impurity of her monthly p	5614
	15:20	" 'Anything she lies on during her p will	5614
	15:25	at a time other than her monthly p or has	5614
	15:25	a discharge that continues beyond her p	5614
	15:25	just as in the days of her p.	5614
	15:26	as is her bed during her monthly p,	5614
	15:26	will be unclean, as during her p.	5614
	15:33	for a woman in her monthly p,	1865+5614
	18:19	during the uncleanness of her monthly p.	5614
	20:18	with a woman during her monthly p	1865
	25: 8	of years amount to a p of forty-nine years.	3427
Nu	6: 5	" 'During the entire p of his vow	3427
	6: 5	be holy until the p of his separation to	3427

Nu	6: 6	Throughout the **p** *of* his separation to	3427
	6: 8	the **p** *of* his separation he is consecrated to	3427
	6:12	for the **p** *of* his separation and must bring	3427
	6:13	when the **p** *of* his separation is over.	3427
Job	1: 5	When a **p** of feasting had run its course,	3427
Eze	18: 6	or lie with a woman *during* her **p.**	5614
	22:10	those who violate women during their **p,**	5614
Da	7:12	but were allowed to live for a **p** of time.)	10221+10232+10530
Ac	1: 3	He appeared to them **over a p** of forty days	1328
	24: 2	"We have enjoyed a **long p** of peace	4498

PERIODS (1) [PERIOD]

1Ch	9:25	and share their duties for **seven-day p.**	2021+3427+8679

PERISH (84) [PERISHABLE, PERISHED, PERISHES, PERISHING]

Ge	6:17	Everything on earth *will* **p.**	1588
	47:19	Why *should we* **p** before your eyes—	4637
Ex	19:21	to see the LORD and many of them **p.**	5877
Lev	26:38	*You will* **p** among the nations;	6
Dt	4:26	that *you will* quickly **p** from the land	6+6
	11:17	and *you will* soon **p** from the good land	6
	28:22	which will plague you until you **p.**	6
	32:25	Young men and young women will **p,**	NIH
Jos	23:13	until you **p** from this good land	6
	23:16	and *you will* quickly **p** from	6
Jdg	5:31	"So *may* all your enemies **p,** O LORD!	6
1Sa	26:10	or he will go into battle and **p.**	6200
2Ki	9: 8	The whole house of Ahab *will* **p.**	6
Est	4:14	but you and your father's family *will* **p.**	6
	4:16	And if *I* **p,** I perish."	6
	4:16	And if I perish, *I* **p."**	6
Job	3: 3	"May *the day of* my birth **p,**	6
	3:11	"Why *did I* not **p** at birth,	4637
	4: 9	at the blast of his anger *they* **p.**	3983
	4:20	unnoticed, *they* **p** forever.	6
	6:18	they go up into the wasteland and **p.**	6
	20: 7	*he will* **p** forever, like his own dung;	6
	34:15	all mankind *would* **p** together	1588
	36:12	*they will* **p** by the sword and die	6296
Ps	1: 6	but the way of the wicked *will* **p.**	6
	9: 3	they stumble and **p** before you.	6
	9:18	nor the hope of the afflicted ever **p.**	6
	10:16	the nations *will* **p** from his land.	6
	37:20	But the wicked *will* **p:**	6
	41: 5	"When will he die and his name **p?"**	6
	49:10	the senseless alike **p** and leave their wealth	6
	49:12	he is like the beasts *that* **p.**	1950
	49:20	like the beasts *that* **p.**	1950
	68: 2	*may* the wicked **p** before God.	6
	71:13	May my accusers **p** in shame;	3983
	73:27	Those who are far from you *will* **p;**	6
	80:16	at your rebuke your *people* **p.**	6
	83:17	*may they* **p** in disgrace.	6
	92: 9	O LORD, surely your enemies *will* **p;**	6
	102:26	They *will* **p,** but you remain;	6
Pr	11:10	when the wicked **p,** there are shouts of joy.	6
	19: 9	and he who pours out lies *will* **p.**	6
	21:28	A false witness *will* **p,**	6
	28:28	when the wicked **p,** the righteous thrive.	6
Isa	1:28	and those who forsake the LORD *will* **p.**	3983
	29:14	the wisdom of the wise *will* **p,**	6
	31: 3	both *will* **p** together.	3983
	41:11	who oppose You will be as nothing and **p.**	6
	57: 1	The righteous **p,** and no one ponders it	6
	60:12	or kingdom that will not serve you *will* **p;**	6
Jer	6:21	neighbors and friends *will* **p."**	6
	8:14	to the fortified cities and **p** there!	1959
	8:14	For the LORD our God *has* **doomed** us **to p**	1959
	10:11	not make the heavens and the earth, *will* **p**	10005
	10:15	when their judgment comes, *they will* **p.**	6
	14:15	Those same prophets *will* **p** by sword	9462
	16: 4	*They will* **p** by sword and famine,	3983
	27:10	I will banish you and *you will* **p.**	6
	27:15	I will banish you and *you will* **p,**	6
	40:15	and the remnant of Judah *to* **p?"**	6
	44:12	*They will* all **p** in Egypt;	9462
	44:27	in Egypt they will **p** by sword and famine	9462
	49:10	relatives and neighbors *will* **p,**	8720
	51:18	when their judgment comes, *they will* **p.**	6
Eze	5:12	of your people will die of the plague or **p**	3983
Jnh	1: 6	will take notice of us, and *we will* not **p."**	6
	3: 9	his fierce anger so that *we will* not **p."**	6
Zec	11: 9	Let the dying die, and the perishing **p.**	3948
	13: 8	"two-thirds will be struck down and **p;**	1588
Lk	13: 3	But unless you repent, *you* too will all **p."**	660
	13: 5	But unless you repent, *you* too will all **p."**	660
	21:18	But not a hair of your head *will* **p.**	660
Jn	3:16	that whoever believes in him *shall* not **p**	660
	10:28	I give them eternal life, and *they shall* never **p;**	660
	11:50	for the people than that the whole nation **p."**	660
Ac	8:20	"May your money **p** with you,	724+1639+1650
	13:41	you scoffers, wonder and **p,**	906
Ro	2:12	the law *will* also **p** apart from the law,	660
Col	2:22	These are all destined to **p** with use,	5785
2Th	2:10	They **p** because they refused to love	NIG
Heb	1:11	They *will* **p,** but you remain;	660
1Pe	1: 4	into an inheritance that **can never p,** spoil	915
2Pe	2:12	and like beasts *they* too *will* **p.**	5780+5785
	3: 9	patient with you, not wanting anyone *to* **p,**	660

PERISHABLE (6) [PERISH]

1Co	15:42	The body that is sown is **p,**	1877+5785
	15:50	nor does the **p** inherit the imperishable.	5785
	15:53	**p** must clothe itself with the imperishable,	5778
	15:54	When the **p** has been clothed with	5778
1Pe	1:18	that it was not *with* **p** *things* such as silver	5778
	1:23	you have been born again, not of **p** seed,	5778

PERISHED (14) [PERISH]

Ge	7:21	Every living thing that moved on the earth **p**	1588
Nu	16:33	*they* **p** and were gone from the community.	6
Dt	2:14	that entire generation of fighting men *had* **p**	9462
	7:20	the survivors who hide from you *have* **p.**	6
2Sa	1:27	The weapons of war *have* **p!"**	6
Job	4: 7	Who, being innocent, *has ever* **p?**	6
Ps	9: 6	even the memory of them *has* **p.**	6
	83:10	*who* **p** at Endor and became like refuse on	9012
	119:92	I would have **p** in my affliction.	6
Jer	7:28	Truth *has* **p;** it has vanished from their lips.	6
	12: 4	the animals and birds *have* **p.**	6200
	49: 7	*Has* counsel **p** from the prudent?	6
La	1: 9	My priests and my elders **p** in the city	1588
Mic	4: 9	*Has* your counselor **p,**	6

PERISHES (5) [PERISH]

Job	4:11	The lion **p** for lack of prey,	6
	8:13	so **p** the hope of the godless.	6
	18:17	The memory of him **p** from the earth;	6
Pr	11: 7	When a wicked man dies, his hope **p;**	6
1Pe	1: 7	which **p** even though refined by fire—	660

PERISHING (11) [PERISH]

Job	31:19	if I have seen *anyone* **p** for lack of clothing,	6
	33:18	his life from **p** by the sword.	6296
Pr	31: 6	Give beer to *those who are* **p,**	6
Ecc	7:15	a righteous man **p** in his righteousness,	6
Isa	27:13	Those *who were* **p** in Assyria	6
Jer	44:18	and *have been* **p** by sword and famine."	9462
Zec	11: 9	Let the dying die, and the **p** perish.	3948
1Co	1:18	the cross is foolishness *to those who are* **p,**	660
2Co	2:15	who are being saved and those who are **p.**	660
	4: 3	it is veiled to those who *are* **p.**	660
2Th	2:10	of evil that deceives those who *are* **p.**	660

PERIZZITES (23)

Ge	13: 7	The Canaanites and **P** were also living in	7254
	15:20	Hittites, **P,** Rephaites,	7254
	34:30	a stench to the Canaanites and **P,**	7254
Ex	3: 8	Amorites, **P,** Hivites and Jebusites.	7254
	3:17	Amorites, **P,** Hivites and Jebusites—	7254
	23:23	**P,** Canaanites, Hivites and Jebusites,	7254
	33: 2	Hittites, **P,** Hivites and Jebusites.	7254
	34:11	Hittites, **P,** Hivites and Jebusites.	7254
Dt	7: 1	Girgashites, Amorites, Canaanites, **P,**	7254
	20:17	the Hittites, Amorites, Canaanites, **P,**	7254
Jos	3:10	**P,** Girgashites, Amorites and Jebusites.	7254
	9: 1	Canaanites, **P,** Hivites and Jebusites)—	7254
	11: 3	Hittites, **P** and Jebusites in the hill country;	7254
	12: 8	Canaanites, **P,** Hivites and Jebusites):	7254
	17:15	for yourselves there in the land of the **P**	7254
	24:11	as did also the Amorites, **P,** Canaanites,	7254
Jdg	1: 4	the LORD gave the Canaanites and **P**	7254
	1: 5	putting to rout the Canaanites and **P.**	7254
	3: 5	Amorites, **P,** Hivites and Jebusites.	7254
1Ki	9:20	from the Amorites, Hittites, **P,** Hivites	7254
2Ch	8: 7	from the Hittites, Amorites, **P,** Hivites	7254
Ezr	9: 1	like those of the Canaanites, Hittites, **P,**	7254
Ne	9: 8	Amorites, **P,** Jebusites and Girgashites.	7254

PERJURERS (2) [PERJURY]

Mal	3: 5	to testify against sorcerers, adulterers and **p,**	2021+4200+8678+9214
1Ti	1:10	*for* slave traders and liars and **p—**	2156

PERJURY (1) [PERJURERS]

Jer	7: 9	commit adultery and **p,**	2021+4200+8678+9214

PERMANENT (4) [PERMANENTLY]

Lev	25:34	it is their **p** possession.	6409
Jos	8:28	So Joshua burned Ai and made it a **p** heap	6409
Jn	8:35	Now a slave *has* no **p place** in the family,	3531
Heb	7:24	he has a **p** priesthood.	563

PERMANENTLY (2) [PERMANENT]

Lev	25:23	" 'The land must not be sold	4200+7552
	25:30	the house in the walled city shall belong **p** to the buyer	2021+4200+7552

PERMISSIBLE (4) [PERMIT]

1Co	6:12	"Everything *is* **p** for me"—but not everything is beneficial.	2003
	6:12	"Everything *is* **p** for me"—but I will not be mastered by anything.	2003
	10:23	"Everything is **p"**—but not everything is beneficial.	2003
	10:23	"Everything is **p"**—but not everything is constructive.	2003

PERMISSION (12) [PERMIT]

Jdg	11:17	'Give us **p** to **go** through your country,'	AIT
1Sa	20: 6	'David **earnestly asked** my **p** to hurry	8626+8626
	20:28	"David **earnestly asked** me **for p** to	8626+8626
Ne	13: 6	Some time later I asked his **p**	4946
Est	9:13	"give the Jews in Susa **p** to carry out	5989
Isa	22:16	and who gave you **p** to cut out a grave	4200
Da	1: 8	asked the chief official **for p** not to defile	1335
Mk	5:13	He gave them **p,** and the evil spirits came	2205
Lk	8:32	and *he* gave them **p.**	2205
Jn	19:38	With Pilate's **p,** he came and took	2205
Ac	21:40	*Having* **received** the commander's **p,**	2205
	26: 1	"You *have* **p** to speak for yourself."	2205

PERMIT (4) [PERMISSIBLE, PERMISSION, PERMITS, PERMITTED, PERMITTING]

Ex	12:23	not **p** the destroyer to enter your houses	5989
Hos	5: 4	"Their deeds *do not* **p** them to return	5989
Ac	24:23	**p** his friends to take care of his needs.	3266+3594
1Ti	2:12	not **p** a woman to teach or to have authority	2205

PERMITS (2) [PERMIT]

Ecc	5:12	abundance of a rich man **p** him no sleep.	5663
1Co	16: 7	to spend some time with you, if the Lord **p.**	2205

PERMITTED (5) [PERMIT]

Ex	19:13	he shall not be **p to live.'**	AIT
Dt	18:14	LORD your God *has* not **p** you *to do* so.	5989
Mt	19: 8	"Moses **p** you to divorce your wives	2205
Mk	10: 4	"Moses **p** a man to write a certificate	2205
2Co	12: 4	things that man *is* not **p** to tell.	2003

PERMITTING (1) [PERMIT]

Heb	6: 3	And God **p,** we will do so.	2205

PERPETUATE (1)

Ps	45:17	I will **p** your **memory** through all	2349+9005

PERPLEXED (5) [PERPLEXITY]

Da	4:19	(also called Belteshazzar) *was* greatly **p**	10724
Lk	9: 7	And he was **p,** because some were saying	1389
Ac	2:12	Amazed and **p,** they asked one another,	1389
2Co	4: 8	**p,** but not in despair;	679
Gal	4:20	because *I am* **p** about you!	679

PERPLEXITY (1) [PERPLEXED]

Lk	21:25	in anguish and **p** at the roaring and tossing	680

PERSECUTE (18) [PERSECUTED, PERSECUTING, PERSECUTION, PERSECUTIONS, PERSECUTOR, PERSECUTORS]

Dt	30: 7	curses on your enemies who hate and **p** you.	8103
Ps	9:13	O LORD, see how my enemies **p** me!	6715
	69:26	For *they* **p** those you wound and talk about	8103
	119:86	help me, for *men* **p** me without cause.	8103
	119:157	Many are the foes *who* **p** me,	8103
	119:161	Rulers **p** me without cause,	8103
Mt	5:11	**p** you and falsely say all kinds of evil	1503
	5:44	and pray for those who **p** you,	1503
Lk	11:49	and others *they* will **p.'**	1503
	21:12	they will lay hands on you and **p** you.	1503
Jn	15:20	they persecuted me, *they will* **p** you also.	1503
Ac	7:52	a prophet your fathers *did* not **p?**	1503
	9: 4	"Saul, Saul, why *do you* **p** me?"	1503
	12: 1	belonged to the church, *intending to* **p** them.	2808
	22: 7	Why *do you* **p** me?'	1503
	26:11	I even went to foreign cities *to* **p** them.	1503
	26:14	'Saul, Saul, why *do you* **p** me?	1503
Ro	12:14	Bless those who **p** you;	1503

PERSECUTED (18) [PERSECUTE]

Mt	5:10	Blessed are those who *are* **p** because	1503
	5:12	the same way *they* **p** the prophets who were	1503
	10:23	When you *are* **p** in one place,	1503
	24: 9	be handed over to be **p** and put to death,	2568
Jn	5:16	things on the Sabbath, the Jews **p** him.	1503
	15:20	If *they* **p** me, they will persecute you also.	1503
Ac	22: 4	I **p** the followers of this Way to their death,	1503
1Co	4:12	*when we are* **p,** we endure it;	1503
	15: 9	because *I* **p** the church of God.	1503
2Co	4: 9	**p,** but not abandoned;	1503
Gal	1:13	how intensely *I* **p** the church of God	1503
	1:23	"The man who formerly **p** us is now	1503
	4:29	the son born in the ordinary way **p** the son	1503
	5:11	why *am I* still *being* **p?**	1503
	6:12	to avoid *being* **p** for the cross of Christ.	1503
1Th	3: 4	we kept telling you that we would be **p.**	2567
2Ti	3:12	a godly life in Christ Jesus *will be* **p,**	1503
Heb	11:37	destitute, **p** and mistreated—	2567

PERSECUTING (4) [PERSECUTE]

Ac	9: 5	"I am Jesus, whom you *are* **p,"** he replied.	1503
	22: 8	'I am Jesus of Nazareth, whom you *are* **p,'**	1503
	26:15	'I am Jesus, whom you *are* **p,'**	1503
Php	3: 6	as for zeal, **p** the church;	1503

PERSECUTION (9) [PERSECUTE]

Mt	13:21	trouble or **p** comes because of the word,	1501
Mk	4:17	trouble or **p** comes because of the word,	1501

Ac	8: 1	On that day a great **p** broke out against	1501
	11:19	Now those who had been scattered by the **p**	2568
	13:50	stirred up **p** against Paul and Barnabas,	1501
Ro	8:35	or hardship or **p** or famine or nakedness	1501
1Th	3: 7	and **p** we were encouraged about you	2568
Heb	10:33	you were publicly exposed to insult and **p**;	2568
Rev	2:10	and *you will* suffer **p** for ten days.	2400+2568

PERSECUTIONS (5) [PERSECUTE]

Mk	10:30	and with them, **p**) and in the age to come,	1501
2Co	12:10	in insults, in hardships, in **p**, in difficulties.	1501
2Th	1: 4	in all the **p** and trials you are enduring.	1501
2Ti	3:11	**p**, sufferings—what kinds of things	1501
	3:11	Iconium and Lystra, the **p** I endured.	1501

PERSECUTOR (1) [PERSECUTE]

| 1Ti | 1:13 | a blasphemer and a **p** and a violent man, | 1502 |

PERSECUTORS (4) [PERSECUTE]

Ps	119:84	When will you punish my **p**?	8103
Jer	15:15	Avenge me on my **p**.	8103
	17:18	Let my **p** be put to shame,	8103
	20:11	so my **p** will stumble and not prevail.	8103

PERSEVERANCE (13) [PERSEVERE]

Ro	5: 3	we know that suffering produces **p**;	5705
	5: 4	**p**, character; and character, hope.	5705
2Co	12:12	were done among you with great **p**.	5705
2Th	1: 4	about your **p** and faith in all	5705
	3: 5	into God's love and Christ's **p**.	5705
Heb	12: 1	let us run with **p** the race marked out for us.	5705
Jas	1: 3	that the testing of your faith develops **p**.	5705
	1: 4	**P** must finish its work so that you may	5705
	5:11	You have heard of Job's **p** and	5705
2Pe	1: 6	and to self-control, **p**;	5705
	1: 6	and to **p**, godliness;	5705
Rev	2: 2	your hard work and your **p**.	5705
	2:19	your love and faith, your service and **p**,	5705

PERSEVERE (2) [PERSEVERANCE, PERSEVERED, PERSEVERES, PERSEVERING]

| 1Ti | 4:16 | **P** in them, because if you do, | 2152 |
| Heb | 10:36 | You need **to p** so that when you have done | 5705 |

PERSEVERED (3) [PERSEVERE]

Heb	11:27	*he* **p** because he saw him who is invisible.	2846
Jas	5:11	we consider blessed those who *have* **p**.	5702
Rev	2: 3	*have* **p** and have endured hardships	2400+5702

PERSEVERES (2) [PERSEVERE]

| 1Co | 13: 7 | always trusts, always hopes, always **p**. | 5702 |
| Jas | 1:12 | Blessed is the man who **p** under trial, | 5702 |

PERSEVERING (1) [PERSEVERE]

| Lk | 8:15 | retain it, and by **p** produce a crop. | 5705 |

PERSIA (29) [PERSIAN, PERSIANS]

2Ch	36:20	until the kingdom of **P** came to power.	7273
	36:22	In the first year of Cyrus king of **P**,	7273
	36:22	of Cyrus king of **P** to make a proclamation	7273
	36:23	"This is what Cyrus king of **P** says:	7273
Ezr	1: 1	In the first year of Cyrus king of **P**,	7273
	1: 1	of Cyrus king of **P** to make a proclamation	7273
	1: 2	"This is what Cyrus king of **P** says:	7273
	1: 8	king of **P** had them brought by Mithredath	7273
	3: 7	as authorized by Cyrus king of **P**.	7273
	4: 3	Cyrus, the king of **P**, commanded us."	7273
	4: 5	king of **P** and down to the reign of Darius	7273
	4: 5	and down to the reign of Darius king of **P**.	7273
	4: 7	And in the days of Artaxerxes king of **P**,	7273
	4: 9	**P**, Erech and Babylon,	10060
	4:24	of the reign of Darius king of **P**.	10594
	6:14	Darius and Artaxerxes, kings of **P**.	10594
	7: 1	during the reign of Artaxerxes king of **P**,	7273
	9: 9	in the sight of the kings of **P**:	7273
Est	1: 3	The military leaders of **P** and Media,	7273
	1:14	of **P** and Media who had special access to	7273
	1:19	be written in the laws of **P** and Media,	7273
	10: 2	the annals of the kings of Media and **P**?	7273
Eze	27:10	of **P**, Lydia and Put served as soldiers	7273
	38: 5	**P**, Cush and Put will be with them,	7273
Da	8:20	the kings of Media and **P**.	7273
	10: 1	In the third year of Cyrus king of **P**,	7273
	10:13	I was detained there with the king of **P**.	7273
	10:20	the prince of **P**, and when I go, the prince	7273
	11: 2	Three more kings will appear in **P**,	7273

PERSIAN (4) [PERSIA]

Ne	12:22	were recorded in the reign of Darius the **P**.	7275
Est	1:18	This very day the **P** and Median women of	7273
Da	6:28	of Darius and the reign of Cyrus the **P**.	10595
	10:13	**P** kingdom resisted me twenty-one days.	7273

PERSIANS (4) [PERSIA]

Da	5:28	and given to the Medes and **P**."	10594
	6: 8	with the laws of the Medes and **P**,	10594
	6:12	with the laws of the Medes and **P**,	10594
	6:15	law of the Medes and **P** no decree or edict	10594

PERSIS (1)

| Ro | 16:12 | Greet my dear friend **P**, | 4372 |

PERSIST (5) [PERSISTED, PERSISTENCE, PERSISTS]

Dt	29:19	though *I* **p** in going my own way."	4213+9244
1Sa	12:25	Yet if *you* **p** in doing evil,	8317+8317
2Ki	17:34	To this day they **p** in their former practices.	6913
Isa	1: 5	Why *do you* **p** in rebellion?	3578
Ro	11:23	And if they *do* not **p** in unbelief,	2152

PERSISTED (3) [PERSIST]

2Ki	2:17	*they* **p** until he was too ashamed to refuse.	7210
	17:22	The Israelites **p** in all the sins of Jeroboam	2143
	17:40	but **p** in their former practices.	3869+6913

PERSISTENCE (1) [PERSIST]

| Ro | 2: 7 | who by **p** in doing good seek glory, honor | 5705 |

PERSISTS (1) [PERSIST]

| Dt | 25: 8 | If *he* **p** in saying, "I do not want to marry | 6641 |

PERSON (102) [PERSON'S, PERSONAL, PERSONALLY, PERSONS]

Ex	12: 4	in accordance with what each **p** will eat.	AIT
	16:16	an omer for each **p** you have in your tent.' "	5883
	16:22	two omers for each **p**—	AIT
	23: 7	not put an innocent or honest **p** to death,	AIT
	36: 1	Oholiab and every skilled **p** to whom	408
	36: 2	and Oholiab and every skilled **p** to whom	408
	38:26	one beka per **p**,	1653
Lev	5: 1	" 'If a **p** sins because he does not speak up	5883
	5: 2	**p** touches anything ceremonially unclean—	5883
	5: 4	" 'Or if a **p** thoughtlessly takes an oath	5883
	5:15	"When a **p** commits a violation	5883
	5:17	a **p** sins and does what is forbidden in any	5883
	7:11	for the fellowship offering a **p** may present	NIH
	7:18	the **p** who eats any of it will	5883
	7:20	that **p** must be cut off from his people.	5883
	7:21	that **p** must be cut off from his people.' "	5883
	7:27	that **p** must be cut off from his people.' "	5883
	13: 4	the infected **p** in isolation for seven days.	5596
	13:12	it covers all the skin of the infected **p**	5596
	13:13	he shall pronounce that **p** clean.	5596S
	13:17	priest shall pronounce the infected **p** clean;	5596
	13:30	the priest shall pronounce that **p** unclean;	2257S
	13:31	infected **p** in isolation for seven days.	5596+5999
	13:36	the **p** is unclean.	2085S
	13:39	that **p** is clean.	2085S
	13:45	**p** with such an infectious disease	AIT
	14: 2	"These are the regulations for the diseased **p**	AIT
	14: 3	If the **p** has been healed of his infectious	7665S
	14: 8	The **p** to be cleansed must wash his clothes,	AIT
	14:30	which the **p** can afford,	2257S
	15: 8	that **p** must wash his clothes and bathe	NIH
	17:10	that **p** who eats blood and will cut him off	5883
	19: 8	that **p** must be cut off from his people.	5883
	20: 6	" 'I will set my face against the **p** who turns	5883
	22: 3	that **p** must be cut off from my presence.	5883
	22: 5	or *any* **p** who makes him unclean,	132
	22:13	No unauthorized **p**, however,	2424
	27: 5	a **p** between the ages of five and twenty,	NIH
	27: 6	a **p** between one month and five years,	NIH
	27: 7	If it is a **p** sixty years old or more,	NIH
	27: 8	he is to present the **p** to the priest,	2257
	27:24	of Jubilee the field will revert to the **p**	2257S
	27:29	" 'No **p** devoted to destruction may	132
Nu	5: 6	is unfaithful to the LORD, that **p** is guilty	5883
	5: 7	to it and give it all to the **p** he has wronged.	889S
	5: 8	But if that **p** has no close relative	408
	9:13	that **p** must be cut off from his people	5883
	15:27	" 'But if just one **p** sins unintentionally,	5883
	15:30	and that **p** must be cut off from his people.	5883
	15:31	that **p** must surely be cut off;	5883
	16: 5	and he will have that **p** come near him.	NIH
	19:13	That **p** must be cut off from Israel.	5883
	19:14	the law that applies when a **p** dies in a tent;	132
	19:17	"For the unclean **p**, put some ashes	AIT
	19:19	to sprinkle the unclean **p** on the third	AIT
	19:19	The **p** being cleansed must wash his clothes	NIH
	19:20	a **p** who is unclean does not purify himself,	408
	19:22	an unclean **p** touches becomes unclean,	AIT
	35: 6	a **p** who has killed someone may flee.	AIT
	35:11	**p** who has killed someone accidentally may flee.	AIT
	35:12	so that a **p** accused of murder may not die	AIT
	35:21	that **p** shall be put to death;	5782S
	35:30	a **p** is to be put to death as a murderer only	5883
Dt	4:42	which *anyone* who *had* killed a **p** could flee	8357
	17: 5	to your city gate and stone that **p** to death.	4392S
	27:25	who accepts a bribe to kill an innocent **p**."	1947S
	29:19	When such a **p** hears the words of this oath,	2257S
Jos	20: 3	so that anyone who kills a **p** accidentally	5883
1Sa	10: 6	and you will be changed into a different **p**.	408
2Sa	3:19	Abner also spoke to the Benjamites in **p**.	265+4928
	6:19	to each **p** in the whole crowd of Israelites,	6639
	14:14	that a banished **p** may not remain estranged	AIT
Est	5:12	"I'm the only **p** Queen Esther invited	NIH
Ps	62:12	Surely you will reward *each* **p** according	408
Pr	24:12	Will he not repay *each* **p** according	132
Jer	5: 1	but *one* **p** who deals honestly and seeks	408
Eze	44:25	not defile himself by going near a dead **p**;	132

Eze	44:25	if the dead **p** was his father or mother,	NIH
Da	11:21	be succeeded by a contemptible **p** who has	AIT
Hag	2:12	"If a **p** carries consecrated meat in the fold	408
	2:13	But I tell you, Do not resist an evil **p**.	AIT
Mt	5:39	search for some worthy **p** there and stay	AIT
	10:11	and then he will reward each **p** according	AIT
	16:27	a dead **p** was being carried out—	AIT
Lk	7:12	a **p** more distinguished than you	1952
	14: 8	but woe to that **p** through whom they come.	AIT
	17: 1	"As for the **p** who hears my words but does	5516
Jn	12:47	"A **p** who has had a bath needs only	3836
	13:10	*to* each **p** according to what he has done."	AIT
Ro	2: 6	in **p** he is unimpressive	3836+3836+4242+5393
2Co	10:10	but "and to your seed," meaning one **p**,	AIT
Gal	3:16	No immoral, impure or greedy **p**—	4431
Eph	5: 5	Such a **p** goes into great detail	NIG
Col	2:18	for a short time (in **p**, not in thought),	4725
1Th	2:17	Warn a divisive **p** once.	476
Tit	3:10	And without doubt the lesser **p** is blessed	AIT
Heb	7: 7	that a **p** is justified by what he does and not	476
Jas	2:24	It corrupts the whole **p**,	5393
	3: 6	in faith will make the sick **p** well;	AIT
	5:15	Any such **p** is the deceiver and	4047
2Jn	1: 7	and each **p** was judged according	AIT
Rev	20:13		

PERSON'S (1) [PERSON]

| Ex | 22:11 | not lay hands on the other **p** property. | AIT |

PERSONAL (7) [PERSON]

Ge	26:26	with Ahuzzath his **p** adviser and Phicol	5335
2Sa	13:17	He called his **p** servant and said,	5853+9250
1Ki	4: 5	a priest and **p** adviser *to* the king;	8291
2Ki	12: 4	the money received from **p** vows and	5883+6886
1Ch	29: 3	now give my **p** treasures of gold and silver	6035
Est	2: 2	the king's **p** attendants proposed,	5853+9250
Ac	12:20	a trusted **p** servant of the king,	2093+3131+3836

PERSONALLY (3) [PERSON]

Ge	43: 9	you can hold me **p** responsible for him.	AIT
Gal	1:22	I was **p** unknown to the churches of Judea	4725
Col	2: 1	and for all who *have* not met me **p**.	1877+3836+3972+4725+4922

PERSONS (8) [PERSON]

Ge	46:26	numbered sixty-six in **p**.	5883
Lev	18:29	such **p** must be cut off from their people.	5883
	27: 2	a special vow to dedicate **p** to the LORD	5883
Nu	31:28	whether **p**, cattle, donkeys, sheep or goats.	132
	31:30	select one out of every fifty, whether **p**,	132
	31:47	Moses selected one out of every fifty **p**	132
Lk	15: 7	over ninety-nine righteous **p** who do	AIT
Ac	4:34	There were no needy **p** among them.	5516

PERSPIRE (1)

| Eze | 44:18 | not wear anything that makes them **p**. | 3472 |

PERSUADE (6) [PERSUADED, PERSUADING, PERSUASION, PERSUASIVE, PERSUASIVELY]

Jdg	19: 3	went to her to **p** her to return.	1819+4213+6584
2Ki	18:30	*Do not let* Hezekiah **p** you to trust	1053
Isa	36:15	*Do not let* Hezekiah **p** you to trust	1053
Ac	18: 4	trying to **p** Jews and Greeks.	4275
	26:28	*you can* **p** me to be a Christian?"	4275
2Co	5:11	to fear the Lord, *we* try to **p** men.	4275

PERSUADED (11) [PERSUADE]

Jdg	19: 7	man got up to go, his father-in-law **p** him,	7210
Pr	25:15	Through patience a ruler *can* be **p**,	7331
Jer	28:15	**p** this nation to trust in lies.	1053
Mt	27:20	the chief priests and the elders **p** the crowd	4275
Lk	20: 6	they are **p** that John was a prophet."	4275
Ac	5:40	His speech **p** them.	4275
	6:11	Then *they* secretly **p** some men to say,	5680
	16:15	And *she* **p** us.	4128
	17: 4	the Jews *were* **p** and joined Paul and Silas,	4275
Ro	4:21	*being* fully **p** that God had power	4442
2Ti	1: 5	*I am* **p**, now lives in you also.	4275

PERSUADING (1) [PERSUADE]

| Ac | 18:13 | "is **p** the people to worship God in ways | 400 |

PERSUASION (1) [PERSUADE]

| Gal | 5: 8 | That kind of **p** does not come from | 4282 |

PERSUASIVE (2) [PERSUADE]

| Pr | 7:21 | With **p** words she led him astray; | 4375 |
| 1Co | 2: 4 | not with wise and **p** words, | 4273 |

PERSUASIVELY (1) [PERSUADE]

| Ac | 19: 8 | arguing **p** about the kingdom of God. | 4275 |

PERTAINING (1)

| 1Ch | 26:32 | for every matter **p** to God and for the | AIT |

PERUDA (1)

| Ezr | 2:55 | the descendants of Sotai, Hassophereth, **P**, | 7243 |

PERVERSE (17) [PERVERT]

Dt	32:20	for they are a **p** generation,	9337
1Sa	20:30	"You son of a **p** and rebellious *woman!*	6390
Ps	101: 4	*Men of* **p** heart shall be far from me;	6836
Pr	2:12	from men whose words are **p,**	9337
	3:32	for the LORD detests a **p** man but takes	4279
	8: 8	none of them is crooked or **p.**	6836
	8:13	evil behavior and **p** speech.	9337
	10:31	but a **p** tongue will be cut out.	9337
	10:32	but the mouth of the wicked only *what is* **p.**	9337
	11:20	The LORD detests *men of* **p** heart	6836
	16:28	A **p** man stirs up dissension,	9337
	17:20	A *man of* **p** heart does not prosper;	6836
	19: 1	a fool whose lips are **p.**	6836
	28: 6	a rich man whose ways are **p,**	6836
	28:18	but he whose ways *are* **p** will suddenly fall.	6835
Mt	17:17	"O unbelieving and **p** generation,"	1406
Lk	9:41	"O unbelieving and **p** generation,"	1406

PERVERSENESS (1) [PERVERT]

Pr	2:14	in doing wrong and rejoice in the **p** of evil,	9337

PERVERSION (4) [PERVERT]

Lev	18:23	to have sexual relations with it; that is a **p.**	9316
	20:12	What they have done is a **p;**	9416
Ro	1:27	in themselves the due penalty *for* their **p.**	4415
Jude	1: 7	to sexual immorality and **p.** 599+2283+3958+4922	

PERVERSITY (2) [PERVERT]

Pr	4:24	Put away **p** from your mouth;	6838
	16:30	He who winks with his eye is plotting **p;**	9337

PERVERT (8) [PERVERSE, PERVERSENESS, PERVERSION, PERVERSITY, PERVERTED, PERVERTING, PERVERTS]

Ex	23: 2	*do* not **p** justice by siding with the crowd,	5742
Lev	19:15	*Do* not **p** justice; do not show partiality 6404+6913	
Dt	16:19	*Do* not **p** justice or show partiality.	5742
Job	8: 3	Does God **p** justice?	6430
	8: 3	*Does* the Almighty **p** what is right?	6430
	34:12	that the Almighty *would* **p** justice.	6430
Pr	17:23	A wicked man accepts a bribe in secret to **p**	5742
Gal	1: 7	and are trying *to* **p** the gospel of Christ.	3570

PERVERTED (4) [PERVERT]

1Sa	8: 3	and accepted bribes and **p** justice.	5742
Job	33:27	'I sinned, and **p** what was right,	6390
Jer	3:21	because *they have* **p** their ways	6390
Hab	1: 4	hem in the righteous, so that justice is **p.**	6823

PERVERTING (1) [PERVERT]

Ac	13:10	you never stop **p** the right ways of the Lord?	1406

PERVERTS (1) [PERVERT]

1Ti	1:10	*for* adulterers and **p,** for slave traders	780

PESTILENCE (4) [PESTILENCES]

Dt	32:24	consuming **p** and deadly plague;	8404
Ps	91: 3	the fowler's snare and from the deadly **p.**	1822
	91: 6	nor the **p** that stalks in the darkness,	1822
Hab	3: 5	**p** followed his steps.	8404

PESTILENCES (1) [PESTILENCE]

Lk	21:11	famines and **p** in various places,	3369

PESTILENT (KJV) See TROUBLEMAKER

PESTLE (1)

Pr	27:22	grinding him like grain with a **p,**	6605

PESTS (1)

Mal	3:11	I will prevent **p** from devouring your crops,	430

PET (1)

Job	41: 5	*Can you* **make a p** of him like a bird	8471

PETER (176) [CEPHAS, PETER'S, SIMON]

Mt	4:18	Simon called **P** and his brother Andrew.	4377
	10: 2	first, Simon (who is called **P**)	4377
	14:28	"Lord, if it's you," **P** replied,	4377
	14:29	Then **P** got down out of the boat,	4377
	15:15	**P** said, "Explain the parable to us."	4377
	16:16	Simon **P** answered, "You are the Christ,	4377
	16:18	I tell you that you are **P,** and on this rock	4377
	16:22	**P** took him aside and began to rebuke him.	4377
	16:23	Jesus turned and said *to* **P,** "Get behind me,	4377
	17: 1	After six days Jesus took with him **P,**	4377
	17: 4	**P** said to Jesus, "Lord, it is good for us	4377
	17:24	came to **P** and asked, "Doesn't your teacher	4377
	17:25	When **P** came into the house,	899S
	17:26	"From others," **P** answered.	NIG
	18:21	Then **P** came to Jesus and asked, "Lord,	4377
	19:27	**P** answered him, "We have left everything	4377
	26:33	**P** replied, "Even if all fall away on account	4377
	26:35	But **P** declared, "Even if I have to die	4377

Mt	26:37	He took **P** and the two sons of Zebedee	4377
	26:40	watch with me for one hour?" he asked **P.**	4377
	26:58	But **P** followed him at a distance,	4377
	26:69	Now **P** was sitting out in the courtyard,	4377
	26:73	those standing there went up to **P** and said,	4377
	26:75	**P** remembered the word Jesus had spoken:	4377
Mk	3:16	Simon (to whom he gave the name **P**);	4377
	5:37	He did not let anyone follow him except **P,**	4377
	8:29	**P** answered, "You are the Christ."	4377
	8:32	**P** took him aside and began to rebuke him.	4377
	8:33	and looked at his disciples, he rebuked **P.**	4377
	9: 2	After six days Jesus took **P,** James and John	4377
	9: 5	**P** said to Jesus, "Rabbi, it is good for us	4377
	10:28	**P** said to him, "We have left everything	4377
	11:21	**P** remembered and said to Jesus, "Rabbi,	4377
	13: 3	Mount of Olives opposite the temple, **P,**	4377
	14:29	**P** declared, "Even if all fall away,	4377
	14:31	But **P** insisted emphatically,	3836S
	14:33	He took **P,** James and John along	4377
	14:37	"Simon," he said *to* **P,** "are you asleep?	4377
	14:54	**P** followed him at a distance,	4377
	14:66	While **P** was below in the courtyard,	4377
	14:67	When she saw **P** warming himself,	4377
	14:70	those standing near said *to* **P,**	4377
	14:72	Then **P** remembered the word Jesus had	4377
	16: 7	But go, tell his disciples and **P,**	4377
Lk	5: 8	When Simon **P** saw this,	4377
	6:14	Simon (whom he named **P**),	4377
	8:45	When they all denied it, **P** said, "Master,	4377
	8:51	not let anyone go in with him except **P,**	4377
	9:20	**P** answered, "The Christ of God."	4377
	9:28	after Jesus said this, he took **P,** John	4377
	9:32	**P** and his companions were very sleepy,	4377
	9:33	**P** said to him, "Master, it is good for us	4377
	12:41	**P** asked, "Lord, are you telling this parable	4377
	18:28	**P** said to him, "We have left all we had	4377
	22: 8	Jesus sent **P** and John, saying,	4377
	22:34	Jesus answered, "I tell you, **P,**	4377
	22:54	**P** followed at a distance.	4377
	22:55	**P** sat down with them.	4377
	22:58	"Man, I am not!" **P** replied.	4377
	22:60	**P** replied, "Man, I don't know what you're talking about!"	
	22:61	The Lord turned and looked straight at **P.**	4377
	22:61	Then **P** remembered the word the Lord had	4377
	24:12	**P,** however, got up and ran to the tomb.	4377
Jn	1:42	Cephas" (which, when translated, is **P**).	4377
	1:44	Philip, like Andrew and **P,** was from	4377
	6:68	Simon **P** answered him, "Lord,	4377
	13: 6	He came to Simon **P,** who said to him,	4377
	13: 8	said **P,** "you shall never wash my feet."	4377
	13: 9	"Then, Lord," Simon **P** replied, "not just	4377
	13:24	Simon **P** motioned to this disciple and said,	4377
	13:36	Simon **P** asked him, "Lord, where are you	4377
	13:37	**P** asked, "Lord, why can't I follow you	4377
	18:10	Then Simon **P,** who had a sword,	4377
	18:11	Jesus commanded **P,** "Put your sword away!	4377
	18:15	Simon **P** and another disciple were following Jesus.	4377
	18:16	but **P** had to wait outside at the door.	4377
	18:16	to the girl on duty there and brought **P** in.	4377
	18:17	the girl at the door asked **P,**	4377
	18:18	**P** also was standing with them,	4377
	18:25	As Simon **P** stood warming himself,	4377
	18:26	of the man whose ear **P** had cut off,	4377
	18:27	Again **P** denied it, and at that moment	4377
	20: 2	So she came running to Simon **P**	4377
	20: 3	So **P** and the other disciple started for	4377
	20: 4	but the other disciple outran **P** and reached	4377
	20: 6	Then Simon **P,** who was behind him,	4377
	21: 2	Simon **P,** Thomas (called Didymus),	4377
	21: 3	Simon **P** told them, and they said,	4377
	21: 7	the disciple whom Jesus loved said *to* **P,**	4377
	21: 7	As soon as Simon **P** heard him say,	4377
	21:11	Simon **P** climbed aboard and dragged	4377
	21:15	Jesus said *to* Simon **P,** "Simon son of John,	4377
	21:17	**P** was hurt because Jesus asked him	4377
	21:19	of death by which **P** would glorify God.	NIG
	21:20	**P** turned and saw that the disciple	4377
	21:21	When **P** saw him, he asked, "Lord,	4377
Ac	1:13	Those present were **P,** John, James and	4377
	1:15	In those days **P** stood up among	4377
	1:20	said **P,** "it is written in the book of Psalms,	NIG
	2:14	Then **P** stood up with the Eleven,	4377
	2:37	they were cut to the heart and said to **P** and	4377
	2:38	**P** replied, "Repent and be baptized,	4377
	3: 1	One day **P** and John were going up to	4377
	3: 3	When he saw **P** and John about to enter,	4377
	3: 4	**P** looked straight at him, as did John.	4377
	3: 4	Then **P** said, "Look at us!"	NIG
	3: 6	Then **P** said, "Silver or gold I do not have,	4377
	3:11	While the beggar held on to **P** and John,	4377
	3:12	When **P** saw this, he said to them:	4377
	4: 1	up *to* **P and John** while they were speaking	899S
	4: 3	They seized **P and John,**	899S
	4: 7	They had **P and John** brought before them	899S
	4: 8	**P,** filled with the Holy Spirit, said to them:	4377
	4:13	When they saw the courage *of* **P** and John	4377
	4:19	**P** and John replied, "Judge for yourselves	4377
	4:23	**P** and John went back to their own people	NIG
	5: 3	Then **P** said, "Ananias, how is it that	4377
	5: 8	**P** asked her, "Tell me, is this the price	4377
	5: 9	**P** said to her, "How could you agree to test	4377
	5:29	**P** and the other apostles replied:	4377
	8:14	they sent **P** and John to them.	4377
	8:17	**P** and John placed their hands on them,	NIG
	8:20	**P** answered: "May your money perish with	4377

Ac	8:25	**P and John** returned to Jerusalem, 3525+3836S	
	9:32	As **P** traveled about the country,	4377
	9:34	"Aeneas," **P** said to him,	4377
	9:38	the disciples heard that **P** was in Lydda,	4377
	9:39	**P** went with them, and when he arrived	4377
	9:40	**P** sent them all out of the room;	4377
	9:40	and seeing **P** she sat up.	4377
	9:43	**P** stayed in Joppa for some time with	NIG
	10: 5	a man named Simon who is called **P.**	4377
	10: 9	**P** went up on the roof to pray.	4377
	10:13	Then a voice told him, "Get up, **P.**	4377
	10:14	"Surely not, Lord!" **P** replied.	4377
	10:17	While **P** was wondering about the meaning	4377
	10:18	as **P** was staying there.	4377
	10:19	While **P** was still thinking about the vision,	4377
	10:21	**P** went down and said to the men,	4377
	10:23	Then **P** invited the men into the house to	NIG
	10:23	The next day **P** started out with them,	NIG
	10:25	As **P** entered the house,	4377
	10:26	But **P** made him get up.	4377
	10:27	**P** went inside and found a large gathering	NIG
	10:32	Send to Joppa for Simon who is called **P.**	4377
	10:34	Then **P** began to speak:	4377
	10:44	While **P** was still speaking these words,	4377
	10:45	who had come with **P** were astonished	4377
	10:46	in tongues and praising God. Then **P** said,	4377
	10:48	Then they asked **P** to stay with them for	899S
	11: 2	So when **P** went up to Jerusalem,	4377
	11: 4	**P** began and explained everything	4377
	11: 7	Then I heard a voice telling me, 'Get up, **P.**	4377
	11:13	'Send to Joppa for Simon who is called **P.**	4377
	12: 3	he proceeded to seize **P** also.	4377
	12: 5	So **P** was kept in prison,	4377
	12: 6	**P** was sleeping between two soldiers,	4377
	12: 7	He struck **P** on the side and woke him up.	4377
	12: 8	And **P** did so.	NIG
	12: 9	**P** followed him out of the prison,	NIG
	12:11	Then **P** came to himself and said,	4377
	12:13	**P** knocked at the outer entrance,	899S
	12:14	"**P** is at the door!"	4377
	12:16	But **P** kept on knocking,	4377
	12:17	**P** motioned with his hand for them to	NIG
	12:18	the soldiers as to what had become of **P.**	4377
	15: 7	**P** got up and addressed them:	4377
1Co	15: 5	and that he appeared *to* **P,**	3064
Gal	1:18	up to Jerusalem to get acquainted with **P**	4377
	2: 7	just as **P** had been to the Jews,	4377
	2: 8	the ministry of **P** as an apostle to the Jews,	4377
	2: 9	**P** and John, those reputed to be pillars,	3064
	2:11	When **P** came to Antioch,	3064
	2:14	I said *to* **P** in front of them all,	3064
1Pe	1: 1	**P,** an apostle of Jesus Christ,	4377
2Pe	1: 1	Simon **P,** a servant and apostle	4377

PETER'S (7) [PETER]

Mt	8:14	When Jesus came into **P** house,	4377
	8:14	he saw **P** mother-in-law lying in bed with	899S
Jn	1:40	Andrew, Simon **P** brother, was one of	4377
	6: 8	Andrew, Simon **P** brother, spoke up,	4377
Ac	5:15	that at least **P** shadow might fall on some	4377
	12: 7	he said, and the chains fell off **P** wrists.	899S
	12:14	When she recognized **P** voice,	4377

PETHAHIAH (4)

1Ch	24:16	the nineteenth to **P,**	7342
Ezr	10:23	Shimei, Kelaiah (that is, Kelita), **P,**	7342
Ne	9: 5	Sherebiah, Hodiah, Shebaniah and **P—**	7342
	11:24	**P** son of Meshezabel,	7342

PETHOR (2)

Nu	22: 5	who was at **P,** near the River,	7335
Dt	23: 4	and they hired Balaam son of Beor from **P**	7335

PETHUEL (1)

Joel	1: 1	of the LORD that came to Joel son of **P.**	7333

PETITION (18) [PETITIONED, PETITIONS]

1Ch	16: 4	to **make p,** to give thanks,	2349
Est	5: 6	"Now what is your **p?**	8629
	5: 7	"My **p** and my request is this:	8629
	5: 8	and if it pleases the king to grant my **p**	8629
	7: 2	"Queen Esther, what is your **p?**	8629
	7: 3	grant me my life—this is my **p.**	8629
	9:12	Now what is your **p?**	8629
Ps	38: T	A psalm of David. A **p.**	2349
	70: T	For the director of music. Of David. A **p.**	2349
Jer	7:16	for this people nor offer any plea or **p**	9525
	11:14	for this people nor offer any plea or **p**	9525
	36: 7	Perhaps they will bring their **p** before	9382
	37:20	Let me bring my **p** before you:	9382
	42: 2	"Please hear our **p** and pray to	9382
	42: 9	to whom you sent me to present your **p,**	9382
Da	9: 3	and pleaded with him in prayer and **p,**	9384
Ac	23:15	you and the Sanhedrin the commander	1872
Php	4: 6	by prayer and **p,** with thanksgiving,	1255

PETITIONED (2) [PETITION]

Ezr	8:23	So we fasted and **p** our God about this,	1335
Ac	25:24	The whole Jewish community *has* **p** me	1961

PETITIONS (2) [PETITION]

Da	9:17	hear the prayers and **p** *of* your servant.	9384

Heb 5: 7 he offered up prayers and **p** with loud cries   2656

PEULLETHAI (1)

1Ch 26: 5 Issachar the seventh and **P** the eighth.   7191

PHALEC (KJV) See PELEG

PHALLU (KJV) See PALLU

PHALTI, PHALTIEL (KJV) See PALTIEL

PHANTOM (1)

Ps 39: 6 Man is a mere **p** as he goes to and fro: 7513

PHANUEL (1)

Lk 2:36 the daughter *of* **P**, of the tribe of Asher.   5750

PHARAOH (214) [PHARAOH'S]

Ge 12:15 they praised her to **P**,   7281
12:17 the LORD inflicted serious diseases on **P**   7281
12:18 So **P** summoned Abram.   7281
12:20 **P** gave orders about Abram to his men,   7281
40: 2 **P** was angry with his two officials,   7281
40:13 Within three days **P** will lift up your head   7281
40:14 to **P** and get me out of this prison.   7281
40:17 all kinds of baked goods for **P**,   7281
40:19 Within three days **P** will lift off your head   7281
41: 1 **P** had a dream: He was standing by   7281
41: 4 Then **P** woke up.   7281
41: 7 Then **P** woke up; it had been a dream.   7281
41: 8 **P** told them his dreams,   7281
41: 9 Then the chief cupbearer said to **P**,   7281
41:10 **P** was once angry with his servants,   7281
41:14 So **P** sent for Joseph,   7281
41:14 he came before **P**.   7281
41:15 **P** said to Joseph, "I had a dream,   7281
41:16 "I cannot do it," Joseph replied to **P**,   7281
41:16 "but God will give **P** the answer he desires."   7281
41:17 Then **P** said to Joseph,   7281
41:25 Then Joseph said to **P**,   7281
41:25 "The dreams of **P** are one and the same.   7281
41:25 God has revealed to **P** what he is about   7281
41:28 "It is just as I said to **P**:   7281
41:28 God has shown **P** what he is about to do.   7281
41:32 the dream was given to **P** in two forms is   7281
41:33 "And now let **P** look for a discerning and   7281
41:34 Let **P** appoint commissioners over the land   7281
41:35 store up the grain under the authority of **P**,   7281
41:37 The plan seemed good to **P** and to all   7281
41:38 So **P** asked them, "Can we find anyone like   7281
41:39 Then **P** said to Joseph, "Since God has   7281
41:41 So **P** said to Joseph, "I hereby put you   7281
41:42 Then **P** took his signet ring from his finger   7281
41:44 Then **P** said to Joseph, "I am Pharaoh,   7281
41:44 Then Pharaoh said to Joseph, "I am **P**,   7281
41:45 **P** gave Joseph the name Zaphenath-Paneah   7281
41:46 when he entered the service of **P** king   7281
41:55 the people cried to **P** for food.   7281
41:55 Then **P** told all the Egyptians,   7281
42:15 As surely as **P** lives, you will not leave   7281
42:16 If you are not, then as surely as **P** lives,   7281
44:18 though you are equal to **P** *himself*.   7281
45: 8 He made me father to **P**,   7281
45:16 **P** and all his officials were pleased.   7281
45:17 **P** said to Joseph, "Tell your brothers,   7281
45:21 as **P** had commanded,   7281
46: 5 and their wives in the carts that **P** had sent   7281
46:31 "I will go up and speak to **P** and will say   7281
46:33 When **P** calls you in and asks,   7281
47: 1 Joseph went and told **P**, "My father and   7281
47: 2 and presented them before **P**.   7281
47: 3 **P** asked the brothers, "What is your   7281
47: 3 servants are shepherds," they replied to **P**,   7281
47: 5 **P** said to Joseph, "Your father and brothers   7281
47: 7 father Jacob in and presented him before **P**.   7281
47: 7 After Jacob blessed **P**,   7281
47: 8 **P** asked him, "How old are you?"   7281
47: 9 And Jacob said to **P**,   7281
47:10 Then Jacob blessed **P** and went out   7281
47:11 the district of Rameses, as **P** directed.   7281
47:19 we with our land will be in bondage to **P**.   7281
47:20 Joseph bought all the land in Egypt for **P**,   7281
47:22 from **P** and had food enough from   7281
47:22 from the allotment **P** gave them.   7281
47:23 and your land today for **P**,   7281
47:24 give a fifth of it to **P**.   7281
47:25 we will be in bondage to **P**."   7281
47:26 that a fifth of the produce belongs to **P**.   7281
50: 4 speak to **P** for me.   7281
50: 6 **P** said, "Go up and bury your father,   7281
Ex 1:11 and Rameses as store cities for **P**.   7281
1:19 The midwives answered **P**,   7281
1:22 Then **P** gave this order to all his people: 7281
2:15 When **P** heard of this, he tried to kill Moses,   7281
2:15 but Moses fled from **P** and went to live   7281
3:10 I am sending you to **P** to bring my people   7281
3:11 to **P** and bring the Israelites out of Egypt?"   7281
4:21 before **P** all the wonders I have given you   7281
4:22 say to **P**, 'This is what the LORD says: 7281
5: 1 to **P** and said, "This is what the LORD,   7281
5: 2 **P** said, "Who is the LORD,   7281
5: 5 Then **P** said, "Look, the people of the land   7281

Ex 5: 6 That same day **P** gave this order to   7281
5:10 "This is what **P** says: 7281
5:15 Israelite foremen went and appealed to **P**:   7281
5:17 **P** said, "Lazy, that's what you are—lazy!   NIH
5:20 When they left **P**,   7281
5:21 a stench to **P** and his officials and have put   7281
5:23 since I went to **P** to speak in your name,   7281
6: 1 "Now you will see what I will do to **P**:   7281
6:11 tell **P** king of Egypt to let the Israelites go   7281
6:12 why would **P** listen to me,   7281
6:13 and Aaron about the Israelites and **P** king   7281
6:27 They were the ones who spoke to **P** king   7281
6:29 Tell **P** king of Egypt everything I tell you."   7281
6:30 why would **P** listen to me?"   7281
7: 1 "See, I have made you like God to **P**,   7281
7: 2 and your brother Aaron is to tell **P** to let   7281
7: 7 when they spoke to **P**.   7281
7: 9 "When **P** says to you, 'Perform a miracle,'   7281
7: 9 and throw it down before **P**,'   7281
7:10 So Moses and Aaron went to **P** and did just   7281
7:10 Aaron threw his staff down in front of **P**   7281
7:11 then summoned wise men and sorcerers,   7281
7:15 Go to **P** in the morning as he goes out to   7281
7:20 of **P** and his officials and struck the water   7281
8: 1 "Go to **P** and say to him, 'This is what   7281
8: 8 **P** summoned Moses and Aaron and said,   7281
8: 9 Moses said to **P**, "I leave to you the honor   7281
8:10 "Tomorrow," **P** said.   NIH
8:12 After Moses and Aaron left **P**,   7281
8:12 about the frogs he had brought on **P**.   7281
8:15 But when **P** saw that there was relief,   7281
8:19 The magicians said to **P**,   7281
8:20 and confront **P** as he goes to the water   7281
8:25 **P** summoned Moses and Aaron and said,   7281
8:28 **P** said, "I will let you go to offer sacrifices   7281
8:29 the flies will leave **P** and his officials   7281
8:29 be sure that **P** does not act deceitfully again   7281
8:30 Moses left **P** and prayed to the LORD,   7281
8:31 The flies left **P** and his officials   7281
8:32 also **P** hardened his heart and would not let   7281
9: 1 "Go to **P** and say to him,   7281
9: 7 **P** sent men to investigate and found that   7281
9: 8 into the air in the presence of **P**.   7281
9:10 from a furnace and stood before **P**.   7281
9:13 confront **P** and say to him,   7281
9:20 Those officials of **P** who feared the word   7281
9:27 Then **P** summoned Moses and Aaron.   7281
9:33 Then Moses left **P** and went out of the city.   7281
9:34 When **P** saw that the rain and hail   7281
10: 1 Then the LORD said to Moses, "Go to **P**,   7281
10: 3 So Moses and Aaron went to **P** and said   7281
10: 6 Then Moses turned and left **P**.   7281
10: 8 Moses and Aaron were brought back to **P**.   7281
10:10 **P** said, "The LORD be with you—   NIH
10:16 **P** quickly summoned Moses and Aaron   7281
10:18 then left **P** and prayed to the LORD.   7281
10:24 Then **P** summoned Moses and said, "Go,   7281
10:28 **P** said to Moses, "Get out of my sight!   7281
11: 1 "I will bring one more plague on **P** and   7281
11: 5 from the firstborn son of **P**,   7281
11: 8 Then Moses, hot with anger, left **P**.   7281
11: 9 "**P** will refuse to listen to you—   7281
11:10 performed all these wonders before **P**, but   7281
12:29 from the firstborn of **P**,   7281
12:30 **P** and all his officials and all   7281
12:31 the night **P** summoned Moses and Aaron   NIH
13:15 When **P** stubbornly refused to let us go,   7281
13:17 When **P** let the people go,   7281
14: 3 **P** will think, 'The Israelites are wandering   7281
14: 4 But I will gain glory for myself through **P**   7281
14: 5 **P** and his officials changed their minds   7281
14: 8 The LORD hardened the heart of King **P**   7281
14:10 As **P** approached, the Israelites looked up,   7281
14:17 And I will gain glory through **P**   7281
14:18 the LORD gain glory through **P**,   7281
14:28 of **P** that had followed the Israelites into   7281
18: 4 he saved me from the sword of **P**."   7281
18: 8 to **P** and the Egyptians for Israel's sake and   7281
18:10 from the hand of the Egyptians and of **P**,   7281
Dt 6:21 tell him: "We were slaves of **P** in Egypt,   7281
6:22 and **P** and his whole household.   7281
7: 8 from the power of **P** king of Egypt.   7281
7:18 the LORD your God did to **P** and   7281
11: 3 both to **P** king of Egypt and   7281
29: 2 that the LORD did in Egypt to **P**,   7281
34:11 to **P** and to all his officials and   7281
1Sa 2:27 when they were in Egypt under **P**?   7281
6: 6 as the Egyptians and **P** did?   7281
1Ki 3: 1 Solomon made an alliance with **P** king   7281
9:16 (**P** king of Egypt had attacked   7281
11:18 they went to Egypt, to **P** king of Egypt,   7281
11:19 **P** was so pleased with Hadad   7281
11:21 Then Hadad said to **P**, "Let me go,   7281
11:22 to your own country?" **P** asked.   7281
2Ki 17: 7 from under the power of **P** king of Egypt.   7281
18:21 Such is **P** king of Egypt to all who depend   7281
23:29 **P** Neco king of Egypt went up to   7281
23:33 **P** Neco put him in chains at Riblah in   7281
23:34 **P** Neco made Eliakim son of Josiah king   7281
23:35 Jehoiakim paid **P** Neco the silver   7281
Ne 9:10 miraculous signs and wonders against **P**,   7281
Ps 135: 9 O Egypt, against **P** and all his servants.   7281
136:15 but swept **P** and his army into the Red Sea;   7281
SS 1: 9 mare harnessed to one of the chariots of **P**.   7281
Isa 19:11 wise counselors of **P** give senseless advice.   7281
19:11 How can you say to **P**,   7281
36: 6 Such is **P** king of Egypt to all who depend   7281

Jer 25:19 **P** king of Egypt, his attendants,   7281
44:30 to hand **P** Hophra king of Egypt over   7281
46: 2 against the army of **P** Neco king of Egypt,   7281
46:17 '**P** king of Egypt is only a loud noise;   7281
46:25 on **P**, on Egypt and her gods and her kings,   7281
46:25 and on those who rely on **P**.   7281
47: 1 the Philistines before **P** attacked Gaza: 7281
Eze 17:17 **P** with his mighty army and great horde   7281
29: 2 against **P** king of Egypt and prophesy   7281
29: 3 " 'I am against you, **P** king of Egypt,   7281
30:21 I have broken the arm of **P** king of Egypt.   7281
30:22 I am against **P** king of Egypt,   7281
30:24 but I will break the arms of **P**,   7281
30:25 but the arms of **P** will fall limp.   7281
31: 2 say to **P** king of Egypt and to his hordes: 7281
31:18 " 'This is **P** and all his hordes,   7281
32: 2 take up a lament concerning **P** king of   7281
32:28 O **P**, will be broken and will lie among   NIH
32:31 "**P**—he and all his army—will see them   7281
32:32 **P** and all his hordes will be laid among   7281
Ac 7:10 to gain the goodwill of **P** king of Egypt;   5755
7:13 and **P** learned about Joseph's family.   5755
Ro 9:17 For the Scripture says to **P**:   5755

PHARAOH'S (56) [PHARAOH]

Ge 12:15 And when **P** officials saw her,   7281
37:36 one of **P** officials, the captain of the guard.   7281
39: 1 an Egyptian who was one of **P** officials,   7281
40: 7 So he asked **P** officials who were   7281
40:11 **P** cup was in my hand,   7281
40:11 squeezed them into **P** cup and put the cup   7281
40:13 and you will put **P** cup in his hand,   7281
40:20 Now the third day was **P** birthday,   7281
40:21 that he once again put the cup into **P** hand,   7281
41:46 And Joseph went out from **P** presence   7281
45: 2 and **P** household heard about it.   7281
45:16 When the news reached **P** palace.   7281
47:14 and he brought it to **P** palace.   7281
47:20 The land became **P**,   4200+7281
47:26 of the priests that did not become **P**.   4200+7281
50: 4 Joseph said to **P** court, "If I have found   7281
50: 7 All **P** officials accompanied him—   7281
Ex 2: 5 **P** daughter went down to the Nile to bathe,   7281
2: 7 Then his sister asked **P** daughter,   7281
2: 9 **P** daughter said to her, "Take this baby   7281
2:10 to **P** daughter and he became her son.   7281
5:14 by **P** slave drivers were beaten   7281
7: 3 But I will harden **P** heart,   7281
7:13 Yet **P** heart became hard and he would   7281
7:14 "**P** heart is unyielding;   7281
7:22 and **P** heart became hard;   7281
8:19 **P** heart was hard and he would not listen,   7281
8:24 Dense swarms of flies poured into **P** palace   7281
9:12 the LORD hardened **P** heart and he would   7281
9:35 So **P** heart was hard and he would not let   7281
10: 7 **P** officials said to him,   7281
10:11 and Aaron were driven out of **P** presence.   7281
10:20 But the LORD hardened **P** heart,   7281
10:27 But the LORD hardened **P** heart,   7281
11: 3 in Egypt by **P** officials and by the people.)   7281
11:10 but the LORD hardened **P** heart,   7281
14: 4 And I will harden **P** heart,   7281
14: 9 The Egyptians—all **P** horses and chariots,   7281
14:23 and all **P** horses and chariots   7281
15: 4 **P** chariots and his army he has hurled into   7281
15: 4 of **P** officers are drowned in the Red Sea.   2257S
15:19 When **P** horses, chariots and horsemen   7281
1Ki 7: 8 a palace like this hall for **P** daughter,   7281
9:24 After **P** daughter had come up from   7281
11: 1 Solomon loved many foreign women
   besides **P** daughter—   7281
11:20 There Genubath lived with **P** *own* children.   7281
1Ch 4:18 the children of **P** daughter Bithiah,   7281
2Ch 8:11 Solomon brought **P** daughter up from   7281
Isa 30: 2 who look for help to **P** protection,   7281
30: 3 But **P** protection will be to your shame,   7281
Jer 37: 5 **P** army had marched out of Egypt,   7281
37: 7 who sent you to inquire of me, '**P** army,   7281
37:11 from Jerusalem because of **P**,   7281
43: 9 at the entrance to **P** palace in Tahpanhes.   7281
Ac 7:21 **P** daughter took him and brought him up   5755
Heb 11:24 to be known as the son *of* **P** daughter.   5755

PHARAOH-NECHO, PHARAOH-NECHOH (KJV) See PHARAOH NECO

PHARES, PHAREZ (KJV) See PEREZ

PHARISEE (12) [PHARISEE'S, PHARISEES]

Mt 23:26 Blind **P**! First clean the inside of the cup   5757
Lk 7:39 When the **P** who had invited him saw this,   5757
11:37 a **P** invited him to eat with him;   5757
11:38 The **P**, noticing that Jesus did not first wash   5757
14: 1 to eat in the house of a prominent **P**,   5757
18:10 one a **P** and the other a tax collector.   5757
18:11 The **P** stood up and prayed about himself: 5757
Ac 5:34 But a **P** named Gamaliel,   5757
23: 6 I am a **P**, the son of a Pharisee.   5757
23: 6 I am a Pharisee, the son *of* a **P**.   5757
26: 5 strictest sect of our religion, I lived as a **P**.   5757
Php 3: 5 in regard to the law, a **P**;   5757

PHARISEE'S (2) [PHARISEE]
Lk	7:36	so he went to the P house and reclined at	5757
	7:37	that Jesus was eating at the P house,	5757

PHARISEES (84) [PHARISEE]
Mt	3: 7	many of the P and Sadducees coming to	5757
	5:20	that of the P and the teachers of the law,	5757
	9:11	When the P saw this,	5757
	9:14	"How is it that we and the P fast,	5757
	9:34	the P said, "It is by the prince of demons	5757
	12: 2	When the P saw this, they said to him,	5757
	12:14	But the P went out and plotted	5757
	12:24	But when the P heard this, they said,	5757
	12:38	the P and teachers of the law said to him,	5757
	15: 1	Then some P and teachers of the law came	5757
	15:12	"Do you know that the P were offended	5757
	16: 1	The P and Sadducees came to Jesus	5757
	16: 6	against the yeast of the P and Sadducees."	5757
	16:11	be on your guard against the yeast of the P	5757
	16:12	the teaching of the P and Sadducees.	5757
	19: 3	Some P came to him to test him.	5757
	21:45	and the P heard Jesus' parables,	5757
	22:15	the P went out and laid plans to trap him	5757
	22:34	silenced the Sadducees, the P got together.	5757
	22:41	While the P were gathered together,	5757
	23: 2	of the law and the P sit in Moses' seat.	5757
	23:13	"Woe to you, teachers of the law and P,	5757
	23:15	"Woe to you, teachers of the law and P,	5757
	23:23	"Woe to you, teachers of the law and P,	5757
	23:25	"Woe to you, teachers of the law and P,	5757
	23:27	"Woe to you, teachers of the law and P,	5757
	23:29	"Woe to you, teachers of the law and P,	5757
	27:62	the chief priests and the P went to Pilate.	5757
Mk	2:16	of the law who were P saw him eating with	5757
	2:18	John's disciples and the P were fasting.	5757
	2:18	and the disciples of the P are fasting,	5757
	2:24	The P said to him, "Look, why are they	5757
	3: 6	Then the P went out and began to plot with	5757
	7: 1	The P and some of the teachers of the law	5757
	7: 3	(The P and all the Jews do not eat	5757
	7: 5	the P and teachers of the law asked Jesus.	5757
	8:11	The P came and began to question Jesus.	5757
	8:15	"Watch out for the yeast of the P and that	5757
	10: 2	Some P came and tested him by asking,	5757
	12:13	the P and Herodians to Jesus to catch him	5757
Lk	5:17	P and teachers of the law, who had come	5757
	5:21	The P and the teachers of the law began	5757
	5:30	But the P and the teachers of the law	5757
	5:33	and so do the disciples of the P,	5757
	6: 2	Some of the P asked, "Why are you doing	5757
	6: 7	The P and the teachers of the law	5757
	7:30	But the P and experts in the law rejected	5757
	7:36	one of the P invited Jesus to have dinner	5757
	11:39	you P clean the outside of the cup	5757
	11:42	"Woe to you P, because you give God	5757
	11:43	"Woe to you P, because you love the most	5757
	11:53	the P and the teachers of the law began	5757
	12: 1	on your guard against the yeast of the P,	5757
	13:31	At that time some P came to Jesus and said	5757
	14: 3	Jesus asked the P and experts in the law,	5757
	15: 2	the P and the teachers of the law muttered,	5757
	16:14	The P, who loved money,	5757
	17:20	having been asked by the P when	5757
	19:39	Some of the P in the crowd said to Jesus,	5757
Jn	1:24	Now some P who had been sent	5757
	3: 1	a man of the P named Nicodemus,	5757
	4: 1	The P heard that Jesus was gaining	5757
	7:32	The P heard the crowd whispering such	
		things about him.	5757
	7:32	and the P sent temple guards to arrest him.	5757
	7:45	guards went back to the chief priests and P,	5757
	7:47	he has deceived you also?" the P retorted.	5757
	7:48	"Has any of the rulers or of the P believed	5757
	8: 3	The teachers of the law and the P brought	5757
	8:13	The P challenged him, "Here you are,	5757
	9:13	to the P the man who had been blind.	5757
	9:15	Therefore the P also asked him	5757
	9:16	Some of the P said, "This man is not from	
		God,	5757
	9:40	Some P who were with him heard him	5757
	11:46	the P and told them what Jesus had done.	5757
	11:47	the chief priests and the P called a meeting	5757
	11:57	the chief priests and P had given orders	5757
	12:19	So the P said to one another, "See,	5757
	12:42	of the P they would not confess their faith	5757
	18: 3	from the chief priests and P.	5757
Ac	15: 5	to the party of the P stood up and said,	5757
	23: 6	of them were Sadducees and the others P,	5757
	23: 7	a dispute broke out between the P and	5757
	23: 8	but the P acknowledge them all.)	5757
	23: 9	the teachers of the law who were P stood	5757

PHAROSH (KJV) See PAROSH

PHARPAR (1)
2Ki	5:12	Abana and P, the rivers of Damascus,	7286

PHARZITES (KJV) See PEREZITE

PHASEAH (KJV) See PASEAH

PHEBE (KJV) See PHOEBE

PHENICE (KJV) See PHOENIX, PHOENICIA

PHENICIA (KJV) See PHOENICIA

PHICHOL (KJV) See PHICOL

PHICOL (3)
Ge	21:22	that time Abimelech and P the commander	7087
	21:32	Abimelech and P the commander	7087
	26:26	with Ahuzzath his personal adviser and P	7087

PHILADELPHIA (2)
Rev	1:11	Thyatira, Sardis, P and Laodicea."	5788
	3: 7	"To the angel of the church in P write:	5788

PHILEMON (1)
Phm	1: 1	To P our dear friend and fellow worker,	5800

PHILETUS (1)
2Ti	2:17	Among them are Hymenaeus and P,	5801

PHILIP (34) [PHILIP'S]
Mt	10: 3	P and Bartholomew; Thomas	5805
Mk	3:18	P, Bartholomew, Matthew, Thomas,	5805
Lk	3: 1	of Galilee, his brother P tetrarch of Iturea	5805
	6:14	his brother Andrew, James, John, P,	5805
Jn	1:43	Finding P, he said to him, "Follow me."	5805
	1:44	P, like Andrew and Peter,	5805
	1:45	P found Nathanael and told him,	5805
	1:46	"Come and see," said P.	5805
	1:48	under the fig tree before P called you."	5805
	6: 5	he said to P, "Where shall we buy bread	5805
	6: 7	P answered him, "Eight months' wages	5805
	12:21	They came to P, who was from Bethsaida	5805
	12:22	P went to tell Andrew;	5805
	12:22	Andrew and P in turn told Jesus.	5805
	14: 8	P said, "Lord, show us the Father and	5805
	14: 9	Jesus answered: "Don't you know me, P,	5805
Ac	1:13	P and Thomas, Bartholomew	5805
	6: 5	also P, Procorus, Nicanor, Timon,	5805
	8: 5	P went down to a city in Samaria	5805
	8: 6	When the crowds heard P and saw	5805
	8:12	But when they believed P as he preached	5805
	8:13	And he followed P everywhere,	5805
	8:26	Now an angel of the Lord said to P,	5805
	8:29	The Spirit told P, "Go to that chariot	5805
	8:30	Then P ran up to the chariot and heard	5805
	8:30	"Do you understand what you are reading?"	
		P asked.	NIG
	8:31	he invited P to come up and sit with him.	5805
	8:34	The eunuch asked P, "Tell me, please,	5805
	8:35	Then P began with that very passage	5805
	8:38	Then both P and the eunuch went down	5805
	8:38	down into the water and P baptized him.	NIG
	8:39	Spirit of the Lord suddenly took P away,	5805
	8:40	P, however, appeared at Azotus	5805
	21: 8	and stayed at the house of P the evangelist,	5805

PHILIP'S (2) [PHILIP]
Mt	14: 3	because of Herodias, his brother P wife,	5805
Mk	6:17	his brother P wife, whom he had married.	5805

PHILIPPI (6) [PHILIPPIANS]
Mt	16:13	to the region of Caesarea P,	5805
Mk	8:27	on to the villages around Caesarea P.	5805
Ac	16:12	From there we traveled to P,	5804
	20: 6	But we sailed from P after the Feast	5804
Php	1: 1	To all the saints in Christ Jesus at P,	5804
1Th	2: 2	suffered and been insulted in P,	5804

PHILIPPIANS (1) [PHILIPPI]
Php	4:15	Moreover, as you P know,	5803

PHILISTIA (8) [PHILISTINE]
Ex	15:14	anguish will grip the people of P.	7148
Ps	60: 8	over P I shout in triumph."	7148
	83: 7	P, with the people of Tyre.	7148
	87: 4	P too, and Tyre, along with Cush—	7148
	108: 9	over P I shout in triumph."	7148
Isa	11:14	They will swoop down on the slopes of P	7149
Joel	3: 4	and Sidon and all you regions of P?	7148
Am	6: 2	and then go down to Gath in P.	7148

PHILISTINE (62) [PHILISTIA, PHILISTINE'S, PHILISTINES]
Ex	13:17	on the road through the P country,	7149
Jos	13: 3	(the territory of the five P rulers in Gaza,	7149
Jdg	14: 1	and saw there a young P woman.	7149
	14: 2	"I have seen a P woman in Timnah;	7149
1Sa	6: 1	had been in P territory seven months,	7149
	6: 4	according to the number of the P rulers,	7149
	6:18	of P towns belonging to the five rulers—	7149
	10: 5	where there is a P outpost.	7149
	13: 3	Jonathan attacked the P outpost at Geba,	7149
	13: 4	"Saul has attacked the P outpost,	7149
	13:17	Raiding parties went out from the P camp	7149
	14: 1	over to the P outpost on the other side."	7149
1Sa	14: 4	to cross to reach the P outpost was a cliff;	7149
	14:11	showed themselves to the P outpost.	7149
	14:19	the tumult in the P camp increased more	7149
	17: 4	came out of the P camp.	7149
	17: 8	Am I not a P, and are you not the servants	7149
	17:10	P said, "This day I defy the ranks of Israel!	7149
	17:16	the P came forward every morning	7149
	17:23	Goliath, the P champion from Gath,	7149
	17:26	be done for the man who kills this P	7149
	17:26	Who is this uncircumcised P	7149
	17:32	"Let no one lose heart on account of this P;	7149
	17:33	"You are not able to go out against this P	7149
	17:36	this uncircumcised P will be like one	7149
	17:37	from the hand of this P."	7149
	17:40	his sling in his hand, approached the P.	7149
	17:41	the P, with his shield bearer in front of him,	7149
	17:43	And the P cursed David by his gods.	7149
	17:45	David said to the P, "You come against me	7149
	17:46	the carcasses of the P army to the birds of	7149
	17:48	As the P moved closer to attack him,	7149
	17:49	and struck the P on the forehead.	7149
	17:50	So David triumphed over the P with a sling	7149
	17:50	a sword in his hand he struck down the P	7149
	17:55	watched David going out to meet the P,	7149
	17:57	as David returned from killing the P,	7149
	18: 6	after David had killed the P,	7149
	18:25	for the bride than a hundred P foreskins."	7149
	18:30	The P commanders continued to go out	7149
	19: 5	in his hands when he killed the P.	7149
	21: 9	"The sword of Goliath the P,	7149
	22:10	and the sword of Goliath the P."	7149
	23: 1	if we go to Keilah against the P forces!"	7149
	27: 7	in P territory a year and four months.	7149
	27:11	as long as he lived in P territory.	7149
	28: 5	When Saul saw the P army, he was afraid;	7149
	29: 2	As the P rulers marched with their units	7149
	29: 4	the P commanders were angry with him	7149
	29: 7	do nothing to displease the P rulers."	7149
	29: 9	nevertheless, the P commanders have said,	7149
2Sa	3:14	for the price of a hundred P foreskins."	7149
	5:17	in front of you to strike the P army."	7149
	21:17	he struck the P down and killed him.	7149
	23:14	and the P garrison was at Bethlehem.	7149
	23:16	three mighty men broke through the P lines,	7149
1Ki	15:27	down at Gibbethon, a P town, while Nadab	7149
	16:15	near Gibbethon, a P town.	7149
1Ch	11:16	and the P garrison was at Bethlehem.	7149
	11:18	So the Three broke through the P lines,	7149
	14:15	in front of you to strike the P army."	7149
	14:16	and they struck down the P army,	7149

PHILISTINE'S (5) [PHILISTINE]
1Sa	17:11	On hearing the P words, Saul and all the	7149
	17:51	the P sword and drew it from the scabbard.	7149
	17:54	the P head and brought it to Jerusalem,	7149
	17:54	and he put the P weapons in his own tent.	2257S
	17:57	with David still holding the P head.	7149

PHILISTINES (210) [PHILISTINE]
Ge	10:14	Casluhites (from whom the P came)	7149
	21:32	of his forces returned to the land of the P.	7149
	21:34	And Abraham stayed in the land of the P	7149
	26: 1	and Isaac went to Abimelech king of the P	7149
	26: 8	Abimelech king of the P looked down	7149
	26:14	and servants that the P envied him.	7149
	26:15	the P stopped up, filling them with earth.	7149
	26:18	the P had stopped up after Abraham died,	7149
Ex	23:31	from the Red Sea to the Sea of the P,	7149
Jos	13: 2	all the regions of the P and Geshurites:	7149
Jdg	3: 3	the five rulers of the P,	7149
	3:31	who struck down six hundred P with	7149
	10: 6	of the Ammonites and the gods of the P.	7149
	10: 7	into the hands of the P and the Ammonites,	7149
	10:11	the Amorites, the Ammonites, the P,	7149
	13: 1	into the hands of the P for forty years.	7149
	13: 5	of Israel from the hands of the P."	7149
	14: 3	Must you go to the uncircumcised P to get	7149
	14: 4	an occasion to confront the P;	7149
	15: 3	a right to get even with the P;	7149
	15: 5	in the standing grain of the P.	7149
	15: 6	When the P asked, "Who did this?"	7149
	15: 6	So the P went up and burned her	7149
	15: 9	The P went up and camped in Judah,	7149
	15:11	"Don't you realize that the P are rulers	7149
	15:12	to tie you up and hand you over to the P."	7149
	15:14	the P came toward him shouting.	7149
	15:20	for twenty years in the days of the P.	7149
	16: 5	The rulers of the P went to her and said,	7149
	16: 8	of the P brought her seven fresh thongs	7149
	16: 9	"Samson, the P are upon you!"	7149
	16:12	"Samson, the P are upon you!"	7149
	16:14	"Samson, the P are upon you!"	7149
	16:18	she sent word to the rulers of the P,	7149
	16:18	the rulers of the P returned with the silver	7149
	16:20	she called, "Samson, the P are upon you!"	7149
	16:21	Then the P seized him,	7149
	16:23	of the P assembled to offer a great sacrifice	7149
	16:27	all the rulers of the P were there,	7149
	16:28	with one blow get revenge on the P	7149
	16:30	"Let me die with the P!"	7149
1Sa	4: 1	Israelites went out to fight against the P.	7149
	4: 1	camped at Ebenezer, and the P at Aphek.	7149
	4: 2	The P deployed their forces to meet Israel,	7149
	4: 2	Israel was defeated by the P,	7149
	4: 3	bring defeat upon us today before the P?	7149

1Sa	4: 6	Hearing the uproar, the **P** asked,	7149
	4: 7	the **P** were afraid. "A god has come	7149
	4: 9	Be strong, **P**! Be men, or you will be subject	7149
	4:10	So the **P** fought, and the Israelites were	7149
	4:17	"Israel fled before the **P**,	7149
	5: 1	After the **P** had captured the ark of God,	7149
	5: 8	the rulers of the **P** and asked them,	7149
	5:11	of the **P** and said, "Send the ark of the god	7149
	6: 2	the **P** called for the priests and the diviners	7149
	6: 4	The **P** asked, "What guilt offering should	NIH
	6:12	of the **P** followed them as far as the border	7149
	6:16	The five rulers of the **P** saw all this and	7149
	6:17	These are the gold tumors the **P** sent as	7149
	6:21	**P** have returned the ark of the LORD.	7149
	7: 3	deliver you out of the hand of the **P**."	7149
	7: 7	the **P** heard that Israel had assembled	7149
	7: 7	the rulers of the **P** came up to attack them.	7149
	7: 7	they were afraid because of the **P**.	7149
	7: 8	he may rescue us from the hand of the **P**."	7149
	7:10	the **P** drew near to engage Israel in battle.	7149
	7:10	the **P** and threw them into such a panic	7149
	7:11	of Mizpah and pursued the **P**,	7149
	7:13	So the **P** were subdued and did	7149
	7:13	the hand of the LORD was against the **P**.	7149
	7:14	from Ekron to Gath that the **P** had captured	7149
	7:14	territory from the power of the **P**.	7149
	9:16	deliver my people from the hand of the **P**.	7149
	12: 9	of Hazor, and into the hands of the **P** and	7149
	13: 3	and the **P** heard about it.	7149
	13: 4	now Israel has become a stench to the **P**."	7149
	13: 5	The **P** assembled to fight Israel,	7149
	13:11	that the **P** were assembling at Micmash,	7149
	13:12	the **P** will come down against me at Gilgal,	7149
	13:16	while the **P** camped at Micmash.	7149
	13:19	because the **P** had said,	7149
	13:20	down to the **P** to have their plowshares,	7149
	13:23	a detachment of **P** had gone out to the pass	7149
	14:11	said the **P**. "The Hebrews are crawling out	7149
	14:13	The **P** fell before Jonathan,	NIH
	14:20	They found the **P** in total confusion,	NIH
	14:21	with the **P** and had gone up with them	7149
	14:22	of Ephraim heard that the **P** were on	7149
	14:30	Would not the slaughter of the **P** have been	7149
	14:31	after the Israelites had struck down the **P**	7149
	14:36	the **P** by night and plunder them till dawn,	7149
	14:37	"Shall I go down after the **P**?	7149
	14:46	Then Saul stopped pursuing the **P**,	7149
	14:47	Edom, the kings of Zobah, and the **P**.	7149
	14:52	of Saul there was bitter war with the **P**,	7149
	17: 1	Now the **P** gathered their forces for war	7149
	17: 2	and drew up their battle line to meet the **P**.	7149
	17: 3	The **P** occupied one hill and the Israelites	7149
	17:19	fighting against the **P**."	7149
	17:21	Israel and the **P** were drawing up their	7149
	17:51	When the **P** saw that their hero was dead,	7149
	17:52	and pursued the **P** to the entrance of Gath	7149
	17:53	the Israelites returned from chasing the **P**,	7149
	18:17	Let the **P** do that!"	7149
	18:21	so that the hand of the **P** may be against him	7149
	18:25	to have David fall by the hands of the **P**.	7149
	18:27	went out and killed two hundred **P**.	7149
	19: 8	and David went out and fought the **P**.	7149
	23: 1	the **P** are fighting against Keilah	7149
	23: 2	saying, "Shall I go and attack these **P**?"	7149
	23: 2	"Go, attack the **P** and save Keilah."	7149
	23: 4	I am going to give the **P** into your hand."	7149
	23: 5	fought the **P** and carried off their livestock.	7149
	23: 5	on the **P** and saved the people of Keilah.	2157S
	23:27	The **P** are raiding the land."	7149
	23:28	pursuit of David and went out to meet the **P**.	7149
	24: 1	After Saul returned from pursuing the **P**,	7149
	27: 1	to escape to the land of the **P**.	7149
	28: 1	In those days the **P** gathered their forces	7149
	28: 4	The **P** assembled and came and set	7149
	28:15	"The **P** are fighting against me,	7149
	28:19	over both Israel and you to the **P**,	7149
	28:19	also hand over the army of Israel to the **P**."	7149
	29: 1	The **P** gathered all their forces at Aphek,	7149
	29: 3	The commanders of the **P** asked,	7149
	29:11	to go back to the land of the **P**,	7149
	29:11	and the **P** went up to Jezreel.	7149
	30:16	from the land of the **P** and from Judah.	7149
	31: 1	Now the **P** fought against Israel;	7149
	31: 2	The **P** pressed hard after Saul and his sons,	7149
	31: 7	And the **P** came and occupied them.	7149
	31: 8	when the **P** came to strip the dead,	7149
	31: 9	of the **P** to proclaim the news in the temple	7149
	31:11	of what the **P** had done to Saul,	7149
2Sa	1:20	lest the daughters of the **P** be glad,	7149
	3:18	from the hand of the **P** and from the hand	7149
	5:17	When the **P** heard that David had been	7149
	5:18	Now the **P** had come and spread out in	7149
	5:19	"Shall I go and attack the **P**?	7149
	5:19	for I will surely hand the **P** over to you."	7149
	5:21	The **P** abandoned their idols there,	NIH
	5:22	the **P** came up and spread out in the Valley	7149
	5:25	the **P** all the way from Gibeon to Gezer.	7149
	8: 1	David defeated the **P** and subdued them,	7149
	8: 1	Metheg Ammah from the control of the **P**.	7149
	8:12	the Ammonites and the **P**, and Amalek.	7149
	19: 9	who rescued us from the hand of the **P**.	7149
	21:12	the **P** had hung them after they struck Saul	7149
	21:15	a battle between the **P** and Israel.	7149
	21:15	down with his men to fight against the **P**,	7149
	21:18	there was another battle with the **P**, at Gob.	7149
	21:19	In another battle with the **P** at Gob,	7149
	23: 9	the **P** gathered [at Pas Dammim] for battle.	7149

2Sa	23:10	struck down the **P** till his hand grew tired	7149
	23:11	When the **P** banded together at a place	7149
	23:12	He defended it and struck the **P** down,	7149
	23:13	a band of **P** was encamped in the Valley	7149
1Ki	4:21	from the River to the land of the **P**,	7149
2Ki	8: 2	and stayed in the land of the **P** seven years.	7149
	8: 3	from the land of the **P** and went to the king	7149
	18: 8	he defeated the **P**, as far as Gaza	7149
1Ch	1:12	Casluhites (from whom the **P** came)	7149
	10: 1	Now the **P** fought against Israel;	7149
	10: 2	The **P** pressed hard after Saul and his sons,	7149
	10: 7	And the **P** came and occupied them.	7149
	10: 8	when the **P** came to strip the dead,	7149
	10: 9	throughout the land of the **P** to proclaim	7149
	10:11	of everything the **P** had done to Saul,	7149
	11:13	at Pas Dammim when the **P** gathered there	7149
	11:13	the troops fled from the **P**.	7149
	11:14	They defended it and struck the **P** down,	7149
	11:15	a band of **P** was encamped in the Valley	7149
	12:19	to David when he went with the **P** to fight	7149
	12:19	and his men did not help the **P** because,	7149
	14: 8	When the **P** heard that David had been	7149
	14: 9	Now the **P** had come and raided the Valley	7149
	14:10	"Shall I go and attack the **P**?	7149
	14:12	The **P** had abandoned their gods there,	NIH
	14:13	Once more the **P** raided the valley;	7149
	18: 1	David defeated the **P** and subdued them,	7149
	18: 1	villages from the control of the **P**,	7149
	18:11	the Ammonites and the **P**, and Amalek.	7149
	20: 4	war broke out with the **P**, at Gezer.	7149
	20: 4	and the **P** were subjugated.	NIH
	20: 5	In another battle with the **P**,	7149
2Ch	9:26	from the River to the land of the **P**,	7149
	17:11	Some **P** brought Jehoshaphat gifts	7149
	21:16	against Jehoram the hostility of the **P** and	7149
	26: 6	the **P** and broke down the walls of Gath,	7149
	26: 6	near Ashdod and elsewhere among the **P**.	7149
	26: 7	God helped him against the **P** and against	7149
	28:18	the **P** had raided towns in the foothills and	7149
Ps	56: T	When the **P** had seized him in Gath.	7149
Isa	2: 6	like the **P** and clasp hands with pagans.	7149
	9:12	and **P** from the west have devoured Israel	7149
	14:29	Do not rejoice, all you **P**,	7148
	14:31	Melt away, all you **P**!	7148
Jer	25:20	to destroy all the kings of the **P**	824+7149
	47: 1	to Jeremiah the prophet concerning the **P**	7149
	47: 4	the day has come to destroy all the **P** and	7149
	47: 4	The LORD is about to destroy the **P**,	7149
Eze	16:27	of your enemies, the daughters of the **P**,	7149
	16:57	and the daughters of the **P**—	7149
	25:15	the **P** acted in vengeance and took revenge	7149
	25:16	about to stretch out my hand against the **P**,	7149
Am	1: 8	till the last of the **P** is dead,"	7149
	9: 7	the **P** from Caphtor and the Arameans	7149
Ob	1:19	the foothills will possess the land of the **P**.	7149
Zep	2: 5	O Canaan, land of the **P**.	7149
Zec	9: 6	and I will cut off the pride of the **P**.	7149

PHILOLOGUS (1)

Ro	16:15	Greet **P**, Julia, Nereus and his sister,	5807

PHILOSOPHER (1) [PHILOSOPHY]

1Co	1:20	Where is the **p** of this age?	5186

PHILOSOPHERS (1) [PHILOSOPHY]

Ac	17:18	*of* Epicurean and Stoic **p** began to dispute	5815

PHILOSOPHY (1) [PHILOSOPHER, PHILOSOPHERS]

Col	2: 8	through hollow and deceptive **p**,	5814

PHINEHAS (25)

Ex	6:25	and she bore him **P**.	7090
Nu	25: 7	When **P** son of Eleazar, the son of Aaron,	7090
	25:11	"**P** son of Eleazar, the son of Aaron,	7090
	31: 6	along with **P** son of Eleazar, the priest,	7090
Jos	22:13	So the Israelites sent **P** son of Eleazar,	7090
	22:30	When **P** the priest and the leaders of	7090
	22:31	And **P** son of Eleazar, the priest,	7090
	22:32	Then **P** son of Eleazar, the priest,	7090
	24:33	to his son **P** in the hill country of Ephraim.	7090
Jdg	20:28	with **P** son of Eleazar,	7090
1Sa	1: 3	where Hophni and **P**, the two sons of Eli,	7090
	2:34	Hophni and **P**, will be a sign to you—	7090
	4: 4	And Eli's two sons, Hophni and **P**,	7090
	4:11	and Eli's two sons, Hophni and **P**, died.	7090
	4:17	Also your two sons, Hophni and **P**,	7090
	4:19	His daughter-in-law, the wife of **P**,	7090
	14: 3	of Ichabod's brother Ahitub son of **P**,	7090
1Ch	6: 4	Eleazar was the father of **P**,	7090
	6: 4	**P** the father of Abishua,	7090
	6:50	Eleazar his son, **P** his son, Abishua his son,	7090
	9:20	In earlier times **P** son of Eleazar was	7090
Ezr	7: 5	the son of **P**, the son of Eleazar,	7090
	8: 2	of the descendants of **P**, Gershom;	7090
	8:33	Eleazar son of **P** was with him,	7090
Ps	106:30	But **P** stood up and intervened,	7090

PHLEGON (1)

Ro	16:14	Greet Asyncritus, **P**, Hermes, Patrobas,	5823

PHOEBE (1)

Ro	16: 1	I commend to you our sister **P**,	5833

PHOENICIA (4) [SYRIAN PHOENICIA]

Isa	23:11	an order concerning **P** that her fortresses	4046
Ac	11:19	with Stephen traveled as far as **P**,	5834
	15: 3	as they traveled through **P** and Samaria,	5834
	21: 2	We found a ship crossing over to **P**,	5834

PHOENIX (1)

Ac	27:12	hoping to reach **P** and winter there.	5837

PHRYGIA (3)

Ac	2:10	**P** and Pamphylia, Egypt and the parts	5867
	16: 6	throughout the region of **P** and Galatia,	5867
	18:23	throughout the region of Galatia and **P**,	5867

PHURAH (KJV) See PURAH

PHUT (KJV) See PUT

PHUVAH (KJV) See PUAH

PHYGELUS (1)

2Ti	1:15	including **P** and Hermogenes.	5869

PHYLACTERIES (1)

Mt	23: 5	They make their **p** wide and the tassels	5873

PHYSICAL (5) [PHYSICALLY]

Da	1: 4	young men without any **p** defect,	4583
Ro	2:28	nor is circumcision merely outward and **p**.	4922
Col	1:22	he has reconciled you by Christ's **p** body	4922
1Ti	4: 8	For **p** training is of some value,	5394
Jas	2:16	but does nothing about his **p** needs,	5393

PHYSICALLY (2) [PHYSICAL]

Ro	2:27	The one who is not circumcised **p** and	1666+5882
1Co	5: 3	I am not **p** present, I am with you in spirit.	5393

PHYSICIAN (2) [PHYSICIANS]

Jer	8:22	Is there no **p** there?	8324
Lk	4:23	'**P**, heal yourself! Do here in your hometown what we have heard	2620

PHYSICIANS (4) [PHYSICIAN]

Ge	50: 2	Then Joseph directed the **p** in his service	8324
	50: 2	So the **p** embalmed him,	8324
2Ch	16:12	help from the LORD, but only from the **p**.	8324
Job	13: 4	you *are* worthless **p**, all of you!	8324

PI HAHIROTH (4)

Ex	14: 2	to turn back and encamp near **P**,	7084
	14: 9	they camped by the sea near **P**,	7084
Nu	33: 7	They left Etham, turned back to **P**,	7084
	33: 8	They left **P** and passed through the sea	7084

PI-BESETH (KJV) See BUBASTIS

PICK (24) [PICKED, PICKERS, PICKS]

Lev	19:10	over your vineyard a second time or **p up**	4377
	27:33	*He must* not **p** out the good from the bad	1329
Dt	23:25	*you may* **p** kernels with your hands,	7786
Ru	2: 2	and **p up** the leftover grain behind anyone	4377
	2:16	the bundles and leave them for *her* to **p up**,	4377
1Ki	20:33	as a good sign and were quick to **p up**	2715
2Ki	5: 7	he is **trying to p** a quarrel with me!"	628
	9:25	"**P** him **up** and throw him on the field	5951
	9:26	then, **p** him **up** and throw him on that plot,	5951
Ps	80:12	so that all who pass by **p** its grapes?	768
Isa	41:16	the wind *will* **p** them **up**,	5951
Eze	24: 5	take the **p** of the flock.	4436
Jnh	1:12	"**P** me **up** and throw me into the sea,"	5951
Mt	7:16	*Do people* **p** grapes from thornbushes,	5198
	12: 1	*to* **p** some heads of grain and eat them.	5504
Mk	2:23	they began *to* **p** some heads of grain.	5504
	8:19	many basketfuls of pieces *did you* **p up?"**	149
	8:20	many basketfuls of pieces *did you* **p up?"**	149
	16:18	*they will* **p up** snakes with their hands;	149
Lk	6: 1	and his disciples *began to* **p** some heads	5504
	6:44	*People do* not **p** figs from thornbushes,	5198
Jn	5: 8	**P up** your mat and walk.	149
	5:11	'**P up** your mat and walk.' "	149
	5:12	"Who is this fellow who told you *to* **p** it **up**	149

PICKED (23) [PICK]

Jdg	1: 7	and big toes cut off *have* **p up** scraps	4377
	4:21	**p up** a tent peg and a hammer	4374
1Sa	20:38	The boy **p up** the arrow and returned	4377
2Sa	4: 4	His nurse **p** him **up** and fled,	5951
1Ki	13:29	prophet **p up** the body of the man of God,	5951
	17:23	Elijah **p up** the child and carried him down	4374
2Ki	2:13	*He* **p up** the cloak that had fallen	8123
	2:16	*the* LORD *has* **p** him **up** and set him down	5951
Eze	29: 5	the open field and not be gathered or **p up**.	7695
Na	2: 5	He summons his **p troops**,	129

Mt	14:20	and the disciples **p** up twelve basketfuls	149
	15:37	the disciples **p** up seven basketfuls	149
	27: 6	The chief priests **p** up the coins and said,	3284
Mk	6:43	and the disciples **p** up twelve basketfuls	149
	8: 8	the disciples **p** up seven basketfuls	149
Lk	9:17	and the disciples **p** up twelve basketfuls	149
	14: 7	The guests **p** the places of honor at the table,	1721
Jn	5: 9	he **p** up his mat and walked.	149
	8:59	At this, *they* **p** up stones to stone him,	149
	10:31	Again the Jews **p** up stones to stone him,	1002
	15: 6	such branches *are* **p** up, thrown into the fire	5051
Ac	20: 9	from the third story and *was* **p** up dead.	149
Rev	18:21	Then a mighty angel **p** up a boulder the size	149

PICKERS (2) [PICK]

Jer	49: 9	If **grape** **p** came to you,	1305
Ob	1: 5	If **grape** **p** came to you,	1305

PICKS (6) [PICK]

Lev	11:25	Whoever **p** up one of their carcasses	5951
	11:28	Anyone *who* **p** up their carcasses must wash	5951
	11:40	Anyone *who* **p** up the carcass must wash	5951
	15:10	whoever **p** up those things must wash his	5951
2Sa	12:31	with saws and with iron **p** and axes.	3044
1Ch	20: 3	with saws and with iron **p** and axes.	3044

PIECE (39) [PIECES]

Ex	15:25	and the LORD showed him a **p** of wood.	6770
	25:19	make the cherubim **of one p** with the cover,	4946
	25:31	buds and blossoms shall be **of one p** with it.	4946
	25:36	The buds and branches shall all be of **one p**	AIT
	27: 2	so that the horns and the altar are **of one p,**	4946
	28: 8	**of one p** with the ephod and	4946
	30: 2	its horns **of one p** with it.	4946
	37: 8	at the two ends he made them **of one p** with	4946
	37:17	buds and blossoms were **of one p** with it.	4946
	37:22	and the branches were all **of one p** with	4946
	37:25	its horns **of one p** with it.	4946
	38: 2	that the horns and the altar were **of one p,**	4946
	39: 5	**of one p** with the ephod and made	4946
Lev	9:13	the burnt offering **p by piece,**	4200+5984
	9:13	the burnt offering **piece by p,**	4200+5984
Jdg	16: 9	as a **p** of string snaps when it comes	5861+7348
	20: 6	into pieces and sent *one* **p** to each region	2023[S]
Ru	4: 3	is selling the **p** of land that belonged	2754
1Sa	2:36	a **p** of silver and a crust of bread and plead,	102
	9:23	"Bring the **p of meat** I gave you,	4950
	24:11	look at this **p** of your robe in my hand!	4053
2Sa	17:13	to the valley until not even a **p** of it can	7656
1Ki	7:24	in two rows in **one p** with the Sea.	3669
	17:11	"And bring me, please, a **p** *of* bread."	7326
2Ch	4: 3	in two rows in **one p** with the Sea.	4609
Job	2: 8	a **p** of broken pottery and scraped himself	3084
	41:29	A club seems to him but a **p of straw;**	7990
	42:11	and each one gave him a **p of silver** and	7988
Pr	28:21	yet a man will do wrong for a **p** *of* bread.	7326
Eze	24: 6	Empty it **p** by piece without casting lots	5984
	24: 6	Empty it piece by piece without casting lots	5984
Am	3:12	the lion's mouth only two leg bones or a **p**	977
Mk	2:21	the **new** **p** will pull away from the old,	AIT
Lk	19:20	I have kept it laid away in a **p** of cloth.	5051
	24:42	They gave him a **p** of broiled fish,	3538
Jn	13:26	the one to whom I will give this **p** of bread	6040
	13:26	Then, dipping the **p** of bread,	6040
	19:23	woven in one **p** from top to bottom.	NIG
Ac	5: 1	also sold a **p** of property.	3228

PIECES (97) [PIECE]

Ge	15:17	torch appeared and passed between the **p.**	1617
	33:19	For a hundred **p** of silver,	7988
	37:33	Joseph has **surely been torn to p.**"	3271+3271
	44:28	*"He has* **surely been torn to p.**"	3271+3271
Ex	22:13	was torn to **p** by a wild animal,	3271+3271
	23:24	**break** their sacred stones **to p.**	8689+8689
	28: 7	It is to have two **shoulder p** attached to two	4190
	28:12	and fasten them on the **shoulder p** *of*	4190
	28:25	to the **shoulder p** *of* the ephod at the front.	4190
	28:27	the bottom of the **shoulder p** on the front of	4190
	29:17	Cut the ram into **p** and wash the inner parts	5984
	29:17	putting them with the head and the *other* **p.**	5984
	32:19	**breaking** them **to p** at the foot of	8689
	39: 4	They made **shoulder p** for the ephod,	4190
	39: 7	Then they fastened them on the **shoulder p**	4190
	39:18	to the **shoulder p** *of* the ephod at the front.	4190
	39:20	the bottom of the **shoulder p** on the front of	4190
Lev	1: 6	to skin the burnt offering and cut it into **p.**	5984
	1: 8	Aaron's sons the priests shall arrange the **p,**	5984
	1:12	He is to cut it into **p,**	5984
	6:21	and present the grain offering broken in **p**	7326
	8:20	He cut the ram into **p** and burned the head,	5984
	8:20	the head, the **p** and the fat.	5984
Nu	24: 8	and **break** their bones **in p;**	1751
Dt	9:17	**breaking** them **to p** before your eyes.	8689
Jos	24:32	for a hundred **p** *of* silver from the sons	7988
Jdg	20: 6	**cut** her **into p** and sent one piece to each	5983
1Sa	11: 7	He took a pair of oxen, **cut** them **into p,**	5983
	11: 7	sent the **p** by messengers throughout Israel,	NIH
1Ki	11:30	and tore it into twelve **p.**	7974
	11:31	"Take ten **p** for yourself,	7974
	18:23	and *let them* **cut** it **into p** and put it on	5983
	18:33	**cut** the bull **into p** and laid it on the wood.	5983
2Ki	11:18	and idols **to p** and killed Mattan the priest	3512
	18: 4	*He* **broke into p** the bronze snake	4198
	23:12	**smashed** them **to p** and threw the rubble	8368

2Ch	25:12	down so that all **were dashed to p.**	1324
	34: 4	he **cut to p** the incense altars that were	1548
	34: 4	These he **broke to p** and scattered over	1990
	34: 7	the idols to powder and **cut to p** all	1548
Job	4:20	and dusk *they* **are broken to p;**	4198
	18: 4	You *who* **tear** yourself **to p** in your anger,	3271
	26:12	by his wisdom *he* **cut Rahab to p**	4730
Ps	2: 9	*you will* **dash** them **to p** like pottery."	5879
	7: 2	and **rip** me **to p** with no one to rescue me.	7293
	29: 5	the LORD **breaks in p** the cedars	8689
	50:22	or *I will* **tear** you **to p,**	3271
	119:72	to me than **thousands** *of* **p** *of* silver	AIT
Isa	13:16	Their infants *will* **be dashed to p**	8187
	24:12	its gate *is* **battered to p.**	4198+8625
	27: 9	to be like chalk stones **crushed to p,**	5879
	30:14	It will **break in p** like pottery,	8691
	30:14	among its **p** not a fragment will be found	4845
	51: 9	Was it not you who **cut Rahab to p,**	2933
Jer	5: 6	*to* **tear to p** any who venture out,	3271
	23:29	like a hammer that **breaks a rock in p?**	7207
	34:18	in two and walked between its **p.**	1440
	34:19	of the land who walked between the **p** *of*	1440
Eze	16:40	who will stone you and **hack** you **to p**	1438
	23:34	you will dash it to **p** and tear your breasts.	3084
	24: 4	Put into it the **p** *of* meat,	5984
	24: 4	all the choice **p**—the leg and the shoulder.	5984
	27:26	But the east wind *will* **break** you **to p** in	8689
Da	2: 5	and interpret it, I will have you cut into **p**	10197
	2:35	the gold *were* **broken to p** at the same time	10182
	2:40	and as iron **breaks** things **to p,**	10671
	2:45	**broke** the iron, the bronze, the clay, the silver and the gold **to p.**	10182
	3:29	into **p** and their houses be turned into piles	10197
Hos	5:14	I *will* **tear** them **to p** and go away;	3271
	6: 1	He *has* **torn** us **to p** but he will heal us;	3271
	6: 5	Therefore *I* **cut** you **in p** with my prophets,	2933
	8: 6	It will **be broken in p,** that calf of Samaria.	8646
Am	6:11	the great house into **p** and the small house	8269
Mic	1: 7	All her idols *will* **be broken to p;**	4198
	3: 3	**break** their bones **in p;**	7200
	4:13	and *you will* **break to p** many nations."	1990
Na	3:10	Her infants *were* **dashed to p** at the head	8187
Zec	11:12	So they paid me **thirty** **p** *of* silver.	AIT
	11:13	the **thirty** **p** *of* silver and threw them into	AIT
Mt	7: 6	and then turn and **tear** you **to p.**	4838
	14:20	picked up twelve basketfuls of **broken p**	3083
	15:37	picked up seven basketfuls *of* **broken p**	3083
	21:44	who falls on this stone *will* **be broken to p,**	5314
	24:51	*He will* **cut** him **to p** and assign him	1497
Mk	6:43	picked up twelve basketfuls of **broken p**	3083
	8: 8	picked up seven basketfuls *of* **broken p**	3083
	8:19	many basketfuls *of* **p** did you pick up?"	3083
	8:20	many basketfuls *of* **p** did you pick up?"	3083
Lk	9:17	picked up twelve basketfuls *of* **broken p**	3083
	12:46	*He will* **cut** him **to p** and assign him	1497
	20:18	who falls on that stone *will* **be broken to p,**	5314
Jn	6:12	"Gather the **p** that are left over.	3083
	6:13	*with* the **p** of the five barley loaves left over	3083
Ac	23:10	Paul *would* **be torn to p** by them.	1400
	27:41	the stern *was* **broken to p** by the pounding	3395
	27:44	The rest were to get there on planks or on **p**	5516
Rev	2:27	he will **dash** them **to p** like pottery'—	5341

PIERCE (9) [PIERCED, PIERCES, PIERCING]

Ex	21: 6	the door or the doorpost and **p** his ear with	8361
Nu	24: 8	with their arrows *they* **p** them.	4730
Job	40:24	or trap him and **p** his nose?	5918
	41: 2	through his nose or **p** his jaw with a hook?	5918
Ps	37:15	But their swords *will* **p** their own hearts,	928+995
	45: 5	Let your sharp arrows **p** the hearts of	928
Pr	12:18	Reckless words **p** like a sword,	4532
Eze	28: 7	and wisdom and **p** your shining splendor.	2726
Lk	2:35	And a sword *will* **p** your own soul too."	1451

PIERCED (16) [PIERCE]

Jdg	5:26	she shattered and **p** his temple.	2737
2Ki	9:24	The arrow **p** his heart and he slumped	3655
Job	26:13	his hand **p** the gliding serpent.	2726
Ps	22:16	*they have* **p** my hands and my feet.	4125
	38: 2	For your arrows *have* **p** me,	928+5737
	40: 6	but my ears *you have* **p;**	4125
Isa	14:19	with *those* **p** by the sword,	3249
	51: 9	who **p** that monster **through?**	2726
	53: 5	But he was **p** for our transgressions,	2726
La	3:13	*He* **p** my heart *with* arrows from his	928+995
Hab	3:14	With his own spear *you* **p** his head	5918
Zec	12:10	They will look on me, the one *they have* **p,**	1991
Jn	19:34	one of the soldiers **p** Jesus' side with a spear	3817
	19:37	"They will look on the one *they have* **p.**"	1708
1Ti	6:10	and **p** themselves with many griefs.	4345
Rev	1: 7	eye will see him, even those who **p** him;	1708

PIERCES (7) [PIERCE]

2Ki	18:21	*which* **p** a man's hand and wounds him	5918
Job	16:13	Without pity, *he* **p** my kidneys and	7114
	20:24	a bronze-tipped arrow **p** him.	2737
	30:17	Night **p** my bones;	5918
Pr	7:23	till an arrow **p** his liver,	7114
Isa	36: 6	*which* **p** a man's hand and wounds him	5918
Jer	4:18	How *it* **p** to the heart!"	5595

PIERCING (1) [PIERCE]

Job	16: 9	my opponent **fastens** on me his **p** eyes.	4323

PIETY (3)

Job	4: 6	Should not your **p** be your confidence	3711
	15: 4	even undermine **p** and hinder devotion	3711
	22: 4	"Is it for your **p** that he rebukes you	3711

PIG (2) [PIG'S, PIGS]

Lev	11: 7	And the **p,** though it has a split hoof	2614
Dt	14: 8	The **p** is also unclean; although it has	2614

PIG'S (2) [PIG]

Pr	11:22	Like a gold ring in a **p** snout is	2614
Isa	66: 3	like one who presents **p** blood,	2614

PIGEON (3) [PIGEONS]

Ge	15: 9	along with a dove and a **young p.**"	1578
Lev	1:14	he is to offer a dove or a young **p.**	3433
	12: 6	a burnt offering and a young **p** or a dove for	3433

PIGEONS (9) [PIGEON]

Lev	5: 7	he is to bring two doves or two young **p** to	3433
	5:11	cannot afford two doves or two young **p,**	3433
	12: 8	she is to bring two doves or two young **p,**	3433
	14:22	and two doves or two young **p,**	3433
	14:30	he shall sacrifice the doves or the young **p,**	3433
	15:14	or two young **p** and come before	3433
	15:29	or two young **p** and bring them to the priest	3433
Nu	6:10	or two young **p** to the priest at the entrance	3433
Lk	2:24	"a pair of doves or two young **p.**"	4361

PIGS (17) [PIG]

Isa	65: 4	who eat the flesh of **p,**	2614
	66:17	in the midst of those who eat the flesh of **p**	2614
Mt	7: 6	do not throw your pearls to **p.**	5956
	8:30	from them a large herd *of* **p** was feeding.	5956
	8:31	send us into the herd *of* **p.**"	5956
	8:32	So they came out and went into the **p,**	5956
	8:33	Those tending the **p** ran off,	NIG
Mk	5:11	herd *of* **p** was feeding on the nearby hillside.	5956
	5:12	"Send us among the **p;**	5956
	5:13	evil spirits came out and went into the **p.**	5956
	5:14	Those tending **the p** ran off	899[S]
	5:16	and told about the **p** as well.	5956
Lk	8:32	A large herd *of* **p** was feeding there on	5956
	8:33	they went into the **p,**	5956
	8:34	those tending the **p** saw what had happened,	NIG
	15:15	who sent him to his fields to feed **p.**	5956
	15:16	with the pods that the **p** were eating.	5956

PILATE (61) [PILATE'S]

Mt	27: 2	led him away and handed him over *to* **P,**	4397
	27:13	Then **P** asked him, "Don't you hear	4397
	27:17	the crowd had gathered, **P** asked them,	4397
	27:19	While **P** was sitting on the judge's seat,	899[S]
	27:22	with Jesus who is called Christ?" **P** asked.	4397
	27:23	What crime has he committed?" asked **P.**	1254+3836[S]
	27:24	When **P** saw that he was getting nowhere,	4397
	27:58	Going to **P,** he asked for Jesus' body.	4397
	27:58	and **P** ordered that it be given to him.	4397
	27:62	chief priests and the Pharisees went to **P.**	4397
	27:65	"Take a guard," **P** answered.	4397
Mk	15: 1	led him away and handed him over *to* **P.**	4397
	15: 2	"Are you the king of the Jews?" asked **P.**	4397
	15: 4	So again **P** asked him,	4397
	15: 5	still made no reply, and **P** was amazed.	4397
	15: 8	The crowd came up and asked **P** to do	NIG
	15: 9	to you the king of the Jews?" asked **P,**	4397
	15:11	to have **P** release Barabbas instead.	NIG
	15:12	the king of the Jews?" **P** asked them.	4397
	15:14	What crime has he committed?" asked **P.**	4397
	15:15	**P** released Barabbas to them.	4397
	15:43	went boldly to **P** and asked for Jesus' body.	4397
	15:44	**P** was surprised to hear that he was already	4397
Lk	3: 1	when Pontius **P** was governor of Judea,	4397
	13: 1	the Galileans whose blood **P** had mixed	4397
	23: 1	whole assembly rose and led him off to **P.**	4397
	23: 3	So **P** asked Jesus, "Are you the king of the Jews?"	4397
	23: 4	then **P** announced to the chief priests and	4397
	23: 6	**P** asked if the man was a Galilean.	4397
	23: 7	they sent him back to **P.**	4397
	23:12	That day Herod and **P** became friends—	4397
	23:13	**P** called together the chief priests,	4397
	23:20	**P** appealed to them again.	4397
	23:24	So **P** decided to grant their demand.	4397
	23:52	Going to **P,** he asked for Jesus' body.	4397
Jn	18:29	So **P** came out to them and asked,	4397
	18:31	**P** said, "Take him yourselves	4397
	18:33	**P** then went back inside the palace,	4397
	18:35	"Am I a Jew?" **P** replied.	4397
	18:37	"You are a king, then!" said **P.**	4397
	18:38	"What is truth?" **P** asked.	4397
	19: 1	Then **P** took Jesus and had him flogged.	4397
	19: 4	Once more **P** came out and said to	4397
	19: 5	**P** said to them, "Here is the man!"	NIG
	19: 6	But **P** answered, "You take him	4397
	19: 8	When **P** heard this, he was even more afraid	4397
	19:10	"Do you refuse to speak to me?" **P** said.	4397
	19:12	From then on, **P** tried to set Jesus free,	4397
	19:13	When **P** heard this, he brought Jesus out	4397
	19:14	"Here is your king," **P** said to the Jews.	NIG
	19:15	"Shall I crucify your king?" **P** asked.	4397

Jn 19:16   Finally P handed him over to them to   *NIG*
    19:19   P had a notice prepared and fastened to   4397
    19:21   The chief priests of the Jews protested *to* P,   4397
    19:22   P answered, "What I have written,   4397
    19:31   they asked P to have the legs broken and   4397
    19:38   Joseph of Arimathea asked P for the body   4397
Ac   3:13   and you disowned him before P,   4397
    4:27   Indeed Herod and Pontius P met together   4397
    13:28   they asked P to have him executed.   4397
1Ti   6:13   while testifying before Pontius P made   4397

PILATE'S (1) [PILATE]
Jn 19:38   With P permission, he came and took   4397

PILDASH (1)
Ge 22:22   Kesed, Hazo, P, Jidlaph and Bethuel."   7109

PILE (11) [PILED, PILES]
Lev 26:30   and p your dead bodies on the lifeless forms   5989
Jos   7:26   Over Achan they heaped up a large p   1643
    8:29   And they raised a large p of rocks over it,   1643
Ru   3: 7   to lie down at the far end of the **grain p.**   6894
Ezr   6:11   to be made a p of rubble,   10470
Job   8:17   around a p of rocks and looks for a place   1643
Jer 50:26   p her up like heaps of grain.   6148
Eze 24: 5   P wood beneath it *for* the bones;   1883
    24: 1   I, too, *will* p the wood **high.**   1540
Lk 14:35   for the soil nor for the **manure p;**   3161
Ac 28: 3   Paul gathered a p of brushwood and,   4436

PILED (8) [PILE]
Ge 31:46   So they took stones and p them *in* a heap,   6913
Ex   8:14   They *were* p into heaps,   7392
    15: 8   the blast of your nostrils the waters **p up.**   6890
Jos   3:16   *It* p up in a heap a great distance away,   7756
Jdg   9:49   *They* p them against the stronghold   8492
2Sa 18:17   a big pit in the forest and **p up** a large heap   5893
2Ch 31: 6   and *they* p them in heaps.   5989
Rev 18: 5   for her sins *are* **p up** to heaven,   3140

PILEHA (KJV) See PILHA

PILES (9) [PILE]
2Ki 10: 8   in two p at the entrance of the city gate   7393
    19:25   fortified cities into p of stone.   1643+5898
Job 27:16   up silver like dust and clothes like p   3922
Isa 37:26   fortified cities into p of stone.   1643+5898
Da   2: 5   and your houses turned into p of rubble,   10470
    3:29   be turned into p of rubble,   10470
Hos 12:11   Their altars will be like p of stones on   1643
Na   3: 3   Many casualties, p *of* dead,   3880
Hab   2: 6   " 'Woe to him *who* **p up** stolen goods   8049

PILGRIMAGE (3)
Ge 47: 9   years of my p are a hundred and thirty.   4472
    47: 9   not equal the years of the p of my fathers."   4472
Ps 84: 5   who have set their hearts on p.   5019

PILGRIMS (KJV) See STRANGERS

PILHA (1)
Ne 10:24   Hallohesh, P, Shobek,   7116

PILLAGE (2) [PILLAGED]
Ezr   9: 7   to p and humiliation at the hand   1023
Jer 50:11   you *who* p my inheritance,   9115

PILLAGED (2) [PILLAGE]
Ob   1: 6   his hidden treasures p!   1239
Na   2:10   She is p, plundered, stripped!   1011

PILLAR (44) [PILLARS]
Ge 19:26   and she became a p of salt.   5907
    28:18   and set it up as a p and poured oil on top   5167
    28:22   and this stone that I have set up as a p will   5167
    31:13   a p and where you made a vow to me.   5167
    31:45   So Jacob took a stone and set it up as a p.   5167
    31:51   and here is this p I have set up between you   5167
    31:52   and this p is a witness,   5167
    31:52   past this heap and p to my side to harm me.   5167
    35:14   a stone p at the place where God had talked   5167
    35:20   Over her tomb Jacob set up a p,   5167
    35:20   and to this day that p marks Rachel's tomb.   5167
Ex 13:21   in a p of cloud to guide them on their way   6647
    13:21   by night in a p of fire to give them light,   6647
    13:22   Neither the p of cloud by day nor the pillar   6647
    13:22   Neither the pillar of cloud by day nor the p   6647
    14:19   the p of cloud also moved from in front   6647
    14:24   the LORD looked down from the p of fire   6647
    33: 9   the p of cloud would come down and stay   6647
    33:10   the people saw the p of cloud standing at   6647
Nu 12: 5   the LORD came down in a p of cloud;   6647
    14:14   and that you go before them with a p of cloud   6647
    14:14   in a pillar of cloud by day and a p of fire   6647
Dt 31:15   the LORD appeared at the Tent in a p   6647
Jdg   9: 6   beside the great tree at the p in Shechem   5164
2Sa 18:18   During his lifetime Absalom had taken a p   5170
    18:18   He named the p after himself,   5170
1Ki   7:21   The p to the south he named Jakin and   6647

2Ki 11:14   standing by the p, as the custom was.   6647
    23: 3   by the p and renewed the covenant in   6647
    25:17   Each p was twenty-seven feet high.   6647
    25:17   The bronze capital on top of one p was four   2257S
    25:17   The other p, with its network, was similar.   6647
2Ch 23:13   standing by his p at the entrance   6641
    34:31   by his p and renewed the covenant in   6641
Ne   9:12   By day you led them with a p of cloud,   6647
    9:12   by night with a p of fire to give them light   6647
    9:19   the p of cloud did not cease to guide them   6647
    9:19   nor the p of fire by night to shine on   6647
Ps 99: 7   He spoke to them from the p of cloud;   6647
Jer   1:18   an iron p and a bronze wall to stand against   6647
    52:22   on top of **the** one p was five cubits high   2257S
    52:22   The other p, with its pomegranates,   6647
1Ti   3:15   the p and foundation of the truth.   5146
Rev   3:12   Him who overcomes I will make a p in   5146

PILLARS (45) [PILLAR]
Ex 24: 4   and set up twelve **stone p** representing   5167
Jdg 16:25   When they stood him among the p,   6647
    16:26   "Put me where I can feel the p that support   6647
    16:29   toward the two central p on which   6647
1Ki   7: 6   of that were p and an overhanging roof.   6647
    7:15   He cast two bronze p,   6647
    7:16   of cast bronze to set on the tops of the p;   6647
    7:17   the capitals on top of the p,   6647
    7:18   to decorate the capitals on top of the p.   6647
    7:19   of the p in the portico were in the shape   6647
    7:20   On the capitals of both p,   6647
    7:21   the p at the portico of the temple.   6647
    7:22   And so the work on the p was completed.   6647
    7:41   two p; the two bowl-shaped capitals on top   6647
    7:41   bowl-shaped capitals on top of the p;   6647
    7:41   bowl-shaped capitals on top of the p;   6647
    7:42   the bowl-shaped capitals on top of the p);   6647
2Ki 25:13   The Babylonians broke up the bronze p,   6647
    25:16   The bronze from the two p,   6647
1Ch 18: 8   the p and various bronze articles.   6647
2Ch   3:15   In the front of the temple he made two p,   6647
    3:16   and put them on top of the p.   6647
    3:17   He erected the p in the front of the temple,   6647
    4:12   two p; the two bowl-shaped capitals on top   6647
    4:12   bowl-shaped capitals on top of the p;   6647
    4:12   bowl-shaped capitals on top of the p;   6647
    4:13   the bowl-shaped capitals on top of the p);   6647
Est   1: 6   to silver rings on marble p.   6647
Job   9: 6   from its place and makes its p tremble.   6647
    26:11   The p of the heavens quake,   6647
Ps   75: 3   it is I who hold its p firm.   6647
  144:12   and our daughters will be like p carved   2312
Pr   9: 1   she has hewn out its seven p.   6647
SS   5:15   His legs are p of marble set on bases   6647
Jer 27:19   the LORD Almighty says about the p,   6647
    43:13   in Egypt he will demolish the **sacred p**   5167
    52:17   The Babylonians broke up the bronze p,   6647
    52:20   The bronze from the two p,   6647
    52:21   Each of the p was eighteen cubits high   6647
Eze 26:11   and your strong p will fall to the ground.   5167
    40:49   and there were p on each side of the jambs.   6647
    42: 6   The rooms on the third floor had no p,   6647
Am   9: 1   "Strike the **tops of the p** so that   4117
Gal   2: 9   Peter and John, those reputed to be p,   5146
Rev 10: 1   and his legs were like fiery p.   5146

PILLED (KJV) See PEELED

PILOT (2)
Ac 27:11   the advice of the p and of the owner of   3237
Jas   3: 4   a very small rudder wherever the p wants   3995

PILTAI (1)
Ne 12:17   of Miniamin's and of Moadiah's, P;   7122

PIN (6)
Jdg 16:13   and tighten it with the p,   3845
    16:14   and tightened it with the p.   3845
    16:14   from his sleep and pulled up the p and   3845
1Sa 18:11   *"I'll* p David to the wall."   5782
    19:10   to p him to the wall with his spear,   5782
    26: 8   Now *let me* p him to the ground   5782

PINE (18) [PINES]
1Ki   5: 8   in providing the cedar and p logs.   1360
    5:10   with all the cedar and p logs he wanted,   1360
    6:15   the floor of the temple with planks of p.   1360
    6:34   He also made two p doors,   1360
    9:11   the cedar and p and gold he wanted.   1360
2Ch   2: 8   p and algum logs from Lebanon,   1360
    3: 5   with p and covered it with fine gold   1360+6770
Ps 104:17   the stork has its home in the p trees.   1360
Isa 14: 8   the p trees and the cedars of Lebanon exult   1360
    19: 8   on the water *will* **p away.**   581
    44:14   or planted a p, and the rain made it grow.   815
    55:13   of the thornbush will grow the p tree,   1360
    60:13   glory of Lebanon will come to you, the p,   1360
Eze 27: 5   They made all your timbers of p trees   1360
    31: 8   nor could the p trees equal its boughs.   1360
Hos 14: 8   I am like a green p tree;   1360
Na   2: 3   the **spears of** p are brandished.   1360
Zec 11: 2   Wail, O p tree, for the cedar has fallen;   1360

PINES (4) [PINE]
1Sa   2: 5   but she who has had many sons p away.   581
2Ki 19:23   its tallest cedars, the choicest of its p.   1360
Isa 37:24   its tallest cedars, the choicest of its p.   1360
    41:19   I will set p in the wasteland,   1360

PINIONS (2)
Dt 32:11   to catch them and carries them on its p.   89
Job 39:13   with the p and feathers *of* the stork.   89

PINON (2)
Ge 36:41   Oholibamah, Elah, P,   7091
1Ch   1:52   Oholibamah, Elah, P,   7091

PINS (KJV) See TENT PEGS

PINT (1)
Jn 12: 3   Then Mary took *about a* p of pure nard,   *3354*

PIPES (4)
Da   3: 5   zither, lyre, harp, p and all kinds of music,   10507
    3:10   p and all kinds of music must fall down   10507
    3:15   zither, lyre, harp, p and all kinds of music,   10507
Zec   4:12   the two gold p that pour out golden oil?"   7574

PIRAM (1)
Jos 10: 3   P king of Jarmuth, Japhia king of Lachish   7231

PIRATHON (2) [PIRATHONITE]
Jdg 12:13   After him, Abdon son of Hillel, *from* P,   7285
    12:15   and was buried at P in Ephraim,   7284

PIRATHONITE (3) [PIRATHON]
2Sa 23:30   Benaiah the P, Hiddai from the ravines   7285
1Ch 11:31   from Gibeah in Benjamin, Benaiah the P,   7285
    27:14   for the eleventh month, was Benaiah the P,   7285

PISGAH (8)
Nu 21:20   in Moab where the top of P overlooks   7171
    23:14   to the field of Zophim on the top of P,   7171
Dt   3:17   below the slopes of P.   7171
    3:27   up to the top of P and look west and north   7171
    4:49   below the slopes of P.   7171
    34: 1   from the plains of Moab to the top of P,   7171
Jos 12: 3   and then southward below the slopes of P.   7171
    13:20   Beth Peor, the slopes of P,   7171

PISHON (1)
Ge   2:11   The name of the first is the P;   7093

PISIDIA (1)
Ac 14:24   After going through P, they came into   *4407*

PISIDIAN (1)
Ac 13:14   From Perga they went on to P Antioch.   *4408*

PISON (KJV) See PISHON

PISPAH (1)
1Ch   7:38   The sons of Jether: Jephunneh, P and Ara.   7183

PISS (KJV) See URINE

PISSETH (KJV) See MALE

PISTACHIO (1)
Ge 43:11   some p nuts and almonds.   1063

PIT (66) [PITS]
Ex 21:33   "If a man uncovers a p or digs one and fails   1014
    21:34   the owner of the p must pay for the loss;   1014
2Sa 18:17   into a big p in the forest and piled up   7074
    23:20   He also went down into a p on a snowy day   1014
1Ch 11:22   He also went down into a p on a snowy day   1014
Job   9:31   you would plunge me into a **slime p** so that   8846
    33:18   to preserve his soul from the p,   8846
    33:22   His soul draws near to the p,   8846
    33:24   'Spare him from going down to the p;   8846
    33:28   from going down to the p,   8846
    33:30   to turn back his soul from the p,   8846
Ps   7:15   into the p he has made.   8846
    9:15   into the p they have dug;   8846
    28: 1   be like those who have gone down to the p.   1014
    30: 3   you spared me from going down into the p.   1014
    30: 9   in my going down to the p?   8846
    35: 7   and without cause dug a p for me,   8846
    35: 8   may they fall into the p, to their ruin.   2023S
    40: 2   He lifted me out of the **slimy p,**   1014+8622
    55:23   down the wicked into the p of corruption;   931
    57: 6   They dug a p in my path—   8864
    69:15   up or the p close its mouth over me.   931
    88: 4   among those who go down to the p;   1014
    88: 6   You have put me in the lowest p,   1014
    94:13   till a p is dug for the wicked.   8846
  103: 4   who redeems your life from the p and   8846

Ps	143: 7	I will be like those who go down to the **p**.	1014
Pr	1:12	like those who go down to the **p**;	1014
	22:14	The mouth of an adulteress is a deep **p**;	8757
	23:27	for a prostitute is a deep **p**	8757
	26:27	If a man digs a **p**, he will fall into it;	8846
Ecc	10: 8	Whoever digs a **p** may fall into it;	1585
Isa	14:15	to the grave, to the depths of the **p**.	1014
	14:19	those who descend to the stones of the **p**.	1014
	24:17	Terror and **p** and snare await you,	7074
	24:18	at the sound of terror will fall into a **p**;	7074
	24:18	whoever climbs out of the **p** will be caught	7074
	30:33	Its **fire p** has been made deep and wide,	4509
	38:17	In your love you kept me from the **p**	8846
	38:18	to the **p** cannot hope for your faithfulness.	1014
Jer	18:20	Yet they have dug a **p** for me.	8757
	18:22	a **p** to capture me and have hidden snares	8757
	48:43	Terror and **p** and snare await you,	7074
	48:44	into a **p**, whoever climbs out of the pit will	7074
	48:44	whoever climbs out of the **p** will be caught	7074
La	3:53	to end my life in a **p** and threw stones	1014
	3:55	O LORD, from the depths of the **p**.	1014
Eze	19: 4	and he was trapped in their **p**.	8846
	19: 8	and he was trapped in their **p**.	8846
	26:20	down with those who go down to the **p**,	1014
	26:20	with those who go down to the **p**,	1014
	28: 8	They will bring you down to the **p**,	8846
	31:14	with those who go down to the **p**.	1014
	31:16	the grave with those who go down to the **p**.	1014
	32:18	with those who go down to the **p**.	1014
	32:23	of the **p** and her army lies around her grave.	1014
	32:24	with those who go down to the **p**;	1014
	32:25	with those who go down to the **p**;	1014
	32:29	with those who go down to the **p**.	1014
	32:30	with those who go down to the **p**.	1014
Jnh	2: 6	But you brought my life up from the **p**,	8846
Zec	9:11	your prisoners from the waterless **p**.	1014
Mt	12:11	a sheep and it falls into a **p** on the Sabbath,	1073
	15:14	leads a blind man, both will fall into a **p**."	1073
Mk	12: 1	dug a **p** for the winepress and	5700
Lk	6:39	Will they not both fall into a **p**?	1073

PITCH (11) [PITCHED]

Ge	6:14	make rooms in it and coat it with **p** inside	4109
Ex	2: 3	for him and coated it with tar and **p**.	2413
	33: 7	to take a tent and **p** it outside the camp	5742
Pr	20:20	his lamp will be snuffed out in **p darkness**.	854+3125
Isa	13:20	no Arab will **p** his **tent** there,	182
	34: 9	Edom's streams will be turned into **p**,	2413
	34: 9	her land will become blazing **p**!	2413
Jer	6: 3	they will **p** their tents around her,	9546
	10:20	now to **p** my tent or to set up my shelter.	5742
Eze	25: 4	up their camps and **p** their tents	5989
Da	11:45	He will **p** his royal tents between the seas	5749

PITCH-DARK (1) [DARK]

Am	5:20	**p**, without a ray of brightness?	695

PITCHED (15) [PITCH]

Ge	12: 8	the hills east of Bethel and **p** his tent,	5742
	13:12	of the plain and **p** his **tents** near Sodom.	182
	26:25	There he **p** his tent,	5742
	31:25	Jacob had **p** his tent in the hill country	9546
	33:19	the plot of ground where he **p** his tent.	5742
	35:21	Israel moved on again and **p** his tent	5742
Jdg	4:11	**p** his tent by the great tree in Zaanannim	5742
	20:19	the Israelites got up and **p camp**	2837
1Sa	17: 1	**They p camp** at Ephes Dammim,	2837
2Sa	6:17	in its place inside the tent that David had **p**	5742
	16:22	So they **p** a tent for Absalom on the roof,	5742
1Ch	15: 1	a place for the ark of God and **p** a tent	5742
	16: 1	and set it inside the tent that David had **p**	5742
2Ch	1: 4	because he had **p** a tent for it in Jerusalem.	5742
Ps	19: 4	In the heavens he has **p** a tent for the sun,	8492

PITCHER (1) [PITCHERS]

Ecc	12: 6	before the **p** is shattered at the spring,	3902

PITCHERS (4) [PITCHER]

Ex	25:29	as its **p** and bowls for the pouring out	7987
	37:16	its plates and dishes and bowls and its **p** for	7987
1Ch	28:17	sprinkling bowls and **p**;	7987
Mk	7: 4	such as the washing of cups, **p** and kettles.)	3829

PITFALLS (2)

Ps	119:85	arrogant dig **p** for me, contrary to your law.	8864
La	3:47	We have suffered terror and **p**,	7074

PITHOM (1)

Ex	1:11	and they built **P** and Rameses as store cities	7351

PITHON (2)

1Ch	8:35	**P**, Melech, Tarea and Ahaz.	7094
	9:41	**P**, Melech, Tahrea and Ahaz.	7094

PITIED (2) [PITY]

Ps	106:46	to be **p** by all who held them captive.	8171
1Co	15:19	we are to be **p more than** all men.	1795

PITIFUL (1) [PITY]

Rev	3:17	you do not realize that you are wretched, **p**,	1795

PITS (5) [PIT]

Ge	14:10	the Valley of Siddim was **full of** tar **p**,	931+931
1Sa	13: 6	among the rocks, and in **p** and cisterns.	7663
Ps	140:10	into **miry p**, never to rise.	4549
Isa	42:22	all of them trapped in **p** or hidden away	2987
Zep	2: 9	a place of weeds and salt **p**,	4838

PITTANCE (1)

Ps	44:12	You sold your people for a **p**,	2104+4202

PITY (44) [PITIED, PITIFUL]

Dt	7:16	*Do not* look on them **with p**	2571+6524
	13: 8	**Show** him no **p**.	2571+6524
	19:13	**Show** him no **p**.	2571+6524
	19:21	**Show** no **p**: life for life,	2571+6524
	25:12	shall cut off her hand. **Show** her no **p**.	2571+6524
2Sa	12: 6	because he did such a thing and **had** no **p**."	2858
2Ch	36:15	because he **had p** on his people and	2798
Job	16:13	Without **p**, he pierces my kidneys	2798
	19:21	"**Have p** on me, my friends, have pity,	2858
	19:21	"Have pity on me, my friends, **have p**,	2858
Ps	72:13	*He will* take **p** on the weak and the needy	2571
	102:14	her very dust **moves** them to **p**.	2858
	109:12	to him or **take p** on his fatherless children.	2858
Ecc	4:10	But **p** the man who falls and has no one	365
Isa	9:17	nor will he **p** the fatherless and widows,	8163
Jer	13:14	*I will* allow no **p** or mercy	2798
	15: 5	"Who *will* have **p** on you, O Jerusalem?	2798
	16: 5	my love and my **p** from this people,"	8171
	20:16	the towns the LORD overthrew without **p**,	5714
	21: 7	he will show them no mercy or **p**	2798
La	2: 2	Without **p** the Lord has swallowed up all	2798
	2:17	He has overthrown you without **p**,	2798
	2:21	you have slaughtered them without **p**.	2798
	3:43	you have slain without **p**.	2798
Eze	5:11	I will not **look** *on* you **with p**	2571+6524
	7: 4	I will not **look** *on* you **with p**	2571+6524
	7: 9	I will not **look** *on* you **with p**	2571+6524
	8:18	I will not **look** on them **with p**	2571+6524
	9: 5	without **showing p** or compassion.	2571+6524
	9:10	I will not **look** *on* you **with p**	2571+6524
	16: 5	No one **looked** on you **with p**	2571+6524
	20:17	Yet I **looked** on them **with p**	2571+6524
	24:14	*I will* not **have p**, nor will I relent.	2571
Joel	2:14	He may turn and **have p** and leave behind	5714
	2:18	for his land and **take p** on his people.	2798
Zec	11: 6	to bring disaster upon you and **showed** no **p**	5714
	11: 6	For *I will* no longer **have p** on the people	2798
Mt	18:27	The servant's master **took p** on him,	5072
Mk	9:22	**take p** on us and help us."	5072
Lk	10:33	and when he saw him, *he* **took p** on him.	5072
	16:24	**have p** on me and send Lazarus to dip	1796
	17:13	"Jesus, Master, **have p** on us!"	1796
1Jn	3:17	and sees his brother in need but **has no p**	3091+3836+5073

PLACE (792) [PLACED, PLACES, PLACING]

Ge	1: 9	under the sky be gathered to one **p**,	5226
	2:21	of the man's ribs and closed up the **p**	9393
	4:25	"God has granted me another child **in p** of	9393
	8: 9	But the dove could find no **p** to set its feet	4955
	13: 3	he went **from p to place** until he came	4200+5023
	13: 3	he went **from place to p** until he came	4200+5023
	13: 3	to the **p** between Bethel and Ai	5226
	18:24	not spare the **p** for the sake of the fifty	5226
	18:26	I will spare the whole **p** for their sake."	5226
	19:13	because we are going to destroy this **p**.	5226
	19:14	He said, "Hurry and get out of this **p**,	5226
	19:27	and returned to the **p** where he had stood	5226
	20:11	'There is surely no fear of God in this **p**,	5226
	21:31	So that **p** was called Beersheba,	5226
	22: 3	he set out for the **p** God had told him about.	5226
	22: 4	looked up and saw the **p** in the distance.	5226
	22: 9	they reached the **p** God had told him about,	5226
	22:14	that **p** The LORD Will Provide.	5226
	24:31	I have prepared the house and a **p** for	5226
	26: 7	the men of that **p** asked him about his wife,	5226
	26: 7	of this **p** might kill me on account	5226
	28:11	When he reached a certain **p**,	5226
	28:16	he thought, "Surely the LORD is in this **p**,	5226
	28:17	"How awesome is this **p**!	5226
	28:19	He called that **p** Bethel.	5226
	29: 3	Then they would return the stone to its **p**	5226
	29:22	the people of the **p** and gave a feast.	5226
	30: 2	"Am I **in the p** of God,	9393
	30:41	Jacob *would* **p** the branches in the troughs	8492
	30:42	he *would* not **p** them there.	8492
	32: 2	So he named that **p** Mahanaim.	5226
	32:30	So Jacob called the **p** Peniel, saying,	5226
	33:17	a **p** for himself and made shelters	1074
	33:17	That is why the **p** is called Succoth.	5226
	35: 7	and he called the **p** El Bethel,	5226
	35:13	up from him at the **p** where he had talked	5226
	35:14	a stone pillar at the **p** where God had talked	5226
	35:15	Jacob called the **p** where God had talked	5226
	39:20	and put him in prison, the **p** where	5226
	42:15	as Pharaoh lives, you will not leave **this** *p*	AIT
	42:27	**p** where they stopped for the night	4869

Ge	43:21	**p** where we stopped for the night	4869
	43:30	Joseph hurried out and looked for a **p**	NIH
	44:33	as my lord's slave **in p** of the boy,	9393
	49:15	When he sees how good is his **resting p** and	4957
	49:30	as a burial **p** from Ephron the Hittite,	299
	50:11	That is why **that p** near the Jordan	2023S
	50:13	which Abraham had bought as a burial **p**	299
	50:19	Am I **in** *the* **p** of God?	9393
	50:25	you must carry my bones up from **this p**."	AIT
Ex	3: 5	"Take off your sandals, for the **p**	5226
	4:24	At a **lodging p** on the way,	4869
	9:19	**bring** your livestock and everything you have in the field **to a p of** shelter,	6395
	9:26	The only **p** it did not hail was the land	9004
	10:23	No one could see anyone else or leave his **p**	9393
	13:19	carry my bones up with you from **this p**."	AIT
	13:22	by night **left** *its* **p** in front of the people.	4631
	14:27	and at daybreak the sea went back to its **p**.	419
	15:17	the **p**, O LORD, you made for your dwelling,	4806
	15:23	(That is why **the p** is called Marah.)	2023S
	16:33	Then **p** it before the LORD to be kept for	5663
	17: 1	**traveling from p to place** as the LORD	5023
	17: 1	**traveling from place to p** as the LORD	5023
	17: 7	And he called the **p** Massah and Meribah	5226
	21:13	he is to flee to a **p** I will designate.	5226
	23:20	and to bring you to the **p** I have prepared.	5226
	25:21	**P** the cover on top of the ark and put in	5989
	26:33	the curtain from the clasps and **p** the ark of	995
	26:33	The curtain will separate the Holy **P** from	7731
	26:33	the Holy Place from the **Most Holy P**.	7731+7731
	26:34	of the Testimony in the **Most Holy P**.	7731+7731
	26:35	**P** the table outside the curtain on	8492
	28:29	"Whenever Aaron enters the **Holy P**,	7731
	28:35	be heard when he enters the **Holy P** before	7731
	28:43	the altar to minister in the **Holy P**,	7731
	29:30	in the **Holy P** is to wear them seven days.	7731
	29:31	and cook the meat in a sacred **p**.	5226
	29:43	and the **p** will be consecrated by my glory.	NIH
	30:18	**P** it between the Tent of Meeting	5989
	30:36	Grind some of it to powder and **p** it in front	5989
	31:11	and fragrant incense for the **Holy P**.	7731
	32:34	Now go, lead the people to **the p** I spoke of,	889S
	33: 1	the LORD said to Moses, "Leave this **p**,	NIH
	33:21	"There is a **p** near me where you may stand	NIH
	40: 3	**P** the ark of the Testimony in it and shield	8492
	40: 5	**P** the gold altar of incense in front of	5989
	40: 6	"**P** the altar of burnt offering in front of	5989
	40: 7	**p** the basin between the Tent of Meeting	5989
	40: 8	set up the tabernacle, he **put** the bases in **p**,	5989
Lev	4:12	the camp to a **p** ceremonially clean,	5226
	4:24	on the goat's head and slaughter it at the **p**	5226
	4:29	the sin offering and slaughter it at the **p** of	5226
	4:33	and slaughter it for a sin offering at the **p**	5226
	6:10	on the altar and **p** them beside the altar.	8492
	6:11	and carry the ashes outside the camp to a **p**	5226
	6:16	it is to be eaten without yeast in a holy **p**;	5226
	6:25	be slaughtered before the LORD in the **p**	5226
	6:26	it is to be eaten in a holy **p**,	5226
	6:27	you must wash it in a holy **p**.	5226
	6:30	to make atonement in the **Holy P** must not	7731
	7: 2	to be slaughtered in the **p** where	5226
	7: 6	but it must be eaten in a holy **p**;	5226
	10:13	Eat it in a holy **p**, because it is your share	5226
	10:14	Eat them in a ceremonially clean **p**;	5226
	10:18	its blood was not taken into the **Holy P**,	7731
	13:19	and in the **p** where the boil was,	5226
	14:13	to slaughter the lamb in the holy **p** where	5226
	14:40	and thrown into an unclean **p** outside	5226
	14:41	into an unclean **p** outside the town.	5226
	14:45	and taken out of the town to an unclean **p**.	5226
	15:31	for defiling my **dwelling p**,	5438
	16: 2	the **Most Holy P** behind the curtain in front	7731
	16:16	make atonement for the **Most Holy P**	7731
	16:17	in to make atonement in the **Most Holy P**	7731
	16:20	making atonement for the **Most Holy P**,	7731
	16:22	on itself all their sins to a solitary **p**;	824
	16:23	on before he entered the **Most Holy P**,	7731
	16:24	in a holy **p** and put on his regular garments.	5226
	16:27	the **Most Holy P** to make atonement, must	7731
	16:33	make atonement for the **Most Holy P**,	5219+7731
	21:11	not enter a **p** where there is a dead body.	NIH
	22:22	*Do not* **p** any of these on the altar as	5989
	24: 9	who are to eat it in a holy **p**,	5226
	26: 1	not **p** a carved stone in your land to bow	5989
	26:11	I will put my **dwelling p** among you,	5438
Nu	2:17	each in his own **p** under his standard.	3338
	3:12	from among the Israelites **in p** of	9393
	3:41	the Levites for me **in p** of all the firstborn	9393
	3:41	and the livestock of the Levites **in p** of all	9393
	3:45	"Take the Levites **in p** of all the firstborn	9393
	3:45	and the livestock of the Levites **in p** of	9393
	4: 6	and **put** the poles **in p**.	8492
	4: 8	and **put** its poles **in p**.	8492
	4:11	and **put** its poles **in p**.	8492
	4:14	*to* **p** on it all the utensils used	5989
	4:14	and **put** its poles **in p**.	8492
	5:18	he shall loosen her hair and **p** in her hands	5989
	6:19	*to* **p** in his hands a boiled shoulder of	5989
	8:16	I have taken them as my own **in p** of	9393
	8:18	the Levites **in p** of all the firstborn sons	9393
	10:12	**traveled from p to place** until the cloud	5023
	10:12	**traveled from place to p** until the cloud	5023
	10:29	"We are setting out for the **p** about which	5226
	10:33	to find them a **p** to rest.	4957
	11: 3	So that **p** was called Taberah,	5226
	11:34	the **p** was named Kibroth Hattaavah,	5226
	13:24	That **p** was called the Valley of Eshcol	5226

Nu	14:40	up to the **p** the LORD promised." 5226
	17: 4	**P** them in the Tent of Meeting in front of 5663
	19: 9	in a ceremonially clean **p** outside the camp. 5226
	20: 5	up out of Egypt to this terrible **p**? 5226
	21: 3	so the **p** was named Hormah. 5226
	22:26	in a narrow **p** where there was no room 5226
	23:13	to another **p** where you can see them; 5226
	23:27	"Come, let me take you to another **p**. 5226
	24:21	"Your **dwelling p** is secure, 4632
	32:14	standing in the **p** of your fathers 9393
	32:17	until we have brought them to their **p**. 5226
	35:15	These six towns will be a **p** of refuge 5236
Dt	1:31	the way you went until you reached this **p**." 5226
	2:12	from before them and settled **in** their p, 9393
	2:21	who drove them **out** and settled in their **p**. 9393
	2:22	and have lived in their **p** to this day. 9393
	2:23	and settled in their **p**.) 9393
	11: 5	in the desert until you arrived at this **p**, 5226
	11:24	Every **p** where you set your foot will 5226
	12: 5	to the **p** the LORD your God will choose 5226
	12: 5	To **that p** you must go; 9004S
	12: 9	not yet reached the **resting p** and 4957
	12:11	the **p** the LORD your God will choose as 5226
	12:14	at the **p** the LORD will choose in one 5226
	12:18	the **p** the LORD your God will choose— 5226
	12:21	the **p** where the LORD your God chooses 5226
	12:26	and go to the **p** the LORD will choose. 5226
	13: 2	or wonder of which he has spoken **takes p**, 995
	14:23	at the **p** he will choose as a dwelling 5226
	14:24	But if that **p** is too distant NIH
	14:24	and cannot carry your tithe (because the **p** 5226
	14:25	and take the silver with you and go to the **p** 5226
	15:20	at the **p** he will choose. 5226
	16: 2	the **p** the LORD will choose as a dwelling 5226
	16: 6	except in the **p** he will choose as a dwelling 5226
	16: 7	at the **p** the LORD your God will choose. 5226
	16:11	at the **p** he will choose as a dwelling 5226
	16:15	the Feast to the LORD your God at the **p** 5226
	16:16	at the **p** he will choose: 5226
	17: 8	to the **p** the LORD your God will choose. 5226
	17:10	to the decisions they give you at the **p** 5226
	17:15	*Do* not a **p** foreigner over you, 5989
	18: 6	and comes in all earnestness to the **p** 5226
	18:22	of the LORD *does* not **take p** or come true, 2118
	23:12	a **p** outside the camp where you can go 3338
	26: 2	the **p** the LORD your God will choose as 5226
	26: 9	to this **p** and gave us this land, 5226
	26:10	**P** the basket before the LORD your God 5663
	26:15	down from heaven, your holy **dwelling p**, 5061
	28:65	no **resting p** for the sole of your foot. 4955
	29: 7	When you reached this **p**, 5226
	31:11	at the **p** he will choose, 5226
	31:26	"Take this Book of the Law and **p** it beside 8492
Jos	1: 3	I will give you every **p** where you set 5226
	4: 3	over with you and put them down at the **p** 4869
	4:18	the waters of the Jordan returned to their **p** 5226
	5: 7	So he raised up their sons in their **p**, 9393
	5: 9	So the **p** has been called Gilgal to this day. 5226
	5:15	for the **p** where you are standing is holy." 5226
	6:23	and put them in a **p** outside the camp NIH
	7:26	Therefore that **p** has been called the Valley 5226
	8: 9	and they went to the **p of ambush** and lay 4422
	8:14	at a **certain p** overlooking the Arabah. 4595
	8:28	heap of ruins, a **desolate p** to this day. 9039
	9:27	and for the altar of the LORD at the **p** 5226
	20: 4	into their city and give him a **p** to live 5226
	24:26	up there under the oak near the **holy p** of 5219
Jdg	2: 5	and they called that **p** Bokim. 5226
	6:20	**p** them on this rock, 5663
	6:37	I *will* a wool fleece on the threshing floor. 3657
	7: 7	Let all the other men go, each to his own **p**. 5226
	9:35	soldiers came out from their **hiding p**. 4422
	15:17	through your country to our own **p**.' 5226
	15:17	and the **p** was called Ramath Lehi. 5226
	15:19	God opened up the **hollow p** in Lehi, 4847
	16: 2	So they surrounded the **p** and lay in wait NIH
	17: 8	that town in search of **some other p** to stay. 889S
	17: 9	he said, "and I'm looking for a **p** to stay." 889S
	18: 1	of the Danites was seeking a **p** of their own 5709
	18: 3	What are you doing in **this p**? AIT
	18:12	This is why the **p** west of Kiriath Jearim 5226
	18:15	the house of the young Levite at Micah's **p** 1074
	19:16	(the men of the **p** were Benjamites), 5226
	20:33	the Israelite ambush charged out of its **p** on 5226
	21:24	the Israelites left **that p** and went home 9004S
Ru	1: 7	the **p** where she had been living and set out 5226
	2:19	the one at whose **p** she had been working. NIH
	3: 4	note the **p** where he is lying. 5226
1Sa	2:20	to **take the p** of the one she prayed for 9393
	3: 2	was lying down in his usual **p**. 5226
	3: 9	So Samuel went and lay down in his **p**. 5226
	5: 3	and put him back in his **p**, 5226
	5:11	let it go back to its own **p**, 5226
	6: 2	Tell us how we should send it back to its **p**." 5226
	6:21	Come down and take it up to your **p**." NIH
	9:12	for the people have a sacrifice at the **high p**. 1195
	9:13	before he goes up to the **high p** to eat. 1195
	9:14	toward them on his way up to the **high p**. 1195
	9:19	"Go up ahead of me to the **high p**, 1195
	9:25	After they came down from the **high p** to 1195
	10: 5	of prophets coming down from the **high p** 1195
	10:13	he went to the **high p**. 1195
	12: 8	of Egypt and settled them in this **p**. 5226
	20:19	go to the **p** where you hid when this trouble 5226
	20:25	He sat in his customary **p** by the wall, 4632
	20:25	but David's **p** was empty. 5226
	20:27	David's **p** was empty again. 5226

1Sa	20:37	to the **p** where Jonathan's arrow had fallen, 5226
	21: 2	I have told them to meet me at a certain **p**. 5226
	23:13	**moving from p to place.** 889+928+2143+2143
	23:13	**moving from place to p.** 889+928+2143+2143
	23:28	why they call this **p** Sela Hammahlekoth. 5226
	26: 5	and went to the **p** where Saul had camped. 5226
	27: 5	let a **p** be assigned to me in one of 5226
	29: 4	to the **p** you assigned him. 5226
2Sa	2:16	So that **p** in Gibeon was called 5226
	2:23	to the **p** where Asahel had fallen and died. 5226
	5:20	So that **p** was called Baal Perazim. 5226
	6: 8	and to this day that **p** is called Perez Uzzah. 5226
	6:17	the LORD and set it in its **p** inside the tent 5226
	7: 6	**moving from p to place** with a tent 2143
	7: 6	**moving from place to p** with a tent 2143
	7:10	a **p** for my people Israel and will plant them 5226
	11:16	he put Uriah at a **p** where he knew 5226
	15:17	and they halted at a **p** some distance away. 1074
	15:25	and let me see it and his **dwelling p** again. 5659
	16: 8	Saul, **in** whose **p** you have reigned. 9393
	17: 9	he is hidden in a cave or some other **p**. 5226
	17:25	over the army **in p** of Joab. 9393
	18: 6	the battle **took p** in the forest of Ephraim. 2118
	19:13	the commander of my army **in p** of Joab.' " 9393
	19:28	but *you* **gave** your servant a **p** among 8883
	21: 5	and *have* no **p** anywhere in Israel, 3656
	21:20	In still another battle, *which* **took p** at Gath, 2118
	22:20	He brought me out into a **spacious p**; 5303
	23:11	When the Philistines banded together at a **p** NIH
1Ki	1:30	and he will sit on my throne in my **p**." 9393
	1:35	and sit on my throne and reign in my **p**. 9393
	3: 4	for that was the most important **high p**, 1195
	3: 7	you have made your servant king in **p** of 9393
	4:28	brought to the **proper** 889+2118+5226+9004
	5: 5	the throne **in** your **p** will build the temple 9393
	5: 9	in rafts by sea to the **p** you specify. 5226
	6:16	an inner sanctuary, the **Most Holy P**. 7731+7731
	7:50	the innermost room, the **Most Holy P**, 7731+7731
	8: 6	to its **p** in the inner sanctuary of the temple, 5226
	8: 6	of the temple, the **Most Holy P**, 7731+7731
	8: 7	The cherubim spread their wings over the **p** 5226
	8: 8	the **Holy P** in front of the inner sanctuary. 7731
	8: 8	but not from outside the Holy **P**; NIH
	8:10	the priests withdrew from the **Holy P**, 7731
	8:13	a **p** for you to dwell forever." 4806
	8:21	I have provided a **p** there for the ark, 5226
	8:29	this **p** of which you said, 'My Name 5226
	8:29	the prayer your servant prays toward this **p**. 5226
	8:30	when they pray toward this **p**. 5226
	8:30	Hear from heaven, your **dwelling p**, 5226
	8:35	toward this **p** and confess your name 5226
	8:39	then hear from heaven, your **dwelling p**, 4806
	8:43	then hear from heaven, your **dwelling p**, 4806
	8:49	then from heaven, your **dwelling p**, 4806
	11: 7	a **high p** for Chemosh the detestable god 1195
	13:16	or drink water with you in this **p**. 5226
	13:22	and drank water in the **p** he told you 5226
	17: 9	I have commanded a widow **in that p** 9004S
	21: 6	I will give you another vineyard **in** its **p**.' 9393
	21: 9	of fasting and seat Naboth in a **prominent p** 8031
	21:12	and seated Naboth in a **prominent p** among 8031
	21:19	the **p** where dogs licked up Naboth's blood, 5226
2Ki	2: 7	the **p** where Elijah and Elisha had stopped NIH
	3:25	was left with its stones in **p**, NIH
	6: 1	the **p** where we meet with you is too small 5226
	6: 2	and let us build a **p** there for us to live." 5226
	6: 6	When he showed him the **p**, 5226
	6: 6	up my camp in such and such a **p**." 5226
	6: 9	"Beware of passing that **p**, NIH
	6:10	king of Israel checked on the **p** indicated by 5226
	11:16	as she reached the **p** *where* the horses enter 2006
	11:19	king then **took** *his* **p** on the royal throne, 3782
	14:21	and made him king in **p** of 9393
	17: 7	*All this* **took p** because the Israelites 2118
	17:11	At every **high p** they burned incense, 1195
	18:25	to attack and destroy this **p** without word 5226
	21:24	and they made Josiah his son king **in** his **p**. 9393
	22:16	to bring disaster on this **p** and its people, 5226
	22:17	my anger will burn against this **p** and will 5226
	22:19	against this **p** and its people, 5226
	22:20	the disaster I am going to bring on this **p**.' " 5226
	23:15	the **high p** made by Jeroboam son of Nebat, 1195
	23:15	even that altar and **high p** he demolished. 1195
	23:15	the **high p** and ground it to powder, 1195
	23:30	and made him king in **p** of his father. 9393
	23:34	of Josiah king in **p** of his father Josiah 9393
	24:17	king in his **p** and changed his name 9393
1Ch	4:41	Then they settled **in** their **p**, 9393
	6:49	all that was done in the **Most Holy P**, 7731+7731
	11:13	a **p** where there was a field full of barley, NIH
	13:11	and to this day that **p** is called Perez Uzzah. 5226
	14:11	So that **p** was called Baal Perazim. 5226
	15: 1	a **p** for the ark of God and pitched a tent 5226
	15: 3	the LORD to the **p** he had prepared for it. 5226
	15:12	to the **p** I have prepared for it. NIH
	16:27	strength and joy in his **dwelling p**. 5226
	16:39	the tabernacle of the LORD at the **high p** 1195
	17: 5	from one **dwelling p** to another. 5438
	17: 9	a **p** for my people Israel and will plant them 5226
	20: 1	In still another battle, *which* **took p** at Gath, 2118
	21:29	at that time on the **high p** at Gibeon. 1195
	23:32	the Tent of Meeting for the **Holy P** and, 7731
	28: 2	to build a house as a **p of rest** for the ark of 4957
	28:11	its inner rooms and the **p** of atonement. 1074
	29:23	on the throne of the LORD as king in **p** of 9393
2Ch	1: 3	and the whole assembly went to the **high p** 1195
	1: 4	to **the p** he had prepared for it, 2021S

2Ch	1: 8	and have made me king **in his p**. 9393
	1:13	to Jerusalem from the **high p** at Gibeon, 1195
	2: 6	except as a **p** to burn sacrifices before him? NIH
	3: 1	the **p** provided by David. 5226
	3: 8	He built the **Most Holy P**, 7731+7731
	3:10	In the Most Holy **P** he made a pair 1074
	4:22	the inner doors to the **Most Holy P** 7731+7731
	5: 7	to its **p** in the inner sanctuary of the temple, 5226
	5: 7	of the temple, the **Most Holy P**, 7731+7731
	5: 9	The cherubim spread their wings over the **p** 5226
	5: 9	but not from outside the Holy **P**; NIH
	5:11	priests then withdrew from the **Holy P**. 7731
	6: 2	a **p** for you to dwell forever." 4806
	6:20	toward this temple day and night, this **p** 5226
	6:20	the prayer your servant prays toward this **p**. 5226
	6:21	when they pray toward this **p**. 5226
	6:21	Hear from heaven, your **dwelling p**; 5226
	6:26	toward this **p** and confess your name 5226
	6:30	then hear from heaven, your **dwelling p**. 4806
	6:33	then hear from heaven, your **dwelling p**, 4806
	6:39	then from heaven, your **dwelling p**, 4806
	6:40	to the prayers offered in this **p**. 5226
	6:41	and come to your **resting p**, 5665
	7:12	and have chosen this **p** for myself as 5226
	7:15	to the prayers offered in this **p**. 5226
	20:24	the **p that overlooks** the desert and looked 5205
	22: 1	Jehoram's youngest son, king **in his p**, 9393
	24:11	the chest and carry it back to its **p**. 5226
	26: 1	made him king **in p** of his father Amaziah 9393
	29: 6	faces away from the LORD's **dwelling p** 5438
	30:27	reached heaven, his holy **dwelling p** 5061
	33:25	and they made Josiah his son king **in his p**. 9393
	34:24	to bring disaster on this **p** and its people— 5226
	34:25	my anger will be poured out on this **p** 5226
	34:27	against this **p** and its people, 5226
	34:28	the disaster I am going to bring on this **p** 5226
	35: 5	in the **holy p** with a group of Levites 7731
	36: 1	and made him king in Jerusalem **in p** of 9393
	36:15	on his people and on his **dwelling p**. 5061
Ezr	1: 4	the people of any **p** where survivors may 5226
	4:15	a **p** of rebellion from ancient times. 10089+10135+10193S
	4:19	and has been a **p** of rebellion 10089+10193S
	6: 3	be rebuilt as a **p** to present sacrifices, 10087
	9: 8	and giving us a **firm p** in his sanctuary, 3845
Ne	1: 9	and bring them to the **p** I have chosen as 5226
	3: 1	They dedicated it and **set** its doors in **p**, 6641
	3: 3	**put** its doors and bolts and bars in **p**. 6641
	3: 6	**put** its doors and bolts and bars in **p**. 6641
	3:13	**put** its doors and bolts and bars in **p**. 6641
	3:14	**put** its doors and bolts and bars in **p**. 6641
	3:15	**putting** its doors and bolts and bars in **p**. 6641
	7: 1	**set** the doors in **p**, 6641
Est	2: 9	and moved her and her maids into the **best p** AIT
	4:14	for the Jews will arise from another **p**, 5226
Job	7:10	his **p** will know him no more. 5226
	8: 6	and restore you to your rightful **p**. 5661
	8:17	of rocks and looks for a **p** among the stones. AIT
	8:18	that **p** disowns it and says, NIH
	9: 6	from its **p** and makes its pillars tremble. 5226
	10:21	before I go to the **p** of no return, NIH
	14:18	and as a rock is moved from its **p**, 5226
	16: 4	if you were **in** my **p**, 9393
	18: 4	Or must the rocks be moved from their **p**? 5226
	18:21	such is the **p** of *one* who knows not God." 5226
	20: 9	his **p** will look on him no more. 5226
	27:21	it sweeps him out of his **p**. 5226
	27:23	in derision and hisses him out of his **p**. 5226
	28: 1	for silver and a **p** where gold is refined. 5226
	30:23	to the **p** appointed for all the living. 1074
	34:22	There is no **dark p**, no deep shadow, 3125
	34:24	the mighty and sets up others **in** their **p**. 9393
	36:16	the jaws of distress to a **spacious p** free 8144
	37: 1	and leaps from its **p**. 5226
	38:10	and set its doors and bars in **p**, 8492
	38:12	or shown the dawn its **p**, 5226
	38:24	to the **p** where the lightning is dispersed, NIH
	38:24	or the **p** where the east winds are scattered NIH
Ps	8: 3	which *you* have **set in p**, 3922
	18:19	He brought me out into a **spacious p**; 5303
	24: 3	Who may stand in his holy **p**? 5226
	26: 8	O LORD, the **p** where your glory dwells 5226
	28: 2	my hands toward your **Most Holy P**. 1808+7731
	31: 8	but have set my feet in a **spacious p**. 5303
	32: 7	You are my **hiding p**; 6260
	33:14	from his dwelling **p** he watches all who live 4806
	40: 2	on a rock and gave me a firm **p to stand**. 892
	41: 8	he will never get up from the **p** NIH
	43: 3	to the **p** where you **dwell**. 5438
	45:16	sons *will* **take the p** of your fathers; 2118+9393
	46: 4	the **holy** *p* where the Most High dwells. AIT
	50: 1	the rising of the sun to the **p** where it **sets**. 4427
	51: 6	you teach me wisdom in the **inmost p**. 6258
	55: 8	I would hurry to my **p** of shelter, 5144
	62: 4	to topple him from his **lofty p**; 8420
	66:12	but you brought us to a **p of abundance**. 8122
	69:25	May their **p** be deserted; 3227
	73:18	Surely *you* **p** them on slippery ground; 8883
	74: 4	Your foes roared in the **p** where you met 4595
	74: 7	the **dwelling p** of your Name. 5438
	74: 8	burned every **p** where God was **worshiped** 4595
	76: 2	his **dwelling p** in Zion. 5104
	84: 1	How lovely is your **dwelling p**, 5438
	84: 3	a **p** near your altar, O LORD Almighty, NIH
	84: 6	they make it a **p** of springs; NIH
	88:12	Are your wonders in the **p** of **darkness**, AIT
	90: 1	you have been our **dwelling p** 5061

Ps 103:16	and its **p** remembers it no more.	5226
104: 8	to the **p** you assigned for them.	5226
109: 8	may another take his **p of leadership.**	7213
113: 3	the rising of the sun to the **p where** it **sets,**	4427
132: 5	till I find a **p** for the LORD,	5226
132: 7	"Let us go to his **dwelling p;**	5438
132: 8	O LORD, and come to your **resting p,**	4957
132:11	"One of your own descendants *I will*	8883
132:14	"This is my **resting p** for ever and ever;	4957
139:15	from you when I was made in the **secret p.**	6260
148: 8	*He* set them **in p** for ever and ever;	6641
Pr 3:19	by understanding he set the heavens **in p;**	3922
8:25	before the mountains were settled **in p,**	3190
8:27	I was there when *he* set the heavens **in p,**	3922
24:15	do not raid his **dwelling p;**	8070
25: 6	and do not claim a **p** among great men;	5226
Ecc 1: 7	To the **p** the streams come from,	5226
3:16	In the **p of** judgment—wickedness	5226
3:16	wickedness was there, in the **p of** justice—	5226
3:20	All go to the same **p;**	5226
4: 1	the oppression that *was* **taking p** under	6913
6: 6	Do not all go to the same **p?**	5226
8:10	and go from the holy **p** and receive praise	5226
11: 3	in the **p** where it falls, there will it lie.	5226
SS 8: 6	**P** me like a seal over your heart,	8492
Isa 3:13	The LORD **takes** *his* **p** in court;	5893
4: 6	and **hiding p** from the storm and rain.	5039
7: 7	" *'It will* not **take p,** it will not happen,	7756
7:23	in every **p** where there were	5226
11:10	and his **p of** rest will be glorious.	4957
13:13	the earth will shake from its **p** at the wrath	5226
14: 2	and bring them to their own **p.**	5226
14:21	Prepare a **p to slaughter** his sons for	4749
14:23	into a **p** *for* owls and into swampland;	4625
16:12	When Moab appears at her **high p,**	1195
18: 4	and will look on from my **dwelling p,**	4806
18: 7	**p** of the Name of the LORD Almighty.	5226
22:16	on the height and chiseling your **resting p**	5438
22:22	*I will* **p** on his shoulder the key to	5989
22:23	I will drive him like a peg into a firm **p;**	5226
22:25	peg driven into the firm **p** will give way;	5226
23:13	The Assyrians *have* **made** it a **p**	3569
28:12	"This is the **resting p,** let the weary rest";	4957
28:12	and, "This is the **p of** repose"—	5276
28:15	a lie our refuge and falsehood *our* **hiding p.**	6259
28:17	and water will overflow your **hiding p.**	6260
28:25	Does he not plant wheat *in* its **p,**	8463
33:21	be like a **p of** broad rivers and streams.	5226
41: 1	let us meet together at the **p of** judgment.	5477
42: 9	See, the former things *have* **taken p,**	995
45: 6	to the **p of** its **setting** men may know there is none besides me.	5115
46: 7	they set it up **in** its **p,** and there it stands.	9393
49:20	'This **p** is too small for us;	5226
51:16	I *who* **set** the heavens **in p,**	5749
54: 2	"Enlarge the **p of** your tent,	5226
57:15	"I live in a high and **holy p,**	AIT
60:13	to adorn the **p of** my sanctuary;	5226
60:13	and I will glorify the **p of** my feet.	5226
60:17	and silver **in p of** iron.	9393
60:17	and iron **in p of** stones.	9393
63:18	while your people possessed your **holy p,**	7731
65:10	the Valley of Achor a **resting p** *for* herds,	8070
66: 1	Where will my **resting p** be?	5226
Jer 2:37	You will also leave *that* **p** with your hands	AIT
3: 2	Is there *any* **p** where you have	AIT
4: 7	He has left his **p** to lay waste your land.	5226
7: 3	and I will let you live in this **p.**	5226
7: 6	and do not shed innocent blood in this **p,**	5226
7: 7	then I will let you live in this **p,**	5226
7:12	now to the **p** in Shiloh where I first made	5226
7:14	the **p** I gave to you and your fathers.	5226
7:20	and my wrath will be poured out on this **p,**	5226
9: 2	in the desert a **lodging p** *for* travelers, so	4869
13: 7	and dug up the belt and took it from the **p**	5226
14:13	I will give you lasting peace in this **p.' "**	5226
16: 2	and have sons or daughters in this **p."**	5226
16: 9	of bride and bridegroom in this **p.**	5226
17:12	is the **p of** our sanctuary.	5226
19: 3	to bring a disaster on this **p** that will make	5226
19: 4	and made this a **p of** foreign gods;	5226
19: 4	and they have filled this **p** with the blood of	5226
19: 6	people will no longer call this **p** Topheth	5226
19: 7	" 'In this **p** I will ruin the plans of Judah	5226
19:12	to this **p** and to those who live here,	5226
19:13	of Judah will be defiled like this **p,**	5226
22: 3	and do not shed innocent blood in this **p.**	5226
22:11	as king of Judah but has gone from this **p:**	5226
22:12	in the **p** where they have led him captive;	5226
23: 4	*I will* **p** shepherds over them	7756
24: 5	whom I sent away from this **p** to the land of	5226
25:35	the leaders of the flock no **p to escape.**	7129
26:23	into the **burial p** of the common people.)	7700
27:22	and restore them to this **p.' "**	5226
28: 3	to this **p** all the articles of the LORD's house	5226
28: 4	to this **p** Jehoiachin son of Jehoiakim king	5226
28: 6	the exiles back to this **p** from Babylon.	5226
28:13	but in its **p** you will get a yoke of iron.	9393
29:10	to bring you back to this **p.**	5226
29:14	the **p** from which I carried you into exile."	5226
29:26	the LORD has appointed you priest **in p** of	9393
30:10	'I will surely save you out of a **distant p,**	8158
30:18	and the palace will stand in its **proper p.**	5477
32:37	to this **p** and let them live in safety.	5226
33:10	'You say about this **p,**	5226
33:12	'In this **p,** desolate and without men	5226
37: 1	he reigned **in p** of Jehoiachin son of	9393

Jer 40: 2	"The LORD your God decreed this disaster for this **p.**	5226
42:18	you will never see this **p** again.'	5226
42:22	famine and plague in the **p** where you want	5226
44:29	to you that I will punish you in this **p,'**	5226
46:27	I will surely save you out of a **distant p,**	8158
49:33	a haunt of jackals, a **desolate p** forever.	9039
50: 6	and hill and forgot their own **resting p.**	8070
51:37	a **p** where no one lives.	NIH
51:62	you have said you will destroy this **p,**	5226
La 1: 3	she finds no **resting p.**	4955
2: 6	he has destroyed his **p of meeting.**	4595
Eze 3:12	the LORD be praised in his **dwelling p!**—	5226
4: 3	**p** it as an iron wall between you and	5989
7:22	and they will desecrate my **treasured p;**	7621
12: 3	and go from where you are to another **p.**	5226
20:29	What is this **high p** you go to?' "	1195
21: 7	*It will* **surely take p,**	2118
21:30	In the **p** where you were created,	5226
25: 5	for camels and Ammon into a **resting p**	5271
26: 5	she will become a **p to spread** fishnets.	5427
26:14	and you will become a **p to spread** fishnets.	5427
26:15	and *the* **slaughter takes p** in you?	2222+2223
26:20	and you will not return or **take** *your* **p** in	3656
34:23	*I will* **p** over them one shepherd.	7756
37:27	My **dwelling p** will be with them;	5438
38:15	You will come from your **p** in the far north,	5226
39: 8	*It will* **surely take p,**	2118
39:11	that day I will give Gog a burial **p** in Israel,	5226
41: 4	said to me, "This is the **Most Holy P."**	7731+7731
41:21	the front of the **Most Holy P** was similar.	7731
41:23	and the **Most Holy P** had double doors.	7731
42:13	for the **p** is holy.	5226
43: 7	"Son of man, this is the **p** *of* my throne and	5226
43: 7	this is the place of my throne and the **p** *for*	5226
45: 3	the sanctuary, the **Most Holy P.**	7731+7731
45: 4	a **p** for their houses as well as a holy place	5226
45: 4	a place for their houses as well as a **holy p**	5219
46:19	and showed me a **p** at the western end.	5226
46:20	"This is the **p** where the priests will cook	5226
Da 2:45	the king what *will* **take p** in the future.	10201
7: 9	"As I looked, "thrones **were set in p,**	10667
8: 8	and in its **p** four prominent horns grew up	9393
8:11	the **p** *of* his sanctuary was brought low.	4806
8:17	he came near the **p where** I was **standing,**	6642
11: 7	from her family line will arise to take her **p.**	4030
11:36	for what has been determined *must* **take p.**	6913
Hos 1:10	In the **p** where it was said to them,	5226
5:15	to my **p** until they admit their guilt.	5226
9:13	like Tyre, planted in a **pleasant p.**	5659
Jnh 4: 5	Jonah went out and sat down at a **p** east of	NIH
Mic 1: 3	The LORD is coming from his **dwelling p;**	5226
1: 5	What is Judah's **high p?** Is it not Jerusalem?	1195
1: 6	a **p** for planting vineyards.	8441
2:10	For this is not your **resting p,**	4957
2:12	the **p** will throng with people.	NIH
Na 2: 5	the protective shield *is* **put in p.**	3922
2:11	the **p** where they **fed** their young,	5337
Zep 1: 4	I will cut off from this **p** every remnant	5226
2: 6	will be a **p** for shepherds and sheep pens.	NIH
2: 9	a **p** *of* weeds and salt pits,	4940
Hag 2: 9	'And in this **p** I will grant peace,'	5226
Zec 3: 7	of my courts, and I will give you a **p**	4544
5:11	the basket will be set there in its **p."**	4807
6:12	and he will branch out from his **p** and build	9393
12: 6	but Jerusalem will remain intact in her **p.**	9393
14:10	be raised up and remain **in** its **p,**	9393
Mal 1: 7	"*You* **p** defiled food on my altar.	5602
1:11	In every **p** incense and pure offerings will	5226
Mt 1:22	All this **took p** to fulfill what the Lord	1181
2: 9	of them until it stopped over **the p where**	4023
2:22	that Archelaus was reigning in Judea **in p**	505
8:20	the Son of Man has no **p** to lay his head."	4544
10:23	When you are persecuted in one **p,**	NIG
12: 9	Going on **from that p,**	1696
12:15	Aware of this, Jesus withdrew **from that p.**	1696
14:13	by boat privately to a solitary **p.**	5536
14:15	and said, "This is a remote **p,**	5536
14:35	when the men *of* that **p** recognized Jesus,	5536
15:21	Leaving **that p,** Jesus withdrew to	1696
15:33	in this **remote p** to feed such a crowd?"	2244
19:13	*to* **p** his hands on them and pray for them.	2202
21: 4	This **took p** to fulfill what was spoken	1181
23: 6	they love the **p of** honor at banquets and	4752
24:15	"So when you see standing in the holy **p**	5536
24:20	that your flight *will* not **take p** in winter or	1181
24:51	and assign him a **p** with the hypocrites,	3538
26:36	with his disciples to a **p** called Gethsemane,	6005
26:52	"Put your sword back in its **p,"**	5536
26:56	But this *has* all **taken p** that the writings of	1181
27: 6	to buy the potter's field as a **burial p**	5438
27:33	to a **p** called Golgotha (which means	5536
27:33	Golgotha (which means The **P** of the Skull).	5536
28: 6	Come and see the **p** where he lay.	5536
Mk 1:35	left the house and went off to a solitary **p,**	5536
6:11	And if any **p** will not welcome you or listen	5536
6:31	"Come with me by yourselves to a quiet **p**	5536
6:32	by themselves in a boat to a solitary **p.**	5536
6:35	"This is a remote **p,"** they said,	5536
7:24	Jesus **left** that **p** and went to the vicinity	1696
7:32	they begged him to **p** his hand on the man.	2202
8: 4	in this **remote p** can anyone get enough bread to feed them?"	2244
9:30	They left **that p** and passed	1696
10: 1	then left **that p** and went into the region	1696
12:41	the **p where** the offerings were put	1126
13:18	Pray that *this will* not **take p** in winter,	1181

Mk 14:32	They went to a **p** called Gethsemane,	6005
15:22	to the **p** called Golgotha (which means	5536
15:22	Golgotha (which means The **P** of the Skull).	5536
16: 6	See the **p** where they laid him.	5536
16:18	*they will* **p** their hands **on** sick people,	2202
Lk 2: 2	that took **p** while Quirinius was governor	NIG
4: 5	to a high **p** and showed him in an instant all	4001
4:17	he found the **p** where it is written:	5536
4:42	At daybreak Jesus went out to a solitary **p.**	5536
6:17	down with them and stood on a level **p.**	5536
9:12	because we are in a remote **p** here."	5536
9:58	the Son of Man has no **p** to lay his head."	4544
10: 1	of him to every town and **p** where he was	5536
10:32	when he came to the **p** and saw him,	5536
11: 1	One day Jesus was praying in a certain **p.**	5536
11:33	and puts it in a **p** where it will be **hidden,**	3219
12:17	I have no **p** to store my crops.'	4024+4544
12:46	and assign him a **p** with the unbelievers.	3538
13:31	"Leave this **p** and go somewhere else.	1949
14: 8	do not take the **p of** honor,	4752
14: 9	you will have to take the least important **p.**	5536
14:10	when you are invited, take the lowest **p,**	5536
14:10	'Friend, move up to a better **p.'**	NIG
16:28	so that they will not also come to this **p**	5536
19:37	near the **p where the road goes down**	2853
21: 7	be the sign that they are about to **take p?"**	1181
21:28	When these things begin to **take p,**	1181
22:40	On reaching the **p,** he said to them,	5536
22:33	When they came to the **p** called the Skull,	5536
23:48	to witness this sight saw what **took p,**	1181
24:21	it is the third day since all this **took p.**	1181
Jn 2: 1	On the third day a wedding **took p** at Cana	1181
4:20	that the **p** where we must worship is	5536
5: 9	on which this **took p** was a Sabbath,	NIG
6:10	There was plenty of grass in that **p,**	5536
6:23	the **p** where the people had eaten the bread	5536
6:20	near the **p where the offerings were put.**	1126
8:35	a slave *has* no **permanent p** in the family,	3531
10:40	to the **p** where John had been baptizing in	5536
10:42	And **in that p** many believed in Jesus.	1695
11:30	at the **p** where Martha had met him.	5536
11:32	When Mary reached **the p where** Jesus was	3963
11:48	and take away both our **p** and our nation."	5536
13:12	he put on his clothes and **returned to** *his* **p.**	404+4099
14: 2	I am going there to prepare a **p** for you.	5536
14: 3	And if I go and prepare a **p** for you,	5536
14: 4	the way to the **p** where I am going."	NIG
18: 2	Now Judas, who betrayed him, knew the **p,**	5536
18:36	But now my kingdom is **from another p."**	1949
19:13	at a **p** known as the Stone Pavement	5536
19:17	he went out to the **p** of the Skull (which	5536
19:20	the **p** where Jesus was crucified was near	5536
19:41	At the **p** where Jesus was crucified,	5536
Ac 1:20	" 'May his **p** be deserted;	2068
1:20	" 'May another take his **p of leadership.'**	2175
2: 1	they were all together **in one p.**	899+2093+3836
2:30	that he would **p** one of his descendants	2767
3:11	in the **p** called Solomon's Colonnade.	NIG
4:31	the **p** where they were meeting was shaken.	5536
6:13	against this holy **p** and against the law.	5536
6:14	Jesus of Nazareth will destroy this **p** and	5536
7: 7	of that country and worship me in this **p.'**	5536
7:33	the **p** where you are standing is holy	5536
7:46	that he might provide a **dwelling p** for	5013
7:49	Or where will my **resting p** be?	5536
9:12	and **p** his hands **on him**	2202
12:17	he said, and then he left for another **p.**	5536
16:13	where we expected to find a **p of** prayer.	4666
16:16	when we were going to the **p of** prayer.	4666
18:23	and traveled **from p to place** throughout	2759
18:23	and traveled **from place to p** throughout	2759
21:28	against our people and our law and this **p.**	5536
21:28	into the temple area and defiled this holy **p.**	5536
26:18	a **p** among those who are sanctified by faith	3102
27: 8	and came to a **p** called Fair Havens,	5536
28:13	to the **p where** he was **staying.**	3825
Ro 2:16	This will take **p** on the day when God	NIG
9:26	that in the very **p** where it was said to them,	5536
15:23	now that there is no more **p** for me to work	5536
1Co 7:17	retain the **p** in life that the Lord	4344
11:18	**In the first p,** I hear that when you come	4754
2Co 7: 3	before that *you* **have such a p** in our hearts	1639
Eph 5: 4	or coarse joking, which *are* **out of p,**	465+4024
6:14	with the breastplate of righteousness **in p,**	1907
Php 2: 9	God **exalted** him **to the highest p**	5671
1Ti 5:24	reaching the **p of** judgment ahead of them;	NIG
2Ti 2:18	that the resurrection *has* already **taken p,**	1181
Phm 1:13	so that he could **take** your **p** in helping me	5642
Heb 2: 6	there is a **p where** someone has testified:	4543
5: 6	And he says in **another** *p,*	AIT
8: 7	no **p** would have been sought for another.	5536
9: 2	this was called the **Holy P.**	41
9: 3	a room called the **Most Holy P,**	41+41
9: 8	that the way into the **Most Holy P** had not	NIG
9:12	but he entered the **Most Holy P** once for all	NIG
9:25	the **Most Holy P** every year with blood	NIG
10:19	the **Most Holy P** by the blood of Jesus,	AIT
11: 8	to go to a **p** he would later receive	5536
13:11	the blood of animals into the **Most Holy P**	AIT
2Pe 1:19	as to a light shining in a dark **p,**	5536
1Jn 1:10	be a liar and his word *has* no **p** in our lives.	1639
Rev 1: 1	to show his servants what must soon **take p.**	1181
1:19	what is now and what will **take p** later.	1181
2: 5	and remove your lampstand from its **p.**	5536
4: 1	and I will show you what must **take p**	1181
6:14	and island was removed from its **p.**	5536

Rev	12: 6	the desert to a p prepared for her by God,	5536
	12: 8	and they lost their p in heaven.	5536
	12:14	that she might fly to the p prepared for her	5536
	13: 6	to slander his name and his **dwelling p**	5008
	16:16	the p that in Hebrew is called Armageddon.	5536
	20:11	and there was no p for them.	5536
	21: 8	their p will be in the fiery lake	3538
	22: 6	the things that must soon **take p.**"	1181

PLACED (87) [PLACE]

Ge	3:24	he p on the east side of the Garden	8905
	22: 6	the burnt offering and p it on his son Isaac,	8492
	28:18	the stone he had p under his head and set it	8492
	30:35	and he p them in the care of his sons.	5989
	30:38	Then he p the peeled branches in all	3657
	50:23	of Makir son of Manasseh were p at birth	3528
	50:26	he was p in a coffin in Egypt.	8492
Ex	2: 3	Then she p the child in it and put it among	8492
	40:20	He took the Testimony and p it in the ark,	5989
	40:22	Moses p the table in the Tent of Meeting on	8492
	40:24	He p the lampstand in the Tent of Meeting	8492
	40:26	Moses p the gold altar in the Tent	8492
	40:30	Then he p the basin between the Tent of Meeting	8492
Lev	8: 8	He p the breastpiece on him and put	8492
	8: 9	Then he p the turban on Aaron's head	8492
Nu	17: 7	Moses p the staffs before the LORD in	5663
Jos	10:24	So they came forward and p their feet	8492
	10:27	the mouth of the cave they p large rocks,	8492
Jdg	7:16	he p trumpets and empty jars in the hands	5989
	8:27	which he p in Ophrah, his town.	3657
1Sa	6:11	They p the ark of the LORD on the cart	8492
	6:15	and p them on the large rock.	8492
2Sa	12:30	and it was p on David's head.	AIT
	15: 2	with a complaint to be p before the king for	995
1Ki	6:27	He p the cherubim inside the innermost	5989
	7: 4	Its **windows** were p high in sets of three,	9209
	7:39	He p five of the stands on the south side of	5989
	7:39	He p the Sea on the south side,	5989
	7:51	and he p them in the treasuries of	5989
	8: 9	the two stone tablets that Moses had p in it	5663
	10: 9	in you and p you on the throne of Israel.	5989
	21: 8	Ahab's name, p his seal on them,	928+2597+3159
2Ki	12: 9	He p it beside the altar,	5989
1Ch	29: 3	and it was p on David's head.	6584
2Ch	4: 6	for washing and p five on the south side	5989
	4: 7	to the specifications for them and p them in	5989
	4: 8	He made ten tables and p them in	5663
	4:10	He p the Sea on the south side,	5989
	5: 1	he p them in the treasuries of God's temple.	5989
	5:10	the two tablets that Moses had p in it	5989
	6:11	There I have p the ark,	8492
	6:13	and had p it in the center of the outer court.	5989
	9: 8	and p you on his throne as king to rule for	5989
	23:18	Then Jehoiada p the oversight of the temple	8492
	24: 8	a chest was made and p outside,	5989
	28:27	but he was not p in the tombs of the kings	995
Ezr	1: 7	from Jerusalem and had p in the temple	5989
Ne	5:15	p a heavy burden on the people	3877
	9:37	to the kings you have p over us.	5989
Est	2: 3	Let them be p under the care of Hegai,	NIH
	6: 8	one with a royal crest p on its head.	5989
Job	6: 2	be weighed and all my misery be p on	5951
	20: 4	ever since man was p on the earth,	8492
Ps	21: 3	and a crown of pure gold on his head.	8883
Jer	24: 1	baskets of figs p in front of the temple of	3585
	37:21	then gave orders for Jeremiah to be p in	7212
Eze	23:41	a table spread before it on which you had p	8492
	32:27	whose swords were p under their heads?	5989
	40:42	On them were p the utensils	5663
	43: 8	When they p their threshold next	5989
Da	2:38	in your hands he has p mankind and	10314
	2:48	p Daniel in a high position	10648
	2:48	the entire province of Babylon and p him	NIH
	5: 7	and have a gold chain p around his neck,	NIH
	5:16	and have a gold chain p around your neck,	NIH
	5:29	a gold chain was p around his neck,	NIH
	6:17	A stone was brought and p over the mouth	10682
Mt	19:15	When he had p his hands **on** them,	2202
	21: 7	p their cloaks on them,	2202
	27:37	Above his head they p the written charge	2202
	27:60	and p it in his own new tomb	5502
Mk	6:56	they p the sick in the marketplaces.	5502
	15:46	and p it in a tomb cut out of rock.	5502
Lk	2: 7	She wrapped him in cloths and p him in	369
	23:53	in linen cloth and p it in a tomb cut in	5502
Jn	3:35	the Son and has p everything in his hands.	1443
	6:27	On him God the Father has p his **seal**	5381
Ac	7:16	and p in the tomb that Abraham had bought	5502
	7:21	When he was p **outside,**	1758
	8:17	Then Peter and John p their hands **on** them,	2202
	9:37	and her body was washed and p in	5502
	13: 3	they p their hands on them	2202
	19: 6	When Paul p his hands **on** them,	2202
	28: 8	p his hands on him and healed him.	2202
Eph	1:22	And God p all things **under** his feet	5718
Rev	1:17	Then he p his right hand on me and said:	5502
	3: 8	I have p before you an open door	1443

PLACES (144) [PLACE]

Ex	10:23	in the p **where** they lived.	4632
Lev	14:28	to put on the same p he put the blood of	5226
	26:30	I will destroy your **high p,**	1195
Nu	24: 5	O Jacob, your **dwelling p,** O Israel!	5438
	33:52	and demolish all their **high p.**	1195
	35:12	They will be p of refuge from the avenger,	6551

Dt	1:33	to search out p for you to camp and	5226
	12: 2	the p on the high mountains and on the hills	5226
	12: 3	and wipe out their names from those p.	5226
	33:29	and you will trample down their **high p.**"	1195
Jdg	5:11	the voice of the singers at the **watering p.**	5393
	19:13	and spend the night in one of those p."	5226
	20: 2	of Israel **took** their p in the assembly of	3656
	20:33	All the men of Israel moved from their p	5226
1Sa	7:16	judging Israel in all those p.	5226
	23:23	the hiding p he uses and come back to me	4676
	30:31	and to those in all the other p where David	5226
1Ki	3: 2	however, were still sacrificing at the **high p,**	1195
	3: 3	and burned incense on the **high p.**	1195
	12:31	Jeroboam built shrines on **high p**	1195
	12:32	at the **high p** he had made.	1195
	13: 2	of the **high p** who now make offerings here,	1195
	13:32	and against all the shrines on the **high p** in	1195
	13:33	for the **high p** from all sorts of people.	1195
	13:33	a priest he consecrated for the **high p.**	1195
	14:23	They also set up for themselves **high p,**	1195
	15:14	Although he did not remove the **high p,**	1195
	22:43	The **high p,** however, were not removed,	1195
2Ki	6:10	so that he was on his guard **in such p.**	9004S
	8:12	"You will set fire to their **fortified p,**	4448
	12: 3	The **high p,** however, were not removed;	1195
	14: 4	The **high p,** however, were not removed;	1195
	15: 4	The **high p,** however, were not removed;	1195
	15:35	The **high p,** however, were not removed;	1195
	16: 4	and burned incense at the **high p,**	1195
	17: 9	to fortified city they built themselves **high p**	1195
	17:29	people of Samaria had made at the **high p.**	1195
	17:32	as priests in the shrines at the **high p.**	1195
	18: 4	He removed the **high p,**	1195
	18:22	isn't he the one whose **high p** and altars	1195
	21: 3	**high p** his father Hezekiah had destroyed;	1195
	23: 5	to burn incense on the **high p** of the towns	1195
	23: 8	of Judah and desecrated the **high p,**	1195
	23: 9	of the **high p** did not serve at the altar of	1195
	23:13	the **high p** that were east of Jerusalem on	1195
	23:19	the **high p** that the kings of Israel had built	1195
	23:20	the priests of those **high p** on the altars	1195
2Ch	8:11	because the p where the ark of the LORD	2156S
	11:15	for the **high p** and for the goat	1195
	14: 3	the foreign altars and the **high p,**	1195
	14: 5	the **high p** and incense altars in every town	1195
	15:17	Although he did not remove the **high p**	1195
	17: 6	furthermore, he removed the **high p** and	1195
	20:33	The **high p,** however, were not removed,	1195
	21:11	had also built **high p** on the hills of Judah	1195
	28: 4	and burned incense at the **high p,**	1195
	28:25	in Judah he built **high p** to burn sacrifices	1195
	31: 1	the **high p** and the altars throughout Judah	1195
	32:12	Hezekiah himself remove this god's **high p**	1195
	33: 3	**high p** his father Hezekiah had demolished;	1195
	33:17	continued to sacrifice at the **high p,**	1195
	33:19	and the sites where he built **high p** and set	1195
	34: 3	to purge Judah and Jerusalem of **high p,**	1195
	35:10	in their p with the Levites in their divisions	6642
	35:15	were in the p prescribed by David, Asaph,	5096
Ezr	3:10	**took** their p to praise the LORD,	6641
	6: 5	are to be returned to their p in the temple	10087
Ne	3: 7	p under the authority of the governor	NIH
	4:13	of the wall at the **exposed p,**	7460
	9: 2	They **stood** in their p and confessed	6641
	12:40	then **took** their p in the house of God;	6641
Job	3:14	p now lying in ruins,	2999
	4:18	If God p no **trust** in his servants,	586
	15:15	If God p no **trust** in his holy ones,	586
	28: 4	in p forgotten by the foot of man;	2021S
	38:20	Can you take them to their p?	1473
Ps	16: 6	for me in **pleasant p;**	AIT
	74:20	haunts of violence fill the **dark p** of the land	4743
	78:58	They angered him with their **high p;**	1195
SS	2:14	in the **hiding p** on the mountainside,	6260
Isa	7:25	p where cattle are **turned loose**	5448
	15: 2	to its **high p** to weep;	1195
	17: 9	will be like p **abandoned** to thickets	AIT
	30:28	he p in the jaws of the peoples a bit	NIH
	32:18	My people will live in peaceful **dwelling p,**	5659
	32:18	in secure homes, in undisturbed **p of rest.**	4957
	34:14	and find for themselves **p of rest.**	4955
	36: 7	isn't he the one whose **high p** and altars	1195
	40: 4	the **rugged** p a plain.	8221
	42:16	before them and make the **rough p** smooth.	5112
	45: 3	riches stored in **secret p,**	5041
	61: 4	and restore the p long **devastated;**	AIT
Jer	7:31	They have built the **high p** of Topheth in	1195
	9:26	and all who live in the desert in distant p.	6991
	17: 3	together with your **high p,**	1195
	17: 6	He will dwell in the **parched p** of the desert	3083
	19: 5	the **high p** of Baal to burn their sons in	1195
	23:24	in **secret p** so that I cannot see him?"	5041
	25:23	Buz and all who are in **distant p;**	6991+7899
	26:10	to the house of the LORD and **took** their p	3782
	29:14	I will gather you from all the nations and p	5226
	32:35	They built **high p** for Baal in the Valley	1195
	48:35	the **high p** and burn incense to their gods,"	1195
	49:10	I will uncover his **hiding p,**	5041
	49:32	those who are in **distant p**	6991+7899
	51:51	because foreigners have entered the **holy p**	5219
Eze	6: 3	and I will destroy your **high p.**	1195
	6: 6	be laid waste and the **high p** demolished,	1195
	6:13	where they offered fragrant incense	5226
	16:16	of your garments to make gaudy **high p,**	1195
	34:12	from all the p where they were scattered on	5226
	34:26	and the p **surrounding** my hill.	AIT
	42:14	on other clothes before they go near **the p**	889S

Eze	43: 7	lifeless idols of their kings at their **high p.**	1195
	46:23	with p **for fire** built all around under	4453
	47:10	be p for **spreading** nets.	5427
Da	4:21	and **having nesting** p in its branches for	10709
Hos	10: 8	The **high p** of wickedness will be destroyed	1195
Joel	3: 7	I am going to rouse them out of the p	5226
Am	4:13	and treads the **high p** of the earth—	1195
	7: 9	"The **high p** of Isaac will be destroyed and	1195
	9:11	I will repair its **broken p,** restore its ruins,	7288
Mic	1: 3	he comes down and treads the **high p** of	1195
Hab	1: 6	across the whole earth to seize **dwelling p**	5438
Mt	8:11	**take** their p at the feast with Abraham,	369
	12:43	it goes through arid p seeking rest and does	5536
	13: 5	Some fell on **rocky p,**	4378
	13:20	on **rocky p** is the man who hears the word	4378
	20:23	These p belong to those for whom	NIG
	24: 7	be famines and earthquakes in various **p.**	5536
Mk	1:45	but stayed outside in lonely p.	5536
	4: 5	Some fell on **rocky p,**	4378
	4:16	Others, like seed sown on **rocky p,**	4378
	10:40	These p belong to those for whom	NIG
	12:39	in the synagogues and the **p of honor**	4752
	13: 8	There will be earthquakes in various p,	5536
Lk	5:16	But Jesus often withdrew to lonely **p**	2245
	8:29	driven by the demon into **solitary p.**	2245
	11:24	it goes through arid p seeking rest and does	5536
	13:29	**take** their p at the feast in the kingdom	369
	14: 7	guests picked the **p of honor at the table,**	4752
	20:46	in the synagogues and the **p of honor**	4752
	21:11	famines and pestilences in various **p,**	5536
Ac	17:26	and the **exact p** where they should live.	3999

PLACING (4) [PLACE]

Ge	48:17	Joseph saw his father p his right hand	8883
2Ki	10:24	"If one of you lets any of the men I am p	995
Ezr	5: 8	with large stones and p the timbers in	10682
Ac	9:17	P his hands **on** Saul, he said,	2202

PLAGUE (84) [PLAGUED, PLAGUES]

Ex	8: 2	I will p your whole country with frogs.	5597
	9: 3	a terrible p on your livestock in the field—	1822
	9:15	and struck you and your people with a p	1822
	10:14	before had there been such a p of locusts,	NIH
	10:17	to take this **deadly p** away from me."	4638
	11: 1	"I will bring one more p on Pharaoh and	5596
	12:13	No destructive p will touch you	5598
	30:12	Then no p will come on them	5598
	32:35	the LORD **struck** the people **with a p**	5597
Lev	26:25	I will send a p among you,	1822
Nu	8:19	so that no p will strike the Israelites	5598
	11:33	and he struck them with a severe p.	4804
	14:12	strike them down with a p and destroy them,	1822
	14:37	were struck down and died of a p	4487
	16:46	the p has started."	5598
	16:47	The p had already started among the people	5598
	16:48	and the p stopped.	4487
	16:49	But 14,700 people died from the p,	4487
	16:50	for the p had stopped.	4487
	25: 8	the p against the Israelites was stopped;	4487
	25: 9	those who died in the p numbered 24,000.	4487
	25:18	when the p came as a result of Peor.	4487
	26: 1	After the p the LORD said to Moses	4487
	31:16	so that a p struck the LORD's people.	4487
Dt	28:21	The LORD will p you with diseases	1815
	28:22	which will p you until you perish.	8103
	32:24	consuming pestilence and deadly p;	7776
Jos	22:17	a p fell on the community of the LORD!	5598
1Sa	6: 4	same p has struck both you and your rulers.	4487
2Sa	24:13	Or three days of p in your land?	1822
	24:15	So the LORD sent a p on Israel from	1822
	24:21	that the p on the people may be stopped."	4487
	24:25	and the p on Israel was stopped.	4487
1Ki	8:37	"When famine or p comes to the land,	1822
1Ch	21:12	days of p in the land,	1822
	21:14	So the LORD sent a p on Israel,	1822
	21:17	not let this p remain on your people."	4487
	21:22	that the p on the people may be stopped.	4487
2Ch	6:28	"When famine or p comes to the land,	1822
	7:13	the land or send a p among my people,	1822
	20: 9	the sword of judgment, or p or famine,	1822
Job	27:15	The p will bury those who survive him,	4638
Ps	78:50	from death but gave them over to the p.	1822
	91: 6	nor the p that destroys at midday;	7776
	106:29	and a p broke out among them.	4487
	106:30	and the p was checked.	4487
Isa	11:22	The LORD **will strike** Egypt **with a p;**	5597
Jer	14:12	with the sword, famine and p."	1822
	21: 6	and they will die of a terrible p.	1822
	21: 7	the people in this city who survive the p,	1822
	21: 9	by the sword, famine or p.	1822
	24:10	and p against them until they are destroyed	1822
	27: 8	the sword, famine and p, declares the LORD,	1822
	27:13	the sword, famine and p with which	1822
	28: 8	disaster and p against many countries	1822
	29:17	and p against them and I will make them	1822
	29:18	famine and p and will make them abhorrent	1822
	32:24	Because of the sword, famine and p,	1822
	32:36	and p it will be handed over to the king	1822
	34:17	to fall by the sword, p and famine.	1822
	38: 2	by the sword, famine or p,	1822
	42:17	by the sword, famine and p;	1822
	42:22	You will die by the sword, famine and p in	1822
	44:13	famine and p, as I punished Jerusalem.	1822
Eze	5:12	of your people will die of the p or perish	1822
	5:17	P and bloodshed will sweep through you,	1822

Jer	6:11	by the sword, famine and **p.**	1822
	6:12	He that is far away will die of the **p,**	1822
	7:15	inside are **p** and famine;	1822
	7:15	the city will be devoured by famine and **p.**	1822
	12:16	of them from the sword, famine and **p,** so	1822
	14:19	a **p** into that land and pour out my wrath	1822
	14:21	sword and famine and wild beasts and **p—**	1822
	28:23	a **p** upon her and make blood flow	1822
	33:27	in strongholds and caves will die of a **p.**	1822
	38:22	I will execute judgment upon him with **p**	1822
Hab	3:5	**P** went before him;	1822
Zec	14:12	the **p** with which the LORD will strike all	4487
	14:15	A similar **p** will strike the horses	4487
	14:18	on them the **p** he inflicts on the nations	4487
Rev	6:8	of the earth to kill by sword, famine and **p,**	2505
	11:6	and to strike the earth with every kind of **p**	4435
	16:21	And they cursed God on account of the **p**	4435
	16:21	because the **p** was so terrible.	4435

PLAGUED (2) [PLAGUE]

Ps	73:5	they **are** not **p** by human ills.	5595
	73:14	All day long I have been **p;**	5595

PLAGUES (16) [PLAGUE]

Ex	5:3	he may strike us with **p** or with the sword."	1822
	9:14	the full force of my **p** against you and	4487
Dt	28:59	the LORD will send fearful **p** on you	4804
1Sa	4:8	the Egyptians with all kinds of **p** in	4804
Hos	13:14	Where, O death, are your **p?**	1822
Am	4:10	"I sent **p** among you as I did to Egypt.	1822
Rev	9:18	of mankind was killed by the three **p**	4435
	9:20	not killed by these **p** still did not repent of	4435
	15:1	seven angels with the seven last **p—**	4435
	15:6	the seven angels with the seven **p.**	4435
	15:8	the temple until the seven **p** of	4435
	16:9	who had control over these **p,**	4435
	18:4	so that you will not receive any of her **p;**	4435
	18:8	in one day her **p** will overtake her:	4435
	21:9	of the seven last **p** came and said to me,	4435
	22:18	God will add to him the **p** described	4435

PLAIN (30) [PLAINLY, PLAINS]

Ge	11:2	they found a **p** in Shinar and settled there.	1326
	13:10	Lot looked up and saw that the whole **p** of	3971
	13:11	So Lot chose for himself the whole **p** of	3971
	13:12	of the **p** and pitched his tents near Sodom.	3971
	19:17	and don't stop anywhere in the **p!**	3971
	19:25	and the entire **p,** including all those living	3971
	19:28	toward all the land of the **p,**	3971
	19:29	So when God destroyed the cities of the **p,**	3971
Jos	17:16	in the **p** have iron chariots.	824+6677
Jdg	1:34	not allowing them to come down into the **p.**	6677
2Sa	18:23	by way of the **p** and outran the Cushite.	3971
1Ki	7:46	in the **p** of the Jordan between Succoth	3971
2Ch	4:17	in the **p** of the Jordan between Succoth	3971
	26:10	in the foothills and in the **p.**	4793
	35:22	but went to fight him on the **p** of Megiddo.	1326
Ne	6:2	in one of the villages on the **p** of Ono."	1326
Isa	40:4	the rugged places a **p.**	1326
	63:14	like cattle that go down to the **p,**	1326
Jer	47:5	O remnant on the **p,**	6677
Eze	3:22	"Get up and go out to the **p,**	1326
	3:23	So I got up and went out to the **p.**	1326
	8:4	as in the vision I had seen in the **p.**	1326
Da	3:1	the **p** of Dura in the province of Babylon.	10117
Hab	2:2	the revelation and **make** it **p** on tablets	930
Zec	12:11	of Hadad Rimmon in the **p** of Megiddo.	1326
Ro	1:19	since what may be known about God is **p**	5745
	1:19	because God has **made** it **p** to them.	5746
2Co	5:11	What we are is **p** to God,	5746
	5:11	and I hope it **is** also **p** to your conscience.	5746
Eph	3:9	to **make p** to everyone the administration	5894

PLAINLY (8) [PLAIN]

Mt	7:23	Then I will **tell** them **p,**	3933
Mk	7:35	and he began to speak **p.**	3987
	8:32	He spoke **p** about this,	4244
Jn	3:21	so that it may be **seen p**	5746
	10:24	If you are the Christ, tell us **p."**	4244
	11:14	So then he told them **p,** "Lazarus is dead,	4244
	16:25	but will tell you **p** about my Father.	4244
2Co	4:2	by **setting forth** the truth **p** we commend	5748

PLAINS (20) [PLAIN]

Nu	22:1	the Israelites traveled to the **p** of Moab	6858
	26:3	So on the **p** of Moab by the Jordan across	6858
	26:63	when they counted the Israelites on the **p**	6858
	31:12	at their camp on the **p** of Moab,	6858
	33:48	of Abarim and camped on the **p** of Moab	6858
	33:49	There on the **p** of Moab they camped along	6858
	33:50	On the **p** of Moab by the Jordan across	6858
	35:1	On the **p** of Moab by the Jordan across	6858
	36:13	through Moses to the Israelites on the **p**	6858
Dt	34:1	from the **p** of Moab to the top of Pisgah.	6858
	34:8	The Israelites grieved for Moses in the **p**	6858
Jos	4:13	over before the LORD to the **p** of Jericho.	6858
	5:10	while camped at Gilgal on the **p** of Jericho,	6858
	13:32	in the **p** of Moab across the Jordan east	6858
Jdg	1:19	to drive the people from the **p,**	6677
1Ki	20:23	But if we fight them on the **p,**	4793
	20:25	so we can fight Israel on the **p.**	4793
2Ki	25:5	and overtook him in the **p** of Jericho.	6858
Jer	39:5	and overtook Zedekiah in the **p** of Jericho.	6858
	52:8	and overtook him in the **p** of Jericho.	6858

PLAITING (KJV) See BRAIDED

PLAN (31) [PLANNED, PLANNING, PLANS]

Ge	11:6	then nothing they **p** to do will be impossible	2372
	41:37	The **p** seemed good to Pharaoh and	1821
Ex	26:30	to the **p** shown you on the mountain.	5477
Nu	33:56	I will do to you what I **p** to do to them.' "	1948
1Sa	18:25	Saul's **p** was to have David fall by	1821
2Sa	17:4	This **p** seemed good to Absalom and to all	1821
1Ch	28:18	He also gave him the **p** for the chariot,	9322
	28:19	in all the details of the **p."**	9322
2Ch	13:8	you **p** to resist the kingdom of the LORD,	606
	30:4	The **p** seemed right both to the king and to	1821
Est	8:3	an end to the evil **p** of Haman the Agagite,	4742
Job	42:2	no **p** of yours can be thwarted.	4659
Ps	64:6	"We have devised a perfect **p!"**	2925
	140:4	protect me from men of violence who **p**	3108
Pr	14:22	But those who **p** what is good find love	3086
	21:30	no **p** that can succeed against the LORD.	6783
Isa	5:19	let the **p** of the Holy One of Israel come,	6783
	8:10	propose your **p,** but it will not stand,	1821
	14:26	the **p** determined for the whole world;	6783
Jer	18:11	for you and devising a **p** against you.	4742
	36:3	about every disaster I **p** to inflict on them,	3108
	49:30	he has devised a **p** against you.	4742
Eze	43:10	Let them consider the **p,**	9422
Am	3:7	without revealing his **p** to his servants	6051
Mic	2:1	Woe to those who **p** iniquity,	3108
	4:12	they do not understand his **p,**	6783
Mt	28:12	with the elders and **devised a p,**	3284+5206
Ac	9:24	but Saul learned of their **p.**	2101
	27:43	and kept them from carrying out their **p.**	1088
Ro	15:24	I **p** to do so when I go to Spain.	NIG
Eph	1:11	having been predestined according to the **p**	4606

PLANE (2)

Ge	30:37	and **p** trees and made white stripes on them	6895
Eze	31:8	the **p** trees compare with its branches—	6895

PLANES (KJV) See CHISELS

PLANK (6) [PLANKS]

Mt	7:3	pay no attention to the **p** in your own eye?	1512
	7:4	the time there is a **p** in your own eye?	1512
	7:5	first take the **p** out of your own eye,	1512
Lk	6:41	pay no attention to the **p** in your own eye?	1512
	6:42	when you yourself fail to see the **p** in your	1512
	6:42	first take the **p** out of your eye,	1512

PLANKS (3) [PLANK]

1Ki	6:9	roofing it with beams and cedar **p.**	8444
	6:15	and covered the floor of the temple with **p**	7521
Ac	27:44	The rest were to get there on **p** or on pieces	4909

PLANNED (22) [PLAN]

2Ki	19:25	In days of old I **p** it;	3670
Ps	40:5	The **things** you **p** for us no one can recount	4742
Pr	30:32	or if you have **p** evil,	2372
Isa	14:24	"Surely, as I have **p,** so it will be,	1948
	19:12	the LORD Almighty has **p** against Egypt.	3619
	22:11	have regard for the One who **p** it long ago.	3670
	23:8	Who **p** this against Tyre,	3619
	23:9	The LORD Almighty **p** it,	3619
	25:1	marvelous things, **things p** long ago.	6783
	37:26	In days of old I **p** it;	3670
	46:11	what I have **p,** that will I do.	3670
Jer	18:8	and not inflict on it the disaster I had **p.**	3108
	49:20	what the LORD has **p** against Edom,	3619+6783
	50:45	the LORD has **p** against Babylon,	3619+6783
La	2:17	The LORD has done what he **p;**	2372
Da	11:17	by his exceptional qualities that the king **p**	10575
Ac	27:42	The soldiers **p** to kill the prisoners	1087+1181
Ro	1:13	that I **p** many times to come to you	4729
2Co	1:15	I **p** to visit you first so	1089
	1:16	I **p** to visit you on my way to Macedonia	NIG
	1:17	When I **p** this, did I do it lightly?	1089
Heb	11:40	God had **p** something better for us so	4587

PLANNING (4) [PLAN]

Ecc	9:10	nor **p** nor knowledge nor wisdom.	3113
Isa	14:24	of what the LORD Almighty is **p**	3619+6783
Jer	26:3	and not bring on them the disaster I was **p**	3108
Mic	2:3	"I am **p** disaster against this people,	3108

PLANS (41) [PLAN]

1Sa	23:10	that Saul **p** to come to Keilah and destroy	1335
2Ki	16:10	with detailed **p** for its construction.	9322
	16:11	with all the **p** that King Ahaz had sent	889S
1Ch	28:2	and I **made p** to build it.	3922
	28:11	Then David gave his son Solomon the **p**	9322
	28:12	the **p** of all that the Spirit had put	9322
Ezr	4:5	and frustrate their **p** during the entire reign	6783
Job	5:12	He thwarts the **p** of the crafty,	4742
	17:11	My days have passed, my **p** are shattered,	2365
	23:14	and many such **p** he still has in store.	2179S
Ps	14:6	You evildoers frustrate the **p** of the poor,	6783
	20:4	of your heart and make all your **p** succeed.	6783
	33:10	The LORD foils the **p** of the nations;	6783
	33:11	But the **p** of the LORD stand firm forever,	6783
	64:5	They encourage each other in evil **p,**	1821
	140:2	who **devise** evil in their hearts and stir	3108

Ps	140:8	do not let their **p** succeed,	2373
	146:4	on that very day their **p** come to nothing.	6955
Pr	12:5	The **p** of the righteous are just,	4742
	15:22	**P** fail for lack of counsel.	4742
	16:1	To man belong the **p** of the heart,	5119
	16:3	and your **p** will succeed.	4742
	16:9	In his heart a man **p** his course,	3108
	19:21	Many are the **p** in a man's heart,	4742
	20:18	Make **p** by seeking advice;	4742
	21:5	The **p** of the diligent lead to profit as surely	4742
Isa	19:3	and I will bring their **p** to nothing;	6783
	29:15	to great depths to hide their **p** from	6783
	30:1	"to those who carry out **p** that are not mine,	6783
	32:8	But the noble man **makes** noble **p,**	3619
Jer	18:12	We will continue with our own **p;**	4742
	18:18	"Come, let's **make p** against Jeremiah;	3108+4742
	19:7	" 'In this place I will ruin the **p** of Judah	6783
	29:11	For I know the **p** I have for you,"	3108+4742
	29:11	"**p** to prosper you and not to harm you,	4742
	29:11	**p** to give you hope and a future.	NIH
Da	11:17	but his **p** will not succeed or help him.	NIH
Hos	11:6	of their gates and put an end to their **p.**	4600
Mt	22:15	the Pharisees went out and **laid p**	3284+5206
Jn	12:10	chief priests **made p** to kill Lazarus as well,	1086
2Co	1:17	Or do I **make** my **p** in a worldly manner so	1086

PLANT (59) [IMPLANTED, PLANTED, PLANTER, PLANTING, PLANTS, REPLANTED, TRANSPLANTED]

Ge	1:29	"I give you every seed-bearing **p** on	6912
	1:30	I give every green **p** for food."	6912
	2:5	and no **p** of the field had yet sprung up,	6912
	9:20	proceeded to **p** a vineyard.	5749
	47:23	here is seed for you so you **can p**	2445
Ex	10:15	Nothing green remained on tree or **p** in all	6912
	15:17	You will bring them in and **p** them on	5749
Lev	19:19	**p** your field with two kinds of **seed.**	2445
	19:23	" 'When you enter the land and **p** any kind	5749
	25:20	if we do not **p** or harvest our crops?"	2445
	25:22	While you **p** during the eighth year,	2445
	26:16	You will **p** seed in vain,	2445
Dt	6:11	vineyards and olive groves you **did** not **p—**	5749
	22:9	Do not **p** two kinds of **seed** in your vineyard	2445
	22:9	if you do, not only the crops you **p** but	2445+2446
	28:30	You will **p** a vineyard, but you will not	5749
	28:39	You will **p** vineyards and cultivate them	5749
Jos	24:13	and olive groves that you **did** not **p.'**	5749
2Sa	7:10	for my people Israel and **will p** them so	5749
1Ki	4:33	He described **p** life, from the cedar of	6770
2Ki	19:29	**p** vineyards and eat their fruit.	5749
1Ch	17:9	for my people Israel and **will p** them so	5749
Job	8:16	like a **well-watered p** in the sunshine,	8183
	14:9	and put forth shoots like a **p.**	5750
Ecc	3:2	a time to **p** and a time to uproot,	5749
	11:4	Whoever watches the wind **will** not **p;**	2445
Isa	17:10	the finest plants and **p** imported vines,	2445
	17:11	and on the morning when you **p** them,	2446
	28:25	Does he not **p** wheat in its place,	8492
	37:30	**p** vineyards and eat their fruit.	5749
	65:21	they will **p** vineyards and eat their fruit.	5749
	65:22	or **p** and others eat.	5749
Jer	1:10	to destroy and overthrow, to build and to **p.**	5749
	24:6	I **will p** them and not uproot them.	5749
	29:5	**p** gardens and eat what they produce.	5749
	29:28	**p** gardens and eat what they produce.' "	5749
	31:5	Again you **will p** vineyards on the hills	5749
	31:5	farmers **will p** them and enjoy their fruit.	5749
	31:27	"when I **will p** the house of Israel and	2445
	31:28	so I **will** watch over them to build and to **p,"**	5749
	32:41	and **will** assuredly **p** them in this land	5749
	35:7	sow seed or **p** vineyards;	5749
	42:10	I **will p** you and not uproot you,	5749
Eze	16:7	I made you grow like a **p** of the field.	7542
	17:22	from the very top of a cedar and **p** it;	5989
	17:22	from its topmost shoots and **p** it on a high	9278
	17:23	the mountain heights of Israel I **will p** it;	9278
	28:26	and will build houses and **p** vineyards;	5749
Hos	2:23	I **will p** her for myself in the land;	2445
Am	9:14	They **will p** vineyards	5749
	9:15	I **will p** Israel in their own land,	5749
Mic	6:15	You **will p** but not harvest;	2445
Zep	1:13	they **will p** vineyards but not drink	5749
Mt	15:13	"Every **p** that my heavenly Father has	5884
Mk	4:31	the smallest seed you **p** in the ground.	5062
Jn	19:29	put the sponge on a stalk of the **hyssop p,**	5727
1Co	15:37	you do not **p** the body that will be,	5062
Jas	1:11	with scorching heat and withers the **p;**	5965
Rev	9:4	not to harm the grass of the earth or any **p**	5952

PLANTED (51) [PLANT]

Ge	2:8	the LORD God had **p** a garden in the east,	5749
	21:33	Abraham **p** a tamarisk tree in Beersheba,	5749
	26:12	Isaac **p** crops in that land and	2445
Lev	11:37	a carcass falls on any seeds that **are to be p,**	2445
Nu	24:6	like aloes **p** by the LORD,	5749
Dt	11:10	where you **p** your seed and irrigated it	2445
	20:6	Has anyone **p** a vineyard and not begun	5749
	21:4	a valley that has not been plowed or **p** and	2445
	29:23	nothing, nothing sprouting,	2445
Jdg	6:3	Whenever the Israelites **p** their crops,	2445
Ps	1:3	He is like a tree **p** by streams of water,	9278
	44:2	the nations and **p** our fathers;	5749
	80:8	you drove out the nations and **p** it.	5749
	80:15	the root your right hand has **p,**	5749
	92:13	**p** in the house of the LORD,	9278

Ps 104:16 the cedars of Lebanon that *he* p. 5749
107:37 They sowed fields and p vineyards, 5749
Ecc 2: 4 I built houses for myself and p vineyards. 5749
2: 5 I made gardens and parks and p all kinds 5749
Isa 5: 2 of stones and p it with the choicest vines. 5749
40:24 No sooner are *they*, 5749
44:14 or p a pine, and the rain made it grow. 5749
60:21 They are the shoot I have p, 4760
Jer 2:21 I *had* p you like a choice vine of sound 5749
11:17 The LORD Almighty, who p you, 5749
12: 2 *You have* p them, and they have taken root; 5749
17: 8 a tree p by the water that sends out its roots 9278
18: 9 a nation or kingdom is to be built up and p, 5749
45: 4 and uproot what *I have* p, 5749
Eze 17: 4 where *he* p it in a city of traders. 8492
17: 5 *He* p it like a willow by abundant water, 8492
17: 7 toward him from the plot where it was p 4760
17: 8 *had been* p in good soil by abundant water 9278
19:10 like a vine in your vineyard p by the water; 9278
19:13 Now *it is* p in the desert, 9278
Hos 9:13 like Tyre, p in a pleasant place. 9278
10:13 But *you have* p wickedness, 3086
Am 5:11 though *you have* p lush vineyards, 5749
Hag 1: 6 *You have* p much, but have harvested little. 2445
Mt 13:31 which a man took and p in his field. 5062
15:13 that my heavenly Father *has not* p will 5885
21:33 There was a landowner who p a vineyard 5885
Mk 4:32 when p, it grows and becomes the largest 5062
12: 1 "A man p a vineyard. 5885
Lk 13: 6 "A man had a fig tree, p in his vineyard, 5885
13:19 which a man took and p in his garden. 965
17: 6 'Be uprooted and p in the sea,' 5885
20: 9 "A man p a vineyard, 5885
1Co 3: 6 I p the seed, Apollos watered it, 5885
Jas 1:21 and humbly accept the word p in you, 1875
Rev 10: 2 *He* p his right foot on the sea 5502

PLANTER (1) [PLANT]
Am 9:13 and the p by the one treading grapes. 2446+5432

PLANTING (5) [PLANT]
Lev 26: 5 and the grape harvest will continue until p, 2446
Isa 28:24 When a farmer plows for p, 2445
61: 3 p of the LORD for the display of his splendor 4760
Mic 1: 6 a place for p vineyards. 4760
Lk 17:28 buying and selling, p and building. 5885

PLANTS (30) [PLANT]
Ge 1:11 seed-bearing p and trees on the land 6912
1:12 p bearing seed according to their kinds 6912
3:18 and you will eat the p of the field. 6912
9: 3 Just as I gave you the green p, 6912
30:14 into the fields and found *some* mandrake p, 1859
Dt 32: 2 like abundant rain on tender p. 6912
2Ki 19:26 They are like p in the field, 6912
Job 8:19 and from the soil other p grow. NIH
40:21 Under the lotus p he lies, 7365
Ps 37: 2 like green p they will soon die away. 3764
104:14 and p for man to cultivate— 6912
144:12 in their youth will be like well-nurtured p, 5745
Pr 31:16 out of her earnings *she* p a vineyard. 5749
SS 4:13 Your p are an orchard of pomegranates 8945
Isa 17:10 the finest p and plant imported vines, 5750
19: 7 also the p along the Nile, 6868
37:27 They are like p in the field, 6912
Da 4:15 with the animals among the p of the earth. 10572
Zec 10: 1 and p of the field to everyone. 6912
Mt 13: 6 the sun came up, the p were scorched, NIG
13: 7 which grew up and choked the p, 899^S
13:32 the largest *of* garden p and becomes a tree, 3303
Mk 4: 6 the sun came up, the p were scorched, NIG
4: 7 which grew up and choked the p, 899^S
4:32 and becomes the largest of all garden p, 3303
Lk 8: 6 p withered because they had no moisture. NIG
8: 7 which grew up with it and choked the p. 899^S
1Co 3: 7 So neither he who p nor he who waters 5885
3: 8 The man who p and the man who waters 5885
9: 7 Who p a vineyard and does not eat 5885

PLASTER (5) [PLASTERED]
Lev 14:42 to replace these and take new clay and p 3212
14:45 its stones, timbers and all the p— 6760
Dt 27: 2 up some large stones and coat them with p. 8487
27: 4 command you today, and coat them with p. 8487
Da 5: 5 a human hand appeared and wrote on the p 10142

PLASTERED (3) [PLASTER]
Lev 14:43 and the house scraped and p, 3212
14:48 not spread after the house *has been* p, 3212
Isa 44:18 their eyes *are* p over so they cannot see, 3220

PLATE (16) [PLATES, PLATTER]
Ex 28:36 "Make a p of pure gold and engrave on it 7488
39:30 They made the p, the sacred diadem, 7488
Lev 8: 9 on Aaron's head and set the gold p, 7488
Nu 7:13 His offering was one silver p weighing 7883
7:19 he brought was one silver p weighing 7883
7:25 His offering was one silver p weighing 7883
7:31 His offering was one silver p weighing 7883
7:37 His offering was one silver p weighing 7883
7:43 His offering was one silver p weighing 7883
7:49 His offering was one silver p weighing 7883
7:55 His offering was one silver p weighing 7883

Nu 7:61 His offering was one silver p weighing 7883
7:67 His offering was one silver p weighing 7883
7:73 His offering was one silver p weighing 7883
7:79 His offering was one silver p weighing 7883
7:85 Each silver p weighed a hundred and thirty shekels, 7883

PLATEAU (10)
Dt 3:10 We took all the towns on the p, 4793
4:43 in the desert p, for the Reubenites; 824+4793
Jos 13: 9 and included the whole p *of* Medeba as far 4793
13:16 and the whole p past Medeba 4793
13:17 to Heshbon and all its towns on the p, 4793
13:21 on the p and the entire realm of Sihon king 4793
20: 8 the desert on the p in the tribe of Reuben, 4793
Jer 21:13 above this valley on the rocky p, declares 4793
48: 8 be ruined and the p destroyed, 4793
48:21 Judgment has come to the p— 4793

PLATES (4) [PLATE]
Ex 25:29 And make its p and dishes of pure gold, 7883
37:16 its p and dishes and bowls and its pitchers 7883
Nu 4: 7 and put on it the p, dishes and bowls, and 7883
7:84 when it was anointed: twelve silver p, 7883

PLATFORM (3)
2Ch 6:13 Now he had made a bronze p, 3963
6:13 He stood on the p and then knelt down 2257^S
Ne 8: 4 Ezra the scribe stood on a high wooden p 4463

PLATTED (KJV) See TWISTED

PLATTER (4) [PLATE]
Mt 14: 8 "Give me here on a p the head of John 4402
14:11 His head was brought in on a p and given 4402
Mk 6:25 now the head of John the Baptist on a p." 4402
6:28 and brought back his head on a p. 4402

PLAY (14) [PLAYED, PLAYERS, PLAYING, PLAYS]
Ge 4:21 the father of all *who* p the harp and flute. 9530
19: 9 and now *he* wants to p the judge! 9149+9149
1Sa 16:16 to search for someone who can p the harp. 5594
16:16 He *will* p when the evil spirit 928+3338+5594
16:18 who knows how *to* p the harp. 5594
16:23 David would take his harp and p. 928+3338+5594
1Ch 25:26 and Benaiah were to p the lyres according NIH
15:21 Jeiel and Azaziah were to p the harps, NIH
16: 5 They were to p the lyres and harps, NIH
Job 40:20 and all the wild animals p nearby. 8471
Ps 33: 3 p skillfully, and shout for joy. 5594
81: 2 p the melodious harp and lyre. NIH
Isa 11: 8 The infant *will* p near the hole of 9130
23:16 p the harp well, sing many a song, 5594

PLAYED (6) [PLAY]
1Sa 10: 5 flutes and harps being p before them, NIH
2Ch 29:28 the singers sang and the trumpeters p. 2955
Pr 30:32 *you have* p the fool and exalted yourself, 5571
Mt 11:17 " 'We p the flute for you, and you did not 884
Lk 7:32 " 'We p the flute for you, and you did not 884
1Co 14: 7 will anyone know what tune *is being* p 884

PLAYERS (2) [PLAY]
Mt 9:23 the ruler's house and saw the flute p and 886
Rev 18:22 flute p and trumpeters, 886

PLAYING (11) [PLAY]
1Sa 18:10 while David *was* p the harp, 928+3338+5594
19: 9 While David *was* p the harp, 928+3338+5594
1Ki 1:40 p flutes and rejoicing greatly, 2727
2Ki 3:15 While the harpist was p, 5594
1Ch 15:28 and the p of lyres and harps. 9048
16:42 the trumpets and cymbals and for the p of NIH
2Ch 5:12 dressed in fine linen and p cymbals, NIH
34:12 skilled in p musical instruments— NIH
Ps 68:25 with them are the maidens p tambourines. 9528
Zec 8: 5 be filled with boys and girls p there." 8471
Rev 14: 2 like that of harpists p their harps. 3068

PLAYS (2) [PLAY]
1Sa 16:17 "Find someone *who* p well and bring him 5594
Eze 33:32 a beautiful voice and p an instrument well, 5594

PLEA (25) [PLEAD, PLEADED, PLEADING, PLEADS, PLEAS]
Ge 30: 6 he has listened to my p and given me 7754
Nu 21: 3 The LORD listened to Israel's p and gave 7754
1Ki 8:28 your servant's prayer and his p for mercy, 9382
8:38 or p is made by any of your people Israel 9382
8:45 hear from heaven their prayer and their p, 9382
8:49 hear their prayer and their p, 9382
8:52 "May your eyes be open to your servant's p 9382
8:52 be open to your servant's plea and to the p 9382
9: 3 the prayer and p you have made before me; 9382
2Ch 6:19 and his p for mercy, 9382
6:29 or p is made by any of your people Israel— 9382
6:35 hear from heaven their prayer and their p, 9382
33:13 by his entreaty and listened to his p; 9382

Job 13: 6 listen to the p of my lips. 8191
35:13 God does not listen to their empty p; 8736
Ps 17: 1 Hear, O LORD, my righteous p; NIH
55: 1 O God, do not ignore my p; 9382
102:17 he will not despise their p. 9525
Pr 6: 3 press your p with your neighbor! 8104
Isa 32: 7 even when the p of the needy is just. 1819
Jer 7:16 for this people nor offer any p or petition 8262
11:14 "Do not pray for this people nor offer any p 8262
La 3:56 You heard my p; 7754
Eze 36:37 Once again *I will* yield to the p of 2011
Lk 18: 3 who kept coming to him with the p, 3306

PLEAD (22) [PLEA]
Jdg 6:31 "Are you going to p Baal's cause? 8189
1Sa 2:36 a piece of silver and a crust of bread and p, 606
1Ki 8:47 and repent and p with you in the land 2858
2Ch 6:37 and p with you in the land of their captivity 2858
Est 4: 8 for mercy and p with him for her people. 1335
Job 8: 5 But if you will look to God and p with 2858
9:15 p with my Judge for mercy. 2858
35: 9 *they* p for relief from the arm of 8775
Ps 43: 1 and p my cause against an ungodly nation; 8189
Isa 1:17 p the case *of* the widow. 8189
45:14 down before you and p with you, saying, 7137
Jer 5:28 not p the case of the fatherless to win it, 1906
7:16 *do not* p with me, for I will not listen to you. 7003
15:11 surely *I will* make your enemies p 7003
27:18 let them p with the LORD Almighty that 7003
30:13 There is no *one to* p your cause, 1906
Da 2:18 to p *for* mercy from the God of heaven 10114
Mic 6: 1 p your case *before* the mountains; 8189
Mk 5:17 Then the people began *to* p with Jesus 4151
Gal 4:12 I p with you, brothers, become like me, 1289
Php 4: 2 I p with Euodia and I plead with Syntyche 4151
4: 2 with Euodia and I p with Syntyche to agree 4151

PLEADED (13) [PLEA]
Ge 42:21 We saw how distressed he was when he p 2858
Dt 3:23 At that time *I* p with the LORD: 2858
2Sa 12:16 David p *with* God for the child. 1335
Est 8: 3 Esther again p with the king. 1819
Da 9: 3 So I turned to the Lord God and p with him 1335
Mt 8:34 *they* p with him to leave their region. 4151
Mk 5:23 and p earnestly with him, 4151
Lk 7: 4 they p earnestly with him, 4151
15:28 So his father went out and p with him. 4151
Ac 2:40 and *he* p with them, 4151
21:12 and the people there p with Paul not to go 4151
2Co 8: 4 *they* urgently p with us for the privilege 1289
12: 8 Three times *I* p with the Lord 4151

PLEADING (5) [PLEA]
Pr 19: 7 Though he pursues them with p, 609
Jer 3:21 the weeping and p of the people of Israel, 9384
38:26 'I *was* p with the king not to send me 5877+9382
Lk 8:41 p with him to come to his house 4151
13:25 you will stand outside knocking and p, 3306

PLEADS (5) [PLEA]
Job 16:21 on behalf of a man he p with God as a man 3519
16:21 he pleads with God as a man p for his friend. NIH
Pr 18:23 A poor man p for mercy, 1819
Isa 59: 4 no *one* p his case with integrity. 9149
Mic 7: 9 until *he* p my case and establishes my right. 8189

PLEAS (2) [PLEA]
2Ch 6:39 hear their prayer and their p, 9382
Isa 19:22 he will respond to their p and heal them. 6983

PLEASANT (20) [PLEASE]
Ge 49:15 and how p *is* his land, 5838
Ps 16: 6 lines have fallen for me in p *places;* 5833
106:24 Then they despised the p land; 2775
133: 1 p it is when brothers live together in unity! 5833
135: 3 sing praise to his name, for that is p. 5833
147: 1 how p and fitting to praise him! 5833
Pr 2:10 and knowledge *will be* p to your soul. 5838
3:17 Her ways are p ways, 5840
16:21 and p words promote instruction. 5518
16:24 P words are a honeycomb, 5840
Isa 30:10 Tell us p *things,* prophesy illusions. 2747
32:12 Beat your breasts for the p fields, 2774
Jer 12:10 they will turn my p field into 2775
31:26 My sleep *had been* p to me. 6844
Hos 4:13 poplar and terebinth, where the shade is p. 3202
9:13 like Tyre, planted in a p place. 5659
Mic 2: 9 of my people from their p homes. 9503
Zec 7:14 how they made the p land desolate.' " 2775
1Th 3: 6 that you always have p memories of us and 19
Heb 12:11 No discipline seems p at the time, 5915

PLEASANTNESS (1) [PLEASE]
Pr 27: 9 and the p of one's friend springs 5518

PLEASE (115) [PLEASANT, PLEASANTNESS, PLEASED, PLEASES, PLEASING, PLEASURE, PLEASURES]
Ge 19: 2 "p turn aside to your servant's house. 5528
19:18 But Lot said to them, "No, my lords, p! 5528
24:14 'P let down your jar that I may have 5528

Ge	24:17	"P give me a little water from your jar."	5528
	24:23	P tell me, is there room	5528
	24:42	p grant success to the journey	5528
	24:43	to her, "P let me drink a little water	5528
	24:45	and I said to her, 'P give me a drink.'	5528
	27:19	P sit up and eat some of my game so	5528
	30:14	"P give me some of your son's mandrakes."	5528
	30:27	"If I have found favor in your eyes, p stay.	5528
	32:29	Jacob said, "P tell me your name."	5528
	33:10	"No, p!" said Jacob.	5528
	33:11	P accept the present that was brought	5528
	34: 8	P give her to him as his wife.	5528
	43:20	"P, sir," they said, "we came down here	1065
	44:18	Then Judah went up to him and said: "P,	1065
	44:33	p let your servant remain here	5528
	47: 4	now, p let your servants settle in Goshen."	5528
	50:17	Now p forgive the sins of the servants of	5528
Ex	4:13	"O Lord, p send someone else to do it."	5528
	21: 8	If she does not p the master	928+6524+8317
	32:32	But now, p forgive their sin—	561
Nu	10:31	But Moses said, "P do not leave us.	5528
	12:11	and he said to Moses, "P, my lord, do	1065+5528
	12:13	"O God, p heal her!"	5528
	20:17	P let us pass through your country.	5528
	23:27	Perhaps it will p God	928+3837+6524
	36: 6	They may marry anyone they p as long as	928+3202+6524
Dt	12:13	not to sacrifice your burnt offerings anywhere you p.	8011
	28:63	so it will p him to ruin and destroy you.	8464
Jos	2:12	p swear to me by the LORD	5528
Jdg	4:19	"P give me some water."	5528
	6:18	P do not go away until I come back	5528
	10:15	but p rescue us now."	5528
	16:28	O God, p strengthen me just once more,	5528
	18: 5	"P inquire of God to learn whether	5528
	19: 6	"P stay tonight and enjoy yourself."	5528
Ru	2: 7	'P let me glean and gather among	5528
1Sa	9:18	"Would you p tell me where	5528
	15:30	But p honor me before the elders	5528
	25: 8	P give your servants and your son David	5528
	25:24	P let your servant speak to you;	5528
	25:28	P forgive your servant's offense.	5528
	28:22	Now p listen to your servant	5528
2Sa	13:13	P speak to the king;	5528
	13:24	Will the king and his officials p join me?"	5528
	13:26	p let my brother Amnon come with us."	5528
	18:22	p let me run behind the Cushite."	5528
1Ki	2:17	So he continued, "P ask King Solomon—	5528
	3:26	"P, my lord, give her the living baby!	1065
	17:11	"And bring me, p, a piece of bread."	5528
	20:32	Ben-Hadad says: 'P let me live.' "	5528
	20:37	and said, "Strike me, p."	5528
2Ki	1:13	"p have respect for my life and the lives	5528
	4:22	"P send me one of the servants and	5528
	5:15	P accept now a gift from your servant."	5528
	5:17	"If you will not," said Naaman, "p let me,	5528
	5:22	P give them a talent of silver and two sets	5528
	6: 3	Won't you p come with your servants?	3283+5528
	18:26	"P speak to your servants in Aramaic,	5528
2Ch	10: 7	to these people and p them and give them	8464
Ne	9:37	over our bodies and our cattle as they p.	8356
Est	3:11	and do with the people as you p.	928+3202+6524
Job	10: 3	Does it p you to oppress me,	3202
	34: 9	a man nothing when he tries to p God.'	8354
Ps	69:31	This will p the LORD more than an ox,	3512
Pr	20:23	and dishonest scales do not p him.	3202
Isa	29:11	say to him, "Read this, p," he will answer,	5528
	29:12	and say, "Read this, p," he will answer,	5528
	36:11	"P speak to your servants in Aramaic,	5528
	44:28	and will accomplish all that I p;	2914
	46:10	and I will do all that I p.	2914
	58: 3	as you p and exploit all your workers.	2914
	58:13	and from doing as you p on my holy day,	2914
	58:13	not doing as you p or speaking idle words,	2914
Jer	6:20	your sacrifices do not p me."	6844
	27: 5	and I give it to anyone I p.	928+3837+6524
	36:15	They said to him, "Sit down, p,	5528
	37: 3	"P pray to the LORD our God for us."	5528
	37:20	But now, my lord the king, p listen.	5528
	40: 4	go wherever you p."	928+2256+3202+3838+6524
	40: 5	or go anywhere else you p."	928+3838+6524
	42: 2	"P hear our petition and pray to the LORD	5528
Da	1:12	"P test your servants for ten days:	5528
Hos	9: 1	nor will their sacrifices p him.	6844
	10:10	When I p, I will punish them;	205
Jnh	1:14	p do not let us die for taking this man's life.	5528
Mk	5:23	P come and put your hands on her so	NIG
Lk	14:18	P excuse me.'	2263+5148
	14:19	P excuse me.'	2263+5148
Jn	5:30	I seek not to p myself but him who sent me.	2525
Ac	8:34	The eunuch asked Philip, "Tell me, p,	1289+5148
	9:38	to him and urged him, "P come at once!"	NIG
	13:15	of encouragement for the people, p speak."	NIG
	21:39	P let me speak to the people."	1289+5148
Ro	8: 8	by the sinful nature cannot p God.	743
	15: 1	of the weak and not to p ourselves.	743
	15: 2	of us should p his neighbor for his good,	743
	15: 3	Christ did not p himself but, as it is written:	743
1Co	7:32	how he can p the Lord.	743
	7:33	how he can p his wife—	743
	7:34	how she can p her husband.	743
	10:33	even as I try to p everybody in every way.	743
2Co	5: 9	So we make it our goal to p him,	1639+2298
Gal	1:10	Or am I trying to p men?	743
	1:10	If I were still trying to p men,	743
	6: 8	The one who sows to p his sinful nature,	NIG

Gal	6: 8	the one who sows to p the Spirit,	NIG
Col	1:10	of the Lord and may p him in every way:	742
1Th	2: 4	We are not trying to p men but God,	743
	4: 1	how to live in order to p God,	743
2Ti	2: 4	he wants to p his commanding officer.	743
Tit	2: 9	to try to p them, not to talk back to them,	2298
Heb	11: 6	without faith it is impossible to p God,	2297

PLEASED (78) [PLEASE]

Ge	45:16	Pharaoh and all his officials were p.	928+3512+6524
	49: 6	and hamstrung oxen as they p.	8356
Ex	33:13	If you are p with me,	928+2834+5162+6524
	33:16	that you are p with me and with your people	928+2834+5162+6524
	33:17	I am p with you and I know you by name."	928+2834+5162+6524
Lev	10:19	Would the LORD have been p if I had eaten	928+6524
Nu	14: 8	If the LORD is p with us,	2911
	24: 1	when Balaam saw that it p the LORD to bless Israel,	928+3201+6524
Dt	21:14	If you are not p with her,	2911
	28:63	as it p the LORD to make you prosper	8464
	33:11	and be p with the work of his hands.	8354
Jos	22:30	Gad and Manasseh had to say, they were p.	928+3512+6524
1Sa	12:22	the LORD was p to make you his own.	3283
	16:22	for I am p with him."	928+2834+5162+6524
	18: 5	This p all the people,	928+3512+6524
	18:20	they told Saul about it, he was p.	928+3837+6524
	18:22	'Look, the king is p with you,	2911
	18:26	he was p to become the king's son-in-law.	928+3837+6524
	29: 6	be p to have you serve with me in the army	928+3202+6524
2Sa	3:36	All the people took note and were p;	928+3512+6524
	3:36	everything the king did p them.	928+3202+6524
	7:29	be p to bless the house of your servant,	3283
	15:26	But if he says, 'I am not p with you,'	2911
	19: 6	be p if Absalom were alive today	928+3838+6524
1Ki	3:10	The Lord was p that Solomon had asked for this.	928+3512+6524
	5: 7	he was greatly p and said,	8523
	9:12	he was not p with them.	928+3837+6524
	11:19	Pharaoh was so p with Hadad that he gave him a sister	928+2834+5162+6524
1Ch	17:27	Now you have been p to bless the house	3283
	28: 4	and from my father's sons he was p	8354
	29:17	you test the heart and are p with integrity.	8354
Ne	2: 6	It p the king to send me; so I set a time.	3512
	9:24	to deal with them as they p.	8356
	12:44	for Judah was p with the ministering priests	8525
Est	1:21	nobles were p with this advice,	928+3512+6524
	2: 9	The girl p him and won his favor.	928+3512+6524
	2:14	not return to the king unless he was p	2911
	5: 2	he was p with her and	928+2834+5951+6524
	8: 5	and if he is p with me,	928+3202+6524
	9: 5	they did what they p to those who hated	8356
Ps	40:13	Be p, O LORD, to save me;	8354
	41:11	I know that you are p with me,	2911
	105:22	as he p and teach his elders wisdom.	5883
Ecc	4:16	But those who came later were not p with	8523
Isa	42:21	It p the LORD for the sake of his	2911
Eze	18:23	am I not p when they turn from their ways	NIH
Da	4:27	O king, be p to accept my advice:	10739
	6: 1	It p Darius to appoint 120 satraps to rule	10739
	8: 4	He did as he p and became great.	8356
Hos	8:13	but the LORD is not p with them.	8354
Jnh	1:14	for you, O LORD, have done as you p."	2911
Mic	6: 7	the LORD be p with thousands of rams,	8354
Mal	1: 8	Would he be p with you?	8354
	1:10	I am not p with you,"	2914
	2:17	who do evil are in the eyes of the LORD, and he is p with them"	2911
Mt	3:17	with him I am well p."	2305
	14: 6	of Herodias danced for them and p Herod	743
	17: 5	with him I am well p.	2305
Mk	1:11	with you I am well p."	2305
	6:22	she p Herod and his dinner guests.	743
Lk	3:22	with you I am well p."	2305
	12:32	for your Father has been p to give you	2305
	23: 8	When Herod saw Jesus, he was greatly p,	5897
Jn	5:21	Son gives life to whom he is p to give it.	2527
Ac	6: 5	This proposal p the whole group.	743
	12: 3	When he saw that this p the Jews,	744+1639
Ro	15:26	For Macedonia and Achaia were p to make	2305
	15:27	They were p to do it,	2305
1Co	1:21	God was p through the foolishness	2305
	10: 5	God was not p with most of them;	2305
Gal	1:15	and called me by his grace, was p	2305
Col	1:19	For God was p to have all his fullness dwell	2305
Heb	10: 6	with burnt offerings and sin offerings you were not p,	2305
	10: 8	nor were you p with them"	2305
	10:38	he shrinks back, I will not be p with him."	2305
	11: 5	he was commended as one who p God.	2297
	13:16	for with such sacrifices God is p.	2297
2Pe	1:17	with him I am well p."	2305

PLEASES (40) [PLEASE]

1Sa	23:20	come down whenever it p you to do so,	205
2Sa	19:27	so do whatever p you.	928+3202+6524
	19:37	Do for him whatever p you."	928+3202+6524

Mt	19:38	I will do for him whatever p you.	928+3202+6524
	24:22	"Let my lord the king take whatever p him	928+3202+6524
1Ch	21:23	Let my lord the king do whatever p him.	928+3202+6524
Ezr	5:17	Now if it p the king, let him issue	10294
Ne	2: 5	"If it p the king and if your servant	3201
	2: 7	I also said to him, "If it p the king,	3201
Est	1:19	"Therefore, if it p the king,	3201
	2: 4	the girl who p the king be queen instead of Vashti.	928+3512+6524
	3: 9	If it p the king, let a decree be issued	3201
	5: 4	"If it p the king," replied Esther,	3201
	5: 8	the king regards me with favor and if it p	3201
	7: 3	O king, and if it p your majesty,	3201
	8: 5	"If it p the king," she said,	3202
	9:13	"If it p the king," Esther answered,	3202
Job	23:13	He does whatever he p.	203
Ps	115: 3	he does whatever p him.	2911
	135: 6	The LORD does whatever p him,	2911
Pr	15: 8	but the prayer of the upright p him.	8356
	21: 1	like a watercourse wherever he p.	2911
Ecc	2:26	To the man who p him, God gives wisdom,	3202
	2:26	to hand it over to the one who p God.	3202
	7:26	The man who p God will escape her,	3202
	8: 3	for he will do whatever he p.	2911
	11: 7	and it p the eyes to see the sun.	3202
Isa	56: 4	who choose what p me and hold fast	2911
Eze	46: 5	is to be as much as he p,	3338+5522
	46:11	with the lambs as much as one p,	3338+5522
Da	4:35	He does as he p with the powers of heaven	10605
	11: 3	with great power and do as he p.	8356
	11:16	The invader will do as he p;	8356
	11:36	"The king will do as he p.	8356
Jn	3: 8	The wind blows wherever it p.	2527
	8:29	for I always do what p him."	744
Eph	5:10	and find out what p the Lord.	1639+2298
Col	3:20	for this p the Lord.	1639+2298
1Ti	2: 3	This is good, and p God our Savior,	621
1Jn	3:22	we obey his commands and do what p him.	744

PLEASING (58) [PLEASE]

Ge	2: 9	that were p to the eye and good for food.	2773
	3: 6	the fruit of the tree was good for food and p	9294
	8:21	The LORD smelled the p aroma and said	5767
Ex	29:18	the LORD, a p aroma, an offering made to	5767
	29:25	along with the burnt offering for a p aroma	5767
	29:41	a p aroma, an offering made to the LORD	5767
Lev	1: 9	an aroma p to the LORD.	5767
	1:13	an aroma p to the LORD.	5767
	1:17	an aroma p to the LORD.	5767
	2: 2	an aroma p to the LORD.	5767
	2: 9	an aroma p to the LORD.	5767
	2:12	not to be offered on the altar as a p aroma.	5767
	3: 5	an aroma p to the LORD.	5767
	3:16	an offering made by fire, a p aroma.	5767
	4:31	on the altar as an aroma p to the LORD.	5767
	6:15	on the altar as an aroma p to the LORD.	5767
	6:21	in pieces as an aroma p to the LORD.	5767
	8:21	a p aroma, an offering made to the LORD	5767
	8:28	a p aroma, an offering made to the LORD	5767
	17: 6	of Meeting and burn the fat as an aroma p	5767
	23:13	to the LORD by fire, a p aroma—	5767
	23:18	an aroma p to the LORD.	5767
	26:31	and I will take no delight in the p aroma	5767
Nu	15: 3	as an aroma p to the LORD—	5767
	15: 7	Offer it as an aroma p to the LORD.	5767
	15:10	an aroma p to the LORD.	5767
	15:13	an offering made by fire as an aroma p	5767
	15:14	an offering made by fire as an aroma p to	5767
	15:24	for a burnt offering as an aroma p to	5767
	18:17	an aroma p to the LORD.	5767
	28: 2	as an aroma p to me.'	5767
	28: 6	at Mount Sinai as a p aroma,	5767
	28: 8	an aroma p to the LORD.	5767
	28:13	This is for a burnt offering, a p aroma,	5767
	28:24	for seven days as an aroma p to	5767
	28:27	a year old as an aroma p to the LORD.	5767
	29: 2	As an aroma p to the LORD,	5767
	29: 6	by fire—a p aroma.	5767
	29: 8	an aroma p to the LORD a burnt offering	5767
	29:13	an offering made by fire as an aroma p to	5767
	29:36	an offering made by fire as an aroma p to	5767
1Sa	29: 9	"I know that you have been as p in my eyes	3202
Ezr	6:10	that they may offer sacrifices to the God	10478
Ps	19:14	and the meditation of my heart be p	8356
	104:34	May my meditation be p to him,	6844
Pr	15:26	but those of the pure are p to him.	5840
	16: 7	When a man's ways are p to the LORD,	8354
	22:18	for it is p when you keep them	5833
SS	1: 3	P is the fragrance of your perfumes;	3202
	4:10	How much more p is your love than wine,	3201
	7: 6	How beautiful you are and how p, O love,	5838
La	2: 4	a foe he has slain all who were p to the eye;	4718
Ro	12: 1	holy and p to God—	2298
	12: 2	his good, p and perfect will.	2298
	14:18	in this way is p to God and approved	2298
Php	4:18	an acceptable sacrifice, p to God.	2298
1Ti	5: 4	for this is p to God.	621
Heb	13:21	and may he work in us what is p to him,	2298

PLEASURE (34) [PLEASE]

Ge	18:12	my master is old, will I now have this p?"	6366
Job	22: 3	What p would it give the Almighty	2914
Ps	5: 4	You are not a God who takes p in evil;	2913

Ps	51:16	*you do* not **take p** in burnt offerings.	8354
	51:18	In your **good p** make Zion prosper;	8356
	109:17	he **found** no **p** in blessing—	2911
	147:10	*His* **p** *is* not in the strength of the horse,	2911
Pr	10:23	A fool finds **p** in evil conduct,	8468
	16:13	Kings take **p** *in* honest lips;	8356
	18: 2	A fool **finds** no **p** in understanding	2911
	21:17	He who loves **p** will become poor;	8525
Ecc	2: 1	with **p** to find out what is good.”	8525
	2: 2	And what does **p** accomplish?”	8525
	2:10	I refused my heart no **p.**	8525
	5: 4	He has no **p** in fools; fulfill your vow.	2914
	7: 4	but the heart of fools is in the house of **p.**	8525
	12: 1	“I find no **p** in them”—	2914
Isa	1:11	*I* have no **p** *in* the blood of bulls	2911
	9:17	the Lord *will* take no **p** in the young men,	8523
Jer	6:10	*they* **find** no **p** in it.	2911
Eze	16:37	with whom *you* **found p,**	6844
	18:23	*Do I* **take** any **p** in the death of the wicked?	2911+2911
	18:32	For I **take** no **p** in the death of anyone,	2911
	33:11	*I* **take** no **p** in the death of the wicked,	2911
Da	4: 2	*It is* my **p** to tell you about the miraculous	10739
Hag	1: 8	so that *I may* **take p** in it and be honored,”	8354
Mal	2:13	or accepts them *with* **p** from your hands.	8356
Mt	11:26	Yes, Father, for this was your **good p.**	2306
Lk	10:21	Yes, Father, for this was your **good p.**	2306
Eph	1: 5	in accordance with his **p** and will—	2306
	1: 9	of his will according to his **good p,**	2306
1Ti	5: 6	the widow who **lives for p** is dead even	5059
2Ti	3: 4	**lovers** of **p** rather than lovers of God—	5798
2Pe	2:13	of **p** is to carouse in broad daylight.	2454

PLEASURES (6) [PLEASE]

Ps	16:11	with eternal **p** at your right hand.	5833
Lk	8:14	riches and **p,** and they do not mature.	2454
Tit	3: 3	by all kinds of passions and **p.**	2454
Heb	11:25	the people of God rather than to enjoy the **p**	656
Jas	4: 3	you may spend what you get on your **p.**	2454
2Pe	2:13	in their **p** while they feast with you.	573

PLEDGE (32) [PLEDGED, PLEDGES]

Ge	38:17	“Will you give me something as a **p**	6860
	38:18	He said, “What **p** should I give you?”	6860
	38:20	in order to get his **p** back from the woman,	6860
Ex	22:26	**take** your neighbor’s cloak **as a p,**	2471+2471
Nu	30: 2	or takes an oath to obligate himself by a **p,**	674
	30: 3	to the Lord or obligates herself by a **p**	674
	30: 4	about her vow or **p** but says nothing to her,	674
	30: 4	then all her vows and every **p**	674
	30:10	a vow or obligates herself by a **p** under oath	674
	30:13	or any sworn **p** to deny herself.	674
Dt	24:10	to get *what* he is **offering** as a **p.**	6287
	24:11	the loan bring the **p** out to you.	6287
	24:12	to sleep with his **p** in your possession.	6287
	24:17	**take** the cloak of the widow **as a p.**	2471
2Ch	34:32	had everyone in Jerusalem and Benjamin **p**	6641
Ezr	10:19	**gave** their hands **in p** to put away their	5989
Job	17: 3	“Give me, O God, the **p** you demand.	6842
	24: 3	**take** the widow’s ox **in p.**	2471
Pr	6: 1	if *you* have **struck** hands **in p** for another,	9546
	11:15	to **strike** hands **in p** is safe.	9364
	17:18	in judgment **strikes** hands **in p** and puts	9546
	20:16	**hold** it **in p** if he does it for a wayward	2471
	22:26	not be a *man who* **strikes** hands **in p** or puts	9546
	27:13	**hold** it **in p** if he does it for a wayward	2471
Eze	17:18	Because *he had* **given** his hand **in p**	5989
	18: 7	returns **what** he **took in p** for a loan.	2481
	18:12	not return **what** he **took in p.**	2478
	18:16	or **require a p for a loan,**	2471+2478
	33:15	gives back **what** he **took in p for a loan,**	2478
Am	2: 8	beside every altar on garments **taken in p.**	2471
1Ti	5:12	because they have broken their first **p.**	4411
1Pe	3:21	but the **p** of a good conscience toward God.	2090

PLEDGED (13) [PLEDGE]

Ge	19:14	*who were* **p to marry** his daughters.	4374
Ex	22:16	seduces a virgin *who is* not **p to be married**	829
Dt	20: 7	*Has* anyone **become p** *to* a woman and	829
	22:23	to meet in a town a virgin **p to be married**	829
	22:25	meet a girl **p to be married** and rapes her,	829
	22:28	to meet a virgin who *is* not **p to be married**	829
	28:30	*You will be* **p to be married** to a woman,	829
2Ki	23: 3	the people *themselves* to the covenant.	6641
1Ch	29:24	**p** their submission to King Solomon.	3338+5989
Mic	7:20	as *you* **p on oath** to our fathers	8678
Mt	1:18	His mother Mary *was* **p to be married**	3650
Lk	1:27	to a virgin **p to be married** to a man	3650
	2: 5	Mary, who *was* **p to be married** to him	3650

PLEDGES (5) [PLEDGE]

Nu	30: 5	none of her vows or the **p** by which she	674
	30: 7	then her vows or the **p** by which she	674
	30:11	then all her vows or the **p** by which she	674
	30:12	or **p** that came from her lips will stand.	674
	30:14	or the **p** binding on her.	674

PLEIADES (3)

Job	9: 9	the **P** and the constellations of the south.	3966
	38:31	“Can you bind the beautiful **P?**	3966
Am	5: 8	the **P** and Orion, who turns blackness	3966

PLENTIFUL (8) [PLENTY]

1Ki	10:27	as **p** as sycamore-fig trees in the foothills.	4200+8044
1Ch	12:40	were **p** supplies of flour, fig cakes,	4200+8044
2Ch	1:15	as **p** as sycamore-fig trees in the foothills.	4200+8044
	9:27	as **p** as sycamore-fig trees in the foothills.	4200+8044
Isa	30:23	that comes from the land will be rich and **p.**	9045
Eze	36:29	and **make** it **p** and will not bring famine	8049
Mt	9:37	“The harvest is **p** but the workers are few.	4498
Lk	10: 2	He told them, “The harvest is **p,**	4498

PLENTIFULLY (1) [PLENTY]

Ge	41:47	of abundance the land produced **p.**	4200+7859

PLENTY (21) [PLENTIFUL, PLENTIFULLY]

Ge	24:25	“We have **p** *of* straw and fodder,	8041
	33: 9	Esau said, “I already have **p,** my brother.	8041
	34:21	the land has **p of room** for them.	3338+8146
2Ch	2: 9	to provide me with **p of lumber,**	4200+8044
	31:10	we have had enough to eat and **p** to spare,	4200+8044
	32: 4	kings of Assyria come and find **p** of water?”	8041
Job	20:22	In the midst of his **p,** distress will overtake	8565
Ps	17:14	their sons **have p,** and they store up wealth	8425
	37:19	in days of famine *they will* **enjoy p.**	8425
Pr	27:27	You will **have p** of goats’ milk to feed you	1896
Jer	44:17	At that time *we* **had p** *of* food	8425
Joel	2:26	*You will* **have p to eat,** until you are full,	430+430
Mic	2:11	‘I will prophesy for you **p** of wine	NIH
Lk	12:19	“You have **p** of good things laid up	4498
Jn	3:23	because there was **p of** water,	4498
	6:10	There was **p** of grass in that place,	4498
Ac	14:17	*he* **provides** you **with p** of food	1855
2Co	8:14	your **p** will supply what they need,	4354
	8:14	in turn their **p** will supply what you need.	4354
Php	4:12	and I know what it is *to* **have p.**	4355
	4:12	whether **living in p** or in want.	4355

PLIED (1) [PLY]

Lk	23: 9	He **p** him with many questions,	2089

PLIGHT (2)

2Ki	7:13	Their **p** will be like that of all the Israelites	NIH
Ps	59: 4	Arise to help me; look on my **p!**	NIH

PLOT (41) [PLOTS, PLOTTED, PLOTTING]

Ge	33:19	the **p** *of* ground where he pitched his tent.	2754
2Ki	9:10	dogs will devour her on the **p of ground**	2750
	9:21	at the **p of ground** *that had* belonged	2754
	9:26	make you pay for it on this **p of ground,**	2754
	9:26	then, pick him up and throw him on that **p,**	2754
	9:36	On the **p of ground** at Jezreel	2750
	9:37	be like refuse on the ground in the **p**	2750
Ne	4:15	of their **p** and that God had frustrated it,	6783
Est	2:22	But Mordecai found out about the **p**	1821
	9:25	when the **p** came to the king’s attention,	2023S
Ps	2: 1	the nations conspire and the peoples **p**	2047
	21:11	Though *they* **p** evil against you	5742
	31:13	against me and **p** to take my life.	2372
	35: 4	may *those who* **p** my ruin be turned back	3108
	37:12	The wicked **p** against the righteous	2372
	38:12	all day long *they* **p** deception.	2047
	64: 6	*They* **p** injustice and say,	2924
	83: 3	*they* **p** against those you cherish.	3619
	83: 5	With one mind *they* **p** together;	3619
Pr	3:29	*Do* not **p** harm against your neighbor,	3086
	12:20	in the hearts of *those who* **p** evil,	3086
	14:22	Do not *those who* **p** evil go astray?	3086
	24: 2	for their hearts **p** violence,	2047
Isa	28:25	barley *in its* **p,** and spelt in its field?	6168
Jer	11:18	Because the Lord revealed their **p** to me,	NIH
	48: 2	in Heshbon *men will* **p** her downfall:	3108
Eze	17: 7	toward him from the **p** *where* it was planted	6870
	17:10	wither away in the **p** *where* it grew?’ ”	6870
Da	11:24	*He will* **p** the overthrow of fortresses—	3108
Hos	7:15	but *they* **p** evil against me.	3108
Mic	2: 1	to *those who* **p** evil on their beds!	7188
Na	1: 9	Whatever *they* **p** against	3108
Zec	8:17	*do* not **p** evil **against** your neighbor,	928+3108+4222
Mk	3: 6	the Pharisees went out and *began to* **p**	1443+5206
Jn	4: 5	near the **p of ground** Jacob had given	6005
Ac	4:25	the nations rage and the peoples **p** in vain?	3509
	14: 5	There was a **p afoot** among the Gentiles	3995
	20: 3	Because the Jews made a **p** against him just	2101
	23:13	More than forty men were involved in this **p**	5350
	23:16	the son of Paul’s sister heard of this **p,**	1909
	23:30	*of* a **p** to be carried out against the man,	2101

PLOTS (12) [PLOT]

Ps	36: 4	Even on his bed he **p** evil;	3108
	52: 2	Your tongue **p** destruction;	3108
Pr	6:14	*who* **p** evil with deceit in his heart—	3086
	16:27	A scoundrel **p** evil,	4125
	24: 8	He who **p** evil will be known as a schemer.	3108
Isa	33:15	who stops his ears against **p** *of* murder	9048
Jer	18:23	you know, O Lord, all their **p** to kill you.	6783
La	3:60	all their **p** against me.	4742
	3:61	all their **p** against me—	4742
Da	11:25	not be able to stand because of the **p** devised	4742

Na	1:11	has one come forth *who* **p** evil against	3108
Ac	20:19	although I was severely tested by the **p** of	2101

PLOTTED (17) [PLOT]

Ge	37:18	*they* **p** to kill him.	5792
2Sa	21: 5	the man who destroyed us and **p** against us	1948
1Ki	15:27	of the house of Issachar **p** against him,	8003
	16: 9	of half his chariots, **p** against him.	8003
	16:16	in the camp heard that Zimri *had* **p** against	8003
2Ki	21:24	the people of the land killed all who *had* **p**	8003
2Ch	24:21	But *they* **p** against him,	8003
	33:25	the people of the land killed all who *had* **p**	8003
Ne	4: 8	They all **p** together to come and fight	8003
Est	9:24	*had* **p** against the Jews to destroy them	3108
Isa	7: 5	and Remaliah’s son *have* **p** your ruin,	3619
Jer	11:19	I did not realize that *they* had **p** against me,	3108+4742
	49:30	“Nebuchadnezzar king of Babylon has **p** against you;	3619+6783
Hab	2:10	*You have* **p** the ruin of many peoples,	3619
Mt	12:14	But the Pharisees went out and **p**	3284+5206
	26: 4	and *they* **p** to arrest Jesus in some sly way	5205
Jn	11:53	So from that day on *they* **p** to take his life.	1086

PLOTTING (5) [PLOT]

1Sa	23: 9	David learned that Saul *was* **p** against him,	2021+3086+8288
Ne	6: 6	that you and the Jews *are* **p** to revolt,	3108
Ps	56: 5	they are always **p** to harm me.	4742
Pr	16:30	He who winks with his eye *is* **p** perversity;	3108
Eze	11: 2	these are the men who *are* **p** evil	3108

PLOUGH (KJV) See PLOW

PLOW (8) [PLOWED, PLOWING, PLOWMAN, PLOWMEN, PLOWS, PLOWSHARES]

Dt	22:10	*Do* not **p** with an ox and a donkey	3086
1Sa	8:12	others to **p** his ground and reap his harvest,	3086
Job	4: 8	*those who* **p** evil and those who sow trouble	3086
Pr	20: 4	A sluggard *does* not **p** in season;	3086
Isa	28:24	does he **p** continually?	NIH
Hos	10:11	I will drive Ephraim, Judah *must* **p,**	3086
Am	6:12	*Does one* **p** there with oxen?	3086
Lk	9:62	to the **p** and looks back is fit for service in	770

PLOWED (8) [PLOW]

Dt	21: 4	to a valley that *has* not **been p** or planted	6268
Jdg	14:18	“If *you* had not **p** with my heifer,	3086
Ps	129: 3	Plowmen *have* **p** my back	3086
Jer	26:18	“ ‘Zion *will* be **p** like a field,	3086
Eze	36: 9	*you will* be **p** and sown,	6268
Hos	10: 4	up like poisonous weeds in a **p** field.	9439
	12:11	be like piles of stones on a **p** field.	9439
Mic	3:12	Zion *will* be **p** like a field,	3086

PLOWING (6) [PLOW]

Ge	45: 6	for the next five years there will not be **p**	3045
Ex	34:21	the **p** season and harvest you must rest.	3045
1Ki	19:19	He *was* **p** with twelve yoke of oxen	3086
	19:21	He burned the **p** equipment to cook	1330
Job	1:14	“The oxen were **p** and the donkeys	3086
Lk	17: 7	“Suppose one of you had a servant **p** or	769

PLOWMAN (2) [PLOW]

Am	9:13	“when the reaper will be overtaken by the **p**	3086
1Co	9:10	when the **p** plows and the thresher threshes,	769

PLOWMEN (1) [PLOW]

Ps	129: 3	**P** have plowed my back and	3086

PLOWS (3) [PLOW]

Ps	141: 7	“As *one* **p** and breaks up the earth,	7114
Isa	28:24	When a farmer **p** for planting,	3086
1Co	9:10	the plowman **p** and the thresher threshes,	769

PLOWSHARES (5) [PLOW]

1Sa	13:20	down to the Philistines to have their **p,**	4739
	13:21	of a shekel for sharpening **p** and mattocks,	4739
Isa	2: 4	into **p** and their spears into pruning hooks.	908
Joel	3:10	Beat your **p** into swords	908
Mic	4: 3	into **p** and their spears into pruning hooks.	908

PLUCK (1) [PLUCKED]

Mk	9:47	And if your eye causes you to sin, **p** it **out.**	1675

PLUCKED (1) [PLUCK]

Ge	8:11	there in its beak was a **freshly p** olive leaf!	3273

PLUMAGE (2)

Eze	17: 3	and full of **p** of varied colors came	5681
	17: 7	with powerful wings and full **p.**	5681

PLUMB (8)

2Ki	21:13	and the **p line** *used against* the house	5487
Isa	28:17	and righteousness the **p line;**	5487
	34:11	the measuring line of chaos and the **p line**	74

Am	7: 7	by a wall that had been built **true to p,**	643
	7: 7	with a **p line** in his hand.	643
	7: 8	"A **p line,**" I replied.	643
	7: 8	a **p line** among my people Israel;	643
Zec	4:10	Men will rejoice when they see the **p line**	74+974

PLUNDER (105) [PLUNDERED, PLUNDERERS]

Ge	34:29	taking as **p** everything in the houses.	1024
	49:27	in the evening he divides the **p."**	8965
Ex	3:22	And so **you will p** the Egyptians."	5911
Nu	14: 3	Our wives and children will be taken as **p.**	1020
	14:31	that you said would be taken as **p,**	1020
	31: 9	**took** all the Midianite herds, flocks and goods **as p.**	1024
	31:11	They took all the **p** and spoils,	8965
	31:12	and **p** to Moses and Eleazar the priest and	8965
	31:32	The **p** remaining from the spoils that	1020
	31:53	Each soldier *had* **taken p** for himself.	1024
Dt	2:35	But the livestock and the **p** *from*	8965
	3: 7	and the **p** *from* their cities we carried off	8965
	13:16	Gather all the **p** *of* the town into the middle	8965
	13:16	and completely burn the town and all its **p**	8965
	20:14	you may take these as **p** for yourselves.	8965
	20:14	the **p** the LORD your God gives you	8965
Jos	7:21	in the **p** a beautiful robe from Babylonia,	8965
	8: 2	that you may carry off their **p** and livestock	8965
	8:27	for themselves the livestock and **p**	8965
	11:14	for themselves all the **p** and livestock	8965
	22: 8	and divide with your brothers the **p**	8965
Jdg	5:19	but they carried off no silver, no **p.**	1299
	5:30	colorful garments as **p** for Sisera,	8965
	5:30	garments for my neck—all this as **p?"**	8965
	8:24	an earring from your **share of the p."**	8965
	8:25	each man threw a ring from his **p** onto it.	8965
1Sa	14:30	of the **p** they took *from* their enemies.	8965
	14:32	They pounced on the **p** and, taking sheep,	8965
	14:36	after the Philistines by night and **p** them	1024
	15:19	Why did you pounce on the **p** and do evil	8965
	15:21	took sheep and cattle from the **p,**	8965
	30:16	the great amount of **p** they had taken from	8965
	30:19	**p** or anything else they had taken.	8965
	30:20	saying, "This is David's **p.**"	8965
	30:22	not share with them the **p** we recovered.	8965
	30:26	he sent some of the **p** to the elders of Judah,	8965
	30:26	"Here is a present for you from the **p** of	8965
2Sa	8:12	the **p** taken from Hadadezer son of Rehob,	8965
	12:30	He took a great quantity of **p** from the city	8965
2Ki	3:23	Now to the **p,** Moab!"	8965
1Ch	20: 2	He took a great quantity of **p** from the city	8965
	26:27	of the **p** taken in battle they dedicated for	8965
2Ch	14:13	of Judah carried off a large amount of **p.**	8965
	15:11	from the **p** they had brought back.	8965
	20:25	and his men went to carry off their **p,**	8965
	20:25	There was so much **p** that it took three days	8965
	24:23	the **p** to their king in Damascus.	8965
	25:13	and carried off great quantities of **p.**	1023
	28: 8	They also took a great deal of **p,**	8965
	28:14	and in the presence of the officials and all	1023
	28:15	the **p** they clothed all who were naked.	8965
Ne	4: 4	Give them over as **p** in a land of captivity.	1023
Est	3:13	the month of Adar, and to **p** their goods.	1024
	8:11	and to **p** the property of their enemies.	1024
	9:10	But they did not lay their hands on the **p.**	1023
	9:15	but they did not lay their hands on the **p.**	1023
	9:16	but did not lay their hands on the **p.**	1023
Ps	68:12	in the camps men divide the **p.**	8965
	109:11	*may* strangers the fruits of his labor.	1024
Pr	1:13	and fill our houses with **p;**	8965
	12:12	The wicked desire the **p** *of* evil men,	5179
	16:19	among the oppressed than to share **p** with	8965
	22:23	and *will* **p** those who plunder them.	5883+7693
	22:23	and will **p** *those who* plunder them.	7693
Isa	3:14	the **p** *from* the poor is in your houses.	1611
	8: 4	and the **p** *of* Samaria will be carried off by	8965
	9: 3	as men rejoice when dividing the **p.**	8965
	10: 6	to seize loot and snatch **p,**	1020
	11:14	together *they will* **p** the people to the east.	1024
	17:14	the lot of *those who* **p** us.	1024
	33: 4	Your **p,** O nations, is harvested as	8965
	33:23	and even the lame will carry off **p.**	1020
	42:22	They have become **p,** with no one	1020
	49:24	Can **p** be taken from warriors,	4917
	49:25	and **p** retrieved from the fierce;	4917
Jer	2:14	Why then has he become **p?**	1020
	15:13	and your treasures I will give away as **p,**	1020
	17: 3	and all your treasures I will give away as **p,**	1020
	20: 5	They will take it away *as* **p** and carry it off	1024
	30:16	*Those who* **p** you will be plundered;	9116
	49:32	Their camels will become **p,**	1020
	50:10	all *who* **p** her will have their fill,"	8964
Eze	7:21	I will hand it all over as **p** to foreigners	1020
	23:46	and give them over to terror and **p.**	1020
	25: 7	and give you as **p** to the nations.	1020
	26: 5	She will become **p** for the nations,	1020
	26:12	*They will* **p** your wealth	8964
	29:19	and **p** the land as pay for his army.	1020+1024
	36: 5	so that they might **p** its pastureland.'	1020
	38:12	I will **p** and loot and turn my hand	8964+8965
	38:13	"Have you come to **p?**	8964+8965
	38:13	and goods and to seize much **p?**'	8965
	39:10	and *they will* **p** those who plundered them	8964
Da	11:24	He will distribute **p,** loot and wealth	1023
Am	3:10	"who hoard **p** and loot in their fortresses."	2805
	3:11	and **p** your fortresses.	1024

Na	2: 9	**P** the silver! Plunder the gold!	1024
	2: 9	**P** the gold! The supply is endless,	1024
	3: 1	full of lies, full of **p,** never without victims!	7294
Hab	2: 8	the peoples who are left *will* **p** you.	8964
Zep	2: 9	The remnant of my people *will* **p** them;	1024
Zec	2: 9	so that their slaves will **p** them.	8965
	14: 1	day of the LORD is coming when your **p** will	8965
Heb	7: 4	Abraham gave him a tenth of the **p!**	215

PLUNDERED (27) [PLUNDER]

Ex	12:36	so *they* **p** the Egyptians.	5911
Jdg	2:14	handed them over to raiders *who* **p** them.	9116
1Sa	14:48	from the hands of *those who had* **p** them.	9115
	17:53	*they* **p** their camp.	9116
2Ki	7:16	Then the people went out and **p** the camp	1024
	21:14	They will be looted and **p** by all their foes	5468
2Ch	14:14	*They* **p** all these villages,	1024
Ps	44:10	and our adversaries *have* **p** us.	9115
	76: 5	Valiant men *lie* **p,**	8964
	89:41	All who pass by *have* **p** him;	9116
Isa	10:13	I **p** their treasures,	9115
	24: 3	completely laid waste and **totally p.**	1024+1024
	42:22	But this is a people **p** and looted,	1024
Jer	30:16	Those who plunder you will be **p;**	5468
	50:10	So Babylonia will be **p;**	8965
	50:37	*They will* be **p.**	1024
Eze	34: 8	so has been **p** and has become food for all	1020
	34:22	and they will no longer be **p.**	1020
	34:28	They will no longer be **p** by the nations,	1020
	36: 4	that have been **p** and ridiculed by the rest of	1020
	39:10	And they will plunder *those who* **p** them	8964
Da	11:33	by the sword or be burned or captured or **p.**	1023
Hos	13:15	His storehouse *will be* **p**	9115
Na	2:10	She is pillaged, **p,** stripped!	4433
Hab	2: 8	Because you *have* **p** many nations,	8964
Zep	1:13	Their wealth will be **p,**	5468
Zec	2: 8	against the nations that *have* **p** you—	8964

PLUNDERERS (2) [PLUNDER]

2Ki	17:20	and gave them into the hands of **p,**	9115
Isa	42:24	and Israel to the **p?**	1024

PLUNGE (6) [PLUNGED]

1Sa	2:14	He would **p** it into the pan or kettle	5782
Job	9:31	you would **p** me into a slime pit so that	3188
Ps	68:23	that *you may* **p** your feet in the blood	8175
Joel	2: 8	*They* **p** through defenses	5877
1Ti	6: 9	and harmful desires that **p** men into ruin	1112
1Pe	4: 4	They think it strange that you *do not* **p** with	5340

PLUNGED (4) [PLUNGE]

Jdg	3:21	drew the sword from his right thigh and **p** it	9546
2Sa	18:14	and **p** them into Absalom's heart	9546
	20:10	and Joab **p** it into his belly,	5782
Rev	16:10	and his kingdom *was* **p into** darkness.	1181

PLUS (2)

Eze	45:12	Twenty shekels **p** twenty-five shekels plus fifteen shekels equal one mina.	NIH
	45:12	Twenty shekels plus twenty-five shekels **p** fifteen shekels equal one mina.	NIH

PLY (1) [PLIED]

Isa	23:17	as a prostitute and *will* **p** her trade with all	2388

POCHERETH (KJV) See POKERETH HAZZEBAIM

POCKET (1)

1Sa	25:29	as from the **p** of a sling.	4090

PODS (2)

2Ki	6:25	a quarter of a cab of *seed* **p** for five shekels.	1807
Lk	15:16	He longed to fill his stomach with the **p**	3044

POETS (2)

Nu	21:27	That is why the **p** say:	5439
Ac	17:28	As some *of* your own **p** have said,	4475

POINT (34) [POINTED, POINTING, POINTS]

Jdg	3:25	They waited to the **p** of embarrassment,	6330
1Sa	7:11	along the way to a **p** below Beth Car.	NIH
	17: 7	and its iron *p* weighed six hundred shekels.	4259
2Sa	13: 2	Amnon became frustrated to the **p** of	4200
2Ki	19: 3	to the **p** of birth and there is no strength	5402
	20: 1	and was **at the p** of death.	4200
2Ch	32:24	and was **at the p** of death.	6330
Ne	3:16	made repairs up to a **p** opposite the tombs	NIH
	3:19	a **p** facing the ascent to the armory as far as	NIH
	3:26	a **p** opposite the Water Gate toward the east	NIH
Job	20:25	the **gleaming p** out of his liver.	1398
Pr	9: 3	calls from the **highest p** *of* the city.	1726+5294
	9:14	on a seat at the **highest p** *of* the city,	5294
Isa	37: 3	to the **p** of birth and there is no strength	5402
	38: 1	and was **at the p** of death.	4200
Jer	17: 1	inscribed with a flint **p,**	7632
Eze	47:20	the boundary to a **p** opposite Lebo Hamath.	NIH
Mt	4: 5	and had him stand on the **highest p** of	4762
	26:38	with sorrow to the **p** of death.	2401

Mk	14:34	with sorrow **to the p** of death,"	2401
Lk	4: 9	and had him stand on the **highest p** of	4762
Jn	7:25	**At that p** some of the people	4036
Ac	26:24	**At this p** Festus interrupted Paul's defense.	1254+4047
Ro	2: 1	for at **whatever** *p* you judge the other,	AIT
1Co	9: 8	**from** a human **p** of view?	476+2848
2Co	5:16	**from** a worldly **p** of view.	2848+4922
	7:11	At **every** *p* you have proved yourselves to	AIT
Php	3:15	And if on **some** *p* you think differently,	5516
1Ti	1: 7	*If you* **p** these things out to the brothers,	5719
2Ti	2: 9	am suffering **even to the p** of being chained	3588
Heb	8: 1	The **p** of what we are saying **is this:**	3049
	12: 4	you have not yet resisted **to the p** of shedding your blood.	3588
Jas	2:10	at just **one** *p* is guilty of breaking all of it.	AIT
Rev	2:10	Be faithful, **even to the p** of death,	948

POINTED (1) [POINT]

Jn	4:44	(Now Jesus himself *had* **p** out that	3455

POINTING (3) [POINT]

Isa	58: 9	with the **p** finger and malicious talk,	8938
Mt	12:49	**P** to his disciples, he said,	899+1753+3836+5931
1Pe	1:11	to which the Spirit of Christ in them *was* **p**	1317

POINTS (3) [POINT]

Ne	4:13	the people behind the lowest **p** of the wall	5226
Ac	25:19	they had some **p of dispute** with him	2427
Ro	15:15	I have written you quite boldly **on some p,**	608+3538

POISED (2)

Job	15:24	like a king **p** to attack,	6969
	37:16	Do you know how the clouds **hang p,**	5146

POISON (10) [POISONED, POISONOUS, POISONS]

Dt	29:18	among you that produces such bitter **p.**	8032
	32:32	Their grapes are filled with **p,**	8032
	32:33	the deadly **p** *of* cobras.	8032
Job	6: 4	my spirit drinks in their **p;**	2779
	20:16	He will suck the **p** *of* serpents;	8032
Ps	140: 3	the **p** of vipers is on their lips.	2779
Am	6:12	But you have turned justice into **p** and	8032
Mk	16:18	and when they drink **deadly p,**	2503+5516
Ro	3:13	"The **p** of vipers is on their lips."	2675
Jas	3: 8	It is a restless evil, full of deadly **p.**	2675

POISONED (4) [POISON]

Jer	8:14	to perish and given us **p** water to drink,	8032
	9:15	people eat bitter food and drink **p** water.	8032
	23:15	make them eat bitter food and drink **p** water,	8032
Ac	14: 2	and **p** their minds against the brothers.	2808

POISONOUS (1) [POISON]

Hos	10: 4	therefore lawsuits spring up like **p weeds** in	8032

POISONS (1) [POISON]

Pr	23:32	In the end it bites like a snake and **p** like	7301

POKERETH-HAZZEBAIM (2)

Ezr	2:57	Shephatiah, Hattil, **P** and Ami	7097
Ne	7:59	Shephatiah, Hattil, **P** and Amon	7097

POLE (20) [POLES]

Nu	13:23	of them carried it on a **p** between them,	4573
	21: 8	"Make a snake and put it up on a **p;**	5812
	21: 9	a bronze snake and put it up on a **p.**	5812
Dt	16:21	Do not set up any wooden **Asherah p**	895
Jdg	6:25	and cut down the **Asherah p** beside it.	895
	6:26	the wood of the **Asherah p** that you cut	895
	6:28	with the **Asherah p** beside it cut down and	895
	6:30	and cut down the **Asherah p** beside it."	895
1Ki	15:13	she had made a repulsive **Asherah p.**	895
	15:13	Asa cut the **p** down and burned it in	5145S
	16:33	Ahab also made an **Asherah p** and did more	895
2Ki	6: 2	where each of us can get a **p;**	7771
	13: 6	**Asherah p** remained standing in Samaria.	895
	17:16	and an **Asherah p.**	895
	21: 3	to Baal and made an **Asherah p,**	895
	21: 7	the carved **Asherah p** he had made	895
	23: 6	the **Asherah p** from the temple of the LORD	895
	23:15	and burned the **Asherah p** also.	895
2Ch	15:16	she had made a repulsive **Asherah p.**	895
	15:16	Asa cut the **p** down, broke it up and	5145S

POLES (56) [POLE]

Ex	25:13	Then make **p** *of* acacia wood	964
	25:14	the **p** into the rings on the sides of the chest	964
	25:15	The **p** are to remain in the rings of this ark;	964
	25:27	to the rim to hold the **p** used in carrying	964
	25:28	Make the **p** *of* acacia wood.	964
	27: 6	Make **p** *of* acacia wood for the altar	964
	27: 7	The **p** are to be inserted into the rings	964
	30: 4	to hold the **p** used to carry it.	964
	30: 5	the **p** of acacia wood and overlay them	964
	34:13	and cut down their **Asherah p.**	895
	35:12	the ark with its **p** and the atonement cover	964

Ex	35:13	with its **p** and all its articles and the bread	964
	35:15	of incense with its **p**, the anointing oil and	964
	35:16	its **p** and all its utensils;	964
	37: 4	Then he made **p** of acacia wood	964
	37: 5	the **p** into the rings on the sides of the ark	964
	37:14	to the rim to hold the **p** used in carrying	964
	37:15	The **p** for carrying the table were made	964
	37:27	to hold the **p** used to carry it.	964
	37:28	the **p** *of* acacia wood and overlaid them	964
	38: 5	They cast bronze rings to hold the **p** for	964
	38: 6	the **p** of acacia wood and overlaid them	964
	38: 7	the **p** into the rings so they would be on	964
	39:35	the ark of the Testimony with its **p** and	964
	39:39	its **p** and all its utensils;	964
	40:20	attached the **p** to the ark and put	964
Nu	4: 6	a cloth of solid blue over that and put the **p**	964
	4: 8	that with hides of sea cows and put its **p**	964
	4:11	that with hides of sea cows and put its **p**	964
	4:14	of hides of sea cows and put its **p** in place.	964
Dt	7: 5	cut down their **Asherah p** and burn their	895
	12: 3	and burn their **Asherah p** in the fire;	895
1Ki	8: 7	the ark and its **carrying p**	964
	8: 8	These **p** were so long that their ends could	964
	14:15	the LORD to anger by making **Asherah p.**	895
	14:23	and **Asherah** on every high hill and	895
2Ki	17:10	They set up sacred stones and **Asherah p**	895
	18: 4	and cut down the **Asherah p.**	895
	23:14	down the **Asherah p** and covered the sites	895
1Ch	15:15	ark of God with the **p** on their shoulders,	4574
2Ch	5: 8	and covered the ark and its **carrying p.**	964
	5: 9	These **p** were so long that their ends,	964
	14: 3	and cut down the **Asherah p**	895
	17: 6	the high places and the **Asherah p**	895
	19: 3	for you have rid the land of the **Asherah p**	895
	24:18	and worshiped **Asherah p** and idols.	895
	31: 1	and cut down the **Asherah p.**	895
	33: 3	to the Baals and made **Asherah p.**	895
	33:19	and set up **Asherah p** and idols	895
	34: 3	**Asherah p**, carved idols and cast images.	895
	34: 4	and smashed the **Asherah p**,	895
	34: 7	he tore down the altars and the **Asherah p**	895
Isa	17: 8	for the **Asherah p** and the incense altars	895
	27: 9	no **Asherah p** or incense altars will be left	895
Jer	17: 2	and **Asherah p** beside the spreading trees	895
Mic	5:14	uproot from among you your **Asherah p**	895

POLISH (1) [POLISHED]

Jer	46: 4	**P** your spears, put on your armor!	5347

POLISHED (9) [POLISH]

2Ch	4:16	the temple of the LORD were of **p** bronze.	5347
Ezr	8:27	darics, and two fine articles of **p** bronze,	7410
SS	5:14	like **p** ivory decorated with sapphires.	6952
Isa	49: 2	a **p** arrow and concealed me in his quiver.	1406
Eze	21: 9	" 'A sword, a sword, sharpened and **p**—	5307
	21:10	**p** to flash like lightning!	5307
	21:11	" 'The sword is appointed to be **p**,	5307
	21:11	it is sharpened and **p**,	5307
	21:28	**p** to consume and to flash like lightning!	5307

POLLUTE (2) [POLLUTED, POLLUTES]

Nu	35:33	" '*Do* not **p** the land where you are.	2866
Jude	1: 8	these dreamers **p** their own bodies,	3620

POLLUTED (4) [POLLUTE]

Ezr	9:11	a land **p** by the corruption of its peoples.	5614
Pr	25:26	a **p** well is a righteous man who gives way	8845
Ac	15:20	telling them to abstain from food **p** by idols,	246
Jas	1:27	to keep oneself **from being p** by the world.	834

POLLUTES (1) [POLLUTE]

Nu	35:33	Bloodshed **p** the land,	2866

POLLUX (1)

Ac	28:11	the **twin gods Castor and P.**	1483

POMEGRANATE (5) [POMEGRANATES]

1Sa	14: 2	on the outskirts of Gibeah under a **p** tree	8232
SS	4: 3	behind your veil are like the halves of a **p.**	8232
	6: 7	behind your veil are like the halves of a **p.**	8232
Joel	1:12	the **p**, the palm and the apple tree—	8232
Hag	2:19	the **p** and the olive tree have	8232

POMEGRANATES (24) [POMEGRANATE]

Ex	28:33	Make **p** *of* blue, purple and scarlet yarn	8232
	28:34	and the **p** are to alternate around the hem of	8232
	39:24	made **p** *of* blue, purple and scarlet yarn	8232
	39:25	around the hem between the **p.**	8232
	39:26	and **p** alternated around the hem of the robe	8232
Nu	13:23	along with some **p** and figs.	8232
	20: 5	It has no grain or figs, grapevines or **p.**	8232
Dt	8: 8	vines and fig trees, **p**, olive oil and honey;	8232
1Ki	7:18	He made **p** in two rows encircling each	8232
	7:20	were the two hundred **p** in rows all around.	8232
	7:42	the four hundred **p** for the two sets	8232
	7:42	for the two sets of network (two rows of **p**	8232
2Ki	25:17	with a network and **p** of bronze all around.	8232
2Ch	3:16	also made a hundred **p** and attached them	8232
	4:13	the four hundred **p** for the two sets	8232
	4:13	for the two sets of network (two rows of **p**	8232
SS	4:13	an orchard of **p** with choice fruits,	8232
	6:11	to see if the vines had budded or the **p** were	8232

SS	7:12	and if the **p** are in bloom—	8232
	8: 2	spiced wine to drink, the nectar of my **p.**	8232
Jer	52:22	with a network and **p** of bronze all around.	8232
	52:22	The other pillar, with its **p**, was similar.	8232
	52:23	There were ninety-six **p** on the sides;	8232
	52:23	of **p** above the surrounding network was	8232

POMP (5)

Isa	8: 7	the king of Assyria with all his **p.**	3883
	10:16	under his **p** a fire will be kindled like	3883
	14:11	All your **p** has been brought down to	1454
	21:16	all the **p** *of* Kedar will come to an end.	3883
Ac	25:23	with great **p** and entered the audience room	5752

PONDER (4) [PONDERED, PONDERS]

Ps	64: 9	the works of God and **p** what he has done.	8505
	119:95	but *I will* **p** your statutes.	1067
Isa	14:16	stare at you, *they* **p** your fate:	1067
	33:18	In your thoughts *you* will **p** the former terror	2047

PONDERED (5) [PONDER]

Ne	5: 7	I **p** them in my mind and then accused	4888
Ps	111: 2	*they* **are p** by all who delight in them.	2011
Ecc	12: 9	*He* **p** and searched out and set	264
Isa	57:11	and have neither remembered me nor **p** this	8492
Lk	2:19	up all these things and **p** them in her heart.	5202

PONDERS (1) [PONDER]

Isa	57: 1	and no one **p** it in his heart;	8492

PONDS (2)

Ex	7:19	over the **p** and all the reservoirs'—	106
	8: 5	over the streams and canals and **p**,	106

PONTIUS (3)

Lk	3: 1	when **P** Pilate was governor of Judea,	4508
Ac	4:27	and **P** Pilate met together with the Gentiles	4508
1Ti	6:13	before **P** Pilate made the good confession,	4508

PONTUS (3)

Ac	2: 9	Judea and Cappadocia, **P** and Asia,	4509
	18: 2	a Jew named Aquila, a native **of P**,	4507
1Pe	1: 1	scattered throughout **P**, Galatia,	4509

POOL (20) [POOLS]

2Sa	2:13	and met them at the **p** *of* Gibeon.	1391
	2:13	down on one side of the **p** and one group	1391
	4:12	and hung the bodies by the **p** in Hebron.	1391
1Ki	22:38	They washed the chariot at a **p** *in* Samaria	1391
2Ki	18:17	at the aqueduct of the Upper **P**,	1391
	20:20	how he made the **p** and the tunnel	1391
Ne	2:14	the Fountain Gate and the King's **P**,	1391
	3:15	also repaired the wall of the **P** *of* Siloam	1391
	3:16	the artificial **p** and the House of the Heroes.	1391
Ps	114: 8	who turned the rock into a **p**,	106+4784
Isa	7: 3	at the end of the aqueduct of the Upper **P**,	1391
	22: 9	you stored up water in the Lower **P**,	1391
	22:11	the two walls for the water of the Old **P**,	1391
	35: 7	The burning sand will become a **p**,	106
	36: 2	at the aqueduct of the Upper **P**,	1391
Jer	41:12	They caught up with him near the great **p**	4784
Na	2: 8	Nineveh is like a **p**,	1391+4784
Jn	5: 2	in Jerusalem near the Sheep Gate a **p**,	3148
	5: 7	"I have no one to help me into the **p** when	3148
	9: 7	the **P** *of* Siloam" (this word means Sent).	3148

POOLS (6) [POOL]

Dt	8: 7	a land with streams and **p** of water,	6524
Ps	84: 6	the autumn rains also cover it with **p.**	1391
	107:35	He turned the desert into **p** of water and	106
SS	7: 4	Your eyes are the **p** of Heshbon by the gate	1391
Isa	41:18	I will turn the desert into **p** of water,	106
	42:15	into islands and dry up the **p.**	106

POOR (177) [IMPOVERISHED, POOREST, POVERTY]

Ex	23: 3	and do not show favoritism to a **p** *man*	1924
	23: 6	"Do not deny justice to your **p** *people*	36
	23:11	Then the **p** *among* your people may get food	36
	30:15	a half shekel and the **p** are not to give less	1924
Lev	14:21	however, he is **p** and cannot afford these,	1924
	19:10	Leave them for the **p** and the alien.	6714
	19:15	do not show partiality to the **p** or favoritism	1924
	23:22	Leave them for the **p** and the alien.	6714
	25:25	" 'If one of your countrymen *becomes* **p**	4575
	25:35	" 'If one of your countrymen *becomes* **p**	4575
	25:39	of your countrymen *becomes* **p** among you	4575
	25:47	and one of your countrymen *becomes* **p**	4575
	27: 8	If anyone making the vow *is* too **p** to pay	4575
Nu	13:20	Is it fertile or **p**?	8136
Dt	15: 4	However, there should be no **p** among you,	36
	15: 7	If there is a **p** *man* among your brothers	36
	15: 7	or tightfisted toward your **p** brother.	36
	15:11	There will always be **p** *people* in the land.	36
	15:11	and toward the **p** and needy in your land.	6714
	24:12	If the man is **p**,	6714
	24:14	not take advantage of a hired man who is **p**	6714
	24:15	because he is **p** and is counting on it.	6714
Ru	3:10	after the younger men, whether rich or **p.**	1924
1Sa	2: 8	raises the **p** from the dust and lifts the needy	1924

1Sa	18:23	I'm only a **p** man and little known."	8133
2Sa	12: 1	one rich and the other **p.**	8133
	12: 3	**p** *man* had nothing except one little ewe	8133
		lamb he had bought.	
	12: 4	that belonged to the **p** man and prepared it	8133
Est	9:22	of food to one another and gifts to the **p.**	36
Job	5:16	**p** have hope, and injustice shuts its mouth.	1924
	20:10	His children must make amends to the **p;**	1924
	20:19	the **p** and left them destitute;	1924
	24: 4	the needy from the path and force all the **p**	6714
	24: 5	the **p** go about their labor of foraging food;	NIH
	24: 9	the infant of the **p** is seized for a debt.	6714
	24:14	murderer rises up and kills the **p** and needy;	6714
	29:12	because I rescued the **p** who cried for help,	6714
	30:25	Has not my soul grieved for the **p**?	36
	31:16	"If I have denied the desires of the **p** or let	1924
	34:19	and does not favor the rich over the **p**,	1924
	34:28	They caused the cry of the **p** to come	1924
Ps	14: 6	You evildoers frustrate the plans of the **p**,	6714
	22:26	The **p** will eat and be satisfied;	6705
	34: 6	This **p** man called, and the LORD heard him;	6714
	35:10	You rescue the **p** from those too strong	6714
	35:10	the **p** and needy from those who rob them."	6714
	37:14	the bow to bring down the **p** and needy,	6714
	40:17	Yet I am **p** and needy;	6714
	49: 2	both low and high, rich and **p** alike;	36
	68:10	O God, you provided for the **p.**	6714
	69:32	The **p** will see and be glad—	6705
	70: 5	Yet I am **p** and needy;	6714
	74:21	may the **p** and needy praise your name.	6714
	82: 3	maintain the rights of the **p** and oppressed.	6714
	86: 1	and answer me, for I am **p** and needy.	6714
	109:16	the **p** and the needy and the brokenhearted.	6714
	109:22	For I am **p** and needy,	6714
	112: 9	He has scattered abroad his gifts to the **p**,	36
	113: 7	raises the **p** from the dust and lifts the needy	1924
	132:15	her **p** will I satisfy with food.	36
	140:12	the **p** and upholds the cause of the needy.	6714
Pr	10: 4	Lazy hands make a *man* **p**,	8133
	10:15	but poverty is the ruin of the **p.**	1924
	13: 7	*another* **pretends to be p**,	8133
	13: 8	but a **p** *man* hears no threat.	8133
	13:23	**p** *man's* field may produce abundant food,	8133
	14:20	The **p** are shunned even by their neighbors,	8133
	14:31	He who oppresses the **p** shows contempt	1924
	17: 5	the **p** shows contempt for their Maker;	8133
	18:23	A **p** *man* pleads for mercy,	8133
	19: 1	a **p** *man* whose walk is blameless than	8133
	19: 4	but a **p** *man's* friend deserts him.	1924
	19: 7	A **p** *man* is shunned by all his relatives—	1924
	19:17	He who is kind to the **p** lends to the LORD,	1924
	19:22	better *to be* **p** than a liar.	8133
	20:13	Do not love sleep or *you will* **grow p;**	3769
	21:13	If a man shuts his ears to the cry of the **p**,	1924
	21:17	He who loves pleasure will become **p;**	4728
	22: 2	Rich and **p** have this in common:	8133
	22: 7	The rich rule over the **p**,	8133
	22: 9	for he shares his food with the **p.**	1924
	22:16	who oppresses the **p** to increase his wealth	1924
	22:22	Do not exploit the **p** because they are poor	1924
	22:22	Do not exploit the **p** because they are poor	1924
	23:21	for drunkards and gluttons *become* **p**,	3769
	28: 3	A ruler who oppresses the **p** is like	1924
	28: 6	a **p** *man* whose walk is blameless than	8133
	28: 8	who will be kind to the **p.**	1924
	28:11	but a **p** *man* who has discernment sees	1924
	28:27	He who gives to the **p** will lack nothing,	8133
	29: 7	The righteous care about justice for the **p**,	1924
	29:13	The **p** *man* and the oppressor have this	8133
	29:14	If a king judges the **p** with fairness,	1924
	30: 9	Or *I may* **become p** and steal,	3769
	30:14	with knives to devour the **p** from the earth,	6714
	31: 9	defend the rights of the **p** and needy."	6714
	31:20	to the **p** and extends her hands to the needy.	6714
Ecc	4:13	Better a **p** but wise youth than an old	5014
	5: 8	If you see the **p** oppressed in a district,	8133
	6: 8	What does a **p** *man* gain by knowing how	6714
	9:15	there lived in that city a man **p** but wise,	5014
	9:15	But nobody remembered that man.	5014
	9:16	But the **p** *man's* wisdom is despised,	5014
Isa	3:14	the plunder from the **p** is in your houses.	6714
	3:15	and grinding the faces of the **p**?"	6714
	10: 2	to deprive the **p** of their rights	1924
	10:30	O Laishah! **P** Anathoth!	6714
	11: 4	with justice he will give decisions for the **p**	6705
	14:30	The **poorest of the p** will find pasture,	1147+1924
	25: 4	You have been a refuge for the **p**,	1924
	26: 6	feet of the oppressed, the footsteps of the **p.**	6714
	32: 7	he makes up evil schemes to destroy the **p**	6714
	40:20	A *man* **too p** to present such an offering	6123
	41:17	"The **p** and needy search for water,	6714
	58: 7	the hungry and to provide the **p** wanderer	6714
	61: 1	to preach good news to the **p.**	6705
Jer	2:34	the lifeblood of the innocent **p**,	36
	5: 4	I thought, "These are only the **p;**	1924
	5:28	they do not defend the rights of the **p.**	36
	22:16	He defended the cause of the **p** and needy,	6714
	24: 2	the other basket had very **p** figs,	8273
	24: 3	**p** ones are so bad they cannot be eaten."	8273
	24: 8	" 'But like the **p** figs,	8273
	29:17	and I will make them like **p** figs that are	9135
	39:10	in the land of Judah some of the **p** people,	1924
Eze	16:49	they did not help the **p** and needy.	6714
	18:12	He oppresses the **p** and needy.	6714
	22:29	they oppress the **p** and needy and mistreat	6714
Am	2: 7	They trample on the heads of the **p** as upon	1924
	4: 1	you women who oppress the **p** and crush	1924

Am	5:11	You trample on the **p** and force him	1924
	5:12	you deprive the **p** of justice in the courts.	36
	8: 4	and do away with the **p** *of* the land,	6714
	8: 6	buying the **p** with silver and the needy for	1924
Zec	7:10	the fatherless, the alien or the **p.**	6714
Mt	5: 3	"Blessed are the **p** in spirit,	4777
	11: 5	and the good news is preached to the **p.**	4777
	19:21	go, sell your possessions and give *to* the **p,**	4777
	26: 9	a high price and the money given *to* the **p."**	4777
	26:11	The **p** you will always have with you,	4777
Mk	10:21	sell everything you have and give *to* the **p,**	4777
	12:42	But a widow came and put two very small	4777
	12:43	this **p** widow has put more into	4777
	14: 5	and the money given *to* the **p."**	4777
	14: 7	The **p** you will always have with you,	4777
Lk	4:18	to preach good news *to* the **p.**	4777
	6:20	"Blessed are you who are **p,**	4777
	7:22	and the good news is preached to the **p.**	4777
	11:41	give what is inside [the dish] **to** the **p,**	1443+1797
	12:33	Sell your possessions and **give to** the **p.**	1443+1797
	14:13	But when you give a banquet, invite the **p,**	4777
	14:21	and alleys of the town and bring in the **p,**	4777
	18:22	Sell everything you have and give *to* the **p,**	4777
	19: 8	now I give half of my possessions *to* the **p,**	4777
	21: 2	He also saw a **p** widow put it two very small	4293
	21: 3	"this **p** widow has put in more than all	4777
Jn	12: 5	and the money given *to* the **p?**	4777
	12: 6	not say this because he cared about the **p**	4777
	12: 8	You will always have the **p** among you,	4777
	13:29	or to give something *to* the **p.**	4777
Ac	9:36	always doing good and **helping the p.**	1797+4472
	10: 4	and **gifts to the p** have come up as	1797
	10:31	and remembered your **gifts to the p.**	1797
	24:17	to bring my people **gifts for the p** and	1797
Ro	15:26	a contribution for the **p** among the saints	4777
1Co	13: 3	If *I* give all I possess **to the p**	6039
	13:12	Now we see but a **p** reflection as in	141+1877
2Co	6:10	**p,** yet making many rich;	4777
	8: 9	yet for your sakes he *became* **p,**	4776
	9: 9	"He has scattered abroad his gifts *to* the **p;**	4288
Gal	2:10	that we should continue to remember the **p,**	4777
Jas	2: 2	a **p** *man* in shabby clothes also comes in.	4777
	2: 3	but say *to* the **p** *man,*	4777
	2: 5	not God chosen those who are **p** in the eyes	4777
	2: 6	But you have insulted the **p.**	4777
Rev	3:17	pitiful, **p,** blind and naked.	4777
	13:16	small and great, rich and **p,** free and slave,	4777

POOREST (6) [POOR]

2Ki	24:14	Only the **p** people of the land were left.	1930
	25:12	behind some of the **p** *people of* the land	1930
Isa	14:30	The **p of the poor** will find pasture,	1147+1924
Jer	40: 7	and children who were the **p** in the land	1930
	52:15	of the **p** people and those who remained in	1930
	52:16	the rest of the **p** *people of* the land to work	1930

POPLAR (3) [POPLARS]

Ge	30:37	however, took fresh-cut branches from **p,**	4242
Isa	44: 4	like **p** trees by flowing streams.	6857
Hos	4:13	under oak, **p** and terebinth,	4242

POPLARS (4) [POPLAR]

Lev	23:40	and palm fronds, leafy branches and **p,**	5707+6857
Job	40:22	The **p** by the stream surround him.	6857
Ps	137: 2	There on the **p** we hung our harps,	6857
Isa	15: 7	over the Ravine of the **P.**	6857

POPULACE (1) [POPULATION]

| 2Ki | 25:11 | the rest of the **p** and those who had gone | 2162 |

POPULATION (1) [POPULACE]

| Pr | 14:28 | A large **p** is a king's glory, | 6639 |

POPULOUS (KJV) See NUMEROUS

PORATHA (1)

| Est | 9: 8 | **P,** Adalia, Aridatha, | 7054 |

PORCH (2) [PORTICO, PORTICOES]

| Jdg | 3:23 | Then Ehud went out to the **p;** | 4997 |
| Joel | 2:17 | weep between the **temple p** and the altar. | 395 |

PORCIUS (1) [FESTUS]

| Ac | 24:27 | Felix was succeeded by **P** Festus, | 4517 |

PORPHYRY (1)

| Est | 1: 6 | and silver on a mosaic pavement of **p,** | 985 |

PORT (1)

| Jnh | 1: 3 | where he found a ship bound for **that p.** | 9576ˢ |

PORTENT (2)

| Ps | 71: 7 | I have become like a **p** to many, | 4603 |
| Isa | 20: 3 | as a sign and **p** against Egypt and Cush, | 4603 |

PORTICO (44) [PORCH]

| 1Ki | 6: 3 | The **p** at the front of the main hall of | 395 |
| | 7: 6 | In front of it was a **p,** | 395 |

1Ki	7:12	of the temple of the LORD with its **p.**	395
	7:19	of the pillars in the **p** were in the shape	395
	7:21	the pillars at the **p** of the temple.	395
1Ch	28:11	the plans for the **p** of the temple,	395
2Ch	3: 4	The **p** at the front of the temple	395
	8:12	that he had built in front of the **p,**	395
	15: 8	of the LORD that was in front of the **p** of	395
	29: 7	the doors of the **p** and put out the lamps.	395
	29:17	of the month they reached the **p** of	395
Eze	8:16	between the **p** and the altar,	395
	40: 7	the **p** facing the temple was one rod deep.	395
	40: 8	Then he measured the **p** of the gateway;	395
	40: 9	The **p** *of* the gateway faced the temple.	395
	40:14	The measurement was up to the **p** facing	395
	40:15	to the far end of its **p** was fifty cubits.	395
	40:16	openings all around, as was the **p;**	395
	40:21	and its **p** had the same measurements	395
	40:22	its **p** and its palm tree decorations had	395
	40:22	with its **p** opposite them.	395
	40:24	He measured its jambs and its **p,**	395
	40:25	and its **p** had narrow openings all around,	395
	40:26	with its **p** opposite them;	395
	40:29	and its **p** had the same measurements as	395
	40:29	and its **p** had openings all around.	395
	40:31	Its **p** faced the outer court;	395
	40:33	and its **p** had the same measurements as	395
	40:33	and its **p** had openings all around.	395
	40:34	Its **p** faced the outer court;	395
	40:36	its projecting walls and its **p,**	395
	40:37	Its **p** faced the outer court;	395
	40:38	with a doorway was by the **p** in each of	395
	40:39	In the **p** *of* the gateway were two tables	395
	40:40	the outside wall of the **p** of the gateway,	395
	40:48	He brought me to the **p** of the temple	395
	40:48	and measured the jambs of the **p;**	395
	40:49	The **p** was twenty cubits wide,	395
	41:15	inner sanctuary and the **p** facing the court,	395
	41:25	a wooden overhang on the front of the **p.**	395
	41:26	of the **p** were narrow windows	395
	44: 3	by way of the **p** *of* the gateway and go out	395
	46: 2	through the **p** of the gateway and stand by	395
	46: 8	he is to go in through the **p** of the gateway,	395

PORTICOES (1) [PORCH]

| Eze | 40:30 | (The **p** of the gateways around | 395 |

PORTION (73) [APPORTIONED, PORTIONS]

Ge	43:34	Benjamin's **p** was five times as much	5368
Lev	2: 2	and burn this as a **memorial p** on the altar.	260
	2: 9	the **memorial p** from the grain offering	260
	2:16	the **memorial p** of the crushed grain and	260
	5:12	as a **memorial p** and burn it on the altar	260
	6:15	and burn the **memorial p** on the altar as	260
	7:35	the **p** of the offerings made to the LORD	5419
	24: 7	as a **memorial p** to represent the bread and	260
Nu	15:19	present a **p** as an offering to the LORD.	8123
	18: 8	and your sons as your **p** and regular share.	5421
	18:28	the LORD's **p** to Aaron the priest.	9556
	18:29	as the LORD's **p** the best and holiest part	9556
Dt	26:13	the **sacred p** and have given it to the Levite,	7731
	26:14	not eaten any of the **sacred p** while I was	5647ˢ
	32: 9	For the LORD's **p** is his people,	2750
	33:21	the leader's **p** was kept for him.	2754
Jos	15:13	Joshua gave to Caleb son of Jephunneh a **p**	2750
	17:14	and one **p** for an inheritance?	2475
	18: 7	however, do not get a **p** among you,	2750
	19: 9	Judah's **p** was more than they needed.	2750
1Sa	1: 5	But to Hannah he gave a double **p**	4950
2Ki	2: 9	"Let me inherit a double **p** of your spirit,"	7023
1Ch	16:18	of Canaan as the **p** you will inherit."	2475
2Ch	30:22	For the seven days they ate their **assigned p**	4595
	31: 4	in Jerusalem to give the **p** due the priests	4987
Ne	12:47	also set aside the **p** for the other Levites,	NIH
	12:47	the **p** for the descendants of Aaron.	NIH
Job	24:18	their **p** of the land is cursed,	2754
Ps	16: 5	you have assigned me my **p** and my cup;	2750
	73:26	the strength of my heart and my **p** forever.	2750
	105:11	of Canaan as the **p** you will inherit."	2475
	119:57	You are my **p,** O LORD;	2750
	142: 5	my **p** in the land of the living."	2750
Isa	17:14	This is the **p** of those who loot us,	2750
	53:12	Therefore *I will* **give** him a **p** among	2745
	57: 6	smooth stones of the ravines are your **p;**	2750
	61: 7	my people will receive a **double p,**	5467
	61: 7	and so they will inherit a **double p**	5467
Jer	6: 3	each tending his own **p."**	3338
	10:16	He who is the **P** of Jacob is not like these,	2750
	13:25	the **p** I have decreed for you,"	4987
	51:19	He who is the **P** of Jacob is not like these,	2750
La	3:24	I say to myself, "The LORD is my **p;**	2750
Eze	44:30	the **first p** of your ground meal so that	AIT
	45: 1	to present to the LORD a **p** of the land as	9556
	45: 4	be the **sacred p** of the land for the priests,	NIH
	45: 6	cubits long, adjoining the sacred **p;**	9556
	45:14	The **prescribed p** of oil,	2976
	48: 1	Dan will have one **p;**	AIT
	48: 2	"Asher will have one **p;**	AIT
	48: 3	"Naphtali will have one **p;**	AIT
	48: 4	"Manasseh will have one **p;**	AIT
	48: 5	"Ephraim will have one **p;**	AIT
	48: 6	"Reuben will have one **p;**	AIT
	48: 7	"Judah will have one **p;**	AIT
	48: 8	**p** you are to present **as a special gift.**	9556
	48: 9	"The **special p** you are to offer to the LORD	9556

Eze	48:10	This will be the sacred **p** for the priests.	9556
	48:12	a special gift to them from the sacred **p** of	9556
	48:12	a most holy **p,** bordering the territory of	NIH
	48:18	on the sacred **p** and running the length of it,	9556
	48:20	The entire **p** will be a square, 25,000	9556
	48:20	the sacred **p,** along with the property of	9556
	48:21	of the area formed by the sacred **p** and	9556
	48:21	cubits of the sacred **p** to the eastern border.	9556
	48:21	the sacred **p** with the temple sanctuary will	9556
	48:23	Benjamin will have one **p;**	AIT
	48:24	"Simeon will have one **p;**	AIT
	48:25	"Issachar will have one **p;**	AIT
	48:26	"Zebulun will have one **p;**	AIT
	48:27	"Gad will have one **p;**	AIT
Zec	2:12	The LORD will inherit Judah as his **p** in	2750
Rev	18: 6	Mix her a **double p** from her own cup.	AIT

PORTIONS (23) [PORTION]

Ge	4: 4	But Abel brought **fat p** from some of	2693
	43:34	**p** were served to them from Joseph's table,	5368
Lev	8:26	on the **fat p** and on the right thigh.	2693
	9:19	But the **fat p** of the ox and the ram—	2693
	9:24	the burnt offering and the **fat p** on	2693
	10:15	the **fat p** of the offerings made by fire,	2693
Jos	19:49	the land into its **allotted p,**	1473
1Sa	1: 4	he would give **p** of the meat	4950
2Ch	7: 7	the grain offerings and the **fat p.**	2693
	31:19	to distribute **p** to every male among them	4950
	35:14	the burnt offerings and the **fat p**	2693
Ne	8:12	to send **p** of food and to celebrate	4950
	12:44	to bring into the storerooms the **p** required	4987
	12:47	the daily **p** for the singers and gatekeepers.	4987
	13:10	that the **p** assigned to the Levites had	4987
Pr	31:15	for her family and **p** for her servant girls.	2976
Ecc	11: 2	Give **p** to seven, yes to eight,	2750
Isa	34:17	He allots their **p;** his hand distributes them	1598
Eze	45: 7	border parallel to one of the tribal **p,**	2750
	47:13	with *two* **p** for Joseph.	2475
	48: 8	to west will equal one of the tribal **p;**	2750
	48:21	of the tribal **p** will belong to the prince,	2750
	48:29	and these will be their **p,"**	4713

PORTRAIT (3)

Mt	22:20	"Whose **p** is this? And whose inscription?"	1635
Mk	12:16	"Whose **p** is this? And whose inscription?"	1635
Lk	20:24	Whose **p** and inscription are on it?"	1635+2400

PORTRAYED (4)

Eze	8:10	and I saw **p** all over the walls all kinds	2977
	23:14	She saw men **p** on a wall,	2977
	23:14	figures of Chaldeans **p** in red,	2980
Gal	3: 1	Before your very eyes Jesus Christ *was* clearly **p** as crucified.	4592

PORTS (1)

| Ac | 27: 2 | a ship from Adramyttium about to sail for **p** | NIG |

POSES (1)

| Jer | 29:27 | who **p** as a prophet among you? | 5547 |

POSITION (21) [POSITIONS]

Ge	40:13	up your head and restore you to your **p,**	4030
	40:21	He restored the chief cupbearer to his **p,**	5482
	41:13	I was restored to my **p,**	4030
Jos	8:19	in the ambush rose quickly from their **p**	5226
Jdg	7:21	each man held his **p** around the camp,	9393
	9:44	to a **p** at the entrance to the city gate.	6641
2Sa	3: 6	**strengthening his own p** in the house of	2616
1Ki	2:35	the army **in Joab's p** and replaced Abiathar	9393
	15:13	from her **p** as queen mother,	1485
	20:22	"**Strengthen** *your* **p** and see what must	2616
2Ch	12: 1	Rehoboam's **p** as king was established	4895
	15:16	Maacah from her **p** as queen mother,	1485
Est	1:19	Also let the king give her **royal p**	4895
	4:14	but that you have come to **royal p** for such	4895
Isa	22:19	and you will be ousted from your **p.**	5096
Da	2:48	the king **placed** Daniel **in a high p**	10648
	5:19	Because of the **high p** he gave him,	10650
Ro	12:16	willing to associate *with people* **of low p.**	5424
Jas	1: 9	ought to take pride in his **high p.**	5737
	1:10	rich should take pride in his **low p,**	5428
2Pe	3:17	of lawless men and fall from your **secure p.**	5113

POSITIONS (23) [POSITION]

Jos	3: 3	to move out from your **p** and follow it.	5226
	8:13	**had** the soldiers **take up** *their* **p—**	8492
	10: 5	up with all their troops and **took up p**	2837
	10:31	he **took up p** against it and attacked it.	2837
	10:34	*they* **took up p** against it and attacked it.	2837
Jdg	9:34	and **took up concealed p** near Shechem	741
	20:20	to fight the Benjamites and **took up battle p**	6885
	20:22	and again **took up** *their* **p**	6885
	20:30	the third day and **took up p** against Gibeah	6885
	20:33	from their places and **took up p**	6885
1Sa	17:20	as the army was going out to its **battle p,**	5120
1Ch	9:22	gatekeepers *had been* **assigned to** their **p**	3569
2Ch	7: 6	The priests took their **p,**	5466
	14:10	and *they* **took up** battle **p** in the Valley	6885
	20:17	**Take up** *your* **p;** stand firm and see	3656
	30:16	their regular **p** as prescribed in the Law	6642
Ecc	10: 6	Fools are put in many **high p,**	5294
Jer	46: 4	**Take** *your* **p** with helmets on!	3656

Jer	46:14	'Take *your* p and get ready,	3656
	50: 9	*They* will take up *their* p against her,	6885
	50:14	"Take up *your* p around Babylon,	6885
Eze	23:24	*they* will take up p against you	8492
Jude	1: 6	not keep their p of authority	794

POSSESS (67) [POSSESSED, POSSESSING, POSSESSION, POSSESSIONS, POSSESSOR]

Ge	24:60	*may* your offspring p the gates	3769
Lev	20:24	But I said to you, "You will p their land;	3769
	25:32	in the Levitical towns, which they p.	299
Nu	27:11	nearest relative in his clan, that *he may* p it.	3769
	33:53	for I have given you the land to p.	3769
	35: 2	in from the inheritance the Israelites will p.	299
	35: 8	the Israelites p are to be given in proportion	299
	35: 8	that every Israelite *will* p the inheritance	3769
Dt	2:31	Now begin to conquer and p his land."	3769
	4:14	that you are crossing the Jordan to p.	3769
	4:26	that you are crossing the Jordan to p.	3769
	5:31	to follow in the land I am giving them to p."	3769
	5:33	in the land that *you will* p.	3769
	6: 1	that you are crossing the Jordan to p,	3769
	7: 1	into the land you are entering to p	3769
	8: 1	and increase and may enter and p the land	3769
	9: 6	giving you this good land to p,	3769
	10:11	and p the land that I swore to their fathers	3769
	11: 8	that you are crossing the Jordan to p,	3769
	11:29	into the land you are entering to p,	3769
	12: 1	the God of your fathers, has given you to p	3769
	15: 4	the LORD your God is giving you to p	3769
	16:20	so that you may live and p the land	3769
	19: 2	the LORD your God is giving you to p.	3769
	19:14	the LORD your God is giving you to p.	3769
	21: 1	the LORD your God is giving you to p,	3769
	23:20	in the land you are entering to p.	3769
	25:19	around you in the land he is giving you to p	3769
	28:21	from the land you are entering to p.	3769
	28:63	from the land you are entering to p.	3769
	30:16	in the land you are entering to p.	3769
	30:18	the Jordan to enter and p.	3769
	31:13	the land you are crossing the Jordan to p."	3769
	32:47	the land you are crossing the Jordan to p."	3769
Jos	22:19	If the land you p is defiled,	299
Jdg	11:24	whatever the LORD our God has given us, we will p.	3769
1Ch	28: 8	that *you may* p this good land and pass it on	3769
Ezr	7:25	wisdom of your God, which you p,	10089+10311
	9:11	to p is a land polluted by the corruption	3769
Ne	9:23	that you told their fathers to enter and p.	3769
Ps	69:35	Then people will settle there and p it;	3769
Pr	8:12	*I* p knowledge and discretion.	5162
Isa	14: 2	of Israel *will* p the nations as menservants	5706
	34:11	The desert owl and screech owl *will* p it;	3769
	34:17	*They will* p it forever and dwell there	3769
	57:13	the land and my holy mountain."	3769
	60:21	and *they will* p the land forever.	3769
	65: 9	from Judah *those who will* p my mountains;	3769
Jer	1: 5	the land you p today."	NIH
	30: 3	to the land I gave their forefathers *to* p,'	3769
	32: 8	Since it is your right to redeem it and p it,	3772
Eze	33:25	*should you* then p the land?	3769
	33:26	*Should you* then p the land?'	3769
	36:12	*They will* p you, and you will	3769
	45: 8	*will* allow the house of Israel to p	5989
Da	7:18	the kingdom and *will* p it forever—	10277
Am	9:12	so that *they may* p the remnant of Edom	3769
Ob	1:17	the house of Jacob *will* p its inheritance.	3769
	1:19	and people from the foothills will p	NIH
	1:19	and Benjamin will p Gilead.	NIH
	1:20	of Israelite exiles who are in Canaan will p	NIH
	1:20	in Sepharad *will* p the towns of the Negev.	3769
Jn	5:39	that by them you p eternal life.	2400
Ac	7: 5	and his descendants after him *would* p	2959
1Co	8: 1	We know that *we* all p knowledge.	2400
	13: 3	If I give all I p to the poor	3836+5639
2Pe	1: 8	you p these qualities in increasing measure,	5639

POSSESSED (13) [POSSESS]

Ps	105:21	master of his household, ruler over all he p,	7871
Isa	63:18	a little while your people p your holy place,	3769
Jer	16:19	"Our fathers p nothing but false gods,	5706
Eze	33:24	yet *he* p the land.	3769
Da	7:22	the time came when they p the kingdom.	10277
Mk	1:23	then a man in their synagogue who was p	NIG
	3:22	"He is p by Beelzebub!	2400
	5:15	p by the legion of **demons**,	1227
	7:25	a woman whose little daughter *was* p by	2400
	9:17	who is p by a spirit that has robbed him	2400
Lk	4:33	In the synagogue there was a man p by	2400
Jn	8:49	"*I am* not p by a demon," said Jesus,	2400
	10:21	not the sayings *of a man* p by a demon.	1227

POSSESSING (1) [POSSESS]

2Co	6:10	having nothing, and yet p everything.	2988

POSSESSION (97) [POSSESS]

Ge	15: 7	to give you this land to take p *of* it."	3769
	15: 8	how can I know that *I will* gain p *of* it?"	3769
	17: 8	I will give as an everlasting p to you	299
	22:17	Your descendants *will* take p *of* the cities	3769
	28: 4	that you *may* take p *of* the land where you	3769
	30:33	Any goat in my p that is not speckled	907

Ge	48: 4	and I will give this land as an everlasting p	299
Ex	6: 8	I will give it to you as a p.	4627
	19: 5	of all nations you will be my **treasured** p.	6035
	22: 4	"If the stolen animal is found alive in his p	3338
	22: 9	In all cases of **illegal** p of an ox,	7322
	23:30	until you have increased enough *to* take p	5706
Lev	14:34	which I am giving you as your p,	299
	25:24	the country that you **hold** as a p,	299
	25:28	the buyer until the Year of Jubilee.	3338
	25:34	it is their permanent p.	299
Nu	13:30	"We should go up and take p of the land,	3769
	21:35	And *they* took p of his land.	3769
	32: 5	be given to your servants as our p.	299
	32:22	this land will be your p before the LORD.	299
	32:29	give them the land of Gilead as their p.	299
	32:30	*they* must **accept** *their* p with you	296
	33:53	Take p of the land and settle in it,	3769
Dt	1: 8	Go in and take p of the land that	3769
	1:21	Go up and take p of it as the LORD,	3769
	1:39	I will give it to them and they *will* take p	3769
	2: 9	to the descendants of Lot as a p."	3772
	2:12	the land the LORD gave them as their p.)	3772
	2:19	not give you p of any land belonging to	3772
	2:19	I have given it as a p to the descendants	3772
	2:24	*to* take p of it and engage him in battle.	3769
	3:18	has given you this land to take p of it.	3769
	3:20	to the p I have given you."	3772
	4: 1	that you may live and may go in and take p	3769
	4: 5	in the land you are entering to take p of it.	3769
	4:22	to cross over and take p of that good land.	3769
	4:47	*They* took p of his land and the land	3769
	7: 6	the earth to be his people, his **treasured** p.	6035
	9: 4	"The LORD has brought me here to take p	3769
	9: 5	that you are going in to take p of their land;	3769
	9:23	and take p of the land I have given you."	3769
	11:11	to take p of is a land of mountains	3769
	11:31	about to cross the Jordan to enter and take p	3769
	14: 2	LORD has chosen you to be his **treasured** p.	6035
	16: 4	be found **in** your p in all your land	4200
	17:14	and *have* taken p of it and settled in it,	3769
	24:12	not go to sleep with his pledge **in** your p.	928
	26: 1	as an inheritance and *have* taken p *of* it	3769
	26:18	his **treasured** p as he promised,	6035
	30: 5	and *you will* take p of it.	3769
	31: 3	and *you will* take p *of* their land.	3769
	32:49	the Israelites as their own p.	299
	33: 4	the p of the assembly of Jacob.	4627
Jos	1:11	the Jordan here to go in and take p *of*	3769
	1:15	until they too *have* taken p of the land that	3769
	12: 6	and the half-tribe of Manasseh to be their p.	3772
	18: 3	before you begin to take p *of* the land that	3769
	19:47	Danites **had difficulty** taking p of	3655+4946
	21:12	to Caleb son of Jephunneh as his p.	299
	21:43	and *they* took p *of* it and settled there.	3769
	23: 5	and *you will* take p *of* their land,	3769
	24: 8	and *you will* took p *of* their land.	3769
Jdg	1:19	*They* took p of the hill country,	3769
	2: 6	they went to take p of the land,	3769
	3:13	and *they* took p of the City of Palms.	3769
	3:28	**taking** p of the fords of the Jordan that led	4334
	8: 6	hands of Zebah and Zalmunna in your p?	3338
	8:15	hands of Zebah and Zalmunna in your p?	3338
1Ki	21:15	up and take p of the vineyard of Naboth	3769
	21:16	down to take p of Naboth's vineyard.	3769
	21:18	where he has gone to take p of it.	3769
2Ch	20:11	of the p you gave us as an inheritance.	3772
Ne	9:15	in and take p of the land you had sworn	3769
	9:24	Their sons went in and took p of the land.	3769
	9:25	*they* took p of houses filled with all kinds	3769
Ps	2: 8	the ends of the earth your p.	299
	73: 9	and their tongues take p of the earth.	2143
	83:12	"Let us take p of the pasturelands of God."	3769
	135: 4	Israel to be his **treasured** p.	6035
Jer	32:23	They came in and took p of it,	3769
	49: 1	Why then *has* Molech taken p of Gad?	3769
Eze	7:24	the most wicked of the nations *to* take p	3769
	11:15	this land was given to us as our p.'	4627
	25: 4	to give you to the people of the East as a p.	4627
	25:10	the East as a p, so that the Ammonites will	4627
	33:24	the land has been given to us as our p.'	4627
	35:10	be ours and *we will* take p of them,"	3769
	36: 2	The ancient heights have become our p." '	4627
	36: 3	from every side so that you became the p of	4627
	36: 5	their hearts they made my land their own p	4627
	44:28	You are to give them no p in Israel;	299
	44:28	I will be their p.	299
	45: 5	as their p for towns to live in.	299
	45: 8	This land will be his p in Israel.	299
Mic	2: 4	my people's p is divided up.	2750
Mal	3:17	in the day when I make up my **treasured** p.	6035
Eph	1:14	the redemption *of* those who are God's p—	4348

POSSESSIONS (38) [POSSESS]

Ge	12: 5	all the p they had accumulated and	8214
	13: 6	for their p were so great that they were	8214
	14:12	Abram's nephew Lot and his p,	8214
	14:16	and brought back his relative Lot and his p,	8214
	15:14	afterward they will come out with great p.	8214
	32:23	he sent over all his p.	889S
	36: 7	Their p were too great for them	8214
	46: 6	and the p they had acquired in Canaan,	8214
Nu	16:32	and all Korah's men and all their p.	8214
Dt	12:11	the **choice** p you have vowed to the LORD.	4436
	18: 8	from the sale of **family** p.	3
Jos	7:11	they have put them with their own p.	3998
Jdg	18:21	their livestock and their p in front of them,	3885

1Ki	13: 8	"Even if you were to give me half your p,	1074
2Ch	31: 3	The king contributed from his own p for	8214
	35: 7	all from the king's own p.	8214
Ezr	8:21	for us and our children, with all our p.	8214
Ne	5:13	of his house and p every man who does	3330
Job	15:29	nor will his p spread over the land.	4978
Pr	12:27	but the diligent man prizes his p.	2104
Ecc	5:19	when God gives any man wealth and p,	5794
	6: 2	God gives a man wealth, p and honor,	5794
Zec	9: 4	But the Lord *will* take away her p	3769
Mt	12:29	a strong man's house and carry off his p	5007
	19:21	go, sell your p and give to the poor,	3836+5639
	24:47	he will put him in charge of all his p.	5639
Mk	3:27	a strong man's house and carry off his p	5007
Lk	11:21	guards his own house, his p are safe.	5639
	12:15	not consist in the abundance of his p."	5639
	12:33	Sell your p and give to the poor.	5639
	12:44	he will put him in charge of all his p.	5639
	16: 1	was accused of wasting his p.	3836+5639
	19: 8	and now I give half of my p to the poor,	5639
Ac	2:45	Selling their p and goods,	3228
	4:32	that any of his p was his own,	5639
2Co	12:14	because what I want is not your p but you.	3836
Heb	10:34	that you yourselves had better and lasting p.	5638
1Jn	3:17	If anyone has material p and sees his	1050

POSSESSOR (1) [POSSESS]

Ecc	7:12	that wisdom preserves the life of its p.	1251

POSSIBLE (19) [POSSIBLY]

Ne	5: 8	"**As far as** p, we have bought back	1896+3869
Mt	19:26	but with God all things are p."	1543
	24:24	deceive even the elect—if that were p.	1543
	26:39	if it is p, may this cup be taken from me.	1543
	26:42	if *it it* is not p for this cup to be taken away	1538
Mk	9:23	"Everything is p for him who believes."	1543
	10:27	all things are p with God."	1543
	13:22	to deceive the elect—if that were p.	1543
	14:35	and prayed that if p the hour might pass from him.	1543+1639
	14:36	Father," he said, "everything is p for you.	1543
Lk	18:27	"What is impossible with men is p	1543
Ac	17:15	and Timothy to join him as **soon** *as* p.	AIT
	20:16	if p, by the day of Pentecost.	1543
	26: 9	that I ought to do all that was p to oppose	NIG
Ro	12:18	If it is p, as far as it depends on you,	1543
	13: 5	not only because of p punishment but also	NIG
1Co	6: 5	Is it p that there is nobody among you wise	4024
	9:19	a slave to everyone, to win as many as p.	NIG
	9:22	so that **by all** p **means** I might save some.	4122

POSSIBLY (3) [POSSIBLE]

Ge	27:37	So what *can I* p do for you, my son?"	AIT
Lk	3:15	in their hearts if John *might* p be the Christ.	AIT
Ro	5: 7	a good man someone might p dare to die.	5440

POST (5) [POSTED, POSTING, POSTS]

Jos	10:18	and p some men there to guard it.	7212
Ecc	10: 4	do not leave your p;	5226
Isa	21: 6	"Go, p a lookout and have him report	6641
	21: 8	every night I stay at my p.	5466
Ac	17: 9	and the others p bond and let them go.	2653

POSTED (6) [POST]

2Ki	10:24	Now Jehu *had* p eighty men outside	8492
	11:18	Then Jehoiada the priest p guards at	8492
Ne	4: 9	to our God and p a guard day and night	6641
	4:16	The officers p themselves behind all	NIH
Isa	22: 7	and horsemen *are* p at the city gates;	8883+8883
	62: 6	*I have* p watchmen on your walls,	7212

POSTERITY (2)

Ps	21:10	their p from mankind.	2446
	22:30	P will serve him; future generations	2446

POSTING (2) [POST]

Ne	4:13	p them by families, with their swords,	6641
Mt	27:66	by putting a seal on the stone and p	NIG

POSTS (42) [POST]

Ex	26:32	on four p of acacia wood overlaid	6647
	26:37	Make gold hooks for this curtain and five p	6647
	27:10	with twenty p and twenty bronze bases and	6647
	27:10	and with silver hooks and bands on the p.	6647
	27:11	with twenty p and twenty bronze bases and	6647
	27:11	and with silver hooks and bands on the p.	6647
	27:12	with ten p and ten bases.	6647
	27:14	with three p and three bases,	6647
	27:15	with three p and three bases.	6647
	27:16	with four p and four bases.	6647
	27:17	All the p around the courtyard are	6647
	35:11	clasps, frames, crossbars, p and bases;	6647
	35:17	of the courtyard with its p and bases, and	6647
	36:36	They made four p of acacia wood for it	6647
	36:38	and they made five p with hooks for them	6647
	36:38	the tops of the p and their bands with gold	2157S
	38:10	with twenty p and twenty bronze bases,	6647
	38:10	and with silver hooks and bands on the p.	6647
	38:11	and had twenty p and twenty bronze bases,	6647
	38:11	with silver hooks and bands on the p.	6647
	38:12	with ten p and ten bases,	6647
	38:12	with silver hooks and bands on the p.	6647

Ex	38:14	with three **p** and three bases,	6647
	38:15	with three **p** and three bases.	6647
	38:17	The bases for the **p** were bronze.	6647
	38:17	The hooks and bands on the **p** were silver,	6647
	38:17	all the **p** of the courtyard had silver bands.	6647
	38:19	with four **p** and four bronze bases.	6647
	38:28	shekels to make the hooks for the **p**,	6647
	38:28	to overlay the tops of **the p**.	2157S
	39:33	its clasps, frames, crossbars, **p** and bases;	6647
	39:40	of the courtyard with its **p** and bases, and	6647
	40:18	inserted the crossbars and set up the **p**.	6647
Nu	3:36	its crossbars, **p**, bases, all its equipment,	6647
	3:37	as the **p** *of* the surrounding courtyard	6647
	4:31	its crossbars, **p** and bases,	6647
	4:32	as the **p** *of* the surrounding courtyard	6647
Jdg	16:3	together with the two **p**,	4647
2Ch	35:15	at each gate did not need to leave their **p**,	6275
Ne	7:3	at their **p** and some near their own houses."	5464
	13:11	and stationed them at their **p**.	6642
SS	3:10	Its **p** he made of silver, its base of gold.	6647

POT (34) [POTS, POTSHERD, POTSHERDS, POTTER, POTTER'S, POTTERS, POTTERY]

Lev	6:28	The clay **p** the meat is cooked in must	3998
	6:28	but if it is cooked in a bronze **p**,	3998
	6:28	but if it is cooked in a bronze pot, the **p** is	NIH
	11:33	If one of them falls into a clay **p**,	3998
	11:33	and you must break the **p**.	2257S
	11:34	on it from such a **p** is unclean,	3998
	11:35	an oven or **cooking p** must be broken up.	3968
	14:5	be killed over fresh water in a clay **p**.	3998
	14:50	of the birds over fresh water in a clay **p**.	3998
	15:12	" 'A clay **p** that the man touches must	3998
Nu	11:8	They cooked it in a **p** or made it into cakes.	7248
Jdg	6:19	the meat in a basket and its broth in a **p**,	7248
1Sa	2:14	into the pan or kettle or caldron or **p**,	7248
2Ki	4:38	"Put on the large **p** and cook some stew	6105
	4:39	he cut them up into the **p** *of* stew,	6105
	4:40	"O man of God, there is death in the **p**!"	6105
	4:41	He put it into the **p** and said,	6105
	4:41	And there was nothing harmful in the **p**.	6105
Job	41:20	from his nostrils as from a boiling **p** over	1857
	41:31	and stirs up the sea like a **p of ointment**.	5350
Ecc	7:6	Like the crackling of thorns under the **p**,	6105
Isa	29:16	Can the **p** say of the potter,	3671
Jer	1:13	"I see a boiling **p**, tilting away from	6105
	18:4	But the **p** he was shaping from the clay	3998
	18:4	so the potter formed it into another **p**,	3998
	22:28	broken **p**, an object no one wants?	6775
Eze	11:3	This city is a **cooking p**,	6105
	11:7	the meat and this city is the **p**,	6105
	11:11	This city will not be a **p** for you,	6105
	24:3	" 'Put on the **cooking p**;	6105
	24:6	to the **p** now encrusted,	6105
	24:11	the empty **p** on the coals till it becomes hot	NIH
Mic	3:3	like flesh for the **p**?"	7831
Zec	14:21	Every **p** in Jerusalem and Judah will	6105

POTENT (1)

Isa	47:9	your many sorceries and all your **p** spells.	6800

POTENTATE (KJV) See RULER

POTIPHAR (4)

Ge	37:36	the Midianites sold Joseph in Egypt to **P**,	7035
	39:1	**P**, an Egyptian who was one of	7035
	39:4	**P** put him in charge of his household,	NIH
	39:5	The blessing of the LORD was on everything **P** had,	2257S

POTIPHERA (3)

Ge	41:45	and gave him Asenath daughter of **P**,	7036
	41:50	to Joseph by Asenath daughter of **P**,	7036
	46:20	to Joseph by Asenath daughter of **P**,	7036

POTS (15) [POT]

Ex	16:3	There we sat around **p** *of* meat and ate all	6105
	27:3	its **p** to remove the ashes, and its shovels,	6105
	38:3	its **p**, shovels, sprinkling bowls.	6105
1Ki	7:45	the **p**, shovels and sprinkling bowls.	6105
2Ki	25:14	They also took away the **p**, shovels,	6105
2Ch	4:11	the **p** and shovels and sprinkling bowls.	6105
	4:16	the **p**, shovels, meat forks	6105
	35:13	and boiled the holy offerings in the **p**,	6105
Ps	58:9	Before your **p** can feel [the heat of]	6105
Isa	65:4	and whose **p** hold broth of unclean meat;	3998
Jer	52:18	They also took away the **p**, shovels,	6105
	52:19	censers, sprinkling bowls, **p**, lampstands,	6105
La	4:2	are now considered as **p** *of* clay,	5574
Zec	14:20	the **cooking p** in the LORD's house will	6105
	14:21	to sacrifice will take some of **the p**	2157S

POTSHERD (3) [POT]

Ps	22:15	My strength is dried up like a **p**,	3084
Isa	45:9	but a **p** among the potsherds on the ground.	3084
Jer	19:2	near the entrance of the **P** Gate.	3068

POTSHERDS (2) [POT]

Job	41:30	His undersides are jagged **p**,	3084
Isa	45:9	but a potsherd among the **p** *on* the ground.	3084

POTTAGE (KJV) See STEW

POTTER (12) [POT]

Isa	29:16	as if the **p** were thought to be like the clay!	3450
	29:16	Can the pot say of the **p**,	3450
	41:25	as if he were a **p** treading the clay.	3450
	45:9	Does the clay say to the **p**,	3450
	64:8	We are the clay, you are the **p**;	3450
Jer	18:4	so the **p** formed it into another pot,	3450
	18:6	can I not do with you as this **p** does?"	3450
	18:6	"Like clay in the hand of the **p**,	3450
	19:1	"Go and buy a clay jar from a **p**.	3450
Zec	11:13	the LORD said to me, "Throw it to the **p**"—	3450
	11:13	into the house of the LORD to the **p**.	3450
Ro	9:21	Does not the **p** have the right to make out	3038

POTTER'S (6) [POT]

Jer	18:2	"Go down to the **p** house,	3450
	18:3	So I went down to the **p** house,	3450
	19:11	and this city just as this **p** jar is smashed	3450
La	4:2	as pots of clay, the work of a **p** hands!	3450
Mt	27:7	the **p** field as a burial place for foreigners.	3038
	27:10	and they used them to buy the **p** field,	3038

POTTERS (1) [POT]

1Ch	4:23	the **p** who lived at Netaim and Gederah;	3450

POTTERY (8) [POT]

2Sa	17:28	and bowls and articles of **p**.	3450
Job	2:8	a **piece of broken p** and scraped himself	3084
Ps	2:9	you will dash them to pieces like **p**."	3450+3998
	31:12	I have become like broken **p**.	3998
Isa	30:14	It will break in pieces like **p**,	3450+5574
Jer	25:34	you will fall and be shattered like fine **p**.	3998
Ro	9:21	lump of clay some **p** for noble purposes	5007
Rev	2:27	he will dash them to pieces like **p**'—	3039+5007

POUCH (2) [POUCHES]

Ge	42:35	in each man's sack was his **p** *of* silver!	7655
1Sa	17:40	put them in the **p** of his shepherd's bag and,	3541

POUCHES (1) [POUCH]

Ge	42:35	they and their father saw the money **p**,	7655

POULTICE (2)

2Ki	20:7	Then Isaiah said, "Prepare a **p** of figs."	1811
Isa	38:21	"Prepare a **p** of figs and apply it to the boil,	1811

POULTRY (1)

Ne	5:18	six choice sheep and *some* **p** were prepared	7606

POUNCE (2) [POUNCED]

1Sa	15:19	Why *did you* **p** on the plunder and do evil	6513
Isa	33:4	like a swarm of locusts *men* **p** on it.	9212

POUNCED (1) [POUNCE]

1Sa	14:32	They **p** on the plunder and, taking sheep,	6513

POUND (1) [POUNDED, POUNDING, POUNDS]

SS	5:4	my heart *began to* **p** for him.	2159

POUNDED (2) [POUND]

2Sa	22:43	I **p** and trampled them like mud in	1990
Hab	3:16	I heard and my heart **p**,	8074

POUNDING (3) [POUND]

Jdg	19:22	**P** on the door, they shouted to the old man	1985
Ps	93:3	the seas have lifted up their **p** waves.	1922
Ac	27:41	and the stern was broken to pieces by the **p**	1040

POUNDS (5) [POUND]

Job	37:1	"At this my heart **p** and leaps	3006
Ps	38:10	My heart **p**, my strength fails me;	6086
Jer	4:19	My heart **p** within me, I cannot keep silent.	2159
Jn	19:39	myrrh and aloes, about **seventy-five p**.	1669+3354
Rev	16:21	of about a **hundred p** each fell upon men.	5418

POUR (78) [DOWNPOUR, OUTPOURED, OUTPOURING, POURED, POURING, POURS]

Ex	4:9	take some water from the Nile and **p** it *on*	9161
	29:12	**p** out the rest of it at the base of the altar.	9161
	30:9	and *do* not **p** a drink offering on it.	5818
	30:32	*Do* not **p** it on men's bodies and do	6057
Lev	2:1	*He is to* **p** oil on it,	3668
	2:6	Crumble it and **p** oil on it;	3668
	4:7	The rest of the bull's blood *he shall* **p** out	9161
	4:18	of the blood *he shall* **p** out at the base of	9161
	4:25	the altar of burnt offering and **p** out the rest	9161
	4:30	the altar of burnt offering and **p** out the rest	9161
	4:34	the altar of burnt offering and **p** out the rest	9161
	14:15	**p** it in the palm of his own left hand,	3668
	14:26	The priest *is to* **p** some of the oil into	3668
Nu	5:15	*He must* not **p** oil on it or put incense on it,	3668
	19:17	into a jar and **p** fresh water over them.	5989

Nu	20:8	and *it will* **p** out its water.	5989
	28:7	**P** out the drink offering to the LORD at	5818
Dt	12:16	**p** it out on the ground like water.	9161
	12:24	**p** it out on the ground like water.	9161
	15:23	**p** it out on the ground like water.	9161
Jdg	6:20	and **p** out the broth."	9161
1Ki	18:33	and **p** it on the offering and on the wood."	3668
2Ki	3:11	*to* **p** water on the hands of Elijah."	3668
	4:4	**P** oil into all the jars, and as each is filled,	3668
	9:3	and **p** the oil on his head and declare,	3668
Job	3:24	my groans **p** out like water.	5988
	10:10	*Did you* not **p** me out like milk and	5988
	15:13	and **p** out such words from your mouth?	3655
	16:20	*as* my eyes **p** out tears to God;	1940
	36:28	the clouds **p** down *their* moisture	5688
Ps	16:4	*I will* not **p** out their libations of blood	5818
	19:2	Day after day *they* **p** forth speech;	5580
	42:4	as *I* **p** out my soul;	9161
	62:8	**p** out your hearts to him,	9161
	69:24	**P** out your wrath on them;	9161
	79:6	**P** out your wrath on the nations that do not	9161
	94:4	*They* **p** out arrogant words;	5580
	104:10	He **makes** springs **p** water into the ravines;	8938
	142:2	*I* **p** out my complaint before him;	9161
Ecc	11:3	*they* **p** rain upon the earth.	8197
Isa	44:3	For *I will* **p** water on the thirsty land,	3668
	44:3	*I will* **p** out my Spirit on your offspring,	3668
	46:6	Some **p** out gold from their bags	2313
Jer	6:11	"**P** it out on the children in the street and	9161
	7:18	*They* **p** out drink offerings to other gods	5818
	10:25	**P** out your wrath on the nations that do not	9161
	14:16	*I will* **p** out on them the calamity	9161
	44:17	of Heaven and *will* **p** out drink offerings	5818
	44:25	to burn incense and **p** out drink offerings	5818
	48:12	"when I will send *men who* **p** from jars,	7579
	48:12	and *they will* **p** her out;	7579
La	2:19	**p** out your heart like water in the presence	9161
Eze	7:8	*I am* about to **p** out my wrath on you	9161
	14:19	a plague into that land and **p** out my wrath	9161
	20:8	So I said I *would* **p** out my wrath on them	9161
	20:13	So I said *I would* **p** out my wrath on them	9161
	20:21	So I said *I would* **p** out my wrath on them	9161
	21:31	*I will* **p** out my wrath upon you	9161
	22:31	So I will **p** out my wrath on them	9161
	24:3	put it on and **p** water into it.	3668
	24:7	*she did* not **p** it on the ground;	9161
	30:15	*I will* **p** out my wrath on Pelusium,	9161
	38:22	*I will* **p** down torrents of rain,	4763
	39:29	for *I will* **p** out my Spirit on the house	9161
Hos	5:10	*I will* **p** out my wrath on them like	9161
	9:4	not **p** out wine offerings to the LORD,	5818
Joel	2:28	*I will* **p** out my Spirit on all people.	9161
	2:29	*I will* **p** out my Spirit in those days.	9161
Mic	1:6	*I will* **p** her stones into the valley	5599
Zep	3:8	the kingdoms and to **p** out my wrath	9161
Zec	4:12	the two gold pipes that **p** out golden oil?"	8197
	12:10	"And *I will* **p** out on the house of David	9161
Mal	3:10	and **p** out so much blessing that you will	8197
Mt	9:17	Neither *do men* **p** new wine	965
	9:17	No, *they* **p** new wine into new wineskins,	965
Ac	2:17	*I will* **p** out my Spirit on all people.	1772
	2:18	*I will* **p** out my Spirit in those days,	1772
Rev	16:1	**p** out the seven bowls of God's wrath on	1772

POURED (94) [POUR]

Ge	28:18	and set it up as a pillar and **p** oil on top	3668
	35:14	and *he* **p** out a drink offering on it;	5818
	35:14	*he also* **p** oil on it.	3668
Ex	8:24	swarms of flies **p** into Pharaoh's palace	995
	9:33	and the rain no *longer* **p** down on the land.	5988
Lev	8:12	He **p** some of the anointing oil on Aaron's	3668
	8:15	He **p** out the rest of the blood at the base of	3668
	9:9	the rest of the blood *he* **p** out at the base of	3668
	21:10	the anointing oil **p** on his head	3668
Dt	12:27	of your sacrifices *must* be **p** beside the altar	9161
Jdg	5:4	the earth shook, the heavens **p**,	5752
	5:4	the clouds **p** down water.	5752
Ru	3:15	*he* **p** into it six **measures** of barley	4499
1Sa	7:6	they drew water and **p** it out before	9161
	10:1	Then Samuel took a flask of oil and **p** it	3668
2Sa	21:10	till the rain **p** down from the heavens on	5988
	23:16	instead, *he* **p** it out before the LORD.	5818
1Ki	13:3	and the ashes on it *will* be **p** out."	9161
	13:5	was split apart and its ashes **p** out	4946+9161
2Ki	4:40	The stew *was* **p** out for the men,	3668
	9:6	Then the prophet **p** the oil on Jehu's head	3668
	16:13	**p** out his drink offering.	5818
1Ch	11:18	instead, *he* **p** it out before the LORD.	5818
2Ch	12:7	My wrath *will* not *be* **p** out on Jerusalem	5988
	34:21	that *is* **p** out on us because our fathers have	5988
	34:25	my anger *will be* **p** out on this place	5988
Job	29:6	the rock **p** out for me streams of olive oil.	3668
Ps	18:42	*I* **p** them out like mud in the streets.	8197
	22:14	*I am* **p** out like water,	9161
	68:8	the heavens **p** down rain, before God,	5752
	77:17	The clouds **p** down water,	2442
	79:3	*They have* **p** out blood like water all	9161
	92:10	fine oils *have been* **p** upon me.	1176
	133:2	It is like precious oil on the head,	NIH
Pr	1:23	*I would have* **p** out my heart to you	5580
	25:20	or like vinegar **p** on soda,	NIH
Ecc	2:19	the work into which *I have* **p** my **effort**	6661
SS	1:3	your name is like perfume **p** out.	8197
Isa	19:14	The LORD *has* **p** into them a spirit	5007
	32:15	till the Spirit *is* **p** upon us from on high,	6867
	42:25	So *he* **p** out on them his burning anger,	9161

Isa 53:12 because *he* p out his life unto death, 6867
57: 6 to them *you have* p out drink offerings 9161
63: 6 and p their blood on the ground." 3718
Jer 1:14 "From the north disaster *will* be p out 7337
7:20 and my wrath *will* be p out on this place, 5988
19:13 and p out drink offerings to other gods.' " 5818
42:18 'As my anger and wrath *have been* p out 5988
42:18 in Jerusalem, so *will* my wrath *be* p out 5988
44: 6 Therefore, my fierce anger *was* p out; 5988
44:19 of Heaven and p out drink offerings to her, 5818
48:11 not p from one jar to another— 8197
La 2: 4 *he has* p out his wrath like fire on the tent 9161
2:11 my heart *is* p out on the ground 9161
4:11 *he has* p out his fierce anger. 9161
Eze 16:36 Because you p out your wealth 9161
20:28 and p out their drink offerings. 5818
22:22 that I the LORD *have* p out my wrath 9161
23: 8 and p out their lust upon her. 9161
24: 7 *She* p it on the bare rock; 8492
36:18 So I p out my wrath on them 9161
Da 9:11 the servant of God, *have been* p out on us, 5988
9:27 the end that is decreed *is* p out on him." 5988
Na 1: 6 His wrath *is* p out like fire; 5988
Zep 1:17 Their blood *will* be p out like dust 9161
Mt 26: 7 which *she* p on his head as he was reclining 2972
26:12 *When* she p this perfume on my body, 965
26:28 blood of the covenant, which *is* p out for 1772
Mk 14: 3 *She* broke the jar and p the perfume **on** 2972
14: 8 p perfume **on** my body beforehand **to prepare** for my burial. 3690
14:24 blood of the covenant, which *is* p out for 1772
Lk 5:38 new wine must be p into new wineskins. 1064
6:38 *will* be p into your lap. 1443
7:38 kissed them and p perfume **on** them. 230
7:46 but she *has* p perfume **on** my feet. 230
22:20 in my blood, which *is* p out for you. 1772
Jn 11: 2 the same one who p perfume **on** the Lord 230
12: 3 *she* p it on Jesus' feet and wiped his feet 230
13: 5 *he* p water into a basin and began 965
Ac 2:33 and *has* p out what you now see and hear. 1772
10:45 of the Holy Spirit *had been* p out even on 1772
Ro 5: 5 because God *has* p out his love 1772
Php 2:17 I am *being* p out like a drink offering 5064
1Ti 1:14 *was* p out on me **abundantly,** 5670
2Ti 4: 6 already *being* p out like a drink offering, 5064
Tit 3: 6 whom *he* p out on us generously 1772
Rev 14:10 which *has been* p full strength into the cup 3042
16: 2 The first angel went and p out his bowl on 1772
16: 3 The second angel p out his bowl on 1772
16: 4 The third angel p out his bowl on the rivers 1772
16: 8 The fourth angel p out his bowl on the sun, 1772
16:10 The fifth angel p out his bowl on 1772
16:12 The sixth angel p out his bowl on 1772
16:17 The seventh angel p out his bowl into 1772

POURING (10) [POUR]

Ex 25:29 and bowls *for the* p out of offerings. 5818
29: 7 the anointing oil and anoint him *by* p it 3668
37:16 pitchers for the p out of drink offerings. 5818
1Sa 1:15 *I was* p out my soul to the LORD. 9161
2Ki 4: 5 the jars to her and she *kept* p. 3668
Jer 32:29 and *by* p out drink offerings to other gods 5818
44:18 of Heaven and p out drink offerings to her, 5818
44:19 like her image and p out drink offerings 5818
Hab 2:15 p it *from* the wineskin till they are drunk, 6203
Lk 10:34 bandaged his wounds, p **on** oil and wine. 2219

POURS (16) [POUR]

Job 12:21 *He* p contempt on nobles and disarms 9161
41:20 Smoke p from his nostrils as from 3655
Ps 75: 8 *he* p it **out,** and all the wicked of the earth 5599
102: T and p out his lament before the LORD. 9161
107:40 *he who* p contempt on nobles 9161
Pr 6:19 a false witness *who* p out lies and 7032
14: 5 but a false witness p out lies. 7032
19: 5 and *he who* p out lies will not go free. 7032
19: 9 and *he who* p out lies will perish. 7032
Jer 6: 7 As a well p out its water, 7981
6: 7 so *she* p out her wickedness. 7981
Am 5: 8 and p them out over the face of the land— 9161
9: 6 and p them **out** over the face of the land— 9161
Mk 2:22 And no one p new wine into old wineskins. 965
2:22 No, he p new wine into new wineskins." NIG
Lk 5:37 And no one p new wine into old wineskins. 965

POURTRAY (KJV) See DRAW

POVERTY (20) [POOR]

Dt 28:48 in nakedness and dire p, 2896
1Sa 2: 7 The LORD *sends* p and wealth; 3769
Pr 6:11 and p will come on you like a bandit 8203
10:15 but p is the ruin of the poor. 8203
11:24 another withholds unduly, but comes to p. 4728
13:18 He who ignores discipline comes to p 8203
14:23 but mere talk leads only to p. 4728
21: 5 to profit as surely as haste leads to p. 4728
22:16 who gives gifts to the rich—both come to p. 4728
24:34 and p will come on you like a bandit 8203
28:19 who chases fantasies will have his fill of p. 8203
28:22 and is unaware that p awaits him. 2895
30: 8 give me neither p nor riches, 8203
31: 7 let them drink and forget their p 8203
Ecc 4:14 or he may have been born in p 8133
Mk 12:44 but she, out *of* her p, put in everything— 5730

Lk 21: 4 of her p put in all she had to live on." 5729
2Co 8: 2 their extreme p welled up in rich generosity. 4775
8: 9 that you *through* his p might become rich. 4775
Rev 2: 9 I know your afflictions and your p— 4775

POWDER (7)

Ex 30:36 Grind some of it to p and place it in front of 1990
32:20 then he ground it to p, 1990
Dt 9:21 and **ground** it to p as fine as dust and 3221+3512
28:24 the rain of your country into dust and p; 85
2Ki 23: 6 to p and scattered the dust over the graves 6760
23:15 the high place and ground it to p, 6760
2Ch 34: 7 to p and cut to pieces all the incense altars 1990

POWER (276) [OVERPOWER, OVERPOWERED, OVERPOWERING, OVERPOWERS, POWERFUL, POWERFULLY, POWERLESS, POWERS]

Ge 31:29 I have the p to harm you; 445+3338
49: 3 excelling in honor, excelling in p. 6435
Ex 1: 8 not know about Joseph, **came to** p in Egypt. 7756
4:21 the wonders I have given you the p to do. 3338
9:16 that I might show you my p and 3946
14:31 the great p the LORD displayed against 3946
15: 6 Your right hand, O LORD, was majestic in p. 3946
15:16 By the p *of* your arm they will be as still as 1524
32:11 of Egypt with great p and a mighty hand? 3946
Nu 14:13 By your p you brought these people up 3946
Dt 7: 8 from the p of Pharaoh king of Egypt. 3338
8:17 "My p and the strength of my hands 3946
9:26 by your **great** p and brought out of Egypt 1542
9:29 by your great p and your outstretched arm." 3946
34:12 For no one has ever shown the mighty p 3338
Jdg 1:35 the p of the house of Joseph increased, 3338
3:12 **gave** Eglon king of Moab p over Israel. 2616
6: 2 the p of Midian was so oppressive, 3338
6: 9 I snatched you from the p *of* Egypt and 3338
14: 6 The Spirit of the LORD **came** upon him **in** p 7502
14:19 the Spirit of the LORD **came** upon him **in** p. 7502
14:19 The Spirit of the LORD **came** upon him **in** p. 7502
1Sa 7:14 the neighboring territory from the p *of* 3338
10: 6 Spirit of the LORD *will* **come** upon you **in** p, 7502
10:10 the Spirit of God **came** upon him **in** p, 7502
10:18 from the p *of* Egypt and all the kingdoms 3338
11: 6 the Spirit of God **came** upon him **in** p, 7502
16:13 Spirit of the LORD **came** upon David **in** p. 7502
1Ki 18:46 The p *of* the LORD **came** upon Elijah 3338
2Ki 13: 3 for a long time he kept them under the p 3338
13: 5 and they escaped from the p *of* Aram. 3338
17: 7 from under the p *of* Pharaoh king of Egypt. 3338
17:36 with mighty p and outstretched arm, 3946
19:26 Their people, drained of p, 3338
1Ch 29:11 and the p and the glory and the majesty and 1476
29:12 In your hands are strength and p to exalt 1476
29:30 together with the details of his reign and p, 1476
2Ch 13:20 Jeroboam did not regain p during the time 3946
20: 6 P and might are in your hand, 3946
20:12 For we have no p to face this vast army 3946
25: 8 for God has the p to help or to overthrow." 3946
32: 7 there is a **greater** p with us than with him. 8041
36:20 until the kingdom of Persia **came to** p. 4887
Est 10: 2 And all his acts of p and might, 9549
Job 6:13 Do I have any p to help myself, NIH
9: 4 His wisdom is profound, his p is vast. 3946
10:16 again **display** *your* **awesome** p against me. 7098
12:13 "To God belong wisdom and p; 1476
21: 7 growing old and increasing in p? 2657
23: 6 Would he oppose me with great p? 3946
24:22 But God drags away the mighty by his p; 3946
26:12 By his p he churned up the sea; 3946
26:14 then can understand the thunder of his p?" 1476
27:11 "I will teach you about the p *of* God; 3338
27:22 as he flees headlong from its p. 3338
30:18 In his great p [God] becomes like clothing 3946
36:22 "God is exalted in his p. 3946
37:23 beyond our reach and exalted in p; 3946
40:16 what p in the muscles of his belly! 226
Ps 20: 6 from his holy heaven with the saving p 1476
22:20 my precious life from the p *of* the dogs. 3338
37:17 for the p *of* the wicked will be broken, 2432
37:33 the LORD will not leave them in their p 3338
63: 2 in the sanctuary and beheld your p 6437
65: 6 who formed the mountains by your p, 3946
66: 3 So great is your p that your enemies cringe 6437
66: 7 He rules forever by his p, 1476
68:28 Summon your p, O God; 6437
68:34 Proclaim the p of God, 6437
68:34 whose p is in the skies. 6437
68:35 of Israel gives p and strength to his people. 6437
71:18 till I declare your p to the next generation, 2432
74:13 you who split open the sea by your p; 6437
77:14 you display your p among the peoples. 6437
78: 4 his p, and the wonders he has done. 6449
78:26 and led forth the south wind by his p. 6437
78:42 They did not remember his p— 3338
89:13 Your arm is endued with p; 1476
89:48 or save himself from the p *of* the grave? 3338
90:11 Who knows the p of your anger? 6437
106: 8 to make his **mighty** p known. 1476
106:42 and subjected them to their p. 3338
111: 6 He has shown his people the p of his works, 3946
145: 6 of the p *of* your awesome works, 6449
147: 5 Great is our Lord and mighty in p; 3946
150: 2 Praise him for his **acts of** p; 1476

Pr 3:27 when it is in your p to act. 445+3338
8:14 I have understanding and p. 1476
11: 7 all he expected from his p comes to nothing. 226
18:21 The tongue has the p *of* life and death, 3338
24: 5 A wise man has **great** p, 6437
28:12 the wicked **rise to** p, men go into hiding. 7756
28:28 the wicked **rise to** p, people go into hiding; 7756
30:26 of little p, yet they make their home in 6786
Ecc 4: 1 p was on the side of their oppressors— 3946
8: 8 No man has p over the wind to contain it; 8954
8: 8 so no one has p over the day of his death. 8950
Isa 10:33 will lop off the boughs with **great** p. 5124
11: 2 the Spirit of counsel and of p, 1476
17: 3 and **royal** p from Damascus. 4930
19: 4 I will hand the Egyptians over to the p *of* 3338
33:13 you who are near, acknowledge my p! 1476
37:27 Their people, drained of p, 3338
40:10 See, the Sovereign LORD comes with p, 2617
40:26 Because of his great p and mighty strength, 226
40:29 the weary and increases the p of the weak. 6800
47:14 even save themselves from the p *of* 3338
63:12 who sent his glorious **arm of** p to be 2432
Jer 10: 6 and your name is mighty in p. 1476
10:12 But God made the earth by his p; 3946
16:21 this time I will teach them my p and might. 3338
18:21 hand them over to the p *of* the sword. 3338
23:10 an evil course and use their p unjustly. 1476
27: 5 With my great p and outstretched arm 3946
32:17 the heavens and the earth by your great p 3946
51:15 "He made the earth by his p; 3946
Eze 13:21 and they will no longer fall prey to your p. 3338
22: 6 who are in you uses his p to shed blood. 2432
26:17 You were a p on the seas, 2617
32:29 despite their p, they are laid with those 1476
32:30 despite the terror caused by their p. 3338
Da 2:20 wisdom and p are his. 10130
2:23 You have given me wisdom and p, 10130
2:37 of heaven has given you dominion and p 10278
4:30 by my mighty p and for the glory 10774
6:27 He has rescued Daniel from the p 10311
7:14 authority, glory and **sovereign** p; 10424
7:26 and his p will be taken away 10717
7:27 p and greatness of the kingdoms under 10717
8: 4 and none could rescue from his p. 3338
8: 7 and none could rescue the ram from his p. 3338
8: 8 at the **height of** his p his large horn was broken off, 6793
8: 9 in p to the south and to the east and toward 3856
8:22 but will not have the same p. 3946
8:24 become very strong, but not by his own p. 3946
8:25 he will be destroyed, but not by human p. 3338
11: 2 When he has **gained** p by his wealth, 2621
11: 3 with great p and do as he pleases. 4938
11: 4 nor will it have the p he exercised, 5445
11: 5 and will rule his own kingdom with great p. 4938
11: 6 but she will not retain her p, 2432+3946
11: 6 and he and his p will not last. 2432
11:16 and will have the p to **destroy** it. 3986
11:23 with only a few people he will rise to p. 6793
11:42 He will extend his p over many countries; 3338
12: 7 When the p of the holy people 3338
Hos 13:14 "I will ransom them from the p *of* the grave; 3338
Mic 2: 1 because it is in their p to do it. 445+3338
3: 8 But as for me, I am filled with p, 3946
7:16 deprived of all their p. 1476
Na 1: 3 LORD is slow to anger and great in p; 3946
Hab 3: 4 where his p was hidden. 6437
Hag 2:22 and shatter the p of the foreign kingdoms. 2620
Zec 3: 4 'Not by might nor by p, but by my Spirit,' 3946
9: 4 and destroy her p on the sea, 2657
Mt 22:29 not know the Scriptures or the p of God. 1539
24:30 with p and great glory. 1539
Mk 5:30 At once Jesus realized that p had gone out 1539
9: 1 the kingdom of God come with p." 1539
12:24 not know the Scriptures or the p of God? 1539
13:26 Son of Man coming in clouds with great p 1539
Lk 1:17 in the spirit and p of Elijah, 1539
1:35 p of the Most High will overshadow you. 1539
4:14 Jesus returned to Galilee in the p of the Spirit, 1539
4:36 With authority and p he gives orders 1539
5:17 And the p of the Lord was present for him 1539
6:19 because p was coming from him 1539
8:46 I know that p has gone out from me." 1539
9: 1 he gave them p and authority 1539
10:19 to overcome all the p of the enemy; 2026
12: 5 has p to throw you into hell. 2026
20:20 over *to* the p and authority of the governor. 794
21:27 the Son of Man coming in a cloud with p 1539
24:49 the city until you have been clothed with p 1539
Jn 13: 3 Father had put all things **under** his p, 1650+5931
17:11 protect them **by the** p *of* your name— 1877
19:10 "Don't you realize I have p either to free 2026
19:11 "You would have no p over me if it were 2026
Ac 1: 8 But you will receive p when the Holy Spirit comes on you; 1539
3:12 Why do you stare at us as if *by* our own p 1539
4: 7 "By what p or what name did you do this?" 1539
4:28 They did what your p and will had 5931
4:33 *With* great p the apostles continued 1539
6: 8 Stephen, a man full of God's grace and p, 1539
8:10 the divine p known as the Great Power." 1539
8:10 the divine power known as the Great **P**." NIG
10:38 Jesus of Nazareth with the Holy Spirit and p 1539
10:38 and healing all who *were* **under the** p of 2872
13:17 in Egypt, with mighty p he led them out of 1098
19:20 of the Lord spread widely and grew in p. 3197

Ac	26:18	and from the p of Satan to God,	2026
Ro	1: 4	the Spirit of holiness was declared with p	1539
	1:16	because it is the p of God for the salvation	1539
	1:20	his eternal p and divine nature—	1539
	4:21	that God had p to do what he had promised.	1543+1639
	9:17	that I might display my p in you and	1539
	9:22	to show his wrath and make his p known,	1543
	15:13	that you may overflow with hope by the p	1539
	15:19	by the p of signs and miracles,	1539
	15:19	through the p of the Spirit.	1539
1Co	1:17	lest the cross of Christ be emptied of its p.	NIG
	1:18	but to us who are being saved it is the p	1539
	1:24	the p of God and the wisdom of God.	1539
	2: 4	but with a demonstration of the Spirit's p,	1539
	2: 5	not rest on man's wisdom, but on God's p.	1539
	4:19	but what p they have.	1539
	4:20	of God is not a matter of talk but of p.	1539
	5: 4	and the p of our Lord Jesus is present,	1539
	6:14	By his p God raised the Lord from	1539
	15:24	after he has destroyed all dominion, authority and p.	1539
	15:43	it is sown in weakness, it is raised in p;	1539
	15:56	and the p of sin is the law.	1539
2Co	4: 7	show that this all-surpassing p is from God	1539
	6: 7	in truthful speech and in the p of God;	1539
	10: 4	they have divine p to demolish strongholds.	1543
	12: 9	for my p is made perfect in weakness."	1539
	12: 9	so that Christ's p may rest on me.	1539
	13: 4	yet he lives by God's p.	1539
	13: 4	yet by God's p we will live with him	1539
Gal	4:29	the son born by the p of the Spirit.	NIG
Eph	1:19	and his incomparably great p for us	1539
	1:19	p is like the working of his mighty strength,	NIG
	1:21	p and dominion, and every title that can	1539
	3: 7	through the working of his p.	1539
	3:16	with p through his Spirit	1539
	3:18	may have p, together with all the saints,	2015
	3:20	according to his p that is at work within us,	1539
	6:10	be strong in the Lord and in his mighty p.	3197
Php	3:10	to know Christ and the p of his resurrection	1539
	3:21	the p that enables him to bring everything	1918
Col	1:11	with all p according to his glorious might	1539
	2:10	who is the head over every p and authority,	794
	2:12	with him through your faith in the p	1918
1Th	1: 5	not simply with words, but also with p,	1539
2Th	1: 9	of the Lord and from the majesty of his p,	2709
	1:11	by his p he may fulfill every good purpose	1539
	2: 7	secret p of lawlessness is already at work;	NIG
2Ti	1: 7	give us a spirit of timidity, but a spirit of p,	1539
	1: 8	suffering for the gospel, by the p of God,	1539
	3: 5	a form of godliness but denying its p.	1539
Heb	2:14	destroy him who holds the p of death—	3197
	7:16	to his ancestry but on the basis of the p of	1539
1Pe	1: 5	through faith are shielded by God's p until	1539
	4:11	be the glory and the p for ever and ever.	3197
	5:11	To him be the p for ever and ever. Amen.	3197
2Pe	1: 3	His divine p has given us everything we need for life and godliness	1539
	1:16	the p and coming of our Lord Jesus Christ,	1539
Jude	1:25	be glory, majesty, p and authority,	3197
Rev	1: 6	to him be glory and p for ever and ever!	3197
	4:11	to receive glory and honor and p,	1539
	5:12	the Lamb, who was slain, to receive p	1539
	5:13	be praise and honor and glory and p,	3197
	6: 4	Its rider was given p to take peace from	NIG
	6: 8	They were given p over a fourth of	2026
	7: 2	to the four angels who had been given p	NIG
	7:12	and honor and p and strength be to our God	1539
	9: 3	down upon the earth and were given p like	2026
	9: 5	They were not given p to kill them,	NIG
	9:10	in their tails they had p to torment people	2026
	9:19	The p of the horses was in their mouths and	2026
	11: 3	And I will give p to my two witnesses,	NIG
	11: 6	These men have p to shut up the sky so	2026
	11: 6	and they have p to turn the waters	2026
	11:17	because you have taken your great p	1539
	12:10	"Now have come the salvation and the p	1539
	13: 2	The dragon gave the beast his p	1539
	13: 7	He was given p to make war against	NIG
	13:14	the signs he was given p to do on behalf of	NIG
	13:15	He was given p to give breath to the image	NIG
	15: 8	from the glory of God and from his p,	1539
	16: 8	sun was given p to scorch people with fire.	NIG
	17:13	and will give their p and authority to	1539
	17:17	by agreeing to give the beast their p to rule,	NIG
	18:10	Woe, O great city, O Babylon, city of p!	2708
	19: 1	and glory and p belong to our God,	1539
	20: 6	The second death has no p over them,	2026

POWERFUL (56) [POWER]

Ge	18:18	surely become a great and p nation,	6786
	26:16	you have become too p for us."	6793
Nu	13:28	But the people who live there are p,	6434
	20:20	against them with a large and p army.	2617
	26: 2	because they are too p for me.	6786
Dt	26: 5	a great nation, and numerous.	6786
Jos	4:24	that the hand of the LORD is p and so	2617
	17:17	"You are numerous and very p.	3946
	23: 9	before you great and p nations.	6786
2Sa	5:10	he became more and more p,	1524+2143+2143+2256
	22:18	He rescued me from my p enemy,	6434
1Ki	19:11	a great and p wind tore the mountains apart	2617
1Ch	11: 9	David became more and more p,	1524+2143+2143+2256

2Ch	17:12	Jehoshaphat became more and more p;	1541+2025+2143+2256+4200+5087+6330
	22: 9	of Ahaziah p enough to retain the kingdom.	3946
	26: 8	because he had become very p.	2616
	26:13	a p force to support the king	3946
	26:15	for he was greatly helped until he became p.	2616
	26:16	But after Uzziah became p,	2621
	27: 6	Jotham grew p because he walked	2616
Ezr	4:20	Jerusalem has had p kings ruling over	10768
	7:28	and all the king's p officials.	1475
Est	9: 4	became more and more p.	1524+2143+2256
Job	5:15	he saves them from the clutches of the p.	2617
	22: 8	though you were a p man, owning land—	2432
	35: 9	they plead for relief from the arm of the p.	8041
Ps	18:17	He rescued me from my p enemy,	6434
	29: 4	The voice of the LORD is p;	3946
Ecc	7:19	Wisdom makes one wise man more p than	6451
	9:14	And a p king came against it,	1524
Isa	27: 1	his fierce, great and p sword,	2617
	28: 2	See, the Lord has one who is p and strong.	2617
Jer	5:27	they have become rich and p	1540
	32:18	O great and p God,	1475
Eze	17: 3	A great eagle with p wings,	1524
	17: 7	with p wings and full plumage.	1524
Da	7: 7	terrifying and frightening and very p.	10768
	11:25	with a large and very p army,	6786
Joel	1: 6	p and without number;	6786
Mic	7: 3	the p dictate what they desire—	1524
Zec	6: 3	the fourth dappled—all of them p.	600
	6: 7	When the p horses went out,	600
	8:22	And many peoples and p nations will come	6786
Mt	3:11	me will come one who is more p than I,	2708
Mk	1: 7	"After me will come one more p than I,	2708
Lk	3:16	But one more p than I will come,	2708
	24:19	p in word and deed before God and all	1543
Ac	7:22	the wisdom of the Egyptians and was p	1543
	9:22	Yet Saul grew more and more p and baffled	1904
2Co	13: 3	but is p among you.	1542
2Th	1: 7	in blazing fire with his p angels.	1539
	2:11	a p delusion so that they will believe the lie	1918
Heb	1: 3	sustaining all things by his p word.	1539
	11:34	and who became p in battle	2708
Jas	5:16	of a righteous man is p and effective.	2710
2Pe	2:11	although they are stronger and more p,	1539

POWERFULLY (1) [POWER]

Col	1:29	his energy, which so p works in me.	1539+1877

POWERLESS (9) [POWER]

Dt	28:32	p to lift a hand.	401+445+4200
2Ch	14:11	you to help the p against the mighty.	401+3946
Ne	5: 5	but we are p,	401+445+3338+4200
Job	26: 2	"How you have helped the p!	3946+4202
Jer	14: 9	like a warrior p to save?	3523+4202
Da	8: 7	The ram was p to stand against him;	3946+4202
	11:15	The forces of the South will be p to resist;	4202
Ro	5: 6	at just the right time, when we were still p,	820
	8: 3	the law was p to do in that it was weakened	105

POWERS (12) [POWER]

Isa	24:21	In that day the LORD will punish the p in	7372
Da	4:35	He does as he pleases with the p of heaven	10264
Mt	13:54	and these miraculous p?"	1539
	14: 2	That is why miraculous p are at work	1539
Mk	6:14	and that is why miraculous p are at work	1539
Ro	8:38	the present nor the future, nor any p,	1539
1Co	12:10	to another miraculous p,	1539+1920
Eph	6:12	against the p of this dark world	3179
Col	1:16	and invisible, whether thrones or p or rulers	3262
	2:15	And having disarmed the p and authorities,	794
Heb	6: 5	the goodness of the word of God and the p	1539
1Pe	3:22	authorities and p in submission to him.	1539

PRACTICALLY (1)

Ac	19:26	in Ephesus and in p the whole province	5385

PRACTICE (31) [PRACTICED, PRACTICES]

Lev	19:26	" 'Do not p divination or sorcery.	5727
Dt	18:14	to those who p sorcery or divination.	6726
1Sa	2:13	Now it was the p of the priests with	5477
	27:11	And such was his p as long as he lived	5477
Ps	52: 2	like a sharpened razor, you who p deceit.	6913
	119:56	This has been my p: I obey your precepts.	AIT
Ecc	8: 8	wickedness will not release those who p it.	1251
Isa	2: 6	they p divination from the Philistines	6726
Jer	6:13	prophets and priests alike, all p deceit.	6913
	8:10	prophets and priests alike, all p deceit.	6913
Eze	13:23	therefore you will no longer see false visions or p divination.	7876+7877
	22:29	p extortion and commit robbery;	6943+6945
	33:31	but they do not put them into p.	6913
	33:32	but do not put them into p.	6913
Hos	7: 1	They p deceit, thieves break into houses,	7188
Mt	7:24	words of mine and puts them into p is like	4472
	7:26	words of mine and does not put them into p	4472
	23: 3	for they do not p what they preach.	4472
Lk	6:47	and hears my words and puts them into p.	4472
	6:49	not put them into p is like a man who built	4472
	8:21	who hear God's word and put it into p."	4472
Ac	16:21	for us Romans to accept or p."	4472
Ro	1:32	but also approve of those who p them.	4556
	3:13	their tongues p deceit."	1514

Ro	12:13	God's people who are in need. P hospitality.	1503
1Co	11:16	we have no other p—nor do the churches	5311
Php	4: 9	or seen in me—put it into p.	4556
1Ti	5: 4	put their religion into p by caring for	2355
Jas	3:16	there you find disorder and every evil p.	4547
Rev	21: 8	those who p magic arts,	5761
	22:15	those who p magic arts,	5761

PRACTICED (10) [PRACTICE]

Lev	18:30	detestable customs that were p before you	6913
Jos	13:22	Balaam son of Beor, who p divination.	7876
2Ki	17:17	They p divination and sorcery	7876+7877
	21: 6	p sorcery and divination,	6726
2Ch	33: 6	p sorcery, divination and witchcraft,	6726
Eze	18:18	because he p extortion,	6943+6945
Mt	23:23	You should have p the latter,	4472
Lk	11:42	You should have p the latter,	4472
Ac	8: 9	a man named Simon had p sorcery in	3405
	19:19	A number who had p sorcery brought their scrolls together	4556

PRACTICES (53) [PRACTICE]

Ex	23:24	or worship them or follow their p.	5126
Lev	18: 3	Do not follow their p.	2978
Dt	18:10	who p divination or sorcery,	7876+7877
	18:12	and because of these detestable p	9359
Jdg	2:19	to give up their evil p and stubborn ways.	5095
1Ki	14:24	the people engaged in all the detestable p	9359
2Ki	17: 8	and followed the p of the nations	2978
	17: 8	as well as the p that the kings of Israel	NIH
	17:19	They followed the p Israel had introduced.	2978
	17:34	To this day they persist in their former p.	5477
	17:40	however, but persisted in their former p.	5477
	21: 2	following the detestable p of the nations	9359
2Ch	17: 4	his commands rather than the p of Israel.	5126
	27: 2	however, continued their corrupt p.	8845
	33: 2	following the detestable p of the nations	9359
	36:14	following all the detestable p of the nations	9359
Ezr	6:21	the unclean p of their Gentile neighbors	3240
	9: 1	peoples with their detestable p,	9359
	9:11	By their detestable p they have filled it	9359
	9:14	peoples who commit such detestable p?	9359
Ps	101: 7	No one who p deceit will dwell	6913
Isa	9:17	He p ungodliness and spreads error	6913
Jer	25: 5	from your evil ways and your evil p,	5095
Eze	5:11	with all your vile images and detestable p,	9359
	6: 9	and for all their detestable p.	9359
	6:11	because of all the wicked and detestable p	9359
	7: 3	and repay you for all your detestable p.	9359
	7: 4	for your conduct and the detestable p	9359
	7: 8	and repay you for all your detestable p.	9359
	7: 9	with your conduct and the detestable p	9359
	12:16	may acknowledge all their detestable p.	9359
	14: 6	and renounce all your detestable p!	9359
	16: 2	confront Jerusalem with her detestable p	9359
	16:22	In all your detestable p	9359
	16:43	to all your other detestable p?	9359
	16:47	and copied their detestable p.	9359
	16:58	of your lewdness and your detestable p,	9359
	20: 4	Then confront them with the detestable p	9359
	20:44	to your evil ways and your corrupt p,	6613
	22: 2	Then confront her with all her detestable p	9359
	23:36	confront them with their detestable p,	9359
	36:31	for your sins and detestable p.	9359
	43: 8	defiled my holy name by their detestable p.	9359
	44: 6	Enough of your detestable p,	9359
	44: 7	In addition to all your other detestable p,	9359
	44:13	the shame of their detestable p.	9359
Mic	6:16	of Omri and all the p of Ahab's house,	5126
Zec	1: 4	'Turn from your evil ways and your evil p.'	5095
	1: 6	to us what our ways and p deserve,	5095
Mt	5:19	in the kingdom of heaven, but whoever p	4472
Col	3: 9	you have taken off your old self with its p	4552
Rev	2: 6	You hate the p of the Nicolaitans,	2240
	22:15	and everyone who loves and p falsehood.	4472

PRAETORIUM (2)

Mt	27:27	into the P and gathered the whole company	4550
Mk	15:16	the palace (that is, the P) and called together	4550

PRAISE (340) [PRAISED, PRAISES, PRAISEWORTHY, PRAISING]

Ge	24:27	"P be to the LORD,	1385
	29:35	"This time I will p the LORD."	3344
	49: 8	"Judah, your brothers will p you;	3344
Ex	15: 2	He is my God, and I will p him,	5658
	18:10	He said, "P be to the LORD,	1385
Lev	19:24	an offering of p to the LORD.	2136
Dt	8:10	p the LORD your God for the good land	1385
	10:21	He is your p; he is your God,	9335
	26:19	He has declared that he will set you in p,	9335
	32: 3	Oh, p the greatness of our God!	2035
Jos	7:19	the God of Israel, and give him the p.	9343
Jdg	5: 2	when the people willingly offer themselves—p the LORD!	1385
	5: 9	P the LORD!	1385
Ru	4:14	"P be to the LORD,	1385
1Sa	25:32	"P be to the LORD, the God of Israel,	1385
	25:39	he said, "P be to the LORD,	1385
2Sa	22: 4	I call to the LORD, who is worthy of p,	2146
	22:47	P be to my Rock!	1385
	22:50	Therefore I will p you, O LORD,	3344
1Ki	1:48	'P be to the LORD, the God of Israel,	1385

1Ki	5: 7	"**P** be to the LORD today,	1385
	8:15	"**P** be to the LORD, the God of Israel,	1385
	8:56	"**P** be to the LORD, who has given rest	1385
	10: 9	**P** be *to* the LORD your God,	1385
1Ch	16: 4	and to **p** the LORD, the God of Israel:	2146
	16: 9	Sing to him, **sing p** to him;	2376
	16:25	great is the LORD and most **worthy of p**;	2146
	16:35	that we may glory in your **p**."	9335
	16:36	**P** be to the LORD, the God of Israel,	1385
	16:36	Then all the people said "Amen" and "**P**	2146
	23: 5	and four thousand *are to* **p** the LORD with	2146
	23:30	also to stand every morning to thank and **p**	2146
	29:10	saying, "**P** be to you, O LORD,	1385
	29:13	and **p** your glorious name.	2146
	29:20	"**P** the LORD your God."	1385
2Ch	2:12	And Hiram added: "**P** be *to* the LORD,	1385
	5:13	to **give p** and thanks to the LORD.	2146
	5:13	they raised their voices in **p** to the LORD	2146
	6: 4	"**P** be to the LORD, the God of Israel,	1385
	8:14	and the Levites to lead the **p** and to assist	2146
	9: 8	**P** be *to* the LORD your God,	1385
	20:21	the LORD and *to* **p** him for the splendor	2146
	20:22	As they began to sing and **p**,	9335
	29:30	the Levites to **p** the LORD with the words	2146
	30:21	by the LORD's instruments of **p**.	6437
Ezr	3:10	took their places to **p** the LORD,	2146
	3:11	With **p** and thanksgiving they sang to	2146
	3:11	And all the people gave a great shout of **p**	2146
	7:27	**P** be *to* the LORD, the God of our fathers,	1385
Ne	9: 5	"Stand up and **p** the LORD your God,	1385
	9: 5	may it be exalted above all blessing and **p**.	9335
	12:24	who stood opposite them to **give p**	2146
	12:46	for the songs of **p** and thanksgiving to God.	9335
Ps	7:17	and *will* **sing p** to the LORD Most High.	2146
	8: 2	of children and infants you have ordained **p**	6437
	9: 1	*I will* **p** you, O LORD,	3344
	9: 2	*I will* **sing p** *to* your name, O Most High.	2376
	16: 7	*I will* **p** the LORD, who counsels me;	1385
	18: 3	I call to the LORD, *who is* **worthy of p**,	2146
	18:46	**P** be to my Rock!	1385
	18:49	Therefore *I will* **p** you among the nations!	3344
	21:13	we will sing and **p** your might.	2376
	22: 3	you are the **p** of Israel.	9335
	22:22	in the congregation *I will* **p** you.	2146
	22:23	*You* who fear the LORD, **p** him!	2146
	22:25	the **theme** of my **p** in the great assembly;	9335
	22:26	they who seek the LORD *will* **p** him—	2146
	26: 7	proclaiming aloud your **p** and telling	9343
	26:12	in the great assembly *I will* **p** the LORD.	1385
	28: 6	**P** be to the LORD,	1385
	30: 4	**p** his holy name.	3344
	30: 9	*Will* the dust **p** you?	3344
	31:21	**P** be to the LORD,	1385
	33: 1	it is fitting for the upright to **p** him.	9335
	33: 2	**P** the LORD with the harp;	3344
	34: 1	his **p** will always be on my lips.	9335
	35:18	among throngs of people *I will* **p** you.	2146
	40: 3	a **hymn** of **p** to our God.	9335
	41:13	**P** be *to* the LORD, the God of Israel,	1385
	42: 5	for *I will* yet **p** him,	3344
	42:11	for *I will* yet **p** him,	3344
	43: 4	*I will* **p** you with the harp, O God,	3344
	43: 5	for *I will* yet **p** him,	3344
	44: 8	and *we will* **p** your name forever.	3344
	45:17	the nations *will* **p** you for ever and ever.	3344
	47: 7	sing to him a **psalm** of **p**.	5380
	48: 1	Great is the LORD, and most **worthy of p**,	2146
	48:10	your **p** reaches to the ends of the earth;	9335
	49:18	and *men* **p** you when you prosper—	3344
	51:15	and my mouth will declare your **p**.	9335
	52: 9	*I will* **p** you forever	3344
	52: 9	I will **p** you in the presence of your saints.	NIH
	54: 6	*I will* **p** your name, O LORD,	3344
	56: 4	In God, whose word *I* **p**, in God I trust;	2146
	56:10	In God, whose word *I* **p**, in the LORD,	2146
	56:10	in the LORD, whose word *I* **p**—	2146
	57: 9	*I will* **p** you, O Lord, among the nations;	3344
	59:17	O my Strength, *I* **sing p** to you;	2376
	61: 8	Then *will I* ever **sing p** *to* your name	2376
	63: 4	*I will* **p** you as long as I live,	1385
	63: 5	with singing lips my mouth *will* **p** you.	2146
	63:11	all who swear by God's name *will* **p** him,	2146
	64:10	*let* all the upright in heart **p** him!	2146
	65: 1	**P** awaits you, O God, in Zion;	9335
	66: 2	make his **p** glorious!	2146
	66: 4	*they* **sing p** to you,	2376
	66: 4	*they* **sing p** *to* your name."	2376
	66: 8	**P** our God, O peoples, let the sound	1385
	66: 8	O peoples, let the sound of his **p** be heard;	9335
	66:17	his **p** was on my tongue.	8128
	66:20	**P** be to God,	1385
	67: 3	*May* the peoples **p** you, O God;	3344
	67: 3	*may* all the peoples **p** you.	3344
	67: 5	*May* the peoples **p** you, O God;	3344
	67: 5	*may* all the peoples **p** you.	3344
	68: 4	Sing to God, **sing p** to his name,	2376
	68:19	**P** be to the Lord, to God our Savior,	1385
	68:26	**P** God in the great congregation;	1385
	68:26	**p** the LORD in the assembly of Israel.	NIH
	68:32	**sing p** to the Lord,	2376
	68:35	**P** be to God!	1385
	69:30	*I will* **p** God's name in song	2146
	69:34	*Let* heaven and earth **p** him,	2146
	71: 6	I will ever **p** you.	9335
	71: 8	My mouth is filled with your **p**,	9335
	71:14	**p** you more and more.	9335
	71:22	*I will* **p** you with the harp	3344

Ps	71:22	*I will* **sing p** to you with the lyre,	2376
	71:23	My lips will shout for joy when *I* **sing p**	2376
	72:18	**P** be *to* the LORD God, the God of Israel,	1385
	72:19	**P** be *to* his glorious name forever;	1385
	74:21	*may* the poor and needy **p** your name.	2146
	75: 9	*I will* **sing p** to the God of Jacob,	2376
	76:10	your wrath against men **brings** you **p**,	3344
	79:13	sheep of your pasture, *will* **p** you forever;	3344
	79:13	to generation we will recount your **p**.	9335
	86:12	*I will* **p** you, O Lord my God,	3344
	88:10	Do those who are dead rise up and **p** you?	3344
	89: 5	The heavens **p** your wonders,	3344
	89:52	**P** be to the LORD forever!	1385
	92: 1	It is good to **p** the LORD and make music	3344
	96: 2	Sing to the LORD, **p** his name;	2146
	96: 4	great is the LORD and most **worthy of p**;	2146
	97:12	and **p** his holy name.	2146
	99: 3	*Let them* **p** your great and awesome name	3344
	100: 4	with thanksgiving and his courts with **p**;	9335
	100: 4	give thanks to him and **p** his name.	1385
	101: 1	to you, O LORD, *I will* **sing p**.	2376
	102:18	a people not yet created *may* **p** the LORD:	2146
	102:21	be declared in Zion and his **p** in Jerusalem	9335
	103: 1	**P** the LORD, O my soul;	1385
	103: 1	all my inmost being, **p** his holy name.	NIH
	103: 2	**P** the LORD, O my soul,	1385
	103:20	**P** the LORD, you his angels,	1385
	103:21	**P** the LORD, all his heavenly hosts,	1385
	103:22	**P** the LORD, all his works everywhere	1385
	103:22	**P** the LORD, O my soul.	1385
	104:33	*I will* **sing p** to my God as long as I live.	2376
	104:35	**P** the LORD, O my soul.	1385
	104:35	**P** the LORD.	2146
	105: 2	Sing to him, **sing p** to him;	2376
	105:45	**P** the LORD.	2146
	106: 1	**P** the LORD.	2146
	106: 2	acts of the LORD or fully declare his **p**?	9335
	106: 5	and join your inheritance in **giving p**.	9335
	106:12	they believed his promises and sang his **p**.	9335
	106:47	to your holy name and glory in your **p**.	9335
	106:48	**P** be to the LORD, the God of Israel,	1385
	106:48	**P** the LORD.	2146
	107:32	and **p** him in the council of the elders.	2146
	108: 3	*I will* **p** you, O LORD,	3344
	109: 1	O God, whom I **p**, do not remain silent,	9335
	109:30	in the great throng *I will* **p** him.	2146
	111: 1	**P** the LORD.	2146
	111:10	To him *belongs* eternal **p**.	9335
	112: 1	**P** the LORD.	2146
	113: 1	**P** the LORD.	2146
	113: 1	**P**, O servants of the LORD,	2146
	113: 1	**p** the name of the LORD.	2146
	113: 9	**P** the LORD.	2146
	115:17	It is not the dead *who* **p** the LORD,	2146
	115:18	**P** the LORD.	2146
	116:19	**P** the LORD.	2146
	117: 1	**P** the LORD, all *you* nations;	2146
	117: 2	**P** the LORD.	2146
	119: 7	*I will* **p** you with an upright heart	3344
	119:12	**P** be *to* you, O LORD;	1385
	119:108	O LORD, the willing **p** of my mouth,	NIH
	119:164	a day *I* **p** you for your righteous laws.	2146
	119:171	May my lips overflow with **p**,	9335
	119:175	Let me live that I *may* **p** you,	2146
	122: 4	to **p** the name of the LORD according to	3344
	124: 6	**P** be *to* the LORD,	1385
	134: 1	**P** the LORD, all *you* servants of the LORD	1385
	134: 2	Lift up your hands in the sanctuary and **p**	1385
	135: 1	**P** the LORD.	2146
	135: 1	**P** the name of the LORD;	2146
	135: 1	Praise the name of the LORD; **p** him,	2146
	135: 3	**P** the LORD, for the LORD is good;	2146
	135: 3	**sing p** to his name, for that is pleasant.	2376
	135:19	O house of Israel, **p** the LORD;	1385
	135:19	O house of Aaron, **p** the LORD;	1385
	135:20	O house of of Levi, **p** the LORD;	1385
	135:20	*you* who fear him, **p** the LORD.	1385
	135:21	**P** be *to* the LORD from Zion,	1385
	135:21	**P** the LORD.	2146
	138: 1	*I will* **p** you, O LORD,	3344
	138: 1	before the "gods" *I will* **sing** your **p**.	2376
	138: 2	and *will* **p** your name for your love	3344
	138: 4	*May* all the kings of the earth **p** you,	3344
	139:14	*I* **p** you because I am fearfully	3344
	140:13	Surely the righteous *will* **p** your name and	3344
	142: 7	that I *may* **p** your name.	3344
	144: 1	**P** be *to* the LORD my Rock,	1385
	145: T	A **psalm** of **p**. Of David.	9335
	145: 1	*I will* **p** your name for ever and ever.	1385
	145: 2	Every day *I will* **p** you	1385
	145: 3	Great is the LORD and most **worthy of p**;	2146
	145:10	All you have made *will* **p** you, O LORD;	3344
	145:21	My mouth will speak in **p** *of* the LORD.	9335
	145:21	*Let* every creature **p** his holy name	1385
	146: 1	**P** the LORD.	2146
	146: 1	**P** the LORD, O my soul.	2146
	146: 2	*I will* **p** the LORD all my life;	2146
	146: 2	*I will* **sing p** to my God as long as I live.	2376
	146:10	**P** the LORD.	2146
	147: 1	**P** the LORD.	2146
	147: 1	how pleasant and fitting to **p** him!	9335
	147:20	**p** your God, O Zion,	2146
	148: 1	**P** the LORD.	2146
	148: 1	**P** the LORD from the heavens,	2146
	148: 1	**p** him in the heights above.	2146

Ps	148: 2	**P** him, all his angels, praise him,	2146
	148: 2	Praise him, all his angels, **p** him,	2146
	148: 3	**P** him, sun and moon, praise him,	2146
	148: 3	Praise him, sun and moon, **p** him,	2146
	148: 4	**P** him, you highest heavens and you waters	2146
	148: 5	*Let them* **p** the name of the LORD,	2146
	148: 7	**P** the LORD from the earth,	2146
	148:13	*Let them* **p** the name of the LORD,	2146
	148:14	the **p** of all his saints, of Israel,	9335
	148:14	**P** the LORD.	2146
	149: 1	**P** the LORD.	2146
	149: 1	his **p** in the assembly of the saints.	9335
	149: 3	*Let them* **p** his name with dancing	2146
	149: 6	May the **p** *of* God be in their mouths and	8128
	149: 9	**P** the LORD.	2146
	150: 1	**P** the LORD.	2146
	150: 1	**P** God in his sanctuary;	2146
	150: 1	**p** him in his mighty heavens.	2146
	150: 2	**P** him for his acts of power;	2146
	150: 2	**p** him for his surpassing greatness.	2146
	150: 3	**P** him with the sounding of the trumpet,	2146
	150: 3	**p** him with the harp and lyre,	2146
	150: 4	**p** him with tambourine and dancing,	2146
	150: 4	**p** him with the strings and flute,	2146
	150: 5	**P** him with the clash of cymbals,	2146
	150: 5	**p** him with resounding cymbals.	2146
	150: 6	*Let* everything that has breath **p** the LORD.	2146
	150: 6	**P** the LORD.	2146
Pr	27: 2	*Let* another **p** you, and	2146
	27:21	but man is tested by the **p** he *receives*.	4545
	28: 4	Those who forsake the law **p** the wicked,	2146
	31:31	*let* her works **bring** her **p** at the city gate.	2146
Ecc	8:10	and **receive p** in the city where they did this.	8655
SS	1: 4	we will **p** your love more than wine.	2349
Isa	12: 1	"I will **p** you, O LORD.	3344
	25: 1	I will exalt you and **p** your name,	3344
	38:18	For the grave cannot **p** you,	3344
	38:18	death cannot **sing** your **p**;	2146
	38:19	they **p** you, as I am doing today;	3344
	42: 8	I will not give my glory to another or my **p**	9335
	42:10	his **p** from the ends of the earth,	9335
	42:12	glory to the LORD and proclaim his **p** in the islands.	9335
	43:21	for myself that they may proclaim my **p**.	9335
	48: 9	the sake of my **p** I hold it back from you,	9335
	57:19	creating **p** *on* the lips of the mourners	5762
	60: 6	and proclaiming the **p** *of* the LORD.	9335
	60:18	and your gates **P**.	9335
	61: 3	a garment of **p** instead of a spirit of despair.	9335
	61:11	and **p** spring up before all nations.	9335
	62: 7	and makes her the **p** of the earth.	9335
	62: 9	but those who harvest it will eat it and **p**	2146
Jer	13:11	'to be my people for my renown and **p**	9335
	17:14	for you are the *one* I **p**.	9335
	20:13	**Give p** *to* the LORD!	2146
	33: 9	**p** and honor before all nations on earth	9335
Da	2:20	"**P** be to the name of God for ever	10122
	2:23	I thank and **p** you, O God of my fathers:	10693
	3:28	"**P** be to the God of Shadrach,	10122
	4:37	**p** and exalt and glorify the King of heaven,	10693
Joel	2:26	and *you will* **p** the name of the LORD	2146
Hab	3: 3	the heavens and his **p** filled the earth.	9335
Zep	3:19	I will give them **p** and honor in every land	9335
	3:20	and **p** among all the peoples of the earth	9335
Zec	11: 5	Those who sell them say, '**P** the LORD,	1385
Mt	5:16	and **p** your Father in heaven.	1519
	11:25	At that time Jesus said, "*I* **p** you, Father,	2018
	21:16	and infants you have ordained **p**'?"	142
Lk	1:68	"**P** be to the Lord,	2329
	5:26	Everyone was amazed and **gave p to** God.	1519
	10:21	"*I* **p** you, Father, Lord of heaven and earth,	2018
	17:18	and give **p** to God except this foreigner?"	1518
	19:37	of disciples began joyfully to **p** God	140
Jn	5:41	"I do not accept **p** from men,	1518
	5:44	How can you believe if you accept **p**	1518
	5:44	the **p** that comes from the only God?	1518
	12:43	for they loved **p** from men more than praise	1518
	12:43	for they loved praise from men more than **p**	1518
Ac	12:23	because Herod did not give **p** to God,	1518
Ro	2:29	Such a man's **p** is not from men,	2047
	15: 7	in order to bring **p** to God.	1518
	15: 9	"Therefore *I will* **p** you among	2018
	15:11	And again, "**P** the Lord, all *you* Gentiles,	140
1Co	4: 5	that time each will receive his **p** from God.	2047
	11: 2	*I* **p** you for remembering me in everything	2046
	11:17	In the following directives *I* **have** no **p**	2046
	11:22	*Shall I* **p** you for this?	2046
2Co	1: 3	**P** be to the God and Father	2329
	9:13	*men* will **p** God for the obedience	1519
Eph	1: 3	**P** be to the God and Father	2329
	1: 6	to the **p** of his glorious grace,	2047
	1:12	might be for the **p** of his glory.	2047
	1:14	to the **p** of his glory.	2047
Php	1:11	to the glory and **p** of God.	2047
1Th	2: 6	We were not looking for **p** from men,	1518
Heb	13:15	to God a sacrifice of **p**—	139
Jas	3: 9	With the tongue *we* **p** our Lord and Father,	2328
	3:10	Out of the same mouth come **p** and cursing.	2330
	5:13	*Let him* **sing songs** of **p**.	6010
1Pe	1: 3	**P** be to the God and Father	2329
	1: 7	be proved genuine and may result in **p**,	2047
	4:16	but **p** God that you bear that name.	1519
Rev	5:12	and strength and honor and glory and **p**!"	2330
	5:13	the throne and to the Lamb be **p** and honor	2330
	7:12	"**P** and glory and wisdom and thanks	2330
	19: 5	"**P** our God, all *you* his servants,	140

PRAISED (45) [PRAISE]

Ge	12:15	*they* p her to Pharaoh,	2146
	24:48	I p the LORD, the God of my master	1385
Jos	22:33	to hear the report and p God.	1385
Jdg	16:24	When the people saw him, *they* p their god,	2146
2Sa	14:25	In all Israel there was not a man so highly p	2146
1Ch	29:10	David p the LORD in the presence of	1385
	29:20	So they all p the LORD,	1385
2Ch	20:19	and Korahites stood up and p the LORD,	2146
	20:26	where they p the LORD.	1385
	30:22	and offered fellowship offerings and p	3344
	31: 8	they p the LORD and blessed his people	NIH
Ne	5:13	"Amen," and p the LORD.	1385
	8: 6	Ezra p the LORD, the great God;	1385
Job	1:21	may the name of the LORD be p."	1385
	36:24	which men *have* p in song.	8876
Ps	113: 2	Let the name of the LORD be p,	1385
	113: 3	the name of the LORD *is to* be p.	2146
Pr	12: 8	A man **is** p according to his wisdom,	2146
	31:30	a woman who fears the LORD *is to* **be p.**	2146
SS	6: 9	the queens and concubines p her.	2146
Isa	63: 7	the *deeds for which* he is to be p,	9335
	64:11	where our fathers p you,	2146
Jer	48: 2	Moab will be p no more;	9335
Eze	3:12	May the glory of the LORD **be** p in his dwelling place!	1385
Da	2:19	Then Daniel p the God of heaven	10122
	4:34	Then *I* p the Most High;	10122
	5: 4	*they* p the gods of gold and silver,	10693
	5:23	*You* p the gods of silver and gold,	10693
Mt	9: 8	they were filled with awe, and *they* p God,	1519
	15:31	And *they* p the God of Israel.	1519
Mk	2:12	This amazed everyone and they p God,	1519
Lk	2:28	Simeon took him in his arms and p God,	2328
	4:15	and everyone p him.	1519
	7:16	They were all filled with awe and p God	1519
	13:13	she straightened up and p God.	1519
	18:43	all the people saw it, *they* also p God.	142+1443
	23:47	seeing what had happened, p God and said,	1519
Ac	11:18	they had no further objections and p God,	1519
	21:20	When they heard this, *they* p God.	1519
Ro	1:25	who is forever p.	2329
	9: 5	who is God over all, forever p!	2329
2Co	8:18	along with him the brother who is p by all	2047
	11:31	who is *to be* p forever,	2329
Gal	1:24	And *they* p God because of me.	1519
1Pe	4:11	so that in all things God *may be* p	1519

PRAISES (19) [PRAISE]

2Sa	22:50	*I will sing* p to your name.	2376
2Ch	23:13	musical instruments were leading the p.	2146
	29:30	So *they* sang p with gladness	2146
	31: 2	to give thanks and to *sing* p at the gates of	2146
Ps	6: 5	Who p you from the grave?	3344
	9:11	Sing p to the LORD, enthroned in Zion;	2376
	9:14	that I may declare your p in the gates of	9335
	18:49	*I will sing* p to your name.	2376
	35:28	and of your p all day long.	9335
	47: 6	Sing p *to* God, sing praises;	2376
	47: 6	Sing praises to God, sing p;	2376
	47: 6	sing p to our King, sing praises.	2376
	47: 6	sing praises to our King, sing p.	2376
	147: 1	How good it is *to sing* p to our God,	2376
Pr	31:28	her husband also, and *he* p her:	2146
Jer	31: 7	Make *your* p heard, and say, 'O LORD,	2146
Ro	15:11	and *sing* p to him, all *you* peoples."	2046
Heb	2:12	of the congregation *I will sing your* p."	5630
1Pe	2: 9	declare the p of him who called you out	746

PRAISEWORTHY (2) [PRAISE]

Ps	78: 4	we will tell the next generation the p deeds	9335
Php	4: 8	if anything is excellent or p—	2047

PRAISING (16) [PRAISE]

1Ch	25: 3	the harp in thanking and p the LORD.	2146
2Ch	7: 6	King David had made for p the LORD	3344
Ps	84: 4	*they are* ever p you.	2146
Lk	1:64	and he began to speak, p God.	2328
	2:13	p God and saying,	140
	2:20	and p God for all the things they had heard	140
	5:25	he had been lying on and went home p God.	1519
	17:15	came back, p God in a loud voice.	1519
	18:43	and followed Jesus, p God.	1519
	24:53	at the temple, p God.	2328
Ac	2:47	p God and enjoying the favor of all	140
	3: 8	walking and jumping, and p God.	140
	3: 9	all the people saw him walking and p God,	140
	4:21	because all the people *were* p God	1519
	10:46	speaking in tongues and p God.	3486
1Co	14:16	If *you are* p God with your spirit,	2328

PRAY (121) [PRAYED, PRAYER, PRAYERS, PRAYING, PRAYS]

Ge	20: 7	and he will p for you and you will live.	7137
	32:11	I p, from the hand of my brother Esau,	5528
Ex	8: 8	"P to the LORD to take the frogs away	6983
	8: 9	the honor of setting the time *for me to* p	6983
	8:28	Now p for me."	6983
	8:29	I will p to the LORD,	6983
	9:28	P to the LORD, for we have had enough	6983
	10:17	Now forgive my sin once more and p to	6983
Nu	21: 7	P that the LORD will take the snakes away	7137
Dt	4: 7	God is near us whenever we p to him?	7924

1Sa	12:19	"P to the LORD your God	7137
	12:23	against the LORD by failing to p for you.	7137
1Ki	8:30	and of your people Israel when *they* p	7137
	8:35	and when *they* p toward this place	7137
	8:44	and when *they* p to the LORD toward	7137
	8:48	and p to you toward the land	7137
	13: 6	"Intercede with the LORD your God and p	7137
2Ki	19: 4	p for the remnant that still survives."	5951+9525
1Ch	17:25	So your servant has found courage to p	7137
2Ch	6:21	and of your people Israel when *they* p	7137
	6:26	and when *they* p toward this place	7137
	6:34	and when *they* p to you toward this city	7137
	6:38	where they were taken, and p toward	7137
	7:14	humble themselves and p and seek my face	7137
Ezr	9: 6	The God of heaven and p for the well-being	10612
Job	22:27	*You will* p to him, and he will hear you,	6983
	42: 8	My servant Job will p for you,	7137
Ps	5: 2	my King and my God, for to you I p.	7137
	32: 6	Therefore *let* everyone who is godly p	7137
	69:13	But I p to you, O LORD,	9525
	72:15	*May* people ever p for him	7137
	122: 6	P *for* the peace of Jerusalem:	8626
Isa	16:12	she goes to her shrine to p, it is to no avail.	7137
	37: 4	p for the remnant that still survives."	5951+9525
	45:20	*who* p to gods that cannot save.	7137
	64: 9	Oh, look upon us, *we* p,	5528
Jer	7:16	not p for this people nor offer any plea	7137
	11:14	"*Do* not p for this people nor offer any plea	7137
	14:11	"*Do* not p for the well-being of this people.	7137
	29: 7	P to the LORD for it,	7137
	29:12	upon me and come and p to me,	7137
	31: 9	they will p as I bring them back.	9384
	37: 3	"Please p to the LORD our God for us."	7137
	42: 2	"Please hear our petition and p to	7137
	42: 3	P that the LORD your God will tell us	NIH
	42: 4	"I *will* certainly p to the LORD your God	7137
	42:20	'P to the LORD our God for us;	7137
Da	9:23	As soon as you began to p,	9384
Mt	5:44	and p for those who persecute you,	4667
	6: 5	"And when *you* p, do not be like the hypocrites,	4667
	6: 5	*to* p standing in the synagogues and on	4667
	6: 6	But when you p, go into your room,	4667
	6: 6	close the door and p to your Father,	4667
	6: 7	And *when you* p, do not keep on babbling	4667
	6: 9	"This, then, is how you *should* p:	4667
	14:23	up on a mountainside by himself *to* p.	4667
	19:13	to place his hands on them and p for them.	4667
	24:20	P that your flight will not take place	4667
	26:36	"Sit here while *I* go over there and p."	4667
	26:41	"Watch and p so that you will not fall	4667
Mk	6:46	he went up on a mountainside *to* p.	4667
	13:18	P that this will not take place in winter,	4667
	14:32	"Sit here while *I* p."	4667
	14:38	Watch and p so that you will not fall	4667
Lk	5:33	"John's disciples often fast and p,	1255+4472
	6:12	to a mountainside *to* p,	4667
	6:28	p for those who mistreat you.	4667
	9:28	and went up onto a mountain *to* p.	4667
	11: 1	"Lord, teach us *to* p,	4667
	11: 2	He said to them, "When *you* p, say:	4667
	18: 1	to show them that they should always p and	4667
	18:10	"Two men went up to the temple *to* p,	4667
	21:36	and p that you may be able to escape all	1289
	22:40	"P that you will not fall into temptation."	4667
	22:46	"Get up and p so that you will not fall	4667
Jn	17: 9	I p for them. I am not praying for the world,	2263
	17:20	I p also for those who will believe in me	NIG
Ac	8:22	of this wickedness and p to the Lord.	1289
	8:24	"P to the Lord for me so	1289
	10: 9	Peter went up on the roof *to* p.	4667
	21: 5	and there on the beach we knelt *to* p.	4667
	26:29	I p God that not only you	323+2377
Ro	1:10	and I p that now at last by God's will	1289
	8:26	We do not know what *we* ought to p *for,*	4667
	15:31	P that I may be rescued from the	NIG
1Co	11:13	*to* p to God with her head uncovered?	4667
	14:13	in a tongue *should* p that he may interpret	4667
	14:14	For if I p in a tongue, my spirit prays,	4667
	14:15	I will p with my spirit,	4667
	14:15	but *I will* also p with my mind;	4667
2Co	13: 7	Now *we* p to God that you will	2377
Eph	1:18	I p also that the eyes of your heart may	NIG
	3:16	I p that out of his glorious riches	NIG
	3:17	And I p that you, being rooted and	NIG
	6:18	And p in the Spirit on all occasions	4667
	6:19	P also for me, that whenever I open my	NIG
	6:19	P that I may declare it fearlessly,	NIG
Php	1: 4	I always p with joy	1255+4472
Col	1: 3	*when we* p for you,	4667
	1:10	And we p this in order that you may live	NIG
	4: 3	And p for us, too,	4667
	4: 4	P that I may proclaim it clearly,	NIG
1Th	3:10	Night and day *we* p most earnestly	1289
	5:17	p continually;	4667
	5:25	Brothers, p for us.	4667
2Th	1:11	With this in mind, *we* constantly p for you,	4667
	1:12	We p this so that the name of our Lord Jesus	NIG
	3: 1	p for us that the message of the Lord	NIG
	3: 2	And p that we may be delivered	NIG
1Ti	5: 5	p and to ask God **for help.**	1255
Phm	1: 6	I p that you may be active in sharing	4667
Heb	13:18	P for us.	4667
	13:19	*to* p so that I may be restored to you	4047+4472S
Jas	5:13	Is any one of you in trouble? *He should* p.	4667
	5:14	He should call the elders of the church *to* p	4667
	5:16	and p for each other so that you may	2377

1Pe	4: 7	and self-controlled so that you can p.	4666
1Jn	5:16	*he should* p and God will give him life.	160
	5:16	I am not saying that he *should* p about that.	2263
3Jn	1: 2	*I* p that you may enjoy good health and	2377
Jude	1:20	most holy faith and p in the Holy Spirit.	4667

PRAYED (68) [PRAY]

Ge	20:17	Then Abraham p to God,	7137
	24:12	Then *he* p, "O LORD,	606
	25:21	Isaac p to the LORD on behalf of his wife,	6983
	32: 9	Then Jacob p, "O God	606
Ex	8:30	Moses left Pharaoh and p to the LORD.	6983
	10:18	then left Pharaoh and p to the LORD.	6983
Nu	11: 2	he p to the LORD and the fire died down.	7137
	21: 7	So Moses p for the people.	7137
Dt	9:20	but at that time *I* p for Aaron too.	7137
	9:26	*I* p to the LORD and said,	7137
Jdg	13: 8	Then Manoah p to the LORD:	6983
	16:28	Then Samson p to the LORD:	7924
1Sa	1:10	Hannah wept much and p to the LORD.	7137
	1:27	*I* p for this child,	7137
	2: 1	Then Hannah p and said:	7137
	2:20	the *one* she p *for* and gave to the LORD."	8629
	8: 6	so he p to the LORD.	7137
	14:41	Then Saul p to the LORD,	606
2Sa	15:31	So David p, "O LORD,	606
1Ki	8:28	which *I have* p before the LORD,	2858
	18:36	the prophet Elijah stepped forward and p:	606
	19: 4	sat down under it and p that he might die.	8626
2Ki	4:33	shut the door on the two of them and p to	7137
	6:17	And Elisha p, "O LORD,	7137
	6:18	Elisha p to the LORD,	7137
	19:15	And Hezekiah p to the LORD:	7137
	20: 2	Hezekiah turned his face to the wall and p	7137
2Ch	30:18	But Hezekiah p for them, saying,	7137
	32:24	*He* p to the LORD,	7137
	33:13	And when *he* p to him,	7137
Ezr	9: 6	and p: "O my God,	606
Ne	1: 4	and fasted and p before the God of heaven.	7137
	2: 4	Then *I* p to the God of heaven,	7137
	4: 9	But *we* p to our God and posted a guard day	7137
	6: 9	[But I p,] "Now strengthen my hands."	NIH
Job	42:10	After Job *had* p for his friends,	7137
Isa	37:15	And Hezekiah p to the LORD:	7137
	37:21	Because *you have* p to me	7137
	38: 2	Hezekiah turned his face to the wall and p	7137
Jer	32:16	*I* p to the LORD:	7137
Da	6:10	a day he got down on his knees and p,	10612
	9: 4	*I* p to the LORD my God and confessed:	7137
Jnh	2: 1	the fish Jonah p to the LORD his God.	7137
	2: 2	he p, "O LORD,	7137
Mt	26:39	he fell with his face to the ground and p,	4667
	26:42	*He* went away a second time and p,	4667
	26:44	and went away once more and p	4667
Mk	1:35	and went off to a solitary place, where *he* p.	4667
	14:35	he fell to the ground and p that if possible	4667
	14:39	Once more *he* went away and p	4667
Lk	5:16	often withdrew to lonely places and p.	4667
	18:11	The Pharisee stood up and p about himself:	4667
	22:32	But I *have* p for you, Simon,	1289
	22:41	knelt down and p,	4667
	22:44	And being in anguish, *he* p more earnestly,	4667
Jn	17: 1	he looked toward heaven and p:	3306
Ac	1:24	*they* p, "Lord, you know everyone's heart.	4667
	4:31	*After* they p, the place where they were	1289
	6: 6	who p and laid their hands on them.	4667
	7:59	While they were stoning him, Stephen p,	2126
	8:15	they p for them that they might receive	4667
	9:40	then he got down on his knees and p.	4667
	10: 2	to those in need and p to God regularly.	1289
	13: 3	So *after they had* fasted and p,	4667
	20:36	he knelt down with all of them and p.	4667
	27:29	from the stern and p for daylight.	2377
Jas	5:17	*He* p earnestly that it would not rain,	4666+4667
	5:18	Again he p, and the heavens gave rain,	4667

PRAYER (106) [PRAY]

Ge	25:21	The LORD **answered** his p,	6983
Ex	9:29	I will spread out my hands in p to the LORD.	NIH
2Sa	7:27	has found courage to **offer** you this p.	7137+9525
	21:14	God **answered** p in behalf of the land.	6983
	24:25	the LORD **answered** p in behalf of the land,	6983
1Ki	8:28	to your servant's p and his plea for mercy,	9525
	8:28	and the p that your servant is praying	9525
	8:29	the p your servant prays toward this place.	9525
	8:38	and when a p or plea is made by any	9525
	8:45	hear from heaven their p and their plea,	9525
	8:49	hear their p and their plea,	9525
	9: 3	"I have heard the p and plea you have made	9525
2Ki	19:20	I have heard *your* p concerning Sennacherib	7137
	20: 5	I have heard your p and seen your tears;	9525
2Ch	6:19	to your servant's p and his plea for mercy,	9525
	6:19	and the p that your servant is praying	9525
	6:20	the p your servant prays toward this place.	9525
	6:29	and when a p or plea is made by any	9525
	6:35	hear from heaven their p and their plea,	9525
	6:39	hear their p and their pleas,	9525
	7:12	"I have heard your p and have chosen this	9525
	30:27	for their p reached heaven,	9525
	32:20	Isaiah son of Amoz cried out *in* p *to* heaven	7137
	33:18	including his p to his God and the words	9525
	33:19	His p and how God was moved	9525
Ezr	8:23	and he **answered** our p.	6983
Ne	1: 6	to hear the p your servant is praying	9525
	1:11	the p *of* this your servant and to the prayer	9525

Ne	1:11	the prayer of this your servant and to the **p**	9525
	11:17	the director who led in thanksgiving and **p**;	9525
Job	16:17	free of violence and my **p** is pure.	9525
	42: 8	and I will accept his **p** and not deal	NIH
	42: 9	and the LORD accepted Job's **p**.	NIH
Ps	4: 1	be merciful to me and hear my **p**.	9525
	6: 9	the LORD accepts my **p**.	9525
	17: T	A **p** of David.	9525
	17: 1	Give ear to my **p**—	9525
	17: 6	give ear to me and hear my **p**.	614
	39:12	"Hear my **p**, O LORD, listen to my cry	9525
	42: 8	a **p** to the God of my life.	9525
	54: 2	Hear my **p**, O God;	9525
	55: 1	Listen to my **p**, O God,	9525
	61: 1	Hear my cry, O God; listen to my **p**.	9525
	65: 2	O you who hear **p**,	9525
	66:19	surely listened and heard my voice in **p**.	9525
	66:20	not rejected my **p** or withheld his love	9525
	84: 8	Hear my **p**, O LORD God Almighty;	9525
	86: T	A **p** of David.	9525
	86: 6	Hear my **p**, O LORD;	9525
	88: 2	May my **p** come before you;	9525
	88:13	in the morning my **p** comes before you.	9525
	90: T	A **p** of Moses the man of God.	9525
	102: T	A **p** of an afflicted man.	9525
	102: 1	Hear my **p**, O LORD;	9525
	102:17	He will respond to the **p** of the destitute;	9525
	109: 4	but I am a man of **p**.	9525
	141: 2	May my **p** be set before you like incense;	9525
	141: 5	my **p** is ever against the deeds of evildoers;	9525
	142: T	When he was in the cave. A **p**.	9525
	143: 1	O LORD, hear my **p**,	9525
Pr	15: 8	but the **p** of the upright pleases him.	9525
	15:29	from the wicked but he hears the **p** of	9525
Isa	1:15	When you spread out your hands in **p**,	NIH
	26:16	they could **barely whisper** a **p**.	4318+7440
	38: 5	I have heard your **p** and seen your tears;	9525
	56: 7	and give them joy in my house of **p**.	9525
	56: 7	for my house will be called a house of **p**.	9525
La	3: 8	I call out or cry for help, he shuts out my **p**.	9525
	3:44	with a cloud so that no **p** can get through.	9525
Da	9: 3	to the Lord God and pleaded with him in **p**	9525
	9:21	while I was still in **p**, Gabriel,	9525
Jnh	2: 7	and my **p** rose to you, to your holy temple.	9525
Hab	3: 1	A **p** of Habakkuk the prophet.	9525
Mt	21:13	" 'My house will be called a house of **p**,'	4666
	21:22	you will receive whatever you ask for in **p**."	4666
Mk	9:29	"This kind can come out only by **p**."	4667
	11:17	" 'My house will be called a house of **p**'	4666
	11:24	whatever you ask for in **p**, believe that you	4667
Lk	1:13	your **p** has been heard.	1255
	19:46	" 'My house will be a house of **p**';	4666
	22:45	When he rose from **p** and went back to	4666
Jn	17:15	*My* **p** is that you take them out of	2263
	17:20	"My **p** is not for them alone.	2263
Ac	1:14	They all joined together constantly in **p**,	4666
	2:42	to the breaking of bread and to **p**.	4666
	3: 1	going up to the temple at the time of **p**—	4666
	4:24	they raised their voices together in **p**	NIG
	6: 4	and will give our attention to **p** and	4666
	10:31	God has heard your **p** and remembered	4666
	14:23	with **p** and fasting, committed them to	4667
	16:13	where we expected to find a **place of p**.	4666
	16:16	when we were going to the **place of p**,	4666
	28: 8	Paul went in to see him and, *after* **p**,	4667
Ro	10: 1	heart's desire and **p** to God for the Israelites	1255
	12:12	patient in affliction, faithful in **p**.	4666
1Co	7: 5	so that you may devote yourselves to **p**.	4666
2Co	13: 9	and our **p** is for your perfection.	2377
Php	1: 9	this is my **p**: that your love may abound	4667
	4: 6	by **p** and petition, with thanksgiving,	4666
Col	4: 2	Devote yourselves to **p**,	4666
	4:12	He is always wrestling in **p** for you,	4666
1Ti	2: 8	to lift up holy hands in **p**,	4667
	4: 5	it is consecrated by the word of God and **p**.	1950
Jas	5:15	And the **p** offered in faith will make	2376
	5:16	The **p** of a righteous man is powerful	1255
1Pe	3:12	and his ears are attentive to their **p**,	1255

PRAYERS (32) [PRAY]

1Ki	8:54	When Solomon had finished all these **p**	9525
1Ch	5:20	He answered their **p**,	6983
2Ch	6:40	and your ears attentive to the **p** *offered*	9525
	7:15	and my ears attentive to the **p** *offered*	9525
Ps	35:13	When my **p** returned to me unanswered,	9525
	72:20	This concludes the **p** of David son of Jesse.	9525
	80: 4	anger smolder against the **p** of your people?	9525
	109: 7	and may his **p** condemn him.	9525
Pr	28: 9	even his **p** are detestable.	9525
Isa	1:15	even if you offer many **p**, I will not listen.	9525
Da	9:17	hear the **p** and petitions of your servant.	9525
Mk	12:40	and for a show **make** lengthy **p**.	4667
Lk	20:47	and for a show **make** lengthy **p**.	4667
Ac	10: 4	"Your **p** and gifts to the poor have come up	4666
Ro	1:10	in my **p** at all times;	4666
2Co	1:11	as you help us *by* your **p**.	1255
	1:11	in answer to the **p** of many.	NIG
	9:14	*in* their **p** for you their hearts will go out	1255
Eph	1:16	remembering you in my **p**.	4666
	6:18	on all occasions with all kinds of **p**	1255
Php	1: 4	In all my **p** for all of you,	1255
	1:19	that through your **p** and the help given by	1255
1Th	1: 2	mentioning you in our **p**.	4666
1Ti	2: 1	I urge, then, first of all, that requests, **p**,	1255
2Ti	1: 3	and day I constantly remember you in my **p**.	1255
Phm	1: 4	as I remember you in my **p**,	4666

Phm	1:22	to be restored to you in answer to your **p**.	4666
Heb	5: 7	offered up **p** and petitions with loud cries	1255
1Pe	3: 7	so that nothing will hinder your **p**.	4666
Rev	5: 8	which are the **p** of the saints.	4666
	8: 3	*with* the **p** of all the saints,	4666
	8: 4	*together with* the **p** of the saints,	4666

PRAYING (36) [PRAY]

Ge	24:15	Before he had finished **p**,	1819
	24:45	"Before I finished **p** in my heart,	1819
1Sa	1:12	As she kept on **p** to the LORD,	7137
	1:13	Hannah *was* **p** in her heart,	1819
	1:16	I have been **p** here out of my great anguish	1819
	1:26	the woman who stood here beside you **p** to	7137
1Ki	8:28	and the prayer that your servant *is* **p**	7137
	8:33	**p** and making supplication to you	7137
2Ch	6:19	that your servant *is* **p** in your presence.	7137
	6:24	**p** and making supplication before you	7137
	7: 1	When Solomon finished **p**,	7137
Ezr	10: 1	While Ezra *was* **p** and confessing,	7137
Ne	1: 6	the prayer your servant *is* **p** before you day	7003
Job	21:15	What would we gain by **p** to him?'	7137
Da	6:11	and found Daniel **p** and asking God	10114
	9:20	While I was speaking and **p**,	7137
Mk	11:25	And when you stand **p**,	4667
Lk	1:10	the assembled worshipers were **p** outside.	4667
	2:37	but worshiped night and day, fasting and **p**.	1255
	3:21	And as he was **p**, heaven was opened	4667
	6:12	and spent the night in **p** to God.	4666
	9:18	Once when Jesus was **p** in private	4667
	9:29	As he *was* **p**, the appearance of his face	4667
	11: 1	One day Jesus was **p** in a certain place.	4667
Jn	17: 9	I am not **p** for the world,	2263
	18: 1	When he had finished **p**,	3306
Ac	9:11	a man from Tarsus named Saul, for he is **p**.	4667
	10:30	"Four days ago I was in my house **p**	4667
	11: 5	"I was in the city of Joppa **p**,	4667
	12: 5	church was earnestly **p** to God for him.	1181+4666
	12:12	many people had gathered and *were* **p**.	4667
	16:25	**p** and singing hymns to God,	4667
	22:17	"When I returned to Jerusalem and *was* **p** at	4667
Ro	15:30	to join me in my struggle by **p** to God	4666
Eph	6:18	and always keep on **p** for all the saints.	1255
Col	1: 9	not stopped **p** for you and asking God	4667

PRAYS (12) [PRAY]

1Ki	8:29	the prayer your servant **p** toward this place.	7137
	8:42	when he comes and **p** toward this temple,	7137
2Ch	6:20	the prayer your servant **p** toward this place.	7137
	6:32	when he comes and **p** toward this temple,	7137
Job	33:26	He **p** to God and finds favor with him,	6983
Isa	44:17	He **p** to it and says, "Save me;	7137
Da	6: 7	the decree that anyone who **p**	10114+10115
	6:12	during the next thirty days anyone who **p**	10114
	6:13	He still **p** three times a day."	10114+10115
1Co	11: 4	Every man *who* **p** or prophesies	4667
	11: 5	And every woman *who* **p** or prophesies	4667
	14:14	For if I pray in a tongue, my spirit **p**,	4667

PREACH (41) [PREACHED, PREACHER, PREACHES, PREACHING]

Isa	61: 1	the LORD has anointed me to **p** good news	1413
Eze	20:46	**p** against the south and prophesy against	5752
	21: 2	set your face against Jerusalem and **p**	5752
Jnh	3: 2	the great city of Nineveh and **p** against it,	7924
Mt	4:17	From that time on Jesus began to **p**,	3062
	10: 7	As you go, **p** this message:	3062+3306
	11: 1	on from there to teach and **p** in the towns	3062
	23: 3	for they do not practice what *they* **p**.	3306
Mk	1:38	so *I can* **p** there also.	3062
	3:14	and that he might send them out to **p**	3062
	16:15	"Go into all the world and **p** the good news	3062
Lk	4:18	because he has anointed me to **p** good news	2294
	4:43	"I must **p** the good news** of the kingdom	2294
	9: 2	and he sent them out to **p** the kingdom	3062
Ac	9:20	to **p** in the synagogues that Jesus is the Son	3062
	10:42	He commanded us to **p** to the people and	3062
	14: 7	where they continued to **p** the good news.	2294
	16:10	that God had called us to **p** the gospel	2294
	20:20	to **p** anything that would be helpful to you	334
Ro	1:15	That is why I am so eager to **p** the gospel	2294
	2:21	You who **p** against stealing, do you steal?	3062
	10:15	And how *can they* **p** unless they are sent?	3062
	15:20	to **p** the gospel where Christ was not known	2294
1Co	1:17	but to **p** the gospel—	2294
	1:23	but we **p** Christ crucified:	3062
	9:14	the Lord has commanded that those who **p**	2859
	9:16	Yet when *I* **p** the gospel, I cannot boast,	2294
	9:16	I cannot boast, for I am compelled to **p**.	NIG
	9:16	Woe to me if *I do* not **p** the gospel!	2294
	9:17	If I **p** voluntarily, I have a reward;	4556S
	15:11	then, it was I or they, this is what we **p**,	3062
2Co	2:12	Now when I went to Troas to **p** the **gospel**	2295
	4: 5	For *we do not* **p** ourselves,	3062
	10:16	*so that* we can **p** the **gospel** in the regions	2294
Gal	1: 8	from heaven *should* **p** a **gospel** other than	2294
	1:16	so that *I might* **p** him among the Gentiles,	2294
	2: 2	the gospel that *I* **p** among the Gentiles.	3062
Eph	3: 8	to **p** to the Gentiles the unsearchable riches	2294
Php	1:15	that some **p** Christ out of envy and rivalry,	3062
	1:17	The former **p** Christ out of selfish ambition,	2859
2Ti	4: 2	**P** the Word; be prepared in season and	3062

PREACHED (47) [PREACH]

Dt	13: 5	he **p** rebellion against the LORD your God,	1819
Jer	28:16	*you have* **p** rebellion against the LORD.' "	1819
	29:32	because *he has* **p** rebellion against me.' "	1819
Mt	11: 5	**the good news is p** to the poor.	2294
	24:14	the kingdom *will be* **p** in the whole world	3062
	26:13	wherever this gospel *is* **p** throughout	3062
Mk	2: 2	and he **p** the word to them.	3281
	6:12	and **p** that people should repent.	3062
	13:10	the gospel must first *be* **p** to all nations.	3062
	14: 9	the gospel *is* **p** throughout the world,	3062
	16:20	the disciples went out and **p** everywhere,	3062
Lk	3:18	the people and **p** the good news to them.	2294
	7:22	**the good news is p** to the poor.	2294
	16:16	**the good news** of the kingdom of God *is being* **p**,	2294
	24:47	forgiveness of sins *will be* **p** in his name	3062
Ac	8: 4	Those who had been scattered **p**	2294
	8:12	*as he* **p** the good news** of the kingdom	2294
	9:27	and how in Damascus *he had* **p** fearlessly	4245
	10:37	in Galilee after the baptism that John **p**—	3062
	13:24	John **p** repentance and baptism to all	4619
	14:21	*They* **p** the good news** in that city and won	2294
	14:25	and *when they had* **p** the word in Perga,	3281
	15:21	For Moses *has been* **p** in every city	2400+3062
	15:35	and many others taught and **p** the word of	2294
	15:36	the towns where *we* **p** the word of the Lord	2859
	26:20	*I* **p** that they should repent and turn to God	550
	28:31	without hindrance he **p** the kingdom of God	3062
1Co	1:21	of **what was p** to save those who believe.	3060
	9:27	so that *after I have* **p** to others,	3062
	15: 1	to remind you of the gospel *I* **p** to you,	2294
	15: 2	if you hold firmly to the word *I* **p** to you.	2294
	15:12	if *it is* **p** that Christ has been raised from	3062
2Co	1:19	who *was* **p** among you by me and Silas	3062
	11: 4	a Jesus other than the Jesus *we* **p**,	3062
Gal	1: 8	a gospel other than the one *we* **p** to you,	2294
	1:11	that the **gospel** I **p** is not something	2294+2295
	4:13	an illness that *I first* **p** the gospel to you.	2294
Eph	2:17	and **p** peace to you who were far away	2294
Php	1:18	from false motives or true, Christ *is* **p**.	2859
1Th	2: 9	a burden to anyone *while we* **p** the gospel	3062
1Ti	3:16	seen by angels, *was* **p** among the nations,	3062
Heb	4: 2	For we also have had **the gospel p** to us,	2294
	4: 6	and those who formerly **had the gospel p**	2294
1Pe	1:12	by those who *have* **p the gospel** to you by	2294
	1:25	And this is the word that *was* **p** to you.	2294
	3:19	also *he* went and **p** to the spirits in prison	3062
	4: 6	For this is the reason **the gospel** *was* **p** even	2294

PREACHER (1) [PREACH]

| 2Pe | 2: 5 | but protected Noah, a **p** of righteousness, | 3061 |

PREACHES (2) [PREACH]

| Ac | 19:13 | "In the name of Jesus, whom Paul **p**, | 3062 |
| 2Co | 11: 4 | For if someone comes to you and **p** | 3062 |

PREACHING (34) [PREACH]

Ezr	6:14	the **p** of Haggai the prophet and Zechariah,	10452
Am	7:16	and stop **p** against the house of Isaac.'	5752
Mt	3: 1	John the Baptist came, **p** in the Desert of	3062
	4:23	**p** the good news of the kingdom,	3062
	9:35	**p** the good news of the kingdom	3062
	12:41	for they repented at the **p** of Jonah,	3060
Mk	1: 4	in the desert region and **p** a baptism	3062
	1:39	**p** in their synagogues	3062
Lk	3: 3	**p** a baptism of repentance for	3062
	4:44	he kept on **p** in the synagogues of Judea.	3062
	9: 6	from village to village, **p** the **gospel**	2294
	11:32	for they repented at the **p** of Jonah,	3060
	20: 1	in the temple courts and **p the gospel,**	2294
Ac	8:25	**p** the gospel in many Samaritan villages.	2294
	8:40	**p** the gospel in all the towns	2294
	16: 6	having been kept by the Holy Spirit from **p**	3281
	17:13	that Paul *was* **p** the word of God at Berea,	2859
	17:18	because Paul *was* **p the good news**	2294
	18: 5	Paul devoted himself exclusively to **p**,	3364+3836
	20:25	of you among whom I have gone about **p**	3062
Ro	1: 9	with my whole heart in **p** the **gospel**	2295
	10:14	can they hear without *someone* **p** to them?	3062
1Co	2: 4	My message and my **p** were not with wise	3060
	9:18	that in **p** the **gospel** I may offer it free	2294
	9:18	and so not make use of my rights in **p** it.	2295
	15:14	our **p** is useless and so is your faith.	3060
2Co	11: 7	in order to elevate you by **p** the **gospel**	2294+2295
Gal	1: 9	**p** to you a **gospel** other than what you	2294
	1:23	now **p** the faith he once tried to destroy."	2294
	2: 7	the task *of* **p the gospel** to the Gentiles,	2295
	5:11	Brothers, if *I am* still **p** circumcision,	3062
1Ti	4:13	to **p** and to teaching.	4155
	5:17	especially those whose work is **p**	1877+3364
Tit	1: 3	to light through the **p** entrusted to me by	3060

PRECEDE (1) [PRECEDED, PRECEDING]

| 1Th | 4:15 | not **p** those who have fallen asleep. | 5777 |

PRECEDED (4) [PRECEDE]

2Ki	17: 2	but not like the kings of Israel who **p** him.	
	21:11	Amorites who **p** him and has led Judah	4200+7156
Jer	28: 8	early times the prophets who **p** you	4200+7156
	34: 5	the former kings who **p** you.	2118+4200+7156

PRECEDING (1) [PRECEDE]

Ne	5:15	the earlier governors—those **p** me—	4200+7156

PRECEPTS (27)

Dt	33:10	He teaches your **p** to Jacob and your law	5477
Ps	19: 8	The **p** *of* the LORD are right,	7218
	103:18	and remember to obey his **p**.	7218
	105:45	they might keep his **p** and observe his laws.	2976
	111: 7	all his **p** are trustworthy.	7218
	111:10	all who follow **his p** have good understanding.	2157S
	119: 4	You have laid down **p** that are to be fully obeyed.	7218
	119:15	I meditate on your **p** and consider	7218
	119:27	Let me understand the teaching of your **p**;	7218
	119:40	How I long for your **p**!	7218
	119:45	for I have sought out your **p**.	7218
	119:56	This has been my practice: I obey your **p**.	7218
	119:63	to all who follow your **p**.	7218
	119:69	I keep your **p** with all my heart.	7218
	119:78	but I will meditate on your **p**.	7218
	119:87	but I have not forsaken your **p**.	7218
	119:93	I will never forget your **p**,	7218
	119:94	I have sought out your **p**.	7218
	119:100	for I obey your **p**.	7218
	119:104	I gain understanding from your **p**;	7218
	119:110	but I have not strayed from your **p**.	7218
	119:128	and because I consider all your **p** right,	7218
	119:134	that I may obey your **p**.	7218
	119:141	I do not forget your **p**.	7218
	119:159	See how I love your **p**;	7218
	119:168	I obey your **p** and your statutes,	7218
	119:173	for I have chosen your **p**.	7218

PRECINCTS (1)

Eze	42:14	Once the priests enter the **holy p**,	7731

PRECIOUS (48)

Ge	30:20	"God has presented me with a **p** gift.	3202
Ex	28:17	Then mount four rows of **p** stones on it.	NIH
	39:10	they mounted four rows of **p** stones on it.	NIH
Dt	33:13	the LORD bless his land with the **p** dew	4458
1Sa	26:21	Because you considered my life **p** today,	3700
2Sa	12:30	and it was set with **p** stones—	3701
1Ki	10: 2	large quantities of gold, and **p** stones—	3701
	10:10	large quantities of spices, and **p** stones.	3701
	10:11	of almugwood and **p** stones.	3701
1Ch	20: 2	and it was set with **p** stones—	3701
	29: 8	Any who had **p** stones gave them to	NIH
2Ch	3: 6	He adorned the temple with **p** stones.	3701
	9: 1	large quantities of gold, and **p** stones—	3701
	9: 9	large quantities of spices, and **p** stones.	3701
	9:10	they also brought algumwood and **p** stones.	3701
	32:27	for his silver and gold and for his **p** stones,	3701
Ezr	8:27	articles of polished bronze, as **p** as gold.	2776
Job	28:16	with **p** onyx or sapphires.	3701
	29:24	the light of my face *was p to them*.	4202+5877
Ps	19:10	They *are* more **p** than gold,	2773
	22:20	my **p** life from the power of the dogs.	3495
	35:17	my **p** life from these lions.	3495
	72:14	for **p** *is* their blood in his sight.	3700
	116:15	**P** in the sight of the LORD is the death	3701
	119:72	The law from your mouth is more **p**	3202
	133: 2	It is like **p** oil poured on the head,	3202
	139:17	How **p** to me are your thoughts, O God!	3700
Pr	3:15	She is more **p** than rubies;	3701
	8:11	for wisdom is more **p** than rubies,	3202
Isa	28:16	a **p** cornerstone for a sure foundation;	3701
	43: 4	Since you are **p** and honored in my sight,	3700
	54:12	and all your walls of **p** stones.	2914
La	4: 2	How the **p** sons of Zion,	3701
Eze	22:25	and **p** things and make many widows	3702
	27:22	of all kinds of spices and **p** stones,	3701
	28:13	every **p** stone adorned you:	3701
Da	11:38	with **p** stones and costly gifts.	3701
1Pe	1:19	but *with* the **p** blood of Christ,	5508
	2: 4	by men but chosen by God and **p** to him—	1952
	2: 6	a chosen and **p** cornerstone,	1952
	2: 7	Now to you who believe, this stone is **p**.	5507
2Pe	1: 1	have received a faith **as p as** ours:	2700
	1: 4	his very great and **p** promises,	5508
Rev	17: 4	with gold, silver, **p** stones and pearls.	5508
	18:12	cargoes of gold, silver, **p** stones and pearls;	5508
	18:16	with gold, silver, **p** stones and pearls!	5508
	21:11	like that of a **very p** jewel,	5508
	21:19	*with* every kind of **p** stone.	5508

PRECISELY (1)

Ac	11: 4	and explained everything to them **p**	NIG

PREDECESSOR (1) [PREDECESSORS]

1Ch	17:13	I took it away from your **p**.	889+2118+4200+7156

PREDECESSORS (2) [PREDECESSOR]

Dt	19:14	neighbor's boundary stone set up by your **p**	8037
Ezr	4:15	may be made in the archives of your **p**.	10003

PREDESTINATE, PREDESTINATED
(KJV) See PREDESTINED

PREDESTINED (4) [DESTINE]

Ro	8:29	**p** to be conformed to the likeness of his Son	4633
	8:30	And those he **p**, he also called;	4633
Eph	1: 5	he **p** us to be adopted as his sons	4633
	1:11	*having been* **p** according to the plan	4633

PREDICTED (5) [PREDICTION]

1Sa	28:17	The LORD has done what he **p**	1819
Ac	7:52	They even killed those who **p** the coming	4615
	11:28	stood up and through the Spirit **p** that	4955
	16:16	**spirit by which** she **p the future**.	4460+4780
1Pe	1:11	when he **p** the sufferings of Christ and	4626

PREDICTING (2) [PREDICTION]

1Ki	22:13	as one man the other prophets are **p** success	1821
2Ch	18:12	as one man the other prophets are **p** success	1821

PREDICTION (1) [PREDICTED, PREDICTING, PREDICTIONS]

Jer	28: 9	sent by the LORD only if his **p** comes true."	1821

PREDICTIONS (2) [PREDICTION]

Isa	44:26	the words of his servants and fulfills the **p**	6783
	47:13	those stargazers who **make p** month	3359

PREEMINENT (1)

Est	10: 3	**p** among the Jews, and held in high esteem	1524

PREFECTS (4)

Da	3: 2	He then summoned the satraps, **p**,	10505
	3: 3	So the satraps, **p**, governors, advisers,	10505
	3:27	**p**, governors and royal advisers crowded	10505
	6: 7	The royal administrators, **p**, satraps,	10505

PREFER (8) [PREFERENCE]

1Ki	21: 2	a better vineyard or, if you **p**,	928+3202+6524
	21: 6	or if you **p**, I will give you another vineyard	2913
Job	7:15	so that I **p** strangling and death,	1047
	36:21	which *you seem to* **p** to affliction.	1047
Jer	8: 3	of this evil nation *will* **p** death to life,	1047
Eze	16:32	*You* **p** strangers to your own husband!	4374
1Co	4:21	What *do you* **p**?	2527
2Co	5: 8	and *would* **p** to be away from the body	2305+3437

PREFERENCE (1) [PREFER]

Dt	21:16	to the son of the wife he loves **in p to**	6584+7156

PREGNANCY (1) [PREGNANT]

Hos	9:11	no birth, no **p**, no conception.	1061

PREGNANT (33) [PREGNANCY]

Ge	4: 1	and *she became* **p** and gave birth to Cain.	2225
	4:17	and *she became* **p** and gave birth to Enoch.	2225
	16: 4	When he knew *she was* **p**,	2225
	16: 4	and now that she knows *she is* **p**,	2225
	19:36	of Lot's daughters *became* **p** by their father.	2225
	21: 2	Sarah *became* **p** and bore a son to Abraham	2225
	25:21	and his wife Rebekah *became* **p**.	2225
	29:32	Leah *became* **p** and gave birth to a son.	2225
	30: 5	and she *became* **p** and bore him a son.	2225
	30:17	*she became* **p** and bore Jacob a fifth son.	2225
	30:23	She *became* **p** and gave birth to a son	2225
	38: 3	*she became* **p** and gave birth to a son,	2225
	38:18	and she *became* **p** by him.	2225
	38:24	and as a result *she is* now **p**."	2226
	38:25	"I am **p** by the man who owns these,"	2226
Ex	2: 2	and *she became* **p** and gave birth to a son.	2225
	21:22	a **p** woman and she gives birth prematurely	2226
Lev	12: 2	'A woman *who becomes* **p** and gives birth	2445
1Sa	4:19	was **p** and near the time of delivery,	2226
2Sa	11: 5	and sent word to David, saying, "I am **p**."	2226
2Ki	4:17	But the woman *became* **p**,	2225
	8:12	and rip open their **p** *women*."	2226
	15:16	and ripped open all the **p** *women*.	2226
1Ch	7:23	and *she became* **p** and gave birth to a son.	2225
Ps	7:14	*He who is* **p** with evil and conceives trouble	2473
Hos	13:16	their **p** *women* ripped open."	2230
Am	1:13	Because he ripped open the **p women**	2226
Mt	24:19	**p women** and nursing mothers!	1143+1877+2400
Mk	13:17	**p women** and nursing mothers!	1143+1877+2400
Lk	1:24	After this his wife Elizabeth *became* **p** and	5197
	21:23	**p women** and nursing mothers!	1143+1877+2400
1Th	5: 3	as labor pains on a **p woman**,	1143+1877+2400
Rev	12: 2	*She was* **p** and cried out in pain	1143+1877+2400

PREMATURELY (1) [MATURE]

Ex	21:22	and she **gives birth p** but there is no	3529+3655

PREPARATION (9) [PREPARE]

Nu	11:18	'Consecrate yourselves **in p** for tomorrow,	4200
Jos	7:13	'Consecrate yourselves **in p** for tomorrow;	NIH
1Sa	23:22	Go and **make** further **p**.	3922
Mt	27:62	The next day, the one after **P Day**,	4187
Mk	15:42	**P Day** (that is, the day before the Sabbath).	4187
Lk	23:54	**P Day**, the Sabbath was about to begin.	4187
Jn	19:14	It was the **day of P** of Passover Week,	4187
	19:31	Now it was the **day of P**,	4187
	19:42	Because it was the Jewish **day of P** and	4187

PREPARATIONS (11) [PREPARE]

1Ch	22: 5	Therefore *I will* **make p** for it."	3922
	22: 5	David **made** extensive **p** before his death.	3922
2Ch	35: 6	*they* **made p** for themselves and for	3922
	35:14	the Levites **made p** for themselves and for	3922
	35:15	their fellow Levites **made** *the* **p** for them.	3922
Mt	26:17	"Where do you want *us to* **make p** for you	2286
Mk	14:12	"Where do you want *us* to go and **make p**	2286
	14:15	**Make p** for us there."	2286
Lk	10:40	distracted by all the **p** that had **to be made**.	1355
	22: 8	"Go and **make p** for us to eat the Passover."	2286
	22:12	**Make p** there."	2286

PREPARE (95) [PREPARATION, PREPARATIONS, PREPARED, PREPARES, PREPARING]

Ge	18: 7	who hurried to **p** it.	6913
	27: 4	**P** me the kind of tasty food I like	6913
	27: 7	and **p** me some tasty food to eat,	6913
	27: 9	so *I can* **p** some tasty food for your father,	6913
	43:16	slaughter an animal and **p** dinner;	3922
Ex	12:16	**p** food for everyone **to eat**—	430
	12:39	of Egypt and did not have time *to* **p** food	6913
	16: 5	the sixth day *they are to* **p** what they bring	3922
	19:15	"**P** yourselves for the third day.	2118+3922
Lev	6:21	**P** it with oil on a griddle;	6913
	6:22	to succeed him as anointed priest *shall* **p** it.	6913
Nu	15: 5	**p** a quarter of a hin of wine as	6913
	15: 6	a ram **p** a grain offering of two-tenths of	6913
	15: 8	" 'When *you* **p** a young bull as	6913
	15:12	Do this for each one, for as many as *you* **p**.	6913
	23: 1	and **p** seven bulls and seven rams for me.	3922
	23:29	and **p** seven bulls and seven rams for me."	3922
	28: 4	**P** one lamb in the morning and the other	6913
	28: 8	**P** the second lamb at twilight,	6913
	28: 8	and drink offering that *you* **p** in	6913
	28:20	With each bull **p** a grain offering	6913
	28:23	**P** these in addition to the regular morning	6913
	28:24	In this way **p** the food for the offering made	6913
	28:31	**P** these together with their drink offerings,	6913
	29: 2	**p** a burnt offering of one young bull,	6913
	29: 3	the bull **p** a grain offering of three-tenths of	NIH
	29: 9	the bull **p** a grain offering of three-tenths of	NIH
	29:14	of the thirteen bulls **p** a grain offering	NIH
	29:17	" 'On the second day **p** twelve young bulls,	NIH
	29:18	**p** their grain offerings and drink offerings	NIH
	29:20	" 'On the third day **p** eleven bulls.	NIH
	29:21	**p** their grain offerings and drink offerings	NIH
	29:23	" 'On the fourth day **p** ten bulls,	NIH
	29:24	**p** their grain offerings and drink offerings	NIH
	29:26	" 'On the fifth day **p** nine bulls,	NIH
	29:27	**p** their grain offerings and drink offerings	NIH
	29:29	" 'On the sixth day **p** eight bulls,	NIH
	29:30	**p** their grain offerings and drink offerings	NIH
	29:32	" 'On the seventh day **p** seven bulls,	NIH
	29:33	**p** their grain offerings and drink offerings	NIH
	29:37	**p** their grain offerings and drink offerings	NIH
	29:39	**p** these for the LORD at your appointed	6913
Jdg	13:15	to stay until *we* **p** a young goat for you."	6913
	13:16	But if *you* **p** a burnt offering,	6913
2Sa	12: 4	to **p** a meal for the traveler who had come	6913
	13: 5	*Let her* **p** the food in my sight	6913
	13: 5	of your brother Amnon and **p** some food	6913
1Ki	18:23	I *will* **p** the other bull and put it on	6913
	18:25	"Choose one of the bulls and **p** it first,	6913
	20:12	and he ordered his men: "**P** to attack."	3922
2Ki	20: 7	Then Isaiah said, "**P** a poultice of figs."	4374
1Ch	22: 2	to **p** dressed stone for building the house	2933
2Ch	31:11	Hezekiah gave orders to **p** storerooms in	3922
	35: 4	**P** *yourselves* by families	3922
	35: 6	consecrate yourselves and **p** [the lambs]	3922
Est	5: 8	to the banquet *I will* **p** for them.	6913
Job	33: 5	**p** *yourself* and confront me.	6885
Ps	23: 5	*You* **p** a table before me in the presence	6885
Isa	8: 9	**P for battle**, and be shattered!	273
	8: 9	**P for battle**, and be shattered!	273
	14:21	**P** a place to slaughter his sons for the sins	3922
	25: 6	the LORD Almighty *will* **p** a feast	6913
	38:21	"**P** a poultice of figs and apply it to	5951
	40: 3	"In the desert **p** the way for the LORD;	7155
	57:14	"Build up, build up, **p** the road!	7155
	62:10	**P** the way for the people.	7155
Jer	6: 4	"**P** *for* battle against her!	7727
	46: 3	"**P** your shields, both large and small,	6885
	51:12	station the watchmen, **p** an ambush!	3922
	51:27	**P** the nations for battle against her;	7727
	51:28	**P** the nations for battle against her—	7727
Eze	7:23	"**P** chains, because the land is full	6913
Da	11:10	His sons *will* **p for war** and assemble	1741
Joel	3: 9	among the nations: "**P** *for* war!	7727
Am	4:12	**p** to meet your God, O Israel."	3922
Mic	3: 5	*they* **p** to wage war against him.	7727
Na	1:14	*I will* **p** your grave, for you are vile."	8492
Mal	3: 1	who will **p** the way before me.	7155
Mt	3: 3	'**P** the way for the Lord,	2286
	11:10	who *will* **p** your way before you.'	2941
	26:12	she did it to **p** me for burial.	1946
Mk	1: 2	who *will* **p** your way"—	2941
	1: 3	'**P** the way for the Lord,	2286
	14: 8	**poured perfume on** my body beforehand **to p** for my burial.	3690
Lk	1:76	on before the Lord *to* **p** the way for him,	2286
	3: 4	'**P** the way for the Lord,	2286
	7:27	who *will* **p** your way before you.'	2941
	17: 8	Would he not rather say, '**P** my supper,	2286

Lk	22: 9	"Where do you want *us to* **p** for it?"	2286
Jn	14: 2	I am going there *to* **p** a place for you.	2286
	14: 3	And if I go and **p** a place for you,	2286
Eph	4:12	to **p** God's people for works of service,	2938
Phm	1:22	**P** a guest room for me,	2286
1Pe	1:13	**p** your minds **for action**;	350+3836+4019
Rev	16:12	to **p** the way for the kings from the East.	2286

PREPARED (79) [PREPARE]

Ge	18: 8	and milk and the calf that *had been* **p**,	6913
	19: 3	*He* **p** a meal for them,	6913
	24:31	I have **p** the house and a place for	7155
	27:14	and she **p** some tasty food,	6913
	27:31	He too **p** some tasty food and brought it	6913
	43:25	*They* **p** their gifts for Joseph's arrival	3922
Ex	23:20	and to bring you to the place *I have* **p**.	3922
Lev	2: 5	If your grain offering is **p** on a griddle,	NIH
	10:12	and eat it **p** *without yeast* beside the altar,	5174
Nu	15:11	*is to be* **p** in this manner.	6913
	23: 4	and Balaam said, "I have **p** seven altars,	6885
	28:24	*it is to be* **p** in addition to	6913
Jos	24: 9	the king of Moab, to fight against Israel,	7756
Jdg	6: 2	the Israelites **p** shelters for themselves	6913
	6:19	Gideon went in, **p** a young goat,	6913
	19: 5	and *he* **p** to leave, but the girl's father said	7756
Ru	1: 6	and her daughters-in-law **p** to return home	7756
2Sa		David **p** a feast for him and his men.	6913
	12: 4	and **p** it for the one who had come to him."	6913
	13:10	And Tamar took the bread *she had* **p**	6913
1Ki	5:18	of Gebal cut and **p** the timber and stone for	3922
	6:19	*He* **p** the inner sanctuary within the temple	3922
	18:26	So they took the bull given them and **p** it.	6913
	20:12	So *they* **p** to attack the city.	8492
2Ki	6:23	So *he* **p** a great **feast** for them,	4127+4130
1Ch	12:33	experienced soldiers **p** for battle	6885
	12:36	experienced soldiers **p** for battle—	6885
	15: 1	*he* **p** a place for the ark of God and pitched	3922
	15: 3	the ark of the LORD to the place *he had* **p**	3922
	15:12	to the place *I have* **p** for it.	3922
2Ch	1:	from Kiriath Jearim to the place he had **p**	3922
	29:19	*We have* **p** and consecrated all the articles	3922
Ezr	1: 5	**p** to go up and build the house of	7756
Ne	5:18	six choice sheep and some poultry **were p**	6913
	8:10	and send some to those *who have* nothing **p**.	3922
Est	5: 4	come today to a banquet *I have* **p** for him."	6913
	5: 5	to the banquet Esther *had* **p**.	6913
	6:14	to the banquet Esther *had* **p**.	6913
	7:10	on the gallows *he had* **p** for Mordecai.	3922
Job	13:18	Now that *I have* **p** my case,	6885
Ps	7:13	*He has* **p** his deadly weapons;	3922
	78:50	*He* **p** a path for his anger;	7142
Pr	9: 2	*She has* **p** her meat and mixed her wine;	3180
	19:29	Penalties **are p** for mockers,	3922
SS	3: 8	**p** for the terrors of the night.	NIH
Isa	30:33	Topheth *has* long *been* **p**;	6885
Eze	28:13	on the day you were created *they* **were p**.	3922
	38: 7	*be* **p**, you and all the hordes gathered	3922
Zep	1: 7	The LORD *has* **p** a sacrifice;	3922
Mt	20:23	for whom *they have been* **p** by my Father."	2286
	22: 2	like a king who **p** a wedding banquet	4472
	22: 4	that *I have* **p** my dinner:	2286
	25:34	the kingdom **p** for you since the creation of	2286
	25:41	into the eternal fire **p** for the devil	2286
	26:19	as Jesus had directed them and **p**	2286
Mk	10:40	to those for whom *they have been* **p**."	2286
	14:16	So *they* **p** the Passover.	2286
Lk	1:17	to make ready a people **p** for the Lord."	2941
	2:31	which *you have* **p** in the sight of all people,	2286
	12:20	Then who will get what *you have* **p**	2286
	22:13	So *they* **p** the Passover.	2286
	23:56	*they* went home and **p** spices and perfumes.	2286
	24: 1	the spices *they had* **p** and went to the tomb.	2286
Jn	19:19	Pilate **had a notice p** and fastened to	1211+5518
Ac	10:10	and *while* the meal *was being* **p**,	4186
Ro	9:22	of his wrath—**p** for destruction?	2936
	9:23	whom *he* **p in advance** for glory—	4602
1Co	2: 9	no mind has conceived what God has **p**	2286
Eph	2:10	which God **p in advance** for us to do.	4602
2Ti	2:21	to the Master and **p** to do any good work.	2286
	4: 2	*be* **p** in season and out of season;	2392
Heb	10: 5	but a body *you* **p** for me;	2936
	11:16	for *he has* **p** a city for them.	2286
1Pe	3:15	Always be **p** to give an answer	2289
Rev	8: 6	the seven trumpets to sound them.	2286
	9: 7	The locusts looked like horses **p** for battle.	2286
	12: 6	The woman fled into the desert to a place **p**	2286
	12:14	so that she might fly to the place **p** for her	NIG
	21: 2	**p** as a bride beautifully dressed	2286

PREPARES (3) [PREPARE]

Ps	50:23	and *he* **p** the way so that I may show him	8492
	85:13	before him and **p** the way for his steps.	8492
Isa	44:16	over it *he* **p** his meal,	430

PREPARING (9) [PREPARE]

1Ch	9:32	of **p** for every Sabbath the bread set out on	3922
Jer	18:11	I *am* **p** a disaster for you and devising a plan	3670
Eze	39:17	from all around to the sacrifice I *am* **p**	2284
	39:19	At the sacrifice *I am* **p** for you,	2284
Am	7: 1	*He was* **p** swarms of locusts after	3670
Mt	4:21	with their father Zebedee, **p** their nets.	2936
Mk	1:19	and his brother John in a boat, **p** their nets.	2936
Lk	14:16	"A certain man *was* **p** a great banquet	4472
Ac	25: 3	*for they were* **p** an ambush to kill him along	4472

PRESBYTERY (KJV) See ELDERS

PRESCRIBED (23)

Lev	5:10	the other as a burnt offering in the **p way**	5477
	9:16	and offered it in the **p** way.	5477
Nu	15:24	with its **p** grain offering and drink offering,	5477
1Sa	2:29	and offering that *I* **p** for my dwelling?	7422
1Ch	15:13	of him about how to do it in the **p** way."	5477
	23:31	in the proper number and in the **way p**	5477
	24:19	according to the **regulations p** *for* them	5477
2Ch	4:20	to burn in front of the inner sanctuary as **p**;	5477
	29:25	the **way p** by David and Gad the king's seer	5184
	30:16	as **p** in the Law of Moses the man of God.	5477
	35:13	the Passover animals over the fire as **p**,	5477
	35:15	were in the places **p** by David, Asaph,	5184
Ezr	3: 4	required number of burnt offerings **p**	3869+5477
	3:10	as **p** by David king of Israel.	3338+6584
	7:23	Whatever the God of heaven has **p**,	10302+10427
Ne	12:24	as **p** by David the man of God.	5184
	12:36	**musical** instruments *[p by]* David	AIT
	13: 5	new wine and oil **p** *for* the Levites,	5184
Est	2:12	of beauty treatments **p** for the women,	2017
	9:27	in the way **p** and at the time appointed.	4181
Job	36:23	Who *has* **p** his ways for him, or said to him,	7212
Eze	45:14	The **p portion** *of* oil,	2976
Heb	8: 4	the gifts **p** by the law.	2848

PRESENCE (202) [PRESENT]

Ge	4:14	and I will be hidden from your **p**;	7156
	4:16	So Cain went out from the LORD's **p**	4200+7156
	23:11	I give it to you in the **p** of my people.	6524
	23:18	in the **p** of all the Hittites who had come to	6524
	27: 7	that I may give you my blessing in the **p** *of*	7156
	27:30	and Jacob had scarcely left his father's **p**,	7156
	31:32	**In the p** of our relatives,	5584
	31:35	my lord, that I cannot stand up in your **p**;	7156
	40:20	and the chief baker in the **p** of his officials.	9348
	41:46	And Joseph went out from Pharaoh's **p**	4200+7156
	45: 1	"Have everyone leave my **p**!"	4946+6584
	45: 3	because they were terrified at his **p**.	7156
	47:10	and went out from his **p**.	4200+7156
Ex	7:20	He raised his staff in the **p** of Pharaoh	6524
	9: 8	and have Moses toss it into the air in the **p**	6524
	10:11	and Aaron were driven out of Pharaoh's **p**.	7156
	18:12	with Moses' father-in-law in the **p** of God.	7156
	25:30	Put the bread of the **P** on this table to be	7156
	28:30	whenever he enters the **p** of the LORD.	4200+7156
	29:11	the LORD's **p** at the entrance to the Tent	7156
	33:14	"My **P** will go with you,	7156
	33:15	"If your **P** does not go with us,	7156
	33:19	proclaim my name, the LORD, in your **p**.	7156
	34:34	whenever he entered the LORD's **p**	4200+7156
	35:13	and all its articles and the bread of the **P**;	7156
	35:20	Then the whole Israelite community withdrew from Moses' **p**,	4200+7156
	39:36	with all its articles and the bread of the **P**;	7156
Lev	9:24	from the **p** of the LORD and consumed	4200+7156
	10: 2	fire came out from the **p** of the LORD	4200+7156
	19:32	" 'Rise in the **p** of the aged,	7156
	22: 3	that person must be cut off from my **p**.	4200+7156
Nu	4: 7	"Over the table of the **P** they are to spread	7156
	6: 9	" 'If someone dies suddenly **in his p**,	6584
	6:11	because he sinned by being in the **p** of	6584
	17: 9	from the LORD's **p** to all the Israelites.	4200+7156
	19: 3	the camp and slaughtered in his **p**.	7156
	20: 9	Moses took the staff from the LORD's **p**,	4200+7156
	27:19	and commission him in their **p**.	6524
Dt	4:37	of Egypt by his **P** and his great strength,	7156
	12: 7	There, in the **p** of the LORD your God,	7156
	12:18	the **p** of the LORD your God at the place	7156
	14:23	and flocks in the **p** of the LORD your God	7156
	14:26	the **p** of the LORD your God and rejoice.	7156
	15:20	and your family are to eat them in the **p** of	7156
	18: 7	who serve there in the **p** of the LORD.	7156
	19:17	the **p** of the LORD before the priests and	7156
	25: 2	down and have him flogged in his **p** with	6524
	25: 9	up to him in the **p** of the elders,	6524
	27: 7	eating them and rejoicing in the **p** of	7156
	29:10	All of you are standing today in the **p** of	7156
	29:15	in the **p** of the LORD our God but also	7156
	31: 7	and said to him in the **p** of all Israel,	6524
	32:51	both of you broke faith with me in the **p** of	9348
Jos	8:32	There, in the **p** of the Israelites,	7156
	10:12	Joshua said to the LORD in the **p**	6524
	18: 6	to me and I will cast lots for you in the **p** *of*	7156
	18: 8	at Shiloh in the **p** of the LORD."	7156
	18:10	then cast lots for them in Shiloh in the **p** of	7156
	19:51	of Israel assigned by lot at Shiloh in the **p**	7156
Ru	4: 4	that you buy it **in the p** of these seated here	5584
	4: 4	and **in the p** of the elders of my people.	5584
1Sa	2:21	the boy Samuel grew up **in the p** of	6640
	2:28	and to wear an ephod in my **p**.	7156
	6:20	"Who can stand in the **p** of the LORD,	7156
	11:15	and confirmed Saul as king in the **p** of	7156
	12: 3	Testify against me **in the p** of the LORD	5584
	16:13	and anointed him in the **p** of his brothers,	7931
	19:24	and also prophesied in Samuel's **p**.	7156
	21: 6	the bread of the **P** that had been removed	7156
	21:13	So he pretended to be insane in their **p**;	6524
	26:20	to the ground far from the **p** of the LORD."	7156
2Sa	3:13	*Do not* **come into** my **p**	906+7156+8011
	22:13	of his **p** bolts of lightning blazed forth.	5584
	24: 4	left the **p** of the king to enroll	4200+7156
1Ki	1:28	So she came *into* the king's **p** and	4200+7156

1Ki	7:48	on which was the bread of the **P**;	7156
	8: 1	Then King Solomon summoned **into** his **p**	448
	8:28	your servant is praying in your **p** this day.	7156
	19:11	"Go out and stand on the mountain in the **p**	7156
2Ki	3:14	for the **p** of Jehoshaphat king of Judah,	7156
	5:27	from Elisha's **p** and he was leprous,	4200+7156
	13:23	to destroy them or banish them from his **p**.	7156
	17:18	with Israel and removed them from his **p**.	7156
	17:20	until he thrust them from his **p**.	7156
	17:23	until the LORD removed them from his **p**,	7156
	22:10	Shaphan read from it in the **p** of the king.	7156
	22:19	you tore your robes and wept in my **p**,	7156
	23: 3	the pillar and renewed the covenant in the **p**	7156
	23:27	"I will remove Judah also from my **p**	7156
	24: 3	in order to remove them from his **p** because	7156
	24:20	and in the end he thrust them from his **p**.	7156
1Ch	12: 1	from the **p** of Saul son of Kish (they were	7156
	24: 6	recorded their names in the **p** of the king	7156
	24:31	in the **p** *of* King David and of Zadok,	7156
	29:10	the LORD in the **p** of the whole assembly,	6524
	29:22	They ate and drank with great joy in the **p**	7156
2Ch	2: 6	on which was the bread of the **P**;	7156
	6:19	that your servant is praying in your **p**.	7156
	20: 9	we will stand in your **p** before this temple	7156
	26:19	the priests in their **p** before the incense altar	7156
	28:14	and plunder in the **p** of the officials and all	7156
	34:18	Shaphan read from it in the **p** of the king.	7156
	34:24	in the book that has been read in the **p** of	7156
	34:27	and tore your robes and wept in my **p**,	7156
	34:31	the covenant in the **p** of the LORD—	7156
Ezr	4:18	and translated **in my p**.	10621
	9:15	of it not one of us can stand in your **p**."	7156
Ne	1:11	by granting him favor in the **p**	7156
	2: 1	I had not been sad in his **p** before;	7156
	4: 2	and in the **p** of his associates and the army	7156
	8: 3	before the Water Gate **in the p** of the men,	5584
Est	1:16	Then Memucan replied in the **p** of the king	7156
	1:19	Vashti is never again to enter the **p**	4200+7156
	2:23	the book of the annals in the **p** of the king.	7156
	3: 7	the **p** of Haman to select a day and month.	7156
	4: 8	to urge her to go **into** the king's **p** to beg	448
	5: 9	nor showed fear **in his p**,	4946
	8: 1	And Mordecai came into the **p** of the king,	7156
	8:15	Mordecai left the king's **p**	4200+7156
Job	1:12	Satan went out from the **p** of the LORD.	7156
	2: 7	from the **p** of the LORD and afflicted Job	7156
	30:11	they throw off restraint in my **p**.	7156
Ps	5: 5	arrogant cannot stand **in your p**;	4200+5584+6524
	9:18	let the nations be judged in your **p**.	7156
	16:11	you will fill me with joy in your **p**,	7156
	18:12	of the brightness of his **p** clouds advanced,	5584
	21: 6	and made him glad with the joy of your **p**.	7156
	23: 5	a table before me **in the p** of my enemies.	5584
	31:20	In the shelter of your **p** you hide them from	7156
	39: 1	as long as the wicked are in my **p**."	5584
	41:12	and set me in your **p** forever.	7156
	51:11	from your **p** or take your Holy Spirit	4200+7156
	52: 9	I will praise you **in the p** of your saints.	5584
	61: 7	May he be enthroned in God's **p** forever;	7156
	89:15	who walk in the light of your **p**, O LORD.	7156
	90: 8	our secret sins in the light of your **p**.	7156
	101: 7	no one who speaks falsely will stand **in my p**.	4200+5584+6524
	102:28	of your servants will live in your **p**;	NIH
	114: 7	Tremble, O earth, at the **p** of the Lord,	4200+7156
	114: 7	at the **p** of the God of Jacob,	4200+7156
	116:14	to the LORD **in the p** of all his people.	2025+5584
	116:18	to the LORD **in the p** of all his people,	2025+5584
	139: 7	Where can I flee from your **p**?	7156
Pr	8:30	rejoicing always in his **p**,	7156
	14:19	Evil men will bow down in the **p** *of*	7156
	18:16	for the giver and ushers him into the **p** *of*	7156
	25: 5	remove the wicked from the king's **p**,	7156
	25: 6	Do not exalt yourself in the king's **p**,	7156
Ecc	8: 3	Do not be in a hurry to leave the king's **p**.	7156
Isa	3: 8	defying his glorious **p**.	6524
	26:17	so were we in your **p**, O LORD.	7156
	63: 9	and the angel of his **p** saved them.	7156
Jer	5:22	"Should you not tremble in my **p**?	7156
	7:15	I will thrust you from my **p**,	7156
	15: 1	Send them away from my **p**!	7156
	23:39	surely forget you and cast you out of my **p**	7156
	28: 1	of the LORD in the **p** of the priests and all	6524
	32:12	in the **p** of my cousin Hanamel and of	6524
	32:13	"In their **p** I gave Baruch these instructions:	6524
	52: 3	and in the end he thrust them from his **p**.	7156
La	2:19	pour out your heart like water **in the p** of the Lord.	5790+7156
Eze	28: 9	in the **p** of those who kill you?	7156
	38:20	the face of the earth will tremble at my **p**.	7156
	44: 3	the gateway to eat in the **p** of the LORD.	7156
	44:12	in the **p** of their idols and made the house	7156
	46: 3	in the **p** of the LORD at the entrance to	7156
Da	2:27	Daniel came into the **p** and I told him	10621
	7:13	the Ancient of Days and was led **into** his **p**.	10621
Hos	6: 2	that we may live in his **p**.	7156
Na	1: 5	The earth trembles at his **p**,	7156
Zec	6: 5	from standing **in the p** of the Lord of	6584
Mal	3:16	in his **p** concerning those who feared	7156
Mk	7:24	yet he could not keep his **p** secret.	NIG
Lk	1:19	I stand **in the p** of God,	1967
	8:47	**In the p** of all the people,	1967
	14:10	Then you will be honored **in the p** of	1967
	15:10	there is rejoicing **in the p** of the angels	1967
	23:14	I have examined him **in your p**	1967
	24:43	and he took it and ate it **in their p**.	1967
Jn	8:38	what I have seen **in the Father's p**,	4123

Jn	12:37	Jesus had done all these miraculous signs in their **p**,	1869
	17: 5	glorify me in your **p** with the glory I had	4123
	20:30	Jesus did many other miraculous signs in	1967
Ac	2:28	will fill me with joy in your **p.**	3552+3836+4725
	10:33	Now we are all here in the **p** of God	1967
	24:21	I shouted as I stood in their **p:**	1877
2Co	4:14	with Jesus and present us with you in his **p.**	NIG
Php	2:12	not only in my **p**, but now much more	4242
1Th	2:19	or the crown in which we will glory **in the p**	1869
	3: 9	the joy we have in the **p** of our God because	1869
	3:13	be blameless and holy in the **p** of our God	4725
2Th	1: 9	and shut out from the **p** of the Lord and	4725
1Ti	6:12	you made your good confession in the **p**	1967
2Ti	2: 2	things you have heard me say in the **p** of	1328
	4: 1	In the **p** of God and of Christ Jesus,	1967
Heb	2:13	in the **p** of the congregation I will sing	3545
	9:24	now to appear for us *in* God's **p.**	4725
2Pe	2:11	against such beings in the **p** of the Lord.	4123
1Jn	3:19	and how we set our hearts at rest in his **p**	1869
Jude	1:24	and to present you before his **glorious p**	1518
Rev	14:10	tormented with burning sulfur in the **p** of	1967
	20:11	Earth and sky fled from his **p,**	4725

PRESENT (153) [EVER-PRESENT, PRESENCE, PRESENTABLE, PRESENTED, PRESENTING, PRESENTS]

Ge	33:11	Please accept the **p** that was brought to you,	1388
Ex	10:25	to have sacrifices and burnt offerings to **p**	6913
	22:14	or dies while the owner is not **p,**	6640
	29: 3	Put them in a basket and **p** them in it—	7928
	34: 2	**P yourself** to me there on top of	5893
Lev	1: 3	*He must* **p** it at the entrance to the Tent	7928
	2: 8	**p** it to the priest, who shall take it to the	7928
	3: 1	he is to **p** before the Lord an animal	7928
	3: 7	he is to **p** it before the Lord.	7928
	3:12	he is to **p** it before the Lord.	7928
	4: 4	*to* **p** the bull at the entrance to the Tent	995
	4:14	as a sin offering and **p** it before the Tent	995
	6:21	and **p** the grain offering broken in pieces as	7928
	7:11	for the fellowship offering a person *may* **p**	7928
	7:13	*to* **p** an offering with cakes of bread shall	7928
	9: 2	and **p** them before the Lord.	7928
	13:19	*he must* **p himself** to the priest.	8011
	14:11	priest who pronounces him clean *shall*	6641
	16: 7	Then he is to take the two goats and **p** them	6641
	17: 4	the Tent of Meeting to **p** it as an offering to	7928
	18:23	A woman *must* not **p** *herself* to an animal	6641
	21: 6	Because they **p** the offerings made to	7928
	21:21	near to **p** the offerings made to the Lord	7928
	22:15	the sacred offerings the Israelites **p** to	8123
	22:19	you must **p** a male without defect from	NIH
	22:22	**p** as a freewill offering an ox or a sheep	6913
	23: 8	For seven days **p** an offering made to	7928
	23:16	**p** an offering of new grain to the Lord.	7928
	23:18	**P** with this bread seven male lambs,	7928
	23:25	but **p** an offering made to the Lord	7928
	23:27	and **p** an offering made to the Lord	7928
	23:36	For seven days **p** offerings made to	7928
	23:36	a sacred assembly and **p** an offering made	7928
	27: 8	he is to **p** the person to the priest,	6641
Nu	3: 6	of Levi and **p** them to Aaron the priest	6641
	6:14	*to* **p** his offerings to the Lord:	7928
	6:16	*to* **p** them before the Lord and make	7928
	6:17	He is to **p** the basket of unleavened bread	6913
	8:11	*to* **p** the Levites before the Lord as	5677
	8:13	of Aaron and his sons and then **p** them as	5677
	9:13	because *he did* not **p** the Lord's offering	7928
	15: 3	and *you* **p** to the Lord offerings made	6913
	15: 4	the one who brings his offering *shall* **p** to	7928
	15:19	**p** a portion as an offering to the Lord.	8123
	15:20	**P** a cake from the first of your	8123+9556
	15:20	of your ground meal and **p** it as an offering	8123
	16:17	and **p** it before the Lord.	7928
	16:17	You and Aaron are to **p** your censers also."	NIH
	18:19	the Israelites **p** to the Lord I give to you	8123
	18:24	the tithes that the Israelites **p** as an offering	8123
	18:26	as your inheritance, *you must* **p** a tenth of	8123
	18:28	In this way you also *will* **p** an offering to	8123
	18:29	*You must* **p** as the Lord's portion	8123
	18:30	'When you **p** the best part,	8123
	28: 2	'See that *you* **p** to me at the appointed time	7928
	28: 3	the offering made by fire that *you are to* **p**	7928
	28:11	**p** to the Lord a burnt offering	7928
	28:19	**P** to the Lord an offering made by fire,	7928
	28:26	when you **p** to the Lord an offering	7928
	28:27	**P** a burnt offering of two young bulls,	7928
	29: 8	**P** as an aroma pleasing to the Lord	7928
	29:13	**P** an offering made by fire as	7928
	29:36	**P** an offering made by fire as	7928
Dt	12:27	**P** your burnt offerings on the altar of	6913
	31:14	and **p yourselves** at the Tent of Meeting,	3656
Jos	7:14	**p yourselves** tribe by tribe.	7928
1Sa	1:22	I will take him and **p** him before	8011
	10:19	So now **p yourselves** before the Lord	3656
	30:26	"Here is a **p** for you from the plunder of	1388
2Sa	14:20	Joab did this to change the **p** situation.	7156
1Ki	18: 1	"Go and **p yourself** to Ahab.	8011
	18: 2	So Elijah went to **p himself** to Ahab.	8011
	18:15	*I will* surely **p myself** to Ahab today."	8011
1Ch	9:18	up to **the p time.**	2178
	16:40	to **p** burnt offerings to the Lord on	6590
2Ch	13:11	and evening *they* **p** burnt offerings	7787
	23:18	to **p** the burnt offerings of the Lord	6590

2Ch	29: 7	not burn incense or **p** any burnt offerings at	6590
	29:29	the king and everyone **p** with him knelt	5162
	30:21	The Israelites who *were* **p**	5162
	34:33	and he had all who *were* **p** in Israel serve	5162
	35:17	The Israelites who **p** celebrated	5162
Ezr	5:16	to the **p** it has been under construction	10363
	6: 3	be rebuilt as a place *to* **p** sacrifices,	10156
	8:25	and all Israel **p** there had donated for	5162
Est	1: 3	the nobles of the provinces were **p.**	4200+7156
Job	1: 6	One day the angels came to **p themselves**	3656
	1: 6	the angels came to **p themselves** before	3656
	2: 1	and Satan also came with them to **p himself**	3656
	23: 7	There an upright man *could* **p** his **case**	3519
Ps	14: 5	God is **p** in the company of the righteous.	928
	56:12	*I will* **p** my thank offerings to you,	8966
	72:10	kings of Sheba and Seba *will* **p** him gifts.	7928
Pr	4: 9	a garland of grace on your head and **p** you	4481
	18:17	In his **p** case seems right,	NIH
Isa	40:20	to **p** *such* **an offering** selects wood	9556
	41:21	**"P** your case," says the Lord.	7928
	45:21	Declare what is to be, **p** it—	5602
Jer	33:18	and *to* **p** sacrifices.' "	6913
	40: 5	and **p** and let him go.	5368
	42: 9	you sent me to **p** your petition,	4200+5877+7156
	44:15	along with all the women who *were* **p**—	6641
Eze	43:27	the priests *are to* **p** your burnt offerings	6913
	45: 1	*to* **p** to the Lord a portion of the land as	8123
	48: 8	to west will be the portion *you are to* **p** as	8123
	48: 9	of this **p** house will be greater than	340
Mk	8: 9	About four thousand men **were p.**	1639
	10:30	as much in this **p** age (homes, brothers,	3814
	14:14	Some of those **p** were saying indignantly	NIG
Lk	2:22	and Mary took him to Jerusalem *to* **p** him	4225
	5:17	the power of the Lord **was p** for him to heal	1639
	12:56	don't know how to interpret this **p** time?	NIG
	13: 1	Now there were some **p** at that time	4205
	22: 6	**when no crowd was p.**	868
Ac	1:13	Those **p** were Peter, John,	NIG
	5:38	Therefore, **in the p** case I advise you:	3814
	21:18	and all the elders *were* **p.**	4134
	23:30	*to* **p** to you their case against him.	3306
	24:17	for the poor and to **p** offerings.	4225
	25:24	"King Agrippa, and all who *are* **p** with us,	5223
Ro	3:26	to demonstrate his justice at the **p** time,	3814
	8:18	I consider that our **p** sufferings	2789+3814+3836
	8:22	of childbirth right up to the **p time.**	3814
	8:38	neither the **p** nor the future, nor any powers,	1931
	11: 5	at the **p** time there is a remnant chosen	3814
	13:11	And do this, understanding the **p time.**	2789
1Co	3:22	or the world or life or death or the **p** or	1931
	5: 3	Even though I *am* not physically **p,**	582
	5: 3	just as if *I were* **p.**	4205
	5: 4	and the power of our Lord Jesus is **p,**	NIG
	7:26	Because of the **p** crisis,	1931
	7:31	this world in its **p** form is passing away.	NIG
2Co	4:14	also raise us with Jesus and **p** us with you	4225
	8:14	At the **p** time your plenty will supply what they need,	3814
	10:11	we will be in our actions *when we are* **p.**	4205
	11: 2	*that I might* **p** you as a pure virgin to him.	4225
Gal	1: 4	to rescue us from the **p** evil age,	1931
	4:25	and corresponds *to the* **p** city of Jerusalem,	3814
Eph	1:21	in the **p** age but also in the one to come.	4047
	5:27	and to **p** her to himself as a radiant church,	4225
Php	4: 6	with thanksgiving, **p** your requests to God.	1192
Col	1:22	*to* **p** you holy in his sight, without blemish	4444
	1:25	**p** to you the word of God **in its fullness**—	4444
	1:28	so that we *may* **p** everyone perfect in Christ.	4225
	2: 5	*I am* **p** with you in spirit and delight to see	1639
1Ti	4: 8	holding promise *for* both the **p** life and	3814
	6:17	in this **p** world not to be arrogant nor	3814
2Ti	2:15	*to* **p** yourself to God as one approved,	4225
Tit	2:12	upright and godly lives in this **p** age,	3814
Heb	9: 9	Yet *at* **p** we do not see everything subject	3814
	9: 9	This is an illustration for the **p** time,	1931
2Pe	3: 7	the **p** heavens and earth are reserved	3814
Jude	1:24	and *to* **p** you before his glorious presence	2705

PRESENTABLE (1) [PRESENT]

1Co	12:24	while our **p** parts need no special treatment.	2363

PRESENTED (56) [PRESENT]

Ge	30:20	"God has **p** me *with* a precious gift.	2272
	43:15	to Egypt and **p** *themselves* to Joseph.	6641
	43:26	*they* **p** to him the gifts they had brought	995
	47: 2	of his brothers and **p** them before Pharaoh.	3657
	47: 7	in and **p** him before Pharaoh.	6641
Ex	29:27	and the thigh that **was p.**	8123+9556
	32: 6	and **p** fellowship offerings.	5602
	35:22	They all **p** their gold as a wave offering to	5677
Lev	7:34	and the thigh that is **p** and have given them	9556
	7:35	and his sons on the day they *were* **p** to serve	7928
	8:14	*He then* **p** the bull for the sin offering,	5602
	8:18	*He then* **p** the ram for the burnt offering,	7928
	8:22	*He then* **p** the other ram,	7928
	10:14	that was waved and the thigh that was **p.**	9556
	10:15	The thigh that was **p** and the breast	9556
	16:10	but the scapegoat *shall* **be p** alive before	6641
	27:11	the animal *must be* **p** to the priest,	6641
Nu	6:20	and waved and the thigh that was **p.**	9556
	7: 3	These *they* **p** before the tabernacle.	7928
	7:10	its dedication and **p** them before the altar.	7928
	8:15	the Levites and **p** them as a wave offering,	5677
	8:21	Then Aaron **p** them as a wave offering	5677
	16:38	for they *were* **p** before the Lord	7928

Nu	18: 8	in charge of the **offerings** **p** to me;	AIT
	28:15	one male goat *is to* **be p** to the Lord as	6913
	31:52	of hundreds that Moses and Eleazar **p** as	8123
Dt	31:14	and **p themselves** at the Tent of Meeting.	3656
Jos	24: 1	and *they* **p themselves** before God.	3656
Jdg	3:17	*He* **p** the tribute to Eglon king of Moab,	7928
	3:18	After Ehud *had* **p** the tribute,	7928
	20:26	that day until evening and **p** burnt offerings	6590
	21: 4	an altar and **p** burnt offerings	6590
1Sa	18:27	and **p the full number** to the king so	4848
2Ki	11:12	he **p** him with a copy of the covenant	NIH
	16:12	he approached it and **p** offerings on it.	6590
1Ch	6:49	the *ones who* **p** offerings on the altar	7787
	16: 1	and *they* **p** burnt offerings	7928
	23:31	and whenever burnt offerings *were* **p** to	6590
	29:21	to the Lord and **p** burnt offerings to him:	6590
2Ch	23:11	they **p** him with a copy of the covenant	NIH
	24:14	burnt offerings were **p** continually in	6590
	28:21	and from the princes and **p** them to the king	5989
	29:24	**p** their blood on the altar **for a sin offering**	2627
Ezr	3: 5	they **p** the regular burnt offerings,	NIH
	10:19	and for their guilt they each **p** a ram from	NIH
Est	8: 2	and **p** it to Mordecai.	5989
Eze	20:28	**p** their fragrant incense and poured out	8492
Da	1:18	the chief official **p** them to Nebuchadnezzar.	995
	2:46	that an offering and incense *be* **p** to him.	10482
Mt	2:11	and **p** him **with** gifts of gold and of incense	4712
Mk	6:28	*He* **p** it to the girl,	1443
Ac	9:41	and the widows and **p** her to them alive.	4225
	24: 2	Tertullus **p** his **case** before Felix:	2989
	25: 2	**appeared** before him and **p the charges**	1872
Ro	3:25	God **p** him as a sacrifice of atonement,	4729

PRESENTING (6) [PRESENT]

Ex	30:20	the altar to minister by **p** an offering made	7787
	35:24	Those **p** an offering of silver	8123
Nu	9: 7	be kept from **p** the Lord's offering with	7928
	18:32	By **p** the best part of it you will not	8123
Eze	46:14	The **p** of this grain offering to the Lord	NIH
Ac	17:19	this new teaching that you are **p?**	3281

PRESENTS (6) [PRESENT]

Lev	6: 5	on the day he **p** his guilt offering.	NIH
	22:18	**p** a gift for a burnt offering to the Lord,	7928
Nu	15:14	an alien or anyone else living among you **p**	6913
Est	9:19	a day for giving **p** to each other.	4950
	9:22	of feasting and joy and giving **p of food**	4950
Isa	66: 3	like one who **p** pig's blood,	NIH

PRESERVE (24) [PRESERVED, PRESERVES]

Ge	19:32	and then lie with him and **p** our family line	2649
	19:34	and lie with him so *we can* **p** our family line	2649
	45: 7	But God sent me ahead of you to **p** for you	8492
Job	33:18	*to* **p** his soul from the pit,	3104
Ps	36: 6	O Lord, *you* **p** both man and beast.	3828
	41: 2	Lord will protect him and **p his life;**	2649
	79:11	of your arm **p** those condemned to die.	3855
	119:25	**p** my life according to your word.	2649
	119:37	**p** my life according to your word.	2649
	119:40	**P** my life in your righteousness.	2649
	119:88	**P** my life according to your love,	2649
	119:107	I have suffered much; **p my life,**	2649
	119:149	**p** my life, O Lord,	2649
	119:154	**p** my life according to your promise.	2649
	119:156	**p** my life according to your laws.	2649
	119:159	See how I love your precepts; **p my life,**	2649
	138: 7	*you* **p** my life;	2649
	143:11	your name's sake, O Lord, **p my life;**	2649
Pr	3:21	**p** sound judgment and discernment,	5915
	5: 2	and your lips *may* **p** knowledge.	5915
Eze	7:13	not one of them *will* **p** his life.	2616
	13:18	the lives of my people but **p** your own?	2649
Mal	2: 7	The lips of a priest *ought to* **p** knowledge,	9068
Lk	17:33	and whoever loses his life *will* **p** it.	2441

PRESERVED (4) [PRESERVE]

2Sa	22:44	*you have* **p** me as the head of nations.	9068
Ps	66: 9	he *has* **p** our lives and kept	928+2021+2645+8492
	119:93	for by them *you have* **p** my life.	2649
Mt	9:17	into new wineskins, and both *are* **p."**	5337

PRESERVES (3) [PRESERVE]

Ps	31:23	The Lord **p** the faithful,	5915
	119:50	Your promise **p** my life.	2649
Ecc	7:12	that wisdom **p** *the life of* its possessor.	2649

PRESIDENTS (KJV) See ADMINISTRATORS

PRESIDES (1)

Ps	82: 1	God **p** in the great assembly;	5893

PRESS (12) [PRESSED, PRESSES, PRESSING, PRESSURE]

Jdg	14:17	because *she* continued to **p** him.	7439
2Sa	11:25	**P** the attack against the city and destroy it.'	2616
Job	33: 6	No, he *would* not **p charges** against me.	8492
Ps	56: 1	all day long *they* **p** their attack.	4315
Pr	6: 3	**p** *your* **plea** *with* your neighbor!	8104

Hos	6: 3	*let us* **p** on to acknowledge him.	8103
Mic	6:15	you *will* **p** olives but not use the oil	2005
Ac	19:38	*They can* **p** charges.	1592
	25: 5	and **p** charges against the man there,	2989
Php	3:12	but *I* **p** on to take hold of that	1503
	3:14	*I* **p** on toward the goal to win the prize	1503
Rev	14:20	and blood flowed out of the **p**,	3332

PRESSED (18) [PRESS]

Ex	27:20	to bring you clear oil of **p** olives for	4184
	29:40	a quarter of a hin of oil from **p** olives,	4184
Lev	24: 2	to bring you clear oil of **p** olives for	4184
Nu	22:25	she **p** close to the wall,	4315
	28: 5	a quarter of a hin of oil from **p** olives.	4184
Jdg	1:28	they **p** the Canaanites into forced labor	8492
	1:35	they too were **p** into forced labor.	NIH
	9:45	that day Abimelech **p** his attack against	4309
1Sa	13: 6	and that their army *was* hard **p**,	5601
	25:18	of raisins and two hundred **cakes of p figs**,	1811
	30:12	of a **cake of p figs** and two cakes of raisins.	1811
	31: 2	The Philistines **p** hard after Saul	1815
1Ki	5:11	to twenty thousand baths of **p** olive oil.	4184
1Ch	10: 2	The Philistines **p** hard after Saul	1815
Mk	5:24	A large crowd followed and **p** around him.	5315
Lk	6:38	A good measure, **p** down,	4390
2Co	4: 8	We are hard **p** on every side,	2567
	8:13	be relieved while you are hard **p**,	2568

PRESSES (2) [PRESS]

Isa	16:10	no one treads out wine at the **p**,	3676
Jer	48:33	the flow of wine from the **p**;	3676

PRESSING (3) [PRESS]

Ex	5:13	The slave drivers *kept* **p** them, saying,	237
Jdg	20:45	*They kept* **p** after the Benjamites as far	1815
Lk	8:45	people are crowding and **p** against you."	632

PRESSURE (3) [PRESS]

Ge	19: 9	*They* **kept bringing p** on Lot	4394+7210
2Co	1: 8	*We were* **under** great **p**,	976
	11:28	the **p** of my concern for all the churches.	2180

PRESUME (1) [PRESUMES, PRESUMPTION, PRESUMPTUOUSLY]

Jas	3: 1	Not many of you should **p** to be teachers,	NIG

PRESUMES (1) [PRESUME]

Dt	18:20	But a prophet who **p** to speak	2326

PRESUMPTION (1) [PRESUME]

Nu	14:44	*in their* **p** they went up toward	6753

PRESUMPTUOUSLY (1)

Dt	18:22	That prophet has spoken **p**.	928+2295

PRETEND (4) [PRETENDED, PRETENDING, PRETENDS, PRETENSE, PRETENSION]

2Sa	13: 5	"Go to bed and **p** to be ill," Jonadab said.	2703
	14: 2	"**P** *you are* in mourning.	61
1Ki	14: 5	**p** to be someone else."	5796
Pr	12: 9	yet have a servant than **p** to be somebody	3877

PRETENDED (5) [PRETEND]

Ge	42: 7	but *he* **p** to be a stranger	5796
1Sa	21:13	So he **p** to be insane in their presence;	3248+9101
2Sa	13: 6	So Amnon lay down and **p** to be ill.	2703
Ps	34: 7	he **p** to be insane before Abimelech,	3248+9101
Lk	20:20	they sent spies, *who* **p** to be honest.	5693

PRETENDING (1) [PRETEND]

Ac	27:30	**p** they were going to lower some anchors	4733

PRETENDS (2) [PRETEND]

Pr	13: 7	*One man* **p** to be rich, yet has nothing;	6947
	13: 7	*another* **p** to be poor, yet has great wealth.	8133

PRETENSE (2) [PRETEND]

1Ki	14: 6	Why this **p**?	5796
Jer	3:10	but only in **p**," declares the LORD.	9214

PRETENSION (1) [PRETEND]

2Co	10: 5	and every **p** that sets itself up against	5739

PRETEXT (2)

Ac	23:15	to bring him before you **on the p of**	6055
	23:20	before the Sanhedrin tomorrow **on the p of**	6055

PREVAIL (6) [PREVAILED, PREVAILS, PREVALENT]

2Ch	14:11	*do not* **let man p** against you."	6806
Isa	54:17	no weapon forged against you *will* **p**,	7503
Jer	5:22	The waves may roll, but they cannot **p**;	3523
	20:10	then *we will* **p** over him	3523
	20:11	so my persecutors will stumble and not **p**.	3523

PREVAILED (4) [PREVAIL]

Jdg	19: 4	the girl's father, **p** upon him to stay;	928+2616
Jer	20: 7	you overpowered me and **p**.	3523
La	1:16	because the enemy *has* **p**."	1504
Lk	23:23	and their shouts **p**.	2996

PREVAILS (3) [PREVAIL]

1Sa	2: 9	"It is not by strength that one **p**;	1504
Pr	19:21	but it is the LORD's purpose *that* **p**.	7756
Hab	1: 4	the law is paralyzed, and justice never **p**.	3655

PREVALENT (1) [PREVAIL]

Jas	1:21	rid of all moral filth and the evil that is so **p**	4353

PREVENT (7) [PREVENTED]

2Sa	14:11	to **p** the avenger of blood **from**	4946
1Ki	15:17	to **p** anyone *from* leaving or entering	1194+5989
2Ch	16: 1	to **p** anyone *from* leaving or entering	1194+5989
Mal	3:11	*I will* **p** pests from devouring your crops,	1721
Jn	18:36	my servants would fight to **p** my arrest by	3590
Ac	27:42	to kill the prisoners **to p** any of them	3590
Rev	7: 1	to **p** any wind **from blowing**	3590+4463

PREVENTED (2) [PREVENT]

Ro	1:13	to come to you (but *have been* **p** from doing	3266
Heb	7:23	since death **p** them **from** continuing	3266

PREVIOUS (3) [PREVIOUSLY]

Nu	6:12	The **p** days do not count,	8037
Jdg	3: 2	not had **p** battle experience):	4200+7156
Gal	1:13	For you have heard of my **p** way of life	4537

PREVIOUSLY (6) [PREVIOUS]

1Sa	14:21	Hebrews who had **p** been with	919+3869+8997
1Ch	6:65	they allotted the **p** named towns.	AIT
Ac	21:29	(*They had* **p** seen Trophimus the Ephesian in the city	1639+4632
Ro	9:29	It is just as Isaiah *said* **p**:	4625
Gal	3:17	not set aside the covenant **p** established	4623
1Th	2: 2	*We had* **p** suffered and been insulted	4634

PREY (29) [PREYS]

Ge	15:11	**birds of p** came down on the carcasses,	6514
	49: 9	you return from the **p**, my son.	3272
	49:27	in the morning he devours the **p**,	6331
Nu	23:24	a lion that does not rest till he devours his **p**	3272
Job	4:11	The lion perishes for lack of **p**,	3272
	9:26	like eagles swooping down on their **p**.	431
	24:21	*They* **p** on the barren and childless woman,	8286
	28: 7	No **bird of p** knows that hidden path,	6514
	38:39	the **p** for the lioness and satisfy the hunger	3272
Ps	17:12	They are like a lion hungry for **p**,	3271
	22:13	Roaring lions **tearing** their **p** open their mouths wide	3271
	104:21	The lions roar for their **p** and seek their food	3272
Isa	5:29	as they seize their **p** and carry it off	3272
	10: 2	making widows their **p** and robbing	8965
	18: 6	be left to the mountain **birds of p** and to	6514
	31: 4	"As a lion growls, a great lion over his **p**—	3272
	46:11	From the east I summon a **bird of p**;	6514
	59:15	and whoever shuns evil **becomes** *a* **p**.	8964
Jer	12: 9	like a speckled **bird of p** that other birds	6514
	12: 9	that other **birds of p** surround and attack?	6514
Eze	13:21	they will no longer fall **p** to your power.	5180
	19: 3	to tear the **p** and he devoured men.	3272
	19: 6	to tear the **p** and he devoured men.	3272
	22:25	within her like a roaring lion tearing its **p**;	3272
	22:27	within her are like wolves tearing their **p**;	3272
Am	3: 4	a lion roar in the thicket when he has no **p**?	3272
Na	2:12	and strangled the **p** for his mate,	NIH
	2:12	with the kill and his dens with the **p**.	3274
	2:13	I will leave you no **p** on the earth.	3272

PREYS (1) [PREY]

Pr	6:26	and the adulteress **p** upon your very life.	7421

PRICE (31) [PRICED, PRICELESS]

Ge	23: 9	to sell it to me for the full **p** as a burial site	4084
	23:13	I will pay the **p** of the field.	4084
	23:16	for him the **p** he had named in the hearing	4084
	34:12	Make the **p** for the bride and the gift	4558
Lev	25:16	you are to increase the **p**,	5239
	25:16	you are to decrease the **p**,	5239
	25:50	The **p** *for* his release is to be based on	4084
	25:51	a larger share of the **p** paid for him.	4084
Nu	18:16	at the redemption **p set** *at* five shekels	6886
Dt	2:28	and water to drink for their **p** in silver.	NIH
1Sa	13:21	The **p** was two thirds of a shekel	NIH
	18:25	king wants no other **p for** *the* bride than	4558
2Sa	3:14	for the **p** of a hundred Philistine foreskins."	NIH
1Ch	21:22	Sell it to me at the full **p**."	4084
	21:24	"No, I insist on paying the full **p**.	4084
Job	28:15	nor can its **p** be weighed in silver.	4697
	28:18	the **p** of wisdom is beyond rubies.	5433
Pr	27:26	and the goats with the **p** of a field.	4697
Isa	45:13	but not for a **p** or reward,	4697
La	4: 2	our wood can be had only at a **p**.	4697
Da	11:39	and will distribute the land at a **p**.	4697

Am	8: 5	the measure, boosting the **p** and cheating	9203
Mic	3:11	her priests teach for a **p**,	4697
Zec	11:13	the handsome **p** at which they priced me!	3702
Mt	26: 9	a **high p** and the money given to the poor."	AIT
	27: 9	**p set on** him by the people of Israel,	5506+5507
Ac	5: 3	the **p** you and Ananias got for the land?"	NIG
	5: 8	"Yes," she said, "that is the **p**."	NIG
	22:28	"I had to pay a big **p** for my citizenship."	3049
1Co	6:20	you were bought *at* a **p**.	5507
	7:23	You were bought *at* a **p**;	5507

PRICED (1) [PRICE]

Zec	11:13	the handsome price at which they **p** me!	3700

PRICELESS (1) [PRICE]

Ps	36: 7	How **p** is your unfailing love!	3701

PRICKS (KJV) See BARBS, GOAD

PRIDE (69) [PROUD]

Lev	26:19	I will break down your stubborn **p** and	1454
2Ki	19:22	and lifted your eyes in **p**?	5294
2Ch	26:16	his **p** led to his downfall.	1467+4213
	32:26	Hezekiah repented of the **p** *of* his heart,	1470
Job	20: 6	Though his **p** reaches to the heavens	8480
	33:17	from wrongdoing and keep him from **p**,	1575
Ps	10: 4	In his **p** the wicked does not seek him;	678+1470
	31:18	with **p** and contempt they speak arrogantly	1452
	47: 4	the **p** of Jacob, whom he loved.	1454
	56: 2	many are attacking me in their **p**.	5294
	59:12	let them be caught in their **p**.	1454
	62:10	in extortion or **take p** in stolen goods;	2038
	73: 6	Therefore **p** is their necklace;	1452
Pr	8:13	I hate **p** and arrogance,	1449
	11: 2	When **p** comes, then comes disgrace,	2295
	13:10	**P** only breeds quarrels,	2295
	16:18	**P** goes before destruction,	1454
	17: 6	and parents are the **p** of their children.	9514
	21:24	he behaves with **overweening p**.	2295+6301
	29:23	A man's **p** brings him low,	1452
Ecc	7: 8	and patience is better than **p**.	1468+8120
Isa	2:11	the arrogant man will be humbled and the **p**	8124
	2:17	be brought low and the **p** *of* men humbled;	8124
	4: 2	be the **p** and glory of the survivors in Israel.	1454
	9: 9	who say with **p** and arrogance of heart,	1452
	10:12	of Assyria for the **willful p** of his heart	1542+7262
	13:11	and will humble the **p** of the ruthless.	1452
	13:19	the glory of the Babylonians' **p**,	1454
	16: 6	We have heard of Moab's **p**—	1454
	16: 6	her overweening **p** and conceit,	1447
	16: 6	her **p** and her insolence—	1454
	23: 9	to bring low the **p** of all glory and	1454
	25:11	God will bring down their **p** despite	1452
	28: 1	the **p** *of* Ephraim's drunkards,	1454
	28: 1	to that city, the **p** of those laid low by wine!	NIH
	28: 3	That wreath, the **p** of Ephraim's drunkards,	1455
	37:23	and lifted your eyes in **p**?	5294
	43:14	in the ships in which they took **p**.	8262
Jer	13: 9	I will make you the everlasting **p** and	1454
	13: 9	the same way I will ruin the **p** of Judah and	1454
	13: 9	of Judah and the great **p** of Jerusalem.	1454
	13:17	I will weep in secret because of your **p**;	1575
	48:29	"We have heard of Moab's **p**—	1454
	48:29	her overweening **p** and conceit,	1450
	48:29	her overweening **pride** and conceit, her **p**	1454
	49:16	and the **p** of your heart have deceived you,	2295
Eze	7:24	I will put an end to the **p** of the mighty,	1454
	16:56	in the day of your **p**,	1454
	24:21	the stronghold in which you take **p**,	1454
	28: 2	"In *the* **p** *of* your heart you say,	1467
	32:12	They will shatter the **p** of Egypt.	1454
Da	4:37	those who walk in **p** he is able to humble.	10136
	5:20	and hardened with **p**,	10225
	11:12	of the South *will be* **filled with p**	4222+8123
Am	6: 8	the **p** *of* Jacob and detest his fortresses;	1454
	8: 7	The LORD has sworn by the **P** of Jacob:	1454
Ob	1: 3	The **p** of your heart has deceived you,	2295
Zep	2:10	in return for their **p**,	1454
	3:11	from this city those who rejoice in their **p**.	1452
Zec	9: 6	and I will cut off the **p** of the Philistines.	1454
	10:11	Assyria's **p** will be brought down	1454
1Co	4: 6	not **take p** in one man over against another.	5881
2Co	5:12	but are giving you an opportunity to take **p**	3017
	5:12	so that you can answer those who **take p**	3016
	7: 4	I take great **p** in you.	3018
	8:24	of your love and the reason for our **p**	3018
Gal	6: 4	Then *he* can take **p** in himself,	3017
Jas	1: 9	in humble circumstances *ought to* **take p**	3016
	1:10	But the one who is rich should take **p**	NIG

PRIEST (478) [PRIEST'S, PRIESTHOOD, PRIESTLY, PRIESTS, PRIESTS']

Ge	14:18	He was **p** of God Most High,	3913
	41:45	of Potiphera, **p** *of* On, to be his wife.	3913
	41:50	by Asenath daughter of Potiphera, **p** of On.	3913
	46:20	by Asenath daughter of Potiphera, **p** of On.	3913
Ex	2:16	Now a **p** *of* Midian had seven daughters,	3913
	3: 1	Now Jethro, the **p** *of* Midian,	3913
	18: 1	**p** *of* Midian and father-in-law of Moses,	3913
	28: 3	so he *may* **serve** me **as p**.	3912
	29:30	The son who succeeds him **as p** and comes	3913
	30:33	whoever puts it on **anyone other than a p**	2424
	31:10	both the sacred garments for Aaron the **p**	3913

Ex	35:19	both the sacred garments for Aaron the **p**	3913
	38:21	the direction of Ithamar son of Aaron, the **p.**	3913
	39:41	both the sacred garments for Aaron the **p**	3913
	40:13	consecrate him so *he may* **serve** me **as p.**	3912
Lev	1: 7	The sons of Aaron the **p** are to put fire on	3913
	1: 9	and the **p** is to burn all of it on the altar.	3913
	1:12	and the **p** shall arrange them,	3913
	1:13	**p** is to bring all of it and burn it on the altar.	3913
	1:15	The **p** shall bring it to the altar,	3913
	1:17	then the **p** shall burn it on the wood that is	3913
	2: 2	The **p** shall take a handful of the fine flour	3913
	2: 8	present it to the **p,** who shall take it to	3913
	2:16	The **p** shall burn the memorial portion of	3913
	3:11	The **p** shall burn them on the altar as food,	3913
	3:16	The **p** shall burn them on the altar as food,	3913
	4: 3	" 'If the anointed **p** sins,	3913
	4: 5	Then the anointed **p** shall take some of	3913
	4: 7	The **p** shall then put some of the blood on	3913
	4:10	Then the **p** shall burn them on the altar	3913
	4:16	Then the anointed **p** is to take some of	3913
	4:20	In this way the **p** will make atonement	3913
	4:25	Then the **p** shall take some of the blood of	3913
	4:26	In this way the **p** will make atonement for	3913
	4:30	Then the **p** is to take some of the blood	3913
	4:31	and the **p** shall burn it on the altar as	3913
	4:31	In this way the **p** will make atonement	3913
	4:34	Then the **p** shall take some of the blood of	3913
	4:35	and the **p** shall burn it on the altar on top of	3913
	4:35	In this way the **p** will make atonement	3913
	5: 6	**p** shall make atonement for him for his sin.	3913
	5: 8	He is to bring them to the **p,**	3913
	5:10	The **p** shall then offer the other as	3913
	5:12	He is to bring it to the **p,**	3913
	5:13	the **p** will make atonement for him for any	3913
	5:13	of the offering will belong to the **p,**	3913
	5:16	of the value to that and give it all to the **p,**	3913
	5:18	to bring to the **p** as a guilt offering a ram	3913
	5:18	In this way the **p** will make atonement	3913
	6: 6	And as a penalty he must bring to the **p,**	3913
	6: 7	the **p** will make atonement for him before	3913
	6:10	The **p** shall then put on his linen clothes,	3913
	6:12	Every morning the **p** is to add firewood	3913
	6:15	The **p** is to take a handful of fine flour	NIH
	6:22	as anointed **p** shall prepare it.	3913
	6:23	of a **p** shall be burned completely;	3913
	6:26	The **p** who offers it shall eat it;	3913
	7: 5	The **p** shall burn them on the altar as	3913
	7: 7	They belong to the **p** who makes atonement	3913
	7: 8	The **p** who offers a burnt offering	3913
	7: 9	on a griddle belongs to the **p** who offers it,	3913
	7:14	it belongs to the **p** who sprinkles the blood	3913
	7:31	The **p** shall burn the fat on the altar,	3913
	7:32	of your fellowship offerings to the **p** as	3913
	7:34	the **p** and his sons as their regular share	3913
	12: 6	the **p** at the entrance to the Tent of Meeting	3913
	12: 8	In this way the **p** will make atonement	3913
	13: 2	he must be brought to Aaron the **p** or to one	3913
	13: 2	the priest or to one of his sons who is a **p.**	3913
	13: 3	The **p** is to examine the sore on his skin,	3913
	13: 3	When the **p** examines him,	3913
	13: 4	the **p** is to put the infected person	3913
	13: 5	the seventh day the **p** is to examine him,	3913
	13: 6	the **p** is to examine him again, and if	3913
	13: 6	the **p** shall pronounce him clean;	3913
	13: 7	after he has shown himself to the **p** to	3913
	13: 7	he must appear before the **p** again.	3913
	13: 8	The **p** is to examine him,	3913
	13: 9	he must be brought to the **p.**	3913
	13:10	The **p** is to examine him,	3913
	13:11	and the **p** shall pronounce him unclean.	3913
	13:12	so far as the **p** can see,	3913
	13:13	the **p** is to examine him,	3913
	13:15	When the **p** sees the raw flesh,	3913
	13:16	he must go to the **p.**	3913
	13:17	The **p** is to examine him,	3913
	13:17	the **p** shall pronounce the infected person	3913
	13:19	he must present himself to the **p.**	3913
	13:20	The **p** is to examine it,	3913
	13:20	the **p** shall pronounce him unclean.	3913
	13:21	But if, when the **p** examines it,	3913
	13:21	**p** is to put him in isolation for seven days.	3913
	13:22	the **p** shall pronounce him unclean;	3913
	13:23	and the **p** shall pronounce him clean.	3913
	13:25	the **p** is to examine the spot,	3913
	13:25	The **p** shall pronounce him unclean;	3913
	13:26	the **p** examines it and there is no white hair	3913
	13:26	**p** is to put him in isolation for seven days.	3913
	13:27	the seventh day the **p** is to examine him,	3913
	13:27	the **p** shall pronounce him unclean;	3913
	13:28	and the **p** shall pronounce him clean;	3913
	13:30	the **p** is to examine the sore, and	3913
	13:30	the **p** shall pronounce that person unclean;	3913
	13:31	if, when the **p** examines this kind of sore,	3913
	13:31	then the **p** is to put the infected person	3913
	13:32	On the seventh day the **p** is to examine	3913
	13:33	and the **p** is to keep him in isolation	3913
	13:34	the seventh day the **p** is to examine the itch,	3913
	13:34	the **p** shall pronounce him clean.	3913
	13:36	the **p** is to examine him, and if	3913
	13:36	the **p** does not need to look for yellow hair;	3913
	13:37	and the **p** shall pronounce him clean.	3913
	13:39	the **p** is to examine them, and if	3913
	13:43	The **p** is to examine him,	3913
	13:44	The **p** shall pronounce him unclean because	3913
	13:49	and must be shown to the **p.**	3913
	13:50	The **p** is to examine the mildew and isolate	3913
	13:53	"But if, when the **p** examines it,	3913

Lev	13:55	the **p** is to examine it,	3913
	13:56	If, when the **p** examines it,	3913
	14: 2	when he is brought to the **p:**	3913
	14: 3	The **p** is to go outside the camp	3913
	14: 4	the **p** shall order that two live clean birds	3913
	14: 5	Then the **p** shall order that one of the birds	3913
	14:11	**p** who pronounces him clean shall present	3913
	14:12	the **p** is to take one of the male lambs	3913
	14:13	the guilt offering belongs to the **p;**	3913
	14:14	The **p** is to take some of the blood of	3913
	14:15	The **p** shall then take some of the log of oil,	3913
	14:17	The **p** is to put some of the oil remaining	3913
	14:18	in his palm the **p** shall put on the head of	3913
	14:19	"Then the **p** is to sacrifice the sin offering	3913
	14:19	the **p** shall slaughter the burnt offering	NIH
	14:23	the **p** at the entrance to the Tent of Meeting,	3913
	14:24	The **p** is to take the lamb for	3913
	14:26	The **p** is to pour some of the oil into	3913
	14:29	in his palm the **p** shall put on the head of	3913
	14:31	In this way the **p** will make atonement	3913
	14:35	of the house must go and tell the **p,**	3913
	14:36	The **p** is to order the house to be emptied	3913
	14:36	the **p** is to go in and inspect the house.	3913
	14:38	the **p** shall go out the doorway of the house	3913
	14:39	the seventh day the **p** shall return to inspect	3913
	14:44	the **p** is to go and examine it and, if	3913
	14:48	"But if the **p** comes to examine it and	3913
	15:14	the Tent of Meeting and give them to the **p.**	3913
	15:15	The **p** is to sacrifice them,	3913
	15:29	the **p** at the entrance to the Tent of Meeting.	3913
	15:30	The **p** is to sacrifice one for a sin offering	3913
	16:32	The **p** who is anointed and ordained	3913
	16:32	to succeed his father as **high p** is	3912
	17: 5	They must bring them to the **p,** that is,	3913
	17: 6	The **p** is to sprinkle the blood against	3913
	19:22	the **p** is to make atonement for him before	3913
	21: 1	**p** must not make himself ceremonially unclean for any of his people	NIH
	21:10	" 'The high **p,** the one among his brothers	3913
	21:21	the **p** who has any defect is to come near	3913
	22:10	the guest of a **p** or his hired worker eat it.	3913
	22:11	But if a **p** buys a slave with money,	3913
	22:12	daughter marries **anyone other than a p,**	2424
	22:14	to the **p** for the offering and add a fifth of	3913
	23:10	the **p** a sheaf of the first grain you harvest.	3913
	23:11	**p** is to wave it on the day after the Sabbath.	3913
	23:20	The **p** is to wave the two lambs before	3913
	23:20	a sacred offering to the LORD for the **p.**	3913
	27: 8	he is to present the person to the **p,**	3913
	27:11	the animal must be presented to the **p,**	3913
	27:12	Whatever value the **p** then sets,	3913
	27:14	the **p** will judge its quality as good or bad.	3913
	27:14	Whatever value the **p** then sets,	3913
	27:18	the **p** will determine the value according to	3913
	27:23	the **p** will determine its value up to	3913
Nu	3: 6	of Levi and present them to Aaron the **p**	3913
	3:32	Levites was Eleazar son of Aaron, the **p.**	3913
	4:16	"Eleazar son of Aaron, the **p,**	3913
	4:28	of Ithamar son of Aaron, the **p,**	3913
	4:33	of Ithamar son of Aaron, the **p."**	3913
	5: 8	to the LORD and must be given to the **p,**	3913
	5: 9	the Israelites brings to the **p** will belong	3913
	5:10	but what he gives to the **p** will belong to	3913
	5:10	to the priest will belong to the **p.'** "	2257S
	5:15	then he is to take his wife to the **p.**	3913
	5:16	" 'The **p** shall bring her and have her stand	3913
	5:18	After the **p** has had the woman stand before	3913
	5:19	Then the **p** shall put the woman under oath	3913
	5:21	the **p** is to put the woman under this curse	3913
	5:23	" 'The **p** is to write these curses on a scroll	3913
	5:25	The **p** is to take from her hands	3913
	5:26	The **p** is then to take a handful of	3913
	5:30	The **p** is to have her stand before	3913
	6:10	the **p** at the entrance to the Tent of Meeting.	3913
	6:11	The **p** is to offer one as a sin offering and	3913
	6:16	" 'The **p** is to present them before	3913
	6:19	the **p** is to place in his hands	3913
	6:20	The **p** shall then wave them before	3913
	6:20	they are holy and belong to the **p,**	3913
	7: 8	of Ithamar son of Aaron, the **p.**	3913
	15:25	The **p** is to make atonement for	3913
	15:28	The **p** is to make atonement before	3913
	16:37	the **p,** to take the censers out of	3913
	16:39	the **p** collected the bronze censers brought	3913
	18:28	the LORD's portion to Aaron the **p.**	3913
	19: 3	Give it to Eleazar the **p;**	3913
	19: 4	Then Eleazar the **p** is to take some	3913
	19: 6	The **p** is to take some cedar wood,	3913
	19: 7	the **p** must wash his clothes	3913
	25: 7	the **p,** saw this, he left the assembly,	3913
	25:11	son of Eliezer, the son of Aaron, the **p,**	3913
	26: 1	to Moses and Eleazar son of Aaron, the **p,**	3913
	26: 3	Moses and Eleazar the **p** spoke with them	3913
	26:63	the **p** when they counted the Israelites on	3913
	26:64	the **p** when they counted the Israelites in	3913
	27: 2	the **p,** the leaders and the whole assembly,	3913
	27:19	Have him stand before Eleazar the **p** and	3913
	27:21	He is to stand before Eleazar the **p,**	3913
	27:22	and had him stand before Eleazar the **p** and	3913
	31: 6	along with Phinehas son of Eleazar, the **p,**	3913
	31:12	and Eleazar the **p** and the Israelite assembly	3913
	31:13	Eleazar the **p** and all the leaders of	3913
	31:21	the **p** said to the soldiers who had gone	3913
	31:26	and Eleazar the **p** and the family heads of	3913
	31:29	to Eleazar the **p** as the LORD's part.	3913
	31:31	So Moses and Eleazar the **p** did as	3913
	31:41	Moses gave the tribute to Eleazar the **p** as	3913

Nu	31:51	and Eleazar the **p** accepted from them	3913
	31:54	Moses and Eleazar the **p** accepted the gold	3913
	32: 2	the **p** and to the leaders of the community,	3913
	32:28	to Eleazar the **p** and Joshua son of Nun and	3913
	33:38	the LORD's command Aaron the **p** went	3913
	34:17	Eleazar the **p** and Joshua son of Nun.	3913
	35:25	until the death of the high **p,**	3913
	35:28	of refuge until the death of the high **p;**	3913
	35:28	after the death of the high **p** may he return	3913
	35:32	before the death of the high **p.**	3913
Dt	10: 6	and Eleazar his son succeeded him *as* **p.**	3912
	17:12	or for the **p** who stands ministering there to	3913
	20: 2	the **p** shall come forward and address	3913
	26: 3	and say to the **p** in office at the time,	3913
	26: 4	The **p** shall take the basket from your hands	3913
Jos	14: 1	which Eleazar the **p,** Joshua son of Nun	3913
	17: 4	They went to Eleazar the **p,**	3913
	19:51	These are the territories that Eleazar the **p,**	3913
	20: 6	until the death of the high **p** who is serving	3913
	21: 1	of the Levites approached Eleazar the **p,**	3913
	21: 4	of Aaron the **p** were allotted thirteen towns	3913
	21:13	the **p** they gave Hebron (a city of refuge	3913
	22:13	the **p,** to the land of Gilead—	3913
	22:30	the **p** and the leaders of the community—	3913
	22:31	And Phinehas son of Eleazar, the **p,**	3913
	22:32	Then Phinehas son of Eleazar, the **p,**	3913
Jdg	17: 5	and installed one of his sons as his **p.**	3913
	17:10	"Live with me and be my father and **p,**	3913
	17:12	and the young man became his **p** and lived	3913
	17:13	since this Levite has become my **p."**	3913
	18: 4	and said, "He has hired me and I am his **p."**	3913
	18: 6	The **p** answered them, "Go in peace.	3913
	18:17	the **p** and the six hundred armed men stood	3913
	18:18	the **p** said to them, "What are you doing?"	3913
	18:19	Come with us, and be our father and **p.**	3913
	18:19	as **p** rather than just one man's household?"	3913
	18:20	Then the **p** was glad.	3913
	18:24	"You took the gods I made, and my **p,**	3913
	18:27	they took what Micah had made, and his **p,**	3913
1Sa	1: 9	the **p** was sitting on a chair by the doorpost	3913
	2:11	before the LORD under Eli the **p.**	3913
	2:13	the servant of the **p** would come with	3913
	2:14	and the **p** would take for himself whatever	3913
	2:15	the servant of the **p** would come and say to	3913
	2:15	"Give the **p** some meat to roast;	3913
	2:28	of all the tribes of Israel to be my **p,**	3913
	2:35	I will raise up for myself a faithful **p,**	3913
	14: 3	the son of Eli, the LORD's **p** in Shiloh.	3913
	14:19	While Saul was talking to the **p,**	3913
	14:19	So Saul said to the **p,**	3913
	14:36	the **p** said, "Let us inquire of God here."	3913
	21: 1	David went to Nob, to Ahimelech the **p.**	3913
	21: 2	David answered Ahimelech the **p,**	3913
	21: 4	But the **p** answered David,	3913
	21: 6	So the **p** gave him the consecrated bread,	3913
	21: 9	The **p** replied, "The sword of Goliath	3913
	22:11	Then the king sent for the **p** Ahimelech son	3913
	23: 9	he said to Abiathar the **p,**	3913
	30: 7	Then David said to Abiathar the **p,**	3913
2Sa	15:27	The king also said to Zadok the **p,**	3913
	20:26	and Ira the Jairite was David's **p.**	3913
1Ki	1: 7	of Zeruiah and with Abiathar the **p,**	3913
	1: 8	But Zadok the **p,** Benaiah son of Jehoiada,	3913
	1:19	the **p** and Joab the commander of the army,	3913
	1:25	of the army and Abiathar the **p.**	3913
	1:26	But me your servant, and Zadok the **p,**	3913
	1:32	King David said, "Call in Zadok the **p,**	3913
	1:34	There have Zadok the **p** and Nathan	3913
	1:38	So Zadok the **p,** Nathan the prophet,	3913
	1:39	Zadok the **p** took the horn of oil from	3913
	1:42	Jonathan son of Abiathar the **p** arrived.	3913
	1:44	The king has sent with him Zadok the **p,**	3913
	1:45	and Zadok the **p** and Nathan	3913
	2:22	for him and for Abiathar the **p** and Joab son	3913
	2:26	To Abiathar the **p** the king said,	3913
	2:35	and replaced Abiathar with Zadok the **p.**	3913
	4: 2	Azariah son of Zadok—the **p;**	3913
	4: 5	a **p** and personal adviser to the king;	3913
	13:33	a **p** he consecrated *for* the high places.	3913
2Ki	11: 9	as Jehoiada the **p** ordered.	3913
	11: 9	and came to Jehoiada the **p.**	3913
	11:15	the **p** ordered the commanders of units of	3913
	11:15	For the **p** had said,	3913
	11:18	and idols to pieces and killed Mattan the **p**	3913
	11:18	Then Jehoiada the **p** posted guards at	3913
	12: 2	the years Jehoiada the **p** instructed him.	3913
	12: 5	Let every **p** receive the money from one of	3913
	12: 7	the **p** and the other priests and asked them,	3913
	12: 9	Jehoiada the **p** took a chest and bored	3913
	12:10	the royal secretary and the high **p** came,	3913
	16:10	and sent to Uriah the **p** a sketch of the altar,	3913
	16:11	So Uriah the **p** built an altar in accordance	3913
	16:15	then gave these orders to Uriah the **p:**	3913
	16:16	the **p** did just as King Ahaz had ordered.	3913
	22: 4	the high **p** and have him get ready	3913
	22: 8	the high **p** said to Shaphan the secretary,	3913
	22:10	"Hilkiah the **p** has given me a book."	3913
	22:12	He gave these orders to Hilkiah the **p,**	3913
	22:14	Hilkiah the **p,** Ahikam, Acbor,	3913
	23: 4	The king ordered Hilkiah the high **p,**	3913
	23:24	the book that Hilkiah the **p** had discovered	3913
	25:18	as prisoners Seraiah the chief **p,**	3913
	25:18	Zephaniah the **p** next in rank and	3913
1Ch	6:10	of Azariah (it was he who **served as p** in	3912
	16:39	the **p** and his fellow priests before	3913
	24: 6	Zadok the **p,** Ahimelech son of Abiathar	3913
	27: 5	was Benaiah son of Jehoiada the **p.**	3913

1Ch	29:22	the LORD to be ruler and Zadok to be **p.**	3913
2Ch	13: 9	and seven rams may become a **p**	3913
	15: 3	without a **p** to teach and without the law.	3913
	19:11	the chief **p** will be over you in any matter	3913
	22:11	and wife of the **p** Jehoiada,	3913
	23: 8	of Judah did just as Jehoiada the **p** ordered.	3913
	23: 8	"he had not released any of the divisions.	3913
	23:14	the **p** sent out the commanders of units of	3913
	23:14	For the **p** had said,	3913
	23:17	the altars and idols and killed Mattan the **p**	3913
	24: 2	the LORD all the years of Jehoiada the **p.**	3913
	24: 6	the king summoned Jehoiada the chief **p**	NIH
	24:11	and the officer of the chief **p** would come	3913
	24:20	upon Zechariah son of Jehoiada the **p.**	3913
	24:25	for murdering the son of Jehoiada the **p,**	3913
	26:17	the **p** with eighty other courageous priests	3913
	26:20	the chief **p** and all the other priests looked	3913
	31:10	and Azariah the chief **p,**	3913
	34: 9	the high **p** and gave him the money	3913
	34:14	Hilkiah the **p** found the Book of the Law of	3913
	34:18	"Hilkiah the **p** has given me a book."	3913
Ezr	2:63	until there was a **p** ministering with	3913
	7: 5	the son of Aaron the chief **p**—	3913
	7:11	the **p** and teacher, a man learned in matters	3913
	7:12	king of kings, To Ezra the **p,**	10347
	7:21	the **p,** a teacher of the Law of the God	10347
	8:33	the hands of Meremoth son of Uriah, the **p.**	3913
	10:10	Then Ezra the **p** stood up and said to them,	3913
	10:16	the **p** selected men who were family heads,	3913
Ne	3: 1	the high **p** and his fellow priests went	3913
	3:20	of the house of Eliashib the high **p.**	3913
	7:65	until there should be a **p** ministering with	3913
	8: 2	the **p** brought the Law before the assembly,	3913
	8: 9	Ezra the **p** and scribe,	3913
	10:38	A **p** descended from Aaron is	3913
	12:26	the governor and of Ezra the **p** and scribe.	3913
	13: 4	Eliashib the **p** had been put in charge of	3913
	13:13	I put Shelemiah the **p,** Zadok the scribe,	3913
	13:28	the high **p** was son-in-law to Sanballat	3913
Ps	110: 4	"You are a **p** forever, in the order of	
		Melchizedek."	3913
Isa	8: 2	the **p** and Zechariah son of Jeberekiah	3913
	24: 2	it will be the same for **p** as for people,	3913
	61:10	as a bridegroom adorns his head *like a* **p,**	3912
Jer	14:18	and **p** have gone to a land they know not.' "	3913
	18:18	for the teaching of the law by the **p** will not	3913
	20: 1	When the **p** Pashhur son of Immer,	3913
	21: 1	and the **p** Zephaniah son of Maaseiah.	3913
	23:11	"Both prophet and **p** are godless;	3913
	23:33	"When these people, or a prophet or a **p,**	3913
	23:34	If a prophet or a **p** or anyone else claims,	3913
	29:25	to Zephaniah son of Maaseiah the **p,**	3913
	29:26	'The LORD has appointed you **p** in place	3913
	29:29	Zephaniah the **p,** however,	3913
	37: 3	of Shelemiah with the **p** Zephaniah son	3913
	52:24	as prisoners Seraiah the chief **p,**	3913
	52:24	the **p** next in rank and	3913
La	2: 6	both king and **p.**	3913
	2:20	Should **p** and prophet be killed in	3913
Eze	1: 3	word of the LORD came to Ezekiel the **p,**	3913
	7:26	the teaching of the law by the **p** will be lost,	3913
	44:21	no **p** is to drink wine when he enters	3913
	44:25	" 'A **p** must not defile himself by going	NIH
	45:19	The **p** is to take some of the blood of	3913
Hos	4: 4	like those who bring charges against a **p.**	3913
Am	7:10	Then Amaziah the **p** *of* Bethel sent	3913
Hag	1: 1	and to Joshua son of Jehozadak, the high **p:**	3913
	1:12	Joshua son of Jehozadak, the high **p,**	3913
	1:14	of Joshua son of Jehozadak, the high **p,**	3913
	2: 2	to Joshua son of Jehozadak, the high **p,**	3913
	2: 4	O Joshua son of Jehozadak, the high **p**	3913
Zec	3: 1	the high **p** standing before the angel of	3913
	3: 8	O high **p** Joshua and your associates seated	3913
	6:11	and set it on the head of the high **p,**	3913
	6:13	And he will be a **p** on his throne.	3913
Mal	2: 7	the lips of a **p** ought to preserve knowledge,	3913
Mt	8: 4	the **p** and offer the gift Moses commanded,	2636
	26: 3	in the palace *of* the high **p,**	797
	26:51	and struck the servant *of* the high **p,**	797
	26:57	the high **p,** where the teachers of the law	797
	26:58	right up to the courtyard of the high **p.**	797
	26:62	Then the high **p** stood up and said to Jesus,	797
	26:63	The high **p** said to him,	797
	26:65	Then the high **p** tore his clothes and said,	797
Mk	1:44	show yourself *to* the **p** and offer	2636
	2:26	In the days of Abiathar the high **p,**	797
	14:47	and struck the servant *of* the high **p,**	797
	14:53	They took Jesus to the high **p,**	797
	14:54	right into the courtyard *of* the high **p.**	797
	14:60	Then the high **p** stood up before them	797
	14:61	Again the high **p** asked him,	797
	14:63	The high **p** tore his clothes.	797
	14:66	of the servant girls *of* the high **p** came by.	797
Lk	1: 5	of Judea there was a **p** named Zechariah,	2636
	1: 8	and he *was* **serving as p** before God,	2634
	5:14	show yourself *to* the **p** and offer	2636
	10:31	A **p** happened to be going down	2636
	22:50	one of them struck the servant *of* the high **p,**	797
	22:54	and took him into the house *of* the high **p.**	797
Jn	11:49	named Caiaphas, who was high **p** that year,	797
	11:51	but as high **p** that year he prophesied	797
	18:13	Caiaphas, the high **p** that year.	797
	18:15	this disciple was known *to* the high **p,**	797
	18:16	who was known *to* the high **p,** came back,	797
	18:19	the high **p** questioned Jesus	797
	18:22	"Is this the way you answer the high **p?**"	797
	18:24	still bound, to Caiaphas the high **p.**	797

Ac	4: 6	Annas the **high p** was there,	797
	5:17	Then the **high p** and all his associates,	797
	5:21	When the **high p** and his associates arrived,	797
	5:27	to be questioned by the **high p.**	797
	7: 1	**high p** asked him, "Are these charges true?"	797
	9: 1	He went to the **high p**	797
	14:13	The **p** of Zeus, whose temple was	2636
	19:14	Seven sons of Sceva, a Jewish **chief p,**	797
	22: 5	the **high p** and all the Council can testify.	797
	23: 2	the **high p** Ananias ordered those standing	797
	23: 4	"You dare to insult God's **high p?**"	797
	23: 5	I did not realize that he was the **high p;**	797
	24: 1	the **high p** Ananias went down to Caesarea	797
Heb	2:17	a merciful and faithful **high p** in service	797
	3: 1	the apostle and **high p** whom we confess,	797
	4:14	since we have a great **high p** who has gone	797
	4:15	For we do not have a **high p** who is unable	797
	5: 1	Every **high p** is selected from among men	797
	5: 5	the glory of becoming a **high p.**	797
	5: 6	"You are a **p** forever, in the order of	
		Melchizedek."	2636
	5:10	and was designated by God to be **high p** in	797
	6:20	He has become a **high p** forever,	797
	7: 1	This Melchizedek was king of Salem and **p**	2636
	7: 3	like the Son of God he remains a **p** forever.	2636
	7:11	why was there still need for another **p**	2636
	7:15	if another **p** like Melchizedek appears,	2636
	7:16	one who has become a **p** not on the basis of	NIG
	7:17	For it is declared: "You are a **p** forever, in	
		the order of Melchizedek."	2636
	7:21	a **p** with an oath when God said to him:	NIG
	7:21	'You are a **p** forever.' "	2636
	7:26	Such a **high p** meets our need—	797
	8: 1	We do have such a **high p,**	797
	8: 3	Every **high p** is appointed to offer both gifts	797
	8: 4	If he were on earth, he would not be a **p,**	2636
	9: 7	But only the **high p** entered the inner room,	797
	9:11	When Christ came as **high p** of the good	797
	9:25	the **high p** enters the Most Holy Place	797
	10:11	Day after day every **p** stands	2636
	10:12	But when this **p** had offered for all time	NIG
	10:21	we have a great **p** over the house of God,	2636
	13:11	The **high p** carries the blood of animals into	797

PRIEST'S (10) [PRIEST]

Lev	6:29	Any male in a **p** family may eat it;	3913
	7: 6	Any male in a **p** family may eat it,	3913
	21: 9	a **p** daughter defiles herself by becoming	3913
	22:10	" 'No one **outside a p family** may eat	2424
	22:12	If a **p** daughter marries anyone other than	3913
	22:13	But if a **p** daughter becomes a widow	3913
Jn	18:10	drew it and struck the **high p** servant,	797
	18:15	he went with Jesus into the **high p** courtyard,	797
	18:26	One of the **high p** servants,	797
Ac	4: 6	and the other men of the **high p** family.	796

PRIESTHOOD (17) [PRIEST]

Ex	29: 9	The **p** is theirs by a lasting ordinance.	3914
	40:15	to a **p** that will continue for all generations	3914
Nu	16:10	but now you are trying to get the **p** too.	3914
	18: 1	the responsibility for offenses against the **p.**	3914
	18: 7	I am giving you the service of the **p** as	3914
	25:13	a covenant of a lasting **p,**	3914
1Ki	2:27	So Solomon removed Abiathar from the **p**	3913
Ezr	2:62	so were excluded from the **p** as unclean.	3914
Ne	7:64	so were excluded from the **p** as unclean.	3914
	13:29	the priestly office and the covenant of the **p**	3914
Lk	1: 9	according to the custom *of* the **p,**	2632
	3: 2	during the **high p** of Annas and Caiaphas,	797
Heb	7:11	through the Levitical **p** (for on the basis	2648
	7:12	For when there is a change of the **p,**	2648
	7:24	he has a permanent **p.**	2648
1Pe	2: 5	into a spiritual house to be a holy **p,**	2633
	2: 9	But you are a chosen people, a royal **p,**	2633

PRIESTLY (8) [PRIEST]

Lev	21:10	to wear the **p** garments,	NIH
Jos	18: 7	**p** service *of* the LORD is their inheritance.	3914
1Sa	2:36	to some **p** office so I can have food	3914
Ezr	2:69	5,000 minas of silver and 100 **p** garments.	3913
Ne	12:12	these were the heads of the **p** families:	3913
	12:12	because they defiled the **p** office and	3913
Lk	1: 5	who belonged to the **p** division of Abijah;	2389
Ro	15:16	the Gentiles *with* the **p** duty of proclaiming	2646

PRIESTS (422) [PRIEST]

Ge	47:22	However, he did not buy the land of the **p,**	3913
	47:26	of the **p** that did not become Pharaoh's.'	3913
Ex	19: 6	for me a kingdom of **p** and a holy nation.'	3913
	19:22	Even the **p,** who approach the LORD,	3913
	19:24	But the **p** and the people must	3913
	28: 1	so they *may* **serve me as p.**	3912
	28: 4	so they *may* **serve me as p.**	3912
	28:41	Consecrate them so *they may* **serve me as p.**	3912
	29: 1	so *they may* **serve me as p:**	3912
	29:44	and his sons to **serve me as p.**	3912
	30:30	so they *may* **serve me as p.**	3912
	31:10	for his sons when *they* **serve as p,**	3912
	35:19	for his sons when *they* **serve as p.**"	3912
	39:41	for his sons when **serving as p.**	3912
	40:15	so *they may* **serve me as p.**	3912
Lev	1: 5	the **p** shall bring the blood and sprinkle it	3913
	1: 8	Aaron's sons the **p** shall arrange the pieces,	3913
	1:11	the **p** shall sprinkle its blood against	3913

Lev	2: 2	and take it to Aaron's sons the **p.**	3913
	3: 2	Then Aaron's sons the **p** shall sprinkle	3913
	7:35	presented to **serve** the LORD **as p.**	3912
	16:33	the **p** and all the people of the community.	3913
	21: 1	"Speak to the **p,** the sons of Aaron,	3913
	21: 5	" 'P must not shave their heads	NIH
	21: 7	because **p** are holy to their God.	2085
	22: 9	" 'The **p** are to keep my requirements so	NIH
	22:15	The **p** must not desecrate	NIH
	27:21	it will become the property of the **p.**	3913
Nu	3: 3	the anointed **p,** who were ordained to serve	3913
	3: 3	who were ordained to **serve as p.**	3912
	3: 4	and Ithamar **served as p** during the lifetime	3912
	3:10	Appoint Aaron and his sons to serve as **p;**	3914
	10: 8	"The sons of Aaron, the **p,**	3913
	18: 7	and your sons may serve as **p** in connection	3914
Dt	17: 9	Go to the **p,** who are Levites,	3913
	17:18	taken from that of the **p,** who are Levites.	3913
	18: 1	The **p,** who are Levites—	3913
	18: 3	the **p** from the people who sacrifice a bull	3913
	19:17	in the presence of the LORD before the **p**	3913
	21: 5	The **p,** the sons of Levi, shall step forward,	3913
	24: 8	be very careful to do exactly as the **p,**	3913
	27: 9	Then Moses and the **p,** who are Levites,	3913
	31: 9	down this law and gave it to the **p,**	3913
Jos	3: 3	and the **p,** who are Levites, carrying it,	3913
	3: 6	Joshua said to the **p,**	3913
	3: 8	the **p** who carry the ark of the covenant:	3913
	3:13	as the **p** who carry the ark of the LORD—	3913
	3:14	the **p** carrying the ark of the covenant went	3913
	3:15	as the **p** who carried the ark reached	3913
	3:17	The **p** who carried the ark of the covenant	3913
	4: 3	the Jordan from right where the **p** stood and	3913
	4: 9	the spot where the **p** who carried the ark of	3913
	4:10	Now the **p** who carried the ark	3913
	4:11	the LORD and the **p** came to the other side	3913
	4:16	the **p** carrying the ark of the Testimony	3913
	4:17	So Joshua commanded the **p,**	3913
	4:18	And the **p** came up out of the river carrying	3913
	6: 4	Have seven **p** carry trumpets of rams' horns	3913
	6: 4	with the **p** blowing the trumpets.	3913
	6: 6	So Joshua son of Nun called the **p** and said	3913
	6: 6	and have seven **p** carry trumpets in front	3913
	6: 8	the seven **p** carrying the seven trumpets	3913
	6: 9	ahead of the **p** who blew the trumpets,	3913
	6:12	up early the next morning and the **p** took up	3913
	6:13	The seven **p** carrying the seven trumpets	3913
	6:16	when the **p** sounded the trumpet blast,	3913
	8:33	the **p,** who were Levites.	3913
	21:19	All the towns for the **p,**	3913
Jdg	18:30	and his sons were **p** for the tribe of Dan	3913
1Sa	1: 3	the two sons of Eli, were **p** of the LORD.	3913
	2:13	Now it was the practice of the **p** with	3913
	5: 5	That is why to this day neither the **p**	3913
	6: 2	for the **p** and the diviners and said,	3913
	22:11	who were the **p** at Nob,	3913
	22:17	"Turn and kill the **p** of the LORD,	3913
	22:17	not willing to raise a hand to strike the **p** *of*	3913
	22:18	"You turn and strike down the **p.**"	3913
	22:19	the town of the **p,** with its men and women,	3913
	22:21	He told David that Saul had killed the **p** *of*	3913
2Sa	8:17	and Ahimelech son of Abiathar were **p;**	3913
	15:35	Won't the **p** Zadok and Abiathar be there	3913
	17:15	Hushai told Zadok and Abiathar, the **p,**	3913
	19:11	to Zadok and Abiathar, the **p:**	3913
	20:25	Zadok and Abiathar were **p;**	3913
1Ki	4: 4	Zadok and Abiathar—**p;**	3913
	8: 3	the **p** took up the ark,	3913
	8: 4	The **p** and Levites carried them up,	3913
	8: 6	The **p** then brought the ark of	3913
	8:10	When the **p** withdrew from the Holy Place,	3913
	8:11	And the **p** could not perform their service	3913
	12:31	and appointed **p** from all sorts of people,	3085
	12:32	And at Bethel he also installed **p** *at*	3913
	13: 2	On you he will sacrifice the **p** of the high	3913
	13:33	once more appointed **p** *for* the high places	3913
2Ki	10:11	his close friends and his **p,**	3913
	10:19	all his ministers and all his **p.**	3913
	12: 4	Joash said to the **p,**	3913
	12: 6	of King Joash the **p** still had not repaired	3913
	12: 7	the priest and the other **p** and asked them,	3913
	12: 8	The **p** agreed that they would	3913
	12: 9	The **p** who guarded the entrance put into	3913
	12:16	it belonged to the **p.**	3913
	17:27	"Have one of the **p** you took captive	3913
	17:28	So one of the **p** who had been exiled	3913
	17:32	to officiate for them as **p** in the shrines at	3913
	19: 2	Shebna the secretary and the leading **p,**	3913
	23: 2	the **p** and the prophets—	3913
	23: 4	the **p** next in rank and the doorkeepers	3913
	23: 5	He did away with the **pagan p** appointed by	4024
	23: 8	Josiah brought all the **p** from the towns	3913
	23: 8	where the **p** had burned incense.	3913
	23: 9	the **p** of the high places did not serve at	3913
	23: 9	with their fellow **p.**	NIH
	23:20	the **p** of those high places on the altars	3913
1Ch	9:10	Of the **p:** Jedaiah; Jehoiarib; Jakin;	3913
	9:13	The **p,** who were heads of families,	278+2157
	9:30	of the **p** took care of mixing the spices.	3913
	13: 2	also to the **p** and Levites who are with them	3913
	15:11	Zadok and Abiathar the **p,**	3913
	15:14	the **p** and Levites consecrated themselves	3913
	15:24	the **p** were to blow trumpets before the ark	3913
	16: 6	the **p** were to blow the trumpets regularly	3913
	16:39	David left Zadok the priest and his fellow **p**	3913
	18:16	and Ahimelech son of Abiathar were **p;**	3913

1Ch 23: 2	as well as the **p** and Levites.	3913
24: 2	so Eleazar and Ithamar **served as** *the* **p.**	3913
24: 6	and the heads of families of the **p** and of	3913
24:31	and the heads of families of the **p** and of	3913
28:13	for the divisions of the **p** and Levites,	3913
28:21	The divisions of the **p** and Levites are ready	3913
2Ch 4: 6	but the Sea was to be used by the **p**	3913
4: 9	He made the courtyard of the **p,**	3913
5: 5	The **p,** who were Levites, carried them up;	3913
5: 7	The **p** then brought the ark of	3913
5:11	The **p** then withdrew from the Holy Place.	3913
5:11	All the **p** who were there had consecrated themselves,	3913
5:12	by 120 **p** sounding trumpets.	3913
5:14	and the **p** could not perform their service	3913
6:41	May your **p,** O LORD God,	3913
7: 2	The **p** could not enter the temple of	3913
7: 6	The **p** took their positions,	3913
7: 6	the **p** blew their trumpets,	3913
8:14	the divisions of the **p** for their duties,	3913
8:14	the **p** according to each day's requirement.	3913
8:15	from the king's commands to the **p** or to	3913
11:13	The **p** and Levites from all their districts	3913
11:14	and his sons had rejected them as **p** of	3912
11:15	And he appointed his own **p** for	3913
13: 9	But didn't you drive out the **p** *of*	3913
13: 9	and make **p** of your own as the peoples	3913
13:10	The **p** who serve the LORD are sons	3913
13:12	His **p** with their trumpets will sound	3913
13:14	The **p** blew their trumpets	3913
17: 8	and the **p** Elishama and Jehoram.	3913
19: 8	**p** and heads of Israelite families	3913
23: 4	of you **p** and Levites who are going on duty	3913
23: 6	of the LORD except the **p** and Levites	3913
23:18	of the LORD in the hands of the **p,**	3913
24: 5	He called together the **p** and Levites	3913
26:17	the priest with eighty other courageous **p** of	3913
26:18	That is for the **p,** the descendants of Aaron,	3913
26:19	at the **p** in their presence before	3913
26:20	the chief priest and all the other **p** looked	3913
29: 4	He brought in the **p** and the Levites,	3913
29:16	The **p** went into the sanctuary of	3913
29:21	The king commanded the **p,**	3913
29:22	and the **p** took the blood and sprinkled it on	3913
29:24	The **p** then slaughtered the goats	3913
29:26	and the **p** with their trumpets.	3913
29:34	The **p,** however, were too few to skin all	3913
29:34	and until other **p** had been consecrated,	3913
29:34	consecrating themselves than the **p** had been	3913
30: 3	not enough **p** had consecrated themselves	3913
30:15	The **p** and the Levites were ashamed	3913
30:16	The **p** sprinkled the blood handed to them	3913
30:21	and **p** sang to the LORD every day,	3913
30:24	great number of **p** consecrated themselves.	3913
30:25	along with the **p** and Levites	3913
30:27	The **p** and the Levites stood to bless	3913
31: 2	Hezekiah assigned the **p** and Levites	3913
31: 2	each of them according to their duties as **p**	3913
31: 4	in Jerusalem to give the portion due the **p**	3913
31: 9	Hezekiah asked the **p** and Levites about	3913
31:15	in the towns of the **p,**	3913
31:15	distributing to their fellow **p** according	NIH
31:17	And they distributed to the **p** enrolled	3913
31:19	As for the **p,** the descendants of Aaron,	3913
34: 5	the bones of the **p** on their altars,	3913
34:30	the **p** and the Levites—	3913
35: 2	the **p** to their duties and encouraged them	3913
35: 8	to the people and the **p** and Levites.	3913
35: 8	**p** twenty-six hundred Passover offerings	3913
35:10	the **p** stood in their places with the Levites	3913
35:11	the **p** sprinkled the blood handed to them,	3913
35:14	for themselves and for the **p,**	3913
35:14	because the **p,** the descendants of Aaron,	3913
35:14	for themselves and for the Aaronic **p.**	3913
35:18	a Passover as did Josiah, with the **p,**	3913
36:14	of the **p** and the people became more	3913
Ezr 1: 5	and the **p** and Levites—	3913
2:36	The **p:** the descendants of Jedaiah	3913
2:61	And from among the **p:**	3913
2:70	The **p,** the Levites, the singers,	3913
3: 2	and his fellow **p** and Zerubbabel son	3913
3: 8	and the rest of their brothers (the **p** and	3913
3:10	the **p** in their vestments and with trumpets,	3913
3:12	the older **p** and Levites and family heads,	3913
6: 9	as requested by the **p** in Jerusalem—	10347
6:16	the **p,** the Levites and the rest of the exiles	10347
6:18	And they installed the **p** in their divisions	10347
6:20	The **p** and Levites had purified themselves	3913
6:20	for their brothers and for themselves.	3913
7: 7	Some of the Israelites, including **p,** Levites,	3913
7:13	including **p** and Levites,	10347
7:16	as the freewill offerings of the people and **p**	10347
7:24	tribute or duty on any of the **p,** Levites,	10347
8:15	I checked among the people and the **p,**	3913
8:24	Then I set apart twelve of the leading **p,**	3913
8:29	before the leading **p** and the Levites and	3913
8:30	Then the **p** and Levites received the silver	3913
9: 1	including the **p** and the Levites,	3913
9: 7	and our **p** have been subjected to the sword	3913
10: 5	the leading **p** and Levites and all Israel	3913
10: 5	Among the descendants of the **p,**	3913
Ne 2:16	yet I had said nothing to the Jews or the **p**	3913
3: 1	and his fellow **p** went to work and rebuilt	3913
3:22	The repairs next to him were made by the **p**	3913
3:28	Above the Horse Gate, the **p** made repairs,	3913
5:12	Then I summoned the **p** and made	3913
7:39	The **p:** the descendants of Jedaiah	3913

Ne 7:63	And from among the **p:**	3913
7:70	50 bowls and 530 garments for **p.**	3913
7:72	minas of silver and 67 garments for **p.**	3913
7:73	The **p,** the Levites, the gatekeepers,	3913
8:13	along with the **p** and the Levites,	3913
9:32	upon our **p** and prophets,	3913
9:34	our **p** and our fathers did	3913
9:38	and our **p** are affixing their seals to it."	3913
10: 8	These were the **p.**	3913
10:28	"The rest of the people—**p,** Levites,	3913
10:34	"We—the **p,** the Levites and the people—	3913
10:36	to the **p** ministering there.	3913
10:37	to the **p,** the first of our ground meal,	3913
10:39	and where the ministering **p,**	3913
11: 3	**p,** Levites, temple servants and descendants	3913
11:10	From the **p:** Jedaiah; the son of Joiarib;	3913
11:20	with the **p** and Levites,	3913
12: 1	These were the **p** and Levites who returned	3913
12: 7	the leaders of the **p** and their associates in	3913
12:22	as well as those of the **p,**	3913
12:30	When the **p** and Levites had purified themselves ceremonially,	3913
12:35	as well as some **p** with trumpets,	3913
12:41	as well as the **p—**	3913
12:44	the portions required by the Law for the **p**	3913
12:44	with the ministering **p** and Levites.	3913
13: 5	as well as the contributions for the **p.**	3913
13:30	the **p** and the Levites of everything foreign,	3913
Job 12:19	He leads **p** away stripped	3913
Ps 78:64	their **p** were put to the sword,	3913
99: 6	Moses and Aaron were among his **p,**	3913
132: 9	May your **p** be clothed with righteousness;	3913
132:16	I will clothe her **p** with salvation,	3913
Isa 28: 7	**P** and prophets stagger from beer	3913
37: 2	and the leading **p,** all wearing sackcloth,	3913
61: 6	And you will be called **p** of the LORD,	3913
66:21	And I will select some of them also to be **p**	3913
Jer 1: 1	one of the **p** at Anathoth in the territory	3913
1:18	its officials, its **p** and the people of the land.	3913
2: 8	The **p** did not ask, 'Where is the LORD?'	3913
2:26	their **p** and their prophets.	3913
4: 9	the **p** will be horrified,	3913
5:31	the **p** rule by their own authority,	3913
6:13	prophets and **p** alike, all practice deceit.	3913
8: 1	the bones of the **p** and prophets,	3913
8:10	prophets and **p** alike, all practice deceit.	3913
13:13	the kings who sit on David's throne, the **p,**	3913
19: 1	of the elders of the people and of the **p**	3913
26: 7	The **p,** the prophets and all	3913
26: 8	to say, the **p,** the prophets and all	3913
26:11	the **p** and the prophets said to the officials	3913
26:16	the officials and all the people said to the **p**	3913
27:16	Then I said to the **p** and all these people,	3913
28: 1	the LORD in the presence of the **p** and all	3913
28: 5	the **p** and all the people who were standing	3913
29: 1	among the exiles and to the **p,**	3913
29:25	and to all the other **p.**	3913
31:14	I will satisfy the **p** with abundance,	3913
32:32	they, their kings and officials, their **p**	3913
33:18	nor will the **p,** who are Levites,	3913
33:21	with the Levites who are **p** ministering	3913
34:19	the **p** and all the people of the land	3913
48: 7	together with his **p** and officials.	3913
49: 3	together with his **p** and officials.	3913
La 1: 4	All her gateways are desolate, her **p** groan,	3913
1:19	My **p** and my elders perished in the city	3913
4:13	of her prophets and the iniquities of her **p,**	3913
4:16	**p** are shown no honor, the elders no favor.	3913
Eze 22:26	Her **p** do violence to my law	3913
40:45	for the **p** who have charge of the temple,	3913
40:46	for the **p** who have charge of the altar.	3913
42:13	the **p** who approach the LORD will eat	3913
42:14	Once the **p** enter the holy precincts,	3913
43:19	a young bull as a sin offering to the **p,**	3913
43:24	and the **p** are to sprinkle salt on them	3913
43:27	the **p** are to present your burnt offerings	3913
44:13	They are not to come near to **serve** me **as p**	3912
44:15	the **p,** who are Levites and descendants	3913
44:22	of Israelite descent or widows of **p.**	3913
44:24	the **p** are to serve as judges and decide it	2156S
44:28	to be the only inheritance they have.	4392S
44:30	of all your special gifts will belong to the **p.**	3913
44:31	The **p** must not eat anything,	3913
45: 4	be the sacred portion of the land for the **p,**	3913
46: 2	The **p** are to sacrifice his burnt offering	3913
46:19	which belonged to the **p,**	3913
46:20	where the **p** will cook the guilt offering and	3913
48:10	This will be the sacred portion for the **p.**	3913
48:11	This will be for the consecrated **p,**	3913
48:13	"Alongside the territory of the **p,**	3913
Hos 4: 6	I also reject you as my **p;**	3912
4: 7	The more the **p** increased,	4392S
4: 9	And it will be: Like people, like **p.**	3913
5: 1	"Hear this, you **p!**	3913
6: 9	so do bands of **p;** they murder	3913
10: 5	and so will its **idolatrous p,**	4024
Joel 1: 9	The **p** are in mourning,	3913
1:13	Put on sackcloth, O **p,** and mourn;	3913
2:17	Let the **p,** who minister before the LORD,	3913
Mic 3:11	her **p** teach for a price,	3913
Zep 1: 4	of the pagan and the **idolatrous p—**	3913
3: 4	Her **p** profane the sanctuary	3913
Hag 2:11	'Ask the **p** what the law says:	3913
2:12	The answered, "No."	3913
2:13	"Yes," the **p** replied, "it becomes defiled."	3913
Zec 7: 3	the **p** of the house of the LORD Almighty	3913
7: 5	"Ask all the people of the land and the **p,**	3913

Mal 1: 6	"It is you, O **p,** who show contempt for my	3913
2: 1	"And now this admonition is for you, O **p.**	3913
Mt 2: 4	the people's **chief p** and teachers of the law,	797
12: 4	but only *for* the **p.**	2636
12: 5	the Sabbath the **p** in the temple desecrate	2636
16:21	**chief p** and teachers of the law,	797
20:18	be betrayed *to* the **chief p** and the teachers	797
21:15	the **chief p** and the teachers of the law saw	797
21:23	the **chief p** and the elders of	797
21:45	When the **chief p** and the Pharisees heard	797
26: 3	Then the **chief p** and the elders of	797
26:14	called Judas Iscariot—went to the **chief p**	797
26:47	the **chief p** and the elders of the people.	797
26:59	The **chief p** and the whole Sanhedrin	797
27: 1	all the **chief p** and the elders of	797
27: 3	the thirty silver coins *to* the **chief p** and	797
27: 6	The **chief p** picked up the coins and said,	797
27:12	When he was accused by the **chief p** and	797
27:20	But the **chief p** and the elders persuaded	797
27:41	In the same way the **chief p,**	797
27:62	the **chief p** and the Pharisees went to Pilate.	797
28:11	the **chief p** everything that had happened.	797
28:12	When the **chief p** had met with the elders	NIG
Mk 2:26	which is lawful only for **p** to eat.	2636
8:31	**chief p** and teachers of the law,	797
10:33	be betrayed *to* the **chief p** and teachers of	797
11:18	The **chief p** and the teachers of	797
11:27	the temple courts, the **chief p,** the teachers	797
14: 1	and the **chief p** and the teachers of	797
14:10	went to the **chief p** to betray Jesus to them.	797
14:43	sent from the **chief p,** the teachers of the law	797
14:53	and all the **chief p,** elders and	797
14:55	The **chief p** and the whole Sanhedrin	797
15: 1	Very early in the morning, the **chief p,**	797
15: 3	The **chief p** accused him of many things.	797
15:10	the **chief p** had handed Jesus over to him.	797
15:11	But the **chief p** stirred up the crowd	797
15:31	the same way the **chief p** and the teachers	797
Lk 6: 4	he ate what is lawful only for **p** to eat.	2636
9:22	**chief p** and teachers of the law,	797
17:14	he said, "Go, show yourselves *to* the **p.**"	2636
19:47	But the **chief p,** the teachers of the law and	797
20: 1	the **chief p** and the teachers of the law,	797
20:19	of the law and the **chief p** looked for a way	797
22: 2	and the **chief p** and the teachers of the law	797
22: 4	And Judas went *to* the **chief p** and	797
22:52	Then Jesus said to the **chief p,**	797
22:66	both the **chief p** and teachers of the law,	797
23: 4	Then Pilate announced to the **chief p** and	797
23:10	The **chief p** and the teachers of the law	797
23:13	Pilate called together the **chief p,**	797
24:20	The **chief p** and our rulers handed him over	797
Jn 1:19	the Jews of Jerusalem sent **p** and Levites	2636
7:32	Then the **chief p** and the Pharisees sent	797
7:45	the temple guards went back to the **chief p**	797
11:47	Then the **chief p** and the Pharisees called	797
11:57	the **chief p** and Pharisees had given orders	797
12:10	**chief p** made plans to kill Lazarus as well,	797
18: 3	and some officials from the **chief p**	797
18:35	and your **chief p** who handed you over	797
19: 6	as the **chief p** and their officials saw him,	797
19:15	the **chief p** answered.	797
19:21	The **chief p** of the Jews protested to Pilate,	797
Ac 4: 1	The **p** and the captain of the temple guard	2636
4:23	that the **chief p** and elders had said to them.	797
5:24	and the **chief p** were puzzled,	797
6: 7	and a large number *of* **p** became obedient	2636
9:14	from the **chief p** to arrest all who call	797
9:21	to take them as prisoners to the **chief p?**"	797
22:30	he released him and ordered the **chief p**	797
23:14	They went to the **chief p** and elders	797
25: 2	the **chief p** and Jewish leaders appeared	797
25:15	the **chief p** and elders of the Jews	797
26:10	On the authority of the **chief p** I put many	797
26:12	and commission *of* the **chief p.**	797
Heb 7: 5	of Levi who become **p** to collect a tenth	2632
7:14	to that tribe Moses said nothing about **p.**	2636
7:20	Others became **p** without any oath,	2636
7:23	Now there have been many of those **p,**	2636
7:27	Unlike the other **high p,**	797
7:28	law appoints as **high p** men who are weak;	797
9: 6	the **p** entered regularly into the outer room	2636
Rev 1: 6	and has made us to be a kingdom and **p**	2636
5:10	to be a kingdom and **p** to serve our God,	2636
20: 6	be **p** of God and of Christ and will reign	2636

PRIESTS' (2) [PRIEST]

Eze 41:10	the [**p'**] rooms were twenty cubits wide all	NIH
42:13	the temple courtyard are the **p' rooms,**	4384+7731

PRIME (3)

1Sa 2:33	your descendants will die **in the p of life.**	408
Job 29: 4	Oh, for the days when I was in my **p,**	3074
Isa 38:10	the **p** *of* my life must I go through the gates	1953

PRINCE (54) [PRINCE'S, PRINCELY, PRINCES, PRINCESS]

Ge 23: 6	You are a mighty **p** among us.	5954
Dt 33:16	on the brow of the **p** *among* his brothers.	5687
49:26	on the brow of the **p** *among* his brothers.	5687
Jdg 8:18	"each one with the bearing of a **p.**"	1201+4889
2Sa 3:38	that a **p** and a great man has fallen	8569
2Ch 11:22	to be the chief **p** among his brothers,	5592
Ezr 1: 8	who counted them out to Sheshbazzar the **p**	5954

Job	31:37	like a p I would approach him.)—	5592
Pr	14:28	but without subjects a p is ruined.	8138
Isa	9: 6	Everlasting Father, P of Peace.	8569
Eze	7:27	the p will be clothed with despair,	5954
	12:10	This oracle concerns the p in Jerusalem and	5954
	12:12	"The p among them will put his things	5954
	21:25	"'O profane and wicked p of Israel,	5954
	30:13	No longer will there be a p in Egypt.	5954
	34:24	my servant David will be p among them.	5954
	37:25	David my servant will be their p forever.	5954
	38: 2	the chief p of Meshech and Tubal;	5954
	38: 3	O Gog, chief p of Meshech and Tubal.	5954
	39: 1	O Gog, chief p of Meshech and Tubal.	5954
	44: 3	The p himself is the only one who may sit	5954
	45: 7	"'The p will have the land bordering	5954
	45:16	in this special gift for the use of the p	5954
	45:17	of the p to provide the burnt offerings.	5954
	45:22	the p is to provide a bull as a sin offering	5954
	46: 2	The p is to enter from the outside through	5954
	46: 4	The burnt offering the p brings to	5954
	46: 8	When the p enters, he is to go in through	5954
	46:10	The p is to be among them,	5954
	46:12	When the p provides a freewill offering to	5954
	46:16	If the p makes a gift from his inheritance	5954
	46:17	then it will revert to the p.	5954
	46:18	The p must not take any of the inheritance	5954
	48:21	and the city property will belong to the p.	5954
	48:21	of the tribal portions will belong to the p,	5954
	48:22	the center of the area that belongs to the p	5954
	48:22	the p will lie between the border of Judah	5954
Da	8:11	It set itself up to be as great as the P of	8569
	8:25	and take his stand against the P of princes.	8569
	10:13	But the p of the Persian kingdom resisted	8569
	10:20	the p of Persia, and when I go, the prince	8569
	10:20	and when I go, the p of Greece will come;	8569
	10:21	against them except Michael, your p.	8569
	11:22	and a p of the covenant will be destroyed.	5592
	12: 1	the great p who protects your people,	8569
Hos	3: 4	will live many days without king or p,	8569
Mt	9:34	"It is by the p of demons that he drives out	807
	12:24	"It is only by the p of demons,	807
Mk	3:22	the p of demons he is driving out demons."	807
Lk	11:15	the p of demons, he is driving out demons."	807
Jn	12:31	now the p of this world will be driven out.	807
	14:30	for the p of this world is coming.	807
	16:11	the p of this world now stands condemned.	807
Ac	5:31	God exalted him to his own right hand as P	795

PRINCE'S (1) [PRINCE]

| SS | 7: 1 | beautiful your sandaled feet, O p daughter! | 5618 |

PRINCELY (1) [PRINCE]

| Ps | 49:14 | in the grave, far from their p mansions. | 2292 |

PRINCES (72) [PRINCE]

Nu	21:18	the well that the p dug, that the nobles of	8569
	22: 8	So the Moabite p stayed with him.	8569
	22:13	up and said to Balak's p,	8569
	22:14	the Moabite p returned to Balak and said,	8569
	22:15	Then Balak sent other p,	8569
	22:21	saddled his donkey and went with the p	8569
	22:35	So Balaam went with the p of Balak.	8569
	22:40	to Balaam and the p who were with him.	8569
	23: 6	with all the p of Moab.	8569
	23:17	with the p of Moab.	8569
Jos	13:21	allied with Sihon—who lived in that	5817
Jdg	5: 2	"When the p in Israel take the lead, when	7278
	5: 9	My heart is with Israel's p,	2980
	5:15	The p of Issachar were with Deborah;	8569
1Sa	2: 8	he seats them with p and has them inherit	5618
2Sa	13:32	not think that they killed all the p;	1201+4889
2Ki	10: 6	Now the royal p, seventy of them,	1201
	10: 7	took the p and slaughtered all seventy	1201+4889
	10: 8	They have brought the heads of the p.	1201+4889
	11: 2	from among the royal p,	1201
2Ch	21: 4	to the sword along with some of the p	8569
	22: 8	he found the p of Judah and the sons	8569
	22:11	the royal p who were about to be murdered	1201
	28:21	from the p and presented them to the king	8569
Est	1: 3	of Persia and Media, the p, and the nobles	7312
	6: 9	to one of the king's most noble p.	8569
Job	34:19	who shows no partiality to p and does	8569
Ps	45:16	you will make them p throughout the land.	8569
	68:27	there the great throng of Judah's p,	8569
	68:27	and there the p of Zebulun and of Naphtali.	8569
	83:11	all their p like Zebah and Zalmunna,	5817
	105:22	to instruct his p as he pleased	8569
	113: 8	he seats them with p,	5618
	113: 8	with the p of their people.	5618
	118: 9	take refuge in the LORD than to trust in p.	5618
	146: 3	Do not put your trust in p, in mortal men,	5618
	148:11	you p and all rulers on earth,	8569
Pr	8:16	by me p govern, and all nobles who rule	8569
	19:10	how much worse for a slave to rule over p!	8569
Ecc	10: 7	while p go on foot like slaves.	8569
	10:16	a servant and whose p feast in the morning.	8569
	10:17	and whose p eat at a proper time—	8569
Isa	23: 8	whose merchants are p,	8569
	34:12	all her p will vanish away.	8569
	40:23	He brings p to naught and reduces	8142
	49: 7	p will see and bow down,	8569
La	1: 6	Her p are like deer that find no pasture;	8569
	2: 2	and its p down to the ground in dishonor.	8569
	2: 9	and her p are exiled among the nations,	8569
	4: 7	Their p were brighter than snow	5687
La	5:12	P have been hung up by their hands;	8569
Eze	19: 1	up a lament concerning the p of Israel	5954
	21:12	it is against all the p of Israel.	5954
	22: 6	"'See how each of the p of Israel who are	5954
	22:25	There is a conspiracy of her p within her	5954
	26:16	Then all the p of the coast will step down	5954
	27:21	the p of Kedar were your customers;	5954
	32:29	"Edom is there, her kings and all her p;	5954
	32:30	"All the p of the north and all	5817
	39:18	of mighty men and drink the blood of the p	5954
	45: 8	my p will no longer oppress my people	5954
	45: 9	You have gone far enough, O p of Israel!	5954
Da	8:25	and take his stand against the Prince of p.	8569
	9: 6	our kings, our p and our fathers,	8569
	9: 8	our p and our fathers are covered	8569
	10:13	Then Michael, one of the chief p,	8569
Hos	7: 3	the p with their lies.	8569
	7: 5	the p become inflamed with wine,	8569
	8: 4	they choose p without my approval.	8606
	13:10	'Give me a king and p'?	8569
Zep	1: 8	the p and the king's sons and all those clad	8569
Rev	6:15	Then the kings of the earth, the p,	3491

PRINCESS (1) [PRINCE]

| Ps | 45:13 | All glorious is the p within | 1426+4889 |

PRINCIPAL (1)

| 1Ch | 9:26 | But the four p gatekeepers, | 1475 |

PRINCIPLE (1) [PRINCIPLES]

| Ro | 3:27 | On what p? On that of observing the law? | 3795 |

PRINCIPLES (4) [PRINCIPLE]

Gal	4: 3	in slavery under the basic p of the world.	5122
	4: 9	to those weak and miserable p?	5122
Col	2: 8	and the basic p of this world rather than	5122
	2:20	Since you died with Christ to the basic p	5122

PRIOR (1)

| Jos | 20: 9 | and not be killed by the avenger of blood p | 6330 |

PRISCILLA (7)

Ac	18: 2	recently come from Italy with his wife P,	4571
	18:18	accompanied by P and Aquila.	4571
	18:19	where Paul left P and Aquila.	1697S
	18:26	When P and Aquila heard him,	4571
Ro	16: 3	Greet P and Aquila,	4571
1Co	16:19	Aquila and P greet you warmly in the Lord,	4571
2Ti	4:19	Greet P and Aquila and the household	4571

PRISON (74) [IMPRISON, IMPRISONED, IMPRISONMENT, IMPRISONMENTS, IMPRISONS, PRISONER, PRISONERS, PRISONS]

Ge	39:20	Joseph's master took him and put him in p,	1074+2021+6045
	39:20	while Joseph was there in the p,	1074+2021+6045
	39:21	granted him favor in the eyes of the p	1074+2021+6045
	39:21	warden.	1074+2021+6045
	39:22	put Joseph in charge of all those held	
		in the p,	1074+2021+6045
	40: 3	in the same p where Joseph was	1074+2021+6045
	40: 5	who were being held in p—	1074+2021+6045
	40:14	to Pharaoh and get me out of this p.	1074
	42:16	the rest of you will be kept in p,	673
	42:19	let one of your brothers stay here in p,	1074+5464
Jdg	16:21	they set him to grinding in the p.	673+1074
	16:25	So they called Samson out of the p,	673+1074
1Ki	22:27	Put this fellow in p and give	1074+2021+3975
2Ki	17: 4	Shalmaneser seized him and put him in p.	1074+3975
	25:27	he released Jehoiachin from p	1074+3975
	25:29	So Jehoiachin put aside his p clothes and	3975
2Ch	16:10	so enraged that he put him in p.	1074+2021+4551
	18:26	Put this fellow in p and give	1074+2021+3975
Job	11:10	and confines you in p and convenes a court,	6037
Ps	66:11	You brought us into p and laid burdens	5181
	142: 7	Set me free from my p,	4993
Ecc	4:14	youth may have come from p to	673+1074+2021
Isa	24:22	they will be shut up in p and be punished	4993
	42: 7	to free captives from p and to release from	4993
Jer	37: 4	for he had not yet been put in p.	1074+2021+3989
	37:15	that they had made into a p.	1074+2021+3975
	37:18	that you have put me in p?	1074+2021+3975
	52:11	he put him in p till the day	1074+2021+7213
	52:31	and freed him from p	1074+2021+3989
	52:33	So Jehoiachin put aside his p clothes and	3975
Eze	19: 9	They put him in p,	5183
Mt	4:12	that John had been put in p,	4140
	5:25	and you may be thrown into p.	5871
	11: 2	John heard in p what Christ was doing,	1303
	14: 3	and bound him and put him in p because	5871
	14:10	and had John beheaded in the p.	5871
	18:30	he went off and had the man thrown into p	5871
	25:36	I was in p and you came to visit me.'	5871
	25:39	When did we see you sick or in p and go	5871
	25:43	I was sick and in p and you did not look	5871
	25:44	or needing clothes or sick or in p,	5871
Mk	1:14	After John was put in p,	4140
	6:17	and had him bound and put in p.	5871
	6:27	The man went, beheaded John in the p,	5871
Mk	15: 7	A man called Barabbas was in p with	1313
Lk	3:20	He locked John up in p.	5871
	12:58	and the officer throw you into p.	5871
	22:33	I am ready to go with you to p and	5871
	23:19	(Barabbas had been thrown into p for	5871
	23:25	the man who had been thrown into p	5871
Jn	3:24	(This was before John was put in p.)	5871
Ac	8: 3	and women and put them in p.	5871
	12: 4	After arresting him, he put him in p,	5871
	12: 5	So Peter was kept in p,	5871
	12: 9	Peter followed him out of the p,	NIG
	12:17	how the Lord had brought him out of p.	5871
	16:23	they were thrown into p,	5871
	16:26	that the foundations of the p were shaken.	1303
	16:26	At once all the p doors flew open,	NIG
	16:27	and when he saw the p doors open,	5871
	16:37	and threw us into p.	5871
	16:39	and escorted them from the p,	NIG
	16:40	After Paul and Silas came out of the p,	5871
	20:23	that p and hardships are facing me.	1301
	22: 4	and women and throwing them into p,	5871
	24:27	a favor to the Jews, he left Paul in p.	1313
	26:10	I put many of the saints in p,	5871
Ro	16: 7	my relatives who have been in p with me.	5257
2Co	11:23	been in p more frequently,	5871
Heb	10:34	You sympathized with those in p	1300
	11:36	while still others were chained and put in p.	1300
	13: 3	Remember those in p as if you were	1300
1Pe	3:19	also he went and preached to the spirits in p	5871
Rev	2:10	devil will put some of you in p to test you,	5871
	20: 7	Satan will be released from his p	5871

PRISONER (21) [PRISON]

Ex	12:29	to the firstborn of the p,	8660
Jdg	15:10	"We have come to take Samson p,"	673
2Ki	24:12	he took Jehoiachin p.	4374
2Ch	33:11	who took Manasseh p,	4334
Isa	22: 3	All you who were caught were taken p	673
Mt	27:15	custom at the Feast to release a p chosen by	1300
	27:16	At that time they had a notorious p,	1300
Mk	15: 6	the custom at the Feast to release a p whom	1300
Jn	18:39	for me to release to you one p at the time of	NIG
Ac	23:18	The centurion said, "Paul, the p,	1300
	25:14	a man here whom Felix left as a p.	1300
	25:27	For I think it is unreasonable to send on a p	1300
Ro	7:23	and making me a p of the law of sin at	170
		work within my members.	170
Gal	3:22	that the whole world is a p of sin,	5168
Eph	3: 1	the p of Christ Jesus for the sake of you	1300
	4: 1	As a p for the Lord, then,	1300
Col	4:10	My fellow p Aristarchus sends his greetings,	5257
2Ti	1: 8	or ashamed of me his p.	1300
Phm	1: 1	Paul, a p of Christ Jesus,	1300
	1: 9	old man and now also a p of Christ Jesus—	1300
	1:23	Epaphras, my fellow p in Christ Jesus,	5257

PRISONERS (32) [PRISON]

Ge	39:20	the place where the king's p were confined.	659
2Ki	25:18	the guard took as p Seraiah the chief priest,	4374
2Ch	28:11	took many of his people as p.	8647+8664
	28:11	Send back your fellow countrymen you have taken as p,	8647+8664
	28:13	"You must not bring those p here,"	8664
	28:14	So the soldiers gave up the p and plunder in	8664
	28:15	The men designated by name took the p,	8664
	28:17	and attacked Judah and carried away p,	8660
Ps	68: 6	he leads forth the p with singing;	659
	79:11	May the groans of the p come before you;	659
	102:20	of the p and release those condemned	659
	107:10	p suffering in iron chains,	659
Isa	24:22	They will be herded together like p bound	660
	51:14	The cowering p will soon be set free;	7579
	61: 1	and release from darkness for the p,	673
Jer	52:24	the guard took as p Seraiah the chief priest,	4374
La	3:34	To crush underfoot all the p in the land,	659
Hab	1: 9	like a desert wind and gather p like sand.	8660
Zec	9:11	I will free your p from the waterless pit.	659
	9:12	Return to your fortress, O p of hope;	659
Lk	4:18	to proclaim freedom for the p and recovery	171
	21:24	by the sword and will be taken as p to all	170
Ac	9: 2	he might take them as p to Jerusalem.	1313
	9:21	And hasn't he come here to take them as p	1313
	16:25	and the other p were listening to them.	1300
	16:27	because he thought the p had escaped.	1300
	22: 5	to bring these people as p to Jerusalem to	1313
	27: 1	Paul and some other p were handed over to	1304
	27:42	to kill the p to prevent any of them	1304
Gal	3:23	we were held by the law,	5864
Heb	13: 3	in prison as if you were their fellow p,	5279

PRISONS (2) [PRISON]

| Isa | 42:22 | trapped in pits or hidden away in p. | 1074+3975 |
| Lk | 21:12 | They will deliver you to synagogues and p, | 5871 |

PRIVATE (4) [PRIVATELY]

Ge	43:30	He went into his p room and wept there.	2540
Dt	25:11	and seizes him by his p parts,	4434
Mt	17:19	the disciples came to Jesus in p and asked,	2625
Lk	9:18	in p and his disciples were with him,	3668

PRIVATELY (10) [PRIVATE]

| 1Sa | 18:22 | "Speak to David p and say, | 928+2021+4319 |

2Sa	3:27	as though to speak with him p.	928+2021+8952
Jer	37:17	where he asked him p,	928+2021+6260
	40:15	said p to Gedaliah in Mizpah,	928+2021+6260
Mt	14:13	withdrew by boat p to a solitary place.	2625+2848
	24: 3	the disciples came to him p.	2625+2848
Mk	9:28	his disciples asked him p,	2625+2848
	13: 3	James, John and Andrew asked him p,	2625+2848
Lk	10:23	he turned to his disciples and said p,	2625+2848
Gal	2: 2	But I did this p to those who seemed	2625+2848

PRIVILEGE (1)

2Co	8: 4	the p of sharing in this service to the saints.	5921

PRIZE (5) [PRIZES]

1Co	9:24	but only one gets the p?	1092
	9:24	Run in such a way as to get the p.	2898
	9:27	I myself will not be disqualified for the p.	NIG
Php	3:14	I press on toward the goal to win the p	1092
Col	2:18	disqualify you for the p.	2857

PRIZES (1) [PRIZE]

Pr	12:27	but the diligent man p his possessions.	3701

PROBE (5)

Dt	13:14	p and investigate it thoroughly.	2983
Job	10: 6	that you must search out my faults and p	2011
	11: 7	Can you p the limits of the Almighty?	5162
Ps	17: 3	you p my heart and examine me at night,	1043
Jer	20:12	the righteous and p the heart and mind,	8011

PROBLEMS (3)

Dt	1:12	how can I bear your p and your burdens	3268
Da	5:12	explain riddles and solve difficult p.	10626
	5:16	and to solve difficult p.	10626

PROCEDURE (2) [PROCEED]

Ecc	8: 5	wise heart will know the proper time and p.	5477
	8: 6	a proper time and p for every matter,	5477

PROCEED (1) [PROCEDURE, PROCEEDED, PROCEEDINGS, PROCESSION]

Ne	12:31	to p on top of the wall to the right,	2143

PROCEEDED (8) [PROCEED]

Ge	9:20	a man of the soil, p to plant a vineyard.	2725
	42:20	This they p to do.	AIT
	44:12	Then the steward p to search,	AIT
2Ki	8: 2	The woman p to do as the man of God said.	7756
	11: 1	she p to destroy the whole royal family.	7756
2Ch	22:10	she p to destroy the whole royal family of	7756
Ne	12:38	The second choir p in the opposite direction	2143
Ac	12: 3	he p to seize Peter also.	4707

PROCEEDINGS (1) [PROCEED]

Ac	24:22	acquainted with the Way, adjourned the p.	327

PROCESSION (11) [PROCEED]

1Sa	10: 5	you will meet a p of prophets coming	2474
	10:10	a p of prophets met him;	2474
Ne	12:36	Ezra the scribe led the p.	2157S
Ps	42: 4	leading the p to the house of God,	4392S
	68:24	Your p has come into view, O God,	2142
	68:24	p of my God and King into the sanctuary.	2142
	118:27	in the festal p up to the horns of the altar.	2504
SS	6:10	majestic as the stars in p?	1839
Isa	60:11	their kings led in triumphal p.	5627
1Co	4: 9	apostles on display at the end of the p,	NIG
2Co	2:14	who always leads us in triumphal p	2581

PROCHORUS (KJV) See PROCORUS

PROCLAIM (85) [PROCLAIMED, PROCLAIMING, PROCLAIMS, PROCLAMATION]

Ex	33:19	and I will p my name, the LORD,	928+7924
Lev	23: 2	which you are to p as sacred assemblies.	7924
	23: 4	the sacred assemblies you are to p	7924
	23:21	On that same day you are to p	7924
	23:37	which you are to p as sacred assemblies	7924
	25:10	Consecrate the fiftieth year and p liberty	7924
Dt	11:29	to p on Mount Gerizim the blessings,	5989
	30:12	to get it and p it to us so we may obey it?"	9048
	30:13	to get it and p it to us so we may obey it?"	9048
	32: 3	I will p the name of the LORD.	7924
1Sa	31: 9	to p the news in the temple of their idols	1413
2Sa	1:20	p it not in the streets of Ashkelon,	1413
1Ki	21: 9	"P a day of fasting and seat Naboth in a	7924
1Ch	10: 9	Philistines to p the news among their idols	1413
	16:23	p his salvation day after day.	1413
Ne	8:15	that they should p this word and spread it	9048
Ps	2: 7	I will p the decree of the LORD:	6218
	9:11	p among the nations what he has done.	5583
	19: 1	the skies p the work of his hands.	5583
	22:31	They will p his righteousness to a people	5583
	30: 9	Will it p your faithfulness?	5583
	40: 9	I p righteousness in the great assembly;	1413
	50: 6	And the heavens p his righteousness,	5583

Ps	64: 9	they will p the works of God	5583
	68:34	P the power of God,	5989
	71:16	I will come and p your mighty acts,	2349
	71:16	I will p your righteousness, yours alone.	NIH
	92: 2	to p your love in the morning	5583
	96: 2	p his salvation day after day.	1413
	97: 6	The heavens p his righteousness,	5583
	106: 2	Who can p the mighty acts of the LORD	4910
	118:17	and will p what the LORD has done.	6218
	145: 6	and I will p your great deeds.	6218
Isa	12: 4	and p that his name is exalted.	2349
	40: 2	and p to her that her hard service has been	7924
	42:12	the LORD and p his praise in the islands.	5583
	43:21	for myself that they may p my praise.	6218
	44: 1	Let him p it.	7924
	44: 8	Did I not p this and foretell it long ago?	9048
	48:20	Announce this with shouts of joy and p it.	9048
	52: 7	who p peace, who bring good tidings,	9048
	52: 7	who bring good tidings, who p salvation,	9048
	61: 1	to p freedom for the captives and release	7924
	61: 2	to p the year of the LORD's favor and	7924
	66:19	They will p my glory among the nations.	5583
Jer	2: 2	"Go and p in the hearing of Jerusalem:	7924
	3:12	Go, p this message toward the north:	7924
	4: 5	"Announce in Judah and p in Jerusalem	7924
	4:16	"Tell this to the nations, p it to Jerusalem:	9048
	5:20	to the house of Jacob and p it in Judah:	9048
	7: 2	and there p this message:	7924
	11: 6	"P all these words in the towns of Judah	7924
	19: 2	There p the words I tell you,	7924
	22: 1	the king of Judah and p this message there:	1819
	31:10	p it in distant coastlands:	5583
	34: 8	in Jerusalem to p freedom for the slaves.	7924
	34:17	So I now p 'freedom' for you,	7924
	46:14	and p it in Migdol;	9048
	46:14	p it also in Memphis and Tahpanhes:	9048
	50: 2	"Announce and p among the nations, lift up	9048
	50: 2	lift up a banner and p it;	9048
Hos	5: 9	the tribes of Israel I p what is certain.	3359
Joel	3: 9	P this among the nations: Prepare for war!	7924
Am	3: 9	P to the fortresses of Ashdod and to	9048
Jnh	3: 2	"Go to the great city of Nineveh and p to it	7924
Mic	3: 5	if one feeds them, they p 'peace';	7924
Zec	1:14	to me said, "P this word:	7924
	1:17	"P further: This is what the LORD Almighty says:	7924
	9:10	He will p peace to the nations.	1819
Mt	10:27	what is whispered in your ear, p from	3062
	12:18	and he will p justice to the nations.	550
Lk	4:18	He has sent me to p freedom for	3062
	4:19	to p the year of the Lord's favor."	3062
	9:60	but you go and p the kingdom of God."	1334
Ac	17:23	as something unknown I am going to p	2859
	20:27	not hesitated to p to you the whole will	334
	26:23	would p light to his own people and	2859
1Co	11:26	you p the Lord's death until he comes.	2859
Col	1:28	We p him, admonishing and teaching	2859
	4: 3	so that we may p the mystery of Christ,	3281
	4: 4	Pray that I may p it clearly, as I should.	5746
1Jn	1: 1	this we p concerning the Word of life.	NIG
	1: 2	and we p to you the eternal life,	550
	1: 3	We p to you what we have seen and heard,	550
Rev	14: 6	eternal gospel to p to those who live	2294+2295

PROCLAIMED (43) [PROCLAIM]

Ex	9:16	that my name might be p in all the earth.	6218
	34: 5	stood there with him and p his name,	928+7924
Dt	1: 3	Moses p to the Israelites all that	1819
	5:22	These are the commandments the LORD p	1819
	9:10	the LORD p to you on the mountain out of	1819
	10: 4	the Ten Commandments he had p to you on	1819
	15: 2	time for canceling debts has been p.	7924
1Ki	16:16	p Omri, the commander of the army, king	4887
	21:12	They p a fast and seated Naboth in a	7924
2Ki	10:20	assembly in honor of Baal." So they p it.	7924
	11:12	with a copy of the covenant and p him king.	4887
	23:16	with the word of the LORD p by the man	1819
	24: 2	the LORD p by his servants the prophets.	1819
2Ch	20: 3	and he p a fast for all Judah.	7924
	23:11	with a copy of the covenant and p him king.	4887
Ezr	8:21	There, by the Ahava Canal, I p a fast,	7924
Est	1:20	Then when the king's edict is p	9048
	2: 8	the king's order and edict had been p,	9048
	2:18	He p a holiday throughout the provinces	6913
Ps	68:11	great was the company of those who p it:	1413
Isa	45: 3	Which of them foretold this and p it to us	9048
	43:12	I have revealed and saved and p—	9048
Jer	32: 2	they would have p my words to my people	9048
	34:15	Each of you p freedom to his countrymen.	7924
	34:17	not p freedom for your fellow countrymen.	7924
	36: 9	before the LORD was p for all the people	7924
Da	3: 4	Then the herald loudly p,	10637
	5:29	and he was p the third highest ruler in	10371
Jnh	3: 4	He p: "Forty more days and Nineveh	7924
Zec	1: 4	to whom the earlier prophets p:	7924
	7: 7	the LORD p through the earlier prophets	7924
Lk	12: 3	the inner rooms will be p from the roofs.	3062
	16:16	Law and the Prophets were p until John.	NIG
Ac	8: 5	Philip went down to a city in Samaria and p	3062
	8:25	When they had testified and p the word of	3281
	13: 5	they p the word of God in the Jewish	2859
	13:38	through Jesus the forgiveness of sins is p	2859
Ro	9:17	in you and that my name might be p in all	1334
	15:19	I have fully p the gospel of Christ.	NIG
1Co	2: 1	with eloquence or superior wisdom as I p	2859
Col	1:23	and that has been p to every creature	3062

2Ti	4:17	be fully p and all the Gentiles might hear it.	NIG
Heb	9:19	When Moses had p every commandment of	3281

PROCLAIMING (19) [PROCLAIM]

Ex	34: 6	And he passed in front of Moses, p,	7924
1Sa	11: 7	"This will be done to the oxen	606
Est	1:22	p in each people's tongue	1819
	6: 9	p before him, 'This is what is done for	7924
	6:11	on horseback through the city streets, p	7924
Ps	26: 7	p aloud your praise and telling of all your	9048
	92:15	p, "The LORD is upright; he is my Rock,	5583
Isa	60: 6	and incense and p the praise of the LORD.	1413
Jer	4:15	p disaster from the hills of Ephraim.	9048
	20: 8	I cry out p violence and destruction.	7924
Mk	1:14	p the good news of God.	3062
Lk	8: 1	p the good news of the kingdom of God.	2294
Ac	4: 2	the apostles were teaching the people and p	2859
	5:42	p the good news that Jesus is the Christ.	2859
Ro	10: 8	that is, the word of faith we are p:	3062
	15:16	the priestly duty of p the gospel of God,	2295
2Th	2: 4	p himself to be God.	617
Rev	5: 2	And I saw a mighty angel p in a loud voice,	3062

PROCLAIMS (2) [PROCLAIM]

Dt	18:22	a prophet p in the name of the LORD does	1819
Na	1:15	of one who brings good news, who p peace!	9048

PROCLAMATION (9) [PROCLAIM]

2Ch	24: 9	A p was then issued in Judah	7754
	30: 5	They decided to send a p throughout Israel,	7754
	36:22	of Persia to make a p throughout his realm	7754
Ezr	1: 1	of Persia to make a p throughout his realm	7754
	10: 7	A p was then issued throughout Judah	7754
Ne	6: 7	even appointed prophets to make this p	7924
Isa	62:11	The LORD has made p to the ends of	9048
Jnh	3: 7	he issued a p in Nineveh.	2410
Ro	16:25	to establish you by my gospel and the p	3060

PROCONSUL (5) [PROCONSULS]

Ac	13: 7	who was an attendant of the p,	478
	13: 7	The p, an intelligent man,	NIG
	13: 8	and tried to turn the p from the faith.	478
	13:12	When the p saw what had happened,	478
	18:12	While Gallio was p of Achaia,	478

PROCONSULS (1) [PROCONSUL]

Ac	19:38	the courts are open and there are p.	478

PROCORUS (1)

Ac	6: 5	also Philip, P, Nicanor, Timon, Parmenas,	4743

PRODDED (1)

Jdg	16:16	With such nagging she p him day after day	552

PRODUCE (42) [PRODUCED, PRODUCES, PRODUCING, PRODUCT, PRODUCTS]

Ge	1:11	Then God said, "Let the land p vegetation:	2012
	1:24	"Let the land p living creatures according	3655
	3:18	It will p thorns and thistles for you,	7541
	38: 8	to her as a brother-in-law to p offspring	7756
	47:26	that a fifth of the p belongs to Pharaoh.	NIH
Ex	5:18	yet you must p your full quota of bricks."	5989
	8:18	But when the magicians tried to p gnats	3655
Dt	8:18	the ability to p wealth,	6913
	11:17	not rain and the ground will yield no p,	3292
	14:22	a tenth of all that your fields p each year.	2446+3655+9311
	14:28	of that year's p and store it in your towns,	9311
	16:13	after you have gathered the p	NIH
	26: 2	take some of the firstfruits of all that you p	995
	26:12	a tenth of all your p in the third year,	9311
	28:33	and labor p, and you will have nothing	7262
Jos	5:11	they ate some of the p of the land:	6289
	5:12	but that year they ate of the p of Canaan.	9311
1Ch	27:27	Zabdi the Shiphmite was in charge of the p	8611S
Job	40:20	The hills bring him their p,	1006
Ps	78:46	their p to the locust,	3330
	105:35	ate up the p of their soil.	7262
Pr	13:23	A poor man's field may p abundant food,	NIH
Isa	5:10	A ten-acre vineyard will p only a bath	6913
Jer	2: 7	into a fertile land to eat its fruit and rich p.	3206
	29: 5	plant gardens and eat what they p,	7262
	29:28	plant gardens and eat what they p.'"	7262
Eze	17:23	so that it would p branches,	6913
	17:23	it will p branches and bear fruit	5951
	36: 8	will p branches and fruit	5989
	48:18	Its p will supply food for the workers of	9311
Hos	8: 7	The stalk has no head; it will p no flour.	6913
Hab	3:17	the olive crop fails and the fields p no food,	6913
Zec	8:12	the ground will p its crops,	5989
Mt	3: 8	P fruit in keeping with repentance.	4472
	3:10	that does not p good fruit will be cut down	4472
	21:43	and given to a people who will p its fruit.	4472
Mk	4:20	hear the word, accept it, and p a crop—	2844
Lk	3: 8	P fruit in keeping with repentance.	4472
	3: 9	that does not p good fruit will be cut down	4472
	8:15	retain it, and by persevering p a crop.	2844
2Ti	2:23	because you know they p quarrels,	1164
Jas	3:12	Neither can a salt spring p fresh water.	4472

PRODUCED (16) [PRODUCE]

Ge	1:12	The land p vegetation:	3655
	41:47	of abundance the land p plentifully.	6913
	41:48	the food p in those seven years	2118
Nu	17: 8	blossomed and p almonds.	1694
Dt	8:17	the strength of my hands *have* p this wealth	6913
2Ch	31: 5	oil and honey and all *that* the fields p.	9311
Eze	17: 6	and p branches and put out leafy boughs.	6913
Mt	13: 8	where *it* p a crop—a hundred, sixty or	1443
Mk	4: 8	*It* came up, grew and p a crop,	1443
Lk	12:16	of a certain rich man p **a good crop.**	2369
Ac	6:13	*They* p false witnesses, who testified,	2705
Ro	7: 8	p in me every kind of covetous desire.	2981
	7:13	*it* p death in me through what was good,	2981
2Co	7:11	See what this godly sorrow *has* p in you:	2981
1Th	1: 3	and Father your work p by **faith,**	AIT
Jas	5:18	and the earth p its crops.	1056

PRODUCES (16) [PRODUCE]

Lev	25: 7	Whatever the land p may be eaten.	9311
Dt	29:18	among you *that* p such bitter poison.	7238
Ne	9:36	and the other **good things** it p.	AIT
Job	37:10	The breath of God p ice,	5989
Pr	30:33	For as churning the milk p butter,	3655
	30:33	and as twisting the nose p blood,	3655
	30:33	so stirring up anger p strife."	3655
Hag	1:11	the oil and whatever the ground p,	3655
Mt	13:23	He p **a crop,** yielding a hundred,	2844
Mk	4:28	All by itself the soil p grain—	2844
Jn	12:24	But if it dies, *it* p many seeds.	5770
Ro	5: 3	we know that suffering p perseverance;	2981
2Co	1: 6	which p in you patient endurance of	1919
Heb	6: 7	in the rain often falling on it and that p	5503
	6: 8	that p thorns and thistles is worthless and	1766
	12:11	*it* p a harvest of righteousness and peace	625

PRODUCING (1) [PRODUCE]

Ge	38: 9	to keep from p offspring for his brother.	5989

PRODUCT (1) [PRODUCE]

Nu	18:30	to you as the p of the threshing floor or	9311

PRODUCTS (5) [PRODUCE]

Ge	43:11	of the **best** p *of* the land in your bags	2380
Isa	45:14	p *of* Egypt and the merchandise of Cush,	3330
Jer	20: 5	all its p, all its valuables and all	3330
Eze	27:16	with you because of your many p;	5126
	27:18	of your many p and great wealth of goods,	5126

PROFANE (12) [PROFANED]

Lev	18:21	for *you* must not p the name of your God.	2725
	19:12	not swear falsely by my name and so p	2725
	21: 6	and *must* not p the name of their God.	2725
	22: 2	so *they* will not p my holy name.	2725
	22:32	*Do* not p my holy name.	2725
Eze	20:39	no longer p my holy name with your gifts	2725
	21:25	" 'O p and wicked prince of Israel,	2729
	22:26	to my law and p my holy things;	2725
Am	2: 7	use the same girl and so p my holy name.	2725
Zep	3: 4	Her priests p the sanctuary and do violence	2725
Mal	1:12	"But you p it by saying of the Lord's table,	2725
	2:10	Why *do* we p the covenant of our fathers	2725

PROFANED (13) [PROFANE]

Lev	20: 3	and p my holy name.	2725
Jer	34:16	you have turned around and p my name;	2725
Eze	13:19	*You* have p me among my people for	2725
	20: 9	from **being** p in the eyes of the nations	2725
	20:14	from **being** p in the eyes of the nations	2725
	20:22	from **being** p in the eyes of the nations	2725
	22:26	so that *I* am p among them.	2725
	36:20	among the nations *they* p my holy name,	2725
	36:21	the house of Israel p among the nations	2725
	36:22	of my holy name, which *you* have p among	2725
	36:23	which *has* **been** p among the nations,	2725
	36:23	the name *you* have p among them.	2725
	39: 7	*I* will no longer **let** my holy name **be** p,	2725

PROFESS (3) [PROFESSED]

1Ti	2:10	for women who p to worship God.	2040
Heb	4:14	let us hold firmly to the faith we p.	3934
	10:23	Let us hold unswervingly to the hope we p,	3934

PROFESSED (1) [PROFESS]

1Ti	6:21	which some *have* p and in doing so have	2040

PROFIT (12) [PROFITABLE, PROFITS]

Lev	25:37	at interest or sell him food at a p.	5270
Job	20:18	he will not enjoy the p *from* his trading.	2657
	35: 3	You ask him, 'What p *is it* to me,	6122
Pr	14:23	All hard work brings a p,	4639
	21: 5	The plans of the diligent lead to p as surely	4639
Ecc	6:11	and how does that p anyone?	3463
	10:11	there is no p for the charmer.	3862
Isa	23:18	Yet her p and her earnings will be set apart	6087
	44:10	which can p him nothing?	3603
2Co	2:17	**peddle** the word of God **for** p.	2836
Php	3: 7	to my I now consider loss for the sake	3046
Jude	1:11	they have rushed *for* p into Balaam's error;	3635

PROFITABLE (3) [PROFIT]

Pr	3:14	for she is more p than silver	3202+6087
	31:18	She sees that her trading is p,	3202
Tit	3: 8	These things are excellent and p	6068

PROFITS (3) [PROFIT]

Job	34: 9	'*It* p a man nothing when he tries to please God.'	6122
Ecc	5: 9	the king *himself* p from the fields.	6268
Isa	23:18	Her p will go to those who live before	6087

PROFLIGATE (1)

Dt	21:20	*He is a* p and a drunkard."	2361

PROFOUND (5)

Job	9: 4	His wisdom is p, his power is vast.	4222
Ps	92: 5	O Lord, how p your thoughts!	6676
Ecc	7:24	it is far off and **most** p—who can discover it?	6678+6678
Ac	24: 3	we acknowledge this with p gratitude.	4246
Eph	5:32	This is a p mystery—	3489

PROGRESS (3) [PROGRESSED]

Ezr	5: 8	*is* **making rapid** p under their direction.	10613
Php	1:25	all of you for your p and joy in the faith,	4620
1Ti	4:15	so that everyone may see your p.	4620

PROGRESSED (1) [PROGRESS]

2Ch	24:13	and the repairs p under them.	6590

PROJECT (3) [PROJECTED, PROJECTING, PROJECTION, PROJECTIONS, PROJECTS]

1Ki	5:16	supervised the p and directed the workmen.	4856
Ne	6: 3	carrying on a great p and cannot go down.	4856
Eze	43:15	and four horns p **upward** from the hearth.	2025+4200+5087

PROJECTED (1) [PROJECT]

1Ki	6: 3	and p ten cubits from the front of the temple	8145

PROJECTING (17) [PROJECT]

1Ki	7:34	one on each corner, p **from** the stand.	4946
Ne	3:25	and the tower p from the upper palace near	3655
	3:26	toward the east and the p tower.	3655
	3:27	from the great p tower to the wall of Ophel.	3655
Eze	40: 7	and the p walls between the alcoves	NIH
	40:10	the faces of the p walls on each side had	382
	40:14	along the faces of the p walls all around	382
	40:16	The alcoves and the p walls inside	382
	40:16	The faces of the p walls were decorated	382
	40:21	its p walls and its portico had	382
	40:26	on the faces of the p walls on each side.	382
	40:29	its p walls and its portico had	382
	40:33	its p walls and its portico had	382
	40:36	its p walls and its portico,	382
	40:48	and its p **walls** were three cubits wide on	4190
	41: 2	and the p **walls** on each side	4190
	41: 3	and the p **walls** on each side	NIH

PROJECTION (2) [PROJECT]

Ex	26:19	for each frame, one under each p.	3338
	36:24	for each frame, one under each p.	3338

PROJECTIONS (2) [PROJECT]

Ex	26:17	with two p set parallel to each other.	3338
	36:22	with two p set parallel to each other.	3338

PROJECTS (2) [PROJECT]

1Ki	9:23	the chief officials in charge of Solomon's p	4856
Ecc	2: 4	I undertook great p: I built houses	5126

PROLONG (5) [PROLONGED]

Dt	5:33	and prosper and p your days in the land	799
Ps	85: 5	*Will you* p your anger through all	5432
Pr	3: 2	for they will p your life many years	802
Isa	53:10	he will see his offspring and p his days,	799
La	4:22	he will not p your exile.	3578

PROLONGED (2) [PROLONG]

Dt	28:59	harsh and p disasters, and severe and	586
Isa	13:22	and her days *will* not **be** p.	5432

PROMINENT (10)

1Ki	21: 9	of fasting and seat Naboth in a p place	8031
	21:12	and seated Naboth in a p place *among*	8031
Est	9: 4	Mordecai was p in the palace;	1524
Isa	9:15	the elders and p men are the head,	5951+7156
Da	8: 5	a goat with a p horn between his eyes came	2607
	8: 8	in its place four p horns grew up toward	2607
Mk	15:43	a p member of the Council,	2363
Lk	14: 1	to eat in the house of a p Pharisee,	807
Ac	17: 4	and not a few p women.	4755
	17:12	*of* p Greek women and many Greek men.	2363

PROMISCUITY (5) [PROMISCUOUS]

Eze	16:25	with increasing p to anyone who passed by.	9373
	16:26	to anger with your increasing p.	9373
	16:29	you increased your p to include Babylonia,	9373
	16:36	and exposed your nakedness in your p	9373
	23:29	Your lewdness and p	9373

PROMISCUOUS (2) [PROMISCUITY]

Dt	22:21	by *being* p while still in her father's house.	2388
Eze	23:19	and more p as she recalled the days	9373

PROMISE (66) [PROMISED, PROMISES]

Ge	47:29	and p that you will show me kindness	NIH
Nu	23:19	*Does he* p and not fulfill?	1819
	30: 6	a **rash** p by which she obligates herself	4439
	30: 8	or the **rash** p by which she obligates herself,	4439
Jos	9:21	So the leaders' p to them *was* kept.	1819
	23:14	Every p has been fulfilled;	1821
	23:15	But just as every good p of the Lord	1821
2Sa	7:25	keep forever the p you have made	1821
1Ki	2: 4	that the Lord may keep his p to me:	1819+1821
	6:12	I will fulfill through you the p I gave	1821
	8:20	"The Lord has kept the p he made:	1821
	8:24	You have kept *your* p to your servant	1819
1Ch	17:23	let the p you have made	1821
2Ch	1: 9	let your p to my father David be confirmed,	1821
	6:10	"The Lord has kept the p he made,	1821
	6:15	You have kept *your* p to your servant	1819
Ne	5:13	every man who does not keep this p.	1821
	9: 8	You have kept your p because you are	1821
	10:30	"We p not to give our daughters	NIH
Ps	77: 8	Has his p failed for all time?	608
	105:42	For he remembered his holy p given	1821
	106:24	they did not believe his p.	1821
	119:38	Fulfill your p to your servant,	614
	119:41	your salvation according to your p;	614
	119:50	Your p preserves my life.	614
	119:58	be gracious to me according to your p.	614
	119:76	according to your p to your servant.	614
	119:82	My eyes fail, looking for your p;	614
	119:116	Sustain me according to your p,	614
	119:123	looking for your righteous p.	614
	119:154	preserve my life according to your p.	614
	119:162	I rejoice in your p like one who finds great spoil.	614
	119:170	deliver me according to your p.	614
Jer	29:10	I will come to you and fulfill my gracious p	1821
	33:14	'when I will fulfill the gracious p I made to	1821
	34: 4	" 'Yet hear the p of the Lord,	1821
	34: 5	*I* myself **make** *this* p,	1819+1821
Ac	2:39	The p is for you and your children and	2039
	7:17	the time drew near for God to fulfill his p	2039
	26: 7	This is **the** p our twelve tribes are hoping	4005S
Ro	4:13	the p that he would be heir of the world,	2039
	4:14	faith has no value and the p is worthless,	2039
	4:16	Therefore, the p comes by faith,	2039
	4:20	not waver through unbelief regarding the p	2039
	9: 8	the children of the p who are regarded	2039
	9: 9	For this was how the p was stated:	2039
Gal	3:14	so that by faith we might receive the p of	2039
	3:17	by God and thus do away with the p.	2039
	3:18	then it no longer depends on a p;	2039
	3:18	gave it to Abraham through a p.	2039
	3:19	the Seed to whom the p referred had come.	2040
	3:29	and heirs according to the p.	2039
	4:23	was born as the result of a p.	2039
	4:28	you, brothers, like Isaac, are children *of* p.	2039
Eph	2:12	and foreigners to the covenants *of* the p,	2039
	3: 6	sharers together in the p in Christ Jesus.	2039
	6: 2	which is the first commandment with a p—	2039
1Ti	4: 8	holding p for both the present life and	2039
2Ti	1: 1	to the p of life that is in Christ Jesus,	2039
Heb	4: 1	since the p of entering his rest still stands,	2039
	6:13	*When* God **made** his p to Abraham,	2040
	11: 9	who were heirs with him *of* the same p.	2039
	11:11	he considered him faithful who *had* **made** the p.	2040
2Pe	2:19	*They* p them freedom, while they	2040
	3: 9	The Lord is not slow in keeping his p,	2039
	3:13	keeping with his p we are looking forward	2041

PROMISED (133) [PROMISE]

Ge	18:19	about for Abraham what *he has* p him."	1819
	21: 1	and the Lord did for Sarah what *he had* p.	1819
	21: 2	at the very time God *had* p him.	1819
	24: 7	and who spoke to me and p me **on oath,**	8678
	28:15	until I have done what *I have* p you."	8678
	50:24	up out of this land to the land *he* p on oath	8678
Ex	12:25	that the Lord will give you as *he* p,	1819
	13:11	as *he* p **on oath** to you and your forefathers,	8678
	32:13	I will give your descendants all this land *I* p them,	606
	33: 1	go up to the land *I* p **on oath** to Abraham,	8678
Lev	19:20	a slave girl p to another man but who has	3072
Nu	10:29	for the Lord *has* p good things to Israel."	1819
	11:12	that *you* p **on oath** to their forefathers?	8678
	14:16	into the land *he* p them **on oath;**	8678
	14:23	of them will ever see the land *I* p **on oath**	8678
	14:40	"We will *go* up on oath to the place the Lord p."	NIH
	32:11	the land *I* p **on oath** to Abraham, Isaac	8678
	32:24	but do what you have p."	3655+4946+7023
Dt	1:11	a thousand times and bless you as *he has* p!	1819
	6: 3	the Lord the God of your fathers, p you.	1819

Dt 6:18 the LORD p on oath to your forefathers, 8678
6:23 the land that *he* p on oath to our forefathers. 8678
8:1 the LORD p on oath to your forefathers. 8678
9:3 as the LORD *has* p you. 1819
9:28 to take them into the land *he had* p them, 1819
11:25 The LORD your God, as *he* p you, 1819
12:20 has enlarged your territory as *he* p you, 1819
13:17 as *he* p on oath to your forefathers, 8678
15:6 your God will bless you as *he has* p, 1819
18:2 LORD is their inheritance, as *he* p them. 1819
19:8 as *he* p on oath to your forefathers, 8678
19:8 and gives you the whole land *he* p them, 1819
26:15 as *you* p on oath to our forefathers, 8678
26:18 his treasured possession as *he* p, 1819
26:19 to the LORD your God, as *he* p. 1819
27:3 the God of your fathers, p you. 1819
28:9 as his holy people, as *he* p you on oath, 8678
29:13 as *he* p you and as he swore to your fathers, 1819
31:20 the land *I* p on oath to their forefathers, 8678
31:21 into the land *I* p them on oath." 8678
31:23 into the land *I* p them on oath, 8678
34:4 "This is the land *I* p on oath to Abraham, 8678
Jos 1:3 as *I* p Moses. 1819
5:6 that *he had* solemnly p their fathers 8678
13:14 are their inheritance, as *he* p them. 1819
13:33 is their inheritance, as *he* p them. 1819
14:10 "Now then, just as the LORD p, 1819
14:12 that the LORD p me that day. 1819
22:4 as *he* p, return to your homes in the land 1819
23:5 as the LORD your God p you. 1819
23:10 LORD your God fights for you, just as *he* p. 1819
Jdg 1:20 As Moses *had* p, Hebron was given to Caleb, 1819
6:36 by my hand as *you have* p— 1819
11:36 Do to me just as you p, 3655+4946+7023
1Sa 2:30 '*I* p that your house and your father's 606+606
25:30 for my master every good thing *he* p 1819
2Sa 3:9 for David what the LORD p him on oath 8678
3:18 For the LORD p David, 606
7:25 Do as *you* p, 1819
7:28 and *you have* p these good things 1819
19:23 And the king p him on oath. 8678
1Ki 2:24 and has founded a dynasty for me as *he* p— 1819
5:12 just as *he had* p him. 1819
8:15 with his own hand has fulfilled what *he* p 1819
8:20 the throne of Israel, just as the LORD p, 1819
8:24 with your mouth *you have* p and 1819
8:26 let your word that *you* p your servant David my father come true. 1819
8:56 to his people Israel just as *he* p. 1819
9:5 as *I* p David your father when I said, 1819
2Ki 8:19 *He had* p to maintain a lamp for David 606
10:10 The LORD has done what *he* p 1819
20:9 that the LORD will do what *he has* p: 1819
1Ch 11:3 as the LORD had p through Samuel. 1821
11:10 over the whole land, as the LORD had p 1821
17:23 house be established forever. Do as *you* p, 1819
17:26 *You have* p these good things 1819
27:23 because the LORD *had* p to make Israel 1819
2Ch 2:15 and barley and the olive oil and wine *he* p, 606
6:4 who with his hands has fulfilled what *he* p 1819
6:10 the throne of Israel, just as the LORD p, 1819
6:15 with your mouth *you have* p and 1819
6:17 that *you* p your servant David come true. 1819
6:42 the *great love* p to David your servant." AIT
21:7 *He had* p to maintain a lamp for him 606
23:3 the LORD p concerning the descendants 1819
Ne 5:12 an oath to do what they had p. 1821
5:13 And the people did as they had p. 1821
Est 4:7 the exact amount of money Haman *had* p 606
Ps 66:14 vows my lips p and my mouth spoke 7198
119:57 *I have* p to obey your words. 606
Isa 38:7 that the LORD will do what *he has* p: 1819
55:3 my faithful *love* p to David. AIT
Jer 32:42 the prosperity *I have* p them. 1819
44:25 what *you* p when you said, 928+1819+7023
44:25 "Go ahead then, do what *you* p! 5624
Mt 14:7 that *he* p with an oath to give her whatever 3933
Mk 6:23 p her **with an oath**," "Whatever you ask 3923
14:11 They were delighted to hear this and p 2040
Lk 2:29 as you have p, you now dismiss 4839
24:49 to send you what my Father has p; 2039
Ac 1:4 but wait for the gift my Father p, 2039
2:30 a prophet and knew that God *had* p him 3923
2:33 from the Father the p Holy Spirit 2039
3:21 as *he* p long ago through his holy prophets. 3281
7:5 But God p him that he and his descendants 2040
13:23 to Israel the Savior Jesus, as *he* p. 2039
13:32 What God p our fathers 1181+2039
13:34 **holy and sure blessings** p to David.' 4008
18:21 But as he left, he p, "I will come back 3306
26:6 hope in what God has p our fathers 1181+2039
Ro 1:2 the gospel he p beforehand through his 4600
4:21 that God had power to do what he *had* p. 2040
2Co 9:5 for the generous gift you *had* p. 4600
11:2 *I* p you to one husband, to Christ, 764
Gal 3:22 that what *was* p, being given through faith 2039
Eph 1:13 with a seal, the p Holy Spirit, 2039
Tit 1:2 p before the beginning of time, 2039
Heb 6:12 and patience inherit **what has been** p. 2039+3836
6:13 Abraham received **what was** p. 2039+3836
6:17 to the heirs *of* **what was** p, 2039+3836
9:15 may receive the p eternal inheritance— 2039
10:23 for he who p is faithful. 2040
10:36 you will receive what he has p. 2039
11:9 By faith he made his home in the p land 2039
11:13 They did not receive the things p; 2039

Heb 11:33 and gained **what was** p; 2039
11:39 yet none of them received **what had been** p. 2039+3836
12:26 but now he has p, 2040
Jas 1:12 that God has p to those who love him. 2040
2:5 the kingdom he p those who love him? 2040
2Pe 3:4 "Where is this 'coming' he p? 2039
1Jn 2:25 this is what he p us—even eternal life. 2039+2040

PROMISES (23) [PROMISE]
Jos 21:45 of all the LORD's good p to the house 1819+1821
23:14 that not one of all the good p the LORD 1821
1Ki 8:25 the p *you* **made** to him when you said, 1819
8:56 has failed of all the good p he gave 1821
1Ch 17:19 and made known all these **great** p. AIT
25:5 They were given him through the p *of* God 1821
2Ch 6:16 the p *you* **made** to him when you said, 1819
Ps 85:8 he p peace to his people, his saints— 1819
106:12 they believed his p and sang his praise. 1821
119:140 Your p have been thoroughly tested, 614
119:148 that I may meditate on your p. 614
145:13 The LORD is faithful to all his p 1821
Hos 10:4 They **make many** p, take false oaths 1819+1821
Ro 9:4 the temple worship and the p, 2039
15:8 to confirm the p made to the patriarchs 2039
2Co 1:20 For no matter how many p God has made, 2039
7:1 Since we have these p, dear friends, 2039
Gal 3:16 The p were spoken to Abraham and 2039
3:21 the law, therefore, opposed to the p of God? 2039
Heb 7:6 and blessed him who had the p. 2039
8:6 and it is founded on better p. 2039
11:17 He who had received the p was about to 2039
2Pe 1:4 his very great and precious p, so that 2041

PROMOTE (7) [PROMOTED, PROMOTES]
Ne 2:10 that someone had come to p the welfare of 1335
Pr 12:20 but joy for *those who* p peace. 3619
16:21 and pleasant words p instruction. 3578
16:23 and his lips p instruction. 3578
Da 5:19 the wanted to p, he promoted; NIH
Hab 1:7 a law to themselves and p their own honor. 3655
1Ti 1:4 These p controversies rather than God's work— 4218

PROMOTED (3) [PROMOTE]
2Ch 28:19 for he had p **wickedness** in Judah 7277
Da 3:30 Then the king p Shadrach, Meshach and 10613
5:19 those he wanted to promote, he p; 10659

PROMOTES (2) [PROMOTE]
Pr 17:9 He who covers over an offense p love, 1335
Gal 2:17 does that mean that Christ p sin? 281+1356

PROMPT (1) [PROMPTED, PROMPTS]
Job 20:2 "My troubled thoughts p me **to answer** 8740

PROMPTED (4) [PROMPT]
Mt 14:8 P by her mother, she said, 4586
Jn 13:2 and the devil *had* already p Judas Iscariot, 965+1650+2840+3836
1Th 1:3 your labor p *by* **love**, your endurance AIT
2Th 1:11 of yours and every act p *by* your **faith**. AIT

PROMPTS (2) [PROMPT]
Ex 25:2 from each man whose heart p him **to give.** 5605
Job 15:5 Your sin p your mouth; 544

PRONE (1)
Ex 32:22 "You know how p these people are **to evil.** 928

PRONOUNCE (30) [PRONOUNCED, PRONOUNCES, PRONOUNCING]
Ge 48:20 "In your name *will* Israel p *this* **blessing:** 1385
Lev 13:3 *shall* p him **ceremonially unclean.** 3237
13:6 the priest *shall* p him **clean;** 3197
13:8 he *shall* p him **unclean.** 3237
13:11 and the priest *shall* p him **unclean.** 3237
13:13 he *shall* p that person **clean.** 3197
13:15 he *shall* p him **unclean.** 3237
13:17 the priest *shall* p the infected person **clean;** 3197
13:20 the priest *shall* p him **unclean.** 3237
13:22 the priest *shall* p him **unclean.** 3237
13:23 and the priest *shall* p him **clean.** 3197
13:25 The priest *shall* p him **unclean;** 3237
13:27 the priest *shall* p him **unclean;** 3237
13:28 and the priest *shall* p him **clean;** 3197
13:30 the priest *shall* p that person **unclean;** 3237
13:34 the priest *shall* p him **clean.** 3197
13:37 and the priest *shall* p him **clean.** 3197
13:44 The priest *shall* p him **unclean** 3237+3237
14:7 of the infectious disease and p him **clean.** 3197
14:48 he *shall* p the house **clean,** 3197
Dt 10:8 to minister and to p **blessings** in his name, 1385
21:5 to minister and to p **blessings** in the name 1385
23:4 in Aram Naharaim to p a **curse on** you. 7837
27:13 stand on Mount Ebal to p **curses:** 7839
Jdg 12:6 because *he* could not p the word correctly, 1819
1Ch 23:13 to minister before him and to p **blessings** 1385
Job 9:20 I were blameless, *it would* p me **guilty,** 6835
Ps 109:17 He loved to p a curse—may it come on him; NIH
Jer 1:16 *I will* p my judgments *on* my people 1819

Jer 4:12 Now I p my judgments against them." 1819

PRONOUNCED (20) [PRONOUNCE]
Lev 13:7 to the priest to be p **clean,** 3200
13:35 in the skin after he is p **clean,** 3200
14:36 nothing in the house *will be* p **unclean.** 3237
Dt 33:1 of God p *on* the Israelites before his death. 1385
Jos 6:26 At that time Joshua p *this* **solemn oath:** 8678
1Ki 20:40 "*You have* p it yourself." 3076
2Ki 23:17 from Judah and p against the altar of Bethel 7924
25:6 where sentence *was* p on him. 907+1819
1Ch 16:12 his miracles, and the judgments he p, 7023
Ps 76:8 From heaven *you* p judgment, 9048
105:5 his miracles, and the judgments he p, 7023
Jer 19:15 around it every disaster *I* p against them, 1819
26:13 not bring the disaster he has p against you. 1819
26:19 not bring the disaster he p against them? 1819
35:17 in Jerusalem every disaster *I* p against them. 1819
36:7 the anger and wrath p against this people 1819
36:31 and the people of Judah every disaster *I* p 1819
39:5 where he p sentence **on** him. 907+1819
52:9 where he p sentence **on** him. 907+1819
Da 7:22 the Ancient of Days came and p judgment 10314

PRONOUNCES (1) [PRONOUNCE]
Lev 14:11 The priest who p him **clean** shall present 3197

PRONOUNCING (1) [PRONOUNCE]
Lev 13:59 for p them **clean** or unclean. 3197

PROOF (7) [PROVE]
Dt 22:14 I did not find p of her **virginity,"** 1436
22:15 shall bring p **that** she was **a virgin** 1436
22:17 here is the p of my daughter's **virginity."** 1436
22:20 and no p of the girl's **virginity** can be 1436
Ac 17:31 *He has* **given** p of this to all men 4218+4411
2Co 8:24 show these men the p of your love 1893
13:3 since you are demanding p that Christ 1509

PROOFS (1) [PROVE]
Ac 1:3 to these men and gave many **convincing p** 5447

PROPER (29) [PROPERLY]
Lev 5:15 one without defect and of the p **value** 6886
5:18 one without defect and of the p **value.** 6886
6:6 one without defect and of the p **value.** 6886
Jdg 6:26 a p kind of altar to the LORD your God on 5120
2Sa 15:3 "Look, your claims are valid and p, 5791
1Ki 4:28 also brought to the p place their quotas 889+2118+5226+9004
1Ch 23:31 before the LORD regularly in the *p* **number** AIT
Ezr 4:14 to the palace and it is not p for us to see 10071
Ps 104:27 to you to give them their food at the p **time.** 6961
145:15 and you give them their food at the p **time.** 6961
Ecc 5:18 Then I realized that it is good and p for 3637
6:3 and does not receive p **burial,** 7690
8:5 will know the p time and **procedure.** 5477
8:6 a p time and **procedure** for every matter, 5477
10:17 and whose princes eat at a *p* **time—** AIT
Jer 30:18 and the palace will stand in its p **place.** 5477
Mt 3:15 it is p for us to do this to fulfill all righteousness." 4560
24:45 to give them their food at **the p time?** 2789
Lk 1:20 which will come true at their **p time."** 2789
12:42 their food allowance at **the p time?** 2789
Ac 1:42 Though they found no p **ground** for 162
1Co 11:13 Is it p for a woman to pray to God 4560
2Co 10:13 however, will not boast beyond p limits, NIG
Gal 6:9 the p time we will reap a harvest if we do 2625
2Th 2:6 so that he may be revealed at the p **time.** 1571
1Ti 2:6 the testimony given in *its* p time. 2625
3:4 that his children obey him with p **respect.** 4246
5:3 Give p recognition to those widows NIG
1Pe 2:17 **Show p respect to** everyone: 5506

PROPERLY (1) [PROPER]
1Ti 1:8 that the law is good if one uses it p. 3789

PROPERTY (65)
Ge 23:4 Sell me *some p* for a burial site here 299
23:18 to Abraham as his p in the presence of all 5239
34:10 Live in it, trade in it, and **acquire** p in it." 296
34:23 Won't their livestock, their p 7871
47:11 and gave them p in the best part of the land, 299
47:27 *They* **acquired** p there and were fruitful 296
Ex 21:21 since the slave is his p. 4084
22:8 has laid hands on the other man's p. 4856
22:9 or any other **lost** *p* about which someone AIT
22:11 not lay hands on the other person's p. 4856
Lev 6:3 or if he finds **lost** p and lies about it, or 8
6:4 entrusted to him, or the **lost** p he found, 8
25:10 each one of you is to return to his **family** p 299
25:13 everyone is to return to his own p. 299
25:25 becomes poor and sells some of his p, 299
25:27 he can then go back to his own p. 299
25:28 and he can then go back to his p. 299
25:33 So the p of the Levites is redeemable— 889S
25:33 the Levites are their p among the Israelites. 299
25:41 and to the p *of* his forefathers. 299
25:45 and they will become your p. 299
25:46 as inherited p and can make them slaves 299
27:21 it will become the p of the priests. 299

Nu	27: 4	Give us **p** among our father's relatives."	299
	27: 7	You must certainly give them **p** as	299
	32:32	but the **p** we inherit will be on this side of	299
	35:28	high priest may he return to his own **p**.	299+824
	36: 4	and their **p** will be taken from the tribal	5709
Dt	21:16	when he wills his **p** to his sons,	889+2118+4200S
Ru	4: 5	maintain the name of the dead with his **p**."	5709
	4: 7	for the redemption and **transfer of p** to become final,	1821+3972+9455
	4: 9	that I have bought from Naomi all **the p**	889S
	4:10	the name of the dead with his **p**,	5709
1Sa	25: 2	who had **p** there at Carmel,	5126
	25:21	all my watching over this fellow's **p** in	889S
1Ki	21:19	not murdered a man and **seized his p**?'	3769
1Ch	7: 1	Now the first to resettle on their own **p**	299
	27:31	the officials in charge of King David's **p**.	8214
	28: 1	the **p** and livestock belonging to the king	8214
2Ch	11:14	even abandoned their pasturelands and **p**,	299
	31: 1	to their own towns and to their own **p**.	299
Ezr	7:26	confiscation of **p**, or imprisonment.	10470
	10: 8	within three days would forfeit all his **p**,	8214
Ne	11: 3	each on his own **p** in the various towns,	299
	11:20	each on his **ancestral p**.	5709
Est	8:11	and to plunder the **p** of their enemies.	8965
Job	5:24	of your **p** and find nothing missing.	5659
Jer	37:12	**get his share of the p** among the people	2745
Eze	45: 6	the city as its **p** an area 5,000 cubits wide	299
	45: 7	by the sacred district and the **p** of the city.	299
	46:16	it is to be their **p** by inheritance.	299
	46:18	driving them off their **p**.	299
	46:18	inheritance out of his own **p**,	299
	46:18	be separated from his **p**.'"	299
	48:20	along with the **p** of the city.	299
	48:21	and the city will belong to the prince.	299
	48:22	So the **p** of the Levites and the property of	299
	48:22	and the **p** of the city will lie in the center of	299
Mt	25:14	called his servants and entrusted his **p**	3836+5639
Lk	15:12	So he divided his **p** between them.	1050
	15:30	of yours who has squandered your **p**	1050
	16:12	not been trustworthy with someone else's **p**,	NIG
	16:12	will give you **p** of your own?	NIG
Ac	5: 1	his wife Sapphira, also sold a **piece of p**.	3228
Heb	10:34	the confiscation of your **p**,	5639

PROPHECIES (4) [PROPHESY]

2Ch	24:27	the many **p** about him, and the record of	5363
1Co	13: 8	But where there are **p**, they will cease;	4735
1Th	5:20	do not treat **p** with contempt.	4735
1Ti	1:18	in keeping with the **p** once made about you,	4735

PROPHECY (20) [PROPHESY]

2Ki	9:25	when the LORD made this **p** about him:	5363
2Ch	9:29	in the **p** of Ahijah the Shilonite and in	5553
	15: 8	the **p** of Azariah son of Oded the prophet,	5553
Eze	14: 9	"'And if the prophet is enticed to utter a **p**,	1821
Da	9:24	to seal up vision and **p** and to anoint	5566
Mt	13:14	In them is fulfilled the **p** of Isaiah:	4735
1Co	12:10	to another miraculous powers, to another **p**,	4735
	13: 2	the **gift of p** and can fathom all mysteries	4735
	14: 1	spiritual gifts, especially the gift of **p**.	4736
	14: 6	or knowledge or **p** or word of instruction?	4735
	14:22	**p**, however, is for believers,	4735
2Th	2: 2	unsettled or alarmed by some **p**,	4460
2Pe	1:20	that no **p** of Scripture came about by	4735
	1:21	never had its origin in the will of man,	4735
Rev	1: 3	the one who reads the words of this **p**,	4735
	19:10	For the testimony of Jesus is the spirit of **p**."	4735
	22: 7	Blessed is he who keeps the words of the **p**	4735
	22:10	not seal up the words of the **p** of this book,	4735
	22:18	the words of the **p** of this book:	4735
	22:19	takes words away from this book of **p**,	4735

PROPHESIED (36) [PROPHESY]

Nu	11:25	When the Spirit rested on them, they **p**,	5547
	11:26	and they **p** in the camp.	5547
1Sa	19:20	upon Saul's men and they also **p**.	5547
	19:21	he sent more men, and they **p** too.	5547
	19:21	Saul sent men a third time, and they also **p**.	5547
	19:24	He stripped off his robes and also **p**	5547
1Ch	25: 2	who **p** under the king's supervision.	5547
	25: 3	of their father Jeduthun, who **p**,	5547
2Ch	20:37	Eliezer son of Dodavahu of Mareshah **p**	5547
Ezr	5: 1	**p** to the Jews in Judah and Jerusalem in	10451
Ne	6:12	but that he had **p** against me because	1819+5553
Jer	2: 8	The prophets **p** by Baal,	5547
	20: 6	to whom you have **p** lies.'"	5547
	23:13	They **p** by Baal and led my people Israel	5547
	23:21	I did not speak to them, yet they have **p**.	5547
	25:13	in this book and **p** by Jeremiah against all	5547
	26:11	to death because he has **p** against this city.	5547
	26:18	"Micah of Moresheth **p** in the days	5547
	26:20	from Kiriath Jearim was another man who **p**	5547
	26:20	he **p** the same things against this city	5547
	28: 6	the LORD fulfill the words you have **p**	5547
	28: 8	who preceded you and me have **p** war,	5547
	29:31	Because Shemaiah has **p** to you,	5547
	37:19	Where are your prophets who **p** to you,	5547
Eze	13:16	those prophets of Israel who **p** to Jerusalem	5547
	37: 7	So **I p** as I was commanded,	5547
	37:10	So **I p** as he commanded me,	5547
	38:17	At that time they **p** for years	5547
Mt	11:13	all the Prophets and the Law **p** until John.	4736
Mk	7: 6	when he **p** about you hypocrites;	4736
Lk	1:67	was filled with the Holy Spirit and **p**:	4736

Jn	11:51	that year he **p** that Jesus would die for	4736
Ac	19: 6	and they spoke in tongues and **p**.	4736
	21: 9	He had four unmarried daughters who **p**.	4736
Jude	1:14	the seventh from Adam, **p** about these men:	4736

PROPHESIES (13) [PROPHESY]

1Ki	22: 8	because he never **p** anything good	5547
	22:18	that he never **p** anything good about me,	5547
2Ch	18: 7	because he never **p** anything good	5547
	18:17	that he never **p** anything good about me,	5547
Jer	28: 9	the prophet who **p** peace will be recognized	5547
Eze	12:27	and he **p** about the distant future.'	5547
Zec	13: 3	And if anyone still **p**, his father and mother	5547
	13: 3	When he **p**, his own parents will stab him.	5547
1Co	11: 4	Every man who prays or **p** with his head	4736
	11: 5	And every woman who prays or **p**	4736
	14: 3	But everyone who **p** speaks to men	4736
	14: 4	but he who **p** edifies the church.	4736
	14: 5	He who **p** is greater than one who speaks	4736

PROPHESY (65) [PROPHECIES, PROPHECY, PROPHESIED, PROPHESIES, PROPHESYING, PROPHET, PROPHET'S, PROPHETESS, PROPHETIC, PROPHETS]

1Sa	10: 6	and you will **p** with them;	5547
Isa	30:10	Tell us pleasant things, **p** illusions.	2600
Jer	5:31	The prophets **p** lies, the priests rule	5547
	11:21	'Do not **p** in the name of the LORD	5547
	14:14	where the LORD had sent him to **p**.	5547
	23:25	the prophets say who **p** lies in my name.	5547
	23:26	who **p** the delusions of their own minds?'	5566
	23:32	I am against those who **p** false dreams,"	5547
	25:30	"Now **p** all these words against them	5547
	26: 9	Why do you **p** in the LORD's name	5547
	26:12	to **p** against this house and this city all	5547
	27:10	They **p** lies to you that will only serve	5547
	27:15	both you and the prophets who **p** to you.'"	5547
	32: 3	saying, "Why do you **p** as you do?	5547
Eze	4: 7	of Jerusalem and with bared arm **p**	5547
	6: 2	the mountains of Israel; **p** against them	5547
	11: 4	Therefore **p** against them;	5547
	11: 4	Therefore prophesy against them; **p**,	5547
	13: 2	**p** against the prophets of Israel who are	5547
	13: 2	to those who **p** out of their own imagination	5566
	13:17	the daughters of your people who **p** out	5547
	13:17	of their own imagination. **P** against them	5547
	20:46	and **p** against the forest of the southland.	5547
	21: 2	**P** against the land of Israel	5547
	21: 9	**p** and say, 'This is what the Lord says:	5547
	21:14	**p** and strike your hands together.	5547
	21:28	"And you, son of man, **p** and say,	5547
	25: 2	against the Ammonites and **p** against them.	5547
	28:21	your face against Sidon; **p** against her	5547
	29: 2	and **p** against him and against all Egypt.	5547
	30: 2	"Son of man, **p** and say:	5547
	34: 2	**p** against the shepherds of Israel;	5547
	34: 2	**p** and say to them:	5547
	35: 2	face against Mount Seir; **p** against it	5547
	36: 1	**p** to the mountains of Israel and say,	5547
	36: 3	Therefore **p** and say, 'This is what	5547
	36: 6	Therefore **p** concerning the land of Israel	5547
	37: 4	"**P** to these bones and say to them,	5547
	37: 9	Then he said to me, "**P** to the breath;	5547
	37: 9	**p**, son of man, and say to it,	5547
	37:12	Therefore **p** and say to them:	5547
	38: 2	of Meshech and Tubal; **p** against him	5547
	38:14	"Therefore, son of man, **p** and say to Gog:	5547
	39: 1	"Son of man, **p** against Gog and say:	5547
Joel	2:28	Your sons and daughters will **p**,	5547
Am	2:12	and commanded the prophets not to **p**.	5547
	3: 8	LORD has spoken—who can but **p**?	5547
	7:13	Don't **p** anymore at Bethel,	5547
	7:15	'Go, **p** to my people Israel.'	5547
	7:16	You say, "'Do not **p** against Israel,	5547
Mic	2: 6	"Do not **p**," their prophets say.	5752
	2: 6	"Do not **p** about these things;	5752
	2:11	'I will **p** for you plenty of wine	5752
Mt	7:22	'Lord, Lord, did we not **p** in your name,	4736
	26:68	and said, "**P** to us, Christ. Who hit you?"	4736
Mk	14:65	struck him with their fists, and said, "**P**!"	4736
Lk	22:64	They blindfolded him and demanded, "**P**!	4736
Ac	2:17	Your sons and daughters will **p**,	4736
	2:18	my Spirit in those days, and they will **p**.	4736
1Co	13: 9	For we know in part and we **p** in part,	4736
	14: 5	but I would rather have you **p**.	4736
	14:31	For you can all **p** in turn so	4736
	14:39	Therefore, my brothers, be eager to **p**,	4736
Rev	10:11	"You must again **p** about many peoples,	4736
	11: 3	and they will **p** for 1,260 days,	4736

PROPHESYING (32) [PROPHESY]

Nu	11:27	"Eldad and Medad are **p** in the camp."	5547
1Sa	10: 5	and they will be **p**.	5547
	10:10	and he joined in their **p**.	5547
	10:11	who had formerly known him saw him **p**	5547
	10:13	Saul stopped **p**, he went to the high place.	5547
	10:18	He was **p** in his house,	5547
	19:20	But when they saw a group of prophets **p**,	5547
	19:23	and he walked along until he came	5547
1Ki	18:29	and they continued their **frantic** until	5547
	18:29	with all the prophets **p** before them.	5547
	22:12	the other prophets were **p** the same thing.	5547

1Ch	25: 1	Heman and Jeduthun for the ministry of **p**,	5547
2Ch	18: 9	with all the prophets **p** before them.	5547
	18:11	the other prophets were **p** the same thing.	5547
Jer	14:14	"The prophets are **p** lies in my name.	5547
	14:14	They are **p** to you false visions, divinations,	5547
	14:15	about the prophets who are **p** in my name:	5547
	14:16	the people they are **p** to will be thrown out	5547
	20: 1	heard Jeremiah **p** these things,	5547
	23:16	not listen to what the prophets are **p** to you;	5547
	27:14	for they are **p** lies to you.	5547
	27:15	'They are **p** lies in my name.	5547
	27:16	They are **p** lies to you.	5547
	29: 9	They are **p** lies to you in my name.	5547
	29:21	who are **p** lies in my name,	5547
Eze	11:13	as I was **p**, Pelatiah son of Benaiah died.	5547
	13: 2	the prophets of Israel who are now **p**.	5547
	37: 7	And as I was **p**, there was a noise,	5547
Am	7:12	Earn your bread there and do your **p** there.	5547
Ro	12: 6	If a man's gift is **p**, let him use it	4735
1Co	14:24	comes in while everybody is **p**,	4736
Rev	11: 6	not rain during the time they are **p**;	4735

PROPHET (238) [PROPHESY]

Ge	20: 7	Now return the man's wife, for he is a **p**,	5566
Ex	7: 1	and your brother Aaron will be your **p**.	5566
Nu	12: 6	"When a **p** of the LORD is among you,	5566
Dt	13: 1	If a **p**, or one who foretells by dreams,	5566
	13: 3	not listen to the words of that **p** or dreamer.	5566
	13: 5	That **p** or dreamer must be put to death,	5566
	18:15	a **p** like me from among your own brothers.	5566
	18:18	I will raise up for them a **p** like you from	5566
	18:19	to my words that the **p** speaks in my name,	NIH
	18:20	But a **p** who presumes to speak in my name	5566
	18:20	a **p** who speaks in the name of other gods,	5566
	18:22	If what a **p** proclaims in the name of	5566
	18:22	That **p** has spoken presumptuously.	5566
	34:10	no **p** has risen in Israel like Moses,	5566
Jdg	6: 8	he sent them a **p**, who said, "This is what	5566
1Sa	3:20	Samuel was attested as a **p** of the LORD.	5566
	9: 9	the **p** of today used to be called a seer.)	5566
	22: 5	But the **p** Gad said to David,	5566
2Sa	7: 2	he said to Nathan the **p**,	5566
	12:25	he sent word through Nathan the **p**	5566
	24:11	of the LORD had come to Gad the **p**,	5566
1Ki	1: 8	Benaiah son of Jehoiada, Nathan the **p**,	5566
	1:10	not invite Nathan the **p** or Benaiah or	5566
	1:22	Nathan the **p** arrived.	5566
	1:23	they told the king, "Nathan the **p** is here."	5566
	1:32	Nathan the **p** and Benaiah son of Jehoiada."	5566
	1:34	the priest and Nathan the **p** anoint him king	5566
	1:38	So Zadok the priest, Nathan the **p**,	5566
	1:44	Nathan the **p**, Benaiah son of Jehoiada,	5566
	1:45	and Nathan the **p** have anointed him king	5566
	11:29	Ahijah the **p** of Shiloh met him on the way,	5566
	13:11	there was a certain old **p** living in Bethel,	5566
	13:15	So the **p** said to him,	NIH
	13:18	The old **p** answered, "I too am a prophet,	NIH
	13:18	The old prophet answered, "I too am a **p**,	5566
	13:20	to the old **p** who had brought him back.	5566
	13:23	the **p** who had brought him back saddled his donkey	5566
	13:25	in the city where the old **p** lived.	5566
	13:26	When the **p** who had brought him back	5566
	13:27	The **p** said to his sons,	NIH
	13:29	**p** picked up the body of the man of God,	5566
	14: 2	Ahijah the **p** is there—	5566
	14:18	through his servant the **p** Ahijah.	5566
	16: 7	through the **p** Jehu son of Hanani to Baasha	5566
	16:12	against Baasha through the **p** Jehu—	5566
	18:36	the **p** Elijah stepped forward and prayed:	5566
	19:16	from Abel Meholah to succeed you as **p**.	5566
	20:13	Meanwhile a **p** came to Ahab king of Israel	5566
	20:14	The **p** replied, "This is what	NIH
	20:14	The **p** answered, "You will."	NIH
	20:22	the **p** came to the king of Israel and said:	5566
	20:36	So the **p** said, "Because you have not obeyed	NIH
	20:37	The **p** found another man and said,	NIH
	20:38	the **p** went and stood by the road waiting	5566
	20:39	the king passed by, **the p** called out to him,	2085S
	20:41	Then the **p** quickly removed the headband	NIH
	22: 7	"Is there not a **p** of the LORD here	5566
2Ki	3:11	"Is there no **p** of the LORD here,	5566
	5: 3	"If only my master would see the **p** who is	5566
	5: 8	and he will know that there is a **p** in Israel."	5566
	5:13	if the **p** had told you to do some great thing,	5566
	5:16	The **p** answered, "As surely as the LORD	NIH
	6:12	"but Elisha, the **p** who is in Israel,	5566
	6:16	"Don't be afraid," the **p** answered.	5566
	9: 1	The **p** Elisha summoned a man from	5566
	9: 4	young man, the **p**, went to Ramoth Gilead.	5566
	14:25	Then the **p** poured the oil on Jehu's head	NIH
	14:25	Jonah son of Amittai, the **p** from Gath Hepher.	5566
	19: 2	to the **p** Isaiah son of Amoz.	5566
	20: 1	The **p** Isaiah son of Amoz went to him	5566
	20:11	Then the **p** Isaiah called upon the LORD,	5566
	20:14	Then Isaiah the **p** went to King Hezekiah	5566
	20:15	The **p** asked, "What did they see	NIH
	23:18	of the **p** who had come from Samaria.	5566
1Ch	17: 1	he said to Nathan the **p**, "Here I am,	5566
	29:29	the records of Nathan the **p** and the records	5566
2Ch	9:29	not written in the records of Nathan the **p**,	5566
	12: 5	the **p** Shemaiah came to Rehoboam	5566
	12:15	the records of Shemaiah the **p** and of Iddo	5566
	13:22	are written in the annotations of the **p** Iddo	5566
	15: 8	the prophecy of Azariah son of Oded the **p**,	5566

2Ch	18: 6	"Is there not a p of the LORD here	5566
	21:12	Jehoram received a letter from Elijah the p,	5566
	25:15	and he sent a p to him, who said,	5566
	25:16	So the p stopped but said,	5566
	26:22	are recorded by the p Isaiah son of Amoz.	5566
	28: 9	a p of the LORD named Oded was there,	5566
	29:25	and Gad the king's seer and Nathan the p;	5566
	32:20	and the p Isaiah son of Amoz cried out	5566
	32:32	in the vision of the p Isaiah son of Amoz in	5566
	35:18	in Israel since the days of the p Samuel;	5566
	36:12	not humble himself before Jeremiah the p,	5566
Ezr	5: 1	Haggai the p and Zechariah the prophet,	10455
	5: 1	Haggai the prophet and Zechariah the p,	10455
	6:14	under the preaching of Haggai the p	10455
Ps	51: T	When the p Nathan came to him	
Isa	3: 2	the judge and p, the soothsayer and elder,	5566
	37: 2	to the p Isaiah son of Amoz.	5566
	38: 1	The p Isaiah son of Amoz went to him	5566
	39: 3	Then Isaiah the p went to King Hezekiah	5566
	39: 4	the p asked, "What did they see	NIH
Jer	1: 5	I appointed you as a p to the nations."	5566
	14:18	Both p and priest have gone to	5566
	20: 2	he had Jeremiah the p beaten and put in	5566
	23:11	"Both p and priest are godless;	5566
	23:28	Let the p who has a dream tell his dream,	5566
	23:33	"When these people, or a p or a priest,	5566
	23:34	If a p or a priest or anyone else claims,	5566
	23:37	This is what you keep saying to a p:	5566
	25: 2	the p said to all the people of Judah and	5566
	28: 1	the p Hananiah son of Azzur,	5566
	28: 5	Then the p Jeremiah replied to	5566
	28: 5	to the p Hananiah before the priests and all	5566
	28: 9	But the p who prophesies peace will	5566
	28:10	the p Hananiah took the yoke off the neck	5566
	28:10	the neck of the p Jeremiah and broke it,	5566
	28:11	At this, the p Jeremiah went on his way.	5566
	28:12	Shortly after the p Hananiah had broken	5566
	28:12	the yoke off the neck of the p Jeremiah,	5566
	28:15	p Jeremiah said to Hananiah the prophet,	5566
	28:15	prophet Jeremiah said to Hananiah the p,	5566
	28:17	Hananiah the p died.	5566
	29: 1	the text of the letter that the p Jeremiah sent	5566
	29:26	you should put any madman who acts like a p into the stocks	5547
	29:27	who poses as a p among you?	5547
	29:29	however, read the letter to Jeremiah the p.	5566
	32: 2	the p was confined in the courtyard of	5566
	34: 6	the p told all this to Zedekiah king	5566
	36: 8	everything Jeremiah the p told him to do;	5566
	36:26	the scribe and Jeremiah the p.	5566
	37: 2	through Jeremiah the p.	5566
	37: 3	to Jeremiah the p with this message:	5566
	37: 6	of the LORD came to Jeremiah the p:	5566
	38: 9	in all they have done to Jeremiah the p.	5566
	38:10	and lift Jeremiah the p out of the cistern	5566
	38:14	for Jeremiah the p and had him brought to	5566
	42: 2	Jeremiah the p and said to him,	5566
	42: 4	"I have heard you," replied Jeremiah the p.	5566
	43: 6	Jeremiah the p and Baruch son of Neriah.	5566
	45: 1	the p told Baruch son of Neriah in	5566
	46: 1	of the LORD that came to Jeremiah the p	5566
	46:13	the LORD spoke to Jeremiah the p about	5566
	47: 1	to Jeremiah the p concerning the Philistines	5566
	49:34	to Jeremiah the p concerning Elam,	5566
	50: 1	through Jeremiah the p concerning Babylon	5566
La	2:20	priest and p be killed in the sanctuary of	5566
Eze	2: 5	they will know that a p has been among	5566
	7:26	They will try to get a vision from the p;	5566
	14: 4	before his face and then goes to a p,	5566
	14: 7	and then goes to a p to inquire of me,	5566
	14: 9	if the p is enticed to utter a prophecy,	5566
	14: 9	I the LORD have enticed that p,	5566
	14:10	the p will be as guilty as the one who	5566
	33:33	then they will know that a p has been	5566
Da	9: 2	of the LORD given to Jeremiah the p,	5566
Hos	9: 7	the p is considered a fool,	5566
	9: 8	The p, along with my God,	5566
	12:13	The LORD used a p to bring Israel up	5566
	12:13	by a p he cared for him.	5566
Am	7:14	"I was neither a p nor a prophet's son,	5566
Mic	2:11	he would be just the p for this people!	5752
Hab	1: 1	The oracle that Habakkuk the p received.	5566
	3: 1	A prayer of Habakkuk the p,	5566
Hag	1: 1	of the LORD came through the p Haggai	5566
	1: 3	of the LORD came through the p Haggai:	5566
	1:12	and the message of the p Haggai,	5566
	2: 1	of the LORD came through the p Haggai:	5566
	2:10	word of the LORD came through the p Haggai:	5566
Zec	1: 1	word of the LORD came to the p Zechariah	5566
	1: 7	word of the LORD came to the p Zechariah	5566
	13: 4	"On that day every p will be ashamed	5566
	13: 5	He will say, 'I am not a p.	5566
Mal	4: 5	I will send you the p Elijah before	5566
Mt	1:22	the Lord had said through the p:	4737
	2: 5	"for this is what the p has written:	4737
	2:15	the Lord had said through the p:	4737
	2:17	through the p Jeremiah was fulfilled:	4737
	3: 3	he who was spoken of through the p Isaiah:	4737
	4:14	what was said through the p Isaiah:	4737
	8:17	what was spoken through the p Isaiah:	4737
	10:41	a p because he is a prophet will receive	4737
	10:41	a prophet because he is a p will receive	4737
	11: 9	Then what did you go out to see? A p?	4737
	11: 9	Yes, I tell you, and more than a p.	4737
	12:17	what was spoken through the p Isaiah:	4737
	12:39	be given it except the sign of the p Jonah.	4737
	13:35	fulfilled what was spoken through the p:	4737

Mt	13:57	and in his own house is a p without honor."	4737
	14: 5	because they considered him a p.	4737
	21: 4	to fulfill what was spoken through the p:	4737
	21:11	the p from Nazareth in Galilee."	4737
	21:26	for they all hold that John was a p."	4737
	21:46	because the people held that he was a p.	4737
	24:15	spoken of through the p Daniel—	4737
	27: 9	by Jeremiah the p was fulfilled:	4737
Mk	1: 2	It is written in Isaiah the p:	4737
	6: 4	and in his own house is a p without honor."	4737
	6:15	And still others claimed, "He is a p,	4737
	11:32	for everyone held that John really was a p.)	4737
Lk	1:76	will be called a p of the Most High;	4737
	3: 4	in the book of the words of Isaiah the p:	4737
	4:17	The scroll of the p Isaiah was handed	4737
	4:24	"no p is accepted in his hometown.	4737
	4:27	with leprosy in the time of Elisha the p,	4737
	7:16	"A great p has appeared among us,"	4737
	7:26	But what did you go out to see? A p?	4737
	7:26	Yes, I tell you, and more than a p.	4737
	7:39	he said to himself, "If this man were a p,	4737
	13:33	for surely no p can die outside Jerusalem!	4737
	20: 6	they are persuaded that John was a p."	4737
	24:19	"He was a p, powerful in word and	467+4737
Jn	1:21	"Are you the P?"	4737
	1:23	John replied in the words of Isaiah the p,	4737
	1:25	nor Elijah, nor the P?"	4737
	4:19	the woman said, "I can see that you are a p.	4737
	4:44	that a p has no honor in his own country.)	4737
	6:14	"Surely this is the P who is to come into	4737
	7:40	"Surely this man is the P."	4737
	7:52	that a p does not come out of Galilee."	4737
	9:17	The man replied, "He is a p."	4737
	12:38	This was to fulfill the word of Isaiah the p:	4737
Ac	2:16	No, this is what was spoken by the p Joel:	4737
	2:30	a p and knew that God had promised him	4737
	3:22	a p like me from among your own people;	4737
	7:37	a p like me from your own people.'	4737
	7:48	As the p says:	4737
	7:52	ever a p your fathers did not persecute?	4737
	8:28	reading the book of Isaiah the p.	4737
	8:30	and heard the man reading Isaiah the p.	4737
	8:34	please, who is the p talking about,	4737
	13: 6	and false p named Bar-Jesus,	6021
	13:20	until the time of Samuel the p.	4737
	21:10	a p named Agabus came down from Judea.	4737
	28:25	when he said through Isaiah the p:	4737
1Co	14:37	If anybody thinks he is a p	4737
Rev	16:13	and out of the mouth of the false p.	6021
	19:20	with him the false p who had performed	6021
	20:10	the beast and the false p had been thrown.	6021

PROPHET'S (5) [PROPHESY]

Am	7:14	"I was neither a prophet nor a p son,	5566
Zec	13: 4	on a p garment of hair in order to deceive.	168
Mt	10:41	a prophet will receive a p reward,	4737
2Pe	1:20	about by the p own interpretation.	NIG
	2:16	and restrained the p madness.	4737

PROPHETESS (8) [PROPHESY]

Ex	15:20	Then Miriam the p, Aaron's sister,	5567
Jdg	4: 4	Deborah, a p, the wife of Lappidoth,	5567
2Ki	22:14	and Asaiah went to speak to the p Huldah,	5567
2Ch	34:22	with him went to speak to the p Huldah,	5567
Ne	6:14	remember also the p Noadiah and the rest	5567
Isa	8: 3	Then I went to the p, and she conceived	5567
Lk	2:36	There was also a p, Anna,	4739
Rev	2:20	that woman Jezebel, who calls herself a p.	4739

PROPHETIC (3) [PROPHESY]

Zec	13: 4	be ashamed of his p vision.	5547
Ro	16:26	and made known through the p writings by	4738
1Ti	4:14	which was given you through a p message	4735

PROPHETS (245) [PROPHESY]

Nu	11:29	I wish that all the LORD's people were p	5566
1Sa	10: 5	you will meet a procession of p coming	5566
	10:10	a procession of p met him;	5566
	10:11	the p, they asked each other, "What is this	5566
	10:11	Is Saul also among the p?"	5566
	10:12	"Is Saul also among the p?"	5566
	19:20	when they saw a group of p prophesying,	5566
	19:24	"Is Saul also among the p?"	5566
	28: 6	not answer him by dreams or Urim or p.	5566
	28:15	either by p or by dreams.	5566
1Ki	18: 4	Jezebel was killing off the LORD's p,	5566
	18: 4	a hundred p and hidden them in two caves,	5566
	18:13	what I did while Jezebel was killing the p	5566
	18:13	a hundred of the LORD's p in two caves,	5566
	18:19	the four hundred and fifty p of Baal and	5566
	18:19	of Baal and the four hundred p of Asherah,	5566
	18:20	throughout all Israel and assembled the p	5566
	18:22	"I am the only one of the LORD's p left,	5566
	18:22	but Baal has four hundred and fifty p.	5566
	18:25	Elijah said to the p of Baal,	5566
	18:40	"Seize the p of Baal.	5566
	19: 1	how he had killed all the p with the sword.	5566
	19:10	and put your p to death with the sword.	5566
	19:14	and put your p to death with the sword.	5566
	20:35	of the LORD one of the sons of the p said	5566
	20:41	of Israel recognized him as one of the p.	5566
	22: 6	So the king of Israel brought together the p	5566
	22:10	with all the p prophesying before them.	5566
	22:12	All the other p were prophesying	5566

1Ki	22:13	the other p are predicting success for	5566
	22:22	be a lying spirit in the mouths of all his p,'	5566
	22:23	a lying spirit in the mouths of all these p	5566
2Ki	2: 3	The company of the p at Bethel came out	5566
	2: 5	The company of the p at Jericho went up	5566
	2: 7	of the company of the p went and stood at	5566
	2:15	The company of the p from Jericho,	5566
	3:13	Go to the p of your father and the prophets	5566
	3:13	Go to the prophets of your father and the p	5566
	4: 1	a man from the company of the p cried out	5566
	4:38	company of the p was meeting with him,	5566
	5:22	the company of the p have just come to me	5566
	6: 1	The company of the p said to Elisha,	5566
	9: 1	from the company of the p and said to him,	5566
	9: 7	of my servants the p and the blood of all	5566
	10:19	Now summon all the p of Baal,	5566
	17:13	and Judah through all his p and seers:	5566
	17:13	I delivered to you through my servants the p	5566
	17:23	had warned through all his servants the p.	5566
	21:10	the LORD said through his servants the p:	5566
	23: 2	people of Jerusalem, the priests and the p—	5566
	24: 2	proclaimed by his servants the p.	5566
1Ch	16:22	do my p no harm."	5566
2Ch	18: 5	So the king of Israel brought together the p	5566
	18: 9	with all the p prophesying before them.	5566
	18:11	All the other p were prophesying	5566
	18:12	the other p are predicting success for	5566
	18:22	be a lying spirit in the mouths of all his p,'	5566
	20:20	in his p and you will be successful."	5566
	24:19	Although the LORD sent p to the people	5566
	29:25	commanded by the LORD through his p.	5566
	36:16	despised his words and scoffed at his p	5566
Ezr	5: 2	the p of God were with them, helping them.	10455
	9:11	through your servants the p when you said:	5566
Ne	6: 7	even appointed p to make this proclamation	5566
	6:14	and the rest of the p who have been trying	5566
	9:26	They killed your p, who had admonished	5566
	9:30	By your Spirit you admonished them through your p,	5566
	9:32	upon our priests and p, upon our fathers	5566
Ps	74: 9	no miraculous signs; no p are left,	5566
	105:15	do my p no harm."	5566
Isa	9:15	the p who teach lies are the tail.	5566
	28: 7	and p stagger from beer and are befuddled	5566
	29:10	He has sealed your eyes (the p);	5566
	30:10	and to the p, "Give us no more visions	2602
	44:25	signs of false p and makes fools of diviners,	967
Jer	2: 8	The p prophesied by Baal,	5566
	2:26	their priests and their p.	5566
	2:30	Your sword has devoured your p like	5566
	4: 9	and the p will be appalled."	5566
	5:13	The p are but wind and the word is not	5566
	5:31	The p prophesy lies,	5566
	6:13	p and priests alike, all practice deceit.	5566
	7:25	and again I sent you my servants the p.	5566
	8: 1	the bones of the priests and p,	5566
	8:10	p and priests alike, all practice deceit.	5566
	13:13	the p and all those living in Jerusalem.	5566
	14:13	Sovereign LORD, the p keep telling them,	5566
	14:14	"The p are prophesying lies in my name.	5566
	14:15	the p who are prophesying in my name:	5566
	14:15	Those same p will perish by sword	5566
	18:18	nor the word from the p.	5566
	23: 9	Concerning the p: My heart is broken	5566
	23:10	The [p] follow an evil course	4392S
	23:13	the p of Samaria I saw this repulsive thing:	5566
	23:14	And among the p of Jerusalem	5566
	23:15	this is what the LORD Almighty says concerning the p:	5566
	23:15	the p of Jerusalem ungodliness has spread	5566
	23:16	not listen to what the p are prophesying	5566
	23:21	I did not send these p,	5566
	23:25	the p say who prophesy lies in my name.	5566
	23:26	in the hearts of these lying p,	5566
	23:30	"I am against the p who steal	5566
	23:31	against the p who wag their own tongues	5566
	25: 4	the LORD has sent all his servants the p	5566
	26: 5	to the words of my servants the p,	5566
	26: 7	the p and all the people heard Jeremiah	5566
	26: 8	the p and all the people seized him	5566
	26:11	the p said to the officials and all the people,	5566
	26:16	the people said to the priests and the p,	5566
	27: 9	So do not listen to your p, your diviners,	5566
	27:14	Do not listen to the words of the p who say	5566
	27:15	both you and the p who prophesy to you.' "	5566
	27:16	Do not listen to the p who say,	5566
	27:18	If they are p and have the word of	5566
	28: 8	From early times the p who preceded you	5566
	29: 1	the priests, the p and all the other people	5566
	29: 8	the p and diviners among you deceive you.	5566
	29:15	LORD has raised up p for us in Babylon,"	5566
	29:19	again and again by my servants the p	5566
	32:32	their kings and officials, their priests and p,	5566
	35:15	Again and again I sent all my servants the p	5566
	37:19	Where are your p who prophesied to you,	5566
	44: 4	Again and again I sent my servants the p,	5566
	50:36	A sword against her false p!	967
La	2: 9	and her p no longer find visions from	5566
	2:14	visions of your p were false and worthless;	5566
	4:13	But it happened because of the sins of her p	5566
Eze	13: 2	the p of Israel who are now prophesying.	5566
	13: 3	to the foolish p who follow their own spirit	5566
	13: 4	Your p, O Israel, are like jackals	5566
	13: 9	be against the p who see false visions	5566
	13:16	those p of Israel who prophesied	5566
	22:28	Her p whitewash these deeds for them	5566

Eze	38:17	of in former days by my servants the **p**	5566
Da	9: 6	not listened to your servants the **p**,	5566
	9:10	laws he gave us through his servants the **p**.	5566
Hos	4: 5	and the **p** stumble with you.	5566
	6: 5	Therefore I cut you in pieces with my **p**,	5566
	12:10	I spoke to the **p**, gave them many visions	5566
Am	2:11	up **p** from among your sons and Nazirites	5566
	2:12	and commanded the **p** not to prophesy.	5566
	3: 7	his plan to his servants the **p**.	5566
Mic	2: 6	"Do not prophesy," their **p** say.	5752
	3: 5	"As for the **p** who lead my people astray,	5566
	3: 6	The sun will set for the **p**,	5566
	3:11	and her **p** tell fortunes for money.	5566
Zep	3: 4	Her **p** are arrogant;	5566
Zec	1: 4	to whom the earlier **p** proclaimed:	5566
	1: 5	And the **p**, do they live forever?	5566
	1: 6	which I commanded my servants the **p**,	5566
	7: 3	of the LORD Almighty and the **p**,	5566
	7: 7	through the earlier **p** when Jerusalem	5566
	7:12	by his Spirit through the earlier **p**.	5566
	8: 9	by the **p** who were there when	5566
	13: 2	both the **p** and the spirit of impurity from	5566
Mt	2:23	was fulfilled what was said through the **p**:	4737
	5:12	the **p** who were before you.	4737
	5:17	to abolish the Law or the **P**;	4737
	7:12	for this sums up the Law and the **P**.	4737
	7:15	"Watch out for **false p**.	6021
	11:13	the **P** and the Law prophesied until John.	4737
	13:17	many **p** and righteous men longed	4737
	16:14	and still others, Jeremiah or one of the **p**."	4737
	22:40	the **P** hang on these two commandments."	4737
	23:29	You build tombs *for* the **p** and decorate	4737
	23:30	with them in shedding the blood *of* the **p**.'	4737
	23:31	of those who murdered the **p**.	4737
	23:34	Therefore I am sending you **p**	4737
	23:37	you who kill the **p** and stone those sent	4737
	24:11	and many **false p** will appear	6021
	24:24	For false Christs and **false p** will appear	6021
	26:56	the writings of the **p** might be fulfilled."	4737
Mk	6:15	like one *of* the **p** of long ago."	4737
	8:28	and still others, one *of* the **p**."	4737
	13:22	and **false p** will appear and perform signs	6021
Lk	1:70	(as he said through his holy **p** of long ago),	4737
	6:23	For that is how their fathers treated the **p**.	4737
	6:26	how their fathers treated the **false p**.	6021
	9: 8	*of* the **p** of long ago had come back to life."	4737
	9:19	*of* the **p** of long ago has come back to life."	4737
	10:24	For I tell you that many **p** and kings wanted	4737
	11:47	because you build tombs *for* the **p**,	4737
	11:48	they killed **the p**, and you build their tombs.	899S
	11:49	'I will send them **p** and apostles,	4737
	11:50	for the blood of all the **p** that has been shed	4737
	13:28	and Jacob and all the **p** in the kingdom	4737
	13:34	you who kill the **p** and stone those sent	4737
	16:16	Law and the **P** were proclaimed until John.	4737
	16:29	'They have Moses and the **P**;	4737
	16:31	'If they do not listen to Moses and the **P**,	4737
	18:31	and everything that is written by the **p**	4737
	24:25	to believe all that the **p** have spoken!	4737
	24:27	And beginning with Moses and all the **P**,	4737
	24:44	the Law of Moses, the **P** and the Psalms."	4737
Jn	1:45	and about whom the **p** also wrote—	4737
	6:45	It is written in the **P**:	4737
	8:52	Abraham died and so did the **p**,	4737
	8:53	He died, and so did the **p**.	4737
Ac	3:18	through all the **p**, saying that his Christ	4737
	3:21	he promised long ago through his holy **p**.	4737
	3:24	"Indeed, all the **p** from Samuel on,	4737
	3:25	of the **p** and of the covenant God made	4737
	7:42	with what is written in the book of the **p**:	4737
	10:43	All the **p** testify about him	4737
	11:27	During this time some **p** came down	4737
	13: 1	In the church at Antioch there were **p**	4737
	13:15	After the reading *from* the Law and the **P**,	4737
	13:27	of the **p** that are read every Sabbath.	4737
	13:40	that what the **p** have said does not happen	4737
	15:15	The words *of* the **p** are in agreement	4737
	15:32	Judas and Silas, who themselves were **p**,	4737
	24:14	with the Law and that is written in the **P**,	4737
	26:22	I am saying nothing beyond what the **p**	4737
	26:27	King Agrippa, do you believe the **p**?	4737
	28:23	from the Law of Moses and from the **P**.	4737
Ro	1: 2	through his **p** in the Holy Scriptures	4737
	3:21	to which the Law and the **P** testify.	4737
	11: 3	they have killed your **p** and torn	4737
1Co	12:28	first of all apostles, second **p**, third teachers,	4737
	12:29	Are all apostles? Are all **p**?	4737
	14:29	Two or three **p** should speak,	4737
	14:32	*of* **p** are subject to the control of prophets.	4737
	14:32	of prophets are subject to the control *of* **p**.	4737
Eph	2:20	on the foundation *of* the apostles and **p**,	4737
	3: 5	by the Spirit to God's holy apostles and **p**.	4737
	4:11	some to be **p**, some to be evangelists,	4737
1Th	2:15	who killed the Lord Jesus and the **p** and	4737
Tit	1:12	Even one of their own **p** has said,	4737
Heb	1: 1	the **p** at many times and in various ways,	4737
	11:32	Jephthah, David, Samuel and the **p**,	4737
Jas	5:10	the **p** who spoke in the name of the Lord.	4737
1Pe	1:10	Concerning this salvation, the **p**,	4737
2Pe	1:19	the word of the **p** made more certain,	4738
	2: 1	there were also **false p** among the people,	6021
	3: 2	past by the holy **p** and the command given	4737
1Jn	4: 1	because many **false p** have gone out into	6021
Rev	10: 7	just as he announced to his servants the **p**."	4737
	11:10	these two **p** had tormented those who live	4737
	11:18	and for rewarding your servants the **p**	4737
	16: 6	the blood of your saints and **p**,	4737

Rev	18:20	Rejoice, saints and apostles and **p**!	4737
	18:24	In her was found the blood *of* **p** and of	4737
	22: 6	The Lord, the God of the spirits *of* the **p**,	4737
	22: 9	with you and with your brothers the **p** and	4737

PROPITIATION (KJV) See ATONEMENT

PROPORTION (4)
Nu	35: 8	given **in p** to the inheritance of each	3869+7023
Dt	16:10	a freewill offering **in p** to the blessings the	
		LORD your God	889+3869+5002
	16:17	of you must bring a gift **in p** to the way	3869
Ro	12: 6	let him use it in **p** to his faith.	381

PROPOSAL (2) [PROPOSE]
Ge	34:18	Their **p** seemed good to Hamor	1821
Ac	6: 5	This **p** pleased the whole group.	3364

PROPOSE (2) [PROPOSAL, PROPOSED]
Dt	1:14	"What *you* **p** to do is good."	1819
Isa	8:10	**p** your plan, but it will not stand,	1819

PROPOSED (4) [PROPOSE]
Ezr	10:16	So the exiles did as was **p**.	NIH
Est	1:21	so the king did as Memucan **p**.	1821
	2: 2	Then the king's personal attendants **p**,	606
Ac	1:23	So *they* **p** two men:	2705

PROPPED (2)
1Ki	22:35	and the king was **p** up in his chariot facing	6641
2Ch	18:34	of Israel **p** *himself* **up** in his chariot facing	6641

PROPRIETY (2)
1Ti	2: 9	dress modestly, with decency and **p**,	5408
	2:15	continue in faith, love and holiness with **p**.	5408

PROSELYTE (KJV) See CONVERT

PROSPECT (1) [PROSPECTS]
Pr	10:28	The **p** of the righteous is joy,	9347

PROSPECTS (1) [PROSPECT]
Job	6:11	What **p**, that I should be patient?	7891

PROSPER (30) [PROSPERED, PROSPERITY, PROSPEROUS, PROSPERS]
Ge	32: 9	and *I will* **make** you **p**,'	3512
	32:12	'*I will* **surely make** you **p**	3512+3512
Dt	5:33	and **p** and prolong your days in the land	3201
	6:24	that we might always **p** and be kept alive,	3202
	28:63	Just as it pleased the LORD to **make** you **p**	3512
	29: 9	so that *you may* **p** in everything you do.	8505
1Ki	2: 3	You **p**, so that *you may* **p** in all you do	8505
2Ch	24:20	You will not **p**.	7503
Ezr	6:14	of the Jews continued to build and **p** under	10613
Ps	49:18	and men praise you when *you* **p**—	3512
	51:18	In your good pleasure **make** Zion **p**;	3512
Pr	11:10	When the righteous **p**, the city rejoices;	3206
	11:25	A generous man *will* **p**;	2014
	17:20	A man of perverse heart *does* not **p**;	3202+5162
	28:13	He who conceals his sins *does* not **p**,	7503
	28:25	but he who trusts in the LORD *will* **p**.	2014
Isa	53:10	the will of the LORD *will* **p** in his hand.	7503
Jer	10:21	not **p** and all their flock is scattered.	8505
	12: 1	Why *does* the way of the wicked **p**?	7503
	22:30	a man *who will* not **p** in his lifetime,	7503
	22:30	for none of his offspring *will* **p**,	7503
	29: 7	because if it prospers, you too will **p**."	8934
	29:11	'plans to **p** you and not to harm you,	8934
Eze	26: 2	now that she lies in ruins *I will* **p**,'	4848
	36:11	past and *will* **make** you **p** more than before.	3201
Da	4: 1	May you **p** greatly!	10720
	6:25	"May you **p** greatly!	10720
	8:25	He *will* cause deceit *to* **p**,	7503
Mal	3:15	Certainly the evildoers **p**,	1215
Ac	13:17	he **made** the people **p** during their stay	5738

PROSPERED (7) [PROSPER]
Ge	39: 2	The LORD was with Joseph and he **p**,	7503
1Ch	29:23	*He* **p** and all Israel obeyed him.	7503
2Ch	14: 7	So they built and **p**.	7503
	31:21	And so *he* **p**.	7503
Da	6:28	So Daniel **p** during the reign of Darius	10613
	8:12	*It* **p** in everything it did,	7503
Hos	10: 1	as his land **p**, he adorned his sacred stones.	3202

PROSPERITY (31) [PROSPER]
Dt	28:11	The LORD will grant you abundant **p**—	3208
	28:47	and gladly in the time of **p**,	3972+8044
	30:15	See, I set before you today life and **p**,	3206
Job	20:21	his **p** will not endure.	3206
	21:13	They spend their years in **p** and go down to	3202
	21:16	But their **p** is not in their own hands,	3206
	22:21	in this way **p** will come to you.	3208
	36:11	they will spend the rest of their days in **p**	3202
Ps	25:13	He will spend his days in **p**,	3202
	72: 3	The mountains will bring **p** to the people,	8934

Ps	72: 7	**p** will abound till the moon is no more.	8934
	73: 3	For I envied the arrogant when I saw the **p**	8934
	106: 5	that I may enjoy the **p** *of* your chosen ones,	3208
	122: 9	I will seek your **p**.	3202
	128: 2	blessings and **p** will be yours.	3202
	128: 5	may you see the **p** *of* Jerusalem,	3206
Pr	3: 2	and bring you **p**.	8934
	8:18	enduring wealth and **p**.	7407
	13:21	but **p** is the reward of the righteous.	3202
	21:21	and love finds life, **p** and honor.	7407
Ecc	6: 3	how long he lives, if he cannot enjoy his **p**	3208
	6: 6	over but fails to enjoy his **p**.	3208
Isa	45: 7	I bring **p** and create disaster;	8934
Jer	17: 6	he will not see **p** when it comes.	3202
	29: 7	seek the **peace and p** *of* the city	8934
	32:42	the **p** I have promised them.	3208
	33: 9	the abundant **p** and peace I provide for it.'	3208
	39:16	against this city through disaster, not **p**.	3208
La	3:17	I have forgotten what **p** is.	3208
Da	4:27	It may be that then your **p** will continue."	10713
Zec	1:17	'My towns will again overflow with **p**,	3202

PROSPEROUS (11) [PROSPER]
Ge	30:43	In this way the man *grew* exceedingly **p**	7287
Dt	30: 5	*He will* **make** you **more p**	3512
	30: 9	the LORD your God will make you most **p**	3208
	30: 9	delight in you and make you **p**,	3202
Jos	1: 8	Then you *will be* **p** and successful.	7503
Jdg	18: 7	their land lacked nothing, *they were*	3769+6807
Job	8: 7	so **p** will your future be.	8436
	42:10	the LORD **made** him **p** again	8654+8740
Ps	10: 5	His ways *are* always **p**;	2656
Da	4: 4	was at home in my palace, contented and **p**.	10670
Zec	7: 7	its surrounding towns were at rest and **p**,	8929

PROSPERS (6) [PROSPER]
Lev	25:26	to redeem it for him but *he* himself **p**	3338+5952
	25:49	Or if he **p**, he may redeem himself.	3338+5952
Ps	1: 3	Whatever he does **p**.	7503
Pr	16:20	Whoever gives heed to instruction **p**,	3202+5162
	19: 8	he who cherishes understanding **p**.	3202+5162
Jer	29: 7	Pray to the LORD for it, because if it **p**,	8934

PROSTITUTE (52) [PROSTITUTE'S, PROSTITUTED, PROSTITUTES, PROSTITUTING, PROSTITUTION]
Ge	34:31	"Should he have treated our sister like a **p**?"	2390
	38:15	Judah saw her, he thought she *was a* **p**,	2390
	38:21	"Where is the **shrine p** who was beside	7728
	38:21	"There hasn't been any **shrine p** here,"	7728
	38:22	'There hasn't been any **shrine p** here.' "	7728
Ex	34:15	for when *they* **p** themselves to their gods	2388
	34:16	and those daughters **p** *themselves*	2388
Lev	17: 7	the goat idols to whom *they* **p** *themselves*.	2388
	19:29	degrade your daughter by **making** her a **p**,	2388
	20: 6	to mediums and spiritists to **p** *himself*	2388
	21: 9	by *becoming a* **p**, she disgraces her father;	2388
Nu	15:39	not **p** yourselves by going after the lusts	2388
Dt	23:17	or woman is to become a **shrine p**.	7728
	23:18	not bring the earnings of a *female* **p** or of	2390
	23:18	of a female prostitute or of a **male p** into	3978
	23:18	these people *will* soon **p** *themselves*	2388
Jos	2: 1	and entered the house of a **p** named Rahab	2390
	6:17	Only Rahab the **p** and all who are with her	2390
	6:25	But Joshua spared Rahab the **p**,	2390
Jdg	11: 1	His father was Gilead; his mother was a **p**.	2390
	16: 1	Samson went to Gaza, where he saw a **p**.	2390
2Ch	21:11	**caused** the people of Jerusalem to **p** *themselves*	2388
	21:13	**led** Judah and the people of Jerusalem **to p** *themselves*,	2388
Pr	6:26	for the **p** reduces you to a loaf of bread,	2390
	7:10	dressed like a **p** and with crafty intent.	2390
	23:27	for a **p** is a deep pit and a wayward wife is	2390
Isa	23:15	to Tyre as in the song of the **p**:	2390
	23:16	walk through the city, O **p** forgotten;	2390
	23:17	to her **hire as a p** and will ply her trade	924
Jer	2:20	every spreading tree you lay down as a **p**.	2390
	3: 1	you have lived *as a* **p** with many lovers—	2388
	3: 3	Yet you have the brazen look of a **p**;	2390
Eze	16:28	and used your fame to *become a* **p**.	2388
	16:30	acting like a brazen **p**!	2390
	16:31	you were unlike a **p**,	2390
	16:33	Every **p** receives a fee,	2390
	16:35	you **p**, hear the word of the LORD!	2390
	23: 7	She gave herself as a **p** to all the elite of	9373
	23:19	when *she* was a **p** in Egypt.	2388
	23:43	**use** her **as a p**, for that is all she is.'	2388+9373
	23:44	As men sleep with a **p**,	2390
Hos	3: 3	not *be a* **p** or be intimate with any man,	2388
	9: 1	the **wages** of a **p** at every threshing floor.	924
Am	7:17	" 'Your wife *will become a* **p** in the city,	2388
1Co	6:15	members of Christ and unite them *with a* **p**?	4520
	6:16	that he who unites himself *with a* **p** is one	4520
Heb	11:31	By faith the **p** Rahab, because she	4520
Jas	2:25	the **p** considered righteous for what she did	4520
Rev	17: 1	the punishment of the great **p**,	4520
	17:15	where the **p** sits, are peoples, multitudes,	4520
	17:16	and the ten horns you saw will hate the **p**.	4520
	19: 2	the great **p** who corrupted the earth	4520

PROSTITUTE'S (1) [PROSTITUTE]
Jos	6:22	"Go into the **p** house and bring her out	2390

PROSTITUTED (5) [PROSTITUTE]

Jdg	2:17	not listen to their judges but p *themselves*	2388
	8:27	All Israel p *themselves* by worshiping it	2388
	8:33	the Israelites again p *themselves* to	2388
1Ch	5:25	the God of their fathers and p *themselves*	2388
Ps	106:39	by their deeds *they* p *themselves.*	2388

PROSTITUTES (20) [PROSTITUTE]

1Ki	3:16	Now two p came to the king and stood	2390
	14:24	There were even *male* **shrine p** in the land;	7728
	15:12	He expelled the *male* **shrine p** from the land	7728
	22:38	at a pool in Samaria (where the p bathed),	2390
	22:46	the *male* **shrine p** who remained there even	7728
2Ki	23: 7	down the quarters of the *male* **shrine p**,	7728
Job	36:14	among *male* **p of the shrines.**	7728
Pr	29: 3	but a companion of p squanders his wealth.	2390
Isa	57: 3	you offspring of adulterers and **p!**	2388
Jer	5: 7	and thronged to the houses of **p.**	2390
Eze	23: 3	*They* became **p** in Egypt,	2388
Hos	4:14	with harlots and sacrifice with **shrine p—**	7728
Joel	3: 3	for my people and traded boys for **p;**	2390
Mic	1: 7	she gathered her gifts from the wages of **p,**	2390
	1: 7	as the wages of p they will again be used."	2390
Mt	21:31	and the p are entering the kingdom of God	4520
	21:32	but the tax collectors and the p did.	4520
Lk	15:30	who has squandered your property with p	4520
1Co	6: 9	nor idolaters nor adulterers nor **male p**	3434
Rev	17: 5	BABYLON THE GREAT THE MOTHER OF **P**	4520

PROSTITUTING (1) [PROSTITUTE]

Lev	20: 5	and all who follow him in p *themselves*	2388

PROSTITUTION (35) [PROSTITUTE]

Ge	38:24	"Your daughter-in-law Tamar *is* **guilty of p,**	2388
Lev	19:29	or the land *will* **turn to p** and be filled	2388
	21: 7	not marry women defiled by p or divorced	2390
	21:14	or a woman defiled by **p,**	2390
Jer	3: 2	You have defiled the land with your **p**	2394
	13:27	and lustful neighings, your shameless **p!**	2394
Eze	16:16	where *you* **carried on** *your* **p.**	2388
	16:17	for yourself male idols and **engaged in p**	2388
	16:20	Was your p not enough?	9373
	16:22	and your p you did not remember the days	9373
	16:26	*You* **engaged in p** with the Egyptians,	2388
	16:28	*You* **engaged in p** with the Assyrians too,	2388
	16:34	So in your p you are the opposite of others;	9373
	16:41	I will put a stop to your **p,**	2388
	23: 3	**engaging in p** from their youth.	2388
	23: 5	"Oholah **engaged in p** while she was still	2388
	23: 8	not give up the p she began in Egypt,	9373
	23:11	p she was more depraved than her sister.	9373
	23:14	"But she carried her p still further.	9373
	23:18	When she carried on her p openly	9373
	23:27	to the lewdness and p you began in Egypt.	2394
	23:29	and the shame of your p will be exposed.	2393
	23:35	the consequences of your lewdness and **p."**	9373
	43: 7	by their p and the lifeless idols	2394
	43: 9	Now let them put away from me their **p** and	2394
Hos	4:10	*they* will **engage in p** but not increase,	2388
	4:11	to **p,** to old wine and new, which take away	2394
	4:12	A spirit of p leads them astray;	2393
	4:13	Therefore your daughters **turn to p**	2388
	4:14	when *they* **turn to p,**	2388
	4:18	*they* **continue** *their* **p;**	2388+2388
	5: 3	Ephraim, *you* have now **turned to p;**	2388
	5: 4	A spirit of p is in their heart;	2393
	6:10	There Ephraim is given to **p**	2394
Na	3: 4	who enslaved nations by her p and peoples	2393

PROSTRATE (11) [PROSTRATED]

Nu	24: 4	who falls **p,** and whose eyes are opened:	5877
	24:16	who falls **p,** and whose eyes are opened:	5877
Dt	9:18	Then once again *I* fell **p** before the LORD	5877
	9:25	*I* lay **p** before the LORD those forty days	5877
2Sa	19:18	he fell **p** before the king	5877
1Ki	18:39	they fell **p** and cried, "The LORD—	6584+7156
1Ch	29:20	they bowed low and fell **p** before the	2556
Isa	15: 3	and in the public squares they all wail, **p**	3718
	51:23	'**Fall p** that we may walk over you.'	8817
Da	2:46	Then King Nebuchadnezzar fell **p**	10049+10542
	8:17	I was terrified and fell **p.**	6584+7156

PROSTRATED (2) [PROSTRATE]

1Sa	24: 8	and **p** himself with his face to the ground.	2556
	28:14	and **p** himself with his face to the ground.	2556

PROTECT (28) [PROTECTED, PROTECTION, PROTECTIVE, PROTECTS]

Nu	35:25	The assembly *must* **p** the one accused	5911
Dt	23:14	to **p** you and to deliver your enemies	5911
2Sa	18:12	'**P** the young man Absalom for my sake.'	9068
Ezr	8:22	the king for soldiers and horsemen to **p** us	6468
Est	8:11	the right to assemble and **p** themselves;	6584+6641
	9:16	also assembled *to* **p** themselves	6584+6641
Ps	12: 5	"*I will* **p** them from those who	928+3829+8883
	12: 7	and **p** us from such people forever.	5915
	20: 1	*may* the name of the God of Jacob **p** you.	8435
	25:21	*may* integrity and uprightness **p** me,	5915
	32: 7	*you will* **p** me from trouble	5915
	40:11	*may* your love and your truth always **p** me.	5915
	41: 2	LORD *will* **p** him and preserve his life;	9068
	59: 1	**p** me from those who rise up against me.	8435

Ps	61: 7	and faithfulness *to* **p** him.	5915
	64: 1	**p** my life from the threat of the enemy.	5915
	69:29	*may* your salvation, O God, **p** me.	8435
	91:14	*I will* **p** him, for he acknowledges my name.	8435
	140: 1	**p** me from men of violence,	5915
	140: 4	**p** me from men of violence who plan	5915
Pr	2:11	Discretion *will* **p** you,	9068
	4: 6	and *she will* **p** you;	9068
	14: 3	but the lips of the wise **p** them.	9068
Jer	49:11	Leave your orphans; *I will* **p** their lives.**	2649
Da	11: 1	I took my stand to support and **p** him.)	5057
Jn	17:11	**p** them by the power of your name—	5498
	17:15	but that *you* **p** them from the evil one.	5498
2Th	3: 3	and he *will* **strengthen and p** you from	5875

PROTECTED (8) [PROTECT]

Jos	24:17	*He* **p** us on our entire journey and among all	9068
1Sa	30:23	He has **p** us and handed over to us	9068
Ezr	8:31	and *he* **p** us from enemies and bandits along	5911
Job	5:21	*You will* be **p** from the lash of the tongue,	2461
Ps	37:28	*They will* be **p** forever,	9068
Mk	6:20	because Herod feared John and **p** him,	5337
Jn	17:12	I **p** them and kept them safe by that name	5498
2Pe	2: 5	but **p** Noah, a preacher of righteousness,	5875

PROTECTION (9) [PROTECT]

Ge	19: 8	they have come under the p of my roof."	7498
Nu	14: 9	Their p is gone, but the LORD is with us.	7498
	32:17	for p *from* the inhabitants of the land.	4946+7156
Jos	20: 3	and find p from the avenger of blood.	5236
Ezr	9: 9	and he has given us a **wall of p** in Judah	1555
Ps	5:11	Spread *your* p over them,	6114
Isa	30: 2	who look for help to Pharaoh's **p,**	5057
	30: 3	But Pharaoh's p will be to your shame,	5057
Mic	1:11	its p is taken from you.	6644

PROTECTIVE (1) [PROTECT]

Na	2: 5	the p **shield** is put in place.	6116

PROTECTS (5) [PROTECT]

Ps	34:20	he **p** all his bones,	9068
	116: 6	The LORD **p** the simplehearted;	9068
Pr	2: 8	the just and **p** the way of his faithful ones.	9068
Da	12: 1	the great prince who **p** your people,	6584+6641
1Co	13: 7	*It* always **p,** always trusts, always hopes,	5095

PROTEST (3) [PROTESTED]

Ecc	5: 6	And *do not* **p** to the [temple] messenger,	606
Ac	13:51	So they shook the dust from their feet in **p**	NIG
	18: 6	he shook out his clothes in **p** and said	NIG

PROTESTED (2) [PROTEST]

Jn	8:41	"We are not illegitimate children," *they.* **p.**	3306
	19:21	The chief priests of the Jews **p** to Pilate,	3306

PROUD (44) [PRIDE, PROUDLY]

Dt	8:14	then your heart *will become* **p**	8123
2Ch	25:19	and now you are arrogant and **p.**	3877
	32:25	But Hezekiah's heart *was* **p** and he did	1467
Job	28: 8	**P beasts** do not set foot on it,	1201+8832
	38:11	here is where your **p** waves halt'?	1454
	39:20	striking terror with his **p** snorting?	2086
	40:11	look at every **p** *man* and bring him low,	1450
	40:12	look at every **p** *man* and humble him,	1450
	41:34	he is king over all that are **p.**"	1201+8832
Ps	31:23	but the **p** he pays back in full.	1452+6913
	36:11	May the foot of the **p** not come against me,	1452
	40: 4	who does not look to the **p,**	8107
	94: 2	pay back to the **p** what they deserve.	1450
	101: 5	whoever has haughty eyes and a **p** heart,	8146
	123: 4	We have endured much ridicule from the **p,**	8633
	131: 1	My heart *is not* **p,** O LORD,	1467
	138: 6	but the **p** he knows from afar.	1469
	140: 5	**P men** have hidden a snare for me;	1450
	140: 8	or their **p** *will become* **p.**	8123
Pr	3:34	He mocks **p mockers** but gives grace to	4370
	15:25	The LORD tears down the **p** *man's* house	1450
	16: 5	The LORD detests all the **p** of heart.	1468
	16:19	to share plunder with the **p.**	1450
	18:12	Before his downfall a man's heart *is* **p,**	1467
	21: 4	Haughty eyes and a **p** heart,	8146
	21:24	The **p** and arrogant man—	2294
Isa	2:12	a day in store for all the **p** and lofty,	1450
Eze	7:20	They were **p** of their beautiful jewelry	1454
	28: 5	of your wealth your heart *has grown* **p.**	1467
	28:17	Your heart *became* **p** on account	1467
	30: 6	and her **p** strength will fail.	1454
	30:18	there her **p** strength will come to an end.	1454
	31:10	and because *it was* **p** of its height,	4222+8123
	33:28	and her **p** strength will come to an end,	1454
Hos	13: 6	they were satisfied, they *became* **p;**	4213+8123
Zec	10: 3	and make them like a **p** horse in battle.	2086
Lk	1:51	he has scattered *those who are* **p**	5662
Ro	12:16	*Do* not *be* **p,** but be willing to	3836+5734+5858
1Co	5: 2	And you are **p!**	5881
	5: 2	not be **p,** and	5881
2Ti	3: 2	**p,** abusive, disobedient to their parents,	5662
Jas	4: 6	"God opposes the **p** but gives grace to	5662
1Pe	5: 5	"God opposes the **p** but gives grace to	5662
Rev	13: 5	a mouth to utter **p** words and blasphemies	3489

PROUDLY (3) [PROUD]

1Sa	2: 3	"Do not keep talking **so p**	1469+1469
Eze	31:14	by the waters *are ever to* **tower p** on high,	1467
Mic	2: 3	You will no longer walk **p,**	8127

PROVE (18) [PROOF, PROOFS, PROVED, PROVES, PROVING]

Ge	44:16	How *can we* **p** our **innocence?**	7405
Job	6:25	But what *do* your arguments **p?**	3519
	24:25	who *can* **p** me **false** and reduce my words	3941
Pr	29:25	Fear of man *will* **p** to be a snare,	5989
	30: 6	or he will rebuke you and **p** *you* **a liar.**	3941
Isa	43: 9	in their witnesses *to* **p** they were **right,**	7405
Jer	17:11	and in the end *he will* **p** to be a fool.	2118
Mic	1:14	The town of Aczib will **p** deceptive to	NIH
Hab	2: 3	it speaks of the end and *will not* **p** false.	3941
Jn	2:18	"What miraculous sign *can you* **show** us to	
		p your authority	1259
	8:46	*Can* any of you **p** me **guilty** of sin?	1794
Ac	24:13	And they cannot **p** to you the charges	4225
	25: 7	charges against him, which they could not **p.**	617
	26:20	and turn to God and **p** their repentance	NIG
1Co	4: 2	who has been given a trust *must* **p** faithful.	2351
2Co	9: 3	in this matter *should* not **p** **hollow,**	3033
Gal	2:18	*I* **p** that I am a lawbreaker,	5319
Heb	9:16	*to* **p** the death of the one who made it,	5770

PROVED (18) [PROVE]

Dt	13:14	And if it is true and *it has* been **p**	3922
	17: 4	If it is true and *it has* been **p**	3922
1Ki	16:22	But Omri's followers **p** *stronger* than those	2616
Job	6:21	Now *you* too *have* **p** to be of no help;	2118
	32:12	But not *one* of you *has* **p** Job **wrong;**	3519
Ps	51: 4	so that *you are* **p** **right** when you speak	7405
	105:19	till the word of the LORD **p** him **true.**	7671
Ecc	2: 1	But that also **p** to be meaningless.	NIH
Mt	11:19	But wisdom *is* **p** **right** by her actions."	1467
Lk	7:35	But wisdom *is* **p** **right** by all her children."	1467
Ro	3: 4	that *you may be* **p** **right** when you speak	1467
2Co	7:11	At every point you *have* **p** yourselves to	5319
	7:14	about you to Titus *has* **p** to be true as well.	1181
	8:22	with them our brother who *has* often **p**	1507
	9:13	by which you *have* **p** yourselves,	1509
Php	2:22	But you know that Timothy *has* **p** himself,	1509
Col	4:11	and *they have* **p** a comfort to me.	1181
1Pe	1: 7	may be **p** **genuine** and may result in praise,	1510

PROVENDER (KJV) See FODDER

PROVERB (9) [PROVERBS]

Ps	49: 4	I will turn my ear to a **p;**	5442
Pr	26: 7	that hang limp is a **p** in the mouth of a fool.	5442
	26: 9	in a drunkard's hand is a **p** in the mouth of	5442
Eze	12:22	what is this **p** you have in the land of Israel:	5442
	12:23	I am going to put an end to this **p,**	5442
	16:44	" 'Everyone who quotes proverbs *will*	
		quote *this* **p**	5439
	18: 2	by quoting this **p** about the land of Israel:	5442
	18: 3	you will no longer quote this **p** in Israel.	5442
Lk	4:23	"Surely you will quote this **p** to me:	4130

PROVERBS (9) [PROVERB]

1Ki	4:32	He spoke three thousand **p**	5442
Job	13:12	Your maxims are **p** *of* ashes;	5442
Pr	1: 1	**p** *of* Solomon son of David, king of Israel:	5442
	1: 6	for understanding **p** and parables,	5442
	10: 1	The **p** *of* Solomon.	5442
	25: 1	These are more **p** *of* Solomon,	5442
Ecc	12: 9	and searched out and set in order many **p.**	5442
Eze	16:44	" 'Everyone who **quotes p** will quote this	5439
2Pe	2:22	Of them the **p** are true:	4231

PROVES (1) [PROVE]

Dt	19:18	and if the witness **p** to be a liar,	NIH

PROVIDE (53) [PROVIDED, PROVIDES, PROVIDING, PROVISION, PROVISIONS]

Ge	22: 8	"God himself *will* **p** the lamb for	8011
	22:14	called that place The LORD Will **P.**	8011
	45:11	*I will* **p** for you there,	3920
	49:16	"Dan *will* **p justice** for his people as one	1906
	49:20	*he will* **p** delicacies fit for a king.	5989
	50:21	*I will* **p** for you and your children."	3920
Ex	21:11	*If he does* not **p** her with these three things,	6913
	27:16	**p** a curtain twenty cubits long, of three,	NIH
Lev	25:24	*you must* **p** for the redemption of the land.	5989
Dt	6:11	with all kinds of good things *you did* not **p,**	4848
	11:15	*I will* **p** grass in the fields for your cattle,	5989
Jdg	21: 7	*can we* **p** wives for those who are left,	6913
	21: 7	*shall we* **p** wives for the men who are left?	6913
2Sa	7:10	And *I will* **p** a place for my people Israel	8492
	19:33	in Jerusalem, and *I will* **p** for you."	3920
1Ki	4: 7	Each one had to **p supplies** *for* one month	3920
	5:17	to **p a foundation** *of* dressed stone for	3569
1Ch	21: 8	And *I will* **p** a place for my people Israel	8492
	22:14	*to* **p** for the temple of the LORD	3922
2Ch	2: 9	to **p** me with plenty of lumber,	3922
Ezr	1: 4	be living *are to* **p** him with silver and gold,	5951
	7:20	*you may* **p** from the royal treasury.	10498
	7:21	the treasurers of Trans-Euphrates *to* **p**	10522
Ne	2: 7	so that *they will* **p** me **safe-conduct**	6296

Ps	65: 9	filled with water to **p** the people with grain,	3922
Pr	27:26	the lambs will **p** you **with** clothing,	4200
Isa	4: 1	and **p** our own clothes;	4252
	43:20	because I **p** water in the desert and streams	5989
	50:11	all you who light fires and **p** yourselves	273
	58: 7	and to **p** the poor wanderer with shelter—	995
	61: 3	and **p** for those who grieve in Zion—	8492
Jer	33: 9	at the abundant prosperity and peace I **p**	6913
Eze	34:29	I will **p** for them a land renowned	7756
	43:25	to **p** a male goat daily for a sin offering;	6913
	43:25	to **p** a young bull and a ram from the flock,	6913
	45:17	to **p** the burnt offerings, grain offerings	NIH
	45:17	He will **p** the sin offerings,	6913
	45:22	to **p** a bull as a sin offering for himself and	6913
	45:23	of the Feast he is to **p** seven bulls	6913
	45:24	He is to **p** as a grain offering an ephah	6913
	46: 7	He is to **p** as a grain offering one ephah	6913
	46:13	" 'Every day you are to **p** a year-old lamb	6913
	46:13	morning by morning you shall **p** it.	6913
	46:14	also to **p** with it morning by morning	6913
Lk	12:33	**P** purses for yourselves that will	
Ac	7:46	that he might **p** a dwelling place for the God	2351
	11:29	to **p** help for the brothers living in Judea.	4287
	23:24	**P** mounts for Paul so that he may	4225
	27: 3	to his friends so they might **p** for his needs.	5593
1Co	10:13	also **p** a way out so that you can stand up	4472
Col	4: 1	**p** your slaves **with** what is right and fair,	4218
1Ti	5: 8	**p** for his relatives, and especially for	4629
Tit	3:14	that they may **p** for daily necessities and	NIG

PROVIDED (40) [PROVIDE]

Ge	22:14	the mountain of the LORD it will **be p.**"	8011
	43:24	and **p** fodder for their donkeys.	5989
	47:12	Joseph also **p** his father and his brothers	3920
Ru	3: 1	where you will **be well p** for?	
1Sa	21: 4	**p** the men have kept themselves from	421+561
2Sa	9:10	your master's grandson may be **p** for.	
			430+2118+4200+2256+4312
	15: 1	Absalom **p** himself with a chariot	6913
	19:32	He had **p** for the king during his stay	3920
	20: 3	He **p** for them, but did not lie with them.	3920
1Ki	8:21	I have **p** a place there for the ark,	8492
	11:18	a house and land and **p** him with food.	606
2Ki	13: 5	The LORD **p** a deliverer for Israel,	5989
1Ch	22: 3	He **p** a large amount of iron to make nails	3922
	22: 4	He also **p** more cedar logs than could	NIH
	23: 5	with the musical instruments I have **p** for	6913
	29: 2	With all my resources I have **p** for	3922
	29: 3	over and above everything I have **p**	3922
	29:16	that we have **p** for building you a temple	3922
	29:19	the palatial structure for which I have **p.**"	3922
2Ch	2: 7	craftsmen, whom my father David **p,**	3922
	3: 1	the place **p** by David.	3922
	26:14	Uzziah **p** shields, spears, helmets,	3922
	28:15	They **p** them **with clothes** and sandals,	4252
	30:24	Hezekiah king of Judah **p** a thousand bulls	8123
	30:24	the officials **p** them with a thousand bulls	8123
	35: 7	Josiah **p** for all the lay people	8123
	35: 9	**p** five thousand Passover offerings	8123
Ne	13: 5	and he had **p** him with a large room	6913
Est	2: 9	he **p** her with her beauty treatments and	5989
Ps	68:10	O God, you **p** for the poor.	3922
	111: 9	He **p** redemption for his people;	8938
Eze	16:19	Also the food I **p** for you—	5989
	46:15	and the oil shall be **p** morning by morning	6913
Jnh	1:17	the LORD **p** a great fish to swallow Jonah,	4948
	4: 6	the LORD God **p** a vine and made it grow	4948
	4: 7	But at dawn the next day God **p** a worm,	4948
	4: 8	God **p** a scorching east wind,	4948
Ro	11:22	**p** that you continue in his kindness.	1569
Gal	4:18	**p** the purpose is good,	NIG
Heb	1: 3	After he had **p** purification for sins,	4472

PROVIDENCE (1)

Job	10:12	and in your **p** watched over my spirit.	7213

PROVIDES (12) [PROVIDE]

Job	24: 5	the wasteland **p** food **for** their children.	4200
	36:31	the way he governs the nations and **p** food	5989
	38:41	Who **p** food for the raven	3922
Ps	111: 5	He **p** food for those who fear him;	5989
	147: 9	He **p** food for the cattle and for	5989
Pr	31:15	she **p** food for her family and portions	5989
Eze	18: 7	to the hungry and **p** clothing for the naked.	4059
	18:16	to the hungry and **p** clothing for the naked.	4059
	46:12	When the prince **p** a freewill offering to	6913
Ac	14:17	he **p** you **with plenty** of food	1855
1Ti	6:17	who richly **p** us **with** everything	4218
1Pe	4:11	he should do it with the strength God **p,**	5961

PROVIDING (5) [PROVIDE]

Ru	2:18	to the aid of his people by **p** food for them,	5989
1Ki	5: 8	and will do all you want in **p** the cedar	NIH
	5: 9	And you are to grant my wish by **p** food	5989
Ne	13: 7	in **p** Tobiah a room in the courts of	6913
Da	4:21	**p** food for all, giving shelter to the beasts of	NIH

PROVINCE (41) [PROVINCES, PROVINCIAL]

Ezr	2: 1	of the **p** who came up from the captivity of	4519
	6: 2	in the citadel of Ecbatana in the **p** of Media,	10406
	6: 6	fellow officials of **that p,**	10191+10468+10526S
	7:16	and gold you may obtain from the **p**	10406

Ne	1: 3	in the **p** are in great trouble and disgrace.	4519
	7: 6	of the **p** who came up from the captivity of	4519
Est	1:22	to **each p** in its own script and	4519
	2: 3	the king appoint commissioners in every **p**	4519
	3:12	They wrote out in the script of **each p** and	
		in the language	2256+4519+4519
	3:14	the edict was to be issued as law in every **p**	4519
	4: 3	In every **p** to which the edict and order of	4519
	8: 9	written in the script of **each p**	2256+4519+4519
	8:11	any nationality or **p** that might attack them	4519
	8:13	the edict was to be issued as law in every **p**	4519
	8:17	In every **p** and in every city,	4519
	9:28	in every **p** and in every town.	2256+4519+4519
Da	2:48	the entire **p** of Babylon and placed him	10406
	2:49	and Abednego administrators over the **p**	10406
	3: 1	on the plain of Dura in the **p** of Babylon.	10406
	3:12	over the affairs of the **p** of Babylon—	10406
	3:30	and Abednego in the **p** of Babylon.	10406
	8: 2	in the citadel of Susa in the **p** of Elam;	4519
Ac	16: 6	from preaching the word in the **p** of Asia.	823
	19:10	in the **p** of Asia heard the word of the Lord.	823
	19:22	he stayed in the **p** of Asia a little longer.	823
	19:26	and in practically the whole **p** of Asia.	823
	19:27	who is worshiped throughout the **p** of Asia	823
	19:31	Even some of the **officials of the p,**	825
	20: 4	Trophimus **from** the **p** of Asia.	824
	20:16	to avoid spending time in the **p** of Asia,	823
	20:18	from the first day I came into the **p** of Asia,	823
	21:27	from the **p** of Asia saw Paul at the temple.	823
	23:34	the letter and asked what **p** he was from.	2065
	24:19	there are some Jews from the **p** of Asia,	823
	25: 1	Three days after arriving in the **p,**	2065
	27: 2	for ports along the coast of the **p** of Asia,	823
Ro	16: 5	the first convert to Christ in the **p** of Asia.	823
1Co	16:19	in the **p** of Asia send you greetings.	823
2Co	1: 8	the hardships we suffered in the **p** of Asia.	823
2Ti	1:15	in the **p** of Asia has deserted me,	823
Rev	1: 4	To the seven churches in the **p** of Asia:	823

PROVINCES (23) [PROVINCE]

Ezr	4:15	troublesome to kings and **p,**	10406
Est	1: 1	the Xerxes who ruled over 127 **p** stretching	4519
	1: 3	and the nobles of the **p** were present.	4519
	1:16	the peoples of all the **p** of King Xerxes,	4519
	2:18	He proclaimed a holiday throughout the **p**	4519
	3: 8	and scattered among the peoples in all the **p**	4519
	3:12	the governors of the **various p**	2256+4519+4519
	3:13	to all the king's **p** with the order to destroy,	4519
	4:11	and the people of the royal **p** know that	4519
	8: 5	to destroy the Jews in all the king's **p.**	4519
	8: 9	of the 127 **p** stretching from India to Cush.	4519
	8:12	to do this in all the **p** of King Xerxes was	4519
	9: 2	in their cities in all the **p** of King Xerxes	4519
	9: 3	And all the nobles of the **p,** the satraps,	4519
	9: 4	his reputation spread throughout the **p,**	4519
	9:12	in the rest of the king's **p?**	4519
	9:16	of the Jews who were in the king's **p**	4519
	9:20	the Jews throughout the **p** of King Xerxes,	4519
	9:30	to all the Jews in the 127 **p** of the kingdom	4519
Ecc	2: 8	and the treasure of kings and **p.**	4519
La	1: 1	among the **p** has now become a slave.	4519
Da	11: 24	When the richest **p** feel secure,	4519
Ac	6: 9	and Alexandria as well as the **p** of Cilicia	3070

PROVINCIAL (7) [PROVINCE]

1Ki	20:14	of the **p** commanders will do it.' "	4519
	20:15	the young officers of the **p** commanders,	4519
	20:17	of the **p** commanders went out first.	4519
	20:19	the **p** commanders marched out of the city	4519
Ne	11: 3	the **p** leaders who settled in Jerusalem	4519
Da	3: 2	magistrates and all the other **p** officials	10406
	3: 3	and all the other **p** officials assembled for	10406

PROVING (3) [PROVE]

Ac	9:22	in Damascus by **p** that Jesus is the Christ.	5204
	17: 3	and **p** that the Christ had to suffer and rise	4192
	18:28	**p** from the Scriptures that Jesus was	2109

PROVISION (4) [PROVIDE]

Ne	13:31	I also made **p** for contributions of wood	NIH
Ps	144:13	be filled with every kind of **p,**	7049
Eze	45:25	he is to **make** the same **p** for sin offerings,	6913
Ro	5:17	those who receive God's **abundant p**	4353

PROVISIONS (19) [PROVIDE]

Ge	42:25	and to give them **p** for their journey.	7476
	45:21	and he also gave them **p** for their journey.	7476
	45:23	and bread and other **p** for his journey.	4648
Jos	9:11	'Take **p** for your journey;	7476
	9:14	of Israel sampled their **p** but did not inquire	7474
Jdg	7: 8	over the **p** and trumpets of the others.	7476
	20:10	to get **p** for the army.	7476
1Sa	22:10	also gave him **p** and the sword of Goliath	7476
2Sa	19:42	**eaten** any of the king's **p?**	430+430
1Ki	4: 7	who supplied **p** for the king and	3920
	4:22	Solomon's daily **p** were thirty cors	4312
	4:27	**supplied p** for King Solomon	3920
	20:27	Israelites also were mustered and **given p,**	3920
1Ch	12:39	for their families had **supplied p** for them.	3922
2Ch	11:23	He gave them abundant **p**	4648
Ps	132:15	I will bless her with abundant **p;**	7474
Pr	6: 8	yet it stores its **p** in summer	4312
Jer	40: 5	the commander gave him **p** and a present	786
Da	11:26	from the king's **p** will try to destroy him;	7329

PROVOCATION (1) [PROVOKE]

Pr	27: 3	but **p** by a fool is heavier than both.	4088

PROVOKE (14) [PROVOCATION, PROVOKED, PROVOKES, PROVOKING]

Dt	2: 5	Do not **p** them **to war,**	1741
	2: 9	not harass the Moabites or **p** them to war,	1741
	2:19	do not harass them or **p** them to war,	1741
	31:29	the sight of the LORD and **p** him to anger	4087
1Ki	16: 2	to sin and to **p** me to anger by their sins.	4087
	16:33	**p** the LORD, the God of Israel, **to anger**	4087
2Ki	23:26	Manasseh had done to **p** him to anger	4087+4088
Job	12: 6	and those who **p** God are secure—	8074
Isa	65: 3	a people who continually **p** me to my	4087
Jer	7:18	to other gods to **p** me to anger.	4087
	25: 6	do not **p** me **to anger** with what your hands	4087
	32:30	but **p** me with what their hands have made,	4087
	44: 8	Why **p** me **to anger** with what your hands	4087
Eze	8:17	and continually **p** me to anger?	4087

PROVOKED (27) [PROVOKE]

Dt	9: 7	how you **p** the LORD your God **to anger**	7911
Jdg	2:12	They **p** the LORD **to anger**	4087
1Sa	1: 7	her rival **p** her till she wept and would	4087
1Ki	14: 9	you have **p** me **to anger** and thrust me	4087
	14:15	because they **p** the LORD **to anger**	4087
	15:30	he **p** the LORD, the God of Israel, **to anger.**	
			4087+4088
	16:13	they **p** the LORD, the God of Israel, **to anger**	4087
	16:26	they **p** the LORD, the God of Israel, **to anger**	4087
	21:22	because you have **p** me **to anger**	4087+4088
	22:53	and **p** the LORD, the God of Israel, **to anger,**	4087
2Ki	17:11	that **p** the LORD **to anger.**	4087
	21:15	in my eyes and have **p** me **to anger** from	4087
	22:17	to other gods and **p** me **to anger** by all	4087
	23:19	that had **p** the LORD **to anger.**	4087
2Ch	28:25	**p** the LORD, the God of his fathers, **to**	
		anger.	4087
	34:25	to other gods and **p** me **to anger** by all	4087
Ps	106:29	they **p** the LORD **to anger**	4087
Ecc	7: 9	Do not be quickly **p** in your spirit,	4087
Jer	8:19	"Why have they **p** me **to anger**	4087
	11:17	of Judah have done evil and **p** me **to anger**	4087
	25: 7	"and you have **p** me with what your hands	4087
	32:29	the houses where the people **p** me **to anger**	4087
	32:32	The people of Israel and Judah have **p** me	4087
	44: 3	They **p** me **to anger** by burning incense	4087
Eze	16:26	and **p** me **to anger** with your	4087
	20:28	made offerings that **p** me **to anger,**	4088
Hos	12:14	But Ephraim has bitterly **p** him **to anger;**	4087

PROVOKES (1) [PROVOKE]

Eze	8: 3	where the idol that **p** to jealousy stood.	7861

PROVOKING (9) [PROVOKE]

Dt	4:25	the LORD your God and **p** him **to anger,**	4087
	9:18	the LORD's sight and so **p** him **to anger.**	4087
1Sa	1: 6	her rival **kept p** her in order to irritate her.	
			1685+4087+4088
1Ki	16: 7	**p** him **to anger** by the things he did,	4087
2Ki	17:17	evil in the eyes of the LORD, **p** him **to anger**	4087
	21: 6	evil in the eyes of the LORD, **p** him **to anger**	4087
2Ch	33: 6	evil in the eyes of the LORD, **p** him **to anger**	4087
Jer	7:19	But am I the one they are **p?**	4087
Gal	5:26	conceited, **p** and envying each other.	4614

PROWL (4) [PROWLED, PROWLING, PROWLS]

Ps	55:10	Day and night they **p** about on its walls;	6015
	59: 6	snarling like dogs, and **p** about the city.	6015
	59:14	snarling like dogs, and **p** about the city.	6015
	104:20	and all the beasts of the forest **p.**	8253

PROWLED (1) [PROWL]

Eze	19: 6	He **p** among the lions,	2143

PROWLING (1) [PROWL]

La	5:18	which lies desolate, with jackals **p** over it.	2143

PROWLS (2) [PROWL]

Job	28: 8	and no lion **p** there.	6334
1Pe	5: 8	Your enemy the devil **p** around like	4344

PRUDENCE (5) [PRUDENT]

Pr	1: 4	for giving **p** to the simple, knowledge	6893
	8: 5	You who are simple, gain **p;**	6893
	8:12	"I, wisdom, dwell together with **p;**	6893
	15: 5	but whoever heeds correction **shows p.**	6891
	19:25	and the simple will **learn p;**	6891

PRUDENT (12) [PRUDENCE]

Pr	1: 3	and **p** life, doing what is right and just	8505
	12:16	but a **p** man overlooks an insult.	6874
	12:23	A **p** man keeps his knowledge to himself,	6874
	13:16	Every **p** man acts out of knowledge,	6874
	14: 8	of the **p** is to give thought to their ways,	6874
	14:15	but a **p** man gives thought to his steps.	6874
	14:18	but the **p** are crowned with knowledge.	6874
	19:14	but a **p** wife is from the LORD.	8505

Pr	22: 3	A p *man* sees danger and takes refuge,	6874
	27:12	The p see danger and take refuge,	6874
Jer	49: 7	Has counsel perished from the p?	1067
Am	5:13	the p *man* keeps quiet in such times,	8505

PRUNE (2) [PRUNED, PRUNES, PRUNING]

Lev	25: 3	and for six years p your vineyards	2377
	25: 4	Do not sow your fields or p your vineyards.	2377

PRUNED (1) [PRUNE]

Isa	5: 6	a wasteland, neither p nor cultivated,	2377

PRUNES (1) [PRUNE]

Jn	15: 2	while every branch that does bear fruit *he* p	2748

PRUNING (4) [PRUNE]

Isa	2: 4	and their spears into p hooks.	4661
	18: 5	he will cut off the shoots with p knives,	4661
Joel	3:10	into swords and your p hooks into spears.	4661
Mic	4: 3	and their spears into p hooks.	4661

PRUNINGHOOKS (KJV) See PRUNING HOOKS

PSALM (61) [PSALMS]

1Ch	16: 7	*this* p of thanks to the LORD:	3344
Ps	3: T	A p of David. When he fled from his son	4660
	4: T	With stringed instruments. A p of David.	4660
	5: T	For flutes. A p of David.	4660
	6: T	According to sheminith. A p of David.	4660
	8: T	According to gittith. A p of David.	4660
	9: T	"The Death of the Son." A p of David.	4660
	12: T	According to sheminith. A p of David.	4660
	13: T	For the director of music. A p of David.	4660
	15: T	A p of David.	4660
	19: T	For the director of music. A p of David.	4660
	20: T	For the director of music. A p of David.	4660
	21: T	For the director of music. A p of David.	4660
	22: T	"The Doe of the Morning." A p of David.	4660
	23: T	A p of David.	4660
	24: T	Of David. A p.	4660
	29: T	A p of David.	4660
	30: T	A p. A song. For the dedication of the temple. Of David.	4660
	31: T	For the director of music. A p of David.	4660
	38: T	A p of David. A petition.	4660
	39: T	For Jeduthun. A p of David.	4660
	40: T	For the director of music. Of David. A p.	4660
	41: T	For the director of music. Of David. A p.	4660
	47: T	Of the Sons of Korah. A p.	4660
	47: 7	sing to him a p of praise.	5380
	48: T	A song. A p of the Sons of Korah.	4660
	49: T	Of the Sons of Korah. A p.	4660
	50: T	A p of Asaph.	4660
	51: T	For the director of music. A p of David.	4660
	62: T	For Jeduthun. A p of David.	4660
	63: T	A p of David. When he was in the Desert	4660
	64: T	For the director of music. A p of David.	4660
	65: T	For the director of music. A p of David.	4660
	66: T	For the director of music. A song. A p.	4660
	67: T	With stringed instruments. A p.	4660
	68: T	Of David. A p.	4660
	73: T	A p of Asaph.	4660
	75: T	"Do Not Destroy." A p of Asaph.	4660
	76: T	With stringed instruments. A p of Asaph.	4660
	77: T	For Jeduthun. Of Asaph. A p.	4660
	79: T	A p of Asaph.	4660
	80: T	Lilies of the Covenant." Of Asaph. A p.	4660
	82: T	A p of Asaph.	4660
	83: T	A song. A p of Asaph.	4660
	84: T	Of the Sons of Korah. A p.	4660
	85: T	Of the Sons of Korah. A p.	4660
	87: T	Of the Sons of Korah. A p. A song.	4660
	88: T	A p of the Sons of Korah.	4660
	92: T	A p. A song. For the Sabbath day.	4660
	98: T	A p.	4660
	100: T	A p. For giving thanks.	4660
	101: T	Of David. A p.	4660
	108: T	A song. A p of David.	4660
	109: T	For the director of music. Of David. A p.	4660
	110: T	Of David. A p.	4660
	139: T	For the director of music. Of David. A p.	4660
	140: T	For the director of music. A p of David.	4660
	141: T	A p of David.	4660
	143: T	A p of David.	4660
	145: T	A p of praise. Of David.	9335
Ac	13:33	As it is written in the second P:	6011

PSALMS (5) [PSALM]

Lk	20:42	David himself declares in the Book *of* P:	6011
	24:44	Law of Moses, the Prophets and the P."	6011
Ac	1:20	said Peter, "it is written in the book *of* P,	6011
Eph	5:19	Speak to one another with p, hymns and	6011
Col	3:16	and as you sing p, hymns and spiritual	6011

PTOLEMAIS (1)

Ac	21: 7	our voyage from Tyre and landed at P,	4767

PUAH (5) [PUITE]

Ge	46:13	Tola, P, Jashub and Shimron.	7026
Ex	1:15	whose names were Shiphrah and P,	7045

Nu	26:23	through P, the Puite clan;	7025
Jdg	10: 1	Tola son of P, the son of Dodo,	7025
1Ch	7: 1	Tola, P, Jashub and Shimron—four in all.	7025

PUBLIC (23) [PUBLICLY]

Lev	5: 1	not speak up when he hears a p charge	460
Dt	13:16	of the town into the middle of the p square	8148
2Sa	21:12	from the p square at Beth Shan,	8148
Job	29: 7	of the city and took my seat in the p square,	8148
Pr	1:20	she raises her voice in the p squares;	8148
	5:16	your streams of water in the p squares?	8148
Isa	15: 3	the roofs and in the p squares they all wail,	8148
Jer	9:21	and the young men from the p squares.	8148
	48:38	in the p squares there is nothing but mourning,	8148
Eze	16:24	and made a lofty shrine in every p square.	8148
	16:31	lofty shrines in every p square,	8148
Am	5:16	and cries of anguish in every p square.	8148
Mt	1:19	**expose** her to p disgrace,	1258
Lk	20:26	to trap him in what he had said there in p.	1883+3295+3836
Jn	7: 4	to become a p figure acts in secret.	1877+4244
Ac	5:18	the apostles and put them in the p jail.	1323
	12: 4	Herod intended to bring him out *for* p trial	3295
	12:21	sat on his throne and **delivered a p** address	1319
	18:28	he vigorously refuted the Jews in p debate,	1323
Ro	16:23	who is the city's **director of** p works,	3874
Col	2:15	he made a p spectacle of them,	4244
1Ti	4:13	devote yourself *to* the p reading	342
Heb	6: 6	**subjecting** him **to** p disgrace.	4136

PUBLICAN (KJV) See PAGANS, TAX COLLECTOR

PUBLICK (KJV) See PUBLIC

PUBLICLY (11) [PUBLIC]

Lk	1:80	in the desert until he **appeared** p to Israel.	345
Jn	7:10	he went also, not p, but in secret.	5747
	7:13	But no one would say anything p about him	4244
	7:26	Here he is, speaking p,	4244
	11:54	Therefore Jesus no longer moved about p	4244
Ac	16:37	"They beat us p without a trial,	1323
	19: 9	they refused to believe and p maligned the Way.	1967+3836+4436
	19:19	scrolls together and burned them p.	1967+4246
	20:20	have taught you p and from house to house.	1323
1Ti	5:20	Those who sin are to be rebuked p,	1967+4246
Heb	10:33	Sometimes *you* were p **exposed** to insult	2518

PUBLISH (1) [PUBLISHED]

Da	6:12	"Did *you* not p a decree that during	10673

PUBLISHED (2) [PUBLISH]

Est	4: 8	which *had* been p in Susa,	5989
Da	6:10	Daniel learned that the decree *had* been p,	10673

PUBLIUS (1)

Ac	28: 7	an estate nearby that belonged *to* P,	4511

PUDENS (1)

2Ti	4:21	Eubulus greets you, and so do P, Linus,	4545

PUFFED (1) [PUFFS]

Hab	2: 4	"See, *he is* p up; his desires are not upright	6752

PUFFS (2) [PUFFED]

1Co	8: 1	Knowledge p up, but love builds up.	5881
Col	2:18	and his unspiritual mind p him up	5881

PUHITES (KJV) See PUTHITES

PUITE (1) [PUAH]

Nu	26:23	through Puah, the P clan;	7027

PUL (2) [TIGLATH-PILESER]

2Ki	15:19	Then P king of Assyria invaded the land,	7040
1Ch	5:26	up the spirit of P king of Assyria (that is,	7040

PULL (15) [PULLED, PULLING, PULLS]

Jdg	3:22	Ehud *did* not p the sword out,	8990
Ru	2:16	p out some stalks for her from the bundles	8963+8963
1Ki	13: 4	so that he could not p it back.	8740
Job	41: 1	"Can *you* p in the leviathan with a fishhook	5432
Jer	13:26	I will p up your skirts over your face	3106
	22:24	I *would* still p you off.	5998
Eze	17: 9	a strong arm or many people to p it up by	5951
	26: 4	the walls of Tyre and p down her towers;	2238
	29: 4	I *will* p you out from among your streams,	6590
Hos	7:12	I *will* p them **down** like birds of the air.	3718
Am	3:11	he will p down your strongholds	3718
Mt	9:16	the patch will p away from the garment,	149
	13:28	'Do you want *us* to go and p them up?'	5198
Mk	2:21	the new piece will p away from the old,	149
Lk	14: 5	will *you* not immediately p him **out?"**	413

PULLED (20) [PULL]

Ge	19:10	the men inside reached out and p Lot back	995
	37:28	his brothers p Joseph up out of the cistern	5432
Jdg	8:17	also p down the tower of Peniel and killed	5997
	16:14	He awoke from his sleep and p up the pin	5825
1Ki	19:13	*he* p his cloak **over** his face and went out	4286
2Ki	23:12	*He* p down the altars the kings	5997
Ezr	6:11	*to* be p from his house and he is to be lifted	10481
	9: 3	p hair from my head and beard and sat	5307
Ne	13:25	I beat some of the men and p out their **hair.**	5307
Job	4:21	**Are** not the cords of their tent p **up,**	5825
Isa	33:20	its stakes *will* never *be* p up,	5825
	38:12	Like a shepherd's tent *you* p my house *has been* p down	5825
	50: 6	my cheeks to *those who* p out my **beard;**	5307
Jer	38:13	and *they* p him **up** with the ropes	5432
Eze	19: 9	With hooks *they* p him into a cage	5989
Mt	13:40	the weeds *are* p up and burned in the fire,	5198
	13:48	the fishermen p it **up** on the shore.	328
	15:13	*will be* p **up** by the roots.	1748
Lk	5:11	So they p their boats **up** on shore,	2864
Ac	11:10	and then *it was* all p up to heaven again.	413

PULLING (2) [PULL]

Mt	13:29	'because *while you are* p the weeds,	5198
2Co	10: 8	for building you up rather than p you **down,**	2746

PULLS (3) [PULL]

Job	20:25	*He* p it out of his back,	8990
Pr	21:22	of the mighty and p **down** the stronghold	3718
Hab	1:15	The wicked foe p all of them **up**	6590

PULSE (KJV) See VEGETABLES

PUNISH (71) [PUNISHED, PUNISHES, PUNISHING, PUNISHMENT, PUNISHMENTS]

Ge	15:14	But I *will* p the nation they serve	1906
Ex	32:34	when the time comes for me *to* p,	7212
	32:34	I *will* p them for their sin."	7212
Lev	26:18	I *will* p you for your sins seven times over	3579
	26:28	and I *myself* will p you	3579
Dt	22:18	the elders shall take the man and p him.	3579
1Sa	15: 2	'I *will* p the Amalekites	7212
2Sa	7:14	I *will* p him with the rod of men,	3519
Job	37:13	He brings the clouds to p men,	8657
Ps	59: 5	rouse yourself to p all the nations;	7212
	89:32	I *will* p their sin with the rod,	7212
	94:10	*Does he who* disciplines nations not p?	3519
	119:84	When *will you* p my persecutors?	5477+6913
	120: 4	He will p you with a warrior's sharp arrows	NIH
Pr	17:26	It is not good *to* p an innocent man,	6740
	23:13	if *you* p him with the rod, he will not die.	5782
	23:14	P him with the rod and save his soul	5782
Isa	10:12	"I *will* p the king of Assyria for	7212
	13:11	I *will* p the world *for* its evil,	7212
	24:21	In that day the LORD *will* p the powers	7212
	26:21	of his dwelling to p the people of the earth	7212
	27: 1	the LORD *will* p with his sword,	7212
	64:12	Will you keep silent and p us	6700
Jer	2:19	Your wickedness *will* p you;	3579
	5: 9	*Should I* not p them for this?"	7212
	5:29	*Should I* not p them for this?"	7212
	6:15	be brought down when *I* p them,"	7212
	9: 9	*Should I* not p them for this?"	7212
	9:25	I *will* p all who are circumcised only	7212
	11:22	'I *will* p them.	7212
	14:10	and p them for their sins."	7212
	21:14	I *will* p you as your deeds deserve,	7212
	23:34	I *will* p that man and his household.	7212
	25:12	I *will* p the king of Babylon	7212
	27: 8	I *will* p that nation with the sword,	7212
	29:32	I *will* surely p Shemaiah the Nehelamite	7212
	30:20	I *will* p all who oppress them.	7212
	36:31	I *will* p him and his children	7212
	44:13	I *will* p those who live in Egypt with	7212
	44:29	to you that I *will* p you in this place,'	7212
	49: 8	on Esau at the time *I* p him.	7212
	50:18	"I *will* p the king of Babylon and his land	7212
	51:44	I *will* p Bel in Babylon	7212
	51:47	the time will surely come when *I* will p	7212
	51:52	"when *I* will p her idols,	7212
La	4:22	Daughter of Edom, *he will* p your sin	7212
Eze	7:11	into a **rod** *to* p wickedness;	AIT
	23:24	and *they* will p you according	9149
	25:17	on them and p them in my wrath.	9350
Hos	1: 4	because I *will* soon p the house of Jehu	7212
	2:13	I *will* p her *for* the days she burned incense	7212
	4: 9	I *will* p both of them *for* their ways	7212
	4:14	not p your daughters when they turn	7212
	8:13	and p their sins:	7212
	9: 9	and p them *for* their sins.	7212
	10:10	When I please, *I will* p them;	3579
	12: 2	he will p Jacob according to his ways	7212
Am	3: 2	therefore *I will* p you *for* all your sins."	7212
	3:14	"On the day I p Israel for her sins,	7212
Hab	1:12	O Rock, *you* have ordained them *to* p.	3519
Zep	1: 8	the day of the LORD's sacrifice *I will* p	7212
	1: 9	that day *I will* p all who avoid stepping	7212
	1:12	and p those who are complacent.	7212
Zec	10: 3	and *I will* p the leaders;	7212
Lk	23:16	I will p him and then release him."	4084
Ac	4:21	They could not decide how *to* p them,	3134

Ac	7: 7	I *will* **p** the nation they serve as slaves,'	3212
2Co	10: 6	be ready *to* **p** every act of disobedience,	1688
1Th	4: 6	The Lord will **p** men for all such sins,	1690
2Th	1: 8	*He will* **p** those who do not know God	1443+1689
1Pe	2:14	by him to **p** those who do wrong and	1689

PUNISHED (34) [PUNISH]

Ge	19:15	you will be swept away when the city is **p.**	6411
	42:21	"Surely we are being **p** because	872
Ex	21:20	dies as a direct result, *he* **must be p,**	5933+5933
	21:21	not *to* **be p** if the slave gets up after a day	5933
Lev	18:25	so I **p** it *for* its sin,	7212
1Sa	28:10	you *will* **not be p** for this."	6411+7936
1Ch	21: 7	evil in the sight of God; so he **p** Israel.	5782
Ezr	7:26	must surely be **p** by death,	10170+10191+10522
	9:13	you *have* **p** us **less** than our sins have deserved	3104+4200+4752
Ps	73:14	I have been **p** every morning.	9350
	99: 8	though you **p** their misdeeds.	5933
Pr	21:11	a mocker *is* **p**, the simple gain wisdom;	6740
Isa	24:22	they will be shut up in prison and **be p**	7212
	26:14	*You* **p** them and brought them to ruin;	7212
	57:17	I was enraged by his sinful greed; *I* **p** him,	5782
Jer	2:30	"In vain *I* **p** your people;	5782
	6: 6	This city *must* **be p**;	7212
	8:12	they will be brought down when they are **p**,	7213
	23:12	on them in the year they are **p**,"	7213
	30:14	as an enemy would and **p** you as would	4592
	44:13	famine and plague, as *I* **p** Jerusalem.	7212
	46:21	the time for them to be **p.**	7213
	50:18	of Babylon and his land as *I* **p** the king	7212
	50:27	the time for them to be **p.**	7213
	50:31	the time for you *to be* **p.**	7212
La	3:39	when **p** for his sins?	2628
Mk	12:40	Such men *will* **be p** most severely."	3210+3284
Lk	20:47	Such men *will* **be p** most severely."	3210+3284
	23:22	*I will* have him **p** and then release him."	4084
	23:41	We are **p** justly, for we are getting what	NIG
Ac	22: 5	people as prisoners to Jerusalem *to be* **p.**	5512
	26:11	one synagogue to another *to* have them **p**,	5512
2Th	1: 9	**be p** with everlasting destruction	1472+5514
Heb	10:29	a man deserves to be **p** who has trampled	5513

PUNISHES (5) [PUNISH]

Ex	34: 7	he **p** the children and their children *for*	7212
Nu	14:18	he **p** the children *for* the sin of the fathers to	7212
Job	34:26	He **p** them for their wickedness	6215
	35:15	that his anger never **p** and he does not take	7212
Heb	12: 6	and *he* **p** everyone he accepts as a son."	3463

PUNISHING (4) [PUNISH]

Ex	20: 5	the LORD your God, am a jealous God, **p**	7212
Dt	5: 9	the LORD your God, am a jealous God, **p**	7212
Jdg	8:16	by **p** them with desert thorns and briers.	NIH
Isa	30:32	the LORD lays on them with his **p** rod will	4592

PUNISHMENT (56) [PUNISH]

Ge	4:13	"My **p** is more than I can bear.	6411
Lev	19:20	there must be **due p.**	1334
1Sa	14:47	he **inflicted p** on them.	8399
2Ki	7: 9	we wait until daylight, **p** will overtake us.	6411
Job	19:29	for wrath will bring **p** *by* the sword,	6411
	21:19	'God stores up a man's **p** for his sons.'	224
Ps	81:15	and their **p** would last forever.	6961
	91: 8	with your eyes and see the **p** *of* the wicked.	8974
	149: 7	to inflict vengeance on the nations and **p** on	9349
Pr	10:16	the income of the wicked brings them **p.**	2633
	16:22	but folly brings **p** to fools.	4592
Isa	53: 5	the **p** *that brought* us peace was upon him,	4592
Jer	4:18	This is your **p.**	8288
	11:15	Can consecrated meat avert [your **p**]?	NIH
	11:23	the men of Anathoth in the year of their **p.**'	7213
	23: 2	not bestowed care on them, I *will* **bestow p**	7212
	32:18	but *bring the* **p** for the fathers' sins	8966
	46:25	*about to* **bring p** on Amon god of Thebes,	7212
	48:44	I will bring upon Moab the year of her **p**,"	7213
La	4: 6	The **p** of my people is greater than that	6411
	4:22	O Daughter of Zion, your **p** will end;	6411
	5: 7	and we bear their **p.**	6411
Eze	5: 8	against you, Jerusalem, and I will inflict **p**	5477
	5:10	I will inflict **p** on you	9150
	5:15	around you when I inflict **p** on you in anger	9150
	11: 9	over to foreigners and inflict **p** on you.	9150
	16:38	to the **p** of women who commit adultery	5477
	16:41	down your houses and inflict **p** on you in	9150
	21:25	whose time of **p** has reached its climax,	6411
	21:29	whose time of **p** has reached its climax.	6411
	23:10	and **p** was inflicted on her.	9144
	23:24	I will turn you over to them for **p**,	5477
	23:45	to the **p** *of* women who commit adultery	5477
	25:11	and I will inflict **p** on Moab.	9150
	28:22	when I inflict **p** on her	9150
	28:26	they will live in safety when I inflict **p**	9150
	30:14	set fire to Zoan and inflict **p** on Thebes.	9150
	30:19	So I will inflict **p** on Egypt,	9150
	32:27	the **p** for their **sins** rested on their bones,	6411
	35: 5	the time their **p** reached its climax,	6411
	39:21	the **p** I inflict and the hand I lay upon them.	5477
Hos	9: 7	The days of **p** are coming,	7213
Zep	3:15	The LORD has taken away your **p**,	5477
Zec	14:19	be the **p** *of* Egypt and the punishment of all	2633
	14:19	of Egypt and the **p** *of* all the nations that do	2633
Mt	25:46	"Then they will go away to eternal **p**,	3136
Lk	12:48	and does things deserving **p** will be beaten	4435

Lk	21:22	For this is the time *of* **p** in fulfillment of all	1689
Ro	13: 4	**agent** of wrath **to bring p** on the wrongdoer	1690
	13: 5	not only because of possible **p** but also	3973
2Co	2: 6	The **p** inflicted on him by the majority	2204
Heb	2: 2	and disobedience received its just **p**,	3632
2Pe	2: 9	*while continuing* their **p.**	3134
1Jn	4:18	because fear has to do with **p.**	3136
Jude	1: 7	of those who suffer the **p** of eternal fire.	1472
Rev	17: 1	the **p** of the great prostitute,	3210

PUNISHMENTS (1) [PUNISH]

Zep	3: 7	nor all *my* **p come** upon her.	7212

PUNITES (KJV) See PUITES

PUNON (2)

Nu	33:42	They left Zalmonah and camped at **P.**	7044
	33:43	They left **P** and camped at Oboth.	7044

PUR (3) [LOT]

Est	3: 7	the month of Nisan, they cast the **p** (that is,	7052
	9:24	the Jews to destroy them and had cast the **p**	7052
	9:26	days were called Purim, from the word **p.**)	7052

PURAH (2)

Jdg	7:10	go down to the camp with your servant **P**	7242
	7:11	So he and **P** his servant went down to	7242

PURCHASE (6) [PURCHASED]

2Ki	22: 6	Also *have* them **p** timber and dressed stone	7864
2Ch	34:11	and builders to **p** dressed stone,	7864
Pr	20:14	then off he goes and boasts about his **p.**	NIH
Jer	32:11	I took the deed of **p**—	5239
	32:14	and unsealed copies of the deed of **p**,	5239
	32:16	of **p** to Baruch son of Neriah, I prayed to	5239

PURCHASED (6) [PURCHASE]

1Ki	10:28	merchants **p** them from Kue.	928+4374+4697
2Ki	12:12	They **p** timber and dressed stone for	7864
2Ch	1:16	merchants **p** them from Kue.	928+4374+4697
Ps	74: 2	Remember the people you **p** of old,	7864
Rev	5: 9	and with your blood *you* **p** men for God	60
	14: 4	They *were* **p** from among men and offered	60

PURE (108) [PUREST, PURIFICATION, PURIFIED, PURIFIER, PURIFIES, PURIFY, PURIFYING, PURITY]

Ex	25:11	Overlay it with **p** gold, both inside and out,	3196
	25:17	"Make an atonement cover of **p** gold—	3196
	25:24	with **p** gold and make a gold molding	3196
	25:29	And make its plates and dishes of **p** gold,	3196
	25:31	a lampstand of **p** gold and hammer it out,	3196
	25:36	hammered out of **p** gold.	3196
	25:38	and trays are to be of **p** gold.	3196
	25:39	of **p** gold is to be used for the lampstand	3196
	28:14	and two braided chains of **p** gold,	3196
	28:22	breastpiece make braided chains of **p** gold,	3196
	28:36	"Make a plate of **p** gold and engrave on it	3196
	30: 3	and all the sides and the horns with **p** gold,	3196
	30:34	and frankincense, all in equal amounts,	2341
	30:35	It is to be salted and **p** and sacred.	3196
	31: 8	the **p** gold lampstand and all its accessories,	3196
	37: 2	He overlaid it with **p** gold,	3196
	37: 6	He made the atonement cover of **p** gold—	3196
	37:11	Then they overlaid it with **p** gold and made	3196
	37:16	And they made from **p** gold the articles for	3196
	37:17	of **p** gold and hammered it out, base	3196
	37:22	hammered out of **p** gold.	3196
	37:23	as its wick trimmers and trays, of **p** gold.	3196
	37:24	from one talent of **p** gold.	3196
	37:26	and all the sides and the horns with **p** gold,	3196
	37:29	the sacred anointing oil and the **p**,	2341
	39:15	they made braided chains of **p** gold,	3196
	39:25	of **p** gold and attached them around	3196
	39:30	out of **p** gold and engraved on it,	3196
	39:37	the **p** gold lampstand with its row of lamps	3196
Lev	24: 4	The lamps on the **p** gold lampstand before	3196
	24: 6	on the table of **p** gold before the LORD.	3196
	24: 7	Along each row put some **p** incense as	2341
2Sa	22:27	to the pure *you* show yourself pure,	1405
	22:27	to the pure *you* **show yourself p,**	1405
1Ki	6:20	He overlaid the inside with **p** gold,	6034
	6:21	the inside of the temple with **p** gold,	6034
	7:49	the lampstands of **p** gold (five on the right	6034
	7:50	the **p** gold basins,	6034
	10:21	of the Forest of Lebanon were **p** gold.	6034
2Ki	25:15	all that were made of **p** gold or silver.	2298+2298
1Ch	28:17	of **p** gold for the forks, sprinkling bowls	3196
2Ch	3: 4	He overlaid the inside with **p** gold.	3196
	4:20	of **p** gold with their lamps, to burn in front	6034
	4:22	the **p** gold wick trimmers,	6034
	9:17	with ivory and overlaid with **p** gold.	3196
	9:20	of the Forest of Lebanon were **p** gold.	6034
Job	4:17	Can a man *be* more **p** than his Maker?	3197
	8: 6	if you are **p** and upright,	2341
	11: 4	'My beliefs are flawless and I am **p**	1338
	14: 4	Who can bring *what is* **p** from the impure?	3196
	15:14	What is man, that *he could be* **p**,	2342
	15:15	if even the heavens *are* not **p** in his sight,	2348
	16:17	of violence and my prayer is **p.**	2341
	25: 4	How *can* one born of woman *be* **p**?	2342

Job	25: 5	and the stars *are* not **p** in his eyes,	2348
	28:19	it cannot be bought with **p** gold.	3196
	31:24	put my trust in gold or said to **p** gold,	4188
	33: 9	'I am **p** and without sin;	2341
Ps	18:26	to the **p** you show yourself pure,	1405
	18:26	to the pure *you* **show yourself p,**	1405
	19: 9	fear of the LORD is **p**, enduring forever.	3196
	19:10	than much **p** gold;	7058
	21: 3	and placed a crown of **p** gold on his head.	7058
	24: 4	He who has clean hands and a **p** heart,	1338
	51:10	Create in me a **p** heart, O God,	3196
	73: 1	*to those who are* **p** in heart.	1338
	73:13	Surely in vain *have I* **kept** my heart **p**;	2342
	119: 9	How *can* a young man **keep** his way **p**?	2342
	119:127	more than **p** gold,	7058
Pr	15:26	but those of the **p** are pleasing to him.	3196
	20: 9	Who can say, "*I have* **kept** my heart **p**;	2342
	20:11	by whether his conduct is **p** and right.	2341
	22:11	He who loves a **p** heart and whose speech	3196
	30:12	those who are **p** in their own eyes and	3196
SS	5:15	pillars of marble set on bases of **p** gold.	7058
Isa	13:12	I will make man scarcer than **p** gold,	7058
	52:11	Come out from it and *be* **p**,	1405
Jer	52:19	all that were made of **p** gold or silver.	2298+2298
Da	2:32	The head of the statue was made of **p** gold,	10294
Hab	1:13	Your eyes are too **p** to look on evil;	3196
Mal	1:11	In every place incense and **p** offerings will	3196
Mt	5: 8	Blessed are the **p** in heart,	2754
Mk	14: 3	very expensive perfume, *made of* **p** nard.	4410
Jn	12: 3	Then Mary took about a pint of **p** nard,	4410
2Co	11: 2	I might present you as a **p** virgin to him.	54
	11: 3	from your sincere and **p** devotion to Christ.	55
Php	1:10	be **p** and blameless until the day of Christ,	1637
	2:15	so that you may become blameless and **p**,	193
	4: 8	whatever is **p**, whatever is lovely,	54
1Ti	1: 5	from a **p** heart and a good conscience and	2754
	5:22	Keep yourself **p.**	54
2Ti	2:22	on the Lord out of a **p** heart.	2754
Tit	1:15	*To* the **p**, all things are pure,	2754
	1:15	To the pure, all things are **p**,	2754
	1:15	and do not believe, nothing is **p.**	2754
	2: 5	to be self-controlled and **p**,	54
Heb	7:26	one who is holy, blameless, **p**,	299
	10:22	and having our bodies washed *with* **p** water.	2754
	13: 4	and the marriage bed kept **p**,	299
Jas	1: 2	Consider it **p** joy, my brothers,	4246
	1:27	Religion that God our Father accepts as **p**	2754
	3:17	that comes from heaven is first of all **p**;	54
1Pe	2: 2	Like newborn babies, crave **p** spiritual milk,	100
1Jn	3: 3	hope in him purifies himself, just as he is **p.**	54
Rev	14: 4	for they kept themselves **p.**	4221
	21:18	and the city of **p** gold, as pure as glass.	2754
	21:18	and the city of pure gold, as **p** as glass.	2754
	21:21	The great street of the city was of **p** gold,	2754

PUREST (1) [PURE]

SS	5:11	His head is **p** gold;	4188+7058

PURGE (16) [PURGED]

Dt	13: 5	*You must* **p** the evil from among you.	1278
	17: 7	*You must* **p** the evil from among you.	1278
	17:12	*You must* **p** the evil from Israel.	1278
	19:13	*You must* **p** from Israel the guilt	1278
	19:19	*You must* **p** the evil from among you.	1278
	21: 9	So you *will* **p** from yourselves the guilt	1278
	21:21	*You must* **p** the evil from among you.	1278
	22:21	*You must* **p** the evil from among you.	1278
	22:22	*You must* **p** the evil from Israel.	1278
	22:24	*You must* **p** the evil from among you.	1278
	24: 7	*You must* **p** the evil from among you.	1278
Jdg	20:13	so that we may put them to death and **p**	1278
2Ch	34: 3	to **p** Judah and Jerusalem of high places,	3197
Pr	20:30	and beatings **p** the inmost being.	NIH
Isa	1:25	*I will* **thoroughly p** away your dross	1342+2021+3869+7671
Eze	20:38	*I will* **p** you of those who revolt and rebel	1405

PURGED (2) [PURGE]

2Ch	34: 5	and so *he* **p** Judah and Jerusalem.	3197
Jer	6:29	the wicked **are** not **p** out.	5998

PURGETH (KJV) See PRUNES

PURIFICATION (10) [PURE]

Lev	12: 4	until the days of her **p** are over.	3198
	12: 6	the days of her **p** for a son or daughter are	3198
Nu	19: 9	the water of cleansing; it is for **p from sin.**	2633
	19:17	put some ashes from the burned **p offering**	2633
1Ch	23:28	the side rooms, the **p** of all sacred things	3200
Ne	12:45	service of their God and the service of **p**,	3200
Lk	2:22	the time of their **p** according to the Law	2752
Ac	21:24	join in their **p** rites and pay their expenses.	49
	21:26	the date when the days *of* **p** would end and	50
Heb	1: 3	After he had provided **p** for sins,	2752

PURIFIED (22) [PURE]

Lev	12: 4	thirty-three days to be **p** from her bleeding.	3200
	12: 5	sixty-six days to be **p** from her bleeding.	3200
Nu	8:15	"After *you have* **p** the Levites	3197
	8:21	The Levites **p themselves** and washed	2627
	31:23	But *it must* also **be p** with the water	2627
2Sa	11: 4	(She had **p herself** from her uncleanness.)	7727
2Ch	29:18	"We have **p** the entire temple of the LORD,	3197

2Ch	30:18	Issachar and Zebulun *had* not p themselves,	3197
Ezr	6:20	The priests and Levites *had* p **themselves**	3197
Ne	12:30	p **themselves** ceremonially,	3197
	12:30	*they* p the people, the gates and the wall.	3197
	13:30	So *I* p the priests and the Levites	3197
Job	1:5	Job would send and **have** them **p.**	7727
Ps	12:6	in a furnace of clay, p seven times.	2423
Eze	43:22	the altar *is to be* p as it was purified with	2627
	43:22	the altar is to be purified as *it was* p with	2627
Da	11:35	refined, p and made spotless until the time	1405
	12:10	Many *will* **be p,** made spotless and refined,	1405
Ac	15:9	for *he* p their hearts by faith.	2751
	21:26	the men and p *himself* along with them.	49
Heb	9:23	the copies of the heavenly things *to be* p	2751
1Pe	1:22	*Now that you have* p yourselves by obeying	49

PURIFIER (1) [PURE]

Mal	3:3	He will sit as a refiner and p *of* silver;	3197

PURIFIES (2) [PURE]

1Jn	1:7	his Son, p us from all sin.	2751
	3:3	hope in him p himself, just as he is pure.	49

PURIFY (29) [PURE]

Ge	35:2	and p **yourselves** and change your clothes.	3197
Ex	29:36	**P** the altar by making atonement for it,	2627
Lev	8:15	on all the horns of the altar *to* p the altar.	2627
	14:49	To p the house he is to take two birds	2627
	14:52	*He* shall p the house with the bird's blood,	2627
Nu	8:7	To p them, do this: Sprinkle the water	3197
	8:7	and so **themselves.**	3197
	8:21	and made atonement for them to p them.	3197
	19:12	he *must* p himself with the water on	2627
	19:12	not p himself on the third and seventh days,	2627
	19:13	of anyone and fails *to* p himself defiles	2627
	19:19	and on the seventh day *he is to* p him.	2627
	19:20	a person who is unclean *does* not **p himself,**	2627
	31:19	and seventh days you *must* **p yourselves**	2627
	31:20	**P** every garment as well	2627
2Ch	29:15	they went in to p the temple of the LORD,	3197
	29:16	into the sanctuary of the LORD *to* p it.	3197
	34:8	to p the land and the temple,	3197
Ne	12:30	I gave orders *to* p the rooms,	3197
	13:22	*to* p **themselves** and go and guard the gates	3197
Isa	66:17	"Those who consecrate and **p themselves**	3197
Eze	43:20	so p the altar and make atonement for it.	2627
	45:18	to take a young bull without defect and p	2627
Zep	3:9	"Then *will I* p the lips of the peoples,	1359+2200
Mal	3:3	*he will* p the Levites and refine them	3197
2Co	7:1	*let us* p ourselves from everything that	2751
Tit	2:14	to redeem us from all wickedness and *to* p	2751
Jas	4:8	and p your hearts, you double-minded.	49
1Jn	1:9	and p us from all unrighteousness.	2751

PURIFYING (1) [PURE]

Eze	43:23	When you have finished p it,	2627

PURIM (5)

Est	9:26	(Therefore these days were called **P,**	7052
	9:28	of **P** should never cease to be celebrated by	7052
	9:29	to confirm this second letter concerning **P.**	7052
	9:31	of **P** at their designated times,	7052
	9:32	about **P,** and it was written down in	7052

PURITY (5) [PURE]

Hos	8:5	How long will they be incapable of **p?**	5931
2Co	6:6	in **p,** understanding, patience and kindness;	55
1Ti	4:12	in life, in love, in faith and in **p.**	48
	5:2	younger women as sisters, with absolute **p.**	48
1Pe	3:2	they see the **p** and reverence of your lives.	54

PURLOINING (KJV) See STEAL

PURPLE (51)

Ex	25:4	**p** and scarlet yarn and fine linen;	763
	26:1	and blue, **p** and scarlet yarn,	763
	26:31	**p** and scarlet yarn and finely twisted linen,	763
	26:36	**p** and scarlet yarn and finely twisted linen	763
	27:16	**p** and scarlet yarn and finely twisted linen	763
	28:5	and blue, **p** and scarlet yarn, and fine linen.	763
	28:6	and of blue, **p** and scarlet yarn,	763
	28:8	and with blue, **p** and scarlet yarn,	763
	28:15	of gold, and of blue, **p** and scarlet yarn,	763
	28:33	**p** and scarlet yarn around the hem of	763
	35:6	**p** and scarlet yarn and fine linen,	763
	35:23	**p** or scarlet yarn or fine linen, or goat hair,	763
	35:25	blue, **p** or scarlet yarn or fine linen.	763
	35:35	**p** and scarlet yarn and fine linen,	763
	36:8	blue, **p** and scarlet yarn,	763
	36:35	**p** and scarlet yarn and finely twisted linen,	763
	36:37	**p** and scarlet yarn and finely twisted linen	763
	38:18	**p** and scarlet yarn and finely twisted linen	763
	38:23	**p** and scarlet yarn and fine linen.)	763
	39:1	From the blue, **p** and scarlet yarn	763
	39:2	and of blue, **p** and scarlet yarn,	763
	39:3	**p** and scarlet yarn and fine linen—	763
	39:5	and with blue, **p** and scarlet yarn,	763
	39:8	of gold, and of blue, **p** and scarlet linen	763
	39:24	**p** and scarlet yarn and finely twisted linen	763
	39:29	blue, **p** and scarlet yarn—	763
Nu	4:13	the bronze altar and spread a **p** cloth over it.	763
Jdg	8:26	the pendants and the **p** garments worn by	763

2Ch	2:7	and in **p,** crimson and blue yarn,	760
	2:14	and with **p** and blue and crimson yarn	763
	3:14	**p** and crimson yarn and fine linen,	763
Est	1:6	with cords of white linen and **p material**	763
	8:15	a large crown of gold and a **p** robe	763
Pr	31:22	she is clothed in fine linen and **p.**	763
SS	3:10	Its seat was upholstered with **p,**	763
Jer	10:9	then dressed in blue and **p**—	763
La	4:5	Those nurtured in **p** now lie on ash heaps.	9355
Eze	27:7	of blue and **p** from the coasts of Elishah.	763
	27:16	they exchanged turquoise, **p** fabric,	763
Da	5:7	in **p** and have a gold chain placed	10066
	5:16	in **p** and have a gold chain placed	10066
	5:29	Daniel was clothed in **p,**	10066
Mk	15:17	They put a **p** robe on him,	4525
	15:20	the **p** robe and put his own clothes on him.	4525
Lk	16:19	a rich man who was dressed in **p**	4525
Jn	19:2	They clothed him in a **p** robe	4526
	19:5	the crown of thorns and the **p** robe,	4526
Ac	16:14	a **dealer in p** cloth from the city	4527
Rev	17:4	The woman was dressed in **p** and scarlet,	4526
	18:12	fine linen, **p,** silk and scarlet cloth;	4525
	18:16	**p** and scarlet, and glittering with gold,	4526

PURPOSE (42) [PURPOSED, PURPOSELY, PURPOSES]

Ex	9:16	But I have raised you up **for this** very **p,**	6288
Lev	7:24	may be used for any other **p,**	4856
1Ch	23:5	the musical instruments I have provided for	
		that p."	2146S
Job	36:5	he is mighty, and firm in his **p.**	4213
Ps	57:2	to God, who fulfills [his **p**] for me.	NIH
	138:8	The LORD will fulfill [his **p**] for me;	NIH
Pr	19:21	but it is the LORD's **p** that prevails.	6783
Isa	10:7	his **p** is to destroy,	4222
	46:10	I say: My **p** will stand,	6783
	46:11	from a far-off land, a man to fulfill my **p.**	6783
	48:14	LORD's chosen ally will carry out his **p**	2914
	49:4	But I said, "I have labored to **no p;**	8198
	55:11	and achieve the **p** for which I sent it.	7503
Jer	15:11	"Surely I will deliver you for a **good p;**	AIT
	51:11	because his **p** is to destroy Babylon.	4659
	51:12	The LORD **will carry out** *his* **p,**	2372
Lk	7:30	in the law rejected God's **p** for themselves,	1087
Ac	2:23	to you by God's set **p** and foreknowledge;	1087
	5:38	For if their **p** or activity is of human origin,	1087
	13:36	"For when David had served God's **p**	1087
Ro	8:28	who have been called according to his **p.**	4606
	9:11	that God's **p** in election might stand:	4606
	9:17	"I raised you up for this very **p,**	1650
1Co	3:8	and the man who waters have one **p,**	1650
2Co	5:5	it is God who has made us **for this** very **p**	1650
Gal	3:19	What, then, was the **p** of the law?	NIG
	4:18	provided the **p** is good,	NIG
Eph	1:11	in conformity with the **p** of his will,	1087
	2:15	His **p** was **to** create in himself one new man	2671
	3:11	to his eternal **p** which he accomplished	4606
	6:22	I am sending him to you **for** this very **p,**	1650
Php	2:2	being one in spirit and **p.**	5858
	2:13	to will and to act according to his **good p.**	2306
Col	2:2	My **p** is **that** they may be encouraged	2671
	4:8	**for the express p** that you may know about	
		our circumstances	899+1650+4047
2Th	1:11	by his power he may fulfill every good **p**	2306
1Ti	2:7	And **for** this **p** I was appointed a herald and	1650
2Ti	1:9	but because of his own **p** and grace.	4606
	3:10	my way of life, my **p,** faith, patience, love,	4606
Heb	6:17	the unchanging nature *of* his **p** very clear	1087
Rev	17:13	They have one **p** and will give their power	1191
	17:17	to accomplish his **p** by agreeing to give	1191

PURPOSED (5) [PURPOSE]

Isa	14:24	and as *I have* **p,** so it will stand.	3619
	14:27	For the LORD Almighty *has* **p,**	3619
Jer	49:20	what *he* has **p** against those who live in	
		Teman:	3108+4742
	50:45	what *he* has **p** against the land of the	
		Babylonians,	3108+4742
Eph	1:9	which *he* **p** in Christ,	4729

PURPOSELY (1) [PURPOSE]

Jn	7:1	**p** staying away from Judea because	2527

PURPOSES (10) [PURPOSE]

Ps	33:10	he thwarts the **p** *of* the peoples,	4742
	33:11	the **p** *of* his heart through all generations.	4742
Pr	20:5	The **p** of a man's heart are deep waters,	6783
Jer	23:20	until he fully accomplishes the **p**	4659
	30:24	until he fully accomplishes the **p**	4659
	32:19	great are your **p** and mighty are your deeds.	6783
	51:29	the LORD's **p** against Babylon stand—	4742
Ro	9:21	of clay some pottery for noble **p** and some	NIG
2Ti	2:20	some are for **noble p** and some for ignoble.	5507
	2:21	he will be an instrument for **noble p,**	5507

PURSE (6) [PURSES]

Pr	1:14	and we will share a common **p"**—	3967
	7:20	He took his **p** filled *with* money and	7655
Hag	1:6	only to put them in a **p** with holes in it."	7655
Lk	10:4	Do not take a **p** or bag or sandals;	964
	22:35	"When I sent you without a **p,**	964
	22:36	He said to them, "But now if you have a **p,**	964

PURSES (3) [PURSE]

Pr	16:30	*he who* **p** his lips is bent on evil.	7975
Isa	3:22	and the capes and cloaks, the **p**	3038
Lk	12:33	Provide **p** for yourselves that will not wear	964

PURSUE (51) [PURSUED, PURSUER, PURSUERS, PURSUES, PURSUING, PURSUIT]

Ex	14:4	and *he will* **p** them.	8103
	15:9	"The enemy boasted, '*I will* **p,**	8103
Lev	26:7	*You will* **p** your enemies,	8103
	26:33	and will draw out my sword and **p** you.	339
Dt	19:6	the avenger of blood *might* **p** him in a rage,	8103
	28:45	*They will* **p** you and overtake you	8103
Jos	8:6	*They will* **p** us until we have lured them	339+3655
	8:16	All the men of Ai were called to **p** them,	8103
	10:19	**P** your enemies, attack them from the rear	8103
1Sa	30:8	"Shall *I* **p** this raiding party?"	8103
	30:8	"**P** them," he answered.	8103
2Sa	17:1	Take your master's men and **p** him,	8103
	20:7	from Jerusalem to **p** Sheba son of Bicri.	8103
	20:13	the men went on with Joab to **p** Sheba son	8103
	24:13	from your enemies while they **p** you?	8103
Job	19:22	Why *do you* **p** me as God does?	8103
Ps	7:1	save and deliver me from all *who* **p** me,	8103
	7:5	then *let* my enemy **p** and overtake me;	8103
	31:15	from my enemies and from *those who* **p** me.	8103
	34:14	seek peace and **p** it.	8103
	35:3	and javelin against *those who* **p** me.	8103
	38:20	with evil slander me when I **p** what is good.	8103
	56:1	O God, for men **hotly p** me;	8634
	56:2	My slanderers **p** me all day long;	8634
	57:3	rebuking *those who* **hotly p** me;	8634
	71:11	**p** him and seize him,	8103
	83:15	so **p** them with your tempest	8103
	142:6	rescue me from *those who* **p** me,	8103
Pr	15:9	but he loves *those who* **p** righteousness.	8103
Isa	51:1	*you who* **p** righteousness and who seek	8103
Jer	2:24	*that* **p** her need not tire themselves;	1335
	9:16	and *I will* **p** them *with* the sword	339+8938
	29:18	*I will* **p** them *with* the sword,	8103
	48:2	the sword *will* **p** you.	339+2143
	49:37	"*I will* **p** them *with* the sword	339+8938
	50:21	**P,** kill and completely destroy them,"	339
La	1:3	All *who* **p** her have overtaken her in	8103
	3:66	**P** them in anger and destroy them from	8103
	5:5	*Those who* **p** us are at our heels;	8103
Eze	5:2	For I will **p** them with drawn sword.	339
	5:12	and a third I will scatter to the winds and **p**	339
	12:14	and I will **p** them with drawn sword.	339
	35:6	over to bloodshed and it *will* **p** you.	8103
	35:6	bloodshed *will* **p** you.	8103
Hos	8:3	an enemy *will* **p** him.	8103
Na	1:8	*he will* **p** his foes into darkness.	8103
Mt	23:34	in your synagogues and **p** from town	1503
Ro	9:30	the Gentiles, who *did* not **p** righteousness,	1503
1Ti	6:11	and **p** righteousness, godliness, faith, love,	1503
2Ti	2:22	and **p** righteousness, faith, love and peace,	1503
1Pe	3:11	he must seek peace and **p** it.	1503

PURSUED (31) [PURSUE]

Ge	31:23	he **p** Jacob *for* seven days and caught up	8103
	35:5	around them so that no one **p** them.	8103
Ex	14:8	so that *he* **p** the Israelites	8103
	14:9	**p** the Israelites and overtook them	8103
	14:23	The Egyptians **p** them,	8103
Jos	8:16	and *they* **p** Joshua and were lured away	8103
	10:10	Israel **p** them *along* the road going up	8103
	11:8	They defeated them and **p** them all the way	8103
	24:6	and the Egyptians **p** them with chariots	8103
Jdg	4:16	But Barak **p** the chariots and army as far	8103
	7:23	and *they* **p** the Midianites.	8103
	7:25	*They* **p** the Midianites and brought	8103
	8:12	fled, but *he* **p** them and captured them,	8103
1Sa	7:11	of Israel rushed out of Mizpah and **p**	8103
	17:52	and **p** the Philistines to the entrance of Gath	8103
2Sa	2:19	to the right nor to the left as *he* **p** him.	339+2143
	2:24	But Joab and Abishai **p** Abner,	8103
	2:28	they no longer **p** Israel,	8103
	20:10	and his brother Abishai **p** Sheba son	8103
	22:38	"*I* **p** my enemies and crushed them;	8103
2Ki	25:5	but the Babylonian army **p** the king	8103
2Ch	13:19	Abijah **p** Jeroboam and took from him	8103
	14:13	Asa and his army **p** them as far as Gerar.	8103
Ps	18:37	"*I* **p** my enemies and overtook them;	8103
Jer	39:5	But the Babylonian army **p** them	8103
	52:8	but the Babylonian army **p** King Zedekiah	8103
La	3:43	covered yourself with anger and **p** us;	8103
Am	1:11	Because he **p** his brother with a sword,	8103
Ro	9:31	*who* **p** a law of righteousness,	1503
	9:32	Because they **p** it not by faith but as if	NIG
Rev	12:13	he **p** the woman who had given birth to	1503

PURSUER (1) [PURSUE]

La	1:6	in weakness they have fled before the **p.**	8103

PURSUERS (7) [PURSUE]

Jos	2:7	and as soon as the **p** had gone out,	8103
	2:16	"Go to the hills so the **p** will not find you.	8103
	2:22	until the **p** had searched all along the road	8103
	8:20	the desert had turned back against their **p.**	8103
Ne	9:11	but you hurled their **p** into the depths,	8103
Isa	30:16	Therefore your **p** will be swift!	8103

La	4:19	Our p were swifter than eagles in the sky;	8103

PURSUES (11) [PURSUE]

Jos	20: 5	If the avenger of blood p him,	8103
Ps	143: 3	The enemy p me, he crushes me to	8103
Pr	11:19	but he who p evil goes to his death.	8103
	13:21	Misfortune p the sinner,	8103
	18: 1	An unfriendly man p selfish ends;	1335
	19: 7	Though he p them with pleading,	8103
	21:21	He who p righteousness and love finds life,	8103
	28: 1	The wicked man flees though no one p,	8103
Isa	41: 3	He p them and moves on unscathed,	8103
Jer	8: 6	Each p his own course like a horse	928+8740
Hos	12: 1	he p the east wind all day	8103

PURSUING (22) [PURSUE]

Ge	14:15	p them as far as Hobah, north of Damascus.	8103
Lev	26:17	you will flee even when no one is p you.	8103
	26:36	even though no one is p them.	8103
	26:37	even though no one is p them.	8103
Dt	11: 4	waters of the Red Sea as they were p you,	8103
Jdg	8: 5	and I am still p Zebah and Zalmunna,	8103
1Sa	14:46	Then Saul stopped p the Philistines,	339
	24: 1	After Saul returned from p the Philistines,	339
	24:14	Whom are you p? A dead dog?	8103
	25:29	though someone is p you to take your life,	8103
	26:18	he added, "Why is my lord p his servant?	8103
2Sa	2:26	order your men to stop p their brothers?"	339
	2:30	from p Abner and assembled all his men.	339
	18:16	and the troops stopped p Israel,	8103
1Ki	22:33	the king of Israel and stopped p him.	339+4946
2Ch	18:32	they stopped p him.	339+4946
Ps	35: 6	with the angel of the LORD p them.	8103
Isa	65: 2	p their own imaginations—	339
Jer	2:33	How skilled you are at p love!	1335
Hos	5:11	trampled in judgment, intent on p idols.	339+2143
1Ti	3: 8	and not p dishonest gain.	153
Tit	1: 7	not violent, not p dishonest gain.	153

PURSUIT (13) [PURSUE]

Ge	14:14	in his household and went in p as far	8103
Jos	2: 7	So the men set out in p of the spies on	8103
	8:17	the city open and went in p of Israel.	8103
Jdg	4:22	Barak came by in p of Sisera,	8103
	8: 4	exhausted yet keeping up the p,	8103
1Sa	17:52	they joined the battle in hot p.	339
	23:25	went into the Desert of Maon in p	8103
	23:28	Then Saul broke off his p of David	8103
	30:10	and four hundred men continued the p.	8103
2Sa	2:23	But Asahel refused to give up the p;	6073
	2:27	the p of their brothers until morning."	339
	17: 1	and set out tonight in p of David.	8103
1Ki	20:20	the Arameans fled, with the Israelites in p.	8103

PUSH (5) [PUSHED, PUSHES, PUSHING]

Dt	15:17	and p it through his ear lobe into the door,	5989
Jos	23: 5	He will p them out before you,	3769
2Ki	4:27	Gehazi came over to p her away,	2074
Ps	44: 5	Through you we p back our enemies;	5590
Jer	46:15	for the LORD will p them down.	2074

PUSHED (7) [PUSH]

Jdg	16:30	Then he p with all his might,	5742
Ps	118:13	I was p back and about to fall,	1890+1890
Isa	16: 2	Like fluttering birds p from the nest,	8938
Zec	5: 8	and he p her back into the basket	8959
	5: 8	p the lead cover down over its mouth.	8959
Ac	7:27	the other p Moses aside and said,	723
	19:33	The Jews p Alexander to the front,	4582

PUSHES (1) [PUSH]

2Co	11:20	advantage of you or p himself forward	2048

PUSHES (Anglicized) See also SHOVES

PUSHING (2) [PUSH]

Joel	2:20	p it into a parched and barren land,	5615
Mk	3:10	with diseases were p forward to touch him.	2158

PUT (1021) [PUTS, PUTTING]

Ge	2: 8	and there he p the man he had formed.	8492
	2:15	and p him in the Garden of Eden to work it	5663
	3:12	"The woman you p here with me—	5989
	3:15	And I will p enmity between you and	8883
	4:15	Then the LORD p a mark on Cain so	8492
	6:13	"I am going to p an end to all people,	995+4200+7156
	6:16	P a door in the side of the ark	8492
	10: 6	Cush, Mizraim, P and Canaan.	7033
	16: 5	I p my servant in your arms,	5989
	21:15	she p the boy under one of the bushes.	8959
	24: 2	"P your hand under my thigh.	8492
	24: 9	So the servant p his hand under the thigh	8492
	24:47	"Then I p the ring in her nose and	8492
	26:11	or his wife shall surely be p to death.	4637+4637
	27:15	and p them on her younger son Jacob.	4252
	28:11	he p it under his head and lay down	8492
	30:36	Then he p a three-day journey	8492
	30:40	and did not p them with Laban's animals.	8883
	31:17	Then Jacob p his children and his wives	5951
	31:34	and p them inside her camel's saddle	8492
Ge	31:37	P it here in front of your relatives	8492
	32:16	He p them in the care of his servants,	5989
	33: 2	He p the maidservants and their children	5989
	34:26	They p Hamor and his son Shechem to	2222
	37:34	p on sackcloth and mourned	928+5516+8492
	38: 7	so the LORD p him to death.	4637
	38:10	so he p him to death also.	4637
	38:19	and p on her widow's clothes again.	4252
	38:28	one of them p out his hand;	5989
	39: 4	Potiphar p him in charge of his household,	7212
	39: 5	time he p him in charge of his household	7212
	39:20	Joseph's master took him and p him	5989
	39:22	So the warden p Joseph in charge	5989
	40: 3	and p them in custody in the house of	5989
	40:11	squeezed them into Pharaoh's cup and p	5989
	40:13	and you will p Pharaoh's cup in his hand,	5989
	40:15	to deserve being p in a dungeon."	8492
	40:21	so that he once again p the cup	5989
	41:33	and p him in charge of the land of Egypt.	8883
	41:41	"I hereby p you in charge of the whole land	5989
	41:42	from his finger and p it on Joseph's finger.	5989
	41:42	He dressed him in robes of fine linen and p	8492
	41:43	Thus he p him in charge of the whole land	5989
	41:48	In each city he p the food grown in	5989
	42:17	And he p them all in custody for three days.	665
	42:25	p each man's silver back in his sack,	8740
	42:37	"You may p both of my sons to death if	4637
	43:11	P some of the best products of the land	4374
	43:12	the silver that was p back into the mouths	8740
	43:18	that was p back into our sacks the first time.	8740
	43:22	We don't know who p our silver	8492
	44: 1	as they can carry, and p each man's silver	8492
	44: 2	Then p my cup, the silver one,	8492
	47: 6	p them in charge of my own livestock."	8492
	47:29	p your hand under my thigh and promise	8492
	48:14	and p it on Ephraim's head,	8883
	48:14	he p his left hand on Manasseh's head,	NIH
	48:18	p your right hand on his head."	8492
	48:20	So he p Ephraim ahead of Manasseh.	8492
Ex	1:11	So they p slave masters over them	8492
	2: 3	and p it among the reeds along the bank of	8492
	3:22	which you will p on your sons	8492
	4: 6	"Put your hand inside your cloak."	995
	4: 6	So Moses p his hand into his cloak,	995
	4: 7	"Now p it back into your cloak," he said.	8740
	4: 7	So Moses p his hand back into his cloak,	8740
	4:15	You shall speak to him and p words	8492
	4:20	them on a donkey and started back	8206
	5:21	and have p a sword in their hand to kill us."	5989
	12: 7	the blood and p it on the sides and tops of	5989
	12:22	and p some of the blood on the top and on	5595
	14:31	feared the LORD and p their trust in him	586
	16:33	"Take a jar and p an omer of manna in it.	5989
	16:34	Aaron p the manna in front of the	5663
	17: 2	Why do you p the LORD to the test?"	5814
	17:12	a stone and p it under him and he sat on it.	8492
	19: 9	and will always p their trust in you."	586
	19:12	P limits for the people around the mountain	1487
	19:12	shall surely be p to death.	4637+4637
	19:23	'P limits around the mountain	1487
	21:12	shall surely be p to death.	4637+4637
	21:14	from my altar and p him to death.	AIT
	21:15	must be p to death.	4637+4637
	21:16	when he is caught must be p to death.	4637+4637
	21:17	must be p to death.	4637+4637
	21:29	and the owner also must be p to death.	4637
	22:19	with an animal must be p to death.	4637+4637
	23: 7	p an innocent or honest person to death,	2222
	24: 6	Moses took half of the blood and p it	8492
	25:16	Then p in the ark the Testimony	5989
	25:21	the cover on top of the ark and p in the ark	5989
	25:25	a handbreadth wide and p a gold molding	6913
	25:30	P the bread of the Presence on this table to	5989
	26:11	Then make fifty bronze clasps and p them	995
	26:34	P the atonement cover on the ark of	5989
	26:35	on the north side of the tabernacle and p	5989
	27: 5	P it under the ledge of the altar so	5989
	28:30	Also p the Urim and the Thummim in	5989
	28:41	After you p these clothes on	4252
	29: 3	P them in a basket and present them in it—	5989
	29: 6	P the turban on his head and attach	8492
	29: 9	and p headbands on them.	2502
	29:12	of the bull's blood and p it on the horns of	5989
	29:20	take some of its blood and p it on the lobes	5989
	29:24	P all these in the hands of Aaron	8492
	30: 6	P the altar in front of the curtain that is	5989
	30:18	and p water in it.	5989
	31:14	who desecrates it must be p to death;	4637+4637
	31:15	must be p to death.	4637+4637
	33: 4	to mourn and no one p on any ornaments.	8883
	33:22	I will p you in a cleft in the rock	8492
	34:33	he p a veil over his face.	5989
	34:35	Then Moses would p the veil back	8740
	35: 2	does any work on it must be p to death.	4637
	37:12	a handbreadth wide and p a gold molding	6913
	37:14	The rings were p close to the rim to hold	NIH
	40: 3	the ark of the Testimony and p the curtain	8492
	40: 7	of Meeting and the altar and p water in it.	5989
	40: 8	up the courtyard around it and p the curtain	5989
	40:18	p the bases in place,	5989
	40:19	over the tabernacle and p the covering over	8492
	40:20	the ark and p the atonement cover over it.	5989
	40:28	Then he p up the curtain at the entrance to	8492
	40:30	and the altar and p water in it for washing,	5989
	40:33	the tabernacle and altar and p up the curtain	5989
Lev	1: 7	of Aaron the priest are to p fire on the altar	5989
	2: 1	pour oil on it, p incense on it	5989
Lev	2:15	P oil and incense on it;	5989
	4: 7	The priest shall then p some of the blood	5989
	4:18	He is to p some of the blood on the horns	5989
	4:25	the sin offering with his finger and p it on	5989
	4:30	of the blood with his finger and p it on	5989
	4:34	the sin offering with his finger and p it on	5989
	5:11	He must not p oil or incense on it,	8492
	6:10	The priest shall then p on his linen clothes,	4252
	6:11	to take off these clothes and p on others,	4252
	8: 7	He p the tunic on Aaron,	5989
	8: 7	clothed him with the robe and p the ephod	5989
	8: 8	on him and p the Urim and Thummim in	5989
	8:13	p tunics on them,	4252
	8:13	tied sashes around them and p headbands	2502
	8:15	and with his finger he p it on all the horns	5989
	8:23	the ram and took some of its blood and p it	5989
	8:24	and p some of the blood on the lobes	5989
	8:26	he p these on the fat portions and on	8492
	8:27	He p all these in the hands of Aaron	5989
	9: 9	the blood and p it on the horns of the altar;	5989
	10: 1	p fire in them and added incense;	5989
	11:32	P it in water;	995
	11:38	But if water has been p on the seed and	5989
	13: 4	p the infected person in isolation	6037
	13:11	He is not to p him in isolation	6037
	13:21	then the priest is to p him in isolation	6037
	13:26	then the priest is to p him in isolation	6037
	13:31	p the infected person in isolation	6037
	14:14	of the blood of the guilt offering and p it on	5989
	14:17	to p some of the oil remaining in his palm	5989
	14:18	the priest shall p on the head of the one to	5989
	14:25	and take some of its blood and p it on	5989
	14:28	to p on the same places he put the blood of	5989
	14:28	to put on the same places he p the blood of	NIH
	14:29	the priest shall p on the head of the one to	5989
	14:34	and I p a spreading mildew in a house in	5989
	16: 4	He is to p on the sacred linen tunic,	4252
	16: 4	to tie the linen sash around him and p on	7571
	16:13	He is to p the incense on the fire before	5989
	16:18	and some of the goat's blood and p it on all	5989
	16:21	p them on the goat's head.	5989
	16:23	and take off the linen garments he p on	4252
	16:24	a holy place and p on his regular garments.	4252
	16:32	He is to p on the sacred linen garments	4252
	19:14	or p a stumbling block in front of the blind,	5989
	19:20	Yet they are not to be p to death,	4637
	19:28	the dead or p tattoo marks on yourselves.	5989
	20: 2	to Molech must be p to death.	4637+4637
	20: 4	to Molech and they fail to p him to death,	4637
	20: 9	he must be p to death.	4637+4637
	20:10	the adulteress must be p to death.	4637+4637
	20:11	and the woman must be p to death;	4637+4637
	20:12	both of them must be p to death.	4637+4637
	20:13	They must be p to death;	4637+4637
	20:15	he must be p to death,	4637+4637
	20:16	he must be p to death,	4637+4637
	20:27	among you must be p to death.	4637+4637
	24: 7	Along each row p some pure incense as	5989
	24:12	They p him in custody until the will of	5663
	24:16	must be p to death.	4637+4637
	24:16	he must be p to death.	4637
	24:17	must be p to death.	4637+4637
	24:21	whoever kills a man must be p to death.	4637
	26:11	I will p my dwelling place among you,	5989
	26:36	a windblown leaf will p them to flight.	8103
	27:29	he must be p to death.	4637+4637
Nu	1:51	who goes near it shall be p to death.	4637
	3:10	approaches the sanctuary must be p to death."	4637
	3:38	was to be p to death.	4637
	4: 6	and p the poles in place.	8492
	4: 7	to spread a blue cloth and p on it the plates,	5989
	4: 8	and p its poles in place.	8492
	4:10	a covering of hides of sea cows and p it on	5989
	4:11	and p its poles in place.	8492
	4:12	that with hides of sea cows and p them on	5989
	4:14	and p its poles in place.	8492
	5:15	He must not pour oil on it or p incense	5989
	5:17	and p some dust from the tabernacle floor	5989
	5:19	p the woman under oath	8678
	5:21	p the woman under this curse of the oath—	8652+8678
	6:18	and p it in the fire that is under the sacrifice	5989
	6:27	"So they will p my name on the Israelites,	8492
	11:11	that you p the burden of all these people	5989
	11:15	p me to death right now—	2222+2222
	11:17	of the Spirit that is on you and p the Spirit	8492
	11:25	the Spirit that was on him and p the Spirit	5989
	11:29	the LORD would p his Spirit on them!"	5989
	14:15	If you p these people to death all at one	4637
	16: 7	and tomorrow p fire and incense in them	5989
	16:17	to take his censer and p incense in it—	5989
	16:18	p fire and incense in it,	5989
	16:21	from this assembly so I can p an end	3983
	16:45	from this assembly so I can p an end	3983
	16:46	"Take your censer and p incense in it,	5989
	17:10	"P back Aaron's staff in front of	8740
	17:10	This will p an end to their grumbling	3983
	18: 7	near the sanctuary must be p to death."	4637
	18: 8	"I myself have p you in charge of	5989
	19: 9	up the ashes of the heifer and p them	5663
	19:17	p some ashes from the burned purification	4374
	20:26	Remove Aaron's garments and p them on	4252
	20:28	and p them on his son Eleazar.	4252
	21: 8	"Make a snake and p it up on a pole;	8492
	21: 9	So Moses made a bronze snake and p it up	8492
	21:24	p him to the sword and took over his land	5782

Nu	22: 6	Now come and **p** a **curse on** these people,	826
	22:11	Now come and **p** a **curse on** them for me.	7686
	22:12	You must not **p** a **curse** on those people,	826
	22:17	and **p** a **curse on** these people for me."	7686
	23: 5	The LORD **p** a message in Balaam's mouth	8492
	23:16	with Balaam and **p** a message in his mouth	8492
	25: 5	"Each of you must be **p** to **death** those	2222
	25:11	that in my zeal I did not **p** an **end** to them.	3983
	25:15	Midianite woman who **was p** to **death** was	5782
	31:23	that can withstand fire **must be p** through	6296
	31:23	be **p** through that water.	6296
	35:16	the murderer **shall be p** to **death.**	4637+4637
	35:17	the murderer **shall be p** to **death.**	4637+4637
	35:18	the murderer **shall be p** to **death.**	4637+4637
	35:19	shall **p** the murderer to **death**;	4637
	35:19	he shall **p** him to **death.**	4637
	35:21	that person **shall be p** to **death**;	4637+4637
	35:21	shall **p** the murderer to **death**	4637
	35:30	to **be p** to **death** as a murderer only on	8357
	35:30	But no one is to **be p** to **death** on	4637
	35:31	**must** surely **be p** to **death.**	4637+4637
Dt	1:41	So every one of you **p** on his weapons,	2520
	2: 5	not even enough to **p** your foot **on.**	4534
	2:25	This very day I will begin to **p** the terror	5989
	9:28	he brought them out to **p** them to **death** in	4637
	10: 2	Then you are to **p** them in the chest."	8492
	10: 5	down the mountain and the tablets in	8492
	11:25	will **p** the terror and fear of you on	5989
	12: 5	among all your tribes to **p** his **Name** there	8492
	12: 7	in everything you have **p** your hand **to,**	5448
	12:18	in everything you **p** your hand **to.**	5448
	12:21	to **p** his Name is too far away from you,	8492
	13: 5	or dreamer must **be p** to **death,**	4637
	13: 9	you **must certainly p** him to **death.**	2222+2222
	13:15	you **must certainly p** to the sword	5782+5782
	14:24	the LORD will choose to **p** his **Name** is	8492
	15:10	and in everything you **p** your hand **to.**	5448
	15:19	**p** the firstborn of your oxen to **work,**	6268
	16: 9	from the time you begin to **p** the sickle to	NIH
	17: 6	a man **shall be p** to **death,**	4637
	17: 6	but no one **shall be p** to **death** on	4637
	17:12	the LORD your God must **be p** to **death.**	4637
	18:18	I will **p** my words in his mouth,	5989
	18:20	of other gods, must **be p** to **death."**	4637
	20:13	**p** to the sword all the men in it.	5782
	21:13	and **p aside** the clothes she was wearing	6073
	21:22	of a capital offense is **p** to **death**	4637
	23:20	in everything you **p** your hand **to** in	5448
	23:24	but do not **p** any in your basket.	5989
	23:25	not **p** a sickle to his standing grain.	5677
	24:16	not **be p** to **death** for their children,	4637
	24:16	nor children **p** to **death** for their fathers;	4637
	26: 2	and **p** them in a basket.	8492
	28: 8	and on everything you **p** your hand **to.**	5448
	28:20	in everything you **p** your hand **to,**	5448
	28:48	He will **p** an iron yoke on your neck	5989
	30: 7	The LORD your God will **p** all these curses	5989
	32:30	or two **p** ten thousand to **flight,**	5674
	32:39	I **p** to **death** and I bring to life,	4637
Jos	1:18	will **be p** to **death.**	4637
	4: 3	over with you and **p** them **down** at the place	5663
	4: 8	where they **p** them **down.**	5663
	6:23	and **p** them in a place outside the camp	5663
	6:24	but they **p** the silver and gold and	5989
	7:11	they have **p** them with their own possessions	8492
	8:24	and when every one of them had **been p** to	5877
	9: 5	The men **p** worn and patched sandals	NIH
	10:24	"Come here and **p** your feet on the necks	8492
	10:28	He **p** the city and its king to the sword	5782
	10:30	and everyone in it Joshua **p** to the sword.	5782
	10:32	and everyone in it he **p** to the sword,	5782
	10:35	They captured it that same day and **p** it to	5782
	10:37	They took the city and **p** it to the sword,	5782
	10:39	and **p** them to the sword.	5782
	11:10	captured Hazor and **p** its king to the sword.	5782
	11:11	Everyone in it they **p** to the sword.	5782
	11:12	and their kings and **p** them to the sword.	5782
	11:14	but all the people they **p** to the sword	5782
	13:22	the Israelites had **p** to the sword Balaam son	2222
	19:47	took it, **p** it to the sword and occupied it.	5782
	24: 7	and he **p** darkness between you and	8492
	24: 9	for Balaam son of Beor to **p** a **curse on** you.	7837
Jdg	1: 8	They **p** the city to the sword and set it	5782
	1:25	and they **p** the city to the sword but spared	5782
	4:18	and she **p** a covering **over** him.	4059
	6:13	now the LORD has abandoned us and **p** us	5989
	6:31	Whoever fights for him shall **be p** to **death**	4637
	9:26	and its citizens **p** their **confidence** in him.	1053
	16:19	Having **p** him to **sleep** on her lap,	3822
	16:26	"**P** me where I can feel the pillars	5663
	17: 4	And they were **p** in Micah's house.	2118
	18:10	and a spacious land that God has **p**	5989
	19:28	the man **p** her on his donkey and set out	4374
	20:13	so that we may **p** them to **death** and purge	4637
	20:37	and **p** the whole city to the sword.	5782
	20:48	of Israel went back to Benjamin and **p** all	5782
	21: 5	should **certainly be p** to **death.**	4637+4637
	21:10	and **p** to the sword those living there,	5782
Ru	3: 3	and **p** on your best clothes.	8492
	3:15	into it six measures of barley and **p** it	8883
1Sa	2: 5	the LORD's will to **p** them to **death.**	4637
	5: 3	They took Dagon and **p** him **back**	8740
	6: 8	the ark of the LORD and **p** it on the cart,	5989
	6: 8	and in a chest beside it **p** the gold objects	8492
	7: 4	So the Israelites **p away** their Baals	6073
	11:12	to us and we will **p** them to **death."**	4637
	11:13	"No one shall **be p** to **death** today.	4637

1Sa	14:26	yet no one **p** his hand to his mouth,	5952
	14:45	and he was not **p** to **death.**	4637
	15: 3	**p** to **death** men and women,	4637
	15:33	And Samuel **p** Agag to **death** before	9119
	17:38	He **p** a coat of armor **on** him	4252
	17:40	**p** them in the pouch of his shepherd's bag	8492
	17:54	and he **p** the Philistine's weapons	8492
	19: 6	David will not **be p** to **death."**	4637
	20:32	"Why should he **be p** to **death?**	4637
	22:19	He also **p** to the sword Nob,	5782
	25:13	"**P** on your swords!"	2520
	25:13	So they **p** on their swords,	2520
	25:13	and David **p** on his.	2520
	26:12	the LORD had **p** them into a deep sleep.	5877
	31:10	They **p** his armor in the temple of	8492
2Sa	3:31	and **p on** sackcloth and walk in mourning	2520
	4:10	I seized him and **p** him to **death** in Ziklag.	2222
	8: 2	Every two lengths of them were **p** to **death,**	4637
	8: 6	He **p** garrisons in the Aramean kingdom	8492
	8:14	He **p** garrisons throughout Edom,	8492
	10:10	He **p** the rest of the men under the command	5989
	11:15	"**P** Uriah in the front line where	2035
	11:16	he **p** Uriah at a place where he knew	5989
	12:20	**p on lotions** and changed his clothes,	6057
	13:18	So his servant **p** her **out** and	2021+2575+3655
	13:19	Tamar **p** ashes on her head and tore	4374
	13:19	She **p** her hand on her head and went away,	8492
	14: 3	And Joab **p** the words in her mouth.	8492
	14: 7	so that we may **p** him to **death** for the life	4637
	14: 7	They would **p out** the only burning coal	3882
	14:19	and who **p** all these words into the mouth	8492
	14:32	let him **p** me to **death."**	4637
	15:14	to overtake us and bring ruin upon us and **p**	5782
	17:23	**p** his house in **order** and then hanged	7422
	18:13	**p** my life **in jeopardy**—	6913+9214
	19:19	May the king **p** it out of his mind.	8492
	19:21	"Shouldn't Shimei **be p** to **death** for this?	4637
	19:22	Should anyone **be p** to **death**	4637
	20: 3	to take care of the palace and **p** them in	5989
	21: 1	because he **p** the Gibeonites to **death.**	4637
	21: 4	the right to **p** anyone in Israel to **death."**	4637
	21: 9	they were **p** to **death** during the first days	4637
	23:23	David **p** him in charge of his bodyguard.	8492
1Ki	1: 1	even when they **p** covers **over** him.	4059
	1: 5	**p** himself forward and said,	5951
	1:38	The Pelethites went down and **p** Solomon	8206
	1:44	and they have **p** him on the king's mule,	8206
	1:51	that he will not **p** his servant to **death**	4637
	2: 8	'I will not **p** you to **death** by the sword.'	4637
	2:24	Adonijah shall **be p** to **death** today!"	4637
	2:26	but I will not **p** you to **death** now,	4637
	2:35	The king **p** Benaiah son of Jehoiada over	5989
	3:20	She **p** him by her breast	8886
	3:20	and **p** her dead son by my breast.	8886
	5: 3	the LORD **p** his enemies under his feet.	5989
	5: 5	'Your son whom I will **p** on the throne	5989
	8: 6	and **p** it beneath the wings of the cherubim.	NIH
	10:17	The king **p** them in the Palace of the Forest	5989
	10:24	to hear the wisdom God had **p** in his heart.	5989
	11:28	he **p** him **in charge** of the whole labor force	7212
	11:36	the city where I chose to **p** my Name.	8492
	12: 4	"Your father **p** a **heavy** yoke on us,	7996
	12: 4	the harsh labor and the heavy yoke he **p**	5989
	12: 9	'Lighten the yoke your father **p** on us'?"	5989
	12:10	'Your father **p** a **heavy** yoke on us,	3877
	14:21	the tribes of Israel in which to **p** his Name.	8492
	18: 9	over to Ahab to **be p** to **death?**	4637
	18:23	and **p** it on the wood but not set fire to it.	8492
	18:23	and **p** it on the wood but not set fire to it.	5989
	18:42	bent down to the ground and **p** his face	8492
	19:10	**p** your prophets to **death** with the sword.	2222
	19:14	**p** your prophets to **death** with the sword.	2222
	19:17	Jehu will **p** to **death** any who escape	4637
	19:17	and Elisha will **p** to **death** any who escape	4637
	21:27	**p** on sackcloth and fasted.	8492
	22:23	"So now the LORD has **p** a lying spirit in	5989
	22:27	**P** this fellow in prison	8492
2Ki	2:20	he said, "and **p** salt in it."	8492
	4: 4	as each is filled, **p** it to **one side.**	5825
	4:10	Let's make a small room on the roof and **p**	8492
	4:38	"**P** on the large pot and cook some stew	9189
	4:41	He **p** it into the pot and said,	8959
	5:24	the servants and **p** them **away** in the house.	7212
	7:17	**p** the officer on whose arm he leaned **in charge** of the gate,	7212
	10: 7	They **p** their heads in baskets and sent them	8492
	10: 8	"**P** them in two piles at the entrance of	8492
	11: 2	She **p** him and his nurse in a bedroom	NIH
	11: 4	and **p** them **under oath** at the temple of	8678
	11: 8	Anyone who approaches your ranks must **be p** to **death.**	4637
	11:12	Jehoiada brought out the king's son and **p**	5989
	11:15	"Bring her out between the ranks and **p** to	4637S
	11:15	"She must not **be p** to **death** in the temple	4637
	11:16	and there she was **p** to **death.**	4637
	12: 9	The priests who guarded the entrance **p** into	5989
	12:10	of the LORD and **p** it **into** bags.	7443
	13:16	Elisha **p** his hands on the king's hands.	8492
	14: 6	**p** the sons of the assassins to **death,**	4637
	14: 6	not **be p** to **death** for their children,	4637
	14: 6	nor children **p** to **death** for their fathers;	4637
	16: 9	to Kir and **p** Rezin to **death.**	4637
	16:14	and **p** it on the north side of the new altar.	5989
	17: 4	and **p** him **in prison.**	673
	18:23	if you can **p** riders on them!	5989
	19: 1	he tore his clothes and **p** on sackcloth	4059
	19: 7	to **p** such a spirit in him that when he hears	5989

2Ki	19:26	are dismayed and **p** to **shame.**	1017
	19:28	I will **p** my hook in your nose and my bit	8492
	19:35	of the LORD went out and **p** to **death**	5782
	20: 1	**P** your house **in order,**	7422
	21: 4	"In Jerusalem I will **p** my Name."	8492
	21: 7	and **p** it in the temple,	8492
	21: 7	I will **p** my Name forever.	8492
	23:33	Pharaoh Neco **p** him in chains at Riblah in	673
	25: 7	Then they **p out** his eyes,	6422
	25:29	So Jehoiachin **p aside** his prison clothes and	9101
1Ch	1: 8	Cush, Mizraim, **P** and Canaan.	7033
	2: 3	so the LORD **p** him to **death.**	4637
	6:31	the men David **p in charge** of the music	3338+6584+6641
	10:10	They **p** his armor in the temple	8492
	10:14	So the LORD **p** him to **death** and turned	4637
	11:25	David **p** him in charge of his bodyguard.	8492
	12:15	and they **p** to **flight** everyone living in	1368
	13:10	down because he had **p** his hand on the ark.	8938
	18: 6	He **p** garrisons in the Aramean kingdom	8492
	18:13	He **p** garrisons in Edom,	8492
	19:11	He **p** the rest of the men under the command	5989
	21:27	and he **p** his sword **back** into its sheath.	8740
	26:32	and King David **p** them **in charge** of	7212
	28:12	the Spirit had **p** in his mind for the courts of	2118
2Ch	3:16	He made interwoven chains and **p** them	5989
	5: 7	and **p** it beneath the wings of the cherubim.	NIH
	6:20	you said you would **p** your Name there.	8492
	9:16	The king **p** them in the Palace of the Forest	5989
	9:23	to hear the wisdom God had **p** in his heart.	5989
	10: 4	"Your father **p** a **heavy** yoke on us,	7996
	10: 4	the harsh labor and the heavy yoke he **p**	5989
	10: 9	'Lighten the yoke your father **p** on us'?"	5989
	10:10	'Your father **p** a **heavy** yoke on us,	3877
	11:11	and **p** commanders in them,	5989
	11:12	He **p** shields and spears in all the cities,	NIH
	12:13	the tribes of Israel in which to **p** his Name.	8492
	14: 7	he said to Judah, "and **p** walls **around** them,	6015
	15:13	the God of Israel, were to **be p** to **death,**	4637
	16:10	he was so enraged that he **p** him in prison.	5989
	17: 2	the fortified cities of Judah and **p** garrisons	5989
	18:22	"So now the LORD has **p** a lying spirit in	5989
	18:26	**P** this fellow in prison	8492
	21: 4	he **p** all his brothers to the sword along	2222
	22: 9	He was brought to Jehu and **p** to **death.**	4637
	22:11	to be murdered and **p** him and his nurse in	5989
	23: 7	enters the temple must **be p** to **death.**	4637
	23:11	the king's son and **p** the crown on him;	5989
	23:14	"Bring her out between the ranks and **p** to	4637S
	23:14	"Do not **p** her to **death** at the temple of	4637
	23:15	and there they **p** her to **death.**	4637
	25: 4	he did not **p** their sons to **death,**	4637
	25: 4	not **be p** to **death** for their children,	AIT
	25: 4	nor children **p** to **death** for their fathers;	AIT
	28:15	All those who were weak they **p** on donkeys	5633
	29: 7	also shut the doors of the portico and **p out**	3882
	33: 7	the carved image he had made and **p** it	8492
	33: 7	I will **p** my Name forever.	8492
	33:11	**p** a hook in his nose,	NIH
	35: 3	"**P** the sacred ark in the temple	5989
	35:24	**p** him in the other chariot he had	8206
	36: 7	the LORD and **p** them in his temple there.	5989
	36:22	throughout his realm and to **p** it in writing:	NIH
Ezr	1: 1	throughout his realm and to **p** it in writing:	NIH
	7:27	who has **p** it into the king's heart	5989
	10: 5	the leading priests and Levites and all Israel **under oath**	8678
	10:19	in pledge to **p away** their wives,	3655
Ne	2:12	I had not told anyone what my God had **p**	5989
	3: 3	**p** its doors and bolts and bars **in place.**	6641
	3: 5	but their nobles would not **p** their shoulders	995
	3: 6	**p** its doors and bolts and bars **in place.**	6641
	3:13	**p** its doors and bolts and bars **in place.**	6641
	3:14	**p** its doors and bolts and bars **in place.**	6641
	4:11	kill them and **p** an end to the work."	8697
	7: 2	I **p in charge** of Jerusalem	7422
	7: 5	So my God **p** it into my heart to assemble	5989
	9:26	they **p** your law behind their backs.	8959
	9:31	in your great mercy you did not **p** an end	6913
	13: 4	Eliashib the priest had **been p** in charge of	5989
	13: 9	then I **p back into** them the equipment of	8740
	13:13	**p** Shelemiah the priest, Zadok the scribe, and a Levite named Pedaiah **in charge of the storerooms**	238+732+6584
Est	2: 8	to the citadel of Susa and **p** under the care	NIH
	3: 9	and I will **p** ten thousand talents of silver	995+4200+9202
	4: 1	**p** on sackcloth and ashes,	4252
	4: 4	for him to **p** on instead of his sackcloth,	4252
	4:11	but one law: that he **be p** to **death.**	4637
	5: 1	Esther **p** on her royal **robes**	4252
	8: 3	She begged him to **p** an end to the evil plan	6296
	9:15	they **p** to **death** in Susa three hundred men,	2222
Job	1:10	"Have you not **p** a **hedge** around him	8455
	1:15	They **p** the servants to the sword,	5782
	1:17	They **p** the servants to the sword,	5782
	7:12	that you **p** me under guard?	8492
	8:17	if you **p away** the sin that is in your hand	8178
	12:18	He takes off the **shackles p** on by kings	AIT
	13:14	Why do I **p** myself **in jeopardy**	928+1414+5951+9094
	14: 6	till he has **p** in his time like a hired man.	8354
	14: 7	it will bud and **p forth** shoots like a plant.	6913
	17: 3	Who else will **p** up security for me?	3338+4200+9546
	29:14	**p on** righteousness **as** my **clothing**;	4252
	30: 1	whose fathers I would have disdained to **p**	8883

Job	31:24	"If *I* have *p* my trust *in* gold or said	8492
	31:35	*p* his indictment **in writing.**	4180
	31:36	*I would p* it on like a crown.	6698
	34:13	Who *p* him **in charge** *of* the whole world?	8492
	40: 4	*I p* my hand over my mouth.	8492
	41: 2	*Can you p* a cord through his nose	8492
	41: 5	or *p* him **on a leash** for your girls?	8003
Ps	8: 6	*you p* everything under his feet:	8883
	22: 4	In you our fathers *p* **their trust;**	1053
	25: 2	*Do* not *let me be p* to shame,	1017
	25: 3	in you *will ever be p* to shame.	1017
	25: 3	be *p* to shame who are treacherous	1017
	25:20	*let me* not *be p* to shame,	1017
	31: 1	*let me never be p* to shame;	1017
	31:17	*Let me* not *be p* to shame, O LORD,	1017
	31:17	the wicked be *p* to shame and lie silent in	1017
	33:22	O LORD, even as *we p our* hope in you.	3498
	35: 4	be disgraced and *p* to shame;	4007
	35:13	I *p* on sackcloth and humbled myself	4230
	35:26	over my distress *be p* to shame	1017
	39: 1	*I will p* a muzzle on my mouth as long as	9068
	40: 3	*He p* a new song in my mouth,	5989
	40: 3	Many will see and fear and *p their* trust in	1053
	40:14	*be p* to shame and confusion;	1017
	42: 5	*P your* hope in God,	3498
	42:11	*P your* hope in God,	3498
	43: 5	*P your* hope in God,	3498
	44: 7	*p* our adversaries **to shame.**	1017
	53: 5	*you p* them to shame,	1017
	69: 6	*may* those who seek you not *be p* to shame	4007
	69:11	when *I p* on sackcloth,	4230+5989
	69:21	*They p* gall in my food	5989
	70: 2	*May* those who seek my life *be p* to shame	1017
	71: 1	*let me* never *be p* to shame.	1017
	71:24	to harm me *have been p* to shame	1017
	78: 7	Then *they would p* their trust in God	8492
	78:18	*They* willfully *p* God **to the test**	5814
	78:31	*he p* **to death** the sturdiest among them,	2222
	78:41	Again and again *they p* God **to the test;**	5814
	78:56	But *they p* God **to the test**	5814
	78:64	their priests *were p* to the sword,	5877
	78:66	*he p* them to everlasting shame.	5989
	85: 4	*p away* your displeasure toward us.	7296
	86:17	my enemies may see it and *be p* to shame,	1017
	88: 6	*You have p* me in the lowest pit,	8883
	89:44	*You have p* **an end** to his splendor	8697
	97: 7	All who worship images *are p* to shame,	1017
	101: 5	*him will I p* to silence;	7551
	101: 8	Every morning *I will p* to silence all	7551
	105:18	his neck *was p* in irons,	995
	106:14	in the wasteland *they p* God **to the test.**	5814
	109:28	when they attack *they will be p* to shame,	1017
	119: 6	Then *I would* not *be p* to shame	1017
	119:31	*do* not *let me be p* to shame.	1017
	119:43	for *I have p* my hope in your laws.	3498
	119:46	before kings and *will* not *be p* to shame,	1017
	119:74	for *I have p* my hope in your word.	3498
	119:78	the arrogant *be p* to shame for wronging me	1017
	119:80	that *I may* not *be p* to shame.	1017
	119:81	but *I have p* my hope in your word.	3498
	119:114	*I have p* my hope in your word.	3498
	119:147	*I have p* my hope in your word.	3498
	127: 5	not *be p* to shame when they contend	1017
	130: 5	my soul waits, and in his word *I p my* hope.	3498
	130: 7	O Israel, *p your* hope in the LORD,	3498
	131: 3	*p your* hope in the LORD both now	3498
	143: 8	for *I have p* my trust in you.	1053
	146: 3	*Do* not *p your* trust in princes,	1053
	147:11	who *p their* hope in his unfailing love.	3498
Pr	4:24	*P away* perversity from your mouth;	6073
	6: 1	*you have p* up security for your neighbor,	6842
	23: 2	and a knife to your throat if you are given	—
	29:24	he is *p* **under oath** and dare not testify.	460+9048
Ecc	10: 6	Fools *are p* in many high positions,	5989
SS	5: 3	*must I p* it on again?	4252
Isa	5:20	who *p* darkness for light and light	8492
	5:20	who *p* bitter for sweet and sweet for bitter.	8492
	7:12	*I will* not *p* the LORD **to the test."**	5814
	8:17	*I will p* my trust in him.	7747
	10: 7	to *p* **an end** to many nations.	4162
	11: 8	young child *p* his hand into the viper's nest.	2063
	13:11	*I will p* **an end** to the arrogance of	8697
	16:10	for *I have p* **an end** to the shouting.	8697
	20: 5	in Egypt will be afraid and *be p* to shame.	1017
	22:12	to tear out your hair and *p on* sackcloth.	2520
	26:11	for your people and *be p* to shame;	1017
	30: 5	*be p* to shame because of a people useless	1017
	31: 8	the sword and their young men *will be p*	2118
	32:11	*p* sackcloth around your waists.	2520
	36: 8	if you can *p* riders on them!	5989
	37: 1	he tore his clothes and *p on* sackcloth	4059
	37: 7	to *p* a spirit in him so that when he hears	5989
	37:27	are dismayed and *p* to shame,	1017
	37:29	*I will p* my hook in your nose and my bit	8492
	37:36	of the LORD went out and *p* to death	5782
	38: 1	*P* your house **in order,**	7422
	38:17	*you have p* all my sins behind your back.	8959
	41:19	*I will p* in the desert the cedar and	5989
	42: 1	*I will p* my Spirit on him	5989
	42: 4	In his law the islands *will p their* hope."	3498
	44:11	*He* and his kind *will be p* to shame.	1017
	45:16	All the makers of idols *will be p* to shame	1017
	45:17	*you will* never *be p* to shame or disgraced,	1017
	45:24	because of you and *be p* to shame.	1017
	49:18	*you will p* them on, like a bride.	8003
	50: 7	and I know *I will* not *be p* to shame.	1017
	51:16	*I have p* my words in your mouth	8492

Isa	51:23	*I will p* it into the hands of your tormentors,	8492
	52: 1	*P on* your garments of splendor,	4252
	57: 8	doorposts *you have p* your pagan symbols.	8492
	59:17	*He p on* righteousness as his breastplate,	4252
	59:17	*he p on* the garments of vengeance	4252+9432
	59:21	that *I have p* in your mouth will not depart	8492
	65:13	but *you will be p* to shame.	1017
	65:15	the Sovereign LORD *will p* you **to death,**	4637
	65:15	Yet *they will be p* to shame.	1017
Jer	1: 9	"Now, *I have p* my words in your mouth.	5989
	4: 1	*p* your detestable idols **out** of my sight	6073
	4: 8	So *p on* sackcloth, lament and wail,	2520
	4:30	Why dress yourself in scarlet and *p on*	6335
	6:21	"I *will p* obstacles before this people.	5989
	6:26	*p on* sackcloth and roll in ashes;	2520
	8: 9	The wise *will be p* to shame;	1017
	13: 1	a linen belt and *p* it around your waist,	8492
	13: 2	and *p* it around my waist.	8492
	15: 9	*I will p* the survivors to the sword	5989
	17:13	all who forsake you *will be p* to shame.	1017
	17:18	*Let* my persecutors *be p* to shame,	1017
	18:21	let their men *be p* to the sword,	2222+4638
	20: 2	he had Jeremiah the prophet beaten and *p*	5989
	20: 4	to Babylon or *p* them to the sword.	5782
	21: 7	*He will p* them to the sword;	5782
	25:31	on all mankind and *p* the wicked to	5989
	26:15	however, that if you *p* me **to death,**	4637
	26:19	anyone else in Judah *p* him **to death?**	4637+4637
	26:21	the king sought to *p* him **to death.**	4637
	26:24	over to the people to be *p* **to death.**	4637
	27: 2	a yoke out of straps and crossbars and *p* it	5989
	28:14	*I will p* an iron yoke on the necks	5989
	29:21	of Babylon, and *he will p* them **to death**	5782
	29:26	you should *p* any madman who acts like	5989
	31:21	"Set up road signs; *p* up guideposts.	8492
	31:33	"*I will p* my law in their minds	5989
	32:14	and *p* them in a clay jar so they will last	5989
	36:20	After they *p* the scroll in the room	7212
	37: 4	for he *had* not yet *been p* in prison.	5989
	37:16	Jeremiah *was p* into a vaulted cell in	995
	37:18	that *you have p* me in prison?"	5989
	38: 4	"This man *should be p* **to death.**	4637
	38: 6	and *p* him into the cistern of Malkijah,	8959
	38: 7	that *they had p* Jeremiah into the cistern.	5989
	38:12	"*P* these old rags and worn-out clothes	8492
	39: 7	Then *he p* out Zedekiah's eyes	6422
	40: 7	and *had p* him **in charge** of the men,	7212
	40:10	and *p* them in your storage jars,	8492
	46: 4	Polish your spears, *p on* your armor!	4252
	46: 9	men of Cush and *P* who carry shields,	7033
	46:24	The Daughter of Egypt *will be p* to shame,	1017
	48: 2	'Come, *let us p* **an end** to that nation.'	4162
	48: 9	*P* salt on Moab, for she will be laid waste;	5989
	48:35	In Moab *I will p* **an end** to those who	8697
	49: 3	*P on* sackcloth and mourn;	2520
	50: 2	Bel *will be p* to shame,	1017
	50: 2	*be p* to shame and her idols filled	1017
	51: 3	nor *let him p* on his armor.	6590
	52:11	Then *he p* out Zedekiah's eyes,	6422
	52:11	where *he p* him in prison till the day	5989
	52:33	So Jehoiachin *p aside* his prison clothes and	9101
La	2:10	on their heads and *p on* sackcloth.	2520
	3:65	*P* a veil over their hearts,	5989
Eze	3:20	and *p* a stumbling block before him,	5989
	4: 1	*p* it in front of you and draw the city	5989
	4: 2	set up camps against it and *p* battering rams	8492
	4: 4	on your left side and *p* the sin of the house	8492
	4: 9	*p* them in a storage jar and use them	5989
	7:18	*They will p on* sackcloth and be clothed	2520
	7:24	*I will p* **an end** to the pride of the mighty,	8697
	9: 4	and *p* a mark on the foreheads of	9338+9344
	10: 7	and *p* it into the hands of the man in linen,	5989
	11:19	I will give them an undivided heart and *p*	5989
	12: 6	*P* them on your shoulder	5951
	12:12	"The prince among them *will p* his things	5951
	12:23	*I am going to p* **an end** to this proverb,	8697
	14: 3	and *p* wicked stumbling blocks	5989
	16: 9	and *p* ointments on you,	6057
	16:10	and *p* leather **sandals on** you.	5836
	16:11	*I p* bracelets on your arms and a necklace	5989
	16:12	and *I p* a ring on your nose,	5989
	16:18	embroidered clothes to *p* on them,	4059
	16:41	*I will p* a stop to your prostitution,	5989
	17: 5	the seed of your land and *p* it in fertile soil.	5989
	17: 6	and *p* out leafy boughs.	8938
	17:16	the king who *p* him on the **throne,**	4887
	18:13	*he will surely be p* to death	4637+4637
	19: 9	*They p* him in prison,	995
	20:17	not destroy them or *p* an end *to* them in	6913
	22:15	and *I will p* **an end** to your uncleanness.	9462
	22:20	in my anger and my wrath and *p* you inside	5663
	23:27	So *I will p* a stop **to** the lewdness	8697
	23:31	so *I will p* her cup into your hand.	5989
	23:40	your eyes and *p on your* jewelry.	6335+6344
	23:42	the rabble, and *they p* bracelets on the arms	5989
	23:48	*I will p* **an end** to lewdness in the land,	8697
	24: 3	"'*P on* the cooking pot;	9189
	24: 3	*p* it on and pour water into it.	9189
	24: 3	*P* into it the pieces of meat.	665
	24: 8	up wrath and take revenge *I p* her blood	5989
	26:13	*I will p* **an end** to your noisy songs,	8697
	26:17	*you p* your terror on all who lived there.	5989
	27:10	and *P* served as soldiers in your army.	7033
	27:31	because of you and *will p on* sackcloth.	2520
	29: 4	But *I will p* hooks in your jaws and make	5989
	30: 5	Cush and *P*, Lydia and all Arabia,	7033
	30:10	"'*I will p* **an end** to the hordes of Egypt	8697

Eze	30:13	"'I will destroy the idols and *p* **an end** *to*	8697
	30:21	It has not been bound up for healing or *p*	8697
	30:24	of Babylon and *p* my sword in his hand,	5989
	30:25	when *I p* my sword into the hand of	5989
	33:31	but *they do* not *p* them **into practice.**	6913
	33:32	but *do* not *p* them **into practice.**	6913
	36:26	a new heart and *p* a new spirit in you;	5989
	36:27	And *I will p* my Spirit in you	5989
	37: 6	*I will p* breath in you,	5989
	37:14	*I will p* my Spirit in you	5989
	37:26	and *I will p* my sanctuary among them	5989
	38: 4	*I p* hooks in your jaws and bring you out	5989
	38: 5	Persia, Cush and *P* will be with them,	7033
	42:13	There *they will p* the most holy offerings	5663
	42:14	to *p on* other clothes before they go near	4252
	43: 9	Now *let them p away* from me	8178
	43:20	You are to take some of its blood and *p* it	5989
	44: 8	*you p* others in charge of my sanctuary.	8492
	44:14	Yet *I will p* them in charge of the duties	5989
	44:19	and *p on* other clothes,	4252
	45:19	the sin offering and *p* it on the doorposts of	5989
Da	1: 2	in Babylonia and *p* in the treasure house	995
	2:13	to *p* the wise men **to death,**	10625
	2:13	and his friends to *p* them **to death.**	10625
	2:14	had gone out to *p* **to death** the wise men	10625
	5:19	Those the king wanted to *p* to death,	NIH
	5:19	wanted to put to death, *he p* to death;	10625
	6: 8	issue the decree and *p* it **in writing**	10375+10673
	6: 9	Darius *p* the decree **in writing.**	10375+10673
	6:13	O king, or to the decree *you p* **in writing.**	10673
	9:24	to *p* **an end** *to* sin, to atone for wickedness,	9462
	9:27	of the 'seven' he will *p* **an end** *to* sacrifice	8697
	11:18	commander *will p* **an end** *to* his insolence	8697
Hos	1: 4	*I will p* **an end** to the kingdom of Israel.	8697
	8: 1	"*P* the trumpet to your lips!	NIH
	10:10	to *p* them **in bonds** for their double sin.	673
	10:11	so *I will p* a yoke on her fair neck.	6296
	11: 6	of their gates and *p* **an end** to their plans.	430
Joel	1:13	*P on* sackcloth, O priests, and mourn;	2520
Am	6: 3	*You p* off the evil day and bring near	5612
Jnh	3: 5	from the greatest to the least, *p on* sackcloth	4252
Mic	7: 5	*p* no **confidence** in a friend.	1053
Na	2: 5	the protective shield *is p* in place.	3922
	3: 9	*P* and Libya were among her allies.	7033
	3:10	and all her great men *were p* in chains.	928+2414+8415
Zep	3:11	that day *you will* not *be p* to shame for all	1017
	3:19	and honor in every land where they were *p*	NIH
Hag	1: 6	*You p on* clothes, but are not warm.	4252
	1: 6	only to *p* them in a purse with holes in it."	NIH
Zec	3: 4	and *I will p* rich garments on you."	4252
	3: 5	Then I said, "*P* a clean turban on his head."	8492
	3: 5	So *they p* a clean turban on his head	8492
	13: 4	*He will* not *p on* a prophet's garment	4252
Mt	4: 7	'*Do* not *p* the Lord your God **to the test.**'	*1733*
	4:12	that John *had been p* in prison,	*4140*
	5:15	Neither do people light a lamp and *p* it	*5502*
	5:15	Instead they *p* it on its stand,	*NIG*
	6:17	*p* oil on your head and wash your face,	*230*
	7:26	and *does* not *p* them **into practice** is like	*4472*
	9:18	But come and *p* your hand on her,	*2202*
	9:25	After the crowd *had been p* outside,	*1675*
	10:21	and *have* them *p* to death.	*2506*
	12:18	*I will p* my Spirit on him,	*5502*
	12:21	In his name the nations *will p their* hope."	*1827*
	12:44	swept clean and *p* **in order.**	*3175*
	14: 3	and bound him and *p* him in prison because	*700*
	15: 4	or mother *must be p* to death.'	*2505+5462*
	17: 4	If you wish, *I will p* up three shelters—	*4472*
	17:17	How long *shall I p* up with you?	*462*
	21:33	*He p* a wall **around** it,	*4363*
	22:44	until *I p* your enemies under your feet." '	*5502*
	23: 4	*They* tie up heavy loads and *p* them on	*2202*
	24: 9	over to be persecuted and *p* to death,	*650*
	24:45	the master *has p* **in charge** of the servants	*2770*
	24:47	*he will p* him **in charge** of all	*2770*
	25:16	*p* his money **to work** and gained five more.	*2237*
	25:21	*I will p you* **in charge** of many things.	*2770*
	25:23	*I will p you* **in charge** of many things.	*2770*
	25:27	you should have *p* my money on deposit	*965*
	25:33	*He will p* the sheep on his right and	*2705*
	26:52	"*P* your sword **back** in its place,"	*695*
	26:53	at once *p at* my disposal more than twelve legions of angels?	*4225*
	26:59	so that *they could p* him **to death.**	*2506*
	27: 1	to the decision to *p* Jesus **to death.**	*2506*
	27: 6	against the law to *p* this into the treasury,	*965*
	27:28	and *p* a scarlet robe on him,	*4363*
	27:28	They *p* a staff in his right hand and knelt	*NIG*
	27:31	and *p* his own clothes on him.	*1907*
	27:31	*p* it on a stick, and offered it to Jesus	*4363*
Mk	1:14	After John *was p* in prison,	*4140*
	4:21	in a lamp to *p* it under a bowl or a bed?	*5502*
	4:21	Instead, don't you *p* it on its stand?	*5502*
	5:23	Please come and *p* your hands on her so	*2202*
	5:40	After he *p* them **all out,**	*1675*
	6:17	and he had him bound and *p* in prison,	*NIG*
	7:10	or mother *must be p* to death.'	*2505+5462*
	7:33	Jesus *p* his fingers into the man's ears.	*965*
	8:23	on the man's eyes and *p* his hands on him,	*2202*
	8:25	Once more Jesus *p* his hands **on**	*2202*
	9: 5	*Let us p* up three shelters—	*4472*
	9:19	How long *shall I p* up with you?	*462*
	10:16	*p* his hands on them and blessed them.	*5502*
	12: 1	*He p* a wall **around** it,	*4363*
	12:36	until *I p* your enemies under your feet." '	*5502*
	12:41	the **place** where the **offerings** were *p*	*1126*

Mk	12:42	and **p** in two very small copper coins,	965
	12:43	this poor widow *has* **p** more into	965
	12:44	**p** in everything—all she had to live on."	965
	13:12	and *have* them **p** to death.	2506
	14:55	so that they could **p** him **to** death,	2506
	15:17	*They* **p** a purple robe on him,	1898
	15:20	and **p** his own clothes **on** him.	1907
	15:36	**p** it on a stick, and offered it to Jesus	4363
Lk	4:12	'*Do* not **p** the Lord your God **to the** test.'"	1733
	5: 3	and asked him *to* **p** out a little from shore.	2056
	5: 4	he said to Simon, "**P** out into deep water,	2056
	6:49	and *does* not **p** them **into practice** is like	4472
	7:46	*You* did not **p** oil on my head,	230
	8:21	hear God's word and **p** it **into practice."**	4472
	9:33	Let us **p** up three shelters—	4472
	9:41	with you and **p up with** you?	462
	10:34	Then *he* **p** the man **on** his own donkey,	2097
	11:25	the house swept clean and **p** in order.	3175
	12:44	he will **p** him **in charge** of all	2770
	13:13	Then *he* **p** his hands **on** her,	2202
	15:22	Bring the best robe and **p** it **on** him.	1907
	15:22	**P** a ring on his finger and sandals	1443
	19:13	'**P** this money **to work,'**	4549
	19:21	not **p** in and reap what you did not sow.'	5502
	19:22	taking out what *I* did not **p** in,	5502
	19:23	then didn't *you* **p** my money on deposit,	1443
	19:35	on the colt and **p** Jesus on it.	2097
	21: 2	He also saw a poor widow **p**	965
	21: 3	"this poor widow *has* **p** in more than all	965
	21: 4	of her poverty **p** in all she had to live on."	965
	21:16	and *they* will **p** some of you **to death.**	2506
	23:26	and **p** the cross on him and made him carry	2202
Jn	2:11	and his disciples **p** *their* **faith** in him.	4409
	3:24	(This was before John was **p** in prison.)	965
	7:31	many in the crowd **p** *their* **faith** in him	4409
	8:20	the **place where** the offerings were **p.**	1126
	8:30	as he spoke, many **p** *their* **faith** in him.	4409
	9: 6	and **p** it **on** the man's eyes.	2222
	9:11	and **p** it **on** my eyes.	2222
	9:15	"He **p** mud on my eyes," the man replied,	2202
	9:22	*would be* **p** out of the synagogue;	697
	11:45	had seen what Jesus did, **p** *their* **faith** in him	4409
	12: 6	he used to help himself to what *was* **p** into it.	965
	12:36	**P** *your* **trust** in the light while you have it,	4409
	12:42	*they* would be **p** out of the synagogue;	697
	13: 3	the Father *had* **p** all things under his power,	1443
	13:12	he **p** on his clothes and returned	3284
	16: 2	*They* will **p** you **out of the** synagogue;	697+4472
	18:11	"**P** your sword away!	965
	19: 2	a crown of thorns and **p** it on his head.	2202
	19:29	**p** the sponge **on** a stalk of the hyssop plant,	4363
	20: 2	we don't know where *they have* **p** him!"	5502
	20:13	"and I don't know where *they have* **p** him."	5502
	20:15	tell me where *you have* **p** him,	5502
	20:25	the nail marks in his hands and **p** my finger	965
	20:25	and **p** my hand into his side,	965
	20:27	he said to Thomas, "**P** your finger here;	5770
	20:27	Reach out your hand and **p** it into my side.	965
Ac	2:23	**p** him **to death** by nailing him to the cross.	359
	3: 2	where he *was* **p** every day to beg	5502
	4: 3	*they* **p** them in jail until the next day.	5502
	4:35	and **p** it at the apostles' feet.	5502
	4:37	the money and **p** it at the apostles' feet.	5502
	5: 2	the rest and **p** it at the apostles' feet.	5502
	5:18	the apostles and **p** them in the public jail.	5502
	5:25	The men *you* **p** in jail are standing in	5502
	5:33	and wanted *to* **p** them **to death.**	359
	5:34	that the men *be* **p** outside for a little while.	4472
	7:53	that was **p** into effect through angels	1408
	8: 3	he dragged off men and women and **p** them	4140
	12: 2	**p** to death with the sword.	359
	12: 4	After arresting him, he **p** him in prison,	5502
	12: 8	"**P** on your **clothes** and sandals."	2439
	14:23	in whom *they had* **p** their **trust.**	4409
	16:11	From Troas we **p** out to sea	343
	16:24	he **p** them in the inner cell	965
	20:10	the young man and **p** *his* **arms around** him.	5227
	21: 1	we **p** out to sea and sailed straight to Cos.	343
	22:29	**p** Paul, a Roman citizen, in chains.	1313
	26:10	the authority of the chief priests I **p** many	2881
	26:10	and *when* they *were* **p** to death,	359
	27: 2	and *we* **p** out to sea.	343
	27: 4	From there we **p** out to sea again	343
	27: 6	for Italy and **p** us on board.	899+1650+1837
	28: 3	*as he* **p** it on the fire, a viper,	2202
	28:11	After three months *we* **p** out to sea in	343
	28:12	We **p** in at Syracuse and stayed there	2864
Ro	6:19	I **p** this in human terms because	474+3306
	7:11	through the commandment **p** me **to death.**	650
	8:13	if by the Spirit *you* **p** **to death** the misdeeds	2506
	9:33	trusts in him *will* never *be* **p** to shame."	2875
	10:11	trusts in him *will* never *be* **p** to shame."	2875
	13:12	So let us **p** aside the deeds of darkness	700
	13:12	the deeds of darkness and **p** on the armor	1907
	14:13	up your mind *not to* **p** any stumbling block	5502
	16:17	and **p** obstacles in your way that are	NIG
1Co	4: 9	God *has* **p** us apostles **on display**	617
	5: 2	with grief and *have* **p** out of your fellowship	149
	9:12	we **p** up with anything rather than hinder	5095
	10:27	eat whatever *is* **p** before you	4192
	13:11	I **p** childish ways **behind** me.	2934
	15:25	until *he has* **p** all his enemies under his feet.	5502
	15:27	For *he* "*has* **p** everything under his feet."	5718
	15:27	that "everything" *has been* **p** under him,	5718
	15:27	who **p** everything **under** Christ.	5718
	15:28	to him who **p** everything **under** him,	5718
2Co	1:22	and **p** his Spirit in our hearts as a deposit,	1443

2Co	2: 5	not to **p** it too severely.	2096
	3:13	who *would* **p** a veil over his face to keep	5502
	6: 3	We **p** no stumbling block in anyone's path,	1443
	8:16	who **p** into the heart of Titus the same	1443
	11: 1	I hope *you will* **p** up with a little of my	462
	11: 4	*you* **p up with** it easily enough.	462
	11:19	*You* gladly **p up with** fools since you are	462
	11:20	even **p up with** anyone who enslaves you	462
Gal	2:16	*have* **p** *our* **faith** in Christ Jesus	4409
	3:19	The law *was* **p** into effect through angels	1411
	3:24	So the law was **p in charge to** lead	4080
Eph	1:10	to be **p** into effect when the times	3873
	2:16	by which he **p** to death their hostility.	650
	4:22	to **p** off your old self,	700
	4:24	and to **p** on the new self,	1907
	4:25	each of you *must* **p** off falsehood	700
	6:11	**P** on the full armor of God so that you can	1907
	6:13	Therefore **p** on the full armor of God,	377
Php	1:16	knowing that *I am* **p** here for the defense of	3023
	3: 3	and who **p** no confidence in the flesh—	4275
	3: 4	*to* **p** confidence in the flesh, I have more:	4275
	4: 9	or seen in me—**p** it **into practice.**	4556
Col	3: 5	**P** to death, therefore, whatever belongs	3739
	3:10	and *have* **p** on the new self,	1907
	3:14	And over all these virtues **p** on love,	NIG
1Th	5: 8	**p** on a mask to cover up greed—	4733
	5:19	*Do* not **p** out the Spirit's fire;	4931
1Ti	4:10	that *we* have **p** our hope in the living God,	1827
	5: 4	**p** their religion into practice by caring for	2355
	5: 9	No widow *may* be **p** on the list of widows	2899
	5:11	not **p** them on such a list.	4148
	6:17	to be arrogant *nor* to **p** their hope in wealth,	1827
	6:17	but to **p** their hope in God,	NIG
2Ti	3: 3	when *men* will not **p up with**	462
Heb	2: 8	and **p** everything **under** his feet."	5718
	2:13	And again, "I *will* **p** my **trust** in him."	1639+4275
	8:10	I *will* **p** my laws in their minds	1443
	9:18	the first covenant *was* not **p** into effect	1590
	10:16	I *will* **p** my laws in their hearts,	1443
	11:36	still others were chained and **p** in prison.	NIG
	11:37	*they* were **p** to death by the sword.	633+1877+5840
Jas	3: 3	When *we* **p** bits into the mouths of horses	965
1Pe	2: 6	in him *will* never *be* **p** to shame."	2875
	3: 5	women of the past who **p** their hope in God	1827
	3:18	He was **p** to death in the body	2506
2Pe	1:14	I know that *I will* soon **p** it **aside,**	629+1639
Rev	2:10	the devil will **p** some of you in prison	965
	2:13	who *was* **p** to death in your city—	650
	3:18	salve *to* **p** on your eyes, so you can see.	1608
	7: 3	the trees until *we* **p** a seal on the foreheads	5381
	17:17	For God *has* **p** it into their hearts	1443

PUTEOLI (1)

Ac	28:13	and on the following day we reached **P.**	4541

PUTHITES (1)

1Ch	2:53	the Ithrites, **P,** Shumathites and Mishraites.	7057

PUTIEL (1)

Ex	6:25	married one of the daughters of **P,**	7034

PUTS (32) [PUT]

Ex	30:33	and whoever **p** it on anyone other than	5989
Lev	16: 4	with water before *he* **p** them **on.**	4252
Nu	22:38	I must speak only what God **p** in my mouth.	8492
	23:12	"Must I not speak what the LORD **p** in	8492
2Sa	22:48	*who* **p** the nations under me,	3718
1Ki	20:11	'One who **p** on *his* armor should not boast	2520
1Ch	22:12	when *he* **p** you **in command** over Israel,	7422
Job	28: 3	*Man* **p** an end to the darkness;	8492
Ps	33: 7	he **p** the deep into storehouses.	5989
Pr	11:15	*He who* **p** up security *for* another will	4135
	17:18	and **p up security** for his neighbor.	6842+6859
	20:16	Take the garment of *one who* **p up security**	6842
	21:29	wicked man **p** up a bold front,	928+6451+7156
	22:26	in pledge or **p up security** for debts;	6842
	25: 8	in the end if your neighbor **p** you to shame?	4007
	27:13	Take the garment of *one who* **p up security**	6842
Eze	14: 4	in his heart and **p** a wicked stumbling block	8492
	14: 7	in his heart and **p** a wicked stumbling block	8492
Mt	7:24	words of mine and **p** them **into practice** is	4472
Mk	4:29	he **p** the sickle to it,	690
	13:34	He leaves his house and **p** his servants	1443
Lk	6:47	hears my words and **p** them **into practice.**	4472
	8:16	a lamp and hides it in a jar or **p** it under	5502
	8:16	Instead, *he* **p** it on a stand,	5502
	9:62	"No one who **p** his hand **to** the plow	2095
	11:33	and **p** it in a place where it will be hidden,	5502
	11:33	Instead *he* **p** it on its stand,	NIG
	12:42	the master **p in charge** of his servants	2770
	15: 5	*he joyfully* **p** it **on** his shoulders	2202
1Ti	5: 5	in need and left all alone **p** *her* **hope** in God	1827
Heb	6:16	the oath confirms what is said and **p** an end	NIG
3Jn	1:10	to do so and **p** them **out** of the church.	1675

PUTTING (28) [PUT]

Ex	29:17	**p** them with the head and the other pieces.	5989
Dt	13: 9	be the first in **p** him **to death,**	4637
	17: 7	be the first in **p** him **to death,**	4637
	20:19	do not destroy its trees by **p** an ax to them,	5616
	26: 6	made us suffer, **p** us to hard labor.	5989
Jos	11:17	struck them down, **p** them **to death.**	4637
Jdg	1: 5	**p** to rout the Canaanites and Perizzites.	5782

Jdg	6:19	**P** the meat in a basket and its broth in	8492
	18:21	**P** their little children, their livestock	8492
1Sa	6:19	**p** seventy of them to death because	5782
	19:13	with a garment and **p** some goats' hair *at*	8492
	28: 8	Saul disguised himself, **p** on other clothes,	4252
1Ki	5: 3	by **p** my Name there forever.	8492
Ne	3:15	**p** its doors and bolts and bars **in place.**	6641
	9:38	**p** it **in writing,** and our leaders,	4180
Job	13:27	on all my paths *by* **p** marks on the soles	2977
Eze	8:17	Look at them **p** the branch to their nose!	8938
	17:13	made a treaty with him, **p** him under oath.	995
Mt	27:66	and made the tomb secure *by* **p** a seal on	5381
Mk	12:41	and watched the crowd **p** their money into	965
Lk	18: 7	Will he keep **p** them off?	3428
	21: 1	Jesus saw the rich **p** their gifts into	965
Jn	12:11	over to Jesus and **p** *their* **faith** in him.	4409
Ac	15:10	*by* **p** on the necks of the disciples a yoke	2202
Col	2:11	in the **p** off of the sinful nature,	589
1Th	5: 8	**p** on faith and love as a breastplate,	1907
Heb	2: 8	In **p** everything **under** him,	5718
2Pe	2: 4	**p** them **into** gloomy dungeons to be held	4140

PUZZLED (2)

Mk	6:20	When Herod heard John, he *was* greatly **p;**	679
Ac	5:24	temple guard and the chief priests *were* **p,**	1389

PYGARG (KJV) See IBEX

PYRRHUS (1)

Ac	20: 4	He was accompanied by Sopater *son of* **P**	4795

Q

QUAIL (4)

Ex	16:13	That evening **q** came and covered the camp,	8513
Nu	11:31	the LORD and drove **q** in from the sea.	8513
	11:32	the people went out and gathered **q.**	8513
Ps	105:40	and he brought them **q** and satisfied them	8513

QUAKE (7) [EARTHQUAKE,
EARTHQUAKES, QUAKED, QUAKING]

Job	26:11	The pillars of the heavens **q,**	8344
Ps	46: 3	and the mountains **q** with their surging.	8321
	75: 3	*When* the earth and all its people **q,**	4570
Isa	64: 2	to your enemies and *cause* the nations *to* **q**	8074
Eze	27:28	The shorelands *will* **q** when you seamen cry	8321
Na	1: 5	The mountains **q** before him and	8321
Rev	16:18	so tremendous was the **q.**	4939

QUAKED (4) [QUAKE]

Jdg	5: 5	The mountains **q** before the LORD,	5688
2Sa	22: 8	"The earth trembled and **q,**	8321
Ps	18: 7	The earth trembled and **q,**	8321
	77:18	the earth trembled and **q.**	8321

QUAKING (3) [QUAKE]

1Sa	13: 7	all the troops with him *were* **q with fear.**	3006
Ps	60: 2	mend its fractures, for *it is* **q.**	4572
Jer	4:24	I looked at the mountains, and *they were* **q;**	8321

QUALIFIED (3)

Da	1: 4	and **q** to serve in the king's palace.	3946
Col	1:12	who *has* **q** you to share in the inheritance of	2655
2Ti	2: 2	to reliable men who will also be **q**	2653

QUALITIES (3) [QUALITY]

Da	6: 3	by his exceptional **q** that the king planned	10658
Ro	1:20	God's **invisible** *q*—his eternal power and divine nature—	AIT
2Pe	1: 8	you possess these **q** in increasing measure,	NIG

QUALITY (5) [QUALITIES]

Lev	27:12	who *will* judge its **q** as good or bad.	6885
	27:14	the priest *will* judge its **q** as good or bad.	6885
1Ki	5:17	from the quarry large blocks of **q** stone	3701
	7:10	with large stones of **good q,**	3701
1Co	3:13	the fire will test **the q** of each man's work.	3961

QUALM (1)

Jude	1:12	eating with you **without the slightest q**—	925

QUANTITIES (9) [QUANTITY]

Ge	41:49	Joseph stored up huge **q** of grain,	2221
1Ki	10: 2	large **q** of gold, and precious stones,	8041
	10:10	large **q** of spices, and precious stones.	2221
1Ch	22:14	of bronze and iron too great to	NIH
	29: 2	all of these in **large q.**	4200+8044
2Ch	9: 1	**large q** of gold, and precious stones—	4200+8044
	9: 9	large **q** of spices, and precious stones.	4200+8044
	25:13	and carried off **great q** of plunder.	8041

Zec 14:14   **great q** *of* gold and silver and   4200+4394+8044

QUANTITY (7) [QUANTITIES]

Lev	19:35	when measuring length, weight or **q.**	5374
Jos	22: 8	and a **great q** *of* clothing—	2221+4394
2Sa	8: 8	King David took a **great q** of bronze.	2221+4394
	12:30	took a **great q** *of* plunder from the city	2221+4394
1Ch	18: 8	David took a great **q** of bronze,	8041
	20: 2	took a **great q** *of* plunder from the city	2221+4394
	23:29	and all **measurements of q** and size.	5374

QUARREL (15) [QUARRELED, QUARRELING, QUARRELS, QUARRELSOME]

Ge	45:24	"Don't **q** on the way!"	8074
Ex	17: 2	Moses replied, "Why *do you* **q** with me?	8189
	21:18	"If men **q** and one hits the other with	8189
Jdg	11:25	*Did he ever* **q** with Israel or fight with them?	8189+8189
2Ki	5: 7	how he is **trying to pick a q** with me!"	628
2Ch	35:21	"What **q** is there **between** you and me,	4200
Pr	15:18	but a patient man calms a **q.**	8190
	17:14	Starting a **q** is like breaching a dam;	4506
	17:19	He who loves a **q** loves sin;	5175
	20: 3	but every fool is **quick to q.**	1679
	26:17	the ears is a passer-by who meddles in a **q**	8190
	26:20	without gossip a **q** dies down.	4506
Mt	12:19	*He will* not **q** or cry out;	2248
2Ti	2:24	And the Lord's servant must not **q;**	3481
Jas	4: 2	*You* **q** and fight.	3481

QUARRELED (7) [QUARREL]

Ge	26:20	of Gerar **q** with Isaac's herdsmen and said,	8189
	26:21	but *they* **q** over that one also;	8189
	26:22	and no *one* **q** over it.	8189
Ex	17: 2	So they **q** with Moses and said,	8189
	17: 7	and Meribah because the Israelites **q** and	8189
Nu	20: 3	They **q** with Moses and said,	8189
	20:13	where the Israelites **q** with the LORD and	8189

QUARRELING (7) [QUARREL]

Ge	13: 7	And **q** arose between Abram's herdsmen	8190
	13: 8	"Let's not have any **q** between you and me,	5312
Isa	58: 4	Your fasting ends in **q** and strife,	8190
Ac	12:20	He had been **q** with the people of Tyre	2595
1Co	3: 3	since there is jealousy and **q** among you,	2251
2Co	12:20	I fear that there may be **q,** jealousy,	2251
2Ti	2:14	before God against **q about words;**	3362

QUARRELS (8) [QUARREL]

Pr	13:10	Pride only breeds **q,**	5175
	20:13	**q** and insults are ended.	1907
Isa	45: 9	"Woe to *him* who **q** with his Maker,	8189
1Co	1:11	that there are **q** among you.	2251
1Ti	6: 4	and **q about words** that result in envy,	3363
2Ti	2:23	because you know they produce **q.**	3480
Tit	3: 9	and arguments and **q** about the law,	3480
Jas	4: 1	What causes fights and **q** among you?	3480

QUARRELSOME (7) [QUARREL]

Pr	19:13	and a **q** wife is like a constant dripping.	4506
	21: 9	of the roof than share a house with a **q** wife.	4506
	21:19	a desert than with a **q** and ill-tempered wife.	4506
	25:24	of the roof than share a house with a **q** wife.	4506
	26:21	so is a **q** man for kindling strife.	4506
	27:15	A **q** wife is like a constant dripping on	4506
1Ti	3: 3	not violent but gentle, **not q,**	285

QUARRIES (2) [QUARRY]

Jos	7: 5	as far as the **stone q** and struck them down	8696
Ecc	10: 9	*Whoever* **q** stones may be injured by them;	5825

QUARRY (3) [QUARRIES]

1Ki	5:17	they **removed from** the **q** large blocks	5825
	6: 7	only blocks dressed at the **q** were used,	5024
Isa	51: 1	to the **q** *from* which you were hewn;	1014+5217

QUART (1) [QUARTS]

Rev	6: 6	saying, "A **q** of wheat for a day's wages,	5955

QUARTER (13) [QUARTERS]

Ex	29:40	with a **q** *of* a hin of oil from pressed olives,	8063
	29:40	and a **q** *of* a hin of wine as a drink offering.	8055
Lev	23:13	its drink offering of a **q** *of* a hin of wine.	8055
Nu	15: 4	of an ephah of fine flour mixed with a **q** *of*	8055
	15: 5	a **q** *of* a hin of wine as a drink offering.	8055
	28: 5	with a **q** *of* a hin of oil from pressed olives,	8055
	28: 7	to be a **q** *of* a hin of fermented drink	8055
	28:14	and with each lamb, a **q** *of* a hin.	8055
1Sa	9: 8	he said, "I have a **q** of a shekel of silver.	8063
2Ki	6:25	a **q** *of* a cab of seed pods for five shekels.	8065
Ne	9: 3	the Law of the LORD their God for a **q** *of*	8055
	9: 3	and spent another **q** in confession and	8055
Zep	1:10	wailing from the **New Q,**	5467

QUARTERS (5) [QUARTER]

2Sa	19:11	has reached the king at his **q?**	1074
2Ki	23: 7	down the **q** of the male shrine prostitutes,	1074
Ne	3:30	made repairs opposite his **living q.**	5969

Isa	11:12	of Judah from the four **q** *of* the earth.	4053
Jer	49:36	against Elam the four winds from the four **q**	7896

QUARTS (1) [QUART]

Rev	6: 6	and three **q** of barley for a day's wages,	5955

QUARTUS (1)

Ro	16:23	and our brother **Q** send you their greetings.	3181

QUATERNIONS (KJV) See SQUADS OF FOUR SOLDIERS

QUEEN (53) [QUEEN'S, QUEENS]

1Ki	10: 1	When the **q** of Sheba heard about the fame	4893
	10: 4	When the **q** of Sheba saw all the wisdom	4893
	10:10	so many spices brought in as those the **q**	4893
	10:13	gave the **q** of Sheba all she desired and	4893
	11:19	of his own wife **Q** Tahpenes, in marriage.	1485
	15:13	from her **position as q mother.**	1485
2Ki	10:13	families of the king and of the **q** mother."	1485
2Ch	9: 1	the **q** of Sheba heard of Solomon's fame,	4893
	9: 3	the **q** of Sheba saw the wisdom of Solomon,	4893
	9: 9	the **q** of Sheba gave to King Solomon.	4893
	9:12	gave the **q** of Sheba all she desired	4893
	15:16	from her **position as q mother,**	1485
Ne	2: 6	Then the king, with the **q** sitting beside him,	8712
Est	1: 9	**Q** Vashti also gave a banquet for	4893
	1:11	to bring before him **Q** Vashti,	4893
	1:12	**Q** Vashti refused to come.	4893
	1:15	what must be done to **Q** Vashti?"	4893
	1:16	"**Q** Vashti has done wrong,	4893
	1:17	'King Xerxes commanded **Q** Vashti to	4893
	2: 4	the girl who pleases the king *be* **q** instead	4887
	2:17	crown on her head and **made** her **q** instead	4887
	2:22	about the plot and told **Q** Esther,	4893
	5: 2	When he saw **Q** Esther standing in	4893
	5: 3	Then the king asked, "What is it, **Q** Esther?	4893
	5:12	"I'm the only person **Q** Esther invited	4893
	7: 1	and Haman went to dine with **Q** Esther,	4893
	7: 2	"**Q** Esther, what is your petition?	4893
	7: 3	Then **Q** Esther answered,	4893
	7: 5	King Xerxes asked **Q** Esther, "Who is he?	4893
	7: 6	Haman was terrified before the king and **q.**	4893
	7: 7	stayed behind to beg **Q** Esther for his life.	4893
	7: 8	even molest the **q** while she is with me	4893
	8: 1	That same day King Xerxes gave **Q** Esther	4893
	8: 7	to **Q** Esther and to Mordecai the Jew,	4893
	9:12	The king said to **Q** Esther,	4893
	9:29	So **Q** Esther, daughter of Abihail,	4893
	9:31	the Jew and **Q** Esther had decreed for them,	4893
Isa	47: 5	no more will you be called **q** *of* kingdoms.	1509
	47: 7	'I will continue forever—the eternal **q!'**	1509
Jer	7:18	cakes of bread for the **Q** *of* Heaven.	4906
	13:18	Say to the king and to the **q mother,**	1485
	29: 2	after King Jehoiachin and the **q** mother,	1485
	44:17	We will burn incense to the **Q** *of* Heaven	4906
	44:18	stopped burning incense to the **Q** *of* Heaven	4906
	44:19	burned incense to the **Q** *of* Heaven	4906
	44:25	drink offerings to the **Q** *of* Heaven.'	4906
La	1: 1	She who was **q** among the provinces has	8576
Eze	16:13	and rose to be a **q.**	4867
Da	5:10	The **q,** hearing the voices of the king	10423
Mt	12:42	The **Q** of the South will rise at the judgment	999
Lk	11:31	The **Q** of the South will rise at the judgment	999
Ac	8:27	Candace, **q** of the Ethiopians.	999
Rev	18: 7	In her heart she boasts, 'I sit as **q;**	999

QUEEN'S (2) [QUEEN]

Est	1:17	For the **q** conduct will become known to all	4893
	1:18	about the **q** conduct will respond to all	4893

QUEENS (4) [QUEEN]

SS	6: 8	Sixty **q** there may be,	4893
	6: 9	the **q** and concubines praised her.	4893
Isa	49:23	and their **q** your nursing mothers.	8576
Jer	44: 9	by your fathers and by the kings and **q**	851S

QUENCH (6) [QUENCHED]

Ps	104:11	the wild donkeys **q** their thirst.	8689
SS	8: 7	Many waters cannot **q** love;	3882
Isa	1:31	with no one to **q** the **fire."**	3882
Jer	4: 4	burn with no *one* to **q** it.	3882
	21:12	burn with no *one* to **q** it.	3882
Am	5: 6	and Bethel will have no *one* to **q** it.	3882

QUENCHED (10) [QUENCH]

2Ki	22:17	burn against this place and *will* not *be* **q.'**	3882
2Ch	34:25	poured out on this place and *will* not *be* **q.'**	3882
Isa	34:10	*It will* not *be* **q** night and day;	3882
	66:24	nor will their fire *be* **q,**	3882
Jer	7:20	and it will burn and not *be* **q.**	3882
	46:10	till it has **q its thirst** with blood.	8115
Eze	20:47	The blazing flame *will* not *be* **q,**	3882
	20:48	LORD have kindled it; *it will* not *be* **q.' "**	3882
Mk	9:48	worm does not die, and the fire *is* not **q.'**	4931
Heb	11:34	**q** the fury of the flames, and escaped	4931

QUESTION (24) [QUESTIONED, QUESTIONING, QUESTIONS]

Jdg	11:12	to the Ammonite king with the **q:**	606

Est	5: 8	Then I will answer the king's **q.**"	1821
Job	38: 3	*I will* **q** you, and you shall answer me.	8626
	40: 7	*I will* **q** you, and you shall answer me.	8626
	42: 4	*I will* **q** you, and you shall answer me.'	8626
Ps	35:11	*they* **q** me on things I know nothing about.	8626
Isa	36:21	*do you* **q** me about my children,	8626
Jer	38:27	officials did come to Jeremiah and **q** him,	8626
Mt	21:24	Jesus replied, "I will also ask you one **q.**	3364
	22:23	came to him with a **q.**	2089
	22:35	an expert in the law, tested him with this **q:**	2089
Mk	8:11	The Pharisees came and began to **q** Jesus.	5184
	11:29	Jesus replied, "I will ask you one **q.**	3364
	12:18	came to him with a **q.**	2089
Lk	3:10	He replied, "I will also ask you a **q.**	3364
	20:27	came to Jesus with a **q.**	2089
	22:23	They began to **q** among themselves which	5184
Jn	8: 6	*They were* using this **q** as a trap,	3306
	18:21	Why **q** me? Ask those who heard me.	2263
Ac	4: 7	before them and *began to* **q** them:	4785
	15: 2	to see the apostles and elders about this **q.**	2427
	15: 6	apostles and elders met to consider this **q.**	3364
	22:29	about to **q** him withdrew immediately.	458
1Ti	3:16	**Beyond all q,** the mystery of godliness	3935

QUESTIONED (11) [QUESTION]

Ge	43: 7	The man **q** us **closely** about ourselves	8626+8626
Jdg	8:14	a young man of Succoth and **q** him,	8626
Ezr	5: 9	*We* **q** the elders and asked them,	10689
Ne	1: 2	and *I* **q** them about the Jewish remnant	8626
Job	21:29	*Have you* never **q** those who travel?	8626
Da	1:20	about which the king **q** them,	1335
Lk	20:21	So the spies **q** him:	2089
Jn	1:25	**q** him, "Why then do you baptize if you are	2263
	18:19	the high priest **q** Jesus about his disciples	2263
Ac	5:27	the Sanhedrin to be **q** by the high priest.	2089
	22:24	*be* flogged and **q** in order to find out why	458

QUESTIONING (1) [QUESTION]

Jn	8: 7	When they kept on **q** him,	2263

QUESTIONS (18) [QUESTION]

Ge	43: 7	We simply answered his **q.**	1821
1Ki	10: 1	she came to test him with **hard q.**	2648
	10: 3	Solomon answered all her **q;**	1821
2Ch	9: 1	to Jerusalem to test him with **hard q.**	2648
	9: 2	Solomon answered all her **q;**	1821
Pr	18:17	till another comes forward and **q** him.	2983
Ecc	7:10	For it is not wise to ask **such q.**	2296S
Mt	22:46	no one dared to **ask** him any more **q.**	2089
Mk	12:34	no one dared **ask** him any more **q.**	2089
Lk	2:46	listening to them and **asking** them **q.**	2089
	11:53	and to **besiege** him **with q,**	694+4309+4498
	20:40	And no one dared to ask him any more **q.**	NIG
	23: 9	*He* plied him with many **q,**	3364
Jn	16:30	not even need to have anyone **ask** you **q.**	2263
Ac	18:15	since it involves **q** about words and names	2427
	23:29	I found that the accusation had to do with **q**	2427
1Co	10:25	in the meat market without **raising q**	373
	10:27	before you without **raising q** of conscience.	373

QUICK (15) [QUICK-TEMPERED, QUICKLY]

Ge	18: 6	"**Q,**" he said, "get three seahs of fine flour	4554
	25:30	He said to Jacob, "**Q,** let me have some	5528
Ex	32: 8	*They have been* **q** to turn away	4554
Jdg	9:48	He ordered the men with him, "**Q!**	4554
1Ki	20:33	men took this as a good sign and *were* **q**	4554
Pr	6:18	feet *that are* **q** to rush into evil,	4554
	20: 3	but every fool is **q to quarrel.**	1679
Ecc	5: 2	*Do not be* **q** with your mouth,	987
Da	1: 4	well informed, **q to understand,**	1067+4529
Jnh	4: 2	That is why I was *so* **q** to flee to Tarshish.	7709
Mal	3: 5	I will be **q** to testify against sorcerers,	4554
Lk	15:22	"But the father said to his servants, '**Q!**	5444
Ac	12: 7	"**Q,** get up!" he said,	1877+5443
	22:18	and saw the Lord speaking. '**Q!**"	5067
Jas	1:19	Everyone should be **q** to listen,	5444

QUICK, QUICKEN (KJV) See also GIVE LIFE, LIVING

QUICK-TEMPERED (3) [QUICK, TEMPER]

Pr	14:17	A **q** *man* does foolish things,	678+7920
	14:29	but a **q** *man* displays folly.	7920+8120
Tit	1: 7	not overbearing, not **q,**	3975

QUICKLY (75) [QUICK]

Ge	19:22	But flee there **q,** because I cannot do	4554
	24:18	and **q** lowered the jar to her hands	4554
	24:20	So *she* **q** emptied her jar into the trough,	4554
	24:46	"She **q** lowered her jar from her shoulder	4554
	27:20	"How did you find it *so* **q,** my son?"	4554
	41:14	and he *was* **q** brought from the dungeon.	8132
	44:11	of them **q** lowered his sack to the ground	4554
	45:13	And bring my father down here **q.**"	4554
Ex	10:16	Pharaoh **q** summoned Moses and Aaron	4554
Dt	4:26	against you this day that you will **q** perish	4554
	7: 4	against you and will **q** destroy you.	4554
	9: 3	and annihilate them **q,**	4554
	9:12	They have turned away **q**	4554
	9:16	You had turned aside **q** from the way that	4554
Jos	2: 5	Go after them **q,**	4554
	8:19	in the ambush rose **q** from their position	4559

Jos	8:19	the city and captured it and **q** set it on fire.	4554
	10: 6	Come up to us **q** and save us!	4559
	23:16	and you will **q** perish from the good land	4559
Jdg	2:17	they **q** turned from the way	4554
1Sa	17:48	David ran **q** toward the battle line	4554
	20:38	Then he shouted, "Hurry! Go **q!**	2590
	23:27	to Saul, saying, "Come **q!**	4554
	25:23	*she* **q** got off her donkey and bowed down	4554
	25:34	if you had not come **q** to meet me,	4554
	25:42	Abigail **q** got on a donkey and,	4554
2Sa	5:24	in the tops of the balsam trees, **move q,**	3077
	15:14	or *he will* **move q** to overtake us	4554
	17:18	the two of them left **q** and went to the house	4559
1Ki	20:41	Then the prophet **q** removed the headband	4554
2Ki	4:22	go to the man of God **q**	8132
2Ch	29:36	because it was done **so q.**	928+7328
	35:13	caldrons and pans and **served** them **q** to all	8132
Job	8:12	they wither **more q than** grass.	4200+7156
Ps	22:19	O my Strength, **come q** to help me.	2590
	31: 2	Turn your ear to me, come **q** to my rescue;	4559
	38:22	**Come q** to help me, O Lord my Savior.	2590
	40:13	O Lord, **come q** to help me.	2590
	69:17	answer me **q,** for I am in trouble.	4554
	70: 1	O Lord, **come q** to help me.	2590
	70: 5	I am poor and needy; **come q** to me, O God.	2590
	71:12	**come q,** O my God, to help me.	2590
	79: 8	may your mercy come **q** to meet us,	4554
	81:14	**how q** would I subdue their enemies	3869+5071
	90:10	for they **q** pass, and we fly away.	2673
	102: 2	when I call, answer me **q.**	4554
	118:12	but they died out as **q** as burning thorns;	NIH
	141: 1	O Lord, I call to you; **come q** to me.	2590
	143: 7	Answer me **q,** O Lord;	4554
Pr	20:21	An inheritance **q gained** at the beginning	987
Ecc	4:12	A cord of three strands is not **q** broken.	928+4559
	7: 9	Do not be **q** provoked in your spirit,	987
	8:11	the sentence for a crime is not **q** carried out,	4559
Isa	58: 8	and your healing will **q** appear;	4554
Jer	9:18	*Let them* **come q** and wail over us	4554
	48:16	her calamity *will* **come q.**	4394+4554
	49:30	"Flee **q** away! Stay in deep caves,	4394
Joel	3:11	Come **q,** all you nations from every side,	6429
Zep	1:14	near and **coming q.**	4394+4554
Mt	5:25	"Settle matters **q** with your	5444
	13: 5	It sprang up **q,** because the soil was shallow.	2311
	13:21	he **q** falls away.	2317
	21:20	"How did the fig tree wither **so q?"**	4202
	28: 7	Then go **q** and tell his disciples.	5444
Mk	1:28	about him spread **q** over the whole region	2317
	4: 5	It sprang up **q,** because the soil was shallow.	2317
	4:17	they **q** fall away.	2317
Lk	14:21	'Go out **q** into the streets and alleys of	5441
	16: 6	sit down **q,** and make it four hundred.'	5441
	18: 8	he will see that they get justice, and **q.**	1877+5443
Jn	11:29	she got up **q** and went to him.	5444
	11:31	noticed how **q** she got up and went out,	5441
	13:27	"What you are about to do, do **q,"**	5441
Gal	1: 6	I am astonished that you are **so q** deserting	5441
2Ti	4: 9	Do your best to come to me **q,**	5441

QUIET (38) [QUIETED, QUIETLY, QUIETNESS]

Ge	25:27	while Jacob was a **q** man,	9447
	34: 5	so he **kept q** *about* it until they came home.	3087
Jdg	3:19	The king said, **"Q!"**	2187
	18:19	They answered him, **"Be q!**	3087
2Sa	13:20	**Be q** now, my sister; he is your brother.	3087
2Ki	11:20	And the city *was* **q,**	9200
1Ch	4:40	and the land was spacious, peaceful and **q.**	8929
	22: 9	and I will grant Israel peace and **q**	9201
2Ch	23:21	And the city *was* **q,**	9200
Ne	5: 8	to us!" *They kept* **q,**	3087
Est	7: 4	*I would have kept* **q,**	3087
Job	6:24	"Teach me, and I *will be* **q;**	3087
Ps	23: 2	he leads me beside **q** waters,	4957
	76: 8	and the land feared and *was* **q—**	9200
	83: 1	*be* not **q,** O God, be not still.	3087
Pr	17: 1	Better a dry crust with **peace and q** than	8932
Ecc	9:17	The **q** words of the wise are more to	5739
Isa	18: 4	"I will remain **q** and will look on	9200
	42:14	*I have been* **q** and held myself back.	3087
	62: 1	for Jerusalem's sake *I will* not remain **q,**	9200
Am	5:13	the prudent man **keeps q** in such times,	1957
Zep	3:17	*he will* **q** you with his love,	3087
Mt	20:31	and told them to be **q,**	4995
Mk	1:25	**"Be q!"** said Jesus sternly.	5821
	4:39	the wind and said to the waves, **"Q!**	4995
	6:31	"Come with me by yourselves to a **q** place	2245
	9:34	But *they kept* **q** because on the way	4995
	10:48	Many rebuked him and told him to be **q,**	4995
Lk	4:35	**"Be q!"** Jesus said sternly.	5821
	18:39	rebuked him and told him to be **q,**	4967
	19:40	"I tell you," he replied, "if they **keep q,**	4995
Ac	12:17	for them *to be* **q** and described how	4967
	19:36	you ought to be **q** and not do anything rash.	2948
	22: 2	they became very **q.**	2484
1Co	14:28	the speaker *should* **keep q** in the church	4967
1Th	4:11	Make it your ambition to **lead a q life,**	2483
1Ti	2: 2	and **q** lives in all godliness and holiness.	2485
1Pe	3: 4	the unfading beauty *of* a gentle and **q** spirit,	2485

QUIETED (2) [QUIET]

Ps	131: 2	But I have stilled and **q** my soul;	1957
Ac	19:35	The city clerk **q** the crowd and said:	2948

QUIETENED (Anglicized) See QUIETED

QUIETLY (7) [QUIET]

Jdg	4:21	a tent peg and a hammer and went **q** to him	928+2021+4319
Ru	3: 7	Ruth approached **q,** uncovered his feet and lay down.	928+2021+4319
Ps	35:20	*those who* **live q** *in* the land.	8091
La	3:26	to wait **q** for the salvation of the Lord.	1876
Eze	24:17	Groan **q;** do not mourn for the dead.	1957
Mt	1:19	he had in mind to divorce her **q.**	3277
Ac	16:37	And now do they want to get rid of us **q?**	3277

QUIETNESS (4) [QUIET]

Job	3:26	I have no peace, no **q;**	9200
Isa	30:15	in **q** and trust is your strength,	9200
	32:17	the effect of righteousness *will be* **q**	9200
1Ti	2:11	A woman should learn in **q** and full submission.	2484

QUIRINIUS (1)

Lk	2: 2	the first census that took place while **Q** was governor of Syria.)	3256

QUITE (5)

2Sa	15:11	as guests and went **q innocently,**	4200+9448
Jn	4:18	What you have just said is **q** true."	NIG
Ro	15:15	I have written you **q boldly**	5529
1Co	16:12	He was **q** unwilling to go now,	4122
1Th	3: 3	You know **q** well that we were destined	NIG

QUIVER (6) [QUIVERED, QUIVERS]

Ge	27: 3	get your weapons—your **q** and bow—	9437
Job	39:23	The **q** rattles against his side,	880
Ps	127: 5	Blessed is the man whose **q** is full of them.	880
Isa	22: 6	Elam takes up the **q,**	880
	49: 2	a polished arrow and concealed me in his **q.**	880
La	3:13	He pierced my heart with arrows from his **q.**	880

QUIVERED (1) [QUIVER]

Hab	3:16	my lips **q** at the sound;	7509

QUIVERS (1) [QUIVER]

Jer	5:16	Their **q** are like an open grave;	880

QUOTA (3) [QUOTAS]

Ex	5: 8	don't reduce the **q.**	NIH
	5:14	"Why didn't you meet your **q** *of* bricks	2976
	5:18	you must produce your **full q** *of* bricks."	9420

QUOTAS (1) [QUOTA]

1Ki	4:28	their **q** of barley and straw for the	3869+5477

QUOTE (4) [QUOTES, QUOTING]

Eze	12:23	and *they will* no longer **q** it in Israel.'	5439
	16:44	" 'Everyone who quotes proverbs *will* **q** *this* **proverb**	5439
	18: 3	you *will* no longer **q** this proverb in Israel.	5439
Lk	4:23	"Surely *you will* **q** this proverb to me:	3306

QUOTES (1) [QUOTE]

Eze	16:44	" 'Everyone who **q** proverbs will quote this proverb	5439

QUOTING (1) [QUOTE]

Eze	18: 2	*by* **q** this proverb about the land of Israel:	5439

R

RAAMAH (5)

Ge	10: 7	Seba, Havilah, Sabtah, **R** and Sabteca.	8311
	10: 7	the sons of **R:** Sheba and Dedan.	8311
1Ch	1: 9	Seba, Havilah, Sabta, **R** and Sabteca.	8309
	1: 9	The sons of **R:** Sheba and Dedan.	8309
Eze	27:22	merchants of Sheba and **R** traded with you;	8311

RAAMIAH (1)

Ne	7: 7	Azariah, **R,** Nahamani, Mordecai, Bilshan,	8313

RAAMSES (KJV) See RAMESES

RABBAH (15)

Dt	3:11	It is still in **R** of the Ammonites.	8051
Jos	13:25	as far as Aroer, near **R;**	8051
	15:60	Kiriath Baal (that is, Kiriath Jearim) and **R**	8051
2Sa	11: 1	the Ammonites and besieged **R.**	8051
	12:26	against **R** *of* the Ammonites and captured	8051

2Sa	12:27	against **R** and taken its water supply.	8051
	12:29	the entire army and went to **R,**	8051
	17:27	of Nahash from **R** of the Ammonites,	8051
1Ch	20: 1	the land of the Ammonites and went to **R**	8051
	20: 1	Joab attacked **R** and left it in ruins.	8051
Jer	49: 2	the battle cry against **R** of the Ammonites;	8051
	49: 3	Cry out, O inhabitants of **R!**	8051
Eze	21:20	against **R** *of* the Ammonites and another	8051
	25: 5	I will turn **R** into a pasture for camels	8051
Am	1:14	I will set fire to the walls of **R**	8051

RABBATH (KJV) See RABBAH

RABBI (16) [RABBONI]

Mt	23: 7	and to have men call them **'R.'**	4806
	23: 8	"But you are not to be called **'R,'**	4806
	26:25	said, "Surely not I, **R?"**	4806
	26:49	Judas said, "Greetings, **R!"**	4806
Mk	9: 5	Peter said to Jesus, **"R,** it is good for us	4806
	10:51	The blind man said, **"R,** I want to see."	4808
	11:21	Peter remembered and said to Jesus, **"R,**	4806
	14:45	Going at once to Jesus, Judas said, **"R!"**	4806
Jn	1:38	They said, **"R"** (which means Teacher),	4806
	1:49	Then Nathanael declared, **"R,**	4806
	3: 2	He came to Jesus at night and said, **"R,**	4806
	3:26	They came to John and said to him, **"R,**	4806
	4:31	Meanwhile his disciples urged him, **"R,**	4806
	6:25	**"R,** when did you get here?"	4806
	9: 2	His disciples asked him, **"R,** who sinned,	4806
	11: 8	"But **R,"** they said, "a short while ago	4806

RABBIM See BATH RABBIM

RABBIT (2)

Lev	11: 6	The **r,** though it chews the cud,	817
Dt	14: 7	not eat the camel, the **r** or the coney.	817

RABBITH (1)

Jos	19:20	**R,** Kishion, Ebez,	8056

RABBLE (2)

Nu	11: 4	The **r** with them began to crave other food,	671
Eze	23:42	the desert along with men from the **r,**	132+8044

RABBONI (1) [RABBI]

Jn	20:16	toward him and cried out in Aramaic, **"R!"**	4808

RABMAG (KJV) See OFFICIAL

RABSARIS (KJV) See CHIEF OFFICER

RABSHAKEH (KJV) See FIELD COMMANDER

RACA (1)

Mt	5:22	Again, anyone who says to his brother, **'R,'**	4819

RACAL (1)

1Sa	30:29	and **R;** to those in the towns of the	8218

RACE (9) [RACED]

Ezr	9: 2	mingled the holy **r** with the peoples around	2446
Ecc	9:11	The **r** is not to the swift or the battle to	5296
Ac	20:24	if only I may finish the **r** and complete	1536
Ro	9: 3	my brothers, those *of* my own **r,**	5150
1Co	9:24	not know that in a **r** all the runners run,	5084
Gal	2: 2	that I was running or *had* **run** my **r** in vain.	5556
	5: 7	You were **running** a good **r.**	5556
2Ti	4: 7	I have finished the **r,** I have kept the faith.	1536
Heb	12: 1	with perseverance the **r** marked out for us.	74

RACED (2) [RACE]

Est	8:14	The couriers, riding the royal horses, **r** out,	987
Jer	12: 5	"If *you have* **r** with men on foot	8132

RACHAB (KJV) See RAHAB

RACHAL (KJV) See RACAL

RACHEL (42) [RACHEL'S]

Ge	29: 6	here comes his daughter **R** with the sheep."	8162
	29: 9	**R** came with her father's sheep,	8162
	29:10	When Jacob saw **R** daughter of Laban,	8162
	29:11	Jacob kissed **R** and began to weep aloud.	8162
	29:12	He had told **R** that he was a relative	8162
	29:16	and the name of the younger was **R.**	8162
	29:17	but **R** was lovely in form, and beautiful.	8162
	29:18	Jacob was in love with **R** and said,	8162
	29:18	in return for your younger daughter **R."**	8162
	29:20	So Jacob served seven years to get **R,**	8162
	29:25	I served you for **R,** didn't I?	8162
	29:28	and then Laban gave him his daughter **R** to	8162
	29:29	Bilhah to his daughter **R** as her maidservant.	8162
	29:30	Jacob lay with **R** also,	8162
	29:30	and he loved **R** more than Leah.	8162
	29:31	he opened her womb, but **R** was barren.	8162

Ge	30: 1	When **R** saw that she was	8162
	30: 6	Then **R** said, "God has vindicated me;	8162
	30: 8	Then **R** said, "I have had a great struggle	8162
	30:14	**R** said to Leah, "Please give me some	8162
	30:15	**R** said, "he can sleep with you tonight	8162
	30:22	Then God remembered **R**;	8162
	30:25	After **R** gave birth to Joseph,	8162
	31: 4	to **R** and Leah to come out to the fields	8162
	31:14	Then **R** and Leah replied,	8162
	31:19	**R** stole her father's household gods.	8162
	31:32	Now Jacob did not know that **R** had stolen	8162
	31:34	Now **R** had taken the household gods	8162
	31:35	**R** said to her father, "Don't be angry,	NIH
	33: 1	**R** and the two maidservants.	8162
	33: 2	and **R** and Joseph in the rear.	8162
	33: 7	Last of all came Joseph and **R**,	8162
	35:16	**R** began to give birth	8162
	35:19	So **R** died and was buried on the way	8162
	35:24	The sons of **R**: Joseph and Benjamin.	8162
	46:19	The sons of Jacob's wife **R**:	8162
	46:22	These were the sons of **R** who were born	8162
	46:25	whom Laban had given to his daughter **R**—	8162
	48: 7	to my sorrow **R** died in the land of Canaan	8162
Ru	4:11	into your home like **R** and Leah,	8162
Jer	31:15	**R** weeping for her children and refusing to	8162
Mt	2:18	**R** weeping for her children and refusing to	*4830*

RACHEL'S (5) [RACHEL]

Ge	30: 7	**R** servant Bilhah conceived again	8162
	31:33	he entered **R** tent.	8162
	35:20	and to this day that pillar marks **R** tomb.	8162
	35:25	The sons of **R** maidservant Bilhah:	8162
1Sa	10: 2	you will meet two men near **R** tomb,	8162

RACKED (2)

Isa	21: 3	At this my body *is* **r** with pain,	4848
La	4: 9	**r** with hunger, they waste away for lack	1991

RADDAI (1)

1Ch	2:14	the fourth Nethanel, the fifth **R**,	8099

RADIANCE (5) [RADIANT]

Job	31:26	in *its* **r** or the moon moving in splendor,	2145
Eze	1:28	so was the **r** around him.	5586
	10: 4	and the court was full of the **r** of the glory	5586
2Co	3:13	at it while the **r** was fading away.	NIG
Heb	1: 3	The Son is the **r** of God's glory and	575

RADIANT (9) [RADIANCE]

Ex	34:29	that his face *was* **r** because he had spoken	7966
	34:30	Israelites saw Moses, his face *was* **r**,	7966
	34:35	they saw that his face *was* **r**.	7966
Ps	19: 8	The commands of the LORD are **r**,	1338
	34: 5	Those who look to him *are* **r**;	5642
SS	5:10	My lover is **r** and ruddy,	7456
Isa	60: 5	Then you will look and *be* **r**,	5642
Eze	43: 2	and the land *was* **r** with his glory.	239
Eph	5:27	and to present her to himself as a **r** church,	*1902*

RAFTERS (2)

Ecc	10:18	If a man is lazy, the **r** sag;	5248
SS	1:17	beams of our house are cedar; our **r** are firs.	8112

RAFTS (2)

1Ki	5: 9	in **r** by sea to the place you specify.	1827
2Ch	2:16	that you need and will float them in **r**	8343

RAGAU (KJV) See REU

RAGE (25) [ENRAGED, OUTRAGEOUS, RAGED, RAGES, RAGING]

Dt	19: 6	avenger of blood might pursue him **in a r**,	2801+4222
2Ki	5:12	So he turned and went off in a **r**.	2779
	19:27	and when you come and go and *how* you **r**	8074
	19:28	Because you **r** against me	8074
2Ch	25:10	and left for home in a **great r**.	678+3034
	28: 9	But you have slaughtered them in a **r**	2408
Est	1:12	he was filled with **r** against Mordecai.	2779
	7: 7	The king got up in a **r**,	2779
Job	15:13	so that you vent your **r** against God	8120
Ps	7: 6	rise up against the **r** of my enemies.	6301
Pr	19:12	A king's **r** is like the roar of a lion,	2408
Isa	7: 4	*they* **r** like the raging sea!	2159
	37:28	and when you come and go and *how* you **r**	8074
	37:29	Because you **r** against me and	8074
	41:11	"All who **r** against you will surely	3013
Jer	51:55	Waves [of enemies] *will* **r** like great waters;	2159
Da	3:13	Furious with **r**, Nebuchadnezzar summoned Shadrach, Meshach and Abednego.	10654
	8: 6	the canal and charged at him in great **r**.	2779
	11:11	of the South will march out *in a* **r** and fight	5352
	11:44	in a great **r** to destroy and annihilate many.	2779
Hab	3: 8	Did your **r** against the sea when you rode	6301
Ac	4:25	the nations **r** and the peoples plot in vain?	*5865*
Gal	5:20	hatred, discord, jealousy, **fits of r**,	*2596*
Eph	4:31	Get rid of all bitterness, **r** and anger,	*2596*
Col	3: 8	anger, **r**, malice, slander,	*2596*

RAGED (5) [RAGE]

1Ki	22:35	All day long the battle **r**,	6590
2Ch	18:34	All day long the battle **r**,	6590
Isa	45:24	All who *have* **r** against him will come	3013
Jer	44: 6	*it* **r** against the towns of Judah and	1277
Am	1:11	because his anger **r** continually	3271

RAGES (4) [RAGE]

Job	40:23	When the river **r**, he is not alarmed;	6943
Ps	50: 3	and around him a **tempest r**.	4394+8548
Pr	19: 3	yet his heart **r** against the LORD.	2406
	29: 9	the fool **r** and scoffs, and there is no peace.	8074

RAGING (9) [RAGE]

2Ch	26:19	While he *was* **r** at the priests	2406
Ps	124: 5	the **r** waters would have swept us away.	2327
Isa	17:12	Oh, the **r** of many nations—	2162
	17:12	they rage like the **r** sea!	2159
	30:30	down with **r** anger and consuming fire,	2408
Jnh	1:15	and the **r** sea grew calm.	2408
Lk	8:24	up and rebuked the wind and the **r** waters;	*3114*
Ac	27:20	and the storm **continued r**,	*2130+3900+4024*
Heb	10:27	of judgment and *of* **r** fire that will consume	*2419*

RAGS (5)

Pr	23:21	and drowsiness clothes them in **r**.	7974
Isa	64: 6	and all our righteous acts are like filthy **r**;	955
Jer	38:11	He took *some* old **r** and worn-out clothes	6080
	38:12	"Put these old **r** and worn-out clothes	6080
1Co	4:11	*we are* **in r**, we are brutally treated,	*1217*

RAGUEL (KJV) See REUEL

RAHAB (14)

Jos	2: 1	of a prostitute named **R** and stayed there.	8147
	2: 3	the king of Jericho sent this message to **R**:	8147
	6:17	Only **R** the prostitute and all who are	8147
	6:23	went in and brought out **R**,	8147
	6:25	But Joshua spared **R** the prostitute,	8147
Job	9:13	even the cohorts of **R** cowered at his feet.	8105
	26:12	by his wisdom he cut **R** to pieces.	8105
Ps	87: 4	"I will record **R** and Babylon	8105
	89:10	You crushed **R** like one of the slain;	8105
Isa	30: 7	Therefore I call her **R** the Do-Nothing.	8105
	51: 9	Was it not you who cut **R** to pieces,	8105
Mt	1: 5	Boaz, whose mother was **R**,	*4829*
Heb	11:31	By faith the prostitute **R**, because she	*4805*
Jas	2:25	even **R** the prostitute considered righteous	*4805*

RAHAM (2)

1Ch	2:44	Shema was the father of **R**,	8165
	2:44	and **R** the father of Jorkeam.	NIH

RAHEL (KJV) See RACHEL

RAID (2) [RAIDED, RAIDERS, RAIDING]

2Sa	3:22	from a **r** and brought with them a great deal	1522
Pr	24:15	*do* not **r** his dwelling place;	8720

RAIDED (7) [RAID]

1Sa	27: 8	and his men went up and **r** the Geshurites,	7320
	30: 1	the Amalekites *had* **r** the Negev and Ziklag.	7320
	30:14	We **r** the Negev of the Kerethites and	7320
1Ch	14: 9	the Philistines had come and **r** the Valley	7320
	14:13	Once more the Philistines **r** the valley;	7320
2Ch	25:13	in the war **r** Judean towns from Samaria	7320
	28:18	the Philistines *had* **r** towns in the foothills	7320

RAIDERS (7) [RAID]

Ge	49:19	"Gad will be attacked by a **band of r**,	1522
Jdg	2:14	over to **r** who plundered them.	9115
	2:16	who saved them out of the hands of these **r**.	9115
2Ki	13:20	Now Moabite **r** used to enter the country	1522
	13:21	suddenly they saw a **band of r**;	1522
	24: 2	Moabite and Ammonite **r** against him.	1522
2Ch	22: 1	king in his place, since the **r**,	1522

RAIDING (11) [RAID]

1Sa	13:17	**R** parties went out from the Philistine camp	8845
	14:15	and those in the outposts and **r parties**—	8845
	23:27	The Philistines *are* **r** the land."	7320
	27:10	"Where *did you go* **r** today?"	7320
	30: 8	"Shall I pursue this **r party**?	1522
	30:15	"Can you lead me down to this **r party**?"	1522
2Sa	4: 2	Now Saul's son had two men who were leaders of **r bands**.	1522
2Ki	6:23	from Aram stopped **r** Israel's territory.	928+995
1Ch	12:18	and made them leaders of his **r bands**.	1522
	12:21	They helped David against **r bands**,	1522
Job	1:17	"The Chaldeans formed three **r parties**	8031

RAIL (1)

Ps	102: 8	*those who* **r** against me use my name as	2147

RAIMENT (KJV) See CLOTHING, DRESS, GARMENT

RAIN (90) [RAINBOW, RAINED, RAINING, RAINS, RAINY]

Ge	2: 5	the LORD God *had* not **sent r** on the earth	4763
	7: 4	Seven days from now I **will send r** on	4763
	7:12	And **r** fell on the earth forty days	1773
	8: 2	and the **r** had stopped falling from the sky.	1773
Ex	9:33	the **r** no longer poured down on the land.	4764
	9:34	that the **r** and hail and thunder had stopped,	4764
	16: 4	"I **will r down** bread from heaven for you.	4763
Lev	26: 4	I will send you **r** in its season,	1773
Dt	11:11	and valleys that drinks **r** from heaven.	4764
	11:14	then I will send **r** *on* your land in its season,	4764
	11:17	not **r** and the ground will yield no produce,	4764
	28:12	to send **r** *on* your land in season and	4764
	28:24	the **r** *of* your country into dust and powder;	4764
	32: 2	like **r** and my words descend like dew,	4764
	32: 2	like **abundant r** on tender plants.	8053
1Sa	12:17	upon the LORD to send thunder and **r**.	4764
	12:18	the LORD sent thunder and **r**.	4764
2Sa	1:21	may you have neither dew nor **r**,	4764
	21:10	till the **r** poured down from the heavens on	4784
	22:12	the dark **r** clouds of the sky.	4784
	23: 4	after **r** that brings the grass from the earth.'	4764
1Ki	8:35	the heavens are shut up and there is no **r**	4764
	8:36	and send **r** on the land you gave	4764
	17: 1	nor **r** in the next few years except	4764
	17: 7	up because there had been no **r** in the land.	1773
	17:14	not run dry until the day the LORD gives **r**	1773
	18: 1	and I will send **r** on the land."	4764
	18:41	for there is the sound of a heavy **r**."	1773
	18:44	and go down before the **r** stops you.' "	1773
	18:45	a heavy **r** came on and Ahab rode off	1773
2Ki	3:17	You will see neither wind nor **r**,	1773
2Ch	6:26	the heavens are shut up and there is no **r**	4764
	6:27	and send **r** on the land you gave	4764
	7:13	I shut up the heavens so that there is no **r**,	4764
Ezr	10: 9	by the occasion and because of the **r**.	1773
Job	5:10	He bestows **r** on the earth;	4764
	20:23	and **r** down his blows upon him.	4763
	28:26	when he made a decree for the **r** and a path	4764
	29:23	and drank in my words as the **spring r**.	4919
	36:27	which distill as **r** to the streams;	4764
	37: 6	'Fall on the earth,' and to the **r** shower,	4764
	38:25	Who cuts a channel for the **torrents of r**,	8852
	38:28	Does the **r** have a father?	4764
Ps	11: 6	On the wicked *he will* **r** fiery coals	4763
	18:11	the dark **r** clouds of the sky.	4784
	68: 8	the heavens **poured down r**, before God,	5752
	72: 6	He will be like **r** falling on a mown field,	4764
	105:32	He turned their **r** into hail,	1773
	135: 7	he sends lightning with the **r** and brings out	4764
	147: 8	the earth with **r** and makes grass grow on	4764
Pr	16:15	his favor is like a **r** cloud in spring.	4919
	25:14	and wind without **r** is a man who boasts	1773
	25:23	As a north wind brings **r**,	1773
	26: 1	Like snow in summer or **r** in harvest,	4764
	28: 3	like a driving **r** that leaves no crops.	4764
Ecc	11: 3	they pour **r** upon the earth.	1773
	12: 2	and the clouds return after the **r**;	1773
Isa	4: 6	and hiding place from the storm and **r**.	4764
	5: 6	command the clouds not to **r** on it."	4763+4764
	28: 2	like a **driving r** and a flooding	2443+4784
	30:23	also send you **r** *for* the seed you sow in	4764
	44:14	or planted a pine, and the **r** made it grow.	1773
	45: 8	"You heavens above, **r down** righteousness;	8319
	55:10	As the **r** and the snow come down	1773
Jer	10:13	with the **r** and brings out the wind	4764
	14: 4	The ground is cracked because there is no **r**	1773
	14:22	the worthless idols of the nations **bring r**?	1772
	51:16	with the **r** and brings out the wind	4764
Eze	1:13	**R** will come in torrents,	1773
	13:13	of **r** will fall with destructive fury.	1773
	22:24	You are a land that *has* **had** no **r** or showers	4763
	38:22	I will pour down torrents of **r**,	1773
Am	4: 7	"I also withheld **r** from you when	1773
	4: 7	*I* **sent** r on one town	1773
	4: 7	One field had **r**; another had none	4763
Zec	10: 1	Ask the LORD for **r** in the springtime;	4764
	10: 1	He gives showers of **r** to men,	1773
	14:17	the LORD Almighty, they will have no **r**.	1773
	14:18	they will have no **r**.	NIH
Mt	5:45	and **sends r** on the righteous and	1101
	7:25	The **r** came down, the streams rose,	1104
	7:27	The **r** came down, the streams rose,	1104
Lk	12:54	immediately you say, 'It's **going to r**,'	2262+3915
Ac	14:17	He has shown kindness by giving you **r**	5624
Heb	6: 7	in the **r** often falling on it and that produces	5624
Jas	5:17	He prayed earnestly that *it would* not **r**,	1101
	5:17	not **r** on the land for three and a half years.	1101
	5:18	Again he prayed, and the heavens gave **r**,	5624
Jude	1:12	They are clouds **without r**,	536
Rev	11: 6	not **r** during the time they are prophesying;	1101

RAINBOW (6) [RAIN]

Ge	9:13	I have set my **r** in the clouds,	8008
	9:14	the earth and the **r** appears in the clouds,	8008
	9:16	Whenever the **r** appears in the clouds,	8008
Eze	1:28	Like the appearance of a **r** in the clouds on	8008
Rev	4: 3	A **r**, resembling an emerald,	2692
	10: 1	with a **r** above his head;	2692

RAINED (5) [RAIN]

Ge	19:24	Then the LORD **r down** burning sulfur	4763
Ex	9:23	So the LORD **r** hail on the land of Egypt;	4763

Ps 78:24 he **r** down manna for the people to eat, 4763
    78:27 He **r** meat **down** on them like dust, 4763
Lk 17:29 fire and sulfur **r** down from heaven 1101

RAINING (1) [RAIN]

Ac 28: 2 a fire and welcomed us all because it was **r** 5624

RAINS (11) [RAIN]

Dt 11:14 both autumn and **spring r,** 4919
Job 24: 8 They are drenched by mountain **r** and hug 2443
Ps 84: 6 the **autumn r** also cover it with pools. 4620
SS   2:11 The winter is past; the **r** are over and gone. 1773
Jer 3: 3 and no **spring r** have fallen. 4919
     5:24 who gives autumn and spring **r** in season, 1773
Hos 6: 3 he will come to us like the **winter r,"** 1773
     6: 3 like the **spring r** that water the earth." 4919
Joel 2:23 for he has given you the **autumn r** 4620
     2:23 both autumn and **spring r,** as before. 4919
Jas 5: 7 for the **autumn** and spring **r.** 4611

RAINY (3) [RAIN]

Ezr 10:13 and it is the **r** season, 1773
Pr 27:15 like a constant dripping on a **r** day; 6039
Eze 1:28 of a rainbow in the clouds on a **r** day, 1773

RAISE (61) [RISE]

Ge   4:20 of those who live in tents and **r** livestock. NIH
Ex 14:16 **R** your staff and stretch out your hand over 8123
    24:11 not **r** his hand against these leaders of 8938
Dt 18:15 The LORD your God *will* **r** up for you 7756
    18:18 *I will* **r** up for them a prophet like you 7756
Jos 6:10 *do* not **r** your voices, 9048
Jdg 8:28 the Israelites *did* not **r** its head again. 5951
1Sa 2:35 *I will* **r** up for myself a faithful priest, 7756
    18:17 "I *will* not **r** a hand against him. 2118
    22:17 not willing to **r** a hand to strike the priests 8938
2Sa 7:12 *I will* **r** up your offspring to succeed you, 7756
1Ki 14:14 "The LORD *will* **r** up for himself a king 7756
    20:25 also **r** an army like the one you lost— 4948
2Ki 4:28 "Didn't I tell you, 'Don't **r** my **hopes'?"** 8922
1Ch 17:11 *I will* **r** up your offspring to succeed you, 7756
Job 38:34 *"Can you* **r** your voice to the clouds 8123
Ps 41:10 **r** me **up,** that I may repay them. 7756
Pr   8: 1 *Does* not understanding **r** her voice? 5989
     8: 4 I **r** my voice to all mankind. NIH
Isa 8: 9 **R** the war **cry,** *you* nations, 8131
    10:15 the ax **r** above him who swings it, 6995
    10:26 and he will **r** his staff over the waters, 5951
    11:12 He *will* **r** a banner for the nations 5951
    13: 2 **R** a banner on a bare hilltop, shout to them; 5951
    14:13 *I will* **r** my throne above the stars of God; 8123
    24:14 They **r** their voices, they shout for joy; 5951
    42: 2 or **r** his voice in the streets. 5951
    42:11 *Let* the desert and its towns **r** their voices; 5951
    42:13 with a shout he *will* **r** the **battle cry** 7658
    45:13 I *will* **r** up Cyrus in my righteousness: 6424
    58: 1 **R** your voice like a trumpet. 8123
    58:12 and *will* **r** up the age-old foundations; 7756
    62:10 **R** a banner for the nations. 8123
Jer 4: 6 **R** the signal to go to Zion! 5951
     6: 1 **R** the signal over Beth Hakkerem! 5951
    23: 5 *I will* **r** up to David a righteous Branch, 7756
    30: 9 whom *I will* **r** up for them. 7756
Eze 26: 8 to your walls and **r** his shields against you. 7756
    27:30 *They will* **r** their voice and cry bitterly 9048
Da 11:11 *who will* **r** a large army, 6641
Hos 5: 8 **R** the battle **cry** in Beth Aven; 8131
Mic 5: 5 *we will* **r** against him seven shepherds, 7756
Zec 1:21 so that no one *could* **r** his head, 5951
     1:21 I *will* surely **r** my hand against them so 5677
    11:16 *to* **r** up a shepherd over the land who will 7756
Mt   3: 9 of these stones God can **r** up children 1586
    10: 8 Heal the sick, **r** the dead, 1586
Lk   3: 8 of these stones God can **r** up children 1586
Jn   2:19 and *I will* **r** it **again** in three days." 1586
     2:20 and *you are going to* **r** it in three days?" 1586
     6:39 but **r** them **up** at the last day. 482
     6:40 and I *will* **r** him up at the last day." 482
     6:44 and I *will* **r** him **up** at the last day. 482
     6:54 and I *will* **r** him **up** at the last day. 482
Ac   3:22 'The Lord your God *will* **r** up for you 482
1Co 6:14 and he *will* **r** us also. 1995
    15:15 not **r** him if in fact the dead are not raised. 1586
2Co 1: 9 also **r** us with Jesus and present us with you 1586
Heb 11:19 Abraham reasoned that God could **r** 1586
Jas 3:18 Peacemakers who sow in peace **r** a harvest NIG
     5:15 the Lord *will* **r** him **up.** 1586

RAISED (127) [RISE]

Ge 14:22 *I have* **r** my hand to the LORD, God Most 8123
           High, Creator of heaven and earth, **and**
           have taken an oath
Ex   7:20 *He* **r** his staff in the presence of Pharaoh 8123
     9:16 But *I have* **r** you **up** for this very purpose, 6641
Nu 14: 1 the people of the community **r** their voices 2256+5951+5989
    20:11 Then Moses **r** his arm and struck 8123
Jos 5: 7 So *he* **r** up their sons in their place, 7756
     8:29 And *they* **r** a large pile of rocks over it, 7756
Jdg 2:16 Then the LORD **r** up judges, 7756
     2:18 the LORD **r** up a judge for them, he was 7756
     3: 9 he **r** up for them a deliverer, 7756
1Sa 4: 5 all Israel **r** such a great **shout** 8131+9558
     4:27 *He* **r** his hand to his mouth, 8740

2Sa 12: 3 *He* **r** it, and it grew up with him 2649
    23: 8 he **r** his spear against eight hundred men, 6424
    23:18 He **r** his spear against three hundred men, 6424
1Ki 11:14 LORD **r** up against Solomon an adversary, 7756
    11:23 And God **r** up against Solomon another 7756
2Ki 3: 4 Now Mesha king of Moab **r** sheep, 5924
    19:22 Against whom *have you* **r** your voice 8123
1Ch 11:11 he **r** his spear against three hundred men, 6424
    11:20 He **r** his spear against three hundred men, 6424
2Ch 5:13 they **r** their voices in praise to the LORD 8123
    13:15 and the men of Judah **r** the **battle cry** 8131
Ne   5: 1 the men and their wives **r** a great outcry 2118
Est 2: 7 of Mordecai to which the king *had* **r** him, 1540
Job 31:21 if *I have* **r** my hand against the fatherless, 5677
Ps 60: 4 *you have* **r** a banner to be unfurled against 5989
    80:15 the son *you have* **r** up for yourself 599
    80:17 the son of man *you have* **r** up for yourself. 599
   148:14 *He has* **r** up for his people a horn, 8123
Isa 2: 2 *it will be* **r** above the hills, 5951
     5:25 his hand *is* **r** and he strikes them down. 5742
    18: 3 when a banner *is* **r** on the mountains, 5951
    23:13 *they* **r** up their siege towers, 7756
    37:23 Against whom *have you* **r** your voice 8123
    40: 4 Every valley *shall* be **r** up, 5951
    49:11 and my highways *will* be **r** up. 8123
    52:13 be **r** and lifted up and highly exalted. 8123
Jer 12: 6 they *have* **r** a loud **cry** against you. 7924
    29:15 "The LORD *has* **r** up prophets for us 7756
La   2: 7 *they have* **r** a shout in the house of 5989
Eze 2: 2 Spirit came into me and **r** me to my feet. 6641
     3:24 Spirit came into me and **r** me to my feet. 6641
    41: 8 that the temple had a **r** base all around it, 1470
Da   4:34 Nebuchadnezzar, **r** my eyes toward heaven, 10475
     7: 5 *It was* **r** up on one of its sides, 10624
     8:18 Then he touched me and **r** me to my feet. 6641
Am   2:11 *I also* **r** up prophets from among your sons 7756
Mic 4: 1 it *will be* **r** above the hills, 5951
Zec 5: 7 Then the cover of lead was **r,** 5951
    14:10 But Jerusalem will be **r** up and remain 8027
Mt 11: 5 the deaf hear, the dead *are* **r,** 1586
    16:21 be killed and on the third day be **r** to life. 1586
    17: 9 the Son of Man *has been* **r** from the dead." 1586
    17:23 and on the third day he will be **r** to life." 1586
    20:19 On the third day he will be **r** to life!" 1586
    27:52 holy people who had died *were* **r** to life. 1586
    27:64 the people that *he has been* **r** from the dead. 1586
Mk   6:14 "John the Baptist *has been* **r** from the dead, 1586
     6:16 *has been* **r** from the dead!" 1586
Lk   1:69 *He has* **r** up a horn of salvation for us in 1586
     7:22 the deaf hear, the dead *are* **r,** 1586
     9: 7 that John *had been* **r** from the dead, 1586
     9:22 be killed and on the third day be **r** to life." 1586
    24: 7 and on the third day be **r** again.' " 482
Jn   2:22 After *he was* **r** from the dead, 1586
    12: 1 whom Jesus *had* **r** from the dead. 1586
    12: 9 whom *he had* **r** from the dead. 1586
    12:17 and **r** him from the dead continued 1586
    21:14 to his disciples *after he was* **r** from 1586
Ac   2:14 **r** his voice and addressed the crowd: 2048
     2:24 But God **r** him **from the dead,** 482
     2:32 God *has* **r** this Jesus **to life,** 482
     3:15 but God **r** him from the dead. 1586
     3:26 *When* God **r** up his servant, 482
     4:10 whom you crucified but whom God **r** from 1586
     4:24 *they* **r** their voices together in prayer 149
     5:30 **r** Jesus **from the dead—** 1586
     9:21 the man who **r** **havoc** in Jerusalem 4514
    10:40 but God **r** him **from the dead** 1586
    13:30 But God **r** him from the dead, 1586
    13:34 The fact that God **r** him from the dead, 482
    13:37 But the one whom God **r** **from the dead** did 1586
    22:22 Then *they* **r** their voices and shouted, 2048
Ro   4:24 in him who **r** Jesus our Lord from the dead. 1586
     4:25 over to death for our sins and *was* **r** to life 1586
     6: 4 just as Christ *was* **r** from the dead through 1586
     6: 9 For we know that *since* Christ *was* **r** from 1586
     7: 4 *to* him who *was* **r** from the dead, 1586
     8:11 *of* him who **r** Jesus from the dead is living 1586
     8:11 he who **r** Christ from the dead will 1586
     8:34 more than that, who *was* **r** **to life—** 1586
     9:17 "*I* **r** you up for this very purpose, 1995
    10: 9 in your heart that God **r** him from the dead, 1586
1Co 6:14 his power God **r** the Lord **from the dead,** 1586
    15: 4 that he *was* **r** on the third day according to 1586
    15:12 if it is preached that Christ *has been* **r** from 1586
    15:13 then not even Christ *has been* **r.** 1586
    15:14 And if Christ *has* not *been* **r,** 1586
    15:15 that he **r** Christ **from the dead.** 1586
    15:15 not raise him if in fact the dead *are* not **r.** 1586
    15:16 For if the dead *are* not **r,** 1586
    15:16 then Christ *has* not *been* **r** either. 1586
    15:17 if Christ *has* not *been* **r,** your faith is futile; 1586
    15:20 But Christ *has* indeed *been* **r** from the dead, 1586
    15:29 If the dead *are* not **r** at all, 1586
    15:32 If the dead *are* not **r,** "Let us eat and drink, 1586
    15:35 someone may ask, "How *are* the dead **r?** 1586
    15:42 is sown in perishable, *it is* **r** imperishable; 1586
    15:43 it is sown in dishonor, *it is* **r** in glory; 1586
    15:43 it is sown in weakness, *it is* **r** in power; 1586
    15:44 sown a natural body, *it is* **r** a spiritual body. 1586
    15:52 the dead *will* be **r** imperishable, 1586
2Co 1: 9 one who **r** the Lord Jesus **from the dead** 1586
     5:15 for him who died for them and *was* **r** again. 1586
Gal 1: 1 who **r** him from the dead— 1586
Eph 1:20 *when* he **r** him from the dead and seated him 1586
     2: 6 And God **r** us **up** with Christ and seated us 5283

Col 2:12 and **r** with him through your faith in 5283
     2:12 who **r** him from the dead. 1586
1Th 1:10 whom *he* **r** from the dead— 1586
2Ti 2: 8 Remember Jesus Christ, **r** from the dead, 1586
Heb 11:35 received back their dead, **r** **to life again.** 414
1Pe 1:21 who **r** him from the dead and glorified him, 1586
Rev 10: 5 and on the land **r** his right hand to heaven. 149

RAISES (8) [RISE]

1Sa 2: 6 he brings down to the grave and **r** up. 6590
     2: 8 *He* **r** the poor from the dust and lifts 7756
Ps 113: 7 *He* **r** the poor from the dust and lifts 7756
Pr   1:20 *she* **r** her voice in the public squares; 5989
Isa 19:16 that the LORD Almighty **r** against them. 5677
Jn   5:21 as the Father **r** the dead and gives them life, 1586
Ac 26: 8 consider it incredible that God **r** the dead? 1586
2Co 1: 9 but on God, who **r** the dead. 1586

RAISIN (2) [RAISINS]

1Ch 12:40 **r** cakes, wine, oil, cattle and sheep, 7540
Hos 3: 1 to other gods and love the sacred **r** cakes." 6694

RAISING (11) [RISE]

Jdg 21: 2 **r** their voices and weeping bitterly. 5951
1Ki 15: 4 in Jerusalem by **r** up a son to succeed him 7756
Ps 55:12 if a foe *were* **r** himself against me, 1540
Jer 4:16 a war cry against the cities of Judah. 5989
Am   7:10 "Amos *is* **r** a **conspiracy** against you in 8003
Hab 1: 6 I *am* **r** up the Babylonians, 7756
Ac 10:29 **without r** any objection. 395
    13:33 their children, *by* **r** up Jesus. 482
    17:31 of this to all men *by* **r** him from the dead." 482
1Co 10:25 in the meat market without **r** **questions** 373
    10:27 without **r** **questions** of conscience. 373

RAISINS (7) [RAISIN]

Nu   6: 3 not drink grape juice or eat **grapes** or **r.** 2256+3313+4300+6694
1Sa 25:18 a hundred **cakes** of **r** and two hundred cakes 7540
    30:12 of a cake of pressed figs and two **cakes** of **r.** 7540
2Sa 6:19 of dates and a **cake** of **r** to each person in 862
    16: 1 a hundred **cakes** of **r,** 7540
1Ch 16: 3 and a **cake** of **r** to each Israelite man 862
SS   2: 5 Strengthen me with **r,** 862

RAKEM (1)

1Ch 7:16 and his sons were Ulam and **R.** 8388

RAKKATH (1)

Jos 19:35 Zer, Hammath, **R,** Kinnereth, 8395

RAKKON (1)

Jos 19:46 Me Jarkon and **R,** 8378

RALLIED (4) [RALLY]

Ge 48: 2 Israel **r** *his* **strength** and sat up on the bed. 2616
Ex 32:26 And all the Levites **r** to him. 665
2Sa 2:25 Then the men of Benjamin **r** behind Abner. 7695
Ac   5:36 and about four hundred men **r** to him. 4679

RALLY (1) [RALLIED]

Isa 11:10 the nations *will* **r** to him, 2011

RAM (101) [RAM'S, RAMS, RAMS']

Ge 15: 9 a goat and a **r,** each three years old, 380
    22:13 up and there in a thicket he saw a **r** caught 380
    22:13 over and took the **r** and sacrificed it as 380
Ex 25: 5 **r** skins dyed red and hides of sea cows; 380
    26:14 for the tent a covering of **r** skins dyed red, 380
    29:17 the **r** into pieces and wash the inner parts 380
    29:18 Then burn the entire **r** on the altar. 380
    29:19 "Take the other **r,** 380
    29:22 "Take from this **r** the fat, the fat tail, 380
    29:22 (This is the **r** *for* the ordination.) 380
    29:26 the breast of the **r** for Aaron's ordination, 380
    29:27 "Consecrate those parts of the ordination **r** 380
    29:31 the **r** *for* the ordination and cook the meat 380
    29:32 and his sons are to eat the meat of the **r** and 380
    29:34 of the **ordination** or any bread is left over 4854
    35: 7 **r** skins dyed red and hides of sea cows; 380
    35:23 **r** skins dyed red or hides of sea cows 380
    36:19 for the tent a covering of **r** skins dyed red, 380
    39:34 of **r** skins dyed red, the covering of hides 380
Lev 5:15 to bring to the LORD as a penalty a **r** from 380
     5:16 for him with the **r** as a guilt offering, 380
     5:18 to bring to the priest as a guilt offering a **r** 380
     6: 6 his guilt offering, **r** from the flock, 380
     8:18 then presented the **r** *for* the burnt offering, 380
     8:19 the **r** and sprinkled the blood against NIH
     8:20 the **r** into pieces and burned the head, 380
     8:21 the whole **r** on the altar as a burnt offering, 380
     8:22 He then presented the other **r,** 380
     8:22 the **r** *for* the ordination. 380
     8:23 the **r** and took some of its blood and put it NIH
           Moses' share of the ordination **r—** 380
     9: 2 a bull calf for your sin offering and a **r** 380
     9: 4 and a **r** for a fellowship offering to sacrifice 380
     9:18 the ox and the **r** as the fellowship offering 380
     9:19 But the fat portions of the ox and the **r—** 380

Lev	16: 3	with a young bull for a sin offering and a **r**	380
	16: 5	a sin offering and a **r** for a burnt offering.	380
	19:21	a **r** to the entrance to the Tent of Meeting	380
	19:22	With the **r** of the guilt offering the priest is	380
Nu	5: 8	with the **r** with which atonement is made	380
	6:14	a **r** without defect for a fellowship offering,	380
	6:17	of unleavened bread and is to sacrifice the **r**	380
	6:19	in his hands a boiled shoulder of the **r**,	380
	7:15	one **r** and one male lamb a year old,	380
	7:21	one **r** and one male lamb a year old,	380
	7:27	one **r** and one male lamb a year old,	380
	7:33	one **r** and one male lamb a year old,	380
	7:39	one **r** and one male lamb a year old,	380
	7:45	one **r** and one male lamb a year old,	380
	7:51	one **r** and one male lamb a year old,	380
	7:57	one **r** and one male lamb a year old,	380
	7:63	one **r** and one male lamb a year old,	380
	7:69	one **r** and one male lamb a year old,	380
	7:75	one **r** and one male lamb a year old,	380
	7:81	one **r** and one male lamb a year old,	380
	15: 6	a **r** prepare a grain offering of two-tenths of	380
	15:11	Each bull or **r**, each lamb or young goat,	380
	23: 2	of them offered a bull and a **r** on each altar.	380
	23: 4	on each altar I have offered a bull and a **r**."	380
	23:14	and offered a bull and a **r** on each altar.	380
	23:30	and offered a bull and a **r** on each altar.	380
	28:11	one **r** and seven male lambs a year old,	380
	28:12	with the **r**, a grain offering of two-tenths of	380
	28:14	with the **r**, a third of a hin;	380
	28:19	one **r** and seven male lambs a year old,	380
	28:20	with the **r**, two-tenths;	380
	28:27	one **r** and seven male lambs a year old as	380
	28:28	with the **r**, two-tenths;	380
	29: 2	one **r** and seven male lambs a year old,	380
	29: 3	with the **r**, two-tenths;	380
	29: 8	one **r** and seven male lambs a year old,	380
	29: 9	with the **r**, two-tenths;	380
	29:36	one **r** and seven male lambs a year old,	380
	29:37	With the bull, the **r** and the lambs,	380
Ru	4:19	Hezron the father of **R**,	8226
	4:19	**R** the father of Amminadab,	8226
1Ch	2: 9	Jerahmeel, **R** and Caleb.	8226
	2:10	**R** was the father of Amminadab,	8226
	2:25	**R** his firstborn, Bunah, Oren,	8226
	2:27	The sons of **R** the firstborn of Jerahmeel:	8226
Ezr	10:19	for their guilt they each presented a **r** from	380
Job	32: 2	the Buzite, of the family of **R**,	8226
Eze	43:23	to offer a young bull and a **r** from the flock,	380
	43:25	you are also to provide a young bull and a **r**	380
	45:24	for each bull and an ephah for each **r**,	380
	46: 4	to be six male lambs and a **r**,	380
	46: 5	The grain offering given with the **r** is to be	380
	46: 6	six lambs and a **r**, all without defect.	380
	46: 7	one ephah with the **r**,	380
	46:11	an ephah with a **r**,	380
Da	8: 3	before me was a **r** with two horns,	380
	8: 4	the **r** as he charged toward the west and	380
	8: 6	the two-horned **r** I had seen standing beside	380
	8: 7	I saw him attack the **r** furiously,	380
	8: 7	striking the **r** and shattering his two horns.	380
	8: 7	The **r** was powerless to stand against him;	380
	8: 7	none could rescue the **r** from his power.	380
	8:20	The two-horned **r** that you saw represents	380
Mt	1: 3	Hezron the father of **R**,	730
	1: 4	**R** the father of Amminadab,	730
Lk	3:33	the son of **R**, the son of Hezron,	730

RAM'S (3) [RAM]

Ex	19:13	the **r horn** sounds a long blast may they go	3413
Ps	81: 3	Sound the **r horn** at the New Moon,	8795
	98: 6	with trumpets and the blast of the **r horn**—	8795

RAMAH (34)

Jos	18:25	Gibeon, **R**, Beeroth,	8230
	19: 8	as far as Baalath Beer (**R** in the Negev).	8230
	19:29	The boundary then turned back toward **R**	8230
	19:36	Adamah, **R**, Hazor,	8230
Jdg	4: 5	the Palm of Deborah between **R** and Bethel	8230
	19:13	to reach Gibeah or **R** and spend the night	8230
1Sa	1:19	and then went back to their home at **R**.	8230
	2:11	Then Elkanah went home to **R**,	8230
	7:17	But he always went back to **R**,	8230
	8: 4	and came to Samuel at **R**.	8230
	15:34	Then Samuel left for **R**,	8230
	16:13	Samuel then went to **R**.	8230
	19:18	at **R** and told him all that Saul had done	8230
	19:19	"David is in Naioth at **R**";	8230
	19:22	for **R** and went to the great cistern at Secu.	8230
	19:22	"Over in Naioth at **R**," they said.	8230
	19:23	So Saul went to Naioth at **R**.	8230
	20: 1	Then David fled from Naioth at **R** and went	8230
	25: 1	and they buried him at his home in **R**.	8230
	28: 3	and buried him in his own town of **R**.	8230
1Ki	15:17	and fortified **R** to prevent anyone	8230
	15:21	he stopped building **R** and withdrew	8230
	15:22	they carried away from **R** the stones	8230
2Ch	16: 1	and fortified **R** to prevent anyone	8230
	16: 5	he stopped building **R**	8230
	16: 6	and they carried away from **R** the stones	8230
Ezr	2:26	of **R** and Geba 621	8230
Ne	7:30	of **R** and Geba 621	8230
	11:33	in Hazor, **R** and Gittaim,	8230
Isa	10:29	**R** trembles; Gibeah of Saul flees.	8230
Jer	31:15	"A voice is heard in **R**, mourning and great	8230
	40: 1	of the imperial guard had released him at **R**.	8230

| Hos | 5: 8 | Sound the trumpet in Gibeah, the horn in **R**. | 8230 |
| Mt | 2:18 | "A voice is heard in **R**, weeping and great | 4821 |

RAMATH LEHI (1) [LEHI]

| Jdg | 15:17 | and the place was called **R**. | 8257 |

RAMATH MIZPAH (1) [MIZPAH]

| Jos | 13:26 | from Heshbon to **R** and Betonim, | 8256 |

RAMATHAIM (1)

| 1Sa | 1: 1 | There was a certain man from **R**, | 8259 |

RAMATHAIM-ZOPHIM (KJV) See
RAMATHAIM, ZUPHITE

RAMATHITE (1) [RAMATH]

| 1Ch | 27:27 | the **R** was in charge of the vineyards. | 8258 |

RAMESES (5)

Ge	47:11	the district of **R**, as Pharaoh directed.	8314
Ex	1:11	and they built Pithom and **R** as store cities	8314
	12:37	The Israelites journeyed from **R** to Succoth.	8314
Nu	33: 3	The Israelites set out from **R** on	8314
	33: 5	The Israelites left **R** and camped at Succoth.	8314

RAMIAH (1)

| Ezr | 10:25 | **R**, Izziah, Malkijah, Mijamin, Eleazar, | 8243 |

RAMOTH (7) [RAMOTH GILEAD, RAMOTH NEGEV]

Dt	4:43	**R** in Gilead, for the Gadites;	8030
Jos	20: 8	**R** in Gilead in the tribe of Gad,	8030
	21:38	**R** in Gilead (a city of refuge	8030
2Ki	8:29	at **R** in his battle with Hazael king of Aram.	8230
1Ch	6:73	**R** and Anem, together with their	8030
	6:80	the tribe of Gad they received **R** in Gilead,	8030
2Ch	22: 6	at **R** in his battle with Hazael king of Aram.	8230

RAMOTH GILEAD (20) [RAMOTH]

1Ki	4:13	in **R** (the settlements of Jair son of	8240
	22: 3	"Don't you know that **R** belongs	8240
	22: 4	with me to fight against **R**?"	8240
	22: 6	"Shall I go to war against **R**,	8240
	22:12	"Attack **R** and be victorious."	8240
	22:15	shall we go to war against **R**,	8240
	22:20	entice Ahab into attacking **R** and going	8240
	22:29	Jehoshaphat king of Judah went up to **R**.	8240
2Ki	8:28	against Hazael king of Aram at **R**.	8240
	9: 1	of oil with you and go to **R**.	8240
	9: 4	young man, the prophet, went to **R**.	8240
	9:14	and all Israel had been defending **R**	8240
2Ch	18: 2	with him and urged him to attack **R**.	8240
	18: 3	"Will you go with me against **R**?"	8240
	18: 5	"Shall we go to war against **R**,	8240
	18:11	"Attack **R** and be victorious,"	8240
	18:14	shall we go to war against **R**,	8240
	18:19	of Israel into attacking **R** and going	8240
	18:28	Jehoshaphat king of Judah went up to **R**.	8240
	22: 5	against Hazael king of Aram in **R**.	8240

RAMOTH NEGEV (1) [RAMOTH]

| 1Sa | 30:27 | who were in Bethel, **R** and Jattir; | 8241 |

RAMP (7) [RAMPS]

2Sa	20:15	They built a **siege r** up to the city,	6149
2Ki	19:32	with shield or build a **siege r** against it.	6149
Job	19:12	they build a **siege r** against me and encamp	2006
Isa	37:33	with shield or build a **siege r** against it.	6149
Eze	4: 2	siege works against it, build a **r** up to it,	6149
	21:22	to build a **r** and to erect siege works.	6149
	26: 8	a **r** up to your walls and raise his shields	6149

RAMPART (1) [RAMPARTS]

| Ps | 91: 4 | his faithfulness will be your shield and **r**. | 6089 |

RAMPARTS (4) [RAMPART]

Ps	48:13	consider well her **r**,	2658
Isa	26: 1	God makes salvation its walls and **r**.	2658
La	2: 8	He made **r** and walls lament;	2658
Hab	2: 1	at my watch and station myself on the **r**;	5189

RAMPS (7) [RAMP]

Job	30:12	they build their **siege r** against me.	369+784
Jer	6: 6	"Cut down the trees and build **siege r**	6149
	32:24	how the **siege r** are built up to take the city.	6149
	33: 4	to be used against the **siege r** and the sword	6149
Eze	17:17	when **r** are built and siege works erected	6149
Da	11:15	of the North will come and build up **siege r**	6149
Hab	1:10	they build **earthen r** and capture them.	6760

RAMS (68) [RAM]

Ge	31:38	nor have I eaten **r** from your flocks.	380
	32:14	two hundred ewes and twenty **r**,	380
Ex	29: 1	a young bull and two **r** without defect.	380
	29: 3	along with the bull and the two **r**.	380
	29:15	"Take one of the **r**,	380
Lev	8: 2	the two **r** and the basket containing bread	380

Lev	23:18	one young bull and two **r**.	380
Nu	7:17	five **r**, five male goats and five male lambs	380
	7:23	five **r**, five male goats and five male lambs	380
	7:29	five **r**, five male goats and five male lambs	380
	7:35	five **r**, five male goats and five male lambs	380
	7:41	five **r**, five male goats and five male lambs	380
	7:47	five **r**, five male goats and five male lambs	380
	7:53	five **r**, five male goats and five male lambs	380
	7:59	five **r**, five male goats and five male lambs	380
	7:65	five **r**, five male goats and five male lambs	380
	7:71	five **r**, five male goats and five male lambs	380
	7:77	five **r**, five male goats and five male lambs	380
	7:83	five **r**, five male goats and five male lambs	380
	7:87	twelve **r** and twelve male lambs a year old,	380
	7:88	to twenty-four oxen, sixty **r**,	380
	23: 1	and prepare seven bulls and seven **r**	380
	23:29	and prepare seven bulls and seven **r**	380
	29:13	two **r** and fourteen male lambs a year old,	380
	29:14	with each of the two **r**, two-tenths;	380
	29:17	two **r** and fourteen male lambs a year old,	380
	29:18	With the bulls, **r** and lambs,	380
	29:20	two **r** and fourteen male lambs a year old,	380
	29:21	With the bulls, **r** and lambs,	380
	29:23	two **r** and fourteen male lambs a year old,	380
	29:24	With the bulls, **r** and lambs,	380
	29:26	two **r** and fourteen male lambs a year old,	380
	29:27	With the bulls, **r** and lambs,	380
	29:29	two **r** and fourteen male lambs a year old,	380
	29:30	With the bulls, **r** and lambs,	380
	29:32	two **r** and fourteen male lambs a year old,	380
	29:33	With the bulls, **r** and lambs,	380
Dt	32:14	with choice **r** of Bashan and	380
1Sa	15:22	and to heed is better than the fat of **r**.	380
2Ki	3: 4	and with the wool of a hundred thousand **r**.	380
1Ch	15:26	seven bulls and seven **r** were sacrificed.	380
	29:21	a thousand **r** and a thousand male lambs,	380
2Ch	13: 9	with a young bull and seven **r** may become	380
	17:11	seven thousand seven hundred **r**—	380
	29:21	They brought seven bulls, seven **r**,	380
	29:22	the **r** and sprinkled their blood on the altar;	380
	29:32	a hundred **r** and two hundred male lambs—	380
Ezr	6: 9	Whatever is needed—young bulls, **r**,	10175
	6:17	two hundred **r**, four hundred male lambs	10175
	7:17	to buy bulls, **r** and male lambs,	10175
	8:35	twelve bulls for all Israel, ninety-six **r**,	380
Job	42: 8	So now take seven bulls and seven **r** and go	380
Ps	66:15	fat animals to you and an offering of **r**;	380
	114: 4	the mountains skipped like **r**,	380
	114: 6	that you skipped like **r**, you hills,	380
Isa	1:11	of **r** and the fat of fattened animals;	380
	34: 6	fat from the kidneys of **r**.	380
	60: 7	the **r** of Nebaioth will serve you;	380
Jer	51:40	like lambs to the slaughter, like **r** and goats.	380
Eze	4: 2	set up camps against it and put **battering r**	4119
	21:22	where he is to set up **battering r**,	4119
	21:22	to set **battering r** against the gates,	4119
	26: 9	He will direct the blows of his **battering r**	7692
	27:21	they did business with you in lambs, **r**	380
	34:17	and between **r** and goats.	380
	39:18	if they were **r** and lambs, goats and bulls—	380
	45:23	to provide seven bulls and seven **r**	380
Mic	6: 7	the Lord be pleased with thousands of **r**,	380

RAMS' (2) [RAM]

| Jos | 6: 4 | carry trumpets of **r horns** in front of the ark. | 3413 |
| 1Ch | 15:28 | with the sounding of **r horns** and trumpets, | 8795 |

RAN (61) [RUN]

Ge	18: 7	Then he **r** to the herd and selected a choice,	8132
	24:20	**r** back to the well to draw more water,	8132
	24:28	The girl **r** and told her mother's household	8132
	29:12	So she **r** and told her father.	8132
	33: 4	Esau **r** to meet Jacob and embraced him;	8132
	39:12	But he left his cloak in her hand and **r** out	5674
	39:15	he left his cloak beside me and **r** out	5674
	39:18	he left his cloak beside me and **r** out of	5674
Ex	4: 3	it became a snake, and he **r** from it.	5674
Nu	11:27	A young man **r** and told Moses,	8132
	16:47	and **r** into the midst of the assembly.	8132
Jos	4:18	to their place at flood stage as before.	2143
	7:22	and they **r** to the tent, and there it was,	8132
	15: 3	Then it **r** past Hezron up to Addar	6296
	15: 8	Then it **r** up the Valley of Ben Hinnom	8132
	15:10	**r** along the northern slope of Mount Jearim	6296
	17: 7	The boundary **r** southward from there	2143
	18:17	and **r** down to the Stone of Bohan son	6590
	19:11	Going west it **r** to Maralah,	6590
	19:34	The boundary **r** west through Aznoth Tabor	8740
Jdg	7:21	all the Midianites **r**, crying out as they fled.	8132
	9:54	So his servant **r** him **through**, and he died.	1991
1Sa	3: 5	And he **r** to Eli and said, "Here I am;	8132
	4:12	a Benjamite **r** from the battle line and went	8132
	10:23	**r** and brought him out,	8132
	17:22	**r** to the battle lines and greeted his brothers.	8132
	17:24	they all **r** from him in great fear.	5674
	17:48	David **r** quickly toward the battle line	8132
	17:51	David **r** and stood over him.	8132
	17:51	their hero was dead, they **turned and r**.	5674
	20:36	As the boy **r**, he shot an arrow beyond him.	8132
2Sa	18:21	down before Joab and **r** off.	8132
	18:23	Then Ahimaaz **r** by way of the plain	8132
1Ki	2:39	two of Shimei's slaves **r** off to Achish son	1368
	18:35	The water **r down** around the altar and	2143
	18:46	he **r** ahead of Ahab all the way to Jezreel.	8132
	19: 3	Elijah was afraid and **r** for his life.	2143

1Ki	19:20	Elisha then left his oxen and **r** after Elijah.	8132
	22:35	The blood from his wound **r** onto the floor	3668
2Ki	7: 7	the camp as it was and **r** for their lives.	5674
	9:10	Then he opened the door and **r.**	5674
Jnh	1: 3	But Jonah **r** away from the LORD	1368
Mt	8:33	Those tending the pigs **r off,**	5771
	27:48	Immediately one of them **r** and got	5556
	28: 8	and **r** to tell his disciples.	5556
Mk	5: 6	he **r** and fell on his knees in front of him.	5556
	5:14	the pigs **r off** and reported this in the town	5771
	6:33	and **r** on foot from all the towns	5340
	6:55	*They* **r** throughout that whole region	4366
	9:15	they were overwhelmed with wonder and **r**	4708
	10:17	a man **r up to** him and fell on his knees	4708
	15:36	One man **r**, filled a sponge	5556
Lk	8:34	*they* **r** off and reported this in the town	5771
	15:20	he **r** to his son, threw his arms around him	5556
	19: 4	So he **r** ahead and climbed	4731
	24:12	Peter, however, got up and **r** to the tomb.	5556
Ac	8:30	Then Philip **r up to** the chariot and heard	4708
	12:14	so overjoyed *she* **r** back without opening it	1661
	19:16	that *they* **r** out of the house naked	1767
	21:32	and soldiers and **r down** to the crowd.	2963
	27:41	the ship struck a sandbar and **r aground.**	2131

RANDOM (3)

1Ki	22:34	But someone drew his bow **at r** and	4200+9448
2Ch	18:33	But someone drew his bow **at r** and	4200+9448
Pr	26:10	an archer who wounds **at r** is he who hires	3972

RANG (2) [RING]

Mt	25: 6	"At midnight the cry **r** out:	1181
1Th	1: 8	The Lord's message **r** out from you	2010

RANGE (5) [RANGES]

Nu	27:12	the Abarim **r** and see the land I have given	NIH
Dt	32:49	into the Abarim **R** to Mount Nebo in Moab,	2215
2Ch	16: 9	For the eyes of the LORD **r** throughout	8763
Isa	32:20	**letting** your cattle and donkeys **r free.**	8079+8938
Zec	4:10	which **r** throughout the earth.)"	8763

RANGES (1) [RANGE]

Job	39: 8	*He* **r** the hills *for* his pasture and searches	9365

RANGING (KJV) See CHARGING

RANK (10) [RANKING, RANKS]

1Sa	18: 5	**gave** him **a high r** in the army.	6584+8492
2Ki	23: 4	the priests **next in r** and the doorkeepers	5467
	25:18	Zephaniah the priest **next in r** and	5467
1Ch	15:18	and with them their brothers **next in r:**	5467
2Ch	31:12	and his brother Shimei was **next in r.**	5467
Est	10: 3	the Jew was **second in r** to King Xerxes,	5467
Isa	3: 3	the captain of fifty and **man of r,**	5951+7156
	5:13	their **men of r** will die of hunger	3883
Jer	52:24	Zephaniah the priest **next in r** and	5467
Eze	23:23	chariot officers and **men of high r,**	7924

RANKING (1) [RANK]

Ac	25:23	with the **high r officers** and the leading men	5941

RANKS (13) [RANK]

1Sa	17: 8	Goliath stood and shouted to the **r** *of* Israel,	5120
	17:10	"This day I defy the **r** of Israel!"	5120
2Ki	11: 8	Anyone who approaches your **r** must be put	8444
	11:15	"Bring her out between the **r** and put to	8444
1Ch	12:38	who volunteered to serve in the **r.**	5120
2Ch	23:14	"Bring her out between the **r** and put to	8444
Job	40:19	He **r** first among the works of God,	NIH
Pr	30:27	yet they advance together **in r;**	2951
Isa	14:31	and there is not a straggler in its **r.**	4596
Jer	46:21	in her **r** are like fattened calves.	7931
	50:37	and chariots and all the foreigners in her **r!**	9348
Joel	2: 8	through defenses without **breaking r.**	1298
Gal	2: 4	false brothers *had* **infiltrated** our **r**	4207+4209

RANSACKED (2)

Ob	1: 6	But how Esau *will* be **r,**	2924
Zec	14: 2	the city will be captured, the houses **r,**	9116

RANSOM (20) [RANSOMED, RANSOMS]

Ex	30:12	a **r** for his life at the time he is counted.	4111
Nu	35:31	not accept a **r** for the life of a murderer,	4111
	35:32	not accept a **r** for anyone who has fled to	4111
Job	5:20	In famine *he will* **r** you from death,	7009
	6:22	**pay a r** for me from your wealth,	8815
	6:23	**r** me from the clutches of the ruthless'?	7009
	33:24	I have found a **r** for him'—	4111
Ps	49: 7	of another or give to God a **r** *for* him—	4111
	49: 8	the **r** *for* a life is costly,	7018
Pr	13: 8	A man's riches may **r** his life,	4111
	21:18	The wicked become a **r** for the righteous,	4111
Isa	43: 3	I give Egypt for your **r,**	4111
	47:11	that *you* cannot **ward off** with a **r;**	4105
	50: 2	Was my arm too short to **r** you?	7014
Jer	31:11	the LORD *will* **r** Jacob and redeem them	7009
Hos	13:14	"*I will* **r** them from the power of	7009
Mt	20:28	and to give his life as a **r** for many."	3389
Mk	10:45	and to give his life as a **r** for many."	3389
1Ti	2: 6	who gave himself as a **r** for all men—	519

Heb	9:15	a **r** to set them free from the sins committed	667

RANSOMED (4) [RANSOM]

Lev	19:20	but *who has* not **been r** or given her freedom,	7009+7009
	27:29	No person devoted to destruction *may* **be r;**	7009
Isa	35:10	and the **r** *of* the LORD will return.	7009
	51:11	The **r** *of* the LORD will return.	7009

RANSOMS (1) [RANSOM]

Ps	55:18	*He* **r** me unharmed from the battle waged	7009

RAPED (5) [RAPES]

Jdg	19:25	and *they* **r** her and abused her throughout	3359
	20: 5	*They* **r** my concubine, and she died.	6700
2Sa	13:14	and since he was stronger than she, *he* **r** her.	2256+6700+8886
	13:32	since the day Amnon **r** his sister Tamar.	6700
Zec	14: 2	the houses ransacked, and the women **r.**	8711

RAPED (Anglicized) See also VIOLATED

RAPES (2) [RAPED]

Dt	22:25	a man happens to meet a girl pledged to be married and **r** her,	2256+2616+6640+8886
	22:28	happens to meet a virgin not pledged to be married and **r** her	2256+6640+8886+9530

RAPHA (7) [BETH RAPHA]

2Sa	21:16	Ishbi-Benob, one of the descendants of **R,**	8335
	21:18	one of the descendants of **R.**	8335
	21:20	He also was descended from **R.**	8335
	21:22	These four were descendants of **R** in Gath,	8335
1Ch	8: 2	Nohah the fourth and **R** the fifth.	8325
	20: 6	He also was descended from **R.**	8325
	20: 8	These were descendants of **R** in Gath,	8325

RAPHAH (1)

1Ch	8:37	**R** was his son, Eleasah his son	8334

RAPHU (1)

Nu	13: 9	from the tribe of Benjamin, Palti son of **R;**	8336

RAPID (1) [RAPIDLY]

Ezr	5: 8	with diligence and *is* **making r progress**	10613

RAPIDLY (2) [RAPID]

Ac	6: 7	of disciples in Jerusalem increased **r,**	5379
2Th	3: 1	that the message of the Lord *may* **spread r**	5556

RARE (4) [RARELY]

1Sa	3: 1	In those days the word of the LORD was **r;**	3701
Pr	20:15	but lips that speak knowledge are a **r** jewel.	3702
	24: 4	with **r** and beautiful treasures.	3701
Isa	13:12	more **r** than the gold of Ophir.	NIH

RARELY (1) [RARE]

Ro	5: 7	Very **r** will anyone die for a righteous man,	3660

RASE (KJV) See TEAR DOWN

RASH (12) [RASHLY]

Lev	13: 2	a swelling or a **r** or a bright spot on his skin	6204
	13: 6	pronounce him clean, it is only a **r.**	5030
	13: 7	But if the **r** does spread in his skin	5030
	13: 8	and if the **r** has spread in the skin,	5030
	13:39	a **harmless r** that has broken out on the skin	993
	14:56	and for a swelling, a **r** or a bright spot,	6204
Nu	30: 6	a **r** promise by which she obligates herself	4439
	30: 8	**r** promise by which she obligates herself,	4439
Ps	106:33	and **r** words came from Moses' lips.	1051
Isa	32: 4	mind of the **r** will know and understand,	4554
Ac	19:36	to be quiet and not do anything **r.**	4637
2Ti	3: 4	**r,** conceited, lovers of pleasure	4637

RASHLY (2) [RASH]

Pr	13: 3	but he *who* **speaks r** will come to ruin.	7316+8557
	20:25	a trap for a man *to* dedicate something **r**	4362

RAT (1) [RATS]

Lev	11:29	the weasel, the **r,** any kind of great lizard,	6572

RATE (1)

Lev	25:50	**based on the r paid** to a hired man	3427+3869

RATHER (69)

Ge	27:12	a curse on myself **r than** a blessing."	2256+4202
Dt	15: 8	**R** be openhanded and freely lend him	3954
Jdg	6:27	he did it at night **r than** in the daytime.	4946
	18:19	as priest **r than** just one man's household?"	196
Ru	2:16	**R,** pull out some stalks for her from	1685+2256
2Sa	6:21	who chose me **r than** your father or anyone	4946
2Ki	1:13	**R,** worship the LORD your God;	561+3954
	20:10	"**R,** have it go back ten steps."	3954+4202
2Ch	17: 4	and followed his commands **r than**	2256+4202
Est	6: 6	that the king *would* **r** honor than me?"	2911

Job	7:15	**r** than this body of mine.	4946
	32: 2	with Job for justifying himself **r than** God.	4946
Ps	52: 3	You love evil **r** than good,	4946
	52: 3	falsehood **r than** speaking the truth.	4946
	84:10	*I* would **r** be a doorkeeper in the house	1047
Pr	8:10	knowledge **r than** choice gold,	4946
	8:19	to choose understanding **r than** silver!	4946
Ecc	5: 1	near to listen **r than** to offer the sacrifice	4946
Jer	7:19	Are they not **r** harming themselves,	2022
	22:10	weep bitterly for him who is exiled,	NIH
La	3: 2	and made me walk in darkness **r than** light;	4202
Eze	16: 5	**R,** you were thrown out into the open field,	2256
	18:23	**R,** am I not pleased when they turn	2022
	33:11	**r** that they turn from their ways and live.	561
		for themselves **r than** for my flock,	4202
Da	3:28	to give up their lives **r than** serve	10379
Hos	6: 6	of God **r than** burnt offerings.	4946
Mt	10: 6	Go **r** to the lost sheep of Israel.	3437
	10:28	**R,** be afraid of the One who can	1254+3437
Mk	7:15	it is what comes out of a man	247
Lk	11:28	"Blessed **r** are those who hear the word	3528
	17: 8	Would he not **r** say, 'Prepare my supper,	247
	18:14	"I tell you that this man, **r than** the other,	4123
Jn	14:10	**R,** it is the Father, living in me,	1254
Ac	4:19	in God's sight to obey you **r than** God.	3437
	5:29	"We must obey God **r than** men!	3437
Ro	1:25	and served created things **r than**	4123
	3:20	**r,** through the law we become conscious	1142
	3:31	**R,** we uphold the law.	247
	6:13	**but r** offer yourselves to God,	247
	11:11	**R,** because of their transgression,	247
	12: 3	**but r** think of yourself with sober judgment,	247
	13:14	**R,** clothe yourselves with the Lord Jesus	247
	15:21	**R,** as it is written:	247
1Co	5: 2	Shouldn't you **r** have been filled with grief	3437
	6: 7	Why not **r** be wronged?	3437
	6: 7	Why not **r** be cheated?	3437
	9:12	with anything **r** than hinder the gospel	2671+3590
	9:15	I would **r** die than have anyone deprive me	3437
	14: 5	but I would **r** have you prophesy.	3437
	14:19	But in the church *I would* **r** speak five intelligible words	2527
2Co	4: 2	**R,** we have renounced secret and	247
	5:12	is seen **r** than in what is in the heart.	2779+3590
	6: 4	**R,** as servants of God	247
	7:12	**but r** that before God you could see	247
	10: 8	for building you up **r than** pulling you	2779+4024
Gal	1:12	**r,** I received it by revelation	247
	4: 9	or **r** are known by God—	3437
	5:13	**r,** serve one another in love.	247
Eph	5: 4	which are out of place, but **r** thanksgiving.	3437
	5:11	deeds of darkness, but **r** expose them.	3437
Col	2: 8	basic principles of this world **r than**	2779+4024
1Ti	1: 4	These promote controversies **r than** God's work—	3437
	4: 7	**r,** train yourself to be godly.	1254
2Ti	3: 4	lovers of pleasure **r** than lovers of God—	3437
Tit	1: 8	**R** he must be hospitable.	247
Heb	11:25	of God **r** than to enjoy the pleasures of sin	3437
	12:13	the lame may not be disabled, but **r** healed.	3437
1Pe	4: 2	**but r** for the will of God.	247

RATIFIED (1)

Jos	9:15	and the leaders of the assembly **r** it **by oath.**	8678

RATIONED (2)

Eze	4:16	The people will eat **r** food in anxiety	928+5486
	4:16	in anxiety and drink **r** water in despair,	928+5374

RATS (5) [RAT]

1Sa	6: 4	"Five gold tumors and five gold **r,**	6572
	6: 5	and of the **r** that are destroying the country,	6572
	6:11	along with it the chest containing the gold **r**	6572
	6:18	of the gold **r** was according to the number	6572
Isa	66:17	of those who eat the flesh of pigs and **r**	6572

RATTLES (1) [RATTLING]

Job	39:23	The quiver **r** against his side,	8261

RATTLING (2) [RATTLES]

Job	41:29	he laughs at the **r** *of* the lance.	8323
Eze	37: 7	a **r** sound, and the bones came together,	8323

RAVAGE (6) [RAVAGED, RAVAGES, RAVAGING]

Ge	41:30	and the famine *will* **r** the land.	3983
Jdg	6: 5	they invaded the land to **r** it.	8845
Ps	80:13	Boars from the forest **r** it and the creatures	4155
Jer	5: 6	a wolf from the desert *will* **r** them,	8720
	5:10	"Go through her vineyards and **r** them,	8845
Eze	26: 8	*He will* **r** your settlements on the mainland	2222

RAVAGED (3) [RAVAGE]

Isa	6:11	and the fields ruined and **r,**	9039
Eze	26: 6	on the mainland *will* be **r** by the sword.	2222
	36: 3	Because *they* **r** and hounded you	9037

RAVAGES (2) [RAVAGE]

Ps	35:17	Rescue my life from their **r,**	8738
Jer	14:18	if I go into the city, I see the **r** *of* famine.	9377

RAVAGING (1) [RAVAGE]
1Ch 21:12 with the angel of the LORD r every part — 8845

RAVEN (6) [RAVENS]
Ge 8:7 and sent out a r, and it kept flying — 6854
Lev 11:15 any kind of r, — 6854
Dt 14:14 any kind of r, — 6854
Job 38:41 Who provides for the r when — 6854
SS 5:11 his hair is wavy and black as a r. — 6854
Isa 34:11 the great owl and the r will nest there. — 6854

RAVENING (1) [RAVENOUS]
Jer 2:30 has devoured your prophets like a r lion. — 8845

RAVENOUS (2) [RAVENING]
Ge 49:27 "Benjamin is a r wolf; — 3271
Ps 57:4 I lie among r beasts— — 4266

RAVENS (5) [RAVEN]
1Ki 17:4 and I have ordered the r to feed you there." — 6854
17:6 The r brought him bread and meat in — 6854
Ps 147:9 and for the young r when they call. — 6854
Pr 30:17 will be pecked out by the r of the valley, — 6854
Lk 12:24 Consider the r: They do not sow or reap, — 3165

RAVIN (KJV) See PREY, RAVENOUS

RAVINE (13) [RAVINES]
Jos 16:8 the border went west to the Kanah R — 5707
17:7 boundary continued south to the Kanah R. — 5707
17:9 of Manasseh was the northern side of the r — 5707
19:11 and extended to the r near Jokneam. — 5707
1Sa 15:5 of Amalek and set an ambush in the r. — 5707
25:20 riding her donkey into a mountain r, — 6260
30:9 with him came to the Besor R, — 5707
30:10 too exhausted to cross the r. — 5707
30:21 and who were left behind at the Besor R. — 5707
1Ki 17:3 turn eastward and hide in the Kerith R, — 5707
17:5 He went to the Kerith R, east of the Jordan, — 5707
Isa 15:7 and stored up they carry away over the R — 5707
Zec 1:8 among the myrtle trees in a r. — 5185

RAVINES (17) [RAVINE]
Nu 21:14 "...Waheb in Suphah and the r, — 5707
21:15 the r that lead to the site of Ar and lie along — 5707
2Sa 23:30 Hiddai from the r of Gaash, — 5707
1Ch 11:32 Hurai from the r of Gaash, — 5707
Job 22:24 your gold of Ophir to the rocks in the r, — 5707
Ps 104:10 He makes springs pour water into the r; — 5707
Isa 7:19 the steep r and in the crevices in the rocks, — 5707
57:5 in the r and under the overhanging crags. — 5707
57:6 the smooth stones of the r are your portion; — 5707
Eze 6:3 mountains and hills, to the r and valleys, — 692
31:12 its branches lay broken in all the r of — 692
32:6 and be filled with your flesh. — 692
34:13 the r and in all the settlements in the land. — 692
35:8 and in your valleys and in all your r. — 692
36:4 mountains and hills, to the r and valleys, — 692
36:6 mountains and hills, to the r and valleys: — 692
Joel 3:18 all the r of Judah will run with water. — 692

RAVING (1)
Jn 10:20 "He is demon-possessed and r mad. — 3419

RAVISH (1) [RAVISHED]
Dt 28:30 but another will take her and r her. — 8711

RAVISHED (3) [RAVISH]
Isa 13:16 houses will be looted and their wives r. — 8711
Jer 3:2 any place where you have not been r? — 8711
La 5:11 Women have been r in Zion, — 6700

RAW (9)
Ex 12:9 Do not eat the meat r or cooked in water, — 5529
Lev 13:10 the hair white and if there is r flesh in — 2645+4695
13:14 But whenever r flesh appears on him, — 2645
13:15 When the priest sees the r flesh, — 2645
13:15 The r flesh is unclean. — 2645
13:16 Should the r flesh change and turn white, — 2645
13:24 or white spot appears in the r flesh of — 4695
1Sa 2:15 boiled meat from you, but only r." — 2645
Eze 29:18 and every shoulder made r. — 5307

RAWBONED (1)
Ge 49:14 "Issachar is a r donkey lying down — 1752

RAY (1) [RAYS]
Am 5:20 pitch-dark, without a r of brightness? — 5586

RAYS (3) [RAY]
Job 3:9 for daylight in vain and not see the first r — 6757
41:18 his eyes are like the r of dawn. — 6757
Hab 3:4 r flashed from his hand, — 7967

RAZOR (7)
Nu 6:5 of separation no r may be used on his head. — 9509
Jdg 13:5 No r may be used on his head, — 4623
16:17 "No r has ever been used on my head," — 4623
1Sa 1:11 and no r will ever be used on his head." — 4623
Ps 52:2 it is like a sharpened r, — 9509
Isa 7:20 In that day the Lord will use a r hired from — 9509
Eze 5:1 and use it as a barber's r to shave your head — 9509

REACH (29) [REACHED, REACHES, REACHING]
Ge 3:22 be allowed to r out his hand and take also — 8938
19:22 I cannot do anything until you r it." — 995
Ex 4:4 "R out your hand and take it by the tail." — 8938
Dt 30:11 not too difficult for you or beyond your r. — 8158
Jos 3:8 'When you r the edge of the Jordan's — 995+6330
10:19 the rear and don't let them r their cities, — 448+995
Jdg 19:13 let's try to r Gibeah or Ramah and spend — 7928
1Sa 10:3 on from there until you r the great tree — 995+6330
14:4 to cross to r the Philistine outpost — 6584
2Sa 5:8 to use the water shaft to r those 'lame and — 5595
15:5 Absalom would r out his hand, — 8938
Job 3:22 with gladness and rejoice when they r — 5162
29:19 My roots will r to the water, — 7337
37:23 The Almighty is beyond our r and exalted — 5162
Ps 32:6 mighty waters rise, they will not r him. — 5595
144:7 R down your hand from on high; — 8938
Isa 11:11 the Lord will r out his hand a second time — 3578S
59:9 and righteousness does not r us. — 5952
65:20 he who fails to r a hundred will — 2627
Eze 31:14 so well-watered are ever to r such — 6641
Am 9:9 and not a pebble will r the ground. — 5877
Mic 5:4 his greatness will r to the ends of the earth. — 6330
Lk 13:32 and on the third day I will r my goal.' — 5457
Jn 20:27 R out your hand and put it into my side. — 5770
Ac 17:27 and perhaps r out for him and find him, — 6027
20:16 for he was in a hurry to r Jerusalem, — 1181+1650
27:12 hoping to r Phoenix and winter there. — 2918
Eph 4:13 until we all r unity in the faith and in — 2918
Rev 12:14 times and half a time, out of the serpent's r. — NIG

REACHED (102) [REACH]
Ge 8:9 He r out his hand and took the dove — 8938
10:19 of Canaan r from Sidon toward Gerar as far — 2118
15:16 as bad as the outcry that has r me. — NIH
18:21 as bad as the outcry that has r me. — 448+995
19:10 men inside r out and pulled Lot back — 3338+8938
19:23 By the time Lot r Zoar, — 995+2025
22:9 they r the place God had told him about, — 448+995
22:10 Then he r out his hand and took the knife — 8938
28:11 When he r a certain place, — 7003
37:18 and before he r them, — 7928
45:16 When the news r Pharaoh's palace — 9048
46:1 and when he r Beersheba, — 995+2025
48:14 But Israel r out his right hand and put it — 8938
50:10 they r the threshing floor of Atad, — 995+6330
Ex 3:9 now the cry of the Israelites has r me, — 448+995
4:4 So Moses r out and took hold of the snake — 8938
16:35 they ate manna until they r the border — 448+995
Nu 13:23 When they r the Valley of Eshcol, — 995+6330
21:23 When he r Jahaz, he fought with Israel. — 995+2025
Dt 1:19 and so we r Kadesh Barnea. — 995+6330
1:20 "You have r the hill country of the Amorites, — 995+6330
1:31 way you went until you r this place." — 995+6330
12:9 yet r the resting place and the inheritance — 448+995
29:7 When you r this place, — 448+995
Jos 3:15 priests who carried the ark r the Jordan — 995+6330
10:20 few who were left r their fortified cities. — 448+995
15:11 along to Mount Baalah and r Jabneel. — 3655
17:10 of Manasseh the sea and bordered Asher — 2118
Jdg 3:21 Ehud r with his left hand, — 8938
5:26 Her hand r for the tent peg, — 8938
7:19 the hundred men with him r the edge — 928+995
16:29 Then Samson r toward — 4369
19:29 When he r home, — 448+995
1Sa 9:5 When they r the district of Zuph, — 928+995
9:16 for their cry has r me." — 995
14:27 so he r out the end of the staff that was — 448+995
15:13 When Samuel r him, Saul said, — 448+995
17:20 He r the camp as the army was going out — 995
30:1 and his men r Ziklag on the third day. — 995
2Sa 6:6 Uzzah r out and took hold of the ark — 8938
19:11 throughout Israel has r the king — 448+995
22:17 "He r down from on high and took hold — 8938
1Ki 2:28 When the news r Joab, — 995+6330
19:8 until he r Horeb, — NIH
2Ki 4:27 she r the man of God at the mountain, — 448+995
4:32 When Elisha r the house, — 995+2025
6:7 Then the man r out his hand and took it. — 8938
7:5 When they r the edge of the camp, — 995+6330
7:8 The men who had leprosy r the edge of — 995+6330
9:18 "The messenger has r them, — 448+995
9:20 The lookout reported, "He has r them, — 995+6330
11:16 So they seized her as she r the place where — 995
19:23 I have r its remotest parts, — 995
19:28 and your insolence has r my ears, — 6590
1Ch 13:9 Uzzah r out his hand to steady the ark, — 8938
2Ch 23:15 So they seized her as she r the entrance — 448+995
29:17 the month they r the portico of the LORD. — 995
30:27 for their prayer r heaven, — 995+4200
Ezr 9:6 and our guilt has r to the heavens. — 1540+6330
Ne 4:1 the wall till all of it r half its height, — 6330+8003
Job 28:22 'Only a rumor of it has r our ears.' — 928+9048
Ps 18:16 He r down from on high and took hold — 8938
Isa 10:14 so my hand r for the wealth of the nations; — NIH
16:8 which once r Jazer and spread toward — 5595
37:24 I have r its remotest heights, — 995
37:29 and because your insolence has r my ears, — 6590
Jer 1:9 Then the LORD r out his hand — 8938
37:13 But when he r the Benjamin Gate, — 928+2118
48:32 they r as far as the sea of Jazer. — 5595
Eze 10:7 Then one of the cherubim r out his hand to — 8938
21:25 whose time of punishment has r its climax, — NIH
21:29 whose time of punishment has r its climax, — NIH
35:5 the time their punishment r its climax, — NIH
40:49 It was r by a flight of stairs, — 448+6590
Da 6:24 And before they r the floor of the den, — 10413
8:10 It grew until it r the host of the heavens, — NIH
Jnh 3:6 When the news r the king of Nineveh, — 5595
Mic 1:9 It has r the very gate of my people, — 5595
Mt 8:3 Jesus r out his hand and touched the man. — 1753
14:31 Immediately Jesus r out his hand — 1753
26:51 one of Jesus' companions r for his sword, — 1753+3836+5931
Mk 1:41 Jesus r out his hand and touched the man. — 1753
11:13 When he r it, he found nothing but leaves, — 2093+2262
15:1 and the whole Sanhedrin, r a decision. — 4472
Lk 1:44 as the sound of your greeting r my ears, — 1181
5:13 Jesus r out his hand and touched the man. — 2093+2262
19:5 When Jesus r the spot, — 2093+2262
Jn 6:21 and immediately the boat r the shore — 1181+2093
11:32 When Mary r the place where Jesus was — 2262
20:4 but the other disciple outran Peter and r — 2262
20:8 who had r the tomb first, also went inside. — 2262
Ac 8:40 in all the towns until he r Caesarea. — 1650+2262
11:22 r the ears of the church at Jerusalem, — 201+1650
16:4 the decisions r by the apostles and elders — 5679
21:8 we r Caesarea and stayed at the house — 1650+2262
21:31 news r the commander of the Roman — 326
21:35 When Paul r the steps, — 1181+2093
27:44 In this way everyone r land in safety. — 2093
28:13 and on the following day we r Puteoli. — 1650+2262
1Co 14:36 Or are you the only people it has r? — 2918
Eph 1:10 the times will have r their fulfillment— — NIG
Jas 5:4 The cries of the harvesters have r the ears — 1656

REACHES (18) [REACH]
Ge 11:4 with a tower that r to the heavens, — 8031
Dt 25:11 and she r out and seizes him — 3338+8938
2Ki 10:2 "As soon as this letter r you, — 448+995
2Ch 32:9 in a rage that r to heaven. — 5595
Job 20:6 Though his pride r to the heavens — 6590
41:26 The sword that r him has no effect, — 5952
Ps 36:5 Your love, O LORD, r to the heavens, — 928
48:10 your praise r to the ends of the earth; — 6584
57:10 your faithfulness r to the skies. — 6330
71:19 Your righteousness r to the skies, O God, — 6330
108:4 your faithfulness r to the skies. — 6330
Isa 8:8 As one r into a nest, — 5162
15:8 their wailing r as far as Eglaim, — NIH
Jer 51:9 for her judgment r to the skies, — 5595
51:53 Even if Babylon r the sky — 6590
Da 4:22 your greatness has grown until it r the sky, — 10413
12:12 Blessed is the one who waits for and r — 5595
2Co 10:13 a field that r even to you. — 2391

REACHETH (KJV) See EXTENDS, PIERCES, REACHES, TOUCHED

REACHING (11) [REACH]
Ge 28:12 with its top r to heaven, — 5595
Ex 25:11 r from the waist to the thigh. — 2118
1Sa 17:49 R into his bag and taking out a stone, — 3338+8938
Ps 57:10 For great is your love, r to the heavens; — 6330
Isa 8:8 passing through it and r up to the neck. — 5595
Mk 11:15 On r Jerusalem, Jesus entered — 1650+2262
Lk 22:37 about me is r its fulfillment." — 2400
22:40 On r the place, he said to them, — 1181+2093
2Co 4:15 grace that is r more and more people may cause thanksgiving — 1328+3836+4429+4498
1Ti 5:24 r the place of judgment ahead of them; — 4575
Rev 1:13 a robe r down to his feet — 4468

READ (77) [READER, READING, READS]
Ex 24:7 Book of the Covenant and r it to the people. — 7924
Dt 17:19 and he is to r it all the days of his life so — 7924
31:11 you shall r this law before them — 7924
Jos 8:34 Joshua r all the words of the law— — 7924
8:35 that Joshua did not r to the whole assembly — 7924
2Ki 5:7 that he took to the king of Israel r: — 606
5:7 As soon as the king of Israel r the letter, — 7924
19:14 the letter from the messengers and r it. — 7924
22:8 He gave it to Shaphan, who r it. — 7924
22:10 And Shaphan r from it in the presence of — 7924
22:16 in the book the king of Judah has r. — 7924
23:2 He r in their hearing all the words of — 7924
2Ch 30:18 the king and from his officials, which r: — 606
34:18 And Shaphan r from it in the presence of — 7924
34:24 the book that has been r in the presence of — 7924
34:30 He r in their hearing all the words of — 7924
Ezr 4:18 The letter you sent us has been r — 10637
4:23 of the letter of King Artaxerxes was r — 10637
5:7 The report they sent him r as follows: — 10374
Ne 8:3 He r it aloud from daybreak till noon — 7924
8:8 They r from the Book of the Law of God, — 7924
8:8 people could understand what was being r. — 5246
8:18 Ezra r from the Book of the Law of God. — 7924
9:3 where they were and r from the Book — 7924
13:1 that day the Book of Moses was r aloud in — 7924
Est 6:1 to be brought in and r to him. — 7924

Isa	29:11	give the scroll to *someone who* can **r**,	3359+6219
	29:11	"**R** this, please," he will answer, "I can't;	7924
	29:12	scroll to someone *who* cannot **r**,	3359+4202+6219
	29:12	and say, "**R** this, please," he will answer,	7924
	29:12	will answer, "I don't **know how to r**."	3359+6219
	34:16	Look in the scroll of the LORD and **r**:	7924
	37:14	the letter from the messengers and **r** it.	7924
Jer	29:29	**r** the letter to Jeremiah the prophet.	7924
	36: 6	on a day of fasting and **r** to the people from	7924
	36: 6	**R** them to all the people of Judah who come	7924
	36: 8	at the LORD's temple *he* **r** the words of	7924
	36:10	Baruch **r** to all the people at the LORD's	7924
	36:13	Micaiah told them everything he had heard	
		Baruch **r** to the people	7924
	36:14	"Bring the scroll from which *you have* **r** to	7924
	36:15	"Sit down, please, and **r** it to us."	7924
	36:15	So Baruch **r** it to them.	7924
	36:21	the room of Elishama the secretary and **r** it	7924
	36:23	Whenever Jehudi *had* **r** three	7924
	51:61	see that *you* **r** all these words **aloud.**	7924
Da	5: 8	but they could not **r** the writing or tell	10637
	5:15	to **r** this writing and tell me what it means,	10637
	5:16	If you can **r** this writing	10637
	5:17	*I will* **r** the writing for the king	10637
Mt	12: 3	"Haven't *you* **r** what David did when he	336
	12: 5	Or haven't *you* **r** in the Law that on	336
	19: 4	"Haven't *you* **r,**" he replied,	336
	21:16	"Yes," replied Jesus, "*have you* never **r**,	336
	21:42	"*Have you* never **r** in the Scriptures:	336
	22:31	*have you* not **r** what God said to you,	336
Mk	2:25	"*Have you* never **r** what David did when he	336
	12:10	Haven't *you* **r** this scripture:	336
	12:26	*have you* not **r** in the book of Moses,	336
	15:26	notice of the charge against him: **r**:	1639+2108
Lk	4:16	And he stood up *to* **r**.	336
	6: 3	"*Have you* never **r** what David did when he	336
	10:26	"How *do you* **r** it?"	336
	23:38	a written notice above him, which **r**:	NIG
Jn	19:19	*It* **r**: JESUS OF NAZARETH, KING OF THE JEWS	
			1211+1639
	19:20	Many of the Jews **r** this sign,	336
Ac	13:27	of the prophets that *are* **r** every Sabbath.	336
	15:21	from the earliest times and *is* **r** in	336
	15:31	The *people* **r** it and were glad	336
	23:34	The governor **r** the letter	336
2Co	1:13	not write you anything *you* cannot **r**	336
	3: 2	on our hearts, known and **r** by everybody.	336
	3:14	when the old covenant *is* **r**,	342
	3:15	Even to this day when Moses *is* **r**,	336
Col	4:16	After this letter *has been* **r** to you,	336
	4:16	also **r** in the church of the Laodiceans and	336
	4:16	that you in turn **r** the letter from Laodicea.	336
1Th	5:27	before the Lord *to have* this letter **r** to all	336

READER (2) [READ]

Mt	24:15	let the **r** understand—	336
Mk	13:14	let the **r** understand—	336

READILY (2) [READY]

Job	4:19	who are crushed **more r than** a moth!	4200+7156
Ro	11:24	how much more **r** will these,	NIG

READINESS (2) [READY]

2Co	7:11	**r to see justice done.**	1689
Eph	6:15	the **r** that comes from the gospel of peace.	2288

READING (8) [READ]

Jer	51:63	When you finish **r** this scroll,	7924
Ac	8:28	on his way home was sitting in his chariot **r**	336
	8:30	up to the chariot and heard the man **r** Isaiah	336
	8:30	"Do you understand what *you are* **r**?"	336
	8:32	The eunuch was **r** this passage of Scripture:	336
	13:15	After the **r** from the Law and the Prophets,	342
Eph	3: 4	*In* **r** this, then, you will be able	336
1Ti	4:13	devote yourself *to* the **public r** of Scripture,	342

READS (2) [READ]

Da	5: 7	"Whoever **r** this writing	10637
Rev	1: 3	the one who **r** the words of this prophecy,	336

READY (94) [ALREADY, READILY, READINESS]

Ge	24:61	Then Rebekah and her maids **got r**	7756
	46:29	Joseph *had* his chariot **made r** and went	673
	46:30	Israel said to Joseph, "Now *I am* **r to die,**	4637
Ex	14: 6	So he **had** his chariot **made r**	673
	17: 4	*They are* almost **r** to **stone** me."	AIT
	19:11	and be **r** by the third day,	3922
	34: 2	Be **r** in the morning,	3922
Nu	4:15	and when the camp *is* **r** to **move**,	AIT
	8:11	they may be **r** to do the work of the LORD.	2118
	32:17	But we *are* **r** to arm ourselves and go ahead	2590
Jos	1: 2	**get r** to cross the Jordan River into	7756
	1:11	'**Get** your supplies **r**.	3922
	22:26	'*Let us* **get r** and build an altar—	6913
1Sa	6: 7	"Now then, **get a new cart r**,	6913
	9:26	"**Get r**, and I will send you on your way."	7756
	9:26	When Saul **got r**,	7756
	25:41	**r** to serve you and wash the feet	NIH
2Sa	15:15	"Your servants are **r** to do whatever	2180
	15:26	'I am not pleased with you,' then I am **r**;	2180
1Ki	1: 5	So he **got** chariots and horses **r**,	6913
2Ki	22: 4	high priest and **have** *him* **get r** the money	9462

1Ch	5:18	**r** for military service—	3655+7372
	7: 4	had 36,000 **men r for battle,**	1522+4878+7372
	7:11	fighting men **r to go out** to war.	3655+7372
	7:40	of men **r for battle,**	928+2021+4878+7372
	12: 8	**r for battle** and able	408+2021+4200+4878+7372
	12:17	*r to have* you **unite** with me.	AIT
	12:25	Simeon, warriors **r for** battle—7,100;	4200
	12:35	men of Dan, **r for** battle—28,600;	6885
	28:21	the priests and Levites are **r** for all the work	NIH
2Ch	25: 5	men **r for military service,**	3655+7372
	26:11	**r to go out** by divisions according	3655+7372
	26:19	a censer in his hand *r* to **burn incense,**	AIT
	29:26	Levites **stood r** with David's instruments,	AIT
Est	3:14	of every nationality so they would be **r** for	6969
	8:13	so that the Jews would be **r** on that day	6969
Job	3: 8	those *who are* **r** to rouse Leviathan.	6969
	18:12	disaster *is* **r** for him when he falls.	3922
	32:19	like new wineskins **r** to **burst.**	1324
Ps	7:13	he **makes r** his flaming arrows.	7188
	59: 4	yet *they are* **r** to attack me.	3922
	119:173	May your hand be **r** to help me,	NIH
Pr	21:31	The horse is **made r** for the day of battle,	3922
	22:18	**have** all of them **r** on your lips.	3922
	24:27	and **get** your fields **r**;	6963
Isa	30:33	it *has* **been made r** for the king.	3922
Jer	1:17	"**Get** yourself **r!**	273+5516
	9: 3	**make r** their tongue like a bow, **to shoot**	2005
	46:14	'Take your positions and **get r**,	3922
La	2: 4	his right hand *is* **r**.	5893
Eze	7:14	the trumpet and **get** everything **r**,	3922
	21:11	**made r** for the hand of the slayer.	5989
	38: 7	" '**Get r**; be prepared,	3922
Da	3:15	if you are **r** to fall down and worship	10577
Hos	2: 9	and my new wine when it is **r**,	4595
Na	2: 3	on the day they are **made r**;	3922
Zec	5:11	When *it is* **r**, the basket will be set there	3922
Mt	22: 4	and everything *is* **r**.	2289
	22: 8	'The wedding banquet is **r**,	2289
	24:44	So you also must be **r**,	2289
	25:10	The virgins who were **r** went in with him to	2289
Mk	3: 9	to **have** a small boat **r** for him,	4674
	14:15	a large upper room, furnished and **r**.	2289
Lk	1:17	to **have** a people prepared for the Lord."	2286
	1:39	that time Mary **got r** and hurried to a town	482
	9:52	a Samaritan village to **get** things **r** for him;	2286
	12:35	"Be **dressed r for service**	3836+4019+4322
	12:38	those servants whose master finds them **r**,	NIG
	12:40	You also must be **r**, because the Son of Man	2289
	12:47	and *does* not **get r** or does	2286
	14:17	'Come, for everything is now **r**.'	2289
	17: 8	**get r** my supper and **wait** on me while I eat	4322
	22:33	I am **r** to go with you to prison and	2289
Jn	8:37	*you are* **r** to kill me.	2426
Ac	16:10	we **got r** at once to leave for Macedonia,	2426
	21:13	I am **r** not only to be bound,	2290
	21:15	we **got r** and went up to Jerusalem.	2171
	23:15	We are **r** to kill him before he gets here."	2289
	23:21	They are **r** now, waiting for your consent	2289
	23:23	"**Get r** a detachment of two hundred	2286
	28:10	in many ways and *when we were* **r** *to* **sail**,	AIT
1Co	3: 2	not solid food, for *you were* not yet **r** for it.	1538
	3: 2	Indeed, *you are* still not **r**.	1538
	14: 8	who *will* **get r** for battle?	4186
2Co	9: 2	that since last year *you* in Achaia were **r**	4186
	9: 3	but that you may be **r**,	4186
	9: 5	Then it will be **r** as a generous gift,	2289
	10: 6	be **r** to punish every act of disobedience,	2090
	12:14	Now I am **r** to visit you for the third time,	2290
Tit	3: 1	to be **r** to do whatever is good,	2289
1Pe	1: 5	until the coming of the salvation that is **r** to	2289
	4: 5	give account *to* him who *is* **r** to judge	2290+2400
Rev	16:15	And the four angels who *had been* **kept r**	2286
	19: 7	and his bride *has* **made** herself **r**.	2286

REAFFIRM (3) [AFFIRM]

1Sa	11:14	to Gilgal and there **r** the kingship."	2542
	20:17	And Jonathan *had* David **r** his oath out	3578
2Co	2: 8	therefore, *to* **r** your love for him.	3263

REAIAH (4)

1Ch	4: 2	**R** son of Shobal was the father of Jahath,	8025
	5: 5	Micah his son, **R** his son, Baal his son,	8025
Ezr	2:47	Giddel, Gahar, **R**,	8025
Ne	7:50	**R**, Rezin, Nekoda,	8025

REAL (3) [REALITIES, REALITY, REALLY]

Jn	6:55	For my flesh is **r** food	239
	6:55	and my blood is **r** drink.	239
1Jn	2:27	and as that anointing is **r**, not counterfeit—	239

REALITIES (1) [REAL]

Heb	10: 1	that are coming—not the **r** themselves.	1635

REALITY (1) [REAL]

Col	2:17	the **r**, however, is found in Christ.	5393

REALIZE (32) [REALIZED, REALIZING]

Ge	42:23	not **r** that Joseph could understand them,	3359
Ex	10: 7	*Do you* not yet **r** that Egypt is ruined?"	3359
Nu	22:34	*I did* not **r** you were standing in the road	3359
Jdg	13:16	not **r** that it was the angel of the LORD.)	3359
	15:11	"Don't *you* **r** that the Philistines are rulers	3359
	20:34	so heavy that the Benjamites *did* not **r** how	3359

1Sa	12:17	And *you will* **r** what an evil thing you did	
			2256+3359+8011
2Sa	2:26	Don't *you* **r** that this will end in bitterness?	3359
	3:38	"*Do you* not **r** that a prince and	3359
Ecc	2:14	*to* **r** that the same fate overtakes them both.	3359
Jer	2:19	Consider then and **r** how evil and bitter it is	8011
	11:19	not **r** that they had plotted against me,	3359
Da	2: 8	you are trying to gain time, because *you* **r**	10255
Hos	7: 2	not **r** that I remember all their evil deeds.	
			606+4200+4222
	7: 9	but he *does* not **r** it.	3359
	11: 3	but *they did* not **r** it was I who healed them.	3359
	14: 9	*He will* **r** these things.	1067
Jn	3:10	*He did* not **r** where it had come from,	3857
	11:50	*You do* not **r** that it is better for you	3357
	12:16	Only after Jesus was glorified *did they* **r**	3630
	13: 7	"You *do* not **r** now what I am doing,	3857
	14:20	that day you *will* **r** that I am in my Father,	1182
	19:10	"Don't *you* **r** I have power either	3857
	20:14	but *she did* not **r** that it was Jesus.	3857
	21: 4	but the disciples *did* not **r** that it was Jesus.	3857
Ac	7:25	Moses thought that his own people *would* **r**	5317
	10:34	"I *now* **r** how true it is that God does	2898
	23: 5	*I did* not **r** that he was the high priest;	3857
1Co	11: 3	*to* **r** that the head of every man is Christ,	3857
2Co	10:11	Such people *should* **r** that what we are	3357
	13: 5	*Do you* not **r** that Christ Jesus is in you—	2105
Rev	3:17	But *you do* not **r** that you are wretched,	3857

REALIZED (29) [REALIZE]

Ge	3: 7	and *they* **r** they were naked;	3359
	28: 8	Esau then **r** how displeasing the Canaanite	8011
Ex	5:19	The Israelite foremen **r** they were in trouble	8011
Jdg	6:22	When Gideon **r** that it was the angel of	8011
	13:21	Manoah **r** that it was the angel of	3359
	20:41	*they* **r** that disaster had come upon them.	8011
Ru	1:18	When Naomi **r** that Ruth was determined	8011
1Sa	3: 8	Eli **r** that the LORD was calling the boy.	1067
	18:28	When Saul **r** that the LORD was	2256+3359+8011
2Sa	10: 6	the Ammonites **r** that they had become	8011
	12:19	and he **r** the child was dead.	1067
	20:12	When *he* **r** that everyone who came up	8011
1Ki	3:15	and he **r** it had been a dream.	2180
1Ch	19: 6	the Ammonites **r** that they had become	8011
Ne	6:12	*I* **r** that God had not sent him,	5795
	6:16	lost their self-confidence, because *they* **r**	3359
Ecc	5:18	Then I **r** that it is good and proper for	8011
SS	6:12	Before *I* **r** it, my desire set me among	3359
Eze	10:20	and *I* **r** that they were cherubim.	3359
Mt	2:16	*When* Herod **r** that he had been outwitted by	3972
Mk	5:30	At once Jesus **r** *that* power had gone out	2105
Lk	1:22	*They* **r** he had seen a vision in the temple,	2105
Jn	4:53	the father **r** that this was the exact time	1182
	6:22	on the opposite shore of the lake **r**	3972
	6:24	Once the crowd **r** that neither Jesus	3972
Ac	4:13	and John and **r** that they were unschooled,	2898
	16:19	the owners of the slave girl **r** that their hope	3972
	19:34	But *when they* **r** he was a Jew,	2105
	22:29	*when he* **r** that he had put Paul,	2105

REALIZING (3) [REALIZE]

Ge	38:16	Not **r** that she was his daughter-in-law,	3359
Est	7: 7	**r** that the king had already decided his fate,	8011
Ro	2: 4	not **r** that God's kindness leads you	51

REALLY (44) [REAL]

Ge	3: 1	he said to the woman, "Did God **r** say,	677+3954
	18:13	Will I **r** have a child, now that I am old?	598+677
	18:24	Will you **r** sweep it away and not spare	677
	20:12	Besides, she **r** is my sister,	593
	26: 9	"She is **r** your wife!	421
	27:21	to know whether *you* **r** are my son Esau	2296
	27:24	"Are you **r** my son Esau?"	2296
	45:12	*that* it is **r** I who am speaking to you.	3954
Lev	25:42	because what he is **r** selling you is	NIH
Nu	22:37	Am I **r** not able to reward you?"	598
Jdg	6:17	give me a sign that it is **r** you talking to me.	NIH
	6:31	If Baal **r** is a god,	3954
	9:15	If you **r** want to anoint me king over you	622+928
	11: 9	*will I* **r** be your head?"	AIT
	14:16	You don't **r** love me.	8370
	15: 3	I will **r** harm them."	3954
1Ki	8:27	"But will God **r** dwell on earth?	598
	18: 7	and said, "Is it **r** you, my lord Elijah?"	2296
2Ch	6:18	"But will God **r** dwell on earth with men?	598
Ecc	3:22	he cannot **r** comprehend it.	AIT
Jer	7: 5	If *you* **r** change your ways and your	3512+3512
	9:26	For all these nations are **r** uncircumcised,	NIH
Zec	7: 5	was it **r** for me that you fasted?"	NIH
Mk	11:32	everyone held that John **r** was a prophet.)	3953
Jn	4:42	that this man **r** is the Savior of the world."	242
	7:26	Have the authorities **r** concluded that he is	242
	8:31	hold to my teaching, you are **r** my disciples.	242
	13:38	"Will you **r** lay down your life for me?	NIG
	14: 7	If you **r** knew me, you would know my	NIG
Ac	7:25	not believing that he **r** was a disciple.	NIG
	12: 9	what the angel was doing was **r** happening;	239
Ro	7: 7	not have known what coveting **r** was if	NIG
1Co	5: 7	How I wish that you **r** had become kings so	1145
	5: 7	a new batch without yeast—as you **r** are.	NIG
	14:25	exclaiming, "God is **r** among you!"	3953
Gal	1: 7	which is **r** no gospel at all.	NIG
	3: 4	if it **r** was for nothing?	1145
Php	1:12	that what has happened to me has **r** served	3437
1Th	3: 8	For now we **r** live,	NIG

1Ti	5: 3	to those widows who *are* r in need.	3953
	5: 5	The widow who is r in need	3953
	5:16	church can help those widows who are r	3953
Jas	2: 8	you r keep the royal law found in Scripture,	3530
1Jn	2:19	but they did not r belong to us.	NIG

REALM (11) [REALMS]

Dt	32:22	one that burns to the r of death below.	8619
Jos	13:21	the entire r of Sihon king of the Amorites,	4931
	13:27	the rest of the r of Sihon king of Heshbon	4931
	13:30	the entire r of Og king of Bashan—	4931
2Ch	36:22	to make a proclamation throughout his r	4895
Ezr	1: 1	to make a proclamation throughout his r	4895
	7:23	Why should there be wrath against the r of	10424
Est	1:20	proclaimed throughout all his vast r,	4895
	2: 3	of his r to bring all these beautiful girls into	4895
Da	11: 9	Then the king of the North will invade the r	4895
Hab	2: 9	to him who builds his r by unjust gain	1074

REALMS (5) [REALM]

Eph	1: 3	who has blessed us in the **heavenly** r	2230
	1:20	at his right hand in the **heavenly** r,	2230
	2: 6	with him in the **heavenly** r in Christ Jesus,	2230
	3:10	the rulers and authorities in the **heavenly** r,	2230
	6:12	spiritual forces of evil in the **heavenly** r.	2230

REAP (30) [REAPED, REAPER, REAPERS, REAPING, REAPS]

Lev	19: 9	" 'When you r the harvest of your land,	7917
	19: 9	*do not* r to the very edges of your field	7917
	23:10	to give you and *you* r its harvest,	7917
	23:22	" 'When you r the harvest of your land,	7917
	23:22	*do not* r to the very edges of your field	7917
	25: 5	*Do not* r what grows of itself or	7907+7917
	25:11	and *do not* r what grows of itself or harvest	7917
1Sa	8:12	others to plow his ground and r his harvest,	7917
2Ki	19:29	But in the third year sow and r,	7917
Job	4: 8	and those who sow trouble r it.	7917
Ps	126: 5	Those who sow in tears *will* r with songs	7917
Ecc	11: 4	whoever looks at the clouds *will* not r.	7917
Isa	37:30	But in the third year sow and r,	7917
Jer	12:13	They will sow wheat but r thorns;	7917
Hos	8: 7	"They sow the wind and r the whirlwind.	7917
	10:12	the fruit of unfailing love,	7917
Mt	6:26	they do not sow or r or store away in barns,	2545
Lk	12:24	Consider the ravens: They do not sow or r,	2545
	19:21	not put in and r what you did not sow.'	2545
Jn	4:38	to r what you have not worked for.	2545
Ro	6:21	What benefit *did you* r at that time from	2400
	6:22	the benefit *you* r leads to holiness,	2400
1Co	9:11	is it too much if we r a material **harvest**	2545
2Co	9: 6	sows sparingly *will* also r sparingly,	2545
	9: 6	sows generously *will* also r generously.	2545
Gal	6: 8	from that nature *will* r destruction;	2545
	6: 8	from the Spirit *will* r eternal life.	2545
	6: 9	for at the proper time *we will* **r a harvest**	2545
Rev	14:15	"Take your sickle and r,	2545
	14:15	because the time *to* r has come,	2545

REAPED (3) [REAP]

Ge	26:12	and the same year r a hundredfold,	5162
Hos	10:13	planted wickedness, you have r evil,	7917
Jn	4:38	and you *have* r **the benefits of** their labor."	1656

REAPER (7) [REAP]

Ps	129: 7	with it the r cannot fill his hands,	7917
Isa	17: 5	a r gathers the standing grain and harvests	7907
Jer	9:22	like cut grain behind the r,	7917
	50:16	and the r with his sickle at harvest.	9530
Am	9:13	the r will be overtaken by the plowman and	7917
Jn	4:36	Even now the r draws his wages,	2545
	4:36	the sower and the r may be glad together.	2545

REAPERS (1) [REAP]

2Ki	4:18	who was with the r.	7917

REAPING (2) [REAP]

Ge	45: 6	not be plowing and r.	7907
Lk	19:22	and r what I did not sow?	2545

REAPPEARS (2) [APPEAR]

Lev	13:57	But if *it* r in the clothing,	6388+8011
	14:43	"If the mildew r in the house	2256+7255+8740

REAPS (4) [REAP]

Pr	11:18	he who sows righteousness r a sure reward.	NIH
	22: 8	He who sows wickedness r trouble,	7917
Jn	4:37	the saying 'One sows and another r' is true.	2545
Gal	6: 7	A man r what he sows.	2545

REAR (17) [REARED, REARING]

Ge	33: 2	and Rachel and Joseph *in the* r.	340
Ex	26:12	that is left over is to hang down at the r *of*	294
Nu	10:25	Finally, as the r **guard** for all the units,	665
Jos	6: 9	and the r **guard** followed the ark.	665
	6:13	the r **guard** followed the ark of the LORD,	665
	10:19	**attack** them **from the** r.	2386
1Sa	29: 2	David and his men were marching at the r	340
1Ki	6:16	He partitioned off twenty cubits at the r *of*	3752
2Ch	13:13	Jeroboam had sent troops around to the r,	339

2Ch	13:14	at both front and r.	294
Ps	83: 2	how your foes r their heads.	5951
Isa	52:12	the God of Israel will be your r guard.	665
	58: 8	glory of the LORD *will be* your r **guard.**	665
Eze	40:13	from the **top of** the r wall	AIT
	41:15	the building facing the courtyard at the r *of*	339
Hos	9:12	Even if *they* r children,	1540
Joel	2:20	into the eastern sea and *those in the* r into	6067

REARED (6) [REAR]

Job	31:18	from my youth I r him as would a father,	1540
Isa	1: 2	"I r children and brought them up,	1540
	23: 4	*I have* neither r sons nor brought	1540
	51:18	the sons *she* r there was none to take her by	1540
La	2:22	those I cared for and r,	8049
Eze	19: 2	among the young lions and r her cubs.	8049

REARING (1) [REAR]

2Ki	10: 6	leading men of the city, *who were* r them.	1540

REASON (58) [REASONABLE, REASONED, REASONING, REASONS]

Ge	2:24	For this r a man will leave his father	4027
	20:10	"What *was your* r for doing this?"	8011
	41:32	The r the dream was given to Pharaoh	6584
1Sa	19: 5	like David by killing him **for no r?"**	2855
Job	2: 3	against him to ruin him **without any r."**	2855
	9:17	a storm and multiply my wounds **for no r.**	2855
	12:24	the leaders of the earth of their r;	4213
	22: 6	from your brothers **for no r;**	2855
Ps	35:19	who hate me **without r** maliciously wink	2855
	38:19	those who hate me **without r** are numerous.	9214
	69: 4	Those who hate me **without r** outnumber	2855
Pr	3:30	Do not accuse a man **for no r—**	2855
Isa	1:18	"Come now, *let us* **r together,"**	3519
Mt	2:10	Looking **for a r** to accuse Jesus,	2671
	19: 3	to divorce his wife for any and every **r?"**	162
	19: 5	**'For this r** a man will leave his father	1915
Mk	2: 5	Some of them were looking **for a r** to	2671
	10: 7	**'For this r** a man will leave his father	1915
Lk	6: 7	the teachers of the law were looking for a r	2671
Jn	1:31	but the r I came baptizing with water	1328+4047
	5:18	the more the Jews tried all the harder	1328+4047
	8:47	The r you do not hear is that you	1328+4047
	10:17	The r my Father loves me is that I lay	1328+4047
	12:27	for this very r I came to this hour.	1328+4047
	12:39	For this r they could not believe,	1328+4047
	15:25	'They hated me **without r.'**	1562
	18:37	In fact, for this r I was born,	1650+4047
Ac	19:40	since there is no r for it."	165
	28:20	For this r I have asked to see you and talk	162
Ro	14: 9	**For this very** r, Christ died	1650+4047
1Co	4:17	For this r I am sending to you Timothy,	1328+4047
	11:10	**For this r**, and because of the angels,	1328+4047
	12:15	not **for that r** cease to be part of the body.	4047+4123
	12:16	not **for that r** cease to be part of the body.	4047+4123
	14:13	**For this r** anyone who speaks in a tongue	1475
2Co	2: 9	The r I wrote you was to see	1142+1650+4047
	8:24	of your love and the r for our pride in you,	NIG
Gal	6:12	The only r they do this is	NIG
Eph	1:15	**For this r**, ever since I heard	1328+4047
	3: 1	**For this r** I, Paul,	4047+5920
	3:14	**For this r** I kneel before the Father,	4047+5920
	5:31	**"For this r** a man will leave his father	505+4047
Col	1: 9	**For this r**, since the day we heard	1328+4047
1Th	3: 5	**For this r**, when I could stand it no longer,	1328+4047
2Th	2:11	**For this r** God sends them	1328+4047
1Ti	1:16	for **that very r** I was shown mercy so	1328+4047
2Ti	1: 6	**For this r** I remind you to fan into flame	162
Tit	1: 5	The r I left you in Crete was	4047+5920
Phm	1:15	Perhaps **the r** he was separated from	1328+4047
Heb	2:17	**For this r** he had to be made like	3854
	9:15	**For this r** Christ is the mediator of	1328+4047
	10: 1	**For this r** it can never,	NIG
Jas	4: 5	Or do you think Scripture says **without r**	3036
1Pe	3:15	to everyone who asks you to give the r for	3364
	4: 6	**For this is the r** the gospel was preached	1650+4047
		even to those	
2Pe	1: 5	**For this very** r, make every effort to add to	899+4047
		your faith goodness;	
1Jn	3: 1	**The r** the world does not know us is	1328+4047
	3: 8	**The r** the Son of God appeared was	1650+4047

REASONABLE (2) [REASON]

Ac	18:14	it would be r for me to listen to you.	2848+3364
	26:25	"What I am saying is true and r.	5408

REASONED (6) [REASON]

Ac	17: 2	on three Sabbath days he r with them from	1363
	17:17	So he r in the synagogue with the Jews and	1363
	18: 4	Every Sabbath he r in the synagogue,	1363
	18:19	He himself went into the synagogue and r	1363
1Co	13:11	I thought like a child, I r like a child.	3357
Heb	11:19	Abraham r that God could raise the dead,	3357

REASONING (1) [REASON]

Job	32:11	while you spoke, I listened to your r;	9312

REASONS (3) [REASON]

1Co	15:32	in Ephesus for merely **human r,**	476
Php	3: 4	though I myself have r for such confidence.	NIG
	3: 4	If anyone else thinks he has r	NIG

REASSIGN (1) [ASSIGN]

Isa	49: 8	the land and to r its desolate inheritances,	5706

REASSURE (2) [ASSURE]

2Ki	25:24	an oath to r them and their men.	NIH
Jer	40: 9	took an oath to r them and their men.	NIH

REASSURED (1) [ASSURE]

Ge	50:21	And *he* r them and spoke kindly to them.	5714

REBA (2)

Nu	31: 8	Zur, Hur and **R**—the five kings of Midian.	8064
Jos	13:21	Evi, Rekem, Zur, Hur and **R**—	8064

REBECCA (KJV) See REBEKAH

REBEKAH (30) [REBEKAH'S]

Ge	22:23	Bethuel became the father of **R.**	8071
	24:15	**R** came out with her jar on her shoulder.	8071
	24:29	Now **R** had a brother named Laban,	8071
	24:30	had heard **R** tell what the man said to her,	8071
	24:45	I finished praying in my heart, **R** came out,	8071
	24:51	Here is **R**; take her and go,	8071
	24:53	of clothing and gave them to **R**;	8071
	24:58	So they called **R** and asked her,	8071
	24:59	So they sent their sister **R** on her way,	8071
	24:60	And they blessed **R** and said to her,	8071
	24:61	Then **R** and her maids got ready	8071
	24:61	So the servant took **R** and left.	8071
	24:64	**R** also looked up and saw Isaac.	8071
	24:67	and he married **R.**	8071
	25:20	when he married **R** daughter of Bethuel	8071
	25:21	and his wife **R** became pregnant.	8071
	25:26	Isaac was sixty years old when **R** gave birth	NIH
	25:28	loved Esau, but **R** loved Jacob.	8071
	26: 7	of this place might kill me on account of **R**,	8071
	26: 8	and saw Isaac caressing his wife **R.**	8071
	26:35	They were a source of grief to Isaac and **R.**	8071
	27: 5	Now **R** was listening as Isaac spoke	8071
	27: 6	**R** said to her son Jacob,	8071
	27:11	Jacob said to **R** his mother,	8071
	27:15	Then **R** took the best clothes	8071
	27:42	**R** was told what her older son Esau had said	8071
	27:46	Then **R** said to Isaac, "I'm disgusted	8071
	28: 5	the Aramean, the brother of **R**,	8071
	29:12	a relative of her father and a son of **R.**	8071
	49:31	there Isaac and his wife **R** were buried,	8071

REBEKAH'S (2) [REBEKAH]

Ge	35: 8	Now Deborah, **R** nurse,	8071
Ro	9:10	but **R** children had one and the same father,	4831

REBEL (18) [REBELLED, REBELLING, REBELLION, REBELLIOUS, REBELS]

Ex	23:21	*Do not* r against him;	5352
Nu	14: 9	Only *do not* r against the LORD.	5277
Dt	1:26	how much more will you r after I die!	NIH
Jos	22:18	" 'If you r against the LORD today,	5277
	22:19	not r against the LORD or against us	5277
	22:29	"Far be it from us to r against the LORD	5277
1Sa	12:14	and *do not* r against his commands, and if	5286
	12:14	and if *you* r against his commands,	5286
2Ki	18:20	that *you* r against me?	5277
Job	24:13	"There are those *who* r *against* the light,	5277
Isa	1:20	but if you resist and r,	5286
	36: 5	that *you* r against me?	5277
	48: 8	you were called a r from birth.	7321
Eze	2: 8	*Do not* r like that rebellious house;	2118+5308
	20:38	I will purge you of those who revolt and r	7321
Da	11:14	men among your own people *will* r	5951
Mt	10:21	children *will* r **against** their parents	2060
Mk	13:12	Children *will* r **against** their parents	2060

REBELLED (52) [REBEL]

Ge	14: 4	but in the thirteenth year *they* r.	5277
Nu	20:24	*both of you* r against my command at	5286
	26: 9	the community officials who r	5897
	26: 9	among Korah's followers when they r	5897
	27:14	the community r at the waters in the Desert	5312
Dt	1:26	*you* r against the command of the LORD	5286
	1:43	*You* r against the LORD's command and	5286
	9:23	But *you* r against the command of	5286
1Sa	22:13	he *has* r against me and lies in wait for me,	7756
1Ki	11:26	Jeroboam son of Nebat r against the king.	3338+8123
	11:27	account of how *he* r against the king:	3338+8123
2Ki	1: 1	After Ahab's death, Moab r against Israel.	7321
	3: 5	of Moab r against the king of Israel.	7321
	3: 7	"The king of Moab *has* r against me.	7321
	8:20	Edom r against Judah and set up their own	7321
	18: 7	*He* r against the king of Assyria and did	5277
	24: 1	But then he changed his mind and r	5277
	24:20	Zedekiah r against the king of Babylon.	5277
2Ch	13: 6	r against his master.	5277
	21: 8	Edom r against Judah and set up its own	7321

2Ch	36:13	*He also* r against King Nebuchadnezzar,	5277
Ne	9:26	they were disobedient and r against you;	5277
Ps	5:10	for *they have* r against you.	5286
	78:40	How often *they* r *against* him in the desert	5286
	78:56	But they put God to the test and r against	5286
	105:28	for *had they* not r against his words?	5286
	106: 7	and *they* r by the sea, the Red Sea.	5286
	106:33	for *they* r against the Spirit of God,	5286
	107:11	for *they had* r *against* the words of God	5286
Isa	1: 2	but they *have* r against me.	7321
	43:27	your spokesmen r against me.	7321
	63:10	Yet they r and grieved his Holy Spirit.	7321
	66:24	the dead bodies of those who r against me;	7321
Jer	2: 8	the leaders r against me.	7321
	2:29	You *have* all r against me,"	7321
	3:13	*you have* r against the LORD your God,	7321
	4:17	because *she has* r against me,' "	5286
	52: 3	Zedekiah r against the king of Babylon.	5277
La	1:18	yet *I* r *against* his command.	5286
	3:42	"We have sinned and r and you have	5286
Eze	2: 3	to a rebellious nation that *has* r against me;	5277
	5: 6	in her wickedness *she has* r against my laws	5286
	17:15	But the king r against him	5277
	20: 8	" 'But *they* r against me and would	5286
	20:13	people of Israel r against me in the desert.	5286
	20:21	" 'But the children r against me:	5286
Da	9: 5	We have been wicked and *have* r;	5277
	9: 9	even though *we have* r against him;	5277
Hos	7:13	because *they have* r against me!	7321
	8: 1	the people have broken my covenant and r	7321
	13:16	because *they have* r against their God.	5286
Heb	3:16	Who were *they* who heard and r?	4176

REBELLING (3) [REBEL]

Ne	2:19	"*Are* you r against the king?"	5277
Ps	78:17	r in the desert *against* the Most High.	5286
Ro	13: 2	against the authority *is* r **against** what God	468

REBELLION (42) [REBEL]

Ex	23:21	he will not forgive your r,	7322
	34: 7	and forgiving wickedness, r and sin.	7322
Lev	16:16	of the uncleanness and r *of* the Israelites,	7322
	16:21	and confess over it all the wickedness and r	7322
Nu	14:18	abounding in love and forgiving sin and r.	7322
Dt	13: 5	because he preached r against the LORD	6240
Jos	22:16	and build yourselves an altar in r	5277
	22:22	If this has been in r or disobedience to	5278
	22:22	If this has been in r or disobedience to	7322
	24:11	that I am not guilty of wrongdoing or r.	7322
1Sa	15:23	For r is like the sin of divination,	5308
1Ki	12:19	So Israel *has been* in r against the house	7321
	16:20	and the r he carried out,	8004
2Ki	8:22	To this day Edom *has been* in r	7321
2Ch	10:19	So Israel *has been* in r against the house	7321
	21:10	To this day Edom *has been* in r	7321
Ezr	4:15	a place of r from ancient times.	10083
	4:19	against kings and has been a place of r	10438
Ne	9:17	and in their r appointed a leader in order	5308
Job	34:37	To his sin he adds r;	7322
Ps	106:43	on r and they wasted away in their sin.	5286
Pr	17:11	An evil man is bent only on r;	5308
Isa	1: 5	Why do you persist in r?	6240
	24:20	upon it is the **guilt** of its r that it falls—	7322
	58: 1	to my people their r and to the house	7322
	59:13	r and treachery against the LORD,	7321
Jer	5: 6	for their r is great	7322
	28:16	you have preached r against the LORD.' "	6240
	29:32	because he has preached r against me.' "	6240
	33: 8	and will forgive all their sins of r	7321
Eze	21:24	by your open r, revealing your sins in all	7322
Da	8:12	Because of r, the host [of the saints] and	7322
	8:13	the r that causes desolation,	7322
Mt	26:55	"Am I **leading a r,** that you have come out	3334
Mk	14:48	"Am I **leading a r,**" said Jesus,	3334
Lk	22:52	who had come for him, "Am I **leading a r,**	3334
	23:14	who *was* **inciting** the people to r.	695
Jn	18:40	Barabbas **had taken part in a r.**	1639+3334
2Th	2: 3	until the r occurs and the man of lawlessness	686
Heb	3: 8	not harden your hearts as you did in the r,	4177
	3:15	not harden your hearts as you did in the r."	4177
Jude	1:11	they have been destroyed *in* Korah's r.	517

REBELLIOUS (42) [REBEL]

Nu	17:10	to be kept as a sign to the r.	1201+5308
Dt	9: 7	you have been r against the LORD.	5286
	9:24	You have been r against the LORD ever	5286
	21:18	If a man has a stubborn and r son who does	5286
	21:20	"This son of ours is stubborn and r.	5286
	31:27	For I know how r and stiff-necked you are.	5308
	31:27	If you have been r against the LORD	5286
1Sa	20:30	"You son of a perverse and r woman!	5280
Ezr	4:12	and are rebuilding that r and wicked city.	10439
	4:15	that this city is a r city,	10439
Ps	25: 7	not the sins of my youth and my r *ways;*	7322
	66: 7	let not the r rise up against him—	6253
	68: 6	but the r live in a sun-scorched land.	6253
	68:18	from men, even from the r—	6253
	78: 8	a stubborn and r generation,	5286
	107:11	through their r ways and suffered affliction	4784
Pr	24:21	my son, and do not join with the r,	9101
	28: 2	When a country is r, it has many rulers,	7322
Isa	30: 9	These are r people, deceitful children,	5308
	50: 5	and I *have* not *been* r,	5286
Jer	5:23	these people have stubborn and r hearts;	5286
La	1:20	for *I have been* **most** r.	5286+5286

Eze	2: 3	to a r nation that has rebelled against me;	5277
	2: 5	or fail to listen—for they are a r house—	5308
	2: 6	though they are a r house.	5308
	2: 7	or fail to listen, for they are r.	5308
	2: 8	Do not rebel like that r house;	5308
	3: 9	though they are a r house."	5308
	3:26	though they are a r house.	5308
	3:27	for they are a r house.	5308
	12: 2	you are living among a r people.	5308
	12: 2	for they are a r people.	5308
	12: 3	though they are a r house.	5308
	12: 9	did not that r house of Israel ask you,	5308
	12:25	For in your days, you r house,	5308
	17:12	"Say to this r house,	5308
	24: 3	Tell this r house a parable and say to them:	5308
	44: 6	Say to the r house of Israel,	5308
Hos	9:15	all their leaders *are* r.	6253
	14: 9	but the r stumble in them.	7321
Zep	3: 1	to the city of oppressors, r and defiled!	5286
Tit	1:10	For there are many r *people,*	538

REBELS (13) [REBEL]

Nu	20:10	and Moses said to them, "Listen, you r,	5286
Jos	1:18	Whoever r against your word and does	5286
1Ki	11:24	the leader of a **band of** r when David	1522
	11:24	the r went to Damascus,	NIH
Isa	1:23	Your rulers *are* r, companions of thieves;	6253
	1:28	But r and sinners will both be broken,	7321
	46: 8	fix it in mind, take it to heart, you r.	7321
	57: 4	Are you not a brood of r,	7322
Jer	6:28	They are all **hardened** r,	6073+6253
Da	8:23	when r have become completely wicked,	7321
Hos	5: 2	The r are deep in slaughter.	8473
Ro	13: 2	he who **against** the authority is rebelling	530
1Ti	1: 9	for the righteous but *for* lawbreakers and r,	538

REBIRTH (1) [BEAR]

Tit	3: 5	through the washing *of* r and renewal by	4098

REBUILD (27) [BUILD]

Jos	6:26	the man who undertakes *to* r this city,	1215
Ezr	5: 2	to work to r the house of God in Jerusalem.	10111
	5: 3	to r this temple and restore this structure?"	10111
	5: 9	to r this temple and restore this structure?"	10111
	5:13	King Cyrus issued a decree to r this house	10111
	5:15	And r the house of God on its site.'	10111
	5:17	in fact issue a decree to r this house of God	10111
	6: 7	the Jews and the Jewish elders r this house	10111
	9: 9	He has granted us new life to r the house	8123
Ne	2: 5	my fathers are buried so that *I can* r it."	1215
	2:17	Come, *let us* r the wall of Jerusalem,	1215
	4:10	so much rubble that we cannot r the wall."	1215
Ps	69:35	for God will save Zion and r the cities	1215
	102:16	For the LORD *will* r Zion and appear	1215
Isa	9:10	but we will r *with* dressed stone;	1215
	45:13	He *will* r my city and set my exiles free,	1215
	58:12	*Your people will* r the ancient ruins	1215
	60:10	"Foreigners *will* r your walls,	1215
	61: 4	*They will* r the ancient ruins and restore	1215
Jer	33: 7	and will r them as they were before.	1215
Da	9:25	the decree to restore and r Jerusalem until	1215
Am	9:14	*they will* r the ruined cities and live	1215
Mal	1: 4	we will r the ruins."	1215+2256+8740
Mt	26:61	the temple of God and r it in three days.' "	3868
Ac	15:16	this I will return and r David's fallen tent.	488
	15:16	Its ruins I will r, and I will restore it,	488
Gal	2:18	If *I* r what I destroyed,	3868+4099

REBUILDING (6) [BUILD]

Ezr	2:68	the r *of* the house of God on its site.	6641
	4:12	from you have gone to Jerusalem and *are* r	10111
	5:11	the God of heaven and earth, and we *are* r	10111
Ne	2:18	They replied, "Let us start r."	1215
	2:20	We his servants will start r, but as for you,	1215
	4: 1	When Sanballat heard that we *were* r	1215

REBUILT (42) [BUILD]

Nu	21:27	"Come to Heshbon and *let it* be r;	1215
	32:37	And the Reubenites r Heshbon,	1215
	32:38	They gave names to the cities *they* r.	1215
Dt	13:16	It is to remain a ruin forever, never *to* be r.	1215
Jdg	18:28	The Danites r the city and settled there.	1215
	21:23	and the r and towns and settled in them.	1215
1Ki	9:17	And Solomon r Gezer.)	1215
	16:34	In Ahab's time, Hiel of Bethel r Jericho.	1215
2Ki	14:22	the *one who* r Elath and restored it to Judah	1215
	15:35	Jotham r the Upper Gate of the temple of	1215
	21: 3	the r the high places his father Hezekiah	1215
	21: 3	had destroyed;	1215+2256+8740
2Ch	8: 2	Solomon r the villages tht Hiram had given	1215
	8: 5	He r Upper Beth Horon and Lower Beth	1215
	24:13	*They* r the temple of God according	6641
	26: 2	the *one who* r Elath and restored it to Judah	1215
	26: 6	He then r towns near Ashdod and elsewhere	1215
	27: 3	Jotham r the Upper Gate of the temple of	1215
	33: 3	He r the high places his father Hezekiah	1215
	33: 3	had demolished;	1215+2256+8740
	33:14	Afterward he r the outer wall of the City	1215
Ezr	4:21	that this city *will* not be r until I so order.	10111
	6: 3	*Let* the temple be r as a place	10111
Ne	3: 1	The Fish Gate *was* r by the sons	1215
	3: 3	They r it and put its doors and bolts	1215
	3:14	He r it and put its doors and bolts and bars	1215

Ne	3:15	He r it, roofing it over and putting its doors	1215
	4: 6	So *we* r the wall till all	1215
	6: 1	of our enemies that *I had* r the wall and not	1215
	7: 1	the wall *had been* r and I had set the doors	1215
	7: 4	and the houses *had* not yet *been* r.	1215
Job	12:14	What he tears down cannot be r;	1215
Isa	25: 2	*it will* never be r.	1215
	44:28	he will say of Jerusalem, "*Let it* be r,"	1215
Jer	30:18	the city *will* be r on her ruins,	1215
	31: 4	I will build you up again and *you will* be r,	1215
	31:38	"when this city *will* be r for me from	1215
Eze	26:14	You *will* never be r,	1215
	36:10	The towns will be inhabited and the ruins r.	1215
	36:33	and the ruins r.	1215
	36:36	the LORD *have* r what was destroyed,	1215
Da	9:25	*It will* be r with streets and a trench,	1215
Zec	1:16	and there my house *will* be r.	1215

REBUKE (61) [REBUKED, REBUKES, REBUKING]

Lev	19:17	R your neighbor **frankly**	3519+3519
Dt	28:20	and r in everything you put your hand to,	4486
Ru	2:16	and don't r her."	1721
1Sa	2:25	however, did not listen to their father's r,	7754
2Sa	22:16	the earth laid bare at the r *of* the LORD,	1722
2Ki	19: 3	a day of distress and r and disgrace,	9349
	19: 4	and that *he will* r him for the words	3519
Job	11: 3	*Will* no *one* r you when you mock?	4007
	13:10	He would **surely** r you	3519+3519
	20: 3	I hear a r *that* dishonors me,	4592
	26:11	pillars of the heavens quake, aghast at his r.	1722
Ps	6: 1	*do* not r me in your anger or discipline me	3519
	18:15	foundations of the earth laid bare at your r,	1722
	38: 1	*do* not r me in your anger or discipline me	3519
	39:11	You r and discipline men for their sin;	9350
	50: 8	*I do* not r you for your sacrifices	3519
	50:21	I will r you and accuse you to your face.	3519
	68:30	R the beast among the reeds,	1721
	76: 6	At your r, O God of Jacob, both horse and	1722
	80:16	at your r your people perish.	1722
	104: 7	But at your r the waters fled,	1722
	119:21	You r the arrogant,	1721
	141: 5	*let him* r me—it is oil on my head.	3519
Pr	1:23	If you had responded to my r,	9350
	1:25	and would not accept my r,	9350
	1:30	not accept my advice and spurned my r,	9350
	3:11	and do not resent his r,	9350
	9: 8	*Do* not r a mocker or he will hate you;	3519
	9: 8	r a wise man and he will love you.	3519
	13: 1	but a mocker does not listen to r.	1722
	15:31	to a life-giving r will be at home among	9350
	17:10	A r impresses a man	1722
	19:25	r a discerning man,	3519
	25:12	an ornament of fine gold is a wise man's r	3519
	27: 5	Better is open r than hidden love.	9350
	30: 6	or *he will* r you and prove you a liar.	3519
Ecc	7: 5	a wise man's r than to listen to the song	1722
Isa	37: 3	a day of distress and r and disgrace,	9349
	37: 4	and that *he will* r him for the words	3519
	50: 2	By a mere r I dry up the sea,	1722
	51:20	with the wrath of the LORD and the r	1722
	54: 9	never to r you again.	1721
	66:15	and his r with flames of fire.	1722
Jer	2:19	your backsliding *will* r you.	3519
Eze	3:26	be silent and unable *to* r them,	3519
	5:15	in anger and in wrath and with stinging r.	9350
Hos	2: 2	"R your mother, rebuke her,	8189
	2: 2	"Rebuke your mother, r her,	8189
Zec	3: 2	"The LORD r you, Satan!	1721
	3: 2	who has chosen Jerusalem, r you!	1721
Mal	2: 3	"Because of you I *will* r your descendants;	1721
Mt	16:22	Peter took him aside and began to r him.	2203
Mk	8:32	Peter took him aside and began *to* r him.	2203
Lk	17: 3	"If your brother sins, r him,	2203
	19:39	"Teacher, r your disciples!"	2203
1Ti	5: 1	*Do* not r an older man **harshly,**	2159
2Ti	4: 2	correct, r and encourage—	2203
Tit	1:13	Therefore, r them sharply,	1794
	2:15	Encourage and r with all authority.	1794
Jude	1: 9	but said, "The Lord r you!"	2203
Rev	3:19	Those whom I love *I* r and discipline.	1794

REBUKED (32) [REBUKE]

Ge	31:42	and last night *he* r you."	3519
	37:10	his father r him and said,	1721
1Sa	24: 7	With these words David r his men and did	9117
1Ch	16:21	for their sake *he* r kings;	3519
Ne	13:11	So *I* r the officials and asked them,	8189
	13:17	*I* r the nobles of Judah and said to them,	8189
	13:25	*I* r them and called curses down on them.	8189
Ps	9: 5	You *have* r the nations and destroyed	1721
	105:14	for their sake *he* r kings:	3519
	106: 9	He r the Red Sea, and it dried up;	1721
Mt	8:26	*he* got up and r the winds and the waves,	2203
	17:18	Jesus r the demon,	2203
	19:13	But the disciples r those who brought them.	2203
	20:31	The crowd r them and told them to	2203
Mk	4:39	*He* got up, r the wind and said to the waves,	2203
	8:33	and looked at his disciples, *he* r Peter.	2203
	9:25	*he* r the evil spirit.	2203
	10:13	but the disciples r them.	2203
	10:48	Many r him and told him to be quiet,	2203
	14: 5	And *they* r her **harshly.**	1839
	16:14	he r them for their lack of faith	3943
Lk	3:19	But *when* John r Herod the tetrarch because	1794

Lk 4:39 So he bent over her and r the fever, 2203
4:41 But he r them and would not allow them 2203
8:24 up and r the wind and the raging waters; 2203
9:42 But Jesus r the evil spirit, 2203
9:55 But Jesus turned and r them, 2203
18:15 When the disciples saw this, they r them. 2203
18:39 Those who led the way r him and told him 2203
23:40 But the other criminal r him. 2203
1Ti 5:20 Those who sin are to be r publicly, 1794
2Pe 2:16 he was r for his wrongdoing by a donkey— 1792+2400

REBUKES (8) [REBUKE]
Job 22:4 "Is it for your piety that he r you 3519
Ps 2:5 Then he r them in his anger 1819
Pr 9:7 whoever r a wicked man incurs abuse. 3519
28:23 He who r a man will in 3519
29:1 after many r will suddenly be destroyed— 9350
Isa 17:13 when he r them they flee far away, 1721
Na 1:4 He r the sea and dries it up; 1721
Heb 12:5 and do not lose heart when he r you, 1794

REBUKING (2) [REBUKE]
Ps 57:3 r those who hotly pursue me; 3070
2Ti 3:16 r, correcting and training in righteousness, 1791

RECAB (13) [RECABITE, RECABITES]
2Sa 4:2 One was named Baanah and the other R; 8209
4:5 Now R and Baanah, 8209
4:6 R and his brother Baanah slipped away. 8209
4:9 David answered R and his brother Baanah, 8209
2Ki 10:15 he came upon Jehonadab son of R, 8209
10:23 Then Jehu and Jehonadab son of R went 8209
1Ch 2:55 the father of the house of R. 8209
Ne 3:14 by Malkijah son of R, 8209
Jer 35:6 Jonadab son of R gave us this command: 8209
35:8 Jonadab son of R commanded us. 8209
35:14 son of R ordered his sons not to drink wine 8209
35:16 of Jonadab son of R have carried out 8209
35:19 'Jonadab son of R will never fail to have 8209

RECABITE (2) [RECAB]
Jer 35:2 the R family and invite them to come to one 8211
35:5 the men of the R family and said to them, 8211

RECABITES (2) [RECAB]
Jer 35:3 the whole family of the R. 8211
35:18 Then Jeremiah said to the family of the R, 8211

RECAH (1)
1Ch 4:12 These were the men of R. 8212

RECALL (1) [RECALLED, RECALLING]
2Pe 3:2 I want you to r the words spoken in the 3630

RECALLED (3) [RECALL]
Isa 63:11 Then his people r the days of old, 2349
Eze 23:19 and more promiscuous as she r the days 2349
Jn 2:22 his disciples r what he had said. 3630

RECALLING (2) [RECALL]
Job 11:16 r it only as waters gone by. 2349
2Ti 1:4 R your tears, I long to see you, 3630

RECAPTURE (1) [CAPTURE]
Eze 14:5 I will do this to r the hearts of the people 9530

RECAPTURED (1) [CAPTURE]
2Ki 13:25 Jehoash son of Jehoahaz r from Ben-Hadad
son of Hazael 2256+4374+8740

RECEDE (1) [RECEDED]
Ge 8:5 The waters continued to r until the tenth 2893

RECEDED (5) [RECEDE]
Ge 8:1 and the waters r. 8896
8:3 The water r steadily from the earth.
2143+2256+8740+8740
8:8 to see if the water had r from the surface of 7837
8:11 Then Noah knew that the water had r from 7837
Rev 6:14 The sky r like a scroll, rolling up, 714

RECEIPT OF CUSTOM (KJV) See TAX
COLLECTOR'S BOOTH, TAX BOOTH

RECEIVE (104) [RECEIVED, RECEIVES, RECEIVING, RECEPTION]
Ge 4:11 to r your brother's blood from your hand. 4374
32:20 when I see him, perhaps he will r me." 5951+7156
Ex 25:2 You are to r the offering for me 4374
25:3 the offerings you are to r from them: 4374
30:16 R the atonement money from the Israelites. 4374
Nu 18:23 They will r no inheritance among 5706+5709
18:26 'When you r from the Israelites. 4374
18:28 from all the tithes you r from the Israelites. 4374
26:54 to r its inheritance according to the number 5989
32:19 We will not r any inheritance with them on 5706

Dt 9:9 up on the mountain to r the tablets of stone, 4374
19:14 in the inheritance you r in the land 5706
33:3 and from you r instruction, 5951
2Ki 12:5 Let every priest r the money from one of 4374
Ne 10:38 the Levites when they r the tithes, 6923
Job 7:11 Why were these knees to r me 7709
35:7 or what does he r from your hand? 4374
Ps 24:5 He will r blessing from the LORD 5951
27:10 the LORD will r me. 665
110:3 the dawn you will r the dew of your youth. 4200
Pr 11:31 If the righteous r their due on earth, 8966
28:10 the blameless will r a good inheritance. 5706
Ecc 6:3 and does not r proper burial, 2118+4200
8:10 and r praise in the city where they did this. 8655
Isa 50:11 This is what you shall r from my hand 2118+4200
61:7 Instead of their shame my people will r NIH
Eze 16:61 and be ashamed when you r your sisters, 4374
Da 2:6 you will r from me gifts and rewards 10618
7:18 But the saints of the Most High will r 10618
11:34 they fall, they will r a little help, 6468+6469
12:13 you will r your allotted inheritance." NIH
Hos 14:2 "Forgive all our sins and r us graciously, 4374
Mt 10:41 a prophet because he is a prophet will r 3284
10:41 because he is a righteous man will r 3284
11:5 The blind r sight, the lame walk, 329
19:29 for my sake will r a hundred times as much 3284
20:10 they expected to r more. 3284
21:22 you will r whatever you ask for 3284
Mk 4:16 hear the word and at once r it with joy. 3284
10:15 anyone who will not r the kingdom 1312
10:30 will fail to r a hundred times as much 3284
Lk 7:22 The blind r sight, the lame walk, 329
8:13 on the rock are the ones who r the word 1312
8:17 anyone who will not r the kingdom 1312
18:30 to r many times as much in this age and, 655
18:42 Jesus said to him, "R your sight; 329
Jn 1:11 but his own did not r him. 4161
3:27 "A man can r only what is given him 3284
7:39 those who believed in him were later to r. 3284
16:24 Ask and you will r, 3284
20:22 "R the Holy Spirit. 3284
Ac 1:8 But you will r power when the Holy Spirit 3284
2:38 And you will r the gift of the Holy Spirit. 3284
7:59 Stephen prayed, "Lord Jesus, r my spirit." 1312
8:15 for them that they might r the Holy Spirit, 3284
8:19 on whom I lay my hands may r the 3284
19:2 "Did you r the Holy Spirit when you 3284
19:3 "Then what baptism did you r?" 966
19:25 "Men, you know we r a good income 1639
20:35 'It is more blessed to give than to r.' " 3284
22:13 'Brother Saul, r your sight!' 329
26:18 so that they may r forgiveness of sins and 3284
Ro 5:17 much more will those who r God's
abundant provision of grace 3284
8:15 not r a spirit that makes you a slave again 3284
11:31 in order that they too may now r mercy as 1796
16:2 to r her in the Lord in a way worthy of 4657
1Co 3:14 he will r his reward. 3284
4:5 that time each will r his praise from God. 1181
4:7 What do you have that you did not r? 3284
4:7 And if you did r it, 3284
9:14 the gospel should r their living from 2409
2Co 5:10 that each one may r what is due him for 3152
6:1 not to r God's grace in vain. 1312
6:17 Touch no unclean thing, and I will r you." 1654
11:4 or if you r a different spirit from 3284
11:16 you do, then r me just as you would a fool, 1312
Gal 1:12 I did not r it from any man, 4161
3:2 Did you r the Spirit by observing the law, 3284
3:14 by faith we might r the promise of the Spirit 3284
4:5 that we might r the full rights of sons. 655
Php 2:19 that I also may be cheered when I r news 1182
Col 3:24 that you will r an inheritance from 655
1Th 5:9 to suffer wrath but to r salvation 4348
1Ti 1:16 believe on him and r eternal life. NIG
2Ti 2:5 he does not r the victor's crown 5110
2:6 be the first to r a share of the crops. 3561
Heb 4:16 so that we may r mercy and find grace 3284
9:15 that those who are called may r the 3284
10:36 you will r what he has promised. 3152
11:8 a place he would later r as his inheritance, 3284
11:13 They did not r the things promised; 3152
11:19 he did r Isaac back from death. 3152
Jas 1:7 not think he will r anything from the Lord; 3284
1:12 he will r the crown of life 3284
4:3 When you ask, you do not r, 3284
1Pe 2:20 how is it to your credit if you r a beating 3139
5:4 you will r the crown of glory 3152
2Pe 1:11 and you will r a rich welcome into 2220
1Jn 3:22 and r from him anything we ask, 3284
Rev 4:11 to r glory and honor and power, 3284
5:12 the Lamb, who was slain, to r power 3284
13:16 to r a mark on his right hand or the 1443
17:12 but who for one hour will r authority 3284
18:4 so that you will not r any of her plagues; 3284

RECEIVED (142) [RECEIVE]
Ge 33:10 now that you have r me favorably. 8354
43:23 I r your silver." 448+995
47:22 because they r a regular allotment 4200
Ex 18:2 his father-in-law Jethro r her 4374
36:3 They r from Moses all the offerings 4374
Nu 23:20 I have r a command to bless; 4374
26:62 because they r no inheritance among them. 5989
32:18 until every Israelite has r his inheritance. 5706
34:14 of Manasseh have r their inheritance. 4374

Nu 34:15 and a half tribes have r their inheritance on 4374
Dt 18:8 even though he has r money from the sale NIH
Jos 13:8 the Reubenites and the Gadites had r 4374
14:1 the areas the Israelites r as an inheritance 5706
14:4 The Levites r no share of the land 5989
16:4 of Joseph, r their inheritance. 5706
17:1 who had r Gilead and Bashan because 2118+4200
17:6 of the tribe of Manasseh r an inheritance 5706
18:2 not yet r their inheritance. 2745
18:7 Manasseh have already r their inheritance 4374
19:9 the Simeonites r their inheritance within 5706
21:7 r twelve towns from the tribes of Reuben, 4200
21:23 Also from the tribe of Dan they r Eltekeh, NIH
21:25 the tribe of Manasseh they r Taanach NIH
1Ki 5:8 "I have r the message you sent me 9048
10:14 that Solomon r yearly was 666 talents, 995+4200
2Ki 12:4 the census, the money r from personal vows AIT
19:9 Now Sennacherib r a report that Tirhakah, 9048
19:14 Hezekiah r the letter from the messengers 4374
20:13 Hezekiah r the messengers 9048
1Ch 6:71 The Gershonites r the following: 4200
6:71 of the half-tribe of Manasseh they r Golan NIH
6:72 from the tribe of Issachar they r Kedesh, NIH
6:74 from the tribe of Asher they r Mashal, NIH
6:76 from the tribe of Naphtali they r Kedesh NIH
6:77 (the rest of the Levites) r the following: 4200
6:77 From the tribe of Zebulun they r Jokneam, NIH
6:78 the Jordan east of Jericho they r Bezer in NIH
6:80 the tribe of Gad they r Ramoth in Gilead, NIH
11:6 and so he r the command. 2118
12:18 So David r them and made them leaders 7691
2Ch 9:13 gold that Solomon r yearly was 666 talents, 995
21:12 Jehoram r a letter from Elijah the prophet,
448+995
Ezr 5:5 to Darius and his written reply be r. 10754
8:30 the priests and Levites r the silver and gold 7691
Est 2:3 and recognition has Mordecai r for this?" 6913
Job 15:18 hiding nothing r from their fathers 4946
Ps 68:18 you r gifts from men, 4374
Isa 37:1 Now Sennacherib r a report that Tirhakah, 9048
37:14 Hezekiah r the letter from the messengers 4374
39:2 Hezekiah r the envoys gladly 6584+8523
40:2 that she has r from the LORD's hand 4374
47:13 counsel you have r has only worn you out! AIT
Hab 1:1 The oracle that Habakkuk the prophet r. 2600
Mt 6:2 they have r their reward in full. 600
6:5 they have r their reward in full. 600
6:16 they have r their reward in full. 600
10:8 Freely you have r, freely give. 3284
13:20 r the seed that fell on the rocky places 5062
13:22 r the seed that fell among the thorns 5062
13:23 r the seed that fell on good soil 5062
15:5 'Whatever help you might otherwise have r NIG
20:9 about the eleventh hour came and each r 3284
20:10 But each one of them also r a denarius, 3284
20:11 When they r it, they began to grumble 3284
20:34 Immediately they r their sight 329
25:16 The man who had r the five talents went 3284
25:18 the man who had r the one talent went off, 3284
25:20 The man who had r the five talents brought 3284
25:24 the man who had r the one talent came. 3284
25:27 that when I returned I would have r it back 3152
Mk 7:11 help you might otherwise have r 6067
10:52 Immediately he r his sight 329
11:24 believe that you have r it, 3284
Lk 6:24 for you have already r your comfort. 600
16:25 in your lifetime you r your good things, 655
16:25 while Lazarus r bad things, NIG
18:43 Immediately he r his sight 329
Jn 1:12 Yet to all who r him, 3284
1:16 of his grace we have all r one blessing 3284
9:15 also asked him how he had r his sight. 329
9:18 that he had been blind and had r his sight 329
10:18 This command I r from my Father." 3284
19:30 When he had r the drink, Jesus said, 3284
Ac 2:33 he has r from the Father the promised 3284
5:3 for yourself some of the money you r for NIG
7:38 and he r living words to pass on to us. 1312
7:45 Having r the tabernacle, 1342
7:53 you who have r the law that was put 3284
8:17 and they r the Holy Spirit. 3284
10:47 They have r the Holy Spirit just 3284
11:1 the Gentiles also had r the word of God. 1312
17:11 for they r the message with great eagerness 1312
17:17 at Jerusalem, the brothers r us warmly. 622
21:40 r the commander's permission, 2205
28:21 "We have not r any letters from Judea 1312
Ro 1:5 we r grace and apostleship to call people 3284
1:27 and r in themselves the due penalty 655
4:11 And he r the sign of circumcision, 3284
4:13 Abraham and his offspring r the promise NIG
5:11 whom we have now r reconciliation. 3284
8:15 you r the Spirit of sonship. 3284
11:30 to God have now r mercy as a result 1796
15:28 that they have r this fruit, NIG
1Co 2:12 We have not r the spirit of the world but 3284
6:19 whom you have r from God? NIG
11:23 For I r from the Lord what I also passed on 4161
15:1 which you r and on which you have taken 4161
15:3 For what I r I passed on to you as of first 4161
2Co 1:12 the comfort we ourselves have r from God. 4151
11:4 a different spirit from the one you r, 3284
11:24 Five times I r from the Jews 3284
Gal 1:12 I r it by revelation from Jesus Christ. NIG
Eph 4:1 a life worthy of the calling you have r. 2813+3104
Php 4:9 Whatever you have learned or r or heard 4161
4:18 I have r full payment and even more; 600

Php	4:18	I am amply supplied, now that *I have* **r**	1312
Col	2: 6	So then, just as *you* **r** Christ Jesus as Lord,	4161
	4:10	*(You have* **r** instructions about him;	3284
	4:17	to it that you complete the work *you have* **r**	4161
1Th	2:13	when *you* **r** the word of God,	4161
2Th	3: 6	according to the teaching *you* **r** from us.	4161
1Ti	3: 6	God created to **be r with** thanksgiving	3562
	4: 4	to be rejected *if it is* **r** with thanksgiving,	3284
Heb	2: 2	and disobedience **r** its just punishment,	3284
	6:15	Abraham **r** what was promised.	2209
	8: 6	But the ministry Jesus *has* **r** is as superior	5593
	10:26	on sinning *after we have* **r** the knowledge of	3284
	10:32	*after you had* **r** the **light,**	5894
	11:17	He who *had* **r** the promises was about	346
	11:35	Women **r** back their dead,	3284
	11:39	none of them **r** what had been promised.	3152
1Pe	2:10	once you *had* **r** **mercy,**	1796
	2:10	but now *you have* **r** **mercy.**	1796
	4:10	Each one should use whatever gift *he has* **r**	3284
2Pe	1: 1	of our God and Savior Jesus Christ *have* **r**	3275
	1:17	For *he* **r** honor and glory from God	3284
1Jn	2:27	anointing *you* **r** from him remains in you,	3284
Rev	2:27	just as I *have* **r** authority from my Father;	3284
	3: 3	therefore, what *you have* **r** and heard;	3284
	17:12	not yet **r** a kingdom,	3284
	19:20	With these signs he had deluded those who	
		had **r** the mark	3284
	20: 4	and *had* not **r** his mark on their foreheads	3284

RECEIVES (21) [RECEIVE]

Job	27:13	heritage a ruthless man **r** from the Almighty	4374
Pr	8:35	For whoever finds me finds life and **r** favor	7049
	18:22	a wife finds what is good and **r** favor from	7049
	27:21	but man is tested by the **praise** he **r**.	AIT
	28:27	to them **r** many curses.	NIH
Eze	16:33	Every prostitute **r** a fee,	4200+5989
Mt	7: 8	For everyone who asks **r**;	3284
	10:40	"He who **r** you receives me,	1312
	10:40	"He who receives you **r** me,	1312
	10:40	he who **r** me receives the one who sent me.	1312
	10:40	he who receives me **r** the one who sent me.	1312
	10:41	Anyone who **r** a prophet because he is	1312
	10:41	and anyone who **r** a righteous man	1312
	13:20	the word and at once **r** it with joy.	3284
Lk	11:10	For everyone who asks **r**;	3284
Ac	10:43	in him **r** forgiveness of sins	3284
Gal	6: 6	who **r** instruction in the word	2994
Heb	6: 7	for whom it is farmed **r** the blessing	3561
Rev	2:17	known only to him who **r** it.	3284
	14: 9	the beast and his image and **r** his mark on	3284
	14:11	or for anyone who **r** the mark of his name."	3284

RECEIVES (Anglicized) See also GETS

RECEIVING (9) [RECEIVE]

2Sa	16:12	with good for the cursing I am **r** today."	NIH
Ac	16:24	Upon **r** such orders,	3284
Ro	9: 4	the covenants, the **r of the law,**	3792
2Co	7:15	**r** him with fear and trembling.	1312
	11: 8	*by* **r** support from them so as to serve you.	3284
Php	4:15	the matter of giving and **r**, except you only;	3331
Heb	12:28	*we are* **r** a kingdom that cannot be shaken,	4161
1Pe	1: 9	for *you are* **r** the goal of your faith,	3152
3Jn	1: 7	**r** no help from the pagans.	3284

RECENT (1) [RECENTLY]

1Ti	3: 6	He must not be a **r convert,**	3745

RECENTLY (4) [RECENT]

Dt	24: 5	If a man has **r** married,	2543
	32:17	*They* **r** the righteous acts of the LORD,	2543+4946+7940
Jer	34:15	**R** you repented and did what is right	2021+3427
Ac	18: 2	who had **r** come from Italy	4711

RECEPTION (1) [RECEIVE]

1Th	1: 9	report what kind of **r** you gave us.	1658

RECESSES (2)

Job	28: 3	he searches the **farthest r** for ore in	3972+9417
	38:16	the sea or walked in the **r** *of* the deep?	2984

RECHAB, RECHABITES (KJV) See RECAB, RECABITE

RECHAH (KJV) See RECAH

RECITE (4) [RECITED, RECITING]

Dt	27:14	Levites *shall* **r** to all the people	606+2256+6699
Jdg	5:11	*They* **r** the righteous acts of the LORD,	5989
Ps	45: 1	a noble theme *as* I **r** my verses for the king;	606
	50:16	"What right have you to **r** my laws	6218

RECITED (1) [RECITE]

Dt	31:30	And Moses **r** the words of this song	1819

RECITING (1) [RECITE]

Dt	32:45	When Moses finished **r** all these words	1819

RECKLESS (5)

Nu	22:32	to oppose you because your path *is a* **r** one	3740
Jdg	9: 4	Abimelech used it to hire **r** adventurers,	8199
Pr	12:18	**R words** pierce like a sword,	1051
	14:16	but a fool is hotheaded and **r**.	1053
Jer	23:32	and lead my people astray with their **r** lies,	7071

RECKONED (7) [RECKONING]

Ge	21:12	through Isaac that your offspring *will* **be r**.	7924
	48: 5	in Egypt before I came to you here will be **r**	NIH
	48: 6	in the territory they inherit *they* **will be r**	7924
Nu	18:27	Your offering *will* **be r** to you as grain	3108
	18:30	*it will* **be r** to you as the product of	3108
Ro	9: 7	through Isaac that your offspring *will* **be r**."	2813
Heb	11:18	through Isaac that your offspring *will* **be r**."	2813

RECKONING (3) [RECKONED]

Isa	10: 3	What will you do on the day of **r**,	7213
Hos	5: 9	Ephraim will be laid waste on the day of **r**.	9349
	9: 7	the days of **r** are at hand.	8936

RECLAIM (1) [CLAIM]

Isa	11:11	a second time to **r** the remnant that is left	7864

RECLAIMED (1) [CLAIM]

Est	8: 2	which *he had* **r** from Haman,	6296

RECLINE (1) [RECLINED, RECLINING]

Lk	12:37	**have** them **r at the table**	369

RECLINED (3) [RECLINE]

Lk	7:36	to the Pharisee's house and **r at the table.**	2884
	11:37	so *he* went in and **r at the table.**	404
	22:14	Jesus and his apostles **r at the table.**	404

RECLINING (7) [RECLINE]

Est	7: 8	on the couch where Esther was **r**.	6584
Mt	26: 7	on his head *as he was* **r at the table.**	367
	26:20	Jesus *was* **r at the table** with the Twelve.	367
Mk	14: 3	**r at the table** in the home of a man known	2879
	14:18	*While* they *were* **r at the table** eating,	367
Jn	12: 2	among those **r at the table** with him.	367
	13:23	whom Jesus loved, was **r** next to him.	367

RECOGNITION (3) [RECOGNIZE]

Est	6: 3	"What honor and **r** has Mordecai received	1525
1Co	16:18	Such men *deserve* **r**.	2105
1Ti	5: 3	**Give** proper **r** to those widows who	5506

RECOGNIZE (16) [RECOGNITION, RECOGNIZED, RECOGNIZES, RECOGNIZING]

Ge	27:23	*He did* not **r** him,	5795
	38:25	"See if *you* **r** whose seal and cord	5795
	42: 8	they *did* not **r** him.	5795
Dt	33: 9	*He did* not **r** his brothers	5795
1Sa	24:11	Now understand and **r** that I am not guilty	8011
Job	2:12	*they* could hardly **r** him;	5795
Mt	7:16	By their fruit *you will* **r** them.	2105
	7:20	Thus, by their fruit *you will* **r** them.	2105
	17:12	and *they* did not **r** him,	2105
Lk	19:44	not **r** the time of God's coming to you."	1182
Jn	1:10	the world *did* not **r** him.	1182
	10: 5	because *they do* not **r** a stranger's voice."	3857
Ac	13:27	and their rulers *did* not **r** Jesus,	51
	27:39	*they* did not **r** the land,	2105
1Jn	4: 2	This is how *you can* **r** the Spirit of God:	1182
	4: 6	how *we* **r** the Spirit of truth and the spirit	1182

RECOGNIZED (24) [RECOGNIZE]

Ge	37:33	*He* **r** it and said, "It is my son's robe!	5795
	38:26	Judah **r** them and said,	5795
	42: 7	soon as Joseph saw his brothers, *he* **r** them,	5795
	42: 8	Although Joseph **r** his brothers,	5795
Jdg	18: 3	they **r** the voice of the young Levite;	5795
Ru	3:14	but got up before anyone *could* **be r**;	5795
1Sa	3:20	**r** that Samuel was attested as a prophet	3359
	26:17	Saul **r** David's voice and said,	5795
1Ki	14: 2	so you won't *be* **r** as the wife of Jeroboam.	3359
	18: 7	Obadiah **r** him, bowed down to the ground,	5795
	20:41	king of Israel **r** him as one of the prophets.	5795
Jer	28: 9	the prophet who prophesies peace *will* **be r**	3359
La	4: 8	*they* **are** not **r** in the streets.	5795
Mt	12:33	for a tree is **r** by its fruit.	1182
	14:35	And *when* the men of that place **r** Jesus,	2105
Mk	6:33	But many who saw them leaving **r** them	2105
	6:54	as they got out of the boat, *people* **r** Jesus.	2105
Lk	6:44	Each tree is **r** by its own fruit.	1182
	24:31	their eyes were opened and *they* **r** him,	2105
	24:35	how Jesus *was* **r** by them when he broke	1182
Ac	3:10	*they* **r** him as the same man who used	2105
	12:14	When she **r** Peter's voice,	2105
Ro	7:13	But in order that sin *might be* **r** as sin,	5743
Gal	2: 9	of fellowship *when they* **r** the grace given	1182

RECOGNIZES (1) [RECOGNIZE]

Job	11:11	Surely he **r** deceitful men;	3359

RECOGNIZING (2) [RECOGNIZE]

Lk	24:16	but they were kept from **r** him.	2105
1Co	11:29	For anyone who eats and drinks without **r**	1359

RECOIL (1) [RECOILS]

Ps	54: 5	*Let* evil **r** on those who slander me;	8740

RECOILS (1) [RECOIL]

Ps	7:16	The trouble he causes **r** on himself;	8740

RECOMMENDATION (1) [RECOMMENDED]

2Co	3: 1	letters *of* **r** to you or from you?	5364

RECOMMENDED (1) [RECOMMENDATION]

Est	6:10	Do not neglect anything *you have* **r**."	1819

RECOMPENSE (2)

Isa	40:10	and his **r** accompanies him.	7190
	62:11	and his **r** accompanies him.' "	7190

RECONCILE (3) [RECONCILED, RECONCILIATION, RECONCILING]

Ac	7:26	*He tried to* **r** them by saying,	1645+1650+5261
Eph	2:16	*to* **r** both of them to God through the cross,	639
Col	1:20	and through him *to* **r** to himself all things,	639

RECONCILED (8) [RECONCILE]

Mt	5:24	First go and *be* **r** to your brother;	1367
Lk	12:58	try hard *to be* **r** to him on the way,	557
Ro	5:10	*we were* **r** to him through the death	2904
	5:10	how much more, *having been* **r**,	2904
1Co	7:11	she must remain unmarried or else *be* **r**	2904
2Co	5:18	who **r** us to himself through Christ	2904
	5:20	on Christ's behalf: *Be* **r** to God.	2904
Col	1:22	now *he has* **r** you by Christ's physical body	639

RECONCILIATION (4) [RECONCILE]

Ro	5:11	through whom we have now received **r**.	2903
	11:15	For if their rejection is the **r** of the world,	2903
2Co	5:18	and gave us the ministry *of* **r**:	2903
	5:19	he has committed to us the message *of* **r**.	2903

RECONCILING (1) [RECONCILE]

2Co	5:19	God was **r** the world to himself in Christ,	2904

RECONSECRATED (1) [CONSECRATE]

Da	8:14	then the sanctuary *will* **be r**."	7405

RECONSIDER (2) [CONSIDER]

Job	6:29	**r**, for my integrity is at stake.	6388+8740
Jer	18:10	then *I will* **r** the good I had intended	5714

RECORD (16) [RECORDED, RECORDER, RECORDS]

1Ch	4:33	And *they* kept a genealogical **r**.	3509
	5: 1	*could* not **be** listed in the genealogical **r**	3509
	7: 7	genealogical **r** listed 22,034 fighting men.	3509
	7: 9	Their genealogical **r** listed the heads	9352
2Ch	24:27	and the **r** of the restoration of the temple	NIH
Ne	7: 5	the genealogical **r** *of* those who had been	6219
Est	6: 1	the **r** of his reign,	1821
Ps	56: 8	**R** my lament; list my tears on your	6218
	56: 8	are they not in your **r**?	6225
	87: 4	"I will **r** Rahab and Babylon	2349
	130: 3	If *you*, O LORD, **kept a r** of sins, O Lord,	9068
Jer	22:30	"**R** this man as if childless,	4180
Eze	24: 2	**r** this date, this very date,	4180+9005
Hos	13:12	his sins are **kept on r**.	7621
Mt	1: 1	A **r** of the genealogy of Jesus Christ the son	1047
1Co	13: 5	it keeps no **r** of wrongs.	3357

RECORDED (22) [RECORD]

Ex	38:21	which *were* **r** at Moses' command by	7212
Nu	33: 2	the LORD's command Moses **r** the stages	4180
Dt	28:61	and disaster not **r** in this Book of the Law,	4180
Jos	24:26	And Joshua **r** these things in the Book of	4180
1Ki	8: 5	*that they* could not **be r** or counted.	6218
1Ch	9: 1	All Israel was listed in the genealogies **r** in	4180
	24: 6	**r** their names in the presence of the king	4180
2Ch	5: 6	*that they* could not **be r** or counted.	6218
	20:34	which *are* **r** in the book of the kings	6590
	26:22	*are* **r** by the prophet Isaiah son of Amoz.	4180
	31:19	all *who* **were r** in the genealogies	3509
Ezr	8:34	and the entire weight **was r** at that time.	4180
Ne	12:22	**were r** in the reign of Darius the Persian.	4180
	12:23	of Eliashib *were* **r** in the book of the annals	4180
Est	2:23	All this *was* **r** in the book of the annals in	4180
	6: 2	It was found *r* there that Mordecai	4180
	9:20	Mordecai **r** these events,	4180
Job	19:23	"Oh, that my words *were* **r**,	4180
Isa	4: 3	all who *are* **r** among the living	4180
Jer	51:60	all that *had* *been* **r** concerning Babylon.	4180
Jn	20:30	which are not **r** in this book.	1211
Rev	20:12	to what they had done as **r** in the books.	1211

RECORDER (9) [RECORD]

2Sa	8:16	Jehoshaphat son of Ahilud *was* r;	4654
	20:24	Jehoshaphat son of Ahilud was r;	4654
1Ki	4: 3	Jehoshaphat son of Ahilud—r;	4654
2Ki	18:18	Joah son of Asaph the r went out to them.	4654
	18:37	and Joah son of Asaph the r went	4654
1Ch	18:15	Jehoshaphat son of Ahilud was r;	4654
2Ch	34: 8	with Joah son of Joahaz, the r,	4654
Isa	36: 3	Joah son of Asaph the r went out to him.	4654
	36:22	Joah son of Asaph the r went to Hezekiah,	4654

RECORDS (35) [RECORD]

Ge	41:49	it was so much that he stopped **keeping r**	6218
Ex	6:16	of the sons of Levi according to their r:	9352
	6:19	the clans of Levi according to their r.	9352
Nu	1:20	by one, according to the r *of* their clans	9352
	1:22	by one, according to the r *of* their clans	9352
	1:24	by name, according to the r of their clans	9352
	1:26	by name, according to the r of their clans	9352
	1:28	by name, according to the r of their clans	9352
	1:30	by name, according to the r of their clans	9352
	1:32	by name, according to the r of their clans	9352
	1:34	by name, according to the r of their clans	9352
	1:36	by name, according to the r of their clans	9352
	1:38	by name, according to the r of their clans	9352
	1:40	by name, according to the r of their clans	9352
	1:42	by name, according to the r of their clans	9352
Ru	4:10	among his family or from the **town** r.	5226+9133
1Ch		(These r are from ancient times.)	1821
	5: 7	listed according to their **genealogical r:**	9352
	5:17	were entered in the **genealogical r**	3509
	26:31	to the **genealogical r** of their families.	9352
	26:31	a search was made in the r,	NIH
	29:29	they are written in the r *of* Samuel the seer,	1821
	29:29	the r *of* Nathan the prophet and the records	1821
	29:29	and the r *of* Gad the seer,	1821
2Ch	9:29	not written in the r *of* Nathan the prophet,	1821
	12:15	the r *of* Shemaiah the prophet and of Iddo	1821
	31:16	**names** were in the **genealogical r—**	3509
	31:17	**enrolled** by their families **in the** **genealogical r**	3509
	31:18	**listed** in *these* **genealogical r.**	3509
	33:19	all are written in the r *of* the seers.	1821
Ezr	2:62	These searched for their family r,	4181
	4:15	In these r you will find that this city	10177+10515
Ne	7:64	These searched for their family, r,	4181
Est	9:32	and it was written down in the r.	6219
Eze	13: 9	or be listed in the r of the house of Israel,	4181

RECOUNT (3) [RECOUNTED]

Ps	40: 5	The things you planned for us no *one can* r	6885
	79:13	to generation *we will* r your praise.	6218
	119:13	With my lips *I* r all the laws that come	6218

RECOUNTED (1) [RECOUNT]

Ps	119:26	*I* r my ways and you answered me;	6218

RECOVER (13) [RECOVERED, RECOVERY]

2Ki	1: 2	to see if *I will* r from this injury."	2649
	8: 8	ask him, 'Will *I* r from this illness?' "	2649
	8: 9	'Will *I* r from this illness?' "	2649
	8:10	'*You will* **certainly** r';	2649+2649
	8:14	told me that *you would* **certainly** r."	2649+2649
	8:29	so King Joram returned to Jezreel to r from	8324
	9:15	but King Joram had returned to Jezreel to r	8324
	20: 1	you are going to die; *you will not* r."	2649
2Ch	14:13	of Cushites fell that they could not r;	4695
	22: 6	to r *from* the wounds they had inflicted	8324
Isa	38: 1	you are going to die; *you will not* r."	2649
	38:21	apply it to the boil, and *he will* r."	2649
Eze	7:13	The seller *will not* r the land he has sold	8740

RECOVERED (12) [RECOVER]

Ge	14:16	*He* r all the goods and brought back	8740
	38:12	When Judah *had* r **from** *his* **grief,**	5714
1Sa	30:18	David r everything the Amalekites had taken,	5911
	30:22	not share with them the plunder *we* r.	5911
2Sa	14:14	which cannot **be** r, so we must die.	665
2Ki	13:25	and so *he* r the Israelite towns.	8740
	14:28	how *he* r for Israel both Damascus	8740
	16: 6	of Aram r Elath for Aram by driving out	8740
	20: 7	so and applied it to the boil, and *he* r.	2649
Jer	41:16	the survivors from Mizpah whom *he had* r	8740
Eze	38: 8	a land *that has* r from war,	8740
Rev	18:14	and splendor have vanished, never *to be* r.'	2351

RECOVERY (4) [RECOVER]

Isa	38: 9	of Judah after his illness and r:	2649+2716+4946
	39: 1	because he had heard of his illness and r.	2616
Lk	4:18	the prisoners and r **of** sight for the blind,	330
Ro	11:11	Did they stumble so as to fall beyond r?	NIG

RECTANGULAR (2)

1Ki	7: 5	All the doorways had r frames,	8062
Eze	41:21	The outer sanctuary had a r doorframe.	8062

RED (54) [REDDISH]

Ge	25:25	The first to come out was r,	145
	25:30	"Quick, let me have some of that r stew!	137

Ex	10:19	the locusts and carried them into the R Sea.	6068
	13:18	around by the desert road toward the R Sea.	6068
	15: 4	are drowned in the R Sea.	6068
	15:22	the R Sea and they went into the Desert	6068
	23:31	from the R Sea to the Sea of the Philistines,	6068
	25: 5	ram skins **dyed** r and hides of sea cows;	131
	26:14	for the tent a covering of ram skins **dyed** r,	131
	35: 7	ram skins **dyed** r and hides of sea cows	131
	35:23	ram skins r or hides of sea cows	131
	36:19	for the tent a covering of ram skins **dyed** r,	131
	39:34	of ram skins **dyed** r, the covering of hides	131
Lev	11:14	the r kite, any kind of black kite,	1798
Nu	14:25	the desert along the route to the R Sea."	6068
	19: 2	Tell the Israelites to bring you a r heifer	137
	21: 4	along the route to the R Sea,	6068
	33:10	They left Elim and camped by the R Sea.	6068
	33:11	the R Sea and camped in the Desert of Sin.	6068
Dt	1:40	the desert along the route to the R Sea."	6068
	2: 1	the desert along the route to the R Sea,	6068
	11: 4	of the R Sea as they were pursuing you,	6068
	14:13	the r kite, the black kite, any kind of falcon,	8012
Jos	2:10	the LORD dried up the water of the R Sea	6068
	4:23	to the R Sea when he dried it up before us	6068
	24: 6	and horsemen as far as the R Sea.	6068
Jdg	11:16	Israel went through the desert to the R Sea	6068
1Ki	9:26	on the shore of the R Sea,	6068
2Ki	3:22	the water looked r—like blood.	137
Ne	9: 9	you heard their cry at the R Sea.	6068
Job	16:16	My face is r with weeping,	2813
Ps	106: 7	and they rebelled by the sea, the R Sea.	6068
	106: 9	He rebuked the R Sea, and it dried up;	6068
	106:22	of Ham and awesome deeds by the R Sea.	6068
	136:13	to him who divided the R Sea asunder	6068
	136:15	swept Pharaoh and his army into the R Sea;	6068
Pr	23:31	Do not gaze at wine when *it is* r,	131
Isa	1:18	though *they are* r as crimson,	131
	63: 2	Why are your garments r,	137
Jer	22:14	panels it with cedar and decorates it in r.	9266
	49:21	their cry will resound to the R Sea.	6068
Eze	23:14	figures of Chaldeans portrayed in r,	9266
Na	2: 3	The shields of his soldiers *are* r;	131
Zec	1: 8	there before me was a man riding a r horse!	137
	1: 8	Behind him were r, brown and white horses.	137
	6: 2	The first chariot had r horses,	137
Mt	16: 2	'It will be fair weather, for the sky *is* r,'	4793
	16: 3	'for the sky *is* r and overcast.'	4793
Ac	7:36	the R Sea and for forty years in the desert.	2261
Heb	11:29	the people passed through the R Sea as	2261
Rev	6: 4	another horse came out, a **fiery r** one.	4794
	6:12	the whole moon turned **blood** r,	135+6055
	9:17	Their breastplates were **fiery** r, dark blue,	4791
	12: 3	an enormous r dragon with seven heads	4794

REDDISH (2) [RED]

Lev	13:49	or any leather article, is greenish or r,	140
	14:37	and if it has greenish or r depressions	140

REDDISH-WHITE (4) [WHITE]

Lev	13:19	a white swelling or r spot appears,	140+4237
	13:24	r or white spot appears in the raw flesh	140+4237
	13:42	But if he has a r sore on his bald head	140+4237
	13:43	on his head or forehead is r like	140+4237

REDEEM (53) [KINSMAN-REDEEMER, KINSMAN-REDEEMERS, REDEEMABLE, REDEEMED, REDEEMER, REDEEMS, REDEMPTION]

Ex	6: 6	and *I will* r you with an outstretched arm	1457
	13:13	R with a lamb every firstborn donkey,	7009
	13:13	but if *you* do not r it, break its neck.	7009
	13:13	R every firstborn among your sons.	7009
	13:15	and r each of my firstborn sons.'	7009
	21:30	he may r his life by paying whatever	7018
	34:20	R the firstborn donkey with a lamb,	7009
	34:20	but if *you* do not r it, break its neck.	7009
	34:20	R all your firstborn sons.	7009
Lev	25:25	and r *what* his countryman has sold.	1457
	25:26	to r it for him but he himself prospers	1457
	25:26	and acquires sufficient means to r it,	1460
	25:29	During that time he may r it.	1460
	25:32	the **right to** r their houses in	1460
	25:48	One of his relatives *may* r him:	1457
	25:49	or any blood relative in his clan *may* r him.	1457
	25:49	Or if he prospers, *he may* r **himself.**	1457
	27:13	If the owner *wishes* to r the animal,	1457+1457
	27:19	who dedicates the field *wishes* to r it,	1457+1457
	27:20	If, however, *he does* not r the field,	1457
	27:27	If he does not r it,	1457
Nu	3:46	*To* r the 273 firstborn Israelites who exceed	7012
	18:15	But *you* **must** r every firstborn son	7009+7009
	18:16	*you must* r them at the redemption price	7009
	18:17	"But *you must* not r the firstborn of an ox,	7009
Ru	3:13	and in the morning if he wants to r, good;	1457
	3:13	to redeem, good; *let him* r.	1457
	4: 4	If *you will* r it, do so.	1457
	4: 4	"I will r it," he said.	1457
	4: 6	"Then I cannot r it because I might	1457
	4: 6	r it yourself.	1457
2Sa	7:23	on earth that God went out to r as a people	7009
1Ch	17:21	on earth whose God went out to r a people	7009
Ps	25:22	R Israel, O God, from all their troubles!	7009
	26:11	r me and be merciful to me.	7009
	31: 5	r me, O LORD, the God of truth.	7009
	44:26	r us because of your unfailing love.	7009

Ps	49: 7	No man *can* r the life of another or	7009+7009
	49:15	But God *will* r my life from the grave;	7009
	69:18	r me because of my foes.	7009
	119:134	R me from the oppression of men,	7009
	119:154	Defend my cause and r me;	1457
	130: 8	*He* himself *will* r Israel from all their sins.	7009
Jer	15:21	of the wicked and r you from the grasp of	7009
	31:11	the LORD will ransom Jacob and r them	1457
	32: 8	Since it is your right to r it and possess it,	1460
Hos	7:13	*to* r them but they speak lies against me.	7009
	13:14	*I will* r them from death.	1457
Mic	4:10	the LORD *will* r you out of the hand	1457
Zec	10: 8	Surely *I will* r them;	7009
Lk	24:21	the one who was going to r Israel.	3390
Gal	4: 5	to r those under law,	1973
Tit	2:14	to r us from all wickedness and to purify	3390

REDEEMABLE (1) [REDEEM]

Lev	25:33	So the property of the Levites *is* r—	1457

REDEEMED (45) [REDEEM]

Ex	15:13	the people you have r.	1457
	21: 8	he must let her be r.	7009
Lev	25:30	If *it is* not r before a full year has passed,	1457
	25:31	They can be r, and they are to be returned	1460
	25:54	" 'Even if *he* is not r in any of these ways,	1457
	27:20	*it can* never be r.	1457
	27:28	or family land—may be sold or r;	1457
	27:33	become holy and cannot be r.' "	1457
Nu	3:49	from those who exceeded the number r by	7009
Dt	7: 8	with a mighty hand and r you from the land	7009
	9:26	your own inheritance that *you* r	7009
	13: 5	who brought you out of Egypt and r you	7009
	15:15	in Egypt and the LORD your God r you.	7009
	21: 8	whom *you have* r, O LORD,	7009
	24:18	and the LORD your God r you from there.	7009
2Sa	7:23	whom *you* r from Egypt?	7009
1Ch	17:21	whom *you* r from Egypt?	7009
Ne	1:10	whom *you* r by your great strength	7009
Job	33:28	*He* r my soul from going down to the pit,	7009
Ps	71:23	I, whom *you have* r.	7009
	74: 2	the tribe of your inheritance, whom *you* r—	1457
	77:15	With your mighty arm *you* r your people,	1457
	78:42	the day *he* r them from the oppressor,	7009
	106:10	from the hand of the enemy *he* r them.	1457
	107: 2	Let the r of the LORD say this—	1457
	107: 2	those *he* r from the hand of the foe,	1457
Isa	1:27	Zion *will* be r with justice,	7009
	29:22	who r Abraham, says to the house of Jacob;	7009
	35: 9	But only the r will walk there,	1457
	43: 1	"Fear not, for *I have* r you;	1457
	44:22	Return to me, for *I have* r you."	1457
	44:23	for the LORD *has* r Jacob,	1457
	48:20	say, "The LORD *has* r his servant Jacob."	1457
	51:10	of the sea so that *he* r might cross over?	1457
	52: 3	and without money *you will* be r."	1457
	52: 9	*he* has r Jerusalem.	1457
	62:12	called the Holy People, the R of the LORD;	1457
	63: 9	In his love and mercy *he* r them;	1457
La	3:58	you took up my case; *you* r my life.	1457
Mic	6: 4	I brought *you* up out of Egypt and r you	7009
Lk	1:68	he has come and *has* r his people.	3391+4472
Gal	3:13	Christ r us **from** the curse of the law	1973
	3:14	He r us in order that the blessing given	NIG
1Pe	1:18	as silver or gold that *you were* r from	3390
Rev	14: 3	who *had been* r from the earth.	60

REDEEMER (17) [REDEEM]

Job	19:25	I know that my R lives,	1457
Ps	19:14	O LORD, my Rock and my R.	1457
	78:35	that God Most High was their R.	1457
Isa	41:14	your R, the Holy One of Israel.	1457
	43:14	your R, the Holy One of Israel:	1457
	44: 6	Israel's King and R, the LORD Almighty:	1457
	44:24	your R, who formed you in the womb:	1457
	47: 4	Our R—the LORD Almighty is his name—	1457
	48:17	your R, the Holy One of Israel:	1457
	49: 7	the R and Holy One of Israel—	1457
	49:26	I, the LORD, am your Savior, your R,	1457
	54: 5	the Holy One of Israel *is* your R;	1457
	54: 8	says the LORD your R.	1457
	59:20	"The R will come to Zion,	1457
	60:16	I, the LORD, am your Savior, your R,	1457
	63:16	our R from of old is your name.	1457
Jer	50:34	Yet their R is strong;	1457

REDEEMS (4) [REDEEM]

Lev	27:15	If the man who dedicates his house r it,	1457
	27:31	If a man r any of his tithe,	1457+1457
Ps	34:22	The LORD r his servants;	7009
	103: 4	who r your life from the pit	1457

REDEMPTION (23) [REDEEM]

Lev	25:24	you must provide for the r of the land.	1460
	25:29	the **right of** r a full year after its sale.	1460
	25:48	the **right of** r after he has sold himself.	1460
	25:51	for his r a larger share of the price paid	1460
	25:52	that and pay for his r accordingly.	1460
Nu	3:48	the r of the additional Israelites to Aaron	7012
	3:49	the r money from those who exceeded	7017
	3:51	the r money to Aaron and his sons,	7012
	18:16	at the r price set at five shekels of silver,	7009
Ru	4: 7	r and transfer of property to become final,	1460
Ps	111: 9	He provided r for his people;	7014

Ps	130: 7	and with him is full **r.**	7014
Isa	63: 4	and the year of my **r** has come.	1453
Lk	2:38	to all who were looking forward to the **r**	3391
	21:28	because your **r** is drawing near."	667
Ro	3:24	through the **r** that came by Christ Jesus.	667
	8:23	our adoption as sons, the **r** of our bodies.	667
1Co	1:30	that is, our righteousness, holiness and **r.**	667
Eph	1: 7	In him we have **r** through his blood,	667
	1:14	the **r** of those who are God's possession—	667
	4:30	you were sealed for the day of **r.**	667
Col	1:14	in whom we have **r,** the forgiveness of sins.	667
Heb	9:12	having obtained eternal **r.**	3391

REDOUND (KJV) See OVERFLOW

REDUCE (7) [REDUCED, REDUCES]

Ex	5: 8	don't **r** the quota.	1757
	5:19	to **r** the number of bricks required of you	1757
2Ki	10:32	In those days the LORD began to **r** the size	7894
Job	11: 3	Will your idle talk **r** men to silence?	3087
	24:25	who can prove me false and **r** my words	8492
Isa	41:15	and **r** the hills to chaff.	8492
Jer	10:24	in your anger, lest you **r** me to nothing.	5070

REDUCED (11) [REDUCE]

Ge	47:21	**r** the people to servitude,	4200+6268+6269
Ex	5:11	but your work will not be **r** at all.' "	1757
Lev	27:18	and its set value will be **r.**	1757
Job	30:19	and I am **r** to dust and ashes.	5439
Ps	79: 1	they have **r** Jerusalem to rubble.	8492
	89:40	through all his walls and **r** his strongholds	8492
	102: 5	Because of my loud groaning I am **r** to skin	1815
Isa	25: 5	as heat is **r** by the shadow of a cloud,	NIH
Eze	16:27	against you and **r** your territory;	1757
	28:18	and I **r** you to ashes on the ground in	5989
Am	5: 5	and Bethel will be **r** to nothing."	NIH

REDUCES (2) [REDUCE]

Pr	6:26	for the prostitute **r** you to a loaf of bread,	6330
Isa	40:23	He brings princes to naught and **r** the rulers	6913

REED (12) [REEDS]

1Ki	14:15	that it will be like a **r** swaying in the water.	7866
2Ki	18:21	that splintered **r** of a staff,	7866
Isa	9:14	both palm branch and **r** in a single day;	109
	19:15	head or tail, palm branch or **r.**	109
	36: 6	that splintered **r** of a staff,	7866
	42: 3	A bruised **r** he will not break,	7866
	58: 5	for bowing one's head like a **r** and for lying	109
Eze	29: 6	" 'You have been a staff of **r** for the house	7866
Mt	11: 7	A **r** swayed by the wind?	2812
	12:20	A bruised **r** he will not break,	2812
Lk	7:24	A **r** swayed by the wind?	2812
Rev	11: 1	a **r** like a measuring rod and was told,	2812

REEDS (10) [REED]

Ge	41: 2	sleek and fat, and they grazed among the **r.**	286
	41:18	fat and sleek, and they grazed among the **r.**	286
Ex	2: 3	the child in it and put it among the **r** along	6068
	2: 5	among the **r** and sent her slave girl to get it.	6068
Job	8:11	Can **r** thrive without water?	286
	40:21	hidden among the **r** in the marsh.	7866
	41:20	as from a boiling pot over a fire of **r.**	109
Ps	68:30	Rebuke the beast among the **r,**	7866
Isa	19: 6	The **r** and rushes will wither,	7866
	35: 7	grass and **r** and papyrus will grow.	7866

REEKED (1)

Ex	8:14	and the land **r** of them.	944

REEL (2) [REELED, REELING, REELS]

Isa	28: 7	also stagger from wine and **r** from beer:	9494
	28: 7	befuddled with wine; they **r** from beer,	9494

REELAIAH (1)

Ezr	2: 2	Nehemiah, Seraiah, **R,** Mordecai, Bilshan,	8305

REELED (1) [REEL]

Ps	107:27	They **r** and staggered like drunken men;	2510

REELING (1) [REEL]

Zec	12: 2	that sends all the surrounding peoples **r.**	8303

REELS (1) [REEL]

Isa	24:20	The earth **r** like a drunkard,	5675+5675

REENTERED (1) [ENTER]

Ne	2:15	and **r** through the Valley Gate.	995+2256+8740

REESTABLISHED (1) [ESTABLISH]

2Ch	29:35	service of the temple of the LORD was **r.**	3922

REFER (1) [REFERRED, REFERRING]

1Jn	5:16	I **r** to those whose sin does not lead	NIG

REFERRED (1) [REFER]

Gal	3:19	the Seed to whom the promise **r** had come.	AIT

REFERRING (2) [REFER]

Ex	4:26	"bridegroom of blood," **r** to circumcision.)	4200
Jn	13:18	"I am not **r** to all of you;	3306

REFINE (3) [REFINED, REFINER, REFINER'S, REFINING]

Jer	9: 7	"See, I will **r** and test them,	7671
Zec	13: 9	I will **r** them like silver and test them	7671
Mal	3: 3	the Levites and **r** them like gold and silver.	2423

REFINED (10) [REFINE]

1Ch	28:18	and the weight of the **r** gold for the altar	2423
	29: 4	and seven thousand talents of **r** silver,	2423
Job	28: 1	for silver and a place where gold is **r.**	2423
Ps	12: 6	like silver **r** in a furnace of clay,	7671
	66:10	you, O God, tested us; you **r** us like silver.	7671
Isa	48:10	See, I have **r** you, though not as silver;	7671
Da	11:35	so that they may be **r,**	7671
	12:10	Many will be purified, made spotless and **r,**	7671
1Pe	1: 7	which perishes even though **r** by fire—	1507
Rev	3:18	I counsel you to buy from me gold **r** in	4792

REFINER (1) [REFINE]

Mal	3: 3	He will sit as a **r** and purifier of silver;	7671

REFINER'S (1) [REFINE]

Mal	3: 2	he will be like a **r** fire or a launderer's soap.	7671

REFINING (1) [REFINE]

Jer	6:29	but the **r** goes on in vain;	7671+7671

REFLECT (3) [REFLECTED, REFLECTION, REFLECTS]

Isa	47: 7	not consider these things or **r** on	2349
2Co	3:18	with unveiled faces all **r** the Lord's glory,	3002
2Ti	2: 7	**R** on what I am saying,	3783

REFLECTED (1) [REFLECT]

Ecc	9: 1	So I **r** on all this and concluded	448+4213+5989

REFLECTION (1) [REFLECT]

1Co	13:12	Now we see but a poor **r** as in a **mirror;**	2269

REFLECTS (3) [REFLECT]

Pr	27:19	As water **r** a face,	2021+2021+4200+7156+7156
	27:19	so a man's heart **r** the man.	132+2021+4200
Ecc	5:20	He seldom **r** on the days of his life,	2349

REFORM (4) [REFORMS]

Jer	7: 3	**R** your ways and your actions,	3512
	18:11	and **r** your ways and your actions.'	3512
	26:13	Now **r** your ways and your actions	3512
	35:15	from your wicked ways and **r** your actions;	3512

REFORMS (1) [REFORM]

Ac	24: 2	and your foresight has brought about **r**	1480

REFRAIN (10) [REFRAINED]

Dt	23:22	But if you **r** from making a vow,	2532
1Sa	18: 8	Saul was very angry; this **r** galled him.	1821
1Ki	22: 6	against Ramoth Gilead, or shall I **r?**"	2532
	22:15	against Ramoth Gilead, or shall I **r?**"	2532
2Ch	18: 5	against Ramoth Gilead, or shall I **r?**"	2532
	18:14	against Ramoth Gilead, or shall I **r?**"	2532
Job	16: 6	and if I **r,** it does not go away.	2532
Ps	37: 8	**R** from anger and turn from wrath;	8332
Ecc	3: 5	a time to embrace and a time to **r,**	8178
2Co	12: 6	But I **r,** so no one will think more	5767

REFRAINED (2) [REFRAIN]

2Sa	12: 4	but the rich man **r** from taking one	2798
Job	29: 9	the chief men **r** from speaking	6806

REFRAINETH (KJV) See HOLDS

REFRESH (7) [REFRESHED, REFRESHES, REFRESHING]

Jdg	19: 5	"**R** yourself with something to eat;	6184
	19: 8	the girl's father said, "**R** yourself.	6184
2Sa	16: 2	to **r** those who become exhausted in	9272
SS	2: 5	**r** me with apples, for I am faint with love.	8331
Jer	31:25	I will **r** the weary and satisfy the faint."	8115
Phm	1:20	**r** my heart in Christ.	399
2Pe	1:13	I think it is right to **r** your memory as long	1444

REFRESHED (10) [REFRESH]

Ge	18: 5	you can be **r** and then go on your way	4213+6184
Ex	23:12	and the alien as well, may be **r.**	5882
2Sa	16:14	And there he **r** himself.	5882
Ps	68: 9	your weary inheritance.	3922
Pr	11:25	he who refreshes others will himself be **r.**	3722
Ro	15:32	**together** with you be **r.**	5265
1Co	16:18	For they **r** my spirit and yours also.	399
2Co	7:13	because his spirit has been **r** by all of you.	399
2Ti	1:16	because he often **r** me and was not ashamed	434

REFRESHES (2) [REFRESH]

Pr	11:25	he who **r** others will himself be refreshed.	8115
	25:13	he **r** the spirit of his masters.	8740

REFRESHING (1) [REFRESH]

Ac	3:19	that times of **r** may come from the Lord,	433

REFUGE (93) [REFUGEES]

Nu	35: 6	the Levites will be cities of **r,**	5236
	35:11	select some towns to be your cities of **r,**	5236
	35:12	They will be places of **r** from the avenger,	5236
	35:13	be your cities of **r.**	5236
	35:14	and three in Canaan as cities of **r.**	5236
	35:15	These six towns will be a **place of r**	5236
	35:25	of blood and send him back to the city of **r**	5236
	35:26	of the city of **r** to which he has fled	5236
	35:28	The accused must stay in his city of **r** until	5236
	35:32	for anyone who has fled to a city of **r** and	5236
Dt	23:15	If a slave has taken **r** with you,	5911
	32:37	are their gods, the rock they took **r** in,	2879
	33:27	The eternal God is your **r,**	5104
Jos	20: 2	the Israelites to designate the cities of **r,**	5236
	21:13	(a city of **r** for one accused of murder),	5236
	21:21	of **r** for one accused of murder) and Gezer,	5236
	21:27	(a city of **r** for one accused of murder) and	5236
	21:32	(a city of **r** for one accused of murder),	5236
	21:38	(a city of **r** for one accused of murder),	5236
Jdg	9:15	come and take **r** in my shade;	2879
Ru	2:12	whose wings you have come to take **r.**"	2879
2Sa	22: 3	my God is my rock, in whom I take **r,**	2879
	22: 3	He is my stronghold, my **r** and my savior—	4960
	22:31	He is a shield for all who take **r** in him.	2879
1Ch	6:57	of Aaron were given Hebron (a city of **r**),	5236
	6:67	they were given Shechem (a city of **r**),	5236
Ps	2:12	Blessed are all who take **r** in him.	2879
	5:11	But let all who take **r** in you be glad;	2879
	7: 1	O LORD my God, I take **r** in you;	2879
	9: 9	The LORD is a **r** for the oppressed,	5369
	11: 1	In the LORD I take **r.**	2879
	14: 6	but the LORD is their **r.**	4726
	16: 1	Keep me safe, O God, for in you I take **r.**	2879
	17: 7	by your right hand those who take **r** in you	2879
	18: 2	my God is my rock, in whom I take **r.**	2879
	18:30	He is a shield for all who take **r** in him.	2879
	25:20	for I take **r** in you.	2879
	31: 1	In you, O LORD, I have taken **r;**	2879
	31: 2	be my rock of **r,** a strong fortress	5057
	31: 4	for you are my **r.**	5057
	31:19	the sight of men on those who take **r** in you.	2879
	34: 8	blessed is the man who takes **r** in him.	2879
	34:22	no one will be condemned who takes **r**	2879
	36: 7	and low among men find **r** in the shadow	2879
	37:40	because they take **r** in him.	2879
	46: 1	God is our **r** and strength,	4726
	57: 1	for in you my soul takes **r.**	2879
	57: 1	I will take **r** in the shadow of your wings	2879
	59:16	my **r** in times of trouble.	4960
	61: 3	For you have been my **r,**	4726
	61: 4	in your tent forever and take **r** in the shelter	2879
	62: 7	he is my mighty rock, my **r.**	4726
	62: 8	for God is our **r.**	4726
	64:10	in the LORD and take **r** in him;	2879
	71: 1	In you, O LORD, I have taken **r;**	2879
	71: 3	Be my rock of **r,** to which I can always go;	5061
	71: 7	but you are my strong **r.**	4726
	73:28	I have made the Sovereign LORD my **r;**	4726
	91: 2	"He is my **r** and my fortress, my God,	4726
	91: 4	and under his wings you will find **r;**	2879
	91: 9	even the LORD, who is my **r—**	4726
	94:22	and my God the rock in whom I take **r.**	4726
	104:18	the crags are a **r** for the coneys.	4726
	118: 8	to take **r** in the LORD than to trust in man.	2879
	118: 9	It is better to take **r** in the LORD than	2879
	119:114	You are my **r** and my shield;	6260
	141: 8	O Sovereign LORD; in you I take **r—**	2879
	142: 4	I have no **r;** no one cares for my life.	4960
	142: 5	I say, "You are my **r,**	4726
	144: 2	my shield, in whom I take **r,**	2879
Pr	14:26	way of the LORD is a **r** for the righteous,	5057
	14:26	and for his children it will be a **r.**	4726
	14:32	but even in death the righteous have a **r.**	2879
	22: 3	A prudent man sees danger and takes **r,**	6259
	27:12	The prudent see danger and take **r,**	6259
	30: 5	he is a shield to those who take **r** in him.	2879
Isa	4: 6	**r** and hiding place from the storm and rain.	4726
	14:32	and in her his afflicted people will find **r.**"	2879
	25: 4	You have been a **r** for the poor,	5057
	25: 4	a **r** for the needy in his distress,	5057
	27: 5	Or else let them come to me for **r;**	4726
	28:15	a lie our **r** and falsehood our hiding place."	4726
	28:17	hail will sweep away your **r,** the lie,	4726
	30: 2	to Egypt's shade for **r,**	4726
	32: 2	be like a shelter from the wind and a **r** from	6260
	33:16	whose **r** will be the mountain fortress.	5369
	57:13	But the man who makes me his **r** will inherit the land	2879
Jer	16:19	my **r** in time of distress,	4960
	17:17	you are my **r** in the day of disaster.	4726
	17:17	Who can enter our **r?**"	5104
Joel	3:16	But the LORD will be a **r** for his people,	4726
Na	1: 7	The LORD is good, a **r** in times of trouble.	5057
	3:11	you will go into hiding and seek **r** from	5057

REFUGEES (2) [REFUGE]

Isa	16: 3	Hide the fugitives, do not betray the **r**.	5610
Jer	50:28	the fugitives and **r** from Babylon declaring	7128

REFUND (1)

Lev	25:27	the value for the years since he sold it and **r**	8740

REFUSAL (1) [REFUSE]

Mk	16:14	for their lack of faith and their **stubborn r**	5016

REFUSE (50) [REFUSAL, REFUSED, REFUSES, REFUSING]

Ge	23: 6	None of us *will* **r** you his tomb	3973
	24:41	be released from my oath even if they **r**	4202
Ex	8: 2	If you **r** to let them go,	4412
	9: 2	If you **r** to let them go and continue	4412
	10: 3	'How long *will you* **r** to humble yourself	4412
	10: 4	If you **r** to let them go,	4412
	11: 9	"Pharaoh will **r** to listen to you—	4202
	16:28	"How long *will you* **r**	4412
Lev	26:21	" 'If you remain hostile toward me and **r**	14+4202
Nu	14:11	How long will they **r** to believe in me,	4202
Dt	20:12	If they **r** to make peace	4202
1Ki	2:16	*Do not* **r** me."	8740
	2:17	ask King Solomon—*he will* not **r** you—	8740
	2:20	"*Do not* **r** me."	8740
	2:20	*I will* not **r** you."	8740
	20: 7	my silver and my gold, *I did* not **r** him."	4979
2Ki	2:17	until he was too ashamed to **r**.	NIH
	9:37	Jezebel's body will lie like **r** on the ground	1961
Job	6: 7	I **r** to touch it; such food makes me ill.	4412
	34:33	when *you* **r** to repent?	4415
Ps	26: 5	the assembly of evildoers and **r** to sit with	4202
	83:10	at Endor and became like **r** on the ground.	1961
	141: 5	My head *will* not **r** it.	5648
Pr	6:35	*he will* **r** the bribe, however great it is.	14+4202
	21: 7	for *they* **r** to do what is right.	4412
	21:25	because his hands **r** to work.	4412
	30: 7	*do not* **r** me before I die:	4979
Isa	5:25	and the dead bodies are like **r** in the streets.	6054
Jer	3: 3	*you* **r** to blush with shame.	4412
	8: 2	but will be like **r** lying on the ground.	1961
	8: 5	They cling to deceit; *they* **r** to return.	4412
	9: 6	in their deceit *they* **r** to acknowledge me,"	4412
	9:22	" 'The dead bodies of men will lie like **r** on	1961
	13:10	who **r** to listen to my words,	4412
	16: 4	but will be like **r** lying on the ground.	1961
	25:28	But if *they* **r** to take the cup from your hand	4412
	25:33	but will be like **r** lying on the ground.	1961
	38:21	But if you **r** to surrender,	4412
La	3:45	You have made us scum and **r** among	4400
Eze	3:27	and whoever will **r** let him refuse:	2534
	3:27	and whoever will refuse *let him* **r**;	2532
Hos	11: 5	not Assyria rule over them because *they* **r**	4412
Mk	6:26	he did not want *to* **r** her.	119
Jn	5:40	yet *you* **r** to come to me to have life.	2527+4024
	19:10	"Do you **r** to speak to me?"	4024
Ac	25:11	*I do* not **r** to die.	4148
1Co	4:13	the **r** of the world.	4370
	16:11	No one, then, *should* **r to accept** him.	2024
Heb	12:25	See to it that *you* do not **r** him who speaks.	4148
Rev	11: 9	on their bodies and **r** them burial.	918+4024

REFUSED (58) [REFUSE]

Ge	37:35	but *he* **r** to be comforted.	4412
	39: 8	But *he* **r**.	4412
	39:10	*he* **r** to go to bed with her or even be	4202+9048
	48:19	But his father **r** and said, "I know, my son,	4412
Ex	4:23	But *you* **r** to let him go,	4412
	13:15	When Pharaoh **stubbornly r** to let us go,	7996
Nu	20:21	Since Edom **r** to let them go	4412
	22:13	the LORD *has* **r** to let me go with you,"	4412
	22:14	"Balaam **r** to come with us."	4412
Dt	2:30	king of Heshbon **r** to let us pass through.	14+4202
Jdg	2:19	They **r** to give up their evil practices	4202
	11:17	also to the king of Moab, and he **r**.	14+4202
1Sa	8:19	But the people **r** to listen to Samuel.	4412
	28:23	He **r** and said, "I will not eat."	4412
2Sa	2:23	But Asahel **r** to give up the pursuit;	4412
	12:17	but *he* **r**, and he would not eat any food	14+4202
	13: 9	but *he* **r** to eat.	4412
	13:14	But *he* **r** to listen to her,	14+4202
	13:16	But *he* **r** to listen to her.	14+4202
	13:25	Absalom urged him, *he still* **r** to go,	4202
	14:29	but Joab **r** to come to him.	4412
	14:29	he sent a second time, but *he* **r** to come.	4412
	23:16	But *he* **r** to drink it;	14+4202
1Ki	12:16	When all Israel saw that the king **r** to listen	4202
	20:35	Strike me with your weapon," but the man **r**	4412
	21: 4	He lay on his bed sulking and **r** to eat.	4202
	21:15	the Jezreelite that *he* **r** to sell you.	4412
	22:49	with your men," but Jehoshaphat **r**.	14+4202
2Ki	5:16	And even though Naaman urged him, *he* **r**.	4412
	15:16	because they **r** to open their gates.	4202
1Ch	11:18	But *he* **r** to drink it;	14+4202
2Ch	10:16	When all Israel saw that the king **r** to listen	4202
Ne	9:17	*They* **r** to listen and failed to remember	4412
	9:29	became stiff-necked and **r** to listen.	4202
Est	1:12	Queen Vashti **r** to come.	4412
	3: 4	Day after day *they* spoke to him but he **r**	4202
Ps	77: 2	and my soul **r** to be comforted.	4412
	78:10	they did not keep God's covenant and **r**	4412
Ecc	2:10	*I* **r** my heart no pleasure.	4979

Jer	5: 3	you crushed them, but *they* **r** correction.	4412
	5: 3	harder than stone and **r** to repent.	4412
	11:10	who **r** to listen to my words.	4412
Zec	7:11	"But they **r** to pay attention;	4412
Mt	18:30	"But he **r**.	2527+4024
	22: 3	but *they* **r** to come.	2527+4024
	27:34	but after tasting it, *he* **r** to drink it.	2527+4024
Lk	15:28	The older brother became angry and **r**	2527+4024
	18: 4	"For some time *he* **r**.	2527+4024
Ac	7:39	"But our fathers **r** to obey him.	2527+4024
	14: 2	But the Jews who **r to believe** stirred up	578
	19: 9	*they* **r to believe** and publicly maligned	578
2Th	2:10	They perish because *they* **r** to love the truth	1312+4024
Heb	11:24	**r** to be known as the son of Pharaoh's	766
	11:35	Others were tortured and **r** to be released,	4148
	12:25	*when they* **r** him who warned them on earth,	4148
Rev	13:15	and cause all who **r to worship** the image to be killed.	3590+4686
	16: 9	but *they* **r to repent** and glorify him.	3566+4024
	16:11	but *they* **r to repent** of what they had done.	3566+4024

REFUSES (7) [REFUSE]

Ex	7:14	*he* **r** to let the people go.	4412
	22:17	father **absolutely r** to give her to him,	4412+4412
Dt	25: 7	"My husband's brother **r** to carry	4412
Pr	11:15	but *whoever* **r** to strike hands	8533
Mt	18:17	If *he* **r to listen** *to* them,	4159
	18:17	and if *he* **r to listen** even *to* the church,	4159
3Jn	1:10	he **r** to welcome the brothers.	4046

REFUSING (4) [REFUSE]

Jer	31:15	Rachel weeping for her children and **r** to	4412
	50:33	captors hold them fast, **r** to let them go.	4412
Da	9:11	and turned away, **r** to obey you.	1194
Mt	2:18	Rachel weeping for her children and **r**	2527+4024

REFUTE (4) [REFUTED]

Job	32: 3	because they had found no **way to r** Job,	5101
	32:13	*let* God **r** him, not man.'	5622
Isa	54:17	*you will* **r** every tongue that accuses you.	8399
Tit	1: 9	and **r** those who oppose it.	1794

REFUTED (1) [REFUTE]

Ac	18:28	he vigorously **r** the Jews in public debate,	1352

REGAIN (5) [GAIN]

1Sa	29: 4	How better *could* he **r** his master's **favor** than	8354
1Ki	12:21	and to **r** the kingdom for Rehoboam son	8740
2Ch	11: 1	and to **r** the kingdom for Rehoboam.	8740
	13:20	Jeroboam *did* not **r** power during	6388+6806
Job	9:18	He would not let me **r** my breath	8740

REGAINED (1) [GAIN]

Ac	9:19	he **r** his strength.	1932

REGARD (50) [REGARDED, REGARDING, REGARDLESS, REGARDS]

Ge	31:15	*Does* he not **r** us *as* foreigners?	3108
Lev	5:15	a violation and sins unintentionally **in r** to	4946
	5:16	for what he has failed to do **in r** to	4946
	11:35	and you *are* to **r** them as unclean.	2118+4200
	19:23	**r** its fruit **as forbidden**,	6887+6889
	21: 8	**R** them **as holy**,	7727
Nu	18:10	You *must* **r** it as holy.	2118+4200
Dt	33: 9	'I have no **r** for them.'	8011
Jos	7: 1	But the Israelites acted unfaithfully **in r** to	928
1Sa	2:12	*they* had no **r** for the LORD.	3359
Ezr	7:14	about Judah and Jerusalem **with r** to	10089
Est	9:31	for themselves and their descendants in **r**	NIH
Job	21:29	*Have you* **paid** no **r** to their accounts—	5795
	34:27	from following him and **had** no **r** for any	8505
	37:24	for *does he* not have **r** for all the wise	8011
Ps	28: 5	Since *they* **show** no **r** for the works of	1067
	41: 1	Blessed is *he who* has **r** for the weak;	8505
	54: 3	men without **r for** God.	4200+5584+8492
	74:20	**Have r for** your covenant,	4200+5564
	86:14	men without **r for** you.	4200+5584+8492
	119:117	*I will* always have **r for** your decrees.	9120
Isa	5:12	*they* have no **r for** the deeds of the LORD,	5564
	8:13	the one *you are to* **r as holy**,	7727
	17: 8	and *they will* have no **r for**	8011
	22:11	or have **r for** the One who made it,	8011
	26:10	of uprightness *they* go on doing evil and **r**	8011
Jer	24: 5	*I* **r** as good the exiles from Judah,	5795
	33:24	no longer **r** them *as* a nation.	2118+4200+7156
Eze	44: 8	Instead of carrying out your **duty** in **r**	AIT
Da	11:37	*He will* **show** no **r** for the gods of his fathers	1067
	11:37	nor *will he* **r** any god,	1067
Am	5:22	*I will* have no **r** for them.	5564
Jn	16: 8	He will convict the world of guilt **in r to** sin	4309
	16: 9	**in r to** sin, because men do not believe	4309
	16:10	**in r to** righteousness, because I am going	4309
	16:11	and **in r to** judgment,	4309
1Co	4: 1	men *ought to* **r** us as servants of Christ and	3357
	14:20	*In r to* **evil** be infants,	AIT
2Co	5:16	now on we **r** no one from a worldly point of	3857
Eph	4:22	**with r to** your former way of life,	2848
Php	3: 5	**in r to** the law, a Pharisee;	2848

Col	1:24	still lacking in **r** to Christ's afflictions	NIG
	2:16	or **with r** to a religious festival,	1877+3538
1Th	5:13	Hold them *in the* **highest r** in love because	5655
2Th	3:15	Yet *do* not **r** him as an enemy,	2451
Heb	7:14	and **in r** to that tribe Moses said nothing	1650
	11:20	and Esau **in r** to their future.	4309
1Pe	4: 6	according to men **in r** to the **body**,	AIT
	4: 6	but live according to God **in r** to the **spirit**.	AIT
	5:12	whom *I* **r** as a faithful brother,	3357

REGARDED (19) [REGARD]

Ex	11: 3	Moses himself was **highly r** in Egypt	1524+4394
Dt	24:13	**r** as a righteous act **in the sight of**	4200+7156
2Sa	16:23	and Absalom **r** all of Ahithophel's advice.	4200
2Ki	5: 1	in the sight of his master and **highly r**,	5951+7156
2Ch	32:23	then on *he* was **highly r** by all the nations.	5951
Job	18: 3	Why *are we* **r** as cattle	3108
	31:26	if *I* have **r** the sun in its radiance or	8011
Isa	40:15	*they* **are** as dust on the scales;	3108
	40:17	*they* **are r** by him as worthless	3108
Da	4:35	the peoples of the earth **are r** as nothing.	10285
Hos	8:12	but *they* **r** them as something alien.	3108
Mk	10:42	"You know that those who are **r** as rulers of	1506
Ac	5:13	though *they* were **highly r** by the people.	3486
Ro	2: 6	not *be* **r** as though they were circumcised?	3357
	9: 8	the children of the promise who *are* **r**	3357
2Co	5:16	Though *we once* **r** Christ in this way,	1182
	6: 8	genuine, yet **r** as impostors;	6055
	6: 9	yet **r** as unknown;	6055
Heb	11:26	*He* **r** disgrace for the sake of Christ as	2451

REGARDING (6) [REGARD]

Lev	5: 1	to testify **r** something he has seen	NIH
Jos	22:20	acted unfaithfully **r** the devoted things	928
Eze	14:22	be consoled **r** the disaster I have brought	6584
	44: 5	concerning all the **regulations r** the temple	AIT
Ro	1: 3	**r** his Son, who as to his human nature was	4309
	4:20	not waver through unbelief **r** the promise	1650

REGARDLESS (1) [REGARD]

2Ch	5:11	**r** of their divisions.	401+4200+9068

REGARDS (4) [REGARD]

Est	5: 8	If the king **r** *me with* favor and	928+5162+6524
	8: 5	"and if he **r** *me with* favor and	4200+5162+7156
Ro	14: 6	He who **r** one day as special,	5858
	14:14	But if anyone **r** something as unclean.	3357

REGEM (1)

1Ch	2:47	The sons of Jahdai: **R**, Jotham, Geshan,	8084

REGEM-MELECH (1)

Zec	7: 2	people of Bethel had sent Sharezer and **R**,	8085

REGENERATION (KJV) See REBIRTH

REGIMENT (2)

Ac	10: 1	in what was known as the Italian **R**.	5061
	27: 1	*who* belonged *to* the Imperial **R**.	5061

REGION (61) [REGIONS]

Ge	10:30	The **r** where they **lived** stretched	4632
	20: 1	on from there into the **r** of the Negev	824
	22: 2	whom you love, and go to the **r** of Moriah.	824
	35:22	While Israel was living in that **r**,	824
	36:20	who were living in the **r**:	824
	45:10	You shall live in the **r** of Goshen and be	824
	46:28	When they arrived in the **r** of Goshen,	824
	46:34	Then you will be allowed to settle in the **r**	824
	47:13	the whole **r** because the famine was severe;	824
	47:27	Now the Israelites settled in Egypt in the **r**	824
Dt	2:18	"Today you are to pass by the **r** of Moab	1473
	3: 4	the whole **r** *of* Argob.	2475
	3:13	(The whole **r** *of* Argob in Bashan used to	2475
	3:14	the whole **r** of Argob as far as the border of	2475
	34: 3	and the **whole r** *from* the Valley of Jericho,	3971
Jos	7: 2	and told them, "Go up and spy out the **r**."	824
	10:40	So Joshua subdued the whole **r**,	824
	10:41	and from the whole **r** of Goshen to Gibeon.	824
	11: 3	and to the Hivites below Hermon in the **r**	824
	11:16	all the Negev, the whole **r** *of* Goshen,	824
	13: 4	the **r** of the Amorites,	1473
	16: 3	the territory of the Japhletites as far as the **r**	1473
	17:12	to live in that **r**.	824
	19:29	and came out at the sea in the **r** of Aczib,	2475
Jdg	4:26	into pieces and sent one piece to each **r**	8441
2Sa	20:14	and through the **entire r** *of* the Berites,	AIT
	24: 6	to Gilead and the **r** *of* Tahtim Hodshi,	824
2Ki	4:38	to Gilgal and there was a famine in that **r**.	824
	10:33	of the Jordan in all the land of Gilead (the **r**	NIH
1Ch	5:10	of the Hagrites throughout the entire **r** east	7156
Ne	3:22	by the priests from the **surrounding r**.	3971
	12:28	also were brought together from the **r**	3971
Ps	78:12	in the **r** of Zoan.	8441
	78:43	his wonders in the **r** *of* Zoan."	8441
Isa	49:12	some from the **r** of Aswan."	824
Eze	47: 8	toward the eastern **r** and goes down into	1666
Mt	3: 5	and all Judea and the whole **r** of the Jordan.	4369
	4:25	and the **r** across the Jordan followed him.	NIG
	8:28	When he arrived at the other side in the **r** of	6001
	8:34	they pleaded with him to leave their **r**.	3990

Mt	9:26	News of this spread through all that **r**.	1178
	9:31	the news about him all over that **r**.	1178
	15:21	Jesus withdrew to the **r** of Tyre and Sidon.	3538
	16:13	to the **r** of Caesarea Philippi,	3538
	19: 1	he left Galilee and went into the **r** of Judea	3990
Mk	1: 4	in the **desert r** and preaching a baptism	2245
	1:28	about him spread quickly over the whole **r**	4369
	5: 1	across the lake to the **r** of the Gerasenes.	6001
	5:17	to plead with Jesus to leave their **r**.	3990
	6:55	throughout that whole **r** and carried the sick	6001
	7:31	down to the Sea of Galilee and into the **r** of	3990
	8:10	the boat with his disciples and went to the **r**	3538
	10: 1	that place and went into the **r** of Judea and	3990
Lk	4:26	to a widow in Zarephath in the **r** of Sidon.	NIG
	8:26	They sailed to the **r** of the Gerasenes,	6001
	8:37	of the **r** of the Gerasenes asked Jesus	4369
Jn	11:54	Instead he withdrew to a **r** near the desert,	6001
Ac	13:49	of the Lord spread through the whole **r**.	6001
	13:50	and expelled them from their **r**.	3990
	16: 6	throughout the **r** of Phrygia and Galatia,	6001
	18:23	throughout the **r** of Galatia and Phrygia,	6001

REGIONS (10) [REGION]

Ge	36:40	by name, according to their clans and **r**:	5226
Jos	13: 2	all the **r** *of* the Philistines and Geshurites:	1666
	13: 6	for all the inhabitants of the **mountain r**	2215
Eze	19: 8	those from **r** round about.	4519
Joel	3: 4	and Sidon and all you **r** *of* Philistia?	1666
Mk	3: 8	**r** across the Jordan and around Tyre	4305
Ro	15:23	for me to work in these **r**,	3107
2Co	10:16	so that we can preach the gospel in the **r**	NIG
	11:10	in the **r** of Achaia will stop this boasting	3107
Eph	4: 9	also descended to the lower, earthly **r**?	3538

REGISTER (3) [REGISTERED, REGISTRATION]

Ps	87: 6	Lord will write in the **r** *of* the peoples:	4180
Lk	2: 3	And everyone went to his own town *to* **r**.	616
	2: 5	He went there *to* **r** with Mary,	616

REGISTERED (5) [REGISTER]

1Ch	9:22	They **were r** by genealogy in their villages.	3509
	23:24	of families as they **were r** under their names	7212
Ezr	8: 1	These are the family heads and *those* **r**	3509
	8: 3	Zechariah, and with him **were r** 150 men;	3509
	8:20	All **were r** by name.	5918

REGISTRATION (1) [REGISTER]

Ne	7: 5	and the common people for **r** by **families**.	3509

REGRET (4)

2Ch	21:20	He passed away, to no one's **r**,	2775
2Co	7: 8	caused you sorrow by my letter, *I* do not **r** it	3564
	7: 8	Though *I did* it—I see that my letter hurt	3564
	7:10	that leads to salvation and leaves **no r**,	294

REGROUPED (1) [GROUP]

2Sa	10:15	they had been routed by Israel, *they* **r**.	665+3480

REGULAR (55) [REGULARLY]

Ge	47:22	because they received a **r allotment**	2976
Ex	29:28	be the **r share** from the Israelites for Aaron	2976
Lev	6:14	It is his **r** share of the offerings made to	6409
	6:20	an ephah of fine flour as a **r** grain offering,	9458
	6:22	It is the Lord's **r** share and is to	6409
	7:34	the priest and his sons as their **r** share from	6409
	7:36	as their **r** share for the generations to come.	6409
	10:15	be the **r** share for you and your children,	6409
	14:32	and who cannot afford the **r** offerings	NIH
	15:19	a woman has her **r flow** *of* blood,	928+1414+2307
	16:24	in a holy place and put on his **r** garments.	NIH
	23: 7	a sacred assembly and do no **r work**.	4856+6275
	23: 8	a sacred assembly and do no **r work**.'	4856+6275
	23:21	a sacred assembly and do no **r work**.	4856+6275
	23:25	Do no **r work**,	4856+6275
	23:35	do no **r work**.	4856+6275
	23:36	the closing assembly; do no **r work**.	4856+6275
	24: 9	of their **r** share of the offerings made to	6409
Nu	4:16	the **r** grain offering and the anointing oil.	9458
	8:25	their **r service** and work no longer.	6275+7372
	18: 8	and your sons as your portion and **r** share.	6409
	18:11	and daughters as your **r** share.	6409
	18:19	and daughters as your **r** share.	6409
	28: 3	as a **r** burnt offering each day.	9458
	28: 6	This is the **r** burnt offering instituted	9458
	28:10	the **r** burnt offering and its drink offering,	9458
	28:15	the **r** burnt offering with its drink offering,	9458
	28:18	a sacred assembly and do no **r work**.	4856+6275
	28:23	in addition to the **r** morning burnt offering,	9458
	28:24	the **r** burnt offering and its drink offering.	9458
	28:25	a sacred assembly and do no **r work**.	4856+6275
	28:26	a sacred assembly and do no **r work**.	4856+6275
	28:31	the **r** burnt offering and its grain offering.	9458
	29: 1	a sacred assembly and do no **r work**.	4856+6275
	29:11	the **r** burnt offering with its grain offering,	9458
	29:12	a sacred assembly and do no **r work**.	4856+6275
	29:16	the **r** burnt offering with its grain offering	9458
	29:19	the **r** burnt offering with its grain offering	9458
	29:22	the **r** burnt offering with its grain offering	9458
	29:25	the **r** burnt offering with its grain offering	9458
	29:28	the **r** burnt offering with its grain offering	9458
	29:31	the **r** burnt offering with its grain offering	9458
Nu	29:34	the **r** burnt offering with its grain offering	9458
	29:35	an assembly and do no **r work**.	4856+6275
	29:38	the **r** burnt offering with its grain offering	9458
2Ki	25:30	the king gave Jehoiachin a **r** allowance	9458
2Ch	30: 3	not been able to celebrate it at the **r** time	2085S
	30:16	up their **positions** as prescribed in the Law	AIT
Ezr	3: 5	they presented the **r** burnt offerings.	9458
Ne	10:33	the **r** grain offerings and burnt offerings;	9458
Job	1: 5	This was Job's **r** custom.	2021+3427+3972
Jer	5:24	who assures us of the **r** weeks of harvest.'	2978
	52:34	of Babylon gave Jehoiachin a **r** allowance	9458
Eze	41:17	and on the walls **at r intervals** all around	4500
	46:15	by morning for a **r** burnt offering.	9458

REGULARLY (15) [REGULAR]

Ex	29:38	to offer on the altar **r** each day:	9458
	29:42	this burnt offering is to be made **r**	9458
	30: 8	the lamps at twilight so incense will burn **r**	9458
Lev	24: 8	to be set out before the Lord **r**,	9458
2Ki	25:29	the rest of his life ate **r** at the king's table.	9458
1Ch	16: 6	to blow the trumpets **r** before the ark of	9458
	16:37	of the Lord to minister there **r**,	9458
	16:40	the Lord on the altar of burnt offering **r**,	9458
	23:31	They were to serve before the Lord **r** in	9458
2Ch	2: 4	for setting out the consecrated bread **r**,	9458
	24:11	did this **r** and collected	928+3427+3427+4200
Jer	52:33	the rest of his life ate **r** at the king's table.	9458
Eze	39:14	" 'Men will be **r** employed to cleanse	1328+4246
Ac	10: 2	to those in need and prayed to God **r**,	1328+4246
Heb	9: 6	priests entered **r** into the outer room	

REGULATED (1) [REGULATION]

Ne	11:23	which **r** their daily activity.	591

REGULATION (3) [REGULATED, REGULATIONS]

Ne	8:18	in accordance with the **r**,	5477
Heb	7:16	not on the basis of a **r** as to his ancestry but	3795
	7:18	The former **r** is set aside	1953

REGULATIONS (45) [REGULATION]

Ex	12:43	"These are the **r** for the Passover:	2978
Lev	6: 9	'These are the **r** for the burnt offering:	9368
	6:14	" 'These are the **r** for the grain offering:	9368
	6:25	'These are the **r** for the sin offering:	9368
	7: 1	" 'These are the **r** for the guilt offering,	9368
	7:11	the **r** for the fellowship offering	9368
	7:37	These, then, are the **r** for the burnt offering,	9368
	11:46	" 'These are the **r** *concerning* animals,	9368
	12: 7	the **r** for the woman who gives birth to	9368
	13:59	the **r** *concerning* contamination by mildew	9368
	14: 2	"These are the **r** *for* the diseased person at	9368
	14:32	These are the **r** *for* anyone who has	9368
	14:54	the **r** for any infectious skin disease,	9368
	14:57	These are the **r** for infectious skin diseases	9368
	15:32	These are the **r** *for* a man with a discharge,	9368
	26:46	and the **r** that the Lord established	9368
Nu	9: 3	in accordance with all its rules and **r**."	5477
	9:12	they must follow all the **r**.	2978
	9:14	so in accordance with its rules and **r**.	5477
	9:14	You must have the same **r** for the alien and	2978
	15:16	The same laws and **r** will apply both to you	5477
	30:16	These are the **r** the Lord gave Moses	2976
	35:24	the avenger of blood according to these **r**.	5477
	36:13	and **r** the Lord gave through Moses to	5477
Dt	12:28	to obey all these **r** I am giving you,	1821
1Sa	10:25	Samuel explained to the people the **r** *of*	5477
1Ki	6:12	carry out my **r** and keep all my commands	5477
	8:58	decrees and **r** he gave our fathers.	5477
2Ki	23: 3	and keep his commands, **r** and decrees	6343
1Ch	6:32	according to the **r** *laid down* for them.	5477
	24:19	according to the **r** *prescribed for* them	5477
2Ch	34:31	and keep his commands, **r** and decrees	6343
Ne	9:13	You gave them **r** and laws that are just	5477
	10:29	**r** and decrees of the Lord our Lord.	5477
Est	9:32	Esther's decree confirmed these **r**	1821
Eze	43:11	its whole design and all its **r** and laws.	2978
	43:11	be faithful to its design and follow all its **r**.	2978
	43:18	be the **r** *for* sacrificing burnt offerings	2978
	44: 5	concerning all the **r** *regarding* the temple of	2978
Lk	1: 6	observing all the Lord's commandments and **r** blamelessly.	1468
Eph	2:15	the law with its commandments and **r**.	1504
Col	2:14	*with* its **r**, that was against us and	1504
	2:23	**Such r** indeed have an appearance	4015S
Heb	9: 1	Now the first covenant had **r** for worship	1468
	9:10	external **r** applying until the time of	1468

REHABIAH (4)

1Ch	23:17	The descendants of Eliezer: **R** was the first.	8152
	23:17	but the sons of **R** were very numerous.	8152
	24:21	for **R**, from his sons: Isshiah was the first.	8153
	26:25	**R** his son, Jeshaiah his son, Joram his son,	8153

REHEARSE (KJV) See RECITE

REHOB (10) [BETH REHOB]

Nu	13:21	the land from the Desert of Zin as far as **R**,	8149
Jos	19:28	to Abdon, **R**, Hammon and Kanah,	8149
	19:30	Ummah, Aphek and **R**.	8149
	21:31	and **R**, together with their pasturelands—	8149
Jdg	1:31	or Aczib or Helbah or Aphek or **R**,	8149

2Sa	8: 3	David fought Hadadezer son of **R**,	8150
	8:12	the plunder taken from Hadadezer son of **R**,	8150
	10: 8	the Arameans of Zobah and **R** and the men	8149
1Ch	6:75	and **R**, together with their pasturelands;	8149
Ne	10:11	Mica, **R**, Hashabiah,	8150

REHOBOAM (50) [REHOBOAM'S]

1Ki	11:43	And **R** his son succeeded him as king.	8154
	12: 1	**R** went to Shechem,	8154
	12: 3	and the whole assembly of Israel went to **R**	8154
	12: 5	**R** answered, "Go away for three days and	NIH
	12: 6	Then King **R** consulted the elders	8154
	12: 8	But **R** rejected the advice the elders gave	NIH
	12:12	and all the people returned to **R**,	8154
	12:17	**R** still ruled over them.	8154
	12:18	King **R** sent out Adoniram,	8154
	12:18	King **R**, however, managed to get into	8154
	12:21	When **R** arrived in Jerusalem,	8154
	12:21	and to regain the kingdom for **R** son	8154
	12:23	"Say to **R** son of Solomon king of Judah,	8154
	12:27	**R** king of Judah.	8154
	12:27	They will kill me and return to King **R**."	8154
	14:21	**R** son of Solomon was king in Judah.	8154
	14:25	In the fifth year of King **R**,	8154
	14:27	So King **R** made bronze shields	8154
	14:30	There was continual warfare between **R**	8154
	14:31	And **R** rested with his fathers	8154
	15: 6	There was war between **R** and Jeroboam	8154
1Ch	3:10	Solomon's son was **R**, Abijah his son,	8154
2Ch	9:31	And **R** his son succeeded him as king.	8154
	10: 1	**R** went to Shechem,	8154
	10: 3	he and all Israel went to **R** and said to him:	8154
	10: 5	**R** answered, "Come back to me	NIH
	10: 6	Then King **R** consulted the elders	8154
	10: 8	But **R** rejected the advice the elders gave	NIH
	10:12	and all the people returned to **R**,	8154
	10:17	**R** still ruled over them.	8154
	10:18	King **R** sent out Adoniram,	8154
	10:18	King **R**, however, managed to get into	8154
	11: 1	When **R** arrived in Jerusalem,	8154
	11: 1	and to regain the kingdom for **R**.	8154
	11: 3	"Say to **R** son of Solomon king of Judah	8154
	11: 5	**R** lived in Jerusalem and built up towns	8154
	11:17	the kingdom of Judah and supported **R** son	8154
	11:18	**R** married Mahalath, who was the daughter	8154
	11:21	**R** loved Maacah daughter of Absalom	8154
	11:22	**R** appointed Abijah son of Maacah to be	8154
	12: 2	in the fifth year of King **R**.	8154
	12: 5	Then the prophet Shemaiah came to **R** and	8154
	12:10	So King **R** made bronze shields	8154
	12:12	Because **R** humbled himself,	2257S
	12:13	King **R** established himself firmly	8154
	12:15	There was continual warfare between **R**	8154
	12:16	**R** rested with his fathers and was buried in	8154
	13: 7	around him and opposed **R** son of Solomon	8154
Mt	1: 7	Solomon the father of **R**,	4850
	1: 7	**R** the father of Abijah,	4850

REHOBOAM'S (3) [REHOBOAM]

1Ki	14:29	As for the other events of **R** reign,	8154
2Ch	12: 1	After **R** position as king was established	8154
	12:15	As for the events of **R** reign,	8154

REHOBOTH (3) [REHOBOTH IR]

Ge	26:22	He named it **R**, saying,	8151
	36:37	from **R** *on* the river succeeded him as king.	8151
1Ch	1:48	from **R** *on* the river succeeded him as king.	8151

REHOBOTH IR (1) [REHOBOTH]

Ge	10:11	where he built Nineveh, **R**, Calah	8155

REHUM (8)

Ezr	2: 2	Bilshan, Mispar, Bigvai, **R** and Baanah):	8156
	4: 8	**R** the commanding officer and Shimshai	10662
	4: 9	**R** the commanding officer and Shimshai	10662
	4:17	To **R** the commanding officer,	10662
	4:23	the letter of King Artaxerxes was read to **R**	10662
Ne	3:17	by the Levites under **R** son of Bani.	8156
	10:25	**R**, Hashabnah, Maaseiah,	8156
	12: 3	Shecaniah, **R**, Meremoth,	8156

REI (1)

1Ki	1: 8	Shimei and **R** and David's special guard did	8298

REIGN (154) [REIGNED, REIGNING, REIGNS]

Ge	37: 8	"*Do you* intend to **r** over us?	4887+4887
Ex	15:18	The Lord *will* **r** for ever and ever."	4887
Dt	17:20	and his descendants **r** a long time **over**	6584
	32:25	in their homes terror will **r**.	NIH
1Sa	8: 9	the king who *will* **r** over them will do."	4887
	8:11	the king who *will* **r** over you will be:	4887
	11:12	'Shall Saul **r** over us?'	4887
2Sa	21: 1	During the **r** *of* David,	3427
1Ki	1:35	and sit on my throne and **r** in my place.	4887
	6: 1	the fourth year of Solomon's **r** over Israel,	4887
	11:41	As for the other events of Solomon's **r**—	NIH
	14:19	The other events of Jeroboam's **r**,	NIH
	14:29	As for the other events of Rehoboam's **r**,	NIH
	15: 1	of the **r** of Jeroboam son of Nebat,	4889
	15: 7	As for the other events of Abijah's **r**,	NIH
	15:23	As for all the other events of Asa's **r**,	NIH

1Ki	15:29	As soon as he *began to* r,	4887
	15:31	As for the other events of Nadab's r,	NIH
	16: 5	As for the other events of Baasha's r,	NIH
	16:11	As soon as he *began to* r and was seated on	4887
	16:14	As for the other events of Elah's r,	NIH
	16:20	As for the other events of Zimri's r,	NIH
	16:27	As for the other events of Omri's r,	NIH
	22:39	As for the other events of Ahab's r,	NIH
	22:45	As for the other events of Jehoshaphat's r,	NIH
	22:46	even after the r of his father Asa.	3427
2Ki	1:18	As for all the other events of Ahaziah's r,	NIH
	8:16	Jehoram son of Jehoshaphat *began his* r	4887
	8:23	As for the other events of Jehoram's r,	NIH
	8:25	of Jehoram king of Judah *began to* r.	4887
	10:34	As for the other events of Jehu's r,	NIH
	11:21	when he *began to* r.	4887
	12:19	As for the other events of the r of Joash,	NIH
	13: 8	As for the other events of the r of Jehoahaz,	NIH
	13:12	As for the other events of the r of Jehoash,	NIH
	13:22	of Aram oppressed Israel throughout the r	3427
	14: 1	of Joash king of Judah *began to* r.	4887
	14:15	As for the other events of the r of Jehoash,	NIH
	14:18	As for the other events of Amaziah's r,	NIH
	14:28	As for the other events of Jeroboam's r,	NIH
	15: 1	of Amaziah king of Judah *began to* r.	4887
	15: 6	As for the other events of Azariah's r,	NIH
	15:11	of Zechariah's r are written in the book of	NIH
	15:15	The other events of Shallum's r,	NIH
	15:18	*During* his entire r he did not turn away	3427
	15:21	As for the other events of Menahem's r,	NIH
	15:26	The other events of Pekahiah's r,	NIH
	15:31	As for the other events of Pekah's r,	NIH
	15:32	of Uzziah king of Judah *began to* r.	4887
	15:36	As for the other events of Jotham's r,	NIH
	16: 1	of Jotham king of Judah *began to* r.	4887
	16:19	As for the other events of the r of Ahaz,	NIH
	18: 1	of Ahaz king of Judah *began to* r.	4887
	18:13	the fourteenth year of King Hezekiah's r,	NIH
	20:20	As for the other events of Hezekiah's r,	NIH
	21:17	As for the other events of Manasseh's r,	NIH
	21:25	As for the other events of Amon's r,	NIH
	22: 3	In the eighteenth year of his r,	4889
	23:28	As for the other events of Josiah's r,	NIH
	23:33	in the land of Hamath so that he *might* not r	4887
	24: 1	During Jehoiakim's r,	3427
	24: 5	As for the other events of Jehoiakim's r,	NIH
	24:12	In the eighth year of the r of the king	4887
	25: 1	So in the ninth year of Zedekiah's r,	4887
1Ch	4:31	These were their towns until the r	NIH
	5:10	During Saul's r they waged war against	3427
	7: 2	During the r *of* David,	3427
	13: 3	for we did not inquire of it during the r	3427
	22: 9	and quiet during his r.	3427
	26:31	fortieth year of David's r a search was made	4895
	29:29	As for the events of King David's r,	NIH
	29:30	together with the details of his r and power,	4895
2Ch	3: 2	in the fourth year of his r.	4895
	9:29	As for the other events of Solomon's r,	NIH
	12:15	As for the events of Rehoboam's r,	NIH
	13: 1	In the eighteenth year of the r *of* Jeroboam	4889
	13:22	The other events of Abijah's r,	NIH
	15:10	of the fifteenth year of Asa's r.	4895
	15:19	until the thirty-fifth year of Asa's r.	4895
	16: 1	the thirty-sixth year of Asa's r Baasha king	4895
	16:11	The events of Asa's r,	NIH
	16:12	of his r Asa was afflicted with a disease	4895
	16:13	in the forty-first year of his r Asa died	4887
	17: 7	of his r he sent his officials Ben-Hail,	4887
	20:34	The other events of Jehoshaphat's r,	NIH
	22: 1	of Jehoram king of Judah *began to* r.	4887
	23: 3	"The king's son *shall* r,	4887
	25:26	As for the other events of Amaziah's r,	NIH
	26:22	The other events of Uzziah's r,	NIH
	27: 7	The other events in Jotham's r,	NIH
	28:26	The other events of his r and all his ways,	NIH
	29: 3	In the first month of the first year of his r,	4887
	32:32	The other events of Hezekiah's r	NIH
	33:18	The other events of Manasseh's r,	NIH
	34: 3	In the eighth year of his r,	4887
	34: 8	In the eighteenth year of Josiah's r,	4887
	35:19	in the eighteenth year of Josiah's r.	4895
	35:26	The other events of Josiah's r and his acts	NIH
	36: 8	The other events of Jehoiakim's r,	NIH
Ezr	4: 5	and frustrate their plans during the entire r	3427
	4: 5	and down to the r *of* Darius king of Persia,	4895
	4: 6	At the beginning of the r *of* Xerxes,	4895
	4:24	to a standstill until the second year of the r	10424
	6:15	in the sixth year of the r *of* King Darius.	10424
	7: 1	during the r *of* Artaxerxes king of Persia,	4895
	8: 1	up with me from Babylon during the r	4895
Ne	12:22	were recorded in the r *of* Darius	4895
Est	1: 3	of his r he gave a banquet for all his nobles	4887
	2:16	in the seventh year of his r	4895
	6: 1	the chronicles, the record of his r,	3427
Ps	68:16	at the mountain where God chooses to r,	3782
Pr	8:15	By me kings r and rulers make laws	4887
Isa	9: 7	He will r on David's throne and	NIH
	24:23	the LORD Almighty *will* r on Mount Zion	4887
	32: 1	a king *will* r in righteousness	4887
	36: 1	the fourteenth year of King Hezekiah's r,	NIH
Jer	1: 2	the r *of* Josiah son of Amon king of Judah,	4887
	1: 3	the r *of* Jehoiakim son of Josiah king	3427
	3: 6	During the r *of* King Josiah,	3427
	23: 5	a King *who will* r wisely	4887
	26: 1	in the r *of* Jehoiakim son of Josiah king	4931
	27: 1	in the r *of* Zedekiah son of Josiah king	4930
	28: 1	early in the r *of* Zedekiah king of Judah,	4930

Jer	33:21	a descendant *to* r on his throne.	4887
	35: 1	the LORD during the r *of* Jehoiakim son	3427
	36: 2	the time I began speaking to you in the r	3427
	49:34	early in the r *of* Zedekiah king of Judah:	4895
	51:59	of Judah in the fourth year of his r.	4887
	52: 4	So in the ninth year of Zedekiah's r,	4887
La	5:19	You, O LORD, r forever;	3782
Da	1: 1	In the third year of the r *of* Jehoiakim king	4895
	2: 1	In the second year of his r,	4895
	5:26	the days of your r and brought it to an end.	10424
	6:28	So Daniel prospered during the r *of* Darius	10424
	6:28	of Darius and the r *of* Cyrus the Persian.	10424
	8: 1	In the third year of King Belshazzar's r, I,	4895
	8:23	"In the latter part of their r,	4895
	9: 2	in the first year of his r,	4887
Hos	1: 1	the r *of* Jeroboam son of Jehoash king	3427
Am	5:15	You put off the evil day and bring near a r	8699
Zep	1: 1	the r *of* Josiah son of Amon king of Judah:	3427
Lk	1:33	he will r over the house of Jacob forever;	996
	3: 1	fifteenth year *of* the r of Tiberius Caesar—	2449
Ac	11:28	(This happened during the r *of* Claudius.)	NIG
Ro	5:17	of the gift of righteousness r in life through	996
	5:21	so also grace *might* r through righteousness	996
	6:12	not *let* sin r in your mortal body so	996
1Co	15:25	For he must r until he has put all his enemies	996
2Ti	2:12	if we endure, *we will* also r *with* him.	5203
Rev	5:10	and *they will* r on the earth."	996
	11:15	and he will r for ever and ever."	996
	11:17	your great power and *have begun to* r.	996
	20: 6	be priests of God and of Christ and *will* r	996
	22: 5	And *they will* r for ever and ever.	996

REIGNED (94) [REIGN]

Ge	36:31	These were the kings who r in Edom	4887
	36:31	in Edom before any Israelite king r:	4887
Nu	21:34	who r in Heshbon."	3782
Dt	1: 4	who r in Heshbon,	3782
	1: 4	who r in Ashtaroth.	3782
	3: 2	who r in Heshbon.	3782
	4:46	who r in Heshbon and was defeated	3782
Jos	9:10	of Heshbon, and Og king of Bashan, who r	NIH
	12: 2	who r in Heshbon.	3782
	12: 4	who r in Ashtaroth and Edrei.	3782
	13:12	who *had* r in Ashtaroth and Edrei	4887
Jdg	4: 2	a king of Canaan, who r in Hazor.	4887
1Sa	13: 1	and he r over Israel [forty-]two years.	4887
2Sa	2:10	and he r two years.	4887
	5: 4	and he r forty years.	4887
	5: 5	In Hebron he r over Judah seven years	4887
	5: 5	and in Jerusalem he r over all Israel	4887
	8:15	David r over all Israel,	4887
	16: 8	in whose place *you have* r.	4887
1Ki	2:11	He *had* r forty years over Israel—	4887
	11:42	Solomon r in Jerusalem	4887
	14:20	He r for twenty-two years and then rested	4887
	14:21	and he r seventeen years in Jerusalem,	4887
	15: 2	and *he* r in Jerusalem three years.	4887
	15:10	and *he* r in Jerusalem forty-one years.	4887
	15:25	and *he* r over Israel two years.	4887
	15:33	and *he* r twenty-four years.	NIH
	16: 8	and r in Tirzah two years.	NIH
	16:15	Zimri r in Tirzah seven days.	4887
	16:23	and *he* r twelve years, six of them in Tirzah.	4887
	16:29	and *he* r in Samaria	4887
	22:42	and *he* r in Jerusalem twenty-five years.	4887
	22:51	and *he* r over Israel two years.	4887
2Ki	3: 1	and *he* r twelve years.	4887
	8:17	and *he* r in Jerusalem eight years.	4887
	8:26	and *he* r in Jerusalem one year.	4887
	10:36	The time that Jehu r over Israel	4887
	12: 1	and *he* r in Jerusalem forty years.	4887
	13: 1	and *he* r seventeen years.	NIH
	13:10	and *he* r sixteen years.	NIH
	14: 2	and *he* r in Jerusalem twenty-nine years.	4887
	14:23	and *he* r forty-one years.	NIH
	15: 2	and *he* r in Jerusalem fifty-two years.	4887
	15: 8	and *he* r six months.	NIH
	15:13	and *he* r in Samaria one month.	4887
	15:17	and *he* r in Samaria ten years.	NIH
	15:23	and *he* r two years.	NIH
	15:27	and *he* r twenty years.	NIH
	15:33	and *he* r in Jerusalem sixteen years.	4887
	16: 2	and *he* r in Jerusalem sixteen years.	NIH
	17: 1	and *he* r nine years.	NIH
	18: 2	and *he* r in Jerusalem twenty-nine years.	4887
	21: 1	and *he* r in Jerusalem fifty-five years.	4887
	21:19	and *he* r in Jerusalem two years.	4887
	22: 1	and *he* r in Jerusalem thirty-one years.	4887
	23:31	and *he* r in Jerusalem three months.	4887
	23:36	and *he* r in Jerusalem eleven years.	4887
	24: 8	and *he* r in Jerusalem three months.	4887
	24:18	and *he* r in Jerusalem eleven years.	4887
1Ch	1:43	These were the kings who r in Edom	4887
	1:43	in Edom before any Israelite king r:	4887
	3: 4	where *he* r seven years and six months.	4887
	3: 4	David r in Jerusalem thirty-three years,	4887
	18:14	David r over all Israel,	4887
2Ch	1:13	And *he* r over Israel.	4887
	9:30	Solomon r in Jerusalem	4887
	12:13	and *he* r seventeen years in Jerusalem,	4887
	13: 2	and *he* r in Jerusalem three years.	4887
	20:31	So Jehoshaphat r over Judah.	4887
	20:31	and *he* r in Jerusalem twenty-five years.	4887
	21: 5	and *he* r in Jerusalem eight years.	4887
	21:20	and *he* r in Jerusalem eight years.	4887
	22: 2	and *he* r in Jerusalem one year.	4887

2Ch	24: 1	and *he* r in Jerusalem forty years.	4887
	25: 1	and *he* r in Jerusalem twenty-nine years.	4887
	26: 3	and *he* r in Jerusalem fifty-two years.	4887
	27: 1	and *he* r in Jerusalem sixteen years.	4887
	27: 8	and *he* r in Jerusalem sixteen years.	4887
	28: 1	and *he* r in Jerusalem sixteen years.	4887
	29: 1	and *he* r in Jerusalem twenty-nine years.	4887
	33: 1	and *he* r in Jerusalem fifty-five years.	4887
	33:21	and *he* r in Jerusalem two years.	4887
	34: 1	and *he* r in Jerusalem thirty-one years.	4887
	36: 2	and *he* r in Jerusalem three months.	4887
	36: 5	and *he* r in Jerusalem eleven years.	4887
	36: 9	and *he* r in Jerusalem three months	4887
	36:11	and *he* r in Jerusalem eleven years.	4887
Est	1: 1	At that time King Xerxes r from his royal	3782
Jer	37: 1	*he* r in place of Jehoiachin son	4887+4889
	52: 1	and *he* r in Jerusalem eleven years.	4887
Ro	5:14	death r from the time of Adam to the time	996
	5:17	death r through that one man,	996
	5:21	just as sin r in death,	996
Rev	20: 4	to life and r with Christ a thousand years.	996

REIGNING (1) [REIGN]

Mt	2:22	But when he heard that Archelaus *was* r	996

REIGNS (18) [REIGN]

1Sa	12:14	and the king who r over you follow	4887
1Ki	15:16	king of Israel throughout their r.	3427
	15:32	king of Israel throughout their r.	3427
1Ch	5:17	in the genealogical records during the r	3427
	16:31	among the nations, "The LORD r!"	4887
Ps	9: 7	The LORD r forever;	3782
	47: 8	God r over the nations;	4887
	93: 1	The LORD r, he is robed in majesty;	4887
	96:10	Say among the nations, "The LORD r."	4887
	97: 1	The LORD r, let the earth be glad;	4887
	99: 1	The LORD r, let the nations tremble;	4887
	146:10	The LORD r forever, your God, O Zion,	4887
Isa	1: 1	that Isaiah son of Amoz saw during the r	3427
	52: 7	who say to Zion, "Your God r!"	4887
Hos	1: 1	during the r *of* Uzziah, Jotham, Ahaz	3427
Mic	1: 1	of Moresheth during the r *of* Jotham, Ahaz	3427
Lk	22:53	But this is your hour—when darkness r."	2026
Rev	19: 6	For our Lord God Almighty r.	996

REIMBURSE (1)

Lk	10:35	I *will* r you for any extra expense	625

REIN (2)

Job	10: 1	therefore *I will* **give free** r to my complaint	6440
Jas	1:26	**keep a tight** r on his tongue,	5902

REINFORCE (1) [REINFORCED, REINFORCEMENTS]

Jer	51:12	**R** the guard, station the watchmen,	2616

REINFORCED (2) [REINFORCE]

2Ch	24:13	according to its original design and r it.	599
	32: 5	He built another wall outside that one and r	2616

REINFORCEMENTS (1) [REINFORCE]

Isa	43:17	the army and r together, and they lay there,	6450

REJECT (32) [REJECTED, REJECTING, REJECTION, REJECTS]

Lev	26:15	and if you r my decrees and abhor my laws	4415
	26:44	*I will* not r them or abhor them so as	4415
1Sa	12:22	the LORD *will* not r his people,	5759
1Ki	9: 7	and *will* r this temple I have consecrated	4946+6584+7156+8938
2Ki	23:27	and *I will* r Jerusalem, the city I chose,	4415
1Ch	28: 9	if you forsake him, *he will* r you forever.	2396
2Ch	6:42	LORD God, *do* not r your anointed one.	7156+8740
	7:20	and *will* r this temple I have consecrated	4946+6584+7156+8959
Job	8:20	"Surely God *does* not r a blameless man	4415
Ps	27: 9	*Do* not r me or forsake me,	5759
	36: 4	and *does* not r what is wrong.	4415
	44:23	*Do* not r us forever.	2396
	77: 7	"Will the Lord r forever?	2396
	88:14	*do you* r me and hide your face from me?	2396
	94:14	For the LORD *will* not r his people;	5759
	119:118	*You* r all who stray from your decrees,	6136
	132:10	*do* not r your anointed one.	7156+8740
Isa	7:15	and honey when he knows enough *to* r	4415
	7:16	But before the boy knows enough *to* r	4415
	31: 7	that day every one of *you* will r the idols	4415
Jer	31:37	be searched out *will* I r all the descendants	4415
	33:26	then *I will* r the descendants of Jacob	4415
Hos	4: 6	*I* also r you as my priests;	4415
	9:17	My God *will* r them because they have	4415
Lk	6:22	and insult you and r your name as evil,	1675
Ac	13:46	Since *you* r it and do not consider yourselves	723
Ro	2: 8	who are self-seeking and who r the truth	578
	11: 1	I ask then: *Did* God r his people?	723
	11: 2	God *did* not r his people,	723
1Th	4: 8	this instruction *does* not r man but God,	119
Tit	1:14	to the commands of those *who* r the truth.	695
Jude	1: 8	r authority and slander celestial beings.	119

REJECTED (79) [REJECT]

Lev	26:43	for their sins because they **r** my laws	4415
Nu	11:20	because *you* have **r** the LORD,	4415
	14:31	in to enjoy the land *you* have **r**.	4415
Dt	32:15	the God who made him and **r**	5571
	32:19	and **r** them because he was angered	5540
1Sa	8: 7	it is not you *they* have **r**,	4415
	8: 7	but *they* have **r** me as their king.	4415
	10:19	But you *have* now **r** your God,	4415
	15:23	*you* have **r** the word of the LORD,	4415
	15:23	he has **r** you as king."	4415
	15:26	*You* have **r** the word of the LORD,	4415
	15:26	the LORD *has* **r** you as king over Israel!"	4415
	16: 1	since I *have* **r** him as king over Israel?	4415
	16: 7	for I *have* **r** him.	4415
1Ki	12: 8	But Rehoboam **r** the advice	6440
	19:10	The Israelites *have* **r** your covenant,	6440
	19:14	The Israelites *have* **r** your covenant,	6440
2Ki	17:15	*They* **r** his decrees and the covenant	4415
	17:20	the LORD **r** all the people of Israel;	4415
2Ch	10: 8	But Rehoboam **r** the advice the elders gave	6440
	11:14	because Jeroboam and his sons *had* **r** them	2396
Ps	43: 2	Why have *you* **r** me?	2396
	44: 9	But now *you* have **r** and humbled us;	2396
	60: 1	*You* have **r** us, O God,	2396
	60:10	*you* who have **r** us and no longer go out	2396
	66:20	not **r** my prayer or withheld his love	6073
	74: 1	Why have *you* **r** us forever, O God?	2396
	78:59	he **r** Israel completely.	4415
	78:67	Then *he* **r** the tents of Joseph,	4415
	89:38	But you have **r**, you have spurned,	2396
	108:11	*you* who have **r** us and no longer go out	2396
	118:22	the builders **r** has become the capstone;	4415
Pr	1:24	But since *you* **r** me when I called	4412
Isa	5:24	for *they* have **r** the law of the LORD	4415
	8: 6	"Because this people *has* **r** the gently	4415
	14:19	of your tomb like a **r** branch;	9493
	30:12	"Because *you* have **r** this message,	4415
	41: 9	I have chosen you and *have* not **r** you.	4415
	49:21	I was exiled and **r**.	6073
	53: 3	He was despised and **r** *by* men,	2534
	54: 6	a wife when married young, only *to* be **r**,"	4415
Jer	2:37	for the LORD *has* **r** those you trust;	4415
	6:19	to my words and have **r** my law.	4415
	6:30	They are called **r** silver,	4415
	6:30	because the LORD *has* **r** them."	4415
	7:29	on the barren heights, for the LORD *has* **r**	4415
	8: 9	Since *they* have **r** the word of the LORD,	4415
	14:19	*Have* you **r** Judah **completely?**	4415+4415
	15: 6	You *have* **r** me," declares the LORD.	5759
	33:24	'The LORD *has* **r** the two kingdoms	4415
La	1:15	Lord *has* **r** all the warriors in my midst;	6136
	2: 7	The Lord *has* **r** his altar	2396
	5:22	unless *you* have **utterly r** us	4415+4415
Eze	5: 6	She *has* **r** my laws and has	4415
	20:13	not follow my decrees but **r** my laws—	4415
	20:16	because *they* **r** my laws and did	4415
	20:24	not obeyed my laws but *had* **r** my decrees	4415
Hos	4: 6	"Because *you* have **r** knowledge,	4415
	8: 3	But Israel *has* **r** what is good;	2396
Am	2: 4	Because *they* have **r** the law of the LORD	4415
Zec	10: 6	They will be as though *I* had not **r** them,	2396
Mt	21:42	the builders **r** has become the capstone;	627
Mk	8:31	of Man must suffer many things and *be* **r**	627
	9:12	of Man must suffer much and *be* **r**?	2022
	12:10	the builders **r** has become the capstone;	627
Lk	7:30	in the law **r** God's purpose for themselves,	119
	9:22	of Man must suffer many things and *be* **r**	627
	17:25	and *be* **r** by this generation.	627
	20:17	the builders **r** has become the capstone'?	627
Ac	4:11	He is " 'the stone *you* builders **r**,	2024
	7:35	"This is the same Moses whom *they* had **r**	766
	7:39	*they* **r** him and in their hearts turned back	723
1Ti	1:19	Some *have* **r** these and	723
	4: 4	to be **r** if it is received with thanksgiving,	612
2Ti	3: 8	who, as far as the faith is concerned, are **r**.	99
Heb	10:28	Anyone who **r** the law of Moses died	119
	12:17	to inherit this blessing, *he was* **r**.	627
1Pe	2: 4	**r** by men but chosen by God and precious	627
	2: 7	the builders **r** has become the capstone,"	627

REJECTING (3) [REJECT]

Dt	31:20	**r** me and breaking my covenant.	5540
1Ki	12:13	**R** the advice given him by the elders,	6440
2Ch	10:13	**R** the advice of the elders,	6440

REJECTION (1) [REJECT]

Ro	11:15	if their **r** is the reconciliation of the world,	613

REJECTS (8) [REJECT]

Isa	33:15	*who* **r** gain from extortion	4415
Lk	10:16	he who **r** you hears me;	119
	10:16	he who **r** you **r** me;	119
	10:16	but he who **r** me rejects him who sent me."	119
	10:16	but he who **r** me rejects him who sent me."	119
Jn	3:36	but whoever **r** the Son will not see life,	578
	12:48	a judge for the one who **r** me and does	119
1Th	4: 8	he who **r** this instruction does	119

REJOICE (133) [JOY]

Lev	23:40	and **r** before the LORD your God	8523
Dt	12: 7	you and your families shall eat and *shall* **r**	8523
	12:12	And there **r** before the LORD your God,	8523
	12:18	*to* **r** before the LORD your God	8523
	14:26	the presence of the LORD your God and **r**.	8523
	16:11	And **r** before the LORD your God at	8523
	26:11	among you *shall* **r** in all the good things	8523
	32:43	**R**, O nations, with his people,	8264
	33:18	"**R**, Zebulun, in your going out, and you,	8523
2Sa	1:20	lest the daughters of the uncircumcised **r**.	6600
1Ch	16:10	the hearts of those who seek the LORD **r**.	8523
	16:31	*Let* the heavens **r**, let the earth be glad;	8523
2Ch	6:41	*may* your saints **r** in your goodness.	8523
	20:27	*given* them **cause to r** over their enemies.	8055
Job	3:22	with gladness and **r** when they reach	8464
	22:19	'The righteous see their ruin and **r**;	8523
Ps	2:11	the LORD with fear and **r** with trembling.	1635
	5:11	those who love your name *may* **r** in you.	6636
	9: 2	I will be glad and **r** in you;	6636
	9:14	of Zion and there **r** in your salvation.	1635
	13: 4	and my foes *will* **r** when I fall.	1635
	14: 7	*let* Jacob **r** and Israel be glad!	1635
	31: 7	I will be glad and **r** in your love,	1635
	32:11	**R** in the LORD and be glad, you righteous;	8523
	33:21	In him our hearts **r**,	8523
	34: 2	let the afflicted hear and **r**.	8055
	35: 9	Then my soul *will* **r** in the LORD	1635
	39:13	that *I* may **r** again before I depart	1158
	40:16	*may* all who seek you **r** and be glad in you;	8464
	51: 8	*let* the bones you have crushed **r**.	1635
	53: 6	*let* Jacob **r** and Israel be glad!	1635
	63:11	But the king *will* **r** in God;	8523
	64:10	*Let* the righteous **r** in the LORD	8523
	66: 6	*come, let* us **r** in him.	8523
	68: 3	the righteous be glad and **r** before God;	6636
	68: 4	and **r** before him.	6600
	70: 4	*may* all who seek you **r** and be glad in you;	8464
	85: 6	that your people *may* **r** in you?	8523
	89:16	*They* **r** in your name all day long;	1635
	89:42	*made* all his enemies **r**.	8055
	96:11	*Let* the heavens **r**, let the earth be glad;	8523
	97: 1	*let* the distant shores **r**.	1635
	97:12	**R** in the LORD, *you* who are righteous,	8523
	104:31	*may* the LORD **r** in his works—	8523
	104:34	*as* I **r** in the LORD.	8523
	105: 3	the hearts of those who seek the LORD **r**.	8523
	107:42	The upright see and **r**,	8523
	109:28	but your servant *will* **r**.	8523
	118:24	*let* us **r** and be glad in it.	1635
	119:14	I **r** in following your statutes	8464
	119:74	*May* those who fear you **r**	8523
	119:162	I **r** in your promise	8464
	149: 2	*Let* Israel **r** in their Maker;	8523
	149: 5	the saints **r** in this honor and sing for joy	6600
Pr	2:14	in doing wrong and **r** in the perverseness	1635
	5:18	and *may* you **r** in the wife of your youth.	8523
	23:16	my inmost being *will* **r**	6600
	23:25	*may* she who gave you birth **r**!	1635
	24:17	when he stumbles, *do* not *let* your heart **r**,	1635
	29: 2	When the righteous thrive, the people **r**;	8523
SS	1: 4	*We* **r** and delight in you;	1635
Isa	9: 3	*they* **r** before you as people rejoice at	8523
	9: 3	they rejoice before you as people **r** at	8525
	9: 3	as *men* **r** when dividing the plunder.	1635
	13: 3	*those who* **r** in my triumph.	6611
	14:29	*Do* not **r**, all you Philistines, that the rod	8055
	25: 9	*let* us **r** and be glad in his salvation."	1635
	29:19	the humble will **r** in the LORD;	8055
	29:19	the needy *will* **r** in the Holy One of Israel.	1635
	30:29	your hearts will **r** as when people go up	8525
	35: 1	the wilderness *will* **r** and blossom.	1635
	35: 2	*it will* **r** greatly and shout for joy.	677+1635+1638
	41:16	But you *will* **r** in the LORD and glory in	1635
	42:11	*let* the settlements where Kedar lives **r**.	NIH
	49:13	**r**, O earth; burst into song, O mountains!	1635
	61: 7	and instead of disgrace *they* will **r**	8264
	62: 5	so *will* your God **r** over you.	8464
	65:13	my servants *will* **r**,	8523
	65:18	be glad and **r** forever *in* what I will create,	1635
	65:19	*I will* **r** over Jerusalem and take delight	1635
	66:10	"**R** with Jerusalem and be glad for her,	8523
	66:10	**r greatly** with her,	5375+8464
	66:14	your heart *will* **r** and you will flourish	8464
Jer	11:15	in your wickedness, then can you **r**?"	6600
	31:12	*they* will **r** in the bounty of the LORD—	5642
	32:41	*I will* **r** in doing them good	8464
	50:11	"Because *you* **r** and are glad,	8523
La	1:21	*they* **r** at what you have done.	8464
	4:21	**R** and be glad, O Daughter of Edom,	8464
Eze	7:12	*Let* not the buyer **r** nor the seller grieve,	8523
	21:10	" 'Shall we **r** in the scepter	8464
Hos	9: 1	*Do* not **r**, O Israel;	8523
Joel	2:21	Be not afraid, O land; be glad and **r**.	8523
	2:23	**r** in the LORD your God,	8523
Am	6:13	*you who* **r** in the conquest of Lo Debar	8524
Ob	1:12	nor **r** over the people of Judah in the day	8523
Hab	3:18	yet I *will* **r** in the LORD,	6600
Zep	3:11	from this city *those who* **r** *in* their pride.	6611
	3:14	Be glad and **r** with all your heart,	6600
	3:17	*he will* **r** over you with singing."	1635
Zec	4:10	*Men will* **r** when they see the plumb line	8523
	9: 9	**R** greatly, O Daughter of Zion!	1635
	10: 7	their hearts *will* **r** in the LORD.	1635
Mt	5:12	**R** and be glad, because great is your reward	5897
Lk	1:14	and many *will* **r** because of his birth,	5897
	6:23	"**R** in that day and leap for joy,	5897
	10:20	*do* not **r** that the spirits submit to you,	5897
	10:20	*r* that your names are written in heaven."	5897
	15: 6	'R with me; I have found my lost sheep.'	5176
	15: 9	'R with me; I have found my lost coin.'	5176
Jn	16:22	but I will see you again and you *will* **r**,	5897

Ro	5: 2	And *we* **r** in the hope of the glory of God.	3016
	5: 3	Not only so, but *we* also **r** in our sufferings,	3016
	5:11	but *we* also **r** in God through our Lord	3016
	12:15	**R** with those who rejoice;	5897
	12:15	Rejoice with *those who* **r**;	5897
	15:10	Again, it says, "**R**, O Gentiles,	2370
2Co	2: 3	by those who ought to **make** me **r**.	5897
Php	1:18	And because of this *I* **r**.	5897
	1:18	Yes, and *I will* continue to **r**,	5897
	2:17	*I* am glad and **r** with all of you.	5176
	2:18	So you too should be glad and **r** with me.	5176
	3: 1	Finally, my brothers, **r** in the Lord!	5897
	4: 4	**R** in the Lord always.	5897
	4: 4	I will say it again: **R**!	5897
	4:10	*I* **r** greatly in the Lord that	5897
Col	1:24	Now *I* **r** in what was suffered for you,	5897
1Pe	1: 8	In this *you* **r** with	22
	4:13	But **r** that you participate in the sufferings	5897
Rev	12:12	Therefore **r**, *you* heavens	2370
	18:20	**R** over her, O heaven!	2370
	18:20	**R**, saints and apostles and prophets!	NIG
	19: 7	*Let* us **r** and be glad and give him glory!	5897

REJOICED (16) [JOY]

1Sa	6:13	*they* **r** at the sight.	8523
2Ki	11:20	and all the people of the land **r**.	8523
1Ch	29: 9	The people **r** at the willing response	8523
	29: 9	David the king also **r** greatly.	8523+8525
2Ch	15:15	All Judah **r** about the oath	8523
	23:21	and all the people of the land **r**.	8523
	29:36	the people **r** at what God had brought about	8523
	30:25	The entire assembly of Judah **r**,	8523
Ne	12:43	The women and children also **r**.	8523
Job	31:25	*if I have* **r** over my great wealth,	8523
	31:29	"If I have **r** at my enemy's misfortune	8523
Ps	122: 1	*I* **r** with those who said to me,	8523
SS	3:11	the day of his wedding, the day his heart **r**.	8525
Eze	35:15	Because you **r** when the inheritance of	8525
Hos	10: 5	*those who had* **r** over its splendor,	1635
Jn	8:56	Your father Abraham **r** at the thought	22

REJOICES (18) [JOY]

1Sa	2: 1	"My heart **r** in the LORD;	6636
Ps	13: 5	my heart **r** in your salvation.	1635
	16: 9	and my tongue **r**;	1635
	21: 1	O LORD, the king **r** in your strength.	8523
	48:11	Mount Zion **r**, the villages of Judah	8523
	97: 8	Zion hears and **r** and the villages of Judah	8523
	119:14	I rejoice in following your statutes as one **r**	NIH
Pr	11:10	When the righteous prosper, the city **r**;	6636
Isa	8: 6	and **r** in Rezin and the son of Remaliah,	5375
	61:10	my soul **r** in my God.	1635
	62: 5	as a bridegroom **r** over his bride,	5375
Eze	35:14	the whole earth **r**, I will make you desolate.	8523
Hab	1:15	and so *he* **r** and is glad.	8523
Lk	1:47	and my spirit **r** in God my Savior,	22
Jn	16:20	and mourn while the world **r**.	5897
Ac	2:26	my heart is glad and my tongue **r**;	22
1Co	12:26	if one part is honored, every part **r with** it.	5176
	13: 6	Love does not delight in evil but **r with**	5176

REJOICING (24) [JOY]

Nu	10:10	Also at your times of **r**—	8525
Dt	27: 7	eating them and **r** in the presence of	8523
2Sa	6:12	of Obed-Edom to the City of David with **r**.	8525
1Ki	1:40	playing flutes and **r** greatly,	8524+8525
2Ki	11:14	of the land were **r** and blowing trumpets.	8524
1Ch	15:25	from the house of Obed-Edom, with **r**.	8525
2Ch	23:13	of the land were **r** and blowing trumpets,	8524
	23:18	with **r** and singing, as David had ordered.	8525
	30:21	for seven days with great **r**,	8525
Ne	12:43	**r** because God had given them great joy.	8523
	12:43	of Jerusalem could be heard far away.	8525
Job	39:21	He paws fiercely, **r** in his strength,	8464
Ps	19: 5	like a champion **r** to run his course.	8464
	30: 5	but **r** comes in the morning.	8262
	105:43	He brought out his people with **r**,	8607
Pr	8:30	**r** always in his presence,	8471
	8:31	**r** in his whole world and delighting	8471
Jer	30:19	of thanksgiving and the sound of **r**.	8471
Eze	25: 6	and stamped your feet, **r** with all the malice	8523
Lk	15: 7	that in the same way there will be more **r**	5915
	15:10	there is **r** in the presence of the angels	5915
Ac	5:41	**r** because they had been counted worthy	5897
	8:39	but went on his way **r**.	5897
2Co	6:10	sorrowful, yet always **r**;	5897

REJOINED (1) [JOIN]

Jdg	14: 9	When *he* **r** his parents, he gave them	448+2143

REKEM (5)

Nu	31: 8	Among their victims were Evi, **R**, Zur,	8390
Jos	13:21	Evi, **R**, Zur, Hur and Reba—	8390
	18:27	**R**, Irpeel, Taralah,	8389
1Ch	2:43	Korah, Tappuah, **R** and Shema.	8390
	2:44	**R** was the father of Shammai.	8390

RELATED (11) [RELATING, RELATION, RELATIONS, RELATIONSHIP, RELATIONSHIPS, RELATIVE, RELATIVES]

Lev	21: 4	people **r** *to* him **by marriage**,	1251
Nu	3:26	and everything **r** *to* their use.	4200

Nu	3:31	the curtain, and **everything** *r to* their use.	AIT
	3:36	and **everything** *r to* their use,	AIT
	4:32	all their equipment and everything **r** to	4200
2Sa	19:42	"We did this because the king is **closely r**	7940
2Ki	8:27	for he was **r by marriage** to Ahab's family.	3163
2Ch	4:16	shovels, meat forks and all **r** articles.	2157S
Est	8: 1	for Esther had told how he was **r** to her.	4200
Ac	19:25	along with the workmen in **r** trades,	5525S
Heb	5: 1	to represent them in matters **r** to God,	NIG

RELATING (1) [RELATED]

Ne	11:24	was the king's agent in all affairs **r** to	4200

RELATION (1) [RELATED]

1Ki	10: 1	the fame of Solomon and his **r to** the name	4200

RELATIONS (34) [RELATED]

Ex	19:15	**Abstain from sexual r.**"	440+448+851+5602
	22:19	"Anyone *who* **has sexual r with**	6640+8886
Lev	18: 6	a close relative to **have sexual r.**	1655+6872
	18: 7	**dishonor** your father **by having sexual r with**	1655+6872
	18: 7	your mother; *do* not **have r with** her.	1655+6872
	18: 8	" '*Do* not **have sexual r with** your father's wife;	1655+6872
	18: 9	" '*Do* not **have sexual r with** your sister,	1655+6872
	18:10	" '*Do* not **have sexual r with** your son's daughter	1655+6872
	18:11	" '*Do* not **have sexual r with** the daughter	1655+6872
	18:12	" '*Do* not **have sexual r with** your father's sister;	1655+6872
	18:13	" '*Do* not **have sexual r with** your mother's sister,	1655+6872
	18:14	*Do* not **dishonor** your father's brother **by** approaching his wife **to have sexual r;**	1655+6872
	18:15	" '*Do* not **have sexual r with** your daughter-in-law.	1655+6872
	18:15	*do* not **have r with** her.	1655+6872
	18:16	" '*Do* not **have sexual r with** your brother's wife;	1655+6872
	18:17	" '*Do* not **have sexual r with** both a woman and her daughter.	1655+6872
	18:17	*Do* not **have sexual r with** either	1655+6872
	18:18	rival wife and **have sexual r with** her	1655+6872
	18:19	**have sexual r** during the uncleanness	1655+6872
	18:20	'*Do* not **have sexual r with**	2446+4200+5989+8888
	18:23	'*Do* not **have sexual r with** an animal	5989+8888
	18:23	to an animal to **have sexual r with** it;	8061
	20:15	'If a man **has sexual r with** an animal,	5989+8888
	20:16	an animal to **have sexual r with** it,	8061
	20:17	and *they* **have sexual r,** it is a disgrace.	906+6872+8011
	20:18	and **has sexual r with** her,	906+1655+6872
	20:19	" '*Do* not **have sexual r with** the sister of either your mother or	1655+6872
Dt	27:21	"Cursed the man *who* **has sexual r with** any animal."	6640+8886
Jdg	4:17	because there were **friendly r** between	8934
1Ki	1: 4	the king **had** no **intimate r with** her.	3359
	5:12	There were **peaceful r** between Hiram	8934
Ro	1:26	Even their women exchanged natural **r**	5979
	1:27	also abandoned natural **r** with women	5979
2Co	1:12	and especially in our **r** with you,	NIG

RELATIONSHIP (3) [RELATED]

Jdg	18: 7	a long way from the Sidonians and had no **r**	1821
	18:28	from Sidon and had no **r** with anyone else.	1821
Ro	2:17	on the law and brag about your **r to** God;	1877

RELATIONSHIPS (1) [RELATED]

Nu	30:16	concerning **r between** a man and his wife,	1068

RELATIVE (22) [RELATED]

Ge	14:14	that his **r** had been taken captive,	278
	14:16	the goods and brought back his **r** Lot	278
	29:12	a **r** *of* her father and a son of Rebekah.	278
	29:15	"Just because you are a **r** *of* mine,	278
Lev	18: 6	" 'No one is to approach any **close r**	1414+8638
	18:12	she is your father's **close r.**	8638
	18:13	because she is your mother's **close r.**	8638
	20:19	for that would dishonor a **close r;**	8638
	21: 2	except for a **close r,**	7940+8638
	25:25	his nearest **r** is to come	1457
	25:49	An uncle or a cousin or any **blood r**	1414+8638
Nu	5: 8	But if that person has no **close r**	1457
	27:11	give his inheritance to the nearest **r**	8638
Ru	2: 1	Now Naomi had a **r** on her husband's side,	4530
	2:20	She added, "That man is our **close r;**	7940
1Ki	16:11	whether **r** or friend.	1457
Jer	23:35	of you keeps on saying to his friend or **r:**	278
	32: 7	**as nearest r** it is your right and **duty**	1460
Am	6:10	And if a **r** who is to burn the bodies comes	1856
Lk	1:36	Even Elizabeth your **r** is going to have	5151
Jn	18:26	a **r** of the man whose ear Peter had cut off,	5150
Ro	16:11	Greet Herodion, my **r.**	5150

RELATIVES (82) [RELATED]

Ge	24: 4	to my country and my own **r** and get a wife	4580
	24:27	the journey to the house of my master's **r.**"	278
	27:37	and have made all his **r** his servants,	278

Ge	31: 3	to the land of your fathers and to your **r,**	4580
	31:23	Taking his **r** with him,	278
	31:25	and Laban and his **r** camped there too.	278
	31:32	In the presence of our **r,**	278
	31:37	Put it here in front of your **r** and mine.	278
	31:46	He said to his **r,** "Gather some stones."	278
	31:54	the hill country and invited his **r** to a meal.	278
	32: 9	'Go back to your country and your **r,**	4580
Lev	10: 6	But your **r,** all the house of Israel,	278
	18:17	they are her **close r.**	8638
	25:48	One of his **r** may redeem him:	278
Nu	27: 4	Give us property among our father's **r.**"	278
	27: 7	as an inheritance among their father's **r.**	278
Jdg	14: 3	among your **r** or among all our people?	278
2Ki	10:13	he met *some of* **r** of Ahaziah king of Judah	278
	10:13	They said, "We are **r** of Ahaziah,	278
1Ch	5: 7	Their **r** by clans, listed according	278
	5:13	Their **r,** by families, were:	278
	7: 5	The **r** who were fighting men belonging	278
	7:22	and his **r** came to comfort him.	278
	8:32	They too lived near their **r** in Jerusalem.	278
	9:38	They too lived near their **r** in Jerusalem.	278
	12:32	with all their **r** under their command;	278
	15: 5	Uriel the leader and 120 **r;**	278
	15: 6	Asaiah the leader and 220 **r;**	278
	15: 7	Joel the leader and 130 **r;**	278
	15: 8	Shemaiah the leader and 200 **r;**	278
	15: 9	Eliel the leader and 80 **r;**	278
	15:10	Amminadab the leader and 112 **r.**	278
	25: 7	Along with their **r—**	278
	25: 9	his sons and **r,** 12 the second to Gedaliah,	278
	25: 9	he and his **r** and sons,	278
	25:10	the third to Zaccur, his sons and **r,** 12	278
	25:11	the fourth to Izri, his sons and **r,** 12	278
	25:12	the fifth to Nethaniah, his sons and **r,** 12	278
	25:13	the sixth to Bukkiah, his sons and **r,** 12	278
	25:14	the seventh to Jesarelah, his sons and **r,** 12	278
	25:15	the eighth to Jeshaiah, his sons and **r,** 12	278
	25:16	the ninth to Mattaniah, his sons and **r,** 12	278
	25:17	the tenth to Shimei, his sons and **r,** 12	278
	25:18	the eleventh to Azarel, his sons and **r,** 12	278
	25:19	the twelfth to Hashabiah, his sons and **r,** 12	278
	25:20	the thirteenth to Shubael, his sons and **r,** 12	278
	25:21	the fourteenth to Mattithiah, his sons and **r,** 12	278
	25:22	the fifteenth to Jerimoth, his sons and **r,** 12	278
	25:23	the sixteenth to Hananiah, his sons and **r,** 12	278
	25:24	seventeenth to Joshbekashah, his sons and **r,**	278
	25:25	the eighteenth to Hanani, his sons and **r,**	278
	25:26	the nineteenth to Mallothi, his sons and **r,**	278
	25:27	the twentieth to Eliathah, his sons and **r,**	278
	25:28	the twenty-first to Hothir, his sons and **r,**	278
	25:29	twenty-second to Giddalti, his sons and **r,**	278
	25:30	twenty-third to Mahazioth, his sons and **r,**	278
	25:31	to Romamti-Ezer, his sons and **r,**	278
	26: 7	his **r** Elihu and Semakiah were	278
	26: 8	and their sons and their **r** were capable men	278
	26: 9	Meshelemiah had sons and **r,**	278
	26:11	The sons and **r** of Hosah were 13 in all.	278
	26:12	just as their **r** had.	278
	26:25	His **r** through Eliezer:	278
	26:26	and his **r** were in charge of all the treasuries	278
	26:28	in the care of Shelomith and his **r.**	—
	26:30	From the Hebronites: Hashabiah and his **r—**	278
	26:32	Jeriah had twenty-seven hundred **r,**	278
2Ch	5:12	Heman, Jeduthun and their sons and **r—**	278
	22: 8	of Judah and the sons of Ahaziah's **r,**	278
Pr	19: 7	A poor man is shunned by all his **r—**	278
Jer	49:10	His children, **r** and neighbors will perish,	278
Eze	11:15	your brothers who are your **blood r** and	408+1460
Mk	6: 4	among his **r** and in his own house is	5150
Lk	1:58	Her neighbors and **r** heard that	5150
	1:61	"There is no one among your **r** who has	5149
	2:44	for him among their **r** and friends.	5150
	14:12	your brothers or **r,** or your rich neighbors;	5150
	21:16	brothers, **r** and friends,	5150
Ac	10:24	and had called together his **r**	5150
Ro	16: 7	my **r** who have been in prison with me.	5150
	16:21	as do Lucius, Jason and Sosipater, my **r.**	5150
1Ti	5: 8	If anyone does not provide for his **r,**	2625

RELEASE (30) [RELEASED, RELEASES]

Lev	14: 7	*he is to* **r** the live bird in the open fields.	8938
	14:53	*to* **r** the live bird in the open fields outside	8938
	16:22	and the man *shall* **r** it in the desert.	8938
	25:50	for his **r** is to be based on the rate paid to	4928
Nu	30: 5	the LORD *will* **r** her because her father	6142
	30: 8	and the LORD *will* **r** her.	6142
	30:12	and the LORD *will* **r** her.	6142
Dt	15:13	And when *you* **r** him,	8938
Ps	25:15	for only he *will* **r** my feet from the snare.	3655
	102:20	of the prisoners and **r** those condemned	7337
Ecc	8: 8	not **r** those who practice it.	4880
Isa	42: 7	to free captives from prison and to **r** from	NIH
	61: 1	for the captives and **r from darkness** for	7223
Mt	27:15	the governor's custom at the Feast *to* **r**	668
	27:17	"Which one do you want *me to* **r** to you:	668
	27:21	of the two do you want *me to* **r** to you?"	668
Mk	15: 6	*to* **r** a prisoner whom the people requested.	668
	15: 9	"Do you want *me to* **r** to you the king of	668
	15:11	the crowd to **have** Pilate **r** Barabbas instead.	668
Lk	4:18	*to* **r** the oppressed,	690+912+1877
	23:16	*I will* punish him and then **r** him."	668
	23:18	**R** Barabbas to us!"	668
	23:20	Wanting *to* **r** Jesus,	668
	23:22	I will have him punished and then **r** him."	668
Jn	18:39	for *me to* **r** to you one prisoner at the time	668

Jn	18:39	Do you want *me to* **r** 'the king of the Jews'?	668
Ac	4:23	*On their* **r,** Peter and John went back	668
	16:35	with the order: "**R** those men."	668
	28:18	They examined me and wanted *to* **r** me,	668
Rev	9:14	"**R** the four angels who are bound at	3395

RELEASED (28) [RELEASE]

Ge	24: 8	then *you will* **be r** from this oath of mine.	5927
	24:41	*you will* **be r** from my oath even	5927
	24:41	*you will* **be r** from my oath.'	5929
Lev	25:41	Then he and his children *are to* **be r,**	3655
	25:54	he and his children *are to* **be r** in the Year	3655
	27:21	When the field *is* **r** in the Jubilee,	3655
Jos	2:20	**be r** from the oath you made us swear."	5929
2Ki	25:27	he **r** Jehoiachin from prison on	5951+8031
2Ch	23: 8	the priest *had* not **r** any of the divisions.	7080
Job	12:14	the man he imprisons cannot **be r.**	7337
Ps	105:20	The king sent and **r** him,	6002
Jer	20: 3	when Pashhur **r** him from the stocks,	6002
	40: 1	of the imperial guard *had* **r** him at Ramah.	8938
	52:31	he **r** Jehoiachin king of Judah and	5951+8031
Mal	4: 2	And you will go out and leap like calves **r**	NIH
Mt	27:26	Then *he* **r** Barabbas to them.	668
Mk	15:15	Pilate **r** Barabbas to them.	668
Lk	23:25	*He* **r** the man who had been thrown	668
Ac	3: 4	and asked that a murderer *be* **r** to you.	5919
	16:36	that *you* and Silas **be r.**	668
	22:30	he **r** him and ordered the chief priests	3395
Ro	7: 2	*she is* **r** from the law of marriage.	2934
	7: 3	she is **r** from that law and is not	1801
	7: 6	we have been **r** from the law so	2934
Heb	11:35	Others were tortured and refused to be **r,**	667
	13:23	that our brother Timothy *has been* **r.**	668
Rev	9:15	and year *were* **r** to kill a third of mankind.	3395
	20: 7	Satan *will* **be r** from his prison	3395

RELEASES (1) [RELEASE]

Lev	16:26	"The *man who* **r** the goat as	8938

RELENT (12) [RELENTED, RELENTS]

Ex	32:12	**r** and do not bring disaster on your	5714
Job	6:29	**R,** do not be unjust;	8740
Ps	7:12	If *he does* not **r,** he will sharpen his sword;	8740
	90:13	**R,** O LORD!	8740
Isa	57: 6	In the light of these things, *should I* **r?**	5714
Jer	4:28	because I have spoken and *will* not **r,**	5714
	18: 8	then *I will* **r** and not inflict on it	5714
	26: 3	Then *I will* **r** and not bring on them	5714
	26:13	Then the LORD *will* **r and not bring**	5714
	26:19	**r,** so that he *did* **not bring** the disaster	5714
Eze	24:14	I will not have pity, nor *will I* **r.**	5714
Jnh	3: 9	God *may* yet **r** and with compassion turn	8740

RELENTED (4) [RELENT]

Ex	32:14	Then the LORD **r and did not** bring	5714
Ps	106:45	and out of his great love he **r.**	5714
Am	7: 3	So the LORD **r.**	5714
	7: 6	So the LORD **r.**	5714

RELENTLESS (1)

Isa	14: 6	subdued nations with **r** aggression.	1172+3104

RELENTS (2) [RELENT]

Joel	2:13	and *he* **r** from sending calamity.	5714
Jnh	4: 2	a God *who* **r** from sending calamity.	5714

RELIABLE (6) [RELY]

1Sa	29: 6	as the LORD lives, you have been **r,**	3838
Pr	22:21	teaching you true and **r** words,	622
Isa	8: 2	of Jeberekiah as **r** witnesses for me."	586
Jer	2:21	like a choice vine of sound and **r** stock.	622
Jn	8:26	But he who sent me is **r,**	239
2Ti	2: 2	*to* **r** men who will also be qualified	4412

RELIANCE (1) [RELY]

Pr	25:19	or a lame foot is **r** *on* the unfaithful in times	4440

RELIED (7) [RELY]

Jdg	20:36	because *they* **r** on the ambush they had set	1053
2Ch	13:18	of Judah were victorious because *they* **r** on	9128
	16: 7	"Because you **r** on the king of Aram and	9128
	16: 8	Yet when you **r** on the LORD,	9128
Ps	71: 6	From birth *I have* **r** on you;	6164
Isa	20: 6	'See what has happened to *those* we **r** on,	4438
	30:12	**r** on oppression and depended on deceit,	1053

RELIEF (20) [RELIEVE]

Ex	8:15	But when Pharaoh saw that there was **r,**	8121
1Sa	8:18	you will cry out **for r** from	4200+4946+7156
	16:23	Then **r** *would* **come** to Saul;	8118
Ezr	9: 8	to our eyes and a little **r** in our bondage.	4695
Est	4:14	and deliverance for the Jews will arise	8119
	9:16	to protect themselves and **get r** from their	5663
	9:22	when the Jews **got r** from their enemies,	5663
Job	16: 5	comfort from my lips *would* **bring** you **r.**	3104
	32:20	I must speak and **find r;**	8118
	35: 9	*they* **plead for r** from the arm of	8775
Ps	4: 1	**Give** me **r** from my distress;	8143
	94:13	you **grant** him **r** from days of trouble,	9200
	143: 1	and righteousness **come to** my **r.**	6699

Isa	1:24	"Ah, *I* will **get** r from my foes	5714
	14:3	the LORD **gives** you r from suffering	5663
La	2:18	give yourself no r, your eyes no rest.	7029
	3:49	My eyes will flow unceasingly, without r,	2198
	3:56	"Do not close your ears to my cry for r."	8121
Mic	1:12	waiting for r, because disaster has come	3202
2Th	1:7	and give r to you who are troubled,	457

RELIES (1) [RELY]
Job	8:14	**what** he r **on** is a spider's web.	4440

RELIEVE (3) [RELIEF, RELIEVED, RELIEVING]
Dt	23:12	the camp where you can go to r yourself.	NIH
	23:13	and when you r **yourself**,	2575+3782
1Sa	24:3	Saul went in to r himself.	906+2257+6114+8079

RELIEVED (2) [RELIEVE]
Job	16:6	"Yet if I speak, my pain **is not** r;	3104
2Co	8:13	Our desire is not that others might be r	457

RELIEVING (1) [RELIEVE]
Jdg	3:24	"He *must be* r himself in the inner room	906+2257+6114+8079

RELIGION (5) [RELIGIOUS]
Ac	25:19	of dispute with him about their own r and	1272
	26:5	that according to the strictest sect of our r,	2579
1Ti	5:4	**put** *their* **r into practice by caring for**	2355
Jas	1:26	he deceives himself and his r is worthless.	2579
	1:27	**R** that God our Father accepts as pure	2579

RELIGIOUS (6) [RELIGION]
Am	5:21	"I hate, I despise your r **feasts**;	2504
	8:10	I will turn your r **feasts** into mourning	2504
Ac	17:22	I see that in every way you are **very** r.	1273
Col	2:16	or with regard to a r **festival,**	2038
Heb	10:11	and **performs** his r **duties,**	3310
Jas	1:26	If anyone considers himself r and yet does	2580

RELISH (1)
Hos	4:8	of my people and r their wickedness.	5883+5951

RELUCTANTLY (1)
2Co	9:7	not r or under compulsion,	1666+3383

RELY (14) [RELIABLE, RELIANCE, RELIED, RELIES]
2Ch	14:11	O LORD our God, for we r on you,	9128
Job	39:11	*Will you* r on him for his great strength?	1053
Isa	10:20	will no longer r on him who struck them	9128
	10:20	down but will truly r on the LORD,	9128
	31:1	who r on horses, who trust in the multitude	9128
	48:2	the holy city and r on the God of Israel—	6164
	50:10	the name of the LORD and r on his God.	9128
	59:4	They r on empty arguments and speak lies;	1053
Jer	46:25	and on those who r on Pharaoh.	1053
Eze	33:26	*You* r on your sword,	6641
Ro	2:17	if *you* r **on** the law and brag	2058
2Co	1:9	that we might not r on ourselves but on God,	1639+4275
Gal	3:10	All who r **on** observing the law are	1639+1666
1Jn	4:16	we know and r **on** the love God has for us.	4409

REMAIN (116) [REMAINDER, REMAINED, REMAINING, REMAINS]
Ge	15:2	what can you give me since I r childless	2143
	24:55	*"Let the girl* r with us ten days or so;	3782
	36:7	too great for them *to* r together;	3782
	44:33	please *let* your servant r here	3782
Ex	8:9	except for *those that* r in the Nile."	8636
	8:11	*they will* r only in the Nile."	8636
	25:15	The poles *are to* r in the rings of this ark;	2118
	34:25	of the sacrifice from the Passover Feast r	4328
Lev	6:9	The burnt offering is *to* r on the altar hearth	NIH
	11:37	that are to be planted, they r clean.	NIH
	22:27	*it is to* r with its mother for seven days.	2118
	25:28	what he sold *will* r in the possession of	2118
	25:51	If many years r, he must pay for his	6388
	25:52	a few years r until the Year of Jubilee,	8636
	26:21	" 'If *you* r hostile toward me and refuse	2143
	27:14	value the priest then sets, so *it will* r.	7756
	27:18	according to the number of years that r	3855
Nu	4:7	the bread that is continually there *is to* r	2118
	9:22	the Israelites *would* r **in camp**	2837
	32:26	our flocks and herds *will* r here in	2118
	33:55	those *you* **allow to** r will become barbs	3855
Dt	3:16	*It is to* r a ruin forever,	2118
	16:4	the evening of the first day r until morning.	4328
	31:26	There *it will* r as a witness against you.	2118
Jos	18:5	Judah *is to* r in its territory on the south	6641
	23:4	the land of the nations that r—	8636
	23:7	Do not associate with these nations that r	8636
	23:12	with the survivors of these nations that r	8636
Jdg	2:23	The LORD *had* **allowed** those nations **to** r;	5663
Ru	1:13	*Would you* r **unmarried** for them?	408+1194+2118+4200+4200+6328
1Sa	16:22	saying, "Allow David *to* r in my service,	6641
2Sa	14:14	that a banished person *may not* r **estranged**	AIT

2Sa	16:18	his I will be, and *I* will r with him.	3782
1Ki	2:45	and David's throne *will* r secure before	2118
1Ch	21:17	but do not let this plague r on your people."	NIH
2Ch	32:10	that you r in Jerusalem under siege?	3782
	33:4	"My Name *will* r in Jerusalem forever."	2118
Est	4:14	For if *you* r **silent** at this time,	3087+3087
Job	29:20	My glory will r fresh in me,	NIH
	37:8	*they* r in their dens.	8905
Ps	28:1	For if *you* r **silent,**	AIT
	30:5	weeping *may* r for a night,	4328
	49:11	Their tombs will r their houses forever,	NIH
	102:26	They will perish, but you r;	6641
	102:27	But you r the same,	NIH
	109:1	O God, whom I praise, *do not* r **silent,**	AIT
	109:15	*May* their sins always r before the LORD,	2118
	125:3	the wicked *will not* r over the land allotted	5663
Pr	2:21	the blameless *will* r in it;	3855
	10:30	but the wicked *will not* r in the land.	8905
Isa	4:3	who r in Jerusalem, will be called holy,	3855
	7:22	All who r in the land will eat curds	3855
	10:4	Nothing *will* r but to cringe among	NIH
	15:9	the fugitives of Moab and upon *those who* r	8642
	17:6	Yet some gleanings *will* r,	8636
	18:4	"*I will* r **quiet** and will look on	AIT
	22:18	and there your splendid chariots will r—	NIH
	46:3	all you *who* r of the house of Israel,	8642
	62:1	for Jerusalem's sake *I will not* r **quiet,**	AIT
Jer	24:8	whether they r in this land or live in Egypt.	8636
	27:11	*I will let* that nation r in its own land to	5663
	27:22	be taken to Babylon and there *they will* r	2118
	29:16	on David's throne and all the people who r	3782
	32:5	where *he will* r until I deal with him,	2118
	51:30	*they* r in their strongholds.	3782
Eze	36:36	the nations around you that r will know	8636
	39:14	others will bury those *that* r on the ground.	3855
	44:2	"This gate *is to* r shut.	2118
	44:2	*It is to* r shut because the LORD,	2118
Da	2:43	be a mixture and *will not* r **united,**	10201
	4:15	r in the ground, in the grass of the field.	10697
	4:23	while its roots r in the ground.	10697
	11:12	yet *he will* not r **triumphant.**	AIT
Hos	9:3	*They* will not r in the LORD's land;	3782
Zec	9:3	*It will* r in his house and destroy it,	4328
	12:6	but Jerusalem will r intact in her place.	6388
	14:10	But Jerusalem will be raised up and r	3782
Jn	1:32	down from heaven as a dove and r on him.	3531
	1:33	down and r is he who will baptize with	3531
	12:34	the Law that the Christ *will* r forever,	3531
	15:4	**R** in me, and I will remain in you.	3531
	15:4	Remain in me, and I will r in you.	NIG
	15:4	bear fruit by itself; *it must* r in the vine.	3531
	15:4	Neither can you bear fruit unless *you* r	3531
	15:6	If anyone *does not* r in me,	3531
	15:7	*you* r in me and my words remain in you,	3531
	15:7	If you remain in me and my words r in you,	3531
	15:9	Now r in my love.	3531
	15:10	*you will* r in my love,	3531
	15:10	and r in his love.	3531
	17:11	*I will* r in the world no longer,	1639
	21:22	"If I want him *to* r alive until I return,	3531
	21:23	"If I want him *to* r alive until I return,	3531
Ac	3:21	He must r in heaven until the time comes	NIG
	11:23	*to* r true to the Lord with all their hearts.	4693
	14:22	and encouraging them *to* r **true to**	1844
Ro	13:8	*Let* no **debt** r **outstanding,**	4053
1Co	7:11	she *must* r unmarried or else be reconciled	3531
	7:20	Each one *should* r in the situation	3531
	7:24	*should* r in the situation God called him to.	3531
	7:26	that it is good for you *to* r as you are.	1639
	13:13	now these three r: faith, hope and love.	3531
	14:34	women *should* r **silent** in the churches.	AIT
Gal	2:5	that the truth of the gospel *might* r with you.	1373
Php	1:24	but it is more necessary for you that I r in	2152
	1:25	Convinced of this, I know that I *will* r,	3531
2Ti	2:13	if we are faithless, he *will* r **faithful,**	3531
Heb	1:11	They will perish, but you r;	1373
	1:12	But you r the same, and your years will	1639
	8:9	they *did* not r **faithful to** my covenant,	1844
	12:27	so that what cannot be shaken *may* r.	3531
1Jn	2:24	also *will* r in the Son and in the Father.	3531
	2:27	just as it has taught you, r in him.	3531
Rev	2:13	Yet *you* r **true to** my name.	3195
	14:12	and faithful to Jesus.	NIG
	17:10	he does come, he must r for a little while.	3531

REMAINDER (1) [REMAIN]
Est	9:16	the r of the Jews who were in the king's	8637

REMAINED (63) [REMAIN]
Ge	18:22	but Abraham r standing before the LORD.	6388
	32:4	with Laban and *have* r there till now.	336
	49:24	But his bow r steady,	3782
Ex	8:31	not a fly r.	8636
	10:15	Nothing green r on tree or plant in all	3855
	17:12	so that his hands r steady till sunset.	2118
	20:21	The people r at a distance,	6641
Lev	10:3	Aaron r silent.	AIT
Nu	9:18	*they* r in camp.	2837
	9:19	the cloud r over the tabernacle a long time,	799
	11:26	Eldad and Medad, *had* r in the camp.	8636
	36:12	and their inheritance r in their father's clan	2118
Jos	4:10	the priests who carried the ark r **standing**	AIT
	5:8	*they* r where they were in camp	3782
	8:17	Not a man r in Ai or Bethel who did not go	8636
Jdg	1:30	who r among them; but they did subject	3782

Jdg	5:17	Asher r on the coast and stayed in his coves	3782
	7:3	men left, while ten thousand r.	8636
	13:2	a wife who was sterile and r **childless.**	3528+4202
	19:4	so *he* r with him three days,	3782
1Sa	5:4	lying on the threshold; only his body r.	8636
	7:2	that the ark r at Kiriath Jearim,	3782
	13:7	Saul r at Gilgal, and all the troops with him	6388
	18:29	and he r his enemy the rest of his days.	2118
	23:18	but David r at Horesh.	3782
2Sa	6:11	the LORD r *in* the house of Obed-Edom	3782
	11:1	But David r in Jerusalem.	3782
	11:12	Uriah r in Jerusalem that day and the next.	3782
1Ki	12:20	Only the tribe of Judah r loyal to the house	2118
	22:46	the male shrine prostitutes who r there even	8636
2Ki	2:22	And the water *has* r **wholesome** to this day,	AIT
	10:11	So Jehu killed everyone in Jezreel who r of	8636
	11:3	*He* r hidden with his nurse at the temple of	2118
	13:6	the Asherah pole r **standing** in Samaria.	AIT
	18:36	people r **silent** and said nothing in reply,	AIT
	25:11	into exile the people who r in the city,	8636
1Ch	12:29	most of whom *had* r **loyal** to Saul's house	AIT
	13:14	of God r with the family of Obed-Edom	3782
	20:1	but David r in Jerusalem.	3782
2Ch	22:9	*He* r hidden with them at the temple of God	2118
Isa	36:21	*people* r **silent** and said nothing in reply,	AIT
Jer	35:11	So *we have* r in Jerusalem."	3782
	37:16	where he r a long time.	3782
	37:21	So Jeremiah r in the courtyard of the guard.	3782
	38:13	Jeremiah r in the courtyard of the guard.	3782
	38:28	and Jeremiah r in the courtyard of	3782
	39:9	into exile to Babylon the people who r in	8636
	39:14	So *he* r among his own people.	3782
	52:15	of the poorest people and those *who* r in	8636
Eze	17:6	but its roots r under it.	2118
Da	1:21	And Daniel r there until the first year	2118
	2:49	while Daniel himself r at the royal court.	NIH
Hos	10:9	O Israel, and there *you have* r.	6641
Mt	11:23	*it would* have r to this day.	3531
	26:63	But Jesus r **silent.**	AIT
Mk	3:4	But they r **silent.**	AIT
	14:61	But Jesus r **silent** and gave no answer.	AIT
Lk	1:22	to them but r unable to speak.	1373
	1:24	and for five months r **in seclusion.**	AIT
	14:4	But they r **silent.**	AIT
Ac	1:14	It r in the land until the time of David,	NIG
	15:35	But Paul and Barnabas r in Antioch,	1417
1Jn	2:19	*they would* have r with us;	3531

REMAINING (15) [REMAIN]
Ex	28:10	six names on one stone and the r six on	3855
Lev	10:12	Moses said to Aaron and his r sons,	3855
	10:16	Aaron's r sons, and asked,	3855
	14:17	to put some of the oil r in his palm on	3856
Nu	31:32	The plunder r *from* the spoils that	3856
Jos	7:6	r there till evening.	NIH
1Ki	9:21	their descendants r in the land,	3855
1Ch	4:43	the r Amalekites who had escaped,	8642
2Ch	8:8	their descendants r in the land,	3855
Ne	11:1	the r nine were to stay in their own towns.	3338
Isa	10:19	And the r trees of his forests will be so few	8637
Jer	27:18	the LORD Almighty that the furnishings r	3855
Eze	25:16	the Kerethites and destroy those r **along**	8642
	48:15	"The r **area,** 5,000 cubits wide and 25,000	3855
Jn	19:23	with the undergarment r.	NIG

REMAINS (45) [REMAIN]
Ex	22:13	bring in the r as evidence and he will not	3274
Lev	11:36	or a cistern for collecting water r clean,	2118
	13:46	as he has the infection he r **unclean.**	3237+3238
	27:17	the value that has been set r.	7756
Nu	15:31	his guilt r on him.' "	NIH
	16:37	to take the censers out of the **smoldering** r	8599
	19:13	his uncleanness r on him.	6388
Dt	24:20	Leave what r for the alien,	NIH
	24:21	Leave what r for the alien,	NIH
Jos	7:26	which r to this day.	NIH
	8:29	which r to this day.	NIH
	13:2	"This is the land that r:	NIH
2Sa	7:2	while the ark of God r in a tent."	3782
1Ki	20:10	if **enough** dust r in Samaria to give each	AIT
2Ki	9:10	of Shaphat r on his shoulders today!"	6641
Ne	9:10	to this day.	3869
Job	19:4	my error r my concern alone.	4328
	34:29	But if he r **silent,** who can condemn him?	AIT
Ps	146:6	the LORD, who r faithful forever.	9068
Pr	29:1	man *who* r **stiff-necked** after many rebukes	AIT
Ecc	1:4	but the earth r forever.	6641
Isa	6:13	And though a tenth r in the land,	6388
	29:8	but he awakens, and his hunger r.	NIH
Eze	32:5	and fill the valleys with your r.	8239
	48:18	What r of the area,	3855
	48:21	"What r on both sides of the area formed	3855
Mic	7:2	not one upright man r.	NIH
Hag	1:4	while this house r a ruin?"	NIH
	1:9	"Because of my house, which r a ruin,	NIH
	2:5	And my Spirit r among you.	6641
Jn	3:36	for God's wrath r on him."	3531
	6:56	and drinks my blood r in me,	3531
	9:41	that you claim you can see, your guilt r.	3531
	12:24	it r only a single seed.	3531
	15:5	*If a man* r in me, and I in him,	3531
1Co	11:21	One r **hungry,** another gets drunk.	AIT
2Co	3:14	for to this day the same veil r when	3531
Heb	4:6	*It still* r that some will enter that rest,	657
	4:9	*There* r, then, a Sabbath-rest for the people	657

Heb	7: 3	like the Son of God he *r* a priest forever.	3531
1Jn	2:24	from the beginning *r* in you.	3531
	2:27	anointing you received from him *r* in you,	3531
	3: 9	because God's seed *r* in him;	3531
	3:14	Anyone who does not love *r* in death.	3531
Rev	3: 2	Strengthen what *r* and is about to die,	3370

REMALIAH (11) [REMALIAH'S]

2Ki	15:25	One of his chief officers, Pekah son of R,	8248
	15:27	of R became king of Israel in Samaria,	8248
	15:30	of Elah conspired against Pekah son of R.	8248
	15:32	In the second year of Pekah son of R king	8248
	15:37	of Aram and Pekah son of R against Judah.)	8248
	16: 1	In the seventeenth year of Pekah son of R,	8248
	16: 5	and Pekah son of R king of Israel marched	8248
2Ch	28: 6	In one day Pekah son of R killed a hundred	8248
Isa	7: 1	and Pekah son of R king of Israel marched	8248
	7: 4	of Rezin and Aram and the son of R.	8248
	8: 6	and rejoices over Rezin and the son of R,	8248

REMALIAH'S (2) [REMALIAH]

Isa	7: 5	Ephraim and R son have plotted your ruin,	8248
	7: 9	and the head of Samaria is only R son.	8248

REMARKABLE (2)

Lk	5:26	"We have seen *r* things today."	4141
Jn	9:30	The man answered, "Now that is *r*!	2515

REMARKED (1) [REMARKING]

Ac	17:18	Others *r*, "He seems to be advocating	NIG

REMARKING (1) [REMARKED]

Lk	21: 5	Some of his disciples *were* r about how	3306

REMEDIES (1) [REMEDY]

Jer	46:11	But you multiply *r* in vain;	8337

REMEDY (6) [REMEDIES]

2Ch	36:16	against his people and there was no *r*.	5340
Pr	6:15	will suddenly be destroyed—without *r*.	5340
	29: 1	will suddenly be destroyed—without *r*.	5340
Isa	3: 7	in that day he will cry out, "I have no *r*.	2502
Jer	30:13	no *r* for your sore, no healing for you.	8337
Mic	2:10	it is ruined, **beyond all r**.	5344

REMEMBER (166) [REMEMBERED, REMEMBERING, REMEMBERS, REMEMBRANCE]

Ge	9:15	I will *r* my covenant between me and you	2349
	9:16	I will see it and *r* the everlasting covenant	2349
	31:50	*r that* God is a witness between you	8011
	40:14	*r* me and show me kindness;	2349
	40:23	chief cupbearer, however, *did not* r Joseph;	2349
Ex	20: 8	"R the Sabbath day by keeping it holy.	2349
	32:13	R your servants Abraham, Isaac and Israel,	2349
	33:13	R that this nation is your people."	8011
Lev	26:42	I will *r* my covenant with Jacob	2349
	26:42	and I will *r* the land.	2349
	26:45	But for their sake I will *r* the covenant	2349
Nu	11: 5	We *r* the fish we ate in Egypt at no cost—	2349
	15:39	at and so you will *r* all the commands of	2349
	15:40	Then you will *r* to obey all my commands	2349
Dt	4:10	R the day you stood before the LORD	NIH
	5:15	R that you were slaves in Egypt and that	2349
	7:18	*r* well what the LORD your God did	2349+2349
	8: 2	R how the LORD your God led you all	2349
	8:18	But *r* the LORD your God,	2349
	9: 7	R this and never forget how you provoked	2349
	9:27	R your servants Abraham, Isaac and Jacob.	2349
	11: 2	R today that your children were not	3359
	15:15	R that you were slaves in Egypt and	2349
	16: 3	so that all the days of your life *you may* r	2349
	16:12	R that you were slaves in Egypt,	2349
	24: 9	R what the LORD your God did to Miriam	2349
	24:18	R that you were slaves in Egypt and	2349
	24:22	R that you were slaves in Egypt.	2349
	25:17	R what the Amalekites did to you along	2349
	32: 7	R the days of old;	2349
Jos	1:13	"R the command that Moses the servant of	2349
	23: 4	R how I have allotted as an inheritance	8011
Jdg	8:34	and *did* not r the LORD their God,	2349
	9: 2	R, I am your flesh and blood."	2349
	16:28	"O Sovereign LORD, *r* me.	2349
1Sa	1:11	look upon your servant's misery and *r* me,	2349
	20:23	*r*, the LORD is witness between you	2180
	25:31	when the LORD has brought my master success, *r* your servant."	2349
2Sa	19:19	*Do not* r how your servant did wrong on	2349
1Ki	2: 8	"And *r*, you have with you Shimei son	2180
2Ki	9:25	how you and I were riding together	2349
	20: 3	"R, O LORD, how I have walked	2349
1Ch	16:12	R the wonders he has done, his miracles,	2349
2Ch	6:42	R the great love promised to David	2349
	24:22	King Joash *did* not r the kindness	2349
Ne	1: 8	"R the instruction you gave your servant Moses,	2349
	4:14	R the Lord, who is great and awesome,	2349
	5:19	R me with favor, O my God,	2349
	6:14	R Tobiah and Sanballat, O my God,	2349
	6:14	*r* also the prophetess Noadiah and the rest	NIH
	9:17	and failed *to* r the miracles you performed	2349

Ne	13:14	R me for this, O my God,	2349
	13:22	R me for this also, O my God,	2349
	13:29	R them, O my God,	2349
	13:31	R me with favor, O my God.	2349
Job	7: 7	R, O God, that my life is but a breath;	2349
	10: 9	R that you molded me like clay.	2349
	14:13	would set a time and then *r* me!	2349
	36:24	R to extol his work,	2349
	41: 8	*you will* r the struggle and never do it again!	2349
Ps	20: 3	*May he* r all your sacrifices	2349
	22:27	All the ends of the earth *will* r and turn to	2349
	25: 6	R, O LORD, your great mercy and love,	2349
	25: 7	R not the sins of my youth	2349
	25: 7	according to your love *r* me,	2349
	42: 4	These things *I* r as I pour out my soul:	2349
	42: 6	therefore *I will* r you from the land of	2349
	63: 6	On my bed *I* r you;	2349
	74: 2	R the people you purchased of old,	2349
	74:18	R how the enemy has mocked you,	2349
	74:22	*r* how fools mock you all day long.	2349
	77:11	*I will* r the deeds of the LORD;	2349
	77:11	yes, *I will* r your miracles of long ago.	2349
	78:42	*They did* not r his power—	2349
	88: 5	whom *you* r no more,	2349
	89:47	R how fleeting is my life.	2349
	89:50	R, Lord, how your servant has been mocked	2349
	103:18	with those who keep his covenant and *r*	2349
	105: 5	R the wonders he has done, his miracles,	2349
	106: 4	R me, O LORD, when you show favor	2349
	106: 7	*they did* not r your many kindnesses	2349
	119:49	R your word to your servant,	2349
	119:52	*I* r your ancient laws, O LORD,	2349
	119:55	In the night *I* r your name, O LORD,	2349
	132: 1	*r* David and all the hardships he endured.	2349
	137: 6	to the roof of my mouth if *I do* not r you,	2349
	137: 7	R, O LORD, what the Edomites did on	2349
	143: 5	*I* r the days of long ago;	2349
Pr	31: 7	and *r* their misery no more.	2349
Ecc	11: 8	But *let him* r the days of darkness,	2349
	12: 1	R your Creator in the days of your youth,	2349
	12: 6	R him—before the silver cord is severed,	NIH
Isa	38: 3	"R, O LORD, how I have walked	2349
	44:21	"R these things, O Jacob,	2349
	46: 8	"R this, fix it in mind, take it to heart,	2349
	46: 9	R the former things, those of long ago;	2349
	54: 4	of your youth and *r* no more the reproach	2349
	64: 5	*who* r your ways.	2349
	64: 9	*do* not r our sins forever.	2349
Jer	2: 2	" 'I r the devotion of your youth,	2349
	14:10	now *r* their wickedness and punish them	2349
	14:21	R your covenant with us and do not break	2349
	15:15	O LORD; *r* me and care for me.	2349
	17: 2	Even their children *r* their altars	2349
	18:20	R that I stood before you and spoke	2349
	31:20	I often speak against him, *I still* r him.	2349+2349
	31:34	and *will* r their sins no more."	2349
	44:21	"Did not the LORD *r* and think about	2349
	51:50	R the LORD in a distant land,	2349
La	3:19	*I* r my affliction and my wandering,	2349
	3:20	*I* well r them, and my soul is	2349+2349
	5: 1	R, O LORD, what has happened to us;	2349
Eze	6: 9	those who escape *will* r me—	2349
	16:22	and your prostitution *you did* not r the days	2349
	16:43	" 'Because *you did* not r the days	2349
	16:60	Yet *I will* r the covenant I made with you	2349
	16:61	Then *you will* r your ways and	2349
	16:63	*you will* r and be ashamed	2349
	20:43	There *you will* r your conduct and all	2349
	23:27	with longing or *r* Egypt anymore.	2349
	36:31	Then *you will* r your evil ways	2349
Da	6:15	"R, O king, that according to the law	10313
Hos	7: 2	not realize that *I* r all their evil deeds.	2349
	8:13	Now *he will* r their wickedness	2349
	9: 9	God *will* r their wickedness	2349
Mic	6: 5	*r* what Balak king of Moab counseled	2349
	6: 5	R [your journey] from Shittim to Gilgal,	NIH
Hab	3: 2	in wrath *r* mercy.	2349
Zec	10: 9	yet in distant lands *they will* r me.	2349
Mal	4: 4	"R the law of my servant Moses,	2349
Mt	5:23	and there *r* that your brother has something	3630
	16: 9	Don't *you* r the five loaves for	3648
	27:63	"*we* r that while he was still alive	3630
Mk	8:18	And don't *you* r?	3648
Lk	1:72	to our fathers and *to* r his holy covenant,	3630
	16:25	"But Abraham replied, 'Son, *r* that	3630
	17:32	R Lot's wife!	3648
	23:42	*r* me when you come into your kingdom."	3630
	24: 6	R how he told you,	3630
Jn	15:20	R the words I spoke to you:	3648
	16: 4	time comes *you will* r that I warned you.	3648
Ac	20:31	R that for three years I never stopped	3648
Ro	1: 9	is my witness how constantly *I* r you	3644+4472
1Co	1:16	*I don't* r if I baptized anyone else.)	3857
2Co	9: 6	R this: Whoever sows sparingly will	1254+4047
Gal	2:10	that *we should continue to* r the poor,	3648
Eph	2:11	*r* that formerly you who are Gentiles	3648
	2:12	*r* that at that time you were separate	NIG
Php	1: 3	I thank my God every time *I* r you.	3644
Col	4:18	R my chains.	3648
1Th	1: 3	*We* continually r before our God	3648
	2: 9	you *r*, brothers, our toil and hardship;	3648
2Th	2: 5	Don't *you* r that when I was with you	3648
2Ti	1: 3	*I* constantly r you in my prayers,	2400+3644
Phm	1: 4	I always thank my God *as* I r you	3644+4472
Heb	8:12	and *will* r their sins no more."	3630
	10:17	and lawless acts *I will* r no more."	3630

Heb	10:32	R those earlier days after you had received	389
	13: 3	R those in prison as if you were their fellow	3630
	13: 7	R your leaders, who spoke the word of God	3648
Jas	5:20	*r* this: Whoever turns a sinner from the	1182
2Pe	1:15	always be able *to* r these things.	3647+4472
Jude	1:17	*r* what the apostles of our Lord Jesus Christ	3630
Rev	2: 5	R the height from which you have fallen!	3648
	3: 3	R, therefore, what you have received	3648

REMEMBERED (56) [REMEMBER]

Ge	8: 1	But God *r* Noah and all the wild animals	2349
	19:29	he *r* Abraham, and he brought Lot out of	2349
	30:22	Then God *r* Rachel; he listened to her	2349
	41:31	The abundance in the land *will* not *be* r,	3359
	42: 9	Then he *r* his dreams about them and said	2349
Ex	2:24	and he *r* his covenant with Abraham,	2349
	3:15	the **name by which** I *am to be* r from generation to generation.	2352
	6: 5	and *I have* r my covenant,	2352
	17:14	a scroll as **something** to be r and make sure	2355
Nu	10: 9	Then *you will be* r by the LORD your God	2349
1Sa	1:19	Hannah his wife, and the LORD *r* her.	2349
Est	2: 1	he *r* Vashti and what she had done	2349
	9:28	These days *should be* r and observed	2349
Job	24:20	evil men *are* no longer r but are broken like	2349
Ps	77: 3	*I* r you, O God, and I groaned;	2349
	77: 6	*I* r my songs in the night.	2349
	78:35	*They* r that God was their Rock,	2349
	78:39	He *r* that they were but flesh,	2349
	83: 4	that the name of Israel *be* r no more."	2349
	98: 3	He has *r* his love and his faithfulness to	2349
	105:42	For he *r* his holy promise given	2349
	106:45	for their sake he *r* his covenant and out	2349
	109:14	*May* the iniquity of his fathers *be* r before	2349
	111: 4	He has caused his wonders to be r;	2352
	112: 6	a righteous man will be r forever.	2352
	136:23	to the *One* who in our low estate	2349
	137: 1	and wept when we *r* Zion.	2349
Ecc	1:11	to come will not be r by those who follow.	2355
	2:16	wise man, like the fool, will not be long r;	2355
	9:15	But nobody *r* that poor man.	2349
Isa	23:16	*you have* not r the Rock, your fortress.	2349
	23:16	sing many a song, so that *you will be* r."	2349
	57:11	and *have* neither r me nor pondered this	2349
	65:17	The former things will not be r,	2349
Jer	3:16	It will never enter their minds or *be* r;	2349
	11:19	that his name *be* r no more."	2349
La	2: 1	not r his footstool in the day of his anger.	2349
Eze	3:20	The righteous things he did *will* not *be* r,	2349
	18:22	of the offenses he has committed *will be* r	2349
	18:24	the righteous things he has done *will be* r.	2349
	21:32	*you will be* r no more;	2349
	25:10	so that the Ammonites *will* not *be* r among	2349
	33:13	the righteous things he has done *will be* r;	2349
	33:16	of the sins he has committed *will be* r	2349
Jnh	2: 7	"When my life was ebbing away, *I* r you,	2349
Zec	13: 2	and *they will be* r no more,"	2349
Mt	26:75	Then Peter *r* the word Jesus had spoken:	3630
Mk	11:21	Peter *r* and said to Jesus, "Rabbi, look!	389
	14:72	Peter *r* the word Jesus had spoken to him:	389
Lk	22:61	Then Peter *r* the word the Lord had spoken	5703
	24: 8	Then *they* r his words.	3630
Jn	2:22	His disciples *r* that it is written:	3630
Ac	10:31	God has heard your prayer and *r* your gifts	3630
	11:16	Then *I* r what the Lord had said:	3630
Rev	16:19	God *r* Babylon the Great and gave her	3630
	18: 5	and God *has* r her crimes.	3648

REMEMBERING (4) [REMEMBER]

Lk	1:54	helped his servant Israel, *r* to be merciful	3630
Ac	20:35	*r* the words the Lord Jesus himself said:	3648
1Co	11: 2	I praise you for *r* me in everything and for	3630
Eph	1:16	*r* you in my prayers.	3644+4472

REMEMBERS (11) [REMEMBER]

1Ch	16:15	*He* r his covenant forever,	2349
Ps	6: 5	No one *r* you when he is dead.	2352
	9:12	For he who avenges blood *r*;	2349
	103:14	*he* r that we are dust.	2349
	103:16	and its place *r* it no more.	5795
	105: 8	*He* r his covenant forever,	2349
	111: 5	*he* r his covenant forever.	2349
	115:12	The LORD *r* us and will bless us:	2349
Isa	43:25	for my own sake, and *r* your sins no more	2349
La	1: 7	and wandering Jerusalem *r* all the treasures	2349
2Co	7:15	*when he* r that you were all obedient,	389

REMEMBRANCE (5) [REMEMBER]

Ecc	1:11	There is no *r* of men of old,	2355
Mal	3:16	A scroll of *r* was written in his presence	2355
Lk	22:19	my body given for you; do this in *r* of me."	390
1Co	11:24	body, which is for you; do this in *r* of me."	390
	11:25	do this, whenever you drink it, in *r* of me."	390

REMETH (1)

Jos	19:21	R, En Gannim, En Haddah	8255

REMIND (11) [REMINDED, REMINDER, REMINDERS, REMINDING]

Nu	16:40	to the Israelites that no one except	2355
1Ki	17:18	to *r* me of my sin and kill my son?"	2349
Eze	21:23	but he *will* r them *of* their guilt	2349
Jn	14:26	will teach you all things and *will* r you *of*	5703

Ro	15:15	as if to **r** you of them **again,**	2057
1Co	4:17	He *will* **r** you of my way of life	389
	15: 1	*I want to* **r** you of the gospel I preached	1192
2Ti	1: 6	For this reason *I* **r** you to fan into flame	389
Tit	3: 1	**R** the people to be subject to rulers	5703
2Pe	1:12	So I will always **r** you of these things.	5703
Jude	1: 5	I want *to* **r** you that the Lord delivered	5703

REMINDED (2) [REMIND]

Ge	41: 9	"Today I *am* **r** of my shortcomings.	2349
2Ti	1: 5	*I have been* **r** of your sincere faith,	3284+5704

REMINDER (5) [REMIND]

Ex	13: 9	on your hand and a **r** on your forehead that	2355
Nu	5:15	a **r** offering to draw attention to guilt.	2355
	5:18	and place in her hands the **r** offering,	2355
Eze	29:16	*be a* **r** of their sin in turning to her for help.	2349
Heb	10: 3	But those sacrifices are an annual **r** of sins,	390

REMINDERS (1) [REMIND]

2Pe	3: 1	both of them as **r** to stimulate you	5704

REMINDING (1) [REMIND]

2Ti	2:14	*Keep* **r** them **of** these things.	5703

REMISSION (KJV) See FORGIVENESS

REMMON (KJV) See RIMMON

REMMON-METHOAR (KJV) See RIMMON, TURNED

REMNANT (65)

Ge	45: 7	to preserve for you a **r** on earth	8642
Dt	3:11	(Only Og king of Bashan was left of the **r**	3856
2Ki	19: 4	Therefore pray for the **r** that still survives."	8642
	19:30	Once more a **r** of the house of Judah	7129
	19:31	For out of Jerusalem will come a **r,**	8642
	21:14	the **r** of my inheritance and hand them over	8642
2Ch	34: 9	Ephraim and the remnant of Israel and	8642
	34:21	inquire of the LORD for me and for the **r** in	8636
	36:20	He carried into exile to Babylon the **r,**	8642
Ezr	9: 8	in leaving us a **r** and giving us a firm place	7129
	9:13	and have given us a **r** like this.	7129
	9:14	leaving us no **r** or survivor?	8642
	9:15	We arc left this day as a **r,**	7129
Ne	1: 2	about the Jewish **r** that survived the exile,	7129
Isa	1: 9	In that day the **r** of Israel,	8637
	10:20	A **r** will return, a remnant of Jacob	8637
	10:21	a **r** *of* Jacob will return to the Mighty God.	8637
	10:22	only a **r** will return.	8637
	11:11	the **r** that is left of his people from Assyria,	8637
	11:16	a highway for the **r** of his people that is left	8637
	17: 3	the **r** of Aram will be like the glory of	8637
	28: 5	a beautiful wreath for the **r** *of* his people.	8637
	37: 4	Therefore pray for the **r** that still survives."	8642
	37:31	Once more a **r** of the house of Judah	7129
	37:32	For out of Jerusalem will come a **r,**	8642
Jer	6: 9	the **r** of Israel as thoroughly as a vine;	8642
	11:23	Not even a **r** will be left to them,	8642
	23: 3	"I myself will gather the **r** of my flock out	8642
	31: 7	save your people, the **r** of Israel.'	8642
	40:11	the king of Babylon had left a **r** in Judah	8642
	40:15	be scattered and the **r** of Judah to perish?"	8642
	42: 2	to the LORD your God for this entire **r,**	8642
	42:15	hear the word of the LORD, O **r** of Judah.	8642
	42:19	"O **r** of Judah, the LORD has told you,	8642
	43: 5	and all the army officers led away all the **r**	8642
	44: 7	and so leave yourselves without a **r?**	8642
	44:12	of the **r** of Judah who were determined to go	8642
	44:14	of the **r** of Judah who have gone to live	8642
	44:28	the whole **r** of Judah who came to live	8642
	47: 4	the **r** *from* the coasts of Caphtor.	8642
	47: 5	O **r** on the plain,	8642
	50:20	for I will forgive the **r** I spare.	8636
	50:26	Completely destroy her and leave her no **r.**	8642
Eze	9: 8	the entire **r** of Israel in this outpouring	8642
	11:13	Will you completely destroy the **r**	8642
Am	5:15	will have mercy on the **r** of Joseph.	8642
	9:12	so that they may possess the **r** of Edom	8642
Mic	2:12	I will surely bring together the **r** of Israel.	8642
	4: 7	I will make the lame a **r,**	8642
	5: 7	The **r** of Jacob will be in the midst	8642
	5: 8	The **r** of Jacob will be among the nations,	8642
	7:18	and forgives the transgression of the **r**	8642
Zep	1: 4	from this place *every* **r** of Baal, the names	8637
	2: 7	It will belong to the **r** of the house	8642
	2: 9	The **r** of my people will plunder them;	8642
	3:13	The **r** of Israel will do no wrong;	8642
Hag	1:12	the whole **r** of the people obeyed the voice	8642
	1:14	and the spirit of the whole **r** of the people.	8642
	2: 2	the high priest, and to the **r** of the people.	8642
Zec	8: 6	to the **r** of this people at that time,	8642
	8:11	not deal with the **r** of this people as I did in	8642
	8:12	as an inheritance for the **r** of this people.	8642
Ac	15:17	that the **r** of men may seek the Lord,	2905
Ro	9:27	only the **r** will be saved.	5698
	11: 5	at the present time there is a **r** chosen	3307

REMORSE (1)

Mt	27: 3	he *was* **seized with r** and returned	3564

REMOTE (7) [REMOTEST]

Jdg	19: 1	a **r** area *in* the hill country of Ephraim took	3752
	19:18	to a **r** area *in* the hill country of Ephraim	3752
Mt	14:15	"This is a **r** place, and it's already	2245
	15:33	in this **r** place to feed such a crowd?"	2244
Mk	6:35	"This is a **r** place," they said,	2245
	8: 4	in this **r** place can anyone get enough bread	2244
Lk	9:12	because we are in a **r** place here."	2245

REMOTEST (3) [REMOTE]

2Ki	19:23	I have reached its **r** parts,	7891
Ne	9:22	allotting to them even the **r** frontiers.	6992
Isa	37:24	I have reached its **r** heights,	7891

REMOVAL (2) [REMOVE]

Isa	27: 9	will be the full fruitage of the **r** of his sin:	6073
1Pe	3:21	not the **r** of dirt **from** the body but	629

REMOVE (54) [REMOVAL, REMOVED, REMOVES, REMOVING]

Ge	30:32	through all your flocks today and **r** from	6073
Ex	12:15	the first day **r** the yeast from your houses,	8697
	27: 3	its pots to **r** the **ashes,** and its shovels,	2014
	33:23	Then *I will* **r** my hand and you will see	6073
Lev	1:16	*to* **r** the crop with its contents and throw it	6073
	3: 4	which *he will* **r** with the kidneys.	6073
	3:10	which *he will* **r** with the kidneys.	6073
	3:15	which *he will* **r** with the kidneys.	6073
	4: 8	*He shall* **r** all the fat from the bull of	8123
	4: 9	which *he will* **r** with the kidneys—	6073
	4:19	*He shall* **r** all the fat from it and burn it on	8123
	4:31	*He shall* **r** all the fat,	6073
	4:35	*He shall* **r** all the fat,	6073
	6:10	and shall **r** the ashes of the burnt offering	8123
	26: 6	*I will* **r** savage beasts from the land,	8697
Nu	4:13	They are to **r** the **ashes** *from* the bronze altar	2014
	20:26	**R** Aaron's garments and put them on his	7320
Jos	7:13	against your enemies until you **r** it.	6073
1Ki	15:14	Although *he did* not **r** the high places,	6073
	20:24	**R** all the kings from their commands	6073
2Ki	23: 4	and the doorkeepers to **r** from the temple of	3655
	23:27	"*I will* **r** Judah also from my presence	6073
	24: 3	to **r** them from his presence because of	6073
2Ch	15:17	Although *he did* not **r** the high places	6073
	29: 5	**R** all defilement from the sanctuary.	3655
	32:12	Hezekiah himself **r** this god's high places	6073
Job	9:34	*someone to* **r** God's rod from me,	6073
	22:23	If *you* **r** wickedness **far** from your tent	8178
Ps	39:10	**R** your scourge from me;	6073
	119:22	**R** from me scorn and contempt,	1655
Pr	25: 4	**R** the dross from the silver,	2048
	25: 5	**r** the wicked from the king's presence,	2048
	27:22	*you will* not **r** his folly from him.	6073
Isa	1:25	and **r** all your impurities.	6073
	25: 8	*he will* **r** the disgrace of his people	6073
	57:14	**R** the obstacles out of the way	8123
	62:10	**R** the stones.	6232
Jer	4:10	to you that *will only serve to* **r** you **far**	8178
	28:16	*about to* **r** you from the face of the earth."	8938
	32:31	and wrath that I *must* **r** it from my sight.	6073
Eze	11:18	return to it and **r** all its vile images	6073
	11:19	*I will* **r** from them their heart of stone	6073
	21:26	Take off the turban, **r** the crown.	8123
	34:10	*I will* **r** them from tending the flock so	8697
	36:26	*I will* **r** from you your heart of stone	6073
Hos	2: 2	*Let her* **r** the adulterous look from her face	6073
	2:17	*I will* **r** the names of the Baals	6073
Zep	3:11	because *I will* **r** from this city those who	6073
	3:18	for the appointed feasts *I will* **r** from you;	665
Zec	3: 9	'and *I will* **r** the sin of this land in a single	4631
	13: 2	"*I will* **r** both the prophets and the spirit	6296
Mt	7: 5	*to* **r** the speck **from** your brother's eye.	1675
Lk	6:42	*to* **r** the speck **from** your brother's eye.	1675
Rev	2: 5	to you and **r** your lampstand from its place.	3075

REMOVED (65) [REMOVE]

Ge	8:13	then **r** the covering from the ark and saw	6073
	30:35	That same day *he* **r** all the male goats	6073
	48:12	Then Joseph **r** them from Israel's knees	3655
Ex	25:15	*they are* not *to be* **r.**	6073
	34:34	*he* **r** the veil until he came out.	6073
Lev	4:10	just as the fat is **r** from the ox sacrificed as	8123
	4:31	as the fat is **r** from the fellowship offering,	6073
	4:35	just as the fat is **r** from the lamb of	6073
	7: 4	which *is to be* **r** with the kidneys.	6073
Nu	10:28	Moses **r** Aaron's garments and put them	7320
Dt	26:13	"*I have* **r** from my house the sacred portion	1278
	26:14	nor *have I* **r** any of it while I was unclean,	1278
Ru	4: 8	And *he* **r** his sandal.	8990
1Sa	21: 6	of the Presence that *had been* **r** from before	6073
2Sa	6: 7	whom *I* **r** from before you.	6073
	20:13	After Amasa had *been* **r** from the road,	3325
1Ki	2:27	So Solomon **r** Abiathar from the priesthood	1763
	5:17	*they* **r** from the **quarry** large blocks	5825
	20:41	Then the prophet quickly **r** the headband	6073
	22:43	The high places, however, *were* not **r,**	6073
2Ki	12: 3	The high places, however, *were* not **r;**	6073
	14: 4	The high places, however, *were* not **r;**	6073
	15: 4	The high places, however, *were* not **r;**	6073
	15:35	The high places, however, *were* not **r;**	6073
	16:17	King Ahaz took away the panels and **r**	6073
	16:17	*He* **r** the Sea from the bronze bulls	3718
	16:18	and **r** the royal entryway outside the temple	NIH

2Ki	17:18	with Israel and **r** them from his presence.	6073
	17:23	until the LORD **r** them from his presence,	6073
	18: 4	He **r** the high places,	6073
	18:22	whose high places and altars Hezekiah **r,**	6073
	23:11	He **r** from the entrance to the temple of	8697
	23:12	He **r** them from there,	NIH
	23:16	he had the bones **r** from them and burned on the altar	2256+4374+8938
	23:19	Josiah **r** and defiled all the shrines at	6073
	23:27	also from my presence as *I* **r** Israel,	6073
	24:13	Nebuchadnezzar **r** all the treasures from	3655
2Ch	14: 3	He **r** the foreign altars and the high places,	6073
	14: 5	He **r** the high places and incense altars	6073
	15: 8	*He* **r** the detestable idols from the whole	6296
	17: 6	he **r** the high places and the Asherah poles	6073
	20:33	The high places, however, *were* not **r,**	6073
	29:19	that King Ahaz **r** in his unfaithfulness	2396
	30:14	*They* **r** the altars in Jerusalem	6073
	33:15	of the foreign gods and **r** the image from	NIH
	34:33	Josiah **r** all the detestable idols from all	6073
Ezr	5:14	even **r** from the temple of Babylon the gold	10485
Job	19: 9	He has stripped me of my honor and **r**	6073
	34:20	the mighty *are* **r** without human hand.	6073
Ps	30:11	*you* **r** my sackcloth and clothed me	7337
	81: 6	"I **r** the burden from their shoulders;	6073
	103:12	*so far has he* **r** our transgressions from us.	8178
Pr	27:25	*When* the hay is **r** and new growth appears	1655
Isa	10:13	*I* **r** the boundaries of nations,	6073
	14:25	and his burden **r** from their shoulders."	6073
	36: 7	whose high places and altars Hezekiah **r,**	6073
	54:10	the mountains be shaken and the hills *be* **r,**	4572
	54:10	be shaken nor my covenant of peace *be* **r,**"	4572
	54:14	Terror will be far **r;**	NIH
Jer	8: 1	of Jerusalem *will be* **r** from their graves.	3655
	28: 3	that Nebuchadnezzar king of Babylon **r**	4374
Eze	24:12	its heavy deposit *has* not *been* **r,**	3655
Jn	20: 1	that the stone *had been* **r** from the entrance.	149
2Co	3:14	*It has* not *been* **r,** because only in Christ is it	365
Rev	6:14	and every mountain and island *was* **r**	3075

REMOVES (1) [REMOVE]

1Sa	17:26	and **r** this disgrace from Israel?	6073

REMOVING (2) [REMOVE]

Ac	13:22	After **r** Saul, he made David their king.	3496
Heb	12:27	The words "once more" indicate the **r**	3557

REMPHAN (KJV) See REPHAN

REND (2)

Isa	64: 1	*you would* **r** the heavens and come down,	7973
Joel	2:13	**R** your heart and not your garments.	7973

RENDER (2) [RENDERING]

Isa	16: 3	"Give us counsel, **r** a decision.	6913
Zec	8:16	**r** true and sound **judgment**	5477+9149

RENDERING (1) [RENDER]

Isa	28: 7	they stumble when **r** decisions.	7133

RENEGADES (1)

Jdg	12: 4	"You Gileadites are **r** from Ephraim	7127

RENEW (8) [RENEWAL, RENEWED, RENEWING]

Ru	4:15	He will **r** your life and sustain you	8740
Ps	51:10	O God, and **r** a steadfast spirit within me.	2542
	104:30	and *you* **r** the face of the earth.	2542
Isa	40:31	who hope in the LORD will **r** their strength.	2736
	41: 1	**Let** the nations **r** their strength!	2736
	61: 4	*they will* **r** the ruined cities	2542
La	5:21	**r** our days as of old	2542
Hab	3: 2	**R** them in our day, in our time	2649

RENEWAL (4) [RENEW]

Job	14:14	I will wait for my **r** to come.	2722
Isa	57:10	You found **r** of your strength,	2652
Mt	19:28	"I tell you the truth, at the **r** of all things,	4098
Tit	3: 5	through the washing of rebirth and **r** by	364

RENEWED (7) [RENEW]

2Ki	23: 3	the pillar and **r** the covenant in the presence	4162
2Ch	34:31	and **r** the covenant in the presence of	4162
Job	33:25	then his flesh is **r** like a child's;	8186
Ps	103: 5	with good things so that your youth is **r** like	2542
2Co	4:16	yet inwardly we *are being* **r** day by day.	363
Php	4:10	that at last you *have* **r** your concern for me.	352
Col	3:10	which *is being* **r** in knowledge in	363

RENEWING (1) [RENEW]

Ro	12: 2	but be transformed *by* the **r** of your mind.	364

RENOUNCE (3) [RENOUNCED, RENOUNCES]

Eze	14: 6	and **r** all your detestable practices!	7156+8740
Da	4:27	**R** your sins by doing what is right,	10596
Rev	2:13	*You did* not **r** your faith in me,	766

RENOUNCED (3) [RENOUNCE]
Ps	89:39	*You have* **r** the covenant with your servant	5545
Mt	19:12	and others *have* **r marriage** because of the kingdom	1571+2335+2336
2Co	4: 2	we have **r** secret and shameful ways;	584

RENOUNCES (1) [RENOUNCE]
Pr	28:13	whoever confesses and **r** them finds mercy.	6440

RENOWN (12) [RENOWNED]
Ge	6: 4	They were the heroes of old, men of **r**.	9005
Ps	102:12	your **r** endures through all generations.	2352
	135:13	your **r**, O LORD, through all generations.	2352
Isa	26: 8	and **r** are the desire of our hearts.	2352
	55:13	This will be for the LORD's **r**,	9005
	63:12	to gain for himself everlasting **r**,	9005
Jer	13:11	'to be my people for my **r** and praise	9005
	32:20	and have gained the **r** that is still yours.	9005
	33: 9	Then this city will bring me **r**, joy,	9005
	49:25	Why has the city of **r** not been abandoned,	9335
Eze	26:17	" 'How you are destroyed, O city of **r**,	2146
Hos	12: 5	the LORD is his **name of r**!	2352

RENOWNED (3) [RENOWN]
Isa	23: 8	whose traders *are* **r** in the earth?	3877
	23: 9	of all glory and to humble all *who are* **r** on	3877
Eze	34:29	I will provide for them a land **r**	4200+9005

RENT (1) [RENTED]
Mt	21:41	"and *he will* **r** the vineyard to other tenants,	1686

RENTED (4) [RENT]
Mt	21:33	Then *he* **r** the vineyard to some farmers	1686
Mk	12: 1	Then *he* **r** the vineyard to some farmers	1686
Lk	20: 9	**r** it to some farmers and went away for	1686
Ac	28:30	Paul stayed there in his own **r house**	3637

REOPENED (1)
Ge	26:18	Isaac **r** the wells that had been	2256+2916+8740

REPAID (9) [PAY]
Ge	44: 4	'Why *have you* **r** good with evil?	8966
Jdg	9:56	Thus God **r** the wickedness that Abimelech	8740
2Sa	16: 8	The LORD *has* **r** you for all the blood	8740
Pr	14:14	faithless *will be* **fully r** for their ways,	8425
Jer	18:20	*Should* good *be* **r** with evil?	8966
Lk	6:34	expecting to be **r** in full.	655
	14:12	and so you will be **r**.	501
	14:14	*be* **r** at the resurrection of the righteous."	500
Col	3:25	Anyone who does wrong *will be* **r**	3152

REPAIR (14) [REPAIRED, REPAIRER, REPAIRING, REPAIRS]
2Ki	12: 5	*be used to* **r** whatever damage is found in	2616
	12: 8	from the people and that they *would* not **r**	2616
	12:12	and dressed stone for the **r** *of* the temple of	2616
	12:14	*who* used it to **r** the temple.	2616
	22: 5	have these men pay the workers who **r**	981+2616
	22: 6	and dressed stone to **r** the temple.	2616
1Ch	26:27	for the **r** of the temple of the LORD.	2616
2Ch	24: 5	to **r** the temple of your God.	2616
	24:12	workers in iron and bronze to **r** the temple.	2616
	34: 8	to **r** the temple of the LORD his God.	2616
Ezr	9: 9	the house of our God and **r** its ruins,	6641
Eze	13: 5	not gone up to the breaks in the wall *to* **r** it	1553
Am	9:11	I will **r** its broken places, restore its ruins,	1553
Na	3:14	tread the mortar, **r** the brickwork!	2616

REPAIRED (24) [REPAIR]
1Ki	18:30	and *he* **r** the altar of the LORD,	8324
2Ki	12: 6	of King Joash the priests *still had* not **r**	2616
2Ch	15: 8	*He* **r** the altar of the LORD that was	2542
	29: 3	of the temple of the LORD and **r** them.	2616
	34:10	the workers *who* **r** and restored the temple.	980
Ne	3: 4	the son of Hakkoz, **r** the next section.	2616
	3: 5	The next section *was* **r** by the men	2616
	3: 6	The Jeshanah Gate *was* **r** by Joiada son	2616
	3: 8	one of the goldsmiths, **r** the next section;	2616
	3: 9	of Jerusalem, **r** the next section.	2616
	3:11	son of Pahath-Moab **r** another section and	2616
	3:12	**r** the next section with the help	2616
	3:13	The Valley Gate *was* **r** by Hanun and	2616
	3:13	also **r** five hundred yards of the wall as far	NIH
	3:14	The Dung Gate *was* **r** by Malkijah son	2616
	3:15	The Fountain Gate *was* **r** by Shallun son	2616
	3:15	He also **r** the wall of the Pool of Siloam,	NIH
	3:19	ruler of Mizpah, **r** another section,	2616
	3:20	of Zabbai zealously **r** another section,	2616
	3:21	the son of Hakkoz, **r** another section,	2616
	3:24	Binnui son of Henadad **r** another section,	2616
	3:27	the men of Tekoa **r** another section,	2616
	3:27	the sixth son of Zalaph, **r** another section.	2616
Jer	19:11	potter's jar is smashed and cannot be **r**.	8324

REPAIRER (1) [REPAIR]
Isa	58:12	you will be called **R of Broken Walls**,	1553

REPAIRING (4) [REPAIR]
2Ki	12: 7	"Why aren't you **r** the damage done to	2616

2Ki	12: 7	but hand it over for **r** the temple."	981
2Ch	32: 5	Then he worked hard **r** all the broken	1215
Ezr	4:12	They are restoring the walls and **r** the	10253

REPAIRS (22) [REPAIR]
2Ch	24:13	and the **r** progressed under them.	776
Ne	3: 4	the son of Meshezabel, **made r,**	2616
	3: 4	to him Zadok son of Baana also **made r.**	2616
	3: 7	*were* **made r** by men from Gibeon	2616
	3: 8	the perfume-makers, **made r** next to that.	2616
	3:10	of Harumaph **made r** opposite his house,	2616
	3:10	of Hashabneiah **made r** next to him.	2616
	3:16	**made r** up to a point opposite the tombs	2616
	3:17	*the r were* **made** by the Levites	2616
	3:17	**carried out r** for his district.	2616
	3:18	*the r were* **made** by their countrymen	2616
	3:22	**r** next to him *were* **made** by the priests	2616
	3:23	and Hasshub **made r** in front of their house;	2616
	3:23	son of Ananiah, **made r** beside his house.	2616
	3:26	of Ophel **made r** up to a point opposite	NIH
	3:28	Above the Horse Gate, the priests **made r,**	2616
	3:29	son of Immer **made r** opposite his house.	2616
	3:29	the guard at the East Gate, **made r.**	2616
	3:30	**made r** opposite his living quarters.	2616
	3:31	**made r** as far as the house of	2616
	3:32	the goldsmiths and merchants **made r.**	2616
	4: 7	the **r** to Jerusalem's walls had gone ahead	776

REPAY (47) [PAY]
Lev	25:28	if he does not acquire the means *to* **r** him,	8740
Dt	7:10	But those who hate him he will **r** to their	8966
	7:10	*to* **r** to their face those who hate him.	8966
	32: 6	Is this the way *you* **r** the LORD,	1694
	32:35	It is mine to avenge; *I will* **r**.	8966
	32:41	and **r** those who hate me.	8966
Ru	2:12	the LORD **r** you for what you have done.	8966
2Sa	3:39	*May* the LORD **r** the evildoer according	8966
	16:12	the LORD will see my distress and **r** me	8740
1Ki	2:32	The LORD *will* **r** him *for* the blood he shed,	6584+8031+8740
	2:44	the LORD *will* **r** you *for* your wrongdoing.	928+8031+8740
Job	21:19	*Let him* **r** the man himself,	8966
Ps	28: 4	**R** them for their deeds and	5989
	28: 4	**r** them for what their hands have done	5989
	35:12	*They* **r** me evil for good	8966
	37:21	The wicked borrow and *do* not **r**,	8966
	38:20	*Those who* **r** my good with evil slander me	8966
	41:10	raise me up, that *I may* **r** them.	8966
	94:23	He will **r** them for their sins	8740
	103:10	not treat us as our sins deserve or **r** us	1694
	109: 5	*They* **r** me evil for good,	8492
	116:12	How *can I* **r** the LORD for all his goodness	8740
Pr	24:12	*Will* he not **r** each person according	8740
Isa	59:18	so *will* he **r** wrath to his enemies	8966
	59:18	he will **r** the islands their due.	8966
Jer	16:18	I *will* **r** them double *for* their wickedness	8966
	25:14	*I will* **r** them according to their deeds and	8966
	50:29	**R** her for her deeds;	8966
	51:24	"Before your eyes *I will* **r** Babylon	8966
	51:56	God of retribution; *he will* **r** in full.	8966+8966
Eze	7: 3	and **r** you for all your detestable practices.	5989
	7: 4	*I will* surely **r** you *for* your conduct and	5989
	7: 8	and **r** you for all your detestable practices.	5989
	7: 9	*I will* **r** you in accordance with your	5989
Hos	4: 9	for their ways and **r** them *for* their deeds.	8740
	12: 2	according to his ways and **r** him according	8740
	12:14	the guilt of his bloodshed and *will* **r** him	8740
Joel	2:25	"I will **r** you *for* the years the locusts	8966
Mt	18:25	and all that he had to **r** **the debt.**	625
Lk	14:14	Although they cannot **r** you,	500
Ro	11:35	ever given to God, *that* God *should* **r** him?"	500
	12:17	*Do* not **r** anyone evil for evil.	625
	12:19	mine to avenge; *I will* **r**," says the Lord.	500
2Ti	4:14	The Lord *will* **r** him for what he has done.	625
Heb	10:30	"It is mine to avenge; *I will* **r**," and again,	500
1Pe	3: 9	*Do* not **r** evil with evil or insult with insult,	625
Rev	2:23	and *I will* **r** each of you according	1443

REPAYING (5) [PAY]
2Ch	6:23	**r** the guilty by bringing down on his own	8740
	20:11	*how* they *are* **r** us by coming to drive us out	1694
Isa	66: 6	the LORD **r** his enemies all they deserve.	8966
Joel	3: 4	*Are* you **r** me *for* something I have done?	8966
1Ti	5: 4	their own family and so **r** their parents	304+625

REPAYMENT (1) [PAY]
Lk	6:34	you lend to those from whom you expect **r**,	3284

REPAYS (3) [PAY]
Job	21:31	Who **r** him for what he has done?	8966
	34:11	*He* **r** a man for what he has done.	8966
Ps	137: 8	happy *is* he who **r** you for what you have	8966

REPEALED (3)
Est	1:19	laws of Persia and Media, *which* cannot *be* **r**	6296
Da	6: 8	the Medes and Persians, which cannot *be* **r.**	10528
	6:12	the Medes and Persians, which cannot *be* **r.**	10528

REPEAT (2) [REPEATED, REPEATEDLY, REPEATS]
2Co	11:16	*I* **r**: Let no one take me for a fool.	3306+4099

REPEATED (8) [REPEAT]
Ge	44: 6	he **r** these words to them.	1819
Jdg	9: 3	When the brothers **r** all this to the citizens	1819
	11:11	And he **r** all his words before the LORD	1819
1Sa	8:21	he **r** it before the LORD.	1819
	11: 5	Then *they* **r** to him what the men	6218
	17:27	*They* **r** to him what they had been saying	606
	18:23	They **r** these words to David.	1819
Heb	10: 1	by the same sacrifices **r** endlessly year	4712[S]

REPEATEDLY (2) [REPEAT]
Jer	46:16	*They will* stumble **r**;	8049
Lk	8:31	And *they* **begged** him **r** not to order them	AIT

REPEATS (2) [REPEAT]
Pr	17: 9	*whoever* **r** the matter separates close friends.	9101
	26:11	so a fool **r** his folly.	9101

REPENT (39) [PENITENT, REPENTANCE, REPENTED, REPENTS]
1Ki	8:47	and **r** and plead with you in the land	8740
2Ch	6:37	and **r** and plead with you in the land	8740
Job	34:33	when you refuse to **r**?	NIH
	36:10	to correction and commands them *to* **r**	8740
	42: 6	Therefore I despise myself and **r** in dust	5714
Isa	59:20	to *those* in Jacob *who* **r** of their sins,"	8740
Jer	5: 3	harder than stone and refused to **r**.	8740
	15:19	"If *you* **r**, I will restore you	8740
Eze	14: 6	'This is what the Sovereign LORD says: **R**!	8740
	18:30	declares the Sovereign LORD. **R**!	8740
	18:32	declares the Sovereign LORD. **R** and live!	8740
Hos	11: 5	over them because they refuse to **r**?	8740
Mt	3: 2	"**R**, for the kingdom of heaven is near."	3566
	4:17	"**R**, for the kingdom of heaven is near."	3566
	11:20	because *they* did not **r**.	3566
	21:32	*you* did not **r** and believe him.	3564
Mk	1:15	**R** and believe the good news!"	3566
	6:12	and preached that *people* should **r**.	3566
Lk	13: 3	But unless *you* **r**, you too will all perish.	3567
	13: 5	But unless *you* **r**, you too will all perish."	3567
	15: 7	righteous persons who do not need *to* **r**.	3567
	16:30	from the dead goes to them, they *will* **r**."	3566
	17: 4	back to you and says, '*I* **r**,' forgive him."	3566
Ac	2:38	Peter replied, "**R** and be baptized,	3566
	3:19	**R**, then, and turn to God,	3566
	8:22	**R** of this wickedness and pray to the Lord.	3566
	17:30	he commands all people everywhere *to* **r**.	3566
	26:20	I preached that they should **r** and turn	3566
Rev	2: 5	**R** and do the things you did at first.	3566
	2: 5	If *you* do not **r**, I will come to you and	3566
	2:16	**R** therefore! Otherwise, I will soon come	3566
	2:21	I have given her time to **r** of her immorality	3566
	2:22	unless *they* **r** of her ways.	3566
	3: 3	received and heard; obey it, and **r**.	3566
	3:19	So be earnest, and **r**.	3566
	9:20	not killed by these plagues still *did* not **r** of	3566
	9:21	Nor *did they* **r** of their murders,	3566
	16: 9	but *they* **refused to r** and glorify him.	3566+4024
	16:11	*they* **refused to r** of what they had done.	3566+4024

REPENTANCE (21) [REPENT]
Isa	30:15	"In **r** and rest is your salvation,	8746
Mt	3: 8	Produce fruit in keeping with **r**.	3567
	3:11	"I baptize you with water for **r**.	3567
Mk	1: 4	a baptism *of* **r** for the forgiveness of sins.	3567
Lk	3: 3	a baptism *of* **r** for the forgiveness of sins.	3567
	3: 8	Produce fruit in keeping with **r**.	3567
	5:32	to call the righteous, but sinners to **r**."	3567
	24:47	**r** and forgiveness of sins will be preached	3567
Ac	5:31	that he might give **r** and forgiveness of sins	3567
	11:18	even the Gentiles **r** unto life."	3567
	13:24	John preached **r** and baptism to all	3567
	19: 4	"John's baptism was a baptism *of* **r**.	3567
	20:21	**turn** to God in **r** and have faith in our Lord	3567
	26:20	to God and prove their **r** by their deeds.	3567
Ro	2: 4	that God's kindness leads you toward **r**?	3567
2Co	7: 9	but because your sorrow led you to **r**.	3567
	7:10	Godly sorrow brings **r** that leads to	3567
2Ti	2:25	that God will grant them **r** leading them to	3567
Heb	6: 1	the foundation of **r** from acts that lead	3567
	6: 6	if they fall away, to be brought back to **r**,	3567
2Pe	3: 9	anyone to perish, but everyone to come to **r**.	3567

REPENTED (9) [REPENT]
2Ch	32:26	Then Hezekiah **r** of the pride of his heart,	4044
Jer	31:19	After I strayed, *I* **r**;	5714
	34:15	Recently you **r** and did what is right	8740
Zec	1: 6	"Then *they* **r** and said,	8740
Mt	11:21	*they* would *have* **r** long ago in sackcloth	3566
	12:41	for *they* **r** at the preaching of Jonah,	3566
Lk	10:13	*they* would *have* **r** long ago,	3566
	11:32	for *they* **r** at the preaching of Jonah,	3566
2Co	12:21	and *have* not **r** of the impurity,	3566

REPENTS (5) [REPENT]
Jer	8: 6	No one **r** of his wickedness, saying,	5714
	18: 8	and if that nation I warned of **r** of its evil,	5714
Lk	15: 7	rejoicing in heaven over one sinner *who* **r**	3566
	15:10	the angels of God over one sinner *who* **r**."	3566

Lk 17: 3 rebuke him, and if *he* **r**, forgive him.   3566

REPHAEL (1)
1Ch 26: 7 Othni, **R**, Obed and Elzabad;   8330

REPHAH (1)
1Ch 7:25 **R** was his son, Resheph his son,   8338

REPHAIAH (5)
1Ch 3:21 Pelatiah and Jeshaiah, and the sons of **R**,   8341
     4:42 Neariah, **R** and Uzziel, the sons of Ishi,   8341
     7: 2 The sons of Tola: Uzzi, **R**, Jeriel, Jahmai,   8341
     9:43 **R** was his son, Eleasah his son and   8341
Ne   3: 9 **R** son of Hur, ruler of a half-district of   8341

REPHAIM (8)
Jos 15: 8 at the northern end of the Valley of **R**.   8329
    18:16 north of the Valley of **R**.   8329
2Sa 5:18 and spread out in the Valley of **R**;   8329
     5:22 up and spread out in the Valley of **R**;   8329
    23:13 was encamped in the Valley of **R**.   8329
1Ch 11:15 was encamped in the Valley of **R**.   8329
    14: 9 and raided the Valley of **R**;   8329
Isa 17: 5 gleans heads of grain in the Valley of **R**.   8329

REPHAIMS (KJV) See REPHAITES

REPHAITES (10)
Ge 14: 5 and defeated the **R** in Ashteroth Karnaim,   8328
    15:20 Hittites, Perizzites, **R**,   8328
Dt   2:11 they too were considered a **R**,   8328
     2:20 (That too was considered a land of the **R**,   8328
     3:11 of Bashan was left of the remnant of the **R**.   8328
     3:13 to be known as a land of the **R**.   8328
Jos 12: 4 Og king of Bashan, one of the last of the **R**,   8328
    13:12 and had survived as one of the last of the **R**,   8328
    17:15 in the land of the Perizzites and **R**."   8328
1Ch 20: 4 Sippai, one of the descendants of the **R**,   8328

REPHAN (1)
Ac   7:43 shrine of Molech and the star of your god **R**,   4818

REPHIDIM (5)
Ex 17: 1 They camped at **R**,   8340
    17: 8 and attacked the Israelites at **R**.   8340
    19: 2 After they set out from **R**,   8340
Nu 33:14 They left Alush and camped at **R**,   8340
    33:15 They left **R** and camped in the Desert   8340

REPLACE (6) [REPLACED]
Lev 14:42 are to take other stones *to* **r** these   448+995+9393
1Ki 14:27 Rehoboam made bronze shields to **r** them   9393
    20:24 and **r** them with other officers.   8492+9393
2Ki 17:24 in the towns of Samaria to **r** the Israelites.   9393
2Ch 12:10 Rehoboam made bronze shields to **r** them   9393
Isa 9:10 but *we will* **r** them *with* cedars."   2736

REPLACED (3) [REPLACE]
1Sa 21: 6 from before the LORD and **r** *by* hot bread   8492
1Ki 2:35 and **r** Abiathar with Zadok the priest.   5989+9393
Da   8:22 The four horns *that* **r** the one   6641+9393

REPLANTED (1) [PLANT]
Eze 36:36 and *have* **r** what was desolate.   5749

REPLENISH (KJV) See FILL

REPLICA (1)
Jos 22:28 Look at the **r** *of* the LORD's altar,   9322

REPLIED (414) [REPLY]
Ge   4: 9 *he* **r**. "Am I my brother's keeper?"   606
    19: 9 "Get out of our way," *they* **r**.   606
    20:11 Abraham **r**, "I said to myself,   606
    21:30 *He* **r**, "Accept these seven lambs   606
    22: 1 "Here I am," *he* **r**.   606
    22: 7 "Yes, my son?" Abraham **r**.   606
    22:11 "Here I am," *he* **r**.   606
    23: 5 The Hittites **r** *to* Abraham,   6699
    23:10 among his people and he **r** *to* Abraham in   6699
    24:40 *"He* **r**, 'The LORD, before whom I have   606
    24:55 But her brother and her mother **r**,   606
    25:31 Jacob **r**, "First sell me your birthright."   606
    27:20 LORD your God gave me success," *he* **r**.   606
    27:24 "I am," *he* **r**.   606
    29: 4 "We're from Haran," *they* **r**.   606
    29: 8 *they* **r**, "until all the flocks are gathered and   606
    29:26 Laban **r**, "It is not our custom here to give   606
    30:31 "Don't give me anything," Jacob **r**.   606
    31:14 Then Rachel and Leah **r**,   6699
    32:26 But Jacob **r**, "I will not let you go   606
    32:29 But *he* **r**, "Why do you ask my name?"   606
    34:13 Jacob's sons **r** deceitfully as they spoke   6699
    34:31 But *they* **r**, "Should he have treated our
             sister like a prostitute?"   606
    37:13 "Very well," *he* **r**.   606
    37:16 *He* **r**, "I'm looking for my brothers.   606
    41:16 "I cannot do it," Joseph **r** *to* Pharaoh,   6699

Ge 42: 7 "From the land of Canaan," they **r**,   606
    42:13 *they* **r**, "Your servants were twelve brothers,   606
    42:22 Reuben **r**, "Didn't I tell you not to sin   6699
    43: 7 *They* **r**, "The man questioned us closely   606
    43:28 *They* **r**, "Your servant our father is still alive   606
    44:16 "What can we say to my lord?" Judah **r**.   606
    46: 2 "Here I am," *he* **r**.   606
    47: 3 servants are shepherds," *they* **r** to Pharaoh,   606
Ex   4: 2 "A staff," *he* **r**.   606
     4:10 Moses **r**, "It will be as you say,   606
     9:29 Moses **r**, "When I have gone out of   606
    10:29 "Just as you say," Moses **r**,   606
    17: 2 Moses **r**, "Why do you quarrel with me?   606
    18:17 Moses' father-in-law **r**, "What you are doing   606
    19:24 The LORD **r**, "Go down and bring Aaron   606
    32:18 Moses **r**: "It is not the sound of victory,   606
    32:33 The LORD **r** to Moses, "Whoever has sinned   606
    33:14 The LORD **r**, "My Presence will go   606
Lev 10:19 Aaron **r** to Moses, "Today they sacrificed   1819
Nu 11:29 Moses **r**, "Are you jealous for my sake?   606
    12:14 The LORD **r** to Moses, "If her father had spit   606
    14:20 The LORD **r**, "I have forgiven them,   606
    20:19 The Israelites **r**: "We will go along the   606
    22:38 "Well, I have come to you now," Balaam **r**.   606
Dt   1:41 Then *you* **r**, "We have sinned against   6699
Jos 2:21 "Agreed," *she* **r**.   606
     5:14 *he* **r**, "but as commander of the army of   606
     5:15 The commander of the LORD's army **r**,   606
     7:20 Achan **r**, "It is true!   6699
     9:19 *She* **r**, "Do me a special favor.   606
    17:16 The people of Joseph **r**,   606
    22:21 the half-tribe of Manasseh **r** *to* the heads of   6699
    24:22 "Yes, we are witnesses," they **r**.   606
Jdg 1:15 *She* **r**, "Do me a special favor.   606
     6:13 Gideon **r**, "if the LORD is with us,   606
     6:17 Gideon **r**, "If now I have found favor   606
     6:31 Joash **r** to the hostile crowd around him,   606
     8: 7 Then Gideon **r**, "Just for that,   606
     8:19 Gideon **r**, "Those were my brothers,   606
     9:11 "But the fig tree **r**, 'Should I give up my   606
     9:36 Zebul **r**, "You mistake the shadows of   606
    10:11 The LORD **r**, "When the Egyptians,   606
    11:10 elders of Gilead **r**, "The LORD is our witness   606
    11:36 *she* **r**, "you have given your word to   606
    12: 5 "Are you an Ephraimite?" If *he* **r**,   606
    13:16 The angel of the LORD **r**, "Even though   606
    13:18 He **r**, "Why do you ask my name?   606
    14: 3 His father and mother **r**,   606
    14:14 *He* **r**, "Out of the eater, something to eat;   606
    14:16 *he* **r**, "so why should I explain it to you?"   606
    16:13 *He* **r**, "If you weave the seven braids   606
    18:24 *He* **r**, "You took the gods I made,   606
    19:12 His master **r**, "No.   606
    20:18 The LORD **r**, "Judah shall go first."   606
Ru   1:16 But Ruth **r**, "Don't urge me to leave you or   606
     2: 6 The foreman **r**, "She is the Moabitess   6699
     2:11 Boaz **r**, "I've been told all about what   6699
     3:10 "The LORD bless you, my daughter," *he* **r**.   606
1Sa 1:15 "Not so, my lord," Hannah **r**,   6699
     4:17 The man who brought the news **r**,   6699
     6: 4 *They* **r**, "Five gold tumors and five gold   606
     9: 6 But the servant **r**, "Look,   606
     9:19 "I am the seer," Samuel **r**.   6699
    10:16 Saul **r**, "He assured us that the donkeys   606
    11: 2 But Nahash the Ammonite **r**,   606
    12: 4 not cheated or oppressed us," *they* **r**.   606
    12:20 "Do not be afraid," Samuel **r**.   606
    13:11 Saul **r**, "When I saw that men were   606
    14:36 "Do whatever seems best to you," *they* **r**.   606
    14:40 "Do what seems best to you," the men **r**.   606
    15:16 "Tell me," Saul **r**.   606
    15:22 But Samuel **r**: "Does the LORD delight in
             burnt offerings   606
    15:30 Saul **r**, "I have sinned.   606
    16: 5 Samuel **r**, "Yes, in peace;   606
    17:33 Saul **r**, "You are not able to go out   606
    17:55 Abner **r**, "As surely as you live, O king,   606
    18:25 Saul **r**, "Say to David,   606
    20: 2 "Never!" Jonathan **r**. "You are not   606
    21: 5 David **r**, "Indeed women have been kept   6699
    21: 9 The priest **r**, "The sword of Goliath   606
    23:21 Saul **r**, "The LORD bless you   606
    26:14 Abner **r**, "Who are you who calls to   6699
    26:17 David **r**, "Yes it is, my lord the king."   606
    28: 2 Achish **r**, "Very well,   606
    29: 3 Achish **r**, "Is this not David,   606
    30:23 David **r**, "No, my brothers,   606
2Sa 7: 3 Nathan **r** to the king, "Whatever you have   606
     7: 5 "Your servant," *he* **r**.   606
     9: 6 "Your servant," *he* **r**.   606
    12:13 Nathan **r**, "The LORD has taken away your   606
    12:19 "Yes," *they* **r**, "he is dead."   606
    13:25 "No, my son," the king **r**.   606
    14:10 The king **r**, "If anyone says anything   606
    14:12 "Speak," *he* **r**.   606
    15:21 But Ittai **r** *to* the king, "As surely as   6699
    17: 7 Hushai **r** *to* Absalom, "The advice   606
    18:12 But the man **r**, "Even if a thousand shekels   606
    18:22 But Joab **r**, "My son,   606
    18:32 The Cushite **r**, "May the enemies of my lord   606
    19:22 David **r**, "What do you and I have   606
    20:20 Joab **r**, "Far be it from me to swallow up   6699
    24: 3 But Joab **r** to the king,   606
    24:24 But the king **r** to Araunah, "No,   606
1Ki 1:52 Solomon **r**, "If he shows himself to be   606
     2:14 "You may say it," *she* **r**.   606
     2:18 "Very well," Bathsheba **r**,   606

1Ki 2:20 The king **r**, "Make it, my mother;   606
    11:22 "Nothing," Hadad **r**, "but do let me go!"   606
    12: 7 *They* **r**, "If today you will be a servant   1819
    12:10 young men who had grown up with him **r**,   1819
    13:14 "I am," *he* **r**.   606
    17:12 *she* **r**, "I don't have any bread—   606
    17:19 "Give me your son," Elijah **r**.   606
    18: 8 "Yes," *he* **r**.   606
    18:18 not made trouble for Israel," Elijah **r**.   606
    19:10 *He* **r**, "I have been very zealous for the LORD   606
    19:14 *He* **r**, "I have been very zealous for the LORD   606
    19:20 "Go back," Elijah **r**.   606
    20: 9 So *he* **r** to Ben-Hadad's messengers,   606
    20:14 The prophet **r**, "This is what   606
    21: 3 But Naboth **r**, "The LORD forbid   606
    22: 4 Jehoshaphat **r** to the king of Israel,   606
    22: 8 not say that," Jehoshaphat **r**.   606
    22:25 Micaiah **r**, "You will find out on   606
2Ki 1: 6 "A man came to meet us," *they* **r**.   606
     1: 8 *They* **r**, "He was a man with a garment   606
     1:12 "If I am a man of God," Elijah **r**,   6699
     2: 3 "Yes, I know," Elisha **r**.   606
     2: 4 And *he* **r**, "As surely as the LORD lives   606
     2: 5 "Yes, I know," *he* **r**,   606
     2: 6 And *he* **r**, "As surely as the LORD lives   606
     2: 9 a double portion of your spirit," Elisha **r**.   606
     2:16 "No," Elisha **r**, "do not send them."   606
     3: 7 "I will go with you," *he* **r**.   606
     4: 2 Elisha **r** to her, "How can I help you?   606
     4: 2 But *her* **r**, "There is not a jar left."   606
     4:13 *She* **r**, "I have a home among my own   606
     5: 5 "By all means, go," the king of Aram **r**.   606
     6: 3 "I will," Elisha **r**.   606
     6:27 The king **r**, "If the LORD does not help you,   606
     7:19 The man of God *had* **r**, "You will see it   606
     8:14 Hazael **r**, "He told me that you would   606
     9: 5 "For you, commander," *he* **r**.   606
     9:11 and the sort of things he says," Jehu **r**.   606
     9:18 What do you have to do with peace?" Jehu **r**.   606
     9:19 Jehu **r**, "What do you have to do with peace   606
     9:22 "How can there be peace," Jehu **r**,   606
    14: 9 of Israel **r** to Amaziah king of Judah: 606+8938
    18:27 But the commander **r**,   606
    20:14 "From a distant land," Hezekiah **r**.   606
    20:19 you have spoken is good," Hezekiah **r**.   606
1Ch 17: 2 Nathan **r** to David, "Whatever you have   606
    21: 3 But Joab **r**, "May the LORD multiply   606
    21:24 But King David **r** to Araunah, "No,   606
2Ch 10: 7 *They* **r**, "If you will be kind to these people   1819
    10:10 with him **r**, "Tell the people who have said   1819
    18: 3 Jehoshaphat **r**, "I am as you are,   606
    18: 7 not say that," Jehoshaphat **r**.   606
    18:24 Micaiah **r**, "You will find out on   606
    25: 9 The man of God **r**, "The LORD can give   606
    25:18 of Israel **r** to Amaziah king of Judah: 606+8938
Ne   2:18 *They* **r**, "Let us start rebuilding."   606
Est 1:16 Then Memucan **r** in the presence of   606
     5: 4 "If it pleases the king," **r** Esther,   606
     5: 7 Esther **r**, "My petition and my request   6699
     8: 7 King Xerxes **r** to Queen Esther and   606
Job 1: 9 "Does Job fear God for nothing?" Satan **r**.   6699
     2: 4 "Skin for skin!" Satan **r**.   6699
     2:10 *He* **r**, "You are talking like a foolish woman   606
     4: 1 Then Eliphaz the Temanite **r**:   6699
     6: 1 Then Job **r**:   6699
     8: 1 Then Bildad the Shuhite **r**:   6699
     9: 1 Then Job **r**:   6699
    11: 1 Then Zophar the Naamathite **r**:   6699
    12: 1 Then Job **r**:   6699
    15: 1 Then Eliphaz the Temanite **r**:   6699
    16: 1 Then Job **r**:   6699
    18: 1 Then Bildad the Shuhite **r**:   6699
    19: 1 Then Job **r**:   6699
    20: 1 Then Zophar the Naamathite **r**:   6699
    21: 1 Then Job **r**:   6699
    22: 1 Then Eliphaz the Temanite **r**:   6699
    23: 1 Then Job **r**:   6699
    25: 1 Then Bildad the Shuhite **r**:   6699
    26: 1 Then Job **r**:   6699
    42: 1 Then Job **r** *to* the LORD: 6699
Isa 36:12 But the commander **r**,   606
    39: 3 "From a distant land," Hezekiah **r**.   606
    39: 8 you have spoken is good," Hezekiah **r**.   606
Jer 1:11 "I see the branch of an almond tree," *I* **r**.   606
    28: 5 Then the prophet Jeremiah **r**   606
    35: 6 But *they* **r**, "We do not drink wine,   606
    36:18 Baruch **r**, "he dictated all these words   606
    37:17 Jeremiah **r**, "you will be handed over to   606
    38:20 "They will not hand you over," Jeremiah **r**.   606
    42: 4 "I have heard you," *r* Jeremiah the prophet.   606
Da   2: 5 The king **r** to the astrologers,   10558
     2: 7 Once more *they* **r**, "Let the king tell   10558
     2:27 Daniel **r**, "No wise man, enchanter,   10558
     3:16 Meshach and Abednego **r** to the king,   10558
     3:24 *They* **r**, "Certainly, O king."   10558
    12: 9 *He* **r**, "Go your way, Daniel,   606
Am   7: 8 "A plumb line," *I* **r**.   606
Jnh 1:12 *he* **r**, "and it will become calm.   606
     4: 4 But the LORD **r**, "Have you any right   606
Hab 2: 2 Then the LORD **r**: "Write down the   606
Hag 2:13 "Yes," the priests **r**, "it becomes defiled."   6699
Zec 4: 5 "No, my lord," *I* **r**.   606
     4:13 *He* **r**, "Do you not know what these are?"   606
     5: 6 *He* **r**, "It is a measuring basket."   606
     5:11 *He* **r**, "To the country of Babylonia to build   606
Mt   2: 5 "In Bethlehem in Judea," they **r**,   3306

Mt	3:15	Jesus r, "Let it be so now;	646
	8: 8	The centurion r, "Lord,	646+5774
	8:20	Jesus r, "Foxes have holes and birds of	3306
	8:26	He r, "You of little faith,	3306
	9:28	"Yes, Lord," they r.	3306
	11: 4	Jesus r, "Go back and report	646
	12:48	He r to him, "Who is my mother,	646
	13:11	He r, "The knowledge of the secrets	646
	13:28	"'An enemy did this,' he r.	5774
	13:51	"Yes," they r.	3306
	14:16	Jesus r, "They do not need to go away.	3306
	14:28	"Lord, if it's you," Peter r,	3306
	15: 3	Jesus r, "And why do you break	646
	15:13	He r, "Every plant that my heavenly	646
	15:26	He r, "It is not right to take the children's	646
	15:34	"Seven," they r, "and a few small fish."	3306
	16: 2	He r, "When evening comes, you say,	646
	16:14	They r, "Some say John the Baptist;	3306
	16:17	Jesus r, "Blessed are you,	646
	17:11	Jesus r, "To be sure, Elijah comes	646
	17:17	Jesus r, "how long shall I stay with you?	3306
	17:20	He r, "Because you have so little faith.	646
	17:25	"Yes, he does," he r.	3306
	19: 4	"Haven't you read," he r,	646
	19: 8	Jesus r, "Moses permitted you to divorce	646
	19:11	Jesus r, "Not everyone can accept this word,	3306
	19:17	ask me about what is good?" Jesus r.	3306
	19:18	Jesus r, " 'Do not murder,	3306
	21:16	"Yes," r Jesus, "have you never read,	3306
	21:21	Jesus r, "I tell you the truth,	646
	21:24	Jesus r, "I will also ask you one question.	646
	21:41	a wretched end," they r, "and he will rent	3306
	22:21	"Caesar's," they r.	3306
	22:29	Jesus r, "You are in error because you do	646
	22:37	Jesus r: " 'Love the Lord your God with all	5774
	22:42	"The son of David," they r.	3306
	25: 9	they r, 'there may not be enough for	646
	25:12	"But he r, 'I tell you the truth,	646
	25:21	"His master r, 'Well done,	5774
	25:23	"His master r, 'Well done,	5774
	25:26	"His master r, 'You wicked, lazy servant!	646
	26:18	He r, "Go into the city to a certain man	3306
	26:23	Jesus r, "The one who has dipped his hand	646
	26:33	Peter r, "Even if all fall away on account	646
	26:50	Jesus r, "Friend, do what you came for."	646
	26:64	"Yes, it is as you say," Jesus r.	3306
	27: 4	"What is that to us?" they r.	3306
	27:11	"Yes, it is as you say," Jesus r.	5774
Mk	1:38	Jesus r, "Let us go somewhere else—	3306
	5: 9	"My name is Legion," he r,	3306
	7: 6	He r, "Isaiah was right when he prophesied	3306
	7:28	she r, "but even the dogs under the table	646
	8: 5	"Seven," they r.	3306
	8:19	"Twelve," they r.	3306
	8:28	They r, "Some say John the Baptist;	3306
	9:12	Jesus r, "To be sure, Elijah does come first,	5774
	9:19	"O unbelieving generation," Jesus r,	646
	9:29	He r, "This kind can come out only	3306
	10: 3	"What did Moses command you?" he r.	646
	10: 5	that Moses wrote you this law," Jesus r.	3306
	10:29	"I tell you the truth," Jesus r,	5774
	10:37	They r, "Let one of us sit at your right and	3306
	11:29	Jesus r, "I will ask you one question.	3306
	12:16	"Caesar's," they r.	3306
	12:24	Jesus r, "Are you not in error	5774
	12:32	"Well said, teacher," the man r.	3306
	13: 2	you see all these great buildings?" r Jesus.	3306
	14:20	"It is one of the Twelve," he r,	646
	15: 2	"Yes, it is as you say," Jesus r.	646
Lk	3:14	He r, "Don't extort money	3306
	7:22	So he r to the messengers,	646
	7:43	Simon r, "I suppose the one who had	646
	8:21	He r, "My mother and brothers are	646
	8:30	he r, because many demons had gone	3306
	9:13	He r, "You give them something to eat."	3306
	9:19	They r, "Some say John the Baptist;	646
	9:41	Jesus r, "how long shall I stay with you	646
	9:58	Jesus r, "Foxes have holes and birds of	3306
	9:59	But the man r, "Lord,	3306
	9:62	Jesus r, "No one who puts his hand to	3306
	10:18	He r, "I saw Satan fall like lightning	3306
	10:26	"What is written in the Law?" he r.	3306
	10:28	"You have answered correctly," Jesus r.	646
	10:37	The expert in the law r,	3306
	11:28	He r, "Blessed rather are those who hear	3306
	11:46	Jesus r, "And you experts in the law,	3306
	12:14	Jesus r, "Man, who appointed me a judge	3306
	13: 8	the man r, 'leave it alone	646
	13:32	He r, "Go tell that fox,	3306
	14:16	Jesus r: "A certain man was preparing a	3306
	15:27	'Your brother has come,' the r,	3306
	16: 6	" 'Eight hundred gallons of olive oil,' he r.	3306
	16: 7	" 'A thousand bushels of wheat,' he r.	3306
	16:25	"But Abraham r, 'Son,	3306
	16:29	"Abraham r, 'They have Moses and	3306
	17: 6	He r, "If you have faith as small as	3306
	17:20	the kingdom of God would come, Jesus r.	646
	17:37	He r, "Where there is a dead body,	3306
	18:27	Jesus r, "What is impossible	3306
	18:41	"Lord, I want to see," he r.	3306
	19:17	"Well done, my good servant!' his master r.	3306
	19:22	"His master r, 'I will judge you	3306
	19:26	"He r, 'I tell you that to everyone who has,	NIG
	19:34	They r, "The Lord needs it."	3306
	19:40	"I tell you," he r, "if they keep quiet,	646
	20: 3	He r, "I will also ask you a question.	646
	20:25	"Caesar's," they r.	3306
Lk	20:34	Jesus r, "The people of this age marry	3306
	21: 8	He r: "Watch out that you are not deceived.	3306
	22:10	He r, "As you enter the city,	3306
	22:33	But he r, "Lord, I am ready to go with you	3306
	22:38	"That is enough," he r.	3306
	22:58	I am not!" Peter r.	5774
	22:60	Peter r, "Man, I don't know what you're talking about!"	3306
	22:70	He r, "You are right in saying I am."	5774
	23: 3	"Yes, it is as you say," Jesus r.	646
	24:19	"About Jesus of Nazareth," they r.	3306
Jn	1:23	John r in the words of Isaiah the prophet,	5774
	1:26	"I baptize with water," John r,	646
	1:39	"Come," he r, "and you will see."	3306
	2: 4	why do you involve me?" Jesus r.	3306
	2:20	The Jews r, "It has taken forty-six years	3306
	3:27	To this John r, "A man can receive only	646
	4:17	"I have no husband," she r.	646
	4:50	Jesus r, "You may go.	3306
	5: 7	the invalid r, "I have no one to help me	646
	5:11	But he r, "The man who made me well said	646
	6:70	Then Jesus r, "Have I not chosen you,	646
	7:12	Others r, "No, he deceives the people."	3306
	7:52	They r, "Are you from Galilee, too?	646
	8:19	not know me or my Father," Jesus r.	646
	8:25	I have been claiming all along," Jesus r.	3306
	8:34	Jesus r, "I tell you the truth,	646
	8:54	Jesus r, "If I glorify myself,	646
	9:11	He r, "The man they call Jesus	646
	9:15	he put mud on my eyes," the man r,	3306
	9:17	The man r, "He is a prophet."	646
	9:25	He r, "Whether he is a sinner or not,	646
	9:34	To this they r, "You were steeped in sin	646
	10:33	r the Jews, "but for blasphemy,	646
	11:12	His disciples r, "Lord, if he sleeps,	3306
	11:34	"Come and see, Lord," they r.	3306
	12: 7	"Leave her alone," Jesus r.	3306
	12:23	Jesus r, "The hour has come for the Son	646
	13: 7	Jesus r, "You do not realize	646
	13: 9	Simon Peter r, "Not just my feet but	3306
	13:36	Jesus r, "Where I am going,	646
	14:23	Jesus r, "If anyone loves me,	646
	18: 5	"Jesus of Nazareth," they r.	3306
	18:17	He r, "I am not."	646
	18:20	"I have spoken openly to the world," Jesus r.	646
	18:23	"If I said something wrong," Jesus r,	646
	18:30	"If he were not a criminal," they r,	646
	18:35	"Am I a Jew?" Pilate r.	646
Ac	2:38	Peter r, "Repent and be baptized,	NIG
	4:19	But Peter and John r, "Judge for yourselves	646
	5:29	Peter and the other apostles r:	646
	7: 2	To this he r: "Brothers and fathers,	5774
	9: 5	Jesus, whom you are persecuting," he r.	NIG
	10:14	"Surely not, Lord!" Peter r.	5774
	10:22	The men r, "We have come from Cornelius	3306
	11: 8	"'I r, 'Surely not, Lord!	3306
	16:31	They r, "Believe in the Lord Jesus,	3306
	19: 3	"John's baptism," they r.	3306
	21:37	"Do you speak Greek?" he r.	5774
	22: 8	whom you are persecuting,' he r.	3306
	22:19	I r, 'these men know that I went	3306
	22:28	"But I was born a citizen," Paul r.	5774
	23: 5	Paul r, "Brothers, I did not realize	5774
	24:10	for him to speak, Paul r:	646
	25:22	He r, "Tomorrow you will hear him."	5774
	26:15	whom you are persecuting,' the Lord r.	3306
	26:25	most excellent Festus," Paul r.	5774
	26:29	Paul r, "Short time or long—	NIG
	28:21	They r, "We have not received any letters	3306

REPLIES (2) [REPLY]

Ne	6:17	and r from Tobiah kept coming to them.	889S
Isa	21:12	The watchman r, "Morning is coming,	606

REPLY (27) [REPLIED, REPLIES]

2Ki	18:36	remained silent and said nothing in r,	6699
Ezr	4:17	The king sent this r: To Rehum	10601
	5: 5	to Darius and his written r be received.	10496
Ne	6: 3	so I sent messengers to them with this r:	606
	6: 8	I sent him this r: "Nothing like what you	606
Est	4:15	Then Esther sent this r to Mordecai:	606
Job	13:22	or let me speak, and you r.	8740
	20: 3	and my understanding inspires me to r.	6699
	32:16	now that they stand there with no r?	6699
	32:20	I must open my lips and r.	6699
	35: 4	"I would like to r to you and to	4863+8740
	40: 4	how can I r to you?	8740
Ps	38:14	whose mouth can offer no r.	9350
Pr	15:23	A man finds joy in giving an apt r—	5101+7023
	16: 1	from the LORD comes the r of the tongue.	5101
Isa	36:21	remained silent and said nothing in r,	6699
Jer	18:12	But they will r, 'It's no use.	606
Joel	2:19	The LORD will r to them:	6699
Mt	22:46	No one could say a word in r,	3306
	25:40	"The King will r, 'I tell you the truth,	646
	25:45	"He will r, 'I tell you the truth,	646
	27:14	But Jesus made no r,	646
Mk	7:29	he told her, "For such a r, you may go;	3364
	15: 5	But Jesus still made no r,	646
Lk	10:30	In r Jesus said: "A man was going down	5696
	13:27	"But he will r, 'I don't know you	3306
Jn	3: 3	Jesus r declared, "I tell you the truth,	646

REPOINTING (1)

1Sa	13:21	sharpening forks and axes and for r goads.	5893

REPORT (48) [REPORTED, REPORTING, REPORTS]

Ge	37: 2	he brought their father a bad r about them.	1804
Nu	13:32	a bad r about the land they had explored.	1804
	14:15	the nations who have heard this r	9051
	14:36	against him by spreading a bad r about it—	1804
	14:37	for spreading the bad r about the land	1804
Dt	1:22	to spy out the land for us and bring back a r	1821
Jos	1:22	And I brought him back a r according	1821
	22:33	to hear the r and praised God.	1821
1Sa	2:24	not a good r that I hear spreading among	9019
2Sa	1: 5	to the young man who brought him the r,	5583
	1:13	to the young man who brought him the r,	5583
	13:30	the r came to David;	9019
	13:33	about the r that all the king's sons are dead.	1821
1Ki	10: 6	"The r I heard in my own country	1821
	10: 7	you have far exceeded the r I heard.	9019
2Ki	6:13	The r came back: "He is in Dothan."	5583
	7: 9	at once and r this to the royal palace.	5583
	19: 7	in him that when he hears a certain r,	9019
	19: 9	Sennacherib received a r that Tirhakah,	9048
1Ch	21: 2	Then r back to me so that I may know	995
2Ch	9: 5	"The r I heard in my own country	1821
	9: 6	you have far exceeded the r I heard.	9019
Ezr	5: 5	a r could go to Darius and his written reply	10302
	5: 7	The r they sent him read as follows:	10601
Ne	6: 7	Now this r will get back to the king;	1821
Est	2:23	the r was investigated and found to be true,	1821
Job	38:35	Do they r to you, 'Here we are'?	606
Ecc	10:20	and a bird on the wing may r what you say.	5583
Isa	21: 6	post a lookout and have him r what he sees.	5583
	23: 5	they will be in anguish at the r from Tyre.	9051
	37: 7	in him so that when he hears a certain r,	9019
	37: 9	Sennacherib received a r that Tirhakah,	9048
Jer	10:22	Listen! The r is coming—	9019
	20:10	"Terror on every side! R him!"	5583
	20:10	Report him! Let's r him!"	5583
	36:16	We must r all these words to the king.	5583+5583
	37: 5	besieging Jerusalem heard the r about them,	9051
Mt	2: 8	As soon as you find him, r to me,	550
	11: 4	"Go back and r to John what you hear	550
	28:14	If this r gets to the governor,	NIG
Lk	7:22	"Go back and r to John what you have seen	550
Jn	11:57	he should r it so that they might arrest him.	3606
Ac	5:24	On hearing this r, the captain of the temple	3364
2Co	6: 8	bad r and good report;	1556
	6: 8	bad report and good r;	2367
Gal	1:23	They only heard the r.	NIG
1Th	1: 9	for they themselves r what kind of reception	550
2Th	2: 2	r or letter supposed to have come from us,	3364

REPORTED (57) [REPORT]

Ge	14:13	One who had escaped came and r this	5583
Ex	6: 9	Moses r this to the Israelites,	1819
	16:22	the community came and r this to Moses.	5583
Nu	13:26	There they r to them and to	1821+8740
	14:39	When Moses r this to all the Israelites,	1819
Dt	1:22	they brought it down to us and r,	1821+8740
Jos	22:32	and Gadites in Gilead and r to the	1821+8740
Jdg	9:25	and this was r to Abimelech.	5583
	9:42	and this was r to Abimelech.	5583
1Sa	11: 4	of Saul and r these terms to the people,	1819
	11: 9	the messengers went and r this to the men	5583
	17:31	What David said was overheard and r	5583
	25:12	When they arrived, they r every word.	5583
2Sa	7:11	Nathan r to David all the words	1819
	18:25	to the king and r it.	5583
	24: 9	Joab r the number of the fighting men to	5989
1Ki	2:30	Benaiah r to the king,	1821+8740
	13:25	and they went and r it in the city where	1819
	18:44	The seventh time the servant r,	606
	20:17	Ben-Hadad had dispatched scouts, who r,	5583
2Ki	7:11	and it was r within the palace.	5583
	7:15	the messengers returned and r to the king.	5583
	9:18	The lookout r, "The messenger has	5583
	9:20	The lookout r, "He has reached them,	5583
	17:26	It was r to the king of Assyria:	1821
	22: 9	went to the king and r to him:	1821+8740
1Ch	17:15	Nathan r to David all the words	1819
	21: 5	Joab r the number of the fighting men	5989
2Ch	29:18	Then they went in to King Hezekiah and r:	606
	34:16	the book to the king and r to him:	1821+8740
Ne	6: 6	"It is r among the nations—	9048
Est	2:22	who in turn r it to the king,	606
	4: 9	and r to Esther what Mordecai had said.	5583
	4:12	When Esther's words were r to Mordecai,	5583
		of those slain in the citadel of Susa was r to	995
Jer	36:20	the king in the courtyard and r everything	5583
Zec	1:11	And they r to the angel of the LORD,	6699
Mt	8:33	went into the town and r all this,	550
	28:11	the city and r to the chief priests everything	550
Mk	5:14	Those tending the pigs ran off and r this in	550
	6:30	around Jesus and r to him all they had done	550
	16:13	These returned and r it to the rest;	550
Lk	8:34	they r it in the town and countryside,	550
	9:10	they r to Jesus what they had done.	1455
	14:21	"The servant came back and r this	550
Ac	4:23	to their own people and r all that	550
	5:22	So they went back and r,	550
	14:27	they gathered the church together and r all	334
	15: 4	to whom they r everything God had done	334
	16:38	The officers r this to the magistrates,	550
	21:19	and in detail what God had done among	2007
	22:26	he went to the commander and r it.	550
	23:22	"Don't tell anyone that you have r this	1872

Ac	28:21	from there *has* r or said anything bad	550
Ro	1: 8	your faith *is being* r all over the world.	2859
	3: 8	as *we are being* **slanderously** r as saying	1059
1Co	5: 1	*It is* actually r that there is sexual immorality among you,	201

REPORTING (1) [REPORT]

Ne	6:19	they kept r to me his good deeds and	606

REPORTS (10) [REPORT]

Ex	23: 1	"Do not spread false r.	9051
Dt	2:25	They will hear r *of* you and will tremble	9051
Jos	9: 9	For we have heard r *of* him:	9053
Ne	6: 6	according to these r you are about	1821
Jer	6:24	We have heard r *about* them,	9053
	50:43	king of Babylon has heard r *about* them,	9051
Da	11:44	But r from the east and the north	9019
Mt	14: 1	At that time Herod the tetrarch heard the r	198
Ac	9:13	"I have heard many r about this man	NIG
	21:24	there is no truth in these r about you,	2994

REPOSE (3) [REPOSES]

Dt	28:65	Among those nations *you will* **find** no r,	8089
Isa	28:12	and, "This is the **place of r**"—	5276
	34:14	the night creatures *will* also r and find	8089

REPOSES (1) [REPOSE]

Pr	14:33	Wisdom r in the heart of the discerning and	5663

REPRESENT (6) [REPRESENTATION, REPRESENTATIVE, REPRESENTATIVES, REPRESENTED, REPRESENTING, REPRESENTS]

Lev	24: 7	to r the bread and to be an offering made to	4200
Jer	40:10	I myself will stay at Mizpah to r you before	6641
Da	8:22	that was broken off r four kingdoms	NIH
Gal	3:20	does not r just one party; but God is one.	NIG
	4:24	for the women r two covenants.	1639
Heb	5: 1	among men and is appointed to r them	NIG

REPRESENTATION (1) [REPRESENT]

Heb	1: 3	of God's glory and the **exact** r of his being,	5917

REPRESENTATIVE (2) [REPRESENT]

Ex	18:19	You must be the people's r before God	NIH
2Sa	15: 3	there is no r of the king to hear you."	907+4946

REPRESENTATIVES (1) [REPRESENT]

2Co	8:23	for our brothers, they are r of the churches	693

REPRESENTED (2) [REPRESENT]

Nu	17: 8	which r the house of Levi,	4200
Jdg	18: 2	These men r all their clans.	4946

REPRESENTING (2) [REPRESENT]

Ex	24: 4	up twelve stone pillars r the twelve tribes	4200
Nu	1:44	each one r his family.	4200

REPRESENTS (1) [REPRESENT]

Da	8:20	The two-horned ram that you saw r the kings	NIH

REPRIMANDED (1)

Jer	29:27	So why *have* you not r Jeremiah	1721

REPROACH (21) [REPROACHED]

Jos	5: 9	"Today I have rolled away the r *of* Egypt	3075
Ne	5: 9	to avoid the r *of* our Gentile enemies?	3075
Job	27: 6	my conscience *will* not r me as long	3070
Ps	44:13	You have made us a r to our neighbors,	3075
	44:16	at the taunts of *those who* r and revile me,	3070
	79: 4	We are **objects of** r to our neighbors,	3075
	79:12	the r they have hurled at you,	3075
Isa	51: 7	the r *of* men or be terrified by their insults.	3075
	54: 4	of your youth and remember no more the r	3075
Jer	15:15	think of how I suffer r for your sake.	3075
	20: 8	insult and r all day long.	7841
	24: 9	a r and a byword, an object of ridicule	3075
	29:18	of cursing and horror, of scorn and r,	3075
	42:18	cursing and horror, of condemnation and r;	3075
	44: 8	of cursing and r among all the nations	3075
	44:12	cursing and horror, of condemnation and r.	3075
	49:13	an object of horror, of r and of cursing;	3075
Eze	5:14	and a r among the nations around you,	3075
	5:15	You will be a r and a taunt,	3075
Zep	3:18	they are a burden and a r to you.	3075
1Ti	3: 2	Now the overseer must be **above** r,	455

REPROACHED (1) [REPROACH]

Job	19: 3	Ten times now *you have* r me;	4007

REPROBATE, REPROBATES (KJV)
See DEPRAVED, FAIL, FAILED, REJECTED, UNFIT

REPROOF, REPROVE (KJV) See

ACCUSE, CONVICT, CORRECT, CORRECTION, DECIDE, EXPOSE, PROVE, REBUKE

REPROVES (1)

Am	5:10	you hate the *one who* r in court	3519

REPTILES (5)

1Ki	4:33	also taught about animals and birds, r	8254
Ac	10:12	as well as r of the earth and birds of the air.	2260
	11: 6	wild beasts, r, and birds of the air.	2260
Ro	1:23	and birds and animals and r.	2260
Jas	3: 7	r and creatures of the sea are being tamed	2260

REPULSE (2) [REPULSIVE]

2Ki	18:24	How *can you* r one officer of the least	7156+8740
Isa	36: 9	How then *can you* r one officer of	7156+8740

REPULSIVE (6) [REPULSE]

1Ki	15:13	because she had made a r Asherah pole.	5145
1Ch	21: 6	because the king's command *was* r to him.	9493
2Ch	15:16	because she had made a r Asherah pole.	5145
Job	33:20	so that his very being **finds** food r	2299
Ps	88: 8	and have made me r to them.	9359
Jer	23:13	the prophets of Samaria I saw this **r thing:**	9524

REPUTATION (4) [REPUTED]

Est	9: 4	his r spread throughout the provinces,	9053
Pr	25:10	and you will never lose your **bad** r.	1804
1Ti	3: 7	He must also have a good r with outsiders,	3456
Rev	3: 1	you have a r of being alive,	3950

REPUTED (1) [REPUTATION]

Gal	2: 9	James, Peter and John, those r to be pillars,	1506

REQUEST (31) [REQUESTED, REQUESTING, REQUESTS]

Ge	19:21	"Very well, I will grant this r too;	1821
Jdg	6:39	*Let me* make just one more r.	1819
	8: 8	up to Peniel and **made** *the* same r of them,	1819
	8:24	And he said, "I *do* **have** one r,	8626+8629
	11:37	But grant me this one r," she said.	1821
1Sa	25:35	heard your words and **granted** your r.	5951+7156
2Sa	12:20	and at his r they served him food,	8626
	14:22	the king has granted his servant's r."	1821
1Ki	2:16	Now *I* have one r **to make**	8626+8629
	2:20	"I **have** one small r **to make**	8626+8629
	2:22	"Why *do* you r Abishag the Shunammite	8626
	2:22	*You might as well* r the kingdom for him—	8626
	2:23	does not pay with his life for this r!	1819+1821
1Ch	4:10	And God granted his r.	8626
Est	5: 3	What *is* your r? Even up to half the	1336
	5: 6	And what *is* your r? Even up to half the	1336
	5: 7	"My petition and my r is this:	1336
	5: 8	to grant my petition and fulfill my r,	1336
	7: 2	What *is* your r? Even up to half the	1336
	7: 3	And spare my people—this is my r.	1336
	9:12	What *is* your r? I will also be granted."	1336
Job	6: 8	"Oh, that I might have my r,	8629
Ps	21: 2	and have not withheld the r of his lips.	830
Da	2:49	at Daniel's r the king appointed Shadrach,	10114
	9:20	and making my r to the LORD my God	9382
Mt	14: 9	he ordered that her r be granted	NIG
	15:28	Your r is granted."	2527
Mk	6:25	the girl hurried in to the king with the r:	160
Jn	12:21	from Bethsaida in Galilee, with a r.	2263
Ac	23:21	waiting for your consent to their r."	NIG
	24: 4	*I would* r that you be kind enough	4151

REQUESTED (5) [REQUEST]

Ex	12:31	Go, worship the LORD as you *have* r.	1819
Ezr	6: 9	as r *by* the priests in Jerusalem—	10397
Jer	42: 4	to the LORD your God as you *have* r;	1821
Mk	15: 6	to release a prisoner whom the *people* r.	4148
Ac	25: 3	They **urgently** r Festus, as a favor	160+4151

REQUESTING (1) [REQUEST]

Ac	16:39	from the prison, r them to leave the city.	2263

REQUESTS (7) [REQUEST]

Ne	2: 8	the king **granted** my r.	5989
Ps	5: 3	in the morning I lay my r before you and	NIH
	20: 5	May the LORD grant all your r.	5399
Da	9:18	We do not make r of you	9384
Eph	6:18	with all kinds of prayers and r.	1255
Php	4: 6	with thanksgiving, present your r to God.	161
1Ti	2: 1	I urge, then, first of all, that r, prayers,	1255

REQUIRE (8) [REQUIRED, REQUIREMENT, REQUIREMENTS, REQUIRES, REQUIRING]

Ex	5: 8	But r them to make the same number	8492
Dt	15: 2	not r **payment** *from* his fellow Israelite	5601
	15: 3	*You may* r **payment** *from* a foreigner,	5601
2Ki	12:15	*They did* not r **an accounting** *from* those	3108
Ps	40: 6	and sin offerings *you did* not r.	8626
Eze	18:16	r **a pledge for a loan.**	2471+2478
	20:40	There *I* will r your offerings	2011

Mic	6: 8	And what *does* the LORD r of you?	2011

REQUIRED (25) [REQUIRE]

Ge	50: 3	for that was the **time** r *for* embalming.	AIT
Ex	5:13	"Complete the **work** r *of* you for each day,	AIT
	5:19	the number of **bricks** r *of* you for each day."	AIT
	22:11	and no **restitution** *is* r.	AIT
	22:13	as evidence and *he* will not *be* r to **pay for**	AIT
Lev	23:37	and drink offerings r *for* each day.	1821
	27:16	to be set according to the amount of **seed** r	AIT
Nu	7: 7	to the Gershonites, as their work r,	7023
	7: 8	to the Merarites, as their work r.	7023
Jos	16:10	of Ephraim but *are* r to do forced labor.	AIT
1Ki	8:31	and *is* r to take an oath	460+928+5957
2Ch	6:22	and *is* r to take an oath	460+928+5957
	24: 6	"Why haven't *you* r the Levites to	2011+6584
	24: 9	that Moses the servant of God had r of	6584
	24:12	to the men who carried out the work r *for*	6275
Ezr	3: 4	the Feast of Tabernacles with the r number	1821
Ne	12:44	to bring into the storerooms the **portions** r	AIT
Jnh	3: 3	very important city—a visit r three days.	NIH
Lk	2:27	for him what the custom of the Law r,	2848
	2:39	and Mary had done everything r **by the Law**	2848
	3:13	"Don't collect any more than you *are* r to,"	1411
Ac	15: 5	"The Gentiles must be circumcised and r	4133
Ro	2:14	do by nature things r **by the law,**	AIT
1Co	4: 2	Now *it is* r that those who have been given	2426
Heb	10: 8	(although the law r them to be made).	2848

REQUIRED (Anglicized) See also OBLIGATED

REQUIREMENT (5) [REQUIRE]

Nu	19: 2	"This is a r *of* the law that	2978
	27:11	This is to be a legal r for the Israelites,	2978
	31:21	"This is the r *of* the law that	2978
2Ch	8:13	to the daily r for offerings commanded	1821
	8:14	the priests according to each day's r.	1821

REQUIREMENTS (19) [REQUIRE]

Ge	26: 5	Abraham obeyed me and kept my r,	5466
Lev	18:30	Keep my r and do not follow any of	5466
	22: 9	"The priests are to keep my r so	5466
Nu	35:29	"'These are to be legal r for you	2978
Dt	11: 1	Love the LORD your God and keep his r,	5466
1Ki	2: 3	and commands, his laws and r,	6343
2Ki	23:24	the r of the law written in the book	1821
1Ch	16:37	according to each day's r.	1821
	29:19	r and decrees and to do everything to build	6343
2Ch	13:11	observing the r *of* the LORD our God.	5466
Jer	5: 4	the way of the LORD, the r *of* their God.	5477
	5: 5	the way of the LORD, the r *of* their God."	5477
	8: 7	But my people do not know the r of	5477
Zec	3: 7	you will walk in my ways and keep my r,	5466
Mal	3:14	What did we gain by carrying out his r	5466
Ac	15:28	with anything beyond the following r:	2055
Ro	2:15	the r of the law are written on their hearts,	2240
	2:26	not circumcised keep the law's r,	1468
	8: 4	that the **righteous** r of the law might	1468

REQUIRES (9) [REQUIRE]

Lev	8:35	for seven days and do what the LORD r,"	5466
Nu	7: 5	to the Levites as each man's work r."	7023
1Ki	2: 3	what the LORD your God r:	5466
2Ki	17:26	what the god of that country r.	5477
	17:26	because the people do not know what he r."	5477
	17:27	what the god of the land r."	5477
Jn	6:28	"What must we do to do the works God r?"	AIT
Heb	7: 5	Now the law r the descendants	1953
	9:22	the law r that nearly everything be cleansed	2848

REQUIRING (1) [REQUIRE]

Lev	22:16	and so bring upon them guilt r **payment.**	873

REQUITE, REQUITED, REQUITING
(KJV) See PAID BACK, PAY, PAYS BACK, REPAY, REPAYING, SHOW THE SAME FAVOR

REREWARD (KJV) See REAR, REAR GUARD

RESCUE (84) [RESCUED, RESCUES, RESCUING]

Ge	37:21	he tried to r him from their hands.	5911
	37:22	to r him from them and take him back	5911
Ex	2:17	and **came to** their r and watered their flock.	3828
	3: 8	to r them from the hand of the Egyptians	5911
Dt	22:27	there was no *one* to r her.	4635
	25:11	of one of them comes to r her husband	5911
	28:29	with no *one* to r you.	4635
	28:31	and no *one* will r them.	3828
Jdg	9:17	risked his life *to* r you from the hand	5911
	10:15	but please r us now."	5911
	18:28	*to* r them because they lived a long way	5911
1Sa	7: 8	that *he may* r us from the hand of	3828
	11: 3	if no *one* comes *to* r us,	4635
	12:21	nor *can they* r you, because they are useless.	5911
	30: 8	overtake them and **succeed in the r."**	5911+5911

2Sa	3:18	'By my servant David I *will* **r** my people Israel	3828
	10:11	then you are to come to my **r**;	3802
	10:11	then I will come to **r** you.	3828
	21:17	Abishai son of Zeruiah **came to** David's **r**;	6468
1Ch	19:12	then you are to **r** me;	9591
	19:12	then *I will* **r** you.	3828
2Ch	32:17	of the other lands *did* not **r** their people	5911
	32:17	the god of Hezekiah *will* not **r** his people	5911
Job	5:19	From six calamities he *will* **r** you;	5911
	10: 7	and that no *one* can **r** me from your hand?	5911
Ps	7: 2	and rip me to pieces with no *one to* **r** me.	5911
	17:13	**r** me from the wicked by your sword.	7117
	22: 8	*let* the LORD **r** him.	7117
	22:21	**R** me from the mouth of the lions;	3828
	25:20	Guard my life and **r** me;	5911
	31: 2	**come** quickly to my **r**;	5911
	35:10	You **r** the poor from those too strong	5911
	35:17	**R** my life from their ravages,	8740
	43: 1	**r** me from deceitful and wicked men.	7117
	50:22	or I will tear you to pieces, with none *to* **r**:	5911
	69:14	**R** me from the mire, do not let me sink;	5911
	69:18	Come near and **r** me;	1457
	71: 2	**R** me and deliver me in your righteousness;	5911
	71:11	for no *one will* **r** him."	5911
	72:14	*He will* **r** them from oppression	1457
	82: 4	**R** the weak and needy;	7117
	91:14	says the LORD, "I *will* **r** him;	7117
	140: 1	**R** me, O LORD, from evil men;	2740
	142: 6	**r** me from those who pursue me,	5911
	143: 9	**R** me from my enemies, O LORD,	7117
	144: 7	and **r** me from the mighty waters,	5911
	144:11	Deliver me and **r** me from the hands	5911
Pr	19:19	if *you* **r** him, you will have to do it again.	5911
	24:11	**R** those being led away to death;	5911
Isa	5:29	and carry it off with no *one to* **r**.	5911
	19:20	and *he will* **r** them.	5911
	31: 5	he will 'pass over' it and *will* **r** it.	4880
	42:22	with no *one to* **r** them;	5911
	46: 2	unable *to* **r** the burden,	4880
	46: 4	I will sustain you and *I will* **r** you.	4880
	50: 2	Do I lack the strength to **r** you?	5911
Jer	1: 8	for I am with you and *will* **r** you,"	5911
	1:19	for I am with you and *will* **r** you,"	5911
	15:20	for I am with you to **r** and save you,"	3828
	21:12	**r** from the hand of his oppressor	5911
	22: 3	**R** from the hand of his oppressor	5911
	39:17	But *I will* **r** you on that day,	5911
Eze	34:10	*I will* **r** my flock from their mouths,	5911
	34:12	*I will* **r** them from all the places	5911
	34:27	of their yoke and **r** them from the hands	5911
Da	3:15	Then what god *will be able to* **r** you	10706
	3:17	and *he will* **r** us from your hand, O king.	10706
	6:14	to **r** Daniel and made every effort	10706
	6:16	whom you serve continually, **r** you!"	10706
	6:20	been able to **r** you from the lions?"	10706
	8: 4	and none *could* **r** from his power.	5911
	8: 7	and none *could* **r** the ram from his power.	5911
Hos	5:14	with no *one to* **r** them.	5911
Mic	5: 8	and no *one* can **r**.	5911
Zep	3:19	*I will* **r** the lame	3828
Zec	11: 6	and *I will* not **r** them from their hands."	5911
Mt	27:43	*Let* God **r** him now if he wants him,	4861
Lk	1:74	*to* **r** us from the hand of our enemies,	4861
Ac	7:25	that God was using him to **r** them,	1443+5401
	26:17	*I will* **r** you from your own people and	1975
Ro	7:24	Who *will* **r** me from this body of death?	4861
Gal	1: 4	who gave himself for our sins to **r** us from	1975
2Ti	4:18	The Lord *will* **r** me from every evil attack	4861
2Pe	2: 9	how *to* **r** godly men from trials and to hold	4861

RESCUED (36) [RESCUE]

Ex	2:19	"An Egyptian **r** us from the shepherds.	5911
	5:23	*you have* not **r** your people **at all.**"	5911+5911
	18:10	who **r** you from the hand of the Egyptians	5911
	18:10	and who **r** the people from the hand of	5911
Nu	10: 9	LORD your God and **r** from your enemies.	3828
Jos	22:31	Now *you have* **r** the Israelites from	5911
Jdg	8:34	who *had* **r** them from the hands	5911
1Sa	11:13	for this day the LORD *has* **r** Israel."	6913+9591
	14:23	So the LORD **r** Israel that day,	3828
	14:45	So the men **r** Jonathan,	7009
	17:35	struck it and **r** the sheep from its mouth.	5911
2Sa	19: 9	he *is* the *one* who **r** us from the hand of	4880
	22:18	*He* **r** me from my powerful enemy,	5911
	22:20	*he* **r** me because he delighted in me.	2740
	22:49	from violent men *you* **r** me.	5911
2Ki	18:34	*have they* **r** Samaria from my hand?	5911
Ne	9:27	*who* **r** them from the hand of their enemies.	3828
Job	29:12	because I **r** the poor who cried for help,	4880
Ps	18:17	*He* **r** me from my powerful enemy,	5911
	18:19	*he* **r** me because he delighted in me.	2740
	18:48	from violent men *you* **r** me,	5911
	81: 7	In your distress you called and *I* **r** you,	2740
	107:20	*he* **r** them from the grave.	4880
Pr	11: 8	The righteous man *is* **r** from trouble,	2740
Isa	36:19	*Have they* **r** Samaria from my hand?	5911
	49:24	or captives **r** *from* the fierce?	4880
Da	3:28	who has sent his angel and **r** his servants!	10706
	6:27	*He has* **r** Daniel from the power of	10706
Mic	4:10	there *you will* be **r**.	5911
Ac	7:10	and **r** him from all his troubles.	1975
	12:11	that the Lord sent his angel and **r** me	1975
	23:27	but *I* came with my troops and **r** him,	1975
Ro	15:31	Pray that *I may be* **r** from the unbelievers	4861
Col	1:13	For he *has* **r** us from the dominion	4861

2Ti	3:11	Yet the Lord **r** me from all of them.	4861
2Pe	2: 7	and if *he* **r** Lot, a righteous man,	4861

RESCUES (5) [RESCUE]

1Sa	14:39	As surely as the LORD who **r** Israel lives,	4635
Pr	12: 6	but the speech of the upright **r** them.	5911
Jer	20:13	*He* **r** the life of the needy from the hands of	5911
Da	6:27	*He* **r** and he saves; he performs signs	10706
1Th	1:10	Jesus, who **r** us from the coming wrath.	4861

RESCUING (1) [RESCUE]

Ex	18: 9	in **r** them from the hand of the Egyptians.	5911

RESEMBLED (3) [RESEMBLING]

Rev	9: 7	and their faces **r** human faces.	6055
	9:17	The heads of the horses **r** the heads	6055
	13: 2	The beast I saw **r** a leopard,	1639+3927

RESEMBLING (1) [RESEMBLED]

Rev	4: 3	A rainbow, **r** an emerald,	3927+3970

RESEN (1)

Ge	10:12	**R**, which is between Nineveh and Calah;	8271

RESENT (1) [RESENTFUL, RESENTMENT, RESENTS]

Pr	3:11	and *do* not **r** his rebuke,	7762

RESENTFUL (1) [RESENT]

2Ti	2:24	kind to everyone, able to teach, **not r**.	452

RESENTMENT (3) [RESENT]

Jdg	8: 3	At this, their **r** against him subsided.	8120
Job	5: 2	**R** kills a fool, and envy slays the simple.	4089
	36:13	"The godless in heart harbor **r**;	678

RESENTS (1) [RESENT]

Pr	15:12	A mocker **r** correction;	170+4202

RESERVE (4) [RESERVED]

Ge	41:36	This food should be **held in r** for	7214
Dt	32:34	not **kept** this **in r** and sealed it in my vaults?	4022
1Ki	19:18	Yet *I* **r** seven thousand in Israel—	8636
Job	38:23	which *I* **r** for times of trouble,	3104

RESERVED (6) [RESERVE]

Ge	27:36	"Haven't *you* **r** any blessing for me?"	724
Isa	26:11	the **fire r** *for* your enemies consume them.	AIT
Ro	11: 4	*have* **r** for myself seven thousand who have not bowed the knee to Baal."	2901
2Pe	2:17	Blackest darkness *is* **r** for them.	5498
	3: 7	the present heavens and earth are **r** for fire,	2564
Jude	1:13	whom blackest darkness *has been* **r** forever.	5498

RESERVOIR (1) [RESERVOIRS]

Isa	22:11	a **r** between the two walls for the water of	5225

RESERVOIRS (2) [RESERVOIR]

Ex	7:19	over the ponds and all the **r'**—	4784+5224
Ecc	2: 6	I made **r** to water groves of	1391+4784

RESETTLE (2) [SETTLE]

1Ch	9: 2	Now the first *to* **r** on their own property	3782
Eze	36:33	*I will* **r** your towns,	3782

RESETTLED (2) [SETTLE]

2Ki	17:26	"The people you deported and **r** in	3782
Eze	38:12	against the **r** ruins and the people gathered	3782

RESHEPH (1)

1Ch	7:25	Rephah was his son, **R** his son,	8405

RESIDE (1) [RESIDENCE, RESIDENT, RESIDENTS, RESIDES]

Job	38:19	And where does darkness **r**?	5226

RESIDENCE (5) [RESIDE]

2Sa	5: 9	then **took up r** in the fortress and called it	3782
1Ch	11: 7	David then **took up r** in the fortress,	3782
Ne	2: 8	the city wall and for the **r** I will occupy?"	1074
Est	2:16	She was taken to King Xerxes in the royal **r**	1074
Da	4:30	Babylon I have built as the royal **r**,	10103

RESIDENT (5) [RESIDE]

Ex	12:45	but a **temporary r** and a hired worker may	9369
Lev	25: 6	the hired worker and **temporary r** who live	9369
	25:35	as you would an alien or a **temporary r**,	9369
	25:40	as a hired worker or a **temporary r**.	9369
	25:47	or a **temporary r** among you becomes rich	9369

RESIDENTS (4) [RESIDE]

Lev	25:45	also buy some of the **temporary r** living	9369
Ne	3:13	by Hanun and the **r** *of* Zanoah.	3782
	7: 3	Also appoint **r** *of* Jerusalem as guards,	3782

Ac	2: 9	**r** of Mesopotamia, Judea and Cappadocia,	2997

RESIDES (3) [RESIDE]

Job	18:15	Fire **r** in his tent;	8905
	41:22	Strength **r** in his neck;	4328
Ecc	7: 9	for anger **r** in the lap of fools.	5663

RESIDUE (KJV) See LEFT, OTHER, REMAINS, REMNANT, REST, SURVIVORS

RESIN (3)

Ge	2:12	**aromatic r** and onyx are also there.)	978
Ex	30:34	**gum r**, onycha and galbanum—	5753
Nu	11: 7	like coriander seed and looked like **r**.	978

RESIST (13) [RESISTED, RESISTS]

Jdg	2:14	they were no longer able to **r**.	4200+6641+7156
2Ki	10: 4	"If two kings *could* not **r** him,	4200+6641+7156
2Ch	13: 7	and not strong enough to **r** them.	7156
	13: 8	you plan to **r** the kingdom of the LORD.	2616
Pr	28: 4	but those who keep the law **r** them.	1741
Isa	1:20	but if *you* **r** and rebel,	4784
Da	11:15	forces of the South will be powerless *to* **r**;	6641
	11:32	the people who know their God *will* firmly **r** him.	6913
Mt	5:39	But I tell you, *Do* not **r** an evil person.	468
Lk	21:15	none of your adversaries will be able to **r**	468
Ac	7:51	You always **r** the Holy Spirit!	528
Jas	4: 7	**R** the devil, and he will flee from you.	468
1Pe	5: 9	**R** him, standing firm in the faith,	468

RESISTED (3) [RESIST]

Job	9: 4	Who *has* **r** him and come out unscathed?	7996
Da	10:13	the prince of the Persian kingdom **r** me	4200+5584+6641
Heb	12: 4	yet **r** to the point of shedding your blood.	510

RESISTS (1) [RESIST]

Ro	9:19	For who **r** his will?"	468

RESOLUTELY (1)

Lk	9:51	Jesus **r** set out for Jerusalem.	3836+4725+5114

RESOLVED (4)

2Ch	20: 3	Jehoshaphat **r** to inquire of the LORD,	5989+7156
Ps	17: 3	*I have* **r** that my mouth will not sin.	2372
Da	1: 8	Daniel **r** not to defile himself	4213+6584+8492
1Co	2: 2	For *I* **r** to know nothing while I was with	3212

RESORT (1) [RESORTED]

Nu	24: 1	he did not **r** to sorcery as at other times,	2143+4200+7925

RESORTED (1) [RESORT]

Jos	9: 4	they **r** to a ruse: They went as a delegation	6913

RESOUND (9) [RESOUNDED, RESOUNDING, RESOUNDS]

1Ch	16:32	*Let* the sea **r**, and all that is in it;	8306
Ps	96:11	*let* the sea **r**, and all that is in it;	8306
	98: 7	*Let* the sea **r**, and everything in it,	8306
	118:15	and victory **r** in the tents of the righteous:	7754
Jer	6: 7	Violence and destruction **r** in her;	9048
	25:31	The tumult *will* **r** to the ends of the earth,	995
	49:21	their cry *will* **r** to the Red Sea.	9048
	50:46	its cry *will* **r** among the nations.	5989
	51:55	the roar of their voices *will* **r**.	5989

RESOUNDED (3) [RESOUND]

2Sa	22:14	the voice of the Most High **r**.	5989
Ps	18:13	the voice of the Most High **r**.	5989
	77:17	the skies **r** *with* thunder;	5989

RESOUNDING (2) [RESOUND]

Ps	150: 5	praise him with **r** cymbals.	9558
1Co	13: 1	I am only a **r** gong or a clanging cymbal.	2490

RESOUNDS (2) [RESOUND]

1Ki	1:45	gone up cheering, and the city **r** with it.	2169
Job	37: 4	When his voice **r**, he holds nothing back.	9048

RESOURCES (1)

1Ch	29: 2	With all my **r** I have provided for	3946

RESPECT (32) [RESPECTABLE, RESPECTED, RESPECTS]

Ge	41:40	Only with **r** to the throne will I be greater	NIH
Lev	19: 3	of *you* must **r** his mother and father,	3707
	19:32	**show r** for the elderly and revere your God.	2075
	22: 2	"Tell Aaron and his sons to **treat with r**	5692
Dt	28:50	a fierce-looking nation without **r** for the old	5951+7156
2Ki	1:13	"please **have r** for my life and	928+3700+6524
	1:14	But now **have r** for my life!"	928+3700+6524
	3:14	if I *did* not **have r** for the presence of	5951
Est	1:20	all the women *will* **r** their husbands,	3702+5989

Pr	11:16	A kindhearted woman gains **r**,	3883
Isa	5:12	no **r** for the work of his hands.	8011
La	5:12	elders **are shown** no **r**.	2075+7156
Mal	1: 6	If I am a master, where is the **r** *due* me?"	4616
Mt	21:37	'*They will* **r** my son,' he said.	1956
Mk	12: 6	saying, '*They will* **r** my son.'	1956
Lk	20:13	perhaps *they will* **r** him.'	1956
Ro	13: 7	if **r**, then respect; if honor, then honor.	5832
	13: 7	if respect, then **r**; if honor, then honor.	5832
Eph	5:33	and the wife *must* **r** her husband.	5828
	6: 5	obey your earthly masters with **r** and fear,	5832
1Th	4:12	so that your daily life may **win the r**	2361
	5:12	*to* **r** those who work hard among you,	3857
1Ti	3: 4	that his children obey him with proper **r**.	4949
	3: 8	likewise, are to be men **worthy of r**,	4948
	3:11	their wives are to be women **worthy of r**,	4948
	6: 1	consider their masters worthy *of* full **r**,	5507
	6: 2	not *to* **show less r** for them	2969
Tit	2: 2	**worthy of r**, self-controlled,	4948
1Pe	2:17	**Show proper r** to everyone:	5506
	2:18	submit yourselves to your masters with all **r**	5832
	3: 7	and treat them with **r** as the weaker partner	5507
	3:15	But do this with gentleness and **r**,	5832

RESPECTABLE (1) [RESPECT]

1Ti	3: 2	self-controlled, **r**, hospitable, able to teach,	3177

RESPECTED (10) [RESPECT]

Dt	1:13	wise, understanding and **r** men from each	3359
	1:15	wise and **r** men, and appointed them	3359
1Sa	9: 6	a man of God; he *is* **highly r**,	3877
	22:14	captain of your bodyguard and **highly r**	3877
Pr	31:23	Her husband **is r** at the city gate,	3359
Isa	32: 5	nor the scoundrel be **highly r**.	8777
	33: 8	its witnesses are despised, no one is **r**.	3108
Ac	10:22	who is **r** by all the Jewish people.	3455
	22:12	a devout observer of the law and highly **r**	3455
Heb	12: 9	and *we* **r** them for it.	1956

RESPECTER (KJV) See FAVORITISM

RESPECTS (2) [RESPECT]

Pr	13:13	but *he who* **r** a command is rewarded.	3707
Ac	25:13	at Caesarea *to* **pay** *their* **r** to Festus.	832

RESPITE (1)

Job	20:20	"Surely he will have no **r** from his craving;	8929

RESPLENDENT (2)

Ps	76: 4	You *are* **r** with light,	239
	132:18	but the crown on his head *will be* **r**."	7437

RESPOND (17) [RESPONDED, RESPONDING, RESPONSE, RESPONSIVE]

1Sa	4:20	But *she did* not **r** or pay any attention.	6699
2Ch	32:25	and he *did* not **r** to the kindness shown him;	8740
Est	1:18	about the queen's conduct *will* **r** to all	606
Ps	102:17	*He will* **r** to the prayer of the destitute;	7155
Pr	29:19	though he understands, he will not **r**.	5101
Isa	14:10	They *will* all **r**, they will say to you,	6699
	19:22	and *he will* **r** to their **pleas** and heal them.	6983
Jer	2:30	*they did* not **r** to correction.	4374
	17:23	and would not listen or **r** to discipline.	4374
	32:33	they would not listen or **r** to discipline.	4374
Hos	2:21	"In that day *I will* **r**,"	6699
	2:21	"*I will* **r** to the skies,	6699
	2:21	and they *will* **r** to the earth;	6699
	2:22	and the earth *will* **r** to the grain,	6699
	2:22	and they *will* **r** to Jezreel.	6699
Ac	16:14	The Lord opened her heart *to* **r** to	4668
Rev	16: 7	And I heard the altar **r**:	3306

RESPONDED (12) [RESPOND]

Ex	19: 8	The people all **r** together,	6699
	24: 3	they **r** *with* one voice,	6699
	24: 7	*They* **r**, "We will do everything	606
Jdg	7:14	His friend **r**, "This can be nothing other	6699
	20:28	The Lord **r**, "Go, for tomorrow I will	606
2Sa	19:43	of Judah **r** even more harshly than the men	1821
Ezr	10:12	The whole assembly **r** with a loud voice:	6699
Ne	8: 6	and all the people lifted their hands and **r**,	6699
Job	9:16	Even if I summoned him and he **r**,	6699
Pr	1:23	If *you had* **r** to my rebuke,	8740
Jer	7:28	not obeyed the Lord its God or **r** to	4374
Lk	20:39	Some of the teachers of the law **r**,	646

RESPONDING (1) [RESPOND]

Ne	12:24	one section **r** to the other,	4200+6645

RESPONSE (8) [RESPOND]

1Ki	18:26	But there was no **r**; no one answered.	7754
	18:29	But there was no **r**, no one answered.	7754
2Ki	4:31	but there was no sound or **r**.	7993
1Ch	29: 9	The people rejoiced at the **willing r**	5605
Job	19: 7	*I* **get** no **r**; though I call for help,	6699
Da	10:12	and I have come in **r** to them.	928
Ro	8:31	What, then, shall we say in **r** to this?	NIG
Gal	2: 2	I went in **r** to a revelation and set before	2848

RESPONSIBILITIES (4) [RESPONSIBLE]

Nu	8:26	how you are to assign the **r** of the Levites."	5466
1Ch	23:32	the Levites carried out their **r** for the Tent	5466
2Ch	31:16	according to their **r** and their divisions.	5466
	31:17	according to their **r** and their divisions.	5466

RESPONSIBILITY (13) [RESPONSIBLE]

Nu	4:27	to them as their **r** all they are to carry.	5466
	18: 1	the **r for offenses** *against* the sanctuary,	6411
	18: 1	the **r for offenses** *against* the priesthood.	6411
	18:23	and bear the **r for offenses** *against* it.	6411
1Ch	9:26	with the **r** for the rooms and treasuries in	6584
	9:31	with the **r** for baking the offering bread.	6584
	15:22	that was his **r** because he was skillful at it.	NIH
Ne	10:32	**assume the r** for carrying out	6584+6641
	10:35	also assume **r** for bringing to the house of	NIH
Mt	27: 4	"That's your **r**."	3972+5148
	27:24	"It is **your r**!"	3972+5148
Ac	6: 3	We will turn this **r** over to them	5970
	18: 6	I am clear of my **r**.	NIG

RESPONSIBLE (45) [RESPONSIBILITIES, RESPONSIBILITY]

Ge	16: 5	"You are **r** for the wrong I am suffering.	6584
	39:22	and he was *made* **r** *for* all	6913
	43: 9	*you can* **hold** me personally **r** *for* him.	1335+3338+4946
Ex	21:19	who struck the blow *will* **not be held r** if	5927
	21:28	the owner of the bull will **not be held r**.	5929
Lev	5: 1	he *will be* **held r**.	5951+6411
	5:17	he is guilty and *will be* **held r**.	5951+6411
	7:18	of it *will be* **held r**.	5951+6411
	17:16	he *will be* **held r**.' "	5951+6411
	19: 8	Whoever eats it *will be* **held r**	5951+6411
	20:17	and *will be* **held r**.	5951+6411
	20:19	both of *you would be* **held r**.	5951+6411
	20:20	They *will be* **held r**;	2628+5951
	24:15	he *will be* **held r**;	2628+5951
Nu	1:53	*to be* **r** for the care of the tabernacle of	9068
	3:25	the Gershonites were **r** for **the care** *of*	5466
	3:28	The Kohathites were **r** for the care of	5466
	3:31	They were **r** for the care of the ark,	5466
	3:32	He was appointed over those who were **r**	5466
	3:38	They were **r** *for* the care of the sanctuary	5466
	7: 9	the holy things, *for* which they were **r**.	6275
	14:37	these men **r** for **spreading** the bad report	AIT
	18: 3	*to be* **r** to you and are to perform all	5466+9068
	18: 4	to join you and *be* **r** for the care of the Tent	9068
	18: 5	*to be* **r** for the care of the sanctuary and	9068
	30:15	then *he is* **r** for her guilt."	5951
	31:30	who *are* **r** *for* the care of the Lord's	9068
	31:47	who *were* **r** *for* the care of the Lord's	9068
Jos	2:19	we will **not be r**.	5929
1Sa	22:22	*I am* **r** for the death of your father's	928+6015
	23:20	and we will be **r** for handing him over to	4200
1Ch	9:13	**r** *for* ministering in the house of God.	4856
	9:19	from his family (the Korahites) were **r**	4856+6275
	9:19	the Tent just as their fathers had been **r** for	6584
	9:33	from other duties because they were **r** for	6584
	16:42	and Jeduthun were **r** for the sounding of	NIH
	26:30	were **r** in Israel west of the Jordan for all	7213
Ne	11:22	who were the singers **r for the service**	4200+5584
	13:10	and singers **r** *for* the service had gone back	6913
	13:13	They were made **r** for distributing	6584
Jnh	1: 7	to find out who is **r** for this calamity."	928+4200+8611
	1: 8	who is **r** for making all this trouble for us?	889+928+4200
Lk	11:50	*be* **held r** for the blood of all the prophets	1699
	11:51	this generation *will be* **held r** for it all.	1699
1Co	7:24	Brothers, each man, as **r** to God,	NIG

RESPONSIVE (2) [RESPOND]

2Ki	22:19	Because your heart was **r** and you humbled	8205
2Ch	34:27	Because your heart was **r** and you humbled	8205

REST (269) [RESTED, RESTING, RESTLESS, RESTS, SABBATH-REST]

Ge	8: 4	of the seventh month the ark **came to r** on	5663
	14:10	men fell into them and the **r** fled to the hills.	8636
	18: 4	and then you may all wash your feet and **r**	9128
	30:36	while Jacob continued to tend the **r**	3855
	30:40	but made the **r** face the streaked	7366S
	42:16	*the* **r** *of* **you** will be kept in prison,	AIT
	42:19	while *the* **r** *of* **you** go and take grain back	AIT
	44: 4	*the* **r** *of* **us** will become my lord's slaves."	AIT
	44:10	*the* **r** *of* **you** will be free from blame."	AIT
	44:17	*The* **r** *of* **you**, go back to your father	AIT
	47:30	but when *I* **r** with my fathers,	8886
	49:26	*Let all these* **r** on the head of Joseph,	2118
Ex	4: 7	it was restored, like the **r** of his flesh.	NIH
	16:23	'Tomorrow is a **day of r**,	8702
	23:12	so that your ox and your donkey *may* **r** and	5663
	29:12	pour out the **r** *of* it at the base of the altar.	3972
	31:15	but the seventh day is a Sabbath of **r**,	8702
	33:14	and *I will* **give** you **r**."	5663
	34:21	but on the seventh day *you shall* **r**;	8697
	34:21	and harvest *you must* **r**.	8697
	35: 2	a Sabbath of **r** to the Lord.	8702
Lev	2: 3	*The* **r** of the grain offering belongs	3855
	2:10	*The* **r** of the grain offering belongs	3855
	4: 7	*The* **r** *of* the bull's blood he shall pour out	3972
	4:12	that is, **all** *the* **r** of the bull—	AIT
Lev	4:18	The **r** of the blood he shall pour out at	3972
	4:25	and pour out the **r** of the blood at the base	NIH
	4:30	and pour out the **r** of the blood at the base	3972
	4:34	and pour out the **r** of the blood at the base	NIH
	5: 9	the **r** of the blood must be drained out at	8636
	5:13	The **r** of the offering will belong to	NIH
	6:16	Aaron and his sons shall eat the **r** of it,	3855
	8:15	He poured out the **r** of the blood at the base	NIH
	8:32	burn up the **r** of the meat and the bread.	3855
	9: 9	of the blood he poured out at the base	NIH
	14: 9	his eyebrows and the **r** of his hair.	3972
	14:18	The **r** of the oil in his palm	3855
	14:29	The **r** of the oil in his palm	3855
	16:31	It is a sabbath of **r**,	8702
	23: 3	but the seventh day is a Sabbath of **r**,	8702
	23:24	to have a **day of r**,	8702
	23:32	It is a sabbath of **r** for you,	8702
	23:39	the first day is a **day of r**,	8702
	23:39	and the eighth day also is a **day of r**.	8702
	25: 4	the land is to have a sabbath of **r**,	8702
	25: 5	The land is to have a year of **r**.	8702
	26:34	then the land *will* **r** and enjoy its sabbaths.	8697
	26:35	the land *will* **have** *the* **r** it did not have	8697
Nu	10:12	the cloud **came to r** in the Desert of Paran.	8905
	10:33	to find them a **place to r**.	4957
	10:36	Whenever it **came to r**, he said, "Return,	5663
	16: 9	of Israel has separated you from the **r** of	NIH
	18:31	You and your households may eat the **r**	NIH
	23:24	not **r** till he devours his prey and drinks	8886
	31:27	in the battle and the **r** of the community.	3972
Dt	3:13	The **r** of Gilead and also all of Bashan,	3856
	3:20	until the Lord **gives r** to your brothers	5663
	5:14	your manservant and maidservant *may* **r**,	5663
	12:10	and *he will* **give** you **r** from all your enemies	5663
	19:20	The **r** *of the people* will hear of this and	8636
	25:19	the Lord your God **gives** you **r** from all	5663
	31:16	"You *are going to* **r** with your fathers,	8886
	33:12	the beloved of the Lord **r** secure in him,	8905
	33:16	*Let all these* **r** on the head of Joseph,	995
Jos	1:13	'The Lord your God *is giving* you **r**	5663
	1:15	until the Lord **gives** them **r**,	5663
	7:25	and after they had stoned **the r**,	4392S
	11:23	Then the land **had r** from war.	9200
	13:27	with the **r** of the realm of Sihon king	3856
	14: 3	the Levites an inheritance among **the r**,	4392S
	14:15	Th⎯n the land **had r** from war.	9200
	17: 2	for the **r** of the people of Manasseh—	3855
	17: 6	to the **r** of the descendants of Manasseh.	3855
	21: 5	The **r** of Kohath's descendants were allotted	3855
	21:20	The **r** of the Kohathite clans of	3855
	21:26	and their pasturelands were given to the **r**	3855
	21:34	(the **r** of the Levites) were given:	3855
	21:40	who *were the* **r** of the Levites, were twelve.	3855
	21:44	The Lord **gave** them **r** on every side,	5663
	22: 4	Lord your God *has* **given** your brothers **r**	5663
	23: 1	and the Lord *had* **given** Israel **r** from all	5663
Jdg	7: 6	All the **r** got down on their knees to drink.	3856
	7: 8	the **r** of the Israelites to their tents but kept	3972S
Ru	1: 9	that each of you will find **r** in the home	4957
	2: 7	except for a short **r** in the shelter."	3782
	3:18	not **r** until the matter is settled today."	9200
1Sa	13: 2	The **r** of the men he sent back	3856
	15:15	but we totally destroyed the **r**."	3463
	18:29	he remained his enemy the **r** of his days.	3972
	18:30	David met with more success than the **r**	3972
2Sa	4: 5	while he *was* **taking** his noonday **r**.	5435+8886
	7: 1	and the Lord *had* **given** him **r** from all	5663
	7:11	also **give** you **r** from all your enemies.	5663
	7:12	When your days are over and *you* **r**	8886
	10:10	the **r** *of* the men under the command	3856
	12:28	Now muster the **r** *of* the troops and besiege	3856
	13:27	so he sent with him Amnon and the **r** *of*	3972
	14: 9	let the blame **r on** me and	6584
	14:17	the word of my lord the king bring me **r**,	4957
1Ki	1:21	as soon as my lord the king is **laid to r**	8886
	2:33	*May* the guilt of their blood **r** on the head	8740
	5: 4	now the Lord my God *has* **given** me **r**	5663
	8:56	who has given **r** to his people Israel just	4957
	12:23	and to the **r** *of* the people,	3856
	20:15	Then he assembled the **r** of the Israelites,	3972
	20:30	The **r** of them escaped to the city of Aphek	3855
	22:46	He rid the land of the **r** of the male shrine	3856
2Ki	13: 7	for the king of Aram had destroyed **the r**	4392S
	25:11	along with the **r** *of* the populace	3856
	25:11	and *for the* **r** *of* his life ate regularly at	3427+3972
1Ch	6:31	of the Lord after the ark **came to r** there.	4955
	6:61	The **r** of Kohath's descendants were allotted	3855
	6:70	to the **r** of the Kohathite clans.	3855
	6:77	(the **r** of the Levites) received the following:	3855
	11: 8	while Joab restored the **r** of the city.	8637
	12:38	All the **r** of the Israelites were also	8642
	13: 2	let us send word far and wide to the **r**	8636
	16:41	and the **r** *of those* chosen and designated	8637
	19:11	the **r** *of* the men under the command	3856
	22: 9	a son who will be a man of **peace and r**,	4957
	22: 9	and *I will* **give** him **r** from all his enemies	5663
	22:18	*has* he not **granted** you **r** on every side?	5663
	23:25	*has* **granted r** to his people and has come	5663
	24:20	As for the **r** of the descendants of Levi:	3855
	28: 2	to build a house as a **place of r** for the ark	4957
2Ch	14: 6	for the Lord **gave** him **r**.	5663
	14: 7	and he has **given** us **r** on every side."	5663
	15:15	So the Lord **gave** them **r** on every side.	5663
	20:30	for his God *had* **given** him **r** on every side.	5663
	24:14	they brought the **r** *of* the money to the king	8637
Ezr	2:70	the **r** of the Israelites settled in their towns.	3972
	3: 8	and the **r** *of* their brothers (the priests and	8637

Ezr	4:3	and the r of the heads of the families	8637
	4:7	and the r of his associates wrote a letter	8637
	4:9	together with the r of their associates—	10692
	4:17	the r of their associates living in Samaria	10692
	6:16	the Levites and the r of the exiles—	10692
	7:18	then do whatever seems best with the r of	10692
Ne	4:14	the officials and the r of the people,	3856
	4:19	the officials and the r of the people,	3856
	6:1	Geshem the Arab and the r of our enemies	3856
	6:14	the r of the prophets who have been trying	3856
	7:72	by the r of the people was 20,000	8642
	7:73	along with certain of the people and the r	3972
	9:28	"But as soon as they were at r,	5663
	10:28	"The r of the people—	8637
	11:1	and the r of the people cast lots	8637
	11:20	The r of the Israelites.	8637
Est	9:12	in the r of the king's provinces?	8637
Job	3:13	I would be asleep and at r	5663
	3:17	and there the weary are at r.	5663
	3:26	I have no r, but only turmoil."	5663
	11:18	you will look about you and take your r	8886
	16:18	may my cry never be laid to r!	5226
	24:23	He may let them r in a feeling of security,	9128
	30:17	my gnawing pains never r.	8886
	36:11	they will spend the r of their days	NIH
Ps	16:9	my body also will r secure,	8905
	33:22	May your unfailing love r upon us,	2118
	55:6	I would fly away and be at r—	8905
	62:1	My soul finds r in God alone;	1875
	62:5	Find r, O my soul, in God alone;	1957
	80:17	Let your hand r on the man	2118
	90:17	the favor of the Lord our God r upon us;	2118
	91:1	will r in the shadow of the Almighty.	4328
	95:11	"They shall never enter my r."	4957
	116:7	Be at r once more, O my soul,	4955
Pr	6:10	a little folding of the hands to r—	8886
	21:16	of understanding comes to r in the company	5663
	24:33	a little folding of the hands to r—	8886
	26:2	an undeserved curse does not come to r.	995
Ecc	2:23	even at night his mind does not r.	8886
	6:5	it has more r than does that man—	5739
	10:4	calmness can lay great errors to r.	5663
SS	1:7	and where you r your sheep at midday.	8069
Isa	11:2	The Spirit of the LORD will r on him—	5663
	11:10	and his place of r will be glorious.	4957
	13:20	no shepherd will r his flocks there.	8069
	14:7	All the lands are at r and at peace;	5663
	23:12	even there you will find no r."	5663
	25:10	of the LORD will r on this mountain;	5663
	28:12	"This is the resting place, let the weary r";	5663
	30:15	"In repentance and r is your salvation,	5739
	32:18	in undisturbed places of r.	4957
	34:14	and find for themselves places of r.	4955
	38:10	the gates of death and be robbed of the r	3856
	44:17	From the r he makes a god, his idol;	8642
	57:2	they find r as they lie in death.	5663
	57:20	which cannot r, whose waves cast up mire	9200
	62:6	who call on the LORD, give yourselves no r,	1954
	62:7	give him no r till he establishes Jerusalem	1954
	63:14	they were given r by the Spirit of	5663
Jer	6:16	and you will find r for your souls.	5273
	31:2	I will come to give r to Israel."	8089
	33:12	be pastures for shepherds to r their flocks.	8069
	39:9	and the r of the people.	3856
	41:10	the r of the people who were in Mizpah—	8642
	45:3	with groaning and find no r.' "	4957
	47:6	'how long till you r?	9200
	47:7	But how can it r when the LORD has	9200
	48:11	"Moab has been at r from youth,	8631
	50:34	so that he may bring r to their land,	8089
	52:15	along with the r of the craftsmen	3856
	52:16	the r of the poorest people of the land	4946
	52:33	and for the r of his life ate regularly at	3427+3972
La	2:18	give yourself no relief, your eyes no r.	1957
	5:5	we are weary and find no r.	5663
Eze	34:18	the r of your pasture with your feet?	3856
	34:18	Must you also muddy the r with your feet?	3855
	36:3	that you became the possession of the r of	8642
	36:4	by the r of the nations around you—	8642
	36:5	against the r of the nations,	8642
	44:30	so that a blessing may r on your household.	5663
	48:23	"As for the r of the tribes:	3856
Da	2:18	not be executed with the r of the wise men	10692
	12:13	You will r, and then at the end of the days	5663
Mic	5:3	and the r of his brothers return to join	3856
Na	3:18	your nobles lie down to r.	8905
Hab	2:5	he is arrogant and never at r.	5657
Zec	1:11	the earth and found the whole world at r	3782
	6:8	the north country have given my Spirit r in	5663
	7:7	and its surrounding towns were at r	3782
	9:1	of Hadrach and will r upon Damascus—	4957
	12:14	and all the r of the clans and their wives.	8636
	14:2	the r of the people will not be taken from	3856
Mt	10:13	let your peace r on it;	2262
	11:28	weary and burdened, and I will give you r.	399
	11:29	and you will find r for your souls.	398
	12:43	through arid places seeking r and does	398
	22:6	The r seized his servants,	3370
	27:49	The r said, "Now leave him alone."	3370
Mk	6:31	to a quiet place and get some r."	399
	6:13	These returned and reported it to the r;	3370
Lk	10:6	your peace will r on him;	2058
	11:24	through arid places seeking r and does	398
	12:26	why do you worry about the r?	3370
Jn	11:16	to the r of the disciples.	5209
Ac	2:3	tongues of fire that separated and came to r	2767
	5:2	brought the r and put it at the apostles' feet.	NIG
Ac	16:17	This girl followed Paul and the r of us,	NIG
	21:18	The next day Paul and the r of us went	NIG
	27:44	The r were to get there on planks or	3370
	28:9	the r of the sick on the island came	3370
1Co	2:5	your faith might not r on men's wisdom,	1639
	7:12	To the r I say this (I, not the Lord):	3370
2Co	7:5	this body of ours had no r,	457
	12:9	so that Christ's power may r on me.	2172
Eph	4:3	Like the r, we were by nature objects	3370
Php	4:3	and the r of my fellow workers,	3370
1Th	4:13	or to grieve like the r of men,' "	3370
Heb	3:11	'They shall never enter my r.' "	2923
	3:18	that they would never enter his r if not	2923
	4:1	the promise of entering his r still stands,	2923
	4:3	Now we who have believed enter that r,	2923
	4:3	'They shall never enter my r.' "	2923
	4:5	'They shall never enter my r."	2923
	4:6	It still remains that some will enter that r,	899S
	4:8	For if Joshua had given them r,	2924
	4:10	for anyone who enters God's r also rests	2923
	4:11	therefore, make every effort to enter that r,	2923
1Pe	4:11	r of his earthly life	2145
1Jn	3:19	set our hearts at r in his presence	4275
Rev	2:24	Now I say to the r of you in Thyatira,	3370
	9:20	The r of mankind that were not killed	3370
	12:17	and went off to make war against the r	3370
	14:11	There is no r day or night	398
	14:13	"they will r from their labor,	399
	19:21	The r of them were killed with the sword	3370
	20:5	(The r of the dead did not come to life until	3370

RESTED (54) [REST]

Ge	2:2	on the seventh day he r from all his work.	8697
	2:3	on it he r from all the work of creating	8697
Ex	16:30	So the people r on the seventh day.	8697
	20:11	but he r on the seventh day.	5663
	31:17	seventh day he abstained from work and r.'	5882
Nu	11:25	When the Spirit r on them,	5663
	11:26	Yet the Spirit r on them,	5663
1Ki	2:10	Then David r with his fathers	8886
	7:3	above the beams that r on the columns—	6584
	7:25	The Sea r on top of them,	6584
	11:21	that David r with his fathers and that Joab	8886
	11:43	Then he r with his fathers and was buried	8886
	14:20	He reigned for twenty-two years and then r	8886
	14:31	And Rehoboam r with his fathers	8886
	15:8	And Abijah r with his fathers	8886
	15:24	Then Asa r with his fathers and was buried	8886
	16:6	Baasha r with his fathers and was buried	8886
	16:28	Omri r with his fathers and was buried	8886
	22:40	Ahab r with his fathers.	8886
	22:50	Then Jehoshaphat r with his fathers	8886
2Ki	8:24	Jehoram r with his fathers and was buried	8886
	10:35	Jehu r with his fathers and was buried	8886
	13:9	Jehoahaz r with his fathers and was buried	8886
	13:13	Jehoash r with his fathers,	8886
	14:16	Jehoash r with his fathers and was buried	8886
	14:22	to Judah after Amaziah r with his fathers.	8886
	14:29	Jeroboam r with his fathers,	8886
	15:7	Azariah r with his fathers,	8886
	15:22	Menahem r with his fathers.	8886
	15:38	Jotham r with his fathers and was buried	8886
	16:20	Ahaz r with his fathers and was buried	8886
	20:21	Hezekiah r with his fathers.	8886
	21:18	Manasseh r with his fathers and was buried	8886
	24:6	Jehoiakim r with his fathers.	8886
2Ch	4:4	The Sea r on top of them,	6584
	9:31	Then he r with his fathers and was buried	8886
	12:16	Rehoboam r with his fathers	8886
	14:1	And Abijah r with his fathers	8886
	16:13	of his reign Asa died and r with his fathers.	8886
	21:1	Then Jehoshaphat r with his fathers	8886
	26:2	to Judah after Amaziah r with his fathers.	8886
	26:23	Uzziah r with his fathers and was buried	8886
	27:9	Jotham r with his fathers and was buried in	8886
	28:27	Ahaz r with his fathers and was buried in	8886
	32:33	Hezekiah r with his fathers and was buried	8886
	33:20	Manasseh r with his fathers and was buried	8886
	36:21	all the time of its desolation it r,	8697
Ezr	8:32	where we r three days.	3782
Est	9:17	on the fourteenth they r and made it a day	5663
	9:18	and then on the fifteenth they r and made it	5663
Eze	32:27	The punishment for their sins r	2118
Am	5:19	though he entered his house and r his hand	6164
Lk	23:56	But they r on the Sabbath in obedience to	2483
Heb	4:4	the seventh day God r from all his work."	2924

RESTING (23) [REST]

Ge	28:12	in which he saw a stairway r on the earth,	5893
	49:15	When he sees how good is his r place and	4957
Dt	12:9	yet reached the r place and the inheritance	4957
	28:65	no r place for the sole of your foot.	4955
1Ki	7:30	each had a basin r on four supports,	4946+9393
2Ki	2:15	said, "The spirit of Elijah is r on Elisha."	5663
	9:16	because Joram was r there	8886
2Ch	6:41	O LORD God, and come to your r place,	5665
Ps	132:8	O LORD, and come to your r place,	4957
	132:14	"This is my r place for ever and ever;	4957
SS	1:13	a sachet of myrrh r between my breasts.	4328
Isa	22:16	on the height and chiseling your r place in	5438
	28:12	"This is the r place, let the weary rest";	4957
	66:1	Where will my r place be?	4957
Jer	50:6	and hill and forgot their own r place.	8070
La	1:3	she finds no r place.	4955
Eze	25:5	for camels and Ammon into a r place	5271
Mic	2:10	For this is not your r place,	4957
Mt	26:45	"Are you still sleeping and r?	399
Mk	14:41	"Are you still sleeping and r?	399
Ac	7:49	Or where will my r place be?	2923
Tit	1:2	and knowledge r on the hope of eternal life,	2093

RESTITUTION (14)

Ex	22:3	"A thief must certainly make r,	8966+8966
	22:5	he must make r from the best of his own	8966
	22:6	one who started the fire must make r.	8966+8966
	22:11	owner is to accept this, and no r is required.	8966
	22:12	he must make r to the owner.	8966
	22:14	he must make r.	8966+8966
Lev	5:16	He must make r for what he has failed to do	8966
	6:5	He must make r in full,	8966
	22:14	he must make r to the priest for the offering	5989
	24:18	the life of someone's animal must make r—	8966
	24:21	Whoever kills an animal must make r,	8966
Nu	5:7	He must make full r for his wrong,	928+8031+8740
	5:8	to whom r can be made for the wrong,	8740
	5:8	the r belongs to the LORD and must	871+8740

RESTLESS (5) [REST]

Ge	4:12	You will be a r wanderer on the earth."	5675
	4:14	I will be a r wanderer on the earth,	5675
	27:40	But when you grow r,	8113
Jer	49:23	troubled like the r sea.	1796
Jas	3:8	It is a r evil, full of deadly poison.	190

RESTORATION (1) [RESTORE]

2Ch	24:27	and the record of the r of the temple of God	3572

RESTORE (61) [RESTORATION, RESTORED, RESTORER, RESTORES, RESTORING]

Ge	40:13	up your head and r you to your position,	8740
Dt	30:3	the LORD your God will r your fortunes	8740
2Sa	8:3	to r his control along the Euphrates River.	8740
	9:7	I will r to you all the land that belonged	8740
2Ch	24:4	Some time later Joash decided to r	2542
	24:12	and carpenters to r the LORD's temple,	2542
Ezr	5:3	to rebuild this temple and r this structure?"	10354
	5:9	to rebuild this temple and r this structure?"	10354
Ne	4:2	Will they r their wall?	6441
Job	8:6	and r you to your rightful place.	8966
Ps	41:3	on his sickbed and r him from his bed	2200
	51:12	R to me the joy of your salvation	8740
	60:1	you have been angry—now r us!	8740
	69:4	I am forced to r what I did not steal.	8740
	71:20	you will r my life again;	2649
	80:3	R us, O God;	8740
	80:7	R us, O God Almighty;	8740
	80:19	R us, O LORD God Almighty;	8740
	85:4	R us again, O God our Savior,	8740
	126:4	R our fortunes, O LORD,	8740
Isa	1:26	I will r your judges as in days of old,	8740
	44:26	and of their ruins, 'I will r them,'	7756
	49:6	to r the tribes of Jacob and bring back those	7756
	49:8	a covenant for the people, to r the land and	7756
	57:18	I will guide him and r comfort to him,	8966
	61:4	They will rebuild the ancient ruins and r	7756
Jer	15:19	I will r you that you may serve me;	8740
	16:15	For I will r them to the land	8740
	27:22	'Then I will bring them back and r them	8740
	30:3	and Judah back from captivity and r them	8740
	30:17	But I will r you to health	6590
	30:18	" 'I will r the fortunes of Jacob's tents	8740
	31:18	R me, and I will return,	8740
	32:44	because I will r their fortunes,	8740
	33:11	For I will r the fortunes of the land	8740
	33:26	For I will r their fortunes	8740
	42:12	on you and r you to your land.'	8740
	48:47	"Yet I will r the fortunes of Moab in days	8740
	49:6	I will r the fortunes of the Ammonites,"	8740
	49:39	"Yet I will r the fortunes of Elam in days	8740
La	1:16	no one to r my spirit.	8740
	5:21	R us to yourself, O LORD,	8740
Eze	16:53	I will r the fortunes of Sodom	8740
Da	9:25	the decree to r and rebuild Jerusalem until	8740
Hos	6:2	on the third day he will r us,	7756
	6:11	"Whenever I would r the fortunes	8740
Joel	3:1	I r the fortunes of Judah and Jerusalem,	8740
Am	9:11	"In that day I will r David's fallen tent.	7756
	9:11	I will repair its broken places, r its ruins,	7756
Na	2:2	The LORD will r the splendor of Jacob	8740
Zep	2:7	he will r their fortunes.	8740
	3:20	of the earth when I r your fortunes	8740
Zec	9:12	even now I announce that I will r twice	8740
	10:6	I will r them because I have compassion	3782
Mt	17:11	Elijah comes and will r all things.	635
Ac	1:6	are you at this time going to r the kingdom	635
	3:21	the time comes for God to r everything,	635
	9:12	and place his hands on him to r his sight."	329
	15:16	Its ruins I will rebuild, and I will r it,	494
Gal	6:1	you who are spiritual should r him gently,	2936
1Pe	5:10	will himself r you and make you strong,	2936

RESTORED (39) [RESTORE]

Ge	40:21	He r the chief cupbearer to his position,	8740
	41:13	I was r to my position,	8740
Ex	4:7	and when he took it out, it was r,	8740

Nu	21:27	let it be rebuilt; *let* Sihon's city **be r.**	3922
1Sa	7:14	from Israel *were* **r** to her,	8740
1Ki	13: 6	and pray for me that my hand *may be* **r.**"	8740
	13: 6	and the king's hand *was* **r** and became	8740
2Ki	5:10	and your flesh *will be* **r** and you will	8740
	5:14	and his flesh *was* **r** and became clean like	8740
	8: 1	to the woman whose son *he had* **r to life,**	2649
	8: 5	**r** the dead to life,	2649
	8: 5	and this is her son whom Elisha **r to life.**"	2649
	14:22	the one who rebuilt Elath and **r** it to Judah	8740
	14:25	the one who **r** the boundaries of Israel	8740
1Ch	11: 8	while Joab **r** the rest of the city.	2649
2Ch	26: 2	the one who rebuilt Elath and **r** it to Judah	8740
	33:16	Then *he* **r** the altar of the LORD	1215
	34:10	the workers who repaired and **r** the temple.	2616
Ezr	4:13	that if this city is built and its walls *are* **r,**	10354
	4:16	that if this city is built and its walls *are* **r,**	10354
Ne	3: 8	*They* **r** Jerusalem as far as the Broad Wall.	6441
Job	22:23	you return to the Almighty, *you will be* **r:**	1215
	33:25	*it is* **r** as in the days of his youth.	8740
	33:26	he *is* **r** by God *to* his righteous state.	8740
Ps	85: 1	*you* **r** the fortunes of Jacob.	8740
Isa	38:16	**You r me to health** and let me live.	2730
Eze	21:27	It *will* not *be* **r** until he comes	2118
Da	4:26	be **r** to you when you acknowledge	10629
	4:34	and my sanity *was* **r.**	10754
	4:36	At the same time that my sanity *was* **r,**	10754
	4:36	and *I* was **r** to my throne and became	10771
Mic	4: 8	the former dominion *will be* **r** to you;	910
Mt	9:30	and their sight *was* **r.**	487
	12:13	he stretched it out and it *was* **completely r,**	635
Mk	3: 5	and his hand *was* **completely r.**	635
	8:25	Then his eyes were opened, his sight *was* **r,**	635
Lk	6:10	He did so, and his hand *was* **completely r.**	635
Phm	1:22	a guest room for me, because I hope to *be* **r**	5919
Heb	13:19	to pray so that *I may be* **r** to you soon.	635

RESTORER (1) [RESTORE]

Isa	58:12	**R** of Streets with Dwellings.	8740

RESTORES (4) [RESTORE]

Ps	14: 7	the LORD **r** the fortunes of his people,	8740
	23: 3	*he* **r** my soul. He guides me in paths of	8740
	53: 6	When God **r** the fortunes of his people,	8740
Mk	9:12	Elijah does come first, and **r** all things.	635

RESTORING (2) [RESTORE]

2Ki	12:12	met all the other expenses of **r** the temple.	2616
Ezr	4:12	*They are* **r** the walls and repairing	10354

RESTRAIN (5) [RESTRAINED, RESTRAINING, RESTRAINT]

1Sa	3:13	and *he* failed *to* **r** them.	3909
Job	9:13	God *does* not **r** his anger;	8740
Jer	2:24	in her heat who *can* **r** her?	8740
	14:10	*they* do not **r** their feet.	3104
	31:16	"**R** your voice from weeping and your eyes	4979

RESTRAINED (6) [RESTRAIN]

Ex	36: 6	so the people **were r** from bringing more,	3973
Est	5:10	Haman **r** himself and went home.	706
Ps	76:10	and the survivors of your wrath *are* **r.**	2520
	78:38	Time after time he **r** his anger and did not	8740
Eze	31:15	and its abundant waters **were r.**	3973
2Pe	2:16	a man's voice and **r** the prophet's madness.	3266

RESTRAINING (3) [RESTRAIN]

Pr	27:16	**r** her is like restraining the wind	7621
	27:16	like **r** the wind or grasping oil with	7621
Col	2:23	they lack any value **in r** sensual indulgence.	4639

RESTRAINT (6) [RESTRAIN]

Job	30:11	they throw off **r** in my presence.	8270
Ps	119:51	The arrogant mock me **without r,**	4394+6330
Pr	17:27	A man of knowledge **uses** words with **r,**	3104
	23: 4	have the wisdom *to* **show r.**	2532
	29:18	the people **cast off r;**	7277
Eze	35:13	against me and spoke against me **without r,**	6984

RESTRICT (1) [RESTRICTED, RESTRICTION]

1Co	7:35	not to **r** you,	1105+2095

RESTRICTED (1) [RESTRICT]

Jer	36: 5	Then Jeremiah told Baruch, "I *am* **r;**	6806

RESTRICTION (1) [RESTRICT]

Job	36:16	of distress to a spacious place free from **r,**	4608

RESTS (9) [REST]

Dt	33:12	one the LORD loves **r** between his shoulders.	8905
2Ch	28:11	for the LORD's fierce anger **r on** you."	6584
	28:13	and his fierce anger **r on** Israel."	6584
	36:21	The land enjoyed its **sabbath r;**	8701
Pr	19:23	Then *one* **r** content, untouched by trouble.	4328
	21:31	but victory **r with** the LORD.	4200
Lk	2:14	peace to men **on whom his favor r.**"	2306
Heb	4:10	for anyone who enters God's rest also **r**	2924
1Pe	4:14	for the Spirit of glory and of God **r** on you.	399

RESULT (28)

Ge	38:24	and **as a r** she is now pregnant."	4200
Ex	21:20	a rod and the slave dies **as a direct r,**	3338+9393
Lev	7:16	the **r** of a vow or is a freewill offering.	NIH
Nu	25:18	when the plague came **as a r** of Peor."	1821+6584
Ezr	9:13	a **r** of our evil deeds and our great guilt,	928
Mic	7:13	as the **r** *of* their deeds.	7262
Mk	1:45	**As a r,** Jesus could no longer enter	6063
Lk	21:13	*This will* **r** in your being witnesses	609
Ac	5:15	**As a r,** people brought the sick into	6063
	25:26	so that *as a* **r** of this investigation	1181
Ro	3: 8	"Let us do evil that good *may* **r**"?	2262
	5:16	not like **the r** of the one man's sin:	1328
	5:18	as **the r** of one trespass was condemnation	1328
	5:18	so also **the r** of one act of righteousness	1328
	6:21	Those things **r** in death!	5465
	6:22	and the **r** is eternal life.	5465
	11:30	mercy *as a r of* their **disobedience,**	AIT
	11:31	now receive mercy *as a r of* God's **mercy**	AIT
1Co	9: 1	Are you not the **r** of my work in the Lord?	NIG
	11:34	you meet together it may not **r** in judgment.	1650
2Co	3: 3	a letter from Christ, the **r** of our ministry,	5679
	9:11	and through us your generosity *will* **r** in	2981
Gal	4:23	by the free woman was born **as the r** of	1328
Php	1:13	**As a r,** it has become clear throughout	6063
2Th	1: 5	as *a* **r** you will be counted worthy of	1650+3836
1Ti	6: 4	quarrels about words that **r** in envy,	1181+1666
1Pe	1: 7	*may be* proved genuine and may **r** in praise,	2351
	4: 2	**As a r,** he does not live the rest	1650+3836

RESURRECTION (40)

Mt	22:23	the Sadducees, who say there is no **r,**	414
	22:28	Now then, at the **r,** whose wife will she be	414
	22:30	the **r** people will neither marry nor be given	414
	22:31	But about the **r** of the dead—	414
	27:53	after Jesus' **r** they went into the holy city	1587
Mk	12:18	Then the Sadducees, who say there is no **r,**	414
	12:23	At the **r** whose wife will she be,	414
Lk	14:14	be repaid at the **r** of the righteous."	414
	20:27	the Sadducees, who say there is no **r,**	414
	20:33	Now then, at the **r** whose wife will she be,	414
	20:35	of taking part in that age and *in* the **r** from	414
	20:36	since they are children *of* the **r.**	414
Jn	11:24	"I know he will rise again in the **r** at	414
	11:25	Jesus said to her, "I am the **r** and the life.	414
Ac	1:22	a witness with us *of his* **r.**"	414
	2:31	he spoke of the **r** of the Christ,	414
	4: 2	the people and proclaiming in Jesus the **r** of	414
	4:33	the apostles continued to testify to the **r** of	414
	17:18	the good news about Jesus and the **r.**	414
	17:32	When they heard about the **r** of the dead,	414
	23: 6	I stand on trial because of my hope *in* the **r**	414
	23: 8	(The Sadducees say that there is no **r,**	414
	24:15	be a **r** of both the righteous and the wicked.	414
	24:21	'It is concerning the **r** of the dead that I am	414
Ro	1: 4	be the Son of God by his **r** from the dead:	414
	6: 5	also be united with him *in* his **r.**	414
1Co	15:12	how can some of you say that there is no **r**	414
	15:13	If there is no **r** of the dead,	414
	15:21	the **r** of the dead comes also through a man.	414
	15:29	Now if there is no **r,**	NIG
	15:42	So will it be with the **r** of the dead.	414
Php	3:10	to know Christ and the power *of* his **r** and	414
	3:11	somehow, to attain to the **r** from the dead.	1983
2Ti	2:18	They say that the **r** has already taken place,	414
Heb	6: 2	the laying on of hands, the **r** of the dead,	414
	11:35	so that they might gain a better **r.**	414
1Pe	1: 3	through the **r** of Jesus Christ from the dead,	414
	3:21	It saves you by the **r** of Jesus Christ,	414
Rev	20: 5	This is the first **r.**	414
	20: 6	holy are those who have part in the first **r.**	414

RETAIN (5) [RETAINS]

2Ch	22: 9	the house of Ahaziah powerful enough to **r**	6806
Da	11: 6	but *she will* not **r** her power,	6806
Lk	8:15	**r** it, and by perseverance produce a crop.	2988
Ro	1:28	not think it worthwhile *to* **r** the knowledge	2400
1Co	7:17	**r** the place in life that the Lord assigned	4344

RETAINS (2) [RETAIN]

Lev	25:29	he **r** the right of redemption a full year	2118
	25:48	he **r** the right of redemption	2118+4200

RETAKE (2) [TAKE]

Jdg	11:26	Why didn't *you* **r** them during that time?	5911
1Ki	22: 3	and yet we are doing nothing *to* **r** it from	4374

RETALIATE (1)

1Pe	2:23	they hurled their insults at him, *he* did not **r;**	518

RETINUE (2)

1Ki	10:13	and returned with her **r** to her own country.	6269
2Ch	9:12	and returned with her **r** to her own country.	6269

RETIRE (1)

Nu	8:25	*they must* **r** from their regular service	8740

RETORTED (1)

Jn	7:47	he has deceived you also?" the Pharisees **r.**	646

RETREAT (5) [RETREATED,

RETREATING, RETREATS]

Jdg	20:32	"Let's **r** and draw them away from the city	5674
Job	41:25	*they* **r** before his thrashing.	2627
Ps	44:10	*You* made us **r** before the enemy,	294+8740
	74:21	*Do* not *let* the oppressed **r** in disgrace;	8740
Da	11: 9	of the South but *will* **r** to his own country.	8740

RETREATED (1) [RETREAT]

2Sa	23: 9	Then the men of Israel **r,**	6590

RETREATING (1) [RETREAT]

Jer	46: 5	They are terrified, *they are* **r,**	294+6047

RETREATS (1) [RETREAT]

Pr	30:30	mighty among beasts, *who* **r** before nothing;	8740

RETRIBUTION (6)

Ps	69:22	may it become **r** and a trap.	8936
Isa	34: 8	a year of **r,** to uphold Zion's cause.	8936
	35: 4	with divine **r** he will come to save you."	1691
	59:18	so will he repay wrath to his enemies and **r**	1691
Jer	51:56	LORD is a God of **r;** he will repay in full.	1692
Ro	11: 9	a stumbling block and a **r** for them.	501

RETRIEVED (1)

Isa	49:25	and plunder **r** *from* the fierce;	4880

RETURN (216) [RETURNED, RETURNING, RETURNS]

Ge	3:19	until you **r** to the ground, since from it you	8740
	3:19	for dust you are and to dust *you will* **r.**"	8740
	8:12	but this time *it* did not **r** to him.	8740
	18:10	"I will surely **r** to you about this time	8740+8740
	18:14	*I will* **r** to you at the appointed time	8740
	20: 7	Now **r** the man's wife, for he is a prophet,	8740
	20: 7	But if you *do* not **r** her,	8740
	28:21	so that *I* **r** safely to my father's house,	8740
	29: 3	Then *they would* **r** the stone to its place	8740
	29:18	"I'll work for you seven years in **r for**	928
	29:27	in **r for** another seven years of work."	928
	30:15	"he can sleep with you tonight in **r for**	9393
	31:30	because *you* longed *to* **r** to your father's	AIT
	43:12	for *you* must **r** the silver that was put back	8740
	44:33	and *let* the boy **r** with his brothers.	6590
	45:17	Load your animals and **r** to the land	995+2143
	49: 9	*you* **r** from the prey, my son.	6590
	50: 5	and bury my father; then *I will* **r.'** "	8740
Ex	4:21	"When you **r** to Egypt,	2143+8740
	13:17	they might change their minds and **r**	8740
	22:26	**r** it to him by sunset,	8740
	33:11	Then Moses *would* **r** to the camp,	8740
Lev	14: 2	*he must* **r** what he has stolen or taken	8740
	14:39	the seventh day the priest *shall* **r** to inspect	8740
	25:10	of *you is to* **r** to his family property	8740
	25:13	" 'In this Year of Jubilee everyone *is to* **r**	8740
Nu	10:36	Whenever it came to rest, he said, "**R,**	8740
	18:21	in Israel as their inheritance in **r for**	2739
	32:18	*We* will not **r** to our homes	8740
	32:22	*you may* **r** and be free from your obligation	8740
	35:28	the high priest *may* he **r** to his own property.	8740
Dt	4:30	then in later days *you will* **r** to	8740
	5:30	"Go, tell them *to* **r** to their tents.	8740
	16: 7	in the morning **r** to your tents.	2143+2256+7155
	17:16	or make the people **r** to Egypt to get more	8740
	23:11	and at sunset *he may* **r** to the camp.	995
	24:13	**R** his cloak to him by sunset so	8740+8740
	30: 2	when you and your children **r** to the LORD	8740
Jos	2:16	until they **r,** and then go on your way."	8740
	18: 4	Then *they will* **r** to me.	995
	18: 8	Then **r** to me, and I will cast lots for you	8740
	22: 4	**r** to your homes in the land that Moses	7155
	22: 8	"**R** to your homes with your great wealth—	8740
	22: 9	the Israelites at Shiloh in Canaan to **r**	8740
Jdg	6:18	the LORD said, "I will wait until you **r.**"	8740
	8: 9	"When I **r** in triumph,	8740
	11:31	the door of my house to meet me when I **r**	8740
	19: 3	to her to persuade her to **r.**	8740
	20: 8	No, not one of *us* will **r** to his house.	6073
Ru	1: 6	*to* **r** home from there.	8740
	1:11	But Naomi said, "**R** home, my daughters.	8740
	1:12	**R** home, my daughters;	8740
1Sa	6: 3	"If you **r** the ark of the god of Israel,	8938
	18: 2	and did not let him **r** to his father's house.	8740
	29: 4	that *he may* **r** to the place you assigned him.	8740
2Sa	1:22	the sword of Saul *did* not **r** unsatisfied.	8740
	12:23	I will go to him, but he *will* not **r** to me."	8740
	15:34	if *you* **r** to the city and say to Absalom,	8740
	17: 3	of the man you seek will mean the **r** of all;	8740
	19:14	They sent word to the king, "**R,**	8740
	19:37	*Let* your servant **r,**	8740
1Ki	11:21	that *I may* **r** to my own country."	2143
	12:27	to *to* King Rehoboam."	8740
	13: 9	or drink water or **r** by the way you came.' "	8740
	13:10	So he took another road and *did* not **r** by	8740
	13:17	not eat bread or drink water there or **r** by	8740
	17:21	*let* this boy's life **r** to him!"	8740
	20:34	"I will **r** the cities my father took	8740
	22:27	but bread and water until I **r** safely.' "	995
	22:28	Micaiah declared, "If *you* ever **r** safely,	8740+8740
2Ki	4:22	go to the man of God quickly and **r.**"	8740
	19: 7	*he will* **r** to his own country,	8740

2Ki	19:28	I will **make** you **r** by the way you came.'	8740
	19:33	By the way that he came *he will* **r**;	8740
2Ch	18:26	but bread and water until I **r** safely.'"	8740
	18:27	Micaiah declared, "If *you* ever **r** safely,	8740+8740
	30: 6	"People of Israel, **r** to the LORD,	8740
	30: 6	that *he may* **r** to you who are left,	8740
	30: 9	If you **r** to the LORD, then your brothers	8740
	30: 9	not turn his face from you if *you* **r** to him."	8740
Ne	1: 9	but if *you* **r** to me and obey my commands,	8740
	7: 5	of those *who had been* the first to **r**.	6590
	9:17	a leader in order to **r** to their slavery.	8740
	9:29	"You warned them to **r** to your law,	8740
Est	2:14	the morning **r** to another part of the harem	8740
	2:14	not **r** to the king unless he was pleased	995+6388
Job	7: 9	he who goes down to the grave *does not* **r**.	6590
	10:21	before I go to the place of no **r**,	8740
	15:31	for he will get nothing in **r**.	9455
	16:22	before I go on the journey of no **r**.	8740
	22:23	If *you* **r** to the Almighty,	8740
	34:15	and man *would* **r** to the dust.	8740
	39: 4	they leave and do not **r**.	8740
Ps	9:17	The wicked **r** to the grave,	8740
	59: 6	*They* **r** at evening, snarling like dogs,	8740
	59:14	*They* **r** at evening, snarling like dogs,	8740
	78:39	a passing breeze *that does not* **r**.	8740
	80:14	**R** to us, O God Almighty!	8740
	85: 8	but *let them* not **r** to folly.	8740
	90: 3	saying, "**R** to dust, O sons of men."	8740
	104:22	they **r** and lie down in their dens,	NIH
	104:29	they die and **r** to the dust.	8740
	109: 4	In **r** for my friendship they accuse me,	8740
	126: 6	*will* **r** with songs of joy,	995+995
	146: 4	their spirit departs, *they* **r** to the ground;	8740
Pr	2:19	None who go to her **r** or attain the paths	8740
Ecc	1: 7	the streams come from, there they **r** again.	2143
	3:20	all come from dust, and to dust all **r**.	8740
	4: 9	because they have a good **r** for their work:	8510
	12: 2	and the clouds **r** after the rain;	8740
Isa	10:21	A remnant *will* **r**, a remnant of Jacob	8740
	10:21	remnant of Jacob will **r** to the Mighty God.	NIH
	10:22	only a remnant *will* **r**.	8740
	13:14	each *will* **r** to his own people,	7155
	23:17	*She will* **r** to her hire as a prostitute	8740
	31: 6	**R** to him you have so greatly revolted	8740
	35:10	and the ransomed of the LORD *will* **r**.	8740
	37: 7	*he will* **r** to his own country,	8740
	37:29	I will **make** you **r** by the way you came.	8740
	37:34	By the way that he came *he will* **r**;	8740
	44:22	**R** to me, for I have redeemed you."	8740
	51:11	The ransomed of the LORD *will* **r**.	8740
	55:10	and *do not* **r** to it without watering the earth	8740
	55:11	*It will* not **r** to me empty,	8740
	63:17	**R** for the sake of your servants,	8740
Jer	3: 1	*should he* **r** to her again?	8740
	3: 1	*would you* now **r** to me?"	8740
	3: 7	that after she had done all this *she would* **r**	8740
	3:10	her unfaithful sister Judah *did not* **r** to me	8740
	3:12	"'**R**, faithless Israel,' declares the LORD,	8740
	3:14	"**R**, faithless people," declares the LORD,	8740
	3:22	"**R**, faithless people; I will cure you of backsliding."	8740
	4: 1	"If *you will* **r**, O Israel, return to me,"	8740
	4: 1	"If *you will* return, O Israel, **r** to me,"	8740
	8: 4	When a man turns away, *does he* not **r**?	8740
	8: 5	*They* cling to deceit; they refuse to **r**.	8740
	14: 3	*They* **r** with their jars unfilled;	8740
	22:10	he will never **r** nor see his native land	8740
	22:11	"He will never **r**.	8740
	22:27	to the land they long to **r** to."	8740
	24: 7	for *they will* **r** to me with all their heart.	8740
	31: 8	a great throng *will* **r**.	8740
	31:16	"*They will* **r** from the land of the enemy.	8740
	31:17	"Your children *will* **r** to their own land.	8740
	31:18	Restore me, and *I will* **r**,	8740
	31:21	**R**, O Virgin Israel, return to your towns.	8740
	31:21	Return, O Virgin Israel, **r** to your towns.	8740
	37: 8	the Babylonians *will* **r** and attack this city;	8740
	44:14	to live in Egypt will escape or survive to **r**	8740
	44:14	to which they long to **r** and live;	8740
	44:14	none *will* **r** except a few fugitives;	8740
	44:28	and **r** *to* the land of Judah from Egypt will	8740
	47: 6	**R** to your scabbard; cease and be still.'	665
	50: 9	skilled warriors *who do not* **r** empty-handed.	8740
	50:16	the sword of the oppressor *let* everyone **r**	7155
La	3:40	and *let us* **r** to the LORD.	8740
	5:21	O LORD, that *we may* **r**;	8740
Eze	11:18	"*They will* **r** to it and remove all its vile	995
	16:55	*will* **r** to what they were before;	8740
	16:55	and you and your daughters *will* **r**	8740
	18:12	*He does not* **r** what he took in pledge.	8740
	21: 5	sword from its scabbard; *it will* not **r** again.'	8740
	21:30	**R** the sword to its scabbard.	8740
	26:20	and you will not **r** or take your place in	8740
	29:14	from captivity and **r** them to Upper Egypt,	8740
	46: 9	to **r** through the gate by which he entered,	8740
Da	10:20	Soon *I will* **r** to fight against the prince	8740
	11:28	of the North *will* **r** *to* his own country.	8740
	11:28	against it and then **r** *to* his own country.	8740
	11:30	*He will* **r** and show favor	8740
Hos	3: 5	Afterward the Israelites *will* **r** and seek	8740
	5: 4	"Their deeds do not permit them to **r**	8740
	6: 1	"Come, *let us* **r** to the LORD.	8740
	7:10	not **r** to the LORD his God or search for him.	8740
	8:13	*They will* **r** *to* Egypt.	8740
	9: 3	Ephraim *will* **r** *to* Egypt	8740
	11: 5	not **r** to Egypt and will not Assyria rule	8740

Hos	12: 6	But you *must* **r** to your God;	8740
	14: 1	**R**, O Israel, to the LORD your God.	8740
	14: 2	Take words with you and **r** to the LORD.	8740
Joel	2:12	"**r** to me with all your heart,	8740
	2:13	**R** to the LORD your God,	8740
	3: 4	*I will* swiftly and speedily **r**	8740
	3: 7	and *I will* **r** on your own heads what you	8740
Ob	1:15	your deeds *will* **r** upon your own head.	8740
Mic	5: 3	of his brothers **r** to join the Israelites.	8740
Zep	2:10	This is what they will get in **r** for	9393
Zec	1: 3	'**R** to me,' declares the LORD Almighty,	8740
	1: 3	'and *I will* **r** to you,'	8740
	1:16	'*I will* **r** to Jerusalem with mercy,	8740
	8: 3	"*I will* **r** to Zion and dwell in Jerusalem.	8740
	9:12	**R** to your fortress, O prisoners of hope;	8740
	10: 9	their children will survive, and *they will* **r**.	8740
Mal	3: 7	Return to me, and *I will* return to you,"	8740
	3: 7	Return to me, and *I will* **r** to you,"	8740
	3: 7	"But you ask, 'How *are we to* **r**?'	8740
Mt	10:13	if it is not, *let* your peace **r** to you.	2188
	12:44	Then it says, '*I will* **r** to the house I left.'	2188
Lk	8:39	"**R** home and tell how much God has done for you."	1650+5715
	10: 6	if not, it *will* **r** to you.	366
	10:35	'Look after him,' he said, 'and when I **r**,	2059
	11:24	Then it says, '*I will* **r** to the house I left.'	5715
	12:36	like men waiting for their master *to* **r**	386+4536
	17:18	Was no one found to **r** and give praise	5715
	19:12	have himself appointed king and then *to* **r**.	5715
Jn	21:22	"If I want him to remain alive until I **r**,	2262
	21:23	"If I want him to remain alive until I **r**,	2262
Ac	13:13	where John left them to **r** to Jerusalem.	5715
	15:16	"'After this I will **r** and rebuild David's	418
	15:33	the brothers with the blessing of peace to **r**	NIG
Ro	9: 9	"At the appointed time *I will* **r**,	2262
1Co	16:11	on his way in peace so that *he may* **r** to me.	2262
2Co	1:23	to spare you that I *did not* **r** to Corinth.	2262
	13: 2	On *my* **r** I will not spare	1650+2262+3836+4099
1Th	3: 9	How can we thank God enough for you in **r**	500
Heb	11:15	they would have had opportunity *to* **r**.	366

RETURNED (185) [RETURN]

Ge	8: 9	so it **r** to Noah in the ark.	8740
	8:11	When the dove **r** to him in the evening,	995
	14:17	After Abram **r** from defeating Kedorlaomer	8740
	18:33	he left, and Abraham **r** home.	8740
	19:27	the next morning Abraham got up and **r** to	NIH
	20:14	and *he* **r** Sarah his wife to him.	8740
	21:32	of his forces **r** to the land of the Philistines.	8740
	22:19	Then Abraham **r** to his servants,	8740
	31:55	Then he left and **r** home.	8740
	32: 6	When the messengers **r** to Jacob, they said,	8740
	35: 9	After Jacob **r** from Paddan Aram,	995
	37:29	When Reuben **r** to the cistern and saw	8740
	42:28	"My silver *has been* **r**,"	8740
	43:10	*we could have* gone and **r** twice."	8740
	44:13	Then they all loaded their donkeys and **r** to	8740
	50:14	After burying his father, Joseph **r** to Egypt,	8740
Ex	2:18	When the girls **r** to Reuel their father,	995
	2:18	"Why *have you* **r** so early today?"	995
	5:22	Moses **r** to the LORD and said, "O Lord,	8740
	18:27	and Jethro **r** to his own country.	2143
Lev	25:28	*It will be* **r** in the Jubilee.	3655
	25:30	*It is not to be* **r** in the Jubilee.	3655
	25:31	and *they are to be* **r** in the Jubilee.	3655
	25:33	and *is to be* **r** in the Jubilee,	3655
Nu	11:30	Then Moses and the elders of Israel **r** to	665
	13:25	the end of forty days *they* **r** from exploring	8740
	14:36	*who* **r** and made the whole community	8740
	16:50	Then Aaron **r** to Moses at the entrance to	8740
	22:14	So the Moabite princes **r** to Balak and said,	995
	24:25	and **r** home and Balak went his own way.	8740
	31:14	who **r** from the battle.	995
Dt	28:31	taken from you and *will not be* **r**.	8740
Jos	2:22	along the road and **r** without finding them.	8740
	4:18	the waters of the Jordan **r** to their place	8740
	6:11	Then the people **r** *to* camp and spent	995
	6:14	around the city once and **r** *to* the camp.	8740
	7: 3	When *they* **r** to Joshua, they said,	8740
	8:24	all the Israelites **r** *to* Ai	8740
	10:15	Then Joshua **r** with all Israel to the camp	8740
	10:21	The whole army then **r** safely to Joshua in	8740
	10:43	Then Joshua **r** with all Israel to the camp	8740
	18: 9	and **r** to Joshua in the camp at Shiloh.	995
	22:32	the leaders **r** to Canaan from their meeting	8740
Jdg	2:19	*the people* **r** *to* ways even more corrupt	8740
	7:15	*He* **r** to the camp of Israel and called out,	8740
	8:13	then **r** from the battle by the Pass of Heres.	8740
	11:34	When Jephthah **r** to his home in Mizpah,	995
	11:39	*she* **r** to her father and he did to her	8740
	14: 2	When *he* **r**, he said to his father and mother,	6590
	15:19	his strength **r** and he revived.	8740
	16:18	the rulers of the Philistines **r** with the silver	6590
	17: 3	When *he* **r** the eleven hundred shekels	8740
	17: 4	So he **r** the silver to his mother,	8740
	18: 8	When *they* **r** to Zorah and Eshtaol,	995
	21:14	So the Benjamites **r** at that time	8740
	21:23	Then *they* **r** to their inheritance and rebuilt	8740
Ru	1:22	So Naomi **r** from Moab accompanied	8740
1Sa	4: 3	When the soldiers **r** to camp,	995
	6:16	of the Philistines saw all this and then **r**	8740
	6:21	Philistines *have* **r** the ark of the LORD.	8740
	17:53	the Israelites **r** from chasing the Philistines,	8740
	17:57	as David **r** from killing the Philistine,	8740
	20:38	The boy picked up the arrow and **r**	995
	24: 1	After Saul **r** from pursuing the Philistines,	8740

1Sa	24:22	Then Saul **r** home, but David	2143
	26:25	David went on his way, and Saul **r** home.	8740
	27: 9	Then *he* **r** to Achish.	8740
2Sa	1: 1	David **r** from defeating the Amalekites	8740
	2:30	Then Joab **r** from pursuing Abner	8740
	3:22	then David's men and Joab **r** from a raid	995
	3:27	Now when Abner **r** *to* Hebron,	8740
	6:20	When David **r** home to bless his household,	8740
	8:13	And David became famous after he **r**	8740
	10:14	So Joab **r** from fighting the Ammonites	8740
	12:31	David and his entire army **r** *to* Jerusalem.	8740
	17:20	*so they* **r** to Jerusalem.	8740
	19:15	the king **r** and went as far as the Jordan	8740
	19:24	the king left until the day *he* **r** safely.	995
	19:39	and Barzillai **r** to his home.	8740
	20: 3	When David **r** to his palace in Jerusalem,	8740
	23:10	The troops **r** to Eleazar,	8740
1Ki	2:41	from Jerusalem to Gath and had **r**,	8740
	3:15	*He* **r** to Jerusalem,	995
	10:13	and **r** with her retinue to her own country.	2143
	10:22	Once every three years it **r**, carrying gold,	995
	12: 2	he **r** from Egypt.	8740
	12:12	and all the people **r** to Rehoboam,	995
	12:20	the Israelites heard that Jeroboam *had* **r**,	8740
	13:19	So the man of God **r** with him and ate	8740
	14:28	afterward *they* **r** them to the guardroom.	8740
	17:22	and the boy's life **r** to him, and he lived.	8740
2Ki	1: 5	When the messengers **r** to the king,	8740
	2:18	When *they* **r** to Elisha,	8740
	2:25	on to Mount Carmel and from there **r**	8740
	3:27	they withdrew and **r** to their own land.	8740
	4:38	Elisha **r** to Gilgal and there was a famine in	8740
	4:39	When *he* **r**, he cut them up into the pot	995
	6:23	and *they* **r** to their master.	2143
	7: 8	*They* **r** and entered another tent	8740
	7:15	the messengers **r** and reported to the king.	8740
	8:14	Then Hazael left Elisha and **r** to his master.	995
	8:29	so King Joram **r** to Jezreel to recover from	8740
	9:15	but King Joram *had* **r** to Jezreel to recover	8740
	14:14	He also took hostages and **r** to Samaria.	8740
	16:11	and finished it before King Ahaz **r**	995
	19:36	*He* **r** to Nineveh and stayed there.	8740
1Ch	16:43	and David **r** **home** to bless his family.	6015
	20: 3	David and his entire army **r** *to* Jerusalem.	8740
2Ch	9:12	and **r** with her retinue to her own country.	2143
	9:21	Once every three years it **r**, carrying gold,	995
	10: 2	he **r** from Egypt.	8740
	10:12	and all the people **r** to Rehoboam,	995
	12:11	afterward *they* **r** them to the guardroom.	8740
	14:15	Then *they* **r** to Jerusalem.	8740
	19: 1	of Judah **r** safely to his palace in Jerusalem,	8740
	20:27	the men of Judah and Jerusalem **r** joyfully	8740
	22: 6	so *he* **r** to Jezreel to recover from	8740
	25:14	When Amaziah **r** from slaughtering	995
	25:24	and **r** to Samaria.	8740
	28: 9	and he went out to meet the army when it **r**	995
	28:15	the City of Palms, and **r** to Samaria.	8740
	31: 1	the Israelites **r** to their own towns and	8740
Ezr	2: 1	to Babylon (*they* **r** to Jerusalem and Judah,	8740
	3: 8	and the Levites and all who *had* **r** from	995
	6: 5	*are to be* **r** to their places in the temple	10754
	6:21	the Israelites who *had* **r** from the exile ate it,	8740
	8:35	Then the exiles who *had* **r**	995
Ne	4:15	we all **r** to the wall, each to his own work.	8740
	7: 6	of Babylon had taken captive (*they* **r**	8740
	8:17	that *had* **r** from exile built booths and lived	8740
	12: 1	These were the priests and Levites who **r**	6590
	13: 6	I *had* **r** to the king.	995
Est	6:12	Afterward Mordecai **r** to the king's gate.	8740
	7: 8	Just as the king **r** from the palace garden to	8740
Ps	35:13	my prayers **r** to me **unanswered,**	2668+8740
	60: T	and when Joab **r** and struck down	8740
Isa	9:13	people *have* not **r** to him who struck them,	8740
	37:37	*He* **r** to Nineveh and stayed there.	8740
Jer	11:10	*They have* **r** to the sins of their forefathers,	8740
	19:14	Jeremiah then **r** from Topheth,	995
Da	2:17	Then Daniel **r** to his house and explained	10016
	4:36	my honor and splendor *were* **r** to me for	10754
	6:18	the king **r** to his palace and spent the night	10016
Am	4: 6	yet *you have* not **r** to me,"	8740
	4: 8	yet *you have* not **r** to me,"	8740
	4: 9	yet *you have* not **r** to me,"	8740
	4:10	yet *you have* not **r** to me,"	8740
	4:11	yet *you have* not **r** to me,"	8740
Zec	4: 1	Then the angel who talked with me **r**	8740
Mt	4:12	*they* **r** to their country by another route.	432
	4:12	John had been put in prison, he **r** to Galilee.	432
	25:19	a long time the master of those servants **r**	2262
	25:27	that when I **r** I would have received it back	2262
	26:40	Then he **r** to his disciples and found them	2262
	26:45	Then he **r** to the disciples and said to them,	2262
	27: 3	with remorse and **r** the thirty silver coins to	5138
Mk	14:37	Then he **r** to his disciples and found them	2262
	16:13	These **r** and reported it to the rest;	599
Lk	1:23	of service was completed, he **r** home.	599
	1:56	for about three months and then **r** home.	5715
	2:20	The shepherds **r**, glorifying and praising	5715
	2:39	*they* **r** to Galilee to their own town	2188
	4: 1	**r** from the Jordan and was led by the Spirit	5715
	4:14	Jesus **r** to Galilee in the power of the Spirit,	5715
	7:10	the men who had been sent **r** to the house	5715
	8:40	Now when Jesus **r**, a crowd welcomed him,	5715
	8:55	Her spirit **r**, and at once she stood up.	2188
	9:10	*When* the apostles **r**, they reported to Jesus	5715
	10:17	The seventy-two **r** with joy and said,	5715
	19:15	"He was made king, however, and **r** home.	1877+2059+3836

Lk	24:33	They got up and r at once to Jerusalem. 5715
	24:52	and r to Jerusalem with great joy. 5715
Jn	4:27	Just then his disciples r and were surprised 2262
	13:12	he put on his clothes and r to his place. 404+4099
	20:17	for I have not yet r to the Father. 326
Ac	1:12	Then they r to Jerusalem from 5715
	8:25	Peter and John r to Jerusalem, 5715
	12:25	they r from Jerusalem, 5715
	14:21	Then they r to Lystra, 5715
	21:6	we went aboard the ship, and they r home. 5715
	22:17	"When I r to Jerusalem and was praying at 5715
	23:32	while they r to the barracks. 5715
Ro	14:9	and r to life so that he might be the Lord 2409
Gal	1:17	into Arabia and later r to Damascus. 5715
1Pe	2:25	but now you have r to the Shepherd 2188

RETURNING (12) [RETURN]

Ge	48:7	As I was r from Paddan, 995
1Sa	7:3	"If you are r to the LORD 8740
	11:5	Just then Saul was r from the fields, 995
	18:6	the men were r home after David had killed 995
2Sa	20:22	each r to his home. NIH
Ecc	1:6	ever r on its course. 8740
Mic	2:8	like men r from battle. 8740
Mk	14:41	R the third time, he said to them, 2262
Lk	2:43	while his parents were r home, 5715
Jn	13:3	and that he had come from God and was r 5632
	20:17	'I am r to my Father and your Father, 326
Heb	7:1	He met Abraham r from the defeat of 5715

RETURNS (11) [RETURN]

Lev	22:13	and she r to live in her father's house as 8740
Pr	3:14	and yields better r than gold. 9311
	26:11	As a dog r to its vomit, 8740
Ecc	12:7	and the dust r to the ground it came from, 8740
	12:7	and the spirit r to God who gave it. 8740
Isa	52:8	When the LORD r to Zion, 8740
Eze	18:7	but r what he took in pledge for a loan. 8740
	33:15	r what he has stolen, 8966
Mt	24:46	whose master finds him doing so when he r. 2262
Lk	12:43	the master finds doing so when he r. 2262
2Pe	2:22	"A dog r to its vomit," and, 2188

REU (6)

Ge	11:18	he became the father of R. 8293
	11:19	And after he became the father of R, 8293
	11:20	When R had lived 32 years, 8293
	11:21	R lived 207 years and had other sons 8293
1Ch	1:25	Eber, Peleg, R, 8293
Lk	3:35	the son of R, the son of Peleg, 4814

REUBEN (56) [REUBENITE, REUBENITES]

Ge	29:32	She named him R, for she said, 8017
	30:14	R went out into the fields 8017
	35:22	R went in and slept with his father's 8017
	35:23	R the firstborn of Jacob, Simeon, Levi, 8017
	37:21	When R heard this, he tried to rescue him 8017
	37:22	R said this to rescue him from them 8017
	37:29	When R returned to the cistern and saw 8017
	42:22	R replied, "Didn't I tell you not to sin 8017
	42:37	Then R said to his father, 8017
	46:8	R the firstborn of Jacob. 8017
	46:9	The sons of R: Hanoch, Pallu, Hezron 8017
	48:5	just as R and Simeon are mine. 8017
	49:3	"R, you are my firstborn, my might, 8017
Ex	1:2	R, Simeon, Levi and Judah; 8017
	6:14	of R the firstborn son of Israel were Hanoch 8017
	6:14	These were the clans of R. 8017
Nu	1:5	from R, Elizur son of Shedeur; 8017
	1:20	From the descendants of R the firstborn son 8017
	1:21	number from the tribe of R was 46,500. 8017
	2:10	of the camp of R under their standard. 8017
	2:10	of the people of R is Elizur son of Shedeur. 8017
	2:16	All the men assigned to the camp of R, 8017
	7:30	the leader of the people of R, 8017
	10:18	The divisions of the camp of R went next, 8017
	13:4	These are their names: from the tribe of R, 8017
	26:5	The descendants of R, the firstborn son 8017
	26:7	These were the clans of R; 8017
	34:14	because the families of the tribe of R, 1201+8018
Dt	27:13	R, Gad, Asher, Zebulun, Dan and Naphtali. 8017
	33:6	"Let R live and not die, 8017
Jos	4:12	The men of R, Gad and the half-tribe of 8017
	13:15	to the tribe of R, clan by clan: 1201+8017
	15:6	to the Stone of Bohan son of R. 8017
	18:7	R and the half-tribe of Manasseh 8017
	18:17	ran down to the Stone of Bohan son of R, 8017
	20:8	the desert on the plateau in the tribe of R, 8017
	21:7	received twelve towns from the tribes of R, 8017
	21:36	from the tribe of R, Bezer, Jahaz, 8017
	22:13	R, Gad and the half-tribe of Manasseh 1201+8017
	22:15	R, Gad and the half-tribe of Manasseh 1201+8017
	22:21	R, Gad and the half-tribe of Manasseh 1201+8017
	22:30	heard what R, Gad and Manasseh had 1201+8017
	22:31	said to R, Gad and Manasseh, 1201+8017
Jdg	5:15	the districts of R there was much searching 8017
	5:16	the districts of R there was much searching 8017
2Ki	10:33	of Gad, and Manasseh), from Aroer by 8018
1Ch	2:1	R, Simeon, Levi, Judah, Issachar, Zebulun, 8017
	5:1	The sons of R the firstborn of Israel (he was 8017
	5:3	the sons of R the firstborn of Israel: 8017
	6:63	from the tribes of R, 8017
	6:78	from the tribe of R across the Jordan east 8017
	12:37	men of R, Gad and the half-tribe of 8018

Eze	48:6	"R will have one portion; 8017
	48:7	it will border the territory of R from east 8017
	48:31	on the north side will be the gate of R, 8017
Rev	7:5	were sealed, from the tribe of R 12,000, 4857

REUBENITE (2) [REUBEN]

Dt	11:6	sons of Eliab the R, 1201+8017
1Ch	11:42	Adina son of Shiza the R, 8018

REUBENITES (30) [REUBEN]

Nu	16:1	the son of Levi, and certain R— 1201+8017
	32:1	The R and Gadites 1201+8017
	32:6	Moses said to the Gadites and R, 1201+8017
	32:25	The Gadites and R said to Moses, 1201+8017
	32:29	He said to them, "If the Gadites and R, 1201+8017
	32:31	The Gadites and R answered, 1201+8017
	32:33	the R and the half-tribe of Manasseh 1201+8017
	32:37	And the R rebuilt Heshbon, 8017
Dt	3:12	the R and the Gadites the territory north 8018
	3:16	But to the R and the Gadites I gave 8018
	4:43	Bezer in the desert plateau, for the R; 8018
	29:8	and gave it as an inheritance to the R, 8018
Jos	1:12	But to the R, the Gadites and the half-tribe 8018
	12:6	of the LORD gave their land to the R, 8018
	13:8	the R and the Gadites had received 8018
	13:23	The boundary of the R was the bank 1201+8017
	13:23	the inheritance of the R, 1201+8017
	22:1	Then Joshua summoned the R, 8018
	22:9	the R, the Gadites and the half-tribe 1201+8017
	22:10	the R, the Gadites and the half-tribe 1201+8017
	22:25	you R and Gadites! 1201+8017
	22:32	the R and Gadites in Gilead and 1201+8017
	22:33	to devastate the country where the R 1201+8017
	22:34	the R and Gadites gave the altar this 1201+8017
1Ch	5:6	Beerah was a leader of the R. 8018
	5:18	The R, the Gadites and the half-tribe 1201+8017
	5:26	who took the R, the Gadites and 8018
	11:42	who was chief of the R, 8018
	26:32	King David put them in charge of the R, 8018
	27:16	over the R: Eliezer son of Zicri; 8018

REUEL (10)

Ge	36:4	to Esau, Basemath bore R, 8294
	36:10	and R, the son of Esau's wife Basemath. 8294
	36:13	The sons of R: 8294
	36:17	The sons of Esau's son R: 8294
	36:17	These were the chiefs descended from R 8294
Ex	2:18	When the girls returned to R their father, 8294
Nu	10:29	Now Moses said to Hobab son of R 8294
1Ch	1:35	Eliphaz, R, Jeush, Jalam and Korah. 8294
	1:37	The sons of R: 8294
	9:8	Meshullam son of Shephatiah, the son of R, 8294

REUMAH (1)

Ge	22:24	His concubine, whose name was R, 8020

REUNITED (1) [UNITE]

Hos	1:11	and the people of Israel will be r, 3481+7695

REVEAL (7) [REVEALED, REVEALER, REVEALING, REVEALS, REVELATION, REVELATIONS]

Nu	12:6	I r myself to him in visions, 3359
1Sa	2:27	'Did I not clearly r myself 1655+1655
Da	2:11	No one can r it to the king except the gods, 10252
	2:47	for you were able to r this mystery." 10144
Mt	11:27	to whom the Son chooses to r him. 636
Lk	10:22	to whom the Son chooses to r him. 636
Gal	1:16	to r his Son in me so that I might preach him 636

REVEALED (62) [REVEAL]

Ge	35:7	because it was there that God r himself 1655
	41:25	God has r to Pharaoh what he is about 5583
Dt	29:29	but the things r belong to us and 1655
1Sa	3:7	The word of the LORD had not yet been r 1655
	3:21	and there he r himself to Samuel 1655
	9:15	the LORD had r this to Samuel: 265+906+1655
2Sa	7:27	you have r this to your servant, saying, 265+1655
2Ki	8:10	but the LORD has r to me that he will 8011
1Ch	17:25	have r to your servant that you will 1655
Est	2:10	Esther had not r her nationality 5583
Ps	98:2	and r his righteousness to the nations. 1655
	147:19	He has r his word to Jacob, 5583
Isa	22:14	The LORD Almighty has r this 1655
	40:5	And the glory of the LORD will be r, 1655
	43:12	I have r and saved and proclaimed— 5583
	53:1	to whom has the arm of the LORD been r? 1655
	56:1	and my righteousness will soon be r. 1655
	65:1	"I r myself to those who did not ask 2011
Jer	11:18	Because the LORD r their plot to me, 3359
	38:21	this is what the LORD has r to me: 8011
Eze	20:5	of the house of Jacob and r myself to them 3359
	20:9	among and in whose sight I had r myself to 3359
Da	2:19	the night the mystery was r to Daniel in 10144
	2:30	As for me, this mystery has been r to me, 10144
Hos	7:1	and the crimes of Samaria r. NIH
Mt	11:25	and r them to little children. 636
	16:17	for this was not r to you by man, 636
Lk	2:26	It had been r to him by the Holy Spirit 5976
	2:35	that the thoughts of many hearts will be r. 636
	10:21	and r them to little children. 636
	17:30	like this on the day the Son of Man is r. 636

Jn	1:31	with water was that he might be r to Israel." 5746
	2:11	He thus r his glory, 5746
	12:38	to whom has the arm of the Lord been r?" 5746
	17:6	"I have r you to those whom you gave me 5746
Ro	1:17	the gospel a righteousness from God is r, 636
	1:18	wrath of God is being r from heaven against 636
	2:5	when his righteous judgment will be r. 637
	8:18	with the glory that will be r in us. 636
	8:19	for the sons of God to be r. 637
	10:20	I r myself to those who did not ask 1181+1871
	16:26	but now r and made known through 5746
1Co	1:7	for our Lord Jesus Christ to be r. 637
	2:10	but God has r it to us by his Spirit. 636
	3:13	It will be r with fire, 636
2Co	4:10	the life of Jesus may also be r in our body. 5746
	4:11	so that his life may be r in our mortal body. 5746
Gal	3:23	locked up until faith should be r. 636
Eph	3:5	in other generations as it has now been r 636
2Th	1:7	This will happen when the Lord Jesus is r 637
	2:3	and the man of lawlessness is r, 636
	2:6	so that he may be r at the proper time. 636
	2:8	And then the lawless one will be r, 636
2Ti	1:10	now been r through the appearing 5746
1Pe	1:5	of the salvation that is ready to be r in 636
	1:7	glory and honor when Jesus Christ is r. 637
	1:12	It was r to them that they were 636
	1:13	be given you when Jesus Christ is r. 637
	1:20	but was r in these last times for your sake. 5746
	4:13	you may be overjoyed when his glory is r. 637
	5:1	also will share in the glory to be r: 636
Rev	15:4	for your righteous acts have been r." 5746

REVEALER (2) [REVEAL]

Da	2:29	the r of mysteries showed you what is 10144
	2:47	and the Lord of kings and a r of mysteries, 10144

REVEALING (2) [REVEAL]

Eze	21:24	r your sins in all that you do— 8011
Am	3:7	without r his plan to his servants 1655

REVEALS (5) [REVEAL]

Nu	23:3	Whatever he r to me I will tell you." 8011
Job	12:22	He r the deep things of darkness 1655
Da	2:22	He r deep and hidden things; 10144
	2:28	there is a God in heaven who r mysteries. 10144
Am	4:13	creates the wind, and r his thoughts to man, 5583

REVELATION (16) [REVEAL]

2Sa	7:17	to David all the words of this entire r. 2612
1Ch	17:15	to David all the words of this entire r. 2606
Pr	29:18	there is no r, the people cast off restraint; 2606
Da	10:1	a r was given to Daniel 1821
Hab	2:2	"Write down the r and make it plain 2606
	2:3	For the r awaits an appointed time; 2606
Lk	2:32	a light for r to the Gentiles and for glory 637
Ro	16:25	to the r of the mystery hidden for long ages 637
1Co	14:6	unless I bring you some r or knowledge 637
	14:26	a r, a tongue or an interpretation. 637
	14:30	a r comes to someone who is sitting down, 636
Gal	1:12	rather, I received it by r from Jesus Christ. 637
	2:2	in response to a r and set before them 637
Eph	1:17	may give you the Spirit of wisdom and r, 637
	3:3	the mystery made known to me by r, 637
Rev	1:1	The r of Jesus Christ, 637

REVELATIONS (2) [REVEAL]

2Co	12:1	I will go on to visions and r from the Lord. 637
	12:7	because of these surpassingly great r, 637

REVELED (1) [REVELRY]

Ne	9:25	they r in your great goodness. 6357

REVELERS (3) [REVELRY]

Isa	5:14	and masses with all their brawlers and r. 6601
	24:8	the noise of the r has stopped, 6611
Jer	15:17	I never sat in the company of r, 8471

REVELING (3) [REVELRY]

1Sa	30:16	drinking and r because of the great amount 2510
Isa	23:12	He said, "No more of your r, 6600
2Pe	2:13	r in their pleasures while they feast 1960

REVELRY (6) [REVELED, REVELERS, REVELING]

Ex	32:6	to eat and drink and got up to indulge in r. 7464
Isa	22:2	O city of tumult and r? 6611
	22:13	But see, there is joy and r, 8525
	23:7	Is this your city of r, the old, old city, 6611
	32:13	of merriment and for this city of r. 6611
1Co	10:7	and got up to indulge in pagan r." 4089

REVENGE (11) [VENGEANCE]

Lev	19:18	" 'Do not seek r or bear a grudge against 5933
Jdg	15:7	I won't stop until I get my r on you." 5933
	16:28	with one blow get r on the Philistines 5933+5934
1Sa	18:25	to take r on his enemies.' " 5933
Ps	44:16	because of the enemy, who is bent on r. 5933
Pr	6:34	he will show no mercy when he takes r. 5934
Jer	20:10	over him and take our r on him." 5935
Eze	24:8	take r I put her blood on the bare rock, 5933+5934

Eze	25:12	'Because Edom took r on the house	5933+5934
	25:15	and took r with malice in their hearts,	5933+5934
Ro	12:19	*Do* not take r, my friends,	1688+4932

REVENUE (4) [REVENUES]

Isa	23: 3	the harvest of the Nile was the r of Tyre,	9311
	33:18	Where is the *one who* took *the* r?	9202
Ro	13: 7	if r, then revenue; if honor, then honor.	5465
	13: 7	if revenue, then r; if honor, then honor.	5465

REVENUES (4) [REVENUE]

1Ki	10:15	the r from merchants and traders and	5006
2Ch	9:14	not including the r brought in by merchants	NIH
Ezr	4:13	and the royal r will suffer.	10063
	6: 8	from the r of Trans-Euphrates,	10402

REVERE (17) [REVERED, REVERENCE, REVERENT, REVERING]

Lev	19:32	for the elderly and r your God.	3707
Dt	4:10	to r me as long as they live in the land	3707
	13: 4	and him *you* must r.	3707
	14:23	to r the LORD your God always.	3707
	17:19	the days of his life so that he may learn to r	3707
	28:58	*do not* r this glorious and awesome name—	3707
Job	37:24	Therefore, men r him,	3707
Ps	22:23	R him, all *you* descendants of Israel!	1593
	33: 8	*let* all the people of the world r him.	1593
	102:15	all the kings of the earth will r your glory.	NIH
Ecc	3:14	God does it so that *men will* r him.	3707
Isa	25: 3	cities of ruthless nations *will* r you.	3707
	59:19	they will r his glory.	NIH
	63:17	and harden our hearts so we do not r you?	3711
Jer	10: 7	Who *should* not r you,	3707
Hos	10: 3	"We have no king because *we did* not r	3707
Mal	4: 2	But for you *who* r my name,	3710

REVERED (4) [REVERE]

Jos	4:14	and *they* r him all the days of his life,	3707
	4:14	just as *they had* r Moses.	3707
2Ki	4: 1	and you know that he r the LORD.	3707
Mal	2: 5	for reverence and he r me and stood in awe	3707

REVERENCE (15) [REVERE]

Lev	19:30	" 'Observe my Sabbaths and *have* r for	3707
	26: 2	" 'Observe my Sabbaths and *have* r for	3707
Jos	5:14	Joshua fell facedown to the ground *in* r,	2556
Ne	5:15	But out of r *for* God I did not act like that.	3711
Ps	5: 7	*in* r will I bow down	3711
Jer	44:10	not humbled themselves or *shown* r,	3707
Da	6:26	of my kingdom people must fear and r	10167
Mal	2: 5	for r and he revered me and stood in awe	4616
Ac	10:25	Cornelius met him and fell at his feet in r.	4686
2Co	7: 1	perfecting holiness out of r for God.	5832
Eph	5:21	Submit to one another out of r for Christ.	5832
Col	3:22	with sincerity of heart and r for the Lord.	5832
Heb	12:28	so worship God acceptably with r and awe,	2325
1Pe	3: 2	they see the purity and r of your lives.	5832
Rev	11:18	and your saints and those who r your name,	5828

REVERENT (4) [REVERE]

Ecc	8:12	who *are* r before God.	3707
Tit	2: 3	teach the older women to be r in	2640
Heb	5: 7	he was heard because of his r submission.	2325
1Pe	1:17	live your lives as strangers here in r fear.	5832

REVERING (2) [REVERE]

| Dt | 8: 6 | walking in his ways and r him. | 3707 |
| Ne | 1:11 | your servants who delight in r your name. | 3707 |

REVERSE (1) [REVERSED]

| Isa | 43:13 | When I act, who *can* r it?" | 8740 |

REVERSED (1) [REVERSE]

| Eze | 7:13 | concerning the whole crowd *will* not *be* r. | 8740 |

REVERT (3)

Lev	27:24	In the Year of Jubilee the field *will* r to	8740
1Ki	12:26	"The kingdom *will* now *likely* r to	8740
Eze	46:17	then *it will* r to the prince.	8697

REVIEW (1)

| Isa | 43:26 | R the past *for* me, | 2349 |

REVILE (5) [REVILED, REVILES]

Ps	10:13	Why *does* the wicked man r God?	5540
	44:16	the taunts of those who reproach and r me,	1552
	55: 3	down suffering upon me and r me	8475
	74:10	*Will* the foe r your name forever?	5540
Ecc	10:20	*Do* not r the king even in your thoughts,	7837

REVILED (1) [REVILE]

| Ps | 74:18 | how foolish people *have* r your name. | 5540 |

REVILES (1) [REVILE]

| Ps | 10: 3 | he blesses the greedy and r the LORD. | 5540 |

REVIVE (5) [REVIVED, REVIVING]

Ps	80:18	r us, and we will call on your name.	2649
	85: 6	*Will* you not r us again,	2649
Isa	57:15	to r the spirit of the lowly and to revive	2649
	57:15	the lowly and to r the heart of the contrite.	2649
Hos	6: 2	After two days *he will* r us;	2649

REVIVED (3) [REVIVE]

Ge	45:27	the spirit of their father Jacob r.	2649
Jdg	15:19	his strength returned and *he* r.	2649
1Sa	30:12	He ate and *was* r,	8120+8740

REVIVING (1) [REVIVE]

| Ps | 19: 7 | law of the LORD is perfect, r the soul. | 8740 |

REVOKE (1) [REVOKED, REVOKING]

| Ps | 132:11 | a sure oath that *he will* not r: | 8740 |

REVOKED (3) [REVOKE]

Est	8: 8	and sealed with his ring *can be* r."	8740
Isa	45:23	in all integrity a word *that will* not *be* r:	8740
Zec	11:11	*It was* r on that day,	7296

REVOKING (1) [REVOKE]

| Zec | 11:10 | r the covenant I had made with all the nations. | 7296 |

REVOLT (7) [REVOLTED, REVOLUTIONS]

Ezr	4:19	a long history of r against kings	10492
Ne	6: 6	that you and the Jews are plotting to r,	5277
Isa	59:13	fomenting oppression and r,	6240
Eze	2: 3	and their fathers *have been* in r against me	7321
	20:38	I will purge you of those *who* r and rebel	5277
Ac	5:37	led a band of people in r.	923
	21:38	a r and led four thousand terrorists out into	415

REVOLTED (4) [REVOLT]

Jdg	9:18	(but today you *have* r against my father's	7756
2Ki	8:22	Libnah r at the same time.	7321
2Ch	21:10	Libnah r at the same time,	7321
Isa	31: 6	to him you have so greatly r *against*,	6240

REVOLUTIONS (1) [REVOLT]

| Lk | 21: 9 | When you hear *of* wars and r, | 189 |

REWARD (55) [REWARDED, REWARDING, REWARDS]

Ge	15: 1	I am your shield, your very great r."	8510
Nu	22:17	I *will* r you handsomely,	3877+3877+4394
	22:37	Am I really not able to r you?"	3877
	24:11	I said *I would* r you handsomely,	3877+3877
1Sa	24:19	*May* the LORD r you well for	8966
2Sa	4:10	r I gave him **for** his news!	1415
	18:22	*that will* bring you a r."	5162
	19:36	but why *should* the king r me in this way?	1694
Job	17: 5	If a man denounces his friends for r,	2750
	34:33	*Should* God then r you on your terms,	8966
Ps	17:14	of this world whose r is in this life.	2750
	19:11	in keeping them there is great r.	6813
	62:12	Surely you *will* r each person according	8966
	127: 3	children a r from him.	8510
Pr	9:12	If you are wise, your wisdom will r you;	4200
	11:18	he who sows righteousness reaps a sure r.	8512
	13:21	but prosperity *is the* r of the righteous.	8966
	19:17	and *he will* r him *for* what he has done.	8966
	25:22	and the LORD *will* r you.	8966
	31:31	Give her the r she has earned,	3338+7262
Ecc	2:10	and this was the r for all my labor.	2750
	9: 5	they have no further r,	8510
Isa	40:10	See, his r is with him,	8510
	45:13	but not for a price or r,	8816
	49: 4	and my r is with my God."	7190
	61: 8	In my faithfulness I *will* r them and	5989+7190
	62:11	See, his r is with him,	8510
Jer	17:10	to r a man according to his conduct,	5989
	32:19	you r everyone according to his conduct	5989
Eze	29:18	Yet he and his army got no r from	8510
	29:20	I have given him Egypt as a r for his efforts	8510
Mt	5:12	because great is your r in heaven,	3635
	5:46	what r will you get?	3635
	6: 1	you will have no r from your Father	3635
	6: 2	they have received their r in full.	3635
	6: 4	who sees what is done in secret, *will* r you.	625
	6: 5	they have received their r in full.	3635
	6: 6	who sees what is done in secret, *will* r you.	625
	6:16	they have received their r in full.	3635
	6:18	who sees what is done in secret, *will* r you.	625
	10:41	a prophet will receive a prophet's r,	3635
	10:41	will receive a righteous man's r.	3635
	10:42	he will certainly not lose his r."	3635
	16:27	and then *he will* r each person according	3635
Mk	9:41	to Christ will certainly not lose his r.	3635
Lk	6:23	because great is your r in heaven.	3635
	6:35	Then your r will be great,	3635
Ac	1:18	(With the r he got for his wickedness,	3635
1Co	3:14	he will receive his r.	3635
	9:17	If I preach voluntarily, I have a r;	3635
	9:18	What then is my r?	3635
Eph	6: 8	that the Lord *will* r everyone	3152
Col	3:24	an inheritance from the Lord as a r.	502

| Heb | 11:26 | because he was looking ahead to his r. | 3632 |
| Rev | 22:12 | I am coming soon! My r is with me, | 3635 |

REWARDED (15) [REWARD]

Ge	30:18	"God *has* r me for giving my maidservant	5989+8510
Nu	24:11	but the LORD has kept you from being r."	3883
Ru	2:12	May you be richly r by the LORD,	5382
2Sa	22:21	to the cleanness of my hands he has r me.	8740
	22:25	The LORD *has* r me according	8740
2Ch	15: 7	for your work will be r."	8510
Ps	18:20	to the cleanness of my hands he has r me.	8740
	18:24	The LORD *has* r me according	8740
	58:11	"Surely the righteous still are r;	7262
Pr	13:13	but he who respects a command *is* r.	8966
	14:14	and the good man r for his.	NIH
Jer	31:16	for your work will be r,"	8510
1Co	3: 8	each *will be* r according to his own labor.	3284+3635
Heb	10:35	your confidence; it will be richly r.	3632
2Jn	1: 8	but that *you may be* r fully.	655+3635

REWARDING (1) [REWARD]

| Rev | 11:18 | *for* r your servants the prophets | 1443+3635+3836 |

REWARDS (5) [REWARD]

1Sa	26:23	The LORD r every man for his righteous	8740
Pr	12:14	as surely as the work of his hands r him.	8740
Da	2: 6	from me gifts and r and great honor.	10454
	5:17	and give your r to someone else.	10454
Heb	11: 6	he r those who earnestly seek him.	1181+3633

REZEPH (2)

| 2Ki | 19:12 | the gods of Gozan, Haran, R and the people | 8364 |
| Isa | 37:12 | the gods of Gozan, Haran, R and the people | 8364 |

REZIA (KJV) See RIZIA

REZIN (10) [REZIN'S]

2Ki	15:37	the LORD began to send R king of Aram	8360
	16: 5	Then R king of Aram and Pekah son	8360
	16: 6	R king of Aram recovered Elath for Aram	8360
	16: 9	He deported its inhabitants to Kir and put R	8360
Ezr	2:48	R, Nekoda, Gazzam,	8360
Ne	7:50	Reaiah, R, Nekoda,	8360
Isa	7: 1	King R of Aram and Pekah son	8360
	7: 4	of R and Aram and of the son of Remaliah.	8360
	7: 8	and the head of Damascus is only R.	8360
	8: 6	of Shiloah and rejoices over R and the son	8360

REZIN'S (1) [REZIN]

| Isa | 9:11 | But the LORD has strengthened R foes | 8360 |

REZON (3)

1Ki	11:23	R son of Eliada,	8139
	11:25	R was Israel's adversary as long	NIH
	11:25	So R ruled in Aram and was hostile	NIH

RHEGIUM (1)

| Ac | 28:13 | From there we set sail and arrived at R. | 4836 |

RHESA (1)

| Lk | 3:27 | the son *of* R, the son of Zerubbabel, | 4840 |

RHODA (1)

| Ac | 12:13 | and a servant girl named R came to answer | 4851 |

RHODES (2)

| Eze | 27:15 | " 'The men of R traded with you, | 8102 |
| Ac | 21: 1 | The next day we went to R and from there | 4852 |

RIB (1) [RIBS]

| Ge | 2:22 | made a woman from the r he had taken out | 7521 |

RIBAI (2)

| 2Sa | 23:29 | Ithai son of R from Gibeah in Benjamin, | 8192 |
| 1Ch | 11:31 | Ithai son of R from Gibeah in Benjamin, | 8192 |

RIBBAND (KJV) See CORD

RIBBON (1)

| SS | 4: 3 | Your lips are like a scarlet r; | 2562 |

RIBLAH (11)

Nu	34:11	from Shepham to R on the east side of Ain	8058
2Ki	23:33	at R in the land of Hamath so that he might	8058
	25: 6	He was taken to the king of Babylon at R,	8058
	25:20	to the king of Babylon at R.	8058
	25:21	There at R, in the land of Hamath,	8058
Jer	39: 5	to Nebuchadnezzar king of Babylon at R in	8058
	39: 6	There at R the king of Babylon slaughtered	8058
	52: 9	He was taken to the king of Babylon at R in	8058
	52:10	There at R the king of Babylon slaughtered	8058
	52:26	to the king of Babylon at R.	8058
	52:27	There at R, in the land of Hamath,	8058

RIBS (2) [RIB]

Ge	2:21	he took one of the man's **r** and closed up	7521
Da	7: 5	it had three **r** in its mouth between its teeth.	10552

RICH (98) [ENRICH, ENRICHED, RICHER, RICHES, RICHEST, RICHLY, RICHNESS]

Ge	14:23	'I made Abram **r**.'	6947
	26:13	The man became **r**,	1540
	49:20	"Asher's food will be **r**;	9045
Ex	30:15	The **r** are not to give more than	6938
Lev	25:47	resident among you becomes **r**	3338+5952
Ru	3:10	after the younger men, whether **r** or poor.	6938
2Sa	12: 1	one **r** and the other poor.	6938
	12: 2	The **r** man had a very large number of sheep	6938
	12: 4	"Now a traveler came to the **r** man,	6938
	12: 4	but the **r** man refrained from taking one	NIH
1Ch	4:40	They found **r**, good pasture,	9045
Job	15:29	He will no longer be **r** and his wealth will	6947
	21:24	his bones **r** with marrow.	9197
	34:19	to princes and does not favor the **r** over	8777
Ps	21: 3	You welcomed him with **r** blessings	3202
	22:29	the **r** of the earth will feast and worship;	2016
	49: 2	both low and high, **r** and poor alike:	6938
	49:16	not be overawed when a man grows **r**, when	6947
	76: 4	more majestic than mountains **r** with game.	AIT
	145: 8	slow to anger and **r** in love.	1524
Pr	10:15	The wealth of the **r** are their fortified city,	6938
	13: 7	One man pretends to be **r**, yet has nothing;	6947
	14:20	but the **r** have many friends.	6938
	18:11	The wealth of the **r** are their fortified city;	6938
	18:23	but a **r** man answers harshly.	6938
	21:17	and oil will never be **r**.	6947
	22: 2	**R** and poor have this in common:	6938
	22: 7	The **r** rule over the poor,	6938
	22:16	and he who gives gifts to the **r**—	6938
	23: 4	Do not wear yourself out to get **r**;	6947
	24:25	and **r** blessing will come upon them.	3202
	28: 6	a **r** man whose ways are perverse.	6938
	28:11	A **r** man may be wise in his own eyes,	6938
	28:20	one eager to get **r** will not go unpunished.	6947
	28:22	A stingy man is eager to get **r**	2104
Ecc	5:12	abundance of a **r** man permits him no sleep.	6938
	10: 6	while the **r** occupy the low ones.	6938
	10:20	or curse the **r** in your bedroom,	6938
Isa	5:17	lambs will feed among the ruins of the **r**.	4671
	25: 6	a feast of **r** food for all peoples, a banquet	9043
	30:23	the food that comes from the land will be **r**	2015
	33: 6	a **r** store of salvation and wisdom	2890
	53: 9	and with the **r** in his death,	6938
Jer	2: 7	a fertile land to eat its fruit and **r** produce.	3206
	5:27	they have become **r** and powerful	6947
	9:23	of his strength or the **r** man boast	6938
	49:19	from Jordan's thickets to a **r** pastureland,	419
	50:44	from Jordan's thickets to a **r** pastureland,	419
	51:13	You who live by many waters and are **r**	8041
Eze	34:14	in a **r** pasture on the mountains of Israel.	9045
	38:12	**r** in livestock and goods,	6913
Hos	12: 8	Ephraim boasts, "I am very **r**;	6947
Mic	2: 8	the **r** robe from those who pass by without	159
	6:12	Her **r** men are violent;	6938
Zec	3: 4	and I will put **r** garments on you."	4711
	11: 3	their **r** pastures are destroyed!	168
	11: 5	'Praise the LORD, I am **r**!'	6947
Mt	19:23	for a **r** man to enter the kingdom of heaven.	4454
	19:24	through the eye of a needle than for a **r** man	4454
	27:57	there came a **r** man from Arimathea,	4454
Mk	10:23	for the **r** to enter the kingdom of God!"	2400+3836+5975
	10:25	through the eye of a needle than for a **r** man	4454
	12:41	Many **r** people threw in large amounts.	4454
Lk	1:53	but has sent the **r** away empty.	4456
	6:24	"But woe to you who are **r**,	4454
	12:16	"The ground of a certain **r** man produced	4454
	12:21	for himself but is not **r** toward God."	4456
	14:12	or your **r** neighbors;	4454
	16: 1	a **r** man whose manager was accused	4454
	16:19	"There was a **r** man who was dressed	4454
	16:21	to eat what fell from the **r** man's table.	4454
	16:22	The **r** man also died and was buried.	4454
	18:24	for the **r** to enter the kingdom of God!	2400+3836+5975
	18:25	through the eye of a needle than for a **r** man	4454
	21: 1	Jesus saw the **r** putting their gifts into	4454
1Co	4: 8	Already you have become **r**!	4456
2Co	6:10	poor, yet making many **r**;	4457
	8: 2	extreme poverty welled up in **r** generosity.	4458
	8: 9	that though he was **r**, yet for your sake	4454
	8: 9	you through his poverty might become **r**.	4456
	9:11	You will be made **r** in every way so	4457
Eph	2: 4	God, who is **r** in mercy,	4454
1Ti	6: 9	to get **r** fall into temptation and a trap and	4456
	6:17	Command those who are **r** in this present	4454
	6:18	to be **r** in good deeds,	4456
Jas	1:10	But the one who is **r** should take pride	4454
	1:11	the **r** man will fade away even	4454
	2: 5	in the eyes of the world to be **r** in faith and	4454
	2: 6	Is it not the **r** who are exploiting you?	4454
	5: 1	Now listen, you **r** people,	4454
2Pe	1:11	and you will receive a **r** welcome into	4455
Rev	2: 9	and your poverty—yet you are **r**!	4454
	3:17	You say, 'I am **r**;	4454
	3:18	so you can become **r**;	4454
	6:15	the princes, the generals, the **r**, the mighty,	4454
	13:16	small and great, **r** and poor, free and slave,	4454
	18: 3	and the merchants of the earth grew **r**	4456
Rev	18:19	all who had ships on the sea became **r**	4456

RICHER (1) [RICH]

Da	11: 2	who will be far **r** than all the others.	6947+6948

RICHES (51) [RICH]

1Ki	3:13	you have not asked for—both **r** and honor—	6948
	10:23	Solomon was greater in **r** and wisdom than	6948
2Ch	1:11	not asked for wealth, **r** or honor, nor for	5794
	1:12	I will also give you wealth, **r** and honor,	5794
	9:22	in **r** and wisdom than all the other kings of	6948
	32:27	Hezekiah had very great **r** and honor,	6948
	32:29	for God had given him very great **r**.	8214
Job	20:15	He will spit out the **r** he swallowed;	2657
	36:18	Be careful that no one entices you by **r**;	6217
Ps	49: 6	in their wealth and boast of their great **r**?	6948
	49:12	But man, despite his **r**, does not endure;	3702
	49:20	A man who has **r** without understanding is	3702
	62:10	though your **r** increase,	2657
	112: 3	Wealth and **r** are in his house,	6948
	119:14	as one rejoices in great **r**.	2104
Pr	3:16	in her left hand are **r** and honor.	6948
	8:18	With me are **r** and honor,	6948
	11:28	Whoever trusts in his **r** will fall,	6948
	13: 8	A man's **r** may ransom his life,	6948
	22: 1	good name is more desirable than great **r**;	6948
	23: 5	Cast but a glance at **r**, and they are gone,	2257S
	27:24	for **r** do not endure forever,	2890
	30: 8	give me neither poverty nor **r**,	6948
Isa	10: 3	Where will you leave your **r**?	3883
	30: 6	the envoys carry their **r** on donkeys' backs,	2657
	45: 3	**r** stored in secret places,	4759
	60: 5	to you the **r** of the nations will come.	2657
	61: 6	and in their **r** you will boast.	3883
Jer	9:23	or the rich man boast of his **r**,	6948
	17:11	the man who gains **r** by unjust means.	6948
	48: 7	Since you trust in your deeds and **r**,	238
	49: 4	you trust in your **r** and say,	238
Da	11:43	the treasures of gold and silver and all the **r**	2776
Joel	2:22	the fig tree and the vine yield their **r**.	2657
Lk	8:14	**r** and pleasures, and they do not mature.	4458
	16:11	who will trust you with true **r**?	NIG
Ro	2: 4	Or do you show contempt for the **r**	4458
	9:23	the **r** of his glory known to the objects	4458
	11:12	if their transgression means **r** for the world,	4458
	11:12	and their loss means **r** for the Gentiles,	4458
	11:12	much greater **r** will their fullness bring!	NIG
	11:33	of the **r** of the wisdom and knowledge	4458
Eph	1: 7	in accordance with the **r** of God's grace	4458
	1:18	the **r** of his glorious inheritance in	4458
	2: 7	the incomparable **r** of his grace,	4458
	3: 8	to the Gentiles the unsearchable **r** of Christ,	4458
	3:16	of his glorious **r** he may strengthen you	4458
Php	4:19	according to his glorious **r** in Christ Jesus.	4458
Col	1:27	the Gentiles the glorious **r** of this mystery,	4458
	2: 2	the full **r** of complete understanding,	4458
Rev	18:14	All your **r** and splendor have vanished,	3353

RICHEST (3) [RICH]

Ps	63: 5	satisfied as with the **r** of foods;	2016+2256+2693
Isa	55: 2	and your soul will delight in the **r** of fare.	2016
Da	11:24	When the **r** provinces feel secure,	5458

RICHLY (10) [RICH]

Ge	37: 3	and he made a **r** ornamented robe for him.	7168
	37:23	the **r** ornamented robe he was wearing—	7168
Dt	15: 4	he will **r** bless you,	1385+1385
Ru	2:12	May you be **r** rewarded by the LORD,	8969
2Sa	13:18	She was wearing a **r** ornamented robe,	7168
Pr	28:20	A faithful man will be **r** blessed,	8041
Ro	10:12	and **r** blesses all who call on him,	4456
Col	3:16	Let the word of Christ dwell in you **r**	4455
1Ti	6:17	who **r** provides us with everything	4455
Heb	10:35	it will be **r** rewarded.	3489

RICHNESS (2) [RICH]

Ge	27:28	of heaven's dew and of earth's **r**—	9044
	27:39	dwelling will be away from the earth's **r**,	9044

RID (32)

Ge	21:10	"Get **r** of that slave woman and her son,	1763
	35: 2	"Get **r** of the foreign gods you have	6073
Ex	8: 9	and your houses may be **r** of the frogs,	4162
Lev	13:58	that has been washed and is **r** of the mildew	6073
Nu	17: 5	I will **r** myself of this constant grumbling	8896
Jdg	9:29	Then I would get **r** of him.	6073
	10:16	Then they got **r** of the foreign gods	6073
1Sa	1:14	Get **r** of your wine."	6073
	7: 3	then **r** yourselves of the foreign gods and	6073
2Sa	4:11	from your hand and **r** the earth of you!"	1278
	13:13	Where could I get **r** of my disgrace?	2143
	14: 7	then we will get **r** of the heir as well.'	9012
1Ki	15:12	from the land and got **r** of all	6073
	22:46	He **r** the land of the rest of the male shrine	1278
2Ki	3: 2	He got **r** of the sacred stone of Baal	6073
	23:24	Josiah got **r** of the mediums and spiritists,	1278
2Ch	15:15	for you have **r** the land of the Asherah poles	1278
	33:15	He got **r** of the foreign gods and removed	6073
Eze	18:31	**R** yourselves of all the offenses	4946+6584+8959
	20: 7	And I said to them, "Each of you, get **r** of	8959
	20: 8	they did not get **r** of the vile images	8959
	34:25	with them and **r** the land of wild beasts so	8697
Zec	11: 8	In one month I got **r** of the three shepherds	3948
Lk	22: 2	looking for some way to get **r** of Jesus,	359
Ac	16:37	now do they want to get **r** of us quietly?	1675
	22:22	"**R** the earth of him!"	149
1Co	5: 7	Get **r** of the old yeast that you may be	1705
Gal	4:30	"Get **r** of the slave woman and her son,	1675
Eph	4:31	Get **r** of all bitterness, rage and anger,	149
Col	3: 8	But now you must **r** yourselves of	700
Jas	1:21	get **r** of all moral filth and the evil that is	700
1Pe	2: 1	**r** yourselves of all malice and all deceit,	700

RIDDEN (4) [RIDE]

Nu	22:30	which you have always **r**, to this day?	8206
Est	6: 8	and a horse the king has **r**,	8206
Mk	11: 2	which no one has ever **r**.	2767
Lk	19:30	which no one has ever **r**.	2767

RIDDLE (8) [RIDDLES]

Jdg	14:12	"Let me tell you a **r**," Samson said to them.	2648
	14:13	"Tell us your **r**," they said.	2648
	14:15	"Coax your husband into explaining the **r**	2648
	14:16	You've given my people a **r**,	2648
	14:17	She in turn explained the **r** to her people.	2648
	14:18	you would not have solved my **r**."	2648
	14:19	to those who had explained the **r**.	2648
Ps	49: 4	with the harp I will expound my **r**:	2648

RIDDLES (3) [RIDDLE]

Nu	12: 8	clearly and not in **r**;	2648
Pr	1: 6	the sayings and **r** of the wise.	2648
Da	5:12	explain **r** and solve difficult problems.	10019

RIDE (13) [RIDDEN, RIDER, RIDERS, RIDES, RIDING, RODE]

Ge	41:43	He had him **r** in a chariot	8206
Dt	32:13	He made him **r** on the heights of the land	8206
Jdg	5:10	"You who **r** on white donkeys,	8206
2Sa	16: 2	for the king's household to **r** on,	8206
	19:26	'I will have my donkey saddled and will **r**	8206
2Ki	10:16	Then he had him **r** along in his chariot.	8206
Ps	45: 4	In your majesty **r** forth victoriously	8206
	66:12	You let men **r** over our heads;	8206
Isa	30:16	You said, 'We will **r** off on swift horses.'	8206
	33:21	No galley with oars will **r** them,	928+2143
	58:14	and I will cause you to **r** on the heights	8206
Jer	6:23	They sound like the roaring sea as they **r**	8206
	50:42	They sound like the roaring sea as they **r**	8206

RIDER (13) [RIDE]

Ge	49:17	so that its **r** tumbles backward.	8206
Ex	15: 1	horse and its **r** he has hurled into the sea.	8206
	15:21	horse and its **r** he has hurled into the sea."	8206
Job	39:18	she laughs at horse and **r**.	8206
Jer	51:21	with you I shatter horse and **r**,	8206
Zec	12: 4	with panic and its **r** with madness,"	8206
Rev	6: 2	Its **r** held a bow, and he was given a crown,	2764+3836
	6: 4	Its **r** was given power to take peace from the earth	2764+3836
	6: 5	Its **r** was holding a pair of scales	2764+3836
	6: 8	Its **r** was named Death,	2764+3836
	19:11	**r** is called Faithful and True.	899+2093+2764
	19:19	against the **r** on the horse and his army.	2764
	19:21	that came out of the mouth of the **r** on	2764

RIDERS (9) [RIDE]

2Sa		the chariots and **r** almost upon him.	1251+7304
2Ki	18:23	if you can put **r** on them!	8206
Isa	21: 7	**r** on donkeys or riders on camels,	8207
	21: 7	riders on donkeys or **r** on camels,	8207
	36: 8	if you can put **r** on them!	8206
Eze	39:20	eat your fill of horses and **r**,	8207
Hag	2:22	horses and their **r** will fall,	8206
Rev	9:17	The horses and **r** I saw in my vision looked like this:	2093+2764+3836
	19:18	men, of horses and their **r**,	899+2093+2764

RIDES (6) [RIDE]

Dt	33:26	who **r** on the heavens to help you and on	8206
Ps	68: 4	extol him who **r** on the clouds—	8206
	68:33	to him who **r** the ancient skies above,	8206
	104: 3	the clouds his chariot and **r** on the wings of	2143
Isa	19: 1	See, the LORD **r** on a swift cloud	8206
Rev	17: 7	of the woman and of the beast she **r**,	1002

RIDGE (1) [RIDGES]

Ge	48:22	the **r** of land I took from the Amorites	8900

RIDGES (1) [RIDGE]

Ps	65:10	You drench its furrows and level its **r**;	1521

RIDICULE (14) [RIDICULED]

Dt	28:37	of horror and an object of scorn and **r** to all	9110
1Ki	9: 7	then become a byword and an object of **r**	9110
2Ki	19: 4	has sent to **r** the living God,	3070
2Ch	7:20	I will make it a byword and an object of **r**	9110
Job	19:18	when I appear, they **r** me.	1819
Ps	123: 4	We have endured much **r** from the proud,	4353
Isa	37: 4	has sent to **r** the living God,	3070
Jer	24: 9	an object of **r** and cursing,	9110
	48:26	let her be an object of **r**.	8468

Jer	48:27	Was not Israel the **object of** your **r**?	8468
	48:39	Moab has become an **object of** r,	8468
Mic	2: 4	In that day *men will* **r** you;	5442+5951
Hab	2: 6	not all of them taunt him with **r** and scorn,	4886
Lk	14:29	everyone who sees it *will* **r** him,	*1850*

RIDICULED (8) [RIDICULE]

Jdg	9:38	Aren't these the men *you* **r**?	4415
2Ch	30:10	but the people scorned and **r** them.	4352
Ne	2:19	they mocked and **r** us.	1022
	4: 1	*He* **r** the Jews,	4352
Jer	20: 7	I am **r** all day long; everyone mocks me.	8468
Eze	36: 4	that have been plundered and **r** by the rest	4353
Hos	7:16	this they *will be* **r** in the land of Egypt.	4352
Lk	23:11	Herod and his soldiers **r** and mocked him.	*2024*

RIDING (15) [RIDE]

Lev	15: 9	" 'Everything the man sits on when **r** will	8206
Nu	22:22	Balaam *was* **r** on his donkey,	8206
1Sa	25:20	As she **came** **r** her donkey into	8206
2Sa	18: 9	He *was* **r** his mule,	8206
	18: 9	while the mule he was **r** kept on going.	9393
2Ki	9:25	how you and I *were* **r** together **in chariots**	8206
Ne	2:12	with me except the one I *was* **r** on.	8206
Est	8:14	The couriers, **r** the royal horses, raced out,	8206
Jer	17:25	and their officials *will* come **r** in chariots	8206
	22: 4	**r** in chariots and on horses,	8206
Eze	38:15	all of them **r** *on* horses, a great horde,	8206
Zec	1: 8	there before me was a man **r** a red horse!	8206
	9: 9	gentle and **r** on a donkey, on a colt,	8206
Mt	21: 5	gentle and **r** on a donkey, on a colt,	*2094*
Rev	19:14	**r** on white horses and dressed in fine linen,	NIG

RIE (KJV) See SPELT

RIFLED (KJV) See RANSACKED

RIFTS (1)

| Jer | 2: 6 | through a land of deserts and **r**, | 8757 |

RIGGING (2)

| Pr | 23:34 | on the high seas, lying on top of the **r**. | 2479 |
| Isa | 33:23 | Your **r** hangs loose: | 2475 |

RIGHT (460) [ARIGHT, RIGHTFUL, RIGHTFULLY, RIGHTLY, RIGHTS]

Ge	4: 7	If *you* **do what is** **r**,	3512
	4: 7	But if *you do* not **do what is** **r**,	3512
	13: 9	If you go to the left, *I'll* **go to the** **r**;	3554
	13: 9	if you go to the **r**, I'll go to the left."	3545
	18:19	of the LORD by doing *what is* **r** and just,	7407
	18:25	Will not the Judge of all the earth do **r**?"	5477
	24:48	on the **r** road to get the granddaughter	622
	43:23	"It's **all r**," he said.	8934
	48:13	Ephraim on his **r** toward Israel's left hand	3545
	48:13	on his left toward Israel's **r** hand,	3545
	48:14	But Israel reached out his **r** hand and put it	3545
	48:17	Joseph saw his father placing his **r** hand	3545
	48:18	put your **r** hand on his head."	3545
Ex	8:26	But Moses said, "That *would* not *be* **r**.	3922
	9:27	"The LORD is **in the r**,	7404
	14:22	a wall of water on their **r** and on their left.	3545
	14:29	a wall of water on their **r** and on their left.	3545
	15: 6	"Your **r** hand, O LORD, was majestic	3545
	15: 6	Your **r** hand, O LORD, was majestic	3545
	15:12	You stretched out your **r** hand and	3545
	15:26	of the LORD your God and do what is **r**	3838
	21: 8	*He has* no **r** to sell her to foreigners,	5440
	29:20	of the **r** ears of Aaron and his sons,	3556
	29:20	on the thumbs of their **r** hands,	3556
	29:20	and on the big toes of their **r** feet.	3556
	29:22	with the fat on them, and the **r** thigh.	3545
Lev	7:32	the **r** thigh of your fellowship offerings to	3545
	7:33	the **r** thigh as his share.	3545
	8:23	and put it on the lobe of Aaron's **r** ear,	3556
	8:23	the thumb of his **r** hand and on the big toe	3556
	8:23	and on the big toe of his **r** foot.	3556
	8:24	of the blood on the lobes of their **r** ears,	3556
	8:24	on the thumbs of their **r** hands and on	3556
	8:24	and on the big toes of their **r** feet.	3556
	8:25	both kidneys and their fat and the **r** thigh.	3545
	8:26	on the fat portions and on the **r** thigh.	3545
	9:21	Aaron waved the breasts and the **r** thigh	3545
	14:14	and put it on the lobe of the **r** ear of the one	3556
	14:14	the thumb of his **r** hand and on the big toe	3556
	14:14	and on the big toe of his **r** foot.	3556
	14:16	dip his **r** forefinger into the oil in his palm,	3556
	14:17	in his palm on the lobe of the **r** ear of	3556
	14:17	the thumb of his **r** hand and on the big toe	3556
	14:17	and on the big toe of his **r** foot,	3556
	14:25	and put it on the lobe of the **r** ear of the one	3556
	14:25	the thumb of his **r** hand and on the big toe	3556
	14:25	and on the big toe of his **r** foot.	3556
	14:27	and with his **r** forefinger sprinkle some of	3556
	14:28	of the **r** ear of the one to be cleansed,	3556
	14:28	be cleansed, on the thumb of his **r** hand and	3556
	14:28	and on the big toe of his **r** foot.	3556
	25:29	the **r** of **redemption** a full year after its sale.	1460
	25:32	the **r** to **redeem** their houses in	1460
	25:48	he retains the **r** of **redemption**	1460
Nu	11:15	put me to death **r** now—	5528
	18:18	the wave offering and the **r** thigh are yours.	3545

Nu	20:17	the king's highway and not turn to the **r** or	3545
	22:26	either to the **r** or to the left.	3545
	22:29	I would kill you **r** now."	6964
	25: 6	to his family a Midianite woman **r** before	4200
	27: 7	"What Zelophehad's daughters are saying is **r**.	4026
	36: 5	of the descendants of Joseph is saying is **r**.	4026
Dt	2:27	we will not turn aside to the **r** or to the left.	3545
	5:32	do not turn aside to the **r** or to the left.	3545
	6:18	Do what is **r** and good in the LORD's	3838
	11: 6	the earth opened its mouth **r** in the middle	NIH
	12:25	because you will be doing what is **r** in	3838
	12:28	and **r** in the eyes of the LORD your God.	3838
	13:18	and doing what is **r** in his eyes.	3838
	17:11	to the **r** or to the left.	3545
	17:20	and turn from the law to the **r** or to the left.	3545
	21: 9	since you have done what is **r** in the eyes of	3838
	21:17	The **r** *of* the firstborn belongs to him.	5477
	28:14	to the **r** or to the left.	3545
Jos	1: 7	do not turn from it to the **r** or to the left,	3545
	4: 3	the Jordan from **r** where the priests stood	2296
	9:25	to us whatever seems good and **r** to you."	3838
	23: 6	without turning aside to the **r** or to the left.	3545
Jdg	3:16	strapped to his **r** thigh under his clothing.	3545
	3:21	the sword from his **r** thigh and plunged it	3545
	4:18	"Come, my lord, come **r** **in**.	448
	5:26	her **r** hand for the workman's hammer.	3545
	7:20	in their **r** hands the trumpets they were	3545
	11:23	what **r** have you to take it over?	NIH
	12: 6	"All **r**, say 'Shibboleth.' "	5528
	14: 3	She's the **r** one for me."	3837
	15: 3	"This time *I* **have a r to get even**	5927
	16:29	his **r** hand on the one and his left hand on	3545
Ru	4: 4	For no one **has the r to do it** except you,	1457S
1Sa	6:12	they did not turn to the **r** or to the left.	3545
	11: 2	on the condition that I gouge out the **r** eye	3545
	12: 3	I will **make** it **r**."	8740
	12:23	I will teach you the way that is good and **r**.	3838
	14:13	with his armor-bearer **r** **behind** him.	339
	14:41	the God of Israel, "Give me the **r** answer."	9459
2Sa	2:14	"All **r**, *let them* do it,"	7756S
	2:19	to the **r** nor to the left as he pursued him.	3545
	2:21	"Turn aside to the **r** or to the left;	3545
	8:15	doing what was just and **r**	7407
	14:19	no one can **turn to the r** or to the left	3554
	16: 6	and the special guard were on David's **r**	3545
	18:11	to the ground **r** **there**?	9004
	19:28	So what **r** do I have to make any more	7407
	20: 9	by the beard with his **r** hand to kiss him.	3545
	21: 4	"We **have** no **r** to demand silver or gold	4200
	21: 4	nor do we **have the r** to put anyone in Israel	4200
	23: 5	"Is not my house **r** with God?	4026
1Ki	1:25	**R** now they are eating and drinking	2180
	2:19	and she sat down at his **r** hand.	3545
	3: 9	and to distinguish between **r** and wrong.	3202
	7:49	the lampstands of pure gold (five on the **r**	3545
	8:36	Teach them the **r** way to live,	3202
	11:33	nor done what is **r** in my eyes,	3838
	11:38	in my ways and do what is **r** in my eyes	3838
	14: 8	doing only what was **r** in my eyes.	3838
	15: 5	For David had done what was **r** in the eyes	3838
	15:11	Asa did what was **r** in the eyes of	3838
	22:19	of heaven standing around him on his **r** and	3545
	22:43	he did what was **r** in the eyes of the LORD.	3838
2Ki	2: 8	The water divided *to the* **r** and to the left,	2178S
	2:14	it divided *to the* **r** and to the left,	2178S
	4:23	"It's **all r**," she said.	8934
	4:26	'Are you **all r**?	8934
	4:26	Is your husband **all r**?	8934
	4:26	Is your child **all r**?' "	8934
	4:26	"Everything is **all r**," she said.	8934
	5:21	"Is everything **all r**?	8934
	5:22	"Everything is **all r**," Gehazi answered.	8934
	7: 9	they said to each other, "We're not doing **r**.	4026
	9:11	"Is everything **all r**?	8934
	10:30	in accomplishing what is **r** in my eyes	3838
	12: 2	Joash did what was **r** in the eyes of the LORD	3838
	12: 9	on the **r** side as one enters the temple of LORD	3545
	14: 3	He did what was **r** in the eyes of the LORD,	3838
	15: 3	He did what was **r** in the eyes of the LORD,	3838
	15:34	He did what was **r** in the eyes of the LORD,	3838
	16: 2	he did not do what was **r** in the eyes of	3838
	17: 9	the LORD their God that were not **r**.	4026
	18: 3	He did what was **r** in the eyes of the LORD	3838
	22: 2	He did what was **r** in the eyes of the LORD	3838
	22: 2	not turning aside to the **r** or to the left.	3545
1Ch	6:39	who served at his **r** hand:	3545
	13: 4	because it seemed **r** to all the people.	3837
	18:14	doing what was just and **r**	7407
2Ch	6:27	Teach them the **r** way to live,	3202
	14: 2	Asa did what was good and **r** in the eyes of	3838
	18:18	with all the host of heaven standing on his **r**	3545
	20:32	he did what was **r** in the eyes of the LORD.	3838
	24: 2	Joash did what was **r** in the eyes of	3838
	25: 2	He did what was **r** in the eyes of the LORD,	3838
	26: 4	He did what was **r** in the eyes of the LORD,	3838
	26:18	"It is not **r** **for** you, Uzziah,	4200
	27: 2	He did what was **r** in the eyes of the LORD,	3838
	28: 1	he did not do what was **r** in the eyes of	3838
	29: 2	He did what was **r** in the eyes of the LORD,	3838
	30: 4	The plan seemed **r** both to the king and to	3837
	31:20	doing what was good and **r** and faithful	3838
	34: 2	not turning aside to the **r** or to the left.	3545
Ezr	10:12	with a loud voice: "You are **r**!	4026
Ne	2:20	in Jerusalem or any claim or **historic r**	2355

Ne	4:11	*we will* **be r** there among them	995
	5: 9	I continued, "What you are doing is not **r**.	3202
	8: 4	Beside him on his **r** stood Mattithiah,	3545
	9:13	and laws that are just and **r**,	622
	12:31	to proceed on top of the wall to the **r**,	3545
Est	5: 2	with favor and **thinks** *it* the **r** thing to do,	4178
	8:11	the **r** to assemble and protect themselves;	NIH
Job	8: 3	Does the Almighty pervert *what* is **r**?	7406
	27: 5	admit you are in the **r**;	7405
	30:12	On my **r** the tribe attacks;	3545
	32: 9	not only the aged who understand *what* is **r**.	5477
	33:12	"But I tell you, in this *you* *are* not **r**,	7405
	33:23	to tell a man *what* is **r** *for* him,	3841
	33:27	'I sinned, and perverted *what* was **r**,	3838
	34: 4	Let us discern for ourselves *what* is **r**;	5477
	34: 6	Although I am **r**, I am considered a liar;	5477
	40:14	to you that your own **r** hand can save you.	3545
	42: 7	you have not spoken of me *what* is **r**,	3922
	42: 8	You have not spoken of me *what* is **r**,	3922
Ps	4: 5	Offer **r** sacrifices and trust in the LORD.	7406
	9: 4	For you have upheld my **r** and my cause;	5477
	16: 8	he is at my **r** hand, I will not be shaken.	3545
	16:11	with eternal pleasures at your **r** hand.	3545
	17: 2	may your eyes see *what* is **r**.	4797
	17: 7	by your **r** hand those who take refuge	3545
	18:35	and your **r** hand sustains me;	3545
	19: 8	The precepts of the LORD are **r**,	3838
	20: 6	with the saving power of his **r** hand.	3545
	21: 8	your **r** hand will seize your foes.	3545
	25: 9	in what is **r** and teaches them his way.	5477
	26:10	whose **r** hands are full of bribes.	3545
	33: 4	For the word of the LORD is **r and true**;	3838
	44: 3	it was your **r** hand, your arm,	3545
	45: 4	let your **r** hand display awesome deeds.	3545
	45: 9	at your **r** hand is the royal bride in gold	3545
	48:10	your **r** hand is filled with righteousness.	3545
	50:16	"What **r** have you to recite my	3870+4200+4537
	51: 4	so that *you are* proved **r** when you speak	7405
	60: 5	Save us and help us with your **r** hand,	3545
	63: 8	your **r** hand upholds me.	3545
	73:23	you hold me by my **r** hand.	3545
	74:11	Why do you hold back your hand, your **r** hand?	3545
	77:10	the years of the **r** hand *of* the Most High."	3545
	78:54	to the hill country his **r** hand had taken.	3545
	80:15	the root your **r** hand has planted,	3545
	80:17	on the man at your **r** hand,	3545
	89:13	your hand is strong, your **r** hand exalted.	3545
	89:25	his **r** hand over the rivers.	3545
	89:42	You have exalted the **r** hand *of* his foes;	3545
	91: 7	ten thousand at your **r** hand,	3545
	98: 1	**r** hand and his holy arm have worked	3545
	99: 4	in Jacob you have done what is just and **r**.	7407
	106: 3	who constantly do *what* is **r**.	7407
	108: 6	Save us and help us with your **r** hand,	3545
	109: 6	let an accuser stand at his **r** hand.	3545
	109:31	he stands at the **r** hand *of* the needy one,	3545
	110: 1	at my **r** hand until I make your enemies	3545
	110: 5	The Lord is at your **r** hand;	3545
	118:15	LORD's **r** hand has done mighty things!	3545
	118:16	The LORD's **r** hand is lifted high;	3545
	118:16	the LORD's **r** hand has done mighty things!"	3545
	119:128	**consider** all your precepts **r**,	3837
	119:137	O LORD, and your laws are **r**.	3838
	119:144	Your statutes are forever **r**;	7406
	121: 5	the LORD is your shade at your **r** hand;	3545
	137: 5	may my **r** hand forget [its skill].	3545
	138: 7	with your **r** hand you save me.	3545
	139:10	your **r** hand will hold me fast.	3545
	142: 4	Look to my **r** and see;	3545
	144: 8	whose **r** hands are deceitful.	3545
	144:11	whose **r** hands are deceitful.	3545
Pr	1: 3	*doing what* is **r** and just and fair;	7406
	2: 9	Then you will understand *what* is **r** and just	7406
	3:16	Long life is in her **r** hand;	3545
	4:27	Do not swerve to the **r** or the left;	3545
	8: 6	I open my lips to speak *what* is **r**.	4797
	8: 9	To the discerning all of them are **r**;	5791
	12:15	The way of a fool seems **r** to him,	3838
	14:12	There is a way that seems **r** to a man,	3838
	16:25	There is a way that seems **r** to a man,	3838
	18:17	The first to present his case seems **r**,	7404
	20:11	by whether his conduct is pure and **r**.	3838
	21: 2	All a man's ways seem **r** to him,	3838
	21: 7	for they refuse to do *what* is **r**.	5477
	21: 7	To do *what* is **r** and just is more acceptable	7407
	23:16	when your lips speak *what* is **r**.	4797
	23:19	**keep** your heart on the **r**	886
Ecc	7:20	a righteous man on earth who does *what* is **r**	3202
	10: 2	The heart of the wise inclines to the **r**,	3545
	12:10	Teacher searched to find **just** the **r** words,	2914
SS	1: 4	*How* **r** they are to adore you!	4797
	2: 6	and his **r** arm embraces me.	3545
	8: 3	under my head and his **r** arm embraces me.	3545
Isa	1: 7	by foreigners **r before** you,	4200+5584
	1:17	learn *to* **do r**!	3512
	7:15	to reject the wrong and choose the **r**.	3202
	7:16	to reject the wrong and choose the **r**,	3202
	9:20	On the **r** they will devour,	3545
	28:26	and teaches him the **r** way.	5477
	30:10	"Give us no more visions of *what* is **r**!	5791
	30:21	Whether *you* **turn to the r** or to the left,	3554
	33:15	and speaks *what* is **r**, who rejects gain	4797
	40:14	and who taught him the **r** way?	5477
	41:10	I will uphold you with my righteous **r** hand.	3545
	41:13	of your **r** hand and says to you, Do not fear;	3545
	41:26	so we could say, 'He was **r**'?	7404

Isa	43: 9	in their witnesses *to* **prove** *they were* r,	7405
	44:20	"Is not this thing in my r hand a lie?"	3545
	45: 1	whose r hand I take hold of to subdue	3545
	45:19	I declare *what* is r.	4797
	48:13	and my r hand spread out the heavens;	3545
	51: 7	"Hear me, you who know *what* is r,	7406
	54: 3	you will spread out to the r and to the left;	3545
	56: 1	"Maintain justice and do *what* is r,	7407
	58: 2	as if they were a nation that does *what* is r	7407
	62: 8	The LORD has sworn by his r hand and	3545
	63:12	of power to be at Moses' r hand,	3545
	64: 5	to the help of those who gladly do r,	7406
Jer	8: 6	but they do not say *what* is r.	4026
	22: 3	Do what is just and r.	7407
	22:15	He did *what* was r and just,	5477
	22:24	were a signet ring on my r hand,	3545
	23: 5	and do what is just and r in the land.	3838
	26:14	with me whatever you think is good and r.	3838
	32: 7	as nearest relative it is your r and duty	5477
	32: 8	it is your r to redeem it and possess it,	5477
	33:15	he will do what is just and r in the land.	7407
	34:15	Recently you repented and did *what* is r	3838
La	2: 3	He has withdrawn his r hand at	3545
	2: 4	his r hand is ready.	3545
Eze	1:10	on the r side each had the face of a lion,	3545
	4: 6	lie down again, this time on your r side,	3556
	18: 5	righteous man who does what is just and r	7407
	18:19	Since the son has done what is just and r	7407
	18:21	and does what is just and r, he will surely	7407
	18:27	and does what is just and r, he will save	7407
	21:16	O sword, slash **to the** r, then to the left,	3554
	21:22	Into his r hand will come the lot	3545
	33:14	from his sin and does what is just and r—	7407
	33:16	He has done what is just and r;	7407
	33:19	and does what is just and r,	7407
	39: 3	make your arrows drop from your r hand.	3545
	45: 9	and oppression and do what is just and r.	7407
Da	4:27	Renounce your sins by doing *what* is r,	10610
	4:37	because everything he does is r	10643
	12: 7	lifted his r hand and his left hand	3545
Hos	14: 9	The ways of the LORD are r;	3838
Am	3:10	"They do not know how to do r,"	5791
Jnh	4: 4	"Have you any r to be angry?"	3512
	4: 9	"*Do* you **have a** r to be angry about	3512
	4:11	a hundred twenty thousand people who	
		cannot tell their r hand from their left,	3545
Mic	3: 9	who despise justice and distort all that is r;	3838
	7: 9	and establishes my r.	5477
Hab	2:16	the LORD's r hand is coming around	3545
Zec	3: 1	Satan standing at his r side to accuse him.	3545
	4: 3	the r *of* the bowl and the other on its left."	3545
	4:11	"What are these two olive trees on the r	3545
	11:17	May the sword strike his arm and his r eye!	3545
	11:17	his r eye totally blinded!"	3545
	12: 6	They will consume r and left all	3545
Mt	5:29	If your r eye causes you to sin,	1288
	5:30	And if your r hand causes you to sin,	1288
	5:39	If someone strikes you on the r cheek,	1288
	6: 3	do not let your left hand know what your r	
		hand is doing,	1288
	11:19	But wisdom **is proved** r by her actions."	1467
	15: 7	Isaiah was r when he prophesied	2822
	15:26	not r to take the children's bread and toss it	2819
	20: 4	and I will pay you whatever is r.'	1465
	20:15	Don't I **have the** r to do what I want	2003
	20:21	of these two sons of mine may sit at your r	1288
	20:23	to sit at my r or left is not for me to grant.	1288
	21: 3	and he will send them r **away."**	2317
	22:17	*Is it* r by pay taxes to Caesar or not?"	2003
	22:26	r **on down** to the seventh.	2401
	22:44	"Sit at my r hand until I put your enemies	1288
	24:33	you know that it is near, r at the door.	2093
	25:33	He will put the sheep on his r and the goats	1288
	25:34	"Then the King will say to those on his r,	1288
	26:58	r **up** to the courtyard of the high priest.	2401
	26:64	sitting at the r hand of the Mighty One	1288
	27:29	They put a staff in his r **hand** and knelt	1288
	27:38	one on his r and one on his left.	1288
Mk	5:15	sitting there, dressed and **in** *his* **r mind;**	5404
	6:25	"I want you to give me r **now** the head	1994
	7: 6	"Isaiah was r when he prophesied	2822
	7:27	not r to take the children's bread and toss it	2819
	10:37	of us sit at your r and the other at your left	1288
	10:40	to sit at my r or left is not for me to grant.	1288
	12:14	*Is it* r for us to pay taxes to Caesar or not?	2003
	12:32	"You are r in saying that God is one	237+2093
	12:36	"Sit at my r **hand** until I put your enemies	1288
	13:29	you know that it is near, r at the door.	2093
	14:54	r **into** the courtyard of the high priest.	
			1650+2276+2401
	14:62	sitting at the r **hand** of the Mighty One	1288
	15:27	one on his r and one on his left.	1288
	16: 5	in a white robe sitting on the r **side**,	1288
	16:19	into heaven and he sat at the r **hand** of God.	1288
Lk	1:11	standing at the r **side** of the altar of incense.	1288
	4:30	But he **walked** r **through** the crowd	1451
	5:19	r in front of Jesus.	NIG
	6: 6	man was there whose r hand was shriveled.	1288
	7:29	**acknowledged that** God's way *was* r,	1467
	7:35	wisdom *is proved* r by all her children."	1467
	8:35	dressed and **in** *his* **r mind;**	5404
	12:57	for yourselves what is r?	1465
	20:21	know that you speak and teach **what** is r,	3987
	20:22	*Is it* r for us to pay taxes to Caesar	2003
	20:42	Lord said to my Lord: "Sit at my r **hand**	1288
	21: 9	but the end will not come r **away."**	2311
	22:50	cutting off his r ear.	1288

Lk	22:69	be seated at the r hand of the mighty God."	1288
	22:70	He replied, "You are r in saying I am."	NIG
	23:33	one on his r, the other on his left.	1288
Jn	1:12	he gave the r to become children of God—	2026
	4:17	to her, "You are r when you say	2822
	7: 6	"The r time for me has not yet come;	2789
	7: 6	for you any time is r.	2289
	7: 8	for me the r time has not yet come."	2789
	7:24	and make a r judgment."	1465
	8:16	But if I do judge, my decisions are r,	240
	8:48	"Aren't we r in saying that you are	2822
	18:10	cutting off his r ear.	1288
	18:31	"But we **have** no r to execute anyone,"	2003
	18:37	"You are r in saying I am a king.	NIG
	21: 6	"Throw your net on the r side of the boat	1288
Ac	2:25	he is at my r **hand,** I will not be shaken.	1288
	2:33	Exalted *to* the r **hand** of God,	1288
	2:34	Lord said to my Lord: "Sit at my r **hand**	1288
	3: 7	Taking him *by* the r **hand**,	1288
	4:19	for yourselves whether it is r in God's sight	1465
	5:31	*to* his own r **hand** as Prince and Savior	1288
	6: 2	not be r for us to neglect the ministry of	744
	7:55	and Jesus standing at the r **hand** of God.	1288
	7:56	and the Son of Man standing at the r **hand**	1288
	8:21	because your heart is not r before God.	2318
	10:35	who fear him and do **what** is r.	1466
	11:11	**"R then** three men who had been sent to me	1994
	13:10	and an enemy of everything that is r!	1466
	13:10	Will you never stop perverting the r ways	2318
	25:11	no one *has for* r to hand me over to them.	1538
Ro	3: 4	that *you may be* **proved** r when you speak	1467
	5: 6	**at just the** r **time,** when we were	2789+2848
	7:21	I want to do good, evil *is* r there with me.	4154
	8:22	of childbirth r **up** to the present time.	948
	8:34	at the r **hand** of God and is also interceding	1288
	9:21	Does not the potter have the r to make out	2026
	12:17	to do what is r in the eyes of everybody.	2819
	13: 3	rulers hold no terror *for* those who do r,	19
	13: 3	do what is r and he will commend you.	19
1Co	7:35	a r *way* in undivided devotion to the Lord.	2363
	7:37	this man also does **the** r **thing.**	2822
	7:38	So then, he who marries the virgin does r,	2822
	9: 4	Don't we **have the** r to food and drink?	2026
	9: 5	the r to take a believing wife along with us,	2026
	9:12	If others have this r of support from you,	2026
	9:12	But we did not use this r.	2026
2Co	5:13	if *we are* **in** *our* **r mind,** it is for you.	5404
	6: 7	of righteousness *in the* r **hand** and in	1288
	8:21	For we are taking pains to do what is r,	2819
	13: 7	the test but that you will do what is r even	2819
Gal	2: 9	and Barnabas the r **hand** of fellowship	1288
Eph	1:20	from the dead and seated him at his r **hand**	1288
	6: 1	obey your parents in the Lord, for this is r.	1465
Php	1: 7	It is r for me to feel this way about all	1465
	4: 8	whatever is noble, whatever is r,	1465
Col	3: 1	where Christ is seated at the r **hand** of God.	1288
	4: 1	provide your slaves with what is r and fair,	1465
2Th	1: 5	that God's judgment is r,	1465
	3: 9	because we do not **have** the r to such help,	2026
	3:13	you, brothers, never tire of **doing what is** r.	2818
Heb	1: 3	he sat down at the r **hand** of the Majesty	1288
	1:13	"Sit at my r **hand** until I make your enemies	1288
	8: 1	a high priest, who sat down at the r **hand** of	1288
	10:12	he sat down at the r **hand** of God.	1288
	12: 2	sat down at the r **hand** of the throne of God.	1288
	13:10	at the tabernacle have no r to eat.	2026
Jas	2: 8	your neighbor as yourself," you are doing r.	2822
1Pe	2:14	and to commend *those* **who do** r.	18
	3: 6	You are her daughters *if you* **do what is** r	16
	3:14	But even if you should suffer for **what is** r,	1466
	3:22	into heaven and is at God's r **hand—**	1288
2Pe	1:13	I think it is r to refresh your memory	1465
1Jn	2:29	everyone who does **what is** r has been born	1466
	3: 7	He who does **what is** r is righteous,	1466
	3: 7	Anyone who does not do **what is** r is not	1466
Rev	1:16	In his r hand he held seven stars,	1288
	1:17	Then he placed his r **hand** on me and said:	1288
	1:20	the seven stars that you saw in my r **hand**	1288
	2: 1	the seven stars in his r **hand** and walks	1288
	2: 7	I will give the r to eat from the tree of life,	NIG
	3:21	the r to sit with me on my throne,	NIG
	5: 1	Then I saw in the r **hand** of him who sat on	1288
	5: 7	came and took the scroll from the r **hand**	1288
	10: 2	He planted his r foot on the sea	1288
	10: 5	and on the land raised his r **hand** to heaven.	1288
	13:16	a mark on his r hand or on his forehead,	1288
	22:11	let him who *does* r continue to do right;	1465
	22:11	let him who does right continue to do r;	1466
	22:14	the r to the tree of life and may go through	2026

RIGHT-HANDED (1) [HAND]

1Ch	12: 2	to shoot arrows or to sling stones r or	3554

RIGHTEOUS (303) [OVERRIGHTEOUS, RIGHTEOUSLY, RIGHTEOUSNESS, RIGHTEOUSNESS']

Ge	6: 9	Noah was a r man,	7404
	7: 1	I have found you r in this generation.	7404
	18:23	"Will you sweep away the r with	7404
	18:24	What if there are fifty r *people* in the city?	7404
	18:24	the place for the sake of the fifty r *people*	7404
	18:25	to kill the r with the wicked,	7404
	18:25	treating the r and the wicked alike.	7404
	18:26	I find fifty r *people* in the city of Sodom,	7404
	18:28	if the number of the r is five less than fifty?	7404

Ge	38:26	"*She is* more r than I,	7405
Ex	23: 8	and twists the words of the r.	7404
Nu	23:10	Let me die the death of the r,	3838
Dt	4: 8	so great as to have such r decrees and laws	7404
	16:19	of the wise and twists the words of the r.	7404
	24:13	be regarded as a r **act** in the sight of	7407
	33:21	he carried out the LORD's r **will,**	7407
Jdg	5:11	They recite the r **acts** *of* the LORD,	7407
	5:11	the r **acts** *of* his warriors in Israel.	7407
1Sa	12: 7	the r **acts** performed by the LORD for you	7407
	24:17	"You are more r than I," he said.	7404
1Ki	3: 6	because he was faithful to you and r	7407
Ezr	9:15	O LORD, God of Israel, you are r!	7404
Ne	9: 8	because you are r.	7404
Job	4:17	'Can a mortal *be* more r than God?	7405
	9: 2	But how *can* a mortal *be* r before God?	7405
	12: 4	though r and blameless!	7405
	15:14	or one born of woman, that *he could be* r?	7405
	17: 9	Nevertheless, the r will hold to their ways,	7404
	22: 3	the Almighty if *you were* r?	7405
	22:19	"The r see their ruin and rejoice;	7404
	22:23	How *then can* a **man** *be* r before God?	7405
	27:17	what he lays up the r will wear,	7404
	32: 1	because he was r in his own eyes.	7404
	33:26	he is restored by God to his r **state.**	7407
	35: 7	If *you are* r, what do you give to him,	7405
	36: 7	He does not take his eyes off the r;	7404
Ps	1: 5	nor sinners in the assembly of the r.	7404
	1: 6	the LORD watches over the way of the r,	7404
	4: 1	Answer me when I call you, O my r God.	7406
	5:12	For surely, O LORD, you bless the r;	7404
	7: 9	O r God, who searches minds and hearts,	7404
	7: 9	of the wicked and make the r secure.	7404
	7:11	God is a r judge,	7404
	11: 3	what can the r do?"	7404
	11: 5	The LORD examines the r,	7404
	11: 7	For the LORD is r, he loves justice;	7404
	14: 5	for God is present in the company of the r.	7404
	15: 2	and who does *what* is r,	7406
	17: 1	Hear, O LORD, my r plea;	7404
	19: 9	of the LORD are sure and altogether r.	7405
	31:18	they speak arrogantly against the r.	7404
	32:11	Rejoice in the LORD and be glad, you r;	7404
	33: 1	Sing joyfully to the LORD, you r;	7404
	34:15	the r and his ears are attentive to their cry;	7404
	34:17	The r cry out, and the LORD hears them;	NIH
	34:19	A r *man* may have many troubles,	7404
	34:21	the foes of the r will be condemned.	7404
	37:12	against the r and gnash their teeth at them;	7404
	37:16	the r have than the wealth of many wicked;	7404
	37:17	but the LORD upholds the r.	7404
	37:21	but the r give generously;	7404
	37:25	yet I have never seen the r forsaken	7404
	37:29	the r will inherit the land and dwell	7404
	37:30	The mouth of the r **man** utters wisdom,	7404
	37:32	The wicked lie in wait for the r,	7404
	37:39	The salvation of the r comes from	7404
	51:19	Then there will be r sacrifices,	7406
	52: 6	The r will see and fear;	7404
	55:22	he will never let the r fall.	7404
	58:10	The r will be glad when they are avenged,	7404
	58:11	"Surely the r still are rewarded;	7404
	64:10	the r rejoice in the LORD and take refuge	7404
	68: 3	may the r be glad and rejoice before God;	7404
	69:28	the book of life and not be listed with the r.	7404
	71:24	will tell of your r **acts** all day long,	7407
	72: 7	In his days the r will flourish;	7404
	75:10	but the horns of the r will be lifted up.	7404
	88:12	or your r **deeds** in the land of oblivion?	7407
	92:12	The r will flourish like a palm tree,	7404
	94:21	the r and condemn the innocent to death.	7404
	97:11	upon the r and joy on the upright in heart.	7404
	97:12	Rejoice in the LORD, you *who* are r,	7404
	112: 4	the gracious and compassionate and r **man.**	7404
	112: 6	a r *man* will be remembered forever.	7404
	116: 5	The LORD is gracious and r;	7404
	118:15	and victory resound in the tents of the r:	7404
	118:20	the LORD through which the r may enter.	7404
	119: 7	with an upright heart as I learn your r laws.	7406
	119:62	to give you thanks for your r laws.	7406
	119:75	I know, O LORD, that your laws are r,	7406
	119:106	that I will follow your r laws.	7406
	119:121	I have done *what* is r and just;	7406
	119:123	looking for your r promise.	7406
	119:137	**R** are you, O LORD,	7404
	119:138	The statutes you have laid down are r;	7406
	119:160	all your r laws are eternal.	7406
	119:164	a day I praise you for your r laws.	7406
	119:172	for all your commands are r.	7406
	125: 3	not remain over the land allotted to the r,	7404
	125: 3	then the r might use their hands to do evil.	7404
	129: 4	But the LORD is r;	7404
	140:13	Surely the r will praise your name and	7404
	141: 5	Let a r **man** strike me—it is a kindness;	7404
	142: 7	Then the r will gather about me because	7404
	143: 2	for no one living *is* r before you.	7405
	145:17	The LORD is r in all his ways and loving	7404
	146: 8	the LORD loves the r.	7404
Pr	2:20	of good men and keep to the paths of the r.	7404
	3:33	but he blesses the home of the r.	7404
	4:18	The path of the r is like the first gleam	7404
	9: 9	a r *man* and he will add to his learning.	7404
	10: 3	the r go hungry but he thwarts the craving	7404
	10: 6	Blessings crown the head of the r,	7404
	10: 7	The memory of the r will be a blessing,	7404
	10:11	The mouth of the r is a fountain of life,	7404
	10:16	The wages of the r bring them life,	7404

Pr	10:20	The tongue of the r is choice silver,	7404
	10:21	The lips of the r nourish many,	7404
	10:24	what the r desire will be granted.	7404
	10:25	but the r stand firm forever.	7404
	10:28	The prospect of the r is joy,	7404
	10:29	way of the LORD is a refuge for the r,	9448
	10:30	The r will never be uprooted.	7404
	10:31	The mouth of the r brings forth wisdom,	7404
	10:32	The lips of the r know what is fitting,	7404
	11: 8	The r man is rescued from trouble,	7404
	11: 9	but through knowledge the r escape.	7404
	11:10	When the r prosper, the city rejoices;	7404
	11:19	The truly r man attains life,	7407
	11:21	but those who are r will go free.	2446+7404
	11:23	The desire of the r ends only in good,	7404
	11:28	but the r will thrive like a green leaf.	7404
	11:30	The fruit of the r is a tree of life,	7404
	11:31	If the r receive their due on earth,	7404
	12: 3	but the r cannot be uprooted.	7404
	12: 5	The plans of the r are just,	7404
	12: 7	but the house of the r stands firm.	7404
	12:10	A r man cares for the needs of his animal,	7404
	12:12	but the root of the r flourishes.	7404
	12:13	but a r man escapes trouble.	7404
	12:21	No harm befalls the r,	7404
	12:26	A r man is cautious in friendship,	7404
	13: 5	The r hate what is false,	7404
	13: 9	The light of the r shines brightly,	7404
	13:21	but prosperity is the reward of the r.	7404
	13:22	but a sinner's wealth is stored up for the r.	7404
	13:25	The r eat to their hearts' content,	7404
	14:19	and the wicked at the gates of the r.	7404
	14:32	but even in death the r have a refuge.	7404
	15: 6	The house of the r contains great treasure,	7404
	15:28	The heart of the r weighs its answers,	7404
	15:29	the wicked but he hears the prayer of the r.	7404
	16:31	it is attained by a r life.	7407
	18:10	the r run to it and are safe.	7404
	20: 7	The r man leads a blameless life;	7404
	21:12	The R One takes note of the house of	7404
	21:15	it brings joy to the r but terror to evildoers.	7404
	21:18	The wicked become a ransom for the r,	7404
	21:26	but the r give without sparing.	7404
	23:24	The father of a r man has great joy;	7404
	24:15	like an outlaw against a r man's house, do	7404
	24:16	for though a r man falls seven times,	7404
	25:26	or a polluted well is a r man who gives way	7404
	28: 1	but the r are as bold as a lion.	7404
	28:12	When the r triumph, there is great elation;	7404
	28:28	but when the wicked perish, the r thrive.	7404
	29: 2	When the r thrive, the people rejoice;	7404
	29: 6	but a r one can sing and be glad.	7404
	29: 7	The r care about justice for the poor,	7404
	29:16	but the r will see their downfall.	7404
	29:27	The r detest the dishonest;	7404
Ecc	3:17	"God will bring to judgment both the r and	7404
	7:15	a r man perishing in his righteousness,	7404
	7:20	not a r man on earth who does what is right	7404
	8:14	r men who get what the wicked deserve,	7404
	8:14	wicked men who get what the r deserve.	7404
	9: 1	that the r and the wise and what they do are	7404
	9: 2	the r and the wicked, the good and the bad,	7404
Isa	3:10	Tell the r it will be well with them,	7404
	10:22	Destruction has been decreed,	
		overwhelming and r.	7407
	24:16	"Glory to the R One."	7404
	26: 2	Open the gates that the r nation may enter,	7404
	26: 7	The path of the r is level;	7404
	26: 7	you make the way of the r smooth.	7404
	41:10	I will uphold you with my r right hand.	7406
	45:21	a r God and a Savior; there is none but me.	7404
	45:25	the descendants of Israel will be found r	7405
	53:11	by his knowledge my r servant will justify	
		many,	7404
	57: 1	r perish, and no one ponders it in his heart;	7404
	57: 1	the r are taken away to be spared from evil.	7404
	60:21	be r and they will possess the land forever.	7404
	64: 6	and all our r acts are like filthy rags;	7407
Jer	3:11	"Faithless Israel is more r than unfaithful	
		Judah.	7405
	4: 2	a truthful, just and r way you swear,	7404
	12: 1	You are always r, O LORD,	7404
	20:12	you who examine the r and probe the heart	7404
	23: 5	"when I will raise up to David a r Branch,	7404
	31:23	'The LORD bless you, O r dwelling,	7406
	33:15	at that time I will make a r Branch sprout	7407
La	1:18	"The LORD is r, yet I rebelled against his	7404
	4:13	who shed within her the blood of the r.	7404
Eze	3:20	when a r man turns from his righteousness	7404
	3:20	The r things he did will not be remembered,	7407
	3:21	the r man not to sin and he does not sin,	7404
	13:22	you disheartened the r with your lies,	7404
	16:51	and have made your sisters seem r	7405
	16:52	they appear more r than you.	7405
	16:52	for you have made your sisters appear r.	7405
	18: 5	a r man who does what is just and right.	7404
	18: 9	That man is r; he will surely live,	7404
	18:20	of the r man will be credited to him,	7404
	18:22	of the r things he has done, he will live.	7407
	18:24	"But if a r man turns from his righteousness	7404
	18:24	None of the r things he had done will	7407
	18:26	If a r man turns from his righteousness	7404
	21: 3	from you both the r and the wicked.	7404
	21: 4	I am going to cut off the r and the wicked,	7404
	23:45	But r men will sentence them to	7404
	33:12	'The righteousness of the r man will	7404
	33:12	The r man, if he sins,	7404

Eze	33:13	If I tell the r man that he will surely live,	7404
	33:13	none of the r things he has done will	7407
	33:18	If a r man turns from his righteousness	7404
Da	9: 7	you are r, but this day we are covered	7404
	9:14	LORD our God is r in everything he does;	7404
	9:16	O Lord, in keeping with all your r acts,	7404
	9:18	not make requests of you because we are r,	7407
Hos	14: 9	the r walk in them,	7404
Am	2: 6	They sell the r for silver,	7404
	5:12	the r and take bribes and you deprive	7404
Mic	6: 5	you may know the r acts of the LORD."	7407
Hab	1: 4	The wicked hem in the r,	7404
	1:13	up those more r than themselves?	7404
	2: 4	but the r will live by his faith—	7404
Zep	3: 5	LORD within her is r; he does no wrong.	7404
Zec	8: 8	be my people, and I will be faithful and r	7407
	9: 9	king comes to you, r and having salvation,	7404
Mal	3:18	the distinction between the r and	7404
Mt	1:19	Because Joseph her husband was a r man	1465
	5:45	and sends rain on the r and the unrighteous.	1465
	9:13	I have not come to call the r, but sinners."	1465
	10:41	and anyone who receives a r man	1465
	10:41	because he is a r man will receive	1465
	10:41	will receive a r man's reward.	1465
	13:17	and r men longed to see what you see	1465
	13:43	the r will shine like the sun in the kingdom	1465
	13:49	and separate the wicked from the r	1465
	23:28	on the outside you appear to people as r but	1465
	23:29	and decorate the graves of the r.	1465
	23:35	And so upon you will come all the r blood	1465
	23:35	of r Abel to the blood of Zechariah son	1465
	25:37	"Then the r will answer him, 'Lord,	1465
	25:46	but the r to eternal life."	1465
Mk	2:17	I have not come to call the r, but sinners."	1465
	6:20	knowing him to be a r and holy man.	1465
Lk	1:17	the disobedient to the wisdom of the r—	1465
	2:25	who was r and devout.	1465
	5:32	I have not come to call the r,	1465
	14:14	be repaid at the resurrection of the r."	1465
	15: 7	over ninety-nine r persons who do not need	1465
	23:47	"Surely this was a r man."	1465
Jn	17:25	"R Father, though the world does	1465
Ac	3:14	and R One and asked that a murderer	1465
	7:52	the coming of the R One?	1465
	10:22	He is a r and God-fearing man,	1465
	22:14	to know his will and to see the R One and	1465
	24:15	a resurrection of both the r and the wicked.	1465
Ro	1:17	"The r will live by faith."	1465
	1:32	Although they know God's r decree	1468
	2: 5	when his r judgment will be revealed.	1464
	2:13	not those who hear the law who are r	1465
	2:13	the law who will be declared r.	1467
	3:10	"There is no one r, not even one;	1465
	3:20	be declared r in his sight by observing	1467
	5: 7	Very rarely will anyone die for a r man,	1465
	5:19	of the one man the many will be made r.	1465
	7:12	and the commandment is holy, r and good.	1465
	8: 4	that the r requirements of the law might	1468
Gal	3:11	because, "The r will live by faith."	1465
1Th	2:10	r and blameless we were among you	1469
1Ti	1: 9	not for the r but for lawbreakers and rebels,	1465
2Ti	4: 8	the r Judge, will award to me on that day—	1465
Tit	3: 5	not because of r things we had done,	1466+1877
Heb	10:38	By faith he will live by faith.	1465
	11: 4	By faith he was commended as a r man,	1465
	12:23	to the spirits of r men made perfect,	1465
Jas	1:20	not bring about the r life that God desires.	1466
	2:21	Was not our ancestor Abraham considered	
		r for what he did	1467
	2:25	the prostitute considered r for what she did	1467
	5:16	prayer of a r man is powerful and effective.	1465
1Pe	3:12	For the eyes of the Lord are on the r	1465
	3:18	the r for the unrighteous, to bring you	1465
	4:18	And, "If it is hard for the r to be saved,	1465
2Pe	2: 7	Lot, a r man, who was distressed by	1465
	2: 8	(for that r man, living among them day	1465
	2: 8	in his r soul by the lawless deeds he saw	1465
1Jn	2: 1	Jesus Christ, the R One.	1465
	2:29	If you know that he is r,	1465
	3: 7	He who does what is right is r,	1465
	3: 7	what is right is righteous, just as he is r.	1465
	3:12	and his brother's were r.	1465
Rev	15: 4	for your r acts have been revealed."	1468
	19: 8	Fine linen stands for the r acts of the saints.	1468

RIGHTEOUSLY (3) [RIGHTEOUS]

Ps	9: 4	you have sat on your throne, judging r,	7406
Isa	33:15	He who walks r and speaks what is right,	7407
Jer	11:20	you who judge r and test the heart	7406

RIGHTEOUSNESS (239) [RIGHTEOUS]

Ge	15: 6	Abram believed the LORD, and he credited	
		it to him as r.	7407
Dt	6:25	he has commanded us, that will be our r."	7407
	9: 4	of this land because of my r."	7407
	9: 5	It is not because of your r or your integrity	7407
	9: 6	it is not because of your r that	7407
	33:19	and there offer sacrifices of r;	7406
1Sa	26:23	The LORD rewards every man for his r	7407
2Sa	22:21	LORD has dealt with me according to my r;	7406
	22:25	LORD has rewarded me according to my r,	7407
	23: 3	'When one rules over men in r,	7404
1Ki	10: 9	to maintain justice and r."	7407
2Ch	9: 8	to maintain justice and r."	7407
Job	27: 6	I will maintain my r and never let go of it;	7407

Job	29:14	I put on r as my clothing;	7406
	35: 8	and your r only the sons of men.	7407
	37:23	in his justice and great r,	7407
Ps	5: 8	in your r because of my enemies—	7406
	7: 8	Judge me, O LORD, according to my r,	7406
	7:17	of his r and will sing praise to the name of	7406
	9: 8	He will judge the world in r;	7406
	17:15	And I—in r I will see your face;	7406
	18:20	LORD has dealt with me according to my r;	7406
	18:24	LORD has rewarded me according to my r,	7406
	22:31	They will proclaim his r to a people	7406
	23: 3	in paths of r for his name's sake.	7406
	31: 1	deliver me in your r.	7406
	33: 5	The LORD loves r and justice;	7406
	35:24	Vindicate me in your r, O LORD my God;	7406
	35:28	of your r and of your praises all day long.	7406
	36: 6	Your r is like the mighty mountains,	7406
	36:10	your r to the upright in heart.	7407
	37: 6	He will make your r shine like the dawn,	7406
	40: 9	I proclaim r in the great assembly;	7406
	40:10	I do not hide your r in my heart;	7407
	45: 4	in behalf of truth, humility and r;	7406
	45: 7	You love r and hate wickedness;	7406
	48:10	your right hand is filled with r.	7406
	50: 6	And the heavens proclaim his r,	7406
	51:14	and my tongue will sing of your r.	7407
	65: 5	You answer us with awesome deeds of r,	7406
	71: 2	Rescue me and deliver me in your r;	7406
	71:15	My mouth will tell of your r,	7406
	71:16	I will proclaim your r, yours alone.	7406
	71:19	Your r reaches to the skies, O God,	7406
	72: 1	O God, the royal son with your r.	7406
	72: 2	He will judge your people in r,	7406
	72: 3	the hills the fruit of r.	7406
	85:10	r and peace kiss each other.	7406
	85:11	and r looks down from heaven.	7406
	85:13	R goes before him and prepares the way	7406
	89:14	R and justice are the foundation	7406
	89:16	they exult in your r.	7406
	94:15	Judgment will again be founded on r,	7406
	96:13	the world in r and the peoples in his truth.	7406
	97: 2	r and justice are the foundation	7406
	97: 6	The heavens proclaim his r,	7406
	98: 2	and revealed his r to the nations.	7406
	98: 9	the world in r and the peoples with equity.	7406
	103: 6	The LORD works r and justice for all	7406
	103:17	and his r with their children's children—	7407
	106:31	to him as r for endless generations to come.	7407
	111: 3	and his r endures forever.	7406
	112: 3	and his r endures forever.	7406
	112: 9	his r endures forever;	7406
	118:19	Open for me the gates of r;	7406
	119:40	Preserve my life in your r.	7406
	119:142	Your r is everlasting and your law is true.	7407
	132: 9	May your priests be clothed with r;	7406
	143: 1	in your faithfulness and r come	7406
	143:11	in your r, bring me out of trouble.	7406
	145: 7	and joyfully sing of your r.	7406
Pr	8:20	I walk in the way of r,	7407
	10: 2	but r delivers from death.	7406
	11: 4	but r delivers from death.	7406
	11: 5	The r of the blameless makes a straight way	7406
	11: 6	The r of the upright delivers them,	7406
	11:18	but he who sows r reaps a sure reward.	7406
	12:28	In the way of r there is life;	7406
	13: 6	R guards the man of integrity,	7406
	14:34	R exalts a nation, but sin is a disgrace	7406
	15: 9	but he loves those who pursue r.	7406
	16: 8	a little with r than much gain with injustice.	7406
	16:12	for a throne is established through r.	7406
	21:21	He who pursues r and love finds life,	7406
	25: 5	his throne will be established through r.	7406
Ecc	7:15	a righteous man perishing in his r,	7406
Isa	1:21	r used to dwell in her—but now murderers!	7406
	1:26	Afterward you will be called the City of R,	7406
	1:27	her penitent ones with r.	7406
	5: 7	for r, but heard cries of distress.	7406
	5:16	holy God will show himself holy by his r.	7406
	9: 7	and upholding it with justice and r from	7406
	11: 4	but with r he will judge the needy,	7406
	11: 5	R will be his belt and faithfulness the sash	7406
	16: 5	and speeds the cause of r.	7406
	26: 9	the people of the world learn r.	7406
	26:10	they do not learn r;	7406
	28:17	I will make justice the measuring line and r	7406
	32: 1	a king will reign in r and rulers will rule	7406
	32:16	Justice will dwell in the desert and r live in	7407
	32:17	The fruit of r will be peace;	7406
	32:17	the effect of r will be quietness	7406
	33: 5	he will fill Zion with justice and r.	7407
	41: 2	calling him in r to his service?	7406
	42: 6	the LORD, have called you in r;	7406
	42:21	of his r to make his law great and glorious.	7406
	45: 8	"You heavens above, rain down r;	7406
	45: 8	let salvation spring up, let r grow with it;	7407
	45:13	I will raise up Cyrus in my r:	7406
	45:24	'In the LORD alone are r and strength.' "	7406
	46:12	you who are far from r.	7406
	46:13	I am bringing my r near, it is not far away;	7406
	48: 1	but not in truth or r—	7406
	48:18	your r like the waves of the sea.	7406
	51: 1	you who pursue r and who seek	7406
	51: 5	My r draws near speedily,	7406
	51: 6	my r will never fail.	7406
	51: 8	But my r will last forever,	7407
	54:14	In r you will be established:	7406
	56: 1	at hand and my r will soon be revealed.	7407

Isa	57:12	I will expose your **r** and your works,	7407
	58: 8	then your **r** will go before you,	7406
	59: 9	and **r** does not reach us.	7407
	59:14	and **r** stands at a distance;	7407
	59:16	and his own **r** sustained him.	7407
	59:17	He put on **r** as his breastplate,	7407
	60:17	peace your governor and **r** your ruler.	7407
	61: 3	They will be called oaks of **r**,	7406
	61:10	of salvation and arrayed me in a robe of **r**,	7407
	61:11	so the Sovereign LORD will make **r**	7407
	62: 1	till her **r** shines out like the dawn,	7406
	62: 2	The nations will see your **r**,	7407
	63: 1	"It is I, speaking in **r**, mighty to save."	7407
Jer	9:24	justice and **r** on earth,	7407
	23: 6	will be called: The LORD Our **R.**	7406
	33:16	will be called: The LORD Our **R.**	7406
Eze	3:20	when a righteous man turns from his **r**	7407
	14:14	they could save only themselves by their **r**,	7407
	14:20	They would save only themselves by their **r.**	7407
	18:20	The **r** of the righteous man will be credited	7407
	18:24	"But if a righteous man turns from his **r**	7407
	18:26	from his **r** and commits sin, he will die	7407
	33:12	'The **r** of the righteous man will	7407
	33:12	be allowed to live because of **his former r.'**	2023S
	33:13	but then he trusts in his **r** and does evil,	7407
	33:18	If a righteous man turns from his **r**	7407
Da	9:24	to bring in everlasting **r**,	7406
	12: 3	and *those who* **lead** many **to r**,	7405
Hos	2:19	I will betroth you in **r** and justice,	7406
	10:12	Sow for yourselves, reap the fruit	7407
	10:12	until he comes and showers **r** on you.	7406
Joel	2:23	for he has given you the autumn rains in **r**.	7407
Am	5: 7	into bitterness and cast **r** to the ground	7407
	5:24	**r** like a never-failing stream!	7407
	6:12	and the fruit of **r** into bitterness—	7407
Mic	7: 9	I will see his **r**.	7407
Zep	2: 3	Seek **r**, seek humility;	7406
Mal	3: 3	Then the LORD will have men who will	
		bring offerings in **r**,	7407
	4: 2	sun of **r** will rise with healing in its wings.	7407
Mt	3:15	it is proper for us to do this to fulfill all **r.**"	1466
	5: 6	Blessed are those who hunger and thirst	
		for **r**,	1466
	5:10	Blessed are those who are persecuted	
		because of **r**,	1466
	5:20	For I tell you that unless your **r** surpasses	1466
	6: 1	not to do your **'acts of r'** before men,	1466
	6:33	But seek first his kingdom and his **r**,	1466
	21:32	to you to show you the way of **r**,	1466
Lk	1:75	in holiness and **r** before him all our days.	1466
	18: 9	To some who were confident of their own **r**	1465
Jn	16: 8	of guilt in regard to sin and **r** and judgment;	1466
	16:10	to **r**, because I am going to the Father,	1466
Ac	24:25	As Paul discoursed on **r**, self-control	1466
Ro	1:17	For in the gospel a **r** from God is revealed,	1466
	1:17	a **r** that is by faith from first to last,	NIG
	3: 5	But if our unrighteousness brings out God's	
		r more clearly,	1466
	3:21	But now a **r** from God, apart from law,	1466
	3:22	This **r** from God comes through faith	1466
	4: 3	and it was credited to him as **r.**"	1466
	4: 5	his faith is credited as **r.**	1466
	4: 6	to whom God credits **r** apart from works:	1466
	4: 9	Abraham's faith was credited to him as **r**.	1466
	4:11	a seal of the **r** that he had by faith	1466
	4:11	in order that **r** might be credited to them.	1466
	4:13	but through the **r** that comes by faith.	1466
	4:22	This is why "it was credited to him as **r.**"	1466
	4:24	to whom God will credit **r—**	NIG
	5:17	of grace and of the gift of **r** reign in life	1466
	5:18	the result of one **act of r** was justification	1468
	5:21	so also grace might reign through **r**	1466
	6:13	of your body to him as instruments of **r**.	1466
	6:16	or to obedience, which leads to **r**?	1466
	6:18	from sin and have become slaves **to r**.	1466
	6:19	so now offer them in slavery **to r** leading	1466
	6:20	you were free *from* the control of **r**,	1466
	8:10	yet your spirit is alive because of **r**.	1466
	9:30	That the Gentiles, who did not pursue **r**,	1466
	9:30	have obtained it, a **r** that is by faith;	1466
	9:31	who pursued a law of **r**, has not attained it.	1466
	10: 3	Since they did not know the **r** that comes	1466
	10: 3	they did not submit *to* God's **r**.	1466
	10: 4	the end of the law so that there may be **r**	1466
	10: 5	Moses describes in this way the **r** that is by	1466
	10: 6	But the **r** that is by faith says:	1466
	14:17	but of **r**, peace and joy in the Holy Spirit,	1466
1Co	1:30	that is, our **r**, holiness and redemption.	1466
2Co	3: 9	more glorious is the ministry that brings **r**!	1466
	5:21	that in him we might become the **r** of God.	1466
	6: 7	with weapons of **r** in the right hand and in	1466
	6:14	what do **r** and wickedness have in common?	1466
	9: 9	his **r** endures forever."	1466
	9:10	and will enlarge the harvest of your **r**.	1466
	11:15	if his servants masquerade as servants of **r**.	1466
Gal	2:21	for if **r** could be gained through the law,	1466
	3: 6	and it was credited to him as **r.**"	1466
	3:21	**r** would certainly have come by the law.	1466
	5: 5	through the Spirit the **r** for which we hope.	1466
Eph	4:24	to be like God in true **r** and holiness.	1466
	5: 9	of the light consists in all goodness, **r**	1466
	6:14	with the breastplate of **r** in place,	1466
Php	1:11	of **r** that comes through Jesus Christ—	1466
	3: 6	as for legalistic **r**, faultless.	1466
	3: 9	a **r** of my own that comes from the law, but	1466
	3: 9	the **r** that comes from God and is by faith.	1466
1Ti	6:11	flee from all this, and pursue **r**, godliness.	1466

2Ti	2:22	Flee the evil desires of youth, and pursue **r**,	1466
	3:16	rebuking, correcting and training in **r**,	1466
	4: 8	there is in store for me the crown *of* **r**,	1466
Heb	1: 8	and **r** will be the scepter of your kingdom.	2319
	1: 9	You have loved **r** and hated wickedness;	1466
	5:13	not acquainted with the teaching *about* **r**.	1466
	7: 2	First, his name means "king of **r**";	1466
	11: 7	and became heir *of* the **r** that comes	1466
	12:11	it produces a harvest *of* **r** and peace	1466
Jas	2:23	and it was credited to him as **r**,"	1466
	3:18	who sow in peace raise a harvest of **r**.	1466
1Pe	2:24	so that we might die to sins and live *for* **r**;	1466
2Pe	1: 1	To those who through the **r** of our God	1466
	2: 5	but protected Noah, a preacher of **r**,	1466
	2:21	for them not to have known the way of **r**,	1466
	3:13	new heaven and a new earth, the home of **r**.	1466

RIGHTFUL (1) [RIGHT]
Job	8: 6	and restore you to your **r** place.	7406

RIGHTFULLY (1) [RIGHT]
Eze	21:27	until he comes to whom it **r** belongs;	5477

RIGHTLY (3) [RIGHT]
Ge	27:36	Esau said, "Isn't he **r** named Jacob?	3954
Jn	13:13	and **r** so, for that is what I am.	2822
2Th	1: 3	to thank God for you, brothers, and **r** so,	545+1639

RIGHTS (18) [RIGHT]
Ex	21: 9	he must grant her the **r** of a daughter.	5477
	21:10	food, clothing and **marital r**.	6703
Dt	21:16	*he must* not **give the r of the firstborn**	1144
1Ch	5: 1	his **r as firstborn** were given to the sons	1148
	5: 2	the **r of the firstborn** belonged	1148
Job	36: 6	but gives the afflicted their **r**.	5477
Ps	82: 3	**maintain** *the* **r** of the poor and oppressed.	7405
Pr	31: 5	and deprive all the oppressed of their **r**.	1907
	31: 8	for the **r** of all who are destitute.	1907
	31: 9	**defend** the **r** of the poor and needy."	1906
Ecc	5: 8	and justice and **r** denied,	7406
Isa	10: 2	the poor of their **r** and withhold justice	1907
Jer	5:28	they do not defend the **r** of the poor.	5477
La	3:35	to deny a man his **r** before the Most High,	5477
1Co	9:15	But I have not used any of these **r**.	NIG
	9:18	so not make use of my **r** in preaching it.	2026
Gal	4: 5	that we might receive the **full r of sons**.	5625
Heb	12:16	sold his **inheritance r** as the oldest son.	4757

RIGID (1)
Mk	9:18	gnashes his teeth and **becomes r**.	3830

RIGOUR (KJV) See RUTHLESSLY

RIM (24) [RIMS]
Ex	25:25	around it a **r** a handbreadth wide and put	4995
	25:25	and put a gold molding on the **r**.	4995
	25:27	to the **r** to hold the poles used in carrying	4995
	37:12	also made around it a **r** a handbreadth wide	4995
	37:12	and put a gold molding on the **r**.	4995
	37:14	to the **r** to hold the poles used in carrying	4995
Dt	2:36	From Aroer on the **r** of the Arnon Gorge,	8557
	4:48	This land extended from Aroer on the **r** of	8557
Jos	12: 2	from Aroer on the **r** of the Arnon Gorge—	8557
	13: 9	from Aroer on the **r** of the Arnon Gorge,	8557
	13:16	from Aroer on the **r** of the Arnon Gorge,	8557
1Ki	7:23	measuring ten cubits from **r** to rim	8557
	7:23	measuring ten cubits from rim to **r**	8557
	7:24	Below the **r**, gourds encircled it—	8557
	7:26	and its **r** was like the rim of a cup,	8557
	7:26	and its rim was like the **r** *of* a cup,	8557
2Ch	4: 2	measuring ten cubits from **r** to rim	8557
	4: 2	measuring ten cubits from rim to **r**	8557
	4: 3	Below **the r**, figures of bulls encircled it—	2257S
	4: 5	and its **r** was like the rim of a cup,	8557
	4: 5	and its rim was like the **r** *of* a cup,	8557
Eze	43:13	with a **r** of one span around the edge.	1473
	43:17	with a **r** of half a cubit and a gutter of—	1473
	43:20	of the upper ledge and all around the **r**,	1473

RIMMON (13) [EN RIMMON, GATH RIMMON, HADAD RIMMON, RIMMON PEREZ]
Jos	15:32	Lebaoth, Shilhim, Ain and **R—**	8234
	19: 7	**R**, Ether and Ashan—	8234
	19:13	it came out at **R** and turned toward Neah.	8234
Jdg	20:45	and fled toward the desert to the rock of **R**,	8234
	20:47	and fled into the desert to the rock of **R**,	8234
	21:13	of peace to the Benjamites at the rock of **R**.	8234
2Sa	4: 2	they were sons of **R** the Beerothite from	8233
	4: 5	the sons of **R** the Beerothite,	8233
	4: 9	the sons of **R** the Beerothite,	8233
2Ki	5:18	When my master enters the temple of **R**	8235
	5:18	when I bow down in the temple of **R**,	8235
1Ch	4:32	Ain, **R**, Token and Ashan—	8234
Zec	14:10	The whole land, from Geba to **R**,	8234

RIMMON PEREZ (2) [PEREZ, RIMMON]
Nu	33:19	They left Rithmah and camped at **R**.	8236
	33:20	They left **R** and camped at Libnah.	8236

RIMMONO (1)
1Ch	6:77	**R** and Tabor, together with their	8237

RIMS (3) [RIM]
1Ki	7:33	**r**, spokes and hubs were all of cast metal.	1461
Eze	1:18	Their **r** were high and awesome,	1461
	1:18	and all four **r** were full of eyes all around.	1461

RING (23) [RANG, RINGED, RINGS]
Ge	24:22	the man took out a gold **nose r** weighing	5690
	24:30	As soon as he had seen the **nose r**,	5690
	24:47	the **r** in her nose and the bracelets	5690
	41:42	Then Pharaoh took his **signet r**	3192
Ex	26:24	and fitted into a single **r**;	3192
	27: 4	a bronze **r** at each of the four corners of	3192
	36:29	to the top and fitted into a single **r**;	3192
Jdg	8:25	each man threw a **r** *from* his plunder onto it.	5690
Est	3:10	So the king took his **signet r** from his finger	3192
	3:12	and sealed with his own **r**.	3192
	8: 2	The king took off his **signet r**,	3192
	8: 8	and seal it with the king's **signet r—**	3192
	8: 8	the king's name and sealed with his **r** can	3192
	8:10	the dispatches with the king's **signet r**,	3192
Job	16:16	deep shadows **r** my eyes;	6584
	42:11	a piece of silver and a gold **r**.	5690
Pr	11:22	Like a gold **r** in a pig's snout is	5690
Jer	22:24	were a **signet r** on my right hand,	2597
Eze	16:12	and I put a **r** in your nose,	5690
Da	6:17	and the king sealed it with his own **signet r**	10536
Hag	2:23	'and I will make you like my **signet r**,	2597
Lk	15:22	Put a **r** on his finger and sandals on his feet.	1234
Jas	2: 2	into your meeting **wearing a gold r**	5993

RINGED (1) [RING]
Job	41:14	**r** about *with* his fearsome teeth?	6017

RINGLEADER (1) [LEAD]
Ac	24: 5	He is a **r** of the Nazarene sect	4756

RINGS (42) [RING]
Ge	35: 4	the foreign gods they had and the **r** in their	5690
Ex	25:12	Cast four gold **r** for it and fasten them	3192
	25:12	with two **r** on one side and two rings on	3192
	25:12	with two rings on one side and two **r** on	3192
	25:14	the poles into the **r** on the sides of the chest	3192
	25:15	The poles are to remain in the **r** of this ark;	3192
	25:26	Make four gold **r** for the table	3192
	25:27	The **r** are to be close to the rim to hold	3192
	26:29	and make gold **r** to hold the crossbars.	3192
	27: 7	into the **r** so they will be on two sides of	3192
	28:23	Make two gold **r** for it and fasten them	3192
	28:24	the two gold chains to the **r** at the corners	3192
	28:26	Make two gold **r** and attach them to	3192
	28:27	Make two more gold **r** and attach them to	3192
	28:28	The **r** of the breastpiece are to be tied to	3192
	28:28	be tied to the **r** of the ephod with blue cord,	3192
	30: 4	Make two gold **r** for the altar below	3192
	35:22	brooches, earrings, **r** and ornaments.	3192
	36:34	and made gold **r** to hold the crossbars.	3192
	37: 3	He cast four gold **r** for it and fastened them	3192
	37: 3	with two **r** on one side and two rings on	3192
	37: 3	with two rings on one side and two **r** on	3192
	37: 5	into the **r** on the sides of the ark to carry it.	3192
	37:13	They cast four gold **r** for the table	3192
	37:14	The **r** were put close to the rim to hold	3192
	37:27	They made two gold **r** below	3192
	38: 5	They cast bronze **r** to hold the poles for	3192
	38: 7	into the **r** so they would be on the sides of	3192
	39:16	gold filigree settings and two gold **r**,	3192
	39:16	and fastened the **r** to two of the corners of	3192
	39:17	They fastened the two gold chains to the **r**	3192
	39:19	They made two gold **r** and attached them to	3192
	39:20	Then they made two more gold **r**	3192
	39:21	the **r** of the breastpiece to the rings of	3192
	39:21	of the breastpiece to the **r** of the ephod	3192
Nu	31:50	armlets, bracelets, **signet r**,	3192
Jdg	8:26	The weight of the gold **r** he asked for came	5690
Est	1: 6	and purple material to silver **r**	1664
Isa	3:21	the **signet r** and nose rings,	3192
	3:21	the signet rings and nose **r**,	5690
Da	6:17	with his own signet ring and with the **r**	10536
Hos	2:13	she decked herself with **r** and jewelry,	5690

RINGSTRAKED (KJV) See STREAKED

RINNAH (1)
1Ch	4:20	Amnon, **R**, Ben-Hanan and Tilon.	8263

RINSED (3) [RINSING]
Lev	6:28	the pot is to be scoured and **r** with water.	8851
	15:12	any wooden article *is to* **be r** with water.	8851
2Ch	4: 6	to be used for the burnt offerings *were*, **r**,	1866

RINSING (1) [RINSED]
Lev	15:11	a discharge touches without **r** his hands	8851

RIOT (3) [RIOTERS, RIOTING, RIOTS]
Mt	26: 5	"or there may be a **r** among the people."	2573
Mk	14: 2	they said, "or the people *may* **r**."	1639+2573
Ac	17: 5	formed a mob and **started** a **r** in the city.	2572

RIOTERS (1) [RIOT]

Ac	21:32	When **the** r saw the commander and	1254+3836ˢ

RIOTING (1) [RIOT]

Ac	19:40	in danger of being charged with r because	5087

RIOTS (2) [RIOT]

Ac	24: 5	stirring up r among the Jews all over the world.	5087
2Co	6: 5	in beatings, imprisonments and r;	189

RIP (3) [RIPPED]

2Ki	8:12	and r open their pregnant women."	1324
Ps	7: 2	like a lion and r me **to pieces** with no one	7293
Hos	13: 8	attack them and r them **open.**	4213+6033+7973

RIPE (13) [RIPEN, RIPENED, RIPENING, RIPENS]

Nu	13:20	(It was the season for the **first** r grapes.)	1137
2Ki	4:42	from the **first** r **grain,**	1137
Isa	28: 4	will be like a **fig** r before harvest—	1136
Joel	3:13	Swing the sickle, for the harvest *is* r.	1418
Am	8: 1	a basket of r **fruit.**	7811
	8: 2	"A basket of r **fruit,"** I answered.	7811
	8: 2	"The **time is** r for my people Israel;	995+7891
Na	3:12	like fig trees with their **first** r **fruit;**	1137
Zec	8: 4	and women **of** r old **age** will sit in	2418
Mk	4:29	As soon as the grain *is* r,	4140
Jn	4:35	They are r for harvest.	3328
Rev	14:15	for the harvest of the earth *is* r."	3830
	14:18	because its grapes *are* r."	196

RIPEN (2) [RIPE]

Ex	9:32	were not destroyed, because they r later.)	689
Jer	24: 2	like those that r **early;**	1136

RIPENED (3) [RIPE]

Ge	40:10	it blossomed, and its clusters r *into* grapes.	1418
Isa	16: 9	The shouts of joy over your r **fruit** and	7811
Jer	48:32	The destroyer has fallen on your r **fruit**	7811

RIPENING (1) [RIPE]

Isa	18: 5	and the flower becomes a r grape,	1694

RIPENS (1) [RIPE]

Hos	2: 9	I will take away my grain when it r,	6961

RIPHATH (2)

Ge	10: 3	Ashkenaz, **R** and Togarmah.	8196
1Ch	1: 6	Ashkenaz, **R** and Togarmah.	8196

RIPPED (3) [RIP]

2Ki	15:16	and r open all the pregnant women.	1324
Hos	13:16	their pregnant women r **open."**	1324
Am	1:13	Because he r **open** the pregnant women	1324

RISE (119) [ARISE, ARISEN, ARISES, AROSE, RAISE, RAISED, RAISES, RAISING, RISEN, RISES, RISING, ROSE, UPRAISED, UPRISING]

Lev	19:32	" **'R** in the presence of the aged,	7756
Nu	10:35	Moses said, **"R up,** O LORD!	7756
	23:24	The people r like a lioness;	7756
	24:17	a scepter *will* r out of Israel.	7756
Dt	28: 7	that the enemies who r up against you will	7756
	28:43	The alien who lives among you *will* r	6590
	32:38	Let them r up to help you!	7756
	33:11	the loins of *those who* r up *against* him;	7756
	33:11	strike his foes till *they* r no more."	7756
Jos	8: 7	*to* r up from ambush and take the city.	7756
Jdg	20:40	column of smoke began to r from the city,	6590
1Sa	9:13	Then the LORD said, **"R** and anoint him;	7756
2Sa	18:32	the king and all who r up to harm you be	7756
	22:39	and *they* could not r;	7756
Ezr	10: 4	**R up;** this matter is in your hands.	7756
Job	14:12	so man lies down and *does* not r;	7756
	20:27	the earth *will* r up against him.	7756
	24:12	The **groans** of the dying r from the city,	AIT
	25: 3	Upon whom *does* his light not r?	7756
Ps	3: 1	How many r up against me!	7756
	7: 6	r up against the rage of my enemies;	5951
	17: 1	it does not r from deceitful lips.	NIH
	17:13	**R up,** O LORD, confront them,	7756
	18:38	I crushed them so that they could not r;	7756
	20: 8	but we r up and stand firm.	7756
	27:12	for false witnesses r up against me,	7756
	32: 6	mighty waters r, they will not reach him.	8852
	35:23	Awake, and r to my defense!	7810
	36:12	thrown down, not able to r!	7756
	44:26	**R up** and help us;	7756
	59: 1	protect me from *those who* r up *against* me.	7756
	66: 7	*let* not the rebellious r up against him.	8123
	74:22	**R up,** O God, and defend your cause;	7756
	82: 8	**R up,** O God, judge the earth,	7756
	88:10	*Do* those who are dead r up and praise you?	7756
	94: 2	**R up,** O Judge of the earth;	5951
	94:16	Who *will* r up for me against the wicked?	7756
	119:62	At midnight *I* r to give you thanks	7756
Ps	119:147	*I* r before dawn and cry for help;	7709
	127: 2	In vain you r early and stay up late,	7756
	135: 7	He **makes** clouds r from the ends of the earth;	6590
	139: 2	You know when I sit and *when* I r;	7756
	139: 9	If *I* r on the wings of the dawn,	5951
	139:21	and abhor *those who* r up *against* you?	7756
	140:10	into miry pits, never *to* r.	7756
Pr	28:12	the wicked r to **power,** men go into hiding.	7756
	28:28	wicked r **to power,** people go into hiding;	7756
Ecc	12: 4	when *men* r up at the sound of birds,	7756
Isa	3: 5	The young *will* r up against the old,	8104
	5:11	to *those who* r **early** in the morning to run	8899
	14: 9	it makes them r from their thrones—	7756
	14:21	to r to inherit the land and cover the earth	7756
	14:22	"I **will** r up against them,"	7756
	24:20	that it falls—never *to* r again.	7756
	26:14	those departed spirits *do* not r.	7756
	26:19	your dead will live; their bodies *will* r.	7756
	28:21	The LORD *will* r up as he did	7756
	31: 2	He *will* r up against the house of	7756
	32: 9	r up and listen to me;	7756
	33: 3	when you r up, the nations scatter.	8129
	34:10	its smoke *will* r forever.	6590
	43:17	and they lay there, never *to* r *again,*	7756
	49: 7	"Kings will see you and r up,	7756
	51:17	**R up,** O Jerusalem, you who have drunk	7756
	52: 2	r up, sit enthroned, O Jerusalem.	7756
	58:10	then your light *will* r in the darkness,	2436
Jer	10:13	he **makes** clouds r from the ends of the earth.	6590
	25:27	and vomit, and fall *to* r no more because of	7756
	46: 8	She says, '*I* will r and cover the earth;	6590
	49:14	**R up** for battle!"	7756
	51:16	he **makes** clouds r from the ends of the earth.	6590
	51:42	The sea will r over Babylon;	6590
	51:64	'So will Babylon sink *to* r no more	7756
Eze	1:20	and the wheels *would* r along with them,	5951
	10:16	when the cherubim spread their wings *to* r	8123
	17:14	brought low, unable *to* r **again,**	5951
Da	2:39	"After you, another kingdom *will* r,	10624
	2:39	*that will* r from the earth.	10624
	11:14	"In those times many *will* r against	6641
	11:23	with only a few people *he will* r to power.	6590
	11:31	"His armed forces *will* r up to desecrate	6641
	12:13	and then at the end of the days *you will* r	6641
Hos	10:14	of battle *will* r against your people, so	7756
Joel	2:20	And its stench will go up; its smell *will* r."	6590
Am	5: 2	never *to* r again, deserted in her own land,	7756
	7: 9	with my sword *I will* r against the house	7756
	8: 8	The whole land *will* r like the Nile;	6590
	8:14	they will fall, never *to* r again."	7756
Ob	1: 1	"**R,** and let us go against her for battle"—	7756
Mic	4:13	"**R** and thresh, O Daughter of Zion,	7756
	7: 8	Though I have fallen, *I* **will** r.	7756
Mal	4: 2	the sun of righteousness *will* r with healing	2436
Mt	5:45	**causes** his sun **to** r on the evil and the good	422
	12:42	Queen of the South *will* r at the judgment	1586
	24: 7	Nation *will* r against nation,	1586
	26:46	**R,** let us go! Here comes my betrayer!"	1586
	27:63	'After three days *I* will r **again.'**	1586
Mk	8:31	be killed and after three days r **again.**	482
	9:31	and after three days *he will* r."	482
	10:34	Three days later *he will* r."	482
	12:25	When the dead r, they will neither marry	482
	13: 8	Nation *will* r against nation,	1586
	14:42	**R!** Let us go! Here comes my betrayer!"	1586
Lk	11:31	of the South *will* r at the judgment with	1586
	17:19	Then he said to him, **"R** and go;	482
	18:33	On the third day *he will* r **again."**	482
	20:37	even Moses showed that the dead r,	1586
	21:10	"Nation *will* r against nation,	1586
	24:38	and why *do* doubts r in your minds?	326
	24:46	The Christ will suffer and r from the dead	482
Jn	5:29	those who have done good will r to live,	414
	5:29	to live, and those who have done evil will r	414
	11:23	"Your brother *will* r **again."**	482
	11:24	"I know *he will* r **again** in the resurrection	482
	20: 9	from Scripture that Jesus had *to* r from	482
Ac	17: 3	that the Christ had to suffer and r from	414
	26:23	as the first to r from the dead,	414
Eph	5:14	"Wake up, O sleeper, r from the dead,	482
1Th	4:16	and the dead in Christ *will* r first.	482

RISEN (16) [RISE]

Ge	19:23	the sun *had* r over the land.	3655
Dt	34:10	no prophet *has* r in Israel like Moses,	7756
2Sa	14: 7	Now the whole clan *has* r up	7756
Eze	47: 5	the water *had* r and was deep enough	1448
Mic	2: 8	Lately my people *have* r up like an enemy.	7756
Mt	11:11	not *anyone greater* than John the Baptist;	1586
	14: 2	He is not here; he *has* r from the dead!	1586
	26:32	But after I *have* r, I will go ahead of you	1586
	28: 6	He is not here; *he has* r, just as he said.	1586
	28: 7	'*He has* r from the dead and is going ahead	1586
Mk	9: 9	until the Son of Man *had* r from the dead.	482
	14:28	But after I *have* r, I will go ahead of you	1586
	16: 6	He *has* r! He is not here.	1586
	16: 6	those who had seen him *after* he had r.	1586
Lk	24: 6	He is not here; *he has* r!	1586
	24:34	Lord *has* r and has appeared to Simon."	1586

RISES (33) [RISE]

Jos	11:17	from Mount Halak, which r *toward* Seir,	6590

Jos	12: 7	to Mount Halak, which r *toward* Seir	6590
Jdg	5:31	be like the sun *when it* r in its strength."	3655
Job	16: 8	my gauntness r up and testifies against me.	7756
	24:14	murderer r up and kills the poor and needy;	7756
	41:25	When he r up, the mighty are terrified;	8420
Ps	19: 6	It r at one end of the heavens	4604
	74:23	of your enemies, *which* r continually.	6590
	104:22	The sun r, and they steal away;	2436
Pr	24:16	*he* r again, but the wicked are brought down	7756
Ecc	1: 5	The sun r and the sun sets,	2436
	1: 5	and hurries back to where it r.	2436
	3:21	the spirit of man r upward and if the spirit	6590
	10: 4	If a ruler's anger r against you,	6590
Isa	2:19	when he r to shake the earth.	7756
	2:21	when he r to shake the earth.	7756
	3:13	*he* r to judge the people.	6641
	30:18	*he* r to show you compassion.	8123
	60: 1	and the glory of the LORD r upon you.	2436
	60: 2	the LORD r upon you	2436
Jer	46: 7	"Who is this *that* r like the Nile,	6590
	46: 8	Egypt r like the Nile,	6590
	48:34	"The sound of their cry r from Heshbon	5989
	51: 9	*it* r as **high** as the clouds.'	5951
Hos	6: 3	As surely as the **sun** r, he will appear;	8840
	7: 4	from the kneading of the dough till it r.	2806
Am	9: 5	the whole land r like the Nile,	6590
Mic	7: 6	a daughter r up against her mother,	7756
Lk	16:31	not be convinced even if someone r from	482
Eph	2:21	and r to become a holy temple in the Lord.	889
Jas	1:11	the sun r with scorching heat and withers	422
2Pe	1:19	until the day dawns and the morning star r	422
Rev	14:11	smoke of their torment r for ever and ever.	326

RISING (20) [RISE]

Ge	19:28	and he saw dense smoke r from the land,	6590
Jos	8:20	and saw the smoke of the city r against	6590
1Ki	18:44	"A cloud as small as a man's hand *is* r	6590
Ps	50: 1	the earth from the r *of* the sun to the place	4667
	113: 3	the r *of* the sun to the place where it sets,	4667
Isa	13:10	The r sun will be darkened and	3655
	30:28	like a rushing torrent, r up to the neck.	2936
	41:25	one from the r sun who calls on my name.	4667
	45: 6	so that from the r *of* the sun to the place	4667
	59:19	and from the r *of* the sun,	4667
Jer	25:32	a mighty storm *is* r from the ends of	6424
	47: 2	"See how the waters *are* r in the north;	6590
Eze	8:11	and a fragrant cloud of incense *was* r.	6590
Mal	1:11	from the r to the setting of the sun.	4667
Mk	9:10	discussing what "r from the dead" meant.	482
	12:26	Now about the dead r—have you not read	1586
Lk	1:78	the r **sun** will come to us from heaven	424
	2:34	to cause the falling and r of many in Israel,	414
	12:54	"When you see a cloud r in the west,	422
Rev	14:20	r as high as the horses' bridles for	NIG

RISK (4) [RISKED, RISKING]

2Sa	17:17	for *they* could not r being seen entering	3523
	23:17	not the blood of men who went **at the** r **of**	928
1Ch	11:19	of these men who went **at the** r **of**	928
La	5: 9	We get our bread **at the** r **of** our lives	928

RISKED (5) [RISK]

Jdg	5:18	The people of Zebulun r their very lives;	3070+4200+4637
	9:17	r his life to rescue you from the hand of Midian	4946+5584+8959
1Ch	11:19	Because they r their lives to bring it back,	928
Ac	15:26	men *who have* r their lives for the name	4140
Ro	16: 4	They r their **lives** for me.	5549+5719

RISKING (1) [RISK]

Php	2:30	r his life to make up for the help you could	4129

RISSAH (2)

Nu	33:21	They left Libnah and camped at **R.**	8267
	33:22	They left **R** and camped at Kehelathah.	8267

RITES (1)

Ac	21:24	Take these men, join in their **purification** r	49

RITHMAH (2)

Nu	33:18	They left Hazeroth and camped at **R.**	8414
	33:19	They left **R** and camped at Rimmon Perez.	8414

RIVAL (4) [RIVALRY]

Lev	18:18	" 'Do not take your wife's sister as a r **wife**	7675
1Sa	1: 6	her r kept provoking her in order	7651
	1: 7	her r provoked her till she wept and would	NIH
Eze	31: 8	cedars in the garden of God *could* not r it,	6669

RIVALRY (1) [RIVAL]

Php	1:15	that some preach Christ out of envy and r,	2251

RIVER (109) [RIVERBANK, RIVERBED, RIVERS]

Ge	2:10	A r watering the garden flowed from Eden;	5643
	2:13	The name of the second r is the Gihon;	5643
	2:14	The name of the third r is the Tigris;	5643
	2:14	And the fourth r is the Euphrates.	5643
	15:18	from the r *of* Egypt to the great river,	5643

Ge	15:18	from the river of Egypt to the great r,	5643
	31:21	he fled with all he had, and crossing the R,	5643
	36:37	from Rehoboth on the r succeeded him	5643
	41: 2	out of the r there came up seven cows,	3284
	41:18	out of the r there came up seven cows,	3284
Ex	2: 5	were walking along the r bank.	3284
	4: 9	the r will become blood on the ground."	3284
	7:18	in the Nile will die, and the r will stink;	3284
	7:21	and the r smelled so bad that	3284
	7:24	they could not drink the water of the r.	3284
	23:31	and from the desert to the R.	5643
Nu	22: 5	who was at Pethor, near the R,	5643
	24: 6	like gardens beside a r,	5643
Dt	1: 7	as far as the great r, the Euphrates.	5643
	3:16	the border) and out to the Jabbok R,	5707
	11:24	from the Euphrates R to the western sea.	5643
Jos	1: 2	to cross the Jordan R into the land I am	NIH
	1: 4	and from the great r, the Euphrates—	5643
	2:23	forded the r and came to Joshua son of Nun	NIH
	3: 8	go and stand in the r.' "	3720
	4:18	the priests came up out of the r carrying the ark of the covenant	3720
	12: 2	to the Jabbok R, which is the border	5707
	13: 3	from the Shihor R on the east of Egypt to	NIH
	24: 2	of Abraham and Nahor, lived beyond the R	5643
	24: 3	from the land beyond the R and led him	5643
	24:14	beyond the R and in Egypt,	5643
	24:15	beyond the R, or the gods of the Amorites,	5643
Jdg	4: 7	and his troops to the Kishon R and give him	5707
	4:13	from Harosheth Haggoyim to the Kishon R.	5707
	5:21	The r Kishon swept them away,	5707
	5:21	the age-old r, the river Kishon.	5707
	5:21	the age-old river, the r Kishon.	5707
2Sa	8: 3	to restore his control along the Euphrates R.	5643
	10:16	Arameans brought from beyond the R;	5643
	17:21	"Set out and cross the r at once;	4784
1Ki	4:21	from the R to the land of the Philistines,	5643
	4:24	over all the kingdoms west of the R,	5643
	14:15	and scatter them beyond the R,	5643
2Ki	17: 6	the Habor R and in the towns of the Medes,	5643
	18:11	on the Habor R and in towns of the Medes.	5643
	23:29	of Egypt went up to the Euphrates R to help	5643
	24: 7	from the Wadi of Egypt to the Euphrates R.	5643
1Ch	1:48	from Rehoboth on the r succeeded him	5643
	5: 9	the desert that extends to the Euphrates R,	5643
	5:26	Habor, Hara and the r of Gozan,	5643
	13: 5	the Shihor R in Egypt to Lebo Hamath,	NIH
	18: 3	establish his control along the Euphrates R	5643
	19:16	Arameans brought from beyond the R,	5643
2Ch	9:26	over all the kings from the R to the land of	5643
Job	40:23	When the r rages, he is not alarmed;	5643
Ps	36: 8	you give them drink from your r of delights.	5707
	46: 4	There is a r whose streams make glad the city of God,	5643
	72: 8	He will rule from sea to sea and from the R	5643
	80:11	its shoots as far as the R.	5643
	83: 9	you did to Sisera and Jabin at the r Kishon,	5707
	105:41	like a r it flowed in the desert.	5643
Isa	7:20	a razor hired from beyond the R—	5643
	8: 7	the mighty floodwaters of the R—	5643
	11:15	sweep his hand over the Euphrates R.	5643
	19: 5	The waters of the r will dry up,	3542
	19: 7	at the mouth of the r.	3284
	48:18	your peace would have been like a r,	5643
	66:12	"I will extend peace to her like a r,	5643
Jer	2:18	to Assyria to drink water from the R?	5643
	46: 2	the Euphrates R by Nebuchadnezzar king	5643
	46: 6	the north by the R Euphrates they stumble	5643
	46:10	in the land of the north by the R Euphrates.	5643
	51:32	the r crossings seized,	5045
La	2:18	let your tears flow like a r day and night;	5707
Eze	1: 1	I was among the exiles by the Kebar R,	5643
	1: 3	the Kebar R in the land of the Babylonians.	5643
	3:15	at Tel Abib near the Kebar R.	5643
	3:23	like the glory I had seen by the Kebar R,	5643
	10:15	creatures I had seen by the Kebar R.	5643
	10:20	the God of Israel by the Kebar R,	5643
	10:22	as those I had seen by the Kebar R.	5643
	43: 3	like the visions I had seen by the Kebar R,	5643
	47: 5	but now it was a r that I could not cross,	5707
	47: 5	a r that no one could cross.	5707
	47: 6	Then he led me back to the bank of the r.	5707
	47: 7	of trees on each side of the r.	5707
	47: 9	creatures will live wherever the r flows.	5707
	47: 9	so where the r flows everything will live.	5707
	47:12	on both banks of the r.	5707
Da	7:10	A r of fire was flowing,	10468
	10: 4	I was standing on the bank of the great r,	5643
	12: 5	of the r and one on the opposite bank.	3284
	12: 6	who was above the waters of the r,	3284
	12: 7	who was above the waters of the r,	3284
Am	5:24	But let justice roll on like a r,	4784
	8: 8	it will be stirred up and then sink like the r	3284
	9: 5	then sinks like the r of Egypt—	3284
Na	2: 6	The r gates are thrown open and	5643
	3: 8	The r was her defense, the waters her wall.	3542
Zec	9:10	from sea to sea and from the R to the ends	5643
Mt	3: 6	they were baptized by him in the Jordan R.	4532
Mk	1: 5	they were baptized by him in the Jordan R.	4532
Ac	16:13	the city gate to the r,	4532
Rev	9:14	at the great r Euphrates."	4532
	12:15	the serpent spewed water like a r,	4532
	12:16	by opening its mouth and swallowing the r	4532
	16:12	angel poured out his bowl on the great r Euphrates,	4532
	22: 1	angel showed me the r of the water of life,	4532
	22: 2	On each side of the r stood the tree of life,	4532

RIVERBANK (1) [RIVER]

Ge	41: 3	and stood beside those on the r.	3284+8557

RIVERBED (2) [RIVER]

Job	14:11	the sea or a r becomes parched and dry,	5643
Isa	19: 5	and the r will be parched and dry.	5643

RIVERS (29) [RIVER]

2Ki	5:12	Abana and Pharpar, the r of Damascus,	5643
Job	20:17	the r flowing with honey and cream.	5643+5707
	28:11	of the r and brings hidden things to light.	5643
Ps	74:15	you dried up the ever flowing r.	5643
	78:16	and made water flow down like r.	5643
	78:44	He turned their r to blood;	3284
	89:25	his right hand over the r.	5643
	98: 8	Let the r clap their hands,	5643
	107:33	He turned r into a desert,	5643
	137: 1	By the r of Babylon we sat and wept	5643
SS	8: 7	r cannot wash it away.	5643
Isa	18: 1	to the land of whirring wings along the r	5643
	18: 2	whose land is divided by r.	5643
	18: 7	whose land is divided by r.	5643
	33:21	be like a place of broad r and streams.	5643
	41:18	I will make r flow on barren heights,	5643
	42:15	I will turn r into islands and dry up	5643
	43: 2	and when you pass through the r,	5643
	50: 2	I turn r into a desert;	5643
Jer	46: 7	like r of surging waters?	5643
	46: 8	like r of surging waters.	5643
Mic	6: 7	with ten thousand r of oil?	5707
Na	1: 4	he makes all the r run dry.	5643
Hab	3: 8	Were you angry with the r, O LORD?	5643
	3: 9	You split the earth with r;	5643
Zep	3:10	From beyond the r of Cush my worshipers,	5643
2Co	11:26	I have been in danger from r,	4532
Rev	8:10	fell from the sky on a third of the r and on	4532
	16: 4	on the r and springs of water,	4532

RIZIA (1)

1Ch	7:39	The sons of Ulla: Arah, Hanniel and R.	8359

RIZPAH (4)

2Sa	3: 7	a concubine named R daughter of Aiah.	8366
	21: 8	the two sons of Aiah's daughter R,	8366
	21:10	R daughter of Aiah took sackcloth	8366
	21:11	David was told what Aiah's daughter R,	8366

ROAD (98) [CROSSROADS, ROADS, ROADSIDE]

Ge	16: 7	the spring that is beside the r to Shur.	2006
	24:48	on the right r to get the granddaughter	2006
	38:14	which is on the r to Timnah.	2006
	38:21	the shrine prostitute who was beside the r	2006
	48: 7	So I buried her there beside the r	2006
Ex	13:17	God did not lead them on the r through	2006
	13:18	around by the desert r toward the Red Sea.	2006
Nu	20:19	"We will go along the main r,	5019
	21: 1	heard that Israel was coming along the r	2006
	21:33	Then they turned and went up along the r	2006
	22:22	of the LORD stood in the r to oppose him.	2006
	22:23	the angel of the LORD standing in the r	2006
	22:23	she turned off the r into a field.	2006
	22:23	Balaam beat her to get her back on the r.	2006
	22:31	the angel of the LORD standing in the r	2006
	22:34	I did not realize you were standing in the r	2006
Dt	1: 2	to Kadesh Barnea by the Mount Seir r.)	2006
	2: 8	We turned from the Arabah r,	2006
	2: 8	and traveled along the desert r of Moab.	2006
	2:27	We will stay on the main r;	2006+2006
	3: 1	Next we turned and went up along the r	2006
	6: 7	at home and when you walk along the r,	2006
	11:19	at home and when you walk along the r,	2006
	11:30	west of the r, toward the setting sun,	2006
	22: 4	or his ox fallen on the r,	2006
	22: 6	you come across a bird's nest beside the r,	2006
	27:18	man who leads the blind astray on the r."	2006
Jos	2: 7	in pursuit of the spies on the r that leads to	2006
	2:22	the pursuers had searched all along the r	2006
	10:10	the r going up to Beth Horon and cut them	2006
	10:11	on the r down from Beth Horon	4618
Jdg	5:10	and you who walk along the r,	2006
	21:19	of the r that goes from Bethel to Shechem,	5019
Ru	1: 7	the r that would take them back to the land	2006
1Sa	4:13	on his chair by the side of the r,	2006
	6:12	keeping on the r and lowing all the way;	5019
	17:52	along the Shaaraim r to Gath and Ekron.	2006
	26: 3	Saul made his camp beside the r on the hill	2006
2Sa	13:34	and saw many people on the r west of him,	2006
	15: 2	by the side of the r leading to the city gate.	2006
	16:13	along the r while Shimei was going along	2006
	20:12	in his blood in the middle of the r,	5019
	20:12	from the r into a field and threw a garment	5019
	20:13	After Amasa had been removed from the r,	2006
1Ki	13:10	So he took another r and did not return by	2006
	13:12	And his sons showed him which r the man	2006
	13:24	a lion met him on the r and killed him,	2006
	13:24	and his body was thrown down on the r,	2006
	13:28	and found the body thrown down on the r,	2006
	20:38	the prophet went and stood by the r waiting	2006
	22:24	As he was walking along the r,	2006
2Ki	6:19	"This is not the r and this is not the city.	2006
	7:15	and they found the whole r strewn with	2006
	9:27	he fled up the r to Beth Haggan.	2006

2Ki	12:20	on the r down to Silla.	3718
	18:17	on the r to the Washerman's Field.	5019
1Ch	26:16	and the Shalleketh Gate on the upper r fell	5019
	26:18	there were four at the r and two at	5019
Ezr	8:22	to protect us from enemies on the r,	2006
Job	30:13	They break up my r;	5986
Pr	26:13	The sluggard says, "There is a lion in the r,	2006
Ecc	10: 3	Even as he walks along the r,	2006
Isa	7: 3	on the r to the Washerman's Field.	5019
	15: 5	on the r to Horonaim they lament their destruction.	2006
	36: 2	on the r to the Washerman's Field.	5019
	51:10	who made a r in the depths of the sea	2006
	57:14	"Build up, build up, prepare the r!	2006
Jer	31:21	"Set up r signs; put up guideposts.	7483
	31:21	the highway, the r that you take.	2006
	48: 5	on the r down to Horonaim anguished cries	4618
	48:19	Stand by the r and watch,	2006
Eze	21:19	Make a signpost where the r branches off	2006
	21:20	Mark out one r for the sword to come	2006
	21:21	of Babylon will stop at the fork in the r,	2006
	21:21	the Hethlon r past Lebo Hamath to Zedad,	2006
	47:15	the Hethlon r to Lebo Hamath;	2006
	48: 1	the Hethlon r to Lebo Hamath;	2006
Hos	6: 9	they murder on the r to Shechem,	2006
Na	2: 1	Guard the fortress, watch the r,	2006
Mt	7:13	and broad is the r that leads to destruction,	3847
	7:14	the gate and narrow the r that leads to life,	3847
	21: 8	on the r, while others cut branches from	3847
	21: 8	from the trees and spread them on the r.	3847
	21:19	Seeing a fig tree by the r,	3847
Mk	9:33	"What were you arguing about on the r?"	3847
	10:52	and followed Jesus along the r.	3847
	11: 8	Many people spread their cloaks on the r,	3847
Lk	9:57	As they were walking along the r,	3847
	10: 4	and do not greet anyone on the r.	3847
	10:31	to be going down the same r,	3847
	19:36	people spread their cloaks on the r.	3847
	19:37	near the place where the r goes down	2853
	24:32	while he talked with us on the r and opened	3847
Ac	8:26	"Go south to the r—the desert road—	3847
	8:26	to the road—the desert—	NIG
	8:36	As they traveled along the r,	3847
	9:17	to you on the r as you were coming here—	3847
	19: 1	Paul took the r through the interior	1451
	26:13	About noon, O king, as I was on the r,	3847

ROADS (17) [ROAD]

Lev	26:22	few in number that your r will be deserted.	2006
Dt	19: 3	Build r to them and divide into three parts	2006
Jdg	5: 6	in the days of Jael, the r were abandoned;	784
	20:31	in the open field and on the r—	5019
	20:32	and draw them away from the city to the r."	5019
	20:45	down five thousand men along the r.	5019
Isa	33: 8	no travelers are on the r.	784
	49: 9	the r and find pasture on every barren hill.	2006
	49:11	I will turn all my mountains into r,	2006
	59: 8	They have turned them into crooked r;	5986
Jer	6:25	Do not go out to the fields or walk on the r,	2006
	18:15	They made them walk in bypaths and on r	2006
La	1: 4	The r to Zion mourn,	2006
Eze	21:19	mark out two r for the sword of the king	2006
	21:21	at the junction of the two r,	2006
Lk	3: 5	The crooked r shall become straight,	NIG
	14:23	'Go out to the r and country lanes	3847

ROADSIDE (6) [ROAD]

Ge	38:16	he went over to her by the r and said,	2006
	49:17	Dan will be a serpent by the r,	2006
Jer	3: 2	By the r you sat waiting for lovers,	2006
Mt	20:30	Two blind men were sitting by the r,	3847
Mk	10:46	was sitting by the r begging.	3847
Lk	18:35	a blind man was sitting by the r begging.	3847

ROAM (4) [ROAMED, ROAMING]

Jdg	11:37	to r the hills and weep with my friends,	2143+2256+3718
Isa	8:21	they will r through the land;	6296
Jer	2:31	Why do my people say, 'We are free to r;	8113
	50: 6	and caused them to r on the mountains.	8740

ROAMED (2) [ROAM]

1Sa	30:31	where David and his men had r.	2143
Job	30: 3	they r the parched land in desolate	6908

ROAMING (3) [ROAM]

Job	1: 7	"From r through the earth and going back	8763
	2: 2	"From r through the earth and going back	8763
Pr	26:13	a fierce lion r the streets!'	NIH

ROAR (38) [ROARED, ROARING, ROARS]

Job	4:10	The lions may r and growl,	8614
	37: 2	Listen to the r of his voice,	8075
	37: 4	After that comes the sound of his r;	8613
Ps	42: 7	to deep in the r of your waterfalls;	7754
	46: 3	though its waters r and foam and	2159
	104:21	The lions r for their prey	8613
Pr	19:12	A king's rage is like the r of a lion,	5638
	20: 2	A king's wrath is like the r of a lion;	5638
Isa	5:29	Their r is like that of the lion,	8614
	5:29	they r like young lions;	8613
	5:30	that day they will r over it like the roaring	5637
	17:12	they r like the roaring of great waters!	8616
	17:13	peoples r like the roar of surging waters,	8616

Isa	17:13	peoples roar like the **r** of surging waters,	8623
	51:15	who churns up the sea so that its waves **r**—	2159
Jer	5:22	they may **r**, but they cannot cross it.	2159
	10:13	he thunders, the waters in the heavens **r**;	2162
	11:16	with the **r** of a mighty storm he will set it	7754
	25:30	" 'The LORD will **r** from on high;	8613
	25:30	from his holy dwelling and **r** **mightily**	8613+8613
	31:35	who stirs up the sea so that its waves **r**—	2159
	51:16	he thunders, the waters in the heavens **r**;	2162
	51:38	Her *people* all **r** like young lions,	8613
	51:55	the **r** of their voices will resound.	8623
Eze	1:24	like the **r** of rushing waters,	7754
	19: 9	so his **r** was heard no longer on	7754
	43: 2	His voice was like the **r** of rushing waters,	7754
Hos	10:14	the **r** of battle will rise against your people,	8623
	11:10	he will **r** like a lion.	8613
Joel	3:16	The LORD will **r** from Zion and thunder	8613
Am	3: 4	a lion **r** in the thicket when he has no prey?	8613
Zec	9:15	They will drink and **r** as with wine;	2159
	11: 3	Listen to the **r** of the lions;	8614
2Pe	3:10	The heavens will disappear **with a r;**	4853
Rev	10: 3	he gave a loud shout like the **r** of a lion.	3681
	14: 2	And I heard a sound from heaven like the **r**	5889
	19: 1	I heard what sounded like the **r** of a	3489+5889
	19: 6	the **r** of rushing waters and like loud peals	5889

ROARED (4) [ROAR]

Ps	74: 4	Your foes **r** in the place where you met	8613
Jer	2:15	Lions *have* **r**; they have growled at him.	8613
Am	3: 8	The lion *has* **r**—who will not fear?	8613
Hab	3:10	the deep **r** and lifted its waves on high.	5989+7754

ROARING (15) [ROAR]

Jdg	14: 5	suddenly a young lion came **r** toward him.	8613
Ps	22:13	**R** lions tearing their prey open their mouths	8613
	65: 7	who stilled the **r** of the seas,	8623
	65: 7	the **r** of their waves,	8623
Pr	28:15	Like a **r** lion or a charging bear is	5637
Isa	5:30	that day they will roar over it like the **r** of	5639
	17:12	they roar like the **r** of great waters!	8623
Jer	6:23	like the **r** sea as they ride on their horses;	2159
	50:42	like the **r** sea as they ride on their horses;	2159
	51:42	its **r** waves will cover her.	2162
Eze	19: 7	in it were terrified by his **r**.	7754+8614
	22:25	within her like a **r** lion tearing its prey;	8613
Zep	3: 3	Her officials are **r** lions,	8613
Lk	21:25	and perplexity at the **r** and tossing of	2492
1Pe	5: 8	like a **r** lion looking for someone to devour.	6054

ROARS (3) [ROAR]

Jer	12: 8	She **r** at me; therefore I hate her.	928+5989+7754
Hos	11:10	When he **r**, his children will come trembling	8613
Am	1: 2	"The LORD **r** from Zion and thunders	8613

ROAST (4) [ROASTED, ROASTS]

Ex	12: 9	but **r** it *over* the fire—	7507
Dt	16: 7	**R** it and eat it at the place	1418
1Sa	2:15	"Give the priest some meat to **r**;	7499
Pr	12:27	The lazy man *does* not **r** his game,	3047

ROASTED (10) [ROAST]

Ex	12: 8	That same night they are to eat the meat **r**	7507
Lev	2:14	offer crushed heads of new grain **r** in	7828
	23:14	not eat any bread, or **r** or new grain,	7833
Jos	5:11	unleavened bread and **r** **grain**.	7828
Ru	2:14	he offered her *some* **r** **grain**.	7833
1Sa	17:17	of **r** **grain** and these ten loaves of bread	7833
	25:18	five dressed sheep, five seahs of **r** **grain**,	7833
2Sa	17:28	flour and **r** **grain**, beans and lentils,	7833
2Ch	35:13	*They* **r** the Passover animals over the fire	1418
Isa	44:19	*I* **r** meat and I ate.	7499

ROASTS (1) [ROAST]

Isa	44:16	he **r** his meat and eats his fill.	7499

ROB (12) [ROBBED, ROBBER, ROBBERS, ROBBERY, ROBBING, ROBS]

Lev	19:13	" 'Do not defraud your neighbor or **r** him.	1608
	26:22	**r** you **of** your **children**,	8897
Jdg	9:25	to ambush and **r** everyone who passed by,	1608
	14:15	Did you invite us here to **r** us?"	3769
Ps	35:10	the poor and needy from *those who* **r** them."	1608
Hos	7: 1	bandits in the streets;	7320
Mal	3: 8	"Will a man **r** God? Yet you rob me.	7693
	3: 8	"Will a man rob God? Yet you **r** me.	7693
	3: 8	"But you ask, 'How do we **r** you?'	7693
Mt	12:29	Then *he can* **r** his house.	1395
Mk	3:27	Then *he can* **r** his house.	1395
Ro	2:22	You who abhor idols, *do you* **r** **temples**?	2644

ROBBED (15) [ROB]

Dt	28:29	day after day you will be oppressed and **r**,	1608
2Sa	17: 8	and as fierce as a wild bear **r** of her **cubs**.	8891
Ps	7: 4	with or without cause *have* **r** my foe—	2740
Pr	4:16	they are **r** of slumber till they make someone fall.	1608
	17:12	a bear **r** of her cubs than a fool in his folly.	8891
Isa	38:10	of death and be **r** of the rest of my years?"	7212
Jer	21:12	of his oppressor the *one who has* been **r**,	1608
	22: 3	of his oppressor the *one who has* been **r**,	1608
Eze	18:18	**r** his brother and did what was wrong	1608+1609

Hos	13: 8	Like a bear **r** of her cubs,	8891
Mk	9:17	by a spirit that has **r** him of speech.	228
Ac	19:27	will *be* **r** of her divine majesty.	2747
	19:37	though they have neither **r** temples	2645
2Co	11: 8	*I* **r** other churches by receiving support	5195
1Ti	6: 5	who *have* been **r** of the truth and who think	691

ROBBER (1) [ROB]

Jn	10: 1	in by some other way, is a thief and a **r**.	3334

ROBBERS (13) [ROB]

Jer	7:11	become a den of **r** to you?	7265
Eze	7:22	**r** will enter it and desecrate it.	7265
Ob	1: 5	"If thieves came to you, if **r** *in* the night—	8720
Mt	21:13	but you are making it a 'den of **r**.' "	3334
	27:38	Two **r** were crucified with him,	3334
	27:44	In the same way the **r** who were crucified	3334
Mk	11:17	But you have made it 'a den of **r**.' "	3334
	15:27	They crucified two **r** with him,	3334
Lk	10:30	when he fell into the hands of **r**.	3334
	10:36	to the man who fell into the hands of **r**?"	3334
	18:11	**r**, evildoers, adulterers—	774
	19:46	but you have made it 'a den of **r**.' "	3334
Jn	10: 8	before me were thieves and **r**,	3334

ROBBERY (5) [ROB]

Isa	61: 8	I hate **r** and iniquity.	1610
Eze	18: 7	*He does* not **commit** **r** but gives	1608+1611
	18:12	*He* **commits** **r**.	1608+1611
	18:16	*He does* not **commit** **r** but gives	1608+1611
	22:29	practice extortion and **commit** **r**;	1608+1610

ROBBING (2) [ROB]

Isa	10: 2	widows their prey and **r** the fatherless.	1024
Mal	3: 9	because you *are* **r** me.	7693

ROBE (61) [ROBED, ROBES]

Ge	37: 3	and he made a richly ornamented **r** for him.	4189
	37:23	they stripped him of his **r**—	4189
	37:23	the richly ornamented **r** he was wearing—	4189
	37:31	Then they got Joseph's **r**,	4189
	37:31	slaughtered a goat and dipped the **r** in	4189
	37:32	the ornamented **r** back to their father	4189
	37:32	Examine it to see whether it is your son's **r**.	4189
	37:33	"It is my son's **r**!	4189
Ex	28: 4	a breastpiece, an ephod, a **r**, a woven tunic,	5077
	28:31	the **r** of the ephod entirely of blue cloth,	5077
	28:33	and scarlet yarn around the hem of the **r**,	2257S
	28:34	to alternate around the hem of the **r**.	5077
	29: 5	the tunic, the **r** of the ephod,	5077
	39:22	the **r** of the ephod entirely of blue cloth—	5077
	39:23	with an opening in the center of the **r** like	5077
	39:24	around the hem of the **r**,	5077
	39:26	the hem of the **r** to be worn for ministering,	5077
Lev	8: 7	clothed him with the **r** and put the ephod	5077
Jos	7:21	in the plunder a beautiful **r** *from* Babylonia,	168
	7:24	took Achan son of Zerah, the silver, the **r**,	168
1Sa	2:19	a little **r** and took it to him when she went	5077
	15:27	Saul caught hold of the hem of his **r**,	5077
	18: 4	the **r** he was wearing and gave it to David,	5077
	24: 4	and cut off a corner of Saul's **r**.	5077
	24: 5	for having cut off a corner of his **r**.	889S
	24:11	look at this piece of your **r** in my hand!	5077
	24:11	the corner of your **r** but did not kill you.	5077
	28:14	"An old man wearing a **r** is coming up,"	5077
2Sa	13:18	She was wearing a richly ornamented **r**,	4189
	13:19	and tore the ornamented **r** she was wearing.	4189
	15:32	his **r** torn and dust on his head.	4189
1Ch	15:27	David was clothed in a **r** of fine linen,	5077
Ne	5:13	also shook out the **folds of** my **r** and said,	2950
Est	6: 8	have them bring a royal **r** the king has worn	4230
	6: 9	Then let the **r** and horse be entrusted to one	4230
	6: 9	*Let them* **r** the man the king delights	4252
	6:10	"Get the **r** and the horse and do just	4230
	6:11	So Haman got the **r** and the horse.	4230
	8:15	a large crown of gold and a purple **r**	9423
Job	1:20	got up and tore his **r** and shaved his head.	5077
	29:14	justice was my **r** and my turban.	5077
SS	5: 3	I have taken off my **r**—	4189
Isa	6: 1	and the **train** of his **r** filled the temple.	8767
	22:21	with your **r** and fasten your sash	4189
	61:10	and arrayed me in a **r** of righteousness,	5077
Mic	2: 8	the rich **r** from those who pass by without	8515
Zec	8:23	of one Jew by the **hem of** his **r** and say,	4053
Mt	27:28	They stripped him and put a scarlet **r**	5948
	27:31	they took off the **r** and put his own clothes	5948
Mk	15:17	They put a **purple** **r** on him,	4525
	15:20	the **purple** **r** and put his own clothes	4525
	16: 5	a young man dressed in a white **r** sitting on	5124
Lk	15:22	Bring the best **r** and put it on him.	5124
	23:11	Dressing him in an elegant **r**,	2264
Jn	19: 2	They clothed him in a purple **r**	2668
	19: 5	the crown of thorns and the purple **r**,	2668
Heb	1:12	You will roll them up like a **r**;	4316
Rev	1:13	a **r** **reaching down to** his **feet**	4468
	6:11	Then each of them was given a white **r**,	5124
	19:13	He is dressed in a **r** dipped in blood,	2668
	19:16	On his **r** and on his thigh he has this name	2668

ROBED (5) [ROBE]

Est	6:11	*He* **r** Mordecai, and led him on horseback	4252
Ps	93: 1	The LORD **reigns**, *he is* **r** in majesty;	4252
	93: 1	the LORD *is* **r** in majesty and is armed	4252

Isa	63: 1	Who is this, **r** in splendor,	4230
Rev	10: 1	*He was* **r** in a cloud,	4314

ROBES (41) [ROBE]

Ge	41:42	He dressed him in **r** of fine linen and put	955
	49:11	his **r** in the blood of grapes.	6078
1Sa	19:24	He stripped off his **r** and also prophesied	955
1Ki	10: 5	the attending servants in their **r**,	4860
	10:25	articles of silver and gold, **r**,	8515
	22:10	Dressed in their royal **r**, the king of Israel	955
	22:30	but you wear your royal **r**."	955
2Ki	5: 7	he tore his **r** and said, "Am I God?	955
	5: 8	that the king of Israel had torn his **r**,	955
	5: 8	"Why have you torn your **r**?	955
	6:30	king heard the woman's words, he tore his **r**.	955
	10:22	"Bring **r** for all the ministers of Baal."	4230
	10:22	So he brought out **r** for them.	4860
	11:14	Then Athaliah tore her **r** and called out,	955
	22:11	the Book of the Law, he tore his **r**.	955
	22:19	you tore your **r** and wept in my presence,	955
2Ch	9: 4	the attending servants in their **r**,	4860
	9: 4	in their **r** and the burnt offerings he made at	4860
	9:24	articles of silver and gold, and **r**,	8515
	18: 9	Dressed in their royal **r**,	955
	18:29	but you wear your royal **r**."	955
	23:13	Athaliah tore her **r** and shouted, "Treason!	955
	34:19	heard the words of the Law, he tore his **r**.	955
	34:27	and tore your **r** and wept in my presence,	955
Est	5: 1	Esther **put on** *her* royal **r** and stood	4252
Job	2:12	and they tore their **r** and sprinkled dust	5077
Ps	45: 8	All your **r** are fragrant with myrrh	955
	133: 2	down upon the collar of his **r**.	4496
Isa	3:22	the **fine r** and the capes and cloaks,	4711
Eze	26:16	from their thrones and lay aside their **r**	5077
Da	3:21	So these men, wearing their **r**, trousers,	10517
	3:27	their **r** were not scorched,	10517
Jnh	3: 6	rose from his throne, took off his **royal r**,	168
Mk	12:38	They like to walk around in **flowing r** and	5124
Lk	20:46	around in **flowing r** and love to be greeted	5124
Ac	9:39	and showing the **r** and other clothing	5945
	12:21	Herod, wearing his royal **r**,	2264
Rev	7: 9	They were wearing white **r** and	5124
	7:13	"These in white **r**—who are they,	5124
	7:14	they have washed their **r** and made them	5124
	22:14	"Blessed are those who wash their **r**,	5124

ROBOAM (KJV) See REHOBOAM

ROBS (2) [ROB]

Pr	19:26	*He who* **r** his father and drives out his	8720
	28:24	*He who* **r** his father or mother and says,	1608

ROCK (117) [ROCKS, ROCKY]

Ge	49:24	because of the Shepherd, the **R** of Israel,	74
Ex	17: 6	I will stand there before you by the **r**	7446
	17: 6	Strike the **r**, and water will come out of it	7446
	33:21	near me where you may stand on a **r**.	7446
	33:22	a cleft in the **r** and cover you with my hand	7446
Nu	20: 8	Speak to that **r** before their eyes	6152
	20: 8	You will bring water out of the **r** for	6152
	20:10	in front of the **r** and Moses said to them,	6152
	20:10	must we bring you water out of this **r**?"	6152
	20:11	and struck the **r** twice with his staff.	6152
	24:21	your nest is set in a **r**;	6152
Dt	8:15	He brought you water out of hard **r**.	7446
	32: 4	He is the **R**, his works are perfect,	7446
	32:13	He nourished him with honey from the **r**,	6152
	32:15	and rejected the **R** his Savior.	7446
	32:18	You deserted the **R**, who fathered you;	7446
	32:30	unless their **R** had sold them,	7446
	32:31	For their **r** is not like our Rock,	7446
	32:31	For their rock is not like our **R**,	7446
	32:37	are their gods, the **r** they took refuge in,	7446
Jdg	6:20	place them on this **r**,	6152
	6:21	Fire flared from the **r**,	7446
	7:25	They killed Oreb at the **r** of Oreb,	7446
	13:19	and sacrificed it on a **r** to the LORD.	7446
	15: 8	down and stayed in a cave in the **r** of Etam.	6152
	15:11	down to the cave in the **r** of Etam and said	6152
	15:13	and led him up from the **r**.	6152
	20:45	toward the desert to the **r** of Rimmon,	6152
	20:47	into the desert to the **r** of Rimmon,	6152
	21:13	an offer of peace to the Benjamites at the **r**	6152
1Sa	2: 2	there is no **R** like our God.	7446
	6:14	and there it stopped beside a large **r**.	74
	6:15	and placed them on the large **r**.	74
	6:18	The large **r**, on which they set the ark of	74
	23:25	to the **r** and stayed in the Desert of Maon.	6152
2Sa	20: 8	While they were at the great **r** in Gibeon,	74
	21:10	and spread it out for herself on a **r**.	7446
	22: 2	He said: "The LORD is my **r**,	6152
	22: 3	my God is my **r**, in whom I take refuge,	7446
	22:32	And who is the **R** except our God?	7446
	22:47	Praise be to my **R**!	7446
	22:47	Exalted be God, the **R**, my Savior!	7446
	23: 3	the **R** of Israel said to me:	7446
1Ch	11:15	to David to the **r** at the cave of Adullam,	7446
Ne	9:15	in their thirst you brought them water from the **r**;	6152
Job	14:18	as a **r** is moved from its place,	7446
	19:24	or engraved in **r** forever!	7446
	28: 9	the **flinty r** and lays bare the roots of	2734
	28:10	He tunnels through the **r**;	7446
	29: 6	the **r** poured out for me streams of olive oil.	7446

Jer	41:24	His chest is hard as **r**,	74
Ps	18: 2	The LORD is my **r**, my fortress and	6152
	18: 2	my God is my **r**, in whom I take refuge.	7446
	18:31	And who is the **R** except our God?	7446
	18:46	Praise be to my **R**!	7446
	19:14	O LORD, my **R** and my Redeemer.	7446
	27: 5	of his tabernacle and set me high upon a **r**.	7446
	28: 1	To you I call, O LORD my **R**;	7446
	31: 2	be my **r** *of* refuge, a strong fortress	7446
	31: 3	Since you are my **r** and my fortress,	6152
	40: 2	on a **r** and gave me a firm place to stand.	6152
	42: 9	I say to God my **R**,	6152
	61: 2	lead me to the **r** that is higher than I.	7446
	62: 2	He alone is my **r** and my salvation;	7446
	62: 6	He alone is my **r** and my salvation;	7446
	62: 7	he is my mighty **r**, my refuge.	7446
	71: 3	Be my **r** *of* refuge, to which I can always go	7446
	71: 3	for you are my **r** and my fortress.	6152
	78:20	When he struck the **r**, water gushed out,	7446
	78:35	They remembered that God was their **R**,	7446
	81:16	with honey from the **r** I would satisfy you."	7446
	89:26	my God, the **R** my Savior.	7446
	92:15	The LORD is upright; he is my **R**,	7446
	94:22	and my God the **r** *in* whom I take refuge.	7446
	95: 1	let us shout aloud to the **R** of our salvation.	7446
	105:41	He opened the **r**, and water gushed out;	7446
	114: 8	who turned the **r** into a pool,	7446
	114: 8	the **hard r** into springs of water.	2734
	144: 1	Praise be to the LORD my **R**,	7446
Pr	30:19	the way of a snake on a **r**,	7446
SS	2:14	My dove in the clefts of the **r**,	6152
Isa	8:14	a stone that causes men to stumble and a **r**	7446
	10:26	he struck down Midian at the **r** of Oreb;	7446
	17:10	you have not remembered the **R**,	7446
	22:16	and chiseling your resting place in the **r**?	6152
	26: 4	the LORD, is the **R** eternal.	7446
	30:29	of the LORD, to the **R** of Israel.	7446
	32: 2	in the desert and the shadow of a great **r** in	6152
	44: 8	No, there is no other **R**; I know not one."	7446
	48:21	he made water flow for them from the **r**;	7446
	48:21	he split the **r** and water gushed out.	7446
	51: 1	Look to the **r** *from which* you were cut and	7446
Jer	23:29	like a hammer that breaks a **r** in pieces?	6152
	51:26	No **r** will be taken from you for	74
Eze	24: 7	She poured it on the bare **r**;	6152
	24: 8	I put her blood on the bare **r**,	6152
	26: 4	and make her a bare **r**.	6152
	26:14	I will make you a bare **r**,	6152
Da	2:34	While you were watching, a **r** was cut out,	10006
	2:35	But the **r** that struck the statue became	10006
	2:45	the meaning of the vision of the **r** cut out of	10006
	2:45	a **r** that broke the iron, the bronze, the clay,	NIH
Hab	1:12	O **R**, you have ordained them to punish.	7446
Zec	12: 3	I will make Jerusalem an immovable **r**.	74
Mt	7:24	a wise man who built his house on the **r**.	4376
	7:25	because it had its foundation on the **r**.	4376
	16:18	and on this **r** I will build my church,	4376
	27:60	that he had cut out of the **r**.	4376
Mk	15:46	and placed it in a tomb **cut out** *of* **r**.	4376
Lk	6:48	down deep and laid the foundation on **r**.	4376
	8: 6	Some fell on **r**, and when it came up,	4376
	8:13	on the **r** are the ones who receive the word	4376
	23:53	and placed it in a tomb **cut in the r**,	3292
Ro	9:33	a stone that causes men to stumble and a **r**	4376
1Co	10: 4	from the spiritual **r** that accompanied them,	4376
	10: 4	and that **r** was Christ.	4376
1Pe	2: 8	to stumble and a **r** that makes them fall."	4376

ROCKS (31) [ROCK]

Dt	8: 9	the **r** are iron and you can dig copper out of	74
Jos	7:26	they heaped up a large pile of **r**,	74
	8:29	And they raised a large pile of **r** over it,	74
	10:18	"Roll large **r** up to the mouth of the cave,	74
	10:27	the mouth of the cave they placed large **r**,	74
1Sa	13: 6	they hid in caves and thickets, among the **r**,	6152
2Sa	18:17	in the forest and piled up a large heap of **r**	74
1Ki	19:11	the mountains apart and shattered the **r**	6152
Job	8:17	around a **pile of r** and looks for a place	1643
	18: 4	Or must the **r** be moved from their place?	7446
	22:24	your gold of Ophir to the **r** in the ravines,	7446
	24: 8	by mountain rains and hug the **r** for lack	7446
	28: 6	sapphires come from its **r**,	74
	30: 6	among the **r** and in holes in the ground.	4091
Ps	78:15	the **r** in the desert and gave them water	7446
	137: 9	and dashes them against the **r**.	6152
Isa	2:10	Go into the **r**, hide in the ground	7446
	2:19	the **r** and to holes in the ground from dread	7446
	2:21	They will flee to caverns in the **r** and to	7446
	7:19	and in the crevices in the **r**,	6152
Jer	4:29	some climb up among the **r**.	4091
	13: 4	and hide it there in a crevice in the **r**."	6152
	16:16	and hill and from the crevices of the **r**,	6152
	48:28	and dwell among the **r**,	6152
	49:16	you who live in the clefts of the **r**,	6152
Ob	1: 3	the clefts of the **r** and make your home on	6152
Na	1: 6	the **r** are shattered before him.	7446
Mt	27:51	The earth shook and the **r** split.	4376
Ac	27:29	that we would be dashed against the **r**,	5536+5550
Rev	6:15	in caves and among the **r** of the mountains.	4376
	6:16	They called *to* the mountains and the **r**,	4376

ROCKY (10) [ROCK]

Nu	23: 9	From the **r** peaks I see them,	7446
Job	39:28	a **r** crag is his stronghold.	6152
Ps	78:16	of a **r** **crag** and made water flow down	6152

Jer	18:14	of Lebanon ever vanish from its **r** slopes?	7446
	21:13	above this valley on the **r** plateau, declares	7446
Am	6:12	Do horses run on the **r** crags?	6152
Mt	13: 5	Some fell on **r** places,	*4378*
	13:20	on **r** places is the man who hears the word	*4378*
Mk	4: 5	Some fell on **r** places,	*4378*
	4:16	Others, like seed sown on **r** places,	*4378*

ROD (51) [RODS]

Ex	21:20	with a **r** and the slave dies as a direct result,	8657
Lev	27:32	that passes under the **shepherd's r—**	8657
1Sa	17: 7	His spear shaft was like a weaver's **r**,	4962
2Sa	7:14	I will punish him with the **r** *of* men,	8657
	23:21	a spear with a shaft like a weaver's **r**.	4962
1Ch	11:23	the Egyptian had a spear like a weaver's **r**	4962
	20: 5	a spear with a shaft like a weaver's **r**.	4962
Job	9:34	someone to remove God's **r** from me,	8657
	21: 9	the **r** *of* God is not upon them.	8657
Ps	23: 4	your **r** and your staff, they comfort me.	8657
	89:32	with the **r**, their iniquity with flogging;	8657
Pr	10:13	but a **r** is for the back of him who lacks judgment,	8657
	13:24	He who spares the **r** hates his son,	8657
	14: 3	A fool's talk brings a **r** to his back,	2643
	22: 8	and the **r** of his fury will be destroyed.	8657
	22:15	**r** of discipline will drive it far from him.	8657
	23:13	you punish him with the **r**, he will not die.	8657
	23:14	with the **r** and save his soul from death.	8657
	26: 3	and a **r** for the backs of fools!	8657
	29:15	The **r** of correction imparts wisdom,	8657
Isa	9: 4	the **r** of their oppressor.	8657
	10: 5	"Woe to the Assyrian, the **r** *of* my anger,	8657
	10:15	As if a **r** were to wield him who lifts it up,	8657
	10:24	who beat you with a **r** and lift up a club	8657
	11: 4	the earth with the **r** *of* his mouth;	8657
	14: 5	LORD has broken the **r** of the wicked,	4751
	14:29	that the **r** that struck you is broken;	8657
	28:27	caraway is beaten out with a **r**,	4751
	30:32	with his punishing **r** will be to the music	4751
La	3: 1	the man who has seen affliction by the **r**	8657
Eze	7:10	Doom has burst forth, the **r** has budded,	4751
	7:11	into a **r** *to punish* wickedness;	4751
	20:37	of you as you pass under my **r**,	8657
	40: 3	a linen cord and a measuring **r** in his hand.	7866
	40: 5	The length of the measuring **r** in	7866
	40: 5	it was one **measuring r** thick	7866
	40: 5	and one **r** high.	7866
	40: 6	it was one **r** deep.	7866
	40: 7	The alcoves for the guards were one **r** long	7866
	40: 7	and one **r** wide,	7866
	40: 7	the temple was one **r** deep.	7866
	41: 8	It was the length of the **r**, six long cubits.	7866
	42:16	the east side with the measuring **r**;	7866
	42:17	five hundred cubits by the measuring **r**.	7866
	42:18	five hundred cubits by the measuring **r**.	7866
	42:19	five hundred cubits by the measuring **r**.	7866
Mic	5: 1	strike Israel's ruler on the cheek with a **r**.	8657
	6: 9	"Heed the **r** and the One who appointed it.	4751
Rev	11: 1	a reed like a **measuring r** and was told,	*4811*
	21:15	a measuring **r** of gold to measure the city,	2812
	21:16	the city *with* the **r** and found it to be 12,000	2812

RODANIM (2)

Ge	10: 4	Elishah, Tarshish, the Kittim and the **R**.	8102
1Ch	1: 7	Elishah, Tarshish, the Kittim and the **R**.	8102

RODE (11) [RIDE]

Jdg	10: 4	He had thirty sons, *who* **r** thirty donkeys.	8206
	12:14	*who* **r** on seventy donkeys.	8206
1Sa	30:17	except four hundred young men who **r** off	8206
1Ki	13:14	and **r** after the man of God.	2143
	18:45	a heavy rain came on and Ahab **r** off	8206
2Ki	9:16	he got into his chariot and **r** to Jezreel.	2143
	9:18	The horseman **r** off to meet Jehu and said,	2143
	9:21	of Israel and Ahaziah king of Judah **r** out,	3655
Est	8:10	*who* **r** fast horses especially bred for	8206
Hab	3: 8	Did you rage against the sea when *you* **r**	8206
Rev	6: 2	he **r** out as a conqueror bent on conquest.	*2002*

RODENTS (1)

Isa	2:20	the **r** and bats their idols of silver and idols	2923

RODS (3) [ROD]

Job	40:18	his limbs like **r** of iron.	4758
SS	5:14	His arms are **r** of gold set with chrysolite.	1664
2Co	11:25	Three times *I was* **beaten with r**,	*4810*

ROE (1) [ROEBUCKS]

Dt	14: 5	the gazelle, the **r** **deer**, the wild goat,	3502

ROEBUCK (KJV) See GAZELLE

ROEBUCKS (1) [ROE]

1Ki	4:23	as well as deer, gazelles, **r** and choice fowl.	3502

ROES (KJV) See GAZELLE

ROGEL See EN ROGEL

ROGELIM (2)

2Sa	17:27	and Barzillai the Gileadite from **R**	8082
	19:31	also came down from **R** to cross the Jordan	8082

ROHGAH (1)

1Ch	7:34	Ahi, **R**, Hubbah and Aram.	8108

ROI See BEER LAHAI ROI

ROLL (14) [ROLLED, ROLLING, ROLLS]

Ge	29: 3	the shepherds *would* **r** the stone away from	1670
Jos	10:18	"**R** large rocks up to the mouth of the cave,	1670
1Sa	14:33	"**R** a large stone over here at once."	1670
Pr	26:27	if a man rolls a stone, *it will* **r** back on him.	8740
Isa	22:18	*He will* **r** you **up tightly** like a ball and throw you	7571+7571+7572
Jer	5:22	The waves *may* **r**, but they cannot prevail;	1723
	6:26	put on sackcloth and **r** in ashes;	7147
	25:34	**r** in the dust, *you* leaders of the flock.	7147
	51:25	**r** you off the cliffs,	1670
Eze	27:30	they will sprinkle dust on their heads and **r**	7147
Am	5:24	But *let* justice **r** on like a river,	1670
Mic	1:10	In Beth Ophrah **r** in the dust.	7147
Mk	16: 3	"Who will **r** the stone **away** from	*653*
Heb	1:12	*You will* **r** them **up** like a robe;	*1813*

ROLLED (15) [ROLL]

Ge	29: 8	the stone *has been* **r** away from the mouth	1670
	29:10	over and **r** the stone away from the mouth	1670
Jos	5: 9	"Today *I have* **r** away the reproach	1670
2Ki	2: 8	**r** it **up** and struck the water with it.	1676
Isa	9: 5	in battle and every garment **r** in blood will	1670
	28:27	nor *is* a cartwheel **r** over cummin;	6015
	34: 4	be dissolved and the sky **r** up like a scroll;	1670
	38:12	Like a weaver *I have* **r** up my life,	7886
Mt	27:60	**r** a big stone **in front of** the entrance	4685
	28: 2	**r** **back** the stone and sat on it.	*653*
Mk	9:20	He fell to the ground and **r** **around**,	*3244*
	15:46	Then *he* **r** a stone against the entrance of	4685
	16: 4	which was very large, *had been* **r** **away**.	*653*
Lk	4:20	Then he **r** up the scroll,	4771
	24: 2	They found the stone **r** **away** from the tomb,	*653*

ROLLER (KJV) See SPLINT

ROLLING (2) [ROLL]

Job	30:14	amid the ruins *they* **come r** in.	1670
Rev	6:14	The sky receded like a scroll, **r** **up**,	*1813*

ROLLS (2) [ROLL]

Pr	26:27	if a *man* **r** a stone, it will roll back on him.	1670
Isa	9:18	so that *it* **r** **upward** *in* a column of smoke.	60

ROMAMTI-EZER (2)

1Ch	25: 4	Hanani, Eliathah, Giddalti and **R**;	8251
	25:31	the twenty-fourth to **R**,	8251

ROMAN (13) [ROME]

Lk	2: 1	a census should be taken of the entire **R** world.	*3876*
Jn	18:28	to the palace of the **R** governor.	NIG
Ac	11:28	famine would spread over the entire **R** world.	*3876*
	16:12	a **R** colony and the leading city of	*3149*
	16:37	even though we are **R** citizens,	476+4871
	16:38	that Paul and Silas were **R** citizens,	4871
	21:31	the commander *of* the **R** troops that	5061
	22:25	for you to flog a **R** citizen who hasn't	476+4871
	22:26	"This man is a **R** citizen."	4871
	22:27	"Tell me, are you a **R** citizen?"	4871
	22:29	a **R** citizen, in chains.	4871
	23:27	for I had learned that he is a **R** citizen.	4871
	25:16	not the **R** custom to hand over any man	4871

ROMANS (3) [ROME]

Jn	11:48	and then the **R** will come and take away	4871
Ac	16:21	advocating customs unlawful for us **R**	*1639+4871*
	28:17	in Jerusalem and handed over to the **R**.	4871

ROME (10) [ROMAN, ROMANS]

Ac	2:10	near Cyrene; visitors from **R**	4871
	18: 2	had ordered all the Jews to leave **R**.	4873
	19:21	he said, "I must visit **R** also."	4873
	23:11	so you must also testify in **R**."	4873
	25:25	to the Emperor I decided to send him to **R**.	NIG
	28:14	And so we came to **R**.	4873
	28:16	When we got to **R**,	4873
Ro	1: 7	To all in **R** who are loved by God and called	4873
	1:15	the gospel also to you who are at **R**.	4873
2Ti	1:17	On the contrary, when he was in **R**,	4873

ROOF (38) [ROOFED, ROOFING, ROOFS]

Ge	6:16	Make a **r** for it and finish the ark to	7415
	19: 8	under the protection of my **r**."	7771
Dt	22: 8	around your **r** so that you may not bring	1511
	22: 8	on your house if someone falls from **the r**.	5647S
Jos	2: 6	to the **r** and hidden them under the stalks	1511
	2: 6	the stalks of flax she had laid out on the **r**.)	1511
	2: 8	she went up on the **r**	1511

Jdg	9:51	in and climbed up on the tower r.	1511
	16:27	on the r were about three thousand men	1511
1Sa	9:25	with Saul on the r of his house.	1511
	9:26	and Samuel called to Saul on the r,	1511
2Sa	11: 2	and walked around on the r of the palace.	1511
	11: 2	From the r he saw a woman bathing.	1511
	16:22	they pitched a tent for Absalom on the r,	1511
	18:24	up to the r of the gateway by the wall.	1511
1Ki	7: 6	of that were pillars and an **overhanging** r.	6264
2Ki	4:10	Let's make a small room on the r and put	7815
	19:26	like grass sprouting on the r,	1511
	23:12	the kings of Judah had erected on the r *near*	1511
Job	29:10	their tongues stuck to the r of their **mouths.**	2674
Ps	22:15	and my tongue sticks to the r of my **mouth;**	4918
	102: 7	I have become like a bird alone on a r.	1511
	129: 6	May they be like grass on the r,	1511
	137: 6	May my tongue cling to the r of my **mouth**	2674
Pr	21: 9	Better to live on a corner of the r than share	1511
	25:24	Better to live on a corner of the r than share	1511
Isa	37:27	like grass sprouting on the r,	1511
La	4: 4	to the r of its **mouth.**	2674
Eze	3:26	to the r of your **mouth** so that you will	2674
Da	4:29	on the r of the royal palace of Babylon,	NIH
Mt	8: 8	not deserve to have you come under my r.	5094
	24:17	Let no one on the r of his **house** go down	1560
Mk	2: 4	they made an opening in the r above Jesus	5094
	13:15	Let no one on the r of his **house** go down	1560
Lk	5:19	the r and lowered him on his mat through	1560
	7: 6	not deserve to have you come under my r.	5094
	17:31	On that day no one who is on the r	1560
Ac	10: 9	Peter went up on the r to pray.	1560

ROOFED (1) [ROOF]

1Ki	7: 3	*It was* r with cedar above the beams	6211

ROOFING (2) [ROOF]

1Ki	6: 9	r it *with* beams and cedar planks.	6211
Ne	3:15	r it *over* and putting its doors and bolts	3233

ROOFS (9) [ROOF]

Ne	8:16	and built themselves booths on their own r,	1511
Isa	15: 3	the r and in the public squares they all wail,	1511
	22: 1	that you have all gone up on the r,	1511
Jer	19:13	where they burned incense on the r to all	1511
	32:29	by burning incense on the r to Baal and	1511
	48:38	On all the r *in* Moab and in the public	1511
Zep	1: 5	those who bow down on the r to worship	1511
Mt	10:27	in your ear, proclaim from the r.	1560
Lk	12: 3	be proclaimed from the r.	1560

ROOM (83) [ROOMS, STOREROOM, STOREROOMS]

Ge	24:23	is there r in your father's house for us	5226
	24:25	as well as r for you to spend the night."	5226
	26:22	"Now the LORD *has* given us r	8143
	34:21	the land has **plenty of** r for them.	3338+8146
	43:30	He went into his **private** r and wept there.	2540
Lev	26:10	to move it out to **make** r for the new.	4946+7156
Nu	22:26	in a narrow place where there was no r	2006
Jdg	3:20	the **upper** r of his summer palace and said,	6608
	3:23	of the **upper** r behind him and locked them.	6608
	3:24	and found the doors of the **upper** r locked.	6608
	3:24	"He must be relieving himself in the **inner** r	2540
	3:25	when he did not open the doors of the r,	6608
	15: 1	He said, "I'm going to my wife's r."	2540
	16: 9	With men hidden in the r,	2540
	16:12	Then, with men hidden in the r,	2540
2Sa	18:33	up to the r *over* the gateway and wept.	6608
1Ki	1:15	to see the aged king in his r,	2540
	6:17	In front of this r was forty cubits long.	1074
	6:27	the cherubim inside the **innermost** r of	AIT
	6:27	touched each other in the middle of the r.	1074
	7:50	for the doors of the innermost r,	1074
	17:19	to the **upper** r where he was staying,	6608
	17:23	the child and carried him down from the r	6608
	20:30	to the city and hid in an **inner** r.	928+2540+2540
	22:25	day you go to hide in an **inner** r.	928+2540+2540
2Ki	1: 2	through the lattice of his **upper** r in Samaria	6608
	4:10	a small r on the roof and put in it a bed and	6608
	4:11	he went up to his r and lay down there.	6608
	4:35	and forth in the r and then got on the bed	1074
	9: 2	and take him into an **inner** r.	928+2540+2540
	23:11	the r *of* an official named Nathan-Melech,	4384
	23:12	on the roof near the **upper** r of Ahaz,	6608
2Ch	18:24	day you go to hide in an **inner** r.	928+2540+2540
Ezr	10: 6	of God and went to the r of Jehohanan son	4384
Ne	2:14	not enough r for my mount to get through;	5226
	3:31	and as far as the r **above** the corner;	6608
	3:32	the corner **above** and the Sheep Gate	6608
	13: 5	with a large r formerly used to store	4384
	13: 7	in providing Tobiah a r in the courts of	5969
	13: 8	all Tobiah's household goods out of the r.	4384
Ps	10: 4	in all his thoughts there is no r for God.	NIH
SS	3: 4	to the r *of* the one who conceived me.	2540
Jer	7:32	in Topheth until there is no more r.	5226
	19:11	in Topheth until there is no more r.	5226
	35: 4	the r *of* the sons of Hanan son of Igdaliah	4384
	35: 4	It was next to the r of the officials,	4384
	36:10	of Gemariah son *of* Shaphan	4384
	36:12	to the secretary's r in the royal palace,	4384
	36:20	in the r *of* Elishama the secretary,	4384
	36:21	of Elishama the secretary and read it	4384
	38:11	with him and went to a r under the treasury	NIH
Eze	40:38	A r with a doorway was by the portico	4384

Eze	40:45	"The r facing south is for	4384
	40:46	and the r facing north is for	4384
	41: 5	it was six cubits thick, and each **side** r	7521
Da	6:10	his **upstairs** r where the windows opened	10547
Joel	2:16	Let the bridegroom leave his r and	2540
Zec	10:10	and *there will* not **be** r **enough** for them.	5162
Mal	3:10	that you will not have r **enough** for it.	1896
Mt	6: 6	But when you pray, go into your r,	5421
Mk	2: 2	So many gathered that *there was* no r left,	6003
	14:14	Where is my **guest** r,	2906
	14:15	He will show you a large **upper** r,	333
Lk	2: 7	because there was no r for them in the inn.	5536
	14:22	but there is still r.'	5536
	22:11	Where is the **guest** r,	2906
	22:12	He will show you a large **upper** r,	333
Jn	8:37	because you *have* no r for my word.	6003
	21:25	even the whole world *would* not *have* r **for**	6003
Ac	1:13	they went **upstairs** to the r where	5673
	9:37	and placed in an **upstairs** r.	5673
	9:39	he arrived he was taken upstairs to the r.	5673
	9:40	Peter sent them all out of the r;	NIG
	20: 8	in the **upstairs** r where we were meeting.	5673
	25:23	with great pomp and entered the **audience** r	211
	26:31	They left the r, and while talking	NIG
Ro	12:19	my friends, but leave r for God's wrath,	5536
2Co	7: 2	**Make** r **for** us in your hearts.	6003
Phm	1:22	Prepare a **guest** r for me,	3825
Heb	9: 2	In its first r were the lampstand,	NIG
	9: 3	Behind the second curtain was a r called	5008
	9: 6	the priests entered regularly into the outer r	5008
	9: 7	But only the high priest entered the inner r,	NIG

ROOMS (49) [ROOM]

Ge	6:14	make r in it and coat it with pitch inside	7860
1Ki	6: 5	in which there were **side** r.	7521
	6:10	And he built the **side** r all along the temple.	3666
	6:29	in both the inner and **outer** r,	AIT
	6:30	**both** the inner and **outer** r	AIT
1Ch	9:26	for the r and treasuries in the house of God.	4384
	9:33	in the r of the temple and were exempt	4384
	23:28	to be in charge of the courtyards, the **side** r,	4384
	28:11	its inner r and the place of atonement.	2540
	28:12	of the LORD and all the surrounding r,	4384
Ne	13: 9	I gave orders to purify the r,	4384
Pr	24: 3	through knowledge its r are filled with rare	2540
Isa	26:20	enter your r and shut the doors behind you;	2540
Jer	22:13	his **upper** r by injustice,	6608
	22:14	a great palace with spacious **upper** r.'	6608
	35: 2	and invite them to come to one of the **side** r	4384
Eze	40:17	There I saw *some* r and a pavement	4384
	40:17	there were thirty r along the pavement.	4384
	40:44	within the inner court, were two r,	4384
	41: 6	The **side** r were on three levels,	7521
	41: 6	to serve as supports for the **side** r,	7521
	41: 7	The **side** r all around the temple were wider	7521
	41: 7	so that the r widened as one went upward.	NIH
	41: 8	forming the foundation of the **side** r.	7521
	41: 9	of the **side** r was five cubits thick.	7521
	41: 9	The open area between the **side** r of	7521
	41:10	the [priests'] r was twenty cubits wide all	4384
	41:11	There were entrances to the **side** r from	7521
	41:26	The **side** r *of* the temple	7521
	42: 1	to the r opposite the temple courtyard	4384
	42: 4	In front of the r was an inner passageway	4384
	42: 5	Now the upper r were narrower,	4384
	42: 5	from the r on the lower and middle floors	NIH
	42: 6	**The** r on the third floor had no pillars,	2177S
	42: 7	There was an outer wall parallel to the r	4384
	42: 7	it extended in front of the r for fifty cubits.	4384
	42: 8	While the row of r on the side next to	4384
	42: 9	The lower r had an entrance on	4384
	42:10	and opposite the outer wall, were r	4384
	42:11	These were like the r on the north;	4384
	42:11	were the doorways of the r on the south.	4384
	42:12	by which one enters **the** r.	5527S
	42:13	and south r facing the temple courtyard are	4384
	42:13	the temple courtyard are the **priests'** r,	4384+7731
	44:19	in and are to leave them in the sacred r,	4384
	46:19	of the gate to the sacred r facing north,	4384
Mt	24:26	or, 'Here he is, in the **inner** r,'	5421
Lk	12: 3	in the ear in the **inner** r will be proclaimed	5421
Jn	14: 2	In my Father's house are many r;	3665

ROOST (1)

Zep	2:14	and the screech owl *will* r on her columns.	4328

ROOSTER (13)

Pr	30:31	a **strutting** r, a he-goat, and a king	2435+5516
Mt	26:34	"this very night, before the r crows,	232
	26:74	Immediately a r crowed.	232
	26:75	"Before the r crows, you will disown me	232
Mk	13:35	or at midnight, or **when the** r **crows,**	231
	14:30	before the r crows twice you yourself will		
		disown me three times."	232
	14:72	Immediately the r crowed the second time.	232
	14:72	"Before the r crows twice you will disown		
		me three times."	232
Lk	22:34	"I tell you, Peter, before the r crows today,	232
	22:60	Just as he was speaking, the r crowed.	232
	22:61	"Before the r crows today,	232
Jn	13:38	I tell you the truth, before the r crows,	232
	18:27	and at that moment a r began to crow.	232

ROOT (35) [ROOTED, ROOTS]

Dt	29:18	make sure there is no r among you	9247
2Ki	19:30	of the house of Judah will take r below	9247
Job	5: 3	I myself have seen a fool **taking** r,	9245
	19:28	since the r of the trouble lies in him,'	9247
	30: 4	and their food was the r of the broom tree.	9247
Ps	80: 9	and *it took* r and filled the land.	9245+9247
	80:15	the r your right hand has planted,	4035
Pr	12:12	but the r of the righteous flourishes.	9247
Isa	11:10	the **R** of Jesse will stand as a banner for	9247
	14:29	the r of that snake will spring up a viper,	9247
	14:30	But your r I will destroy by famine;	9247
	27: 6	In days to come Jacob *will* **take** r,	9245
	37:31	of the house of Judah will take r below	9247
	40:24	no sooner *do they* **take** r in the ground	1614+9245
	53: 2	and like a r out of dry ground.	9247
Jer	12: 2	and *they have* **taken** r;	9245
Hos	9:16	Ephraim is blighted, their r is withered,	9247
Mal	4: 1	"Not a r or a branch will be left to them.	9247
Mt	3:10	The ax is already at the r of the trees,	4844
	13: 6	and they withered because they had no r.	4844
	13:21	since he has no r, he lasts only a short time.	4844
	13:29	*you may* r **up** the wheat with them.	1748
Mk	4: 6	and they withered because they had no r.	4844
	4:17	they have no r, they last only a short time.	4844
Lk	3: 9	The ax is already at the r of the trees,	4844
	8:13	they hear it, but they have no r.	4844
Ro	11:16	if the r is holy, so are the branches.	4844
	11:17	in the nourishing sap *from* the olive r,	4844
	11:18	You do not support the r,	4844
	11:18	but the r supports you.	4844
	15:12	Isaiah says, "The **R** of Jesse will spring up,	4844
1Ti	6:10	the love of money is a r of all kinds of evil.	4844
Heb	12:15	the grace of God and that no bitter r grows	4844
Rev	5: 5	the **R** of David, has triumphed.	4844
	22:16	I am the **R** and the Offspring of David,	4844

ROOTED (2) [ROOT]

Eph	3:17	that you, *being* r and established in love,	4845
Col	2: 7	r and built up in him, strengthened in	4845

ROOTS (21) [ROOT]

Jdg	5:14	whose r were in Amalek;	9247
Job	8:17	it entwines its r around a pile of rocks	9247
	14: 8	Its r may grow old in the ground	9247
	18:16	His r dry up below	9247
	28: 9	and lays bare the r of the mountains.	9247
	29:19	My r will reach to the water,	9247
Isa	5:24	so their r will decay and their flowers	9247
	11: 1	from his r a Branch will bear fruit.	9247
Jer	17: 8	the water that sends out its r by the stream.	9247
Eze	17: 6	but its r remained under it.	9247
	17: 7	now sent out its r toward him from the plot	9247
	17: 9	or many people to pull it up by the r.	9247
	31: 7	for its r went down to abundant waters.	9247
Da	4:15	But let the stump and its r,	10743
	4:23	while its r remain in the ground.	10743
	4:26	with its r means that your kingdom will	10743
Hos	14: 5	cedar of Lebanon he will send down his r;	9247
Am	2: 9	I destroyed his fruit above and his r below.	9247
Jnh	2: 6	To the r *of* the mountains I sank down;	7893
Mt	15:13	not planted *will be* **pulled up by the** r.	1748
Mk	11:20	they saw the fig tree withered from the r.	4844

ROPE (6) [ROPES]

Ex	28:14	braided chains of pure gold, like a r,	6310
	28:22	braided chains of pure gold, like a r.	6310
	39:15	braided chains of pure gold, like a r.	6310
Jos	2:15	So she let them down by a r through	2475
Job	41: 1	or tie down his tongue with a r?	2475
Isa	3:24	instead of a sash, a r;	5940

ROPES (28) [ROPE]

Ex	35:18	and for the courtyard, and their r;	4798
	39:40	the r and tent pegs for the courtyard,	4798
Nu	3:26	the tabernacle and altar, and the r—	4798
	3:37	with their bases, tent pegs and r.	4798
	4:26	the r and all the equipment used	4798
	4:32	with their bases, tent pegs, r,	4798
Jdg	15:13	with two new r and led him up from	6310
	15:14	The r on his arms became like charred flax,	6310
	16:11	"If anyone ties me securely with new r	6310
	16:12	Delilah took new r and tied him with them.	6310
	16:12	But he snapped **the** r off his arms as	4392S
2Sa	17:13	then all Israel will bring r to that city,	2475
1Ki	20:31	around our waists and r around our heads.	2475
	20:32	and r around their heads, they went to	2475
Job	39: 5	Who untied his r?	4593
Ps	119:61	Though the wicked bind me with r,	2475
Isa	5:18	and wickedness as with cart r,	6310
	33:20	nor any of its r broken.	2475
Jer	10:20	My tent is destroyed; all its r are snapped.	4798
	38: 6	They lowered Jeremiah by r into	2475
	38:11	and let them down with r to Jeremiah in	2475
	38:12	under your arms to pad the r."	2475
	38:13	with the r and lifted him out of the cistern.	2475
Eze	3:25	And you, son of man, they will tie with r;	6310
	4: 8	up with r so that you cannot turn	6310
Ac	27:17	they passed r under the ship itself	1069
	27:32	the soldiers cut the r that held the lifeboat	5389
	27:40	in the sea and at the same time untied the r	2415

ROSE (62) [RISE]

Ge	7:18	The waters **r** and increased greatly on	1504
	7:19	They **r** greatly on the earth,	1504
	7:20	The waters **r** and covered the mountains to	1504
	23: 3	Then Abraham **r** from beside his dead wife	7756
	23: 7	Then Abraham **r** and bowed down before	7756
	32:31	The sun **r** above him as he passed Peniel,	2436
	37: 7	in the field when suddenly my sheaf **r**	7756
Ex	32: 6	So the next day the people **r** early	8899
	33: 8	all the people **r** and stood at the entrances	7756
Nu	16: 2	and **r** up against Moses.	7756
Jos	8:19	in the ambush **r** quickly from their position	7756
Jdg	3:20	As the king **r** from his seat,	7756
	6:38	Gideon **r** early the next day;	8899
	9:43	he **r** to attack them.	7756
	10: 1	the son of Dodo, **r** to save Israel.	7756
	19: 8	when he **r** to go, the girl's father said,	8899
	20: 8	All the people **r** as one man, saying,	7756
1Sa	5: 3	the people of Ashdod **r** early the next day,	8899
	5: 4	But the following morning when they **r**,	8899
	9:26	They **r** about daybreak and Samuel called	8899
2Sa	18:31	from all who **r** up against you."	7756
	22: 9	Smoke **r** from his nostrils;	6590
1Ki	1:49	all Adonijah's guests **r** in alarm	7756
	8:54	he **r** from before the altar of the LORD,	7756
	18:45	the sky grew black with clouds, the wind **r**,	NIH
2Ki	3:24	the Israelites **r** up and fought them	7756
	8:21	but he **r** up and broke through by night;	7756
1Ch	21: 1	Satan **r** up against Israel and incited David	6641
	28: 2	King David **r** to his feet and said:	7756
2Ch	20:23	The men of Ammon and Moab **r** up against	6641
	21: 9	but he **r** up and broke through by night.	7756
Ezr	9: 5	I **r** from my self-abasement,	7756
	10: 5	So Ezra **r** and put the leading priests	7756
Est	5: 9	that he neither **r** nor showed fear	7756
Job	29: 8	and stepped aside and the old men **r**	7756
Ps	18: 8	Smoke **r** from his nostrils;	6590
	76: 9	O God, **r** up to judge,	7756
	78:21	and his wrath **r** against Israel,	6590
	78:31	God's anger **r** against them;	6590
SS	2: 1	I am a **r** of Sharon, a lily of the valleys.	2483
Eze	1:19	the living creatures **r** from the ground,	5951
	1:19	from the ground, the wheels also **r**.	5951
	1:21	and when the creatures **r** from the ground,	5951
	1:21	the wheels **r** along with them,	5951
	10: 4	Then the glory of the LORD **r** from above	8123
	10:15	Then the cherubim **r** upward.	8250
	10:17	and when the cherubim **r**,	8123
	10:17	when the cherubim rose, they **r** with them,	8250
	10:19	the cherubim spread their wings and **r** from	8250
	16:13	You became very beautiful and **r** to be	7503
Jnh	1: 7	LORD, and my prayer **r** to you,	995
	3: 6	he **r** from his throne,	7756
	4: 8	When the sun **r**, God provided a scorching	2436
Mt	7:25	The rain came down, the streams **r**,	2262
	7:27	The rain came down, the streams **r**,	2262
Mk	16: 9	When Jesus **r** early on the first day of	482
Lk	22:45	When he **r** from prayer and went back to	482
	23: 1	whole assembly **r** and led him off to Pilate.	482
Ac	10:41	by us who ate and drank with him after he **r**	482
	26:30	The king **r**, and with him the governor	482
1Th	4:14	We believe that Jesus died and **r** again and	482
Rev	9: 2	smoke **r** from it like the smoke from	326

ROSH (1)

Ge	46:21	Ashbel, Gera, Naaman, Ehi, **R**, Muppim,	8033

ROT (7) [ROTS, ROTTED, ROTTEN]

Pr	10: 7	but the name of the wicked will **r**.	8372
Isa	40:20	an offering selects wood that will not **r**.	8372
	50: 2	their fish **r** for lack of water and die	944
Hos	5:12	like to the people of Judah.	8373
Zec	14:12	Their flesh will **r** while they are still	5245
	14:12	their eyes will **r** in their sockets,	5245
	14:12	and their tongues will **r** in their mouths.	5245

ROTS (1) [ROT]

Pr	14:30	gives life to the body, but envy **r** the bones.	8373

ROTTED (1) [ROT]

Jas	5: 2	Your wealth has **r**, and moths have eaten	4960

ROTTEN (2) [ROT]

Job	13:28	"So man wastes away like something **r**,	8373
	41:27	like straw and bronze like **r** wood.	8375

ROUGH (4) [ROUGHER, ROUGHS]

Isa	40: 4	the **r** ground shall become level,	6815
	42:16	and make the **r** places smooth.	5112
Lk	3: 5	the **r** ways smooth.	5550
Jn	6:18	and the waters grew **r**.	1444

ROUGHER (2) [ROUGH]

Jnh	1:11	The sea was getting **r and rougher**.	2143+2256+6192
	1:11	The sea was getting **rougher and r**.	2143+2256+6192

ROUGHS (1) [ROUGH]

Isa	44:13	he **r** it **out** with chisels and marks it	6913

ROUND (6) [ROUNDED, ROUNDS]

Jdg	7:13	"A **r** loaf of barley bread came tumbling	7501
1Ki	7:31	This opening was **r**,	6318
	7:31	The panels of the stands were square, not **r**.	6318
Ecc	1: 6	**r** and round it goes,	6015
	1: 6	round and **r** it goes,	6015
Eze	19: 8	those from regions **r about**.	6017

ROUND (Anglicized) See also AROUND

ROUNDABOUT (1) [AROUND]

2Ki	3: 9	After a **r** march of seven days,	6015

ROUNDED (3) [ROUND]

1Ki	10:19	and its back had a **r** top.	6318
SS	7: 2	a **r** goblet that never lacks blended wine.	6044
Ac	17: 5	so they **r** up some bad characters from	4689

ROUNDS (2) [ROUND]

SS	3: 3	as they **made** their **r** in the city.	6015
	5: 7	as they **made** their **r** in the city.	6015

ROUSE (12) [AROUSE, AROUSED, AROUSES, ROUSED, ROUSES]

Ge	49: 9	like a lioness—who dares to **r** him?	7756
Nu	23:24	they **r themselves** like a lion that does	5951
	24: 9	like a lioness—who dares to **r** them?	7756
Job	3: 8	those who are ready to **r** Leviathan.	6424
	8: 6	even now he will **r** himself on your behalf	6424
	41:10	No one is fierce enough to **r** him.	6424
Ps	44:23	Why do you sleep? **R** yourself!	7810
	59: 5	**r** yourself to punish all the nations;	6424
Isa	28:21	he will **r** himself as in the Valley	8074
Joel	3: 7	I am going to **r** them out of the places	6424
	3: 9	**R** the warriors!	6424
Zec	9:13	I will **r** your sons, O Zion,	6424

ROUSED (5) [ROUSE]

Job	14:12	men will not awake or **be r** from their sleep.	6424
SS	8: 5	Under the apple tree I **r** you;	6424
Eze	7: 6	It has **r** itself against you.	7810
Joel	3:12	"Let the nations **be r**;	6424
Zec	2:13	he has **r himself** from his holy dwelling."	6424

ROUSES (1) [ROUSE]

Isa	14: 9	it **r** the spirits of the departed	6424

ROUT (3) [ROUTED, ROUTING, ROUTS]

Jdg	1: 5	**putting to r** the Canaanites and Perizzites.	5782
Ps	92:11	my ears have heard the **r**	NIH
	144: 6	shoot your arrows and **r** them.	2169

ROUTE (8) [ROUTES]

Nu	14:25	and set out toward the desert along the **r** to	2006
	21: 4	They traveled from Mount Hor along the **r**	2006
Dt	1:22	and bring back a report about the **r** we are	2006
	1:40	and set out toward the desert along the **r** to	2006
	2: 1	and set out toward the desert along the **r** to	2006
Jdg	8:11	up by the **r** of the nomads east of Nobah	2006
2Ki	3: 8	"By what **r** shall we attack?"	2006
Mt	2:12	they returned to their country by another **r**.	3847

ROUTED (13) [ROUT]

Ge	14:15	to attack them and he **r** them,	5782
Jos	7: 4	but they were **r** by the men of Ai,	5674
	7: 8	that Israel has been **r** by its enemies?	2200+6902
Jdg	4:15	the LORD **r** Sisera and all his chariots	2169
1Sa	7:10	panic that they were **r** before the Israelites.	5597
2Sa	10:15	Arameans saw that they had been **r** by Israel,	5597
	22:15	bolts of lightning and **r** them.	2169
2Ki	14:12	Judah was **r** by Israel,	5597
1Ch	19:16	Arameans saw that they had been **r** by Israel,	5597
2Ch	13:15	God **r** Jeroboam and all Israel	5597
	25:22	Judah was **r** by Israel,	5597
Ps	18:14	great bolts of lightning and **r** them.	2169
Heb	11:34	in battle and **r** foreign armies.	3111

ROUTES (1) [ROUTE]

Job	6:18	Caravans turn aside from their **r**;	2006

ROUTING (1) [ROUT]

Jdg	8:12	and captured them, **r** their entire army.	3006

ROUTS (1) [ROUT]

Jos	23:10	One of you **r** a thousand,	8103

ROVERS (KJV) See RAIDING

ROVING (1)

Ecc	6: 9	the eye sees than the **r** of the appetite.	2143

ROW (15) [ROWED, ROWS]

Ex	28:17	In the first **r** there shall be a ruby,	3215
	28:18	in the second **r** a turquoise, a sapphire and	3215
	28:19	in the third **r** a jacinth, an agate and	3215
	28:20	in the fourth **r** a chrysolite, and	3215
	39:10	In the first **r** there was a ruby,	3215
	39:11	in the second **r** a turquoise, a sapphire and	3215
	39:12	in the third **r** a jacinth, an agate and	3215
	39:13	in the fourth **r** a chrysolite.	3215
	39:37	the pure gold lampstand with its **r** of lamps	5120
Lev	24: 6	Set them in two rows, six in each **r**,	5121
	24: 7	Along each **r** put some pure incense as	5121
1Ki	7: 3	forty-five beams, fifteen to a **r**.	3215
Eze	42: 8	While the **r** of rooms on the side next to	NIH
	42: 8	the **r** on the side nearest the sanctuary was	NIH
Jnh	1:13	the men did their best to **r** back to land.	3168

ROWED (1) [ROW]

Jn	6:19	When they had **r** three or three and	1785

ROWERS (KJV) See OARSMEN

ROWING (KJV) See AT THE OARS

ROWS (11) [ROW]

Ex	28:17	Then mount four **r** of precious stones on it.	3215
	39:10	Then they mounted four **r**	3215
Lev	24: 6	Set them in two **r**, six in each row,	5121
1Ki	7: 2	and thirty high, with four **r**	3215
	7:18	in two **r** encircling each network	3215
	7:20	pomegranates in **r** all around.	3215
	7:24	The gourds were cast in two **r** in one piece	3215
	7:42	of network (two **r** of pomegranates	3215
2Ch	4: 3	The bulls were cast in two **r** in one piece	3215
	4:13	of network (two **r** of pomegranates	3215
Job	41:15	His back has **r** of shields tightly sealed	692

ROYAL (136) [ROYALTY]

Jos	10: 2	like one of the **r** cities;	4930
	11:12	Joshua took all these **r** cities and their kings	4889
	13:31	and Ashtaroth and Edrei (the **r** cities of Og	4931
1Sa	27: 5	Why should your servant live in the **r** city	4930
2Sa	8:18	and David's sons were **r** advisers.	3913
	12:26	the Ammonites and captured the **r** citadel.	4867
	14:26	two hundred shekels by the **r** standard.	4889
1Ki	1: 9	all the men of Judah who were **r** officials,	4889
	1:46	Solomon has taken his seat on the **r** throne.	4867
	1:47	the **r** officials have come	4889
	4: 7	for the king and the **r** household.	2257S
	5: 9	by providing food for my **r** household."	NIH
	9: 1	the temple of the LORD and the **r** palace,	4889
	9: 5	I will establish your **r** throne	4930
	9:10	of the LORD and the **r** palace—	4889
	10:12	of the LORD and for the **r** palace,	4889
	10:13	what he had given her out of his **r** bounty.	4889
	10:28	the **r** merchants purchased them from Kue.	4889
	11: 3	He had seven hundred wives of **r** birth	8576
	11:14	from the **r** line of Edom.	4889
	11:20	whom Tahpenes brought up in the **r** palace.	7281
	14:26	and the treasures of the **r** palace.	4889
	14:27	on duty at the entrance to the **r** palace.	4889
	16:18	the citadel of the **r** palace and set the palace	4889
	22:10	Dressed in their **r** robes,	NIH
	22:30	but you wear your **r** robes."	NIH
2Ki	7: 9	at once and report this to the **r** palace."	4889
	10: 6	Now the **r** princes, seventy of them,	4889
	11: 1	to destroy the whole **r** family.	4930
	11: 2	from among the **r** princes,	4889
	11: 5	a third of you guarding the **r** palace,	4889
	11:19	king then took his place on the **r** throne,	4889
	12:10	the **r** secretary and the high priest came,	4889
	12:18	temple of the LORD and of the **r** palace,	4889
	14:14	and in the treasuries of the **r** palace.	4889
	15:25	in the citadel of the **r** palace at Samaria.	4889
	16: 8	the **r** palace and sent it as a gift to the king	4889
	16:18	the **r** entryway outside the temple of	4889
	18:15	and in the treasuries of the **r** palace.	4889
	24:13	of the LORD and from the **r** palace,	4889
	25: 9	the **r** palace and all the houses	4889
	25:19	of the fighting men and five **r** advisers.	4889
	25:25	the son of Elishama, who was of **r** blood,	4867
1Ch	27:25	of Adiel was in charge of the **r** storehouses.	4889
	27:34	Joab was the commander of the **r** army.	4889
	29:25	and bestowed on him **r** splendor such	4895
2Ch	1:16	the **r** merchants purchased them from Kue.	4889
	2: 1	for the Name of the LORD and a **r** palace	4895
	7:11	the temple of the LORD and the **r** palace,	4889
	7:18	I will establish your **r** throne,	4895
	9:11	temple of the LORD and for the **r** palace,	4889
	12: 9	and the treasures of the **r** palace.	4889
	12:10	on duty at the entrance to the **r** palace.	4889
	18: 9	Dressed in their **r** robes,	NIH
	18:29	but you wear your **r** robes."	NIH
	22:10	to destroy the whole **r** family of the house	4930
	22:11	from among the **r** princes who were about	4889
	23: 5	a third of you at the **r** palace and a third at	4889
	23:20	and seated the king on the **r** throne,	4930
	24:11	the **r** secretary and the officer of	4889
	26:11	Hananiah, one of the **r** officials.	4889
	28:21	the LORD and from the **r** palace and from	4889
Ezr	4:13	and the **r** revenues will suffer.	10421
	4:22	to the detriment of the **r interests**?	10421
	5:17	be made in the **r** archives of Babylon to see	10421
	6: 4	The costs are to be paid by the **r** treasury.	10421
	6: 8	to be fully paid out of the **r** treasury,	10421
	7:20	you may provide from the **r** treasury.	10421
	8:36	the king's orders to the **r** satraps and to	4889

Est	1: 2	from his **r** throne in the citadel of Susa,	4895
	1: 7	and the **r** wine was abundant,	4895
	1: 9	the women in the **r** palace of King Xerxes.	4895
	1:11	Queen Vashti, wearing her **r** crown,	4895
	1:19	let him issue a **r** decree and let it be written	4895
	1:19	Also let the king give her **r position**	4895
	2:16	in the **r** residence in the tenth month,	4895
	2:17	So he set a **r** crown on her head	4895
	2:18	and distributed gifts with **r** liberality.	4889
	3: 2	the **r** officials at the king's gate knelt down	4889
	3: 3	Then the **r** officials at the king's gate	4889
	3: 9	of silver into the **r** treasury for the men	4889
	3:12	the **r** secretaries were summoned	4889
	4: 7	to pay into the **r** treasury for the destruction	4889
	4:11	and the people of the **r** provinces know that	4889
	4:14	that you have come to **r position** for such	4895
	5: 1	on her **r** robes and stood in the inner court	4895
	5: 1	The king was sitting on his **r** throne in	4895
	6: 8	have them bring a **r** robe the king has worn	4895
	6: 8	one with a **r** crest placed on its head.	4895
	8: 9	At once the **r** secretaries were summoned—	4889
	8:14	The couriers, riding the **r** horses, raced out,	350
	8:15	the king's presence wearing **r** garments	4895
Ps	45: 9	at your right hand is the **r** bride in gold	8712
	72: 1	O God, and **r** to the king your righteousness.	NIH
SS	6:12	my desire set me among the **r** chariots	5618
	7: 5	Your hair is like **r** tapestry;	NIH
Isa	17: 3	and **r power** from Damascus;	4930
	60:16	of nations and be nursed at **r** breasts.	4889
	62: 3	a **r** diadem in the hand of your God.	4867
Jer	21:11	"Moreover, say to the **r** house of Judah,	4889
	26:10	they went up from the **r** palace to the house	4889
	32: 2	in the courtyard of the guard in the **r** palace	4889
	33: 4	the **r** palaces of Judah that have been torn	4889
	36:12	to the secretary's room in the **r** palace,	4889
	38: 7	a Cushite, an official in the **r** palace,	4889
	39: 8	The Babylonians set fire to the **r** palace and	4889
	41: 1	who was of **r** blood and had been one of	4867
	43:10	he will spread his **r canopy** above them.	9188
	52:13	the **r** palace and all the houses	4889
	52:25	the fighting men, and seven **r** advisers.	4889
Eze	17:13	a member of the **r** family and made a treaty	4867
Da	1: 3	in some of the Israelites from the **r** family	4867
	1: 8	to defile himself with the **r** food and wine,	4889
	1:13	that of the young men who eat the **r** food,	4889
	1:15	of the young men who ate the **r** food.	4889
	2:49	Daniel himself remained at the **r** court.	10421
	3:27	and **r** advisers crowded around them.	10421
	4:29	on the roof of the **r** palace of Babylon,	10424
	4:30	Babylon I have built as the **r** residence,	10424
	4:31	Your **r authority** has been taken from you.	10424
	5: 5	near the lampstand in the **r** palace.	10421
	5:20	from his **r** throne and stripped of his glory.	10424
	6: 7	The **r** administrators, prefects, satraps,	10421
	6:12	and spoke to him about his **r** decree:	10421
	11: 6	together with her **r** escort and her father	NIH
	11:20	a tax collector to maintain the **r** splendor.	4895
	11:45	He will pitch his **r** tents between the seas at	683
Hos	5: 1	Listen, O **r** house!	4889
Jnh	3: 6	he rose from his throne, took off his **r robes,**	168
Hag	2:22	I will overturn **r** thrones and shatter	4930
Zec	14:10	the Tower of Hananel to the **r** winepresses.	4889
Jn	4:46	a certain **r official** whose son lay sick	997
	4:49	The **r official** said, "Sir, come down before	997
Ac	12:21	Herod, wearing his **r** robes,	997
Jas	2: 8	If you really keep the **r** law found	997
1Pe	2: 9	you are a chosen people, a **r** priesthood,	994

ROYALTY (1) [ROYAL]

Da	11:21	who has not been given the honor of **r.**	4895

RUB (1) [RUBBED]

Lk	6: 1	**r** them in their hands and eat the kernels.	*6041*

RUBBED (3) [RUB]

2Sa	1:21	the shield of Saul—no longer **r** with oil.	5417
Eze	16: 4	nor **were** *you* **r with salt** or	4873+4873
	29:18	every head **was r bare** and every shoulder	7942

RUBBISH (1)

Php	3: 8	I consider them **r,** that I may gain Christ	*5032*

RUBBLE (16)

2Ki	23:12	smashed them to pieces and threw the **r**	6760
Ezr	6:11	his house is to be made a **pile of r.**	10470
Ne	4: 2	stones back to life from those heaps of **r—**	6760
	4:10	so much **r** that we cannot rebuild the wall."	6760
Job	15:28	houses crumbling to **r,**	1643
Ps	79: 1	they have reduced Jerusalem to **r.**	6505
Isa	25: 2	You have made the city a **heap of r,**	1643
Jer	26:18	Jerusalem will become a **heap of r,**	6505
Eze	26: 4	I will scrape away her **r** and make her	6760
	26:12	timber and **r** into the sea.	6760
Da	2: 5	and your houses turned into **piles of r.**	10470
	3:29	and their houses be turned into **piles of r,**	10470
Mic	1: 6	"Therefore I will make Samaria a **heap of r,**	6505
	3:12	Jerusalem will become a **heap of r,**	6505
Zep	1: 3	The wicked will have only **heaps of r**	4843
	2:14	**r** will be in the doorways,	2997

RUBIES (8) [RUBY]

Job	28:18	the price of wisdom is beyond **r.**	7165
Pr	3:15	She is more precious than **r;**	7165

Pr	8:11	for wisdom is more precious than **r,**	7165
	20:15	Gold there is, and **r** in abundance,	7165
	31:10	She is worth far more than **r.**	7165
Isa	54:12	I will make your battlements of **r,**	3905
La	4: 7	their bodies more ruddy than **r,**	7165
Eze	27:16	coral and **r** for your merchandise.	3905

RUBY (3) [RUBIES]

Ex	28:17	In the first row there shall be a **r,**	138
	39:10	In the first row there was a **r,**	138
Eze	28:13	**r,** topaz and emerald, chrysolite,	138

RUDDER (1) [RUDDERS]

Jas	3: 4	they are steered by a very small **r** wherever	*4382*

RUDDERS (1) [RUDDER]

Ac	27:40	the ropes that held the **r.**	*4382*

RUDDY (4)

1Sa	16:12	He was **r,** with a fine appearance	145
	17:42	**r** and handsome, and he despised him.	145
SS	5:10	My lover is radiant and **r,**	137
La	4: 7	their bodies more **r** than rubies,	131

RUDE (1)

1Co	13: 5	*It is* not **r,** it is not self-seeking,	*858*

RUDIMENTS (KJV) See BASIC PRINCIPLES

RUE (1)

Lk	11:42	**r** and all other kinds of garden herbs,	*4379*

RUFUS (2)

Mk	15:21	Simon, the father *of* Alexander and **R,**	*4859*
Ro	16:13	Greet **R,** chosen in the Lord,	*4859*

RUGGED (4)

Ps	68:15	**r** are the mountains of Bashan.	1493
	68:16	Why gaze in envy, O **r** mountains,	1493
SS	2:17	a gazelle or like a young stag on the **r** hills.	1441
Isa	40: 4	the **r** places a plain.	8221

RUGS (2)

Isa	21: 5	They set the tables, they spread the **r,**	7620
Eze	27:24	embroidered work and multicolored **r**	1710

RUHAMAH (KJV) See LOVED ONE

RUIN (82) [RUINED, RUINING, RUINS]

Nu	11:15	and do not let me face my own **r.**"	8288
	14:20	but he will come to **r** at last."	7
	14:24	but they too will come to **r.**"	7
Dt	11: 4	how the LORD **brought** lasting **r** *on* them.	6
	13:16	It is to remain a **r** forever,	9424
	28:20	and **come to** sudden **r** because of	6
	28:63	so it will please him to **r** and destroy you.	6
2Sa	15:14	to overtake us and bring **r** upon us and put	8288
	16: 8	You have come to **r** because you are a man	8288
2Ki	3:19	and **r** every good field with stones."	3872
2Ch	34:11	kings of Judah had **allowed to fall into r.**	8845
Est	6:13	*you will* **surely come to r!**"	5877+5877
	9:24	(that is, the lot) for their **r** and destruction.	2169
Job	2: 3	though you incited me against him to **r** him	1180
	22:19	"The righteous see their **r** and rejoice;	NIH
	31: 3	Is it not **r** for the wicked,	369
Ps	9: 6	Endless **r** has overtaken the enemy,	2999
	35: 4	may those who plot my **r** be turned back	8288
	35: 8	may **r** overtake them by surprise—	8739
	35: 8	may they fall into the pit, to their **r.**	8739
	38:12	those who would harm me talk of my **r;**	2095
	40:14	may all who desire my **r** be turned back	8288
	52: 5	**bring** you **down** to everlasting **r:**	5997
	64: 8	against them and **bring** them **to r;**	4173
	70: 2	may all who desire my **r** be turned back	8288
	73:18	you cast them down to **r.**	5397
Pr	3:25	of sudden disaster or of the **r** that overtakes	8739
	5:14	I have come to the brink of utter **r** in	8273
	10: 8	but a chattering fool **comes to r.**	4231
	10:10	and a chattering fool **comes to r.**	4231
	10:14	but the mouth of a foolish invites **r.**	4745
	10:15	but poverty is the **r** of the poor.	4745
	10:29	but it is the **r** of those who do evil.	4745
	13: 3	but he who speaks rashly will come to **r.**	4745
	18:24	A man of many companions *may* **come to r,**	8318
	19:13	A foolish son is his father's **r,**	2095
	21:12	**brings** the wicked **to r.**	2021+4200+6156+8273
	26:28	and a flattering mouth works **r.**	4510
	31: 3	your vigor on *those who* **r** kings.	4681
SS	2:15	the little foxes *that* **r** the vineyards,	2472
Isa	7: 5	and Remaliah's son have plotted your **r,**	8288
	23:13	its fortresses bare and turned it into a **r.**	5143
	24: 1	he will **r** its face and scatter its inhabitants	6390
	25: 2	the fortified town a **r,**	5143
	26:14	and **brought** them **to r;**	9012
	51:19	**r** and destruction, famine and sword—	8719
	59: 7	**r** and destruction mark their ways.	8719
	60:18	nor **r** or destruction within your borders,	8719
Jer	12:10	Many shepherds *will* **r** my vineyard	8845

Jer	13: 9	the same way *I will* **r** the pride of Judah	8845
	19: 7	" 'In this place *I will* **r** the plans of Judah	1327
	22: 5	that this palace will become a **r.**' "	2999
	25: 9	horror and scorn, and an everlasting **r.**	2999
	25:18	to make them a **r** and an object of horror	2999
	27:17	Why should this city become a **r?**"	2999
	38: 4	the good of these people but their **r.**"	8288
	48:18	up against you and **r** your fortified cities.	8845
	49:13	a **r** and an object of horror, of reproach and	9014
La	3:47	and pitfalls, **r** and destruction."	8643
Eze	5:14	"I will make you a **r** and a reproach among	2999
	21:27	A **r!** A ruin! I will make it a ruin!	6392
	21:27	A ruin! A **r!** I will make it a ruin!	6392
	21:27	A ruin! A ruin! I will make it a **r!**	6392
	23:33	the cup of **r** and desolation,	9014
	29:10	the land of Egypt a **r** and a desolate waste	2999
Hos	2:12	*I will* **r** her vines and her fig trees,	9037
	4:14	without understanding *will* **come to r!**	4231
Am	5: 9	and brings the fortified city to **r),**	8719
	6:16	but you do not grieve over the **r** of Joseph.	8691
Mic	6:13	to **r** you because of your sins.	9037
	6:16	over to **r** and your people to derision;	9014
Hab	2: 9	to escape the clutches of **r!**	8273
	2:10	You have plotted the **r** of many peoples,	7896
Zep	1:15	a day of trouble and **r,**	5409
	2:15	What a **r** she has become,	9014
Hag	1: 4	while this house remains a **r?**"	2992
	1: 9	"Because of my house, which remains a **r,**	2992
Ro	3:16	**r** and misery mark their ways,	*5342*
1Ti	6: 9	and harmful desires that plunge men into **r**	*3897*
Rev	17:16	bring her *to* **r** and leave her naked;	2246
	18:17	In one hour such great wealth *has been* **brought to r!**'	2246
	18:19	In one hour *she has been* **brought to r!**	2246

RUINED (44) [RUIN]

Ge	41:36	the country *may* not be **r** by the famine."	4162
Ex	8:24	and throughout Egypt the land **was r** by	8845
	10: 7	Do you not yet realize that Egypt *is* **r?**"	6
Dt	28:51	or lambs of your flocks until you are **r.**	6
Jdg	6: 4	the land and **r** the crops all the way to Gaza	8845
Job	15:28	he will inhabit **r** towns and houses	3948
Ps	109:10	may they be driven from their **r** homes.	2999
Pr	14:28	but without subjects a prince is **r.**	4745
Isa	3:14	"It is you *who have* **r** my vineyard;	1278
	6: 5	"*I am* **r!** For I am a man of unclean lips,	1950
	6:11	the cities **lie r** and without inhabitant,	8615
	6:11	the houses are left deserted and the fields **r**	8615
	15: 1	Ar in Moab *is* **r,** destroyed in a night!	1950
	15: 1	Kir in Moab *is* **r,** destroyed in a night!	1950
	24:10	The **r** city lies desolate;	9332
	49:19	"Though you *were* **r** and made desolate	2999
	60:12	*it will be* utterly **r.**	2990+2990
	61: 4	the **r** cities that have been devastated	2997
Jer	4:13	Woe to us! We are **r!**	8720
	4:27	"The whole land will be **r,**	9039
	9:12	Why *has* the land *been* **r** and laid waste like	6
	9:19	'How **r** we are!	8720
	13: 7	but now it *was* **r** and completely useless.	8845
	48: 1	"Woe to Nebo, for *it will* **be r.**	8720
	48: 8	*be* **r** and the plateau destroyed,	6
Eze	6: 6	your idols smashed and **r,**	8697
	29:12	will lie desolate forty years among **r** cities.	2990
	30: 7	and their cities will lie among **r** cities.	2990
	36:38	the **r** cities be filled with flocks of people.	2992
Joel	1: 7	my vines and my fig trees.	4200+7914
	1:10	The fields *are* **r,** the ground is dried up;	8720
Am	7: 9	and the sanctuaries of Israel will be **r;**	2990
	9:14	they will rebuild the **r** cities and live	9037
Mic	2: 4	'We are utterly **r;**	8720+8720
	2:10	because it is defiled, it is **r,**	2256+2472+2472
Na	2: 2	and *have* **r** their vines.	8845
Zep	1:11	all who trade with silver *will* be **r.**	4162
Zec	11: 2	the stately trees are **r!**	8720
	11: 3	the lush thicket of the Jordan *is* **r!**	8720
Mt	9:17	wine will run out and the wineskins *will* be **r.**	660
	12:25	kingdom divided against itself *will* be **r,**	2246
Mk	2:22	both the wine and the wineskins *will* be **r.**	660
Lk	5:37	wine will run out and the wineskins *will* be **r.**	660
	11:17	kingdom divided against itself *will* be **r,**	2246

RUINING (1) [RUIN]

Tit	1:11	*because they are* **r** whole households	*426*

RUINS (57) [RUIN]

Lev	26:31	cities into **r** and lay waste your sanctuaries,	2999
	26:33	and your cities will lie in **r.**	2999
Jos	8:28	and made it a permanent **heap of r,**	9424
1Ki	18:30	the altar of the LORD, which *was* in **r.**	2238
1Ch	20: 1	Joab attacked Rabbah and **left** it in **r.**	2238
2Ch	34: 6	and in the **r** around them,	2999
Ezr	9: 9	the house of our God and repair its **r,**	2999
Ne	2: 3	where my fathers are buried lies in **r,**	2992
	2:17	Jerusalem lies in **r,**	2992
Job	3:14	**places** now **lying in r,**	2999
	30:14	amid the **r** they come rolling in.	8739
Ps	74: 3	Turn your steps toward these everlasting **r,**	5397
	89:40	and reduced his strongholds to **r.**	4745
	102: 6	like an owl among the **r.**	2999
Pr	19: 3	A man's own folly **r** his life,	6156
	24:31	and the stone wall *was* in **r.**	2238
Ecc	4: 5	The fool folds his hands and **r** himself.	430
Isa	3: 6	take charge of this **heap of r!**"	4843
	5:17	lambs will feed among the **r** of the rich.	2999
	17: 1	be a city but will become a heap of **r.**	5142

Isa 24:12 city is left in **r**, its gate is battered to pieces. 9014
44:26 'They shall be built,' and of their **r**, 2999
51: 3 and will look with compassion on all her **r**; 2999
52: 9 songs of joy together, you **r** of Jerusalem, 2999
58:12 Your people will rebuild the ancient **r** 2999
61: 4 They will rebuild the ancient **r** and restore 2999
64:11 and all that we treasured lies in **r**. 2999
Jer 4: 7 Your towns *will* lie in **r** 5898
4:20 the whole land lies in **r**. 8720
4:26 all its towns lay in **r** before the LORD, 5997
9:11 "I will make Jerusalem a **heap of r**, 1643
9:19 because our houses *are* in **r**.'" 8959
30:18 the city will be rebuilt on her **r**, 9424
44: 2 Today they lie deserted and in **r** 2999
44: 6 the desolate **r** they are today. 9039
46:19 for Memphis will be laid waste and lie in **r** 5898
49: 2 it will become a mound of **r**, 9039
49:13 and all its towns will be in **r** forever." 2999
51:37 Babylon will be a **heap of r**, 1643
Eze 13: 4 O Israel, are like jackals among **r**. 2999
26: 2 now that *she* lies in **r** I will prosper,' 2990
26:20 dwell in the earth below, as in ancient **r**, 2999
33:24 in those **r** in the land of Israel are saying, 2999
33:27 as I live, those who are left in the **r** will fall 2999
35: 4 I will turn your towns into **r** and you will 2999
36: 4 to the ravines and valleys, to the desolate **r** 2999
36:10 towns will be inhabited and the **r** rebuilt 2999
36:33 and the **r** will be rebuilt. 2999
36:35 the cities that were lying in **r**, 2992
38:12 the resettled **r** and the people gathered from 2999
Joel 1:17 The storehouses *are* in **r**, 9037
Am 9:11 I will repair its broken places, restore its **r**, 2232
Na 3: 7 'Nineveh *is* in **r**—who will mourn for her?' 8720
Zep 2: 4 be abandoned and Ashkelon left in **r**. 9039
Mal 1: 4 we will rebuild the **r**." 2999
Ac 15:16 Its **r** I will rebuild, and I will restore it, 2940
2Ti 2:14 and only **r** those who listen. 2953

RULE (87) [RULED, RULER, RULER'S, RULERS, RULES, RULING]

Ge 1:26 and *let them* **r** over the fish of the sea and 8097
1:28 **R** over the fish of the sea and the birds of 8097
3:16 and he *will* **r** over you." 8097
37: 8 *Will you* **actually** **r** us?" 5440+5440
Lev 25:43 *Do* not **r** over them ruthlessly, 8097
25:46 not **r** over your fellow Israelites ruthlessly. 8097
25:53 to it that his owner *does* not **r** over 8097
26:17 those who hate you will **r** over you, 8097
Dt 15: 6 *You* will **r** over many nations 5440
15: 6 many nations but none *will* **r** over you. 5440
19: 4 the **r** *concerning* the man who kills another 1821
Jdg 8:22 The Israelites said to Gideon, "**R** over us," 5440
8:23 Gideon told them, "I *will* not **r** over you, 5440
8:23 nor *will* my son **r** over you. 5440
8:23 The LORD *will* **r** over you." 5440
9: 2 *to have* all seventy of Jerub-Baal's sons 5440
13:12 to be the **r** *for* the boy's life and work?" 5477
1Sa 12:12 'No, we want a king *to* **r** over us'— 4887
14:47 After Saul had assumed **r** over Israel, 4867
2Sa 3:21 you *may* **r** over all that your heart desires." 4887
19:10 whom we anointed *to* **r** over us, 6584
1Ki 2:12 and his **r** was firmly established. 4895
5: 7 for he has given David a wise son to **r** over 6584
8:16 I have chosen David to **r** my people Israel. 2118+6584
11:37 you will **r** over all that your heart desires; 4887
2Ch 6: 5 I have chosen David to **r** my people Israel. 2118+6584
7:18 'You shall never fail to have a man *to* **r** 5440
9: 8 and placed you on his throne as king to **r** NIH
20: 6 You **r** over all the kingdoms of the nations. 5440
Ne 9:37 *They* **r** over our bodies and our cattle 5440
Ps 2: 9 *You will* **r** them with an iron scepter; 8286
7: 7 **R** over them from on high; 3782
19:13 *may they* not **r** over me. 5440
49:14 The upright *will* **r** over them in 8097
67: 4 for *you* **r** the peoples justly and guide 9149
72: 8 *He will* **r** from sea to sea and from 8097
89: 9 You **r** over the surging sea; 5440
110: 2 *you will* **r** in the midst of your enemies. 8097
119:133 *let* no sin **r** over me. 8948
Pr 8:16 and all nobles *who* **r** on earth. 9149
12:24 Diligent hands *will* **r**, 5440
17: 2 wise servant *will* **r** over a disgraceful son, 5440
19:10 much worse for a slave *to* **r** over princes! 5440
22: 7 The rich **r** over the poor, 5440
29: 2 when the wicked **r**, the people groan. 5440
Isa 3:12 oppress my people, women **r** over them. 5440
14: 2 of their captors and **r** over their oppressors. 8097
19: 4 and a fierce king *will* **r** over them," 5440
28:10 For it is: Do and do, do and do, **r** on rule, 7742
28:10 For it is: Do and do, do and do, rule on **r**, 7742
28:10 **r** on rule; a little here, a little there." 7742
28:10 rule on **r**; a little here, a little there." 7742
28:13 Do and do, do and do, **r** on rule, 7742
28:13 Do and do, do and do, rule on **r**, 7742
28:13 do and do, rule on rule, **r** on rule; 7742
28:13 do and do, rule on rule, rule on **r**; 7742
28:14 you scoffers *who* **r** this people in Jerusalem, 5440
32: 1 in righteousness and rulers *will* **r** 8606
52: 5 and *those who* **r** them mock," 5440
Jer 5:31 the priests **r** by their own authority, 8097
22:30 on the throne of David **r** anymore 5440
33:26 and will not choose one of his sons *to* **r** 5440
51:28 and all the countries they **r**, 4939
La 5: 8 Slaves **r** over us, and there is none to free us 5440

Eze 20:33 *I will* **r** over you with a mighty hand and 4887
29:15 that it *will* never again **r** over the nations. 8097
Da 2:39 one of bronze, *will* **r** over the whole earth. 10715
6: 1 It pleased Darius to appoint 120 satraps to **r** 10542
7: 6 and it was given **authority to r**. 10717
11: 3 *who will* **r** *with* great power and do as 5440
11: 5 *will* **r** his own kingdom with great power. 5440
Hos 11: 5 to Egypt and will not Assyria **r** over them 4889
Mic 4: 7 The LORD *will* **r** over them in Mount Zion 4887
5: 6 They *will* **r** the land of Assyria with 8286
Zec 6:13 be clothed with majesty and will sit and **r** 5440
9:10 His **r** will extend from sea to sea and from 5445
Ro 13: 9 are summed up in this one **r**: 3364
15:12 one who will arise *to* **r** over the nations; 806
1Co 7:17 the **r** *I lay down* in all the churches. 1411
Gal 6:16 Peace and mercy to all who follow this **r**, 2834
Eph 1:21 far above all **r** and authority, 794
Col 3:15 Let the peace of Christ **r** in your hearts, 1093
2Th 3:10 we were with you, *we* **gave** you this **r**: 4133
Rev 2:27 '*He will* **r** them with an iron scepter; 4477
12: 5 who will **r** all the nations with an iron 4477
17:17 to give the beast their power to **r**, 993
19:15 "*He will* **r** them with an iron scepter." 4477

RULED (31) [RULE]

Jos 12: 2 *He* **r** from Aroer on the rim of 5440
12: 3 also **r** over the eastern Arabah from the Sea NIH
12: 5 *He* **r** over Mount Hermon, Salecah, 5440
13:10 king of the Amorites, who **r** in Heshbon, 4887
13:21 king of the Amorites, who **r** at Heshbon. 4887
Jdg 11:19 who **r** in Heshbon, and said to him, 4889
Ru 1: 1 In the days when the judges **r**, 9149
1Ki 4: 1 So King Solomon **r** over all Israel. 2118+4889
4:21 And Solomon **r** over all the kingdoms from 5440
4:24 For he **r** over all the kingdoms west of 8097
9:19 and throughout all the territory he **r**. 4939
11:25 So Rezon **r** in Aram and was hostile 4887
12:17 Rehoboam *still* **r** over them. 4887
14:19 Jeroboam's reign, his wars and how *he* **r**, 4887
22:47 was then no king in Edom; a deputy **r**. 4889
2Ki 11: 3 the LORD for six years while Athaliah **r** 4887
1Ch 4:22 who **r** in Moab and Jashubi Lehem. 1249
29:27 over Israel forty years— 4887
2Ch 8: 6 and throughout all the territory he **r**. 4939
9:26 He **r** over all the kings from the River to 5440
10:17 Rehoboam *still* **r** over them. 4887
22:12 for six years while Athaliah **r** the land. 4887
Ne 9:28 to the hand of their enemies so that *they* **r** 8097
Est 1: 1 the Xerxes who **r** *over* 127 provinces 4887
Ps 106:41 and their foes **r** over them. 5440
Ecc 1:16 wisdom more than anyone who has **r** over 6584
Isa 26:13 other lords besides you *have* **r** over us, 1249
63:19 but *you have* not **r** over them, 5440
Jer 34: 1 in the empire he **r** were fighting 3338+4939
Eze 34: 4 *You have* **r** them harshly and brutally. 8097
Ac 13:21 of the tribe of Benjamin, who **r** forty years. NIG

RULER (85) [RULE]

Ge 34: 2 son of Hamor the Hivite, the **r** *of* that area, 5954
45: 8 of his entire household and **r** of all Egypt. 5440
45:26 In fact, he *is* **r** of all Egypt." 5440
Ex 2:14 "Who made you **r** and judge over us? 8569
22:28 "Do not blaspheme God or curse the **r** 5954
Nu 24:19 A **r** will come out of Jacob and destroy 8097
2Sa 5: 2 and you will become their.'" 5592
6:21 from his house when he appointed me **r** 5592
7: 8 the flock to be **r** over my people Israel. 5592
1Ki 1:35 I have appointed him **r** over Israel 5592
11:34 I have made him **r** all the days of his life 5954
22:26 the **r** of the city and to Joash the king's son 8569
1Ch 5: 2 the strongest of his brothers and a **r** came 5592
11: 2 and you will become their.'" 5592
17: 7 to be **r** over my people Israel. 5592
29:12 you *are* the **r** of all things. 5440
29:22 the LORD to be **r** and Zadok to be priest. 5592
2Ch 18:25 to Amon the **r** of the city and to Joash 8569
34: 8 of Azaliah and Maaseiah the **r** of the city, 8569
Ne 3: 9 **r** of a half-district of Jerusalem, 8569
3:12 **r** of a half-district of Jerusalem, 8569
3:14 **r** of the district of Beth Hakkerem. 8569
3:15 **r** of the district of Mizpah. 8569
3:16 **r** of a half-district of Beth Zur. 8569
3:17 Hashabiah, **r** *of* half the district of Keilah, 8569
3:18 **r** of the other half-district of Keilah. 8569
3:19 **r** *of* Mizpah, repaired another section, 8569
Est 1:22 be **r** over his own household. 8606
Ps 8: 6 *You* **made** him **r** over the works 5440
82: 7 you will fall like every other **r**." 8569
105:20 the **r** *of* peoples set him free. 5440
105:21 **r** over all he possessed, 5440
Pr 6: 7 It has no commander, no overseer or **r**, 5440
17: 7 how much worse lying lips to a **r**! 5618
19: 6 Many curry favor with a **r**, 5618
23: 1 When you sit to dine with a **r**, 5440
25:15 Through patience a **r** can be persuaded, 7903
28: 3 A **r** who oppresses the poor is like 1505+8031
28:16 A tyrannical **r** lacks judgment, 5592
29:12 If a **r** listens to lies, all his officials 5440
29:26 Many seek an audience with a **r**, 5440
Ecc 9:17 to be heeded than the shouts of a **r** of fools. 5440
10: 5 the sort of error that arises from a **r**: 8954
Isa 16: 1 Send lambs as tribute to the **r** *of* the land, 5440
60:17 and righteousness your **r**. 5601
Jer 30:21 their **r** will arise from among them. 5440
51:46 violence in the land and of **r** against ruler. 5440

Jer 51:46 violence in the land and of ruler against **r**. 5440
Eze 28: 2 say to the **r** of Tyre, 5592
31:11 I handed it over to the **r** *of* the nations, 380
Da 2:38 *he has* **made** you **r** over them all. 10715
2:48 He **made** him **r** over the entire province 10715
5: 7 *be* **made** the third highest **r** in the kingdom. 10715
5:16 *be* **made** the third highest **r** in the kingdom. 10715
5:29 and he was proclaimed the third highest **r** 10718
9: 1 who *was* **made** **r** over the Babylonian 4887
9:25 the **r**, comes, there will be seven 'sevens,' 5592
9:26 of the **r** who will come will destroy the city 5592
Am 2: 3 I will destroy her **r** and kill all her officials 9149
Mic 5: 1 They will strike Israel's **r** on the cheek with 9149
5: 2 of you will come for me one who will be **r** 5440
7: 3 the **r** demands gifts, the judge accepts 8569
Hab 1:14 like sea creatures that have no **r**. 5440
Zec 10: 4 from him the battle bow, from him every **r**. 5601
Mt 2: 6 for out of you will come a **r** who will be 2451
9:18 a **r** came and knelt before him and said, 807
Mk 5:35 from the house of Jairus, the **synagogue r.** 801
5:36 Jesus told the **synagogue r,** 801
5:38 to the home *of* the **synagogue r,** 801
Lk 8:41 a man named Jairus, a **r** of the synagogue, 807
8:49 from the house of Jairus, the **synagogue r,** 807
13:14 the **synagogue r** said to the people, 801
18:18 A certain **r** asked him, "Good teacher, 807
Ac 7:10 so he made him **r** over Egypt 2451
7:18 nothing about Joseph, **became r** of Egypt. 482
7:27 'Who made you **r** and judge over us? 807
7:35 'Who made you **r** and judge?' 807
7:35 *to be* their **r** and deliverer by God himself, 807
18: 8 Crispus, the **synagogue r,** 801
18:17 on Sosthenes the **synagogue r** and beat him 801
23: 5 not speak evil about the **r** of your people.'" 807
Eph 2: 2 of this world and *of* the **r** of the kingdom 807
1Ti 6:15 God, the blessed and only **R,** 1541
Rev 1: 5 and the **r** of the kings of the earth. 807
3:14 the **r** of God's creation. 794

RULER'S (5) [RULE]

Ge 49:10 nor the **r** **staff** from between his feet, 2980
Ecc 10: 4 If a **r** anger rises against you, 5440
Eze 19:11 Its branches were strong, fit for a **r** scepter. 5440
19:14 on it fit for a **r** scepter.' 5440
Mt 9:23 the **r** house and saw the flute players and 807

RULERS (83) [RULE]

Ge 17:20 He will be the father of twelve **r**, 5954
25:16 the names of the twelve tribal **r** according 5954
Jos 13: 3 (the territory of the five Philistine **r** 6249
Jdg 5: 3 the five **r** of the Philistines, 6249
5: 3 Listen, you **r**! 8142
15:11 "Don't you realize that the Philistines *are* **r** 5440
16: 5 The **r** of the Philistines went to her 6249
16: 8 Then the **r** of the Philistines brought her 6249
16:18 she sent word to the **r** of the Philistines, 6249
16:18 So the **r** of the Philistines returned with 6249
16:23 the **r** of the Philistines assembled to offer 6249
16:27 all the **r** of the Philistines were there, 6249
16:30 and down came the temple on the **r** and all 6249
1Sa 5: 8 the **r** of the Philistines and asked them, 6249
5:11 the **r** of the Philistines and said, "Send 6249
6: 4 according to the number of the Philistine **r**, 6249
6: 4 both you and your **r**. 6249
6:12 The **r** of the Philistines followed them 6249
6:16 The five of the Philistines saw all this 6249
6:18 of Philistine towns belonging to the five **r**— 6249
7: 7 the **r** of the Philistines came up 6249
29: 2 As the Philistine **r** marched with their units 6249
29: 6 but the **r** don't approve of you. 6249
29: 7 do nothing to displease the Philistine **r**." 6249
2Sa 7: 7 to any of their **r** whom I commanded 8657
1Ch 12:19 after consultation, their **r** sent him away. 6249
2Ch 23:20 the **r** of the people and all the people of 5440
32:31 by the **r** of Babylon to ask him about 8569
Job 3:15 with **r** who had gold, 8569
Ps 2: 2 the **r** gather together against the LORD 8142
2:10 be warned, you **r** of the earth. 9149
58: 1 Do you **r** indeed speak justly? 380
76:12 He breaks the spirit of **r**; 5592
105:30 which went up into the bedrooms of their **r**. 4889
110: 6 heaping up the dead and crushing the **r** of 8031
119:23 Though **r** sit together and slander me, 8569
119:161 **R** persecute me without cause, 8569
141: 6 their **r** will be thrown down from the cliffs, 9149
148:11 you princes and all **r** on earth, 9149
Pr 8:15 By me kings reign and **r** make laws 8142
28: 2 a country is rebellious, it has many **r**, 8569
31: 4 kings to drink wine, not for **r** to crave beer, 8142
Ecc 7:19 Wisdom makes one wise man more powerful than ten **r** in a city. 8954
Isa 1:10 you **r** of Sodom; listen to the law 7903
1:23 Your **r** are rebels, companions of thieves; 8569
14: 5 the rod of the wicked, the scepter of the **r**, 5440
16: 8 The **r** of the nations have trampled down 1251
32: 1 in righteousness and **r** will rule 8569
40:23 and reduces the **r** of this world to nothing. 9149
41:25 He treads on **r** as if they were mortar, 6036
49: 7 to the servant of **r**: 5440
Da 7:27 and all **r** will worship and obey him." 10717
9:12 against us and against our **r** by bringing 9149
11:39 *He will* **make** them **r** over many people 5440
Hos 4:18 their **r** dearly love shameful ways. 4482
7: 7 hot as an oven; they devour their **r**. 9149
13:10 Where are your **r** in all your towns, 9149

Mic	3: 1	you **r** *of* the house of Israel.	7903
	3: 9	you **r** *of* the house of Israel,	7903
Hab	1:10	They deride kings and scoff at **r.**	8142
Zep	3: 3	her **r** are evening wolves,	9149
Mt	2: 6	by no means least among the **r** of Judah;	2450
	20:25	"You know that the **r** of the Gentiles lord it	807
Mk	5:22	Then one *of* the **synagogue r**, named Jairus,	801
	10:42	as **r** of the Gentiles lord it over them,	806
Lk	1:52	down **r** from their thrones but has lifted up	1541
	12:11	before synagogues, **r** and authorities, do	794
	23:13	the chief priests, the **r** and the people,	807
	23:35	and the **r** even sneered at him.	807
	24:20	and our **r** handed him over to be sentenced	807
Jn	7:48	of the **r** or *of* the Pharisees believed in him?	807
Ac	4: 5	The next day the **r**, elders and teachers	807
	4: 8	"**R** and elders of the people!	807
	4:26	the **r** gather together against the Lord and	807
	13:15	the **synagogue r** sent word to them, saying,	801
	13:27	The people of Jerusalem and their **r** did	807
Ro	13: 3	For **r** hold no terror for those who do right,	807
1Co	2: 6	wisdom of this age or *of* the **r** of this age,	807
	2: 8	None *of* the **r** of this age understood it,	807
Eph	3:10	be made known *to* the **r** and authorities in	794
	6:12	but against the **r**, against the authorities,	794
Col	1:16	whether thrones or powers or **r**	794
Tit	3: 1	Remind the people to be subject *to* **r**	794

RULES (20) [RULE]

Nu	9: 3	with all its **r** and regulations."	2978
	9:14	so in accordance with its **r** and regulations.	2978
	15:15	the same **r** for you and for the alien living	2978
2Sa	23: 3	'When *one* **r** over men in righteousness,	5440
	23: 3	*when he* **r** in the fear of God,	5440
1Ki	21:18	Ahab king of Israel, who **r** in Samaria.	NIH
2Ch	30:19	even if he is not clean **according to the r**	3869
Ps	22:28	to the LORD and *he* **r** over the nations.	5440
	59:13	the ends of the earth that God **r** over Jacob.	5440
	66: 7	*He* **r** forever by his power,	5440
	103:19	and his kingdom **r** over all.	5440
Isa	29:13	of me is made up only of **r** taught by men.	5184
	40:10	and his arm **r** for him.	5440
Da	4:26	when you acknowledge that Heaven **r.**"	10718
Mt	15: 9	their teachings are but **r** taught by men."	1945
Mk	7: 7	their teachings are but **r** taught by men.'	1945
Lk	22:26	and the one who **r** like the one who serves.	2451
Col	2:20	*do you* **submit** to its **r:**	1505
2Ti	2: 5	unless he competes **according to the r.**	3789
Rev	17:18	The woman you saw is the great city that **r** over the kings	993+2400

RULING (8) [RULE]

Jdg	14: 4	for at that time they *were* **r** over Israel.)	5440
1Ki	3:27	Then the king gave *his* **r:**	6699
	15:18	the king of Aram, who *was* **r** in Damascus.	3782
2Ch	16: 2	king of Aram, who *was* **r** in Damascus.	3782
Ezr	4:20	Jerusalem has had powerful kings **r** over	10718
Job	34:30	to keep a godless man from **r**,	4887
Pr	28:15	or a charging bear is a wicked man **r** over	5440
Jn	3: 1	a member of the Jewish **r** council.	807

RUMAH (1)

| 2Ki | 23:36 | daughter of Pedaiah; she was from **R.** | 8126 |

RUMBLE (1) [RUMBLING, RUMBLINGS]

| Jer | 47: 3 | at the noise of enemy chariots and the **r** | 2162 |

RUMBLING (3) [RUMBLE]

Job	37: 2	to the **r** that comes from his mouth.	2049
Eze	3:12	and I heard behind me a loud **r** sound—	8323
	3:13	the wheels beside them, a loud **r** sound.	8323

RUMBLINGS (4) [RUMBLE]

Rev	4: 5	**r** and peals of thunder.	5889
	8: 5	and there came peals of thunder, **r**,	5889
	11:19	And there came flashes of lightning, **r**,	5889
	16:18	Then there came flashes of lightning, **r**,	5889

RUMOR (5) [RUMORS]

Job	28:22	'Only a **r** of it has reached our ears.'	9051
Jer	51:46	*one* **r** comes this year, another the next,	9019
Eze	7:26	and **r** upon rumor.	9019
	7:26	and rumor upon **r.**	9019
Jn	21:23	the **r** spread among the brothers	3364

RUMORS (4) [RUMOR]

Jer	51:46	not lose heart or be afraid when **r** are heard	9019
	51:46	the next, **r** of violence in the land and	NIH
Mt	24: 6	You will hear of wars and **r** of wars,	198
Mk	13: 7	When you hear of wars and **r** of wars,	198

RUMP (KJV) See FAT TAIL

RUN (73) [OUTRAN, OVERRAN,
    OVERRUN, RAN, RUNNER, RUNNERS,
    RUNNING, RUNS]

Ge	19:20	Look, here is a town near enough to **r** to,	5674
	31:27	Why *did you* **r** off secretly	1368
	39:13	in her hand and *had* **r** out of the house,	5674
Ex	23:27	I will make all your enemies turn their backs and **r.**	NIH

Lev	26:36	*They will* **r** as though fleeing from	5674
Nu	34: 7	**r a line** from the Great Sea to Mount Hor	9292
	34:10	**r a line** from Hazar Enan to Shepham.	204
Jos	7:12	and **r** because they have been made liable	NIH
Ru	3:10	You *have* not **r** after the younger men,	2143
1Sa	8:11	and they will **r** in front of his chariots.	8132
	14:22	that the Philistines *were* **on the r**,	5674
	19:11	"If you don't **r** *for* your life tonight,	4880
	20:36	"**R** and find the arrows I shoot."	8132
	21:13	and **letting** saliva **r down** his beard.	3718
	31: 4	"Draw your sword and **r** me **through**,	1991
	31: 4	and **r** me **through** and abuse me."	1991
2Sa	15: 1	a chariot and horses and with fifty men *to* **r**	8132
	18:19	"Let me **r** and take the news to the king that	8132
	18:22	please *let me* **r** behind the Cushite."	8132
	18:23	He said, "Come what may, *I want to* **r.**"	8132
	18:23	So Joab said, "**R!**"	8132
1Ki	1: 5	with fifty men *to* **r** ahead of him.	8132
	17:14	be used up and the jug of oil *will* not **r dry**	2893
	17:16	not used up and the jug of oil *did* not **r**, dry,	2893
2Ki	4:26	**R** to meet her and ask her,	8132
	4:29	take my staff in your hand and **r.**	2143
	5:20	*I will* **r** after him and get something	8132
	9: 3	Then open the door and **r**; don't delay!"	5674
1Ch	10: 4	"Draw your sword and **r** me **through**,	1991
Ne	6:11	But I said, "Should a man like me **r** away?	1368
Job	1: 5	When a period of feasting *had* **r** *its* course,	5938
	39:18	spreads her **feathers** to **r**,	928+2021+5257+5294
Ps	16: 4	sorrows of those will increase *who* **r** after	4554
	19: 5	like a champion rejoicing to **r** his course.	8132
	119:32	*I* **r** in the path of your commands,	8132
Pr	4:12	when *you* **r**, you will not stumble.	8132
	18:10	the righteous **r** to it and are safe.	8132
Isa	5:11	in the morning *to* **r** after their drinks,	8103
	7:25	and *where* sheep **r.**	5330
	8: 7	overflow all its channels, **r** over all its banks	2143
	10: 3	To whom *will you* **r** for help?	5674
	40:31	*they will* **r** and not grow weary,	8132
Jer	2:23	*I have* not **r** after the Baals'?	2143
	2:25	**Do not r** until your feet are bare	4979
	17:16	not **r** away from being your shepherd,	237
	23:21	yet they *have* **r** with their message;	8132
	48: 6	**R** *for* your lives!	4880
	51: 6	**R** *for* your lives!	4880
	51:45	**R** *for* your lives!	4880
	51:45	**R** from the fierce anger of the LORD.	NIH
Eze	47:15	the north side it will **r** from the Great Sea	NIH
	47:18	"On the east side the boundary will **r**	NIH
	47:19	the south side it will **r** from Tamar as far as	NIH
	48:28	of Gad *will* **r** south from Tamar to	2118
Joel	2: 9	*they* **r** along the wall.	8132
	3:18	all the ravines of Judah *will* **r** *with* water.	2143
Am	6:12	*Do* horses **r** on the rocky crags?	8132
Na	1: 4	*he* **makes** all the rivers **r dry**.	2990
Hab	2: 2	on tablets so that a herald *may* **r** with it.	8132
Zec	2: 4	"**R**, tell that young man,	8132
Mt	6:32	For the pagans **r** after all these things,	2118
	9:17	the wine *will* **r** out and the wineskins will	1772
Lk	5:37	the wine *will* **r** out and the wineskins will	1772
Jn	10: 5	*they will* **r** away from him because they do	5771
Ac	27:17	that *they would* **r aground** on the sandbars	1738
	27:26	we must **r aground** on some island."	1738
	27:39	where they decided *to* **r** the ship **aground**	2034
1Co	9:24	not know that in a race all the runners, **r**,	5556
	9:24	**R** in such a way as to get the prize.	5556
	9:26	*I do* not **r** like a man running aimlessly;	5556
Gal	2: 2	that I was running or *had* **r** *my* **race** in vain.	5556
Php	2:16	the day of Christ that *I* did not **r** or labor	5556
Heb	12: 1	and *let us* **r** with perseverance	5556

RUNNER (1) [RUN]

| Job | 9:25 | "My days are swifter than a **r**; | 8132 |

RUNNERS (1) [RUN]

| 1Co | 9:24 | Do you not know that in a race all the **r** run, | 5556 |

RUNNING (30) [RUN]

Ge	16: 8	"I'm **r** away from my mistress Sarai,"	1368
	31:20	by not telling him he *was* **r away.**	1368
Ex	32:25	Moses saw that the people *were* **r** wild and	7277
Lev	21:20	or **r** sores or damaged testicles.	3539
	22:22	anything with warts or festering or **r sores.**	3539
Jos	8: 6	'They are **r** away from us as they did	5674
2Sa	3:29	without *someone who has a* **r** sore or	2307
	18:24	As he looked out, he saw a man **r** alone.	8132
	18:26	Then the watchman saw another man **r**,	8132
	18:26	"Look, another man **r** alone!"	8132
2Ki	5:21	When Naaman saw him **r** toward him,	8132
2Ch	23:12	the noise of the people **r** and cheering	8132
Ps	133: 2	**r down** on the beard,	3718
	133: 2	**r down** on Aaron's beard,	NIH
Pr	5:15	**r water** from your own well.	5689
Jer	2:23	You are a swift she-camel **r here and there**,	2006+8592
Eze	45: 7	**r** lengthwise from the western to	NIH
	48:18	on the sacred portion and **r** the length of it,	NIH
	48:21	Both these areas **r** the length of	NIH
Jnh	1:10	(They knew he *was* **r** away from	1368
Mk	9:25	When Jesus saw that a crowd *was* **r** to	2192
Lk	6:38	pressed down, shaken together and **r over**,	5658
	17:23	*Do not* **go r off after** them.	599+1503+3593
Jn	20: 2	So *she* came **r** to Simon Peter and	5556
	20: 4	Both *were* **r**, but the other disciple outran Peter	5556
Ac	3:11	all the people were astonished and **came r**	5340

Ac	21:30	and the people came **r** from all directions.	5282
1Co	9:26	I do not **r** like a man aimlessly;	NIG
Gal	2: 2	that *I was* **r** or had run my race in vain.	5556
	5: 7	*You were* **r** a good **race.**	5556

RUNS (8) [RUN]

Ge	2:14	it **r** along the east side of Asshur.	2143
2Sa	18:27	the first one **r** like Ahimaaz son of Zadok."	5297
Ps	147:15	his word **r** swiftly.	8132
Eze	16:34	**r** after you *for* your **favors.**	339+2388
Lk	12:30	For the pagan world **r** after all such things,	2118
Jn	10:12	he abandons the sheep and **r** away.	5771
	10:13	The man **r** away because he is a hired hand	NIG
2Jn	1: 9	Anyone who **r** ahead and does not continue	4575

RURAL (1)

| Est | 9:19 | That is why **r** Jews—those living in villages | 7253 |

RUSE (1)

| Jos | 9: 4 | resorted to a **r:** They went as a delegation | 6893 |

RUSH (6) [RUSHED, RUSHES, RUSHING]

Jdg	21:21	then **r** from the vineyards and each	3655
Pr	1:16	for their feet **r** into sin,	8132
	6:18	feet that are quick to **r** into evil,	8132
Isa	59: 7	Their feet **r** into sin;	8132
Jer	49: 3	**r** here and there inside the walls,	8763
Joel	2: 9	*They* **r** upon the city;	9212

RUSHED (15) [RUSH]

Jos	8:19	from their position and **r forward.**	8132
Jdg	9:44	and the companies with him **r forward** to	7320
	9:44	Then two companies **r** upon those in	7320
1Sa	7:11	of Israel **r** out of Mizpah and pursued	3655
2Sa	19:17	They **r** to the Jordan, where the king was.	7502
Est	6:12	But Haman **r** home, with his head covered	1894
Mt	8:32	the whole herd **r** down the steep bank into	3994
Mk	5:13	the herd **r** down the steep bank into the lake	3994
Lk	8:33	the herd **r** down the steep bank into the lake	3994
Ac	7:57	at the top of their voices, *they* all **r** at him,	3994
	14:14	*they* tore their clothes and **r** out into	1737
	16:29	**r** in and fell trembling before Paul	1659
	17: 5	They **r** to Jason's house in search of Paul	2392
	19:29	and **r** as one man into the theater.	3994
Jude	1:11	*they have* **r** for profit into Balaam's error;	1772

RUSHES (3) [RUSH]

Dt	32:35	disaster is near and their doom **r** upon them.	2590
Job	16:14	*he* **r** at me like a warrior.	8132
Isa	19: 6	The reeds and **r** will wither,	6068

RUSHING (11) [RUSH]

Jdg	5:15	**r** after him into the valley.	8938
Job	20:28	**r** waters on the day of God's wrath.	5599
Isa	30:28	His breath *is* like a **r** torrent,	8851
Eze	1:24	His voice was like the roar of **r** waters,	8041
	43: 2	like the roar of **r** waters,	8041
Mic	1: 4	like water **r** down a slope.	5599
Na	2: 4	**r back and forth** through the squares.	9212
Rev	1:15	his voice was like the sound *of* **r** waters.	4498
	9: 9	of many horses and chariots **r** into battle.	5556
	14: 2	*of* **r** waters and like a loud peal of thunder.	4498
	19: 6	like the roar of **r** waters and like loud peals	4498

RUST (2)

| Mt | 6:19 | where moth and **r** destroy, | 1111 |
| | 6:20 | where moth and **r** do not destroy, | 1111 |

RUTH (21)

Ru	1: 4	one named Orpah and the other **R.**	8134
	1:14	but **R** clung to her.	8134
	1:16	But **R** replied, "Don't urge me to leave you	8134
	1:18	that **R** was determined to go with her,	2085S
	1:22	from Moab accompanied by **R**	8134
	2: 2	And **R** the Moabitess said to Naomi,	8134
	2: 8	Boaz said to **R**, "My daughter, listen to me.	8134
	2:17	So **R** gleaned in the field until evening.	NIH
	2:18	**R** also brought out and gave her	NIH
	2:19	Then **R** told her mother-in-law about	NIH
	2:21	Then **R** the Moabitess said,	8134
	2:22	Naomi said to **R** her daughter-in-law,	8134
	2:23	So **R** stayed close to the servant girls	NIH
	3: 5	"I will do whatever you say," **R** answered.	NIH
	3: 7	**R** approached quietly, uncovered his feet	NIH
	3: 9	"I am your servant **R**," she said.	8134
	3:16	When **R** came to her mother-in-law,	NIH
	4: 5	from Naomi and from **R** the Moabitess,	8134
	4:10	I have also acquired **R** the Moabitess,	8134
	4:13	So Boaz took **R** and she became his wife.	8134
Mt	1: 5	Obed, whose mother was **R**,	4858

RUTHLESS (20) [RUTHLESSLY]

Job	6:23	ransom me from the clutches of the **r**'?	6883
	15:20	the **r** through all the years stored up	6883
	27:13	*a* man receives from the Almighty:	6883
Ps	35:11	**R** witnesses come forward;	2805
	37:35	I have seen a wicked and **r** man flourishing	6883
	54: 3	**r** men seek my life—	6883
	86:14	a band of **r** men seeks my life—	6883
Pr	11:16	but **r** *men* gain only wealth.	6883

Isa	13:11	and will humble the pride of the **r**.	6883
	25: 3	cities of **r** nations will revere you.	6883
	25: 4	the **r** is like a storm driving against a wall	6883
	25: 5	so the song of the **r** is stilled.	6883
	29: 5	the **r** hordes like blown chaff.	6883
	29:20	The **r** will vanish,	6883
Eze	28: 7	the *most* **r** of nations;	6883
	30:11	He and his army—the *most* **r** of nations—	6883
	31:12	the *most* **r** of foreign nations cut it down	6883
	32:12	the *most* **r** of all nations.	6883
Hab	1: 6	that **r** and impetuous people,	5253
Ro	1:31	they are senseless, faithless, heartless, **r**.	*446*

RUTHLESSLY (6) [RUTHLESS]

Ex	1:13	and worked them **r**.	928+7266
	1:14	the Egyptians used them **r**.	928+7266
Lev	25:43	Do not rule over them **r**, but fear your God.	928+7266
	25:46	not rule over your fellow Israelites **r**.	928+7266
	25:53	that his owner does not rule over him **r**.	928+7266
Job	30:21	You turn on me **r**;	425+4200

S

SABACHTHANI (2)

Mt	27:46	in a loud voice, "Eloi, Eloi, lama **s**?"—	*4876*
Mk	15:34	in a loud voice, "Eloi, Eloi, lama **s**?"—	*4876*

SABAOTH (KJV) See ALMIGHTY

SABBATH (133) [SABBATHS]

Ex	16:23	a holy **S** to the LORD.	8701
	16:25	"because today is a **S** to the LORD.	8701
	16:26	but on the seventh day, the **S**,	8701
	16:29	that the LORD has given you the **S**;	8701
	20: 8	"Remember the **S** day by keeping it holy.	8701
	20:10	seventh day is a **S** to the LORD your God.	8701
	20:11	Therefore the LORD blessed the **S** day	8701
	31:14	" 'Observe the **S**, because it is holy to you.	8701
	31:15	but the seventh day is a **S** of rest,	8701
	31:15	Whoever does any work on the **S** day must	8701
	31:16	The Israelites are to observe the **S**,	8701
	35: 2	a **S** of rest to the LORD	8701
	35: 3	in any of your dwellings on the **S** day."	8701
Lev	16:31	It is a **s** of rest,	8701
	23: 3	but the seventh day is a **S** of rest,	8701
	23: 3	wherever you live, it is a **S** to the LORD.	8701
	23:11	priest is to wave it on the day after the **S**.	8701
	23:15	" 'From the day after the **S**,	8701
	23:16	up to the day after the seventh **S**,	8701
	23:32	It is a **s** of rest for you,	8701
	23:32	*you are to* **observe** *your* **s**."	8697+8701
	24: 8	before the LORD regularly, **S** after Sabbath,	928+928+2021+2021+3427+3427+8701+8701
	24: 8	before the LORD regularly, **Sabbath after S**,	928+928+2021+2021+3427+3427+8701+8701
	25: 2	the land itself **must observe a s**	8697+8701
	25: 4	in the seventh year the land is to have a **s**	8701
	25: 4	a sabbath of rest, a **s** to the LORD.	8701
	25: 6	during the **s** year will be food for you—	8701
	26:34	the land will enjoy its **s** years all the time	8701
Nu	15:32	gathering wood on the **S** day.	8701
	28: 9	" 'On the **S** day, make an offering of two	8701
	28:10	the burnt offering for **every S**,	928+8701+8701
Dt	5:12	"Observe the **S** day by keeping it holy,	8701
	5:14	seventh day is a **S** to the LORD your God.	8701
	5:15	commanded you to observe the **S** day.	8701
2Ki	4:23	"It's not the New Moon or the **S**."	8701
	11: 5	that are going on duty on the **S**—	8701
	11: 7	that normally go off **S** duty are all to guard	8701
	11: 9	the **S** and those who were going off duty—	8701
	16:18	the **S** canopy that had been built at	8701
1Ch	9:32	*for* **every S** the bread set out on the table.	8701+8701
2Ch	23: 4	on the **S** are to keep watch at the doors,	8701
	23: 8	the **S** and those who were going off duty—	8701
	36:21	The land enjoyed its **s rests**;	8701
Ne	9:14	You made known to them your holy **S**	8701
	10:31	or grain to sell on the **S**,	8701
	10:31	from them on the **S** or on any holy day.	8701
	13:15	treading winepresses on the **S**	8701
	13:15	bringing all this into Jerusalem on the **S**.	8701
	13:16	and selling them in Jerusalem on the **S** to	8701
	13:17	you are doing—desecrating the **S** day?	8701
	13:18	wrath against Israel by desecrating the **S**."	8701
	13:19	on the gates of Jerusalem before the **S**,	8701
	13:19	and not opened until the **S** was over.	8701
	13:19	be brought in on the **S** day.	8701
	13:21	that time on they no longer came on the **S**.	8701
	13:22	the gates in order to keep the **S** day holy.	8701
Ps	92: T	A psalm. A song. For the **S** day.	8701
Isa	56: 2	who keeps the **S** without desecrating it,	8701
	56: 6	all who keep the **S** without desecrating it	8701
	58:13	"If you keep your feet from breaking the **S**	8701
	58:13	if you call the **S** a delight and	8701

Isa	66:23	to another and from *one* **S** to another,	8701
Jer	17:21	Be careful not to carry a load on the **S** day	8701
	17:22	of your houses or do any work on the **S**,	8701
	17:22	but keep the **S** day holy,	8701
	17:24	through the gates of this city on the **S**,	8701
	17:24	the **S** day holy by not doing any work on it,	8701
	17:27	the **S** day holy by not carrying any load	8701
	17:27	the gates of Jerusalem on the **S** day,	8701
Eze	46: 1	the six working days, but on the **S** day and	8701
	46: 4	on the **S** day is to be six male lambs and	8701
	46:12	as he does on the **S** day.	8701
Hos	2:11	her **S** days—all her appointed feasts.	8701
Am	8: 5	**S** be ended that we may market wheat?"—	8701
Mt	12: 1	through the grainfields *on the* **S**.	4879
	12: 2	Your disciples are doing what is unlawful on the **S**."	4879
	12: 5	*on the* **S** the priests in the temple desecrate	4879
	12: 8	For the Son of Man is Lord of the **S**."	4879
	12:10	"Is it lawful to heal *on the* **S**?"	4879
	12:11	a sheep and it falls into a pit *on the* **S**,	4879
	12:12	Therefore it is lawful to do good *on the* **S**."	4879
	24:20	not take place in winter or *on the* **S**.	4879
	28: 1	**After the S**, at dawn on the first day	4067+4879
Mk	1:21	and when the **S** came,	4879
	2:23	**One S** Jesus was going through	1877+3836+4879
	2:24	are they doing what is unlawful on the **S**?"	4879
	2:27	he said to them, "The **S** was made for man,	4879
	2:27	not man for the **S**.	4879
	2:28	So the Son of Man is Lord even *of the* **S**."	4879
	3: 2	to see if he would heal him *on the* **S**.	4879
	3: 4	"Which is lawful *on the* **S**: to do good or	4879
	6: 2	When the **S** came, he began to teach	4879
	15:42	(that is, the **day before the S**).	4640
	16: 1	When the **S** was over, Mary Magdalene	4879
Lk	4:16	on the **S** day he went into the synagogue,	4879
	4:31	and on the **S** began to teach the people.	4879
	6: 1	**One S** Jesus was going through	1877+4879
	6: 2	"Why are you doing what is unlawful on the **S**?	4879
	6: 5	"The Son of Man is Lord *of the* **S**."	4879
	6: 6	On another **S** he went into the synagogue	4879
	6: 7	to see if he would heal on the **S**,	4879
	6: 9	"I ask you, which is lawful *on the* **S**:	4879
	13:10	On a **S** Jesus was teaching in one of	4879
	13:14	because Jesus had healed *on the* **S**,	4879
	13:14	be healed on those days, not *on the* **S**."	4879
	13:15	the **S** untie his ox or donkey from the stall	4879
	13:16	*on the* **S** day from what bound her?"	4879
	14: 1	One **S**, when Jesus went to eat in the house	4879
	14: 3	"Is it lawful to heal *on the* **S** or not?"	4879
	14: 5	or an ox that falls into a well on the **S** day,	4879
	23:54	and the **S** was about to begin.	4879
	23:56	the **S** in obedience to the commandment.	4879
Jn	5: 9	The day on which this took place was a **S**,	4879
	5:10	"It is the **S**; the law forbids you to carry	4879
	5:16	Jesus was doing these things on the **S**,	4879
	5:18	not only was he breaking the **S**,	4879
	7:22	you circumcise a child on the **S**.	4879
	7:23	Now if a child can be circumcised on the **S**	4879
	7:23	for healing the whole man on the **S**?	4879
	9:14	and opened the man's eyes was a **S**.	4879
	9:16	for he does not keep the **S**."	4879
	19:31	and the next day was to be a special **S**.	4879
	19:31	the bodies left on the crosses during the **S**,	4879
Ac	1:12	a **S** day's walk from the city.	1584+2400+3847+4879
	13:14	*On the* **S** they entered the synagogue	4879
	13:27	of the prophets that are read every **S**.	4879
	13:42	about these things on the next **S**.	4879
	13:44	the next **S** almost the whole city gathered	4879
	15:21	and is read in the synagogues on every **S**."	4879
	16:13	*On the* **S** we went outside the city gate	2465+3836+4879
	17: 2	on three **S days** he reasoned with them from	4879
	18: 4	Every **S** he reasoned in the synagogue,	4879
Col	2:16	a New Moon celebration or a **S day**.	4879

SABBATH-REST (1) [REST]

Heb	4: 9	then, a **S** for the people of God;	4878

SABBATHS (30) [SABBATH]

Ex	31:13	'You must observe my **S**.	8701
Lev	19: 3	and you must observe my **S**.	8701
	19:30	" 'Observe my **S** and have reverence	8701
	23:38	to those for the LORD's **S** and in addition	8701
	25: 8	" 'Count off seven **s** of years—	8701
	25: 8	that the seven **s** of years amount to a period	8701
	26: 2	" 'Observe my **S** and have reverence	8701
	26:34	then the land will rest and enjoy its **s**.	8701
	26:35	not have during the **s** you lived in it.	8701
	26:43	and will enjoy its **s** while it lies desolate	8701
1Ch	23:31	on **S** and at New Moon festivals and	8701
2Ch	2: 4	and evening and on **S** and New Moons and	8701
	8:13	for offerings commanded by Moses for **S**,	8701
	31: 3	and for the burnt offerings on the **S**,	8701
Ne	10:33	for the offerings on the **S**,	8701
Isa	1:13	New Moons, **S** and convocations—	8701
	56: 4	"To the eunuchs who keep my **S**,	8701
La	2: 6	The LORD has made Zion forget her appointed feasts and her **S**;	8701
Eze	20:12	Also I gave them my **S** as a sign between us,	8701
	20:13	and they utterly desecrated my **S**.	8701
	20:16	and desecrated my **S**.	8701
	20:20	Keep my **S** holy, that they may be a sign	8701
	20:21	and they desecrated my **S**.	8701

Eze	20:24	and desecrated my **S**,	8701
	22: 8	and desecrated my **S**.	8701
	22:26	they shut their eyes to the keeping of my **S**,	8701
	23:38	and desecrated my **S**.	8701
	44:24	and they are to keep my **S** holy.	8701
	45:17	the New Moons and the **S**—	8701
	46: 3	On the **S** and New Moons the people of	8701

SABEANS (4)

Job	1:15	and the **S** attacked and carried them off.	8644
Isa	45:14	the merchandise of Cush, and those tall **S**—	6014
Eze	23:42	**S** were brought from the desert along	6014
Joel	3: 8	and they will sell them to the **S**,	8645

SABTA (1)

1Ch	1: 9	Seba, Havilah, **S**, Raamah and Sabteca.	6029

SABTAH (1)

Ge	10: 7	Seba, Havilah, **S**, Raamah and Sabteca.	6030

SABTECA (2)

Ge	10: 7	Seba, Havilah, Sabtah, Raamah and **S**.	6031
1Ch	1: 9	Seba, Havilah, Sabta, Raamah and **S**.	6031

SACAR (2)

1Ch	11:35	Ahiam son of **S** the Hararite,	8511
	26: 4	**S** the fourth, Nethanel the fifth,	8511

SACHET (1)

SS	1:13	a **s** of myrrh resting between my breasts.	7655

SACK (10) [SACKS]

Ge	42:25	to put each man's silver back in his **s**,	8566
	42:27	for the night one of them opened his **s**	8566
	42:27	and he saw his silver in the mouth of his **s**.	623
	42:28	"Here it is in my **s**."	623
	42:35	in each man's **s** was his pouch of silver!	8566
	43:21	in the mouth of his **s**.	623
	44: 2	put each man's silver in the mouth of his **s**.	623
	44: 2	in the mouth of the youngest one's **s**,	623
	44:11	of them quickly lowered his **s** to the ground	623
	44:12	And the cup was found in Benjamin's **s**.	623

SACKBUT (KJV) See LYRE

SACKCLOTH (49)

Ge	37:34	on **s** and mourned for his son many days.	8566
Lev	11:32	whether it is made of wood, cloth, hide or **s**.	8566
2Sa	3:31	and put on **s** and walk in mourning in front	8566
	21:10	of Aiah took **s** and spread it out for herself	8566
1Ki	20:31	of Israel with **s** around our waists and ropes	8566
	20:32	Wearing **s** around their waists and ropes	8566
	21:27	he tore his clothes, put on **s** and fasted.	8566
	21:27	He lay in **s** and went around meekly.	8566
2Ki	6:30	and there, underneath, he had **s** on his body.	8566
	19: 1	he tore his clothes and put on **s** and went	8566
	19: 2	and the leading priests, all wearing **s**, to	8566
1Ch	21:16	Then David and the elders, clothed in **s**,	8566
Ne	9: 1	fasting and wearing **s** and having dust	8566
Est	4: 1	he tore his clothes, put on **s** and ashes,	8566
	4: 2	no one clothed in **s** was allowed to enter it.	8566
	4: 3	Many lay in **s** and ashes.	8566
	4: 4	for him to put on instead of his **s**,	8566
Job	16:15	"I have sewed **s** over my skin	8566
Ps	30:11	you removed my **s** and clothed me with joy,	8566
	35:13	I put on **s** and humbled myself with fasting.	8566
	69:11	when I put on **s**, people make sport of me.	8566
Isa	3:24	instead of fine clothing, **s**;	4680+8566
	15: 3	In the streets they wear **s**;	8566
	20: 2	the **s** from your body and the sandals	8566
	22:12	to tear out your hair and put on **s**.	8566
	32:11	**put s around** your waists.	2520
	37: 1	he tore his clothes and put on **s** and went	8566
	37: 2	and the leading priests, all wearing **s**,	8566
	50: 3	with darkness and make **s** its covering."	8566
	58: 5	like a reed and for lying on **s** and ashes?	8566
Jer	4: 8	So put on **s**, lament and wail,	8566
	6:26	O my people, put on **s** and roll in ashes;	8566
	48:37	and every waist is covered with **s**.	8566
	49: 3	Put on **s** and mourn;	8566
La	2:10	on their heads and put on **s**.	8566
Eze	7:18	They will put on **s** and be clothed	8566
	27:31	because of you and will put on **s**.	8566
Da	9: 3	in fasting, and in **s** and ashes.	8566
Joel	1: 8	in **s** grieving for the husband of her youth.	8566
	1:13	Put on **s**, O priests, and mourn;	NIH
	1:13	Come, spend the night in **s**,	8566
Am	8:10	of you wear **s** and shave your heads.	8566
Jnh	3: 5	from the greatest to the least, put on **s**.	8566
	3: 6	covered himself with **s** and sat down in	8566
	3: 8	But let man and beast be covered with **s**.	8566
Mt	11:21	they would have repented long ago in **s**	4884
Lk	10:13	sitting in **s** and ashes.	4884
Rev	6:12	The sun turned black like **s** made	4884
	11: 3	for 1,260 days, clothed in **s**."	4884

SACKED (1)

2Ki	15:16	*He* **s** Tiphsah and ripped open all the	5782

SACKS (10) [SACK]

Ge	42:35	As they were emptying their s,	8566
	43:12	that was put back into the mouths of your s.	623
	43:18	that was put back into our s the first time.	623
	43:21	for the night we opened our s and each	623
	43:22	We don't know who put our silver in our s."	623
	43:23	has given you treasure in your s;	623
	44: 1	"Fill the men's s with as much food	623
	44: 8	inside the mouths of our s.	623
Jos	9: 4	with worn-out s and old wineskins,	8566
1Sa	9: 7	The food in our s is gone.	3998

SACRED (131)

Ex	12:16	On the first day hold a s assembly,	7731
	23:24	and break their s stones to pieces.	5167
	28: 2	Make s garments for your brother Aaron,	7731
	28: 4	They are to make these s garments	7731
	28:38	in the s gifts the Israelites consecrate,	7731
	29: 6	on his head and attach the s diadem to	7731
	29:29	"Aaron's s garments will belong	7731
	29:31	and cook the meat in a s place.	7705
	29:33	because they are s.	7731
	29:34	It must not be eaten, because it is s.	7731
	30:25	Make these into a s anointing oil,	7731
	30:25	It will be the s anointing oil.	7731
	30:31	to be my s anointing oil for the generations	7731
	30:32	It is s, and you are to consider it sacred.	7731
	30:32	It is sacred, and you are to consider it s.	7731
	30:35	It is to be salted and pure and s.	7731
	31:10	both the s garments for Aaron the priest and	7731
	34:13	smash their s stones and cut down	5167
	35:19	both the s garments for Aaron the priest and	7731
	35:21	for all its service, and for the s garments.	7731
	37:29	also made the s anointing oil and the pure,	7731
	39: 1	They also made s garments for Aaron,	7731
	39:30	They made the plate, the s diadem,	7731
	39:41	both the s garments for Aaron the priest and	7731
	40:13	Then dress Aaron in the s garments,	7731
Lev	8: 9	the s diadem, on the front of it,	7731
	12: 4	not touch anything s or go to the sanctuary	7731
	16: 4	He is to put on the s linen tunic,	7731
	16: 4	These are s garments;	7731
	16:32	He is to put on the s linen garments	7731
	22: 2	the s offerings the Israelites consecrate	7731
	22: 3	the s offerings that the Israelites consecrate	7731
	22: 4	not eat the s offerings until he is cleansed.	7731
	22: 6	the s offerings unless he has bathed himself	7731
	22: 7	and after that he may eat the s offerings.	7731
	22:10	a priest's family may eat the s offering,	7731
	22:12	she may not eat any of the s contributions.	7731
	22:14	"If anyone eats a s offering by mistake,	7731
	22:15	the s offerings the Israelites present to	7731
	22:16	by allowing them to eat the s offerings and	7731
	23: 2	which you are to proclaim as s assemblies.	7731
	23: 3	a day of s assembly.	7731
	23: 4	the s assemblies you are to proclaim	7731
	23: 7	a s assembly and do no regular work.	7731
	23: 8	And on the seventh day hold a s assembly	7731
	23:20	a s offering to the LORD for the priest.	7731
	23:21	a s assembly and do no regular work.	7731
	23:24	a day of rest, a s assembly commemorated	7731
	23:27	Hold a s assembly and deny yourselves,	7731
	23:35	The first day is a s assembly;	7731
	23:36	a s assembly and present an offering made	7731
	23:37	as s assemblies for bringing offerings made	7731
	26: 1	up an image or a s stone for yourselves,	5167
Nu	5: 9	All the s contributions the Israelites bring to	7731
	5:10	Each man's s gifts are his own,	7731
	28:18	a s assembly and do no regular work.	7731
	28:25	On the seventh day hold a s assembly	7731
	28:26	hold a s assembly and do no regular work.	7731
	29: 1	of the seventh month hold a s assembly.	7731
	29: 7	of this seventh month hold a s assembly.	7731
	29:12	hold a s assembly and do no regular work.	7731
Dt	7: 5	down their altars, smash their s stones,	5167
	12: 3	down their altars, smash their s stones	5167
	16:22	and do not erect a s stone,	5167
	26:13	the s portion and have given it to	7731
	26:14	not eaten any of the s portion while I was	5647S
Jos	6:19	and the articles of bronze and iron are s to	7731
1Ki	1:39	from the s tent and anointed Solomon.	NIH
	8: 4	of Meeting and all the s furnishings in it.	7731
	14:23	high places, s stones and Asherah poles	5167
2Ki	3: 2	He got rid of the s stone of Baal	5167
	10:26	They brought the s stone out of the temple	5167
	10:27	They demolished the s stone of Baal	5167
	12: 4	the money that is brought as s offerings to	7731
	12:18	of Judah took all the s objects dedicated	7731
	17:10	They set up s stones and Asherah poles	5167
	18: 4	smashed the s stones and cut down	5167
	23:14	the s stones and cut down the Asherah poles	5167
1Ch	16:42	of the other instruments for s song.	466
	22:19	of the LORD and the s articles belonging	7731
	23:28	of all s things and the performance	7731
2Ch	5: 5	of Meeting and all the s furnishings in it.	7731
	14: 3	smashed the s stones and cut down	5167
	24: 7	of God and had used even its s objects for	7731
	31: 1	smashed the s stones and cut down	5167
	35: 3	the s ark in the temple that Solomon son	7731
Ezr	2:63	not to eat any of the most s food until	7731+7731
	3: 5	for all the appointed s feasts of the LORD,	7727
	8:30	and s articles that had been weighed out to	NIH
	8:33	and gold and the s articles into the hands	NIH
Ne	7:65	not to eat any of the most s food until	7731+7731
	8: 9	"This day is s to the LORD your God.	7705

Ne	8:10	This day is s to our Lord.	7705
	8:11	saying, "Be still, for this is a s day.	7705
Ps	89:20	with my s oil I have anointed him.	7731
Isa	1:29	"You will be ashamed because of the s oaks	381
	14:13	on the utmost heights of the s mountain.	7600
	64:10	Your s cities have become a desert;	7731
	65: 5	for I am too s for you!'	7727
Jer	31:23	O righteous dwelling, O s mountain.'	7731
	43:13	in Egypt he will demolish the s pillars	5167
La	4: 1	The s gems are scattered at the head	7731
Eze	44:19	in and are to leave them in the s rooms,	7731
	45: 1	the land as a district, 25,000 cubits long	7731
	45: 3	In the s district, measure off a section	NIH
	45: 4	be the s portion of the land for the priests,	7731
	45: 6	cubits long, adjoining the s portion;	7731
	45: 7	by the s district and the property of the city.	7731
	46:19	of the gate to the s rooms facing north,	7731
	48:10	This will be the s portion for the priests.	7731
	48:12	be a special gift to them from the s portion	NIH
	48:18	the s portion and running the length of it,	7731
	48:20	portion, along with the property of	7731
	48:21	of the area formed by the s portion and	7731
	48:21	cubits of s portion to the eastern border,	NIH
	48:21	the s portion with the temple sanctuary will	7731
Hos	3: 1	to other gods and love the s raisin cakes."	862
	3: 4	without sacrifice or s stones,	5167
	10: 1	his land prospered, he adorned his s stones.	5167
	10: 2	and destroy their s stones.	5167
Joel	1:14	Declare a holy fast; call a s assembly.	6809
	2:15	declare a holy fast, call a s assembly.	6809
Mic	5:13	and your s stones from among you;	5167
Zec	14:20	the LORD's house will be like the s bowls	4670
Mt	7: 6	"Do not give dogs what is s;	41
	23:17	gold, or the temple that makes the gold s?	39
	23:19	the gift, or the altar that makes the gift s?	39
Ro	14: 5	One man considers one day more s than	NIG
		another;	
1Co	3:17	God's temple is s, and you are that temple.	41
2Pe	1:18	when we were with him on the s mountain.	41
	2:21	the s command that was passed on to them.	41

SACRIFICE (166) [SACRIFICED, SACRIFICES, SACRIFICING]

Ge	22: 2	S him there as a burnt offering on one of	6590
	31:54	He offered a s there in the hill country	2285
Ex	5: 3	'Let us go and s to our God.'	2284
	5:17	'Let us go and s to the LORD.'	2284
	8:25	"Go, s to your God here in the land."	2284
	12:27	'It is the Passover s to the LORD,	2285
	13:15	This is why I s to the LORD	2284
	20:24	and s on it your burnt offerings	2284
	23:18	"Do not offer the blood of a s to me along	2285
	29:36	S a bull each day as a sin offering	6913
	29:41	S the other lamb at twilight with	6913
	34:15	to their gods and s to them,	2284
	34:25	"Do not offer the blood of a s to me along	2285
	34:25	of the s from the Passover Feast remain	2285
Lev	3: 3	s made to the LORD by fire:	852
	3: 9	s made to the LORD by fire:	852
	7:16	the s shall be eaten on the day he offers it,	2285
	7:17	of the s left over till the third day must	2285
	7:29	the LORD is to bring part of it as his s to	7933
	9: 4	a ram for a fellowship offering to s before	2284
	9: 7	"Come to the altar and s your sin offering	6913
	9: 7	s the offering that is for the people	6913
	14:19	to s the sin offering and make atonement	6913
	14:30	he shall s the doves or the young pigeons,	6913
	15:15	The priest is to s them,	6913
	15:30	The priest is to s one for a sin offering and	6913
	16: 9	to the LORD and s it for a sin offering.	6913
	16:24	and s the burnt offering for himself and	6913
	17: 5	and s them as fellowship offerings	2284
	17: 5	who offers a burnt offering or s	2285
	17: 9	the entrance to the Tent of Meeting to s it to	6913
	19: 5	"When you a fellowship offering to	2284
	19: 5	s it in such a way that it will be accepted	2284
	19: 6	It shall be eaten on the day you s it or on	2285
	22:29	"When you s a thank offering to	2284
	22:29	s it in such a way that it will be accepted	2284
	23:12	you must s as a burnt offering to	6913
	23:19	Then s one male goat for a sin offering	6913
Nu	6:17	and is to s the ram as a fellowship offering	6913
	6:17	and put it in the fire that is under the s of	
	7:88	for the s of the fellowship offering came	2285
	15: 5	for the burnt offering or the s,	2285
	15: 8	a young bull as a burnt offering or s,	2285
Dt	12:13	not to s your burnt offerings anywhere you	
		please.	6590
	15:21	you must not s it to the LORD your God.	2284
	16: 2	S as the Passover to the LORD your God	2284
	16: 4	of the meat you s on the evening of	2284
	16: 5	You must not s the Passover in any town	2284
	16: 6	There you must s the Passover in	2284
	17: 1	Do not s to the LORD your God an ox or	2284
	18: 3	from the people who s a bull or	2284+2285
	27: 7	S fellowship offerings there,	2284
Jos	22:23	or to s fellowship offerings on it,	6913
Jdg	11:31	and I will s it as a burnt offering."	6590
	16:23	the Philistines assembled to offer a great s	2285
1Sa	1: 3	to worship and s to the LORD Almighty	2284
	1: 4	Whenever the day came for Elkanah to s,	2284
	1:21	up with all his family to offer the annual s	2285
	2:13	the people that whenever anyone offered a s	2285
	2:19	up with her husband to offer the annual s.	2285
	2:29	Why do you scorn my s and offering	2285
	3:14	of Eli's house will never be atoned for by s	2285

1Sa	9:12	for the people have a s at the high place.	2285
	9:13	because he must bless the s;	2285
	10: 8	down to you to s burnt offerings	6590
	15:15	and cattle to s to the LORD your God,	2284
	15:21	in order to s them to the LORD your God	2284
	15:22	To obey is better than s,	2285
	16: 2	'I have come to s to the LORD.'	2285
	16: 3	Invite Jesse to the s,	2285
	16: 5	I have come to s to the LORD.	2284
	16: 5	Consecrate yourselves and come to the s	2285
	16: 5	and his sons and invited them to the s.	2285
	20: 6	because an annual s is being made there	2285
	20:29	because our family is observing a s in	2285
2Sa	24:24	not s to the LORD my God burnt offerings	6590
1Ki	8:63	Solomon offered a s of fellowship offerings	2284
	13: 2	On you he will s the priests of the high	2284
	18:29	until the time for the evening s,	4966+6590
	18:36	At the time of s, the prophet Elijah	4966+6590
	18:38	fire of the LORD fell and burned up the s,	6592
2Ki	3:20	about the time for offering the s,	4966
	3:27	and offered him as a s on the city wall.	6592
	10:19	I am going to hold a great s for Baal.	2285
	17:35	serve them or s to them.	2284
	23:10	so no one could use it to s his son	6296
1Ch	21:24	or s a burnt offering that costs me nothing."	6590
2Ch	7: 5	a s of twenty-two thousand head of cattle	2285
	28:23	I will s to them so they will help me."	2284
	29:27	the order to s the burnt offering on the altar.	6590
	29:28	the s of the burnt offering was completed.	NIH
	33:17	however, continued to s at the high places,	2284
Ezr	3: 2	the God of Israel to s burnt offerings on it,	6590
	7:17	and s them on the altar of the temple	10638
	9: 4	And I sat there appalled until the evening s.	4966
	9: 5	Then, at the evening s,	4966
Job	1: 5	in the morning he would s a burnt offering	6590
	42: 8	to my servant Job and s a burnt offering	6590
Ps	27: 6	at his tabernacle will I s with shouts	2284+2285
	40: 6	S and offering you did not desire,	2285
	50: 5	who made a covenant with me by s."	2285
	50:14	S thank offerings to God,	2284
	51:16	You do not delight in s, or I would bring it;	2285
	54: 6	I will s a freewill offering to you;	2284
	66:15	I will s fat animals to you and	6590+6592
	107:22	Let them s thank offerings and tell	2284
	116:17	I will s a thank offering to you and call	2284
	141: 2	up of my hands be like the evening s.	4966
Pr	15: 8	The LORD detests the s of the wicked,	2285
	21: 3	more acceptable to the LORD than s.	2285
	21:27	The s of the wicked is detestable—	2285
Ecc	5: 1	to listen rather than to offer the s of fools,	2285
Isa	34: 6	For the LORD has a s in Bozrah and	2285
	57: 5	you s your children in the ravines and under	8821
Jer	32:35	in the Valley of Ben Hinnom to s their sons	6296
	46:10	will offer s in the land of the north by	2285
Eze	20:26	the s of every firstborn—	6296
	20:31	the s of your sons in the fire—	6296
	39:17	from all around to the s I am preparing	2285
	39:17	the great s on the mountains of Israel.	2285
	39:19	At the s I am preparing for you,	2285
	43:24	on them and s them as a burnt offering to	6590
	46: 2	The priests are to s his burnt offering	6913
Da	8:11	it took away the daily s from him,	9458
	8:12	and the daily s were given over	9458
	8:13	the vision concerning the daily s,	9458
	9:21	about the time of the evening s.	4966
	9:27	In the middle of the 'seven' he will put an	
		end to s	2285
	11:31	and will abolish the daily s.	9458
	12:11	the time that the daily s is abolished and	9458
Hos	3: 4	without s or sacred stones,	2285
	4:13	They s on the mountaintops	2284
	4:14	with harlots and s with shrine prostitutes—	2284
	6: 6	For I desire mercy, not s,	2285
	12:11	Do they s bulls in Gilgal?	2284
	13: 2	"They offer human s and kiss	2284
Jnh	1:16	a s to the LORD and made vows to him.	2285
	2: 9	with a song of thanksgiving, will s to you.	2284
Zep	1: 7	The LORD has prepared a s;	2285
	1: 8	On the day of the LORD's s I will punish	2285
Zec	14:21	and all who come to s will take some of	2284
Mal	1: 8	When you bring blind animals for s,	2284
	1: 8	When you s crippled or diseased animals,	5602
Mt	9:13	'I desire mercy, not s.'	2602
	12: 7	'I desire mercy, not s,'	2602
Mk	14:12	it was customary to s the Passover lamb,	2604
Lk	2:24	and to offer a s in keeping with what is said	2602
Ro	3:25	God presented him as a s of atonement	2663
1Co	10:19	s offered to an idol is anything,	1628
	10:28	"This has been offered in s,"	2638
Eph	5: 2	for us as a fragrant offering and s to God.	2602
Php	2:17	the s and service coming from your faith,	2602
	4:18	an acceptable s, pleasing to God.	NIG
Heb	9:26	to do away with sin by the s of himself.	2602
	10: 5	"S and offering you did not desire,	2602
	10:10	we have been made holy through the s of	
		the body of Jesus Christ	4714
	10:12	for all time one s for sins,	2602
	10:14	by one s he has made perfect forever those	
		who are being made holy.	4714
	10:18	there is no longer any s for sin.	4714
	10:26	no s for sins is left,	2602
	11: 4	By faith Abel offered God a better s than	2602
	11:17	when God tested him, offered Isaac as a s.	4712
	11:17	was about to s his one and only son,	4712
	13:15	let us continually offer to God a s of praise	2602
1Jn	2: 2	He is the atoning s for our sins,	2662
	4:10	and sent his Son as an atoning s	2662

SACRIFICED (68) [SACRIFICE]

Ge	8:20	*he* **s** burnt offerings on it.	6590
	22:13	the ram and **s** it as a burnt offering instead	6590
Ex	24: 5	and **s** young bulls as fellowship offerings to	2284
	32: 6	the people rose early and **s** burnt offerings	6590
	32: 8	They have bowed down to it and **s** to it	2284
Lev	4:10	just as the fat is removed from the ox **s** *as*	2285
	9:22	And *having* **s** the sin offering,	6913
	10:19	"Today *they* **s** their sin offering	7928
	18:21	" 'Do not give any of your children to *be* **s**	6296
Nu	7:17	to be **s** as a fellowship offering.	2285
	7:23	to be **s** as a fellowship offering.	2285
	7:29	to be **s** as a fellowship offering.	2285
	7:35	to be **s** as a fellowship offering.	2285
	7:41	to be **s** as a fellowship offering.	2285
	7:47	to be **s** as a fellowship offering.	2285
	7:53	to be **s** as a fellowship offering.	2285
	7:59	to be **s** as a fellowship offering.	2285
	7:65	to be **s** as a fellowship offering.	2285
	7:71	to be **s** as a fellowship offering.	2285
	7:77	to be **s** as a fellowship offering.	2285
	7:83	to be **s** as a fellowship offering.	2285
	22:40	Balak **s** cattle and sheep,	2284
Dt	32:17	*They* **s** to demons, which are not God—	2284
Jos	8:31	and **s** fellowship offerings.	2284
Jdg	6:28	beside it cut down and the second bull **s** on	6590
	13:19	and **s** it on a rock to the LORD.	6590
1Sa	6:14	the cart and **s** the cows as a burnt offering	6590
	11:15	There *they* **s** fellowship offerings before	2284
2Sa	6:13	he **s** a bull and a fattened calf.	2284
	6:17	and David **s** burnt offerings	6590
	24:25	to the LORD there and **s** burnt offerings	6590
1Ki	1: 9	Adonijah then **s** sheep,	2284
	1:19	He has **s** great numbers of cattle,	2284
	1:25	down and **s** great numbers of cattle,	2284
	3:15	of the Lord's covenant and **s** burnt offerings	6590
	9:25	a year Solomon **s** burnt offerings	6590
2Ki	16: 3	of the kings of Israel and even **s** his son in	6296
	17:17	*They* **s** their sons and daughters in the fire.	6296
	21: 6	He **s** his own son in the fire,	6296
1Ch	15:26	seven bulls and seven rams *were* **s.**	2284
	21:26	to the LORD there and **s** burnt offerings	6590
2Ch	8:12	Solomon **s** burnt offerings to the LORD,	6590
	15:11	At that time *they* **s** to the LORD	2284
	28: 3	the Valley of Ben Hinnom and **s** his sons in	1277
	33: 6	He **s** his sons in the fire in the Valley	6296
	33:16	of the LORD and **s** fellowship offerings	2284
	34: 4	over the graves of those *who had* **s** to them.	2284
Ezr	3: 3	on its foundation and **s** burnt offerings on it	6590
	8:35	from captivity **s** burnt offerings to the God	7928
Ps	106:37	*They* **s** their sons and their daughters	2284
	106:38	whom *they* **s** to the idols of Canaan,	2284
Eze	16:20	to me and **s** them as food to the idols.	2284
	16:21	You slaughtered my children and **s** them to thc idols,	928+5989+6296
	23:37	*they* even **s** their children,	6296
	23:39	On the very day they **s** their children	8821
Hos	11: 2	*They* **s** to the Baals and they burned incense	2284
Lk	22: 7	on which the Passover lamb had *to be* **s.**	2604
Ac	15:29	You are to abstain from **food s** to idols,	1628
	21:25	they should abstain from **food s** to idols,	1628
1Co	5: 7	For Christ, our Passover lamb, *has been* **s.**	2604
	8: 1	Now about **food s** to idols:	1628
	8: 4	So then, about eating **food s** to idols?	1628
	8: 7	of it as having been **s** to an idol.	NIG
	8:10	to eat what *has been* **s** to idols?	1628
Heb	7:27	**He s** for their sins once for all	4472S
	9:28	so Christ *was* **s** once to take away the sins	4712
Rev	2:14	to sin by eating **food s** to idols and	1628
	2:20	and the eating of **food s** to idols.	1628

SACRIFICES (142) [SACRIFICE]

Ge	46: 1	he offered **s** to the God of his father Isaac.	2285
Ex	3:18	to **offer s** to the LORD our God.'	2284
	5: 3	to **offer s** to the LORD our God,	2284
	8: 8	and I will let your people go to **offer s** to	2284
	8:26	The **s** we **offer** the LORD our God would	2284
	8:26	we **offer s** that are detestable in their eyes,	2284
	8:27	to **offer s** to the LORD our God,	2284
	8:28	to **offer s** to the LORD your God in	2284
	8:29	by not letting the people go to **offer s** to	2284
	10:25	to have **s** and burnt offerings to present to	2285
	18:12	brought a burnt offering and other **s** to God,	2285
	22:20	"Whoever **s** to any god other than	2284
	34:15	they will invite you and you will eat their **s.**	2285
Lev	17: 3	Any Israelite who **s** an ox,	8821
	17: 5	to the LORD the **s** they are now making in	2285
	17: 7	They must no longer offer any of their **s** to	2285
	23:37	**s** and drink offerings required for each day.	2285
Nu	15: 3	whether burnt offerings or **s,**	2285
	25: 2	who invited them to the **s** *to* their gods.	2285
Dt	12: 6	there bring your burnt offerings and **s,**	2285
	12:11	your burnt offerings and **s,**	2285
	12:27	of yours must be poured beside the altar of	2285
	12:31	**burn** their sons and daughters in the fire *as* **s** to their gods.	8596
	18:10	among you who **s** his son or daughter in	6296
	32:38	the gods who ate the fat of their **s** and drank	2285
	33:19	and there offer **s** *of* righteousness;	2285
Jos	22:26	but not for burnt offerings or **s.'**	2285
	22:27	**s** and fellowship offerings.	2285
	22:28	not for burnt offerings and **s,**	2285
	22:29	grain offerings and **s,**	2285
Jdg	2: 5	There *they* **offered s** to the LORD.	2284
1Sa	6:15	and **made s** to the LORD.	2284+2285

1Sa	15:22	the LORD delight in burnt offerings and **s**	2285
2Sa	15:12	While Absalom was offering **s,**	2285
	15:24	and Abiathar **offered s** until all	6590
1Ki	3: 3	except that he **offered s** and burned incense	2284
	3: 4	The king went to Gibeon to **offer s,**	2284
	8:62	the king and all Israel with him offered **s**	2285
	11: 8	who burned incense and **offered s**	2284
	12:27	If these people go up to offer **s** at the temple	2285
	12:32	and **offered s** on the altar.	6590
	12:33	*he* **offered s** on the altar he had built	6590
	22:43	and the people continued *to* **offer s**	2284
2Ki	5:17	and **s** to any other god but the LORD.	2285
	10:24	they went in to make **s** and burnt offerings.	2285
	12: 3	*to* **offer s** and burn incense there.	2284
	14: 4	*to* **offer s** and burn incense there.	2284
	15: 4	*to* **offer s** and burn incense there.	2284
	15:35	*to* **offer s** and burn incense there.	2284
	16: 4	**He offered s** and burned incense at	2284
	16:15	the blood of the burnt offerings and **s.**	2285
	17:31	**burned** their children in the fire **as s**	8596
	17:36	down and to him **offer s.**	2284
1Ch	21:28	he **offered s** there.	2284
	23:13	to **offer s** before the LORD,	2284
	29:21	The next day *they* **made s** to the LORD	2284+2285
	29:21	and other **s** in abundance for all Israel.	2285
2Ch	2: 6	except as a place to **burn s** before him?	7787
	7: 1	and consumed the burnt offering and the **s,**	2285
	7: 4	the king and all the people offered **s** before	2285
	7:12	this place for myself as a temple for **s.**	2285
	11:16	followed the Levites to Jerusalem to **offer s**	2284
	25:14	bowed down to them and **burned s** to them.	7787
	28: 3	He **burned s** in the Valley of Ben Hinnom	7787
	28: 4	*He* **offered s** and burned incense at	2284
	28:23	*He* **offered s** to the gods of Damascus,	2284
	28:25	in Judah he built high places to **burn s**	7787
	29:31	Come and bring **s** and thank offerings to	2285
	29:31	the assembly brought **s** and thank offerings,	2285
	29:33	The animals consecrated as **s** amounted	NIH
	32:12	before one altar and **burn s** on it'?	7787
	33:22	Amon worshiped and **offered s** to all	2284
Ezr	3: 3	both the morning and evening **s.**	6592
	3: 5	the New Moon **s** and the sacrifices for all	NIH
	3: 5	and the **s** for all the appointed sacred feasts	NIH
	6: 3	the temple be rebuilt as a place to present **s,**	10157
	6:10	so that *they* may **offer s** pleasing to the God	10638
Ne	4: 2	*Will they* **offer s?**	2284
	12:43	And on that day they offered great **s,**	2285
Ps	4: 5	Offer right **s** and trust in the LORD.	2285
	20: 3	May he remember all your **s**	4966
	50: 8	for your **s** or your burnt offerings,	2285
	50:23	*He who* **s** thank offerings honors me,	2284
	51:17	The **s** *of* God are a broken spirit;	2285
	51:19	Then there will be righteous **s,**	2285
	106:28	of Peor and ate **s** *offered to* lifeless gods;	2285
Ecc	9: 2	those who **offer s** and those who do not.	2284
Isa	1:11	multitude of your **s**—what are they to me?"	2285
	19:21	with **s** and grain offerings;	2285
	43:23	nor honored me with your **s.**	2285
	43:24	or lavished on me the fat of your **s.**	2285
	56: 7	Their burnt offerings and **s** will be accepted	2285
	57: 7	there you went up to offer your **s.**	2285
	65: 3	**offering s** in gardens and burning incense	2284
	65: 7	"Because *they* **burned s** on the mountains	7787
	66: 3	*whoever* **s** a bull is like one who kills a man,	8821
Jer	6:20	your **s** do not please me."	2284
	7:21	to your other **s** and eat the meat yourselves!	2285
	7:22	about burnt offerings and **s,**	2285
	17:26	bringing burnt offerings and **s,**	2285
	19: 4	*they* have **burned s** in it to gods	7787
	33:18	to burn grain offerings and to present **s.' "**	2285
Eze	20:28	there they offered their **s,**	2285
	20:40	along with all your holy **s.**	NIH
	40:41	on which the **s** *were* **slaughtered.**	8821
	40:42	the burnt offerings and the other **s.**	2285
	44:11	they may slaughter the burnt offerings and **s**	2285
	44:15	they are to stand before me to **offer s** of fat	7928
	46:24	at the temple will cook the **s** *of* the people."	2285
Hos	4:19	and their **s** will bring them shame.	2285
	8:13	They offer **s** given to me and they eat	2285
	9: 4	nor will their **s** please him.	2285
	9: 4	Such **s** will be to them like the bread	NIH
Am	4: 4	Bring your **s** every morning,	2285
	5:25	"Did you bring me **s** and offerings	2285
Hab	1:16	Therefore *he* **s** to his net and burns incense	2284
Mal	1:13	or diseased animals and offer them as **s,**	4966
	1:14	but then a blemished animal to the Lord.	2284
	2: 3	the offal from your **festival s,**	2504
Mk	1:44	show yourself to the priest and **offer** the **s**	4712
	12:33	love your neighbor as yourself is more important than all burnt offerings and **s."**	2602
Lk	5:14	show yourself to the priest and **offer** the **s**	4712
	13: 1	whose blood Pilate had mixed with their **s.**	2602
Ac	7:41	They brought **s** to it and held a celebration	2602
	7:42	" 'Did you bring me **s** and offerings	2602
	14:13	and the crowd wanted *to* **offer s** to them.	2604
Ro	12: 1	to offer your bodies as living **s,**	2602
1Co	10:18	Do not those who eat the **s** participate in	2602
	10:20	**s** of pagans *are* **offered**	2604
Heb	5: 1	to offer gifts and **s** for sins.	2602
	5: 3	This is why he has to **offer s**	4712
	7:27	he does not need to offer **s** day after day,	2602
	8: 3	to offer both gifts and **s,**	2602
	9: 9	the gifts and **s** being offered were not able	2602
	9:23	to be purified with these **s,**	NIG
	9:23	*with* better **s** than these.	2602
	10: 1	*by* the same **s** repeated endlessly year	2602
	10: 3	But those **s** are an annual reminder of sins,	NIG

Heb	10: 8	First he said, "**S** and offerings,	2602
	10:11	again and again he offers the same **s,**	2602
	13:16	for *with* such **s** God is pleased.	2602
1Pe	2: 5	offering spiritual **s** acceptable to God	2602

SACRIFICING (12) [SACRIFICE]

1Sa	2:15	and say to the man who *was* **s,** "Give	2284
	7:10	While Samuel was **s** the burnt offering,	6590
2Sa	6:18	After he had finished **s** the burnt offerings	6590
1Ki	3: 2	however, *were* still **s** at the high places,	2284
	8: 5	**s** so many sheep and cattle that they could	2284
	12:32	**s** to the calves he had made.	2284
1Ch	16: 2	After David had finished **s**	6590
2Ch	5: 6	**s** so many sheep and cattle that they could	2284
	35:14	*were* **s** the burnt offerings and	6590
Ezr	4: 2	we seek your God and *have been* **s** to him	2284
Eze	43:18	for **s** burnt offerings and sprinkling blood	6590
Ac	14:18	the crowd from **s** to them.	2604

SACRILEGE   (KJV) See ROB TEMPLES

SAD (9) [SADDENED, SADNESS]

Ge	40: 7	"Why are your faces *so* **s** today?"	8273
Ne	2: 1	I had not been **s** in his presence before;	8273
	2: 2	"Why does your face **look** *so* **s**	8273
	2: 2	Why *should* my face not **look s** when	8317
Ecc	7: 3	because a **s** face is good for the heart.	8278
Mt	19:22	the young man heard this, he went away **s,**	3382
	26:22	They *were* very **s** and began to say	3382
Mk	10:22	went away **s,** because he had great wealth.	3382
Lk	18:23	When he heard this, he became **very s,**	4337

SADDENED (1) [SAD]

Mk	14:19	They were **s,** and one by one they said	3382

SADDLE (5) [SADDLEBAGS, SADDLED]

Ge	31:34	inside her camel's **s** and was sitting on them	4121
Jdg	5:10	sitting on your **s blankets,**	4496
1Ki	13:13	he said to his sons, "**S** the donkey for me."	2502
	13:27	"**S** the donkey for me," and they did so.	2502
Eze	27:20	" 'Dedan traded in **s** blankets with you.	8210

SADDLEBAGS (1) [SADDLE]

Ge	49:14	donkey lying down between **two s.**	5478

SADDLED (10) [SADDLE]

Ge	22: 3	Abraham got up and **s** his donkey.	2502
Nu	22:21	**s** his donkey and went with the princes	2502
Jdg	19:10	with his two **s** donkeys and his concubine.	2502
2Sa	16: 1	He had a string of donkeys **s** and loaded	2502
	17:23	he **s** his donkey and set out for his house	2502
	19:26	'*I will* have my donkey **s** and will ride	2502
1Ki	2: 40	he **s** his donkey and went to Achish at Gath	2502
	13:13	And when *they had* **s** the donkey for him,	2502
	13:23	the prophet who had brought him back **s** his donkey	2502
2Ki	4:24	*She* **s** the donkey and said to her servant,	2502

SADDUCEES (14)

Mt	3: 7	and **S** coming to where he was baptizing,	4881
	16: 1	and **S** came to Jesus and tested him	4881
	16: 6	against the yeast of the Pharisees and **S.**"	4881
	16:11	against the yeast *of* the Pharisees and **S.**"	4881
	16:12	against the teaching of the Pharisees and **S.**	4881
	22:23	the **S,** who say there is no resurrection,	4881
	22:34	Hearing that Jesus had silenced the **S,**	4881
Mk	12:18	Then the **S,** who say there is no resurrection,	4881
Lk	20:27	*of* the **S,** who say there is no resurrection,	4881
Ac	4: 1	of the temple guard and the **S** came up	4881
	5:17	who were members of the party of the **S,**	4881
	23: 6	of them were **S** and the others Pharisees,	4881
	23: 7	*between* the Pharisees and the **S,**	4881
	23: 8	(The **S** say that there is no resurrection,	4881

SADNESS (1) [SAD]

Ne	2: 2	This can be nothing but **s** *of* heart."	8278

SADOC   (KJV) See ZADOK

SAFE (28) [SAVE]

Dt	29:19	"I will be **s,** even though I persist in going	8934
1Sa	20: 7	he says, 'Very well,' then your servant is **s.**	8934
	20:21	as surely as the LORD lives, you are **s;**	8934
	22:23	You will be **s** with me."	5466
2Sa	18:29	"Is the young man Absalom **s?**"	8934
	18:32	"Is the young man Absalom **s?**"	8934
2Ch	15: 5	In those days it was not **s** to travel about,	8934
Ezr	8:21	before our God and ask him for a **s** journey	3838
Job	21: 9	Their homes are **s** and free from fear;	8934
Ps	12: 7	you *will* **keep** us **s** and protect us	9068
	16: 1	**Keep** me **s,** O God, for in you I take refuge.	9068
	27: 5	of trouble he *will* **keep** me **s** in his dwelling;	7621
	31:20	in your dwelling you **keep** them **s**	7621
	37: 3	dwell in the land and enjoy **s** pasture.	575
Pr	11:15	to strike hands in pledge *is* **s.**	1053
	18:10	the righteous run to it and *are* **s.**	8435
	20:28	Love and faithfulness **keep** a king **s;**	5915
	28:18	He whose walk is blameless is **kept s,**	3828
	28:26	but he who walks in wisdom is **kept s.**	4880
	29:25	but whoever trusts in the LORD **is kept s.**	8435

Jer	7:10	and say, *"We are s"*—safe to do all these	5911
	7:10	s to do all these detestable things?	NIH
	12: 5	If you stumble in s country,	8934
	12:12	no one will be s.	8934
Lk	11:21	his own house, his possessions are s.	1645+1877
	15:27	because he has him back s and sound.'	5617
Jn	17:12	and **kept** them s by that name you gave me.	5875
1Jn	5:18	the one who was born of God keeps him s,	5498

SAFE-CONDUCT (1) [CONDUCT]

Ne	2: 7	that *they will* **provide** me s until I arrive	6296

SAFEGUARD (1) [GUARD]

Php	3: 1	and it is a s for you.	855

SAFEKEEPING (2) [KEEP]

Ex	22: 7	or goods for s and they are stolen from	9068
	22:10	to his neighbor for s and it dies or is injured	9068

SAFELY (18) [SAVE]

Ge	19:16	and of his two daughters and led them s out	5663
	28:21	so that I return s to my father's house,	928+8934
	33:18	he arrived s at the city of Shechem	8969
Lev	25:18	and you will live s in the land.	1055+4200
Jos	10:21	whole army then returned s to Joshua	928+8934
1Sa	20:13	not let you know and send you away s.	4200+8934
2Sa	19:24	the king left until the day he returned s.	928+8934
	19:30	my lord the king has arrived home s."	928+8934
1Ki	22:27	but bread and water until I return s.' "	928+8934
	22:28	Micaiah declared, "If you ever return s,	928+8934
2Ch	18:26	but bread and water until I return s.' "	928+8934
	18:27	Micaiah declared, "If you ever return s,	928+8934
	19: 1	Jehoshaphat king of Judah returned s	928+8934
Ps	78:53	guided them s, so they were unafraid;	1055+4200
Zec	8:10	No one could go about his business s	
		because of his enemy,	2021+4200+8934
Ac	23:24	that *he may be* taken s to Governor Felix."	1407
	28: 1	Once s on shore, we found out that	1407
2Ti	4:18	from every evil attack and *will* **bring** me s	5392

SAFETY (34) [SAVE]

Ge	43: 9	I myself *will* **guarantee** his s;	6842
	44:32	Your servant **guaranteed** the boy's s	6842
Lev	25:19	and you will eat your fill and live there in s.	1055
	26: 5	the food you want and live in s	1055
Dt	12:10	around you so that you will live *in* s.	1055
	33:28	So Israel will live *in* s alone;	1055
Jdg	18: 7	that the people were living in s,	1055
1Ki	4:25	from Dan to Beersheba, lived in s,	1055
Job	5: 4	His children are far from s,	3829
	5:11	and those who mourn are lifted to s.	3829
	11:18	about you and take your rest in s.	1055
	30:15	my s vanishes like a cloud.	3802
Ps	4: 8	O LORD, make me dwell in s.	1055
	141:10	while I pass by in s.	NIH
Pr	1:33	but whoever listens to me will live *in* s and	1055
	3:23	Then you will go on your way in s,	1055
Isa	14:30	and the needy will lie down in s.	1055
Jer	4: 6	**Flee for** s without delay!	6395
	6: 1	"**Flee for** s, people of Benjamin!	6395
	23: 6	be saved and Israel will live in s.	1055
	32:37	to this place and let them live in s.	1055
	33:16	be saved and Jerusalem will live in s.	1055
Eze	28:26	They will live there in s	1055
	28:26	they will live in s when I inflict punishment	1055
	34:25	in the desert and sleep in the forests in s.	1055
	34:28	They will live in s,	1055
	38: 8	and now all of them live in s.	1055
	38:14	when my people Israel are living in s,	1055
	39: 6	and on those who live in s in the coastlands,	1055
	39:26	toward me when they lived in s in their land	1055
Hos	2:18	so that all may lie down in s.	1055
Zep	2:15	This is the carefree city that lived in s.	1055
Ac	27:44	In this way everyone reached land in s.	1407
1Th	5: 3	While people are saying, "Peace and s,"	854

SAFFRON (1)

SS	4:14	nard and s, calamus and cinnamon,	4137

SAG (1)

Ecc	10:18	If a man is lazy, the rafters s;	4812

SAHADUTHA See JEGAR SAHADUTHA

SAID (3187) [SAY]

Ge	1: 3	And God s, "Let there be light,"	606
	1: 6	And God s, "Let there be an expanse	606
	1: 9	And God s, "Let the water under the sky	606
	1:11	And God s, "Let the land produce vegetation:	606
	1:14	And God s, "Let there be lights in	606
	1:20	And God s, "Let the water teem	606
	1:22	God blessed them and s,	606
	1:24	And God s, "Let the land produce	606
	1:26	Then God s, "Let us make man	606
	1:28	God blessed them and s to them,	606
	1:29	Then God s, "I give you every seed-bearing	606
	2:18	The LORD God s, "It is not good for the man	606
	2:23	The man s, "This is now bone of my bones	606
	3: 1	*He* s to the woman, "Did God really say,	606
	3: 2	The woman s to the serpent, "We may eat	606
	3: 4	not surely die," the serpent s to the woman.	606

Ge	3:11	*he* s, "Who told you that you were naked?	606
	3:12	The man s, "The woman you put here	606
	3:13	Then the LORD God s to the woman,	606
	3:13	The woman s, "The serpent deceived me,	606
	3:14	So the LORD God s to the serpent,	606
	3:16	To the woman *he* s, "I will greatly increase	606
	3:17	To Adam *he* s, "Because you listened	606
	3:22	And the LORD God s, "The man has now	606
	4: 1	*She* s, "With the help of the LORD	606
	4: 6	the LORD s to Cain, "Why are you angry?	606
	4: 8	Now Cain s to his brother Abel,	606
	4: 9	Then the LORD s to Cain, "Where is your	606
	4:10	The LORD s, "What have you done?	606
	4:13	Cain s to the LORD, My punishment	606
	4:15	But the LORD s to him, "Not so;	606
	4:23	Lamech s to his wives, "Adah and Zillah,	606
	5:29	He named him Noah and s,	606
	6: 3	the LORD s, "My Spirit will not contend	606
	6: 7	So the LORD s, "I will wipe mankind,	606
	6:13	So God s to Noah, "I am going to put an end	606
	7: 1	The LORD then s to Noah,	606
	8:15	Then God s to Noah,	1819
	8:21	the pleasing aroma and s in his heart:	606
	9: 8	God s to Noah and to his sons with him:	606
	9:12	God s, "This is the sign of the covenant	606
	9:17	So God s to Noah, "This is the sign	606
	9:25	*he* s, "Cursed be Canaan!	606
	9:26	He also s, "Blessed be the LORD,	606
	10: 9	that is why *it* is s, "Like Nimrod,	606
	11: 3	*They* s to each other, "Come,	606
	11: 4	Then *they* s, "Come, let us build ourselves	606
	11: 6	The LORD s, "If as one people speaking	606
	12: 1	The LORD *had* s to Abram,	606
	12: 7	The LORD appeared to Abram and s,	606
	12:11	*he* s to his wife Sarai,	606
	12:18	"What have you done to me?" *he* s.	606
	13: 8	So Abram s to Lot,	606
	13:14	The LORD s to Abram after Lot had parted	606
	14:21	The king of Sodom s to Abram,	606
	14:22	But Abram s to the king of Sodom,	606
	15: 2	But Abram s, "O Sovereign LORD,	606
	15: 3	Abram s, "You have given me no children;	606
	15: 5	He took him outside and s,	606
	15: 5	*he* s to him, "So shall your offspring be."	606
	15: 7	*He* also s to him, "I am the LORD,	606
	15: 8	But Abram s, "O Sovereign LORD,	606
	15: 9	So the LORD s to him, "Bring me a heifer,	606
	15:13	Then the LORD s to him, "Know for certain	606
	15:18	LORD made a covenant with Abram and s,	606
	16: 2	so she s to Abram,	606
	16: 2	Abram agreed to **what** Sarai s.	7754
	16: 5	Then Sarai s to Abram,	606
	16: 6	"Your servant is in your hands," Abram s.	606
	16: 8	And *he* s, "Hagar, servant of Sarai,	606
	16:11	The angel of the LORD also s to her:	606
	16:13	"You are the God who sees me," for *she* s,	606
	17: 1	the LORD appeared to him and s,	606
	17: 3	Abram fell facedown, and God s to him,	1819
	17: 9	Then God s to Abraham, "As for you,	606
	17:15	God also s to Abraham, "As for Sarai	606
	17:17	he laughed and s to himself, "Will a son	606
	17:18	And Abraham s to God, "If only Ishmael	606
	17:19	Then God s, "Yes,	606
	18: 3	*He* s, "If I have found favor in your eyes,	606
	18: 6	*he* s, "get three seahs of fine flour	606
	18: 9	"There, in the tent," *he* s.	606
	18:10	Then the LORD s, "I will surely return	606
	18:13	Then the LORD s to Abraham,	606
	18:15	Sarah was afraid, so she lied and s,	606
	18:15	But *he* s, "Yes, you did laugh."	606
	18:17	the LORD s, "Shall I hide from Abraham	606
	18:20	the LORD s, "The outcry against Sodom	606
	18:23	Then Abraham approached him and s:	606
	18:26	The LORD s, "If I find fifty righteous people	606
	18:28	"If I find forty-five there," *he* s,	606
	18:29	*He* s, "For the sake of forty, I will not do it."	606
	18:30	Then *he* s, "May the Lord not be angry,	606
	18:31	Abraham s, "Now that I have been so bold	606
	18:31	*He* s, "For the sake of twenty,	606
	18:32	Then *he* s, "May the Lord not be angry,	606
	19: 2	*he* s, "please turn aside	606
	19: 7	and s, "No, my friends.	606
	19: 9	And *they* s, "This fellow came here as	606
	19:12	The two men s to Lot,	606
	19:14	*He* s, "Hurry and get out of this place,	606
	19:17	*one of them* s, "Flee for your lives!	606
	19:18	But Lot s to them, "No, my lords, please!	606
	19:21	*He* s to him, "Very well,	606
	19:31	the older daughter s to the younger,	606
	19:34	The next day the older daughter s to	606
	20: 2	and there Abraham s of his wife Sarah,	606
	20: 3	in a dream one night and s to him, "You are	606
	20: 4	Abimelech had not gone near her, so *he* s,	606
	20: 6	Then God s to him in the dream, "Yes,	606
	20: 9	Then Abimelech called Abraham in and s,	606
	20:11	Abraham replied, "*I* s to myself,	606
	20:13	*I* s to her, 'This is how you can show your	606
	20:15	And Abimelech s, "My land is before you;	606
	20:16	To Sarah *he* s, "I am giving your brother	606
	21: 1	LORD was gracious to Sarah as *he had* s,	606
	21: 6	Sarah s, "God has brought me laughter,	606
	21: 7	"Who *would have* s to Abraham	4910
	21:10	*she* s to Abraham, "Get rid of that slave	606
	21:12	But God s to him, "Do not be so distressed	606
	21:17	of God called to Hagar from heaven and s	606
	21:22	the commander of his forces s to Abraham,	606
	21:24	Abraham s, "I swear it."	606

Ge	21:26	But Abimelech s, "I don't know who	606
	22: 1	*He* s to him, "Abraham!"	606
	22: 2	Then God s, "Take your son,	606
	22: 5	He s to his servants, "Stay here	606
	22: 7	Isaac spoke up and s to his father Abraham,	606
	22: 7	"The fire and wood are here," Isaac s,	606
	22:12	"Do not lay a hand on the boy," *he* s.	606
	22:14	And to this day *it* is s,	606
	22:16	and s, "I swear by myself, declares	606
	23: 3	and spoke to the Hittites. *He* s,	606
	23: 8	*He* s to them, "If you are willing	1819
	23:11	"No, my lord," *he* s.	606
	23:13	and *he* s to Ephron in their hearing,	1819
	24: 2	He s to the chief servant in his household,	606
	24: 6	not take my son back there," Abraham s.	606
	24:17	The servant hurried to meet her and s,	606
	24:18	"Drink, my lord," *she* s,	606
	24:19	After she had given him a drink, *she* s,	606
	24:30	and had heard Rebekah tell what the man s	1819
	24:31	you who are blessed by the LORD," *he* s.	606
	24:33	Then food was set before him, but *he* s,	606
	24:33	"Then tell us," [Laban] s.	606
	24:34	So s, "I am Abraham's servant.	606
	24:37	my master made me swear an oath, and s,	606
	24:42	"When I came to the spring today, *I* s,	606
	24:45	and *I* s to her, 'Please give me a drink.'	606
	24:46	lowered her jar from her shoulder and s,	606
	24:47	"*She* s, 'The daughter of Bethuel son	606
	24:52	Abraham's servant heard **what** they s,	1821
	24:54	When they got up the next morning, *he* s,	606
	24:56	But *he* s to them, "Do not detain me,	606
	24:57	Then *they* s, "Let's call the girl and ask her	606
	24:58	"I will go," *she* s.	606
	24:60	And they blessed Rebekah and s to her,	606
	25:22	and *she* s, "Why is this happening to me?"	606
	25:23	The LORD s to her, "Two nations are in	606
	25:30	He s to Jacob, "Quick, let me have some	606
	25:32	"Look, I am about to die," Esau s.	606
	25:33	But Jacob s, "Swear to me first."	606
	26: 2	The LORD appeared to Isaac and s,	606
	26: 7	*he* s, "She is my sister,"	606
	26: 9	So Abimelech summoned Isaac and s,	606
	26:10	Abimelech s, "What is this you have done	606
	26:16	Abimelech s to Isaac, "Move away from us;	606
	26:20	with Isaac's herdsmen and s,	606
	26:24	the LORD appeared to him and s,	606
	26:28	so we s, 'There ought to be	606
	26:32	*They* s, "We've found water!"	606
	27: 1	he called for Esau his older son and s	606
	27: 2	Isaac s, "I am now an old man	606
	27: 6	Rebekah s to her son Jacob,	606
	27:11	Jacob s to Rebekah his mother,	606
	27:13	His mother s to him, "My son,	606
	27:18	He went to his father and s, "My father."	606
	27:19	Jacob s to his father, "I am Esau	606
	27:21	Then Isaac s to Jacob, "Come near	606
	27:22	who touched him and s,	606
	27:25	Then *he* s, "My son,	606
	27:26	Then his father Isaac s to him, "Come here,	606
	27:27	he blessed him and s, "Ah,	606
	27:31	Then *he* s to him, "My father,	606
	27:33	Isaac trembled violently and s,	606
	27:34	he burst out with a loud and bitter cry and s	606
	27:35	But *he* s, "Your brother came deceitfully	606
	27:36	Esau s, "Isn't he rightly named Jacob?	606
	27:38	Esau s to his father, "Do you have only one	606
	27:41	He s to himself, "The days of mourning	606
	27:42	**what** her older son Esau had s,	1821
	27:42	she sent for her younger son Jacob and s	606
	27:46	Then Rebekah s to Isaac,	606
	28:13	There above it stood the LORD, and *he* s:	606
	28:17	He was afraid and s, "How awesome	606
	29: 5	*He* s to them, "Do you know Laban,	606
	29: 6	"Yes, he is," *they* s,	606
	29: 7	"Look," *he* s, "the sun is still high;	606
	29:14	Then Laban s to him, "You are my own	606
	29:15	Laban s to him, "Just because you are a	606
	29:18	Jacob was in love with Rachel and s,	606
	29:19	Laban s, "It's better that I give her	606
	29:21	Then Jacob s to Laban, "Give me my wife.	606
	29:25	So Jacob s to Laban,	606
	29:32	She named him Reuben, for *she* s,	606
	29:33	and when she gave birth to a son *she* s,	606
	29:34	and when she gave birth to a son *she* s,	606
	29:35	and when she gave birth to a son *she* s,	606
	30: 1	So *she* s to Jacob, "Give me children,	606
	30: 2	Jacob became angry with her and s,	606
	30: 3	*she* s, "Here is Bilhah, my maidservant.	606
	30: 6	Then Rachel s, "God has vindicated me;	606
	30: 8	Then Rachel s, "I have had a great struggle	606
	30:11	Then Leah s, "What good fortune!"	606
	30:13	Then Leah s, "How happy I am!	606
	30:14	Rachel s to Leah, "Please give me some	606
	30:15	But *she* s to her, Wasn't it enough	606
	30:15	"Very well," Rachel s,	606
	30:16	"You must sleep with me," *she* s.	606
	30:18	Then Leah s, "God has rewarded me	606
	30:20	Then Leah s, "God has presented me with	606
	30:23	and gave birth to a son and s,	606
	30:24	She named him Joseph, and s,	606
	30:25	Jacob s to Laban, "Send me on my way	606
	30:27	But Laban s to him, "If I have found favor	606
	30:29	Jacob s to him, "You know how I have	606
	30:34	"Agreed," s Laban.	606
	30:34	"Let it be as you have s."	1821
	31: 3	Then the LORD s to Jacob,	606
	31: 5	*He* s to them, "I see that your father's	606

Ge 31: 8	If *he* s, 'The speckled ones will	606
31: 8	and if *he* s, 'The streaked ones	606
31:11	The angel of God s to me in the dream,	606
31:12	And *he* s, 'Look up and see that all	606
31:24	the Aramean in a dream at night and s	606
31:26	Laban s to Jacob, "What have you done?	606
31:29	last night the God of your father s to me,	606
31:35	Rachel s to her father, "Don't be angry,	606
31:46	He s to his relatives, "Gather some stones."	606
31:48	Laban s, "This heap is a witness	606
31:49	It was also called Mizpah, because *he* s,	606
31:51	Laban also s to Jacob, "Here is this heap,	606
32: 2	When Jacob saw them, *he* s,	606
32: 6	the messengers returned to Jacob, *they* s,	606
32: 9	O Lord, s to me, 'Go back	606
32:12	But you *have*, 'I will surely make you	606
32:16	each herd by itself, and s to his servants,	606
32:26	the man s, "Let me go, for it is daybreak."	606
32:28	Then the man s, 'Your name will no longer	606
32:29	Jacob s, "Please tell me your name."	8626
33: 8	"To find favor in your eyes, my lord," *he* s.	606
33: 9	Esau s, "I already have plenty, my brother.	606
33:10	"No, please!" s Jacob.	606
33:12	Then Esau s, "Let us be on our way;	606
33:13	But Jacob s to him, "My lord knows	606
33:15	Esau s, "Then let me leave some	606
34: 4	And Shechem s to his father Hamor,	606
34: 8	But Hamor s to them,	1819
34:11	Shechem s to Dinah's father and brothers,	606
34:14	*They* s to them, "We can't do such a thing;	606
34:19	lost no time in doing what *they* s,	1821
34:21	"These men are friendly toward us," *they* s.	606
34:30	Then Jacob s to Simeon and Levi,	606
35: 1	Then God s to Jacob, "Go up to Bethel	606
35: 2	So Jacob s to his household and	606
35:10	God s to him, "Your name is Jacob,	606
35:11	And God s to him, "I am God Almighty;	606
35:17	the midwife s to her, "Don't be afraid,	606
37: 6	*He* s to them, "Listen to this dream I had:	606
37: 8	His brothers s to him,	606
37: 8	because of his dream and **what** he had s.	1821
37: 9	"Listen," *he* s, "I had another dream,	606
37:10	his father rebuked him and s,	606
37:13	and Israel s to Joseph, "As you know,	606
37:14	So *he* s to him, "Go and see if all is well	606
37:19	*they* s to each other.	606
37:21	"Let's not take his life," *he* s.	606
37:22	Reuben s this to rescue him from them	606
37:26	Judah s to his brothers,	606
37:30	He went back to his brothers and s,	606
37:32	to their father and s, "We found this.	606
37:33	He recognized it and s, "It is my son's	606
37:35	*he* s, "in mourning will I go down to	606
38: 8	Then Judah s to Onan,	606
38:11	Judah then s to his daughter-in-law Tamar,	606
38:16	he went over to her by the roadside and s,	606
38:17	a young goat from my flock," *he* s.	606
38:18	*He* s, "What pledge should I give you?"	606
38:21	been any shrine prostitute here," *they* s.	606
38:22	So he went back to Judah and s,	606
38:22	Besides, the men who lived there s,	606
38:23	Then Judah s, "Let her keep what she has,	606
38:24	Judah s, "Bring her out	606
38:25	by the man who owns these," *she* s.	606
38:26	Judah recognized them and s,	606
38:28	and tied it on his wrist and s,	606
38:29	his brother came out, and *she* s,	606
39: 7	master's wife took notice of Joseph and s,	606
39:12	She caught him by his cloak and s,	606
39:14	"Look," *she* s to them,	606
40: 8	Then Joseph s to them,	606
40: 9	*He* s to him, "In my dream I saw	606
40:12	"This is what it means," Joseph s to him.	606
40:16	*he* s to Joseph, "I too had a dream:	606
40:18	"This is what it means," Joseph s.	6699
40:22	had s to them **in** *his* **interpretation.**	7354
41: 9	Then the chief cupbearer s to Pharaoh,	1819
41:15	Pharaoh s to Joseph, "I had a dream,	606
41:15	But I have heard *it* s of you that	606
41:17	Then Pharaoh s to Joseph, "In my dream	1819
41:25	Then Joseph s to Pharaoh,	606
41:28	"It is just as *I* s to Pharaoh:	1819
41:39	Then Pharaoh s to Joseph, "Since God	606
41:41	So Pharaoh s to Joseph, "I hereby put you	606
41:44	Then Pharaoh s to Joseph, "I am Pharaoh,	606
41:51	Joseph named his firstborn Manasseh and s,	NIH
41:52	The second son he named Ephraim and s,	NIH
41:54	famine began, just as Joseph had s.	606
42: 1	grain in Egypt, he s to his sons,	606
42: 9	his dreams about them and s to them,	606
42:12	*he* s to them. "You have come to see	606
42:14	Joseph s to them, "It is just as I told you:	606
42:18	On the third day, Joseph s to them,	606
42:21	*They* s to one another,	606
42:28	*he* s to his brothers.	606
42:28	to each other trembling and s,	606
42:29	that had happened to them. *They* s,	606
42:31	But *we* s to him, 'We are honest men;	606
42:33	the man who is lord over the land s to us,	606
42:36	Their father Jacob s to them,	606
42:37	Then Reuben s to his father.	606
42:38	But Jacob s, "My son will not go	606
43: 2	their father s to them, "Go back	606
43: 3	But Judah s to him, "The man warned us	606
43: 5	because the man s to us,	606
43: 8	Then Judah s to Israel his father,	606
43:11	Then their father Israel s to them,	606

Ge 43:16	*he* s to the steward of his house,	606
43:20	*they* s, "we came down here the first time	606
43:23	"It's all right," *he* s.	606
43:27	and then *he* s, "How is your aged father	606
43:29	*he* s, "God be gracious to you, my son."	606
43:31	controlling himself, s, "Serve the food."	606
44: 2	And he did as Joseph s.	1819
44: 4	from the city when Joseph s to his steward,	606
44: 7	But *they* s to him, "Why does my lord say	606
44:10	"Very well, then," *he* s.	606
44:15	Joseph s to them, "What is this	606
44:17	But Joseph s, "Far be it from me to do such	606
44:18	Then Judah went up to him and s:	606
44:21	"Then *you* s to your servants,	606
44:22	And *we* s to my lord,	606
44:24	**what** my lord had s.	1821
44:25	"Then our father s, 'Go back	606
44:26	But *we* s, 'We cannot go down.	606
44:27	"Your servant my father s to us,	606
44:28	One of them went away from me, and *I* s,	606
44:32	I s, 'If I do not bring him back to you,	606
45: 3	Joseph s to his brothers, "I am Joseph!	606
45: 4	Then Joseph s to his brothers,	606
45: 4	When they had done so, *he* s,	606
45:17	Pharaoh to Joseph, "Tell your brothers,	606
45:24	and as they were leaving *he* s to them,	606
45:27	when they told him everything Joseph had s	1819
45:28	And Israel s, "I'm convinced!	606
46: 2	to Israel in a vision at night and s,	606
46: 3	"I am God, the God of your father," *he* s.	606
46:30	Israel s to Joseph, "Now I am ready to die,	606
46:31	Then Joseph s to his brothers and to his	606
47: 4	*They* also s to him, "We have come	606
47: 5	Pharaoh s to Joseph, "Your father and	606
47: 9	And Jacob s to Pharaoh, "The years of my	606
47:15	all Egypt came to Joseph and s,	606
47:16	"Then bring your livestock," s Joseph.	606
47:18	they came to him the following year and s,	606
47:23	Joseph s to the people,	606
47:25	"You have saved our lives," *they* s.	606
47:29	he called for his son Joseph and s to him,	606
47:30	"I will do as you say," *he* s.	606
47:31	"Swear to me," *he* s.	606
48: 3	Jacob s to Joseph, "God Almighty appeared	606
48: 4	and s to me, 'I am going to make you	606
48: 9	Joseph s to his father.	606
48: 9	Then Israel s, "Bring them to me	606
48:11	Israel s to Joseph, "I never expected	606
48:15	Then he blessed Joseph and s,	606
48:18	Joseph s to him, "No, my father,	606
48:19	But his father refused and s, "I know,	606
48:20	He blessed them that day and s,	606
48:21	Then Israel s to Joseph, "I am about to die,	606
49: 1	Then Jacob called for his sons and s:	606
49:28	and this is what their father s to them	1819
50: 4	Joseph s to Pharaoh's court,	1819
50: 5	'My father made me swear an oath and s,	606
50: 6	Pharaoh s, "Go up and bury your father,	606
50:11	of Atad, *they* s, "The Egyptians are holding	606
50:15	that their father was dead, *they* s, "What	606
50:18	"We are your slaves," *they* s.	606
50:19	But Joseph s to them, "Don't be afraid.	606
50:24	Joseph s to his brothers, "I am about to die.	606
50:25	the sons of Israel swear an oath and s,	606
Ex 1: 9	"Look," *he* s to his people,	606
1:15	of Egypt s to the Hebrew midwives,	606
2: 6	"This is one of the Hebrew babies," *she* s.	606
2: 9	Pharaoh's daughter s to her,	606
2:14	*The man* s, "Who made you ruler and judge	606
3: 4	And Moses s, "Here I am."	606
3: 5	"Do not come any closer," God s.	606
3: 6	Then *he* s, "I am the God of your father,	606
3: 7	The Lord s, "I have indeed seen	606
3:11	But Moses s to God, "Who am I,	606
3:12	And God s, "I will be with you.	606
3:13	Moses s to God, "Suppose I go	606
3:14	God s to Moses, "I AM WHO I AM.	606
3:15	God also s to Moses, "Say to the Israelites,	606
3:16	appeared to me and s,	606
4: 2	Then the Lord s to him, "What is that	606
4: 3	The Lord s, "Throw it on the ground."	606
4: 4	Then the Lord s to him, "Reach out your	606
4: 5	s the Lord, "is so that they may believe	NIH
4: 6	Then the Lord s, "Put your hand inside	606
4: 7	"Now put it back into your cloak," *he* s.	606
4: 8	Then the Lord s, "If they do not believe	NIH
4:10	Moses s to the Lord, "O Lord,	606
4:11	The Lord s to him, "Who gave man his	606
4:13	But Moses s, "O Lord,	606
4:14	anger burned against Moses and *he* s,	606
4:18	to Jethro his father-in-law and s to him,	606
4:18	Jethro s, "Go, and I wish you well."	606
4:19	Now the Lord *had* s to Moses in Midian,	606
4:21	The Lord s to Moses, "When you return	606
4:25	a bridegroom of blood to me," *she* s.	606
4:26	(At that time *she* s "bridegroom of blood,"	606
4:27	The Lord s to Aaron, "Go into the desert	606
4:30	the Lord *had* s to Moses.	1819
5: 1	to Pharaoh and s, "This is what the Lord,	606
5: 2	Pharaoh s, "Who is the Lord,	606
5: 3	Then *they* s, "The God of the Hebrews	606
5: 4	But the king of Egypt s, "Moses and Aaron,	606
5: 5	Then Pharaoh s, "Look,	606
5:10	the foremen went out and s to the people,	606
5:17	Pharaoh s, "Lazy, that's what you are—	606
5:21	and *they* s, "May the Lord look upon you	606
5:22	Moses returned to the Lord and s,	606

Ex 6: 1	Then the Lord s to Moses, "Now you will	606
6: 2	God also s to Moses, "I am the Lord.	1819
6:10	Then the Lord s to Moses,	1819
6:12	But Moses s to the Lord,	1819
6:26	and Moses to whom the Lord s,	606
6:29	he s to him, "I am the Lord.	1819
6:30	But Moses s to the Lord, "Since I speak	606
7: 1	Then the Lord s to Moses, "See,	606
7: 8	The Lord s to Moses and Aaron,	606
7:13	just as the Lord *had* s.	1819
7:14	Then the Lord s to Moses,	606
7:19	The Lord s to Moses, "Tell Aaron,	606
7:22	just as the Lord *had* s.	1819
8: 1	Then the Lord s to Moses, "Go to Pharaoh	606
8: 5	Then the Lord s to Moses, "Tell Aaron,	606
8: 8	summoned Moses and Aaron and s,	606
8: 9	Moses s to Pharaoh, "I leave to you the	606
8:10	"Tomorrow," Pharaoh s.	606
8:15	just as the Lord *had* s.	1819
8:16	Then the Lord s to Moses, "Tell Aaron,	606
8:19	The magicians s to Pharaoh,	606
8:19	just as the Lord *had* s.	1819
8:20	Then the Lord s to Moses, "Get up early	606
8:25	summoned Moses and Aaron and s,	606
8:26	But Moses s, "That would not be right.	606
8:28	Pharaoh s, "I will let you go	606
9: 1	Then the Lord s to Moses, "Go to Pharaoh	606
9: 5	The Lord set a time and s,	606
9: 8	Then the Lord s to Moses and Aaron,	606
9:12	just as the Lord *had* s to Moses.	1819
9:13	Then the Lord s to Moses, "Get up early	606
9:22	Then the Lord s to Moses, "Stretch out	606
9:27	"This time I have sinned," *he* s to them.	606
9:35	just as the Lord *had* s through Moses.	1819
10: 1	Then the Lord s to Moses, "Go to Pharaoh	606
10: 3	So Moses and Aaron went to Pharaoh and s	606
10: 7	Pharaoh's officials s to him,	606
10: 8	"Go, worship the Lord your God," *he* s.	606
10:10	Pharaoh s, "The Lord be with you—	606
10:12	And the Lord s to Moses,	606
10:16	summoned Moses and Aaron and s,	606
10:21	Then the Lord s to Moses, "Stretch out	606
10:24	Then Pharaoh summoned Moses and s,	606
10:25	But Moses s, "You must allow us	606
10:28	Pharaoh s to Moses, "Get out of my sight!	606
11: 1	Now the Lord *had* s to Moses,	606
11: 4	So Moses s, "This is what the Lord says:	606
11: 9	The Lord *had* s to Moses, "Pharaoh will	606
12: 1	The Lord s to Moses and Aaron in Egypt,	606
12:21	the elders of Israel and s to them,	606
12:31	summoned Moses and Aaron and s,	606
12:32	Take your flocks and herds, as *you have* s,	1819
12:33	"For otherwise," *they* s, "we will all die!"	606
12:43	The Lord s to Moses and Aaron,	606
13: 1	The Lord s to Moses,	1819
13: 3	Then Moses s to the people,	606
13:17	For God s, "If they face war,	606
13:19	He *had* s, "God will surely come to your aid	606
14: 1	Then the Lord s to Moses,	1819
14: 5	changed their minds about them and s,	606
14:11	*They* s to Moses, "Was it because	606
14:15	Then the Lord s to Moses, "Why are you	606
14:25	And the Egyptians s, "Let's get away	606
14:26	Then the Lord s to Moses,	606
15:26	*He* s, "If you listen carefully to the voice of	606
16: 3	The Israelites s to them,	606
16: 4	Then the Lord s to Moses, "I will rain down	606
16: 6	So Moses and Aaron s to all the Israelites,	606
16: 8	Moses also s, "You will know that it was	606
16:11	The Lord s to Moses,	1819
16:15	the Israelites saw it, *they* s to each other,	606
16:15	Moses s to them, "What is it?"	606
16:19	Then Moses s to them,	606
16:23	*He* s to them, "This is what the Lord	606
16:25	"Eat it today," Moses s,	606
16:28	Then the Lord s to Moses, "How long	606
16:32	Moses s, "This is what the Lord has	606
16:33	So Moses s to Aaron, "Take a jar	606
17: 2	So they quarreled with Moses and s,	606
17: 3	*They* s, "Why did you bring us up out	606
17: 9	Moses s to Joshua, "Choose some of	606
17:14	Then the Lord s to Moses, "Write this	606
17:16	*He* s, "For hands were lifted up to the throne	606
18: 3	One son was named Gershom, for Moses s,	606
18: 4	for he s, "My father's God was my helper;	NIH
18:10	He s, "Praise be to the Lord,	606
18:14	the people, *he* s, "What is this you are doing	606
18:24	to his father-in-law and did everything *he* s.	606
19: 3	the mountain and s, "This is what you are	606
19: 8	"We will do everything the Lord *has* s."	1819
19: 9	The Lord s to Moses, "I am going to come	606
19: 9	told the Lord **what** the people had s.	1821
19:10	the Lord s to Moses, "Go to the people	606
19:15	Then *he* s to the people, "Prepare yourselves	606
19:21	and the Lord s to him, "Go down and warn	606
19:23	Moses s to the Lord, "The people cannot	606
20:19	and s to Moses, "Speak to us yourself	606
20:20	Moses s to the people, "Do not be afraid.	606
20:22	Lord s to Moses, "Tell the Israelites this:	606
23:13	"Be careful to do everything *I have* s	606
24: 1	Then *he* s to Moses, "Come up	606
24: 3	"Everything the Lord *has* s we will do."	1819
24: 4	down everything the Lord had s.	1821
24: 7	"We will do everything the Lord *has* s;	1819
24: 8	sprinkled it on the people and s,	606
24:12	The Lord s to Moses, "Come up to me	606
24:14	*He* s to the elders, "Wait here for us	606

Ex 25:1	The LORD s to Moses,	1819
30:11	Then the LORD s to Moses,	1819
30:17	Then the LORD s to Moses,	1819
30:22	Then the LORD s to Moses,	1819
30:34	Then the LORD s to Moses,	606
31:1	Then the LORD s to Moses,	1819
31:12	Then the LORD s to Moses,	606
32:1	they gathered around Aaron and s, "Come,	606
32:4	Then *they* s, "These are your gods,	606
32:7	Then the LORD s to Moses, "Go down,	1819
32:8	down to it and sacrificed to it and *have* s,	606
32:9	"I have seen these people," the LORD s	606
32:11	he s, "why should your anger burn	606
32:17	he s to Moses, "There is the sound of war	606
32:21	He s to Aaron, "What did these people do	606
32:23	They s to me, 'Make us gods	606
32:26	he stood at the entrance to the camp and s,	606
32:27	Then he s to them, "This is what the LORD	606
32:29	Then Moses s, "You have been set apart to	606
32:30	The next day Moses s to the people,	606
32:31	So Moses went back to the LORD and s,	606
33:1	Then the LORD s to Moses, "Leave this	1819
33:5	For the LORD *had* s to Moses,	606
33:12	Moses s to the LORD, "You have been telling	606
33:12	You *have* s, 'I know you by name	606
33:15	Then Moses s to him, "If your Presence	606
33:17	And the LORD s to Moses, "I will do	606
33:18	Then Moses s, "Now show me your glory."	606
33:19	And the LORD s, "I will cause all	606
33:20	But," he s, "you cannot see my face,	606
33:21	Then the LORD s, "There is a place	606
34:1	The LORD s to Moses, "Chisel out two	606
34:9	if I have found favor in your eyes," he s,	606
34:10	Then the LORD s: "I am making a covenant	606
34:27	Then the LORD s to Moses, "Write down	606
35:1	the whole Israelite community and s to them,	606
35:4	Moses s to the whole Israelite community,	606
35:30	Then Moses s to the Israelites, "See,	606
36:5	and s to Moses, "The people are bringing	606
40:1	Then the LORD s to Moses:	1819
Lev 1:1	from the Tent of Meeting. He s,	606
4:1	The LORD s to Moses,	1819
5:14	The LORD s to Moses:	1819
6:1	The LORD s to Moses:	1819
6:8	The LORD s to Moses:	1819
6:19	The LORD also s to Moses,	1819
6:24	The LORD s to Moses,	1819
7:22	The LORD s to Moses,	1819
7:28	The LORD s to Moses,	1819
8:1	The LORD s to Moses,	1819
8:5	Moses s to the assembly, "This is what	606
8:31	Moses then s to Aaron and his sons,	606
9:2	*He* s to Aaron, "Take a bull calf	606
9:6	Then Moses s, "This is what	606
9:7	Moses s to Aaron, "Come to the altar	606
10:3	Moses then s to Aaron, "This is what	606
10:3	what the LORD spoke of when *he* s:	606
10:4	and s to them, "Come here.	606
10:6	Then Moses s to Aaron and his sons	606
10:7	So they did as Moses s.	1821
10:8	Then the LORD s to Aaron,	1819
10:12	Moses s to Aaron and his remaining sons,	1819
11:1	The LORD s to Moses and Aaron,	1819
12:1	The LORD s to Moses,	1819
13:1	The LORD s to Moses and Aaron,	1819
14:1	The LORD s to Moses,	1819
14:33	The LORD s to Moses and Aaron,	1819
15:1	The LORD s to Moses and Aaron,	1819
16:2	The LORD s to Moses: "Tell your brother	606
17:1	The LORD s to Moses,	1819
17:14	That is why *I have* s to the Israelites,	606
18:1	The LORD s to Moses,	1819
19:1	The LORD s to Moses,	1819
20:1	The LORD s to Moses,	1819
20:24	*I* s to you, "You will possess their land;	606
21:1	The LORD s to Moses,	1819
21:16	The LORD s to Moses,	1819
22:1	The LORD s to Moses,	1819
22:17	The LORD s to Moses,	1819
22:26	The LORD s to Moses,	1819
23:1	The LORD s to Moses,	1819
23:9	The LORD s to Moses,	1819
23:23	The LORD s to Moses,	1819
23:26	The LORD s to Moses,	1819
23:33	The LORD s to Moses,	1819
24:1	The LORD s to Moses:	1819
24:13	Then the LORD s to Moses:	1819
25:1	The LORD s to Moses on Mount Sinai,	1819
27:1	The LORD s to Moses,	1819
Nu 1:1	after the Israelites came out of Egypt. He s:	606
1:48	The LORD *had* s to Moses,	1819
2:1	The LORD s to Moses and Aaron:	1819
3:5	The LORD s to Moses,	1819
3:11	The LORD also s to Moses,	1819
3:14	The LORD s to Moses in the Desert	1819
3:40	The LORD s to Moses, "Count all the	606
3:44	The LORD also s to Moses,	1819
4:1	The LORD s to Moses and Aaron,	1819
4:17	The LORD s to Moses and Aaron,	1819
4:21	The LORD s to Moses,	1819
5:1	The LORD s to Moses,	1819
5:5	The LORD s to Moses,	1819
5:11	Then the LORD s to Moses,	1819
6:1	The LORD s to Moses,	1819
6:22	The LORD s to Moses,	1819
7:4	The LORD s to Moses,	606
7:11	For the LORD *had* s to Moses,	606

Nu 8:1	The LORD s to Moses,	1819
8:5	The LORD s to Moses:	1819
8:23	The LORD s to Moses,	1819
9:1	after they came out of Egypt. He s,	606
9:7	and s to Moses,	606
9:9	Then the LORD s to Moses,	606
10:1	The LORD s to Moses:	1819
10:29	Now Moses s to Hobab son of Reuel	606
10:29	for the place about which the LORD s,	606
10:31	But Moses s, "Please do not leave us.	606
10:35	Whenever the ark set out, Moses s,	606
10:36	Whenever it came to rest, he s, "Return,	606
11:1	again the Israelites started wailing and s,	606
11:16	The LORD s to Moses: "Bring me seventy	606
11:21	But Moses s, "Here I am	606
11:24	told the people **what** the LORD had s.	1821
11:28	spoke up and s, "Moses, my lord,	606
12:4	At once the LORD s to Moses,	606
12:6	*he* s, "Listen to my words:	606
12:11	and he s to Moses, "Please, my lord,	606
13:1	The LORD s to Moses,	1819
13:17	Moses sent them to explore Canaan, he s,	606
13:30	the people before Moses and s,	606
13:31	But the men who had gone up with him s,	606
13:32	about the land they had explored. They s,	606
14:2	and the whole assembly s to them,	606
14:4	And *they* s to each other,	606
14:7	and s to the entire Israelite assembly.	606
14:11	The LORD s to Moses, "How long	606
14:13	Moses s to the LORD, "Then the Egyptians	606
14:26	The LORD s to Moses and Aaron:	1819
14:31	for your children that *you* s would be taken	606
14:40	"We have sinned," they s.	606
14:41	But Moses s, "Why are you disobeying	606
15:1	The LORD s to Moses,	1819
15:17	The LORD s to Moses,	1819
15:35	the LORD s to Moses, "The man must die.	606
15:37	The LORD s to Moses,	606
16:3	to oppose Moses and Aaron and s to them,	606
16:5	Then *he* s to Korah and all his followers:	1819
16:8	Moses also s to Korah, "Now listen,	606
16:12	But *they* s, "We will not come!	606
16:15	Then Moses became very angry and s to	606
16:16	Moses s to Korah, "You and all your	606
16:20	The LORD s to Moses and Aaron,	1819
16:23	Then the LORD s to Moses,	1819
16:28	Then Moses s, "This is how you will know	606
16:36	The LORD s to Moses,	1819
16:41	You have killed the LORD's people," *they* s.	606
16:44	and the LORD s to Moses,	1819
16:46	Then Moses s to Aaron, "Take your censer	606
16:47	So Aaron did as Moses s,	1819
17:1	The LORD s to Moses,	1819
17:10	The LORD s to Moses, "Put back Aaron's	606
17:12	The Israelites s to Moses, "We will die!	606
18:1	The LORD s to Aaron, "You, your sons	1819
18:8	Then the LORD s to Aaron,	1819
18:20	The LORD s to Aaron, "You will have no	606
18:24	That is why *I* s concerning them:	606
18:25	The LORD s to Moses,	1819
19:1	The LORD s to Moses and Aaron:	1819
20:3	They quarreled with Moses and s,	606
20:7	The LORD s to Moses,	1819
20:10	in front of the rock and Moses s to them,	606
20:12	But the LORD s to Moses and Aaron,	606
20:23	the LORD s to Moses and Aaron,	606
21:5	and s, "Why have you brought us up out	NIH
21:7	The people came to Moses and s,	606
21:8	The LORD s to Moses, "Make a snake	606
21:16	the well where the LORD s to Moses,	606
21:34	The LORD s to Moses, "Do not be afraid	606
22:4	The Moabites s to the elders of Midian,	606
22:5	Balak s: "A people has come out of Egypt;	606
22:7	they told him **what** Balak had s.	1821
22:8	"Spend the night here," Balaam s to them,	606
22:10	Balaam s to God, "Balak son of Zippor,	606
22:12	God s to Balaam, "Do not go with them.	606
22:13	The next morning Balaam got up and s	606
22:14	Moabite princes returned to Balak and s,	606
22:16	They came to Balaam and s:	606
22:20	That night God came to Balaam and s,	606
22:28	donkey's mouth, and *she* s to Balaam,	606
22:30	The donkey s to Balaam, "Am I not	606
22:30	"No," he s.	606
22:34	Balaam s to the angel of the LORD,	606
22:35	The angel of the LORD s to Balaam,	606
22:37	Balak s to Balaam, "Did I not send you	606
23:1	Balaam s, "Build me seven altars here,	606
23:2	Balak did as Balaam s,	1819
23:3	Then Balaam s to Balak, "Stay here	606
23:4	God met with him, and Balaam s,	606
23:5	put a message in Balaam's mouth and s,	606
23:7	'Come,' he s, 'curse Jacob for me;	NIH
23:11	Balak s to Balaam, "What have you done	606
23:13	Then Balak s to him, "Come with me	606
23:15	Balaam s to Balak, "Stay here	606
23:16	and put a message in his mouth and s,	606
23:23	*It will* now *be* s of Jacob and of Israel.	606
23:25	Then Balak s to Balaam, "Neither curse them	606
23:27	Then Balak s to Balaam, "Come.	606
23:29	Balaam s, "Build me seven altars here,	606
23:30	Balak did as Balaam had s,	606
24:10	He struck his hands together and s to him,	606
24:11	*I* s I would reward you handsomely,	606
25:4	The LORD s to Moses, "Take all the leaders	606
25:5	So Moses s to Israel's judges,	606
25:10	The LORD s to Moses,	1819

Nu 25:16	The LORD s to Moses,	1819
26:1	After the plague the LORD s to Moses	606
26:3	Eleazar the priest spoke with them and s,	606
26:52	The LORD s to Moses,	1819
27:2	the leaders and the whole assembly, and s,	606
27:6	and the LORD s to him,	606
27:12	Then the LORD s to Moses, "Go up	606
27:15	Moses s to the LORD,	1819
27:18	So the LORD s to Moses, "Take Joshua	606
28:1	The LORD s to Moses,	1819
30:1	Moses s to the heads of the tribes of Israel:	1819
30:2	but must do everything he s.	3655+4946+7023
31:1	The LORD s to Moses,	1819
31:3	So Moses s to the people, "Arm some of	1819
31:21	Then Eleazar the priest s to the soldiers	606
31:25	The LORD s to Moses,	1819
31:49	and s to him, "Your servants have counted	606
32:2	and to the leaders of the community, and s,	606
32:5	in your eyes," *they* s, "let this land be given	606
32:6	Moses s to the Gadites and Reubenites,	606
32:16	Then they came up to him and s,	606
32:20	Moses s to them, "If you will do this—	606
32:25	The Gadites and Reubenites s to Moses,	606
32:29	He s to them, "If the Gadites and	606
32:31	servants will do what the LORD *has* s.	1819
32:50	across from Jericho the LORD s to Moses,	1819
34:1	The LORD s to Moses,	1819
34:16	The LORD s to Moses,	1819
35:1	across from Jericho, the LORD s to Moses,	1819
35:9	Then the LORD s to Moses:	1819
36:2	They s, "When the LORD commanded my	606
Dt 1:6	The LORD our God s to us at Horeb,	1819
1:9	At that time *I* s to you, "You are too heavy	606
1:20	Then *I* s to you, "You have reached	606
1:22	Then all of you came to me and s,	606
1:27	You grumbled in your tents and s,	606
1:29	Then *I* s to you, "Do not be terrified;	606
1:34	When the LORD heard **what** you s,	1821+7754
1:37	LORD became angry with me also and s,	606
1:39	And the little ones that *you* s would	606
1:42	But the LORD s to me, "Tell them,	606
2:2	Then the LORD s to me,	606
2:9	Then the LORD s to me, "Do not harass	606
2:13	And the LORD s, "Now get up and cross	NIH
2:17	the LORD s to me,	1819
2:31	The LORD s to me, "See, I have begun	606
3:2	The LORD s to me, "Do not be afraid of him,	606
3:26	"That is enough," the LORD s.	606
4:10	when he s to me, "Assemble the people	606
5:1	Moses summoned all Israel and s:	606
5:5	did not up the mountain.) And he s:	606
5:24	*you* s, "The LORD our God has shown us	606
5:28	when you spoke to me and the LORD s	606
5:28	"I have heard what this people s to you.	1819
5:28	Everything *they* s was good.	1819
6:19	your enemies before you, as the LORD s.	1819
9:2	You know about them and have heard it s:	NIH
9:13	And the LORD s to me, "I have seen this	606
9:23	he s, "Go up and take possession of the land	606
9:25	the LORD *had* s he would destroy you.	606
9:26	I prayed to the LORD and s,	606
10:1	At that time the LORD s to me.	606
10:11	"Go," the LORD s to me.	606
13:12	If you hear *it* s about one of the towns	606
18:16	on the day of the assembly when you s,	606
18:17	The LORD s to me: "What they say is good.	606
22:17	Now he has slandered her and s,	606
27:9	who are Levites, s to all Israel, "Be silent,	1819
28:68	a journey *I* s you should never make again.	606
29:2	Moses summoned all the Israelites and s	606
31:2	The LORD *has* s to me, "You shall not cross	606
31:3	cross over ahead of you, as the LORD s.	1819
31:7	and s to him in the presence of all Israel,	606
31:14	The LORD s to Moses, "Now the day	606
31:16	And the LORD s to Moses:	606
32:20	"I will hide my face from them," he s,	606
32:26	*I* s I would scatter them and blot out	606
32:46	he s to them, "Take to heart all the words	606
33:2	He s: "The LORD came from Sinai	606
33:7	And this he s about Judah:	606
33:8	About Levi he s:	606
33:9	He s of his father and mother,	606
33:12	About Benjamin he s:	606
33:13	About Joseph he s:	606
33:18	About Zebulun he s:	606
33:20	About Gad he s:	606
33:22	About Dan he s:	606
33:23	About Naphtali he s:	606
33:24	About Asher he s:	606
34:4	Then the LORD s to him, "This is the land	606
34:4	Abraham, Isaac and Jacob when I s,	606
34:5	as the LORD had s.	7023
Jos 1:1	the LORD s to Joshua son of Nun,	606
1:12	and the half-tribe of Manasseh, Joshua s,	606
2:1	"Go, look over the land," he s.	606
2:4	She s, "Yes, the men came to me,	606
2:9	and s to them, "I know that the LORD has	606
2:16	Now *she had* s to them,	606
2:17	The men s to her, "This oath you made us	606
2:24	They s to Joshua, "The LORD has	606
3:6	Joshua s to the priests, "Take up the ark	606
3:7	And the LORD s to Joshua, "Today I will	606
3:9	Joshua s to the Israelites, "Come here	606
4:1	crossing the Jordan, the LORD s to Joshua.	606
4:5	and s to them, "Go over before the ark	606
4:15	Then the LORD s to Joshua.	606
4:21	*He* s to the Israelites, "In the future	606

Jos	5: 2	At that time the LORD s to Joshua,	606
	5: 9	Then the LORD s to Joshua,	606
	6: 2	Then the LORD s to Joshua, "See,	606
	6: 6	of Nun called the priests and s to them,	606
	6:22	Joshua s to the two men who had spied out	606
	7: 3	When they returned to Joshua, they s	606
	7: 7	And Joshua s, "Ah, Sovereign LORD,	606
	7:10	The LORD s to Joshua, "Stand up!	606
	7:19	Then Joshua s, "My son,	606
	7:25	Joshua s, "Why have you brought this	606
	8: 1	the LORD s to Joshua, "Do not be afraid;	606
	8:18	Then the LORD s to Joshua, "Hold out	606
	9: 6	at Gilgal and s to him and the men of Israel,	606
	9: 7	The men of Israel s to the Hivites,	606
	9: 8	"We are your servants," they s to Joshua.	606
	9:11	and all those living in our country s to us,	606
	9:22	Joshua summoned the Gibeonites and s,	1819
	10: 4	up and help me attack Gibeon," he s,	606
	10: 8	The LORD s to Joshua, "Do not be afraid	606
	10:12	Joshua s to the LORD in the presence	1819
	10:18	he s, "Roll large rocks up to the mouth of	606
	10:22	Joshua s, "Open the mouth of the cave	606
	10:24	he summoned all the men of Israel and s to	606
	10:25	Joshua s to them, "Do not be afraid;	606
	11: 6	The LORD s to Joshua, "Do not be afraid	606
	13: 1	the LORD s to him, "You are very old,	606
	14: 6	and Caleb son of Jephunneh the Kenizzite s	606
	14: 6	"You know what the LORD s to Moses	1819
	14:10	for forty-five years since the time he s this	1819
	14:12	I will drive them out just as he s."	1819
	15:16	Caleb s, "I will give my daughter Acsah	606
	17: 4	Joshua son of Nun, and the leaders and s,	606
	17:14	The people of Joseph s to Joshua,	1819
	17:17	But Joshua s to the house of Joseph—	606
	18: 3	So Joshua s to the Israelites:	606
	20: 1	Then the LORD s to Joshua:	1819
	21: 2	at Shiloh in Canaan and s to them,	1819
	22: 2	and s to them, "You have done all that	606
	22:15	the half-tribe of Manasseh—they s to them:	1819
	22:26	"That is why we s, 'Let us get ready	606
	22:28	"And we s, 'If they ever say this to us,	606
	22:31	the priest, s to Reuben, Gad and Manasseh,	606
	23: 2	and s to them: "I am old and well advanced	606
	24: 2	Joshua s to all the people, "This is what	606
	24:19	Joshua s to the people, "You are not able	606
	24:21	But the people s to Joshua, "No!	606
	24:22	Then Joshua s, "You are witnesses	606
	24:23	s Joshua, "throw away the foreign gods	NIH
	24:24	And the people s to Joshua,	606
	24:27	he s to all the people.	606
	24:27	It has heard all the words the LORD has s	1819
Jdg	1: 3	of Judah s to the Simeonites their brothers,	606
	1: 7	Then Adoni-Bezek s, "Seventy kings	606
	1:12	Caleb s, "I will give my daughter Acsah	606
	1:24	a man coming out of the city and they s	606
	2: 1	up from Gilgal to Bokim and s,	606
	2: 1	I s, 'I will never break my covenant	606
	2:20	LORD was very angry with Israel and s,	606
	3:19	near Gilgal he himself turned back and s,	606
	3:19	The king s, "Quiet!"	606
	3:20	the upper room of his summer palace and s,	606
	3:24	They s, "He must be relieving himself in	606
	4: 6	of Abinoam from Kedesh in Naphtali and s	606
	4: 8	Barak s to her, "If you go with me,	606
	4: 9	"Very well," Deborah s,	606
	4:14	Then Deborah s to Barak, "Go!	606
	4:18	Jael went out to meet Sisera and s to him,	606
	4:19	"I'm thirsty," he s.	606
	4:22	she s, "I will show you the man	606
	5:23	'Curse Meroz,' s the angel of the LORD.	606
	6: 8	who s, "This is what the LORD,	606
	6:10	I s to you, 'I am the LORD your God;	606
	6:12	he s, "The LORD is with you,	606
	6:13	that our fathers told us about when they s,	606
	6:14	The LORD turned to him and s,	606
	6:18	the LORD s, "I will wait until you return."	606
	6:20	The angel of God s to him, "Take the meat	606
	6:23	But the LORD s to him, "Peace!	606
	6:25	That same night the LORD s to him,	606
	6:36	Gideon s to God, "If you will save Israel	606
	6:37	will save Israel by my hand, as you s."	1819
	6:39	Then Gideon s to God, "Do not be angry	606
	7: 2	The LORD s to Gideon, "You have too many	606
	7: 4	But the LORD s to Gideon, "There are still	606
	7: 7	LORD s to Gideon, "With the three hundred	606
	7: 9	During that night the LORD s to Gideon,	606
	8: 5	He s to the men of Succoth, "Give my troops	606
	8: 6	But the officials of Succoth s,	606
	8: 9	So he s to the men of Peniel,	606
	8:15	Gideon came and s to the men of Succoth,	606
	8:20	Turning to Jether, his oldest son, he s,	606
	8:21	Zebah and Zalmunna s, "Come,	606
	8:22	The Israelites s to Gideon, "Rule over us—	606
	8:24	And he s, "I do have one request,	606
	9: 1	to his mother's brothers in Shechem and s	1819
	9: 3	for they s, "He is our brother."	606
	9: 8	They s to the olive tree, 'Be our king.'	606
	9:10	"Next, the trees s to the fig tree,	606
	9:12	trees s to the vine, 'Come and be our king.'	606
	9:14	"Finally all the trees s to the thornbush,	606
	9:15	"The thornbush s to the trees,	606
	9:28	Then Gaal son of Ebed s,	606
	9:30	of the city heard what Gaal son of Ebed s,	1821
	9:36	When Gaal saw them, he s to Zebul, "Look,	606
	9:38	Then Zebul s to him,	606
	9:38	"Where is your big talk now, you who s,	606
	10:15	But the Israelites s to the LORD,	606

Jdg	10:18	of the people of Gilead s to each other,	606
	11: 2	in our family," they s, "because you are	606
	11: 6	"Come," they s, "be our commander,	606
	11: 7	Jephthah s to them, "Didn't you hate me	606
	11: 8	The elders of Gilead s to him,	606
	11:19	who ruled in Heshbon, and s to him,	606
	11:37	But grant me this one request," she s.	606
	11:38	"You may go," he s.	606
	12: 1	crossed over to Zaphon and s to Jephthah,	606
	12: 4	down because the Ephraimites had s,	606
	12: 5	and whenever a survivor of Ephraim s,	606
	12: 6	they s, "All right, say 'Shibboleth.' "	606
	12: 6	If he s, "Sibboleth," because he could	606
	13: 3	of the LORD appeared to her and s,	606
	13: 7	But he s to me, 'You will conceive	606
	13:11	When he came to the man, he s,	606
	13:11	"I am," he s.	606
	13:15	Manoah s to the angel of the LORD,	606
	13:22	"We are doomed to die!" he s to his wife.	606
	14: 2	he returned, he s to his father and mother,	5583
	14: 3	But Samson s to his father, "Get her for me.	606
	14:12	tell you a riddle," Samson s to them.	606
	14:13	"Tell us your riddle," they s.	606
	14:15	On the fourth day, they s to Samson's wife,	606
	14:18	on the seventh day the men of the town s	606
	14:18	Samson s to them, "If you had not plowed	606
	15: 1	He s, "I'm going to my wife's room."	606
	15: 2	he s, "that I gave her to your friend.	606
	15: 3	Samson s to them, "This time I have a right	606
	15: 7	Samson s to them, "Since you've acted like	606
	15:11	down to the cave in the rock of Etam and s	606
	15:12	They s to him, "We've come to tie you up	606
	15:12	Samson s, "Swear to me	606
	15:16	Then Samson s, "With a donkey's jawbone	606
	16: 5	rulers of the Philistines went to her and s,	606
	16: 6	So Delilah s to Samson, "Tell me the secret	606
	16:10	Delilah s to Samson, "You have made a fool	606
	16:11	He s, "If anyone ties me securely	606
	16:13	Delilah then s to Samson, "Until now,	606
	16:15	Then she s to him, "How can you say,	606
	16:17	on my head," he s, "because I have been	606
	16:26	Samson s to the servant who held his hand,	606
	16:30	Samson s, "Let me die with the Philistines!"	606
	17: 2	s to his mother, "The eleven hundred	606
	17: 2	Then his mother s, "The LORD bless you,	606
	17: 3	she s, "I solemnly consecrate my silver to	606
	17: 9	he s, "and I'm looking for a place to stay."	606
	17:10	Then Micah s to him, "Live with me and	606
	17:13	And Micah s, "Now I know that	606
	18: 4	for him, and s, "He has hired me	NIH
	18: 5	Then they s to him, "Please inquire of God	606
	18:14	the land of Laish s to their brothers,	606
	18:18	the priest s to them, "What are you doing?"	606
	18:23	the Danites turned and s to Micah,	606
	19: 5	but the girl's father s to his son-in-law,	606
	19: 6	Afterward the girl's father s,	606
	19: 8	when he rose to go, the girl's father s,	606
	19: 9	his father-in-law, the girl's father, s,	606
	19:11	the servant s to his master, "Come,	606
	19:20	welcome at my house," the old man s.	606
	19:23	The owner of the house went outside and s	606
	19:28	He s to her, "Get up; let's go."	606
	19:30	Everyone who saw it s, "Such a thing	606
	20: 3	Then the Israelites s, "Tell us how this	606
	20: 4	the husband of the murdered woman, s,	6699
	20:18	They s, "Who of us shall go first to fight	606
	20:23	They s, "Shall we go up again to battle	606
	20:39	the men of Israel (about thirty), and they s,	606
	21: 3	one tribe is cut off from Israel," they s.	606
	21:11	"This is what you are to do," they s.	606
	21:16	And the elders of the assembly s,	606
	21:17	they s, "so that a tribe of Israel will not	606
Ru	1: 8	Then Naomi s to her two daughters-in-law,	606
	1:10	and s to her, "We will go back with you	606
	1:11	But Naomi s, "Return home, my daughters.	606
	1:15	s Naomi, "your sister-in-law is going back	606
	2: 2	And Ruth the Moabitess s to Naomi,	606
	2: 2	Naomi s to her, "Go ahead, my daughter."	606
	2: 7	She s, 'Please let me glean and gather	606
	2: 8	Boaz s to Ruth, "My daughter, listen to me.	606
	2:13	to find favor in your eyes, my lord," she s.	606
	2:14	At mealtime Boaz s to her, "Come over	606
	2:19	the man I worked with today is Boaz," she s.	606
	2:20	Naomi s to her daughter-in-law.	606
	2:21	Then Ruth the Moabitess said,	606
	2:21	Ruth the Moabitess said, "He even s to me,	606
	2:22	Naomi s to Ruth her daughter-in-law,	606
	3: 1	One day Naomi her mother-in-law s to her,	606
	3: 9	"I am your servant Ruth," she s.	606
	3:14	and he s, "Don't let it be known that	606
	3:15	He also s, "Bring me the shawl	606
	3:18	Then Naomi s, "Wait, my daughter,	606
	4: 1	Boaz s, "Come over here, my friend,	606
	4: 2	took ten of the elders of the town and s,	606
	4: 3	Then he s to the kinsman-redeemer,	606
	4: 4	"I will redeem it," he s.	606
	4: 5	Then Boaz s, "On the day you buy the land	606
	4: 6	At this, the kinsman-redeemer s,	606
	4: 8	So the kinsman-redeemer s to Boaz,	606
	4:11	Then the elders and all those at the gate s,	606
	4:14	The women s to Naomi: "Praise be	606
	4:17	women living there s, "Naomi has a son."	606
1Sa	1:14	and s to her, "How long will you keep on	606
	1:18	She s, "May your servant find favor	606
	1:22	She s to her husband, "After the boy is	606
	1:26	and she s to him, "As surely as you live,	606
	2: 1	Then Hannah prayed and s: "My heart	606

1Sa	2:16	If the man s to him,	606
	2:23	he s to them, "Why do you do such things?	606
	2:27	a man of God came to Eli and s to him,	606
	3: 5	And he ran to Eli and s, "Here I am;	606
	3: 5	But Eli s, "I did not call;	606
	3: 6	And Samuel got up and went to Eli and s,	606
	3: 6	"My son," Eli s, "I did not call;	606
	3: 8	and Samuel got up and went to Eli and s,	606
	3:10	Then Samuel s, "Speak,	606
	3:11	And the LORD s to Samuel:	606
	3:16	but Eli called him and s,	606
	3:17	"What was it he s to you?"	1819
	3:18	Then Eli s, "He is the LORD;	606
	4: 7	"A god has come into the camp," they s.	606
	4:20	the women attending her s, "Don't despair;	1819
	4:22	She s, "The glory has departed from Israel,	606
	5: 7	of Ashdod saw what was happening, they s,	606
	5:11	of the Philistines and s, "Send the ark of	606
	6: 2	for the priests and the diviners and s,	606
	7: 3	And Samuel s to the whole house of Israel,	606
	7: 5	Then Samuel s, "Assemble all Israel	606
	7: 8	They s to Samuel, "Do not stop crying out	606
	8: 5	They s to him, "You are old,	606
	8: 6	But when they s, "Give us a king	606
	8:11	He s, "This is what the king who will reign	606
	8:19	"No!" they s. "We want a king over us.	606
	8:21	When Samuel heard all that the people s,	1821
	8:22	Then Samuel s to the men of Israel,	606
	9: 3	and Kish s to his son Saul,	606
	9: 5	Saul s to the servant who was with him,	606
	9: 7	Saul s to his servant, "If we go,	606
	9: 8	he s, "I have a quarter of a shekel of silver.	606
	9:10	"Good," Saul s to his servant.	606
	9:17	the LORD s to him, "This is the man	6699
	9:23	Samuel s to the cook, "Bring the piece	606
	9:24	Samuel s, "Here is what has been kept	606
	9:24	from the time I s, 'I have invited guests.' "	606
	9:27	Samuel s to Saul, "Tell the servant to go on	606
	10:14	"Looking for the donkeys," he s.	606
	10:15	Saul's uncle s, "Tell me what Samuel said	606
	10:15	"Tell me what Samuel s to you."	606
	10:16	not tell his uncle what Samuel had s about	606
	10:18	and s to them, "This is what the LORD,	606
	10:19	And you have s, 'No, set a king over us.'	606
	10:22	And the LORD s, "Yes, he has hidden	606
	10:24	Samuel s to all the people, "Do you see	606
	10:27	But some troublemakers s,	606
	11: 1	and all the men of Jabesh s to him,	606
	11: 3	The elders of Jabesh s to him,	606
	11: 5	to him what the men of Jabesh had s.	1821
	11:10	They s to the Ammonites,	606
	11:12	The people then s to Samuel,	606
	11:13	But Saul s, "No one shall be put	606
	11:14	Then Samuel s to the people, "Come,	606
	12: 1	Samuel s to all Israel, "I have listened	606
	12: 1	"I have listened to everything you s to me	606
	12: 5	Samuel s to them, "The LORD is witness	606
	12: 5	"He is witness," they s.	606
	12: 6	Then Samuel s to the people,	606
	12:10	They cried out to the LORD and s,	606
	12:12	you s to me, 'No, we want a king to rule	606
	12:19	The people all s to Samuel,	606
	13: 3	trumpet blown throughout the land and s,	606
	13: 9	So he s, "Bring me the burnt offering and	606
	13:13	"You acted foolishly," Samuel s.	606
	13:19	because the Philistines had s,	606
	14: 1	One day Jonathan son of Saul s to	606
	14: 6	Jonathan s to his young armor-bearer,	606
	14: 7	that you have in mind," his armor-bearer s.	606
	14: 8	Jonathan s, "Come, then;	606
	14:11	s the Philistines. "The Hebrews are crawling	606
	14:12	So Jonathan s to his armor-bearer,	606
	14:17	Then Saul s to the men who were with him,	606
	14:18	Saul s to Ahijah, "Bring the ark of God."	606
	14:19	Saul s to the priest, "Withdraw your hand."	606
	14:29	Jonathan s, "My father has made trouble	606
	14:33	Then someone s to Saul, "Look,	5583
	14:33	"You have broken faith," he s.	606
	14:34	Then he s, "Go out among the men	606
	14:36	Saul s, "Let us go down after the Philistines	606
	14:36	the priest s, "Let us inquire of God here."	606
	14:38	Saul therefore s, "Come here,	606
	14:39	But not one of the men s a word.	6699
	14:40	Saul then s to all the Israelites,	606
	14:42	Saul s, "Cast the lot between me	606
	14:43	Then Saul s to Jonathan,	606
	14:44	Saul s, "May God deal with me,	606
	14:45	the men s to Saul, "Should Jonathan die—	606
	15: 1	Samuel s to Saul, "I am the one	606
	15: 6	Then he s to the Kenites, "Go away,	606
	15:13	When Samuel reached him, Saul s,	606
	15:14	But Samuel s, "What then is this bleating	606
	15:16	"Stop!" Samuel s to Saul.	606
	15:16	"Let me tell you what the LORD s	1819
	15:17	Samuel s, "Although you were once small	606
	15:20	"But I did obey the LORD," Saul s.	606
	15:24	Then Saul s to Samuel, "I have sinned.	606
	15:26	But Samuel s to him, "I will not go back	606
	15:28	Samuel s to him, "The LORD has torn	606
	15:32	Then Samuel s, "Bring me Agag king of	606
	15:33	But Samuel s, "As your sword has made	606
	16: 1	The LORD s to Samuel, "How long	606
	16: 2	But Samuel s, "How can I go?	606
	16: 2	The LORD s, "Take a heifer with you	606
	16: 4	Samuel did what the LORD s.	1819
	16: 7	But the LORD s to Samuel, "Do not consider	606
	16: 8	But Samuel s, "The LORD has not chosen	606

1Sa	16: 9	then had Shammah pass by, but Samuel s,	606
	16:10	but Samuel s to him, "The LORD has not	606
	16:11	Samuel s, "Send for him;	606
	16:12	Then the LORD s, "Rise and anoint him;	606
	16:15	Saul's attendants s to him, "See,	606
	16:17	So Saul s to his attendants,	606
	16:19	Then Saul sent messengers to Jesse and s,	606
	17:10	Then the Philistine s, "This day I defy	606
	17:17	Now Jesse s to his son David,	606
	17:29	"Now what have I done?" s David.	606
	17:31	What David s was overheard and reported	1819
	17:32	David s to Saul, "Let no one lose heart	606
	17:34	But David s to Saul, "Your servant	606
	17:37	Saul s to David, "Go,	606
	17:39	"I cannot go in these," he s to Saul,	606
	17:43	He s to David, "Am I a dog,	606
	17:44	he s, "and I'll give your flesh to the birds of	606
	17:45	David s to the Philistine, "You come against	606
	17:55	he s to Abner, commander of the army,	606
	17:56	The king s, "Find out whose son this young	606
	17:58	David s, "I am the son of your servant Jesse	606
	18:17	Saul s to David, "Here is my older daughter	606
	18:17	For Saul s to himself, "I will not raise a hand	606
	18:18	But David s to Saul, "Who am I,	606
	18:21	So Saul s to David, "Now you have	606
	18:23	But David s, "Do you think it is	606
	18:24	Saul's servants told him what David had s,	1819
	19: 4	and s to him, "Let not the king do wrong	606
	19:14	Michal s, "He is ill."	606
	19:17	Saul s to Michal, "Why did you deceive me	606
	19:17	Michal told him, "He s to me,	606
	19:22	"Over in Naioth at Ramah," they s.	606
	20: 3	But David took an oath and s,	606
	20: 3	and he has s to himself,	606
	20: 4	Jonathan s to David, "Whatever you want	606
	20: 5	So David s, "Look, tomorrow is	606
	20: 9	"Never!" Jonathan s.	606
	20:11	Jonathan s, "let's go out into the field."	606
	20:12	Then Jonathan s to David:	606
	20:18	Then Jonathan s to David:	606
	20:26	Saul s nothing that day, for he thought,	1819
	20:27	Then Saul s to his son Jonathan,	606
	20:29	He s, 'Let me go,	606
	20:30	Saul's anger flared up at Jonathan and he s	606
	20:36	and he s to the boy, "Run and find the arrows	606
	20:40	to the boy and s, "Go, carry them back	606
	20:42	Jonathan s to David, "Go in peace,	606
	21: 2	with a certain matter and s to me,	606
	21: 9	David s, "There is none like it;	606
	21:11	But the servants of Achish s to him,	606
	21:14	Achish s to his servants, "Look at the man!	606
	22: 3	to Mizpah in Moab and s to the king	606
	22: 5	But the prophet Gad s to David,	606
	22: 7	Saul s to them, "Listen, men of Benjamin!	606
	22: 9	who was standing with Saul's officials, s,	6699
	22:12	Saul s, "Listen now, son of Ahitub."	606
	22:13	Saul s to him, "Why have you conspired	606
	22:16	But the king s, "You will surely die,	606
	22:22	Then David s to Abiathar:	606
	23: 3	But David's men s to him,	606
	23: 7	and he s, "God has handed him over to me,	606
	23: 9	he s to Abiathar the priest,	606
	23:10	David s, "O LORD, God of Israel,	606
	23:11	And the LORD s, "He will."	606
	23:12	And the LORD s, "They will."	606
	23:17	"Don't be afraid," he s.	606
	23:19	up to Saul at Gibeah and s,	606
	24: 4	The men s, "This is the day	606
	24: 4	the day the LORD spoke of when he s	606
	24: 6	He s to his men, "The LORD forbid	606
	24: 9	He s to Saul, "Why do you listen	606
	24:10	I s, 'I will not lift my hand	606
	24:17	"You are more righteous than I," he s.	606
	25: 5	So he sent ten young men and s to them,	606
	25:13	David s to his men, "Put on your swords!"	606
	25:21	David had just s, "It's been useless—	606
	25:24	She fell at his feet and s:	606
	25:32	David s to Abigail, "Praise be to the LORD,	606
	25:35	what she had brought him and s, "Go home	606
	25:39	David heard that Nabal was dead, he s,	606
	25:40	His servants went to Carmel and s	1819
	25:41	down with her face to the ground and s,	606
	26: 1	The Ziphites went to Saul at Gibeah and s,	606
	26: 6	"I'll go with you," s Abishai.	606
	26: 8	Abishai s to David,	606
	26: 9	David s to Abishai, "Don't destroy him!	606
	26:10	As surely as the LORD lives," he s,	606
	26:15	David's, "You're a man, aren't you?	606
	26:17	Saul recognized David's voice and s,	606
	26:19	in the LORD's inheritance and have s,	606
	26:21	Then Saul s, "I have sinned.	606
	26:25	Then Saul s to David, "May you be blessed,	606
	27: 5	Then David s to Achish,	606
	27:12	Achish trusted David and s to himself,	606
	28: 1	Achish s to David,	606
	28: 2	David s, "Then you will see	606
	28: 7	Saul then s to his attendants,	606
	28: 7	"There is one in Endor," they s.	606
	28: 8	"Consult a spirit for me," he s,	606
	28: 9	But the woman s to him,	606
	28:11	"Bring up Samuel," he s.	606
	28:12	she cried out at the top of her voice and s	606
	28:13	The king s to her, "Don't be afraid.	606
	28:13	The woman s, "I see a spirit coming up out	606
	28:14	a robe is coming up," she s.	606
	28:15	Samuel s to Saul, "Why have you disturbed	606
	28:15	"I am in great distress," Saul s.	606

1Sa	28:16	Samuel s, "Why do you consult me,	606
	28:21	and saw that he was greatly shaken, she s,	606
	28:23	He refused and s, "I will not eat."	606
	29: 4	commanders were angry with him and s,	606
	29: 6	So Achish called David and s to him,	606
	29: 9	the Philistine commanders have s,	606
	30: 7	Then David s to Abiathar the priest,	606
	30:13	He s, "I am an Egyptian,	606
	30:22	among David's followers s,	6699
	31: 4	Saul s to his armor-bearer,	606
2Sa	1: 4	He s, "The men fled from the battle.	606
	1: 5	Then David s to the young man	606
	1: 6	the young man s, "and there was Saul,	606
	1: 7	he called out to me, and I s,	606
	1: 9	he s to me, 'Stand over me and kill me!	606
	1:13	David s to the young man who brought him	606
	1:15	Then David called one of his men and s,	606
	1:16	For David had s to him,	606
	1:16	mouth testified against you when you s,	606
	2: 1	The LORD s, "Go up.	606
	2:14	Then Abner s to Joab,	606
	2:14	"All right, let them do it," Joab s.	606
	2:21	Then Abner s to him,	606
	3: 7	And Ish-Bosheth s to Abner,	606
	3: 8	of what Ish-Bosheth s and he answered,	1821
	3:13	"Good," s David.	606
	3:16	Then Abner s to him, "Go back home!"	606
	3:17	with the elders of Israel and s,	606
	3:21	Then Abner s to David,	606
	3:24	So Joab went to the king and s,	606
	3:28	Later, when David heard about this, he s,	606
	3:31	David s to Joab and all the people with him,	606
	3:38	Then the king s to his men,	606
	4: 8	of Ish-Bosheth to David at Hebron and s to	606
	5: 1	of Israel came to David at Hebron and s,	606
	5: 2	And the LORD s to you,	606
	5: 6	The Jebusites s to David,	606
	5: 8	On that day, David s,	606
	5:20	He s, "As waters break out,	606
	6: 9	of the LORD that day and s,	606
	6:20	of Saul came out to meet him and s,	606
	6:21	David s to Michal, "It was before	606
	7: 2	he s to Nathan the prophet,	606
	7:18	in and sat before the LORD, and he s:	606
	9: 2	and the king s to him, "Are you Ziba?"	606
	9: 6	David s, "Mephibosheth!"	606
	9: 7	"Don't be afraid," David s to him,	606
	9: 8	Mephibosheth bowed down and s,	606
	9: 9	Saul's servant, s to him,	606
	9:11	Then Ziba s to the king,	606
	10: 3	the Ammonite nobles s to Hanun their lord,	606
	10: 5	The king s, "Stay at Jericho	606
	10:11	Joab s, "If the Arameans are too strong	606
	11: 3	The man s, "Isn't this Bathsheba,	606
	11: 8	Then David s to Uriah, "Go down to your	606
	11:11	Uriah s to David, "The ark and Israel	606
	11:12	Then David s to him, "Stay here	606
	11:23	The messenger s to David,	606
	12: 1	When he came to him, he s,	606
	12: 5	with anger against the man and s to Nathan,	606
	12: 7	Then Nathan s to David, "You are the man!	606
	12:13	Then David s to Nathan, "I have sinned	606
	13: 4	Amnon s to him, "I'm in love with Tamar,	606
	13: 5	to bed and pretend to be ill," Jonadab s.	606
	13: 6	the king came to see him, Amnon s to him,	606
	13: 9	"Send everyone out of here," Amnon s.	606
	13:10	Then Amnon s to Tamar, "Bring the food	606
	13:11	he grabbed her and s, "Come to bed	606
	13:12	she s to him.	606
	13:15	Amnon s to her, "Get up and get out!"	606
	13:16	she s to him. "Don't force me.	606
	13:17	he called his personal servant and s,	606
	13:20	Her brother Absalom s to her,	606
	13:22	Absalom never s a word to Amnon,	1819
	13:24	Absalom went to the king and s,	606
	13:26	Then Absalom, "If not,	606
	13:32	s, "My lord should not think	6699
	13:35	Jonadab s to the king, "See,	606
	13:35	it has happened just as your servant s."	1821
	14: 2	He s to her, "Pretend you are in mourning.	606
	14: 4	and she s, "Help me, O king!"	606
	14: 5	She s, "I am indeed a widow;	606
	14: 8	The king s to the woman, "Go home,	606
	14: 9	But the woman from Tekoa s to him,	606
	14:11	She s, "Then let the king invoke	606
	14:11	"As surely as the LORD lives," he s,	606
	14:12	Then the woman s, "Let your servant speak	606
	14:13	The woman s, "Why then have you devised	606
	14:18	Then the king s to the woman,	6699
	14:18	"Let my lord the king speak," the woman s.	606
	14:21	The king s to Joab, "Very well, I will do it.	606
	14:22	Joab s, "Today your servant knows	606
	14:24	the king s, "He must go to his own house;	606
	14:30	Then he s to his servants, "Look,	606
	14:31	to Absalom's house and he s to him,	606
	14:32	Absalom s to Joab, "Look,	606
	14:32	"Look, I sent word to you and s,	606
	15: 7	Absalom s to the king, "Let me go to Hebron	606
	15: 9	The king s to him, "Go in peace."	606
	15:14	Then David s to all his officials who were	606
	15:19	The king s to Ittai the Gittite,	606
	15:22	David s to Ittai, "Go ahead, march on."	606
	15:25	Then the king s to Zadok,	606
	15:27	The king also s to Zadok the priest,	606
	15:33	David s to him, "If you go with me,	606
	16: 3	Ziba s to him, "He is staying in Jerusalem,	606
	16: 4	Then the king s to Ziba,	606

2Sa	16: 4	"I humbly bow," Ziba s.	606
	16: 7	As he cursed, Shimei s, "Get out, get out,	606
	16: 9	Then Abishai son of Zeruiah s to the king,	606
	16:10	But the king s, "What do you and I have	606
	16:10	he is cursing because the LORD s to him,	606
	16:11	David then s to Abishai and all his officials,	606
	16:16	went to Absalom and s to him,	606
	16:18	Hushai to Absalom, "No,	606
	16:20	Absalom s to Ahithophel,	606
	17: 1	Ahithophel s to Absalom,	606
	17: 5	But Absalom s, "Summon also Hushai	606
	17: 6	When Hushai came to him, Absalom s,	606
	17:14	Absalom and all the men of Israel s,	606
	17:21	They s to him, "Set out and cross the river	606
	17:29	For they s, "The people have become hungry	606
	18: 3	But the men s, "You must not go out;	606
	18:11	Joab s to the man who had told him this,	606
	18:14	Joab s, "I'm not going to wait like this	606
	18:19	Now Ahimaaz son of Zadok s,	606
	18:21	Then Joab s to a Cushite, "Go,	606
	18:22	Ahimaaz son of Zadok again s to Joab,	606
	18:23	He s, "Come what may, I want to run."	NIH
	18:23	So Joab s, "Run!"	606
	18:25	The king s, "If he is alone,	606
	18:26	The king s, "He must be bringing good news	606
	18:27	The watchman s, "It seems to me that	606
	18:27	"He's a good man," the king s.	606
	18:28	the king with his face to the ground and s,	606
	18:30	The king s, "Stand aside and wait here."	606
	18:31	Then the Cushite arrived and s,	606
	18:33	As he went, he s: "O my son Absalom!	606
	19: 2	because on that day the troops heard it s,	606
	19: 5	Joab went into the house to the king and s,	606
	19:11	since what is being is throughout Israel	1821
	19:19	and s to him, "May my lord not hold me	606
	19:21	Then Abishai son of Zeruiah s,	6699
	19:23	the king s to Shimei, "You shall not die."	606
	19:26	He s, "My lord the king,	606
	19:26	since I your servant am lame, I s,	606
	19:29	The king s to him, "Why say more?	606
	19:30	Mephibosheth s to the king,	606
	19:33	The king s to Barzillai,	606
	19:38	The king s, "Kimham shall cross over	606
	20: 4	Then the king s to Amasa,	606
	20: 6	David s to Abishai,	606
	20: 9	Joab s to Amasa, "How are you,	606
	20:11	of Joab's men stood beside Amasa and s,	606
	20:17	She s, "Listen to what your servant has	606
	20:17	"I'm listening," he s.	606
	20:21	The woman s to Joab,	606
	21: 1	The LORD s, "It is on account of Saul	606
	21: 6	So the king s, "I will give them to you."	606
	21:16	s he would kill David.	606
	22: 2	He s: "The LORD is my rock,	606
	23: 3	the Rock of Israel s to me:	1819
	23:15	David longed for water and s, "Oh,	606
	23:17	O LORD, to do this!" he s.	606
	24: 2	So the king s to Joab and the army	606
	24:10	and he s to the LORD, "I have sinned	606
	24:13	So Gad went to David and s to him,	5583
	24:14	David s to Gad, "I am in deep distress.	606
	24:16	and s to the angel who was afflicting	606
	24:17	he s to the LORD, "I am the one	606
	24:18	that day Gad went to David and s to him,	606
	24:21	Araunah s, "Why has my lord	606
	24:22	Araunah s to David, "Let my lord the king	606
	24:23	Araunah also s to him,	606
1Ki	1: 2	So his servants s to him,	606
	1: 5	put himself forward and s, "I will be king."	606
	1:14	will come in and confirm what you have s."	1821
	1:17	She s to him, "My lord,	606
	1:24	Nathan s, "Have you, my lord the king,	606
	1:28	Then King David s, "Call in Bathsheba."	6699
	1:31	s, "May my lord King David live forever!"	606
	1:32	King David s, "Call in Zadok the priest,	606
	1:33	he s to them: "Take your lord's servants	606
	1:42	Adonijah s, "Come in.	606
	1:48	and s, 'Praise be to the LORD, the God	606
	1:53	and Solomon s, "Go to your home."	606
	2: 2	about to go the way of all the earth," he s.	606
	2:15	"As you know," he s,	606
	2:16	"You may make it," she s.	606
	2:20	to make of you," she s.	606
	2:21	So she s, "Let Abishag the Shunammite	606
	2:26	To Abiathar the priest the king s,	606
	2:30	the tent of the LORD and s to Joab,	606
	2:36	Then the king sent for Shimei and s to him,	606
	2:38	as my lord the king has s."	1819
	2:42	the king summoned Shimei and s to him,	606
	2:42	At that time you s to me,	606
	2:44	The king also s to Shimei,	606
	3: 5	and God s, "Ask for whatever you want me	606
	3:11	So God s to him, "Since you have asked	606
	3:17	One of them s, "My lord,	606
	3:22	The other woman s, "No!	606
	3:23	The king s, "This one says,	606
	3:24	Then the king s, "Bring me a sword."	606
	3:26	with compassion for her son and s to	606
	3:26	other s, "Neither I nor you shall have him.	606
	5: 5	when he s, 'Your son whom I will put on	606
	5: 7	he was greatly pleased and s,	606
	8:12	Then Solomon s, "The LORD has said	606
	8:12	"The LORD has s that he would dwell in	606
	8:15	Then he s: "Praise be to the LORD	606
	8:15	to my father David. For he s,	606
	8:18	But the LORD s to my father David,	606
	8:23	and s: "O LORD, God of Israel,	606

Ref	Text	Num
1Ki 8:25	the promises you made to him when you s,	606
8:29	this place of which you s,	606
9: 3	The LORD s to him: "I have heard	606
9: 5	as I promised David your father when I s,	606
10: 6	She s to the king, "The report I heard	606
11:11	So the LORD s to Solomon,	606
11:21	Then Hadad s to Pharaoh, "Let me go,	606
11:31	Then he s to Jeroboam, "Take ten pieces	606
12: 3	of Israel went to Rehoboam and s to him:	1819
12:10	"Tell these people who have s to you,	1819
12:12	as the king had s, "Come back to me	1819
12:14	and s, "My father made your yoke heavy;	1819
12:28	He s to the people, "It is too much for you	606
13: 4	from the altar and s, "Seize him!"	606
13: 6	Then the king s to the man of God,	6699
13: 7	The king s to the man of God,	1819
13:11	They also told their father what he had s to	1819
13:13	So he s to his sons, "Saddle the donkey	606
13:15	So the prophet s to him,	606
13:16	The man of God s, "I cannot turn back	606
13:18	angel s to me by the word of the LORD:	1819
13:26	of it, he s, "It is the man of God who defied	606
13:27	The prophet s to his sons,	1819
13:30	and they mourned over him and s, "Oh,	NIH
13:31	After burying him, he s to his sons,	606
14: 2	and Jeroboam s to his wife,	606
14: 4	So Jeroboam's wife did what he s and went	NIH
14: 6	he s, "Come in, wife of Jeroboam.	606
14:18	as the LORD had s through his servant	1819+1821
15:19	between me and you," he s, "as there was	606
17: 1	from Tishbe in Gilead, s to Ahab,	606
17:13	Elijah s to her, "Don't be afraid.	606
17:13	Go home and do as you have s.	1821
17:18	She s to Elijah, "What do you have against	606
17:23	He gave him to his mother and s, "Look,	606
17:24	Then the woman s to Elijah,	606
18: 5	Ahab had s to Obadiah,	606
18: 7	and s, "Is it really you, my lord Elijah?"	606
18:15	Elijah s, "As the LORD Almighty lives,	606
18:17	When he saw Elijah, he s to him,	606
18:21	Elijah went before the people and s,	606
18:21	But the people s nothing.	6699
18:22	Then Elijah s to them,	606
18:24	all the people s, "What you say is good."	6699
18:25	Elijah s to the prophets of Baal,	606
18:27	to taunt them. "Shout louder!" he s.	606
18:30	Then Elijah s to all the people,	606
18:33	Then he s to them, Fill your large jars	606
18:34	"Do it again," he s, and they did it again.	606
18:41	And Elijah s to Ahab, "Go, eat and drink,	606
18:43	"There is nothing there," he s.	606
18:43	Seven times Elijah s, "Go back."	606
18:44	So Elijah s, "Go and tell Ahab,	606
19: 4	"I have had enough, LORD," he s.	606
19: 5	All at once an angel touched him and s,	606
19: 7	a second time and touched him and s,	606
19:11	The LORD s, "Go out and stand on	606
19:13	Then a voice to him, "What are you doing	606
19:15	The LORD s to him, "Go back	606
19:20	he s, "and then I will come with you."	606
20: 5	The messengers came again and s,	606
20: 7	the elders of the land and s to them,	606
20:18	He s, "If they have come out for peace,	606
20:22	the prophet came to the king of Israel and s,	606
20:31	His officials s to him, "Look,	606
20:32	they went to the king of Israel and s,	606
20:33	your brother Ben-Hadad!" they s.	606
20:33	"Go and get him," the king s.	606
20:34	[Ahab s,] "On the basis of a treaty	NIH
20:35	the sons of the prophets s to his companion.	606
20:36	So the prophet s, "Because you have not	606
20:37	The prophet found another man and s,	606
20:39	someone came to me with a captive and s,	606
20:40	"That is your sentence," the king of Israel s.	606
20:42	He s to the king, "This is what the LORD	606
21: 2	Ahab s to Naboth, "Let me have your	1819
21: 4	Naboth the Jezreelite had s,	1819+1821+2021
21: 6	"Because I s to Naboth the Jezreelite,	1819
21: 6	he s, 'I will not give you my vineyard.' "	606
21: 7	Jezebel his wife s, "Is this how you act	606
21:15	she s to Ahab, "Get up and take	606
21:20	Ahab s to Elijah, "So you have found me,	606
22: 3	The king of Israel had s to his officials,	606
22: 5	But Jehoshaphat also s to the king of Israel,	606
22: 9	of Israel called one of his officials and s,	606
22:12	they s, "for the LORD will give it into	606
22:13	to summon Micaiah s to him,	1819
22:14	But Micaiah s, "As surely as the LORD lives,	606
22:16	The king s to him, "How many times	606
22:17	the LORD s, 'These people have no master.	606
22:18	The king of Israel s to Jehoshaphat,	606
22:20	And the LORD s, 'Who will entice Ahab	606
22:21	stood before the LORD and s,	606
22:22	spirit in the mouths of all his prophets,' he s.	606
22:22	succeed in enticing him,' s the LORD.	606
22:30	The king of Israel s to Jehoshaphat,	606
22:49	At that time Ahaziah son of Ahab s	606
2Ki 1: 3	angel of the LORD to Elijah the Tishbite,	1819
1: 6	"And he s to us, 'Go back	606
1: 8	The king s, "That was Elijah the Tishbite."	606
1: 9	and s to him, "Man of God, the king says,	1819
1:11	The captain s to him, "Man of God,	6699
1:15	The angel of the LORD s to Elijah:	1819
2: 2	Elijah s to Elisha, "Stay here;	606
2: 2	But Elisha s, "As surely as the LORD lives	606
2: 4	Then Elijah s to him, "Stay here, Elisha;	606
2: 6	Then Elijah s to him, "Stay here;	606

Ref	Text	Num
2Ki 2: 9	When they had crossed, Elijah s to Elisha,	606
2:10	"You have asked a difficult thing," Elijah s,	606
2:15	s, "The spirit of Elijah is resting on Elisha."	606
2:16	they s, "we your servants have fifty able men	606
2:17	So he s, "Send them."	606
2:18	he s to them, "Didn't I tell you not to go?"	606
2:19	The men of the city s to Elisha, "Look,	606
2:20	"Bring me a new bowl," he s,	606
2:23	"Go on up, you baldhead!" they s.	606
3:12	Jehoshaphat s, "The word of the LORD is	606
3:13	Elisha s to the king of Israel,	606
3:14	Elisha s, "As surely as the LORD Almighty	606
3:16	and he s, "This is what the LORD says:	606
3:23	"That's blood!" they s.	606
4: 2	she s, "except a little oil."	606
4: 3	Elisha s, "Go around and ask all your	606
4: 6	When all the jars were full, she s to her son,	606
4: 7	She went and told the man of God, and he s,	606
4: 9	She s to her husband, "I know that this man	606
4:12	He s to his servant Gehazi,	606
4:13	Elisha s to him, "Tell her,	606
4:14	Gehazi s, "Well, she has no son	606
4:15	Then Elisha s, "Call her."	606
4:16	"About this time next year," Elisha s,	606
4:19	My head!" he s to his father.	606
4:22	She called her husband and s,	606
4:23	"It's all right," she s.	606
4:24	the donkey and s to her servant, "Lead on;	606
4:25	the man of God s to his servant Gehazi,	606
4:26	"Everything is all right," she s.	606
4:27	but the man of God, "Leave her alone!	606
4:28	for a son, my lord?" she s.	606
4:29	Elisha s to Gehazi,	606
4:30	But the child's mother s,	606
4:36	Elisha summoned Gehazi and s,	606
4:36	When she came, he s, "Take your son."	606
4:38	he s to his servant,	606
4:41	Elisha s, "Get some flour."	606
4:41	He put it into the pot and s,	606
4:42	"Give it to the people to eat," Elisha s.	606
5: 3	She s to her mistress,	606
5: 4	and told him what the girl from Israel had s.	1819
5: 7	he tore his robes and s, "Am I God?	606
5:11	But Naaman went away angry and s,	606
5:13	Naaman's servants went to him and s,	1819
5:15	He stood before him and s,	606
5:17	"If you will not," s Naaman, "please let me,	606
5:19	"Go in peace," Elisha s.	606
5:20	the servant of Elisha the man of God, s	606
5:23	"By all means, take two talents," s Naaman.	606
5:26	But Elisha s to him, "Was not my spirit with	606
6: 1	The company of the prophets s to Elisha,	606
6: 2	And he s, "Go."	606
6: 3	Then one of them s, "Won't you please come	606
6: 7	"Lift it out," he s.	606
6: 8	After conferring with his officers, he s,	606
6:12	my lord the king," s one of his officers,	606
6:20	After they entered the city, Elisha s,	606
6:28	She answered, "This woman s to me,	606
6:29	The next day I s to her,	606
6:31	He s, "May God deal with me,	606
6:32	but before he arrived, Elisha s to the elders,	606
6:33	king] s, "This disaster is from the LORD.	606
7: 1	Elisha s, "Hear the word of the LORD.	606
7: 2	the king was leaning s to the man of God,	6699
7: 3	They s to each other, "Why stay here	606
7: 6	so that they s to one another, "Look,	606
7: 9	Then they s to each other,	606
7:12	up in the night and s to his officers,	606
7:16	as the LORD had s.	1821
7:18	It happened as the man of God had s to	1819
7:19	The officer had s to the man of God, "Look,	6699
8: 1	Now Elisha had s to the woman whose son	1819
8: 2	to do as the man of God s.	1821
8: 4	the servant of the man of God, and had s,	1819
8: 5	Gehazi s, "This is the woman,	606
8: 6	assigned an official to her case and s to him,	606
8: 8	he s to Hazael, "Take a gift with you	606
8: 9	He went in and stood before him, and s,	606
8:13	Hazael s, "How could your servant,	606
9: 1	the company of the prophets and s to him,	606
9: 5	a message for you, commander," he s.	606
9:12	"That's not true!" they s.	606
9:12	Jehu s, "Here is what he told me:	606
9:15	Jehu s, "If this is the way you feel,	606
9:18	The horseman rode off to meet Jehu and s,	606
9:19	When he came to them he s,	606
9:25	Jehu s to Bidkar, his chariot officer,	606
9:33	"Throw her down!" Jehu s.	606
9:34	"Take care of that cursed woman," he s,	606
9:36	They went back and told Jehu, who s,	606
10: 1	the guardians of Ahab's children. He s,	606
10: 4	But they were terrified and s,	606
10: 9	He stood before all the people and s,	606
10:13	They s, "We are relatives of Ahaziah,	606
10:15	Jehu greeted him and s,	606
10:15	"If so," s Jehu, "give me your hand."	NIH
10:16	Jehu s, "Come with me and see my zeal for	606
10:18	and s to them, "Ahab served Baal a little;	606
10:20	Jehu s, "Call an assembly in honor of Baal."	606
10:22	And Jehu s to the keeper of the wardrobe,	606
10:23	Jehu s to the ministers of Baal,	606
10:30	The LORD s to Jehu, "Because you have done	606
11:15	For the priest had s, "She must not be put	606
12: 4	Joash s to the priests, "Collect all the money	606
13:15	Elisha s, "Get a bow and some arrows,"	606
13:16	he s to the king of Israel.	606

Ref	Text	Num
2Ki 13:17	"Open the east window," he s.	606
13:17	"Shoot!" Elisha s, and he shot.	606
13:18	Then he s, "Take the arrows,"	606
13:19	The man of God was angry with him and s,	606
14:27	since the LORD had not s he would blot out	1819
17:12	worshiped idols, though the LORD had s,	606
18:19	The field commander s to them,	606
18:26	Shebna and Joah s to the field commander,	606
18:36	remained silent and s nothing in reply,	6699
18:37	told him what the field commander had s.	1821
19: 6	Isaiah s to them, "Tell your master,	606
19:23	And you have s, "With my many chariots	606
20: 1	of Amoz went to him and s, "This is what	606
20: 7	Then Isaiah s, "Prepare a poultice of figs."	606
20:10	shadow to go forward ten steps," s Hezekiah.	606
20:15	everything in my palace," Hezekiah.	606
20:16	Then Isaiah s to Hezekiah.	606
21: 4	of which the LORD had s,	606
21: 7	of which the LORD had s to David and	606
21:10	The LORD s through his servants	1819
22: 3	to the temple of the LORD. He s:	606
22: 8	the high priest s to Shaphan the secretary,	606
22:15	She s to them, "This is what the LORD,	606
23:17	The men of the city s,	606
23:18	"Leave it alone," he s.	606
23:27	So the LORD s, "I will remove Judah also	606
23:27	and this temple, about which I s,	606
25:24	be afraid of the Babylonian officials," he s.	606
1Ch 10: 4	Saul s to his armor-bearer,	606
11: 1	came together to David at Hebron and s,	606
11: 2	And the LORD your God s to you,	606
11: 5	s to David, "You will not get	606
11: 6	David had s, "Whoever leads the attack on	606
11:17	David longed for water and s, "Oh,	606
11:19	that I should do this!" he s.	606
12:17	David went out to meet them and s to them,	6699
12:18	and he s: "We are yours, O David!	NIH
12:19	They s, "It will cost us our heads	606
12:23	as the LORD had s:	7023
13: 2	He then s to the whole assembly of Israel,	606
14:11	He s, "As waters break out,	606
15: 2	Then David s, "No one but the Levites	606
15:12	He s to them, "You are the heads of	606
16:36	Then all the people s "Amen" and "Praise	606
17: 1	he s to Nathan the prophet, "Here I am,	606
17:16	in and sat before the LORD, and he s:	606
19: 3	the Ammonite nobles s to Hanun,	606
19: 5	The king s, "Stay at Jericho	606
19:12	Joab s, "If the Arameans are too strong	606
21: 2	So David s to Joab and the commanders of	606
21: 8	Then David s to God, "I have sinned	606
21: 9	The LORD s to Gad, David's seer,	1819
21:11	So Gad went to David and s to him,	606
21:13	David s to Gad, "I am in deep distress.	606
21:15	and s to the angel who was destroying	606
21:17	David s to God, "Was it not I	606
21:22	David s to him, "Let me have the site	606
21:23	Araunah s to David, "Take it!	606
22: 1	Then David s, "The house of	606
22: 5	David s, "My son Solomon is young	606
22: 7	David s to Solomon: "My son,	606
22:11	as he s you would.	1819
22:18	He s to them, "Is not the LORD your God	NIH
23: 4	David s, "Of these, twenty-four thousand	NIH
23:25	For David had s, "Since the LORD,	606
28: 2	King David rose to his feet and s:	606
28: 3	But God s to me, 'You are not to build	606
28: 6	He s to me: 'Solomon your son is the one	606
28:19	David s, "I have in writing from the hand	NIH
28:20	David also s to Solomon his son,	606
29: 1	Then King David s to the whole assembly:	606
29:20	Then David s to the whole assembly,	606
2Ch 1: 7	That night God appeared to Solomon and s	606
1:11	God s to Solomon, "Since this is your heart's	606
6: 1	Then Solomon s, "The LORD has said	606
6: 1	"The LORD has s that he would dwell in	606
6: 4	Then he s: "Praise be to the LORD,	606
6: 4	to my father David. For he s,	606
6: 8	But the LORD s to my father David,	606
6:14	He s: "O LORD, God of Israel,	606
6:16	the promises you made to him when you s,	606
6:20	which you s you would put your Name there	606
7:12	the LORD appeared to him at night and s:	606
7:18	with David your father when I s,	606
8:11	for her, for he s, "My wife must not live in	606
9: 5	She s to the king, "The report I heard	606
9: 6	not believe what they s until I came and	1821
10: 3	and all Israel went to Rehoboam and s,	1819
10:10	"Tell the people who have s to you,	1819
10:12	as the king had s, "Come back to me	1819
10:14	and s, "My father made your yoke heavy;	1819
12: 5	and he s to them, "This is what the LORD	606
12: 6	and the king humbled themselves and s,	606
13: 4	in the hill country of Ephraim, and s,	606
13:22	what he did and what he s,	1821
14: 7	"Let us build up these towns," he s to Judah,	606
14:11	Asa called to the LORD his God and s,	606
15: 2	He went out to meet Asa and s to him,	606
16: 3	between me and you," he s, "as there was	606
16: 7	the seer came to Asa king of Judah and s	606
18: 4	But Jehoshaphat also s to the king of Israel,	606
18: 8	of Israel called one of his officials and s,	606
18:11	they s, "for the LORD will give it into	606
18:12	to summon Micaiah s to him,	1819
18:13	But Micaiah s, "As surely as the LORD lives,	606
18:15	The king s to him, "How many times	606
18:16	the LORD s, 'These people have no master	606

2Ch	18:17	The king of Israel s to Jehoshaphat, 606
	18:19	And the LORD s, 'Who will entice Ahab 606
	18:20	stood before the LORD and s, 606
	18:21	spirit in the mouths of all his prophets,' he s. 606
	18:21	succeed in enticing him,' s the LORD. 606
	18:29	The king of Israel s to Jehoshaphat, 606
	19: 2	went out to meet him and s to the king, 606
	20: 6	and s: "O LORD, God of our fathers, 606
	20:15	He s: "Listen, King Jehoshaphat 606
	20:20	As they set out, Jehoshaphat stood and s, 606
	21:12	a letter from Elijah the prophet, which s: 606
	22: 9	They buried him, for they s, 606
	23: 3	Jehoiada s to them, "The king's son 606
	23:14	and s to them: "Bring her out 606
	23:14	For the priest had s, "Do not put her 606
	24: 5	the priests and Levites and s to them, 606
	24: 6	the chief priest and s to him, 606
	24:20	He stood before the people and s, 606
	24:22	but killed his son, who s as he lay dying, 606
	25: 7	But a man of God came to him and s, 606
	25:15	and he sent a prophet to him, who s, 606
	25:16	the king s to him, "Have we appointed you 606
	25:16	So the prophet stopped but s, 606
	26:18	They confronted him and s, 606
	26:23	for people s, "He had leprosy." 606
	28: 9	He s to them, "Because the LORD, 606
	28:13	not bring those prisoners here," they s, 606
	29: 5	and s: "Listen to me, 606
	29:31	Then Hezekiah s, "You have now dedicated 6699
	32: 4	and find plenty of water?" they s. 606
	32: 8	what Hezekiah the king of Judah s. 1821
	33: 4	of which the LORD had s, 606
	33: 7	of which God had s to David and 606
	34:15	Hilkiah s to Shaphan the secretary, 6699
	34:23	She s to them, "This is what the LORD, 606
	35: 3	He s to the Levites, who instructed all Israel 606
	35:22	He would not listen to what Neco had s 1821
Ezr	4: 2	and to the heads of the families and s, 606
	8:28	I s to them, "You as well as these articles 606
	9: 1	the leaders came to me and s, 606
	9:11	your servants the prophets when you s: 606
	10: 2	one of the descendants of Elam, s to Ezra, 6699
	10:10	Then Ezra the priest stood up and s to them, 606
Ne	1: 3	They s to me, "Those who survived the exile 606
	1: 5	Then I s: "O LORD, God of heaven, 606
	2: 3	but I s to the king, "May the king live forever 606
	2: 4	The king s to me, "What is it you want?" 606
	2: 7	I also s to him, "If it pleases the king, 606
	2:16	yet I had s nothing to the Jews or the priests 5583
	2:17	I s to them, "You see the trouble we are in: 606
	2:18	upon me and what the king had s to me. 606
	4: 2	he s, "What are those feeble Jews doing? 606
	4: 3	s, "What they are building— 606
	4:10	Meanwhile, the people in Judah s, 606
	4:11	Also our enemies s, "Before they know it 606
	4:14	I stood up and s to the nobles, the officials 606
	4:19	Then I s to the nobles, the officials 606
	4:22	At that time I also s to the people, 606
	5: 8	and s: "As far as possible, 606
	5:12	"We will give it back," they s. 606
	5:13	I also shook out the folds of my robe and s, 606
	5:13	At this the whole assembly s, "Amen," 606
	6:10	He s, "Let us meet in the house of God, 606
	6:11	But I s, "Should a man like me run away? 606
	6:19	and then telling me what I s. 1821
	7: 3	I s to them, "The gates of Jerusalem 606
	8: 9	the people s to them all, 606
	8:10	Nehemiah s, "Go and enjoy choice food 606
	9: 5	Shebaniah and Pethahiah—s: 606
	9:18	for themselves an image of a calf and s, 606
	13:17	I rebuked the nobles of Judah and s 606
	13:21	But I warned them and s, 606
	13:25	an oath in God's name and s: NIH
Est	3: 8	Then Haman s to King Xerxes, 606
	3:11	"Keep the money," the king s to Haman, 606
	4: 9	reported to Esther what Mordecai had s. 1821
	5: 5	"Bring Haman at once," the king s, 606
	5:14	His wife Zeresh and all his friends s to him, 606
	6: 4	The king s, "Who is in the court?" 606
	6:13	His advisers and his wife Zeresh s to him, 606
	7: 5	Esther s, "The adversary and enemy is 606
	7: 9	one of the eunuchs attending the king, s, 606
	7: 9	The king s, "Hang him on it!" 606
	8: 5	"If it pleases the king," she s, 606
	9:12	The king s to Queen Esther, 606
Job	1: 7	The LORD s to Satan, "Where have you come 606
	1: 8	the LORD s to Satan, "Have you considered 606
	1:12	The LORD s to Satan, "Very well, then, 606
	1:14	a messenger came to Job and s, 606
	1:16	another messenger came and s, 606
	1:17	another messenger came and s, 606
	1:18	yet another messenger came and s, 606
	1:21	and s: "Naked I came from my mother's 606
	2: 2	the LORD s to Satan, "Where have you come 606
	2: 3	the LORD s to Satan, "Have you considered 606
	2: 6	The LORD s to Satan, "Very well, then, 606
	2: 9	His wife s to him, "Are you still holding on 606
	2:10	In all this, Job did not sin in what he s. 8557
	2:13	No one s a word to him, 1819
	3: 2	He s: 6699
	3: 3	and the night it was s, 'A boy is born!' 606
	6:22	Have I ever s, 'Give something 606
	21:19	[It is s,] 'God stores up a man's punishment NIH
	22:17	They s to God, 'Leave us alone! 606
	28:28	And he s to man, 'The fear of the Lord— 606
	31:24	"If I have put my trust in gold or s to pure 606
	31:31	if the men of my household have never s, 606

Job	32: 6	So Elihu son of Barakel the Buzite s: 6699
	33: 8	"But you have s in my hearing— 606
	34: 1	Then Elihu s: 6699
	35: 1	Then Elihu s: 6699
	36: 2	that there is more to be s in God's behalf. 4863
	36:23	or s to him, 'You have done wrong'? 606
	38: 1	LORD answered Job out of the storm. He s: 606
	38:11	when I s, 'This far you may come 606
	40: 1	The LORD s to Job: 6699
	42: 4	["You s,] 'Listen now, and I will speak; NIH
	42: 7	After the LORD had s these things to Job, 1819
	42: 7	he s to Eliphaz the Temanite, 606
Ps	2: 7	He s to me, "You are my Son; 606
	16: 2	I s to the LORD, "You are my Lord; 606
	18: T	from the hand of Saul. He s: 606
	30: 6	I felt secure, I s, "I will never be shaken." 606
	31:22	In my alarm I s, "I am cut off 606
	32: 5	I s, "O LORD, have mercy on me; 606
	38:16	For I s, "Do not let them gloat 606
	39: 1	I s, "I will watch my ways 606
	40: 7	Then I s, "Here I am, I have come— 606
	41: 4	I s, "O LORD, have mercy on me; 606
	54: T	When the Ziphites had gone to Saul and s, 606
	55: 6	I s, "Oh, that I had the wings of a dove! 606
	73:15	If I had s, "I will speak thus," 606
	74: 8	They s in their hearts, "We will crush them 606
	82: 6	"I s, 'You are "gods"; 606
	83:12	who s, "Let us take possession of 606
	87: 3	Glorious things are s of you, O city of God: 1819
	87: 5	Indeed, of Zion it will be s, 606
	89: 3	You s, "I have made a covenant NIH
	89:19	to your faithful people you s: 606
	94:18	When I s, "My foot is slipping," 606
	95:10	I s, "They are a people whose hearts go astray, 606
	102:24	So I s: "Do not take me away, O my God, 606
	106:23	So he s he would destroy them— 606
	116:10	therefore I s, "I am greatly afflicted." 1819
	116:11	And in my dismay I s, "All men are liars." 606
	122: 1	I rejoiced with those who s to me, 606
	126: 2	Then it was s among the nations, 606
	137: 3	they s, "Sing us one of the songs of Zion!" NIH
Pr	4: 4	he taught me and s, "Lay hold of my words 606
	6: 2	you have been trapped by what you s, 609+7023
	7:13	and with a brazen face she s: 606
Ecc	2: 2	"Laughter," I s, "is foolish. 606
	2:15	I s in my heart, "This too is meaningless." 1819
	7:23	All this I tested by wisdom and I s, 606
	9:16	So I s, "Wisdom is better than strength." 606
SS	2:10	My lover spoke and s to me, "Arise, 606
	7: 8	I s, "I will climb the palm tree; 606
Isa	6: 1	With it he touched my mouth and s, "See, 606
	6: 8	And I s, "Here am I. 606
	6: 8	He s, "Go and tell this people: 606
	6:11	Then I s, "For how long, O Lord?" 606
	7: 3	Then the LORD s to Isaiah, "Go out, 606
	7:12	But Ahaz s, "I will not ask; 606
	7:13	Isaiah s, "Hear now, you house of David! 606
	8: 1	The LORD s to me, "Take a large scroll 606
	8: 3	And the LORD s to me, "Name him 606
	8:11	not to follow the way of this people. He s: 606
	14:13	You s in your heart, "I will ascend 606
	20: 2	He s to him, "Take off the sackcloth 606
	20: 3	Then the LORD s, "Just as my servant Isaiah 606
	22: 4	Therefore I s, "Turn away from me; 606
	23:12	He s, "No more of your reveling, 606
	24:16	But I s, "I waste away, I waste away! 606
	28:12	to whom he s, "This is the resting place, let 606
	30:16	You s, 'No, we will flee on horses.' 606
	30:16	You s, 'We will ride off on swift horses.' NIH
	36: 4	The field commander s to them, 606
	36:11	Shebna and Joah s to the field commander, 606
	36:21	remained silent and s nothing in reply, 6699
	36:22	told him what the field commander had s. 1821
	37: 6	Isaiah s to them, "Tell your master 606
	37:24	And you have s, 'With my many chariots 606
	38: 1	Isaiah son of Amoz went to him and s, 606
	38:10	I s, "In the prime of my life must I go 606
	38:11	I s, "I will not again see the LORD, 606
	38:21	Isaiah had s, "Prepare a poultice of figs 606
	39: 4	everything in my palace," Hezekiah s. 606
	39: 5	Then Isaiah s to Hezekiah, 606
	40: 6	And I s, "What shall I cry?" 606
	41: 9	I s, 'You are my servant'; 606
	45:19	I have not s to Jacob's descendants, 606
	46:11	What I have s, that will I bring about; 1819
	47: 7	You s, 'I will continue forever— 606
	47:10	in your wickedness and s, 606
	49: 3	He s to me, "You are my servant, Israel, 606
	49: 4	But I s, "I have labored to no purpose; 606
	49:14	But Zion s, "The LORD has forsaken me, 606
	51:23	your tormentors, who s to you, 'Fall prostrate 606
	57:14	And it will be s: "Build up, build up, 606
	63: 8	He s, "Surely they are my people, 606
	65: 1	I s, 'Here am I, here am I.' 606
	66: 5	have s, 'Let the LORD be glorified, 606
Jer	1: 6	"Ah, Sovereign LORD," I s, 606
	1: 7	But the LORD s to me, "Do not say, 606
	1: 9	and touched my mouth and s to me, 606
	1:12	The LORD s to me, "You have seen correctly 606
	1:14	The LORD s to me, "From the north disaster 606
	2:20	you s, 'I will not serve you!' 606
	2:25	But you s, 'It's no use! 606
	3: 6	the LORD s to me, "Have you seen what 606
	3:11	The LORD s to me, "Faithless Israel is more 606
	3:19	"I myself s,' 'How gladly I would treat 606
	4:10	Then I s, "Ah, Sovereign LORD, 606

Jer	5:12	they s, "He will do nothing! 606
	6:16	But you s, 'We will not walk in it.' 606
	6:17	I appointed watchmen over you and s, NIH
	6:17	But you s, 'We will not listen.' 606
	9:13	The LORD s, "It is because they have 606
	10:19	Yet I s to myself, "This is my sickness, 606
	11: 4	I s, 'Obey me and do everything I command 606
	11: 6	The LORD s to me, "Proclaim all these words 606
	11: 9	the LORD s to me, "There is a conspiracy 606
	13: 1	This is what the LORD s to me: 606
	13: 6	Many days later the LORD s to me, 606
	14:11	Then the LORD s to me, "Do not pray for 606
	14:13	But I s, "Ah, Sovereign LORD, 606
	14:14	Then the LORD s to me, "The prophets 606
	15: 1	Then the LORD s to me: "Even if Moses 606
	15:11	The LORD s, "Surely I will deliver you 606
	17:19	This is what the LORD s to me: 606
	18:18	They s, "Come, let's make plans 606
	19:14	the LORD's temple and s to all the people, 606
	20: 3	from the stocks, Jeremiah s to him, 606
	21: 1	priest Zephaniah son of Maaseiah. They s: 606
	22:21	but you s, 'I will not listen!' 606
	25: 2	the prophet s to all the people of Judah and 1819
	25: 5	They s, "Turn now, each of you, 606
	25:15	the LORD, the God of Israel, s to me: 606
	26: 8	and all the people seized him and s, 606
	26:11	the priests and the prophets s to the officials 606
	26:12	Then Jeremiah s to all the officials and all 606
	26:16	the people s to the priests and the prophets, 606
	26:17	the elders of the land stepped forward and s 606
	27: 2	This is what the LORD s to me: 606
	27:12	I s, "Bow your neck under the yoke of 606
	27:16	Then I s to the priests and all these people, 1819
	28: 1	s to me in the house of the LORD in 606
	28: 6	He s, "Amen! 606
	28:11	and he s before all the people, "This is what 606
	28:15	Then the prophet Jeremiah s to Hananiah 606
	29: 3	to King Nebuchadnezzar in Babylon. It s: 606
	29:25	You s to Zephaniah, 606
	32: 6	Jeremiah s, "The word of the LORD came 606
	32: 8	"Then, just as the LORD had s, 1821
	32: 8	to me in the courtyard of the guard and s, 606
	32:24	What you s has happened, as you now see. 1819
	34:13	out of the land of slavery. I s, 606
	35: 5	before the men of the Recabite family and s 606
	35:11	we s, 'Come, we must go to Jerusalem 606
	35:15	They s, "Each of you must turn 606
	35:18	Jeremiah s to the family of the Recabites, 606
	36:15	They s to him, "Sit down, please, 606
	36:16	they looked at each other in fear and s to 606
	36:19	Then the officials s to Baruch, 606
	36:29	You burned that scroll and s, 606
	37:13	the son of Hananiah, arrested him and s, 606
	37:14	"That's not true!" Jeremiah s. 606
	37:18	Then Jeremiah s to King Zedekiah, 606
	38: 1	telling all the people when he s, 606
	38: 4	Then the officials s to the king, 606
	38: 8	Ebed-Melech went out of the palace and s 1819
	38:12	Ebed-Melech the Cushite s to Jeremiah, 606
	38:14	the king s to Jeremiah. "Do not hide 606
	38:15	Jeremiah s to Zedekiah, 606
	38:17	Then Jeremiah s to Zedekiah, 606
	38:19	King Zedekiah s to Jeremiah, 606
	38:24	Then Zedekiah s to Jeremiah, 606
	38:25	'Tell us what you s to the king and what 1819
	38:25	to the king and what the king s to you; 1819
	38:27	So they s no more to him, 3087
	40: 2	the guard found Jeremiah, he s to him, 606
	40: 3	he has done just as he s he would. 1819
	40: 9	be afraid to serve the Babylonians," he s. 606
	40:14	and s to him, "Don't you know that 606
	40:15	Then Johanan son of Kareah s privately 606
	40:16	of Ahikam s to Johanan son of Kareah, 606
	41: 6	When he met them, he s, 606
	41: 8	ten of them s to Ishmael, "Don't kill us! 606
	42: 2	Jeremiah the prophet and s to him, 606
	42: 5	Then they s to Jeremiah, 606
	42: 9	He s to them, "This is what the LORD, 606
	42:20	and s, 'Pray to the LORD our God for us; 606
	43: 2	and all the arrogant men s to Jeremiah, 606
	44: 4	who s, 'Do not do this detestable thing 606
	44:15	in Lower and Upper Egypt, s to Jeremiah, 6699
	44:17	We will certainly do everything we s we would: 3655+4946+7023
	44:20	Then Jeremiah s to all the people, 606
	44:24	Then Jeremiah s to all the people, 606
	44:25	when you s, 'We will certainly carry out 606
	45: 3	You s, 'Woe to me! 606
	45: 4	[The LORD s,] "Say this to him: NIH
	50: 7	their enemies s, 'We are not guilty, 606
	51:61	He s to Seraiah, "When you get to Babylon, 606
	51:62	you have s you will destroy this place, 1819
La	3:57	and you s, "Do not fear." 606
Eze	2: 1	He s to me, "Son of man, 606
	2: 3	He s: "Son of man, 606
	3: 1	And he s to me, "Son of man, 606
	3: 3	Then he s to me, "Son of man, 606
	3: 4	He then s to me: "Son of man, 606
	3:10	And he s to me, "Son of man, 606
	3:22	and he s to me, "Get up and go out 606
	3:24	He spoke to me and s: "Go, shut yourself 606
	4:13	The LORD s, "In this way the people 606
	4:14	Then I s, "Not so, Sovereign LORD! 606
	4:15	he s, "I will let you bake your bread 606
	4:16	He then s to me: "Son of man, 606
	8: 5	Then he s to me, "Son of man, 606
	8: 6	And he s to me, "Son of man, 606

Eze	8: 8	*He* s to me, "Son of man,	606
	8: 9	And *he* s to me, "Go in and see	606
	8:12	*He* s to me, "Son of man,	606
	8:13	*he* s, "You will see them doing things	606
	8:15	*He* s to me, "Do you see this, son of man?	606
	8:17	*He* s to me, "Have you seen this,	606
	9: 4	and s to him, "Go throughout the city	606
	9: 5	As I listened, *he* s to the others,	606
	9: 7	Then *he* s to them, "Defile the temple	606
	10: 2	The LORD s to the man clothed in linen,	606
	11: 2	The LORD s to me, "Son of man,	606
	11:15	of whom the people of Jerusalem *have* s,	606
	16: 6	as you lay there in your blood *I* s to you,	606
	20: 5	With uplifted hand I s to them,	606
	20: 7	And *I* s to them, "Each of you,	606
	20: 8	So *I* s I would pour out my wrath on them	606
	20:13	So *I* s I would pour out my wrath on them	606
	20:18	*I* s to their children in the desert,	606
	20:21	So *I* s I would pour out my wrath on them	606
	20:29	Then *I* s to them: What is this high place	606
	20:49	Then *I* s, "Ah, Sovereign LORD!	606
	23:36	The LORD s to me: "Son of man,	606
	23:43	*I* s about the one worn out by adultery,	606
	24:20	So *I* s to them, "The word of the LORD came	606
	25: 3	Because you s "Aha!"	606
	25: 8	'Because Moab and Seir s, "Look,	606
	26: 2	because Tyre *has* s of Jerusalem, 'Aha!	606
	29: 9	" 'Because *you* s, "The Nile is mine;	606
	33:21	from Jerusalem came to me and s,	606
	35:10	" 'Because you *have* s, "These two nations	606
	35:12	the contemptible things *you have* s against	606
	35:12	You s, "They have been laid waste	606
	36: 2	The enemy s of you, "Aha!	606
	36:20	for *it was* s of them, 'These are the LORD's	606
	37: 3	*I* s, "O Sovereign LORD,	606
	37: 4	Then *he* s to me, "Prophesy to these bones	606
	37: 9	Then *he* s to me, "Prophesy to the breath;	606
	37:11	Then *he* s to me: "Son of man,	606
	40: 4	The man s to me, "Son of man,	1819
	40:45	*He* s to me, "The room facing south	1819
	41: 4	*He* s to me, "This is the Most Holy Place."	606
	41:22	The man s to me, "This is the table	1819
	42:13	Then *he* s to me, "The north and south	606
	43: 7	*He* s: "Son of man,	606
	43:18	Then *he* s to me, "Son of man,	606
	44: 2	LORD s to me, "This gate is to remain shut.	606
	44: 5	The LORD s to me, "Son of man,	606
	46:20	*He* s to me, "This is the place	606
	46:24	*He* s to me, "These are the kitchens	606
	47: 8	*He* s to me, "This water flows	606
Da	1:11	Daniel then s to the guard whom	606
	2: 3	he s to them, "I have had a dream	606
	2:20	and s: "Praise be to the name of God	10042
	2:24	and s to him, "Do not execute	10042
	2:25	took Daniel to the king at once and s,	10042
	2:47	The king s to Daniel, "Surely your God is	10558
	3: 9	*They* s to King Nebuchadnezzar, "O king,	10558
	3:14	and Nebuchadnezzar s to them,	10558
	3:25	*He* s, "Look! I see four men	10558
	3:28	Nebuchadnezzar s, "Praise be to the God	10558
	4: 9	I s, "Belteshazzar, chief of the magicians,	NIH
	4:19	So the king s, "Belteshazzar,	10558
	4:30	he s, "Is not this the great Babylon	10558
	4:33	Immediately *what* had been s	10418
	5: 7	astrologers and diviners to be brought and s	10558
	5:10	"O king, live forever!" she s.	10558
	5:13	and the king s to him, "Are you Daniel,	10558
	6: 5	Finally these men s,	10042
	6: 6	as a group to the king and s:	10042
	6:13	Then *they* s to the king, "Daniel,	10558
	6:15	the men went as a group to the king and s	10042
	6:16	So the king s to Daniel, "May your God,	10558
	7: 2	Daniel s: "In my vision at night	10558
	8:13	and another holy one s to him,	606
	8:14	*He* s to me, "It will take 2,300 evenings	606
	8:17	"Son of man," *he* s to me,	606
	8:19	*He* s: "I am going to tell you what will	606
	9:22	He instructed me and s to me, "Daniel,	1819
	10:11	*He* s, "Daniel, you who are highly esteemed,	606
	10:11	when he s this to me, I stood up trembling.	1819
	10:16	I s to the one standing before me,	606
	10:19	O man highly esteemed," *he* s.	606
	10:19	I was strengthened and s, "Speak, my lord,	1819
	10:20	So *he* s, "Do you know why I have come	606
	12: 7	*One of them* s to the man clothed in linen,	606
Hos	1: 2	the LORD s to him, "Go, take to yourself	606
	1: 4	Then the LORD s to Hosea,	606
	1: 6	Then the LORD s to Hosea,	606
	1: 9	Then the LORD s, "Call him Lo-Ammi,	606
	1:10	In the place where *it was* s to them,	606
	2: 5	She s, 'I will go after my lovers,	606
	2:12	which *she* s were her pay from her lovers;	606
	3: 1	The LORD s to me, "Go, show your love	606
	13: 2	*It is* s of these people,	606
	13:10	of whom *you* s, 'Give me a king	606
Joel	2:32	will be deliverance, as the LORD *has* s,	606
Am	1: 2	*He* s: "The LORD roars from Zion	606
	7: 3	"This will not happen," the LORD s.	606
	7: 6	the Sovereign LORD s.	606
	7: 8	Then the Lord s, "Look,	606
	7:12	Amaziah s to Amos, "Get out, you seer!	606
	7:15	from tending the flock and s to me,	606
	8: 2	Then the LORD s to me, "The time is ripe	606
	9: 1	the Lord standing by the altar, and *he* s:	606
Jnh	1: 6	The captain went to him and s,	606
	1: 7	Then the sailors s to each other, "Come,	606
	2: 2	*He* s: "In my distress I called to the	606

Jnh	2: 4	I s, 'I have been banished from your sight;	606
	4: 2	this not **what** I s when I was still at home?	1821
	4: 8	He wanted to die, and s,	606
	4: 9	But God s to Jonah, "Do you have any right	606
	4: 9	"I do," *he* s.	606
	4:10	But the LORD s, "You have been concerned	606
Mic	2: 7	*Should it* be s, O house of Jacob:	606
	3: 1	Then *I* s, "Listen, you leaders of Jacob,	606
	7:10	*she who* s to me, "Where is the LORD	606
Zep	2:15	She s to herself, "I am,	606
	3: 7	*I* s to the city, 'Surely you will fear me	606
Hag	2:13	Then Haggai s, "If a person defiled	606
	2:14	Then Haggai s, " 'So it is with this people	6699
Zec	1: 6	"Then they repented and s,	606
	1:12	Then the angel of the LORD s,	6699
	1:14	Then the angel who was speaking to me s,	606
	2: 4	and s to him: "Run, tell that young man,	606
	3: 2	The LORD s to Satan, "The LORD rebuke you	606
	3: 4	The angel s to those who were standing	6699
	3: 4	Then *he* s to Joshua, "See,	606
	3: 5	Then *I* s, "Put a clean turban on his head."	606
	4: 6	So *he* s to me, "This is the word of the LORD	6699
	4:13	"No, my lord," *I* s.	606
	4:14	So *he* s, "These are the two who are anointed	606
	5: 3	And *he* s to me, "This is the curse	606
	5: 5	to me came forward and s to me,	606
	5: 8	*He* s, "This is wickedness,"	606
	6: 7	And *he* s, "Go throughout the earth!"	606
	11: 9	and s, "I will not be your shepherd.	606
	11:13	LORD s to me, "Throw it to the potter"—	606
	11:15	Then the LORD s to me,	606
Mal	3:13	"You *have* s harsh *things* against me,"	1821
	3:13	you ask, 'What *have we* s against you?'	1819
	3:14	*"You have* s, 'It is futile to serve God.	606
Mt	1:20	the Lord appeared to him in a dream and s,	3306
	1:22	to fulfill what the Lord *had* s through	3306
	2: 8	*He* sent them to Bethlehem and s,	3306
	2:13	up," *he* s, "take the child and his mother	3306
	2:15	so was fulfilled what the Lord *had* s through	3306
	2:17	Then what *was* s through the prophet	3306
	2:20	and s, "Get up, take the child and his	3306
	2:23	So was fulfilled what *was* s through	3306
	3: 7	*he* s to them: "You brood of vipers!	3306
	3:17	And a voice from heaven s, "This is my Son	3306
	4: 3	The tempter came to him and s,	3306
	4: 6	"If you are the Son of God," *he* s,	3306
	4: 9	"All this I will give you," *he* s,	3306
	4:10	Jesus s to him, "Away from me, Satan!	3306
	4:14	to fulfill what *was* s through the prophet	3306
	4:19	"Come, follow me," Jesus s,	3306
	5:21	that *it was* s to the people long ago,	3306
	5:27	"You have heard that *it was* s,	3306
	5:31	"It has been s, 'Anyone who divorces	3306
	5:33	that *it was* s to the people long ago,	3306
	5:38	"You have heard that *it was* s,	3306
	5:43	"You have heard that *it was* s,	3306
	8: 2	came and knelt before him and s,	3306
	8: 3	"I am willing," *he* s.	3306
	8: 4	Then Jesus s to him, "See that you don't tell	3306
	8: 6	*he* s, "my servant lies at home paralyzed	3306
	8: 7	Jesus s to him, "I will go and heal him."	3306
	8:10	and s to those following him,	3306
	8:13	Then Jesus s to the centurion, "Go!	3306
	8:19	a teacher of the law came to him and s,	3306
	8:21	Another disciple s to him, "Lord,	3306
	8:32	*He* s to them, "Go!"	3306
	9: 2	*he* s to the paralytic, "Take heart, son;	3306
	9: 3	of the teachers of the law s to themselves,	3306
	9: 4	Knowing their thoughts, Jesus s,	3306
	9: 6	Then *he* s to the paralytic, "Get up,	3306
	9:12	On hearing this, Jesus s,	3306
	9:18	a ruler came and knelt before him and s,	3306
	9:21	*She* s to herself, "If I only touch his cloak,	3306
	9:22	"Take heart, daughter," *he* s,	3306
	9:24	*he* s, "Go away. The girl is not dead	3306
	9:29	Then he touched their eyes and s,	3306
	9:33	The crowd was amazed and s,	3306
	9:34	Pharisees s, "It is by the prince of demons	3306
	9:37	Then *he* s to his disciples,	3306
	11:25	At that time Jesus s, "I praise you, Father,	3306
	12: 2	When the Pharisees saw this, *they* s to him,	3306
	12:11	He s to them, "If any of you has a sheep	3306
	12:13	*he* s to the man, "Stretch out your hand."	3306
	12:23	All the people were astonished and s,	3306
	12:24	But when the Pharisees heard this, *they* s,	3306
	12:25	Jesus knew their thoughts and s to them,	3306
	12:38	of the Pharisees and teachers of the law s	3306
	12:49	Pointing to his disciples, *he* s,	3306
	13:27	"The owner's servants came to him and s,	3306
	13:36	His disciples came to him and s,	3306
	13:52	He s to them, "Therefore every teacher	3306
	13:57	But Jesus s to them,	3306
	14: 2	and *he* s to his attendants, "This is John	3306
	14: 8	Prompted by her mother, she s,	5774
	14:15	the disciples came to him and s,	3306
	14:18	"Bring them here to me," he s.	3306
	14:26	"It's a ghost," *they* s, and cried out in fear.	3306
	14:27	But Jesus immediately s to them:	3281+3306
	14:29	"Come," he s.	3306
	14:31	"You of little faith," *he* s,	3306
	15: 4	For God s, 'Honor your father and mother'	3306
	15:10	Jesus called the crowd to him and s,	3306
	15:15	Peter s, "Explain the parable to us."	3306
	15:25	"Lord, help me!" she s.	3306
	15:27	she s, "but even the dogs eat the crumbs	3306
	15:32	Jesus called his disciples to him and s,	3306
	16: 6	"Be careful," Jesus s to them.	3306

Mt	16: 7	discussed this among themselves and s,	3306
	16:22	to rebuke him. "Never, Lord!" he s.	NIG
	16:23	Jesus turned and s to Peter, "Get behind me,	3306
	16:24	Then Jesus s to his disciples,	3306
	17: 4	Peter s to Jesus, "Lord, it is good for us	3306
	17: 5	a voice from the cloud s, "This is my Son,	3306
	17: 7	"Get up," *he* s.	3306
	17:15	"Lord, have mercy on my son," *he* s.	3306
	17:22	he s to them, "The Son of Man is going to	3306
	17:26	"Then the sons are exempt," Jesus s to him.	5774
	18: 3	And *he* s: "I tell you the truth,	3306
	18:32	'You wicked servant,' *he* s,	3306
	19: 5	and s, 'For this reason a man will leave	3306
	19:10	The disciples s to him,	3306
	19:14	Jesus s, "Let the little children come to me,	3306
	19:20	"All these I have kept," the young man s.	3306
	19:23	Then Jesus s to his disciples,	3306
	19:26	Jesus looked at them and s,	3306
	19:28	Jesus s to them, "I tell you the truth,	3306
	20: 7	*"He* s to them, 'You also go and work	3306
	20: 8	the owner of the vineyard s to his foreman,	3306
	20:12	*they* s, 'and you have made them equal	3306
	20:17	the twelve disciples aside and s to them,	3306
	20:21	*She* s, "Grant that one of these two sons	3306
	20:22	Jesus s to them. "Can you drink from the cup	3306
	20:23	Jesus s to them, "You will indeed drink	3306
	20:25	Jesus called them together and s,	3306
	21:13	"It is written," *he* s to them,	3306
	21:19	Then *he* s to it, "May you never bear fruit	3306
	21:25	They discussed it among themselves and s,	3306
	21:27	Then he s, "Neither will I tell you	5774
	21:28	He went to the first and s, 'Son,	3306
	21:30	"Then the father went to the other son and s	3306
	21:31	Jesus s to them, "I tell you the truth,	3306
	21:37	'They will respect my son,' *he* s.	3306
	21:38	tenants saw the son, *they* s to each other,	3306
	21:42	Jesus s to them, "Have you never read in	3306
	22: 4	"Then he sent some more servants and s,	3306
	22: 8	"Then *he* s to his servants,	3306
	22:16	*they* s, "we know you are a man	3306
	22:18	But Jesus, knowing their evil intent, s,	3306
	22:21	Then *he* s to them, "Give to Caesar what is	3306
	22:24	*they* s, "Moses told us that if a man dies	3306
	22:31	have you not read what God s to you,	3306
	22:43	*He* s to them, "How is it then that David,	3306
	22:44	" 'The Lord s to my Lord:	3306
	23: 1	Jesus s to the crowds and to his disciples:	3281
	24: 3	"Tell us," *they* s, "when will this happen,	3306
	25: 8	The foolish ones s to the wise,	3306
	25:11	others also came. 'Sir! Sir!' *they* s.	3306
	25:20	*he* s, 'you entrusted me with five talents.	3306
	25:22	*he* s, 'you entrusted me with two talents;	3306
	25:24	*he* s, 'I knew that you are a hard man,	3306
	26: 1	*he* s to his disciples, "Sit here while I go	3306
	26: 5	"But not during the Feast," *they* s,	3306
	26:10	Aware of this, Jesus s to them,	3306
	26:21	And while they were eating, *he* s,	3306
	26:25	Judas, the one who would betray him, s,	3306
	26:35	And all the other disciples s the same.	3306
	26:36	and *he* s to them, "Sit here while I go over	3306
	26:38	*he* s to them, "My soul is overwhelmed	3306
	26:45	he returned to the disciples and s to them,	3306
	26:49	Going at once to Jesus, Judas s, "Greetings,	3306
	26:52	Jesus s to him, "for all who draw the sword	3306
	26:55	At that time Jesus s to the crowd,	3306
	26:61	and declared, "This fellow s, 'I am able	5774
	26:62	the high priest stood up and s to Jesus,	3306
	26:63	The high priest s to him,	3306
	26:65	Then the high priest tore his clothes and s,	3306
	26:68	and s, "Prophesy to us,	3306
	26:69	also were with Jesus of Galilee," she s.	3306
	26:70	"I don't know what you're talking about,"	
		he s.	3306
	26:71	another girl saw him and s to the people	3306
	26:73	those standing there went up to Peter and s,	3306
	27: 4	"I have sinned," *he* s,	3306
	27: 6	The chief priests picked up the coins and s,	3306
	27:24	"I am innocent of this man's blood," *he* s.	3306
	27:29	"Hail, king of the Jews!" *they* s.	3306
	27:42	"He saved others," *they* s,	3306
	27:43	for *he* s, 'I am the Son of God.' "	3306
	27:47	*they* s, "He's calling Elijah."	3306
	27:49	The rest s, "Now leave him alone.	3306
	27:63	*they* s, "we remember that while he was	3306
	27:63	that while he was still alive that deceiver s,	3306
	28: 5	The angel s to the women, "Do not be afraid	3306
	28: 6	He is not here; he has risen, just as *he* s.	3306
	28: 9	"Greetings," *he* s.	3306
	28:10	Then Jesus s to them, "Do not be afraid.	3306
	28:18	Then Jesus came to them and s,	3281
Mk	1:15	"The time has come," *he* s.	3306
	1:17	"Come, follow me," Jesus s,	3306
	1:25	s Jesus **sternly**. "Come out of him!"	2203
	1:41	"I am willing," *he* s.	3306
	2: 5	*he* s to the paralytic, "Son, your sins are	3306
	2: 8	and *he* s to them, "Why are you thinking	3306
	2:10	*He* s to the paralytic,	3306
	2:17	On hearing this, Jesus s to them,	3306
	2:24	The Pharisees s to him, "Look,	3306
	2:27	Then *he* s to them, "The Sabbath was made	3306
	3: 3	Jesus s to the man with the shriveled hand,	3306
	3: 5	s to the man, "Stretch out your hand."	3306
	3:21	they went to take charge of him, for *they* s,	3306
	3:22	the law who came down from Jerusalem s,	3306
	3:30	He s this because they were saying,	NIG
	3:34	at those seated in a circle around him and s,	3306
	4: 2	by parables, and in his teaching s:	3306

Mk	4: 9	Then Jesus s, "He who has ears to hear, 3306
	4:11	But to those on the outside everything is s NIG
	4:13	Jesus s to them, "Don't you understand 3306
	4:21	*He* s to them, "Do you bring in a lamp 3306
	4:26	*He* also s, "This is what the kingdom 3306
	4:30	Again *he* s, "What shall we say 3306
	4:35	*he* s to his disciples, "Let us go over 3306
	4:38	The disciples woke him and s to him, 3306
	4:39	rebuked the wind and s to the waves, 3306
	4:40	*He* s to his disciples, "Why are you so afraid 3306
	5: 8	For Jesus *had* s to him, "Come out 3306
	5:19	Jesus did not let him, but s, 3306
	5:34	He s to her, "Daughter, your faith 3306
	5:35	"Your daughter is dead," *they* s. 3306
	5:36	Ignoring what *he* s, Jesus told 3281
	5:39	*He* went in and s to them, 3306
	5:41	He took her by the hand and s to her, 3306
	6: 4	Jesus s to them, "Only in his hometown, 3306
	6:15	Others s, "He is Elijah." 3306
	6:16	But when Herod heard this, *he* s, "John, 3306
	6:22	The king s to the girl, "Ask me for anything 3306
	6:24	*She* went out and s to her mother, 3306
	6:31	*he* s to them, "Come with me 3306
	6:35	"This is a remote place," *they* s, 3306
	6:37	*They* s to him, "You give them something 3306
	6:38	When they found out, *they* s, "Five— 3306
	6:50	Immediately he spoke to them and s, 3306
	7: 9	And *he* s to them: "You have a fine way 3306
	7:10	For Moses s, 'Honor your father 3306
	7:14	Again Jesus called the crowd to him and s, 3306
	7:34	up to heaven and with a deep sigh s to him, 3306
	7:37	"He has done everything well," *they* s. 3306
	8: 1	Jesus called his disciples to him and s, 3306
	8:12	He sighed deeply and s, 3306
	8:16	They discussed this with one another and s, 3306
	8:21	*He* s to them, "Do you still not understand?" 3306
	8:24	*He* looked up and s, "I see people; 3306
	8:33	"Get behind me, Satan!" *he* s. 3306
	8:34	to him along with his disciples and s: 3306
	9: 1	And *he* s to them, "I tell you the truth, 3306
	9: 5	Peter s to Jesus, "Rabbi, it is good for us 3306
	9:23	" 'If you can'?" s Jesus. 3306
	9:25	"You deaf and mute spirit," *he* s, 3306
	9:26	so much like a corpse that many s, 3306
	9:31	*He* s to them, "The Son of Man is going to 3306
	9:35	Jesus called the Twelve and s, 3306
	9:36	Taking him in his arms, *he* s to them, 3306
	9:38	s John, "we saw a man driving out demons 5774
	9:39	"Do not stop him," Jesus s. 3306
	10: 4	They s, "Moses permitted a man to write 3306
	10:14	"Let the little children come 3306
	10:21	"One thing you lack," *he* s. 3306
	10:23	Jesus looked around and s to his disciples, 3306
	10:24	But Jesus s again, "Children, how hard it is 3306
	10:26	even more amazed, and s to each other, 3306
	10:27	Jesus looked at them and s, 3306
	10:28	Peter s to him, "We have left everything 3306
	10:33	"We are going up to Jerusalem," he s, NIG
	10:35	"we want you to do for us 3306
	10:38	"You don't know what you are asking," Jesus s. 3306
	10:39	Jesus s to them, "You will drink the cup 3306
	10:42	Jesus called them together and s, 3306
	10:49	Jesus stopped and s, "Call him." 3306
	10:51	The blind man s, "Rabbi, I want to see." 3306
	10:52	"Go," s Jesus, "your faith has healed you." 3306
	11:14	Then *he* s to the tree, 3306
	11:17	as he taught them, *he* s, "Is it not written: 3306
	11:21	Peter remembered and s to Jesus, "Rabbi, 3306
	11:31	They discussed it among themselves and s, 3306
	11:33	Jesus s, "Neither will I tell you 3306
	12: 7	"But the tenants s to one another, 3306
	12:14	*They* came to him and s, "Teacher, 3306
	12:17	Then Jesus s to them, "Give to Caesar what 3306
	12:19	*they* s, "Moses wrote for us that if 3306
	12:26	how God s, 'I am the God of 3306
	12:32	"Well s, teacher," the man replied. 2822
	12:34	*he* s to him, "You are not far from the 3306
	12:36	" 'The Lord s to my Lord: 3306
	12:38	As he taught, Jesus s, "Watch out for 3306
	12:43	Calling his disciples to him, Jesus s, 3306
	13: 1	one of his disciples s to him, "Look, 3306
	13: 5	Jesus s to them: "Watch out that no one 3306
	14: 2	"But not during the Feast," *they* s, 3306
	14: 6	"Leave her alone," s Jesus. 3306
	14:18	he s, "I tell you the truth, 3306
	14:19	and one by one they s to him, 3306
	14:24	which is poured out for many," *he* s to them. 3306
	14:31	And all the others s the same. 3306
	14:32	and Jesus s to his disciples, 3306
	14:34	sorrow to the point of death," *he* s to them. 3306
	14:36	*he* s, "everything is possible for you. 3306
	14:37	"Simon," *he* s to Peter, "are you asleep? 3306
	14:41	Returning the third time, *he* s to them, 3306
	14:45	Going at once to Jesus, Judas s, "Rabbi!" 3306
	14:48	"Am I leading a rebellion," s Jesus, 3306
	14:62	"I am," s Jesus. 3306
	14:65	struck him with their fists, and s, 3306
	14:67	also were with that Nazarene, Jesus," *she* s. 3306
	14:68	he s, and went out into the entryway. NIG
	14:69	*she* s again to those standing around, 3306
	14:70	those standing near s to Peter, 3306
	15:31	"He saved others," *they* s, 3306
	15:35	*they* s, "Listen, he's calling Elijah." 3306
	15:36	if Elijah comes to take him down," *he* s. 3306
	15:39	*he* s, "Surely this man was the Son of God!" 3306
	16: 6	"Don't be alarmed," *he* s. 3306

Mk	16: 8	*They* s nothing to anyone, 3306
	16:15	*He* s to them, "Go into all the world 3306
Lk	1:13	But the angel s to him: "Do not be afraid, 3306
	1:25	"The Lord has done this for me," *she* s. 3306
	1:28	The angel went to her and s, "Greetings, 3306
	1:30	But the angel s to her, "Do not be afraid, 3306
	1:36	and she who *was* s to be barren is 2813
	1:38	"May it be to me as you have s." 4839
	1:45	the Lord *has* s to her will be accomplished!" 3281
	1:46	And Mary s: "My soul glorifies the Lord 3306
	1:55	even as he s to our fathers." 3281
	1:60	but his mother spoke up and s, 3306
	1:61	*They* s to her, "There is no one among your 3306
	1:70	*he* s through his holy prophets of long ago), 3281
	2:10	But the angel s to them, "Do not be afraid. 3306
	2:15	the shepherds s to one another, 3281
	2:18	at what the shepherds s to them. 3281
	2:24	in keeping with what *is* s in the Law of 3281
	2:33	and mother marveled at what *was* s 3281
	2:34	Then Simeon blessed them and s to Mary, 3306
	2:48	His mother s to him, "Son, 3306
	3: 7	John s to the crowds coming out to 3306
	4: 3	The devil s to him, "If you are the Son of 3306
	4: 6	And he s to him, "I will give you all their 3306
	4: 9	"If you are the Son of God," *he* s, 3306
	4:23	Jesus s to them, "Surely you will quote 3306
	4:35	s **sternly**, "Come out of him!" 2203
	4:36	the people were amazed and s to each other, 5196
	4:43	But he s, "I must preach the good news of 3306
	5: 4	he s to Simon, "Put out into deep water, 3306
	5: 8	he fell at Jesus' knees and s, 3306
	5:10	Then Jesus s to Simon, "Don't be afraid; 3306
	5:13	"I am willing," *he* s. 3306
	5:20	When Jesus saw their faith, *he* s, "Friend, 3306
	5:24	*He* s to the paralyzed man, "I tell you, 3306
	5:26	They were filled with awe and s, 3306
	5:27	"Follow me," Jesus s to him, 3306
	5:33	They s to him, "John's disciples often fast 3306
	6: 5	Then Jesus s to them, "The Son of Man 3306
	6: 8	and s to the man with the shriveled hand, 3306
	6: 9	Then Jesus s to them, "I ask you, 3306
	6:10	then s to the man, "Stretch out your hand." 3306
	6:20	Looking at his disciples, *he* s: 3306
	7: 9	*he* s, "I tell you, I have not found such 3306
	7:13	his heart went out to her and *he* s, 3306
	7:14	He s, "Young man, I say to you, get up!" 3306
	7:16	prophet has appeared among us," *they* s. 3306
	7:20	When the men came to Jesus, *they* s, 3306
	7:39	*he* s to himself, "If this man were a prophet, 3306
	7:40	"Tell me, teacher," *he* s. 5774
	7:43	"You have judged correctly," Jesus s. 3306
	7:44	Then *he* turned toward the woman and s 5774
	7:48	Jesus s to her, "Your sins are forgiven." 3306
	7:50	Jesus s to the woman, 3306
	8: 8	When he s this, he called out, 3306
	8:10	He s, "The knowledge of the secrets of 3306
	8:22	One day Jesus s to his disciples, 3306
	8:45	When they all denied it, Peter s, "Master, 3306
	8:46	But Jesus s, "Someone touched me; 3306
	8:48	Then he s to her, "Daughter, 3306
	8:49	"Your daughter is dead," *he* s. 3306
	8:50	Hearing this, Jesus s to Jairus, 646
	8:52	"Stop wailing," Jesus s. 3306
	8:54	But he took her by the hand and s, 5888
	9: 9	But Herod s, "I beheaded John. 3306
	9:12	the Twelve came to him and s, 3306
	9:14	But he s to his disciples, "Have them sit 3306
	9:22	And *he* s, "The Son of Man must suffer 3306
	9:23	Then he s to them all: 3306
	9:28	About eight days after Jesus s this, NIG
	9:33	Peter s to him, "Master, it is good for us 3306
	9:43	*he* s to his disciples, 3306
	9:48	Then *he* s to them, "Whoever welcomes 3306
	9:49	s John, "we saw a man driving out demons 3306
	9:50	"Do not stop him," Jesus s, 3306
	9:57	a man s to him, "I will follow you 3306
	9:59	*He* s to another man, "Follow me." 3306
	9:60	Jesus s to him, "Let the dead bury their own 3306
	9:61	Still another s, "I will follow you, Lord; 3306
	10:17	The seventy-two returned with joy and s, 3306
	10:21	full of joy through the Holy Spirit, s, 3306
	10:23	he turned to his disciples and s privately, 3306
	10:30	In reply Jesus s: "A man was going down 3306
	10:35	'Look after him,' *he* s, 'and when I return, 3306
	10:39	at the Lord's feet listening to what *he* s. 3364
	11: 1	he finished, one of his disciples s to him, 3306
	11: 2	*He* s to them, "When you pray, say: 3306
	11: 5	Then *he* s to them, "Suppose one of you 3306
	11:15	But some of them s, "By Beelzebub, 3306
	11:17	Jesus knew their thoughts and s to them: 3306
	11:29	As the crowds increased, Jesus s, 3306
	11:39	Then the Lord s to him, "Now then, 3306
	11:49	Because of this, God in his wisdom s, 3306
	12: 3	What *you have* s in the dark will be heard 3306
	12:13	Someone in the crowd s to him, "Teacher, 3306
	12:15	Then he s to them, "Watch out! 3306
	12:18	"Then he s, 'This is what I'll do. 3306
	12:20	"But God s to him, 'You fool! 3306
	12:22	Then Jesus s to his disciples: 3306
	12:54	*He* s to the crowd: "When you see a cloud 3306
	13: 7	So he s to the man who took care of 3306
	13:12	he called her forward and s to her, 3306
	13:14	the synagogue ruler s to the people, 3306
	13:17	When he s this, all his opponents were 3306
	13:23	He s to them, 3306
	13:31	Pharisees came to Jesus and s to him, 3306
	14:12	Then Jesus s to his host, 3306

Lk	14:15	he s to Jesus, "Blessed is the man who 3306
	14:18	The first s, 'I have just bought a field, 3306
	14:19	"Another s, 'I have just bought five yoke 3306
	14:20	"Still another s, 'I just got married, 3306
	14:22	" 'Sir,' the servant s, 'what you ordered 3306
	14:25	and turning to them *he* s: 3306
	15:12	The younger one s to his father, 'Father, 3306
	15:17	"When he came to his senses, *he* s, 5774
	15:21	"The son s to him, 'Father, I have sinned 3306
	15:22	"But the father s to his servants, 'Quick! 3306
	15:31	" 'My son,' the father s, 3306
	16: 3	"The manager s to himself, 3306
	16:15	*He* s to them, "You are the ones who justify 3306
	16:30	" 'No, father Abraham,' he s, 3306
	16:31	"*He* s to him, 'If they do not listen to Moses 3306
	17: 1	Jesus s to his disciples: 3306
	17: 5	apostles s to the Lord, "Increase our faith!" 3306
	17:14	When he saw them, *he* s, "Go, 3306
	17:19	Then *he* s to him, "Rise and go; 3306
	17:22	Then *he* s to his disciples, 3306
	18: 2	*He* s: "In a certain town there was a judge 3306
	18: 4	But finally *he* s to himself, 3306
	18: 6	And the Lord s, "Listen to what the unjust 3306
	18:13	but beat his breast and s, 'God, 3306
	18:16	But Jesus called the children to him and s, 3306
	18:21	I have kept since I was a boy," *he* s. 3306
	18:22	When Jesus heard this, *he* s to him, 3306
	18:24	Jesus looked at him and s, 3306
	18:28	Peter s to him, "We have left all we had 3306
	18:29	"I tell you the truth," Jesus s to them, 3306
	18:42	Jesus s to him, "Receive your sight; 3306
	19: 5	he looked up and s to him, "Zacchaeus, 3306
	19: 8	But Zacchaeus stood up and s to the Lord, 3306
	19: 9	Jesus s to him, "Today salvation has come 3306
	19:12	*He* s: "A man of noble birth went 3306
	19:13	'Put this money to work,' *he* s, 3306
	19:16	"The first one came and s, 'Sir, 3306
	19:18	"The second came and s, 'Sir, 3306
	19:20	"Then another servant came and s, 'Sir, 3306
	19:24	"Then *he* s to those standing by, 3306
	19:25	" 'Sir,' *they* s, 'he already has ten!' 3306
	19:28	*After* Jesus *had* s this, he went on ahead, 3306
	19:39	of the Pharisees in the crowd s to Jesus, 3306
	19:42	and s, "If you, even you, had only known 3306
	19:46	"It is written," *he* s to them, 3306
	20: 2	authority you are doing these things," *they* s. 3306
	20: 5	They discussed it among themselves and s, 3306
	20: 8	Jesus s, "Neither will I tell you 3306
	20:13	owner of the vineyard s, 'What shall I do? 3306
	20:14	'This is the heir,' *they* s. 3306
	20:19	When the people heard this, *they* s, 3306
	20:20	hoped to catch Jesus in **something he** s 3364
	20:23	through their duplicity and s to them, 3306
	20:25	He s to them, "Then give to Caesar what is 3306
	20:26	to trap him in **what** he had s there in public. 4839
	20:28	*they* s, "Moses wrote for us that if 3306
	20:39	the teachers of the law responded, "Well s, 3306
	20:41	Then Jesus s to them, "How is it that 3306
	20:42	" 'The Lord s to my Lord: 3306
	20:45	Jesus s to his disciples, 3306
	21: 3	"I tell you the truth," *he* s, 3306
	21: 5	and with gifts dedicated to God. But Jesus s, 3306
	21:10	Then *he* s to them: "Nation will rise against 3306
	22:15	And *he* s to them, "I have eagerly desired to 3306
	22:17	After taking the cup, he gave thanks and s, 3306
	22:25	Jesus s to them, "The kings of the Gentiles 3306
	22:36	*He* s to them, "But now if you have a purse, 3306
	22:38	The disciples s, "See, Lord, 3306
	22:40	On reaching the place, *he* s to them, 3306
	22:49	to happen, *they* s, "Lord, should we strike 3306
	22:52	Then Jesus s to the chief priests, 3306
	22:56	*She* looked closely at him and s, 3306
	22:57	"Woman, I don't know him," *he* s. 3306
	22:58	A little later someone else saw him and s, 5774
	22:65	*they* s many other insulting things to him. 3306
	22:67	"If you are the Christ," *they* s, "tell us." 3306
	22:71	Then they s, "Why do we need any more testimony? 3306
	23:14	and s to them, "You brought me this man 3306
	23:28	Jesus turned and s to them, 3306
	23:34	Jesus s, "Father, forgive them, 3306
	23:35	*They* s, "He saved others; 3306
	23:37	and s, "If you are the king of the Jews, 3306
	23:40	"Don't you fear God," *he* s, 5774
	23:42	Then *he* s, "Jesus, remember me 3306
	23:46	*When he had* s this, he breathed his last. 3306
	23:47	and s, "Surely this was a righteous man." 3306
	24: 5	but the *men* s to them, "Why do you look 3306
	24:23	a vision of angels, who s he was alive. 3306
	24:24	and found it just as the women *had* s, 3306
	24:25	He s to them, "How foolish you are, 3306
	24:27	he **explained** to them **what** *was* s 1450
	24:36	Jesus himself stood among them and s, 3306
	24:38	*He* s to them, "Why are you troubled, 3306
	24:40	*When he had* s this, he showed them 3306
	24:44	*He* s to them, "This is what I told you 3306
Jn	1:15	saying, "This was he *of* whom *I* s, 3306
	1:21	*He* s, "I am not. 3306
	1:22	Finally *they* s, "Who are you? 3306
	1:29	toward him and s, "Look, the Lamb of God, 3306
	1:30	This is the one I meant when I s, 3306
	1:36	When he saw Jesus passing by, *he* s, "Look, 3306
	1:38	*They* s, "Rabbi" (which means Teacher), 3306
	1:40	of the two who heard what John had s NIG
	1:42	Jesus looked at him and s, "You are Simon 3306
	1:43	Finding Philip, he s to him, "Follow me." 3306
	1:46	"Come and see," s Philip. 3306

Jn 1:47   *he* s of him, "Here is a true Israelite,   3306
1:50   Jesus s, "You believe because I told you   3306
2: 3   Jesus' mother s to him,   3306
2: 5   His mother s to the servants,   3306
2: 7   Jesus s to the servants,   3306
2:10   and s, "Everyone brings out the choice wine   3306
2:16   To those who sold doves *he* s,   3306
2:22   his disciples recalled what *he had* s.   3306
3: 2   He came to Jesus at night and s, "Rabbi,   3306
3:10   "You are Israel's teacher," s Jesus,   646
3:26   They came to John and s to him, "Rabbi,   3306
3:28   You yourselves can testify that *I* s,   3306
4: 7   Jesus s to her, "Will you give me a drink?"   3306
4: 9   The Samaritan woman s to him,   3306
4:11   the woman s, "you have nothing to draw   3306
4:15   The woman s to him, "Sir,   3306
4:17   Jesus s to her, "You are right   3306
4:18   What *you have* just s is quite true."   3306
4:19   the woman s, "I can see that you are   3306
4:25   The woman s, "I know that Messiah"   3306
4:28   the woman went back to the town and s to   3306
4:32   But *he* s to them, "I have food to eat   3306
4:33   Then his disciples s to each other,   3306
4:34   s Jesus, "is to do the will of him who sent   3306
4:42   *They* s to the woman, "We no longer   3306
4:42   just because of what you s;   3282
4:49   The royal official s, "Sir, come down   3306
4:52   *they* s to him, "The fever left him   3306
4:53   the exact time at which Jesus *had* s to him,   3306
5: 8   Then Jesus s to him, "Get up!   3306
5:10   the Jews s to the man who had been healed,   3306
5:11   "The man who made me well s to me,   3306
5:14   Later Jesus found him at the temple and s   3306
5:17   Jesus s to them, "My Father is always   646
6: 5   *he* s to Philip, "Where shall we buy bread   3306
6:10   Jesus s, "Have the people sit down."   3306
6:12   *he* s to his disciples, "Gather the pieces   3306
6:20   But *he* s to them, "It is I; don't be afraid."   3306
6:32   Jesus s to them, "I tell you the truth,   3306
6:34   *they* s, "from now on give us this bread."   3306
6:41   to grumble about him because *he* s,   3306
6:42   *They* s, "Is this not Jesus, the son of Joseph,   3306
6:53   Jesus s to them, "I tell you the truth,   3306
6:59   *He* s this while teaching in the synagogue   3306
6:60   On hearing this, many of his disciples s,   3306
6:61   Jesus s to them, "Does this offend you?   3306
7: 3   Jesus' brothers s to him,   3306
7: 9   *Having* s this, he stayed in Galilee.   3306
7:12   Some s, "He is a good man."   3306
7:21   Jesus s to them, "I did one miracle,   3306
7:31   *They* s, "When the Christ comes,   3306
7:33   Jesus s, "I am with you for only a short time   3306
7:35   The Jews s to one another,   3306
7:36   What did he mean when *he* s,   3306
7:37   Jesus stood and s in a loud voice,   3306
7:38   as the Scripture *has* s,   3306
7:40   On hearing his words, *some* of the people s,   3306
7:41   Others s, "He is the Christ."   3306
8: 4   and s to Jesus, "Teacher, this woman   3306
8: 7   he straightened up and s to them,   3306
8:11   "No one, sir," she s.   3306
8:12   When Jesus spoke again to the people, *he* s,   3306
8:21   Once more Jesus s to them,   3306
8:28   So Jesus s, "When you have lifted up   3306
8:31   To the Jews who had believed him, Jesus **s,**   3306
8:39   "If you were Abraham's children," s Jesus,   3306
8:42   Jesus s to them, "If God were your Father,   3306
8:49   "I am not possessed by a demon," s Jesus,   646
8:55   If *I* s did not, I would be a liar like you,   3306
8:57   not yet fifty years old," the Jews s to him,   3306
9: 3   s Jesus, "but this happened so that the work   646
9: 6   *Having* s this, he spit on the ground,   3306
9: 9   Others s, "No, he only looks like him."   3306
9:12   "I don't know," *he* s.   3306
9:16   Some of the Pharisees s, "This man is not   3306
9:22   His parents s this because they were afraid   3306
9:23   That was why his parents s, "He is of age;   3306
9:24   "Give glory to God," *they* s.   3306
9:28   Then they hurled insults at him and s,   3306
9:35   *he* s, "Do you believe in the Son of Man?"   3306
9:37   Jesus s, "You have now seen him;   3306
9:38   Then the man s, "Lord, I believe,"   5774
9:39   Jesus s, "For judgment I have come   3306
9:41   Jesus s, "If you were blind,   3306
10: 7   Therefore Jesus s again, "I tell you the truth,   3306
10:20   Many of them s, "He is demon-possessed   3306
10:21   But others s, "These are not the sayings of   3306
10:32   but Jesus s to them, "I have shown you   646
10:34   '*I have* s you are gods'?   3306
10:36   you accuse me of blasphemy because *I* s,   3306
10:41   *They* s, "Though John never performed   3306
10:41   all that John s about this man was true."   3306
11: 4   When he heard this, Jesus **s,**   3306
11: 7   Then *he* s to his disciples,   3306
11: 8   they s, "a short while ago the Jews tried   3306
11:11   After *he had* s this, he went on to tell them,   3306
11:16   Then Thomas (called Didymus) s to the rest   3306
11:21   "Lord," Martha s to Jesus,   3306
11:23   Jesus s to her, "Your brother will rise again.   3306
11:25   Jesus s to her, "I am the resurrection   3306
11:28   And *after she had* s this,   3306
11:28   "The Teacher is here," *she* s,   3306
11:32   she fell at his feet and s, "Lord,   3306
11:36   Then the Jews s, "See how he loved him!"   3306
11:37   But some of them s, "Could not he who   3306
11:39   "Take away the stone," *he* s.   3306
11:39   "But, Lord," s Martha, the sister of the dead   3306

Jn 11:40   Then Jesus s, "Did I not tell you that   3306
11:41   Then Jesus looked up and s, "Father,   3306
11:42   but *I* s this for the benefit of the people   3306
11:43   When *he had* s this, Jesus called in a loud   3306
11:44   Jesus s to them, "Take off the grave clothes   3306
12:19   So the Pharisees s to one another, "See,   3306
12:21   "Sir," *they* s, "we would like to see Jesus."   3306
12:29   and heard it s it had thundered;   3306
12:29   others s an angel had spoken to him.   3306
12:30   Jesus s, "This voice was for your benefit,   3306
12:33   *He* s this to show the kind of death   3306
12:41   Isaiah s this because he saw Jesus' glory   3306
13: 6   He came to Simon Peter, *who* s to him,   3306
13: 8   s Peter, "you shall never wash my feet."   3306
13:11   that was why *he* s not every one was clean.   3306
13:21   *After he had* s this, Jesus was troubled   3306
13:24   Simon Peter motioned to this disciple and **s,**   NIG
13:28   at the meal understood why Jesus s this   3306
13:31   When he was gone, Jesus s,   3306
14: 5   Thomas s to him, "Lord, we don't know   3306
14: 8   Philip s, "Lord, show us the Father and   3306
14:22   Then Judas (not Judas Iscariot) s, "But,   3306
14:26   and will remind you of everything I *have* s   3306
16: 6   Because I *have* s these things,   3281
16:15   That is why *I* s the Spirit will take   3306
16:17   *Some* of his disciples s to one another,   3306
16:19   so *he* s to them, "Are you asking   3306
16:19   when I s, 'In a little while you will see me   3306
16:29   Jesus' disciples s, "Now you are speaking   3306
17: 1   After Jesus s this, he looked toward heaven   3281
18: 5   "I am he," Jesus s.   3306
18: 5   When Jesus s, "I am he,"   3306
18: 7   And they s, "Jesus of Nazareth."   3306
18:20   *I* s nothing in secret.   3281
18:21   Surely they know what I s."   3306
18:22   When Jesus s this, one of the officials   3306
18:23   "If *I* s something wrong," Jesus replied,   3281
18:31   Pilate s, "Take him yourselves   3306
18:36   Jesus s, "My kingdom is not of this world.   646
18:37   "You are a king, then!" s Pilate.   3306
18:38   and s, "I find no basis for a charge   3306
19: 4   Once more Pilate came out and s to   3306
19: 5   Pilate s to them, "Here is the man!"   3306
19:10   "Do you refuse to speak to me?" Pilate s.   3306
19:14   "Here is your king," Pilate s to the Jews.   3306
19:24   "Let's not tear it," *they* s to one another.   3306
19:24   that the scripture might be fulfilled which s,   3306
19:26   *he* s to his mother, "Dear woman,   3306
19:28   Jesus s, "I am thirsty."   3306
19:30   When he had received the drink, Jesus s,   3306
20: 2   the one Jesus loved, and s,   3306
20:13   "They have taken my Lord away," *she* s,   3306
20:15   "Woman," *he* s, "why are you crying?   3306
20:15   Thinking he was the gardener, she s, "Sir,   3306
20:16   Jesus s to her, "Mary."   3306
20:17   Jesus s, "Do not hold on to me,   3306
20:18   And she told them that *he had* s these things   3306
20:19   Jesus came and stood among them and s,   3306
20:20   *After he* s this, he showed them his hands   3306
20:21   Again Jesus s, "Peace be with you!   3306
20:22   And with that he breathed on them and s,   3306
20:25   But he s to them, "Unless I see the nail   3306
20:26   Jesus came and stood among them and s,   3306
20:27   Then *he* s to Thomas, "Put your finger here;   3306
20:28   Thomas s to him, "My Lord and my God!"   3306
21: 3   Simon Peter told them, and *they* s,   3306
21: 6   He s, "Throw your net on the right side of   3306
21: 7   the disciple whom Jesus loved s to Peter,   3306
21:10   Jesus s to them, "Bring some of the fish   3306
21:12   Jesus s to them, "Come and have breakfast."   3306
21:15   Jesus s to Simon Peter, "Simon son of John,   3306
21:15   Lord," *he* s, "you know that I love you."   3306
21:15   Jesus s, "Feed my lambs."   3306
21:16   Again Jesus s, "Simon son of John,   3306
21:16   Jesus s, "Take care of my sheep.   3306
21:17   The third time *he* s to him,   3306
21:17   *He* s, "Lord, you know all things;   3306
21:17   Jesus s, "Feed my sheep.   3306
21:19   Jesus s this to indicate the kind of death   3306
21:19   Then *he* s to him, "Follow me!"   3306
21:20   against Jesus at the supper and *had* s,   3306
21:23   he only s, "If I want him to remain alive   NIG

Ac 1: 7   *He* s to them: "It is not for you to know   3306
1: 9   *After he* s this, he was taken up   3306
1:11   "Men of Galilee," they s,   3306
1:16   and s, "Brothers, the Scripture had to   3306
1:20   s Peter, "it is written in the book of Psalms,   NIG
2:13   Some, however, made fun of them and s,   3306
2:25   David s about him: " 'I saw the Lord   3306
2:34   and yet he s, " 'The Lord said to my Lord: 3306
2:34   and yet he said, " 'The Lord s to my Lord: 3306
2:37   they were cut to the heart and s to Peter and   3306
3: 4   Then Peter s, "Look at us!"   3306
3: 6   Then Peter s, "Silver or gold I do not have,   3306
3:12   When Peter saw this, *he* s to them: 646
3:22   For Moses s, 'The Lord your God will raise   3306
3:25   *He* s to Abraham, 'Through your offspring   3306
4: 8   Peter, filled with the Holy Spirit, s to them: 3306
4:23   the chief priests and elders *had* s to them.   3306
4:24   "Sovereign Lord," *they* s,   3306
5: 3   Then Peter s, "Ananias, how is it that Satan   3306
5: 8   "Yes," she s, "that is the price."   3306
5: 9   Peter s to her, "How could you agree to test   NIG
5:20   "Go, stand in the temple courts," *he* s,   3306
5:25   Then someone came and s, "Look!   550
5:28   not to teach in this name," *he* s.   3306
6: 2   gathered all the disciples together and s,   3306

Ac 7: 3   God s, 'and go to the land I will show you.'   3306
7: 7   God s, 'and afterward they will come out of   3306
7:27   the other pushed Moses aside and s,   3306
7:33   the Lord s to him, 'Take off your sandals;   3306
7:56   *he* s, "I see heaven open and the Son   3306
7:60   When *he had* s this, he fell asleep.   3306
8: 6   they all paid close attention *to what* he s.   3306
8:19   and s, "Give me also this ability so   3306
8:24   so that nothing you s may happen   3306
8:26   Now an angel of the Lord s to Philip,   3281
8:31   "How can I," he s,   3306
8:36   they came to some water and the eunuch s,   5774
9:15   But the Lord s to Ananias, "Go!   3306
9:17   Placing his hands on Saul, *he* s,   3306
9:34   "Aeneas," Peter s to him,   3306
9:40   Turning toward the dead woman, *he* s,   3306
10: 3   who came to him and s, "Cornelius!"   3306
10:19   the Spirit s to him, "Simon,   3306
10:21   Peter went down and s to the men,   3306
10:26   "Stand up," *he* s, "I am only a man myself."   3306
10:28   *He* s to them: "You are well aware   5774
10:31   s, 'Cornelius, God has heard your prayer   5774
10:46   and praising God. Then Peter s,   646
11: 3   and s, "You went into the house   3306
11:16   Then I remembered what the Lord *had* s: 3306
12: 7   *he* s, and the chains fell off Peter's wrists.   3306
12: 8   Then the angel s to him,   3306
12:11   Then Peter came to himself and s,   3306
12:15   she kept insisting that it was so, they s,   3306
12:17   *he* s, and then he left for another place.   3306
13: 2   the Holy Spirit s, "Set apart for me   3306
13: 9   looked straight at Elymas and s,   3306
13:16   Paul motioned with his hand and s: 3306
13:25   As John was completing his work, *he* s: 3306
13:40   the prophets *have* s does not happen to you: 3306
14:22   to enter the kingdom of God," they s.   NIG
15: 5   to the party of the Pharisees stood up and s,   3306
15:24   troubling your minds *by what they* s.   3364
15:32   s much to encourage and strengthen   3364
15:36   Some time later Paul s to Barnabas,   3306
16:15   *she* s, "come and stay at my house."   3306
16:18   so troubled that *he* turned around and s to   3306
16:20   brought them before the magistrates and s,   3306
16:37   But Paul s to the officers: 5774
17: 3   proclaiming to you is the Christ," he s.   NIG
17:11   to see if *what* Paul s was true.   4047S
17:18   They s this because Paul was preaching   NIG
17:19   where *they* s to him,   3306
17:22   up in the meeting of the Areopagus and s: 5774
17:28   As some of your own poets *have* s,   3306
17:32   some of them sneered, but others s,   3306
18: 6   he shook out his clothes in protest and s   3306
18:14   Gallio s to the Jews, "If you Jews were   3306
19: 4   Paul s, "John's baptism was a baptism   3306
19:21   "After I have been there," *he* s,   3306
19:25   with the workmen in related trades, and s: 3306
19:35   The city clerk quieted the crowd and s: 5774
19:41   *After he had* s this, he dismissed the   3306
20: 1   s good-by and set out for Macedonia.   832
20:10   "Don't be alarmed," *he* s.   3306
20:18   When they arrived, *he* s to them: 3306
20:35   the words the Lord Jesus himself s: 3306
20:36   *When he had* s this, he knelt down   3306
21:11   tied his own hands and feet with it and s,   3306
21:14   we gave up and s, "The Lord's will be done.   3306
21:20   Then *they* s to Paul: 3306
21:40   to them in Aramaic: 4715
22: 2   they became very quiet. Then Paul s: 5774
22:10   " 'Get up,' the Lord s,   3306
22:13   He stood beside me and s, 'Brother Saul,   3306
22:14   "Then he s: 'The God of our fathers   3306
22:18   he s to me. 'Leave Jerusalem   NIG
22:21   "Then the Lord s to me, 'Go;   3306
22:22   The crowd listened to Paul until he s this.   NIG
22:25   Paul s to the centurion standing there,   3306
22:28   Then the commander s,   646
23: 1   Paul looked straight at the Sanhedrin and s,   3306
23: 3   Then Paul s to him, "God will strike you,   3306
23: 4   Those who were standing near Paul s,   3306
23: 7   *When he s* this, a dispute broke out   3306
23: 9   nothing wrong with this man," *they* s.   3306
23:11   the Lord stood near Paul and s,   3306
23:14   to the chief priests and elders and s,   3306
23:17   Paul called one of the centurions and s,   5774
23:18   The centurion s, "Paul, the prisoner,   5774
23:20   *He* s: "The Jews have agreed to ask   3306
23:35   *he* s, "I will hear your case   5774
24:22   "When Lysias the commander comes," *he* s,   3306
24:25   Felix was afraid and s, "That's enough   646
25: 9   wishing to do the Jews a favor, s to Paul,   3306
25:14   He s: "There is a man here   3306
25:22   Then Agrippa s to Festus, "I would like   NIG
25:24   Festus s: "King Agrippa,   5774
26: 1   Agrippa s to Paul, "You have permission   5774
26:22   the prophets and Moses s would happen——   3281
26:28   Then Agrippa s to Paul,   NIG
26:31   and while talking with one another, *they* s,   3281
26:32   Agrippa s to Festus, "This man could have   5774
27:11   instead of listening to what Paul s.   3306
27:21   Paul stood up before them and s: 3306
27:24   and s, 'Do not be afraid. Paul.   3306
27:31   Paul s to the centurion and the soldiers,   3306
27:33   "For the last fourteen days," *he* s,   3306
27:35   *After he* s this, he took some bread   3306
28: 4   *they* s to each other,   3306
28: 6   they changed their minds and s he was   3306
28:17   When they had assembled, Paul s to them: 3306

Ac	28:21	from there has reported or s anything bad	3281
	28:24	Some were convinced by what he s,	3306
	28:25	to your forefathers when he s through Isaiah	3306
Ro	4:18	just as it had been s to him,	3306
	7: 7	if the law had not s, "Do not covet."	3306
	9:26	in the very place where it was s to them,	3306
	9:29	It is just as Isaiah s previously:	4625
	15:18	the Gentiles to obey God by what I have s	3364
1Co	6:16	it is s, "The two will become one flesh."	5774
	11:24	he broke it and s, "This is my body,	3306
	14:29	the others should weigh carefully what is s.	NIG
2Co	2:13	So I s good-by to them and went on	698
	4: 6	who s, "Let light shine out of darkness,"	3306
	6:16	As God has s: "I will live with them	3306
	7: 3	I have s before that you have such a place	4625
	7:14	But just as everything we s to you was true,	3281
	9: 3	as I s you would be.	3306
	12: 9	But he s to me, "My grace is sufficient	3306
Gal	1: 9	As we have already s, so now I say again:	4625
	2:14	I s to Peter in front of them all,	3306
Eph	5:14	This is why it is s: "Wake up, O sleeper,	3306
Tit	1:12	Even one of their own prophets has s,	3306
Heb	3: 5	to what would be s in the future.	3281
	3:10	with that generation, and I s,	3306
	3:15	As has just been s: "Today,	1877+3306+3836
	4: 3	just as God has s, "So I declared on oath	3306
	4: 7	as was s before: "Today, if you hear his	4625
	5: 5	But God s to him, "You are my Son;	3281
	6:16	the oath confirms what is s and puts an end	NIG
	7:13	He of whom these things are s belonged to	3306
	7:14	to that tribe Moses s nothing about priests.	3281
	7:15	And what we have s is even more clear	NIG
	7:21	a priest with an oath when God s to him:	3306
	8: 8	But God found fault with the people and s:	3306
	9:20	He s, "This is the blood of the covenant,	3306
	10: 5	when Christ came into the world, he s:	3306
	10: 7	Then I s, 'Here I am—it is written about me	3306
	10: 8	First he s, "Sacrifices and offerings,	3306
	10: 9	Then he s, "Here I am, I have come to do	3306
	10:30	we know him who s, "It is mine to avenge;	3306
	11:18	even though God had s to him,	3281
	12:21	The sight was so terrifying that Moses s,	3306
	13: 5	because God has s, "Never will I leave you;	3306
Jas	2:11	For he who s, "Do not commit adultery,"	3306
	2:11	also s, "Do not murder."	3306
Jude	1: 9	but s, "The Lord rebuke you!"	3306
	1:18	They s to you, "In the last times	3306
Rev	1:11	which s: "Write on a scroll what you see	3306
	1:17	Then he placed his right hand on me and s:	3306
	4: 1	speaking to me like a trumpet s,	3306
	5: 5	one of the elders s to me, "Do not weep!	3306
	5:14	The four living creatures s, "Amen,"	3306
	7:14	And he s, "These are they who have come	3306
	9:14	It s to the sixth angel who had the trumpet,	3306
	10: 4	up what the seven thunders have s and do	3281
	10: 6	the sea and all that is in it, and s,	NIG
	10: 9	He s to me, "Take it and eat it.	3306
	11:15	loud voices in heaven, which s:	3306
	14: 7	He s in a loud voice, "Fear God and give	3306
	14: 8	A second angel followed and s, "Fallen!	3306
	14: 9	A third angel followed them and s in	3306
	17: 1	the seven bowls came and s to me,	3281
	17: 7	angel s to me: "Why are you astonished?	3306
	17:15	Then the angel s to me, "The waters	3306
	18:21	and threw it into the sea, and s:	3281
	19: 9	Then the angel s to me, "Write:	3306
	19:10	But he s to me, "Do not do it!	3306
	21: 5	He who was seated on the throne s,	3306
	21: 5	Then he s, "Write this down,	3306
	21: 6	He s to me: "It is done.	3306
	21: 9	of the seven last plagues came and s to me,	3281
	22: 6	The angel s to me, "These words	3306
	22: 9	But he s to me, "Do not do it!	3306

SAIL (18) [FORESAIL, SAILED, SAILING, SAILORS]

1Ki	22:48	but they never set s—they were wrecked	2143
	22:49	said to Jehoshaphat, "Let my men s with	
		your men,"	641+928+2021+2143
2Ch	20:37	and were not able to set s to trade.	2143
Isa	33:21	no mighty ship will s them.	6296
	33:23	mast is not held secure, the s is not spread.	5812
Eze	27: 7	from Egypt was your s and served	5155
Ac	18:21	Then he set s from Ephesus.	343
	20: 3	a plot against him just as he was about to s	343
	20:15	The next day we set s from there	676
	20:16	to s past Ephesus to avoid spending time	4179
	21: 2	went on board and set s.	343
	27: 1	When it was decided that we would s	676
	27: 2	to s for ports along the coast of the province	4434
	27:12	the majority decided that we should s on,	343
	27:21	you should have taken my advice not to s	343
	27:24	the lives of all who s with you.'	4434
	28:10	in many ways and when we were ready to s,	343
	28:13	From there we set s and arrived	4311

SAILED (19) [SAIL]

1Ki	9:28	They s to Ophir and brought back	995
2Ch	8:18	to Ophir and brought back four hundred	995
Jnh	1: 3	and s for Tarshish to flee from the LORD.	995
Lk	8:23	As they s, he fell asleep.	4434
	8:26	They s to the region of the Gerasenes,	2929
Ac	13: 4	went down to Seleucia and s from there	676
	13:13	Paul and his companions s to Perga	343
	14:26	From Attalia they s back to Antioch,	676

Ac	15:39	Barnabas took Mark and s for Cyprus,	1739
	16:11	From Troas we put out to sea and s straight	2312
	18:18	Then he left the brothers and s for Syria,	1739
	18:18	Before he s, he had his hair cut off	NIG
	20: 6	But we s from Philippi after the Feast	1739
	20:13	on ahead to the ship and s for Assos,	343
	21: 1	we put out to sea and s straight to Cos.	2312
	21: 3	we s on to Syria.	4434
	27: 5	When we had s across the open sea off	1386
	27: 7	s to the lee of Crete, opposite Salome.	5709
	27:13	so they weighed anchor and s along	4162

SAILING (2) [SAIL]

Ac	27: 6	the centurion found an Alexandrian ship s	4434
	27: 9	and s had already become dangerous	4452

SAILORS (7) [SAIL]

1Ki	9:27	s who knew the sea—	408+641
Eze	27: 9	the sea and their s came alongside to trade	4876
Jnh	1: 5	All the s were afraid and each cried out	4876
	1: 7	Then the s said to each other, "Come,	NIH
Ac	27:27	s sensed they were approaching land.	3731
	27:30	the s let the lifeboat down into the sea,	3731
Rev	18:17	and all who travel by ship, the s,	3731

SAINTS (69)

1Sa	2: 9	He will guard the feet of his s,	2883
2Ch	6:41	may your s rejoice in your goodness.	2883
Ps	16: 3	As for the s who are in the land,	7705
	30: 4	Sing to the LORD, you s of his;	2883
	31:23	Love the LORD, all his s!	2883
	34: 9	Fear the LORD, you his s,	7705
	52: 9	I will praise you in the presence of your s.	2883
	79: 2	the flesh of your s to the beasts of the earth.	2883
	85: 8	he promises peace to his people, his s—	2883
	116:15	in the sight of the LORD is the death of his s.	2883
	132: 9	may your s sing for joy."	2883
	132:16	and her s will ever sing for joy.	2883
	145:10	your s will extol you.	2883
	148:14	the praise of all his s, of Israel,	2883
	149: 1	his praise in the assembly of the s.	2883
	149: 5	the s rejoice in this honor and sing for joy	2883
	149: 9	This is the glory of all his s.	2883
Da	7:18	But the s of the Most High will receive	10620
	7:21	this horn was waging war against the s	10620
	7:22	and pronounced judgment in favor of the s	10620
	7:25	against the Most High and oppress his s	10620
	7:25	The s will be handed over to him for a time,	NIH
	7:27	will be handed over to the s,	10620
	8:12	Because of rebellion, the host [of the s]	NIH
Ac	9:13	and all the harm he has done to your s	41
	9:32	he went to visit the s in Lydda.	41
	26:10	of the chief priests I put many of the s	41
Ro	1: 7	who are loved by God and called to be s:	41
	8:27	the Spirit intercedes for the s in accordance	41
	15:25	to Jerusalem in the service of the s there.	41
	15:26	a contribution for the poor among the s	41
	15:31	be acceptable to the s there,	41
	16: 2	the s and to give her any help she may need	41
	16:15	and Olympas and all the s with them.	41
1Co	6: 1	for judgment instead of before the s?	41
	6: 2	not know that the s will judge the world?	41
	14:33	As in all the congregations of the s,	41
	16:15	to the service of the s.	41
2Co	8: 4	together with all the s throughout Achaia.	41
	8: 4	of sharing in this service to the s.	41
	9: 1	to write to you about this service to the s.	41
	13:13	All the s send their greetings.	41
Eph	1: 1	To the s in Ephesus,	41
	1:15	the Lord Jesus and your love for all the s,	41
	1:18	of his glorious inheritance in the s,	41
	3:18	together with all the s,	41
	6:18	and always keep on praying for all the s.	41
Php	1: 1	To all the s in Christ Jesus at Philippi,	41
	4:21	Greet all the s in Christ Jesus.	41
	4:22	All the s send you greetings,	41
Col	1: 4	and of the love you have for all the s—	41
	1:12	in the inheritance of the s in the kingdom	41
	1:26	but is now disclosed to the s.	41
1Ti	5:10	washing the feet of the s,	41
Phm	1: 5	in the Lord Jesus and your love for all the s.	41
	1: 7	brother, have refreshed the hearts of the s.	41
Jude	1: 3	faith that was once for all entrusted to the s.	41
Rev	5: 8	which are the prayers of the s.	41
	8: 3	with the prayers of all the s,	41
	8: 4	together with the prayers of the s,	41
	11:18	your servants the prophets and your s	41
	13: 7	against the s and to conquer them.	41
	13:10	and faithfulness on the part of the s.	41
	14:12	of the s who obey God's commandments	41
	16: 6	for they have shed the blood of your s	41
	17: 6	woman was drunk with the blood of the s,	41
	18:20	Rejoice, s and apostles and prophets!	41
	18:24	the blood of prophets and of the s,	41
	19: 8	for the righteous acts of the s.)	41

SAKE (105) [SAKES]

Ge	12:13	be treated well for your s and my life will	6288
	12:16	He treated Abram well for her s,	6288
	18:24	and not spare the place for the s of	5100
	18:26	I will spare the whole place for them."	6288
	18:29	He said, "For the s of forty,	6288
	18:31	He said, "For the s of twenty,	6288
	18:32	He answered, "For the s of ten,	6288

Ge	26:24	of your descendants for the s of	6288
Ex	18: 8	and the Egyptians for Israel's s	128+6584
Lev	26:45	But for their s I will remember	4200
Nu	11:29	Moses replied, "Are you jealous for my s?	4200
Jos	23: 3	to all these nations for your s;	4946+7156
1Sa	12:22	For the s of his great name the LORD will	6288
2Sa	5:12	exalted his kingdom for the s of his people	6288
	7:21	For the s of your word and according	6288
	9: 1	I can show kindness for Jonathan's s?"	6288
	9: 7	surely show you kindness for the s of	6288
	18: 5	with the young man Absalom for my s."	4200
	18:12	'Protect the young man Absalom for my s.'	4200
1Ki	11:12	for the s of David your father,	5100
	11:13	will give him one tribe for the s of David	5100
	11:13	and for the s of Jerusalem,	5100
	11:32	But for the s of my servant David and	5100
	11:34	of his life for the s of David my servant,	5100
	15: 4	for David's s the LORD his God gave him	5100
2Ki	8:19	for the s of his servant David,	5100
	19:34	for my s and for the sake of David	5100
	19:34	and for the s of David my servant."	5100
	20: 6	I will defend this city for my s and for	5100
	20: 6	and for the s of my servant David.' "	5100
1Ch	17: 19	highly exalted for the s of his people Israel.	6288
	16:21	for their s he rebuked kings:	6584
	17:19	For the s of your servant and according	6288
Ne	10:28	from the neighboring peoples for the s	448
Job	18: 4	is the earth to be abandoned for your s?	5100
Ps	23: 3	in paths of righteousness for his name's s.	5100
	25:11	For the s of your name, O LORD,	5100
	31: 3	for the s of your name lead and guide me.	5100
	44:22	Yet for your s we face death all day long;	6584
	69: 7	For I endure scorn for your s,	6584
	79: 9	and forgive our sins for your name's s!	5100
	105:14	for their s he rebuked kings:	6584
	106: 8	Yet he saved them for his name's s,	5100
	106:45	for their s he remembered his covenant	4200
	109:21	deal well with me for your name's s;	5100
	122: 8	For the s of my brothers and friends,	5100
	122: 9	For the s of the house of the LORD our God	5100
	132:10	For the s of David your servant,	6288
	143:11	For your name's s, O LORD,	5100
Isa	37:35	for my s and for the sake of David	5100
	37:35	and for the s of David my servant!"	5100
	42:21	the LORD for the s of his righteousness	5100
	43:14	"For your s I will send to Babylon	5100
	43:25	blots out your transgressions, for my own s,	5100
	45: 4	For the s of Jacob my servant,	5100
	48: 9	For my own name's s I delay my wrath;	5100
	48: 9	the s of my praise I hold it back from you,	NIH
	48:11	For my own s, for my own sake, I do this.	5100
	48:11	For my own sake, for my own, I do this.	5100
	62: 1	For Zion's s I will not keep silent,	5100
	62: 1	for Jerusalem's s I will not remain quiet,	5100
	63:17	Return for the s of your servants,	5100
Jer	14: 7	do something for the s of your name.	5100
	14:21	For the s of your name do not despise us;	5100
	15:15	think of how I suffer reproach for your s.	6584
Eze	20: 9	But for the s of my name I did what would	5100
	20:14	But for the s of my name I did what would	5100
	20:22	and for the s of my name I did what would	5100
	20:44	when I deal with you for my name's s and	5100
	36:22	It is not for your s, O house of Israel,	5100
	36:22	but for the s of my holy name,	4200
	36:32	to know that I am not doing this for your s,	5100
Da	9:17	For your s, O Lord, look with favor	5100
	9:19	For your s, O my God, do not delay,	5100
Mt	10:39	whoever loses his life for my s will find it.	1915
	15: 3	of God for the s of your tradition?	1328
	15: 6	the word of God for the s of your tradition.	1328
	19:29	or children or fields for my s will receive	1915
	24:22	for the s of the elect those days will	1328
Mk	13:20	But for the s of the elect,	1328
Lk	18:29	or children for the s of the kingdom of God	1915
Jn	11:15	and for your s I am glad I was not there,	1328
Ro	1: 5	Through him and for his name's s,	5642
	8:36	"For your s we face death all day long;	1915
	9: 3	from Christ for the s of my brothers,	5642
	14:20	not destroy the work of God for the s of	1915
1Co	9:23	I do all this for the s of the gospel,	1328
	10:28	both for the s of the man who told you and	1328
	10:28	man who told you and for conscience' s—	NIG
2Co	2:10	in the sight of Christ for your s,	1328
	4: 5	and ourselves as your servants for Jesus' s.	1328
	4:11	being given over to death for Jesus' s,	1328
	5:13	it is for the s of God;	AIT
	12:10	That is why, for Christ's s, I delight in	5642
Eph	3: 1	of Christ Jesus for the s of you Gentiles—	5642
Php	3: 7	now consider loss for the s of Christ.	1328
	3: 8	for whose s I have lost all things.	1328
Col	1:24	for the s of his body, which is the church.	5642
1Th	1: 5	how we lived among you for your s.	1328
2Ti	2:10	Therefore I endure everything for the s of	1328
Tit	1:11	and that for the s of dishonest gain.	5920
Heb	11:26	He regarded disgrace for the s of Christ as	AIT
1Pe	1:20	was revealed in these last times for your s.	1328
	2:13	Submit yourselves for the Lord's s	1328
3Jn	1: 7	It was for the s of the Name	5642

SAKES (1) [SAKE]

2Co	8: 9	yet for your s he became poor,	1328

SAKIA (1)

1Ch	8:10	Jeuz, S and Mirmah. These were his sons,	8499

SALAH (KJV) See SHELAH

SALAMIS (1)
Ac 13: 5 When they arrived at S,   *4887*

SALATHIEL (KJV) See SHEALTIEL

SALCAH, SALCHAH (KJV) See
SALECAH

SALE (4) [SELL]
Lev 25:29 of redemption a full year after its s.   4928
Dt 18: 8 though he has received **money from** the s   4928
28:68 **offer yourselves for** s to your enemies   4835
Ps 44:12 gaining nothing from their s.   4697

SALECAH (4)
Dt 3:10 and all Bashan as far as S and Edrei,   6146
Jos 12: 5 He ruled over Mount Hermon, S,   6146
13:11 and all Bashan as far as S—   6146
1Ch 5:11 next to them in Bashan, as far as S: 6146

SALEM (4)
Ge 14:18 king of S brought out bread and wine.   8970
Ps 76: 2 His tent is in S, his dwelling place in Zion.   8970
Heb 7: 1 This Melchizedek was king of S and priest   4889
7: 2 "king of S" means "king of peace."   4889

SALES (1) [SELL]
Ac 4:34 brought the money *from* the s   *4405*

SALIM (1)
Jn 3:23 John also was baptizing at Aenon near S,   4890

SALIVA (2)
1Sa 21:13 of the gate and letting s run down his beard.   8202
Jn 9: 6 made some mud with the s,   *4770*

SALLAI (1)
Ne 11: 8 and his followers, Gabbai and S—928 men.   6144

SALLU (3) [SALLU'S]
1Ch 9: 7 S son of Meshullam, the son of Hodaviah,   6132
Ne 11: 7 S son of Meshullam, the son of Joed,   6132
12: 7 S, Amok, Hilkiah   6139

SALLU'S (1) [SALLU]
Ne 12:20 of S, Kallai; of Amok's, Eber;   6139

SALMA (2)
1Ch 2:51 S the father of Bethlehem,   8514
2:54 The descendants of S: 8514

SALMON (7)
Ru 4:20 Nahshon the father of S,   8517
4:21 S the father of Boaz,   8517
1Ch 2:11 Nahshon was the father of S,   8517
2:11 S the father of Boaz,   8517
Mt 1: 4 Nahshon the father of S,   *4891*
1: 5 S the father of Boaz,   *4891*
Lk 3:32 the son *of* S, the son of Nahshon,   *4885*

SALMONE (1)
Ac 27: 7 we sailed to the lee of Crete, opposite S.   *4892*

SALOME (2)
Mk 15:40 of James the younger and of Joses, and S.   *4897*
16: 1 and S bought spices so that they might go   *4897*

SALT (46) [SALTED, SALTINESS, SALTY]
Ge 14: 3 in the Valley of Siddim (the S Sea).   4875
19:26 and she became a pillar of s.   4875
Lev 2:13 Season all your grain offerings with s.   4875
2:13 the s of the covenant of your God out   4875
2:13 add s to all your offerings.   4875
Nu 18:19 It is an everlasting covenant of s before   4875
34: 3 from the end of the S Sea,   4875
34:12 along the Jordan and end at the S Sea.   4875
Dt 3:17 to the Sea of the Arabah (the S Sea),   4875
29:23 The whole land will be a burning waste of s   4875
Jos 3:16 (the S Sea) was completely cut off.   4875
12: 3 to the Sea of the Arabah (the S Sea),   4875
15: 2 the bay at the southern end of the S Sea,   4875
15: 5 the S Sea as far as the mouth of the Jordan.   4875
15:62 the City of S and En Gedi—   4875
18:19 at the northern bay of the S Sea,   4875
Jdg 9:45 he destroyed the city and scattered s over it.   4875
2Sa 8:13 in the Valley of S.   4875
2Ki 2:20 he said, "and put s in it."   4875
2:21 and threw the s into it, saying, "This is what   4875
14: 7 the Valley of S and captured Sela in battle,   4875
1Ch 18:12 in the Valley of S.   4875
2Ch 13: 5 his descendants forever by a covenant of s?   4875
25:11 and led his army to the Valley of S,   4875
Ezr 6: 9 and wheat, s, wine and oil,   10420

Ezr 7:22 and s without limit.   10420
Job 6: 6 Is tasteless food eaten without s,   4875
30: 4 In the brush they gathered s **herbs**,   4865
39: 6 the s **flats** as his habitat.   4877
Ps 60: T in the Valley of S.   4875
107:34 and fruitful land into a s **waste**,   4877
Jer 17: 6 in a s land where no one lives.   4877
48: 9 Put s on Moab, for she will be laid waste;   7490
Eze 16: 4 nor **were you rubbed with** s or   4873+4873
43:24 to sprinkle s on them and sacrifice them as   4875
47: 9 and makes the s water fresh;   NIH
47:11 they will be left for s.   4875
Zep 2: 9 a place of weeds and s pits,   4875
Mt 5:13 "You are the s of the earth.   229
5:13 But if the s loses its saltiness,   229
Mk 9:50 "S is good, but if it loses its saltiness,   229
9:50 Have s in yourselves,   229
Lk 14:34 "S is good, but if it loses its saltiness,   229
Col 4: 6 be always full of grace, seasoned *with* s,   229
Jas 3:11 Can both fresh water and s **water** flow from   *4395*
3:12 Neither can a s **spring** produce fresh water.   266

SALTED (2) [SALT]
Ex 30:35 *It is to* **be** s and pure and sacred.   4873
Mk 9:49 Everyone *will be* s with fire.   245

SALTINESS (3) [SALT]
Mt 5:13 But if the salt **loses its** s,   *3701*
Mk 9:50 "Salt is good, but if it loses its s,   *383*
Lk 14:34 "Salt is good, but if it **loses its** s,   *3701*

SALTY (3) [SALT]
Mt 5:13 how *can it be* **made** s again?   245
Mk 9:50 how *can you* **make** it s again?   789
Lk 14:34 how *can it be* **made** s again?   789

SALU (1)
Nu 25:14 the Midianite woman was Zimri son of S,   6140

SALUTATION, SALUTATIONS (KJV)
See GREETED, GREETING

SALUTE, SALUTED, SALUTETH (KJV)
See CALL, GREET, GREETED,
GREETINGS, GREETS, PAY RESPECTS

SALVATION (122) [SAVE]
Ex 15: 2 he has become my s.   3802
2Sa 22: 3 my shield and the horn of my s.   3829
23: 5 Will he not bring to fruition my s   3829
1Ch 16:23 proclaim his s day after day.   3802
2Ch 6:41 O Lord God, be clothed with s,   9591
Ps 9:14 of Zion and there rejoice in your s.   3802
13: 5 my heart rejoices in your s.   3802
14: 7 that s for Israel would come out of Zion!   3802
18: 2 He is my shield and the horn of my s,   3829
27: 1 The Lord is my light and my s—   3829
28: 8 a fortress of s for his anointed one.   3802
35: 3 Say to my soul, "I am your s."   3802
35: 9 in the Lord and delight in his s.   3802
37:39 The s of the righteous comes from   9591
40:10 I speak of your faithfulness and s.   9591
40:16 may those who love your s always say,   9591
50:23 so that I may show him the s of God."   3829
51:12 of your s and grant me a willing spirit,   3829
53: 6 that s for Israel would come out of Zion!   3802
62: 1 my s comes from him.   3802
62: 2 He alone is my rock and my s;   3802
62: 6 He alone is my rock and my s;   3802
62: 7 My s and my honor depend on God;   3829
67: 2 your s among all nations.   3802
69:13 O God, answer me with your sure s.   3829
69:27 do not let them share in your s.   7407
69:29 may your s, O God, protect me.   3802
70: 4 may those who love your s always say,   3802
71:15 of your s all day long,   9591
74:12 you bring s upon the earth.   3802
85: 7 O Lord, and grant us your s.   3829
85: 9 Surely his s is near those who fear him,   3829
91:16 and show him my s."   3802
95: 1 let us shout aloud to the Rock of our s.   3829
96: 2 proclaim his s day after day.   3802
98: 1 and his holy arm *have* **worked** s for him.   3828
98: 2 The Lord has made his s known   3802
98: 3 of the earth have seen the s of our God.   3802
116:13 of s and call on the name of the Lord.   3802
118:14 he has become my s.   3802
118:21 you have become my s.   3802
119:41 your s according to your promise;   9591
119:81 My soul faints with longing for your s,   9591
119:123 My eyes fail, looking for your s,   3802
119:155 S is far from the wicked,   3802
119:166 I wait for your s, O Lord,   3802
119:174 I long for your s, O Lord,   3802
132:16 I will clothe her priests with s,   3829
149: 4 he crowns the humble with s.   3802
Isa 12: 2 God is my s; I will trust and not be afraid.   3802
12: 2 and my song; he has become my s."   3802
12: 3 you will draw water from the wells of s.   3802
25: 9 let us rejoice and be glad in his s."   3802
26: 1 God makes s its walls and ramparts.   3802

Isa 26:18 We have not brought s to the earth;   3802
30:15 "In repentance and rest *is* your s,   3828
33: 2 our s in time of distress.   3802
33: 6 rich store of s and wisdom and knowledge;   3802
45: 8 Let the earth open wide, let s spring up,   3829
45:17 by the Lord with an everlasting s;   9591
46:13 and my s will not be delayed.   9591
46:13 I will grant s to Zion, my splendor to Israel.   9591
49: 6 that you may bring my s to the ends of the   3802
49: 8 and in the day of s I will help you;   3802
51: 5 my s is on the way,   3829
51: 6 But my s will last forever,   3802
51: 8 my s through all generations."   3802
52: 7 who bring good tidings, who proclaim s,   3802
52:10 and all the ends of the earth will see the s   3802
56: 1 and do what is right, for my s is close   3802
59:16 so his own arm **worked** s for him,   3828
59:17 and the helmet of s on his head;   3802
60:18 but you will call your walls S   3802
61:10 with garments of s and arrayed me in a robe   3829
62: 1 her s like a blazing torch.   3802
63: 5 so my own arm **worked** s for me,   3828
Jer 3:23 in the Lord our God is the s *of* Israel.   9591
La 3:26 to wait quietly for the s of the Lord.   9591
Jnh 2: 9 S comes from the Lord."   3802
Zec 9: 9 king comes to you, righteous and **having** s,   3828
Lk 1:69 of s for us in the house of his servant David   5401
1:71 s from our enemies and from the hand   5401
1:77 the knowledge of s through the forgiveness   5401
2:30 For my eyes have seen your s,   5403
3: 6 And all mankind will see God's s.' "   5403
19: 9 "Today s has come to this house,   5401
Jn 4:22 for s is from the Jews.   5401
Ac 4:12 S is found in no one else,   5401
13:26 to us that this message of s has been sent.   5401
13:47 you may bring s to the ends of the earth.' "   5401
28:28 that God's s has been sent to the Gentiles,   5403
Ro 1:16 of God for the s of everyone who believes: 5401
11:11 s has come to the Gentiles   5401
13:11 because our s is nearer now than   5401
2Co 1: 6 it is for your comfort and s;   5401
6: 2 and in the day of s I helped you."   5401
6: 2 now is the day of s.   5401
7:10 that leads to s and leaves no regret,   5401
Eph 1:13 the word of truth, the gospel *of* your s.   5401
6:17 the helmet *of* s and the sword of the Spirit,   5403
Php 2:12 to work out your s with fear and trembling,   5401
1Th 5: 8 and the hope *of* s as a helmet.   5401
5: 9 to receive s through our Lord Jesus Christ.   5401
2Ti 2:10 that they too may obtain the s that is   5401
3:15 which are able to make you wise for s   5401
Tit 2:11 the grace of God that brings s has appeared   5403
Heb 1:14 to serve those who will inherit s?   5401
2: 3 if we ignore such a great s?   5401
2: 3 This s, which was first announced by   NIG
2:10 should make the author of their s perfect   5401
5: 9 the source *of* eternal s for all who obey him   5401
6: 9 things that accompany s.   5401
9:28 to bring s to those who are waiting for him.   5401
1Pe 1: 5 by God's power until the coming of the s   5401
1: 9 the goal of your faith, the s of your souls.   5401
1:10 Concerning this s, the prophets,   5401
2: 2 so that by it you may grow up in your s,   5401
2Pe 3:15 in mind that our Lord's patience means s,   5401
Jude 1: 3 to write to you about the s we share,   5401
Rev 7:10 "S belongs to our God,   5401
12:10 "Now have come the s and the power and   5401
19: 1 S and glory and power belong to our God,   5401

SALVE (1)
Rev 3:18 and s to put on your eyes, so you can see.   *3141*

SAMARIA (119) [SAMARITAN, SAMARITANS]
1Ki 13:32 in the towns of S will certainly come true."   9076
16:24 of S from Shemer for two talents of silver   9076
16:24 calling it S, after Shemer,   9076
16:28 with his fathers and was buried in S.   9076
16:29 in S over Israel twenty-two years.   9076
16:32 in the temple of Baal that he built in S.   9076
18: 2 Now the famine was severe in S,   9076
20: 1 he went up and besieged S and attacked it.   9076
20:10 if enough dust remains in S to give each   9076
20:17 who reported, "Men are advancing from S."   9076
20:34 as my father did in S."   9076
20:43 the king of Israel went to his palace in S   9076
21: 1 close to the palace of Ahab king of S.   9076
21:18 Ahab king of Israel, who rules in S.   9076
22:10 by the entrance of the gate of S,   9076
22:37 So the king died and was brought to S,   9076
22:38 a pool in S (where the prostitutes bathed),   9076
22:51 of Ahab became king of Israel in S in   9076
2Ki 1: 2 of his upper room in S and injured himself.   9076
1: 3 and meet the messengers of the king of S   9076
2:25 and from there returned to S.   9076
3: 1 of Ahab became king of Israel in S in   9076
3: 6 So at that time King Joram set out from S   9076
5: 3 would see the prophet who is in S!   9076
6:19 And he led them to S.   9076
6:20 and there they were, inside S.   9076
6:24 marched up and laid siege to S.   9076
7: 1 of barley for a shekel at the gate of S."   9076
7:18 of barley for a shekel at the gate of S."   9076
10: 1 in S seventy sons of the house of Ahab.   9076
10: 1 So Jehu wrote letters and sent them to S: 9076

2Ki	10:12	Jehu then set out and went toward S. 9076
	10:17	When Jehu came to S, he killed all who 9076
	10:35	with his fathers and was buried in S. 9076
	10:36	over Israel in S was twenty-eight years. 9076
	13: 1	of Jehu became king of Israel in S, 9076
	13: 6	the Asherah pole remained standing in S. 9076
	13: 9	with his fathers and was buried in S. 9076
	13:10	of Jehoahaz became king of Israel in S 9076
	13:13	Jehoash was buried in S with the kings 9076
	14:14	He also took hostages and returned to S. 9076
	14:16	with his fathers and was buried in S with 9076
	14:23	of Jehoash king of Israel became king in S, 9076
	15: 8	of Jeroboam became king of Israel in S, 9076
	15:13	and he reigned in S one month. 9076
	15:14	of Gadi went from Tirzah up to S. 9076
	15:14	He attacked Shallum son of Jabesh in S, 9076
	15:17	and he reigned in S ten years. 9076
	15:23	of Menahem became king of Israel in S, 9076
	15:25	in the citadel of the royal palace at S. 9076
	15:27	of Remaliah became king of Israel in S, 9076
	17: 1	of Elah became king of Israel in S, 9076
	17: 5	against S and laid siege to it for three years. 9076
	17: 6	of Assyria captured S and deported 9076
	17:24	in the towns of S to replace the Israelites. 9076
	17:24	They took over S and lived in its towns. 9076
	17:26	in the towns of S do not know what the god 9076
	17:27	the priests you took captive from S go back 9004S
	17:28	exiled from S came to live in Bethel 9076
	17:29	up in the shrines the people of S had made 9085
	18: 9	of Assyria marched against S and laid siege 9076
	18:10	S was captured in Hezekiah's sixth year, 9076
	18:34	Have they rescued S from my hand? 9076
	21:13	against S and the plumb line used against 9076
	23:18	of the prophet who had come from S. 9076
	23:19	in the towns of S that had provoked 9076
2Ch	18: 2	he went down to visit Ahab in S. 9076
	18: 9	by the entrance to the gate of S, 9076
	22: 9	while he was hiding in S. 9076
	25:13	in the war raided Judean towns from S 9076
	25:24	and returned to S. 9076
	28: 8	which they carried back to S. 9076
	28: 9	to meet the army when it returned to S 9076
	28:15	the City of Palms, and returned to S. 9076
Ezr	4:10	and settled in the city of S and elsewhere 10726
	4:17	of the rest of their associates living in S 10726
Ne	4: 2	of his associates and the army of S, 9076
Isa	7: 9	The head of Ephraim is S, 9076
	7: 9	and the head of S is only Remaliah's son. 9076
	8: 4	and the plunder of S will be carried off by 9076
	9: 9	Ephraim and the inhabitants of S— 9076
	10: 9	and S like Damascus? 9076
	10:10	images excelled those of Jerusalem and S— 9076
	10:11	as I dealt with S and her idols?' " 9076
	36:19	Have they rescued S from my hand? 9076
Jer	23:13	the prophets of S I saw this repulsive thing: 9076
	31: 5	you will plant vineyards on the hills of S; 9076
	41: 5	and S, bringing grain offerings and incense 9076
Eze	16:46	Your older sister was S, 9076
	16:51	S did not commit half the sins you did. 9076
	16:53	of Sodom and her daughters and of S 9076
	16:55	and S with her daughters, will return 9076
	23: 4	Oholah is S, and Oholibah is Jerusalem. 9076
	23:33	the cup of your sister S. 9076
Hos	7: 1	and the crimes of S revealed. 9076
	8: 5	Throw out your calf-idol, O S! 9076
	8: 6	It will be broken in pieces, that calf of S. 9076
	10: 5	in S fear for the calf-idol of Beth Aven. 9076
	10: 7	S and its king will float away like a twig on 9076
	13:16	The people of S must bear their guilt, 9076
Am	3: 9	yourselves on the mountains of S; 9076
	3:12	those who sit in S on the edge of their beds 9076
	4: 1	you cows of Bashan on Mount S, 9076
	6: 1	and to you who feel secure on Mount S, 9076
	8:14	They who swear by the shame of S, or say, 9076
Ob	1:19	the fields of Ephraim and S, 9076
Mic	1: 1	the vision he saw concerning S? 9076
	1: 5	What is Jacob's transgression? Is it not S? 9076
	1: 6	"Therefore I will make S a heap of rubble, 9076
Lk	17:11	Jesus traveled along the border between S 4899
Jn	4: 4	Now he had to go through S. 4899
	4: 5	So he came to a town in S called Sychar, 4899
Ac	1: 8	in Jerusalem, and in all Judea and S, 4899
	8: 1	throughout Judea and S, 4899
	8: 5	a city in S and proclaimed the Christ there. 4899
	8: 9	in the city and amazed all the people of S. 4899
	8:14	in Jerusalem heard that S had accepted 4899
	9:31	Galilee and S enjoyed a time of peace. 4899
	15: 3	as they traveled through Phoenicia and S, 4899

SAMARITAN (8) [SAMARIA]

Lk	9:52	into a S village to get things ready for him; 4901
	10:33	S, as he traveled, came where the man was; 4901
	17:16	and thanked him—and he was a S. 4901
Jn	4: 7	When a S woman came to draw water, 4899
	4: 9	The S woman said to him, 4902
	4: 9	"You are a Jew and I am a S woman. 4902
	8:48	"Aren't we right in saying that you are a S 4901
Ac	8:25	preaching the gospel in many S villages. 4901

SAMARITANS (5) [SAMARIA]

Mt	10: 5	The Gentiles or enter any town of the S. 4901
Jn	4: 9	(For Jews do not associate with S.) 4901
	4:22	You S worship what you do not know; NIG
	4:39	of the S from that town believed in him 4901
	4:40	So when the S came to him, 4901

SAME (267)

Ge	11: 6	the s language they have begun to do this, 285
	17:26	both circumcised on that s day. 6795
	21:23	as an alien the s kindness I have shown 3869
	26:12	the s year reaped a hundredfold, 2085
	26:18	the s names his father had given them. 3869
	30:35	That s day he removed all the male goats 2085
	32:19	the s thing to Esau when you meet him. 3869
	40: 3	in the s prison where Joseph was confined. NIH
	40: 5	had a dream the s night, 285
	41:11	Each of us had a dream the s night, 285
	41:25	"The dreams of Pharaoh are one and the s. 285
	41:26	it is one and the s dream. 285
Ex	5: 6	That s day Pharaoh gave this order to 2085
	5: 8	make the s number of bricks as before; 889
	6:26	It was this s Aaron and Moses to whom 2085
	6:27	It was the s Moses and Aaron. 2085
	7:11	also did the s things by their secret arts; 4027
	7:22	But the Egyptian magicians did the s things 4027
	8: 7	But the magicians did the s things 4027
	12: 8	That s night they are to eat the meat roasted 2296
	12:12	"On that s night I will pass through Egypt 2296
	12:49	The s law applies to the native-born and to 285
	22:30	Do the s with your cattle and your sheep. 4027
	23:11	Do the s with your vineyard 4027
	25:33	the s for all six branches extending from 4027
	26: 2	All the curtains are to be the s size— 285
	26: 3	and do the s with the other five. 2489S
	26: 4	the s with the end curtain in the other set. 4027
	26: 8	All eleven curtains are to be the s size— 285
	29:41	the s grain offering and its drink offering as 3869
	30:32	and do not make any oil with the s formula. 4017
	34:16	lead your sons to do the s. 339+466+2177+2388S
	36: 9	All the curtains were the s size— 285
	36:10	and did the s with the other 285+285+448+2489S
	36:11	and the s was done with the end curtain in 4027
	36:15	All eleven curtains were the s size— 285
	37:19	the s for all six branches extending from 4027
Lev	7: 7	" 'The s law applies to the sin offering 285
	14:28	to put on the s places he put the blood of NIH
	16:16	He is to do the s for the Tent of Meeting, 4027
	18: 9	born in the s home or elsewhere. 1074+4580
	22:28	a cow or a sheep and its young on the s day. 285
	22:30	It must be eaten that s day; 2085
	23:21	On that s day you are to proclaim 6795
	24:22	You are to have the s law for the alien and 285
Nu	2:17	That s day he is to consecrate his head. 4027
	6:11	they came to Moses and Aaron that s day 2085
	9: 6	they came to Moses and Aaron that s day 2085
	9:14	You must have the s regulations for 285
	10: 7	but not with the s. signal." AIT
	13:33	and we looked the s to. 4027
	15:15	the s rules for you and for the alien living 285
	15:15	the alien shall be the s before the LORD: 3869
	15:16	The s laws and regulations will apply both 285
	15:29	One and the s law applies to everyone 285
	26: 9	The s Dathan and Abiram were 2085
	28: 8	along with the s kind of grain offering 3869
Dt	2:22	the s for the descendants of Esau, 889+3869
	3:21	the s to all the kingdoms over there 4027
	7:19	The LORD your God will do the s to all 4027
	12:30	We will do the s." 4027
	15:17	Do the s for your maidservant. 4027
	21:23	Be sure to bury him that s day, 2085
	22: 3	Do the s if you find your brother's donkey 4027
	27:11	the s day Moses commanded the people: 2085
	32:48	On that s day the LORD told Moses, 6795
Jos	6:15	around the city seven times in the s manner, 2296
	7: 6	The elders of Israel did the s, NIH
	10:35	They captured it that s day and put it to 2085
Jdg	6:25	That s night the LORD said to him, 2085
	8: 8	to Peniel and made the s request of them, 3869
1Sa	2:34	they will both die on the s day. 285
	4:12	That s day a Benjamite ran from 2085
	6: 4	because the s plague has struck both you 285
	6:16	and then returned that s day to Ekron. 2085
	12:18	and that s day the LORD sent thunder 2085
	17:30	and brought up the s matter, 3869
	28:25	That s night they got up and left. 2085
	30:24	to be the s as that of him who went down to 3869
	31: 6	and all his men died together that s day. 2085
2Sa	2: 6	the s favor because you have done this. 2296
	16: 5	from the s clan as Saul's family came out AIT
1Ki	3:17	This woman and I live in the s house. 285
	6:33	In the s way he made four-sided jambs 4027
	7:18	He did the s for each capital. 4027
	7:37	in the s molds and were identical in size 285
	8:64	On that s day the king consecrated 2085
	11: 8	He did the s for all his foreign wives, 4027
	13: 3	That s day the man of God gave a sign: 2085
	22:12	other prophets were prophesying the s thing. 4027
2Ki	4:17	about that s time she gave birth to a son, 2296
	8:22	Libnah revolted at the s time. 2085
1Ch	23:30	They were to do the s in the evening 4027
	24:31	were treated the s as those of the 4200+6645
2Ch	16:10	At the s time Asa brutally oppressed some 2085
	18:11	other prophets were prophesying the s thing. 4027
	21:10	Libnah revolted at the s time, 2085
	27: 5	The Ammonites brought him the s amount 2296S
	35:12	They did the s with the cattle. 4027
Ne	5: 5	Although we are of the s flesh and blood as 3869
	6: 4	Four times they sent me the s message, 3869
	6: 5	and each time I gave them the s answer. 3869
	6: 5	sent his aide to me with the s message, 3869
	9: 1	On the twenty-fourth day of the s month, 2296
	13:18	Didn't your forefathers do the s things, 3907

Est	1:18	to all the king's nobles in the s way. NIH
	8: 1	That s day King Xerxes gave Queen Esther 2085
	9:11	of Susa was reported to the king that s day. 2085
Job	9:22	It is all the s; that is why I say, 285
	31:15	the s one form us both within our mothers? 285
Ps	102:27	But you remain the s, 285
Ecc	2:14	that the s fate overtakes them both. 285
	3:19	the s fate awaits them both: 285
	3:19	All have the s breath; 285
	3:20	All go to the s place; 285
	6: 6	Do not all go to the s place? 285
	9: 3	The s destiny overtakes all. 285
Isa	24: 2	it will be the s for priest as for people, 3869
Jer	13: 9	'In the s way I will ruin the pride of Judah 3970
	14:15	Those s prophets will perish by sword 2156
	26:20	s things against this land as 3869
	27:12	the s message to Zedekiah king of Judah. 3869
	28: 1	In the fifth month of that s year, 2085
	28:11	'In the s way will I break the yoke 3970
	28:17	In the seventh month of that s year, 2085
Eze	4: 5	s number of days as the years of their sin. 4200
	10:22	the s appearance as those I had seen by NIH
	18:24	and does the s detestable things 3869
	21:19	both starting from the s country. 285
	23: 2	daughters of the s mother. 285
	23:13	both went the s way. 285
	23:38	At that s time they defiled my sanctuary 2085
	40:10	the three had the s measurements, 285
	40:10	on each side had the s measurements. 285
	40:21	and its portico had the s measurements as 3869
	40:22	the s measurements as those of 3869
	40:24	and they had the s measurements as 3869
	40:28	it had the s measurements as the others. 3869
	40:29	and its portico had the s measurements as 3869
	40:32	it had the s measurements as the others. 3869
	40:33	and its portico had the s measurements as 3869
	40:35	It had the s measurements as the others, 3869
	42:11	they had the s length and width, 3869
	44: 3	of the gateway and go out the s way." 2257S
	45:11	The ephah and the bath are to be the s size, 285
	45:20	to do the s on the seventh day of the month 4027
	45:25	to make the s provision for sin offerings, 3869
	46: 8	and he is to come out the s way. 2257S
	46:22	the courts in the four corners was the s size. 285
Da	2:35	the gold were broken to pieces at the s time 10248
	4:36	At the s time that my sanity was restored, 10192S
	8:22	but will not have the s power, 2257S
	11:27	will sit at the s table and lie to each other, 285
Am	2: 7	Father and son use the s girl AIT
	9: 7	Israelites the s to me as the Cushites? 3869
Zec	6:10	Go the s day to the house of Josiah son 2085
Mt	5:12	for in the s way they persecuted 4048
	5:16	In the s way, let your light shine 4048
	5:19	and teaches others to do the s will 4048
	7: 2	For in the s way you judge others, 3210S
	13: 1	That s day Jesus went out of the house 1697
	17:12	In the s way the Son of Man is going 2779+4048
	18:14	In the s way your Father in heaven is 4048
	20: 5	and the ninth hour and did the s thing. 6058
	20:14	the man who was hired last the s as 2779+6055
	21:30	to the other son and said the s thing. 6058
	21:36	and the tenants treated them the s way. 6058
	22:23	That s day the Sadducees, 1697
	23:28	In the s way, on the outside you appear 4048
	26:35	And all the other disciples said the s. 3931
	26:44	saying the s thing. 899
	27:41	In the s way the chief priests, 3931
	27:44	In the s way the robbers who were crucified 899
Mk	12:21	It was the s with the third. 6058
	14:31	And all the others said the s. 6058
	14:39	and prayed the s thing. 899
	15:31	In the s way the chief priests and 3931
Lk	3:11	and the one who has food should do the s." 3931
	10:31	to be going down the s road, 1697
	14:33	In the s way, any of you who does not 4048
	15: 7	in the s way there will be more rejoicing 4048
	15:10	In the s way, I tell you, there is rejoicing 4048
	17:28	"It was the s in the days of Lot. 2777+3931
	20:31	and in the s way the seven died, 6058
	22:20	In the s way, after supper he took the cup, 6058
	23:40	"since you are under the s sentence? 899
	24:13	Now that s day two of them were going to 899
Jn	6:11	He did the s with the fish. 3931
	9: 8	the s man who used to sit and beg?" NIG
	11: 2	the s one who poured perfume on the Lord NIG
	12:42	Yet at the s time many even among 3940
	21:13	and did the s with the fish. 3931
Ac	1:11	This s Jesus, who has been taken from you 4047
	1:11	will come back in the s way you have seen him go 4005+5573
	3:10	they recognized him as the s man who used 899
	7:35	this Moses whom they rejected with NIG
	11:17	if God gave them the s gift as he gave us, 2698
	24:15	I have the s hope in God as these men 2779+4005
	24:26	At the s time he was hoping that Paul 275
	27:40	in the sea and at the s time untied the ropes 275
Ro	1:27	In the s way the men also abandoned 3931
	2: 1	you who pass judgment do the s things, 899
	2: 3	judgment on them and yet do the s things, 899
	3:30	and the uncircumcised through that s faith. 3836
	4: 6	David says the s thing when he 2749+2779
	6:11	In the s way, count yourselves dead to sin 4048
	8:26	In the s way, the Spirit helps us 6058
	9:10	Rebekah's children had one and the s father, NIG
	9:21	have the right to make out of the s lump 899
	10:12	the s Lord is Lord of all and richly blesses 899

Ro 12: 4 members do not all have the s function,   899
1Co 2:11 **In the s way** no one knows the thoughts of
           God except the Spirit   2779+4048
     7: 4 **In the s way,** the husband's body does not   3931
     9: 8 Doesn't the Law say **the s thing?**   4047
     9:14 **In the s way,** the Lord has commanded   4048
    10: 3 They all ate the s spiritual food   899
    10: 4 and drank the s spiritual drink;   899
    11:25 **In the s way,** after supper he took the cup, 6058
    12: 4 different kinds of gifts, but the s Spirit.   899
    12: 5 different kinds of service, but the s Lord.   899
    12: 6 but the s God works all of them in all men.   899
    12: 8 of knowledge by means of the s Spirit,   899
    12: 9 to another faith by the s Spirit,   899
    12:11 the work of one and the s Spirit,   899
    15: 6 five hundred of the brothers **at the s time,** 2384
    15:39 All flesh is not the s: 899
2Co 1: 6 endurance *of* the s sufferings we suffer.   899
     1:17 so that in the s breath I say,   NIG
     3:14 for to this day the s veil remains when   899
     4:13 With that s spirit of faith we also believe   899
     8:16 into the heart of Titus the s concern I have   899
    12:18 act *in* the s spirit and follow the same   899
    12:18 in the same spirit and **follow the s course?** 2717
Gal 4:29 **It is the s** now.   2779+4048
Eph 5:28 **In this s way,** husbands ought to love   2779+4048
     6: 9 And masters, treat your slaves in the **s way.** 899
Php 1:30 through the s struggle you saw I had,   899
     2: 2 being like-minded, having the s love,   899
     2: 5 Your attitude should be the s as that   NIG
     3: 1 It is no trouble for me to write the **s things** 899
1Th 2:14 the s *things* those churches suffered from   899
1Ti 3: 6 and fall under the s judgment as the devil.   NIG
     3:11 **In the s way,** their wives are to be worthy   6058
     5:25 **In the s way,** good deeds are obvious,   6058
Heb 1:12 But you remain the s,   899
     2:11 who are made holy are of **the s family.**   1651
     6:11 to show this s diligence to the very end,   899
     9:21 **In the s way,** he sprinkled with the blood   3931
    10: 1 *by* the s sacrifices repeated endlessly year   899
    10:11 again and again he offers the s sacrifices,   899
    11: 9 who were heirs with him *of* the s promise.   899
    13: 8 Jesus Christ is the s yesterday and today   899
Jas 1:11 **In the s way,** the rich man will fade away   4048
     2:17 **In the s way,** faith by itself,   4048
     2:25 **In the s way,** was not even Rahab   3931
     3:10 of the s mouth come praise and cursing.   899
     3:11 and salt water flow from the s spring?   899
1Pe 3: 1 in **the s way** be submissive to your
           husbands   3931
     3: 7 in **the s way** be considerate as you live   3931
     4: 1 arm yourselves also with the s attitude,   899
     4: 4 with them into the s flood of dissipation,   899
     5: 5 in **the s way** be submissive to those   3931
     5: 9 the world are undergoing the s *kind*   899
2Pe 3: 7 *By* the s word these present heavens   899
     3:16 He writes **the s way** in all his letters, 2779+6055
Jude 1: 8 **In the very s way,** these dreamers pollute   3931

SAMGAR (1)

Jer 39: 3 Nergal-Sharezer of S, Nebo-Sarsekim a   6161

SAMGAR-NEBO (KJV) See SAMGAR, NEBO-SARSEKIM

SAMLAH (4)

Ge   36:36 S from Masrekah succeeded him as king.   8528
     36:37 When S died, Shaul from Rehoboth on   8528
1Ch   1:47 S from Masrekah succeeded him as king.   8528
      1:48 When S died, Shaul from Rehoboth on   8528

SAMOS (1)

Ac   20:15 The day after that we crossed over to S,   4904

SAMOTHRACE (1)

Ac   16:11 we put out to sea and sailed straight for S, 4903

SAMPLE (1) [SAMPLED]

Pr   23:30 who go to s bowls of mixed wine.   2983

SAMPLED (1) [SAMPLE]

Jos   9:14 The men of Israel s their provisions but did 4374

SAMSON (37) [SAMSON'S]

Jdg 13:24 gave birth to a boy and named him S.   9088
     14: 1 S went down to Timnah and saw there   9088
     14: 3 But S said to his father, "Get her for me. 9088
     14: 5 S went down to Timnah together   9088
     14:10 And S made a feast there,   9088
     14:12 "Let me tell you a riddle," S said to them. 9088
     14:18 S said to them, "If you had not plowed   NIH
     15: 1 S took a young goat and went   9088
     15: 3 S said to them, "This time I have a right   9088
     15: 6 "S, the Timnite's son-in-law,   9088
     15: 7 S said to them, "Since you've acted like   9088
     15:10 "We have come to take S prisoner,"   9088
     15:11 the cave in the rock of Etam and said to S, 9088
     15:12 S said, "Swear to me that you won't kill me 9088
     15:16 Then S said, "With a donkey's jawbone I
            have made donkeys of them.   9088
     15:19 When S drank, his strength returned   NIH

Jdg 15:20 S led Israel for twenty years in the days of NIH
     16: 1 One day S went to Gaza,   9088
     16: 2 The people of Gaza were told, "S is here!" 9088
     16: 3 But S lay there only until the middle of   9088
     16: 6 So Delilah said to S, "Tell me the secret   9088
     16: 7 S answered her, "If anyone ties me   9088
     16: 9 "S, the Philistines are upon you!"   9088
     16:10 Delilah said to S, "You have made a fool   9088
     16:12 "S, the Philistines are upon you!"   9088
     16:13 Delilah then said to S, "Until now,   9088
     16:14 Again she called to him, "S,   9088
     16:20 "S, the Philistines are upon you!"   9088
     16:23 "Our god has delivered S, our enemy.   9088
     16:25 they shouted, "Bring out S to entertain us." 9088
     16:25 So they called S out of the prison,   9088
     16:26 S said to the servant who held his hand,   9088
     16:27 men and women watching S perform.   9088
     16:28 Then S prayed to the LORD,   9088
     16:29 S reached toward the two central pillars   9088
     16:30 S said, "Let me die with the Philistines!" 9088
Heb 11:32 Barak, S, Jephthah, David, Samuel and   4907

SAMSON'S (3) [SAMSON]

Jdg 14:15 On the fourth day, they said to S wife   9088
     14:16 Then S wife threw herself on him, sobbing, 9088
     14:20 And S wife was given to the friend   9088

SAMUEL (140) [SAMUEL'S]

1Sa 1:20 She named him S, saying,   9017
     2:18 But S was ministering before the LORD—   9017
     2:21 the boy S grew up in the presence of   9017
     2:26 And the boy S continued to grow in stature   9017
     3: 1 The boy S ministered before the LORD   9017
     3: 3 and S was lying down in the temple of   9017
     3: 4 Then the LORD called S.   9017
     3: 4 S answered, "Here I am."   NIH
     3: 6 Again the LORD called, "S!"   9017
     3: 6 And S got up and went to Eli and said,   9017
     3: 7 Now S did not yet know the LORD: 9017
     3: 8 The LORD called S a third time,   9017
     3: 8 and S got up and went to Eli and said,   NIH
     3: 9 So Eli told S, "Go and lie down,   9017
     3: 9 So S went and lay down in his place.   9017
     3:10 calling as at the other times, "S!   9017
     3:10 at the other times, "Samuel! S!   9017
     3:10 Then S said, "Speak, for your servant is   9017
     3:11 And the LORD said to S: 9017
     3:15 S lay down until morning and then opened   9017
     3:16 but Eli called him and said, "S,   9017
     3:16 S answered, "Here I am."   NIH
     3:18 So S told him everything,   9017
     3:19 The LORD was with S as he grew up,   9017
     3:20 to Beersheba recognized that S was attested 9017
     3:21 and there he revealed himself to S   9017
     7: 3 And S said to the whole house of Israel,   9017
     7: 5 Then S said, "Assemble all Israel   9017
     7: 6 And S was leader of Israel at Mizpah.   9017
     7: 8 They said to S, "Do not stop crying out   9017
     7: 9 Then S took a suckling lamb and offered it   9017
     7:10 While S was sacrificing the burnt offering, 9017
     7:12 Then S took a stone and set it up   9017
     7:15 S continued as judge over Israel all   9017
     8: 1 When S grew old, he appointed his sons   9017
     8: 4 of Israel gathered together and came to S   9017
     8: 6 a king to lead us," this displeased S;   9017
     8:10 S told all the words of the LORD to   9017
     8:19 But the people refused to listen to S.   9017
     8:21 When S heard all that the people said,   9017
     8:22 Then S said to the men of Israel,   9017
     9:14 and as they were entering it, there was S,   9017
     9:15 the LORD had revealed this to S: 9017
     9:17 When S caught sight of Saul,   9017
     9:18 Saul approached S in the gateway   9017
     9:19 "I am the seer," S replied.   9017
     9:22 Then S brought Saul and his servant into   9017
     9:23 S said to the cook, "Bring the piece of meat 9017
     9:24 S said, "Here is what has been kept   NIH
     9:24 And Saul dined with S that day.   9017
     9:25 S talked with Saul on the roof of his house. NIH
     9:26 about daybreak and S called to Saul on   9017
     9:26 he and S went outside together.   9017
     9:27 S said to Saul, "Tell the servant to go on   9017
    10: 1 Then S took a flask of oil and poured it   9017
    10: 9 As Saul turned to leave S,   9017
    10:14 not to be found, we went to S."   9017
    10:15 "Tell me what S said to you."   9017
    10:16 not tell his uncle what S had said about   9017
    10:17 S summoned the people of Israel to   9017
    10:20 S brought all the tribes of Israel near   9017
    10:24 S said to all the people,   9017
    10:25 S explained to the people the regulations of 9017
    10:25 Then S dismissed the people,   9017
    11: 7 of anyone who does not follow Saul and S."   9017
    11:12 The people then said to S,   9017
    11:14 Then S said to the people, "Come,   9017
    12: 1 S said to all Israel, "I have listened   9017
    12: 5 S said to them, "The LORD is witness   NIH
    12: 6 Then S said to the people,   9017
    12:18 sent Jerub-Baal, Barak, Jephthah and S,   9017
    12:18 Then S called upon the LORD,   9017
    12:18 people stood in awe of the LORD and of S.   9017
    12:19 The people all said to S,   9017
    12:20 "Do not be afraid," S replied.   9017
    13: 8 He waited seven days, the time set by S;   9017
    13: 8 but S did not come to Gilgal,   9017

1Sa 13:10 S arrived, and Saul went out to greet him. 9017
     13:11 "What have you done?" asked S.   9017
     13:13 "You acted foolishly," S said.   9017
     13:15 Then S left Gilgal and went up to Gibeah   9017
     15: 1 S said to Saul, "I am the one the LORD sent 9017
     15:10 Then the word of the LORD came to S: 9017
     15:11 S was troubled, and he cried out to   9017
     15:12 Early in the morning S got up and went   9017
     15:13 When S reached him, Saul said,   9017
     15:14 But S said, "What then is this bleating   9017
     15:16 "Stop!" S said to Saul.   9017
     15:17 S said, "Although you were once small   9017
     15:22 But S replied: "Does the LORD delight in
            burnt offerings and   9017
     15:24 Then Saul said to S, "I have sinned.   9017
     15:26 S said to him, "I will not go back with you. 9017
     15:27 As S turned to leave,   9017
     15:28 S said to him, "The LORD has torn   9017
     15:31 So S went back with Saul,   9017
     15:32 Then S said, "Bring me Agag king of   9017
     15:33 But S said, "As your sword has made
            women childless,   9017
     15:33 And S put Agag to death before the LORD   9017
     15:34 Then S left for Ramah,   9017
     15:35 Until the day S died, he did not go to see 9017
     15:35 though S mourned for him.   9017
     16: 1 The LORD said to S, "How long will you   9017
     16: 2 But S said, "How can I go?   9017
     16: 4 S did what the LORD said.   9017
     16: 5 S replied, "Yes, in peace;   NIH
     16: 6 S saw Eliab and thought,   NIH
     16: 7 But the LORD said to S, "Do not consider   9017
     16: 8 and had him pass in front of S.   9017
     16: 8 But S said, "The LORD has not chosen   NIH
     16: 9 then had Shammah pass by, but S said,   NIH
     16:10 Jesse had seven of his sons pass before S, 9017
     16:10 but S said to him, "The LORD has not   9017
     16:11 S said, "Send for him;   9017
     16:13 So S took the horn of oil and anointed him 9017
     16:13 S then went to Ramah.   9017
     19:18 he went to S at Ramah and told him all   9017
     19:18 he and S went to Naioth and stayed there.   9017
     19:20 with S standing there as their leader,   9017
     19:22 And he asked, "Where are S and David?"   9017
     25: 1 Now S died, and all Israel assembled   9017
     28: 3 Now S was dead, and all Israel mourned   9017
     28:11 "Bring up S," he said.   9017
     28:12 When the woman saw S, she cried out   9017
     28:14 Then Saul knew it was S,   9017
     28:15 S said to Saul, "Why have you disturbed me 9017
     28:16 S said, "Why do you consult me,   9017
1Ch   6:27 Elkanah his son and S his son.   9017
      6:28 The sons of S: Joel the firstborn   9017
      6:33 the musician, the son of Joel, the son of S, 9017
      7: 2 Rephaiah, Jeriel, Jahmai, Ibsam and S—   9017
      9:22 to their positions of trust by David and S 9017
     11: 3 as the LORD had promised through S.   9017
     26:28 And everything dedicated by S the seer and 9017
     29:29 they are written in the records of S the seer, 9017
2Ch 35:18 in Israel since the days of the prophet S; 9017
Ps   99: 6 S was among those who called   9017
Jer 15: 1 if Moses and S were to stand before me,   9017
Ac   3:24 "Indeed, all the prophets from S on,   4905
     13:20 God gave them judges until the time of S   4905
Heb 11:32 Jephthah, David, S and the prophets,   4905

SAMUEL'S (4) [SAMUEL]

1Sa   4: 1 And S word came to all Israel.   9017
      7:13 Throughout S lifetime, the hand of the LORD 9017
     19:24 and also prophesied in S presence.   9017
     28:20 filled with fear because of S words.   9017

SANBALLAT (10)

Ne   2:10 When S the Horonite and Tobiah   6172
      2:19 But when S the Horonite,   6172
      4: 1 When S heard that we were rebuilding   6172
      4: 7 But when S, Tobiah, the Arabs,   6172
      6: 1 When word came to S, Tobiah,   6172
      6: 2 S and Geshem sent me this message: 6172
      6: 5 S sent his aide to me with the same message 6172
      6:12 because Tobiah and S had hired him.   6172
      6:14 Remember Tobiah and S, O my God,   6172
     13:28 the high priest was son-in-law to S   6172

SANCTIFIED (10) [SANCTIFY]

Jn   17:19 that they too *may be* truly s.   39+1639
Ac   20:32 an inheritance among all those who *are* s. 39
     26:18 and a place among those who *are* s by faith 39
Ro   15:16 s by the Holy Spirit.   39
1Co   1: 2 to those s in Christ Jesus and called to   39+1639
      6:11 But you were washed, *you were* s,   39
      7:14 For the unbelieving husband *has been* s   39
      7:14 and the unbelieving wife *has been* s   39
1Th   4: 3 It is God's will that you should be s: 40
Heb 10:29 the blood of the covenant that s *him,*   39

SANCTIFY (4) [SANCTIFIED, SANCTIFYING]

Jn   17:17 S them by the truth; your word is truth.   39
     17:19 For them I s myself, that they too may be   39
1Th   5:23 God of peace, s you through and through.   39
Heb   9:13 s them so that they are outwardly clean.   39

SANCTIFYING (2) [SANCTIFY]

2Th	2:13	to be saved through the s work of the Spirit	40
1Pe	1: 2	through the s work of the Spirit,	40

SANCTUARIES (4) [SANCTUARY]

Lev	26:31	into ruins and lay waste your s,	5219
Eze	7:24	and their s will be desecrated.	5219
	28:18	dishonest trade you have desecrated your s.	5219
Am	7: 9	be destroyed and the s of Israel will	5219

SANCTUARY (177) [SANCTUARIES]

Ex	15:17	you made for your dwelling, the s, O Lord,	5219
	25: 8	"Then have them make a s for me,	5219
	30:13	according to the s shekel.	7731
	30:24	all according to the s shekel—	7731
	35:19	garments worn for ministering in the s—	7731
	36: 1	of constructing the s are to do the work just	7731
	36: 3	to carry out the work of constructing the s.	7731
	36: 4	the work on the s left their work	7731
	36: 6	as an offering for the s."	7731
	38:24	on the s was 29 talents and 730 shekels,	7731
	38:24	according to the s shekel.	7731
	38:25	shekels, according to the s shekel—	7731
	38:26	half a shekel, according to the s shekel,	7731
	38:27	the bases for the s and for the curtain—	7731
	39: 1	garments for ministering in the s.	7731
	39:41	garments worn for ministering in the s,	7731
Lev	4: 6	in front of the curtain of the s.	7731
	5:15	according to the s shekel.	7731
	10: 4	away from the front of the s."	7731
	10:17	the sin offering in the s area?	7731
	10:18	you should have eaten the goat in the s area,	7731
	12: 4	not touch anything sacred or go to the s	5219
	16: 3	"This is how Aaron is to enter the s area:	7731
	19:30	and have reverence for my s.	5219
	20: 3	to Molech, he has defiled my s	5219
	21:12	nor leave the s of his God or desecrate it,	5219
	21:23	and so desecrate my s.	5219
	26: 2	and have reverence for my s.	5219
	27: 3	according to the s shekel;	7731
	27:25	to be set according to the s shekel.	7731
Nu	3:10	anyone else who approaches the s must	NIH
	3:28	responsible for the care of the s.	7731
	3:31	the articles of the s used in ministering,	7731
	3:32	responsible for the care of the s.	7731
	3:38	They were responsible for the care of the s	5219
	3:38	Anyone else who approached the s was to	NIH
	3:47	according to the s shekel.	7731
	3:50	shekels, according to the s shekel.	7731
	4:12	the articles used for ministering in the s,	7731
	4:19	and his sons are to go into the s and assign	NIH
	7:13	both according to the s shekel,	7731
	7:19	both according to the s shekel,	7731
	7:25	both according to the s shekel,	7731
	7:31	both according to the s shekel,	7731
	7:37	both according to the s shekel,	7731
	7:43	both according to the s shekel,	7731
	7:49	both according to the s shekel,	7731
	7:55	both according to the s shekel,	7731
	7:61	both according to the s shekel,	7731
	7:67	both according to the s shekel,	7731
	7:73	both according to the s shekel,	7731
	7:79	both according to the s shekel,	7731
	7:85	according to the s shekel.	7731
	7:86	according to the s shekel.	7731
	8:19	the Israelites when they go near the s."	7731
	18: 1	the responsibility for offenses against the s,	5219
	18: 3	near the furnishings of the s or the altar,	7731
	18: 5	to be responsible for the care of the s and	7731
	18: 7	Anyone else who comes near the s must	NIH
	18:16	according to the s shekel,	7731
	19:20	because he has defiled the s of the LORD.	5219
	28: 7	the drink offering to the LORD at the s.	7731
	31: 6	who took with him articles from the s and	7731
Jos	22:27	we will worship the LORD at his s	4200+7156S
1Ki	6: 5	the main hall and inner s he built a structure	1808
	6:16	to form within the temple an inner s,	1808
	6:19	the inner s within the temple to set the ark	1808
	6:20	The inner s was twenty cubits long,	1808
	6:21	across the front of the inner s,	1808
	6:22	the altar that belonged to the inner s.	1808
	6:23	In the inner s he made a pair of cherubim	1808
	6:31	of the inner s he made doors of olive wood	1808
	7:49	in front of the inner s);	1808
	8: 6	to its place in the inner s of the temple,	1808
	8: 8	in front of the inner s, but not from outside	1808
1Ch	9:29	and all the other articles of the s,	7731
	22:19	Begin to build the s of the LORD God,	5219
	24: 5	for there were officials of the s and officials	7731
	28:10	to build a temple as a s.	5219
2Ch	4:20	to burn in front of the inner s as prescribed;	1808
	5: 7	to its place in the inner s of the temple,	1808
	5: 9	could be seen from in front of the inner s,	1808
	20: 8	They have lived in it and have built in it a s	5219
	26:18	Leave the s, for you have been unfaithful;	5219
	29: 5	Remove all defilement from the s.	7731
	29: 7	or present any burnt offerings at the s to	7731
	29:16	The priests went into the s of the LORD	1074
	29:21	for the s and for Judah.	5219
	30: 8	Come to the s, which he has consecrated	5219
	30:19	not clean according to the rules of the s."	7731
	36:17	with the sword in the s.	1074+5219
Ezr	9: 8	and giving us a firm place in his s,	5226+7731
Ne	10:39	where the articles for the s are kept and	5219
Ps	15: 1	LORD, who may dwell in your s?	185

Ps	20: 2	from the s and grant you support from Zion.	7731
	60: 6	God has spoken from his s:	7731
	63: 2	in the s and beheld your power	7731
	68:17	the Lord [has come] from Sinai into his s.	7731
	68:24	procession of my God and King into the s.	7731
	68:35	You are awesome, O God, in your s;	5219
	73:17	till I entered the s of God;	5219
	74: 3	the enemy has brought on the s.	7731
	74: 7	They burned your s to the ground;	5219
	78:69	He built his s like the heights,	5219
	96: 6	strength and glory are in his s.	5219
	102:19	"The LORD looked down from his s	7731
	108: 7	God has spoken from his s:	7731
	114: 2	Judah became God's s, Israel his dominion.	7731
	134: 2	Lift up your hands in the s and praise	7731
	150: 1	Praise God in his s;	7731
Isa	8:14	and he will be a s;	5219
	60:13	to adorn the place of my s;	5219
	62: 9	in the courts of my s."	7731
	63:18	our enemies have trampled down your s.	5219
Jer	17:12	is the place of our s.	5219
La	1:10	she saw pagan nations enter her s—	5219
	2: 7	rejected his altar and abandoned his s.	5219
	2:20	Should priest and prophet be killed in the s	5219
Eze	5:11	because you have defiled my s with all	5219
	8: 6	things that will drive me far from my s?	5219
	9: 6	Begin at my s."	5219
	11:16	for a little while I have been a s for them in	5219
	21: 2	against Jerusalem and preach against the s.	5219
	23:38	At that same time they defiled my s	5219
	23:39	they entered my s and desecrated it.	5219
	24:21	I am about to desecrate my s—	5219
	25: 3	over my s when it was desecrated and over	5219
	37:26	and I will put my s among them forever.	5219
	37:28	when my s is among them forever.' "	5219
	41: 1	Then the man brought me to the outer s	2121
	41: 2	He also measured the outer s;	NIH
	41: 3	Then he went into the inner s and measured	7163
	41: 4	And he measured the length of the inner s,	2257S
	41: 4	across the end of the outer s.	2121
	41:15	The outer s, the inner sanctuary and	2121
	41:15	the inner s and the portico facing the court,	7164
	41:17	the entrance to the inner s and on the walls	1074
	41:17	around the inner and outer s	7164
	41:20	on the wall of the outer s.	2121
	41:21	The outer s had a rectangular doorframe,	2121
	41:23	Both the outer s and the Most Holy Place	2121
	41:25	of the outer s were carved cherubim	2121
	42: 8	the row on the side nearest the s	2121
	43:21	of the temple area outside the s.	5219
	44: 1	to the outer gate of the s,	5219
	44: 5	of the temple and all the exits of the s.	5219
	44: 7	in heart and flesh into my s,	5219
	44: 8	you put others in charge of my s.	5219
	44: 9	in heart and flesh is to enter my s,	5219
	44:11	They may serve in my s,	5219
	44:15	of my s when the Israelites went astray	5219
	44:16	They alone are to enter my s;	5219
	44:27	the day he goes into the inner court of the s	7731
	44:27	of the sanctuary to minister in the s,	7731
	45: 2	section 500 cubits square is to be for the s,	7731
	45: 3	In it will be the s, the Most Holy Place.	7731
	45: 4	the s and who draw near to minister before	5219
	45: 4	as well as a holy place for the s.	5219
	45:18	without defect and purify the s.	5219
	47:12	because the water from the s flows to them.	5219
	48: 8	the s will be in the center of it.	5219
	48:10	the center of it will be the s of the LORD.	5219
	48:21	the sacred portion with the temple s will be	5219
Da	8:11	and the place of his s was brought low.	5219
	8:13	and the surrender of the s and of the host	7731
	8:14	then the s will be reconsecrated."	7731
	9:17	O Lord, look with favor on your desolate s.	5219
	9:26	will destroy the city and the s.	7731
Am	7:13	because this is the king's s and the temple	7731
Zep	3: 4	Her priests profane the s and do violence to	7731
Mal	2:11	Judah has desecrated the s the LORD loves,	7731
Lk	11:51	who was killed between the altar and the s.	3875
Heb	6:19	It enters the inner s behind the curtain,	NIG
	8: 2	and who serves in the s,	41
	8: 5	They serve at a s that is a copy and shadow	3302
	9: 1	for worship and also an earthly s.	41
	9:24	For Christ did not enter a man-made s	41

SAND (29) [SANDY]

Ge	22:17	in the sky and as the s on the seashore.	2567
	32:12	and will make your descendants like the s	2567
	41:49	like the s of the sea;	2567
Ex	2:12	he killed the Egyptian and hid him in the s.	2567
Dt	33:19	on the treasures hidden in the s."	2567
Jos	11: 4	as numerous as the s on the seashore.	2567
Jdg	7:12	be counted than the s on the seashore.	2567
1Sa	13: 5	as numerous as the s on the seashore.	2567
2Sa	17:11	as numerous as the s on the seashore—	2567
1Ki	4:20	and Israel were as numerous as the s on	2567
	4:29	of understanding as measureless as the s on	2567
Job	6: 3	surely outweigh the s of the seas—	2567
	29:18	my days as numerous as the grains of s.	2567
	39:14	on the ground and lets them warm in the s,	6760
Ps	78:27	flying birds like s on the seashore.	2567
	139:18	they would outnumber the grains of s.	2567
Pr	27: 3	Stone is heavy and s a burden,	2567
Isa	10:22	O Israel, be like the s by the sea,	2567
	35: 7	The burning s will become a pool,	9220
	48:19	descendants would have been like the s,	2567
Jer	5:22	I made the s a boundary for the sea,	2567

Isa	15: 8	more numerous than the s of the sea.	2567
	33:22	as measureless as the s on the seashore.' "	2567
Hos	1:10	"Yet the Israelites will be like the s on	2567
Hab	1: 9	a desert wind and gather prisoners like s.	2567
Mt	7:26	like a foolish man who built his house on s.	302
Ro	9:27	the number of the Israelites be like the s by	302
Heb	11:12	the stars in the sky and as countless as the s	302
Rev	20: 8	In number they are like the s on	302

SANDAL (6) [SANDALED, SANDALS]

Ge	14:23	not even a thread or the thong of a s,	5837
Ru	4: 7	one party took off his s and gave it to	5837
	4: 8	And he removed his s.	5837
Ps	60: 8	upon Edom I toss my s;	5837
	108: 9	upon Edom I toss my s;	5837
Isa	5:27	not a s thong is broken.	5837

SANDALED (1) [SANDAL]

SS	7: 1	How beautiful your s feet,	928+2021+5837

SANDALS (28) [SANDAL]

Ex	3: 5	"Take off your s, for the place	5837
	12:11	into your belt, your s on your feet	5837
Dt	25: 9	take off one of his s, spit in his face and say,	5837
	29: 5	nor did the s on your feet.	5837
Jos	5:15	"Take off your s, for the place	5837
	9: 5	The men put worn and patched s	5837
	9:13	And our clothes and s are worn out by	5837
1Ki	2: 5	around his waist and the s on his feet.	5837
2Ch	28:15	They provided them with clothes and s,	5836
Isa	11:15	so that men can cross over in s.	5837
	20: 2	from your body and the s from your feet."	5837
Eze	16:10	an embroidered dress and put leather s on	5836
	24:17	Keep your turban fastened and your s	5837
	24:23	on your heads and your s on your feet.	5837
Am	2: 6	and the needy for a pair of s.	5837
	8: 6	with silver and the needy for a pair of s,	5837
Mt	3:11	whose s I am not fit to carry.	5687
	10:10	or extra tunic, or s or a staff;	5687
Mk	1: 7	of whose s I am not worthy to stoop down	5687
	6: 9	Wear s but not an extra tunic.	4908
Lk	3:16	thongs of whose s I am not worthy to untie.	5687
	10: 4	Do not take a purse or bag or s;	5687
	15:22	Put a ring on his finger and s on his feet.	5687
	22:35	"When I sent you without purse, bag or s,	5687
Jn	1:27	the thongs of whose s I am not worthy	5687
Ac	7:33	the Lord said to him, 'Take off your s;	5687
	12: 8	"Put on your clothes and s."	4908+5686
	13:25	whose s I am not worthy to untie.'	5687

SANDBAR (1) [SANDBARS]

Ac	27:41	the ship struck a s and ran aground.	1458+5536

SANDBARS (1) [SANDBAR]

Ac	27:17	they would run aground on the s of Syrtis,	5358

SANDY (1) [SAND]

Ac	27:39	but they saw a bay with a s beach,	129

SANG (24) [SING]

Ex	15: 1	Then Moses and the Israelites s this song to	8876
	15:21	Miriam s to them: "Sing to the LORD,	6702
Nu	21:17	Then Israel s this song: "Spring up, O well!	8876
Jdg	5: 1	and Barak son of Abinoam s this song:	8876
1Sa	18: 7	As they danced, they s	6702
	29: 5	the David they s about in their dances:	6702
2Sa	3:33	The king s this lament for Abner:	7801
	22: 1	David s to the LORD the words of this song	1819
2Ch	5:13	in praise to the LORD and s:	9048
	29:28	the singers s and the trumpeters played.	8876
	29:30	So they s praises with gladness	2146
	30:21	and priests s to the LORD every day,	2146
Ezr	3:11	and thanksgiving they s to the LORD:	6702
Ne	12:42	The choirs s under the direction	9048
Job	38: 7	while the morning stars s together and all	8264
Ps	7: T	which he s to the LORD concerning Cush,	8876
	18: T	He s to the LORD the words of this song	1819
	106:12	they believed his promises and s his praise.	8876
Mt	11:17	we s a dirge, and you did not mourn.'	2577
Lk	7:32	we s a dirge, and you did not cry."	2577
Rev	5: 9	And they s a new song: "You are worthy	106
	5:12	In a loud voice they s: "Worthy is the Lamb	3306
	14: 3	And they s a new song before the throne	106
	15: 3	and s the song of Moses the servant of God	106

SANHEDRIN (19)

Mt	5:22	'Raca,' is answerable to the S.	5284
	26:59	and the whole S were looking for false	5284
Mk	14:55	and the whole S were looking for evidence	5284
	15: 1	the teachers of the law and the whole S,	5284
Jn	11:47	and the Pharisees called a meeting of the S.	5284
Ac	4:15	from the S and then conferred together.	5284
	5:21	they called together the S—	5284
	5:27	the S to be questioned by the high priest.	5284
	5:34	stood up in the S and ordered that the men	5284
	5:41	The apostles left the S,	5284
	6:12	and brought him before the S.	5284
	6:15	in the S looked intently at Stephen,	5284
	22:30	the chief priests and all the S to assemble.	5284
	23: 1	Paul looked straight at the S and said,	5284
	23: 6	called out in the S, "My brothers,	5284
	23:15	the S petition the commander to bring him	5284

Ac 23:20 to bring Paul before the S tomorrow on 5284
 23:28 so I brought him to their S. 5284
 24:20 in me when I stood before the S— 5284

SANITY (2)
Da 4:34 and my s was restored. 10430
 4:36 At the same time that my s was restored, 10430

SANK (12) [SINK]
Ge 42:28 Their hearts s and they turned to each other 3655
Ex 15: 5 *they* s to the depths like a stone. 3718
 15:10 *They* s like lead in the mighty waters. 7510
Nu 21:18 that the nobles of the people s— 4125
Jdg 3:22 Even the handle s in after the blade, 995
 5:27 At her feet he s, he fell; there he lay. 4156
 5:27 At her feet *he* s, he fell; 4156
 5:27 where *he* s, there he fell—dead. 4156
1Sa 17:49 The stone s into his forehead, 3190
SS 5: 6 My heart s at his departure. 3655
Jer 38: 6 and Jeremiah s **down** into the mud. 3190
Jnh 2: 6 To the roots of the mountains *I* s **down**; 3718

SANK (Anglicized) See also MELTED

SANNAH See KIRIATH SANNAH

SANSANNAH (1)
Jos 15:31 Ziklag, Madmannah, S, 6179

SAP (2) [SAPPED]
Hos 7: 9 Foreigners s his strength, 430
Ro 11:17 now share in the nourishing s from the olive *NIG*

SAPH (1)
2Sa 21:18 that time Sibbecai the Hushathite killed S, 6198

SAPHIR (KJV) See SHAPHIR

SAPPED (2) [SAP]
Ps 32: 4 my strength **was** s as in the heat of summer. 2200
La 1:14 and the Lord *has* s my strength. 4173

SAPPHIRA (1)
Ac 5: 1 together with his wife S, 4912

SAPPHIRE (7) [SAPPHIRES]
Ex 24:10 like a pavement made of s, 6209
 28:18 a s and an emerald; 6209
 39:11 a s and an emerald; 6209
Eze 1:26 what looked like a throne of s, 74+6209
 10: 1 the likeness of a throne of s above 74+6209
 28:13 onyx and jasper, s, turquoise and beryl. 6209
Rev 21:19 first foundation was jasper, the second s, 4913

SAPPHIRES (5) [SAPPHIRE]
Job 28: 6 s come from its rocks, 6209
 28:16 with precious onyx or s. 6209
SS 5:14 like polished ivory decorated with s. 6209
Isa 54:11 your foundations with s. 6209
La 4: 7 their appearance like s. 6209

SARAH (38) [SARAH'S, SARAI]
Ge 17:15 her name will be S. 8577
 17:17 Will S bear a child at the age of ninety?" 8577
 17:19 "Yes, but your wife S will bear you a son, 8577
 17:21 Isaac, whom S will bear to you 8577
 18: 6 So Abraham hurried into the tent to S. 8577
 18: 9 "Where is your wife S?" 8577
 18:10 and S your wife will have a son." 8577
 18:10 S was listening at the entrance to the tent, 8577
 18:11 and S were already old and well advanced 8577
 18:11 and S was past the age of childbearing. 8577
 18:12 So S laughed to herself as she thought, 8577
 18:13 "Why did S laugh and say, 8577
 18:14 next year and S will have a son." 8577
 18:15 S was afraid, so she lied and said, 8577
 20: 2 and there Abraham said of his wife S, 8577
 20: 2 Then Abimelech king of Gerar sent for S 8577
 20:14 and he returned S his wife to him. 8577
 20:16 To S he said, "I am giving your brother 8577
 20:18 because of Abraham's wife S. 8577
 21: 1 LORD was gracious to S as he had said, 8577
 21: 1 LORD did for S what he had promised. 8577
 21: 2 S became pregnant and bore a son 8577
 21: 3 the name Isaac to the son S bore him. 8577
 21: 6 S said, "God has brought me laughter, 8577
 21: 7 to Abraham that S would nurse children? 8577
 21: 9 But S saw that the son whom Hagar 8577
 21:12 Listen to whatever S tells you, 8577
 23: 1 S lived to be a hundred and twenty-seven 8577
 23: 2 and Abraham went to mourn for S and 8577
 23:19 Afterward Abraham buried his wife S in 8577
 24:36 My master's wife S has borne him a son 8577
 24:67 into the tent of his mother S, 8577
 25:10 There Abraham was buried with his wife S. 8577
 49:31 There Abraham and his wife S were buried, 8577
Isa 51: 2 your father, and to S, who gave you birth. 8577
Ro 9: 9 and S will have a son. 4925
Heb 11:11 he was past age—and S herself was barren 4925

1Pe 3: 6 like S, who obeyed Abraham 4925

SARAH'S (2) [SARAH]
Ge 25:12 whom S maidservant, Hagar the Egyptian, 8577
Ro 4:19 and that S womb was also dead. 4925

SARAI (15) [SARAH]
Ge 11:29 The name of Abram's wife was S, 8584
 11:30 Now S was barren; she had no children. 8584
 11:31 and his daughter-in-law S, 8584
 12: 5 He took his wife S, his nephew Lot, 8584
 12:11 he said to his wife S, 8584
 12:17 because of Abram's wife S. 8584
 16: 1 Now S, Abram's wife, had borne him no 8584
 16: 2 Abram agreed to what S said. 8584
 16: 3 S his wife took her Egyptian maidservant 8584
 16: 5 Then S said to Abram, 8584
 16: 6 S mistreated Hagar; so she fled from her. 8584
 16: 8 And he said, "Hagar, servant of S, 8584
 16: 8 "I'm running away from my mistress S," 8584
 17:15 "As for S your wife, 8584
 17:15 you are no longer to call her S; 8584

SARAPH (1)
1Ch 4:22 the men of Cozeba, and Joash and S, 8598

SARDINE (KJV) See CARNELIAN

SARDIS (3)
Rev 1:11 Thyatira, S, Philadelphia and Laodicea." 4915
 3: 1 "To the angel of the church in S write: 4915
 3: 4 Yet you have a few people in S who have 4915

SARDITES (KJV) See SEREDITE

SARDIUS (KJV) See RUBY

SARDONYX (1)
Rev 21:20 the fifth s, the sixth carnelian, 4918

SAREPTA (KJV) See ZAREPHATH

SARGON (1)
Isa 20: 1 commander, sent by S king of Assyria, 6236

SARID (2)
Jos 19:10 of their inheritance went as far as S. 8587
 19:12 It turned east from S toward the sunrise to 8587

SARON (KJV) See SHARON

SARSECHIM (KJV) See NEBO-SARSEKIM

SARUCH (KJV) See SERUG

SASH (9) [SASHES]
Ex 28: 4 a robe, a woven tunic, a turban and a s. 77
 28:39 The s is to be the work of an embroiderer. 77
 39:29 The s was of finely twisted linen and blue, 77
Lev 8: 7 tied the s around him, 77
 16: 4 he is to tie the linen s around him and put 77
Isa 3:24 instead of a s, a rope; 2514
 11: 5 and faithfulness the s *around* his waist. 258
 22:21 and fasten your s around him 77
Rev 1:13 and with a golden s around his chest. 2438

SASHES (6) [SASH]
Ex 28:40 and headbands for Aaron's sons, 77
 29: 9 Then tie s on Aaron and his sons. 77
Lev 8:13 tied s around them and put headbands 77
Pr 31:24 and supplies the merchants with s, 2512
Isa 3:20 the headdresses and ankle chains and s, 8005
Rev 15: 6 and wore golden s around their chests. 2438

SAT (99) [SIT]
Ge 21:16 Then she went off and s **down** nearby, 3782
 21:16 *as she* s there nearby, she began to sob. 3782
 37:25 As *they* s **down** to eat their meal, 3782
 38:14 and then s **down** at the entrance to Enaim, 3782
 48: 2 Israel rallied his strength and s **up** on 3782
Ex 2:15 where he s **down** by a well. 3782
 12:29 Pharaoh, who s on the throne, 3782
 16: 3 There we s around pots of meat and ate all 3782
 17:12 a stone and put it under him and *he* s on it. 3782
 32: 6 Afterward *they* s **down** to eat and drink 3782
Lev 15: 6 with a discharge s on must wash his clothes 3782
Jdg 6:11 The angel of the LORD came and s **down** 3782
 19: 6 of them s **down** to eat and drink together. 3782
 19:15 They went and s in the city square, 3782
 20:26 and there they s weeping before 3782
 21: 2 where *they* s before God until evening, 3782
Ru 2:14 When *she* s **down** with the harvesters, 3782
 4: 1 up to the town gate and s there. 3782
 4: 1 So he went over and s **down**. 3782
1Sa 20:24 the king s **down** to eat. 3782
 20:25 He s in his customary place by the wall, 3782

1Sa 20:25 and Abner s next to Saul, 3782
 28:23 up from the ground and s on the couch. 3782
2Sa 2:13 One group s **down** on one side of the pool 3782
 7:18 in and s before the LORD, and he said: 3782
 19:28 a place among *those who* s at your table. 430
1Ki 2:12 So Solomon s on the throne, 3782
 2:19 down to her and s **down** on his throne. 3782
 2:19 and *she* s **down** at his right hand. 3782
 19: 4 He came to a broom tree, s **down** under it 3782
 21:13 and s opposite him and brought charges 3782
2Ki 4:20 the boy s on her lap until noon, 3782
1Ch 17:16 in and s before the LORD, and he said: 3782
 29:23 So Solomon s on the throne of the LORD 3782
Ezr 9: 3 from my head and beard and s **down** 3782
 9: 4 And I s there appalled until 3782
 10:16 the first day of the tenth month *they* s **down** 3782
Ne 1: 4 *I* s **down** and wept. 3782
Est 3:15 The king and Haman s **down** to drink, 3782
Job 2: 8 and scraped himself with it as he s among 3782
 2:13 Then *they* s on the ground with him 3782
 29:25 the way for them and s as their chief; 3782
Ps 107:10 *Some* s in darkness and the deepest gloom, 3782
 137: 1 By the rivers of Babylon *we* s and wept 3782
Jer 3: 2 By the roadside *you* s **waiting** for lovers, 3782
 3: 2 s like a nomad in the desert. NIH
 15:17 *I* never s in the company of revelers, 3782
 15:17 *I* s alone because your hand was on me 3782
Eze 3:15 *I* s among them for seven days— 3782
 14: 1 the elders of Israel came to me and s **down** 3782
 20: 1 and *they* s **down** in front of me. 3782
 23:41 *You* s on an elegant couch, 3782
Jnh 3: 6 covered himself with sackcloth and s **down** 3782
 4: 5 Jonah went out and s **down** at a place east 3782
 4: 5 s in its shade and waited to see 3782
Zec 5: 7 and there in the basket s a woman! 3782
Mt 5: 1 he went up on a mountainside and s **down**. 2767
 13: 1 went out of the house and s by the lake. 2764
 13: 2 around him that he got into a boat and s 2764
 13:48 Then they s **down** and collected 2767
 15:29 he went up on a mountainside and s **down**. 2764
 21: 7 and Jesus s on them. 2125
 26:55 Every day *I* s in the temple courts 2757
 26:58 *He* entered and s **down** with the guards 2764
 28: 2 rolled back the stone and s on it. 2764
Mk 2: 1 that he got into a boat and s in it out on 2764
 6:40 So *they* s **down** in groups of hundreds 404
 11: 7 threw their cloaks over it, he s on it. 2767
 12:41 Jesus s **down** opposite the place where 2767
 14:54 There *he* s with the guards 1639+5153
 16:19 up into heaven and *he* s at the right hand 2767
Lk 4:20 gave it back to the attendant and s **down**. 2767
 5: 3 Then he s **down** and taught the people from 2767
 7:15 The dead man s **up** and began to talk, 361
 9:15 The disciples did so, and everybody s **down**. 2884
 10:39 who s at the Lord's feet listening 4149
 22:55 of the courtyard and *had* s **down together**, 5154
 22:55 Peter s **down** with them. 2764
Jn 4: 6 s **down** by the well. 2757
 6: 3 went up on a mountainside and s **down** 2764
 6:10 and the men s **down**, about five thousand 404
 8: 2 and he s **down** to teach them. 2767
 12:14 Jesus found a young donkey and s upon it, 2767
 19:13 he brought Jesus out and s **down** on 2767
Ac 9:40 and seeing Peter *she* s **up**. 361
 12:21 wearing his royal robes, s on his throne 2767
 13:14 they entered the synagogue and s **down**. 2767
 14: 8 In Lystra *there* s a man crippled in his feet, 2764
 16:13 We s **down** and began to speak to 2767
1Co 10: 7 "The people s **down** to eat and drink and got 2767
Heb 1: 3 he s **down** at the right hand of the Majesty 2767
 8: 1 We do have such a high priest, who s **down** 2767
 10:12 he s **down** at the right hand of God. 2767
 12: 2 and s **down** at the right hand of the throne 2767
Rev 3:21 as I overcame and s **down** with my Father 2767
 4: 3 And the one who s there had the appearance 2764
 5: 1 Then I saw in the right hand *of* him who s 2764
 5: 7 the scroll from the right hand *of* him who s 2764

SATAN (53) [SATAN'S]
1Ch 21: 1 S rose up against Israel and incited David 8477
Job 1: 6 and S also came with them. 8477
 1: 7 The LORD said to S, "Where have you come 8477
 1: 7 S answered the LORD, "From roaming 8477
 1: 8 the LORD said to S, "Have you considered 8477
 1: 9 Job fear God for nothing?" S replied. 8477
 1:12 the LORD said to S, "Very well, then, 8477
 1:12 Then S went out from the presence of 8477
 2: 1 and S also came with them 8477
 2: 2 the LORD said to S, "Where have you come 8477
 2: 2 S answered the LORD, "From roaming 8477
 2: 3 the LORD said to S, "Have you considered 8477
 2: 4 "Skin for skin!" S replied. 8477
 2: 6 The LORD said to S, "Very well, then, 8477
 2: 6 So S went out from the presence of 8477
Zec 3: 1 S standing at his right side to accuse him. 8477
 3: 2 The LORD said to S, "The LORD rebuke you, 8477
 3: 2 "The LORD rebuke you, 8477
Mt 4:10 Jesus said to him, "Away from me, S! 4928
 12:26 If S drives out Satan, 4928
 12:26 If Satan drives out S, 4928
 16:23 and said to Peter, "Get behind me, S! 4928
Mk 1:13 forty days, being tempted by S. 4928
 3:23 "How can S drive out Satan? 4928
 3:23 "How can Satan drive out S? 4928
 3:26 And if S opposes himself and is divided, 4928

Mk	4:15	S comes and takes away the word	4928
	8:33	"Get behind me, S!" he said.	4928
Lk	10:18	"I saw S fall like lightning from heaven.	4928
	11:18	If S is divided against himself,	4928
	13:16	this woman, whom S has kept bound	4928
	22: 3	Then S entered Judas, called Iscariot,	4928
	22:31	Simon, S has asked to sift you as wheat.	4928
Jn	13:27	S entered into him.	4928
Ac	5: 3	how is it that S has so filled your heart	4928
	26:18	and from the power of S to God,	4928
Ro	16:20	of peace will soon crush S under your feet.	4928
1Co	5: 5	hand this man over to S,	4928
	7: 5	Then come together again so that S will	4928
2Co	2:11	in order that S might not outwit us.	4928
	11:14	S himself masquerades as an angel of light.	4928
	12: 7	a messenger of S, to torment me.	4928
1Th	2:18	but S stopped us.	4928
2Th	2: 9	in accordance with the work of S displayed	4928
1Ti	1:20	whom I have handed over to S to be taught	4928
	5:15	in fact already turned away to follow S.	4928
Rev	2: 9	but are a synagogue of S.	4928
	2:13	where you live—where S has his throne.	4928
	2:13	in your city—where S lives.	4928
	3: 9	of S, who claim to be Jews though they are	4928
	12: 9	that ancient serpent called the devil, or S,	4928
	20: 2	that ancient serpent, who is the devil, or S,	4928
	20: 7	S will be released from his prison	4928

SATAN'S (1) [SATAN]

Rev	2:24	have not learned S so-called deep secrets	4928

SATED (1) [SATISFY]

La	3:15	with bitter herbs and s me with gall.	8115

SATIATE, SATIATED (KJV) See SATISFY, SATISFIED

SATISFACTION (4) [SATISFY]

Est	5:13	But all this gives me no s as long as I see	8750
Ecc	2:24	to eat and drink and find s in his work.	3202
	3:13	and find s in all his toil—	3202
	5:18	to find s in his toilsome labor under the sun	3208

SATISFIED (42) [SATISFY]

Ex	18:23	and all these people will go home s."	928+8934
Lev	10:20	Moses heard this, he was s.	928+3512+6524
	26:26	You will eat, but you will not be s.	8425
Dt	6:11	then when you eat and are s,	8425
	8:10	When you have eaten and are s,	8425
	8:12	Otherwise, when you eat and are s,	8425
	11:15	and you will eat and be s.	8425
	14:29	in your towns may come and eat and be s,	8425
	26:12	so that they may eat in your towns and be s.	8425
Ps	17:15	I will be s with seeing your likeness.	8425
	22:26	The poor will eat and be s;	8425
	59:15	wander about for food and howl if not s.	8425
	63: 5	My soul will be s as with the richest	8425
	104:13	the earth is s by the fruit of his work.	8425
	104:28	they are s with good things.	8425
	105:40	and he brought them quail and s them with	8425
Pr	13: 4	but the desires of the diligent are fully s.	2014
	18:20	with the harvest from his lips he is s.	8425
	27:20	Death and Destruction are never s,	8425
	30:15	"There are three things that are never s,	8425
	30:16	land, which is never s with water, and fire,	8425
Ecc	5:10	whoever loves wealth is never s	NIH
	6: 7	yet his appetite is never s.	4848
Isa	9:20	on the left they will eat, but not be s.	8425
	53:11	he will see the light [of life] and be s;	8425
	66:11	and be s at her comforting breasts;	8425
Jer	46:10	The sword will devour till it is s,	8425
	50:19	be s on the hills of Ephraim and Gilead.	8425
Eze	16:28	and even after that, you still were not s.	8425
	16:29	but even with this you were not s.	8425
	27:33	you s many nations;	8425
Hos	13: 6	When I fed them, they were s;	8425
	13: 6	when they were s, they became proud;	8425
Mic	6:14	You will eat but not be s;	8425
Hab	2: 5	as the grave and like death is never s,	8425
Mt	14:20	They all ate and were s,	5963
	15:37	They all ate and were s.	5963
Mk	6:42	They all ate and were s,	5963
	8: 8	The people ate and were s.	5963
Lk	6:21	who hunger now, for you will be s.	5963
	9:17	They all ate and were s,	5963
3Jn	1:10	Not s with that, he refuses to welcome	758

SATISFIES (3) [SATISFY]

Ps	103: 5	who s your desires with good things so	8425
	107: 9	for he s the thirsty and fills the hungry	8425
	147:14	He grants peace to your borders and s you	8425

SATISFY (18) [SATED, SATISFACTION, SATISFIED, SATISFIES]

Job	38:27	to s a desolate wasteland and make it sprout	8425
	38:39	for the lioness and s the hunger of the lions	4848
Ps	81:16	with honey from the rock I would s you."	8425
	90:14	S us in the morning with your unfailing love	8425
	91:16	With long life will I s him	8425
	132:15	her poor will I s with food.	8425
	145:16	and s the desires of every living thing.	8425
Pr	5:19	may her breasts s you always,	8115

Pr	6:30	to s his hunger when he is starving.	4848
Isa	55: 2	and your labor on what does not s?	8429
	58:10	in behalf of the hungry and s the needs of	8425
	58:11	he will s your needs in a sun-scorched land	8425
Jer	31:14	I will s the priests with abundance,	8115
	31:25	I will refresh the weary and s the faint."	4848
Eze	7:19	not s their hunger or fill their stomachs	8425
Joel	2:19	new wine and oil, enough to s you fully;	8425
Mt	28:14	we will s him and keep you out of trouble."	4275
Mk	15:15	Wanting to s the crowd,	2653+4472

SATRAPS (13)

Ezr	8:36	delivered the king's orders to the royal s	346
Est	3:12	Haman's orders to the king's s,	346
	8: 9	Mordecai's orders to the Jews, and to the s,	346
	9: 3	And all the nobles of the provinces, the s,	346
Da	3: 2	He then summoned the s, prefects,	10026
	3: 3	So the s, prefects, governors, advisers,	10026
	3:27	and the s, prefects, governors	10026
	6: 1	It pleased Darius to appoint 120 s to rule	10026
	6: 2	The s were made accountable to them so	10026
	6: 3	and the s by his exceptional qualities that	10026
	6: 4	and the s tried to find grounds for charges	10026
	6: 6	the administrators and the s went as a group	10026
	6: 7	The royal administrators, prefects, s,	10026

SATYRS (KJV) See WILD GOATS

SAUL (373) [SAUL'S]

1Sa	9: 2	He had a son named S,	8620
	9: 3	and Kish said to his son S,	8620
	9: 5	S said to the servant who was with him,	8620
	9: 7	S said to his servant, "If we go,	8620
	9:10	"Good," S said to his servant.	8620
	9:15	Now the day before S came,	8620
	9:17	When Samuel caught sight of S,	8620
	9:18	S approached Samuel in the gateway	8620
	9:21	S answered, "But am I not a Benjamite,	8620
	9:22	Then Samuel brought S and his servant	8620
	9:24	with what was on it and set it in front of S.	8620
	9:24	And S dined with Samuel that day.	8620
	9:25	Samuel talked with S on the roof	8620
	9:26	about daybreak and Samuel called to S on	8620
	9:26	When S got ready, he and Samuel went	8620
	9:27	Samuel said to S, "Tell the servant to go on	8620
	10: 9	As S turned to leave Samuel,	2257S
	10:11	Is S also among the prophets?"	8620
	10:12	"Is S also among the prophets?"	8620
	10:13	After S stopped prophesying,	NIH
	10:16	S replied, "He assured us that	8620
	10:21	Finally S son of Kish was chosen.	8620
	10:26	S also went to his home in Gibeah,	8620
	10:27	But S kept silent.	NIH
	11: 4	of S and reported these terms to the people,	8620
	11: 5	Just then S was returning from the fields,	8620
	11: 6	When S heard their words,	8620
	11: 7	the oxen of anyone who does not follow S	8620
	11: 8	When S mustered them at Bezek,	NIH
	11:11	The next day S separated his men	8620
	11:12	'Shall S reign over us?'	8620
	11:13	But S said, "No one shall be put	8620
	11:15	and confirmed S as king in the presence of	8620
	11:15	and S and all the Israelites held	8620
	13: 1	S was [thirty] years old when he became	8620
	13: 2	S chose three thousand men from Israel;	8620
	13: 3	Then S had the trumpet blown throughout	8620
	13: 4	"S has attacked the Philistine outpost,	8620
	13: 4	people were summoned to join S at Gilgal.	8620
	13: 7	S remained at Gilgal,	8620
	13: 9	And S offered up the burnt offering.	NIH
	13:10	and S went out to greet him.	8620
	13:11	S replied, "When I saw that the men were	8620
	13:15	and S counted the men who were with him.	8620
	13:16	S and his son Jonathan and the men	8620
	13:22	on the day of the battle not a soldier with S	8620
	13:22	only S and his son Jonathan had them.	8620
	14: 1	One day Jonathan son of S said to	8620
	14: 2	S was staying on the outskirts of Gibeah	8620
	14:17	Then S said to the men who were with him,	8620
	14:18	S said to Ahijah, "Bring the ark of God."	8620
	14:19	While S was talking to the priest,	8620
	14:19	S said to the priest, "Withdraw your hand."	8620
	14:20	Then S and all his men assembled	8620
	14:21	over to the Israelites who were with S	8620
	14:24	S had bound the people under an oath,	8620
	14:33	Then someone said to S, "Look,	8620
	14:35	Then S built an altar to the LORD;	8620
	14:36	S said, "Let us go down after	8620
	14:37	So S asked God, "Shall I go down after	8620
	14:38	S therefore said, "Come here,	8620
	14:40	Then S said to all the Israelites,	NIH
	14:41	Then S prayed to the LORD,	8620
	14:41	And Jonathan and S were taken by lot,	8620
	14:42	S said, "Cast the lot between me	8620
	14:43	Then S said to Jonathan,	8620
	14:44	S said, "May God deal with me,	8620
	14:45	the men said to S, "Should Jonathan die—	8620
	14:46	Then S stopped pursuing the Philistines,	8620
	14:47	After S had assumed rule over Israel,	8620
	14:52	All the days of S there was bitter war with	8620
	14:52	whenever S saw a mighty or brave man,	8620
	15: 1	said to S, "I am the one the LORD sent	8620
	15: 4	So S summoned the men	8620
	15: 5	S went to the city of Amalek and set	8620
	15: 7	Then S attacked the Amalekites all the way	8620

1Sa	15: 9	But S and the army spared Agag and	8620
	15:11	"I am grieved that I have made S king,	8620
	15:12	Samuel got up and went to meet S,	8620
	15:12	but he was told, "S has gone to Carmel.	8620
	15:13	When Samuel reached him, S said,	8620
	15:15	S answered, "The soldiers brought them	8620
	15:16	"Stop!" Samuel said to S.	8620
	15:16	"Tell me," S replied.	NIH
	15:20	"But I did obey the LORD," S said.	8620
	15:24	Then S said to Samuel, "I have sinned.	8620
	15:27	S caught hold of the hem of his robe,	NIH
	15:30	S replied, "I have sinned.	NIH
	15:31	So Samuel went back with S,	8620
	15:31	and S worshiped the LORD.	8620
	15:34	S went up to his home in Gibeah of Saul.	8620
	15:34	Saul went up to his home in Gibeah of S.	8620
	15:35	he did not go to see S again,	8620
	15:35	that he had made S king over Israel.	8620
	16: 1	"How long will you mourn for S,	8620
	16: 2	S will hear about it and kill me."	8620
	16:14	Spirit of the LORD had departed from S,	8620
	16:17	So S said to his attendants,	8620
	16:19	Then S sent messengers to Jesse and said,	8620
	16:19	and sent them with his son David to S.	8620
	16:21	David came to S and entered his service.	8620
	16:21	S liked him very much,	NIH
	16:22	Then S sent word to Jesse, saying,	8620
	16:23	the spirit from God came upon S,	8620
	16:23	Then relief would come to S;	8620
	17: 2	S and the Israelites assembled and camped	8620
	17: 8	and are you not the servants of S?	8620
	17:11	S and all the Israelites were dismayed	8620
	17:13	Jesse's three oldest sons had followed S to	8620
	17:14	The three oldest followed S,	8620
	17:15	and forth from S to tend his father's sheep	8620
	17:19	They are with S and all the men of Israel in	8620
	17:31	was overheard and reported to S,	8620
	17:31	and S sent for him.	NIH
	17:32	to S, "Let no one lose heart on account	8620
	17:33	S replied, "You are not able to go out	8620
	17:34	But David said to S, "Your servant	8620
	17:37	S said to David, "Go, and the LORD be	8620
	17:38	Then S dressed David in his own tunic.	8620
	17:39	"I cannot go in these," he said to S,	8620
	17:55	As S watched David going out to meet	8620
	17:57	Abner took him and brought him before S,	8620
	17:58	"Whose son are you, young man?" S asked	8620
	18: 1	After David had finished talking with S,	8620
	18: 2	that day S kept David with him and did	8620
	18: 5	Whatever S sent him to do,	8620
	18: 5	so successfully that S gave him a high rank	8620
	18: 6	from all the towns of Israel to meet King S	8620
	18: 7	"S has slain his thousands,	8620
	18: 8	S was very angry; this refrain galled him.	8620
	18: 9	that time on S kept a jealous eye on David.	8620
	18:10	from God came forcefully upon S.	8620
	18:10	S had a spear in his hand	8620
	18:12	S was afraid of David, because the LORD	8620
	18:12	the LORD was with David but had left S.	8620
	18:15	When S saw how successful he was,	8620
	18:17	S said to David, "Here is my older daughter	8620
	18:17	S said to himself, "I will not raise a hand	8620
	18:18	But David said to S, "Who am I,	8620
	18:20	and when they told S about it,	8620
	18:21	So S said to David, "Now you have	8620
	18:22	Then S ordered his attendants:	8620
	18:25	S replied, "Say to David,	8620
	18:27	Then S gave him his daughter Michal	8620
	18:28	When S realized that the LORD was with	8620
	18:29	S became still more afraid of him,	8620
	19: 1	S told his son Jonathan and all	8620
	19: 2	"My father S is looking for a chance	8620
	19: 4	of David to S his father and said to him,	8620
	19: 6	S listened to Jonathan and took this oath:	8620
	19: 7	He brought him to S, and David was with	8620
	19: 7	and David was with S as before.	2257S
	19:10	an evil spirit from the LORD came upon S	8620
	19:10	S tried to pin him to the wall	8620
	19:10	but David eluded him as S drove the spear	8620
	19:11	S sent men to David's house to watch it	8620
	19:14	When S sent the men to capture David,	8620
	19:15	Then S sent the men back to see David	8620
	19:17	S said to Michal, "Why did you deceive me	8620
	19:18	at Ramah and told him all that S had done	8620
	19:19	Word came to S: "David is in Naioth	8620
	19:21	S was told about it, and he sent more men,	8620
	19:21	S sent men a third time,	8620
	19:23	So S went to Naioth at Ramah.	NIH
	19:24	"Is S also among the prophets?"	8620
	20:25	opposite Jonathan, and Abner sat next to S,	8620
	20:26	S said nothing that day, for he thought,	8620
	20:27	Then S said to his son Jonathan,	8620
	20:33	But S hurled his spear at him to kill him.	8620
	21:10	from S and went to Achish king of Gath.	8620
	21:11	" 'S has slain his thousands,	8620
	22: 6	Now S heard that David and his men	8620
	22: 6	And S, spear in hand, was seated	8620
	22: 7	S said to them, "Listen, men of Benjamin!	8620
	22:12	S said, "Listen now, son of Ahitub."	8620
	22:13	S said to him, "Why have you conspired	8620
	22:21	that S had killed the priests of the LORD.	8620
	22:22	I knew he would be sure to tell S.	8620
	23: 7	S was told that David had gone to Keilah.	8620
	23: 8	And S called up all his forces for battle,	8620
	23: 9	When David learned that S was plotting	8620
	23:10	that S plans to come to Keilah and destroy	8620
	23:11	Will S come down, as your servant has	8620

1Sa 23:12 of Keilah surrender me and my men to S?" 8620
23:13 When S was told that David had escaped 8620
23:14 Day after day S searched for him, 8620
23:15 that S had come out to take his life. 8620
23:17 "My father S will not lay a hand on you. 8620
23:17 Even my father S knows this." 8620
23:19 The Ziphites went up to S at Gibeah 8620
23:21 S replied, "The LORD bless you 8620
23:24 they set out and went to Ziph ahead of S. 8620
23:25 S and his men began the search, 8620
23:25 When S heard this, he went into the Desert 8620
23:26 S was going along one side of 8620
23:26 hurrying to get away from S. 8620
23:26 As S and his forces were closing in 8620
23:27 a messenger came to S, 8620
23:28 Then S broke off his pursuit of David 8620
24: 1 After S returned from pursuing 8620
24: 2 So S took three thousand chosen men 8620
24: 3 and S went in to relieve himself. 8620
24: 7 and did not allow them to attack S. 8620
24: 7 And S left the cave and went his way. 8620
24: 8 went out of the cave and called out to S, 8620
24: 8 When S looked behind him, 8620
24: 9 He said to S, "Why do you listen 8620
24:16 When David finished saying this, S asked, 8620
24:22 So David gave his oath to S. 8620
24:22 Then S returned home, but David 8620
25:44 But S had given his daughter Michal, 8620
26: 1 The Ziphites went to S at Gibeah and said, 8620
26: 2 So S went down to the Desert of Ziph, 8620
26: 3 S made his camp beside the road on the hill 8620
26: 3 he saw that S had followed him there, 8620
26: 4 and learned that S had definitely arrived. 8620
26: 5 and went to the place where S had camped. 8620
26: 5 He saw where S and Abner son of Ner, 8620
26: 5 S was lying inside the camp, 8620
26: 6 will go down into the camp with me to S?" 8620
26: 7 and there was S, lying asleep 8620
26:17 S recognized David's voice and said, 8620
26:21 Then S said, "I have sinned. 8620
26:25 Then S said to David, "May you be blessed 8620
26:25 and S returned home. 8620
27: 1 be destroyed by the hand of S. 8620
27: 1 Then S will give up searching 8620
27: 4 S was told that David had fled to Gath, 8620
28: 3 S had expelled the mediums and spiritists 8620
28: 4 while S gathered all the Israelites and set 8620
28: 5 S saw the Philistine army, he was afraid; 8620
28: 7 S then said to his attendants, 8620
28: 8 So S disguised himself, 8620
28: 9 "Surely you know what S has done. 8620
28:10 S swore to her by the LORD, 8620
28:12 at the top of her voice and said to S, 8620
28:12 you deceived me? You are S!" 8620
28:14 Then S knew it was Samuel, 8620
28:15 Samuel said to S, "Why have you disturbed 8620
28:15 "I am in great distress," S said. 8620
28:20 Immediately S fell full length on 8620
28:21 to S and saw that he was greatly shaken, 8620
28:25 Then she set it before S and his men, 8620
29: 3 who was an officer of S king of Israel?" 8620
29: 3 and from the day he left S until now, NIH
29: 5 " 'S has slain his thousands, 8620
31: 2 The Philistines pressed hard after S 8620
31: 3 The fighting grew fierce around S, 8620
31: 4 S said to his armor-bearer, 8620
31: 4 so S took his own sword and fell on it. 8620
31: 5 the armor-bearer saw that S was dead, 8620
31: 6 S and his three sons and his armor-bearer 8620
31: 7 that the Israelite army had fled and that S 8620
31: 8 they found S and his three sons fallen 8620
31:11 of what the Philistines had done to S, 8620
31:12 the bodies of S and his sons from the wall 8620
2Sa 1: 1 After the death of S, David returned 8620
1: 4 And S and his son Jonathan are dead." 8620
1: 5 that S and his son Jonathan are dead?" 8620
1: 6 "and there was S, leaning on his spear, 8620
1:12 till evening for S and his son Jonathan, 8620
1:17 David took up this lament concerning S 8620
1:21 the shield of S—no longer rubbed with oil. 8620
1:22 the sword of S did not return unsatisfied. 8620
1:23 "S and Jonathan—in life they were loved 8620
1:24 "O daughters of Israel, weep for S, 8620
2: 4 of Jabesh Gilead who had buried S, 8620
2: 5 for showing this kindness to S your master 8620
2: 7 for S your master is dead, 8620
2: 8 of S and brought him over to Mahanaim. 8620
2:10 Ish-Bosheth son of S was forty years old 8620
2:12 with the men of Ish-Bosheth son of S, 8620
2:15 for Benjamin and Ish-Bosheth son of S, 8620
3: 1 between the house of S and the house 8620
3: 1 the house of S grew weaker and weaker. 8620
3: 6 During the war between the house of S and 8620
3: 6 his own position in the house of S. 8620
3: 7 Now S had had a concubine named Rispah 8620
3: 8 the house of your father S and to his family 8620
3:10 the house of S and establish David's throne 8620
3:13 unless you bring Michal daughter of S 8620
3:14 sent messengers to Ish-Bosheth son of S, 8620
4: 1 of S heard that Abner had died in Hebron, 8620
4: 4 (Jonathan son of S had a son who was lame 8620
4: 4 when the news about S and Jonathan came 8620
4: 8 "Here is the head of Ish-Bosheth son of S, 8620
4: 8 the king against S and his offspring." 8620
4:10 when a man told me, 'S is dead,' 8620
5: 2 In the past, while S was king over us, 8620
6:16 Michal daughter of S watched from 8620

2Sa 6:20 Michal daughter of S came out to meet him 8620
6:23 And Michal daughter of S had no children 8620
7:15 as I took it away from S, 8620
9: 1 "Is there anyone still left of the house of S 8620
9: 3 of S to whom I can show God's kindness?" 8620
9: 6 the son of S, came to David, 8620
9: 7 that belonged to your grandfather S, 8620
9: 9 that belonged to S and his family. 8620
12: 7 and I delivered you from the hand of S. 8620
16: 8 the blood you shed in the household of S, 8620
21: 1 of S and his blood-stained house; 8620
21: 2 but S in his zeal for Israel and Judah 8620
21: 4 to demand silver or gold from S 8620
21: 6 before the LORD at Gibeah of S— 8620
21: 7 Mephibosheth son of Jonathan, the son of S, 8620
21: 7 between David and Jonathan son of S. 8620
21: 8 whom she had borne to S, 8620
21:12 of S and his son Jonathan from the citizens 8620
21:12 after they struck S down on Gilboa.) 8620
21:13 of S and his son Jonathan from there, 8620
21:14 the bones of S and his son Jonathan in 8620
22: 1 of all his enemies and from the hand of S. 8620
1Ch 8:33 Kish the father of S, 8620
8:33 and S the father of Jonathan, Malki-Shua, 8620
9:39 Kish the father of S, 8620
9:39 and S the father of Jonathan, Malki-Shua, 8620
10: 2 The Philistines pressed hard after S 8620
10: 3 The fighting grew fierce around S, 8620
10: 4 S said to his armor-bearer, 8620
10: 4 so S took his own sword and fell on it. 8620
10: 5 the armor-bearer saw that S was dead, 8620
10: 6 So S and his three sons died, 8620
10: 7 and that S and his sons had died, 8620
10: 8 they found S and his sons fallen 8620
10:11 of everything the Philistines had done to S, 8620
10:12 and took the bodies of S and his sons 8620
10:13 S died because he was unfaithful to 8620
11: 2 In the past, even while S was king, 8620
12: 1 banished from the presence of S son of Kish 8620
12: 2 they were kinsmen of S from the tribe 8620
12:19 with the Philistines to fight against S. 8620
12:19 if he deserts to his master S.") 8620
13: 3 not inquire of it during the reign of S." 8620
15:29 Michal daughter of S watched from 8620
26:28 by Samuel the seer and by S son of Kish, 8620
Ps 18: T of all his enemies and from the hand of S. 8620
52: T the Edomite had gone to S and told him: 8620
54: T When the Ziphites had gone to S and said, 8620
57: T When he had fled from S into the cave. 8620
59: T When S had sent men to watch David's 8620
Isa 10:29 Ramah trembles; Gibeah of S flees. 8620
Ac 7:58 at the feet of a young man named S. 4930
8: 1 S was there, giving approval to his death. 4930
8: 3 But S began to destroy the church. 4930
9: 1 S was still breathing out murderous threats 4930
9: 4 "S, Saul, why do you persecute me?" 4910
9: 4 "Saul, why do you persecute me?" 4910
9: 5 "Who are you, Lord?" S asked. NIG
9: 7 with S stood there speechless; 899S
9: 8 S got up from the ground, 4930
9:11 and ask for a man from Tarsus named S, 4930
9:17 Placing his hands on S, he said, 899S
9:17 he said, "Brother S, the Lord— 4930
9:19 S spent several days with the disciples NIG
9:22 Yet S grew more and more powerful 4930
9:24 but S learned of their plan. 4930
9:27 how S on his journey had seen the Lord NIG
9:28 So S stayed with them and moved NIG
11:25 Barnabas went to Tarsus to look for S, 4930
11:26 for a whole year Barnabas and S met with 899S
11:30 their gift to the elders by Barnabas and S. 4930
12:25 Barnabas and S had finished their mission, 4930
13: 1 up with Herod (the tetrarch) and S. 4930
13: 2 "Set apart for me Barnabas and S for 4930
13: 7 sent for Barnabas and S because he wanted 4930
13: 9 Then S, who was also called Paul, 4930
13:21 and he gave them S son of Kish, 4930
13:22 After removing S, he made David their king 899S
22: 7 and heard a voice say to me, 'S! 4910
22: 7 and heard a voice say to me, 'Saul! S! 4910
22:13 He stood beside me and said, 'Brother S, 4910
26:14 'S, Saul, why do you persecute me? 4910
26:14 'Saul, S, why do you persecute me? 4910

SAUL'S (43) [SAUL]

1Sa 9: 3 belonging to S father Kish were lost, 8620
10: 1 and poured it on S head and kissed him, 2257S
10: 9 God changed S heart, 2257S
10:14 Now S uncle asked him and his servant, 8620
10:15 S uncle said, "Tell me what Samuel said 8620
13: 8 and S men began to scatter. 2021S
14:16 S lookouts at Gibeah in Benjamin saw 4200+8620
14:49 S sons were Jonathan, Ishvi and 8620
14:50 the commander of S army was Abner son 8620
14:50 and Ner was S uncle. 8620
14:51 S father Kish and Abner's father Ner were 8620
16:15 S attendants said to him, "See, 8620
17:12 S time he was old and well advanced 8620
18: 5 and S officers as well. 8620
18:19 when the time came for Merab, S daughter, 8620
18:20 S daughter Michal was in love with David, 8620
18:24 S servants told him what David had said, 8620
18:30 more success than the rest of S officers, 8620
19:20 upon S men and they also prophesied. 8620
20:30 S anger flared up at Jonathan and he said 8620

1Sa 21: 7 Now one of S servants was there that day, 8620
21: 7 Doeg the Edomite, S head shepherd. 4200+8620
22: 9 who was standing with S officials, said, 8620
23:16 And S son Jonathan went to David 8620
24: 4 and cut off a corner of S robe. 4200+8620
26:12 the spear and water jug near S head, 8620
2Sa 2: 1 the third day a man arrived from S camp, 8620
2: 8 the commander of S army, 4200+8620
4: 2 Now S son had two men who were leaders 8620
9: 2 a servant of S household named Ziba. 8620
9: 9 Then the king summoned Ziba, S servant, 8620
16: 5 from the same clan as S family came out 8620
19:17 the steward of S household, 8620
19:24 Mephibosheth, S grandson, 8620
21: 8 with the five sons of S daughter Merab, 8620
21:11 Rizpah, S concubine, had done, 8620
21:14 in the tomb of S father Kish, 2257S
1Ch 5:10 During S reign they waged war against 8620
12:23 to David at Hebron to turn S kingdom over 8620
12:29 men of Benjamin, S kinsmen—3,000 8620
12:29 of whom had remained loyal to S house 8620
Ac 9:18 something like scales fell from S eyes, 899S

SAVAGE (2)

Lev 26: 6 I will remove s beasts from the land, 8273
Ac 20:29 s wolves will come in among you and will 987

SAVE (190) [SAFE, SAFELY, SAFETY, SALVATION, SAVED, SAVES, SAVING, SAVIOR]

Ge 32:11 S me, I pray, from the hand of my brother 5911
45: 5 because it was to s lives that God sent me 4695
45: 7 and to s your lives by a great deliverance. 2649
Ex 16:23 S whatever is left and keep it 5663
Nu 31:18 but s for yourselves every girl who has
never slept with a man. 2649
Dt 4:42 into one of these cities and s his life. 2649
19: 4 and flees there to s his life— 2649
19: 5 to one of these cities and s his life. 2649
Jos 2:13 and that you will s us from death." 5911
10: 6 Come up to us quickly and s us! 3828
Jdg 6:14 in the strength you have and s Israel out 3828
6:15 Gideon asked, "how can I s Israel? 3828
6:31 Are you trying to s him? 3828
6:36 "If you will s Israel by my hand 3828
6:37 then I will know that you will s Israel 3828
7: 7 I will s you and give the Midianites 3828
10: 1 the son of Dodo, rose to s Israel. 3828
10:12 did I not s you from their hands? 3828
10:13 so I will no longer s you. 3828
10:14 Let them s you when you are in trouble!" 3828
10:14 you didn't s me out of their hands, 3828
1Sa 4: 3 and s us from the hand of our enemies." 3828
10:27 "How can this fellow s us?" 3828
23: 2 "Go, attack the Philistines and s Keilah." 3828
2Sa 22: 3 from violent men you s me. 3828
22:28 You s the humble, 3828
22:42 but there was no one to s them— 4635
1Ki 1:12 how you can s your own life and the life 4880
2Ki 16: 7 up and s me out of the hand of the king 4880
18:35 has been able to s his land from me? 5911
19:34 I will defend this city and s it, 3828
1Ch 16:35 Cry out, "S us, O God our Savior; 3828
2Ch 20: 9 and you will hear us and s us.' 3828
25:15 not s their own people from your hand?" 5911
32:11 'The LORD our God will s us from 5911
32:14 has been able to s his people from me? 5911
Ne 2: 8 like me go into the temple to s his life? 2649
Job 20:20 he cannot s himself by his treasure. 4880
22:29 then he will s the downcast. 3828
40:14 to you that your own right hand can s you. 3828
Ps 6: 4 s me because of your unfailing love. 3828
7: 1 s and deliver me from all who pursue me, 3828
17: 7 the wonder of your great love, you who s 3828
17:14 by your hand s me from such men, NIH
18:27 You s the humble, 3828
18:41 but there was no one to s them— 3828
20: 9 O LORD, s the king! 3828
22:21 s me from the horns of the wild oxen. 6699
28: 9 S your people and bless your inheritance; 3828
31: 2 a strong fortress to s me. 3828
31:16 s me in your unfailing love. 3828
33:17 despite all its great strength it cannot s. 4880
39: 8 S me from all my transgressions; 5911
40:13 Be pleased, O LORD, to s me; 5911
51:14 S me from bloodguilt, O God, 5911
54: 1 S me, O God, by your name; 3828
59: 2 Deliver me from evildoers and s me 3828
60: 5 S us and help us with your right hand, 3828
69: 1 S me, O God, for the waters have come up 3828
69:35 for God will s Zion and rebuild the cities 3828
70: 1 Hasten, O God, to s me; 5911
71: 2 turn your ear to me and s me. 3828
71: 3 give the command to s me, 3828
72: 4 the people and s the children of the needy; 3828
72:13 on the weak and the needy and s the needy 3828
76: 9 to s all the afflicted of the land. 3828
80: 2 Awaken your might; come and s us. 3802
86: 2 s your servant who trusts in you. 3828
86:16 grant your strength to your servant and s 3828
89:48 or s himself from the power of the grave? 4880
91: 3 Surely he will s you from the fowler's 5911
106: 4 come to my aid when you s them, 3802
106:47 S us, O LORD our God, 3828
108: 6 S us and help us with your right hand, 3828

Ps	109:26	s me in accordance with your love.	3828
	109:31	to s his life from those who condemn him.	3828
	116: 4	"O LORD, s me!"	4880
	118:25	s us; O LORD, grant us success.	3828
	119:94	S me, for I am yours;	3828
	119:146	s me and I will keep your statutes.	3828
	120: 2	S me, O LORD, from lying lips and	5911
	138: 7	*with* your right hand *you* s me.	3828
	146: 3	in mortal men, who cannot s.	9591
Pr	2:12	Wisdom *will* s you from the ways	5911
	2:16	It *will* s you also from the adulteress,	5911
	23:14	with the rod and s his soul from death.	5911
Isa	33:22	it is he *who will* s us.	3828
	35: 4	divine retribution he will come to s you."	3828
	36:20	has been able to s his land from me?	5911
	37:35	"I will defend this city and s it,	3828
	38:20	The LORD *will* s me,	3828
	44:17	He prays to it and says, "S me;	5911
	44:20	*he* cannot s himself, or say,	5911
	45:20	who pray to gods *that* cannot s.	5911
	46: 7	*it* cannot s him from his troubles.	3828
	47:13	*let them* s you from what is coming	3828
	47:14	They cannot even s themselves from	5911
	47:15	there is not *one that can* s you.	3828
	49:25	and your children I *will* s.	3828
	57:13	*let* your collection [of idols] s you!	5911
	59: 1	the arm of the LORD is not too short *to s,*	3828
	63: 1	speaking in righteousness, mighty to s."	3828
Jer	2:27	they say, 'Come and s us!'	3828
	2:28	*if they can* s you when you are in trouble?	3828
	14: 9	like a warrior powerless to s?	3828
	15:20	for I am with you to rescue and s you,"	5911
	15:21	"I *will* s you from the hands of the wicked	3828
	17:14	s me and I will be saved,	3828
	30:10	'I *will* surely s you out of a distant place,	3828
	30:11	I am with you and *will* s you,'	3828
	31: 7	s your people, the remnant of Israel.'	3828
	39:18	*I will* s you; you will not fall	4880+4880
	42:11	with you and *will* s you and deliver you	3828
	46:27	I *will* surely s you out of a distant place,	3828
La	4:17	for a nation *that could* not s us.	3828
Eze	3:18	from his evil ways in order to s his **life**,	2649
	7:19	to s them in the day of the LORD's wrath.	5911
	13:21	I will tear off your veils and s my people	5911
	13:22	from their evil ways and so s their **lives**,	2649
	13:23	*I will* s my people from your hands.	5911
	14:14	were in it, they *could* s only themselves	5911
	14:16	not s their own sons or daughters.	5911
	14:18	not s their own sons or daughters.	5911
	14:20	*they could* s neither son nor daughter.	5911
	14:20	They *would* s only themselves	5911
	18:27	does what is just and right, he *will* s his life.	2649
	33:12	of the righteous man *will* not s him	5911
	34:22	*I will* s my flock,	3828
	36:29	*I will* s you from all your uncleanness.	3828
	37:23	for *I will* s them from all their sinful	3828
Da	3:17	the God we serve is able to s us from it,	10706
	3:29	for no other god can s in this way."	10489
	6:14	made every effort until sundown to s him.	10489
Hos	1: 7	and *I will* s them—not by bow,	3828
	13:10	Where is your king, that *he may* s you?	3828
	14: 3	Assyria cannot s us;	3828
Am	2:14	and the warrior *will* not s his life.	4880
	2:15	and the horseman *will* not s his life.	4880
Mic	2: 3	from which *you* cannot s yourselves.	4631
	6:14	You will store up but s nothing,	7117
	6:14	what *you* s I will give to the sword.	7117
Hab	1: 2	but *you do* not s?	3828
	3:13	to s your anointed one.	3829
Zep	1:18	to s them on the day of the LORD's wrath.	5911
	3:17	*he is* mighty to s.	3828
Zec	8: 7	"I *will* s my people from the countries of	3828
	8:13	O Judah and Israel, so *will I* s you,	3828
	9:16	The LORD their God *will* s them on	3828
	10: 6	"I *will* strengthen the house of Judah and s	3828
	12: 7	"The LORD *will* s the dwellings	3828
Mt	1:21	he *will* s his people from their sins."	5392
	8:25	and woke him, saying, "Lord, s us!	5392
	14:30	beginning to sink, cried out, "Lord, s me!"	5392
	16:25	For whoever wants *to* s his life will lose it,	5392
	27:40	and build it in three days, s yourself!	5392
	27:42	they said, "but he can't s himself!	5392
	27:49	Let's see if Elijah comes *to* s him.	5392
Mk	3: 4	*to* s life or to kill?"	5392
	8:35	For whoever wants *to* s his life will lose it,	5392
	8:35	for me and for the gospel *will* s it.	5392
	15:30	come down from the cross and s yourself!"	5392
	15:31	they said, "but he can't s himself!	5392
Lk	6: 9	*to* s life or to destroy it?"	5392
	9:24	For whoever wants *to* s his life will lose it,	5392
	9:24	but whoever loses his life for me *will* s it.	5392
	19:10	to seek and *to* s what was lost."	5392
	23:35	*let him* s himself if he is the Christ of God,	5392
	23:37	"If you are the king of the Jews, s yourself."	5392
	23:39	S yourself and us!"	5392
Jn	3:17	but *to* s the world through him.	5392
	12: 7	that *she should* s this perfume for the day	5498
	12:27	'Father, s me from this hour'?	5392
	12:47	not come to judge the world, but *to* s it.	5392
Ac	2:40	and he pleaded with them, "S yourselves	5392
Ro	11: 14	my own people to envy and s some of them.	5392
1Co	1:21	*to* s those who believe.	5392
	7:16	wife, whether *you will* s your husband?	5392
	7:16	husband, whether *you will* s your wife?	5392
	9:22	that by all possible means *I might* s some.	5392
2Co	12:14	not have *to* s up for their parents,	2564
1Ti	1:15	Jesus came into the world *to* s sinners—	5392
1Ti	4:16	*you will* s both yourself and your hearers.	5392
Heb	5: 7	to the one who could s him from death,	5392
	7:25	*to* s completely those who come to God	5392
	11: 7	in holy fear built an ark to s his family.	5401
Jas	1:21	the word planted in you, which can s you.	5392
	2:14	Can such faith s him?	5392
	4:12	the one who is able *to* s and destroy.	5392
	5:20	of his way *will* s him from death and cover	5392
Jude	1:23	snatch others from the fire and s them;	5392

SAVED (109) [SAVE]

Ge	47:25	*"You have* s our **lives**," they said.	2649
Ex	14:30	the LORD s Israel from the hands of	3828
	16:24	So *they* s it until morning,	5663
	18: 4	*he* s me from the sword of Pharaoh."	5911
	18: 8	the way and how the LORD *had* s them.	5911
Dt	33:29	Who is like you, a people s by the LORD?	3828
Jos	9:26	So Joshua s them from the Israelites,	5911
Jdg	2:16	*who* s them out of the hands of these raiders.	3828
	2:18	with the judge and s them out of the hands	3828
	3: 9	Caleb's younger brother, *who* s them.	3828
	3:31	He too s Israel.	3828
	7: 2	against me that her own strength *has* s her,	3828
	8:22	*you have* s us out of the hand of Midian."	3828
1Sa	23: 5	the Philistines and s the people of Keilah.	3828
2Sa	19: 5	who have just s your life and the lives	4880
	22: 4	and *I am* s from my enemies.	3828
2Ki	14:27	*he* s them by the hand of Jeroboam son	3828
2Ch	32:22	So the LORD s Hezekiah and the people	3828
Job	26: 2	How *you have* s the arm that is feeble!	3828
Ps	18: 3	and *I am* s from my enemies.	3828
	22: 5	They cried to you and *were* s;	4880
	33:16	No king is s by the size of his army;	3828
	34: 6	he s him out of all his troubles.	3828
	80: 3	your face shine upon us, that *we may* be s.	3828
	80: 7	your face shine upon us, that *we may* be s.	3828
	80:19	your face shine upon us, that *we may* be s.	3828
	106: 8	Yet *he* s them for his name's sake,	3828
	106:10	*He* s them from the hand of the foe;	3828
	106:21	They forgot the God *who* s them,	3828
	107:13	and *he* s them from their distress.	3828
	107:19	and *he* s them from their distress.	3828
	116: 6	when I was in great need, *he* s me.	3828
Ecc	9:15	and *he* s the city by his wisdom.	4880
Isa	25: 9	we trusted in him, and *he* s us.	3828
	43:12	I have revealed and s and proclaimed—	3828
	45:17	But Israel *will be* s by the LORD with	3828
	45:22	"Turn to me and *be* s,	3828
	63: 9	and the angel of his presence s them.	3828
	64: 5	How then *can we* be s?	3828
Jer	4:14	wash the evil from your heart and *be* s.	3828
	8:20	the summer has ended, and we *are* not s."	3828
	17:14	save me and *I will* be s,	3828
	23: 6	In his days Judah *will* be s	3828
	30: 7	but *he will* be s out of it.	3828
	33:16	In those days Judah *will* be s	3828
Eze	3:19	but you *will have* s yourself.	5911
	3:21	and you *will have* s yourself.	5911
	14:16	They alone *would* be s,	5911
	14:18	They alone *would* be s.	5911
	33: 5	*he would have* s himself.	4880
	33: 9	but you *will have* s yourself.	5911
Joel	2:32	calls on the name of the LORD *will* be s;	5911
Am	3:12	so *will* the Israelites be s,	5911
Mt	10:22	he who stands firm to the end *will be* s.	5392
	19:25	"Who then *can be* s?"	5392
	24:13	he who stands firm to the end *will be* s.	5392
	27:42	*"He* s others," they said,	5392
Mk	10:26	"Who then *can be* s?"	5392
	13:13	he who stands firm to the end *will be* s.	5392
	15:31	*"He* s others," they said,	5392
	16:16	Whoever believes and is baptized *will be* s,	5392
Lk	7:50	"Your faith *has* s you; go in peace."	5392
	8:12	so that *they may* not believe and be s.	5392
	13:23	*are* only a few people *going to* be s?"	5392
	18:26	"Who then *can be* s?"	5392
	23:35	They said, *"He* s others;	5392
Jn	2:10	but you *have* the best till now."	5498
	5:34	but I mention it that you *may be* s.	5392
	10: 9	whoever enters through me *will be* s.	5392
Ac	2:21	on the name of the Lord *will be* s.'	5392
	2:47	the Lord added to their number daily those who *were being* s.	5392
	4:12	given to men by which we must be s."	5392
	11:14	and all your household *will be* s."	5392
	15: 1	taught by Moses, you cannot *be* s."	5392
	15:11	the grace of our Lord Jesus that *we are* s,	5392
	16:17	who are telling you the way to *be* s."	5401
	16:30	"Sirs, what must I do to *be* s?"	5392
	16:31	believe in the Lord Jesus, and *you will be* s	5392
	27:20	we finally gave up all hope *of being* s.	5392
	27:31	you cannot *be* s."	5392
Ro	5: 9	*be* s from God's wrath through him!	5392
	5:10	*shall we be* s through his life!	5392
	8:24	For in this hope *we were* s.	5392
	9:27	only the remnant *will be* s.	5392
	10: 1	for the Israelites is that they may *be* s.	1650+5401
	10: 9	raised him from the dead, *you will be* s.	5392
	10:10	your mouth that you confess and *are* s.	1650+5401
	10:13	calls on the name of the Lord *will be* s."	5392
	11:26	And so all Israel *will be* s, as it is written:	5392
1Co	1:18	but *to* us who *are being* s it is the power	5392
	3:15	*he himself will be* s,	5392
	5: 5	and his spirit s on the day of the Lord.	5392
	10:33	so that *they may* be s.	5392
	15: 2	By this gospel *you are* s,	5392
2Co	2:15	of Christ among those who *are being* s	5392
Eph	2: 5	it is by grace *you have been* s.	1639+5392
	2: 8	For it is by grace *you have been* s,	1639+5392
Php	1:28	but that you will be s—and that by God.	5401
	2:16	to the Gentiles so that *they may* be s.	5392
2Th	2:10	to love the truth and so *be* s.	5392
	2:13	from the beginning God chose you to *be* s	5401
1Ti	2: 4	who wants all men *to be* s and to come to	5392
	2:15	women *will be* s through childbearing—	5392
2Ti	1: 9	who *has* s us and called us to a holy life—	5392
Tit	3: 5	*he* s us, not because of righteous things	5392
	3: 5	He s us through the washing of rebirth	NIG
Heb	10:39	of those who believe and are s.	1650+4348+6034
1Pe	3:20	eight in all, *were* s **through** water,	1407
	4:18	And, "If it is hard for the righteous *to be* s,	5392

SAVES (20) [SAVE]

1Sa	10:19	who s you out of all your calamities	3828
	17:47	not by sword or spear that the LORD s;	3828
Job	5:15	*He* s the needy from the sword	3828
	5:15	he s them from the clutches of	NIH
Ps	7:10	*who* s the upright in heart.	3828
	18:48	*who* s me from my enemies.	7117
	20: 6	Now I know that the LORD s his anointed;	3828
	34:18	and s those who are crushed in spirit.	3828
	37:40	from the wicked and s them,	3828
	51:14	O God, the God who s me,	9591
	55:16	But I call to God, and the LORD s me.	3828
	57: 3	He sends from heaven and s me,	3828
	68:20	Our God is a God who s;	4636
	88: 1	O LORD, the God who s me,	3802
	145:19	he hears their cry and s them.	3828
Pr	14:25	A truthful witness s lives,	5911
Da	6:27	He rescues and *he* s;	10489
Am	3:12	"As a shepherd s from the lion's mouth	5911
1Pe	3:21	symbolizes baptism that now s you also—	5392
	3:21	It s you by the resurrection of Jesus Christ,	NIG

SAVING (5) [SAVE]

Ge	50:20	is now being done, the s *of* many lives.	2649
1Sa	14: 6	Nothing can hinder the LORD from s,	3828
Ps	20: 6	from his holy heaven with the s power	3829
	22: 1	Why are you so far from s me,	3802
1Co	16: 2	in keeping with his income, s it up, so that	NIG

SAVIOR (55) [SAVE]

Dt	32:15	and rejected the Rock his S.	3802
2Sa	22: 3	He is my stronghold, my refuge and my s—	4635
	22:47	Exalted be God, the Rock, my S!	3829
1Ch	16:35	Cry out, "Save us, O God our S;	3829
Ps	18:46	Exalted be God my S!	3829
	24: 5	and vindication from God his S.	3829
	25: 5	for you are God my S,	3829
	27: 9	O God my S.	3829
	38:22	Come quickly to help me, O Lord my S.	9591
	42: 5	in God, for I will yet praise him, my S	3802
	42:11	my S and my God.	3802
	43: 5	my S and my God.	3802
	65: 5	O God our S, the hope of all the ends of the	3829
	68:19	Praise be to the Lord, to God our S,	3802
	79: 9	Help us, O God our S,	3829
	85: 4	Restore us again, O God our S,	3829
	89:26	my God, the Rock my S.'	3802
Isa	17:10	You have forgotten God your S;	3829
	19:20	he will send them a s and defender,	4635
	43: 3	your God, the Holy One of Israel, your S;	4635
	43:11	and apart from me there is no s.	4635
	45:15	O God and S of Israel.	4635
	45:21	a righteous God and a S;	4635
	49:26	the LORD, am your S, your Redeemer,	4635
	60:16	the LORD, am your S, your Redeemer,	4635
	62:11	the Daughter of Zion, 'See, your S comes!'	3829
	63: 8	and so he became their S.	4635
Jer	14: 8	O Hope of Israel, its S in times of distress,	4635
Hos	13: 4	no S except me.	4635
Mic	7: 7	I wait for God my S;	3829
Hab	3:18	I will be joyful in God my S.	3829
Lk	1:47	and my spirit rejoices in God my S,	5400
	2:11	in the town of David a S has been born	5400
Jn	4:42	that this man really is the S of the world."	5400
Ac	5:31	to his own right hand as Prince and S	5400
	13:23	God has brought to Israel the S Jesus,	5400
Eph	5:23	his body, of which he is the S.	5400
Php	3:20	And we eagerly await a S from there,	5400
1Ti	1: 1	*of* God our S and *of* Christ Jesus our hope,	5400
	2: 3	This is good, and pleases God our S,	5400
	4:10	who is the S of all men,	5400
2Ti	1:10	through the appearing of our S,	5400
Tit	1: 3	to me by the command of God our S,	5400
	1: 4	the Father and Christ Jesus our S.	5400
	2:10	the teaching *about* God our S attractive.	5400
	2:13	appearing *of* our great God and S,	5400
	3: 4	kindness and love of God our S appeared,	5400
	3: 6	through Jesus Christ our S,	5400
2Pe	1: 1	and Jesus Christ have received a faith	5400
	1:11	of our Lord and S Jesus Christ.	5400
	2:20	and S Jesus Christ and are again entangled	5400
	3: 2	and the command given by our Lord and S	5400
	3:18	*of* our Lord and S Jesus Christ.	5400
1Jn	4:14	that the Father has sent his Son to be the S	5400
Jude	1:25	*to* the only God our S be glory,	5400

SAVOUR (KJV) See AROMA

SAVOURY (KJV) See TASTY

SAW (604) [SEE]

Ge	1: 4	God s that the light was good,	8011
	1:10	And God s that it was good.	8011
	1:12	And God s that it was good.	8011
	1:18	And God s that it was good.	8011
	1:21	And God s that it was good.	8011
	1:25	And God s that it was good.	8011
	1:31	God s all that he had made,	8011
	3: 6	When the woman s that the fruit of	8011
	6: 2	the sons of God s that the daughters	8011
	6: 5	The Lord s how great man's wickedness	8011
	6:12	God s how corrupt the earth had become,	8011
	8:13	from the ark and s that the surface of	8011
	9:22	s his father's nakedness and told his two	8011
	12:14	the Egyptians s that she was a very beautiful	8011
	12:15	And when Pharaoh's officials s her,	8011
	13:10	Lot looked up and s that the whole plain of	8011
	18: 2	up and s three men standing nearby.	8011
	18: 2	When he s them, he hurried from the	8011
	19: 1	When he s them, he got up to meet them	8011
	19:28	and he s dense smoke rising from the land,	8011
	21: 9	But Sarah s that the son whom Hagar	8011
	21:19	Then God opened her eyes and she s a well	8011
	22: 4	On the third day Abraham looked up and s	8011
	22:13	up and there in a thicket he s a ram caught	8011
	24:63	he s camels approaching.	8011
	24:64	Rebekah also looked up and s Isaac.	8011
	26: 8	and s Isaac caressing his wife Rebekah.	8011
	26:28	"We s clearly that the Lord was	8011+8011
	28:12	a dream in which he s a stairway resting on	2180
	29: 2	There he s a well in the field,	8011
	29:10	When Jacob s Rachel daughter of Laban,	8011
	29:31	the Lord s that Leah was not loved,	8011
	30: 1	When Rachel s that she was not bearing	8011
	30: 9	Leah s that she had stopped having children,	8011
	31:10	up and s that the male goats mating with	2180
	32: 2	When Jacob s them, he said,	8011
	32:25	the man s that he could not overpower him,	8011
	32:30	saying, "It is because I s God face to face,	8011
	33: 5	Then Esau looked up and s the women	8011
	34: 2	s her, he took her and violated her.	8011
	37: 4	When his brothers s that their father loved	8011
	37:18	But they s him in the distance,	8011
	37:25	up and s a caravan of Ishmaelites coming	8011
	37:29	the cistern and s that Joseph was not there,	2180
	38:14	For she s that, though Shelah had now	8011
	38:15	When Judah s her, he thought she was	8011
	39: 3	When his master s that the Lord was	8011
	39:13	When she s that he had left his cloak	8011
	40: 6	he s that they were dejected.	8011
	40: 9	"In my dream I s a vine in front of me,	2180
	40:16	the chief baker s that Joseph had given	8011
	41:22	"In my dreams I also s seven heads	8011
	42: 7	As soon as Joseph s his brothers,	8011
	42:21	We s how distressed he was	8011
	42:27	and he s his silver in the mouth of his sack.	8011
	42:35	they and their father s the money pouches,	8011
	43:16	When Joseph s Benjamin with them,	8011
	43:29	looked about and s his brother Benjamin,	8011
	45:27	and when he s the carts Joseph had sent	8011
	48: 8	When Israel s the sons of Joseph, he asked,	8011
	48:17	Joseph s his father placing his right hand	8011
	50:11	When the Canaanites who lived there s	8011
	50:15	When Joseph's brothers s that their father	8011
	50:23	and s the third generation of Ephraim's	8011
Ex	2: 2	When she s that he was a fine child,	8011
	2: 5	She s the basket among the reeds	8011
	2: 6	She opened it and s the baby.	8011
	2:11	He s an Egyptian beating a Hebrew,	8011
	2:13	and s two Hebrews fighting.	2180
	3: 2	Moses s that though the bush was	8011
	3: 4	the Lord s that he had gone over to look,	8011
	8:15	But when Pharaoh s that there was relief,	8011
	9:34	When Pharaoh s that the rain and hail	8011
	14:30	and Israel s the Egyptians lying dead on	8011
	14:31	And when the Israelites s the great power	8011
	16:15	When the Israelites s it,	8011
	18:14	When his father-in-law s all that Moses	8011
	20:18	the people s the thunder and lightning	8011
	20:18	and lightning and heard the trumpet and s	NIH
	24:10	and s the God of Israel.	8011
	24:11	they s God, and they ate and drank.	2600
	32: 1	When the people s that Moses was so long	8011
	32: 5	When Aaron s this, he built an altar	8011
	32:19	When Moses approached the camp and s	8011
	32:25	Moses s that the people were running wild	8011
	33:10	the people s the pillar of cloud standing at	8011
	34:30	When Aaron and all the Israelites s Moses,	8011
	34:35	they s that his face was radiant.	8011
	39:43	the work and s that they had done it just as	2180
Lev	9:24	And when all the people s it,	8011
Nu	12:10	toward her and s that she had leprosy;	2180
	13:28	We even s descendants of Anak there.	8011
	13:32	All the people we s there are of great size.	8011
	13:33	We s the Nephilim there (the descendants	8011
	14:22	not one of the men who s my glory and	8011
	17: 8	of the Testimony and s that Aaron's staff,	2180
	22: 2	of Zippor s all that Israel had done to	8011
	22:23	When the donkey s the angel of the Lord	8011
	22:25	the donkey s the angel of the Lord,	8011
	22:27	the donkey s the angel of the Lord,	8011

Nu	22:31	and he s the angel of the Lord standing in	8011
	22:33	The donkey s me and turned away	8011
	22:41	and from there he s part of the people.	8011
	24: 1	when Balaam s that it pleased the Lord	8011
	24: 2	and s Israel encamped tribe by tribe,	8011
	24:20	Balaam s Amalek and uttered his oracle:	8011
	24:21	Then he s the Kenites and uttered his oracle:	8011
	25: 7	the priest, s this, he left the assembly,	8011
	32: 1	s that the lands of Jazer and Gilead	8011
Dt	1:28	We even s the Anakites there.' "	8011
	1:31	There you s how the Lord your God	8011
	4: 3	You s with your own eyes what	8011
	4:12	the sound of words but s no form;	8011
	4:15	You s no form of any kind the day	8011
	7:19	You s with your own eyes the great trials,	8011
	9:16	I s that you had sinned against	2180
	10:21	and awesome wonders you s	8011
	11: 2	that your children were not the ones who s	8011
	11: 5	not your children who s what he did for you	NIH
	11: 7	that s all these great things	8011
	26: 7	Lord heard our voice and s our misery,	8011
	29: 3	With your own eyes you s those great trials,	8011
	29:17	You s among them their detestable images	8011
	32:19	The Lord s this and rejected them	8011
Jos	5:13	he looked up and s a man standing in front	8011
	7:21	When I s in the plunder a beautiful robe	8011
	8:14	When the king of Ai s this,	8011
	8:20	The men of Ai looked back and s the smoke	2180
	8:21	and all Israel s that the ambush had taken	8011
	9: 1	You s with your own eyes what I did to	8011
Jdg	1:24	the spies s a man coming out of the city	8011
	3:25	There they s their lord fallen to the floor,	2180
	9:36	When Gaal s them, he said to Zebul, "Look,	8011
	9:43	he s the people coming out of the city,	8011
	9:55	the Israelites s that Abimelech was dead,	8011
	11:35	When he s her, he tore his clothes	8011
	12: 3	When I s that you wouldn't help,	8011
	14: 1	Samson went down to Timnah and s there	8011
	16: 1	where he s a prostitute.	8011
	16:18	Delilah s that he had told her everything,	8011
	16:24	When the people s him,	8011
	17: 6	everyone did as he s fit.	928+6524
	18: 7	where they s that the people were living	8011
	19: 3	and when her father s him,	8011
	19:17	When he looked and s the traveler in	8011
	19:30	Everyone who s it said,	8011
	20:36	the Benjamites s that they were beaten.	8011
	20:40	and s the smoke of the whole city going up	2180
	21:25	everyone did as he s fit.	928+6524
Ru	2:18	and her mother-in-law s how much she	8011
1Sa	2:32	the men of Ashdod s what was happening,	8011
	6:13	and when they looked up and s the ark,	8011
	6:16	of the Philistines s all this and then returned	8011
	10:11	had formerly known him s him prophesying	8011
	10:14	"But when we s they were not to be found,	8011
	12:12	"But when you s that Nahash king of	8011
	13: 6	of Israel s that their situation was critical	8011
	13:11	"When I s that the men were scattering,	8011
	14:16	Saul's lookouts at Gibeah in Benjamin s	8011
	14:26	they s the honey oozing out,	2180
	14:52	whenever Saul s a mighty or brave man,	8011
	16: 6	Samuel s Eliab and thought,	8011
	17:24	When the Israelites s the man,	8011
	17:42	over and s that he was only a boy,	8011
	17:51	the Philistines s that their hero was dead,	8011
	18:15	When Saul s how successful he was,	8011
	19: 5	and you s it and were glad.	8011
	19:20	they s a group of prophets prophesying,	8011
	22: 9	"I s the son of Jesse come to Ahimelech son	8011
	25:23	When Abigail s David,	8011
	26: 3	When he s that Saul had followed him there,	8011
	26: 5	He s where Saul and Abner son of Ner,	8011
	26:12	No one s or knew about it,	8011
	28: 5	Saul s the Philistine army, he was afraid;	8011
	28:12	When the woman s Samuel,	8011
	28:21	to Saul and s that he was greatly shaken,	8011
	31: 5	the armor-bearer s that Saul was dead,	8011
	31: 7	the valley and those across the Jordan s that	8011
2Sa	1: 7	When he turned around and s me,	8011
	6:16	when she s King David leaping and dancing	8011
	10: 9	Joab s that there were battle lines in front	8011
	10:14	When the Ammonites s that the Arameans	8011
	10:15	the Arameans s that they had been routed	8011
	10:19	of Hadadezer s that they had been defeated	8011
	11: 2	From the roof he s a woman bathing.	8011
	13:34	and s many people on the road west of him,	8011
	17:18	But a young man s them and told Absalom.	8011
	17:23	When Ahithophel s that his advice had	8011
	18:10	When one of the men s this, he told Joab,	8011
	18:10	"I just s Absalom hanging in an oak tree."	8011
	18:11	"What? You s him? Why didn't you strike	8011
	18:24	As he looked out, he s a man running alone.	8011
	18:26	Then the watchman s another man running,	8011
	18:29	"I s great confusion just as Joab was about	8011
	20:12	and the man s that all the troops came to	8011
	24:17	When David s the angel who was striking	8011
	24:20	When Araunah looked and s the king	8011
1Ki	3:21	I s that it wasn't the son I had borne."	2180
	3:28	because they s that he had wisdom	8011
	4:27	s to it that nothing was lacking.	6372
	7: 9	to size and trimmed with a s on their inner	4490
	10: 4	When the queen of Sheba s all the wisdom	8011
	10: 7	not believe these things until I came and s	8011
	11:28	and when Solomon s how well	8011
	12:16	When all Israel s that the king refused	8011
	13:25	by s the body thrown down there,	8011
	16:18	When Zimri s that the city was taken,	8011

1Ki	18:17	When he s Elijah, he said to him,	8011
	18:39	When all the people s this,	8011
	22:17	"I s all Israel scattered on the hills	8011
	22:19	I s the Lord sitting on his throne	8011
	22:32	the chariot commanders s Jehoshaphat,	8011
	22:33	the chariot commanders s that he was not	8011
2Ki	2:12	Elisha s this and cried out, "My father!	8011
	2:12	And Elisha s him no more.	8011
	3:26	the king of Moab s that the battle had gone	8011
	4:25	When he s her in the distance,	8011
	5:21	When Naaman s him running toward him,	8011
	6:17	and he looked and s the hills full of horses	2180
	6:21	When the king of Israel s them,	8011
	9:17	in Jezreel s Jehu's troops approaching,	8011
	9:22	When Joram s Jehu he asked,	8011
	9:26	'Yesterday I s the blood of Naboth and	8011
	9:27	king of Judah s what had happened,	8011
	11: 1	When Athaliah the mother of Ahaziah s	8011
	12:10	Whenever they s that there was	8011
	13: 4	for he s how severely the king of Aram	8011
	13:21	suddenly they s a band of raiders;	8011
	16:10	He s an altar in Damascus and sent to Uriah	8011
	16:12	the king came back from Damascus and s	8011
	20:15	"They s everything in my palace,"	8011
	23:16	and when he s the tombs that were there on	8011
1Ch	10: 5	the armor-bearer s that Saul was dead,	8011
	10: 7	When all the Israelites in the valley that	8011
	15:29	she s King David dancing and celebrating,	8011
	19:10	Joab s that there were battle lines in front	8011
	19:15	When the Ammonites s that the Arameans	8011
	19:16	the Arameans s that they had been routed	8011
	19:19	of Hadadezer s that they had been defeated	8011
	21:15	the Lord s it and was grieved because of	8011
	21:16	up and s the angel of the Lord standing	8011
	21:20	he turned and s the angel;	8011
	21:21	and when Araunah looked and s him,	8011
	21:28	when David s that the Lord had answered	8011
2Ch	7: 3	the Israelites s the fire coming down and	8011
	9: 3	queen of Sheba s the wisdom of Solomon,	8011
	9: 6	until I came and s with my own eyes.	8011
	10:16	When all Israel s that the king refused	NIH
	12: 7	the Lord s that they humbled themselves,	8011
	13:14	and s that they were being attacked at	2180
	15: 9	when they s that the Lord his God was	8011
	18:16	"I s all Israel scattered on the hills	8011
	18:18	I s the Lord sitting on his throne	8011
	18:31	the chariot commanders s Jehoshaphat,	8011
	18:32	when the chariot commanders s that he was	8011
	20:24	they s only dead bodies lying on	2180
	22:10	When Athaliah the mother of Ahaziah s	8011
	24:11	the king's officials and they s that there was	8011
	26:20	they s that he had leprosy on his forehead,	2180
	31: 8	and his officials came and s the heaps,	8011
Ezr	3:12	wept aloud when they s the foundation	928+6524
Ne	9: 9	"You s the suffering of our forefathers	8011
	13:15	In those days I s men in Judah treading	8011
	13:23	in those days I s men of Judah who had	8011
Est	2:15	Esther won the favor of everyone who s her.	8011
	3: 5	When Haman s that Mordecai would	8011
	5: 2	When he s Queen Esther standing in	8011
	5: 9	But when he s Mordecai at the king's gate	8011
Job	2:12	When they s him from a distance,	906+5951+6524
	2:13	because they s how great his suffering was.	8011
	3:16	like an infant who never s the light of day?	8011
	8:18	'I never s you.'	8011
	10:18	I wish I had died before any eye s me.	8011
	20: 9	The eye that s him will not see him again;	8812
	29: 8	the young men s me and stepped aside and	8011
	29:11	and those who s me commended me,	8011
	32: 5	But when he s that the three men had	8011
	42:16	he s his children and their children to	8011
Ps	31: 7	for you s my affliction and knew	8011
	48: 5	they s [her] and were astounded;	8011
	73: 3	the arrogant when I s the prosperity of	8011
	77:16	The waters s you, O God,	8011
	77:16	O God, the waters s you and writhed;	8011
	107:24	They s the works of the Lord,	8011
	139:16	your eyes s my unformed body.	8011
Pr	7: 7	I s among the simple,	8011
	24:32	and learned a lesson from what I s:	8011
Ecc	2:13	I s that wisdom is better than folly,	8011
	3:16	And I s something else under the sun:	8011
	3:22	So I s that there is nothing better for	8011
	4: 1	Again I looked and s all the oppression	8011
	4: 1	I s the tears of the oppressed—	2180
	4: 4	And I s that all labor and all achievement	8011
	4: 7	Again I s something meaningless under	8011
	4:15	I s that all who lived and walked under	8011
	6: 5	it never s the sun or knew anything,	8011
	8: 9	All this I s, as I applied my mind	8011
	8:10	Then too, I s the wicked buried—	8011
	8:17	then I s all that God has done.	8011
	9:13	I also s under the sun this example	8011
SS	6: 9	The maidens s her and called her blessed;	8011
Isa	1: 1	that Isaiah son of Amoz s during the reigns	2600
	2: 1	This is what Isaiah son of Amoz s	2600
	5: 7	And he looked for justice, but s bloodshed;	2180
	6: 1	I s the Lord seated on a throne,	8011
	10:15	or the s boast against him who uses it?	5373
	13: 1	that Isaiah son of Amoz s:	2600
	22: 9	you s that the City of David had many	8011
	39: 4	"They s everything in my palace,"	8011
	59:16	He s that there was no one,	8011
Jer	3: 7	and her unfaithful sister Judah s it.	8011
	3: 8	Yet I s that her unfaithful sister Judah had	8011
	18: 3	and I s him working at the wheel.	2180

Jer	23:13	prophets of Samaria I s this repulsive thing:	8011
	39: 4	and all the soldiers s them, they fled;	8011
	41:13	with him s Johanan son of Kareah and	8011
	44: 2	You s the great disaster I brought	8011
La	1:10	she s pagan nations enter her sanctuary—	8011
Eze	1: 1	the heavens were opened and I s visions	8011
	1: 4	I s a windstorm coming out of the north—	2180
	1:15	I s a wheel on the ground	2180
	1:27	I s that from what appeared to be his waist	8011
	1:28	When I s it, I fell facedown,	8011
	2: 9	I looked, and I s a hand stretched out to me.	2180
	8: 2	I looked, and I s a figure like that of a man.	2180
	8: 5	the gate of the altar I s this idol of jealousy.	2180
	8: 7	I looked, and I s a hole in the wall.	2180
	8: 8	I dug into the wall and s a doorway there.	NIH
	8:10	and I s portrayed all over the walls all kinds	2180
	8:14	and I s women sitting there,	2180
	9: 2	And I s six men coming from the direction	2180
	10: 1	and I s the likeness of a throne of sapphire	2180
	10: 9	and I s beside the cherubim four wheels,	2180
	11: 1	and I s among them Jaazaniah son	8011
	13:16	and s visions of peace for her	2600+2606
	16: 6	" 'Then I passed by and s you kicking about	8011
	16: 8	and s that you were old enough for love,	2180
	19: 5	" 'When she s her hope unfulfilled,	8011
	20:28	and they s any high hill or any leafy tree,	8011
	23:11	"Her sister Oholibah s this,	8011
	23:13	I s that she too defiled herself;	8011
	23:14	She s men portrayed on a wall,	8011
	23:16	As soon as she s them,	5260+6524
	37: 2	and I s a great many bones on the floor of	2180
	40: 3	and I s a man whose appearance was	2180
	40: 5	I s a wall completely surrounding	2180
	40:17	There I s some rooms and a pavement	2180
	40:24	to the south side and I s a gate facing south.	2180
	41: 8	I s that the temple had a raised base all	8011
	43: 2	and I s the glory of the God	2180
	43: 3	The vision I s was like the vision	8011
	44: 4	and s the glory of the LORD filling	2180
	46:21	and I s in each corner another court.	2180
	47: 1	and I s water coming out from under	2180
	47: 7	I s a great number of trees on each side of	2180
Da	2:26	"Are you able to tell me what I s	10255
	2:41	as you s that the feet and toes were partly	10255
	2:41	even as you s iron mixed with clay.	10255
	2:43	as you s the iron mixed with baked clay,	10255
	3:27	They s that the fire had not harmed	10255
	4:10	the visions I s while lying in my bed:	10646
	4:13	"In the visions I s while lying in my bed,	10646
	4:20	The tree you s, which grew large and	10255
	4:23	"You, O king, s a messenger, a holy one,	10255
	8: 2	In my vision I s myself in the citadel	8011
	8: 7	I s him attack the ram furiously,	8011
	8:20	The two-horned ram that you s represents	8011
	10: 7	I, Daniel, was the only one who s the vision;	8011
Hos	5:13	"When Ephraim s his sickness,	8011
	9:10	when I s your fathers,	8011
Am	1: 1	what he s concerning Israel two years	2600
	9: 1	I s the Lord standing by the altar,	8011
Jnh	3:10	When God s what they did and	8011
Mic	1: 1	the vision he s concerning Samaria	2600
Hab	3: 7	I s the tents of Cushan in distress,	8011
	3:10	the mountains s you and writhed.	8011
Hag	2: 3	'Who of you is left who s this house	8011
Mt	2: 2	We s his star in the east and have come	3972
	2:10	When they s the star, they were overjoyed.	3972
	2:11	they s the child with his mother Mary,	3972
	3: 7	But when he s many of the Pharisees	3972
	3:16	and he s the Spirit of God descending like	3972
	4:18	the Sea of Galilee, he s two brothers,	3972
	4:21	he s two other brothers,	3972
	5: 1	Now when he s the crowds,	3972
	8:14	he s Peter's mother-in-law lying in bed with	3972
	8:18	When Jesus s the crowd around him,	3972
	8:34	And when they s him, they pleaded	3972
	9: 2	When Jesus s their faith,	3972
	9: 8	When the crowd s this,	3972
	9: 9	he s a man named Matthew sitting at	3972
	9:11	When the Pharisees s this,	3972
	9:22	Jesus turned and s her.	3972
	9:23	the ruler's house and s the flute players and	3972
	9:36	When he s the crowds, he had compassion	3972
	12: 2	When the Pharisees s this, they said to him,	3972
	14:14	When Jesus landed and s a large crowd,	3972
	14:26	the disciples s him walking on the lake,	3972
	14:30	But when he s the wind, he was afraid and,	1063
	15:31	The people were amazed when they s	1063
	17: 8	they s no one except Jesus.	3972
	18:31	the other servants s what had happened,	3972
	20: 3	and s others standing in the marketplace	3972
	21:15	of the law s the wonderful things he did and	3972
	21:20	When the disciples s this, they were amazed.	3972
	21:32	And even after you s this,	3972
	21:38	"But when the tenants s the son,	3972
	26: 8	When the disciples s this,	3972
	26:71	where another girl s him and said to	3972
	27: 3	s that Jesus was condemned,	3972
	27:24	When Pilate s that he was getting nowhere,	3972
	27:54	with him who were guarding Jesus s	3972
	28:17	When they s him, they worshiped him;	3972
Mk	1:10	he s heaven being torn open and	3972
	1:16	he s Simon and his brother Andrew casting	3972
	1:19	he s James son of Zebedee	3972
	2: 5	When Jesus s their faith,	3972
	2:14	he s Levi son of Alphaeus sitting at	3972
	2:16	who were Pharisees s him eating with the	3972
	3:11	Whenever the evil spirits s him,	2555

Mk	5: 6	When he s Jesus from a distance,	3972
	5:15	they s the man who had been possessed by	2555
	5:38	Jesus s a commotion,	2555
	6:33	many who s them leaving recognized them	3972
	6:34	When Jesus landed and s a large crowd,	3972
	6:48	He s the disciples straining at the oars,	3972
	6:49	but when they s him walking on the lake,	3972
	6:50	because they all s him and were terrified.	3972
	7: 2	s some of his disciples eating food	3972
	8:25	and he s everything clearly.	1838
	9: 8	they no longer s anyone with them	3972
	9:14	they s a large crowd around them and	3972
	9:15	As soon as all the people s Jesus,	3972
	9:20	When the spirit s Jesus,	3972
	9:25	When Jesus s that a crowd was running to	3972
	9:38	"we s a man driving out demons	3972
	10:14	When Jesus s this, he was indignant.	3972
	11:20	they s the fig tree withered from the roots.	3972
	12:34	When Jesus s that he had answered wisely,	3972
	14:67	When she s Peter warming himself,	3972
	14:69	When the servant girl s him there,	3972
	15:39	heard his cry and s how he died, he said,	3972
	15:47	the mother of Joses s where he was laid.	2555
	16: 4	when they looked up, they s that the stone,	2555
	16: 5	they s a young man dressed in	3972
Lk	1:12	When Zechariah s him, he was startled	3972
	2:48	When his parents s him, they were astonished.	3972
	5: 2	he s at the water's edge two boats,	3972
	5: 8	When Simon Peter s this,	3972
	5:12	When he s Jesus, he fell with his face to	3972
	5:20	When Jesus s their faith, he said, "Friend,	3972
	5:27	Jesus went out and s a tax collector by	2517
	7:13	When the Lord s her, his heart went out	3972
	7:39	the Pharisee who had invited him s this,	3972
	8:28	When he s Jesus, he cried out	3972
	8:34	the pigs s what had happened,	3972
	9:32	they s his glory and the two men standing	3972
	9:49	"we s a man driving out demons	3972
	9:54	When the disciples James and John s this,	3972
	10:18	"I s Satan fall like lightning from heaven.	2555
	10:31	and when he s the man,	3972
	10:32	when he came to the place and s him,	3972
	10:33	and when he s him, he took pity on him.	3972
	13:12	When Jesus s her, he called her forward	3972
	15:20	his father s him and was filled	3972
	16:23	he looked up and s Abraham far away,	3972
	17:14	When he s them, he said, "Go,	3972
	17:15	One of them, when he s he was healed,	3972
	18:15	When the disciples s this,	3972
	18:43	all the people s it, they also praised God.	3972
	19: 7	All the people s this and began to mutter,	3972
	19:41	As he approached Jerusalem and s the city,	3972
	20:14	tenants s him, they talked the matter over.	3972
	20:23	He s through their duplicity and said	2917
	21: 1	Jesus s the rich putting their gifts into	3972
	21: 2	He also s a poor widow put	3972
	22:49	When Jesus' followers s what was going	3972
	22:56	A servant girl s him seated there in	3972
	22:58	A little later someone else s him and said,	3972
	23: 8	When Herod s Jesus, he was greatly pleased,	3972
	23:48	to witness this sight s what took place,	2555
	23:55	and s the tomb and how his body was laid	2517
	24:12	he s the strips of linen lying by themselves,	1063
	24:37	thinking they s a ghost.	2555
Jn	1:29	The next day John s Jesus coming	1063
	1:32	"I s the Spirit come down from heaven as	2517
	1:36	When he s Jesus passing by, he said, "Look,	1838
	1:38	Jesus s them following and asked,	2517
	1:39	So they went and s where he was staying,	3972
	1:47	When Jesus s Nathanael approaching,	3972
	1:48	"I s you while you were still under	3972
	1:50	"You believe because I told you I s you	3972
	2:23	at the Passover Feast, many people s	2555
	5: 6	When Jesus s him lying there and learned	3972
	6: 2	of people followed him because they s	2555
	6: 5	up and s a great crowd coming toward him,	2517
	6:14	After the people s the miraculous sign	3972
	6:19	they s Jesus approaching the boat,	2555
	6:26	not because you s miraculous signs but	3972
	8:56	he s it and was glad."	3972
	9: 1	he s a man blind from birth.	3972
	11:32	the place where Jesus was and s him,	3972
	11:33	When Jesus s her weeping,	3972
	12:41	Isaiah said this because he s Jesus' glory	3972
	16:19	Jesus s that they wanted to ask him	1182
	19: 6	as the chief priests and their officials s him,	3972
	19:26	When Jesus s his mother there,	3972
	19:35	The man who s it has given testimony,	3972
	20: 1	and s that the stone had been removed from	1063
	20: 6	He s the strips of linen lying there,	2555
	20: 8	He s and believed.	3972
	20:12	and s two angels in white, seated where	2555
	20:14	turned around and s Jesus standing there,	2555
	20:20	The disciples were overjoyed when they s	3972
	21: 9	they s a fire of burning coals there with fish	1063
	21:20	Peter turned and s that the disciple	1063
	21:21	When Peter s him, he asked, "Lord,	3972
Ac	2: 3	They s what seemed to be tongues of fire	3972
	2:25	" 'I s the Lord always before me.	4632
	3: 3	When he s Peter and John about to enter,	3972
	3: 9	the people s him walking and praising God,	3972
	3:12	When Peter s this, he said to them:	3972
	4:13	When they s the courage of Peter and John	2555
	6:15	and they s that his face was like the face of	3972
	7:24	He s one of them being mistreated by	3972
	7:31	When he s this, he was amazed at the sight.	3972

Ac	7:55	looked up to heaven and s the glory of God,	3972
	8: 6	When the crowds heard Philip and s	1063
	8:13	by the great signs and miracles he s.	2555
	8:18	When Simon s that the Spirit was given at	3972
	9:35	and Sharon s him and turned to the Lord.	3972
	10: 3	He distinctly s an angel of God,	3972
	10:11	He s heaven opened and something like	2555
	11: 5	and in a trance I s a vision.	3972
	11: 5	I s something like a large sheet being let	NIG
	11: 6	I looked into it and s four-footed animals of	3972
	11:23	and s the evidence of the grace of God,	3972
	12: 3	When he s that this pleased the Jews,	3972
	12:16	and when they opened the door and s him,	3972
	13:12	When the proconsul s what had happened,	3972
	13:45	When the Jews s the crowds,	3972
	14: 9	s that he had faith to be healed	3972
	14:11	When the crowd s what Paul had done,	3972
	16:27	and when he s the prison doors open,	3972
	21:27	some Jews from the province of Asia s Paul	2517
	21:32	When the rioters s the commander	3972
	22: 9	My companions s the light,	2517
	22:18	and s the Lord speaking.	3972
	26:13	I s a light from heaven,	3972
	27:39	but they s a bay with a sandy beach,	2917
	28: 4	When the islanders s the snake hanging	3972
Gal	1:19	I s none of the other apostles—	3972
	2: 7	they s that I had been entrusted with	3972
	2:14	When I s that they were not acting in line	3972
Php	1:30	through the same struggle you s I had,	3972
Heb	3: 9	and for forty years s what I did.	3972
	11:13	they only s them and welcomed them from	3972
	11:23	because they s he was no ordinary child,	3972
	11:27	because he s him who is invisible.	3972
2Pe	2: 8	by the lawless deeds he s and heard)—	1062
Rev	1: 2	who testifies to everything he s—	3972
	1:12	I turned I s seven golden lampstands,	3972
	1:17	When I s him, I fell at his feet	3972
	1:20	the seven stars that you s in my right hand	3972
	5: 1	Then I s in the right hand of him who sat	3972
	5: 2	And I s a mighty angel proclaiming in	3972
	5: 6	Then I s a Lamb, looking as if	3972
	6: 9	I s under the altar the souls of those	3972
	7: 1	After this I s four angels standing at	3972
	7: 2	I s another angel coming up from the east,	3972
	8: 2	I s the seven angels who stand before God,	3972
	9: 1	and I s a star that had fallen from the sky	3972
	9:17	and riders I s in my vision looked like this:	3972
	10: 1	Then I s another mighty angel coming	2555
	11:11	and terror struck those who s them.	3972
	12:13	When the dragon s that he had been hurled	3972
	13: 1	And I s a beast coming out of the sea.	3972
	13: 2	The beast I s resembled a leopard,	3972
	13:11	I s another beast, coming out of the earth.	3972
	14: 6	Then I s another angel flying in midair,	3972
	15: 1	I s in heaven another great and marvelous	3972
	15: 2	And I s what looked like a sea of glass	3972
	16:13	I s three evil spirits that looked like frogs;	3972
	17: 3	There I s a woman sitting on	3972
	17: 6	I s that the woman was drunk with	3972
	17: 6	When I s her, I was greatly astonished.	3972
	17: 8	The beast, which you s, once was,	3972
	17:12	"The ten horns you s are ten kings who have	3972
	17:15	the angel said to me, "The waters you s,	3972
	17:16	The beast and the ten horns you s will hate	3972
	17:18	The woman you s is the great city	3972
	18: 1	After this I s another angel coming down	3972
	19:11	I s heaven standing open and there	3972
	19:17	And I s an angel standing in the sun,	3972
	19:19	Then I s the beast and the kings of	3972
	20: 1	I s an angel coming down out of heaven,	3972
	20: 4	I s thrones on which were seated	3972
	20: 4	And I s the souls of those who had been	NIG
	20:11	Then I s a great white throne	3972
	20:12	And I s the dead, great and small,	3972
	21: 1	Then I s a new heaven and a new earth,	3972
	21: 2	I s the Holy City, the new Jerusalem,	3972
	22: 8	am the one who heard and s these things.	1063

SAWDUST (2)

Mt	7: 3	at the speck of s in your brother's eye	2847
Lk	6:41	at the speck of s in your brother's eye	2847

SAWED (1) [SAWS]

| Heb | 11:37 | They were stoned; they were s in two; | 4569 |

SAWN (Anglicized) See SAWED

SAWS (2) [SAWED]

2Sa	12:31	consigning them to labor with s and	4490
1Ch	20: 3	consigning them to labor with s and	4490

SAY (921) [SAID, SAYING, SAYINGS, SAYS]

Ge	3: 1	He said to the woman, "Did God really s,	606
	3: 3	but God did s, 'You must not eat fruit	606
	12:12	When the Egyptians see you, they will s,	606
	12:13	S you are my sister,	606
	12:19	Why did you s, 'She is my sister,'	606
	14:23	so that you will never be able to s,	606
	18: 5	"Very well," they answered, "do as you s."	1819
	18:13	"Why did Sarah laugh and s,	606
	20: 5	Did he not s to me, 'She is my sister,'	606
	20: 5	and didn't she also s, 'He is my brother'?	606
	20:13	Everywhere we go, s of me,	606
	24:14	May it be that when I s to a girl,	606

Ge	24:33	until I have told you **what I have to s.**"	1821
	24:43	a maiden comes out to draw water and *I* s	606
	24:50	we can s nothing to you one way or	1819
	26: 7	because he was afraid to s,	606
	26: 9	Why *did you* s, 'She is my sister'?"	606
	27: 6	I overheard your father s	1819
	27:13	Just do what I s; go and get them for me."	7754
	27:43	Now then, my son, do **what** I s:	7754
	31:24	"Be careful not *to* s anything to Jacob,	1819
	31:29	'Be careful not *to* s anything to Jacob,	1819
	32: 4	"This is what *you are to* s"	606
	32:18	then *you are to* s,	606
	32:19	"*You are to* s the same thing to Esau	1819
	32:20	And be sure *to* s,	606
	37:17	"I heard *them* s, 'Let's go to Dothan.' "	606
	37:20	into one of these cisterns and s *that*	606
	43: 7	How were we to know *he would* s,	606
	44: 4	when you catch up with them, s to them,	606
	44: 7	"Why *does* my lord s such things?	1819
	44:10	then," he said, "let it be as you s.	1821
	44:16	"What *can we* s to my lord?"	606
	44:16	"What *can we* s?	1819
	45: 9	Now hurry back to my father and s to him,	606
	46:31	up and speak to Pharaoh and *will* s to him,	606
	47:30	"I will do as you s," he said.	1821
	50:17	'This is what *you are to* s to Joseph:	606
Ex	3:13	"Suppose I go to the Israelites and s	606
	3:14	This is what *you are to* s to the Israelites:	606
	3:15	God also said to Moses, **"S** to the Israelites,	606
	3:16	assemble the elders of Israel and s to them,	606
	3:18	to go to the king of Egypt and s to him,	606
	4: 1	not believe me or listen to me and s,	606
	4:12	and will teach you what *to* s."	1819
	4:22	Then s to Pharaoh, 'This is what	606
	4:28	the LORD had sent him to s,	1821
	6: 6	"Therefore, s to the Israelites:	606
	7: 2	You *are to* s everything I command you,	1819
	7: 9	'Perform a miracle,' then s to Aaron,	606
	7:16	Then s to him, 'The LORD,	606
	7:16	has sent me to s to you:	606
	8: 1	"Go to Pharaoh and s to him,	606
	8:10	Moses replied, "It will be as you s,	1821
	8:20	to the water and s to him, 'This is what	606
	9: 1	"Go to Pharaoh and s to him,	1819
	9:13	confront Pharaoh and s to him,	606
	10:29	"Just as *you* s," Moses replied,	1819
	13:14	s to him, 'With a mighty hand	606
	14:12	Didn't *we* s to you in Egypt,	1819+1821
	16: 9	**"S** to the entire Israelite community,	606
	19: 3	*to* s to the house of Jacob and what you are	606
	23:22	to what he says and do all that *I* s,	1819
	30:31	s to him, 'This is to be	1819
	31:13	**"S** to the Israelites, 'You must observe	1819
	32:12	Why *should* the Egyptians s,	606
Lev	1: 2	"Speak to the Israelites and s to them:	606
	4: 2	"Speak to the Israelites: 'When anyone sins	1819
	6:25	**"S** to Aaron and his sons:	1819
	7:23	**"S** to the Israelites: 'Do not eat any	1819
	7:29	**"S** to the Israelites: 'Anyone who brings	1819
	9: 3	Then s to the Israelites: 'Take a male goat	1819
	11: 2	**"S** to the Israelites: 'Of all the animals	1819
	12: 2	**"S** to the Israelites: 'A woman who	1819
	15: 2	"Speak to the Israelites and s	606
	17: 2	and his sons and to all the Israelites and s	606
	17: 8	**"S** to them: 'Any Israelite	606
	17:12	Therefore *I* s to the Israelites,	606
	18: 2	"Speak to the Israelites and s to them:	606
	19: 2	the entire assembly of Israel and s to them:	606
	20: 2	**"S** to the Israelites: 'Any Israelite	606
	21: 1	the sons of Aaron, and s to them:	606
	21:17	**"S** to Aaron: 'For the generations to come	1819
	22: 3	**"S** to them: 'For the generations to come,	606
	22:18	and his sons and to all the Israelites and s	606
	23: 2	"Speak to the Israelites and s to them:	606
	23:10	"Speak to the Israelites and s to them:	606
	23:24	**"S** to the Israelites: 'On the first day	1819
	23:34	**"S** to the Israelites: 'On the fifteenth day	1819
	24:15	S to the Israelites: 'If anyone curses	1819
	25: 2	"Speak to the Israelites and s to them:	606
	27: 2	"Speak to the Israelites and s to them:	606
Nu	5: 6	**"S** to the Israelites: 'When a man or woman	1819
	5:12	"Speak to the Israelites and s to them:	606
	5:19	the woman under oath and s to her,	606
	5:22	" Then the woman *is to* s, "Amen.	606
	6: 2	"Speak to the Israelites and s to them:	606
	6:23	to bless the Israelites. S to them:	606
	8: 2	"Speak to Aaron and s to him,	606
	11:21	and you s, 'I will give them meat to eat for	606
	11:23	or not *what* I will come true for you."	1821
	14:15	who have heard this report about you *will* s,	606
	14:28	to you the very things I heard *you* s:	1819
	15: 2	"Speak to the Israelites and s to them:	606
	15:18	"Speak to the Israelites and s to them:	606
	15:38	"Speak to the Israelites and s to them:	606
	16:24	**"S** to the assembly, 'Move away from	1819
	18:26	"Speak to the Levites and s to them:	606
	18:30	**"S** to the Levites: 'When you present	606
	21:21	Israel sent messengers to s to Sihon king of	606
	21:27	That is why the poets s:	606
	22:17	and do whatever *you* s.	606
	22:38	"But can I s just anything?	1819
	23:17	Balak asked him, "What *did* the LORD s?"	1819
	24:13	and I *must* s only what the LORD says'?	1819
	27: 8	**"S** to the Israelites, 'If a man dies	1819
	28: 2	"Give this command to the Israelites and s	606
	28: 3	S to them: 'This is the offering made by fire	606
	33:51	"Speak to the Israelites and s to them:	606

Nu	34: 2	"Command the Israelites and s to them:	606
	35:10	"Speak to the Israelites and s to them:	606
Dt	1:28	*They* s, 'The people are stronger	606
	4: 6	who will hear about all these decrees and s,	606
	7:17	*You may* s to yourselves,	606
	8:17	*You may* s to yourself, "My power and my	606
	9: 4	*do* not s to yourself, "The LORD has	606
	9:28	country from which you brought us *will* s,	606
	12:20	and you crave meat and s,	606
	17:14	settled in it, and you s, "Let us set a king	606
	18:17	"What *they* s is good.	1819
	18:20	not commanded him to s,	1819
	18:21	*You may* s to yourselves,	606
	20: 3	*He shall* s: "Hear, O Israel,	606
	20: 5	The officers *shall* s to the army:	1819
	21:20	*They shall* s to the elders,	606
	22:16	The girl's father *will* s to the elders,	606
	25: 7	to the elders at the town gate and s,	606
	25: 9	spit in his face and s,	606
	26: 3	and s to the priest in office at the time,	606
	26:13	Then s to the LORD your God:	606
	27:15	all the people *shall* s, "Amen!"	606+2256+6699
	27:16	Then all the people *shall* s, "Amen!"	606
	27:17	Then all the people *shall* s, "Amen!"	606
	27:18	Then all the people *shall* s, "Amen!"	606
	27:19	Then all the people *shall* s, "Amen!"	606
	27:20	Then all the people *shall* s, "Amen!"	606
	27:21	Then all the people *shall* s, "Amen!"	606
	27:22	Then all the people *shall* s, "Amen!"	606
	27:23	Then all the people *shall* s, "Amen!"	606
	27:24	Then all the people *shall* s, "Amen!"	606
	27:25	Then all the people *shall* s, "Amen!"	606
	27:26	Then all the people *shall* s, "Amen!"	606
	28:67	In the morning *you will* s,	606
	32:27	lest the adversary misunderstand and s,	606
	32:37	*He will* s: "Now where are their gods,	606
Jos	2:21	"Let it be as you s."	1821
	6:10	*do* not s a word until the day I tell you to shout!"	3655+4946+7023
	7: 8	O Lord, what *can I* s,	606
	8: 6	for *they will* s, 'They are running away	606
	9:11	go and meet them and s to them,	606
	22:24	that some day your descendants *might* s	606
	22:27	not *be able to* s to ours,	606
	22:28	"And we said, 'If *they* ever s this to us,	606
	22:30	Gad and Manasseh *had to* s,	1819
Jdg	4:20	'Is anyone here?' s 'No.' "	606
	7: 4	If *I* s, 'This one shall go with you,'	606
	7: 4	but if *I* s, 'This one shall not go with you,'	606
	9:29	*I would* s to Abimelech,	606
	9:54	your sword and kill me, so that *they* can't s,	606
	11:10	we will certainly do as you s."	1821
	12: 6	"All right, s 'Shibboleth.' "	606
	16:15	Then she said to him, "How *can you* s,	606
	18:19	**Don't s a word.**	3338+6584+7023+8492
	21:22	*we will* s to them,	606
Ru	3: 5	"I will do whatever *you* s," Ruth answered.	606
1Sa	1: 8	Elkanah her husband *would* s to her,	606
	2:15	the servant of the priest would come and s	606
	3: 9	"Go and lie down, and if he calls you, s,	606
	9: 9	*he would* s, "Come, let us go to the seer,"	606
	9:21	Why *do you* s such a thing to me?"	1819
	10: 2	*They will* s to you, 'The donkeys you set out	606
	11: 9	**"S** to the men of Jabesh Gilead,	606
	13: 9	If *they* s to us, 'Wait there until we come	606
	14:10	But if *they* s, 'Come up to us,'	606
	16: 2	"Take a heifer with you and s,	606
	18:22	"Speak to David privately and s, 'Look,	606
	18:25	Saul replied, **"S** to David,	606
	19:24	This is why *people* s, "Is Saul also among	606
	20:21	Then I will send a boy and s, 'Go,	NIH
	20:21	If *I* s to him, 'Look,	606+606
	20:22	But if *I* s to the boy, 'Look,	606
	24: 9	"Why do you listen *when* men s,	606
	25: 6	S to him: 'Long life to you!	606
	25:24	*what* your servant has to s.	1821
	27:10	David *would* s, "Against the Negev	606
	27:11	"They might inform on us and s,	606
	30:24	Who will listen to **what** you s?	1821
2Sa	2: 5	to the men of Jabesh Gilead *to* s to them,	606
	3:11	Ish-Bosheth did not dare to s another word	8740
	3:12	on his behalf to s to David,	606
	5: 8	That is why *they* s, "The 'blind and lame'	606
	7: 7	*did I* ever s to any of their rulers	1819+1821
	7:20	"What more *can* David s to you?	1819
	7:26	Then men *will* s, 'The LORD Almighty	606
	11:21	If he asks you this, then s to him, 'Also,	606
	11:22	David everything Joab had sent him to s.	NIH
	11:25	David told the messenger, **"S** this to Joab:	606
	11:25	S this to encourage Joab."	NIH
	13: 5	s to him, 'I would like my sister Tamar	606
	13:28	in high spirits from drinking wine and *I* s	606
	14: 7	*they* s, 'Hand over the one who struck	606
	14:15	"And now I have come to s this to my lord	1819
	15: 3	Then Absalom *would* s to him, "Look,	606
	15:10	throughout the tribes of Israel to s,	606
	15:10	then s, 'Absalom is king in Hebron.' "	606
	15:34	if you return to the city and s to Absalom,	606
	17: 5	so we can hear what he has to s."	7023
	17: 9	whoever hears about it *will* s,	606
	19:10	So why *do you* s **nothing** *about* bringing	3087
	19:13	And s to Amasa, 'Are you not my own	606
	19:29	The king said to him, "Why s more?	1819+1821
	20:17	*what* your servant *has to* s."	1821
	20:18	continued, "Long ago *they* **used to** s,	1819+1819
1Ki	1:13	Go in to King David and s to him,	606
	2:14	he added, "I have **something to** s to you."	1821

2Sa	2:14	"*You may* s it," she replied.	1819
	2:38	**"What** you s is good.	1821
	2:42	**'What** you s is good.	1821
	8:47	in the land of their conquerors and s,	606
	9: 8	by will be appalled and will scoff and s,	606
	12: 9	How should we answer these people who s	1819
	12:23	**"S** to Rehoboam son of Solomon king	606
	18:11	now you tell me to go to my master and s,	606
	18:14	now you tell me to go to my master and s,	606
	18:24	all the people said, "What you s is good."	1821
	19: 2	So Jezebel sent a messenger to Elijah to s,	606
	20: 4	The king of Israel answered, "Just as you s,	1821
	21:19	S to him, 'This is what the LORD says:	1819
	21:19	s to him, 'This is what the LORD says:	1819
	22: 8	"The king *should* not s that,'	606
	22:27	and s, 'This is what the king says:	606
2Ki	5:10	Elisha sent a messenger to s to him, "Go,	606
	5:22	"My master sent me to s,	606
	7: 4	If *we* s, 'We'll go into the city'—	606
	8:10	Elisha answered, "Go and s to him,	606
	8:14	"What *did* Elisha s to you?"	606
	9:37	so that no *one* will be able to s,	606
	10: 5	and we will do anything you s.	606
	16: 7	to s to Tiglath-Pileser king of Assyria,	606
	18:20	You s you have strategy and military	NIH
	18:22	And if *you* s to me,	606
	18:27	to s these things, and not to the men sitting	1819
	19:10	**"S** to Hezekiah king of Judah:	606
	20:14	"What *did* those men s,	606
1Ch	16:31	*let them* s among the nations,	606
	17: 6	*did I* ever s to any of their leaders	1819+1821
	17:18	"What more can David s to you	NIH
	17:24	Then men *will* s, 'The LORD Almighty,	606
2Ch	6:37	with you in the land of their captivity and s,	606
	7:21	all who pass by will be appalled and s,	606
	10: 9	How should we answer these people who s	1819
	11: 3	**"S** to Rehoboam son of Solomon king	606
	18: 7	"The king *should* not s that,"	606
	18:26	and s, 'This is what the king says:	606
	25:19	*You* s *to yourself* that you have defeated	606
Ezr	8:17	to s to Iddo and his kinsmen,	1819
	9:10	now, O our God, what *can we* s after this?	606
	10:12	We must do as you s.	1821
Ne	5: 8	because they could find nothing to s.	1821
	5:12	We will do as you s."	606
Est	1:17	so they will despise their husbands and s,	606
	4:10	Then she instructed him *to* s to Mordecai,	7422
Job	6:26	Do you mean to correct **what** I s,	4863
	8: 2	"How long *will you* s such things?	4910
	9:12	Who *can* s to him, 'What are you doing?'	606
	9:22	It is all the same; that is why *I* s,	606
	9:27	If I s, 'I will forget my complaint,	606
	10: 2	*I will* s to God: Do not condemn me,	606
	11: 4	*You* s to God, 'My beliefs are flawless	606
	13:17	let your ears take in **what** I s.	289
	17:12	in the face of darkness they s,	NIH
	17:14	if *I* s to corruption, 'You are my father,'	7924
	19:28	"If *you* s, 'How we will hound him,	606
	20: 7	those who have seen him *will* s,	606
	21:14	Yet *they* s to God, 'Leave us alone!	606
	21:28	*You* s, 'Where now is the great man's house,	606
	22:13	Yet *you* s, 'What does God know?	606
	22:29	When men are brought low and s,	606
	23: 5	and consider what *he would* s.	606
	28:22	Destruction and Death s,	606
	32: 7	that the three men had nothing more to s,	5101
	32:10	"Therefore *I* s: Listen to me;	606
	32:13	*Do* not s, 'We have found wisdom;	606
	32:15	and *have* no more *to* s;	6699
	32:17	I too *will* **have** my s;	2750+6699
	33: 1	pay attention to everything I s.	1821
	33:24	to him and s, 'Spare him from going down	606
	33:32	If you have **anything to** s, answer me;	4863
	34:16	listen to what I s.	4863
	34:34	wise men who hear me s to me,	606
	35: 2	*You* s, 'I will be cleared by God.'	606
	35:14	will he listen *when you* s that you do	606
	37:19	"Tell us what *we should* s to him;	606
	40: 5	twice, but I will s no more."	NIH
Ps	2: 3	"Let us break their chains," they s,	NIH
	10:13	Why *does he* s to himself,	606
	11: 1	How then *can you* s to me: "Flee like a bird	606
	13: 4	my enemy *will* s, "I have overcome him,"	606
	31:14	*I* s, "You are my God."	606
	35: 3	S to my soul, "I am your salvation."	606
	35:21	They gape at me and s, "Aha!	606
	35:25	or s, "We have swallowed him up."	606
	35:27	*may they* always s, "The LORD be exalted,	606
	40:15	May those *who* s to me, "Aha!	606
	40:16	*may* those who love your salvation always s,	606
	41: 5	My enemies s of me in malice,	606
	41: 5	while men s to me all day long,	606
	42: 9	*I* s to God my Rock, "Why have you forgotten me?	606
	58:11	Then men *will* s, "Surely the righteous	606
	59: 7	and they s, "Who can hear us?"	NIH
	64: 5	*they* s, "Who will see them?"	606
	64: 6	They plot injustice and s,	NIH
	66: 3	S to God, "How awesome are your deeds!	606
	70: 3	May those *who* s to me, "Aha!	606
	70: 4	*may* those who love your salvation always s,	606
	71:11	They s, "God has forsaken him.	606
	73:11	*They* s, "How can God know?	606
	75: 2	*You* s, "I choose the appointed time;	NIH
	75: 4	To the arrogant *I* s, 'Boast no more,	606
	79:10	Why *should* the nations s,	606
	83: 4	*they* s, "let us destroy them as a nation,	606

Ps	85: 8	I will listen to what God the LORD *will* s;	1819
	87: 4	and will s, 'This one was born in Zion.' "	NIH
	91: 2	*I will* s of the LORD,	606
	94: 7	They s, "The LORD does not see;	606
	96:10	S among the nations, "The LORD reigns."	606
	106:48	*Let* all the people s, "Amen!"	606
	107: 2	*Let* the redeemed of the LORD s this—	606
	115: 2	Why *do* the nations s,	606
	118: 2	*Let* Israel s: "His love endures forever."	606
	118: 3	*Let* the house of Aaron s:	606
	118: 4	*Let* those who fear the LORD s:	606
	119:82	I s, "When will you comfort me?"	606
	122: 8	sake of my brothers and friends, *I will* s,	1819
	124: 1	had not been on our side—*let* Israel s—	606
	129: 1	oppressed me from my youth—*let* Israel s—	606
	129: 8	*May* those who pass by not s,	606
	139:11	*If I* s, "Surely the darkness will hide me	606
	140: 6	*I* s to you, "You are my God."	606
	141: 7	[They will s,] "As one plows and breaks up	NIH
	142: 5	I cry to you, O LORD; *I* s,	606
Pr	1:11	If *they* s, "Come along with us;	606
	3:28	*Do* not s to your neighbor,	606
	4:10	Listen, my son, accept **what** I s	609
	4:20	My son, pay attention to **what** I s;	1821
	5: 7	do not turn aside from **what** I s.	609+7023
	5:12	*You will* s, "How I hated discipline!	606
	7: 4	S to wisdom, "You are my sister,"	606
	7:24	pay attention to **what** I s.	609+7023
	8: 6	Listen, for *I have* worthy things *to* s;	1819
	20: 9	Who can s, "I have kept my heart pure;	606
	20:22	*Do* not s, "I'll pay you back	606
	23:35	"They hit me," you will s,	NIH
	24: 7	at the gate he has nothing *to* s.	7023+7337
	24:12	If *you* s, "But we knew nothing	606
	24:29	not s, "I'll do to him as he has done to me;	606
	25: 7	it is better for him *to* s to you,	606
	30: 9	and disown you and s,	606
	30:15	four *that* never s, 'Enough!':	606
Ecc	1: 8	things are wearisome, more than one can s.	1819
	1:10	Is there anything of which *one can* s,	606
	5: 6	be angry at **what** you s and destroy the work	7754
	6: 3	and does not receive proper burial, *I* s that	606
	7:10	*Do* not s, "Why were the old days better	606
	7:21	not pay attention to every word *people* s,	1819
	8: 2	Obey the king's command, I s,	NIH
	8: 4	a king's word is supreme, who *can* s to him,	606
	8:14	This too, *I* s, is meaningless."	606
	10:20	a bird on the wing may report **what** you s.	1821
	12: 1	and the years approach when *you will* s,	606
Isa	2: 3	Many peoples will come and s, "Come,	606
	3: 6	and s, "You have a cloak,	NIH
	4: 1	and s, "We will eat our own food	606
	5:19	to those *who* s, "Let God hurry,	606
	7: 4	S to him, 'Be careful,	606
	8: 4	Before the boy knows how *to* s 'My father'	7924
	9: 9	*who* s with pride and arrogance of heart,	606
	10:12	he will s, "I will punish the king of Assyria	NIH
	10:29	They go over the pass, and s,	NIH
	12: 1	In that day *you will* s: "I will praise you,	606
	12: 4	In that day *you will* s: "Give thanks to	606
	14: 8	the cedars of Lebanon exult over you and s,	NIH
	14:10	They will all respond, *they will* s to you,	606
	19:11	How *can* you s to Pharaoh,	606
	20: 6	the people who live on this coast *will* s,	606
	22:13	"Let us eat and drink," *you* s,	NIH
	22:15	"Go, s to this steward, to Shebna,	NIH
	25: 9	In that day *they will* s,	606
	28:23	pay attention and hear **what** I s.	614
	29:11	and s to him, "Read this, please,"	606
	29:12	and s, "Read this, please," he will answer,	606
	29:16	*Shall* what is formed s to him who formed	606
	29:16	*Can* the pot s of the potter,	606
	30:10	*They* s to the seers, "See no more visions!"	606
	30:22	like a menstrual cloth and s to them,	606
	32: 9	hear **what** I have *to* s!	614
	33:24	No one living in Zion *will* s, "I am ill";	606
	35: 4	s to those with fearful hearts,	606
	36: 5	You s you have strategy	NIH
	36: 7	And if *you* s to me,	606
	36:12	to s these things, and not to the men sitting	1819
	37:10	"S to Hezekiah king of Judah:	606
	38:15	But what *can I* s?	1819
	39: 3	"What *did* those men s,	606
	40: 9	s to the towns of Judah,	606
	40:27	Why *do* you s, O Jacob, and complain,	606
	41:26	so *we could* s, 'He was right?'	606
	42:17	those who trust in idols, who s to images,	606
	42:22	with no *one* to s, "Send them back."	606
	43: 6	*I will* s to the north, 'Give them up!	606
	43: 9	so that others may hear and s, "It is true."	606
	44: 5	One *will* s, 'I belong to the LORD';	606
	44:19	the knowledge or understanding to s, "Half	606
	44:20	he cannot save himself, or s,	606
	44:28	he *will* s of Jerusalem, "Let it be rebuilt,"	606
	45: 9	*Does* the clay s to the potter,	606
	45: 9	Does your work s, 'He has no hands'?	NIH
	45:24	*They will* s of me,	606
	46:10	what is still to come. I s:	606
	47:10	and knowledge mislead you when *you* s	606
	48: 5	that *you could* not s, 'My idols did them';	606
	48: 7	So *you* cannot s, 'Yes, I knew them.'	606
	48:20	Send it out to the ends of the earth; s,	606
	49: 9	to s to the captives,	606
	49:20	during your bereavement *will* yet s	606
	49:21	Then *you will* s in your heart,	606
	51:16	and *who* s to Zion, 'You are my people.' "	606
	52: 7	who proclaim salvation, *who* s to Zion,	606

Isa	56: 3	who has bound himself to the LORD s,	606
	57:10	but *you would* not s, 'It is hopeless.'	606
	58: 3	'Why have we fasted,' *they* s,	NIH
	58: 9	you will cry for help, and *he will* s:	606
	62:11	"S to the Daughter of Zion, 'See,	606
	65: 5	who s, 'Keep away;	606
	65: 8	and *men* s, 'Don't destroy it, there is	606
Jer	1: 7	But the LORD said to me, "*Do* not s,	606
	1: 7	to and s whatever I command you.	1819
	1:17	up and s to them whatever I command you.	1819
	2:23	"How *can* you s, 'I am not defiled,'	606
	2:27	*They* s to wood, 'You are my father,'	606
	2:27	yet when they are in trouble, *they* s,	606
	2:31	Why *do* my people s, 'We are free to roam;	606
	2:35	*you* s, 'I am innocent.'	606
	2:35	I will pass judgment on you because you s,	606
	3:16	declares the LORD, "men will no longer s,	606
	4: 5	in Judah and proclaim in Jerusalem and s:	606
	4: 5	Cry aloud and s: 'Gather together!	606
	5: 2	Although *they* s, 'As surely as the LORD	606
	5:13	so let what they s be done to them."	NIH
	5:24	*They do* not s to themselves,	606
	6:14	'Peace, peace,' they s,	606
	7: 4	*Do* not trust in deceptive words and s,	606
	7:10	which bears my Name, and s,	606
	7:28	Therefore s to them, 'This is the nation	606
	8: 4	"S to them, 'This is what the LORD says:	606
	8: 6	but *they do* not s what is right.	1819
	8: 8	" 'How *can* you s, "We are wise,	606
	8:11	"Peace, peace," they s,	606
	9:22	S, "This is what the LORD declares:	1819
	13:12	"S to them: 'This is what the LORD,	606
	13:12	And if *they* s to you,	606
	13:18	S to the king and to the queen mother,	606
	13:21	What *will you* s when [the LORD] sets	606
	16:14	"when *men* will no longer s,	606
	16:15	but they will s, 'As surely as the LORD	NIH
	16:19	from the ends of the earth and s,	606
	17:20	S to them, 'Hear the word of the LORD,	606
	18:11	"Now therefore s to the people of Judah	606
	19: 3	and s, 'Hear the word of the LORD	606
	19:11	and s to them, 'This is what the LORD	606
	20: 9	But if *I* s, "I will not mention him or speak	606
	21:11	"Moreover, s to the royal house of Judah,	NIH
	21:13	you who s, "Who can come against us?	606
	23: 7	"when *people* will no longer s,	606
	23: 8	but they will s, 'As surely as the LORD	NIH
	23:17	the stubbornness of their hearts *they* s,	606
	23:25	the prophets s who prophesy lies	606
	23:25	They s, 'I had a dream!	606
	23:33	s to them, 'What oracle?	606
	25:30	against them and s to them:	606
	26: 4	S to them, 'This is what the LORD says:	606
	26: 8	the LORD had commanded him to s,	1819
	27: 4	and s, 'This is what the LORD Almighty,	606
	27:14	to the words of the prophets who s to you,	606
	27:16	Do not listen to the prophets who s,	606
	28: 7	to what I *have* to s in your hearing and in	1819
	29:15	*You may* s, "The LORD has raised	606
	31: 7	Make your praises heard, and s,	606
	31:29	"In those days *people will* no longer s,	606
	32: 3	You s, 'This is what the LORD says:	606
	32: 7	is going to come to you and s,	606
	32:25	you, O Sovereign LORD, s to me,	606
	32:43	be bought in this land of which you s,	606
	33:10	'You s about this place,	606
	36:14	the son of Cushi, to s to Baruch,	606
	38:22	Those *women will* s to you:	606
	38:25	and they come to you and s,	606
	38:27	the king had ordered him to s.	1821
	42:13	if you s, 'We will not stay in this land,'	606
	42:14	and if you s, 'No, we will go and live in	606
	43: 2	The LORD our God has not sent you to s,	606
	43:10	Then s to them, 'This is what	606
	45: 4	[The LORD said,] "S this to him:	606
	46:16	*They will* s, 'Get up, let us go back	606
	48:14	"How *can* you s, 'We are warriors,	606
	48:17	s, 'How broken is the mighty scepter,	606
	49: 4	you trust in your riches and s,	NIH
	49:14	An envoy was sent to the nations to s,	NIH
	50: 2	keep nothing back, but s,	606
	51:35	s the inhabitants of Zion.	606
	51:62	Then s, 'O LORD, you have said you will	606
	51:64	Then s, 'So will Babylon sink to rise no more	606
La	2:12	*They* s to their mothers, "Where is bread	606
	2:13	What *can I* s for you?	6386
	2:16	they scoff and gnash their teeth and s,	606
	3:18	So *I* s, "My splendor is gone and all	606
	3:24	I s *to* myself, "The LORD is my portion;	606
	3:41	and our hands to God in heaven, and s:	NIH
	4:15	*people* among the nations s,	606
Eze	2: 4	S to them, 'This is what	606
	2: 6	*Do* not be afraid of **what** *they* s	1821
	2: 8	you, son of man, listen to what I s to you.	1819
	3:11	S to them, 'This is what the Sovereign LORD	606
	3:18	When I s to a wicked man,	606
	3:27	I will open your mouth and *you shall* s	606
	6: 3	and s: 'O mountains of Israel,	606
	8:12	*They* s, 'The LORD does not see us;	606
	9: 9	*They* s, 'The LORD has forsaken the land;	606
	11: 3	*They* s, 'Will it not soon be time	606
	11: 5	and he told me *to* s:	606
	11:16	"Therefore s: 'This is what the Sovereign LORD says:	606
	11:17	"Therefore s: 'This is what the Sovereign LORD says:	606

Eze	12:10	"S to them, 'This is what the Sovereign LORD says:	606
	12:11	S to them, 'I am a sign to you.'	606
	12:19	S to the people of the land:	606
	12:23	S to them, 'This is what the Sovereign LORD says:	606
	12:23	S to them, 'The days are near	1819
	12:25	I will fulfill *whatever I* s,	1819+1821
	12:28	"Therefore s to them, 'This is what	606
	12:28	whatever *I* s will be fulfilled,	1819+1821
	13: 2	S to those who prophesy out	606
	13: 6	They s, "The LORD declares,"	606
	13: 7	and uttered lying divinations when you s,	606
	13:15	*I will* s to you, "The wall is gone	606
	13:18	s, 'This is what the Sovereign LORD says:	606
	14: 6	"Therefore s to the house of Israel,	606
	14:17	I bring a sword against that country and s,	606
	16: 3	s, 'This is what the Sovereign LORD says	606
	17: 3	S to them, 'This is what the Sovereign LORD says:	606
	17: 9	"S to them, 'This is what the Sovereign LORD says:	606
	17:12	"S to this rebellious house,	606
	17:12	S to them: 'The king of Babylon went to	606
	18:25	*you* s, 'The way of the Lord is not just.'	606
	19: 2	and s: " 'What a lioness was your mother	606
	20: 3	speak to the elders of Israel and s to them,	606
	20: 5	and s to them: 'This is what the Sovereign LORD says:	606
	20:27	speak to the people of Israel and s to them,	606
	20:30	"Therefore s to the house of Israel:	606
	20:32	" 'You s, "We want to be like the nations,	606
	20:47	S to the southern forest:	606
	21: 3	and s to her: 'This is what the LORD says:	606
	21: 7	*you shall* s, 'Because of the news	606
	21: 9	and s, 'This is what the Lord says:	606
	21:28	"And you, son of man, prophesy and s,	606
	22: 3	and s: 'This is what the Sovereign LORD says:	606
	22:24	s to the land, 'You are a land that has had no	606
	22:28	*They* s, 'This is what	606
	24: 3	Tell this rebellious house a parable and s	606
	24:21	S to the house of Israel, 'This is what	606
	25: 3	S to them, 'Hear the word of the Sovereign	606
	26:17	up a lament concerning you and s to you:	606
	27: 3	S to Tyre, situated at the gateway to	606
	27: 3	" 'You s, O Tyre, "I am perfect in beauty."	606
	28: 2	"Son of man, s to the ruler of Tyre,	606
	28: 2	" 'In the pride of your heart *you* s,	606
	28: 9	*Will you then* s, "I am a god,"	606+606
	28:12	a lament concerning the king of Tyre and s	606
	28:22	and s: 'This is what the Sovereign LORD says:	606
	29: 3	Speak to him and s: 'This is what	606
	29: 3	*You* s, "The Nile is mine;	606
	30: 2	"Son of man, prophesy and s:	606
	30: 2	" 'Wail and s, "Alas for that day!"	NIH
	31: 2	s to Pharaoh king of Egypt and	606
	32: 2	concerning Pharaoh king of Egypt and s	606
	32:19	S to them, 'Are you more favored than others?	NIH
	32:21	within the grave the mighty leaders *will* s	1819
	33: 2	speak to your countrymen and s to them:	606
	33: 8	When I s to the wicked, 'O wicked man,	606
	33:10	"Son of man, s to the house of Israel,	606
	33:11	S to them, 'As surely as I live,	606
	33:12	son of man, s to your countrymen,	606
	33:14	And if I s to the wicked man,	606
	33:17	"Yet your countrymen s,	606
	33:20	Yet, O house of Israel, *you* s,	606
	33:25	Therefore s to them, 'This is what	606
	33:27	"S this to them: 'This is what the Sovereign	606
	34: 2	prophesy and s to them: 'This is what	606
	35: 3	s: 'This is what the Sovereign LORD says:	606
	36: 1	prophesy to the mountains of Israel and s,	606
	36: 3	Therefore prophesy and s, 'This is what	606
	36: 6	of Israel and s to the mountains and hills, to	606
	36:13	Because *people* s to you,	606
	36:22	"Therefore s to the house of Israel,	606
	36:35	*They* will s, 'This land that was laid waste	606
	37: 4	"Prophesy to these bones and s to them,	606
	37: 9	prophesy, son of man, and s to it,	606
	37:11	*They* s, 'Our bones are dried up	606
	37:12	Therefore prophesy and s to them:	606
	37:19	s to them, 'This is what the Sovereign	1819
	37:21	and s to them, 'This is what the Sovereign	1819
	38: 3	s: 'This is what the Sovereign LORD says:	606
	38:11	*You* will s, "I will invade a land	606
	38:13	of Tarshish and all her villages *will* s	606
	38:14	son of man, prophesy and s to Gog:	606
	39: 1	"Son of man, prophesy against Gog and s:	606
	44: 6	S to the rebellious house of Israel,	606
Da	3:29	or language who s anything against the God	10042
	4:35	No one can hold back his hand or s to him:	10042
	5:11	your father the king, I s—	NIH
	11:36	and *will* s unheard-of things against	1819
Hos	2: 1	"S of your brothers, 'My people,'	606
	2: 7	Then *she will* s, 'I will go back to my	606
	2:23	*I will* s to those called 'Not my people,'	606
	2:23	and *they will* s, 'You are my God.' "	606
	10: 3	Then *they will* s, "We have no king	606
	10: 8	*they will* s to the mountains, "Cover us!"	606
	14: 2	S to him: "Forgive all our sins	606
	14: 3	*We will* never again s 'Our gods'	606
Joel	2:17	*Let* them s, "Spare your people, O LORD.	606
	2:17	Why *should they* s among the peoples,	606
	3:10	*Let* the weakling s, "I am strong!"	606

Am	4: 1	and crush the needy and s to your husbands,	606
	5:14	will be with you, just as *you* s he is.	606
	6:10	and he says, "No," then *he will* s, "Hush!	606
	6:13	in the conquest of Lo Debar and s,	606
	7:16	You s, " 'Do not prophesy against Israel,	606
	8:14	or s, 'As surely as your god lives, O Dan,'	606
	9:10	all those who s, 'Disaster will not overtake	606
Ob	1: 1	An envoy was sent to the nations to s,	NIH
	1: 3	you *who* s to yourself, 'Who can bring me	606
Mic	2: 6	"Do not prophesy," their **prophets** s.	5752
	3:11	Yet they lean upon the LORD and s,	606
	4: 2	Many nations will come and s, "Come,	606
	4:11	They s, "Let her be defiled,	606
	1	let the hills hear **what** *you* **have to** s.	7754
Na	3: 7	All who see you will flee from you and s,	606
Hab	2: 1	I will look to see what *he will* s to me,	1819
Zep	3:16	On that day *they will* s to Jerusalem,	606
Hag	1: 2	"These people s, 'The time has not	606
Zec	8:21	of one city will go to another and s,	606
	8:23	of one Jew by the hem of his robe and s,	606
	11: 5	Those who sell them s, 'Praise the LORD,	606
	12: 5	the leaders of Judah *will* s in their hearts,	606
	13: 3	to whom he was born, *will* s to him,	606
	13: 5	*He will* s, 'I am not a prophet.	606
	13: 9	*I will* s, 'They are my people,'	606
	13: 9	'They are my people,' and they *will* s,	606
Mal	1: 4	Edom *may* s, "Though we have been crushed	606
	1: 5	You will see it with your own eyes and s,	606
	1:13	And *you* s, 'What a burden!'	606
Mt	3: 9	And do not think you can s to yourselves,	3306
	5:11	persecute you and falsely s all kinds of evil	3306
	7: 4	How can *you* s to your brother,	3306
	7:22	Many *will* s to me on that day, 'Lord,	3306
	8: 8	But just s the word, and my servant	3306
	8: 9	I s to my servant, 'Do this,' and he does it."	NIG
	8:11	*I* s to you that many will come from	3306
	9: 5	to s, 'Your sins are forgiven,' or to say,	3306
	9: 5	or to s, 'Get up and walk'?	3306
	10:19	not worry about what *to* s or how to say it.	3281
	10:19	not worry about what to say or how to s it.	NIG
	10:19	At that time you will be given what *to* s,	3281
	11:18	and *they* s, 'He has a demon.'	3306
	11:19	and drinking, and *they* s, 'Here is a glutton	3306
	12:34	how can you who are evil s anything good?	3281
	13:34	*he did* not s anything to them without using	3281
	15: 5	But you s that if a man says to his father	3306
	16: 2	He replied, "When evening comes, *you* s,	3306
	16:13	"Who *do* people s the Son of Man is?"	3306
	16:14	They replied, "Some s John the Baptist;	NIG
	16:14	"Some say John the Baptist; others s Elijah;	NIG
	16:15	"Who *do you* s I am?"	3306
	17:10	of the law s that Elijah must come first?"	3306
	17:20	*you* can s to this mountain,	3306
	21: 5	"S to the Daughter of Zion,	J306
	21:21	but also *you can* s to this mountain, 'Go,	3306
	21:25	"If we s, 'From heaven,' he will ask,	3306
	21:26	But if *we* s, 'From men'—	3306
	22:23	*who* s there is no resurrection,	3306
	22:46	No one could s a word **in reply,**	646
	23:16	You s, 'If anyone swears by the temple,	3306
	23:18	You also s, 'If anyone swears by the altar,	NIG
	23:30	And *you* s, 'If we had lived in the days	3306
	23:39	you will not see me again until *you* s,	3306
	25:34	"Then the King *will* s to those on his right,	3306
	25:41	"Then *he will* s to those on his left,	3306
	26:22	and began *to* s to him one after the other,	3306
	26:54	that s it must happen in this way?"	NIG
	26:64	"Yes, it is as you s," Jesus replied.	3306
	26:64	"But *I* s to all of you:	3306
	27:11	"Yes, it is as you s," Jesus replied.	3306
	28:13	*"You are to* s, 'His disciples came	3306
Mk	2: 9	Which is easier: *to* s to the paralytic,	3306
	2: 9	or to s, 'Get up, take your mat and walk'?	3306
	4:30	s the kingdom of God **is like,**	3929
	4:34	*He did* not s anything to them without using	3281
	5:41	(which means, "Little girl, *I* s to you,	3306
	7:11	But you s that if a man says to his father	3306
	8:27	"Who *do* people s I am?"	3306
	8:28	They replied, "Some s John the Baptist;	NIG
	8:28	"Some say John the Baptist; others s Elijah;	NIG
	8:29	"Who *do you* s I am?"	3306
	9: 6	(He did not know what *to* s,	646
	9:11	of the law s that Elijah must come first?"	3306
	9:39	the next moment s anything **bad about** me,	2800
	11:14	And his disciples heard him s it.	NIG
	11:31	"If *we* s, 'From heaven,' he will ask,	3306
	11:32	But if *we* s, 'From men'...."	3306
	12:18	Sadducees *who* s there is no resurrection,	3306
	12:35	"How is it that the teachers of the law s that	3306
	13:11	do not worry beforehand about what *to* s.	3281
	13:11	Just s whatever is given you at the time,	3281
	13:37	What *I* s to you, I say to everyone:	3306
	13:37	What I say to you, *I* s to everyone:	3306
	14:14	S to the owner of the house he enters,	3306
	14:40	They did not know what *to* s to him.	646
	14:58	"We heard him s, 'I will destroy this	3306
	15: 2	"Yes, it is as you s," Jesus replied.	3306
Lk	3: 8	And do not begin *to* s to yourselves,	3306
	5: 5	because you s so, I will let down the nets."	4839
	5:23	*to* s, 'Your sins are forgiven,' or to say,	3306
	5:23	to say, 'Your sins are forgiven,' or *to* s,	3306
	6:42	How can *you* s to your brother, 'Brother,	3306
	6:46	'Lord, Lord,' and do not do what *I* s?	3306
	7: 6	when the centurion sent friends *to* s to him:	3306
	7: 7	s the word, and my servant will be healed.	3306
	7: 8	I s to my servant, 'Do this,' and he does it."	NIG
	7:14	He said, "Young man, *I* s to you, get up!"	3306

Lk	7:33	and *you* s, 'He has a demon.'	3306
	7:34	and drinking, and *you* s, 'Here is a glutton	3306
	7:49	The other guests began *to* s among	3306
	9:18	"Who *do* the crowds s I am?"	3306
	9:19	They replied, "Some s John the Baptist;	NIG
	9:19	"Some say John the Baptist; others s Elijah;	NIG
	9:20	"Who *do you* s I am?"	3306
	9:61	but first let me go back and s good-by	698
	10: 5	"When you enter a house, first s,	3306
	10:10	go into its streets and s,	3306
	11: 2	He said to them, "When you pray, s:	3306
	11: 9	"So I s to you: Ask and it will be given	3306
	11:18	I s this because you claim	NIG
	11:45	*when you* s these things, you insult us also."	3306
	11:54	waiting to catch him in something he **might** s.	1666+3836+5125
	12:11	defend yourselves or what *you will* s,	3306
	12:12	at that time what *you* should s."	3306
	12:19	And *I'll* s to myself,	3306
	12:54	immediately *you* s, 'It's going to rain,'	3306
	12:55	And when the south wind blows, *you* s,	3306
	13:26	"Then *you will* s, 'We ate and drank	3306
	13:35	you will not see me again until *you* s,	3306
	14: 6	And they had nothing *to* s.	503
	14: 9	both of you *will* come and s to you,	3306
	14:10	*he will* s to you, 'Friend,	3306
	15:18	and go back to my father and s to him:	3306
	17: 6	*you can* s to this mulberry tree,	3306
	17: 7	Would *he* s to the servant when he comes in	3306
	17: 8	*Would he* not rather s, 'Prepare my supper,	3306
	17:10	*should* s, 'We are unworthy servants,	3306
	17:21	nor *will people* s, 'Here it is,'	3306
	19:14	and sent a delegation after him *to* s,	3306
	20: 5	"If we s, 'From heaven,' he will ask,	3306
	20: 6	But if *we* s, 'From men,'	3306
	20:27	who s there is no resurrection,	515
	20:41	"How is it that *they* s the Christ is the Son	3306
	22:11	and s to the owner of the house,	3306
	23: 3	"Yes, it is as you s," Jesus replied.	3306
	23:29	For the time will come when *you will* s,	3306
	23:30	Then " 'they will s to the mountains,	3306
Jn	1:22	What *do you* s about yourself?"	3306
	1:37	When the two disciples heard him s this,	3281
	4:17	when *you* s you have no husband.	3306
	4:35	*Do* you not s, 'Four months more and then	3306
	5:47	how are you going to believe what I s?"	4839
	6:14	*they* began to s, "Surely this is the Prophet	3306
	6:42	can he now s, 'I came down from heaven'?"	3306
	6:65	*He* went on *to* s, "This is why I told you	3306
	7:13	But no one *would* s anything publicly	3281
	7:42	not the Scripture s that the Christ will come	3306
	8: 5	Now what *do you* s?"	3306
	8:26	"I have much *to* s in judgment of you.	3281
	8:33	How *can you* s that we shall be set free?"	3306
	8:43	Because you are unable to hear what I s.	3364
	8:52	yet you s that if anyone keeps your word,	3306
	9:17	"What *have* you *to* s about him?"	3306
	9:19	"Is this the one you s was born blind?	3306
	9:40	with him heard him s this and asked,	NIG
	11:51	*He* did not s this on his own,	3306
	12: 6	not s this because he cared about the poor	3306
	12:27	my heart is troubled, and what *shall I* s?	3306
	12:34	so how *can* you s, 'The Son of Man must	3306
	12:49	commanded me what *to* s and how to say it.	3306
	12:49	commanded me what to say and how *to* s it.	3281
	12:50	So whatever I s is just what	3281
	12:50	the Father has told me *to* s."	3281
	14: 9	How can you s, 'Show us the Father'?	3306
	14:10	The words I s to you are not just my own.	3306
	14:11	Believe me when I s that I am in the Father	NIG
	14:28	"You heard me s, 'I am going away	3306
	16:12	"I have much more *to* s to you,	3306
	17:13	but I s these things while I am still in	3281
	21: 7	As soon as Simon Peter heard him s,	NIG
	21:23	But Jesus *did* not s that he would not die;	3306
Ac	2:14	listen carefully to what I s.	4839
	4:14	there was nothing they could s.	515
	6:11	they secretly persuaded some men *to* s,	3306
	6:14	For we have heard him s that this Jesus	3306
	9: 4	to the ground and heard a voice s to him,	3306
	10:22	so that he could hear what you have to s."	4839
	11:13	an angel appear in his house and s,	3306
	17:18	"What is this babbler trying *to* s?"	3306
	19:13	*They would* s, "In the name of Jesus,	3306
	21:37	"May I s something to you?"	3306
	22: 7	to the ground and heard a voice s to me,	3306
	23: 8	Sadducees s that there is no resurrection,	3306
	28:26	" 'Go to this people and s, "You will	3306
Ro	2:22	You *who* s that people should	3306
	3: 5	what *shall we* s? That God is unjust	3306
	3: 8	Why not s—as we are being slanderously reported	NIG
	3: 8	as saying and as some claim that we s—	3306
	4: 1	What then *shall we* s that Abraham,	3306
	4: 3	What *does* the Scripture s?	3306
	6: 1	What *shall we* s, then? Shall we go on	3306
	7: 7	What *shall we* s, then? Is the law sin?	3306
	8:31	What, then, *shall we* s in response to this?	3306
	9:14	What then *shall we* s? Is God unjust?	3306
	9:19	One of *you will* s to me:	3306
	9:20	*"Shall* what is formed s to him who formed	3306
	9:30	What then *shall we* s? That the Gentiles,	3306
	10: 6	*"Do* not s in your heart, 'Who will ascend	3306
	10: 8	But what *does it* s? "The word is near you;	3306
	11:19	*You will* s then, "Branches were broken off	3306
	12: 3	the grace given me *I* s to every one of you:	3306
1Co	1:15	so no one *can* s that you were baptized	3306

1Co	6: 5	*I* s this to shame you.	3306
	7: 6	*I* s this as a concession, not as a command.	3306
	7: 8	Now to the unmarried and the widows *I* s:	3306
	7:12	To the rest *I* s this (I, not the Lord):	3306
	9: 8	*Do I* s this merely from a human point	3281
	9: 8	Doesn't the Law s the same thing?	3306
	10:15	judge for yourselves what *I* s.	5774
	11:22	What *shall I* s to you?	3306
	12: 3	"Jesus be cursed," and no one can s,	3306
	12:15	If the foot *should* s, "Because I am not	3306
	12:16	And if the ear *should* s, "Because I am not	3306
	12:21	The eye cannot s to the hand,	3306
	12:21	And the head cannot s to the feet,	NIG
	14:16	who do not understand s "Amen"	3306
	14:23	not s that you are out of your mind?	3306
	14:26	What then *shall we* s, brothers?	1639
	15:12	some of you s that there is no resurrection of	3281
	15:34	*I* s this to your shame.	3281
2Co	1:17	so that in the same breath I s, "Yes, yes"	NIG
	5: 8	We are confident, I s, and would prefer	NIG
	7: 3	*I do* not s this to condemn you;	3306
	9: 4	not *to* s anything **about** you—	3306
	10:10	For *some* s, "His letters are weighty	5774
	12: 6	is warranted by what I do or s.	201+1609+1666
Gal	1: 9	As we have already said, so now *I* s again:	3306
	3:16	The Scripture *does* not s "and to seeds,"	3306
	4:30	But what *does* the Scripture s?	3306
	5:16	So *I* s, live by the Spirit,	3306
Php	3:18	before and now s again even with tears,	3306
	4: 4	*I will* s it again: Rejoice!	3306
1Th	1: 8	we do not need *to* s anything **about** it,	3281
2Ti	2: 2	And the things you have heard **me** s	1609+4123
	2:18	s that the resurrection has already taken place,	3306
	4: 3	to s what their itching ears want to hear.	NIG
Tit	2: 8	because they have nothing bad *to* s	3306
	2:12	It teaches us to s **"No"** to ungodliness	766
Heb	1: 5	For to which of the angels *did* God ever s,	3306
	1:13	To which of the angels *did* God ever s,	3306
	5:11	We have much *to* s about this,	3306
	7: 9	**One might even** s that Levi,	2229+3306+6055
	9:11	that is *to* s, not a part of this creation.	NIG
	11:14	People who s such things show	3306
	11:32	And what more *shall I* s?	3306
	13: 6	So we s with confidence,	3306
Jas	1:13	When tempted, no one *should* s,	3306
	2: 3	to the man wearing fine clothes and s,	3306
	2: 3	but s to the poor man, "You stand there"	3306
	2:18	But someone *will* s, "You have faith;	3306
	4:13	Now listen, *you* who s, "Today or tomorrow	3306
	4:15	Instead, *you ought to* s, "If it is the Lord's	3306
2Pe	3: 4	*They will* s, "Where is this 'coming' he promised?	3306
Rev	2: 9	of those who s they are Jews and are not,	3306
	2:24	Now *I* s to the rest of you in Thyatira,	3306
	3:17	*You* s, 'I am rich; I have acquired wealth	3306
	4:10	lay their crowns before the throne and s:	3306
	6: 1	of the four living creatures s in a voice	3306
	6: 3	I heard the second living creature s,	3306
	6: 5	I heard the third living creature s, "Come!"	3306
	6: 7	the voice of the fourth living creature s,	3306
	10: 4	but I heard a voice from heaven s,	3306
	12:10	Then I heard a loud voice in heaven s:	3306
	14:13	I heard a voice from heaven s, "Write:	3306
	16: 5	I heard the angel in charge of the waters s:	3306
	18: 4	Then I heard another voice from heaven s:	3306
	18:14	"They *will* s, 'The fruit you longed	NIG
	22:17	The Spirit and the bride s, "Come!"	3306
	22:17	And *let* him who hears s, "Come!"	3306

SAYING (285) [SAY]

Ge	4:25	s, "God has granted me another child	NIH
	9: 1	God blessed Noah and his sons, s to them,	606
	14:19	s, "Blessed be Abram by God Most High,	606
	19:15	the angels urged Lot, s, "Hurry!	606
	24: 7	to me and promised me on oath, s,	606
	24:21	**Without** s **a word,** the man watched her	3087
	24:27	s, "Praise be to the LORD, the God	606
	26:22	He named it Rehoboth, s,	606
	28:20	Then Jacob made a vow, s,	606
	31: 1	Jacob heard that Laban's sons *were* s,	1821
	32:30	So Jacob called the place Peniel, s,	NIH
	39:19	s, "This is how your slave treated me,"	606
	50:16	So they sent word to Joseph, s,	606
Ex	2:10	She named him Moses, s,	606
	2:22	and Moses named him Gershom, s,	606
	5:13	The slave drivers kept pressing them, s,	606
	5:17	That is why you keep s,	606
	11: 8	bowing down before me and s, 'Go,	606
	15:24	So the people grumbled against Moses, s,	606
	17: 7	and because they tested the LORD s,	606
	33: 1	s, 'I will give it to your descendants.'	606
Lev	8:31	s, 'Aaron and his sons are to eat it.'	606
Nu	11:20	s, "Why did we ever leave Egypt?" '"	606
	16:31	As soon as he finished s all this,	1819
	20:14	from Kadesh to the king of Edom, s:	NIH
	27: 7	*What* Zelophehad's daughters *are* s is right.	1819
	30:14	He confirms them by s **nothing** to	3087
	36: 5	of the descendants of Joseph *is* s is right.	1819
Dt	1: 5	Moses began to expound this law, s,	606
	2:26	king of Heshbon offering peace and s,	606
	12:30	s, "How do these nations serve their gods?	606
	13: 6	entices you, s, "Let us go and worship	606
	13:13	their town astray, s, "Let us go and worship	606
	22:14	a bad name, s, "I married this woman,	606
	25: 8	If he persists in s, "I do not want to marry	606

Dt	33:27	He will drive out your enemy before you, s,	606
Jos	9:22	"Why did you deceive us by s,	606
	22: 8	s, "Return to your homes	606
Jdg	5:29	indeed, she **keeps** s to herself,	609+8740
	6:32	s, "Let Baal contend with him,"	606
	7:11	and listen to what *they are* s.	1819
	7:13	"I had a dream," *he was* s.	606
	7:24	throughout the hill country of Ephraim, s,	606
	8:15	about whom you taunted me by s,	606
	9:31	to Abimelech, s, "Gaal son of Ebed	606
	11:15	s: "This is what Jephthah says:	606
	11:17	to the king of Edom, s, 'Give us permission	606
	16: 2	They made no move during the night, s,	606
	16:23	s, "Our god has delivered Samson,	606
	16:24	people saw him, they praised their god, s,	606
	20: 8	All the people rose as one man, s,	606
	20:12	throughout the tribe of Benjamin, s, "What	606
	20:32	While the Benjamites *were* s,	606
	20:32	the Israelites *were* s, "Let's retreat	606
	21:20	So they instructed the Benjamites, s,	606
Ru	3:17	s, 'Don't go back to your mother-in-law	606
1Sa	1:11	And she made a vow, s,	606
	1:20	She named him Samuel, s,	NIH
	2:20	Eli would bless Elkanah and his wife, s,	606
	4:21	She named the boy Ichabod, s,	606
	6:21	s, "The Philistines have returned the ark of	606
	7:12	He named it Ebenezer, s,	606
	8: 7	"Listen to all that the people *are* s to you;	606
	10: 1	s, "Has not the LORD anointed you leader	606
	10:12	So it became a s: "Is Saul also among the	5442
	14:24	s, "Cursed be any man who eats food	606
	14:28	the army under a strict oath, s, "Cursed	606
	15:18	And he sent you on a mission, s,	606
	16:22	Then Saul sent word to Jesse, s,	606
	17:25	Now the Israelites *had been* s,	606
	17:27	They repeated to him what they had been s	1821
	18:11	s to himself, "I'll pin David to the wall."	606
	20:16	s, "May the LORD call David's enemies	NIH
	20:42	of the LORD, s, 'The LORD is witness	606
	23: 2	s, "Shall I go and attack these Philistines?"	606
	23:27	a messenger came to Saul, s,	606
	24:13	As the old s goes, 'From evildoers come	5442
	24:16	When David finished s this, Saul asked,	1819
	30:20	s, "This is David's plunder."	606
	30:26	who were his friends, s,	606+4200
2Sa	3:35	but David took an oath, s,	606
	7: 4	the word of the LORD came to Nathan, s:	606
	7:27	you have revealed this to your servant, s,	606
	11: 5	and sent word to David, s,	606
	12:27	Joab then sent messengers to David, s,	606
	19: 9	s, "The king delivered us from the hand	606
	19:41	of Israel were coming to the king and s	606
	21:17	Then David's men swore to him, s,	606
	24: 1	and he incited David against them, s,	606
1Ki	1:25	and drinking with him and s,	606
	1:47	to congratulate our lord King David, s,	606
	8:55	of Israel in a loud voice, s:	606
	18:31	s, "Your name shall be Israel."	606
	20: 2	s, "This is what Ben-Hadad says:	606
	21:13	the people, s, "Naboth has cursed both God	606
2Ki	1: 2	So he sent messengers, s,	606
	2:21	s, "This is what the LORD says:	606
	10: 6	Then Jehu wrote them a second letter, s,	606
	11: 5	He commanded them, s,	606
	18:22	s to Judah and Jerusalem,	606
1Ch	4: 9	His mother had named him Jabez, s,	606
	17: 3	the word of God came to Nathan, s,	606
	29:10	s, "Praise be to you, O LORD,	606
2Ch	5:13	"He is good; his love endures forever."	NIH
	7: 6	s, "His love endures forever."	NIH
	20: 8	in it a sanctuary for your Name, s,	606
	20:21	as they went out at the head of the army, s:	606
	20:37	s, "Because you have made an alliance	606
	30:18	But Hezekiah prayed for them, s,	606
	32:12	s to Judah and Jerusalem,	606
	32:17	the God of Israel, and s this against him:	606
	35:21	But Neco sent messengers to him, s,	606
Ne	1: 8	s, 'If you are unfaithful, I will scatter you	606
	2:20	I answered them *by* s, "The God of heaven	606
	5: 2	Some *were* s, "We and our sons	606
	5: 3	Others *were* s, "We are mortgaging our fields,	606
	5: 4	Still others *were* s, "We have had to borrow	606
	6: 8	"Nothing like what you *are* s is happening;	606
	8:11	The Levites calmed all the people, s,	NIH
Job	22:19	the innocent mock them, s,	NIH
Ps	2: 5	and terrifies them in his wrath, s,	NIH
	3: 2	Many *are* s of me, "God will not deliver	NIH
	39: 2	**not** *even* s anything good,	3120
	41: 7	they imagine the worst for me, s,	NIH
	42:10	s to me all day long, "Where is your God?"	NIH
	52: 6	they will laugh at him, s,	NIH
	78:19	They spoke against God, s,	606
	90: 3	You turn men back to dust, s,	606
Isa	6: 8	Then I heard the voice of the Lord s,	606
	7: 5	Remaliah's son have plotted your ruin, s,	606
	19:25	The LORD Almighty will bless them, s,	606
	30:21	your ears will hear a voice behind you, s,	606
	36: 7	s to Judah and Jerusalem,	606
	45:14	s, 'Surely God is with you,	NIH
	47: 8	lounging in your security and s to yourself,	NIH
Jer	1: 4	The word of the LORD came to me, s,	606
	4:10	and Jerusalem by s, 'You will have peace,'	606
	4:31	stretching out her hands and s, "Alas!	NIH
	8: 6	No one repents of his wickedness, s,	606
	11: 7	I warned them again and again, s,	606
	11:19	s, "Let us destroy the tree and its fruit;	NIH

Jer	11:21	and s, 'Do not prophesy in the name of	606
	12: 4	Moreover, *the people are* s,	606
	12:16	s, 'As surely as the LORD lives'—	NIH
	14:15	I did not send them, yet they *are* s,	606
	17:15	They **keep** s to me, "Where is the word	606
	18:19	hear **what** my accusers are s!	7754
	20:10	All my friends are waiting for me to slip, s,	NIH
	20:15	s, "A child is born to you—a son!"	606
	23:17	*They* **keep** s to those who despise me,	606+606
	23:35	of *you* keeps on s to his friend or relative:	606
	23:37	This is what *you* keep s to a prophet:	606
	31: 3	The LORD appeared to us in the past, s:	NIH
	31:34	or a man his brother, s, 'Know the LORD,'	606
	32: 3	s, "Why do you prophesy as you do?	606
	32:36	"You *are* s about this city, 'By the sword,	606
	33:11	s, "Give thanks to the LORD Almighty,	606
	33:24	not noticed that these people *are* s,	1819
	35:12	word of the LORD came to Jeremiah, s:	606
	38: 4	by the things *he is* s to them.	1819
	40:16	*What you are* s about Ishmael is not true."	1819
Eze	9:11	s, "I have done as you commanded."	606
	11: 5	That is what *you are* s, O house of Israel,	606
	12:27	the house of Israel *is* s, 'The vision he sees	606
	13:10	" 'Because they lead my people astray, s,	606
	20:49	They *are* s of me, 'Isn't he just telling	606
	33:10	'This is what *you are* s:	606
	33:24	in those ruins in the land of Israel *are* s,	606
	33:30	s to each other, 'Come and hear	1819
Da	4:23	coming down from heaven and s,	10042
	10:15	While he *was* s this to me,	1819
	12: 7	s, "It will be for a time,	NIH
Am	7: 8	For this is what Amos *is* s:	606
	8: 5	s, "When will the New Moon be over	606
Hab	2: 6	s, " 'Woe to him who piles up stolen goods	606
Mal	1: 7	s that the LORD's table is contemptible.	606
	1:12	you profane it by s *of* the Lord's table,	606
	2:17	By s, "All who do evil are good in the eyes	606
Mt	3: 2	and s, "Repent, for the kingdom	3306
	3:14	But John tried to deter him, s,	3306
	5: 2	and he began to teach them, s,	3306
	6:31	So do not worry, s, 'What shall we eat?'	3306
	7:28	When Jesus had finished s these things,	3364
	8:25	The disciples went and woke him, s, "Lord,	3306
	9:18	*While he was* s this, a ruler came	3281
	13: 3	he told them many things in parables, s:	3306
	14: 4	for John *had been* s to him:	3306
	14:33	s, "Truly you are the Son of God."	3306
	19: 1	When Jesus had finished s these things,	3364
	21: 2	s to them, "Go to the village ahead of you,	3306
	21:16	"Do you hear what these children *are* s?"	3306
	22: 1	Jesus spoke to them again in parables, s:	3306
	26: 1	When Jesus had finished s all these things,	3364
	26:26	s, "Take and eat; this is my body."	3306
	26:27	gave thanks and offered it to them, s,	3306
	26:44	prayed the third time, s the same thing.	3306
	27:40	and s, "You who are going to destroy	3306
Mk	2:12	s, "We have never seen anything like this!"	3306
	3:30	He said this because *they were* s,	3306
	6:14	*Some were* s, "John the Baptist has been raised from the dead,	3306
	6:18	For John *had been* s to Herod,	3306
	7:19	(In s this, Jesus declared all foods "clean.")	NIG
	8:26	Jesus sent him home, s,	3306
	11: 2	s to them, "Go to the village ahead of you,	3306
	12: 6	He sent him last of all, s,	3306
	12:32	in s that God is one and there is no other	3306
	14: 4	Some of those present were s **indignantly**	24
	14:22	and gave it to his disciples, s, "Take it;	3306
	15:29	shaking their heads and s, "So!	3306
Lk	2:13	appeared with the angel, praising God and s,	3306
	2:28	took him in his arms and praised God, s:	3306
	2:50	But they did not understand what *he was* s	3281
	4:21	and he began by s to them,	3306
	7: 1	When Jesus had finished s all this in	4839
	8:24	The disciples went and woke him, s,	3306
	8:38	but Jesus sent him away, s,	3306
	9: 7	because some *were* s that John	3306
	9:33	(He did not know what *he was* s.)	3306
	9:35	A voice came from the cloud, s,	3306
	11:27	As Jesus *was* s these things,	3306
	12: 1	Jesus began to speak first to his disciples, s:	NIG
	14:30	s, 'This fellow began to build and was	3306
	19:29	he sent two of his disciples, s to them,	3306
	22: 8	Jesus sent Peter and John, s,	3306
	22:19	s, "This is my body given for you;	3306
	22:20	after the supper he took the cup, s,	3306
	22:70	He replied, "You are right in s I am."	3306
	23: 2	And they began to accuse him, s,	3306
	24:34	and s, "It is true! The Lord has risen	3306
Jn	1:15	s, "This was he of whom I said,	3306
	3: 7	You should not be surprised at *my* s,	3306
	4:37	the s 'One sows and another reaps' is true.	3364
	7:26	and *they are* **not** s a word to him.	3306+4029
	8:48	"Aren't we right in s that you are	3306
	10:24	The Jews gathered around him, s,	3306
	16:17	What does he mean by s,	3306+4005
	16:18	We don't understand what *he is* s."	3281
	16:26	*I am* **not** s that I will ask the Father	3306
	18:25	He denied it, s, "I am not."	3306
	18:37	"You are right in s I am a king.	3306
	19: 3	s, "Hail, king of the Jews!"	3306
Ac	3:18	s that his Christ would suffer.	NIG
	7:26	He tried to reconcile them by s, 'Men,	3306
	11:18	s, "So then, God has granted even	3306
	13:15	the synagogue rulers sent word to them, s,	3306
	13:45	talked abusively against what Paul *was* s.	3281
	17: 7	s that there is another king,	3306

Ac	21: 6	*After* s good-by to each other,	571
	26:14	and I heard a voice s to me in Aramaic,	3306
	26:22	*I am* s nothing beyond what the prophets	3306
	26:25	"What *I am* s is true and reasonable.	710
Ro	3: 8	as we are being slanderously reported as s	NIG
	4: 9	*We have been* s that Abraham's faith	3306
1Co	4: 6	learn from us the meaning of the s,	NIG
	7:35	*I am* s this for your own good,	3306
	11:25	after supper he took the cup, s,	3306
	14: 9	how will anyone know what *you are* s?	3281
	14:11	not grasp the meaning *of* what **someone is** s,	5889
	14:16	since he does not know what *you are* s?	3306
	15:54	then the s that is written will come true:	3364
Gal	4: 1	What *I am* s is that as long as the heir is	3306
Php	4:11	*I am* **not** s this because I am in need,	3306
1Th	5: 3	While *people are* s, "Peace and safety,"	3306
2Th	2: 2	s that the day of the Lord has already come.	NIG
1Ti	1:15	a trustworthy s that deserves full acceptance	3364
	3: 1	Here is a trustworthy s:	3364
	4: 9	a trustworthy s that deserves full acceptance	3364
	5:13	s things they ought not to.	3281
2Ti	2: 7	Reflect on what *I am* s,	3306
	2:11	Here is a trustworthy s:	3364
Tit	3: 8	This is a trustworthy s.	3364
Heb	6:14	s, "I will surely bless you	3306
	8: 1	The point of what *we are* s is this:	3306
	8:11	or a man his brother, s, 'Know the Lord,'	3306
2Pe	1:17	s, "This is my Son, whom I love;	NIG
1Jn	5:16	*I am* **not** s that he should pray about that.	3306
Rev	4: 8	Day and night they never stop s:	3306
	6: 6	s, "A quart of wheat for a day's wages,	3306
	7:12	s: "Amen! Praise and glory	3306
	11:12	Then they heard a loud voice from heaven s	3306
	11:17	s: "We give thanks to you,	3306
	16: 1	Then I heard a loud voice from the temple s	3306
	16:17	a loud voice from the throne, s,	3306
	19: 5	Then a voice came from the throne, s:	3306
	21: 3	And I heard a loud voice from the throne s,	3306

SAYINGS (10) [SAY]

Ps	49:13	and of their followers, who approve their s.	7023
Pr	1: 6	the s and riddles *of* the wise.	1821
	22:17	Pay attention and listen to the s *of* the wise;	1821
	22:20	Have I not written thirty s for you,	NIH
	22:20	s of counsel and knowledge,	NIH
	24:23	These also are s of the wise:	NIH
	30: 1	The s *of* Agur son of Jakeh—	1821
	31: 1	The s *of* King Lemuel:	1821
Ecc	12:11	their **collected** s like firmly embedded	670+1251
Jn	10:21	"These are not the s of a man possessed by	4839

SAYS (742) [SAY]

Ge	24:14	and *she* s, 'Drink, and I'll water your camels	606
	24:44	and if *she* s to me, 'Drink, and I'll water	606
	32: 4	'Your servant Jacob s,	606
	45: 9	'This is what your son Joseph s:	606
Ex	4:22	say to Pharaoh, 'This is what the LORD s:	606
	5: 1	This is what the LORD, the God of Israel, s:	606
	5:10	"This is what Pharaoh s:	606
	7: 9	"When Pharaoh s to you,	1819
	7:17	This is what the LORD s:	606
	8: 1	'This is what the LORD s:	606
	8:20	'This is what the LORD s:	606
	9: 1	the LORD, the God of the Hebrews, s:	606
	9:13	the LORD, the God of the Hebrews, s:	606
	10: 3	the LORD, the God of the Hebrews, s:	606
	11: 4	So Moses said, "This is what the LORD s:	606
	22: 9	lost property about which **somebody** s,	606
	23:21	Pay attention to him and listen to **what** he s.	7754
	23:22	If you listen carefully to **what** he s	7754
	32:27	s: 'Each man strap a sword to his side.	606
Nu	20:14	"This is what your brother Israel s:	606
	21:14	the Book of the Wars of the LORD s:	606
	22:16	"This is what Balak son of Zippor s:	606
	23:26	I must do whatever the LORD s?"	1819
	24:13	and I must say only what the LORD s'?	1819
	30: 4	about her vow or pledge but s **nothing**	3087
	30: 7	about it but s **nothing** to her,	3087
	30:11	but s **nothing** to her and does not forbid her,	3087
	30:14	But if her husband s **nothing** to her *about* it	3087+3087
	32:27	fight before the LORD, just as our lord s."	1819
Dt	5:27	and listen to all that the LORD our God s.	606
	13: 2	which he has spoken takes place, and *he* s,	606
	15:16	But if your servant s to you,	606
Jos	7:13	the God of Israel, s:	606
	22:16	"The whole assembly of the LORD s:	606
	24: 2	the LORD, the God of Israel, s:	606
Jdg	6: 8	the LORD, the God of Israel, s:	606
	11:15	"This is what Jephthah s:	606
1Sa	2:27	"This is what the LORD s:	606
	9: 6	and everything *he* s comes true.	1819
	10:18	the LORD, the God of Israel, s:	606
	15: 2	This is what the LORD Almighty s:	606
	20: 7	*he* s, 'Very well,' then your servant is safe.	606
2Sa	7: 5	'This is what the LORD s:	606
	7: 8	'This is what the LORD Almighty s:	606
	12: 7	the LORD, the God of Israel, s:	606
	12:11	"This is what the LORD s:	606
	14:10	"If anyone s anything to you,	1819
	14:13	When the king s this,	1819
	14:17	"And now your servant s,	1819
	14:19	to the left from anything my lord the king s.	1819
	15:26	But if he s, 'I am not pleased with you,'	606
	17: 6	Should we do what he s?	1821

Ref	Text	Num
2Sa 24:12	'This is what the LORD **s**:	606
1Ki 1:51	*He* **s**, 'Let King Solomon swear to me today	606
2:30	"The king **s**, 'Come out!' "	606
2:31	the king commanded Benaiah, "Do as *he* **s**.	1819
3:23	The king said, "This one **s**,	606
3:23	while that one **s**, 'No!	606
11:31	this is what the LORD, the God of Israel, **s**:	606
12:24	'This is what the LORD **s**:	606
13: 2	This is what the LORD **s**:	606
13:21	'This is what the LORD **s**:	606
14: 7	this is what the LORD, the God of Israel, **s**:	606
17:14	this is what the LORD, the God of Israel, **s**:	606
20: 2	saying, "This is what Ben-Hadad **s**:	606
20: 5	"This is what Ben-Hadad **s**:	606
20:13	"This is what the LORD **s**:	606
20:14	"This is what the LORD **s**:	606
20:28	"This is what the LORD **s**:	606
20:32	"Your servant Ben-Hadad **s**:	606
20:42	"This is what the LORD **s**:	606
21:19	Say to him, 'This is what the LORD **s**:	606
21:19	say to him, 'This is what the LORD **s**:	606
21:23	"And also concerning Jezebel the LORD **s**:	1819
22:11	'This is what the LORD **s**:	606
22:27	'This is what the king **s**:	606
2Ki 1: 4	Therefore this is what the LORD **s**:	606
1: 6	'This is what the LORD **s**:	606
1: 9	"Man of God, the king **s**, 'Come down!' "	1819
1:11	"Man of God, this is what the king **s**,	606
1:16	'This is what the LORD **s**:	606
2:21	saying, "This is what the LORD **s**:	606
3:16	'This is what the LORD **s**:	606
3:17	For this is what the LORD **s**:	606
4:43	For this is what the LORD **s**:	606
7: 1	This is what the LORD **s**:	606
9: 3	'This is what the LORD **s**:	606
9: 6	This is what the LORD, the God of Israel, **s**:	606
9:11	know the man and the **sort of things he s**,"	8490
9:12	"This is what the LORD **s**:	606
9:18	"This is what the king **s**:	606
9:19	"This is what the king **s**:	606
18:19	what the great king, the king of Assyria **s**:	606
18:29	This is what the king **s**:	606
18:30	in the LORD when he **s**, 'The LORD will	606
18:31	This is what the king of Assyria **s**:	606
18:32	for he is misleading you when he **s**,	606
19: 3	They told him, "This is what Hezekiah **s**:	606
19: 6	'This is what the LORD **s**:	606
19:10	god you depend on deceive you when he **s**,	606
19:20	"This is what the LORD, the God of Israel, **s**:	606
19:32	"Therefore this is what the LORD **s**	606
20: 1	"This is what the LORD **s**:	606
20: 5	the LORD, the God of your father David, **s**:	606
20:17	Nothing will be left, **s** the LORD.	606
21:12	this is what the LORD, the God of Israel, **s**:	606
22:15	"This is what the LORD, the God of Israel, **s**:	606
22:16	'This is what the LORD **s**:	606
22:18	**s** concerning the words you heard:	606
1Ch 17: 4	'This is what the LORD **s**:	606
17: 7	'This is what the LORD Almighty **s**:	606
21:10	'This is what the LORD **s**:	606
21:11	'This is what the LORD **s**:	606
2Ch 11: 4	'This is what the LORD **s**:	606
12: 5	"This is what the LORD **s**,	606
18:10	"This is what the LORD **s**:	606
18:13	I can tell him only what my God **s**."	606
18:26	'This is what the king **s**:	606
20:15	This is what the LORD **s** to you:	606
21:12	the God of your father David, **s**:	606
24:20	"This is what God **s**:	606
32:10	This is what Sennacherib king of Assyria **s**:	606
32:11	When Hezekiah **s**, 'The LORD our God will save us	606
34:23	"This is what the LORD, the God of Israel, **s**:	606
34:24	'This is what the LORD **s**:	606
34:26	**s** concerning the words you heard:	606
36:23	"This is what Cyrus king of Persia **s**:	606
Ezr 1: 2	"This is what Cyrus king of Persia **s**:	606
Ne 6: 6	and Geshem **s** it is true—	606
Job 8:18	that place disowns it and **s**,	NIH
28:14	The deep **s**, 'It is not in me';	606
28:14	the sea **s**, 'It is not with me.'	606
33:27	Then he comes to men and **s**, 'I sinned,	606
34: 5	"Job **s**, 'I am innocent,	606
34: 9	For *he* **s**, 'It profits a man nothing	606
34:18	Is he not the *One* who **s** to kings,	606
34:31	"Suppose *a man* **s** to God,	606
35:10	But no *one* **s**, 'Where is God my Maker,	606
37: 6	*He* **s** to the snow, 'Fall on the earth,'	606
Ps 10: 6	*He* **s** to himself, "Nothing will shake me;	606
10:11	*He* **s** to himself, "God has forgotten;	606
12: 4	that **s**, "We will triumph with our tongues;	606
12: 5	I will now arise," **s** the LORD.	606
14: 1	The fool **s** in his heart, "There is no God."	606
27: 8	My heart **s** of you, "Seek his face!"	606
50:16	But to the wicked, God **s**:	606
53: 1	The fool **s** in his heart, "There is no God."	606
68:22	Lord **s**, "I will bring them from Bashan;	606
81: 6	He **s**, "I removed the burden	NIH
91:14	"Because he loves me," **s** the LORD,	NIH
110: 1	The LORD **s** to my Lord:	5536
Pr 9: 4	*she* **s** to those who lack judgment.	606
9:16	*she* **s** to those who lack judgment.	606
20:14	it's no good!" **s** the buyer;	606
22:13	The sluggard **s**, "There is a lion outside!"	606
23: 7	"Eat and drink," *he* **s** to you,	606
24:24	*Whoever* **s** to the guilty,	606
26:13	The sluggard **s**, "There is a lion in the road,	606
Pr 26:19	is a man who deceives his neighbor and **s**,	606
28:24	He who robs his father or mother and **s**,	606
30:16	and fire, *which* never **s**, 'Enough!'	606
30:20	She eats and wipes her mouth and **s**,	606
Ecc 1: 2	Meaningless!" **s** the Teacher.	606
7:27	"Look," **s** the Teacher,	606
12: 8	Meaningless!" **s** the Teacher.	606
Isa 1:11	what are they to me?" **s** the LORD.	606
1:18	let us reason together," **s** the LORD.	606
3:16	The LORD **s**, "The women of Zion are	606
7: 7	Yet this is what the Sovereign LORD **s**:	606
10: 8	'Are not my commanders all kings?' *he* **s**.	606
10:13	For *he* **s**: " 'By the strength of my hand	606
10:24	the Lord, the LORD Almighty, **s**:	606
16:14	But now the LORD **s**:	1819
18: 4	This is what the LORD **s** to me:	606
21: 6	This is what the Lord **s** to me:	606
21:16	This is what the Lord **s** to me:	606
22:14	**s** the Lord, the LORD Almighty.	606
22:15	the Lord, the LORD Almighty, **s**:	606
28:16	So this is what the Sovereign LORD **s**:	606
29:13	The Lord **s**: "These people come near to	606
29:22	**s** to the house of Jacob:	606
30:12	this is what the Holy One of Israel **s**:	606
30:15	Sovereign LORD, the Holy One of Israel, **s**:	606
31: 4	This is what the LORD **s** to me:	606
33:10	"Now will I arise," **s** the LORD.	606
36: 4	what the great king, the king of Assyria, **s**:	606
36:14	This is what the king **s**:	606
36:15	in the LORD *when* he **s**, 'The LORD will	606
36:16	This is what the king of Assyria **s**:	606
36:18	not let Hezekiah mislead you *when* he **s**,	606
37: 3	They told him, "This is what Hezekiah **s**:	606
37: 6	'This is what the LORD **s**:	606
37:10	god you depend on deceive you *when* he **s**,	606
37:21	This is what the LORD, the God of Israel, **s**:	606
37:33	"Therefore this is what the LORD **s**	606
38: 1	'This is what the LORD **s**:	606
38: 5	the God of your father David, **s**:	606
39: 6	Nothing will be left, **s** the LORD.	606
40: 1	Comfort, comfort my people, **s** your God.	606
40: 6	A voice **s**, "Cry out."	606
40:25	Or who is my equal?" **s** the Holy One.	606
41: 6	each helps the other and **s** to his brother,	606
41: 7	*He* **s** of the welding, "It is good."	606
41:13	who takes hold of your right hand and **s**	606
41:21	"Present your case," **s** the LORD.	606
41:21	"Set forth your arguments," **s** Jacob's King.	606
42: 5	This is what God the LORD **s**—	606
43: 1	But now, this is what the LORD **s**—	606
43:14	This is what the LORD **s**—	606
43:16	This is what the LORD **s**—	606
44: 2	This is what the LORD **s**—	606
44: 6	"This is what the LORD **s**—	606
44:16	He also warms himself and **s**, "Ah!	606
44:17	He prays to it and **s**, "Save me;	606
44:24	"This is what the LORD **s**—	606
44:26	who **s** of Jerusalem, 'It shall be inhabited,'	606
44:27	who **s** to the watery deep,	606
44:28	who **s** of Cyrus, 'He is my shepherd	606
45: 1	"This is what the LORD **s** to his anointed,	606
45:10	Woe to *him who* **s** to his father,	606
45:11	"This is what the LORD **s**—	606
45:13	**s** the LORD Almighty."	606
45:14	This is what the LORD **s**:	606
45:18	For this is what the LORD **s**—	606
45:18	but formed it to be inhabited—he **s**:	NIH
48:17	This is what the LORD **s**—	606
48:22	"There is no peace," **s** the LORD,	606
49: 5	And now the LORD **s**—	606
49: 6	*he* **s**: "It is too small a thing for you	606
49: 7	This is what the LORD **s**—	606
49: 8	This is what the LORD **s**:	606
49:22	This is what the Sovereign LORD **s**:	606
49:25	But this is what the LORD **s**:	606
50: 1	This is what the LORD **s**:	606
51:22	This is what your Sovereign LORD **s**,	606
52: 3	For this is what the LORD **s**:	606
52: 4	For this is what the Sovereign LORD **s**:	606
54: 1	of her who has a husband," **s** the LORD.	606
54: 6	only to be rejected," **s** your God.	606
54: 8	**s** the LORD your Redeemer.	606
54:10	**s** the LORD, who has compassion on you.	606
56: 1	This is what the LORD **s**:	606
56: 4	For this is what the LORD **s**:	606
57:15	For this is what the high and lofty *One* **s**—	606
57:19	peace, to those far and near," **s** the LORD.	606
57:21	"There is no peace," **s** my God,	606
59:21	this is my covenant with them," **s** the LORD.	606
59:21	from this time on and forever," **s** the LORD.	606
65: 7	and the sins of your fathers," **s** the LORD.	606
65: 8	This is what the LORD **s**:	606
65:13	the Sovereign LORD **s**:	606
65:25	on all my holy mountain," **s** the LORD.	606
66: 1	This is what the LORD **s**:	606
66: 9	and not give delivery?" **s** the LORD.	606
66: 9	when I bring to delivery?" **s** your God.	606
66:12	For this is what the LORD **s**:	606
66:20	and on mules and camels," **s** the LORD.	606
66:21	of them also to be priests and Levites," **s**	606
66:23	and bow down before me," **s** the LORD.	606
Jer 2: 5	This is what the LORD **s**:	606
4: 3	the LORD **s** to the men of Judah and	606
4:27	This is what the LORD **s**:	606
5:14	the LORD God Almighty **s**:	606
6: 6	This is what the LORD Almighty **s**:	606
6: 9	This is what the LORD Almighty **s**:	606
Jer 6:15	down when I punish them," **s** the LORD.	606
6:16	This is what the LORD **s**:	606
6:21	Therefore this is what the LORD **s**:	606
6:22	This is what the LORD **s**:	606
7: 3	the God of Israel, **s**:	606
7:20	the Sovereign LORD **s**:	606
7:21	the God of Israel, **s**:	606
8: 4	"Say to them, 'This is what the LORD **s**:	606
8:12	be brought down when they are punished, **s**	606
9: 7	the LORD Almighty **s**:	606
9:15	the God of Israel, **s**:	606
9:17	This is what the LORD Almighty **s**:	606
9:23	This is what the LORD **s**:	606
10: 1	Hear what the LORD **s** to you,	1819
10: 2	This is what the LORD **s**:	606
10:18	For this is what the LORD **s**:	606
11: 3	the God of Israel, **s**:	606
11:11	Therefore this is what the LORD **s**:	606
11:21	"Therefore this is what the LORD **s** about	606
11:22	the LORD Almighty **s**:	606
12:14	This is what the LORD **s**:	606
13: 1	This is what the LORD **s** to me:	606
13:12	the God of Israel, **s**:	606
13:13	then tell them, 'This is what the LORD **s**:	606
14:10	the LORD **s** about this people:	606
14:15	this is what the LORD **s** about	606
15: 2	tell them, 'This is what the LORD **s**:	606
15:19	Therefore this is what the LORD **s**:	606
16: 3	For this is what the LORD **s** about the sons	606
16: 5	For this is what the LORD **s**:	606
16: 9	the God of Israel, **s**:	606
17: 5	This is what the LORD **s**:	606
17:21	This is what the LORD **s**:	606
18:11	'This is what the LORD **s**: Look!	606
18:13	Therefore this is what the LORD **s**:	606
18:18	and pay no attention to anything he **s**."	1821
19: 1	This is what the LORD **s**:	606
19: 3	the God of Israel, **s**: Listen!	606
19:11	'This is what the LORD Almighty **s**:	606
19:15	the God of Israel, **s**: 'Listen!	606
20: 4	For this is what the LORD **s**:	606
21: 4	the God of Israel, **s**:	606
21: 8	tell the people, 'This is what the LORD **s**:	606
21:12	this is what the LORD **s**:	606
22: 1	This is what the LORD **s**:	606
22: 3	This is what the LORD **s**:	606
22: 6	the LORD **s** about the palace of the king	606
22:11	the LORD **s** about Shallum son of Josiah,	606
22:14	He **s**, 'I will build myself a great palace	606
22:18	Therefore this is what the LORD **s**:	606
22:30	This is what the LORD **s**:	606
23: 2	**s** to the shepherds who tend my people:	606
23:15	this is what the LORD Almighty **s**	606
23:16	This is what the LORD Almighty **s**:	606
23:17	'The LORD **s**: You will have peace.'	1819
23:38	this is what the LORD **s**:	606
24: 5	the God of Israel, **s**:	606
24: 8	so bad they cannot be eaten,' **s** the LORD,	606
25: 8	Therefore the LORD Almighty **s** this:	606
25:27	the God of Israel, **s**:	606
25:28	'This is what the LORD Almighty **s**:	606
25:32	This is what the LORD Almighty **s**:	606
26: 2	"This is what the LORD **s**:	606
26: 4	Say to them, 'This is what the LORD **s**:	606
26:18	'This is what the LORD Almighty **s**:	606
27: 4	the God of Israel, **s**:	606
27:16	"This is what the LORD **s**:	606
27:19	the LORD Almighty **s** about the pillars,	606
27:21	**s** about the things that are left in the house	606
28: 2	the God of Israel, **s**:	606
28:11	"This is what the LORD **s**:	606
28:13	'This is what the LORD **s**:	606
28:14	the God of Israel, **s**:	606
28:16	Therefore, this is what the LORD **s**:	606
29: 4	**s** to all those I carried into exile	606
29: 8	the God of Israel, **s**:	606
29:10	This is what the LORD **s**:	606
29:16	the LORD **s** about the king who sits	606
29:17	this is what the LORD Almighty **s**:	606
29:21	**s** about Ahab son of Kolaiah	606
29:25	the God of Israel, **s**:	606
29:31	'This is what the LORD **s** about Shemaiah	606
29:32	this is what the LORD **s**:	606
30: 2	the God of Israel, **s**:	606
30: 3	to possess,' **s** the LORD."	606
30: 5	"This is what the LORD **s**:	606
30:12	"This is what the LORD **s**:	606
30:18	"This is what the LORD **s**:	606
31: 2	This is what the LORD **s**:	606
31: 7	This is what the LORD **s**:	606
31:15	This is what the LORD **s**:	606
31:16	This is what the LORD **s**:	606
31:23	the God of Israel, **s**:	606
31:35	This is what the LORD **s**,	606
31:37	This is what the LORD **s**:	606
32: 3	You say, 'This is what the LORD **s**:	606
32:14	the God of Israel, **s**:	606
32:15	the God of Israel, **s**:	606
32:28	Therefore, this is what the LORD **s**:	606
32:36	the God of Israel, **s**:	606
32:42	"This is what the LORD **s**:	606
33: 2	"This is what the LORD **s**, he who made	606
33: 4	**s** about the houses in this city and	606
33:10	"This is what the LORD **s**:	606
33:11	the land as they were before,' **s** the LORD.	606
33:12	"This is what the LORD Almighty **s**:	606
33:13	of the one who counts them," **s** the LORD.	606

Ref	Text	Num
Jer 33:17	For this is what the LORD s:	606
33:20	"This is what the LORD s:	606
33:25	This is what the LORD s:	606
34: 2	the God of Israel, s:	606
34: 2	'This is what the LORD s:	606
34: 4	This is what the LORD s concerning you:	606
34:13	the God of Israel, s:	606
34:17	"Therefore, this is what the LORD s:	606
35:13	the God of Israel, s:	606
35:17	the God of Israel, s: 'Listen!	606
35:18	the God of Israel, s:	606
35:19	the God of Israel, s:	606
36:29	'This is what the LORD s:	606
36:30	the LORD s about Jehoiakim king	606
37: 7	the God of Israel, s:	606
37: 9	"This is what the LORD s:	606
38: 2	'This is what the LORD s:	606
38: 3	And this is what the LORD s:	606
38:17	the God of Israel, s:	606
39:16	the God of Israel, s:	606
42: 4	the LORD s and will keep nothing back	6699
42: 9	to present your petition, s:	606
42:15	the God of Israel, s:	606
42:18	the God of Israel, s:	606
42:20	tell us everything he s and we will do it.'	606
43:10	the God of Israel, s:	606
44: 2	the God of Israel, s:	606
44: 7	the God of Israel, s:	606
44:11	the God of Israel, s:	606
44:25	the God of Israel, s:	606
44:26	'I swear by my great name,' s the LORD,	606
44:30	This is what the LORD s:	606
45: 2	the God of Israel, s to you, Baruch:	606
45: 4	'This is what the LORD s:	606
46: 8	*She* s, 'I will rise and cover the earth;	606
46:25	The LORD Almighty, the God of Israel, s:	606
47: 2	This is what the LORD s:	606
48: 1	s: "Woe to Nebo, for it will be ruined.	606
48:40	This is what the LORD s: "Look!	606
49: 1	This is what the LORD s:	606
49: 2	out those who drove her out," s the LORD.	606
49: 7	This is what the LORD Almighty s:	606
49:12	This is what the LORD s:	606
49:18	s the LORD, "so no one will live there;	606
49:28	This is what the LORD s:	606
49:35	This is what the LORD Almighty s:	606
50:18	the God of Israel, s:	606
50:33	This is what the LORD Almighty s:	606
51: 1	This is what the LORD s:	606
51:33	the God of Israel, s:	606
51:35	those who live in Babylonia," s Jerusalem.	606
51:36	Therefore, this is what the LORD s:	606
51:58	This is what the LORD Almighty s:	606
Eze 2: 4	'This is what the Sovereign LORD s.'	606
3:11	'This is what the Sovereign LORD s,'	606
3:27	'This is what the Sovereign LORD s.'	606
5: 5	"This is what the Sovereign LORD s:	606
5: 7	this is what the Sovereign LORD s:	606
5: 8	this is what the Sovereign LORD s:	606
6: 3	the Sovereign LORD s to the mountains	606
6:11	" 'This is what the Sovereign LORD s:	606
7: 2	this is what the Sovereign LORD s to	606
7: 5	"This is what the Sovereign LORD s:	606
11: 5	"This is what the LORD s:	606
11: 7	the Sovereign LORD s:	606
11:16	'This is what the Sovereign LORD s:	606
11:17	'This is what the Sovereign LORD s:	606
12:10	the Sovereign LORD s about those living	606
12:19	'This is what the Sovereign LORD s:	606
12:23	'This is what the Sovereign LORD s:	606
12:28	'This is what the Sovereign LORD s:	606
13: 3	This is what the Sovereign LORD s:	606
13: 8	this is what the Sovereign LORD s:	606
13:13	this is what the Sovereign LORD s:	606
13:18	'This is what the Sovereign LORD s:	606
13:20	this is what the Sovereign LORD s:	606
14: 4	'This is what the Sovereign LORD s:	606
14: 6	'This is what the Sovereign LORD s:	606
14:21	"For this is what the Sovereign LORD s:	606
15: 6	this is what the Sovereign LORD s:	606
16: 3	the Sovereign LORD s to Jerusalem:	606
16:36	This is what the Sovereign LORD s:	606
16:59	" 'This is what the Sovereign LORD s:	606
17: 3	'This is what the Sovereign LORD s:	606
17: 9	'This is what the Sovereign LORD s:	606
17:19	this is what the Sovereign LORD s:	606
17:22	" 'This is what the Sovereign LORD s:	606
18:29	Yet the house of Israel s,	606
20: 3	'This is what the Sovereign LORD s:	606
20: 5	'This is what the Sovereign LORD s:	606
20:27	'This is what the Sovereign LORD s:	606
20:30	'This is what the Sovereign LORD s:	606
20:39	'This is what the Sovereign LORD s:	606
20:47	This is what the Sovereign LORD s:	606
21: 3	'This is what the LORD s:	606
21: 9	prophesy and say, 'This is what the Lord s:	606
21:24	'this is what the Sovereign LORD s:	606
21:26	this is what the Sovereign LORD s:	606
21:28	'This is what the Sovereign LORD s about	606
22: 3	'This is what the Sovereign LORD s:	606
22:19	this is what the Sovereign LORD s:	606
22:28	'This is what the Sovereign LORD s'—	606
23:22	this is what the Sovereign LORD s:	606
23:28	"For this is what the Sovereign LORD s:	606
23:32	'This is what the Sovereign LORD s:	606
23:35	this is what the Sovereign LORD s:	606
23:46	"This is what the Sovereign LORD s:	606

Ref	Text	Num
Eze 24: 3	'This is what the Sovereign LORD s:	606
24: 6	" 'For this is what the Sovereign LORD s:	606
24: 9	this is what the Sovereign LORD s:	606
24:21	'This is what the Sovereign LORD s:	606
25: 3	This is what the Sovereign LORD s:	606
25: 6	For this is what the Sovereign LORD s:	606
25: 8	'This is what the Sovereign LORD s:	606
25:12	'This is what the Sovereign LORD s:	606
25:13	this is what the Sovereign LORD s:	606
25:15	'This is what the Sovereign LORD s:	606
25:16	this is what the Sovereign LORD s:	606
26: 3	this is what the Sovereign LORD s:	606
26: 7	"For this is what the Sovereign LORD s:	606
26:15	"This is what the Sovereign LORD s	606
26:19	"This is what the Sovereign LORD s:	606
27: 3	'This is what the Sovereign LORD s:	606
28: 2	'This is what the Sovereign LORD s:	606
28: 6	this is what the Sovereign LORD s:	606
28:12	'This is what the Sovereign LORD s:	606
28:22	'This is what the Sovereign LORD s:	606
28:25	" 'This is what the Sovereign LORD s:	606
29: 3	'This is what the Sovereign LORD s:	606
29: 8	this is what the Sovereign LORD s:	606
29:13	" 'Yet this is what the Sovereign LORD s:	606
29:19	this is what the Sovereign LORD s:	606
30: 2	'This is what the Sovereign LORD s:	606
30: 6	" 'This is what the LORD s:	606
30:10	" 'This is what the Sovereign LORD s:	606
30:13	" 'This is what the Sovereign LORD s:	606
30:22	this is what the Sovereign LORD s:	606
31:10	" 'This is what the Sovereign LORD s:	606
31:15	" 'This is what the Sovereign LORD s:	606
32: 3	" 'This is what the Sovereign LORD s:	606
32:11	" 'For this is what the Sovereign LORD s:	606
33:25	'This is what the Sovereign LORD s:	606
33:27	'This is what the Sovereign LORD s:	606
34: 2	'This is what the Sovereign LORD s:	606
34:10	This is what the Sovereign LORD s:	606
34:11	" 'For this is what the Sovereign LORD s:	606
34:17	'This is what the Sovereign LORD s:	606
34:20	the Sovereign LORD s to them:	606
35: 3	'This is what the Sovereign LORD s:	606
35:14	This is what the Sovereign LORD s:	606
36: 2	'This is what the Sovereign LORD s:	606
36: 3	'This is what the Sovereign LORD s:	606
36: 4	the Sovereign LORD s to the mountains	606
36: 5	this is what the Sovereign LORD s:	606
36: 6	'This is what the Sovereign LORD s:	606
36: 7	'This is what the Sovereign LORD s:	606
36:13	" 'This is what the Sovereign LORD s:	606
36:22	'This is what the Sovereign LORD s:	606
36:33	" 'This is what the Sovereign LORD s:	606
36:37	'This is what the Sovereign LORD s:	606
37: 5	the Sovereign LORD s to these bones:	606
37: 9	'This is what the Sovereign LORD s:	606
37:12	'This is what the Sovereign LORD s:	606
37:19	'This is what the Sovereign LORD s:	606
37:21	'This is what the Sovereign LORD s:	606
38: 3	'This is what the Sovereign LORD s:	606
38:10	" 'This is what the Sovereign LORD s:	606
38:14	'This is what the Sovereign LORD s:	606
38:17	" 'This is what the Sovereign LORD s:	606
39: 1	'This is what the Sovereign LORD s:	606
39:17	this is what the Sovereign LORD s:	606
39:25	the Sovereign LORD s:	606
43:18	this is what the Sovereign LORD s:	606
44: 6	'This is what the Sovereign LORD s:	606
44: 9	This is what the Sovereign LORD s:	606
45: 9	" 'This is what the Sovereign LORD s:	606
45:18	" 'This is what the Sovereign LORD s:	606
46: 1	" 'This is what the Sovereign LORD s:	606
46:16	" 'This is what the Sovereign LORD s:	606
47:13	This is what the Sovereign LORD s:	606
Am 1: 3	This is what the LORD s:	606
1: 5	of Aram will go into exile to Kir," s	606
1: 6	This is what the LORD s:	606
1: 8	s the Sovereign LORD.	606
1: 9	This is what the LORD s:	606
1:11	This is what the LORD s:	606
1:13	This is what the LORD s:	606
1:15	he and his officials together," s the LORD.	606
2: 1	This is what the LORD s:	606
2: 3	and kill all her officials with him," s	606
2: 4	This is what the LORD s:	606
2: 6	This is what the LORD s:	606
3:11	this is what the Sovereign LORD s:	606
3:12	This is what the LORD s:	606
5: 3	This is what the Sovereign LORD s:	606
5: 4	This is what the LORD s to the house	606
5:16	the LORD God Almighty, s:	606
5:17	for I will pass through your midst," s	606
5:27	beyond Damascus," s the LORD,	606
6:10	and he s, "No," then he will say, "Hush!	606
7:17	Therefore this is what the LORD s:	606
9:15	s the LORD your God.	606
Ob	the Sovereign LORD s about Edom—	606
Mic 2: 3	Therefore, the LORD s:	606
2:11	If a liar and deceiver comes and s,	NIH
3: 5	This is what the LORD s:	606
6: 1	Listen to what the LORD s:	606
Na 1:12	This is what the LORD s:	606
Hab 2:19	Woe to *him who* s to wood, 'Come to life!'	606
Zep 3:20	before your very eyes," s the LORD.	606
Hag 1: 2	This is what the LORD Almighty s:	606
1: 5	Now this is what the LORD Almighty s:	606
1: 7	This is what the LORD Almighty s:	606
1: 8	in it and be honored," s the LORD.	606

Ref	Text	Num
Hag 2: 6	"This is what the LORD Almighty s:	606
2: 7	s the LORD Almighty.	606
2: 9	s the LORD Almighty.	606
2:11	"This is what the LORD Almighty s:	606
2:11	'Ask the priests what the law s:	606
Zec 1: 3	This is what the LORD Almighty s:	606
1: 3	s the LORD Almighty.	606
1: 4	This is what the LORD Almighty s:	606
1:14	This is what the LORD Almighty s:	606
1:16	"Therefore, this is what the LORD s:	606
1:17	This is what the LORD Almighty s:	606
2: 8	For this is what the LORD Almighty s:	606
3: 7	"This is what the LORD Almighty s:	606
3: 9	s the LORD Almighty,	5536
4: 6	but by my Spirit,' s the LORD Almighty.	606
5: 3	for according to what it s on one side,	NIH
5: 3	and according to what it s on the other,	NIH
6:12	this is what the LORD Almighty s:	606
7: 9	"This is what the LORD Almighty s:	606
7:13	I would not listen," s the LORD Almighty.	606
8: 2	This is what the LORD Almighty s:	606
8: 3	This is what the LORD s:	606
8: 4	This is what the LORD Almighty s:	606
8: 6	This is what the LORD Almighty s:	606
8: 7	This is what the LORD Almighty s:	606
8: 9	This is what the LORD Almighty s:	606
8:14	This is what the LORD Almighty s:	606
8:14	s the LORD Almighty,	606
8:19	This is what the LORD Almighty s:	606
8:20	This is what the LORD Almighty s:	606
8:23	This is what the LORD Almighty s:	606
11: 4	This is what the LORD my God s:	606
Mal 1: 2	"I have loved you," s the LORD.	606
1: 2	the LORD s. "Yet I have loved Jacob,	5536
1: 4	But this is what the LORD Almighty s:	606
1: 6	s the LORD Almighty.	606
1: 8	s the LORD Almighty.	606
1: 9	s the LORD Almighty.	606
1:10	s the LORD Almighty.	606
1:11	s the LORD Almighty.	606
1:13	s the LORD Almighty.	606
1:13	accept them from your hands?" s the LORD.	606
1:14	I am a great king," s the LORD Almighty,	606
2: 2	s the LORD Almighty,	606
2: 4	s the LORD Almighty,	606
2: 8	s the LORD Almighty.	606
2:16	s the LORD God of Israel,	606
2:16	s the LORD Almighty.	606
3: 1	will come," s the LORD Almighty.	606
3: 5	s the LORD Almighty.	606
3: 7	s the LORD Almighty.	606
3:10	Test me in this," s the LORD Almighty,	606
3:11	s the LORD Almighty.	606
3:12	s the LORD Almighty.	606
3:13	said harsh things against me," s the LORD.	606
3:17	s the LORD Almighty,	606
4: 1	s the LORD Almighty.	606
4: 3	s the LORD Almighty.	606
Mt 5:22	Again, anyone who s to his brother, 'Raca,'	3306
5:22	But anyone who s, 'You fool!'	3306
7:21	"Not everyone who s to me, 'Lord, Lord,'	3306
12:44	Then *it* s, 'I will return to the house I left.'	3306
15: 5	But you say that if a man s to his father	3306
21: 3	If anyone s anything to you,	3306
22:43	calls him 'Lord'? For he s,	NIG
24:23	At that time if anyone s to you, 'Look,	3306
24:48	But suppose that servant is wicked and s	3306
26:18	'The Teacher s: My appointed time is near.	3306
Mk 7:11	But you say that if a man s to his father	3306
11:23	if anyone s to this mountain, 'Go,	3306
11:23	but believes that what *he* s will happen,	3281
13:21	At that time if anyone s to you, 'Look,	3306
Lk 4:12	Jesus answered, "It s: 'Do	3306
5:39	for he s, 'The old is better.' "	3306
11: 5	and he goes to him at midnight and s,	3306
11:24	Then *it* s, 'I will return to the house I left.'	3306
12:45	But suppose the servant s to himself,	3306
15: 6	and neighbors together and s, 'Rejoice	3306
15: 9	and neighbors together and s, 'Rejoice	3306
17: 4	and seven times comes back to you and s,	3306
18: 6	"Listen to what the unjust judge s.	3306
Jn 8:22	Is that why he s, 'Where I go,	3306
8:47	He who belongs to God hears what God s.	4839
12:39	because, as Isaiah s elsewhere:	3306
19:37	as another scripture s, "They will look on	3306
Ac 2:17	God s, I will pour out my Spirit	3306
7:48	As the prophet s:	3306
7:49	house will you build for me? s the Lord.	3306
15:17	the Gentiles who bear my name, s the Lord,	3306
19:26	*He* s that man-made gods are no gods at all.	3306
21:11	"The Holy Spirit s, 'In this way	3306
Ro 3:19	Now we know that whatever the law s,	3306
3:19	*it* s to those who are under the law,	3281
4: 6	David s the same thing when he speaks of	NIG
9:15	For he s to Moses, "I will have mercy	3306
9:17	For the Scripture s to Pharaoh:	3306
9:25	As he s in Hosea: "I will call them	3306
10: 6	But the righteousness that is by faith s:	3306
10:11	As the Scripture s, "Anyone who trusts	3306
10:16	For Isaiah s, "Lord, who has believed	3306
10:19	Moses s, "I will make you envious	3306
10:20	And Isaiah boldly s, "I was found	3306
10:21	But concerning Israel he s,	3306
11: 2	Scripture s in the poassage **about** Elijah—	3306
11: 9	David s: "May their table become a snare	3306
12:19	I will repay," s the Lord.	3306
14:11	" 'As surely as I live,' s the Lord,	3306

Ro	15:10	Again, *it* s, "Rejoice, O Gentiles,	3306
	15:12	Isaiah s, "The Root of Jesse will spring up,	3306
1Co	1:12	One of you s, "I follow Paul";	3306
	3: 4	For when one s, "I follow Paul,"	3306
	9:10	Surely *he* s this for us, doesn't he?	3306
	10:28	But if anyone s to you,	3306
	12: 3	who is speaking by the Spirit of God s,	3306
	14:13	that he may interpret what he s.	NIG
	14:21	then they will not listen to me," s the Lord.	3306
	14:34	but must be in submission, as the Law s.	3306
	15:27	when *it* s that "everything" has been put	3306
2Co	6: 2	For *he* s, "In the time of my favor	3306
	6: 17	from them and be separate, s the Lord.	3306
	6:18	s the Lord Almighty."	3306
Gal	4:21	you are not aware of what the law s?	NIG
Eph	4: 8	This is why *it* s: "When he ascended	3306
1Ti	4: 1	The Spirit clearly s that in later times	3306
	5:18	For the Scripture s, "Do not muzzle	3306
Heb	1: 6	*he* s, "Let all God's angels worship him."	3306
	1: 7	In speaking of the angels *he* s,	3306
	1: 8	But about the Son *he* s, "Your throne,	NIG
	1:10	He also s, "In the beginning, O Lord,	NIG
	2:12	*He* s, "I will declare your name	3306
	2:13	And again *he* s, "Here am I,	NIG
	3: 7	So, as the Holy Spirit s: "Today, if you	3306
	4: 5	And again in the passage above *he* s,	NIG
	5: 6	And *he* s in another place,	3306
	10:15	Spirit also testifies about this. First *he* s:	3306
	10:16	with them after that time, s the Lord.	3306
Jas	1:22	and so deceive yourselves. Do what it s.	NIG
	1:23	to the word but does not do what it s is like	NIG
	2:16	*If* one of you s to him, "Go,	3306
	2:23	And the scripture was fulfilled that s,	3306
	3: 2	If anyone is never at fault in **what** he s,	3364
	4: 5	Or do you think Scripture s without reason	3306
	4: 6	That is why Scripture s: "God opposes	3306
1Pe	2: 6	For in Scripture *it* s: "See, I lay a stone	4321
1Jn	2: 4	The man who s, "I know him,"	3306
	4:20	If anyone s, "I love God,"	3306
Rev	1: 8	s the Lord God, "who is, and who was,	3306
	2: 7	let him hear what the Spirit s to the churches	3306
	2:11	let him hear what the Spirit s to the churches	3306
	2:17	let him hear what the Spirit s to the churches	3306
	2:29	let him hear what the Spirit s to the churches	3306
	3: 6	let him hear what the Spirit s to the churches	3306
	3:13	let him hear what the Spirit s to the churches	3306
	3:22	let him hear what the Spirit s to the churches	3306
	14:13	s the Spirit, "they will rest from their labor,	3306
	22:20	He who testifies to these things s, "Yes,	3306

SCAB, SCABBED (KJV) See FESTERING SORES, RASH, RUNNING SORES, SORES

SCABBARD (5)

1Sa	17:51	and drew it from the s.	9509
Jer	47: 6	Return to your s; cease and be still.'	9509
Eze	21: 3	I will draw my sword from its s and cut off	9509
	21: 5	I the LORD have drawn my sword from its s;	9509
	21:30	Return the sword to its s.	9509

SCABS (1)

Job	7: 5	My body is clothed with worms and s,	1599+6760

SCAFFOLD (KJV) See PLATFORM

SCALE (4) [SCALES]

1Sa	17: 5	his head and wore a **coat of s armor**	7989+9234
2Sa	22:30	with my God *I can* s a wall.	1925
Ps	18:29	with my God *I can* s a wall.	1925
Joel	2: 7	*they* s walls like soldiers.	6590

SCALES (25) [SCALE]

Lev	11: 9	you may eat any that have fins and s.	7989
	11:10	that do not have fins and s—	7989
	11:12	the water that does not have fins and s is to	7989
	19:36	Use honest s and honest weights,	4404
Dt	14: 9	you may eat any that has fins and s.	7989
	14:10	that does not have fins and s you may	7989
Job	6: 2	and all my misery be placed on the s!	4404
	31: 6	let God weigh me in honest s	4404
Pr	11: 1	The LORD abhors dishonest s,	4404
	16:11	Honest s and balances are from the LORD;	4404
	20:23	and dishonest s do not please him.	4404
Isa	40:12	or weighed the mountains on the s and	7144
	40:15	they are regarded as dust on the s;	4404
	46: 6	and weigh out silver on the s,	7866
Jer	32:10	and weighed out the silver on the s.	4404
Eze	5: 1	take a **set of s** and divide up the hair.	4404+5486
	29: 4	the fish of your streams stick to your s.	7989
	29: 4	with all the fish sticking to your s.	7989
	45:10	You are to use accurate s,	4404
Da	5:27	You have been weighed on the s	10396
Hos	12: 7	The merchant uses dishonest s;	4404
Am	8: 5	the price and cheating with dishonest s,	4404
Mic	6:11	Shall I acquit a man with dishonest s,	4404
Ac	9:18	something like s fell from Saul's eyes,	3318
Rev	6: 5	Its rider was holding a **pair of s** in his hand.	2433

SCALL (KJV) See SORE

SCALP (1) [SCALPS]

Lev	13:41	If he has lost his hair from the front of his s	7156

SCALPS (1) [SCALP]

Isa	3:17	the LORD will make their s bald."	7327

SCANT (KJV) See SHORT

SCAPEGOAT (4) [GOAT]

Lev	16: 8	for the LORD and the other for the **s**.	6439
	16:10	But the goat chosen by lot as the s shall	6439
	16:10	by sending it into the desert as a s.	6439
	16:26	a s must wash his clothes and bathe himself	6439

SCAR (2)

Lev	13:23	it is only a s *from* the boil,	7648
	13:28	it is only a s *from* the burn.	7648

SCARCE (2) [SCARCELY, SCARCER, SCARCITY]

Dt	8: 9	not *be* s and you will lack nothing;	430+928+5017
Eze	4:17	for food and water *will be* s.	2893

SCARCELY (4) [SCARCE]

Ge	27:30	and Jacob had s left his father's presence,	421
Job	29:24	When I smiled at them, they s believed it;	4202
SS	3: 4	S had I passed them when I found	3869+5071
Lk	9:39	It s *ever* leaves him and is destroying him.	3653

SCARCER (1) [SCARCE]

Isa	13:12	*I will* **make** man s than pure gold,	3700

SCARCITY (2) [SCARCE]

Pr	6:11	like a bandit and s like an armed man.	4728
	24:34	like a bandit and s like an armed man.	4728

SCARECROW (1)

Jer	10: 5	Like a s *in* a melon patch,	9473

SCARLET (49)

Ge	38:28	a s **thread** and tied it on his wrist and said,	9106
	38:30	who had the s **thread** on his wrist,	9106
Ex	25: 4	purple and s **yarn**, and fine linen;	9106+9357
	26: 1	purple and s **yarn**,	9106+9357
	26:31	and s **yarn** and finely twisted linen,	9106+9357
	26:36	and s **yarn** and finely twisted linen—	9106+9357
	27:16	and s **yarn** and finely twisted linen—	9106+9357
	28: 5	purple and s **yarn**, and fine linen.	9106+9357
	28: 6	and of blue, purple and s **yarn**,	9106+9357
	28: 8	and with blue, purple and s **yarn**,	9106+9357
	28:15	gold, and of blue, purple and s **yarn**,	9106+9357
	28:33	and s **yarn** around the hem of the robe,	9106+9357
	35: 6	purple and s **yarn**, and fine linen;	9106+9357
	35:23	or s **yarn** or fine linen, or goat hair,	9106+9357
	35:25	blue, purple or s **yarn** or fine linen.	9106+9357
	35:35	purple and s **yarn**, and fine linen,	9106+9357
	36: 8	purple and s **yarn**,	9106+9357
	36:35	and s **yarn** and finely twisted linen,	9106+9357
	36:37	and s **yarn** and finely twisted linen—	9106+9357
	38:18	and s **yarn** and finely twisted linen—	9106+9357
	38:23	purple and s **yarn** and fine linen.)	9106+9357
	39: 1	and s **yarn** they made woven garments	9106+9357
	39: 2	and of blue, purple and s **yarn**,	9106+9357
	39: 3	purple and s **yarn** and finely twisted	9106+9357
	39: 5	and with blue, purple and s **yarn**,	9106+9357
	39: 8	of gold, and of blue, purple and s **yarn**,	9106+9357
	39:24	and s **yarn** and finely twisted linen	9106+9357
	39:29	purple and s **yarn**—	9106+9357
Lev	14: 4	s **yarn** and hyssop be brought for the	9106+9357
	14: 6	the s **yarn** and the hyssop	9106+9357
	14:49	s **yarn** and hyssop.	9106+9357
	14:51	hyssop, the s **yarn** and the live bird,	9106+9357
	14:52	cedar wood, the hyssop and the s **yarn**.	9106+9357
Nu	4: 8	Over these they are to spread a s cloth,	9106+9357
	19: 6	hyssop and s **wool** and throw them	9106+9357
Jos	2:18	you have tied this s cord in the window	9106
	2:21	And she tied the s cord in the window.	9106
2Sa	1:24	who clothed you in s and finery,	9106
Pr	31:21	for all of them are clothed in s.	9106
SS	4: 3	Your lips are like a s ribbon;	9106
Isa	1:18	"Though your sins are like s,	9106
Jer	4:30	Why dress yourself in s and put on jewels	9106
Na	2: 3	the warriors *are* **clad in s**.	9443
Mt	27:28	They stripped him and put a s robe on him,	3132
Heb	9:19	s wool and branches of hyssop,	3132
Rev	17: 3	There I saw a woman sitting on a s beast	3132
	17: 4	The woman was dressed in purple and s,	3132
	18:12	fine linen, purple, silk and s cloth;	3132
	18:16	purple and s, and glittering with gold,	3132

SCATTER (39) [SCATTERED, SCATTERING, SCATTERS]

Ge	49: 7	*I will* s them in Jacob and disperse them	2745
Lev	26:33	*I will* s you among the nations	2430
Nu	16:37	and s the coals some distance away, for	2430
Dt	4:27	The LORD *will* s you among the peoples,	7046
	28:64	the LORD *will* s you among all nations,	7046
	32:26	I said *I would* s them and blot out	6990
1Sa	13: 8	and Saul's men *began to* s.	7046

1Ki	14:15	that he gave to their forefathers and s them	2430
Ne	1: 8	I *will* s you among the nations,	7046
Ps	68:30	S the nations who delight in war.	1029
	106:27	among the nations and s them throughout	2430
	144: 6	Send forth lightning and s [the enemies];	7046
Ecc	3: 5	a time to s stones and a time to gather them,	8959
Isa	24: 1	he will ruin its face and s its inhabitants—	7046
	28:25	does he not sow caraway and s cummin?	2450
	33: 3	when you rise up, the nations s.	5880
Jer	9:16	I *will* s them among nations	7046
	13:24	"I *will* s you like chaff driven by	7046
	18:17	I *will* s them before their enemies;	7046
	30:11	the nations among which *I* s you,	7046
	46:28	the nations among which *I* s you,	5615
	49:32	I *will* s to the winds those who are	2430
	49:36	I *will* s them to the four winds,	2430
Eze	5: 2	And s a third to the wind.	2430
	5:10	and *will* s all your survivors to the winds.	2430
	5:12	a third *I will* s to the winds and pursue	2430
	6: 5	I *will* s your bones around your altars.	2430
	10: 2	from among the cherubim and s them over	2450
	12:14	I *will* s to the winds all those	2430
	12:15	among the nations and s them through	2430
	20:23	among the nations and s them through	2430
	22:15	the nations and s you through the countries;	2430
	29:12	the Egyptians among the nations and s them	2430
	30:23	the Egyptians among the nations and s them	2430
	30:26	the Egyptians among the nations and s them	2430
Da	4:14	strip off its leaves and s its fruit.	10095
Hab	3:14	when his warriors stormed out to s us,	7046
Zec	1:21	against the land of Judah to s its people."	2430
	10: 9	Though *I* s them among the peoples,	2445

SCATTERED (85) [SCATTER]

Ge	9:19	from them came the people who were s *over*	5880
	10:18	Later the Canaanite clans s	7046
	11: 4	for ourselves and not *be* s over the face of	7046
	11: 8	So the LORD s them from there over all	7046
	11: 9	From there the LORD s them over the face	7046
Ex	5:12	the people s all over Egypt to gather stubble	7046
	32:20	to powder, s it on the water and made	2430
Nu	10:35	*May* your enemies *be* s;	7046
Dt	30: 3	from all the nations where he s you.	7046
Jdg	9:45	he destroyed the city and s salt *over* it.	2445
1Sa	11:11	Those who survived *were* s,	7046
	30:16	and there they were, s over the countryside,	5759
2Sa	17:19	the opening of the well and s grain over it.	8848
	22:15	He shot arrows and s [the enemies],	7046
1Ki	22:17	"I saw all Israel s on the hills like sheep	7046
2Ki	23: 6	to powder and s the dust over the graves of	8959
	25: 5	were separated from him and s,	7046
2Ch	18:16	"I saw all Israel s on the hills like sheep	7046
	34: 4	These he broke to pieces and s over	2450
Est	3: 8	"There is a certain people dispersed and s	7233
Job	4:11	and the cubs of the lioness *are* s.	7233
	18:15	burning sulfur is s over his dwelling.	2430
	38:24	or the place where the east winds *are* s over	7046
Ps	18:14	He shot his arrows and s [the enemies],	7046
	44:11	be devoured like sheep and *have* s us among	2430
	53: 5	God s the bones of those who attacked you;	7061
	68: 1	May God arise, *may* his enemies *be* s;	7046
	68:14	When the Almighty s the kings in the land,	7298
	89:10	with your strong arm *you* s your enemies.	7061
	92: 9	all evildoers *will* **be s**.	7233
	112: 9	*He* has s **abroad** his gifts to the poor,	7061
	141: 7	so our bones *have been* s at the mouth of	7061
Isa	11:12	he will assemble the s *people* of Judah	7046
Jer	3:13	*you have* s your favors to foreign gods	7061
	10:21	not prosper and all their flock *is* s.	7046
	23: 2	"Because you *have* s my flock	7046
	31:10	'He who s Israel will gather them	2430
	40:12	all the countries where *they had* **been s**.	5615
	40:15	*to be* s and the remnant of Judah to perish?"	7046
	43: 5	from all the nations where *they had* **been s**.	5615
	50:17	a s flock that lions have chased away.	7061
	52: 8	*were* separated from him and s,	7046
La	4: 1	The sacred gems *are* s at the head	9161
Eze	6: 8	the sword when you *are* s among the lands	2430
	11:16	the nations and s them among the countries,	7046
	11:17	from the countries where *you have* **been s**.	7046
	17:21	and the survivors *will be* s to the winds.	7298
	20:34	from the countries where *you have* **been s**—	7046
	20:41	from the countries where *you have* **been s**,	7046
	28:25	from the nations where *they have* **been s**,	7046
	29:13	from the nations where *they were* s.	7046
	34: 5	*they were* s because there was no shepherd,	7046
	34: 5	when *they were* s they became food for all	7046
	34: 6	They *were* s over the whole earth,	7046
	34:12	after his s flock when he is with them,	7298
	34:12	from all the places where *they were* s on	7046
	36:19	and *they were* s through the countries;	2430
Da	9: 7	the countries where *you have* s us because	5615
Joel	3: 2	for *they* s my people among the nations	7061
Na	3:18	Your people *are* s on the mountains	7056
Zep	3:10	my s people, will bring me offerings.	7046
	3:19	the lame and gather those *who have* **been s**.	5615
Zec	1:19	"These are the horns that s Judah,	2430
	1:21	"These are the horns that s Judah so	2430
	2: 6	*I have* s you to the four winds of heaven,"	7298
	7:14	'*I have* s them **with a whirlwind**	6192
	13: 7	and the sheep *will be* s,	7046
Mt	25:24	and gathering where *you have* not s **seed**.	1399
	25:26	and gather where I have not s **seed**?	1399
	26:31	and the sheep of the flock *will be* s.'	1399
Mk	14:27	and the sheep *will be* s.'	1399

Lk	1:51	he has s those who are proud	1399
Jn	2:15	he s the coins of the money changers	1772
	7:35	go where our **people live s among**	1402+3836
	11:52	for that nation but also for the s children	1399
	16:32	and has come, when you will be s,	5025
Ac	5:37	and all his followers were s.	1399
	8: 1	the apostles were s throughout Judea	1401
	8: 4	Those who had been s preached	1401
	11:19	Now those who had been s by	1401
1Co	10: 5	their bodies were s over the desert.	2954
2Co	9: 9	"He has s abroad" his gifts to the poor;	5025
Jas	1: 1	To the twelve tribes s among the nations:	1402
1Pe	1: 1	in the world, s throughout Pontus,	1402

SCATTERING (5) [SCATTER]

1Sa	13:11	"When I saw that the men were s,	5880
Jer	23: 1	to the shepherds who are destroying and s	7046
Mt	13: 4	As he was s the seed,	5062
Mk	4: 4	As he was s the seed,	5062
Lk	8: 5	As he was s the seed,	5062

SCATTERS (7) [SCATTER]

Job	36:30	See how he s his lightning about him,	7298
	37:11	he s his lightning through them.	7046
Ps	147:16	He spreads the snow like wool and s	7061
Mt	12:30	and he who does not gather with me s.	5025
Mk	4:26	A man's seed on the ground.	965
Lk	11:23	and he who does not gather with me, s.	5025
Jn	10:12	Then the wolf attacks the flock and s it.	5025

SCENE (1)

| Mk | 9:25 | that a crowd was running to the s, | NIG |

SCENT (2)

| Job | 14: 9 | yet at the s of water it will bud | 8194 |
| | 39:25 | He **catches the** s of battle from afar, | 8193 |

SCEPTER (27) [SCEPTERS]

Ge	49:10	The s will not depart from Judah,	8657
Nu	24:17	a s will rise out of Israel.	8657
Est	4:11	to this is for the king to extend the gold s	9222
	5: 2	and held out to her the gold s that was	9222
	5: 2	and touched the tip of the s.	9222
	8: 4	the gold s to Esther and she arose and stood	9222
Ps	2: 9	You will rule them with an iron s;	8657
	45: 6	a s of justice will be the scepter	8657
	45: 6	of justice will be the s of your kingdom.	8657
	60: 7	Ephraim is my helmet, Judah my s.	2980
	108: 8	Ephraim is my helmet, Judah my s.	2980
	110: 2	The LORD will extend your mighty s	4751
	125: 3	The s of the wicked will not remain over	8657
Isa	14: 5	the s of the rulers,	8657
	30:31	with his s he will strike them down.	8657
Jer	48:17	say, 'How broken is the mighty s,	4751
Eze	19:11	Its branches were strong, fit for a ruler's s	8657
	19:14	on it fit for a ruler's s.'	8657
	21:10	in the s of my son [Judah]?	8657
	21:13	And what if the s [of Judah],	8657
Am	1: 5	and the one who holds the s in Beth Eden.	8657
	1: 8	and the one who holds the s in Ashkelon.	8657
Zec	10:11	down and Egypt's s will pass away.	8657
Heb	1: 8	and righteousness will be the s	4811
Rev	2:27	'He will rule them with an iron s;	4811
	12: 5	who will rule all the nations with an iron s.	4811
	19:15	"He will rule them with an iron s."	4811

SCEPTERS (1) [SCEPTER]

| Nu | 21:18 | the nobles with s and staffs." | 2980 |

SCEVA (1)

| Ac | 19:14 | Seven sons of S, a Jewish chief priest, | 5005 |

SCHEME (4) [SCHEMER, SCHEMES, SCHEMING]

Est	9:25	that the evil s Haman had devised against	4742
Ecc	7:25	to search out wisdom and the s of things	3113
	7:27	to another to discover the s of things—	3113
Eze	38:10	and you will devise an evil s.	4742

SCHEMER (1) [SCHEME]

| Pr | 24: 8 | who plots evil will be known as a s. | 1251+4659 |

SCHEMES (20) [SCHEME]

Ex	21:14	a man s and kills another man deliberately,	2326
Job	5:13	and the s of the wily are swept away.	6783
	10: 3	while you smile on the s of the wicked?	6783
	18: 7	his own s throw him down.	6783
	21:27	the s by which you would wrong me.	4659
Ps	10: 2	who are caught in the s he devises.	4659
	21:11	and devise **wicked** s, they cannot succeed;	4659
	26:10	in whose hands are **wicked** s,	2365
	37: 7	when they carry out their **wicked** s.	4659
	119:150	Those who devise **wicked** s are near,	2365
Pr	1:31	and be filled with the fruit of their s.	4600
	6:18	a heart that devises wicked s,	4742
	24: 9	s of folly are sin, and men detest a mocker.	2365
Ecc	7:29	but men have gone into search of many s."	3115
	8:11	of the people are filled with s to do wrong.	NIH
Isa	32: 7	he makes up **evil** s to destroy the poor	2365
Jer	6:19	disaster on this people, the fruit of their s,	4742

Jer	11:15	in my temple as she works out her **evil** s	4659
2Co	2:11	For we are not unaware of his s.	3784
Eph	6:11	take your stand against the devil's s.	3497

SCHEMING (2) [SCHEME]

| Ne | 6: 2 | But they were s to harm me; | 3108 |
| Eph | 4:14 | and craftiness of men in their deceitful s. | 3497 |

SCHISM (KJV) See DIVISION

SCHOLAR (1)

| 1Co | 1:20 | Where is the wise man? Where is the s? | 1208 |

SCHOOL (KJV) See LECTURE HALL

SCHOOLMASTER (KJV) See SUPERVISION, PUT IN CHARGE

SCIENCE (KJV) See KNOWLEDGE

SCOFF (10) [SCOFFED, SCOFFERS, SCOFFING, SCOFFS]

1Ki	9: 8	all who pass by will be appalled and will s	9239
Ps	59: 8	you s at all those nations.	4352
	73: 8	They s, and speak with malice;	4610
Jer	19: 8	all who pass by will be appalled and will s	9239
	49:17	all who pass by will be appalled and will s	9239
	50:13	and s because of all her wounds.	9239
La	2:15	they s and shake their heads at the Daughter	9239
	2:16	they s and gnash their teeth and say,	9239
Hab	1:10	They deride kings and s at rulers.	5377
Zep	2:15	All who pass by her s and shake their fists.	9239

SCOFFED (1) [SCOFF]

| 2Ch | 36:16 | despised his words and s at his prophets | 9506 |

SCOFFERS (4) [SCOFF]

Isa	28:14	you s who rule this people in Jerusalem.	408+4371
Ac	13:41	you s, wonder and perish,	2970
2Pe	3: 3	that in the last days s will come,	1851
Jude	1:18	there will be s who will follow their own ungodly desires."	1851

SCOFFING (1) [SCOFF]

| 2Pe | 3: 3 | s and following their own evil desires. | 1848 |

SCOFFS (2) [SCOFF]

| Ps | 2: 4 | in heaven laughs; the Lord s at them. | 4352 |
| Pr | 29: 9 | the fool rages and s, and there is no peace. | 8471 |

SCOOP (1) [SCOOPED, SCOOPING, SCOOPS]

| Pr | 6:27 | Can a man s fire into his lap | 3149 |

SCOOPED (1) [SCOOP]

| Jdg | 14: 9 | which he s out with his hands and ate | 8098 |

SCOOPING (1) [SCOOP]

| Isa | 30:14 | for taking coals from a hearth or s water out | 3106 |

SCOOPS (1) [SCOOP]

| Ps | 7:15 | and s it **out** falls into the pit he has made. | 2916 |

SCORCH (1) [SCORCHED, SCORCHING, SUN-SCORCHED]

| Rev | 16: 8 | sun was given power to s people with fire. | 3009 |

SCORCHED (11) [SCORCH]

Ge	41: 6	thin and s by the east wind.	8728
	41:23	withered and thin and s by the east wind.	8728
	41:27	so are the seven worthless heads of grain s	8728
2Ki	19:26	s before it grows up.	8729
Pr	6:28	on hot coals without his feet **being** s?	3917
Isa	9:19	of the LORD Almighty the land will be s	6977
	37:27	s before it grows up.	8729
Eze	20:47	from south to north will be s by it.	7646
Da	3:27	their robes were not s,	10731
Mt	13: 6	when the sun came up, the plants were s	3009
Mk	4: 6	when the sun came up, the plants were s,	3009

SCORCHING (8) [SCORCH]

Dt	28:22	with s heat and drought,	3031
Ps	11: 6	a s wind will be their lot.	2363
Pr	16:27	and his speech is like a s fire.	7647
Isa	11:15	with a s wind he will sweep his hand over	6522
Jer	4:11	"A s wind from the barren heights in	7456
Jnh	4: 8	God provided a s east wind,	3046
Jas	1:11	sun rises with s heat and withers the plant;	3014
Rev	7:16	sun will not beat upon them, nor any s **heat.**	3008

SCORN (38) [SCORNED, SCORNFULLY, SCORNING, SCORNS]

| Dt | 28:37 | of horror and an **object of** s and ridicule | 5442 |

1Sa	2:29	Why do you s my sacrifice and offering	1246
2Ch	29: 8	an object of dread and horror and s,	9240
Job	16:10	they strike my cheek in s and unite together	3075
	19:18	Even the little boys s me;	4415
	34: 7	who drinks s like water?	4353
Ps	39: 8	do not make me the s of fools.	3075
	44:13	the s and derision of those around us.	4353
	64: 8	who see them will **shake their heads in** s	5653
	69: 7	For I endure s for your sake,	3075
	69:10	When I weep and fast, I must endure s;	3075
	69:20	S has broken my heart	3075
	71:13	to harm me be covered with s and disgrace.	3075
	79: 4	of s and derision to those around us.	4353
	89:41	he has become the s of his neighbors.	3075
	109:25	I am an **object of** s to my accusers;	3075
	119:22	Remove from me s and contempt,	3075
Pr	23: 9	for he will s the wisdom of your words.	996
Isa	43:28	to destruction and Israel to s.	1526
Jer	18:16	an **object of** lasting s;	9241
	19: 8	and make it an **object of** s;	9240
	25: 9	and make them an object of horror and s,	9240
	25:18	and an object of horror and s and cursing,	9240
	29:18	cursing and horror, of s and reproach,	9240
	48:27	that you **shake your head in** s	5653
	51:37	a haunt of jackals, an object of horror and s,	9240
Eze	22: 4	Therefore I will make you an **object of** s to	3075
	23:32	it will bring s and derision,	7465
	34:29	in the land or bear the s of the nations.	4009
	36: 6	because you have suffered the s of	4009
	36: 7	the nations around you will also suffer s.	4009
	36:15	the s of the peoples or cause your nation	3075
Da	9:16	and your people an **object of** s to all those	3075
Joel	2:17	not make your inheritance an **object of** s,	3075
	2:19	never again will I make you an **object of** s	3075
Mic	6:16	you will bear the s of the nations."	3075
Hab	2: 6	of them taunt him with ridicule and s,	2648
Gal	4:14	you did not treat me with contempt or s.	1746

SCORNED (7) [SCORN]

2Ch	30:10	but the people s and ridiculed them.	8471
Est	3: 6	he s **the idea** of killing only Mordecai.	928+1022+6524
Ps	22: 6	s by men and despised by the people.	3075
	69:19	You know how I am s,	3075
SS	8: 7	it would be **utterly** s.	996+996
Eze	16:31	because you s payment.	7840
	16:57	you are now s by the daughters of Edom	3075

SCORNFULLY (1) [SCORN]

| Job | 34:37 | s he **claps** his **hands** among us | 6215 |

SCORNING (1) [SCORN]

| Heb | 12: 2 | s its shame, and sat down at the right hand | 2969 |

SCORNS (2) [SCORN]

| Pr | 13:13 | He who s instruction will pay for it, | 996 |
| | 30:17 | that s obedience to a mother, | 996 |

SCORPION (5) [SCORPIONS]

Nu	34: 4	cross south of S Pass,	6832
Jos	15: 3	crossed south of S Pass,	6832
Jdg	1:36	of the Amorites was from S Pass to Sela	6832
Lk	11:12	Or if he asks for an egg, will give him a s?	5026
Rev	9: 5	like that of the sting of a s when it strikes	5026

SCORPIONS (9) [SCORPION]

Dt	8:15	with its venomous snakes and s.	6832
1Ki	12:11	I will scourge you with s.' "	6832
	12:14	I will scourge you with s.' "	6832
2Ch	10:11	I will scourge you with s.' "	6832
	10:14	I will scourge you with s."	6832
Eze	2: 6	around you and you live among s.	6832
Lk	10:19	and s and to overcome all the power of	5026
Rev	9: 3	and were given power like that of s of	5026
	9:10	They had tails and stings like s,	5026

SCOUNDREL (4) [SCOUNDREL'S, SCOUNDRELS]

2Sa	16: 7	get out, you man of blood, you s!	408+1175+2021
Pr	6:12	A s and villain, who goes about with	132+1175
	16:27	A s plots evil, and his speech is like	408+1175
Isa	32: 5	nor the s highly respected.	3964

SCOUNDREL'S (1) [SCOUNDREL]

| Isa | 32: 7 | The s methods are wicked, | 3964 |

SCOUNDRELS (3) [SCOUNDREL]

1Ki	21:10	But seat two s opposite him	1175+1201
	21:13	Then two s came and sat opposite him	1175+1201
2Ch	13: 7	Some worthless s gathered around him	1175+1201

SCOURED (1)

| Lev | 6:28 | the pot is to **be** s and rinsed with water. | 5347 |

SCOURGE (8) [SCOURGED]

1Ki	12:11	I will s you with scorpions.' "	3579
	12:14	I will s you with scorpions.' "	3579
2Ch	10:11	I will s you with scorpions.' "	NIH
	10:14	I will s you with scorpions."	NIH

Job	9:23	When a s brings sudden death,	8765
Ps	39:10	Remove your s from me;	5596
Isa	28:15	When an overwhelming s sweeps by,	8765
	28:18	When the overwhelming s sweeps by,	8765

SCOURGED (4) [SCOURGE]

1Ki	12:11	My father s you with whips;	3579
	12:14	My father s you with whips;	3579
2Ch	10:11	My father s you with whips;	3579
	10:14	My father s you with whips;	3579

SCOURGES, SCOURGETH, SCOURGING, SCOURGINGS (KJV)
See FLOG, FLOGGED, FLOGGING, LASH, PUNISHES, PUNISHMENT, SCOURGE, WHIP, WHIPS

SCOUTS (2)

1Sa	26: 4	he sent out s and learned that Saul	8078
1Ki	20:17	Now Ben-Hadad had dispatched s,	NIH

SCRAPE (1) [SCRAPED]

Eze	26: 4	*I will* s away her rubble and make her	6081

SCRAPED (4) [SCRAPE]

Lev	14:41	**have** all the inside walls of the house s	7909
	14:41	and the material that *is off* dumped into	7894
	14:43	and the house s and plastered,	7894
Job	2: 8	a piece of broken pottery and s **himself**	1740

SCRAPS (2)

Jdg	1: 7	and big toes cut off *have* **picked up** s	4377
Eze	13:19	for a few handfuls of barley and s *of* bread.	7336

SCRAWNY (1)

Ge	41:19	s and very ugly and lean.	1924

SCRAWNY (Anglicized) See also RAWBONED

SCREAM (2) [SCREAMED, SCREAMS]

Ge	39:15	he heard me s **for help**,	2256+7754+7924+8123
Dt	22:24	in a town and *did* not s **for help**,	7590

SCREAMED (3) [SCREAM]

Ge	39:14	He came in here to sleep with me, but *I* s.	928+1524+7754+7924
	39:18	as soon as I s **for help**,	2256+7754+7924+8123
Dt	22:27	and though the betrothed girl s,	7590

SCREAMS (1) [SCREAM]

Lk	9:39	A spirit seizes him and *he* suddenly s;	3189

SCREECH (4)

Lev	11:16	the s **owl**, the gull, any kind of hawk,	9379
Dt	14:15	the s **owl**, the gull, any kind of hawk,	9379
Isa	34:11	The desert owl and s **owl** will possess it;	7887
Zep	2:14	and the s **owl** will roost on her columns.	7887

SCRIBE (11) [SCRIBE'S, SCRIBES]

1Ch	24: 6	The s Shemaiah son of Nethanel, a Levite,	6221
	27:32	was a counselor, a man of insight and a s.	6221
Ne	8: 1	They told Ezra the s to bring out the Book	6221
	8: 4	the s stood on a high wooden platform built	6221
	8: 9	Ezra the priest and s,	6221
	8:13	gathered around Ezra the s to give attention	6221
	12:26	the governor and of Ezra the priest and s.	6221
	12:36	Ezra the s led the procession.	6221
	13:13	I put Shelemiah the priest, Zadok the s,	6221
Jer	36:26	to arrest Baruch the s and Jeremiah	6221
	36:32	and gave it to the s Baruch son of Neriah,	6221

SCRIBE'S (1) [SCRIBE]

Jer	36:23	a s knife and threw them into the firepot,	6221

SCRIBES (3) [SCRIBE]

1Ch	2:55	and the clans of s who lived at Jabez:	6221
2Ch	34:13	of the Levites were secretaries, s	8853
Jer	8: 8	the lying pen of the s has handled it falsely?	6221

SCRIP (KJV) See BAG

SCRIPT (5)

Ezr	4: 7	in Aramaic s and in the Aramaic language.	4181
Est	1:22	to each province in its own s and	4181
	3:12	the s *of* each province and in the language	4181
	8: 9	in the s *of* each province and the language	4181
	8: 9	to the Jews in their own s and language.	4181

SCRIPTURE (33) [SCRIPTURES]

Mk	12:10	Haven't you read this s:	1210
Lk	4:21	"Today this s is fulfilled in your hearing."	1210
Jn	2:22	the S and the words that Jesus had spoken.	1210
	7:38	Whoever believes in me, as the S has said,	1210

Jn	7:42	not the S say that the Christ will come	1210
	10:35	and the S cannot be broken—	1210
	13:18	But this is to fulfill the s:	1210
	17:12	to destruction so that S would be fulfilled.	1210
	19:24	that the s might be fulfilled which said,	1210
	19:28	and so that the S would be fulfilled,	1210
	19:36	These things happened so that the s would	1210
	19:37	as another s says, "They will look on the	1210
	20: 9	not understand from S that Jesus had to rise	1210
Ac	1:16	the S had to be fulfilled which	1210
	8:32	The eunuch was reading this passage *of* S:	1210
	8:35	with that very passage *of* S and told him	1210
Ro	4: 3	What does the S say?	1210
	9:17	For the S says to Pharaoh: "I raised you up	1210
	10:11	As the S says, "Anyone who trusts in him	1210
	11: 2	the S says in the passage about Elijah—	1210
Gal	3: 8	The S foresaw that God would justify	1210
	3:16	The S does not say "and to seeds,"	NIG
	3:22	But the S declares that the whole world is	1210
	4:30	But what does the S say?	1210
1Ti	4:13	devote yourself to the public reading of S,	NIG
	5:18	For the S says, "Do not muzzle the ox	1210
2Ti	3:16	All S is God-breathed and is useful	1210
Jas	2: 8	If you really keep the royal law found in S,	1210
	2:23	And the s was fulfilled that says,	1210
	4: 5	Or do you think S says without reason that	1210
	4: 6	That is why S says: "God opposes the proud	NIG
1Pe	2: 6	For in S it says: "See, I lay a stone in Zion,	1210
2Pe	1:20	that no prophecy *of* S came about by	1210

SCRIPTURES (21) [SCRIPTURE]

Da	9: 2	I, Daniel, understood from the S,	6219
Mt	21:42	"Have you never read in the S:	1210
	22:29	in error because you do not know the S or	1210
	26:54	the S be fulfilled that say it must happen	1210
Mk	12:24	not in error because you do not know the S	1210
	14:49	But the S must be fulfilled."	1210
Lk	24:27	to them what was said in all the S	1210
	24:32	with us on the road and opened the S	1210
	24:45	so they could understand the S.	1210
Jn	5:39	the S because you think that	1210
	5:39	These are the S that testify about me,	NIG
Ac	17: 2	he reasoned with them from the S,	1210
	17:11	and examined the S every day to see	1210
	18:24	with a thorough knowledge of the S.	1210
	18:28	from the S that Jesus was the Christ.	1210
Ro	1: 2	through his prophets in the Holy S	1210
	15: 4	*of* the S we might have hope.	1210
1Co	15: 3	Christ died for our sins according to the S,	1210
	15: 4	on the third day according to the S,	1210
2Ti	3:15	from infancy you have known the holy S,	1207
2Pe	3:16	as they do the other S,	1210

SCROLL (66) [SCROLLS]

Ex	17:14	on a s as something to be remembered	6219
Nu	5:23	" 'The priest is to write these curses on a s	6219
Dt	17:18	he is to write for himself on a s a copy	6219
Jos	18: 9	They wrote its description on a s,	6219
1Sa	10:25	He wrote them down on a s and deposited it	6219
Ezr	6: 2	A s was found in the citadel of Ecbatana in	10399
Job	19:23	that they were written on a s,	6219
Ps	40: 7	it is written about me in the s.	4479+6219
	56: 8	Record my lament; list my tears on your s—	5532
Isa	8: 1	"Take a large s and write on it with	1663
	29:11	but words sealed in a s.	6219
	29:11	if you give **the** s to someone who can read,	2257S
	29:12	you give the s to someone who cannot read,	6219
	29:18	the deaf will hear the words of the s,	6219
	30: 8	inscribe it on a s,	6219
	34: 4	be dissolved and the sky rolled up like a s;	6219
	34:16	Look in the s *of* the LORD and read:	6219
Jer	36: 2	"Take a s and write on it all	4479+6219
	36: 4	Baruch wrote them on the s.	4479+6219
	36: 6	and read to the people from the s the words	4479
	36: 8	the words of the LORD from the s.	6219
	36:10	the words of Jeremiah from the s.	6219
	36:11	the words of the LORD from the s,	6219
	36:13	Baruch read to the people from the s,	4479
	36:14	"Bring the s from which you have read to	4479
	36:14	son of Neriah went to them with the s	4479
	36:18	and I wrote them in ink on the s."	4479
	36:20	After they put the s in the room of Elishama	4479
	36:21	The king sent Jehudi to get the s,	4479
	36:23	three or four columns of the s,	NIH
	36:23	until the entire s was burned in the fire.	4479
	36:25	urged the king not to burn the s,	4479
	36:27	the king burned the s containing the words	4479
	36:28	"Take another s and write on it all	4479
	36:28	on it all the words that were on the first s,	4479
	36:29	You burned that s and said,	4479
	36:32	So Jeremiah took another s and gave it to	4479
	36:32	Baruch wrote on it all the words of the s	6219
	45: 1	a s the words Jeremiah was then dictating:	6219
	51:60	a s about all the disasters that would come	6219
	51:63	When you finish reading this s,	6219
Eze	2: 9	In it was a s,	4479+6219
	3: 1	eat what is before you, eat this s;	4479
	3: 2	and he gave me the s to eat.	4479
	3: 3	eat this s I am giving you	4479
Da	12: 4	up and seal the words of the s until the time	6219
Zec	5: 1	and there before me was a flying s!	4479
	5: 2	I answered, "I see a flying s,	4479
Mal	3:16	A s of remembrance was written	6219
Lk	4:17	The s of the prophet Isaiah was handed	1046
	4:20	Then he rolled up the s,	1046

Heb	9:19	and sprinkled the s and all the people.	1046
	10: 7	it is written about me in the s—	1046
Rev	1:11	"Write on a s what you see and send it to	1046
	5: 1	on the throne a s with writing on both sides	1046
	5: 2	to break the seals and open the s?"	1046
	5: 3	on earth or under the earth could open the s	1046
	5: 4	to open the s or look inside.	1046
	5: 5	He is able to open the s and its seven seals."	1046
	5: 7	He came and took the s from the right hand	NIG
	5: 9	"You are worthy to take the s and	1046
	6:14	The sky receded like a s, rolling up,	1046
	10: 2	He was holding a **little** s.	1044
	10: 8	"Go, take the s that lies open in the hand of	1046
	10: 9	and asked him to give me the **little** s.	1044
	10:10	I took the **little** s from the angel's hand	1044

SCROLLS (3) [SCROLL]

Ac	19:19	A number who had practiced sorcery brought their s together	1047
	19:19	When they calculated the value **of the** s,	899S
2Ti	4:13	and my s, especially the parchments.	1046

SCULPTURED (1)

2Ch	3:10	he made a pair of s cherubim and	5126+7589

SCUM (2)

La	3:45	You have made us s and refuse among	6082
1Co	4:13	Up to this moment we have become the s of	4326

SCURVY (KJV) See FESTERING SORE

SCYTHIAN (1)

Col	3:11	barbarian, S, slave or free, but Christ is all,	5033

SEA (353) [SEAFARERS, SEAMEN, SEAS, SEASHORE]

Ge	1:21	the great **creatures of the** s and every living	9490
	1:26	and let them rule over the fish of the s and	3542
	1:28	over the fish of the s and the birds of the air	3542
	9: 2	and upon all the fish of the s;	3542
	14: 3	in the Valley of Siddim (the Salt S).	3542
	32:12	like the sand of the s,	3542
	41:49	like the sand of the s;	3542
Ex	10:19	the locusts and carried them into the Red S.	3542
	13:18	by the desert road toward the Red S.	3542
	14: 2	between Migdol and the s.	3542
	14: 2	They are to encamp by the s,	3542
	14: 9	and overtook them as they camped by the s	3542
	14:16	over the s to divide the water so that	3542
	14:16	so that the Israelites can go through the s	3542
	14:21	Moses stretched out his hand over the s,	3542
	14:21	that night the LORD drove the s back with	3542
	14:22	Israelites went through the s on dry ground,	3542
	14:23	and horsemen followed them into the s.	3542
	14:26	the s so that the waters may flow back over	3542
	14:27	Moses stretched out his hand over the s,	3542
	14:27	and at daybreak the s went back to its place.	3542
	14:27	and the LORD swept them into the s.	3542
	14:28	that had followed the Israelites into the s.	3542
	14:29	Israelites went through the s on dry ground,	3542
	15: 1	and its rider he has hurled into the s.	3542
	15: 4	and his army he has hurled into the s.	3542
	15: 4	officers are drowned in the Red S.	3542
	15: 8	deep waters congealed in the heart of the s.	3542
	15:10	and the s covered them.	3542
	15:19	chariots and horsemen went into the s,	3542
	15:19	the LORD brought the waters of the s back	3542
	15:19	but the Israelites walked through the s on	3542
	15:21	and its rider he has hurled into the s."	3542
	15:22	the Red S and they went into the Desert	3542
	20:11	the s, and all that is in them,	3542
	23:31	the Red S to the Sea of the Philistines,	3542
	23:31	the Red Sea to the S *of* the Philistines,	3542
	25: 5	ram skins dyed red and hides of s **cows**;	9391
	26:14	and over that a covering of hides of s **cows**.	9391
	35: 7	ram skins dyed red and hides of s **cows**;	9391
	35:23	or hides of s **cows** brought them.	9391
	36:19	and over that a covering of hides of s **cows**.	9391
	39:34	of hides of s **cows** and the shielding curtain;	9391
Nu	4: 6	they are to cover this with hides of s **cows**,	9391
	4: 8	that with hides of s **cows** and put its poles	9391
	4:10	a covering of hides of s **cows** and put it on	9391
	4:11	that with hides of s **cows** and put its poles	9391
	4:12	cover that with hides of s **cows** and put them	9391
	4:14	of hides of s **cows** and put its poles in place.	9391
	4:25	and the outer covering of **hides of s cows**,	9391
	11:22	the fish in the s were caught for them?"	3542
	11:31	the LORD and drove quail in from the s.	3542
	13:29	and the Canaanites live near the s and along	3542
	14:25	the desert along the route to the Red S."	3542
	21: 4	along the route to the Red S,	3542
	33: 8	and passed through the s into the desert,	3542
	33:10	They left Elim and camped by the Red S.	3542
	33:11	the Red S and camped in the Desert of Sin.	3542
	34: 3	from the end of the Salt S.	3542
	34: 5	join the Wadi of Egypt and end at the S.	3542
	34: 6	be the coast of the Great S.	3542
	34: 7	run a line from the Great S to Mount Hor	3542
	34:11	along the slopes east of the S *of* Kinnereth.	3542
	34:12	along the Jordan and end at the Salt S.	3542
Dt	1:40	the desert along the route to the Red S."	3542
	2: 1	the desert along the route to the Red S,	3542
	3:17	from Kinnereth to the S *of* the Arabah	3542

Dt	3:17	to the Sea of the Arabah (the Salt S),	3542
	4:49	as far as the S of the Arabah,	3542
	11: 4	of the Red S as they were pursuing you,	3542
	11:24	from the Euphrates River to the western s.	3542
	30:13	Nor is it beyond the s,	3542
	30:13	the s to get it and proclaim it to us	3542
	34: 2	all the land of Judah as far as the western s,	3542
Jos	1: 4	to the Great S on the west.	3542
	2:10	the LORD dried up the water of the Red S	3542
	3:16	while the water flowing down to the S of	3542
	3:16	(the Salt S) was completely cut off.	3542
	4:23	to the Red S when he dried it up before us	3542
	9: 1	the Great S as far as Lebanon (the kings of	3542
	12: 3	the S of Kinnereth to the S of the Arabah	3542
	12: 3	the Sea of Kinnereth to the S of the Arabah	3542
	12: 3	to the Sea of the Arabah (the Salt S),	3542
	13:27	up to the end of the S of Kinnereth).	3542
	15: 2	the bay at the southern end of the Salt S,	3542
	15: 4	the Wadi of Egypt, ending at the s.	3542
	15: 5	the Salt S as far as the mouth of the Jordan.	3542
	15: 5	the bay of the s at the mouth of the Jordan.	3542
	15:11	The boundary ended at the s.	3542
	15:12	the coastline of the Great S.	3542
	15:47	of Egypt and the coastline of the Great S.	3542
	16: 3	and on to Gezer, ending at the s.	3542
	16: 6	and continued to the s.	3542
	16: 8	to the Kanah Ravine and ended at the s.	3542
	17: 9	of the ravine and ended at the s.	3542
	17:10	The territory of Manasseh reached the s	3542
	18:19	at the northern bay of the Salt S,	3542
	19:29	turned toward Hosah and came out at the s	3542
	23: 4	the Jordan and the Great S in the west.	3542
	24: 6	out of Egypt, you came to the s,	3542
	24: 6	and horsemen as far as the Red S.	3542
	24: 7	the s over them and covered them.	3542
Jdg	11:16	Israel went through the desert to the Red S	3542
2Sa	22:16	the s were exposed and the foundations of	3542
1Ki	5: 9	down from Lebanon to the s,	3542
	5: 9	in rafts by s to the place you specify.	3542
	7:23	He made the S of cast metal,	3542
	7:24	in two rows in one piece with the S.	3542
	7:25	The S stood on twelve bulls,	NIH
	7:25	The S rested on top of them,	3542
	7:39	He placed the S on the south side,	3542
	7:44	the S and the twelve bulls under it;	3542
	9:26	on the shore of the Red S.	3542
	9:27	sailors who knew the s—	3542
	10:22	of trading ships at s along with the ships	3542
	18:43	"Go and look toward the s,"	3542
	18:44	as a man's hand is rising from the s."	3542
2Ki	14:25	from Lebo Hamath to the S of the Arabah,	3542
	16:17	He removed the S from the bronze bulls	3542
	25:13	and the bronze S that were at the temple of	3542
	25:16	the S and the movable stands,	3542
1Ch	16:32	Let the s resound, and all that is in it;	3542
	18: 8	which Solomon used to make the bronze S,	3542
2Ch	2:16	and will float them in rafts by s down	3542
	4: 2	He made the S of cast metal,	3542
	4: 3	in two rows in one piece with the S.	3542
	4: 4	The S stood on twelve bulls,	NIH
	4: 4	The S rested on top of them,	3542
	4: 6	but the S was to be used by the priests	3542
	4:10	He placed the S on the south side,	3542
	4:15	the S and the twelve bulls under it;	3542
	8:18	men who knew the s.	3542
	20: 2	from the other side of the S.	3542
Ezr	3: 7	so that they would bring cedar logs by s	3542
Ne	9: 9	you heard their cry at the Red S.	3542
	9:11	You divided the s before them,	3542
Job	7:12	Am I the s, or the monster of the deep,	3542
	9: 8	and treads on the waves of the s.	3542
	11: 9	the earth and wider than the s.	3542
	12: 8	or let the fish of the s inform you.	3542
	14:11	from the s or a riverbed becomes parched	3542
	26:12	By his power he churned up the s;	3542
	28:14	the s says, 'It is not with me.'	3542
	36:30	bathing the depths of the s.	3542
	38: 8	the s behind doors when it burst forth from	3542
	38:16	"Have you journeyed to the springs of the s	3542
	41:31	like a boiling caldron and stirs up the s like	3542
Ps	8: 8	the birds of the air, and the fish of the s,	3542
	18:15	the s were exposed and the foundations of	4784
	33: 7	He gathers the waters of the s into jars;	3542
	46: 2	the mountains fall into the heart of the s,	3542
	66: 6	He turned the s into dry land,	3542
	68:22	I will bring them from the depths of the s,	3542
	72: 8	from s to sea and from the River to the ends	3542
	72: 8	from sea to s and from the River to the ends	3542
	74:13	It was you who split open the s	3542
	77:19	Your path led through the s,	3542
	78:13	He divided the s and led them through;	3542
	78:53	but the s engulfed their enemies.	3542
	80:11	It sent out its boughs to the S,	3542
	89: 9	You rule over the surging s;	3542
	89:25	I will set his hand over the s,	3542
	93: 4	mightier than the breakers of the s—	3542
	95: 5	The s is his, for he made it,	3542
	96:11	let the s resound, and all that is in it;	3542
	98: 7	Let the s resound, and everything in it,	3542
	104:25	There is the s, vast and spacious,	3542
	106: 7	and they rebelled by the s, the Red Sea,	3542
	106: 7	and they rebelled by the sea, the Red S.	3542
	106: 9	He rebuked the Red S, and it dried up;	3542
	106:22	of Ham and awesome deeds by the Red S.	3542
	107:23	Others went out on the s in ships;	3542
	107:29	the waves of the s were hushed.	2157S
	114: 3	s looked and fled, the Jordan turned back;	3542

Ps	114: 5	Why was it, O s, that you fled, O Jordan,	3542
	136:13	to him who divided the Red S asunder	3542
	136:15	and his army into the Red S;	3542
	139: 9	if I settle on the far side of the s,	3542
	146: 6	the s, and everything in them—	3542
	148: 7	you great s creatures and all ocean depths,	9490
Pr	8:29	the s its boundary so the waters would	3542
Ecc	1: 7	All streams flow into the s,	3542
	1: 7	yet the s is never full.	3542
Isa	5:30	over it like the roaring of the s.	3542
	9: 1	by the way of the s, along the Jordan—	3542
	10:22	O Israel, be like the sand by the s,	3542
	11: 9	of the LORD as the waters cover the s.	3542
	11:11	from Hamath and from the islands of the s.	3542
	11:15	up the gulf of the Egyptian s;	3542
	16: 8	and went as far as the s.	3542
	17:12	they rage like the raging s!	3542
	18: 2	which sends envoys by s in papyrus boats	3542
	21: 1	An oracle concerning the Desert by the S:	3542
	23: 4	O fortress of the s, for the sea has spoken:	3542
	23: 4	O fortress of the sea, for the s has spoken:	3542
	23:11	over the s and made its kingdoms tremble.	3542
	24:15	the God of Israel, in the islands of the s.	3542
	27: 1	he will slay the monster of the s.	3542
	42:10	you who go down to the s,	3542
	43:16	he who made a way through the s,	3542
	48:18	your righteousness like the waves of the s.	3542
	50: 2	By a mere rebuke I dry up the s,	3542
	51:10	Was it not you who dried up the s,	3542
	51:10	who made a road in the depths of the s so	3542
	51:15	up the s so that its waves roar—	3542
	57:20	But the wicked are like the tossing s,	3542
	63:11	is he who brought them through the s,	3542
Jer	5:22	I made the sand a boundary for the s,	3542
	6:23	They sound like the roaring s as they ride	3542
	15: 8	more numerous than the sand of the s.	3542
	25:22	the kings of the coastlands across the s;	3542
	27:19	about the pillars, the S, the movable stands	3542
	31:35	who stirs up the s so that its waves roar—	3542
	46:18	like Carmel by the s.	3542
	48:32	Your branches spread as far as the s;	3542
	48:32	they reached as far as the s of Jazer.	3542
	49:21	their cry will resound to the Red S.	3542
	49:23	troubled like the restless s.	3542
	50:42	They sound like the roaring s as they ride	3542
	51:36	up her s and make her springs dry.	3542
	51:42	The s will rise over Babylon;	3542
	52:17	and the bronze S that were at the temple of	3542
	52:20	the S and the twelve bronze bulls under it,	3542
La	2:13	Your wound is as deep as the s.	3542
Eze	26: 3	like the s casting up its waves.	3542
	26: 5	Out in the s she will become a place	3542
	26:12	timber and rubble into the s.	3542
	26:17	O city of renown, peopled by men of the s!	4784
	26:18	in the s are terrified at your collapse.'	3542
	27: 3	situated at the gateway to the s,	3542
	27: 9	of the s and their sailors came alongside	3542
	27:25	with heavy cargo in the heart of the s.	3542
	27:26	to pieces in the heart of the s.	3542
	27:27	on board will sink into the heart of the s on	3542
	27:32	like Tyre, surrounded by the s?"	3542
	27:34	by the s in the depths of the waters;	3542
	38:20	The fish of the s, the birds of the air,	3542
	39:11	of those who travel east toward the S.	3542
	47: 8	where it enters the S.	3542
	47: 8	When it empties into the S,	3542
	47:10	like the fish of the Great S.	3542
	47:15	the north side it will run from the Great S	3542
	47:17	The boundary will extend from the s	3542
	47:18	to the eastern s and as far as Tamar.	3542
	47:19	along the Wadi [of Egypt] to the Great S.	3542
	47:20	the Great S will be the boundary to	3542
	48:28	along the Wadi [of Egypt] to the Great S.	3542
Da	7: 2	of heaven churning up the great s.	10322
	7: 3	from the others, came up out of the s.	10322
Hos	4: 3	of the air and the fish of the s are dying.	3542
Joel	2:20	into the eastern s and those in the rear into	3542
	2:20	and those in the rear into the western s.	3542
Am	5: 8	of the s and pours them out over the face of	3542
	8:12	from s to sea and wander from north to east,	3542
	8:12	from sea to s and wander from north to east,	3542
	9: 3	from me at the bottom of the s,	3542
	9: 6	of the s and pours them out over the face of	3542
Jnh	1: 4	Then the LORD sent a great wind on the s,	3542
	1: 5	the cargo into the s to lighten the ship.	3542
	1: 9	who made the s and the land."	3542
	1:11	The s was getting rougher and rougher.	3542
	1:11	to you to make the s calm down for us?"	3542
	1:12	"Pick me up and throw me into the s,"	3542
	1:13	for the s grew even wilder than before.	3542
	1:15	and the raging s grew calm.	3542
Mic	7:12	from Egypt to the Euphrates and from s	3542
	7:12	to the Euphrates and from sea to s and	3542
	7:19	into the depths of the s.	3542
Na	1: 4	He rebukes the s and dries it up;	3542
Hab	1:14	You have made men like fish in the s,	3542
	1:14	like s creatures that have no ruler.	8254
	2:14	as the waters cover the s.	3542
	3: 8	Did you rage against the s when you rode	3542
	3:15	You trampled the s with your horses,	3542
Zep	1: 3	the birds of the air and the fish of the s,	3542
	2: 5	Woe to you who live by the s,	3542
	2: 6	The land by the s,	3542
Hag	2: 6	the sea and the dry land.	3542
Zec	9: 4	and destroy her power on the s,	3542
	9:10	from s to sea and from the River to the ends	3542
	9:10	from sea to s and from the River to the ends	3542

Zec	10:11	They will pass through the s of trouble;	3542
	10:11	the surging s will be subdued and all	3542
	14: 8	to the eastern s and half to the western sea,	3542
	14: 8	to the eastern sea and half to the western s,	3542
Mt	4:15	the way to the s, along the Jordan,	2498
	4:18	As Jesus was walking beside the S	2498
	15:29	Jesus left there and went along the S	2498
	18: 6	and to be drowned in the depths of the s.	2498
	21:21	'Go, throw yourself into the s,'	2498
	23:15	over land and s to win a single convert,	2498
Mk	1:16	As Jesus walked beside the S of Galilee,	2498
	7:31	to the S of Galilee and into the region of	2498
	9:42	be better for him to be thrown into the s	2498
	11:23	'Go, throw yourself into the s,'	2498
Lk	17: 2	to be thrown into the s with a millstone tied	2498
	17: 6	'Be uprooted and planted in the s,'	2498
	21:25	at the roaring and tossing of the s.	2498
Jn	6: 1	to the far shore of the S of Galilee (that is,	2498
	6: 1	(that is, the S of Tiberias),	NIG
	21: 1	by the S of Tiberias.	2498
Ac	4:24	the heaven and the earth and the s,	2498
	7:36	the Red S and for forty years in the desert.	2498
	10: 6	whose house is by the s."	2498
	10:32	Simon the tanner, who lives by the s.'	2498
	14:15	and earth and s and everything in them.	2498
	16:11	From Troas we put out to s	343
	21: 1	we put out to s and sailed straight to Cos.	343
	27: 2	and we put out to s.	343
	27: 4	From there we put out to s again	343
	27: 5	When we had sailed across the open s off	4283
	27:17	they lowered the s anchor and let the ship	5007
	27:27	across the Adriatic S,	102
	27:30	the sailors let the lifeboat down into the s,	2498
	27:38	the ship by throwing the grain into the s.	2498
	27:40	the s and at the same time untied the ropes	2498
	28: 4	for though he escaped from the s,	2498
	28:11	After three months we put out to s in	343
Ro	9:27	of the Israelites be like the sand by the s,	2498
1Co	10: 1	and that they all passed through the s.	2498
	10: 2	into Moses in the cloud and in the s.	2498
2Co	11:25	I spent a night and a day in the open s,	1113
	11:26	in danger in the country, in danger at s;	2498
Heb	11:29	the people passed through the Red S as	2498
Jas	1: 6	he who doubts is like a wave of the s,	2498
	3: 7	and creatures of the s are being tamed	1879
Jude	1:13	They are wild waves of the s,	2498
Rev	4: 6	the throne there was what looked like a s	2498
	5:13	under the earth and on the s, and all that is	2498
	7: 1	from blowing on the land or on the s or	2498
	7: 2	to harm the land and the s:	2498
	7: 3	"Do not harm the land or the s or the trees	2498
	8: 8	all ablaze, was thrown into the s.	2498
	8: 8	A third of the s turned into blood,	2498
	8: 9	a third of the living creatures in the s died,	2498
	10: 2	on the s and his left foot on the land,	2498
	10: 5	Then the angel I had seen standing on the s	2498
	10: 6	and the s and all that is in it, and said,	2498
	10: 8	of the angel who is standing on the s and on	2498
	12:12	But woe to the earth and the s,	2498
	13: 1	And the dragon stood on the shore of the s.	2498
	13: 1	And I saw a beast coming out of the s.	2498
	14: 7	the earth, the s and the springs of water."	2498
	15: 2	like a s of glass mixed with fire and,	2498
	15: 2	standing beside the s, those who had been	2498
	16: 3	on the s, and it turned into blood like that	2498
	16: 3	and every living thing in the s died.	2498
	18:17	"Every s captain, and all who travel	3237
	18:17	and all who earn their living from the s,	2498
	18:19	on the s became rich through her wealth!	2498
	18:21	of a large millstone and threw it into the s,	2498
	20:13	The s gave up the dead that were in it,	2498
	21: 1	and there was no longer any s.	2498

SEAFARERS (1) [SEA]

Isa	23: 2	of Sidon, whom the s have enriched.	3542+6296

SEAH (3) [SEAHS]

2Ki	7: 1	a s of flour will sell for a shekel	6006
	7:16	So a s of flour sold for a shekel,	6006
	7:18	a s of flour will sell for a shekel	6006

SEAHS (6) [SEAH]

Ge	18: 6	"get three s of fine flour and knead it	6006
1Sa	25:18	five dressed sheep, five s of roasted grain,	6006
1Ki	18:32	around it large enough to hold two s	6006
2Ki	7: 1	for a shekel and two s of barley for a shekel	6006
	7:16	and two s of barley sold for a shekel,	6006
	7:18	for a shekel and two s of barley for a shekel	6006

SEAL (35) [SEALED, SEALING, SEALS]

Ge	38:18	"Your s and its cord,	2597
	38:25	"See if you recognize whose s and cord	3160
Ex	28:11	the way a gem cutter engraves a s.	2597
	28:21	each engraved like a s with the name of one	2597
	28:36	of pure gold and engrave on it as on a s:	2597
	39: 6	like a s with the names of the sons of Israel.	2597
	39:14	each engraved like a s with the name of one	2597
	39:30	like an inscription on a s:	2597
1Ki	21: 8	placed his s on them,	928+2597+3159
Est	8: 8	and s it with the king's signet ring—	3159
Job	38:14	The earth takes shape like clay under a s;	2597
Ps	40: 7	I do not s my lips, as you know, O LORD.	3973
SS	8: 6	Place me like a s over your heart,	2597
	8: 6	like a s on your arm;	2597

Isa 8:16 Bind up the testimony and **s** up the law 3159
Da 8:26 but **s** up the vision, 6258
9:24 to **s** up vision and prophecy and to anoint 3159
12:4 close up and **s** the words of the scroll until 3159
Mt 27:66 the tomb secure *by* putting a **s** on the stone 5381
Jn 6:27 On him God the Father *has* placed his **s** 5381
Ro 4:11 a **s** of the righteousness that he had by faith 5382
1Co 9:2 you are the **s** of my apostleship in the Lord. 5382
2Co 1:22 **set** his **s** of ownership on us, 5381
Eph 1:13 *you* were **marked** in him with a **s**, 5381
Rev 6:3 When the Lamb opened the second **s**, 5382
6:5 When the Lamb opened the third **s**, 5382
6:7 When the Lamb opened the fourth **s**, 5382
6:9 When he opened the fifth **s**, 5382
6:12 I watched as he opened the sixth **s**. 5382
7:2 having the **s** of the living God. 5382
7:3 the trees until *we* **put** a **s** on the foreheads 5381
8:1 When he opened the seventh **s**, 5382
9:4 not have the **s** of God on their foreheads. 5382
10:4 but I heard a voice from heaven say, "**S** up 5381
22:10 "*Do* not **s** up the words of the prophecy 5381

SEALED (23) [SEAL]

Dt 32:34 "Have I not kept this in reserve and **s** it 3159
Ne 10:1 Those *who* **s** it were: 3159
Est 3:12 in the name of King Xerxes himself and **s** 3159
8:8 in the king's name and **s** with his ring 3159
8:10 **s** the dispatches with the king's signet ring, 3159
Job 14:17 My offenses *will* be **s** up in a bag; 3159
41:15 of shields tightly **s together**; 2597+6037
SS 4:12 you are a spring enclosed, a **s** fountain. 5835
Isa 29:10 He has **s** your eyes (the prophets); 6794
29:11 is nothing but words **s** in a scroll. 3159
29:11 he will answer, "I can't; it is **s**." 3159
Jer 32:10 I signed and **s** the deed, had it witnessed, 3159
32:11 the **s** *copy* containing the terms 3159
32:14 both the **s** and unsealed copies of the deed 3159
32:44 and **s** witnessed in the territory 3159
Da 6:17 and the king **s** it with his own signet ring 10291
12:9 the words are closed up and **s** until the time 3159
Eph 4:30 with whom *you* were **s** for the day 3159
2Ti 2:19 **s** with this inscription: "The Lord 2400+5382
Rev 5:1 a scroll with writing on both sides and **s** 2958
7:4 I heard the number *of* those who were **s**; 5381
7:5 From the tribe of Judah 12,000 *were* **s**, 5381
20:3 and locked and **s** it over him, 5381

SEALING (1) [SEAL]

Dt 29:12 with you this day and **s** with an oath, NIH

SEALS (7) [SEAL]

Ne 9:38 and our priests *are* **affixing** their **s** to it." 3159
Job 9:7 he **s** off the light of the stars. 1237+3159
Rev 5:1 on both sides and sealed *with* seven **s**. 5382
5:2 "Who is worthy to break the **s** and open 5382
5:5 He is able to open the scroll and its seven **s**. 5382
5:9 to take the scroll and to open its **s**, 5382
6:1 as the Lamb opened the first of the seven **s**. 5382

SEAM (2) [SEAMS]

Ex 28:27 the **s** just above the waistband of the ephod. 4678
39:20 the **s** just above the waistband of the ephod. 4678

SEAMEN (4) [SEA]

Eze 27:8 O Tyre, were aboard as your **s**. 2480
27:27 your mariners, **s** and shipwrights 2480
27:28 shorelands will quake when your **s** cry out. 2480
27:29 the mariners and all the **s** will stand on 2480+3542

SEAMLESS (1)

Jn 19:23 This garment was **s**, woven in one piece 731

SEAMS (1) [SEAM]

Eze 27:9 on board as shipwrights to caulk your **s**. 981

SEARCH (48) [SEARCHED, SEARCHES, SEARCHING]

Ge 44:12 Then the steward *proceeded to* **s**, 2924
Dt 1:33 to **s out** places for you to camp and 9365
Jdg 17:8 that town *in* **s** of some other place to stay. 5162
1Sa 16:16 *to* **s** for someone who can play the harp. 1335
23:25 Saul and his men began the **s**, 1335
26:2 to **s** there for David. 1335
2Sa 5:17 they went up in full force to **s** for him, 1335
1Ki 2:40 to Achish at Gath in **s** of his slaves. 1335
20:6 to send my officials *to* **s** your palace and 2924
1Ch 4:39 of the valley in **s** of pasture for their flocks. 1335
14:8 they went up in full force to **s** for him, 1335
26:31 David's reign a **s** *was* **made** in the records, 2011
2Ch 22:9 He then **went** in **s** of Ahaziah, 1335
Ezr 4:15 so that a **s** *may be* **made** 10118
4:19 I issued an order and a **s** *was* **made**, 10118
5:17 *let* a **s** be **made** in the royal archives 10118
Est 2:2 Let a **s** be **made** for beautiful young virgins 1335
Job 3:21 *who* **s** for it more than for hidden treasure, 2916
7:21 *you will* **s** for me, but I will be no more." 8838
10:6 that *you must* **s out** my faults and probe 1335
Ps 4:4 **s** your hearts and be silent. 606+928
139:23 **S** me, O God, and know my heart; 2983
Pr 2:4 for silver and **s** for it as for hidden treasure, 2924
25:2 to **s out** a matter is the glory of kings. 2983

Ecc 3:6 a time to **s** and a time to give up, 1335
7:25 *to* **s out** wisdom and the scheme of things 1335
7:29 but men *have* **gone** in **s** of many schemes." 1335
8:17 Despite all his efforts to **s** *it* **out**, 1335
SS 3:2 *I will* **s** for the one my heart loves. 1335
Isa 41:12 Though *you* **s** for your enemies, 1335
41:17 "The poor and needy **s** for water, 1335
Jer 5:1 and consider, **s** through her squares, 1335
17:10 "I the LORD **s** the heart and examine 2983
50:20 "**s** *will* be made for Israel's guilt, 1335
La 1:11 All her people groan *as they* **s** for bread; 1335
Eze 34:8 and because my shepherds *did not* **s** for 2011
34:11 I myself *will* **s** for my sheep and look 2011
34:16 *I will* **s** for the lost and bring back 1335
39:14 the seven months *they* will begin their **s**. 2983
Hos 7:10 not return to the LORD his God or **s** for 1335
Zep 1:12 At that time *I will* **s** Jerusalem with lamps 2924
Mt 2:8 "Go and **make** a careful **s** for the child. 2004
2:13 for Herod is going to **s** for the child 2426
10:11 **s** for some worthy person there and stay 2004
Lk 11:41 the house and **s** carefully until she finds it? 2426
Jn 6:24 the boats and went to Capernaum in **s** of 2426
Ac 12:19 Herod had a **thorough** **s** **made for** him 2118
17:5 They rushed to Jason's house in **s** of Paul 2426

SEARCHED (22) [SEARCH]

Ge 31:34 Laban **s through** everything in the tent 5491
31:35 So he **s** but could not find 2924
31:37 Now that *you have* **s through** all my goods, 5491
Jos 2:22 until the pursuers *had* **s** all along the road 1335
1Sa 23:14 Day after day Saul **s** for him, 1335
27:4 he no longer **s** for him. 1335
2Sa 17:20 The men **s** but found no one, 1335
1Ki 1:3 **s** throughout Israel *for* a beautiful girl 1335
2Ki 2:17 *who* **s** for three days but did not find him. 1335
Ezr 2:62 These **s** *for* their family records, 1335
6:1 and *they* **s** in the archives stored in 10118
Ne 7:64 These **s** *for* their family records, 1335
Ps 139:1 *you have* **s** me and you know me. 2983
Ecc 12:9 and **s out** and set in order many proverbs. 2983
12:10 The Teacher **s** to find just the right words, 2983
Jer 31:37 of the earth below be **s out** will I reject all 2983
La 1:19 in the city while *they* **s** for food 1335
Eze 20:6 of Egypt into a land *I had* **s out** for them, 9365
34:4 not brought back the strays or **s** for the lost. 1335
34:6 and no one **s** or looked for them. 2011
2Ti 1:17 *he* **s** hard **for** me until he found me. 2426
1Pe 1:10 **s intently and with the greatest care,** 1699+2001+2779

SEARCHES (11) [SEARCH]

1Ch 28:9 for the LORD **s** every heart 2011
Job 28:3 *he* **s** the farthest recesses **for** ore 2983
28:11 *He* **s** the sources of the rivers 2924
39:8 for his pasture and **s** for any green thing. 2011
Ps 7:9 O righteous God, *who* **s** minds and hearts, 1043
Pr 11:27 but evil comes to him *who* **s** for it. 2011
20:27 the lamp of the LORD **s** the spirit of a man; 2924
20:27 it **s** out his inmost being. NIH
Ro 8:27 And he who **s** our hearts knows the mind of 2236
1Co 2:10 The Spirit **s** all things, 2236
Rev 2:23 that I am he who **s** hearts and minds, 2236

SEARCHING (8) [SEARCH]

Jdg 5:15 In the districts of Reuben there was much **s** 2984
5:16 In the districts of Reuben there was much **s** 2984
1Sa Saul will give up **s** for me anywhere 1335
Job 32:11 while *you were* **s** for words, 2983
Ecc 7:28 while I *was* **s** but not finding— 1335
Am 8:12 **s** for the word of the LORD, 1335
Lk 2:48 Your father and I *have been* anxiously **s** for 2426
2:49 "Why *were* you **s** for me?" 2426

SEARED (2) [SEARING]

1Ti 4:2 consciences *have been* **s** **as with a hot iron.** 3013
Rev 16:9 They *were* **s** by the intense heat 3009

SEARING (1) [SEARED]

Ps 38:7 My back is filled with **s pain**; 7828

SEAS (29) [SEA]

Ge 1:10 and the gathered waters he called "**s**." 3542
1:22 in number and fill the water in the **s**, 3542
Lev 11:9 the creatures living in the water of the **s** and 3542
11:10 But all creatures in the **s** or streams that do 3542
Dt 33:19 they will feast on the abundance of the **s**, 3542
Ne 9:6 the **s** and all that is in them. 3542
Job 6:3 It would surely outweigh the sand of the **s**— 3542
Ps 8:8 all that swim the paths of the **s**. 3542
24:2 the **s** and established it upon the waters. 3542
65:5 the ends of the earth and of the farthest **s**, 3542
65:7 who stilled the roaring of the **s**, 3542
69:34 the **s** and all that move in them, 3542
78:15 and gave them water as abundant as the **s**; 9333
93:3 The **s** have lifted up, O LORD, 5643
93:3 O LORD, the **s** have lifted up their voice; 5643
93:3 the **s** have lifted up their pounding waves. 5643
135:6 in the **s** and all their depths. 3542
Pr 23:34 be like one sleeping on the **high s**, 3542+4213
30:19 the way of a ship on the **high s**, 3542+4213
Isa 60:5 the wealth on the **s** will be brought to you, 3542
Eze 26:17 You were a power on the **s**, 3542
27:4 Your domain was on the **high s**; 3542+4213

Eze 27:26 Your oarsmen take you out to the high **s**. 4784
27:33 When your merchandise went out on the **s**, 3542
28:2 on the throne of a god in the heart of the **s**." 3542
28:8 a violent death in the heart of the **s**. 3542
32:2 in the **s** thrashing about in your streams, 3542
Da 11:45 He will pitch his royal tents between the **s** 3542
Jnh 2:3 into the very heart of the **s**, 3542

SEASHORE (13) [SEA]

Ge 22:17 in the sky and as the sand on the **s**. 3542+8557
49:13 "Zebulun will live by the **s** and 2572+3542
Jos 11:4 as numerous as the sand on the **s**. 3542+8557
Jdg 7:12 be counted than the sand on the **s**. 3542+8557
1Sa 13:5 as numerous as the sand on the **s**. 3542+8557
2Sa 17:11 as numerous as the sand on the **s**— 3542
1Ki 4:20 as numerous as the sand on the **s**; 3542
4:29 as measureless as the sand on the **s** 3542+8557
Ps 78:27 flying birds like sand on the **s**. 3542
Jer 33:22 and as measureless as the sand on the **s**.'" 3542
Hos 1:10 the Israelites will be like the sand on the **s**, 3542
Heb 11:12 as countless as the sand on the **s**. 2498+3836+5927
Rev 20:8 In number they are like the sand *on* the **s**. 2498

SEASON (20) [SEASONED, SEASONS]

Ge 31:10 "In breeding **s** I once had a dream 6961
Ex 34:21 the **plowing s** and harvest you must rest. 3045
Lev 2:13 **S** all your grain offerings with salt. 4873
26:4 I will send you rain in its **s**, 6961
Nu 28:2 (It was the **s** for the first ripe grapes.) 3427
Dt 11:14 then I will send rain on your land in its **s**, 6961
28:12 in **s** and to bless all the work of your hands. 6961
Ezr 10:13 and it is the rainy **s**; 6961
Job 5:26 like sheaves gathered in **s**. 6961
6:17 but that cease to flow in the dry **s**, 6961
Ps 1:3 in **s** and whose leaf does not wither. 6961
Pr 20:4 A sluggard does not plow in **s**; 3074
Ecc 3:1 and a **s** for every activity under heaven: 6961
SS 2:12 the **s** *of* singing has come, 6961
Jer 5:24 who gives autumn and spring rains in **s**, 6961
Eze 34:26 I will send down showers in **s**; 6961
Mk 11:13 because it was not the **s** for figs. 2789
2Ti 4:2 be prepared **in s** and out of season; 2323
4:2 be prepared in season and **out of s**; 178
Tit 1:3 and at his **appointed s** he brought his word 2789

SEASONED (1) [SEASON]

Col 4:6 be always full of grace, **s** with salt, 789

SEASONS (7) [SEASON]

Ge 1:14 as signs to mark **s** and days and years, 4595
Job 38:32 in their **s** or lead out the Bear with its cubs? 6961
Ps 104:19 The moon marks off the **s**, 4595
Jer 8:7 the stork in the sky knows her **appointed s**, 4595
Da 2:21 He changes times and **s**; 10232
Ac 14:17 from heaven and crops in *their* **s**; 2789
Gal 4:10 and months and **s** and years! 2789

SEAT (26) [SEATED, SEATING, SEATS]

Ex 18:13 The next day Moses took *his* **s** to serve 3782
Jdg 3:20 As the king rose from his **s**, 4058
1Sa 20:18 because your **s** will be empty. 4632
2Sa 19:8 king got up and took *his* **s** in the gateway. 3782
1Ki 1:46 Solomon *has* **taken** *his* **s** on the royal 3782
10:19 On both sides of the **s** were armrests, 5226+8699
21:9 "Proclaim a day of fasting and **s** Naboth in 3782
21:10 But **s** two scoundrels opposite him 3782
2Ki 25:28 and gave him a **s of honor** higher than those 4058
2Ch 9:18 On both sides of the **s** were armrests, 5226+8699
Est 3:1 and giving him a **s of honor** higher than that 4058
Job 29:7 the city and took my **s** in the public square, 4632
Ps 1:1 or stand in the way of sinners or sit in the **s** 4632
Pr 9:14 on a **s** *at* the highest point of the city, 4058
31:23 he **takes** his **s** among the elders of the land. 3782
SS 3:10 Its **s** was upholstered with purple, 5323
Isa 22:23 be a **s** *of* honor for the house of his father. 4058
Jer 52:32 and gave him a **s of honor** higher than those 4058
Da 7:9 and the Ancient of Days **took** *his* **s**. 10338
Mt 23:2 of the law and the Pharisees sit in Moses' **s**. 2756
27:19 While Pilate was sitting on the **judge's s**, 1037
Lk 14:9 'Give this man your **s**.' 5536
Jn 19:13 down on the **judge's s** at a place known as 1037
Ro 14:10 we will all stand before God's **judgment s**. 1037
2Co 5:10 before the **judgment s** of Christ, 1037
Jas 2:3 "Here's a good **s** for you," 2764

SEATED (29) [SEAT]

Ge 43:33 The men *had been* **s** before him in the order 3782
Ru 4:4 of these **s** here and in the presence of 3782
1Sa 9:22 his servant into the hall and **s** them 5226+5989
22:6 *was* **s** under the tamarisk tree on the hill 3782
1Ki 16:11 As soon as he began to reign and *was* **s** on 3782
21:12 and **s** Naboth in a prominent place among 3782
2Ch 23:20 through the Upper Gate and **s** the king on 3782
Ps 47:8 God *is* **s** on his holy throne. 3782
Isa 6:1 I saw the Lord **s** on a throne, 3782
Da 7:10 court *was* **s**, and the books were opened. 10338
Zec 3:8 O high priest Joshua and your associates **s** 3782
Mk 3:34 at those **s** in a circle around him and said, 2764
Lk 22:56 A servant girl saw him **s** there in 2764
22:69 be **s** at the right hand of the mighty God." 2764
Jn 6:11 and distributed *to* those who *were* **s** 367
12:15 your king is coming, **s** on a donkey's colt." 2764
20:12 **s** where Jesus' body had been, 2757

Ac	20: 9	S in a window *was* a young man named	2757
Eph	1:20	from the dead and s him at his right hand in	2767
	2: 6	and s us **with** him in the heavenly realms	5154
Col	3: 1	where Christ is s at the right hand of God.	2764
Rev	4: 4	and so on them *were* twenty-four elders.	2764
	11:16	who *were* s on their thrones before God,	2764
	14:14	s on the cloud *was* one "like a son of man"	2764
	14:16	So he who was s on the cloud swung his	2764
	19: 4	who *was* s on the throne.	2764
	20: 4	*were* s those who had been given authority	2767
	20:11	a great white throne and him who *was* s	2764
	21: 5	He who *was* s on the throne said,	2764

SEATING (2) [SEAT]

1Ki	10: 5	the s *of* his officials, the attending servants	4632
2Ch	9: 4	the s *of* his officials, the attending servants	4632

SEATS (7) [SEAT]

1Sa	2: 8	he s them with princes and has them inherit	3782
Ps	113: 8	he s them with princes, with the princes of	3782
Jer	39: 3	of the king of Babylon came and **took** s in	3782
Mt	23: 6	the **most important** s in the synagogues;	4751
Mk	12:39	the **most important** s in the synagogues and	4751
Lk	11:43	because you love the **most important** s in	4751
	20:46	the **most important** s in the synagogues and	4751

SEAWEED (1) [WEED]

Jnh	2: 5	s was wrapped around my head.	6068

SEBA (4)

Ge	10: 7	S, Havilah, Sabtah, Raamah and Sabteca.	6013
1Ch	1: 9	S, Havilah, Sabta, Raamah and Sabteca.	6013
Ps	72:10	kings of Sheba and S will present him gifts.	6013
Isa	43: 3	Cush and S in your stead.	6013

SEBAM (1)

Nu	32: 3	Heshbon, Elealeh, S, Nebo and Beon—	8423

SEBAT (KJV) See SHEBAT

SECACAH (1)

Jos	15:61	In the desert: Beth Arabah, Middin, S,	6117

SECHU (KJV) See SECU

SECLUSION (1)

Lk	1:24	and for five months *remained* **in** s.	4332

SECOND (163) [TWO]

Ge	1: 8	and there was morning—the s day.	9108
	2:13	The name of the s river is the Gihon;	9108
	7:11	on the seventeenth day of the s month—	9108
	8:14	the s month the earth was completely dry.	9108
	22:15	to Abraham from heaven a s **time**	9108
	30: 7	and bore Jacob a s son.	9108
	30:12	Leah's servant Zilpah bore Jacob a s son.	9108
	32:19	He also instructed the s,	9108
	41: 5	He fell asleep again and had a s dream:	9108
	41:52	The s son he named Ephraim and said,	9108
Ex	4: 8	they may believe the s.	340
	16: 1	of the s month after they had come out	9108
	25:19	on one end and the s cherub on the other;	285
	25:35	a s bud under the second pair,	NIH
	25:35	a second bud under the s pair,	NIH
	28:18	in the s row a turquoise, a sapphire and	9108
	37: 8	on one end and the s cherub on the other;	285
	37:21	a s bud under the second pair,	NIH
	37:21	a second bud under the s pair,	NIH
	39:11	in the s row a turquoise, a sapphire and	9108
	40:17	the first day of the first month in the s year.	9108
Lev	19:10	**go over** your vineyard a s **time**	6618
Nu	1: 1	of Sinai on the first day of the s month of	9108
	1: 1	of the s year after the Israelites came out	9108
	1:18	on the first day of the s month.	9108
	2:16	They will set out s.	9108
	7:18	On the s day Nethanel son of Zuar,	9108
	8: 8	to take a s young bull for a sin offering.	9108
	9: 1	of the s year after they came out of Egypt.	9108
	9:11	on the fourteenth day of the s month	9108
	10: 6	At the sounding of a s blast,	9108
	10:11	On the twentieth day of the s month of	9108
	10:11	of the second month of the s year,	9108
	28: 8	Prepare the s lamb at twilight,	9108
	29:17	" 'On the s day prepare twelve young bulls,	9108
Dt	24: 3	and her s husband dislikes her	340
	24:20	*do* not **go over the branches a** s **time.**	339+6994
Jos	6:14	the s day they marched around the city once	9108
	10:32	and Joshua took it on the s day.	9108
	19: 1	The s lot came out for the tribe of Simeon.	9108
Jdg	6:25	"Take the s bull from your father's herd,	9108
	6:26	offer the s bull as a burnt offering.	9108
	6:28	beside it cut down and the s bull sacrificed	9108
	20:24	Israelites drew near to Benjamin the s day.	9108
1Sa	8: 2	and the name of his s was Abijah,	5467
	17:13	the s, Abinadab; and the third, Shammah.	5467
	18:21	a s *opportunity* to become my son-in-law."	9109
	20:27	But the next day, the s day *of* the month,	9108
	20:34	on that s day of the month he did not eat,	9108
	23:17	and I will be s to you.	5467
2Sa	3: 3	his s, Kileab the son of Abigail the widow	5467

2Sa	14:29	So he sent a s time, but he refused to come.	9108
1Ki	6: 1	in the month of Ziv, the s month,	9108
	6:25	The s cherub also measured ten cubits,	9108
	9: 2	the LORD appeared to him a s **time**,	9108
	15:25	of Israel in the s year of Asa king of Judah,	9109
	19: 7	The angel of the LORD came back a s **time**	9108
2Ki	1:17	Joram succeeded him as king in the s year	9109
	9:19	So the king sent out a s horseman.	9108
	10: 6	Then Jehu wrote them a s letter, saying,	9108
	14: 1	the s year of Jehoash son of Jehoahaz king	9109
	15:32	In the s year of Pekah son of Remaliah king	9109
	19:29	and the s year what springs from that.	9108
	22:14	She lived in Jerusalem, in the **S District.**	5467
1Ch	2:13	the s son was Abinadab, the third Shimea,	9108
	3: 1	the s, Daniel the son of Abigail of Carmel;	9108
	3:15	Johanan the firstborn, Jehoiakim the s son,	9108
	5:12	Shapham the s, then Janai and Shaphat,	5467
	6:28	Joel the firstborn and Abijah the s son.	9108
	8: 1	Ashbel the s son, Aharah the third,	9108
	8:39	Jeush the s son and Eliphelet the third.	9108
	12: 9	Obadiah the s **in command**, Eliab the third,	9108
	16: 5	Zechariah s, then Jeiel, Shemiramoth,	5467
	23:11	Jahath was the first and Ziza the s,	9108
	23:19	Jeriah the first, Amariah the s,	9108
	23:20	Micah the first and Isshiah the s.	9108
	24: 7	the s to Jedaiah,	9108
	24:23	Jeriah the first, Amariah the s,	9108
	25: 9	the s to Gedaliah, he and his relatives and	9108
	26: 2	Zechariah the firstborn, Jediael the s,	9108
	26: 4	Shemaiah the firstborn, Jehozabad the s,	9108
	26:11	the s, Tabaliah the third and Zechariah	9108
	27: 4	of the division for the s month was Dodai	9108
	29:22	Solomon son of David as king a s **time**,	9108
2Ch	3: 2	on the s day of the second month in	9108
	3: 2	the s month in the fourth year of his reign.	9108
	3:12	of the s cherub was five cubits long	337
	21:19	at the end of the s year, his bowels came out	9109
	27: 5	the same amount also in the s and third	9108
	28: 7	and Elkanah, s *to* the king.	5467
	30: 2	to celebrate the Passover in the s month.	9108
	30:13	of Unleavened Bread in the s month.	9108
	30:15	on the fourteenth day of the s month.	9108
	34:22	She lived in Jerusalem, in the **S District.**	5467
Ezr	3: 8	In the s month of the second year	9108
	3: 8	of the s year after their arrival at the house	9108
	4:24	until the s year of the reign of Darius king	10775
Ne	8:13	On the s day of the month,	9108
	11: 9	of Hassenuah was over the **S District** of	5467
	11:17	Bakbukiah, s among his associates;	5467
	12:38	The s choir proceeded in	9108
Est	2:19	When the virgins were assembled a s **time,**	9108
	7: 2	as they were drinking wine on that s day,	9108
	9:29	to confirm this s letter concerning Purim.	9108
	10: 3	the Jew was s **in rank** to King Xerxes,	5467
Job	42:14	the s Keziah and the third Keren-Happuch.	9108
Isa	11:11	a s **time** to reclaim the remnant that is left	9108
	37:30	and the s year what springs from that.	9108
Jer	1:13	word of the LORD came to me a s **time:**	9108
	33: 1	word of the LORD came to him a s **time:**	9108
Eze	10:14	the s the face of a man,	9108
	43:22	"On the s day you are to offer a male goat	9108
Da	2: 1	In the s year of his reign,	9109
	7: 5	"And there before me was a s beast,	10765
Am	7: 1	and just as the s **crop** was coming up.	4381
Jnh	3: 1	word of the LORD came to Jonah a s **time:**	9108
Na	1: 9	trouble will not come a s **time.**	AIT
Hag	1: 1	In the s year of King Darius	9109
	1:15	of the sixth month in the s year	9109
	2:10	in the s year of Darius,	9108
	2:20	to Haggai a s **time** on the twenty-fourth day	9108
Zec	1: 1	In the eighth month of the s year of Darius,	9109
	1: 7	in the s year of Darius,	9109
	6: 2	The first chariot had red horses, the s black,	9108
	11:14	Then I broke my s staff called Union,	9108
Mt	22:26	The same thing happened to the s	1311
	22:39	And the s is like it:	1311
	26:42	went away a s **time** and prayed,	1311+1666+4099
Mk	12:21	The s one married the widow,	1311
	12:31	s is this: 'Love your neighbor as yourself.'	1311
	14:72	the rooster crowed the s **time.**	1311+1666
Lk	12:38	even if he comes in the s or third watch of	1311
	16: 7	"Then he asked the s,	NIG
	19:18	"The s came and said, 'Sir,	1311
	20:30	The s	1311
Jn	3: 4	a s **time** into his mother's womb to	1309
	4:54	This was the s miraculous sign that Jesus performed,	1311+4099
	9:24	A s **time** they summoned the man	1311+1666
Ac	7:13	On their s **visit,** Joseph told his brothers	1311
	10:15	The voice spoke to him a s **time**	1311+1666+4099
	11: 9	the voice spoke from heaven a s **time**	1311+1666
	12:10	They passed the first and s guards and came	1311
	13:33	As it is written in the s Psalm:	1311
1Co	12:28	first of all apostles, s prophets, third	1309
	15:47	the s man from heaven.	1311
2Co	13: 2	a warning when I was with you a s **time.**	1309
Tit	3:10	and then warn him a s *time.*	1311
Heb	9: 3	Behind the s curtain was a room called	1311
	9:28	will appear a s **time,** not to bear sin,	1311+1666
	10: 9	He sets aside the first to establish the s.	1311
2Pe	3: 1	Dear friends, this is now my s letter to you.	1311
Rev	2:11	not be hurt at all by the s death.	1311
	4: 7	the s was like an ox,	1311
	6: 3	When the Lamb opened the s seal,	1311
	6: 3	I heard the s living creature say, "Come!"	1311
	8: 8	The s angel sounded his trumpet,	1311
	11:14	The s woe has passed;	1311

Rev	14: 8	A s angel followed and said, "Fallen!	1311
	16: 3	The s angel poured out his bowl on the sea,	1311
	20: 6	The s death has no power over them,	1311
	20:14	The lake of fire is the s death.	1311
	21: 8	This is the s death."	1311
	21:19	first foundation was jasper, the s sapphire,	1311

SECOND-IN-COMMAND (1) [COMMAND]

Ge	41:43	He had him ride in a chariot as his s,	5467

SECRET (44) [SECRETLY, SECRETS]

Ex	7:11	also did the same things by their s **arts:**	4268
	7:22	the same things by their s **arts,**	4319
	8: 7	the same things by their s **arts;**	4319
	8:18	to produce gnats by their s **arts,**	4319
Dt	27:15	and sets it up in s."	6260
	29:29	The s *things* belong to the LORD our God,	6259
Jdg	3:19	"I have a s message for you, O king."	6260
	16: 5	showing you the s of his great strength	928+4537
	16: 6	"Tell me the s of your great strength	928+4537
	16: 9	So the s of his strength was not discovered.	NIH
	16:15	a fool of me and haven't told me the s	928+4537
2Sa	12:12	You did it in s, but I will do this thing	6260
	15:10	Absalom sent s **messengers** throughout	8078
Est	2:20	But Esther *had* **kept** s her family background	401+5583
Ps	10: 8	watching **in** s for his victims.	7621
	90: 8	our s sins in the light of your presence.	6623
	101: 5	Whoever slanders his neighbor in s,	6260
	139:15	from you when I was made in the s **place.**	6260
Pr	9:17	food eaten in s is delicious!"	6260
	11:13	but a trustworthy man keeps a s.	1821
	17:23	a bribe in s to pervert the course of justice.	2668
	21:14	A gift given in s soothes anger,	6260
Isa	45: 3	riches stored in s **places,**	5041
	45:19	I have not spoken in s,	6260
	48:16	I have not spoken in s;	6260
	65: 4	and spend their nights **keeping** s **vigil;**	5915
Jer	13:17	I will weep in s because of your pride;	5041
	23:24	in s **places** so that I cannot see him?"	5041
Eze	28: 3	Is no s hidden from you?	6259
Mt	6: 4	so that your giving may be in s.	3220
	6: 4	your Father, who sees what is done in s,	3220
	6: 6	your Father, who sees what is done in s,	3220
	6:18	your Father, who sees what is done in s,	3224
Mk	4:11	"The s of the kingdom of God	3696
	7:24	yet he could not **keep** his presence s.	3291
Jn	7: 4	to become a public figure acts in s.	3220
	7:10	he went also, not publicly, but in s.	3220
	18:20	I said nothing in s.	3220
1Co	2: 7	No, we speak of God's s wisdom,	1877+3696
	4: 1	as those entrusted with the s *things* of God.	3696
2Co	4: 2	we have renounced s and shameful ways;	3696
Eph	5:12	to mention what the disobedient do *in* s.	3225
Php	4:12	I *have* **learned** the s of being content	3679
2Th	2: 7	s power of lawlessness is already at work;	3696

SECRETARIES (4) [SECRETARY]

1Ki	4: 3	and Ahijah, sons of Shisha—s;	6221
2Ch	34:13	Some of the Levites were s,	6221
Est	3:12	the first month the royal s were summoned.	6221
	8: 9	At once the royal s were summoned—	6221

SECRETARY (32) [SECRETARIES, SECRETARY'S]

2Sa	8:17	of Abiathar were priests; Seraiah was s;	6221
	20:25	Sheva was s; Zadok and Abiathar were	6221
2Ki	12:10	the royal s and the high priest came,	6221
	18:18	the palace administrator, Shebna the s,	6221
	18:37	Shebna the s and Joah son of Asaph	6221
	19: 2	Shebna the s and the leading priests,	6221
	22: 3	King Josiah sent the s,	6221
	22: 8	the high priest said to Shaphan the s,	6221
	22: 9	the s went to the king and reported to him:	6221
	22:10	Then Shaphan the s informed the king,	6221
	22:12	the s and Asaiah the king's attendant:	6221
	25:19	He also took the s who was chief officer	6221
1Ch	18:16	of Abiathar were priests; Shavsha was s;	6221
2Ch	24:11	the royal s and the officer of the chief priest	6221
	26:11	to their numbers as mustered by Jeiel the s	6221
	34:15	Hilkiah said to Shaphan the s,	6221
	34:18	Then Shaphan the s informed the king,	6221
	34:20	the s and Asaiah the king's attendant:	6221
Ezr	4: 8	the s wrote a letter against Jerusalem	10516
	4: 9	and Shimshai the s, together with the rest	10516
	4:17	the commanding officer, Shimshai the s and	10516
	4:23	and Shimshai the s and their associates,	10516
Isa	36: 3	the palace administrator, Shebna the s,	6221
	36:22	the palace administrator, Shebna the s,	6221
	37: 2	Shebna the s, and the leading priests,	6221
Jer	36:10	of Gemariah son of Shaphan the s,	6221
	36:12	Elishama the s, Delaiah son of Shemaiah,	6221
	36:20	the scroll in the room of Elishama the s,	6221
	36:21	from the room of Elishama the s and read it	6221
	37:15	in the house of Jonathan the s,	6221
	37:20	to the house of Jonathan the s,	6221
	52:25	He also took the s who was chief officer	6221

SECRETARY'S (1) [SECRETARY]

Jer	36:12	to the s room in the royal palace, where all	6221

SECRETLY (16) [SECRET]

Ge	31:27	Why did you run off s and deceive me?	2461

Dt	13: 6	your closest friend s entices you,	928+2021+6260
	27:24	man who kills his neighbor s."	928+2021+6260
	28:57	to eat them s during the siege	928+2021+6260
Jos	2: 1	Then Joshua son of Nun s sent two spies	3089
2Sa	21:12	*(They had* **taken** them s from the public	1704
2Ki	17: 9	The Israelites s **did** things against	2901
Job	4:12	"A word **was brought** to me,	1704
	13:10	if you s showed partiality.	928+2021+6260
	31:27	so that my heart was s enticed	928+2021+6260
Jer	38:16	King Zedekiah swore this oath s	928+2021+6260
Mt	2: 7	the Magi s and found out from them	3277
Jn	19:38	but s because he feared the Jews.	3221
Ac	6:11	Then *they* s persuaded some men to say,	5680
2Pe	2: 1	They *will* s **introduce** destructive heresies,	4206
Jude	1: 4	*have* s **slipped in** among you.	4208

SECRETS (7) [SECRET]

Job	11: 6	and disclose to you the s *of* wisdom,	9502
Ps	44:21	since he knows the s *of* the heart?	9502
Mt	13:11	"The knowledge of the s of the kingdom	3696
Lk	8:10	the s of the kingdom of God has been given	3696
Ro	2:16	on the day when God will judge men's s	3220
1Co	14:25	and the s of his heart will be laid bare.	3220
Rev	2:24	have not learned Satan's so-called deep s	NIG

SECT (5)

Lk	5:30	**who belonged to their** s complained	899
Ac	24: 5	He is a ringleader *of* the Nazarene s	146
	24:14	the Way, which they call a s.	146
	26: 5	according to the strictest s of our religion,	146
	28:22	people everywhere are talking against this s.	146

SECTION (20) [SECTIONS]

2Ki	14:13	a s about six hundred feet long.	NIH
2Ch	25:23	a s about six hundred feet long.	NIH
Ne	3: 2	men of Jericho built the **adjoining** s,	3338+6584
	3: 4	the son of Hakkoz, repaired the **next** s.	3338+6584
	3: 5	The **next** s was repaired by the men	3338+6584
	3: 8	of the goldsmiths, repaired the **next** s;	3338+6584
	3: 9	repaired the **next** s.	3338+6584
	3:11	of Pahath-Moab repaired another s and	4500
	3:12	**next** s with the help of his daughters.	3338+6584
	3:19	ruler of Mizpah, repaired another s,	4500
	3:20	of Zabbai zealously repaired another s,	4500
	3:21	the son of Hakkoz, repaired another s,	4500
	3:24	Binnui son of Henadad repaired another s,	4500
	3:27	the men of Tekoa repaired another s,	4500
	3:30	the sixth son of Zalaph, repaired another s.	4500
	12:24	*one* s responding to the other,	5464
Eze	42: 3	the s twenty cubits from the inner court and	NIH
	42: 3	from the inner court and in the s opposite	NIH
	45: 2	a s 500 cubits square is to be for	NIH
	45: 3	measure off a s 25,000 cubits long	NIH

SECTIONS (3) [SECTION]

1Ki	22:34	and hit the king of Israel between the s	1817
2Ch	18:33	and hit the king of Israel between the s	1817
	32: 5	repairing all the **broken** s of the wall	AIT

SECU (1)

1Sa	19:22	and went to the great cistern at **S**.	8497

SECUNDUS (1)

Ac	20: 4	Aristarchus and **S** from Thessalonica,	4941

SECURE (40) [SECURED, SECURELY, SECURES, SECURITY]

Nu	24:21	"Your dwelling place is s,	419
Dt	33:12	the beloved of the LORD rest s in him,	1055
	33:28	Jacob's spring is s in a land of grain	NIH
Jdg	18: 7	like the Sidonians, unsuspecting and s.	1053
1Ki	2:45	and David's throne will remain s before	3922
Job	5: 4	You will know that your tent is s;	8934
	11:18	*You will be* s, because there is hope;	1053
	12: 6	and those who provoke God are s—	1058
	21:23	completely s and at ease,	8916
	40:23	he is s, though the Jordan should surge	1053
Ps	9: 7	of the wicked and **make** the righteous s.	3922
	16: 5	you *have* **made** my lot s.	9461
	16: 9	my body also will rest s,	1055
	30: 6	I **felt** s, I said, "I will never be shaken."	8930
	48: 8	God **makes** her s forever.	3922
	112:8	His heart is s, he will have no fear;	6164
	122: 6	"*May* those who love you **be** s.	8922
Pr	14:26	He who fears the LORD has a s fortress,	4440
	20:28	through love his throne *is* **made** s.	6184
	27:24	and a crown is not s for all generations.	NIH
	29:14	his throne *will* always **be** s.	3922
Isa	32: 9	you daughters *who* **feel** s,	1053
	32:10	a year you *who* **feel** s will tremble;	1053
	32:11	shudder, you daughters *who* **feel** s!	1053
	32:18	in s homes, in undisturbed places of rest.	4440
	33:23	mast *is* not **held** s, the sail is not spread.	2616
Jer	22:21	I warned you when you **felt** s,	8932
Eze	34:27	the people will be s in their land.	1055
Da	8:25	When they **feel** s, he will destroy many	8932
	11:21	the kingdom when its people **feel** s,	8932
	11:24	When the richest provinces **feel** s,	8932
Am	6: 1	and to *you who* **feel** s on Mount Samaria,	1053
Zec	1:15	with the nations that **feel** s.	8633
	14:11	Jerusalem will be s.	1055
Mt	27:64	So give the order for the tomb *to be* **made** s	856

Mt	27:65	**make** the tomb as s as you know how."	856
	27:66	and **made** the tomb s by putting a seal on	856
Ac	27:16	we were hardly able to make the lifeboat s.	4331
Heb	6:19	as an anchor for the soul, firm and s.	1010
2Pe	3:17	and fall from your s **position**.	5113

SECURED (2) [SECURE]

2Sa	23: 5	arranged and s in every part?	9068
Ac	12:20	*Having* s **the support** of Blastus,	4275

SECURELY (8) [SECURE]

Jdg	16:11	"If *anyone* **ties** me s with new ropes	673+673
1Sa	12:11	so that you lived s.	1055
	25:29	my master will be **bound** s in the bundle	7674
1Ki	2:24	he who has established me s on the throne	3782
Pr	8:28	above and **fixed** s the fountains of the deep,	6451
	10: 9	The man of integrity walks s,	1055
Mic	5: 4	And *they will* **live** s,	3782
Ac	5:23	the jail s locked, with the guards	854+1877+4246

SECURES (1) [SECURE]

Ps	140:12	that the LORD s justice for the poor	6913

SECURITY (20) [SECURE]

Dt	24: 6	*Do not* **take** a pair of millstones—not even	
		the upper one—as s for a debt,	2471
	24: 6	**taking** a man's livelihood as s.	2471
2Ki	20:19	not be peace and s in my lifetime?"	622
Job	17: 3	Who else *will* **put up** s *for* me?	3338+4200+9546
	18:14	the s of his tent and marched off to the king	4440
	22: 6	*You* **demanded** s *from* your brothers	2471
	24:23	He may let them rest in a **feeling** of s,	1055
	31:24	or said to pure gold, 'You are my s,'	4440
Ps	122: 7	May there be peace within your walls and s	8932
Pr	6: 1	if *you have* **put up** s for your neighbor,	6842
	11:15	He who **puts up** s *for* another will	6842
	17:18	and **puts up** s for his neighbor.	6842+6859
	20:16	Take the garment of *one who* **puts up** s *for*	6842
	22:26	in pledge or **puts up** s for debts;	6842
	27:13	Take the garment of *one who* **puts up** s *for*	6842
Isa	39: 8	"There will be peace and s in my lifetime."	622
	47: 8	lounging in your s and saying to yourself,	1055
Jer	30:10	Jacob will again have peace and s,	8631
	33: 6	will let them enjoy abundant peace and s.	622
	46:27	Jacob will again have peace and s,	8631

SEDITION (1)

Ezr	4:19	and has been a place of rebellion and s.	10083

SEDITIONS (KJV) See DISSENSIONS

SEDUCE (1) [SEDUCED, SEDUCES, SEDUCTIVE]

2Pe	2:14	*they* s the unstable;	1284

SEDUCED (1) [SEDUCE]

Pr	7:21	she s him with her smooth talk.	5615

SEDUCES (1) [SEDUCE]

Ex	22:16	"If a man s a virgin who is not pledged to	7331

SEDUCTIVE (2) [SEDUCE]

Pr	2:16	from the wayward wife with her s words,	2744
	7: 5	from the wayward wife with her s words.	2744

SEE (796) [NEARSIGHTED, SAW, SEEING, SEEN, SEES, SIGHT, SIGHTING, SIGHTLESS, SIGHTS]

Ge	2:19	to the man to s what he would name them;	8011
	8: 8	a dove to s if the water had receded from	8011
	9:16	*I will* s it and remember	8011
	9:23	*they would* not s their father's nakedness.	8011
	11: 5	But the LORD came down to s the city	8011
	12:12	When the Egyptians s you, they will say,	8011
	13:15	All the land that you s I will give to you	8011
	18:16	s them **on their way**.	8938
	18:21	down and s if what they have done is as bad	8011
	24:13	S, I am standing beside this spring,	2180
	24:43	S, I am standing beside this spring;	2180
	27: 1	so weak that *he could* no longer s,	8011
	31: 5	"I s that your father's attitude toward me is	8011
	31:12	and s that all the male goats mating with	8011
	31:32	s for yourself whether there is anything	5795
	31:43	All you s is mine.	8011
	32:20	later, when *I* s him,	7156+8011
	33:10	For *to* s your face is like seeing the face	8011
	37:14	"Go and s if all is well with your brothers	8011
	37:20	Then *we'll* s what comes of his dreams."	8011
	37:32	**Examine** it *to* s whether it is your son's	
		robe."	5795
	38:25	"*S if you* **recognize** whose seal and cord	AIT
	42: 9	to s where our land is unprotected."	8011
	42:12	to s where our land is unprotected."	8011
	42:16	be tested to s if you are telling the truth.	NIH
	43: 3	not s my face again unless your brother is	8011
	43: 5	not s my face again unless your brother is	8011
	44:21	down to me so *I can* s him for myself.'	6524+8492
	44:23	*you will* not s my face again.'	8011
	44:26	We cannot s the man's face	8011

Ge	44:34	*Do not let me* s the misery that would come	8011
	45:12	"*You can* s **for yourselves**,	4013+6524+8011
	45:28	I will go and s him before I die."	8011
	48:10	and he could hardly s.	8011
	48:11	"I never expected *to* s your face again,"	8011
	48:11	God *has* **allowed** me *to* s your children too.	8011
Ex	2: 4	a distance to s what would happen to him.	3359
	3: 3	"I will go over and s this strange sight—	8011
	4:18	in Egypt *to* s if any of them are still alive."	8011
	4:21	s that you perform before Pharaoh all	8011
	6: 1	*you will* s what I will do to Pharaoh:	8011
	7: 1	Then the LORD said to Moses, "**S**,	8011
	10:23	No one *could* s anyone else	8011
	10:28	The day you s my face you will s	8011
	12:13	and when *I* s the blood, I will pass over	8011
	12:23	*he will* s the blood on the top and sides of	8011
	14:13	Stand firm and *you will* s the deliverance	8011
	14:13	The Egyptians you s today you will never	8011
	14:13	you s today *you will* never s again.	8011
	16: 4	s whether they will follow my instructions.	NIH
	16: 7	and in the morning *you will* s the glory of	8011
	16:32	to come, so *they can* s the bread I gave you	8011
	19:21	not force their way through to s the LORD	8011
	21:19	s that *he* **is completely healed**.	8324+8324
	23: 5	*If you* s the donkey of someone who hates	8011
	23: 8	for a bribe blinds *those who* s and twists	7221
	23:20	"**S**, I am sending an angel ahead of you	2180
	25:40	**S** that you make them according to	8011
	31: 2	"**S**, I have chosen Bezalel son of Uri,	8011
	33:20	But," he said, "you cannot s my face,	8011
	33:20	for no one *may* s me and live."	8011
	33:23	and *you will* s my back;	8011
	34:10	among *will* s how awesome is the work	8011
	35:30	Then Moses said to the Israelites, "**S**,	8011
Lev	13:12	so far as the priest can s,	5260+6524
	25:53	you must s *to* it that his owner does	4200+6524
Nu	4:18	"*S* that the Kohathite tribal clans *are* not	
		cut off	AIT
	11: 6	we never s anything but this manna!"	448+6524
	11:23	*You will* now s whether or	8011
	13:18	S what the land is like and whether	8011
	14:23	not one of them *will ever* s the land	8011
	14:23	treated me with contempt *will ever* s it.	8011
	23: 9	From the rocky peaks *I* s them,	8011
	23: 9	I s a people who live apart and do	2176
	23:13	to another place where *you can* s them;	8011
	23:13	*you will* s only a part but not all of them.	8011
	23:23	'**S** what God has done!'	NIH
	24:17	"*I* s him, but not now;	8011
	27:12	up this mountain in the Abarim range and s	8011
	28: 2	'**S** that you present to me at the appointed	9068
	32:11	of Egypt *will* s the land I promised on oath	8011
Dt	1: 8	S, I have given you this land.	8011
	1:21	S, the LORD your God has given you	8011
	1:35	"Not a man of this evil generation *shall* s	8011
	1:36	He *will* s it, and I will give him	8011
	2:24	S, I have given into your hand Sihon	8011
	2:31	The LORD said to me, "**S**,	8011
	3:25	Let me go over and s the good land beyond	8011
	3:28	to inherit the land that *you will* s."	8011
	4: 5	S, I have taught you decrees and laws as	8011
	4:19	when you look up to the sky and s the sun,	8011
	4:28	which cannot s or hear or eat or smell.	8011
	11:26	S, I am setting before you today a blessing	8011
	12:32	S that you do all I command you;	9068
	18:16	nor s this great fire anymore,	8011
	20: 1	to war against your enemies and s horses	8011
	21: 7	nor *did* our eyes s it done.	8011
	22: 1	*you* s your brother's ox or sheep straying,	8011
	22: 4	If *you* s your brother's donkey	8011
	23:14	not s among you anything indecent	8011
	28:10	on earth *will* s that you are called by	8011
	28:34	The sights *you* s will drive you mad.	8011
	28:67	and the sights that your eyes *will* s.	8011
	29: 4	a mind that understands or eyes that s	8011
	29:22	from distant lands *will* s the calamities	8011
	30:15	S, I set before you today life	8011
	32:20	he said, "and s what their end will be;	8011
	32:39	"S now that I myself am He!	8011
	32:52	*you will* s the land only from a distance;	8011
	34: 4	*I have* **let** you s it with your eyes,	8011
Jos	3: 3	"When you s the ark of the covenant of	8011
	3:11	S, the ark of the covenant of the Lord of all	2180
	5: 6	to them that they *would* not s the land	8011
	6: 2	Then the LORD said to Joshua, "**S**,	8011
	8: 8	S *to* it; you have my orders."	8011
	9:12	But now s how dry and moldy it is.	2180
	9:13	but s how cracked they are.	2180
	24:27	"**S**!" he said to all the people.	2180
Jdg	1:24	we will s that you *are* **treated** well."	AIT
	2:22	to test Israel and s whether they would keep	NIH
	3: 4	the Israelites to s whether they would obey	3359
	13: 4	Now s *to* it that you drink no wine	9068
	14:10	Now his father went down to s the woman.	NIH
	16: 5	"*S if you can* **lure** him into showing you	AIT
1Sa	2:32	and *you will* s distress in my dwelling,	5564
	3: 2	so weak that he could barely s,	8011
	3:11	And the LORD said to Samuel: "**S**,	2180
	4:15	so that he could not s.	8011
	10:24	"*Do you* s the man the LORD has chosen?	8011
	12:13	s, the LORD has set a king over you.	2180
	12:16	and s this great thing the LORD is about	8011
	14: 8	over toward the men and **let** them s *us*.	1655
	14:17	"Muster the forces and s who has left us."	8011
	14:29	S how my eyes brightened when I tasted	8011
	15:35	he did not go to s Saul again,	8011
	16:15	Saul's attendants said to him, "**S**,	2180

1Sa 17:18	S how your brothers are	7212	
17:25	"Do you s how this man keeps coming out?"	8011	
19:15	Then Saul sent the men back to s David	8011	
20:29	let me get away to s my brothers.'	8011	
24:11	S, my father, look at this piece of your robe	8011	
25:17	Now think it over and s what you can do,	8011	
25:25	I did not s the men my master sent.	8011	
28: 2	"Then you will s for yourself	3359	
28:13	What do you s?"	8011	
28:13	"I s a spirit coming up out of the ground."	8011	
2Sa 3:13	of Saul when you come to s me."	8011	
13: 5	"When your father comes to s you,	8011	
13: 6	When the king came to s him,	8011	
13:34	"I s men in the direction of Horonaim,	8011	
13:35	Jonadab said to the king, "S,	2180	
14:24	he must not s my face."	8011	
14:24	to his own house and did not s the face of	8011	
14:32	Now then, I want to s the king's face,	8011	
15: 4	I would s that he gets justice."	7405	
15:25	he will bring me back and let me s it	8011	
16:12	be that the LORD will s my distress	8011	
19: 6	I s that you would be pleased	3359	
24: 3	and may the eyes of my lord the king s it.	8011	
1Ki 1:15	So Bathsheba went to s the aged king	NIH	
1:48	who has allowed my eyes to s a successor	8011	
9:12	to s the towns that Solomon had given him,	8011	
11:31	'S, I am going to tear the kingdom out	2180	
14: 4	Now Ahijah could not s;	8011	
15:19	S, I am sending you a gift of silver	2180	
20: 7	"S how this man is looking for trouble!	2256+3359+8011	
20:13	'Do you s this vast army?	8011	
20:22	and s what must be done,	2256+3359+8011	
22: 2	of Judah went down to s the king of Israel.	NIH	
2Ki 1: 2	to s if I will recover from this injury."	NIH	
1:14	S, fire has fallen from heaven	2180	
2:10	if you s me when I am taken from you,	8011	
2:19	this town is well situated, as you can s,	8011	
3:17	You will s neither wind nor rain,	8011	
5: 3	"If only my master would s	4200+7156	
5: 7	S how he is trying to pick a quarrel with me!"	2256+3359+8011	
6:17	"O LORD, open his eyes so he may s."	8011	
6:20	open the eyes of these men so they can s."	8011	
6:32	to the elders, "Don't you s	8011	
7: 2	"You will s it with your own eyes,"	8011	
7:19	"You will s it with your own eyes,"	8011	
8:29	down to Jezreel to s Joram son of Ahab,	8011	
9:16	of Judah had gone down to s him.	8011	
9:17	he called out, "I s some troops coming."	8011	
10:16	with me and s my zeal for the LORD."	8011	
10:19	S that no one is missing,	NIH	
10:23	"Look around and s that no servants of	8011	
13:14	Jehoash king of Israel went down to s him	NIH	
19:16	open your eyes, O LORD, and s;	8011	
20:15	"What did they s in your palace?"	8011	
22:20	not s all the disaster I am going to bring	8011	
23:17	"What is that tombstone I s?"	8011	
1Ch 12:17	the God of our fathers s it and judge you."	8011	
2Ch 16: 3	S, I am sending you silver and gold.	2180	
20:11	S how they are repaying us by coming	2180	
20:17	stand firm and s the deliverance	8011	
22: 6	down to Jezreel to s Joram son of Ahab	8011	
24:22	the LORD s this and call you to account."	8011	
29: 8	as you can s with your own eyes.	8011	
30: 7	an object of horror, as you s.	8011	
34:28	not s all the disaster I am going to bring	8011	
Ezr 4:14	to the palace and it is not proper for us to s	10255	
5:17	to s if King Cyrus did in fact issue a decree	NIH	
Ne 2:17	I said to them, "You s the trouble we are in:	8011	
4:11	"Before they know it or s us,	8011	
8: 5	All the people could s him	4200+6524	
9:36	"But s, we are slaves today,	2180	
Est 3: 4	to s whether Mordecai's behavior would	8011	
5:13	as long as I s that Jew Mordecai sitting at	8011	
8: 6	can I bear to s disaster fall on my people?	8011	
8: 6	How can I bear to s the destruction	8011	
Job 3: 9	for daylight in vain and not s the first rays	8011	
6:21	you s something dreadful and are afraid.	8011	
7: 7	my eyes will never s happiness again.	8011	
7: 8	eye that now sees me will s me no longer;	8800	
9:11	When he passes me, I cannot s him;	8011	
10: 4	Do you s as a mortal sees?	8011	
14:21	if they are brought low, he does not s it.	1067	
17:15	Who can s any hope for me?	8800	
19:26	yet in my flesh I will s God;	2600	
19:27	I myself will s him with my own eyes—	2600	
20: 9	The eye that saw him will not s him again;	NIH	
21: 8	They s their children established	4200+7156	
21:20	Let his own eyes s his destruction;	8011	
22:11	why it is so dark you cannot s,	8011	
22:12	And s how lofty are the highest stars!	8011	
22:14	so he does not s us as he goes about in	8011	
22:19	"The righteous s their ruin and rejoice;	8011	
23: 9	he is at work in the north, I do not s him;	296	
24:15	he thinks, 'No eye will s me,'	8800	
28:10	his eyes s all its treasures.	8011	
31: 4	not s my ways and count my every step?	8011	
34:26	where everyone can s them,	8011	
34:29	If he hides his face, who can s him?	8800	
34:32	Teach me what I cannot s;	2600	
35: 5	Look up at the heavens and s;	8011	
35:14	when you say that you do not s him,	8800	
36:30	S how he scatters his lightning about him,	2176	
Ps 9:13	s how my enemies persecute me!	8011	
10:14	But you, O God, do s trouble and grief;	8011	
11: 7	upright men will s his face.	2600	

Ps 14: 2	of men to s if there are any who understand,	8011	
16:10	nor will you let your Holy One s decay.	8011	
17: 2	may your eyes s what is right.	2600	
17:15	in righteousness I will s your face;	2600	
22: 7	All who s me mock me;	8011	
25:19	S how my enemies have increased and	8011	
27:13	I will s the goodness of the LORD in	8011	
31:11	those who s me on the street flee from me.	8011	
34: 8	Taste and s that the LORD is good;	8011	
34:12	and desires to s many good days,	8011	
36: 9	in your light we s light.	8011	
36:12	S how the evildoers lie fallen—	9004	
37:34	when the wicked are cut off, you will s it.	8011	
40: 3	Many will s and fear and put their trust in	8011	
40:12	my sins have overtaken me, and I cannot s.	8011	
41: 6	Whenever one comes to s me,	8011	
46: 8	Come and s the works of the LORD,	2600	
49: 9	he should live on forever and not s decay.	8011	
49:10	For all can s that wise men die;	8011	
49:19	who will never s the light [of life].	8011	
50:18	When you s a thief, you join with him;	8011	
52: 6	The righteous will s and fear;	8011	
53: 2	of men to s if there are any who understand,	8011	
55: 9	for I s violence and strife in the city.	8011	
58: 8	like a stillborn child, may they not s the sun.	2600	
59: 3	S how they lie in wait for me!	2180	
59: 7	S what they spew from their mouths—	2180	
64: 5	they say, "Who will s them?"	8011	
64: 8	all who s them will shake their heads	8011	
66: 5	Come and s what God has done,	8011	
69:23	be darkened so they cannot s,	8011	
69:32	The poor will s and be glad—	8011	
71:20	Though you have made me troubles,	8011	
80:14	Look down from heaven and s!	8011	
83: 2	S how your enemies are astir,	2180	
86:17	my enemies may s it and be put to shame,	8011	
89:48	What man can live and not s death,	8011	
91: 8	You will only observe with your eyes and s	8011	
94: 7	They say, "The LORD does not s;	8011	
94: 9	Does he who formed the eye not s?	5564	
97: 6	and all the peoples s his glory.	8011	
107:42	The upright s and rejoice,	8011	
109:25	when they s me, they shake their heads.	8011	
112:10	The wicked man will s and be vexed,	8011	
115: 5	but cannot speak, eyes, but they cannot s;	8011	
119:18	that I may s wonderful things in your law.	5564	
119:74	who fear you rejoice when they s me,	8011	
119:96	To all perfection I s a limit;	8011	
119:159	S how I love your precepts;	8011	
128: 5	may you s the prosperity of Jerusalem;	8011	
128: 6	may you live to s your children's children.	8011	
135:16	but cannot speak, eyes, but they cannot s;	8011	
139:24	S if there is any offensive way in me,	8011	
142: 4	Look to my right and s;	8011	
Pr 20:12	Ears that hear and eyes that s—	8011	
22:29	Do you s a man skilled in his work?	2600	
23:33	Your eyes will s strange sights	8011	
24:18	or the LORD will s and disapprove	8011	
26:12	Do you s a man wise in his own eyes?	8011	
27:12	The prudent s danger and take refuge,	8011	
29:16	but the righteous will s their downfall.	8011	
29:20	Do you s a man who speaks in haste?	2600	
Ecc 2: 3	to s what was worthwhile for men to do	8011	
2:24	This too, I s, is from the hand of God,	8011	
3:18	so that they may s that they are like	8011	
3:22	to s what will happen after him?	8011	
5: 8	If you s the poor oppressed in a district,	8011	
7:11	is a good thing and benefits those who s	8011	
11: 7	and it pleases the eyes to s the sun.	8011	
11: 9	of your heart and whatever your eyes s,	5260	
SS 2:11	S! The winter is past;	2180	
6:11	to s if the vines had budded or	8011	
7:12	the vineyards to s if the vines have budded,	8011	
Isa 1:21	S how the faithful city has become a harlot!	377	
3: 1	S now, the Lord, the LORD Almighty,	2180	
5:19	let him hasten his work so we may s it.	8011	
5:30	he will s darkness and distress;	2180	
6: 7	With it he touched my mouth and said, "S,	2180	
6:10	Otherwise they might s with their eyes,	8011	
8:22	the earth and s only distress and darkness	2180	
10:33	S, the Lord, the LORD Almighty,	2180	
13: 9	S, the day of the LORD is coming—	2180	
13:17	S, I will stir up against them the Medes,	2180	
14:16	Those who s you stare at you,	8011	
17: 1	An oracle concerning Damascus: "S,	2180	
18: 3	you will s it, and when a trumpet sounds,	8011	
19: 1	An oracle concerning Egypt: S,	2180	
20: 6	'S what has happened to those we relied	2180	
21: 3	I am bewildered by what I s.	8011	
22:13	But s, there is joy and revelry,	2180	
24: 1	S, the LORD is going to lay waste	2180	
26:11	your hand is lifted high, but they do not s it.	2600	
26:11	Let them s your zeal for your people and	2600	
26:21	S, the LORD is coming out	2180	
28: 2	S, the Lord has one who is powerful	2180	
28:16	"S, I lay a stone in Zion, a tested stone,	2180	
29:18	and darkness the eyes of the blind will s.	8011	
29:23	When they s among them their children,	8011	
30:10	They say to the seers, "S no more visions!"	8011	
30:10	with your own eyes you will s them.	8011	
30:27	S, the Name of the LORD comes	2180	
30:30	and will make them s his arm coming down	8011	
32: 1	S, a king will reign in righteousness	2176	
32: 3	Then the eyes of those who s will no longer	8011	
33:17	Your eyes will s the king in his beauty	2600	
33:19	You will s those arrogant people no more,	8011	
33:20	your eyes will s Jerusalem,	8011	

Isa 34: 5	s, it descends in judgment on Edom,	2180	
35: 2	they will s the glory of the LORD,	8011	
37:17	open your eyes, O LORD, and s;	8011	
38:11	I said, "I will not again s the LORD,	8011	
39: 4	"What did they s in your palace?"	8011	
40: 5	and all mankind together will s it.	8011	
40:10	S, the Sovereign LORD comes	2180	
40:10	S, his reward is with him,	2180	
41:15	"S, I will make you into a threshing sledge,	2180	
41:20	so that people may s and know,	8011	
41:29	S, they are all false!	2176	
42: 9	S, the former things have taken place,	2180	
42:18	"Hear, you deaf; look, you blind, and s!	8011	
43:19	S, I am doing a new thing!	2180	
44: 16	I am warm; I s the fire."	2180	
44:18	over so they cannot s,	8011	
48:10	S, I have refined you, though not as silver;	2180	
49: 7	"Kings will s you and rise up,	8011	
49: 7	princes will s and bow down,	NIH	
49:12	S, they will come from afar—	2180	
49:16	S, I have engraved you on the palms	2176	
49:22	"S, I will beckon to the Gentiles	2180	
51:22	"S, I have taken out of your hand the cup	2180	
52: 8	they will s it with their own eyes.	8011	
52:10	the earth will s the salvation of our God.	8011	
52:13	S, my servant will act wisely;	2180	
52:15	For what they were not told, they will s,	8011	
53:10	he will s his offspring	8011	
53:11	he will s the light [of life] and be satisfied;	8011	
54:16	"S, it is I who created the blacksmith	2180	
55: 4	S, I have made him a witness to	2176	
58: 7	when you s the naked, to clothe him,	8011	
60: 2	S, darkness covers the earth	2180	
61: 9	All who s them will acknowledge	8011	
62: 2	The nations will s your righteousness,	8011	
62:11	"Say to the Daughter of Zion, 'S,	2180	
62:11	S, his reward is with him,	2180	
63:15	from heaven and s from your lofty throne,	8011	
65: 6	"S, it stands written before me:	2180	
66: 5	that we may s your joy!'	8011	
66:14	When you s this, your heart will rejoice	8011	
66:15	S, the LORD is coming with fire,	2180	
66:18	and they will come and s my glory.	8011	
Jer 1:10	S, today I appoint you over nations	8011	
1:11	"What do you s, Jeremiah?"	8011	
1:11	"I s the branch of an almond tree,"	8011	
1:12	s that my word is fulfilled."	AIT	
1:13	"What do you s?"	8011	
1:13	"I s a boiling pot,	8011	
2:10	s if there has ever been anything like this:	8011	
2:23	S how you behaved in the valley;	8011	
3: 2	"Look up to the barren heights and s.	8011	
4:21	How long must I s the battle standard	8011	
5:12	we will never s sword or famine.	8011	
5:21	who have eyes but do not s,	8011	
7:12	and s what I did to it because of	8011	
7:17	not s what they are doing in the towns	8011	
8:17	"S, I will send venomous snakes	2180	
9: 7	"S, I will refine and test them,	2180	
9:15	"S, I will make this people eat bitter food	2180	
11:20	let me s your vengeance upon them,	8011	
12: 3	you s me and test my thoughts about you.	8011	
12: 4	"He will not s what happens to us."	8011	
13:20	and s those who are coming from the north.	8011	
14:13	'You will not s the sword or suffer famine.	8011	
14:18	I s those slain by the sword;	2180	
14:18	I s the ravages of famine.	2180	
16:12	S how each of you is following	8011	
17: 6	he will not s prosperity when it comes.	8011	
20: 4	with your own eyes you will s them fall by	8011	
20:12	let me s your vengeance upon them,	8011	
20:18	to s trouble and sorrow and to end my days	8011	
21: 8	S, I am setting before you the way of life	2180	
22:10	nor s his native land again.	8011	
22:12	he will not s this land again."	8011	
23:18	of the LORD to s or to hear his word?	8011	
23:19	S, the storm of the LORD will burst out	2180	
23:24	in secret places so that I cannot s him?"	8011	
24: 3	the LORD asked me, "What do you s,	2180	
25:29	S, I am beginning to bring disaster on	2180	
29:32	nor will he s the good things I will do	8011	
30: 6	Ask and s: Can a man bear children?	8011	
30: 6	Then why do I s every strong man	8011	
30:23	S, the storm of the LORD will burst out	2180	
31: 8	S, I will bring them from the land of	2180	
32: 4	to face and s him with his own eyes.	8011	
32:24	"S how the siege ramps are built up to take	2180	
32:24	What you said has happened, as you now s.	8011	
34: 3	You will s the king of Babylon	8011	
42: 2	For as you now s, though we were once many,	6524+8011	
42:14	not war or hear the trumpet or be hungry	8011	
42:18	you will never s this place again.'	8011	
44:23	disaster has come upon you, as you now s."	NIH	
46: 5	What do I s?	2180	
47: 2	"S how the waters are rising in the north;	2180	
49:35	"S, I will break the bow of Elam,	2180	
50:31	"S, I am against you, O arrogant one,"	2180	
51: 1	This is what the LORD says: "S,	2180	
51:36	"S, I will defend your cause	2180	
51:61	s that you read all these words aloud.	8011	
La 1:12	Look around and s,	8011	
1:20	"S, O LORD, how distressed I am!	8011	
2:16	we have lived to s it,"	8011	
3:36	would not the Lord s such things?	8011	
3:51	What I s brings grief to my soul because	6524	
5: 1	look, and s our disgrace.	8011	

Eze
8:6 do you s what they are doing— 8011
8:6 But you will s things that are 8011
8:9 "Go in and s the wicked 8011
8:12 They say, 'The LORD does not s us; 8011
8:13 "You will s them doing things that are 8011
8:15 He said to me, "Do you s this, son of man? 8011
8:15 You will s things that are even more 8011
9:9 the LORD does not s." 8011
12:2 They have eyes to s but do not see and ears 8011
12:2 but do not s and ears to hear but do not hear, 8011
12:6 Cover your face so that you cannot s 8011
12:12 He will cover his face so that he cannot s 2021+4200+6524+8011
12:13 but he will not s it, and there he will die. 8011
13:9 be against the prophets who s false visions 2600
13:23 therefore you will no longer s false visions 2600
14:22 when you s their conduct and their actions, 8011
14:23 when you s their conduct and their actions, 8011
16:37 and they will s all your nakedness. 8011
20:48 Everyone will s that I the LORD have kindled 8011
22:6 "S how each of the princes 2180
32:31 will s them and he will be consoled 8011
34:20 S, I myself will judge between 2180
39:21 the nations will s the punishment I inflict 8011
40:4 Tell the house of Israel everything you s." 8011
47:6 He asked me, "Son of man, do you s this?" 8011

Da
1:10 Why should he s you looking worse than 8011
1:13 in accordance with what you s." 8011
3:25 I s four men walking around in the fire, 10255
5:23 which cannot s or hear or understand. 10255
9:18 open your eyes and s the desolation of 8011
10:7 the men with me did not s it, 8011

Joel
2:28 your young men will s visions. 8011
3:7 "S, I am going to rouse them out of 2180

Am
3:9 s the great unrest within her and 8011
7:8 LORD asked me, "What do you s, Amos?" 8011
7:8 "What do you s, Amos?" 8011

Ob
1:2 "S, I will make you small among 2180

Jnh
4:5 and waited to s what would happen to 8011

Mic
7:9 I will s his righteousness. 8011
7:10 Then my enemy will s it and will 8011
7:10 My eyes will s her downfall; 8011
7:16 Nations will s and be ashamed, 8011

Na
3:7 All who s you will flee from you and say, 8011

Hab
2:1 I will look to s what he will say to me, 8011
2:4 "S, he is puffed up; 2180

Hag
1:9 "You expected much, but s, 2180

Zec
1:9 Then he said to Joshua, "S, 8011
3:9 S, the stone I have set in front of Joshua! 2180
4:2 He asked me, "What do you s?" 8011
4:2 "I s a solid gold lampstand with a bowl at 8011
4:10 when they s the plumb line in the hand 8011
5:2 He asked me, "What do you s?" 8011
5:2 I answered, "I s a flying scroll, 8011
5:5 up and s what this is that is appearing." 8011
9:5 Ashkelon will s it and fear; 8011
9:9 S, your king comes to you, 2180
10:2 diviners s visions that lie; 2600
10:7 Their children will s it and be joyful; 8011

Mal
1:5 You will s it with your own eyes and say, 8011
3:1 "S, I will send my messenger, 2180
3:10 "and s if I will not throw open NIH
3:18 And you will again s the distinction 8011
3:1 "S, I will send you the prophet Elijah 2180

Mt
5:8 Blessed are the pure in heart, for they will s 3972
5:8 God. 3972
5:16 that they may s your good deeds 3972
6:28 S how the lilies of the field grow. 2908
7:5 and then you will s clearly to remove 1332
8:4 "S that you don't tell anyone. 3972
9:30 "S that no one knows about this." 3972
11:4 and report to John what you hear and s: 1063
11:7 "What did you go out into the desert to s? 2517
11:8 If not, what did you go out to s? 3972
11:9 Then what did you go out to s? 3972
12:22 so that he could both talk and s. 1063
12:38 we want to s a miraculous sign from you." 3972
13:13 "Though seeing, they do not s; 1063
13:15 Otherwise they might s with their eyes, 3972
13:16 But blessed are your eyes because they s, 1063
13:17 to s what you see but did not see it, 3972
13:17 to see what you see but did not see it, 1063
13:17 to see what you see but did not s it, 3972
15:17 "Don't you s that whatever enters 3783
16:28 before they s the Son of Man coming 3972
18:10 "S that you do not look down on one 3972
18:10 that their angels in heaven always s the face 1063
21:5 'S, your king comes to you, 2627
22:11 "But when the king came in to s the guests, 2517
23:5 "Everything they do is done for men to s: 2517
23:39 you will not s me again until you say, 3972
24:2 "Do you s all these things?" 1063
24:6 but s to it that you are not alarmed. 3972
24:15 "So when you s standing in the holy place 3972
24:25 S, I have told you ahead of time. 2627
24:30 They will s the Son of Man coming on 3972
24:33 Even so, when you s all these things, 3972
25:20 S, I have gained five more.' 3972
25:22 s, I have gained two more.' 3972
25:25 S, here is what belongs to you.' 3972
25:37 when did we s you hungry and feed you, 3972
25:38 When did we s you a stranger and invite you 3972
25:39 When did we s you sick or in prison and go 3972
25:44 when did we s you hungry or thirsty or 3972
26:58 down with the guards to s the outcome. 3972
26:64 In the future you will s the Son 3972
27:49 Let's s if Elijah comes to save him." 3972

Mt
28:6 Come and s the place where he lay. 3972
28:7 There you will s him.' 3972
28:10 there they will s me." 3972

Mk
1:44 "S that you don't tell this to anyone. 3972
3:2 to s if he would heal him on the Sabbath. NIG
5:14 people went out to s what had happened. 3972
5:31 "You s the people crowding against you," 1063
5:32 around to s who had done it. 3972
6:38 he asked. "Go and s." 3972
7:18 "Don't you s that nothing that enters a man 3783
8:17 Do you still not s or understand? 3783
8:18 Do you have eyes but fail to s, 1063
8:23 Jesus asked, "Do you s anything?" 1063
8:24 He looked up and said, "I s people; 1063
9:1 not taste death before they s the kingdom 3972
10:51 The blind man said, "Rabbi, I want to s." 329
13:2 "Do you s all these great buildings? 1063
13:14 "When you s 'the abomination 3972
13:26 "At that time men will s the Son 3972
13:29 so, when you s these things happening, 3972
14:62 "And you will s the Son of Man sitting at 3972
15:4 S how many things they are accusing you 3972
15:24 they cast lots to s what each would get. NIG
15:32 that we may s and believe." 3972
15:36 Let's s if Elijah comes to take him down," 3972
16:6 S the place where they laid him. 3972
16:7 There you will s him, 3972

Lk
2:15 "Let's go to Bethlehem and s this thing 3972
3:6 And all mankind will s God's salvation.' " 3972
6:7 to s if he would heal on the Sabbath. NIG
6:42 when you yourself fail to s the plank 1063
6:42 and then you will s clearly to remove 1332
7:24 "What did you go out into the desert to s? 2517
7:25 If not, what did you go out to s? 3972
7:26 But what did you go out to s? 3972
7:44 "Do you s this woman? 1063
8:10 so that, " 'though seeing, they may not s; 1063
8:16 so that those who come in can s the light. 1063
8:19 Jesus' mother and brothers came to s him, NIG
8:20 standing outside, wanting to s you." 3972
8:35 people went out to s what had happened. 3972
9:9 And he tried to s him. 3972
9:27 not taste death before they s the kingdom 3972
10:23 "Blessed are the eyes that s what you see. 1063
10:23 "Blessed are the eyes that see what you s. 1063
10:24 and kings wanted to s what you see but did 3972
10:24 and kings wanted to see what you s but did 1063
10:24 to see what you see but did not s it, 3972
11:33 so that those who come in may s the light. 1063
11:35 S to it, then, that the light within you is 5023
12:54 "When you s a cloud rising in the west, 3972
13:28 when you s Abraham, Isaac and Jacob 3972
13:35 you will not s me again until you say, 3972
14:18 and I must go and s it. 3972
14:28 the cost to s if he has enough money 1623
17:22 when you will long to s one of the days of 3972
17:22 but you will not s it. 3972
18:5 s that she gets justice, 1688
18:8 I tell you, he will s that they get justice, NIG
18:41 "Lord, I want to s," he replied. 329
19:3 he wanted to s who Jesus was, 3972
19:4 and climbed a sycamore-fig tree to s him, 3972
21:6 "As for what you s here, the time will 2555+4047
21:20 "When you s Jerusalem being surrounded 3972
21:27 At that time they will s the Son of Man 3972
21:30 you can s for yourselves and know 1063
21:31 so, when you s these things happening, 3972
22:38 The disciples said, "S, Lord, 2627
23:8 a long time had been wanting to s him. 3972
23:8 he hoped to s him perform some miracle. 3972
23:15 as you can s, he has done nothing to deserve 2627
24:24 but him they did not s." 3972
24:39 Touch me and s; a ghost does not have flesh 3972
24:39 as you s I have." 2555

Jn
1:33 'The man on whom you s the Spirit come 3972
1:39 "Come," he replied, "and you will s." 3972
1:46 "Come and s," said Philip. 3972
1:50 You shall s greater things than that." 3972
1:51 you shall s heaven open, 3972
3:3 no one can s the kingdom of God 3972
3:36 but whoever rejects the Son will not s life, 3972
4:19 "I can s that you are a prophet. 2555
4:29 s a man who told me everything I ever did. 3972
4:48 "Unless you people s miraculous signs 3972
5:14 "S, you are well again. 3972
6:30 then will you give that we may s it 3972
6:62 What if you s the Son of Man ascend to 2555
7:3 so that your disciples may s 2555
8:51 he will never s death." 2555
9:11 So I went and washed, and then I could s." 329
9:15 "and I washed, and now I s." 1063
9:19 How is it that now he can s?" 1063
9:21 But how he can s now, 1063
9:25 I was blind but now I s!" 1063
9:39 so that the blind will s 1063
9:39 and those who s will become blind." 1063
9:41 you claim you can s, your guilt remains. 1063
11:34 "Come and s, Lord," they replied. 3972
11:36 Then the Jews said, "S how he loved him!" 3972
11:40 you would s the glory of God?" 3972
12:9 only because of him but also to s Lazarus, 3972
12:15 s, your king is coming, 2627
12:19 So the Pharisees said to one another, "S, 2555
12:21 they said, "we would like to s Jesus." 3972
12:40 so they can neither s with their eyes, 3972
14:19 long, the world will not s me anymore, 2555
14:19 but you will s me. 2555

Jn
16:10 where you can s me no longer; 2555
16:16 "In a little while you will s me no more, 2555
16:16 then after a little while you will s me." 3972
16:17 'In a little while you will s me no more, 2555
16:17 and then after a little while you will s me,' 3972
16:19 'In a little while you will s me no more, 2555
16:19 then after a little while you will s me'? 3972
16:22 I will s you again and you will rejoice, 3972
16:30 Now we can s that you know all things and 3857
17:24 and to s my glory, the glory you have given 2555
18:26 "Didn't I s you with him in 3972
20:25 "Unless I s the nail marks in his hands 3972
20:27 "Put your finger here; s my hands. 3972

Ac
2:17 your young men will s visions, 3972
2:27 nor will you let your Holy One s decay. 3972
2:31 nor did his body s decay. 3972
2:33 and has poured out what you now s 1063
3:16 this man whom you s 2555
3:16 as you can s. 595+5148
4:14 But since they could s 1063
7:56 "I s heaven open and the Son 2555
8:23 For I s that you are full of bitterness 3972
8:39 and the eunuch did not s him again, 3972
9:7 they heard the sound but did not s anyone. 2555
9:9 he opened his eyes he could s nothing. 1063
9:17 so that you may s again and be filled with 329
9:18 and he could s again. 329
13:11 you will be unable to s the light 1063+3590
13:35 'You will not let your Holy One s decay.' 3972
13:37 from the dead did not s decay. 3972
15:2 s the apostles and elders about 4309
15:36 of the Lord and s how they are doing." NIG
17:11 and examined the Scriptures every day to s NIG
17:16 he was greatly distressed to s that 2555
17:22 s that in every way you are very religious. 2555
18:2 Paul went to s them, NIG
19:26 And you s and hear 2555
20:25 the kingdom will ever s me again. 3972
20:38 that they would never s his face again. 2555
21:18 and the rest of us went to s James, NIG
21:20 Then they said to Paul: "You s, brother, 2555
22:12 "A man named Ananias came to s me. NIG
22:13 at that very moment I was able to s him. 329
22:14 to s the Righteous One and to hear words 3972
25:24 all who are present with us, you s this man! 2555
26:7 This is the promise our twelve tribes are 2918
26:7 hoping to s fulfilled 2918
27:10 I can s that our voyage is going to be 2555
28:8 Paul went in to s him and, after prayer, NIG
28:20 For this reason I have asked to s you 3972
28:27 Otherwise they might s with their eyes, 3972
28:30 and welcomed all who came to s him. NIG

Ro
1:11 I long to s you so that I may impart 3972
5:6 You s, at just the right time, 1142
7:23 but I s another law at work in the members 1063
9:33 As it is written: "S, I lay in Zion a stone 2627
11:8 not s and ears so that they could not hear, 1063
11:10 be darkened so they cannot s, 1063
15:21 not told about him will s, 3972
15:23 for many years to s you, 2262+4639

1Co
3:12 Now we s but a poor reflection as in 1063
13:12 then we shall s face to face. NIG
16:7 I do not want to s you now and make only 3972
16:10 s to it that he has nothing to fear 1063

2Co
2:9 to s if you would stand the test and 1182
4:4 so that they cannot s the light of the gospel 878
7:8 I s that my letter hurt you, 1063
7:11 S what this godly sorrow has produced 2627
7:11 readiness to s justice done. 1689
7:12 that before God you could s for yourselves 5746
7:13 we were especially delighted to s NIG
8:7 s that you also excel in everything— AIT
8:24 so that the churches can s it. 4725S
13:5 Examine yourselves to s whether you are in NIG
13:7 Not that people will s that we have stood 5743

Gal
1:17 to Jerusalem to s those who were apostles 4639
6:11 S what large letters I use as I write to you 3972

Php
1:27 whether I come and s you or only hear 3972
2:23 to send him as soon as I s how things go 927
2:28 that when you s him again you may be glad 3972

Col
2:5 and delight to s how orderly you are and 1063
2:8 S to it that no one takes you captive 1063
4:16 s that it is also read in the church of 4472
4:17 "S to it that you complete the work 1063

1Th
2:17 we made every effort to s you, 3972
3:6 of us and that you long to s us, 3972
3:6 just as we also long to s you. NIG
3:10 that we may s you again 3972

1Ti
3:4 manage his own family well and s that 4613
4:15 so that everyone may s your progress. 5745
6:16 whom no one has seen or can s. 3972

2Ti
1:4 Recalling your tears, I long to s you, 3972

Tit
3:13 the lawyer and Apollos on their way and s NIG

Heb
2:8 at present we do not s everything subject 3972
2:9 But we s Jesus, who was made a lower 1063
3:12 S to it, brothers, that none of you has 1063
3:19 So we s that they were not able to enter, 1063
8:5 "S to it that you make everything 3972
10:25 all the more as you s the Day approaching. 1063
11:1 for and certain of what we do not s. 1063
12:14 without holiness no one will s the Lord. 3972
12:15 S to it that no one misses the grace of God 2174
12:16 S that no one is sexually immoral, NIG
12:25 S to it that you do not refuse him 1063
13:23 I will come with him to s you. 3972

Jas
2:22 You s that his faith and his actions 1063
2:24 You s that a person is justified by what he 3972

Jas	5: 7	**S** how the farmer waits for the land	2627
1Pe	1: 8	and *even though you do* not s him now,	3972
	2: 6	For in Scripture it says: "**S,** I lay a stone in	2627
	2:12	they may s your good deeds	2227
	3: 2	*when they* s the purity and reverence	2227
	3:10	and s good days must keep his tongue	3972
2Pe	1:15	to s that after my departure you will always	NIG
1Jn	2:24	*S that* what you have heard from the	
		beginning **remains** in you.	AIT
	3: 2	for *we shall* s him as he is.	3972
	4: 1	the spirits to s whether they are from God,	NIG
3Jn	1:14	I hope *to* s you soon,	3972
Jude	1:14	"**S,** the Lord is coming with thousands	2627
Rev	1: 7	and every eye *will* s him,	3972
	1:11	"Write on a scroll what *you* s and send it to	1063
	1:12	around *to* s the voice that was speaking	1063
	3: 8	**S,** I have placed before you an open door	2627
	3:18	and salve to put on your eyes, so *you can* s.	1063
	5: 5	**S,** the Lion of the tribe of Judah,	2627
	9:20	idols that cannot s or hear or walk.	1063
	17: 8	of the world will be astonished *when they* s	1063
	18: 9	with her and shared her luxury s the smoke	1063
	18:18	*When they* s the smoke of her burning,	1063
	21:22	*I did* not s a temple in the city,	3972
	22: 4	*They will* s his face, and his name will be	3972

SEED (81) [SEED-BEARING, SEEDS, SEEDTIME]

Ge	1:11	and trees on the land that bear fruit with s	2446
	1:12	plants bearing s according to their kinds	2446
	1:12	and trees bearing fruit with s in it according	2446
	1:29	every tree that has fruit with s in it.	2445+2446
	47:19	Give us s so that we may live and not die,	2446
	47:23	here is s for you so you can plant	2446
	47:24	The other four-fifths you may keep as s *for*	2446
Ex	16:31	like coriander s and tasted like wafers made	2446
Lev	11:38	But if water has been put on the s and	2445
	19:19	not **plant** your field **with** two kinds of s.	2446
	26:16	You will plant s in vain,	2446
	27:16	according to the amount of s *required*	2446
	27:16	of silver to a homer of barley s.	2446
Nu	11: 7	The manna was like coriander s and looked	2446
	24: 7	their s will have abundant water.	2446
Dt	11:10	where you planted your s and irrigated it	2446
	22: 9	*Do* not **plant** two kinds of s in your	2445
	28:38	You will sow much s in the field	2446
1Ki	18:32	large enough to hold two seahs of s.	2446
2Ki	6:25	a quarter of a cab of s pods for five shekels.	1807
Ps	126: 6	goes out weeping, carrying **s to sow,**	2446+5433
Ecc	11: 6	Sow your s in the morning,	2446
Isa	5:10	a homer of s only an ephah of grain."	2446
	6:13	so the holy s will be the stump in the land."	2446
	30:23	He will also send you rain for the s you sow	2446
	32:20	*sowing* your s by every stream,	2445
	55:10	that it yields s for the sower and bread for	2446
Jer	35: 7	sow s or plant vineyards;	2446
Eze	17: 5	the s *of* your land and put it in fertile soil.	2446
Hag	2:19	Is there yet any s left in the barn?	2446
Zec	8:12	"The s will grow well,	2446
Mt	13: 4	"A farmer went out *to* **sow** his s.	5062
	13: 4	As he *was* **scattering** the s,	5062
	13: 7	Other s fell among thorns,	NIG
	13: 8	Still other s fell on good soil,	NIG
	13:19	This is the s **sown** along the path.	5062
	13:20	received the s **that fell** on rocky places	5062
	13:22	received the s **that fell** among the thorns	5062
	13:23	received the s **that fell** on good soil	5062
	13:24	of heaven is like a man who sowed good s	5065
	13:27	'Sir, didn't you sow good s in your field?	5065
	13:31	kingdom of heaven is like a mustard s,	3133
	13:37	"The one who sowed the good s is the Son	5065
	13:38	good s stands for the sons of the kingdom.	5065
	17:20	if you have faith as small as a mustard s,	3133
	25:24	where *you* have not **scattered** s.	1399
	25:26	and gather where *I have* not **scattered** s?	1399
Mk	4: 3	"Listen! A farmer went out *to* **sow** his s.	5062
	4: 4	As he *was* **scattering the** s,	5062
	4: 7	Other s fell among thorns,	NIG
	4: 8	Still other s fell on good soil.	NIG
	4:15	Some people are like s along the path,	5062
	4:16	Others, like s **sown** on rocky places,	5062
	4:18	Still others, like s **sown** among thorns,	5062
	4:20	Others, like s **sown** on good soil,	5062
	4:26	A man scatters s on the ground.	5078
	4:27	the s sprouts and grows,	5078
	4:31	It is like a mustard s,	3133
	4:31	the smallest s you plant in the ground.	5065
Lk	8: 5	"A farmer went out *to* **sow** his s.	5078
	8: 5	As he *was* **scattering the** s,	5078
	8: 7	Other s fell among thorns,	NIG
	8: 8	Still other s fell on good soil.	NIG
	8:11	The s is the word of God.	5078
	8:14	The s that fell among thorns stands	NIG
	8:15	But the s on good soil stands for those with	NIG
	13:19	It is like a mustard s,	3133
	17: 6	"If you have faith as small as a mustard s,	3133
	12:24	it remains only a single s.	NIG
1Co	3: 6	I planted the s, Apollos watered it,	NIG
	9:11	If we *have* **sown** spiritual s among you,	5062
	15:37	but just a s, perhaps of wheat or of	3133
	15:38	to each kind *of* s he gives its own body.	5065
2Co	9:10	Now he who supplies s to the sower	5078
	9:10	and increase your store of s and will	3836+5078
Gal	3:16	spoken to Abraham and *to* his s.	5065
	3:16	meaning many people, but "and *to* your s,"	5065
	3:19	of transgressions until the **S** to whom	5065

Gal	3:29	then you are Abraham's s,	5065
1Pe	1:23	not of perishable s, but of imperishable,	5076
1Jn	3: 9	because God's s remains in him;	5065

SEED-BEARING (2) [SEED]

Ge	1:11	s plants and trees on the land that bear	2445+2446
	1:29	"I give you every s plant on the face	2445+2446

SEEDS (7) [SEED]

Lev	11:37	If a carcass falls on any s that are to	2433+2446
Nu	6: 4	not even the s or skins.	3079
Isa	61:11	the sprout come up and a garden causes s	2433
Joel	1:17	The s are shriveled beneath the clods.	7237
Mt	13:32	Though it is the smallest of all your s,	5065
Jn	12:24	But if it dies, it produces many s.	2843
Gal	3:16	The Scripture does not say "and *to* s,"	5065

SEEDTIME (1) [SEED]

Ge	8:22	long as the earth endures, s and harvest,	2446

SEEING (29) [SEE]

Ge	33:10	to see your face is like s the face of God,	8011
Ex	2:12	Glancing this way and that and s no one,	8011
Nu	35:23	or, without s him, drops a stone on him	8011
Jdg	13:20	**S** this, Manoah and his wife fell	8011
	18:26	s that they were too strong for him,	8011
2Sa	14:28	in Jerusalem without s the king's face.	8011
Ps	17:15	I will be satisfied with s your likeness.	NIH
Ecc	1: 8	The eye never has enough of s,	8011
	8:16	his eyes not s sleep day or night—	8011
Isa	6: 9	*be* **ever** s, but never perceiving.'	8011+8011
	28: 7	they stagger when s **visions,**	8015
Hos	9:10	it was like s the early fruit on the fig tree.	NIH
Mt	13:13	"Though s, they do not see;	1063
	13:14	you will be **ever** s but never perceiving.	
			1063+1063
	15:31	the lame walking and the blind s.	1063
	21:19	**S** a fig tree by the road,	3972
Mk	4:12	" 'they may be **ever** s but never perceiving,	
			1063+1063
	5:22	**S** Jesus, he fell at his feet	3972
	11:13	**S** in the distance a fig tree in leaf,	3972
Lk	8:10	so that, " 'though s, they may not see;	1063
	8:47	woman, s that she could not go unnoticed,	3972
	23:47	The centurion, s what had happened,	3972
Jn	8:56	at the thought of s my day;	3972
	9: 7	man went and washed, and came home s.	1063
Ac	2:31	**S** what was ahead, he spoke of the	4632
	9:40	She opened her eyes, and s Peter she sat up.	3972
	12: 9	he thought he was seeing a vision.	1063
	28: 6	a long time and s nothing unusual happen	2555
	28:26	*you will be* **ever** s but never perceiving."	
			1063+1063

SEEK (128) [SEEKING, SEEKS, SELF-SEEKING, SOUGHT]

Ex	18:15	the people come to me to s God's **will.**	2011
Lev	19:18	not s **revenge** or bear a grudge against one	5933
	19:31	not turn to mediums or s **out** spiritists.	1335
Dt	4:29	if from there *you* s the LORD your God,	1335
	12: 5	But *you are to* s the place	2011
	23: 6	*Do* not s a treaty of friendship with them	2011
2Sa	17: 3	of the man you s will mean the return of all;	1335
1Ki	22: 5	"First s the counsel of the LORD."	2011
1Ch	16:10	of *those who* s the LORD rejoice.	1335
	16:11	s his face always.	1335
	28: 9	If *you* s him, he will be found by you;	2011
2Ch	7:14	and pray and s my face and turn	1335
	14: 4	He commanded Judah to s the LORD,	2011
	15: 2	If *you* s him, he will be found by you,	2011
	15:12	They entered into a covenant to s	2011
	15:13	All who *would* not s the LORD,	2011
	16:12	even in his illness *he did* not s **help** from	1335
	18: 4	"First s the counsel of the LORD."	2011
	20: 4	of Judah came together to s **help** from	1335
	20: 4	from every town in Judah to s him.	2011
	34: 3	he began to s the God of his father David.	2011
Ezr	4: 2	*we* s your God and have been sacrificing	2011
	6:21	of their Gentile neighbors in order to s	2011
	9:12	*Do* not s a treaty of friendship with them	2011
Ps	4: 2	you love delusions and s false gods?	1335
	9:10	have never forsaken *those who* s you.	2011
	10: 4	In his pride the wicked does not s him;	2011
	14: 2	any who understand, *any who* s God.	1335
	22:26	*they who* s the LORD will praise him—	2011
	24: 6	Such is the generation of *those who* s him,	2011
	24: 6	*who* s your face, O God of Jacob.	1335
	27: 4	this is what *I* s: that I may dwell in	1335
	27: 4	upon the beauty of the LORD and to s him	1329
	27: 8	My heart says of you, "**S** his face!"	1335
	27: 8	Your face, LORD, *I will* s.	1335
	34:10	*those who* s the LORD lack no good thing.	2011
	34:14	s peace and pursue it.	1335
	35: 4	May *those who* s my life be disgraced	1335
	38:12	*Those who* s my life set their traps,	1335
	40:14	*May all who* s to take my life be put	1335
	40:16	But may all *who* s you rejoice and be glad	1335
	45:12	men of wealth *will* s your **favor.**	2704+7156
	53: 2	any who understand, *any who* s God.	2011
	54: 3	ruthless men s my life—	1335
	63: 1	you are my God, **earnestly** *I* s you;	8838
	63: 9	They *who* s my life will be destroyed;	1335
	69: 4	*those who* s **to destroy** me.	7551

Ps	69: 6	may *those who* s you not be put to shame	1335
	69:32	you who s God, may your hearts live!	2011
	70: 2	May *those who* s my life be put to shame	1335
	70: 4	But may all *who* s you rejoice and be glad	1335
	78:34	Whenever God slew them; *they would* s him	2011
	83:16	with shame so that *men will* s your name,	1335
	104:21	The lions roar for their prey and s their food	1335
	105: 3	of *those who* s the LORD rejoice.	1335
	105: 4	s his face always.	1335
	119: 2	and s him with all their heart.	2011
	119:10	*I* s you with all my heart;	2011
	119:155	for *they do* not s **out** your decrees.	2011
	119:176	**S** your servant, for I have not forgotten	1335
	122: 9	*I will* s your prosperity.	1335
Pr	8:17	and *those who* s me find me.	8838
	18:15	the ears of the wise s **out.**	1335
	25:27	nor is it honorable to s one's own honor.	2984
	28: 5	*those who* s the LORD understand it fully.	1335
	29:10	a man of integrity and s to kill the upright.	1335
	29:26	Many s **an audience with** a ruler,	1335+7156
Isa	1:17	**S** justice, encourage the oppressed.	2011
	31: 1	or s **help** *from* the LORD.	2011
	45:19	to Jacob's descendants, '**S** me in vain.'	1335
	51: 1	you who pursue righteousness and *who* s	1335
	55: 6	**S** the LORD while he may be found;	2011
	58: 2	For day after day *they* s me out;	2011
	65: 1	I was found by *those who* did not s me.	1335
	65:10	for my people who s me.	2011
Jer	4:30	Your lovers despise you; *they* s your life.	1335
	19: 7	at the hands of *those who* s their lives,	1335
	19: 9	on them by the enemies *who* s their lives.'	1335
	21: 7	and to their enemies *who* s their lives.	1335
	22:25	to *those who* s your life, those you fear—	1335
	26:19	the LORD and his **favor?**	906+2704+7156
	29: 7	s the peace and prosperity of the city	2011
	29:13	*You will* s me and find me	1335
	29:13	when *you* s me with all your heart.	2011
	34:20	over to their enemies *who* s their lives.	1335
	34:21	over to their enemies *who* s their lives,	1335
	44:30	of Egypt over to his enemies *who* s his life,	1335
	45: 5	then s great things for yourself?	1335
	45: 5	**S** them not.	1335
	46:26	over to *those who* s their lives,	1335
	49:37	before *those who* s their lives;	1335
	50: 4	of Judah together will go in tears to s	1335
Eze	7:25	When terror comes, *they will* s peace,	1335
	21:21	to s **an omen:** He will cast lots	7876+7877
Hos	3: 5	Afterward the Israelites will return and s	1335
	5: 6	with their flocks and herds to s the LORD,	1335
	5:15	And *they will* s my face;	1335
	5:15	in their misery *they will* **earnestly** s me."	8838
	10:12	for it is time to s the LORD,	2011
Am	5: 4	"**S** me and live;	2011
	5: 5	*do* not s Bethel, do not go to Gilgal,	2011
	5: 6	**S** the LORD and live;	2011
	5:14	**S** good, not evil, that you may live.	2011
Na	3:11	you will go into hiding and s refuge from	1335
Zep	1: 6	from following the LORD and neither s	1335
	2: 3	**S** the LORD, all you humble of the land,	1335
	2: 3	**S** righteousness, seek humility;	1335
	2: 3	Seek righteousness, s humility;	1335
Zec	8:21	the LORD and s the LORD Almighty.	2011
	8:22	to Jerusalem to s the LORD Almighty and	1335
	11:16	or s the young, or heal the injured,	1335
Mal	2: 7	from his mouth *men should* s instruction—	1335
Mt	6:33	s first his kingdom and his righteousness,	2426
	7: 7	s and you will find;	2426
Lk	11: 9	s and you will find;	2426
	12:31	But s his kingdom, and these things will be	2426
	19:10	For the Son of Man came *to* s and to save	2426
Jn	5:30	and my judgment is just, for *I* s not to please	2426
Ac	15:17	that the remnant of men *may* s the Lord,	1699
	17:27	God did this so that men would s him	2426
Ro	2: 7	by persistence in doing good s glory,	2426
	10:20	"I was found by those who *did* not s me;	2426
1Co	7:27	Are you married? *Do* not s a divorce.	2426
	10:24	Nobody *should* s his own good,	2426
Gal	2:17	"If, *while we* s to be justified in Christ,	2426
Heb	11: 6	that he rewards those who **earnestly** s him.	1699
1Pe	3:11	*he must* s peace and pursue it.	2426
Rev	9: 6	During those days men *will* s death,	2426

SEEKING (25) [SEEK]

Jdg	14: 4	who *was* s an occasion to confront	1335
	18: 1	in those days the tribe of the Danites *was* s	1335
1Sa	22:23	*man who is* s your life is seeking mine also.	1335
	22:23	man who is seeking your life *is* s mine also.	1335
1Ki	12:28	s **advice,** the king made two golden calves.	3619
2Ki	16: 5	I will use the bronze altar for s **guidance."**	1329
1Ch	22:19	Now devote your heart and soul to s	2011
2Ch	11:16	tribe of Israel who set their hearts on s	1335
	12:14	because he had not set his heart on s	2011
	19: 3	and have set your heart on s God."	2011
	30:19	who sets his heart on s God—	2011
Est	9: 2	to attack *those* s their destruction.	1335
Ps	37:32	in wait for the righteous, s their very lives;	1335
Pr	20:18	Make plans by s advice;	NIH
Jer	11:21	of Anathoth who *are* s your life and saying,	1335
	38: 4	This man *is* not s the good of these people	2011
	38:16	over to those who *are* s your life."	1335
	44:30	the enemy *who was* s his life.' "	1335
Mal	2:15	Because *he was* s godly offspring.	1335
	3: 1	the Lord you *are* s will come to his temple;	1335
Mt	12:43	it goes through arid places s rest and does	2426
Lk	11:24	it goes through arid places s rest and does	2426
Jn	8:50	*I am* not s glory for myself;	2426

Ac 13:11   s someone to lead him by the hand.   2426
1Co 10:33   not s my own good but the good of many,   2426

SEEKS (14) [SEEK]

Job 39:29   From there he s out his food;   2916
Ps 86:14   a band of ruthless men s my life—   1335
Pr 11:27   He who s good finds goodwill,   8838
14: 6   The mocker s wisdom and finds none,   1335
15:14   The discerning heart s knowledge,   1335
Isa 16: 5   in judging justice and speeds the cause   2011
56:11   each s his own gain.   4200
Jer 5: 1   but one person who deals honestly and s   1335
La 2:10   to the one who s him;   2011
Mt 7: 8   who asks receives; he who s finds;   2426
Lk 11:10   who asks receives; he who s finds;   2426
Jn 4:23   the kind of worshipers the Father s.   2426
8:50   there is one who s it, and he is the judge.   2426
Ro 3:11   no one who understands, no one who s God.   1699

SEEM (18) [SEEMED, SEEMS]

Lev 13:31   it does not s to be more than skin deep   5260
Ne 9:32   do not let all this hardship s trifling   AIT
Job 8: 7   Your beginnings will s humble,   2118
36:21   which you s to prefer to affliction.   AIT
Pr 16: 2   All a man's ways s innocent to him,   928+6524
21: 2   All a man's ways s right to him,   928+6524
Isa 5:28   their horses' hoofs s like flint,   3108
29:17   and the fertile field s like a forest?   3108
58: 2   they s eager to know my ways,   AIT
58: 2   They ask me for just decisions and s eager   AIT
Eze 16:51   made your sisters s righteous by all these   7405
21:23   It will s like a false omen   928+2118+6524
Hag 2: 3   Does it not s to you like nothing?   928+4017+6524
Zec 8: 6   "It may s marvelous to the remnant   928+6524
8: 6   but will it s marvelous to me?"   928+6524
1Co 12:22   that s to be weaker are indispensable,   1506
2Co 10: 9   not want to s to be trying to frighten you   1506
13: 7   even though we may s to have failed.   6055

SEEMED (17) [SEEM]

Ge 29:20   but they s like only a few days to him   928+2118+6524
34:18   Their proposal s good to Hamor   928+6524
41:37   The plan s good to Pharaoh and   928+6524
Nu 13:33   We s like grasshoppers in our own eyes,   2118
Dt 1:23   The idea s good to me;   928+6524
2Sa 3:19   it is impossible for him to do anything   928+6524
17: 4   This plan s good to Absalom and to all   928+6524
1Ch 13: 4   because it s right to all the people.   928+6524
2Ch 30: 4   The plan s right both to the king and to   928+6524
Jer 18: 4   shaping it as s best to him.   928+6524
Lk 1: 3   it s good also to me to write   1506
24:11   their words s to them like nonsense.   5743
Ac 2: 3   They saw what s to be tongues of fire   6059
15:28   It s good to the Holy Spirit and to us not   1506
Gal 2: 2   to those who s to be leaders,   1506
2: 6   As for those who s to be important—   1506
Rev 13: 3   One of the heads of the beast s to have had   6055

SEEMLY (KJV) See FITTING

SEEMS (23) [SEEM]

Jos 9:25   to us whatever s good and right to you.   928+6524
24:15   if serving the LORD s undesirable to you,   928+6524
1Sa 1:23   "Do what s best to you,"   928+6524
11:10   can do to us whatever s good to you."   928+6524
14:36   "Do whatever s best to you."   928+6524
14:40   "Do whatever s best to you," the men   928+6524
2Sa 15:26   him do to me whatever s good to him."   928+6524
18: 4   "I will do whatever s best to you."   928+6524
18:27   "It s to me that the first one runs   8011
1Ch 13: 2   "If it is good to you and if it is the will of   NIH
Ezr 7:18   then do whatever s best with the rest of   10320
Est 8: 8   in behalf of the Jews as s best to you,   928+6524
Job 15:21   when all s well, marauders attack him.   NIH
41:29   A club s to him but a piece of straw;   3108
Pr 12:15   The way of a fool s right in his own,   928+6524
14:12   There is a way that s right to a man,   4200+7156
16:25   There is a way that s right to a man,   4200+7156
18:17   The first to present his case s right,   NIH
Isa 32:15   and the fertile field s like a forest.   3108
Ac 17:18   "He s to be advocating foreign gods."   1506
1Co 4: 9   For it s to me that God has put us apostles   1506
16: 4   If it s advisable for me to go also,   AIT
Heb 12:11   No discipline s pleasant at the time,   1506

SEEN (218) [SEE]

Ge 16:13   "I have now s the One who sees me."   8011
24:30   As soon as he had s the nose ring,   8011
29:32   "It is because the LORD has s my misery.   8011
31:12   for I have s all that Laban has been doing   8011
31:42   But God has s my hardship and the toil   8011
41:19   I had never s such ugly cows in all the land   8011
44:28   And I have not s him since.   8011
45:13   in Egypt and about everything you have s.   8011
46:30   since I have s for myself that you   7156+8011
Ex 3: 7   "I have indeed s the misery of my people in Egypt.   8011+8011
3: 9   and I have s the way the Egyptians are   8011
3:16   I have watched over you and have s   7212+7212
4:31   about them and had s their misery,   8011
10: 5   the face of the ground so that it cannot be s.   8011

Ex 10: 6   nor your forefathers have ever s from   8011
13: 7   with yeast in it is to be s among you,   8011
13: 7   nor shall any yeast be s anywhere   8011
19: 4   'You yourselves have s what I did to Egypt,   8011
20:22   'You have s for yourselves that I have   8011
32: 9   "I have s these people,"   8011
33:23   but my face must not be s."   8011
34: 3   with you or be s anywhere on the mountain;   8011
Lev 5: 1   to testify regarding something he has s   8011
14:35   'I have s something that looks like mildew   8011
Nu 14:14   O LORD, have been s face to face,   8011
23:21   "No misfortune is s in Jacob,   5564
27:13   After you have s it,   8011
Dt 1:19   dreadful desert that you have s,   8011
3:21   "You have s with your own eyes all that   8011
4: 9   the things your eyes have s or let them slip   8011
5:24   Today we have s that a man can live even   8011
9:13   the LORD said to me, "I have s this people,   8011
29: 2   Your eyes have s all that the LORD did   8011
Jos 23: 3   You yourselves have s everything   8011
Jdg 2: 7   and who had s all the great things   8011
5: 8   or spear was s among forty thousand   8011
6:22   I have s the angel of the LORD face   8011
9:48   Do what you have s me do!"   8011
13:22   "We have s God!"   8011
14: 2   "I have s a Philistine woman in Timnah,   8011
18: 9   We have s that the land is very good.   8011
19:30   "Such a thing has never been s or done,   8011
1Sa 16:18   "I have s a son of Jesse of Bethlehem   8011
23:22   and who has s him there.   8011
24:10   This day you have s with your own eyes   8011
2Sa 17:17   they could not risk being s entering the city.   8011
18:21   "Go, tell the king what you have s."   8011
1Ki 6:18   Everything was cedar; no stone was to be s.   8011
8: 8   so long that their ends could be s from   8011
10:12   or s since that day.)   8011
2Ki 14:26   The LORD had s how bitterly everyone   8011
20: 5   I have heard your prayer and s your tears;   8011
23:24   the other detestable things s in Judah   8011
1Ch 29:17   And now I have s with joy how willingly   8011
2Ch 5: 9   could be s from in front of the inner   8011
9:11   Nothing like them had ever been s in Judah.   8011
Ezr 3:12   who had s the former temple,   8011
Est 9:26   in this letter and because of what they had s   8011
Job 5: 3   I myself have s a fool taking root,   8011
13: 1   "My eyes have s all this,   8011
15:17   let me tell you what I have s,   2600
20: 7   those who have s him will say,   8011
27:12   You have all s this yourselves.   2600
28: 7   no falcon's eye has s it.   8812
31:19   if I have s anyone perishing for lack of   8011
36:25   All mankind has s it;   2600
38:17   Have you s the gates of the shadow   8011
38:22   of the snow or s the storehouses of the hail,   8011
42: 5   heard of you but now my eyes have s you.   8011
Ps 35:21   With our own eyes we have s it."   8011
35:22   O LORD, you have s this; be not silent.   8011
37:25   yet I have never s the righteous forsaken   8011
37:35   I have s a wicked and ruthless man   8011
48: 8   so have we s in the city of the LORD   8011
63: 2   I have s you in the sanctuary   2600
77:19   though your footprints were not s.   3359
90:15   for as many years as we have s trouble.   8011
92:11   My eyes have s the defeat of my   5564
95: 9   though they had s what I did.   8011
98: 3   of the earth have s the salvation of our God.   8011
Pr 25: 7   than for him to s you with your eyes   8011
Ecc 1:14   I have s all the things that are done under   8011
3:10   I have s the burden God has laid on men.   8011
4: 3   who has not s the evil that is done under   8011
5:13   I have s a grievous evil under the sun: 8011
6: 1   I have s another evil under the sun,   8011
7:15   In this meaningless life of mine I have s   8011
9:11   I have s something else under the sun: 8011
10: 5   There is an evil I have s under the sun,   8011
10: 7   I have s slaves on horseback,   8011
SS 3: 3   "Have you s the one my heart loves?"   8011
Isa 6: 5   and my eyes have s the King,   8011
9: 2   The people walking in darkness have s   8011
38: 5   I have heard your prayer and s your tears;   8011
41: 5   The islands have s it and fear;   8011
42:20   You have s many things,   8011
57:18   I have s his ways, but I will heal him;   8011
58: 3   they say, 'and you have not s it?'   8011
64: 4   no eye has s any God besides you,   8011
66: 8   Who has ever s such things?   8011
66:19   not heard of my fame or s my glory.   8011
Jer 1:12   "You have s correctly,   8011
3: 6   "Have you s what faithless Israel has done?   8011
13:26   over your face that your shame may be s—   8011
13:27   I have s your detestable acts on the hills   8011
23:14   of Jerusalem I have s something horrible: 8011
La 1: 8   for they have s her nakedness;   8011
3: 1   I am the man who has s affliction by the rod   8011
3:59   You have s, O LORD, the wrong done to me.   8011
3:60   You have s the depth of their vengeance,   8011
Eze 3:23   like the glory I had s by the Kebar River,   8011
8: 4   as in the vision I had s in the plain.   8011
8:12   have you s what the elders of the house   8011
8:17   said to me, "Have you s this, son of man?   8011
10: 8   of the cherubim could be s what looked like   8011
10:15   These were the living creatures I had s by   8011
10:20   the living creatures I had s beneath the God   8011
10:22   same appearance as those I had s by   8011
11:24   Then the vision I had s went up from me,   8011
13: 3   follow their own spirit and have s nothing!   8011
13: 7   Have you not s false visions   2600

Eze 16:50   I did away with them as you have s.   8011
43: 3   The vision I saw was like the vision I had s   8011
43: 3   like the visions I had s by the Kebar River,   8011
Da 8: 6   toward the two-horned ram I had s standing   8011
9:21   the man I had s in the earlier vision,   8011
11:19   he will stumble and fall, to be s no more.   5162
Hos 6:10   I have s a horrible thing in the house   8011
9:13   I have s Ephraim, like Tyre,   8011
Mt 2: 9   the star they had s in the east went ahead   3972
4:16   the people living in darkness have s   3972
6: 1   before men, to be s by them.   2517
6: 5   and on the street corners to be s by men.   5743
9:33   like this has ever been s in Israel."   5743
17: 9   "Don't tell anyone what you have s,   3969
Mk 2:12   "We have never s anything like this!"   3972
5:16   Those who had s it told the people   3972
9: 9   to tell anyone what they had s until the Son   3972
16:11   that Jesus was alive and that she had s him,   2517
16:14   to believe those who had s him   2517
Lk 1:22   They realized he had s a vision in the temple,   3972
2:17   When they had s him, they spread the word   3972
2:20   for all the things they had heard and s,   3972
2:26   not die before he had s the Lord's Christ.   3972
2:30   For my eyes have s your salvation,   3972
5:26   "We have s remarkable things today."   3972
7:22   to John what you have s and heard: 3972
8:36   Those who had s it told the people how   3972
9:36   and told no one at that time what they had s.   3972
19:37   loud voices for all the miracles they had s: 3972
24:23   told us that they had s a vision of angels,   3972
Jn 1:14   We have s his glory, the glory of the One   2517
1:18   No one has ever s God,   3972
1:34   I have s and I testify that this is the Son   3972
3:11   and we testify to what we have s,   3972
3:21   so that it may be s plainly that what he has   5746
3:32   He testifies to what he has s and heard,   3972
4:45   They had s all that he had done in Jerusalem   3972
5:37   have never heard his voice nor s his form,   3972
6:36   you have s me and still you do not believe.   3972
6:46   No one has s the Father except the one   3972
6:46   only he has s the Father.   3972
8:38   I am telling you what I have s in   3972
8:57   "and you have s Abraham!"   3972
9: 8   who had formerly s him begging asked,   2555
9:37   Jesus said, "You have now s him;   3972
11:45   and had s what Jesus did,   2517
14: 7   you do know him and have s him."   3972
14: 9   Anyone who has s me has seen the Father.   3972
14: 9   Anyone who has seen me has s the Father.   3972
15:24   But now they have s these miracles,   3972
20:18   with the news: "I have s the Lord!"   3972
20:25   disciples told him, "We have s the Lord!"   3972
20:29   told him, "Because you have s me,   3972
20:29   blessed are those who have not s and   3972
Ac 4:20   in the same way you have s him go   2517
4:20   about what we have s and heard."   3972
7:34   I have indeed s the oppression of my people in Egypt.   3972+3972
7:44   according to the pattern he had s.   3972
9:12   In a vision he has s a man named Ananias   3972
9:27   He told them how Saul on his journey had s   3972
10:40   on the third day and caused him to be s.   1871
10:41   He was not s by all the people,   NIG
11:13   how he had s an angel appear in his house   3972
13:31   and for many days he was s   3972
16:10   After Paul had s the vision,   3972
21:29   (They had previously s Trophimus   1639+4632
22:15   to all men of what you have s and heard.   3972
26:16   and as a witness of what you have s of me   3972
Ro 1:20   and divine nature—have been clearly s,   2775
8:24   But hope that is s is no hope at all.   1063
1Co 2: 9   However, as it is written: "No eye has s,   3972
9: 1   Have I not s Jesus our Lord?   3972
2Co 4:18   So we fix our eyes not on what is s,   1063
4:18   For what is s is temporary,   1063
5:12   in what is s rather than in what is in   4725
Php 4: 9   or s in me—put it into practice.   3972
Col 2:18   into great detail about what he has s,   3972
1Ti 3:16   a body, was vindicated by the Spirit, was s   3972
6:16   whom no one has s or can see.   3972
Heb 11: 3   so that what is s was not made out   1063
11: 7   when warned about things not yet s,   1063
Jas 5:11   of Job's perseverance and have s what   3972
1Pe 1: 8   Though you have not s him, you love him;   3972
1Jn 1: 1   which we have s with our eyes,   3972
1: 2   we have s it and testify to it,   3972
1: 3   We proclaim to you what we have s   3972
2: 8   its truth is s in him and you,   NIG
3: 6   to sin has either s him or known him.   3972
4:12   No one has ever s God;   2517
4:14   And we have s and testify that   2517
4:20   whom he has s, cannot love God,   3972
4:20   cannot love God, whom he has not s.   3972
3Jn 1:11   who does what is evil has not s God.   3972
Rev 1:19   "Write, therefore, what you have s,   3972
10: 5   the angel I had s standing on the sea and on   3972
11:19   and within his temple was s the ark   3972
22: 8   And when I had heard and s them,   1063

SEER (21) [SEER'S, SEERS]

1Sa 9: 9   he would say, "Come, let us go to the s,"   8014
9: 9   the prophet of today used to be called a s.)   8014
9:11   and they asked them, "Is the s here?"   8014
9:19   "I am the s," Samuel replied.   8014
2Sa 15:27   said to Zadok the priest, "Aren't you a s?   8014

2Sa	24:11	to Gad the prophet, David's **s**:	2602
1Ch	9:22	of trust by David and Samuel the **s**.	8014
	21: 9	The LORD said to Gad, David's **s**,	2602
	25: 5	All these were sons of Heman the king's **s**.	2602
	26:28	And everything dedicated by Samuel the **s**	8014
	29:29	in the records of Samuel the **s**,	8014
	29:29	the prophet and the records of Gad the **s**,	2602
2Ch	9:29	the Shilonite and in the visions of Iddo the **s**	2602
	12:15	of Shemaiah the prophet and of Iddo the **s**	2602
	16: 7	At that time Hanani the **s** came to Asa king	8014
	16:10	Asa was angry with the **s** because of this;	8014
	19: 2	Jehu the **s**, the son of Hanani, went out	2602
	29:25	by David and Gad the king's **s** and Nathan	2602
	29:30	the words of David and of Asaph the **s**.	2602
	35:15	Asaph, Heman and Jeduthun the king's **s**.	2602
Am	7:12	Amaziah said to Amos, "Get out, you **s**!	2602

SEER'S (1) [SEER]

1Sa	9:18	please tell me where the **s** house is?"	8014

SEERS (6) [SEER]

2Ki	17:13	and Judah through all his prophets and **s**:	2602
2Ch	33:18	to his God and the words the **s** spoke to him	2602
	33:19	all are written in the records of the **s**.	2602
Isa	29:10	he has covered your heads (the **s**).	2602
	30:10	They say to the **s**, "See no more visions!"	8014
Mic	3: 7	The **s** will be ashamed and the diviners	2602

SEES (52) [SEE]

Ge	16:13	"You are the God *who* **s** me," for she said,	8024
	16:13	"I have now seen the *One who* **s** me."	8011
	44:31	**s** that the boy isn't there, he will die.	8011
	49:15	When *he* **s** how good is his resting place and	8011
Ex	4:14	and his heart will be glad when *he* **s** you.	8011
Lev	13: 5	if *he* **s** that the sore is unchanged and	928+6524
	13:15	When the priest **s** the raw flesh,	8011
Nu	12: 8	*he* **s** the form of the LORD.	5564
	24: 3	the oracle of one whose eye **s clearly**,	9280
	24: 4	who **s** a vision from the Almighty,	2600
	24:15	the oracle of one whose eye **s clearly**,	9280
	24:16	*who* **s** a vision from the Almighty,	2600
Dt	12: 8	everyone as he **s** fit,	928+6524
	32:36	when *he* **s** their strength is gone	8011
Job	7: 8	eye *that now* **s** me will see me no longer;	8011
	10: 4	Do you see as a mortal **s**?	8011
	11:11	and when *he* **s** evil, does he not take note?	8011
	28:24	the ends of the earth and **s** everything under	8011
	33:26	*he* **s** God's face and shouts for joy;	8011
	34:21	*he* **s** their every step.	8011
Ps	10:11	he covers his face and never **s**."	8011
	33:13	the LORD looks down and **s** all mankind;	8011
	97: 4	the earth **s** and trembles.	8011
Pr	22: 3	A prudent man **s** danger and takes refuge,	8011
	28:11	a poor man who has discernment **s through**	2983
	31:18	*She* **s** that her trading is profitable.	3247
Ecc	6: 9	Better *what* the eye **s** than the roving of	5260
Isa	11: 3	not judge by **what** he **s** with his eyes,	5260
	21: 6	a lookout and have him report what *he* **s**.	8011
	21: 7	When *he* **s** chariots with teams of horses,	8011
	28: 4	as someone **s** it and takes it in his hand,	8011
	29:15	in darkness and think, "Who **s** us?	8011
	47:10	and have said, 'No one **s** me.'	8011
La	3:50	the LORD looks down from heaven and **s**.	8011
Eze	12:27	vision he **s** is for many years from now,	2600
	18:14	a son *who* **s** all the sins his father commits,	8011
	18:14	and though *he* **s** them, he does not do such	8011
	33: 3	and *he* **s** the sword coming against the land	8011
	33: 6	the watchman **s** the sword coming and does	8011
	39:15	the land and *one of them* **s** a human bone,	8011
Mt	6: 4	your Father, who **s** what is done in secret,	1063
	6: 6	your Father, who **s** what is done in secret,	1063
	6:18	your Father, who **s** what is done in secret,	1063
Lk	14:29	everyone who **s** it will ridicule him,	2555
Jn	5:19	he can do only what *he* **s** his Father doing,	1063
	10:12	So when *he* **s** the wolf coming,	2555
	11: 9	for *he* **s** by this world's light.	1063
	12:45	he looks at me, *he* **s** the one who sent me.	2555
	14:17	because *it* neither **s** him nor knows him.	2555
1Co	8:10	with a weak conscience **s** you who have this knowledge eating	3972
1Jn	3:17	and **s** his brother in need but has no pity	2555
	5:16	If anyone **s** his brother commit a sin	3972

SEGUB (3)

1Ki	16:34	at the cost of his youngest son **S**,	8437
1Ch	2:21	and she bore him **S**.	8437
	2:22	**S** was the father of Jair,	8437

SEIR (39)

Ge	14: 6	and the Horites in the hill country of **S**,	8541
	32: 3	of him to his brother Esau in the land of **S**,	8541
	33:14	until I come to my lord in **S**."	8541
	33:16	that day Esau started on his way back to **S**.	8541
	36: 8	Edom) settled in the hill country of **S**.	8541
	36: 9	of the Edomites in the hill country of **S**.	8541
	36:20	These were the sons of **S** the Horite,	8543
	36:21	of **S** in Edom were Horite chiefs.	8543
	36:30	according to their divisions, in the land of **S**.	8541
Nu	24:18	Edom will be conquered; **S**, his enemy,	8541
Dt	1: 2	to Kadesh Barnea by the Mount **S** road.)	8541
	1:44	and beat you down from **S** all the way	8541
	2: 1	around the hill country of **S**.	8541
	2: 4	the descendants of Esau, who live in **S**.	8541
	2: 5	I have given Esau the hill country of **S**	8541

Dt	2: 8	the descendants of Esau, who live in **S**.	8541
	2:12	Horites used to live in **S**,	8541
	2:22	the descendants of Esau, who lived in **S**,	8541
	2:29	the descendants of Esau, who live in **S**,	8541
	33: 2	from Sinai and dawned over them from **S**;	8541
Jos	11:17	which rises toward **S**,	8541
	12: 7	toward **S** (their lands Joshua gave as	8541
	15:10	from Baalah to Mount **S**,	8542
	24: 4	I assigned the hill country of **S** to Esau,	8541
Jdg	5: 4	"O LORD, when you went out from **S**,	8541
1Ch	1:38	The sons of **S**: Lotan, Shobal, Zibeon,	8543
	4:42	invaded the hill country of **S**.	8541
2Ch	20:10	and Mount **S**, whose territory you would	8541
	20:22	and Mount **S** who were invading Judah,	8541
	20:23	against the men from Mount **S** to destroy	8541
	20:23	finished slaughtering the men from **S**,	8541
	25:11	where he killed ten thousand men of **S**.	8541
	25:14	the gods of the people of **S**.	8541
Isa	21:11	Someone calls to me from **S**, "Watchman,	8541
Eze	25: 8	'Because Moab and **S** said, "Look,	8541
	35: 2	set your face against Mount **S**;	8541
	35: 3	I am against you, Mount **S**,	8541
	35: 7	I will make Mount **S** a desolate waste	8541
	35:15	You will be desolate, O Mount **S**,	8541

SEIRAH (1)

Jdg	3:26	He passed by the idols and escaped to **S**.	8545

SEIZE (29) [SEIZED, SEIZES, SEIZING, SEIZURES]

Ge	43:18	and **s** us as slaves and take our donkeys."	4374
Jdg	7:24	"Come down against the Midianites and **s**	4334
	21:21	the vineyards and each of you **s** a wife from	2642
1Ki	13: 4	from the altar and said, "**S** him!"	9530
	18:40	"**S** the prophets of Baal.	9530
	20: 6	*They will* **s** everything you value	928+3338+8492
1Ch	7:21	when they went down to **s** their livestock,	4374
Job	3: 6	That night—may thick darkness **s** it;	4374
Ps	21: 8	your right hand *will* **s** your foes.	5162
	71:11	pursue him and **s** him,	9530
	109:11	*May* a creditor **s** all he has;	5943
Isa	3: 6	A man *will* **s** one of his brothers	9530
	5:29	as *they* **s** their prey and carry it off	296
	10: 6	to **s** loot and snatch plunder,	8964
	13: 8	**Terror** *will* **s** *them*, pain	987
	21: 3	pangs **s** me, like those of a woman in labor;	296
Jer	12:14	"As for all my wicked neighbors who **s**	5595
Eze	38:13	and goods and to **s** much plunder?" '	8964
Da	11: 6	He will also **s** their gods,	NIH
	11:21	and *he will* **s** it through intrigue.	2616
Am	9: 3	there I will hunt them down and **s** them,	4374
Ob	1:13	nor **s** their wealth in the day	8938
Mic	2: 2	They covet fields and **s** them, and houses,	1608
Hab	1: 6	across the whole earth to **s** dwelling places	3769
Zec	14:13	Each man *will* **s** the hand of another,	2616
Jn	7:30	At this they tried *to* **s** him,	4389
	7:44	Some wanted *to* **s** him,	4389
	10:39	Again they tried *to* **s** him,	4389
Ac	12: 3	he proceeded *to* **s** Peter also.	5197

SEIZED (53) [SEIZE]

Ge	14:11	The four kings **s** all the goods of Sodom	4374
	21:25	of water that Abimelech's servants *had* **s**.	1608
	34:28	*They* **s** their flocks and herds and donkeys	4374
Ex	15:15	leaders of Moab *will be* **s** with trembling,	296
Jdg	12: 6	*they* **s** him and killed him at the fords of	296
	16:21	Then the Philistines **s** him,	296
1Sa	17:35	When it turned on me, *I* **s** it by its hair,	2616
2Sa	4:10	I **s** him and put him to death in Ziklag.	296
	10: 4	So Hanun **s** David's men,	4374
1Ki	18:40	*They* **s** them, and Elijah had them brought	9530
	21:19	not murdered a man and **s** his **property**?'	3769
2Ki	11:16	So *they* **s** her as she reached the place	3338+8492
	17: 4	Shalmaneser **s** him and put him in prison.	6806
1Ch	5:21	*They* **s** the livestock of the Hagrites—	8647
	19: 4	So Hanun **s** David's men, shaved them,	4374
2Ch	23:15	*they* **s** her as she reached the entrance	3338+8492
Est	8:17	because fear of the Jews *had* **s** them.	5877+6584
	9: 3	because fear of Mordecai *had* **s** them.	5877+6584
Job	4:14	fear and trembling **s** me	7925
	16:12	*he* **s** me by the neck and crushed me.	296
	18:20	men of the east *are* **s** with horror.	296
	20:19	*he has* **s** houses he did not build.	1608
	24: 9	the infant of the poor *is* **s for a debt**.	2471
Ps	48: 6	Trembling **s** them there,	296
	56: T	When the Philistines *had* **s** him in Gath.	296
Isa	10:10	As my hand **s** the kingdoms of the idols,	5162
Jer	26: 8	the prophets and all the people **s** him	9530
	49:24	anguish and pain *have* **s** her,	296
	51:32	the river crossings **s**, the marshes set on fire,	9530
	51:41	the boast of the whole earth **s**!	9530
Mt	21:35	"The tenants **s** his servants;	3284
	22: 6	The rest **s** his servants,	3195
	26:50	**s** Jesus and arrested him.	2093+2095+3836+5931
	27: 3	he *was* **s with remorse** and returned	3564
Mk	14: 3	But they **s** him, beat him and sent him away	3284
	14:46	men **s** Jesus and arrested him.	2095+3836+5931
	14:51	When *they* **s** him,	3195
Lk	8:29	Many times *it had* **s** him,	5275
	23:26	led him away, *they* **s** Simon from Cyrene,	2138
Jn	7:30	Yet no one **s** him, because his time *had* not	4389
Ac	4: 3	*They* **s** Peter and John,	2095+3836+5931
	5: 5	great fear **s** all who heard what had happened.	1181+2093

Ac	5:11	Great fear **s** the whole church	1181+2093
	6:12	*They* **s** Stephen and brought him before	5275
	16:19	they **s** Paul and Silas and dragged them into	2138
	19:17	they *were* all **s with fear**,	2158+5832
	19:29	The people **s** Gaius and Aristarchus,	5275
	21:27	They stirred up the whole crowd and **s** him,	2093+2095+3836+5931
	23:27	This man *was* **s** by the Jews and they were	5197
	24: 6	tried to desecrate the temple, so *we* **s** him.	3195
	26:21	the Jews **s** me in the temple courts and tried	5197
1Co	10:13	No temptation *has* **s** you except what is common to man.	3284
Rev	20: 2	*He* **s** the dragon, that ancient serpent,	3195

SEIZES (8) [SEIZE]

Dt	25:11	and **s** him by his private parts,	2616
Job	18: 9	A trap **s** him by the heel;	296
	21: 6	I am terrified; trembling **s** my body.	296
Ps	137: 9	*he* who **s** your infants and dashes them	296
Pr	26:17	Like *one who* **s** a dog by the ears is	2616
Mic	4: 9	pain **s** you like that of a woman in labor?	2616
Mk	9:18	Whenever *it* **s** him, it throws him to the	2898
Lk	9:39	A spirit **s** him and he suddenly screams;	3284

SEIZING (4) [SEIZE]

Lk	22:54	Then **s** him, they led him away	5197
Ac	21:30	**S** Paul, they dragged him from the temple,	2138
Ro	7: 8	But sin, **s** the opportunity afforded by	3284
	7:11	For sin, **s** the opportunity afforded by	3284

SEIZURES (2) [SEIZE]

Mt	4:24	the demon-possessed, those *having* **s**,	4944
	17:15	"He *has* **s** and is suffering greatly.	4944

SELA (4) [SELA HAMMAHLEKOTH]

Jdg	1:36	the Amorites was from Scorpion Pass to **S**	6153
2Ki	14: 7	the Valley of Salt and captured **S** in battle,	6153
Isa	16: 1	from **S**, across the desert,	6153
	42:11	Let the people of **S** sing for joy;	6153

SELA HAMMAHLEKOTH (1) [SELA]

1Sa	23:28	That is why they call this place **S**.	6154

SELAH (74)

Ps	3: 2	"God will not deliver him." **S**	6138
	3: 4	he answers me from his holy hill. **S**	6138
	3: 8	blessing be on your people. **S**	6138
	4: 2	love delusions and seek false gods? **S**	6138
	4: 4	search your hearts and be silent. **S**	6138
	7: 5	make me sleep in the dust. **S**	6138
	9:16	by the work of their hands. Higgaion. **S**	6138
	9:20	nations know they are but men. **S**	6138
	20: 3	and accept your burnt offerings. **S**	6138
	21: 2	not withheld the request of his lips. **S**	6138
	24: 6	who seek your face, O God of Jacob. **S**	6138
	24:10	he is the King of glory. **S**	6138
	32: 4	in the heat of summer. **S**	6138
	32: 5	you forgave the guilt of my sin. **S**	6138
	32: 7	surround me with songs of deliverance. **S**	6138
	39: 5	each man's life is but a breath. **S**	6138
	39:11	each man is but a breath. **S**	6138
	44: 8	we will praise your name forever. **S**	6138
	46: 3	mountains quake with their surging. **S**	6138
	46: 7	the God of Jacob is our fortress. **S**	6138
	46:11	the God of Jacob is our fortress. **S**	6138
	47: 4	the pride of Jacob, whom he loved. **S**	6138
	48: 8	God makes her secure forever. **S**	6138
	49:13	who approve their sayings. **S**	6138
	49:15	he will surely take me to himself. **S**	6138
	50: 6	for God himself is judge. **S**	6138
	52: 3	rather than speaking the truth. **S**	6138
	52: 5	uproot you from the land of the living. **S**	6138
	54: 3	men without regard for God. **S**	6138
	55: 7	and stay in the desert. **S**	6138
	55:19	will hear and afflict them—**S**	6138
	57: 3	rebuking those who hotly pursue me; **S**	6138
	57: 6	fallen into it themselves. **S**	6138
	59: 5	mercy to wicked traitors. **S**	6138
	59:13	that God rules over Jacob. **S**	6138
	60: 4	against the bow. **S**	6138
	61: 4	the shelter of your wings. **S**	6138
	62: 4	in their hearts they curse. **S**	6138
	62: 8	God is our refuge. **S**	6138
	66: 4	sing praise to your name." **S**	6138
	66: 7	rise up against him. **S**	6138
	66:15	will offer bulls and goats. **S**	6138
	67: 1	and make his face shine upon us, **S**	6138
	67: 4	the nations of the earth. **S**	6138
	68: 7	through the wasteland, **S**	6138
	68:19	bears our burdens. **S**	6138
	68:32	sing praise to the Lord, **S**	6138
	75: 3	who hold its pillars firm. **S**	6138
	76: 3	the weapons of war. **S**	6138
	76: 9	the afflicted of the land. **S**	6138
	77: 3	and my spirit grew faint. **S**	6138
	77: 9	in anger withheld his compassion?" **S**	6138
	77:15	descendants of Jacob and Joseph. **S**	6138
	81: 7	at the waters of Meribah. **S**	6138
	82: 2	show partiality to the wicked? **S**	6138
	83: 8	to the descendants of Lot. **S**	6138
	84: 4	they are ever praising you. **S**	6138
	84: 8	listen to me, O God of Jacob. **S**	6138
	85: 2	and covered all their sins. **S**	6138

Ps	87: 3	O city of God: S	6138
	87: 6	"This one was born in Zion." S	6138
	88: 7	overwhelmed me with all your waves. S	6138
	88:10	rise up and praise you? S	6138
	89: 4	throne firm through all generations.' " S	6138
	89:37	faithful witness in the sky." S	6138
	89:45	with a mantle of shame. S	6138
	89:48	the power of the grave? S	6138
	140: 3	poison of vipers is on their lips. S	6138
	140: 5	set traps for me along my path. S	6138
	140: 8	or they will become proud. S	6138
	143: 6	soul thirsts for you like a parched land. S	6138
Hab	3: 3	the Holy One from Mount Paran. S	6138
	3: 9	you called for many arrows. S	6138
	3:13	you stripped him from head to foot. S	6138

SELDOM (2)
Pr	25:17	S *set* foot in your neighbor's house—	3700
Ecc	5:20	He s reflects on the days of his life,	2221+4202

SELECT (6) [SELECTED, SELECTS]
Ex	12:21	at once and s the animals for your families	4374
	18:21	But s capable men from all the people—	2600
Nu	31:30	s one out of every fifty, whether persons,	4374
	35:11	s some towns to be your cities of refuge,	7936
Est	3: 7	in the presence of Haman to s a day and a	
		month.	3427+3427+4200+4946
Isa	66:21	And *I will* s some of them also to	4374

SELECTED (12) [SELECT]
Ge	18: 7	Then he ran to the herd and s a choice,	4374
	32:13	and from what he had with him *he's* a gift	4374
Ex	21: 8	the master who *has* s her for himself,	3585
Nu	18: 6	*I myself have* s your fellow Levites from	4374
	31:47	Moses s one out of every fifty persons	4374
Dt	1:23	*I* s twelve of you, one man from each tribe.	4374
2Sa	10: 9	so *he* s some of the best troops in Israel	1047
2Ki	7:14	So *they* s two chariots with their horses,	4374
1Ch	19:10	so *he* s some of the best troops in Israel	1047
Ezr	10:16	the priest s men who were family heads,	976
Est	2: 9	to her seven maids s from the king's palace	8011
Heb	5: 1	Every high priest *is* s from among men	3284

SELECTS (3) [SELECT]
Ex	21: 9	If *he* s her for his son,	3585
Pr	31:13	*She* s wool and flax and works	2011
Isa	40:20	to present such an offering s wood that will	1047

SELED (2)
1Ch	2:30	The sons of Nadab: S and Appaim.	6135
	2:30	S died without children.	6135

SELEUCIA (1)
Ac	13: 4	down to S and sailed from there to Cyprus.	4942

SELF (9) [HERSELF, HIMSELF, ITSELF, MYSELF, ONESELF, OURSELVES, SELFISH, SELVES, THEMSELVES, YOURSELF, YOURSELVES]
Ex	32:13	to whom you swore by **your own** s:	3870
Lk	9:25	and yet lose or forfeit **his** very s?	1571
Ro	6: 6	that our old s was crucified with him so that	476
Eph	4:22	to put off your old s,	476
	4:24	and to put on the new s,	476
Col	3: 9	since you have taken off your old s	476
	3:10	and have put on the new s,	NIG
Phm	1: 19	to mention that you owe me **your very** s.	4932
1Pe	3: 4	it should be that of your inner s,	476+2840+3836

SELF-ABASEMENT (1)
Ezr	9: 5	at the evening sacrifice, I rose from my s,	9504

SELF-CONDEMNED (1) [CONDEMN]
Tit	3:11	such a man is warped and sinful; he is s.	896

SELF-CONFIDENCE (1) [CONFIDENCE]
Ne	6:16	were afraid and **lost** their s,	928+4394+5877+6524

SELF-CONFIDENT (1) [CONFIDENCE]
2Co	11:17	In this s boasting I am not talking as	5712

SELF-CONTROL (7) [CONTROL]
Pr	25:28	down is a man who lacks s.	4200+5110+8120
Ac	24:25	righteousness, s and the judgment to come,	1602
1Co	7: 5	not tempt you because of your **lack of** s.	202
Gal	5:23	gentleness and s. Against such things	1602
2Ti	3: 3	unforgiving, slanderous, **without** s, brutal,	203
2Pe	1: 6	and to knowledge, s;	1602
	1: 6	and to s, perseverance;	1602

SELF-CONTROLLED (11) [CONTROL]
1Th	5: 6	who are asleep, but *let us be* alert and s.	3768
	5: 8	since we belong to the day, *let us be* s,	3768
1Ti	3: 2	the husband of but one wife, temperate, s,	5409
Tit	1: 8	**who is** s, upright, holy and disciplined.	5409
	2: 2	worthy of respect, s, and sound in faith,	5409
	2: 5	to be s and pure, to be busy at home,	5409
	2: 6	encourage the young men *to be* s.	5404

Tit	2:12	and to live s, upright and godly lives	5407
1Pe	1:13	prepare your minds for action; *be* s;	3768
	4: 7	*be* clear minded and s so that you can pray.	3768
	5: 8	*Be* s and alert.	3768

SELF-DISCIPLINE (1) [DISCIPLINE]
2Ti	1: 7	but a spirit of power, of love and *of* s.	5406

SELF-IMPOSED (1) [IMPOSE]
Col	2:23	with their s **worship**,	1615

SELF-INDULGENCE (2) [INDULGE]
Mt	23:25	but inside they are full of greed and s.	202
Jas	5: 5	You have lived on earth in luxury and s.	5059

SELF-SEEKING (2) [SEEK]
Ro	2: 8	for those who are s and who reject the truth	2249
1Co	13: 5	It is not rude, *it is* not s,	1571+2426+3836

SELFISH (7) [SELF]
Ps	119:36	toward your statutes and not toward s **gain.**	1299
Pr	18: 1	An unfriendly man pursues s **ends;**	9294
Gal	5:20	discord, jealousy, fits of rage, s **ambition,**	2249
Php	1:17	The former preach Christ out of s **ambition,**	2249
	2: 3	of s **ambition** or vain conceit,	2249
Jas	3:14	if you harbor bitter envy and s **ambition**	2249
	3:16	For where you have envy and s **ambition,**	2249

SELFSAME (KJV) See SAME, VERY

SELL (39) [SALE, SALES, SELLER, SELLERS, SELLING, SELLS, SOLD]
Ge	23: 4	S me some property for a burial site here	5989
	23: 9	so *he will* s me the cave of Machpelah,	5989
	23: 9	Ask him *to* s it to me for the full price as	5989
	25:31	Jacob replied, "First s me your birthright."	4835
	37:27	*let's* s him to the Ishmaelites and	4835
	47:16	"*I will* s you food in exchange	5989
	47:22	That is why *they did* not s their land.	4835
Ex	21: 8	He has no right to s her to foreigners,	4835
	21:35	*to* s the live one and divide both the money	4835
Lev	25: 14	" 'If *you* s **land** to one of your	4835+4928
	25:15	*to* s to you on the basis of the number	4835
	25:37	at interest or s him food at a profit.	5989
Dt	2:28	S us food to eat and water to drink	8690
	14:21	or you *may* s it to a foreigner.	4835
	21:14	*You* **must** not s her or treat her as a slave,	928+2021+4084+4835+4835
1Ki	21: 6	'S me your vineyard;	928+4084+5989
	21:15	that he refused to s you.	928+4084+5989
2Ki	4: 7	"Go, s the oil and pay your debts.	4835
	7: 1	a seah of flour will s for a shekel	NIH
	7:18	a seah of flour *will* s **for** a shekel	928+2118
1Ch	21:22	S it to me at the full price."	5989
Ne	10:31	or grain to s on the Sabbath,	4835
Pr	11:26	but blessing crowns *him who is willing to* s.	8690
	23:23	Buy the truth and *do* not s it;	4835
Isa	50: 1	Or to which of my creditors *did I* s you?	4835
Eze	30:12	I will dry up the streams of the Nile and s	4835
	48:14	*They must* not s or exchange any of it.	4835
Joel	3: 8	*I will* s your sons and daughters to	4835
	3: 8	and *they will* s them to the Sabeans,	4835
Am	2: 6	They s the righteous for silver,	4835
	8: 5	be over that *we may* s grain, and the Sabbath	8690
Zec	11: 5	*Those who* s them say, 'Praise the LORD,	4835
Mt	19:21	go, s your possessions and give to the poor,	4797
	25: 9	go to those who s oil and buy some	4797
Mk	10:21	s everything you have and give to the poor,	4797
Lk	12:33	S your possessions and give to the poor.	4797
	18:22	S everything you have and give to the poor,	4797
	22:36	s your cloak and buy one.	4797
Rev	13:17	so that no one could buy or s unless he had	4797

SELLER (3) [SELL]
Isa	24: 2	for mistress as for maid, for s as for buyer,	4835
Eze	7:12	Let not the buyer rejoice nor the s grieve,	4835
	7:13	The s will not recover the land he has sold	4835

SELLERS (1) [SELL]
Ne	13:20	or twice the merchants and s *of* all kinds	4835

SELLING (16) [SELL]
Ge	25:33	an oath to him, s his birthright to Jacob.	4835
	45: 5	not be angry with yourselves for s me here,	4835
Lev	25:16	he *is* really s you is the number of crops.	4835
Ru	4: 3	*is* s the piece of land that belonged	4835
Ne	5: 8	Now you are s your brothers,	4835
	13:15	I warned them against s food on that day.	4835
	13:15	of merchandise and s them in Jerusalem on	4835
Am	8: 6	s even the sweepings with the wheat.	8690
Mt	21:12	drove out all who *were* buying and s there.	60
	21:12	and the benches *of* those who s doves.	4797
Mk	11:15	driving out those who were buying and s	60
	11:15	and the benches *of* those who s doves,	4797
Lk	17:28	buying and s, planting and building.	4797
	19:45	and began driving out those who *were* s.	4797
Jn	2:14	In the temple courts he found men s cattle,	4797
Ac	2:45	S their possessions and goods,	4405

SELLS (10) [SELL]
Ex	21: 7	"If a man s his daughter as a servant,	4835
	21:16	and either s him or still has him	4835
	22: 1	an ox or a sheep and slaughters it or s it,	4835
Lev	25:25	and s some of his property,	4835
	25:29	" 'If a man s a house in a walled city,	4835
	25:39	among you and s himself to you,	4835
	25:47	and s himself to the alien living among you	4835
Dt	15:12	s himself to you and serves you six years,	4835
	24: 7	and treats him as a slave or s him,	4835
Pr	31:24	She makes linen garments and s them,	4835

SELVEDGE (KJV) See END

SELVES (1) [SELF]
Ro	6:19	because you are weak *in* your **natural** s.	4922

SEM (KJV) See SHEM

SEMAKIAH (1)
1Ch	26: 7	his relatives Elihu and S were	6165

SEMEIN (1)
Lk	3:26	the son of Mattathias, the son *of* S,	4946

SEMEN (6)
Ge	38: 9	with his brother's wife, he spilled his s on	NIH
Lev	15:16	" 'When a man has an emission of s,	2446
	15:17	Any clothing or leather that has s on it must	2446
	15:18	with a woman and there is an emission of s,	2446
	15:32	unclean by an emission of s,	2446
	22: 4	or by anyone who has an emission of s,	2446

SENAAH (2)
Ezr	2:35	of S 3,630	6171
Ne	7:38	of S 3,930	6171

SENATE (KJV) See FULL ASSEMBLY

SEND (264) [SENDING, SENDS, SENT]
Ge	7: 4	Seven days from now I *will* s rain on	4763
	24: 7	he *will* s his angel before you so	8938
	24:40	*will* s his angel with you and	8938
	24:54	"S me **on my way** to my master."	8938
	24:56	S me **on** my **way** so I may go to my master.	8938
	27:45	*I'll* s **word** *for* you to come back	8938
	30:25	"S me **on** my **way** so I can go back	8938
	31:27	so *I could* s you **away** with joy and singing	8938
	37:13	Come, *I am going to* s you to them."	8938
	38:17	"I'll s you a young goat from my flock,"	8938
	38:17	something as a pledge until you s it?"	8938
	38:23	After all, *I did* s her this young goat,	8938
	42: 4	But Jacob *did* not s Benjamin,	8938
	42:16	S one of your number to get your brother;	8938
	43: 4	If *you will* s our brother along with us,	8938
	43: 5	But if you will not s him,	8938
	43: 8	"S the boy along with me and we will go	8938
Ex	4:13	"O Lord, please s someone else to do it."	8938
	8:21	I *will* s swarms of flies on you	8938
	9:14	or this time I *will* s the full force of my	8938
	9:18	at this time tomorrow I *will* s the worst	4763
	23:27	"I *will* s my terror ahead of you and throw	8938
	23:28	I *will* s the hornet ahead of you to drive	8938
	33: 2	I *will* s an angel before you and drive out	8938
	33:12	not let me know whom *you will* s	8938
	33:15	*do* not s us **up** from here.	6590
Lev	16:21	He *shall* s the goat **away** into the desert in	8938
	25:21	I *will* s you such a blessing in the sixth year	7422
	26: 4	I *will* s you rain in its season,	5989
	26:22	I *will* s wild animals against you,	8938
	26:25	I *will* s a plague among you,	8938
Nu	5: 2	*to* s **away** from the camp anyone who has	8938
	5: 3	S away male and female alike;	8938
	5: 3	s them outside the camp so they will	8938
	13: 2	"S some men to explore the land	8938
	13: 2	From each ancestral tribe s one	8938
	22:37	"*Did I* not s you an **urgent** summons?	8938+8938
	31: 4	S into battle a thousand men from each of	8938
	35:25	and s him **back** to the city of refuge	8740
Dt	1:22	"*Let us* s men ahead to spy out the land	8938
	7:20	the LORD your God *will* s the hornet	8938
	11:14	*I will* s rain on your land in its season,	5989
	15:13	*do* not s him away empty-handed.	8938
	19:12	the elders of his town *shall* s **for** him,	8938
	28: 8	The LORD *will* s a blessing	7422
	28:12	to s rain on your land in season and	5989
	28:20	The LORD *will* s on you curses,	8938
	28:59	the LORD *will* s **fearful** plagues on you	7098
	28:68	The LORD *will* s you **back** in ships	8740
	32:24	*I will* s wasting famine against them,	8938
	32:24	I *will* s against them the fangs of wild	NIH
Jos	1:16	and wherever *you* s us we will go.	8938
	7: 3	S two or three thousand men to take it	6590
	7: 3	*I will* s them **out** to make a survey of	6590
Jdg	20:38	with the ambush that they *should* s **up**	6590
1Sa	5:11	"S the ark of the god of Israel **away**;	8938
	6: 2	how *we should* s it **back** to its place."	8938
	6: 3	*do* not s it **away** empty,	8938
	6: 3	**by all means** s a guilt offering to him.	8740+8938
	6: 4	"What guilt offering *should we* s to him?"	8740
	6: 6	not s the Israelites **out** so they could go	8938

1Sa	6: 8	S it on its way,	8938
	9:16	"About this time tomorrow I will s you	8938
	9:26	s you on your way."	8938
	11: 3	so we can s messengers throughout Israel;	8938
	12:17	I will call upon the LORD to s thunder	5989
	16:11	Samuel said, "S for him;	2256+4374+8938
	16:19	"S me your son David,	8938
	19:17	and s my enemy away so that he escaped?"	8938
	20:12	will I not s you word and let you know?	8938
	20:13	not let you know and s you away safely.	8938
	20:21	Then I will s a boy and say, 'Go,	8938
	20:31	Now s and bring him to me,	8938
	29: 4	"S the man back, that he may return	8740
2Sa	11: 6	"S me Uriah the Hittite."	8938
	11:12	and tomorrow I will s you back.	8938
	13: 9	"S everyone out of here," Amnon said.	3655
	14:29	for Joab in order to s him to the king,	8938
	14:32	'Come here so I can s you to the king	8938
	15:36	S them to me with anything you hear."	8938
	17:16	Now s a message immediately	8938
	18:29	as Joab was about to s the king's servant	8938
	19:31	and to s him on his way from there.	8938
1Ki	8:36	and s rain on the land you gave your people	5989
	8:44	wherever you s them, and when they pray	8938
	18: 1	and I will s rain on the land."	5989
	20: 6	to s my officials to search your palace and	8938
	22:26	s him back to Amon the ruler of the city	8740
2Ki	2:16	"No," Elisha replied, "do not s them."	8938
	2:17	So he said, "S them."	8938
	4:22	"Please s me one of the servants and	8938
	5: 5	"I will s a letter to the king of Israel."	8938
	5: 7	Why does this fellow s someone to me to	8938
	6:13	"so I can s men and capture him."	8938
	7:13	let us s them to find out what happened."	8938
	9:17	S him to meet them and ask,	8938
	15:37	the LORD began to s Rezin king of Aram	8938
1Ch	13: 2	let us s word far and wide to the rest	8938
2Ch	2: 3	"S me cedar logs as you did	NIH
	2: 7	"S me, therefore, a man skilled to work	8938
	2: 8	"S me also cedar, pine and algum logs	8938
	2:15	"Now let my lord s his servants the wheat	8938
	6:27	and s rain on the land you gave your people	5989
	6:34	wherever you s them, and when they pray	8938
	7:13	or s a plague among my people,	8938
	18:25	s him back to Amon the ruler of the city	8740
	28:11	S back your fellow countrymen you have	8740
	30: 5	to s a proclamation throughout Israel,	6296
Ezr	5:17	let the king s us his decision in this matter.	10714
	10: 3	before our God to s away all these women	3655
Ne	2: 5	let him s me to the city in Judah	8938
	2: 6	It pleased the king to s me; so I set a time.	8938
	8:10	s some to those who have nothing prepared.	8938
	8:12	to s portions of food and to celebrate	8938
Job	1: 5	Job would s and have them purified.	8938
	14:20	change his countenance and s him away.	8938
	21:11	They s forth their children as a flock;	8938
	38:35	Do you s the lightning bolts on their way?	8938
Ps	20: 2	May he s you help from the sanctuary	8938
	43: 3	S forth your light and your truth,	8938
	104:30	When you s your Spirit, they are created,	8938
	144: 6	S forth lightning and scatter	1397+1398
Pr	10:26	so is a sluggard to those who s him.	8938
	14:22	for those two will s sudden destruction	7756
	25:13	a trustworthy messenger to those who s him;	8938
SS	7:13	The mandrakes s out their fragrance,	5989
Isa	6: 8	"Whom shall I s?	8938
	6: 8	"Here am I. S me!"	8938
	10: 6	I s him against a godless nation,	8938
	10:16	will s a wasting disease upon his sturdy	8938
	16: 1	S lambs as tribute to the ruler of the land,	8938
	19:20	he will s them a savior and defender,	8938
	30:23	also s you rain for the seed you sow in	5989
	34: 3	their dead bodies will s up a stench;	6590
	42:19	and deaf like the messenger I s?	8938
	42:22	with no one to say, "S them back."	8740
	43:14	"For your sake I will s to Babylon	8938
	48:20	S it out to the ends of the earth;	3655
	66:19	and I will s some of those who survive to	8938
Jer	1: 7	You must go to everyone I s you to	8938
	2:10	s to Kedar and observe closely;	8938
	8:17	I will s venomous snakes among you,	8938
	9:17	s for the most skillful of them.	8938
	14: 3	The nobles s their servants for water;	8938
	14:15	I did not s them, yet they are saying,	8938
	14:22	Do the skies themselves s down showers?	5989
	15: 1	S them away from my presence!	8938
	15: 3	"I will s four kinds of destroyers	7212
	16:16	"But now I will s for many fishermen,"	8938
	16:16	After that I will s for many hunters,	8938
	22: 7	I will s destroyers against you,	7727
	23:21	I did not s these prophets.	8938
	23:32	yet I did not s or appoint them.	8938
	24:10	I will s the sword,	8938
	25:15	the nations to whom I s you drink it.	8938
	25:16	and go mad because of the sword I will s	8938
	25:27	because of the sword I will s among you.'	8938
	27: 3	then s word to the kings of Edom, Moab,	8938
	29:17	"I will s the sword,	8938
	29:31	"S this message to all the exiles:	8938
	29:31	even though I did not s him,	8938
	37:20	Do not s me back to the house of Jonathan	8740
	38:26	not to s me back to Jonathan's house	8740
	43:10	I will s for my servant	2256+4374+8938
	48:12	"when I will s men who pour from jars,	8938
	51: 2	I will s foreigners to Babylon	8938
	51:27	s up horses like a swarm of locusts,	6590
	51:53	I will s destroyers against her,"	907+995+4946

Eze	5:17	I will s famine and wild beasts	8938
	13:11	and I will s hailstones hurtling down,	5989
	14:13	to cut off its food supply and s famine	8938
	14:15	"Or if I s wild beasts through that country	6296
	14:19	"Or if I s a plague into that land	8938
	14:21	How much worse will it be when I s	8938
	28:23	I will s a plague upon her	8938
	34:26	I will s down showers in season;	3718
	39: 2	and s you against the mountains of Israel.	995
	39: 6	I will s fire on Magog and	8938
Da	11:20	"His successor will s out a tax collector	6296
Hos	8:14	But I will s fire upon their cities	8938
Joel	3: 6	you might s them far from their homeland.	8178
Am	1: 4	I will s fire upon the house of Hazael	8938
	1: 7	I will s fire upon the walls of Gaza	8938
	1:10	I will s fire upon the walls of Tyre	8938
	1:12	I will s fire upon Teman	8938
	2: 2	I will s fire upon Moab that will consume	8938
	2: 5	I will s fire upon Judah that will consume	8938
	5:27	Therefore I will s you into exile	1655
	8:11	I will s a famine through the land—	8938
Zec	5: 4	'I will s it out, and it will enter the house	3655
Mal	2: 2	"I will s a curse upon you,	8938
	3: 1	"See, I will s my messenger,	8938
	4: 5	I will s you the prophet Elijah before	8938
Mt	8:31	s us into the herd of pigs."	690
	9:38	to s out workers into his harvest field."	1675
	11:10	" 'I will s my messenger ahead of you,	690
	13:41	The Son of Man will s out his angels,	690
	14:15	S the crowds away,	668
	15:23	"S her away, for she keeps crying out	668
	15:32	I do not want to s them away hungry,	668
	19: 7	a certificate of divorce and s her away?"	668
	21: 3	and he will s them right away."	690
	24:31	And he will s his angels with	690
Mk	1: 2	"I will s my messenger ahead of you,	690
	3:14	be with him and that he might s them out	690
	5:10	and again not to s them out of the area.	690
	5:12	"S us among the pigs,"	4287
	6:36	S the people away so they can go to	668
	8: 3	If I s them home hungry,	668
	10: 4	a certificate of divorce and s her away."	668
	11: 3	and will s it back here shortly.' "	690
	12: 6	"He had one left to s, a son,	NIG
	13:27	And he will s his angels and gather	690
Lk	7:27	" 'I will s my messenger ahead of you,	690
	9:12	"S the crowd away so they can go to	668
	10: 2	to s out workers into his harvest field.	1675
	11:49	"I will s them prophets and apostles,	690
	14:32	he will s a delegation while the other is still	690
	16:24	have pity on me and s Lazarus to dip the tip	4287
	16:27	father, s Lazarus to my father's house,	4287
	20:13	I will s my son, whom I love;	4287
	24:49	to s you what my Father has promised;	690
Jn	3:17	For God did not s his Son into the world	690
	13:20	whoever accepts anyone I s accepts me;	4287
	14:26	whom the Father will s in my name,	4287
	15:26	whom I will s to you from the Father,	4287
	16: 7	but if I go, I will s him to you.	4287
Ac	3:20	and that he may s the Christ,	690
	7:34	Now come, I will s you back to Egypt.'	690
	7:37	'God will s you a prophet like me	482
	7:43	Therefore I will s you into exile'	3579
	10: 5	Now s men to Joppa to bring back	4287
	10:32	S to Joppa for Simon who is called Peter.	4287
	11:13	'S to Joppa for Simon who is called Peter.	690
	15:22	of their own men and s them to Antioch	4287
	15:25	to choose some men and s them to you	4287
	22:21	I will s you far away to the Gentiles.' "	1990
	24:25	When I find it convenient, I will s for you."	3559
	25:21	I ordered him held until I could s him	402
	25:25	to the Emperor I decided to s him to Rome.	4287
	25:27	to s on a prisoner without specifying	4287
Ro	16:16	All the churches of Christ s greetings.	832
	16:23	our brother Quartus s you their greetings.	832
1Co	1:17	For Christ did not s me to baptize,	690
	16: 3	and s them with your gift to Jerusalem.	4287
	16:11	S him on his way in peace	4636
	16:19	in the province of Asia s you greetings.	832
	16:20	All the brothers here s greetings.	832
2Co	1:16	have you s me on my way to Judea.	4636
	13:13	All the saints s their greetings.	832
Php	2:19	in the Lord Jesus to s Timothy to you soon,	4287
	2:23	to s him as soon as I see how things go	4287
	2:25	But I think it is necessary to s back	4287
	2:28	Therefore I am all the more eager to s him,	4287
	4:21	The brothers who are with me s greetings.	832
	4:22	All the saints s you greetings,	832
Col	4:14	Luke, the doctor, and Demas s greetings.	832
Tit	3:12	As soon as I s Artemas or Tychicus to you,	4287
Heb	13:24	Those from Italy s you their greetings.	832
2Jn	1:13	of your chosen sister s their greetings.	832
3Jn	1: 6	s them on their way in a manner worthy	4636
	1:14	The friends here s their greetings.	832
Rev	1:11	"Write on a scroll what you see and s it to	4287

SENDING (44) [SEND]

Ge	32: 5	Now I am s this message to my lord,	8938
	32:20	"I will pacify him with these gifts I am s on	2143
Ex	3:10	I am s you to Pharaoh to bring my people	8938
	23:20	I am s an angel ahead of you to guard you	8938
Lev	16:10	to be used for making atonement by s it into	8938
Jdg	6:14	Am I not s you?"	8938
1Sa	6: 8	beside it put the gold objects you are s back	8740
	16: 1	I am s you to Jesse of Bethlehem.	8938

2Sa	10: 3	by s men to you to express sympathy?	8938
	13:16	"S me away would be	8938
1Ki	15:19	See, I am s you a gift of silver and gold.	8938
2Ki	1: 6	that you are s men to consult Baal-Zebub,	8938
	5: 6	"With this letter I am s my servant Naaman	8938
	6:32	you see how this murderer is s someone	8938
1Ch	19: 3	by s men to you to express sympathy?	8938
2Ch	2: 3	"I am s you Huram-Abi, a man of great skill	8938
	16: 3	See, I am s you silver and gold.	8938
Ezr	4:14	we are s this message to inform the king,	10714
Ne	6:17	of Judah were s many letters to Tobiah,	2143
Pr	26: 6	or drinking violence is the s of a message	8938
Jer	42: 6	whom we are s you, so that it will go well	8938
Eze	2: 3	"Son of man, I am s you to the Israelites,	8938
	2: 4	to whom I am s you are obstinate	8938
	17:15	by s his envoys to Egypt to get horses and	8938
Joel	2:13	"I am s you grain, new wine and oil,	NIH
	2:19	a God who relents from s calamity.	NIH
Jnh	4: 2	a God who relents from s calamity.	NIH
Mt	10:16	I am s you out like sheep among wolves.	690
	23:34	I am s you prophets and wise men	690
Lk	10: 3	I am s you out like lambs among wolves.	690
Jn	20:21	As the Father has sent me, I am s you."	4287
Ac	11:30	s their gift to the elders by Barnabas	690
	15:27	Therefore we are s Judas and Silas	690
	26:17	I am s you to them	690
Ro	8: 3	God did by s his own Son in the likeness	4287
1Co	4:17	For this reason I am s to you Timothy,	4287
2Co	8:18	And we are s along with him the brother	5225
	8:22	In addition, we are s with them our brother	5225
	9: 3	But I am s the brothers in order that	4287
Eph	6:22	I am s him to you for this very purpose,	4287
Col	4: 8	I am s him to you for the express purpose	4287
Phm	1:12	I am s him—who is my very heart—back	402
Rev	1: 1	by s his angel to his servant John,	690
	11:10	and will celebrate by s each other gifts,	4287

SENDS (30) [SEND]

Dt	24: 1	gives it to her and s her from his house,	8938
	24: 3	gives it to her and s her from his house,	8938
	28:48	you will serve the enemies the LORD s	8938
1Sa	2: 7	The LORD s poverty and wealth;	3769
Job	5:10	he s water upon the countryside.	8938
	12:24	he s them wandering through a trackless	9494
	37: 3	and s it to the ends of the earth.	NIH
Ps	57: 3	He s from heaven and saves me,	8938
	57: 3	God s his love and his faithfulness.	8938
	135: 7	he s lightning with the rain and brings out	6913
	147:15	He s his command to the earth;	8938
	147:18	He s his word and melts them;	8938
Isa	18: 2	which s envoys by sea in papyrus boats	8938
Jer	10:13	He s lightning with the rain and brings out	6913
	17: 8	the water that s out its roots by the stream.	8938
	42: 5	with everything the LORD your God s you	8938
	51:16	He s lightning with the rain and brings out	6913
Hos	12: 1	with Assyria and s olive oil to Egypt.	3297
Joel	2:23	He s you abundant showers,	3718
Zec	12: 2	to make Jerusalem a cup that s all	AIT
Mt	5:45	s rain on the righteous and the unrighteous.	1101
Ro	16:21	my fellow worker, s his greetings to you,	832
	16:23	s you his greetings.	832
Col	4:10	Aristarchus s you his greetings,	832
	4:11	Jesus, who is called Justus, also s greetings.	NIG
	4:12	and a servant of Christ Jesus, s greetings.	832
2Th	2:11	For this reason God s them a powerful	4287
Tit	3:15	Everyone with me s you greetings.	832
Phm	1:23	prisoner in Christ Jesus, s you greetings,	832
1Pe	5:13	together with you, s you her greetings,	832

SENEH (1)

1Sa	14: 4	one was called Bozez, and the other S.	6175

SENIR (4) [HERMON]

Dt	3: 9	the Amorites call it S.)	8536
1Ch	5:23	that is, to S (Mount Hermon).	8536
SS	4: 8	from the top of S, the summit of Hermon,	8536
Eze	27: 5	of pine trees from S;	8536

SENNACHERIB (15) [SENNACHERIB'S]

2Ki	18:13	S king of Assyria attacked all	6178
	19: 7	Now S received a report that Tirhakah,	NIH
	19:16	listen to the words S has sent to insult	6178
	19:20	I have heard your prayer concerning S king	6178
	19:36	So S king of Assyria broke camp	6178
2Ch	32: 1	S king of Assyria came and invaded Judah.	6178
	32: 2	When Hezekiah saw that S had come and	6178
	32: 9	when S king of Assyria and all his forces	6178
	32:10	"This is what S king of Assyria says:	6178
	32:22	from the hand of S king of Assyria	6178
Isa	36: 1	S king of Assyria attacked all	6178
	37: 9	Now S received a report that Tirhakah,	NIH
	37:17	listen to all the words S has sent to insult	6178
	37:21	to me concerning S king of Assyria,	6178
	37:37	So S king of Assyria broke camp	6178

SENNACHERIB'S (1) [SENNACHERIB]

2Ch	32:16	S officers spoke further against the LORD	2257S

SENSE (5) [SENSED, SENSELESS, SENSES, SENSIBLE, SENSITIVE, SENSITIVITY]

Dt	32:28	They are a nation without s,	6783

Job	39:17	with wisdom or give her a share of **good s**.	1069
Ecc	10: 3	the fool lacks **s** and shows everyone	4213
1Co	12:17	where would the **s of hearing** be?	198
	12:17	where would the **s of smell** be?	4018

SENSED (1) [SENSE]

Ac	27:27	the sailors **s** they were approaching land.	5706

SENSELESS (13) [SENSE]

Ps	49:10	and the **s** alike perish and leave their wealth	1280
	73:22	I was **s** and ignorant; I was a brute beast	1280
	92: 6	The **s** man does not know,	1280
	94: 8	Take heed, you **s** ones among the people;	1279
Isa	19:11	wise counselors of Pharaoh **give s** advice.	1279
Jer	4:22	They are **s** children;	6119
	5:21	you foolish and **s** people,	401+4213
	10: 8	*They are* all **s** and foolish.	1279
	10:14	Everyone *is* **s** and without knowledge;	1279
	10:21	The shepherds *are* **s** and do not inquire of	1279
	51:17	"Every man *is* **s** and without knowledge;	1279
Hos	7:11	easily deceived and **s**—	401+4213
Ro	1:31	they are **s**, faithless, heartless, ruthless.	852

SENSES (3) [SENSE]

Lk	15:17	"When he came to **his s**, he said,	1571
1Co	15:34	**Come back to** *your* **s** as you ought,	1729
2Ti	2:26	that *they will* **come to** *their* **s** and escape	392

SENSIBLE (2) [SENSE]

Job	18: 2	**Be s**, and then we can talk.	1067
1Co	10:15	I speak *to* **s people**;	5861

SENSITIVE (3) [SENSE]

Dt	28:54	Even the most gentle and **s** man	6697
	28:56	The most gentle and **s** *woman* among you—	6697
	28:56	so **s** and gentle that she would not venture	6695

SENSITIVITY (1) [SENSE]

Eph	4:19	*Having* **lost all s**, they have given themselves	556

SENSUAL (2) [SENSUALITY]

Col	2:23	lack any value in restraining **s** indulgence.	4922
1Ti	5:11	**s desires overcome their dedication to**	2952

SENSUALITY (1) [SENSUAL]

Eph	4:19	they have given themselves over *to* **s** so as	816

SENT (654) [SEND]

Ge	2: 5	the LORD God *had* not **s** rain on the earth	4763
	8: 1	and he **s** a wind over the earth,	6296
	8: 7	and **s** out a raven, and it kept flying	8938
	8: 8	Then *he* **s** out a dove to see if	8938
	8:10	He waited seven more days and again **s** out	8938
	8:12	and **s** the dove out again,	8938
	12:20	and *they* **s** him on his way,	906+8938
	19:13	against his people is so great that he *has* **s** us	8938
	20: 2	Then Abimelech king of Gerar **s** for Sarah	8938
	21:14	on her shoulders and then **s** her **off**	8938
	24:59	**s** their sister Rebekah **on her way**,	8938
	25: 6	the sons of his concubines and **s** them **away**	8938
	26:27	you were hostile to me and **s** me **away**?"	8938
	26:29	but always treated you well and **s** you **away**	8938
	26:31	Then Isaac **s** them **on their way**,	8938
	27:42	*she* **s** for her younger son Jacob	2256+7924+8938
	28: 5	Then Isaac **s** Jacob **on** *his* **way**,	8938
	28: 6	*had* **s** him to Paddan Aram to take a wife	8938
	31: 4	So Jacob **s word** to Rachel and Leah to come out	2256+7924+8938
	31:42	surely *have* **s** me **away** empty-handed.	8938
	32: 3	Jacob **s** messengers ahead of him	8938
	32:18	They are a gift **s** to my lord Esau,	8938
	32:23	After *he had* **s** them **across** the stream,	6296
	32:23	he **s over** all his possessions.	6296
	37:14	*he* **s** him **off** from the Valley of Hebron.	8938
	38:20	Meanwhile Judah **s** the young goat	8938
	38:25	she **s a message** to her father-in-law.	8938
	41: 8	so *he* **s for** all the magicians and wise men	2256+7924+8938
	41:14	So Pharaoh **s for** Joseph,	2256+7924+8938
	44: 3	the men **were s** on *their* **way** with their	8938
	45: 5	because it was to save lives *that* God **s** me	8938
	45: 7	But God **s** me ahead of you to preserve	8938
	45: 8	then, it was not you *who* **s** me here, but God.	8938
	45:23	And this is what *he* **s** to his father:	8938
	45:24	Then *he* **s** his brothers **away**,	8938
	45:27	the carts Joseph *had* **s** to carry him back,	8938
	46: 5	carts that Pharaoh *had* **s** to transport him.	8938
	46:28	Now Jacob **s** Judah ahead of him to Joseph	8938
	50:16	So *they* **s word** to Joseph, saying,	7422
Ex	2: 5	the reeds and **s** her slave girl to get it.	8938
	3:12	the sign to you that it is I *who have* **s** you:	8938
	3:13	'The God of your fathers *has* **s** me to you,'	8938
	3:14	'I AM *has* **s** me to you.' "	8938
	3:15	the God of Jacob—*has* **s** me to you.'	8938
	4:28	the LORD *had* **s** him to say,	8938
	5:22	Is this why *you* **s** me?	8938
	7:16	God of the Hebrews, *has* **s** me to say to you:	8938
	9: 7	Pharaoh **s** men to investigate and found that	8938
	9:23	the LORD **s** thunder and hail,	5989
	18: 2	After Moses *had* **s away** his wife Zipporah,	8933
	18: 6	Jethro *had* **s word** to him,	606

Ex	18:27	Moses **s** his father-in-law **on** *his* **way**,	8938
	24: 5	Then *he* **s** young Israelite men,	8938
	36: 6	**s** this word **throughout** the camp:	6296
Lev	26:41	toward them so that *I* **s** them into the land	995
Nu	5: 4	*they* **s** them outside the camp.	8938
	13: 3	the LORD's command Moses **s** them **out**	8938
	13:16	the names of the men Moses **s** to explore	8938
	13:17	When Moses **s** them to explore Canaan,	8938
	13:27	"We went into the land *to* which *you* **s** us,	8938
	14:36	So the men Moses *had* **s** to explore the land,	8938
	16:28	the LORD *has* **s** me to do all these things	8938
	16:29	then the LORD *has* not **s** me.	8938
	20:14	Moses **s** messengers from Kadesh to	8938
	20:16	and **s** an angel and brought us out of Egypt.	8938
	21: 6	LORD **s** venomous snakes among them;	8938
	21:21	Israel **s** messengers to say to Sihon king of	8938
	21:32	After Moses *had* **s** spies to Jazer,	8938
	22: 5	**s** messengers to summon Balaam son	8938
	22:10	king of Moab, **s** me *this* **message:**	8938
	22:15	Then Balak **s** other princes,	8938
	24:12	"Did I not tell the messengers *you* **s** me,	8938
	31: 6	Moses **s** them into battle,	8938
	32: 8	This is what your fathers did when I **s** them	8938
Dt	2:26	of Kedemoth *I* **s** messengers to Sihon king	8938
	6:22	the LORD **s** miraculous signs	5989
	9:23	the LORD **s** you out from Kadesh Barnea,	8938
	24: 5	not *be* **s** to war or have any other duty laid	3655
	34:11	and wonders the LORD **s** him to do	8938
Jos	2: 1	of Nun secretly **s** two spies from Shittim.	8938
	2: 3	the king of Jericho **s** *this* **message** to Rahab:	8938
	2:21	So *she* **s** them **away** and they departed.	8938
	6:17	because she hid the spies *we* **s**.	8938
	6:25	the men Joshua *had* **s** as spies to Jericho—	8938
	7: 2	Now Joshua **s** men from Jericho to Ai,	8938
	7:22	So Joshua **s** messengers,	8938
	8: 3	of his best fighting men and **s** them **out**	8938
	8: 9	Then Joshua **s** them **off,**	8938
	10: 6	then **s** word to Joshua in the camp at Gilgal:	8938
	11: 1	*he* **s word** to Jobab king of Madon,	8938
	14: 7	when Moses the servant of the LORD **s** me	8938
	14:11	as strong today as the day Moses **s** me **out;**	8938
	22: 6	Then Joshua blessed them and **s** them **away,**	8938
	22: 7	When Joshua **s** them home,	8938
	22:13	So the Israelites **s** Phinehas son of Eleazar,	8938
	22:14	With him they **s** ten of the chief men,	NIH
	24: 5	" 'Then *I* **s** Moses and Aaron,	8938
	24: 9	*he* **s for** Balaam son of Beor to put a curse on you.	2256+4200+7924+8938
	24:12	*I* **s** the hornet ahead of you,	8938
	24:28	Then Joshua **s** the people **away,**	8938
Jdg	1:23	When they **s** *men* **to spy out** Bethel	9365
	3:15	The Israelites **s** him with tribute	8938
	3:18	*he* **s** on their **way** the men who had	8938
	4: 6	*She* **s for** Barak son of Abinoam from Kedesh	2256+4200+7924+8938
	6: 8	he **s** a prophet, who said,	8938
	6:35	He **s** messengers throughout Manasseh,	8938
	7: 8	So Gideon **s** the rest of the Israelites	8938
	7:24	Gideon **s** messengers throughout	8938
	9:23	God **s** an evil spirit between Abimelech and	8938
	9:31	Under cover *he* **s** messengers to Abimelech,	8938
	11:12	Then Jephthah **s** messengers to	8938
	11:14	Jephthah **s** back messengers to	8938
	11:17	Israel **s** messengers to the king of Edom,	8938
	11:17	*They* **s** also to the king of Moab,	8938
	11:19	"Then Israel **s** messengers to Sihon king of	8938
	11:28	to the message Jephthah **s** him.	8938
	13: 8	let the man of God *you* **s** to us come again	8938
	16:18	*she* **s** word to the rulers of the Philistines,	8938
	18: 2	So the Danites **s** five warriors from Zorah	8938
	19:25	and **s** her outside to them,	3655
	19:29	and **s** them into all the areas of Israel.	8938
	20: 6	into pieces and **s** one piece to each region	8938
	20:12	The tribes of Israel **s** men throughout	8938
	21:10	assembly **s** twelve thousand fighting men	8938
	21:13	the whole assembly **s** an offer of peace to	8938
1Sa	4: 4	So the people **s** men to Shiloh,	8938
	4:13	the whole town **s** up a cry.	2410
	5:10	So *they* **s** the ark of God to Ekron.	8938
	6:17	These are the gold tumors the Philistines **s**	8740
	6:21	Then *they* **s** messengers to the people	8938
	11: 7	and **s** the pieces by messengers	8938
	12: 8	and the LORD **s** Moses and Aaron,	8938
	12:11	Then the LORD **s** Jerub-Baal, Barak,	8938
	12:18	and that same day the LORD **s** thunder	5989
	13: 2	rest of the men *he* **s** back to their homes.	8938
	14:15	It was a **panic** *s* by God.	AIT
	15: 1	the one the LORD **s** to anoint you king	8938
	15:18	And **s** you on a mission, saying,	8938
	16:12	So *he* **s** and had him brought in.	8938
	16:19	Then Saul **s** messengers to Jesse and said,	8938
	16:20	a young goat and **s** them with his son David	8938
	16:22	Then Saul **s word** to Jesse, saying,	8938
	17:31	and Saul **s for** him.	4374
	18: 5	Whatever Saul **s** him to do,	8938
	18:13	So he **s** David **away** from him	6073
	19:11	Saul **s** men to David's house to watch it and	8938
	19:14	When Saul **s** the men to capture David,	8938
	19:15	Then Saul **s** the men **back** to see David	8938
	19:20	so he **s** men to capture him.	8938
	19:21	Saul was told about it, and *he* **s** more men,	8938
	19:21	Saul **s** men a third time,	8938
	20:22	because the LORD *has* **s** you **away**.	8938
	22:11	king **s for** the priest Ahimelech	4200+7924+8938
	25: 5	So he **s** ten young men and said to them,	8938
	25:14	"David's messengers from the desert	8938
	25:25	I did not see the men my master **s**.	8938

1Sa	25:32	who *has* **s** you today to meet me.	8938
	25:39	Then David **s** word to Abigail,	8938
	25:40	"David *has* **s** us to you to take you	8938
	26: 4	he **s** out scouts and learned that Saul	8938
	30:26	he **s** some of the plunder to the elders	8938
	30:27	He **s** it to those who were in Bethel,	NIH
	31: 9	and *they* **s** messengers throughout the land	8938
2Sa	2: 5	he **s** messengers to the men	8938
	3:12	Then Abner **s** messengers on his behalf	8938
	3:14	Then David **s** messengers to Ish-Bosheth	8938
	3:21	David **s** Abner **away,** and he went in peace.	8938
	3:22	because David *had* **s** him **away,**	8938
	3:23	and that the king *had* **s** him **away**	8938
	3:26	Joab then left David and **s** messengers	8938
	5:11	Hiram king of Tyre **s** messengers to David,	8938
	8:10	he **s** his son Joram to King David	8938
	10: 2	So David **s** a delegation to express his	8938
	10: 3	Hasn't David **s** them to you to explore	8938
	10: 4	and **s** them **away.**	8938
	10: 5	*he* **s** messengers to meet the men,	8938
	10: 7	David **s** Joab **out** with the entire army	8938
	11: 1	David **s** Joab **out** with the king's men and	8938
	11: 3	and David **s** someone to find out about her.	8938
	11: 4	Then David **s** messengers to get her.	8938
	11: 5	The woman conceived and **s word** to David,	2256+5583+8938
	11: 6	So David **s** *this* **word** to Joab:	8938
	11: 6	And Joab **s** him to David.	8938
	11: 8	and a gift from the king *was* **s** after him.	3655
	11:14	a letter to Joab and **s** it with Uriah.	8938
	11:18	Joab **s** David a full account of the battle.	8938
	11:22	he told David everything Joab *had* **s** him	8938
	12: 1	The LORD **s** Nathan to David.	8938
	12:25	*he* **s word** through Nathan the prophet	8938
	12:27	Joab then **s** messengers to David, saying,	8938
	13: 7	David **s** word to Tamar at the palace:	8938
	13:27	so *he* **s** with him Amnon and the rest of	8938
	14: 2	So Joab **s** someone to Tekoa and had	8938
	14:29	Then Absalom **s for** Joab in order	8938
	14:29	he **s** a second time, but he refused to come.	8938
	14:32	"Look, *I* **s word** to you and said,	8938
	15:10	Then Absalom **s** secret messengers	8938
	15:12	he also **s for** Ahithophel the Gilonite,	8938
	18: 2	David **s** the troops **out**—	8938
	19:11	King David **s** this message to Zadok	8938
	19:14	*They* **s word** to the king, "Return,	8938
	24:13	how I should answer the *one who* **s** me."	8938
	24:15	So the LORD **s** a plague on Israel from	5989
1Ki	1:44	The king *has* **s** with him Zadok the priest,	8938
	1:53	Then King Solomon **s** men,	8938
	2:36	Then the king **s for** Shimei and said to him,	2256+4200+7924+8938
	4:34	**s** by all the kings of the world,	907+4946
	5: 1	*he* **s** his envoys to Solomon,	8938
	5: 2	Solomon **s back** this message to Hiram:	8938
	5: 8	So Hiram **s** word to Solomon:	8938
	5: 8	"I have received the message *you* **s** me	8938
	5:14	*He* **s** them **off** to Lebanon in shifts	8938
	7:13	King Solomon **s** to Tyre and brought Huram	8938
	8:66	On the following day *he* **s** the people **away.**	8938
	9:14	Hiram *had* **s** to the king 120 talents of gold.	8938
	9:27	And Hiram **s** his men—sailors who knew	8938
	12: 3	So *they* **s for** Jeroboam,	2256+4200+7924+8938
	12:18	King Rehoboam **s** out Adoniram,	8938
	12:20	*they* **s** and called him to the assembly	8938
	14: 6	I *have* **been s** to you *with* bad news.	8938
	15:18	He entrusted it to his officials and **s** them	8938
	15:20	and **s** the commanders of his forces against	8938
	18:10	where my master *has* not **s** someone to look	8938
	18:20	So Ahab **s word** throughout all Israel	8938
	19: 2	So Jezebel **s** a messenger to Elijah to say,	8938
	20: 2	*He* **s** messengers into the city to Ahab king	8938
	20: 5	'*I* **s** to demand your silver and gold,	8938
	20: 7	When *he* **s for** my wives and my children,	8938
	20:10	Ben-Hadad **s** another message to Ahab:	8938
	21: 8	and **s** them to the elders and nobles	8938
	21:14	Then *they* **s** word to Jezebel:	8938
2Ki	1: 2	So he **s** messengers, saying to them,	8938
	1: 6	to the king who **s** you and tell him,	8938
	1: 9	Then *he* **s** to Elijah a captain	8938
	1:11	At this the king **s** to Elijah another captain	8938
	1:13	the king **s** a third captain with his fifty men.	8938
	1:16	to consult that *you have* **s** messengers	8938
	2: 2	the LORD *has* **s** me to Bethel."	8938
	2: 4	the LORD *has* **s** me to Jericho."	8938
	2: 6	the LORD *has* **s** me to the Jordan."	8938
	2:17	And *they* **s** fifty men,	8938
	3: 7	*He* also **s** this message to Jehoshaphat king	8938
	5: 8	*he* **s** him this message:	8938
	5:10	Elisha **s** a messenger to say to him, "Go,	8938
	5:22	"My master **s** me to say,	8938
	5:24	*He* **s** the men **away** and they left.	8938
	6: 9	of God **s** word to the king of Israel:	8938
	6:14	Then *he* **s** horses and chariots and	8938
	6:23	*he* **s** them **away,**	8938
	6:32	The king **s** a messenger ahead,	8938
	7:14	the king **s** them after the Aramean army.	8938
	8: 9	of Aram *has* **s** me to ask,	8938
	9:19	So the king **s** out a second horseman.	8938
	10: 1	Jehu wrote letters and **s** them *to* Samaria:	8938
	10: 5	the elders and the guardians **s** this message	8938
	10: 7	They put their heads in baskets and **s** them	8938
	10:21	Then he **s word** throughout Israel,	8938
	11: 4	In the seventh year Jehoiada **s for** the commanders	2256+4374+8938
	12:18	and he **s** them **to** Hazael king of Aram,	8938
	14: 8	Then Amaziah **s** messengers to Jehoash son	8938

2Ki	14: 9	"A thistle in Lebanon s a message to	8938
	14:19	but *they* s men after him to Lachish	8938
	16: 7	Ahaz s messengers to say	8938
	16: 8	the royal palace and s it as a gift to the king	8938
	16:10	He saw an altar in Damascus and s to Uriah	8938
	16:11	with all the plans that King Ahaz *had* s	8938
	17: 4	for *he had* s envoys to So king of Egypt,	8938
	17:25	so he s lions among them	8938
	17:26	*He has* s lions among them,	8938
	18:14	So Hezekiah king of Judah s this message	8938
	18:17	of Assyria with his supreme commander,	8938
	18:27	that my master s me to say these things, and	8938
	19: 2	*He* s Eliakim the palace administrator,	8938
	19: 4	*has* s to ridicule the living God,	8938
	19: 9	So he again s messengers to Hezekiah	8938
	19:16	to the words Sennacherib *has* s to insult	8938
	19:20	Then Isaiah son of Amoz s a message	8938
	20:12	of Babylon s Hezekiah letters and a gift,	8938
	22: 3	King Josiah s the secretary,	8938
	22:15	Tell the man who s you to me,	8938
	22:18	who s you to inquire of the Lord,	8938
	24: 2	The Lord s Babylonian, Aramean,	8938
	24: 2	*He* s them to destroy Judah.	8938
1Ch	6:15	s Judah and Jerusalem **into exile**	1655
	10: 9	and s **messengers** throughout the land of	8938
	12:19	after consultation, their rulers s him **away**.	8938
	14: 1	Hiram king of Tyre s messengers to David,	8938
	18:10	he s his son Hadoram to King David	8938
	19: 2	So David s a delegation to express his	8938
	19: 4	and s them **away.**	8938
	19: 5	*he* s messengers to meet them,	8938
	19: 6	and the Ammonites s a thousand talents	8938
	19: 8	David s Joab **out** with the entire army	8938
	19:16	routed by Israel, *they* s messengers	8938
	21:12	how I should answer the *one who* s me."	8938
	21:14	So the Lord s a plague on Israel,	5989
	21:15	And God s an angel to destroy Jerusalem.	8938
2Ch	2: 3	Solomon s this message to Hiram king	8938
	2: 3	for my father David when *you* s him cedar	8938
	7:10	of the seventh month *he* s the people	8938
	8:18	And Hiram s him ships commanded	8938
	10: 3	So *they* s for Jeroboam, 2256+4200+7924+8938	
	10:18	King Rehoboam s **out** Adoniram,	8938
	13:13	Jeroboam *had* s troops **around** to the rear,	6015
	16: 2	and s it to Ben-Hadad king of Aram,	8938
	16: 4	and s the commanders of his forces against	8938
	17: 7	of his reign *he* s his officials Ben-Hail,	8938
	23:14	the priest s *out* the commanders of units of	3655
	24:19	the Lord s prophets to the people	8938
	24:23	*They* s all the plunder to their king	8938
	25:10	to him from Ephraim and s them home.	2143
	25:13	the troops that Amaziah *had* s **back**	8740
	25:15	and s a prophet to him, who said,	8938
	25:17	*he* s this challenge to Jehoash son	8938
	25:18	"A thistle in Lebanon s a message to	8938
	25:27	but *they* s men after him to Lachish	8938
	28:16	At that time King Ahaz s to the king	8938
	30: 1	Hezekiah s **word** to all Israel and Judah and	8938
	32: 9	he s his officers to Jerusalem	8938
	32:21	And the Lord s an angel,	8938
	32:31	But when envoys *were* s by the rulers	8938
	34: 8	*he* s Shaphan son of Azaliah and Maaseiah	8938
	34:22	the king had s with him went to speak to	NIH
	34:23	Tell the man who s you to me,	8938
	34:26	who s you to inquire of the Lord,	8938
	35:21	But Neco s messengers to him, saying,	8938
	36:10	King Nebuchadnezzar s *for* him	8938
	36:15	s **word** to them through his messengers	8938
Ezr	4:11	(This is a copy of the letter *they* s him.)	10714
	4:17	The king s this reply:	10714
	4:18	The letter *you* s us has been read	10714
	5: 6	s to King Darius.	10714
	5: 7	The report *they* s him read as follows:	10714
	6:13	because of the decree King Darius *had* s,	10714
	7:14	*You are* s by the king and his seven	10714
	8:17	and *I* s them to Iddo, the leader in	7422
Ne	2: 9	also s army officers and cavalry with me.	8938
	6: 2	Sanballat and Geshem s me this message:	8938
	6: 3	so *I* s messengers to them with this reply:	8938
	6: 4	Four times *they* s me the same message,	8938
	6: 5	Sanballat s his aide to me with the same	8938
	6: 8	*I* s him this reply:	8938
	6:12	I realized that God *had* not s him,	8938
	6:19	And Tobiah s letters to intimidate me.	8938
	9:10	*You* s miraculous signs and wonders	5989
Est	1:22	*He* s dispatches to all parts of the kingdom,	8938
	3:13	Dispatches *were* s by couriers to all	8938
	4: 4	*She* s clothes *for* him to put on instead	8938
	4:13	he s **back** this answer:	8740
	4:15	Then Esther s this reply to Mordecai:	8740
	8:10	and s them by mounted couriers,	8938
	9:20	and s e letters to all the Jews throughout	8938
	9:30	And Mordecai s letters to all the Jews in	8938
Job	22: 9	And *you* s widows **away** empty-handed	8938
Ps	59: T	When Saul *had* s men to watch David's	8938
	78:25	*he* s them all the food they could eat.	8938
	78:45	*He* s swarms of flies that devoured them,	8938
	78:61	*He* s [the ark of] his might into captivity,	5989
	80:11	It s **out** its boughs to the Sea,	8938
	105:17	and *he* s a man before them—	8938
	105:20	The king s and released him,	8938
	105:26	*He* s Moses his servant, and Aaron,	8938
	105:28	*He* s darkness and made the land dark—	8938
	106:15	but s a wasting disease upon them	8938
	107:20	*He* s **forth** his word and healed them;	8938
	135: 9	*He* s his signs and wonders into your midst,	8938
Pr	9: 3	*She has* s **out** her maids,	8938

Pr	17:11	a merciless official *will* be s against him.	8938
	22:21	can give sound answers to *him who* s you?	8938
Isa	6:12	until the Lord *has* s everyone **far away**	8178
	9: 8	The Lord *has* s a message against Jacob;	8938
	20: 1	s by Sargon king of Assyria,	8938
	36: 2	the king of Assyria s his field commander	8938
	36:12	that my master s me to say these things, and	8938
	37: 2	*He* s Eliakim the palace administrator,	8938
	37: 4	*has* s to ridicule the living God,	8938
	37: 9	he s messengers to Hezekiah with this word:	8938
	37:17	to all the words Sennacherib *has* s to insult	8938
	37:21	Then Isaiah son of Amoz s a message	8938
	39: 1	of Babylon s Hezekiah letters and a gift,	8938
	48:16	Sovereign Lord *has* s me, with his Spirit.	8938
	50: 1	of divorce with which *I* s her **away?**	8938
	50: 1	because of your transgressions your mother	
		was s **away.**	8938
	55:11	and achieve the purpose for which *I* s it.	8938
	57: 9	*You* s your ambassadors far away;	8938
	61: 1	*He has* s me to bind up the brokenhearted,	8938
	63:12	*who* s his glorious arm of power to be	2143
Jer	3: 8	and s her **away** because of all her adulteries.	8938
	7:25	again and again *I* s you my servants	8938
	14:14	not s them or appointed them or spoken	8938
	19:14	where the Lord *had* s him to prophesy,	8938
	21: 1	when King Zedekiah s to him Pashhur son	8938
	24: 5	from Judah, whom *I* s **away** from this place	8938
	25: 4	though the Lord *has* s all his servants	8938
	25:17	the nations to whom he s me drink it:	8938
	26: 5	whom *I have* s to you again and again	8938
	26:12	"The Lord s me to prophesy	8938
	26:15	for in truth the Lord *has* s me to you	8938
	26:22	however, s Elnathan son of Acbor to Egypt,	8938
	27:15	'*I have* not s them,' declares the Lord.	8938
	28: 9	as one truly s *by* the Lord only	8938
	28:15	The Lord *has* not s you,	8938
	29: 1	that the prophet Jeremiah s from Jerusalem	8938
	29: 3	of Judah s to King Nebuchadnezzar	8938
	29: 9	*I have* not s them," declares the Lord.	8938
	29:19	"words that *I* s to them again and again	8938
	29:20	all you exiles whom *I have* s **away**	8938
	29:25	You s letters in your own name to all	8938
	29:28	he s this message to us in Babylon:	8938
	35:15	and again *I* s all my servants the prophets	8938
	36:14	all the officials s Jehudi son of Nethaniah,	8938
	36:21	The king s Jehudi to get the scroll,	8938
	37: 3	s Jehucal son of Shelemiah with	8938
	37: 7	who s you to inquire of me,	8938
	37:17	Then King Zedekiah s *for* him	8938
	38:14	Then King Zedekiah s *for* Jeremiah	8938
	39:14	s and had Jeremiah taken out of	8938
	40:14	of the Ammonites *has* s Ishmael son	8938
	42: 9	to whom *you* s me to present your petition,	8938
	42:20	when *you* s me to the Lord your God	8938
	42:21	the Lord your God in all *he* s me	8938
	43: 1	the Lord *had* s him to tell them—	8938
	43: 2	The Lord our God *has* not s you to say,	8938
	44: 4	and again *I* s my servants the prophets,	8938
	49:14	An envoy *was* s to the nations to say,	8938
La	1:13	"From on high *he* s fire,	8938
	1:13	s it **down** into my bones.	3718
Eze	3: 5	not **being** s to a people of obscure speech	8938
	3: 6	Surely if *I had* s you to them,	8178
	11:16	Although *I* s them **far away** among	8178
	13: 6	when the Lord *has* not s them;	8938
	17: 7	The vine now s **out** its roots toward him	4102
	23:16	she lusted after them and s messengers	8938
	23:40	"*They* even s messengers for men who came	8938
	31: 4	around its base and s their channels to all	8938
	39:28	I s them **into exile** among the nations,	1655
Da	2:13	and *men were* s *to* **look for** Daniel	AIT
	3:28	who *has* s his angel and rescued his	10714
	5:24	Therefore he s the hand that wrote	10714
	6:22	My God s his angel, and shut the mouths	10714
	6:22	and stand up, for *I have* now **been** s to you."	8938
Hos	5:13	s to the great king **for help.**	8938
Joel	2:25	my great army that *I* s among you.	8938
Am	4: 7	*I* s **rain** on one town,	4763
	4:10	"*I* s plagues among you as I did to Egypt.	8938
	7:10	of Bethel s a message to Jeroboam king	8938
Ob	1: 1	An envoy *was* s to the nations to say, "Rise,	8938
Jnh	1: 4	Then the Lord s a great wind on the sea,	3214
Mic	6: 4	*I* s Moses to lead you,	8938
Hag	1:12	because the Lord their God *had* s him.	8938
Zec	1:10	the ones the Lord *has* s to go throughout	8938
	2: 8	"After he has honored me and *has* s me	8938
	2: 9	that the Lord Almighty *has* s me.	8938
	2:11	that the Lord Almighty *has* s me to you.	8938
	4: 9	that the Lord Almighty *has* s me to you.	8938
	6:15	that the Lord Almighty *has* s me to you.	8938
	7: 2	The people of Bethel *had* s Sharezer	8938
	7:12	to the words that the Lord Almighty *had* s	8938
Mal	2: 4	that *I have* s you this admonition so	8938
Mt	2: 8	He s them to Bethlehem and said,	4287
	10: 5	These twelve Jesus s **out** with the following	690
	10:40	receives me receives the one who s me.	690
	11: 2	what Christ was doing, *he* s his disciples	4287
	14:35	*they* s **word** to all the surrounding country,	690
	15:24	"*I was* s only to the lost sheep of Israel."	690
	15:39	*After* Jesus *had* s the crowd **away,**	668
	20: 2	for the day and s them into his vineyard.	690
	21: 1	Jesus s two disciples,	690
	21:34	*he* s his servants to the tenants	690
	21:36	he s other servants to them,	690
	21:37	Last of all, *he* s his son to them.	690
	22: 3	*He* s his servants to those who had been	690
	22: 4	"Then *he* s some more servants and said,	690

Mt	22: 7	He s his army and destroyed those	4287
	22:16	*They* s their disciples to him along with	690
	23:37	you who kill the prophets and stone those s	690
	26:47	s from the chief priests and the elders of	NIG
	27:19	his wife s him this **message:**	690
Mk	1:12	At once the Spirit s him **out** into the desert,	1675
	1:43	Jesus s him **away** at once with a strong	1675
	3:31	*they* s someone in to call him.	690
	6: 7	he s them **out** two by two	690
	6:27	So he immediately s an executioner	690
	9:37	not welcome me but the one who s me."	690
	11: 1	Jesus s two of his disciples,	690
	12: 2	At harvest time he s a servant to the tenants	690
	12: 3	beat him and s him **away** empty-handed.	690
	12: 4	Then *he* s another servant to them;	690
	12: 5	*He* s still another, and that one they killed.	690
	12: 5	He s many others; some of them they beat,	NIG
	12: 6	he s him last of all, saying,	690
	12:13	Later *they* s some of the Pharisees	690
	14:13	So *he* s two of his disciples, telling them,	690
	14:43	s from the chief priests,	NIG
Lk	1:19	and *I have been* s to speak to you and	690
	1:26	God s the angel Gabriel to Nazareth,	690
	1:53	but *has* s the rich **away** empty.	1990
	4:18	He *has* s me to proclaim freedom for	690
	4:26	Yet Elijah *was* not s to any of them,	4287
	4:43	because that is why *I was* s."	690
	7: 3	of Jesus and s some elders of the Jews	690
	7: 6	from the house when the centurion s friends	4287
	7:10	Then the men who *had been* s returned to	4287
	7:19	*he* s them to the Lord to ask,	4287
	7:20	"John the Baptist s us to you to ask,	690
	8:38	but Jesus s him **away,** saying,	668
	9: 2	and *he* s them **out** to preach the kingdom	690
	9:48	welcomes me welcomes the one who s me.	690
	9:52	And *he* s messengers on ahead,	690
	10: 1	and s them two by two ahead of him	690
	10:16	he who rejects me rejects him who s me."	690
	13:34	you who kill the prophets and stone those s	690
	14: 4	he healed him and s him **away.**	668
	14:17	At the time of the banquet *he* s his servant	690
	15:15	*who* s him to his fields to feed pigs.	4287
	19:14	and s a delegation after him to say,	690
	19:15	Then *he* s **for** the servants	3306+5888
	19:29	*he* s two of his disciples, saying to them,	690
	19:32	Those who *were* s ahead went	690
	20:10	At harvest time *he* s a servant to the tenants	690
	20:10	and s him **away** empty-handed.	1990
	20:11	*He* s another servant,	4287+4707
	20:11	and s **away** empty-handed.	1990
	20:12	*He* s still a third,	4287+4707
	20:20	Keeping a close watch on him, *they* s spies,	690
	22: 8	Jesus s Peter and John, saying,	690
	22:35	"When *I* s you without purse,	690
	23: 7	Herod's jurisdiction, he s him to Herod,	402
	23:11	*they* s him **back** to Pilate.	402
	23:15	Neither has Herod, for *he* s him **back** to us;	402
Jn	1: 6	There came a man *who was* s from God;	690
	1:19	the Jews of Jerusalem s priests and Levites	690
	1:22	an answer to those *who* s us.	4287
	1:24	Now some Pharisees who had been s	690
	1:33	except that the one who s me to baptize	4287
	3:28	'I am not the Christ but am s ahead of him.'	690
	3:34	the one whom God *has* s speaks the words	690
	4:34	*of* him who s me and to finish his work.	4287
	4:38	I s you to reap what you have	690
	5:23	not honor the Father, who s him.	4287
	5:24	and believes him who s me has eternal life	4287
	5:30	not to please myself but him who s me.	4287
	5:33	"You *have* s to John and he has testified to	690
	5:36	testifies that the Father *has* s me.	690
	5:37	the Father *who* s me has himself testified	4287
	5:38	for you do not believe the one he s.	4287
	6:29	to believe in the one he *has* s."	690
	6:38	but to do the will *of* him who s me.	4287
	6:39	And this is the will *of* him who s me,	4287
	6:44	unless the Father who s me draws him,	4287
	6:57	the living Father s me and I live because of	690
	7:16	It comes *from* him who s me.	4287
	7:18	for the honor *of* the one who s him is a man	4287
	7:28	but he who s me is true.	4287
	7:29	because I am from him and he s me."	690
	7:32	the Pharisees s temple guards to arrest him.	690
	7:33	and then I go to the one who s me.	4287
	8:16	I stand with the Father, who s me.	4287
	8:18	my other witness is the Father, who s me."	4287
	8:26	But he who s me is reliable,	4287
	8:29	The one who s me is with me;	4287
	8:42	I have not come on my own; but he s me.	4287
	9: 4	we must do the work *of* him who s me.	4287
	9: 7	the Pool of Siloam" (this word means S).	690
	9:18	and had received his sight until *they* s **for**	5888
	10:36	the Father set apart as his very own and s	690
	11: 3	So the sisters s word to Jesus, "Lord,	690
	11:42	that they may believe that you s me."	690
	12:44	but in the one who s me.	4287
	12:45	he looks at me, he sees the one who s me.	4287
	12:49	the Father who s me commanded me what	4287
	13:16	messenger greater than the one who s him.	4287
	13:20	accepts me accepts the one who s me."	4287
	14:24	they belong to the Father who s me.	4287
	15:21	for they do not know the One who s me.	4287
	16: 5	"Now I am going to him who s me,	4287
	17: 3	and Jesus Christ, whom *you have* s.	690
	17: 8	and they believed that you s me.	690

Jn	17:18	As *you* s me into the world,	690
	17:18	I *have* s them into the world.	690
	17:21	the world may believe that you *have* s me.	690
	17:23	that you s me and have loved them even	690
	17:25	and they know that you *have* s me.	690
	18:24	Then Annas s him, still bound,	690
	20:21	As the Father *has* s me, I am sending you."	690
Ac	3:26	*he* s him first to you to bless you	690
	5:21	and s to the jail for the apostles.	690
	7: 4	God s him to this land where you are	3579
	7:12	*he* s our fathers on their first visit.	690
	7:14	Joseph s *for* his father Jacob	690+3559
	7:35	He *was* s to be their ruler and deliverer	690
	8:14	*they* s Peter and John to them.	690
	9:17	*has* s me so that you may see again and	690
	9:30	down to Caesarea and s him *off* to Tarsus.	1990
	9:38	*they* s two men to him and urged him,	690
	9:40	Peter s them all out of the room;	1675
	10: 8	that had happened and s them to Joppa.	690
	10:17	the men s by Cornelius found out	690
	10:20	go with them, for I *have* s them."	690
	10:29	So *when I was* s *for*, I came	3569
	10:29	May I ask why *you* s for me?"	3569
	10:33	So *I* s for you immediately;	4287
	10:36	You know the message God s to the people	690
	11:11	"Right then three men *who had been* s to me	690
	11:22	and *they* s Barnabas to Antioch.	1990
	12:11	without a doubt that the Lord s his angel	1990
	13: 3	placed their hands on them and s them *off*.	668
	13: 4	s on *their* way by the Holy Spirit,	1734
	13: 7	s *for* Barnabas and Saul because he wanted	4673
	13:15	the synagogue rulers s word to them,	690
	13:26	that this message of salvation *has been* s.	1990
	15: 3	The church s *them on their* way,	4636
	15:23	With them *they* s *the following letter:*	1211
	15:30	The men *were* s off and went down	668
	15:33	*they were* s *off* by the brothers who	668
	15:33	of peace to return to those who *had* s them.	690
	16:35	the magistrates s their officers to the jailer	690
	17:10	brothers s Paul and Silas *away* to Berea.	1734
	17:14	The brothers immediately s Paul to	1990
	19:22	*He* s two of his helpers,	690
	19:31	s him a message begging him not to venture	4287
	20: 1	Paul s *for* the disciples and,	3569
	20:17	Paul s to Ephesus for the elders of the church.	4287
	23:18	s *for* me and asked me to bring this young	4673
	23:30	*I* s him to you at once.	4287
	24:24	*He* s *for* Paul and listened to him	3569
	24:26	so he s *for* him frequently and talked	3569
	28:28	to know that God's salvation *has been* s to	690
Ro	10:15	how can they preach unless *they are* s?	690
2Co	1:17	with sincerity, like men s from God.	NIG
	12:17	through any of the men *I* s you?	690
	12:18	to go to you and *I* s our brother *with* him.	5273
Gal	1: 1	s not from men nor by man,	NIG
	4: 4	the time had fully come, God s his Son,	1990
	4: 6	God s the Spirit of his Son into our hearts,	1990
Php	2:25	whom you s to take care of my needs.	NIG
	4:16	*you* s me aid again and again when I was	4287
	4:18	from Epaphroditus the gifts you s.	NIG
1Th	3: 2	*We* s Timothy, who is our brother	4287
	3: 5	*I* s to find out about your faith.	4287
2Ti	4:12	*I* s Tychicus to Ephesus.	690
Heb	1:14	Are not all angels ministering spirits s	690
Jas	2:25	and s them *off* in a different direction?	1675
1Pe	1:12	to you by the Holy Spirit s from heaven.	690
	2: 14	*who are* s by him to punish those who do	4287
2Pe	2: 4	when they sinned, but s them **to hell**,	5434
1Jn	4: 9	He s his one and only Son into the world	690
	4:10	but that he loved us and s his Son as	690
	4:14	the Father *has* s his Son to be the Savior of	690
Rev	5: 6	which are the seven spirits of God s *out*	690
	22: 6	s his angel to show his servants the things	690
	22:16	*have* s my angel to give you this testimony	4287

SENTENCE (12) [SENTENCED]

1Ki	20:40	"That is your s," the king of Israel said.	5477
2Ki	25: 6	where s was pronounced on him.	5477
Ps	149: 9	to carry out the s written against them.	5477
Ecc	8:11	the s for a crime is not quickly carried out,	7330
Jer	39: 5	where he pronounced s on him.	5477
	52: 9	where he pronounced s on him.	5477
Eze	16:38	*I will* s you *to* the punishment	9149
	23:45	But righteous men *will* s them *to*	9149
Lk	he said, "since you are under the same s?	3210
Ac	13:28	found no proper ground *for* a **death s,**	2505
Ro	9:28	For the Lord will carry out his s on earth	3364
2Co	1: 9	Indeed, in our hearts we felt the s of death.	645

SENTENCED (3) [SENTENCE]

Jer	26:11	be s *to* death because he has prophesied	5477
	26:16	"This man should not be s *to* death!	5477
Lk	24:20	to be s to death, and they crucified him;	3210

SENTENCES (KJV) See INTRIGUE, RIDDLES

SENTRIES (1)

Ac	12: 6	and s stood guard at the entrance.	5874

SENUAH (KJV) See HASSENUAH

SEORIM (1)

1Ch	24: 8	the third to Harim, the fourth to S,	8556

SEPARATE (26) [SEPARATED, SEPARATES, SEPARATION]

Ge	1: 6	between the waters *to* s water from water."	976
	1:14	in the expanse of the sky to s the day from	976
	1:18	and to s light from darkness.	976
	30:40	Thus he made s flocks for himself and	963+4200
Ex	26:33	The curtain *will* s the Holy Place from	976
Lev	15:31	'*You must* **keep** the Israelites s from things	5692
Nu	16:21	"S yourselves from this assembly	976
Jdg	7: 5	"S those who lap the water	963+3657+4200
2Sa	14: 6	and no *one was* there to s them.	1068+5911
1Ki	5: 9	There *I will* s them and you can take them	5879
2Ki	2:11	He lived in a s house.	2931
2Ch	26:21	He lived in a s house—	2931
Ezr	9: 1	*have* not **kept themselves** s from	976
	10:11	S yourselves from the peoples around you	976
Eze	42:20	to s the holy from the common.	976
Mt	13:49	The angels will come and s the wicked	976
	19: 6	what God has joined together, *let* man not **s.**	6004
	25:32	and *he will* s the people one from another	928
Mk	10: 9	what God has joined together, *let* man not s.	928
Jn	20: 7	by itself, s *from* the linen.	3552+4024
Ro	8:35	Who *shall* s us from the love of Christ?	6004
	8:39	be able *to* s us from the love of God that is	6004
1Co	7:10	A wife *must* not s from her husband.	6004
2Co	6:17	"Therefore come out from them and *be* s,	928
Gal	2:12	he began to draw back and s himself from	928
Eph	2:12	remember that at that time you were s **from**	6006

SEPARATED (19) [SEPARATE]

Ge	1: 4	and he s the light from the darkness.	976
	1: 7	So God made the expanse and s the water	976
	2:10	from there *it was* s into four headwaters.	7233
	25:23	two peoples from within you *will be* s;	7233
Nu	16: 9	the God of Israel *has* s you from the rest of	976
1Sa	11:11	The next day Saul s his men	8492
2Ki	2:11	horses of fire appeared and s the two	1068+7233
	25: 5	All his soldiers were s *from* him	4946+6584
1Ch	24: 5	David s them **into divisions**	2745
Ezr	6:21	who s *themselves* from the unclean	976
Ne	4:19	and we *are* widely s from each other along	7233
	9: 2	*Those of* Israelite descent *had* s **themselves**	976
	10:28	temple servants and all who s **themselves**	976
Isa	59: 2	your iniquities *have* s you from your God;	976
Jer	52: 8	All his soldiers were s *from* him	4946+6584
Eze	46:18	so that none of my people *will be* s	7046
Ac	2: 3	to be tongues of fire *that* s and came to rest	1374
Eph	4:18	in their understanding and s from the life	558
Phm	1:15	Perhaps the reason he was s **from** you for	6004

SEPARATES (5) [SEPARATE]

Ru	1:17	if anything but death s you and me."	7233
Pr	16:28	and a gossip s close friends.	7233
	17: 9	whoever repeats the matter s close friends.	7233
Eze	14: 7	in Israel s *himself* from me and sets up idols	5692
Mt	25:32	from another as a shepherd s the sheep from	928

SEPARATION (10) [SEPARATE]

Nu	6: 2	a vow of s to the LORD as a Nazirite,	5687
	6: 5	vow of s no razor may be used on his head.	5694
	6: 5	He must be holy until the period of his s	5693
	6: 6	of his s to the LORD he must not go near	5693
	6: 7	the **symbol of** his s *to* God is on his head.	5694
	6: 8	of his s he is consecrated to the LORD.	5694
	6:12	for the period of his s and must bring	5694
	6:12	because he became defiled during his s.	5694
	6:13	when the period of his s is over.	5694
	6:21	to the LORD in accordance with his s,	5694

SEPHAR (1)

Ge	10:30	stretched from Mesha toward S,	6223

SEPHARAD (1)

Ob	1:20	from Jerusalem who are in S will possess	6224

SEPHARVAIM (6) [SEPHARVITES]

2Ki	17:24	and S and settled them in the towns	6226
	17:31	and Anammelech, the gods of S.	6226
	18:34	Where are the gods of S, Hena and Ivvah?	6226
	19:13	the king of Arpad, the king of the city of S,	6226
Isa	36:19	Where are the gods of S?	6226
	37:13	the king of Arpad, the king of the city of S,	6226

SEPHARVITES (1) [SEPHARVAIM]

2Ki	17:31	and the S burned their children in the fire	6227

SEPHER See KIRIATH SEPHER

SEPULCHRE, SEPULCHRES (KJV) See GRAVE, GRAVES, TOMB, TOMBS

SERAH (3) [TIMNATH SERAH]

Ge	46:17	Their sister was S.	8580
Nu	26:46	(Asher had a daughter named S.)	8580
1Ch	7:30	Their sister was S.	8580

SERAIAH (18) [SERAIAH'S]

2Sa	8:17	of Abiathar were priests; S was secretary;	8588
2Ki	25:18	of the guard took as prisoners S	8588
	25:23	S son of Tanhumeth the Netophathite,	8588
1Ch	4:13	The sons of Kenaz: Othniel and S.	8588
	4:14	S was the father of Joab,	8588
	4:35	Jehu son of Joshibiah, the son of S,	8588
	6:14	Azariah the father of S,	8588
	6:14	and S the father of Jehozadak.	8588
Ezr	2: 2	Nehemiah, S, Reelaiah, Mordecai, Bilshan,	8588
	7: 1	Ezra son of S, the son of Azariah,	8588
Ne	10: 2	S, Azariah, Jeremiah,	8588
	11:11	S son of Hilkiah,	8588
	12: 1	of Shealtiel and with Jeshua: S,	8588
Jer	36:26	S son of Azriel and Shelemiah son	8589
	40: 8	the sons of Kareah, S son of Tanhumeth,	8588
	51:59	to the staff officer S son of Neriah,	8588
	51:61	He said to S, "When you get to Babylon,	8588
	52:24	of the guard took as prisoners S	8588

SERAIAH'S (1) [SERAIAH]

Ne	12:12	of S family, Meraiah; of Jeremiah's,	8588

SERAPHS (2)

Isa	6: 2	Above him were s, each with six wings:	8597
	6: 6	of the s flew to me with a live coal	8597

SERAPHIMS (KJV) See SERAPHS

SERED (2) [SEREDITE]

Ge	46:14	The sons of Zebulun: S, Elon and Jahleel.	6237
Nu	26:26	through S, the Seredite clan;	6237

SEREDITE (1) [SERED]

Nu	26:26	through Sered, the S clan;	6238

SERGIUS (1) [PAULUS]

Ac	13: 7	an attendant of the proconsul, S Paulus.	4950

SERIOUS (8) [SERIOUSNESS]

Ge	12:17	the LORD inflicted s diseases on Pharaoh	1524
Ex	21:22	but there is no s **injury,**	656
	21:23	But if there is s **injury,**	656
Dt	15:21	is lame or blind, or has any s flaw,	8273
Jer	6:14	wound of my people as though *it were* not s	7837
	8:11	wound of my people as though *it were* not s	7837
Ac	18:14	about some misdemeanor or s crime,	4505
	25: 7	bringing many s charges against him,	987

SERIOUSNESS (1) [SERIOUS]

Tit	2: 7	In your teaching show integrity, s	4949

SERPENT (17) [SERPENT'S, SERPENTS]

Ge	3: 1	Now the s was more crafty than any of	5729
	3: 2	The woman said to the s,	5729
	3: 4	the s said to the woman.	5729
	3:13	The woman said, "The s deceived me,	5729
	3:14	So the LORD God said to the s,	5729
	49:17	Dan will be a s by the roadside,	5729
Job	26:13	his hand pierced the gliding s.	5729
Ps	91:13	you will trample the great lion and the s	9490
Isa	14:29	its fruit will be a darting, **venomous s.**	8597
	27: 1	Leviathan the gliding s,	5729
	27: 1	Leviathan the coiling s;	5729
Jer	46:22	a fleeing s as the enemy advances in force;	5729
	51:34	Like a s he has swallowed us	9490
Am	9: 3	there I will command the s to bite them.	5729
Rev	12: 9	that ancient s called the devil, or Satan,	4058
	12:15	Then from his mouth the s spewed water	4058
	20: 2	He seized the dragon, that ancient s,	4058

SERPENT'S (4) [SERPENT]

Ps	140: 3	They make their tongues as sharp as a s;	5729
Isa	65:25	but dust will be the s food.	5729
2Co	11: 3	as Eve was deceived by the s cunning,	899+4058
Rev	12:14	times and half a time, out of the s reach.	4058

SERPENTS (3) [SERPENT]

Dt	32:33	Their wine is the venom of s,	9490
Job	20:14	it will become the venom of s within him.	7352
	20:16	He will suck the poison of s;	7352

SERUG (6)

Ge	11:20	he became the father of S.	8578
	11:21	And after he became the father of S,	8578
	11:22	When S had lived 30 years,	8578
	11:23	S lived 200 years and had other sons	8578
1Ch	1:26	S, Nahor, Terah	8578
Lk	3:35	the son of S, the son of Reu,	4952

SERVANT (516) [MAIDSERVANT, MAIDSERVANTS, MANSERVANT, MENSERVANTS, SERVANT'S, SERVANTS, SERVANTS']

Ge	15: 3	so a s *in* my household will be my heir."	1201
	16: 5	I put my s in your arms,	9148
	16: 6	"Your s is in your hands," Abram said.	9148

Ge	16: 8	And he said, "Hagar, s of Sarai,	9148
	18: 3	my lord, do not pass your s by.	6269
	18: 5	now that you have come to your s."	6269
	18: 7	tender calf and gave it to a s,	5853
	19:19	Your s has found favor in your eyes,	6269
	24: 2	He said to the chief s in his household,	6269
	24: 5	The s asked him, "What if the woman	6269
	24: 9	So the s put his hand under the thigh	6269
	24:10	s took ten of his master's camels and left,	6269
	24:14	the one you have chosen for your s Isaac.	6269
	24:17	The s hurried to meet her and said,	6269
	24:34	So he said, "I am Abraham's s.	6269
	24:52	When Abraham's heard what they said,	6269
	24:53	the s brought out gold and silver jewelry	6269
	24:59	along with her nurse and Abraham's s	6269
	24:61	So the s took Rebekah and left.	6269
	24:65	and asked the s, "Who is that man	6269
	24:65	"He is my master," the s answered.	6269
	24:66	Then the s told Isaac all he had done.	6269
	26:24	for the sake of my s Abraham."	6269
	29:24	And Laban gave his s girl Zilpah	9148
	29:29	Laban gave his s girl Bilhah	9148
	30: 4	So she gave him her s Bilhah as a wife.	9148
	30: 7	Rachel's s Bilhah conceived again	9148
	30:10	Leah's s Zilpah bore Jacob a son.	9148
	30:12	Leah's s Zilpah bore Jacob a second son.	9148
	32: 4	'Your s Jacob says, I have been staying	6269
	32:10	and faithfulness you have shown your s.	6269
	32:18	'They belong to your s Jacob.	6269
	32:20	'Your s Jacob is coming behind us.' "	6269
	33: 5	children God has graciously given your s."	6269
	33:14	So let my lord go on ahead of his s,	6269
	41:12	a s of the captain of the guard.	6269
	43:28	"Your s our father is still alive and well."	6269
	44:18	my lord, let your s speak a word to my lord.	6269
	44:18	Do not be angry with your s,	6269
	44:24	When we went back to your s my father,	6269
	44:27	"Your s my father said to us,	6269
	44:30	with us when I go back to your s my father	6269
	44:32	Your s guaranteed the boy's safety	6269
	44:33	please let your s remain here	6269
Ex	4:10	past nor since you have spoken to your s.	6269
	14:31	put their trust in him and in Moses his s.	6269
	21: 2	"If you buy a Hebrew s,	6269
	21: 5	"But if the s declares,	6269
	21: 6	Then he will be his s for life.	6268
	21: 7	"If a man sells his daughter as a s,	6269
	21:26	he must let the s go free to compensate for	5647S
	21:27	he must let the s go free to compensate for	5647S
Nu	11:11	"Why have you brought this trouble on your s?	6269
	12: 7	But this is not true of my s Moses;	6269
	12: 8	not afraid to speak against my s Moses?"	6269
	14:24	because my s Caleb has a different spirit	6269
Dt	3:24	to show to your s your greatness	6269
	15:16	But if your s says to you,	NIH
	15:17	and he will become your s for life.	6269
	15:18	not consider it a hardship to set your s free,	2257S
	34: 5	And Moses the s of the LORD died there	6269
Jos	1: 1	the death of Moses the s of the LORD,	6269
	1: 2	"Moses my s is dead.	6269
	1: 7	to obey all the law my s Moses gave you;	6269
	1:13	"Remember the command that Moses the s	6269
	1:15	the s of the LORD gave you east of	6269
	5:14	What message does my Lord have for his s?	6269
	8:31	Moses the s of the LORD had commanded	6269
	8:33	as Moses the s of the LORD had formerly	6269
	9:24	LORD your God had commanded his s Moses	6269
	11:12	Moses the s of the LORD had commanded.	6269
	11:15	As the LORD commanded his s Moses,	6269
	12: 6	Moses, the s of the LORD,	6269
	12: 6	Moses the s of the LORD gave their land to	6269
	13: 8	as he, the s of the LORD, had assigned	6269
	14: 7	I was forty years old when Moses the s of	6269
	18: 7	Moses the s of the LORD gave it to them."	6269
	22: 2	"You have done all that Moses the s of	6269
	22: 4	to your homes in the land that Moses the s	6269
	22: 5	that Moses the s of the LORD gave you:	6269
	24:29	Joshua son of Nun, the s of the LORD,	6269
Jdg	2: 8	Joshua son of Nun, the s of the LORD,	6269
	7:10	go down to the camp with your s Purah	5853
	7:11	and Purah his s went down to the outposts	5853
	9:54	So his s ran him through, and he died.	5853
	15:18	"You have given your s this great victory.	6269
	16:26	Samson said to the s who held his hand,	5853
	19: 3	He had with him his s and two donkeys.	5853
	19: 9	the man, with his concubine and his s,	5853
	19:11	the s said to his master, "Come,	5853
Ru	2: 8	Stay here with my s girls.	5855
	2:13	and have spoken kindly to your s—	9148
	2:13	the standing of one of your s girls."	9148
	2:23	the s girls of Boaz to glean until the barley	5855
	3: 2	with whose s girls you have been,	5855
	3: 9	I am your s Ruth," she said.	563
1Sa	1:11	and not forget your s but give her a son,	563
	1:16	Do not take your s for a wicked woman;	563
	1:18	"May your s find favor in your eyes."	9148
	2:13	the s of the priest would come with	5853
	2:15	the s of the priest would come and say to	5853
	2:16	the s would then answer, "No,	NIH
	3: 9	'Speak, LORD, for your s is listening.' "	6269
	3:10	"Speak, for your s is listening."	6269
	9: 5	Saul said to the s who was with him,	5853
	9: 6	But he replied, "Look, in this town	NIH
	9: 7	Saul said to his s, "If we go,	5853
	9: 8	The s answered him again.	5853

1Sa	9:10	"Good," Saul said to his s.	5853
	9:22	Then Samuel brought Saul and his s into	5853
	9:27	"Tell the s to go on ahead of us"—	5853
	9:27	and the s did so—	NIH
	10:14	Now Saul's uncle asked him and his s,	5853
	17:32	your s will go and fight him."	6269
	17:34	"Your s has been keeping his father's sheep.	6269
	17:36	Your s has killed both the lion and the bear;	6269
	17:58	the son of your s Jesse of Bethlehem."	6269
	19: 4	"Let not the king do wrong to his s David;	6269
	20: 7	If he says, 'Very well,' then your s is safe.	6269
	20: 8	As for you, show kindness to your s,	6269
	22: 8	that my son has incited my s to lie in wait	6269
	22:15	Let not the king accuse your s or any	6269
	22:15	for your s knows nothing at all	6269
	23:10	your s has heard definitely that Saul plans	6269
	23:11	Will Saul come down, as your s has heard?	6269
	23:11	O LORD, God of Israel, tell your s."	6269
	25:24	Please let your s speak to you;	563
	25:24	hear what your s has to say.	563
	25:25	But as for me, your s, I did not see the men	563
	25:27	which your s has brought to my master,	9148
	25:31	when the LORD has brought my master success, remember your s."	563
	25:39	He has kept his s from doing wrong	6269
	26:18	he added, "Why is my lord pursuing his s?	6269
	27: 5	Why should your s live in the royal city	6269
	27:12	the Israelites, that he will be my s forever."	6269
	28: 2	for yourself what your s can do."	6269
	28:22	to your s and let me give you some food	9148
	29: 8	"What have you found against your s from	6269
2Sa	3:18	'By my s David I will rescue my people	6269
	7: 5	"Go and tell my s David, 'This is what	6269
	7: 8	"Now then, tell my s David,	6269
	7:19	about the future of the house of your s.	6269
	7:20	For you know your s, O Sovereign LORD.	6269
	7:21	and made it known to your s.	6269
	7:25	concerning your s and his house.	6269
	7:26	And the house of your s David will	6269
	7:27	you have revealed this to your s, saying,	6269
	7:27	So your s has found courage	6269
	7:28	have promised these good things to your s.	6269
	7:29	be pleased to bless the house of your s,	6269
	7:29	the house of your s will be blessed forever."	6269
	9: 2	a s of Saul's household named Ziba.	6269
	9: 2	"Your s," he replied.	6269
	9: 6	"Your s," he replied.	6269
	9: 8	"What is your s, that you should notice	6269
	9: 9	Then the king summoned Ziba, Saul's s,	5853
	9:11	"Your s will do whatever my lord	6269
	9:11	the king commands his s to do."	6269
	11:21	'Also, your s Uriah the Hittite is dead.' "	6269
	11:24	Moreover, your s Uriah the Hittite is dead."	6269
	13:17	He called his personal s and said,	5853+9250
	13:18	So his s put her out and bolted the door	9250
	13:24	"Your s has had shearers come.	6269
	13:35	it has happened just as your s said."	6269
	14: 6	I your s had two sons.	9148
	14: 7	the whole clan has risen up against your s;	9148
	14:12	"Let your s speak a word to my lord	9148
	14:15	Your s thought, 'I will speak to the king;	9148
	14:15	perhaps he will do what his s asks.	563
	14:16	Perhaps the king will agree to deliver his s	563
	14:17	"And now your s says,	9148
	14:19	it was your s Joab who instructed me	9148
	14:19	all these words into the mouth of your s.	9148
	14:20	Your s Joab did this to change	6269
	14:22	"Today your s knows that he has found	6269
	15: 2	"Your s is from one of the tribes of Israel."	6269
	15: 8	While your s was living at Geshur in Aram,	6269
	15:21	there will your s be."	6269
	15:34	'I will be your s, O king;	6269
	15:34	I was your father's s in the past,	6269
	15:34	but now I will be your s,'	6269
	17:17	A s girl was to go and inform them,	9148
	18:29	as Joab was about to send the king's s	6269
	18:29	your s, but I don't know what it was."	6269
	19:19	Do not remember how your s did wrong on	6269
	19:20	For I your s know that I have sinned,	6269
	19:26	"My lord the king, since I your s am lame,	6269
	19:26	But Ziba my s betrayed me.	6269
	19:27	he has slandered your s to my lord the king.	6269
	19:28	but you gave your s a place	6269
	19:35	Can your s taste what he eats and drinks?	6269
	19:35	Why should your s be an added burden	6269
	19:36	Your s will cross over the Jordan with	6269
	19:37	Let your s return, that I may die in my own	6269
	19:37	But here is your s Kimham.	6269
	20:17	She said, "Listen to what your s has to say."	563
	24:10	take away the guilt of your s.	6269
	24:21	"Why has my lord the king come to his s?"	6269
1Ki	1:13	did you not swear to me your s:	563
	1:17	swore to me your s by the LORD your God:	563
	1:19	but he has not invited Solomon your s.	6269
	1:26	But me your s, and Zadok the priest,	6269
	1:26	and your s Solomon he did not invite.	6269
	1:51	not put his s to death with the sword.' "	6269
	2:38	Your s will do as my lord the king	6269
	3: 6	"You have shown great kindness to your s,	6269
	3: 7	you have made your s king in place	6269
	3: 8	Your s is here among the people	6269
	3: 9	So give your s a discerning heart	6269
	3:20	from my side while I your s was asleep.	563
	8:24	to your s David my father;	6269
	8:25	keep for your s David my father	6269
	8:26	promised your s David my father come true.	6269
	8:28	the cry and the prayer that your s is praying	6269

1Ki	8:29	so that you will hear the prayer your s prays	6269
	8:30	Hear the supplication of your s and	6269
	8:53	just as you declared through your s Moses.	6269
	8:56	good promises he gave through his s Moses.	6269
	8:59	that he may uphold the cause of his s and	6269
	8:66	for his s David and his people Israel.	6269
	11:13	for the sake of David my s and for the sake	6269
	11:32	But for the sake of my s David and the city	6269
	11:34	of his life for the sake of David my s,	6269
	11:36	so that David my s may always have a lamp	6269
	11:38	as David my s did, I will be with you.	6269
	12: 7	"If today you will be a s to these people	6269
	14: 8	but you have not been like my s David,	6269
	14:18	as the LORD had said through his s	6269
	15:29	of the LORD given through his s Ahijah	6269
	18: 9	"that you are handing your s over to Ahab	6269
	18:12	Yet I your s have worshiped the LORD	6269
	18:36	God in Israel and that I am your s	6269
	18:43	"Go and look toward the sea," he told his s.	5853
	18:44	The seventh time the s reported,	NIH
	19: 3	he left his s there,	5853
	20: 9	'Your s will do all you demanded	6269
	20:32	"Your s Ben-Hadad says:	6269
	20:39	"Your s went into the thick of the battle,	6269
	20:40	While your s was busy here and there,	6269
2Ki	4: 1	"Your s my husband is dead,	6269
	4: 2	"Your s has nothing there at all," she said,	9148
	4:12	He said to his s Gehazi,	5853
	4:16	"Don't mislead your s, O man of God!"	9148
	4:19	His father told a s, "Carry him to his mother	5853
	4:20	the s had lifted him up and carried him	NIH
	4:24	She saddled the donkey and said to her s,	5853
	4:25	the man of God said to his s Gehazi,	5853
	4:38	he said to his s, "Put on the large pot	5853
	4:43	this before a hundred men?" his s asked.	9250
	5: 6	"With this letter I am sending my s Naaman	6269
	5:15	Please accept now a gift from your s."	6269
	5:17	said Naaman, "please let me, your s,	6269
	5:17	your s will never again make burnt offerings	6269
	5:18	But may the LORD forgive your s	6269
	5:18	may the LORD forgive your s for this."	6269
	5:20	the s of Elisha the man of God,	5853
	5:25	"Your s didn't go anywhere,"	6269
	6:15	When the s of the man of God got up	9250
	6:15	what shall we do?" the s asked.	5853
	8: 4	the s of the man of God, and had said,	5853
	8:13	Hazael said, "How could your s,	6269
	8:19	Nevertheless, for the sake of his s David,	6269
	9:36	that he spoke through his s Elijah	6269
	10:10	what he promised through his s Elijah."	6269
	14:25	spoken through his s Jonah son of Amittai,	6269
	16: 7	"I am your s and vassal.	6269
	18:12	that Moses the s of the LORD commanded.	6269
	19:34	for my sake and for the sake of David my s.	6269
	20: 6	for my sake and for the sake of my s David.	6269
	21: 8	that my s Moses gave them."	6269
1Ch	2:34	He had an Egyptian s named Jarha.	6269
	2:35	his daughter in marriage to his s Jarha,	6269
	6:49	that Moses the s of God had commanded.	6269
	16:13	O descendants of Israel his s,	6269
	17: 4	"Go and tell my s David, 'This is what	6269
	17: 7	"Now then, tell my s David,	6269
	17:17	about the future of the house of your s.	6269
	17:18	say to you for honoring your s?	6269
	17:18	For you know your s,	6269
	17:19	sake of your s and according to your will,	6269
	17:23	concerning your s and his house	6269
	17:24	And the house of your s David will	6269
	17:25	have revealed to your s that you will build	6269
	17:25	So your s has found courage to pray to you.	6269
	17:26	have promised these good things to your s.	6269
	17:27	of your s, that it may continue forever	6269
	21: 8	I beg you, take away the guilt of your s.	6269
2Ch	1: 3	which Moses the LORD's s had made in	6269
	6:15	to your s David my father;	6269
	6:16	keep for your s David my father	6269
	6:17	that you promised your s David come true.	6269
	6:19	the cry and the prayer that your s is praying	6269
	6:20	the prayer your s prays toward this place.	6269
	6:21	Hear the supplications of your s and	6269
	6:42	the great love promised to David your s."	6269
	24: 6	the s of the LORD and by the assembly	6269
	24: 9	to the LORD the tax that Moses the s	6269
	32:16	the LORD God and against his s Hezekiah.	6269
Ne	1: 6	the prayer your s is praying before you day	6269
	1: 7	decrees and laws you gave your s Moses.	6269
	1: 8	the instruction you gave your s Moses,	6269
	1:11	to the prayer of this your s and to the prayer	6269
	1:11	Give your s success today	6269
	2: 5	and if your s has found favor in his sight,	6269
	9:14	decrees and laws through your s Moses.	6269
	10:29	the Law of God given through Moses the s	6269
Job	1: 8	"Have you considered my s Job?	6269
	2: 3	"Have you considered my s Job?	6269
	19:16	I summon my s, but he does not answer,	6269
	42: 7	spoken of me what is right, as my s Job has.	6269
	42: 8	to my s Job and sacrifice a burnt offering	6269
	42: 8	My s Job will pray for you,	6269
	42: 8	spoken of me what is right, as my s Job has.	6269
Ps	18: T	Of David the s of the LORD.	6269
	19:11	By them is your s warned;	6269
	19:13	Keep your s also from willful sins;	6269
	27: 9	do not turn your s away in anger;	6269
	31:16	Let your face shine on your s;	6269
	35:27	who delights in the well-being of his s."	6269
	36: T	Of David the s of the LORD.	6269
	69:17	Do not hide your face from your s;	6269

Ps	78:70	He chose David his s and took him from	6269
	86: 2	save your s who trusts in you.	
	86: 4	Bring joy to your s, for to you, O Lord,	6269
	86:16	grant your strength to your s and save	6269
	89: 3	I have sworn to David my s,	6269
	89:20	I have found David my s;	6269
	89:39	with your s and have defiled his crown in	6269
	89:50	Lord, how your s has been mocked,	6269
	105: 6	O descendants of Abraham his s,	6269
	105:26	He sent Moses his s, and Aaron,	6269
	105:42	his holy promise given to his s Abraham.	6269
	109:28	but your s will rejoice.	6269
	116:16	O LORD, truly I am your s;	6269
	116:16	I am your s, the son of your maidservant;	6269
	119:17	Do good to your s, and I will live;	6269
	119:23	your s will meditate on your decrees.	6269
	119:38	Fulfill your promise to your s,	6269
	119:49	Remember your word to your s,	6269
	119:65	Do good to your s according to your word,	6269
	119:76	according to your promise to your s.	6269
	119:84	How long must your s wait?	6269
	119:124	Deal with your s according to your love	6269
	119:125	I am your s; give me discernment	6269
	119:135	upon your s and teach me your decrees.	6269
	119:140	and your s loves them.	6269
	119:176	Seek your s, for I have not forgotten	6269
	132:10	For the sake of David your s,	6269
	136:22	an inheritance to his s Israel;	6269
	143: 2	Do not bring your s into judgment,	6269
	143:12	destroy all my foes, for I am your s.	6269
	144:10	who delivers his s David from the deadly	6269
Pr	11:29	and the fool will be s to the wise.	6269
	12: 9	be a nobody and yet have a s than pretend	6269
	14:35	A king delights in a wise s,	6269
	14:35	but a shameful s incurs his wrath.	NIH
	17: 2	A wise s will rule over a disgraceful son,	6269
	22: 7	and the borrower is s to the lender.	6269
	27:27	and to nourish your s girls.	5855
	29:19	A s cannot be corrected by mere words;	6269
	29:21	If a man pampers his s from youth,	6269
	30:10	"Do not slander a s to his master,	6269
	30:22	a s who becomes king,	6269
	31:15	for her family and portions for her s girls.	5855
Ecc	7:21	or you may hear your s cursing you—	6269
	10: 7	a s and whose princes feast in the morning.	5853
Isa	16:14	a s bound by contract would count them,	8502
	20: 3	"Just as my s Isaiah has gone stripped	6269
	21:16	as a s bound by contract would count it,	8502
	22:20	"In that day I will summon my s,	6269
	24: 2	for master as for s, for mistress as for maid,	6269
	37:35	my sake and for the sake of David my s!"	6269
	41: 8	"But you, O Israel, my s, Jacob,	6269
	41: 9	I said, 'You are my s';	6269
	42: 1	"Here is my s, whom I uphold,	6269
	42:19	Who is blind but my s,	6269
	42:19	blind like the s of the LORD?	6269
	43:10	"and my s whom I have chosen,	6269
	44: 1	"But now listen, O Jacob, my s, Israel,	6269
	44: 2	Do not be afraid, O Jacob, my s, Jeshurun,	6269
	44:21	O Jacob, for you are my s, O Israel.	6269
	44:21	I have made you, you are my s;	6269
	45: 4	For the sake of Jacob my s,	6269
	48:20	"The LORD has redeemed his s Jacob."	6269
	49: 3	He said to me, "You are my s, Israel,	6269
	49: 5	in the womb to be his s to bring Jacob back	6269
	49: 6	"It is too small a thing for you to be my s	6269
	49: 7	to the s of rulers: "Kings will see you	6269
	50:10	the LORD and obeys the word of his s?	6269
	52:13	See, my s will act wisely;	6269
	53:11	by his knowledge my righteous s will justify many,	6269
Jer	2:14	Is Israel a s, a slave by birth?	6269
	25: 9	of the north and my s Nebuchadnezzar king	6269
	27: 6	to my s Nebuchadnezzar king of Babylon;	6269
	30:10	" 'So do not fear, O Jacob my s;	6269
	33:21	then my covenant with David my s—	6269
	33:22	of David my s and the Levites who minister	6269
	33:26	the descendants of Jacob and David my s	6269
	43:10	for my s Nebuchadnezzar king of Babylon,	6269
	46:27	"Do not fear, O Jacob my s,	6269
	46:28	Do not fear, O Jacob my s,	6269
Eze	28:25	which I gave to my s Jacob.	6269
	34:23	my s David, and he will tend them;	6269
	34:24	and my s David will be prince among them.	6269
	37:24	" 'My s David will be king over them,	6269
	37:25	in the land I gave to my s Jacob,	6269
	37:25	and David my s will be their prince forever.	6269
	46:17	the s may keep it until the year of freedom;	2257S
Da	6:20	"Daniel, s of the living God, has your God,	10523
	9:11	the s of God, have been poured out on us,	6269
	9:17	hear the prayers and petitions of your s.	6269
	10:17	How can I, your s, talk with you, my lord?	6269
Hag	2:23	my s Zerubbabel son of Shealtiel,'	6269
Zec	3: 8	I am going to bring my s, the Branch.	6269
Mal	1: 6	"A son honors his father, and a s his master.	6269
	4: 4	"Remember the law of my s Moses,	6269
Mt	8: 6	"my s lies at home paralyzed and	4090
	8: 8	just say the word, and my s will be healed.	4090
	8: 9	I say to my s, 'Do this,' and he does it."	1528
	8:13	And his s was healed at that very hour.	4090
	10:24	nor a s above his master.	1528
	10:25	and the s like his master.	1528
	12:18	"Here is my s whom I have chosen,	4090
	18:26	"The s fell on his knees before him.	1528
	18:28	"But when that s went out,	1528
	18:29	"His fellow s fell to his knees	5281
	18:32	"Then the master called the s in.	899S

Mt	18:32	'You wicked s,' he said,	1528
	18:33	on your fellow s just as I had on you?'	5281
	20:26	to become great among you must be your s,	1356
	23:11	The greatest among you will be your s.	1356
	24:45	"Who then is the faithful and wise s,	1528
	24:46	for that s whose master finds him doing so	1528
	24:48	But suppose that s is wicked and says	1528
	24:50	of that s will come on a day when he does	1528
	25:21	'Well done, good and faithful s!	1528
	25:23	'Well done, good and faithful s!	1528
	25:26	"His master replied, 'You wicked, lazy s!	1528
	25:30	And throw that worthless s outside,	1528
	26:51	and struck the s of the high priest,	1528
	26:69	and a s girl came to him.	4087
Mk	9:35	he must be the very last, and the s of all."	1356
	10:43	to become great among you must be your s,	1356
	12: 2	a s to the tenants to collect from them some	1528
	12: 4	Then he sent another s to them;	1528
	14:47	near drew his sword and struck the s of	1528
	14:66	of the s girls of the high priest came by.	4087
	14:69	When the s girl saw him there,	4087
Lk	1:38	"I am the Lord's s," Mary answered.	1527
	1:48	been mindful of the humble state of his s.	1527
	1:54	He has helped his s Israel,	4090
	1:69	for us in the house of his s David	4090
	2:29	you now dismiss your s in peace.	1528
	7: 2	There a centurion's s, whom his master	1528
	7: 3	asking him to come and heal his s.	1528
	7: 7	But say the word, and my s will be healed.	4090
	7: 8	I say to my s, 'Do this,' and he does it."	1528
	7:10	to the house and found the s well.	1528
	12:43	for that s whom the master finds doing so	1528
	12:45	But suppose the s says to himself,	1528
	12:46	of that s will come on a day when he does	1528
	12:47	"That s who knows his master's will	1528
	14:17	At the time of the banquet he sent his s	1528
	14:21	"The s came back and reported this	1528
	14:21	became angry and ordered his s,	1528
	14:22	the s said, 'what you ordered has been done,	1528
	14:23	"Then the master told his s,	1528
	16:13	"No s can serve two masters.	3860
	17: 7	of you had a s plowing or looking after	1528
	17: 7	to the s when he comes in from the field,	899S
	17: 9	the s because he did what he was told	1528
	19:17	" 'Well done, my good s!	1528
	19:20	"Then another s came and said, 'Sir,	NIG
	19:22	by your own words, you wicked s!	1528
	20:10	At harvest time he sent a s to the tenants	1528
	20:11	He sent another s,	1528
	22:50	one of them struck the s of the high priest,	1528
	22:56	A s girl saw him seated there in	4087
Jn	12:26	and where I am, my s also will be.	1356
	13:16	no s is greater than his master,	1528
	15:15	a s does not know his master's business.	1528
	15:20	'No s is greater than his master.'	1528
	18:10	drew it and struck the high priest's s,	1528
Ac	3:13	has glorified his s Jesus.	4090
	3:26	When God raised up his s,	4090
	4:25	the mouth of your s, our father David:	4090
	4:27	to conspire against your holy s Jesus,	4090
	4:30	through the name of your holy s Jesus."	4090
	12:13	and a s girl named Rhoda came to answer	4087
	12:20	Blastus, a trusted personal s of the king,	2093+3131+3836
	26:16	I have appeared to you to appoint you as a s	5677
Ro	1: 1	Paul, a s of Christ Jesus,	1528
	13: 4	For he is God's s to do you good.	1356
	13: 4	He is God's s, an agent of wrath	1356
	14: 4	Who are you to judge someone else's s?	3860
	15: 8	For I tell you that Christ has become a s of	1356
	16: 1	a s of the church in Cenchrea.	1356
Gal	1:10	I would not be a s of Christ.	1528
Eph	3: 7	I became a s of this gospel by the gift	1356
	6:21	the dear brother and faithful s in the Lord,	1356
Php	2: 7	taking the very nature of a s,	1528
Col	1: 7	from Epaphras, our dear fellow s,	5281
	1:23	and of which I, Paul, have become a s.	1356
	1:25	I have become its s by the commission	1356
	4: 7	a faithful minister and fellow s in the Lord.	5281
2Ti	2:24	And the Lord's s must not quarrel;	1528
Tit	1: 1	Paul, a s of God and an apostle of Jesus Christ for the faith	1528
Heb	3: 5	Moses was faithful as a s in all God's	2544
Jas	1: 1	James, a s of God and of the Lord Jesus	1528
2Pe	1: 1	Simon Peter, a s and apostle of Jesus Christ,	1528
Jude	1: 1	Jude, a s of Jesus Christ and a brother of James,	1528
Rev	1: 1	by sending his angel to his s John,	1528
	15: 3	and sang the song of Moses the s of God	1528
	19:10	fellow s with you and with your brothers	5281
	22: 9	fellow s with you and with your brothers	5281

SERVANT'S (12) [SERVANT]

Ge	19: 2	he said, "please turn aside to your s house.	6269
1Sa	1:11	if you will only look upon your s misery	563
	25:28	Please forgive your s offense,	563
	26:19	the king listen to his s words.	6269
2Sa	14:22	because the king has granted his s request."	6269
1Ki	8:28	to your s prayer and his plea for mercy,	6269
	8:52	"May your eyes be open to your s plea and	6269
2Ki	6:17	Then the LORD opened the s eyes,	5853
2Ch	6:19	to your s prayer and his plea for mercy,	6269
Ps	119:122	Ensure your s well-being;	6269
Mt	18:27	The s master took pity on him,	1528
Jn	18:10	(The s name was Malchus.)	1528

SERVANTS (264) [SERVANT]

Ge	21:25	of water that Abimelech's s had seized.	6269
	22: 3	with him two of his s and his son Isaac.	5853
	22: 5	He said to his s, "Stay here with the donkey	5853
	22:19	Then Abraham returned to his s,	5853
	26:14	He had so many flocks and herds and s that	6276
	26:15	So all the wells that his father's s had dug	6269
	26:19	Isaac's s dug in the valley and discovered	6269
	26:25	and there his s dug a well.	6269
	26:32	That day Isaac's s came and told him about	6269
	27:37	and have made all his relatives his s,	6269
	32:16	He put them in the care of his s,	6269
	32:16	each herd by itself, and said to his s,	6269
	39:11	and none of the household s was inside.	408
	39:14	she called her household s.	408
	41:10	Pharaoh was once angry with his s,	6269
	42:10	"Your s have come to buy food.	6269
	42:11	Your s are honest men, not spies."	6269
	42:13	they replied, "Your s were twelve brothers,	6269
	44: 7	be it from your s to do anything like that!	6269
	44: 9	If any of your s is found to have it,	6269
	44:19	My lord asked his s, 'Do you have a father	6269
	44:21	"Then you said to your s, 'Bring him down	6269
	44:23	But you told your s, 'Unless your youngest	6269
	44:31	Your s will bring the gray head	6269
	46:34	'Your s have tended livestock	6269
	47: 3	"Your s are shepherds,"	6269
	47: 4	So now, please let your s settle in Goshen."	6269
	50:17	the sins of the s of the God of your father."	6269
Ex	5:15	"Why have you treated your s this way?	6269
	5:16	Your s are given no straw, yet we are told,	6269
	5:16	Your s are being beaten,	6269
	32:13	Remember your s Abraham, Isaac and	6269
Lev	25:42	Because the Israelites are my s,	6269
	25:55	for the Israelites belong to me as s.	6269
	25:55	They are my s, whom I brought out of	6269
Nu	31:49	and his two s were with him.	5853
	32: 4	"Your s have counted the soldiers	6269
	32: 4	and your s have livestock.	6269
	32: 5	be given to your s as our possession.	6269
	32:25	"We your s will do as our lord commands.	6269
	32:27	But your s, every man armed for battle,	6269
	32:31	"Your s will do what the LORD has said.	6269
Dt	9:27	Remember your s Abraham, Isaac and	6269
	32:36	on his s when he sees their strength is gone	6269
	32:43	for he will avenge the blood of his s;	6269
Jos	9: 8	"We are your s," they said to Joshua.	6269
	9: 9	"Your s have come from a very distant	6269
	9:11	"We are your s; make a treaty with us.' "	6269
	9:24	"Your s were clearly told how	6269
	10: 6	"Do not abandon your s.	6269
Jdg	3:24	the s came and found the doors of	6269
	6:27	of his s and did as the LORD told him.	6269
	19:19	and bread and wine for ourselves your s—	6269
1Sa	9: 3	of the s with you and go and look for	5853
	12:19	"Pray to the LORD your God for your s so	6269
	16:16	Let our lord command his s here to search	6269
	16:18	One of the s answered,	5853
	17: 8	and are you not the s of Saul?	6269
	18:24	Saul's s told him what David had said,	6269
	21: 7	Now one of Saul's s was there that day,	6269
	21:11	But the s of Achish said to him,	6269
	21:14	Achish said to his s, "Look at the man!	6269
	22:14	"Who of all your s is as loyal as David,	6269
	25: 8	Ask your own s and they will tell you.	5853
	25: 8	Please give your s and your son David	6269
	25:10	Nabal answered David's s,	6269
	25:10	Many s are breaking away from their	6269
	25:14	One of the s told Nabal's wife Abigail:	5853
	25:19	Then she told her s, "Go on ahead;	5853
	25:40	His s went to Carmel and said to Abigail,	6269
	25:41	and wash the feet of my master's s."	6269
	29:10	along with your master's s who have come	6269
2Sa	6:20	of his s as any vulgar fellow would!"	6269
	9:10	You and your sons and your s are to farm	6269
	9:10	(Now Ziba had fifteen sons and twenty s.)	6269
	9:12	the members of Ziba's household were s	6269
	11: 9	to the palace with all his master's s and did	6269
	11:13	to sleep on his mat among his master's s;	6269
	11:24	Then the archers shot arrows at your s from	6269
	12:18	David's s were afraid to tell him that	6269
	12:19	David noticed that his s were whispering	6269
	12:21	His s asked him, "Why are you acting this	6269
	13:31	all his s stood by with their clothes torn.	6269
	13:36	too, and all his s wept very bitterly.	6269
	14:30	Then he said to his s, "Look,	6269
	14:30	So Absalom's s set the field on fire.	6269
	14:31	"Why have your s set my field on fire?"	6269
	15:15	"Your s are ready to do whatever our lord	6269
	19:17	and his fifteen sons and twenty s.	6269
1Ki	1: 2	So his s said to him,	6269
	1:27	without letting his s know who should sit	6269
	1:33	"Take your lord's s with you	6269
	8:23	with your s who continue wholeheartedly	6269
	8:32	Judge between your s,	6269
	8:36	from heaven and forgive the sin of your s,	6269
	10: 5	the attending s in their robes,	9250
	12: 7	they will always be your s."	6269
2Ki	1:13	and the lives of these fifty men, your s!	6269
	2:16	they said, "we your s have fifty able men.	6269
	4:22	of the s and a donkey so I can go to the man	5853
	5:13	Naaman's s went to him and said,	5853
	5:23	He gave them to two of his s,	5853
	5:24	from the s and put them away in the house.	4392S
	6: 3	"Won't you please come with your s?"	6269
	9: 7	of my s the prophets and the blood of all	6269

2Ki	9: 7	and the blood of all the LORD's s shed	6269
	9:28	His s took him by chariot to Jerusalem	6269
	10: 5	"We are your s and we will do anything	6269
	10:23	and see that no s of the LORD are here	6269
	17:13	and that I delivered to you through my s	6269
	17:23	as he had warned through all his s	6269
	18:26	"Please speak to your s in Aramaic,	6269
	21:10	The LORD said through his s the prophets:	6269
	23:30	Josiah's s brought his body in a chariot	6269
	24: 2	the word of the LORD proclaimed by his s	6269
1Ch	9: 2	priests, Levites and temple s.	5987
2Ch	2:10	I will give your s, the woodsmen who cut	6269
	2:15	"Now let my lord send his s the wheat	6269
	6:14	with your s who continue wholeheartedly	6269
	6:23	Judge between your s,	6269
	6:27	from heaven and forgive the sin of your s,	9250
	9: 4	the attending s in their robes,	9250
	10: 7	they will always be your s."	6269
	36:20	and they became s to him and his sons until	6269
Ezr	2:43	The temple s: the descendants of Ziha,	5987
	2:55	The descendants of the s of Solomon:	6269
	2:58	The temple s and the descendants of	5987
	2:58	the descendants of the s of Solomon 392	6269
	2:70	and the temple s settled in their own towns,	5987
	4:11	To King Artaxerxes, From your s,	10523
	5:11	the s of the God of heaven and earth,	10523
	7: 7	Levites, singers, gatekeepers and temple s,	5987
	7:24	temple s or other workers at this house	10497
	8:17	the temple s in Casiphia,	5987
	8:20	They also brought 220 of the temple s—	5987
	9:11	through your s the prophets when you said:	6269
Ne	1: 6	before you day and night for your s,	6269
	1:10	"They are your s and your people,	6269
	1:11	and to the prayer of your s who delight	6269
	2:20	We his s will start rebuilding,	6269
	3:26	the temple s living on the hill	5987
	3:31	of the temple s and the merchants, opposite	5987
	7:46	The temple s: the descendants of Ziha,	5987
	7:57	The descendants of the s of Solomon:	6269
	7:60	The temple s and the descendants of	5987
	7:60	the descendants of the s of Solomon 392	6269
	7:73	the singers and the temple s,	5987
	10:28	temple s and all who separated themselves	5987
	11: 3	temple s and descendants	5987
	11: 3	of Solomon's s lived in the towns of Judah,	6269
	11:21	The temple s lived on the hill of Ophel,	5987
Job	1: 3	and had a large number of s.	6276
	1:15	They put the s to the sword,	5853
	1:16	the sky and burned up the sheep and the s,	5853
	1:17	They put the s to the sword,	5853
	4:18	If God places no trust in his s,	6269
Ps	34:22	The LORD redeems his s;	6269
	69:36	the children of his s will inherit it,	6269
	79: 2	They have given the dead bodies of your s	6269
	79:10	the outpoured blood of your s.	6269
	90:13	Have compassion on your s.	6269
	90:16	May your deeds be shown to your s,	6269
	102:14	For her stones are dear to your s;	6269
	102:28	of your s will live in your presence;	6269
	103:21	you his s who do his will.	9250
	104: 4	flames of fire his s.	9250
	105:25	to conspire against his s.	6269
	113: 1	Praise, O s of the LORD,	6269
	134: 1	all you s of the LORD who minister	6269
	135: 1	praise him, you s of the LORD,	6269
	135: 9	O Egypt, against Pharaoh and all his s.	6269
	135:14	and have compassion on his s.	6269
Isa	36:11	"Please speak to your s in Aramaic,	6269
	44:26	of his s and fulfills the predictions	6269
	54:17	This is the heritage of the s of the LORD,	6269
	63:17	Return for the sake of your s,	6269
	65: 8	so will I do in behalf of my s;	6269
	65: 9	and there will my s live.	6269
	65:13	"My s will eat, but you will go hungry;	6269
	65:13	my s will drink, but you will go thirsty;	6269
	65:13	my s will rejoice, but you will be put	6269
	65:14	My s will sing out of the joy of their hearts,	6269
	65:15	but to his s he will give another name.	6269
	66:14	of the LORD will be made known to his s,	6269
Jer	7:25	and again I sent you my s the prophets.	6269
	14: 3	The nobles send their s for water;	7582
	25: 4	The LORD has sent all his s the prophets	6269
	26: 5	not listen to the words of my s the prophets,	6269
	29:19	that I sent to them again and again by my s	6269
	35:15	Again and again I sent all my s the prophets	6269
	44: 4	Again and again I sent my s the prophets,	6269
Eze	38:17	the one I spoke of in former days by my s	6269
Da	1:12	to one of his s, you may keep it until	6269
	1:12	"Please test your s for ten days:	6269
	1:13	and treat your s in accordance with what	6269
	2: 4	Tell your s the dream,	10523
	2: 7	"Let the king tell his s the dream,	10523
	3:26	s of the Most High God, come out!	10523
	3:28	who has sent his angel and rescued his s!	10523
	9: 6	We have not listened to your s the prophets,	6269
	9:10	or kept the laws he gave us through his s	6269
Joel	2:29	Even on my s, both men and women,	6269
Am	3: 7	without revealing his plan to his s	6269
Zec	1: 6	which I commanded my s the prophets,	6269
Mt	13:27	"The owner's s came to him and said, 'Sir,	1528
	13:28	"The s asked him, 'Do you want us to go	1528
	18:23	to settle accounts with his s.	1528
	18:28	one of his fellow s who owed him	5281
	18:31	When the other s saw what had happened,	5281
	21:34	he sent his s to the tenants	1528
	21:35	"The tenants seized his s;	1528
	21:36	Then he sent other s to them,	1528

Mt	22: 3	He sent his s to those who had been invited	1528
	22: 4	"Then he sent some more s and said,	1528
	22: 6	The rest seized his s, mistreated them and	1528
	22: 8	"Then he said to his s,	1528
	22:10	So the s went out into the streets	1528
	24:45	in charge of the s in his household	3859
	24:49	then begins to beat his fellow s and to eat	5281
	25:14	who called his s and entrusted his property	1528
	25:19	a long time the master of those s returned	1528
Mk	13:34	He leaves his house and puts his s	1528
Lk	1: 2	from the first were eyewitnesses and s of	5677
	12:37	those s whose master finds them watching	1528
	12:38	for those s whose master finds them ready,	NIG
	12:42	of his s to give them their food allowance at	2542
	15:22	"But the father said to his s, 'Quick!	1528
	15:26	of the s and asked him what was going on.	4090
	17:10	should say, 'We are unworthy s;	1528
	19:13	of his s and gave them ten minas.	1528
	19:15	for the s to whom he had given the money,	1528
Jn	2: 5	His mother said to the s,	1356
	2: 7	Jesus said to the s, "Fill the jars with water"	899S
	2: 9	the s who had drawn the water knew.	1356
	4:51	his s met him with the news	1528
	15:15	I no longer call you s,	1528
	18:18	and the s and officials stood around	1528
	18:26	One of the high priest's s,	1528
	18:36	my s would fight to prevent my arrest by	5677
Ac	2:18	Even on my s, both men and women,	1528
	4:29	consider their threats and enable your s	1528
	10: 7	of his s and a devout soldier who was one	3860
	16:17	"These men are s of the Most High God,	1528
Ro	13: 6	for the authorities are God's s,	3313
1Co	3: 5	Only s, through whom you came	1356
	4: 1	men ought to regard us as s of Christ and	5677
2Co	4: 5	and ourselves as your s for Jesus' sake.	1528
	6: 4	as s of God we commend ourselves	1356
	11:15	if his s masquerade as servants of	1356
	11:15	servants masquerade as s of righteousness.	1356
	11:23	Are they s of Christ?	1356
Php	1: 1	Paul and Timothy, s of Christ Jesus,	1528
Heb	1: 7	his s flames of fire.	3313
1Pe	2:16	live as s of God.	1528
Rev	1: 1	to show his s what must soon take place.	1528
	2:20	By her teaching she misleads my s	1528
	6:11	of their fellow s and brothers who were to	5281
	7: 3	until we put a seal on the foreheads of the s	1528
	10: 7	just as he announced to his s the prophets."	1528
	11:18	and for rewarding your s the prophets	1528
	19: 2	He has avenged on her the blood of his s."	1528
	19: 5	"Praise our God, all you his s,	1528
	22: 3	and his s will serve him.	1528
	22: 6	sent his angel to show his s the things	1528

SERVANTS' (2) [SERVANT]

Ge	44:16	God has uncovered your s' guilt.	6269
	47: 4	and your s' flocks have no pasture.	4200+6269

SERVE (219) [SERVED, SERVES, SERVICE, SERVICES, SERVING, SERVITUDE]

Ge	1:14	and let them s as signs to mark seasons	2118
	15:14	the nation they s as slaves,	5647
	25:23	and the older will s the younger."	6268
	27:29	May nations s you and peoples bow down	6268
	27:40	by the sword and you will s your brother.	6268
	31:44	and let it s as a witness between us."	2118
	43:31	controlling himself, said, "S the food."	8492
Ex	14:12	let us s the Egyptians'?	6268
	14:12	for us to s the Egyptians than to die in	6268
	18:13	to s as judge for the people	9149
	18:22	Have them s as judges for the people	9149
	21: 2	he is to s you for six years.	6268
	28: 1	so they may s me as priests.	3912
	28: 3	so he may s me as priest.	3912
	28: 4	so they may s me as priests.	3912
	28:41	so they may s me as priests.	3912
	29: 1	so they may s me as priests:	3912
	29:44	and his sons to s me as priests.	3912
	30:30	so they may s me as priests.	3912
	31:10	for his sons when they s as priests,	3912
	35:19	for his sons when they s as priests.	3912
	40:13	consecrate him so he may s me as priest.	3912
	40:15	so they may s me as priests.	3912
Lev	7:35	s the LORD as priests.	3912
Nu	1: 3	or more who are able to s in the army.	3655
	1:20	to s in the army were listed by name,	3655
	1:22	to s in the army were counted and listed	3655
	1:24	to s in the army were listed by name,	3655
	1:26	to s in the army were listed by name,	3655
	1:28	to s in the army were listed by name,	3655
	1:30	to s in the army were listed by name,	3655
	1:32	to s in the army were listed by name,	3655
	1:34	to s in the army were listed by name,	3655
	1:36	to s in the army were listed by name,	3655
	1:38	to s in the army were listed by name,	3655
	1:40	to s in the army were listed by name,	3655
	1:42	to s in the army were listed by name,	3655
	1:45	to s in Israel's army were counted	3655
	3: 3	who were ordained to s as priests,	3655
	3:10	Appoint Aaron and his sons to s as priests;	9068
	4: 3	s in the work in the Tent of Meeting.	6913+7372
	4:23	s in the work at the Tent of Meeting,	7371+7372
	4:30	to s in the work at the Tent of Meeting.	7372
	4:35	to s in the work in the Tent of Meeting,	7372
	4:39	to s in the work at the Tent of Meeting,	7372

Nu	4:43	to s in the work at the Tent of Meeting,	7372
	18: 7	and your sons may s as priests in connection	9068
	26: 2	or more who are able to s in the army	3655
Dt	6:13	s him only and take your oaths in his name.	6268
	7: 4	from following me to s other gods,	6268
	7:16	on them with pity and do not s their gods,	6268
	10:12	to love him, to s the LORD your God	6268
	10:20	Fear the LORD your God and s him.	6268
	11:13	to love the LORD your God and to s him	6268
	12:30	saying, "How do these nations s their gods?	6268
	13: 4	s him and hold fast to him.	6268
	18: 7	like all his fellow Levites who s there in	6641
	28:47	not s the LORD your God joyfully	6268
	28:48	you will s the enemies the LORD sends	6268
Jos	4: 6	to s as a sign among you.	2118
	9:23	to s as woodcutters and water carriers for	6269
	22: 5	to him and to s him with all your heart	6268
	23: 7	You must not s them or bow down to them.	6268
	23:16	go and s other gods and bow down to them,	6268
	24:14	the LORD and s him with all faithfulness.	6268
	24:14	and s the LORD.	6268
	24:15	for yourselves this day whom you will s.	6268
	24:15	me and my household, we will s the LORD."	6268
	24:16	to forsake the LORD to s other gods!	6268
	24:18	We too will s the LORD,	6268
	24:19	"You are not able to s the LORD.	6268
	24:20	you forsake the LORD and s foreign gods,	6268
	24:21	We will s the LORD."	6268
	24:22	that you have chosen to s the LORD."	6268
	24:24	"We will s the LORD our God	6268
Jdg	9:28	S the men of Hamor, Shechem's father!	6268
	9:28	Why should we s Abimelech?	6268
	18:19	Isn't it better that you s a tribe and	2118+4200
1Sa	7: 3	to the LORD and s him only,	6268
	8:11	will take your sons and make them s	4200+8492
	12:10	and we will s you.'	6268
	12:14	If you fear the LORD and s and obey him	6268
	12:20	but s the LORD with all your heart.	6268
	12:24	and s him faithfully with all your heart;	6268
	17: 9	you will become our subjects and s us."	6268
	18:17	only s me bravely and fight the battles of	2118
	25:41	ready to s you and wash the feet	9148
	26:19	and have said, 'Go, s other gods.'	6268
	29: 6	I would be pleased to have you s	995+2256+3655
2Sa	16:19	Furthermore, whom should I s?	6268
	16:19	Should I not s the son?	4200+7156
	16:19	your father, so I will s you."	2118+4200+7156
1Ki	9: 6	to s other gods and worship them,	6268
	9:27	to s in the fleet with Solomon's men.	NIH
	12: 4	and we will s you."	6268
	12: 7	to these people and s them and give them	6268
	16:31	and began to s Baal and worship him.	6268
	17: 1	God of Israel, lives, whom I s,	4200+6641+7156
	18:15	"As the LORD Almighty lives, whom I s,	4200+6641+7156
2Ki	3:14	as the LORD Almighty lives, whom I s,	4200+6641+7156
	4:41	"S it to the people to eat."	3668
	5:16	"As surely as the LORD lives, whom I s,	4200+6641+7156
	10:18	Jehu will s him much.	6268
	17:35	s them or sacrifice to them.	6268
	18: 7	the king of Assyria and did not s him.	6268
	23: 9	of the high places did not s at the altar of	6590
	25:24	down in the land and s the king of Babylon,	6268
1Ch	12:38	were fighting men who volunteered to s	6370
	23:31	They were to s before the LORD regularly	NIH
	28: 9	and s him with wholehearted devotion and	6268
2Ch	7:19	to s other gods and worship them,	6268
	10: 4	and we will s you.	6268
	13:10	The priests who s the LORD are sons	9250
	19: 9	"You must s faithfully and wholeheartedly	6913
	19:11	the Levites will s as officials before you.	8853
	29:11	to stand before him and s him,	9250
	30: 8	s the LORD your God,	6268
	33:16	and told Judah to s the LORD,	6268
	34:33	had all who were present in Israel s	6641
	35: 3	Now s the LORD your God	6268
Ne	4:22	so they can s us as guards by night	2118
	9:35	not s you or turn from their evil ways.	6268
Est	1: 8	to s each man what he wished.	6913
Job	21:15	Who is the Almighty, that we should s him?	6268
	36:11	If they obey and s him,	6268
	39: 9	"Will the wild ox consent to s you?	6268
Ps	2:11	S the LORD with fear and rejoice	6268
	22:30	Posterity will s him;	6268
	72:11	down to him and all nations will s him.	6268
	119:91	for all things s you.	6269
Pr	22:29	He will s before kings;	3656
	22:29	he will not s before obscure men.	3656
Isa	56: 6	to the LORD to s him, to love the name of	9250
	60: 7	the rams of Nebaioth will s you;	9250
	60:10	and their kings will s you.	9250
	60:12	or kingdom that will not s you will perish;	6268
Jer	2:20	you said, 'I will not s you!'	6268
	5:19	so now you will s foreigners in a land	6268
	11:10	They have followed other gods to s them,	6268
	13:10	after other gods to s and worship them, will	6268
	15:19	I will restore you that you may s me;	4200+6641+7156
	16:13	there you will s other gods day and night,	6268
	25: 6	Do not follow other gods to s	6268
	25:11	and these nations will s the king	6268
	27: 6	All nations will s him and his son	6268
	27: 7	not s Nebuchadnezzar king of Babylon	6268
	27: 9	'You will not s the king of Babylon.'	6268
	27:10	that will only s to remove you far	AIT

Jer	27:11	the yoke of the king of Babylon and s him,	6268
	27:12	s him and his people, and you will live.	6268
	27:13	that will not s the king of Babylon,	6268
	27:14	'You will not s the king of Babylon,'	6268
	27:17	S the king of Babylon, and you will live.	6268
	28:14	to make them s Nebuchadnezzar king	6268
	28:14	and they will s him.	6268
	30:9	they will s the LORD their God	6268
	35:15	do not follow other gods to s them.	6268
	35:19	fail to have a man to s me.'"	4200+6641+7156
	40:9	"Do not be afraid to s the Babylonians,"	6268
	40:9	down in the land and s the king of Babylon,	6268
Eze	20:32	who s wood and stone."	9250
	20:39	Go and s your idols, every one of you!	6268
	20:40	the entire house of Israel will s me,	6268
	27:25	of Tarshish s as carriers for your wares.	AIT
	41:6	the wall of the temple to s as supports for	2118
	44:11	They may s in my sanctuary,	2118
	44:11	and stand before the people and s them.	9250
	44:13	They are not to come near to s me as priests	3912
	44:24	the priests are to s as judges and decide it	6641
	45:5	Levites, who s in the temple,	9250
	47:12	Their fruit will s for food and their leaves	2118
Da	1:4	and qualified to s in the king's palace.	6641
	3:12	They neither s your gods nor worship	10586
	3:14	that you do not s my gods or worship	10586
	3:17	the God we s is able to save us from it,	10586
	3:18	that we will not s your gods or worship	10586
	3:28	to give up their lives rather than s	10586
	6:16	"May your God, whom you s continually,	10586
	6:20	has your God, whom you s continually,	10586
Zep	3:9	the LORD and s him shoulder to shoulder.	6268
Zec	4:14	"These are the two who are anointed to s the Lord	6584+6641
Mal	3:14	"You have said, 'It is futile to s God.	6268
	3:18	between those who s God	6268
Mt	4:10	the Lord your God, and s him only.' "	3302
	6:24	"No one can s two masters.	1526
	6:24	You cannot s both God and Money.	1526
	20:28	to be served, but to s, and to give his life	1354
Mk	10:45	to be served, but to s, and to give his life	1354
Lk	1:74	and to enable us to s him without fear	3302
	4:8	the Lord your God and s him only.' "	3302
	12:37	he will dress himself to s,	4322
	16:13	"No servant can s two masters.	1526
	16:13	You cannot s both God and Money."	1526
Ac	7:7	I will punish the nation they s as slaves,'	1526
	26:7	to see fulfilled as they earnestly s God day	3302
	27:23	of the God whose I am and whom I s stood	3302
Ro	1:9	God, whom I s with my whole heart	3302
	7:6	from the law so that we s in the new way of	1526
	9:12	"The older will s the younger."	1526
	12:7	If it is serving, let him s;	1355
1Co	9:13	and those who s at the altar share	4204
2Co	11:8	receiving support from them so as to s you.	1355
	13:4	we will live with him to s you.	1650
Gal	5:13	rather, s one another in love.	1526
Eph	6:7	S wholeheartedly, as if you were serving	1526
1Th	1:9	from idols to s the living and true God,	1526
1Ti	3:10	let them s as deacons.	1354
	6:2	Instead, they are to s them even better,	1526
2Ti	1:3	I thank God, whom I s,	3302
Heb	1:14	to s those who will inherit salvation?	1355
	8:5	They s at a sanctuary that is a copy	3302
	9:14	so that we may s the living God!	3302
1Pe	4:10	Each one should use whatever gift he has received to s others,	1354
	5:2	not greedy for money, but eager to s;	NIG
Jude	1:7	They s as an example of those who suffer	4618
Rev	1:6	to be a kingdom and priests to s his God	NIG
	5:10	to be a kingdom and priests to s our God,	NIG
	7:15	the throne of God and s him day and night	3302
	22:3	and his servants will s him.	3302

SERVED (70) [SERVE]

Ge	29:20	So Jacob s seven years to get Rachel,	6268
	29:25	I s you for Rachel, didn't I?	6268
	30:26	wives and children, for whom I have s you,	6268
	43:32	They s him by himself,	8492
	43:34	portions were s to them from Joseph's table,	5951
Ex	18:26	They s as judges for the people at all times.	9149
	38:8	the women who s at the entrance to the Tent of Meeting.	7371+7371
Nu	3:4	and Ithamar s as priests during the lifetime	3912
	4:37	of all those in the Kohathite clans who s in	6268
	4:41	in the Gershonite clans who s at the Tent	6268
	26:10	And they s as a warning sign.	2118
Jos	24:15	whether the gods your forefathers s beyond	6268
	24:31	Israel s the LORD throughout the lifetime	6268
Jdg	2:7	The people s the LORD throughout	6268
	2:11	in the eyes of the LORD and s the Baals.	6268
	2:13	because they forsook him and s Baal and	6268
	3:6	daughters to their sons, and s their gods.	6268
	3:7	The LORD their God and s the Baals and	6268
	10:6	They s the Baals and the Ashtoreths,	6268
	10:6	forsook the LORD and no longer s him,	6268
	10:13	But you have forsaken me and s other gods,	6268
	10:16	of the foreign gods among them and s	6268
1Sa	2:22	and how they slept with the women who s	7371
	7:4	Baals and Ashtoreths, and s the LORD only.	6268
	8:2	and they s at Beersheba.	9149
	12:10	we have forsaken the LORD and s the Baals	6268
2Sa	12:20	and at his request they s him food,	8492
	13:9	Then she took the pan and s him the bread,	3668
	16:19	Just as I s your father, so I will serve you."	6268
1Ki	11:17	some Edomite officials who had s his father.	6269

1Ki	12:6	the elders who had s his father Solomon	907+6641+7156
	22:53	He s and worshiped Baal and provoked	6268
2Ki	5:2	and she s Naaman's wife.	2118+4200+7156
	10:18	"Ahab s Baal a little;	6268
	17:33	also s their own gods in accordance with	6268
1Ch	6:10	of Azariah (it was he who s as priest in	3912
	6:33	Here are the men who s,	6641
	6:39	who s at his right hand:	6641
	23:24	or more who s in the temple of the LORD.	6275
	24:2	so Eleazar and Ithamar s as the priests.	3912
	27:1	and their officers, who s the king in all	9250
2Ch	10:6	the elders who had s his father Solomon	4200+6641+7156
	17:19	These were the men who s the king,	9250
	35:13	caldrons and pans and s them quickly to all	8132
Ne	12:26	They s in the days of Joiakim son	NIH
Est	1:7	Wine was s in goblets of gold,	9197
	1:10	the seven eunuchs who s him—	9250
Jer	5:19	and s foreign gods in your own land,	6268
	8:2	and s and which they have followed	6268
	16:11	'and followed other gods and s	6268
	22:9	and have worshiped and s other gods.' "	6268
	34:14	After he has s you six years,	6268
	52:12	who s the king of Babylon,	4200+6641+7156
Eze	27:9	was your sail and s as your banner;	2118
	27:10	Lydia and Put s as soldiers in your army.	2118
	44:12	But because they s them in the presence	9250
Hos	12:12	Israel s to get a wife,	6268
Mt	20:28	as the Son of Man did not come to be s,	1354
Mk	10:45	even the Son of Man did not come to be s,	1354
Jn	12:2	Martha s, while Lazarus was among those	1354
	13:2	The evening meal was being s,	NIG
Ac	1:16	Judas, who s as guide for those who	1181
	13:36	"For when David had s God's purpose	5676
	17:25	And he is not s by human hands,	2543
	20:19	I s the Lord with great humility and	1526
Ro	1:25	and s created things rather than the Creator	3302
Php	1:12	that what has happened to me has really s	2262
	2:22	with his father he has s with me in the work	1526
1Ti	3:13	Those who have s well gain an excellent	1354
Heb	7:13	and no one from that tribe has ever s at	4668

SERVES (11) [SERVE]

Dt	15:12	sells himself to you and s you six years,	6268
Mal	3:17	a man spares his son who s him.	6268
Lk	22:26	and the one who rules like the one who s.	1354
	22:27	one who is at the table or the one who s?	1354
	22:27	But I am among you as one who s.	1354
Jn	12:26	Whoever s me must follow me;	1354
	12:26	My Father will honor the one who s me.	1354
Ro	14:18	because anyone who s Christ in this way	1526
1Co	9:7	Who s as a soldier at his own expense?	5129
Hcb	8:2	and who s in the sanctuary,	3313
1Pe	4:11	If anyone s, he should do it with the strength	1354

SERVICE (76) [SERVE]

Ge	41:46	when he entered the s of Pharaoh king of Egypt.	4200+6641+7156
	50:2	Then Joseph directed the physicians in his s	6269
Ex	27:19	All the other articles used in the s of	6275
	30:16	the Israelites and use it for the s of the Tent	6275
	35:21	for all its s, and for the sacred garments.	6275
Nu	4:24	the s of the Gershonite clans as they work	6275
	4:26	and all the equipment used in its s.	6275
	4:27	All their s, whether carrying or doing	6275
	4:28	the s of the Gershonite clans at the Tent	6275
	4:31	as they perform s at the Tent of Meeting:	6275
	4:33	the s of the Merarite clans as they work at	6275
	8:25	retire from their regular s and work	6275+7372
	18:7	I am giving you the s of the priesthood as	6275
Dt	15:18	to set your servant free, because	6269
Jos	18:7	because the priestly s of the LORD is their	3914
1Sa	14:52	or brave man, he took him into his s.	665
	16:21	David came to Saul and entered his s.	4200+6641+7156
	16:22	"Allow David to remain in my s,	4200+7156
1Ki	8:11	And the priests could not perform their s	9250
2Ki	25:14	the bronze articles used in the temple s.	9250
1Ch	5:18	men ready for military s—	3655+7372
	9:18	of the articles used in the temple s;	6275
	23:26	or any of the articles used in its s."	6275
	23:28	to help Aaron's descendants in the s of	6275
	23:32	for the s of the temple of the LORD.	6275
	25:1	list of the men who performed this s:	6275
	26:30	of the LORD and for the king's s.	6275
	28:1	the commanders of the divisions in the s of	9250
	28:13	well as for all the articles to be used in its s.	6275
	28:14	used in various kinds of s,	2256+6275+6275
	28:14	used in various kinds of s:	2256+6275+6275
	28:20	until all the work for the s of the temple of	6275
2Ch	5:14	not perform their s because of the cloud,	9250
	17:16	volunteered himself for the s of the LORD,	5605
	24:14	articles for the s and for the burnt offerings,	9250
	25:5	there were three hundred thousand men ready for military s,	3655+7372
	29:35	So the s of the temple of the LORD	6275
	30:22	who showed good understanding of the s of	4200
	31:21	that he undertook in the s of God's temple	6275
	35:2	to their duties and encouraged them in the s	6275
	35:10	The s was arranged and the priests stood	6275
	35:16	the entire s of the LORD was carried out	6275
Ezr	10:25	the Levites in their groups for the s of God	10525
Ne	10:32	of a shekel each year for the s of the house	6275
	11:22	who were the singers responsible for the s	4856

Ne	12:45	They performed the s of their God and	5466
	12:45	of their God and the s of purification.	5466
	13:10	for the s had gone back to their own fields.	4856
Job	7:1	"Does not man have hard s on earth?	7372
	14:14	of my hard s I will wait for my renewal	7372
Isa	40:2	to her that her hard s has been completed,	7372
	41:2	calling him in righteousness to his s?	8079
Jer	52:18	the bronze articles used in the temple s.	9250
Eze	44:16	to minister before me and perform my s.	5466
Da	1:5	they were to enter the king's s.	4200+6641+7156
	1:19	so they entered the king's s.	4200+6641+7156
Lk	1:23	When his time of s was completed,	3311
	9:62	and looks back is fit for s in the kingdom	2310
	12:35	"Be dressed ready for s and	3836+4019+4322
Jn	16:2	kills you will think he is offering a s to God.	3301
Ro	12:1	I glory in Christ Jesus in my s to God.	NIG
	15:25	I am on my way to Jerusalem in the s of	1354
	15:31	that my s in Jerusalem may be acceptable to	1355
1Co	12:5	There are different kinds of s,	1355
	16:15	and they have devoted themselves to the s	1355
2Co	8:4	with us for the privilege of sharing in this s	1355
	8:18	by all the churches for his s to the gospel.	NIG
	9:1	to write to you about this s to the saints.	1355
	9:12	This s that you perform	1355+3311+3836+4047
	9:13	the s by which you have proved yourselves,	1355
Eph	4:12	to prepare God's people for works of s,	1355
Php	2:17	the sacrifice and s coming from your faith,	3311
1Ti	1:12	me faithful, appointing me to his s.	1355
	6:2	those who benefit from their s are believers,	2307
Heb	2:17	a merciful and faithful high priest in s	NIG
Rev	2:19	your s and perseverance,	1355

SERVICES (3) [SERVE]

Ex	14:5	let the Israelites go and have lost their s!"	6268
Ne	10:32	stood opposite them in the s.	5466
	13:14	done for the house of my God and its s.	5464

SERVILE (KJV) See REGULAR

SERVING (28) [SERVE]

Ex	39:41	the garments for his sons when s as priests.	3912
Nu	4:47	to do the work of s and carrying the Tent	6275
	8:25	in return for the work they do while s at	6275
Dt	28:14	following other gods and s them.	6268
Jos	20:6	until the death of the high priest who is s at	2118
	24:15	if s the LORD seems undesirable to you,	6268
Jdg	2:19	and s and worshiping them.	6268
	10:10	forsaking our God and s the Baals."	6268
1Sa	8:8	forsaking me and s other gods,	6268
1Ki	9:9	other gods, worshiping and s them—	6268
	12:8	who had grown up with him and were s him.	4200+6641+7156
2Ki	17:41	they were s their idols.	6268
1Ch	28:13	the work of s in the temple of the LORD,	6275
2Ch	7:22	other gods, worshiping and s them—	6268
	10:8	who had grown up with him and were s him.	4200+6641+7156
	12:8	the difference between s me and serving	6275
	12:8	the difference between serving me and s	6275
Eze	44:11	of the gates of the temple and s in it;	9250
	48:11	who were faithful in s me and did	5466
Lk	1:8	on duty and he was s as priest before God,	2634
Ro	12:7	If it is s, let him serve;	1355
	12:11	but keep your spiritual fervor, s the Lord.	1526
	16:18	For such people are not s our Lord Christ,	1526
Eph	6:7	as if you were s the Lord, not men,	NIG
Col	3:24	It is the Lord Christ you are s.	1526
2Ti	2:4	No one s as a soldier gets involved	5129
1Pe	1:12	that they were not s themselves, but you,	1354
	5:2	that is under your care, s as overseers—	2174

SERVITOR (KJV) See SERVANT

SERVITUDE (1) [SERVE]

Ge	47:21	Joseph reduced the people to s,	4200+6268+6269

SET (610) [SETS, SETTING, SETTINGS]

Ge	1:17	God s them in the expanse of the sky	5989
	8:9	the dove could find no place to s its feet	4955
	9:13	I have s my rainbow in the clouds,	5989
	11:31	and together they s out from Ur of	3655
	12:4	when he s out from Haran.	3655
	12:5	and they s out for the land of Canaan,	3655
	12:9	Then Abram s out and continued toward	5825
	13:11	of the Jordan and s out toward the east.	5825
	15:17	When the sun had s and darkness had fallen,	995
	18:8	and s these before them.	5989
	21:14	He s them on her shoulders and	8492
	21:28	Abraham s apart seven ewe lambs from	5893
	21:29	of these seven ewe lambs you have s apart	5893
	22:3	he s out for the place God had told him	2143
	22:19	and they s off together for Beersheba.	2143
	24:10	He s out for Aram Naharaim	7756
	24:33	Then food was s before him, but he said,	8492
	28:10	Jacob left Beersheba and s out for Haran.	2143
	28:11	for the night because the sun had s.	995
	28:18	and s it up as a pillar and poured oil on top	8492
	28:22	and this stone that I have s up as a pillar	8492
	30:40	s apart the young of the flock by themselves,	7233
	31:45	So Jacob took a stone and s it up as a pillar.	8123
	31:51	and here is this pillar I have s up	3721
	33:20	There he s up an altar and called it	5893

Ge 34: 8 "My son Shechem *has* his heart s on your 3137
35: 5 Then *they* s out, and the terror of God 5825
35:14 Jacob s up a stone pillar at the place 5893
35:20 Over her tomb Jacob s up a pillar, 5893
43: 9 not bring him back to you and s him here 3657
46: 1 So Israel s out with all that was his, 5825
49:21 a doe s free that bears beautiful fawns. 8938
Ex 9: 5 The LORD s a time and said, 8492
9:17 You still s yourself against my people 6147
16: 1 The whole Israelite community s out from 5825
17: 1 The whole Israelite community s out from 5825
19: 2 After *they* s out from Rephidim, 5825
19: 7 the people and s before them all the words 8492
19:23 the mountain and s it **apart as holy.' "** 7727
21: 1 the laws *you are to* s before them: 8492
24: 4 and s up twelve stone pillars representing NIH
24:13 Then Moses s out with Joshua his aide, 7756
25:37 "Then make its seven lamps and s them **up** 6590
26: 4 along the edge of the end curtain in one s, 2501
26: 4 the same with the end curtain in the other s. 4678
26: 5 on the end curtain of the other s, 4678
26: 9 five of the curtains together **into one s** 963+4200
26: 9 and the other six **into another s.** 963+4200
26:10 the edge of the end curtain in one s and also 2501
26:10 the edge of the end curtain in the other s. 2501
26:17 two projections s **parallel** to each other. 8917
26:30 "S **up** the tabernacle according to the plan 7756
31: 5 to cut and s stones, to work in wood, 4848
32:29 "You *have been* s **apart** to the LORD 3338+4848
35:33 to cut and s stones, to work in wood, 4848
36:11 along the edge of the end curtain in one s, 4678
36:11 with the end curtain in the other s. 4678
36:12 on the end curtain of the other s, 4678
36:16 into one set and the other six into another s. 963
36:16 into one set and the other six into *another* s. 963
36:17 the edge of the end curtain in one s and also 4678
36:17 the edge of the end curtain in the other s. 2501
36:22 with two projections s **parallel** 8917
40: 2 "S **up** the tabernacle, the Tent of Meeting, 7756
40: 4 Bring in the table and s **out** what belongs 6885
40: 4 bring in the lampstand and s **up** its lamps. 6590
40: 8 S **up** the courtyard around it and put 8492
40:17 So the tabernacle *was* s **up** on the first day 7756
40:18 When Moses s **up** the tabernacle, 7756
40:18 inserted the crossbars and s **up** the posts. 7756
40:23 s out the bread on it before the LORD, 6885+6886
40:25 and s **up** the lamps before the LORD, 6590
40:29 He s the altar of burnt offering near 8492
40:33 Then Moses s **up** the courtyard around 7756
40:36 above the tabernacle, *they would* s **out;** 5825
40:37 *they did* not s out—until the day it lifted. 5825
Lev 8: 9 on Aaron's head and s the gold plate, 8492
17:10 *I will* s my face against that person who 5989
20: 3 *I will* s my face against that man 5989
20: 5 *I will* s my face against that man 8492
20: 6 " '*I will* s my face against the person 5989
20:24 who *has* s you **apart** from the nations 976
20:25 those which *I have* s **apart** as unclean 976
20:26 and *I have* s you **apart** from the nations to 976
24: 6 S them in two rows, six in each row, 8492
24: 8 *to be* s before the LORD regularly, 6885
26: 1 " 'Do not make idols or s **up** an image or 7756
26:17 *I will* s my face against you so 5989
27: 3 s the value of a male between the ages 2118
27: 4 s her value at thirty shekels. 2118
27: 5 s the value of a male at twenty shekels and 2118
27: 6 s the value of a male at five shekels 2118
27: 7 s the value of a male at fifteen shekels and 2118
27: 8 who *will* s *the* **value** for him according 6885
27:16 its value *is to be* s according to 2118
27:17 the value that has been s remains. NIH
27:18 and its s **value** will be reduced. 6886
27:25 *to be* s according to the sanctuary shekel, 2118
27:27 he may buy it back at its s **value,** 6886
27:27 it is to be sold at its s **value.** 6886
Nu 1:51 and whenever the tabernacle *is to be* s **up,** 2837
1:52 The Israelites *are to* s **up** their **tents** 2837
1:53 *to* s **up** their **tents** around the tabernacle of 2837
2: 9 They will s out first. 5825
2:16 They will s out second. 5825
2:17 of the Levites *will* s out in the middle of 5825
2:17 *They will* s out in the same order 5825
2:24 They will s out third. 5825
2:31 They will s out last, under their standards. 5825
2:34 and that is the way *they* s **out,** 5825
3:13 *I* s **apart** for myself every firstborn 7727
8: 2 'When you s **up** the seven lamps, 6590
8: 3 he s **up** the lamps so that they faced forward 6590
8:14 In this way *you are to* s the Levites **apart** 976
8:17 *I* s them **apart** for myself. 7727
9:15 the Tent of the Testimony, *was* s **up,** 7756
9:17 from above the Tent, the Israelites s **out;** 5825
9:18 the LORD's command the Israelites s **out,** 5825
9:19 the LORD's order and *did not* s **out.** 5825
9:20 and then at his command *they would* s **out.** 5825
9:21 when it lifted in the morning, *they* s **out.** 5825
9:21 whenever the cloud lifted, *they* s **out.** 5825
9:22 would remain in camp and not s **out;** 5825
9:22 but when it lifted, *they would* s **out.** 5825
9:23 and at the LORD's command *they* s **out.** 5825
10: 2 and for *having* the camps s **out.** 5023
10: 5 the tribes camping on the east *are to* s **out.** 5825
10: 6 the camps on the south *are to* s **out.** 5825
10:12 the Israelites s **out** from the Desert of Sinai 5825
10:13 *They* s **out,** this first time, 5825
10:17 and Merarites, who carried it, s **out.** 5825
10:21 Kohathites s **out,** carrying the holy things. 5825

Nu 10:21 *to be* s **up** before they arrived. 7756
10:25 the divisions of the camp of Dan s **out,** 5825
10:28 for the Israelite divisions as *they* s **out.** 5825
10:33 So *they* s **out** from the mountain of 5825
10:34 over them by day when they s **out** from 5825
10:35 Whenever the ark s **out,** Moses said, 5825
14:25 and s **out** *toward* the desert along the route 5825
16: 3 Why then *do you* s yourselves above 5951
18:11 *whatever* is s **aside** *from* the gifts of all 9556
18:16 at the redemption **price** s *at* five shekels 6886
18:19 Whatever is s **aside** *from* the holy offerings 9556
20:22 The whole Israelite community s **out** 5825
21:11 Then *they* s **out** from Oboth and camped 5825
21:13 *They* s **out** from there and camped 5825
24:21 your nest *is* s in a rock; 8492
31:28 s **apart** as tribute for the LORD one out 8123
31:42 which Moses s **apart** from that of 2936
33: 3 The Israelites s **out** from Rameses on 5825
Dt 1:13 and *I will* s them over you." 8492
1:19 *we* s **out** from Horeb and went toward 5825
1:36 and his descendants the land he s *his* **feet** 2005
1:40 and s **out** toward the desert *along* the route 5825
2: 1 and s **out** toward the desert *along* the route 5825
2:24 "S **out** now and cross the Arnon Gorge. AIT
4:41 Moses s **aside** three cities east of the Jordan, 976
4:44 the law Moses s before the Israelites. 8492
5:21 not s *your* **desire on** your neighbor's house 203
7: 7 The LORD *did* not s *his* **affection** on you 3137
7:26 will be s **apart for** destruction. 3051
7:26 for it is s **apart for** destruction. 3051
10: 8 At that time the LORD s **apart** the tribe 976
10:15 Yet the LORD s *his* **affection** on your 3137
11:24 Every place where *you* s your foot will 2005
14:22 Be sure to s **aside** a tenth of all 6923+6923
15:18 a hardship *to* s your servant **free,** 2930+8938
15:19 S **apart** for the LORD your God every 7727
firstborn male
16:21 not s **up** any wooden Asherah pole beside 5749
17:14 "Let *us* s a king over us like all the nations 8492
19: 2 then s **aside** for yourselves three cities 976
19: 7 This is why I command you *to* s **aside** 976
19: 9 then you are to s **aside** three more cities. NIH
19:14 move your neighbor's boundary stone s **up** 1487
26: 4 from your hands and s it **down** in front of 5663
26:19 He has declared that he *will* s you 5989
27: 2 s **up** some large stones and coat them 7756
27: 4 s **up** these stones on Mount Ebal, 7756
28: 1 the LORD your God *will* s you high 5989
28:36 and the king you s over you to 7756
30: 1 and curses *I have* s before you come 5989
30:15 *I* s before you today life and prosperity, 5989
30:19 that *I have* s before you life and death, 5989
32: 8 *he* s **up** boundaries for the peoples 5893
32:22 and its harvests and s **afire** the foundations 4265
Jos 1: 3 every place where *you* s your foot, 2005
2: 7 So the men s **out in pursuit** of the spies *on* 8103
3: 1 the Israelites s **out** from Shittim and went 5265
3:13 s foot in the Jordan, its waters flowing 5663
4: 9 Joshua s **up** the twelve stones that had been 7756
4:18 No sooner *had* they s their feet on 5998
4:20 And Joshua s **up** at Gilgal 7756
6:26 at the cost of his youngest *will he* s **up** 5893
8: 2 S **an ambush** behind the city." 8492
8: 4 You *are to* s **an ambush** behind the city. 741
8: 8 When you have taken the city, s it **on fire.** 836+928+2021+3675
8:11 *They* s **up camp** north of Ai, 2837
8:12 and s them in ambush between Bethel 8492
8:14 that an **ambush** *had been* s against him 741
8:19 and captured it and quickly s it **on fire.** 836+928+2021+3675
9:17 So the Israelites s **out** and on 5825
16: 9 that were s **aside** for the Ephraimites within 4426
18: 1 of the Israelites gathered at Shiloh and s **up** 8905
20: 7 So *they* s **apart** Kedesh in Galilee in 7727
24:26 a large stone and s it **up** there under the oak 7756
Jdg 1: 8 They put the city to the sword and s it 8938
6:18 and bring my offering and s it before you." 5663
8:33 *They* s **up** Baal-Berith as their god 8492
9:25 to him these citizens of Shechem s men on 8492
9:34 and all his troops s **out** by night and took 7756
9:43 into three companies and s **an ambush** in 741
9:49 against the stronghold and s it **on fire** over 836+928+2021+3675
9:52 the entrance to the tower to s it **on fire,** 836+928+2021+8596
13: 5 to be a **Nazirite,** *s* apart *to* God from birth, AIT
16:17 "because I have been a **Nazirite** *s apart* AIT
16:21 they s *him* to grinding in the prison. 2118
18:11 s **out** from Zorah and Eshtaol. 5825
18:12 On their way *they* s **up camp** 2837
18:30 the Danites s **up** for themselves the idols, 7756
19:14 sun s as they neared Gibeah in Benjamin. 995
19:28 the man put her on his donkey and s **out** 2143
20:29 Then Israel s **an ambush** around Gibeah. 8492
20:36 on the ambush *they had* s near Gibeah. 8492
20:48 the towns they came across *they* s **on fire.** 8938
Ru 1: 7 where she had been living and s **out** on 2143
1Sa 2: 8 upon them *he has* s the world. 8883
4:15 and whose eyes *were* s so that he could 7756
5: 2 into Dagon's temple and s it beside Dagon. 3657
6:18 on which *they* s the ark of the LORD, 5663
7:12 and s it **up** between Mizpah and Shen. 8492
9:10 So *they* s **out** for the town where the man 2143
9:24 when what was on it and s it in front of Saul. 8492
9:24 it *was* s **aside** for you for this occasion, 9068

1Sa 10: 2 'The donkeys *you* s **out** to look for 2143
10:19 And you have said, 'No, s a king over us.' 8492
12: 1 to me and *have* s a king over you. 4887+4889
12:13 see, the LORD *has* s a king over you. 5989
13: 8 the **time** s by Samuel; 4595
13:11 that you did not come at the s **time,** 3427+4595
15: 5 of Amalek and s **an ambush** in the ravine. 741
15:12 There he *has* s **up** a monument 5893
17:20 loaded up and s **out,** as Jesse had directed. 2143
21: 5 as usual whenever I s **out.** 3655
23:24 *they* s **out** and went to Ziph ahead of Saul. 7756
24: 2 from all Israel and s **out** to look for David 2143
26: 5 Then David s **out** and went to the place 7756
28: 4 and came and s **up camp** at Shunem, 2837
28: 4 the Israelites and s **up camp** at Gilboa. 2837
28: 9 Why *have* you s a **trap** for my life to bring 5943
28:25 Then *she* s it before Saul and his men, 5602
2Sa 4: 5 s **out** for the house of Ish-Bosheth, 2143
6: 2 and all his men s **out** from Baalah of Judah 2143
6: 3 *They* s the ark of God on a new cart 8206
6:17 They brought the ark of the LORD and s it 3657
11:22 The messenger s **out,** and when he arrived 2143
12:30 and it was s **with** precious stones— NIH
14:30 Go and s it **on fire."** 836+928+2021+3675
14:30 s the field **on fire.** 836+928+2021+3675
14:31 s my field **on fire?"** 836+928+2021+3675
15:16 The king s **out,** with his entire household 3655
15:17 So the king s **out,** with all the people 3655
15:24 *They* s **down** the ark of God, 3668
17: 1 and s **out** tonight in pursuit of David. 7756
17:21 "S **out** and cross the river at once; 7756
17:22 So David and all the people with him s **out** 7756
17:23 and s **out** for his house in his hometown. 2143
17:23 he took longer than the time the king *had* s 3585
1Ki 1:33 and s Solomon my son on my own mule 8206
5: 6 for your men whatever wages you s. 606
6:19 the inner sanctuary within the temple to s 5989
7: 8 the palace in which he was to live, s 337+2021+2958
farther back,
7:16 of cast bronze to s on the tops of the pillars; 5989
9:16 He *had* s it **on fire.** 836+928+2021+8596
11:18 *They* s **out** from Midian and went to Paran. 7756
12:29 One he s **up** in Bethel, and the other in Dan. 8492
14:12 When you s foot in your city, 995
14:23 They also s **up** for themselves high places, 1215
16:18 and s the palace **on fire** around him. 836+928+2021+8596
16:32 *He* s **up** an altar for Baal in the temple 7756
16:34 and *he* s **up** its gates at the cost of his 5893
18:23 and put it on the wood but not s **fire** to it. 8492
18:23 and put it on the wood but not s **fire** *to it.* 8492
19:21 Then *he* s **out** to follow Elijah 7756
20:16 *They* s **out** at noon while Ben-Hadad and 3655
20:34 "You *may* s **up** your own market areas 8492
20:34 "On the basis of a treaty *I will* s you **free."** 8938
20:42 *'You have* s **free** a man 3338+4946+8938
22:48 but *they* never s **sail—** 2143
2Ki 2:16 and s him **down** on some mountain or 8959
3: 6 at that time King Joram s **out** from Samaria 3655
3: 9 of Israel s **out** with the king of Judah and 2143
4:25 So *she* s **out** and came to the man of God 2143
4:43 "How *can I* s this before a hundred men?" 5989
4:44 Then *he* s it before them, 5989
6: 8 "I will s **up** my camp in such and such 9381
6:22 S food and water before them so 8492
8:12 "You will s **fire to** their fortified places, 836+928+2021+8938
8:20 and s **up** its own king. 4887+4889
10: 3 and s him on his father's throne. 8492
10:12 Jehu then s **out** and went toward Samaria. 995
16:17 the bronze bulls that supported it and s it on 5989
17:10 *They* s **up** sacred stones and Asherah poles 5893
17:29 and s them **up** in the shrines the people 5663
20: 5 *He* s **fire** to the temple of the LORD, 8596
1Ch 9:32 the bread s **out on the table.** 5121
16: 1 They brought the ark of God and s it inside 3657
17:14 *I will* s him over my house 6641
20: 2 and it was s **with** precious stones— 928
23:13 Aaron *was* s **apart,** he and his descendants 976
23:29 the bread s **out on the table,** 5121
25: 1 s **apart** some of the sons of Asaph, 976
2Ch 11:16 from every tribe of Israel who s their hearts 5989
12:14 He did evil because *he had* not s *his* heart 3922
13:11 They s **out** the bread on the ceremonially 5121
19: 3 the Asherah poles and *have* s your heart on 3922
20:20 As they s **out,** Jehoshaphat stood and said, 3655
20:22 the LORD s ambushes against the men 5989
20:33 and the people still *had not* s their hearts on 3922
20:37 and were not able to s **sail** to trade. 2143
21: 8 and s **up** its own king. 4887+4889
25:14 *He* s them **up** as his own gods, 6641
28:24 the doors of the LORD's temple and s **up** 6913
29:12 Then these Levites s **to work:** 7756
33:19 the sites where he built high places and s **up** 6641
35:12 *They* s **aside** the burnt offerings to give 6073
35:20 when Josiah *had* s the temple **in order,** 3922
36:19 *They* s **fire to** God's temple and broke 8596
Ezr 4: 4 around them s *out to* **discourage** AIT
5: 2 s **to work** to rebuild the house of God in 10221+10624+10742
Jerusalem.
8:24 *I* s **apart** twelve of the leading priests, 976
8:31 the twelfth day of the first month *we* s **out** 5825
10:14 married a foreign woman come at a s **time,** 2374
Ne 2: 6 pleased the king to send me; so *I* s a time. 5989
2:12 *I* s **out** during the night with a few men. 7756
3: 1 They dedicated it and s its doors **in place,** 6641
6: 1 though up to that time *I had* not s the doors 6641

Ne	7: 1	and *I* s the doors **in place,**	6641
	10:33	the bread *is* **out** on the table;	5121
	10:34	to the house of our God at s times each year	2374
	12:47	s **aside** the portion for the other Levites,	7727
	12:47	and the Levites s **aside** the portion for	7727
Est	2:17	So *he* s a royal crown on her head	8492
Job	2:11	they s **out** from their homes	995
	14: 5	and *have* s limits he cannot exceed.	6913
	14:13	If only *you would* s me a time and	8883
	24: 1	the Almighty not s times for judgment?	7621
	28: 8	Proud beasts *do* not s foot on it,	2005
	38: 6	On what **were** its footings s,	3190
	38:10	and s its doors and bars **in place,**	8492
	38:33	*Can you* s up [God's] dominion over	8492
Ps	4: 3	that the LORD *has* s **apart** the godly	7111
	8: 1	*You have* s your glory above the heavens.	5989
	8: 3	which *you have* s **in place,**	3922
	11: 2	*they* s their arrows against the strings	3922
	16: 8	I *have* the LORD always before me.	8751
	27: 5	his tabernacle and s me **high** upon a rock.	8123
	31: 4	Free me from the trap that *is* s for me,	3243
	31: 8	over to the enemy but *have* s my feet in	6641
	38:12	Those who seek my life s *their* **traps,**	5943
	40: 2	*he* s my feet on a rock and gave me	7756
	41:12	In my integrity *you* uphold me and s me	5893
	45: 7	therefore God, your God, has s you	NIH
	62:10	*do* not s your heart on them.	8883
	69:22	the table s before them become a snare;	NIH
	74: 4	*they* s up their standards as signs.	8492
	74:17	It was *you* who s all the boundaries of	5893
	78:60	the tent *he had* s up among men.	8905
	81: 6	their hands *were* s **free** from the basket.	6296
	84: 5	who have s their hearts **on** pilgrimage.	928
	85: 3	*You* s **aside** all your wrath and turned	665
	87: 1	He has s his foundation on the holy	NIH
	88: 5	I am s **apart** with the dead,	2930
	89:25	I *will* s his hand over the sea,	8492
	90: 8	*You have* s our iniquities before you,	8883
	101: 3	I *will* s before my eyes no vile thing.	8883
	104: 5	He s the earth on its foundations;	3569
	104: 9	*You* s a boundary they cannot cross;	8492
	105:20	the ruler of peoples s him **free.**	7337
	119:30	I *have* s my **heart** on your laws.	8751
	119:32	for *you have* s my heart **free.**	8143
	119:110	The wicked *have* s a snare for me,	5989
	119:112	My heart *is* s on keeping your decrees to	5742
	132:17	a horn grow for David and s **up** a lamp	6885
	140: 5	the cords of their net and *have* s traps for me	8883
	141: 2	*May* my prayer be s before you like incense;	3922
	141: 3	**S** a guard over my mouth, O LORD;	8883
	141: 9	from the **traps** s *by* evildoers.	AIT
	142: 7	**S** me **free** from my prison,	3655
	148: 6	He s them **in place** for ever and ever;	6641
Pr	1:15	*do* not s foot on their paths;	4979
	3:19	by understanding *he* s the heavens **in place;**	3922
	4: 9	*She will* s a garland of grace on your head	5989
	4:14	*Do* not s **foot** on the path of the wicked	995
	7: 9	as the dark of night s in.	NIH
	8:27	I was there when *he* s the heavens **in place,**	3922
	9: 2	*she has* also s her table.	6885
	22:28	not move an ancient boundary stone s **up**	6913
	25:17	**Seldom** s foot in your neighbor's house—	AIT
	30:14	and whose jaws are s with knives to devour	NIH
Ecc	3:11	He *has* also s eternity in the hearts of men;	5989
	12: 9	and s **in order** many proverbs.	9545
SS	5:14	His arms are rods of gold s with chrysolite.	4848
	5:15	His legs are pillars of marble s on bases	3569
	6:12	my desire s me *among* the royal chariots	8492
Isa	5: 2	*though you* s **out** the finest plants	5749
	17:11	though on the day you s them **out,**	5750
	21: 5	They s the tables, they spread the rugs,	6885
	23:18	and her earnings will be s **apart** for	7731
	27: 4	I *would* s them all **on fire.**	7455
	28: 1	s on the head of a fertile valley—	NIH
	28: 4	s on the head of a fertile valley,	6584
	29: 3	and s **up** my siege works against you.	7756
	33:12	like cut thornbushes *they will* be s **ablaze.**	
		836+928+2021+3675	
	40:20	a skilled craftsman to s **up** an idol that will	3922
	41:19	I *will* s pines in the wasteland,	8492
	41:21	"**S** forth your arguments,"	5602
	43: 2	the flames *will* not s you **ablaze.**	1277
	45:13	and s my exiles **free,**	8938
	46: 7	*they* s it **up** in its place, and there it stands.	5663
	50: 7	Therefore *have* I s my face like flint,	8492
	50:11	and of the torches *you have* s **ablaze.**	1277
	51:14	cowering prisoners *will* soon be s **free;**	7337
	51:16	I who s the heavens **in place,**	5749
	58: 6	cords of the yoke, *to* s the oppressed free	8938
	60:20	Your sun *will* never s again,	995
	63:11	is he *who* s his Holy Spirit among them,	8492
	66:19	"I *will* s a sign among them,	8492
Jer	1: 5	before you were born *I* s you **apart;**	7727
	1:15	and s **up** their thrones in the entrance of	5989
	4: 7	a destroyer of nations *has* s **out.**	5825
	5:26	and like *those who* s traps to catch men.	5893
	7:30	*They have* s **up** their detestable idols in	8492
	9:13	which *I* s before them,	5989
	10:20	now to pitch my tent or *to* s **up** my shelter.	7756
	11:13	and the altars *you have* s **up** to burn incense	8492
	11:16	of a mighty storm *he will* s it **on fire,**	836+3675
	12: 3	**S** them **apart** for the day of slaughter!	7727
	15: 9	Her sun *will* s while it is still day;	995
	22:17	and your heart are s only **on** dishonest gain,	6584
	26: 4	follow my law, which *I have* s before you,	5989
	31:21	"**S** up road signs; put up guideposts.	5893
	31:29	and the children's teeth *are* s **on edge.'**	7733

Jer	31:30	his own teeth *will be* s **on edge.**	7733
	32:29	come in and s it **on fire;**	836+928+2021+3675
	32:34	*They* s **up** their abominable idols in	8492
	34:10	They agreed, and s them **free.**	8938
	34:16	the male and female slaves *you had* s free	8938
	35: 5	Then *I* s bowls full of wine and some cups	5989
	39: 8	The Babylonians s **fire to** the royal palace	
		836+928+2021+8596	
	41:10	and s **out** to cross over to the Ammonites.	2143
	43:10	of Babylon, and *I will* s his throne	8492
	43:12	*He will* s **fire** to the temples of the gods 836+3675	
	44:10	the decrees *I* s before you and your fathers.	5989
	49: 2	its surrounding villages *will be* s **on fire.**	
		836+928+2021+3675	
	49:27	"I *will* s **fire** to the walls of Damascus; 836+3675	
	49:38	I *will* s my throne in Elam	8492
	50:24	I s a **trap** for you, O Babylon,	3704
	51:30	Her dwellings *are* s **on fire;**	3675
	51:32	the marshes s **on fire,** 836+928+2021+8596	
	51:39	I *will* s **out** a feast for them	8883
	51:58	and her high gates s **on fire;** 836+928+2021+3675	
	52:13	*He* s **fire** to the temple of the LORD,	8596
Eze	4: 2	s **up** camps against it and put battering rams	5989
	4:10	and eat it at s times.	4946+6330+6961+6961
	4:11	and drink it at s **times.**	4946+6330+6961+6961
	5: 1	a s of scales and divide up the hair.	4404+5486
	5: 5	which *I have* s in the center of the nations,	8492
	6: 2	s your face against the mountains of Israel;	8492
	12: 3	s **out** and go from where you are	1655
	13:17	s your face against the daughters of your	8492
	13:20	I *will* s **free** the people that you ensnare	8938
	14: 3	these men *have* s **up** idols in their hearts	6590
	14: 8	I *will* s my face against that man	5989
	15: 7	I *will* s my face against them.	5989
	15: 7	And when I s my face against them,	8492
	17: 2	s **forth** an allegory and tell the house	2554
	18: 2	and the children's teeth *are* s **on edge'?**	7733
	20: 7	of the vile images you have s your eyes on,	NIH
	20: 8	of the vile images they had s their eyes on,	NIH
	20:46	s your face toward the south;	8492
	20:47	*I am about to* s **fire** to you,	836+3675
	21: 2	s your face against Jerusalem and preach	8492
	21:22	where he is to s **up** battering rams,	8492
	21:22	to s battering rams against the gates,	8492
	24:11	Then s the empty pot on the coals	6641
	25: 2	s your face against the Ammonites	8492
	25: 4	*They will* s **up** their camps	3782
	26: 8	*he will* s **up** siege works against you,	5989
	28:21	s your face against Sidon;	8492
	29: 2	s your face against Pharaoh king of Egypt	8492
	30: 8	when I s **fire** to Egypt and all her helpers	5989
	30:14	s fire to Zoan and inflict punishment	5989
	30:16	I *will* s fire to Egypt;	5989
	35: 2	s your face against Mount Seir;	8492
	37: 1	of the LORD and s me in the middle of	5663
	38: 2	s your face against Gog,	8492
	39:15	he *will* s **up** a marker beside it until	1215
	40: 2	of Israel and s me on a very high mountain,	5663
	48:20	**As a special gift** *you will* s **aside**	8123
Da	1:18	of the time *by* the king to bring them in,	606
	2:44	the God of heaven *will* s **up** a kingdom	10624
	3: 1	and s it **up** on the plain of Dura in	10624
	3: 2	to the dedication of the image he *had* s **up.**	10624
	3: 3	image that King Nebuchadnezzar *had* s **up,**	10624
	3: 5	gold that King Nebuchadnezzar has s **up.**	10624
	3: 7	gold that King Nebuchadnezzar *had* s **up.**	10624
	3:12	But there are some Jews whom *you have* s	10431
	3:12	the image of gold *you have* s **up."**	10624
	3:14	or worship the image of gold *I have* s **up?**	10624
	3:18	the image of gold *you have* s **up."**	10624
	5:23	*you have* s *yourself* **up** against the Lord	10659
	6: 3	that the king planned to s him over	10624
	7: 9	"As I looked, "thrones *were* s **in place,**	10667
	7:25	and try to change the s **times** and the laws.	10232
	8:11	*It* s *itself* **up** to be as **great** as the Prince	1540
	9:27	he will s **up** an abomination that causes	NIH
	10:10	A hand touched me and s me **trembling**	5675
	10:12	that *you* s your mind to gain understanding	5989
	11:28	be s **against** the holy covenant.	6584
	11:31	Then *they will* s **up** the abomination	5989
	11:44	and *he will* s **out** in a great rage to destroy	3655
	12:11	that causes desolation *is* s **up,**	5989
Hos	8: 4	They s **up** kings without my consent;	4887
Am	1:14	I *will* s **fire** to the walls of Rabbah 836+3675	
	3: 5	on the ground where no snare has been s?	NIH
Ob	1: 7	those who eat your bread *will* s a trap	8492
	1:18	and *they will* s it **on fire** and consume it.	1944
Mic	3: 6	The sun *will* s for the prophets,	995
Hab	2: 9	by unjust gain to s his nest on high,	8492
Zec	3: 9	See, the stone *I have* s in front of Joshua!	5989
	5:11	the basket *will* be s there in its place."	5663
	6:11	and s it on the head of the high priest,	8492
	12: 9	On that day *I will* s **out** to destroy all	1335
Mal	2: 2	*you do* not s your heart to honor my name,"	8492
	2: 2	*you have* not s your heart to honor me.	8492
	4: 1	that day that is coming *will* s them **on fire,"**	4265
Mt	27: 9	price s on him by the people of Israel, 5506+5507	
	27:29	a crown of thorns and s it on his head.	2202
Mk	6:41	to his disciples to s **before** the people.	4192
	8: 6	and gave them to his disciples to s **before**	4192
	15:17	a crown of thorns and s it on him.	4363
Lk	8:22	So they got into a boat and s **out.**	343
	9: 6	they s **out** and went from village to village,	2002
	9:16	to the disciples to s **before** the people.	4192
	9:51	Jesus resolutely s **out** for Jerusalem.	4513
	10: 8	eat what is s before you.	4192
	11: 6	and I have nothing *to* s before him.'	4192

Lk	12:29	not s *your* **heart** on what you will eat	2426
	13:12	*you are* s **free** from your infirmity."	668
	13:16	be s **free** on the Sabbath day	3395
	15:13	s **off** for a distant country	623
	15:18	I will s **out** and go back to my father	482
Jn	5:45	on whom your **hopes are** s.	1827
	6:17	where they got into a boat and s **off** across	2262
	8:32	and the truth *will* s you **free."**	1802
	8:33	How can you say that we shall be s **free?"**	1801
	10:36	the Father s **apart** as his very own and sent	39
	13:15	*I have* s you an example that you should do	1443
	19:12	From then on, Pilate tried to s Jesus **free,**	668
Ac	1: 7	to know the times or dates the Father *has* s	5502
	2:23	*by* God's purpose and foreknowledge;	3988
	7:34	and have come down *to* s them **free.**	1975
	13: 2	"**S apart** for me Barnabas and Saul for	928
	16:34	his house and s a **meal before** them; 4192+5544	
	17:26	and he determined the times for them and	4705
	17:31	For *he has* s a day when he will judge	2705
	18:21	Then *he* s **sail** from Ephesus.	343
	18:23	Paul s **out** from there and traveled	2002
	20: 1	said good-by and s **out** for Macedonia.	2002
	20:15	The next day we s **sail** from there	676
	21: 2	went on board and s **sail.**	343
	26:32	"This man could *have been* s **free** if he had	668
	28:13	From there we s **sail** and arrived	4311
Ro	1: 1	to be an apostle and s **apart** for the gospel	928
	6:18	*You have been* s **free** from sin	1802
	6:22	But now *that you have been* s **free** from sin	1802
	8: 2	of the Spirit of life s me **free** from the law	1802
	8: 5	the sinful nature *have their* **minds** s on what	5858
	8: 5	with the Spirit have their **minds** s on what	NIG
1Co	16: 2	one of you *should* s **aside** a sum of money	5502
2Co	1:10	On him *we have* s our **hope**	1827
	1:22	s his **seal of ownership** on us,	5381
Gal	1:15	who s me **apart** from birth and called me	928
	2: 2	to a revelation and s **before** them the gospel	423
	2:21	I *do* not s **aside** the grace of God,	119
	3:15	Just as no one *can* s **aside** or add to	119
	3:17	*does* not s **aside** the covenant previously	218
	4: 2	and trustees until the **time** s by his father.	4607
	5: 1	It is for freedom that Christ *has* s us **free.**	1802
Php	4:15	when *I* s **out** from Macedonia,	2002
Col	3: 1	s *your* **hearts** on things above,	2426
	3: 2	**S** *your* **minds** on things above, not on	5858
1Ti	4:12	an example for the believers in speech,	1181
Tit	2: 7	In everything s them an example	4218
Heb	1: 9	therefore God, your God, has s you	NIG
	4: 7	Therefore God again s a certain day,	3988
	7:18	The former regulation is s **aside**	120
	7:26	blameless, pure, s **apart** from sinners,	6004
	8: 2	the true tabernacle s **up** by the Lord,	4381
	9: 2	A tabernacle *was* s **up.**	2941
	9:15	that he has died as a ransom to s them free	NIG
	12: 2	for the joy s **before** him endured the cross,	4618
Jas	3: 5	Consider what a great forest *is* s **on fire** by	409
	3: 6	and *is* itself s **on fire** by hell.	5824
1Pe	1:13	s *your* **hope** fully on the grace to	1827
	3:15	But in your hearts s **apart** Christ as Lord.	39
1Jn	3:19	and how *we* s our hearts **at rest**	4275
Rev	13:14	He ordered them *to* s **up** an image in honor	4472
	20: 3	he must *be* s **free** for a short time.	3395

SETH (9)

Ge	4:25	she gave birth to a son and named him S,	9269
	4:26	S also had a son, and he named him Enosh,	9269
	5: 3	in his own image; and he named him S.	9269
	5: 4	After S was born, Adam lived 800 years	9269
	5: 6	When S had lived 105 years,	9269
	5: 7	S lived 807 years and had other sons	9269
	5: 8	Altogether, S lived 912 years,	9269
1Ch	1: 1	Adam, S, Enosh,	9269
Lk	3:38	the son of S, the son of Adam,	4953

SETHUR (1)

Nu	13:13	from the tribe of Asher, S son of Michael;	6256

SETS (46) [SET]

Ge	45:22	shekels of silver and five s *of* clothes.	2722
Ex	36:13	to fasten the *two* s *of* **curtains** together so	AIT
Lev	27:12	Whatever value the priest then s,	NIH
	27:14	Whatever **value** the priest then s,	6885
Dt	27:15	craftsman's hands—and s it **up** in secret."	8492
Jdg	14:12	linen garments and thirty s *of* clothes.	2722
	14:13	linen garments and thirty s *of* clothes."	2722
2Sa	2: 5	or anything else before the one *who* s me!"	995
	22:49	*who* s me **free** from my enemies.	3655
1Ki	7: 4	Its windows were placed high in s *of* three,	3215
	7: 5	they were in the front part in s of three,	7193
	7:41	the **two** s *of* network decorating	AIT
	7:42	for the **two** s *of* network (two rows	AIT
2Ki	5: 5	six thousand shekels of gold and ten s	2722
	5:22	Please give them a talent of silver and two s	2722
	5:23	silver in two bags, with two s *of* clothing.	2722
2Ch	4:12	the **two** s *of* network decorating	AIT
	4:13	for the **two** s *of* network (two rows	AIT
	30:19	*who* s his heart on seeking God—	3922
Job	5:11	The lowly he s on high,	8492
	34:24	the mighty and s **up** others in their places.	6641
	41:21	His breath s coals **ablaze.**	4265
Ps	50: 1	the rising of the sun to the **place where** it s.	4427
	68: 6	God s the lonely in families,	3782
	83:14	s the mountains **ablaze,**	4265
	113: 3	the rising of the sun to the **place where** it s,	4427
	146: 7	The LORD s prisoners **free,**	6002

Pr	31:17	*She* s about her **work** vigorously;	2520+5516
Ecc	1:5	The sun rises and the sun s,	995
Isa	9:18	s the forest thickets **ablaze**,	3675
	30:33	like a stream of burning sulfur, s it **ablaze**.	1277
	64:2	*when* fire s twigs **ablaze** and causes water	7706
Jer	9:8	but in his heart *he* s a trap for him.	8492
	13:21	What will you say when [the LORD] s over	7212
Eze	14:4	When any Israelite s up idols in his heart	6590
	14:7	in Israel separates himself from me and s up	6590
Da	2:21	*he* s up kings and deposes them.	10624
	4:17	and gives them to anyone he wishes and s	10624
	5:21	of men and s over them anyone he wishes.	10624
Am	9:6	and s its foundation on the earth, who calls	3569
Jn	8:36	the Son s you free, you will be free indeed.	1802
2Co	10:5	*that* s *itself* up against the knowledge	2048
2Th	2:4	so that he s *himself* up in God's temple,	2767
1Ti	3:1	If anyone s his **heart on being** an overseer,	3977
Heb	10:9	He s **aside** the first to establish the second.	359
Jas	3:6	s the whole course of his life **on fire**,	5824

SETTER (KJV) See ADVOCATING

SETTING (23) [SET]

Ge	15:12	As the sun *was* s, Abram fell into a deep sleep,	995
Ex	8:9	leave to you the honor of s **the time** for me to pray	4200+5503
Nu	7:1	When Moses finished s **up** the tabernacle,	7756
	10:6	The blast will be the signal for s **out**.	5023
	10:29	"We *are* s **out** for the place about which	5825
Dt	4:8	and laws as this body of laws I *am* s	5989
	11:26	I *am* s before you today a blessing and	5989
	11:30	west of the road, toward the s sun,	4427
	11:32	you obey all the decrees and laws I *am* s	5989
	26:12	you have finished s **aside a tenth**	5130+6923
2Sa	2:24	and *as* the sun *was* s, they came	995
1Ki	22:36	As the sun *was* s, a cry spread	995
2Ch	2:4	for s **out the consecrated bread** regularly,	NIH
	29:18	table for s **out the consecrated bread,**	5121
Ps	118:5	and he answered by s me **free**.	5303
Isa	45:6	to the **place** of its s men may know there is none besides me.	5115
Jer	21:8	See, I *am* s before you the way of life and	5989
Am	7:8	I *am* s a **plumb** line among my people Israel;	8492
Mal	1:11	from the rising to the s *of* the sun.	4427
Mk	7:9	a fine way of s **aside** the commands of God	119
Lk	4:40	*When* the sun *was* s, the people brought	1544
1Co	10:6	as examples to keep us from s our **hearts on**	2122
2Co	4:2	by s **forth** the truth **plainly** we commend	5748

SETTINGS (12) [SET]

Ex	28:11	Then mount the stones in gold filigree s	6015
	28:13	Make gold **filigree** s	5401
	28:14	like a rope, and attach the chains to the s.	5401
	28:20	Mount them in gold **filigree** s.	8687
	28:25	the other ends of the chains to the two s,	5401
	39:6	in gold filigree s and engraved them like	6015
	39:13	They were mounted in gold **filigree** s.	4853
	39:16	They made two gold **filigree** s	5401
	39:18	the other ends of the chains to the two s,	5401
1Ch	29:2	as well as onyx for the s, turquoise,	4854
Pr	25:11	like apples of gold in s *of* silver.	5381
Eze	28:13	Your s and mountings were made of gold;	4856+9513

SETTLE (43) [RESETTLE, RESETTLED, SETTLED, SETTLEMENT, SETTLEMENTS, SETTLES]

Ge	34:10	*You can* s among us;	3782
	34:16	*We'll* s among you and become one people	3782
	34:23	and *they'll* s among us."	3782
	35:1	"Go up to Bethel and s there,	3782
	46:34	*be allowed to* s in the region of Goshen,	3782
	47:4	please *let* your servants s in Goshen."	3782
	47:6	s your father and your brothers in the best	3782
Nu	33:53	Take possession of the land and s in it,	3782
Dt	8:12	when you build fine houses and s **down,**	3782
	12:10	But you will cross the Jordan and s in	3782
Jdg	18:1	a place of their own where they *might* s,	3782
2Ki	25:24	"S **down** in the land and serve the king	3782
2Ch	19:8	the law of the LORD and to s disputes.	NIH
Job	3:5	*may* a cloud s over it;	8905
Ps	69:35	Then *people will* s there and possess it;	3782
	107:4	finding no way to a city **where** they could s,	4632
	107:7	a straight way to a city **where** they could s.	4632
	107:36	and they founded a city **where** they could s.	4632
	139:9	if *I* s on the far side of the sea,	8905
Isa	2:4	and *will* s disputes for many peoples.	3519
	7:19	and s in the steep ravines and	5663
	14:1	and *will* s them in their own land.	5663
	23:7	whose feet have taken her to s in far-off	1591
	54:3	and s in their desolate cities.	3782
Jer	29:5	"Build houses and s **down;**	3782
	29:28	Therefore build houses and s **down;**	3782
	40:9	"S **down** in the land and serve the king	3782
	42:15	to go to Egypt and you do go to s there,	1591
	42:17	to Egypt to s there will die by the sword,	1591
	42:22	in the place where you want to go to s."	1591
	43:2	'You must not go to Egypt to s there.'	1591
	44:12	determined to go to Egypt to s there.	1591
Eze	32:4	**let** all the birds of the air s on you	8905
	32:14	Then *I will* **let** her waters s	9205
	36:11	*I will s people* **on** you as in the past	3782

Eze	37:14	and *I will* s you in your own land.	5663
Hos	11:11	*I will* s them in their homes,"	3782
Mic	4:3	between many peoples and *will* s disputes	3519
Na	3:17	like swarms of locusts that s in the walls on	2837
Mt	5:25	"S matters quickly with your	1639+2333
	18:23	like a king who wanted *to* s accounts	5256
Ac	18:15	s the matter yourselves.	3972
2Th	3:12	to s **down** and earn the bread they eat.	2484+3552

SETTLED (72) [SETTLE]

Ge	11:2	they found a plain in Shinar and s there.	3782
	11:31	But when they came to Haran, *they* s there.	3782
	19:30	Lot and his two daughters left Zoar and s	3782
	25:18	His descendants s in the area from Havilah	8905
	26:17	in the Valley of Gerar and s there.	3782
	36:8	Edom) s in the hill country of Seir.	3782
	47:11	So Joseph s his father and his brothers	3782
	47:27	Now the Israelites s in Egypt in the region	3782
Ex	10:6	from the day they s in this land till now.' ''	2118
	10:14	and s **down** in every area of the country	5663
	16:35	until they came to a land *that was* s;	3782
	22:11	between them *will be* s *by* the taking of	2118
	24:16	the glory of the LORD s on Mount Sinai.	8905
	40:35	the Tent of Meeting because the cloud *had* s	8905
Nu	9:17	wherever the cloud s,	8905
	11:9	When the dew s on the camp at night,	3718
	21:31	So Israel s in the land of the Amorites.	3782
	22:5	the face of the land and *have* s next to me.	3782
	31:10	the towns where the Midianites had s,	4632
	32:40	and *they* s there.	3782
Dt	2:12	from before them and s in their place,	3782
	2:21	who drove them out and s in their place.	3782
	2:23	from Caphtor destroyed them and s	3782
	12:29	But when you have driven them out and s	3782
	17:14	and have taken possession of it and s in it,	3782
	19:1	and when you have driven them out and s	3782
	26:1	and have taken possession of it and s in it,	3782
Jos	19:47	*They* s in Leshem and named it Dan	3782
	19:50	And he built up the town and s there.	3782
	21:43	and they took possession of it and s there.	3782
Jdg	7:12	The other eastern peoples *had* s in the valley,	5877
	11:3	So Jephthah fled from his brothers and s in	3782
	18:28	The Danites rebuilt the city and s there.	3782
	21:23	and rebuilt the towns and s in them.	3782
Ru	3:18	not rest until the matter *is* s today."	3983
1Sa	12:8	of Egypt and s them in this place.	3782
	27:3	David and his men s in Gath with Achish.	3782
2Sa	2:3	and *they* s in Hebron and its towns.	3782
	7:1	After the king *was* s in his palace and	3782
	20:18	'Get your answer at Abel,' and that s *it*.	9462
1Ki	11:24	where *they* s and took control.	3782
2Ki	17:6	*He* s them in Halah, in Gozan	3782
	17:24	and Sepharvaim and s them in the towns	3782
	17:29	in the several towns where they s,	3782
	18:11	to Assyria and s them in Halah,	5663
1Ch	4:41	Then *they* s in their place,	3782
	5:8	*They* s in the area from Aroer to Nebo	3782
	5:23	*they* s in the land from Bashan	3782
	17:1	After David *was* s in his palace,	3782
2Ch	8:2	and s Israelites in them.	3782
	15:9	and Simeon *who had* s among them,	1591
Ezr	2:70	the gatekeepers and the temple servants s	3782
	2:70	the rest of the Israelites s in their towns.	NIH
	3:1	and the Israelites had s in their towns,	NIH
	4:10	and honorable Ashurbanipal deported and s	10338
Ne	7:73	the Israelites, s in their own towns.	3782
	7:73	and the Israelites had s in their towns,	NIH
	11:1	the leaders of the people s in Jerusalem,	3782
	11:3	the provincial leaders who s in Jerusalem	3782
	11:36	of the divisions of the Levites of Judah s	NIH
Ps	68:10	Your people s in it, and from your bounty,	3782
	78:55	he s the tribes of Israel in their homes.	8905
Pr	8:25	before the mountains **were** s in place,	3190
Isa	29:1	Ariel, Ariel, the city where David s!	2837
Eze	31:13	All the birds of the air s on the fallen tree,	8905
	47:22	for yourselves and for the aliens who *have* s	1591
Zec	7:7	Negev and the western foothills *were* s?' ''	3782
Mt	25:19	returned and s **accounts** with them.	3364+5256
Ac	7:4	"So he left the land of the Chaldeans and s	2997
	7:29	where he s *as* a **foreigner** and had two sons.	4230
	19:39	*it must be* s in a legal assembly.	2147
1Co	7:37	who *has* s **the matter** in his own mind,	1612+2705

SETTLEMENT (2) [SETTLE]

Isa	27:10	an abandoned s, forsaken like the desert;	5659
Mt	18:24	As he began the s, a man who owed him	5256

SETTLEMENTS (29) [SETTLE]

Ge	25:16	the twelve tribal rulers according to their s	2958
	36:43	to their s in the land they occupied.	4632
Nu	21:25	and all its **surrounding** s.	1426
	21:32	the Israelites captured its **surrounding** s	1426
	32:41	a descendant of Manasseh, captured their s	2557
	32:42	and its **surrounding** s and called it Nobah	1426
Jos	13:30	all the s *of* Jair in Bashan, sixty towns,	2557
	15:45	Ekron, with its **surrounding** s and villages;	1426
	15:47	Ashdod, its **surrounding** s and villages;	1426
	15:47	and Gaza, its s and villages,	1426
	17:11	together with their **surrounding** s (the third	1426
	17:16	and its s and those in the Valley of Jezreel."	1426
Jdg	1:27	or Megiddo and their **surrounding** s,	1426
	1:26	the **surrounding** s and those towns along	1426
1Ki	4:13	in Ramoth Gilead (the s *of* Jair son	2557
1Ch	2:23	as well as Kenath with its **surrounding** s—	1426
	4:33	These were their s.	4632

1Ch	6:54	These were the locations of their s allotted	4632
	7:28	Their lands and s included Bethel	4632
Ne	11:25	in Kiriath Arba and its **surrounding** s,	1426
	11:25	in Dibon and its s,	1426
	11:27	in Hazar Shual, in Beersheba and its s,	1426
	11:28	in Ziklag, in Meconah and its s,	1426
	11:30	and in Azekah and its s.	1426
	11:31	Aija, Bethel and its s,	1426
Isa	42:11	let the s where Kedar lives rejoice.	2958
Eze	26:6	and her s on the mainland will be ravaged	1426
	26:8	He will ravage your s on the mainland with	1426
	34:13	in the ravines and in all the s *in* the land.	4632

SETTLES (4) [SETTLE]

2Sa	17:12	we will fall on him as dew s on the ground.	5877
Ps	113:9	*He* s the barren woman in her home as	3782
Pr	18:18	Casting the lot s disputes	8697
Eze	47:23	In whatever tribe the alien s,	1591

SEVEN (391) [SEVENFOLD, SEVENS, SEVENTH]

Ge	4:15	he will suffer vengeance s times over."	8679
	4:24	If Cain is avenged s times,	8679
	7:2	s of every kind of clean animal,	8679+8679
	7:3	and also s of every kind of bird,	8679+8679
	7:4	S days from now I will send rain on	8679
	7:10	And after the s days the floodwaters came	8679
	8:10	He waited s more days and again sent out	8679
	8:12	He waited s more days and sent	8679
	21:28	Abraham set apart s ewe lambs from	8679
	21:29	of these s ewe lambs you have set apart	8679
	21:30	"Accept these s lambs from my hand as	8679
	29:18	"I'll work for you s years in return	8679
	29:20	So Jacob served s years to get Rachel,	8679
	29:27	in return for another s years of work."	8679
	29:30	And he worked for Laban another s years.	8679
	31:23	he pursued Jacob for s days and caught up	8679
	33:3	and bowed down to the ground s times	8679
	41:2	when out of the river there came up s cows,	8679
	41:3	After them, s other cows, ugly and gaunt,	8679
	41:4	that were ugly and gaunt ate up the s sleek,	8679
	41:5	S heads of grain, healthy and good,	8679
	41:6	s other heads of grain sprouted—	8679
	41:7	of grain swallowed up the s healthy,	8679
	41:18	when out of the river there came up s cows,	8679
	41:19	After them, s other cows came up—	8679
	41:20	ugly cows ate up the s fat cows that came	8679
	41:22	"In my dreams I also saw s heads of grain,	8679
	41:23	After them, s other heads sprouted—	8679
	41:24	of grain swallowed up the s good heads.	8679
	41:26	The s good cows are seven years,	8679
	41:26	The seven good cows are s years,	8679
	41:26	the s good heads of grain are seven years;	8679
	41:26	the seven good heads of grain are s years;	8679
	41:27	The s lean, ugly cows that came	8679
	41:27	that came up afterward are s years, and	8679
	41:27	the s worthless heads of grain scorched by	8679
	41:27	They are s years of famine.	8679
	41:29	S years of great abundance are coming	8679
	41:30	but s years of famine will follow them.	8679
	41:34	of Egypt during the s years of abundance.	8679
	41:36	during the s years of famine that will come	8679
	41:47	During the s years of abundance	8679
	41:48	in those s years of abundance in Egypt	8679
	41:53	The s years of abundance in Egypt came to	8679
	41:54	and the s years of famine began,	8679
	46:25	to his daughter Rachel—s in all.	8679
Ex	2:16	Now a priest of Midian had s daughters,	8679
	7:25	S days passed after the LORD struck	8679
	12:15	For s days you are to eat bread made	8679
	12:19	For s days no yeast is to be found	8679
	13:6	For s days eat bread made without yeast	8679
	13:7	Eat unleavened bread during those s days;	8679
	22:30	Let them stay with their mothers for s days,	8679
	23:15	for s days eat bread made without yeast,	8679
	25:37	"Then make its s lamps and set them up	8679
	29:30	in the Holy Place is to wear them s days.	8679
	29:35	taking s days to ordain them.	8679
	29:37	For s days make atonement for the altar	8679
	34:18	For s days eat bread made without yeast,	8679
	37:23	They made its s lamps,	8679
Lev	4:6	the blood and sprinkle some of it s times	8679
	4:17	the LORD s times in front of the curtain.	8679
	8:11	of the oil on the altar s times,	8679
	8:33	to the Tent of Meeting for s days,	8679
	8:33	for your ordination will last s days.	8679
	8:35	for s days and do what the LORD requires,	8679
	12:2	be ceremonially unclean for s days.	8679
	13:4	the infected person in isolation for s days.	8679
	13:5	to keep him in isolation another s days.	8679
	13:21	priest is to put him in isolation for s days.	8679
	13:26	priest is to put him in isolation for s days.	8679
	13:31	the infected person in isolation for s days.	8679
	13:33	to keep him in isolation another s days.	8679
	13:50	and isolate the affected article for s days.	8679
	13:54	Then he is to isolate it for another s days.	8679
	14:7	s times he shall sprinkle the one to	8679
	14:8	but he must stay outside his tent for s days.	8679
	14:16	sprinkle some of it before the LORD s times.	8679
	14:27	from his palm s times before the LORD.	8679
	14:38	of the house and close it up for s days.	8679
	14:51	and sprinkle the house s times.	8679
	15:13	he is to count off s days	8679
	15:19	of her monthly period will last s days,	8679
	15:24	he will be unclean for s days;	8679

Lev 15:28 she must count off s days, 8679
16:14 of it with his finger s times before 8679
16:19 of the blood on it with his finger s times 8679
22:27 it is to remain with its mother for s days. 8679
23: 6 for s days you must eat bread made 8679
23: 8 For s days present an offering made to 8679
23:15 count off s full weeks. 8679
23:18 Present with this bread s male lambs, 8679
23:34 Tabernacles begins, and it lasts for s days. 8679
23:36 For s days present offerings made to 8679
23:39 the festival to the LORD for s days; 8679
23:40 before the LORD your God for s days. 8679
23:41 to the LORD for s days each year. 8679
23:42 Live in booths for s days: 8679
25: 8 " 'Count off s sabbaths of years— 8679
25: 8 sabbaths of years—s times seven years— 8679
25: 8 sabbaths of years—seven times s years— 8679
25: 8 the s sabbaths of years amount to a period 8679
26:18 punish you for your sins s times over. 8679
26:21 I will multiply your afflictions s times 8679
26:24 afflict you for your sins s times over. 8679
26:28 punish you for your sins s times over. 8679
Nu 8: 2 'When you set up the s lamps, 8679
12:14 not have been in disgrace for s days? 8679
12:14 Confine her outside the camp for s days; 8679
12:15 confined outside the camp for s days, 8679
13:22 (Hebron had been built s years before Zoan 8679
19: 4 on his finger and sprinkle it s times toward 8679
19:11 of anyone will be unclean for s days. 8679
19:14 in it will be unclean for s days, 8679
19:16 will be unclean for s days. 8679
23: 1 one ram and s male lambs a year old, 8679
23: 1 and prepare s bulls and seven rams for me." 8679
23: 1 and prepare seven bulls and s rams for me." 8679
23: 4 and Balaam said, "I have prepared s altars, 8679
23:14 and there he built s altars and offered a bull 8679
23:29 Balaam said, "Build me s altars here, 8679
23:29 and prepare s bulls and seven rams for me." 8679
23:29 and prepare seven bulls and s rams for me." 8679
28:11 one ram and s male lambs a year old, 8679
28:17 for s days eat bread made without yeast, 8679
28:19 one ram and s male lambs a year old, 8679
28:21 and with each of the s lambs, one-tenth. 8679
28:24 for s days as an aroma pleasing to 8679
28:27 one ram and s male lambs a year old as 8679
28:29 and with each of the s lambs, one-tenth. 8679
29: 2 one ram and s male lambs a year old, 8679
29: 4 and with each of the s lambs, one-tenth. 8679
29: 8 one ram and s male lambs a year old, 8679
29:10 and with each of the s lambs, one-tenth. 8679
29:12 a festival to the LORD for s days. 8679
29:32 " 'On the seventh day prepare s bulls, 8679
29:36 one ram and s male lambs a year old, 8679
31:19 stay outside the camp s days. 8679
Dt 7: 1 s nations larger and stronger than you— 8679
15: 1 of every s years you must cancel debts. 8679
16: 3 but for s days eat unleavened bread, 8679
16: 4 in all your land for s days. 8679
16: 9 Count off s weeks from the time you begin 8679
16:13 the Feast of Tabernacles for s days 8679
16:15 For s days celebrate the Feast to the LORD 8679
28: 7 from one direction but flee from you in s. 8679
28:25 from one direction but flee from them in s, 8679
31:10 "At the end of every s years, 8679
Jos 6: 4 Have s priests carry trumpets 8679
6: 4 march around the city s times, 8679
6: 6 and have s priests carry trumpets in front 8679
6: 8 the s priests carrying the seven trumpets 8679
6: 8 the seven priests carrying the s trumpets 8679
6:13 The s priests carrying the seven trumpets 8679
6:13 the trumpets went forward, 8679
6:15 around the city s times in the same manner, 8679
6:15 on that day they circled the city s times. 8679
18: 2 there were still s Israelite tribes who had 8679
18: 5 You are to divide the land into s parts. 8679
18: 6 descriptions of the s parts of the land, 8679
18: 9 town by town, in s parts. 8679
Jdg 6: 1 and for s years he gave them into the hands 8679
6:25 the one s years old. 8679
12: 9 Ibzan led Israel s years. 8679
14:12 the answer within the s days of the feast, 8679
14:17 She cried the whole s days of the feast. 8679
16: 7 "If anyone ties me with s fresh thongs 8679
16: 8 of the Philistines brought her s fresh thongs 8679
16:13 "If you weave the s braids of my head into 8679
16:13 Delilah took the s braids of his head, 8679
16:19 a man to shave off the s braids of his hair, 8679
20:15 to s hundred chosen men from those living 8679
20:16 Among all these soldiers there were s 8679
hundred chosen men who were left-handed, 8679
Ru 4:15 and who is better to you than s sons, 8679
1Sa 2: 5 She who was barren has borne s children, 8679
6: 1 in Philistine territory s months, 8679
10: 8 but you must wait s days until I come 8679
11: 3 "Give us s days so we can send messengers 8679
13: 8 He waited s days, the time set by Samuel; 8679
16:10 Jesse had s of his sons pass before Samuel, 8679
31:13 and they fasted s days. 8679
2Sa 2:11 of Judah was s years and six months. 8679
5: 5 In Hebron he reigned over Judah s years 8679
8: 4 s thousand charioteers and twenty thousand 8679
10:18 and David killed s hundred of their 8679
21: 6 let s of his male descendants be given to us 8679
21: 9 All s of them fell together; 8679
1Ki 2:11 s years in Hebron and thirty-three in 8679
6: 6 and the third floor s. 8679
6:38 He had spent s years building it. 8679

1Ki 7:17 s for each capital. 8679
8:65 before the LORD our God for s days 8679
8:65 for seven days and s days more, 8679
11: 3 He had s hundred wives of royal birth 8679
16:15 Zimri reigned in Tirzah s days. 8679
18:43 S times Elijah said, "Go back." 8679
19:18 Yet I reserve s thousand in Israel— 8679
20:29 For s days they camped opposite each other, 8679
2Ki 3: 9 After a roundabout march of s days, 8679
3:26 with him s hundred swordsmen to break 8679
4:35 The boy sneezed s times 8679
5:10 "Go, wash yourself s times in the Jordan, 8679
5:14 and dipped himself in the Jordan s times, 8679
8: 1 a famine in the land that will last s years." 8679
8: 2 in the land of the Philistines s years. 8679
8: 3 the s years she came back from the land of 8679
11:21 Joash was s years old when he began 8679
24:16 the entire force of s thousand fighting men, 8679
1Ch 3:24 where he reigned s years and six months. 8679
3:24 Delaiah and Anani—s in all. 8679
5:13 Zia and Eber—s in all. 8679
10:12 and they fasted s days. 8679
11:23 was s and a half feet tall. 564+928+2021+2822
15:26 s bulls and seven rams were sacrificed. 8679
15:26 seven bulls and s rams were sacrificed. 8679
18: 4 s thousand charioteers and twenty thousand 8679
19:18 and David killed s thousand of their 8679
29: 4 and s thousand talents of refined silver, 8679
29:27 s in Hebron and thirty-three in Jerusalem. 8679
2Ch 7: 8 for s days, and all Israel with him— 8679
7: 9 the dedication of the altar for s days and 8679
7: 9 and the festival for s days more. 8679
13: 9 and s rams may become a priest of what are 8679
15:11 to the LORD s hundred head of cattle 8679
15:11 of cattle and s thousand sheep and goats. 8679
17:11 s thousand seven hundred rams 8679
17:11 seven thousand s hundred rams 8679
17:11 s thousand seven hundred goats. 8679
17:11 and seven thousand s hundred goats. 8679
24: 1 Joash was s years old 8679
29:21 They brought s bulls, seven rams, 8679
29:21 They brought seven bulls, s rams, 8679
29:21 s male lambs and seven male goats as 8679
29:21 seven male lambs and s male goats as 8679
30:21 the Feast of Unleavened Bread for s days 8679
30:22 the s days they ate their assigned portion 8679
30:23 to celebrate the festival s more days; 8679
30:23 for another s days they celebrated joyfully. 8679
30:24 a thousand bulls and s thousand sheep 8679
35:17 the Feast of Unleavened Bread for s days. 8679
Ezr 6:22 For s days they celebrated with joy 8679
7:14 You are sent by the king and his s advisers 10696
Ne 8:18 They celebrated the feast for s days, 8679
Est 1: 5 the king gave a banquet, lasting s days, 8679
1:10 the s eunuchs who served him— 8679
1:14 and Memucan, the s nobles of Persia 8679
2: 9 He assigned to her s maids selected from 8679
Job 1: 2 He had s sons and three daughters, 8679
1: 3 and he owned s thousand sheep, 8679
2:13 with him for s days and seven nights. 8679
2:13 with him for seven days and s nights. 8679
5:19 in s no harm will befall you. 8679
42: 8 So now take s bulls and seven rams and go 8679
42: 8 So now take seven bulls and s rams and go 8679
42:13 And he also had s sons and three daughters. 8685
Ps 12: 6 in a furnace of clay, purified s times. 8679
79:12 into the laps of our neighbors s times 8679
119:164 S times a day I praise you 8679
Pr 6:16 s that are detestable to him: 8679
9: 1 she has hewn out its s pillars. 8679
24:16 for though a righteous man falls s times, 8679
26:16 than s men who answer discreetly. 8679
26:25 for s abominations fill his heart. 8679
Ecc 11: 2 Give portions to s, yes to eight, 8679
Isa 4: 1 that day s women will take hold of one man 8679
11:15 up into s streams so that men can cross over 8679
30:26 and the sunlight will be s times brighter, 8679
30:26 like the light of s full days, 8679
Jer 15: 9 of s will grow faint and breathe her last. 8679
52:25 and s royal advisers 8679
Eze 3:15 I sat among them for s days— 8679
3:16 of s days the word of the LORD came 8679
39: 9 For s years they will use them for fuel. 8679
39:12 " 'For s months the house of Israel will 8679
39:14 of the s months they will begin their search. 8679
40:22 S steps led up to it, 8679
40:26 S steps led up to it, 8679
41: 3 on each side of it were s cubits wide. 8679
43:25 "For s days you are to provide 8679
43:26 For s days they are to make atonement for 8679
44:26 After he is cleansed, he must wait s days. 8679
45:21 Passover, a feast lasting s days, 8651
45:23 during the s days of the Feast he is 8679
45:23 of the Feast he is to provide s bulls 8679
45:23 to provide seven bulls and s rams 8679
45:25 " 'During the s days of the Feast, 8679
Da 3:19 the furnace heated s times hotter than usual 10696
4:16 till s times pass by for him. 10696
4:23 until s times pass by for him.' 10696
4:25 S times will pass by for you 10696
4:32 S times will pass by for you 10696
9:25 the ruler, comes, there will be s 'sevens,' 8679
9:27 a covenant with many for one 's.' 8651
9:27 In the middle of the 's' he will put an end 8651
Mic 5: 5 we will raise against him s shepherds, 8679
Zec 3: 9 There are s eyes on that one stone, 8679
4: 2 with a bowl at the top and s lights on it, 8679

Zec 4: 2 with s channels to the lights. 8679
4:10 "(These s are the eyes of the LORD, 8679
Mt 12:45 s other spirits more wicked than itself, 2231
15:34 "S," they replied, "and a few small fish." 2231
15:36 Then he took the s loaves and the fish, 2231
15:37 the disciples picked up s basketfuls 2231
16:10 Or the s loaves for the four thousand, 2231
18:21 when he sins against me? Up to s times?" 2232
18:22 Jesus answered, "I tell you, not s times, 2232
22:25 Now there were s brothers among us. 2231
22:28 whose wife will she be of the s, 2231
Mk 8: 5 "S," they replied. 2231
8: 6 When he had taken the s loaves 2231
8: 8 the disciples picked up s basketfuls 2231
8:20 I broke the s loaves for the four thousand, 2231
8:20 They answered, "S." 2231
12:20 Now there were s brothers. 2231
12:22 In fact, none of the s left any children. 2231
12:23 since the s were married to her?" 2231
16: 9 out of whom he had driven s demons. 2231
Lk 2:36 with her husband s years after her marriage, 2231
8: 2 from whom s demons had come out; 2231
11:26 takes s other spirits more wicked than itself, 2231
17: 4 If he sins against you s times in a day, 2232
17: 4 and s times comes back to you and says, 2232
20:29 Now there were s brothers. 2231
20:31 and in the same way the s died, 2231
20:33 since the s were married to her?" 2231
24:13 about s miles from Jerusalem. 2008+5084
Ac 6: 3 choose s men from among you 2231
13:19 he overthrew s nations in Canaan 2231
19:14 S sons of Sceva, a Jewish chief priest, 2231
20: 6 Troas, where we stayed s days. 2231
21: 4 we stayed with them s days. 2231
21: 8 Philip the evangelist, one of the S. 2231
21:27 When the s days were nearly over, 2231
Ro 11: 4 for myself s thousand who have not bowed 2233
Heb 11:30 had marched around them for s days. 2231
2Pe 2: 5 a preacher of righteousness, and s others; NIG
Rev 1: 4 To the s churches in the province of Asia: 2231
1: 4 and from the s spirits before his throne, 2231
1:11 and send it to the s churches: 2231
1:12 when I turned I saw s golden lampstands, 2231
1:16 In his right hand he held s stars, 2231
1:20 of the s stars that you saw in my right hand 2231
1:20 and of the s golden lampstands is this: 2231
1:20 s stars are the angels of the seven churches, 2231
1:20 seven stars are the angels of the s churches, 2231
1:20 the s lampstands are the seven churches. 2231
1:20 the seven lampstands are the s churches. 2231
2: 1 the words of him who holds the s stars 2231
2: 1 and walks among the s golden lampstands: 2231
3: 1 of him who holds the s spirits of God and 2231
3: 1 the seven spirits of God and the s stars. 2231
4: 5 Before the throne, s lamps were blazing. 2231
4: 5 These are the s spirits of God. 2231
5: 1 on both sides and sealed with s seals. 2231
5: 5 He is able to open the scroll and its s seals." 2231
5: 6 He had s horns and seven eyes, 2231
5: 6 He had seven horns and s eyes, 2231
5: 6 which are the s spirits of God sent out 2231
6: 1 as the Lamb opened the first of the s seals. 2231
8: 2 I saw the s angels who stand before God, 2231
8: 2 and to them were given s trumpets. 2231
8: 6 Then the s angels who had 2231
8: 6 the trumpets prepared to sound them. 2231
10: 3 the voices of the s thunders spoke. 2231
10: 4 the s thunders spoke, I was about to write; 2231
10: 4 up what the s thunders have said and do 2231
11:13 S thousand people were killed in 2231
12: 3 an enormous red dragon with s heads 2231
12: 3 and ten horns and s crowns on his heads. 2231
13: 1 He had ten horns and s heads, 2231
15: 1 s angels with the seven last plagues— 2231
15: 1 seven angels with the s last plagues. 2231
15: 6 Out of the temple came the s angels with 2231
15: 6 the seven angels with the s plagues. 2231
15: 7 the s angels seven golden bowls filled with 2231
15: 7 the seven angels s golden bowls filled with 2231
15: 8 the temple until the s plagues of 2231
15: 8 of the s angels were completed. 2231
16: 1 from the temple saying to the s angels, 2231
16: 1 the s bowls of God's wrath on the earth." 2231
17: 1 the s angels who had the seven bowls came 2231
17: 1 the seven angels who had the s bowls came 2231
17: 3 with blasphemous names and had s heads 2231
17: 7 which has the s heads and ten horns. 2231
17: 9 The s heads are seven hills on which 2231
17: 9 The seven heads are s hills on which 2231
17:10 They are also s kings. 2231
17:11 to the s and is going to his destruction. 2231
21: 9 the s angels who had the seven bowls full 2231
21: 9 the seven angels who had the s bowls full 2231
21: 9 of the s last plagues came and said to me, 2231

SEVEN-DAY (2) [DAY]

Ge 50:10 a s period of mourning for his father. 3427+8679
1Ch 9:25 share their duties for s periods. 2021+3427+8679

SEVENFOLD (1) [SEVEN]

Pr 6:31 Yet if he is caught, he must pay s, 8679

SEVENS (4) [SEVEN]

Da 9:24 "Seventy 's' are decreed for your people 8651
9:25 the ruler, comes, there will be seven 's,' 8651

Da	9:25	will be seven 'sevens,' and sixty-two 's.'	8651
	9:26	After the sixty-two 's,' the Anointed One	8651

SEVENTEEN (8) [SEVENTEENTH]

Ge	37: 2	Joseph, a young man of s,	6926+8679
	47:28	Jacob lived in Egypt s years,	6926+8679
Jdg	8:26	gold rings he asked for came to s hundred	547+2256+4395+8679
		shekels,	
1Ki	14:21	and he reigned s years in Jerusalem,	6926+8679
2Ki	13: 1	and he reigned s years.	6926+8679
1Ch	26:30	s hundred able men—	547+2256+4395+8679
2Ch	12:13	and he reigned s years in Jerusalem,	6926+8679
Jer	32: 9	and weighed out for him s shekels of silver.	
			2256+6927+8679

SEVENTEENTH (6) [SEVENTEEN]

Ge	7:11	on the s day of the second month—	6925+8679
	8: 4	on the s day of the seventh month the ark	
		came to rest	6925+8679
1Ki	22:51	s year of Jehoshaphat king of Judah,	6926+8679
2Ki	16: 1	the s year of Pekah son of Remaliah,	6926+8679
1Ch	24:15	the s to Hezir, the eighteenth to	6925+8679
	25:24	the s to Joshbekashah,	6925+8679

SEVENTH (116) [SEVEN]

Ge	2: 2	By the s day God had finished the work	8668
	2: 2	so on the s day he rested from all his work.	8668
	2: 3	God blessed the s day and made it holy,	8668
	8: 4	and on the seventeenth day of the s month	8668
Ex	12:15	the first day through the s must be cut off	8668
	12:16	and another one on the s day.	8668
	13: 6	on the s day hold a festival to the LORD.	8668
	16:26	but on the s day, the Sabbath,	8668
	16:27	some of the people went out on the s day	8668
	16:29	to stay where he is on the s day;	8668
	16:30	So the people rested on the s day.	8668
	20:10	s day is a Sabbath to the LORD your God.	8668
	20:11	but he rested on the s day.	8668
	21: 2	But in the s year, he shall go free,	8668
	23:11	during the s year let the land lie unplowed	8668
	23:12	but on the s day do not work,	8668
	24:16	the s day the LORD called to Moses from	8668
	31:15	but the s day is a Sabbath of rest,	8668
	31:17	and on the s day he abstained from work	8668
	34:21	but on the s day you shall rest;	8668
	35: 2	but the s day shall be your holy day,	8668
Lev	13: 5	On the s day the priest is to examine him,	8668
	13: 6	the s day the priest is to examine him again,	8668
	13:27	On the s day the priest is to examine him,	8668
	13:32	the s day the priest is to examine the sore,	8668
	13:34	the s day the priest is to examine the itch,	8668
	13:51	On the s day he is to examine it,	8668
	14: 9	On the s day he must shave off all his hair;	8668
	14:39	the s day the priest shall return to inspect	8668
	16:29	the s month you must deny yourselves and	8668
	23: 3	but the s day is a Sabbath of rest,	8668
	23: 8	And on the s day hold a sacred assembly	8668
	23:16	up to the day after the s Sabbath,	8668
	23:24	of the s month you are to have a day of rest,	8668
	23:27	"The tenth day of this s month is the Day	8668
	23:34	'On the fifteenth day of the s month	8668
	23:39	of the s month, after you have gathered	8668
	23:41	celebrate it in the s month.	8668
	25: 4	in the s year the land is to have a sabbath	8668
	25: 9	on the tenth day of the s month;	8668
	25:20	"What will we eat in the s year if we do	8668
Nu	6: 9	the day of his cleansing—the s day.	8668
	7:48	On the s day Elishama son of Ammihud,	8668
	19:12	the water on the third day and on the s day;	8668
	19:12	not purify himself on the third and s days,	8668
	19:19	the unclean person on the third and s days,	8668
	19:19	and on the s day he is to purify him.	8668
	28:25	On the s day hold a sacred assembly	8668
	29: 1	"'On the first day of the s month hold	8668
	29: 7	"'On the tenth day of this s month hold	8668
	29:12	"'On the fifteenth day of the s month,	8668
	29:32	"'On the s day prepare seven bulls,	8668
	31:19	and s days you must purify yourselves	8668
	31:24	the s day wash your clothes and you will	8668
Dt	5:14	s day is a Sabbath to the LORD your God.	8668
	15: 9	"The s year, the year for canceling debts,	8679
	15:12	in the s year you must let him go free.	8668
	16: 8	and on the s day hold an assembly to the	8668
Jos	6: 4	On the s day, march around the city seven	8668
	6:15	On the s day, they got up at daybreak	8668
	6:16	The s time around, when the priests	8668
	19:40	The s lot came out for the tribe of Dan,	8668
Jdg	14:17	So on the s day he finally told her,	8668
	14:18	the s day the men of the town said to him,	8668
2Sa	12:18	On the s day the child died.	8668
1Ki	8: 2	in the month of Ethanim, the s month.	8668
	18:44	The s time the servant reported,	8668
	20:29	and on the s day the battle was joined.	8668
2Ki	11: 4	In the s year Jehoiada sent for	8668
	12: 1	In the s year of Jehu, Joash became king,	8679
	18: 9	the s year of Hoshea son of Elah king	8668
	25: 8	On the s day of the fifth month,	8679
	25:25	In the s month, however,	8668
1Ch	2:15	the sixth Ozem and the s David.	8668
	12:11	Attai the sixth, Eliel the s,	8668
	24:10	the s to Hakkoz, the eighth to Abijah,	8668
	25:14	the s to Jesarelah, his sons and relatives, 12	8668
	26: 3	Jehohanan the sixth and Eliehoenai the s.	8668
	26: 5	Issachar the s and Peullethai the eighth.	8668
	27:10	The s, for the seventh month,	8668

1Ch	27:10	The seventh, for the s month,	8668
2Ch	5: 3	at the time of the festival in the s month.	8668
	7:10	the twenty-third day of the s month he sent	8668
	23: 1	In the s year Jehoiada showed his strength.	8668
	31: 7	the third month and finished in the s month.	8668
Ezr	3: 1	When the s month came and	8668
	3: 6	On the first day of the s month they began	8668
	7: 7	also came up to Jerusalem in the s year	8679
	7: 8	in Jerusalem in the fifth month of the s year	8668
Ne	7:73	When the s month came and	8668
	8: 2	the s month Ezra the priest brought the Law	8668
	8:14	in booths during the feast of the s month	8668
	10:31	Every s year we will forgo working the land	8668
Est	1:10	On the s day, when King Xerxes was	8668
	2:16	in the s year of his reign.	8679
Jer	28:17	In the s month of that same year,	8668
	34:14	'Every s year each of you must free any	8679
	41: 1	In the s month Ishmael son of Nethaniah,	8668
	52:28	in the s year, 3,023 Jews;	8679
Eze	20: 1	In the s year, in the fifth month	8668
	30:20	in the first month on the s day,	8679
	45:20	to do the same on the s day of the month	8679
	45:25	in the s month on the fifteenth day,	8679
Hag	2: 1	On the twenty-first day of the s month,	8668
Zec	7: 5	and mourned in the fifth and s months for	8668
	8:19	s and tenth months will become joyful	8668
Mt	22:26	right on down to the s.	2231
Jn	4:52	"The fever left him yesterday at the s hour."	1575
Heb	4: 4	about the s day in these words:	1575
	4: 4	on the s day God rested from all his work."	1575
Jude	1:14	Enoch, the s from Adam,	1575
Rev	8: 1	When he opened the s seal,	1575
	10: 7	the s angel is about to sound his trumpet,	1575
	11:15	The s angel sounded his trumpet,	1575
	16:17	The s angel poured out his bowl into	1575
	21:20	the sixth carnelian, the s chrysolite,	1575

SEVENTY (58) [70]

Ge	46:27	which went to Egypt, were s in all.	8679
	50: 3	And the Egyptians mourned for him s days.	8679
Ex	1: 5	The descendants of Jacob numbered s	8679
	15:27	twelve springs and s palm trees,	8679
	24: 1	and s of the elders of Israel.	8679
	24: 9	and the s elders of Israel went up	8679
Nu	7:13	silver sprinkling bowl weighing s shekels,	8679
	7:19	silver sprinkling bowl weighing s shekels,	8679
	7:25	silver sprinkling bowl weighing s shekels,	8679
	7:31	silver sprinkling bowl weighing s shekels,	8679
	7:37	silver sprinkling bowl weighing s shekels,	8679
	7:43	silver sprinkling bowl weighing s shekels,	8679
	7:49	silver sprinkling bowl weighing s shekels,	8679
	7:55	silver sprinkling bowl weighing s shekels,	8679
	7:61	silver sprinkling bowl weighing s shekels,	8679
	7:67	silver sprinkling bowl weighing s shekels,	8679
	7:73	silver sprinkling bowl weighing s shekels,	8679
	7:79	silver sprinkling bowl weighing s shekels,	8679
	7:85	and each sprinkling bowl s shekels.	8679
	11:16	"Bring me s of Israel's elders who are	8679
	11:24	He brought together s of their elders	8679
	11:25	on him and put the Spirit on the s elders.	8679
	33: 9	twelve springs and s palm trees,	8679
Dt	10:22	who went down into Egypt were s in all,	8679
Jdg	1: 7	"S kings with their thumbs	8679
	8:30	He had s sons of his own,	8679
	9: 2	to have all s of Jerub-Baal's sons rule	8679
	9: 4	They gave him s shekels of silver from	2231
	9: 5	and on one stone murdered his s brothers.	8679
	9:18	murdered his s sons on a single stone,	8679
	9:24	that the crime against Jerub-Baal's s sons,	8679
	9:56	to his father by murdering his s brothers.	8679
	12:14	who rode on s donkeys.	8679
1Sa	6:19	putting s of them to death	8679
2Sa	24:15	and s thousand of the people from Dan	8679
1Ki	5:15	Solomon had s thousand carriers	8679
2Ki	10: 1	in Samaria s sons of the house of Ahab.	8679
	10: 6	Now the royal princes, s of them,	8679
	10: 7	the princes and slaughtered all s of them.	8679
1Ch	21: 5	including four hundred and s thousand	8679
	21:14	and s thousand men of Israel fell dead.	8679
2Ch	2: 2	He conscripted s thousand men as carriers	8679
	29:32	the assembly brought was s bulls,	8679
	36:21	the years were completed in fulfillment of	8679
Ps	90:10	The length of our days is s years—	8679
Isa	23:15	that time Tyre will be forgotten for s years,	8679
	23:15	But at the end of these s years,	8679
	23:17	At the end of s years, the LORD will deal	8679
Jer	25:11	will serve the king of Babylon s years.	8679
	25:12	"But when the s years are fulfilled,	8679
	29:10	"When s years are completed for Babylon,	8679
Eze	8:11	In front of them stood s elders of the house	8679
	41:12	on the west side was s cubits wide.	8679
Da	9: 2	desolation of Jerusalem would last s years.	8679
	9:24	"S 'sevens' are decreed for your people	8679
Zec	1:12	you have been angry with these s years?"	8679
	7: 5	and seventh months for the past s years,	8679
Ac	23:23	s horsemen and two hundred spearmen	1573

SEVENTY-FIVE (7) [75]

Ge	12: 4	Abram was s years old when he set out	
		from Haran.	2256+2822+8679
	25: 7	Abraham lived a hundred and s years.	
			2256+2822+8679
Est	5:14	"Have a gallows built, s feet high,	564+2822
	7: 9	gallows s feet high stands by Haman's	564+2822
	9:16	They killed s thousand of them	2256+2822+8679

Jn	19:39	of myrrh and aloes, about s pounds.	1669+3354
Ac	7:14	Jacob and his whole family, s in all.	1573+4297

SEVENTY-SEVEN (4)

Ge	4:24	then Lamech s times."	2256+8679+8679
Jdg	8:14	the names of the s officials	2256+8679+8679
Ezr	8:35	ninety-six rams, s male lambs	2256+8679+8679
Mt	18:22	I tell you, not seven times, but s times.	1574+2231

SEVENTY-TWO (2) [72]

Lk	10: 1	After this the Lord appointed s others	1545+1573
	10:17	The s returned with joy and said,	1545+1573

SEVERAL (7)

2Ki	17:29	own gods in the s towns where they settled,	AIT
Da	8:27	was exhausted and lay ill for s days.	AIT
	11:13	and after s years, he will advance with a	AIT
Ac	9:19	Saul spent s days with the disciples	5516
	16:12	And we stayed there s days.	5516
	24:17	"After an absence of s years,	4498
	24:24	S days later Felix came with his wife	5516

SEVERE (22) [SEVERELY]

Ge	12:10	there for a while because the famine was s.	3878
	41:31	the famine that follows it will be so s.	3878
	41:56	for the famine was s throughout Egypt.	2616
	41:57	because the famine was s in all the world.	2616
	43: 1	Now the famine was still s in the land.	3878
	47: 4	because the famine is s in Canaan	2616
	47:13	region because the famine was s;	3878+4394
	47:20	because the famine was too s for them.	2616
Nu	11:33	and he struck them with a s plague.	4394+8041
Dt	28:59	and s and lingering illnesses.	8273
1Ki	18: 2	Now the famine was s in Samaria,	2617
2Ki	25: 3	so s that there was no food for the people	2616
2Ch	16:12	Though his disease was s,	2025+4200+5087
Jer	52: 6	so s that there was no food for the people	2616
Mt	4:24	those suffering s pain,	992
Lk	4:25	and a half years and there was a s famine	3489
	15:14	there was a s famine in that whole country,	2708
Ac	11:28	that a s famine would spread over	3489
2Co	8: 2	Out of the most s trial,	1509+2568
1Th	1: 6	in spite of s suffering,	4498
Rev	11:13	that very hour there was a s earthquake and	3489
	16:18	peals of thunder and a s earthquake.	3489

SEVERED (1) [SEVERING]

Ecc	12: 6	before the silver cord is s,	8178

SEVERELY (22) [SEVERE]

Ru	1:17	May the LORD deal with me, be it ever so s,	3578
1Sa	3:17	May God deal with you, be it ever so s,	3578
	14:44	"May God deal with me, be it ever so s,	3578
	20:13	may the LORD deal with David, be it ever so s,	3578
	25:22	May God deal with David, be it ever so s,	3578
2Sa	3: 9	May God deal with Abner, be it ever so s,	3578
	3:35	"May God deal with me, be it ever so s,	3578
	19:13	May God deal with me, be it ever so s,	3578
1Ki	2:23	"May God deal with me, be it ever so s,	3578
	19: 2	May the gods deal with me, be it ever so s,	3578
	20:10	May the gods deal with me, be it ever so s,	3578
2Ki	6:31	"May God deal with me, be it ever so s,	3578
	13: 4	the king of Aram was oppressing	4315+4316
2Ch	24:25	they left Joash s wounded.	8041
Ps	118:18	The LORD has chastened me s,	3579+3579
Mk	12:40	Such men will be punished most s."	4358
Lk	20:47	Such men will be punished most s."	4358
Ac	16:23	After they had been s flogged,	4498
	20:19	although I was s tested by the plots of	AIT
2Co	2: 5	to some extent—not to put it too s.	2096
	11:23	been flogged more s,	5649
Heb	10:29	How much more s do you think a man	5937

SEVERING (2) [SEVERED]

Lev	1:17	by the wings, not s it completely,	976
	5: 8	from its neck, not s it completely,	976

SEW (1) [SEWED, SEWS]

Eze	13:18	Woe to the women who s magic charms	9529

SEWED (2) [SEW]

Ge	3: 7	so they's fig leaves together	9529
Job	16:15	"I have s sackcloth over my skin	9529

SEWS (3) [SEW]

Mt	9:16	"No one s a patch of unshrunk cloth on	2095
Mk	2:21	"No one s a patch of unshrunk cloth on	2165
Lk	5:36	from a new garment and s it on an old one.	2095

SEX (2) [SEXUAL, SEXUALLY]

Ge	19: 5	to us so that we can have s with them."	3359
Jdg	19:22	to your house so we can have s with him."	3359

SEXUAL (47) [SEX]

Ex	19:15	Abstain from s relations."	440+448+851+5602
	22:19	Anyone who has relations with	6640+8886
Lev	18: 6	any close relative to have s relations.	1655+6872
	18: 7	Do not dishonor your father by having s	
		relations with your mother.	1655+6872

Lev 18: 8   " '*Do* not **have s** relations with your father's wife;   1655+6872
  18: 9   " '*Do* not **have s** relations with your sister,   1655+6872
  18:10   " '*Do* not **have s** relations with your son's daughter   1655+6872
  18:11   " '*Do* not **have s** relations with the daughter of your father's wife   1655+6872
  18:12   " '*Do* not **have s** relations with your father's sister;   1655+6872
  18:13   " '*Do* not **have s** relations with your mother's sister,   1655+6872
  18:14   " '*Do* not **dishonor** your father's brother **by** approaching his wife **to have s** relations;   1655+6872
  18:15   " '*Do* not **have s** relations with your daughter-in-law.   1655+6872
  18:16   " '*Do* not **have s** relations with your brother's wife;   1655+6872
  18:17   " '*Do* not **have s** relations with both a woman and her daughter.   1655+6872
  18:17   *Do* not **have s** relations with either   1655+6872
  18:18   a rival wife and **have s** relations   1655+6872
  18:19   to **have s** relations during the uncleanness of her monthly period.   1655+6872
  18:20   " '*Do* not **have s** relations with your neighbor's wife   2446+4200+5989+8888
  18:23   not **have s** relations with an animal   5989+8888
  18:23   to an animal to **have s** relations with it;   8061
  20:15   a man **has s** relations with an animal,   5989+8888
  20:16   an animal to **have s** relations with it,   8061
  20:17   and *they* **have s** relations,   906+6872+8011
  20:18   and **has s** relations with her,   906+1655+6872
  20:19   " '*Do* not **have s** relations with the sister of either your mother   1655+6872
Nu 25: 1   the men began to **indulge in s** immorality   2388
Dt 27:21   "Cursed is the man *who* **has s** relations with any animal."   6640+8886
Mt 15:19   murder, adultery, **s** immorality, theft,   4518
Mk 7:21   come evil thoughts, **s** immorality, theft,   4518
Ac 15:20   by idols, from **s** immorality, from the meat   4518
  15:29   strangled animals and *from* **s** immorality.   4518
  21:25   strangled animals and from **s** immorality."   4518
Ro 1:24   of their hearts to **s** impurity for   174
  13:13   not *in* **s** immorality and debauchery,   3130
1Co 5: 1   that there is **s** immorality among you, and   4518
  6:13   The body is not *meant for* **s** immorality,   4518
  6:18   Flee from **s** immorality.   4518
  10: 8   *We* should not **commit s** immorality,   4519
2Co 12:21   have not repented of the impurity, **s** sin   4518
Gal 5:19   **s** immorality, impurity and debauchery;   4518
Eph 5: 3   not be even a hint of **s** immorality,   4518
Col 3: 5   **s** immorality, impurity, lust,   4518
1Th 4: 3   that you should avoid **s** immorality;   4518
Jude 1: 7   **gave** themselves **up to s** immorality   1745
Rev 2:14   and by **committing s** immorality.   4519
  2:20   misleads my servants into **s** immorality and   4519
  9:21   their **s** immorality or their thefts.   4519

SEXUALLY (8) [SEX]

1Co 5: 9   not to associate with **s** immoral *people*—   4521
  5:11   a brother but is **s** immoral or greedy,   4521
  6: 9   the **s** immoral nor idolaters nor adulterers   4521
  6:18   but he who **sins s** sins against his own body.   4519
Heb 12:16   See that no one *is* **s** immoral,   4521
  13: 4   the adulterer and all the **s** immoral.   4521
Rev 21:8   the vile, the murderers, the **s** immoral,   4521
  22:15   the **s** immoral, the murderers,   4521

SHAALABBIN (1)

Jos 19:42   **S**, Aijalon, Ithlah,   9125

SHAALBIM (2)

Jdg 1:35   to hold out in Mount Heres, Aijalon and **S**,   9124
1Ki 4: 9   **S**, Beth Shemesh and Elon Bethhanan;   9124

SHAALBONITE (2)

2Sa 23:32   Eliahba the **S**, the sons of Jashen, Jonathan   9126
1Ch 11:33   Azmaveth the Baharumite, Eliahba the **S**,   9126

SHAALIM (1)

1Sa 9: 4   They went on into the district of **S**,   9127

SHAAPH (2)

1Ch 2:47   Jotham, Geshan, Pelet, Ephah and **S**.   9131
  2:49   to **S** the father of Madmannah and to Sheva   9131

SHAARAIM (3)

Jos 15:36   **S**, Adithaim and Gederah   9139
1Sa 17:52   Their dead were strewn along the **S** road   9139
1Ch 4:31   Hazar Susim, Beth Biri and **S**.   9139

SHAASHGAZ (1)

Est 2:14   of the harem to the care of **S**,   9140

SHABBETHAI (3)

Ezr 10:15   supported by Meshullam and **S** the Levite,   8703
Ne 8: 7   Jeshua, Bani, Sherebiah, Jamin, Akkub, **S**,   8703
  11:16   **S** and Jozabad, two of the heads of   8703

SHABBY (1)

Jas 2: 2   and a poor man in **s** clothes also comes in.   4865

SHACHIA (KJV) See SAKIA

SHACKLES (12)

Jdg 16:21   Binding him with bronze **s**,   AIT
2Ki 25: 7   with **bronze s** and took him to Babylon.   5733
2Ch 33:11   with **bronze s** and took him to Babylon.   5733
  36: 6   and bound him with **bronze s** to take him   5733
Job 12:18   He takes off the **s** *put on by* kings and ties   4591
  13:27   You fasten my feet in **s**;   6040
  33:11   He fastens my feet in **s**;   6040
Ps 105:18   They bruised his feet with **s**,   3890
  149: 8   their nobles with **s** *of* iron,   3890
Jer 39: 7   and bound him with **bronze s** to take him   5733
  52:11   with **bronze s** and took him to Babylon,   5733
Na 1:13   from your neck and tear your **s** away."   4593

SHADE (19)

Jdg 9:15   come and take refuge in my **s**;   7498
Ne 8:15   palms and **s** trees, to make booths"—   6290
Ps 80:10   The mountains were covered with its **s**,   7498
  121: 5   the LORD is your **s** at your right hand;   7498
SS 2: 3   I delight to sit in his **s**,   7498
Isa 4: 6   be a shelter and **s** from the heat of the day,   7498
  25: 4   from the storm and a **s** from the heat.   7498
  30: 2   to Egypt's **s** for refuge.   7498
  30: 3   Egypt's **s** will bring you disgrace.   7498
Jer 4:30   Why **s** your eyes with paint?   7973
Eze 17:23   they will find shelter in the **s**   7498
  31: 6   all the great nations lived in its **s**.   7498
  31:12   of the earth came out from under its **s**   7498
  31:17   Those who lived in its **s**,   7498
Hos 4:13   where the **s** is pleasant.   7498
  14: 7   Men will dwell again in his **s**.   7498
Jnh 4: 5   sat in its **s** and waited to see what would   7498
  4: 6   to give **s** for his head to ease his discomfort,   7498
Mk 4:32   that the birds of the air can perch in its **s**."   5014

SHADOW (40) [SHADOWS]

2Ki 20: 9   Shall the **s** go forward ten steps,   7498
  20:10   for the **s** to go forward ten steps,"   7498
  20:11   the **s** go back the ten steps it had gone down   7498
1Ch 29:15   Our days on earth are like a **s**,   7498
Job 3: 5   and **deep s** claim it once more;   7516
  8: 9   and our days on earth are but a **s**.   7498
  10:21   to the land of gloom and **deep s**,   7516
  10:22   of deepest night, of **deep s** and disorder,   7516
  14: 2   like a fleeting **s**, he does not endure.   7498
  17: 7   my whole frame is but a **s**.   7498
  34:22   There is no dark place, no **deep s**,   7516
  38:17   Have you seen the gates of the **s of death**?   7516
  40:22   The lotuses conceal him in their **s**;   7498
Ps 17: 8   hide me in the **s** *of* your wings   7498
  23: 4   I walk through the valley of the **s of death**,   7516
  36: 7   and low among men find refuge in the **s**   7498
  57: 1   I will take refuge in the **s** of your wings   7498
  63: 7   I sing in the **s** *of* your wings.   7498
  91: 1   Most High will rest in the **s** *of* the Almighty.   7498
  102:11   My days are like the evening **s**;   7498
  109:23   I fade away like an evening **s**;   7498
  144: 4   his days are like a fleeting **s**.   7498
Ecc 6:12   days he passes through like a **s**?   7498
  8:13   and their days will not lengthen like a **s**.   7498
Isa 9: 2   on those living in the land of the **s of death**   7516
  16: 3   Make your **s** like night—at high noon.   7498
  25: 5   as heat is reduced by the **s** of a cloud,   7498
  32: 2   like streams of water in the desert and the **s**   7498
  34:15   for her young under the **s** *of* her wings;   7498
  38: 8   I will make the **s** cast by the sun go back   7498
  49: 2   in the **s** *of* his hand he hid me;   7498
  51:16   and covered you with the **s** *of* my hand—   7498
Jer 48:45   "In the **s** *of* Heshbon the fugitives stand   7498
La 4:20   We thought that under his **s** we would live   7498
Mt 4:16   on those living in the land of the **s** of death   5014
Lk 1:79   on those living in darkness and in the **s**   5014
Ac 5:15   at least Peter's **s** might fall on some of them   5014
Col 2:17   These are a **s** of the things that were   5014
Heb 8: 5   at a sanctuary that is a copy and **s** of what is   5014
  10: 1   a **s** of the good things that are coming—   5014

SHADOWS (11) [SHADOW]

Jdg 9:36   "You mistake the **s** *of* the mountains   7498
Ne 13:19   When *evening* **s** fell *on* the gates   7511
Job 7: 2   Like a slave longing for the **evening s**,   7498
  12:22   of darkness and brings **deep s** into the light.   7516
  16:16   **deep s** ring my eyes;   7516
Ps 11: 2   the strings to shoot from the **s** at the upright   694
SS 2:17   Until the day breaks and the **s** flee, turn,   7498
  4: 6   Until the day breaks and the **s** flee,   7498
Isa 59: 9   for brightness, but we walk in **deep s**.   696
Jer 6: 4   and the **s** *of* evening grow long.   7498
Jas 1:17   who does not change like shifting **s**.   684

SHADRACH (14)

Da 1: 7   the name Belteshazzar; to Hananiah, **S**;   8731
  2:49   at Daniel's request the king appointed **S**,   10701
  3:12   **S**, Meshach and Abednego—   10701
  3:13   Nebuchadnezzar summoned **S**,   10701
  3:14   "Is it true, **S**, Meshach and Abednego,   10701
  3:16   **S**, Meshach and Abednego replied to   10701

Da 3:19   Then Nebuchadnezzar was furious with **S**,   10701
  3:20   in his army to tie up **S**, Meshach and   10701
  3:22   the fire killed the soldiers who took up **S**,   10701
  3:26   "**S**, Meshach and Abednego, servants of   10701
  3:26   So **S**, Meshach and Abednego came out of   10701
  3:28   "Praise be to the God of **S**, Meshach and   10701
  3:29   against the God of **S**, Meshach and   10701
  3:30   Then the king promoted **S**, Meshach and   10701

SHAFT (9)

Ex 25:31   of pure gold and hammer it out, base and **s**;   7866
  37:17   and hammered it out, base and **s**;   7866
1Sa 17: 7   His spear **s** was like a weaver's rod,   6770
2Sa 5: 8   the Jebusites will have to use the **water s**   7562
  21:19   a spear with a **s** like a weaver's rod.   6770
  23: 7   a tool of iron or the **s** *of* a spear;   6770
1Ch 20: 5   a spear with a **s** like a weaver's rod.   6770
Job 28: 4   Far from where people dwell he cuts a **s**,   5707
Rev 9: 1   The star was given the key *to* the **s** of   5853

SHAGEE (1)

1Ch 11:34   Jonathan son of **S** the Hararite,   8707

SHAGGY (1)

Da 8:21   The **s** goat is the king of Greece,   8537

SHAHAR   See ZERETH SHAHAR

SHAHARAIM (1)

1Ch 8: 8   Sons were born to **S** in Moab   8844

SHAHAZUMAH (1)

Jos 19:22   The boundary touched Tabor, **S** and   8833

SHAKE (31) [SHAKEN, SHAKES, SHAKING, SHOOK]

Jdg 16:20   "I'll go out as before and **s** myself free."   5850
Ne 5:13   "In this way *may* God **s** out of his house   5850
Job 4:14   and **made** all my bones **s**.   7064
  16: 4   against you and **s** my head at you.   5675
  38:13   the earth by the edges and **s** the wicked out   5850
Ps 10: 6   He says to himself, "Nothing *will* **s** me;   4572
  44:14   the peoples **s** their heads at us.   4954
  64: 8   who see them *will* **s** *their* heads in scorn.   5653
  99: 1   between the cherubim, *let* the earth **s**.   5667
  109:25   when they see me, *they* **s** their heads.   5675
Isa 2:19   when he rises to **s** the earth.   6907
  2:21   when he rises to **s** the earth.   6907
  5.25   The mountains **s**, and the dead bodies are   8074
  10:32   *they will* **s** their fist at the mount of   5677
  13:13   the earth *will* **s** from its place at the wrath   8321
  24:18   the foundations of the earth **s**.   8321
  52: 2   **S** off** your dust; rise up, sit enthroned,   5850
Jer 18:16   by will be appalled and *will* **s** their heads.   5653
  48:27   that *you* **s** *your* **head in scorn**   5653
La 2:15   they scoff and **s** their heads at the Daughter   5675
Am 9: 1   of the pillars so that the thresholds **s**.   8321
  9: 9   and *I will* **s** the house of Israel among all   5675
Zep 2:15   All who pass by her scoff and **s** their fists.   5675
Hag 2: 6   while *I will* once more **s** the heavens and   8321
  2: 7   *I will* **s** all nations,   8321
  2:21   that *I will* **s** the heavens and the earth.   8321
Mt 10:14   **s** the dust **off** your feet when you leave   1759
Mk 6:11   **s** the dust **off** your feet when you leave,   1759
Lk 6:48   torrent struck that house but could not **s** it,   4888
  9: 5   **s** the dust **off** your feet when you leave   701
Heb 12:26   "Once more *I will* **s** not only the earth but   4940

SHAKEN (33) [SHAKE]

1Sa 28:21   to Saul and saw that *he* **was** greatly **s**,   987
2Sa 18:33   The king *was* **s**.   8074
Ne 5:13   So may such a man be **s** out and emptied!"   5850
Job 34:20   the people **are s** and they pass away;   1723
Ps 15: 5   He who does these things *will* never **be s**.   4572
  16: 8   he is at my right hand, *I* will not **be s**.   4572
  21: 7   of the Most High *he will* not **be s**.   4572
  30: 6   I felt secure, I said, "*I* will never **be s**."   4572
  60: 2   *You have* **s** the land and torn it open;   8321
  62: 2   he is my fortress, *I* will never **be s**.   4572
  62: 6   he is my fortress, *I* will not **be s**.   4572
  82: 5   all the foundations of the earth **are s**.   4572
  109:23   *I am* **s** **off** like a locust;   5850
  112: 6   Surely *he will* never **be s**;   4572
  125: 1   *which* cannot **be s** but endures forever.   4572
Isa 7: 2   so the hearts of Ahaz and his people *were* **s**,   5675
  7: 2   as the trees of the forest *are* **s** by the wind.   4572+4572
  24:19   the earth **is thoroughly s**.   4572+4572
  54:10   mountains *be* **s** and the hills be removed,   4631
  54:10   yet my unfailing love for you *will* not **be s**   4631
Am 9: 9   of Israel among all the nations as grain is **s**   5675
Na 3:12   when *they are* **s**, the figs fall into the mouth   5675
Mt 24:29   and the heavenly bodies *will be* **s**.'   4888
Mk 13:25   and the heavenly bodies *will be* **s**.'   4888
Lk 6:38   pressed down, **s together** and running over,   4888
  21:26   for the heavenly bodies *will be* **s**.   4888
Ac 2:25   he is at my right hand, *I* will not **be s**.   4888
  4:31   the place where they were meeting *was* **s**.   4888
  16:26   that the foundations of the prison *were* **s**.   4888
Heb 12:27   the removing of what *can* be **s**—   4888
  12:27   so that what cannot *be* **s** may remain.   4888
  12:28   a kingdom that **cannot be s**,   810

Rev 6:13 as late figs drop from a fig tree *when* s by   4940

SHAKES (6) [SHAKE]
Job 9: 6 He s the earth from its place   8074
    15:25 because *he* s his fist at God   5742
Ps 29: 8 The voice of the LORD s the desert;   2655
    29: 8 the LORD s the Desert of Kadesh.   2655
Isa 30:28 He s the nations in the sieve of destruction;   5677
Joel 2:10 Before them the earth s, the sky trembles,   8074

SHAKING (3) [SHAKE]
Ps 22: 7 they hurl insults, s their heads: 5675
Mt 27:39 by hurled insults at him, s their heads   3075
Mk 15:29 s their heads and saying, "So!   3075

SHALIM (KJV) See SHAALIM

SHALISHA (1)
1Sa 9: 4 of Ephraim and through the area around S,   8995

SHALISHAH See BAAL SHALISHAH

SHALL (467) See Index of Articles Etc.

SHALLEKETH (1)
1Ch 26:16 The lots for the West Gate and the S Gate   8962

SHALLOW (2)
Mt 13: 5 It sprang up quickly, because the soil *was* s.   958+2400+3590
Mk 4: 5 It sprang up quickly, because the soil was s.   958+3590

SHALLUM (25) [SHALLUM'S]
2Ki 15:10 S son of Jabesh conspired against   8935
    15:13 S son of Jabesh became king in the   8935
    15:14 He attacked S son of Jabesh in Samaria,   8935
    22:14 who was the wife of S son of Tikvah,   8935
1Ch 2:40 Sismai the father of S,   8935
    2:41 S the father of Jekamiah,   8935
    3:15 Zedekiah the third, S the fourth.   8935
    4:25 S was Shaul's son,   8935
    6:12 Zadok the father of S,   8935
    6:13 S the father of Hilkiah,   8935
    9:17 The gatekeepers: S, Akkub, Talmon,   8935
    9:17 and their brothers, S their chief   8935
    9:19 S son of Kore, the son of Ebiasaph,   8935
    9:31 the firstborn son of S the Korahite,   8935
2Ch 28:12 of Meshillemoth, Jehizkiah son of S,   8935
    34:22 who was the wife of S son of Tokhath,   8935
Ezr 2:42 the descendants of S, Ater, Talmon,   8935
    7: 2 the son of S, the son of Zadok,   8935
    10:24 From the gatekeepers: S, Telem and Uri.   8935
    10:42 S, Amariah and Joseph.   8935
Ne 3:12 S son of Hallohesh,   8935
    7:45 the descendants of S, Ater, Talmon,   8935
Jer 22:11 the LORD says about S son of Josiah,   8935
    32: 7 of S your uncle is going to come to you   8935
    35: 4 which was over that of Maaseiah son of S   8935

SHALLUM'S (1) [SHALLUM]
2Ki 15:15 The other events of S reign,   8935

SHALLUN (1)
Ne 3:15 The Fountain Gate was repaired by S son   8937

SHALMAI (2)
Ezr 2:46 Hagab, S, Hanan,   8978
Ne 7:48 Lebana, Hagaba, S,   8978

SHALMAN (1)
Hos 10:14 as S devastated Beth Arbel on the day   8986

SHALMANESER (3) [SHALMANESER'S]
2Ki 17: 3 S king of Assyria came up   8987
    17: 4 S seized him and put him in prison.   855+4889S
    18: 9 S king of Assyria marched against Samaria   8987

SHALMANESER'S (1) [SHALMANESER]
2Ki 17: 3 Hoshea, who had been S vassal   2257+4200S

SHAMA (1)
1Ch 11:44 S and Jeiel the sons of Hotham   9052

SHAMARIAH (KJV) See SHEMARIAH

SHAMBLES (KJV) See MEAT MARKET

SHAME (128) [ASHAMED, SHAMED, SHAMEFUL, SHAMEFULLY, SHAMELESS, SHAMELESSLY, SHAMING]
Ge 2:25 were both naked, and *they* felt no s.   1017
Dt 32: 5 to their s they are no longer his children,   4583
1Sa 20:30 sided with the son of Jesse to your own s   1425

1Sa 20:30 to the s of the mother who bore you?   1425+6872
2Ki 19:26 are dismayed and put to s.   1017
Job 8:22 Your enemies will be clothed in s,   1425
    10:15 I am full of s and drowned in my affliction.   7830
    11:15 then you will lift up your face without s;   4583
Ps 4: 2 O men, will you turn my glory into s?   4009
    25: 2 *Do not let me* be put to s,   1017
    25: 3 whose hope is in you *will* ever *be* put to s;   1017
    25: 3 *be* put to s who are treacherous   1017
    25:20 *let me* not be put to s,   1017
    31: 1 *let me* never *be* put to s;   1017
    31:17 *Let me* not *be* put to s, O LORD,   1017
    31:17 the wicked *be* put to s and lie silent in   1017
    34: 5 their faces *are* never covered with s.   2917
    35: 4 be disgraced and put to s;   4007
    35:26 over my distress be put to s and confusion;   1017
    35:26 over me be clothed with s and disgrace.   1425
    40:14 to take my life be put to s and confusion;   1017
    40:15 be appalled at their own s.   1425
    44: 7 put our adversaries to s.   1017
    44:15 and my face is covered with s   1425
    53: 5 *you* put them to s, for God despised them.   1017
    69: 6 *may* those who seek you not *be* put to s   4007
    69: 7 and s covers my face.   4009
    70: 2 *May* those who seek my life *be* put to s   1017
    70: 3 turn back because of their s.   1425
    71: 1 *let me* never *be* put to s.   1017
    71:13 May my accusers perish *in* s;   1017
    71:24 to harm me *have been* put to s   1017
    78:66 he put them to everlasting s.   3075
    83:16 with s so that men will seek your name,   7830
    86:17 my enemies may see it and *be* put to s,   1017
    89:45 you have covered him with a mantle of s.   1019
    97: 7 All who worship images *are* put to s,   1017
    109:28 when they attack *they will be* put to s,   1017
    109:29 be clothed with disgrace and wrapped in s   1425
    119: 6 Then *I* would not *be* put to s   1017
    119:31 *do not let* me be put to s.   1017
    119:46 before kings and *will* not *be* put to s,   1017
    119:78 the arrogant *be* put to s for wronging me   1017
    119:80 that *I may* not *be* put to s.   1017
    127: 5 not *be* put to s when they contend   1017
    129: 5 May all who hate Zion be turned back *in* s.   1017
    132:18 I will clothe his enemies with s,   1425
Pr 3:35 but fools he holds up to s.   7830
    6:33 and his s will never be wiped away;   3075
    13: 5 but the wicked bring s and disgrace.   944
    13:18 ignores discipline comes to poverty and s,   7830
    18: 3 and with s comes disgrace.   7830
    18:13 that is his folly and his s.   4009
    19:26 a son *who* brings s and disgrace.   1017
    25: 8 in the end if your neighbor puts you to s?   4007
    25:10 or he who hears it *may* s you   2873
Isa 20: 4 with buttocks bared—*to* Egypt's s.   6872
    20: 5 in Egypt will be afraid and put to s.   1017
    26:11 for your people and *be* put to s;   1017
    30: 3 But Pharaoh's protection will be to your s,   1425
    30: 5 *be* put to s because of a people useless   1017
    30: 5 but only s and disgrace."   1425
    37:27 are dismayed and put to s.   1017
    42:17 will be turned back *in* utter s,   1017+1425
    44: 9 they are ignorant, *to their own* s.   1017
    44:11 He and his kind *will be* put to s;   1017
    45:16 All the makers of idols *will be* put to s   1017
    45:17 *you* will never *be* put to s or disgraced,   1017
    45:24 will come to him and *be* put to s.   1017
    47: 3 be exposed and your s uncovered.   3075
    50: 7 and I know *I* will not *be* put to s.   1017
    54: 4 "Do not be afraid; *you* will not suffer s.   1017
    54: 4 the s *of* your youth and remember no more   1425
    61: 7 Instead of their s my people will receive   1425
    65:13 but you *will be* put to s.   1017
    66: 5 Yet they *will be* put to s.   1017
Jer 3: 3 you refuse *to* blush with s.   4007
    3:25 Let us lie down in our s,   1425
    6:15 No, *they* have no s at all;   1017+1017
    7:19 harming themselves, to their own s?   1425
    8: 9 The wise *will be* put to s;   1017
    8:12 No, *they* have no s at all;   1017+1017
    9:19 How great *is* our s!   1017
    12:13 So bear the s of your harvest because of   1017
    13:26 over your face that your s may be seen—   7830
    17:13 all who forsake you *will be* put to s.   1017
    17:18 *Let* my persecutors *be* put to s,   1017
    17:18 but *keep* me from s;   1017
    20:18 and sorrow and to end my days in s?   1017
    23:40 everlasting s that will not be forgotten."   4010
    46:12 The nations will hear of your s;   7830
    46:24 The Daughter of Egypt *will be* put to s,   1017
    48:39 How Moab turns her back *in* s!   1017
    50: 2 Bel *will be* put to s,   1017
    50: 2 *be* put to s and her idols filled with terror.'   1017
    51:51 and s covers our faces,   4009
Eze 7:18 be covered with s and their heads will   1019
    23:29 the s of your prostitution will be exposed.   6872
    32:24 They bear their s with those who go down   4009
    32:25 they bear their s with those who go down to   4009
    32:30 and bear their s with those who go down to   4009
    39:26 They will forget their s and all   4009
    44:13 the s of their detestable practices.   4009
Da 9: 7 but this day we are covered with s—   1425
    9: 8 with s because we have sinned against you.   1425
    12: 2 others to s and everlasting contempt.   3075
Hos 4:19 and their sacrifices will bring them s.   1017
Am 8:14 They who swear by the s of Samaria,   873
Ob 1:10 you will be covered with s;   1019
Mic 1:11 Pass on in nakedness and s,   1425

Mic 7:10 and will be covered with s,   1019
Na 3: 5 and the kingdoms your s.   7830
Hab 2:16 You will be filled with s instead of glory.   7830
Zep 3: 5 yet the unrighteous know no s.   1425
    3:11 that day *you will* not *be* put to s for all   1017
    3:19 in every land where they were put to s.   1425
Ro 9:33 who trusts in him *will* never *be* put to s."   2875
    10:11 who trusts in him *will* never *be* put to s."   2875
1Co 1:27 the foolish things of the world to s the wise;   2875
    1:27 God chose the weak things of the world to s   2875
    4:14 I am not writing this *to* s you,   1956
    6: 5 I say this to s you.   1959
    15:34 I say this to your s.   1959
2Co 11:21 To my s I admit that we were too weak   871+2848
Php 3:19 and their glory is in their s.   158
Heb 12: 2 endured the cross, scorning its s,   158
1Pe 2: 6 who trusts in him *will* never *be* put to s."   2875
Jude 1:13 wild waves of the sea, foaming up their s;   158

SHAMED (5) [SHAME]
Ps 69:19 how I am scorned, disgraced and s;   4009
Jer 10:14 every goldsmith *is* s by his idols.   1017
    51:17 every goldsmith *is* s by his idols.   1017
Joel 2:26 never again *will* my people be s.   1017
    2:27 never again *will* my people *be* s.   1017

SHAMEFACEDNESS (KJV) See DECENCY

SHAMEFUL (15) [SHAME]
1Sa 20:34 at his father's s treatment *of* David.   4007
Job 31:11 that would have been s, a sin to be judged.   2365
Pr 14:35 but a s servant incurs his wrath.   1017
Jer 3:24 From our youth s gods have consumed   1425
    11:13 to that s god Baal are as many as the streets   1425
Hos 4:18 their rulers dearly love s ways.   7830
    6: 9 the road to Shechem, committing s crimes.   2365
    9:10 they consecrated themselves to that s idol   1425
Zep 2: 1 gather together, O s nation,   4083+4202
Ro 1:26 of this, God gave them over to s lusts.   871
2Co 4: 2 we have renounced secret and s ways;   158
Eph 5:12 For it is s even to mention what   156
2Pe 2: 2 Many will follow their s *ways*   816
Rev 3:18 so you can cover your s nakedness;   158
    21:27 will anyone who does what is s or deceitful,   1007

SHAMEFULLY (4) [SHAME]
Eze 22:11 another s defiles his daughter-in-law,   928+2365
Mk 12: 4 on the head and treated him s.   870
Lk 20:11 and treated s and sent away empty-handed.   869
Rev 16:15 he may not go naked and be s exposed."   859

SHAMELESS (1) [SHAME]
Jer 13:27 and lustful neighings, your s prostitution!   2365

SHAMELESSLY (1) [SHAME]
Job 19: 3 reproached me; s you attack me.   1017+4202

SHAMER (KJV) See SHEMER, SHOMER

SHAMGAR (2)
Jdg 3:31 After Ehud came S son of Anath,   9011
    5: 6 "In the days of S son of Anath,   9011

SHAMHUTH (1)
1Ch 27: 8 was the commander S the Izrahite.   9016

SHAMING (1) [SHAME]
Hab 2:10 s your own house and forfeiting your life.   1425

SHAMIR (4)
Jos 15:48 In the hill country: S, Jattir, Socoh,   9034
Jdg 10: 1 He lived in S, in the hill country of Ephraim   9034
    10: 2 then he died, and was buried in S.   9034
1Ch 24:24 from the sons of Micah: S.   9033

SHAMMA (1)
1Ch 7:37 Bezer, Hod, S, Shilshah, Ithran and Beera.   9007

SHAMMAH (9)
Ge 36:13 Nahath, Zerah, S and Mizzah.   9015
    36:17 Chiefs Nahath, Zerah, S and Mizzah.   9015
1Sa 16: 9 Jesse then had S pass by, but Samuel said,   9015
    17:13 and the third, S.   9015
2Sa 23: 9 to him was S son of Agee the Hararite.   9007
    23:12 S took his stand in the middle of the field.   NIH
    23:25 S the Harodite, Elika the Harodite,   9015
    23:33 son of S the Hararite,   9015
1Ch 1:37 Nahath, Zerah, S and Mizzah.   9015

SHAMMAI (5) [SHAMMAI'S]
1Ch 2:28 The sons of Onam: S and Jada.   9025
    2:28 The sons of S: Nadab and Abishur.   9025
    2:44 Rekem was the father of S.   9025
    2:45 The son of S was Maon,   9025
    4:17 S and Ishbah the father of Eshtemoa.   9025

SHAMMAI'S (1) [SHAMMAI]
1Ch 2:32 The sons of Jada, S brother: 9025

SHAMMOTH (1)
1Ch 11:27 S the Harorite, Helez the Pelonite, 9021

SHAMMUA (6)
Nu 13: 4 from the tribe of Reuben, S son of Zaccur; 9018
2Sa 5:14 S, Shobab, Nathan, Solomon, 9018
1Ch 3: 5 S, Shobab, Nathan and Solomon. 9055
14: 4 S, Shobab, Nathan, Solomon, 9018
Ne 11:17 and Abda son of S, the son of Galal, 9018
12:18 of Bilgah's, S; of Shemaiah's, Jehonathan; 9018

SHAMSHERAI (1)
1Ch 8:26 S, Shehariah, Athaliah, 9091

SHAN See BETH SHAN

SHAPE (12) [SHAPED, SHAPES, SHAPING]
Ex 32: 4 made it into an idol cast in the s of a calf, 6319
32: 8 an idol cast in the s of a calf. 6319
Dt 4:16 an idol, an image of any s, 6166
9:16 an idol cast in the s of a calf. 6319
1Ki 6:25 two cherubim identical in size and s. 7893
7:19 of the pillars in the portico were in the s 5126
7:22 The capitals on top were in the s of lilies. 5126
7:23 the Sea of cast metal, circular in s, 6017+6318
7:37 and were identical in size and s. 7893
2Ki 17:16 two idols cast in the s of calves,
2Ch 4: 2 the Sea of cast metal, circular in s, 6017+6318
Job 38:14 The earth takes s like clay under a seal; 2200

SHAPED (5) [SHAPE]
Ex 25:33 Three cups s like almond flowers 5481
25:34 four cups s like almond flowers 5481
37:19 Three cups s like almond flowers 5481
37:20 four cups s like almond flowers 5481
Job 10: 8 "Your hands s me and made me. 6771

SHAPES (4) [SHAPE]
Isa 44:10 Who s a god and casts an idol, 3670
44:12 he s an idol with hammers, 3670
44:13 He s it in the form of man, 6913
Jer 10: 3 and a craftsman s it with his chisel. 3338+5126

SHAPHAM (1)
1Ch 5:12 S the second, then Janai and Shaphat, 9171

SHAPHAN (30)
2Ki 22: 3 S son of Azaliah, the son of Meshullam, 9177
22: 8 the high priest said to S the secretary, 9177
22: 8 He gave it to S, who read it. 9177
22: 9 Then S the secretary went to the king 9177
22:10 Then S the secretary informed the king, 9177
22:10 S read from it in the presence of the king. 9177
22:12 Ahikam son of S, Acbor son of Micaiah, 9177
22:12 S the secretary and Asaiah 9177
22:14 S and Asaiah went to speak to 9177
25:22 Gedaliah son of Ahikam, the son of S, 9177
2Ch 34: 8 he sent S son of Azaliah and Maaseiah 9177
34:15 Hilkiah said to S the secretary, 9177
34:15 He gave it to S. 9177
34:16 then S took the book to the king 9177
34:18 Then S the secretary informed the king, 9177
34:18 S read from it in the presence of the king. 9177
34:20 Ahikam son of S, Abdon son of Micah, 9177
34:20 S the secretary and Asaiah 9177
Jer 26:24 Ahikam son of S supported Jeremiah, 9177
29: 3 He entrusted the letter to Elasah son of S 9177
36:10 From the room of Gemariah son of S 9177
36:11 Micaiah son of Gemariah, the son of S, 9177
36:12 Elnathan son of Acbor, Gemariah son of S, 9177
39:14 the son of S, to take him back to his home. 9177
40: 5 Gedaliah son of Ahikam, the son of S, 9177
40: 9 Gedaliah son of Ahikam, the son of S, 9177
40:11 the son of S, as governor over them, 9177
41: 2 the son of S, with the sword, 9177
43: 6 Gedaliah son of Ahikam, the son of S, 9177
Eze 8:11 and Jaazaniah son of S was standing 9177

SHAPHAT (8)
Nu 13: 5 from the tribe of Simeon, S son of Hori; 9151
1Ki 19:16 of S from Abel Meholah to succeed you 9151
19:19 from there and found Elisha son of S. 9151
2Ki 6:31 "Elisha son of S is here. 9151
6:31 of S remains on his shoulders today!" 9151
1Ch 3:22 Hattush, Igal, Bariah, Neariah and S, 9151
5:12 Shapham the second, then Janai and S, 9151
27:29 S son of Adlai was in charge of the herds in 9151

SHAPHER (KJV) See SHEPHER

SHAPHIR (1)
Mic 1:11 in nakedness and shame, you who live in S. 9160

SHAPING (2) [SHAPE]
Jer 18: 4 the pot he was s from the clay was marred 6913

Jer 18: 4 into another pot, s it as seemed best to him. 6913

SHARAI (1)
Ezr 10:40 Macnadebai, Shashai, S, 9232

SHARAIM (KJV) See SHAARAIM

SHARAR (1)
2Sa 23:33 Ahiam son of S the Hararite, 9243

SHARE (102) [SHARED, SHARERS, SHARES, SHARING]
Ge 14:24 the s that belongs to the men who went 2750
14:24 Let them have their s." 2750
21:10 slave woman's son will never s in the inheritance with my son Isaac." 3769
31:14 "Do we still have any s in the inheritance 2750
Ex 12: 4 they must s one with their nearest neighbor, 4374
18:22 because they will s it with you. 5951
29:26 and it will be your s. 4950
29:28 the regular s from the Israelites for Aaron 2976
Lev 6:17 as their s of the offerings made to me 2750
6:18 It is his regular s of the offerings made to 2976
6:22 It is the LORD's regular s and is to 2976
7:33 the right thigh as his s. 4950
7:34 the priest and his sons as their regular s 2976
7:36 to them as their regular s for the generations 2978
8:29 Moses' s of the ordination ram— 4950
10:13 because it is your s and your sons' share of 2976
10:13 because it is your share and your sons' s of 2976
10:14 to you and your children as your s of 2976
10:15 be the regular s for you and your children, 2976
19:17 so you will not s in his guilt. 5951+6584
24: 9 of their regular s of the offerings made to 2976
25:51 a larger s of the price paid for him. 4946
Nu 10:32 we will s with you whatever good things 3512
18: 8 and your sons as your portion and regular s. 2976
18:11 and daughters as your regular s. 2976
18:19 and daughters as your regular s. 2976
18:20 nor will you have any s among them; 2750
18:20 I am your s and your inheritance among 2750
31:29 from their half s and give it to Eleazar 4734
31:36 The half s of those who fought in 2750
Dt 10: 9 the Levites have no s or inheritance 2750
18: 3 This is the s due the priests from 5477
18: 8 He is to s equally in their benefits, 430
21:17 as the firstborn by giving him a double s 7023
Jos 14: 4 The Levites received no s of the land 2750
17: 5 Manasseh's s consisted of ten tracts 2475
19: 9 of the Simeonites was taken from the s 2475
22:19 and s the land with us. 296
22:25 You have no s in the LORD.' 2750
22:27 'You have no s in the LORD.' 2750
Jdg 8:24 an earring from your s of the plunder." 8965
1Sa 26:19 They have now driven me from my s in 6202
30:22 not s with them the plunder we recovered. 5989
30:24 The s of the man who stayed with 2750
30:24 All will s alike." 2745
2Sa 20: 1 "We have no s in David, 2750
1Ki 12:16 "What s do we have in David, 2750
1Ch 9:25 s their duties for seven-day periods. 465+6640
2Ch 10:16 "What s do we have in David, 2750
Ne 2:20 you have no s in Jerusalem or any claim 2750
Job 39:17 with wisdom or give her a s of good sense. 2745
Ps 68:23 the tongues of your dogs have their s." 4945
69:27 do not let them s in your salvation. 995
106: 5 that I may s in the joy of your nation 8523+8525
Pr 1:14 and we will s a common purse"— 2118+4200
1:14 and no one else can s its joy. 6843
16:19 among the oppressed than to s plunder with 2745
17: 2 and will s the inheritance as one of 2745
21: 9 on a corner of the roof than s a house with 2490
25:24 to live on a corner of the roof than s a house 2490
Ecc 9: 2 All s a common destiny— 889+3869+4200
Isa 58: 7 Is it not to s your food with the hungry and 7271
Jer 37:12 get his s of the property among the people 2745
Eze 18:19 the son not s the guilt of his father?' 928+5951
18:20 The son will not s the guilt of the father, 928+5951
18:20 nor will the father s the guilt of the son. 928+5951
Am 7: 1 after the king's s had been harvested and AIT
Mt 21:41 give him his s of the crop at harvest time." 625
25:21 Come and s your master's happiness!' NIG
25:23 Come and s your master's happiness!' NIG
Lk 3:11 "The man with two tunics should s with 3556
15:12 'Father, give me my s of the estate.' 2095+3538
Ac 8:21 You have no part or s in this ministry. 3102
Ro 8:17 with Christ, if indeed we s in his sufferings 5224
8:17 in order that we may also s in his glory. 5280
11:17 and now s in the nourishing sap 1181+5171
12:13 S with God's people who are in need. 3125
15:27 to s with them their material blessings. 3310
1Co 9:13 at the altar s in what is offered on the altar? 5211
9:23 that I may s in its blessings. 1181+5171
2Co 1: 7 because we know that just as you s 1639+3128
1: 7 so also you s in our comfort. NIG
2: 3 that you would all s my joy. NIG
Gal 4:30 slave woman's son will never s in the inheritance with the free woman's 3099
6: 6 in the word must s all good things 3125
Eph 1: 7 all of you s in God's grace with me. 1639+5171
Php 4:14 Yet it was good of you to s in my troubles. 5170
Col 1:12 to s in the inheritance of the saints in 3535
1Th 2: 8 so much that we were delighted to s with 3556

2Th 2:14 that you might s in the glory 4348
1Ti 5:22 and do not s in the sins of others. 3125
6:18 and to be generous and willing to s. 3127
2Ti 2: 6 be the first to receive a s of the crops. 3561
Heb 3: 1 holy brothers, who s in the heavenly calling, 3581
3:14 to s in Christ if we hold firmly till the end 3581
12:10 that we may s in his holiness. 3561
13:16 not forget to do good and to s with others, 3126
1Pe 5: 1 and one who also will s in the glory to 3128
Jude 1: 3 to write to you about the salvation we s, 3123
Rev 18: 4 so that you will not s in her sins, 5170
22:19 from him his s in the tree of life and in 3538

SHARED (12) [SHARE]
2Sa 12: 3 It s his food, drank from his cup 430
1Ki 2:26 s all my father's hardships. 889+928+6700+6700
Ps 41: 9 whom I trusted, he who s my bread, 430
Pr 5:17 never to be s with strangers. 907
Lk 1:58 and they s her joy. 5176
Ac 1:17 and s in this ministry." 3102+3275+3836
4:32 but they s everything they had. 3123
Ro 15:27 For if the Gentiles have s in the Jews' 3125
Php 4:15 not one church s with me in the matter 3125
Heb 2:14 he too s in their humanity so that 3576
6: 4 who have s in the Holy Spirit, 1181+3581
Rev 18: 9 with her and s her luxury see the smoke 5139

SHARERS (1) [SHARE]
Eph 3: 6 s together in the promise in Christ Jesus. 5212

SHARES (5) [SHARE]
2Sa 19:43 "We have ten s in the king; 3338
Pr 22: 9 for he s his food with the poor. 5989
Jn 13:18 'He who s my bread has lifted up his heel 5592
19:23 dividing them into four s, 3538+4472
2Jn 1:11 Anyone who welcomes him s in his wicked 3125

SHAREZER (3)
2Ki 19:37 his sons Adrammelech and S cut him down 8570
Isa 37:38 his sons Adrammelech and S cut him down 8570
Zec 7: 2 of Bethel had sent S and Regem-Melech, 8570

SHARING (6) [SHARE]
Job 31:17 not s it with the fatherless— 430+4946
1Co 9:10 to do so in the hope of s in the harvest. 3576
2Co 8: 4 with us for the privilege of s in this service 3126
9:13 and for your generosity in s with them and 3126
Php 3:10 and the fellowship of s in his sufferings, 3126
Phm 1: 6 that you may be active in s your faith, 3126

SHARON (7) [SHARONITE]
1Ch 5:16 and on all the pasturelands of S as far 9227
27:29 in charge of the herds grazing in S. 9227
SS 2: 1 I am a rose of S, a lily of the valleys. 9227
Isa 33: 9 S is like the Arabah, 9227
35: 2 the splendor of Carmel and S; 9227
65:10 S will become a pasture for flocks, 9227
Ac 9:35 and S saw him and turned to the Lord. 4926

SHARONITE (1) [SHARON]
1Ch 27:29 the S was in charge of the herds grazing 9228

SHARP (19) [SHARPEN, SHARPENED, SHARPENING, SHARPENS, SHARPER, SHARPLY]
Ps 45: 5 Let your s arrows pierce the hearts of 9111
57: 4 whose tongues are s swords. 2521
120: 3 punish you with a warrior's s arrows. 9111
140: 3 They make their tongues as s as a serpent's; 9111
Pr 5: 4 s as a double-edged sword. 2521
25:18 Like a club or a sword or a s arrow is 9111
Isa 5:28 Their arrows are s, all their bows are strung; 9111
41:15 new and s, with many teeth. 3023
Eze 5: 1 take a sword and use it as a barber's razor 2521
28:24 who are painful briers and s thorns. 3872
Ac 15: 2 and Barnabas into s dispute and debate 3900+4024
15:39 a s disagreement that they parted company. 4237
Rev 1:16 of his mouth came a s double-edged sword. 3955
2:12 These are the words of him who has the s, 3955
14:14 a crown of gold on his head and a s sickle. 3955
14:17 and he too had a s sickle. 3955
14:18 in a loud voice to him who had the s sickle, 3955
14:18 "Take your s sickle and gather the clusters 3955
19:15 Out of his mouth comes a s sword with 3955

SHARPEN (4) [SHARP]
Dt 32:41 when I s my flashing sword 9111
Ps 7:12 If he does not relent, he will s his sword; 4323
64: 3 They s their tongues like swords 9111
Jer 51:11 "S the arrows, take up the shields! 1406

SHARPENED (6) [SHARP]
1Sa 13:20 mattocks, axes and sickles s. 4323
Ps 52: 2 it is like a razor, you who practice deceit. 4323
Isa 49: 2 He made my mouth like a sharp 2521
Eze 21: 9 " 'A sword, a sword, s and polished— 2523
21:10 s for the slaughter, polished to flash 2523
21:11 it is s and polished, made ready for the hand 2523

SHARPENING (2) [SHARP]
1Sa	13:21	of a shekel for s plowshares and mattocks,	7201
	13:21	and a third of a shekel for s forks and axes	NIH

SHARPENS (2) [SHARP]
Pr	27:17	As iron s iron, so one man sharpens another.	2527
	27:17	As iron sharpens iron, so one man s another.	2527

SHARPER (1) [SHARP]
Heb	4:12	S than any double-edged sword,	5533

SHARPLY (3) [SHARP]
Jdg	8: 1	And they criticized him s.	928+2622
Jn	6:52	Jews began to argue s among themselves,	3481
Tit	1:13	Therefore, rebuke them s,	705

SHARPNESS (KJV) See HARSH

SHARUHEN (1)
Jos	19: 6	Beth Lebaoth and S—	9226

SHASHAI (1)
Ezr	10:40	Macnadebai, S, Sharai,	9258

SHASHAK (2)
1Ch	8:14	Ahio, S, Jeremoth,	9265
	8:25	Iphdeiah and Penuel were the sons of S.	9265

SHATTER (13) [SHATTERED, SHATTERING, SHATTERS]
Isa	30:31	The voice of the LORD will s Assyria;	3169
Jer	49:37	I will s Elam before their foes,	3169
	51:20	with you I s nations,	5879
	51:21	with you I s horse and rider,	5879
	51:21	with you I s chariot and driver,	5879
	51:22	with you I s man and woman,	5879
	51:22	with you I s old man and youth,	5879
	51:22	with you I s young man and maiden,	5879
	51:23	with you I s shepherd and flock,	5879
	51:23	with you I s farmer and oxen,	5879
	51:23	with you I s governors and officials.	5879
Eze	32:12	They will s the pride of Egypt,	8720
Hag	2:22	and s the power of the foreign kingdoms.	9012

SHATTERED (24) [SHATTER]
Ex	15: 6	Your right hand, O LORD, s the enemy.	8320
Jdg	5:26	she s and pierced his temple.	4730
	10: 8	who that year s and crushed them.	8320
1Sa	2:10	those who oppose the LORD will be s.	3169
1Ki	19:11	the mountains apart and s the rocks before	8689
Job	16:12	All was well with me, but he s me;	7297
	17:11	My days have passed, my plans are s,	5998
Ps	48: 7	You destroyed them like ships of Tarshish s	NIH
	105:33	and fig trees and s the trees of their country.	8689
Ecc	12: 6	before the pitcher is s at the spring,	8689
Isa	7: 8	Ephraim will be too s to be a people.	3169
	8: 9	Raise the war cry, you nations, and be s!	3169
	8: 9	Prepare for battle, and be s!	3169
	8: 9	Prepare for battle, and be s!	3169
	9: 4	you have s the yoke that burdens them,	3169
	21: 9	All the images of its gods lie s on	8689
	30:14	so mercilessly that among its pieces not	4198
Jer	25:34	you will fall and be s like fine pottery.	9518
	48: 1	the stronghold will be disgraced and s.	3169
	48:20	Moab is disgraced, for she is s.	3169
	48:39	"How s she is! How they wail!	3169
	50:23	and s is the hammer of the whole earth!	8689
Eze	27:34	Now you are s by the sea in the depths of	8689
Na	1: 6	the rocks are s before him.	5997

SHATTERING (1) [SHATTER]
Da	8: 7	striking the ram and s his two horns.	8689

SHATTERS (2) [SHATTER]
Job	34:24	Without inquiry he s the mighty and sets	8318
Ps	46: 9	he breaks the bow and s the spear,	7915

SHAUL (9) [SHAUL'S, SHAULITE]
Ge	36:37	S from Rehoboth on the river	8620
	36:38	When S died, Baal-Hanan son	8620
	46:10	Zohar and S the son of a Canaanite woman.	8620
Ex	6:15	Zohar and S the son of a Canaanite woman.	8620
Nu	26:13	through S, the Shaulite clan.	8620
1Ch	1:48	S from Rehoboth on the river	8620
	1:49	When S died, Baal-Hanan son	8620
	4:24	Nemuel, Jamin, Jarib, Zerah and S;	8620
	6:24	Uriel his son, Uzziah his son and S his son.	8620

SHAUL'S (1) [SHAUL]
1Ch	4:25	Shallum was S son,	2257S

SHAULITE (1) [SHAUL]
Nu	26:13	through Shaul, the S clan.	8621

SHAVE (19) [SHAVED]
Lev	14: 8	s off all his hair and bathe with water;	1662
	14: 9	the seventh day he must s off all his hair;	1662
	14: 9	he must s his head, his beard,	1662
	21: 5	" 'Priests must not s their heads or	7942+7947
	21: 5	their heads or s off the edges of their beards	1662
Nu	6: 9	he must s his head on the day	1662
	6:18	the Nazirite must s off the hair	1662
	8: 7	then have them s their whole bodies	6296+9509
Dt	14: 1	s the front of your heads for the dead,	7947+8492
	21:12	into your home and have her s her head,	1662
Jdg	16:19	a man to s off the seven braids of his hair,	1662
Isa	7:20	to s your head and the hair of your legs,	1662
Jer	16: 6	and no one will cut himself or s his head	7942
	47: 5	Gaza will s her head in mourning;	995+7947
Eze	5: 1	and use it as a barber's razor to s your head	6296
	27:31	They will s their heads because of you	7942+7947
	44:20	not s their heads or let their hair grow long,	1662
Am	8:10	you wear sackcloth and s your heads.	6584+7942
Mic	1:16	S your heads in mourning for the	1605+7942

SHAVED (16) [SHAVE]
Ge	41:14	When he had s and changed his clothes,	1662
Lev	13:33	he must be s except for the diseased area,	1662
Nu	6:19	Nazirite has s off the hair of his dedication,	1662
Jdg	16:17	If my head were s, my strength would leave	1662
	16:22	to grow again after it had been s.	1662
2Sa	10: 4	s off half of each man's beard,	1662
1Ch	19: 4	So Hanun seized David's men, s them,	1662
Job	1:20	Job got up and tore his robe and s his head.	1605
Isa	15: 2	Every head is s and every beard cut off.	7947
Jer	2:16	the men of Memphis and Tahpanhes have s	8286
	41: 5	eighty men who had s off their beards,	1662
	48:37	Every head is s and every beard cut off;	7947
Eze	7:18	with shame and their heads will be s.	7947
Ac	21:24	so that they can have their heads s.	3834
1Co	11: 5	it is just as though her head were s.	3834
	11: 6	for a woman to have her hair cut or s off,	3834

SHAVEH (1) [SHAVEH KIRIATHAIM]
Ge	14:17	to meet him in the Valley of S (that is,	8753

SHAVEH KIRIATHAIM (1) [KIRIATHAIM, SHAVEH]
Ge	14: 5	the Zuzites in Ham, the Emites in S	8754

SHAVSHA (1)
1Ch	18:16	of Abiathar were priests; S was secretary;	8807

SHAWL (1) [SHAWLS]
Ru	3:15	the s you are wearing and hold it out."	4762

SHAWLS (1) [SHAWL]
Isa	3:23	and the linen garments and tiaras and s.	8100

SHE (1011) [HER, HERS, HERSELF, SHE'S]
See Index of Articles Etc.

SHE'S (1) [SHE]
Jdg	14: 3	S the right one for me."	2085

SHE-CAMEL (1) [CAMEL]
Jer	2:23	You are a swift s running here and there,	1149

SHEAF (6) [SHEAVES]
Ge	37: 7	when suddenly my s rose and stood upright,	524
Lev	23:10	a s of the first grain you harvest.	6684
	23:11	to wave the s before the LORD so it will	6684
	23:12	On the day you wave the s,	6684
	23:15	day you brought the s of the wave offering,	6684
Dt	24:19	in your field and you overlook a s,	6684

SHEAL (1)
Ezr	10:29	Malluch, Adaiah, Jashub, S and Jeremoth.	8627

SHEALTIEL (13)
1Ch	3:17	of Jehoiachin the captive: S his son,	8630
Ezr	3: 2	son of S and his associates began to build	8630
	3: 8	Zerubbabel son of S,	8630
	5: 2	of S and Jeshua son of Jozadak set to work	10691
Ne	12: 1	with Zerubbabel son of S and with Jeshua:	8630
Hag	1: 1	the prophet Haggai to Zerubbabel son of S,	8630
	1:12	Then Zerubbabel son of S,	9003
	1:14	up the spirit of Zerubbabel son of S,	9003
	2: 2	"Speak to Zerubbabel son of S,	9003
	2:23	my servant Zerubbabel son of S,'	8630
Mt	1:12	Jeconiah was the father of S,	4886
	1:12	S the father of Zerubbabel,	4886
Lk	3:27	the son of Zerubbabel, the son of S,	4886

SHEAR (3) [SHEARED, SHEARER, SHEARERS, SHEARING, SHEEP-SHEARING, SHEEPSHEARERS, SHORN]
Ge	31:19	When Laban had gone to s his sheep,	1605
	38:13	on his way to Timnah to s his sheep,"	1605
Dt	15:19	and do not s the firstborn of your sheep.	1605

SHEAR-JASHUB (1)
Isa	7: 3	"Go out, you and your son S,	8639

SHEARED (1) [SHEAR]
Isa	22:25	it will be s off and will fall,	1548

SHEARER (1) [SHEAR]
Ac	8:32	and as a lamb before the s is silent,	3025

SHEARERS (3) [SHEAR]
1Sa	25:11	and the meat I have slaughtered for my s,	1605
2Sa	13:24	"Your servant has had s come.	1605
Isa	53: 7	and as a sheep before her s is silent,	1605

SHEARIAH (2)
1Ch	8:38	Azrikam, Bokeru, Ishmael, S,	9138
	9:44	Azrikam, Bokeru, Ishmael, S,	9138

SHEARING (4) [SHEAR]
Ge	38:12	to the men who were s his sheep,	1605
Dt	18: 4	the first wool from the s of your sheep,	1600
1Sa	25: 2	which he was s in Carmel.	1605
	25: 4	he heard that Nabal was s sheep.	1605

SHEATH (3) [SHEATHED]
2Sa	20: 8	at his waist was a belt with a dagger in its s.	9509
	20: 8	he stepped forward, it dropped out of its s.	NIH
1Ch	21:27	and he put his sword back into its s.	5620

SHEATHED (1) [SHEATH]
Ps	68:13	the wings of [my] dove are s with silver,	2902

SHEAVES (9) [SHEAF]
Ge	37: 7	We were binding s of grain out in the field	524
	37: 7	while your s gathered around mine	524
Ru	2: 7	'Please let me glean and gather among the s	6684
	2:15	"Even if she gathers among the s,	6684
Job	24:10	like s gathered in season.	1538
	24:10	they carry the s, but still go hungry.	6684
Ps	126: 6	return with songs of joy, carrying s with him.	524
Mic	4:12	he who gathers them like s to the threshing	6658
Zec	12: 6	like a flaming torch among s.	6658

SHEBA (34)
Ge	10: 7	The sons of Raamah: S and Dedan.	8644
	10:28	Obal, Abimael, S,	8644
	25: 3	Jokshan was the father of S and Dedan;	8644
Jos	19: 2	It included: Beersheba (or S), Moladah,	8681
2Sa	20: 1	Now a troublemaker named S son of Bicri,	8680
	20: 2	of Israel deserted David to follow S son	8680
	20: 6	to Abishai, "Now S son of Bicri	8680
	20: 7	from Jerusalem to pursue S son of Bicri	8680
	20:10	and his brother Abishai pursued S son	8680
	20:10	the men went on with Joab to pursue S son	8680
	20:14	S passed through all the tribes of Israel	NIH
	20:15	the troops with Joab came and besieged S	2257S
	20:21	A man named S son of Bicri,	8680
	20:22	and they cut off the head of S son of Bicri	8680
1Ki	10: 1	When the queen of S heard about the fame	8644
	10: 4	When the queen of S saw all the wisdom	8644
	10:10	the queen of S gave to King Solomon.	8644
	10:13	the queen of S all she desired and asked	8644
1Ch	1: 9	The sons of Raamah: S and Dedan.	8644
	1:22	Obal, Abimael, S,	8644
	1:32	The sons of Jokshan: S and Dedan.	8644
	5:13	Michael, Meshullam, S, Jorai, Jacan,	8680
2Ch	9: 1	the queen of S heard of Solomon's fame,	8644
	9: 3	queen of S saw the wisdom of Solomon,	8644
	9: 9	the queen of S gave to King Solomon.	8644
	9:12	queen of S all she desired and asked for;	8644
Job	6:19	The traveling merchants of S look in hope.	8644
Ps	72:10	kings of S and Seba will present him gifts.	8644
	72:15	May gold from S be given him.	8644
Isa	60: 6	And all from S will come,	8644
Jer	6:20	about incense from S or sweet calamus	8644
Eze	27:22	" 'The merchants of S and Raamah traded	8644
	27:23	Canneh and Eden and the merchants of S,	8644
	38:13	S and Dedan and the merchants of Tarshish	8644

SHEBAH (KJV) See SHIBAH

SHEBAM (KJV) See SEBAM

SHEBANIAH (6)
1Ch	15:24	S, Joshaphat, Nethanel, Amasai, Zechariah,	8677
Ne	9: 4	Jeshua, Bani, Kadmiel, S, Bunni,	8676
	9: 5	Sherebiah, Hodiah, S and Pethahiah—	8676
	10: 4	Hattush, S, Malluch,	8676
	10:10	S, Hodiah, Kelita, Pelaiah, Hanan,	8676
	10:12	Zaccur, Sherebiah, S,	8676

SHEBAT (1)
Zec	1: 7	the eleventh month, the month of S,	8658

SHEBER (1)
1Ch	2:48	the mother of S and Tirhanah.	8693

SHEBNA (9)

2Ki	18:18	the palace administrator, **S** the secretary,	8675
	18:26	**S** and Joah said to the field commander,	8675
	18:37	**S** the secretary and Joah son of Asaph	8674
	19: 2	**S** the secretary and the leading priests,	8674
Isa	22:15	"Go, say to this steward, to **S**,	8674
	36: 3	the palace administrator, **S** the secretary,	8674
	36:11	**S** and Joah said to the field commander,	8674
	36:22	the palace administrator, **S** the secretary,	8674
	37: 2	**S** the secretary, and the leading priests,	8674

SHEBUEL   (KJV) See SHUBAEL

SHECANIAH (10) [SHECANIAH'S]

1Ch	3:21	of Arnan, of Obadiah and of **S**.	8908
	3:22	The descendants of **S**:	8908
	24:11	the ninth to Jeshua, the tenth to **S**,	8909
2Ch	31:15	and **S** assisted him faithfully in the towns	8909
Ezr	8: 3	of the descendants of **S**;	8908
	8: 5	**S** son of Jahaziel, and with him 300 men;	8908
	10: 2	Then **S** son of Jehiel,	8908
Ne	3:29	Next to him, Shemaiah son of **S**,	8908
	6:18	since he was son-in-law to **S** son of Arah,	8908
	12: 3	**S**, Rehum, Meremoth,	8908

SHECANIAH'S (1) [SHECANIAH]

Ne	12:14	of Malluch's, Jonathan; of **S**, Joseph;	8908

SHECHEM (62) [SHECHEM'S, SHECHEMITE]

Ge	12: 6	as the site of the great tree of Moreh at **S**.	8901
	33:18	of **S** in Canaan and camped within sight of	8901
	33:19	the sons of Hamor, the father of **S**,	8902
	34: 2	When **S** son of Hamor the Hivite,	8902
	34: 4	And **S** said to his father Hamor,	8902
	34: 7	because **S** had done a disgraceful thing	NIH
	34: 8	"My son **S** has his heart set on your	8902
	34:11	Then **S** said to Dinah's father and brothers,	8902
	34:13	as they spoke to **S** and his father Hamor.	8902
	34:18	seemed good to Hamor and his son **S**.	8902
	34:20	and his son **S** went to the gate of their city	8902
	34:24	with Hamor and his son **S**,	8902
	34:26	They put Hamor and his son **S** to the sword	8902
	35: 4	and Jacob buried them under the oak at **S**.	8901
	37:12	to graze their father's flocks near **S**,	8901
	37:13	your brothers are grazing the flocks near **S**.	8901
	37:14	When Joseph arrived at **S**,	8901
Nu	26:31	through **S**, the Shechemite clan;	8903
Jos	17: 2	the clans of Abiezer, Helek, Asriel, **S**,	8903
	17: 7	from Asher to Micmethath east of **S**.	8901
	20: 7	**S** in the hill country of Ephraim;	8901
	21:21	hill country of Ephraim they were given **S**	8901
	24: 1	assembled all the tribes of Israel at **S**.	8901
	24:25	at **S** he drew up for them decrees and laws.	8901
	24:32	at **S** in the tract of land that Jacob bought	8901
	24:32	sons of Hamor, the father of **S**.	8902
Jdg	8:31	His concubine, who lived in **S**,	8901
	9: 1	to his mother's brothers in **S** and said	8901
	9: 2	"Ask all the citizens of **S**, 'Which is better	8901
	9: 3	repeated all this to the citizens of **S**,	8901
	9: 6	the citizens of **S** and Beth Millo gathered	8901
	9: 6	at the pillar in **S** to crown Abimelech king.	8901
	9: 7	"Listen to me, citizens of **S**,	8901
	9:18	of **S** because he is your brother)—	8901
	9:20	citizens of **S** and Beth Millo,	8901
	9:20	citizens of **S** and Beth Millo,	8901
	9:23	between Abimelech and the citizens of **S**,	8901
	9:24	and on the citizens of **S**,	8901
	9:25	of **S** set men on the hilltops to ambush	8901
	9:26	of Ebed moved with his brothers into **S**,	8901
	9:28	"Who is Abimelech, and who is **S**,	8902
	9:31	to **S** and are stirring up the city against you.	8901
	9:34	and took up concealed positions near **S**	8901
	9:39	the citizens of **S** and fought Abimelech.	8901
	9:41	Zebul drove Gaal and his brothers out of **S**.	8901
	9:42	The next day the people of **S** went out to	NIH
	9:46	of **S** went into the stronghold of the temple	8901
	9:49	So all the people in the tower of **S**,	8901
	9:57	the men of **S** pay for all their wickedness.	8901
	21:19	of the road that goes from Bethel to **S**,	8901
1Ki	12: 1	Rehoboam went to **S**,	8901
	12:25	Then Jeroboam fortified **S** in the hill	8901
1Ch	6:67	hill country of Ephraim they were given **S**	8901
	7:19	Ahian, **S**, Likhi and Aniam.	8903
	7:28	and **S** and its villages all the way to Ayyah	8901
2Ch	10: 1	Rehoboam went to **S**,	8901
Ps	60: 6	"In triumph I will parcel out **S**	8901
	108: 7	"In triumph I will parcel out **S**	8901
Jer	41: 5	and cut themselves came from **S**,	8901
Hos	6: 9	they murder on the road to **S**,	8901
Ac	7:16	Their bodies were brought back to **S**	5374
	7:16	of Hamor at **S** for a certain sum of money.	5374

SHECHEM'S (3) [SHECHEM]

Ge	34: 6	**S** father Hamor went out to talk with Jacob.	8902
	34:26	to the sword and took Dinah from **S** house	8902
Jdg	9:28	Serve the men of Hamor, **S** father!	8902

SHECHEMITE (1) [SHECHEM]

Nu	26:31	through Shechem, the **S** clan;	8904

SHED (46) [SHEDDING, SHEDS]

Ge	9: 6	by man **shall** his blood **be s**;	9161
	37:22	"Don't **s** any blood.	9161
Lev	17: 4	he has **s** blood and must be cut off	9161
Nu	35:33	for the land on which blood *has been* **s**,	9161
	35:33	except by the blood of the *one who* **s** it.	9161
Dt	19:10	Do this so that innocent blood *will* not **be s**	9161
	21: 7	"Our hands *did* not **s** this blood,	9161
2Sa	16: 8	the **blood** you **s** *in* the household of Saul,	1947
1Ki	2:31	the guilt of the innocent blood that Joab **s**.	9161
	2:32	**LORD** will repay him for the blood he **s**,	NIH
2Ki	9: 7	blood of all the **LORD's** servants **s by**	3338+4946
	21:16	Manasseh also **s** so much innocent blood	9161
1Ch	22: 8	'You have **s** much blood	9161
	22: 8	because *you* have **s** much blood on	9161
	28: 3	you are a warrior and *have* **s** blood.'	9161
Ps	97:11	Light **is s** upon the righteous and joy on	2445
	106:38	*They* **s** innocent blood,	9161
Pr	1:16	they are swift to **s** blood,	9161
	6:17	a lying tongue, hands *that* **s** innocent blood,	9161
Isa	26:21	The earth will disclose the **blood** *s*	AIT
	59: 7	they are swift to **s** innocent blood.	9161
Jer	7: 6	or the widow and *do* not **s** innocent blood	9161
	22: 3	and *do* not **s** innocent blood in this place.	9161
La	4:13	who **s** within her the blood of the righteous.	9161
Eze	16:38	who commit adultery and *who* **s** blood;	9161
	21:32	your blood will be **s** in your land,	NIH
	22: 4	because of the blood *you* have **s**	9161
	22: 6	in you uses his power to **s** blood.	9161
	22:12	In you men accept bribes to **s** blood;	9161
	22:13	and the blood *you* had **s** in your midst.	2118
	22:27	they **s** blood and kill people	9161
	23:45	and **s** blood, because they are adulterous	9161
	24: 7	" 'For the blood she **s** is in her midst:	NIH
	24:16	Yet do not lament or weep *or* **s** any tears.	995
	33:25	in it and look to your idols and **s** blood,	9161
	36:18	because *they* had **s** blood in the land	9161
Joel	3:19	in whose land *they* **s** innocent blood.	9161
Mic	7: 2	All men lie in wait to **s** blood;	NIH
Hab	2: 8	For you have **s** man's blood;	NIH
	2:17	For you have **s** man's blood;	NIH
Mt	23:35	the righteous blood *that has been* **s**	1772
Lk	11:50	the blood of all the prophets *that has been* **s**	1772
Ac	22:20	the blood of your martyr Stephen *was* **s**,	1772
Ro	3:15	"Their feet are swift to **s** blood;	1772
Col	1:20	peace through his blood, **s** on the cross.	NIG
Rev	16: 6	for *they* have **s** the blood of your saints	1772

SHEDDING (12) [SHED]

Dt	19:13	from Israel the **guilt of s** innocent **blood**,	1947
	21: 9	yourselves the **guilt of s** innocent **blood**,	1947
Jdg	9:24	the **s** of their **blood**, might be avenged	1947
1Ki	2: 5	**s** their blood in peacetime as if in battle,	8492
2Ki	24: 4	*including* the **s** of innocent blood.	9161
Job	15:33	like an olive tree **s** its blossoms.	8959
Jer	22:17	on **s** innocent blood and on oppression	9161
Eze	22: 3	by **s** blood in her midst and defiles herself	9161
	22: 9	In you are slanderous men bent on **s** blood;	9161
Mt	23:30	not have taken part with them in **s** the blood	NIG
Heb	9:22	and without the **s of blood** there is no forgiveness.	136
	12: 4	yet resisted to the point of **s** your **blood**.	135

SHEDEUR (5)

Nu	1: 5	from Reuben, Elizur son of **S**;	8725
	2:10	of the people of Reuben is Elizur son of **S**.	8725
	7:30	On the fourth day Elizur son of **S**,	8725
	7:35	This was the offering of Elizur son of **S**.	8725
	10:18	Elizur son of **S** was in command.	8725

SHEDS (2) [SHED]

Ge	9: 6	"Whoever **s** the blood of man, by man	9161
Eze	18:10	*who* **s** blood or does any of these other	9161

SHEEP (204) [SHEEP'S, SHEEPSKINS]

Ge	12:16	and Abram acquired **s** and cattle,	7366
	20:14	Then Abimelech brought **s** and cattle	7366
	21:27	So Abraham brought **s** and cattle	7366
	24:35	He has given him **s** and cattle,	7366
	29: 2	with three flocks of **s** lying near it because	7366
	29: 3	from the well's mouth and water the **s**.	7366
	29: 6	here comes his daughter Rachel with the **s**."	7366
	29: 7	Water the **s** and take them back to pasture."	7366
	29: 8	Then we will water the **s**."	7366
	29: 9	Rachel came with her father's **s**,	7366
	29:10	his mother's brother, and Laban's **s**,	7366
	29:10	of the well and watered his uncle's **s**.	7366
	30:32	from them every speckled or spotted **s**,	8445
	31:19	When Laban had gone to shear his **s**,	7366
	31:38	Your **s** and goats have not miscarried,	8161
	32: 5	I have cattle and donkeys, **s and goats**,	7366
	38:12	to the men who were shearing his **s**,	7366
	38:13	on his way to Timnah to shear his **s**,"	7366
	47:17	their **s and goats**, their cattle and	5238+7366
Ex	9: 3	and on your cattle and **s and goats**.	7366
	12: 5	you may take them from the **s** or the goats.	3897
	20:24	your **s and goats** and your cattle.	7366
	22: 1	a man steals an ox or a **s** and slaughters it	8445
	22: 1	of cattle for the ox and four **s** for the sheep.	7366
	22: 1	of cattle for the ox and four sheep for the **s**.	8445
	22: 4	whether ox or donkey or **s**—	8445
	22: 9	a donkey, an **s**, a garment,	8445
	22:10	a **s** or any other animal to his neighbor	8445
	22:30	Do the same with your cattle and your **s**.	7366

Lev	1:10	from either the **s** or the goats,	4166
	7:23	not eat any of the fat of cattle, **s** or goats.	4166
	22:19	**s** or goats in order that it may be accepted	4166
	22:23	present as a freewill offering an ox or a **s**	8445
	22:28	a cow or a **s** and its young on the same day.	8445
	27:26	whether an ox or a **s**, it is the **LORD's**.	8445
Nu	18:17	a **s** or a goat; they are holy.	4166
	22:40	Balak sacrificed cattle and **s**,	7366
	27:17	so the **LORD's** people will not be like **s**	7366
	31:28	cattle, donkeys, **s or goats**.	7366
	31:30	cattle, donkeys, **s, goats or** other animals.	7366
	31:32	that the soldiers took was 675,000 **s**,	7366
	31:36	in the battle was: 337,500 **s**,	7366
	31:43	the community's half—was 337,500 **s**,	7366
Dt	14: 4	the ox, the **s**, the goat,	4166+8445
	14: 5	the ibex, the antelope and the **mountain s**.	2378
	14:26	cattle, **s**, wine or other fermented drink,	7366
	15:19	and do not shear the firstborn of your **s**.	7366
	17: 1	an ox or a **s** that has any defect or flaw in it,	8445
	18: 3	from the people who sacrifice a bull or a **s**:	8445
	18: 4	the first wool from the shearing of your **s**,	7366
	22: 1	If you see your brother's ox or **s** straying,	8445
	28:31	Your **s** will be given to your enemies,	7366
Jos	6:21	young and old, cattle, **s** and donkeys.	8445
	7:24	donkeys and **s**, his tent and all that he had,	7366
Jdg	6: 4	neither **s** nor cattle nor donkeys.	8445
1Sa	14:32	They pounced on the plunder and, taking **s**,	7366
	14:34	'Each of you bring me your cattle and **s**,	8445
	15: 3	cattle and **s**, camels and donkeys.' "	7366
	15: 9	the **s** and cattle, the fat calves and lambs—	7366
	15:14	"What then is this bleating of **s** in my ears?	7366
	15:15	the best of the **s** and cattle to sacrifice to	7366
	15:21	The soldiers took **s** and cattle from	7366
	16:11	Jesse answered, "but he is tending the **s**."	7366
	16:19	who is with the **s**."	7366
	17:15	and forth from Saul to tend his father's **s**	7366
	17:28	And with whom did you leave those few **s**	7366
	17:34	servant has been keeping his father's **s**.	7366
	17:34	a lion or a bear came and carried off a **s**	8445
	17:35	struck it and rescued the **s** from its mouth.	NIH
	22:19	and its cattle, donkeys and **s**.	8445
	24: 3	He came to the **s** pens along the way;	7366
	25: 2	a thousand goats and three thousand **s**,	7366
	25: 4	he heard that Nabal was shearing **s**.	7366
	25:16	the time we were herding our **s** near them.	7366
	25:18	five dressed **s**, five seahs of roasted grain,	7366
	27: 9	but took a and cattle, donkeys and camels,	7366
2Sa	12: 2	The rich man had a very large number of **s**	7366
	12: 4	of his own **s** or cattle to prepare a meal for	7366
	17:29	and curds, **s**, and cheese from cows' milk	7366
	24:17	These are but **s**. What have they done?	7366
1Ki	1: 9	Adonijah then sacrificed **s**,	7366
	1:19	and **s**, and has invited all the king's sons,	7366
	1:25	of cattle, fattened calves, and **s**.	7366
	4:23	and a hundred **s and goats**,	7366
	8: 5	so many **s** and cattle that they could not	7366
	8:63	a hundred and twenty thousand **s and goats**.	7366
2Ki	3: 4	Now Mesha king of Moab **raised s**,	5924
1Ch	5:21	two hundred fifty thousand **s**,	7366
	12:40	oil, cattle and **s**, for there was joy in Israel.	7366
	21:17	These are but **s**. What have they done?	7366
2Ch	5: 6	so many **s** and cattle that they could not	7366
	7: 5	a hundred and twenty thousand **s and goats**.	7366
	14:15	and carried off droves of **s and goats**	7366
	15:11	of cattle and seven thousand **s and goats**	7366
	18: 2	Ahab slaughtered many **s** and cattle for him	7366
	18:16	"I saw all Israel scattered on the hills like **s**	7366
	29:33	and three thousand **s and goats**.	7366
	30:24	and seven thousand **s and goats** for	7366
	30:24	and ten thousand **s and goats**.	7366
	35: 7	a total of thirty thousand **s** and goats	3897+7366
Ne	3: 1	to work and rebuild the **S** Gate.	7366
	3:32	the room above the corner and the **S** Gate	7366
	5:18	Each day one ox, six choice **s**	7366
	12:39	as far as the **S** Gate.	7366
Job	1: 3	and he owned seven thousand **s**,	7366
	1:16	fell from the sky and burned up the **s**	7366
	30: 1	disdained to put with my **s** dogs.	7366
	31:20	for warming him with the fleece from my **s**,	3897
	42:12	He had fourteen thousand **s**,	7366
Ps	44:11	to be devoured like **s** and have scattered us	7366
	44:22	we are considered as **s** to be slaughtered.	7366
	49:14	Like **s** they are destined for the grave,	7366
	74: 1	Why does your anger smolder against the **s**	7366
	78:52	he led them like **s** through the desert.	6373
	78:70	and took him from the **s** pens;	7366
	78:71	from tending the **s** he brought him to be	6402
	79:13	Then we your people, the **s** *of* your pasture,	7366
	100: 3	we are his people, the **s** of his pasture.	7366
	119:176	I have strayed like a lost **s**.	8445
	144:13	Our **s** will increase by thousands,	7366
SS	1: 7	and where you rest your **s** at midday,	NIH
	1: 8	of the **s** and graze your young goats by	7366
	4: 2	Your teeth are like a flock of **s just shorn**,	7892
	6: 6	Your teeth are like a flock of **s** coming up	8161
Isa	5:17	Then **s** will graze as in their own pasture;	3897
	7:25	cattle are turned loose and where **s** run.	8445
	13:14	like **s** without a shepherd,	7366
	22:13	slaughtering of cattle and killing of **s**,	7366
	43:23	not brought me **s** for burnt offerings,	8445
	53: 6	We all, like **s**, have gone astray,	7366
	53: 7	and as a **s** before its shearers is silent,	8161
Jer	12: 3	Drag them off like **s** to be butchered!	7366
	13:20	the **s** of which you boasted?	7366
	23: 1	and scattering the **s** of my pasture!"	7366
	50: 6	"My people have been lost **s**;	7366

Eze	25: 5	and Ammon into a resting place for **s**.	7366
	34: 6	My **s** wandered over all the mountains and	7366
	34:11	I myself will search for my **s** and look	7366
	34:12	so will I look after my **s**.	7366
	34:15	I myself will tend my **s** and have them lie	7366
	34:17	I will judge between *one* **s** and another,	8445
	34:20	See, I myself will judge between the fat **s**	8445
	34:20	between the fat sheep and the lean **s**.	8445
	34:21	butting all the weak **s** with your horns	NIH
	34:22	I will judge between *one* **s** and another.	8445
	34:31	You my **s**, the sheep of my pasture,	7366
	34:31	You my sheep, the **s** *of* my pasture,	7366
	36:37	I will make their people as numerous as **s**,	7366
	45:15	Also one **s** is to be taken from every flock	8445
Hos	12:12	and to pay for her *he* **tended s**.	9068
Joel	1:18	even the flocks of **s** are suffering.	7366
Mic	2:12	I will bring them together like **s** *in* a pen,	7366
	5: 8	like a young lion among flocks of **s**,	7366
Hab	3:17	though there are no **s** in the pen	7366
Zep	2: 6	will be a place for shepherds and **s** pens.	7366
Zec	10: 2	the people wander like **s** oppressed for lack	7366
	11:16	but will eat the meat of the **choice s**,	1374
	13: 7	and the **s** will be scattered,	7366
Mt	9:36	like **s** without a shepherd.	4585
	10: 6	Go rather to the lost **s** of Israel.	4585
	10:16	I am sending you out like **s** among wolves.	4585
	12:11	"If any of you has a **s** and it falls into a pit	4585
	12:12	How much more valuable is a man *than* a **s**!	4585
	15:24	"I was sent only to the lost **s** of Israel."	4585
	18:12	If a man owns a hundred **s**,	4585
	18:13	about **that one s** than about the ninety-nine	899S
	25:32	from another as a shepherd separates the **s**	4585
	25:33	He will put the **s** on his right and the goats	4585
	26:31	and the **s** of the flock will be scattered.'	4585
Mk	6:34	they were like **s** without a shepherd.	4585
	14:27	and the **s** will be scattered.'	4585
Lk	15: 4	"Suppose one of you has a hundred **s**	4585
	15: 4	in the open country and go after the lost **s**	NIG
	15: 6	I have found my lost **s**.'	4585
	17: 7	a servant plowing or **looking after** the **s**.	4477
Jn	2:14	found men selling cattle, **s** and doves,	4585
	2:15	from the temple area, both **s** and cattle;	4585
	5: 2	Now there is in Jerusalem near the **S Gate**	4583
	10: 1	the man who does not enter the **s** pen by	4585
	10: 2	by the gate is the shepherd of his **s**.	4585
	10: 3	and the **s** listen to his voice.	4585
	10: 3	He calls his own **s** by name	4585
	10: 4	and his **s** follow him	4585
	10: 7	"I tell you the truth, I am the gate *for* the **s**.	4585
	10: 8	but the **s** did not listen to them.	4585
	10:11	good shepherd lays down his life for the **s**.	4585
	10:12	not the shepherd who owns the **s**.	4585
	10:12	he abandons the **s** and runs away.	4585
	10:13	a hired hand and cares nothing for the **s**.	4585
	10:14	I know my **s** and my sheep know me—	NIG
	10:14	I know my sheep and my **s** know me—	NIG
	10:15	and I lay down my life for the **s**.	4585
	10:16	I have other **s** that are not of this sheep pen.	4585
	10:16	I have other sheep that are not of this **s pen**.	885
	10:26	do not believe because you are not my **s**.	4585
	10:27	My **s** listen to my voice;	4585
	21:16	Jesus said, "Take care of my **s**."	4585
	21:17	Jesus said, "Feed my **s**.	4585
Ac	8:32	"He was led like a **s** to the slaughter,	4585
Ro	8:36	we are considered as **s** to be slaughtered."	4585
Heb	13:20	Lord Jesus, that great Shepherd *of* the **s**,	4585
1Pe	2:25	For you were like **s** going astray,	4585
Rev	18:13	fine flour and wheat; cattle and **s**;	4585

SHEEP'S (1) [SHEEP]

Mt	7:15	They come to you in **s** clothing,	4585

SHEEP-SHEARING (1) [SHEAR]

1Sa	25: 7	" 'Now I hear that *it is* **s time**.	1605

SHEEPCOTE (KJV) See PASTURE, SHEEP PENS

SHEEPFOLD (KJV) See CAMPFIRES, SHEEP PEN, SHEEP PENS

SHEEPMASTER (KJV) See RAISED SHEEP

SHEEPSHEARERS (1) [SHEAR]

2Sa	13:23	when Absalom's **s** were at Baal Hazor near	1605

SHEEPSKINS (1) [SHEEP]

Heb	11:37	They went about in **s** and goatskins,	3603

SHEER (1)

Isa	28:19	of this message will bring **s** terror.	8370

SHEERAH (1) [UZZEN SHEERAH]

1Ch	7:24	His daughter was **S**,	8641

SHEET (4) [SHEETS]

Isa	25: 7	the **s** that covers all nations;	5012
Ac	10:11	and something like a large **s** being let down	3855
	10:16	and immediately the **s** was taken back	5007
	11: 5	like a large **s** being let down from heaven	3855

SHEETS (2) [SHEET]

Ex	39: 3	They hammered out **thin s** of gold	7063
Nu	16:38	Hammer the censers into **s** to overlay	7063

SHEHARIAH (1)

1Ch	8:26	Shamsherai, **S**, Athaliah,	8843

SHEKEL (41) [SHEKELS]

Ex	30:13	to those already counted is to give a half **s**,	9203
	30:13	according to the sanctuary **s**,	9203
	30:13	This half **s** is an offering to the LORD.	9203
	30:15	to give more than a half **s** and the poor are	9203
	30:24	all according to the sanctuary **s**—	9203
	38:24	according to the sanctuary **s**.	9203
	38:25	shekels, according to the sanctuary **s**—	9203
	38:26	half a **s**, according to the sanctuary shekel	9203
	38:26	half a shekel, according to the sanctuary **s**,	9203
Lev	5:15	according to the sanctuary **s**.	9203
	27: 3	according to the sanctuary **s**,	9203
	27:25	to be set according to the sanctuary **s**,	9203
	27:25	twenty gerahs to the **s**.	9203
Nu	3:47	according to the sanctuary **s**,	9203
	3:50	shekels, according to the sanctuary **s**.	9203
	7:13	both according to the sanctuary **s**,	9203
	7:19	both according to the sanctuary **s**,	9203
	7:25	both according to the sanctuary **s**,	9203
	7:31	both according to the sanctuary **s**,	9203
	7:37	both according to the sanctuary **s**,	9203
	7:43	both according to the sanctuary **s**,	9203
	7:49	both according to the sanctuary **s**,	9203
	7:55	both according to the sanctuary **s**,	9203
	7:61	both according to the sanctuary **s**,	9203
	7:67	both according to the sanctuary **s**,	9203
	7:73	both according to the sanctuary **s**,	9203
	7:79	both according to the sanctuary **s**,	9203
	7:85	according to the sanctuary **s**.	9203
	7:86	according to the sanctuary **s**.	9203
	18:16	according to the sanctuary **s**,	9203
1Sa	9: 8	he said, "I have a quarter of a **s** *of* silver.	9203
	13:21	**two thirds of a s** for sharpening plowshares	7088
	13:21	a third of a **s** for sharpening forks and axes	NIH
2Ki	7: 1	for a **s** and two seahs of barley for a shekel	9203
	7: 1	for a shekel and two seahs of barley for a **s**	9203
	7:16	So a seah of flour sold for a **s**,	9203
	7:16	and two seahs of barley sold for a **s**,	9203
	7:18	for a **s** and two seahs of barley for a shekel	9203
	7:18	for a shekel and two seahs of barley for a **s**	9203
Ne	10:32	of a **s** each year for the service of the house	9203
Eze	45:12	The **s** is to consist of twenty gerahs.	9203

SHEKELS (105) [SHEKEL]

Ge	20:16	"I am giving your brother a thousand **s**	NIH
	23:15	the land is worth four hundred **s** *of* silver,	9203
	23:16	four hundred **s** *of* silver,	9203
	24:22	and two gold bracelets weighing ten **s**.	NIH
	37:28	for twenty **s** of silver to the Ishmaelites,	NIH
	45:22	but to Benjamin he gave three hundred **s**	NIH
Ex	21:32	the owner must pay thirty **s** of silver to	9203
	30:23	500 **s** of liquid myrrh, half as much (that is,	NIH
	30:23	(that is, 250 s) of fragrant cinnamon,	NIH
	30:23	250 **s** of fragrant cane,	NIH
	30:24	500 **s** of cassia—	NIH
	38:24	on the sanctuary was 29 talents and 730 **s**,	9203
	38:25	1,775 **s**, according to the sanctuary shekel—	9203
	38:28	1,775 **s** to make the hooks for the posts,	9203
	38:29	wave offering was 70 talents and 2,400 **s**.	9203
Lev	27: 3	and sixty at fifty **s** of silver, according to	9203
	27: 4	and if it is a female, set her value at thirty **s**.	9203
	27: 5	at twenty **s** and of a female at ten shekels.	9203
	27: 5	at twenty shekels and of a female at ten **s**.	9203
	27: 6	the value of a male at five **s** *of* silver and	9203
	27: 6	and that of a female at three **s** *of* silver.	9203
	27: 7	at fifteen **s** and of a female at ten shekels.	9203
	27: 7	at fifteen shekels and of a female at ten **s**.	9203
	27:16	fifty **s** *of* silver to a homer of barley seed.	9203
Nu	3:47	collect five **s** for each one,	9203
	3:50	**s**, according to the sanctuary shekel.	NIH
	7:13	plate weighing a hundred and thirty **s**,	NIH
	7:13	silver sprinkling bowl weighing seventy **s**,	9203
	7:14	one gold dish weighing ten **s**, filled	NIH
	7:19	plate weighing a hundred and thirty **s**,	NIH
	7:19	silver sprinkling bowl weighing seventy **s**,	9203
	7:20	one gold dish weighing ten **s**, filled	NIH
	7:25	plate weighing a hundred and thirty **s**,	NIH
	7:25	silver sprinkling bowl weighing seventy **s**,	9203
	7:26	one gold dish weighing ten **s**, filled	NIH
	7:31	plate weighing a hundred and thirty **s**,	NIH
	7:31	silver sprinkling bowl weighing seventy **s**,	9203
	7:32	one gold dish weighing ten **s**, filled	NIH
	7:37	plate weighing a hundred and thirty **s**,	NIH
	7:37	silver sprinkling bowl weighing seventy **s**,	9203
	7:38	one gold dish weighing ten **s**, filled	NIH
	7:43	plate weighing a hundred and thirty **s**,	NIH
	7:43	silver sprinkling bowl weighing seventy **s**,	9203
	7:44	one gold dish weighing ten **s**, filled	NIH
	7:49	plate weighing a hundred and thirty **s**,	NIH
	7:49	silver sprinkling bowl weighing seventy **s**,	9203
	7:50	one gold dish weighing ten **s**, filled	NIH
	7:55	plate weighing a hundred and thirty **s**,	NIH
	7:55	silver sprinkling bowl weighing seventy **s**,	9203
	7:56	one gold dish weighing ten **s**, filled	NIH
	7:61	plate weighing a hundred and thirty **s**,	NIH
	7:61	silver sprinkling bowl weighing seventy **s**,	9203
	7:62	one gold dish weighing ten **s**, filled	NIH
	7:67	plate weighing a hundred and thirty **s**,	NIH
	7:67	silver sprinkling bowl weighing seventy **s**,	9203
	7:68	one gold dish weighing ten **s**, filled	NIH
	7:73	plate weighing a hundred and thirty **s**,	NIH
	7:73	silver sprinkling bowl weighing seventy **s**,	9203
	7:74	one gold dish weighing ten **s**, filled	NIH
	7:79	plate weighing a hundred and thirty **s**,	NIH
	7:79	silver sprinkling bowl weighing seventy **s**,	9203
	7:80	one gold dish weighing ten **s**, filled	NIH
	7:85	plate weighing a hundred and thirty **s**,	NIH
	7:85	and each sprinkling bowl seventy **s**.	NIH
	7:85	silver dishes weighed two thousand four	
		hundred **s**,	NIH
	7:86	with incense weighed ten **s** each,	NIH
	7:86	dishes weighed a hundred and twenty **s**.	NIH
	18:16	the redemption price set at five **s** of silver,	9203
	31:52	as a gift to the LORD weighed 16,750 **s**.	9203
Dt	22:19	They shall fine him a hundred **s** of silver	NIH
	22:29	he shall pay the girl's father fifty **s** of silver.	NIH
Jos	7:21	two hundred **s** *of* silver and a wedge	9203
	7:21	and a wedge of gold weighing fifty **s**,	9203
Jdg	8:26	for came to seventeen hundred **s**,	NIH
	9: 4	They gave him seventy **s** of silver from	NIH
	16: 5	of us will give you eleven hundred **s**	NIH
	17: 2	"The eleven hundred **s** of silver	NIH
	17: 3	the eleven hundred **s** of silver to his mother,	NIH
	17: 4	and she took two hundred **s** of silver	NIH
	17:10	and I'll give you ten **s** of silver a year,	NIH
1Sa	17: 5	of bronze weighing five thousand **s**;	9203
	17: 7	and its iron point weighed six hundred **s**.	9203
2Sa	14:26	and its weight was two hundred **s** by	9203
	18:11	Then I would have had to give you ten **s**	NIH
	18:12	"Even if a thousand **s** were weighed out	4084
	21:16	bronze spearhead weighed three hundred **s**	NIH
	24:24	the oxen and paid fifty **s** of silver for them.	9203
1Ki	10:29	from Egypt for six hundred **s** of silver,	NIH
2Ki	5: 5	six thousand **s** of gold and ten sets	NIH
	6:25	a donkey's head sold for eighty **s** of silver,	NIH
	6:25	a quarter of a cab of seed pods for five **s**.	4084
	15:20	Every wealthy man had to contribute fifty **s**	9203
1Ch	21:25	So David paid Araunah six hundred **s**	9203
2Ch	1:17	from Egypt for six hundred **s** of silver,	NIH
	3: 9	The gold nails weighed fifty **s**.	9203
Ne	5:15	on the people and took forty **s** of silver	9203
SS	8:11	Each was to bring for its fruit a thousand **s**	NIH
	8:12	the thousand **s** are for you, O Solomon,	NIH
Isa	7:23	a thousand vines worth a thousand silver **s**,	NIH
Jer	32: 9	and weighed out for him seventeen **s**	9203
Eze	4:10	Weigh out twenty **s** of food to eat each day	9203
	45:12	Twenty **s** plus twenty-five shekels plus	
		fifteen shekels equal one mina.	9203
	45:12	Twenty shekels plus twenty-five **s** plus	
		fifteen shekels equal one mina.	9203
	45:12	Twenty shekels plus twenty-five shekels	
		plus fifteen **s** equal one mina.	9203
Hos	3: 2	for fifteen **s** of silver and about a homer and	NIH

SHELAH (19) [SHELANITE]

Ge	10:24	Arphaxad was the father of **S**,	8941
	10:24	and **S** the father of Eber.	8941
	11:12	he became the father of **S**.	8941
	11:13	And after he became the father of **S**,	8941
	11:14	When **S** had lived 30 years,	8941
	11:15	**S** lived 403 years and had another son	8941
	38: 5	to still another son and named him **S**.	8925
	38:11	until my son **S** grows up."	8925
	38:14	she saw that, though **S** had now grown up,	8925
	38:26	since I wouldn't give her to my son **S**."	8925
	46:12	The sons of Judah: Er, Onan, **S**,	8925
Nu	26:20	through **S**, the Shelanite clan;	8925
1Ch	1:18	Arphaxad was the father of **S**,	8941
	1:18	and **S** the father of Eber.	8941
	1:24	Shem, Arphaxad, **S**,	8941
	2: 3	The sons of Judah: Er, Onan and **S**.	8925
	4:21	The sons of **S** son of Judah:	8925
Ne	11: 5	the son of Zechariah, a descendant **of S**.	8989
Lk	3:35	the son of Eber, the son of **S**,	4885

SHELANITE (1) [SHELAH]

Nu	26:20	through Shelah, the **S** clan;	8989

SHELEMIAH (10)

1Ch	26:14	The lot for the East Gate fell to **S**.	8983
Ezr	10:39	**S**, Nathan, Adaiah,	8982
	10:41	Azarel, **S**, Shemariah,	8983
Ne	3:30	Next to him, Hananiah son of **S**,	8982
	13:13	I put **S** the priest, Zadok the scribe,	8982
Jer	36:14	the son of **S**, the son of Cushi,	8983
	36:26	Seraiah son of Azriel and **S** son of Abdeel	8983
	37: 3	of **S** with the priest Zephaniah son	8982
	37:13	whose name was Irijah son of **S**,	8982
	38: 1	Gedaliah son of Pashhur, Jehucal son of **S**,	8983

SHELEPH (2)

Ge	10:26	Joktan was the father of Almodad, **S**,	8991
1Ch	1:20	Joktan was the father of Almodad, **S**,	8991

SHELESH (1)

1Ch	7:35	Zophah, Imna, **S** and Amal.	8994

SHELISHIYAH See EGLATH SHELISHIYAH

SHELOMI (1)
Nu	34:27	Ahihud son of S, the leader from the tribe	8979

SHELOMITH (8)
Lev	24:11	(His mother's name was S,	8985
1Ch	3:19	S was their sister.	8985
	23:18	The sons of Izhar: S was the first.	8984
	26:25	Joram his son, Zicri his son and S his son.	8984
	26:26	S and his relatives were in charge of all	8984
	26:28	in the care of S and his relatives.	8984
2Ch	11:20	who bore him Abijah, Attai, Ziza and S.	8984
Ezr	8:10	S son of Josiphiah, and with him 160 men;	8984

SHELOMOTH (3)
1Ch	23: 9	The sons of Shimei: S, Haziel and Haran—	8977
	24:22	S; from the sons of Shelomoth: Jahath.	8977
	24:22	from the sons of S: Jahath.	8977

SHELTER (24) [SHELTERED, SHELTERS]
Ex	9:19	**bring** your livestock and everything you have in the field **to a place of** s,	6395
Dt	32:38	*Let them* give you s!	2118+6261
Ru	2: 7	except for a short rest in the s."	1074
1Ch	28:18	and s the ark of the covenant of the LORD.	6114
Job	24: 8	and hug the rocks for lack of s.	4726
Ps	27: 5	in the s *of* his tabernacle and set me high	6260
	31:20	the s *of* your presence you hide them from	6260
	55: 8	I would hurry to my **place of** s,	5144
	61: 4	in your tent forever and take refuge in the s	6260
	91: 1	He who dwells in the s *of* the Most High	6260
Ecc	7:12	Wisdom is a s as money is a shelter,	7498
	7:12	Wisdom is a shelter as money is a s,	7498
Isa	1: 8	The Daughter of Zion is left like a s in	6109
	4: 6	be a s and shade from the heat of the day,	6109
	16: 4	be their s from the destroyer."	6260
	25: 4	s from the storm and a shade from the heat.	4726
	32: 2	Each man will be like a s *from* the wind and	4675
	58: 7	and to provide the poor wanderer with s—	1074
Jer	4:20	my tents are destroyed, my s in a moment.	3749
	4:20	now to pitch my tent or to set up my s.	3749
Eze	17:23	*they will* **find** s in the shade	8905
Da	4:12	Under it the beasts of the field **found** s,	10300
	4:21	*giving* s to the beasts of the field,	10163
Jnh	4: 5	There he made himself a s,	6109

SHELTERED (1) [SHELTER]
Zep	2: 3	perhaps *you will* **be** s on the day of the	6259

SHELTERS (6) [SHELTER]
Ge	33:17	for himself and made s for his livestock.	6109
Jdg	6: 2	the Israelites prepared s for themselves	4953
Jer	49:29	their s will be carried off	3749
Mt	17: 4	If you wish, I will put up three s—	5008
Mk	9: 5	Let us put up three s—	5008
Lk	9:33	Let us put up three s—	5008

SHELUMIEL (5)
Nu	1: 6	from Simeon, S son of Zurishaddai;	8981
	2:12	The leader of the people of Simeon is S son	8981
	7:36	On the fifth day S son of Zurishaddai,	8981
	7:41	the offering of S son of Zurishaddai.	8981
	10:19	S son of Zurishaddai was over the division	8981

SHEM (20)
Ge	5:32	he became the father of S,	9006
	6:10	Noah had three sons: S, Ham and Japheth.	9006
	7:13	On that very day Noah and his sons, S,	9006
	9:18	of Noah who came out of the ark were S,	9006
	9:23	But S and Japheth took a garment	9006
	9:26	"Blessed be the LORD, the God of S!	9006
	9:26	May Canaan be the slave of S.	4564S
	9:27	may Japheth live in the tents of S,	9006
	10: 1	This is the account of S, Ham and Japheth,	9006
	10:21	Sons were also born to S,	9006
	10:21	S was the ancestor of all the sons of Eber.	2085S
	10:22	The sons of S: Elam, Asshur,	9006
	10:31	the sons of S by their clans and languages,	9006
	11:10	This is the account of S.	9006
	11:10	when S was 100 years old,	9006
	11:11	S lived 500 years and had other sons	9006
1Ch	1: 4	The sons of Noah: S, Ham and Japheth.	9006
	1:17	The sons of S: Elam, Asshur,	9006
	1:24	S, Arphaxad, Shelah,	9006
Lk	3:36	the son of Arphaxad, the son *of* S,	4954

SHEMA (6)
Jos	15:26	Amam, S, Moladah,	9054
1Ch	2:43	Korah, Tappuah, Rekem and S.	9050
	2:44	S was the father of Raham,	9050
	5: 8	the son of S, the son of Joel,	9050
	8:13	and Beriah and S,	9050
Ne	8: 4	S, Anaiah, Uriah, Hilkiah and Maaseiah;	9050

SHEMAAH (1)
1Ch	12: 3	and Joash the sons of S the Gibeathite;	9057

SHEMAIAH (39) [SHEMAIAH'S]
1Ki	12:22	word of God came to S the man of God:	9061
1Ch	3:22	S and his sons: Hattush, Igal,	9061
	4:37	the son of Shimri, the son of S.	9061
	5: 4	S his son, Gog his son, Shimei his son,	9061
	9:14	S son of Hasshub, the son of Azrikam,	9061
	9:16	Obadiah son of S, the son of Galal, the son	9061
	15: 8	S the leader and 200 relatives;	9061
	15:11	Joel, S, Eliel and Amminadab the Levites.	9061
	24: 6	The scribe S son of Nethanel, a Levite,	9061
	26: 4	Obed-Edom also had sons: S the firstborn,	9061
	26: 6	His son S also had sons,	9061
	26: 7	The sons of S: Othni, Rephael,	9061
2Ch	11: 2	of the LORD came to S the man of God:	9062
	12: 5	Then the prophet S came to Rehoboam and	9061
	12: 7	this word of the LORD came to S:	9061
	12:15	in the records of S the prophet and of Iddo	9061
	17: 8	With them were certain Levites—S,	9062
	29:14	the descendants of Jeduthun, S and Uzziel.	9061
	31:15	Eden, Miniamin, Jeshua, S,	9061
	35: 9	Also Conaniah along with S and Nethanel,	9062
Ezr	8:13	whose names were Eliphelet, Jeuel and S,	9061
	8:16	So I summoned Eliezer, Ariel, S, Elnathan,	9061
	10:21	Maaseiah, Elijah, S, Jehiel and Uzziah.	9061
	10:31	Eliezer, Ishijah, Malkijah, S, Shimeon,	9061
Ne	3:29	Next to him, S son of Shecaniah,	9061
	6:10	One day I went to the house of S son	9061
	10: 8	Bilgai and S. These were the priests.	9061
	11:15	S son of Hasshub, the son of Azrikam,	9061
	12: 6	S, Joiarib, Jedaiah,	9061
	12:34	Judah, Benjamin, S, Jeremiah,	9061
	12:35	the son of S, the son of Mattaniah,	9061
	12:36	S, Azarel, Milalai, Gilalai, Maai, Nethanel,	9061
	12:42	S, Eleazar, Uzzi, Jehohanan, Malkijah,	9061
Jer	26:20	(Now Uriah son of S from Kiriath Jearim	9062
	29:24	Tell S the Nehelamite,	9062
	29:31	the LORD says about S the Nehelamite:	9061
	29:31	Because S has prophesied to you,	9061
	29:32	I will surely punish S the Nehelamite	9061
	36:12	Elishama the secretary, Delaiah son of S,	9062

SHEMAIAH'S (1) [SHEMAIAH]
Ne	12:18	of Bilgah's, Shammua; of S, Jehonathan;	9061

SHEMARIAH (4)
1Ch	12: 5	Bealiah, S and Shephatiah the Haruphite;	9080
2Ch	11:19	She bore him sons: Jeush, S and Zaham.	9079
Ezr	10:32	Benjamin, Malluch and S.	9079
	10:41	Azarel, Shelemiah, S,	9079

SHEMEBER (1)
Ge	14: 2	Shinab king of Admah, S king of Zeboiim,	9008

SHEMED (1)
1Ch	8:12	Eber, Misham, S (who built Ono and Lod	9013

SHEMER (3)
1Ki	16:24	of Samaria from S for two talents of silver	9070
	16:24	calling it Samaria, after S,	9070
1Ch	6:46	the son of Bani, the son of S,	9070

SHEMESH (1) See BETH SHEMESH, EN SHEMESH, IR SHEMESH
Jos	15: 7	along to the waters of **En** S and came	6539+9087

SHEMIDA (3) [SHEMIDAITE]
Nu	26:32	through S, the Shemidaite clan;	9026
Jos	17: 2	Helek, Asriel, Shechem, Hepher and S.	9026
1Ch	7:19	The sons of S were:	9026

SHEMIDAITE (1) [SHEMIDA]
Nu	26:32	through Shemida, the S clan;	9027

SHEMINITH (3)
1Ch	15:21	play the harps, directing according to s.	9030
Ps	6: T	According to s. A Psalm of David.	9030
	12: T	According to s. A Psalm of David.	9030

SHEMIRAMOTH (4)
1Ch	15:18	Zechariah, Jaaziel, S, Jehiel, Unni, Eliab,	9035
	15:20	Aziel, S, Jehiel, Unni, Eliab,	9035
	16: 5	Zechariah second, then Jeiel, S, Jehiel,	9035
2Ch	17: 8	Shemaiah, Nethaniah, Zebadiah, Asahel, S,	9035

SHEMUEL (1)
Nu	34:20	S son of Ammihud, from the tribe	9017

SHEN (1)
1Sa	7:12	and set it up between Mizpah and S.	9095

SHENAZZAR (1)
1Ch	3:18	S, Jekamiah, Hoshama and Nedabiah.	9100

SHENIR (KJV) See SENIR

SHEPHAM (2)
Nu	34:10	run a line from Hazar Enan to S.	9172
	34:11	from S to Riblah on the east side of Ain	9172

SHEPHATIAH (13)
2Sa	3: 4	the fifth, S the son of Abital;	9152
1Ch	3: 3	S the son of Abital;	9152
	9: 8	and Meshullam son of S, the son of Reuel,	9152
	12: 5	Bealiah, Shemariah and S the Haruphite;	9153
	27:16	S son of Maacah;	9153
2Ch	21: 2	Zechariah, Azariahu, Michael and S.	9153
Ezr	2: 4	of S 372	9152
	2:57	S, Hattil, Pokereth-Hazzebaim and Ami	9152
	8: 8	of the descendants of S, Zebadiah son	9152
Ne	7: 9	of S 372	9152
	7:59	S, Hattil, Pokereth-Hazzebaim and Amon	9152
	11: 4	the son of S, the son of Mahalalel,	9152
Jer	38: 1	S son of Mattan, Gedaliah son of Pashhur,	9152

SHEPHER (2)
Nu	33:23	left Kehelathah and camped at Mount S.	9184
	33:24	They left Mount S and camped at Haradah.	9184

SHEPHERD (62) [SHEPHERD'S, SHEPHERDED, SHEPHERDESS, SHEPHERDS]
Ge	48:15	the God who *has been* my s all my life	8286
	49:24	because of the S, the Rock of Israel,	8286
Nu	27:17	not be like sheep without a s."	8286
1Sa	17:20	in the morning David left the flock with a s,	9068
	21: 7	he was Doeg the Edomite, Saul's head s.	8286
2Sa	5: 2	'You *will* s my people Israel,	8286
	7: 7	whom I commanded to s my people Israel,	8286
1Ki	22:17	on the hills like sheep without a s,	8286
1Ch	11: 2	'You *will* s my people Israel,	8286
	17: 6	whom I commanded to s my people,	8286
2Ch	18:16	on the hills like sheep without a s,	8286
Ps	23: 1	The LORD *is* my s, I shall not be in want.	8286
	28: 9	*be* their s and carry them forever.	8286
	78:71	he brought him to *be* the s of his people	8286
	80: 1	Hear us, O S of Israel,	8286
Ecc	12:11	firmly embedded nails—given by one S.	8286
Isa	13:14	like sheep without a s,	7695
	13:20	no s will rest his flocks there.	8286
	40:11	He tends his flock like a s:	8286
	44:28	'He is my s and will accomplish all	8286
	61: 5	Aliens *will* s your flocks;	8286
	63:11	with the s *of* his flock?	8286
Jer	17:16	I have not run away from *being* your s;	8286
	31:10	and will watch over his flock like a s.'	8286
	43:12	As a s wraps his garment around him,	8286
	49:19	And what s can stand against me?"	8286
	50:44	And what s can stand against me?"	8286
	51:23	with you I shatter s and flock,	8286
Eze	34: 5	they were scattered because *there was* no s,	8286
	34: 8	because my flock lacks a s and	8286
	34:12	a s looks after his scattered flock when he is	8286
	34:16	I *will* s the flock with justice.	8286
	34:23	I will place over them one s,	8286
	34:23	he will tend them and be their s.	8286
	37:24	and they will all have one s.	8286
Am	3:12	"As a s saves from the lion's mouth only	8286
		but I was a s, and I also took care of	1012
Mic	5: 4	and s *his* flock in the strength of the LORD	8286
	7:14	S your people with your staff,	8286
Zec	10: 2	like sheep oppressed for lack of a s.	8286
	11: 9	"I will not *be* your s.	8286
	11:15	"Take again the equipment of a foolish s.	8286
	11:16	up a s over the land who will not care for	8286
	11:17	"Woe to the worthless s,	8286
	13: 7	"Awake, O sword, against my s,	8286
	13: 7	the s, and the sheep will be scattered,	8286
Mt	2: 6	a ruler who *will* **be** the s of	4477
	9:36	like sheep without a s.	4478
	25:32	the people one from another as a s separates	4478
	26:31	" 'I will strike the s, and the sheep will be	4478
Mk	6:34	because they were like sheep without a s.	4478
	14:27	" 'I will strike the s, and the sheep will be	4478
Jn	10: 2	The man who enters by the gate is the s	4478
	10:11	"I am the good s.	4478
	10:11	The good s lays down his life for the sheep.	4478
	10:12	hired hand is not the s who owns the sheep.	4478
	10:14	"I am the good s; I know my sheep	4478
	10:16	and there shall be one flock and one s.	4478
Heb	13:20	our Lord Jesus, that great S of the sheep,	4478
1Pe	2:25	to the S and Overseer of your souls.	4478
	5: 4	And when the **Chief** S appears,	799
Rev	7:17	at the center of the throne *will* be their s;	4477

SHEPHERD'S (3) [SHEPHERD]
Lev	27:32	that passes under the s rod—	8657
1Sa	17:40	put them in the pouch of his s bag and,	8286
Isa	38:12	a s tent my house has been pulled down	8286

SHEPHERDED (1) [SHEPHERD]
Ps	78:72	And David s them with integrity of heart;	8286

SHEPHERDESS (1) [SHEPHERD]
Ge	29: 9	with her father's sheep, for she *was* a s.	8286

SHEPHERDS (50) [SHEPHERD]
Ge	29: 3	the s would roll the stone away from	NIH
	29: 4	Jacob asked the s, "My brothers,	2157S
	46:32	The men *are* s; they tend livestock,	7366+8286

Ge	46:34	all **s** are detestable to the Egyptians."	7366+8286
	47: 3	"Your servants are **s**,"	7366+8286
Ex	2:17	Some **s** came along and drove them away,	8286
	2:19	"An Egyptian rescued us from the **s**.	8286
Nu	14:33	Your children will be **s** here for forty years,	8286
1Sa	25: 7	When your **s** were with us,	8286
2Ki	10:12	At Beth Eked of the **S**,	8286
SS	1: 8	by the tents of the **s**.	8286
Isa	31: 4	though a whole band of **s** is called together	8286
	56:11	They **are s** who lack understanding,	8286
Jer	3:15	Then I will give you **s** after my own heart,	8286
	6: 3	**S** with their flocks will come against her;	8286
	10:21	The **s** are senseless and do not inquire of	8286
	12:10	Many **s** will ruin my vineyard and trample	8286
	22:22	The wind will drive all your **s** away,	8286
	23: 1	to the **s** who are destroying and scattering	8286
	23: 2	says to the **s** who tend my people:	8286
	23: 4	I will place **s** over them who will tend them	8286
	25:34	Weep and wail, you **s**;	8286
	25:35	The **s** will have nowhere to flee,	8286
	25:36	Hear the cry of the **s**,	8286
	33:12	be pastures for **s** to rest their flocks.	8286
	50: 6	their **s** have led them astray	8286
Eze	34: 2	prophesy against the **s** *of* Israel;	8286
	34: 2	Woe to the **s** *of* Israel who only take care	8286
	34: 2	Should not **s** take care of the flock?	8286
	34: 7	you **s**, hear the word of the LORD:	8286
	34: 8	because my **s** did not search for my flock	8286
	34: 9	O **s**, hear the word of the LORD:	8286
	34:10	the **s** and will hold them accountable	8286
	34:10	so that the **s** can no longer feed themselves.	8286
Am	1: 1	words of Amos, one of the **s** of Tekoa—	5924
	1: 2	the pastures of the **s** dry up,	8286
Mic	5: 5	we will raise against him seven **s**,	8286
Na	3:18	O king of Assyria, your **s** slumber;	8286
Zep	2: 6	will be a place for **s** and sheep pens.	8286
Zec	10: 3	"My anger burns against the **s**,	8286
	11: 3	Listen to the wail of the **s**;	8286
	11: 5	Their own **s** do not spare them.	8286
	11: 8	In one month I got rid of the three **s**.	8286
Lk	2: 8	there were **s** living out in the fields nearby,	4478
	2:15	the **s** said to one another,	4478
	2:18	at what the **s** said to them.	4478
	2:20	The **s** returned, glorifying and praising God	4478
Ac	20:28	**Be s** of the church of God,	4477
1Pe	5: 2	**Be s** of God's flock that is under your care,	4477
Jude	1:12	**s** who feed only themselves.	4477

SHEPHO (2)

Ge	36:23	Alvan, Manahath, Ebal, **S** and Onam.	9143
1Ch	1:40	Alvan, Manahath, Ebal, **S** and Onam.	9143

SHEPHUPHAN (1)

1Ch	8: 5	Gera, **S** and Huram.	9146

SHERAH (KJV) See SHEERAH

SHERD, SHERDS (KJV) See FRAGMENT, PIECES

SHEREBIAH (8) [SHEREBIAH'S]

Ezr	8:18	they brought us **S**, a capable man,	9221
	8:24	of the leading priests, together with **S**,	9221
Ne	8: 7	The Levites—Jeshua, Bani, **S**, Jamin,	9221
	9: 4	Shebaniah, Bunni, **S**, Bani and Kenani—	9221
	9: 5	Jeshua, Kadmiel, Bani, Hashabneiah, **S**,	9221
	10:12	Zaccur, **S**, Shebaniah,	9221
	12: 8	Kadmiel, **S**, Judah, and also Mattaniah,	9221
	12:24	leaders of the Levites were Hashabiah, **S**,	9221

SHEREBIAH'S (1) [SHEREBIAH]

Ezr	8:18	the son of Israel, and **S** sons and brothers,	2257S

SHERESH (1)

1Ch	7:16	His brother was named **S**,	9246

SHEREZER (KJV) See SHAREZER

SHERIFFS (KJV) See MAGISTRATES

SHESHACH (2)

Jer	25:26	all of them, the king of **S** will drink it too.	9263
	51:41	"How **S** will be captured,	9263

SHESHAI (3)

Nu	13:22	**S** and Talmai, the descendants of Anak,	9259
Jos	15:14	**S**, Ahiman and Talmai—	9259
Jdg	1:10	and defeated **S**, Ahiman	9259

SHESHAN (4)

1Ch	2:31	Ishi, who was the father of **S**.	9264
	2:31	**S** was the father of Ahlai.	9264
	2:34	**S** had no sons—only daughters.	9264
	2:35	**S** gave his daughter in marriage	9264

SHESHBAZZAR (4)

Ezr	1: 8	who counted them out to **S** the prince	9256
	1:11	**S** brought all these along when the exiles	9256

Ezr	5:14	King Cyrus gave them to a man named **S**,	10746
	5:16	So this **S** came and laid the foundations of	10746

SHETH (1)

Nu	24:17	the skulls of all the sons of **S**.	9269

SHETHAR (1)

Est	1:14	Carshena, **S**, Admatha, Tarshish, Meres,	9285

SHETHAR-BOZENAI (4)

Ezr	5: 3	and **S** and their associates went to them	10750
	5: 6	and **S** and their associates,	10750
	6: 6	and **S** and you, their fellow officials	10750
	6:13	and **S** and their associates carried it out	10750

SHEVA (2)

2Sa	20:25	**S** was secretary; Zadok and Abiathar	8737
1Ch	2:49	and to **S** the father of Macbenah and Gibea.	8737

SHEWBREAD (KJV) See BREAD OF THE PRESENCE

SHIBAH (1)

Ge	26:33	He called it **S**, and to this day the name	8683

SHIBBOLETH (1)

Jdg	12: 6	they said, "All right, say '**S**.' "	8672

SHIBMAH (KJV) See SIBMAH

SHICRON (KJV) See SHIKKERON

SHIELD (51) [SHIELDED, SHIELDING, SHIELDS]

Ge	15: 1	I am your **s**, your very great reward."	4482
Ex	40: 3	the ark of the Testimony in it and **s** the ark	6114
Dt	13: 8	do not spare him or **s** him.	4059
	33:29	He is your **s** and helper	4482
Jdg	5: 8	a **s** or spear was seen among forty thousand	4482
1Sa	17: 7	His **s** bearer went ahead of him,	7558
	17:41	with his **s** bearer in front of him,	7558
2Sa	1:21	For there the **s** *of* the mighty was defiled,	4482
	1:21	the **s** *of* Saul—no longer rubbed with oil.	4482
	22: 3	my **s** and the horn of my salvation.	4482
	22:31	He is a **s** for all who take refuge in him.	4482
	22:36	You give me your **s** *of* victory;	4482
1Ki	10:16	six hundred bekas of gold went into each **s**.	7558
	10:17	with three minas of gold in each **s**.	4482
2Ki	19:32	He will not come before it *with* **s** or build	4482
1Ch	5:18	able-bodied men who could handle **s**	4482
	12: 8	for battle and able to handle the **s** and spear.	7558
	12:24	carrying **s** and spear—6,800 armed for	7558
2Ch	9:15	of hammered gold went into each **s**.	7558
	9:16	with three hundred bekas of gold in each **s**.	4482
	25: 5	able to handle the spear and **s**,	7558
Job	15:26	against him with a thick, strong **s**.	4482
Ps	3: 3	But you are a **s** around me, O LORD;	4482
	5:12	with your favor as with a **s**.	7558
	7:10	My **s** is God Most High,	4482
	18: 2	He is my **s** and the horn of my salvation.	4482
	18:30	He is a **s** for all who take refuge in him.	4482
	18:35	You give me your **s** *of* victory;	4482
	28: 7	The LORD is my strength and my **s**;	4482
	33:20	he is our help and our **s**.	4482
	35: 2	Take up **s** and buckler;	4482
	59:11	But do not kill them, O Lord our **s**,	4482
	84: 9	Look upon our **s**, O God;	4482
	84:11	For the LORD God is a sun and **s**;	4482
	89:18	Indeed, our **s** belongs to the LORD,	4482
	91: 4	his faithfulness will be your **s** and rampart.	7558
	115: 9	trust in the LORD—he is their help and **s**.	4482
	115:10	trust in the LORD—he is their help and **s**.	4482
	115:11	trust in the LORD—he is their help and **s**.	4482
	119:114	You are my refuge and my **s**;	4482
	144: 2	my stronghold and my deliverer, my **s**,	4482
Pr	2: 7	he is a **s** to those whose walk is blameless,	4482
	30: 5	he is a **s** to those who take refuge in him.	4482
Isa	22: 6	Kir uncovers the **s**.	4482
	31: 5	the LORD Almighty *will* **s** Jerusalem;	1713
	31: 5	he *will* **s** it and deliver it,	1713
	37:35	He will not come before it *with* **s** or build	4482
Na	2: 5	the **protective s** is put in place.	6116
Zec	9:15	and the LORD Almighty *will* **s** them.	1713
	12: 8	that day the LORD *will* **s** those who live	1713
Eph	6:16	In addition to all this, take up the **s** of faith,	2599

SHIELDED (3) [SHIELD]

Ex	40:21	and hung the shielding curtain and **s** the ark	6114
Dt	32:10	*He* **s** him and cared for him;	6015
1Pe	1: 5	through faith *are* **s** by God's power until	5864

SHIELDING (3) [SHIELD]

Ex	39:34	of hides of sea cows and the **s** curtain;	5009
	40:21	and hung the **s** curtain and shielded the ark	5009
Nu	4: 5	in and take down the **s** curtain and cover	5009

SHIELDS (43) [SHIELD]

Ex	35:12	the curtain that **s** it;	5009

Dt	33:12	for *he* **s** him all day long,	2910
2Sa	8: 7	the gold **s** that belonged to the officers	8949
1Ki	10:16	King Solomon made two hundred **large s**	7558
	10:17	He also made three hundred **small s**	4482
	14:26	including all the gold **s** Solomon had made.	4482
	14:27	So King Rehoboam made bronze **s**	4482
	14:28	the guards bore **the s**,	4392S
2Ki	11:10	and **s** that had belonged to King David and	8949
1Ch	12:34	37,000 men carrying **s** and spears;	7558
	18: 7	David took the gold **s** carried by the officers	8949
2Ch	9:15	King Solomon made two hundred **large s**	7558
	9:16	He also made three hundred **small s**	4482
	11:12	He put **s** and spears in all the cities,	7558
	12: 9	including the gold **s** Solomon had made.	4482
	12:10	So King Rehoboam made bronze **s**	4482
	12:11	the guards went with him, bearing **the s**,	4392S
	14: 8	equipped with **large s** and with spears,	7558
	14: 8	armed with **small s** and with bows.	4482
	17:17	men with 200,000 men armed with bows and **s**;	4482
	23: 9	the large and **small s** that had belonged	8949
	26:14	Uzziah provided **s**, spears, helmets,	4482
	32: 5	also made large numbers of weapons and **s**.	4482
	32:27	spices, **s** and all kinds of valuables.	4482
Ne	4:16	the other half were equipped with spears, **s**,	4482
Job	41:15	of **s** tightly sealed together;	4482
Ps	46: 9	he burns the **s** with fire.	6317
	76: 3	the **s** and the swords, the weapons of war.	4482
	140: 7	*who* **s** my head in the day of battle—	6114
SS	4: 4	on it hang a thousand **s**,	4482
	4: 4	all of them a **s** of warriors.	8949
Isa	21: 5	Get up, you officers, oil the **s**!	4482
Jer	46: 3	**s**, both large and **small**,	4482
	46: 9	men of Cush and Put who carry **s**,	4482
	51:11	"Sharpen the arrows, take up the **s**!	8949
Eze	23:24	with large and **small s** and with helmets,	4482
	26: 8	up to your walls and raise his **s** against you.	7558
	27:10	They hung their **s** and helmets	4482
	27:11	They hung their **s** around your walls;	8949
	38: 4	and a great horde with large and **small s**,	4482
	38: 5	all with **s** and helmets,	4482
	39: 9	the **small** and large **s**,	4482
Na	2: 3	The **s** *of* his soldiers are red;	4482

SHIFTING (1) [SHIFTS, SHIFTLESS]

Jas	1:17	who does not change like **s** shadows.	5572

SHIFTLESS (1) [SHIFTING]

Pr	19:15	and the **s** man goes hungry.	8244

SHIFTS (1) [SHIFTING]

1Ki	5:14	to Lebanon in **s** of ten thousand a month,	2722

SHIGGAION (1)

Ps	7: T	A **s** of David, which he sang to the LORD	8710

SHIGIONOTH (1)

Hab	3: 1	A prayer of Habakkuk the prophet. On **s**.	8710

SHIHON (KJV) See SHION

SHIHOR (4) [SHIHOR LIBNATH]

Jos	13: 3	from the **S** River on the east of Egypt to	8865
1Ch	13: 5	the **S** River *in* Egypt to Lebo Hamath,	8865
Isa	23: 3	the great waters came the grain of the **S**;	8865
Jer	2:18	to Egypt to drink water from the **S**?	8865

SHIHOR LIBNATH (1) [SHIHOR]

Jos	19:26	the boundary touched Carmel and **S**.	8866

SHIKKERON (1)

Jos	15:11	toward **S**, passed along to Mount Baalah	8914

SHILHI (2)

1Ki	22:42	mother's name was Azubah daughter of **S**.	8944
2Ch	20:31	mother's name was Azubah daughter of **S**.	8944

SHILHIM (1)

Jos	15:32	**S**, Ain and Rimmon—	8946

SHILLEM (3) [SHILLEMITE]

Ge	46:24	Jahziel, Guni, Jezer and **S**.	8973
Nu	26:49	through **S**, the Shillemite clan.	8973
1Ch	7:13	Jahziel, Guni, Jezer and **S**—	8973

SHILLEMITE (1) [SHILLEM]

Nu	26:49	through Shillem, the **S** clan.	8980

SHILOAH (1)

Isa	8: 6	the gently flowing waters of **S** and rejoices	8942

SHILOH (32) [TAANATH SHILOH]

Jos	18: 1	at **S** and set up the Tent of Meeting there.	8926
	18: 8	and I will cast lots for you here at **S** in	8926
	18: 9	and returned to Joshua in the camp at **S**.	8926
	18:10	then cast lots for them in **S** in the presence	8926
	19:51	the tribal clans of Israel assigned by lot at **S**	8926
	21: 2	at **S** in Canaan and said to them,	8926

Jos 22: 9 the Israelites at S in Canaan to return 8926
   22:12 the whole assembly of Israel gathered at S 8926
Jdg 18:31 all the time the house of God was in S. 8926
   21:12 they took them to the camp at S in Canaan. 8926
   21:19 the annual festival of the LORD in S, 8931
   21:21 When the girls of S come out to join in 8870
   21:21 a wife from the girls of S and go to the land 8870
1Sa 1: 3 and sacrifice to the LORD Almighty at S, 8926
   1: 9 finished eating and drinking in S, 8926
   1:24 to the house of the LORD at S. 8931
   2:14 the Israelites who came to S. 8926
   3:21 The LORD continued to appear at S, 8926
   4: 3 the ark of the LORD's covenant from S, 8926
   4: 4 So the people sent men to S, 8926
   4:12 from the battle line and went to S, 8926
   14: 3 the son of Eli, the LORD's priest in S. 8931
1Ki 2:27 the word the LORD had spoken at S about 8926
   11:29 and Ahijah the prophet of S met him on 8872
   14: 2 Then go to S. Ahijah the prophet is there— 8926
   14: 4 and went to Ahijah's house in S. 8926
Ps 78:60 He abandoned the tabernacle of S, 8931
Jer 7:12 the place in S where I first made a dwelling 8870
   7:14 what I did to S I will now do to the house 8931
   26: 6 like S and this city an object of cursing 8926
   26: 9 be like S and this city will be desolate 8931
   41: 5 and cut themselves came from Shechem, S 8926

SHILONI (KJV) See SHELAH

SHILONITE (4) [SHILONITES]

1Ki 12:15 of Nebat through Ahijah the S. 8872
   15:29 through his servant Ahijah the S— 8872
2Ch 9:29 of Ahijah the S and in the visions of Iddo 8872
   10:15 of Nebat through Ahijah the S. 8872

SHILONITES (1) [SHILONITE]

1Ch 9: 5 Of the S: Asaiah the firstborn and his sons. 8872

SHILSHAH (1)

1Ch 7:37 Bezer, Hod, Shamma, S, Ithran and Beera. 8996

SHIMEA (4)

1Ch 2:13 the second son was Abinadab, the third S, 9055
   6:30 S his son, Haggiah his son 9055
   6:39 Asaph son of Berekiah, the son of S, 9055
   20: 7 When he taunted Israel, Jonathan son of S, 9055

SHIMEAH (4)

2Sa 13: 3 a friend named Jonadab son of S, 9056
   13:32 But Jonadab son of S, David's brother, 9056
   21:21 When he taunted Israel, Jonathan son of S, 9056
1Ch 8:32 who was the father of S. 9009

SHIMEAM (1)

1Ch 9:38 Mikloth was the father of S. 9010

SHIMEATH (2) [SHIMEATHITES]

2Ki 12:21 of S and Jehozabad son of Shomer, 9064
2Ch 24:26 son of S an Ammonite woman, 9064

SHIMEATHITES (1) [SHIMEATH]

1Ch 2:55 the Tirathites, S and Sucathites. 9065

SHIMEI (44) [SHIMEI'S, SHIMEITES]

Ex 6:17 by clans, were Libni and S. 9059
Nu 3:18 of the Gershonite clans: Libni and S. 9059
2Sa 16: 5 His name was S son of Gera, 9059
   16: 7 As he cursed, S said, "Get out, get out, 9059
   16:13 along the road while S was going along 9059
   19:16 S son of Gera, the Benjamite 9059
   19:18 When S son of Gera crossed the Jordan, 9059
   19:21 "Shouldn't S be put to death for this? 9059
   19:23 So the king said to S, "You shall not die." 9059
1Ki 1: 8 S and Rei and David's special guard did 9059
   2: 8 you have with you S son of Gera, 9059
   2:36 Then the king sent for S and said to him, 9059
   2:38 S answered the king, "What you say is good 9059
   2:38 And S stayed in Jerusalem for a long time. 9059
   2:39 and S was told, "Your slaves are in Gath." 9059
   2:40 So S went away and brought 9059
   2:41 When Solomon was told that S had gone 9059
   2:42 the king summoned S and said to him, 9059
   2:44 The king also said to S, 9059
   2:46 he went out and struck S down 2257S
1Ch 3:19 The sons of Pedaiah: Zerubbabel and S. 9059
   4:26 Zaccur his son and S his son. 9059
   4:27 S had sixteen sons and six daughters, 9059
   5: 4 Shemaiah his son, Gog his son, S his son, 9059
   6:17 of Gershon: Libni and S. 9059
   6:29 Mahli, Libni his son, S his son, 9059
   6:42 the son of Zimmah, the son of S, 9059
   8:21 Beraiah and Shimrath were the sons of S. 9059
   23: 7 to the Gershonites: Ladan and S. 9059
   23: 9 The sons of S: Shelomoth, Haziel and 9059
   23:10 sons of S: Jahath, Ziza, Jeush and Beriah. 9059
   23:10 These were the sons of S—four in all. 9059
   25: 3 Gedaliah, Zeri, Jeshaiah, S, 9059
   25:17 the tenth to S, his sons and relatives, 12 9059
   27:27 S the Ramathite was in charge of 9059

2Ch 29:14 the descendants of Heman, Jehiel and S; 9059
   31:12 and his brother S was next in rank. 9059
   31:13 under Conaniah and S his brother, 9059
Ezr 10:23 Jozabad, S, Kelaiah (that is, Kelita), 9059
   10:33 Zabad, Eliphelet, Jeremai, Manasseh and S. 9059
   10:38 From the descendants of Binnui: S, 9059
Est 2: 5 named Mordecai son of Jair, the son of S, 9059
Zec 12:13 the clan of S and their wives, 9060

SHIMEI'S (1) [SHIMEI]

1Ki 2:39 two of S slaves ran off to Achish son 4200+9059

SHIMEITES (1) [SHIMEI]

Nu 3:21 the clans of the Libnites and S; 9060

SHIMEON (1)

Ezr 10:31 Eliezer, Ishijah, Malkijah, Shemaiah, S, 9058

SHIMHI, SHIMI (KJV) See SHIMEI

SHIMITES (KJV) See SHIMEITES

SHIMMA (KJV) See SHIMEA

SHIMMERING (1)

Isa 18: 4 like S heat in the sunshine, 7456

SHIMON (1)

1Ch 4:20 The sons of S: Amnon, Rinnah, Ben-Hanan 8873

SHIMRATH (1)

1Ch 8:21 Beraiah and S were the sons of Shimei. 9086

SHIMRI (4)

1Ch 4:37 the son of S, the son of Shemaiah. 9078
   11:45 Jediael son of S, his brother Joha 9078
   26:10 S the first (although he was not the 9078
2Ch 29:13 the descendants of Elizaphan, S and Jeiel; 9078

SHIMRITH (1)

2Ch 24:26 and Jehozabad, son of S a Moabite woman. 9083

SHIMRON (5) [SHIMRONITE, SHIMRON MERON]

Ge 46:13 Tola, Puah, Jashub and S. 9075
Nu 26:24 through S, the Shimronite clan, 9075
Jos 11: 1 to the kings of S and Acshaph, 9074
   19:15 Included were Kattath, Nahalal, S, 9074
1Ch 7: 1 Tola, Puah, Jashub and S—four in all. 9075

SHIMRON MERON (1) [SHIMRON]

Jos 12:20 the king of S one the king of Acshaph one 9077

SHIMRONITE (1) [SHIMRON]

Nu 26:24 through Shimron, the S clan, 9084

SHIMSHAI (4)

Ezr 4: 8 Rehum the commanding officer and S 10729
   4: 9 and S the secretary, together with the rest 10729
   4:17 the commanding officer, S the secretary 10729
   4:23 and S the secretary and their associates, 10729

SHINAB (1)

Ge 14: 2 S king of Admah, Shemeber king of 9098

SHINAR (4)

Ge 10:10 Erech, Akkad and Calneh, in S. 824+9114
   11: 2 they found a plain in S and settled 824+9114
   14: 1 At this time Amraphel king of S, 9114
   14: 9 Amraphel king of S and Arioch king 9114

SHINE (36) [SHINES, SHINING, SHONE]

Nu 6:25 the LORD make his face s upon you and 239
Ne 9:19 by night to s on the way they were to take. 239
Job 3: 4 may no light s upon it. 3649
   9: 7 He speaks to the sun and it does not s; 2436
   22:28 and light will s on your ways. 5585
   33:30 that the light of life may s on him. 239
Ps 4: 6 Let the light of your face s upon us, 5951
   31:16 Let your face s on your servant; 239
   37: 6 make your righteousness s like the dawn, 3655
   67: 1 and bless us and make his face s upon us, 239
   80: 1 between the cherubim, s forth 3649
   80: 3 make your face s upon us, 239
   80: 7 make your face s upon us, 239
   80:19 make your face s upon us, 239
   94: 1 O God who avenges, s forth. 3649
   104:15 oil to make his face s, 7413
   118:27 and he has made his light s upon us. 239
   119:135 Make your face s upon your servant 239
   139:12 the night will s like the day, 239
Isa 30:26 The moon will s like the sun, 240+2118
   60: 1 "Arise, s, for your light has come, 239
   60:19 nor will the brightness of the moon s 239
Jer 31:35 he who appoints the sun by day, to s by 239

Jer 31:35 and stars to s by night, who stirs up the sea 239
Da 12: 3 Those who are wise will s like 2301
Joel 2:10 and the stars no longer s. 665+5586
   3:15 and the stars no longer s. 665+5586
Mt 5:16 let your light s before men, 3290
   13:43 Then the righteous will s like the sun in 1719
Lk 1:79 to s on those living in darkness and in 2210
2Co 4: 6 who said, "Let light s out of darkness," 3290
   4: 6 made his light s in our hearts to give us 3290
Eph 5:14 and Christ will s on you." 2213
Php 2:15 in which you s like stars in the universe 5743
Rev 18:23 of a lamp will never s in you again. 5743
   21:23 not need the sun or the moon to s on it, 5743

SHINES (5) [SHINE]

Ps 50: 2 From Zion, perfect in beauty, God s forth. 3649
Pr 13: 9 The light of the righteous s brightly, 8523
Isa 62: 1 till her righteousness s out like the dawn, 3655
Lk 11:36 as when the light of a lamp s on you." 5894
Jn 1: 5 The light s in the darkness. 5743

SHINING (12) [SHINE]

2Ki 3:22 the sun was s on the water. 2436
Ps 68:13 its feathers with s gold." 3768
   148: 3 sun and moon, praise him, all you s stars. 240
Pr 4:18 s ever brighter till the full light of day. 239+2143+2256
Eze 28: 7 and wisdom and pierce your s splendor. 3650
   32: 8 All the s lights in the heavens I will darken 240
Lk 23:45 for the sun stopped s. 1722
Ac 10:30 a man in s clothes stood before me 3287
2Pe 1:19 as to a light s in a dark place, 5743
1Jn 2: 8 and the true light is already s. 5743
Rev 1:16 like the sun s in all its brilliance. 5743
   15: 6 They were dressed in clean, s linen 3287

SHION (1)

Jos 19:19 Hapharaim, S, Anaharath, 8858

SHIP (28) [SHIP'S, SHIPS, SHIPWRIGHTS]

Pr 30:19 the way of a s on the high seas, 641
Isa 2:16 every trading s and every stately vessel 641+9576
   33:21 no mighty s will sail there. 7469
Jnh 1: 3 where he found a s bound for that port. 641
   1: 4 a violent storm arose that the s threatened 641
   1: 5 the cargo into the sea to lighten the s. NIH
Ac 20:13 on ahead to the s and sailed for Assos, 4450
   20:38 Then they accompanied him to the s. 4450
   21: 2 We found a s crossing over to Phoenicia, 4450
   21: 3 where our s was to unload its cargo. 4450
   21: 6 we went aboard the s, 4450
   27: 2 We boarded a s from Adramyttium about 4450
   27: 6 an Alexandrian s sailing for Italy and put us 4450
   27:10 to be disastrous and bring great loss to s 4450
   27:11 of the pilot and of the owner of the s. 3729
   27:15 The s was caught by the storm and could 4450
   27:17 under the s itself to hold it together. 4450
   27:17 the sea anchor and let the s be driven along. NIG
   27:22 only the s will be destroyed. 4450
   27:30 In an attempt to escape from the s, 4450
   27:31 "Unless these men stay with the s, 4450
   27:38 they lightened the s by throwing the grain 4450
   27:39 where they decided to run the s aground 4450
   27:41 But the s struck a sandbar and ran aground. 3730
   27:44 to get there on planks or on pieces of the s. 4450
   28:11 to sea in a s that had wintered in the island. 4450
   28:11 It was an Alexandrian s with the figurehead NIG
Rev 18:17 and all who travel by s, the sailors, 4434

SHIP'S (1) [SHIP]

Ac 27:19 they threw the s tackle overboard 4450

SHIPHI (1)

1Ch 4:37 and Ziza son of S, the son of Allon, 9181

SHIPHMITE (1)

1Ch 27:27 Zabdi the S was in charge of the produce of 9175

SHIPHRAH (1)

Ex 1:15 whose names were S and Puah, 9186

SHIPHTAN (1)

Nu 34:24 Kemuel son of S, the leader from the tribe 9154

SHIPMASTER (KJV) See CAPTAIN

SHIPMEN (KJV) See SAILORS

SHIPPING (KJV) See BOATS

SHIPS (30) [SHIP]

Ge 49:13 by the seashore and become a haven for s; 641
Nu 24:24 S will come from the shores of Kittim; 7469
      The LORD will send you back in s 641
Jdg 5:17 And Dan, why did he linger by the s? 641
1Ki   King Solomon also built s at Ezion Geber, 639
   10:11 (Hiram's s brought gold from Ophir, 639
   10:22 The king had a fleet of trading s at sea 639+9576
   10:22 at sea along with the s of Hiram. 639

SHIPWRECK – SHORTLY (column 1)

1Ki 22:48	a **fleet of trading** s to go to Ophir	641+9576
2Ch 8:18	And Hiram sent him s commanded	641
9:21	The king had a **fleet of trading** s manned	
	by Hiram's men.	641+2143+9576
20:36	He agreed with him to construct a **fleet of**	
	trading s.	641+2143+4200+9576
20:37	The s were wrecked and were not able	641
Ps 48: 7	like s of Tarshish shattered by an east wind.	641
104:26	There the s go to and fro, and the leviathan,	641
107:23	Others went out on the sea in s;	641
Pr 31:14	She is like the merchant s,	641
Isa 23: 1	Wail, O s of Tarshish!	641
23:14	Wail, you s of Tarshish!	641
43:14	in the s in which they took pride.	641
60: 9	in the lead are the s of Tarshish,	641
Eze 27: 9	All the s of the sea and their sailors	641
27:25	" 'The s of Tarshish serve as carriers	641
27:29	the oars will abandon their s;	641
30: 9	from me in s to frighten Cush out	7469
Da 11:30	S of the western coastlands will oppose him,	7469
11:40	and cavalry and a great **fleet of** s.	641
Jas 3: 4	Or take s as an example.	4450
Rev 8: 9	and a third of the s were destroyed.	4450
18:19	where all who had s on the sea became rich	4450

SHIPWRECK (1) [WRECKED]
Eze 27:27	the heart of the sea on the day of your s.	5147

SHIPWRECKED (2) [WRECKED]
2Co 11:25	once I was stoned, three times I was s,	3728
1Ti 1:19	and so have s their faith.	3728

SHIPWRIGHTS (2) [SHIP]
Eze 27: 9	on board as s to caulk your seams.	NIH
27:27	your mariners, seamen and s,	981+2616

SHISHA (1)
1Ki 4: 3	and Ahijah, sons of S—	8881

SHISHAK (7)
1Ki 11:40	but Jeroboam fled to Egypt, to S the king,	8882
14:25	S king of Egypt attacked Jerusalem.	8882
2Ch 12: 2	S king of Egypt attacked Jerusalem in	8882
12: 5	of S, and he said to them, "This is what	8882
12: 5	therefore, I now abandon you to S.' "	8882
12: 7	not be poured out on Jerusalem through S.	8882
12: 9	When S king of Egypt attacked Jerusalem,	8882

SHITRAI (1)
1Ch 27:29	S the Sharonite was in charge of the herds	8855

SHITTAH　See BETH SHITTAH

SHITTIM (4) [ABEL SHITTIM]
Nu 25: 1	While Israel was staying in S,	8850
Jos 2: 1	of Nun secretly sent two spies from S.	8850
3: 1	the Israelites set out from S and went to	8850
Mic 6: 5	Remember [your journey] from S to Gilgal,	8850

SHIVERS　(KJV) See PIECES

SHIZA (1)
1Ch 11:42	Adina son of S the Reubenite,	8862

SHOA (1)
Eze 23:23	the men of Pekod and S and Koa,	8778

SHOBAB (4)
2Sa 5:14	Shammua, S, Nathan, Solomon,	8744
1Ch 2:18	These were her sons: Jesher, S and Ardon.	8744
3: 5	Shammua, S, Nathan and Solomon.	8744
14: 4	Shammua, S, Nathan, Solomon,	8744

SHOBACH (2)
2Sa 10:16	they went to Helam, with S the commander	8747
10:18	He also struck down S the commander	8747

SHOBAI (2)
Ezr 2:42	Hatita and S 139	8662
Ne 7:45	Hatita and S 138	8662

SHOBAL (9)
Ge 36:20	Lotan, S, Zibeon, Anah,	8748
36:23	The sons of S: Alvan, Manahath,	8748
36:29	These were the Horite chiefs: Lotan, S,	8748
1Ch 1:38	The sons of Seir: Lotan, S, Zibeon, Anah,	8748
1:40	The sons of S: Alvan, Manahath,	8748
2:50	S the father of Kiriath Jearim,	8748
2:52	of S the father of Kiriath Jearim were:	8748
4: 1	Perez, Hezron, Carmi, Hur and S.	8748
4: 2	Reaiah son of S was the father of Jahath,	8748

SHOBEK (1)
Ne 10:24	Hallohesh, Pilha, S,	8749

SHOBI (1)
2Sa 17:27	S son of Nahash from Rabbah of	8661

SHOCHO, SHOCO　(KJV) See SOCO

SHOCHOH　(KJV) See SOCOH

SHOCKED (1) [SHOCKING, SHOCKS]
Eze 16:27	who were s by your lewd conduct.	4007

SHOCKING (1) [SHOCKED]
Jer 5:30	"A horrible and s **thing** has happened in	9136

SHOCKS (2) [SHOCKED]
Ex 22: 6	so that it burns s **of grain** or standing grain,	1538
Jdg 15: 5	He burned up the s and standing grain,	1538

SHOD　(KJV) See FITTED, SANDALS, WEAR

SHOE, SHOE'S, SHOES　(KJV) See SANDAL, SANDALED, SANDALS, UNSANDALED

SHOELATCHET　(KJV) See THONG

SHOHAM (1)
1Ch 24:27	Beno, S, Zaccur and Ibri.	8733

SHOMER (3)
2Ki 12:21	of Shimeath and Jehozabad son of S.	9071
1Ch 7:32	S and Hotham and of their sister Shua.	9071
7:34	The sons of S: Ahi, Rohgah, Hubbah	9071

SHONE (6) [SHINE]
Dt 33: 2	he s **forth** from Mount Paran.	3649
Job 29: 3	when his lamp s upon my head and	2145
Mt 17: 2	His face s like the sun,	3290
Lk 2: 9	and the glory of the Lord s **around** them,	4334
Ac 12: 7	an angel of the Lord appeared and a light s	3290
Rev 21:11	It s **with** the **glory** of God,	1518+2400

SHOOK (18) [SHAKE]
Jdg 5: 4	the earth s, the heavens poured,	8321
1Sa 4: 5	a great shout that the ground s.	2101
14:15	and raiding parties—and the ground s.	8074
2Sa 22: 8	the foundations of the heavens s;	8074
1Ki 1:40	so that the ground s with the sound.	1324
Ne 5:13	I also s **out** the folds of my robe and said,	5850
Ps 18: 7	and the foundations of the mountains s;	8074
68: 8	the earth s, the heavens poured down rain,	8321
Isa 6: 4	and thresholds s and the temple was filled	5675
14:16	"Is this the man **who** s the earth	8074
Hab 3: 6	He stood, and s the earth;	4571
Mt 27:51	The earth s and the rocks split.	4940
28: 4	so afraid of him that **they** s and became	4940
Mk 1:26	The evil spirit s the man **violently**	5057
Ac 13:51	So they s the dust **from** their feet in protest	1759
18: 6	he s **out** his clothes in protest and said	1759
28: 5	But Paul s the snake **off** into the fire	701
Heb 12:26	At that time his voice s the earth,	4888

SHOOT (24) [SHOOTING, SHOOTS, SHOT]
1Sa 20:20	I will s three arrows to the side of it,	3721
20:36	"Run and find the arrows I s."	3721
2Sa 11:20	Didn't you know they would s **arrows** from	3721
2Ki 13:17	"S!" Elisha said, and he shot.	3721
19:32	not enter this city or s an arrow here.	3721
1Ch 12: 2	to s arrows or to sling stones	928+2021+8008
2Ch 26:15	and on the corner defenses to s arrows	3721
Job 41:19	from his mouth; sparks of fire s **out**.	4880
Ps 11: 2	they set their arrows against the strings to s	3721
64: 4	They s from ambush at the innocent man;	3721
64: 4	they s at him suddenly, without fear.	3721
64: 7	But God will s them with arrows;	3721
144: 6	s your arrows and rout them.	8938
Isa 11: 1	A s will come up from the stump of Jesse;	2643
37:33	not enter this city or s an arrow here.	3721
53: 2	He grew up before him like a **tender** s,	3437
60:21	They are the s I have planted,	5916
Jer 9: 3	**make ready** their tongue like a bow, **to** s	2005
50:14	S at her! Spare no arrows,	3343
Eze 5:16	When I s at you with my deadly and	8938
5:16	I will s to destroy you.	8938
17: 4	he broke off its topmost s and carried it	3566
17:22	I myself will take a s from the very top **of**	7550
Ro 11:17	and you, though a **wild olive** s,	66

SHOOTING (2) [SHOOT]
1Sa 20:20	as though I were s at a target.	8938
Pr 26:18	a madman s firebrands or deadly arrows	3721

SHOOTS (12) [SHOOT]
2Ki 19:26	like **tender** green s,	3764
Job 8:16	spreading its s over the garden;	3438
14: 7	and its **new** s will not fail.	3438

Job 14: 9	the scent of water it will bud and put forth s	7908
15:30	a flame will wither his s,	3438
Ps 80:11	its s as far as the River.	3438
128: 3	be like olive s around your table.	9277
Isa 16: 8	Their s spread out and went as far as	8943
18: 5	he will cut off the s with pruning knives,	2360
37:27	like **tender** green s, like grass sprouting	3764
Eze 17:22	from its topmost s and plant it on a high	3438
Hos 14: 6	his **young** s will grow.	3438

SHOPHACH (2)
1Ch 19:16	with S the commander of Hadadezer's army	8791
19:18	also killed S the commander of their army.	8791

SHOPHAN　See ATROTH SHOPHAN

SHORE (18) [ASHORE, SHORES]
Ex 14:30	the Egyptians lying dead on the s.	3542+8557
1Ki 9:26	on the s of the Red Sea.	8557
Eze 27:29	and all the seamen will stand on the s.	824
47:10	Fishermen will stand along **the** s;	2257S
Zep 2:11	The nations on every s will worship him,	362
Mt 13: 2	while all the people stood on the s.	129
13:48	the fishermen pulled it up on the s.	129
Mk 4: 1	while all the people were along the s at	1178
Lk 5: 3	and asked him to put out a little from s.	1178
5: 3	So they pulled their boats up on s,	1178
Jn 6: 1	**to the far** s of the Sea of Galilee (that is,	4305
6:21	and immediately the boat reached the s	1178
6:22	the crowd that had stayed on the **opposite** s	4305
21: 4	Early in the morning, Jesus stood on the s,	129
21: 8	for they were not far from s,	1178
Ac 27:13	and sailed **along the** s of Crete.	839
28: 1	Once safely on s, we found out that	NIG
Rev 13: 1	And the dragon stood on the s of the sea.	302

SHORELANDS (1) [LAND]
Eze 27:28	The s will quake when your seamen cry out.	4494

SHORES (4) [SHORE]
Nu 24:24	Ships will come from the s of Kittim;	3338
Est 10: 1	throughout the empire, to its **distant** s.	362+3542
Ps 72:10	and of **distant** s will bring tribute to him;	362
97: 1	let the distant s rejoice.	362

SHORN (1) [SHEAR]
SS 4: 2	Your teeth are like a flock of **sheep just** s,	7892

SHORT (33) [SHORTENED, SHORTER, SHORTLY]
Nu 11:23	"Is the LORD's arm **too** s?	7918
Ru 2: 7	except for a s rest in the shelter."	5071
1Sa 2:31	when I will cut s your strength and	1548
21:15	Am I so s of madmen that you have	2894
2Sa 16: 1	When David had gone a s distance beyond	5071
19:36	the Jordan with the king for a s distance,	5071
Job 17: 1	My spirit is broken, my days **are** cut s,	2403
Ps 89:45	You have cut s the days of his youth;	7918
102:23	he cut s my days.	7918
Pr 10:27	but the years of the wicked **are** cut s.	7918
Isa 28:20	The bed **is** too s to stretch out on,	7918
29:17	**In a very** s time, will not	4663+5071+6388
50: 2	Was my arm too s to ransom you?	7918+7918
59: 1	the arm of the LORD is not too s to save,	7918
Mic 6:10	your ill-gotten treasures and the s ephah,	8137
Mt 13:21	since he has no root, he lasts **only a** s **time**.	4672
24:22	If those days **had** not **been** cut s,	3143
Mk 4:17	they have no root, they last **only a** s **time**.	4672
13:20	If the Lord **had** not **cut** s those days,	3143
Lk 19: 3	but being a s **man** he could not,	2461+3625+3836
Jn 7:33	Jesus said, "I am with you for only a s time,	3625
11: 8	"a **while ago** the Jews tried to stone you,	3814
Ac 26:28	that in such a s time you can persuade me to	3900
26:29	Paul replied, "S **time** or long—	1877+3900
27:28	A s time later they took soundings again	1099
Ro 3:23	for all have sinned and **fall** s of the glory	5728
1Co 7:29	What I mean, brothers, is that the time is s.	5319
1Th 2:17	we were torn away from you for a s time	6052
Heb 4: 1	of you be found to **have fallen** s of it.	5728
11:25	to enjoy the pleasures of sin **for a** s **time**.	4672
13:22	for I have written you only a s letter.	1099+1328
Rev 12:12	because he knows that his time **is** s."	2400+3900
20: 3	After that, he must be set free **for** a s time.	3625

SHORT-SIGHTED　(Anglicized) See NEARSIGHTED

SHORTCOMINGS (1)
Ge 41: 9	"Today I am reminded of my s.	2628

SHORTENED (2) [SHORT]
Mt 24:22	the sake of the elect those days **will be** s.	3143
Mk 13:20	whom he has chosen, he has s them.	3143

SHORTER (1) [SHORT]
Ex 13:17	the Philistine country, though that was s.	7940

SHORTLY (2) [SHORT]
Jer 28:12	S after the prophet Hananiah had broken	339

Mk 11: 3 Lord needs it and will send it back here **s.**'" *2317*

SHOT (9) [SHOOT]

Ge	49:23	*they* **s** at him with hostility.	8046
Ex	19:13	He shall surely be stoned or **s with arrows;**	3721+3721
1Sa	20:36	As the boy ran, he **s** an arrow beyond him.	3721
2Sa	11:24	Then the archers **s arrows** at your servants	3721
	22:15	He **s** arrows and scattered [the enemies],	8938
2Ki	9:24	Then Jehu drew his bow and **s** Joram	5782
	13:17	"Shoot!" Elisha said, and he **s.**	3721
2Ch	35:23	Archers **s** King Josiah,	3721
Ps	18:14	He **s** his arrows and scattered [the enemies],	8938

SHOULD (371) [SHOULDN'T]

Ge	20: 9	have done things to me that **s** not **be done.**"	AIT
	27:45	Why **s** I **lose** both of you in one day?"	AIT
	29:15	**s** you **work for** me for nothing?	AIT
	29:15	Tell me what your wages **s** be."	NIH
	34: 7	a **thing that s** not **be done.**	AIT
	34:31	"She have **treated** our sister like	AIT
	38:18	He said, "What pledge **s I give** you?"	AIT
	41:35	*They s* **collect** all the food	AIT
	41:36	This food **s** be held in reserve for	AIT
	46:34	you **s answer,** 'Your servants have tended	AIT
	47:15	Why **s we die** before your eyes?	AIT
	47:19	Why **s we perish** before your eyes—	AIT
Ex	3:11	that **I s** go to Pharaoh and bring	AIT
	5: 2	that **I s** **obey** him and let Israel go?	AIT
	16: 7	that **you s grumble** against us?"	AIT
	32:11	"why **s** your anger **burn**	AIT
	32:12	Why **s** the Egyptians **say,**	AIT
Lev	10:18	you **s** have **eaten** the goat in	AIT
	13:16	**S** the raw flesh change and **turn**	AIT
	24:12	of the LORD be **made clear** to them.	AIT
	27:10	if he **s substitute** one animal for another,	AIT
Nu	9: 7	**s** we **be kept** from presenting the LORD's	AIT
	10:31	You know where we **s camp** in the desert,	AIT
	13:30	"We **s** go up and take possession of	6590+6590
	14: 4	We **s choose** a leader and go back to Egypt."	AIT
	15:34	it was not clear what **s** be done to him.	AIT
	16:11	Who is Aaron that **you s grumble**	AIT
	16:40	of Aaron **s come** to burn incense before	AIT
	20: 4	that we and our livestock **s die** here?	AIT
	23:19	God is not a man, that he **s lie,**	AIT
	23:19	nor a son of man, that he **s change his mind.**	AIT
	27: 4	**s** our father's name **disappear** from his clan	AIT
Dt	1:33	and to show you the way **you s go.**	AIT
	5:25	But now, why **s we die?**	AIT
	15: 4	However, *there s* be no poor among you,	AIT
	16:16	No man **s appear** before the LORD	AIT
	20:19	that **you s besiege** them?	AIT
	28:68	on a journey I said you **s** never **make again.**	AIT
Jdg	8: 6	Why **s we give** bread to your troops?"	AIT
	8:15	Why **s we give** bread to your exhausted men?	AIT
	9: 9	olive tree answered, 'S I **give up** my oil,	AIT
	9:11	the fig tree replied, 'S I **give up** my fruit,	AIT
	9:13	the vine answered, 'S I **give up** my wine,	AIT
	9:28	that we **s** be **subject to** him?	AIT
	9:28	Why **s we serve** Abimelech?	AIT
	9:32	the night you and your men **s come** and lie	AIT
	9:38	'Who is Abimelech that we **s** be **subject to**	AIT
	11:34	who **s come out** to meet him	AIT
	14:16	he replied, "so *why s* I **explain** it to you?"	AIT
	20:38	that they **s send up** a great cloud of smoke	AIT
	21: 3	**s** one tribe be **missing** from Israel	AIT
	21: 5	**s certainly be put to death.**	AIT
Ru	3: 1	**s I** not **try to find** a home for you,	AIT
	4: 4	**s bring** the matter to your **attention**	AIT
1Sa	6: 2	Tell us how we **s send** it **back** to its place."	AIT
	6: 4	"What guilt offering **s we send** to him?"	AIT
	9:13	*you s* **find** him about this time."	AIT
	12:23	that **I s sin** against the LORD by failing	AIT
	14:45	But the men said to Saul, "S Jonathan **die**—	AIT
	15:29	he is not a man, that he **s change his mind.**"	AIT
	17:26	that he **s defy** the armies of the living God?	AIT
	18:18	that **I s become** the king's son-in-law?"	AIT
	19:17	Why **s I kill** you?' "	AIT
	20:32	**s** he **be put to death?**	AIT
	24: 6	that **I s do** such a thing to my master,	AIT
	25:11	Why **s I take** my bread and water,	AIT
	26:11	But the LORD forbid that **I s lay** a hand	AIT
	27: 5	Why **s** your servant **live** in the royal city	AIT
2Sa	2:22	Why **s I strike** you down?	AIT
	3:33	"S Abner have **died** as the lawless die?	AIT
	4:11	**s I** not now **demand** his blood from your	AIT
	9: 8	that **you s notice** a dead dog like me?"	AIT
	12:23	But now that he is dead, why **s I fast?**	AIT
	13:12	Such a thing **s** not **be done** in Israel!	AIT
	13:25	"All of us **s** not **go;**	AIT
	13:26	"Why **s** he **go with you?**"	AIT
	13:32	"My lord **s** not **think** that they killed all	AIT
	13:33	the king **s** not be **concerned about**	AIT
	15:19	"Why **s you come** along with us?	AIT
	16: 9	**s** this dead dog **curse** my lord	AIT
	16:19	Furthermore, whom **s I serve?**	AIT
	16:19	**S** I not serve the son?	NIH
	16:20	What **s we do?**"	AIT
	17: 6	**S** we **do** what he says?	AIT
	17: 9	If he **s attack** your troops first,	AIT
	19:11	the elders of Judah, 'Why **s you** be the last	AIT
	19:12	So why **s you** be the last to bring back	AIT
	19:22	**S** anyone **be put to death** in Israel today?	AIT
	19:34	that **I s** go up *to* Jerusalem with the king?	AIT
	19:35	Why **s** your servant **be** an added burden	AIT

2Sa	19:36	but why **s** the king **reward** me *in* this way?	AIT
	24:13	think it over and decide how **I s answer**	AIT
1Ki	1:27	without letting his servants know who **s sit**	AIT
	12: 9	How **s we answer** these people who say	AIT
	20:11	'One who puts on his armor **s** not **boast**	AIT
	20:42	a man I had **determined s die.**	3051
	21: 3	"The LORD forbid that **I s give** you	AIT
	22: 8	"The king **s** not **say** that,"	AIT
2Ki	6:33	Why **s I wait** for the LORD any longer?"	AIT
	7: 2	*even if* the LORD **s open** the floodgates	AIT
	7:19	*even if* the LORD **s open** the floodgates	AIT
	13:19	"You **s** have **struck** the ground five	AIT
1Ch	11:19	"God forbid that **I s do** this!"	AIT
	11:19	"S I **drink** the blood of these men who went	AIT
	12:32	the times and knew what Israel **s do**—	AIT
	21: 3	Why **s he bring** guilt on Israel?"	AIT
	21:12	how **s I answer** the one who sent me."	AIT
	22: 5	for the LORD **s** be of **great** magnificence	AIT
	29:14	we **s** be **able** to give as generously as this?	AIT
2Ch	10: 9	How **s we answer** these people who say	AIT
	18: 7	"The king **s** not **say** that,"	AIT
	19: 2	"S you **help** the wicked and love those who	AIT
	24: 9	in Judah and Jerusalem that they **s bring** to	AIT
	32: 4	"Why **s** the kings of Assyria **come**	AIT
Ezr	4:12	The king **s know** that the Jews who came up	AIT
	4:13	the king **s know** that if this city is built	AIT
	5: 8	The king **s know** that we went to the district	AIT
	7:23	Why **s there** be wrath against the realm of	AIT
Ne	2: 3	Why **s** my face not **look sad**	AIT
	6:11	"S a man like me **run away?**	AIT
	6:11	Or **s** one like me go into the temple	AIT
	7:65	until there **s** be a priest ministering with	NIH
	8:15	and that they **s proclaim** this word	AIT
	13: 1	or Moabite **s** ever be **admitted** into	AIT
Est	1:22	in each people's tongue that every man **s** be	AIT
	6: 6	"What **s** be **done** for the man whom the king	AIT
	9:25	**s come back** onto his own head,	AIT
	9:25	he and his sons **s** be **hanged** on the gallows.	AIT
	9:27	**s** without **fail** observe these two days every	AIT
	9:28	These days **s** be **remembered** and observed	AIT
	9:28	of Purim **s** never **cease** to be celebrated by	AIT
	9:28	**s** the memory of them **die out**	AIT
Job	4: 6	**S** not your piety be your confidence	NIH
	6:11	that **I s still hope?**	AIT
	6:11	What prospects, that **I s** be **patient?**	AIT
	6:14	"A despairing man **s** have the devotion	NIH
	9:29	why **s I struggle** in vain?	AIT
	19:29	*you s* **fear** the sword yourselves;	AIT
	21: 4	Why **s I** not **be impatient?**	AIT
	21:15	Who is the Almighty, that we **s serve** him?	AIT
	32: 7	I thought, 'Age **s speak;**	AIT
	32: 7	advanced years **s teach** wisdom.'	AIT
	33: 7	No fear of me **s alarm** you,	AIT
	33: 7	nor **s** my hand **be heavy** upon you.	AIT
	34:23	that they **s come** before him for judgment.	AIT
	34:33	**S** God then **reward** you on your terms,	AIT
	37:19	"Tell us what we **s say** to him;	AIT
	37:20	**S** he be **told** that I want to speak?	AIT
	40:23	the Jordan **s surge** against his mouth.	AIT
Ps	32: 8	and teach you in the way **you s go;**	AIT
	49: 5	Why **s I fear** when evil days come,	AIT
	49: 9	he **s live** on forever and not see decay.	AIT
	79:10	Why **s** the nations **say,**	AIT
	143: 8	Show me the way **I s go,**	AIT
Pr	5:16	**S** your **springs overflow**	AIT
	16:10	and his mouth **s** not **betray** justice.	AIT
	22: 6	a child **in the way** he **s go,**	2006+6584+7023
Ecc	5: 6	Why **s** God **be angry** at what you say	AIT
	7: 2	the living **s take** this to heart.	AIT
SS	1: 7	Why **s I** be like a veiled woman beside	AIT
Isa	1: 5	Why **s you** be **beaten** anymore?	AIT
	8:19	**s** not a people **inquire of** their God?	AIT
	48:10	who directs you in the way **you s go.**	AIT
	53: 2	in his appearance that we **s desire** him.	AIT
	57: 6	In the light of these things, **s I relent?**	AIT
Jer	3: 1	**s** he **return** to her again?	AIT
	5: 7	"Why **s I forgive** you?	AIT
	5: 9	**S I** not **punish** them for this?"	AIT
	5: 9	"S I not **avenge** myself on such a nation	AIT
	5:22	**S you** not **fear** me?"	AIT
	5:22	"S you not **tremble** in my presence?	AIT
	5:29	**S I** not **punish** them for this?"	AIT
	5:29	"S I not **avenge** myself on such a nation	AIT
	9: 9	**S I** not **punish** them for this?"	AIT
	9: 9	"S I not **avenge** myself on such a nation	AIT
	10: 7	Who **s** not **revere** you,	AIT
	13:12	Every wineskin **s be filled** *with* wine.'	AIT
	13:12	that every wineskin **s be filled** *with* wine?'	AIT
	18:20	**S good be repaid** with evil?	AIT
	26:11	"This man **s** be sentenced to death	NIH
	26:16	"This man **s** not be sentenced to death!"	NIH
	27:17	Why **s** this city **become** a ruin?	AIT
	29:26	*you s* **put** any madman who acts like	AIT
	32:35	that they **s do** such a detestable thing and	AIT
	38: 4	**s** be put to death.	AIT
	40:15	Why **s** he **take** your life and cause all	AIT
	42: 3	where we **s go** and what we **should do.**	AIT
	42: 3	where we should go and what we **s do.**"	AIT
	45: 5	**S** you then **seek** great things for yourself?	AIT
	49:12	**s** you **go unpunished?**	AIT
La	2:20	**S** women **eat** their offspring,	AIT
	2:20	the priest and prophet **be killed**	AIT
	3:39	Why **s** any living man **complain**	AIT
Eze	13:19	have killed those who **s** not **have died**	AIT
	13:19	and have spared those who **s** not **live.**	AIT
	14: 3	**S I** let them **inquire of** me at all?	AIT

Eze	16:16	*Such things* **s** not **happen,**	AIT
	16:16	nor **s** they ever **occur.**	AIT
	33:25	**s** you then **possess** the land?	AIT
	33:26	**S** you then **possess** the land?'	AIT
	34: 2	**S** not shepherds **take care of** the flock?	AIT
Da	1:10	Why **s** he see you looking worse than	AIT
	6: 7	that the king **s issue** an edict and enforce	AIT
Hos	1: 6	that **I s** be **at all forgive** them.	AIT
Joel	2:17	Why **s** they **say** among the peoples,	AIT
Ob	1:12	You **s** not **look down on** your brother	AIT
	1:13	You **s** not **march** through the gates	AIT
	1:14	You **s** not **wait** at the crossroads to cut	AIT
Jnh	1:11	"What **s we do** to you to make the sea calm	AIT
	4:11	**S** I not **be concerned** about that great city?"	AIT
Mic	2: 7	**S** it **be said,** O house of Jacob:	AIT
	3: 1	**S** you not **know** justice.	AIT
Zec	7: 3	"S I **mourn** and fast in the fifth month,	AIT
Mal	1:13	**s I accept** them from your hands?"	AIT
		and from his mouth *men* **s seek** instruction	AIT
Mt	6: 9	"This, then, is how you **s pray:**	*AIT*
	11: 3	or **s we expect** someone else?"	*AIT*
	18:14	that any of these little ones **s be lost.**	AIT
	18:34	until he **s pay back** all he owed.	AIT
	19:12	The one who can accept this **s accept** it."	AIT
	23:23	You **s** have practiced the latter,	*1256*
	25:27	you **s** have put my money on deposit with	*1256*
Mk	6:12	and preached that *people* **s repent.**	*AIT*
	12:15	**S** we **pay** or shouldn't we?"	AIT
Lk	1:43	that the mother of my Lord **s come** to me?	*AIT*
	2: 1	that a **census s be taken** of the entire	*AIT*
	3:10	"What **s we do** then?" the crowd asked.	*AIT*
	3:11	"The man with two tunics **s share** with	*AIT*
	3:11	and the one who has food **s do** the same."	*AIT*
	3:12	"Teacher," they asked, "what **s we do?**"	*AIT*
	3:14	"And what **s we do?**"	*AIT*
	7:19	or **s we expect** someone else?"	*AIT*
	7:20	or **s we expect** someone else?' "	*AIT*
	11:42	You **s** have practiced the latter	*1256*
	12: 5	But I will show you whom *you s* **fear:**	AIT
	12:12	at that time what *you* **s say.**	*1256*
	13: 7	Why **s** it **use up** the soil?'	*AIT*
	13:16	Then **s** not this woman,	*1256*
	17:10	**s say,** 'We are unworthy servants;	*AIT*
	17:31	**s go down** to get them.	*AIT*
	17:31	no one in the field **s** go back for anything.	*AIT*
	18: 1	to show them that they **s** always pray and	*1256*
	22:26	greatest among you **s be** like the youngest,	*AIT*
	22:49	"Lord, **s we strike** with our swords?"	*AIT*
Jn	3: 7	You **s** not be **surprised** at my saying,	*AIT*
	11:57	he **s report** it so that they might arrest him.	*AIT*
	12: 7	that *she* **s save** this perfume for the day	*AIT*
	12:46	so that no one who believes in me **s stay**	*AIT*
	13:14	you also **s** wash one another's feet.	*4053*
	13:15	an example that *you* **s do** as I have done	*AIT*
Ac	4:28	and will had decided beforehand **s happen.**	*AIT*
	10:28	that **I s** not **call** any man impure	*AIT*
	15:19	that *we* **s** not **make it difficult for**	*AIT*
	15:20	Instead *we* **s write** to them,	*AIT*
	17:26	that *they* **s inhabit** the whole earth;	*AIT*
	17:26	and the exact places where they **s** live.	NIG
	17:29	*we* **s** not think that the divine being is	*4053*
	21:25	that they **s abstain from** food sacrificed	*AIT*
	24:20	who are here **s state** what crime they found	*AIT*
	26: 8	Why **s** any of you **consider** it incredible	*AIT*
	26:20	I preached that they **s repent** and turn	NIG
	27:12	the majority decided that we **s sail** on,	*AIT*
	27:21	"Men, you **s** have taken my advice not	*1256*
Ro	2:22	that people **s** not **commit adultery,**	*AIT*
	6: 6	that *we* **s** no longer **be slaves to sin—**	*AIT*
	11:35	*that* God **s repay** him?"	*AIT*
	14: 5	Each one **s** be **fully convinced** in his own	*AIT*
	15: 2	of us **s please** his neighbor for his good,	*AIT*
1Co	3:10	But each one **s be careful** how he builds.	*AIT*
	3:18	he **s become** a "fool" so that he may	
		become wise.	*AIT*
	7: 2	each man **s have** his own wife,	*AIT*
	7: 3	The husband **s fulfill** his marital duty	*AIT*
	7: 9	*they* **s marry,** for it is better to marry than	*AIT*
	7:17	**s retain the place in life** that the Lord	*AIT*
	7:18	He **s** not **become uncircumcised.**	*AIT*
	7:18	He **s** not **be circumcised.**	*AIT*
	7:20	Each one **s remain** in the situation which	*AIT*
	7:24	**s remain** in the situation God called him to.	*AIT*
	7:29	now on those who have wives **s live** as if	*AIT*
	7:36	he **s do** as he wants.	*AIT*
	7:36	*They* **s get married.**	*AIT*
	9:14	**s receive** *their* **living** from the gospel.	*AIT*
	10: 8	**s** not **commit sexual immorality,**	*AIT*
	10: 9	*We* **s** not **test** the Lord,	*AIT*
	10:24	Nobody **s seek** his own good,	*AIT*
	10:29	For why **s** my freedom **be judged**	*AIT*
	11: 6	*she* **s** have her hair **cut off;**	*AIT*
	11: 6	**she s cover** her head.	*AIT*
	11:34	If anyone is hungry, he **s eat** at home,	*AIT*
	12:15	If the foot **s say,** "Because I am not a hand,	*AIT*
	12:16	And if the ear **s say,** "Because I am not	*AIT*
	12:25	so that *there* **s** be no division in the body,	*AIT*
	12:25	but that its parts **s** have equal **concern**	*AIT*
	14:13	in a tongue **s pray** that he may interpret	*AIT*
	14:27	**s** speak, one at a time,	NIG
	14:28	**s keep quiet** in the church and speak	*AIT*
	14:29	Two or three prophets **s speak,**	*AIT*
	14:29	the others **s weigh carefully** what is said.	*AIT*
	14:30	the first speaker **s stop.**	*AIT*
	14:34	women **s** *remain* silent in the churches.	*AIT*
	14:35	*they* **s ask** their own husbands at home;	*AIT*
	14:40	But everything **s** be **done** in a fitting	*AIT*

1Co	16: 2	each one of you *s* **set aside** a sum of money	AIT
	16:11	No one, then, *s* **refuse to accept** him.	AIT
2Co	2: 3	so that when I came I *s* not be **distressed**	AIT
	5:15	that those who live *s* no longer **live**	AIT
	9: 3	in this matter *s* not **prove hollow**,	AIT
	9: 7	Each man *s* give what he has decided	NIG
	10: 7	he *s* **consider** again that we belong	AIT
	10:11	Such people *s* **realize** that what we are	AIT
	12: 6	Even if I *s* **choose** to boast,	AIT
	12:14	children *s* not **have** to save up	4053
Gal	1: 8	from heaven *s* **preach a gospel** other than	AIT
	2: 9	They agreed that we *s* go to the Gentiles.	NIG
	2:10	that we *s* **continue to remember** the poor,	NIG
	3:23	locked up until faith *s* be revealed.	3516
	6: 1	you who are spiritual *s* **restore** him gently.	AIT
	6: 4	Each one *s* test his own actions.	AIT
	6: 5	for each one *s* **carry** his own load.	AIT
Eph	3:10	of God *s* be made **known** to the rulers	AIT
	5: 4	Nor *s* there be obscenity,	NIG
	5:24	so also wives *s* submit to their husbands	NIG
	6:20	Pray that I may declare it fearlessly, as I *s*.	1256
Php	2: 4	you *s* **look** not only to your own interests,	AIT
	2: 5	Your **attitude** *s* be the same as that	AIT
	2:10	that at the name of Jesus every knee *s* **bow**,	2828
	2:18	So you too *s* be **glad** and rejoice with me.	AIT
	3:15	are mature *s* **take such a view of things.**	AIT
Col	4: 1	that is how *you s* **stand firm** in the Lord,	AIT
	4: 4	Pray that I may proclaim it clearly, as I *s*.	1256
1Th	4: 3	It is God's will that you be sanctified:	NIG
	4: 3	that you *s* avoid sexual immorality;	NIG
	4: 4	of you *s* learn to control his own body in	NIG
	4: 6	in this matter no one *s* wrong his brother	NIG
	5: 4	in darkness so that this day *s* **surprise** you	AIT
1Ti	2:11	A woman *s* **learn** in quietness	AIT
	5: 4	these *s* **learn** first of all to put their religion	AIT
	5:16	she *s* **help** them and not let the church	NIG
	6: 1	of slavery *s* **consider** their masters worthy	AIT
2Ti	2: 6	The hardworking farmer *s* be the first	1256
	4:15	*You* too *s* be **on your guard against**	AIT
Tit	2:15	These, then, are the things *you s* **teach.**	AIT
Heb	2:10	*s* **make** the author of their salvation **perfect**	AIT
	12: 9	How much more *s we* **submit** to the Father	AIT
	13: 4	Marriage *s* be honored by all,	NIG
Jas	1: 5	If any of you lacks wisdom, *he s* **ask** God,	AIT
	1: 7	That man *s* not **think** he will receive anything from the Lord;	AIT
	1:10	But the one who is rich *s* take pride	NIG
	1:13	When tempted, no one *s* **say**,	AIT
	1:19	Everyone *s* be quick to listen,	AIT
	3: 1	Not many of you presume to be teachers,	NIG
	3:10	My brothers, this *s* not be.	5973
	5:13	Is any one of you in trouble? *He s* **pray.**	AIT
	5:14	*He s* **call** the elders of the church to pray	AIT
	5:19	if one of you *s* **wander** from the truth	AIT
	5:19	the truth and someone *s* **bring** him **back**,	AIT
1Pe	2:15	doing good *you s* **silence** the ignorant **talk**	AIT
	2:21	that *you s* **follow** in his steps.	AIT
	3: 3	Your beauty *s* not **come** from outward	AIT
	3: 4	Instead, it *s* be that of your inner self,	NIG
	3:14	But even if *you s* **suffer** for what is right,	AIT
	4:10	Each one *s* use whatever gift he has received	NIG
	4:11	he *s* do it as one speaking the very words	NIG
	4:11	he *s* do it with the strength God provides,	NIG
	4:15	it *s* not be as a murderer or thief	NIG
	4:19	to God's will *s* **commit** themselves	AIT
1Jn	3: 1	that *we s* be **called** children of God!	AIT
	3:11	*We s* **love** one another.	AIT
	5:16	he *s* **pray** and God will give him life.	AIT
	5:16	I am not saying that *he s* **pray** about that.	AIT

SHOULDER (25) [SHOULDERS]

Ge	24:15	Rebekah came out with her jar on her *s*.	8900
	24:45	Rebekah came out, with her jar on her *s*.	8900
	24:46	"She quickly lowered her jar from her *s*	NIH
	49:15	he will bend his *s* to the burden and submit	8900
Ex	28: 7	It is to have two *s* **pieces** attached to two	4190
	28:12	and fasten them on the *s* **pieces** *of* the ephod	4190
	28:25	attaching them to the *s* **pieces** *of* the ephod	4190
	28:27	attach them to the bottom of the *s* **pieces**	4190
	39: 4	They made *s* **pieces** for the ephod,	4190
	39: 7	Then they fastened them on the *s* **pieces** *of*	4190
	39:18	attaching them to the *s* **pieces** *of* the ephod	4190
	39:20	to the bottom of the *s* **pieces** on the front of	4190
Nu	6:19	the priest is to place in his hands a boiled *s*	2432
Dt	18: 3	the *s*, the jowls and the inner parts.	2432
Jos	4: 5	Each of you is to take up a stone on his *s*,	8900
Job	31:22	then let my arm fall from the *s*,	8900
	31:36	Surely I would wear it on my *s*,	8900
Isa	22:22	I will place on his *s* the key to the house	8900
Eze	12: 6	Put them on your *s* as they are watching	4190
	12:12	among them will put his things on his *s*	4190
	24: 4	the choice pieces—the leg and the *s*.	4190
	29:18	and every *s* made raw.	4190
	34:21	Because you shove with flank and *s*,	4190
Zep	3: 9	the LORD and serve him *s* **to shoulder.**	285+8900
	3: 9	the LORD and serve him **shoulder to** *s*.	285+8900

SHOULDERS (24) [SHOULDER]

Ge	9:23	took a garment and laid it across their *s*;	8900
	21:14	on her *s* and then sent her off with the boy.	8900
Ex	12:34	on their *s* in kneading troughs wrapped	8900
	28:12	on his *s* as a memorial before the LORD.	4190
Nu	7: 9	because they were to carry on their *s*	4190
Dt	33:12	one the LORD loves rests between his *s*."	4190
Jdg	9:48	some branches which he lifted to his *s*.	8900

Jdg	16: 3	He lifted them to his *s* and carried them to	4190
2Ki	6:31	of Shaphat remains on his *s* today!"	NIH
	9:24	and shot Joram between the *s*.	2432
1Ch	15:15	the ark of God with the poles on their *s*,	4190
2Ch	35: 3	It is not to be carried about on your *s*.	4190
Ne	3: 5	but their nobles would not put their *s* to	7418
Ps	81: 6	"I removed the burden from their *s*;	8900
Isa	9: 4	the bar across their *s*, the rod of their	8900
	9: 6	and the government will be on his *s*.	8900
	10:27	from your *s*, their yoke from your neck;	8900
	14:25	and his burden removed from their *s*."	8900
	46: 7	They lift it to their *s* and carry it;	4190
	49:22	and carry your daughters on their *s*.	4190
Eze	12: 7	carrying them on my *s* while they watched.	4190
	29: 7	you splintered and you tore open their *s*;	4190
Mt	23: 4	up heavy loads and put them on men's *s*,	6049
Lk	15: 5	when he finds it, he joyfully puts it on his *s*	6049

SHOULDN'T (7) [NOT, SHOULD]

2Sa	19:21	"S Shimei be put to death for this?	4202
Ne	5: 9	S you walk in the fear of our God to avoid	4202
Mt	18:33	S you have had mercy on your fellow	1256+4024
Mk	12:15	Should we pay or *s* we?"	3590
Ac	8:36	Why *s* I be baptized?"	3266
1Co	5: 2	S you rather have been filled with grief	4049
	9:12	*s* we have it all the more?	4024

SHOUT (61) [SHOUTED, SHOUTING, SHOUTS]

Nu	23:21	the *s* of the King is among them.	9558
Jos	6: 5	*have* all the people **give a** loud *s*;	8131+9558
	6:10	not say a word until the day I tell you to *s*	8131
	6:10	until the day I tell you to shout. Then *s!*"	8131
	6:16	Joshua commanded the people, "S!	8131
	6:20	when the people **gave a** loud *s*,	8131+9558
Jdg	7:18	from all around the camp blow yours and *s*,	606
1Sa	4: 5	**raised** such **a** great *s* that the ground	8131+9558
	17:52	of Israel and Judah surged forward with a *s*	8131
1Ki	1:34	Blow the trumpet and *s*,	606
	18:27	began to taunt them. "S louder!"	928+7754+7924
Ezr	3:11	all the people **gave a** great *s* of praise	8131+9558
Job	3: 7	may no *s* of joy be heard in it.	8265
	3:18	no longer hear the slave driver's *s*.	7754
	39: 7	he does not hear a driver's *s*.	9583
	39:25	the *s* of commanders and the battle cry.	8308
Ps	20: 5	We will *s* for joy when you are victorious	8264
	33: 3	play skillfully, and *s* for joy.	9558
	35:27	in my vindication *s* for joy and gladness;	8264
	47: 1	*s* to God with cries of joy.	8131
	60: 8	over Philistia I *s* in triumph."	8131
	65:13	*they s* for joy and sing.	8131
	66: 1	S with joy to God, all the earth!	8131
	71:23	My lips *will s* for joy when I sing praise	8264
	81: 1	*s* aloud to the God of Jacob!	8131
	95: 1	*let us s* aloud to the Rock	8131
	98: 4	S for joy to the LORD, all the earth,	8131
	98: 6	*s* for joy before the LORD, the King.	8264
	100: 1	S for joy to the LORD, all the earth.	8131
	108: 9	over Philistia I *s* in triumph."	8131
Isa	12: 6	S aloud and sing for joy, people of Zion,	7412
	13: 2	a banner on a bare hilltop, *s* to them;	7754+8123
	24:14	They raise their voices, *they s* for joy;	8264
	26:19	wake up and *s* for joy.	8264
	35: 2	it will rejoice greatly and *s* for joy.	8264
	35: 6	and the mute tongue *s* for joy.	8264
	40: 9	lift up your voice with a *s*, lift it up,	3946
	42: 2	He will not *s* or cry out,	7590
	42:11	*let them s* from the mountaintops.	7423
	42:13	*with a s* he will raise the battle cry	8131
	44:23	*s* aloud, O earth beneath.	8131
	49:13	S for joy, O heavens;	8264
	52: 8	together *they s* for joy.	8264
	54: 1	burst into song, *s* for joy,	7412
	58: 1	"S it aloud, do not hold back.	928+1744+7924
Jer	25:30	*He will s* like those who tread the grapes,	2116
	25:30	*s* against all who live on the earth.	6699
	31: 7	*s* for the foremost of the nations.	7412
	31:12	and *s* for joy on the heights of Zion;	8264
	49:29	*Men will s* to them, 'Terror on every side!'	7924
	50:15	S against her on every side!	8131
	51:14	and *they will s* in triumph over you.	2116+6702
	51:39	so that *they s* with laughter—	6600
	51:48	in them *will s* for joy over Babylon,	8264
La	2: 7	*a s* in the house of the LORD as on the day	7754
Eze	8:18	Although *they s* in my ears, I will not listen	1524+7754+7924
Zep	3:14	Sing, O Daughter of Zion; *s* aloud,	8131
Zec	2:10	"S and be glad, O Daughter of Zion.	8264
	9: 9	S, Daughter of Jerusalem!	8131
Mk	10:47	he began *to s*, "Jesus, Son of David,	3189
Rev	10: 3	*he gave a* loud *s* like the roar of a lion.	3189+5889

SHOUTED (53) [SHOUT]

Ge	41:43	and *men s* before him, "Make way!"	7924
Lev	9:24	*they s* for joy and fell facedown.	8264
Jos	6:20	When the trumpets sounded, the people *s*,	8131
Jdg	7:20	*they s*, "A sword for the LORD and for	7924
	9: 7	on the top of Mount Gerizim and *s* to them,	2256+5951+7754+7924
	16:25	While they were in high spirits, *they s*,	606
	18:23	As *they s* after them, the Danites turned	7924
	19:22	*they s* to the old man who owned the house,	606
1Sa	10:24	Then the people *s*, "Long live the king!"	8131
	14:12	The men of the outpost *s* to Jonathan	6699

1Sa	17: 8	Goliath stood and *s* to the ranks of Israel,	7924
	17:23	from his lines and *s* his usual defiance,	1819
	20:38	Then he *s*, "Hurry!"	7924
2Sa	20: 1	He sounded the trumpet and *s*,	606
1Ki	1:39	the trumpet and all the people *s*,	606
	18:26	"O Baal, answer us!" they *s*.	606
	18:28	So *they s* louder and slashed	928+7754+7924
2Ki	7:11	The gatekeepers *s* the news,	7924
	9:13	Then they blew the trumpet and *s*,	606
	11:12	and the people clapped their hands and *s*,	606
2Ch	23:11	They anointed him and *s*,	606
	23:13	Athaliah tore her robes and *s*, "Treason!	606
Ezr	3:12	many others to his *s*.	928+7754+8123+9558
Job	30: 5	*s* at as if they were thieves.	8131
	38: 7	and all the angels *s* for joy?	8131
Isa	21: 8	And the lookout *s*, "Day after day, my lord,	7924
Da	3:26	the opening of the blazing furnace and *s*,	10558
Mt	8:29	do you want with us, Son of God?" *they s*.	3189
	20:30	*they s*, "Lord, Son of David,	3189
	20:31	but they *s* all the louder, "Lord,	3189
	21: 9	ahead of him and those that followed *s*,	3189
	27:23	But they *s* all the louder, "Crucify him!"	3189
Mk	9:24	*He s* at the top of *his* voice,	3189
	10:48	but he *s* **all the more**, "Son of David, have mercy on me!"	3189+3437+4498
	11: 9	ahead and those who followed *s*,	3189
	15:13	"Crucify him!" they *s*.	3189
	15:14	But they *s* all the louder, "Crucify him!"	3189
Lk	23:18	but he *s* all the more, "Son of David,	3189
Jn	18:40	*They s* back, "No, not him!	3198
	19: 6	and their officials saw him, *they s*,	3198
	19:15	But they *s*, "Take him away!	3198
Ac	12:22	They *s*, "This is the voice of a god,	2215
	14:11	in the Lycaonian language,	2048+3836+5889
	16:28	Paul *s*, "Don't harm yourself!	3489+5888+5889
	19:33	some of the crowd *s* instructions to him.	NIG
	19:34	all *s* in unison for about two hours:	1181+3189
	21:34	in the crowd *s* one thing and some another,	2215
	22:22	Then they raised their voices and *s*,	3306
	24:21	unless it was this one thing I *s* as I stood	3189
	26:24	"You are out of your mind, Paul!" he *s*.	3489+3836+5774+5889
Rev	10: 3	When *he s*, the voices of the seven thunders	3189
	18: 2	With a mighty voice *he s*: "Fallen!	3189
	19: 3	And again *they s*: "Hallelujah!	3306

SHOUTING (27) [SHOUT]

Ex	32:17	Joshua heard the noise of the people *s*,	8275
Nu	16:34	*s*, "The earth is going to swallow us too!"	606
Jdg	15:14	the Philistines came toward him *s*.	8131
1Sa	4: 6	What's all this *s* in the Hebrew camp?	7754+9558
	17:20	to its battle positions, *s* the war cry.	8131
2Ki	9:27	Jehu chased him, *s*, "Kill him too!"	606
2Ch	15:14	with *s* and with trumpets and horns.	9558
Isa	16:10	for I have put an end to the *s*.	2116
Zep	1:14	the *s* of the warrior there.	7658
Mt	21:15	and the children *s* in the temple area,	3189
Lk	4:41	demons came out of many people, *s*,	3198
	8:28	*s* at the top of *his* voice,	3306+3489+5889
	23:21	But they *kept s*, "Crucify him!	2215
Jn	12:13	and went out to meet him, *s*, "Hosanna!	3198
	19:12	but the Jews *kept s*, "If you let this man go,	3198
Ac	14:14	and rushed out into the crowd, *s*:	3189
	16:17	This girl followed Paul and the rest of us, *s*,	3189
	17: 6	before the city officials, *s*: "These men	1066
	19:28	they were furious and *began s*:	3189
	19:32	Some *were s* one thing, some another.	3189
	21:28	*s*, "Men of Israel, help us!	3189
	21:36	The crowd that followed *kept s*,	3189
	22:23	As *they were s* and throwing off their cloaks	3198
	22:24	to find out why the *people were s* at him	2215
	25:24	*s* that he ought not to live any longer.	1066
Rev	19: 1	the roar of a great multitude in heaven *s*:	3306
	19: 6	and like loud peals of thunder, *s*:	3306

SHOUTS (22) [SHOUT]

2Sa	6:15	brought up the ark of the LORD with *s*	9558
1Ch	15:28	the ark of the covenant of the LORD with *s*,	9558
Ezr	3:13	No one could distinguish the sound of the *s*	9558
Job	8:21	with laughter and your lips with *s* of joy.	9558
	33:26	he sees God's face and *s* for joy;	9558
Ps	5:11	will I sacrifice with *s* of joy;	9558
	42: 4	with *s* of joy and thanksgiving	7754+8262
	47: 5	God has ascended amid *s* of joy,	9558
	105:43	his chosen ones with *s* of joy;	8262
	118:15	S of joy and victory resound in the tents of	8262
Pr	11:10	when the wicked perish, there are *s* of joy.	8262
Ecc	9:17	be heeded than the *s* of a ruler of fools.	2411
Isa	16: 9	The *s* of joy over your ripened fruit and	2116
	16:10	no one sings or is in the vineyards.	8131
	31: 4	against him, he is not frightened by their *s*	7754
	48:20	with *s* of joy and proclaim it.	7754+8262
Jer	48:33	no one treads them with *s* of joy.	2116
	48:33	there are *s*, they are not shouts of joy.	2116
	48:33	there are shouts, they are not *s* of joy.	2116
Zec	4: 7	Then he will bring out the capstone to *s*	9583
Lk	23:23	But *with* loud *s* they insistently demanded	5889
	23:23	that he be crucified, and their *s* prevailed.	5889

SHOVE (1) [SHOVES]

Eze	34:21	Because *you s* with flank and shoulder,	2074

SHOVEL (1) [SHOVELS]

Isa	30:24	spread out with fork and *s*.	4665

SHOVELS (9) [SHOVEL]

Ex	27: 3	its pots to remove the ashes, and its **s**,	3582
	38: 3	its pots, **s**, sprinkling bowls.	3582
Nu	4:14	meat forks, **s** and sprinkling bowls.	3582
1Ki	7:40	the basins and **s** and sprinkling bowls.	3582
	7:45	**s** and sprinkling bowls.	3582
2Ki	25:14	They also took away the pots, **s**,	3582
2Ch	4:11	the pots and **s** and sprinkling bowls.	3582
	4:16	**s**, meat forks and all related articles.	3582
Jer	52:18	They also took away the pots, **s**,	3582

SHOVES (2) [SHOVE]

Nu	35:20	anyone with malice aforethought **s** another	2074
	35:22	if without hostility *someone* suddenly **s** another	2074

SHOW (200) [SHOWED, SHOWING, SHOWN, SHOWS]

Ge	12: 1	and go to the land *I will* **s** you.	8011
	20:13	'This is how *you can* **s** your love to me:	6913
	21:23	**S** to me and the country where you are	6913
	24:12	and **s** kindness to my master Abraham.	6913
	24:49	Now if you will **s** kindness and faithfulness	6913
	40:14	remember me and **s** me kindness;	6913
	47:29	and promise that *you will* **s** me kindness	6913
Ex	9:16	that *I might* **s** you my power and	8011
	18:20	and **s** them the way to live and	3359
	23: 3	and *do* not **s** **favoritism** to a poor man	2075
	25: 9	like the pattern *I will* **s** you.	8011
	33:18	Then Moses said, "Now **s** me your glory."	8011
Lev	10: 3	" 'Among those who approach me *I will* **s** myself holy;	7727
	19:15	*do* not **s** **partiality** to the poor or	5951+7156
	19:32	**s** respect for the elderly	2075
Nu	16: 5	the LORD will **s** who belongs to him	3359
Dt	1:17	*Do* not **s** **partiality** in judging;	5795+7156
	1:33	and to **s** you the way you should go.	8011
	3:24	to **s** to your servant your greatness	8011
	4: 6	this will **s** your wisdom and understanding	6524
	7: 2	and **s** them no **mercy**.	2858
	13: 8	**S** him no **pity**.	2571+6524
	13:17	*he will* **s** you mercy, have compassion	5989
	15: 9	*you do* not **s** ill will toward your needy brother	6524+8317
	16:19	*Do* not pervert justice or **s** **partiality**.	5795+7156
	19:13	**S** him no **pity**.	2571+6524
	19:21	**S** no **pity**: life for life, eye for eye,	2571+6524
	25:12	shall cut off her hand. **S** her no **pity**.	2571+6524
Jos	2:12	by the LORD that *you will* **s** kindness	6913
Jdg	1:24	"**S** us how to get into the city	8011
	4:22	"*I will* **s** you the man you're looking for."	8011
	8:35	*They* also failed to **s** kindness to the family	6913
	13:1	not **s** himself again to Manoah and his wife,	8011
Ru	1: 8	*May* the LORD **s** kindness to you,	6913
1Sa	16: 3	and I *will* **s** you what to do.	3359
	20: 8	As for *you*, **s** kindness to your servant,	6913
	20:14	But **s** me unfailing kindness like that of	6913
2Sa	2: 6	now **s** you kindness and faithfulness,	6913
	2: 6	and I too *will* **s** you the same favor	6913
	9: 1	of Saul to whom *I can* **s** kindness	6913
	9: 3	of Saul to whom *I can* **s** God's kindness?"	6913
	9: 7	"for *I will* **surely** **s** you kindness for	6913+6913
	10: 2	"*I will* **s** kindness to Hanun son of Nahash,	6913
	12:14	*you have* **made** the enemies of the LORD **s** **utter contempt,**	5540+5540
	16:17	"Is this the love *you* **s** your friend?	907
	22:26	"To the faithful *you* **s** **yourself faithful,**	2874
	22:26	to the blameless *you* **s** **yourself blameless,**	9462
	22:27	to the pure *you* **s** **yourself pure,**	1405
	22:27	but to the crooked *you* **s** **yourself shrewd.**	7349
1Ki	2: 2	"So be strong, **s** *yourself* a man,	2118+4200
	2: 7	"But **s** kindness to the sons of Barzillai	6913
	8:50	cause their conquerors to **s** them **mercy;**	8163
2Ki	20:13	that Hezekiah *did* not **s** them.	8011
	20:15	among my treasures that *I did* not **s** them."	8011
1Ch	19: 2	"*I will* **s** kindness to Hanun son of Nahash,	6913
Ezr	2:59	not **s** that their families were descended	5583
Ne	7:61	not **s** that their families were descended	5583
	13:22	**s** mercy to me according to your great love.	2571
Est	4: 8	to **s** *to* Esther and explain it to her,	8011
Job	6:24	**s** me where I have been wrong.	1067
	13: 8	*Will* you **s** him **partiality?**	5951+7156
	13:23	**S** me my offense and my sin.	3359
	24:21	and *to* the widow **s** no **kindness.**	3512
	32:21	*I will* **s** **partiality** to no one,	5951+7156
	36: 2	with me a little longer and *I will* **s** you	2555
	37:13	or to water his earth and **s** his love.	NIH
Ps	4: 6	"Who *can* **s** us any good?"	8011
	17: 7	**S** the **wonder** of your great love,	7098
	18:25	To the faithful *you* **s** **yourself faithful,**	2874
	18:25	to the blameless *you* **s** **yourself blameless,**	9462
	18:26	to the pure *you* **s** **yourself pure,**	1405
	18:26	but to the crooked *you* **s** **yourself shrewd.**	7349
	25: 4	**S** me your ways, O LORD,	3359
	28: 5	Since *they* **s** no **regard** for the works of	1067
	39: 4	"**S** me, O LORD, my life's end and	3359
	50:23	and he prepares the way so that *I may* **s** him	8011
	59: 5	**s** no **mercy** to wicked traitors.	2858
	68:28	**s** us *your* **strength**, O God,	6451
	77: 7	*Will* he never **s** his **favor** again?	8354
	82: 2	unjust and **s** **partiality** *to* the wicked?	5951+7156
	85: 7	**S** us your unfailing love, O LORD,	8011
	88:10	*Do you* **s** your **wonders** to the dead?	6913
	91:16	and **s** him my salvation."	8011

Ps	102:13	for it is time to **s** favor *to* her;	2858
	106: 4	when you **s** favor to your people,	NIH
	143: 8	**S** me the way I should go,	3359
Pr	6:34	*he will* **s** no **mercy** when he takes revenge.	2798
	23: 4	have the wisdom *to* **s** **restraint.**	2532
	24:23	*To* **s** **partiality** in judging is not good:	5795+7156
	28:21	*To* **s** **partiality** is not good—	5795+7156
SS	2:14	**s** me your face, let me hear your voice;	8011
Isa	5:16	and the holy God *will* **s** **himself holy**	7727
	13:10	their constellations *will* not **s** their light.	2145
	19:12	*Let them* **s** you and make known what	5583
	30:18	he rises to **s** you **compassion.**	8163
	39: 2	that Hezekiah *did* not **s** them.	8011
	39: 4	among my treasures that *I did* not **s** them."	8011
	60:10	in favor *I will* **s** you **compassion.**	8163
Jer	6:23	they are cruel and **s** no **mercy.**	8163
	15: 6	I can no longer **s** **compassion.**	5714
	16: 5	do not go to mourn or **s** **sympathy,**	5653
	16:13	for *I will* **s** you no favor.'	5989
	18:17	*I will* **s** them my back and not my face in	8011
	21: 7	*he will* **s** them no **mercy** or pity	2571
	32:18	You **s** love to thousands but bring	6913
	42:12	*I will* **s** you compassion so	5989
La	3:32	he brings grief, *he will* **s** **compassion,**	8163
Eze	20:41	and *I will* **s** **myself holy** among you in	7727
	28:22	on her and **s** myself holy within her.	7727
	28:25	*I will* **s** **myself holy** among them in	7727
	36:23	*I will* **s** the **holiness** of my great name,	7727
	36:23	when I **s** **myself holy** through you	7727
	38:16	when I **s** **myself holy** through you	7727
	38:23	so *I will* **s** **my greatness** and my holiness,	1540
	39:27	*I will* **s** **myself holy** through them in	7727
	40: 4	to everything I *am going to* **s** you,	8011
	44:23	**s** them **how to distinguish** between the	3359
Da	1: 9	God had caused the official to **s** favor	4200+7156
	11:30	and **s** favor to those who forsake	1067
	11:37	He *will* **s** no **regard** for the gods	1067
Hos	1: 6	for *I will* no longer **s** love to the house	8163
	1: 7	Yet *I will* **s** love to the house of Judah;	8163
	2: 4	*I will* not **s** *my* **love** to her children,	8163
	2:23	*I will* **s** *my* **love** to the one I called	8163
	3: 1	"Go, **s** *your* **love** to your wife again,	170
Joel	2:30	*I will* **s** wonders in the heavens and on	5989
Mic	7:15	*I will* **s** them my wonders."	8011
	7:18	but delight to **s** mercy.	NIH
	7:20	and **s** mercy to Abraham,	5989
Na	3: 5	*I will* **s** the nations your nakedness and	8011
Zec	1: 9	"*I will* **s** you what they are."	1892
	7: 9	**s** mercy and compassion to one another.	6913
Mal	1: 6	O priests, *who* **s** **contempt** *for* my name.	1022
Mt	6: 16	to **s** men they are fasting.	5743
	8: 4	But go, **s** yourself to the priest and	1259
	16: 1	and tested him by asking him *to* **s** them	2109
	18:15	sins against you, go and **s** him his **fault,**	1794
	21:32	to you to **s** you the way of righteousness,	NIG
	22:19	**S** me the coin used for paying the tax."	2109
Mk	1:44	But go, **s** yourself to the priest and	1259
	12:40	and *for* a **s** make lengthy prayers.	4733
	14:15	He *will* **s** you a large upper room,	1259
Lk	1:72	*to* **s** mercy to our fathers and	4472
	5:14	**s** yourself to the priest and offer	1259
	6:47	*I will* **s** you what he is like who comes	5683
	12: 5	But *I will* **s** you whom you should fear:	5683
	17:14	he said, "Go, **s** yourselves to the priests."	2109
	18: 1	a parable to **s** them **that** they should	3836+4639
	20:21	and that *you do* not **s** **partiality** but	3284+4725
	20:24	**S** me a denarius.	1259
	20:47	and *for* a **s** make lengthy prayers.	4733
	22:12	He *will* **s** you a large upper room,	1259
Jn	2:18	"What miraculous sign *can you* **s** us to prove your authority	1259
	5:20	to your amazement *he will* **s** him	1259
	7: 4	**s** yourself to the world."	5746
	12:33	*to* **s** the kind of death he was going to die.	4955
	14: 8	**s** us the Father and that will be enough	1259
	14: 9	How can you say, 'S us the Father'?	1259
	14:21	and I too *will* love him and **s** myself	1872
	14:22	why do you intend to **s** yourself to us and	1872
Ac	1:24	**S** us which of these two you have chosen	344
	2:19	*I will* **s** wonders in the heaven above	1443
	7: 3	'and go to the land *I will* **s** you.'	1259
	9:16	I *will* **s** him how much he must suffer	5683
	10:34	that God *does* not **s** **favoritism**	1639+4720
	26:16	of me and what *I will* **s** you.	3972
Ro	2: 4	Or *do you* **s** **contempt** for the riches	2969
	2:11	For God *does* not **s** **favoritism.**	1639+4721
	2:15	since they **s** **that** the requirements of	1892
	9:22	to **s** his wrath and make his power known,	1892
1Co	11:19	**s** which of you have God's approval.	1181+5745
	12:31	now *I will* **s** you the most excellent way.	1259
2Co	3: 3	*You* **s** that you are a letter from Christ,	5746
	4: 2	But we have this treasure in jars of clay to **s**	NIG
	8:19	the Lord himself and *to* **s** our eagerness	NIG
	8:24	Therefore **s** these men the proof	1892
	11:30	of the things that **s** my weakness.	NIG
Eph	2: 7	in order that in the coming ages *he might* **s**	1892
Php	4:10	but you had no opportunity to **s** it.	NIG
1Ti	6: 2	not *to* **s** less **respect** for them	2969
2Ti	1:16	*May* the Lord **s** mercy to the household	1443
Tit	2: 7	In your teaching **s** integrity,	NIG
	2:10	but to **s** **that** they can be fully trusted,	1892
	3: 2	and to **s** true humility toward all men.	1892
Heb	6:11	*to* **s** this same diligence to the very end,	1892
	13:11	People who say such things **s** *that*	1872
Jas	2: 1	as believers in our glorious Lord Jesus Christ, don't **s** **favoritism.**	1877+4721
	2: 3	If *you* **s** **special attention** to the man	2098

Jas	2: 9	But if *you* **s** **favoritism**, you sin	4719
	2:18	**S** me your faith without deeds,	1259
	2:18	and I *will* **s** you my faith by what I do.	1259
	3:13	*let him* **s** it by his good life.	1259
1Pe	2:17	**S** proper **respect to** everyone:	5506
3Jn	1: 8	therefore *to* **s** **hospitality to** such men so	5696
Jude	1:23	to others **s** mercy, mixed with fear—	1796
Rev	1: 1	*to* **s** his servants what must soon take place.	1259
	4: 1	and I *will* **s** you what must take place	1259
	17: 1	*I will* **s** you the punishment of the great	1259
	21: 9	"Come, *I will* **s** you the bride,	1259
	22: 6	sent his angel *to* **s** his servants the things	1259

SHOWED (59) [SHOW]

Ge	39:21	he **s** him kindness and granted him favor in	5742
Ex	15:25	and the LORD **s** him a piece of wood.	3723
Nu	13:26	the whole assembly and **s** them the fruit of	8011
	20:13	and where *he* **s** **himself holy** among them.	7727
Dt	4:36	On earth he **s** you his great fire,	8011
	34: 1	There the LORD **s** him the whole land—	8011
Jdg	1:25	So *he* **s** them, and they put the city to the	8011
Ru	3:10	greater than that which you **s** earlier:	NIH
1Sa	14:11	So both of them **s** **themselves** to	1655
	15: 6	for you **s** kindness to all the Israelites	6913
2Sa	10: 2	just as his father **s** kindness to me."	6913
1Ki	3: 3	Solomon *his* **love** for the LORD	170
	13:12	And his sons **s** him which it road the man	8011
2Ki	6: 4	When *he* **s** him the place,	8011
	11: 4	Then *he* **s** them the king's son.	8011
	13:23	and had compassion and **s** **concern for**	448+7155
	20:13	and **s** them all that was in his storehouses—	8011
1Ch	19: 2	because his father **s** kindness to me."	6913
2Ch	23: 1	In the seventh year Jehoiada **s** *his* **strength.**	2616
	30:22	who **s** good **understanding** of the	8505+8507
Est	5: 9	and observed that he neither rose nor **s** **fear**	2316
Job	10:12	*You* gave me life and **s** me kindness,	6913
	13:10	if *you* secretly **s** **partiality.**	5951+7156
Ps	31:21	for *he* **s** his **wonderful** love to me	7098
	85: 1	*You* **favor** to your land, O LORD;	8354
Isa	39: 2	and **s** them what was in his storehouses—	8011
	40:14	that taught him knowledge or **s** him	3359
	47: 6	and **s** them no mercy.	8492
Jer	11:18	at that time *he* **s** me what they were doing.	8011
	24: 1	the LORD **s** me two baskets of figs placed	8011
	36:24	who heard all these words **s** no **fear,**	7064
Eze	35:11	the anger and jealousy *you* **s** in your hatred	6913
	39:26	the **unfaithfulness** *they* **s** toward me	5085+5086
	46:19	and **s** me a place at the western end.	2180
Da	2:29	of mysteries **s** you what is going to happen.	10313
Am	7: 1	This is what the Sovereign LORD **s** me:	8011
	7: 4	This is what the Sovereign LORD **s** me:	8011
	7: 7	This is what *he* **s** me:	8011
	8: 1	This is what the Sovereign LORD **s** me:	8011
Mic	6: 8	He has **s** you, O man, what is good.	5583
Zec	1:20	Then the LORD **s** me four craftsmen.	8011
	3: 1	Then *he* **s** me Joshua the high priest	8011
	8:14	to bring disaster upon you and **s** no **pity**	5714
Mt	4: 8	and **s** him all the kingdoms of the world	1259
Lk	4: 5	up to a high place and **s** him in an instant all	1259
	20:37	even Moses **s** that the dead rise,	3606
	24:40	he **s** them his hands and feet.	1259
Jn	13: 1	*he* now **s** them the full extent of *his* **love.**	26
	20:20	he **s** them his hands and side.	1259
Ac	1: 3	*he* himself to these men	4225
	15: 8	**s** that he accepted them by giving	3455
	15:14	how God at first **s** *his* **concern** by taking	2170
	18:17	But Gallio **s** no **concern** whatever.	3508
	20:35	I **s** you that by this kind	5683
	28: 2	The islanders **s** us unusual kindness.	4218
1Jn	2:19	but their going **s** that none of them belonged	5746
	2:19	This is how God **s** his love among us:	5746
Rev	21:10	and **s** me the Holy City, Jerusalem,	1259
	22: 1	the angel **s** me the river of the water of life,	1259

SHOWER (2) [SHOWERING, SHOWERS]

Job	37: 6	and to the rain **s**, 'Be a mighty downpour.'	1773
Isa	45: 8	let the clouds **s** it **down.**	5688

SHOWERING (1) [SHOWER]

2Sa	16:13	and throwing stones at him and **s** him	6759

SHOWERS (15) [SHOWER]

Dt	32: 2	like **s** on new grass,	8540
Job	29:23	for me as for **s** and drank in my words as	4764
	36:28	down their moisture and abundant **s** fall	8319
Ps	65:10	you soften it with **s** and bless its crops.	8053
	68: 9	You gave abundant **s**, O God;	1773
	72: 6	like **s** watering the earth.	8053
Jer	3: 3	Therefore the **s** have been withheld,	8053
	14:22	Do the skies themselves send down **s**?	8053
Eze	22:24	'You are a land that has had no rain or **s** in	1775
	34:26	I will send down **s** in season;	1773
	34:26	there will be **s** of blessing.	1773
Hos	10:12	until he comes and **s** righteousness on you.	3722
Joel	2:23	He sends you **abundant s,**	1773
Mic	5: 7	like **s** on the grass,	8053
Zec	10: 1	He gives *of* rain to men,	4764

SHOWING (13) [SHOW]

Ex	20: 6	but **s** love to a thousand [generations]	6913
Dt	5:10	but **s** love to a thousand [generations]	6913
Jdg	16: 5	into **s** *you* the secret of his great strength.	8011
Ru	2:20	not **stopped s** his kindness *to* the living and	6440
2Sa	2: 5	"The LORD bless you for **s** this kindness	6913

Eze   9: 5   without **s** pity or compassion.   2571+6524
Da   1: 4   **s aptitude** for every kind of learning,   8505
Jn   15: 8   **s** yourselves to be my disciples.   NIG
Ac   9:39   and **s** him the robes and other clothing   2109
Ro   12: 8   if it is **s mercy**, let him do it cheerfully.   1796
1Ti   5:10   such as bringing up children, **s hospitality,**   3827
Heb   9: 8   The Holy Spirit *was* **s** by this that the way   1317
Rev   22: 8   at the feet of the angel who *had been* **s** them   1259

SHOWN (56) [SHOW]

Ge   19:19   and you have **s** great kindness to me   6913
   21:23   as an alien the same kindness *I* have **s**   6913
   24:14   that you have **s** kindness to my master.”   6913
   32:10   and faithfulness *you* have **s** your servant.   6913
   41:28   God *has* **s** Pharaoh what he is about to do.   8011
Ex   25:40   to the pattern **s** you on the mountain.   8011
   26:30   the tabernacle according to the plan **s** *you*   8011
   27: 8   be made just as you *were* **s** on the mountain.   8011
Lev   13: 7   after *he has* **s** himself to the priest   8011
   13:49   it is a spreading mildew and *must* be **s** to   8011
Nu   8: 4   like the pattern the LORD *had* **s** Moses.   8011
Dt   4:35   You *were* **s** these things so   8011
   5:24   “The LORD our God *has* **s** us his glory   8011
   34:12   For no one has ever **s** the mighty power   NIH
Jos   2:12   because *I* have **s** kindness to you.   6913
Jdg   13:23   nor **s** us all these things or   8011
Ru   1: 8   as *you* have **s** to your dead and to me.   6913
1Ki   3: 6   “You *have* **s** great kindness to your servant,   6913
2Ki   8:13   “The LORD *has* **s** me that you will become   8011
2Ch   1: 8   “You *have* **s** great kindness to David   6913
   24:22   the kindness Zechariah’s father Jehoiada
       had **s** him   6913
   30: 9   and your children will be **s** compassion   NIH
   32:25   not respond to the **kindness** *s* him;   AIT
Ezr   9: 9   *He has* **s** us kindness in the sight of the
       kings   5742
Job   38:12   or **s** the dawn its place,   3359
   38:17   *Have* the gates of death *been* **s** to you?   1655
Ps   48: 3   *he has* **s** himself to be her fortress.   3359
   60: 3   *You have* **s** your people desperate times;   8011
   78:11   the wonders he *had* **s** them.   8011
   90:16   *May your* deeds *be* **s** to your servants,   8011
   111: 6   *He has* **s** his people the power of his works,   5583
Isa   21: 2   A dire vision *has been* **s** to me: 5583
   26:10   Though **grace is s** to the wicked,   2858
   66:14   but *his* **fury** *will be* **s** to his foes.   2404
Jer   44:10   not humbled themselves or **s reverence,**   3707
   44:25   You and your wives have **s**   4848
La   4:16   priests *are* **s** no **honor**, the elders no   5951+7156
   5:12   elders *are* **s** no **respect.**   2075+7156
Eze   11:25   the exiles everything the LORD *had* **s** me.   8011
Da   2:28   *He has* **s** King Nebuchadnezzar what will   10313
   2:45   “The great God *has* **s** the king what will   10313
Mal   1: 6   ‘How have we **s contempt** *for* your name?’   1022
   2: 9   but *have* **s partiality** in matters of   5951+7156
Mt   5: 7   Blessed are the merciful, for they *will be* **s**
       mercy.   1796
Lk   1:25   “In these days *he has* **s** his **favor**   2078
   1:58   that the Lord *had* **s** her **great** mercy,   3486
Jn   10:32   “*I have* **s** you many great miracles from   1259
Ac   4: 9   an **act of kindness s** to a cripple   2307
   10:28   But God *has* **s** me that I should not call   1259
   14:17   *He has* **kindness** by giving you rain   14
1Co   3:13   his work will be **s** for what it is,   5745
1Ti   1:13   *I was* a **mercy** because I acted in ignorance   1796
   1:16   for that very reason *I was* **s mercy** so that   1796
Heb   6:10   the love *you have* **s** him as you have helped   1892
   8: 5   to the pattern **s** you on the mountain.”   1259
Jas   2:13   without mercy will be **s** to anyone who has   NIG

SHOWS (16) [SHOW]

Dt   10:17   **s** no **partiality** and accepts no bribes.   5951+7156
   17:12   The man who **s** contempt for the judge or   6913
2Sa   22:51   *he* **s** unfailing kindness to his anointed,   6913
1Ki   1:52   “If *he* **s** himself to be a worthy man,   2118+4200
Job   34:19   who **s** no **partiality** *to* princes and   5951+7156
Ps   18:50   *he* **s** unfailing kindness to his anointed,   6913
   123: 2   till he **s** us his **mercy.**   2858
Pr   10:17   He who heeds discipline **s** the way to life,   NIH
   11:22   a beautiful woman *who* **s** no discretion.   6073
   12:16   A fool **s** his annoyance at once,   3359
   14:31   He who oppresses the poor **s contempt**   3070
   15: 5   but whoever heeds correction **s prudence.**   6891
   17: 5   the poor **s contempt** *for* their Maker;   3070
Ecc   10: 3   fool lacks sense and **s** everyone how stupid   606
Isa   27:11   and their Creator **s** them no **favor.**   2858
Jn   5:20   Father loves the Son and **s** him all he does.   1259

SHRED (KJV) See CUT UP

SHREWD (5) [SHREWDLY]

2Sa   13: 3   Jonadab was a very **s** man.   2682
   22:27   but to the crooked *you* **show yourself s.**   7349
Ps   18:26   but to the crooked *you* **show yourself s.**   7349
Mt   10:16   be as **s** as snakes and as innocent as doves.   5861
Lk   16: 8   the people of this world are *more* **s**   5642+5861

SHREWDLY (2) [SHREWD]

Ex   1:10   *we must* **deal s** with them or they will   2681
Lk   16: 8   dishonest manager because he had acted **s.**   5862

SHRIEK (1) [SHRIEKED, SHRIEKS]

Mk   1:26   and came out of him *with* a **s.**   3489+5888+5889

SHRIEKED (1) [SHRIEK]

Mk   9:26   The spirit **s**, convulsed him violently   *3189*

SHRIEKS (1) [SHRIEK]

Ac   8: 7   With **s**, evil spirits came out of many,   *1066+3489+5889*

SHRINE (17) [SHRINES]

Ge   38:21   “Where is the **s prostitute** who was beside   7728
   38:21   “There hasn’t been any **s prostitute** here,”   7728
   38:22   ‘There hasn’t been any **s prostitute** here.’ ”   7728
Dt   23:17   or woman is to become a **s prostitute.**   7728
Jdg   17: 5   Now this man Micah had a **s,**   466+1074
1Ki   14:24   There were even *male* **s prostitutes** in   7728
   15:12   He expelled the *male* **s prostitutes** from   7728
   22:46   the *male* **s prostitutes** who remained there   7728
2Ki   10:25   the bodies out and then entered the **inner s**   6551
   23: 7   the quarters of the *male* **s prostitutes,**   7728
Isa   16:12   she goes to her **s** to pray, it is to no avail.   5219
   44:13   that it may dwell in a **s.**   1074
Eze   8:12   each at the **s** *of* his own idol?   2540
   16:24   and made a **lofty s** in every public square.   8229
Hos   4:14   with harlots and sacrifice with **s prostitutes**   7728
Am   5:26   You have lifted up the **s** *of* your king,   6109
Ac   7:43   You have lifted up the **s** of Molech and   *5008*

SHRINES (15) [SHRINE]

1Ki   12:31   Jeroboam built **s** *on* high places   1074
   13:32   the altar in Bethel and against all the **s** *on*   1074
2Ki   17:29   up in the **s** the people of Samaria had made   1074
   17:32   to officiate for them as priests in the **s** *at*   1074
   23: 8   He broke down the **s** at the gates—   1195
   23:19   and defiled all the **s** *at* the high places that   1074
Job   36:14   among *male* **prostitutes** of the **s.**   7728
Eze   16:25   of every street you built your **lofty s**   8229
   16:31   of every street and made your **lofty s**   8229
   16:39   and destroy your **lofty s.**   8229
   18: 6   He does not eat at the **mountain s** or   2215
   18:11   “He eats at the **mountain s.**   2215
   18:15   “He does not eat at the **mountain s** or   2215
   22: 9   in you are those who eat at the **mountain s**   2215
Ac   19:24   who made silver **s** of Artemis,   *3724*

SHRINK (2) [SHRINKS]

Heb   10:39   not *of* those who **s back** and are destroyed,   *5714*
Rev   12:11   they did not love their lives so much as to **s**   NIG

SHRINKS (1) [SHRINK]

Heb   10:38   if *he* **s back**, I will not be pleased with him.   *5713*

SHRIVEL (2) [SHRIVELED]

Isa   64: 6   we all **s up** like a leaf,   5570
Eze   19:12   The east wind **made** *it* **s,**   3312

SHRIVELED (9) [SHRIVEL]

1Ki   13: 4   hand he stretched out toward the man **s up,**   3312
Isa   34: 4   like **s** figs from the fig tree.   5570
La   4: 8   Their skin *has* **s** on their bones;   7594
Joel   1:17   The seeds *are* **s** beneath the clods.   6308
Mt   12:10   and a man with a **s** hand was there.   *3831*
Mk   3: 1   and a man with a **s** hand was there.   *3830*
   3: 3   Jesus said to the man with the **s** hand,   *3831*
Lk   6: 6   a man was there whose right hand was **s.**   *3831*
   6: 8   and said to the man with the **s** hand,   *3831*

SHROUD (2) [SHROUDED]

Job   40:13   **s** their faces in the grave.   2502
Isa   25: 7   the **s** that enfolds all peoples, the sheet   4287

SHROUDED (2) [SHROUD]

Job   19: 8   *he has* **s** my paths *in* darkness.   8492
Ecc   6: 4   and in darkness its name **is s.**   4059

SHRUB (1)

Ge   2: 5   and no **s** *of* the field had yet appeared   3972+8489

SHUA (4)

Ge   38: 2   the daughter of a Canaanite man named **S.**   8781
   38:12   long time Judah’s wife, the daughter of **S,**   8781
1Ch   2: 3   a Canaanite woman, the daughter of **S.**   8781
   7:32   Shomer and Hotham and of their sister **S.**   8783

SHUAH (2)

Ge   25: 2   Jokshan, Medan, Midian, Ishbak and **S.**   8756
1Ch   1:32   Jokshan, Medan, Midian, Ishbak and **S.**   8756

SHUAL (2) [HAZAR SHUAL]

1Sa   13:17   toward Ophrah in the vicinity of **S,**   8787
1Ch   7:36   The sons of Zophah: Suah, Harnepher, **S,**   8786

SHUBAEL (6)

1Ch   23:16   descendants of Gershom: **S** was the first.   8649
   24:20   **S;** from the sons of Shubael: Jehdeiah.   8742
   24:20   from the sons of **S:** Jehdeiah.   8742
   25: 4   Mattaniah, Uzziel, **S** and Jerimoth;   8649
   25:20   the thirteenth to **S,**   8742
   26:24   **S,** a descendant of Gershom son of Moses,   8649

SHUDDER (7)

Isa   19:16   *They will* **s** with fear at the uplifted hand   3006
   32:11   **s,** *you* daughters who feel secure!   8074
Jer   2:12   O heavens, and **s** with great horror,”   8547
Eze   12:18   and **s** in fear as you drink your water.   8077
   27:35   their kings **s with horror,**   8547
   32:10   and their kings *will* **s** with horror because   8547
Jas   2:19   Even the demons believe that—and **s.**   *5857*

SHUHAH’S (1)

1Ch   4:11   Kelub, **S** brother, was the father of Mehir,   8758

SHUHAM (1) [SHUHAMITE]

Nu   26:42   through **S,** the Shuhamite clan.   8761

SHUHAMITE (2) [SHUHAM]

Nu   26:42   through Shuham, the **S** clan.   8762
   26:43   All of them were **S** clans;   8762

SHUHITE (5)

Job   2:11   Bildad the **S** and Zophar the Naamathite,   8760
   8: 1   Then Bildad the **S** replied: 8760
   18: 1   Then Bildad the **S** replied: 8760
   25: 1   Then Bildad the **S** replied: 8760
   42: 9   the **S** and Zophar the Naamathite did what   8760

SHULAMMITE (2)

SS   6:13   Come back, come back, O **S;**   8769
   6:13   on the **S** as on the dance of Mahanaim?   8769

SHUMATHITES (1)

1Ch   2:53   the Ithrites, Puthites, **S** and Mishraites.   9092

SHUN (2) [SHUNNED, SHUNS]

Job   28:28   and to **s** evil is understanding.’ ”   6073
Pr   3: 7   fear the LORD and **s** evil.   6073

SHUNAMMITE (8)

1Ki   1: 3   Abishag, a **S,** and brought her to the king.   8774
   1:15   where Abishag the **S** was attending him.   8774
   2:17   to give me Abishag the **S** as my wife.”   8774
   2:21   “Let Abishag the **S** be given in marriage   8774
   2:22   “Why do you request Abishag the **S**   8774
2Ki   4:12   he said to his servant Gehazi, “Call the **S.**”   8774
   4:25   “Look! There’s the **S!**   8774
   4:36   and said, “Call the **S.**”   8774

SHUNEM (3)

Jos   19:18   territory included: Jezreel, Kesulloth, **S,**   8773
1Sa   28: 4   and came and set up camp at **S,**   8773
2Ki   4: 8   One day Elisha went to **S.**   8773

SHUNI (2) [SHUNITE]

Ge   46:16   the sons of Gad: Zephon, Haggi, **S,**   8771
Nu   26:15   through **S,** the Shunite clan   8771

SHUNITE (1) [SHUNI]

Nu   26:15   through Shuni, the **S** clan;   8772

SHUNNED (3) [SHUN]

Job   1: 1   he feared God and **s** evil.   6073
Pr   5: 7   The poor *are* **s** even by their neighbors,   8533
   19: 7   A poor man *is* **s** by all his relatives—   8533

SHUNS (4) [SHUN]

Job   1: 8   a man who fears God and **s** evil.”   6073
   2: 3   a man who fears God and **s** evil.   6073
Pr   14:16   A wise man fears the LORD and **s** evil,   6073
Isa   59:15   and *whoever* **s** evil becomes a prey.   6073

SHUPHAM (1) [SHUPHAMITE]

Nu   26:39   through **S,** the Shuphamite clan;   8792

SHUPHAMITE (1) [SHUPHAM]

Nu   26:39   through Shupham, the **S** clan;   8793

SHUPPIM (1)

1Ch   26:16   on the upper road fell to **S** and Hosah.   9157

SHUPPITES (2)

1Ch   7:12   The **S** and Huppites were the descendants   9158
   7:15   a wife from among the Huppites and **S.**   9158

SHUR (6)

Ge   16: 7   the spring that is beside the road to **S.**   8804
   20: 1   and lived between Kadesh and **S.**   8804
   25:18   in the area from Havilah to **S,**   8804
Ex   15:22   they went into the Desert of **S.**   8804
1Sa   15: 7   the way from Havilah to **S,**   8804
   27: 8   in the land extending to **S** and Egypt.)   8804

SHUSHAN (KJV) See SUSA

SHUT (54) [SHUTS]

Ge	7:16	Then the LORD s him in.	6037
	19: 6	to meet them and s the door behind him	6037
	19:10	and pulled Lot back into the house and s	6037
Dt	11:17	and he will s the heavens so that it will	6806
Jos	2: 7	pursuers had gone out, the gate was s.	6037
	6: 1	Now Jericho was tightly s up	2256+6037+6037
Jdg	3:23	he s the doors of the upper room behind him	6037
1Sa	12: 3	a bribe to make me s my eyes?	6623
1Ki	8:35	the heavens are s up and there is no rain	6806
2Ki	4: 4	Then go inside and s the door behind you	6037
	4: 5	She left him and afterward s the door	6037
	4:21	then s the door and went out.	6037
	4:33	s the door on the two of them and prayed to	6037
	6:32	shut the door and hold it s against him.	4315
	6:32	s the door and hold it shut against him.	6037
2Ch	6:26	the heavens are s up and there is no rain	6806
	7:13	I s up the heavens so that there is no rain,	6806
	28:24	He s the doors of the LORD's temple	6037
	29: 7	also s the doors of the portico and put out	6037
Ne	6:10	who was s in at his home.	6806
	7: 3	have them s the doors and bar them.	1589
	13:19	I ordered the doors to be s and not opened	6037
Job	3:10	for it did not s the doors of the womb	6037
	24:16	but by day they s themselves in;	3159
	38: 8	"Who s up the sea behind doors	6114
Ps	107:42	but all the wicked s their mouths.	7890
Isa	22:22	what he opens no one can s,	6037
	24:22	they will be s up in prison and be punished	6037
	26:20	enter your rooms and s the doors	6037
	45: 1	before him so that gates will not be s:	6037
	52:15	kings will s their mouths because of him.	7890
	60:11	they will never be s, day or night,	6037
Jer	13:19	The cities in the Negev will be s up,	6037
	20: 9	a fire s up in my bones.	6806
Eze	3:24	"Go, s yourself inside your house.	6037
	22:26	and they s their eyes to the keeping	6623
	44: 1	the one facing east, and it was s.	6037
	44: 2	"This gate is to remain s.	6037
	44: 2	It is to remain s because the LORD,	6037
	46: 1	of the inner court facing east is to be s on	6037
	46: 2	but the gate will not be s until evening.	6037
	46:12	after he has gone out, the gate will be s.	6037
Da	6:22	and he s the mouths of the lions.	10506
Mal	1:10	that one of you would s the temple doors,	6037
Mt	23:13	You s the kingdom of heaven in men's faces	3091
	25:10	And the door was s.	3091
Lk	4:25	the sky was s for three and a half years	3091
Ac	21:30	and immediately the gates were s.	3091
2Th	1: 9	and s out from the presence of the Lord and	NIG
Heb	11:33	who s the mouths of lions,	5852
Rev	3: 7	What he opens no one can s,	3091
	3: 8	before you an open door that no one can s.	3091
	11: 6	These men have power to s up the sky so	3091
	21:25	On no day will its gates ever be s,	3091

SHUTHELAH (4) [SHUTHELAHITE]

Nu	26:35	through S, the Shuthelahite clan;	8811
	26:36	These were the descendants of S:	8811
1Ch	7:20	S, Bered his son, Tahath his son,	8811
	7:21	Zabad his son and S his son.	8811

SHUTHELAHITE (1) [SHUTHELAH]

Nu	26:35	through Shuthelah, the S clan;	9279

SHUTS (6) [SHUT]

Job	5:16	poor have hope, and injustice s its mouth.	7890
Pr	21:13	If a man s his ears to the cry of the poor,	357
Isa	22:22	and what he s no one can open.	6037
	33:15	and s his eyes against contemplating evil—	6794
La	3: 8	he s out my prayer.	8608
Rev	3: 7	and what he s no one can open.	3091

SHUTTLE (1)

Job	7: 6	"My days are swifter than a weaver's s,	756

SHY (1)

Job	39:22	he does not s away from the sword.	8740

SIA (1)

Ne	7:47	Keros, S, Padon,	6103

SIAHA (1)

Ezr	2:44	Keros, S, Padon,	6104

SIBBECAI (4)

2Sa	21:18	At that time S the Hushathite killed Saph,	6021
1Ch	11:29	S the Hushathite, Ilai the Ahohite,	6021
	20: 4	At that time S the Hushathite killed Sippai,	6021
	27:11	for the eighth month, was S the Hushathite,	6021

SIBBOLETH (1)

Jdg	12: 6	"S," because he could not pronounce	6027

SIBMAH (5)

Nu	32:38	(these names were changed) and S.	8424
Jos	13:19	S, Zereth Shahar on the hill in the valley,	8424
Isa	16: 8	The fields of Heshbon wither, the vines of S	8424
	16: 9	as Jazer weeps, for the vines of S.	8424
Jer	48:32	as Jazer weeps, O vines of S.	8424

SIBRAIM (1)

Eze	47:16	Berothah and S (which lies on the border	6028

SICK (43) [SICKNESS, SICKNESSES]

Pr	13:12	Hope deferred makes the heart s,	2703
Isa	10:18	as when a s man wastes away.	5823
	19:10	and all the wage earners will be s at heart.	108
Eze	34: 4	not strengthened the weak or healed the s	2703
Mt	8:16	with a word and healed all the s.	2400+2809
	9:12	healthy who need a doctor, but the s.	2400+2809
	10: 8	Heal the s, raise the dead,	820
	12:15	and he healed all their s,	NIG
	14:14	had compassion on them and healed their s.	779
	14:35	People brought all their s to him	2400+2809
	14:36	to let the s just touch the edge of his cloak,	NIG
	25:36	I was s and you looked after me,	820
	25:39	When did we see you s or in prison and go	820
	25:43	I was s and in prison and you did not look	822
	25:44	or a stranger or needing clothes or s or	822
Mk	1:32	Jesus and his s and demon-possessed.	2400+2809
	2:17	healthy who need a doctor, but the s.	2400+2809
	6: 5	except lay his hands on a few s people	779
	6:13	and anointed many s people with oil	779
	6:55	whole region and carried the s on mats	2400+2809
	6:56	they placed the s in the marketplaces.	820
	16:18	they will place their hands on s people,	779
Lk	5:17	the Lord was present for him to heal the s.	NIG
	5:31	healthy who need a doctor, but the s.	2400+2809
	7: 2	was s and about to die.	2400+2809
	9: 2	the kingdom of God and to heal the s.	822
	10: 9	Heal the s who are there and tell them,	822
Jn	4:46	a certain royal official whose son lay s	820
	6: 2	miraculous signs he had performed on the s.	820
	11: 1	Now a man named Lazarus was s.	820
	11: 2	whose brother Lazarus now lay s,	820
	11: 3	"Lord, the one you love is s."	820
	11: 6	Yet when he heard that Lazarus was s,	820
Ac	5:15	the s into the streets and laid them on beds	822
	5:16	bringing their s and those tormented	822
	9:37	About that time she became s and died,	820
	19:12	that had touched them were taken to the s,	820
	28: 8	His father was s in bed,	2879
	28: 9	the s on the island came and were cured.	819+2400
1Co	11:30	many among you are weak and s,	779
2Ti	4:20	and I left Trophimus in Miletus.	820
Jas	5:14	Is any one of you s?	820
	5:15	offered in faith will make the s person well;	2827

SICHEM (KJV) See SHECHEM

SICKBED (1) [BED]

Ps	41: 3	The LORD will sustain him on his s	1867+6911

SICKLE (12) [SICKLES]

Dt	16: 9	from the time you begin to put the s to	3058
	23:25	you must not put a s to his standing grain.	3058
Jer	50:16	and the reaper with his s at harvest.	4478
Joel	3:13	Swing the s, for the harvest is ripe.	4478
Mk	4:29	as the grain is ripe, he puts the s to it,	1535
Rev	14:14	a crown of gold on his head and a sharp s	1535
	14:15	"Take your s and reap,	1535
	14:16	on the cloud swung his s over the earth,	1535
	14:17	and he too had a sharp s.	1535
	14:18	in a loud voice to him who had the sharp s,	1535
	14:18	"Take your sharp s and gather the clusters	1535
	14:19	The angel swung his s on the earth,	1535

SICKLES (1) [SICKLE]

1Sa	13:20	mattocks, axes and s sharpened.	3058

SICKNESS (11) [SICK]

Ex	23:25	I will take away s from among you,	4701
Dt	28:61	of s and disaster not recorded in this Book	2716
Pr	18:14	A man's spirit sustains him in s,	4700
Jer	6: 7	her s and wounds are ever before me.	2716
	10:19	Yet I said to myself, "This is my s,	2716
Hos	5:13	"When Ephraim saw his s,	2716
Mt	4:23	and healing every disease and s among	3433
	9:35	and healing every disease and s.	3433
	10: 1	and to heal every disease and s.	3433
Lk	4:40	to Jesus all who had various kinds of s,	820+3798
Jn	11: 4	Jesus said, "This s will not end in death.	819

SICKNESSES (2) [SICK]

Lk	5:15	to hear him and to be healed of their s.	819
	7:21	many who had diseases, s and evil spirits,	3465

SIDDIM (3)

Ge	14: 3	in the Valley of S (the Salt Sea).	8443
	14: 8	up their battle lines in the Valley of S	8443
	14:10	Now the Valley of S was full of tar pits,	8443

SIDE (293) [ASIDE, BESIDE, FIVE-SIDED, FOUR-SIDED, SIDED, SIDES, SIDEWALLS, SIDING]

Ge	2:14	It runs along the east s of Asshur.	AIT
	3:24	the east s of the Garden of Eden cherubim	AIT
	6:16	a door in the s of the ark and make lower,	7396
	31:52	not go past this heap to your s to harm you	AIT
	31:52	past this heap and pillar to my s to harm me.	AIT
Ex	3: 1	the far s of the desert and came to Horeb,	339
	14:20	the cloud brought darkness to the one s	NIH
	14:20	to the one side and light to the other s;	NIH
	17:12	one on one s, one on the other—	2296S
	25:12	with two rings on one s and two rings on	7521
	25:32	three on one s and three on the other.	7396
	26:18	Make twenty frames for the south s of	6991
	26:20	For the other s, the north side	7521
	26:20	the north s of the tabernacle,	6991
	26:26	for the frames on one s of the tabernacle,	7521
	26:27	five for those on the other s,	7521
	26:35	the curtain on the north s of the tabernacle	7521
	26:35	the lampstand opposite it on the south s.	7521
	27: 9	The south s shall be a hundred cubits long	6991
	27:11	The north s shall also be a hundred cubits	6991
	27:14	to be on one s of the entrance,	4190
	27:15	to be on the other s,	4190
	32:27	'Each man strap a sword to his s.	3751
	36:23	They made twenty frames for the south s of	6991
	36:25	For the other s, the north side	7521
	36:25	the north s of the tabernacle,	6991
	36:31	for the frames on one s of the tabernacle,	7521
	36:32	five for those on the other s,	7521
	37: 3	with two rings on one s and two rings on	7521
	37:18	three on one s and three on the other.	7396
	38: 9	The south s was a hundred cubits long	6991
	38:11	The north s was also a hundred cubits long	6991
	38:14	Curtains fifteen cubits long were on one s	4190
	38:15	the other s of the entrance to the courtyard,	4190
	40:22	in the Tent of Meeting on the north s of	3751
	40:24	of Meeting opposite the table on the south s	3751
Lev	1:11	the north s of the altar before the LORD,	3751
	1:15	its blood shall be drained out on the s of	7815
	1:16	with its contents and throw it to the east s	7815
	5: 9	the blood of the sin offering against the s of	7815
	13:55	the mildew has affected one s or the other.	7949S
Nu	3:29	to camp on the south s of the tabernacle.	3751
	3:35	to camp on the north s of the tabernacle.	3751
	32:19	on the other s of the Jordan,	2134+2256+4946+6298
	32:19	to us on the east s of the Jordan."	4946+6298
	32:32	property we inherit will be on this s of	4946+6298
	34: 3	"'Your southern s will include some of	6991
	34:11	to Riblah on the east s of Ain and continue	AIT
	34:12	to its boundaries on every s.'"	6017
	34:15	on the east s of the Jordan of Jericho,	6298
	35: 5	measure three thousand feet on the east s,	6991
	35: 5	three thousand on the south s,	6991
	35:14	Give three on this s of the Jordan and three	6298
	36:11	their cousins on their father's s.	1201+1856
Jos	4:11	and the priests came to the other s	6296
	7: 7	to stay on the other s of the Jordan!	6298
	12: 1	including all the eastern s of the Arabah:	AIT
	12: 7	on the west s of the Jordan, from Baal Gad	6298
	13:27	of Sihon king of Heshbon (the east s of	6298
	17: 9	the northern s of the ravine and ended at	AIT
	18: 7	on the east s of the Jordan.	6298
	18:12	On the north s their boundary began at	6991
	18:14	the western s and came out at Kiriath Baal	6991
	18:14	This was the western s.	6991
	18:15	The southern s began at the outskirts	6991
	18:20	the boundary on the eastern s.	6991
	20: 8	On the east s of the Jordan	6298
	21:44	The LORD gave them rest on every s,	6017
	22: 4	of the LORD gave you on the other s of	6298
	22: 7	the tribe Joshua gave land on the west s of	6298
	22:11	near the Jordan on the Israelite s,	6298
Jdg	8:34	hands of all their enemies on every s.	4946+6017
	10: 8	the Israelites on the east s of the Jordan	6298
	11:18	along the eastern s of the country of Moab,	NIH
	11:18	and camped on the other s of the Arnon.	6298
Ru	2: 1	Naomi had a relative on her husband's s,	4200
1Sa	4:13	there was Eli sitting on his chair by the s of	3338
	4:18	Eli fell backward off his chair by the s of	3338
	12:11	from the hands of your enemies on every s,	6017
	14: 1	over to the Philistine outpost on the other s.	6298
	14: 4	On each s of the pass	2021+2021+2296+2296+4946+4946+4946+4946+6298+6298
	14:47	he fought against their enemies on every s:	6017
	20:20	I will shoot three arrows to the s of it,	7396
	20:21	'Look, the arrows are on this s of you;	2178
	20:41	David got up from the south s	7396
	22:17	Then the king ordered the guards at his s:	6584
	23:26	Saul was going along one s of	7396
	23:26	and David and his men were on the other s,	7396
	26:13	Then David crossed over to the other s	6298
2Sa	2:13	down on one s of the pool and one group	2296S
	2:13	of the pool and one group on the other s.	2296S
	2:16	and thrust his dagger into his opponent's s,	7396
	3: 8	"Am I a dog's head—on Judah's s?	4200
	13:34	coming down the s of the hill.	7396
	13:34	direction of Horonaim, on the s of the hill."	7396
	15: 2	He would get up early and stand by the s of	3338
1Ki	3:20	from my s while I your servant was asleep.	725
	5: 4	on every s, and there is no adversary	6017
	6: 5	in which there were s rooms.	7521
	6: 8	to the lowest floor was on the south s of the temple.	4190
	6:10	he built the s rooms all along the temple.	3666
	7:28	They had s panels attached to uprights.	4995
	7:30	cast with wreaths on each s.	6298
	7:39	He placed five of the stands on the south s	4190
	7:39	He placed the Sea on the south s,	4190
2Ki	4: 4	as each is filled, put it to one s."	5825
	6:11	of us is on the s of the king of Israel?"	448
	9:32	"Who is on my s?	907
	10: 6	"If you are on my s and will obey me,	4200
	11:11	the altar and the temple, from the south s to	4190

2Ki	11:11	the south side to the north s of the temple.	4190
	12: 9	on the right s as one enters the temple of	NIH
	16:14	and put it on the north s of the new altar.	3751
	16:17	the s panels and removed the basins from	4995
1Ch	18:17	chief officials at the king's s.	3338
	22: 9	from all his enemies on every s.	4946+6017
	22:18	he not granted you rest on every s?	4946+6017
	23:28	be in charge of the courtyards, the s rooms,	4384
2Ch	4: 6	for washing and placed five on the south s	AIT
	4: 7	five on the south s and five on the north.	AIT
	4: 8	five on the south s and five on the north.	AIT
	4:10	He placed the Sea on the south s,	4190
	5:12	stood on the east s of the altar,	AIT
	14: 7	and he has given us rest on every s."	4946+6017
	15:15	the LORD gave them rest on every s.	4946+6017
	20: 2	from the other s of the Sea.	6298
	20:30	his God had given him rest on every s.	4946+6017
	23:10	the altar and the temple, from the south s to	4190
	23:10	the south side to the north s of the temple.	4190
	29: 4	assembled them in the square on the east s	AIT
	32:22	He took care of them on every s.	4946+6017
	32:30	and channeled the water down to the west s	AIT
Ne	4: 3	Tobiah the Ammonite, who was at his s,	725
	4:18	of the builders wore his sword at his s	5516
Job	15:10	The gray-haired and the aged are on our s,	928
	18:11	Terrors startle him on every s	1157
	19:10	He tears me down on every s till I am gone;	6017
	21:26	S by side they lie in the dust,	3480
	21:26	Side by s they lie in the dust,	3480
	33:23	if there is an angel on his s as a mediator,	6584
	39:23	The quiver rattles against his s,	6584
Ps	3: 6	drawn up against me on every s.	6017
	31:13	there is terror on every s;	4946+6017
	45: 3	Gird your sword upon your s,	3751
	91: 7	A thousand may fall at your s,	7396
	97: 3	and consumes his foes on every s.	6017
	118:11	They surrounded me on every s,	6015
	124: 1	If the LORD had not been on our s—	4200
	124: 2	not been on our s when men attacked us,	4200
	139: 9	if I settle on the far s of the sea,	344
Pr	8:30	Then I was the craftsman at his s.	725
Ecc	4: 1	power was on the s of their oppressors—	3338
SS	3: 8	each with his sword at his s,	3751
Jer	4:19	and there is terror on every s.	4946+6017
	20:10	"Terror on every s!	4946+6017
	35: 2	to come to one of the s rooms of the house	4384
	46: 5	and there is terror on every s,"	4946+6017
	49:29	'Terror on every s!'	4946+6017
	49:32	on them from every s,"	6298
	50:15	Shout against her on every s!	6017
	51: 2	they will oppose her on every s in	4946+6017
La	2:22	against me terrors on every s.	4946+6017
Eze	1:10	on the right s each had the face of a lion,	NIH
	1:11	the wing of another creature on either s,	NIH
	4: 4	on your left s and put the sin of the house	7396
	4: 4	for the number of days you lie on your s.	2257S
	4: 6	lie down again, this time on your right s,	7396
	4: 8	that you cannot turn from one s to the other	7396
	4: 9	during the 390 days you lie on your s.	7396
	9: 2	in linen who had a writing kit at his s.	5516
	9: 3	in linen who had the writing kit at his s	5516
	9:11	the writing kit at his s brought back word,	5516
	10: 3	the cherubim were standing on the south s	AIT
	10:16	the wheels did not leave their s.	725
	21:14	closing in on them from every s.	2539
	23:22	against you from every s—	6017
	23:24	up positions against you on every s	6017
	27:11	and Helech manned your walls on every s;	6017
	28:23	with the sword against her on every s.	4946+6017
	36: 3	and hounded you from every s so	4946+6017
	40: 2	on whose south s were some buildings	AIT
	40:10	Inside the east gate were three alcoves on each s;	2256+4946+4946+7024+7024
	40:10	projecting walls on each s had the same	2256+4946+4946+7024+7024
	40:19	a hundred cubits on the east s as well as on	AIT
	40:21	Its alcoves—three on each s—	2256+4946+4946+7024+7024
	40:24	to the south s and I saw a gate facing south.	2006
	40:26	the faces of the projecting walls on each s.	2256+4946+4946+7024+7024
	40:27	to the outer gate on the south s;	2006
	40:32	on the east s, and he measured the gateway;	2006
	40:34	palm trees decorated the jambs on either s,	2256+4946+4946+7024+7024
	40:37	palm trees decorated the jambs on either s,	2256+4946+4946+7024+7024
	40:39	portico of the gateway were two tables on each s,	2256+4946+4946+7024+7024
	40:40	on the other s of the steps were two tables.	4190
	40:41	So there were four tables on one s of	7024
	40:44	at the s of the north gate and facing south,	4190
	40:44	at the s of the south gate and facing north.	4190
	40:48	they were five cubits wide on either s.	2256+4946+4946+7024+7024
	40:48	its projecting walls were three cubits wide on either s.	2256+4946+4946+7024+7024
	40:49	there were pillars on each s of the jambs.	2256+4946+4946+7024+7024
	41: 1	width of the jambs was six cubits on each s.	2256+4946+4946+7024+7024
	41: 2	and the projecting walls on each s	2256+4946+4946+7024+7024
	41: 3	on each s of it were seven cubits wide.	NIH
	41: 5	it was six cubits thick, and each s room	7521
	41: 6	The s rooms were on three levels,	7521
	41: 6	to serve as supports for the s rooms,	7521

Eze	41: 7	The s rooms all around the temple	7521
	41: 8	forming the foundation of the s rooms.	7521
	41: 9	of the s rooms was five cubits thick.	7521
	41: 9	The open area between the s rooms of	7521
	41:11	on the west s was seventy cubits wide.	6991
	41:12	including its galleries on each s;	2256+4946+4946+7024+7024
	41:19	the palm tree on one s and the face of a lion	7024
	41:26	with palm trees carved on each s.	2256+4946+4946+7024+7024
	41:26	The s rooms of the temple also had	7521
	42: 1	and opposite the outer wall on the north s.	AIT
	42: 8	While the row of rooms on the s next to	NIH
	42: 8	the row on the s nearest the sanctuary was	NIH
	42: 9	on the east s as one enters them from	AIT
	42:10	On the south s along the length of the wall	2006
	42:16	the east s with the measuring rod;	8120
	42:17	He measured the north s;	8120
	42:18	He measured the west s;	8120
	42:19	Then he turned to the west s and measured;	8120
	45: 7	the land bordering each s of the area formed by	2256+2296+2296+4946+4946S
	45: 7	the west s and eastward from the east side,	6991
	45: 7	the west side and eastward from the east s,	6991
	46:19	through the entrance at the s of the gate to	4190
	47: 1	down from under the south s of the temple,	4190
	47: 2	and the water was flowing from the south s.	4190
	47: 7	I saw a great number of trees on each s of the river.	2256+2296+2296+4946+4946S
	47:15	the north s it will run from the Great Sea by	6991
	47:18	"On the east s the boundary will run	6991
	47:19	the south s it will run from Tamar as far as	6991
	47:20	"On the west s, the Great Sea	6991
	48: 1	be part of its border from the east s to	AIT
	48: 1	from the east side to the west s.	AIT
	48:10	It will be 25,000 cubits long on the north s,	AIT
	48:10	10,000 cubits wide on the west s,	AIT
	48:10	10,000 cubits wide on the east s,	AIT
	48:10	and 25,000 cubits long on the south s.	AIT
	48:16	the north s 4,500 cubits,	6991
	48:16	the south s 4,500 cubits, the east side 4,500	6991
	48:16	the east s 4,500 cubits,	6991
	48:16	and the west s 4,500 cubits.	6991
	48:18	will be 10,000 cubits on the east s and	AIT
	48:18	10,000 cubits on the west s.	AIT
	48:20	25,000 cubits on each s.	928
	48:23	from the east s to the west side.	6991
	48:23	from the east side to the west s.	6991
	48:30	Beginning on the north s, which is 4,500	6991
	48:31	on the north s will be the gate of Reuben,	AIT
	48:32	"On the east s, which is 4,500 cubits long,	6991
	48:33	"On the south s, which measures 4,500	6991
	48:34	"On the west s, which is 4,500 cubits long,	6991
Joel	3:11	all you nations from every s,	4946+6017
	3:12	to judge all the nations on every s.	4946+6017
Zec	5: 3	Satan standing at his right s to accuse him.	NIH
	5: 3	for according to what it says on one s,	2296S
Mt	8:18	he gave orders to cross to the other s of	4305
	8:28	the other s in the region of the Gadarenes,	4305
	14:22	and go on ahead of him to the other s,	4305
	19: 1	into the region of Judea to the other s of	4305
Mk	4:35	"Let us go over to the other s."	4305
	5:21	over by boat to the other s of the lake,	4305
	8:13	into the boat and crossed to the other s.	4305
	16: 5	in a white robe sitting on the right s,	1288
Lk	1:11	at the right s of the altar of incense.	1288
	8:22	"Let's go over to the other s of the lake."	4305
	10:31	he passed by on the other s.	524
	10:32	passed by on the other s.	524
	16:22	and the angels carried him to Abraham's s.	3146
	16:23	Abraham far away, with Lazarus by his s.	3146
	19:43	and hem you in on every s.	4119
Jn	1:18	who is at the Father's s,	3146
	1:28	This all happened at Bethany on the other s	4305
	3:26	was with you on the other s of the Jordan	4305
	6:25	When they found him on the other s of	4305
	18: 1	On the other s there was an olive grove,	3963S
	18:37	Everyone on the s of truth listens to me."	NIG
	19:18	one on each s and Jesus in the middle.	1949+1949+2779
	19:34	of the soldiers pierced Jesus' s with a spear,	4433
	20:20	he showed them his hands and s.	4433
	20:25	and put my hand into his s,	4433
	20:27	Reach out your hand and put it into my s.	4433
	21: 6	"Throw your net on the right s of the boat	3538
Ac	12: 7	He struck Peter on the s and woke him up.	4433
2Co	4: 8	We are hard pressed on every s,	AIT
Php	4: 3	help these women who have contended at my s in the cause of the gospel,	5254
2Ti	4:17	Lord stood at my s and gave me strength,	4225
Heb	10:33	at other times you stood side by s	3128
	10:33	at other times you stood side by s	3128
Rev	22: 2	On each s of the river stood the tree of life,	1696+1949+2779

SIDED (4) [SIDE]

1Sa	20:30	you have s with the son of Jesse	1047+4200
	22:17	because they too have s with David.	3338+6640
2Ch	11:13	from all their districts throughout Israel s	3656
Ac	14: 4	some s with the Jews, others with	1639+5250

SIDES (50) [SIDE]

Ex	12: 7	to take some of the blood and put it on the s	9109
	12:22	on the top and on both s of the doorframe.	9109

Ex	12:23	the blood on the top and s of the doorframe	9109
	25:14	the poles into the rings on the s of the chest	7396
	25:32	Six branches are to extend from the s of	7396
	26:13	a cubit longer on both s;	2256+2296+2296+4946S
	26:13	the s of the tabernacle so as to cover it.	7396
	27: 7	be on two s of the altar when it is carried.	7521
	29:16	and sprinkle it against the altar on all s.	6017
	29:20	sprinkle blood against the altar on all s.	6017
	30: 3	Overlay the top and all the s and the horns	7815
	30: 4	two on opposite s—to hold the poles	7396+7521
	32:15	They were inscribed on both s,	6298
	37: 5	into the rings on the s of the ark to carry it.	7521
	37:18	Six branches extended from the s of	7396
	37:26	and all the s and the horns with pure gold,	7815
	37:27	two on opposite s—to hold the poles	7396+7521
	38: 7	into the rings so they would be on the s of	7521
Lev	1: 5	against the altar on all s at the entrance to	6017
	1:11	against the altar on all s.	6017
	3: 2	the blood against the altar on all s.	6017
	3: 8	against the altar on all s.	6017
	3:13	the blood against the altar on all s.	6017
	7: 2	to be sprinkled against the altar on all s.	6017
	8:19	the blood against the altar on all s.	6017
	8:24	against the altar on all s.	6017
	9:12	he sprinkled it against the altar on all s.	6017
	9:18	he sprinkled it against the altar on all s.	6017
	19:27	" 'Do not cut the hair at the s of your head	6991
Nu	22:24	between two vineyards, with walls on both s.	2256+2296+2296+4946+4946S
	33:55	in your eyes and thorns in your s.	7396
Jos	8:22	caught in the middle, with Israelites on both s.	2256+2296+2296+4946+4946S
	8:33	were standing on both s of the ark of the covenant	2256+2296+2296+4946+4946S
	18:20	of the clans of Benjamin on all s.	6017
Jdg	2: 3	be [thorns] in your s and their gods will be	7396
1Ki	4:24	and had peace on all s.	4946+6017+6298
	5: 3	waged against my father David from all s,	6015
	10:19	On both s of the seat were armrests,	2256+2296+2296+4946+4946S
1Ch	9:24	The gatekeepers were on the four s:	8120
2Ch	9:18	On both s of the seat were armrests,	2256+2296+2296+4946+4946S
Job	11: 6	for true wisdom has two s.	4101
Jer	52:23	were ninety-six pomegranates on the s;	8120
Eze	1: 8	on their four s they had the hands of a man.	8063
	2:10	On both s of it were written words of lament and mourning	294+2256+7156
	40:18	It abutted the s of the gateways and was	4190
	41:22	its corners, its base and its s were of wood.	7815
	42:20	So he measured the area on all four s.	8120
	48:21	"What remains on both s of the area formed by	2256+2296+2296+4946+4946S
Da	7: 5	It was raised up on one of its s,	10680
Rev	5: 1	a scroll with writing on both s	2277+2779+3957

SIDEWALLS (1) [SIDE]

Eze	41:26	the s of the portico were narrow windows	4190

SIDING (1) [SIDE]

Ex	23: 2	do not pervert justice by s with the crowd,	5742

SIDON (32) [GREATER SIDON, SIDONIANS]

Ge	10:15	Canaan was the father of S his firstborn,	7477
	10:19	and the borders of Canaan reached from S	7477
	49:13	his border will extend toward S.	7477
Jdg	1:31	or S or Ahlab or Aczib or Helbah or Aphek	7477
	10: 6	and the gods of Aram, the gods of S,	7477
	18:28	a long way from S and had no relationship	7477
2Sa	24: 6	and on to Dan Jaan and around toward S.	7477
1Ki	17: 9	at once to Zarephath of S and stay there.	7477
1Ch	1:13	Canaan was the father of S his firstborn,	7479
Ezr	3: 7	and oil to the people of S and Tyre,	7479
Isa	23: 2	of the island and you merchants of S,	7477
	23: 4	Be ashamed, O S, and you,	7477
	23:12	O Virgin Daughter of S, now crushed!	7477
Jer	25:22	all the kings of Tyre and S;	7477
	27: 3	and S through the envoys who have come	7477
	47: 4	to cut off all survivors who could help Tyre and S.	7477
Eze	27: 8	Men of S and Arvad were your oarsmen;	7477
	28:21	"Son of man, set your face against S;	7477
	28:22	" 'I am against you, O S,	7477
Joel	3: 4	and S and all you regions of Philistia?	7477
Zec	9: 2	which borders on it, and upon Tyre and S,	7477
Mt	11:21	in you had been performed in Tyre and S,	4972
	11:22	be more bearable for Tyre and S on the day	4972
	15:21	to the region of Tyre and S.	4972
Mk	3: 8	across the Jordan and around Tyre and S.	4972
	7:31	the vicinity of Tyre and went through S,	4972
Lk	4:26	to a widow in Zarephath in the region of S.	4972
	6:17	and from the coast of Tyre and S,	4972
	10:13	in you had been performed in Tyre and S,	4972
	10:14	But it will be more bearable for Tyre and S	4972
Ac	12:20	with the people of Tyre and S;	4973
	27: 3	The next day we landed at S;	4972

SIDONIANS (15) [SIDON]

Dt	3: 9	(Hermon is called Sirion by the S;	7479
Jos	13: 4	from Arah of the S as far as Aphek,	7479
	13: 6	Misrephoth Maim, that is, all the S,	7479
Jdg	3: 3	all the Canaanites, the S,	7479
	10:12	the S, the Amalekites and the Maonites	7479

Jdg 18: 7	like the **S**, unsuspecting and secure.	7479
18: 7	from the **S** and had no relationship	7479
1Ki 5: 6	so skilled in felling timber as the **S**."	7479
11: 1	Ammonites, Edomites, **S** and Hittites.	7479
11: 5	followed Ashteroth the goddess of the **S**,	7479
11:33	worshiped Ashteroth the goddess of the **S**,	7479
16:31	of Ethbaal king of the **S**,	7479
2Ki 23:13	for Ashtoreth the vile goddess of the **S**,	7479
1Ch 22: 4	for the **S** and Tyrians had brought large	7479
Eze 32:30	of the north and all the **S** are there;	7479

SIEGE (49) [BESIEGE, BESIEGED, BESIEGES, BESIEGING, SIEGEWORKS]

Dt 20:12	engage you in battle, **lay s** to that city.	7443
20:19	When *you* **lay s** to a city for a long time,	7443
20:20	not fruit trees and use them to build **s works**	5189
28:52	*They will* **lay s** to all the cities	7674
28:53	enemy will inflict on you during the **s**,	5189
28:55	on you during the **s** of all your cities.	5189
28:57	to eat them secretly during the **s** and in	5189
2Sa 11:16	So while Joab *had* the city **under s**,	9068
20:15	They built a **s** ramp up to the city,	6149
1Ki 16:17	from Gibbethon and **laid s** to Tirzah.	7443
2Ki 6:24	and marched up and **laid s** to Samaria.	7443
6:25	*the* **s** lasted so long that a donkey's head	7443
17: 5	marched against Samaria and **laid s** to it	7443
18: 9	against Samaria and **laid s** to it.	7443
19:32	with shield or build a **s** ramp against it.	6149
24:10	Jerusalem and **laid s** *to* it,	928+995+2021+5189
25: 1	the city and built **s works** all around it.	1911
25: 2	The city was kept under **s** until	5189
2Ch 32: 1	He **laid s** to the fortified cities,	2837+6584
32: 9	and all his forces were laying **s** to Lachish,	NIH
32:10	that you remain in Jerusalem under **s**?	5189
Job 19:12	they build a **s** ramp against me and encamp	2006
30:12	they build their **s** ramps against me.	369+784
Isa 1: 8	in a field of melons, like a city **under s**.	7443
21: 2	Elam, attack! Media, **lay s!**	7443
23:13	they raised up their **s towers**,	1032
29: 3	and set up my **s works** against you.	5193
37:33	with shield or build a **s** ramp against it.	6149
Jer 6: 6	"Cut down the trees and build **s ramps**	6149
10:17	to leave the land, you who live under **s**.	5189
19: 9	during the stress of the **s** imposed on them	5189
32:24	The **s ramps** are built up to take the city.	6149
33: 4	torn down to be used against the **s ramps**	6149
39: 1	with his whole army and **laid s** to it.	7443
52: 4	the city and built **s works** all around it.	1911
52: 5	The city was kept under **s** until the	5189
Eze 4: 2	Then **lay s** to it: Erect siege works	5189
4: 2	lay siege to it: Erect **s works** against it,	1911
4: 3	It will be under **s**, and you shall besiege it.	5189
4: 7	Turn your face toward the **s** of Jerusalem	5189
4: 8	until you have finished the days of your **s**.	5189
5: 2	When the days of your **s** come to an end,	5189
17:17	and **s works** erected to destroy many lives.	1911
21:22	to build a ramp and to erect **s works**.	1911
24: 2	because the king of Babylon *has* **laid s**	6164
26: 8	he will set up **s works** against you,	1911
Da 11:15	the North will come and build up **s ramps**	6149
Mic 5: 1	O city of troops, for a **s** is laid against us.	5189
Na 3:14	Draw water for the **s**, strengthen your	5189

SIEGEWORKS (1) [SIEGE]

Ecc 9:14	surrounded it and built huge **s** against it.	5189

SIEVE (2)

Isa 30:28	the nations in the **s** of destruction;	5864
Am 9: 9	the nations as grain is shaken in a **s**,	3895

SIFT (2)

Jdg 7: 4	and *I will* **s** them for you there.	7671
Lk 22:31	Simon, Satan has asked *to* **s** you as wheat.	4985

SIGH (1) [SIGHED, SIGHING]

Mk 7:34	up to heaven and **with a deep s** said to him,	5100

SIGHED (1) [SIGH]

Mk 8:12	He **s** deeply and said,	417+3836+4460

SIGHING (5) [SIGH]

Job 3:24	For **s** comes to me instead of food;	635
Ps 5: 1	O LORD, consider my **s**.	2052
38: 9	my **s** is not hidden from you.	635
Isa 35:10	and sorrow and **s** will flee away.	635
51:11	and sorrow and **s** will flee away.	635

SIGHT (143) [SEE]

Ge 6:11	Now the earth was corrupt in God's **s**	7156
33:18	and camped **within s** of the city.	907+7156
38: 7	was wicked in the LORD's **s**;	6524
38:10	What he did was wicked in the LORD's **s**;	6524
43:30	Deeply moved **at the s** of his brother.	448
Ex 3: 3	"I will go over and see this strange **s**—	5260
4:11	Who gives him **s** or makes him blind?	7221
10:28	Pharaoh said to Moses, "Get out of **my s!**	AIT
17: 6	So Moses did this in the **s** of the elders	6524
19:11	on Mount Sinai in the **s** *of* all the people.	6524
40:38	in the **s** *of* all the house of Israel	6524
Lev 10: 3	the **s** of all the people I will be honored.' "	7156
26:16	and fever that will destroy your **s**	6524

Lev 26:45	in the **s** *of* the nations to be their God.	6524
Nu 20:12	in me enough to honor me as holy in the **s**	6524
20:27	They went up Mount Hor in the **s** *of*	6524
32:13	who had done evil in the **s** was gone.	6524
Dt 6:18	right and good in the LORD's **s**,	6524
9:18	doing what was evil in the LORD's **s** and	6524
24:13	**regarded** as a righteous act **in the s** of	4200+7156
31:29	upon you because you will do evil in the **s**	6524
34:12	the awesome deeds that Moses did in the **s**	6524
Jos 4:14	That day the LORD exalted Joshua in the **s**	6524
1Sa 2:17	was very great in the LORD's **s**,	907+7156
6:13	saw the ark, they rejoiced at the **s**.	8011
9:17	When Samuel **caught s** of Saul,	8011
2Sa 6:20	in the **s** of the slave girls of his servants	6524
7:19	And as if this were not enough in your **s**,	6524
7:29	that it may continue forever in your **s**;"	7156
10:12	The LORD will do what is good **in his s**."	6524
13: 5	in my **s** so I may watch her and then eat it	6524
13: 6	and make some special bread in my **s**,	6524
13: 8	made the bread in his **s** and baked it.	6524
16:22	with his father's concubines in the **s**	6524
22:25	according to my cleanness in his **s**.	6524
1Ki 14: 5	his **s** was gone because of his age.	6524
2Ki 5: 1	in the **s** of his master and highly regarded,	7156
1Ch 2: 3	was wicked in the LORD's **s**;	6524
17:17	And as if this were not enough in your **s**,	6524
17:27	that it may continue forever in your **s**;	7156
19:13	The LORD will do what is good **in his s**."	6524
21: 7	This command was also evil in the **s**	6524
22: 5	and splendor **in the s** *of* all the nations.	4200
22: 8	shed much blood on the earth in my **s**,	7156
28: 8	in the **s** *of* all Israel and of the assembly of	6524
29:15	We are aliens and strangers in your **s**,	7156
29:25	in the **s** *of* all Israel and bestowed	6524
Ezr 9: 9	He has shown us kindness in the **s** of	7156
Ne 4: 5	and if your servant has found favor in his **s**,	7156
4: 5	or blot out their sins from your **s**,	4200+7156
9:28	they again did what was evil in your **s**.	7156
Job 11: 4	and I am pure in your **s**.'	6524
18: 3	as cattle and considered stupid in your **s**?	6524
41: 9	the mere **s** of him is overpowering.	5260
Ps 18:24	to the cleanness of my hands in his **s**.	6524
19:14	of my heart be pleasing in your **s**,	7156
31:19	which you bestow **in the s** of men	5584
31:22	"I am cut off from your **s!**"	6524
51: 4	and done what is evil in your **s**,	6524
72:14	for precious is their blood in his **s**.	6524
78:12	He did miracles **in the s** *of* their fathers in	5584
90: 4	in your **s** are like a day that has just gone	6524
116:15	Precious in the **s** *of* the LORD is the death	6524
146: 8	the LORD **gives s** *to* the blind,	7219
Pr 3: 4	and a good name in the **s** *of* God and man.	6524
3:21	do not let them out of your **s**;	6524
4:21	Do not let them out of your **s**,	6524
29:13	The LORD **gives s** *to* the eyes of both.	239
Isa 1:16	Take your evil deeds out of my **s!**	7156
5:21	in their own eyes and clever in their own **s**.	7156
31: 9	at **s** of the battle standard their commanders will panic,"	NIH
43: 4	you are precious and honored in my **s**,	6524
52:10	his holy arm in the **s** *of* all the nations,	6524
59:12	For our offenses are many in your **s**,	5584
65:12	evil in my **s** and chose what displeases me."	6524
66: 4	evil in my **s** and chose what displeases me."	6524
Jer 4: 1	out of my **s** and no longer go astray,	7156
18:10	it does evil in my **s** and does not obey me,	6524
18:23	or blot out their sins from your **s**.	4200+7156
31:36	if these decrees vanish from my **s**,"	4200+7156
32:30	but evil in my **s** from their youth;	6524
32:31	and wrath that I must remove it from my **s**.	7156
34:15	and did what is right in my **s**;	6524
Eze 4:12	bake it in the **s** of the people,	6524
4:17	They will be appalled at the **s** of each other	NIH
5: 8	and I will inflict punishment on you in the **s**	6524
5:14	in the **s** *of* all who pass by.	6524
16:41	and inflict punishment on you in the **s**	6524
20: 9	and in whose **s** I had revealed myself to	6524
20:14	in whose **s** I had brought them out.	6524
20:22	in whose **s** I had brought them out.	6524
20:41	among you in the **s** *of* the nations.	6524
28:18	in the **s** *of* all who were watching.	6524
28:25	among them in the **s** *of* the nations.	6524
36:17	a woman's monthly uncleanness in my **s**.	7156
36:34	of lying desolate in the **s** *of* all who pass	6524
38:23	and I will make myself known in the **s**	6524
39:27	through them in the **s** *of* many nations.	6524
Da 6:22	because I was found innocent **in his s**.	10621
Joel 2: 6	At the **s** of them, nations are in anguish;	7156
Jnh 2: 4	I said, 'I have been banished from your **s**;	6524
Hag 2:14	with this people and this nation in my **s**,'	7156
Mt 9:30	and their **s** was restored.	4057
11: 5	The blind **receive s**, the lame walk,	329
20:33	"Lord," they answered, "we want our **s**."	4057
20:34	Immediately *they* **received** *their* **s**	329
Mk 8:25	his eyes were opened, his **s** was restored,	NIG
10:52	Immediately he **received his s**	329
Lk 1: 6	Both of them were upright **in the s** of God,	1883
1:15	for he will be great **in the s** of the Lord.	1967
2:31	which you have prepared in the **s** of all	4725
4:18	for the prisoners and **recovery of s** for	330
7:21	and gave **s** to many who were blind.	1063
7:22	The blind **receive s**, the lame walk,	329
16:15	among men is detestable **in God's s**.	1967
18:42	Jesus said to him, **"Receive** *your* **s**;	329
18:43	Immediately he **received his s**	329
23:48	to witness this **s** saw what took place,	2556
24:31	and he disappeared from their **s**.	NIG

Jn 9:15	also asked him how *he had* **received** *his* **s**.	329
9:18	he had been blind and *had* **received s**	329
Ac 1: 9	and a cloud hid him from their **s**.	4057
4:19	for yourselves whether it is right *in* God's **s**	1967
7:31	When he saw this, he was amazed at the **s**.	3969
9:12	place his hands on him to **restore** *his* **s**."	329
22:13	'Brother Saul, **receive** *your* **s**!'	329
28:15	*At the* **s** of these men Paul thanked God	3972
Ro 2:13	not those who hear the law who are righteous **in God's s**,	2536+3836+4123
3:20	declared righteous **in his s** by observing	899+1967
4:17	He is our father **in the s** of God,	2978
1Co 3:19	this world is foolishness **in God's s**.	2536+4123
2Co 2:10	I have forgiven in the **s** of Christ	4725
4: 2	to every man's conscience in the **s** of God.	1967
5: 7	We live by faith, not by **s**.	1626
12:19	We have been speaking **in the s** of God	2978
Eph 1: 4	the world to be holy and blameless in his **s**.	2979
Col 1:22	through death to present you holy **in his s**,	2979
1Ti 5:21	**in the s** of God and Christ Jesus and	1967
6:13	**In the s** of God, who gives life to everything	1967
Heb 4:13	in all creation is hidden from God's **s**	1967
12:21	The **s** was so terrifying that Moses said,	5751
1Pe 3: 4	which is of great worth **in God's s**.	1967
Rev 3: 2	not found your deeds complete **in the s** of	1967

SIGHTING (1) [SEE]

Ac 21: 3	*After* **s** Cyprus and passing to the south	428

SIGHTLESS (1) [SEE]

Isa 29: 9	blind yourselves and *be* **s**;	9129

SIGHTS (3) [SEE]

Dt 28:34	The **s** you see will drive you mad.	5260+6524
28:67	the terror that will fill your hearts and the **s**	5260
Pr 23:33	Your eyes *will* see strange **s**	AIT

SIGN (87) [SIGNED, SIGNS]

Ge 9:12	"This is the **s** *of* the covenant I am making	253
9:13	be the **s** *of* the covenant between me and	253
9:17	the **s** *of* the covenant I have established	253
17:11	the **s** *of* the covenant between me and you.	253
49: 3	my might, the **first s** *of* my strength,	AIT
Ex 3:12	the **s** to you that it is I who have sent you:	253
4: 8	or pay attention to the first **miraculous s**,	253
8:23	This **miraculous s** will occur tomorrow.' "	253
12:13	be a **s** for you on the houses where you are;	253
13: 9	This observance will be for you like a **s**	253
13:16	And it will be like a **s** on your hand and	253
31:13	a **s** between me and you for the generations	253
31:17	a **s** between me and the Israelites forever,	253
Nu 16:38	Let them be a **s** to the Israelites."	253
17:10	to be kept as a **s** to the rebellious.	253
26:10	And they served as a **warning s**.	5812
Dt 13: 1	and announces to you a **miraculous s**	253
13: 2	if the **s** or wonder of which he has spoken	253
21:17	the first **s** of his father's **strength**.	226
28:46	They will be a **s** and a wonder to you	253
Jos 2:12	Give me a sure **s**	253
4: 6	to serve as a **s** among you.	253
Jdg 6:17	give me a **s** that it is really you talking	253
1Sa 2:34	Hophni and Phinehas, will be a **s** to you—	253
2:34	be our **s** that the LORD has given them	253
1Ki 13: 3	That same day the man of God gave a **s**:	4603
13: 3	"This is the **s** the LORD has declared:	4603
13: 5	according to the **s** given by the man of God	4603
20:33	The men **took** *this* **as a good s**	5727
2Ki 19:29	"This will be the **s** for you, O Hezekiah:	253
20: 8	be the **s** that the LORD will heal me and	253
20: 9	"This is the LORD's **s** to you that	253
2Ch 32:24	and gave him a **miraculous s**.	4603
32:31	about the **miraculous s** that had occurred in	4603
Job 31:35	I **s** now my defense—	9338
Ps 86:17	Give me a **s** of your goodness,	253
Isa 7:11	"Ask the LORD your God for a **s**;	253
7:14	the Lord himself will give you a **s**:	253
19:20	be a **s** and witness to the LORD Almighty	253
20: 3	as a **s** and portent against Egypt and Cush,	253
37:30	"This will be the **s** for you, O Hezekiah:	253
38: 7	" 'This is the LORD's **s** to you that	253
38:22	be the **s** that I will go up to the temple of	253
55:13	for an everlasting **s**, which will not be	253
66:19	"I will set a **s** among them,	253
Jer 44:29	be the **s** to you that I will punish you	253
Eze 4: 3	This will be a **s** to the house of Israel.	253
12: 6	I have made you a **s** to the house of Israel."	4603
12:11	Say to them, 'I am a **s** *to* you.'	4603
20:12	Also I gave them my Sabbaths as a **s**	253
20:20	that they may be a **s** between us.	253
24:24	Ezekiel will be a **s** *to* you;	4603
24:27	So you will be a **s** to them,	4603
Mt 12:38	we want to see a **miraculous s** from you."	4956
12:39	generation asks for a **miraculous s!**	4956
12:39	But none will be given it except the **s** of	4956
16: 1	asking him to show them a **s** from heaven.	4956
16: 4	generation looks for a **miraculous s**,	4956
16: 4	none will be given it except the **s** of Jonah."	4956
24: 3	and what will be the **s** of your coming and	4956
24:30	the **s** of the Son of Man will appear in	4956
Mk 8:11	they asked him for a **s** from heaven.	4956
8:12	does this generation ask for a **miraculous s**?	4956
8:12	I tell you the truth, no **s** will be given to it."	4956
13: 4	the **s** that they are all about to be fulfilled?"	4956

Lk	2:12	This will be a **s** to you:	4956
Lk	2:34	and to be a **s** that will be spoken against,	4956
	11:16	Others tested him by asking for a **s**	4956
	11:29	It asks for a **miraculous s**,	4956
	11:29	none will be given it except the **s** of Jonah.	4956
	11:30	For as Jonah was a **s** to the Ninevites,	4956
	21: 7	be the **s** that they are about to take place?"	4956
Jn	2:18	"What **miraculous s** can you show us	4956
	4:54	This was the second **miraculous s**	4956
	6:14	After the people saw the **miraculous s**	4956
	6:30	"What **miraculous s** then will you give	4956
	10:41	John never performed a **miraculous s**,	4956
	12:18	that he had given this **miraculous s**,	4956
	19:20	Many of the Jews read this **s**,	5518
	19:20	and the **s** was written in Aramaic,	NIG
Ro	4:11	And he received the **s** of circumcision,	4956
1Co	11:10	the woman ought to have a **s** of authority	NIG
	14:22	Tongues, then, are a **s**, not for believers	4956
Php	1:28	a **s** to them that they will be destroyed, but	1893
Rev	12: 1	A great and **wondrous s** appeared in heaven	4956
	12: 3	Then another **s** appeared in heaven:	4956
	15: 1	in heaven another great and marvelous **s**:	4956

SIGNAL (7) [SIGNALED, SIGNALING, SIGNALS]

Nu	10: 6	The blast *will be the* **s** for setting out.	9546
	10: 7	blow the trumpets, but not *with the same* **s**.	8131
Jer	4: 6	Raise the **s** to go to Zion!	5812
	6: 1	Raise the **s** over Beth Hakkerem!	5368
Zec	10: 8	*I will* **s** for them and gather them in.	9239
Mt	26:48	the betrayer had arranged a **s** with them:	4956
Mk	14:44	the betrayer had arranged a **s** with them:	5361

SIGNALED (1) [SIGNAL]

Lk	5: 7	So *they* **s** their partners in the other boat	2916

SIGNALING (1) [SIGNAL]

Nu	31: 6	from the sanctuary and the trumpets for **s**.	9558

SIGNALS (1) [SIGNAL]

Pr	6:13	**s** with his feet and motions with his fingers,	4911

SIGNED (3) [SIGN]

Jer	32:10	*I* **s** and sealed the deed, had it witnessed,	4180
	32:12	and of the witnesses who *had* **s** the deed and	4180
	32:44	and deeds *will be* **s**, sealed and witnessed	4180

SIGNET (10)

Ge	41:42	Then Pharaoh took his **s** ring	3192
Nu	31:50	armlets, bracelets, **s** rings,	3192
Est	3:10	So the king took off his **s** ring from his finger	3192
	8: 2	The king took off his **s** ring,	3192
	8: 8	and seal it with the king's **s** ring—	3192
	8:10	sealed the dispatches with the king's **s** ring,	3192
Isa	3:21	the **s** rings and nose rings,	3192
Jer	22:24	were a **s** ring on my right hand,	2597
Da	6:17	and the king sealed it with his own **s** ring	10536
Hag	2:23	'and I will make you like my **s** ring,	2597

SIGNIFICATION (KJV) See MEANING

SIGNIFY (KJV) See GIVE NOTICE, PETITION, POINTING, SPECIFYING

SIGNPOST (1)

Eze	21:19	a **s** where the road branches off to the city.	3338

SIGNS (76) [SIGN]

Ge	1:14	as **s** to mark seasons and days and years,	253
Ex	4: 9	if they do not believe these two **s** or listen	253
	4:17	so you can perform **miraculous s** with it."	253
	4:28	the **miraculous s** he had commanded him	253
	4:30	He also performed the **s** before the people,	253
	7: 3	and though I multiply my **miraculous s**	253
	10: 1	so that I may perform these **miraculous s**,	253
	10: 2	the Egyptians and how I performed my **s**	253
Nu	14:11	of all the **miraculous s** I have performed	253
	14:22	the **miraculous s** I performed in Egypt and	253
Dt	4:34	by testings, by **miraculous s** and wonders,	253
	6:22	the LORD sent **miraculous s** and wonders,	253
	7:19	the **miraculous s** and wonders,	253
	11: 3	the **s** he performed and the things he did in	253
	26: 8	with great terror and with **miraculous s**	253
	29: 3	those **miraculous s** and great wonders.	253
	34:11	who did all those **miraculous s** and wonders	253
Jos	24:17	performed those great **s** before our eyes.	253
1Sa	10: 7	Once these **s** are fulfilled,	253
	10: 9	and all these **s** were fulfilled that day.	253
Ne	9:10	You sent **miraculous s** and wonders	253
Ps	74: 4	they set up their standards as **s**.	253
	74: 9	We are given no **miraculous s**;	253
	78:43	the day he displayed his **miraculous s**	253
	105:27	They performed his **miraculous s**	253
	135: 9	He sent his **s** and wonders into your midst,	253
Isa	8:18	We are **s** and symbols in Israel from	253
	44:25	the **s** *of* false prophets and makes fools	253
Jer	10: 2	or be terrified by **s** in the sky,	253
	31:21	"Set up **road s**; put up guideposts.	7483
	32:20	You performed **miraculous s** and wonders	253
	32:21	Israel out of Egypt with **s** and wonders,	253

Da	4: 2	about the **miraculous s** and wonders that	10084
Da	4: 3	How great are his **s**,	10084
	6:27	he performs **s** and wonders in the heavens	10084
Mt	16: 3	but you cannot interpret the **s** of the times.	4956
	24:24	and perform great **s** and miracles to deceive	4956
Mk	13:22	and perform **s** and miracles to deceive	4956
	16:17	these **s** will accompany those who believe:	4956
	16:20	with them and confirmed his word by the **s**	4956
Lk	1:22	for he *kept* **making** **s** to them	1377+1639
	1:62	Then *they* made **s** to his father,	1935
	21:11	and fearful events and great **s** from heaven.	4956
	21:25	"There will be **s** in the sun, moon and stars.	4956
Jn	2:11	This, the first *of* his **miraculous s**,	4956
	2:23	people saw the **miraculous s** he was doing	4956
	3: 2	the **miraculous s** you are doing if God were	4956
	4:48	"Unless you people see **miraculous s**	4956
	6: 2	the **miraculous s** he had performed on	4956
	6:26	not because you saw **miraculous s** but	4956
	7:31	Christ comes, will he do more **miraculous s** than this man?"	4956
	9:16	"How can a sinner do such **miraculous s**?"	4956
	11:47	this man performing many **miraculous s**	4956
	12:37	after Jesus had done all these **miraculous s**	4956
	20:30	Jesus did many other **miraculous s** in	4956
Ac	2:19	the heaven above and **s** on the earth below,	4956
	2:22	by God to you *by* miracles, wonders and **s**,	4956
	2:43	**miraculous s** were done by	4956
	4:30	and perform **miraculous s** and wonders	4956
	5:12	The apostles performed many **miraculous s**	4956
	6: 8	did great wonders and **miraculous s** among	4956
	7:36	of Egypt and did wonders and **miraculous s**	4956
	8: 6	and saw the **miraculous s** he did,	4956
	8:13	by the great **s** and miracles he saw.	4956
	14: 3	by enabling them to do **miraculous s**	4956
	15:12	and Paul telling about the **miraculous s**	4956
Ro	15:19	by the power *of* **s** and miracles,	4956
1Co	1:22	Jews demand **miraculous s** and Greeks	4956
2Co	12:12	**s**, wonders and miracles—	4956
2Th	2: 9	of counterfeit miracles, **s** and wonders,	4956
Heb	2: 4	God also testified to it *by* **s**,	4956
Rev	13:13	And he performed great and **miraculous s**,	4956
	13:14	the **s** he was given power to do on behalf of	4956
	16:14	of demons performing **miraculous s**,	4956
	19:20	the **miraculous s** on his behalf.	4956
	19:20	With these **s** he had deluded those who had received the mark of the beast	NIG

SIHON (34) [SIHON'S]

Nu	21:21	Israel sent messengers to say to **S** king of	6095
	21:23	But **S** would not let Israel pass	6095
	21:26	the city of **S** king of the Amorites,	6095
	21:28	a blaze from the city of **S**.	6095
	21:29	his daughters as captives to **S** king of	6095
	21:34	Do to him what you did to **S** king of	6095
	32:33	of **S** king of the Amorites and the kingdom	6095
Dt	1: 4	This was after he had defeated **S** king of	6095
	2:24	I have given into your hand **S** the Amorite,	6095
	2:26	of Kedemoth I sent messengers to **S** king	6095
	2:30	But **S** king of Heshbon refused	6095
	2:31	I have begun to deliver **S** and his country	6095
	2:32	When **S** and all his army came out	6095
	3: 2	Do to him what you did to **S** king of	6095
	3: 6	as we had done with **S** king of Heshbon,	6095
	4:46	in the land of **S** king of the Amorites,	6095
	29: 7	**S** king of Heshbon and Og king	6095
	31: 4	to them what he did to **S** and Og,	6095
Jos	2:10	and what you did to **S** and Og,	6095
	9:10	**S** king of Heshbon, and Og king of Bashan,	6095
	12: 2	**S** king of the Amorites,	6095
	12: 5	and half of Gilead to the border of **S** king	6095
	13:10	all the towns of **S** king of the Amorites,	6095
	13:21	the entire realm of **S** king of the Amorites,	6095
	13:21	princes allied with **S**—	6095
	13:27	the rest of the realm of **S** king of Heshbon	6095
Jdg	11:19	"Then Israel sent messengers to **S** king of	6095
	11:20	**S**, however, did not trust Israel to pass	6095
	11:21	gave **S** and all his men into Israel's hands,	6095
1Ki	4:19	(the country of **S** king of the Amorites and	6095
Ne	9:22	over the country of **S** king of Heshbon and	6095
Ps	135:11	**S** king of the Amorites, Og king of Bashan	6095
	136:19	**S** king of the Amorites	6095
Jer	48:45	a blaze from the midst of **S**;	6095

SIHON'S (1) [SIHON]

Nu	21:27	let it be rebuilt; let **S** city be restored.	6095

SIHOR (KJV) See SHIHOR

SILAS (21)

Ac	15:22	and **S**, two men who were leaders among	4976
	15:27	Therefore we are sending Judas and **S**	4976
	15:32	Judas and **S**, who themselves were prophets,	4976
	15:40	but Paul chose **S** and left,	4976
	16:19	they seized Paul and **S** and dragged them	4976
	16:22	in the attack against **Paul and S**,	899S
	16:25	About midnight Paul and **S** were praying	4976
	16:29	in and fell trembling before Paul and **S**.	4976
	16:36	that you and **S** be released	NIG
	16:38	that Paul and **S** were Roman citizens,	NIG
	16:40	After Paul and **S** came out of the prison,	NIG
	17: 4	were persuaded and joined Paul and **S**,	4976
	17: 5	to Jason's house in search of **Paul and S**	899S
	17:10	the brothers sent Paul and **S** away to Berea.	4976
	17:14	but **S** and Timothy stayed at Berea.	4976

	17:15	for **S** and Timothy to join him as soon	4976
Ac	18: 5	When **S** and Timothy came from	4976
2Co	1:19	who was preached among you by me and **S**	4977
1Th	1: 1	Paul, **S** and Timothy, To the church of	4977
2Th	1: 1	Paul, **S** and Timothy, To the church of	4977
1Pe	5:12	With the help of **S**, whom I regard	4977

SILENCE (17) [SILENCED, SILENCES, SILENT]

Job	11: 3	*Will* your idle talk **reduce** men *to* **s**?	3087
	29:21	**waiting in s** for my counsel.	1957
Ps	8: 2	to **s** the foe and the avenger.	8697
	94:17	I would soon have dwelt in the **s of death**.	1872
	101: 5	him *will I* **put** to **s**;	7551
	101: 8	Every morning *I* will **put** to **s** all the wicked	7551
	115:17	those who go down to **s**,	1872
	143:12	In your unfailing love, **s** my enemies;	7551
Isa	22: 5	You the uproar of foreigners;	4044
	47: 5	"Sit *in* **s**, go into darkness,	1876
Jer	51:55	he will **s** her noisy din.	6
La	2:10	of Zion sit on the ground *in* **s**;	1949
	3:28	Let him sit alone *in* **s**,	1957
Am	8: 3	many bodies—flung everywhere! **S**!"	2187
Ac	19:33	for **s** in order to make a defense before	NIG
1Pe	2:15	by doing good *you should* **s** the ignorant **talk** of foolish men.	5821
Rev	8: 1	there was **s** in heaven for about half an hour.	4968

SILENCED (13) [SILENCE]

Nu	13:30	Caleb **s** the people before Moses and said,	2188
1Sa	2: 9	but the wicked *will be* **s** in darkness.	1957
Job	23:17	Yet *I am* not **s** by the darkness,	7551
Ps	31:18	*Let* their lying lips be **s**,	519
	63:11	while the mouths of liars *will be* **s**.	6126
Jer	47: 5	Ashkelon will be **s**.	1949
	48: 2	You too, O Madmen, will be **s**;	1957
	49:26	all her soldiers *will be* **s** in that day,"	1959
	50:30	all her soldiers *will be* **s** in that day,"	1957
Eze	27:32	"Who was ever **s** like Tyre,	1951
Mt	22:34	Hearing that Jesus *had* **s** the Sadducees,	5821
Ro	3:19	*be* **s** and the whole world held accountable	5852
Tit	1:11	They must *be* **s**, because they are ruining	2187

SILENCES (1) [SILENCE]

Job	12:20	He **s** the lips of trusted advisers	6073

SILENT (59) [SILENCE]

Lev	10: 3	Aaron remained **s**.	1957
Dt	27: 9	said to all Israel, "*Be* **s**, O Israel, and listen!	6129
1Sa	10:27	But Saul kept **s**.	3087
2Ki	18:36	people remained **s** and said nothing in reply,	3087
Est	4:14	For if *you* remain **s** at this time,	3087+3087
Job	7:11	"Therefore I *will not* keep **s**;	3104+7023
	13: 5	If only *you would be* **altogether s**!	3087+3087
	13:13	"Keep **s** and let me speak;	3087
	13:19	If so, *I will* be **s** and die.	3087
	31:34	that *I* kept **s** and would not go outside	1957
	32:16	Must I wait, now that *they are* **s**,	1819+4202
	33:31	*be* **s**, and I will speak.	3087
	33:33	*be* **s**, and I will teach you wisdom."	3087
	34:29	if he remains **s**, who can condemn him?	9200
Ps	4: 4	search your hearts and be **s**.	1957
	22: 2	by night, and am not **s**.	1875
	28: 1	For if *you* remain **s**,	3120
	30:12	that my heart may sing to you and not be **s**.	1957
	31:17	the wicked be put to shame and *lie* **s** in	1957
	32: 3	When *I* kept **s**, my bones wasted away	3087
	35:22	O LORD, you have seen this; *be* not **s**.	3087
	39: 2	But *when I was* **s** and still,	519
	39: 9	*I was* **s**; I would not open my mouth,	519
	50: 3	Our God comes and *will* not be **s**;	3087
	50:21	These things you have done and *I* kept **s**;	3087
	83: 1	O God, do not keep **s**;	1954
	109: 1	O God, whom *I* praise, *do* not remain **s**,	3087
Pr	17:28	Even a fool is thought wise if *he* keeps **s**,	3087
Ecc	3: 7	a time to *be* **s** and a time to speak,	3120
Isa	23: 2	*Be* **s**, *you* people of the island	1957
	24: 8	the joyful harp *is* **s**.	2532
	36:21	*people* remained **s** and said nothing in reply,	3087
	41: 1	"*Be* **s** before me, you islands!	3087
	42:14	"For a long time *I* have kept **s**,	3120
	53: 7	and as a sheep before her shearers *is* **s**,	519
	57:11	not because *I* have *been* **s** that you do	3120
	62: 1	For Zion's sake *I* will not keep **s**,	3120
	62: 6	*they* will never be **s** day or night.	3120
	64:12	*Will* you keep **s** and punish us	3120
	65: 6	*I* will not keep **s** but will pay back in full;	3120
Jer	4:19	My heart pounds within me, *I* cannot keep **s**.	3087
Eze	3:26	of your mouth so that *you will be* **s**	519
	24:27	with him and *will* no longer be **s**.	519
	33:22	mouth was opened and *I was* no longer **s**.	519
Hab	1:13	Why *are you* **s** while the wicked swallow	3087
	2:20	*let* all the earth be **s** before him."	2187
Zep	1: 7	*Be* **s** before the Sovereign LORD,	2187
Mt	26:63	But Jesus *remained* **s**.	4995
Mk	3: 4	But they *remained* **s**.	4995
	14:61	But Jesus *remained* **s** and gave no answer.	4995
Lk	1:20	now you will be **s** and not able to speak	4495
	14: 4	But they *remained* **s**.	2483
	20:26	astonished by his answer, *they became* **s**.	4967
Ac	11:18	and as a lamb before the shearer is **s**,	936
	15:12	The whole assembly *became* **s**.	4967
	18: 9	keep on speaking, *do* not be **s**.	4995
	21:40	When they were *all* **s**,	4498+4968

1Co 14:34 women *should remain* s in the churches. 4967
1Ti 2:12 or have authority over a man; she must be s. 2484

SILK (1)
Rev 18:12 fine linen, purple, s and scarlet cloth; 4986

SILLA (1)
2Ki 12:20 at Beth Millo, on the road down to S. 6133

SILLY (KJV) See SENSELESS, SIMPLE, WEAK-WILLED

SILOAH (KJV) See SILOAM

SILOAM (4)
Ne 3:15 He also repaired the wall of the Pool of S, 8940
Lk 13: 4 when the tower in S fell on them— 4978
Jn 9: 7 in the Pool of S" (this word means Sent). 4978
9:11 He told me to go to S and wash. 4978

SILVER (343)
Ge 13: 2 wealthy in livestock and in s and gold. 4084
20:16 a thousand shekels of s. 4084
23:15 the land is worth four hundred shekels of s, 4084
23:16 four hundred shekels of s, 4084
24:35 s and gold, menservants and maidservants, 4084
24:53 the servant brought out gold and s jewelry 4084
33:19 For a hundred **pieces of s**, 7988
37:28 for twenty shekels of s to the Ishmaelites, 4084
42:25 to put each man's s back in his sack. 4084
42:27 and he saw his s in the mouth of his sack. 4084
42:28 "My s has been returned," 4084
42:35 in each man's sack was his pouch of s! 4084
43:12 Take double the amount of s with you, 4084
43:12 for you must return the s that was put back 4084
43:15 the gifts and double the amount of s, 4084
43:18 of the s that was put back into our sacks 4084
43:21 and each of us found his s— 4084
43:22 We have also brought additional s with us 4084
43:22 We don't know who put our s 4084
43:23 I received your s." 4084
44: 1 put each man's s in the mouth of his sack. 4084
44: 2 Then put my cup, the s one, 4084
44: 2 along with the s *for* his grain." 4084
44: 8 of Canaan the s we found inside the mouths 4084
44: 8 So why would we steal s or gold 4084
45:22 of s and five sets of clothes. 4084
Ex 3:22 for articles of s and gold and for clothing," 4084
11: 2 to ask their neighbors for articles of s 4084
12:35 the Egyptians for articles of s and gold and 4084
20:23 not make for yourselves gods of s or gods 4084
21:32 the owner must pay thirty shekels of s to 4084
22: 7 "If a man gives his neighbor s or goods 4084
25: 3 gold, s and bronze; 4084
26:19 and make forty s bases to go under them— 4084
26:21 and two more s bases—two under each frame. 4084
26:25 be eight frames and sixteen s bases— 4084
26:32 with gold and standing on four s bases. 4084
27:10 and twenty bronze bases and with s hooks 4084
27:11 and twenty bronze bases and with s hooks 4084
27:17 around the courtyard are to have s bands 4084
31: 4 to make artistic designs for work in gold, s 4084
35: 5 to bring to the LORD an offering of gold, s 4084
35:24 of s or bronze brought it as an offering to 4084
35:32 to make artistic designs for work in gold, s 4084
36:24 and made forty s bases to go under them— 4084
36:26 and forty s bases—two under each frame. 4084
36:30 sixteen s bases—two under each frame. 4084
36:36 for them and cast their four s bases. 4084
38:10 and with s hooks and bands on the posts. 4084
38:11 with s hooks and bands on the posts. 4084
38:12 with s hooks and bands on the posts. 4084
38:17 The hooks and bands on the posts were s, 4084
38:17 and their tops were overlaid with s; 4084
38:17 all the posts of the courtyard had s bands. 4084
38:19 Their hooks and bands were s, 4084
38:19 and their tops were overlaid with s. 4084
38:25 The s *obtained from* those of 4084
38:27 The 100 talents of s were used to cast 4084
Lev 5:15 without defect and of the proper value in s, 4084
27: 3 and sixty at fifty shekels of s, according to 4084
27: 6 the value of a male at five shekels of s and 4084
27: 6 and that of a female at three shekels of s. 4084
27:16 fifty shekels of s to a homer of barley seed. 4084
Nu 3:50 the Israelites he collected s weighing 1,365 4084
7:13 His offering was one s plate weighing 4084
7:13 one s sprinkling bowl weighing seventy 4084
7:19 offering he brought was one s plate 4084
7:19 one s sprinkling bowl weighing seventy 4084
7:25 His offering was one s plate weighing 4084
7:25 one s sprinkling bowl weighing seventy 4084
7:31 His offering was one s plate weighing 4084
7:31 one s sprinkling bowl weighing seventy 4084
7:37 His offering was one s plate weighing 4084
7:37 one s sprinkling bowl weighing seventy 4084
7:43 His offering was one s plate weighing 4084
7:43 one s sprinkling bowl weighing seventy 4084
7:49 His offering was one s plate weighing 4084
7:49 one s sprinkling bowl weighing seventy 4084
7:55 His offering was one s plate weighing 4084
7:55 one s sprinkling bowl weighing seventy 4084
7:61 His offering was one s plate weighing 4084
7:61 one s sprinkling bowl weighing seventy 4084

7:67 His offering was one s plate weighing 4084
Nu 7:67 one s sprinkling bowl weighing seventy 4084
7:73 His offering was one s plate weighing 4084
7:73 one s sprinkling bowl weighing seventy 4084
7:79 His offering was one s plate weighing 4084
7:79 one s sprinkling bowl weighing seventy 4084
7:84 when it was anointed: twelve s plates, 4084
7:84 twelve s sprinkling bowls 4084
7:85 Each s plate weighed a hundred and thirty 4084
7:85 the s dishes weighed two thousand four hundred shekels. 4084
10: 2 "Make two trumpets of hammered s, 4084
18:16 the redemption price set at five shekels of s, 4084
22:18 if Balak gave me his palace filled with s 4084
24:13 if Balak gave me his palace filled with s 4084
31:22 Gold, s, bronze, iron, tin, lead 4084
Dt 2: 6 to pay them in s for the food you eat and 4084
2:28 to eat and water to drink for their price in s. 4084
7:25 Do not covet the s and gold on them, 4084
8:13 and flocks grow large and your s 4084
14:25 then exchange your tithe for s, 4084
14:25 and take the s with you and go to the place 4084
14:26 Use the s to buy whatever you like: 4084
17:17 He must not accumulate large amounts of s 4084
22:19 They shall fine him a hundred shekels of s 4084
22:29 the girl's father fifty shekels of s. 4084
29:17 idols of wood and stone, of s and gold. 4084
Jos 6:19 All the s and gold and the articles of bronze 4084
6:24 but they put the s and gold and the articles 4084
7:21 two hundred shekels of s and a wedge 4084
7:21 with the s underneath." 4084
7:22 hidden in his tent, with the s underneath. 4084
7:24 took Achan son of Zerah, the s, the robe, 4084
22: 8 with large herds of livestock, with s, gold, 4084
24:32 that Jacob bought for a hundred **pieces of s** 7988
Jdg 5:19 but they carried off no s, no plunder. 4084
9: 4 They gave him seventy shekels of s from 4084
16: 5 will give you eleven hundred shekels of s." 4084
16:18 of the Philistines returned with the s 4084
17: 2 of s that were taken from you and 4084
17: 2 I have that s with me; I took it." 4084
17: 3 the eleven hundred shekels of s 4084
17: 3 "I solemnly consecrate my s to the LORD 4084
17: 4 So he returned the s to his mother, 4084
17: 4 and she took two hundred shekels of s 4084
17:10 and I'll give you ten shekels of s a year, 4084
1Sa 2:36 down before him for a piece of s and a crust 4084
9: 8 he said, "I have a quarter of a shekel of s. 4084
2Sa 8:10 with him articles of s and gold and bronze. 4084
8:11 as he had done with the s and gold from all 4084
18:11 to give you ten shekels of s and 4084
21: 4 "We have no right to demand s or gold 4084
24:24 and the oxen and paid fifty shekels of s 4084
1Ki 7:51 the s and gold and the furnishings— 4084
10:21 Nothing was made of s, 4084
10:21 because s was considered of little value NIH
10:22 s and ivory, and apes and baboons. 4084
10:25 articles of s and gold, robes, 4084
10:27 The king made s as common in Jerusalem 4084
10:29 from Egypt for six hundred shekels of s, 4084
15:15 the temple of the LORD the s and gold and 4084
15:18 the s and gold that was left in the treasuries 4084
15:19 See, I am sending you a gift of s and gold. 4084
16:24 of Samaria from Shemer for two talents of s 4084
20: 3 'Your s and gold are mine, 4084
20: 5 'I sent to demand your s and gold, 4084
20: 7 my s and my gold, I did not refuse him." 4084
20:39 or you must pay a talent of s.' 4084
2Ki 5: 5 taking with him ten talents of s, 4084
5:22 Please give them a talent of s and two sets 4084
5:23 then tied up the two talents of s in two bags, 4084
6:25 for eighty shekels of s, 4084
7: 8 They ate and drank, and carried away s, 4084
12:13 not spent for making s basins, 4084
12:13 of gold or s for the temple of the LORD; 4084
14:14 the gold and s and all the articles found in 4084
15:19 a thousand talents of s to gain his support 4084
15:20 to contribute fifty shekels of s to be given 4084
16: 8 And Ahaz took the s and gold found in 4084
18:14 of Judah three hundred talents of s 4084
18:15 the s that was found in the temple of 4084
20:13 the s, the gold, the spices and the fine oil— 4084
23:33 a levy of a hundred talents of s and a talent 4084
23:35 Jehoiakim paid Pharaoh Neco the s and 4084
23:35 he taxed the land and exacted the s and gold 4084
25:15 all that were made of pure gold or s. 4084+4084
1Ch 18:10 of articles of gold and s and bronze. 4084
18:11 with the s and gold he had taken 4084
19: 6 the Ammonites sent a thousand talents of s 4084
22:14 a million talents of s, 4084
22:16 in gold and s, bronze and iron— 4084
28:14 and the weight of s for all the silver articles NIH
28:14 and the weight of silver for all the s articles 4084
28:15 of s for each silver lampstand and its lamps, 4084
28:15 of silver for each s lampstand and its lamps, NIH
28:16 the weight of s for the silver tables; 4084
28:16 the weight of silver for the s tables; 4084
28:17 the weight of s for each silver dish; 4084
28:17 the weight of silver for each s dish; NIH
29: 2 gold for the gold work, s for the silver, 4084
29: 2 gold for the gold work, silver for the s, 4084
29: 3 for the temple of my God, over and 4084
29: 4 and seven thousand talents of refined s, 4084
29: 5 for the gold work and the s *work*, 4084
29: 7 ten thousand talents of s, 4084
2Ch 1:15 The king made s and gold as common 4084
1:17 from Egypt for six hundred shekels of s, 4084

2: 7 a man skilled to work in gold and s, 4084
2Ch 2:14 He is trained to work in gold and s, 4084
5: 1 the s and gold and all the furnishings— 4084
9:14 of the land brought gold and s to Solomon. 4084
9:20 Nothing was made of s, 4084
9:20 because s was considered of little value NIH
9:21 s and ivory, and apes and baboons. 4084
9:24 articles of s and gold, and robes, 4084
9:27 The king made s as common in Jerusalem 4084
15:18 into the temple of God the s and gold and 4084
16: 2 the s and gold out of the treasuries of 4084
16: 3 See, I am sending you s and gold. 4084
17:11 gifts and s as tribute, and 4084
21: 3 Their father had given them many gifts of s 4084
24:14 also dishes and other objects of gold and s. 4084
25: 6 from Israel for a hundred talents of s. 4084
25:24 the gold and s and all the articles found in 4084
27: 5 a hundred talents of s, 4084
32:27 and he made treasuries for his s and gold 4084
36: 3 a levy of a hundred talents of s and a talent 4084
Ezr 1: 4 now be living are to provide him with s 4084
1: 6 with articles of s and gold, 4084
1: 9 gold dishes 30 s dishes 1,000 4084
1: 9 gold dishes 30 silver dishes 1,000's pans 29 NIH
1:10 gold bowls 30 matching s bowls 410 4084
1:11 there were 5,400 articles of gold and of s. 4084
2:69 5,000 minas of s and 100 priestly garments. 4084
5:14 the gold and s articles of the house of God, 10362
6: 5 the gold and s articles of the house of God, 10362
7:15 to take with you the s and gold that the king 10362
7:16 with all the s and gold you may obtain from 10362
7:18 with the rest of the s and gold, 10362
7:22 up to a hundred talents of s, 10362
8:25 and I weighed out to them the offering of s 4084
8:26 I weighed out to them 650 talents of s, 4084
8:26 s articles weighing 100 talents, 4084
8:28 The s and gold are a freewill offering to 4084
8:30 Then the priests and Levites received the s 4084
8:33 the s and gold and the sacred articles into 4084
Ne 5:15 on the people and took forty shekels of s 4084
7:71 drachmas of gold and 2,200 minas of s. 4084
7:72 minas of s and 67 garments for priests. 4084
Est 1: 6 of white linen and purple material to s rings 4084
1: 6 and s on a mosaic pavement of porphyry, 4084
3: 9 and I will put ten thousand talents of s into 4084
Job 3:15 who filled their houses with s. 4084
22:25 the choicest s for you. 4084
27:16 up s like dust and clothes like piles of clay, 4084
27:17 and the innocent will divide his s. 4084
28: 1 for s and a place where gold is refined. 4084
28:15 nor can its price be weighed in s. 4084
42:11 and each one gave him a **piece** of s and 7988
Ps 12: 6 like s refined in a furnace of clay, 4084
66:10 you, O God, tested us; you refined us like s. 4084
68:13 the wings of [my] dove are sheathed with s, 4084
68:30 Humbled, may it bring bars of s. 4084
105:37 laden with s and gold, 4084
115: 4 But their idols are s and gold, 4084
119:72 to me than thousands of pieces of s 4084
135:15 The idols of the nations are s and gold, 4084
Pr 2: 4 and if you look for it as for s 4084
3:14 for she is more profitable than s 4084
8:10 Choose my instruction instead of s, 4084
8:19 what I yield surpasses choice s. 4084
10:20 The tongue of the righteous is choice s, 4084
16:16 to choose understanding rather than s! 4084
17: 3 The crucible for s and the furnace for gold, 4084
22: 1 to be esteemed is better than s or gold. 4084
25: 4 Remove the dross from the s, 4084
25:11 like apples of gold in settings of s. 4084
27:21 The crucible for s and the furnace for gold, 4084
Ecc 2: 8 I amassed s and gold for myself, 4084
12: 6 before the s cord is severed, 4084
SS 1:11 of gold, studded with s. 4084
3:10 Its posts he made of s, its base of gold. 4084
8: 9 we will build towers of s on her. 4084
8:11 to bring for its fruit a thousand shekels of s. 4084
Isa 1:22 Your s has become dross, 4084
2: 7 Their land is full of s and gold; 4084
2:20 and bats their idols of s and idols of gold, 4084
7:23 a thousand s shekels, 4084
13:17 not care for s and have no delight in gold. 4084
30:22 with s and your images covered with gold; 4084
31: 7 of s and gold your sinful hands have made. 4084
39: 2 the s, the gold, the spices, the fine oil, 4084
40:19 with gold and fashions s chains for it. 4084
46: 6 from their bags and weigh out s on 4084
48:10 See, I have refined you, though not as s; 4084
60: 9 with their s and gold, 4084
60:17 and s in place of iron, 4084
Jer 6:30 They are called rejected s, 4084
10: 4 They adorn it with s and gold; 4084
10: 9 Hammered s is brought from Tarshish 4084
32: 9 for him seventeen shekels of s. 4084
32:10 and weighed out the s on the scales. 4084
32:25 'Buy the field with s and have 4084
32:44 Fields will be bought for s, 4084
52:19 all that were made of pure gold or s. 4084+4084
Eze 7:19 They will throw their s into the streets, 4084
7:19 Their s and gold will not be able 4084
16:13 So you were adorned with gold and s; 4084
16:17 the jewelry made of my gold and s, 4084
22:18 They are but the dross of s. 4084
22:20 As men gather s, copper, iron, 4084
22:22 As s is melted in a furnace, 4084
27:12 they exchanged s, iron, tin and lead 4084
28: 4 and amassed gold and s in your treasuries. 4084

	38:13	to carry off s and gold,	4084
Da	2:32	its chest and arms of s,	10362
	2:35	the s and the gold were broken to pieces at	10362
	2:45	the clay, the s and the gold to pieces.	10362
	5: 2	to bring in the gold and s goblets	10362
	5: 4	they praised the gods of gold and s,	10362
	5:23	You praised the gods of s and gold,	10362
	11: 8	of s and gold and carry them off to Egypt.	4084
	11:38	to his fathers he will honor with gold and s,	4084
	11:43	the treasures of gold and s and all the riches	4084
Hos	2: 8	who lavished on her the s and gold—	4084
	3: 2	So I bought her for fifteen shekels of s and	4084
	8: 4	With their s and gold they make idols	4084
	9: 6	Their treasures of s will be taken over	4084
	2: 8	for themselves from their s,	4084
Joel	3: 5	For you took my s and my gold	4084
Am	2: 6	They sell the righteous for s,	4084
	8: 6	with s and the needy for a pair of sandals,	4084
Na	2: 9	Plunder the s!	4084
Hab	2:19	It is covered with gold and s;	4084
Zep	1:11	all who trade with s will be ruined.	4084
	1:18	Neither their s nor their gold will be able	4084
Hag	2: 8	'The s is mine and the gold is mine,'	4084
Zec	6:10	"Take [s and gold] from the exiles Heldai,	NIH
	6:11	Take the s and gold and make a crown,	4084
	9: 3	she has heaped up s like dust,	4084
	11:12	So they paid me thirty pieces of s.	4084
	11:13	the thirty pieces of s and threw them into	4084
	13: 9	I will refine them like s and test them	4084
	14:14	great quantities of gold and s and clothing.	4084
Mal	3: 3	He will sit as a refiner and purifier of s;	4084
	3: 3	the Levites and refine them like gold and s.	4084
Mt	10: 9	along any gold or s or copper in your belts;	738
	26:15	So they counted out for him thirty s coins.	736
	27: 3	with remorse and returned the thirty s coins	736
	27: 9	"They took the thirty s coins,	736
Lk	10:35	The next day he took out two s coins	1324
	15: 8	a woman has ten s coins and loses one.	1534
Ac	3: 6	Then Peter said, "S or gold I do not have,	736
	17:29	the divine being is like gold or s or stone—	738
	19:24	who made s shrines of Artemis,	735
	20:33	not coveted anyone's s or gold or clothing.	736
1Co	3:12	s, costly stones, wood, hay or straw,	738
2Ti	2:20	of gold and s, but also of wood and clay;	735
Jas	5: 3	Your gold and s are corroded.	738
1Pe	1:18	not with perishable things such as s or gold	736
Rev	9:20	s, bronze, stone and wood—	735
	18:12	s, precious stones and pearls;	738

SILVERSMITH (3)

Jdg	17: 4	shekels of silver and gave them to a s,	7671
Pr	25: 4	and out comes material for the s;	7671
Ac	19:24	A s named Demetrius.	737

SIMEON (43) [SIMEONITE, SIMEONITES]

Ge	29:33	So she named him S.	9058
	34:25	two of Jacob's sons, S and Levi,	9058
	34:30	Then Jacob said to S and Levi,	9058
	35:23	Reuben the firstborn of Jacob, S, Levi,	9058
	42:24	He had S taken from them and bound	9058
	42:36	Joseph is no more and S is no more,	9058
	43:23	Then he brought S out to them.	9058
	46:10	The sons of S: Jemuel, Jamin, Ohad,	9058
	48: 5	just as Reuben and S are mine.	9058
	49: 5	"S and Levi are brothers—	9058
Ex	1: 2	Reuben, S, Levi and Judah,	9058
	6:15	The sons of S were Jemuel, Jamin, Ohad,	9058
	6:15	These were the clans of S.	9058
Nu	1: 6	from S, Shelumiel son of Zurishaddai;	9058
	1:22	From the descendants of S:	9058
	1:23	number from the tribe of S was 59,300.	9058
	2:12	The tribe of S will camp next to them.	9058
	2:12	of S is Shelumiel son of Zurishaddai.	9058
	7:36	the leader of the people of S,	9058
	10:19	over the division of the tribe of S,	1201+9058
	13: 5	from the tribe of S, Shaphat son of Hori;	9058
	26:12	The descendants of S by their clans were:	9058
	26:14	These were the clans of S;	9063
	34:20	from the tribe of S;	1201+9058
Dt	27:12	S, Levi, Judah, Issachar,	9058
Jos	19: 1	second lot came out for the tribe of S,	1201+9058
	21: 4	from the tribes of Judah, S and Benjamin.	9063
	21: 9	S they allotted the following towns	1201+9058
1Ch	2: 1	Reuben, S, Levi, Judah, Issachar, Zebulun,	9058
	4:24	The descendants of S:	9058
	6:65	S and Benjamin they allotted	1201+9058
	12:25	men of S, warriors ready for battle—	9058
2Ch	15: 9	and S who had settled among them,	9058
	34: 6	In the towns of Manasseh, Ephraim and S,	9058
Eze	48:24	"S will have one portion;	9058
	48:25	it will border the territory of S from east	9058
	48:33	the gate of S, the gate of Issachar and	9058
Lk	2:25	there was a man in Jerusalem called S,	5208
	2:28	S took him in his arms and praised God,	899S
	2:34	Then S blessed them and said to Mary,	5208
	3:30	the son of S, the son of Judah,	5208
Ac	13: 1	Barnabas, S called Niger,	5208
Rev	7: 7	from the tribe of S 12,000,	5208

SIMEONITE (1) [SIMEON]

Nu	25:14	the leader of a S family.	9063

SIMEONITES (8) [SIMEON]

Jos	19: 8	the inheritance of the tribe of the S,	1201+9058

	19: 9	S was taken from the share of Judah,	1201+9058
Jos	19: 9	So the S received their inheritance	1201+9058
Jdg	1: 3	men of Judah said to the S their brothers	9058
	1: 3	So the S went with them.	9058
	1:17	of Judah went with the S their brothers	9058
1Ch	4:42	And five hundred of these S,	1201+9058
	27:16	over the S: Shephatiah son of Maacah;	9063

SIMILAR (10) [SIMILARLY]

1Ki	7: 8	set farther back, was s in design.	3869
2Ki	25:17	The other pillar, with its network, was s.	3869
Jer	36:32	And many s words were added to them.	3869
	52:22	with its pomegranates, was s.	3869
Eze	41:21	one at the front of the Most Holy Place	
		was s.	2021+3869+5260
	42:11	with s exits and dimensions.	3869
	42:11	S to the doorways on the north	3869
Zec	14:15	A s plague will strike the horses and mules,	4027
Mk	4:33	With many s parables Jesus spoke the word	5525
Jude	1: 7	In a s way, Sodom and Gomorrah	3927

SIMILARLY (4) [SIMILAR]

2Ch	3:12	S one wing of the second cherub	2256
1Co	7:22	s, he who was a free man	3931
2Ti	2: 5	S, if anyone competes as an athlete,	1254
Tit	2: 6	S, encourage the young men to be	6058

SIMON (74) [PETER, SIMON'S]

Mt	4:18	S called Peter and his brother Andrew.	4981
	10: 2	first, S (who is called Peter)	4981
	10: 4	S the Zealot and Judas Iscariot,	4981
	13:55	and aren't his brothers James, Joseph, S	4981
	16:16	S Peter answered, "You are the Christ,	4981
	16:17	"Blessed are you, S son of Jonah,	4981
	17:25	"What do you think, S?"	4981
	26: 6	the home of a man known as S the Leper,	4981
	27:32	they met a man from Cyrene, named S,	4981
Mk	1:16	he saw S and his brother Andrew casting	4981
	1:29	and John to the home of S and Andrew.	4981
	1:36	S and his companions went to look for him,	4981
	3:16	S (to whom he gave the name Peter);	4981
	3:18	of Alphaeus, Thaddaeus, S the Zealot	4981
	6: 3	Joseph, Judas and S?	4981
	14: 3	the table in the home of a man known as S	4981
	14:37	"S," he said to Peter, "are you asleep?	4981
	15:21	A certain man from Cyrene, S,	4981
Lk	4:38	the synagogue and went to the home of S.	4981
	5: 3	the boats, the one belonging to S,	1639+4981
	5: 4	he said to S, "Put out into deep water,	4981
	5: 5	S answered, "Master, we've worked hard	4981
	5: 8	When S Peter saw this,	4981
	5:10	Then Jesus said to S, "Don't be afraid;	4981
	6:14	S (whom he named Peter),	4981
	6:15	S who was called the Zealot,	4981
	7:40	Jesus answered him, "S,	4981
	7:43	S replied, "I suppose the one who had	4981
	7:44	he turned toward the woman and said to S,	4981
	22:31	"S, Simon, Satan has asked to sift you	4981
	22:31	S, Satan has asked to sift you as wheat.	4981
	22:32	But I have prayed for you, S,	NIG
	23:26	they seized S from Cyrene,	4981
	24:34	The Lord has risen and has appeared to S."	4981
Jn	1:40	Andrew, S Peter's brother,	4981
	1:41	to find his brother S and tell him,	4981
	1:42	"You are S son of John.	4981
	6: 8	Andrew, S Peter's brother, spoke up,	4981
	6:68	S Peter answered him, "Lord,	4981
	6:71	(He meant Judas, the son of S Iscariot,	4981
	13: 2	Judas Iscariot, son of S, to betray Jesus.	4981
	13: 6	He came to S Peter, who said to him,	4981
	13: 9	"Then, Lord," S Peter replied,	4981
	13:24	S Peter motioned to this disciple and said,	4981
	13:26	he gave it to Judas Iscariot, son of S.	4981
	13:36	S Peter asked him, "Lord,	4981
	18:10	Then S Peter, who had a sword,	4981
	18:15	S Peter and another disciple were following	
		Jesus.	4981
	18:25	As S Peter stood warming himself,	4981
	20: 2	So she came running to S Peter and	4981
	20: 6	Then S Peter, who was behind him,	4981
	21: 2	S Peter, Thomas (called Didymus),	4981
	21: 3	"I'm going out to fish," S Peter told them,	4981
	21: 7	As soon as S Peter heard him say,	4981
	21:11	S Peter climbed aboard and dragged	4981
	21:15	Jesus said to S Peter, "Simon son of John,	4981
	21:15	Jesus said to Simon Peter, "S son of John,	4981
	21:16	Again Jesus said, "S son of John,	4981
	21:17	third time he said to him, "S son of John,	4981
Ac	1:13	James son of Alphaeus and S the Zealot,	4981
	8: 9	a man named S had practiced sorcery in	4981
	8:13	S himself believed and was baptized.	4981
	8:18	When S saw that the Spirit was given at	4981
	8:24	Then S answered, "Pray to the Lord for me	4981
	9:43	for some time with a tanner named S.	4981
	10: 5	a man named S who is called Peter.	4981
	10: 6	He is staying with S the tanner,	4981
	10:18	asking if S who was known	NIG
	10:19	"S, three men are looking for you.	NIG
	10:32	Send to Joppa for S who is called Peter.	4981
	10:32	He is a guest in the home of S the tanner,	4981
	11:13	'Send to Joppa for S who is called Peter.	4981
	15:14	S has described to us how God	5208
2Pe	1: 1	S Peter, a servant and apostle	5208

SIMON'S (4) [SIMON]

Mk	1:30	S mother-in-law was in bed with a fever,	4981
Lk	4:38	Now S mother-in-law was suffering from	4981
	5:10	the sons of Zebedee, S partners.	4981
Ac	10:17	where S house was and stopped at the gate.	4981

SIMPLE (21) [SIMPLEHEARTED, SIMPLY]

Ex	18:22	the s cases they can decide themselves.	7785
	18:26	but the s ones they decided themselves.	7785
2Ki	20:10	"It is a s matter for the shadow to go	7837
Job	5: 2	and envy slays the s.	7331
Ps	19: 7	are trustworthy, making wise the s.	7343
	119:130	it gives understanding to the s.	7343
Pr	1: 4	for giving prudence to the s, knowledge	7343
	1:22	"How long will you s ones love your	
		simple ways?	7343
	1:22	"How long will you simple ones love your	
		s ways?	7344
	1:32	For the waywardness of the s will kill them,	7343
	7: 7	I saw among the s, I noticed among the	7343
	8: 5	You are s, gain prudence;	7343
	9: 4	"Let all who are s come in here!"	7343
	9: 6	Leave your s ways and you will live;	7344
	9:16	"Let all who are s come in here!"	7343
	14:15	A s man believes anything,	7343
	14:18	The s inherit folly,	7343
	19:25	and the s will learn prudence;	7343
	21:11	a mocker is punished, the s gain wisdom;	7343
	22: 3	but the s keep going and suffer for it.	7343
	27:12	but the s keep going and suffer for it.	7343

SIMPLEHEARTED (1) [SIMPLE, HEART]

Ps	116: 6	The LORD protects the s;	7343

SIMPLY (5) [SIMPLE]

Ge	43: 7	We s answered his questions.	6584+7023
Mt	5:37	S let your 'Yes' be 'Yes,' and your 'No,'	1254
Ac	2: 2	they had s been baptized into the name of	3668
1Co	9:17	I am s discharging the trust committed	NIG
1Th	1: 5	our gospel came to you not s with words,	3668

SIMRI (KJV) See SHIMRI

SIN (473) [SIN'S, SINFUL, SINFULNESS, SINNED, SINNER, SINNER'S, SINNERS, SINNING, SINS]

Ge	4: 7	s is crouching at your door;	2633
	15:16	for the s of the Amorites has not yet reached	6411
	18:20	and Gomorrah is so great and their s so	2633
	31:36	"What s have I committed	2633
	39: 9	then could I do such a wicked thing and s	2627
	42:22	"Didn't I tell you not to s against the boy?	2627
Ex	10:17	Now forgive my s once more and pray to	2633
	16: 1	from Elim and came to the Desert of S,	6097
	17: 1	set out from the Desert of S,	6097
	20: 5	the children for the s of the fathers to	6411
	23:33	or they will cause you to s against me,	2627
	29:14	It is a s offering.	2633
	29:36	Sacrifice a bull each day as a s offering	2633
	30:10	with the blood of the atoning s offering for	2633
	32:21	that you led them into such great s?"	2631
	32:30	"You have committed a great s.	2627+2631
	32:30	perhaps I can make atonement for your s."	2633
	32:31	what a great s these people have	
		committed!	2627+2631
	32:32	But now, please forgive their s—	2633
	32:34	I will punish them for their s."	2633
	34: 7	and forgiving wickedness, rebellion and s.	10258
	34: 7	and their children for the s of the fathers to	6411
	34: 9	forgive our wickedness and our s,	2633
Lev	4: 3	a young bull without defect as a s offering	2633
	4: 3	as a sin offering for the s he has committed.	2633
	4: 8	the fat from the bull of the s offering—	2633
	4:14	they become aware of the s they committed,	2633
	4:14	a s offering and present it before the Tent	2633
	4:20	as he did with the bull for the s offering.	2633
	4:21	This is the s offering for the community.	2633
	4:23	he is made aware of the s he committed,	2633
	4:24	It is a s offering.	2633
	4:25	the s offering with his finger and put it on	2633
	4:26	make atonement for the man's s,	2633
	4:28	he is made aware of the s he committed,	2633
	4:28	as his offering for the s he committed	2633
	4:29	the s offering and slaughter it at the place	2633
	4:32	"If he brings a lamb as his offering,	2633
	4:33	and slaughter it for a s offering at the place	2633
	4:34	the s offering with his finger and put it on	2633
	4:35	for him for the s he has committed,	2633
	5: 6	as a penalty for the s he has committed,	2633
	5: 6	or goat from the flock as a s offering;	2633
	5: 6	make atonement for him for his s.	2633
	5: 7	to the LORD as a penalty for his s—	2627
	5: 7	one for a s offering and the other for	2633
	5: 8	the one for the s offering.	2633
	5: 9	the blood of the s offering against the side	2633
	5: 9	It is a s offering.	2633
	5:10	for him for the s he has committed,	2633
	5:11	for his s a tenth of an ephah of fine flour for	2627
	5:11	of an ephah of fine flour for a s offering.	2633
	5:11	because it is a s offering.	2633
	5:12	It is a s offering.	2633
	6: 3	he commits any such s that people may do	2627

Lev	6:17	Like the s offering and the guilt offering,	2633
	6:25	the regulations for the s offering:	2633
	6:25	The s offering is to be slaughtered before	2633
	6:30	But any s offering whose blood is brought	2633
	7:7	both the s offering and the guilt offering:	2633
	7:37	the grain offering, the s offering,	2633
	8:2	the bull for the s offering,	2633
	8:14	then presented the bull for the s offering,	2633
	9:2	"Take a bull calf for your s offering and	2633
	9:3	'Take a male goat for a s offering,	2633
	9:7	to the altar and sacrifice your s offering	2633
	9:8	and slaughtered the calf as a s offering	2633
	9:10	of the liver from the s offering,	2633
	9:15	He took the goat for the people's s offering	2633
	9:15	and offered it for a s offering	2627
	9:22	having sacrificed the s offering	2633
	10:16	about the goat of the s offering and found	2633
	10:17	"Why didn't you eat the s offering in	2633
	10:19	"Today they sacrificed their s offering	2633
	10:19	if I had eaten the s offering today?"	2633
	12:6	a young pigeon or a dove for a s offering.	2633
	12:8	and the other for a s offering.	2633
	14:13	in the holy place where the s offering and	2633
	14:13	the s offering, the guilt offering belongs to	2633
	14:19	the s offering and make atonement for	2633
	14:22	one for a s offering and the other for	2633
	14:31	one as a s offering and the other as	2633
	15:15	the one for a s offering and the other for	2633
	15:30	to sacrifice one for a s offering and the	2633
	16:3	a s offering and a ram for a burnt offering.	2633
	16:5	a s offering and a ram for a burnt offering.	2633
	16:6	for his own s offering to make atonement	2633
	16:9	the LORD and sacrifice it for a s offering.	2633
	16:11	for his own s offering to make atonement	2633
	16:11	to slaughter the bull for his own s	2633
	16:15	then slaughter the goat for the s offering	2633
	16:25	He shall also burn the fat of the s offering,	2633
	16:27	The bull and the goat for the s offerings,	2633
	18:25	so I punished it for its s,	6411
	19:22	the LORD for the s he has committed,	2633
	19:22	and his s will be forgiven.	2633
	23:19	for a s offering and two lambs,	2633
	26:41	and they pay for their s,	6411
Nu	5:7	and must confess the s he has committed.	2633
	5:31	bear the consequences of her s.'	6411
	6:11	to offer one as a s offering and the other as	2633
	6:14	without defect for a s offering,	2633
	6:16	before the LORD and make the s offering	2633
	7:16	one male goat for a s offering;	2633
	7:22	one male goat for a s offering;	2633
	7:28	one male goat for a s offering;	2633
	7:34	one male goat for a s offering;	2633
	7:40	one male goat for a s offering;	2633
	7:46	one male goat for a s offering;	2633
	7:52	one male goat for a s offering;	2633
	7:58	one male goat for a s offering;	2633
	7:64	one male goat for a s offering;	2633
	7:70	one male goat for a s offering;	2633
	7:76	one male goat for a s offering;	2633
	7:82	one male goat for a s offering;	2633
	7:87	goats were used for the s offering.	2633
	8:8	a second young bull for a s offering.	2633
	8:12	a s offering to the LORD and the other for	2633
	9:13	bear the consequences of his s.	2628
	12:11	the s we have so foolishly committed.	2633
	14:18	in love and forgiving s and rebellion.	6411
	14:18	the children for the s of the fathers to	6411
	14:19	forgive the s of these people,	6411
	15:24	and a male goat for a s offering.	2633
	15:25	an offering made by fire and a s offering.	2633
	15:27	a year-old female goat for a s offering.	2633
	18:9	whether grain or s or guilt offerings,	2633
	18:22	or they will bear the consequences of their s	2628
	19:9	it is for purification from s.	2633
	27:3	but he died for his own s and left no sons.	2628
	28:15	be presented to the LORD as a s offering.	2633
	28:22	as a s offering to make atonement for you.	2633
	29:5	as a s offering to make atonement for you.	2633
	29:11	Include one male goat as a s offering,	2633
	29:11	in addition to the s offering for atonement	2633
	29:16	Include one male goat as a s offering,	2633
	29:19	Include one male goat as a s offering,	2633
	29:22	Include one male goat as a s offering,	2633
	29:25	Include one male goat as a s offering,	2633
	29:28	Include one male goat as a s offering,	2633
	29:31	Include one male goat as a s offering,	2633
	29:34	Include one male goat as a s offering,	2633
	29:38	Include one male goat as a s offering,	2633
	32:23	be sure that your s will find you out.	2633
	33:11	the Red Sea and camped in the Desert of S.	6097
	33:12	the Desert of S and camped at Dophkah.	6097
Dt	5:9	the children for the s of the fathers to	6411
	9:18	because of all the s you had committed,	2633
	9:27	their wickedness and their s.	2633
	15:9	and you will be found guilty of s.	2628
	20:18	you will s against the LORD your God.	2627
	22:26	she has committed no s deserving death.	2628
	23:21	of you and you will be guilty of s.	2628
	24:4	Do not bring s upon the land	2627
	24:15	and you will be guilty of s.	2628
	24:16	each is to die for his own s.	2628
Jos	22:17	Was not the s of Peor enough for us?	6411
	22:17	not cleansed ourselves from that s,	NIH
	22:20	not the only one who died for his s.' "	6411
1Sa	2:17	This s of the young men was very great in	2633
	3:13	because of the s he knew about;	6411
	12:23	from me that I should s against the LORD	2627

1Sa	14:34	Do not s against the LORD by eating meat	2627
	14:38	let us find out what s has been committed today.	2633
	15:23	For rebellion is like the s of divination,	2633
	15:25	forgive my s and come back with me,	2633
2Sa	12:13	"The LORD has taken away your s.	2633
	22:24	before him and have kept myself from s.	6411
1Ki	8:34	then hear from heaven and forgive the s	2633
	8:35	confess your name and turn from their s	2633
	8:36	then hear from heaven and forgive the s	2633
	8:46	"When they s against you—	2627
	8:46	for there is no one who does not s—	2627
	12:30	And this thing became a s;	2633
	13:34	This was the s of the house of Jeroboam	2633
	15:26	in the ways of his father and in his s,	2633
	15:34	in the ways of Jeroboam and in his s,	2633
	16:2	caused my people Israel to s	2627
	16:19	of Jeroboam and in the s he had committed	2633
	16:26	of Jeroboam son of Nebat and in his s,	2633
	17:18	to remind me of my s and kill my son?"	6411
	21:22	to anger and have caused Israel to s.'	2627
	22:52	who caused Israel to s.	2627
2Ki	12:16	from the guilt offerings and s offerings was	2633
	17:21	and caused them to commit a great s.	2631
	21:11	and has led Judah into s with his idols.	2627
	21:16	the s that he had caused Judah to commit,	2633
	21:17	including the s he committed,	2633
	23:15	who had caused Israel to s—	2627
2Ch	6:25	then hear from heaven and forgive the s	2633
	6:26	confess your name and turn from their s	2633
	6:27	then hear from heaven and forgive the s	2633
	6:36	"When they s against you—	2627
	6:36	for there is no one who does not s—	2627
	7:14	from heaven and will forgive their s	2633
	19:10	to warn them not to s against the LORD;	870
	19:10	Do this, and you will not s.	870
	28:13	Do you intend to add to our s and guilt?	2633
	29:21	and seven male goats as a s offering for	2633
	29:23	the s offering were brought before the king	2633
	29:24	presented their blood on the altar for a s offering	2627
	29:24	the burnt offering and the s offering	2633
Ezr	6:17	as a s offering for all Israel,	10260
	8:35	as a s offering, twelve male goats.	2633
Ne	6:13	to intimidate me so that I would commit a s	2627
	10:33	for s offerings to make atonement	2633
	13:26	even he was led into s by foreign women.	2627
Job	1:22	not s by charging God with wrongdoing.	2627
	2:10	In all this, Job did not s in what he said.	2627
	8:4	gave them over to the penalty of their s.	7322
	10:6	and probe after my s—	2633
	11:6	God has even forgotten some of your s.	6411
	11:14	the s that is in your hand and allow no evil	224
	13:23	Show me my offense and my s.	2633
	14:16	but not keep track of my s.	2633
	14:17	you will cover over my s;	6411
	15:5	Your s prompts your mouth,	6411
	31:11	a s to be judged.	6411
	31:30	to s by invoking a curse against his life—	2627
	31:33	if I have concealed my s as men do,	7322
	33:9	'I am pure and without s;	7322
	34:37	To his s he adds rebellion;	2633
	35:6	If you s, how does that affect him?	2627
Ps	4:4	In your anger do not s;	2627
	17:3	I have resolved that my mouth will not s.	6296
	18:23	before him and have kept myself from s.	6411
	32:2	the man whose s the LORD does not count	6411
	32:5	Then I acknowledged my s to you and did	2633
	32:5	and you forgave the guilt of my s.	2633
	36:2	to detect or hate his s.	6411
	38:3	bones have no soundness because of my s.	2633
	38:18	I am troubled by my s.	2633
	39:1	and keep my tongue from s;	2627
	39:11	You rebuke and discipline men for their s;	6411
	40:6	burnt offerings and s offerings you did	2631
	51:2	and cleanse me from my s.	2633
	51:3	and my s is always before me.	2633
	59:3	against me for no offense or s of mine,	2633
	66:18	If I had cherished s in my heart,	224
	78:17	But they continued to s against him,	2627
	89:32	I will punish their s with the rod,	7322
	106:43	and they wasted away in their s.	6411
	109:14	the s of his mother never be blotted out.	2633
	119:11	in my heart that I might not s against you.	2627
	119:133	let no s rule over me.	224
Pr	1:16	for their feet rush into s,	8273
	5:22	the cords of his s hold him fast.	2633
	10:19	When words are many, s is not absent.	7322
	14:9	Fools mock at making amends for s,	871
	14:34	but s is a disgrace to any people.	2633
	16:6	love and faithfulness s is atoned for;	6411
	17:19	He who loves a quarrel loves s;	7322
	20:9	I am clean and without s"?	2633
	21:4	the lamp of the wicked, are s!	2633
	24:9	The schemes of folly are s,	2633
	29:6	An evil man is snared by his own s,	7322
	29:16	When the wicked thrive, so does s,	7322
Ecc	5:6	Do not let your mouth lead you into s.	2627
Isa	3:9	they parade their s like Sodom;	2633
	5:18	Woe to those who draw s along with cords	6411
	6:7	and your s atoned for."	2633
	22:14	"Till your dying day this s will not	6411
	27:9	be the full fruitage of the removal of his s:	2633
	30:1	but not by my Spirit, heaping s upon sin;	2633
	30:1	but not by my Spirit, heaping sin upon sin;	2633
	30:13	this s will become for you like a high wall,	6411
	40:2	that her s has been paid for,	6411

Isa	53:12	For he bore the s of many,	2628
	59:7	Their feet rush into s;	8273
	64:5	But when we continued to s against them,	2627
Jer	9:3	They go from one s to another;	8288
	9:7	for what else can I do because of the s	NIH
	16:10	What s have we committed against	2633
	16:17	nor is their s concealed from my eyes.	6411
	16:18	for their wickedness and their s,	2633
	17:1	"Judah's s is engraved with an iron tool,	2633
	17:3	because of s throughout your country.	2633
	31:30	Instead, everyone will die for his own s;	6411
	32:35	a detestable thing and so make Judah s.	2627
	33:8	the s they have committed against me	6411
	36:3	I will forgive their wickedness and their s."	2633
La	2:14	they did not expose your s	6411
	4:22	he will punish your s.	6411
Eze	3:18	that wicked man will die for his s,	6411
	3:19	he will die for his s;	6411
	3:20	you did not warn him, he will die for his s.	2633
	3:21	if you do warn the righteous man not to s	2627
	3:21	not to sin and he does not s,	2627
	4:4	on your left side and put the s of the house	6411
	4:4	You are to bear their s for the number	6411
	4:5	of days as the years of their s.	6411
	4:5	So for 390 days you will bear the s of	6411
	4:6	and bear the s of the house of Judah.	6411
	4:17	and will waste away because of their s.	6411
	7:19	for it has made them stumble into s.	6411
	9:9	"The s of the house of Israel	6411
	16:49	" 'Now this was the s of your sister Sodom:	6411
	18:17	He withholds his hand from s	6404
	18:17	He will not die for his father's s;	6411
	18:18	But his father will die for his own s,	6411
	18:24	from his righteousness and commits s	6404
	18:26	from his righteousness and commits s	6404
	18:26	of the s he has committed he will die.	6404
	18:30	then s will not be your downfall.	6411
	29:16	but will be a reminder of their s in turning	6411
	33:6	man will be taken away because of his s,	6411
	33:8	that wicked man will die for his s,	6411
	33:9	he will die for his s,	6411
	33:14	from his s and does what is just and right—	2633
	39:23	of Israel went into exile for their s,	6411
	40:39	on which the burnt offerings, s offerings	2633
	42:13	the s offerings and the guilt offerings—	2633
	43:19	You are to give a young bull as a s offering	2633
	43:21	You are to take the bull for the s offering	2633
	43:22	a male goat without defect for a s offering,	2633
	43:25	a male goat daily for a s offering;	2633
	44:10	must bear the consequences of their s.	6411
	44:12	and made the house of Israel fall into s,	6411
	44:12	must bear the consequences of their s,	6411
	44:27	he is to offer a s offering for himself,	2633
	44:29	the s offerings and the guilt offerings;	2633
	45:17	He will provide the s offerings,	2633
	45:19	the s offering and put it on the doorposts of	2633
	45:22	a bull as a s offering for himself and for all	2633
	45:23	and a male goat for a s offering,	2633
	45:25	to make the same provision for s offerings,	2633
	46:20	the s offering and bake the grain offering,	2633
Da	9:20	confessing my s and the sin of my people	2633
	9:20	and the s of my people Israel	2633
	9:24	to put an end to s, to atone for wickedness,	2633
Hos	5:5	even Ephraim, stumble in their s;	6411
	8:11	Ephraim built many altars for s offerings,	2627
	10:8	it is the s of Israel.	2633
	10:10	to put them in bonds for their double s.	6411
	12:8	not find in me any iniquity or s."	2628
	13:2	Now they s more and more;	2627
Am	4:4	"Go to Bethel and s;	7321
	4:4	go to Gilgal and s yet more.	7321
Mic	1:13	the beginning of s to the Daughter of Zion,	2633
	3:8	to Jacob his transgression, to Israel his s.	2633
	6:7	the fruit of my body for the s of my soul?	2633
	7:18	Who is a God like you, who pardons s	6411
Zec	3:4	"See, I have taken away your s,	6411
	3:9	and I will remove the s of this land in	6411
	13:1	to cleanse them from s and impurity.	2633
Mal	2:6	and turned many from s.	6411
Mt	5:29	If your right eye causes you to s,	4997
	5:30	And if your right hand causes you to s,	4997
	6:14	you forgive men when they s against you,	4183
	12:31	every s and blasphemy will be forgiven	281
	13:41	of his kingdom everything that causes s	4998
	18:6	anyone causes one of these little ones who believe in me to s,	4997
	18:7	the things that cause people to s!	4998
	18:7	If your hand or your foot causes you to s,	4997
	18:9	And if your eye causes you to s,	4997
	23:32	the measure of the s of your forefathers!	NIG
Mk	3:29	he is guilty of an eternal s."	280
	9:42	anyone causes one of these little ones who believe in me to s,	4997
	9:43	If your hand causes you to s, cut it off.	4997
	9:45	And if your foot causes you to s, cut it off.	4997
	9:47	if your eye causes you to s, pluck it out.	4997
Lk	17:1	that cause people to s are bound to come,	4998
	17:2	to cause one of these little ones to s.	4997
Jn	1:29	who takes away the s of the world!	281
	8:7	"If any one of you is without s,	387
	8:11	and leave your life of s."	279+3600
	8:21	and you will die in your s.	281
	8:34	everyone who sins is a slave to s.	281
	8:46	Can any of you prove me guilty of s?	281
	9:34	"You were steeped in s at birth;	281
	9:41	you would not be guilty of s;	281+2400
	15:22	they would not be guilty of s.	281+2400

Jn	15:22	however, they have no excuse for their s.	281
	15:24	*they would* not be guilty of s.	281+2400
	16: 8	of guilt in regard to s and righteousness	281
	16: 9	in regard to s, because men do not believe	281
	19:11	is guilty of a greater s."	281+2400
Ac	7:60	"Lord, do not hold this s against them."	281
	8:23	of bitterness and captive to s."	94
Ro	2:12	All who s apart from the law will	279
	2:12	and all who s under the law will be judged	279
	3: 9	that Jews and Gentiles alike are all under s.	281
	3:20	through the law we become conscious of s.	281
	4: 8	the man whose s the Lord will never count	281
	5:12	as s entered the world through one man,	281
	5:12	through s, and in this way death came	281
	5:13	before the law was given, s was in the world.	281
	5:13	But s is not taken into account when there is	281
	5:14	even over those who *did* not s by breaking	279
	5:16	not like the result of the one man's s:	279
	5:16	The judgment followed one s	NIG
	5:20	But where s increased, grace increased	281
	5:21	just as s reigned in death,	281
	6: 2	We died to s; how can we live in it	281
	6: 6	so that the body *of* s might be done away	281
	6: 6	that we should no longer be slaves *to* s—	281
	6: 7	anyone who has died has been freed from s.	281
	6:10	The death he died, he died *to* s once for all;	281
	6:11	count yourselves dead *to* s but alive to God	281
	6:12	not let s reign in your mortal body so	281
	6:13	Do not offer the parts of your body *to* s,	281
	6:14	For s shall not be your master,	281
	6:15	*Shall we* s because we are not under law	279
	6:16	whether you are slaves to s,	281
	6:17	though you used to be slaves *to* s,	281
	6:18	from s and have become slaves	281
	6:20	When you were slaves *to* s,	281
	6:22	But now that you have been set free from s	281
	6:23	For the wages *of* s is death,	281
	7: 7	Is the law s? Certainly not!	281
	7: 7	not have known **what** s was except through	281
	7: 8	But s, seizing the opportunity afforded by	281
	7: 8	For apart from law, s is dead.	281
	7: 9	s sprang to life and I died.	281
	7:11	For s, seizing the opportunity afforded by	281
	7:13	in order that s might be recognized as sin,	281
	7:13	in order that sin might be recognized as s,	281
	7:13	through the commandment s might become utterly sinful.	281
	7:14	but I am unspiritual, sold as a slave to s.	281
	7:17	but it is s living in me.	281
	7:20	but it is s living in me that does it.	281
	7:23	the law *of* s at work within my members.	281
	7:25	in the sinful nature a slave to the law *of* s.	281
	8: 2	Spirit of life set me free from the law *of* s	281
	8: 3	the likeness of sinful man to be a s **offering**.	281
	8: 3	And so he condemned s in sinful man,	281
	8:10	your body is dead because of s,	281
	14:23	that does not come from faith is s.	281
1Co	8:12	*When you* s against your brothers	279
	8:12	*you* s against Christ.	279
	8:13	I eat **causes** my brother *to* **fall into** s,	4997
	15:56	The sting of death is s,	281
	15:56	and the power *of* s is the law.	281
2Co	5:21	God made him who had no s to be sin	281
	5:21	God made him who had no sin to be s	281
	11: 7	Was it a s for me to lower myself	281+4472
	11:29	Who is **led into** s, and I do not inwardly	4997
	12:21	the impurity, **sexual** s and debauchery	4518
Gal	2:17	does that mean that Christ **promotes** s?	281+1356
	2:17	that the whole world is a prisoner of s,	281
	6: 1	Brothers, if someone is caught in a s,	4183
Eph	4:26	"In your anger *do* not s":	279
1Ti	5:20	Those who are to be rebuked publicly,	279
Heb	4:15	just as we are—yet was without s.	281
	9:26	at the end of the ages to do away **with** s by	281
	9:28	he will appear a second time, not to bear s,	281
	10: 6	and s **offerings** you were not pleased.	281+4309
	10: 8	burnt offerings and s **offerings** you did	281+4309
	10:18	there is no longer any sacrifice for s.	281
	11:25	to enjoy the pleasures *of* s for a short time.	281
	12: 1	and the s that so easily entangles,	281
	12: 4	In your struggle against s,	281
	13:11	into the Most Holy Place as a s **offering**,	281
Jas	1:15	desire has conceived, it gives birth to s;	281
	1:15	and s, when it is full-grown,	281
	2: 9	*you* s and are convicted by the law	281+2237
1Pe	2:22	"He committed no s, and no deceit was	281
	4: 1	who has suffered in his body is done with s.	281
1Jn	1: 7	blood of Jesus, his Son, purifies us from all s.	281
	1: 8	If we claim to be **without** s,	281+4024
	2: 1	I write this to you so that *you will* not s.	279
	2: 1	But if anybody *does* s,	279
	3: 4	in fact, s is lawlessness.	281
	3: 5	And in him is no s.	281
	3: 6	No one who *continues to* s has either seen	279
	3: 9	No one who is born of God *will continue* to s,	281+4472
	5:16	If anyone sees his brother **commit a** s	279+281
	5:16	*to* those whose s does not lead to death.	279
	5:16	There is a s that leads to death.	281
	5:17	All wrongdoing is s,	281
	5:17	and there is a s that does not lead to death.	281
	5:18	anyone born of God *does* not *continue to* s;	279
Rev	2:14	the Israelites to s by eating food sacrificed	NIG

SIN'S (1) [SIN]

Heb	3:13	of you may be hardened by s deceitfulness.	281

SINA (KJV) See SINAI

SINAI (39) [HOREB]

Ex	16: 1	which is between Elim and S,	6099
	19: 1	they came to the Desert of S.	6099
	19: 2	they entered the Desert of S,	6099
	19:11	the Lord will come down on Mount S in	6099
	19:18	Mount S was covered with smoke,	6099
	19:20	of Mount S and called Moses to the top of	6099
	19:23	"The people cannot come up Mount S,	6099
	24:16	glory of the Lord settled on Mount S.	6099
	31:18	speaking to Moses on Mount S,	6099
	34: 2	and then come up on Mount S.	6099
	34: 4	the first ones and went up Mount S early in	6099
	34:29	down from Mount S with the two tablets of	6099
	34:32	the Lord had given him on Mount S.	6099
Lev	7:38	which the Lord gave Moses on Mount S	6099
	7:38	to the Lord, in the Desert of S.	6099
	25: 1	The Lord said to Moses on Mount S,	6099
	26:46	that the Lord established on Mount S	6099
	27:34	the Lord gave Moses on Mount S for	6099
Nu	1: 1	of S on the first day of the second month of	6099
	1:19	And so he counted them in the Desert of S:	6099
	3: 1	the Lord talked with Moses on Mount S.	6099
	3: 4	before him in the Desert of S.	6099
	3:14	to Moses in the Desert of S,	6099
	9: 1	of S in the first month of the second year	6099
	9: 5	of S at twilight on the fourteenth day of	6099
	10:12	of S and traveled from place to place until	6099
	26:64	the Israelites in the Desert of S.	6099
	28: 6	instituted at Mount S as a pleasing aroma,	6099
	33:15	and camped in the Desert of S.	6099
	33:16	of S and camped at Kibroth Hattaavah.	6099
Dt	33: 2	from S and dawned over them from Seir;	6099
Jdg	5: 5	the One of S, before the Lord,	6099
Ne	9:13	"You came down on Mount S;	6099
Ps	68: 8	before God, the One of S, before God,	6099
	68:17	Lord [has come] from S into his sanctuary.	6099
Ac	7:30	a burning bush in the desert near Mount S.	4982
	7:38	to him on Mount S, and with our fathers;	4982
Gal	4:24	from Mount S and bears children who are	4982
	4:25	for Mount S in Arabia and corresponds to	4982

SINCE (266)

Ge	3:19	s from it you were taken;	3954
	4:25	s Cain killed him."	3954
	14:12	s he was living in Sodom.	2256
	15: 2	what can you give me s I remain childless	2256
	26:27	you were hostile to me	2256
	38:26	s I wouldn't give her to my son	3954+4027+6584
	41:39	"S God has made all this known to you,	339
	42:23	s he was using an interpreter.	3954
	44:28	And I have not seen him s.	2178+6330
	46:30	s I have seen for myself	339
	47:16	s your money is gone."	561
	47:18	the fact that s our money is gone	561
Ex	4:10	nor s you have spoken to your servant.	255+4946
	5:23	**Ever** s I went to Pharaoh to speak	255+4946
	6:12	s I speak with faltering lips?"	2256
	6:30	"S I speak with faltering lips,	2176
	9:24	land of Egypt s it had become a nation.	255+4946
	9:31	s the barley had headed and the flax was	3954
	10:11	s that's what you have been asking for."	3954
	21:21	s the slave is his property.	3954
	23:21	s my Name is in him.	3954
Lev	10:18	S its blood was not taken into	2176
	11:11	**And** s you are to detest them,	2256
	13:13	S it has all turned white, he is clean.	NIH
	21: 3	on him s she has no husband—	889
	25:15	on the basis of the number of years s	339
	25:27	the **years** s he sold it and refund the balance	AIT
	27:26	s the firstborn already belongs to	889
Nu	5:13	(s there is no witness against her	2256
	11:28	who had been Moses' aide s youth,	4946
	14:25	S the Amalekites and Canaanites are living	2256
	20:21	S Edom refused to let them go	2256
	22:20	"S these men have come to summon you,	561
	35:23	then s he was not his enemy and he did	2256
Dt	3:27	s you are not going to cross this Jordan.	3954
	9:24	the Lord **ever** s I have known you.	3427+4946
	12: 9	s you have not yet reached the resting place	3954
	19: 6	s he did it to his neighbor	3954
	21: 9	s you have done what is right in the eyes of	3954
	21:14	s you have dishonored her.	889+9393
	34:10	S **then,** no prophet has risen in Israel	6388
Jos	3: 4	s you have never been this way before.	3954
	5: 6	s they had not obeyed the Lord.	889
	7:26	called the Valley of Achor **ever** s.	2021+2021+2296+3427+6330
	10:14	a day like it before or s,	339
	13:14	s the offerings made by fire to the Lord,	NIH
	14:10	he has kept me alive for forty-five years s	4946
	14:14	belonged to Caleb of Jephunneh the Kenizzite **ever** s,	2021+2021+2296+3427+6330
	15:19	S you have given me land in the Negev,	3954
Jdg	1:15	S you have given me land in the Negev,	3954
	11:23	"Now s the Lord, the God of Israel,	2256
	15: 7	"S you've acted like this,	561
	16:17	a Nazirite set apart to God s birth.	4946
	17:13	s this Levite has become my priest."	3954
	18: 7	And s their land lacked nothing,	3954
	19:23	S this man is my guest,	339+889
	19:30	not s the day the Israelites came up out	4946
	21: 7	s we have taken an oath by the Lord not	2256
	21:18	s we Israelites have taken this oath:	3954
Jdg	21:22	s you did not give your daughters	3954
Ru	2:11	mother-in-law s the death of your husband	339
	3: 9	s you are a kinsman-redeemer."	3954
1Sa	16: 1	s I have rejected him as king over Israel?	2256
	21: 6	s there was no bread there except the bread	3954
	25: 8	s we come at a festive time.	3954
	25:26	"Now s the Lord has kept you,	2256
	27: 6	belonged to the kings of Judah **ever** s.	2021+2021+2296+3427+6330
2Sa	7:11	and have done **ever** s the time	4946
	13:14	**and** s he was stronger than she,	2256
	13:32	Absalom's expressed intention **ever** s	4946
	19:11	to bring the king back to his palace, s	2256
	19:26	s I your servant am lame,	3954
1Ki	3:11	"S you have asked for this and not	889+3610
	8:16	'S the day I brought my people Israel out	4946
	8:39	s you know his heart (for you alone know	889
	10:12	or seen s that day.)	6330
	11:11	"S this is your attitude and you have	889+3610
	18:12	worshiped the Lord s my youth.	4946
	18:25	s there are so many of you.	3954
	21: 2	s it is close to my palace.	3954
2Ki	10: 2	s your master's sons are with you	2256
	14:27	And s the Lord had not said	2256
	18:26	s we understand it.	3954
	23:22	Not s the days of the judges who led Israel,	4946
1Ch	17:10	and have done **ever** s the time	4946
	23:25	For David had said, "S the Lord,	NIH
2Ch	1:11	"S this is your heart's desire and you	889+3610
	1:11	and s you have not asked for a long life but	1685
	2: 6	s the heavens, even the highest heavens,	3954
	6: 5	'S the day I brought my people out	4946
	6:30	s you know his heart (for you alone know	889
	12: 7	"S they have humbled themselves,	NIH
	14: 6	s the land was at peace.	3954
	14:14	s there was much booty there.	3954
	22: 1	king in his place, s the raiders,	3954
	28:23	for he thought, "S the gods of the kings	3954
	30:17	S many in the crowd had	3954
	30:26	for s the days of Solomon son	4946
	31:10	"S the people began to bring their	4946
	35:18	in Israel s the days of the prophet Samuel,	4946
Ezr	4: 2	and have been sacrificing to him s the time	4946
	4:14	Now s we are under obligation to the palace	10168+10353+10619
Ne	6:18	s he was son-in-law to Shecaniah son	3954
Est	1:13	S it was customary for the king	3954
	4:11	But thirty days have passed s I was called	4202
	6:13	and his wife Zeresh said to him, "S	561
Job	9:29	S I am already found guilty,	NIH
	19:28	s the root of the trouble lies in him,'	2256
	20: 4	**ever** s man was placed on the earth,	4974
	21:22	s he judges even the highest?	2256
	30: 2	s their vigor had gone from them?	NIH
Ps	22: 8	Let him deliver him, s he delights in him."	3954
	28: 5	S they show no regard for the works of	3954
	31: 3	S you are my rock and my fortress,	3954
	35: 7	S they hid their net for me without cause	3954
	44:21	s he knows the secrets of the heart?	3954
	45: 2	s God has blessed you forever.	4027+6584
	71: 5	my confidence s my youth.	4946
	71:17	S my youth, O God, you have taught me,	4946
Pr	1:24	**But** s you rejected me when I called	3610
	1:25	s you ignored all my advice and would	2256
	1:29	S they hated knowledge and did not	3954+9393
	1:30	s they would not accept my advice	NIH
	6: 3	s you have fallen into your neighbor's	3954
	17:16	s he has no desire to get wisdom?	2256
Ecc	5:16	s he toils for the wind?	8611
	8: 4	S a king's word is supreme,	889+928
	8: 7	S no man knows the future,	3954
	9: 6	and their jealousy have **long** s vanished;	3893
Isa	7:17	a time unlike any s Ephraim broke away from Judah—	3427+4200+4946
	36:11	s we understand it.	3954
	40:21	not understood s the earth was founded?	NIH
	43: 4	S you are precious and honored	889+4946
	44: 7	and lay out before me what has happened s	4946
	46: 3	whom I have upheld s you were conceived,	4974
	46: 3	and have carried s your birth.	4974
	47:12	which you have labored at s childhood.	4946
	47:15	with and trafficked with s childhood.	4946
	64: 4	S ancient times no one has heard,	4946
Jer	8: 9	S they have rejected the word of	2180
	8:21	S my people are crushed, I am crushed;	6584
	32: 8	S it is your right to redeem it	3954
	44:18	But **ever** s we stopped burning incense	255+4946
	48: 7	S you trust in your deeds and riches,	3610+3954
	50:15	S this is the vengeance of the Lord,	3954
Eze	3: 20	S you did not warn him,	3954
	18:19	S the son has done what is just and right	2256
	23:35	S you have forgotten me and thrust me	3610
	33: 5	S he heard the sound of the trumpet but did	NIH
	33:25	S you eat meat with the blood still in it	NIH
	35: 6	S you did not hate bloodshed,	561
Da	10:12	S the first day that you set your mind	4946
	10:19	my lord, s you have given me strength."	3954
Hos	10: 9	"S the days of Gibeah, you have sinned,	4946
Mic	1: 7	S she gathered her gifts from the wages	3954
Hab	2:18	s a man has carved it?	3954
Zec	7: 3	the land has been my livelihood s	4946
Mal	3: 7	**Ever** s the time of your forefathers	4200+4946
Mt	13:21	s he has no root, he lasts only a short time.	NIG
	13:35	I will utter things hidden s the creation of	608
	18:25	*S he was* not **able** to pay,	AIT
	22:25	and *s he* had no children,	AIT
	22:28	s all of them were married to her?"	1142

Mt	25:34	the kingdom prepared for you s the creation	608
	27: 6	s it is blood money."	2075
Mk	2: 4	S they could not get him to Jesus because	AIT
	4:17	But s they have no root,	NIG
	8: 1	S they had nothing to eat,	NIG
	10:20	"all these I have kept s I was a boy."	1666
	11:11	but s it was already late,	AIT
	12:23	s the seven were married to her?"	1142
Lk	1: 3	s I myself have carefully investigated	NIG
	1:34	Mary asked the angel, "s I am a virgin?"	2075
	11:50	of all the prophets that has been shed s	608
	12:26	S you cannot do this very little thing,	1623
	16:16	S that time, the good news of the kingdom	608
	18:21	"All these I have kept s I was a boy,"	1666
	19: 4	Jesus was coming that way.	4022
	20:33	s the seven were married to her?"	1142
	20:36	s they are children of the resurrection.	4022
	23:40	"s you are under the same sentence?	4022
	24:21	it is the third day s all this took place.	608+4005
Jn	5:47	But s you do not believe what he wrote,	1623
	7: 4	S you are doing these things,	1623
	7:39	s Jesus was not yet been glorified.	4022
	13:29	S Judas had charge of the money,	2075
	19:42	of Preparation and s the tomb was nearby,	4022
Ac	4:14	But s they could see the man	AIT
	13:46	S you reject it and do not consider	2076
	17:29	"Therefore s we are God's offspring,	AIT
	18:15	But s it involves questions about words	1623
	19:36	Therefore, s these facts are undeniable,	AIT
	19:40	s there is no reason for it."	AIT
	21:34	s the commander could not get at the truth	AIT
	22:30	s the commander wanted to find out	AIT
	25:14	S they were spending many days there,	6055
	26: 4	the way I have lived ever s I was a child,	1666
	27:12	S the harbor was unsuitable to winter in,	AIT
Ro	1:19	s what may be known about God is plain	1484
	1:20	For s the creation of the world	608
	1:28	s they did not think it worthwhile to retain	2777
	2:15	s they show that the requirements of	NIG
	3:30	s there is only one God,	1642
	4:19	s he was about a hundred years old—	AIT
	5: 1	s we have been justified through faith,	AIT
	5: 9	S we have now been justified by his blood,	AIT
	6: 9	For we know that s Christ was raised from	AIT
	10: 3	S they did not know the righteousness	AIT
	15:23	and s I have been longing for many years	AIT
1Co	1:21	For s in the wisdom of God the world	2076
	3: 3	For s there is jealousy and quarreling	3963
	7: 2	But s there is so much immorality,	1328
	8: 7	and s their conscience is weak, it is defiled.	NIG
	11: 7	s he is the image and glory of God;	2075
	14:12	S you are eager to have spiritual gifts,	2075
	14:16	s he does not know what you are saying?	2076
	15:21	For s death came through a man,	2076
2Co	3:12	s we have such a hope, we are very bold.	AIT
	4: 1	Therefore, s through God's mercy we have this ministry,	2777
	5:11	S, then, we know what it is to fear the Lord,	AIT
	7: 1	S we have these promises, dear friends,	AIT
	8: 6	s he had earlier made a beginning,	2777
	9: 2	that last year you in Achaia were ready	608
	11:18	S many are boasting in the way	2075
	11:19	You gladly put up with fools s you are	AIT
	13: 3	s you are demanding proof	2075
Gal	4: 7	and s you are a son,	1623
	5:25	S we live by the Spirit,	1623
Eph	1:15	ever s I heard about your faith in	AIT
	6: 9	s you know that he who is both their Master	AIT
Php	1: 7	s I have you in my heart;	1328
	1:30	s you are going through the same struggle	2400
Col	1: 6	just as it has been doing among you s	608+4005
	1: 9	s the day we heard about you,	608
	2:20	S you died with Christ to the basic principles of this world,	1623
	3: 1	S, then, you have been raised with Christ,	1623
	3: 9	s you have taken off your old self	AIT
	3:15	s as members of one body you were called	NIG
	3:24	s you know that you will receive	AIT
1Th	3: 8	s you are standing firm in the Lord.	1569
	5: 8	But s we belong to the day,	AIT
Tit	1: 7	S an overseer is entrusted with God's work,	1142
Heb	2:14	S the children have flesh and blood,	2075
	4: 1	s the promise of entering his rest still stands,	AIT
	4: 3	And yet his work has been finished s	608
	4:14	s we have a great high priest who has gone	AIT
	5: 2	s he himself is subject to weakness.	2075
	6:13	there was no one greater for him to swear	1328+3836
	7:23	s death prevented them from	AIT
	9:26	s to suffer many times since the creation of	608
	10:13	S that time he waits for his enemies to	3370+3836
	10:19	s we have confidence to enter the Most Holy	AIT
	10:21	and s we have a great priest over the house	NIG
	12: 1	s we are surrounded by such a great cloud	AIT
	12:28	s we are receiving a kingdom that cannot	AIT
1Pe	1:17	S you call on a Father who judges each	1623
	4: 1	Therefore, s Christ suffered in his body,	AIT
2Pe	3: 4	Ever s our fathers died,	608+4005
	3: 4	everything goes on as it has s the beginning	608
	3:11	S everything will be destroyed	AIT
	3:14	s you are looking forward to	AIT
	3:17	dear friends, s you already know this,	AIT
1Jn	1: 1	which you have had s the beginning.	608
	4:11	Dear friends, s God so loved us,	1623
Rev	3:10	S you have kept my command	4022
	16:18	No earthquake like it has ever occurred s man has been on the earth.	608+4005

SINCERE (11) [SINCERITY, SINCERELY]

Da	11:34	and many who are not s will join them.	2761
Ac	2:46	and ate together with glad and s hearts,	911
Ro	12: 9	Love must be s.	537
2Co	6: 6	in the Holy Spirit and in s love;	537
	11: 3	from your s and pure devotion to Christ.	605
1Ti	1: 5	and a good conscience and a faith.	537
	3: 8	are to be men worthy of respect, s,	1474+3590
2Ti	1: 5	I have been reminded of your s faith,	537
Heb	10:22	near to God with a s heart in full assurance	240
Jas	3:17	of mercy and good fruit, impartial and s.	537
1Pe	1:22	by obeying the truth so that you have s love	537

SINCERELY (2) [SINCERE]

Job	33: 3	my lips s speak what I know.	1359
Php	1:17	preach Christ out of selfish ambition, not s,	56

SINCERITY (6) [SINCERE]

1Co	5: 8	the bread of s and truth.	1636
2Co	1:12	in the holiness and s that are from God.	1636
	2:17	in Christ we speak before God with s,	1636
	8: 8	to test the s of your love by comparing it	1188
Eph	6: 5	with respect and fear, and with s of heart,	605
Col	3:22	with s of heart and reverence for the Lord.	605

SINEWS (4)

Job	10:11	and knit me together with bones and s?	1630
	40:17	the s of his thighs are close-knit.	1630
Isa	48: 4	the s of your neck were iron,	1630
Col	2:19	and held together by its ligaments and s,	5278

SINFUL (54) [SIN]

Dt	9:21	Also I took that s thing of yours,	2633
Ps	36: 4	he commits himself to a s course and	3202+4202
	38: 5	and are loathsome because of my s folly.	222
	51: 5	Surely I was s at birth,	6411
	51: 5	s from the time my mother conceived me.	2628
Pr	12:13	An evil man is trapped by his s talk,	7322
Isa	1: 4	Ah, s nation, a people loaded with guilt,	2627
	31: 7	of silver and gold your s hands have made.	2628
	57:17	I was enraged by his s greed;	6411
Eze	37:23	save them from all their s backsliding,	2627
Hos	9:15	Because of their s deeds,	8278
Am	9: 8	the Sovereign LORD are on the s kingdom.	2629
Mk	8:38	in this adulterous and s generation,	283
Lk	5: 8	I am a s man!"	283
	7:37	When a woman who had lived a s life in	283
	24: 7	be delivered into the hands of s men,	283
Ro	1:24	over in the s desires of their hearts	2123
	7: 5	when we were controlled by the s nature,	4922
	7: 5	the s passions aroused by the law were	281
	7:13	commandment sin might become utterly s.	283
	7:18	lives in me, that is, in my s nature.	4922
	7:25	but in the s nature a slave to the law of sin.	4922
	8: 3	in that it was weakened by the s nature,	4922
	8: 3	in the likeness of s man to be a sin offering.	281
	8: 3	And so he condemned sin in s man,	4922
	8: 4	to the s nature but according to the Spirit.	4922
	8: 5	to the s nature have their minds set on what	4922
	8: 6	The mind of s man is death,	4922
	8: 7	s mind is hostile to God.	4922
	8: 8	by the s nature cannot please God.	4922
	8: 9	are controlled not by the s nature but by	4922
	8:12	but it is not to the s nature,	4922
	8:13	For if you live according to the s nature,	4922
	13:14	how to gratify the desires of the s nature.	4922
1Co	5: 5	so that the s nature may be destroyed	4922
Gal	5:13	use your freedom to indulge the s nature;	4922
	5:16	not gratify the desires of the s nature.	4922
	5:17	For the s nature desires what is contrary to	4922
	5:17	the Spirit what is contrary to the s nature.	4922
	5:19	The acts of the s nature are obvious:	4922
	5:24	to Christ Jesus have crucified the s nature	4922
	6: 8	The one who sows to please his s nature,	4922
Eph	2: 3	of our s nature and following its desires	4922
Col	2:11	in the putting off of the s nature,	4922
	2:13	and in the uncircumcision of your s nature,	4922
1Ti	1: 9	ungodly and s, the unholy and irreligious;	283
Tit	3:11	be sure that such a man is warped and s;	279
Heb	3:11	See to it, brothers, that none of you has a s,	4505
	12: 3	from s men, so that you will not grow weary	283
1Pe	2:11	to abstain from s desires,	4920
2Pe	2:10	of the s nature and despise authority.	4922
	2:18	to the lustful desires of s human nature,	4922
1Jn	2:16	the cravings of s man,	4922
	3: 8	He who does what is s is of the devil,	281

SINFULNESS (1) [SIN]

Ps	36: 1	concerning the s of the wicked:	7322

SING (122) [SANG, SINGER, SINGERS, SINGING, SINGS, SONG, SONGS, SUNG]

Ex	15: 1	"I will s to the LORD.	8876
	15:21	"S to the LORD, for he is highly exalted.	8876
Nu	21:17	O well! S about it,	6702
Dt	31:19	the Israelites and have them s it,	928+7023+8492
Jdg	5: 3	I will s to the LORD, I will sing;	8876
	5: 3	I will sing to the LORD, I will s;	NIH
1Sa	21:11	the one they s about in their dances?	6702
2Sa	22:50	I will s praises to your name.	2376
1Ch	15:16	their brothers as singers to s joyful songs,	928+4200+7754+8123+9048
1Ch	16: 9	S to him, sing praise to him;	8876
	16: 9	Sing to him, s praise to him;	2376
	16:23	S to the LORD, all the earth;	8876
	16:33	Then the trees of the forest will s,	NIH
	16:33	they will s for joy before the LORD,	8264
2Ch	20:21	to s to the LORD and to praise him for	8876
	20:22	As they began to s and praise,	8876
	31: 2	to give thanks and to s praises	2146
Job	21:12	They s to the music of tambourine and harp;	5951
	29:13	I made the widow's heart s.	8264
Ps	5:11	let them ever s for joy.	8264
	7:17	and will s praise to the name of the LORD	2376
	9: 2	I will s praise to your name,	2376
	9:11	S praises to the LORD, enthroned in Zion;	2376
	13: 6	I will s to the LORD,	8876
	18:49	I will s praises to your name.	2376
	21:13	we will s and praise your might.	8876
	27: 6	I will s and make music to the LORD.	8876
	30: 4	S to the LORD, you saints of his;	2376
	30:12	my heart may s to you and not be silent.	2376
	32:11	s, all you who are upright in heart!	8264
	33: 1	S joyfully to the LORD,	8264
	33: 3	S to him a new song;	8876
	47: 6	Sing praises to God, sing praises;	2376
	47: 6	Sing praises to God, s praise;	2376
	47: 6	s praises to our King, sing praises.	2376
	47: 6	sing praises to our King, s praises.	2376
	47: 7	s to him a psalm of praise.	2376
	51:14	my tongue will s of your righteousness.	8264
	57: 7	I will s and make music.	8876
	57: 9	I will s of you among the peoples,	2376
	59:16	But I will s of your strength,	8876
	59:16	in the morning I will s of your love;	8264
	59:17	O my Strength, I s praise to you;	2376
	61: 8	Then will I ever s praise to your name	2376
	63: 7	I s in the shadow of your wings.	8264
	65:13	they shout for joy and s.	8876
	66: 2	S the glory of his name;	2376
	66: 4	they s praise to you,	2376
	66: 4	they s praise to your name."	2376
	67: 4	May the nations be glad and s for joy,	8264
	68: 4	S to God, sing praise to his name,	8876
	68: 4	Sing to God, s praise to his name,	2376
	68:32	S to God, O kingdoms of the earth,	8876
	68:32	s praise to the Lord,	2376
	71:22	I will s praise to you with the lyre,	2376
	71:23	My lips will shout for joy when I s praise	2376
	75: 9	I will s praise to the God of Jacob.	2376
	81: 1	S for joy to God our strength;	8264
	87: 7	As they make music they will s,	8876
	89: 1	I will s of the LORD's great love forever;	8876
	89:12	Tabor and Hermon s for joy at your name.	8264
	90:14	we may s for joy and be glad all our days.	8264
	92: 4	I s for joy at the works of your hands.	8264
	95: 1	Come, let us s for joy to the LORD;	8264
	96: 1	S to the LORD a new song;	8876
	96: 1	s to the LORD, all the earth.	8876
	96: 2	S to the LORD, praise his name;	8876
	96:12	all the trees of the forest will s for joy;	8264
	96:13	they will s before the LORD,	NIH
	98: 1	S to the LORD a new song,	8876
	98: 1	let the mountains s together for joy;	8264
	98: 9	let them s before the LORD,	NIH
	101: 1	I will s of your love and justice;	8876
	101: 1	to you, O LORD, I will s praise.	2376
	104:12	they s among the branches.	5989+7754
	104:33	I will s to the LORD all my life;	8876
	104:33	I will s praise to my God as long as I live.	2376
	105: 2	S to him, sing praise to him;	8876
	105: 2	Sing to him, s praise to him;	2376
	108: 1	I will s and make music with all my soul.	8876
	108: 3	I will s of you among the peoples.	2376
	119:172	May my tongue s of your word,	6702
	132: 9	may your saints s for joy."	8264
	132:16	and her saints will ever s for joy.	8264+8264
	135: 3	s praise to his name, for that is pleasant.	2376
	137: 3	they said, "S us one of the songs of Zion!"	8876
	137: 4	How can we s the songs of the LORD	8876
	138: 1	before the "gods" I will s your praise.	2376
	138: 5	May they s of the ways of the LORD,	8876
	144: 9	I will s a new song to you, O God;	8876
	145: 7	and joyfully s of your righteousness.	8264
	146: 2	I will s praise to my God as long as I live.	2376
	147: 1	How good it is to s praises to our God,	2376
	147: 7	S to the LORD with thanksgiving;	6702
	149: 1	S to the LORD a new song,	8876
	149: 5	in this honor and s for joy on their beds.	8264
Pr	29: 6	but a righteous one can s and be glad.	8264
Isa	5: 1	I will s for the one I love a song	8876
	12: 5	S to the LORD, for he has done glorious	2376
	12: 6	Shout aloud and s for joy, people of Zion,	8264
	23:16	play the harp well, s many a song,	NIH
	27: 2	In that day—"S about a fruitful vineyard;	6702
	30:29	And you will s as on the night you celebrate	8877
	38:18	death cannot s your praise;	2146
	38:20	and we will s with stringed instruments all	5594
	42:10	to the LORD a new song,	8876
	42:11	Let the people of Sela s for joy;	8264
	44:23	S for joy, O heavens,	8264
	54: 1	"S, O barren woman, you who never bore	8264
	65:14	My servants will s out of the joy	8264
Jer	20:13	S to the LORD!	8876
	31: 7	"S with joy for Jacob;	8264
Hos	2:15	There she will s as in the days	6702
Zep	3:14	S, O Daughter of Zion;	8264
Ro	15: 9	I will s hymns to your name."	6010
	15:11	and s praises to him, all you peoples."	2046

1Co 14:15	*I will* s with my spirit,	6010
14:15	but *I* will also s with my mind.	6010
Eph 5:19	S and make music in your heart to the Lord,	106
Col 3:16	and *as you* s psalms, hymns and	106
Heb 2:12	of the congregation *I will* s your **praises."**	5630
Jas 5:13	Let him s songs of praise.	6010

SINGED (1)
Da 3:27	nor was a hair of their heads s;	10283

SINGER (1) [SING]
2Sa 23: 1	by the God of Jacob, Israel's s *of* songs:	5834

SINGERS (31) [SING]
Jdg 5:11	the voice of the s at the watering places.	2952
2Sa 19:35	the voices of *men* and women s?	8876
1Ch 15:16	of the Levites to appoint their brothers as s	8876
15:27	and as were the s, and Kenaniah.	8876
2Ch 5:13	The trumpeters and s joined in unison,	8876
23:13	and blowing trumpets, and s	8876
29:28	while the s sang and the trumpeters played.	8877
35:25	the *men* and women s commemorate Josiah	8876
Ezr 2:41	The s: the descendants of Asaph 128	8876
2:65	and they also had 200 *men* and women s.	8876
2:70	The priests, the s,	8876
7: 7	Levites, s, gatekeepers and temple servants,	8876
7:24	Levites, s, gatekeepers, temple servants	10234
10:24	From the s: Eliashib.	8876
Ne 7: 1	and the s and the Levites were appointed.	8876
7:44	The s: the descendants of Asaph 148	8876
7:67	they also had 245 *men* and women s.	8876
7:73	the s and the temple servants,	8876
10:28	priests, Levites, gatekeepers, s,	8876
10:39	the gatekeepers and the s stay.	8876
11:22	who *were* the s responsible for the service	8876
11:23	The s were under the king's orders,	8876
12:28	The s also were brought together from 1201+8876	
12:29	for the s had built villages for themselves	8876
12:45	as did also the s and gatekeepers.	8876
12:46	there had been directors for the s and for	8876
12:47	the daily portions for the s and gatekeepers.	8876
13: 5	for the Levites, s and gatekeepers, as well	8876
13:10	and that all the s and s responsible	8876
Ps 68:25	In front are the s, after them the musicians;	8876
Ecc 2: 8	I acquired *men* and women s,	8876

SINGING (20) [SING]
Ge 31:27	with joy and s to the music of tambourines	8877
Ex 32:18	it is the sound of s that I hear."	6702
1Sa 18: 6	the towns of Israel to meet King Saul with s	8876
1Ch 15:22	the head Levite was in charge of the s;	5362
15:27	who was in charge of the s *of* the choirs.	5362
2Ch 23:18	with rejoicing and s, as David had ordered.	8877
29:27	s *to* the LORD began also,	8877
Ps 63: 5	with s lips my mouth will praise you.	8265
68: 6	he leads forth the prisoners with s;	3938
98: 5	with the harp and the sound of s,	2379
SS 2:12	the season of s has come,	2369
Isa 14: 7	they break into s.	8262
24:16	From the ends of the earth we hear s:	2369
35:10	They will enter Zion with s;	8262
51: 3	thanksgiving and the sound of s.	2379
51:11	They will enter Zion with s;	8262
Am 8:10	into mourning and all your s into weeping.	8877
Zep 3:17	he will rejoice over you with s."	8262
Ac 16:25	and Silas *were* praying and s **hymns** to God,	5630
Rev 5:13	and all that is in them, s:	3306

SINGLE (24) [SINGLED, SINGLENESS]
Ge 41: 5	were growing on a s stalk.	285
41:22	full and good, growing on a s stalk.	285
Ex 23:29	But I will not drive them out in a s year,	285
26:24	and fitted into a s ring;	285
36:29	the way to the top and fitted into a s ring;	285
Nu 11:23	they cut off a branch bearing a s cluster	285
Dt 29:21	the LORD *will* s him *out* from all	976
Jdg 9:18	murdered his seventy sons on a s stone,	285
1Ki 16:11	He did not spare a **male,**	AIT
Est 3:13	on a s day, the thirteenth day of the month	285
Isa 9:14	both palm branch and reed in a s day;	285
10:17	a s day it will burn and consume his thorns	285
47: 9	on a s day: loss of children and widowhood.	285
Eze 37:19	making them a s stick of wood,	285
Zec 3: 9	I will remove the sin of this land in a s day.	285
Mt 6:27	Who of you by worrying can add a s hour	1651
23:15	over land and sea to win a s convert,	1651
27:14	not even to a s charge—	1651
Lk 12:25	Who of you by worrying can add a s hour	1651
Jn 12:24	it remains **only a** s seed.	3668
Ac 27:34	of you will lose a s hair from his head."	NIG
Gal 5:14	law is summed up in a s command:	1651
Heb 12:16	who for a s meal sold his inheritance rights	1651
Rev 21:21	each gate made of a s pearl.	1651

SINGLED (1) [SINGLE]
1Ki 8:53	For you s them *out* from all the nations of	976

SINGLENESS (1) [SINGLE]
Jer 32:39	I will give them s of heart and action,	285

SINGS (3) [SING]
Pr 25:20	is *one* who s songs to a heavy heart.	8876

Isa 16:10	no *one* s or shouts in the vineyards;	8264
Eze 33:32	nothing more than one who s love songs	NIH

SINITES (2)
Ge 10:17	Hivites, Arkites, S,	6098
1Ch 1:15	Hivites, Arkites, S,	6098

SINK (8) [SANK, SINKING, SINKS, SUNK]
Dt 28:43	but you *will* s lower and lower.	3718
Ps 69: 2	*I* s in the miry depths,	3190
69:14	Rescue me from the mire, *do* not *let me* s;	3190
Jer 51:64	'So will Babylon s to rise no more because	9205
Eze 27:27	on board *will* s into the heart of the sea on	5877
Am 9: 5	it will be stirred up and then s like the river	9205
Mt 14:30	beginning *to* s, cried out, "Lord, save me!"	2931
Lk 5: 7	both boats so full that they *began to* s.	1112

SINK (Anglicized) See also MELT WITH FEAR

SINKING (1) [SINK]
Ac 20: 9	*who was* s into a deep sleep as Paul talked	2965

SINKS (2) [SINK]
Isa 5:24	and as dry grass s **down** in the flames,	8332
Am 9: 5	then s like the river of Egypt—	9205

SINNED (89) [SIN]
Ex 9:27	"This time *I have* s," he said to them.	2627
9:34	and thunder had stopped, he s again:	2627
10:16	"*I have* s against the LORD your God	2627
32:33	"Whoever *has* s against me I will blot out	2627
Lev 5: 5	he must confess in what way *he has* s	2627
Nu 6:11	to make atonement for him because *he* s	2627
14:40	"We have s," they said.	2627
16:38	of the men who s at the cost of their lives.	2629
21: 7	"*We* s when we spoke against the LORD	2627
22:34	to the angel of the LORD, "*I have* s.	2627
Dt 1:41	you replied, "*We have* s against the LORD.	2627
9:16	that *you had* s against the LORD your God;	2627
Jos 7:11	Israel *has* s; they have violated my covenant	2627
7:20	*I have* s against the LORD,	2627
Jdg 10:10	"We have s against you,	2627
10:15	the Israelites said to the LORD, "We have s.	2627
1Sa 7: 6	"*We have* s against the LORD."	2627
12:10	to the LORD and said, '*We have* s;	2627
15:24	Then Saul said to Samuel, "*I have* s.	2627
15:30	Saul replied, "*I have* s.	2627
26:21	Then Saul said, "*I have* s.	2627
2Sa 12:13	"*I have* s against the LORD."	2627
19:20	For I your servant know that I *have* s,	2627
24:10	"*I have* s greatly in what I have done.	2627
24:17	"*I am the one who has* s and done wrong.	2627
1Ki 8:33	an enemy because *they have* s against you,	2627
8:35	because your people *have* s against you,	2627
8:47	'We have s, we have done wrong,	2627
8:50	who *have* s against you;	2627
8:46	of the LORD and s more than all those	8317
2Ki 17: 7	because the Israelites *had* s against	2627
1Ch 21: 8	"*I have* s greatly by doing this.	2627
21:17	I am the one who *has* s and done wrong.	2627
2Ch 6:24	an enemy because *they have* s against you	2627
6:26	because your people *have* s against you,	2627
6:37	'*We have* s, we have done wrong	2627
6:39	who *have* s against you.	2627
Ezr 10:13	because we have s greatly in this thing.	7321
Ne 9:29	*They* s against your ordinances,	2627
13:26	like these that Solomon king of Israel s?	2627
Job 1: 5	"Perhaps my children *have* s	2627
7:20	If *I have* s, what have I done to you,	2627
8: 4	When your children s against him,	2627
10:14	If *I* s, you would be watching me	2627
24:19	the grave snatches away *those who have* s.	2627
33:27	Then he comes to men and says, '*I* s,	2627
36: 9	that they have s arrogantly.	7322
Ps 41: 4	heal me, for *I have* s against you."	2627
51: 4	*have I* s and done what is evil in your sight,	2627
106: 6	*We have* s, even as our fathers did;	2627
Isa 42:24	against whom *we have* s?	2627
43:27	Your first father s;	2627
Jer 2:35	because you say, '*I have* not s.'	2627
3:25	*We have* s against the LORD our God,	2627
8:14	because *we have* s against him.	2627
14: 7	*we have* s against you.	2627
14:20	*we have* indeed s against you.	2627
40: 3	because *you people* s against the LORD	2627
44:23	and *have* s against the LORD and have	2627
50: 7	for *they* s against the LORD,	2627
50:14	for *she has* s against the LORD.	2627
La 1: 8	Jerusalem *has* s **greatly** and	2627+2628
3:42	"We *have* s and rebelled and you have	7321
5: 7	Our fathers s and are no more,	2627
5:16	Woe to us, for *we have* s!	2627
Eze 28:16	with violence, and *you* s.	2627
Da 9: 5	*we have* s and done wrong.	2627
9: 8	with shame because *we have* s against you.	2627
9:11	because *we have* s against you.	2627
9:15	*we have* s, we have done wrong.	2627
Hos 4: 7	the more *they* s against me;	2627
10: 9	"Since the days of Gibeah, *you have* s,	2627
Mic 7: 9	Because *I have* s against him,	2627
Zep 1:17	because *they have* s against the LORD.	2627
Mt 27: 4	"*I have* s," he said,	279

Lk 15:18	*I have* s against heaven and against you.	279
15:21	*I have* s against heaven and against you.	279
Jn 9: 2	His disciples asked him, "Rabbi, who s,	279
9: 3	"Neither this man nor his parents s,"	279
Ro 3:23	all *have* s and fall short of the glory of God,	279
5:12	death came to all men, because all s—	279
1Co 7:28	But if you do marry, *you* have not s;	279
7:28	and if a virgin marries, *she* has not s.	279
2Co 12:21	be grieved over many who *have* s **earlier**	4579
13: 2	not spare those who s **earlier** or any of	4579
Heb 3:17	Was it not *with* those who s,	279
Jas 5:15	If *he has* s, he will be forgiven.	281+1639+4472
2Pe 2: 4	For if God did not spare angels *when they* s,	279
1Jn 1:10	If we claim *we have* not s,	279

SINNER (20) [SIN]
Pr 11:31	how much more the ungodly and the s!	2627
13: 6	but wickedness overthrows the s.	2633
13:21	Misfortune pursues the s,	2629
Ecc 2:26	but to the s he gives the task of gathering	2627
7:26	but the s she will ensnare.	2627
9: 2	As it is with the good man, so with the s;	2627
9:18	but one s destroys much good.	2627
Lk 7:39	what kind of woman she is—that she is a s."	283
15: 7	in heaven over one s who repents than	283
15:10	the angels of God over one s who repents."	283
18:13	'God, have mercy on me, a s.'	283
19: 7	"He has gone to be the guest of a 's.'"	283+467
Jn 9:16	"How can a s do such miraculous signs?"	283+476
9:24	"We know this man is a s."	283
9:25	He replied, "Whether he is a s or not,	283
Ro 3: 7	why am I still condemned as a s?"	283
1Co 14:24	**convinced** by all that he is a s	1794
1Ti 2:14	woman who was deceived and became a s.	4126
Jas 5:20	turns a s from the error of his way will save	283
1Pe 4:18	what will become of the ungodly and the s?"	283

SINNER'S (1) [SIN]
Pr 13:22	but a s wealth is stored up for the righteous.	2627

SINNERS (44) [SIN]
Nu 32:14	"And here you are, a brood of s,	2629
Ps 1: 1	in the way of s or sit in the seat of mockers.	2629
1: 5	nor s in the assembly of the righteous.	2629
25: 8	therefore he instructs s in his ways.	2629
26: 9	Do not take away my soul along with s,	2629
37:38	But all s will be destroyed;	7321
51:13	and s will turn back to you.	2629
104:35	But may s vanish from the earth and	2629
Pr 1:10	My son, if s entice you,	2629
23:17	Do not let your heart envy s,	2629
Isa 1:28	But rebels and s will both be broken,	2629
13: 9	the land desolate and destroy the s within it.	2629
33:14	The s in Zion are terrified;	2629
Am 9:10	All the s *among* my people will die by	2629
Mt 9:10	many tax collectors and "s" came and ate	283
9:11	with tax collectors and 's'?"	283
9:13	I have not come to call the righteous, but s."	283
11:19	a friend *of* tax collectors and "s." '	283
26:45	Son of Man is betrayed into the hands *of* s.	283
Mk 2:15	many tax collectors and "s" were eating	283
2:16	with the "s" and tax collectors,	283
2:16	with tax collectors and 's'?"	283
2:17	I have not come to call the righteous, but s."	283
14:41	Son of Man is betrayed into the hands *of* s.	283
Lk 5:30	and drink with tax collectors and 's'?"	283
5:32	to call the righteous, but s to repentance."	283
6:32	Even 's' love those who love them.	283
6:33	Even 's' do that.	283
6:34	Even 's' lend to 'sinners,'	283
6:34	Even 'sinners' lend to 's,'	283
7:34	a friend of tax collectors and "s." '	283
13: 2	that these Galileans were worse than all	283
15: 1	the tax collectors and "s" were all gathering	283
15: 2	"This man welcomes s and eats with them."	283
Jn 9:31	We know that God does not listen to s.	283
Ro 5: 8	While we were still s, Christ died for us.	283
5:19	of the one man the many were made s,	283
Gal 2:15	Jews by birth and not 'Gentile s'	283
2:17	it becomes evident that we ourselves are s,	283
1Ti 1:15	Christ Jesus came into the world to save s—	283
1:16	so that in me, the worst of s,	NIG
Heb 7:26	set apart from s, exalted above the heavens.	283
Jas 4: 8	Wash your hands, *you* s,	283
Jude 1:15	the harsh words ungodly s have spoken	283

SINNING (20) [SIN]
Ge 13:13	of Sodom were wicked and were s greatly	2629
20: 6	and so I have kept you from s against me.	2627
Ex 20:20	be with you to keep *you* from s."	2627
Nu 15:28	for the one who erred by s unintentionally,	2630
32:23	*you will be* s against the LORD;	2627
1Sa 14:33	the men *are* s against the LORD	2627
Job 35: 3	and what do I gain by not s?'	2633
Ps 78:32	In spite of all this, *they* kept on s;	2627
Jer 9: 5	they weary themselves with s.	6390
Hos 8:11	these have become altars for s.	2627
Jn 5:14	Stop s or something worse may happen	279
Ro 6: 1	on s so that grace may increase?	281
1Co 7:36	He is not s. They should get married.	279
11:27	be **guilty of** s against the body and blood	1944
15:34	to your senses as you ought, and stop s;	279
Heb 10:26	*on* s after we have received the knowledge	279
2Pe 2:14	eyes full of adultery, they never stop s;	281

1Jn	3: 6	No one who lives in him *keeps on* s.	279
	3: 8	the devil *has been* s from the beginning.	279
	3: 9	he cannot *go on* s, because he has been born	279

SINS (292) [SIN]

Ge	50:17	I ask you to forgive your brothers the s and	7322
	50:17	Now please forgive the s *of* the servants of	7322
Lev	4: 2	'When anyone s unintentionally	2627
	4: 3	" 'If the anointed priest s,	2627
	4:13	Israelite community s **unintentionally**	8706
	4:22	" 'When a leader s unintentionally	2627
	4:27	of the community s unintentionally	2627
	5: 1	" 'If a person s because he does not speak	2627
	5:13	for any of these s he has committed,	2633
	5:15	a violation and s unintentionally in regard	2627
	5:17	"If a person s and does what is forbidden	2627
	6: 2	"If anyone s and is unfaithful to the LORD	2627
	6: 4	he thus s and becomes guilty,	2627
	16:16	whatever their s have been.	2633
	16:21	all their s—and put them on the goat's head.	2633
	16:22	The goat will carry on itself all their s to	6411
	16:30	you will be clean from all your s.	2633
	16:34	to be made once a year for all the s *of*	2633
	26:18	punish you for your s seven times over.	2633
	26:21	seven times over, as your s deserve.	2633
	26:24	afflict you for your s seven times over.	2633
	26:28	punish you for your s seven times over.	2633
	26:39	of their enemies because of their s;	6411
	26:39	of their fathers' s they will waste away.	6411
	26:40	if they will confess their s and the sins	6411
	26:40	if they will confess their sins and the s	6411
	26:43	for their s because they rejected my laws	6411
Nu	14:34	for your s and know what it is like	6411
	15:27	" 'But if just one person s unintentionally,	2627
	15:29	everyone *who* s **unintentionally**,	928+6913+8705
	15:30	anyone *who* s **defiantly**,	928+3338+6913+8123
	16:22	the entire assembly when only one man s?"	2627
	16:26	be swept away because of all their s."	2633
Jos	24:19	not forgive your rebellion and your s.	2633
1Sa	2:25	If a man s against another man,	2627
	2:25	but if a man s against the LORD,	2627
	12:19	for we have added to all our other s the evil	2633
1Ki	14:16	because of the s Jeroboam has committed	2633
	14:22	By the s they committed they stirred	2633
	15: 3	He committed all the s his father had done	2633
	15:30	because of the s Jeroboam had committed	2633
	16: 2	and to provoke me to anger by their s.	2633
	16:13	because of all the s Baasha and his son	2633
	16:19	because of the s he had committed,	2633
	16:31	to commit the s of Jeroboam son of Nebat,	2633
2Ki	3: 3	he clung to the s *of* Jeroboam son of Nebat,	2633
	10:29	not turn away from the s *of* Jeroboam the	2628
	10:31	not turn away from the s of Jeroboam,	2633
	13: 2	by following the s of Jeroboam son of	2633
	13: 6	But they did not turn away from the s *of*	2633
	13:11	and did not turn away from any of the s	2633
	14: 6	each is to die for his own s."	2628
	14:24	and did not turn away from any of the s	2633
	15: 9	not turn away from the s of Jeroboam son	2633
	15:18	not turn away from the s of Jeroboam son	2633
	15:24	not turn away from the s of Jeroboam son	2633
	15:28	not turn away from the s of Jeroboam son	2633
	17:22	the s of Jeroboam and did not turn away	2633
	21:11	of Judah has committed these **detestable s.**	9359
	24: 3	of the s of Manasseh and all he had done,	2633
2Ch	25: 4	each is to die for his own s."	2628
	28:10	But aren't you also **guilty of** s against	873
	33:19	as well as all his s and unfaithfulness,	2633
Ezr	9: 6	because our s are higher than our heads	6411
	9: 7	Because of our s, we and our kings	6411
	9:13	you have punished us less than our s have deserved	6411
Ne	1: 6	I confess the s we Israelites,	2633
	4: 5	not cover up their guilt or blot out their s	2633
	9: 2	and confessed their s and the wickedness	2633
	9:37	Because of our s, its abundant harvest goes	2633
Job	7:21	not pardon my offenses and forgive my s?	6411
	13:23	How many wrongs and s have I committed?	2633
	13:26	and make me inherit the s of my youth.	6411
	22: 5	Are not your s endless?	6411
	31:28	then these also would be s to be judged,	6411
	35: 6	your s are many, what does that do to him?	7322
Ps	5:10	Banish them for their many s,	7322
	19:13	Keep your servant also from **willful s**;	2294
	25: 7	the s *of* my youth and my rebellious ways;	2633
	25:18	and my distress and take away all my s.	2633
	32: 1	are forgiven, whose s are covered.	2631
	40:12	my s have overtaken me, and I cannot see.	6411
	51: 9	from my s and blot out all my iniquity.	2633
	59:12	For the s *of* their mouths,	2633
	65: 3	When we were overwhelmed by s,	1821+6411
	68:21	hairy crowns of those who go on in their s.	871
	79: 8	Do not hold against us the s of the fathers;	6411
	79: 9	and forgive our s for your name's sake.	2633
	85: 2	of your people and covered all their s.	2633
	90: 8	our secret s in the light of your presence.	NIH
	94:23	He will repay them for their s	224
	103: 3	who forgives all your s and heals all your	6411
	103:10	not treat us as our s deserve or repay us	2628
	109:15	May their s always remain before	NIH
	130: 3	If you, O LORD, kept a record of s,	6411
	130: 8	redeem Israel from all their s.	6411
Pr	14:21	He who despises his neighbor s,	2627
	28:13	He who conceals his s does not prosper,	7322
	29:22	and a hot-tempered one commits many s.	7322
Ecc	7:20	on earth who does what is right and never s.	2627

Isa	1:18	"Though your s are like scarlet,	2628
	13:11	the world for its evil, the wicked for their s.	6411
	14:21	a place to slaughter his sons for the s	6411
	26:21	to punish the people of the earth for their s.	6411
	33:24	s of those who dwell there will be forgiven.	6411
	38:17	you have put all my s behind your back.	2628
	40: 2	the LORD's hand double for all her s.	2633
	43:24	But you have burdened me with your s	2633
	43:25	and remembers your s no more.	2633
	44:22	your s like the morning mist.	2633
	50: 1	Because of your s you were sold;	6411
	58: 1	and to the house of Jacob their s.	2633
	59: 2	your s have hidden his face from you,	2633
	59:12	and our s testify against us.	2633
	59:20	to those in Jacob who repent of their s,"	7322
	64: 6	all like the wind our s sweep us away.	6411
	64: 7	and made us waste away because of our s.	6411
	64: 9	do not remember our s forever.	6411
	65: 7	both your s and the sins of your fathers,"	6411
	65: 7	both your sins and the s *of* your fathers,"	6411
Jer	2:13	"My people have committed two s:	8288
	5:25	your s have deprived you of good.	2633
	11:10	to the s *of* their forefathers,	6411
	13:22	it is because of your many s	6411
	14: 7	Although our s testify against us,	6411
	14:10	and punish them for their s."	2633
	15:13	of all your s throughout your country.	2633
	18:23	not forgive their crimes or blot out their s	2633
	30:14	your guilt is so great and your s so many.	2633
	30:15	and many s I have done these things to you.	2633
	31:34	and will remember their s no more."	2633
	32:18	the fathers' s into the laps of their children	6411
	33: 8	and will forgive all their s of rebellion	6411
	50:20	and for the s *of* Judah,	2633
	51: 6	Do not be destroyed because of her s.	6411
La	1: 5	because of her many s.	7322
	1:14	"My s have been bound into a yoke;	7322
	1:22	with me because of all my s.	7322
	3:39	when **punished for** his s?	2628
	4:13	of the s *of* her prophets and the iniquities	2633
Eze	7:13	Because of their s, not one of them	6411
	7:16	each because of his s.	6411
	14:11	defile themselves anymore with all their s.	7322
	14:13	a country s against me by being unfaithful	2627
	16:51	Samaria did not commit half the s you did.	2633
	16:52	Because your s were even more vile than theirs,	2633
	18: 4	The soul who s is the one who will die.	2627
	18:14	a son who sees all the s his father commits,	2633
	18:20	The soul who s is the one who will die.	2627
	18:21	from all the s he has committed	2633
	18:24	of and because of the s he has committed,	2633
	21:24	revealing your s in all that you do—	2633
	23:49	the **consequences** of your s *of* idolatry.	2628
	24:23	of your s and groan among yourselves.	6411
	28:18	By your many s and dishonest trade	6411
	32:27	The **punishment for** their s rested	6411
	33:10	"Our offenses and s weigh us down,	2633
	33:12	The righteous man, if he s,	2627
	33:16	the s he has committed will be remembered	2633
	36:31	and you will loathe yourselves for your s	6411
	36:33	On the day I cleanse you from all your s,	6411
	43:10	that they may be ashamed of their s.	6411
	45:20	for anyone *who* s **unintentionally** or	8706
Da	4:27	Renounce your s by doing what is right,	10259
	9:13	the LORD our God by turning from our s	6411
	9:16	Our s and the iniquities of our fathers	2628
Hos	4: 8	They feed on the s of my people	2633
	7: 1	the s *of* Ephraim are exposed and	6411
	7: 2	Their s engulf them;	5095
	8:13	their wickedness and punish their s:	2633
	9: 7	Because your s are so many	6411
	9: 9	wickedness and punish them for their s.	2633
	13:12	his s are kept on record.	2633
	14: 1	Your s have been your downfall!	6411
	14: 2	"Forgive all our s and receive us graciously,	6411
Am	1: 3	"For three s *of* Damascus, even for four,	7322
	1: 6	"For three s *of* Gaza, even for four,	7322
	1: 9	"For three s *of* Tyre, even for four,	7322
	1:11	"For three s *of* Edom, even for four,	7322
	1:13	"For three s *of* Ammon, even for four,	7322
	2: 1	"For three s *of* Moab, even for four,	7322
	2: 4	"For three s *of* Judah, even for four,	7322
	2: 6	"For three s *of* Israel, even for four,	7322
	3: 2	therefore I will punish you for all your s."	6411
	3:14	"On the day I punish Israel for her s,	7322
	5:12	and how great your s.	2633
Mic	1: 5	because of the s of the house of Israel.	2633
	6:13	to ruin you because of your s.	2633
	7:19	you will tread our s underfoot	6411
Mt	1:21	he will save his people from their s."	281
	3: 6	Confessing their s, they were baptized	281
	6:15	But if you do not forgive men their s,	4183
	6:15	your Father will not forgive your s.	4183
	9: 2	your s are forgiven."	281
	9: 5	to say, 'Your s are forgiven,' or to say,	281
	9: 6	of Man has authority on earth to forgive s."	281
	18:15	When your brother s against you,	279
	18:21	when *he* s against me?	279
	26:28	for many for the forgiveness *of* s.	281
Mk	1: 4	of repentance for the forgiveness *of* s.	281
	1: 5	Confessing their s, they were baptized	281
	2: 5	"Son, your s are forgiven."	281
	2: 7	Who can forgive s but God alone?"	281
	2: 9	'Your s are forgiven,' or to say, 'Get up,	281
	2:10	of Man has authority on earth to forgive s."	281
	3:28	all the s and blasphemies of men will	280
	11:25	Father in heaven may forgive you your s."	4183

Lk	1:77	through the forgiveness *of* their s,	281
	3: 3	of repentance for the forgiveness *of* s.	281
	5:20	he said, "Friend, your s are forgiven."	281
	5:21	Who can forgive s but God alone?"	281
	5:23	to say, 'Your s are forgiven,' or to say,	281
	5:24	of Man has authority on earth to forgive s."	281
	7:47	I tell you, her many s have been forgiven—	281
	7:48	Jesus said to her, "Your s are forgiven."	281
	7:49	"Who is this who even forgives s?"	281
	11: 4	Forgive us our s, for we also forgive	281
	11: 4	we also forgive everyone *who* s against us.	4053
	17: 3	"If your brother s, rebuke him,	279
	17: 4	If *he* s against you seven times in a day,	279
	24:47	and repentance and forgiveness *of* s will	281
Jn	8:24	I told you that you would die in your s;	281
	8:24	you will indeed die in your s."	281
	8:34	everyone who s is a slave to sin.	281+3836+4472
	20:23	you forgive anyone his s, they are forgiven;	281
Ac	2:38	for the forgiveness *of* your s.	281
	3:19	so that your s may be wiped out,	281
	5:31	and forgiveness of s to Israel.	281
	10:43	in him receives forgiveness *of* s	281
	13:38	the forgiveness *of* s is proclaimed to you.	281
	22:16	Get up, be baptized and wash your s away,	281
	26:18	that they may receive forgiveness *of* s and	281
Ro	3:25	the s committed beforehand unpunished—	280
	4: 7	are forgiven, whose s are covered.	281
	4:25	over to death for our s and was raised to life	4183
	11:27	with them when I take away their s."	281
1Co	6:18	other s a man commits are outside his body,	280
	6:18	but he who **sexually** sins against his own	4519
	6:18	who sins sexually s against his own body.	279
	15: 3	that Christ died for our s according to	281
	15:17	you are still in your s.	281
2Co	5:19	not counting men's s against them.	4183
Gal	1: 4	who gave himself for our s to rescue us	281
Eph	1: 7	through his blood, the forgiveness *of* s,	4183
	2: 1	*in* your transgressions and s,	281
Col	1:14	we have redemption, the forgiveness *of* s.	281
	2:13	When you were dead in your s and in	4183
	2:13	He forgave us all our s,	4183
1Th	2:16	In this way they always heap up their s to	281
	4: 6	The Lord will punish men for all such s,	4047S
1Ti	5:22	and do not share in the s of others.	281
	5:24	The s of some men are obvious,	281
	5:24	the s of others trail behind them.	NIG
2Ti	3: 6	who are loaded down *with* s and are swayed	281
Heb	1: 3	After he had provided purification *for* s,	281
	2:17	and that he might make atonement for the s	281
	5: 1	to offer gifts and sacrifices for s.	281
	5: 3	to offer sacrifices for his own s.	281
	5: 3	as well as for the s of the people.	NIG
	7:27	first for his own s, and then for the sins of	281
	7:27	and then for the s of the people.	NIG
	7:27	He sacrificed for their s once for all	NIG
	8:12	and will remember their s no more."	281
	9: 7	s the people had **committed in ignorance**.	52
	9:15	to set them free *from* the s committed under	4126
	9:28	to take away the s of many people;	281
	10: 2	would no longer have felt guilty *for* their s.	281
	10: 3	an annual reminder *of* s,	281
	10: 4	the blood of bulls and goats to take away s.	281
	10:11	which can never take away s.	281
	10:12	offered for all time one sacrifice for s,	281
	10:17	s and lawless acts I will remember no	281
	10:26	no sacrifice for s is left,	281
Jas	4:17	he ought to do and doesn't do it, s.	281+1639
	5:16	Therefore confess your s to each other	281
	5:20	from death and cover over a multitude *of* s.	281
1Pe	2:24	He himself bore our s in his body on	281
	2:24	so that we might die *to* s and live	281
	3:18	For Christ died for s once for all,	281
	4: 8	because love covers over a multitude *of* s.	281
2Pe	1: 9	that he has been cleansed *from* his past s.	281
1Jn	1: 9	If we confess our s, he is faithful and just	281
	1: 9	and will forgive us our s and purify us	281
	2: 2	He is the atoning sacrifice for our s,	281
	2: 2	and not only for ours but also for the s of	NIG
	2:12	because your s have been forgiven	281
	3: 4	Everyone who s breaks the law;	281+3836+4472
	3: 5	so that he might take away our s.	281
	4:10	as an atoning sacrifice for our s.	281
Rev	1: 5	and has freed us from our s by his blood,	281
	18: 4	so that you will not share *in* her s,	281
	18: 5	for her s are piled up to heaven,	281

SION (KJV) See SIYON, ZION

SIPHMOTH (1)

1Sa	30:28	to those in Aroer, S, Eshtemoa	8560

SIPPAI (1)

1Ch	20: 4	that time Sibbecai the Hushathite killed S,	6205

SIR (26) [SIRS]

Ge	23: 6	"S, listen to us. You are a mighty prince	123
	43:20	s," they said, "we came down here	123
Jdg	6:13	"But s," Gideon replied,	123
Mt	13:27	and said, 'S, didn't you sow good seed	3261
	21:30	He answered, 'I will, s,' but he did not go.	3261
	25:11	"Later the others also came. 'S!	3261
	25:11	"Later the others also came. 'Sir! S!'	3261
	27:63	"S," they said, "we remember that	3261
Lk	13: 8	" 'S,' the man replied,	3261

Lk	13:25	'S, open the door for us.'	3261
	14:22	" 'S,' the servant said,	3261
	19:16	"The first one came and said, 'S,	3261
	19:18	"The second came and said, 'S,	3261
	19:20	"Then another servant came and said, 'S,	3261
	19:25	" 'S,' they said, 'he already has ten!'	3261
Jn	4:11	"S," the woman said, "you have nothing	3261
	4:15	The woman said to him, "S,	3261
	4:19	"S," the woman said, "I can see that you are	3261
	4:49	The royal official said, "S,	3261
	5: 7	"S," the invalid replied,	3261
	6:34	"S," they said, "from now	3261
	8:11	"No one, s," she said.	3261
	9:36	"Who is he, s?"	3261
	12:21	"S," they said, "we would like to see Jesus."	3261
	20:15	Thinking he was the gardener, she said, "S,	3261
Rev	7:14	I answered, "S, you know."	3261

SIRAH (1)

2Sa	3:26	they brought him back from the well of S.	6241

SIRION (2) [HERMON]

Dt	3: 9	(Hermon is called S by the Sidonians;	8590
Ps	29: 6	S like a young wild ox.	8590

SIRS (1) [SIR]

Ac	16:30	He then brought them out and asked, "S,	3261

SISAMAI   (KJV) See SISMAI

SISERA (20) [SISERA'S]

Jdg	4: 2	The commander of his army was S,	6102
	4: 7	I will lure S, the commander of Jabin's	6102
	4: 9	the LORD will hand S over to a woman."	6102
	4:12	When they told S that Barak son	6102
	4:13	S gathered together his nine hundred iron chariots	6102
	4:14	the LORD has given S into your hands.	6102
	4:15	the LORD routed S and all his chariots	6102
	4:15	S abandoned his chariot and fled on foot.	6102
	4:16	All the troops of S fell by the sword;	6102
	4:17	S, however, fled on foot to the tent of Jael,	6102
	4:18	Jael went out to meet S and said to him,	6102
	4:22	Barak came by in pursuit of S,	6102
	4:22	and there lay S with the tent peg	6102
	5:20	from their courses they fought against S.	6102
	5:26	She struck S, she crushed his head,	6102
	5:30	colorful garments as plunder for S,	6102
1Sa	12: 9	so he sold them into the hand of S,	6102
Ezr	2:53	Barkos, S, Temah,	6102
Ne	7:55	Barkos, S, Temah,	6102
Ps	83: 9	you did to S and Jabin at the river Kishon,	6102

SISERA'S (1) [SISERA]

Jdg	5:28	"Through the window peered S mother;	6102

SISMAI (2)

1Ch	2:40	Eleasah the father of S,	6183
	2:40	S the father of Shallum,	6183

SISTER (106) [SISTER-IN-LAW, SISTER'S, SISTERS]

Ge	4:22	Tubal-Cain's s was Naamah.	295
	12:13	Say you are my s, so that I will be treated	295
	12:19	Why did you say, 'She is my s,'	295
	20: 2	said of his wife Sarah, "She is my s."	295
	20: 5	Did he not say to me, 'She is my s,'	295
	20:12	Besides, she really is my s,	295
	24:59	So they sent their s Rebekah on her way,	295
	24:60	"Our s, may you increase to thousands	295
	25:20	the Aramean from Paddan Aram and s	295
	26: 7	"She is my s," because he was afraid to say,	295
	26: 9	Why did you say, 'She is my s'?"	295
	28: 9	the s of Nebaioth and daughter	295
	30: 1	she became jealous of her s.	295
	30: 8	"I have had a great struggle with my s,	295
	34:13	Because their s Dinah had been defiled,	295
	34:14	we can't give our s to a man who is	295
	34:17	we'll take our s and go."	1426
	34:27	the city where their s had been defiled.	295
	34:31	"Should he have treated our s like	295
	36: 3	also Basemath daughter of Ishmael and s	295
	36:22	Timna was Lotan's s.	295
	46:17	Their s was Serah.	295
Ex	2: 4	His s stood at a distance	295
	2: 7	Then his s asked Pharaoh's daughter,	295
	6:20	Amram married his s Jochebed,	1860
	6:23	daughter of Amminadab and s of Nahshon,	295
	15:20	Then Miriam the prophetess, Aaron's s,	295
Lev	18: 9	" 'Do not have sexual relations with your s,	295
	18:11	born to our father; she is your s.	295
	18:12	sexual relations with your father's s;	295
	18:13	sexual relations with your mother's s,	295
	18:18	" 'Do not take your wife's s as a rival wife	295
	20:17	" 'If a man marries his s,	295
	20:17	He has dishonored his s and will	295
	20:19	the s of either your mother or your father,	295
	21: 3	or an unmarried s who is dependent on him	295
Nu	6: 7	or mother or brother or s dies,	295
	25:18	in the affair of Peor and their s Cozbi,	295
	26:59	Moses and their s Miriam.	295

Dt	27:22	"Cursed is the man who sleeps with his s,	295
Jdg	15: 2	Isn't her younger s more attractive?	295
2Sa	13: 1	the beautiful s of Absalom son of David.	295
	13: 2	of illness on account of his s Tamar,	295
	13: 4	Tamar, my brother Absalom's s."	295
	13: 5	'I would like my s Tamar to come	295
	13: 6	"I would like my s Tamar to come	295
	13:11	"Come to bed with me, my s."	295
	13:20	Be quiet now, my s; he is your brother.	295
	13:22	because he had disgraced his s Tamar.	295
	13:32	since the day Amnon raped his s Tamar.	295
	17:25	the daughter of Nahash and s of Zeruiah	295
1Ki	11:19	so pleased with Hadad that he gave him a s	295
	11:20	The s of Tahpenes bore him	295
2Ki	11: 2	the daughter of King Jehoram and s	295
1Ch	1:39	Timna was Lotan's s.	295
	3: 9	And Tamar was their s.	295
	3:19	Shelomith was their s.	295
	4: 3	Their s was named Hazzelelponi.	295
	4:19	The sons of Hodiah's wife, the s of Naham:	295
	7:18	His s Hammoleketh gave birth to Ishhod,	295
	7:30	Their s was Serah.	295
	7:32	Shomer and Hotham and of their s Shua.	295
2Ch	22:11	of the priest Jehoiada, was Ahaziah's s,	295
Job	17:14	and to the worm, 'My mother' or 'My s,'	295
Pr	7: 4	Say to wisdom, "You are my s,"	295
SS	4: 9	You have stolen my heart, my s, my bride;	295
	4:10	delightful is your love, my s, my bride!	295
	4:12	You are a garden locked up, my s,	295
	5: 1	I have come into my garden, my s,	295
	5: 2	My lover is knocking: "Open to me, my s,	295
	8: 8	We have a young s,	295
	8: 8	for our s for the day she is spoken for?	295
Jer	3: 7	and her unfaithful s Judah saw it.	295
	3: 8	that her unfaithful s Judah had no fear;	295
	3:10	her unfaithful s Judah did not return to me	295
	22:18	'Alas, my brother! Alas, my s!'	295
Eze	16:45	and you are a true s of your sisters,	295
	16:46	Your older s was Samaria,	295
	16:46	and your younger s, who lived to the south	295
	16:48	your s Sodom and her daughters	295
	16:49	" 'Now this was the sin of your s Sodom:	295
	16:56	You would not even mention your s Sodom	295
	22:11	and another violates his s,	295
	23: 4	and her s was Oholibah.	295
	23:11	"Her s Oholibah saw this,	295
	23:11	lust and prostitution she was more depraved than her s.	295
	23:18	just as I had turned away from her s.	295
	23:31	You have gone the way of your s;	295
	23:33	the cup of your s Samaria.	295
	23:42	on the arms of **the woman and her s**	2177S
	44:25	son or daughter, brother or unmarried s,	295
Mt	12:50	in heaven is my brother and s and mother."	80
Mk	3:35	God's will is my brother and s and mother."	80
Lk	10:39	She had a s called Mary,	80
	10:40	don't you care that my s has left me to do	80
Jn	11: 1	the village of Mary and her s Martha.	80
	11: 5	Jesus loved Martha and her s and Lazarus.	80
	11:28	she went back and called her s Mary aside.	80
	11:39	Lord," said Martha, the s of the dead man,	80
	19:25	his mother's s, Mary the wife of Clopas,	80
Ac	23:16	when the son of Paul's s heard of this plot,	80
Ro	16: 1	I commend to you our s Phoebe,	80
	16:15	Greet Philologus, Julia, Nereus and his s,	80
Phm	1: 2	to Apphia our s,	80
Jas	2:15	Suppose a brother or s is without clothes	80
2Jn	1:13	of your chosen s send their greetings.	80

SISTER'S (4) [SISTER]

Ge	24:30	and the bracelets on his s arms,	295
	29:13	Jacob, his s son, he hurried to meet him.	295
1Ch	7:15	His s name was Maacah.	295
Eze	23:32	"You will drink your s cup,	295

SISTER-IN-LAW (1) [SISTER]

Ru	1:15	"your s is going back to her people	3304

SISTERS (19) [SISTER]

Jos	2:13	my father and mother, my brothers and s,	295
1Ch	2:16	Their s were Zeruiah and Abigail.	295
Job	1: 4	and they would invite their three s to eat	295
	42:11	and s and everyone who had known him	295
Eze	16:45	and you are a true sister of your s,	295
	16:51	and have made your s seem righteous	295
	16:52	have furnished some justification for your s.	295
	16:52	for you have made your s appear righteous.	295
	16:55	And your s, Sodom with her daughters	295
	16:61	and be ashamed when you receive your s,	295
Hos	2: 1	and of your s, 'My loved one.'	295
Mt	13:56	Aren't all his s with us?	80
	19:29	or s or father or mother or children or fields	80
Mk	6: 3	Aren't his s here with us?"	80
	10:29	or s or mother or father or children or fields	80
	10:30	brothers, s, mothers, children and fields—	80
Lk	14:26	his wife and children, his brothers and s—	80
Jn	11: 3	So the s sent word to Jesus, "Lord,	80
1Ti	5: 2	and younger women as s,	80

SISTRUMS (1)

2Sa	6: 5	lyres, tambourines, s and cymbals.	4983

SIT (106) [SAT, SITS, SITTING]

Ge	27:19	Please s up and eat some of my game so	3782

Ge	27:31	"My father, s up and eat some of my game,	7756
Ex	18:14	Why do you alone s as judge,	3782
Nu	32: 6	to war while you s here?	3782
Dt	6: 7	Talk about them when you s at home and	3782
	11:19	talking about them when you s at home and	3782
Ru	4: 1	"Come over here, my friend, and s down."	3782
	4: 2	"S here," and they did so.	3782
1Sa	16:11	we will not s down until he arrives."	6015
1Ki	1:13	and he will s on my throne'?	3782
	1:17	and he will s on my throne.'	3782
	1:20	to learn from you who will s on the throne	3782
	1:24	and that he will s on your throne?	3782
	1:27	who should s on the throne of my lord	3782
	1:30	and he will s on my throne in my place."	3782
	1:35	and s on my throne and reign in my place.	3782
	3: 6	I have given him a son to s on his throne this very day.	3782
	8:20	and now I s on the throne of Israel,	3782
	8:25	to have a man to s before me on the throne	3782
2Ki	10:30	your descendants will s on the throne	3782
	15:12	"Your descendants will s on the throne	3782
1Ch	28: 5	he has chosen my son Solomon to s on	3782
2Ch	6:10	and now I s on the throne of Israel,	3782
	6:16	'You shall never fail to have a man to s before me on the throne of Israel,	3782
Ps	1: 1	of sinners or s in the seat of mockers.	3782
	26: 4	I do not s with deceitful men,	3782
	26: 5	the assembly of evildoers and refuse to s	3782
	69:12	Those who s at the gate mock me,	3782
	80: 1	you who s enthroned between the cherubim	3782
	102:12	But you, O LORD, s enthroned forever;	3782
	110: 1	"S at my right hand until I make your	3782
	119:23	Though rulers s together and slander me,	3782
	132:12	then their sons will s on your throne	3782
	132:14	here I will s enthroned,	3782
	139: 2	You know when I s and when I rise;	3782
Pr	23: 1	When you s to dine with a ruler,	3782
SS	2: 3	I delight to s in his shade,	3782
Isa	3:26	destitute, she will s on the ground.	3782
	14:13	I will s enthroned on the mount	3782
	16: 5	in faithfulness a man will s on it—	3782
	42: 7	and to release from the dungeon those who s	3782
	47: 1	"Go down, s in the dust,	3782
	47: 1	s on the ground without a throne,	3782
	47: 5	"S in silence, go into darkness,	3782
	47:14	here is no fire to s by.	3782
	52: 2	rise up, s enthroned, O Jerusalem;	3782
	65: 4	who s among the graves	3782
Jer	13:13	in this land, including the kings who s	3782
	16: 8	a house where there is feasting and s down	3782
	17:25	then kings who s on David's throne	3782
	22: 2	you who s on David's throne—	3782
	22: 4	then kings who s on David's throne	3782
	22:30	of his offspring will prosper, none will s	3782
	33:17	'David will never fail to have a man to s on	3782
	36:15	They said to him, "S down, please,	3782
	36:30	He will have no one to s on the throne	3782
	48:18	"Come down from your glory and s on	3782
La	2:10	of the Daughter of Zion s on the ground	3782
	3:28	Let him s alone in silence,	3782
Eze	26:16	they will s on the ground,	3782
	28: 2	I s on the throne of a god in the heart of	3782
	33:31	and s before you to listen to your words,	3782
	44: 3	prince himself is the only one who may s	3782
Da	7:26	" 'But the court will s,	10338
	11:27	will s at the same table and lie to each	NIH
Joel	3:12	for there I will s to judge all the nations	3782
Am	3:12	so will the Israelites be saved, those who s	3782
Mic	4: 4	Every man will s under his own vine and	3782
	7: 8	Though I s in darkness,	3782
Zec	3:10	of you will invite his neighbor to s	NIH
	6:13	be clothed with majesty and will s and rule	3782
	8: 4	and women of ripe old age will s in	3782
Mal	3: 3	He will s as a refiner and purifier of silver;	3782
Mt	14:19	And he directed the people to s down on	369
	15:35	He told the crowd to s down on the ground.	404
	19:28	you who have followed me will also s	2764
	20:21	of mine may s at your right and the other	2767
	20:23	but to s at my right or left is not for me	2767
	22:44	"S at my right hand until I put your	2764
	23: 2	"The teachers of the law and the Pharisees	2767
	25:31	he will s on his throne in heavenly glory.	2767
	26:36	"S here while I go over there and pray."	2767
Mk	6:39	**have** all the people s down	369
	8: 6	He told the crowd to s down on the ground.	404
	10:37	"Let one of us s at your right and the other	2767
	10:40	but to s at my right or left is not for me	2767
	12:36	"S at my right hand until I put your	2764
	14:32	"S here while I pray."	2767
Lk	9:14	"Have them s down in groups of about	2884
	14:28	not first s down and estimate the cost to see	2767
	14:31	Will he not first s down	2767
	16: 6	s down quickly, and make it four hundred."	2767
	17: 7	'Come along now and s down to eat'?	404
	20:42	"S at my right hand	2764
	22:30	and drink at my table in my kingdom and s	2764
Jn	6:10	Jesus said, "Have the people s down."	404
	9: 8	the same man who used to s and beg?	2764
Ac	2:34	"S at my right hand	2764
	3:10	as the same man who used to s begging at	2764
	8:31	So he invited Philip to come up and s	2767
	23: 3	You s there to judge me according to	2764
1Co	9: 3	to those who s in judgment on me.	373
Heb	1:13	"S at my right hand	2764
Jas	2: 3	"You stand there" or "S on the floor	2764
Rev	3:21	the right to s with me on my throne,	2767
	18: 7	In her heart she boasts, 'I s as queen;	2764

SITE (13) [SITES]

Ge	12: 6	as far as the s of the great tree of Moreh	5226
	23: 4	for a **burial** s here so I can bury my dead."	7700
	23: 9	to sell it to me for the full price as a burial s	299
	23:20	to Abraham by the Hittites as a burial s.	299
Nu	21:15	the ravines that lead to the s of Ar and lie	8699
1Ki	6: 7	at the temple s while it was being built.	NIH
1Ch	17: 5	I have moved from one **tent** s to another,	185
	21:22	the s of your threshing floor so I can build	5226
	21:25	six hundred shekels of gold for the s.	5226
Ezr	2:68	the rebuilding of the house of God on its s.	4806
	5:15	And rebuild the house of God on its s.'	10087
	6: 7	rebuild this house of God on its s.	10087
Zec	14:10	from the Benjamin Gate to the s of	5226

SITES (2) [SITE]

2Ki	23:14	down the Asherah poles and covered the s	5226
2Ch	33:19	and the s where he built high places and set	5226

SITH (KJV) See SINCE

SITHRI (1)

Ex	6:22	of Uzziel were Mishael, Elzaphan and S.	6262

SITNAH (1)

Ge	26:21	over that one also; so he named it S.	8479

SITS (27) [SIT]

Ex	11: 5	of Pharaoh, who s on the throne,	3782
Lev	15: 4	and anything he s on will be unclean.	3782
	15: 6	Whoever s on anything that the man with	3782
	15: 9	the man s on when riding will be unclean,	5323
	15:20	and anything she s on will be unclean.	3782
	15:22	Whoever touches anything she s on	3782
	15:26	and anything she s on will be unclean.	3782
Est	6:10	Mordecai the Jew, who s at the king's gate.	3782
Ps	29:10	The LORD s **enthroned** over the flood;	3782
	99: 1	he s **enthroned** between the cherubim,	3782
	113: 5	the One who s **enthroned** on high,	3782
Pr	9:14	She s at the door of her house,	3782
	20: 8	When a king s on his throne to judge,	3782
Isa	28: 6	a spirit of justice to him who s in judgment,	3782
	40:22	He s **enthroned** above the circle of the earth	3782
Jer	29:16	the king who s on David's throne and all	3782
Mt	19:28	the Son of Man s on his glorious throne,	2767
	23:22	by God's throne and by the one who s on it.	2764
Rev	4: 9	to him who s on the throne and who lives	2764
	4:10	down before him who s on the throne,	2764
	5:13	"To him who s on the throne and to	2764
	6:16	and hide us from the face of him who s on	2764
	7:10	who s on the throne, and to the Lamb."	2764
	7:15	and he who s on the throne	2764
	17: 1	great prostitute, who s on many waters.	2764
	17: 9	on which the woman s.	2764
	17:15	where the prostitute s, are peoples,	2764

SITTING (75) [SIT]

Ge	18: 1	while he was s at the entrance to his tent in	3782
	19: 1	and Lot was s in the gateway of the city.	3782
	23:10	Ephron the Hittite was s among his people	3782
	31:34	inside her camel's saddle and was s	3782
Lev	15:23	Whether it is the bed or anything she was s	3782
Dt	22: 6	and the mother is s on the young or on	8069
Jdg	3:20	then approached him while he was s alone	3782
		s on your saddle blankets,	3782
1Sa	1: 9	the priest was s on a chair by the doorpost	3782
	4:13	there was Eli s on his chair by the side of	3782
	19: 9	the LORD came upon Saul as he was s	3782
2Sa	18:24	While David was s between the inner	3782
	19: 8	"The king is s in the gateway,"	3782
1Ki	13:14	He found him s under an oak tree	3782
	13:20	While they were s at the table,	3782
	22:10	and Jehoshaphat king of Judah were s	3782
	22:19	the LORD s on his throne with all the host	3782
2Ki	1: 9	who was s on the top of a hill,	3782
	6:32	Now Elisha was s in his house,	3782
	6:32	and the elders were s with him.	3782
	9: 5	he found the army officers s together.	3782
	18:27	and not to the men s on the wall—	3782
2Ch	18: 9	and Jehoshaphat king of Judah were s	3782
	18:18	the LORD s on his throne with all the host	3782
Ezr	10: 9	all the people were s in the square before	3782
Ne	2: 6	Then the king, with the queen s beside him,	3782
Est	2:19	Mordecai was s at the king's gate.	3782
	2:21	the time Mordecai was s at the king's gate,	3782
	5: 1	The king was s on his royal throne in	3782
	5:13	that Jew Mordecai s at the king's gate."	3782
Isa	36:12	and not to the men s on the wall—	3782
Jer	8:14	"Why are we s here?	3782
	32:12	the Jews s in the courtyard of the guard.	3782
	36:12	where all the officials were s:	3782
	36:22	It was the ninth month and the king was s in	3782
	38: 7	While the king was s in the Benjamin Gate,	3782
La	3:63	S or standing, they mock me in their songs.	3782
Eze	8: 1	while I was s in my house and the elders	3782
	8: 1	in my house and the elders of Judah were s	3782
	8:14	and I saw women s there,	3782
Mt	9: 9	he saw a man named Matthew s at	2764
	11:16	They are like children s in the marketplaces	2764
	20:30	Two blind men were s by the roadside,	2764
	24: 3	As Jesus was s on the Mount of Olives,	2764
	26:64	In the future you will see the Son of Man s	2764

Mt	26:69	Now Peter was s out in the courtyard,	2764
	27:19	While Pilate was s on the judge's seat,	2764
	27:36	s **down**, they kept watch over him there.	2764
	27:61	and the other Mary were s there opposite	2764
Mk	2: 6	Now some teachers of the law were s there,	2764
	2:14	of Alphaeus s at the tax collector's booth.	2764
	3:32	A crowd was s around him,	2764
	5:15	s there, dressed and in his right mind;	2764
	9:35	S **down**, Jesus called the Twelve and said,	2767
	10:46	was s by the roadside begging.	2764
	13: 3	As Jesus was s on the Mount of Olives,	2764
	14:62	"And you will see the Son of Man s at	2764
	16: 5	a young man dressed in a white robe s on	2764
Lk	2:46	in the temple courts, s among the teachers,	2757
	5:17	from Judea and Jerusalem, were s there.	2764
	5:27	by the name of Levi s at his tax booth.	2764
	7:32	They are like children s in the marketplace	2764
	8:35	s at Jesus' feet, dressed and	2764
	10:13	s in sackcloth and ashes.	2764
	18:35	a blind man was s by the roadside begging.	2764
Jn	2:14	and others s at tables exchanging money.	2764
Ac	2: 2	the whole house where they were s.	2764
	6:15	All who were s in the Sanhedrin	2757
	8:28	and on his way home was s in his chariot	2764
	26:30	the governor and Bernice and those s **with**	5153
1Co	14:30	revelation comes to someone who is s **down**	2764
Jas	2: 3	but s **in judgment** on it.	3216
Rev	4: 2	a throne in heaven with someone s on it.	2764
	14:15	and called in a loud voice to him who was s	2764
	17: 3	There I saw a woman s on a scarlet beast	2764

SITUATED (3) [SITUATION]

2Ki	2:19	our lord, this town is well s, as you can see,	4632
Eze	27: 3	Say to Tyre, s at the gateway to the sea,	3782
Na	3: 8	Are you better than Thebes, s on the Nile,	3782

SITUATION (9) [SITUATED, SITUATIONS]

Ge	31:40	This was my s: The heat consumed me	AIT
1Sa	13: 6	of Israel saw that their s was critical and	NIH
2Sa	14:20	Joab did this to change the present s.	1821
Da	2: 9	hoping the s will change.	10530
	6:17	so that Daniel's s might not be changed.	10606
Mt	19:10	"If this is the s between a husband and wife,	162
1Co	7:20	in the s which he was in when God called	3104
	7:24	should remain in **the** s God called him to.	4005
Php	4:12	of being content in any and **every** s,	AIT

SITUATIONS (1) [SITUATION]

2Ti	4: 5	But you, keep your head in **all** s,	AIT

SIVAN (1)

Est	8: 9	of the third month, the month of S.	6094

SIX (126) [SIXTH]

Ge	7: 6	Noah was s hundred years old when	9252
	7:11	In the hundredth year of Noah's life,	9252
	8:13	of the first month of Noah's s hundred	9252
	30:20	because I have borne him s sons."	9252
	31:41	for your two daughters and s years	9252
Ex	12:37	There were about s hundred thousand men	9252
	14: 7	He took s hundred of the best chariots,	9252
	16:26	S days you are to gather it,	9252
	20: 9	S days you shall labor	9252
	20:11	in s days the LORD made the heavens and	9252
	21: 2	he is to serve you for s years.	9252
	23:10	"For s years you are to sow your fields	9252
	23:12	"S days do your work,	9252
	24:16	For s days the cloud covered the mountain,	9252
	25:32	S branches are to extend from the sides of	9252
	25:33	the same for all s branches extending from	9252
	25:35	the third pair—s branches in all.	9252
	26: 9	into one set and the other s into another set.	9252
	26:22	Make s frames for the far end, that is,	9252
	28:10	s names on one stone and the remaining six	9252
	28:10	six names on one stone and the remaining s	9252
	31:15	For s days, work is to be done,	9252
	31:17	in s days the LORD made the heavens and	9252
	34:21	"S days you shall labor,	9252
	35: 2	For s days, work is to be done, but	9252
	36:16	into one set and the other s into another set.	9252
	36:27	They made s frames for the far end, that is,	9252
	37:18	S branches extended from the sides of	9252
	37:19	the same for all s branches extending from	9252
	37:21	the third pair—s branches in all.	9252
Lev	23: 3	" 'There are s days when you may work,	9252
	24: 6	Set them in two rows, s in each row,	9252
	25: 3	For s years sow your fields,	9252
	25: 3	and for s years prune your vineyards	9252
Nu	7: 3	before the LORD s covered carts	9252
	11:21	"Here I am among s hundred thousand men	9252
	35: 6	"S of the towns you give the Levites will	9252
	35:13	These s towns you give will be your cities	9252
	35:15	These s towns will be a place of refuge	9252
Dt	3:11	thirteen feet long and s **feet** wide.	564+752
	5:13	S days you shall labor	9252
	15:12	sells himself to you and serves you s years,	9252
	15:18	to you these s years has been worth twice	9252
	16: 8	For s days eat unleavened bread and on	9252
Jos	6: 3	Do this for s days.	9252
	6:14	They did this for s days.	9252
	15:59	s towns and their villages.	9252
	15:62	s towns and their villages.	9252
Jdg	3:31	who struck down s hundred Philistines with	9252
	12: 7	Jephthah led Israel s years.	9252

Jdg	18:11	s hundred men from the clan of the Danites,	9252
	18:16	The s hundred Danites, armed for battle,	9252
	18:17	and the s hundred armed men stood at	9252
	20:47	But s hundred men turned and fled into	9252
Ru	3:15	he poured into it s measures of barley	9252
	3:17	"He gave me these s measures of barley,	9252
1Sa	13: 5	s thousand charioteers, and soldiers as	9252
	13:15	They numbered about s hundred.	9252
	14: 2	With him were about s hundred men,	9252
	17: 7	its iron point weighed s hundred shekels	9252
	23:13	about s hundred in number,	9252
	27: 2	the s hundred men with him left and went	9252
	30: 9	and the s hundred men with him came to	9252
2Sa	2:11	of Judah was seven years and s months.	9252
	5: 5	over Judah seven years and s months.	9252
	6:13	the ark of the LORD had taken s steps,	9252
	15:18	s hundred Gittites who had accompanied	9252
	21:20	with s fingers on each hand and six toes	9252
	21:20	with six fingers on each hand and s toes	9252
1Ki	6: 6	the middle floor s cubits and	9252
	10:16	s hundred bekas of gold went	9252
	10:19	The throne had s steps,	9252
	10:20	Twelve lions stood on the s steps,	9252
	10:29	from Egypt for s hundred shekels of silver,	9252
	11:16	the Israelites stayed there for s months,	9252
	16:23	s of them in Tirzah.	9252
2Ki	5: 5	s thousand shekels of gold and ten sets	9252
	11: 3	the LORD for s years while Athaliah ruled	9252
	13:19	the ground five or s times;	9252
	14:13	**about s hundred feet** long.	564+752+4395
	15: 8	and he reigned s months.	9252
1Ch	3: 4	These s were born to David in Hebron,	9252
	3: 4	where he reigned seven years and s months.	9252
	3:22	and Shaphat—s in all.	9252
	4:27	Shimei had sixteen sons and s daughters,	9252
	8:38	Azel had s sons,	9252
	9:44	Azel had s sons,	9252
	20: 6	with s fingers on each hand and six toes	9252
	20: 6	with six fingers on each hand and s toes	9252
	21:25	So David paid Araunah s hundred shekels	9252
	23: 4	of the LORD and s thousand are to	9252
	25: 3	Shimei, Hashabiah and Mattithiah, s in all,	9252
	26:17	There were s Levites a day on the east,	9252
2Ch	1:17	from Egypt for s hundred shekels of silver,	9252
	3: 8	inside with s hundred talents of fine gold.	9252
	9:15	s hundred bekas of hammered gold went	9252
	9:18	The throne had s steps,	9252
	9:19	Twelve lions stood on the s steps,	9252
	22:12	with them at the temple of God for s years	9252
	25:23	**about s hundred feet** long.	564+752+4395
	29:33	to s hundred bulls and three thousand sheep	9252
Ne	5:18	Each day one ox, s choice sheep	9252
Est	2:12	s months with oil of myrrh and six	9252
	2:12	with oil of myrrh and s with perfumes	9252
Job	5:19	From s calamities he will rescue you;	9252
	42:12	s thousand camels, a thousand yoke of oxen	9252
Pr	6:16	There are s things the LORD hates,	9252
Isa	6: 2	were seraphs, each with s wings;	9252
Jer	34:14	After he has served you s years,	9252
Eze	9: 2	And I saw s men coming from the direction	9252
	40: 5	in the man's hand was s long cubits,	9252
	40:12	and the alcoves were s cubits square.	9252
	41: 1	of the jambs was s cubits on each side.	9252
	41: 3	The entrance was s cubits wide,	9252
	41: 5	it was s cubits thick,	9252
	41: 8	It was the length of the rod, s long cubits.	9252
	46: 1	to be shut on the s working days,	9252
	46: 4	the Sabbath day is to be s male lambs and	9252
	46: 6	s lambs and a ram, all without defect.	9252
Mt	17: 1	After s days Jesus took with him Peter,	1971
Mk	9: 2	After s days Jesus took Peter,	1971
Lk	13:14	"There are s days for work.	1971
Jn	2: 6	Nearby stood s stone water jars,	1971
	12: 1	S days before the Passover,	1971
Ac	11:12	These s brothers also went with me,	1971
Rev	4: 8	of the four living creatures had s wings	1971

SIXSCORE (KJV) See 120

SIXTEEN (18) [SIXTEENTH]

Ge	46:18	to his daughter Leah—s in all.	6926+9252
Ex	26:25	be eight frames and s silver bases—	6925+9252
	36:30	eight frames and s silver bases—	6925+9252
Jos	15:41	s towns and their villages.	6926+9252
	19:22	There were s towns and their villages.	6926+9252
2Ki	13:10	and he reigned s years.	6926+9252
	14:21	who was s years old,	6926+9252
	15: 2	was s years old when he became king,	6926+9252
	15:33	and he reigned in Jerusalem s years.	6926+9252
	16: 2	and he reigned in Jerusalem s years.	6926+9252
1Ch	4:27	Shimei had s sons and six daughters,	6925+9252
	24: 4	s heads of families	6925+9252
2Ch	13:21	had twenty-two sons and s daughters.	6926+9252
	26: 1	who was s years old,	6926+9252
	26: 3	Uzziah was s years old	6926+9252
	27: 1	and he reigned in Jerusalem s years.	6926+9252
	27: 8	and he reigned in Jerusalem s years.	6926+9252
	28: 1	and he reigned in Jerusalem s years.	6926+9252

SIXTEENTH (3) [SIXTEEN]

1Ch	24:14	the fifteenth to Bilgah, the s to Immer,	6925+9252
	25:23	the s to Hananiah, his sons and	6925+9252
2Ch	29:17	on the s day of the first month.	6925+9252

SIXTH (44) [SIX]

Ge	1:31	and there was morning—the s day.	9261
	30:19	and bore Jacob a s son.	9261
Ex	16: 5	On the s day they are to prepare	9261
	16:22	the s day, they gathered twice as much—	9261
	16:29	that is why on the s day he gives you bread	9261
	26: 9	the s curtain double at the front of the tent.	9261
Lev	25:21	I will send you such a blessing in the s year	9261
Nu	7:42	On the s day Eliasaph son of Deuel,	9261
	29:29	" 'On the s day prepare eight bulls,	9261
Jos	19:32	s lot came out for Naphtali, clan by clan:	9261
2Sa	3: 5	and the s, Ithream the son	9261
2Ki	18:10	Samaria was captured in Hezekiah's s year,	9252
1Ch	2:15	the s Ozem and the seventh David.	9261
	3: 3	and the s, Ithream, by his wife Eglah.	9261
	12:11	Attai the s, Eliel the seventh,	9261
	24: 9	the fifth to Malkijah, the s to Mijamin,	9261
	25:13	the s to Bukkiah, his sons and relatives,	9261
	26: 3	Jehohanan the s and Eliehoenai the seventh.	9261
	26: 5	the s, Issachar the seventh and Peullethai	9261
	27: 9	The s, for the sixth month,	9261
	27: 9	The sixth, for the s month,	9261
Ezr	6:15	in the s year of the reign of King Darius.	10747
Ne	3:30	and Hanun, the s son of Zalaph,	9261
Eze	4:11	Also measure out a s of a hin of water	9261
	8: 1	In the s year, in the sixth month	9261
	8: 1	in the s month on the fifth day,	9261
	45:13	a s of an ephah from each homer of wheat	9261
	45:13	an ephah from each homer of wheat and a s	9257
	46:14	consisting of a s of an ephah with a third of	9261
Hag	1: 1	on the first day of the s month,	9261
	1:15	on the twenty-fourth day of the s month in	9261
Mt	20: 5	about the s hour and the ninth hour and did	1761
	27:45	From the s hour until the ninth hour	1761
Mk	15:33	At the s hour darkness came over	1761
Lk	1:26	in the s month, God sent the angel Gabriel	1761
	1:36	to be barren is in her s month.	1761
	23:44	It was now about the s hour,	1761
Jn	4: 6	It was about the s hour.	1761
	19:14	about the s hour.	1761
Rev	6:12	I watched as he opened the s seal.	1761
	9:13	The s angel sounded his trumpet,	1761
	9:14	It said to the s angel who had the trumpet,	1761
	16:12	The s angel poured out his bowl on	1761
	21:20	the s carnelian, the seventh chrysolite,	1761

SIXTY (28) [60]

Ge	25:26	Isaac was s years old when Rebekah	9252
Lev	27: 3	and s at fifty shekels of silver, according to	9252
	27: 7	If it is a person s years old or more,	9252
Nu	7:88	to twenty-four oxen, s rams,	9252
	7:88	s male goats and sixty male lambs	9252
	7:88	sixty male goats and s male lambs	9252
Dt	3: 4	There was not one of the s cities that we did	9252
Jos	13:30	the settlements of Jair in Bashan, s towns,	9252
2Sa	3: 9	and s Benjamites who were with Abner.	9252
1Ki	4:13	in Bashan and its s large walled cities	9252
	4:22	of fine flour and s cors of meal,	9252
	6: 2	for the LORD was s cubits long,	9252
2Ki	25:19	of conscripting the people of the land and s	9252
1Ch	2:21	when he was s years old.)	9252
	2:23	with its surrounding settlements—s towns.)	9252
2Ch	3: 3	the temple of God was s cubits long	9252
	11:21	he had eighteen wives and s concubines,	9252
	11:21	twenty-eight sons and s daughters.	9252
	12: 3	and s thousand horsemen and	9252
SS	3: 7	escorted by s warriors, the noblest of Israel,	9252
	6: 8	S queens there may be,	9252
Jer	52:25	of conscripting the people of the land and s	9252
Eze	40:14	of the gateway—s cubits.	9252
Mt	13: 8	s or thirty times what was sown.	2008
	13:23	s or thirty times what was sown.	2008
Mk	4: 8	s, or even a hundred times."	2008
	4:20	s or even a hundred times what was sown."	2008
1Ti	5: 9	on the list of widows unless she is over s,	2008

SIXTY-EIGHT (1)

1Ch	16:38	and his s associates to minister	2256+9046+9252

SIXTY-FIVE (1) [65]

Isa	7: 8	Within s years Ephraim will	2256+2822+9252

SIXTY-SIX (2)

Ge	46:26	numbered s persons.	2256+9252+9252
Lev	12: 5	Then she must wait s days to be purified	2256+9252+9252

SIXTY-TWO (3) [62]

Da	5:31	at the age of s.	10221+10749+10775
	9:25	seven 'sevens,' and s 'sevens.'	2256+9109+9252
	9:26	After the s 'sevens,'	2256+9109+9252

SIYON (1) [HERMON]

Dt	4:48	on the rim of the Arnon Gorge to Mount S	8481

SIZE (15)

Ex	26: 2	All the curtains are to be the same s—	4500
	26: 8	All eleven curtains are to be the same s—	4500
	36: 9	All the curtains were the same s.	4500
	36:15	All eleven curtains were the same s.	4500
Nu	13:32	All the people we saw there are of great s.	4500
1Ki	6:25	for the two cherubim were identical in s	4500

1Ki	7: 9	blocks of high-grade stone cut to s	4500
	7:11	Above were high-grade stones, cut to s,	4500
	7:37	in the same molds and were identical in s	4500
2Ki	10:32	the LORD began to reduce the s of Israel.	7894
1Ch	23:29	and all measurements of quantity and s.	4500
Ps	33:16	No king is saved by the s of his army;	8044
Eze	45:11	ephah and the bath are to be the same s,	9420
	46:22	in the four corners was the same s.	4500
Rev	18:21	a mighty angel picked up a boulder the s of	6055

SKETCH (1)

2Ki	16:10	and sent to Uriah the priest a s of the altar,	1952

SKIES (21) [SKY]

Dt	28:24	down from the s until you are destroyed.	9028
Job	26: 7	the northern [s] over empty space;	NIH
	26:13	By his breath the s became fair;	9028
	37:18	can you join him in spreading out the s,	8836
	37:21	the s after the wind has swept them clean.	8836
Ps	19: 1	the s proclaim the work of his hands.	8385
	36: 5	your faithfulness to the s.	8836
	57:10	your faithfulness reaches to the s.	8836
	68:33	to him who rides the ancient s above,	9028+9028
	68:34	whose power is in the s.	8836
	71:19	Your righteousness reaches to the s, O God,	5294
	77:17	the s resounded with thunder;	8836
	78:23	Yet he gave a command to the s above	8836
	89: 6	the s above can compare with the LORD?	8836
	108: 4	your faithfulness reaches to the s,	8836
	148: 4	and you waters above the s.	9028
Jer	14:22	Do the s themselves send down showers?	9028
	51: 9	for her judgment reaches to the s,	9028
Hos	2:21	"I will respond to the s,	9028
Mt	11:23	Capernaum, will you be lifted up to the s?	4041
Lk	10:15	Capernaum, will you be lifted up to the s?	4041

SKILL (13) [SKILLED, SKILLFUL, SKILLFULLY, SKILLS]

Ex	31: 3	with s, ability and knowledge in all kinds	2683
	31: 3	Also I have given s to all the craftsmen	2683
	35:26	and had the s spun the goat hair.	2683
	35:31	with s, ability and knowledge in all kinds	2683
	35:35	s to do all kinds of work as craftsmen,	2683+4213
	36: 1	to whom the LORD has given s and ability	2683
2Ch	2:13	Huram-Abi, a man of great s,	1069+2682+3359
Ps	137: 5	may my right hand forget [its s].	NIH
Ecc	2:19	into which I have poured my effort and s	2681
	2:21	do his work with wisdom, knowledge and s,	4179
	10:10	but s will bring success.	2683
Eze	28: 5	By your great s in trading you have	2683
Ac	17:29	an image made by man's design and s.	5492

SKILLED (35) [SKILL]

Ex	26: 1	worked into them by a s craftsman.	3110
	26:31	worked into it by a s craftsman.	3110
	28: 3	s men to whom I have given wisdom	2682+4213
	28: 6	the work of a s craftsman.	3110
	28:15	the work of a s craftsman.	3110
	35:10	"All who are s among you are to come	2682+4213
	35:25	Every s woman spun with her hands	2682+4213
	36: 1	Oholiab and every s person to whom	2682+4213
	36: 2	Oholiab and every s person to whom	2682+4213
	36: 4	So all the s craftsmen who were doing all	2682
	36: 8	All the s men among the workmen	2682+4213
	36: 8	worked into them by a s craftsman.	3110
	36:35	worked into it by a s craftsman.	3110
	39: 3	the work of a s craftsman.	3110
	39: 8	the work of a s craftsman.	3110
1Ki	7:14	we have no one so s in felling timber	3359
	7:14	Huram was highly s and experienced	2683
1Ch	22:15	as well as men s in every kind of work	2682
	25: 7	all of them trained and s in music for	1067
	28:21	and every willing man s	2683
2Ch	2: 7	a man s to work in gold and silver,	2682
	2: 7	and Jerusalem with my s craftsmen,	2682
	2: 8	that your men are s in cutting timber there.	3359
	34:12	who were s in playing musical instruments	1067
Job	32:22	for if I were s in flattery,	3359
Pr	22:29	Do you see a man s in his work?	4542
Isa	3: 3	craftsman and clever enchanter.	2682
	40:20	He looks for a s craftsman to set up an idol	2682
Jer	2:33	How s you are at pursuing love!	2006+3512
	4:22	They are s in doing evil;	2682
	10: 9	all made by s workers.	2682
	50: 9	Their arrows will be s warriors who do	8505
Eze	21:31	I will hand you over to brutal men, men s	3093
	27: 8	your s men, O Tyre, were aboard as your	2682
Mic	7: 3	Both hands are s in doing evil;	3512

SKILLFUL (8) [SKILL]

Ge	25:27	and Esau became a s hunter,	3359
1Ch	15:22	that was his responsibility because he was s	1067
2Ch	26:15	by s men for use on the towers and on	3110
Ps	45: 1	my tongue is the pen of a s writer.	4542
	58: 5	however s the enchanter may be.	2681
	78:72	with s hands he led them.	9312
Jer	9:17	send for the most s of them.	2682
Zec	9: 2	though they are very s.	2681

SKILLFULLY (5) [SKILL]

Ex	28: 8	Its s woven waistband is to be like it—	682
	29: 5	the ephod on him by its s woven waistband.	NIH
	39: 5	Its s woven waistband was like it—	682

Lev	8: 7	the ephod to him by its s woven waistband;	3109
Ps	33: 3	play s, and shout for joy.	3512

SKILLS (1) [SKILL]

Dt	33:11	Bless all his s, O Lord,	2657

SKIM (1)

Job	9:26	They s past like boats of papyrus,	2736

SKIMPING (1)

Am	8: 5	s the measure, boosting the price	7781

SKIN (75) [SKINNED, SKINS, SMOOTH-SKINNED]

Ge	3:21	The LORD God made garments of s	6425
	21:14	and a s of water and gave them to Hagar.	2827
	21:15	When the water in the s was gone,	2827
	21:19	and filled the s with water and gave the boy	2827
	27:11	and I'm a man with smooth s.	AIT
Lev	1: 6	He is to s the burnt offering and cut it	7320
	13: 2	or a rash or a bright spot on his s	1414+6425
	13: 2	that may become an infectious s disease,	7669
	13: 3	priest is to examine the sore on his s,	1414+6425
	13: 3	sore appears to be more than s deep,	1414+6425
	13: 3	it is an infectious s disease.	7669
	13: 4	on his s is white but does not appear	1414+6425
	13: 4	to be more than s deep and the hair in it has	6425
	13: 5	and has not spread in the s,	6425
	13: 6	sore has faded and has not spread in the s,	6425
	13: 7	in his s after he has shown himself to	6425
	13: 8	and if the rash has spread in the s,	6425
	13: 9	"When anyone has an infectious s disease,	7669
	13:10	in the s that has turned the hair white and	6425
	13:11	it is a chronic s disease and	7669
	13:12	"If the disease breaks out all over his s and,	6425
	13:12	it covers all the s of the infected person	6425
	13:18	"When someone has a boil on his s	1414+6425
	13:20	and if it appears to be more than s deep and	6425
	13:20	an infectious s disease that has broken out	7669
	13:21	not more than s deep and has faded,	6425
	13:22	If it is spreading in the s,	6425
	13:24	"When someone has a burn on his s	1414+6425
	13:25	and it appears to be more than s deep,	6425
	13:25	it is an infectious s disease.	7669
	13:26	in the spot and if it is not more than s deep	6425
	13:27	and if it is spreading in the s,	6425
	13:27	it is an infectious s disease.	7669
	13:28	in the s but has faded, it is a swelling from	6425
	13:30	and if it appears to be more than s deep and	6425
	13:31	it does not seem to be more than s deep	6425
	13:32	not appear to be more than s deep,	6425
	13:34	and if it has not spread in the s and appears	6425
	13:34	and appears to be no more than s deep,	6425
	13:35	in the s after he is pronounced clean,	6425
	13:36	and if the itch has spread in the s,	6425
	13:38	or woman has white spots on the s,	1414+6425
	13:39	that has broken out on the s;	6425
	13:43	like an infectious s disease,	1414+6425
	14: 3	of his infectious s disease	7669
	14:32	for anyone who has an infectious s disease	7669
	14:54	the regulations for any infectious s disease,	7669
	14:57	infectious s diseases and mildew.	7669
	22: 4	has an infectious s disease or	7665
Nu	5: 2	has an infectious s disease	7665
Jdg	4:19	She opened a s of milk, gave him a drink,	5532
1Sa	1:24	an ephah of flour and a s of wine,	5574
	10: 3	and another a s of wine.	5574
	16:20	a s of wine and a young goat and sent them	5532
2Sa	16: 1	a hundred cakes of figs and a s of wine.	5574
2Ch	29:34	were too few to s all the burnt offerings;	7320
Job	2: 4	"S for skin!" Satan replied.	6425
	2: 4	"Skin for s!" Satan replied.	6425
	7: 5	my s is broken and festering.	6425
	10:11	with s and flesh and knit me together	6425
	16:15	over my s and buried my brow in the dust.	1654
	18:13	It eats away parts of his s;	6425
	19:20	I am nothing but s and bones;	1414+2256+6425
	19:20	I have escaped with only the s of my teeth.	6425
	19:26	And after my s has been destroyed,	6425
	30:30	My s grows black and peels;	6425
Ps	102: 5	of my loud groaning I am reduced to s	1414
Jer	13:23	Can the Ethiopian change his s or	6425
La	3: 4	He has made my s and my flesh grow old	1414
	4: 8	Their s has shriveled on their bones;	6425
	5:10	Our s is hot as an oven,	6425
Eze	37: 6	upon you and cover you with s;	6425
	37: 8	on them and s covered them,	6425
Mic	3: 2	who tear the s from my people and the flesh	6425
	3: 3	strip off their s and break their bones	6425

SKINK (1)

Lev	11:30	the wall lizard, the s and the chameleon.	2793

SKINNED (1) [SKIN]

2Ch	35:11	while the Levites s the animals.	7320

SKINS (11) [SKIN]

Ex	25: 5	ram s dyed red and hides of sea cows;	6425
	26:14	for the tent a covering of ram s dyed red,	6425
	35: 7	ram s dyed red and hides of sea cows;	6425
	35:23	ram s dyed red or hides of sea cows	6425
	36:19	for the tent a covering of ram s dyed red,	6425

Ex	39:34	of ram s dyed red, the covering of hides	6425
Nu	6: 4	not even the seeds or s.	2293
1Sa	25:18	two s *of* wine, five dressed sheep,	5574
Mt	9:17	If they do, the s will burst,	829
Mk	2:22	If he does, the wine will burst the s,	829
Lk	5:37	If he does, the new wine will burst the s,	829

SKIP (1) [SKIPPED]
Ps	29: 6	*He* makes Lebanon s like a calf,	8376

SKIPPED (2) [SKIP]
Ps	114: 4	the mountains s like rams,	8376
	114: 6	that *you* s like rams, you hills, like lambs?	8376

SKIRTED (1) [SKIRTS]
Jdg	11:18	s the lands of Edom and Moab,	6015

SKIRTS (5) [SKIRTED]
Isa	47: 2	Lift up your s, bare your legs,	8670
Jer	13:22	that your s have been torn off	8767
	13:26	I will pull up your s over your face	8767
La	1: 9	Her filthiness clung to her s;	8767
Na	3: 5	"I will lift your s over your face.	8767

SKULL (6) [SKULLS]
Jdg	9:53	on his head and cracked his s.	1653
2Ki	9:35	they found nothing except her s,	1653
Mt	27:33	Golgotha (which means The Place *of* the S).	3191
Mk	15:22	Golgotha (which means The Place *of* the S).	3191
Lk	23:33	When they came to the place called the S,	3191
Jn	19:17	he went out to the place of the S (which	3191

SKULLS (2) [SKULL]
Nu	24:17	the s of all the sons of Sheth.	7721
Jer	48:45	the s of the noisy boasters.	7721

SKY (74) [SKIES]
Ge	1: 8	God called the expanse "s."	9028
	1: 9	"Let the water under the s be gathered	9028
	1:14	be lights in the expanse of the s to separate	9028
	1:15	in the expanse of the s to give light on	9028
	1:17	in the expanse of the s to give light on	9028
	1:20	above the earth across the expanse of the s."	9028
	8: 2	and the rain had stopped falling from the s.	9028
	22:17	in the s and as the sand on the seashore.	9028
	26: 4	in the s and will give them all these lands,	9028
Ex	9:22	the s so that hail will fall all over Egypt—	9028
	9:23	Moses stretched out his staff toward the s,	9028
	10:21	toward the s so that darkness will spread	9028
	10:22	Moses stretched out his hand toward the s,	9028
	24:10	made of sapphire, clear as the s itself.	9028
	32:13	as numerous as the stars in the s	9028
Lev	26:19	down your stubborn pride and make the s	9028
Dt	1:10	as many as the stars in the s.	9028
	1:28	the cities are large, with walls up to the s.	9028
	4:19	when you look up to the s and see the sun,	9028
	9: 1	with large cities that have walls up to the s.	9028
	10:22	as numerous as the stars in the s.	9028
	17: 3	to the sun or the moon or the stars of the s,	9028
	28:23	The s over your head will be bronze,	9028
	28:62	as numerous as the stars in the s will be left	9028
Jos	8:20	the smoke of the city rising against the s,	9028
	10:11	large hailstones down on them from the s,	9028
	10:13	the middle of the s and delayed going down	9028
Jdg	20:40	of the whole city going up into the s.	9028
2Sa	22:12	the dark rain **clouds of the s**.	6265+8836
1Ki	18:45	Meanwhile, the s grew black with clouds,	9028
1Ch	27:23	as numerous as the stars in the s,	9028
Ne	9:23	as numerous as the stars in the s,	9028
Job	1:16	"The fire of God fell from the s and burned	9028
Ps	18:11	the dark rain **clouds of the s**.	6265+8836
	89:37	the faithful witness in the s."	8836
	147: 8	He covers the s with clouds;	9028
Pr	23: 5	surely sprout wings and fly off to the s like	9028
	30:19	the way of an eagle in the s,	9028
Isa	34: 4	be dissolved and the s rolled up like	9028
	50: 3	I clothe the s with darkness	9028
Jer	4:25	every bird in the s had flown away.	9028
	8: 7	stork in the s knows her appointed seasons,	9028
	10: 2	the nations or be terrified by signs in the s,	9028
	33:22	before me as countless as the stars of the s	9028
	51:53	the s and fortifies her lofty stronghold,	9028
La	4:19	pursuers were swifter than eagles in the s;	9028
Da	4:11	and strong and its top touched the s;	10723
	4:20	with its top touching the s,	10723
	4:22	until it reaches the s,	10723
Joel	2:10	the earth shakes, the s trembles, the sun	9028
	3:16	the earth and the s will tremble.	9028
Na	3:16	till they are more than the stars of the s,	9028
Mt	16: 2	'It will be fair weather, for the s is red,'	4041
	16: 3	for the s is red and overcast.'	4041
	16: 3	how to interpret the appearance *of* the s,	4041
	24:29	the stars will fall from the s,	4041
	24:30	of the Son of Man will appear in the s,	4041
	24:30	Son of Man coming on the clouds *of* the s,	4041
Mk	13:25	the stars will fall from the s,	4041
Lk	4:25	the s was shut for three and a half years	4041
	12:56	the appearance *of* the earth and the s.	4041
	17:24	and lights up the s from one end to	4041
Ac	1:10	They were looking intently up into the s	4041
	1:11	"why do you stand here looking into the s?	4041
Heb	11:12	*in* the s and as countless as the sand on	4041

Rev	6:13	and the stars *in* the s fell to earth,	4041
	6:14	The s receded like a scroll, rolling up,	4041
	8:10	fell from the s and on a third of the rivers and	4041
	9: 1	and I saw a star that had fallen from the s to	4041
	9: 2	The sun and s were darkened by the smoke	113
	11: 6	These men have power to shut up the s so	4041
	12: 4	of the stars *out of* the s and flung them to	4041
	16:21	From the s huge hailstones of about	4041
	20:11	Earth and s fled from his presence,	4041

SLACK (1)
Pr	18: 9	One who is s in his work is brother	8332

SLAIN (61) [SLAY]
Dt	21: 1	If a man is found s, lying in a field	2728
	32:42	the blood of the s and the captives,	2728
Jos	11: 6	hand all of them over to Israel, s.	2728
	13:22	In addition to *those* s in battle,	2728
Jdg	16:24	and multiplied our s."	2728
1Sa	18: 7	"Saul has s his thousands,	5782
	21:11	" 'Saul has s his thousands,	5782
	29: 5	" 'Saul has s his thousands,	5782
	31: 1	and many fell s on Mount Gilboa.	2728
2Sa	1:19	O Israel, lies s on your heights.	2728
	1:22	From the blood of the s,	2728
	1:25	Jonathan lies s on your heights.	2728
2Ki	11:20	because Athaliah *had been* s with the sword	4637
1Ch	5:22	and many others fell s,	2728
	10: 1	and many fell s on Mount Gilboa.	2728
2Ch	23:21	because Athaliah *had been* s with the sword.	4637
Est	9:11	The number of those s in the citadel	2222
Job	39:30	and where the s are, there is he."	2728
Ps	88: 5	like the s who lie in the grave,	2728
	89:10	You crushed Rahab like *one of* the s;	2728
Pr	7:26	her s are a mighty throng.	2222
Isa	10: 4	among the captives or fall among the s.	2222
	14:19	you are covered with the s,	2222
	22: 2	Your s were not killed by the sword,	2728
	26:21	she will conceal her s no longer.	2728
	34: 3	Their s will be thrown out,	2728
	66:16	and many will be those s *by* the LORD.	2728
Jer	9: 1	I would weep day and night for the s	2222
	14:18	I see *those* s *by* the sword;	2728
	18:21	their young men *by* the sword in battle.	5782
	25:33	At that time *those* s *by* the LORD will	2728
	51: 4	They will fall down s in Babylon,	2728
	51:47	be disgraced and her s will all lie fallen	2728
	51:49	"Babylon must fall because of Israel's s,	2728
	51:49	as the s *in* all the earth have fallen because	2728
La	2: 4	Like a foe *he has* s all who were pleasing to	2222
	2:21	*You have* s them in the day of your anger;	2222
	3:43	*you have* s without pity.	2222
Eze	6: 7	Your people will fall s among you,	2728
	6:13	when their *people* lie s among their idols	2728
	9: 7	the temple and fill the courts with the s."	2728
	21:29	on the necks of the wicked who are to be s,	2728
	28:23	The s will fall within her,	2728
	30: 4	When the s fall in Egypt,	2728
	30:11	against Egypt and fill the land with the s.	2728
	32:22	she is surrounded by the graves of all her s,	2728
	32:23	in the land of the living are s,	2728
	32:24	All of them are s, fallen by the sword.	2728
	32:25	A bed is made for her among the s,	2728
	32:25	they are laid among the s.	2728
	32:30	the s in disgrace despite the terror caused	2728
	35: 8	I will fill your mountains with the s;	2728
	37: 9	O breath, and breathe into these s,	2222
Da	5:30	king of the Babylonians, was s,	10625
	7:11	until the beast was s and its body destroyed	10625
Zep	2:12	O Cushites, will be s *by* my sword."	2728
Rev	5: 6	I saw a Lamb, looking as if *it had been* s,	5377
	5: 9	and to open its seals, because *you were* s,	5377
	5:12	"Worthy is the Lamb, who *was* s,	5377
	6: 9	the altar the souls of *those who had been* s	5377
	13: 8	to the Lamb that *was* s from the creation of	5377

SLANDER (27) [SLANDERED, SLANDERER, SLANDERERS, SLANDERING, SLANDEROUS, SLANDEROUSLY, SLANDERS]
Lev	19:16	about **spreading** s among your people.	8215
Ps	15: 3	and *has* no s on his tongue,	8078
	31:13	For I hear the s *of* many;	1804
	38:20	with evil s me when I pursue what is good.	8476
	41: 6	he speaks falsely, while his heart gathers s;	224
	50:20	and s your own mother's son.	1984+5989
	54: 5	Let evil recoil on *those who* s me;	8806
	59:10	and will let me gloat over *those who* s me.	8806
	119:23	Though rulers sit together and s me,	1819
Pr	10:18	and whoever spreads s is a fool.	1804
	30:10	"Do not s a servant to his master,	4387
Jer	6:28	hardened rebels, going about to s.	8215
Eze	36: 3	the object of people's malicious talk and s,	1804
Mt	15:19	sexual immorality, theft, false testimony, s.	1060
Mk	7:22	lewdness, envy, s, arrogance and folly.	1060
2Co	12:20	factions, s, gossip, arrogance and disorder.	2896
Eph	4:31	rage and anger, brawling and s,	1060
Col	3: 8	s, and filthy language from your lips.	1060
1Ti	5:14	and to give the enemy no opportunity for s.	3367
Tit	3: 2	*to* s no one, to be peaceable and considerate	1059
Jas	4:11	Brothers, *do* not s one another.	2895
1Pe	2: 1	hypocrisy, envy, and s of every kind.	2896
	3:16	in Christ may be ashamed of their s.	2895
2Pe	2:10	not afraid to s celestial beings;	1059

Jude	1: 8	reject authority and s celestial beings.	1059
Rev	2: 9	the s of those who say they are Jews and are	1060
	13: 6	and *to* s his name and his dwelling place	1059

SLANDERED (5) [SLANDER]
Dt	22:17	Now he *has* s her and said,	1821+6613+8492
2Sa	19:27	*he has* s your servant to my lord the king.	8078
Ps	35:15	*They* s me without ceasing.	7973
1Co	4:13	*when we are* s, we answer kindly.	1555
1Ti	6: 1	God's name and our teaching *may* not *be* s.	1059

SLANDERER (2) [SLANDER]
Jer	9: 4	and every friend a s.	2143+8215
1Co	5:11	an idolater or a s, a drunkard or a swindler.	3368

SLANDERERS (5) [SLANDER]
Ps	56: 2	My s pursue me all day long;	8806
	140:11	Let s not be established in the land;	408+4383
Ro	1:30	s, God-haters, insolent, arrogant	2897
1Co	6:10	nor s nor swindlers will inherit the kingdom	3368
Tit	2: 3	not to be s or addicted to much wine,	1333

SLANDERING (1) [SLANDER]
Jas	2: 7	the ones who *are* s the noble name of him	1059

SLANDEROUS (4) [SLANDER]
Eze	22: 9	In you are s men bent on shedding blood;	8215
2Ti	3: 3	unforgiving, s, without self-control, brutal,	1333
2Pe	2:11	not bring s accusations against such beings	1061
Jude	1: 9	not dare to bring a s accusation against him,	1060

SLANDEROUSLY (1) [SLANDER]
Ro	3: 8	as *we are being* s **reported** as saying and	1059

SLANDERS (2) [SLANDER]
Dt	22:14	s her and gives her a bad name,	1821+6613+8492
Ps	101: 5	*Whoever* s his neighbor in secret,	4387

SLANG (KJV) See SLUNG

SLAPPED (3) [SLAPS]
1Ki	22:24	went up and s Micaiah in the face.	5782
2Ch	18:23	went up and s Micaiah in the face.	5782
Mt	26:67	struck him with their fists. Others s him	4824

SLAPS (1) [SLAPPED]
2Co	11:20	pushes himself forward or s you in the face.	1296

SLASH (1) [SLASHED]
Eze	21:16	O sword, s to the right, then to the left,	2523

SLASHED (2) [SLASH]
1Ki	18:28	and s **themselves** with swords and spears,	1517
Jer	48:37	every hand is s and every waist is covered	1523

SLAUGHTER (63) [SLAUGHTERED, SLAUGHTERING, SLAUGHTERS]
Ge	43:16	s an animal and prepare dinner;	3180
Ex	12: 6	of the community of Israel *must* s them	8821
	12:21	for your families and s the Passover lamb.	8821
	29:11	S it in the LORD's presence at	8821
	29:16	S it and take the blood and sprinkle it	8821
	29:20	S it, take some of its blood and put it on	8821
Lev	1: 5	*to* s the young bull before the LORD,	8821
	1:11	*to* s it at the north side of the altar before	8821
	3: 2	of his offering and s it at the entrance to	8821
	3: 8	on the head of his offering and s it in front	8821
	3:13	to lay his hand on its head and s it in front	8821
	4: 4	to lay his hand on its head and s it before	8821
	4:24	to lay his hand on the goat's head and s it at	8821
	4:29	and s it at the place of the burnt offering.	8821
	4:33	and s it for a sin offering at the place where	8821
	14:13	*He is to* s the lamb in the holy place where	8821
	14:13	the priest *shall* s the burnt offering	8821
	14:25	*He shall* s the lamb for the guilt offering	8821
	16:11	*he is to* s the bull for his own sin offering.	8821
	16:15	"He shall then s the goat for the sin offering	8821
	22:28	*Do* not s a cow or a sheep and its young on	8821
Dt	12:15	*you may* s your animals in any of your	2284
	12:21	*you may* s animals from the herds	2284
1Sa	14: 9	The s was very great;	4804
	14:30	Would not the s of the Philistines have been	4804
	14:34	and s them here and eat them.	8821
2Sa	17: 9	a s among the troops who follow Absalom.'	4487
2Ch	35: 6	S the Passover lambs,	8821
Est	7: 4	for destruction and s and annihilation.	2222
Pr	7:22	like an ox going to the s,	3181
	24:11	hold back those staggering toward s.	2223
Isa	14:21	Prepare a **place** to s his sons for the sins	4749
	30:25	In the day of great s, when the towers fall,	2223
	34: 2	he will give them over to s.	3181
	34: 6	a sacrifice in Bozrah and a great s in Edom.	3181
	53: 7	he was led like a lamb to the s,	3181
	65:12	and you will all bend down for the s;	3181
Jer	7:32	but the Valley of S, for they will bury	2224
	11:19	I had been like a gentle lamb led to the s;	3180
	12: 3	Set them apart for the day of s!	2224
	19: 6	but the Valley of S.	2224

Jer	48:15	her finest young men will go down in the s, 3181
	50:27	let them go down to the s! 3181
	51:40	"I will bring them down like lambs to the s, 3181
Eze	9: 6	S old men, young men and 2222+4200+5422
	21:10	sharpened for the s, polished to flash 3180+3181
	21:14	It is a sword for s—a sword for great 2728
	21:14	a sword for great s, 2728
	21:15	the sword for s at all their gates. 18
	21:15	it is grasped for s. 3181
	21:22	to give the command to s, 8358
	21:28	" 'A sword, drawn for the s, 3181
	26:15	wounded groan and the s takes place 2222+2223
	34: 3	with the wool and s the choice animals, 2284
	44:11	they may s the burnt offerings and sacrifices 8821
Da	11:12	with pride and will s many thousands, 5877
Hos	5: 2	The rebels are deep in s. 8823
Ob	1: 9	mountains will be cut down in the s. 7780
Zec	11: 4	"Pasture the flock marked for s. 2224
	11: 5	Their buyers s them and go unpunished. 2222
	11: 7	So I pastured the flock marked for s, 2224
Ac	8:32	"He was led like a sheep to the s, 5375
Jas	5: 5	fattened yourselves in the day of s. 5375

SLAUGHTERED (52) [SLAUGHTER]

Ge	37:31	s a goat and dipped the robe in the blood. 8821
Lev	4:15	and the bull shall be s before the LORD. 8821
	4:24	the burnt offering is s before the LORD. 8821
	4:33	at the place where the burnt offering is s. 8821
	6:25	to be s before the LORD in the place 8821
	6:25	in the place the burnt offering is s; 8821
	7: 2	The guilt offering is to be s in the place 8821
	7: 2	in the place where the burnt offering is s, 8821
	8:15	Moses s the bull and took some of 8821
	8:19	Then Moses s the ram and sprinkled 8821
	8:23	Moses s the ram and took some of its blood 8821
	9: 8	So Aaron came to the altar and s the calf as 8821
	9:12	Then he s the burnt offering. 8821
	9:15	and s it and offered it for a sin offering 8821
	9:18	He s the ox and the ram as 8821
	14:13	the sin offering and the burnt offering are s. 8821
Nu	11:22	if flocks and herds were s for them? 8821
	14:16	so he s them in the desert.' 8821
	19: 3	it is to be taken outside the camp and s 8821
Dt	28:31	Your ox will be s before your eyes, 3180
Jdg	15: 8	He attacked them viciously and s many 4804
1Sa	1:25	When they had s the bull, 8821
	11:11	into the camp of the Ammonites and s them 5782
	14:34	brought his ox that night and s it there. 8821
	25:11	and the meat I have s for my shearers, 3180
1Ki	18:40	down to the Kishon Valley and s there. 8821
	19:21	He took his yoke of oxen and s them. 2284
2Ki	3:23	kings must have fought and s each other. 5782
	3:24	And the Israelites invaded the land and s 5782
	10: 7	these men took the princes and s all seventy 8821
	10:14	and s them by the well of Beth Eked— 8821
	23:20	Josiah s all the priests of those high places 2284
2Ch	2: 8	Ahab s many sheep and cattle for him and 2284
	28: 9	But you have s them in a rage that reaches 2222
	29:22	So they s the bulls, and the priests took 8821
	29:22	next they s the rams and sprinkled 8821
	29:22	then they s the lambs and sprinkled 8821
	29:24	then s the goats and presented their blood 8821
	30:15	They s the Passover lamb on 8821
	35: 1	and the Passover lamb was s on 8821
	35:11	The Passover lambs were s. 8821
Ezr	6:20	The Levites s the Passover lamb for all 8821
Ps	44:22	we are considered as sheep to be s. 3186
Jer	25:34	For your time to be s has come; 3180
	39: 6	the king of Babylon s the sons of Zedekiah 8821
	41: 7	and the men who were with him s them 8821
	52:10	the king of Babylon s the sons of Zedekiah 8821
La	2:21	you have s them without pity. 3180
Eze	16:21	You s my children and sacrificed them to 8821
	40:39	sin offerings and guilt offerings were s 8821
	40:41	on which the sacrifices were s. 8821
Ro	8:36	we are considered as sheep to be s." 5375

SLAUGHTERED (Anglicized) See also BUTCHERED

SLAUGHTERING (5) [SLAUGHTER]

1Sa	7:11	s them along the way to a point below 5782
2Ch	20:23	After they finished s the men from Seir, NIH
	25:14	When Amaziah returned from s 5782
Isa	22:13	s of cattle and killing of sheep, 2222
Eze	40:42	the utensils for s the burnt offerings and 8821

SLAUGHTERS (1) [SLAUGHTER]

Ex	22: 1	"If a man steals an ox or a sheep and s it 3180

SLAVE (89) [ENSLAVE, ENSLAVED, ENSLAVES, ENSLAVING, SLAVERY, SLAVES, SLAVING]

Ge	9:26	May Canaan be the s of Shem. 6269
	9:27	and may Canaan be his s." 6269
	20:17	healed Abimelech, his wife and his s girls 563
	21:10	"Get rid of that s woman and her son, 563
	21:10	for that s woman's son will never share in 563
	39:17	"That Hebrew s you brought us came to me 6269
	39:19	saying, "This is how your s treated me," 6269
	44:10	found to have it will become my s; 6269
	44:17	found to have the cup will become my s. 6269
Ge	44:33	as my lord's s in place of the boy, 6269
Ex	1:11	So they put s masters over them 4989
	2: 5	the reeds and sent her s girl to get it. 563
	3: 7	because of their s drivers, 5601
	5: 6	to the s drivers and foremen in charge of 5601
	5:10	the s drivers and the foremen went out 5601
	5:13	The s drivers kept pressing them, saying, 5601
	5:14	by Pharaoh's s drivers were beaten 5601
	11: 5	to the firstborn son of the s girl, 9148
	12:44	Any s you have bought may eat of it 6269
	21:20	a man beats his male or female's with a rod 6269
	21:20	or female slave with a rod and the s dies as NIH
	21:21	but he is not to be punished if the s gets up NIH
	21:21	since the s is his property. 2085S
	21:32	If the bull gores a male or female s, 6269
	21:32	shekels of silver to the master of the s, 6269S
	23:12	s born in your household, 563+1201
Lev	19:20	with a woman who is a s girl promised 9148
	22:11	But if a priest buys a s with money, 5883
	22:11	or if a s is born in his household, NIH
	22:11	that s may eat his food. 2085S
	25:39	do not make him work as a s. 6269+6275
Dt	21:14	You must not sell her or treat her as a s, 6683
	23:15	If a s has taken refuge with you, 6269
	24: 7	treats him as a s or sells him, 6683
	32:36	and no one is left, s or free. 6806
Jdg	9:18	and made Abimelech, the son of his s girl, 563
1Sa	30:13	"I am an Egyptian, the s of an Amalekite. 6269
2Sa	6:20	in the sight of the s girls of his servants 563
	6:22	But by these s girls you spoke of, 563
1Ki	9:21	Solomon conscripted for his s labor force, 6268
	14:10	every last male in Israel—s or free. 6806
	21:21	every last male in Israel—s or free. 6806
2Ki	9: 8	every last male in Israel—s or free. 6806
	14:26	whether s or free, was suffering; 6806
2Ch	8: 8	Solomon conscripted for his s labor force, 4989
Job	3:18	they no longer hear the s driver's shout. 5601
	3:19	and the s is freed from his master. 6269
	7: 2	Like a s longing for the evening shadows, 6269
	41: 4	with you for you to take him as your s 6269
Ps	105:17	Joseph, sold as a s. 6269
Pr	12:24	but laziness ends in s labor. 4989
	19:10	much worse for a s to rule over princes! 6269
Jer	2:14	Is Israel a servant, a s by birth? 1074+3535
La	1: 1	among the provinces has now become a s. 4989
Na	2: 7	Its s girls moan like doves and beat 563
Mt	20:27	whoever wants to be first must be your s— 1528
Mk	10:44	whoever wants to be first must be s of all. 1528
Jn	8:34	everyone who sins is a s to sin. 1528
	8:35	a s has no permanent place in the family, 1528
Ac	7:13	they sold him as a s into Egypt. NIG
	16:16	we were met by a s girl who had a spirit 4087
	16:19	When the owners of the s girl realized 899S
Ro	7:14	but I am unspiritual, sold as a s to sin. NIG
	7:25	I myself in my mind am a s to God's law, 1526
	7:25	but in the sinful nature a s to the law of sin. NIG
	8:15	not receive a spirit that makes you a s again 1525
1Co	7:21	Were you a s when you were called? 1528
	7:22	For he who was a s when he was called by 1528
	7:22	a free man when he was called is Christ's s. 1528
	9:19	I make myself a s to everyone, 1530
	9:27	I beat my body and make it my s so that 1524
	12:13	whether Jews or Greeks, s or free— 1528
Gal	3:28	There is neither Jew nor Greek, s nor free, 1528
	4: 1	he is no different from a s, 1528
	4: 7	So you are no longer a s, but a son; 1528
	4:22	one by the s woman and the other by 4087
	4:23	the s woman was born in the ordinary way; 4087
	4:30	"Get rid of the s woman and her son, 4087
	4:30	for the s woman's son will never share in 4087
	4:31	we are not children of the s woman, 4087
Eph	6: 8	whether he is s or free. 1528
Col	3:11	s or free, but Christ is all, and is in all. 1528
1Ti	1:10	for s traders and liars and perjurers— 435
Phm	1:16	no longer as a s, but better than a slave, 1528
	1:16	but better than a s, as a dear brother. 1528
2Pe	2:19	a man is a s to whatever has mastered him. 1530
Rev	6:15	and every s and every free man hid in caves 1528
	13:16	small and great, rich and poor, free and s, 1528
	19:18	and the flesh of all people, free and s, 1528

SLAVERY (24) [SLAVE]

Ex	2:23	The Israelites groaned in their s 6275
	2:23	for help because of their s went up to God. 6275
	13: 3	out of Egypt, out of the land of s, 6269
	13:14	out of Egypt, out of the land of s. 6269
	20: 2	out of Egypt, out of the land of s. 6269
Dt	5: 6	out of Egypt, out of the land of s. 6269
	6:12	out of Egypt, out of the land of s. 6269
	7: 8	and redeemed you from the land of s, 6269
	8:14	out of Egypt, out of the land of s. 6269
	13: 5	and redeemed you from the land of s; 6269
	13:10	out of Egypt, out of the land of s. 6269
Jos	24:17	out of Egypt, from that land of s, 6269
Jdg	6: 8	out of Egypt, out of the land of s. 6269
Ne	5: 5	to subject our sons and daughters to s. 6269
	9: 17	a leader in order to return to their s. 6285
Jer	34:13	out of Egypt, out of the land of s. 6269
Mic	6: 4	and redeemed you from the land of s. 6269
Ro	6:19	the parts of your body in s to impurity and 1529
	6:19	so now offer them in s to righteousness. 1529
Gal	4: 3	we were in s under the basic principles of 1530
	4:25	because she is in s with her children. 1526
	5: 1	be burdened again by a yoke of s. 1525
1Ti	6: 1	of s should consider their masters worthy 1528
Heb	2:15	free those who all their lives were held in s 1525

SLAVES (71) [SLAVE]

Ge	9:25	The lowest of s will he be to his brothers." 6269+6269
	15:14	But I will punish the nation they serve as s, 6268
	20:14	and male and female s and gave them 6269
	43:18	and seize us as s and take our donkeys." 6269
	44: 9	and the rest of us will become my lord's s." 6269
	44:16	We are now my lord's s— 6269
	50:18	"We are your s," they said. 6269
Ex	6: 6	I will free you from being s to them, 6275
	9:20	to bring their s and their livestock inside. 6269
	9:21	of the LORD left their s and livestock in 6269
Lev	25:42	they must not be sold as s. 6269
	25:44	" 'Your male and female s are to come 6269
	25:44	from them you may buy s. 563+2256+6269
	25:46	as inherited property and can make them s 6268
	26:13	of Egypt so that you would no longer be s 6269
Dt	5:15	Remember that you were s in Egypt and 6269
	6:21	tell him: "We were s of Pharaoh in Egypt, 6269
	15:15	Remember that you were s in Egypt and 6269
	16:12	Remember that you were s in Egypt, 6269
	24:18	Remember that you were s in Egypt and 6269
	24:22	Remember that you were s in Egypt. 6269
	28:68	to your enemies as male and female s, 6269
	28:68	and you yourselves will become his s. 6269
1Sa	8:17	and you yourselves will become his s. 6269
1Ki	2:39	two of Shimei's s ran off to Achish son 6269
	2:39	and Shimei was told, "Your s are in Gath." 6269
	2:40	to Achish at Gath in search of his s. 6269
	2:40	and brought the s back from Gath. 6269
	9:22	But Solomon did not make s of any of 6269
2Ki	4: 1	to take my two boys as his s." 6269
2Ch	8: 9	not make s of the Israelites for his work; 6269
	28:10	make the men and women of Judah and Jerusalem your s. 3899+6269
Ezr	9: 9	Though we are s, 6269
Ne	9:36	"But see, we are s today, 6269
	9:36	s in the land you gave our forefathers 6269
Est	7: 4	sold as male and female s, 6269
Ps	123: 2	of s look to the hand of their master, 6269
Ecc	2: 7	I bought male and female s 6269
	2: 7	and had other s who were born NIH
	10: 7	I have seen s on horseback, 6269
	10: 7	while princes go on foot like s. 6269
Jer	34: 8	in Jerusalem to proclaim freedom for the s. 2002
	34: 9	to free his Hebrew s, both male 6269
	34:10	they would free their male and female s 6269
	34:11	took back the s they had freed 2256+6269+9148
	34:16	the male and female s you had set free 6269
	34:16	to become your s again. 2256+6269+9148
La	5: 8	S rule over us, and there is none to free us 6269
Eze	27:13	they exchanged s and articles of bronze 132+5883
Zec	2: 9	so that their s will plunder them. 6269
Jn	8:33	and have never been s of anyone. 1526
Ac	7: 6	But I will punish the nation they serve as s,' 1526
Ro	6: 6	that we should no longer be s to sin— 1526
	6:16	to someone to obey him as s, you are slaves 1528
	6:16	you are s to the one whom you obey— 1528
	6:16	whether you are s to sin, NIG
	6:17	though you used to be s to sin, 1528
	6:18	and have become s to righteousness. 1530
	6:20	When you were s to sin, 1528
	6:22	from sin and have become s to God, 1530
1Co	7:23	do not become s of men. 1528
Gal	2: 4	in Christ Jesus and to make us s. 2871
	4: 8	you were s to those who by nature are 1526
	4:24	and bears children who are to be s: 1525
Eph	6: 5	S, obey your earthly masters with respect 1528
	6: 6	but like s of Christ, 1528
	6: 9	And masters, treat your s in the same way. 899S
Col	3:22	S, obey your earthly masters in everything; 1528
	3:22	I provide your s with what is right and fair, 1528
Tit	2: 9	Teach s to be subject to their masters 1528
1Pe	2:18	S, submit yourselves to your masters 3860
2Pe	2:19	while they themselves are s of depravity— 1528

SLAVING (1) [SLAVE]

Lk	15:29	All these years I've been s for you 1526

SLAY (16) [SLAIN, SLAYER, SLAYS, SLEW]

Ge	22:10	and took the knife to s his son. 8821
Job	13:15	Though he s me, yet will I hope in him; 7779
Ps	34:21	Evil will s the wicked; 4637
	37:14	to s those whose ways are upright. 3180
	94: 6	They s the widow and the alien; 2222
	139:19	If only you would s the wicked, O God! 7779
Isa	11: 4	the breath of his lips he will s the wicked. 4637
	14:30	it will s your survivors. 2222
	27: 1	he will s the monster of the sea. 2222
Jer	33: 5	of the men I will s in my anger and wrath. 5782
Eze	6: 4	I will s your people in front of your idols. 5877
	28: 9	not a god, in the hands of those who s you. 2726
Hos	2: 3	and s her with thirst. 4637
	9:16	I will s their cherished offspring." 4637
Am	9: 4	there I will command the sword to s them. 2222
Rev	6: 4	the earth and to make men s each other. 5377

SLAYER (2) [SLAY]

Eze	21:11	made ready for the hand of the s. 2222
Hos	9:13	But Ephraim will bring out their children to the s." 2222

SLAYS (1) [SLAY]

Job	5: 2	Resentment kills a fool, and envy s the simple. 4637

SLEDGE (3) [SLEDGES]
Job	41:30	leaving a trail in the mud like a **threshing s**.	3023
Isa	28:27	Caraway is not threshed with a **s**,	3023
	41:15	"See, I will make you into a **threshing s**,	4617

SLEDGES (3) [SLEDGE]
2Sa	24:22	and here are **threshing s** and ox yokes for	4617
1Ch	21:23	the **threshing s** for the wood,	4617
Am	1: 3	she threshed Gilead with a *having* iron teeth,	3023

SLEEK (6)
Ge	41: 2	seven cows, **s** and fat, and they grazed	3637+5260
	41: 4	ugly and gaunt ate up the seven **s**,	3637+5260
	41:18	seven cows, fat and **s**, and they grazed	3637+9307
Dt	32:15	filled with food, he became heavy and **s**.	4170
Jer	5:28	and have grown fat and **s**.	6950
Eze	34:16	but the **s** and the strong I will destroy.	9045

SLEEP (73) [ASLEEP, SLEEPER, SLEEPING, SLEEPLESS, SLEEPS, SLEEPY, SLEPT]
Ge	2:21	the man to fall into a **deep s**;	9554
	15:12	Abram fell into a **deep s**,	9554
	16: 2	Go, **s** with my maidservant;	448+995
	28:11	he put it under his head and **lay down to s**.	8886
	28:16	When Jacob awoke from his **s**, he thought,	9104
	30: 3	**S** with her so that she can bear children	448+995
	30:15	"he can **s** with you tonight in return	6640+8886
	30:16	"You must **s** with me," she said.	448+995
	31:40	and **s** fled from my eyes.	9104
	38:16	"Come now, *let me* **s** with you."	448+995
	38:16	what will you give me **to s with** you?"	448+995
	38:26	And *he* did not **s** with her again.	3359
	39:14	He came in here to **s** with me,	6640+8886
Ex	22:27	What else *will* he **s** in?	8886
Dt	24:12	*do* not **go to s** with his pledge	8886
	24:13	to him by sunset so that he *may* **s** in it.	8886
Jdg	16:14	He awoke from his **s** and pulled up the pin	9104
	16:19	*Having* put him to **s** on her lap,	3822
	16:20	He awoke from his **s** and thought,	9104
1Sa	26:12	the LORD had put them into a **deep s**.	9554
2Sa	3: 7	"Why *did you* **s** with my father's"	448+995
	11:13	the evening Uriah went out to **s** on his mat	8886
Est	6: 1	That night the king could not **s**;	9104
Job	4:13	when **deep s** falls on men,	9554
	14:12	not awake or be roused from their **s**.	9104
	31:10	and *may* other men **s** with her.	4156+6584
	33:15	when **deep s** falls on men as they slumber	9554
Ps	3: 5	I lie down and **s**;	3822
	4: 8	I will lie down and **s** in peace,	3822
	7: 5	to the ground and **make** me **s** in the dust.	8905
	13: 3	or I *will* **s** in death;	3822
	44:23	Awake, O Lord! Why *do you* **s**?	3822
	68:13	Even while *you* **s** among the campfires,	8886
	76: 5	*they* **s** their last sleep;	5670
	76: 5	they sleep their last **s**;	9104
	78:65	Then the Lord awoke as from **s**,	3825
	90: 5	You sweep men away in the **s of death;**	9104
	121: 4	over Israel will neither slumber nor **s**.	3822
	127: 2	for he grants **s** to those he loves.	9097
	132: 4	I will allow no **s** to my eyes,	9104
Pr	3:24	when you lie down, your **s** will be sweet.	9104
	4:16	For *they* cannot **s** till they do evil;	3822
	6: 4	Allow no **s** to your eyes,	9104
	6: 9	When will you get up from your **s**?	9104
	6:10	A little **s**, a little slumber,	9104
	6:22	when you **s**, they will watch over you;	8886
	19:15	Laziness brings on **deep s**,	9554
	20:13	Do not love **s** or you will grow poor;	9104
	24:33	A little **s**, a little slumber, a little folding of	9104
Ecc	5:12	The **s** of a laborer is sweet,	9104
	5:12	abundance of a rich man permits him no **s**.	3822
	8:16	his eyes not seeing **s** day or night—	9104
Isa	29:10	LORD has brought over you a **deep s**:	8120+9554
	56:10	they lie around and dream, they love to **s**.	5670
Jer	31:26	My **s** had been pleasant to me.	9104
	51:39	then **s** forever and not awake,"	3822+9104
	51:57	*they will* **s** forever and not awake,"	3822+9104
Eze	23:44	As men's **s** with a prostitute,	448+995
	34:25	so that they may live in the desert and **s** in	3822
Da	2: 1	his mind was troubled and he could not **s**.	9104
	6:18	And he could not **s**.	10733
	8:18	*I was* **in a deep s**, with my face to the	8101
	10: 9	**fell into a deep s**, my face to the ground.	8101
	12: 2	Multitudes *who* **s** in the dust of the earth	3825
Jnh	1: 5	and **fell into a deep s**.	8101
	1: 6	"How can you **s**?	8101
Zec	4: 1	as a man is wakened from his **s**.	9104
Jn	11:13	his disciples thought he meant **natural s**.	
			3122+3836+3836+5678
Ac	20: 9	*into* a deep **s** as Paul talked on and on.	5678
1Co	15:51	I tell you a mystery: *We* will not all **s**,	3121
2Co	11:27	and **have** often **gone without s**;	71+1877
1Th	5: 7	For those who **s**, sleep at night,	2761
	5: 7	For those who sleep, **s** at night,	2761

SLEEPER (1) [SLEEP]
Eph	5:14	This is why it is said: "Wake up, O **s**,	2761

SLEEPING (22) [SLEEP]
Ge	2:21	while *he was* **s**, he took one of the man's	3822
Nu	5:13	*by* **s** with another man,	907+2446+8886+8887

Nu	5:20	*by* **s** with a man other than your husband"—	
			928+5989+8888
Dt	22:22	is found **s with** another man's wife,	6640+8886
Jdg	16:13	So *while he was* **s**, Delilah took	3822
	19: 4	eating and drinking, and **s** there.	4328
1Sa	26:12	They *were* all **s**, because the LORD had put	3825
1Ki	18:27	Maybe he is **s** and must be awakened."	3825
Pr	23:34	You will be like *one* **s** on the high seas.	8886
Mt	8:24	But Jesus *was* **s**.	2761
	13:25	But *while* everyone *was* **s**,	1877+4111
	26:40	to his disciples and found them **s**,	2761
	26:43	he again found them **s**,	2761
	26:45	*"Are you* still **s** and resting?*	2761
Mk	4:38	Jesus was in the stern, **s** on a cushion.	2761
	13:36	do not let him find you **s**.	2761
	14:37	to his disciples and found them **s**.	2761
	14:40	he again found them **s**,	2761
	14:41	he said to them, *"Are you* still **s** and resting?	2761
Lk	22:46	"Why *are you* **s**?"	2761
Ac	12: 6	Peter was **s** between two soldiers,	3121
2Pe	2: 3	and their destruction *has* not *been* **s**.	3818

SLEEPLESS (1) [SLEEP]
2Co	6: 5	in hard work, **s nights** and hunger;	71

SLEEPS (15) [SLEEP]
Ex	22:16	a virgin who is not pledged to be married	
		and **s with** her,	6640+8886
Lev	14:47	Anyone *who* **s** or eats in the house	8886
	19:20	" 'If a man **s with** a woman who is a slave	
		girl	907+2446+8886+8887
	20:11	" 'If a man **s with** his father's wife,	907+8886
	20:12	" 'If a man **s with** his daughter-in-law,	907+8886
	20:20	" 'If a man **s with** his aunt,	907+8886
Dt	22:23	pledged to be married and *he* **s with**	6640+8886
	27:20	the man *who* **s with** his father's wife,	6640+8886
	27:22	is the man *who* **s with** his sister,	6640+8886
	27:23	man *who* **s with** his mother-in-law."	6640+8886
Pr	6:29	So is he *who* **s with** another man's wife;	448+995
	10: 5	*he who* **s** during harvest is a disgraceful son.	8101
Isa	5:27	not one slumbers or **s**;	3822
Mk	4:27	Night and day, whether *he* **s** or gets up,	2761
Jn	11:12	His disciples replied, "Lord, if *he* **s**,	3121

SLEEPY (1) [SLEEP]
Lk	9:32	Peter and his companions were **very s**,	976+5678

SLEET (1)
Ps	78:47	with hail and their sycamore-figs with **s**.	2857

SLEIGHT (KJV) See SCHEMING

SLEPT (21) [SLEEP]
Ge	16: 4	*He* **s** with Hagar, and she conceived.	448+995
	19: 8	I have two daughters who *have* never **s with**	3359
	26:10	men might well have **s with** your wife,	907+8886
	30: 4	Jacob **s with** her,	448+995
	30:16	So *he* **s** with her that night.	6640+8886
	35:22	**s with** his father's concubine Bilhah,	907+8886
	38:18	So he gave them to her and **s with** her,	448+995
Nu	5:19	"If no other man *has* **s with** you	907+8886
	31:17	And kill every woman *who has* **s with** a	
		man,	408+3359+4200+5435
	31:18	every girl who *has* never **s with**	3359+5435
	31:35	who *had* never **s with** a man.	2351+3359+5435
Dt	22:22	both the man who **s with** her and	6640+8886
Jdg	21:12	in Jabesh Gilead four hundred young women	
		who *had* never **s with**	2351+3359+4200+5435
1Sa	2:22	how *they* **s with** the women who served	907+8886
2Sa	11: 4	She came to him, and *he* **s with** her.	6640+8886
	11: 9	But Uriah *at* the entrance to the palace	8886
	12: 3	drank from his cup and even **s** in his arms.	8886
SS	5: 2	I **s** but my heart was awake.	3825
Eze	23: 8	when during her youth men **s with** her,	907+8886
	23:44	And *they* **s with** her.	448+995
	23:44	so *they* **s with** those lewd women,	448+995

SLEW (1) [SLAY]
Ps	78:34	Whenever God **s** them, they would seek him	2222

SLIGHTEST (1)
Jude	1:12	eating with you **without the s** qualm—	925

SLIDE (KJV) See SLIP, WAVERING

SLIME (1) [SLIMY]
Job	9:31	you would plunge me into a **s** pit so that	8846

SLIMEPITS (KJV) See TAR PITS

SLIMY (1) [SLIME]
Ps	40: 2	He lifted me out of the **s** pit,	1014+8622

SLING (6) [SLINGS, SLUNG]
Jdg	20:16	each of whom *could* **s** a stone at a hair and	7843
1Sa	17:40	with his **s** in his hand, approached the	7845
	17:50	over the Philistine with a **s** and a stone;	7845
	25:29	hurl away as from the pocket of a **s**.	7845
1Ch	12: 2	to shoot arrows or to **s stones**	74+928+2021

Pr	26: 8	a stone in a **s** is the giving of honor to	5275

SLINGS (1) [SLING]
2Ki	3:25	but **men armed with s** surrounded it	7847

SLINGSTONES (3) [STONE]
2Ch	26:14	bows and **s** for the entire army.	74+7845
Job	41:28	**s** are like chaff to him.	74+7845
Zec	9:15	They will destroy and overcome with **s**.	74+7845

SLIP (7) [SLIPPED, SLIPPERY, SLIPPING, SLIPS]
Dt	4: 9	or let them **s** from your heart as long	6073
	32:35	In due time their foot *will* **s**;	4572
1Sa	27: 1	and I *will* **s** out of his hand."	4880
2Ki	9:15	don't *let* anyone **s out** of the city to go	3655
Ps	37:31	his feet *do* not **s**.	5048
	121: 3	He will not let your foot **s**—	4572
Jer	20:10	All my friends are waiting for me to **s**,	7520

SLIPPED (6) [SLIP]
2Sa	4: 6	Then Recab and his brother Baanah **s away**.	4880
Ps	17: 5	my feet *have* not **s**.	4572
	73: 2	But as for me, my feet *had* almost **s**;	5742
Jn	5:13	for Jesus *had* **s away** into the crowd	1728
2Co	11:33	from a window in the wall and **s through**	1767
Jude	1: 4	*have* **secretly s** in among you.	4208

SLIPPERY (3) [SLIP]
Ps	35: 6	may their path be dark and **s**,	2761
	73:18	Surely you place them on **s** *ground;*	2747
Jer	23:12	"Therefore their path will become **s**;	2761

SLIPPING (4) [SLIP]
Job	12: 5	as the fate of *those* whose feet *are* **s**.	5048
Ps	66: 9	and kept our feet from **s**.	4572
	94:18	When I said, "My foot *is* **s**," your love,	4572
Jn	8:59	**s away from** the temple grounds.	2002

SLIPS (1) [SLIP]
Ps	38:16	exalt themselves over me when my foot **s**."	4572

SLOPE (9) [SLOPES]
Jos	15: 8	the southern **s** of the Jebusite city (that is,	4190
	15:10	ran along the northern **s** *of* Mount Jearim	4190
	15:11	It went to the northern **s** *of* Ekron,	4190
	18:12	the northern **s** *of* Jericho and headed west	4190
	18:13	From there it crossed to the south **s** *of* Luz	4190
	18:16	the Hinnom Valley along the southern **s** *of*	4190
	18:18	the northern **s** *of* Beth Arabah and on down	4190
	18:19	then went to the northern **s** *of* Beth Hoglah	4190
Mic	1: 4	like water rushing down a **s**.	4618

SLOPES (12) [SLOPE]
Nu	21:15	and the **s** *of* the ravines that lead to the site	844
	34:11	along the **s** *east of* the Sea of Kinnereth.	4190
Dt	3:17	below the **s** *of* Pisgah.	844
	4:49	below the **s** *of* Pisgah.	844
	33: 2	from his **mountain s**.	850
Jos	7: 5	and struck them down on the **s**.	4618
	10:40	the western foothills and the **mountain s**,	844
	12: 3	and then southward below the **s** *of* Pisgah.	844
	12: 8	the **mountain s**, the desert and the Negev—	844
	13:20	the **s** *of* Pisgah, and Beth Jeshimoth	844
Isa	11:14	They will swoop down on the **s** *of* Philistia	4190
Jer	18:14	of Lebanon ever vanish from its rocky **s**?	8442

SLOTHFUL (KJV) See HESITATE, LACKING, LAZINESS, LAZY, SLACK, SLUGGARD

SLOW (19) [SLOWLY, SLOWNESS]
Ex	4:10	I am **s** *of* speech and tongue."	3878
	34: 6	gracious God, **s** *to* anger, abounding in love	800
Nu	14:18	'The LORD is **s** *to* anger, abounding in love	800
Dt	7:10	he will not be **s** *to* repay.	336
	23:21	*do* not be **s** *to* pay it,	336
2Ki	9:17	don't **s down** for me unless	4200+6806+8206
Ne	9:17	**s** *to* anger and abounding in love.	800
Ps	86:15	gracious God, **s** *to* anger, abounding in love	800
	103: 8	**s** *to* anger, abounding in love.	800
	145: 8	**s** *to* anger and rich in love.	800
Joel	2:13	**s** *to* anger and abounding in love,	800
Jnh	4: 2	**s** *to* anger and abounding in love,	800
Na	1: 3	LORD is **s** *to* anger and great in power;	800
Lk	24:25	and *how* **s** of heart to believe all that	1096
Ac	27: 7	*We* made **s headway** for many days	1095
Heb	5:11	but it is hard to explain because you are **s**	3821
Jas	1:19	**s** to speak and slow to become angry,	1096
	1:19	slow to speak and **s** to become angry,	1096
2Pe	3: 9	The Lord *is* not **s** in keeping his promise,	1094

SLOWLY (1) [SLOW]
Ge	33:14	I move along **s** at the pace of the droves	351+4200

SLOWNESS (1) [SLOW]
2Pe	3: 9	The Lord is not slow in keeping his	
		promise, as some understand **s**.	1097

SLUG (1)

Ps 58: 8 Like a s melting away as it moves along, 8671

SLUGGARD (13) [SLUGGARD'S]

Pr	6: 6	Go to the ant, you s;	6789
	6: 9	How long will you lie there, you s?	6789
	10:26	so is a s to those who send him.	6789
	13: 4	The s craves and gets nothing,	6789
	15:19	The way of the s is blocked with thorns,	6789
	19:24	The s buries his hand in the dish;	6789
	20: 4	A s does not plow in season;	6789
	22:13	The s says, "There is a lion outside!"	6789
	24:30	I went past the field of the s,	6789
	26:13	The s says, "There is a lion in the road,	6789
	26:14	so a s turns on his bed.	6789
	26:15	The s buries his hand in the dish;	6789
	26:16	The s is wiser in his own eyes than	6789

SLUGGARD'S (1) [SLUGGARD]

Pr 21:25 The s craving will be the death of him, 6789

SLUMBER (10) [SLUMBERS]

Job	33:15	when deep sleep falls on men as they s	9484
Ps	121: 3	he who watches over you will not s;	5670
	121: 4	he who watches over Israel will neither s	5670
	132: 4	no s to my eyelids,	9484
Pr	4:16	of s till they make someone fall.	9104
	6: 4	no s to your eyelids.	9484
	6:10	a little s, a little folding of the hands to rest	9484
	24:33	a little s, a little folding of the hands to rest	9484
Na	3:18	O king of Assyria, your shepherds s;	5670
Ro	13:11	for you to wake up from your s,	5678

SLUMBERS (1) [SLUMBER]

Isa 5:27 not one s or sleeps; 5670

SLUMPED (1)

2Ki 9:24 The arrow pierced his heart and he s down 4156

SLUNG (2) [SLING]

| 1Sa | 17: 6 | a bronze javelin was s on his back. | 1068+4190 |
| | 17:49 | he s it and struck the Philistine on the | 7843 |

SLUR (1)

Ps 15: 3 and casts no s on his fellowman, 3075

SLY (3)

Pr	25:23	so a s tongue brings angry looks.	6260
Mt	26: 4	to arrest Jesus in some s way and kill him.	1515
Mk	14: 1	some s way to arrest Jesus and kill	1515+1877

SMALL (70) [SMALLER, SMALLEST]

Ge	19:20	town near enough to run to, and it is s.	5203
	19:20	Let me flee to it—it is very s, isn't it?	5203
Ex	12: 4	If any household is too s for a whole lamb,	5070
Nu	22:18	not do anything great or s to go beyond	7783
Dt	1:17	hear both s and great alike.	7785
	25:14	measures in your house—one large, one s.	7783
Jos	17:15	"and if the hill country of Ephraim is too s	237
1Sa	15:17	you were once s in your own eyes,	7785
	18:23	a s matter to become the king's son-in-law?	7829
	20: 2	my father doesn't do anything, great or s,	7785
	20:35	He had a s boy with him,	7785
1Ki	2:20	"I have one s request to make of you,"	7783
	8:64	altar before the LORD was too s to hold	7785
	10:17	He also made three hundred s shields	4482
	17:13	But first make a s cake of bread for me	7783
	18:44	as s as a man's hand is rising from the sea."	7783
	20:27	like two flocks of goats,	3105
	22:31	"Do not fight with anyone, s or great,	7785
2Ki	4:10	a s room on the roof and put in it a bed and	7783
	6: 1	the place where we meet with you is too s	7639
2Ch	9:16	He also made three hundred s shields	4482
	14: 8	armed with s shields and with bows.	4482
	15:13	were to be put to death, whether s or great,	7785
	18:30	"Do not fight with anyone, s or great,	7785
	23: 9	the large and s shields that had belonged	8949
	36:18	from the temple of God, both large and s,	7783
Job	3:19	The s and the great are there,	7785
Ps	104:25	living things both large and s.	7783
	115:13	who fear the LORD—s and great alike.	7783
	148:10	s creatures and flying birds,	8254
Pr	24:10	how s is your strength!	7639
	30:24	"Four things on earth are s,	7783
Ecc	9:14	a s city with only a few people in it.	7783
Isa	49: 6	"It is too s a thing for you to	7837
	49:19	now you will be too s for your people,	7674
	49:20	'This place is too s for us;	7639
Jer	46: 3	"Prepare your shields, both large and s,	4482
	49:15	"Now I will make you s among the nations,	7785
Eze	23:24	with large and s shields and with helmets.	4482
	38: 4	and a great horde with large and s shields,	4482
	39: 9	the s and large shields, the bows and	4482
Da	8: 9	which started s but grew in power to	7582
Am	6:11	the great house into pieces and the s house	7785
	7: 2	How can Jacob survive? He is so s!"	7785
	7: 5	How can Jacob survive? He is so s!"	7785
Ob	1: 2	I will make you s among the nations;	7785
Mic	5: 2	though you are s among the clans of Judah,	7582
Zec	4:10	"Who despises the day of s things?	7783
Mt	7:14	But s is the gate and narrow the road	5101

Mt	15:34	"Seven," they replied, "and a few s fish."	2715
	17:20	if you have faith as s as a mustard seed,	NIG
Mk	3: 9	to have a s boat ready for him,	4449
	8: 7	They had a few s fish as well;	2715
	12:42	and put in two very s copper coins,	3321
Lk	17: 6	"If you have faith as s as a mustard seed,	NIG
	19:17	trustworthy in a very s matter,	1788
	21: 2	in two very s copper coins.	3321
Jn	6: 9	"Here is a boy with five s barley loaves	3209
	6: 9	with five small barley loaves and two s fish,	4066
Ac	12:18	there was no s commotion among	3900
	26:22	and so I stand here and testify to s	3625
	27:16	to the lee of a s island called Cauda,	3761
Jas	3: 4	by a very s rudder wherever the pilot wants	1788
	3: 5	Likewise the tongue is a s part of the body,	3625
	3: 5	a great forest is set on fire by a s spark.	2462
Rev	11:18	reverence your name—both s and great—	3625
	13:16	He also forced everyone, s and great,	3625
	19: 5	you who fear him, both s and great!"	3625
	19:18	free and slave, s and great."	3625
	20:12	And I saw the dead, great and s,	3625

SMALLER (7) [SMALL]

Nu	26:54	and to a s group a smaller one;	5071
	26:54	and to a smaller group a s one;	5070
	26:56	by lot among the larger and s groups."	5071
	33:54	and to a s group a smaller one.	5071
	33:54	and to a smaller group a s one.	5070
Eze	42: 5	so they were s in floor space than those on	724
	43:14	and from the s ledge up to	7783

SMALLEST (5) [SMALL]

1Sa	9:21	a Benjamite, from the s tribe of Israel,	7783
Isa	60:22	become a thousand, the s a mighty nation.	7582
Mt	5:18	not the s letter, not the least stroke of a pen,	2740
	13:32	Though it is the s of all your seeds,	3625
Mk	4:31	which is the s seed you plant in the ground.	3625

SMART (KJV) See SUFFER

SMASH (7) [SMASHED, SMASHES]

Ex	34:13	s their sacred stones and cut down	8689
Dt	7: 5	down their altars, s their sacred stones,	8689
	12: 3	s their sacred stones and burn their	8689
Jer	13:14	I will s them one against the other,	5879
	19:11	I will s this nation and this city just	8689
	48:12	they will empty her jars and s her jugs.	5879
Am	6:11	and he will s the great house into pieces	5782

SMASHED (14) [SMASH]

Jdg	7:20	blew the trumpets and s the jars.	8689
2Ki	11:18	They s the altars and idols to pieces	8689
	18: 4	s the sacred stones and cut down	8689
	23:12	s them to pieces and threw the rubble into	8368
	23:14	Josiah s the sacred stones and cut down	8689
2Ch	14: 3	s the sacred stones and cut down	8689
	23:17	They s the altars and idols	8689
	31: 1	s the sacred stones and cut down	8689
	34: 4	and s the Asherah poles,	8689
Ps	74: 6	They s all the carved paneling	2150
Jer	19:11	and this city just as this potter's jar is s	8689
Eze	6: 4	and your incense altars will be s;	8689
	6: 6	your idols s and ruined,	8689
Da	2:34	on its feet of iron and clay and s them.	10182

SMASHES (1) [SMASH]

Da 2:40 for iron breaks and s everything— 10290

SMEAR (1) [SMEARED]

Job 13: 4 You, however, s me with lies; 3260

SMEARED (1) [SMEAR]

Ps 119:69 Though the arrogant have s me with lies, 3260

SMELL (11) [SMELLED]

Ge	27:27	Isaac caught the s of his clothes,	8193+8194
	27:27	the s of my son is like the smell of a field	8194
	27:27	the s of a field that the LORD has blessed.	8194
Ex	16:20	but it was full of maggots and began to s.	944
Dt	4:28	which cannot see or hear or eat or s.	8193
Ps	115: 6	but cannot hear, noses, but they cannot s;	8193
Ecc	10: 1	As dead flies give perfume a bad s,	944+5580
Da	3:27	and there was no s of fire on them.	10666
Joel	2:20	And its stench will go up; its s will rise."	7462
1Co	12:17	where would the sense of s be?	4018
2Co	2:16	To the one we are the s of death;	4011

SMELLED (2) [SMELL]

| Ge | 8:21 | The LORD s the pleasing aroma and said | 8193 |
| Ex | 7:21 | the river s so bad that the Egyptians could | 944 |

SMELTED (1)

Job 28: 2 and copper is s from ore. 3668

SMILE (2) [SMILED]

| Job | 9:27 | I will change my expression, and s,' | 1158 |
| | 10: 3 | while you s on the schemes of the wicked? | 3649 |

SMILED (1) [SMILE]

Job 29:24 When I s at them, they scarcely believed it; 8471

SMITE (1) [SMITTEN]

Dt 33:11 S the loins of those who rise up 4730

SMITTEN (1) [SMITE]

Isa 53: 4 stricken by God, s by him, and afflicted. 5782

SMOKE (47) [SMOKING]

Ge	19:28	and he saw dense s rising from the land,	7798
	19:28	like s from a furnace.	7798
Ex	19:18	Mount Sinai was covered with s,	6939
	19:18	The s billowed up from it like smoke from	6940
	19:18	The smoke billowed up from it like s from	6940
	20:18	the trumpet and saw the mountain in s,	6942
Lev	16:13	and the s of the incense will conceal	6727
Jos	8:20	The men of Ai looked back and saw the s	6940
	8:21	and that s was going up from the city,	6940
Jdg	20:38	that they should send up a great cloud of s	6940
	20:40	the column of s began to rise from the city,	6940
	20:40	and saw the s of the whole city going up	5368
2Sa	22: 9	S rose from his nostrils;	6940
Job	41:20	S pours from his nostrils as from	6940
Ps	18: 8	S rose from his nostrils;	6940
	37:20	they will vanish—vanish like s.	6940
	68: 2	As s is blown away by the wind,	6940
	102: 3	For my days vanish like s;	6940
	104:32	who touches the mountains, and they s.	6939
	119:83	Though I am like a wineskin in the s,	7798
	144: 5	touch the mountains, so that they s.	6939
Pr	10:26	As vinegar to the teeth and s to the eyes,	6940
SS	3: 6	up from the desert like a column of s,	6940
Isa	4: 5	over those who assemble there a cloud of s	6940
	6: 4	and the temple was filled with s.	6940
	9:18	so that it rolls upward in a column of s.	6940
	14:31	A cloud of s comes from the north,	6940
	30:27	with burning anger and dense clouds of s;	5366
	34:10	its s will rise forever.	6940
	51: 6	the heavens will vanish like s,	6940
	65: 5	Such people are s in my nostrils,	6940
Hos	13: 3	like s escaping through a window.	6940
Joel	2:30	blood and fire and billows of s.	6940
Na	2:13	"I will burn up your chariots in s,	6940
Ac	2:19	blood and fire and billows of s.	2837
Rev	8: 4	The s of the incense,	2837
	9: 2	s rose from it like the smoke from	2837
	9: 2	from it like the s from a gigantic furnace.	2837
	9: 2	The sun and sky were darkened by the s	2837
	9: 3	of the s locusts came down upon the earth	2837
	9:17	of their mouths came fire, s and sulfur.	2837
	9:18	s and sulfur that came out of their mouths.	2837
	14:11	s of their torment rises for ever and ever.	2837
	15: 8	the temple was filled with s from the glory	2837
	18: 9	with her and shared her luxury see the s	2837
	18:18	When they see the s of her burning,	2837
	19: 3	The s from her goes up for ever and ever."	2837

SMOKING (1) [SMOKE]

Ge 15:17 a s firepot with a blazing torch appeared 6940

SMOLDER (2) [SMOLDERING, SMOLDERS]

| Ps | 74: 1 | Why does your anger s against the sheep | 6939 |
| | 80: 4 | how long will your anger s against | 6939 |

SMOLDERING (4) [SMOLDER]

Nu	16:37	the censers out of the s remains and scatter	8599
Isa	7: 4	because of these two s stubs of firewood—	6942
	42: 3	and a s wick he will not snuff out.	3910
Mt	12:20	and a s wick he will not snuff out,	5606

SMOLDERS (1) [SMOLDER]

Hos 7: 6 Their passion s all night; 3822

SMOOTH (11) [SMOOTH-SKINNED, SMOOTHER, SMOOTHLY, SMOOTHS]

Ge	27:11	and I'm a man with s skin.	2747
	27:16	She also covered his hands and the s part	2753
1Sa	17:40	chose five s stones from the stream,	2752
Ps	55:21	His speech is as s as butter,	2744
Pr	6:24	from the s tongue of the wayward wife.	2753
	7:21	she seduced him with her s talk.	2749
Isa	26: 7	make the way of the righteous s.	7142
	42:16	before them and make the rough places s.	4793
	57: 6	the s stones of the ravines are your portion;	2747
Lk	3: 5	shall become straight, the rough ways s.	3308
Ro	16:18	By s talk and flattery they deceive	5981

SMOOTH-SKINNED (2) [SKIN, SMOOTH]

| Isa | 18: 2 | swift messengers, to a people tall and s, | 5307 |
| | 18: 7 | a people tall and s, from a people feared far | 5307 |

SMOOTHER (1) [SMOOTH]

Pr 5: 3 and her speech is s than oil; 2747

SMOOTHLY (1) [SMOOTH]

Pr 23:31 in the cup, when it goes down s! 928+4797

SMOOTHS (1) [SMOOTH]
Isa 41: 7   and *he who* **s** *with* the hammer spurs   2744

SMYRNA (2)
Rev 1:11   to Ephesus, **S**, Pergamum, Thyatira, Sardis,   5044
    2: 8   "To the angel of the church in **S** write: 5044

SNAIL (KJV) See SKINK, SLUG

SNAKE (24) [SNAKES]
Ex 4: 3   on the ground and it became a **s**,   5729
    4: 4   Moses reached out and took hold of **the s**   2257S
    7: 9   and it will become a **s**."   9490
    7:10   and it became a **s**.   9490
    7:12   down his staff and it became a **s**.   9490
    7:15   the staff that was changed into a **s**.   5729
Nu 21: 8   "Make a **s** and put it up on a pole;   8597
    21: 9   So Moses made a bronze **s** and put it up on   5729
    21: 9   when anyone was bitten by a **s** and looked   5729
    21: 9   by a snake and looked at the bronze **s**,   5729
2Ki 18: 4   into pieces the bronze **s** Moses had made,   5729
Ps 58: 4   Their venom is like the venom of a **s**,   5729
Pr 23:32   In the end it bites like a **s** and poisons like   5729
    30:19   the way of a **s** on a rock,   5729
Ecc 10: 8   through a wall may be bitten by a **s**.   5729
    10:11   If a **s** bites before it is charmed,   5729
Isa 14:29   the root of that **s** will spring up a viper,   5729
Am 5:19   on the wall only to have a **s** bite him.   5729
Mic 7:17   They will lick dust like a **s**,   5729
Mt 7:10   Or if he asks for a fish, will give him a **s**?   4058
Lk 11:11   ask for a fish, will give him a **s** instead?   4058
Jn 3:14   Just as Moses lifted up the **s** in the desert,   4058
Ac 28: 4   the **s** hanging from his hand, they said   2563
    28: 5   But Paul shook the **s** off into the fire   2563

SNAKES (11) [SNAKE]
Nu 21: 6   the LORD sent venomous **s** among them;   5729
    21: 7   the LORD will take the **s** away from us."   5729
Dt 8:15   with its venomous **s** and scorpions.   5729
Isa 30: 6   of adders and darting **s**,   8597
Jer 8:17   "See, I will send venomous **s** among you,   5729
Mt 10:16   be as shrewd as **s** and as innocent as doves.   4058
    23:33   *"You* **s**! You brood of vipers!   4058
Mk 16:18   they will pick up **s** with their hands;   4058
Lk 10:19   I have given you authority to trample on **s**   4058
1Co 10: 9   and were killed by **s**.   4058
Rev 9:19   for their tails were like **s**,   4058

SNAPPED (3) [SNAPS]
Jdg 16: 9   But *he* **s** the thongs as easily as a piece   5998
    16:12   But *he* **s** the ropes off his arms as   5998
Jer 10:20   My tent is destroyed; all its ropes **are s**.   5998

SNAPS (1) [SNAPPED]
Jdg 16: 9   as a piece of string **s** when it comes close to   5998

SNARE (35) [ENSNARE, ENSNARED, SNARED, SNARES]
Ex 10: 7   "How long will this man be a **s** to us?   4613
    23:33   of their gods will certainly be a **s** to you."   4613
    34:12   or they will be a **s** among you.   4613
Dt 7:16   for that will be a **s** to you.   4613
Jdg 2: 3   in your sides and their gods will be a **s**   4613
    8:27   and it became a **s** to Gideon and his family.   4613
1Sa 18:21   "so that she may be a **s** to him and so that   4613
Job 18: 9   a **s** holds him fast.   7545
Ps 25:15   for only he will release my feet from the **s**.   8407
    69:22   May the table set before them become a **s**;   7062
    91: 3   Surely he will save you from the fowler's **s**   7062
    106:36   which became a **s** to them.   4613
    119:110   The wicked have set a **s** for me,   7062
    124: 7   like a bird out of the fowler's **s**;   7062
    124: 7   **s** has been broken, and we have escaped.   7062
    140: 5   Proud men have hidden a **s** for me;   7062
    142: 3   the path where I walk men have hidden a **s**   7062
Pr 6: 5   like a bird from the **s** *of* the fowler.   3338
    7:23   like a bird darting into a **s**,   7062
    18: 7   and his lips are a **s** *to* his soul.   4613
    21: 6   a fleeting vapor and a deadly **s**.   1335
    29:25   Fear of man will prove to be a **s**,   4613
Ecc 7:26   the woman who is a **s**,   5178
    9:12   or birds are taken in a **s**,   7062
Isa 8:14   of Jerusalem he will be a trap and a **s**.   4613
    24:17   Terror and pit and **s** await you,   7062
    24:18   of the pit will be caught in a **s**.   7062
Jer 5:26   in wait like **men who s birds** and   3687
    48:43   Terror and pit and **s** await you,   7062
    48:44   of the pit will be caught in a **s**;   7062
Eze 12:13   and he will be caught in my **s**;   5180
    17:20   and he will be caught in my **s**.   5180
Hos 5: 1   You have been a **s** at Mizpah,   7062
Am 3: 5   on the ground where no **s** has been set?   4613
Ro 11: 9   "May their table become a **s** and a trap,   4075

SNARED (4) [SNARE]
Pr 3:26   and will keep your foot from being **s**.   4335
    29: 6   An evil man is **s** by his own sin,   4613
Isa 8:15   *they will* **be s** and captured.   3704
    28:13   be injured and **s** and captured.   3704

SNARES (13) [SNARE]
Jos 23:13   they will become **s** and traps for you,   7062
2Sa 22: 6   the **s** *of* death confronted me.   4613
Job 22:10   That is why **s** are all around you,   7062
    30:12   *they* **lay s** *for* my feet,   8938
    34:30   from laying **s** *for* the people.   4613
Ps 18: 5   the **s** *of* death confronted me.   4613
    64: 5   they talk about hiding their **s**;   4613
    141: 9   Keep me from the **s** they have laid for me,   7062
Pr 13:14   turning a man from the **s** *of* death.   4613
    14:27   turning a man from the **s** *of* death.   4613
    22: 5   In the paths of the wicked lie thorns and **s**,   7062
Jer 18:22   a pit to capture me and have hidden **s**   7062
Hos 9: 8   yet **s** await him on all his paths,   3687+7062

SNARLING (2)
Ps 59: 6   **s** like dogs, and prowl about the city.   2159
    59:14   **s** like dogs, and prowl about the city.   2159

SNATCH (9) [SNATCHED, SNATCHES]
Job 24:19   heat and drought **s** *away* the melted snow,   1608
    30:22   *You* **s** me *up* and drive me before the wind;   5951
Ps 52: 5   *He will* **s** you *up* and tear you   3149
    119:43   Do not **s** the word of truth from my mouth,   5911
Isa 3:18   that day the Lord *will* **s** *away* their finery: 6073
    10: 6   to seize loot and **s** plunder,   1024
Jn 10:28   no one *can* **s** them out of my hand.   773
    10:29   no one can **s** them out of my Father's hand.   773
Jude 1:23   **s** others from the fire and save them;   773

SNATCHED (10) [SNATCH]
Jdg 6: 9   *I* **s** you from the power of Egypt and from   5911
2Sa 23:21   *He's* the spear from the Egyptian's hand   1608
1Ch 11:23   *He* **s** the spear from the Egyptian's hand   1608
Job 24: 9   The fatherless child *is* **s** from the breast;   1608
    29:17   the fangs of the wicked and **s** the victims   8959
Pr 22:27   your very bed *will be* **s** from under you.   4374
Joel 1: 5   for *it has* **been s** from your lips.   4162
Am 4:11   You were like a burning stick **s** from   5911
Zec 3: 2   Is not this man a burning stick **s** from   5911
Rev 12: 5   her child *was* **s** *up* to God and to his throne.   773

SNATCHES (4) [SNATCH]
Job 9:12   If *he* **s** *away*, who can stop him?   3166
    24:19   so the grave **s** away those who have sinned.   NIH
    27:20   a tempest **s** him *away* in the night.   1704
Mt 13:19   and **s** *away* what was sown in his heart.   773

SNEER (1) [SNEERED, SNEERING, SNEERS]
Isa 57: 4   At whom *do you* **s** and stick out your   7023+8143

SNEERED (2) [SNEER]
Lk 23:35   and the rulers even **s** at him.   1727
Ac 17:32   some of them **s**, but others said,   5949

SNEERING (1) [SNEER]
Lk 16:14   heard all this and *were* **s** at Jesus.   1727

SNEERS (1) [SNEER]
Ps 10: 5   *he* **s** at all his enemies.   7032

SNEEZED (1)
2Ki 4:35   The boy **s** seven times and opened his eyes.   2453

SNIFF (1) [SNIFFING]
Mal 1:13   and *you* **s** *at it* **contemptuously,"**   5870

SNIFFING (1) [SNIFF]
Jer 2:24   **s** the wind in her craving—   8634

SNORTING (3) [SNORTS]
Job 39:20   striking terror with his proud **s**?   5724
    41:18   His **s** throws out flashes of light;   6490
Jer 8:16   **s** of the enemy's horses is heard from Dan;   5725

SNORTS (1) [SNORTING]
Job 39:25   At the blast of the trumpet *he* **s**, 'Aha!'   606

SNOUT (1)
Pr 11:22   Like a gold ring in a pig's **s** is   678

SNOW (20) [SNOWS, SNOWY]
Ex 4: 6   it was leprous, like **s**.   8920
Nu 12:10   there stood Miriam—leprous, like **s**.   8920
2Ki 5:27   he was leprous, as white as **s**.   8920
Job 6:16   by thawing ice and swollen with melting **s**,   8920
    24:19   heat and drought snatch away the melted **s**,   8920
    37: 6   He says to the **s**, 'Fall on the earth,'   8920
    38:22   "Have you entered the storehouses of the **s**   8920
Ps 51: 7   wash me, and I will be whiter than **s**.   8920
    68:14   *it was like* **s fallen** on Zalmon.   8919
    147:16   He spreads the **s** like wool and scatters   8920
    148: 8   and hail, **s** and clouds, stormy winds   8920
Pr 25:13   Like the coolness of **s** at harvest time is   8920
    26: 1   Like **s** in summer or rain in harvest,   8920
Isa 1:18   they shall be as white as **s**;   8920
    55:10   the rain and the **s** come down from heaven,   8920
Jer 18:14   Does the **s** *of* Lebanon ever vanish   8920
La 4: 7   Their princes were brighter than **s**   8920
Da 7: 9   His clothing was as white as **s**;   10758
Mt 28: 3   and his clothes were white as **s**.   5946
Rev 1:14   white like wool, as white as **s**,   5946

SNOWS (1) [SNOW]
Pr 31:21   When it **s**, she has no fear for her household   8920

SNOWY (2) [SNOW]
2Sa 23:20   down into a pit on a **s** day and killed a lion.   8920
1Ch 11:22   down into a pit on a **s** day and killed a lion.   8920

SNUFF (3) [SNUFFED]
Isa 42: 3   and a smoldering wick *he will* not **s** *out*.   3882
Eze 32: 7   When I **s** you *out*, I will cover the heavens   3882
Mt 12:20   and a smoldering wick *he will* not **s** *out*,   4931

SNUFFDISHES (KJV) See TRAYS

SNUFFED (6) [SNUFF]
Job 18: 5   "The lamp of the wicked *is* **s** out;   1980
    21:17   the lamp of the wicked **s** out?   1980
Pr 13: 9   but the lamp of the wicked is **s** out.   1980
    20:20   his lamp *will be* **s** out in pitch darkness.   1980
    24:20   and the lamp of the wicked *will be* **s** out.   1980
Isa 43:17   extinguished, **s** *out* like a wick: 3882

SNUFFERS (KJV) See WICK TRIMMERS

SO (1 of 3003) For SO as a Conjunction, See Index of Articles Etc. (See Introduction p. xi)
2Ki 17: 4   for he had sent envoys to **S** king of Egypt,   6046

SO-CALLED (2) [CALL]
1Co 8: 5   For even if there are **s** gods,   3306
Rev 2:24   have not learned Satan's **s** deep secrets   3306+6055

SOAKED (4) [SOAK]
2Ki 8:15   he took a thick cloth, **s** it in water   3188
Isa 34: 3   the mountains *will be* **s** with their blood,   5022
    34: 7   and the dust *will be* **s** with fat.   2014
Jn 19:29   so they **s** a sponge in it, put the sponge on   3550

SOAP (3)
Job 9:30   with **s** and my hands with washing soda,   8921
Jer 2:22   with soda and use an abundance of **s**,   1383
Mal 3: 2   be like a refiner's fire or a launderer's **s**.   1383

SOAR (4) [SOARED]
Job 39:27   *Does* the eagle **s** at your command   1467
Isa 40:31   *They will* **s** *on* wings like eagles;   6590
Jer 49:22   An eagle *will* **s** and swoop down,   6590
Ob 1: 4   Though *you* **s** like the eagle   1467

SOARED (2) [SOAR]
2Sa 22:11   *he* **s** on the wings of the wind.   1797
Ps 18:10   *he* **s** on the wings of the wind.   1797

SOB (1) [SOBBING]
Ge 21:16   And as she sat there nearby, she began *to* **s**.   1134

SOBBING (1) [SOB]
Jdg 14:16   Samson's wife threw herself on him, **s**,   1134

SOBER (2)
1Sa 25:37   when Nabal *was* **s**,   2021+3516+3655+4946
Ro 12: 3   of yourself with **s** **judgment,**   5404

SOBRIETY (KJV) See PROPRIETY

SOCHO (KJV) See SOCO

SOCHOH (KJV) See SOCOH

SOCKET (3) [SOCKETS]
Ge 32:25   he touched the **s** *of* Jacob's hip so   4090
    32:32   the tendon attached to the **s** *of* the hip,   4090
    32:32   because the **s** *of* Jacob's hip was touched   4090

SOCKETS (3) [SOCKET]
1Ki 6:34   each having two leaves *that* **turned in s**.   1664
    7:50   gold **s** for the doors of the innermost room,   7327
Zec 14:12   their eyes will rot in their **s**,   2986

SOCO (3)
1Ch 4:18   Heber the father of **S**,   8459
2Ch 11: 7   Beth Zur, **S**, Adullam,   8459
    28:18   Aijalon and Gederoth, as well as **S**,   8459

SOCOH (5)
Jos 15:35   Jarmuth, Adullam, **S**, Azekah,   8458

Jos	15:48	In the hill country: Shamir, Jattir, S,	8458
1Sa	17: 1	for war and assembled at S in Judah.	8458
	17: 1	between S and Azekah.	8458
1Ki	4:10	in Arubboth (S and all the land	8458

SOD, SODDEN (KJV) See BOILED, COOKED, COOKING

SODA (3)

Job	9:30	with soap and my hands with **washing** s,	1342
Pr	25:20	or like vinegar poured on s,	6003
Jer	2:22	Although you wash yourself with s and use	6003

SODERING (KJV) See WELDING

SODI (1)

Nu	13:10	from the tribe of Zebulun, Gaddiel son of S;	6052

SODOM (47)

Ge	10:19	and then toward S, Gomorrah,	6042
	13:10	(This was before the LORD destroyed S	6042
	13:12	of the plain and pitched his tents near S.	6042
	13:13	of S were wicked and were sinning greatly	6042
	14: 2	went to war against Bera king of S,	6042
	14: 8	Then the king of S, the king of Gomorrah,	6042
	14:10	when the kings of S and Gomorrah fled,	6042
	14:11	The four kings seized all the goods of S	6042
	14:12	since he was living in S.	6042
	14:17	of S came out to meet him in the Valley	6042
	14:21	The king of S said to Abram,	6042
	14:22	But Abram said to the king of S,	6042
	18:16	they looked down toward S,	6042
	18:20	"The outcry against S and Gomorrah is	6042
	18:22	The men turned away and went toward S,	6042
	18:26	fifty righteous people in the city of S,	6042
	19: 1	The two angels arrived at S in the evening,	6042
	19: 4	all the men from every part of the city of S	6042
	19:24	down burning sulfur on S and Gomorrah—	6042
	19:28	He looked down toward S and Gomorrah,	6042
Dt	29:23	be like the destruction of S and Gomorrah,	6042
	32:32	Their vine comes from the vine of S and	6042
Isa	1: 9	we would have become like S,	6042
	1:10	the word of the LORD, you rulers of S;	6042
	3: 9	they parade their sin like S;	6042
	13:19	will be overthrown by God like S	6042
Jer	23:14	They are all like S to me;	6042
	49:18	As S and Gomorrah were overthrown,	6042
	50:40	As God overthrew S and Gomorrah along	6042
La	4: 6	of my people is greater than that of S,	6042
Eze	16:46	the south of you with her daughters, was S.	6042
	16:48	the Sovereign LORD, your sister S	6042
	16:49	" 'Now this was the sin of your sister S:	6042
	16:53	the fortunes of S and her daughters and	6042
	16:55	S with her daughters and Samaria	6042
	16:56	You would not even mention your sister S	6042
Am	4:11	"I overthrew some of you as I overthrew S	6042
Zep	2: 9	"surely Moab will become like S,	6042
Mt	10:15	be more bearable *for* S and Gomorrah	1178+5047
	11:23	in you had been performed in S,	5047
	11:24	*for* S on the day of judgment than for	1178+5047
Lk	10:12	be more bearable on that day *for* S than for	5047
	17:29	But the day Lot left S,	5047
Ro	9:29	we would have become like S,	5047
2Pe	2: 6	*of* S and Gomorrah by burning them	5047
Jude	1: 7	S and Gomorrah and the surrounding towns	5047
Rev	11: 8	which is figuratively called S and Egypt,	5047

SODOMA (KJV) See SODOM

SODOMITE, SODOMITES (KJV) See MALE SHRINE PROSTITUTES, SHRINE PROSTITUTE

SOFT (KJV) See FAINT, FINE, GENTLE, SOFTEN

SOFTEN (1)

Ps	65:10	*you* s it with showers and bless its crops.	4570

SOIL (38) [SOILED]

Ge	4: 2	Abel kept flocks, and Cain worked the s.	141
	4: 3	of the s as an offering to the LORD.	141
	9:20	Noah, a man of the s, proceeded to plant	141
Ex	23:19	"Bring the best of the firstfruits of your s to	141
	34:26	"Bring the best of the firstfruits of your s to	141
Lev	26:20	because your s will not yield its crops,	824
	27:30	from the s or fruit from the trees, belongs to	824
Nu	13:20	How is the s?	824
Dt	26: 2	that you produce from the s of the land	141
	26:10	now I bring the firstfruits of the s that you,	141
1Ki	18:38	the wood, the stones and the s,	6760
2Ch	26:10	for he loved the s.	141
Job	5: 6	For hardship does not spring from the s,	6760
	8:19	and from the s other plants grow.	6760
	14: 8	in the ground and its stump die in the s,	6760
	14:19	and torrents wash away the s,	824+6760
	21:33	The s *in* the valley is sweet to him;	8073
Ps	37:35	like a green tree in its **native** s,	275
	105:35	ate up the produce of their s.	141

SS	5: 3	*must I* s them again?	3245
Isa	28:24	on breaking up and harrowing the s?	141
	30:24	and donkeys that work the s will eat fodder	141
	61:11	For as the s makes the sprout come up and	824
Eze	17: 5	the seed of your land and put it in fertile s.	8441
	17: 8	in good s by abundant water so	8441
Mt	13: 5	where it did not have much s.	1178
	13: 5	because the s was shallow.	1178
	13: 8	Still other seed fell on good s,	1178
	13:23	on good s is the man who hears the word	1178
Mk	4: 5	where it did not have much s.	1178
	4: 5	because the s was shallow.	1178
	4: 8	Still other seed fell on good s.	1178
	4:20	Others, like seed sown on good s,	1178
	4:28	All by itself the s produces grain—	1178
Lk	8: 8	Still other seed fell on good s.	1178
	8:15	But the seed on good s stands for those with	1178
	13: 7	Why should it use up the s?'	1178
	14:35	for the s nor for the manure pile;	1178

SOILED (1) [SOIL]

Rev	3: 4	in Sardis who *have* not s their clothes.	3662

SOJOURN, SOJOURNED, SOJOURNER, SOJOURNERS, SOJOURNETH, SOJOURNING (KJV) See ALIEN, ALIENS, DWELL, GUEST, LIVE, LIVED, LIVES, LIVING, SETTLED, STAY, STAYED, STAYING, TEMPORARY RESIDENT

SOLACE (KJV) See ENJOY

SOLD (69) [SELL]

Ge	31:15	Not only *has he* s us,	4835
	37:28	of the cistern and s him for twenty shekels	4835
	37:36	Midianites s Joseph in Egypt to Potiphar,	4835
	41:56	Joseph opened the storehouses and s **grain**	8690
	42: 6	the *one who* s **grain** to all its people.	8690
	45: 4	the *one you* s into Egypt!	4835
	47:20	The Egyptians, one and all, s their fields,	4835
Ex	22: 3	*he must* **be** s to pay for his theft.	4835
Lev	25:23	" 'The land *must* not **be** s permanently,	4835
	25:25	**what** his countryman has s.	4928
	25:27	since he s it and refund the balance to	4928
	25:27	the balance to the man to whom *he* s it;	4835
	25:28	**what** he s will remain in the possession of	4928
	25:33	that is, a house s in any town they hold—	4928
	25:34	to their towns *must* not **be** s;	4835
	25:42	*they* **must** not **be** s as slaves.	4835+4929
	25:48	of redemption after *he has* s **himself**.	4835
	25:50	to count the time from the year he s **himself**	4835
	27:20	or if *he has* s it to someone else,	4835
	27:27	*it is to* **be** s at its set value.	4835
	27:28	*may* **be** s or redeemed;	4835
Dt	32:30	unless their Rock *had* s them,	4835
Jdg	2:14	*He* s them to their enemies all around,	4835
	3: 8	against Israel so that *he* s them into	4835
	4: 2	the LORD s them into the hands of Jabin,	4835
	10: 7	*He* s them into the hands of the Philistines	4835
1Sa	12: 9	so *he* s them into the hand of Sisera,	4835
1Ki	21:20	"because *you have* s **yourself** to do evil in	4835
	21:25	who s **himself** to do evil in the eyes of	4835
2Ki	6:25	a donkey's head s for eighty shekels	928+2118
	7:16	So a seah of flour s **for** a shekel,	928+2118
	7:16	and two seahs of barley s for a shekel,	NIH
	17:17	and sorcery and s **themselves** to do evil in	4835
Ne	5: 8	we have bought back our Jewish brothers who **were** s	4835
	5: 8	only for *them to* **be** s **back** to us!"	4835
Est	7: 4	and my people *have* **been** s for destruction	4835
	7: 4	If *we had* merely **been** s as male	4835
Ps	44:12	*You* s your people for a pittance,	4835
	105:17	Joseph, s as a slave.	4835
Isa	50: 1	Because of your sins *you* **were** s;	4835
	52: 3	"You *were* s for nothing,	4835
Jer	34:14	free any fellow Hebrew who *has* s **himself**	4835
Eze	7:13	not recover the **land** he s as long as	4928
Hos	8: 9	Ephraim *has* s *herself* to lovers.	9479
	8:10	Although *they have* s **themselves** among	9479
Joel	3: 3	*they* s girls for wine that they might drink.	4835
	3: 6	*You* s the people of Judah and Jerusalem to	4835
	3: 7	of the places to which *you* s them,	4835
Am	1: 6	and s them to Edom,	6037
	1: 9	Because she s whole communities	6037
Mt	10:29	*Are* not two sparrows s for a penny?	4797
	13:44	in his joy went and s all he had and bought	4797
	13:46	and s everything he had and bought it.	4405
	18:25	and all that he had *be* s to repay the debt.	4405
	26: 9	"This perfume could *have* **been** s at	4405
Mk	14: 5	It could have *been* s for more than	4405
Lk	12: 6	*Are* not five sparrows s for two pennies?	4797
Jn	2:16	*To* those who s doves he said,	4797
	12: 5	"Why wasn't this perfume s and	4405
Ac	4:34	those who owned lands or houses s them,	4797
	4:37	s a field he owned and brought the money	4797
	5: 1	also s a piece of property.	4797
	5: 4	Didn't it belong to you before it was s?	NIG
	5: 4	And *after it was* s,	4405
	7: 9	*they* s him as a slave into Egypt.	625
Ro	7:14	but I am unspiritual, s as a slave to sin.	4405
1Co	10:25	Eat anything s in the meat market	4797

Heb	12:16	for a single meal s his inheritance rights as	625
Rev	18:15	The merchants who s these things	NIG

SOLDIER (13) [SOLDIERS]

Nu	31:53	Each s had taken plunder for himself.	408+7372
1Sa	13:22	So on the day of the battle not a s with Saul	6639
2Sa	17:10	Then even the **bravest** s,	1201+2657
2Ki	5: 1	He was a **valiant** s, but he had leprosy.	1475+2657
2Ch	17:17	From Benjamin: Eliada, a **valiant** s,	1475+2657
Am	2:15	the fleet-footed s will not get away,	2257S
Ac	10: 7	of his servants and a devout s who was one	5132
	28:16	to live by himself, with a s to guard him.	5132
1Co	9: 7	Who **serves as** a s at his own expense?	5129
Php	2:25	my brother, fellow worker and **fellow** s,	5369
2Ti	2: 3	Endure hardship with us like a good s	5132
	2: 4	No one **serving as** a s gets involved	5129
Phm	1: 2	*to* Archippus our **fellow** s and to	5369

SOLDIERS (79) [SOLDIER]

Nu	31:21	said to the s who had gone into battle,	408+7372
	31:27	the s who took part in the battle and	4878+9530
	31:28	From the s who fought in the battle,	408+4878
	31:32	from the spoils that the s took was	6639+7372
	31:49	"Your servants have counted the s	408+4878
Jos	8:13	They had the s take up their positions—	6639
	17: 1	because the Makirites were **great** s.	408+4878
Jdg	9:35	and his s came out from their hiding place.	6639
	20: 2	four hundred thousand s armed	408+8081
	20:16	Among all these s there were seven hundred chosen men who were left-handed,	6639
1Sa	4: 3	When the s returned to camp,	6639
	4:10	Israel lost thirty thousand foot s.	8081
	13: 5	s as numerous as the sand on the seashore.	6639
	14:28	Then one of the s told him,	6639
	15: 4	two hundred thousand foot s	8081
	15:15	"The s brought them from the Amalekites;	6639
	15:21	The s took sheep and cattle from	6639
	26: 7	Abner and the s were lying around him.	6639
2Sa	3:23	When Joab and all the s with him arrived,	7372
	8: 4	and twenty thousand foot s.	408+8081
	10: 6	they hired twenty thousand Aramean foot s	8081
	10:18	and forty thousand of their foot s.	8081
	11: 7	how the s were and how the war was going.	6639
1Ki	20:29	on the Aramean **foot** s in one day.	8081
2Ki	13: 7	ten chariots and ten thousand foot s,	8081
	25: 5	All his s were separated from him	2657
1Ch	12:33	**experienced** s prepared for battle	3655+7372
	12:38	**experienced** s prepared for battle—	3655+7372
	18: 4	and twenty thousand foot s.	408+8081
	19:18	and forty thousand of their **foot** s.	408+8081
2Ch	28: 6	and twenty thousand s in Judah—	1201+2657
	28:14	So the s gave up the prisoners and plunder	2741
Ezr	8:22	the king for s and horsemen to protect us	2657
Jer	38: 4	He is discouraging the s who are left	408+4878
	39: 4	and all the s saw them, they fled;	408+4878
	41: 3	as the Babylonian s who were there.	408+4878
	41:16	the s, women, children	408+1505+4878
	49:26	all her s will be silenced in that day,"	408+4878
	50:30	all her s will be silenced in that day,"	408+4878
	51:32	marshes set on fire, and the s terrified."	408+4878
	52: 8	All his s were separated from him	2657
Eze	27:10	Lydia and Put served as s in your army.	408+4878
	27:27	your merchants and all your s,	408+4878
	39:20	mighty men and s of every kind,'	408+4878
Da	3:20	some of the **strongest** s in his army	10132+10264
	3:22	the fire killed the s who took up Shadrach,	10131
Joel	2: 7	they scale walls like s.	408+4878
Na	2: 3	The shields of his s are red;	1475
Mt	8: 9	a man under authority, with s under me.	5132
	27:27	Then the governor's s took Jesus into	5132
	27:27	and gathered the whole **company of** s	5061
	28:12	they gave the s a large sum of money,	5132
	28:15	So the s took the money and did	3836S
Mk	15:16	The s led Jesus away into the palace	5132
	15:16	called together the whole **company of** s.	5061
Lk	3:14	Then some s asked him,	5129
	7: 8	a man under authority, with s under me.	5132
	23:11	Herod and his s ridiculed and mocked him.	5128
	23:36	The s also came up and mocked him.	5132
Jn	18: 3	a **detachment of** s and some officials from	5061
	18:12	the **detachment of** s with its commander	5061
	19: 2	The s twisted together a crown of thorns	5132
	19:16	So the s took charge of Jesus.	NIG
	19:23	When the s crucified Jesus,	5132
	19:24	So this is what the s did.	5132
	19:32	The s therefore came and broke the legs of	5132
	19:34	*of* the s pierced Jesus' side with a spear,	5132
Ac	12: 4	be guarded by four squads *of* four s each.	5132
	12: 6	Peter was sleeping between two s,	5132
	12:18	there was no small commotion among the s	5132
	21:32	He at once took some officers and s and ran	5132
	21:32	the rioters saw the commander and his s,	5132
	21:35	so great he had to be carried by the s.	5132
	21:37	As the s were about to take Paul into	NIG
	23:23	"Get ready a detachment of two hundred s,	5132
	23:31	So the s, carrying out their orders,	5132
	27:31	Then Paul said *to* the centurion and the s,	5132
	27:42	So the s cut the ropes that held the lifeboat	5132
	27:42	The s planned to kill the prisoners	5132

SOLE (4) [SOLES]

Dt	28:56	to touch the ground with the s *of* her foot.	4090
	28:65	no resting place for the s *of* your foot.	4090
2Sa	14:25	to the s *of* his foot there was no blemish	4090
Isa	1: 6	From the s *of* your foot to the top	4090

SOLEMN (5) [SOLEMNLY]

Ge	50:11	"The Egyptians are holding a s ceremony	3878
Jos	6:26	**pronounced** *this* s oath:	8678
Jdg	21: 5	a s oath that anyone who failed to assemble	1524
Eze	16: 8	**gave** you *my* s oath	8678
Ac	23:14	*"We have* **taken a** s **oath** not to eat	353+354

SOLEMNITIES, SOLEMNITY (KJV) See
APPOINTED FEASTS, FEAST, FESTIVAL, FESTIVALS

SOLEMNLY (7) [SOLEMN]

Ge	43: 3	said to him, "The man **warned** us s,	6386+6386
Dt	1:34	he was angry and s **swore:**	8678
	4:21	and *he* s **swore** that I would not cross	8678
	32:46	the words I *have* s **declared** to you this day,	6386
Jos	5: 6	he *had* s **promised** their fathers to give us,	8678
Jdg	17: 3	*"I* s **consecrate** my silver to the LORD	7727+7727
1Sa	8: 9	but **warn** them s and let them know	6386+6386

SOLES (7) [SOLE]

Dt	28:35	spreading from the s *of* your feet to the top	4090
2Ki	19:24	With the s *of* my feet I have dried up all	4090
Job	2: 7	from the s *of* his feet to the top of his head.	4090
	13:27	on all my paths by putting marks on the s	9247
Isa	37:25	With the s *of* my feet I have dried up all	4090
Eze	43: 7	of my throne and the place for the s	4090
Mal	4: 3	be ashes under the s *of* your feet on the day	4090

SOLID (7)

Nu	4: 6	a cloth of s blue over that and put the poles	4003
2Ch	4:21	and lamps and tongs (they were s gold);	4816
Zec	4: 2	a s gold lampstand with a bowl at the top	3972
1Co	3: 2	I gave you milk, not s **food,**	1109
2Ti	2:19	God's s foundation stands firm,	5104
Heb	5:12	You need milk, not s **food!**	5104
	5:14	But s food is for the mature,	5104

SOLITARY (6)

Lev	16:22	on itself all their sins to a s place;	10141
Mt	14:13	he withdrew by boat privately to a s place.	2245
Mk	1:35	left the house and went off to a s place.	2245
	6:32	by themselves in a boat to a s place.	2245
Lk	4:42	At daybreak Jesus went out to a s place.	2245
	8:29	by the demon into s **places.**	2245

SOLOMON (248) [SOLOMON'S]

2Sa	5:14	Shammua, Shobab, Nathan, S,	8976
	12:24	and they named him S.	8976
1Ki	1:10	or the special guard or his brother S.	8976
	1:12	and the life of your son S.	8976
	1:13	"Surely S your son shall be king after me,	8976
	1:17	'S your son shall be king after me,	8976
	1:19	but he has not invited S your servant.	8976
	1:21	and my son S will be treated as criminals."	8976
	1:26	and your servant he did not invite.	8976
	1:30	S your son shall be king after me,	8976
	1:33	and set S my son on my own mule	8976
	1:34	'Long live King S!'	8976
	1:37	with S to make his throne even greater than	8976
	1:38	and the Pelethites went down and put S	8976
	1:39	of oil from the sacred tent and anointed S.	8976
	1:39	"Long live King S!"	8976
	1:43	"Our lord King David has made S king.	8976
	1:46	S has taken his seat on the royal throne.	8976
	1:50	But Adonijah, in fear of S,	8976
	1:51	Then S was told, 'Adonijah is afraid	8976
	1:51	of King S and is clinging to the horns of	8976
	1:51	'Let King S swear to me today that he will	8976
	1:52	S replied, "If he shows himself to be	8976
	1:53	Then King S sent men,	8976
	1:53	and bowed down to King S,	8976
	1:53	and S said, "Go to your home."	8976
	2: 1	he gave a charge to S his son.	8976
	2:12	So S sat on the throne of his father David,	8976
	2:17	So he continued, "Please ask King S—	8976
	2:19	When Bathsheba went to King S to speak	8976
	2:22	King S answered his mother,	8976
	2:23	Then King S swore by the LORD:	8976
	2:25	So King S gave orders to Benaiah son	8976
	2:27	So S removed Abiathar from	8976
	2:29	King S was told that Joab had fled to	8976
	2:29	Then S ordered Benaiah son of Jehoiada,	8976
	2:41	When S was told that Shimei had gone	8976
	2:45	But King S will be blessed,	8976
	3: 1	S made an alliance with Pharaoh king	8976
	3: 3	S showed his love for the LORD	8976
	3: 4	and S offered a thousand burnt offerings on	8976
	3: 5	the LORD appeared to S during the night	8976
	3: 6	S answered, "You have shown great kindness to your servant,	8976
	3:10	The Lord was pleased that S had asked	8976
	3:15	Then S awoke—and he realized it had been a dream.	8976
	4: 1	So King S ruled over all Israel.	8976
	4: 7	S also had twelve district governors	8976
	4:11	(he was married to Taphath daughter of S);	8976
	4:15	(he had married Basemath daughter of S);	8976
	4:21	And S ruled over all the kingdoms from	8976
	4:26	S had four thousand stalls for chariot horses	8976
	4:27	supplied provisions for King S	8976
	4:29	God gave S wisdom and very great insight,	8976

1Ki	5: 1	that S had been anointed king	2257S
	5: 1	he sent his envoys to S,	8976
	5: 2	S sent back this message to Hiram:	8976
	5: 8	So Hiram sent word to S:	8976
	5:10	In this way Hiram kept S supplied with all	8976
	5:11	and S gave Hiram twenty thousand cors	8976
	5:11	S continued to do this for Hiram year	8976
	5:12	The LORD gave S wisdom,	8976
	5:12	peaceful relations between Hiram and S,	8976
	5:13	King S conscripted laborers	8976
	5:15	S had seventy thousand carriers	8976
	5:18	The craftsmen of S and Hiram and the men	8976
	6: 2	The temple that King S built for	8976
	6:11	The word of the LORD came to S:	8976
	6:14	So S built the temple and completed it.	8976
	6:21	S covered the inside of the temple	8976
	7: 1	It took S thirteen years, however,	8976
	7: 8	S also made a palace like this hall	8976
	7:13	King S sent to Tyre and brought Huram,	8976
	7:14	to King S and did all the work assigned	8976
	7:40	the work he had undertaken for King S in	8976
	7:45	that Huram made for King S for the temple	8976
	7:47	S left all these things unweighed,	8976
	7:48	S also made all the furnishings that were in	8976
	7:51	the work King S had done for the temple of	8976
	8: 1	Then King S summoned into his presence	8976
	8: 2	the men of Israel came together to King S	8976
	8: 5	and King S and the entire assembly	8976
	8:12	Then S said, "The LORD has said	8976
	8:22	Then S stood before the altar of the LORD	8976
	8:54	When S had finished all these prayers	8976
	8:63	S offered a sacrifice of fellowship offerings	8976
	8:65	So S observed the festival at that time,	8976
	9: 1	When S had finished building the temple of	8976
	9:10	during which S built these two buildings—	8976
	9:11	King S gave twenty towns in Galilee	8976
	9:12	to see the towns that S had given him,	8976
	9:15	of the forced labor King S conscripted	8976
	9:17	And S rebuilt Gezer.	8976
	9:21	these S conscripted for his slave labor	8976
	9:22	But S did not make slaves of any of	8976
	9:24	the City of David to the palace S had built	NIH
	9:25	a year S sacrificed burnt offerings	8976
	9:26	King S also built ships at Ezion Geber,	8976
	9:28	which they delivered to King S.	8976
	10: 1	the fame of S and his relation to the name	8976
	10: 2	she came to S and talked with him about all	8976
	10: 3	S answered all her questions;	8976
	10: 4	the queen of Sheba saw all the wisdom of S	8976
	10:10	the queen of Sheba gave to King S	8976
	10:13	King S gave the queen of Sheba all she	8976
	10:14	that S received yearly was 666 talents,	8976
	10:16	King S made two hundred large shields	8976
	10:23	King S was greater in riches	8976
	10:24	The whole world sought audience with S	8976
	10:26	S accumulated chariots and horses;	8976
	11: 1	King S, however, loved many foreign women besides Pharaoh's daughter—	8976
	11: 2	Nevertheless, S held fast to them in love.	8976
	11: 4	As S grew old, his wives turned his heart	8976
	11: 6	So S did evil in the eyes of the LORD;	8976
	11: 7	S built a high place for Chemosh	8976
	11: 9	with S because his heart had turned away	8976
	11:10	he had forbidden S to follow other gods,	2257S
	11:10	S did not keep the LORD's command.	NIH
	11:11	So the LORD said to S,	8976
	11:14	LORD raised up against S an adversary,	8976
	11:23	God raised up against S another adversary,	2257S
	11:25	Israel's adversary as long as S lived,	8976
	11:27	S had built the supporting terraces	8976
	11:28	and when S saw how well	8976
	11:40	S tried to kill Jeroboam,	8976
	11:41	not written in the book of the annals of S?	8976
	11:42	S reigned in Jerusalem over all Israel	8976
	12: 2	where he had fled from King S),	8976
	12: 6	the elders who had served his father S	8976
	12:21	the kingdom for Rehoboam son of S.	8976
	14:21	"Say to Rehoboam son of S king of Judah,	8976
	14:21	Rehoboam son of S was king in Judah.	8976
	14:26	including all the gold shields S had made.	8976
2Ki	21: 7	to David and to his son S,	8976
	23:13	the ones S king of Israel had built	8976
	24:13	that S king of Israel had made for	8976
	25:16	which S had made for the temple of	8976
1Ch	3: 5	Shammua, Shobab, Nathan and S.	8976
	6:10	in the temple S built in Jerusalem),	8976
	6:32	until S built the temple of the LORD	8976
	14: 4	Shammua, Shobab, Nathan, S,	8976
	18: 8	which S used to make the bronze Sea,	8976
	22: 5	"My son S is young and inexperienced,	8976
	22: 6	for his son S and charged him to build	8976
	22: 7	David said to S: "My son,	8976
	22: 9	His name will be S,	8976
	22:17	the leaders of Israel to help his son S.	8976
	23: 1	he made his son S king over Israel.	8976
	28: 5	he has chosen my son S to sit on the throne	8976
	28: 6	'S your son is the one who will build	8976
	28: 9	"And you, my son S,	8976
	28:11	Then David gave his son S the plans for	8976
	28:20	David also said to S his son,	8976
	29: 1	"My son S, the one whom God has chosen,	8976
	29:19	give my son S the wholehearted devotion	8976
	29:22	Then they acknowledged S son of David	8976
	29:23	So S sat on the throne of the LORD	8976
	29:24	pledged their submission to King S.	8976
	29:25	The LORD highly exalted S in the sight	8976
	29:28	His son S succeeded him as king.	2976

2Ch	1: 1	S son of David established himself firmly	8976
	1: 2	Then S spoke to all Israel—	8976
	1: 3	and S and the whole assembly went to	8976
	1: 5	S and the assembly inquired of him there.	8976
	1: 6	S went up to the bronze altar before	8976
	1: 7	That night God appeared to S and said	8976
	1: 8	S answered God, "You have shown great kindness to David	8976
	1:11	God said to S, "Since this is your heart's	8976
	1:13	S went to Jerusalem from	8976
	1:14	S accumulated chariots and horses;	8976
	2: 1	S gave orders to build a temple for	8976
	2: 3	S sent this message to Hiram king of Tyre:	8976
	2:11	Hiram king of Tyre replied by letter to S:	8976
	2:17	S took a census of all the aliens who were	8976
	3: 1	Then S began to build the temple of	8976
	3: 3	The foundation S laid for building	8976
	4:11	the work he had undertaken for King S in	8976
	4:16	that Huram-Abi made for King S for	8976
	4:18	All these things that S made amounted to	8976
	4:19	S also made all the furnishings that were	8976
	5: 1	the work S had done for the temple of	8976
	5: 2	Then S summoned to Jerusalem the elders	8976
	5: 6	and King S and the entire assembly	8976
	6: 1	Then S said, "The LORD has said	8976
	6:12	Then S stood before the altar of the LORD	NIH
	7: 1	When S finished praying,	8976
	7: 5	And King S offered a sacrifice	8976
	7: 7	S consecrated the middle part of	8976
	7: 8	So S observed the festival at that time	8976
	7:10	the LORD had done for David and S and	8976
	7:11	When S had finished the temple of	8976
	8: 1	during which S built the temple of	8976
	8: 2	S rebuilt the villages that Hiram	8976
	8: 3	S then went to Hamath Zobah	8976
	8: 8	these S conscripted for his slave labor	8976
	8: 9	But S did not make slaves of the Israelites	8976
	8:11	S brought Pharaoh's daughter up from	8976
	8:12	S sacrificed burnt offerings to the LORD,	8976
	8:17	Then S went to Ezion Geber and Elath on	8976
	8:18	which they delivered to King S.	8976
	9: 1	to S and talked with him about all she had	8976
	9: 2	S answered all her questions;	8976
	9: 3	the queen of Sheba saw the wisdom of S,	8976
	9: 9	the queen of Sheba gave to King S.	8976
	9:10	and the men of S brought gold from Ophir;	8976
	9:12	King S gave the queen of Sheba all she	8976
	9:13	that S received yearly was 666 talents,	8976
	9:14	of the land brought gold and silver to S.	8976
	9:15	King S made two hundred large shields	8976
	9:22	King S was greater in riches	8976
	9:23	of the earth sought audience with S to hear	8976
	9:25	S had four thousand stalls for horses	8976
	9:30	S reigned in Jerusalem over all Israel	8976
	10: 2	where he had fled from King S),	8976
	10: 6	the elders who had served his father S	8976
	11: 3	"Say to Rehoboam son of S king of Judah	8976
	11:17	supported Rehoboam son of S three years,	8976
	11:17	the ways of David and S during this time.	8976
	12: 9	including the gold shields S had made.	8976
	13: 6	an official of S son of David,	8976
	13: 7	of S when he was young and indecisive	8976
	30:26	for since the days of S son of David king	8976
	33: 7	to David and to his son S,	8976
	35: 3	"Put the sacred ark in the temple that S on	8976
	35: 4	by David king of Israel and by his son S.	8976
Ezr	2:55	The descendants of the servants of S:	8976
	2:58	the descendants of the servants of S	392
Ne	7:57	The descendants of the servants of S:	8976
	7:60	the descendants of the servants of S	392
	12:45	to the commands of David and his son S.	8976
	13:26	because of marriages like these that S king	8976
Ps	72: T	Of S.	8976
	127: T	A song of ascents. Of S.	8976
Pr	1: 1	proverbs of S son of David, king of Israel:	8976
	10: 1	The proverbs of S:	8976
	25: 1	These are more proverbs of S,	8976
SS	1: 5	like the tent curtains of S.	8976
	3: 9	King S made for himself the carriage;	8976
	3:11	and look at King S wearing the crown,	8976
	8:11	S had a vineyard in Baal Hamon;	8976
	8:12	the thousand shekels are for you, O S,	8976
Jer	52:20	which King S had made for the temple of	8976
Mt	1: 6	David was the father of S,	5048
	1: 7	S the father of Rehoboam,	5048
	6:29	not even S in all his splendor was dressed	5048
	12:42	and now one greater than S is here.	5048
Lk	11:31	and now one greater than S is here.	5048
	12:27	not even S in all his splendor was dressed	5048
Ac	7:47	But it was S who built the house for him.	5048

SOLOMON'S (41) [SOLOMON]

1Ki	1:11	Then Nathan asked Bathsheba, S mother,	8976
	1:47	'May your God make S name more famous	8976
	2:13	went to Bathsheba, S mother.	8976
	2:46	now firmly established in S hands.	8976
	4:21	and were S subjects all his life.	8976
	4:22	S daily provisions were thirty cors	8976
	4:25	During S lifetime Judah and Israel,	8976
	4:30	S wisdom was greater than the wisdom	8976
	4:34	of all nations came to listen to S wisdom,	8976
	5: 7	When Hiram heard S message,	8976
	6: 1	in the fourth year of S reign over Israel,	8976
	9:16	as a wedding gift to his daughter, S wife.	8976
	9:23	chief officials in charge of S projects	4200+8976
	9:27	to serve in the fleet with S men.	8976

1Ki	10:21	All King S goblets were gold,	8976
	10:21	was considered of little value in S days.	8976
	10:28	S horses were imported from Egypt	4200+8976
	11:26	He was one of S officials,	4200+8976
	11:31	out of S hand and give you ten tribes.	8976
	11:33	and laws as David, S father, did.	2257S
	11:34	not take the whole kingdom out of S hand;	2257S
	11:40	and stayed there until S death.	8976
	11:41	As for the other events of S reign—	8976
1Ch	3:10	S son was Rehoboam, Abijah his son,	8976
2Ch	1:16	S horses were imported from Egypt	4200+8976
	8:10	They were also King S chief officials	4200+8976
	8:16	All S work was carried out,	8976
	8:18	with S men, sailed to Ophir	8976
	9:1	When the queen of Sheba heard of S fame,	8976
	9:20	All King S goblets were gold,	8976
	9:20	silver was considered of little value in S day	8976
	9:28	S horses were imported from Egypt	4200+8976
	9:29	As for the other events of S reign,	8976
Ne	11:3	of S servants lived in the towns of Judah,	8976
SS	1:1	S Song of Songs.	4200+8611+8976
	3:7	It is S carriage, escorted by	4200+8611+8976
Mt	12:42	the ends of the earth to listen to S wisdom,	5048
Lk	11:31	the ends of the earth to listen to S wisdom,	5048
Jn	10:23	in the temple area walking in S Colonnade.	5048
Ac	3:11	to them in the place called S Colonnade.	5048
	5:12	to meet together in S Colonnade.	5048

SOLVE (2) [SOLVED]

Da	5:12	explain riddles and s difficult problems.	10742
	5:16	interpretations and to s difficult problems.	10742

SOLVED (1) [SOLVE]

Jdg	14:18	you would not have s my riddle."	5162

SOMBER (1)

Mt	6:16	do not look s as the hypocrites do,	1181+5034

SOME (568) [SOMEBODY, SOMEHOW, SOMEONE, SOMEONE'S, SOMETHING, SOMETIMES, SOMEWHAT, SOMEWHERE]

Ge	3:6	she took s and ate it.	4946
	3:6	She also gave s to her husband,	NIH
	3:12	she gave me s fruit from the tree,	4946
	4:3	Cain brought s of the fruits of the soil	4946
	4:4	But Abel brought fat portions from s of	4946
	8:20	taking s of all the clean animals	4946
	9:21	When he drank s of its wine,	4946
	14:10	s of the men fell into them	AIT
	18:6	flour and knead it and bake s bread."	AIT
	18:8	then brought s curds and milk and the calf	AIT
	21:14	the next morning Abraham took s food and	AIT
	22:1	S time later God tested Abraham.	
			339+465+1821+2021+2021
	22:20	S time later Abraham was told,	
			339+465+1821+2021+2021
	23:4	Sell me s property for a burial site here	AIT
	25:29	Once when Jacob was cooking s stew,	AIT
	25:30	"Quick, let me have s of that red stew!	4946
	25:34	Then Jacob gave Esau s bread	AIT
	25:34	some bread and s lentil stew.	AIT
	27:3	to the open country to hunt s wild game	AIT
	27:7	'Bring me s game and prepare me	AIT
	27:7	and prepare me s tasty food to eat,	AIT
	27:9	I can prepare s tasty food for your father,	AIT
	27:14	and she prepared s tasty food,	AIT
	27:19	Please sit up and eat s of my game so	4946
	27:25	"My son, bring me s of your game to eat,	4946
	27:25	and he brought s wine and he drank.	AIT
	27:31	He too prepared s tasty food	AIT
	27:31	"My father, sit up and eat s of my game,	4946
	29:19	that I give her to you than to s other man.	AIT
	30:14	the fields and found s mandrake plants,	AIT
	30:14	"Please give me s of your son's mandrakes.	4946
	30:21	S time later she gave birth to a daughter	339
	31:46	He said to his relatives, "Gather s stones."	AIT
	32:16	and keep s space between the herds."	AIT
	33:15	"Then let me leave s of my men with you."	4946
	35:16	While they were still s distance	824+2021+3896
	36:6	s distance from his brother Jacob.	4946+7156
	37:33	S ferocious animal has devoured him.	NIH
	40:1	S time later, the cupbearer and the baker	
			339+465+1821+2021+2021
	40:4	After they had been in custody for s time,	3427
	42:2	Go down there and buy s for us,	NIH
	43:11	Put s of the best products of the land	4946
	43:11	a little balm and a little honey, s spices	AIT
	43:11	s pistachio nuts and almonds.	AIT
	45:19	Take s carts from Egypt for your children	AIT
	48:1	S time later Joseph was told,	
			339+465+1821+2021+2021
Ex	2:17	S shepherds came along	2021S
	4:9	take s water from the Nile and pour it on	4946
	10:26	We have to use s of them in worshiping	4946
	12:7	to take s of the blood and put it on the sides	4946
	12:10	if s is left till morning, you must burn it.	4946
	12:22	the basin and put s of the blood on the top	4946
	16:17	s gathered much, some little.	AIT
	16:17	some gathered much, s little.	NIH
	16:20	s of them paid no attention to Moses;	408S
	16:27	s of the people went out on the seventh day	4946
	17:5	with you s of the elders of Israel and take	4946
	17:9	"Choose s of our men and go out to fight	AIT

Ex	18:19	now to me and I will give you s advice,	AIT
	29:12	Take s of the bull's blood and put it on	4946
	29:20	take s of its blood and put it on the lobes of	4946
	29:21	And take s of the blood on the altar	4946
	29:21	and s of the anointing oil and sprinkle it	4946
	30:36	Grind s of it to powder and place it in front	4946
	33:7	outside the camp s distance away.	4946+8178
	34:16	And when you choose s of their daughters	4946
Lev	4:5	Then the anointed priest shall take s of	4946
	4:6	the blood and sprinkle s of it seven times	4946
	4:7	The priest shall then put s of the blood on	4946
	4:16	to take s of the bull's blood into the Tent	4946
	4:18	He is to put s of the blood on the horns of	4946
	4:25	Then the priest shall take s of the blood of	4946
	4:30	Then the priest is to take s of the blood	4946
	4:34	Then the priest shall take s of the blood of	4946
	5:9	to sprinkle s of the blood of the sin offering	4946
	8:11	He sprinkled s of the oil on	4946
	8:12	He poured s of the anointing oil	4946
	8:15	the bull and took s of the blood,	AIT
	8:23	the ram and took s of its blood and put it on	4946
	8:24	and put s of the blood on the lobes	4946
	8:30	Then Moses took s of the anointing oil	4946
	8:30	of the anointing oil and s of the blood from	4946
	11:4	" 'There are s that only chew the cud	AIT
	11:21	s winged creatures that walk on all	3972+4946
	11:40	Anyone who eats s of the carcass	4946
	14:4	that two live clean birds and s cedar wood,	AIT
	14:14	to take s of the blood of the guilt offering	4946
	14:15	The priest shall then take s of the log of oil,	4946
	14:16	and with his finger sprinkle s of it before	4946
	14:17	to put s of the oil remaining in his palm on	4946
	14:25	for the guilt offering and take s of its blood	4946
	14:26	The priest is to pour s of the oil into	4946
	14:27	and with his right forefinger sprinkle s of	4946
	14:28	S of the oil in his palm he is to put on	4946
	14:49	to take two birds and s cedar wood,	AIT
	16:14	He is to take s of the bull's blood and	4946
	16:14	then he shall sprinkle s of it	4946
	16:18	He shall take s of the bull's blood	4946
	16:18	of the bull's blood and s of the goat's blood	4946
	16:19	He shall sprinkle s of the blood on it	4946
	24:7	Along each row put s pure incense as	AIT
	25:25	and sells s of his property,	4946
	25:45	also buy s of the temporary residents living	4946
Nu	2:2	the Tent of Meeting s distance from it,	5584
	5:17	Then he shall take s holy water in a clay jar	NIH
	5:17	and put s dust from the tabernacle floor into	4946
	9:6	But s of them could not celebrate	408S
	11:1	and consumed s of the outskirts of	928
	13:2	"Send s men to explore the land of Canaan,	AIT
	13:20	Do your best to bring back s of the fruit of	4946
	13:23	along with s pomegranates and figs.	4946
	16:37	and scatter the coals s distance away, for	2134
	19:6	Then Eleazar the priest is to take s	4946
	19:6	The priest is to take s cedar wood,	AIT
	19:17	put s ashes from the burned purification	4946
	19:18	to take s hyssop, dip it in the water	AIT
	21:1	he attacked the Israelites and captured s	4946
	22:40	and gave s to Balaam and	NIH
	27:20	Give him s of your authority so	4946
	30:15	he nullifies them s time after he hears	339
	31:3	"Arm s of your men to go to war	907+4946
	34:3	" 'Your southern side will include s of	4946
	35:11	select s towns to be your cities of refuge,	AIT
Dt	1:13	Choose s wise, understanding	AIT
	1:25	Taking with them s of the fruit of the land,	4946
	12:20	"I would like s meat,"	AIT
	26:2	take s of the firstfruits of all	4946
	27:2	set up s large stones and coat them	AIT
Jos	2:2	S of the Israelites have come here tonight	408S
	5:11	they ate s of the produce of the land:	4946
	7:1	of the tribe of Judah, took s of them.	4946
	7:11	They have taken s of the devoted things;	4946
	10:18	and post s men there to guard it.	AIT
	22:24	that s day your descendants might say	4737
Jdg	4:19	"Please give me s water."	5071
	5:14	S came from Ephraim,	NIH
	8:5	"Give my troops s bread;	AIT
	9:48	He took an ax and cut off s branches,	AIT
	11:4	S time later, when the Ammonites made	
		war on Israel,	3427+4946
	14:8	S time later, when he went back	3427+4946
	14:8	In it was a swarm of bees and s honey,	AIT
	14:9	he gave them s, and they too ate it.	NIH
	16:4	S time later, he fell in love	339+4027
	17:5	and s idols and installed one of his sons	AIT
	17:8	that town in search of s other place to stay.	889S
	18:22	When they had gone s distance	8178
	18:25	or s hot-tempered men will attack you,	AIT
	19:22	s of the wicked men of the city surrounded	408S
Ru	2:14	Have s bread and dip it in	4946
	2:14	he offered her s roasted grain.	AIT
	2:14	She ate all she wanted and had s left over.	3855
	2:16	pull out s stalks for her from the bundles	NIH
1Sa	2:15	"Give the priest s meat to roast;	AIT
	2:36	to s priestly office so I can have food	285
	6:19	down s of the men of Beth Shemesh,	928
	8:12	S he will assign to be commanders	NIH
	9:11	they met s girls coming out to draw water,	AIT
	10:27	But s troublemakers said,	AIT
	13:7	S Hebrews even crossed the Jordan to	AIT
	14:14	and his armor-bearer killed s twenty men in	3869
	14:24	if the men had eaten today s of	4946
	17:18	and bring back s assurance from them.	AIT
	19:13	with a garment and putting s goats' hair at	2021S
	19:16	and at the head was s goats' hair.	2021S

1Sa	21:4	there is s consecrated bread here—	AIT
	24:10	S urged me to kill you, but I spared you;	AIT
	26:13	on top of the hill s distance away;	4946+8158
	28:22	and let me give you s food so you may eat	7326
	28:24	She took s flour, kneaded it and	AIT
	30:9	where s stayed behind,	3855
	30:26	he sent s of the plunder to the elders	4946
2Sa	2:14	s of the young men get up and	AIT
	3:17	"For s time you have wanted to make	
		David your king.	1685+1685+8997+9453
	4:6	of the house as if to get s wheat,	AIT
	10:9	selected s of the best troops in Israel	3972+4946
	11:17	s of the men in David's army fell;	4946
	11:24	and s of the king's men died.	4946
	13:6	and make s special bread in my sight,	9109S
	13:7	of your brother Amnon and prepare s food	2021S
	13:8	She took s dough, kneaded it,	2021S
	15:17	and they halted at a place s distance away.	5305
	17:9	now, he is hidden in a cave or s other place.	285S
1Ki	7:10	s measuring ten cubits and some eight.	74S
	7:10	some measuring ten cubits and s eight.	74S
	11:17	with s Edomite officials who had served his	
		father.	4946
	13:25	S people who passed by saw the body	AIT
	14:3	s cakes and a jar of honey, and go to him.	AIT
	17:7	S time later the brook dried up	3427
	17:17	S time later the son	339+465+1821+2021+2021
	18:5	Maybe we can find s grass to keep	AIT
	20:20	on horseback with s of his horsemen.	AIT
	21:1	S time later there was an incident	
			339+465+1821+2021+2021
2Ki	2:16	down on s mountain or in some valley."	285
	2:16	down on some mountain or in a valley."	285
	2:23	s youths came out of the town and jeered	AIT
	4:38	"Put on the large pot and cook s stew	AIT
	4:39	He gathered s of its gourds and filled	4946
	4:41	Elisha said, "Get s flour."	AIT
	4:42	along with s heads of new grain.	AIT
	4:43	'They will eat and have s left over.' "	AIT
	4:44	and they ate and had s left over,	AIT
	5:13	prophet had told you to do s great thing,	AIT
	5:19	After Naaman had traveled s distance,	824+3896
	6:24	S time later, Ben-Hadad king	339+4027
	7:8	and took s things from it and hid them also.	NIH
	7:13	"Have s men take five of the horses	AIT
	9:17	he called out, "I see s troops coming."	AIT
	9:33	and s of her blood spattered the wall and	4946
	10:13	he met s relatives of Ahaziah king	AIT
	13:15	Elisha said, "Get a bow and s arrows,"	AIT
	13:21	while s Israelites were burying a man,	AIT
	17:25	among them and they killed s of	928
	20:18	And s of your descendants,	4946
	25:12	behind s of the poorest people of the land	4946
1Ch	4:40	S Hamites had lived there formerly.	4946
	6:66	S of the Kohathite clans were given	4946
	9:2	in their own towns were s Israelites,	AIT
	9:28	S of them were in charge of	4946
	9:30	But s of the priests took care of mixing	4946
	9:32	S of their Kohathite brothers were	4946
	12:8	S Gadites defected to David	4946
	12:16	s men from Judah also came	AIT
	12:19	S of the men of Manasseh defected	4946
	16:4	He appointed s of the Levites to minister	4946
	19:10	selected s of the best troops in Israel	3972+4946
	25:1	set apart s of the sons of Asaph,	4200
	26:27	S of the plunder taken in battle	4946
2Ch	11:23	dispersing s of his sons throughout	3972+4946
	13:7	Indeed, there was s good in Judah.	1821
	13:7	S worthless scoundrels gathered	408S
	16:10	the same time Asa brutally oppressed s of	4946
	17:11	S Philistines brought Jehoshaphat gifts	4946
	18:2	S years later he went down	4200+7891+9102
	19:3	There is, however, s good in you,	1821
	19:8	Jehoshaphat appointed s of the Levites,	4946
	20:1	with s of the Meunites came to make war	4946
	20:2	S men came and told Jehoshaphat,	AIT
	20:19	Then s Levites from the Kohathites	2021S
	21:4	to the sword along with s of the princes	4946
	24:4	S time later Joash decided to restore	339+4027
	28:12	Then s of the leaders in Ephraim—	408S
	28:21	Ahaz took s of the things from the temple	2745
	30:11	Nevertheless, s men of Asher,	AIT
	32:21	s of his sons cut him down with the sword.	4946
	34:13	S of the Levites were secretaries,	4946
Ezr	2:68	s of the heads of the families	4946
	2:70	along with s of the other people,	4946
	7:7	S of the Israelites, including priests,	4946
	9:2	They have taken s of their daughters	4946
	10:44	and s of them had children by these wives.	4946
Ne	—	came from Judah with s other men,	AIT
	1:4	For s days I mourned and fasted and prayed	AIT
	4:13	Therefore I stationed s of the people	AIT
	5:2	S were saying, "We and our sons	889S
	5:5	S of our daughters have already been	
		enslaved,	4946
	5:18	and s poultry were prepared for me,	AIT
	7:3	s at their posts and some near their own	AIT
	7:3	at their posts and s near their own houses."	408S
	7:70	S of the heads of the families	4946+7921
	7:71	S of the heads of the families gave to	4946
	8:10	send s to those who have nothing prepared.	4950S
	11:3	in Jerusalem (now s Israelites,	AIT
	11:25	s of the people of Judah lived	4946
	11:36	S of the divisions of the Levites	4946
	12:35	as well as s priests with trumpets,	4946
	13:6	S time later I asked his permission	3427
	13:19	I stationed s of my own men at the gates so	4946

Ne	13:25	I beat s of the men	4946
Job	11: 6	God has even forgotten s of your sin.	4946
	39:15	that s wild animal may trample them.	NIH
Ps	20: 7	S trust in chariots and some in horses,	465
	20: 7	Some trust in chariots and s in horses,	465
	107: 4	S wandered in desert wastelands,	AIT
	107:10	S sat in darkness and the deepest gloom,	AIT
	107:17	S became fools through their rebellious	AIT
Pr	1:11	let's waylay s harmless soul;	NIH
Ecc	5:14	or wealth lost through s misfortune,	AIT
Isa	1: 9	LORD Almighty had left us s survivors,	3869+5071
	17: 6	Yet s gleanings will remain,	4946
	39: 7	And s of your descendants,	4946
	43:12	I, and not s foreign god among you.	AIT
	44:15	s of it he takes and warms himself,	4946
	46: 6	S pour out gold from their bags	2021S
	49:12	s from the north, some from the west,	465
	49:12	some from the north, s from the west,	NIH
	49:12	s from the region of Aswan."	465
	65: 8	'Don't destroy it, there is yet s good in it,'	AIT
	66:19	and I will send s of those who survive to	4946
	66:21	And I will select s of them also to	4946
Jer	4:29	S go into the thickets;	AIT
	4:29	s climb up among the rocks.	AIT
	19: 1	Take along s of the elders of the people and	4946
	26:17	S of the elders of the land stepped forward	408S
	26:22	along with s other men.	AIT
	35: 5	Then I set bowls full of wine and s cups	AIT
	35: 5	and said to them, "Drink s wine."	AIT
	38:11	He took s old rags and worn-out clothes	AIT
	39:10	the guard left behind in the land of Judah s	4946
	43: 9	take s large stones with you and bury them	AIT
	52:15	of the guard carried into exile s of	4946
Eze	6: 8	" 'But I will spare s,	NIH
	6: 8	for s of you will escape the sword	4200
	10: 7	He took up s of it and put it into the hands	NIH
	14: 1	S of the elders of Israel came to me and sat	408S
	14:22	Yet there will be s survivors—	3855
	16:16	You took s of your garments	4946
	16:52	furnished s justification for your sisters.	AIT
	17: 5	' 'He took s of the seed of your land	4946
	20: 1	s of the elders of Israel came to inquire of	408S
	39:14	S will go throughout the land and,	AIT
	40: 2	on whose south side were s buildings	AIT
	40:17	There I saw s rooms and a pavement	AIT
	43:20	You are to take s of its blood and put it on	4946
	45:19	to take s of the blood of the sin offering	4946
Da	1: 2	with s of the articles from the temple	4946+7921
	1: 3	in s of the Israelites from the royal family	4946
	1: 6	Among these were s from Judah:	1201S
	2:41	it will have s of the strength of iron in it,	10427
	3: 8	At this time s astrologers came forward	10131S
	3:12	But there are s Jews whom you have set	10131S
	3:20	and commanded s of the strongest soldiers	10131S
	8:10	and it threw s of the starry host down to	4946
	11: 6	After s years, they will become allies.	AIT
	11: 8	For s years he will leave the king of	AIT
	11:35	S of the wise will stumble,	4946
	12: 2	s to everlasting life, others to shame	465
Am	4: 1	"Bring us s drinks!"	AIT
	4:11	"I overthrew s of you	928
Hag	2:12	and that fold touches s bread or stew,	2021S
	2:12	s wine, oil or other food,	2021S
Zec	14:21	and all who come to sacrifice will take s of	4946
Mt	8:30	S distance from them a large herd	3426
	9: 2	S men brought to him a paralytic,	AIT
	9: 3	s of the teachers of the law said	5516
	10:11	search for s worthy person there and stay	5516
	12: 1	to pick s heads of grain and eat them.	NIG
	12:38	Then s of the Pharisees and teachers of	5516
	13: 4	s fell along the path,	3525+4005
	13: 5	S fell on rocky places,	257+1254
	14:15	to the villages and buy themselves s food."	NIG
	15: 1	Then s Pharisees and teachers of the law	
	16:14	They replied, "S say John the Baptist;	3525+3836
	16:28	s who are standing here will not taste death	5516
	19: 3	S Pharisees came to him to test him.	NIG
	19:12	For s are eunuchs because they were born	4015
	21:33	the vineyard to s farmers and went away on	NIG
	22: 4	"Then he sent s more servants and said,	257
	23:34	S of them you will kill and crucify;	1666
	25: 8	'Give us s of your oil;	1666
	25: 9	go to those who sell oil and buy s	NIG
	26: 4	and they plotted to arrest Jesus in s sly way	NIG
	27:47	When s of those standing there heard this,	5516
	28:11	s of the guards went into the city	5516
	28:17	they worshiped him; but s doubted.	3836
Mk	2: 3	S men came, bringing to him a paralytic,	NIG
	2: 6	s teachers of the law were sitting there,	5516
	2:18	S people came and asked Jesus,	AIT
	2:23	they began to pick s heads of grain.	3836
	2:26	And he also gave s to his companions."	NIG
	3: 2	S of them were looking for a reason	5516
	4: 4	s fell along the path,	3525+4005
	4: 5	S fell on rocky places,	257
	4:15	S people are like seed along the path,	4047
	5:35	s men came from the house of Jairus,	AIT
	6:14	S were saying, "John the Baptist has been	AIT
	6:31	to a quiet place and get s rest.	3900
	7: 1	The Pharisees and s of the teachers of	
	7: 2	saw s of his disciples eating food	5516
	7:32	There s people brought to him	AIT
	8: 3	s of them have come a long distance."	5516
	8:22	and s people brought a blind man	AIT
	8:28	They replied, "S say John the Baptist;	NIG
	9: 1	s who are standing here will not taste death	5516
	10: 2	S Pharisees came and tested him by asking,	NIG
Mk	11: 5	s people standing there asked,	5516
	12: 1	the vineyard to s farmers and went away on	NIG
	12: 2	from them s of the fruit of the vineyard.	NIG
	12: 5	s of them they beat, others they killed.	3525+4005
	12:13	Later they sent s of the Pharisees	5516
	14: 1	for s sly way to arrest Jesus and kill him.	4802
	14: 4	S of those present were saying indignantly	5516
	14:57	Then s stood up and gave this false	5516
	14:65	Then s began to spit at him;	5516
	15:35	When s of those standing near heard this,	5516
	15:40	S women were watching from a distance.	NIG
	15:46	So Joseph bought s linen cloth,	NIG
Lk	3:14	Then s soldiers asked him,	NIG
	5:18	S men came carrying a paralytic on a mat	NIG
	6: 1	his disciples began to pick s heads of grain,	3836
	6: 2	S of the Pharisees asked,	5516
	6: 4	And he also gave s to his companions."	NIG
	7: 3	of Jesus and sent s elders of the Jews	NIG
	8: 2	and also s women who had been cured	NIG
	8: 5	s fell along the path;	3525+4005
	8: 6	S fell on rock, and when it came up,	2283
	9: 7	because s were saying	5516
	9:19	They replied, "S say John the Baptist;	NIG
	9:27	s who are standing here will not taste death	5516
	11:15	But s of them said, "By Beelzebub,	5516
	11:49	s of whom they will kill	2779
	13: 1	Now there were s present at	5516
	13:31	that time s Pharisees came to Jesus and said	5516
	18: 4	"For s time he refused.	5989
	18: 9	To s who were confident	5516
	19:39	S of the Pharisees in the crowd said	5516
	20: 9	to s farmers and went away for a long time.	NIG
	20:10	to the tenants so they would give him s of	608
	20:27	S of the Sadducees,	5516
	20:39	S of the teachers of the law responded,	5516
	21: 5	S of his disciples were remarking about	5516
	21:16	and they will put s of you to death.	1666
	22: 2	were looking for s way to get rid	3836+4802
	23: 8	he hoped to see him perform s miracle.	5516
	24:22	In addition, s of our women amazed us.	5516
	24:24	Then s of our companions went to the tomb	5516
Jn	1:24	Now s Pharisees who had been sent	NIG
	2: 8	"Now draw s out and take it to the master	1417
	3:22	where he spent s time with them,	1417
	3:25	An argument developed between s of	1666
	5: 1	S time later, Jesus went up to Jerusalem	3552+4047
	6: 1	S time after this, Jesus crossed	3552
	6:23	Then s boats from Tiberias landed near	257
	6:64	Yet there are s of you who do not believe."	5516
	7:12	S said, "He is a good man."	3525+3836
	7:25	At that point s of the people	5516
	7:40	s of the people said,	AIT
	7:44	S wanted to seize him,	5516
	9: 6	made s mud with the saliva,	NIG
	9: 9	S claimed that he was.	257
	9:11	"The man they call Jesus made s mud	NIG
	9:16	S of the Pharisees said,	5516
	9:40	S Pharisees who were with him heard him	3836
	10: 1	but climbs in by s other way,	NIG
	11:37	But s of them said,	5516
	11:46	But s of them went to the Pharisees	5516
	12:20	Now there were s Greeks	5516
	13:29	s thought Jesus was telling him	5516
	16:17	S of his disciples said to one another,	AIT
	18: 3	a detachment of soldiers and s officials	NIG
	21: 6	of the boat and you will find s."	NIG
	21: 9	with fish on it, and s bread.	NIG
	21:10	"Bring s of the fish you have just caught."	608
Ac	2:13	S, however, made fun of them and said,	2283
	5: 3	for yourself s of the money you received for	608
	5:15	that at least Peter's shadow might fall on s	5516
	5:36	S time ago Theudas appeared,	2465+3836+4047+4574
	6:11	Then they secretly persuaded s men to say,	NIG
	8: 9	Now for s time a man named Simon	4732
	8:36	they came to s water and the eunuch said,	5516
	9:19	and after taking s food,	NIG
	9:43	for s time with a tanner named Simon.	2653
	10:23	s of the brothers from Joppa went along.	5516
	11:20	S of them, however, men from Cyprus	5516
	11:27	During this time s prophets came down	NIG
	12: 1	that King Herod arrested s who belonged to	5516
	14: 4	s sided with the Jews,	3525+3836
	15: 1	Then s Jews came down from Antioch	NIG
	15: 1	S men came down from Judea to Antioch	5516
	15: 2	along with s other believers,	5516
	15: 5	Then s of the believers who belonged to	5516
	15: 7	you know that s time ago God	608+792+2465
	15:22	to choose s of their own men and send them	NIG
	15:24	We have heard that s went out from us	5516
	15:25	to choose s men and send them to you	NIG
	15:33	After spending s time there,	NIG
	15:36	S time later Paul said to Barnabas,	5516
	17: 4	S of the Jews were persuaded	5516
	17: 4	up s bad characters from the marketplace,	NIG
	17: 6	they dragged Jason and s other brothers	5516
	17:18	S of them asked,	5516
	17:20	You are bringing s strange ideas to our ears,	5516
	17:28	As s of your own poets have said,	5516
	17:32	s of them sneered, but others said,	3525+4005
	18:14	about s misdemeanor or serious crime,	5516
	18:18	Paul stayed on in Corinth for s time.	2653
	18:23	After spending s time in Antioch,	5516
	19: 1	There he found s disciples	5516
	19: 9	But s of them became obstinate,	5516
	19:13	S Jews who went around driving out	NIG
Ac	19:31	Even s of the officials of the province,	5516
	19:32	S were shouting one thing, some another.	3525
	19:32	Some were shouting one thing, s another.	257
	19:33	s of the crowd shouted instructions to	AIT
	21:16	S of the disciples from Caesarea	NIG
	21:27	s Jews from the province of Asia saw Paul	3836
	21:32	at once took s officers and soldiers and ran	NIG
	21:34	S in the crowd shouted one thing	257
	21:34	the crowd shouted one thing and s another,	NIG
	21:38	the desert s time ago?"	2465+3836+4047+4574
	23: 6	that s of them were Sadducees	1651+3538+3836
	23: 9	and s of the teachers of the law	5516
	24: 1	down to Caesarea with s of the elders and	5516
	24:19	there are s Jews from the province of Asia,	5516
	24:23	under guard but to give him s freedom	NIG
	25: 5	Let s of your leaders come with me	3836
	25:19	they had s points of dispute with him	5516
	27: 1	and s other prisoners were handed over to	5516
	27:26	we must run aground on s island."	5516
	27:30	to lower s anchors from the bow.	NIG
	27:34	Now I urge you to take s food.	NIG
	27:35	he took s bread and gave thanks to God	NIG
	27:36	and ate s food themselves.	NIG
	28:14	There we found s brothers who invited us	NIG
	28:24	S were convinced by what he said,	3525+3836
Ro	1:11	to you s spiritual gift to make you strong—	5516
	3: 3	What if s did not have faith?	5516
	3: 8	as saying and as s claim that we say—	5516
	9:21	of clay s pottery for noble purposes	3525+4005
	9:21	noble purposes and s for common use?	1254+4005
	11:14	to envy and save s of them.	5516
	11:17	If s of the branches have been broken off,	5516
	15:15	written you quite boldly on s points,	608+3538
1Co	1:11	My brothers, s from Chloe's	NIG
	4:18	S of you have become arrogant,	5516
	6:11	And that is what s of you were.	5516
	8: 7	S people are still so accustomed to idols	5516
	9:22	so that by all possible means I might save s.	5516
	10: 7	Do not be idolaters, as s of them were;	5516
	10: 8	as s of them did—and in one day	5516
	10: 9	as s of them did—and were killed	5516
	10:10	And do not grumble, as s of them did—	5516
	10:27	If s unbeliever invites you to a meal	5516
	11:18	and to s extent I believe it.	5516
	14: 6	unless I bring you s revelation	2445
	14:23	s who do not understand or some	2626
	14:23	not understand or s unbelievers come in,	NIG
	15: 6	though s have fallen asleep.	5516
	15:12	how can s of you say	5516
	15:34	for there are s who are ignorant of God—	5516
	16: 7	I hope to spend s time with you,	5516
2Co	2: 5	to s extent—not to put it too	247+608+3538
	3: 1	Or do we need, like s people,	5516
	10: 2	as I expect to be toward s people who think	5516
	10:10	For s say, "His letters are weighty	AIT
	10:12	with s who commend themselves.	5516
Gal	1: 7	Evidently s people are throwing you	5516
	2: 4	s false brothers had infiltrated our ranks	4015
Eph	4:11	It was he who gave s to be apostles,	3525
	4:11	s to be prophets, some to be evangelists,	1254
	4:11	some to be prophets, s to be evangelists,	1254
	4:11	and s to be pastors and teachers,	1254
Php	1:15	that s preach Christ out of envy and rivalry,	5516
	3:15	And if on s point you think differently,	5516
1Th	3: 5	I was afraid that in s way the tempter	4803
2Th	2: 2	unsettled or alarmed by s prophecy,	NIG
	3:11	We hear that s among you are idle.	5516
1Ti	1: 6	S have wandered away from these	5516
	1:19	S have rejected these and	5516
	4: 1	that in later times s will abandon the faith	5516
	4: 8	For physical training is of s value,	3900
	5:15	S have in fact already turned away	5516
	5:24	The sins of s men are obvious,	5516
	6:10	S people, eager for money,	5516
	6:21	which s have professed and in	5516
2Ti	2:18	and they destroy the faith of s.	5516
	2:20	s are for noble purposes and some	3525+4005
	2:20	for noble purposes and s for ignoble.	1254+4005
Phm	1:20	I may have s benefit from you in the Lord;	NIG
Heb	4: 6	It still remains that s will enter that rest,	5516
	10:25	s are in the habit of doing,	5516
	11:36	S faced jeers and flogging,	2283
	13: 2	so doing s people have entertained angels	5516
2Pe	3: 9	as s understand slowness.	5516
	3:16	His letters contain s things that are hard	5516
2Jn	1: 4	It has given me great joy to find s of	1666
3Jn	1: 3	to have s brothers come and tell	NIG
Rev	2:10	devil will put s of you in prison to test you,	1666
	2:17	I will give s of the hidden manna.	AIT

SOMEBODY (5) [BODY, SOME]

Ex	22: 9	any other lost property about which s says,	AIT
Pr	12: 9	and yet have a servant than pretend to be s	3877
Ac	5:36	Theudas appeared, claiming to be s,	5516
Gal	6: 3	without comparing himself to s else,	2283
Heb	9:17	a will is in force only when s has died;	NIG

SOMEHOW (5) [HOW, SOME]

Ro	11:14	the hope that I may s arouse my own people	4803
1Co	12: 2	s or other you were influenced	323+6055
2Co	11: 3	your minds may s be led astray	NIG
Gal	4:11	that s I have wasted my efforts on you.	4803
Php	3:11	and so, s, to attain to the resurrection	1623+4803

SOMEONE (120) [ONE, SOME]

Ex	4:13	"O Lord, please send s else to do it."	928+3338^S
	12:30	for there was not a house without s dead.	AIT
	23: 5	the donkey of s who hates you fallen down	AIT
Lev	2: 1	" 'When s brings a grain offering to	5883
	13:18	"When s has a boil on his skin and it heals,	2257
	13:24	"When s has a burn on his skin and	NIH
	15: 8	with the discharge spits on s who is clean,	2021
	27:20	or if he has sold it to s else,	408
Nu	6: 9	" 'If s dies suddenly in his presence,	4637^S
	19:16	the open who touches s who has been killed	2021
	19:16	s who has died a natural death,	AIT
	19:18	or a grave or s who has been killed	2021^S
	19:18	or s who has died a natural death.	2021^S
	35: 6	a person who has killed s may flee.	NIH
	35:11	who has killed s accidentally may flee.	5883
	35:16	" 'If a man strikes s with an iron object so	2084
	35:17	and he strikes s so that he dies,	2084
	35:18	and he hits s so that he dies,	2084
	35:22	without hostility s suddenly shoves another	AIT
	36: 8	in any Israelite tribe must marry s	285
Dt	20: 5	in battle and s else may dedicate it.	408
	20: 6	or he may die in battle and s else enjoy it.	408
	20: 7	in battle and s else marry her."	408
	22: 8	on your house if s falls from	2021+5877^S
	22:26	of s who attacks and murders his neighbor,	408
Jos	20: 9	who killed s accidentally could flee	5883
Jdg	7:14	"If s comes by and asks you,	408
	6:31	he can defend himself when s breaks down	AIT
Ru	2:22	in s else's field you might be harmed."	337
1Sa	14:33	Then s said to Saul, "Look,	AIT
	16:16	to search for s who can play the harp.	408
	16:17	"Find s who plays well and bring him	408
	17:30	He then turned away to s else and brought	337
	25:29	though s is pursuing you to take your life,	132
	26:15	S came to destroy your lord	285+2021+6639
2Sa	3:29	s who has a running sore	AIT
	11: 3	and David sent s to find out about her.	NIH
	14: 2	So Joab sent s to Tekoa and had	NIH
	23:15	that s would get me a drink of water from	4769
1Ki	14: 5	she will pretend to be s else."	5796
	18:10	my kingdom where my master has not sent s	NIH
	20:39	and s came to me with a captive and said,	408
	22:34	But s drew his bow at random and hit	408
2Ki	5: 7	Why does this fellow send s to me to	408
	6:32	how this murderer is sending s	NIH
1Ch	11:17	that s would get me a drink of water from	4769
	19: 5	s came and told David about the men,	AIT
2Ch	18:33	But s drew his bow at random and hit	408
Ne	2:10	that s had come to promote the welfare of	132
Est	1:19	to s else who is better than she.	8295
Job	4: 2	"If s ventures a word with you,	AIT
	9:33	only there were s to arbitrate between us,	AIT
	9:34	s to remove God's rod from me,	AIT
	31:35	that I had s to hear me!	AIT
Pr	4:16	robbed of slumber till they make s fall.	NIH
	27: 2	s else, and not your own lips.	5799
Ecc	2:21	then he must leave all he owns to s who has	132
Isa	21:11	S calls to me from Seir, "Watchman,	AIT
	28: 4	as s sees it and takes it in his hand,	2021+8011^S
	29:11	if you give the scroll to s who can read,	AIT
	29:12	if you give the scroll to s who cannot read,	889
Eze	43: 6	I heard s speaking to me from inside	NIH
Da	5:17	and give your rewards to s else.	10025
Zec	13: 6	If s asks him, 'What are these wounds	AIT
Mt	5:39	If s strikes you on the right cheek,	4015
	5:40	if s wants to sue you and take your tunic,	3836
	5:41	If s forces you to go one mile,	4015
	11: 3	or should we expect s else?"	2283
	12:47	S told him, "Your mother	5516
Mk	3:31	Standing outside, they sent s in to call him.	NIG
Lk	6:29	If s strikes you on one cheek,	3836
	6:29	If s takes your cloak,	3836
	7:19	or should we expect s else?"	257
	7:20	or should we expect s else?' "	257
	8:20	S told him, "Your mother	NIG
	8:46	But Jesus said, "S touched me;	5516
	8:49	s came from the house of Jairus,	5516
	11:22	s stronger attacks and overpowers him,	AIT
	12:13	S in the crowd said to him, "Teacher,	5516
	13:23	S asked him, "Lord, are only	5516
	14: 8	"When s invites you to a wedding feast,	5516
	16:12	not been trustworthy with s else's property,	259
	16:30	'but if s from the dead goes to them,	5516
	16:31	they will not be convinced even if s rises	5516
	22:58	A little later s else saw him and said,	AIT
Jn	4:33	"Could s have brought him food?"	5516
	5: 7	s else goes down ahead of me."	257
	5:43	but if s else comes in his own name,	257
	21:18	and s else will dress you and lead you	257
Ac	5:25	Then s came and said, "Look!	5516
	8: 9	He boasted that he was s great,	5516
	8:31	he said, "unless s explains it to me?"	5516
	8:34	prophet talking about, himself or s else?"	5516
	13:11	s to lead him by the hand.	5933
	13:41	would never believe, even if s told you.' "	5516
Ro	2: 1	you who pass judgment on s else,	NIG
	3: 7	S might argue, "If my falsehood enhances	
		God's truthfulness	NIG
	5: 7	for a good man s might possibly dare to die.	5516
	6:16	to s to obey him as slaves, you are slaves to	4005
	10:14	can they hear without s preaching to them?	AIT
	14: 4	Who are you to judge s else's servant?	259
	14:20	for a man to eat anything that causes s else	NIG
	15:20	not be building on s else's foundation.	259
1Co	3:10	and s else is building on it.	257
	14:11	not grasp the meaning of what s is saying,	5889
	14:24	s who does not understand comes in	2626
	14:27	one at a time, and s must interpret,	1651
	14:30	revelation comes to s who is sitting down,	257
	15:35	But s may ask, "How are the dead raised?	5516
2Co	11: 4	For if s comes to you and preaches	3836
Gal	6: 1	Brothers, if s is caught in a sin,	476^S
Heb	2: 6	But there is a place where s has testified:	5516
	3: 4	For every house is built by s,	5516
	5:12	you need s to teach you the elementary	5516
	6:16	Men swear by s greater than themselves,	AIT
Jas	2:18	s will say, "You have faith; I have deeds."	5516
	5:19	from the truth and s should bring him back,	5516
1Pe	5: 8	like a roaring lion looking for s to devour.	5516
Rev	1:13	and among the lampstands was s "like a son	NIG
	4: 2	a throne in heaven with s sitting on it.	AIT

SOMEONE'S (3) [ONE, SOME]

Lev	3: 1	" 'If s offering is a fellowship offering,	2257
	24:18	the life of s animal must make restitution—	NIH
Pr	1:11	let's lie in wait for s blood,	NIH

SOMETHING (110) [SOME, THING]

Ge	18: 5	Let me get you s to eat,	4312+7326
	30:30	when may I do s for my own household?"	AIT
	38:17	"Will you give me s as a pledge	NIH
Ex	2:20	Invite him to have s to eat."	4312^S
	10: 6	s neither your fathers	889
	17:14	a scroll as s to be remembered	2355
	24:10	s like a pavement made of sapphire,	AIT
Lev	5: 1	to testify regarding s he has seen or learned	NIH
	6: 2	by deceiving his neighbor about s entrusted	7214
	7:21	If anyone touches s unclean—	3972
	11:32	When one of them dies and falls on s,	2257^S
	14:35	'I have seen s that looks like mildew	NIH
	14:57	to determine when s is clean or unclean.	2021^S
	22: 4	also be unclean if he touches s defiled by	3972
	27:14	" 'If a man dedicates his house as s holy to	7731
	27:23	on that day as s holy to the LORD.	7731
Nu	11: 8	And it tasted like s made with olive oil.	4382
	16:30	if the LORD brings about s totally new,	1375
	18:10	Eat it as s most holy; every male shall eat it.	2021^S
	35:20	or throws s at him intentionally so	NIH
	35:22	or throws s at him unintentionally	3972+3998
Dt	8:16	s your fathers had never known,	889
	23:13	of your equipment have s to dig with,	3845
	24: 1	because he finds s indecent about her,	1821
Jdg	14:14	He replied, "Out of the eater, s to eat;	4407
	14:14	out of the strong, s sweet."	AIT
	18: 9	Aren't you going to do s?	3120
	19: 5	"Refresh yourself with s to eat;	4312+7326
	19:21	they had s to eat and drink.	AIT
Ru	3: 8	the middle of the night s startled the man,	AIT
1Sa	1:18	Then she went her way and ate s,	NIH
	3:11	I am about to do s in Israel that will make	1821
	20:26	"S must have happened	5247
2Sa	3:35	Then they all came and urged David to eat s	4312^S
	12:18	He may do s desperate."	8288
	13: 5	like my sister Tamar to come and give me s	4312^S
1Ki	1:27	Is this s my lord the king has done	1821
	2:14	Then he added, "I have s to say to you."	1821
	13: 7	"Come home with me and have s to eat,	6184
	17:13	and then make s for yourself and your son.	NIH
2Ki	5:20	I will run after him and get s from him."	4399
Job	6:21	you see s dreadful and are afraid.	3170
	6:22	Have I ever said, 'Give s on my behalf,	NIH
	13:28	"So man wastes away like s rotten,	8373
Pr	20:25	for a man to dedicate s rashly and only later	NIH
Ecc	1:10	This is s new"?	2085^S
	3:16	And I saw s else under the sun:	6388
	4: 7	Again I saw s meaningless under the sun:	AIT
	8:14	There is s else meaningless that occurs	NIH
	9:11	I have seen s else under the sun:	8740
Isa	41:23	Do s, whether good or bad,	AIT
Jer	7:31	s I did not command,	889
	14: 7	O LORD, do s for the sake of your name.	6913
	19: 5	s I did not command or mention,	889
	23:14	of Jerusalem I have seen s horrible:	9136
	38:14	"I am going to ask you s,"	1821
Eze	15: 5	how much less can it be made into s useful	4856
Da	6: 5	unless it has s to do with the law	10089
Hos	4: 7	exchanged their Glory for s disgraceful.	AIT
	8:12	but they regarded them as s alien.	AIT
Joel	3: 4	Are you repaying me for s I have done?	1691
Hab	1: 5	to do s in your days that you would	7189
Mt	5:23	and there remember that your brother has s	5516
	14:16	You give them s to eat."	NIG
	25:35	For I was hungry and you gave me s to eat,	NIG
	25:35	I was thirsty and you gave me s to drink,	NIG
	25:37	or thirsty and give you s to drink?	NIG
Mk	5:43	and told them to give her s to eat.	5516
	6:36	and villages and buy themselves s to eat."	5515
	6:37	But he answered, "You give them s to eat."	NIG
Lk	7:40	"Simon, I have s to tell you."	5516
	8:55	Then Jesus told them to give her s to eat.	NIG
	9:13	He replied, "You give them s to eat."	NIG
	11:54	waiting to catch him in s he might say.	5516
	20:20	s he said so that they might hand him over	3364
Jn	4:31	his disciples urged him, "Rabbi, eat s."	NIG
	5:14	Stop sinning or s worse may happen	5516
	13:29	or to give s to the poor.	5516
	18:23	said s wrong," Jesus replied,	NIG
Ac	3: 5	expecting to get s from them.	5516
	9:18	s like scales fell from Saul's eyes,	NIG
	10:10	He became hungry and wanted s to eat,	NIG

Ac	10:11	and s like a large sheet being let down	5516
	11: 5	I saw s like a large sheet being let down	5516
	13:41	for I am going to do s in your days	2240
	17:23	as s unknown I am going to proclaim	AIT
	21:37	"May I say s to you?"	5516
	23:17	he has s to tell him."	5516
	23:18	to you because he has s to tell you."	5516
	25:26	as a result of this investigation I may have s	5515
Ro	4: 2	he had s to boast about—	3017
	12:20	if he is thirsty, give him s to drink.	NIG
	14:14	But if anyone regards s as unclean,	5516
1Co	7:30	those who buy s, as if it were not theirs	NIG
	8: 2	The man who thinks he knows s does not	5516
	10:30	because of s I thank God for?	4005
	14:35	If they want to inquire about s,	5516
	14:37	perhaps of wheat or of s else.	5516
2Co	11: 9	And when I was with you and needed s,	NIG
Gal	1:11	s that man made up.	476+2848
	6: 3	If anyone thinks he is s when he is nothing,	5516
Eph	4:28	doing s useful with his own hands,	3836
	4:28	he may have s to share with those in need.	NIG
Php	2: 6	equality with God as s to be grasped,	772
Heb	8: 3	for this one also to have s to offer.	5516
	11:40	God had planned s better for us so	5516
Jas	4: 2	You want s but don't get it.	NIG
1Pe	4:12	as though s strange were happening to you.	AIT
Rev	8: 8	and s like a huge mountain, all ablaze,	NIG
	9: 7	On their heads they wore s like crowns	6055

SOMETIME (KJV) See ONCE

SOMETIMES (3) [SOME]

Nu	9:20	S the cloud was over the tabernacle	889+3780
	9:21	S the cloud stayed only from evening	889+3780
Heb	10:33	S you were publicly exposed to insult	3525+4047

SOMEWHAT (1) [SOME, WHAT]

2Co	10: 8	even if I boast s freely about the authority	5516

SOMEWHERE (4) [SOME, WHERE]

Isa	45:19	from s in a land of darkness;	5226
Mk	1:38	Jesus replied, "Let us go s else—	250
Lk	13:33	"Leave this place and go s else.	NIG
Heb	4: 4	For s he has spoken about the seventh day	4543

SON (2331) [GRANDSON, GRANDSONS, SON'S, SON-IN-LAW, SONS, SONS', SONS-IN-LAW, SONSHIP]

Ge	4:17	and he named it after his s Enoch.	1201
	4:22	Zillah also had a s, Tubal-Cain,	3528
	4:25	she gave birth to a s and named him Seth,	1201
	4:26	Seth also had a s, and he named him Enosh.	1201
	5: 3	he had a s in his own likeness,	3528
	5:28	Lamech had lived 182 years, he had a s.	1201
	9:24	and found out what his youngest s had done	1201
	11:31	Terah took his s Abram,	1201
	11:31	his grandson Lot s of Haran,	1201
	11:31	the wife of his s Abram,	1201
	15: 4	but a s coming from your own body will	889^S
	16:11	now with child and you will have a s.	1201
	16:15	So Hagar bore Abram a s,	1201
	16:15	the name Ishmael to the s she had borne.	1201
	17:16	I will bless her and will surely give you a s	1201
	17:17	a s be born to a man a hundred years old?	3528
	17:19	"Yes, but your wife Sarah will bear you a s,	1201
	17:23	that very day Abraham took his s Ishmael	1201
	17:25	and his s Ishmael was thirteen;	1201
	17:26	and his s Ishmael were both circumcised on	1201
	18:10	and Sarah your wife will have a s."	1201
	18:14	and Sarah will have a s."	1201
	19:37	The older daughter had a s,	1201
	19:38	The younger daughter also had a s,	1201
	21: 2	and bore a s to Abraham in his old age,	1201
	21: 3	the name Isaac to the s Sarah bore him.	1201
	21: 4	When his s Isaac was eight days old,	1201
	21: 5	when his s Isaac was born to him.	1201
	21: 7	Yet I have borne him a s in his old age."	1201
	21: 9	the s whom Hagar the Egyptian had borne	1201
	21:10	"Get rid of that slave woman and her s,	1201
	21:10	for that slave woman's s will never share in	1201
	21:10	in the inheritance with my s Isaac."	1201
	21:11	because it concerned his s.	1201
	21:13	the s of the maidservant into a nation also,	1201
	22: 2	Then God said, "Take your s,	1201
	22: 2	God said, "Take your son, your only s,	3495
	22: 3	of his servants and his s Isaac.	1201
	22: 6	and placed it on his s Isaac,	1201
	22: 7	"Yes, my s?" Abraham replied.	1201
	22: 7	the lamb for the burnt offering, my s."	1201
	22: 9	He bound his s Isaac and laid him on	1201
	22:10	and took the knife to slay his s.	1201
	22:12	you have not withheld from me your s,	1201
	22:12	from me your son, your only s."	3495
	22:13	as a burnt offering instead of his s.	1201
	22:16	and have not withheld your s,	1201
	22:16	not withheld your son, your only s,	3495
	23: 8	to me and intercede with Ephron s of Zohar	1201
	24: 3	not get a wife for my s from the daughters	1201
	24: 4	and get a wife for my s Isaac."	1201
	24: 5	Shall I then take your s back to	1201
	24: 6	that you do not take my s back there,"	1201
	24: 7	that you can get a wife for my s from there.	1201
	24: 8	Only do not take my s back there."	1201

Ge	24:15	the daughter of Bethuel s of Milcah,	1201
	24:24	the s that Milcah bore to Nahor."	1201
	24:36	My master's wife Sarah has borne him a s	1201
	24:37	not get a wife for my s from the daughters	1201
	24:38	and get a wife for my s.'	1201
	24:40	a wife for my s from my own clan and	1201
	24:44	the LORD has chosen for my master's s.'	1201
	24:47	'The daughter of Bethuel s of Nahor,	1201
	24:48	of my master's brother for his s.	1201
	24:51	let her become the wife of your master's s,	1201
	25: 5	and sent them away from his s Isaac to	1201
	25: 9	the field of Ephron s of Zohar the Hittite,	1201
	25:11	God blessed his s Isaac,	1201
	25:12	This is the account of Abraham's s Ishmael,	1201
	25:19	This is the account of Abraham's s Isaac.	1201
	27: 1	he called for Esau his older s and said	1201
	27: 1	and said to him, "My s."	1201
	27: 5	as Isaac spoke to his s Esau.	1201
	27: 6	Rebekah said to her s Jacob,	1201
	27: 8	my s, listen carefully	1201
	27:13	His mother said to him, "My s,	1201
	27:15	the best clothes of Esau her older s,	1201
	27:15	and put them on her younger s Jacob.	1201
	27:17	to her s Jacob the tasty food and	1201
	27:18	"Yes, my s," he answered.	1201
	27:20	Isaac asked his s,	1201
	27:20	"How did you find it so quickly, my s?"	1201
	27:21	"Come near so I can touch you, my s,	1201
	27:21	to know whether you really are my s Esau	1201
	27:24	"Are you really my s Esau?"	1201
	27:25	Then he said, "My s,	1201
	27:26	"Come here, my s, and kiss me."	1201
	27:27	the smell of my s is like the smell of a field	1201
	27:32	"I am yours," he answered, "your firstborn s.	1201
	27:37	So what can I possibly do for you, my s?"	1201
	27:42	Rebekah was told what her older s Esau	1201
	27:42	she sent for her younger s Jacob and said	1201
	27:43	Now then, my s, do what I say:	1201
	28: 5	to Laban s of Bethuel the Aramean,	1201
	28: 9	and daughter of Ishmael s of Abraham,	1201
	29:12	a relative of her father and a s of Rebekah.	1201
	29:13	his sister's s, he hurried to meet him.	1201
	29:32	Leah became pregnant and gave birth to a s.	1201
	29:33	and when she gave birth to a s she said,	1201
	29:34	and when she gave birth to a s she said,	1201
	29:35	and when she gave birth to a s she said,	1201
	30: 5	and she became pregnant and bore him a s.	1201
	30: 6	he has listened to my plea and given me a s.	1201
	30: 7	and bore Jacob a second s.	1201
	30:10	Leah's servant Zilpah bore Jacob a s.	1201
	30:12	servant Zilpah bore Jacob a second s	1201
	30:17	and bore Jacob a fifth s.	1201
	30:19	and bore Jacob a sixth s.	1201
	30:23	She became pregnant and gave birth to a s	1201
	30:24	"May the LORD add to me another s."	1201
	34: 2	When Shechem s of Hamor the Hivite,	1201
	34: 8	"My s Shechem has his heart set	1201
	34:18	to Hamor and his s Shechem.	1201
	34:20	So Hamor and his s Shechem went to	1201
	34:24	with Hamor and his s Shechem,	1201
	34:26	They put Hamor and his s Shechem to	1201
	35:17	"Don't be afraid, for you have another s."	1201
	35:18	she named her s Ben-Oni,	2257S
	36:10	Eliphaz, the s of Esau's wife Adah,	1201
	36:10	and Reuel, the s of Esau's wife Basemath.	1201
	36:12	Esau's s Eliphaz also had	1201
	36:17	The sons of Esau's s Reuel:	1201
	36:32	Bela s of Beor became king of Edom.	1201
	36:33	Jobab s of Zerah from Bozrah	1201
	36:35	When Husham died, Hadad s of Bedad,	1201
	36:38	Baal-Hanan s of Acbor succeeded him	1201
	36:39	When Baal-Hanan s of Acbor died,	1201
	37:34	and mourned for his s many days.	1201
	37:35	down to the grave to my s."	1201
	38: 3	she became pregnant and gave birth to a s,	1201
	38: 4	and gave birth to a s and named him Onan.	1201
	38: 5	to still another s and named him Shelah.	1201
	38:11	until my s Shelah grows up."	1201
	38:26	since I wouldn't give her to my s Shelah."	1201
	41:52	The second s he named Ephraim and said,	NIH
	42:38	"My s will not go down there with you;	1201
	43:29	his own mother's s, he asked,	1201
	43:29	he said, "God be gracious to you, my s."	1201
	44:20	a young s born to him in his old age.	3529
	45: 9	'This is what your s Joseph says:	1201
	45:28	My s Joseph is still alive.	1201
	46:10	and Shaul the s of a Canaanite woman.	1201
	46:23	The s of Dan: Hushim.	1201
	47:29	he called for his s Joseph and said to him,	1201
	48: 2	"Your s Joseph has come to you,"	1201
	48:19	his father refused and said, "I know, my s,	1201
	49: 9	you return from the prey, my s.	1201
	50:23	of Makir s of Manasseh were placed	1201
Ex	2: 2	she became pregnant and gave birth to a s.	1201
	2:10	to Pharaoh's daughter and he became her s.	1201
	2:22	Zipporah gave birth to a s,	1201
	4:22	Israel is my firstborn s,	1201
	4:23	"Let my s go, so he may worship me."	1201
	4:23	so I will kill your firstborn s.'"	1201
	6:14	the firstborn s of Israel were Hanoch	AIT
	6:15	and Shaul the s of a Canaanite woman.	1201
	6:25	Eleazar s of Aaron married one of	1201
	11: 5	Every firstborn s in Egypt will die,	AIT
	11: 5	from the firstborn s of Pharaoh,	AIT
	11: 5	to the firstborn s of the slave girl,	AIT
	13: 8	On that day tell your s,	1201
	13:14	"In days to come, when your s asks you,	1201

Ex	18: 3	One s was named Gershom, for Moses said,	NIH
	20:10	neither you, nor your s or daughter,	1201
	21: 9	If he selects her for his s,	1201
	21:31	This law also applies if the bull gores a s	1201
	29:30	The s who succeeds him as priest	1201
	31: 2	I have chosen Bezalel s of Uri,	1201
	31: 2	the s of Hur, of the tribe of Judah,	1201
	31: 6	I have appointed Oholiab s of Ahisamach,	1201
	33:11	but his young aide Joshua s of Nun did	1201
	35:30	the LORD has chosen Bezalel s of Uri,	1201
	35:30	the s of Hur, of the tribe of Judah,	1201
	35:34	And he has given both him and Oholiab s	1201
	38:21	the Levites under the direction of Ithamar s	1201
	38:22	(Bezalel s of Uri, the son of Hur,	1201
	38:22	(Bezalel son of Uri, the s of Hur,	1201
	38:23	with him was Oholiab s of Ahisamach, of	1201
Lev	6:22	The s who is to succeed him	1201
	7:33	The s of Aaron who offers the blood and	1201
	12: 2	to a s will be ceremonially unclean	2351
	12: 6	"'When the days of her purification for a s	1201
	21: 2	his s or daughter, his brother,	1201
	24:10	Now the s of an Israelite mother and	1201
	24:11	The s of the Israelite woman blasphemed	1201
Nu	1: 5	from Reuben, Elizur s of Shedeur;	1201
	1: 6	from Simeon, Shelumiel s of Zurishaddai;	1201
	1: 7	from Judah, Nahshon s of Amminadab;	1201
	1: 8	from Issachar, Nethanel s of Zuar;	1201
	1: 9	from Zebulun, Eliab s of Helon;	1201
	1:10	from Ephraim, Elishama s of Ammihud;	1201
	1:10	from Manasseh, Gamaliel s of Pedahzur;	1201
	1:11	from Benjamin, Abidan s of Gideoni;	1201
	1:12	from Dan, Ahiezer s of Ammishaddai;	1201
	1:13	from Asher, Pagiel s of Ocran;	1201
	1:14	from Gad, Eliasaph s of Deuel;	1201
	1:15	from Naphtali, Ahira s of Enan."	1201
	1:20	the descendants of Reuben the firstborn s	AIT
	2: 3	of Judah is Nahshon s of Amminadab.	1201
	2: 5	of the people of Issachar is Nethanel s	1201
	2: 7	the people of Zebulun is Eliab s of Helon.	1201
	2:10	of the people of Reuben is Elizur s	1201
	2:12	of Simeon is Shelumiel s of Zurishaddai.	1201
	2:14	of the people of Gad is Eliasaph s of Deuel.	1201
	2:18	of Ephraim is Elishama s of Ammihud.	1201
	2:20	of Manasseh is Gamaliel s of Pedahzur.	1201
	2:22	of the people of Benjamin is Abidan s	1201
	2:25	of Dan is Ahiezer s of Ammishaddai.	1201
	2:27	of the people of Asher is Pagiel s of Ocran.	1201
	2:29	the people of Naphtali is Ahira s of Enan.	1201
	3:24	of the Gershonites was Eliasaph s of Lael.	1201
	3:30	of the Kohathite clans was Elizaphan s	1201
	3:32	of the Levites was Eleazar s of Aaron,	1201
	3:35	the Merarite clans was Zuriel s of Abihail;	1201
	4:16	"Eleazar s of Aaron, the priest,	1201
	4:28	under the direction of Ithamar s of Aaron,	1201
	4:33	of Meeting under the direction of Ithamar s	1201
	7: 8	under the direction of Ithamar s of Aaron,	1201
	7:12	the first day was Nahshon s of Amminadab	1201
	7:17	the offering of Nahshon s of Amminadab.	1201
	7:18	On the second day Nethanel s of Zuar,	1201
	7:23	This was the offering of Nethanel s	1201
	7:24	On the third day, Eliab s of Helon,	1201
	7:29	the offering of Eliab s of Helon.	1201
	7:30	On the fourth day Elizur s of Shedeur,	1201
	7:35	the offering of Elizur s of Shedeur.	1201
	7:36	the fifth day Shelumiel s of Zurishaddai,	1201
	7:41	the offering of Shelumiel s of Zurishaddai.	1201
	7:42	On the sixth day Eliasaph s of Deuel,	1201
	7:47	the offering of Eliasaph s of Deuel.	1201
	7:48	the seventh day Elishama s of Ammihud,	1201
	7:53	the offering of Elishama s of Ammihud.	1201
	7:54	On the eighth day Gamaliel s of Pedahzur,	1201
	7:59	the offering of Gamaliel s of Pedahzur.	1201
	7:60	On the ninth day Abidan s of Gideoni,	1201
	7:65	the offering of Abidan s of Gideoni.	1201
	7:66	the tenth day Ahiezer s of Ammishaddai,	1201
	7:71	the offering of Ahiezer s of Ammishaddai.	1201
	7:72	On the eleventh day Pagiel s of Ocran,	1201
	7:77	This was the offering of Pagiel s of Ocran.	1201
	7:78	On the twelfth day Ahira s of Enan,	1201
	7:83	This was the offering of Ahira s of Enan.	1201
	10:14	Nahshon s of Amminadab was	1201
	10:15	Nethanel s of Zuar was over the division of	1201
	10:16	and Eliab s of Helon was over the division	1201
	10:18	Elizur s of Shedeur was in command.	1201
	10:19	Shelumiel s of Zurishaddai was over	1201
	10:20	and Eliasaph s of Deuel was over	1201
	10:22	Elishama s of Ammihud was in command.	1201
	10:23	Gamaliel s of Pedahzur was over	1201
	10:24	and Abidan s of Gideoni was over	1201
	10:25	Ahiezer s of Ammishaddai was	1201
	10:26	Pagiel s of Ocran was over the division of	1201
	10:27	and Ahira s of Enan was over the division	1201
	10:29	Now Moses said to Hobab s of Reuel	1201
	11:28	Joshua s of Nun,	1201
	13: 4	Shammua s of Zaccur;	1201
	13: 5	Shaphat s of Hori;	1201
	13: 6	Caleb s of Jephunneh;	1201
	13: 7	from the tribe of Issachar, Igal s of Joseph;	1201
	13: 8	Hoshea s of Nun;	1201
	13: 9	Palti s of Raphu;	1201
	13:10	Gaddiel s of Sodi;	1201
	13:11	Gaddi s of Susi;	1201
	13:12	Ammiel s of Gemalli;	1201
	13:13	Sethur s of Michael;	1201
	13:14	Nahbi s of Vophsi;	1201
	13:15	from the tribe of Gad, Geuel s of Maki.	1201
	13:16	(Moses gave Hoshea s of Nun the name	1201

Nu	14: 6	Joshua s of Nun and Caleb son	1201
	14: 6	of Nun and Caleb s of Jephunneh,	1201
	14:30	except Caleb s of Jephunneh	1201
	14:30	of Jephunneh and Joshua s of Nun.	1201
	14:38	only Joshua s of Nun and Caleb son	1201
	14:38	of Nun and Caleb s of Jephunneh survived.	1201
	16: 1	Korah s of Izhar, the s of Kohath,	1201
	16: 1	Korah son of Izhar, the s of Kohath,	1201
	16: 1	the s of Levi, and certain Reubenites—	1201
	16: 1	sons of Eliab, and On s of Peleth—	1201
	16:37	"Tell Eleazar s of Aaron, the priest, to take	1201
	18:15	But you must redeem every firstborn s	132
	20:25	Get Aaron and his s Eleazar and take them	1201
	20:26	on his s Eleazar, for Aaron will be gathered	1201
	20:28	and put them on his s Eleazar.	1201
	22: 2	Now Balak s of Zippor saw all	1201
	22: 4	So Balak s of Zippor,	1201
	22: 5	messengers to summon Balaam s of Beor,	1201
	22:10	Balaam said to God, "Balak s of Zippor,	1201
	22:16	"This is what Balak s of Zippor says:	1201
	23:18	hear me, s of Zippor.	1201
	23:19	that he should lie, nor a s of man,	1201
	24: 3	"The oracle of Balaam s of Beor,	1201
	24:15	"The oracle of Balaam s of Beor,	1201
	25: 7	When Phinehas s of Eleazar,	1201
	25: 7	Phinehas son of Eleazar, the s of Aaron,	1201
	25:11	"Phinehas s of Eleazar, the son of Aaron,	1201
	25:11	the s of Aaron, the priest,	1201
	25:14	the Midianite woman was Zimri s of Salu,	1201
	26: 1	the LORD said to Moses and Eleazar s	1201
	26: 5	the firstborn s of Israel, were:	AIT
	26: 8	The s of Pallu was Eliab,	1201
	26:33	(Zelophehad s of Hepher had no sons;	1201
	26:65	and not one of them was left except Caleb s	1201
	26:65	of Jephunneh and Joshua s of Nun.	1201
	27: 1	The daughters of Zelophehad s of Hepher,	1201
	27: 1	the s of Gilead, the son of Makir,	1201
	27: 1	the s of Makir, the son of Manasseh,	1201
	27: 1	the son of Makir, the s of Manasseh,	1201
	27: 1	to the clans of Manasseh s of Joseph.	1201
	27: 4	from his clan because he had no s?	1201
	27: 8	'If a man dies and leaves no s,	1201
	27:18	"Take Joshua s of Nun,	1201
	31: 6	along with Phinehas s of Eleazar,	1201
	31: 8	They also killed Balaam s of Beor with	1201
	32:12	not one except Caleb s of Jephunneh	1201
	32:12	of Jephunneh the Kenizzite and Joshua s	1201
	32:28	to Eleazar the priest and Joshua s of Nun	1201
	32:33	and the half-tribe of Manasseh s of Joseph	1201
	32:39	of Makir s of Manasseh went to Gilead,	1201
	34:17	Eleazar the priest and Joshua s of Nun.	1201
	34:19	Caleb s of Jephunneh,	1201
	34:20	Shemuel s of Ammihud, from the tribe	1201
	34:21	Elidad s of Kislon, from the tribe	1201
	34:22	Bukki s of Jogli, the leader from the tribe	1201
	34:23	Hanniel s of Ephod, the leader from	1201
	34:23	from the tribe of Manasseh s of Joseph;	1201
	34:24	Kemuel s of Shiphtan, the leader from	1201
	34:24	from the tribe of Ephraim s of Joseph;	NIH
	34:25	Elizaphan s of Parnach, the leader from	1201
	34:26	Paltiel s of Azzan, the leader from the tribe	1201
	34:27	Ahihud s of Shelomi, the leader from	1201
	34:28	Pedahel s of Ammihud,	1201
	36: 1	The family heads of the clan of Gilead s	1201
	36: 1	the s of Manasseh,	1201
	36:12	the clans of the descendants of Manasseh s	1201
Dt	1:31	as a father carries his s,	1201
	1:36	except Caleb s of Jephunneh.	1201
	1:38	But your assistant, Joshua s of Nun,	1201
	5:14	neither you, nor your s or daughter,	1201
	6:20	In the future, when your s asks you,	1201
	8: 5	in your heart that as a man disciplines his s,	1201
	10: 6	and Eleazar his s succeeded him as priest.	1201
	13: 6	or your s or daughter, or the wife you love,	1201
	18:10	among you who sacrifices his s or daughter	1201
	21:15	but the firstborn is the s of the wife he does	1201
	21:16	of the firstborn to the s of the wife he loves	1201
	21:16	the s of the wife he does not love.	1201
	21:17	the s of his unloved wife as the firstborn	1201
	21:17	That s is the first sign of his father's	2085S
	21:18	a stubborn and rebellious s who does	1201
	21:20	"This s of ours is stubborn and rebellious.	1201
	23: 4	and they hired Balaam s of Beor	1201
	25: 5	and one of them dies without a s,	1201
	25: 6	The first s she bears shall carry on	AIT
	28:56	the husband she loves and her own s	1201
	31:23	The LORD gave this command to Joshua s	1201
	32:44	with Joshua s of Nun and spoke all	1201
	34: 9	Now Joshua s of Nun was filled with	1201
Jos	1: 1	the LORD said to Joshua s of Nun,	1201
	2: 1	Then Joshua s of Nun secretly sent two	1201
	2:23	to Joshua s of Nun and told him everything	1201
	6: 6	So Joshua s of Nun called the priests	1201
	6:26	"At the cost of his firstborn s will he lay	AIT
	7: 1	Achan s of Carmi, the son of Zimri,	1201
	7: 1	Achan son of Carmi, the s of Zimri,	1201
	7: 1	the s of Zerah, of the tribe of Judah,	1201
	7:18	and Achan s of Carmi, the son of Zimri,	1201
	7:18	and Achan son of Carmi, the s of Zimri,	1201
	7:18	the s of Zerah, of the tribe of Judah,	1201
	7:19	Then Joshua said to Achan, "My s,	1201
	7:24	took Achan s of Zerah, the silver, the robe,	1201
	13:22	the Israelites had put to the sword Balaam s	1201
	13:31	the descendants of Makir s of Manasseh—	1201
	14: 1	Joshua s of Nun and the heads of	1201
	14: 6	and Caleb s of Jephunneh	1201
	14:13	Then Joshua blessed Caleb s of Jephunneh	1201

Jos	14:14	to Caleb s of Jephunneh the Kenizzite ever	1201
	15: 6	of Beth Arabah to the Stone of Bohan s	1201
	15:13	Joshua gave to Caleb s of Jephunneh	1201
	15:17	Othniel s of Kenaz, Caleb's brother,	1201
	17: 2	the other male descendants of Manasseh s	1201
	17: 3	Now Zelophehad s of Hepher,	1201
	17: 3	Zelophehad son of Hepher, the s of Gilead,	1201
	17: 3	the s of Makir, the son of Manasseh,	1201
	17: 3	the son of Makir, the s of Manasseh,	1201
	17: 4	Joshua s of Nun, and the leaders and said,	1201
	18:17	down to the Stone of Bohan s of Reuben.	1201
	19:49	the Israelites gave Joshua s of Nun	1201
	19:51	Joshua s of Nun and the heads of	1201
	21: 1	Joshua s of Nun, and the heads of	1201
	21:12	to Caleb s of Jephunneh as his possession.	1201
	22:13	So the Israelites sent Phinehas s of Eleazar,	1201
	22:20	When Achan s of Zerah acted unfaithfully	1201
	22:31	And Phinehas s of Eleazar, the priest,	1201
	22:32	Then Phinehas s of Eleazar, the priest,	1201
	24: 9	When Balak s of Zippor, the king of Moab,	1201
	24: 9	for Balaam s of Beor to put a curse on you.	1201
	24:29	After these things, Joshua s of Nun,	1201
	24:33	And Eleazar s of Aaron died	1201
	24:33	which had been allotted to his s Phinehas in	1201
Jdg	1:13	Othniel s of Kenaz, Caleb's younger	1201
	2: 8	Joshua s of Nun, the servant of the LORD,	1201
	3: 9	Othniel s of Kenaz, Caleb's younger	1201
	3:11	until Othniel s of Kenaz died.	1201
	3:15	the s of Gera the Benjamite.	1201
	3:31	After Ehud came Shamgar s of Anath,	1201
	4: 6	for Barak s of Abinoam from Kedesh	1201
	4:12	that Barak s of Abinoam had gone up	1201
	5: 1	and Barak s of Abinoam sang this song:	1201
	5: 6	"In the days of Shamgar s of Anath,	1201
	5:12	your captives, O s of Abinoam.'	1201
	6:11	where his s Gideon was threshing wheat in	1201
	6:29	they were told, "Gideon s of Joash did it."	1201
	6:30	"Bring out your s	1201
	7:14	be nothing other than the sword of Gideon s	1201
	8:13	Gideon s of Joash then returned from	1201
	8:20	Turning to Jether, his oldest s, he said,	AIT
	8:22	you, your s and your grandson—	1201
	8:23	nor will my s rule over you.	1201
	8:29	Jerub-Baal s of Joash went back home	1201
	8:31	who lived in Shechem, also bore him a s,	1201
	8:32	Gideon s of Joash died at a good old age	1201
	9: 1	Abimelech s of Jerub-Baal went	1201
	9: 5	But Jotham, the youngest s of Jerub-Baal,	1201
	9:18	Abimelech, the s of his slave girl,	1201
	9:26	Now Gaal s of Ebed moved with his	1201
	9:28	Then Gaal s of Ebed said,	1201
	9:28	Isn't he Jerub-Baal's s,	1201
	9:30	of the city heard what Gaal s of Ebed said,	1201
	9:31	"Gaal s of Ebed and his brothers	1201
	9:35	Now Gaal s of Ebed had gone out	1201
	9:57	The curse of Jotham s of Jerub-Baal came	1201
	10: 1	Tola s of Puah, the son of Dodo,	1201
	10: 1	the s of Dodo, rose to save Israel.	1201
	11: 2	"because you are the s of another woman."	1201
	11:25	Are you better than Balak s of Zippor,	1201
	11:34	for her he had neither s nor daughter.	1201
	12:13	After him, Abdon s of Hillel,	1201
	12:15	Then Abdon s of Hillel died,	1201
	13: 3	but you are going to conceive and have a s.	1201
	13: 5	you will conceive and give birth to a s.	1201
	13: 7	'You will conceive and give birth to a s.	1201
	17: 2	"The LORD bless you, my s!"	1201
	17: 3	for my s to make a carved image and	1201
	18:30	and Jonathan s of Gershom,	1201
	18:30	Gershom, the s of Moses,	1201
	20:28	with Phinehas s of Eleazar,	1201
	20:28	the s of Aaron, ministering before it.)	1201
Ru	4:13	and she gave birth to a s.	1201
	4:17	women living there said, "Naomi has a s."	1201
1Sa	1: 1	whose name was Elkanah s of Jeroham,	1201
	1: 1	the s of Elihu, the son of Tohu,	1201
	1: 1	the son of Elihu, the s of Tohu,	1201
	1: 1	the son of Tohu, the s of Zuph.	1201
	1:11	not forget your servant but give her a s,	408+2446
	1:20	and gave birth to a s.	1201
	1:23	the woman stayed at home and nursed her s	1201
	3: 6	"My s," Eli said, "I did not call;	1201
	3:16	but Eli called him and said, "Samuel, my s."	1201
	4:16	Eli asked, "What happened, my s?"	1201
	4:20	you have given birth to a s."	1201
	7: 1	on the hill and consecrated Eleazar his s	1201
	9: 1	whose name was Kish s of Abiel,	1201
	9: 1	the s of Zeror, the son of Becorath,	1201
	9: 1	the son of Zeror, the s of Becorath,	1201
	9: 1	the s of Aphiah of Benjamin.	1201
	9: 2	He had a s named Saul,	1201
	9: 3	and Kish said to his s Saul,	1201
	10: 2	"What shall I do about my s?"'	1201
	10:11	"What is this that has happened to the s	1201
	10:21	Finally Saul s of Kish was chosen.	1201
	13:16	Saul and his s Jonathan and the men	1201
	13:22	only Saul and his s Jonathan had them.	1201
	14: 1	One day Jonathan s of Saul said to	1201
	14: 3	He was a s of Ichabod's brother Ahitub son	1201
	14: 3	Ichabod's brother Ahitub s of Phinehas,	1201
	14: 3	the s of Eli, the LORD's priest in Shiloh.	1201
	14:39	even if it lies with my s Jonathan,	1201
	14:40	I and Jonathan my s will stand over here."	1201
	14:42	the lot between me and Jonathan my s."	1201
	14:50	the commander of Saul's army was Abner s	1201
	16:18	a s of Jesse of Bethlehem who knows how	1201
	16:19	"Send me your s David,	1201
1Sa	16:20	and sent them with his s David to Saul.	1201
	17:12	the s of an Ephrathite named Jesse,	1201
	17:17	Now Jesse said to his s David,	1201
	17:55	"Abner, whose s is that young man?"	1201
	17:56	"Find out whose s this young man is."	1201
	17:58	"Whose s are you, young man?"	1201
	17:58	the s of your servant Jesse of Bethlehem."	1201
	19: 1	Saul told his s Jonathan and all	1201
	20:27	Then Saul said to his s Jonathan,	1201
	20:27	"Why hasn't the s of Jesse come to	1201
	20:30	"You s of a perverse and rebellious woman!	1201
	20:31	As long as the s of Jesse lives on this earth,	1201
	22: 7	Will the s of Jesse give all of you fields	1201
	22: 8	when my s makes a covenant with the son	1201
	22: 8	son makes a covenant with the s of Jesse.	1201
	22: 8	or tells me that my s has incited my servant	1201
	22: 9	the s of Jesse come to Ahimelech son	1201
	22: 9	of Jesse come to Ahimelech s of Ahitub	1201
	22:11	the king sent for the priest Ahimelech s	1201
	22:12	Saul said, "Listen now, s of Ahitub."	1201
	22:13	you and my s of Jesse,	1201
	22:20	Abiathar, a s of Ahimelech son of Ahitub,	1201
	22:20	Abiathar, a son of Ahimelech s of Ahitub,	1201
	23: 6	(Now Abiathar s of Ahimelech had brought	1201
	23:16	And Saul's s Jonathan went to David	1201
	24:16	"Is that your voice, David my s?"	1201
	25: 8	and your s David whatever you can find	1201
	25:10	Who is this s of Jesse?	1201
	25:44	to Paltiel s of Laish, who was from Gallim.	1201
	26: 5	He saw where Saul and Abner s of Ner,	1201
	26: 6	the Hittite and Abishai s of Zeruiah,	1201
	26:14	He called out to the army and to Abner s	1201
	26:17	"Is that your voice, David my s?"	1201
	26:21	Come back, David my s.	1201
	26:25	"May you be blessed, my s David;	1201
	27: 2	and went over to Achish s of Maoch king	1201
	30: 7	s of Ahimelech, "Bring me the ephod."	1201
2Sa	1: 4	And Saul and his s Jonathan are dead."	1201
	1: 5	that Saul and his s Jonathan are dead?"	1201
	1:12	till evening for Saul and his s Jonathan,	1201
	1:13	"I am the s of an alien, an Amalekite,"	1201
	1:17	concerning Saul and his s Jonathan,	1201
	2: 8	Meanwhile, Abner s of Ner,	1201
	2: 8	had taken Ish-Bosheth s of Saul	1201
	2:10	Ish-Bosheth s of Saul was forty years old	1201
	2:12	Abner s of Ner, together with the men of	1201
	2:12	with the men of Ish-Bosheth s of Saul,	1201
	2:13	Joab s of Zeruiah and David's men	1201
	2:15	twelve men for Benjamin and Ish-Bosheth s	1201
	3: 2	His firstborn was Amnon the s of Ahinoam	NIH
	3: 3	Kileab the s of Abigail the widow of Nabal	NIH
	3: 3	the s of Maacah daughter of Talmai king	1201
	3: 4	Adonijah the s of Haggith;	1201
	3: 4	the fifth, Shephatiah the s of Abital;	1201
	3: 5	Ithream the s of David's wife Eglah.	NIH
	3:14	to Ish-Bosheth s of Saul,	1201
	3:15	from her husband Paltiel s of Laish.	1201
	3:23	he was told that Abner s of Ner had come	1201
	3:25	You know Abner s of Ner;	1201
	3:28	concerning the blood of Abner s of Ner.	1201
	3:37	in the murder of Abner s of Ner.	1201
	4: 1	When Ish-Bosheth s of Saul heard	1201
	4: 2	Saul's s had two men who were leaders	1201
	4: 4	(Jonathan s of Saul had a son who was lame	1201
	4: 4	(Jonathan son of Saul had a s who was lame	1201
	4: 8	"Here is the head of Ish-Bosheth s of Saul,	1201
	7:14	I will be his father, and he will be my s.	1201
	8: 3	David fought Hadadezer s of Rehob,	1201
	8:10	he sent his s Joram to King David	1201
	8:12	the plunder taken from Hadadezer s	1201
	8:16	Joab s of Zeruiah was over the army;	1201
	8:16	Jehoshaphat s of Ahilud was recorder;	1201
	8:17	Zadok s of Ahitub and Ahimelech son	1201
	8:17	and Ahimelech s of Abiathar were priests;	1201
	8:18	Benaiah s of Jehoiada was over	1201
	9: 3	"There is still a s of Jonathan;	1201
	9: 4	"He is at the house of Makir s of Ammiel	1201
	9: 5	from the house of Makir s of Ammiel	1201
	9: 6	When Mephibosheth s of Jonathan,	1201
	9: 6	the s of Saul, came to David,	1201
	9:12	Mephibosheth had a young s named Mica,	1201
	10: 1	and his s Hanun succeeded him as king.	1201
	10: 2	"I will show kindness to Hanun s	1201
	11:21	Who killed Abimelech s of Jerub-Besheth?	1201
	11:27	and she became his wife and bore him a s.	1201
	12:14	the s born to you will die."	1201
	12:24	She gave birth to a s,	1201
	13: 1	Amnon s of David fell in love with Tamar,	1201
	13: 1	the beautiful sister of Absalom s of David.	1201
	13: 3	Now Amnon had a friend named Jonadab s	1201
	13: 4	"Why do you, the king's s,	1201
	13:25	"No, my s," the king replied.	1201
	13:32	But Jonadab s of Shimeah,	1201
	13:37	and went to Talmai s of Ammihud,	1201
	13:37	King David mourned for his s every day.	1201
	14: 1	Joab s of Zeruiah knew that	1201
	14:11	so that my s will not be destroyed."	1201
	14:13	king has not brought back his banished s?	NIH
	14:16	to cut off both me and my s from	1201
	15:27	with your s Ahimaaz and Jonathan son	1201
	15:27	son your son Ahimaaz and Jonathan s	1201
	15:36	Ahimaaz s of Zadok and Jonathan son	NIH
	15:36	Ahimaaz son of Zadok and Jonathan s	NIH
	16: 5	His name was Shimei s of Gera,	1201
	16: 8	the kingdom over to your s Absalom.	1201
	16: 9	Then Abishai s of Zeruiah said to the king,	1201
2Sa	16:11	"My s, who is of my own flesh,	1201
	16:19	Should I not serve the s?	1201
	17:25	Amasa was the s of a man named Jether,	1201
	17:27	Shobi s of Nahash from Rabbah of	1201
	17:27	and Makir s of Ammiel from Lo Debar,	1201
	18: 2	under Joab's brother Abishai s of Zeruiah,	1201
	18:12	not lift my hand against the king's s.	1201
	18:18	"I have no s to carry on the memory	1201
	18:19	Now Ahimaaz s of Zadok said,	1201
	18:20	because the king's s is dead."	1201
	18:22	Ahimaaz s of Zadok again said to Joab,	1201
	18:22	But Joab replied, "My s,	1201
	18:27	to me that the first one runs like Ahimaaz s	1201
	18:33	As he went, he said: "O my s Absalom!	1201
	18:33	My s, my son Absalom!	1201
	18:33	My son, my s Absalom!	1201
	18:33	O Absalom, my s, my son!	1201
	18:33	O Absalom, my son, my s!"	1201
	19: 2	"The king is grieving for his s."	1201
	19: 4	"O my s Absalom!	1201
	19: 4	O Absalom, my s, my son!	1201
	19: 4	O Absalom, my son, my s!"	1201
	19:16	Shimei s of Gera, the Benjamite	1201
	19:18	When Shimei s of Gera crossed the Jordan,	1201
	19:21	Then Abishai s of Zeruiah said,	1201
	20: 1	a troublemaker named Sheba s of Bicri,	1201
	20: 1	no part in Jesse's s!	1201
	20: 2	of Israel deserted David to follow Sheba s	1201
	20: 6	to Abishai, "Now Sheba s of Bicri	1201
	20: 7	from Jerusalem to pursue Sheba s of Bicri.	1201
	20:10	and his brother Abishai pursued Sheba s	1201
	20:13	on with Joab to pursue Sheba s of Bicri.	1201
	20:21	A man named Sheba s of Bicri,	1201
	20:22	the head of Sheba s of Bicri and threw it	1201
	20:23	Benaiah s of Jehoiada was over	1201
	20:24	Jehoshaphat s of Ahilud was recorder;	1201
	21: 7	The king spared Mephibosheth s of	1201
	21: 7	son of Jonathan, the s of Saul,	1201
	21: 7	the LORD between David and Jonathan s	1201
	21: 8	to Adriel s of Barzillai the Meholathite.	1201
	21:12	of Saul and his s Jonathan from the citizens	1201
	21:13	of Saul and his s Jonathan from there,	1201
	21:14	the bones of Saul and his s Jonathan in	1201
	21:17	But Abishai s of Zeruiah came	1201
	21:19	Elhanan s of Jaare-Oregim	1201
	21:21	he taunted Israel, Jonathan s of Shimeah,	1201
	23: 1	"The oracle of David s of Jesse,	1201
	23: 9	to him was Eleazar s of Dodai the Ahohite.	1201
	23:11	Next to him was Shammah s of Agee	1201
	23:18	of Joab s of Zeruiah was chief of the Three.	1201
	23:20	Benaiah s of Jehoiada was a valiant fighter	1201
	23:22	the exploits of Benaiah s of Jehoiada;	1201
	23:24	Elhanan s of Dodo from Bethlehem,	1201
	23:26	Ira s of Ikkesh from Tekoa,	1201
	23:29	Heled s of Baanah the Netophathite.	1201
	23:29	Ithai s of Ribai from Gibeah in Benjamin,	1201
	23:33	s of Shammah the Hararite,	1201
	23:33	Ahiam s of Sharar the Hararite,	1201
	23:34	Eliphelet s of Ahasbai the Maacathite,	1201
	23:34	Eliam s of Ahithophel the Gilonite.	1201
	23:36	Igal s of Nathan from Zobah,	1201
	23:36	Nathan from Zobah, the s of Hagri,	1201
	23:37	the armor-bearer of Joab s of Zeruiah,	1201
1Ki	1: 7	Adonijah conferred with Joab s of Zeruiah	1201
	1: 8	Zadok the priest, Benaiah s of Jehoiada,	1201
	1:11	Adonijah, the s of Haggith,	1201
	1:12	and the life of your s Solomon.	1201
	1:13	"Surely Solomon your s shall be king	1201
	1:17	'Solomon your s shall be king after me,	1201
	1:21	I and my s Solomon will be treated	1201
	1:26	and Benaiah s of Jehoiada,	1201
	1:30	Solomon your s shall be king after me,	1201
	1:32	the prophet and Benaiah s of Jehoiada."	1201
	1:33	and set Solomon my s on my own mule	1201
	1:36	Benaiah s of Jehoiada answered the king,	1201
	1:38	Nathan the prophet, Benaiah s of Jehoiada,	1201
	1:42	Jonathan s of Abiathar the priest arrived.	1201
	1:44	Nathan the prophet, Benaiah s of Jehoiada,	1201
	2: 1	he gave a charge to Solomon his s.	1201
	2: 5	"Now you yourself know what Joab s	1201
	2: 5	Abner s of Ner and Amasa son of Jether.	1201
	2: 5	Abner son of Ner and Amasa s of Jether.	1201
	2: 8	you have with you Shimei s of Gera,	1201
	2:13	Now Adonijah, the s of Haggith,	1201
	2:22	and for Abiathar the priest and Joab s	1201
	2:25	So King Solomon gave orders to Benaiah s	1201
	2:29	Solomon ordered Benaiah s of Jehoiada	1201
	2:32	Both of them—Abner s of Ner,	1201
	2:32	and Amasa s of Jether,	1201
	2:34	So Benaiah s of Jehoiada went up	1201
	2:35	The king put Benaiah s of Jehoiada over	1201
	2:39	two of Shimei's slaves ran off to Achish s	1201
	2:46	Then the king gave the order to Benaiah s	1201
	3: 6	a s to sit on his throne this very day.	1201
	3:19	"During the night this woman's s died	1201
	3:20	up in the middle of the night and took my s	1201
	3:20	and put her dead s by my breast.	1201
	3:21	The next morning, I got up to nurse my s—	1201
	3:21	I saw that it wasn't the s I had borne."	1201
	3:22	The living one is my s;	1201
	3:23	'My s is alive and your son is dead,'	1201
	3:23	'My son is alive and your s is dead,'	1201
	3:23	Your s is dead and mine is alive.' "	1201
	3:26	The woman whose s was alive was filled	1201
	3:26	with compassion for her s and said to	1201
	4: 2	Azariah s of Zadok—	1201
	4: 3	Jehoshaphat s of Ahilud—	1201

Ref		Text	Num
1Ki	4: 4	Benaiah s of Jehoiada—commander in chief	1201
	4: 5	Azariah s of Nathan—in charge of	1201
	4: 5	Zabud s of Nathan—a priest and	1201
	4: 6	Adoniram s of Abda—in charge of	1201
	4:12	Baana s of Ahilud—in Taanach and	1201
	4:13	(the settlements of Jair s of Manasseh	1201
	4:14	Ahinadab s of Iddo—in Mahanaim;	1201
	4:16	Baana s of Hushai—in Asher and	1201
	4:17	Jehoshaphat s of Paruah—in Issachar;	1201
	4:18	Shimei s of Ela—in Benjamin;	1201
	4:19	Geber s of Uri—in Gilead	1201
	5: 5	'Your s whom I will put on the throne	1201
	5: 7	a wise s to rule over this great nation."	1201
	8:19	your s, who is your own flesh and blood—	1201
	11:12	I will tear it out of the hand of your s.	1201
	11:20	of Tahpenes bore him a s named Genubath,	1201
	11:23	another adversary, Rezon s of Eliada,	1201
	11:26	Jeroboam s of Nebat rebelled against	1201
	11:36	I will give one tribe to his s so	1201
	11:43	Rehoboam his s succeeded him as king.	1201
	12: 2	When Jeroboam s of Nebat	1201
	12:15	to Jeroboam s of Nebat through Ahijah	1201
	12:16	what part in Jesse's s?	1201
	12:21	and to regain the kingdom for Rehoboam s	1201
	12:23	to Rehoboam s of Solomon king of Judah,	1201
	13: 2	'A s named Josiah will be born to the house	1201
	14: 1	that time Abijah s of Jeroboam became ill,	1201
	14: 5	to ask you about her s,	1201
	14:20	And Nadab his s succeeded him as king.	1201
	14:21	Rehoboam s of Solomon was king	1201
	14:31	And Abijah his s succeeded him as king.	1201
	15: 1	of the reign of Jeroboam s of Nebat,	1201
	15: 4	a lamp in Jerusalem by raising up a s	1201
	15: 8	And Asa his s succeeded him as king.	1201
	15:18	to Ben-Hadad s of Tabrimmon,	1201
	15:18	the s of Hezion, the king of Aram,	1201
	15:24	Jehoshaphat his s succeeded him as king.	1201
	15:25	Nadab s of Jeroboam became king of Israel	1201
	15:27	Baasha s of Ahijah of the house of	1201
	15:33	Baasha s of Ahijah became king	1201
	16: 1	of the LORD came to Jehu s of Hanani	1201
	16: 3	like that of Jeroboam s of Nebat.	1201
	16: 6	And Elah his s succeeded him as king.	1201
	16: 7	the prophet Jehu s of Hanani to Baasha	1201
	16: 8	Elah s of Baasha became king of Israel,	1201
	16:13	and his s Elah had committed	1201
	16:21	half supported Tibni s of Ginath for king,	1201
	16:22	than those of Tibni s of Ginath.	1201
	16:26	in all the ways of Jeroboam s of Nebat and	1201
	16:28	And Ahab his s succeeded him as king.	1201
	16:29	Ahab s of Omri became king of Israel,	1201
	16:30	Ahab s of Omri did more evil in the eyes of	1201
	16:31	to commit the sins of Jeroboam s of Nebat,	1201
	16:34	at the cost of his **firstborn** s Abiram,	AIT
	16:34	at the cost of his **youngest** s Segub,	AIT
	16:34	the word of the LORD spoken by Joshua s	1201
	17:12	for myself and my s, that we may eat it—	1201
	17:13	make something for yourself and your s.	1201
	17:17	the s of the woman who owned	1201
	17:18	to remind me of my sin and kill my s?"	1201
	17:19	"Give me your s," Elijah replied.	1201
	17:20	by causing her s to die?"	1201
	17:23	"Look, your s is alive!"	1201
	19:16	anoint Jehu s of Nimshi king over Israel,	1201
	19:16	and anoint Elisha s of Shaphat	1201
	19:19	from there and found Elisha s of Shaphat.	1201
	21:22	like that of Jeroboam s of Nebat and that	1201
	21:22	of Nebat and that of Baasha s of Ahijah,	1201
	21:29	on his house in the days of his s."	1201
	22: 8	He is Micaiah s of Imlah."	1201
	22: 9	"Bring Micaiah s of Imlah at once."	1201
	22:11	Now Zedekiah s of Kenaanah	1201
	22:24	Then Zedekiah s of Kenaanah went up	1201
	22:26	of the city and to Joash the king's s	1201
	22:40	And Ahaziah his s succeeded him as king.	1201
	22:41	Jehoshaphat s of Asa became king of Judah	1201
	22:49	At that time Ahaziah s of Ahab said	1201
	22:50	And Jehoram his s succeeded him.	1201
	22:51	Ahaziah s of Ahab became king of Israel	1201
	22:52	and mother and in the ways of Jeroboam s	1201
2Ki	1:17	Because Ahaziah had no s,	1201
	1:17	of Jehoram s of Jehoshaphat king of Judah.	1201
	3: 1	Joram s of Ahab became king of Israel	1201
	3: 3	to the sins of Jeroboam s of Nebat,	1201
	3:11	"Elisha s of Shaphat is here.	1201
	3:27	Then he took his firstborn s,	1201
	4: 6	she said to her s, "Bring me another one."	1201
	4:14	"Well, she has no s and her husband is old."	1201
	4:16	"you will hold a s in your arms."	1201
	4:17	about that same time she gave birth to a s,	1201
	4:28	"Did I ask you for a s, my lord?"	1201
	4:36	When she came, he said, "Take your s."	1201
	4:37	Then she took her s and went out.	1201
	6:28	'Give up your s so we may eat him today,	1201
	6:28	and tomorrow we'll eat my s.'	1201
	6:29	So we cooked my s and ate him.	1201
	6:29	'Give up your s so we may eat him,'	1201
	6:31	if the head of Elisha s of Shaphat remains	1201
	8: 1	the woman whose s he had restored to life,	1201
	8: 5	the woman whose s Elisha had brought back	1201
	8: 5	this is her s whom Elisha restored to life."	1201
	8: 9	"Your s Ben-Hadad king of Aram	1201
	8:16	In the fifth year of Joram s of Ahab king	1201
	8:16	Jehoram s of Jehoshaphat began his reign	1201
	8:24	And Ahaziah his s succeeded him as king.	1201
	8:25	In the twelfth year of Joram s of Ahab king	1201
	8:25	Ahaziah s of Jehoram king of Judah began	1201

Ref		Text	Num
2Ki	8:28	Ahaziah went with Joram s of Ahab to war	1201
	8:29	Then Ahaziah s of Jehoram king	1201
	8:29	down to Jezreel to see Joram s of Ahab,	1201
	9: 2	look for Jehu s of Jehoshaphat.	1201
	9: 2	Jehoshaphat, the s of Nimshi.	1201
	9: 9	of Jeroboam s of Nebat and like the house	1201
	9: 9	and like the house of Baasha s of Ahijah.	1201
	9:14	So Jehu s of Jehoshaphat,	1201
	9:14	Jehu son of Jehoshaphat, the s of Nimshi,	1201
	9:20	The driving is like that of Jehu s	1201
	9:29	(In the eleventh year of Joram s of Ahab,	1201
	10:15	he came upon Jehonadab s of Recab,	1201
	10:23	Then Jehu and Jehonadab s of Recab went	1201
	10:29	not turn away from the sins of Jeroboam s	1201
	10:35	And Jehoahaz his s succeeded him as king.	1201
	11: 1	of Ahaziah saw that her s was dead,	1201
	11: 2	took Joash s of Ahaziah and stole him away	1201
	11: 4	Then he showed them the king's s.	1201
	11:12	Jehoiada brought out the king's s and put	1201
	12:21	The officials who murdered him were Jozabad s of Shimeath	1201
	12:21	of Shimeath and Jehozabad s of Shomer.	1201
	12:21	And Amaziah s of Amaziah king of Judah.	1201
	13: 1	of Joash s of Ahaziah king of Judah,	1201
	13: 1	Jehoahaz s of Jehu became king of Israel	1201
	13: 2	by following the sins of Jeroboam s	1201
	13: 3	of Aram and Ben-Hadad his s.	1201
	13: 9	And Jehoash his s succeeded him as king.	1201
	13:10	Jehoash s of Jehoahaz became king	1201
	13:11	of the sins of Jeroboam s of Nebat,	1201
	13:24	Ben-Hadad his s succeeded him as king.	1201
	13:25	Then Jehoash s of Jehoahaz recaptured	1201
	13:25	of Jehoahaz recaptured from Ben-Hadad s	1201
	14: 1	of Jehoash s of Jehoahaz king of Israel,	1201
	14: 1	Amaziah s of Joash king of Judah began	1201
	14: 8	to Jehoash s of Jehoahaz, the son	1201
	14: 8	the s of Jehu, king of Israel,	1201
	14: 9	'Give your daughter to my s in marriage.'	1201
	14:13	the s of Joash, the son of Ahaziah,	1201
	14:13	s of Ahaziah, at Beth Shemesh.	1201
	14:16	And Jeroboam his s succeeded him as king.	1201
	14:17	Amaziah s of Joash king of Judah lived	1201
	14:17	for fifteen years after the death of Jehoash s	1201
	14:23	of Amaziah s of Joash king of Judah,	1201
	14:23	Jeroboam s of Jehoash king of Israel	1201
	14:24	of the sins of Jeroboam s of Nebat,	1201
	14:25	through his servant Jonah s of Amittai,	1201
	14:27	he saved them by the hand of Jeroboam s	1201
	14:29	And Zechariah his s succeeded him as king.	1201
	15: 1	Azariah s of Amaziah king of Judah began	1201
	15: 5	the king's s had charge of the palace	1201
	15: 7	And Jotham his s succeeded him as king.	1201
	15: 8	Zechariah s of Jeroboam became king	1201
	15: 9	not turn away from the sins of Jeroboam s	1201
	15:10	Shallum s of Jabesh conspired against	1201
	15:13	Shallum s of Jabesh became king in	1201
	15:14	Then Menahem s of Gadi went from Tirzah	1201
	15:14	He attacked Shallum s of Jabesh	1201
	15:17	Menahem s of Gadi became king of Israel,	1201
	15:18	not turn away from the sins of Jeroboam s	1201
	15:22	And Pekahiah his s succeeded him as king.	1201
	15:23	Pekahiah s of Menahem became king	1201
	15:24	not turn away from the sins of Jeroboam s	1201
	15:25	Pekah s of Remaliah, conspired against	1201
	15:27	Pekah s of Remaliah became king of Israel	1201
	15:28	not turn away from the sins of Jeroboam s	1201
	15:30	Then Hoshea s of Elah conspired against	1201
	15:30	conspired against Pekah s of Remaliah.	1201
	15:30	in the twentieth year of Jotham s of Uzziah.	1201
	15:32	of Pekah s of Remaliah king of Israel,	1201
	15:32	Jotham s of Uzziah king of Judah began	1201
	15:37	and Pekah s of Remaliah against Judah.)	1201
	15:38	And Ahaz his s succeeded him as king.	1201
	16: 1	In the seventeenth year of Pekah s	1201
	16: 1	Ahaz s of Jotham king of Judah began	1201
	16: 3	the kings of Israel and even sacrificed his s	1201
	16: 5	of Aram and Pekah s of Remaliah king	1201
	16:20	And Hezekiah his s succeeded him as king.	1201
	17: 1	Hoshea s of Elah became king of Israel	1201
	17:21	they made Jeroboam s of Nebat their king.	1201
	18: 1	In the third year of Hoshea s of Elah king	1201
	18: 1	Hezekiah s of Ahaz king of Judah began	1201
	18: 9	the seventh year of Hoshea s of Elah king	1201
	18:18	and Eliakim s of Hilkiah	1201
	18:18	and Joah s of Asaph the recorder went out	1201
	18:26	Then Eliakim s of Hilkiah,	1201
	18:37	Then Eliakim s of Hilkiah	1201
	18:37	Shebna the secretary and Joah s of Asaph	1201
	19: 2	to the prophet Isaiah s of Amoz.	1201
	19:20	Then Isaiah s of Amoz sent a message	1201
	19:37	Esarhaddon his s succeeded him as king.	1201
	20: 1	The prophet Isaiah s of Amoz went to him	1201
	20:12	At that time Merodach-Baladan s of	1201
	20:21	And Manasseh his s succeeded him as king.	1201
	21: 6	He sacrificed his own s in the fire,	1201
	21: 7	to David and to his Solomon,	1201
	21:18	And Amon his s succeeded him as king.	1201
	21:24	they made Josiah his s king in his place.	1201
	21:26	And Josiah his s succeeded him as king.	1201
	22: 3	Shaphan s of Azaliah,	1201
	22: 3	Azaliah, the s of Meshullam,	1201
	22:12	Ahikam s of Shaphan,	1201
	22:12	Acbor s of Micaiah, Shaphan the secretary	1201
	22:14	who was the wife of Shallum s of Tikvah,	1201
	22:14	the s of Harhas, keeper of the wardrobe.	1201
	23:10	to sacrifice his s or daughter in the fire	1201
	23:15	the high place made by Jeroboam s of	1201

Ref		Text	Num
2Ki	23:30	And the people of the land took Jehoahaz s	1201
	23:34	Pharaoh Neco made Eliakim s of Josiah	1201
	24: 6	Jehoiachin his s succeeded him as king.	1201
	25:22	king of Babylon appointed Gedaliah s of	1201
	25:22	son of Ahikam, the s of Shaphan,	1201
	25:23	Ishmael s of Nethaniah,	1201
	25:23	Ishmael son of Nethaniah, Johanan s	1201
	25:23	Seraiah s of Tanhumeth the Netophathite,	1201
	25:23	Jaazaniah the s of the Maacathite,	1201
	25:25	however, Ishmael s of Nethaniah,	1201
	25:25	the s of Elishama, who was of royal blood,	1201
1Ch	1:41	The s of Anah: Dishon.	1201
	1:43	Bela s of Beor, whose city was named	1201
	1:44	Jobab s of Zerah from Bozrah	1201
	1:46	When Husham died, Hadad s of Bedad,	1201
	1:49	Baal-Hanan s of Acbor succeeded him	1201
	2: 7	The s of Carmi: Achar, who brought trouble	1201
	2: 8	The s of Ethan: Azariah.	1201
	2:13	the second s was Abinadab,	NIH
	2:18	Caleb s of Hezron had children	1201
	2:31	The s of Appaim: Ishi,	1201
	2:42	the father of Ziph, and his s Mareshah,	1201
	2:45	The s of Shammai was Maon,	1201
	3: 1	The firstborn s was Amnon the s of Ahinoam	NIH
	3: 1	second, Daniel the s of Abigail of Carmel;	NIH
	3: 2	the s of Maacah daughter of Talmai king	1201
	3: 2	the fourth, Adonijah the s of Haggith;	1201
	3: 3	Shephatiah the s of Abital;	NIH
	3:10	Solomon's s was Rehoboam,	1201
	3:10	Abijah his s, Asa his son.	1201
	3:10	Asa his s, Jehoshaphat his son,	1201
	3:10	Asa his son, Jehoshaphat his s,	1201
	3:11	Jehoram his s, Ahaziah his son,	1201
	3:11	Ahaziah his s, Joash his son,	1201
	3:11	Ahaziah his son, Joash his s,	1201
	3:12	Amaziah his s, Azariah his son,	1201
	3:12	Azariah his s, Jotham his son,	1201
	3:12	Azariah his son, Jotham his s,	1201
	3:13	Ahaz his s, Hezekiah his son,	1201
	3:13	Hezekiah his s, Manasseh his son,	1201
	3:13	Hezekiah his son, Manasseh his s,	1201
	3:14	Amon his s, Josiah his son.	1201
	3:14	Amon his son, Josiah his s.	1201
	3:15	Jehoiakim the second s, Zedekiah the third,	NIH
	3:16	Jehoiachin his s, and Zedekiah.	1201
	3:17	of Jehoiachin the captive: Shealtiel his s,	1201
	4: 2	Reaiah s of Shobal was the father	1201
	4: 8	and of the clans of Aharhel s of Harum.	1201
	4:15	The sons of Caleb s of Jephunneh:	1201
	4:15	The s of Elah: Kenaz.	1201
	4:21	The sons of Shelah s of Judah:	1201
	4:25	Shallum was Shaul's s,	1201
	4:25	Mibsam his s and Mishma his son.	1201
	4:25	Mibsam his son and Mishma his s.	1201
	4:26	Hammuel his s, Zaccur his son	1201
	4:26	Zaccur his s and Shimei his son.	1201
	4:26	Zaccur his son and Shimei his s.	1201
	4:34	Meshobab, Jamlech, Joshah s of Amaziah,	1201
	4:35	Jehu s of Joshibiah, the son of Seraiah,	1201
	4:35	Jehu son of Joshibiah, the s of Seraiah,	1201
	4:35	the son of Seraiah, the s of Asiel,	1201
	4:37	and Ziza s of Shiphi,	1201
	4:37	the s of Allon, the son of Jedaiah,	1201
	4:37	the s of Jedaiah, the son of Shimri,	1201
	4:37	the s of Shimri, the son of Shemaiah.	1201
	4:37	the son of Shimri, the s of Shemaiah.	1201
	5: 1	to the sons of Joseph s of Israel;	1201
	5: 4	The descendants of Joel: Shemaiah his s,	1201
	5: 4	Shemaiah his son, Gog his s,	1201
	5: 4	Gog his son, Shimei his s,	1201
	5: 5	Micah his s, Reaiah his son, Baal his son,	1201
	5: 5	Micah his son, Reaiah his s, Baal his son,	1201
	5: 5	Micah his son, Reaiah his son, Baal his s,	1201
	5: 6	and Beerah his s, whom Tiglath-Pileser	1201
	5: 8	and Bela s of Azaz, the son of Shema,	1201
	5: 8	the s of Shema, the son of Joel.	1201
	5: 8	the son of Shema, the s of Joel.	1201
	5:14	These were the sons of Abihail s of Huri,	1201
	5:14	the s of Jaroah, the son of Gilead,	1201
	5:14	the s of Gilead, the son of Michael,	1201
	5:14	the s of Michael, the son of Jeshishai,	1201
	5:14	the son of Michael, the s of Jeshishai,	1201
	5:14	the son of Jeshishai, the s of Jahdo,	1201
	5:14	the son of Jahdo, the s of Buz.	1201
	5:15	Ahi s of Abdiel, the son of Guni,	1201
	5:15	Ahi son of Abdiel, the s of Guni,	1201
	6:20	Libni his s, Jehath his son, Zimmah his son,	1201
	6:20	Libni his son, Jehath his s, Zimmah his son,	1201
	6:20	Libni his son, Jehath his son, Zimmah his s,	1201
	6:21	Joah his s, Iddo his son, Zerah his son	1201
	6:21	Iddo his s, Zerah his son	1201
	6:21	Zerah his s and Jeatherai his son.	1201
	6:21	Zerah his son and Jeatherai his s.	1201
	6:22	Amminadab his s, Korah his son,	1201
	6:22	Amminadab his son, Korah his s,	1201
	6:22	Korah his son, Assir his s,	1201
	6:23	Elkanah his s, Ebiasaph his son,	1201
	6:23	Ebiasaph his s, Assir his son,	1201
	6:23	Ebiasaph his son, Assir his s,	1201
	6:24	Tahath his s, Uriel his son, Uzziah his son	1201
	6:24	Uriel his s, Uzziah his son	1201
	6:24	Uzziah his s and Shaul his son.	1201
	6:24	Uzziah his son and Shaul his s.	1201
	6:26	Elkanah his s, Zophai his son,	1201
	6:26	Zophai his s, Nahath his son,	1201
	6:26	Zophai his son, Nahath his s,	1201
	6:27	Eliab his s, Jeroham his son,	1201

1Ch	6:27	Jeroham his s, Elkanah his son,	1201
	6:27	Elkanah his s and Samuel his son.	1201
	6:27	Elkanah his son and Samuel his s.	1201
	6:28	Joel the firstborn and Abijah the second s.	NIH
	6:29	Mahli, Libni his s, Shimei his son,	1201
	6:29	Mahli, Libni his son, Shimei his s,	1201
	6:29	Libni his son, Shimei his son, Uzzah his s,	1201
	6:30	Shimea his s, Haggiah his son	1201
	6:30	Haggiah his s and Asaiah his son.	1201
	6:30	Haggiah his son and Asaiah his s.	1201
	6:33	Heman, the musician, the s of Joel,	1201
	6:33	the son of Joel, the s of Samuel,	1201
	6:34	the s of Elkanah, the son of Jeroham,	1201
	6:34	the s of Jeroham, the son of Eliel,	1201
	6:34	the son of Jeroham, the s of Eliel,	1201
	6:34	the son of Eliel, the s of Toah,	1201
	6:35	the s of Zuph, the son of Elkanah,	1201
	6:35	the s of Elkanah, the son of Mahath,	1201
	6:35	the son of Elkanah, the s of Mahath,	1201
	6:35	the son of Mahath, the s of Amasai,	1201
	6:36	the s of Elkanah, the son of Joel,	1201
	6:36	the s of Joel, the son of Azariah,	1201
	6:36	the s of Azariah, the son of Zephaniah,	1201
	6:36	the son of Azariah, the s of Zephaniah,	1201
	6:37	the s of Tahath, the son of Assir,	1201
	6:37	the s of Assir, the son of Ebiasaph,	1201
	6:37	the s of Ebiasaph, the son of Korah,	1201
	6:37	the son of Ebiasaph, the s of Korah,	1201
	6:38	the s of Izhar, the son of Kohath, the son	1201
	6:38	the s of Kohath, the son of Levi,	1201
	6:38	the son of Kohath, the s of Levi,	1201
	6:38	the son of Levi, the s of Israel;	1201
	6:39	Asaph s of Berekiah, the son of Shimea,	1201
	6:39	Asaph son of Berekiah, the s of Shimea,	1201
	6:40	the s of Michael, the son of Baaseiah,	1201
	6:40	the s of Baaseiah, the son of Malkijah,	1201
	6:40	the son of Baaseiah, the s of Malkijah,	1201
	6:41	the s of Ethni, the son of Zerah,	1201
	6:41	the s of Zerah, the son of Adaiah,	1201
	6:41	the son of Zerah, the s of Adaiah,	1201
	6:42	the s of Ethan, the son of Zimmah,	1201
	6:42	the s of Zimmah, the son of Shimei,	1201
	6:42	the son of Zimmah, the s of Shimei,	1201
	6:43	the s of Jahath, the son of Gershon, the son	1201
	6:43	the s of Gershon, the son of Levi;	1201
	6:43	the son of Gershon, the s of Levi;	1201
	6:44	Ethan s of Kishi, the son of Abdi,	1201
	6:44	Ethan son of Kishi, the s of Abdi,	1201
	6:44	the son of Abdi, the s of Malluch,	1201
	6:45	the s of Hashabiah, the son of Amaziah,	1201
	6:45	the s of Amaziah, the son of Hilkiah,	1201
	6:45	the son of Amaziah, the s of Hilkiah,	1201
	6:46	the s of Amzi, the son of Bani,	1201
	6:46	the s of Bani, the son of Shemer,	1201
	6:46	the son of Bani, the s of Shemer,	1201
	6:47	the s of Mahli, the son of Mushi,	1201
	6:47	the s of Mushi, the son of Merari,	1201
	6:47	the son of Mushi, the s of Merari,	1201
	6:47	the son of Merari, the s of Levi.	1201
	6:50	Eleazar his s, Phinehas his son,	1201
	6:50	Eleazar his s, Phinehas his son,	1201
	6:50	Phinehas his son, Abishua his s,	1201
	6:51	Bukki his s, Uzzi his son, Zerahiah his son,	1201
	6:51	Bukki his s, Uzzi his son, Zerahiah his son,	1201
	6:51	Bukki his son, Uzzi his son, Zerahiah his s,	1201
	6:52	Meraioth his s, Amariah his son,	1201
	6:52	Amariah his s, Ahitub his son,	1201
	6:52	Amariah his son, Ahitub his s,	1201
	6:53	Zadok his s and Ahimaaz his son.	1201
	6:53	Zadok his son and Ahimaaz his s.	1201
	6:56	around the city were given to Caleb s	1201
	7: 3	The s of Uzzi: Izrahiah.	1201
	7:10	The s of Jediael: Bilhan.	1201
	7:16	Makir's wife Maacah gave birth to a s	1201
	7:17	The s of Ulam: Bedan.	1201
	7:17	These were the sons of Gilead s of Makir,	1201
	7:17	son of Makir, the s of Manasseh.	1201
	7:20	Shuthelah, Bered his s, Tahath his son,	1201
	7:20	Shuthelah, Bered his son, Tahath his s,	1201
	7:20	Eleadah his s, Tahath his son,	1201
	7:20	Eleadah his son, Tahath his s,	1201
	7:21	Zabad his s and Shuthelah his son.	1201
	7:21	Zabad his son and Shuthelah his s.	1201
	7:23	she became pregnant and gave birth to a s.	1201
	7:25	Rephah was his s, Resheph his son,	1201
	7:25	Rephah was his son, Resheph his s,	NIH
	7:25	Resheph his son, Telah his s,	1201
	7:25	Telah his son, Tahan his s,	1201
	7:26	Ladan his s, Ammihud his son,	1201
	7:26	Ammihud his s, Elishama his son,	1201
	7:26	Ammihud his son, Elishama his s,	1201
	7:27	Nun his s and Joshua his son.	1201
	7:27	Nun his son and Joshua his s.	1201
	7:29	The descendants of Joseph s of Israel lived	1201
	8: 1	Ashbel the second s, Aharah the third,	NIH
	8:30	and his firstborn s was Abdon,	1201
	8:34	The s of Jonathan: Merib-Baal.	1201
	8:37	Raphah was his s,	1201
	8:37	Eleasah his s and Azel his son.	1201
	8:37	Eleasah his son and Azel his s.	1201
	8:39	Jeush the second s and Eliphelet the third.	NIH
	9: 4	Uthai s of Ammihud, the son of Omri,	1201
	9: 4	the s of Omri, the son of Imri,	1201
	9: 4	the son of Omri, the s of Imri,	1201
	9: 4	the son of Imri, the s of Bani,	1201
	9: 4	a descendant of Perez s of Judah.	1201
	9: 7	Sallu s of Meshullam, the son of Hodaviah,	1201

1Ch	9: 7	Sallu son of Meshullam, the s of Hodaviah,	1201
	9: 7	the son of Hodaviah, the s of Hassenuah;	1201
	9: 8	Ibneiah s of Jeroham;	1201
	9: 8	Elah s of Uzzi, the son of Micri,	1201
	9: 8	Elah son of Uzzi, the s of Micri;	1201
	9: 8	and Meshullam s of Shephatiah,	1201
	9: 8	the s of Reuel, the son of Ibnijah.	1201
	9: 8	the son of Reuel, the s of Ibnijah.	1201
	9:11	Azariah s of Hilkiah, the son of Meshullam,	1201
	9:11	the s of Meshullam, the son of Zadok,	1201
	9:11	the son of Meshullam, the s of Zadok,	1201
	9:11	the s of Meraioth, the son of Ahitub,	1201
	9:11	the son of Meraioth, the s of Ahitub,	1201
	9:12	Adaiah s of Jeroham, the son of Pashhur,	1201
	9:12	the s of Pashhur, the son of Malkijah;	1201
	9:12	the son of Pashhur, the s of Malkijah;	1201
	9:12	and Maasai s of Adiel, the son of Jahzerah,	1201
	9:12	and Maasai son of Adiel, the s of Jahzerah,	1201
	9:12	the son of Jahzerah, the s of Meshullam,	1201
	9:12	the s of Meshillemith, the son of Immer.	1201
	9:12	the son of Meshillemith, the s of Immer.	1201
	9:14	Of the Levites: Shemaiah s of Hasshub,	1201
	9:14	the s of Azrikam, the son of Hashabiah,	1201
	9:14	the son of Azrikam, the s of Hashabiah,	1201
	9:15	Heresh, Galal and Mattaniah s of Mica,	1201
	9:15	the s of Zicri, the son of Asaph;	1201
	9:15	the son of Zicri, the s of Asaph;	1201
	9:16	Obadiah s of Shemaiah, the son of Galal,	1201
	9:16	the s of Galal, the son of Jeduthun;	1201
	9:16	the son of Galal, the s of Jeduthun;	1201
	9:16	and Berekiah s of Asa, the son of Elkanah,	1201
	9:16	and Berekiah son of Asa, the s of Elkanah,	1201
	9:19	Shallum s of Kore, the son of Ebiasaph,	1201
	9:19	Shallum son of Kore, the s of Ebiasaph,	1201
	9:19	the s of Ebiasaph, the son of Korah,	1201
	9:20	In earlier times Phinehas s of Eleazar was	1201
	9:21	Zechariah s of Meshelemiah was	1201
	9:31	the firstborn s of Shallum the Korahite,	NIH
	9:36	and his firstborn s was Abdon,	1201
	9:40	The s of Jonathan: Merib-Baal,	1201
	9:43	Rephaiah was his s,	1201
	9:43	Eleasah his s and Azel his son.	1201
	9:43	Eleasah his son and Azel his s.	1201
	10:14	and turned the kingdom over to David s	1201
	11: 6	Joab s of Zeruiah went up first,	1201
	11:12	to him was Eleazar s of Dodai the Ahohite,	1201
	11:22	Benaiah s of Jehoiada was a valiant fighter	1201
	11:24	the exploits of Benaiah s of Jehoiada;	1201
	11:26	Elhanan s of Dodo from Bethlehem;	1201
	11:28	Ira s of Ikkesh from Tekoa,	1201
	11:30	Heled s of Baanah the Netophathite,	1201
	11:31	Ithai s of Ribai from Gibeah in Benjamin,	1201
	11:34	Jonathan s of Shagee the Hararite,	1201
	11:35	Ahiam s of Sacar the Hararite,	1201
	11:35	Eliphal s of Ur,	1201
	11:37	Hezro the Carmelite, Naarai s of Ezbai,	1201
	11:38	Mibhar s of Hagri,	1201
	11:39	the armor-bearer of Joab s of Zeruiah,	1201
	11:41	Uriah the Hittite, Zabad s of Ahlai,	1201
	11:42	Adina s of Shiza the Reubenite,	1201
	11:43	Hanan s of Maacah,	1201
	11:45	Jediael s of Shimri,	1201
	12: 1	from the presence of Saul s of Kish	1201
	12:18	We are with you, O s of Jesse!	1201
	15:17	So the Levites appointed Heman s of Joel;	1201
	15:17	from his brothers, Asaph s of Berekiah;	1201
	15:17	from their brothers the Merarites, Ethan s	1201
	16:38	Obed-Edom s of Jeduthun, and also Hosah,	1201
	17:13	I will be his father, and he will be my s.	1201
	18:10	he sent his s Hadoram to King David	1201
	18:12	Abishai s of Zeruiah struck down	1201
	18:15	Joab s of Zeruiah was over the army;	1201
	18:15	Jehoshaphat s of Ahilud was recorder;	1201
	18:16	Zadok s of Ahitub and Ahimelech son	1201
	18:16	and Ahimelech s of Abiathar were priests;	1201
	18:17	Benaiah s of Jehoiada was over	1201
	19: 1	and his son succeeded him as king.	1201
	19: 2	"I will show kindness to Hanun s	1201
	20: 5	Elhanan s of Jair killed Lahmi the brother	1201
	20: 7	he taunted Israel, Jonathan s of Shimea,	1201
	22: 5	"My s Solomon is young and inexperienced	1201
	22: 6	for his s Solomon and charged him to build	1201
	22: 7	David said to Solomon: "My s,	1201
	22: 9	But you will have a s who will be a man	1201
	22:10	He will be my s, and I will be his father.	1201
	22:11	"Now, my s, the LORD be with you,	1201
	22:17	the leaders of Israel to help his s Solomon.	1201
	23: 1	he made his s Solomon king over Israel.	1201
	24: 6	The scribe Shemaiah s of Nethanel,	1201
	24: 6	Zadok the priest, Ahimelech s of Abiathar	1201
	24:24	The s of Uzziel: Micah;	1201
	24:26	The s of Jaaziah: Beno.	1201
	24:29	From Kish: the s of Kish: Jerahmeel.	1201
	26: 1	Meshelemiah s of Kore,	1201
	26: 6	His s Shemaiah also had sons,	1201
	26:14	Then lots were cast for his s Zechariah,	1201
	26:24	a descendant of Gershom s of Moses,	1201
	26:25	Rehabiah his s, Jeshaiah his son,	1201
	26:25	Rehabiah his son, Jeshaiah his s,	1201
	26:25	Jeshaiah his son, Joram his s,	1201
	26:25	Zicri his s and Shelomith his son.	1201
	26:25	Zicri his son and Shelomith his s.	1201
	26:28	by Samuel the seer and by Saul s of Kish,	1201
	26:28	Abner s of Ner and Joab son of Zeruiah,	1201
	26:28	Abner son of Ner and Joab s of Zeruiah,	1201
	27: 2	was Jashobeam s of Zabdiel.	1201
	27: 5	was Benaiah s of Jehoiada the priest.	1201

1Ch	27: 6	His s Ammizabad was in charge	1201
	27: 7	his s Zebadiah was his successor.	1201
	27: 9	was Ira the s of Ikkesh the Tekoite.	1201
	27:16	over the Reubenites: Eliezer s of Zicri;	1201
	27:16	over the Simeonites: Shephatiah s of Maacah;	1201
	27:17	over Levi: Hashabiah s of Kemuel;	1201
	27:18	over Issachar: Omri s of Michael;	1201
	27:19	over Zebulun: Ishmaiah s of Obadiah;	1201
	27:19	over Naphtali: Jerimoth s of Azriel;	1201
	27:20	over the Ephraimites: Hoshea s of Azaziah;	1201
	27:20	of Manasseh: Joel s of Pedaiah;	1201
	27:21	Manasseh in Gilead: Iddo s of Zechariah;	1201
	27:21	over Benjamin: Jaasiel s of Abner;	1201
	27:22	over Dan: Azarel s of Jeroham.	1201
	27:24	Joab s of Zeruiah began to count the men	1201
	27:25	Azmaveth s of Adiel was in charge of	1201
	27:25	Jonathan s of Uzziah was in charge of	1201
	27:26	Ezri s of Kelub was in charge of	1201
	27:29	Shaphat s of Adlai was in charge of	1201
	27:32	Jehiel s of Hacmoni took care of	1201
	27:34	by Jehoiada s of Benaiah and by Abiathar.	1201
	28: 5	he has chosen my s Solomon to sit on	1201
	28: 6	'Solomon your s is the one who will build	1201
	28: 6	for I have chosen him to be my s,	1201
	28: 9	"And you, my s Solomon,	1201
	28:11	Then David gave his s Solomon the plans	1201
	28:20	David also said to Solomon his s,	1201
	29: 1	to the whole assembly: "My s Solomon,	1201
	29:19	give my s Solomon wholehearted devotion	1201
	29:22	Then they acknowledged Solomon s	1201
	29:26	David s of Jesse was king over all Israel.	1201
	29:28	His s Solomon succeeded him as king.	1201
2Ch	1: 1	Solomon s of David established himself firmly over his kingdom,	1201
	1: 5	But the bronze altar that Bezalel s of Uri,	1201
	1: 5	the s of Hur, had made was in Gibeon	1201
	2:12	He has given King David a wise s,	1201
	6: 9	your s, who is your own flesh and blood—	1201
	9:29	the seer concerning Jeroboam s of Nebat?	1201
	9:31	Rehoboam his s succeeded him as king.	1201
	10: 2	When Jeroboam s of Nebat heard this	1201
	10:15	to Jeroboam s of Nebat through Ahijah	1201
	10:16	what part in Jesse's s?	1201
	11: 3	to Rehoboam s of Solomon king of Judah	1201
	11:17	of Judah and supported Rehoboam s	1201
	11:18	who was the daughter of David's s Jerimoth	1201
	11:18	the daughter of Jesse's s Eliab.	1201
	11:22	Rehoboam appointed Abijah s of Maacah	1201
	12:16	And Abijah his s succeeded him as king.	1201
	13: 6	Yet Jeroboam s of Nebat,	1201
	13: 6	an official of Solomon s of David,	1201
	13: 7	and opposed Rehoboam s of Solomon	1201
	14: 1	Asa his s succeeded him as king,	1201
	15: 1	The Spirit of God came upon Azariah s	1201
	15: 8	and the prophecy of Azariah s of Oded	1201
	17: 1	Jehoshaphat his s succeeded him as king	1201
	17:16	Amasiah s of Zicri,	1201
	18: 7	He is Micaiah s of Imlah."	1201
	18: 8	"Bring Micaiah s of Imlah at once."	1201
	18:10	Now Zedekiah s of Kenaanah	1201
	18:23	Then Zedekiah s of Kenaanah went up	1201
	18:25	of the city and to Joash the king's s,	1201
	19: 2	Jehu the seer, the s of Hanani,	1201
	19:11	and Zebadiah s of Ishmael,	1201
	20:14	of the LORD came upon Jahaziel s	1201
	20:14	the s of Benaiah, the son of Jeiel,	1201
	20:14	the s of Jeiel, the son of Mattaniah,	1201
	20:14	the son of Jeiel, the s of Mattaniah,	1201
	20:34	in the annals of Jehu s of Hanani,	1201
	20:37	Eliezer s of Dodavahu	1201
	21: 1	And Jehoram his s succeeded him as king.	1201
	21: 3	to Jehoram because he was his firstborn s.	AIT
	21:17	Not a s was left to him except Ahaziah,	1201
	22: 1	Jehoram's youngest s, king in his place,	1201
	22: 1	So Ahaziah s of Jehoram king of Judah	1201
	22: 5	with Joram s of Ahab king of Israel to war	1201
	22: 6	Then Ahaziah s of Jehoram king of Judah	1201
	22: 6	down to Jezreel to see Joram s of Ahab	1201
	22: 7	he went out with Joram to meet Jehu s	1201
	22: 9	for they said, "He was a s of Jehoshaphat,	1201
	22:10	of Ahaziah saw that her s was dead,	1201
	22:11	took Joash s of Ahaziah and stole him away	1201
	23: 1	Azariah s of Jeroham,	1201
	23: 1	Ishmael s of Jehohanan,	1201
	23: 1	son of Jehohanan, Azariah s of Obed,	1201
	23: 1	Maaseiah s of Adaiah,	1201
	23: 1	and Elishaphat s of Zicri.	1201
	23: 3	"The king's s shall reign,	1201
	23:11	the king's s and put the crown on him;	1201
	24:20	of God came upon Zechariah s of Jehoiada	1201
	24:22	but killed his s, who said as he lay dying,	1201
	24:25	against him for murdering the s of Jehoiada	1201
	24:26	s of Shimeath an Ammonite woman,	1201
	24:26	s of Shimrith a Moabite woman.	1201
	24:27	And Amaziah his s succeeded him as king.	1201
	25:17	he sent this challenge to Jehoash s	1201
	25:17	the s of Jehu, king of Israel:	1201
	25:18	'Give your daughter to my s in marriage.'	1201
	25:23	the s of Joash, the son of Ahaziah,	1201
	25:23	the s of Ahaziah, at Beth Shemesh.	1201
	25:25	Amaziah s of Joash king of Judah lived	1201
	25:25	for fifteen years after the death of Jehoash s	1201
	26:21	Jotham his s had charge of the palace	1201
	26:22	are recorded by the prophet Isaiah s	1201
	26:23	And Jotham his s succeeded him as king.	1201
	27: 9	And Ahaz his s succeeded him as king.	1201
	28: 6	In one day Pekah s of Remaliah killed	1201

2Ch 28: 7	killed Maaseiah the king's s,	1201
28:12	Azariah s of Jehohanan,	1201
28:12	Berekiah s of Meshillemoth,	1201
28:12	Jehizkiah s of Shallum,	1201
28:12	and Amasa s of Hadlai—	1201
28:27	And Hezekiah his s succeeded him as king.	1201
29:12	from the Kohathites, Mahath s of Amasai	1201
29:12	Mahath son of Amasai and Joel s	1201
29:12	from the Merarites, Kish s of Abdi	1201
29:12	of Abdi and Azariah s of Jehallelel;	1201
29:12	Joah s of Zimmah and Eden son of Joah;	1201
29:12	Joah son of Zimmah and Eden s of Joah;	1201
30:26	since the days of Solomon s of David king	1201
31:14	Kore s of Imnah the Levite,	1201
32:20	and the prophet Isaiah s of Amoz cried out	1201
32:32	the prophet Isaiah s of Amoz in the book of	1201
32:33	And Manasseh his s succeeded him as king.	1201
33: 7	to David and to his s Solomon,	1201
33:20	And Amon his s succeeded him as king.	1201
33:25	they made Josiah his s king in his place.	1201
34: 8	he sent Shaphan s of Azaliah and Maaseiah	1201
34: 8	with Joah s of Joahaz, the recorder,	1201
34:20	Ahikam s of Shaphan,	1201
34:20	Abdon s of Micah, Shaphan the secretary	1201
34:22	who was the wife of Shallum s of Tokhath,	1201
34:22	the s of Hasrah, keeper of the wardrobe.	1201
35: 3	in the temple that Solomon s of David king	1201
35: 4	of Israel and by his s Solomon.	1201
36: 1	And the people of the land took Jehoahaz s	1201
36: 8	Jehoiachin his s succeeded him as king.	1201
Ezr 3: 2	Then Jeshua s of Jozadak	1201
3: 2	and his fellow priests and Zerubbabel s	1201
3: 8	Zerubbabel s of Shealtiel,	1201
3: 8	Jeshua s of Jozadak and the rest of their	1201
5: 2	Then Zerubbabel s of Shealtiel and	10120
5: 2	and Jeshua s of Jozadak set to work	10120
7: 1	Ezra s of Seraiah, the son of Azariah,	1201
7: 1	Ezra son of Seraiah, the s of Azariah,	1201
7: 1	the son of Azariah, the s of Hilkiah,	1201
7: 2	the s of Shallum, the son of Zadok,	1201
7: 2	the s of Zadok, the son of Ahitub,	1201
7: 2	the son of Zadok, the s of Ahitub,	1201
7: 3	the s of Amariah, the son of Azariah,	1201
7: 3	the s of Azariah, the son of Meraioth,	1201
7: 3	the son of Azariah, the s of Meraioth,	1201
7: 4	the s of Zerahiah, the son of Uzzi,	1201
7: 4	the s of Uzzi, the son of Bukki,	1201
7: 4	the son of Uzzi, the s of Bukki,	1201
7: 5	the s of Abishua, the son of Phinehas,	1201
7: 5	the s of Phinehas, the son of Eleazar,	1201
7: 5	the son of Phinehas, the s of Eleazar,	1201
7: 5	the s of Aaron the chief priest—	1201
8: 4	Eliehoenai s of Zerahiah,	1201
8: 5	Shecaniah s of Jahaziel,	1201
8: 6	Ebed s of Jonathan, and with him 50 men;	1201
8: 7	Jeshaiah s of Athaliah,	1201
8: 8	Zebadiah s of Michael,	1201
8: 9	Obadiah s of Jehiel, and with him 218 men;	1201
8:10	Shelomith s of Josiphiah, and	1201
8:11	Zechariah s of Bebai, and	1201
8:12	Johanan s of Hakkatan,	1201
8:18	from the descendants of Mahli s of Levi,	1201
8:18	the s of Israel, and Sherebiah's sons	1201
8:33	into the hands of Meremoth s of Uriah,	1201
8:33	Eleazar s of Phinehas was with him,	1201
8:33	so were the Levites Jozabad s of Jeshua	1201
8:33	of Jeshua and Noadiah s of Binnui.	1201
10: 2	Then Shecaniah s of Jehiel,	1201
10: 6	to the room of Jehohanan s of Eliashib.	1201
10:15	Only Jonathan s of Asahel and	1201
10:15	Only Jonathan son of Asahel and Jahzeiah s	1201
10:18	of Jeshua s of Jozadak, and his brothers:	1201
Ne 1: 1	The words of Nehemiah s of Hacaliah:	1201
3: 2	and Zaccur s of Imri built next to them.	1201
3: 4	Meremoth s of Uriah, the son of Hakkoz	1201
3: 4	Meremoth son of Uriah, the s of Hakkoz,	1201
3: 4	Next to him Meshullam s of Berekiah,	1201
3: 4	the s of Meshezabel, made repairs,	1201
3: 4	to him Zadok s of Baana also made repairs.	1201
3: 6	The Jeshanah Gate was repaired by Joiada s	1201
3: 6	of Paseah and Meshullam s of Besodeiah.	1201
3: 8	Uzziel s of Harhaiah, one of the goldsmiths,	1201
3: 9	Rephaiah s of Hur,	1201
3:10	Adjoining this, Jedaiah s of Harmaph	1201
3:10	and Hattush s of Hashabneiah made repairs	1201
3:11	Malkijah s of Harim and Hasshub son	1201
3:11	Malkijah son of Harim and Hasshub s	1201
3:12	Shallum s of Hallohesh,	1201
3:14	The Dung Gate was repaired by Malkijah s	1201
3:15	by Shallun s of Col-Hozeh,	1201
3:16	Beyond him, Nehemiah s of Azbuk,	1201
3:17	by the Levites under Rehum s of Bani.	1201
3:18	by their countrymen under Binnui s	1201
3:19	Next to him, Ezer s of Jeshua,	1201
3:20	Next to him, Baruch s of Zabbai	1201
3:21	Next to him, Meremoth s of Uriah,	1201
3:21	the s of Hakkoz, repaired another section,	1201
3:23	and next to them, Azariah s of Maaseiah,	1201
3:23	Azariah son of Maaseiah, the s of Ananiah,	1201
3:24	Next to him, Binnui s of Henadad	1201
3:25	and Palal s of Uzai worked opposite	1201
3:25	Next to him, Pedaiah s of Parosh	1201
3:29	Next to them, Zadok s of Immer	1201
3:29	Next to him, Shemaiah s of Shecaniah,	1201
3:30	Next to him, Hananiah s of Shelemiah,	1201
3:30	and Hanun, the sixth s of Zalaph,	1201
3:30	Next to them, Meshullam s of Berekiah	1201

Ne 6:10	One day I went to the house of Shemaiah s	1201
6:10	the s of Mehetabel,	1201
6:18	he was son-in-law to Shecaniah s of Arah,	1201
6:18	and his s Jehohanan had married	1201
6:18	the daughter of Meshullam s of Berekiah.	1201
8:17	the days of Joshua s of Nun until that day,	1201
10: 1	Nehemiah the governor, the s of Hacaliah.	1201
10: 9	The Levites: Jeshua s of Azaniah,	1201
11: 4	Athaiah s of Uzziah, the son of Zechariah,	1201
11: 4	Athaiah son of Uzziah, the s of Zechariah,	1201
11: 4	the s of Amariah, the son of Shephatiah,	1201
11: 4	the s of Shephatiah, the son of Mahalalel,	1201
11: 4	the s of Mahalalel, a descendant of Perez;	1201
11: 5	and Maaseiah s of Baruch,	1201
11: 5	the s of Col-Hozeh, the son of Hazaiah,	1201
11: 5	the son of Col-Hozeh, the s of Hazaiah,	1201
11: 5	the son of Hazaiah, the s of Adaiah,	1201
11: 5	the s of Joiarib, the son of Zechariah,	1201
11: 5	the s of Zechariah, a descendant of Shelah.	1201
11: 7	Sallu s of Meshullam, the son of Joed,	1201
11: 7	Sallu son of Meshullam, the s of Joed,	1201
11: 7	the s of Pedaiah, the son of Kolaiah,	1201
11: 7	the s of Kolaiah, the son of Maaseiah,	1201
11: 7	the son of Kolaiah, the s of Maaseiah,	1201
11: 7	the son of Maaseiah, the s of Ithiel,	1201
11: 7	the son of Ithiel, the s of Jeshaiah,	1201
11: 9	Joel s of Zicri was their chief officer,	1201
11: 9	and Judah s of Hassenuah was over	1201
11:10	From the priests: Jedaiah; the s of Joiarib;	1201
11:11	Seraiah s of Hilkiah,	1201
11:11	the s of Meshullam, the son of Zadok,	1201
11:11	the son of Meshullam, the s of Zadok,	1201
11:11	the s of Meraioth, the son of Ahitub,	1201
11:11	the son of Meraioth, the s of Ahitub,	1201
11:12	Adaiah s of Jeroham, the son of Pelaliah,	1201
11:12	Adaiah son of Jeroham, the s of Pelaliah,	1201
11:12	the s of Amzi, the son of Zechariah,	1201
11:12	the s of Zechariah, the son of Pashhur,	1201
11:12	the son of Zechariah, the s of Pashhur,	1201
11:12	the son of Pashhur, the s of Malkijah,	1201
11:13	Amashsai s of Azarel, the son of Ahzai,	1201
11:13	Amashsai son of Azarel, the s of Ahzai,	1201
11:13	the s of Meshillemoth, the son of Immer,	1201
11:13	the son of Meshillemoth, the s of Immer,	1201
11:14	Their chief officer was Zabdiel s	1201
11:15	From the Levites: Shemaiah s of Hasshub,	1201
11:15	the s of Azrikam, the son of Hashabiah,	1201
11:15	the son of Azrikam, the s of Hashabiah,	1201
11:15	the son of Hashabiah, the s of Bunni;	1201
11:17	Mattaniah s of Mica, the son of Zabdi,	1201
11:17	the s of Zabdi, the son of Asaph,	1201
11:17	the son of Zabdi, the s of Asaph,	1201
11:17	and Abda s of Shammua, the son of Galal,	1201
11:17	and Abda son of Shammua, the s of Galal,	1201
11:17	the son of Galal, the s of Jeduthun.	1201
11:22	of the Levites in Jerusalem was Uzzi s	1201
11:22	the s of Hashabiah, the son of Mattaniah,	1201
11:22	the son of Hashabiah, the s of Mattaniah,	1201
11:22	the son of Mattaniah, the s of Mica.	1201
11:24	Pethahiah s of Meshezabel,	1201
11:24	one of the descendants of Zerah s of Judah,	1201
12: 1	and Levites who returned with Zerubbabel s	1201
12:23	of Johanan s of Eliashib were recorded in	1201
12:24	Jeshua s of Kadmiel, and their associates,	1201
12:26	They served in the days of Joiakim s of	1201
12:26	son of Jeshua, the s of Jozadak,	1201
12:35	and also Zechariah s of Jonathan,	1201
12:35	the s of Shemaiah, the son of Mattaniah,	1201
12:35	the son of Shemaiah, the s of Mattaniah,	1201
12:35	the son of Mattaniah, the s of Micaiah,	1201
12:35	the son of Micaiah, the s of Zaccur,	1201
12:35	the son of Zaccur, the s of Asaph,	1201
12:45	the commands of David and his s Solomon.	1201
13:13	of the storerooms and made Hanan s	1201
13:13	the s of Mattaniah, their assistant,	1201
13:28	One of the sons of Joiada s of Eliashib	1201
Est 2: 5	of Benjamin, named Mordecai s of Jair,	1201
2: 5	the s of Shimei, the son of Kish,	1201
2: 5	the son of Shimei, the s of Kish,	1201
3: 1	King Xerxes honored Haman s of	1201
3:10	and gave it to Haman s of Hammedatha,	1201
8: 5	that Haman s of Hammedatha,	1201
9:10	the ten sons of Haman s of Hammedatha,	1201
9:24	For Haman s of Hammedatha, the Agagite,	1201
Job 25: 6	a s of man, who is only a worm!"	1201
32: 2	But Elihu s of Barakel the Buzite	1201
32: 6	So Elihu s of Barakel the Buzite said:	1201
Ps 2: 7	He said to me, "You are my S;	1201
2:12	Kiss the S, lest he be angry and you	1337
3: T	When he fled from his s Absalom.	1201
8: 4	the s of man that you care for him?	1201
9: T	To [the tune of] "The Death of the S."	1201
50:20	and slander your own mother's s.	1201
72: 1	O God, the royal s with your righteousness.	1201
72:20	This concludes the prayers of David s of	1201
80:15	the s you have raised up for yourself.	1201
80:17	the s of man you have raised up	1201
86:16	and save the s of your maidservant.	1201
116:16	the s of your maidservant;	1201
144: 3	the s of man that you think of him?	1201
Pr 1: 1	The proverbs of Solomon s of David,	1201
1: 8	my s, to your father's instruction and do	1201
1:10	My s, if sinners entice you,	1201
1:15	my s, do not go along with them, do	1201
2: 1	My s, if you accept my words and store	1201
3: 1	My s, do not forget my teaching,	1201
3:11	My s, do not despise the Lord's discipline	1201

Pr 3:12	as a father the s he delights in.	1201
3:21	My s, preserve sound judgment	1201
4:10	Listen, my s, accept what I say,	1201
4:20	My s, pay attention to what I say;	1201
5: 1	My s, pay attention to my wisdom,	1201
5:20	Why be captivated, my s, by an adulteress?	1201
6: 1	My s, if you have put up security	1201
6: 3	my s, to free yourself,	1201
6:20	My s, keep your father's commands and do	1201
7: 1	My s, keep my words and store	1201
10: 1	A wise s brings joy to his father,	1201
10: 1	but a foolish s grief to his mother.	1201
10: 5	who gathers crops in summer is a wise s,	1201
10: 5	sleeps during harvest is a disgraceful s.	1201
13: 1	A wise s heeds his father's instruction,	1201
13:24	He who spares the rod hates his s,	1201
15:20	A wise s brings joy to his father,	1201
17: 2	wise servant will rule over a disgraceful s,	1201
17:21	To **have** a fool for a s brings grief;	3528
17:25	A foolish s brings grief to his father	1201
19:13	A foolish s is his father's ruin,	1201
19:18	Discipline your s, for in that there is hope;	1201
19:26	a s who brings shame and disgrace.	1201
19:27	Stop listening to instruction, my s,	1201
23:15	My s, if your heart is wise,	1201
23:19	Listen, my s, and be wise,	1201
23:24	he who **has** a wise s delights in him.	3528
23:26	My s, give me your heart	1201
24:13	Eat honey, my s, for it is good;	1201
24:21	Fear the Lord and the king, my s,	1201
27:11	Be wise, my s, and bring joy to my heart;	1201
28: 7	He who keeps the law is a discerning s,	1201
29:17	Discipline your s, and he will give you	
	peace;	1201
30: 1	The sayings of Agur s of Jakeh—	1201
30: 4	What is his name, and the name of his s?	1201
31: 2	"O my s, O son of my womb, O son	1337
31: 2	O s of my womb, O son of my vows,	1337
31: 2	O son of my womb, O s of my vows,	1337
Ecc 1: 1	The words of the Teacher, s of David,	1201
4: 8	he had neither s nor brother.	1201
5:14	so that when he has a s there is nothing left	1201
12:12	my s, of anything in addition to them.	1201
Isa 1: 1	that Isaiah s of Amoz saw during the reigns	1201
2: 1	This is what Isaiah s of Amoz saw	1201
7: 1	When Ahaz s of Jotham, the son of Uzziah,	1201
7: 1	When Ahaz son of Jotham, the s of Uzziah,	1201
7: 1	of Aram and Pekah s of Remaliah king	1201
7: 3	"Go out, you and your s Shear-Jashub,	1201
7: 4	and Aram and of the s of Remaliah.	1201
7: 5	and Remaliah's s have plotted your ruin,	1201
7: 6	and make the s of Tabeel king over it."	1201
7: 9	the head of Samaria is only Remaliah's s.	1201
7:14	be with child and will give birth to a s,	1201
8: 2	the priest and Zechariah s of Jeberekiah	1201
8: 3	and she conceived and gave birth to a s.	1201
8: 6	of Shiloah and rejoices over Rezin and the s	1201
9: 6	For to us a child is born, to us a s is given,	1201
13: 1	An oracle concerning Babylon that Isaiah s	1201
14:12	O morning star, s of the dawn!	1201
20: 2	that time the Lord spoke through Isaiah s	1201
22:20	my servant, Eliakim s of Hilkiah.	1201
36: 3	Eliakim s of Hilkiah the palace	1201
36: 3	and Joah s of Asaph the recorder went out	1201
36:22	Then Eliakim s of Hilkiah the palace	1201
36:22	and Joah s of Asaph the recorder went	1201
37: 2	to the prophet Isaiah s of Amoz.	1201
37:21	Then Isaiah s of Amoz sent a message	1201
37:38	Esarhaddon his s succeeded him as king.	1201
38: 1	The prophet Isaiah s of Amoz went to him	1201
39: 1	At that time Merodach-Baladan s of	1201
66: 7	the pains come upon her, she delivers a s.	2351
Jer 1: 1	The words of Jeremiah s of Hilkiah,	1201
1: 2	in the thirteenth year of the reign of Josiah s	1201
1: 3	of Jehoiakim s of Josiah king of Judah,	1201
1: 3	of Zedekiah s of Josiah king of Judah,	1201
6:26	mourn with bitter wailing as for an **only** s,	3495
15: 4	of the earth because of what Manasseh s	1201
20: 1	When the priest Pashhur s of Immer,	1201
20:15	"A child is born to you—a s!"	2351
21: 1	when King Zedekiah sent to him Pashhur s	1201
21: 1	and the priest Zephaniah s of Maaseiah.	1201
22:11	the Lord says about Shallum s of Josiah,	1201
22:18	about Jehoiakim s of Josiah king of Judah:	1201
22:24	Jehoiachin s of Jehoiakim king of Judah,	1201
24: 1	After Jehoiachin s of Jehoiakim king	1201
25: 1	of Judah in the fourth year of Jehoiakim s	1201
25: 3	from the thirteenth year of Josiah s	1201
26: 1	in the reign of Jehoiakim s of Josiah king	1201
26:20	(Now Uriah s of Shemaiah from	1201
26:22	sent Elnathan s of Acbor to Egypt,	1201
26:24	Ahikam s of Shaphan supported Jeremiah,	1201
27: 1	in the reign of Zedekiah s of Josiah king	1201
27:20	and his s and his grandson until the time	1201
27:20	not take away when he carried Jehoiachin s	1201
28: 1	the prophet Hananiah s of Azzur,	1201
28: 4	to this place Jehoiachin s of Jehoiakim king	1201
29: 3	the letter to Elasah s of Shaphan and	1201
29: 3	of Shaphan and to Gemariah s of Hilkiah,	1201
29:21	about Ahab s of Kolaiah and Zedekiah son	1201
29:21	about Ahab son of Kolaiah and Zedekiah s	1201
29:25	to Zephaniah s of Maaseiah the priest,	1201
31: 9	and Ephraim is my **firstborn** s.	AIT
31:20	Is not Ephraim my dear s,	1201
32: 7	Hanamel s of Shallum your uncle is going	1201
32:12	and I gave this deed to Baruch s of Neriah,	1201
32:12	Baruch son of Neriah, the s of Mahseiah,	1201

Jer	32:16	the deed of purchase to Baruch s of Neriah,	1201
	35: 1	the LORD during the reign of Jehoiakim s	1201
	35: 3	So I went to get Jaazaniah s of Jeremiah,	1201
	35: 3	the s of Habazziniah, and his brothers	1201
	35: 4	the room of the sons of Hanan s of Igdaliah	1201
	35: 4	of Maaseiah s of Shallum the doorkeeper.	1201
	35: 6	because our forefather Jonadab s	1201
	35: 8	We have obeyed everything our forefather	
		Jonadab s of Recab commanded	1201
	35:14	'Jonadab s of Recab ordered his sons not	1201
	35:16	of Jonadab s of Recab have carried out	1201
	35:19	'Jonadab s of Recab will never fail to have	1201
	36: 1	of Jehoiakim s of Josiah king of Judah,	1201
	36: 4	So Jeremiah called Baruch s of Neriah,	1201
	36: 8	Baruch s of Neriah did everything Jeremiah	1201
	36: 9	the fifth year of Jehoiakim s of Josiah king	1201
	36:10	From the room of Gemariah s of Shaphan	1201
	36:11	When Micaiah s of Gemariah,	1201
	36:11	the s of Shaphan, heard all the words	1201
	36:12	Delaiah s of Shemaiah,	1201
	36:12	of Shemaiah, Elnathan s of Acbor,	1201
	36:12	Gemariah s of Shaphan,	1201
	36:12	Zedekiah s of Hananiah,	1201
	36:14	all the officials sent Jehudi s of Nethaniah,	1201
	36:14	the s of Shelemiah, the son of Cushi,	1201
	36:14	the son of Shelemiah, the s of Cushi,	1201
	36:14	So Baruch s of Neriah went to them with	1201
	36:26	Jerahmeel, a s of the king,	1201
	36:26	Seraiah s of Azriel and Shelemiah son	1201
	36:26	and Shelemiah s of Abdeel to arrest Baruch	1201
	36:32	and gave it to the scribe Baruch s	1201
	37: 1	Zedekiah s of Josiah was made king	1201
	37: 1	in place of Jehoiachin s of Jehoiakim.	1201
	37: 3	sent Jehucal s of Shelemiah with	1201
	37: 3	of Shelemiah with the priest Zephaniah s	1201
	37:13	whose name was Irijah s of Shelemiah,	1201
	37:13	the s of Hananiah, arrested him and said,	1201
	38: 1	Shephatiah s of Mattan,	1201
	38: 1	Gedaliah s of Pashhur,	1201
	38: 1	Jehucal s of Shelemiah,	1201
	38: 1	of Shelemiah, and Pashhur s of Malkijah	1201
	38: 6	the king's s, which was in the courtyard of	1201
	39:14	They turned him over to Gedaliah s of	1201
	39:14	the s of Shaphan,	1201
	40: 5	"Go back to Gedaliah s of Ahikam,	1201
	40: 5	the s of Shaphan, to take him back	1201
	40: 6	So Jeremiah went to Gedaliah s of Ahikam	1201
	40: 7	of Babylon had appointed Gedaliah s of	1201
	40: 8	Ishmael s of Nethaniah,	1201
	40: 8	Seraiah s of Tanhumeth,	1201
	40: 8	and Jaazaniah the s of the Maacathite,	1201
	40: 9	Gedaliah s of Ahikam, the son of Shaphan,	1201
	40: 9	Gedaliah son of Ahikam, the s of Shaphan,	1201
	40:11	and had appointed Gedaliah s of Ahikam,	1201
	40:11	of Shaphan, as governor over them,	1201
	40:13	Johanan s of Kareah and all	1201
	40:14	of the Ammonites has sent Ishmael s	1201
	40:14	But Gedaliah s of Ahikam did	1201
	40:15	Then Johanan s of Kareah said privately	1201
	40:15	and kill Ishmael s of Nethaniah,	1201
	40:16	But Gedaliah s of Ahikam said	1201
	40:16	of Ahikam said to Johanan s of Kareah,	1201
	41: 1	the seventh month Ishmael s of Nethaniah,	1201
	41: 1	the s of Elishama, who was of royal blood	1201
	41: 1	with ten men to Gedaliah s of Ahikam	1201
	41: 2	Ishmael s of Nethaniah and	1201
	41: 2	up and struck down Gedaliah s of Ahikam,	1201
	41: 2	the s of Shaphan, with the sword,	1201
	41: 6	Ishmael s of Nethaniah went out	1201
	41: 6	he said, "Come to Gedaliah s of Ahikam."	1201
	41: 7	Ishmael s of Nethaniah and	1201
	41: 9	Ishmael s of Nethaniah filled it with	1201
	41:10	imperial guard had appointed Gedaliah s	1201
	41:10	Ishmael s of Nethaniah took them captive	1201
	41:11	When Johanan s of Kareah and all	1201
	41:11	all the crimes Ishmael s of Nethaniah	1201
	41:12	and went to fight Ishmael s of Nethaniah.	1201
	41:13	with him saw Johanan s of Kareah and	1201
	41:14	and went over to Johanan s of Kareah.	1201
	41:15	But Ishmael s of Nethaniah and eight	1201
	41:16	Then Johanan s of Kareah and all	1201
	41:16	recovered from Ishmael s of Nethaniah	1201
	41:16	after he had assassinated Gedaliah s	1201
	41:18	They were afraid of them because Ishmael s	1201
	41:18	of Nethaniah had killed Gedaliah s	1201
	42: 1	including Johanan s of Kareah	1201
	42: 1	of Kareah and Jezaniah s of Hoshaiah,	1201
	42: 8	So he called together Johanan s of Kareah	1201
	43: 2	Azariah s of Hoshaiah and Johanan son	1201
	43: 2	Azariah son of Hoshaiah and Johanan s	1201
	43: 3	But Baruch s of Neriah is inciting you	1201
	43: 4	So Johanan s of Kareah and all	1201
	43: 5	Johanan s of Kareah and all	1201
	43: 6	the imperial guard had left with Gedaliah s	1201
	43: 6	the s of Shaphan, and Jeremiah the prophet	1201
	43: 6	and Jeremiah the prophet and Baruch s of	1201
	45: 1	the prophet told Baruch s of Neriah in	1201
	45: 1	of Neriah in the fourth year of Jehoiakim s	1201
	46: 2	of Jehoiakim s of Josiah king of Judah:	1201
	51:59	to the staff officer Seraiah s of Neriah,	1201
	51:59	the s of Mahseiah, when he went to Babylon	1201
Eze	1: 3	Ezekiel the priest, the s of Buzi,	1201
	2: 1	He said to me, "S of man, stand up	1201
	2: 3	He said: "S of man, I am sending you	1201
	2: 6	And you, s of man, do not be afraid of them	1201
	2: 8	you, s of man, listen to what I say to you.	1201
	3: 1	And he said to me, "S of man,	1201

Eze	3: 3	Then he said to me, "S of man,	1201
	3: 4	He then said to me: "S of man,	1201
	3:10	And he said to me, "S of man,	1201
	3:17	"S of man, I have made you a watchman	1201
	3:25	And you, s of man, they will tie with ropes;	1201
	4: 1	"Now, s of man, take a clay tablet,	1201
	4:16	He then said to me: "S of man,	1201
	5: 1	s of man, take a sharp sword and use it as	1201
	6: 2	"S of man, set your face against	1201
	7: 2	"S of man, this is what the Sovereign	1201
	8: 5	Then he said to me, "S of man,	1201
	8: 6	And he said to me, "S of man,	1201
	8: 8	He said to me, "S of man,	1201
	8:11	and Jaazaniah s of Shaphan was standing	1201
	8:12	He said to me, "S of man,	1201
	8:15	He said to me, "Do you see this, s of man?	1201
	8:17	"Have you seen this, s of man?	1201
	11: 1	and I saw among them Jaazaniah s	1201
	11: 1	of Azzur and Pelatiah s of Benaiah,	1201
	11: 2	The LORD said to me, "S of man,	1201
	11: 4	prophesy against them; prophesy, s of man."	1201
	11:13	Pelatiah s of Benaiah died.	1201
	11:15	"S of man, your brothers—	1201
	12: 2	"S of man, you are living among	1201
	12: 3	"Therefore, s of man, pack your belongings	1201
	12: 9	"S of man, did not that rebellious house	1201
	12:18	"S of man, tremble as you eat your food,	1201
	12:22	"S of man, what is this proverb you have	1201
	12:27	"S of man, the house of Israel is saying,	1201
	13: 2	"S of man, prophesy against the prophets	1201
	13:17	"Now, s of man, set your face against	1201
	14: 3	"S of man, these men have set up idols	1201
	14:13	"S of man, if a country sins against me	1201
	14:20	they could save neither s nor daughter.	1201
	15: 2	"S of man, how is the wood of	1201
	16: 2	"S of man, confront Jerusalem	1201
	17: 2	"S of man, set forth an allegory and tell	1201
	18: 4	the father as well as the s—	1201
	18:10	"Suppose he has a violent s,	1201
	18:14	"But suppose this s has a son who sees all	NIH
	18:14	a s who sees all the sins his father commits,	1201
	18:19	the s not share the guilt of his father?'	1201
	18:19	Since the s has done what is just and right	1201
	18:20	The s will not share the guilt of the father,	1201
	18:20	nor will the father share the guilt of the s.	1201
	20: 3	"S of man, speak to the elders of Israel	1201
	20: 4	Will you judge them, s of man?	1201
	20:27	s of man, speak to the people of Israel	1201
	20:46	"S of man, set your face toward the south;	1201
	21: 2	"S of man, set your face against Jerusalem	1201
	21: 6	"Therefore groan, s of man!	1201
	21: 9	"S of man, prophesy and say, 'This is what	1201
	21:10	in the scepter of my s [Judah]?	1201
	21:12	Cry out and wail, s of man,	1201
	21:14	"So then, s of man,	1201
	21:19	"S of man, mark out two roads for	1201
	21:28	"And you, s of man, prophesy and say,	1201
	22: 2	"S of man, will you judge her?	1201
	22:18	"S of man, the house of Israel has become	1201
	22:24	"S of man, say to the land, 'You are a land	1201
	23: 2	"S of man, there were two women,	1201
	23:36	The LORD said to me, "S of man,	1201
	24: 2	"S of man, record this date, this very date,	1201
	24:16	"S of man, with one blow I am about	1201
	24:25	"And you, s of man,	1201
	25: 2	"S of man, set your face against	1201
	26: 2	"S of man, because Tyre has said	1201
	27: 2	"S of man, take up a lament	1201
	28: 2	"S of man, say to the ruler of Tyre,	1201
	28:12	"S of man, take up a lament concerning	1201
	28:21	"S of man, set your face against Sidon;	1201
	29: 2	"S of man, set your face against Pharaoh	1201
	29:18	"S of man, Nebuchadnezzar king	1201
	30: 2	"S of man, prophesy and say:	1201
	30:21	"S of man, I have broken the arm	1201
	31: 2	"S of man, say to Pharaoh king of Egypt	1201
	32: 2	"S of man, take up a lament	1201
	32:18	"S of man, wail for the hordes of Egypt	1201
	33: 2	"S of man, speak to your countrymen,	1201
	33: 7	"S of man, I have made you a watchman	1201
	33:10	"S of man, say to the house of Israel,	1201
	33:12	s of man, say to your countrymen,	1201
	33:24	"S of man, the people living in those ruins	1201
	33:30	"As for you, s of man,	1201
	34: 2	"S of man, prophesy against the shepherds	1201
	35: 2	"S of man, set your face against Mount Seir	1201
	36: 1	"S of man, prophesy to the mountains	1201
	36:17	"S of man, when the people	1201
	37: 3	He asked me, "S of man,	1201
	37: 9	prophesy, s of man, and say to it,	1201
	37:11	Then he said to me: "S of man,	1201
	37:16	"S of man, take a stick of wood and write	1201
	38: 2	"S of man, set your face against Gog, of	1201
	38:14	s of man, prophesy and say to Gog:	1201
	39: 1	"S of man, prophesy against Gog and say:	1201
	39: 1	"S of man, this is what the Sovereign	1201
	40: 4	The man said to me, "S of man,	1201
	43: 7	He said: "S of man, this is the place	1201
	43:10	"S of man, describe the temple to	1201
	43:18	Then he said to me, "S of man,	1201
	44: 5	The LORD said to me, "S of man,	1201
	44:25	s or daughter, brother or unmarried sister,	1201
	47: 6	He asked me, "S of man, do you see this?"	1201
Da	3:25	and the fourth looks like a s of the gods."	10120
	5:22	"But you his s, O Belshazzar,	10120
	7:13	before me was one like a s of man,	10120
	8:17	"S of man," he said to me,	1201

Da	9: 1	the first year of Darius s of Xerxes (a Mede	1201
Hos	1: 1	the LORD that came to Hosea s of Beeri	1201
	1: 1	of Jeroboam s of Jehoash king of Israel:	1201
	1: 3	and she conceived and bore him a s.	1201
	1: 8	Gomer had another s.	1201
	11: 1	I loved him, and out of Egypt I called my s.	1201
Joel	1: 1	The word of the LORD that came to Joel s	1201
Am	1: 1	and Jeroboam s of Jehoash was king	1201
	2: 7	Father and s use the same girl and	408
	7:14	"I was neither a prophet nor a prophet's s,	1201
	8:10	an only s and the end of it like a bitter day.	3495
Jnh	1: 1	of the LORD came to Jonah s of Amittai:	1201
Mic	6: 5	of Moab counseled and what Balaam s	1201
	7: 6	For a s dishonors his father,	1201
Zep	1: 1	that came to Zephaniah s of Cushi, the son	1201
	1: 1	the s of Gedaliah, the son of Amariah,	1201
	1: 1	the s of Amariah, the son of Hezekiah,	1201
	1: 1	the son of Amariah, the s of Hezekiah,	1201
	1: 1	during the reign of Josiah s of Amon king	1201
Hag	1: 1	through the prophet Haggai to Zerubbabel s	1201
	1: 1	and to Joshua s of Jehozadak,	1201
	1:12	Then Zerubbabel s of Shealtiel,	1201
	1:12	Joshua s of Jehozadak, the high priest,	1201
	1:14	up the spirit of Zerubbabel s of Shealtiel,	1201
	1:14	and the spirit of Joshua s of Jehozadak,	1201
	2: 2	"Speak to Zerubbabel s of Shealtiel,	1201
	2: 2	to Joshua s of Jehozadak, the high priest,	1201
	2: 4	'Be strong, O Joshua s of Jehozadak,	1201
	2:23	my servant Zerubbabel s of Shealtiel,'	1201
Zec	1: 1	the LORD came to the prophet Zechariah s	1201
	1: 1	Zechariah son of Berekiah, the son of Iddo:	1201
	1: 7	the LORD came to the prophet Zechariah s	1201
	1: 7	Zechariah son of Berekiah, the s of Iddo.	1201
	6:10	Go the same day to the house of Josiah s	1201
	6:11	high priest, Joshua s of Jehozadak.	1201
	6:14	and Hen s of Zephaniah as a memorial in	1201
	12:10	for him as one grieves for a firstborn s.	AIT
Mal	1: 6	"A s honors his father,	1201
	3:17	a man spares his s who serves him.	1201
Mt	1: 1	of Jesus Christ the s of David, the son	5626
	1: 1	the son of David, the s of Abraham:	5626
	1:20	"Joseph s of David, do not be afraid	5626
	1:21	She will give birth to a s,	5626
	1:23	to a s, and they will call him Immanuel"—	5626
	1:25	with her until she gave birth to a s.	5626
	2:15	"Out of Egypt I called my s."	5626
	3:17	a voice from heaven said, "This is my S,	5626
	4: 3	"If you are the S of God,	5626
	4: 6	"If you are the S of God," he said,	5626
	4:21	James s of Zebedee and his brother John.	3836
	7: 9	"Which of you, if his s asks for bread,	5626
	8:20	the S of Man has no place to lay his head."	5626
	8:29	"What do you want with us, S of God?"	5626
	9: 2	"Take heart, s; your sins are forgiven."	5451
	9: 6	that the S of Man has authority on earth	5626
	9:27	"Have mercy on us, S of David!"	5626
	10: 2	James s of Zebedee, and his brother John;	3836
	10: 3	James s of Alphaeus, and Thaddaeus;	3836
	10:23	through the cities of Israel before the S	5626
	10:37	anyone who loves his s or daughter more	5626
	11:19	The S of Man came eating and drinking,	5626
	11:27	No one knows the s except the Father,	5626
	11:27	the Father except the S and those to whom	5626
	11:27	the Son and those to whom the S chooses	5626
	12: 8	For the S of Man is Lord of the Sabbath."	5626
	12:23	"Could this be the S of David?"	5626
	12:32	Anyone who speaks a word against the S	5626
	12:40	so the S of Man will be three days	5626
	13:37	"The one who sowed the good seed is the S	5626
	13:41	The S of Man will send out his angels,	5626
	13:55	"Isn't this the carpenter's s?	5626
	14:33	saying, "Truly you are the S of God."	5626
	15:22	"Lord, S of David, have mercy on me!	5626
	16:13	"Who do people say the S of Man is?"	5626
	16:16	"You are the Christ, the S of the living	
		God."	5626
	16:17	"Blessed are you, Simon s of Jonah,	980
	16:27	For the S of Man is going to come	5626
	16:28	the S of Man coming in his kingdom."	5626
	17: 5	"This is my S, whom I love;	5626
	17: 9	until the S of Man has been raised from	5626
	17:12	In the same way the S of Man is going	5626
	17:15	"Lord, have mercy on my s," he said.	5626
	17:22	"The S of Man is going to be betrayed into	5626
	19:28	the S of Man sits on his glorious throne,	5626
	20:18	and the S of Man will be betrayed to	5626
	20:28	as the S of Man did not come to be served,	5626
	20:30	"Lord, S of David, have mercy on us!"	5626
	20:31	"Lord, S of David, have mercy on us!"	5626
	21: 9	"Hosanna to the S of David!"	5626
	21:15	"Hosanna to the S of David,	5626
	21:28	He went to the first and said, 'S,	5451
	21:30	to the other s and said the same thing.	NIG
	21:37	Last of all, he sent his s to them.	5626
	21:37	'They will respect my s,' he said.	5626
	21:38	"But when the tenants saw the s,	5626
	22: 2	a wedding banquet for his s.	5626
	22:42	Whose s is he?"	5626
	22:42	"The s of David," they replied.	NIG
	22:45	how can he be his s?"	5626
	23:15	you make him twice as much a s of hell	5626
	23:35	to the blood of Zechariah s of Berekiah,	5626
	24:27	so will be the coming of the S of Man.	5626
	24:30	the sign of the S of Man will appear in	5626
	24:30	They will see the S of Man coming on	5626
	24:36	not even the angels in heaven, nor the S,	5626
	24:37	so it will be at the coming of the S of Man.	5626

Mt	24:39	how it will be at the coming of the S of Man	5626
	24:44	because the S of Man will come at an hour	5626
	25:31	"When the S of Man comes in his glory,	5626
	26: 2	and the S of Man will be handed over to	5626
	26:24	The S of Man will go just as it is written	5626
	26:24	woe to that man who betrays the S of Man!	5626
	26:45	and the S of Man is betrayed into the hands	5626
	26:63	Tell us if you are the Christ, the S of God."	5626
	26:64	the future you will see the S of Man sitting	5626
	27:40	if you are the S of God!"	5626
	27:43	for he said, 'I am the S of God.' "	5626
	27:54	"Surely he was the S of God!"	5626
	28:19	the name of the Father and of the S and of	5626
Mk	1: 1	the gospel about Jesus Christ, the S of God.	5626
	1:11	"You are my S, whom I love;	5626
	1:19	he saw James s of Zebedee	3836
	2: 5	"S, your sins are forgiven."	5451
	2:10	that the S of Man has authority on earth	5626
	2:14	he saw Levi s of Alphaeus sitting at	3836
	2:28	the S of Man is Lord even of the Sabbath."	5626
	3:11	"You are the S of God."	5626
	3:17	James s of Zebedee and his brother John	3836
	3:18	Thomas, James s of Alphaeus, Thaddaeus,	3836
	5: 7	Jesus, S of the Most High God?	5626
	6: 3	Isn't this Mary's s and the brother of James,	5626
	8:31	that the S of Man must suffer many things	5626
	8:38	the S of Man will be ashamed of him	5626
	9: 7	"This is my S, whom I love.	5626
	9: 9	until the S of Man had risen from the dead.	5626
	9:12	that the S of Man must suffer much and	5626
	9:17	"Teacher, I brought you my s,	5626
	9:31	"The S of Man is going to be betrayed into	5626
	10:33	"and the S of Man will be betrayed to	5626
	10:45	the S of Man did not come to be served,	5626
	10:46	Bartimaeus (that is, the S of Timaeus),	5626
	10:47	"Jesus, S of David, have mercy on me!"	5626
	10:48	but he shouted all the more, "S of David,	5626
	12: 6	"He had one left to send, a s,	5626
	12: 6	saying, 'They will respect my s.'	5626
	12:35	of the law say that the Christ is the s	5626
	12:37	How then can he be his s?"	5626
	13:26	"At that time men will see the S of Man	5626
	13:32	not even the angels in heaven, nor the S,	5626
	14:21	The S of Man will go just as it is written	5626
	14:21	woe to that man who betrays the S of Man!	5626
	14:41	the S of Man is betrayed into the hands	5626
	14:61	the S of the Blessed One?"	5626
	14:62	"And you will see the S of Man sitting at	5626
	15:39	"Surely this man was the S of God!"	5626
Lk	1:13	Your wife Elizabeth will bear you a s,	5626
	1:31	You will be with child and give birth to a s,	5626
	1:32	He will be great and will be called the S of	5626
	1:35	the holy one to be born will be called the S	5626
	1:57	she gave birth to a s.	5626
	2: 7	and she gave birth to her firstborn, a s.	5626
	2:48	His mother said to him, "S,	5451
	3: 2	of God came to John s of Zechariah in	5626
	3:22	"You are my S, whom I love;	5626
	3:23	He was the s, so it was thought, of Joseph,	5626
	3:23	so it was thought, of Joseph, the s of Heli,	3836
	3:24	the s of Matthat, the son of Levi,	3836
	3:24	the s of Levi, the son of Melki,	3836
	3:24	the s of Melki, the son of Jannai,	3836
	3:24	the s of Jannai, the son of Joseph,	3836
	3:24	the son of Jannai, the s of Joseph,	3836
	3:25	the s of Mattathias, the son of Amos,	3836
	3:25	the s of Amos, the son of Nahum,	3836
	3:25	the son of Amos, the s of Nahum,	3836
	3:25	the son of Nahum, the s of Esli,	3836
	3:25	the s of Esli, the s of Naggai,	3836
	3:26	the s of Maath, the son of Mattathias	3836
	3:26	the s of Mattathias, the son of Semein,	3836
	3:26	the son of Mattathias, the s of Semein,	3836
	3:26	the son of Semein, the s of Josech,	3836
	3:26	the son of Josech, the s of Joda,	3836
	3:27	the s of Joanan, the son of Rhesa,	3836
	3:27	the s of Rhesa, the son of Zerubbabel,	3836
	3:27	the s of Zerubbabel, the son of Shealtiel,	3836
	3:27	the son of Zerubbabel, the s of Shealtiel,	3836
	3:27	the son of Shealtiel, the s of Neri,	3836
	3:28	the s of Melki, the son of Addi,	3836
	3:28	the s of Addi, the son of Cosam,	3836
	3:28	the s of Cosam, the son of Elmadam,	3836
	3:28	the son of Cosam, the s of Elmadam,	3836
	3:28	the son of Elmadam, the s of Er,	3836
	3:29	the s of Joshua, the son of Eliezer,	3836
	3:29	the s of Eliezer, the son of Jorim,	NIG
	3:29	the s of Jorim, the son of Matthat,	3836
	3:29	the s of Jorim, the son of Matthat,	3836
	3:29	the son of Matthat, the s of Levi,	3836
	3:30	the s of Simeon, the son of Judah,	3836
	3:30	the s of Judah, the son of Joseph,	3836
	3:30	the s of Joseph, the son of Jonam,	3836
	3:30	the s of Jonam, the son of Eliakim,	3836
	3:30	the son of Jonam, the s of Eliakim,	3836
	3:31	the s of Melea, the son of Menna,	3836
	3:31	the s of Menna, the son of Mattatha,	3836
	3:31	the son of Menna, the s of Mattatha,	3836
	3:31	the s of Mattatha, the son of Nathan,	3836
	3:31	the son of Mattatha, the s of Nathan,	3836
	3:31	the son of Nathan, the s of David,	3836
	3:32	the s of Jesse, the son of Obed,	3836
	3:32	the s of Obed, the son of Boaz,	3836
	3:32	the s of Boaz, the son of Salmon,	3836
	3:32	the s of Salmon, the son of Nahshon,	3836
	3:32	the son of Salmon, the s of Nahshon,	3836
	3:33	the s of Amminadab, the son of Ram,	3836
	3:33	the s of Ram, the son of Hezron,	3836

Lk	3:33	the s of Hezron, the son of Perez,	3836
	3:33	the son of Hezron, the s of Perez,	3836
	3:33	the son of Perez, the s of Judah,	3836
	3:34	the s of Jacob, the son of Isaac,	3836
	3:34	the s of Isaac, the son of Abraham,	3836
	3:34	the s of Abraham, the son of Terah,	3836
	3:34	the son of Abraham, the s of Terah,	3836
	3:34	the son of Terah, the s of Nahor,	3836
	3:35	the s of Serug, the son of Reu,	3836
	3:35	the s of Reu, the son of Peleg,	3836
	3:35	the s of Peleg, the son of Eber,	3836
	3:35	the s of Eber, the son of Shelah,	3836
	3:35	the son of Eber, the s of Shelah,	3836
	3:36	the s of Cainan, the son of Arphaxad,	3836
	3:36	the s of Arphaxad, the son of Shem,	3836
	3:36	the son of Arphaxad, the s of Shem,	3836
	3:36	the s of Noah, the son of Lamech,	3836
	3:36	the son of Noah, the s of Lamech,	3836
	3:37	the s of Methuselah, the son of Enoch,	3836
	3:37	the s of Enoch, the son of Jared,	3836
	3:37	the s of Jared, the son of Mahalalel,	3836
	3:37	the s of Mahalalel, the son of Kenan,	3836
	3:37	the son of Mahalalel, the s of Kenan,	3836
	3:38	the s of Enosh, the son of Seth,	3836
	3:38	the s of Seth, the son of Adam,	3836
	3:38	the son of Seth, the s of Adam,	3836
	3:38	the son of Adam, the s of God.	3836
	4: 3	"If you are the S of God,	5626
	4: 9	"If you are the S of God," he said,	5626
	4:22	"Isn't this Joseph's s?"	5626
	4:41	shouting, "You are the S of God!"	5626
	5:24	that the S of Man has authority on earth	5626
	6: 5	"The S of Man is Lord of the Sabbath."	5626
	6:15	Thomas, James s of Alphaeus,	271
	6:16	Judas s of James,	AIT
	6:22	because of the S of Man.	5626
	7:12	only s of his mother, and she was a widow.	5626
	7:34	The S of Man came eating and drinking,	5626
	8:28	Jesus, S of the Most High God?	5626
	9:22	"The S of Man must suffer many things	5626
	9:26	the S of Man will be ashamed of him	5626
	9:35	"This is my S, whom I have chosen;	5626
	9:38	"Teacher, I beg you to look at my s,	5626
	9:41	Bring your s here."	5626
	9:44	The S of Man is going to be betrayed into	5626
	9:58	the S of Man has no place to lay his head."	5626
	10:22	No one knows who the S is except	5626
	10:22	the S and those to whom the Son chooses	5626
	10:22	the S and those to whom the S chooses	5626
	11:11	if your s asks for a fish,	5626
	11:30	will the S of Man be to this generation.	5626
	12: 8	the S of Man will also acknowledge him	5626
	12:10	against the S of Man will be forgiven,	5626
	12:40	because the S of Man will come at an hour	5626
	12:53	father against s and son against father,	5626
	12:53	father against son and s against father,	5626
	14: 5	"If one of you has a s or an ox that falls into	5626
	15:13	the younger s got together all he had,	5626
	15:19	I am no longer worthy to be called your s;	5626
	15:20	he ran to his s, threw his arms around him	NIG
	15:21	"The s said to him, 'Father, I have sinned	5626
	15:21	I am no longer worthy to be called your s.'	5626
	15:24	this s of mine was dead and is alive again;	5626
	15:25	"Meanwhile, the older s was in the field.	5626
	15:30	when this s of yours who has squandered	5626
	15:31	" 'My s,' the father said,	5451
	16:25	"But Abraham replied, 'S,	5451
	17:22	to see one of the days of the S of Man,	5626
	17:24	For the S of Man in his day will be like	5626
	17:26	also will it be in the days of the S of Man.	5626
	17:30	"It will be just like this on the day the S of	5626
	18: 8	However, when the S of Man comes,	5626
	18:31	that is written by the prophets about the S	5626
	18:38	He called out, "Jesus, S of David,	5626
	18:39	but he shouted all the more, "S of David,	5626
	19: 9	because this man, too, is a s of Abraham.	5626
	19:10	For the S of Man came to seek and	5626
	20:13	I will send my s, whom I love;	5626
	20:41	"How is it that they say the Christ is the S	5626
	20:44	How then can he be his s?"	5626
	21:27	the S of Man coming in a cloud with power	5626
	21:36	that you may be able to stand before the S	5626
	22:22	The S of Man will go as it has been decreed	5626
	22:48	are you betraying the S of Man with	5626
	22:69	the S of Man will be seated at the right hand	5626
	22:70	"Are you then the S of God?"	5626
	24: 7	'The S of Man must be delivered into	5626
		seen and I testify that this is the S of God."	5626
Jn	1:34	"You are Simon s of John.	5626
	1:42	Jesus of Nazareth, the s of Joseph."	5626
	1:45	"Rabbi, you are the S of God;	5626
	1:49	ascending and descending on the S of Man.	5626
	1:51	who came from heaven—the S of Man.	5626
	3:13	so the S of Man must be lifted up,	5626
	3:14	the world that he gave his one and only S,	5626
	3:16	For God did not send his S into the world	5626
	3:17	in the name of God's one and only S.	5626
	3:18	The Father loves the S and has placed	5626
	3:35	Whoever believes in the S has eternal life,	5626
	3:36	but whoever rejects the S will not see life,	5626
	3:36	of ground Jacob had given to his s Joseph.	5626
	4: 5	a certain royal official whose s lay sick	5626
	4:46	and begged him to come and heal his s,	5626
	4:47	"Your s will live."	5626
	4:50	as to the time when his s got better,	NIG
	4:52	"Your s will live."	5626
	4:53	the S can do nothing by himself;	5626
	5:19		

Jn	5:19	whatever the Father does the S also does.	5626
	5:20	loves the S and shows him all he does.	5626
	5:21	so the S gives life to whom he is pleased	5626
	5:22	but has entrusted all judgment to the S,	5626
	5:23	that all may honor the S just as they honor	5626
	5:23	not honor the S does not honor the Father,	5626
	5:25	when the dead will hear the voice of the S	5626
	5:26	he has granted the S to have life in himself.	5626
	5:27	to judge because he is the S of Man.	5626
	6:27	which the S of Man will give you.	5626
	6:40	that everyone who looks to the S	5626
	6:42	"Is this not Jesus, the s of Joseph,	5626
	6:53	unless you eat the flesh of the S of Man	5626
	6:62	What if you see the S of Man ascend to	5626
	6:71	(He meant Judas, the s of Simon Iscariot,	AIT
	8:28	"When you have lifted up the S of Man,	5626
	8:35	but a s belongs to it forever.	5626
	8:36	the S sets you free, you will be free indeed.	5626
	9:19	"Is this your s?"	5626
	9:20	"We know he is our s,"	5626
	9:35	he said, "Do you believe in the S of Man?"	5626
	10:36	blasphemy because I said, 'I am God's S'?	5626
	11: 4	that God's S may be glorified through it."	5626
	11:27	believe that you are the Christ, the S of God,	5626
	12:23	"The hour has come for the S of Man to	5626
	12:34	'The S of Man must be lifted up'?	5626
	12:34	Who is this 'S of Man'?"	5626
	13: 2	Judas Iscariot, s of Simon, to betray Jesus.	AIT
	13:26	he gave it to Judas Iscariot, s of Simon.	AIT
	13:31	the S of Man glorified and God is glorified	5626
	13:32	God will glorify the S in himself,	899S
	14:13	so that the S may bring glory to the Father.	5626
	17: 1	The time has come. Glorify your S,	5626
	17: 1	that your S may glorify you.	5626
	19: 7	because he claimed to be the S of God."	5626
	19:26	"Dear woman, here is your s,"	5626
	20:31	believe that Jesus is the Christ, the S of God	5626
	21:15	"Simon s of John, do you truly love me	AIT
	21:16	Again Jesus said, "Simon s of John,	AIT
	21:17	"Simon s of John, do you love me?"	AIT
Ac	1:13	James s of Alphaeus and Simon the Zealot,	AIT
	1:13	and Judas s of James.	AIT
	4:36	apostles called Barnabas (which means S of	
		Encouragement),	5626
	7:21	and brought him up as her own s.	5626
	7:56	and the S of Man standing at the right hand	5626
	9:20	the synagogues that Jesus is the S of God.	5626
	13:21	and he gave them Saul s of Kish,	5626
	13:22	'I have found David s of Jesse a man	3836
	13:33	" 'You are my S; today I have become your	5626
	20: 4	by Sopater s of Pyrrhus from Berea,	AIT
	23: 6	I am a Pharisee, the s of a Pharisee.	5626
	23:16	the s of Paul's sister heard of this plot,	5626
Ro	1: 3	regarding his S, who as to human nature	5626
	1: 4	to be the S of God by his resurrection from	5626
	1: 9	in preaching the gospel of his S,	5626
	5:10	to him through the death of his S,	5626
	8: 3	by sending his own S in the likeness	5626
	8:29	to be conformed to the likeness of his S,	5626
	8:32	He who did not spare his own S,	5626
	9: 9	and Sarah will have a s."	5626
1Co	1: 9	with his S Jesus Christ our Lord,	5626
	4:17	Timothy, my s whom I love,	5451
	15:28	then the S himself will be made subject	5626
2Co	1:19	For the S of God, Jesus Christ,	5626
Gal	1:16	to reveal his S in me so that I might preach	5626
	2:20	I live by faith in the S of God,	5626
	4: 4	the time had fully come, God sent his S,	5626
	4: 6	God sent the Spirit of his S into our hearts,	5626
	4: 7	So you are no longer a slave, but a s;	5626
	4: 7	you are a s, God has made you also an heir.	5626
	4:23	His s by the slave woman was born	3525+3836S
	4:23	but his s by the free woman was born	3836S
	4:29	At that time the s born in the ordinary way	3836S
	4:29	the s born by the power of the Spirit.	3836S
	4:30	"Get rid of the slave woman and her s,	5626
	4:30	for the slave woman's s will never share in	5626
	4:30	in the inheritance with the free woman's s."	5626
Eph	4:13	in the faith and in the knowledge of the S	5626
Php	2:22	as a s with his father he has served with me	5451
Col	1:13	into the kingdom of the S he loves,	5626
1Th	1:10	for his S from heaven, whom he raised	5626
1Ti	1: 2	To Timothy my true s in the faith:	5451
	1:18	my s, I give you this instruction in keeping	5451
2Ti	1: 2	To Timothy, my dear s:	5451
	2: 1	then, my s, be strong in the grace that is	5451
Tit	1: 4	To Titus, my true s in our common faith:	5451
Phm	1:10	I appeal to you for my s Onesimus,	5451
	1:10	who became my s while I was in chains.	NIG
Heb	1: 2	last days he has spoken to us by his S,	5626
	1: 3	The S is the radiance of God's glory and	4005S
	1: 5	"You are my S; today I have become your	5626
	1: 5	"I will be his Father, and he will be my S"?	5626
	1: 8	But about the S he says, "Your throne,	5626
	2: 6	the s of man that you care for him?	5626
	3: 6	Christ is faithful as a s over God's house.	5626
	4:14	Jesus the S of God, let us hold firmly to	5626
	5: 5	But God said to him, "You are my S;	5626
	5: 8	Although he was a s, he learned obedience	5626
	6: 6	to their loss they are crucifying the S	5626
	7: 3	the S of God he remains a priest forever.	5626
	7:28	which came after the law, appointed the S,	5626
	10:29	to be punished who has trampled the S	5626
	11:17	about to sacrifice his one and only s,	3666
	11:24	to be known as the s of Pharaoh's daughter.	5626
	12: 5	"My s, do not make light of the Lord's	5626
	12: 6	and he punishes everyone he accepts as a s."	5626

Heb	12: 7	For what s is not disciplined by his father?	5626
	12:16	sold his **inheritance rights as the oldest s**.	4757
Jas	2:21	for what he did when he offered his s Isaac	5626
1Pe	5:13	and so does my s Mark.	5626
2Pe	1:17	saying, "This is my S, whom I love;	5626
	2:15	to follow the way of Balaam s of Beor,	3836
1Jn	1: 3	with the Father and with his S,	5626
	1: 7	and the blood of Jesus, his S, purifies us	5626
	2:22	he denies the Father and the S.	5626
	2:23	No one who denies the S has the Father;	5626
	2:23	whoever acknowledges the S has the Father	5626
	2:24	also will remain in the S and in the Father.	5626
	3: 8	The reason the S of God appeared was	5626
	3:23	to believe in the name of his S,	5626
	4: 9	He sent his one and only S into the world	5626
	4:10	but that he loved us and sent his S as	5626
	4:14	the Father has sent his S to be the Savior of	5626
	4:15	If anyone acknowledges that Jesus is the S	5626
	5: 5	Only he who believes that Jesus is the S	5626
	5: 9	which he has given about his S.	5626
	5:10	in the S of God has this testimony	5626
	5:10	the testimony God has given about his S.	5626
	5:11	and this life is in his S.	5626
	5:12	He who has the S has life;	5626
	5:12	not have the S of God does not have life.	5626
	5:13	to you who believe in the name of the S	5626
	5:20	We know also that the S of God has come	5626
	5:20	even in his S Jesus Christ.	5626
2Jn	1: 3	and from Jesus Christ, the Father's S, will	5626
	1: 9	the teaching has both the Father and the S.	5626
Rev	1:13	was someone "like a s of man,"	5626
	2:18	These are the words of the S of God,	5626
	12: 5	She gave birth to a s, a male child,	5626
	14:14	on the cloud was one "like a s of man" with	5626
	21: 7	and I will be his God and he will be my s.	5626

SON'S (12) [SON]

Ge	30:14	give me some of your s mandrakes."	1201
	30:15	Will you take my s mandrakes too?"	1201
	30:15	in return for your s mandrakes."	1201
	30:16	"I have hired you with my s mandrakes.	1201
	37:32	Examine it to see whether it is your s robe."	1201
	37:33	He recognized it and said, "It is my s robe!	1201
Ex		cut off her s foreskin and touched	1201
Lev	18:10	sexual relations with your s daughter	1201
	18:15	She is your s wife; do not have sexual	1201
	18:17	with either her s daughter or her daughter's	1201
2Sa	14:11	"not one hair of your s head will fall to	1201
1Ki	11:35	from his s hands and give you ten tribes.	1201

SON-IN-LAW (11) [SON]

Jdg	15: 6	they were told, "Samson, the Timnite's s,	3163
	19: 5	but the girl's father said to his,	3163
1Sa	18:18	that I should become the king's s?"	3163
	18:21	a second opportunity to become my s."	3161
	18:22	now become his s.' "	3161
	18:23	a small matter to become the king's s?	3161
	18:26	he was pleased to become the king's s.	3161
	18:27	so that he might become the king's s.	3161
	22:14	the king's s, captain of your bodyguard	3163
Ne	6:18	since he was s to Shecaniah son of Arah,	3163
	13:28	the high priest was s to Sanballat	3163

SONG (81) [SING]

Ex	15: 1	Then Moses and the Israelites sang this s to	8878
	15: 2	The LORD is my strength and my s;	2379
Nu	21:17	Then Israel sang this s: "Spring up, O well!	8878
Dt	31:19	down for yourselves this s and teach it to	8878
	31:21	this s will testify against them,	8878
	31:22	So Moses wrote down this s that day	8878
	31:30	the words of this s from beginning to end in	8878
	32:44	of Nun and spoke all the words of this s in	8878
Jdg	5: 1	and Barak son of Abinoam **sang** this s:	8876
	5:12	Wake up, wake up, break out in s!	8877
2Sa	22: 1	words of this s when the LORD delivered	8878
1Ch	16:42	of the other instruments for sacred s.	8877
Job	30: 9	"And now their sons **mock me in** s;	5593
	36:24	which men have **praised in** s.	8876
Ps	18: T	He sang to the LORD the words of this s	8878
	28: 7	for joy and I will give thanks to him in s.	8877
	30: T	A psalm. A s.	8877
	33: 3	Sing to him a new s;	8877
	40: 3	He put a new s in my mouth,	8877
	42: 8	at night his s is with me—	8877
	45: T	A maskil. A wedding s.	8877
	46: T	According to alamoth. A s.	8877
	48: T	A s. A psalm of the Sons of Korah.	8877
	65: T	A psalm of David. A s.	8877
	66: T	For the director of music. A s. A psalm.	8877
	67: T	With stringed instruments. A psalm. A s.	8877
	68: T	Of David. A psalm. A s.	8877
	69:12	and I am the s of the drunkards.	5593
	69:30	in s and glorify him with thanksgiving.	8877
	75: T	A psalm of Asaph. A s.	8877
	76: T	A psalm of Asaph. A s.	8877
	83: T	A s. A psalm of Asaph.	8877
	87: T	Of the Sons of Korah. A psalm. A s.	8877
	88: T	A psalm of the Sons of Korah.	8877
	92: T	A psalm. A s. For the Sabbath day.	8877
	95: 2	and extol him with **music and** s.	2369
	96: 1	Sing to the LORD a new s;	8877
	98: 1	Sing to the LORD a new s;	8877
	98: 4	burst into **jubilant** s with music;	8264
	108: T	A s. A psalm of David.	8877
	118:14	The LORD is my strength and my s;	2379

Ps	119:54	the **theme of** my s wherever I lodge.	2369
	120: T	A s of ascents.	8877
	121: T	A s of ascents.	8877
	122: T	A s of ascents. Of David.	8877
	123: T	A s of ascents.	8877
	124: T	A s of ascents. Of David.	8877
	125: T	A s of ascents.	8877
	126: T	A s of ascents.	8877
	127: T	A s of ascents. Of Solomon.	8877
	128: T	A s of ascents.	8877
	129: T	A s of ascents.	8877
	130: T	A s of ascents.	8877
	131: T	A s of ascents. Of David.	8877
	132: T	A s of ascents.	8877
	133: T	A s of ascents. Of David.	8877
	134: T	A s of ascents.	8877
	144: 9	I will sing a new s to you, O God;	8877
	149: 1	Sing to the LORD a new s,	8877
Ecc	7: 5	a wise man's rebuke than to listen to the s	8877
SS	1: 1	Solomon's S of Songs.	8877
Isa	5: 1	for the one I love a s about his vineyard:	8878
	12: 2	the LORD, is my strength and my s;	2379
	23:15	to Tyre as in the s of the prostitute:	8878
	23:16	play the harp well, sing many a s,	8877
	24: 9	No longer do they drink wine with a s;	8877
	25: 5	so the s of the ruthless is stilled.	2369
	26: 1	In that day this s will be sung in the land	8877
	42:10	Sing to the LORD a new s,	8877
	44:23	Burst into s, you mountains,	8262
	49:13	burst into s, O mountains!	8262
	54: 1	burst into s, shout for joy,	8262
	55:12	the mountains and hills will burst into s	8262
La	3:14	**mock** me in s all day long.	5593
Jnh	2: 9	But I, with a s of thanksgiving,	7754
Mic	2: 4	they will taunt you with this **mournful** s:	5631
Rev	5: 9	And they sang a new s: "You are worthy	6046
	14: 3	And they sang a new s before the throne	6046
	14: 3	No one could learn the s except the 144,000	6046
	15: 3	and sang the s of Moses the servant of God	6046
	15: 3	the servant of God and the s of the Lamb:	6046

SONGS (36) [SING]

1Sa	18: 6	with **joyful** s and with tambourines	8525
2Sa	6: 5	with s and with harps, lyres, tambourines,	8877
	23: 1	by the God of Jacob, Israel's singer of s:	2369
1Ki	4:32	and his s numbered a thousand and five.	8877
1Ch	13: 8	with s and with harps, lyres, tambourines,	8877
	15:16	as singers to **sing** joyful s,	928+4200+7754+8123+9048
Ne	12: 8	was in charge of the s of thanksgiving.	2117
	12:27	with s **of thanksgiving** and with the music	9343
	12:46	for the s of praise and thanksgiving to God.	8877
Job	35:10	who gives s in the night,	2369
Ps	32: 7	and surround me with s of deliverance.	8260
	65: 8	and evening fades you **call forth** s **of joy**.	8264
	77: 6	I remembered my s in the night.	5593
	78:63	and their maidens **had** no **wedding** s;	2146
	100: 2	come before him with **joyful** s.	8265
	107:22	and tell of his works with s **of joy**.	8262
	126: 2	our tongues with s **of joy**.	8262
	126: 5	who sow in tears will reap	8262
	126: 6	will return with s **of joy**,	8262
	137: 3	for there our captors asked us for s,	1821+8877
	137: 3	our tormentors demanded a joy;	NIH
	137: 3	they said, "Sing us one of the s of Zion!"	8877
	137: 4	How can we sing the s of the LORD while	8877
Pr	25:20	is one who sings s to a heavy heart.	8877
Ecc	12: 4	but all their s grow faint;	1426+8877
SS	1: 1	Solomon's Song of S.	8877
Isa	52: 9	Burst into s **of joy** together,	8264
Jer	30:19	From them will come s **of thanksgiving** and	9343
La	3:63	they **mock** me in s.	4947
Eze	26:13	I will put an end to your noisy s,	8877
	33:32	nothing more than one who sings love s	8877
Am	5:23	Away with the noise of your s!	8877
	8: 3	"the s in the temple will turn to wailing.	8878
Eph	5:19	with psalms, hymns and spiritual s.	6046
Col	3:16	and spiritual s with gratitude in your hearts	6046
Jas	5:13	*Let him* **sing** s **of praise**.	6010

SONS (878) [SON]

Ge	5: 4	Adam lived 800 years and had other s	1201
	5: 7	Seth lived 807 years and had other s	1201
	5:10	Enosh lived 815 years and had other s	1201
	5:13	Kenan lived 840 years and had other s	1201
	5:16	Mahalalel lived 830 years and had other s	1201
	5:19	Jared lived 800 years and had other s	1201
	5:22	with God 300 years and had other s	1201
	5:26	Methuselah lived 782 years and had other s	1201
	5:30	Lamech lived 595 years and had other s	1201
	6: 2	the s of God saw that the daughters	1201
	6: 4	the s of God went to the daughters of men	1201
	6:10	Noah had three s: Shem, Ham and Japheth.	1201
	6:18	you and your s and your wife	1201
	7: 7	And Noah and his s and his wife	1201
	7:13	On that very day Noah and his s, Shem,	1201
	7:13	with his wife and the wives of his three s,	1201
	8:16	and your wife and your s and their wives.	1201
	8:18	with his s and his wife and his sons' wives.	1201
	9: 1	Then God blessed Noah and his s,	1201
	9: 8	God said to Noah and to his s with him:	1201
	9:18	The s of Noah who came out of the ark	1201
	9:19	These were the three s of Noah,	1201
	10: 1	Shem, Ham and Japheth, Noah's s,	1201
	10: 1	who themselves had s after the flood.	1201

Ge	10: 2	The s of Japheth:	1201
	10: 3	The s of Gomer:	1201
	10: 4	The s of Javan:	1201
	10: 6	The s of Ham:	1201
	10: 7	The s of Cush:	1201
	10: 7	The s of Raamah: Sheba and Dedan.	1201
	10:20	the s of Ham by their clans and languages,	1201
	10:21	S were also **born** to Shem,	AIT
	10:21	Shem was the ancestor of all the s of Eber.	1201
	10:22	The s of Shem:	1201
	10:23	The s of Aram:	1201
	10:25	Two s were born to Eber:	1201
	10:29	All these were s of Joktan.	1201
	10:31	the s of Shem by their clans and languages,	1201
	10:32	These are the clans of Noah's s,	1201
	11:11	Shem lived 500 years and had other s	1201
	11:13	Arphaxad lived 403 years and had other s	1201
	11:15	Shelah lived 403 years and had other s	1201
	11:17	Eber lived 430 years and had other s	1201
	11:19	Peleg lived 209 years and had other s	1201
	11:21	Reu lived 207 years and had other s	1201
	11:23	Serug lived 200 years and had other s	1201
	11:25	Nahor lived 119 years and had other s	1201
	19:12	sons-in-law, s or daughters.	1201
	22:20	she has borne s to your brother Nahor:	1201
	22:23	Milcah bore **these** eight s to	AIT
	22:24	whose name was Reumah, also **had** s:	3528
	25: 4	The s of Midian were Ephah, Epher,	1201
	25: 6	the s of his concubines and sent them away	1201
	25: 9	His s Isaac and Ishmael buried him in	1201
	25:13	These are the names of the s of Ishmael,	1201
	25:16	These were the s of Ishmael,	1201
	27:29	and may the s of your mother bow down	1201
	29:34	because I have borne him three s."	1201
	30:20	because I have borne him six s."	1201
	30:35	and he placed them in the care of his s.	1201
	31: 1	Jacob heard that Laban's s were saying,	1201
	32:22	and his eleven s and crossed the ford of	3529
	33:19	he bought from the s of Hamor,	1201
	34: 5	his s were in the fields with his livestock;	1201
	34: 7	Now Jacob's s had come in from the fields	1201
	34:13	Jacob's s replied deceitfully as they spoke	1201
	34:25	two of Jacob's s, Simeon and Levi,	1201
	34:27	The s of Jacob came upon the dead bodies	1201
	35:22	Jacob had twelve s:	1201
	35:23	The s of Leah: Reuben the firstborn	1201
	35:24	The s of Rachel: Joseph and Benjamin.	1201
	35:25	The s of Rachel's maidservant Bilhah:	1201
	35:26	The s of Leah's maidservant Zilpah:	1201
	35:26	These were the s of Jacob,	1201
	35:29	And his s Esau and Jacob buried him.	1201
	36: 5	These were the s of Esau,	1201
	36: 6	and s and daughters and all the members	1201
	36:10	These are the names of Esau's s:	1201
	36:11	The s of Eliphaz:	1201
	36:13	The s of Reuel:	1201
	36:14	The s of Esau's wife Oholibamah daughter	1201
	36:15	The s of Eliphaz the firstborn of Esau:	1201
	36:17	The s of Esau's son Reuel:	1201
	36:18	The s of Esau's wife Oholibamah:	1201
	36:19	These were the s of Esau (that is, Edom),	1201
	36:20	These were the s of Seir the Horite,	1201
	36:21	These s of Seir in Edom were Horite chiefs.	1201
	36:22	The s of Lotan: Hori and Homam.	1201
	36:23	The s of Shobal:	1201
	36:24	The s of Zibeon: Aiah and Anah.	1201
	36:26	The s of Dishon:	1201
	36:27	The s of Ezer: Bilhan, Zaavan and Akan.	1201
	36:28	The s of Dishan: Uz and Aran.	1201
	37: 2	the s of Bilhah and the sons of Zilpah,	1201
	37: 2	the sons of Bilhah and the s of Zilpah,	1201
	37: 3	of his *other* s, because he had been born	1201
	37:35	All his s and daughters came to comfort him	1201
	41:50	two s were born to Joseph by Asenath	1201
	42: 1	there was grain in Egypt, he said to his s,	1201
	42: 5	So Israel's s were among those who went	1201
	42:11	We are all the s of one man,	1201
	42:13	the s of one man,	1201
	42:32	We were twelve brothers, s of one father.	1201
	42:37	"You may put both of my s to death if I do	1201
	44:20	and he is the only one of his mother's s left,	NIH
	44:27	'You know that my wife bore me **two** s.	AIT
	45:21	So the s of Israel did this.	1201
	46: 5	and Israel's s took their father Jacob	1201
	46: 7	with him to Egypt his s and grandsons	1201
	46: 8	These are the names of the s of Israel	1201
	46: 9	The s of Reuben: Hanoch, Pallu,	1201
	46:10	The s of Simeon: Jemuel, Jamin,	1201
	46:11	The s of Levi: Gershon, Kohath and Merari.	1201
	46:12	The s of Judah: Er, Onan, Shelah,	1201
	46:12	The s of Perez: Hezron and Hamul.	1201
	46:13	The s of Issachar: Tola, Puah,	1201
	46:14	The s of Zebulun: Sered, Elon and Jahleel.	1201
	46:15	the s Leah bore to Jacob in Paddan Aram,	1201
	46:15	These s and daughters of his were	1201
	46:16	The s of Gad: Zephon, Haggi, Shuni,	1201
	46:17	The s of Asher: Imnah, Ishvah,	1201
	46:17	The s of Beriah: Heber and Malkiel.	1201
	46:19	The s of Jacob's wife Rachel:	1201
	46:21	The s of Benjamin: Bela, Beker,	1201
	46:22	These were the s of Rachel who were born	1201
	46:24	The s of Naphtali: Jahziel, Guni,	1201
	46:25	These were the s born to Jacob by Bilhah,	1201
	48: 1	the two s who had been born to Joseph	1201
	48: 5	your two s born to you in Egypt	1201
	48: 8	When Israel saw the s of Joseph, he asked,	1201

Ge 48: 9 "They are the s God has given me here," 1201
48:10 So Joseph brought his s close to him, 4392S
49: 1 Then Jacob called for his s and said: 1201
49: 2 "Assemble and listen, s of Jacob; 1201
49: 8 your father's s will bow down to you. 1201
49:33 to his s, he drew his feet up into 1201
50:12 Jacob's s did as he had commanded them: 1201
50:25 And Joseph made the s of Israel swear 1201
Ex 1: 1 the names of the s of Israel who went 1201
3:22 which you will put on your s and daughters. 1201
4:20 So Moses took his wife and s, 1201
6:14 The s of Reuben the firstborn son 1201
6:15 The s of Simeon were Jemuel, Jamin, 1201
6:16 of the s of Levi according to their records: 1201
6:17 The s of Gershon, by clans, 1201
6:18 The s of Kohath were Amram, Izhar, 1201
6:19 The s of Merari were Mahli and Mushi. 1201
6:21 The s of Izhar were Korah, 1201
6:22 The s of Uzziel were Mishael, 1201
6:24 The s of Korah were Assir, 1201
10: 9 with our s and daughters, 1201
13:13 Redeem every firstborn among your s. 1201
13:15 and redeem each of my firstborn s.' 1201
13:19 with him because Joseph had made the s 1201
18: 3 and her two s. 1201
18: 5 together with Moses' s and wife, 1201
18: 6 to you with your wife and her two s." 1201
21: 4 a wife and she bears him s or daughters, 1201
22:29 "You must give me the firstborn of your s. 1201
27:21 and his s are to keep the lamps burning 1201
28: 1 along with his s Nadab and Abihu, 1201
28: 4 for your brother Aaron and his s, 1201
28: 9 and engrave on them the names of the s 1201
28:11 of the s of Israel on the two stones the way 1201
28:12 of the ephod as memorial stones for the s 1201
28:21 one for each of the names of the s of Israel, 1201
28:29 the names of the s of Israel over his heart 1201
28:40 sashes and headbands for Aaron's s, 1201
28:41 on your brother Aaron and his s, 1201
28:43 his s must wear them whenever they enter 1201
29: 4 Then bring Aaron and his s to the entrance 1201
29: 8 Bring his s and dress them in tunics 1201
29: 9 Then tie sashes on Aaron and his s. 1201
29: 9 this way you shall ordain Aaron and his s. 1201
29:10 and his s shall lay their hands on its head. 1201
29:15 and his s shall lay their hands on its head. 1201
29:19 and his s shall lay their hands on its head. 1201
29:20 of the right ears of Aaron and his s, 1201
29:21 on Aaron and his garments and on his s 1201
29:21 Then he and his s and their garments will 1201
29:24 Put all these in the hands of Aaron and his s 1201
29:27 that belong to Aaron and his s: 1201
29:28 from the Israelites for Aaron and his s. 1201
29:32 and his s are to eat the meat of the ram and 1201
29:35 his s everything I have commanded you, 1201
29:44 and will consecrate Aaron and his s 1201
30:19 and his s are to wash their hands and feet 1201
30:30 and his s and consecrate them 1201
31:10 and his s to make for his s when they serve 1201
32: 2 your s and your daughters are wearing, 1201
32:29 you were against your own s and brothers, 1201
34:16 of their daughters as wives for your s 1201
34:16 they will lead your s to do the same. 1201
34:20 Redeem all your firstborn s. 1201
35:19 and the garments for his s when they serve 1201
39: 6 like a seal with the names of the s of Israel. 1201
39: 7 of the ephod as memorial stones for the s 1201
39:14 one for each of the names of the s of Israel, 4392S
39:27 For Aaron and his s, 1201
39:41 and the garments for his s when serving 1201
40:12 "Bring Aaron and his s to the entrance to 1201
40:14 Bring his s and dress them in tunics. 1201
40:31 and Moses and Aaron and his s used it 1201
Lev 1: 5 and then Aaron's s the priests shall bring 1201
1: 7 The s of Aaron the priest are to put fire on 1201
1: 8 Then Aaron's s the priests shall arrange 1201
1:11 the altar before the LORD, and Aaron's s 1201
2: 2 and take it to Aaron's s the priests. 1201
2: 3 to Aaron and his s; 1201
2:10 to Aaron and his s; 1201
3: 2 Then Aaron's s the priests shall sprinkle 1201
3: 5 Then Aaron's s are to burn it on the altar 1201
3: 8 Then Aaron's s shall sprinkle its blood 1201
3:13 Then Aaron's s shall sprinkle its blood 1201
6: 9 "Give Aaron and his s this command: 1201
6:14 Aaron's s are to bring it before the LORD, 1201
6:16 Aaron and his s shall eat the rest of it, 1201
6:20 the offering Aaron and his s are to bring to 1201
6:25 "Say to Aaron and his s: 1201
7:10 belongs equally to all the s of Aaron. 1201
7:31 but the breast belongs to Aaron and his s. 1201
7:34 the priest and his s as their regular share 1201
7:35 by fire that were allotted to Aaron and his s 1201
8: 2 "Bring Aaron and his s, 1201
8: 6 and his s forward and washed them 1201
8:13 Then he brought Aaron's s forward, 1201
8:14 Aaron and his s laid their hands on its head. 1201
8:18 Aaron and his s laid their hands on its head. 1201
8:22 Aaron and his s laid their hands on its head. 1201
8:24 Moses also brought Aaron's s forward 1201
8:27 of Aaron and his s and waved them before 1201
8:30 on Aaron and his garments and on his s 1201
8:30 and his s and their garments. 1201
8:31 Moses then said to Aaron and his s, 1201
8:31 saying, 'Aaron and his s are to eat it.' 1201
8:36 So Aaron and his s did everything 1201
9: 1 and his s and the elders of Israel. 1201

Lev 9: 9 His s brought the blood to him, 1201
9:12 His s handed him the blood, 1201
9:18 His s handed him the blood, 1201
10: 1 Aaron's s Nadab and Abihu took their censers, 1201
10: 4 s of Aaron's uncle Uzziel, 1201
10: 6 Then Moses said to Aaron and his Eleazar 1201
10: 9 "You and your s are not to drink wine 1201
10:12 Moses said to Aaron and his remaining s, 1201
10:14 and your s and your daughters may eat 1201
10:16 Aaron's remaining s, and asked, 1201
13: 2 to Aaron the priest or to one of his s who is 1201
16: 1 the death of the two s of Aaron who died 1201
17: 2 to Aaron and his s and to all the Israelites 1201
21: 1 "Speak to the priests, the s of Aaron, 1201
21:24 to Aaron and his s and to all the Israelites. 1201
22: 2 "Tell Aaron and his s to treat with respect 1201
22:18 to Aaron and his s and to all the Israelites 1201
24: 9 It belongs to Aaron and his s, 1201
26:29 of your s and the flesh of your daughters. 1201
Nu 1:10 from the s of Joseph: from Ephraim 1201
1:32 From the s of Joseph: From the 1201
3: 2 of the s of Aaron were Nadab the firstborn 1201
3: 3 Those were the names of Aaron's s, 1201
3: 4 They had no s; 1201
3: 9 Give the Levites to Aaron and his s; 1201
3:10 Appoint Aaron and his s to serve as priests; 1201
3:17 These were the names of the s of Levi: 1201
3:38 Moses and Aaron and his s were to camp to 1201
3:48 the additional Israelites to Aaron and his s." 1201
3:51 the redemption money to Aaron and his s, 1201
4: 5 Aaron and his s are to go in and take down 1201
4:15 and his s have finished covering 1201
4:19 Aaron and his s are to go into the sanctuary 1201
4:27 under the direction of Aaron and his s. 1201
6:23 "Tell Aaron and his s, 1201
8:13 the Levites stand in front of Aaron and his s 1201
8:18 the Levites in place of all the firstborn s AIT
8:19 as gifts to Aaron and his s to do the work at 1201
8:22 under the supervision of Aaron and his s. 1201
10: 8 "The s of Aaron, the priests, 1201
16: 1 Dathan and Abiram, s of Eliab, 1201
16:12 Dathan and Abiram, s of Eliab. 1201
18: 1 your s and your father's family are to bear 1201
18: 1 and you and your s alone are to bear 1201
18: 2 and your s minister before the Tent of 1201
18: 7 But only you and your s may serve 1201
18: 8 to you and your s as your portion 1201
18: 9 that part belongs to you and your s. 1201
18:11 I give this to you and your s and daughters 1201
18:19 to the LORD I give to you and your s 1201
21:29 given up his s as fugitives and his daughters 1201
21:35 together with his s and his whole army, 1201
24:17 the skulls of all the s of Sheth. 1201
26: 9 and the s of Eliab were Nemuel, 1201
26:19 Er and Onan were s of Judah, 1201
26:33 (Zelophehad son of Hepher had no s; 1201
27: 3 but he died for his own sin and left no s. 1201
Dt 2:33 together with his s and his whole army. 1201
7: 3 Do not give your daughters to their s 1201
7: 3 or take their daughters for your s, 1201
7: 4 for they will turn your s away 1201
11: 6 s of Eliab the Reubenite. 1201
12:12 you, your s and daughters, 1201
12:18 you, your s and daughters, 1201
12:31 even burn their s and daughters in the fire 1201
16:11 you, your s and daughters, 1201
16:14 you, your s and daughters, 1201
21: 5 The priests, the s of Levi, 1201
21:15 both bear him s but the firstborn is the son 1201
21:16 when he wills his property to his s, 1201
28:32 Your s and daughters will be given 1201
28:41 You will have s and daughters but you will 1201
28:53 the flesh of the s and daughters 1201
31: 9 to the priests, the s of Levi, 1201
32: 8 according to the number of the s of Israel. 1201
32:19 because he was angered by his s 1201
33:24 "Most blessed of s is Asher; 1201
Jos 5: 7 So he raised up their s in their place, 1201
7:24 the gold wedge, his s and daughters, 1201
13:31 for half of the s of Makir, clan by clan. 1201
14: 4 the s of Joseph had become two tribes— 1201
17: 3 had no s but only daughters. 1201
17: 6 received an inheritance among the s. 1201
24: 4 but Jacob and his s went down to Egypt. 1201
24:32 for a hundred pieces of silver from the s 1201
Jdg 1:20 who drove from it the three s of Anak. 1201
3: 6 and gave their own daughters to their s, 1201
8:19 my brothers, the s of my own mother. 1201
8:30 He had seventy s of his own, 1201
9: 2 to have all seventy of Jerub-Baal's s rule 1201
9: 5 seventy brothers, the s of Jerub-Baal. 1201
9:18 murdered his seventy s on a single stone, 1201
9:24 the crime against Jerub-Baal's seventy s, 1201
10: 4 He had thirty s, who rode thirty donkeys. 1201
11: 2 Gilead's wife also bore him s, 1201
12: 9 He had thirty s and thirty daughters. 1201
12: 9 for his s he brought in thirty young women 1201
12:14 He had forty s and thirty grandsons, 1201
17: 5 and some idols and installed one of his s 1201
17:11 the young man was to him like one of his s 1201
18:30 and his s were priests for the tribe of Dan 1201
Ru 1: 1 together with his wife and two s, 1201
1: 2 and the names of his two s were Mahlon 1201
1: 3 died, and she was left with her two s. 1201
1: 5 and Naomi was left without her two s 3529
1:11 Am I going to have any more s, 1201

Ru 1:12 a husband tonight and then gave birth to s— 1201
4:15 and who is better to you than seven s, 1201
1Sa 1: 3 Hophni and Phinehas, the two s of Eli, 1201
1: 4 to his wife Peninnah and to all her s 1201
1: 8 Don't I mean more to you than ten s?" 1201
2: 5 but she who has had many s pines away. 1201
2:12 Eli's s were wicked men; 1201
2:21 and gave birth to three s and two daughters. 1201
2:22 heard about everything his s were doing 1201
2:24 my s; it is not a good report that I hear 1201
2:25 His s, however, did not listen NIH
2:29 Why do you honor your s more than me 1201
2:34 " 'And what happens to your two s, 1201
3:13 his s made themselves contemptible, 1201
4: 4 And Eli's two s, Hophni and Phinehas, 1201
4:11 and Eli's two s, Hophni and Phinehas, died. 1201
4:17 Also your two s, Hophni and Phinehas, 1201
8: 1 he appointed his s as judges for Israel. 1201
8: 3 But his s did not walk in his ways. 1201
8: 5 and your s do not walk in your ways; 1201
8:11 He will take your s and make them serve 1201
12: 2 and my s are here with you. 1201
14:49 Saul's s were Jonathan, Ishvi and 1201
14:51 and Abner's father Ner were s of Abiel. 1201
16: 1 I have chosen one of his s to be king." 1201
16: 5 and his s and invited them to the sacrifice. 1201
16:10 Jesse had seven of his s pass 1201
16:11 "Are these all the s you have?" 5853
17:12 Jesse had eight s, and in Saul's time 1201
17:13 Jesse's three oldest s had followed Saul to 1201
28:19 tomorrow you and your s will be with me. 1201
30: 3 and s and daughters taken captive. 1201
30: 6 each one was bitter in spirit because of his s 1201
31: 2 pressed hard after Saul and his s, 1201
31: 2 and they killed his s Jonathan, 1201
31: 6 So Saul and his three s and his armor-bearer 1201
31: 7 and that Saul and his s had died, 1201
31: 8 and his three s fallen on Mount Gilboa. 1201
31:12 the bodies of Saul and his s from the wall 1201
2Sa 2:18 The three s of Zeruiah were there: 1201
3: 2 S were born to David in Hebron: 1201
3:39 these s of Zeruiah are too strong for me. 1201
4: 2 they were s of Rimmon the Beerothite from 1201
4: 5 the s of Rimmon the Beerothite, 1201
4: 9 the s of Rimmon the Beerothite, 1201
5:13 and more s and daughters were born to him. 1201
6: 3 Uzzah and Ahio, s of Abinadab, 1201
8:18 and David's s were royal advisers. 1201
9:10 and your s and your servants are to farm 1201
9:10 Ziba had fifteen s and twenty servants.) 1201
9:11 at David's table like one of the king's s. 1201
13:23 he invited all the king's s to come there. 1201
13:27 and the rest of the king's s. 1201
13:29 Then all the king's s got up, 1201
13:30 "Absalom has struck down all the king's s; 1201
13:33 the report that all the king's s are dead. 1201
13:35 "See, the king's s are here; 1201
13:36 the king's s came in, wailing loudly. 1201
14: 6 I your servant had two s. 1201
14:27 Three s and a daughter were born 1201
15:27 You and Abiathar take your two s with you. 1201
15:36 Their two s, Ahimaaz son of Zadok, 1201
16:10 and I have in common, you s of Zeruiah? 1201
19: 5 and the lives of your s and daughters and 1201
19:17 and his fifteen s and twenty servants. 1201
19:22 and I have in common, you s of Zeruiah? 1201
21: 8 the two s of Aiah's daughter Rizpah, 1201
21: 8 with the five s of Saul's daughter Merab, 1201
23:32 the s of Jashen, Jonathan 1201
1Ki 1: 9 He invited all his brothers, the king's s, 1201
1:19 and sheep, and has invited all the king's s, 1201
1:25 He has invited all the king's s, 1201
2: 7 the s of Barzillai of Gilead and let them be 1201
4: 3 and Ahijah, s of Shisha— 1201
4:31 Calcol and Darda, the s of Mahol. 1201
8:25 if only your s are careful in all they do 1201
9: 6 if you or your s turn away from me and do 1201
13:11 whose s came and told him all that the man 1201
13:12 And his s showed him which road the man 1201
13:13 So he said to his s, "Saddle the donkey 1201
13:27 The prophet said to his s, "When I die, 1201
13:31 After burying him, he said to his s, 1201
20:35 the s of the prophets said to his companion, 1201
2Ki 4: 4 and shut the door behind you and your s. 1201
4: 5 the door behind her and her s, 1201
4: 7 You and your s can live on what is left." 1201
9:26 the blood of Naboth and the blood of his s, 1201
10: 1 in Samaria seventy s of the house of Ahab. 1201
10: 2 since your master's s are with you 1201
10: 3 the best and most worthy of your master's s 1201
10: 6 take the heads of your master's s and come 1201
14: 6 Yet he did not put the s of the assassins 1201
17:17 They sacrificed their s and daughters in the 1201
19:37 his s Adrammelech and Sharezer cut him 1201
25: 7 the s of Zedekiah before his eyes. 1201
1Ch 1: 4 The s of Noah: Shem, Ham and Japheth. 1201
1: 5 The s of Japheth: Gomer, Magog, Madai, 1201
1: 6 The s of Gomer: Ashkenaz, 1201
1: 7 The s of Javan: Elishah, Tarshish, 1201
1: 8 s of Ham: Cush, Mizraim, Put and Canaan. 1201
1: 9 The s of Cush: Seba, Havilah, 1201
1: 9 The s of Raamah: Sheba and Dedan. 1201
1:17 The s of Shem: Elam, Asshur, 1201
1:17 The s of Aram: Uz, Hul, Gether 1201
1:19 Two s were born to Eber: 1201
1:23 All these were s of Joktan. 1201
1:28 The s of Abraham: Isaac and Ishmael. 1201

1Ch 1:31 These were the s of Ishmael. 1201
1:32 The s born to Keturah, 1201
1:32 The s of Jokshan: Sheba and Dedan. 1201
1:33 The s of Midian: Ephah, Epher, 1201
1:34 The s of Isaac: Esau and Israel. 1201
1:35 The s of Esau: Eliphaz, Reuel, 1201
1:36 The s of Eliphaz: Teman, Omar, 1201
1:37 The s of Reuel: Nahath, Zerah, 1201
1:38 The s of Seir: Lotan, Shobal, 1201
1:39 The s of Lotan: Hori and Homam. 1201
1:40 The s of Shobal: Alvan, Manahath, 1201
1:40 The s of Zibeon: Aiah and Anah. 1201
1:41 The s of Dishon: Hemdan, Eshban, 1201
1:42 The s of Ezer: Bilhan, Zaavan and Akan. 1201
1:42 The s of Dishan: Uz and Aran. 1201
2:1 These were the s of Israel. 1201
2:3 The s of Judah: Er, Onan and Shelah. 1201
2:4 Judah had five s in all. 1201
2:5 The s of Perez: Hezron and Hamul. 1201
2:6 The s of Zerah: Zimri, Ethan, 1201
2:9 The s born to Hezron were: 1201
2:16 Zeruiah's three s were Abishai, 1201
2:18 These were her s: Jesher, Shobab 1201
2:25 The s of Jerahmeel the firstborn of Hezron: 1201
2:27 The s of Ram the firstborn of Jerahmeel: 1201
2:28 The s of Onam: Shammai and Jada. 1201
2:28 The s of Shammai: Nadab and Abishur. 1201
2:30 The s of Nadab: Seled and Appaim. 1201
2:32 The s of Jada, Shammai's brother: 1201
2:33 The s of Jonathan: Peleth and Zaza. 1201
2:34 Sheshan had no s—only daughters. 1201
2:42 The s of Caleb the brother of Jerahmeel: 1201
2:43 The s of Hebron: Korah, Tappuah, 1201
2:47 The s of Jahdai: Regem, Jotham, 1201
2:50 The s of Hur the firstborn of Ephrathah: 1201
3:1 These were the s of David born to him 1201
3:9 All these were the s of David, 1201
3:9 besides his s by his concubines. 1201
3:15 The s of Josiah: Johanan the firstborn, 1201
3:19 The s of Pedaiah: Zerubbabel and Shimei. 1201
3:19 The s of Zerubbabel: Meshullam and 1201
3:21 and the s of Rephaiah, of Arnan, 1201
3:22 Shemaiah and his s: 1201
3:23 The s of Neariah: Elioenai, Hizkiah 1201
3:24 The s of Elioenai: Hodaviah, 1201
4:3 These were the s of Etam: 1201S
4:7 The s of Helah: Zereth, Zohar, Ethnan, 1201
4:13 The s of Kenaz: Othniel and Seraiah. 1201
4:13 The s of Othniel: Hathath and Meonothai. 1201
4:15 The s of Caleb son of Jephunneh: 1201
4:16 The s of Jehallelel: Ziph, Ziphah, 1201
4:17 The s of Ezrah: Jether, Mered, 1201
4:19 The s of Hodiah's wife, 1201
4:20 The s of Shimon: Amnon, Rinnah, 1201
4:21 The s of Shelah son of Judah: 1201
4:27 Shimei had sixteen s and six daughters, 1201
4:42 Neariah, Rephaiah and Uzziel, the s of Ishi, 1201
5:1 The s of Reuben the firstborn 1201
5:1 his rights as firstborn were given to the s 1201
5:3 the s of Reuben the firstborn of Israel: 1201
5:14 These were the s of Abihail son of Huri, 1201
6:1 s of Levi: Gershon, Kohath and Merari. 1201
6:2 The s of Kohath: Amram, Izhar, 1201
6:3 The s of Aaron: Nadab, Abihu, 1201
6:16 s of Levi: Gershon, Kohath and Merari. 1201
6:17 These are the names of the s of Gershon: 1201
6:18 The s of Kohath: Amram, Izhar, 1201
6:19 The s of Merari: Mahli and Mushi. 1201
6:28 The s of Samuel: Joel the firstborn 1201
6:33 together with their s: 1201
7:1 The s of Issachar: Tola, Puah, 1201
7:2 The s of Tola: Uzzi, Rephaiah, 1201
7:3 The s of Izrahiah: Michael, Obadiah, 1201
7:6 Three s of Benjamin: Bela, Beker NIH
7:7 The s of Bela: Ezbon, Uzzi, 1201
7:8 The s of Beker: Zemirah, Joash, 1201
7:8 All these were the s of Beker. 1201
7:10 The s of Bilhan: Jeush, Benjamin, 1201
7:11 All these s of Jediael were heads 1201
7:13 The s of Naphtali: Jahziel, Guni, 1201
7:16 and his s were Ulam and Rakem. 1201
7:17 These were the s of Gilead son of Makir, 1201
7:19 The s of Shemida were: 1201
7:30 The s of Asher: Imnah, Ishvah, 1201
7:31 The s of Beriah: Heber and Malkiel. 1201
7:33 The s of Japhlet: Pasach, Bimhal 1201
7:33 These were Japhlet's s. 1201
7:34 The s of Shomer: Ahi, Rohgah, 1201
7:35 The s of his brother Helem: 1201
7:36 The s of Zophah: Suah, Harnepher, 1201
7:38 The s of Jether: Jephunneh, 1201
7:39 The s of Ulla: Arah, Hanniel and Rizia. 1201
8:3 The s of Bela were: Addar, Gera, Abihud, 1201
8:8 S were born to Shaharaim in Moab NIH
8:10 These were his s, heads of families. 1201
8:12 The s of Elpaal: Eber, Misham, 1201
8:16 Ishpah and Joha were the s of Beriah. 1201
8:18 Izliah and Jobab were the s of Elpaal. 1201
8:21 Beraiah and Shimrath were the s of Shimei. 1201
8:25 Iphdeiah and Penuel were the s of Shashak. 1201
8:27 Elijah and Zicri were the s of Jeroham. 1201
8:35 The s of Micah: Pithon, Melech, 1201
8:38 Azel had six s, and these were their names: 1201
8:38 All these were the s of Azel. 1201
8:39 The s of his brother Eshek: 1201
8:40 The s of Ulam were brave warriors who could handle the bow. 1201

1Ch 8:40 They had many s and grandsons— 1201
9:5 Asaiah the firstborn and his s. 1201
9:41 The s of Micah: Pithon, Melech, 1201
9:44 Azel had six s, and these were their names: 1201
9:44 These were the s of Azel. 1201
10:2 pressed hard after Saul and his s, 1201
10:2 and they killed his s Jonathan, 1201
10:6 So Saul and his three s died, 1201
10:7 and that Saul and his s had died, 1201
10:8 and his s fallen on Mount Gilboa. 1201
10:12 and his s and brought them to Jabesh. 1201
11:34 the s of Hashem the Gizonite, 1201
11:44 and Jeiel the s of Hotham the Aroerite, 1201
11:46 Jeribai and Joshaviah the s of Elnaam, 1201
12:3 and Joash the s of Shemaah the Gibeathite; 1201
12:3 Jeziel and Pelet the s of Azmaveth; 1201
12:7 and Zebadiah the s of Jeroham from Gedor. 1201
14:3 the father of more s and daughters. 1201
16:13 O s of Jacob, his chosen ones. 1201
16:42 The s of Jeduthun were stationed at 1201
17:11 to succeed you, one of your own s, 1201
18:17 and David's s were chief officials at 1201
21:20 his four s who were with him hid 1201
23:6 into groups corresponding to the s of Levi: 1201
23:8 The s of Ladan: Jehiel the first, 1201
23:9 The s of Shimei: Shelomoth, 1201
23:10 And the s of Shimei: Jahath, Ziza, 1201
23:10 These were the s of Shimei—four in all. 1201
23:11 but Jeush and Beriah did not have many s; 1201
23:12 The s of Kohath: Amram, Izhar, 1201
23:13 The s of Amram: Aaron and Moses. 1201
23:14 The s of Moses the man of God were 1201
23:15 The s of Moses: Gershom and Eliezer. 1201
23:17 Eliezer had no other s, 1201
23:17 but the s of Rehabiah were very numerous. 1201
23:18 The s of Izhar: Shelomith was the first. 1201
23:19 The s of Hebron: Jeriah the first, 1201
23:20 The s of Uzziel: Micah the first 1201
23:21 The s of Merari: Mahli and Mushi. 1201
23:21 The s of Mahli: Eleazar and Kish. 1201
23:22 Eleazar died without having s, 1201
23:22 Their cousins, the s of Kish, married them. 1201
23:23 The s of Mushi: Mahli, Eder 1201
24:1 These were the divisions of the s of Aaron: 1201
24:1 The s of Aaron were Nadab, Abihu, 1201
24:2 and they had no s, 1201
24:20 from the s of Amram: Shubael; 1201
24:20 from the s of Shubael: Jehdeiah. 1201
24:21 Rehabiah, from his s: Isshiah was the first. 1201
24:22 from the s of Shelomoth: Jahath. 1201
24:23 The s of Hebron: Jeriah the first, 1201
24:24 from the s of Micah: Shamir. 1201
24:25 from the s of Isshiah: Zechariah. 1201
24:26 The s of Merari: Mahli and Mushi. 1201
24:27 The s of Merari: from Jaaziah: 1201
24:28 From Mahli: Eleazar, who had no s. 1201
24:30 the s of Mushi: Mahli, Eder and Jerimoth. 1201
25:1 set apart some of the s of Asaph, 1201
25:2 From the s of Asaph: Zaccur, Joseph, 1201
25:2 The s of Asaph were under the supervision 1201
25:3 As for Jeduthun, from his s: 1201
25:4 As for Heman, from his s: 1201
25:5 All these were s of Heman the king's seer. 1201
25:5 God gave Heman fourteen s 1201
25:9 fell to Joseph, his s and relatives, 1201
25:9 to Gedaliah, he and his relatives and s, 1201
25:10 the third to Zaccur, his s and relatives, 1201
25:11 the fourth to Izri, his s and relatives, 1201
25:12 the fifth to Nethaniah, his s and relatives, 1201
25:13 the sixth to Bukkiah, his s and relatives, 1201
25:14 the seventh to Jesarelah, his s and relatives, 1201
25:15 the eighth to Jeshaiah, his s and relatives, 1201
25:16 the ninth to Mattaniah, his s and relatives, 1201
25:17 the tenth to Shimei, his s and relatives, 1201
25:18 the eleventh to Azarel, his s and relatives, 1201
25:19 the twelfth to Hashabiah, his s and relatives, 1201
25:20 thirteenth to Shubael, his s and relatives, 1201
25:21 fourteenth to Mattithiah, his s and relatives, 1201
25:22 fifteenth to Jerimoth, his s and relatives, 1201
25:23 sixteenth to Hananiah, his s and relatives, 1201
25:24 to Joshbekashah, his s and relatives, 1201
25:25 eighteenth to Hanani, his s and relatives, 1201
25:26 nineteenth to Mallothi, his s and relatives, 1201
25:27 twentieth to Eliathah, his s and relatives, 1201
25:28 to Hothir, his s and relatives, 1201
25:29 to Giddalti, his s and relatives, 1201
25:30 to Mahazioth, his s and relatives, 1201
25:31 to Romamti-Ezer, his s and relatives, 1201
26:1 one of the s of Asaph. 1201
26:2 Meshelemiah had s: Zechariah the firstborn, 1201
26:4 Obed-Edom also had s: 1201
26:6 His son Shemaiah also had s, 1201
26:7 The s of Shemaiah: Othni, 1201
26:8 they and their s and their relatives 1201
26:9 Meshelemiah had s and relatives, 1201
26:10 Hosah the Merarite had s: 1201
26:11 The s and relatives of Hosah were 13 in all. 1201
26:15 and the lot for the storehouse fell to his s. 1201
26:22 the s of Jehieli. 1201
26:29 and his s were assigned duties away from 1201
27:32 of Hacmoni took care of the king's s. 1201
28:1 to the king and his s, 1201
28:4 and from my father's s he was pleased 1201
28:5 Of all my s—and the LORD has given me 1201
29:24 as well as all of King David's s, 1201
2Ch 5:12 Jeduthun and their s and relatives— 1201
6:16 if only your s are careful in all they do 1201

2Ch 11:14 and his s had rejected them as priests of 1201
11:19 She bore him s: 1201
11:21 twenty-eight s and sixty daughters. 1201
11:23 of his s throughout the districts of Judah 1201
13:9 the s of Aaron, and the Levites, 1201
13:10 The priests who serve the LORD are s 1201
13:21 and had twenty-two s and sixteen daughters. 1201
21:2 Jehoram's brothers, the s of Jehoshaphat, 1201
21:2 All these were s of Jehoshaphat king 1201
21:14 to strike your people, your s, your wives 1201
21:17 together with his s and wives. 1201
22:1 had killed all the older s. NIH
22:8 of Judah and the s of Ahaziah's relatives, 1201
23:11 and his s brought out the king's son and put 1201
24:3 and he had s and daughters. 1201
24:7 Now the s of that wicked woman Athaliah 1201
24:27 The account of his s, 1201
25:4 Yet he did not put their s to death, 1201
28:3 of Ben Hinnom and sacrificed his s in 1201
28:8 two hundred thousand wives, s and 1201
29:9 by the sword and why our s and daughters 1201
29:11 My s, do not be negligent now, 1201
31:18 and the s and daughters of 1201
32:21 of his s cut him down with the sword. 3665+5055
33:6 He sacrificed his s in the fire in the Valley 1201
36:20 and his s until the kingdom of Persia came 1201
Ezr 3:2 Jeshua and his s and brothers and Kadmiel 1201
3:9 and his s (descendants of Hodaviah) and 1201
3:9 and the s of Henadad and their sons— 1201
3:9 of Henadad and their s and brothers— 1201
3:10 the Levites (the s of Asaph) with cymbals, 1201
6:10 for the well-being of the king and his s. 10120
7:23 against the realm of the king and of his s? 10120
8:18 and Sherebiah's s and brothers, 18 men; 1201
9:2 as wives for themselves and their s, 1201
9:12 in marriage to their s or take their daughters 1201
9:12 or take their daughters for your s. 1201
Ne 3:3 The Fish Gate was rebuilt by the s 1201
4:14 your s and your daughters, 1201
5:2 "We and our s and daughters are numerous; 1201
5:5 as our countrymen and though our s are 1201
5:5 yet we have to subject our s and daughters 1201
9:23 You made their s as numerous as the stars 1201
9:24 Their s went in and took possession of 1201
10:9 Binnui of the s of Henadad, Kadmiel, 1201
10:28 and all their s and daughters who are able 1201
10:30 around us or take their daughters for our s. 1201
10:36 we will bring the firstborn of our s and 1201
13:25 your daughters in marriage to their s, 1201
13:25 in marriage for your s or for yourselves. 1201
13:28 One of the s of Joiada son of Eliashib 1201
Est 5:11 to them about his vast wealth, his many s, 1201
9:10 the ten s of Haman son of Hammedatha, 1201
9:12 the ten s of Haman in the citadel of Susa. 1201
9:13 let Haman's ten s be hanged on gallows." 1201
9:14 and they hanged the ten s of Haman. 1201
9:25 and his s should be hanged on the gallows. 1201
Job 1:2 He had seven s and three daughters, 1201
1:4 His s used to take turns holding feasts 1201
1:13 when Job's s and daughters were feasting 1201
1:18 "Your s and daughters were feasting 1201
14:21 If his s are honored, he does not know it; 1201
21:19 up a man's punishment for his s.' 1201
30:9 "And now their s mock me in song; 4392S
35:8 and your righteousness only the s of men. 1201
42:13 he also had seven s and three daughters. 1201
Ps 11:4 He observes the s of men; 1201
14:2 down from heaven on the s of men to see 1201
17:14 their s have plenty, and they store up wealth 1201
42:T A maskil of the S of Korah. 1201
44:T Of the S of Korah. 1201
45:T Of the S of Korah. 1201
45:16 Your s will take the place of your fathers; 1201
46:T Of the S of Korah. 1201
47:T Of the S of Korah. 1201
48:T A song. A psalm of the S of Korah. 1201
49:T Of the S of Korah. 1201
53:2 down from heaven on the s of men to see 1201
69:8 an alien to my own mother's s; 1201
82:6 you are all s of the Most High.' 1201
84:T Of the S of Korah. 1201
85:T Of the S of Korah. 1201
87:T Of the S of Korah. A psalm. A song. 1201
88:T A psalm of the S of Korah. 1201
89:30 "If his s forsake my law and do 1201
90:3 saying, "Return to dust, O s of men." 1201
105:6 O s of Jacob, his chosen ones. 1201
106:37 They sacrificed their s and their daughters 1201
106:38 the blood of their s and daughters, 1201
127:3 S are a heritage from the LORD, 1201
127:4 of a warrior are s born in one's youth. 1201
128:3 your s will be like olive shoots 1201
132:12 if your s keep my covenant and 1201
132:12 then their s will sit on your throne for ever 1201
144:12 Then our s in their youth will be 1201
Pr 1:8 Listen, my s, to a father's instruction; 1201
5:7 Now then, my s, listen to me; 1201
7:24 Now then, my s, listen to me; 1201
8:32 "Now then, my s, listen to me; 1201
SS 1:6 My mother's s were angry with me 1201
Isa 14:21 Prepare a place to slaughter his s for 1201
23:4 I have neither reared s nor brought 1033
37:38 his s Adrammelech and Sharezer cut him 1201
43:6 Bring my s from afar and my daughters 1201
49:17 Your s hasten back, 1201
49:18 all your s gather and come to you. 4392S
49:22 they will bring your s in their arms 1201

Isa	51:12	the s of men, who are but grass, 1201
	51:18	the s she bore there was none to guide her; 1201
	51:18	the s she reared there was none to take her 1201
	51:20	Your s have fainted; 1201
	54:13	All your s will be taught by the LORD, 1201
	56: 5	and a name better than s and daughters; 1201
	57: 3	come here, you s of a sorceress, 1201
	60: 4	your s come from afar, 1201
	60: 9	bringing your s from afar, 1201
	60:14	The s of your oppressors will come bowing 1201
	62: 5	so will your s marry you; 1201
	63: 8	s who will not be false to me"; 1201
Jer	3:19	" 'How gladly would I treat you like s 1201
	3:24	and herds, their s and daughters. 1201
	5:17	devour your s and daughters; 1201
	6:21	Fathers and s alike will stumble over them; 1201
	7:31	in the Valley of Ben Hinnom to burn their s 1201
	10:20	My s are gone from me and are no more; 1201
	11:22	their s and daughters by famine. 1201
	13:14	fathers and s alike, declares the LORD. 1201
	14:16	their s or their daughters. 1201
	16: 2	and have s or daughters in this place." 1201
	16: 3	For this is what the LORD says about the s 1201
	19: 5	the high places of Baal to burn their s in 1201
	19: 9	I will make them eat the flesh of their s 1201
	29: 6	Marry and have s and daughters; 1201
	29: 6	for your s and give your daughters 1201
	29: 6	so that they too may have s and daughters. 1201
	32:35	to sacrifice their s and daughters to Molech, 1201
	33:26	and will not choose one of his s to rule over 2446
	35: 3	and his brothers and all his s— 1201
	35: 4	the room of the s of Hanan son of Igdaliah 1201
	35: 8	Neither we nor our wives nor our s 1201
	35:14	of Recab ordered his s not to drink wine 1201
	39: 6	of Babylon slaughtered the s of Zedekiah 1201
	40: 8	Johanan and Jonathan the s of Kareah, 1201
	40: 8	the s of Ephai the Netophathite, 1201
	48:46	your s are taken into exile 1201
	49: 1	"Has Israel no s? 1201
	52:10	of Babylon slaughtered the s of Zedekiah 1201
La	4: 2	How the precious s of Zion, 1201
Eze	14:16	not save their own s or daughters. 1201
	14:18	not save their own s or daughters. 1201
	14:22	s and daughters who will be brought out 1201
	16:20	" 'And you took your s and daughters 1201
	20:31	the sacrifice of your s in the fire— 1201
	23: 4	They were mine and gave birth to s 1201
	23:10	took away her s and daughters 1201
	23:25	They will take away your s and daughters, 1201
	23:47	they will kill their s and daughters and burn 1201
	24:21	The s and daughters you left 1201
	24:25	and their s and daughters as well— 1201
	40:46	These are the s of Zadok, 1201
	46:16	from his inheritance to one of his s, it will 1201
	46:17	His inheritance belongs to his s only; 1201
	46:18	He is to give his s their inheritance out 1201
Da	11:10	His s will prepare for war and assemble 1201
Hos	1:10	they will be called 's of the living God.' 1201
Joel	2:28	Your s and daughters will prophesy, 1201
	3: 8	I will sell your s and daughters to 1201
Am	2:11	also raised up prophets from among your s 1201
	7:17	your s and daughters will fall by the sword. 1201
Zep	1: 8	and the king's s and all those clad 1201
Zec	9:13	I will rouse you s, O Zion, 1201
	9:13	O Zion, against your s, O Greece, 1201
Mt	5: 9	for they will be called s of God. 5626
	5:45	that you may be s of your Father in heaven. 5626
	13:38	good seed stands for the s of the kingdom. 5626
	13:38	The weeds are the s of the evil one, 5626
	17:25	from their own s or from others?" 5626
	17:26	"Then the s are exempt," Jesus said to him. 5626
	20:20	of Zebedee's s came to Jesus with her sons 5626
	20:20	of Zebedee's sons came to Jesus with her s 5626
	20:21	of these two s of mine may sit at your right 5626
	21:28	There was a man who had two s. 5451
	26:37	and the two s of Zebedee along with him, 5626
	27:56	and the mother of Zebedee's s. 5626
Mk	3:17	which means s of Thunder); 5626
	10:35	Then James and John, the s of Zebedee, 5626
Lk	5:10	the s of Zebedee, Simon's partners. 5626
	6:35	and you will be s of the Most High, 5626
	15:11	"There was a man who had two s. 5626
Jn	4:12	as did also his s and his flocks and herds?" 5626
	12:36	so that you may become s of light." 5626
	21: 2	the s of Zebedee, and the two other AIT
Ac	2:17	Your s and daughters will prophesy, 5626
	7:16	that Abraham had bought from the s 5626
	7:29	he settled as a foreigner and had two s. 5626
	19:14	Seven s of Sceva, a Jewish chief priest, 5626
Ro	8:14	by the Spirit of God are s of God. 5626
	8:19	in eager expectation for the s of God to 5626
	8:23	as we wait eagerly for our adoption as s, 5625
	9: 4	Theirs is the adoption as s; 5625
	9:26	they will be called 's of the living God.' " 5626
2Co	6:18	and you will be my s and daughters, 5626
Gal	3:26	You are all s of God through faith 5626
	4: 5	that we might receive the full rights of s. 5625
	4: 6	Because you are s, God sent the Spirit 5626
	4:22	For it is written that Abraham had two s, 5626
Eph	1: 5	to be adopted as his s through Jesus Christ, 5625
1Th	5: 5	You are all s of the light and sons of 5626
	5: 5	You are all sons of the light and s of 5626
Heb	2:10	In bringing many s to glory, 5626
	11:21	blessed each of Joseph's s, 5626
	12: 5	of encouragement that addresses you as s: 5626
	12: 7	God is treating you as s. 5626
	12: 8	you are illegitimate children and not true s. 5626

SONS-IN-LAW (3) [SON]

Ge	19:12	s, sons or daughters, or anyone else in 3163
	19:14	So Lot went out and spoke to his s, 3163
	19:14	But his s thought he was joking. 3163

SONS' (5) [SON]

Ge	6:18	and your wife and your s' wives with you. 1201
	7: 7	and his s' wives entered the ark to escape 1201
	8:18	with his sons and his wife and his s' wives. 1201
	46:26	not counting his s' wives— 1201
Lev	10:13	because it is your share and your s' share of 1201

SONSHIP (1) [SON]

Ro	8:15	but you received the Spirit of s. 5625

SOON (105) [SOONER]

Ge	19:17	As s as they had brought them out, 3869
	24:30	As s as he had seen the nose ring, 3869
	29:13	As s as Laban heard the news about Jacob, 3869
	34: 7	in from the fields as s as they heard 3869
	39:18	But as s as I screamed for help, 3869
	40:10	As s as it budded, it blossomed, 3869
	41:32	and God will do it s. 4554
	42: 7	As s as Joseph saw his brothers, 2256
	46:29	As s as Joseph appeared before him, 2256
Ex	8:29	Moses answered, "As s as I leave you, 2180
Nu	16:31	As s as he finished saying all this, 3869
Dt	11:17	and you will s perish from the good land 4559
	31:16	these people will s prostitute themselves 7756
Jos	2: 7	and as s as the pursuers had gone out, 889+3869
	3:13	And as s as the priests who carry the ark of 3869
	3:15	Yet as s as the priests who carried 3869
	4:11	and as s as all of them had crossed, 889+3869
	8:19	As s as he did this, 3869
1Sa	9:13	As s as you enter the town, 3869+4027
	17:57	As s as David returned from killing 3869
	29:10	and leave in the morning as s as it is light." 2256
2Sa	5:24	As s as you hear the sound of marching in 3869
	15:10	"As s as you hear the sound of the trumpets, 3869
	19:41	S all the men of Israel were coming to 2180
	22:45	as s as they hear me, they obey me. 4200
1Ki	1:21	as s as my lord the king is laid to rest 3869
	14:17	As s as she stepped over the threshold of NIH
	15:29	As s as he began to reign, 3869
	16:11	As s as he began to reign and was seated on 928
	20:36	as s as you leave me a lion will kill you." 2180
	21:15	As s as Jezebel heard 3869
2Ki	7: 9	As s as the king of Israel read the letter, 3869
	10: 2	"As s as this letter reaches you, 3869
	10:25	As s as Jehu had finished making 3869
1Ch	14:15	As s as you hear the sound of marching in 3869
2Ch	12: 7	but will s give them deliverance. 3869+5071
	31: 5	As s as the order went out, 3869
Ezr	4:23	As s as the copy of the letter 10008+10168+10427
Ne	9:28	"But as s as they were at rest, 3869
Est	7: 8	As s as the word left the king's mouth, NIH
Job	7:21	For I will s lie down in the dust; 6964
	32:22	my Maker would s take me away. 3869+5071
Ps	18:44	as s as they hear me, they obey me; 4200
	37: 2	for like the grass they will s wither, 4559
	37: 2	like green plants they will s die away. NIH
	37:36	but he s passed away and was no more; AIT
	94:17	I would s have dwelt in the silence of death. 3869+5071
	106:13	But they s forgot what he had done and did 4554
Isa	10:25	Very s my anger against you will end 4663+5071+6388
	28: 4	as s as someone sees it and takes it 889
	30:19	As s as he hears, he will answer you. 3869
	51:14	The cowering prisoners will s be set free; 4554
	56: 1	and my righteousness will s be revealed. NIH
Jer	26: 8	But as s as Jeremiah finished telling all 3869
	27:16	not listen to the prophets who say, 'Very s 4559
	51:33	the time to harvest her will s come." 5071+6388
Eze	11: 3	'Will it not s be time to build houses?' 928+7940
	16:47	in all your ways you s became more depraved than they. 3869+5071+7775
	23:16	As s as she saw them, 4200
	36: 8	for they will s come home. 7928
Da	3: 5	As s as you hear the sound of the horn, 10002+10089+10168+10530
	3: 7	as s as they heard the sound of the horn, 10002+10168+10232+10341
	9:23	As s as you began to pray, 928
	10:20	S I will return to fight against the prince 6964
Hos	1: 4	I will punish the house of Jehu 5071+6388
Mt	2: 8	As s as you find him, report to me, 2054
	3:16	As s as Jesus was baptized, 2317
	24:32	As s as its twigs get tender 4020
Mk	1:29	As s as they left the synagogue, 2317
	4:15	As s as they hear it, 2317+4020
	4:29	As s as the grain is ripe, 2317+4020
	6:54	As s as they got out of the boat, 2317
	7:25	In fact, as s as she heard about him, 2317
	9:15	As s as all the people saw Jesus, 2317
	13:28	As s as its twigs get tender 2453+4020
Lk	1:44	As s as the sound of your greeting 6055
	7:11	S afterward, Jesus went to 1877+2009+3836
Jn	13:27	As s as Judas took the bread, 5538
	13:30	As s as Judas had taken the bread, 2317
	19: 6	As s as the chief priests and their officials 4021
	21: 7	s as Simon Peter heard him say, AIT
Ac	17:10	As s as it was night, 2311
	17:15	and Timothy to join him as s as possible. 5441

Ac	19:29	S the whole city was in an uproar. 2779
	25: 4	and I myself am going there s. 1877+5443
Ro	16:20	The God of peace will s crush Satan under your feet. 1877+5443
1Co	4:19	But I will come to you very s, 5441
Php	2:19	in the Lord Jesus to send Timothy to you s, 5441
	2:23	to send him as s as I see how things go 323+6055
	2:24	in the Lord that I myself will come s. 5441
1Ti	3:14	Although I hope to come to you s, 1877+5443
Tit	3:12	As s as I send Artemas or Tychicus to you, 4020
Heb	8:13	what is obsolete and aging will s disappear. 1584
	13:19	to pray so that I may be restored to you s. 5441
	13:23	If he arrives s, I will come with him to see 5441
2Pe	1:14	because I know that I will s put it aside, 5442
3Jn	1:14	I hope to see you s, 2311
Rev	1: 1	to show his servants what must s take place. 1877+5443
	2:16	I will s come to you and will fight 5444
	3:11	I am coming s. Hold on to what you have, 5444
	11:14	the third woe is coming s. 5444
	22: 6	the things that must s take place." 1877+5443
	22: 7	"Behold, I am coming s! 5444
	22:12	"Behold, I am coming s! 5444
	22:20	"Yes, I am coming s." 5444

SOONER (6) [SOON]

Jos	4:18	No s had they set their feet on the dry ground than the waters 3869
Jdg	8:33	No s had Gideon died than 889+3869
Isa	40:24	No s are they planted, 677+1153
	40:24	no s are they sown, 677+1153
	40:24	no s do they take root in the ground, 677+1153
	66: 8	no s is Zion in labor than she gives birth 1685

SOOT (3)

Ex	9: 8	of s from a furnace and have Moses toss it 7086
	9:10	So they took s from a furnace and stood 7086
La	4: 8	But now they are blacker than s; 8818

SOOTHED (1) [SOOTHES, SOOTHING]

Isa	1: 6	not cleansed or bandaged or s with oil. 8216

SOOTHES (1) [SOOTHED]

Pr	21:14	A gift given in secret s anger, 4092

SOOTHING (1) [SOOTHED]

Ps	55:21	his words are more s than oil, 8216

SOOTHSAYER (1) [SOOTHSAYERS']

Isa	3: 2	the judge and prophet, the s and elder, 7876

SOOTHSAYERS' (1) [SOOTHSAYER]

Jdg	9:37	from the direction of the s' tree." 6726

SOP (KJV) See PIECE OF BREAD

SOPATER (1)

Ac	20: 4	He was accompanied by S son of Pyrrhus 5396

SOPE (KJV) See LAUNDERER'S SOAP

SOPHERETH (1)

Ne	7:57	the descendants of Sotai, S, Perida, 6072

SORCERER (2) [SORCERY]

Ac	13: 6	There they met a Jewish s and false prophet 3407
	13: 8	But Elymas the s (for that is what his name 3407

SORCERERS (4) [SORCERY]

Ex	7:11	Pharaoh summoned wise men and s, 4175
Jer	27: 9	your mediums or your s who tell you, 4177
Da	2: 2	the magicians, enchanters, s and astrologers 4175
Mal	3: 5	I will be quick to testify against s, 4175

SORCERESS (2) [SORCERY]

Ex	22:18	"Do not allow a s to live. 4175
Isa	57: 3	"But you—come here, you sons of a s, 6726

SORCERIES (3) [SORCERY]

Isa	47: 9	of your many s and all your potent spells. 4176
	47:12	your magic spells and with your many s, 4176
Na	3: 4	alluring, the mistress of s, 4176

SORCERY (10) [SORCERER, SORCERERS, SORCERESS, SORCERIES]

Lev	19:26	" 'Do not practice divination or s. 6726
Nu	23:23	There is no s against Jacob, 5728
	24: 1	he did not resort to s as at other times, 5728
Dt	18:10	who practices divination or s, 6726
	18:14	to those who practice s or divination. 6726
2Ki	17:17	and s and sold themselves to do evil in 5727
	21: 6	practiced s, divination 6726
2Ch	33: 6	practiced s, divination and witchcraft, 6726
Ac	8: 9	a man named Simon had practiced s in 3405
	19:19	who had practiced s brought their scrolls 4319

SORE (14) [SORES]

Lev	13: 3	The priest is to examine the s on his skin,	5596
	13: 3	and if the hair in the s has turned white and	5596
	13: 3	the sore has turned white and the s appears	5596
	13: 5	that the s is unchanged and has not spread	5596
	13: 6	s has faded and has not spread in the skin,	5596
	13:29	"If a man or woman has a s on the head or	5596
	13:30	to examine the s, and if it appears to	5596
	13:31	priest examines **this kind of** s,	2021+5596+5999
	13:32	the priest is to examine the s,	5596
	13:42	if he has a reddish-white s on his bald head	5596
	13:43	and if the swollen s on his head	5596
	13:44	because of the s on his head.	5596
2Sa	3:29	be without *someone who has a* **running** s	2307
Jer	30:13	no remedy for your s, no healing for you.	4649

SOREK (1)

Jdg	16: 4	the Valley of S whose name was Delilah.	8604

SORELY (KJV) See ANGUISH, BITTERNESS

SORES (13) [SORE]

Lev	13:17	and if the s have turned white,	5596
	21:20	or **running** s or damaged testicles.	3539
	22:22	with warts or festering or **running** s.	3539
Dt	28:27	**festering** s and the itch,	1734
Job	2: 7	the LORD and afflicted Job with painful s	8825
Isa	1: 6	only wounds and welts and open s,	4804
	3:17	the Lord *will* **bring** s on the heads of	8558
Hos	5:13	Ephraim saw his sickness, and Judah his s,	4649
	5:13	not able to heal your s.	4649
Lk	16:20	a beggar named Lazarus, **covered with** s	1815
	16:21	Even the dogs came and licked his s.	1814
Rev	16: 2	and ugly and painful s broke out on	1814
	16:11	of heaven because of their pains and their s,	1814

SORROW (36) [SORROWFUL, SORROWS]

Ge	42:38	down to the grave in s."	3326
	44:31	of our father down to the grave in s.	3326
	48: 7	to my s Rachel died in the land of Canaan	NIH
Est	9:22	the month when their s was turned into joy	3326
Ps	6: 7	My eyes grow weak with s;	4088
	13: 2	with my thoughts and every day have s	3326
	31: 9	my eyes grow weak with s,	4088
	90:10	yet their span is but trouble and s,	224
	107:39	by oppression, calamity and s;	3326
	116: 3	I was overcome by trouble and s.	3326
	119:28	My soul is weary with s;	9342
Pr	23:29	Who has woe? Who has s?	16
Ecc	1:18	For with much wisdom comes much s;	4088
	7: 3	S is better than laughter,	4088
Isa	35:10	and s and sighing will flee away.	3326
	51:11	and s and sighing will flee away.	3326
	60:20	and your days of s will end.	65
Jer	8:18	O my Comforter in s,	3326
	20:18	to see trouble and s and to end my days	3326
	31:12	and they will s no more.	1790
	31:13	and joy instead of s.	3326
	45: 3	The LORD has added s to my pain;	3326
Eze	23:33	You will be filled with drunkenness and s,	3326
Mt	26:38	"My soul is **overwhelmed with** s to the point of death.	4337
Mk	14:34	"My soul is **overwhelmed with** s to the point of death,"	4337
Lk	22:45	he found them asleep, exhausted from s.	3383
Ro	9: 2	I have great s and unceasing anguish	3383
2Co	2: 7	he will not be overwhelmed *by* excessive s.	3383
	7: 7	your **deep** s, your ardent concern for me,	3851
	7: 8	Even if *I* **caused** you s by my letter,	3382
	7: 9	but because *your* s led you to repentance.	3382
	7:10	Godly s brings repentance that leads	3383
	7:10	but worldly s brings death.	3383
	7:11	See what this godly s has produced in you:	3382
Php	2:27	to spare me s upon sorrow.	3383
	2:27	to spare me sorrow upon s.	3383

SORROWFUL (3) [SORROW]

Mt	26:37	and he began *to be* s and troubled.	3382
2Co	6:10	s, yet always rejoicing;	3382
	7: 9	For *you became* s as God intended and	3382

SORROWS (4) [SORROW]

Ps	16: 4	The s *of* those will increase who run	6780
Isa	53: 3	a man of s, and familiar with suffering.	4799
	53: 4	he took up our infirmities and carried our s,	4799
Zep	3:18	The s for the appointed feasts I will remove	5652

SORRY (2)

Ex	2: 6	He was crying, and *she* **felt** s for him.	2798
2Co	7: 9	not because *you were* **made** s,	3382

SORT (4) [SORTS]

2Ki	9:11	and the **s of things** he says,"	8490
Ecc	10: 5	the s *of* error that arises from a ruler:	3869
2Th	2:10	and in **every** s of evil that deceives those	AIT
Rev	18:12	**every** s of citron wood,	AIT

SORTS (5) [SORT]

1Ki	12:31	and appointed priests from **all** s	7896

1Ki	13:33	for the high places from **all** s *of* people.	7896
2Ki	17:32	appointed **all** s *of* their own *people*	4946+7896
Pr	1:13	we will get **all** s *of* valuable things	AIT
1Co	14:10	Undoubtedly there are all s *of* languages in	1169

SOSIPATER (1)

Ro	16:21	as do Lucius, Jason and S, my relatives.	5399

SOSTHENES (2)

Ac	18:17	on S the synagogue ruler and beat him	5398
1Co	1: 1	and our brother S,	5398

SOTAI (2)

Ezr	2:55	the descendants of S, Hassophereth,	6055
Ne	7:57	the descendants of S, Sophereth, Perida,	6055

SOTTISH (KJV) See SENSELESS

SOUGHT (37) [SEEK]

Ex	32:11	Moses s **the favor of** the LORD his God.	906+2704+7156
1Sa	7: 2	and all the people of Israel mourned and s	NIH
	13:12	*I have* not s the LORD's **favor.'**	2704+7156
	13:14	the LORD *has* s **out** a man	1335
2Sa	21: 1	so David s the face of the LORD.	1335
1Ki	10:24	The whole world s audience with Solomon	1335
2Ki	13: 4	Jehoahaz s the LORD's **favor,**	906+2704+7156
2Ch	9:23	the earth s audience with Solomon to hear	1335
	14: 7	because *we have* s the LORD our God;	2011
	14: 7	*we* s him and he has given us rest	2011
	15: 4	and s him, and he was found by them.	1335
	15:15	They s God eagerly,	1335
	17: 4	but s the God of his father	2011
	22: 9	who s the LORD with all his heart."	2011
	25:20	because *they* s the gods of Edom.	2011
	26: 5	He s God during the days of Zechariah,	2011
	26: 5	As long as he s the LORD,	2011
	31:21	he s his God and worked wholeheartedly.	2011
	33:12	In his distress *he* s **the favor of**	906+2704+7156
Ne	12:27	the Levites *were* s **out** from	1335
Ps	34: 4	I s the LORD, and he answered me;	2011
	77: 2	When I was in distress, *I* s the Lord;	2011
	119:45	for *I have* s **out** your precepts.	2011
	119:58	*I have* s your face with all my heart;	2704
	119:94	*I have* s **out** your precepts.	2011
Isa	9:13	nor *have they* s the LORD Almighty.	2011
	62:12	and you will be called S **After,**	2011
Jer	26:21	the king s to put him to death.	1335
Eze	25:15	with ancient hostility s to destroy Judah,	NIH
	26:21	*You will be* s, but you will never again	1335
Da	4:36	My advisers and nobles s me **out,**	10114
	9:13	*we have* not s **the favor of** the LORD our God	906+2704+7156
Ac	12:20	they now joined together and s **an audience**	4205
Ro	10: 3	from God and s to establish their own,	2426
	11: 7	What Israel s **so earnestly** it did not obtain,	2118
Heb	11: 7	no place would *have been* s for another.	2426
	12:17	though *he* s the blessing with tears.	1699

SOUL (129) [SOULS]

Dt	4:29	with your heart and with all your s.	5883
	6: 5	with all your heart and with all your s and	5883
	10:12	with all your heart and with all your s,	5883
	11:13	with all your heart and with all your s—	5883
	13: 3	with all your heart and with all your s.	5883
	26:16	with all your heart and with all your s.	5883
	30: 2	with all your heart and with all your s,	5883
	30: 6	with all your heart and with all your s,	5883
	30:10	with all your heart and with all your s.	5883
Jos	22: 5	with all your heart and all your s."	5883
Jdg	5:21	March on, my s; be strong!	5883
1Sa	1:10	In bitterness of s Hannah wept much and	5883
	1:15	I was pouring out my s to the LORD.	5883
	14: 7	I am with you **heart and** s."	3869+4222
1Ki	2: 4	before me with all their heart and s,	5883
	8:48	to you with all their heart and s in the land	5883
2Ki	23: 3	and decrees with all his heart and all his s,	5883
	23:25	and with all his s and with all his strength,	5883
1Ch	22:19	Now devote your heart and s to seeking	5883
2Ch	6:38	to you with all their heart and s in the land	5883
	15:12	with all their heart and s.	5883
	34:31	and decrees with all his heart and all his s,	5883
Job	3:20	and life to the bitter of s,	5883
	7:11	I will complain in the bitterness of my s.	5883
	10: 1	and speak out in the bitterness of my s.	5883
	21:25	Another man dies in bitterness of s,	5883
	27: 2	who has made me taste bitterness of s,	5883
	30:25	Has not my s grieved for the poor?	5883
	33:18	to preserve his s from the pit,	5883
	33:20	and his s loathes the choicest meal.	5883
	33:22	His s draws near to the pit,	5883
	33:28	He redeemed my s from going down to	5883
	33:30	to turn back his s from the pit,	5883
Ps	6: 3	My s is in anguish.	5883
	11: 5	and those who love violence his s hates.	5883
	19: 7	law of the LORD is perfect, reviving the s.	5883
	23: 3	he restores my s.	5883
	24: 4	up his s to an idol or swear by what is false.	5883
	25: 1	To you, O LORD, I lift up my s.	5883
	26: 9	Do not take away my s along with sinners,	5883
	31: 7	and knew the anguish of my s.	5883
	31: 9	my s and my body with grief.	5883

Ps	34: 2	My s will boast in the LORD;	5883
	35: 3	Say to my s, "I am your salvation."	5883
	35: 9	Then my s will rejoice in the LORD	5883
	35:12	for good and leave my s forlorn.	5883
	42: 1	so my s pants for you, O God.	5883
	42: 2	My s thirsts for God, for the living God.	5883
	42: 4	as I pour out my s:	5883
	42: 5	Why are you downcast, O my s?	5883
	42: 6	My s is downcast within me;	5883
	42:11	Why are you downcast, O my s?	5883
	43: 5	Why are you downcast, O my s?	5883
	57: 1	for in you my s takes refuge.	5883
	57: 8	Awake, my s!	3883
	62: 1	My s finds rest in God alone;	5883
	62: 5	O my s, in God alone;	5883
	63: 1	my s thirsts for you, my body longs for you,	5883
	63: 5	My s will be satisfied as with the richest	5883
	63: 8	My s clings to you;	5883
	77: 2	and my s refused to be comforted.	5883
	84: 2	My s yearns, even faints,	5883
	86: 4	for you, O Lord, I lift up my s.	5883
	88: 3	For my s is full of trouble	5883
	94:19	your consolation brought joy to my s.	5883
	103: 1	Praise the LORD, O my s;	5883
	103: 2	Praise the LORD, O my s,	5883
	103:22	Praise the LORD, O my s.	5883
	104: 1	Praise the LORD, O my s.	5883
	104:35	Praise the LORD, O my s.	5883
	108: 1	I will sing and make music with all my s.	3883
	116: 7	Be at rest once more, O my s,	5883
	116: 8	O LORD, have delivered my s from death,	5883
	119:20	My s is consumed with longing	5883
	119:28	My s is weary with sorrow;	5883
	119:81	My s faints with longing for your salvation,	5883
	130: 5	I wait for the LORD, my s waits,	5883
	130: 6	My s waits for the Lord more than	5883
	131: 2	But I have stilled and quieted my s;	5883
	131: 2	like a weaned child is my s within me.	5883
	143: 6	my s thirsts for you like a parched land.	5883
	143: 8	for to you I lift up my s.	5883
	146: 1	Praise the LORD, O my s.	5883
Pr	1:11	let's waylay some **harmless** s;	2855+5929
	2:10	and knowledge will be pleasant to your s.	5883
	13:19	A longing fulfilled is sweet to the s,	5883
	16:24	sweet to the s and healing to the bones.	5883
	18: 7	and his lips are a snare to his s.	5883
	19: 8	He who gets wisdom loves his own s;	5883
	22: 5	he who guards his s stays far from them.	5883
	23:14	with the rod and save his s from death.	5883
	24:14	Know also that wisdom is sweet to your s;	5883
	25:25	a weary s is good news from a distant land.	5883
	29:17	he will bring delight to your s.	5883
Isa	1:14	and your appointed feasts my s hates.	5883
	26: 9	My s yearns for you in the night;	5883
	38:15	because of this anguish of my s.	5883
	53:11	After the suffering of his s,	5883
	55: 2	and your s will delight in the richest of fare.	5883
	55: 3	hear me, that your s may live.	5883
	61:10	my s rejoices in my God.	5883
Jer	32:41	in this land with all my heart and s.	5883
La	3:20	and my s is downcast within me.	5883
		What I see brings grief to my s because	5883
Eze	18: 4	For every **living** s belongs to me,	5883
	18: 4	The s who sins is the one who will die.	5883
	18:20	The s who sins is the one who will die.	5883
	27:31	with anguish of s and with bitter mourning.	5883
Mic	6: 7	the fruit of my body for the sin of my s?	5883
Mt	10:28	the body but cannot kill the s.	6034
	10:28	of the One who can destroy both s and body	6034
	16:26	gains the whole world, yet forfeits his s?	6034
	16:26	a man give in exchange for his s?	6034
	22:37	and with all your s and with all your mind.'	6034
	26:38	"My s is overwhelmed with sorrow	6034
Mk	8:36	to gain the whole world, yet forfeit his s?	6034
	8:37	a man give in exchange for his s?	6034
	12:30	with all your s and with all your mind and	6034
	14:34	"My s is overwhelmed with sorrow	6034
Lk	1:46	And Mary said: "My s glorifies the Lord	6034
	2:35	And a sword will pierce your own s too."	6034
	10:27	with all your heart and with all your s	6034
1Th	5:23	s and body be kept blameless at the coming	6034
Heb	4:12	it penetrates even to dividing s and spirit,	6034
	6:19	We have this hope as an anchor *for* the s,	6034
1Pe	2:11	which war against your s.	6034
2Pe	2: 8	was tormented in his righteous s by	6034
3Jn	1: 2	even as your s is getting along well.	6034

SOULS (10) [SOUL]

Job	24:12	and the s *of* the wounded cry out for help.	5883
Pr	11:30	and he who wins s is wise.	5883
Isa	66: 3	and their s delight in their abominations;	5883
Jer	6:16	and you will find rest for your s.	5883
Mt	11:29	and you will find rest *for* your s.	6034
1Pe	1: 9	goal of your faith, the salvation of your s.	6034
	2:25	to the Shepherd and Overseer *of* your s.	6034
Rev	6: 9	the altar the s of those who had been slain	6034
	18:13	and bodies and s of men.	6034
	20: 4	the s of those who had been beheaded	6034

SOUND (124) [FINE-SOUNDING, SOUNDED, SOUNDING, SOUNDINGS, SOUNDNESS, SOUNDS]

Ge	3: 8	and his wife heard the s of the LORD God	7754
Ex	19:19	and the s *of* the trumpet grew louder	7754
	28:35	The s *of* the bells will be heard	7754

Ex	32:17	"There is the s of war in the camp."	7754
	32:18	replied: "It is not the s of victory,	6702+7754
	32:18	it is not the s of defeat;	6702+7754
	32:18	it is the s of singing that I hear."	7754
Lev	25: 9	on the Day of Atonement s the trumpet	6296
	26:36	that the s of a windblown leaf will put them	8131
Nu	10: 9	s a blast on the trumpets.	8131
	10:10	to s the trumpets over your burnt offerings	9546
	29: 1	It is a day for you to s the trumpets.	9558
Dt	4:12	You heard the s of words but saw no form;	7754
Jos	6: 5	When you hear them a long blast on	5432
	6:20	and at the s of the trumpet,	7754
Jdg	11:34	dancing to the s of tambourines!	NIH
1Sa	20:12	I will surely s out my father by this time	2983
2Sa	5:24	as you hear the s of marching in the tops of	7754
	6:15	the ark of the LORD with shouts and the s	7754
	15:10	"As soon as you hear the s of the trumpets,	7754
1Ki	1:40	so that the ground shook with the s	7754
	1:41	On hearing the s of the trumpet,	7754
	14: 6	when Ahijah heard the s of her footsteps at	7754
	18:41	for there is the s of a heavy rain."	7754
2Ki	4:31	there was no s or response.	7754
	6:32	Is not the s of his master's footsteps	7754
	7: 6	to hear the s of chariots and horses and	7754
	7:10	not a s of anyone—	7754
1Ch	14:15	as you hear the s of marching in the tops of	7754
	15:19	and Ethan were to s the bronze cymbals;	9048
	16: 5	Asaph was to s the cymbals,	9048
2Ch	13:12	with their trumpets will s the battle cry	8131
	13:15	At the s of their battle cry,	8131
Ezr	3:13	the s of the shouts of joy from the sound	7754
	3:13	of the shouts of joy from the s of weeping,	7754
	3:13	And the s was heard far away.	7754
Ne	4:20	Wherever you hear the s of the trumpet,	7754
	12:43	s of rejoicing in Jerusalem could be heard	9048
Job	21:12	they make merry to the s of the flute.	7754
	30:31	and my flute to the s of wailing.	7754
	37: 4	After that comes the s of his roar;	7754
Ps	66: 8	O peoples, let the s of his praise be heard;	7754
	81: 3	S the ram's horn at the New Moon,	9546
	98: 5	with the harp and the s of singing,	7754
	104: 7	at the s of your thunder they took to flight;	7754
	115: 7	nor can they utter a s with their throats.	2047
Pr	3:21	preserve s judgment and discernment,	9370
	4: 2	I give you s learning,	3202
	8:14	Counsel and s judgment are mine;	9370
	18: 1	he defies all s judgment.	9370
	22:21	so that you can give s answers	622
Ecc	12: 4	the doors to the street are closed and the s	7754
	12: 4	when men rise up at the s of birds,	7754
Isa	6: 4	At the s of their voices the doorposts	7754
	24:18	Whoever flees at the s of terror will fall	7754
	27:13	And in that day a great trumpet will s.	9546
	51: 3	thanksgiving and the s of singing.	7754
	65:19	the s of weeping and of crying will	7754
	66: 6	It is the s of the LORD repaying his enemies	7754
Jer	2:21	like a choice vine of s and reliable stock.	3972
	4: 5	'S the trumpet throughout the land!'	9546
	4:19	For I have heard the s of the trumpet,	7754
	4:21	the battle standard and hear the s of	7754
	4:29	At the s of horsemen and archers	7754
	6: 1	S the trumpet in Tekoa!	9546
	6:17	'Listen to the s of the trumpet!'	7754
	6:23	They s like the roaring sea as they ride	7754
	9:19	The s of wailing is heard from Zion:	7754
	25:10	s of millstones and the light of the lamp.	7754
	30:19	of thanksgiving and the s of rejoicing.	7754
	47: 3	at the s of the hoofs of galloping steeds,	7754
	48:34	"The s of their cry rises from Heshbon	9048
	49: 2	"when I will s the battle cry	9048
	49:21	At the s of their fall the earth will tremble;	7754
	50:42	They s like the roaring sea as they ride	7754
	50:46	At the s of Babylon's capture	7754
	51:54	"The s of a cry comes from Babylon,	7754
	51:54	of great destruction from the land of	NIH
Eze	1:24	I heard the s of their wings,	7754
	3:12	and I heard behind me a loud rumbling s—	7754
	3:13	the s of the wings of the living creatures	7754
	3:13	against each other and the s of the wheels	7754
	3:13	the wheels beside them, a loud rumbling s.	7754
	10: 5	The s of the wings of the cherubim could	7754
	21:22	to slaughter, to s the battle cry,	7754+8123
	26:15	the coastlands tremble at the s of your fall,	7754
	31:16	at the s of its fall when I brought it down to	7754
	33: 5	Since he heard the s of the trumpet but did	7754
	37: 7	a rattling s, and the bones came together,	8323
Da	3: 5	As soon as you hear the s of the horn,	10631
	3: 7	as soon as they heard the s of the horn,	10631
	3:10	that everyone who hears the s of the horn,	10631
	3:15	Now when you hear the s of the horn, flute,	10631
	10: 6	and his voice like the s of a multitude.	7754
Hos	5: 8	"S the trumpet in Gibeah,	9546
Joel	2: 1	s the alarm on my holy hill.	8131
Hab	3:16	my lips quivered at the s;	7754
Zec	8:16	and render true and s judgment	8934
	9:14	The Sovereign LORD will s the trumpet;	9546
Mt	12:13	completely restored, just as s as the other.	5618
Lk	1:44	as the s of your greeting reached my ears,	5889
	15:27	because he has him back safe and s.'	5617
Jn	3: 8	You hear its s, but you cannot tell where	5889
Ac	2: 2	s like the blowing of a violent wind came	2491
	2: 6	When they heard this s,	1181+5889
	9: 7	they heard the s but did not see anyone.	5889
	20: 9	When he was s asleep,	608+2965+3836+5678
1Co	14: 8	Again, if the trumpet does not s a clear call,	1443
	15:52	For the trumpet will s, the dead will be	4895
1Ti	1:10	whatever else is contrary to s doctrine	5617
1Ti	6: 3	to the s instruction of our Lord Jesus Christ	5617
2Ti	1:13	keep as the pattern of s teaching,	5617
	4: 3	when men will not put up with s doctrine.	5617
Tit	1: 9	that he can encourage others by s doctrine	5617
	1:13	so that they will be s in the faith	5617
	2: 1	in accord with s doctrine.	5617
	2: 2	and s in faith, in love and in endurance.	5617
Rev	1:15	his voice was like the s of rushing waters.	5889
	8: 6	the seven trumpets prepared to s them.	4895
	9: 9	the s of their wings was like the thundering	5889
	10: 7	the seventh angel is about to s his trumpet,	4895
	14: 2	And I heard a s from heaven like the roar	5889
	14: 2	The s I heard was like that of harpists	5889
	18:22	The s of a millstone will never be heard	5889

SOUNDED (23) [SOUND]

Lev	25: 9	Then have the trumpet s everywhere on	6296
Nu	10: 3	When both are s, the whole community	9546
	10: 4	If only one is s, the leaders—	9546
	10: 5	When a trumpet blast is s,	9546
Jos	6:16	when the priests s the trumpet blast,	9546
	6:20	When the trumpets s, the people shouted,	9546
Jdg	7:22	When the three hundred trumpets s,	9546
2Sa	18:16	Then Joab s the trumpet,	9546
	20: 1	He s the trumpet and shouted,	9546
	20:22	So he s the trumpet,	9546
1Ki	1:39	Then they s the trumpet and all	9546
Ne	4:18	the man who s the trumpet stayed with me.	9546
Rev	6: 6	Then I heard what s like a voice among	NIG
	8: 7	The first angel s his trumpet,	4895
	8: 8	The second angel s his trumpet,	4895
	8:10	The third angel s his trumpet,	4895
	8:12	The fourth angel s his trumpet,	4895
	8:13	because of the trumpet blasts about to be s	4895
	9: 1	The fifth angel s his trumpet,	4895
	9:13	The sixth angel s his trumpet,	4895
	11:15	The seventh angel s his trumpet,	4895
	19: 1	After this I heard what s like the roar of	6055
	19: 6	Then I heard what s like a great multitude,	5889

SOUNDING (8) [SOUND]

Nu	10: 6	At the s of a second blast,	9546
Jos	6: 9	All this time the trumpets were s.	9546
	6:13	while the trumpets kept s.	9546
1Ch	15:28	with s of rams' horns and trumpets,	7754
	16:42	and Jeduthun were responsible for the s of	9048
2Ch	5:12	by 120 priests s trumpets.	2955
Ps	47: 5	the LORD amid the s of trumpets.	7754
	150: 3	Praise him with the s of the trumpet,	9547

SOUNDINGS (2) [SOUND]

Ac	27:28	They took s and found that the water was	1075
	27:28	A short time later they took s again	1075

SOUNDNESS (3) [SOUND]

Ps	38: 3	my bones have no s because of my sin.	8934
Isa	1: 6	to the top of your head there is no s—	5507
Tit	2: 8	and s of speech that cannot be condemned,	5618

SOUNDS (10) [SOUND]

Ex	19:13	ram's horn s a long blast may they go	5432
Job	15:21	Terrifying s fill his ears;	7754
	39:24	he cannot stand still when the trumpet s.	7754
Isa	18: 3	and when a trumpet s, you will hear it.	9546
Jer	7:34	the s of joy and gladness and to the voices	7754
	16: 9	and in your days I will bring an end to the s	7754
	25:10	from them the s of joy and gladness,	7754
	33:11	the s of joy and gladness, the voices	7754
Am	3: 6	When a trumpet s in a city,	9546
1Co	14: 7	in the case of lifeless things that make s,	5889

SOUR (6)

Job	20:14	yet his food will turn s in his stomach;	NIH
Jer	31:29	'The fathers have eaten s grapes,	1235
	31:30	whoever eats s grapes—	1235
Eze	18: 2	" 'The fathers eat s grapes,	1235
Rev	10: 9	It will turn your stomach s,	4393
	10:10	when I had eaten it, my stomach turned s.	4393

SOURCE (6) [SOURCES]

Ge	26:35	a s of grief to Isaac and Rebekah.	5289+8120
Lev	20:18	he has exposed the s of her flow,	5227
Ps	80: 6	You have made us a s of contention	4506
Isa	28: 6	a s of strength to those who turn back	1476
Eze	29:16	be a s of confidence for the people of Israel	4440
Heb	5: 9	he became the s of eternal salvation	165

SOURCES (2) [SOURCE]

Job	28:11	the s of the rivers and brings hidden things	4441
Jer	18:14	from distant s ever cease to flow?	2424

SOUTH (126) [SOUTHERN, SOUTHERNMOST, SOUTHLAND, SOUTHWARD]

Ge	13:14	where you are and look north and s,	2025+5582
	28:14	to the north and to the s.	5582
Ex	26:18	Make twenty frames for the s side of	2025+2025+5582+9402
	26:35	the lampstand opposite it on the s side.	2025+9402
	27: 9	s side shall be a hundred cubits	2025+5582+9402
Ex	36:23	They made twenty frames for the s side of	2025+5582+9402
	38: 9	s side was a hundred cubits long	2025+5582+9402
	40:24	opposite the table on the s side	2025+5582
Nu	2:10	On the s will be the divisions of the camp	9402
	3:29	to camp on the s side of the tabernacle.	2025+9402
	10: 6	the camps on the s are to set out.	9402
	34: 4	cross s of Scorpion Pass,	5582
	34: 4	on to Zin and go s of Kadesh Barnea.	5582
	35: 5	three thousand on the s side,	5582
Dt	3:27	Pisgah and look west and north and s	2025+9402
	33: 2	with myriads of holy ones from the s,	3545
Jos	11: 2	in the Arabah s of Kinnereth,	5582
	13: 4	from the s, all the land of the Canaanites,	9402
	15: 1	to the Desert of Zin in the extreme s.	5582+9402
	15: 3	crossed s of Scorpion Pass,	5582
	15: 3	continued on to Zin and went over to the s	5582
	15: 7	which faces the Pass of Adummim s	4946+5582
	17: 9	continued to the Kanah Ravine.	2025+5582
	17:10	On the s the land belonged to Ephraim,	5582
	18: 5	the s and the house of Joseph in its territory	5582
	18:13	From there it crossed to the slope of Luz	5582
	18:13	down to Ataroth Addar on the hill s	4946+5582
	18:14	on the s the boundary turned south along	5582
	18:14	on the south boundary turned s	2025+5582
	18:19	at the mouth of the Jordan in the s.	5582
	19:34	It touched Zebulun on the s,	5582
Jdg	21: 9	and to the s of Lebonah."	5582
1Sa	14: 5	the other to the s toward Geba.	5582
	20:41	David got up from the s side	5582
	23:19	on the hill of Hakilah, s of Jeshimon?	3545+4946
	23:24	in the Arabah s of Jeshimon.	3545
2Sa	24: 5	s of the town in the gorge,	3545
1Ki	6: 8	to the lowest floor was on the s side of	3556
	7:21	to the s he named Jakin and the one to	3556
	7:25	three facing s and three facing east.	2025+5582
	7:39	placed five of the stands on the s side	3545+4946
	7:39	He placed the Sea on the s side,	3556
2Ki	11:11	the temple, from the s side to the north side	3556
	23:13	that were east of Jerusalem on the s of	3545
1Ch	9:24	east, west, north and s,	2025+5582
	26:15	The lot for the S Gate fell to Obed-Edom,	5582
	26:17	four a day on the s and	2025+5582
2Ch	3:17	one to the s and one to the north.	3545
	3:17	to the s he named Jakin and the one to	3556
	4: 4	three facing s and three facing east.	2025+5582
	4: 6	for washing and placed five on the s side	3545
	4: 7	five on the s side and five on the north.	3545
	4: 8	five on the s side and five on the north.	3545
	4:10	He placed the Sea on the s side,	3556
	4:10	the temple, from the s side to the north side	3556
Job	9: 9	the Pleiades and the constellations of the s.	9402
	23: 9	he turns to the s, I catch no glimpse of him.	3545
	37:17	when the land lies hushed under the s wind,	1999
	39:26	and spread his wings toward the s?	9402
Ps	78:26	from the heavens and led forth the s wind	9402
	89:12	You created the north and the s;	3545
	107: 3	from east and west, from north and s.	3542
Ecc	1: 6	wind blows to the s and turns to the north,	1999
	11: 3	Whether a tree falls to the s or to the north,	1999
SS	4:16	Awake, north wind, and come, s wind!	9402
Isa	43: 6	and to the s, 'Do not hold them back.'	5582
Eze	10: 3	the cherubim were standing on the s side of	3545
	16:46	and your younger sister, who lived to the s	3545
	20:46	set your face toward the s;	2025+9402
	20:46	against the s and prophesy against the forest	1999
	20:47	from s to north will be scorched by it,	5582
	21: 4	be unsheathed against everyone from s	5582
	40: 2	on whose s side were some buildings	4946+5582
	40:24	to the s side and I saw a gate facing south.	1999
	40:24	to the south side and I saw a gate facing s.	1999
	40:27	The inner court also had a gate facing s,	1999
	40:27	to the outer gate on the s side;	1999
	40:28	the s gate, and he measured the south gate;	1999
	40:28	and he measured the s gate;	1999
	40:44	at the side of the north gate and facing s,	1999
	40:44	at the side of the s gate and facing north.	1999
	40:45	"The room facing s is for	1999
	41:11	one on the north and another on the s;	1999
	42:10	On the s side along the length of the wall of	1999
	42:12	were the doorways of the rooms on the s.	1999
	42:13	and s rooms facing the temple courtyard are	1999
	42:18	He measured the s side;	1999
	46: 9	to worship is to go out the s gate;	5582
	46: 9	by the s gate is to go out the north gate.	5582
	47: 1	down from under the s side of the temple,	3556
	47: 1	of the temple, s of the altar.	4946+5582
	47: 2	and the water was flowing from the s side.	3556
	47:19	"On the s side it will run from Tamar	5582+9402
	47:19	will be the s boundary.	2025+2025+5582+9402
	48:10	25,000 cubits long on the s side.	5582
	48:16	the north side 4,500 cubits, the s side 4,500	5582
	48:17	250 cubits on the s, 250 cubits on the east,	5582
	48:28	will run s from Tamar to the waters	2025+9402
	48:33	"On the s side, which measures 4,500	5582
Da	8: 4	toward the west and the north and the s.	5582
	8: 9	in power to the s and to the east and toward	5582
	11: 5	"The king of the S will become strong,	5582
	11: 6	The daughter of the king of the S will go to	5582
	11: 9	of the S but will retreat to his own country.	5582
	11:11	of the S will march out in a rage and fight	5582
	11:12	the king of the S will be filled with pride	2257S
	11:14	many will rise against the king of the S.	5582
	11:15	The forces of the S will be powerless	5582
	11:17	an alliance with the king of the S.	2257S
	11:25	and courage against the king of the S.	5582
	11:25	The king of the S will wage war with	5582

Da	11:29	the S again, but this time the outcome will	5582
	11:40	the king of the S will engage him in battle,	5582
Zec	6: 6	one with the dappled horses toward the s."	9402
	9:14	he will march in the storms of the s,	9402
	14: 4	and half moving s.	2025+5582
	14:10	from Geba to Rimmon, s of Jerusalem,	5582
Mt	12:42	*of* the S will rise at the judgment	3803
Lk	11:31	the S will rise at the judgment with the men	3803
	12:55	And when the s wind blows, you say,	3803
	13:29	from east and west and north and s,	3803
Ac	8:26	"Go s to the road—	3540
	21: 3	and passing to the s of it,	2381
	27:13	When a gentle s **wind** began to blow,	3803
	28:13	The next day the s **wind** came up,	3803
Rev	21:13	three on the s and three on the west.	3803

SOUTHEAST (2) [EAST]

1Ki	7:39	at the s corner of the temple.	2025+5582+7711
2Ch	4:10	at the s corner.	2025+2025+5582+7711

SOUTHERN (11) [SOUTH]

Nu	34: 3	" 'Your s side will include some of	5582
	34: 3	your s boundary will start from the end of	5582
Jos	15: 2	Their s boundary started from the bay at	5582
	15: 2	the bay at the s end of the Salt Sea,	2025+5582
	15: 4	This is their s boundary.	5582
	15: 8	Valley of Ben Hinnom along the s	4946+5582
	18:15	The s side began at the outskirts	2025+5582
	18:16	along the s slope of the Jebusite city	2025+5582
	18:19	This was the s boundary.	5582
Eze	20:47	Say to the s forest:	5582
	48:28	"The s boundary of Gad will run	448+5582+6991

SOUTHERNMOST (1) [SOUTH, MOST]

Jos	15:21	The s towns of the tribe of Judah in	4946+7895

SOUTHLAND (2) [SOUTH]

Isa	21: 1	Like whirlwinds sweeping through the s,	5582
Eze	20:46	prophesy against the forest of the s.	5582+8441

SOUTHWARD (3) [SOUTH]

Dt	33:23	he will inherit s to the lake."	1999
Jos	12: 3	and then s below the slopes of Pisgah.	4946+9402
	17: 7	The boundary ran s from there	448+2021+3545

SOUTHWEST (1) [WEST]

Ac	27:12	facing both s and northwest.	3355

SOVEREIGN (303) [SOVEREIGNTY]

Ge	15: 2	But Abram said, "O S LORD,	151
	15: 8	But Abram said, "O S LORD,	151
Ex	23:17	the men are to appear before the S LORD.	123
	34:23	to appear before the S LORD,	123
Dt	3:24	"O S LORD, you have begun to show	151
	9:26	"O S LORD, do not destroy your people,	151
Jos	7: 7	And Joshua said, "Ah, S LORD,	151
Jdg	6:22	he exclaimed, "Ah, S LORD!	151
	16:28	"O S LORD, remember me.	151
2Sa	7:18	"Who am I, O S LORD,	151
	7:19	O S LORD, you have also spoken about	151
	7:19	of dealing with man, O S LORD?	151
	7:20	For you know your servant, O S LORD.	151
	7:22	"How great you are, O S LORD!	151
	7:28	O S LORD, you are God!	151
	7:29	for you, O S LORD, have spoken,	151
1Ki	2:26	of the S LORD before my father David	151
	8:53	O S LORD, brought our fathers out	151
Ps	68:20	the S LORD comes escape from death.	151
	71: 5	For you have been my hope, O S LORD,	151
	71:16	and proclaim your mighty acts, O S LORD;	151
	73:28	I have made the S LORD my refuge;	151
	109:21	But you, O S LORD, deal well with me	151
	140: 7	O S LORD, my strong deliverer,	151
	141: 8	But my eyes are fixed on you, O S LORD;	151
Isa	7: 7	Yet this is what the S LORD says:	151
	25: 8	The S LORD will wipe away the tears	151
	28:16	So this is what the S LORD says:	151
	30:15	This is what the S LORD,	151
	40:10	See, the S LORD comes with power,	151
	48:16	the S LORD has sent me, with his Spirit.	151
	49:22	This is what the S LORD says:	151
	50: 4	The S LORD has given me	151
	50: 5	The S LORD has opened my ears,	151
	50: 7	Because the S LORD helps me,	151
	50: 9	It is the S LORD who helps me.	151
	51:22	This is what your S LORD says,	151
	52: 4	For this is what the S LORD says:	151
	56: 8	The S LORD declares—	151
	61: 1	The Spirit of the S LORD is on me,	151
	61:11	so the S LORD will make righteousness	151
	65:13	Therefore this is what the S LORD says:	151
	65:15	the S LORD will put you to death,	151
Jer	1: 6	"Ah, S LORD," I said,	151
	2:22	declares the S LORD.	151
	4:10	Then I said, "Ah, S LORD,	151
	7:20	the S LORD says:	151
	14:13	But I said, "Ah, S LORD,	151
	32:17	S LORD, you have made the heavens and	151
	32:25	you, O S LORD, say to me,	151
	44:26	"As surely as the S LORD lives."	151
	50:25	for the S LORD Almighty has work to do	151
Eze	2: 4	'This is what the S LORD says.'	151

Eze	3:11	'This is what the S LORD says,'	151
	3:27	'This is what the S LORD says.'	151
	4:14	Then I said, "Not so, S LORD!	151
	5: 5	"This is what the S LORD says:	151
	5: 7	"Therefore this is what the S LORD says:	151
	5: 8	"Therefore this is what the S LORD says:	151
	5:11	declares the S LORD,	151
	6: 3	hear the word of the S LORD.	151
	6: 3	the S LORD says to the mountains	151
	6:11	" 'This is what the S LORD says:	151
	7: 2	this is what the S LORD says to the land	151
	7: 5	"This is what the S LORD says: Disaster!	151
	8: 1	of the S LORD came upon me there.	151
	9: 8	crying out, "Ah, S LORD!	151
	11: 7	"Therefore this is what the S LORD says:	151
	11: 8	declares the S LORD.	151
	11:13	in a loud voice, "Ah, S LORD!	151
	11:16	"This is what the S LORD says:	151
	11:17	"This is what the S LORD says:	151
	11:21	declares the S LORD."	151
	12:10	'This is what the S LORD says:	151
	12:19	the S LORD says about those living	151
	12:23	'This is what the S LORD says:	151
	12:25	declares the S LORD.' "	151
	12:28	'This is what the S LORD says:	151
	12:28	declares the S LORD.' "	151
	13: 3	This is what the S LORD says:	151
	13: 8	the S LORD says:	151
	13: 8	I am against you, declares the S LORD.	151
	13: 9	you will know that I am the S LORD.	151
	13:13	the S LORD says:	151
	13:16	declares the S LORD." '	151
	13:18	'This is what the S LORD says:	151
	13:20	the S LORD says:	151
	14: 4	'This is what the S LORD says:	151
	14: 6	'This is what the S LORD says: Repent!	151
	14:11	declares the S LORD.' "	151
	14:14	declares the S LORD.	151
	14:16	declares the S LORD,	151
	14:18	declares the S LORD,	151
	14:20	declares the S LORD, even if Noah,	151
	14:21	"For this is what the S LORD says:	151
	14:23	declares the S LORD."	151
	15: 6	"Therefore this is what the S LORD says:	151
	15: 8	declares the S LORD."	151
	16: 3	the S LORD says to Jerusalem:	151
	16: 8	declares the S LORD.	151
	16:14	declares the S LORD.	151
	16:19	declares the S LORD.	151
	16:23	Woe to you, declares the S LORD.	151
	16:30	declares the S LORD.	151
	16:36	This is what the S LORD says:	151
	16:43	declares the S LORD,	151
	16:48	As surely as I live, declares the S LORD,	151
	16:59	" 'This is what the S LORD says:	151
	16:63	declares the S LORD.' "	151
	17: 3	'This is what the S LORD says:	151
	17: 9	'This is what the S LORD says:	151
	17:16	surely as I live, declares the S LORD,	151
	17:19	the S LORD says:	151
	17:22	" 'This is what the S LORD says:	151
	18: 3	"As surely as I live, declares the S LORD,	151
	18: 9	he will surely live, declares the S LORD.	151
	18:23	declares the S LORD.	151
	18:30	declares the S LORD.	151
	18:32	declares the S LORD.	151
	20: 3	'This is what the S LORD says:	151
	20: 3	declares the S LORD.'	151
	20: 5	'This is what the S LORD says:	151
	20:27	'This is what the S LORD says:	151
	20:30	'This is what the S LORD says:	151
	20:31	As surely as I live, declares the S LORD,	151
	20:33	As surely as I live, declares the S LORD,	151
	20:36	so I will judge you, declares the S LORD.	151
	20:39	this is what the S LORD says:	151
	20:40	declares the S LORD,	151
	20:44	declares the S LORD.' "	151
	20:47	This is what the S LORD says:	151
	20:49	Then I said, "Ah, S LORD!	151
	21: 7	declares the S LORD."	151
	21:13	declares the S LORD.'	151
	21:24	"Therefore this is what the S LORD says:	151
	21:26	this is what the S LORD says:	151
	21:28	the S LORD says about the Ammonites	151
	22: 3	'This is what the S LORD says:	151
	22:12	declares the S LORD.	151
	22:19	Therefore this is what the S LORD says:	151
	22:28	'This is what the S LORD says'—	151
	22:31	declares the S LORD."	151
	23:22	Oholibah, this is what the S LORD says:	151
	23:28	"For this is what the S LORD says:	151
	23:32	"This is what the S LORD says:	151
	23:34	I have spoken, declares the S LORD.	151
	23:35	"Therefore this is what the S LORD says:	151
	23:46	"This is what the S LORD says:	151
	23:49	you will know that I am the S LORD."	151
	24: 3	'This is what the S LORD says:	151
	24: 6	" 'For this is what the S LORD says:	151
	24: 9	"Therefore this is what the S LORD says:	151
	24:14	declares the S LORD.' "	151
	24:21	'This is what the S LORD says:	151
	24:24	you will know that I am the S LORD.'	151
	25: 3	'Hear the word of the S LORD.	151
	25: 3	This is what the S LORD says:	151
	25: 6	For this is what the S LORD says:	151
	25: 8	'This is what the S LORD says:	151
	25:12	'This is what the S LORD says:	151

Eze	25:13	therefore this is what the S LORD says:	151
	25:14	declares the S LORD.' "	151
	25:15	"This is what the S LORD says:	151
	25:16	therefore this is what the S LORD says:	151
	26: 3	therefore this is what the S LORD says:	151
	26: 5	for I have spoken, declares the S LORD.	151
	26: 7	"For this is what the S LORD says:	151
	26:14	declares the S LORD.	151
	26:15	"This is what the S LORD says to Tyre:	151
	26:19	"This is what the S LORD says:	151
	26:21	declares the S LORD."	151
	27: 3	'This is what the S LORD says:	151
	28: 2	'This is what the S LORD says:	151
	28: 6	"Therefore this is what the S LORD says:	151
	28:10	I have spoken, declares the S LORD.' "	151
	28:12	'This is what the S LORD says:	151
	28:22	'This is what the S LORD says:	151
	28:24	they will know that I am the S LORD.	151
	28:25	" 'This is what the S LORD says:	151
	29: 3	'This is what the S LORD says:	151
	29: 8	the S LORD says:	151
	29:13	" 'Yet this is what the S LORD says:	151
	29:16	they will know that I am the S LORD.' "	151
	29:19	Therefore this is what the S LORD says:	151
	29:20	declares the S LORD.	151
	30: 2	'This is what the S LORD says:	151
	30: 6	declares the S LORD.	151
	30:10	" 'This is what the S LORD says:	151
	30:13	" 'This is what the S LORD says:	151
	30:22	Therefore this is what the S LORD says:	151
	31:10	" 'Therefore this is what the S LORD says:	151
	31:15	" 'This is what the S LORD says:	151
	31:18	declares the S LORD.' "	151
	32: 3	" 'This is what the S LORD says:	151
	32: 8	declares the S LORD.	151
	32:11	" 'For this is what the S LORD says:	151
	32:14	declares the S LORD.	151
	32:16	declares the S LORD."	151
	32:31	declares the S LORD.	151
	32:32	declares the S LORD."	151
	33:11	'As surely as I live, declares the S LORD,	151
	33:25	'This is what the S LORD says:	151
	33:27	'This is what the S LORD says:	151
	34: 2	'This is what the S LORD says:	151
	34: 8	declares the S LORD,	151
	34:10	This is what the S LORD says:	151
	34:11	" 'For this is what the S LORD says:	151
	34:15	declares the S LORD.	151
	34:17	my flock, this is what the S LORD says:	151
	34:20	" 'Therefore this is what the S LORD says	151
	34:30	are my people, declares the S LORD.	151
	34:31	declares the S LORD.' "	151
	35: 3	'This is what the S LORD says:	151
	35: 6	declares the S LORD,	151
	35:11	declares the S LORD,	151
	35:14	This is what the S LORD says:	151
	36: 2	This is what the S LORD says:	151
	36: 3	'This is what the S LORD says:	151
	36: 4	hear the word of the S LORD.	151
	36: 4	the S LORD says to the mountains	151
	36: 5	this is what the S LORD says:	151
	36: 6	'This is what the S LORD says:	151
	36: 7	Therefore this is what the S LORD says:	151
	36:13	" 'This is what the S LORD says:	151
	36:14	declares the S LORD.	151
	36:15	declares the S LORD.' "	151
	36:22	'This is what the S LORD says:	151
	36:23	declares the S LORD,	151
	36:32	declares the S LORD.	151
	36:33	" 'This is what the S LORD says:	151
	36:37	"This is what the S LORD says:	151
	37: 3	I said, "O S LORD, you alone know."	151
	37: 5	the S LORD says to these bones:	151
	37: 9	'This is what the S LORD says:	151
	37:12	'This is what the S LORD says:	151
	37:19	'This is what the S LORD says:	151
	37:21	'This is what the S LORD says:	151
	38: 3	'This is what the S LORD says:	151
	38:10	" 'This is what the S LORD says:	151
	38:14	'This is what the S LORD says:	151
	38:17	" 'This is what the S LORD says:	151
	38:18	declares the S LORD.	151
	38:21	declares the S LORD.	151
	39: 1	'This is what the S LORD says:	151
	39: 5	for I have spoken, declares the S LORD.	151
	39: 8	declares the S LORD.	151
	39:10	declares the S LORD.	151
	39:13	declares the S LORD.	151
	39:17	this is what the S LORD says:	151
	39:20	declares the S LORD.	151
	39:25	"Therefore this is what the S LORD says:	151
	39:29	declares the S LORD."	151
	44: 6	'This is what the S LORD says:	151
	44: 9	This is what the S LORD says:	151
	44:12	declares the S LORD.	151
	44:15	declares the S LORD.	151
	44:27	declares the S LORD.	151
	45: 9	" 'This is what the S LORD says:	151
	45: 9	declares the S LORD.	151
	45:15	declares the S LORD.	151
	45:18	" 'This is what the S LORD says:	151
	46: 1	" 'This is what the S LORD says:	151
	46:16	" 'This is what the S LORD says:	151
	47:13	This is what the S LORD says:	151

Eze	47:23	declares the S LORD.	151
	48:29	declares the S LORD.	151
Da	4:17	living may know that the Most High is s	10718
	4:25	that the Most High is s over the kingdoms	10718
	4:32	that the Most High is s over the kingdoms	10718
	5:21	the Most High God is s over the kingdoms	10718
	7:14	He was given authority, glory and s power;	10424
Am	1: 8	says the S LORD.	151
	3: 7	Surely the S LORD does nothing without	151
	3: 8	The S LORD has spoken—	151
	3:11	Therefore this is what the S LORD says:	151
	4: 2	The S LORD has sworn by his holiness:	151
	4: 5	declares the S LORD.	151
	5: 3	This is what the S LORD says:	151
	6: 8	The S LORD has sworn by himself—	151
	7: 1	This is what the S LORD showed me:	151
	7: 2	I cried out, "S LORD, forgive!	151
	7: 4	This is what the S LORD showed me:	151
	7: 4	The S LORD was calling for judgment	151
	7: 5	I cried out, "S LORD, I beg you, stop!	151
	7: 6	will not happen either," the S LORD said.	151
	8: 1	This is what the S LORD showed me:	151
	8: 3	"In that day," declares the S LORD,	151
	8: 9	"In that day," declares the S LORD,	151
	8:11	declares the S LORD,	151
	9: 8	of the S LORD are on the sinful kingdom.	151
Ob	1: 1	the S LORD says about Edom—	151
Mic	1: 2	that the S LORD may witness against you,	151
Hab	3:19	The S LORD is my strength;	151
Zep	1: 7	Be silent before the S LORD.	151
Zec	9:14	The S LORD will sound the trumpet;	151
Lk	2:29	"S Lord, as you have promised, you	1305
Ac	4:24	"S Lord," they said, "you made the heaven	1305
2Pe	2: 1	denying the s Lord who bought them—	1305
Jude	1: 4	and deny Jesus Christ our only S and Lord.	1305
Rev	6:10	"How long, S Lord, holy and true,	1305

SOVEREIGNTY (2) [SOVEREIGN]

| Da | 5:18 | Most High God gave your father Nebuchadnezzar s and greatness | 10424 |
| | 7:27 | the s, power and greatness of the kingdoms | 10424 |

SOW (31) [SOWED, SOWER, SOWING, SOWN, SOWS]

Ex	23:10	"For six years you are to s your fields	2445
	23:16	with the firstfruits of the crops you s	2445
Lev	25: 3	For six years s your fields,	2445
	25: 4	not s your fields or prune your vineyards.	2445
	25:11	not s and do not reap what grows of itself	2445
Dt	28:38	You will s much seed in the field	3655
2Ki	19:29	But in the third year s and reap,	2445
Job	4: 8	and those who s trouble reap it.	2445
Ps	126: 5	Those who s in tears will reap with songs	2445
	126: 6	goes out weeping, carrying seed to s,	2446+5433
Ecc	11: 6	S your seed in the morning,	2445
Isa	28:25	does he not s caraway and scatter cummin?	7046
	30:23	also send you rain for the seed you s in	2445
	37:30	But in the third year s and reap,	2445
Jer	4: 3	up your unplowed ground and do not s	2445
	12:13	They will s wheat but reap thorns;	2445
	35: 7	s seed or plant vineyards;	2445
Hos	8: 7	"They s the wind and reap the whirlwind.	2445
	10:12	S for yourselves righteousness,	2445
Mt	6:26	they do not s or reap or store away in barns,	5062
	13: 3	"A farmer went out to s his seed.	5062
	13:27	'Sir, didn't you s good seed in your field?	5062
Mk	4: 3	"Listen! A farmer went out to s his seed.	5062
Lk	8: 5	"A farmer went out to s his seed.	5062
	12:24	Consider the ravens: They do not s or reap,	5062
	19:21	not put in and reap what you did not s.'	5062
	19:22	and reaping what I did not s?	5062
1Co	15:36	What you s does not come to life	5062
	15:37	When you s, you do not plant the body	5062
Jas	3:18	Peacemakers who s in peace raise a harvest	5062
2Pe	2:22	and, "A s that is washed goes back to her	5725

SOWED (4) [SOW]

Ps	107:37	They s fields and planted vineyards	2445
Mt	13:24	of heaven is like a man who s good seed	5062
	13:25	his enemy came and s weeds among	2178
	13:37	"The one who s the good seed is the Son	5062

SOWER (5) [SOW]

Isa	55:10	so that it yields seed for the s and bread for	2445
Jer	50:16	Cut off from Babylon the s,	2445
Mt	13:18	then to what the parable of the s means:	5062
Jn	4:36	the s and the reaper may be glad together.	5062
2Co	9:10	to the s and bread for food will also supply	5062

SOWING (1) [SOW]

| Isa | 32:20 | s your seed by every stream, | 2445 |

SOWN (23) [SOW]

Job	31: 8	then may others eat what I have s,	2445
Isa	19: 7	Every s field along the Nile will become	4669
	40:24	no sooner are they s,	2445
Jer	2: 2	through the desert, through a land not s	2445
Eze	36: 9	you will be plowed and s,	2445
Mt	13: 8	a hundred, sixty or thirty times what was s.	NIG
	13:19	and snatches away what was s in his heart.	5062
	13:19	This is the seed s along the path.	5062
	13:23	sixty or thirty times what was s."	NIG
	25:24	where you have not s and gathering	5062

Mt	25:26	that I harvest where I have not s and gather	5062
Mk	4:15	along the path, where the word is s.	5062
	4:15	and takes away the word that was s in them.	5062
	4:16	Others, like seed s on rocky places,	5062
	4:18	Still others, like seed s among thorns,	5062
	4:20	Others, like seed s on good soil,	5062
	4:20	sixty or even a hundred times what was s."	NIG
Lk	8: 8	a hundred times more than was s."	NIG
1Co	9:11	If we have s spiritual seed among you,	5062
	15:42	The body that is s is perishable,	5062
	15:43	it is s in dishonor, it is raised in glory;	5062
	15:43	it is s in weakness, it is raised in power;	5062
	15:44	it is s a natural body, it is raised a spiritual	5062

SOWS (10) [SOW]

Pr	11:18	he who s righteousness reaps a sure reward.	2445
	22: 8	He who s wickedness reaps trouble,	2445
Mt	13:39	and the enemy who s them is the devil.	5062
Mk	4:14	The farmer s the word.	5062
Jn	4:37	the saying 'One s and another reaps' is true.	5062
2Co	9: 6	Whoever s sparingly will also reap	5062
	9: 6	and whoever s generously will also reap	5062
Gal	6: 7	A man reaps what he s.	5062
	6: 8	The one who s to please his sinful nature,	5062
	6: 8	the one who s to please the Spirit,	5062

SPACE (10) [SPACIOUS]

Ge	32:16	and keep some s between the herds."	8119
Ex	25:37	up on it so that they light the s in front of it.	6298
1Sa	26:13	there was a wide s between them.	5226
1Ki	7:36	on the panels, in every available s,	5113
Job	26: 7	the northern [skies] over empty s;	9332
Isa	5: 8	to field till no s is left and you live alone in	5226
	49:20	give us more s to live in.'	5602
Eze	41:17	In the s above the outside of the entrance to	NIH
	42: 5	the galleries took more s from them than	430
	42: 6	so they were smaller in floor s than those	824

SPACIOUS (11) [SPACE]

Ex	3: 8	a good and s land, a land flowing with milk	8146
Jdg	18:10	a land that God has put into your hands,	3338+8146
2Sa	22:20	He brought me out into a s place;	5303
1Ch	4:40	and the land was s, peaceful and quiet.	3338+8146
Ne	7: 4	Now the city was large and s,	3338+8146
	9:35	in the s and fertile land you gave them,	8146
Job	36:16	from the jaws of distress to a s place free	8144
Ps	18:19	He brought me out into a s place.	5303
	31: 8	but have set my feet in a s place.	5303
	104:25	There is the sea, vast and s,	3338+8146
Jer	22:14	a great palace with s upper rooms.'	8118

SPAIN (2)

| Ro | 15:24 | I plan to do so when I go to S. | 5056 |
| | 15:28 | I will go to S and visit you on the way. | 5056 |

SPAN (9)

Ex	23:26	I will give you a full life s.	3427+5031
	28:16	square—a s long and a span wide—	2455
	28:16	square—a span long and a s wide—	2455
	39: 9	It was square—a s long and a span wide—	2455
	39: 9	It was square—a span long and a s wide—	2455
Ps	39: 5	of my years is as nothing before you.	2698
	90:10	yet their s is but trouble and sorrow,	8145
Isa	23:15	for seventy years, the s of a king's life.	3427
Eze	43:13	with a rim of one s around the edge.	2455

SPARE (48) [SPARED, SPARES, SPARING, SPARINGLY]

Ge	18:24	Will you really sweep it away and not s	5951
	18:26	I will s the whole place for their sake."	5951
Dt	13: 8	Do not s him or shield him.	2798
Jos	2:13	that you will s the lives of my father	2649
	22:22	do not s us this day.	3828
Jdg	6: 4	the way to Gaza and did not s a living thing	8636
1Sa	15: 3	Do not s them; put to death men and women	2798
2Sa	21: 2	the Israelites had sworn to [s] them,	NIH
1Ki	16:11	He did not s a single male,	8636
	20:31	Perhaps he will s your life."	2649
2Ki	7: 4	If they s us, we live;	2649
2Ch	31:10	we have had enough to eat and plenty to s,	3855
Est	4:11	the gold scepter to him and s his life.	2649
	7: 3	And s my people—this is my request.	NIH
Job	2: 6	but you must s his life."	9068
	33:24	'S him from going down to the pit;	7021
Ps	78:50	he did not s them from death but gave them	3104
Pr	20:13	stay awake and you will have food to s.	8425
Isa	9:19	no one will s his brother.	2798
	47: 3	I will take vengeance; I will s no one."	7003
Jer	50:14	S no arrows, for she has sinned against	2798
	50:20	for I will forgive the remnant I s.	8636
	51: 3	Do not s her young men;	2798
Eze	5:11	I will not look on you with pity or s you.	2798
	6: 8	" "But I will s some, for some of you	3855
	7: 4	I will not look on you with pity or s you;	2798
	7: 9	I will not look on you with pity or s you;	2798
	8:18	I will not look on them with pity or s them.	2798
	9:10	not look on them with pity or s them,	2798
	12:16	I will s a few of them from the sword,	3855
Da	5:19	those he wanted to s, he spared;	NIH
Joel	2:17	Let them say, "S your people, O LORD.	2571
Am	7: 8	I will s them no longer.	6296
	8: 2	I will s them no longer.	6296

Zec	11: 5	Their own shepherds do not s them.	2798
Mal	3:17	I will s them, just as in compassion a man	2798
Lk	15:17	of my father's hired men have food to s,	4355
Ac	20:29	in among you and will not s the flock.	5767
	27:43	But the centurion wanted to s Paul's life	1407
Ro	8:32	He who did not s his own Son,	5767
	11:21	For if God did not s the natural branches,	5767
	11:21	he will not s you either.	5767
1Co	7:28	and I want to s you this.	5767
2Co	1:23	as my witness that it was in order to s you	5767
	13: 2	not s those who sinned earlier or any of	5767
Php	2:27	to s me sorrow upon sorrow.	2400+3590
2Pe	2: 4	if God did not s angels when they sinned,	5767
	2: 5	not s the ancient world when he brought	5767

SPARED (26) [SPARE]

Ge	12:13	for your sake and my life will be s because	2649
	19:20	Then my life will be s."	2649
	32:30	and yet my life was s."	5911
Ex	1:27	of the Israelites in Egypt and s our homes	5911
Nu	22:33	but I would have s her."	2649
Jos	6:17	with her in her house shall be s,	2649
	6:25	But Joshua s Rahab the prostitute,	2649
Jdg	1:25	they put the city to the sword but s the man	8938
	8:19	the LORD lives, if you had s their lives,	2649
	21:14	of Jabesh Gilead who had been s.	2649
1Sa	2:33	be s only to blind your eyes with tears and	NIH
	15: 9	But Saul and the army s Agag and the best	2798
	15:15	they s the best of the sheep and cattle	2798
	24:10	Some urged me to kill you, but I s you;	2571
2Sa	21: 7	The king s Mephibosheth son of Jonathan,	2798
2Ki	23:18	So they s his bones and those of	4880
2Ch	36:17	and s neither young man nor young woman,	2798
Job	21:30	the evil man is s from the day of calamity,	3104
Ps	30: 3	you s me from going down into the pit.	2649
Isa	57: 1	righteous are taken away to be s from	4946+7156
Jer	38:17	of the king of Babylon, your life will be s	2649
	38:20	and your life will be s.	2649
Eze	15:	he that survives and is s will die of famine.	5915
	13:19	not have died and have s those who should	2649
Da	5:19	those he wanted to spare, he s;	10262
Ac	27:21	you would have s yourselves this damage	3045

SPARES (2) [SPARE]

| Pr | 13:24 | He who s the rod hates his son, | 3104 |
| Mal | 3:17 | just as in compassion a man s his son | 2798 |

SPARING (4) [SPARE]

Ge	19:19	great kindness to me in s my life.	2649
Jos	11:11	destroyed them, not s anything that breathed	3855
	11:14	destroyed them, not s anyone that breathed.	8636
Pr	21:26	but the righteous give without s.	3104

SPARINGLY (2) [SPARE]

| 2Co | 9: 6 | Whoever sows s will also reap sparingly, | 5768 |
| | 9: 6 | Whoever sows sparingly will also reap s, | 5768 |

SPARK (2) [SPARKS]

| Isa | 1:31 | man will become tinder and his work a s; | 5773 |
| Jas | 3: 5 | a great forest is set on fire by a small s. | 4786 |

SPARKLE (1) [SPARKLED, SPARKLES, SPARKLING]

| Zec | 9:16 | They will s in his land like jewels in a crown | 5824 |

SPARKLED (2) [SPARKLE]

| Eze | 1:16 | They s like chrysolite, | 6524 |
| | 10: 9 | the wheels like chrysolite. | 6524 |

SPARKLES (1) [SPARKLE]

| Pr | 23:31 | when it is red, when it s in the cup, | 5989+6524 |

SPARKLING (2) [SPARKLE]

| Isa | 54:12 | of rubies, your gates of s jewels, | 74+734 |
| Eze | 1:22 | an expanse, s like ice, and awesome. | 6524 |

SPARKS (2) [SPARK]

| Job | 5: 7 | to trouble as surely as s fly upward. | 1201+8404 |
| | 41:19 | stream from his mouth; s of fire shoot out. | 3958 |

SPARROW (2) [SPARROWS]

| Ps | 84: 3 | Even the s has found a home, | 7606 |
| Pr | 26: 2 | Like a fluttering s or a darting swallow, | 7606 |

SPARROWS (4) [SPARROW]

Mt	10:29	Are not two s sold for a penny?	5141
	10:31	you are worth more than many s.	5141
Lk	12: 6	Are not five s sold for two pennies?	5141
	12: 7	you are worth more than many s.	5141

SPAT (Anglicized) See SPIT

SPATTERED (3)

Lev	6:27	and if any of the blood is s on a garment,	5684
2Ki	9:33	of her blood s the wall and the horses	5684
Isa	63: 3	their blood s my garments,	5684

SPEAK (322) [SPEAKER, SPEAKING, SPEAKS, SPOKE, SPOKEN, SPOKESMAN, SPOKESMEN]

Ge	18:27	that I have been so bold as to s to the Lord,	1819
	18:30	"May the Lord not be angry, but *let me* s.	1819
	18:31	that I have been so bold as to s to the Lord,	1819
	18:32	but *let me* s just once more.	1819
	19:21	I will not overthrow the town *you* s of.	1819
	34:20	of their city *to* s to their fellow townsmen.	1819
	37: 4	they hated him and could not s a kind *word*	1819
	44:18	*let* your servant s a word to my lord.	1819
	46:31	"I will go up and s to Pharaoh and will say	5583
	50: 4	s to Pharaoh for me.	1819
Ex	4:12	I will help you s and will teach you what	7023
	4:14	I know he can s well.	1819+1819
	4:15	*You shall* s to him and put words	1819
	4:15	both of you s and will teach you what to do.	7023
	4:16	He will s to the people for you,	1819
	5:23	since I went to Pharaoh to s in your name,	1819
	6:12	since I s with faltering lips?"	NIH
	6:30	"Since I s with faltering lips,	NIH
	19: 6	the words *you are to* s to the Israelites."	1819
	19: 7	the LORD had commanded him to s.	NIH
	20:19	"S to us yourself and we will listen.	1819
	20:19	But *do not have* God s to us or we will die."	1819
	29:42	There I will meet you and s to you;	1819
	33:11	The LORD *would* s to Moses face to face,	1819
	34:34	the LORD's presence to s with him,	1819
	34:35	over his face until he went in to s with	1819
Lev	1: 2	"S to the Israelites and say to them:	1819
	5: 1	" 'If a person sins because *he does* not s up	5583
	15: 2	"S to the Israelites and say to them:	1819
	17: 2	"S to Aaron and his sons and to all	1819
	18: 2	"S to the Israelites and say to them:	1819
	19: 2	"S to the entire assembly of Israel and say	1819
	21: 1	"S to the priests, the sons of Aaron,	606
	22:18	"S to Aaron and his sons and to all	1819
	23: 2	"S to the Israelites and say to them:	1819
	23:10	"S to the Israelites and say to them:	1819
	25: 2	"S to the Israelites and say to them:	1819
	27: 2	"S to the Israelites and say to them:	1819
Nu	5:12	"S to the Israelites and say to them:	1819
	6: 2	"S to the Israelites and say to them:	1819
	7:89	the Tent of Meeting to s with the LORD,	1819
	8: 2	"S to Aaron and say to him,	1819
	11:17	I will come down and s with you there,	1819
	12: 6	I s to him in dreams.	1819
	12: 8	With him I s face to face,	1819
	12: 8	not afraid to s against my servant Moses?"	1819
	15: 2	"S to the Israelites and say to them:	1819
	15:18	"S to the Israelites and say to them:	1819
	15:38	"S to the Israelites and say to them:	1819
	17: 2	"S to the Israelites and get twelve staffs	1819
	18:26	"S to the Levites and say to them:	1819
	20: 8	S to that rock before their eyes	1819
	22:35	but s only what I tell you."	1819
	22:38	I must s only what God puts	1819
	23:12	not s what the LORD puts in my mouth?"	1819
	23:19	*Does* he s and then not act?	606
	33:51	"S to the Israelites and say to them:	1819
	35:10	"S to the Israelites and say to them:	1819
Dt	3:26	"Do not s to me anymore about this matter.	1819
	18:20	But a prophet who presumes to s	1819
	31:28	so that I can s these words in their hearing	1819
	32: 1	Listen, O heavens, and I will s;	1819
Jdg	20: 7	s up and give your verdict."	1821
1Sa	2: 3	or *let* your mouth s such arrogance,	3655
	3: 9	'S, LORD, for your servant is listening.' "	1819
	3:10	Then Samuel said, "S, for your servant	1819
	17:29	said David. "Can't I even s?"	1821
	18:22	"S to David privately and say, 'Look,	1819
	19: 3	I'll s to him about you	1819
	25:24	Please *let* your servant s to you;	1819
2Sa	3:27	as though to s with him privately.	1819
	13:13	Please s to the king;	1819
	14: 3	go to the king and s these words to him."	1819
	14:12	"Let your servant s a word to my lord	1819
	14:12	"S," he replied.	1819
	14:15	'I will s to the king;	1819
	14:18	"Let my lord the king s," the woman said.	1819
	19:43	the first to s of bringing back our king?"	1821
	20:16	Tell Joab to come here so I can s to him."	1819
1Ki	2:18	"I will s to the king for you."	1819
	2:19	to King Solomon to s to him for Adonijah,	1819
	22:13	with theirs, and s favorably."	1819
	22:24	go when he went from me to s to you?"	1819
2Ki	2: 3	Elisha replied, "but *do* not s of it."	3120
	2: 5	I know," he replied, "but *do* not s of it."	3120
	4:13	Can we s on your behalf to the king or	1819
	6:12	tells the king of Israel the very words *you* s	1819
	18:20	but *you* s only empty words.	606
	18:26	"Please s to your servants in Aramaic,	1819
	18:26	Don't s to us in Hebrew in the hearing of	1819
2Ch	18:12	with theirs, and s favorably."	1819
	18:23	go when he went from me to s to you?"	1819
	34:22	the king had sent with him went *to* s to	1819
Ne	13:24	not know how to s the language of Judah.	1819
Est	6: 4	the outer court of the palace to s to the king	606
Job	7:11	I will s out in the anguish of my spirit,	1819
	9:35	Then I *would* s up without fear of him,	1819
	10: 1	to my complaint and s out in the bitterness	1819
	11: 5	Oh, how I wish that God *would* s,	1819
	12: 8	or s to the earth, and it will teach you,	8488
	13: 3	*to* s to the Almighty and to argue my case	1819

Job	13: 7	*Will you* s wickedly on God's behalf?	1819
	13: 7	*Will you* s deceitfully for him?	1819
	13:13	"Keep silent and *let me* s;	1819
	13:22	summon me and I will answer, or *let me* s,	1819
	16: 4	I also *could* s like you,	1819
	16: 6	"Yet if I s, my pain is not relieved;	1819
	21: 3	Bear with me while I s,	1819
	27: 4	my lips *will* not s wickedness,	1819
	32: 7	I thought, 'Age *should* s;	1819
	32:20	I *must* s and find relief;	1819
	33: 3	my lips sincerely s what I know.	4910
	33:14	For God *does* s—now one way, now	1819
	33:16	he may s in their ears and terrify them	1655
	33:31	be silent, and I will s.	1819
	33:32	s up, for I want you to be cleared.	1819
	37:20	Should he be told that I *want to* s?	1819
	41: 3	s to you *with* gentle *words*?	1819
	41:12	"I will not *fail to* s of his limbs,	3087
	42: 4	'Listen now, and I will s;	1819
Ps	5: 9	*with* their tongue *they* s deceit.	2744
	12: 2	their flattering lips s with deception.	1819
	17:10	and their mouths s with arrogance.	1819
	28: 3	*who* s cordially with their neighbors	1819
	31:18	with pride and contempt they s arrogantly	1819
	35:20	*They do* not s peaceably,	1819
	35:28	My tongue *will* s of your righteousness	2047
	40: 5	*were I to* s and tell of them,	5583
	40:10	I s of your faithfulness and salvation.	606
	49: 3	My mouth *will* s words of wisdom;	1819
	50: 7	O my people, and I will s, O Israel:	1819
	50:20	*You* s continually against your brother	1819
	51: 4	when you s and justified when you judge.	1819
	58: 1	*Do you* rulers indeed s justly?	1819
	58: 3	the womb they are wayward and s lies.	1819
	71:10	For my enemies s against me;	606
	73: 8	They scoff, and s with malice;	1819
	73:15	If I had said, "I will s thus,"	6218
	75: 5	*do* not s with outstretched neck.' "	1819
	77: 4	I was too troubled *to* s.	1819
	109:20	to those *who* s evil of me.	1819
	115: 5	They have mouths, but cannot s, eyes,	1819
	119:46	I *will* s of your statutes before kings	1819
	120: 7	but when I s, they are for war.	1819
	135:16	They have mouths, but cannot s, eyes,	1819
	139:20	*They s* of you with evil intent;	606
	145: 5	*They will* s of the glorious splendor	1819
	145:11	of your kingdom and s *of* your might,	1819
	145:21	My mouth *will* s in praise of the LORD.	1819
Pr	6:22	when you awake, they *will* s to you.	8488
	8: 6	I open my lips to s what is right.	NIH
	16:10	The lips of a king s as an oracle,	NIH
	20:15	but *lips that* s knowledge are a rare jewel.	AIT
	23: 9	*Do* not s to a fool,	1819
	23:16	when your lips s what is right.	1819
	31: 8	"S up for **those who cannot speak**	7023+7337
	31: 8	up for **those who cannot** s *for themselves,*	522
	31: 9	S up and judge fairly;	7023+7337
Ecc	3: 7	a time to be silent and a time to s,	1819
Isa	8:20	If *they do* not s according to this word,	606
	19:18	in Egypt *will* s the language of Canaan	1819
	28:11	and strange tongues God *will* s	1819
	29: 4	Brought low, *you will* s from the ground;	1819
	36: 5	but *you* s only empty words.	606
	36:11	"Please s to your servants in Aramaic,	1819
	36:11	Don't s to us in Hebrew in the hearing of	1819
	40: 2	S tenderly to Jerusalem,	1819
	41: 1	Let them come forward and s;	1819
	44: 9	**Those who** would s up for	6332
	45:19	I, the LORD, s the truth;	1819
	53: 8	And who *can* s of his descendants?	8488
	59: 4	They rely on empty arguments and s lies;	1819
Jer	1: 6	I said, "I do not know how to s;	1819
	1: 7	So I will go to the leaders and s *to* them;	1819
	6:10	To whom *can* I s and give warning?	1819
	10: 5	their idols cannot s;	1819
	12: 1	Yet I *would* s with you about your justice:	1819
	12: 6	though *they* s well of you.	1819
	14:17	"S this word to them:	606
	20: 8	Whenever I s, I cry out proclaiming violence	1819
	20: 9	"I will not mention him or s any more	1819
	23:16	*They* s visions from their own minds,	1819
	23:21	I *did* not s to them,	1819
	23:28	the one who has my word s it faithfully.	1819
	26: 2	the LORD's house and s to all the people	1819
	26: 7	the people heard Jeremiah s these words in	1819
	26:15	to you to s all these words in your hearing."	1819
	31:20	I often s against him, I still remember him.	1819
	32: 4	and *will* s with him face to face	1819
	34: 3	and he *will* s *with* you face to face.	1819
	48:27	in scorn whenever *you* s of her?	1821
La	3:37	Who *can* s and have it happen if	606
Eze	2: 1	stand up on your feet and I *will* s to you."	1819
	2: 7	*You must* s my words to them,	1819
	3: 1	then go and s to the house of Israel."	1819
	3: 4	the house of Israel and s my words to them.	1819
	3:10	and take to heart all the words I s to you.	1819
	3:11	to your countrymen in exile and s to them.	1819
	3:17	so hear the word I s and give them warning	4946+7023
	3:18	or s out to dissuade him from his evil ways	1819
	3:22	and there I will s to you.	1819
	3:27	But when I s to you,	1819
	12:25	But I the LORD *will* s what I will,	1819
	14: 4	Therefore s to them and tell them,	1819
	20: 3	s to the elders of Israel and say to them,	1819
	20:27	s to the people of Israel and say to them,	1819

Eze	24:27	*you will* s with him and will no longer	1819
	29: 3	S to him and say:	1819
	33: 2	s to your countrymen and say to them:	1819
	33: 7	so hear the word I s and give them warning	4946+7023
	33: 8	not s out to dissuade him from his ways,	1819
	36: 6	I s in my jealous wrath	1819
Da	7:25	He will s against the Most High	10418+10425
	10:11	the words I am *about to* s to you,	1819
	10:16	and I opened my mouth and *began to* s.	1819
	10:19	I was strengthened and said, "S, my lord,	1819
Hos	1: 2	the LORD began *to* s through Hosea,	1819
	2:14	I will lead her into the desert and s tenderly	1819
	7:13	to redeem them but they s lies against me.	1819
Mic	6:12	and their tongues s deceitfully.	928+7023
Hab	2:18	he makes idols that **cannot** s.	522
Zep	3:13	*they will* s no lies, nor will deceit be found	1819
Hag	2: 2	"S to Zerubbabel son of Shealtiel,	606
Zec	8:16	S the truth to each other,	1819
	10: 2	The idols s deceit, diviners see visions	1819
Mt	10:27	I tell you in the dark, s in the daylight;	3306
	11: 7	Jesus began *to* s to the crowd about John:	3306
	12:46	stood outside, wanting to s to him.	3281
	12:47	standing outside, wanting *to* s to you."	3281
	13:10	"Why *do you* s to the people in parables?"	3281
	13:13	This is why I s to them in parables:	3281
	17:25	Jesus was the first *to* s.	3306
Mk	1:34	but he would not let the demons s	3281
	7:35	and he *began* to s plainly.	3281
	7:37	even makes the deaf hear and the mute s."	3281
	12: 1	He then began *to* s to them in parables:	3281
	16:17	*they will* s in new tongues;	3281
Lk	1:19	*to* s to you and to tell you this good news.	3281
	1:20	and not able *to* s until the day this happens,	3281
	1:22	When he came out, he could not s to them.	3281
	1:22	to them but remained **unable** to s.	3273
	1:64	and he *began* to s, praising God.	3281
	4:41	and would not allow them to s,	3281
	6:26	Woe to you when all men s well *of* you,	3306
	7:24	Jesus began *to* s to the crowd about John:	3306
	8:10	but to others I s in parables, so that,	NIG
	12: 1	Jesus began *to* s first to his disciples,	3306
	20:21	we know that *you* s and teach what is right,	3306
Jn	3:11	I tell you the truth, *we* s of what we know,	3281
	3:12	will you believe if I s of heavenly things?	3306
	4:26	Jesus declared, "I who is *to* s am he."	3281
	7:17	from God or whether I s on my own.	3281
	8:28	that I do nothing on my own but s just what	3281
	9:21	He is of age; he *will* s for himself."	3281
	10:25	miracles I do in my Father's name s for me,	3455
	12:49	For I *did* not s of my own accord,	3281
	14:30	I *will* not s with you much longer,	3281
	16:13	He *will* not s on his own;	3281
	16:13	he *will* s only what he hears,	3281
	19:10	"Do you refuse *to* s to me?"	3281
Ac	1: 4	which you have heard me s about.	NIG
	2: 4	with the Holy Spirit and began *to* s	3281
	4:17	we must warn these men *to* s no longer	3281
	4:18	not *to* s or teach at all in the name of Jesus.	5779
	4:29	and enable your servants *to* s your word	3281
	5:40	Then they ordered them not *to* s in	3281
	6:11	"We have heard Stephen s words	3281
	8:33	Who *can* s *of* his descendants?	1455
	10:34	Then Peter **began to** s:	487+3306+3836+5125
	11:15	"As I began to s, the Holy Spirit came on	3281
	11:20	went to Antioch and *began to* s to Greeks	3281
	13:15	of encouragement for the people, please s."	3306
	13:42	the people invited them *to* s further **about**	3281
	13:46	"We had to s the word of God to you first.	3281
	16:13	*to* s to the women who had gathered there.	3281
	18:14	Just as Paul was about to s,	487+3836+5125
	18:26	He began to s *boldly* in the synagogue.	4245
	21:37	"Do you s Greek?"	1182
	21:39	Please let me s to the people."	3281
	22: 2	When they heard *him* s to them in Aramaic,	4715
	23: 5	not s evil **about** the ruler of your people.' "	3306
	24:10	When the governor motioned for him *to* s,	3306
	25:18	When his accusers got up to s,	NIG
	26: 1	"You have permission *to* s for yourself."	3306
	26:26	and I *can* s freely to him.	3281
Ro	3: 4	when you s and prevail when you judge."	3364
	9: 1	I s the truth in Christ—	3306
	15:18	I will not venture *to* s of anything except	3281
1Co	2: 6	s a message of wisdom among the mature,	3281
	2: 7	No, *we* s of God's secret wisdom,	3281
	2:13	This is what *we* s, not in words taught us by	3281
	10:15	I s to sensible people; judge for yourselves	3306
	12:30	Do all s in tongues? Do all interpret?	3281
	13: 1	If I s in the tongues of men and of angels,	3281
	14: 2	in a tongue *does* not s to men but to God.	3281
	14: 5	like every one of you *to* s in tongues,	3281
	14: 6	brothers, if I come to you and s in tongues,	3281
	14: 9	*you* s intelligible words with your tongue,	1443
	14:18	that I s in tongues more than all of you.	3281
	14:19	I would rather s five intelligible words	3281
	14:21	and through the lips of foreigners I *will* s	3281
	14:27	should s, one at a time, and someone must	NIG
	14:28	in the church and s to himself and God.	3281
	14:29	Two or three prophets *should* s,	3281
	14:34	They are not allowed *to* s,	3281
	14:35	for it is disgraceful for a woman *to* s in	3281
2Co	2:17	in Christ *we* s before God with sincerity,	3281
	4:13	of faith we also believe and therefore s,	3281
	6:13	I s as to my children—	3306
Eph	4:25	and s truthfully to his neighbor,	3281
	5:19	S to one another with psalms, hymns and	3281
Php	1:14	*to* s the word of God more courageously	3281

1Th 2: 4 we s as men approved by God to 3281
Heb 6: 9 Even though we s like this, dear friends, 3281
Jas 1:19 slow to s and slow to become angry, 3281
2:12 S and act as those who are going to 3281
1Pe 3:16 s maliciously against your good behavior 2092
1Jn 4: 5 therefore s from the viewpoint of the world, 3281
3Jn 1:12 We also s well of him, 3455
Jude 1:10 Yet these men s abusively against 1059
Rev 13:15 so that it could s and cause all who refused 3281

SPEAKER (5) [SPEAK]

Ac 14:12 because he was the chief s. 3364
1Co 14:11 I am a foreigner to the s, 3281
14:28 the s should keep quiet in the church NIG
14:30 the first s should stop. NIG
2Co 11: 6 I may not be a trained s, but I do have 3364

SPEAKING (102) [SPEAK]

Ge 11: 6 "If as one people s the same language NIH
17:22 When he had finished s with Abraham, 1819
18:33 the LORD had finished s with Abraham, 1819
45:12 that it is really I who am s to you. 1819
Ex 16:10 While Aaron was s to the whole Israelite 1819
19: 9 so that the people will hear me s with you 1819
31:18 When the LORD finished s to Moses 1819
34:33 When Moses finished s to them, 1819
Nu 7:89 he heard the voice s to him from between 1819
Dt 4:33 the voice of God s out of fire, 1819
5:26 the voice of the living God s out of fire, 1819
20: 9 the officers have finished s to the army, 1819
Jdg 15:17 When he finished s, he threw away 1819
1Sa 17:23 heard him s with the men, 1819
2Sa 13:36 As he finished s, the king's sons came in, 1819
1Ki 1:22 While she was still s with the king, 1819
1:42 Even as he was s, Jonathan son of 1819
2Ch 25:16 While he was still s, the king said to him, 1819
Job 1:16 While he was still s, another messenger 1819
1:17 While he was still s, another messenger 1819
1:18 While he was still s, yet another messenger 1819
4: 2 But who can keep from s? 4863
29: 9 refrained from s and covered their mouths 4863
32: 4 Now Elihu had waited before s to Job 1821
Ps 34:13 from evil and your lips from s lies. 1819
52: 3 falsehood rather than s the truth. 1819
Isa 58:13 and not doing as you please or s idle words, 1819
63: 1 "It is I, s in righteousness, mighty to save." 1819
65:24 while they are still s I will hear. 1819
Jer 36: 2 from the time I began s to you in the reign 1819
Eze 1:28 and I heard the voice of one s. 1819
2: 2 and I heard him s to me. 1819
43: 6 I heard someone s to me from inside 1819
Da 7:11 of the boastful words the horn was s. 10425
8:13 Then I heard a holy one s, 1819
8:18 While he was s to me, I was in a deep sleep, 1819
9:20 While I was s and praying, 1819
10: 9 Then I heard him s, 1821+7754
Zec 1:14 Then the angel who was s to me said, 1819
1:19 I asked the angel who was s to me, 1819
2: 3 The angel who was s to me left, 1819
5: 5 the angel who was s to me came forward 1819
5:10 I asked the angel who was s to me. 1819
6: 4 I asked the angel who was s to me. 1819
Mt 10:20 for it will not be you s, but the Spirit 3281
10:20 but the Spirit of your Father s through you. 3281
15:31 when they saw the mute s, 3281
17: 5 While he was still s, a bright cloud 3281
22:43 "How is it then that David, s by the Spirit, 3306
26:47 While he was still s, Judas, 3281
Mk 5:35 While Jesus was still s, some men came 3281
12:36 David himself, s by the Holy Spirit, NIG
13:11 for it is not you s, but the Holy Spirit. 3281
14:43 Just as he was s, Judas, one of the Twelve, 3281
Lk 5: 4 When he had finished s, he said to Simon, 3281
8:49 While Jesus was still s, someone came 3281
9:34 While he was s, a cloud appeared 3306
11:37 When Jesus had finished s, 3281
22:47 While he was still s a crowd came up, 3281
22:60 Just as he was s, the rooster crowed. 3281
Jn 7:26 Here he is, s publicly, and they are not 3281
9:37 in fact, he is the one s with you." 3281
11:13 Jesus had been s of his death, 3306
12:36 When he had finished s, 3281
16:25 "Though I have been s figuratively, 3281
16:29 "Now you are s clearly and without figures 3281
Ac 2: 6 each one heard them s in his own language. 3281
2: 7 "Are not all these men who are s Galileans? 3281
4: 1 and John while they were s to the people. 3281
4:20 For we cannot help s about what we 3281+3590
6:13 "This fellow never stops s against this 3281
9:28 s boldly in the name of the Lord. 4245
10:44 While Peter was still s these words, 3281
10:46 For they heard them s in tongues 3281
14: 3 s boldly for the Lord, 4245
14: 9 He listened to Paul as he was s. 3281
18: 9 keep on s, do not be silent. 3281
20: 2 s many words of encouragement to 4151
22: 9 not understand the voice of him who was s 3281
22:18 and saw the Lord s. 3306
Ro 7: 1 for I am s to men who know the law— 3281
1Co 1: 5 in all your s and in all your knowledge— 3364
12: 3 Therefore I tell you that no one who is s by 3281
12:10 s in different kinds of tongues, 1185
12:28 those s in different kinds of tongues. 1185
13: 1 You will just be s into the air. 3281
14:39 and do not forbid s in tongues. 3281

2Co 10:10 and his s amounts to nothing." 3364
11:21 I am s as a fool—I also dare to boast about. 3306
12: 6 I would be s the truth. 3306
12:19 We have been s in the sight of God as those 3281
13: 3 that Christ is s through me. 3281
Eph 4:15 Instead, s the truth in love, 238
1Th 2:16 from s to the Gentiles so that they may 3281
Heb 1: 7 In s of the angels he says, NIG
2: 5 about which we are s. 3281
11:19 the dead, and figuratively s, 1877+4130
12:19 to a trumpet blast or to such a voice s words NIG
1Pe 4:11 he should do it as one s the very words NIG
2Pe 3:16 s in them of these matters. 3281
Rev 1:12 I turned around to see the voice that was s 3281
4: 1 And the voice I had first heard s to me like 3281

SPEAKS (51) [SPEAK]

Ex 33:11 face to face, as a man s with his friend. 1819
Dt 5:24 that a man can live even if God s with him. 1819
18:19 my words that the prophet s in my name, 1819
18:20 a prophet who s in the name of other gods, 1819
1Sa 16:18 He s well and is a fine-looking man. 1821
Job 7: 5 He s to the sun and it does not shine; 606
34:35 'Job s without knowledge; 1819
36:15 he s to them in their affliction, 265+1655
Ps 15: 2 who s the truth from his heart 1819
37:30 and his tongue s what is just. 1819
41: 6 he s falsely, while his heart gathers slander; 1819
50: 1 s and summons the earth from the rising of 1819
101: 7 no one who s falsely will stand 1819
Pr 8: 7 My mouth s what is true, 2047
13: 3 but he who s rashly will come to ruin. 7316+8557
16:13 they value a man who s the truth. 1819
29:20 Do you see a man who s in haste? 1821
31:26 She s with wisdom, 7023+7337
Isa 9:17 every mouth s vileness. 1819
32: 6 the fool s folly, his mind is busy with evil: 1819
33:15 and s what is right, who rejects gain 1819
Jer 9: 5 and no one s the truth. 1819
9: 8 tongue is a deadly arrow; it s with deceit. 1819
9: 8 With his mouth each s cordially 1819
Eze 10: 5 like the voice of God Almighty when he s. 1819
Hab 2: 3 it s of the end and will not prove false. 7032
Mt 12:32 Anyone who s a word against the Son 3306
12:32 but anyone who s against the Holy Spirit 3306
12:34 the overflow of the heart the mouth s. 3281
Lk 5:21 "Who is this fellow who s blasphemy? 3281
6:45 out of the overflow of his heart his mouth s. 3281
12:10 And everyone who s a word against the Son 3306
Jn 3:31 and s as one from the earth. 3281
3:34 For the one whom God has sent s the words 3281
7:18 When he s on his own does so to gain honor 3281
8:44 When he lies, he s his native language, 3281
Ro 6: 4 when he s of the blessedness of the man 3306
1Co 14: 2 For anyone who s in a tongue does 3281
14: 3 But everyone who prophesies s to men 3281
14: 4 He who s in a tongue edifies himself, 3281
14: 5 He who prophesies is greater than one who s in tongues, 3281
14:13 For this reason anyone who s in a tongue 3281
14:23 and everyone s in tongues, 3281
14:27 If anyone s in a tongue, two— 3281
Heb 11: 4 by faith he still s, even though he is dead. 3281
12:24 the sprinkled blood that s a better word than 3281
12:25 See to it that you do not refuse him who s. 3281
Jas 4:11 Anyone who s against his brother 2895
4:11 against his brother or judges him s against 2895
1Pe 4:11 If anyone s, he should do it as one speaking 3281
1Jn 2: 1 one who s to the Father in our defense— 4156

SPEAR (47) [SPEARHEAD, SPEARMEN, SPEARS]

Nu 25: 7 he left the assembly, took a s in his hand 8242
25: 8 He drove the s through both of them— NIH
Jdg 5: 8 or s was seen among forty thousand 8242
1Sa 13:22 and Jonathan had a sword or s in his hand; 2851
17: 7 His s shaft was like a weaver's rod, 2851
17:45 against me with sword and s and javelin, 2851
17:47 not by sword or s that the LORD saves; 2851
18:10 Saul had a s in his hand 2851
19: 9 as he was sitting in his house with his s 2851
19:10 Saul tried to pin him to the wall with his s, 2851
19:10 but David eluded him as Saul drove the s 2851
20:33 But Saul hurled his s at him to kill him. 2851
21: 8 "Don't you have a s or a sword here? 2851
22: 6 And Saul, s in hand, 2851
26: 7 with his s stuck in the ground near his head. 2851
26: 8 to the ground with one thrust of my s; 2851
26:11 the s and water jug that are near his head, 2851
26:12 the s and water jug near Saul's head, 2851
26:16 Where are the king's s and water jug 2851
26:22 "Here is the king's s," David answered. 2851
2Sa 1: 6 "and there was Saul, leaning on his s, 2851
2:23 the butt of his s into Asahel's stomach, 2851
2:23 and the s came out through his back. 2851
21:19 a s with a shaft like a weaver's rod. 2851
23: 7 a tool of iron or the shaft of a s; 2851
23: 8 he raised his s against eight hundred men, 2851
23:18 He raised his s against three hundred men, 2851
23:21 Although the Egyptian had a s in his hand, 2851
23:21 He snatched the s from the Egyptian's hand 2851
23:21 and killed him with his own s. 2851
1Ch 11:11 he raised his s against three hundred men 2851
11:20 He raised his s against three hundred men, 2851
11:23 the Egyptian had a s like a weaver's rod 2851

1Ch 11:23 He snatched the s from the Egyptian's hand 2851
11:23 and killed him with his own s. 2851
12: 8 and able to handle the shield and s. 8242
12:24 men of Judah, carrying shield and s— 8242
20: 5 a s with a shaft like a weaver's rod. 2851
2Ch 25: 5 able to handle the s and shield. 8242
Job 39:23 along with the flashing s and lance. 2851
41:26 nor does the s or the dart or the javelin. 2851
Ps 35: 3 Brandish s and javelin against those who 2851
46: 9 he breaks the bow and shatters the s, 2851
Jer 6:23 They are armed with bow and s, 3959
Hab 3:11 at the lightning of your flashing s. 2851
3:14 With his own s you pierced his head 4751
Jn 19:34 of the soldiers pierced Jesus' side with a s, 3365

SPEARHEAD (1) [SPEAR]

2Sa 21:16 bronze s weighed three hundred shekels 7802

SPEARMEN (1) [SPEAR]

Ac 23:23 seventy horsemen and two hundred s to go 1287

SPEARS (21) [SPEAR]

1Sa 13:19 the Hebrews will make swords or s!" 2851
1Ki 18:28 and slashed themselves with swords and s, 8242
2Ki 11:10 Then he gave the commanders the s 2851
1Ch 12:34 men carrying shields and s; 2851
2Ch 11:12 He put shields and s in all the cities, 8242
14: 8 equipped with large shields and with s, 8242
23: 9 the commanders of units of a hundred the s 2851
26:14 Uzziah provided shields, s, helmets, 8242
Ne 4:13 with their swords, s and bows. 8242
4:16 while the other half were equipped with s, 8242
4:21 the work with half the men holding s, 8242
Job 41: 7 with harpoons or his head with fishing s? 7528
Ps 57: 4 men whose teeth are s and arrows, 2851
Isa 2: 4 and their s into pruning hooks. 2851
Jer 46: 4 Polish your s, put on your armor! 8242
50:42 They are armed with bows and s; 3959
Eze 39: 9 the bows and arrows, the war clubs and s 8242
Joel 3:10 into swords and your pruning hooks into s. 8242
Mic 4: 3 and their s into pruning hooks. 2851
Na 2: 3 the s of pine are brandished. 1360
3: 3 flashing swords and glittering s! 2851

SPECIAL (33) [ESPECIALLY]

Ge 47: 6 know of any among them with s ability, 2657
Lev 22:21 to the LORD to fulfill a s vow, 5624+7098
27: 2 'If anyone makes a s vow to dedicate 5624+7098
Nu 6: 2 or woman wants to make a s vow, 5623+7098
15: 3 for s vows or freewill offerings 5624+7098
15: 8 for a s vow or a fellowship offering to 5624+7098
Dt 12: 6 your tithes and s gifts, 3338+9556
12:11 your tithes and s gifts, 3338+9556
12:17 or your freewill offerings or s gifts. 3338+9556
Jos 15:19 She replied, "Do me a s favor. 1388
Jdg 1:15 She replied, "Do me a s favor. 1388
2Sa 13: 6 and make some s bread in my sight, 4221+4223
16: 6 the s guard were on David's right and left. 1475
1Ki 1: 8 and David's s guard did not join Adonijah. 1475
1:10 or the s guard or his brother Solomon. 1475
Est 1:14 Persia and Media who had s access to 7156+8011
2: 9 with her beauty treatments and s food. 4950
Jer 13:21 those you cultivated as your s allies? 8031
Eze 44:30 of all your s gifts will belong to the priests. 9556
45:13 "This is the s gift you are to offer: 9556
45:16 of the land will participate in this s gift for 9556
48: 8 portion you are to present as a s gift. 9556
48: 9 "The s portion you are to offer to 9556
48:12 be a s gift to them from the sacred portion 9557
48:20 As a s gift you will set aside 8123
Jn 19:31 and the next day was to be a s Sabbath. 3489
Ro 14: 6 He who regards one day as s, NIG
1Co 12:23 less honorable we treat with s honor. 4358
12:23 unpresentable are treated with s modesty, 4358
12:24 our presentable parts need no s treatment. 5507
Gal 4:10 You are observing s days and months NIG
2Th 3:14 take s note of him. 4957
Jas 2: 3 If you show s attention to 2098

SPECIFIC (1) [SPECIFY]

Nu 4:32 to each man the s things he is to carry. 3998+5466

SPECIFICATIONS (2) [SPECIFY]

1Ki 6:38 finished in all its details according to its s. 5477
2Ch 4: 7 according to the s for them and placed them 5477

SPECIFIED (9) [SPECIFY]

Lev 27: 8 is too poor to pay the s amount, 6886
Nu 29: 6 grain offerings and drink offerings as s. 5477
29:18 drink offerings according to the number s. 5477
29:21 drink offerings according to the number s. 5477
29:24 drink offerings according to the number s. 5477
29:27 drink offerings according to the number s. 5477
29:30 drink offerings according to the number s. 5477
29:33 drink offerings according to the number s. 5477
29:37 drink offerings according to the number s. 5477

SPECIFY (1) [SPECIFIC, SPECIFICATIONS, SPECIFIED, SPECIFYING]

1Ki 5: 9 float them in rafts by sea to the place you s. 8938

SPECIFYING (1) [SPECIFY]
Ac	25:27	to send on a prisoner without s the charges	4955

SPECK (6) [SPECKLED]
Mt	7: 3	at the s of sawdust in your brother's eye	2847
	7: 4	'Let me take the s out of your eye,'	2847
	7: 5	then you will see clearly to remove the s	2847
Lk	6:41	at the s of sawdust in your brother's eye	2847
	6:42	'Brother, let me take the s out of your eye,'	2847
	6:42	then you will see clearly to remove the s	2847

SPECKLED (10) [SPECK]
Ge	30:32	from them every s or spotted sheep,	5923
	30:32	and every spotted or s goat.	5923
	30:33	in my possession that is not s or spotted,	5923
	30:35	and all the s or spotted female goats	5923
	30:39	that were streaked or s or spotted.	5923
	31: 8	If he said, 'The s ones will be your wages,'	5923
	31: 8	then all the flocks gave birth to s young;	5923
	31:10	with the flock were streaked, s or spotted.	5923
	31:12	with the flock are streaked, s or spotted,	5923
Jer	12: 9	to me like a bird of prey that other birds	7380

SPECTACLE (4)
Eze	28:17	I made a s of you before kings.	8019
Na	3: 6	treat you with contempt and make you a s.	8024
1Co	4: 9	We have been made a s to the whole	2519
Col	2:15	he made a public s of them,	1258

SPED (1) [SPEED]
Eze	1:14	The creatures s back and forth like flashes	8351

SPEECH (33) [SPEECHES]
Ge	11: 1	world had one language and a common s.	1821
Ex	4:10	I am slow of s and tongue."	7023
Ps	19: 2	Day after day they pour forth s;	608
	19: 3	There is no s or language where their voice	608
	55: 9	O Lord, confound their s,	4383
	55:21	His s is smooth as butter,	7023
Pr	1:21	gateways of the city she makes her s:	606+609
	5: 3	and her s is smoother than oil;	2674
	8:13	evil behavior and perverse s.	7023
	12: 6	but the s of the upright rescues them.	7023
	16:27	and his s is like a scorching fire.	8557
	22:11	and whose s is gracious will have the king	8557
	26:25	Though his s is charming,	7754
Ecc	5: 3	the s of a fool when there are many words.	7754
Isa	18: 2	an aggressive nation of strange s,	7743+7743
	18: 7	an aggressive nation of strange s,	7743+7743
	29: 4	your s will mumble out of the dust.	614
	29: 4	out of the dust your s will whisper.	614
	33:19	those people of an obscure s,	8557
Jer	5:15	whose s you do not understand.	1819+4537
Eze	3: 5	people of obscure s and difficult language,	8557
	3: 6	peoples of obscure s and difficult language,	8557
Mk	9:17	by a spirit that has robbed him of s.	228
Jn	10: 6	Jesus used this figure of s,	4231
	16:29	and without figures of s.	4231
Ac	5:40	His s persuaded them.	NIG
	7:22	of the Egyptians and was powerful in s	3364
2Co	6: 7	in truthful s and in the power of God;	3364
	8: 7	in faith, in s, in knowledge,	3364
1Ti	4:12	but set an example for the believers in s,	3364
Tit	2: 8	soundness of s that cannot be condemned,	3364
1Pe	3:10	from evil and his lips from deceitful s.	3281
2Pe	2:16	by a donkey—a beast without s—	936

SPEECHES (4) [SPEECH]
Job	15: 3	useless words, with s that have no value?	4863
	16: 3	Will your long-winded s never end?	1821
	16: 4	I could make fine s against you	928+2488+4863
	18: 2	"When will you end these s?	4863

SPEECHLESS (3)
Da	10:15	with my face toward the ground and was s.	519
Mt	22:12	The man was s.	5821
Ac	9: 7	The men traveling with Saul stood there s;	1917

SPEED (2) [SPED, SPEED, SPEEDS]
Ro	9:28	his sentence on earth with s and finality."	5335
2Pe	3:12	forward to the day of God and s its coming.	5067

SPEEDILY (3) [SPEED]
Isa	5:26	Here they come, swiftly and s!	7824
	51: 5	My righteousness draws near s,	NIH
Joel	3: 4	I will swiftly and s return on your own	4559

SPEEDS (1) [SPEED]
Isa	16: 5	justice and s the cause of righteousness.	4542

SPELL (1) [SPELLS]
Rev	18:23	By your magic s all the nations were led	5758

SPELLS (4) [SPELL]
Dt	18:11	or casts s, or who is a medium or	2489+2490
Isa	47: 9	your many sorceries and all your potent s.	2490
	47:12	"Keep on, then, with your magic s and	2490
Mic	5:12	and you will no longer cast s.	6726

SPELT (3)
Ex	9:32	The wheat and s, however,	4081
Isa	28:25	barley in its plot, and s in its field?	4081
Eze	4: 9	beans and lentils, millet and s;	4081

SPEND (42) [SPENDING, SPENT]
Ge	19: 2	You can wash your feet and s the night and	4328
	19: 2	"we will s the night in the square."	4328
	24:23	in your father's house for us to s the night?	4328
	24:25	as well as room for you to s the night."	4328
Nu	22: 8	"S the night here," Balaam said to them,	4328
Dt	32:23	upon them and s my arrows against them.	3983
Jdg	16: 1	went in to s the night with her.	448+995
	19: 9	S the night here; the day is nearly over.	4328
	19:11	at this city of the Jebusites and s the night."	4328
	19:13	to reach Gibeah or Ramah and s the night."	4328
	19:15	There they stopped to s the night.	4328
	19:20	Only don't s the night in the square."	4328
	20: 4	to Gibeah in Benjamin to s the night.	4328
2Sa	17: 8	he will not s the night with the troops.	4328
	17:16	not s the night at the fords in the desert;	4328
1Ch	9:27	They would s the night stationed around	4328
Ne	13:21	"Why do you s the night by the wall?	4328
Job	21:13	They s their years in prosperity and go	3983
	24: 7	Lacking clothes, they s the night naked;	4328
	31:32	but no stranger had to s the night in	4328
	36:11	they will s the rest of their days	3983
Ps	25:13	He will s his days in prosperity,	4328
Pr	31: 3	do not s your strength on women,	5989
SS	7:11	let us s the night in the villages.	4328
Isa	55: 2	Why s money on what is not bread,	9202
	58:10	if you s yourselves in behalf of the hungry	7049
	65: 4	and s their nights keeping secret vigil;	4328
Eze	6:12	So will I s my wrath upon them.	3983
	7: 8	on you and s my anger against you;	3983
	13:15	So I will s my wrath against the wall and	3983
	20: 8	and s my anger against them in Egypt.	3983
	20:21	and s my anger against them in the desert.	3983
Joel	1:13	Come, s the night in sackcloth,	4328
Mk	6:37	to go and s that much on bread and give it	60
Lk	21:37	and each evening he went out to s the night	887
Ac	18:20	they asked him to s more time	2093+3531+5989
	28:14	who invited us to s a week with them.	2152
1Co	16: 7	I hope to s some time with you,	2152+5989
2Co	12:15	So I will very gladly s for you everything	1251
Jas	4: 3	you may s what you get on your pleasures.	1251
	4:13	s a year there, carry on business	4472

SPENDING (5) [SPEND]
Ac	15:33	After s some time there,	4472
	18:23	After s some time in Antioch,	4472
	20:16	to avoid s time in the province	1181+5990
	25: 6	After s eight or ten days with them,	1417
	25:14	Since they were s many days there,	1417

SPENT (33) [SPEND]
Ge	24:54	and drank and s the night there.	4328
	31:54	After they had eaten, they s the night there.	4328
	32:13	He s the night there,	4328
	32:21	but he himself s the night in the camp.	4328
Lev	26:20	Your strength will be s in vain,	9462
Dt	1:46	all the time you s there.	3782
Jos	6:11	to camp and s the night there.	4328
	8: 9	but Joshua s that night with the people.	4328
Jdg	18: 2	where they s the night.	4328
2Sa	12:16	and s the nights lying on the ground.	4328
	14: 2	a woman who has s many days grieving	AIT
1Ki	5:14	so that they s one month in Lebanon	2118
	6:38	He had s seven years building it.	AIT
	19: 9	There he went into a cave and s the night.	4328
2Ki	12:13	was not s for making silver basins.	4946+6913
1Ch	12:39	The men s three days there with David,	2118
Ne	3: 5	s another quarter in confession	AIT
	13:20	of goods s the night outside Jerusalem.	4328
Pr	5:11	when your flesh and body are s.	3983
Isa	49: 4	I have s my strength in vain and	3983
Eze	5:13	And when I have s my wrath upon them,	3983
Da	6:18	to his palace and s the night without eating	10102
Mt	21:17	to Bethany, where he s the night.	887
Mk	5:26	of many doctors and had s all she had,	1251
Lk	6:12	and s the night praying to God.	1381+1639
	15:14	After he had s everything,	1251
Jn	1:39	and s that day with him.	3531
	3:22	where they s some time with them,	1417
Ac	9:19	Saul s several days with the disciples	1181
	14: 3	and Barnabas a considerable time there,	1417
	17:21	foreigners who lived there s their time doing nothing	2320
2Co	11:25	I s a night and a day in the open sea,	4472
1Pe	4: 3	For you have s enough time in the	NIG

SPEW (3) [SPEWED]
Ps	59: 7	See what they s from their mouths—	5580
	59: 7	they s out swords from their lips,	NIH
Jer	51:44	and make him s out what he has swallowed.	3655+4946+7023

SPEWED (3) [SPEW]
Jer	51:34	and then has s us out.	5615
Rev	12:15	Then from his mouth the serpent s water	965
	12:16	that the dragon had s out of his mouth.	965

SPICE (4) [SPICED, SPICES]
SS	4:10	the fragrance of your perfume than any s!	1411
	5: 1	I have gathered my myrrh with my s.	1411
	5:13	like beds of s yielding perfume.	1411
Rev	18:13	and s, of incense, myrrh and frankincense,	319

SPICE-LADEN (1) [LOAD]
SS	8:14	or like a young stag on the s mountains.	1411

SPICED (1) [SPICE]
SS	8: 2	I would give you s wine to drink,	8380

SPICERY (KJV) See SPICES

SPICES (32) [SPICE]
Ge	37:25	Their camels were loaded with s,	5780
	43:11	a little balm and a little honey, some s	5780
Ex	25: 6	s for the anointing oil and for	1411
	30:23	"Take the following fine s:	1411
	30:34	Lord said to Moses, "Take fragrant s—	6160
	35: 8	s for the anointing oil and for	1411
	35:28	also brought s and olive oil for the light and	1411
1Ki	10: 2	with camels carrying s,	1411
	10:10	large quantities of s, and precious stones.	1411
	10:10	so many s brought in as those the queen	1411
	10:25	weapons and s, and horses and mules.	1411
2Ki	20:13	the silver, the gold, the s and the fine oil—	1411
1Ch	9:29	and the oil, incense and s.	1411
	9:30	of the priests took care of mixing the s.	1411
2Ch	9: 1	with camels carrying s,	1411
	9: 9	large quantities of s, and precious stones.	1411
	9: 9	There had never been such s as those	1411
	9:24	weapons and s, and horses and mules.	1411
	16:14	They laid him on a bier covered with s	1411
	32:27	s, shields and all kinds of valuables.	1411
Ps	75: 8	a cup full of foaming wine mixed with s;	5008
SS	4: 6	with myrrh and incense made from all the s	86
	4:14	with myrrh and aloes and all the finest s.	1411
	6: 2	to the beds of s, to browse in the gardens	1411
Isa	39: 2	the silver, the gold, the s, the fine oil,	1411
Eze	24:10	Cook the meat well, mixing in the s;	5350
	27:22	of all kinds of s and precious stones,	1411
Mt	23:23	You give a tenth of your s—mint,	2455
Mk	16: 1	and Salome bought s so that they might go	808
Lk	23:56	Then they went home and prepared s	808
	24: 1	the women took the s they had prepared	808
Jn	19:40	the two of them wrapped it, with the s,	808

SPIDER (KJV) See LIZARD

SPIDER'S (2)
Job	8:14	what he relies on is a s web.	6571
Isa	59: 5	the eggs of vipers and spin a s web.	6571

SPIED (4) [SPY]
Jos	6:22	Joshua said to the two men who had s out	8078
	7: 2	So the men went up and s out Ai.	8078
Jdg	18:14	Then the five men who had s out the land	8078
	18:17	The five men who had s out the land went	8078

SPIES (17) [SPY]
Ge	42: 9	about them and said to them, "You are s!	8078
	42:11	Your servants are honest men, not s."	8078
	42:14	as I told you: You are s!	8078
	42:16	then as surely as Pharaoh lives, you are s!"	8078
	42:31	'We are honest men; we are not s.	8078
	42:34	to me so I will know that you are not s	8078
Nu	21:32	After Moses had sent s to Jazer,	8078
Jos	2: 1	Joshua son of Nun secretly sent two s	408+8078
	2: 7	the s on the road that leads to the fords of	2157S
	2: 8	Before the s lay down for the night,	2156S
	6:17	because she hid the s we sent.	4855
	6:25	the men Joshua had sent as s to Jericho—	8078
Jdg	1:24	the s saw a man coming out of the city	9068
Lk	20:20	Keeping a close watch on him, they sent s,	1588
	20:21	So he questioned him:	NIG
Heb	11:31	Rahab, because she welcomed the s,	2946
Jas	2:25	when she gave lodging to the s	34

SPIKENARD (KJV) See NARD

SPILLED (4) [SPILLS]
Ge	38: 9	with his brother's wife, he s his semen on	8845
2Sa	14:14	Like water s on the ground,	5599
	20:10	and his intestines s out on the ground.	9161
Ac	1:18	and all his intestines s out.	1772

SPILLS (1) [SPILLED]
Job	16:13	he pierces my kidneys and s my gall on	9161

SPIN (3) [SPINDLE, SPUN]
Isa	59: 5	the eggs of vipers and s a spider's web.	755
Mt	6:28	They do not labor or s.	3756
Lk	12:27	They do not labor or s.	3756

SPINDLE (1) [SPIN]
Pr	31:19	the distaff and grasps the s with her fingers.	7134

SPIRIT (533) [SPIRIT'S, SPIRITIST, SPIRITISTS, SPIRITS, SPIRITUAL, SPIRITUALLY]

Ge	1: 2	the S of God was hovering over the waters.	8120
	6: 3	"My S will not contend with man forever,	8120
	41:38	one in whom is the s of God?"	8120
	45:27	the s of their father Jacob revived.	8120
Ex	31: 3	and I have filled him with the S of God,	8120
	35:31	and he has filled him with the S of God,	8120
Nu	11:17	of the S that is on you and put the Spirit	8120
	11:17	of the Spirit that is on you and put the S	NIH
	11:25	the S that was on him and put the Spirit on	8120
	11:25	on him and put the S on the seventy elders.	NIH
	11:25	When the S rested on them,	8120
	11:26	Yet the S also rested on them,	8120
	11:29	that the LORD would put his S on them!"	8120
	14:24	because my servant Caleb has a different s	8120
	24: 2	the S of God came upon him	8120
	27:18	a man in whom is the s,	8120
Dt	2:30	LORD your God had made his s stubborn	8120
	34: 9	of Nun was filled with the s of wisdom	8120
Jdg	3:10	The S of the LORD came upon him,	8120
	6:34	the S of the LORD came upon Gideon,	8120
	9:23	God sent an evil s between Abimelech and	8120
	11:29	the S of the LORD came upon Jephthah.	8120
	13:25	and the S of the LORD began to stir him	8120
	14: 6	The S of the LORD came upon him	8120
	14:19	the S of the LORD came upon him in power.	8120
	15:14	The S of the LORD came upon him	8120
1Sa	10: 6	The S of the LORD will come upon you	8120
	10:10	the S of God came upon him in power,	8120
	11: 6	the S of God came upon him in power,	8120
	16:13	from that day on the S of the LORD came	8120
	16:14	S of the LORD had departed from Saul,	8120
	16:14	an evil s from the LORD tormented him.	8120
	16:15	"See, an evil s from God is tormenting you.	8120
	16:16	when the evil s from God comes upon you,	8120
	16:23	Whenever the s from God came upon Saul,	8120
	16:23	and the evil s would leave him.	8120
	18: 1	Jonathan became one in s with David,	5883
	18:10	an evil s from God came forcefully	8120
	19: 9	an evil s from the LORD came upon Saul	8120
	19:20	the S of God came upon Saul's men	8120
	19:23	But the S of God came even upon him,	8120
	28: 8	"Consult a s for me," he said,	200
	28:13	"I see a s coming up out of the ground."	466
2Sa	13:39	the s of the king longed to go to Absalom,	5883
	23: 2	"The S of the LORD spoke through me;	8120
1Ki	18:12	where the S of the LORD may carry you	8120
	22:21	Finally, a s came forward,	8120
	22:22	a lying s in the mouths of all his prophets,'	8120
	22:23	a lying s in the mouths of all these prophets	8120
	22:24	"Which way did the s from the LORD go	8120
2Ki	2: 9	"Let me inherit a double portion of your s,"	8120
	2:15	said, "The s of Elijah is resting on Elisha."	8120
	2:16	the S of the LORD has picked him up	8120
	5:26	not my s with you when the man got down	4213
	19: 7	to put such a s in him that when he hears	8120
1Ch	5:26	stirred up the s of Pul king of Assyria	8120
	12:18	Then the S came upon Amasai,	8120
	28:12	that the S had put in his mind for the courts	8120
2Ch	15: 1	The S of God came upon Azariah son	8120
	18:20	Finally, a s came forward,	8120
	18:21	a lying s in the mouths of all his prophets,'	8120
	18:22	the LORD has put a lying s in the mouths	8120
	18:23	"Which way did the s from the LORD go	8120
	20:14	Then the S of the LORD came upon	8120
	24:20	the S of God came upon Zechariah son	8120
Ne	9:20	You gave your good S to instruct them.	8120
	9:30	By your S you admonished them	8120
Job	4:15	A s glided past my face,	8120
	6: 4	my s drinks in their poison;	8120
	7:11	I will speak out in the anguish of my s,	8120
	10:12	and in your providence watched over my s.	8120
	17: 1	My s is broken, my days are cut short,	8120
	26: 4	And whose s spoke from your mouth?	5972
	31:39	without payment or broken the s	5883
	32: 8	But it is the s in a man,	8120
	32:18	and the s within me compels me;	8120
	33: 4	The S of God has made me;	8120
	34:14	and he withdrew his s and breath,	8120
Ps	31: 5	Into your hands I commit my s;	8120
	32: 2	against him and in whose s is no deceit.	8120
	34:18	and saves those who are crushed in s.	8120
	51:10	O God, and renew a steadfast s within me.	8120
	51:11	from your presence or take your Holy S	8120
	51:12	of your salvation and grant me a willing s,	8120
	51:17	The sacrifices of God are a broken s;	8120
	73:21	my heart was grieved and my s embittered,	4000
	76:12	He breaks the s of rulers;	8120
	77: 3	I mused, and my s grew faint.	8120
	77: 6	My heart mused and my s inquired:	8120
	104:30	When you send your S, they are created,	8120
	106:33	for they rebelled against the S of God,	8120
	139: 7	Where can I go from your S?	8120
	142: 3	When my s grows faint within me,	8120
	143: 4	So my s grows faint within me;	8120
	143: 7	O LORD; my s fails.	8120
	143:10	may your good S lead me on level ground.	8120
	146: 4	their s departs, they return to the ground;	8120
Pr	15: 4	but a deceitful tongue crushes the s.	8120
	15:13	but heartache crushes the s.	8120
	16:18	a haughty s before a fall.	8120
	16:19	be lowly in s and among the oppressed than	8120

Pr	17:22	but a crushed s dries up the bones.	8120
	18:14	A man's s sustains him in sickness,	8120
	18:14	but a crushed s who can bear?	8120
	20:27	The lamp of the LORD searches the s of	5972
	25:13	he refreshes the s of his masters.	5883
	29:23	but a man of lowly s gains honor.	8120
Ecc	3:21	if the s of man rises upward and if the spirit	8120
	3:21	and if the s of the animal goes down	8120
	7: 9	Do not be quickly provoked in your s,	8120
	12: 7	and the s returns to God who gave it.	8120
Isa	4: 4	from Jerusalem by a s of judgment and	8120
	4: 4	by a spirit of judgment and a s of fire.	8120
	11: 2	The S of the LORD will rest on him—	8120
	11: 2	the S of wisdom and of understanding,	8120
	11: 2	the S of counsel and of power,	8120
	11: 2	and of power, the S of knowledge and of	8120
	19:14	The LORD has poured into them a s	8120
	26: 9	in the morning my s longs for you.	8120
	28: 6	a s of justice to him who sits in judgment,	8120
	29:24	in s will gain understanding;	8120
	30: 1	but not by my S, heaping sin upon sin;	8120
	31: 3	their horses are flesh and not s.	8120
	32:15	till the S is poured upon us from on high,	8120
	34:16	and his S will gather them together.	8120
	37: 7	to put a s in him so that when he hears	8120
	38:16	and my s finds life in them too.	8120
	42: 1	I will put my S on him	8120
	44: 3	I will pour out my S on your offspring,	8120
	48:16	Sovereign LORD has sent me, with his S.	8120
	54: 6	a wife deserted and distressed in s—	8120
	57:15	with him who is contrite and lowly in s,	8120
	57:15	the s of the lowly and to revive the heart of	8120
	57:16	the s of man would grow faint before me—	8120
	59:21	"My S, who is on you,	8120
	61: 1	The S of the Sovereign LORD is on me,	8120
	61: 3	garment of praise instead of a s of despair.	8120
	63:10	Yet they rebelled and grieved his Holy S.	8120
	63:11	is he who set his Holy S among them,	8120
	63:14	they were given rest by the S of the LORD.	8120
	65:14	of heart and wail in brokenness of s.	8120
	66: 2	he who is humble and contrite in s,	8120
Jer	51: 1	up the s of a destroyer against Babylon and	8120
La	1:16	no one to restore my s.	5883
Eze	1:12	Wherever the s would go, they would go,	8120
	1:20	Wherever the s would go, they would go,	8120
	1:20	s of the living creatures was in the wheels.	8120
	1:21	s of the living creatures was in the wheels.	8120
	2: 2	the S came into me and raised me	8120
	3:12	Then the S lifted me up,	8120
	3:14	The S then lifted me up and took me away,	8120
	3:14	in bitterness and in the anger of my s,	8120
	3:24	S came into me and raised me to my feet.	8120
	8: 3	The S lifted me up between earth	8120
	10:17	the s of the living creatures was in them.	8120
	11: 1	Then the S lifted me up and brought me to	8120
	11: 5	Then the S of the LORD came upon me,	8120
	11:19	an undivided heart and put a new s in them;	8120
	11:24	The S lifted me up and brought me to	8120
	11:24	in Babylonia in the vision given by the S.	8120
	13: 3	the foolish prophets who follow their own s	8120
	18:31	and get a new heart and a new s.	8120
	21: 7	every s will become faint	8120
	36:26	I will give you a new heart and put a new s	8120
	36:27	And I will put my S in you and move you	8120
	37: 1	by the S of the LORD and set me in	8120
	37:14	I will put my S in you and you will live,	8120
	39:29	I will pour out my S on the house of Israel,	8120
	43: 5	Then the S lifted me up and brought me	8120
Da	4: 8	and the s of the holy gods is in him.)	10658
	4: 9	I know that the s of the holy gods is in you,	10658
	4:18	because the s of the holy gods is in you."	10658
	5:11	a man in your kingdom who has the s of	10658
	5:14	I have heard that the s of the gods is in you	10658
	7:15	"I, Daniel, was troubled in s,	10658
Hos	4:12	A s of prostitution leads them astray;	8120
	5: 4	A s of prostitution is in their heart;	8120
Joel	2:28	I will pour out my S on all people.	8120
	2:29	I will pour out my S in those days.	8120
Mic	2: 7	"Is the S of the LORD angry?	8120
	3: 8	with the S of the LORD,	8120
Hag	1:14	up the s of Zerubbabel son of Shealtiel,	8120
	1:14	and the s of Joshua son of Jehozadak,	8120
	1:14	the s of the whole remnant of the people.	8120
	2: 5	And my S remains among you.	8120
Zec	4: 6	'Not by might nor by power, but by my S,'	8120
	6: 8	the north country have given my S rest in	8120
	7:12	that the LORD Almighty had sent by his S	8120
	12: 1	and who forms the s of man within him,	8120
	12:10	of Jerusalem a s of grace and supplication.	8120
	13: 2	"I will remove both the prophets and the s	8120
Mal	2:15	In flesh and s they are his.	8120
	2:15	So guard yourself in your s,	8120
	2:16	So guard yourself in your s,	8120
Mt	1:18	to be with child through the Holy S.	4460
	1:20	what is conceived in her is from the Holy S.	4460
	3:11	He will baptize you with the Holy S and	4460
	3:16	and he saw the S of God descending like	4460
	4: 1	Then Jesus was led by the S into the desert	4460
	5: 3	"Blessed are the poor in s,	4460
	10:20	the S of your Father speaking through you.	4460
	12:18	I will put my S on him,	4460
	12:28	But if I drive out demons by the S of God,	4460
	12:31	but the blasphemy against the S will not	4460
	12:32	against the Holy S will not be forgiven,	4460
	12:43	"When an evil s comes out of a man,	4460
	22:43	speaking by the S, calls him 'Lord'?	4460
	26:41	The s is willing, but the body is weak."	4460

Mt	27:50	he gave up his s.	4460
	28:19	and of the Son and of the Holy S,	4460
Mk	1: 8	but he will baptize you with the Holy S."	4460
	1:10	and the S descending on him like a dove.	4460
	1:12	At once the S sent him out into the desert,	4460
	1:23	who was possessed by an evil s cried out,	4460
	1:26	The evil s shook the man violently	4460
	2: 8	Immediately Jesus knew in his s	4460
	3:29	against the Holy S will never be forgiven;	4460
	3:30	"He has an evil s."	4460
	5: 2	an evil s came from the tombs to meet him.	4460
	5: 8	"Come out of this man, you evil s!"	4460
	7:25	by an evil s came and fell at his feet.	4460
	9:17	who is possessed by a s that has robbed him	4460
	9:18	I asked your disciples to drive out the s,	899S
	9:20	When the s saw Jesus,	4460
	9:25	he rebuked the evil s.	4460
	9:25	"You deaf and mute s," he said,	4460
	9:26	The s shrieked, convulsed him violently	NIG
	12:36	David himself, speaking by the Holy S,	4460
	13:11	for it is not you speaking, but the Holy S.	4460
	14:38	The s is willing, but the body is weak.	4460
Lk	1:15	and he will be filled with the Holy S even	4460
	1:17	in the s and power of Elijah,	4460
	1:35	"The Holy S will come upon you,	4460
	1:41	and Elizabeth was filled with the Holy S.	4460
	1:47	and my s rejoices in God my Savior,	4460
	1:67	with the Holy S and prophesied:	4460
	1:80	the child grew and became strong in s;	4460
	2:25	and the Holy S was upon him.	4460
	2:26	to him by the Holy S that he would not die	4460
	2:27	Moved by the S, he went into the temple	4460
	3:16	He will baptize you with the Holy S and	4460
	3:22	and the Holy S descended on him	4460
	4: 1	Jesus, full of the Holy S, returned from	4460
	4: 1	and was led by the S in the desert,	4460
	4:14	returned to Galilee in the power of the S,	4460
	4:18	"The S of the Lord is on me,	4460
	4:33	a man possessed by a demon, an evil s.	4460
	8:29	For Jesus had commanded the evil s	4460
	8:55	Her s returned, and at once she stood up.	4460
	9:39	A s seizes him and he suddenly screams;	4460
	9:42	But Jesus rebuked the evil s,	4460
	10:21	full of joy through the Holy S, said,	4460
	11:13	the Holy S to those who ask him!"	4460
	11:24	"When an evil s comes out of a man,	4460
	12:10	against the Holy S will not be forgiven.	4460
	12:12	for the Holy S will teach you at that time	4460
	13:11	by a s for eighteen years.	4460
	23:46	"Father, into your hands I commit my s."	4460
Jn	1:32	the S come down from heaven as a dove	4460
	1:33	'The man on whom you see the S come	4460
	1:33	who will baptize with the Holy S.'	4460
	3: 5	unless he is born of water and the S.	4460
	3: 6	but the S gives birth to spirit.	4460
	3: 6	but the Spirit gives birth to s.	4460
	3: 8	So it is with everyone born of the S."	4460
	3:34	for God gives the S without limit.	4460
	4:23	the Father in s and truth,	4460
	4:24	God is s, and his worshipers must worship	4460
	4:24	and his worshipers must worship in s and	4460
	6:63	S gives life; the flesh counts for nothing.	4460
	6:63	The words I have spoken to you are s	4460
	7:39	By this he meant the S,	4460
	7:39	Up to that time the S had not been given,	4460
	11:33	he was deeply moved in s and troubled.	4460
	13:21	Jesus was troubled in s and testified,	4460
	14:17	the S of truth. The world cannot accept him,	4460
	14:26	But the Counselor, the Holy S,	4460
	15:26	S of truth who goes out from the Father,	4460
	16:13	But when he, the S of truth, comes,	4460
	16:15	the S will take from what is mine	NIG
	19:30	he bowed his head and gave up his s.	4460
	20:22	"Receive the Holy S.	4460
Ac	1: 2	after giving instructions through the Holy S	4460
	1: 5	be baptized with the Holy S."	4460
	1: 8	when the Holy S comes on you;	4460
	1:16	the Holy S spoke long ago through	4460
	2: 4	All of them were filled with the Holy S	4460
	2: 4	in other tongues as the S enabled them.	4460
	2:17	I will pour out my S on all people.	4460
	2:18	I will pour out my S in those days,	4460
	2:33	from the Father the promised Holy S	4460
	2:38	you will receive the gift of the Holy S.	4460
	4: 8	Peter, filled with the Holy S, said to them:	4460
	4:25	You spoke by the Holy S through	4460
	4:31	And they were all filled with the Holy S	4460
	5: 3	the Holy S and have kept for yourself some	4460
	5: 9	could you agree to test the S of the Lord?	4460
	5:32	and so is the Holy S, whom God has given	4460
	6: 3	to be full of the S and wisdom.	4460
	6: 5	a man full of faith and of the Holy S;	4460
	6:10	not stand up against his wisdom or the S	4460
	7:51	You always resist the Holy S!	4460
	7:55	But Stephen, full of the Holy S,	4460
	7:59	Stephen prayed, "Lord Jesus, receive my s."	4460
	8:15	that they might receive the Holy S,	4460
	8:16	Holy S had not yet come upon any of them;	NIG
	8:17	and they received the Holy S.	4460
	8:18	When Simon saw that the S was given at	4460
	8:19	I lay my hands may receive the Holy S."	4460
	8:29	The S told Philip, "Go to that chariot	4460
	8:39	S of the Lord suddenly took Philip away,	4460
	9:17	and be filled with the Holy S."	4460
	9:31	and encouraged by the Holy S,	4460
	10:19	the S said to him, "Simon, three men are	4460
	10:38	anointed Jesus of Nazareth with the Holy S	4460

Ac	10:44	Holy S came on all who heard the message.	4460
	10:45	of the Holy S had been poured out even on	4460
	10:47	They have received the Holy S just	4460
	11:12	The S told me to have no hesitation	4460
	11:15	the Holy S came on them as he had come	4460
	11:16	but you will be baptized with the Holy S.'	4460
	11:24	full of the Holy S and faith,	4460
	11:28	stood up and through the S predicted that	4460
	13: 2	the Holy S said, "Set apart for me	4460
	13: 4	sent on their way by the Holy S,	4460
	13: 9	filled with the Holy S,	4460
	13:52	with joy and with the Holy S.	4460
	15: 8	that he accepted them by giving the Holy S	4460
	15:28	It seemed good to the Holy S and to us not	4460
	16: 6	by the Holy S from preaching the word in	4460
	16: 7	but the S of Jesus would not allow them to.	4460
	16:16	s by which she predicted the future.	4460+4780
	16:18	that he turned around and said to the s,	4460
	16:18	At that moment the s left her.	NIV
	19: 2	the Holy S when you believed?"	4460
	19: 2	not even heard that there is a Holy S."	4460
	19: 6	the Holy S came on them,	4460
	19:15	the evil s answered them, "Jesus I know,	4460
	19:16	the man who had the evil s jumped on them	4460
	20:22	"And now, compelled by the S,	4460
	20:23	that in every city the Holy S warns me	4460
	20:28	the Holy S has made you overseers.	4460
	21: 4	Through the S they urged Paul not to go on	4460
	21:11	"The Holy S says, 'In this way,	4460
	23: 9	if a s or an angel has spoken to him?"	4460
	28:25	"The Holy S spoke the truth to your	4460
Ro	1: 4	the S of holiness was declared with power	4460
	2:29	by the S, not by the written code.	4460
	5: 5	his love into our hearts by the Holy S,	4460
	7: 6	so that we serve in the new way of the S,	4460
	8: 2	the S of life set me free from the law of sin	4460
	8: 4	to the sinful nature but according to the S.	4460
	8: 5	with the S have their minds set on what	4460
	8: 5	minds set on what the S desires.	4460
	8: 6	mind controlled by the S is life and peace;	4460
	8: 9	not by the sinful nature but by the S,	4460
	8: 9	if the S of God lives in you.	4460
	8: 9	if anyone does not have the S of Christ,	4460
	8:10	yet your s is alive because of righteousness.	4460
	8:11	And if the S of him who raised Jesus from	4460
	8:11	to your mortal bodies through his S.	4460
	8:13	if by the S you put to death the misdeeds of	4460
	8:14	because those who are led by the S	4460
	8:15	not receive a s that makes you a slave again	4460
	8:15	but you received the S of sonship.	4460
	8:16	The S himself testifies with our spirit	4460
	8:16	with our s that we are God's children.	4460
	8:23	who have the firstfruits of the S,	4460
	8:26	the S helps us in our weakness.	4460
	8:26	the S himself intercedes for us with groans	4460
	8:27	knows the mind of the S,	4460
	8:27	because the S intercedes for the saints	NIV
	9: 1	my conscience confirms it in the Holy S—	4460
	11: 8	"God gave them a s of stupor,	4460
	14:17	peace and joy in the Holy S,	4460
	15: 5	give you a s of unity among	899+3836+5858
	15:13	with hope by the power of the Holy S.	4460
	15:16	sanctified by the Holy S.	4460
	15:19	and miracles, through the power of the S.	4460
	15:30	and by the love of the S,	4460
1Co	2:10	but God has revealed it to us by his S.	4460
	2:10	The S searches all things,	4460
	2:11	the thoughts of a man except the man's s	4460
	2:11	the thoughts of God except the S of God.	4460
	2:12	We have not received the s of the world but	4460
	2:12	of the world but the S who is from God,	4460
	2:13	but in words taught by the S,	4460
	2:14	The man without the S does not accept	6035
	2:14	not accept the things that come from the S	4460
	3:16	and that God's S lives in you?	4460
	4:21	or in love and with a gentle s?	4460
	5: 3	I am with you in s.	4460
	5: 4	of our Lord Jesus and I am with you in s,	4460
	5: 5	be destroyed and his s saved on the day of	4460
	6:11	of the Lord Jesus and by the S	4460
	6:17	with the Lord is one with him in s.	4460
	6:19	that your body is a temple of the Holy S,	4460
	7:34	be devoted to the Lord in both body and s.	4460
	7:40	and I think that I too have the S of God.	4460
	12: 3	that no one who is speaking by the S	4460
	12: 3	"Jesus is Lord," except by the Holy S.	4460
	12: 4	different kinds of gifts, but the same S.	4460
	12: 7	of the S is given for the common good.	4460
	12: 8	through the S the message of wisdom,	4460
	12: 8	of knowledge by means of the same S,	4460
	12: 9	to another faith by the same S,	4460
	12: 9	to another gifts of healing by that one S,	4460
	12:11	the work of one and the same S,	4460
	12:13	For we were all baptized by one S	4460
	12:13	and we were all given the one S to drink.	4460
	14: 2	he utters mysteries with his s.	4460
	14:14	For if I pray in a tongue, my s prays,	4460
	14:15	I will pray with my s,	4460
	14:15	I will sing with my s,	4460
	14:16	If you are praising God with your s,	4460
	15:45	the last Adam, a life-giving s.	4460
	16:18	For they refreshed my s and yours also.	4460
2Co	1:22	and put his S in our hearts as a deposit,	4460
	3: 3	with ink but with the S of the living God,	4460
	3: 6	not of the letter but of the S;	4460
	3: 6	for the letter kills, but the S gives life.	4460
	3: 8	of the S be even more glorious?	4460

2Co	3:17	Now the Lord is the S,	4460
	3:17	and where the S of the Lord is,	4460
	3:18	which comes from the Lord, who is the S.	4460
	4:13	With that same s of faith we also believe	4460
	5: 5	for this very purpose and has given us the S	4460
	6: 6	in the Holy S and in sincere love;	4460
	7: 1	that contaminates body and s,	4460
	7:13	his s has been refreshed by all of you.	4460
	11: 4	a different s from the one you received,	4460
	12:18	in the same s and follow the same course?	4460
	13:14	fellowship of the Holy S be with you all.	4460
Gal	3: 2	Did you receive the S by observing	4460
	3: 3	After beginning with the S,	4460
	3: 5	Does God give you his S	4460
	3:14	might receive the promise of the S.	4460
	4: 6	God sent the S of his Son into our hearts,	4460
	4: 6	the S who calls out, "Abba, Father."	NIV
	4:29	the son born by the power of the S.	4460
	5: 5	the S the righteousness for which we hope.	4460
	5:16	So I say, live by the S,	4460
	5:17	desires what is contrary to the S,	4460
	5:17	the S what is contrary to the sinful nature.	4460
	5:18	But if you are led by the S,	4460
	5:22	But the fruit of the S is love, joy, peace,	4460
	5:25	Since we live by the S,	4460
	5:25	let us keep in step with the S.	4460
	6: 8	the one who sows to please the S,	4460
	6: 8	from the S will reap eternal life.	4460
	6:18	of our Lord Jesus Christ be with your s,	4460
Eph	1:13	with a seal, the promised Holy S,	4460
	1:17	the S of wisdom and revelation,	4460
	2: 2	the s who is now at work	4460
	2:18	both have access to the Father by one S.	4460
	2:22	a dwelling in which God lives by his S.	4460
	3: 5	the S to God's holy apostles and prophets.	4460
	3:16	through his S in your inner being,	4460
	4: 3	to keep the unity of the S through the bond	4460
	4: 4	There is one body and one S—	4460
	4:30	And do not grieve the Holy S of God,	4460
	5:18	Instead, be filled with the S.	4460
	6:17	of salvation and the sword of the S,	4460
	6:18	in the S on all occasions with all kinds	4460
Php	1:19	and the help given by the S of Jesus Christ,	4460
	1:27	I will know that you stand firm in one s,	4460
	2: 1	if any fellowship with the S,	4460
	2: 2	being one in s and purpose.	5249
	3: 3	we who worship by the S of God,	4460
	4:23	of the Lord Jesus Christ be with your s.	4460
Col	1: 8	and who also told us of your love in the S.	4460
	2: 5	in s and delight to see how orderly you are	4460
1Th	1: 5	with the Holy S and with deep conviction.	4460
	1: 6	with the joy given by the Holy S.	4460
	4: 8	who gives you his Holy S.	4460
	5:23	May your whole s, soul and body be kept	4460
2Th	2:13	through the sanctifying work of the S and	4460
1Ti	3:16	was vindicated by the S,	4460
	4: 1	The S clearly says that in later times	4460
2Ti	1: 7	For God did not give us a s of timidity,	4460
	1: 7	but a s of power, of love and	NIV
	1:14	the help of the Holy S who lives in us.	4460
	4:22	The Lord be with your s.	4460
Tit	3: 5	of rebirth and renewal by the Holy S,	4460
Phm	1:25	of the Lord Jesus Christ be with your s.	4460
Heb	2: 4	of the Holy S distributed according	4460
	3: 7	So, as the Holy S says: "Today,	4460
	4:12	it penetrates even to dividing soul and s,	4460
	6: 4	who have shared in the Holy S,	4460
	9: 8	The Holy S was showing by this that	4460
	9:14	the eternal S offered himself unblemished	4460
	10:15	The Holy S also testifies to us about this.	4460
	10:29	and who has insulted the S of grace?	4460
Jas	2:26	As the body without the s is dead,	4460
	4: 5	without reason that the s he caused to live	4460
1Pe	1: 2	through the sanctifying work of the S,	4460
	1:11	and circumstances to which the S of Christ	4460
	1:12	to you by the Holy S sent from heaven.	4460
	3: 4	the unfading beauty of a gentle and quiet s,	4460
	3:18	in the body but made alive by the S,	4460
	4: 6	but live according to God in regard to the s.	4460
	4:14	for the S of glory and of God rests on you.	4460
2Pe	1:21	as they were carried along by the Holy S.	4460
1Jn	3:24	We know it by the S he gave us.	4460
	4: 1	Dear friends, do not believe every s,	4460
	4: 2	how you can recognize the S of God:	4460
	4: 2	Every s that acknowledges that Jesus Christ	4460
	4: 3	but every s that does not acknowledge Jesus	4460
	4: 3	This is the s of the antichrist,	NIV
	4: 6	This is how we recognize the S of truth and	4460
	4: 6	the Spirit of truth and the s of falsehood.	4460
	4:13	because he has given us of his S.	4460
	5: 6	And it is the S who testifies,	4460
	5: 6	because the S is the truth.	4460
	5: 8	the S, the water and the blood;	4460
Jude	1:19	and do not have the S.	4460
	1:20	and pray in the Holy S.	4460
Rev	1:10	On the Lord's Day I was in the S,	4460
	2: 7	let him hear what the S says to the churches.	4460
	2:11	let him hear what the S says to the churches.	4460
	2:17	let him hear what the S says to the churches.	4460
	2:29	let him hear what the S says to the churches.	4460
	3: 6	let him hear what the S says to the churches.	4460
	3:13	let him hear what the S says to the churches.	4460
	3:22	let him hear what the S says to the churches.	4460
	4: 2	At once I was in the S,	4460
	14:13	says the S, "they will rest from their labor,	4460
	17: 3	Then the angel carried me away in the S	4460
	18: 2	for demons and a haunt for every evil s,	4460

Rev	19:10	the testimony of Jesus is the s of prophecy."	4460
	21:10	in the S to a mountain great and high,	4460
	22:17	The S and the bride say, "Come!"	4460

SPIRIT'S (2) [SPIRIT]

1Co	2: 4	but with a demonstration of the S power,	4460
1Th	5:19	Do not put out the S fire;	4460

SPIRITIST (2) [SPIRIT]

Lev	20:27	" 'A man or woman who is a medium or s	3362
Dt	18:11	or who is a medium or s or who consults	3362

SPIRITISTS (9) [SPIRIT]

Lev	19:31	" 'Do not turn to mediums or seek out s,	3362
	20: 6	the person who turns to mediums and s	3362
1Sa	28: 3	Saul had expelled the mediums and s from	3362
	28: 9	He has cut off the mediums and s from	3362
2Ki	21: 6	and consulted mediums and s.	3362
	23:24	Josiah got rid of the mediums and s,	3362
2Ch	33: 6	and consulted mediums and s.	3362
Isa	8:19	men tell you to consult mediums and s,	3362
	19: 3	spirits of the dead, the mediums and the s.	3362

SPIRITS (47) [SPIRIT]

Nu	16:22	"O God, God of the s of all mankind,	8120
	27:16	the God of the s of all mankind,	8120
Jdg	16:25	While they were in high s,	3201+4213
Ru	3: 7	and drinking and was in good s,	3512+4213
1Sa	25:36	He was in high s and very drunk.	3201+4213
2Sa	13:28	When Amnon is in high s	3201+4213
Est	1:10	King Xerxes was in high s from wine,	3201+4213
	5: 9	that day happy and in high s.	3201+4213
Ps	78: 8	whose s were not faithful to him.	8120
Pr	2:18	to death and her paths to the s of the dead.	8327
Isa	14: 9	the s of the departed to greet you—	8327
	19: 3	the idols and the s of the dead,	356
	26:14	those departed s do not rise.	8327
Zec	6: 5	"These are the four s of heaven,	8120
Mt	8:16	the s with a word and healed all the sick.	4460
	10: 1	to drive out evil s and to heal every disease	4460
	12:45	seven other s more wicked than itself,	4460
Mk	1:27	He even gives orders to evil s	4460
	3:11	Whenever the evil s saw him,	4460
	5:13	the evil s came out and went into the pigs.	4460
	6: 7	by two and gave them authority over evil s.	4460
Lk	4:36	and power he gives orders to evil s	4460
	6:18	Those troubled by evil s were cured,	4460
	7:21	who had diseases, sicknesses and evil s,	4460
	8: 2	who had been cured of evil s and diseases:	4460
	10:20	do not rejoice that the s submit to you,	4460
	11:26	takes seven other s more wicked than itself,	4460
Ac	5:16	and those tormented by evil s,	4460
	8: 7	With shrieks, evil s came out of many,	4460
	19:12	and the evil s left them.	4460
	19:13	around driving out evil s tried to invoke	2020
	23: 8	and that there are neither angels nor s,	4460
1Co	12:10	to another distinguishing between s,	4460
	14:32	The s of prophets are subject to the control	4460
1Ti	4: 1	and follow deceiving s and things taught	4460
Heb	1:14	Are not all angels ministering s sent	4460
	12: 9	to the Father of our s and live!	4460
	12:23	to the s of righteous men made perfect,	4460
1Pe	3:19	also he went and preached to the s	4460
1Jn	4: 1	test the s to see whether they are from God,	4460
Rev	1: 4	and from the seven s before his throne,	4460
	3: 1	of him who holds the seven s of God and	4460
	4: 5	These are the seven s of God.	4460
	5: 6	which are the seven s of God sent out	4460
	16:13	I saw three evil s that looked like frogs;	4460
	16:14	They are s of demons performing	4460
	22: 6	The Lord, the God of the s of the prophets,	4460

SPIRITUAL (30) [SPIRIT]

Ro	1:11	to you some s gift to make you strong—	4461
	7:14	We know that the law is s;	4461
	12: 1	this is your s act of worship.	3358
	12:11	but keep your s fervor, serving the Lord.	4460
	15:27	have shared in the Jews' s blessings,	4461
1Co	1: 7	not lack any s gift as you eagerly wait	5922
	2:13	expressing s truths in spiritual words.	4461
	2:13	expressing spiritual truths in s words.	4461
	2:15	The s man makes judgments	4461
	3: 1	not address you as s but as worldly—	4461
	9:11	If we have sown s seed among you,	4461
	10: 3	They all ate the same s food	4461
	10: 4	and drank the same s drink;	4461
	10: 4	from the s rock that accompanied them,	4461
	12: 1	Now about s gifts, brothers,	4461
	14: 1	the way of love and eagerly desire s gifts.	4461
	14:12	Since you are eager to have s gifts,	4460
	15:44	sown a natural body, it is raised a s body.	4461
	15:44	a natural body, there is also a s body.	4461
	15:46	The s did not come first, but the natural,	4461
	15:46	but the natural, and after that the s.	4461
Gal	6: 1	you who are s should restore him gently.	4461
Eph	1: 3	the heavenly realms with every s blessing	4461
	5:19	with psalms, hymns and s songs.	4461
	6:12	the s forces of evil in the heavenly realms.	4461
Col	1: 9	through all s wisdom and understanding.	4461
	3:16	and s songs with gratitude in your hearts	4461
1Pe	2: 2	Like newborn babies, crave pure s milk,	3358
	2: 5	into a s house to be a holy priesthood,	4461
	2: 5	offering s sacrifices acceptable to God	4461

SPIRITUALLY (2) [SPIRIT]
1Co	2:14 because they are s discerned.	4462
	14:37 anybody thinks he is a prophet or s gifted,	4461

SPIT (15) [SPITS, SPITTING]
Nu	12:14 "If her father had s in her face,	3762+3762
Dt	25: 9 one of his sandals, s in his face and say,	3762
Job	17: 6 a man in whose face people s.	9531
	20:15 He will s out the riches he swallowed;	7794
	30:10 they do not hesitate to s in my face.	8371
Mt	26:67 Then they s in his face and struck him	1870
	27:30 They s on him, and took the staff and	1870
Mk	7:33 Then he s and touched the man's tongue.	4772
	8:23 When he had s on the man's eyes	4772
	10:34 who will mock him and s on him,	1870
	14:65 Then some began to s at him;	1870
	15:19 on the head with a staff and s on him.	1870
Lk	18:32 They will mock him, insult him, s on him,	1870
Jn	9: 6 Having said this, he s on the ground,	4772
Rev	3:16 I am about to s you out of my mouth.	1840

SPITE (15)
Lev	26:23 " 'If in s of these things you do	928
	26:27 " 'If in s of this you still do not listen to me	928
	26:44 Yet in s of this, when they are in the land	1685
Nu	14:11 in s of all the miraculous signs	928
Dt	1:32 In s of this, you did not trust in the LORD	928
Ezr	10: 2 But in s of this, there is still hope for Israel.	6584
Ne	5:18 In s of all this, I never demanded the food	6640
Job	23: 2 his hand is heavy in s of my groaning.	6584
Ps	78:32 In s of all this, they kept on sinning;	928
	78:32 in s of his wonders, they did not believe.	928
Isa	47: 9 in s of your many sorceries	928
Jer	2:34 Yet in s of all this	6584
	3:10 In s of all this, her unfaithful sister Judah	928
1Th	1: 6 in s of severe suffering, you welcomed	1877
	2: 2 tell you his gospel in s of strong opposition.	NIG

SPITS (1) [SPIT]
Lev	15: 8 the discharge s on someone who is clean,	8394

SPITTING (1) [SPIT]
Isa	50: 6 I did not hide my face from mocking and s.	8371

SPLENDID (3) [SPLENDOR]
Isa	22:18 and there your s chariots will remain—	3883
Eze	17: 8 bear fruit and become a s vine.'	168
	17:23 and bear fruit and become a s cedar.	129

SPLENDOR (76) [SPLENDID]
1Ch	16:27 S and majesty are before him;	2086
	16:29 worship the LORD in the s of his holiness.	2079
	22: 5 be of great magnificence and fame and s in	9514
	29:11 and the glory and the majesty and the s,	2086
	29:25 and bestowed on him royal such	2086
2Ch	20:21 for the s of his holiness as they went out at	2079
Est	1: 4 the vast wealth of his kingdom and the s	3702
Job	13:11 Would not his s terrify you?	8420
	31:23 for fear of his s I could not do such things.	8420
	31:26 in its radiance and the moon moving in s,	3701
	37:22 Out of the north he comes in golden s;	NIH
	40:10 Then adorn yourself with glory and s,	1470
Ps	21: 5 you have bestowed on him s and majesty.	2086
	29: 2 worship the LORD in the s of his holiness.	2079
	45: 3 clothe yourself with s and majesty.	2086
	49:16 when the s of his house increases;	3883
	49:17 his s will not descend with him.	3883
	71: 8 declaring your s all day long.	9514
	78:61 his s into the hands of the enemy.	9514
	89:44 to his s and cast his throne to the ground.	3199
	90:16 your s to their children.	2077
	96: 6 S and majesty are before him;	2086
	96: 9 the LORD in the s of his holiness.	2079
	104: 1 you are clothed with s and majesty.	2086
	145: 5 of the glorious s of your majesty,	2077
	145:12 of your mighty acts and the glorious s	2077
	148:13 his s is above the earth and the heavens.	2086
Pr	4: 9 and present you with a crown of s."	9514
	16:31 Gray hair is a crown of s;	9514
	20:29 gray hair the s of the old.	2077
Isa	2:10 of the LORD and the s of his majesty!	2077
	2:19 of the LORD and the s of his majesty,	2077
	2:21 of the LORD and the s of his majesty,	2077
	10:18 The s of his forests and fertile fields	3883
	16:14 Moab's s and all her many people	3883
	35: 2 the s of Carmel and Sharon;	2077
	35: 2 the glory of the LORD, the s of our God.	2077
	46:13 I will grant salvation to Zion, my s to Israel.	9514
	49: 3 Israel, in whom I will display my s."	6995
	52: 1 Put on your garments of s, O Jerusalem,	9514
	55: 5 for he has endowed you with s."	6995
	60: 9 for he has endowed you with s.	6995
	60:21 work of my hands, for the display of my s.	6995
	61: 3 of the LORD for the display of his s.	6995
	62: 3 be a crown of s in the LORD's hand,	9514
Jer	22:18 'Alas, my master! Alas, his s!'	2086
La	1: 6 All the s has departed from the Daughter	2077
	2: 1 down the s of Israel from heaven to earth;	9514
	3:18 "My s is gone and all that I had hoped from	5905
Eze	16:14 s I had given you made your beauty perfect,	2077
	27:10 and helmets on your walls, bringing you s.	2077
Eze	28: 7 and wisdom and pierce your shining s.	3650
	28:17 corrupted your wisdom because of your s.	3650
	31:18 be compared with you in s and majesty?	3883
Da	4:36 my honor and s were returned to me for	10228
	5:18 and greatness and glory and s.	10199
	11:20 a tax collector to maintain the royal s.	2078
Hos	10: 5 those who had rejoiced over its s,	3883
	14: 6 His s will be like an olive tree,	2086
Na	2: 2 The LORD will restore the s of Jacob like	1454
	2: 2 the splendor of Jacob like the s of Israel,	1454
Hab	3: 4 His s was like the sunrise;	5586
Mt	4: 8 the kingdoms of the world and their s.	1518
	6:29 not even Solomon in all his s was dressed	1518
Lk	4: 6 "I will give you all their authority and s,	1518
	9:31 appeared in glorious s, talking with Jesus.	1518
	12:27 not even Solomon in all his s was dressed	1518
1Co	15:40 but the s of the heavenly bodies is one kind,	1518
	15:40 and the s of the earthly bodies is another.	NIG
	15:41 The sun has one kind of s,	1518
	15:41 and star differs from star in s.	1518
2Th	2: 8 the breath of his mouth and destroy by the s	2211
Rev	18: 1 and the earth was illuminated by his s.	1518
	18:14 All your riches and s have vanished,	3287
	21:24 kings of the earth will bring their s into it.	1518

SPLINT (1)
Eze	30:21 or put in a s so as to become strong enough	3151

SPLINTERED (3)
2Ki	18:21 depending on Egypt, that s reed of a staff,	8368
Isa	36: 6 depending on Egypt, that s reed of a staff,	8368
Eze	29: 7 you s and you tore open their shoulders;	8368

SPLIT (24) [SPLITS]
Lev	11: 3 a s hoof completely divided and that chews	7271
	11: 4 the cud or only have a s hoof,	7271
	11: 4 does not have a s hoof; it is ceremonially	7271
	11: 5 does not have a s hoof; it is unclean for you.	7271
	11: 6 does not have a s hoof; it is unclean for you.	7271
	11: 7 though it has a s hoof completely divided,	7271
	11:26 a s hoof not completely divided or that does	7271
Nu	16:31 the ground under them s apart	1324
Dt	14: 6 a s hoof divided in two and that chews	7271
	14: 7 a s hoof divided you may	7271
	14: 7 they do not have a s hoof;	7271
	14: 8 although it has a s hoof,	7271
1Ki	13: 3 The altar will be s apart and the ashes	7973
	13: 5 the altar was s apart and its ashes poured	7973
	16:21 people of Israel were s into two factions;	2745
Ps	74:13 It was you who s open the sea	7297
	78:15 He s the rocks in the desert	1324
Isa	24:19 is broken up, the earth is s asunder,	7297+7297
	48:21 he s the rock and water gushed out.	1324
Mic	1: 4 and the valleys s apart,	1324
Hab	3: 9 You s the earth with rivers;	1324
Zec	14: 4 and the Mount of Olives will be s in two	1324
Mt	27:51 The earth shook and the rocks s.	5387
Rev	16:19 The great city s into three parts,	1181

SPLITS (1) [SPLIT]
Ecc	10: 9 whoever s logs may be endangered by them.	1324

SPOIL (3) [DESPOIL, SPOILS]
Ps	119:162 in your promise like one who finds great s.	8965
Jer	30:16 all who make s of you I will despoil.	1024
1Pe	1: 4 an inheritance that can never perish, s or	299

SPOILS (10) [SPOIL]
Ex	15: 9 I will divide the s;	8965
Nu	31:11 They took all the plunder and s,	4917
	31:12 s and plunder to Moses and Eleazar	4917
	31:27 the s between the soldiers who took part in	4917
	31:32 the s that the soldiers took was 675,000	4917
Jdg	5:30 'Are they not finding and dividing the s;	8965
Isa	33:23 Then an abundance of s will be divided and	8965
	53:12 and he will divide the s with the strong,	8965
Lk	11:22 the man trusted and divides up the s.	5036
Jn	6:27 Do not work for food that s,	660

SPOKE (184) [SPEAK, SPOKES]
Ge	16:13 She gave this name to the LORD who s	1819
	18:27 Then Abraham s up again:	6699
	18:29 Once again he s to him,	1819
	19:14 So Lot went out and s to his sons-in-law,	1819
	22: 7 Isaac s up and said to his father Abraham,	606
	23: 3 beside his dead wife and s to the Hittites.	1819
	24: 7 and who s to me and promised me on oath,	1819
	27: 5 Now Rebekah was listening as Isaac s	1819
	34: 3 and he loved the girl and s tenderly to her.	1819
	34:13 as they s to Shechem and his father Hamor.	1819
	39:10 And though she s to Joseph day after day,	1819
	42: 7 to be a stranger and s harshly to them.	1819
	42:24 but then turned back and s to them again,	1819
	42:30 over the land harshly to us and treated us	1819
	43:19 So they went up to Joseph's steward and s	1819
	46: 2 God s to Israel in a vision at night and said,	606
	50:21 he reassured them and s kindly to them.	1819
Ex	6:13 the LORD s to Moses and Aaron about	1819
	6:27 They were the ones who s to Pharaoh king	1819
	6:28 Now when the LORD s to Moses in Egypt,	1819
	7: 7 and Aaron eighty-three when they s to	1819
	19:19 Then Moses s and the voice of God	1819
Ex	20: 1 And God s all these words:	1819
	32:34 lead the people to the place I s of,	1819
	33: 9 while the LORD s with Moses.	1819
	34:31 and he s to them.	1819
Lev	1: 1 The LORD called to Moses and s to him	1819
	10: 3 the LORD s of when he said:	1819
	16: 1 The LORD s to Moses after the death of	1819
	24:23 Then Moses s to the Israelites.	1819
Nu	1: 1 The LORD s to Moses in the Tent	1819
	7:89 And he s with him.	1819
	9: 1 The LORD s to Moses in the Desert	1819
	11:25 the LORD came down in the cloud and s	1819
	11:28 s up and said, "Moses, my lord, stop them!"	6699
	17: 6 So Moses s to the Israelites,	1819
	21: 5 they s against God and against Moses,	1819
	21: 7 "We sinned when we s against the LORD	1819
	26: 3 and Eleazar the priest s with them and said,	1819
	36: 1 came and s before Moses and the leaders,	1819
Dt	1: 3 These are the words Moses s to all Israel in	1819
	4:12 Then the LORD s to you out of the fire.	1819
	4:15 the day the LORD s to you at Horeb out of	1819
	5: 4 The LORD s to you face to face out of	1819
	5:28 The LORD heard you when you s to me	1819
	31: 1 Then Moses s these words	1819
	32:44 with Joshua son of Nun and s all the words	1819
Jdg	9:37 But Gaal s up again:	1819
1Sa	3:12 carry out against Eli everything I s	1819
	9:17 "This is the man I s to you about;	606
	19: 4 Jonathan s well of David to Saul his father	1819
	24: 6 the day the LORD s of when he said	NIH
2Sa	3:19 Abner also s to the Benjamites in person.	1819
	6:22 But by these slave girls you s of,	606
	12:18 we s to David but he would not listen to us.	1819
	21: 2 The king summoned the Gibeonites and s	606
	23: 2 "The Spirit of the LORD s through me;	1819
	23: 3 The God of Israel s,	606
1Ki	4:32 He s three thousand proverbs	1819
	9:36 "This is the word of the LORD that he s	1819
2Ki	25:28 He s kindly to him and gave him a seat	1819
1Ch	21: 9 Then the LORD s to the angel,	606
2Ch	1: 2 Then Solomon s to all Israel—	606
	30:22 Hezekiah s encouragingly to all	1819
	32:16 Sennacherib's officers s further against	1819
	32:19 They s about the God of Jerusalem	1819
	33:10 The LORD s to Manasseh and his people,	1819
	33:18 to his God and the words the seers s to him	1819
	34:27 when you heard what he s against this place	1821
	36: 2 who is the word of the LORD.	4946+7023
Ne	9:13 you s to them from heaven.	1819
	13:24 of their children s the language of Ashdod	1819
Est	1:13 he s with the wise men who understood	606
	3: 4 Day after day they s to him but he refused	606
	7: 9 who s up to help the king."	1819
	10: 3 of his people and s up for the welfare of all	1819
Job	26: 4 And whose spirit s from your mouth?	3655
	29:11 Whoever heard me s well of me,	887
	29:22 After I had spoken, they s no more;	NIH
	32:11 I waited while you s,	1821
	40: 5 I s once, but I have no answer—	1821
	40: 6 Then the LORD s to Job out of the storm:	6699
	42: 3 Surely I s of things I did not understand,	5583
Ps	33: 9 For he s, and it came to be;	606
	39: 3 then I s with my tongue:	1819
	66:14 vows my lips promised and my mouth s	1819
	78:19 They s against God, saying,	1819
	89:19 Once you s in a vision,	1819
	99: 7 He s to them from the pillar of cloud;	1819
	105:31 He s, and there came swarms of flies,	606
	105:34 He s, and the locusts came,	606
	107:25 For he s and stirred up a tempest	606
SS	2:10 My lover s and said to me, "Arise,	6699
Isa	7:10 Again the LORD s to Ahaz.	1819
	8: 5 The LORD s to me again:	1819
	8:11 The LORD s to me with his strong hand	606
	20: 2 at that time the LORD s through Isaiah son	1819
	65:12 I s but you did not listen.	1819
	66: 4 when I called, no one answered, when I s,	1819
Jer	7:13 I s to you again and again,	1819
	7:22 of Egypt and s to them,	1819
	18:20 that I stood before you and s in their behalf	1819
	30: 4 the LORD s concerning Israel and Judah:	1819
	35:17 I s to them, but they did not listen;	1819
	46:13 the message the LORD s to Jeremiah	1819
	50: 1 the LORD s through Jeremiah the prophet	1819
	52:32 He s kindly to him and gave him a seat	1819
Eze	2: 2 As he s, the Spirit came into me	1819
	3:24 He s to me and said:	1819
	24:18 So I s to the people in the morning,	1819
	35:13 You boasted against me and s against me	1821
	38:17 Are you not the one I s of in former days	1819
Da	2:14 Daniel s to him with wisdom and tact.	10754
	6:12 So they went to the king and s to him	10042
	7: 8 of a man and a mouth that s boastfully,	10425
	7:20 that had eyes and a mouth that s boastfully,	10425
	9: 6 who s in your name to our kings,	1819
	10:19 When he s to me, I was strengthened	1819
Hos	12:10 I s to the prophets, gave them many visions	1819
	13: 1 When Ephraim s, men trembled;	1819
Zec	1:13 So the LORD s kind and comforting words	6699
Mt	9:33 the man who had been mute s.	3281
	13:34 Jesus s all these things to the crowd	3281
	22: 1 Jesus s to them again in parables, saying:	3306
Mk	3:23 Jesus called them and s to them in parables:	3306
	4:33 With many similar parables Jesus s	3281
	6:50 Immediately he s to them and said,	3281
	8:32 He s plainly about this,	3281
Lk	1:60 but his mother s up and said,	646

Lk	2:38	she gave thanks to God and s about	3281

Lk 2:38 she gave thanks to God and s about 3281
4:22 All s well of him and were amazed at 3455
9:11 and s to them about the kingdom of God, 3281
9:31 They s about his departure, 3306
11:14 the man who had been mute s, 3281
23:22 For the third time he s to them: "Why?" 3306
Jn 6: 8 Andrew, Simon Peter's brother, s up, 3306
7:46 "No one ever s the way this man does," 3281
8:12 When Jesus s again to the people, he said, 3281
8:20 He s these words while teaching in 3281
8:30 Even as he s, many put their faith in him. 3281
9:29 We know that God s to Moses, 3281
11:49 who was high priest that year, s up, 3306
12:34 The crowd s up, "We have heard from the 646
12:41 because he saw Jesus' glory and s 3281
12:48 very word which I s will condemn him 3281
15:20 Remember the words I s to you: 3281
18:16 s to the girl on duty there 3306
18:23 But if I s the truth, why did you strike me?" NIV
Ac 1: 3 to them over a period of forty days and s 3306
1:16 the Holy Spirit s long ago through 4625
2:31 he s of the resurrection of the Christ, 3281
4:25 You s by the Holy Spirit through the mouth 3306
4:31 with the Holy Spirit and s the word 3281
6:10 or the Spirit by whom he s. 3281
7: 6 God s to him in this way: 3281
7:38 the angel who s to him on Mount Sinai, and 3281
10: 7 When the angel who s to him had gone, 3281
10:15 The voice s to him a second time, NIG
11: 9 "The voice s from heaven a second time, 646
14: 1 There they s so effectively that 3281
15:13 When they finished, James s up: 646
16: 2 at Lystra and Iconium s well of him. 3455
16:32 Then they s the word of the Lord to him 3281
18: 9 One night the Lord s to Paul in a vision: 3306
18:25 and he s with great fervor and taught 3281
19: 6 and they s in tongues and prophesied. 3281
19: 8 and s boldly there for three months, 4245
20: 7 Paul s to the people and, 1363
24:24 He sent for Paul and listened to him as he s NIG
28:25 "The Holy Spirit s the truth to your 3281
Heb 1: 1 In the past God s to our forefathers through 3281
4: 7 when a long time later he s through David, 3306
11: 4 when God s well of his offerings. 3455
11:22 s about the exodus of the Israelites 3648
13: 7 who s the word of God to you. 3281
Jas 5:10 the prophets who s in the name of the Lord. 3281
1Pe 1:10 who s of the grace that was to come to you, 4736
1:12 when they s of the things that have NIG
2Pe 1:21 but men s from God as they were carried 3281
2:16 who s with a man's voice and restrained 5779
Rev 10: 3 the voices of the seven thunders s. 3281
10: 4 the seven thunders s, I was about to write; 3281
10: 8 the voice that I had heard from heaven s 3281
13:11 horns like a lamb, but he s like a dragon. 3281

SPOKEN (160) [SPEAK]

Ex 4:10 past nor since you have s to your servant. 1819
20:22 'You have seen for yourselves that I have s 1819
34:29 that his face was radiant because he had s 1819
Nu 12: 2 "Has the Lord s only through Moses?" 1819
12: 2 "Hasn't he also s through us?" 1819
14:35 I, the Lord, have s, 1819
Dt 13: 2 or wonder of which he has s takes place, 1819
18:21 a message has not been s by the Lord?" 1819
18:22 that is a message the Lord has not s. 1819
18:22 That prophet has s presumptuously. 1819
Jos 6: 8 When Joshua had s to the people, 606
Jdg 2: 4 the angel of the Lord had s these things 1819
Ru 2:13 and have s kindly to your servant— 1819+4213+6584
2Sa 2:27 "As surely as God lives, if you had not s, 1819
7:19 also s about the future of the house 1819
7:29 for you, O Sovereign Lord, have s, 1819
1Ki 2:27 the Lord had s at Shiloh about the house 1819
12:15 the word the Lord had s to Jeroboam son 1819
14:11 the Lord has s!" 1819
16:12 the word of the Lord s against Baasha 1819
16:34 the word of the Lord s by Joshua son 1819
17:16 in keeping with the word of the Lord s 1819
22:28 the Lord has not s through me." 1819
2Ki 1:17 to the word of the Lord that Elijah had s. 1819
2:22 according to the word Elisha had s. 1819
10:10 a word the Lord has s against the house 1819
10:17 according to the word of the Lord s 1819
14:25 s through his servant Jonah son of Amittai, 1819
15:12 of the Lord s to Jehu was fulfilled: 1819
19:21 the word that the Lord has s against him: 1819
20:19 of the Lord you have s is good," 1819
22: 7 the Lord when you heard what I have s 1819
1Ch 17:17 you have s about the future of the house 1819
21:19 up in obedience to the word that Gad had s 1819
2Ch 10:15 the word the Lord had s to Jeroboam son 1819
18:27 the Lord has not s through me." 1819
36:21 in fulfillment of the word of the Lord s 7023
36:22 in order to fulfill the word of the Lord s 7023
Ezr 1: 1 in order to fulfill the word of the Lord s 7023
Job 9:15 not enough for you, words s gently to you? AIT
21: 3 and after I have s, mock on. 1819
29:22 After I had s, they spoke no more; 1821
42: 7 because you have not s of me what is right, 1819
42: 8 You have not s of me what is right, 1819
Ps 60: 6 God has s from his sanctuary: 1819
62:11 One thing God has s, two things I have 1819
108: 7 God has s from his sanctuary: 1819
109: 2 they have s against me with lying tongues. 1819

Ps 141: 6 that my words were well s. NIH
Pr 25:11 A word aptly s is like apples of gold 1819
SS 8: 8 for our sister for the day she is s for? 1819
Isa 1: 2 For the mouth of the Lord has s. 1819
1:20 For the mouth of the Lord has s. 1819
16:13 the Lord has already s concerning Moab. 1819
21:17 The Lord, the God of Israel, has s. 1819
22:25 The Lord has s. 1819
23: 4 O fortress of the sea, for the sea has s: 606
24: 3 The Lord has s this word. 1819
25: 8 The Lord has s. 1819
37:22 the word the Lord has s against him: 1819
38:15 He has s to me, and he himself has done this 606
39: 8 of the Lord you have s is good," 1819
40: 5 For the mouth of the Lord has s." 1819
45:19 I have not s in secret, 1819
48:15 I, even I, have s; yes, I have called him. 1819
48:16 "From the first announcement I have not s 1819
58:14 The mouth of the Lord has s. 1819
59: 3 Your lips have s lies. 1819
Jer 4:28 because I have s and will not relent, 1819
5:14 "Because the people have s these words, 1819
13:15 do not be arrogant, for the Lord has s. 1819
14:14 I have not sent them or appointed them or s 1819
23:35 or 'What has the Lord s?' 1819
23:37 or 'What has the Lord s?' 1819
25: 3 of the Lord has come to me and I have s 1819
25:13 that land all the things I have s against it, 1819
26:16 He has s to us in the name of the Lord 1819
29:23 and in my name have s lies, 1819+1821
30: 2 in a book all the words I have s to you. 1819
35:14 But I have s to you again and again, 1819
36: 2 and write on it all the words I have s to you 1819
36: 4 the words the Lord had s to him, 1819
37: 2 the Lord had s through Jeremiah 1819
44:16 not listen to the message you have s to us in 1819
48: 8 because the Lord has s. 606
Eze 5:13 they will know that I the Lord have s 1819
5:15 I the Lord have s. 1819
5:17 I the Lord have s. 1819
13: 7 though I have not s? 1819
17:21 you will know that I the Lord have s." 1819
17:24 " 'I the Lord have s, and I will do it.' " 1819
21:17 I the Lord have s." 1819
21:32 for I the Lord have s.' " 1819
22:14 I the Lord have s, and I will do it. 1819
22:28 when the Lord has not s. 1819
23:34 I have s, declares the Sovereign Lord. 1819
24:14 " 'I the Lord have s. 1819
26: 5 for I have s, declares the Sovereign Lord. 1819
26:14 for I the Lord have s, 1819
28:10 I have s, declares the Sovereign Lord.' " 1819
30:12 I the Lord have s. 1819
34:24 I the Lord have s. 1819
36: 5 In my burning zeal I have s against the rest 1819
36:36 I the Lord have s, and I will do it. 1819
37:14 you will know that I the Lord have s, 1819
39: 5 You will fall in the open field, for I have s, 1819
39: 8 This is the day I have s of. 1819
Da 9:12 You have fulfilled the words s against us 1819
Joel 3: 8 The Lord has s. 1819
Am 3: 1 the Lord has s against you, O people 1819
3: 8 The Sovereign Lord has s— 1819
Ob 1:18 the Lord has s. 1819
Mic 4: 4 for the Lord Almighty has s. 1819+7023
Zec 8: 9 "You who now hear these words s by 7023
Mt 3: 3 This is he who was s of through 3306
8:17 This was to fulfill what was s through 3306
12:17 This was to fulfill what was s through 3306
12:36 for every careless word they have s. 3306
13:35 So was fulfilled what was s through 3306+3306
21: 4 This took place to fulfill what was s through 3306
24:15 s of through the prophet Daniel— 3306
26:65 "He has s blasphemy! 1059
26:75 Peter remembered the word Jesus had s: 3306
27: 9 Then what was s by Jeremiah 3306
Mk 12:12 to arrest him because they knew he had s 3306
14:72 the word Jesus had s to him: 3306
16:19 After the Lord Jesus had s to them, 3281
Lk 2:34 and to be a sign that will be s against, 515
9:36 When the voice had s, 1181
20:19 knew he had s this parable against them. 3306
22:61 the word the Lord had s to him: 3306
24:25 to believe all that the prophets have s! 3281
Jn 2:21 But the temple he had s of was his body. 3306
2:22 the Scripture and the words that Jesus had s. 3306
3:12 I have s to you of earthly things 3306
6:63 The words I have s to you are spirit 4487
12:29 others said an angel had s to him. 3281
14:25 "All this I have s while still with you. 3281
15: 3 because of the word I have s to you. 3281
15:22 If I had not come and s to them, 3281
18: 9 that the words he had s would be fulfilled: 3306
18:20 "I have s openly to the world, 3281
18:32 the words Jesus had s indicating the kind 3306
Ac 2:16 No, this is what was s by the prophet Joel: 3306
3:24 as many as have s, have foretold these days. 3281
9:27 the Lord and that the Lord had s to him, 3281
23: 9 "What if a spirit or an angel has s to him?" 3281
Ro 14:16 what you consider good to be s of as evil. 1059
2Co 1:20 And so through him the "Amen" is s by us NIG
4:13 It is written: "I believed"; therefore I have s. 3281
6:11 We have s freely to you, 487+3836+5125
Gal 3: 8 The promises were s to Abraham and 3306
Heb 1: 2 in these last days he has s to us by his Son, 3281
2: 2 For if the message s by angels was binding, 3281
4: 4 For somewhere he has s about the seventh 3306

Heb 4: 8 not have s later about another day. 3281
12:19 that no further word be s to them, 3364+4707
2Pe 3: 2 the words s in the past by the holy prophets 4625
3Jn 1:12 Demetrius is well s of by everyone— 3455
Jude 1:15 the harsh words ungodly sinners have s 3281

SPOKES (1) [SPOKE]

1Ki 7:33 rims, s and hubs were all of cast metal. 3140

SPOKESMAN (1) [SPEAK, MAN]

Jer 15:19 you will be my s. 3869+7023

SPOKESMEN (1) [SPEAK, MAN]

Isa 43:27 your s rebelled against me. 4885

SPONGE (4)

Mt 27:48 Immediately one of them ran and got a s. 5074
Mk 15:36 One man ran, filled a s with wine vinegar, 5074
Jn 19:29 so they soaked a s in it, 5074
19:29 put the s on a stalk of the hyssop plant, NIG

SPONTANEOUS (1)

Phm 1:14 favor you do will be s and not forced. 1730+2848

SPOON, SPOONS (KJV) See DISH, DISHES

SPORT (3)

Ge 39:14 has been brought to us to make s of us! 7464
39:17 brought us came to me to make s of me, 7464
Ps 69:11 people make s of me. 2118+4200+5442

SPORTING (KJV) See CARESSING, REVELING

SPOT (17) [SPOTLESS, SPOTS, SPOTTED]

Lev 13: 2 a swelling or a rash or a bright s on his skin 994
13: 4 If the s on his skin is white but does 994
13:19 a white swelling or reddish-white s appears, 994
13:23 if the s is unchanged and has not spread, 994
13:24 and a reddish-white or white s appears in 994
13:25 the priest is to examine the s, 994
13:26 and there is no white hair in the s and if it is 994
13:28 the s is unchanged and has not spread in 994
14:56 and for a swelling, a rash or a bright s, 994
Jos 4: 9 in the middle of the Jordan at the s where 9393
2Sa 2:23 He fell there and died on the s. 9393
2Ki 5:11 over the s and cure me of my leprosy. 5226
Job 8:18 But when it is torn from its s, 5226
Isa 28: 8 with vomit and there is not a s without filth. 5226
46: 7 From that s it cannot move. 5226
Lk 19: 5 When Jesus reached the s, 5536
1Ti 6:14 to keep this command without s or blame 834

SPOTLESS (3) [SPOT]

Da 11:35 and made s until the time of the end, 4235
12:10 Many will be purified, made s and refined, 4235
2Pe 3:14 make every effort to be found s, 834

SPOTS (3) [SPOT]

Lev 13:38 a man or woman has white s on the skin, 994
13:39 and if the s are dull white, 994
Jer 13:23 change his skin or the leopard its s? 2494

SPOTTED (8) [SPOT]

Ge 30:32 from them every speckled or s sheep, 3229
30:32 every dark-colored lamb and every s 3229
30:33 in my possession that is not speckled or s, 3229
30:35 the male goats that were streaked or s, 3229
30:35 and all the speckled or s female goats 3229
30:39 that were streaked or speckled or s, 3229
31:10 with the flock were streaked, speckled or s. 1353
31:12 with the flock are streaked, speckled or s, 1353

SPOUSE (KJV) See BRIDE

SPRANG (4) [SPRING]

Jnh 4:10 It s up overnight and died overnight. 2118
Mt 13: 5 It s up quickly, because the soil was shallow 1984
Mk 4: 5 It s up quickly, because the soil was shallow 1984
Ro 7: 9 sin s to life and I died. 348

SPREAD (156) [OUTSPREAD, SPREADING, SPREADS, WIDESPREAD]

Ge 10: 5 (From these the maritime peoples s out 7233
10:32 From these the nations s out over the earth 7233
28:14 you will s out to the west and to the east, 7287
41:56 the famine had s over the whole country, 2118
Ex 1:12 the more they multiplied and s; 7287
9:29 I will s out my hands in prayer to 7298
9:33 He s out his hands toward the Lord; 7298
10:21 toward the sky so that darkness will s 2118
23: 1 "Do not s false reports. 5951
25:20 to have their wings s upward, 7298
29: 2 and wafers s with oil. 5417
37: 9 The cherubim had their wings s upward, 7298

Ex	40:19	Then *he* s the tent over the tabernacle	7298
Lev	2: 4	wafers made without yeast and s with oil.	5417
	7:12	wafers made without yeast and s with oil,	5417
	13: 5	that the sore is unchanged and *has* not s in	7313
	13: 6	the sore has faded and *has* not s in the skin,	7313
	13: 7	But if the rash *does* s in his skin	7313+7313
	13: 8	and if the rash *has* s in the skin,	7313
	13:23	But if the spot is unchanged and *has* not s,	7313
	13:28	and *has* not s in the skin but has faded, it is	7313
	13:32	the itch *has* not s and there is no yellow hair	7313
	13:34	and if it *has* not s in the skin and appears to	7313
	13:35	But if the itch *does* s in the skin	7313+7313
	13:36	and if the itch *has* s in the skin,	7313
	13:51	and if the mildew *has* s in the clothing,	7313
	13:53	the mildew *has* not s in the clothing,	7313
	13:55	even though it *has* not s, it is unclean.	7313
	14:39	If the mildew *has* s on the walls,	7313
	14:44	if the mildew *has* s in the house,	7313
	14:48	to examine it and the mildew *has* not s after	7313
Nu	4: 6	s a cloth of solid blue over that and put	7298
	4: 7	of the Presence *they are to* s a blue cloth	7298
	4: 8	Over these *they* are to s a scarlet cloth,	7298
	4:11	*to* s a blue cloth and cover that with hides	7298
	4:13	the bronze altar and s a purple cloth over it.	7298
	4:14	Over it *they are to* s a covering of hides	7298
	6:15	and wafers s with oil.	5417
	11:32	*they* s them out all around the camp.	8848+8848
	13:32	And *they* s among the Israelites	3655
	24: 6	"Like valleys *they* s out,	5742
Jos	6:27	and his fame s throughout the land.	2118
	7:23	and all the Israelites and s them *out* before	3668
Jdg	8:25	"S the corner of your garment over me,	7298
	20:37	s out and put the whole city to the sword.	5432
Ru	3: 9	"S the corner of your garment over me,	7298
1Sa	4: 2	and *as* the battle s, Israel was defeated	5759
2Sa	5:18	Now the Philistines had come and s out in	5759
	5:22	up and s out in the Valley of Rephaim;	5759
	17:19	a covering and s it *out* over the opening of	7298
	18: 8	The battle s out over the whole	7046
	21:10	of Aiah took sackcloth and s it *out*	5742
1Ki	4:31	his fame s to all the surrounding nations.	2118
	6:27	with their wings s out.	7298
	8: 7	The cherubim s their wings over the place	7298
	8:22	s out his hands *toward* heaven	7298
	8:54	with his hands s out *toward* heaven.	7298
	22:36	a cry s through the army:	6296
2Ki	8:15	in water and s it over the king's face,	7298
	9:13	and took their cloaks and s them under him	8492
	19:14	the LORD and s it *out* before the LORD.	7298
1Ch	14:17	So David's fame s throughout every land,	3655
	28:18	*that* s their wings and shelter the ark of	7298
2Ch	5: 8	The cherubim s their wings over the place	7298
	6:12	assembly of Israel and s out his hands.	7298
	6:13	and s out his hands toward heaven.	7298
	26: 8	and his fame s as far as the border of Egypt,	2143
	26:15	His fame s far and wide,	3655
Ezr	9: 5	with my hands s out to the LORD my God	7298
Ne	4:19	"The work is extensive and s out,	8146
	8:15	that they should proclaim this word and s it	6296
Est	9: 4	his reputation s throughout the provinces,	2143
Job	1:10	so that his flocks and herds *are* s throughout	7287
	15:29	nor *will* his possessions s over the land.	5742
	17:13	if *I* s out my bed in darkness,	8331
	39:26	by your wisdom and s his wings toward	7298
Ps	5:11	S *your* protection over them,	6114
	44:20	the name of our God or s *out* our hands to	7298
	57: 6	*They* s a net for my feet;	3922
	78:19	saying, "Can God s a table in the desert?	6885
	88: 9	*I* s out my hands to you.	8848
	105:39	*He* s out a cloud as a covering,	7298
	136: 6	who s out the earth upon the waters,	8392
	140: 5	*they have* s out the cords of their net	7298
	143: 6	*I* s out my hands to you;	7298
Pr	1:17	How useless *to* s a net in full view of all	2430
	15: 7	The lips of the wise s knowledge;	2430
SS	1:12	my perfume s its fragrance.	5989
	2:13	the blossoming vines s their fragrance.	5989
	4:16	that its fragrance *may* s abroad.	5688
Isa	1:15	When you s *out* your hands in prayer,	7298
	14:11	maggots *are* s beneath you	3667
	16: 8	which once reached Jazer and s *toward*	9494
	16: 8	Their shoots s out and went as far as	5759
	21: 5	They set the tables, they s the rugs,	7596
	25:11	*They will* s *out* their hands in it,	7298
	30:24	s out with fork and shovel.	2430
	33:23	mast is not held secure, the sail *is not* s.	7298
	37:14	the LORD and s it *out* before the LORD.	7298
	42: 5	and stretched them out, *who* s *out* the earth	8392
	44:24	*who* s out the earth by myself,	8392
	48:13	and my right hand s out the heavens;	3253
	54: 3	*you will* s *out* to the right and *to* the left;	7287
	65:11	who s a table for Fortune and fill bowls	6885
Jer	23:15	the prophets of Jerusalem ungodliness *has* s	3655
	43:10	*he* will s his royal canopy above them.	5742
	48:32	Your branches s as far as the sea;	6296
La	1:13	*He* s a net for my feet and turned me back.	7298
Eze	1:11	Their wings *were* s *out* upward;	7233
	1:22	S above the heads of the living creatures	5742
	5: 4	A fire *will* s from there to the whole house	3655
	10:16	and when the cherubim s their wings to rise	5951
	10:19	the cherubim s their wings and rose from	5951
	11:22	with the wheels beside them, s their wings,	5951
	12:13	*I will* s my net for him,	7298
	16: 8	*I* s the corner of my garment over you	7298
	16:14	And your fame s among the nations	3655
	17:20	*I will* s my net for him,	7298
	19: 8	*They* s their net for him,	7298

Eze	19:14	Fire s from one of its main branches	3655
	23:41	a table s before it on which you had placed	6885
	26: 5	she will become a place to s fishnets,	5427
	26:14	you will become a place to s fishnets.	5427
	30:13	and *I will* s fear throughout the land.	5989
	32: 5	*I will* s your flesh on the mountains	5989
	32:23	All who *had* s terror in the land of	5989
	32:24	All who *had* s terror in the land of	5989
	32:25	their terror *had* s in the land of the living,	5989
	32:26	by the sword because *they* s their terror in	5989
	32:32	*I had* him s terror in the land of the living,	5989
Hos	5: 1	a net s *out* on Tabor.	7298
Mal	2: 3	*I will* s on your faces the offal	2430
Mt	4:24	News about him s all over Syria,	599
	9:26	News of this s through all that region.	2002
	9:31	But they went out and s the news about	1424
	21: 8	A very large crowd s their cloaks on	5143
	21: 8	from the trees and s them on the road.	5143
Mk	1:28	about him s quickly over the whole region	2002
	11: 8	Many people s their cloaks on the road,	5143
	11: 8	others s branches they had cut in the fields.	NIG
Lk	2:17	*they* s the word concerning what had been	1192
	4:14	about him s through the whole countryside.	2002
	4:37	And the news about him s throughout	1744
	5:15	Yet the news about him s all the more,	1451
	7:17	This news about Jesus s throughout Judea	2002
	19:36	*people* s their cloaks on the road.	5716
Jn	12:17	from the dead *continued to* s the word.	3455
	21:23	the rumor s among the brothers	2002
Ac	6: 7	So the word of God s.	889
	11:28	that a severe famine would s over	1639
	12:24	word of God continued to increase and s.	4437
	13:49	of the Lord s through the whole region.	1422
	19:20	In this way the word of the Lord s widely	889
2Th	3: 1	that the message of the Lord *may* s rapidly	5556
2Ti	2:17	Their teaching *will* s like gangrene.	2400+3786
Rev	7:15	on the throne *will* s *his* tent over them.	5012

SPREADING (41) [SPREAD]

Lev	13:22	If *it is* s in the skin,	7313+7313
	13:27	and if *it is* s in the skin,	7313+7313
	13:49	a s mildew and must be shown to the priest.	7669
	13:57	or in the leather article, it *is* s,	7255
	14:34	and I put a s mildew in a house	5596+7669
	19:16	not go about a s slander among your people.	8215
Nu	14:36	against him by a s bad report about it—	3655
	14:37	these men *responsible for* s the bad report	3655
Dt	12: 2	on the hills and under every s tree where	8316
	28:35	s *from* the soles of your feet to the top	AIT
Jdg	15: 9	and camped in Judah, s *out* near Lehi.	5759
1Sa	2:24	it is not a good report that I hear s among	6296
1Ki	8:38	and s his hands toward this temple—	7298
	14:23	on every high hill and under every s tree.	8316
2Ki	16: 4	on the hilltops and under every s tree.	8316
	17:10	on every high hill and under every s tree.	8316
2Ch	6:29	and s *out* his hands toward this temple—	7298
	28: 4	on the hilltops and under every s tree.	8316
Job	8:16	s its shoots over the garden;	3655
	26: 9	the full moon, s his clouds over it.	7299
	37:18	*can you* join him in s *out* the skies,	8392
Pr	29: 5	Whoever flatters his neighbor *is* a net	7298
Isa	18: 5	and cut down and take away the s branches.	5746
	57: 5	among the oaks and under every s tree;	8316
Jer	2:20	and under every s tree you lay down as	8316
	3: 6	up on every high hill and under every s tree	8316
	3:13	to foreign gods under every s tree,	8316
	17: 2	and Asherah poles beside the s trees and on	8316
	25:32	Disaster *is* s from nation to nation;	3655
	48:40	s its wings over Moab.	7298
	49:22	s its wings over Bozrah.	7298
Eze	6:13	under every s tree and every leafy oak—	8316
	17: 6	and it sprouted and became a low, s vine.	6243
	31: 5	because of abundant waters.	8938
	31: 7	It was majestic in beauty, with its s boughs,	802
	47:10	there will be places for s nets.	5427
Hos	10: 1	Israel *was* a s vine; he brought forth fruit	1328
Joel	2: 2	Like dawn s across the mountains a large	7298
Mk	1:45	and began to talk freely, s the news.	1424
Ac	4:17	to stop *this* thing from s any further among	1376
1Th	3: 2	and God's fellow worker in s the gospel	2295

SPREADS (12) [SPREAD]

Ex	22: 6	"If a fire breaks out and s *into* thornbushes	5162
Dt	32:11	*that* s its wings to catch them	7298
Job	26: 7	He s out the northern [skies] over empty	5742
	36:29	Who can understand how he s out	5155
	39:18	s *her* feathers to run,	928+2021+5257+5294
Ps	41: 6	then he goes out and s it abroad.	1819
	147:16	He s the snow like wool and scatters	5989
Pr	10:18	and *whoever* s slander is a fool.	3655
Isa	25:11	as a swimmer s *out* his hands to swim.	7298
	32: 6	He practices ungodliness and s error	1819
	40:22	and s them *out* like a tent to live in.	5501
2Co	2:14	and through us s everywhere the fragrance	5746

SPRIG (1)

Eze	17:22	a tender s from its topmost shoots	AIT

SPRING (61) [SPRANG, SPRINGING, SPRINGS, SPRINGTIME, SPRUNG, WELLSPRING]

Ge	16: 7	found Hagar near a s in the desert;	2021+4784+6524
	16: 7	it was the s that *is* beside the road to Shur.	6524

Ge	24:13	See, I am standing beside this s,	4784+6524
	24:16	She went down to the s,	6524
	24:29	and he hurried out to the man at the s.	6524
	24:30	by the camels near the s.	6524
	24:42	"When I came to the s today, I said,	6524
	24:43	See, I am standing beside the s	4784+6524
	24:45	She went down to the s and drew water,	6524
	49:22	a fruitful vine near a s,	6524
Lev	11:36	A s, however, or a cistern for collecting	5078
Nu	21:17	Then Israel sang this song: "S up, O well!	6590
Dt	11:14	both autumn and s rains,	4919
	33:28	Jacob's s is secure in a land of grain	6524
Jos	15: 9	toward the s *of* the waters of Nephtoah,	5078
	18:15	and the boundary came out at the s of	5078
Jdg	7: 1	and all his men camped at the s *of* Harod.	6524
	15:19	So the s was called En Hakkore,	2023S
1Sa	29: 1	and Israel camped by the s in Jezreel.	6524
2Sa	11: 1	In the s, at the time when kings go off	9102+9588
1Ki	20:22	because next s the king	2021+9102+9588
	20:26	The next s Ben-Hadad mustered	9102+9588
2Ki	2:21	Then he went out to the s and threw	4604+4784
	13:20	to enter the country every s.	995+9102
1Ch	20: 1	In the s, at the time when kings go off to	6961+9102+9588
2Ch	32:30	the Gihon s and channeled the water down	4784
	33:14	west of the Gihon s in the valley,	NIH
	36:10	In the s, King Nebuchadnezzar sent	9102+9588
Job	5: 6	For hardship *does* not s from the soil,	3655
	29:23	and drank in my words as the s rain.	4919
Ps	92: 7	that though the wicked s up like grass	7255
Pr	16:15	his favor is like a rain cloud in s.	4919
	25:26	Like a muddied s or a polluted well is	5078
Ecc	4: 4	and all achievement s from man's envy	NIH
	12: 6	before the pitcher is shattered at the s,	4432
SS	4:12	you are a s enclosed, a sealed fountain.	5078
Isa	14:29	the root of that snake *will* s up a viper,	3655
	42: 9	before *they* s *into being* I announce them	7541
	44: 4	*They will* s up like grass in a meadow,	7541
	45: 8	Let the earth open wide, *let* salvation s up,	7238
	58:11	like a s whose waters never fail.	4604+4784
	61:11	*will make* righteousness and praise s up	7541
Jer	2:13	have forsaken me, the s *of* living water,	5227
	3: 3	and no s rains have fallen.	4919
	5:24	who gives autumn and s rains in season,	4919
	9: 1	a s *of water* and my eyes a fountain	4919
	15:18	like a s that fails?	4784
	17:13	forsaken the LORD, the s *of* living water.	5227
Hos	6: 3	like the s rains that water the earth."	4919
	10: 4	therefore lawsuits s up like poisonous	7255
	13:15	his s will fail and his well dry up.	5227
Joel	2:23	both autumn and s rains, as before.	4919
Am	3: 5	*Does* a trap s up from the earth	6590
Jn	4:14	the water I give him will become in him a s	4380
Ro	15:12	Isaiah says, "The Root of Jesse will s up,	NIG
Col	1: 5	and love that s from the hope that is stored	NIG
1Th	2: 3	the appeal we make does not s from error	NIG
Jas	3:11	and salt water flow from the same s?	3956
	3:12	Neither can a salt s produce fresh water.	266
	5: 7	how patient he is for the autumn and s rains.	4069
Rev	21: 6	to drink without cost from the s of the water	4380

SPRINGING (1) [SPRING]

Dt	33:22	"Dan is a lion's cub, s out of Bashan."	2397

SPRINGS (43) [SPRING]

Ge	7:11	the s *of* the great deep burst forth,	5078
	8: 2	Now the s *of* the deep and the floodgates of	5078
	36:24	the hot s in the desert while he was grazing	3553
Ex	15:27	Elim, where there were twelve s and	4784+6524
Nu	33: 9	Elim, where there were twelve s and	4784+6524
Dt	8: 7	with s flowing in the valleys and hills;	9333
Jos	15:19	give me also s *of* water."	1657
	15:19	So Caleb gave her the upper and lower s.	1657
Jdg	1:15	give me also s *of* water."	1657
	1:15	Then Caleb gave her the upper and lower s.	1657
1Ki	18: 5	"Go through the land to all the s and	4784+5078
2Ki	3:19	stop up all the s, and ruin every	4784+5078
	3:25	stopped up all the s and cut down	4784+5078
	19:29	and the second year what s from *that.*	6084
2Ch	32: 3	the water from the s outside the city,	6524
	32: 4	and they blocked all the s and the stream	5078
Job	14: 2	He s up like a flower and withers away;	3655
	38:16	the s *of* the sea or walked in the recesses of	5569
Ps	74:15	It was you who opened up s and streams;	5078
	84: 6	they make it a place of s;	5078
	85:11	Faithfulness s forth from the earth,	7541
	90: 6	though in the morning *it* s up new,	7437
	104:10	He makes s pour water into the ravines;	5078
	107:33	flowing s into thirsty ground,	4604+4784
	107:35	the parched ground into flowing s;	4604+4784
	114: 8	the hard rock into s *of* water.	5078
Pr	5:16	Should your s overflow in the streets,	5078
	8:24	when there were no s abounding	5078
	27: 9	of one's friend s from his earnest counsel.	NIH
Isa	35: 7	the thirsty ground bubbling s.	4432+4784
	37:30	and the second year what s from *that.*	8826
	41:18	and s within the valleys.	5078
	41:18	and the parched ground into s.	4604+4784
	43:19	Now it s *up;* do you not perceive it?	7541
	49:10	and lead them beside s *of* water.	4432
Jer	51:36	I will dry up her sea and make her s dry.	5227
Eze	31: 4	deep s made it grow tall;	9333
	31:15	down to the grave I covered the deep s	9333
2Pe	2:17	These men are s without water	4380
Rev	7:17	he will lead them to s of living water.	4380

Rev	8:10	a third of the rivers and on the **s** of water—	4380
	14: 7	the earth, the sea and the **s** of water."	4380
	16: 4	his bowl on the rivers and **s** of water,	4380

SPRINGTIME (1) [SPRING]

Zec	10: 1	Ask the LORD for rain in the **s**;	4919+6961

SPRINKLE (31) [SPRINKLED, SPRINKLES, SPRINKLING]

Ex	29:16	and take the blood and **s** it against the altar	2450
	29:20	Then **s** blood against the altar on all sides.	2450
	29:21	and **s** it on Aaron and his garments and	5684
Lev	1: 5	the priests shall bring the blood and **s** it	2450
	1:11	the priests *shall* **s** blood against the altar	2450
	3: 2	Then Aaron's sons the priests *shall* **s**	2450
	3: 8	Then Aaron's sons *shall* **s** its blood against	2450
	3:13	Then Aaron's sons *shall* **s** its blood against	2450
	4: 6	into the blood and **s** some of it seven times	5684
	4:17	and **s** it before the LORD seven times	5684
	5: 9	*to* **s** some of the blood of the sin offering	5684
	14: 7	Seven times *he shall* **s** the one to	5684
	14:16	and with his finger **s** some of it before	5684
	14:27	with his right forefinger **s** some of the oil	5684
	14:51	and **s** the house seven times.	5684
	16:14	the bull's blood and with his finger **s** it on	5684
	16:14	then *he shall* **s** some of it	5684
	16:15	*He shall* **s** it on the atonement cover and	5684
	16:19	*He shall* **s** some of the blood on it	5684
	17: 6	The priest *is to* **s** the blood against	2450
Nu	8: 7	**S** the water of cleansing on them;	5684
	18:17	**S** their blood on the altar and burn their fat	2450
	19: 4	on his finger and **s** it seven times toward	5684
	19:18	the tent and all the furnishings	5684
	19:18	He must also **s** anyone who has touched	NIH
	19:	*to* **s** the unclean person on the third	5684
2Ki	16:15	**S** on the altar all the blood of	2450
Isa	52:15	so *will he* **s** many nations,	5684
Eze	27:30	*they will* **s** dust on their heads and roll	6590
	36:25	*I will* **s** clean water on you,	2450
	43:24	*to* **s** salt on them and sacrifice them as	8959

SPRINKLED (26) [SPRINKLE]

Ex	24: 6	and the other half *he* **s** on the altar.	2450
	24: 8	**s** it on the people and said,	2450
Lev	7: 2	and its blood *is to be* **s** against the altar	2450
	8:11	*He* **s** some of the oil on the altar	5684
	8:19	the ram and **s** the blood against the altar	2450
	8:24	he **s** blood against the altar on all sides.	2450
	8:30	and **s** them on Aaron and his garments and	5684
	9:12	and *he* **s** it against the altar on all sides.	2450
	9:18	and *he* **s** it against the altar on all sides.	2450
Nu	19:13	water of cleansing *has* not been **s** on him,	2450
	19:20	water of cleansing *has* not been **s** on him,	2450
Jos	7: 6	and **s** dust on their heads.	6590
2Ki	16:13	and **s** the blood of his fellowship offerings	2450
2Ch	29:22	priests took the blood and **s** it on the altar;	2450
	29:22	the rams and **s** their blood on the altar;	2450
	29:22	the lambs and **s** their blood on the altar.	2450
	30:16	The priests **s** the blood handed to them by	2450
	35:11	and the priests **s** the blood handed to them,	2450
Job	2:12	and they tore their robes and **s** dust	2450
La	2:10	*they have* **s** dust on their heads and put	6590
Hos	7: 9	His hair *is* **s** with gray,	2450
Heb	9:13	and bulls and the ashes of a heifer **s** on	4822
	9:19	and **s** the scroll and all the people.	4822
	9:21	*he* **s** with the blood both the tabernacle	4822
	10:22	*having* our hearts **s** to cleanse us from	4822
	12:24	to the **s** blood that speaks a better word than	4823

SPRINKLES (2) [SPRINKLE]

Lev	7:14	it belongs to the priest who **s** the blood of	2450
Nu	19:21	"The *man who* **s** the water of cleansing must	5684

SPRINKLING (32) [SPRINKLE]

Ex	27: 3	**s** bowls, meat forks and firepans.	4670
	38: 3	its pots, shovels, **s** bowls,	4670
Nu	4:14	meat forks, shovels and **s** bowls.	4670
	7:13	one silver **bowl** weighing seventy shekels,	4670
	7:19	one silver **bowl** weighing seventy shekels,	4670
	7:25	one silver **bowl** weighing seventy shekels,	4670
	7:31	one silver **bowl** weighing seventy shekels,	4670
	7:37	one silver **bowl** weighing seventy shekels,	4670
	7:43	one silver **bowl** weighing seventy shekels,	4670
	7:49	one silver **bowl** weighing seventy shekels,	4670
	7:55	one silver **bowl** weighing seventy shekels,	4670
	7:61	one silver **bowl** weighing seventy shekels,	4670
	7:67	one silver **bowl** weighing seventy shekels,	4670
	7:73	one silver **bowl** weighing seventy shekels,	4670
	7:79	one silver **bowl** weighing seventy shekels,	4670
	7:84	twelve silver plates, twelve silver **bowls**	4670
	7:85	and each **s bowl** seventy shekels.	4670
1Ki	7:40	the basins and shovels and **s** bowls.	4670
	7:45	the pots, shovels and **s** bowls.	4670
	7:50	**s** bowls, dishes and censers;	4670
2Ki	12:13	wick trimmers, **s** bowls,	4670
	25:15	the censers and **s** bowls—	4670
1Ch	28:17	shovels and pitchers;	4670
2Ch	4: 8	He also made a hundred gold **s** bowls.	4670
	4:11	the pots and shovels and **s** bowls.	4670
	4:22	the pots, dishes and censers;	4670
Jer	52:18	shovels, wick trimmers, **s** bowls,	4670
	52:19	censers, **s** bowls, pots, lampstands,	4670
Eze	43:18	and **s** blood upon the altar when it is built:	2450

Zec	9:15	be full like a **bowl used for s** the corners of	4670
Heb	11:28	By faith he kept the Passover and the **s** of	4717
1Pe	1: 2	for obedience to Jesus Christ and **s** by his	4823

SPROUT (8) [SPROUTED, SPROUTING, SPROUTS]

Nu	17: 5	staff belonging to the man I choose *will* **s**,	7255
Job	5: 6	nor *does* trouble **s** from the ground.	7541
	14: 7	If it is cut down, *it will* **s** again,	2736
	38:27	to satisfy a desolate wasteland and **make** it **s**	7541
Pr	23: 5	for *they will* **surely s** wings and fly off	6913+6913
Isa	61:11	the **s** come up and a garden causes seeds	7542
Jer	33:15	*I will* **make** a righteous Branch **s**	7541
Lk	21:30	When *they* **leaves**, you can see	4582

SPROUTED (5) [SPROUT]

Ge	41: 6	After them, seven other heads of grain **s**—	7541
	41:23	After them, seven other heads **s**—	7541
Nu	17: 8	*had* not only **s** but had budded,	7255
Eze	17: 6	and *it* **s** and became a low,	7541
Mt	13:26	When the wheat **s** and formed heads,	1056

SPROUTING (3) [SPROUT]

Dt	29:23	nothing planted, nothing **s**,	7541
2Ki	19:26	like **grass s** on the roof,	AIT
Isa	37:27	like **grass s** on the roof,	AIT

SPROUTS (1) [SPROUT]

Mk	4:27	the seed **s** and grows,	1056

SPRUNG (1) [SPRING]

Ge	2: 5	and no plant of the field *had* yet **s** up,	7541

SPUE, SPUED (KJV) See SPIT, VOMIT, VOMITED

SPUN (3) [SPIN]

Ex	35:25	Every skilled woman **s** with her hands	3211
	35:25	with her hands and brought **what** she had **s**	4757
	35:26	and had the skill **s** the goat hair.	3211

SPUNGE (KJV) See SPONGE

SPUR (1) [SPURRED, SPURS]

Heb	10:24	we may **s** one another **on** toward love	1650+4237

SPURN (1) [SPURNED, SPURNS]

Job	10: 3	*to* **s** the work of your hands,	4415

SPURNED (6) [SPURN]

Ps	89:38	you have **s**, you have been very angry	4415
Pr	1:30	not accept my advice and **s** my rebuke,	5540
	5:12	How my heart **s** correction!	5540
Isa	1: 4	*they have* **s** the Holy One of Israel	5540
	5:24	and **s** the word of the Holy One of Israel.	5540
La	2: 6	in his fierce anger *he has* **s** both king	5540

SPURNS (1) [SPURN]

Pr	15: 5	A fool **s** his father's discipline,	5540

SPURRED (3) [SPUR]

Est	3:15	**S** on by the king's command,	1894
	8:14	raced out, **s** on by the king's command.	1894
Isa	9:11	against them and *has* **s** their enemies **on**.	6056

SPURS (1) [SPUR]

Isa	41: 7	the hammer **s** on him who strikes the anvil.	NIH

SPY (9) [SPIED, SPIES, SPYING]

Dt	1:22	"Let us send men ahead *to* **s** out the land	2916
Jos	2: 2	come here tonight to **s** out the land."	2916
	2: 3	they have come to **s** out the whole land."	2916
	7: 2	"Go up and **s** out the region."	8078
Jdg	1:23	When they **sent** *men* to **s** out Bethel	9365
	18: 2	and Eshtaol to **s** out the land and explore it.	8078
2Sa	10: 3	the city and **s** it **out** and overthrow it?"	8078
1Ch	19: 3	and **s** out the country and overthrow it?"	8078
Gal	2: 4	*to* **s** on the freedom we have in Christ Jesus	2945

SPYING (2) [SPY]

Ge	42:30	treated us as though we *were* **s** on the land.	8078
Jos	6:23	So the young men who *had done the* **s** went	8078

SQUADS (1)

Ac	12: 4	be guarded *by* **four s** of four soldiers each.	5482

SQUALL (2)

Mk	4:37	A furious **s** came up,	449+3278
Lk	8:23	A **s** came down on the lake,	449+3278

SQUANDERED (2) [SQUANDERS]

Lk	15:13	for a distant country and there **s** his wealth	1399
	15:30	this son of yours who *has* **s** your property	2983

SQUANDERS (1) [SQUANDERED]

Pr	29: 3	but a companion of prostitutes **s** his wealth.	6

SQUARE (32) [SQUARES]

Ge	19: 2	"we will spend the night in the **s**."	8148
Ex	27: 1	it is to be **s**, five cubits long	8062
	28:16	It is to be **s**—a span long and a span wide	8062
	30: 2	It is to be **s**, a cubit long and a cubit wide,	8062
	37:25	*It was* **s**, a cubit long and a cubit wide,	8062
	38: 1	*it was* **s**, five cubits long	8062
	39: 9	It was **s**—a span long and a span wide	8062
Dt	13:16	of the town into the middle of the **public s**	8148
Jdg	19:15	They went and sat in the city **s**,	8148
	19:17	he looked and saw the traveler in the city **s**,	8148
	19:20	Only don't spend the night in the **s**."	8148
2Sa	21:12	from the **public s** *at* Beth Shan,	8148
1Ki	7:31	The panels of the stands *were* **s**, not round.	8062
2Ch	29: 4	assembled them in the **s** *on* the east side	8148
	32: 6	and assembled them before him in the **s** *at*	8148
Ezr	10: 9	all the people were sitting in the **s** *before*	8148
Ne	8: 1	as one man in the **s** before the Water Gate.	8148
	8: 3	the **s** before the Water Gate in the presence	8148
	8:16	and in the **s** *by* the Water Gate and the one	8148
Est	4: 6	to Mordecai in the **open s** *of* the city	8148
Job	29: 7	the city and took my seat in the **public s**,	8148
Eze	16:24	and made a lofty shrine in every **public s**.	8148
	16:31	made your lofty shrines in every **public s**.	8148
	40:12	and the alcoves were six cubits **s**.	2256+4946+4946+7024+7024
	40:47	Then he measured the court: *It was* **s**—	8062
	41:22	and two cubits **s**;	802+2256+8145
	43:16	The altar hearth *is* **s**,	448+752+8062+8063
	43:17	The upper ledge also is **s**,	448+752+8063
	45: 2	a section 500 cubits **s** is to be for	8062
	48:20	The entire portion will be a **s**, 25,000 cubits	8055
Am	5:16	and cries of anguish in every **public s**.	8148
Rev	21:16	The city was laid out like a **s**,	5481

SQUARES (9) [SQUARE]

Pr	1:20	she raises her voice in the **public s**;	8148
	5:16	your streams of water in the **public s**?	8148
	7:12	now in the **s**, at every corner she lurks.)	8148
SS	3: 2	through its streets and **s**;	8148
Isa	15: 3	the roofs and in the **public s** they all wail,	8148
Jer	5: 1	search through her **s**.	8148
	9:21	and the young men from the **public s**.	8148
	48:38	the **public s** there is nothing but mourning,	8148
Na	2: 4	rushing back and forth through the **s**.	8148

SQUEEZED (2)

Ge	40:11	**s** them into Pharaoh's cup and put the cup	8469
Jdg	6:38	he **s** the fleece and wrung out the dew—	2318

STAB (1) [STABBED]

Zec	13: 3	his own parents *will* **s** him.	1991

STABBED (4) [STAB]

2Sa	3:27	Joab **s** him *in* the stomach, and he died.	5782
	4: 6	and *they* **s** him in the stomach.	5782
	4: 7	After *they* **s** and killed him,	5782
	20:10	Without being **s** again, Amasa died.	NIH

STABILITY (1)

Pr	29: 4	By justice a king **gives** a country **s**,	6641

STABLE (KJV) See FIRMLY ESTABLISHED, PASTURE

STABLISH, STABLISHED, STABLISHETH (KJV) See ESTABLISH, ESTABLISHED, ESTABLISHES, FULFILL, SET IN PLACE, STAND FIRM, STRENGTHEN, STRENGTHENED

STACHYS (1)

Ro	16: 9	and my dear friend **S**.	5093

STACKS (KJV) See SHOCKS

STACTE (KJV) See GUM RESIN

STADIA (2)

Rev	14:20	the horses' bridles for a distance of 1,600 **s**	5084
	21:16	be 12,000 **s** in length, and as wide and high	5084

STAFF (67) [FLAGSTAFF, STAFFS]

Ge	32:10	I had only my **s** when I crossed this Jordan,	5234
	38:18	and the **s** in your hand," she answered.	4751
	38:25	whose seal and cord and **s** these are."	4751
	47:31	as he leaned on the top of his **s**.	4751
	49:10	nor the **ruler's s** from between his feet,	2980
Ex	4: 2	"A **s**," he replied.	4751
	4: 4	of the snake and it turned back into a **s**	4751
	4:17	But take this **s** in your hand	4751
	4:20	And he took the **s** *of* God in his hand.	4751
	7: 9	'Take your **s** and throw it down	4751

Ex	7:10	Aaron threw his s down in front of Pharaoh	4751
	7:12	Each one threw down his s and it became	4751
	7:12	But Aaron's s swallowed up their staffs.	4751
	7:15	in your hand the s that was changed into	4751
	7:17	With the s that is in my hand I will strike	4751
	7:19	'Take your s and stretch out your hand over	4751
	7:20	He raised his s in the presence of Pharaoh	4751
	8: 5	'Stretch out your hand with your s over	4751
	8:16	'Stretch out your s and strike the dust of	4751
	8:17	with the s and struck the dust of the ground,	4751
	9:23	Moses stretched out his s toward the sky,	4751
	10:13	So Moses stretched out his s over Egypt,	4751
	12:11	on your feet and your s in your hand.	5234
	14:16	Raise your s and stretch out your hand over	4751
	17: 5	in your hand the s with which you struck	4751
	17: 9	of the hill with the s of God in my hands."	4751
	21:19	up and walks around outside with his s;	5475
Nu	17: 2	Write the name of each man on his s.	4751
	17: 3	On the s of Levi write Aaron's name,	4751
	17: 3	be one s for the head of each ancestral tribe.	4751
	17: 5	The s belonging to the man I choose	4751
	17: 6	and Aaron's s was among them.	4751
	17: 8	of the Testimony and saw that Aaron's s,	4751
	17: 9	and each man took his own s.	4751
	17:10	"Put back Aaron's s in front of the Testimony,	4751
	20: 8	"Take the s, and you and your brother	4751
	20: 9	the s from the LORD's presence,	4751
	20:11	and struck the rock twice with his s.	4751
	22:27	and he was angry and beat her with his s.	5234
Jdg	5:14	Zebulun those who bear a commander's s.	8657
	6:21	With the tip of the s that was in his hand,	5475
1Sa	14:27	the s that was in his hand and dipped it into	4751
	14:43	a little honey with the end of my s.	4751
	17:40	Then he took his s in his hand,	5234
2Ki	4:29	take my s in your hand and run.	5475
	4:29	Lay my s on the boy's face."	5475
	4:31	on ahead and laid the s on the boy's face,	5475
	18:21	that splintered reed of a s,	5475
2Ch	32: 3	and military s about blocking off the water	1475
Ps	23: 4	your rod and your s, they comfort me.	5475
Isa	10:26	and he will raise his s over the waters,	4751
	36: 6	that splintered reed of a s,	5475
Jer	48:17	how broken the glorious s!'	5234
	51:59	to the s officer Seraiah son of Neriah,	4957
Eze	12:14	his s and all his troops—	6469
	29: 6	" 'You have been a s of reed for the house	5475
Mic	7:14	Shepherd your people with your s,	8657
Zec	11:10	Then I took my s called Favor and broke it,	5234
	11:14	Then I broke my second s called Union,	5234
Mt	10:10	or extra tunic, or sandals or a s;	4811
	27:29	They put a s in his right hand and knelt	2812
	27:30	the s and struck him on the head again	2812
Mk	6: 8	"Take nothing for the journey except a s—	4811
	15:19	on the head with a s and spit on him.	2812
Lk	9: 3	no s, no bag, no bread, no money,	4811
Heb	9: 4	Aaron's s that had budded,	4811
	11:21	worshiped as he leaned on the top of his s.	4811

STAFFS (7) [STAFF]

Ex	7:12	But Aaron's staff swallowed up their s.	4751
Nu	17: 2	to the Israelites and get twelve s from them,	4751
	17: 6	and their leaders gave him twelve s,	4751
	17: 7	Moses placed the s before the LORD in	4751
	17: 9	the s from the LORD's presence to all	4751
	21:18	the nobles with scepters and s."	5475
Zec	11: 7	Then I took two s and called one Favor and	5234

STAG (3)

SS	2: 9	My lover is like a gazelle or a young s.	385+6762
	2:17	and be like a gazelle or like a young s	385+6762
	8:14	and be like a gazelle or like a young s	385+6762

STAGE (2) [STAGES]

Jos	3:15	Jordan is at flood s all during harvest.	1536+3972+4848+6584
	4:18	and ran at flood s as before.	1536+3972+6584

STAGES (4) [STAGE]

Nu	33: 1	the s in the journey of the Israelites	5023
	33: 2	Moses recorded the s in their journey.	4604
	33: 2	This is their journey by s:	4604
Eze	41: 7	the temple was built in ascending s,	2025+2025+4200+4200+5087+5087

STAGGER (12) [STAGGERED, STAGGERING, STAGGERS]

Job	12:25	he makes them s like drunkards.	9494
Ps	60: 3	you have given us wine that makes us s.	9570
Isa	19:14	they make Egypt s in all that she does;	9494
	28: 7	these also s from wine and reel from beer:	8706
	28: 7	and prophets s from beer and are befuddled	8706
	28: 7	they s when seeing visions,	8706
	29: 9	but not from wine, but not from beer.	5675
	51:17	to its dregs the goblet that makes men s.	9570
	51:22	of your hand the cup that made you s;	9570
Jer	25:16	they will s and go mad because of	1723
La	5:13	boys s under loads of wood.	4173
Am	8:12	Men will s from sea to sea and wander	5675

STAGGERED (3) [STAGGER]

Ps	107:27	They reeled and s like drunken men;	5675
Isa	21: 3	I am s by what I hear,	6390

Am	4: 8	People s from town to town for water	5675

STAGGERING (2) [STAGGER]

1Sa	25:31	not have on his conscience the s burden of needless bloodshed	2256+4842+7050
Pr	24:11	hold back those s toward slaughter.	4572

STAGGERS (2) [STAGGER]

Isa	3: 8	Jerusalem s, Judah is falling;	4173
	19:14	as a drunkard s around in his vomit.	9494

STAIN (2) [STAINED]

Jer	2:22	the s of your guilt is still before me,"	4187
Eph	5:27	without s or wrinkle or any other blemish,	5070

STAINED (6) [STAIN]

1Ki	2: 5	with that blood s the belt around his waist	5989
Isa	59: 3	For your hands are s with blood,	1458
	63: 1	from Bozrah, with his garments s crimson?	2808
	63: 3	and I s all my clothing.	1458
Hos	6: 8	s with footprints of blood.	AIT
Jude	1:23	even the clothing s by corrupted flesh.	5071

STAIRS (2) [DOWNSTAIRS, STAIRWAY, UPSTAIRS]

Ne	9: 4	Standing on the s were the Levites—	5090
Eze	40:49	It was reached by a flight of s,	5092

STAIRWAY (5) [STAIRS]

Ge	28:12	He had a dream in which he saw a s resting	6150
1Ki	6: 8	a s led up to the middle level and	4294
2Ki	20:11	the ten steps it had gone down on the s	5092
Isa	38: 8	the ten steps it has gone down on the s	5092
Eze	41: 7	A s went up from the lowest floor to	NIH

STAKE (1) [STAKES]

Job	6:29	reconsider, for my integrity is at s.	928

STAKES (2) [STAKE]

Isa	33:20	its s will never be pulled up,	3845
	54: 2	lengthen your cords, strengthen your s.	3845

STALK (6) [STALKED, STALKS]

Ge	41: 5	were growing on a single s.	7866
	41:22	full and good, growing on a single s.	7866
Job	10:16	you s me like a lion and again display your	7421
Hos	8: 7	The s has no head; it will produce no flour.	7850
Mk	4:28	first the s, then the head,	5965
Jn	19:29	put the sponge on a s of the hyssop plant,	NIG

STALKED (2) [STALK]

La	4:18	Men s us at every step,	7421
Eze	32:27	of these warriors had s through the land of	NIH

STALKS (3) [STALK]

Jos	2: 6	up to the roof and hidden them under the s	6770
Ru	2:16	pull out some s for her from the bundles	NIH
Ps	91: 6	nor the pestilence that s in the darkness,	2143

STALL (3) [STALLS]

Ps	50: 9	from your s or of goats from your pens,	1074
Mal	4: 2	and leap like calves released from the s.	5272
Lk	13:15	from the s and lead it out to give it water?	5764

STALL-FED (1) [FEED]

1Ki	4:23	ten head of s cattle, twenty of pasture-fed	1374

STALLIONS (3)

Jer	5: 8	They are well-fed, lusty s,	6061
	8:16	of their s the whole land trembles.	52
	50:11	a heifer threshing grain and neigh like s,	52

STALLS (4) [STALL]

1Ki	4:26	Solomon had four thousand s for chariot	774
2Ch	9:25	Solomon had four thousand s for horses	774
	32:28	and he made s for various kinds of cattle,	774
Hab	3:17	no sheep in the pen and no cattle in the s,	8348

STAMMERING (1)

Isa	32: 4	and the s tongue will be fluent and clear.	6589

STAMP (1) [STAMPED]

Eze	6:11	Strike your hands together and s your feet	8392

STAMPED (1) [STAMP]

Eze	25: 6	you have clapped your hands and s your feet	8392

STANCHED (KJV) See STOPPED

STAND (257) [STANDING, STANDS, STOOD]

Ge	31:35	that I cannot s up in your presence;	7756
Ex	9:11	The magicians could not s before Moses	6641
	14:13	S firm and you will see the deliverance	3656

Ex	17: 6	I will s there before you by the rock	6641
	17: 9	Tomorrow I will s on top of the hill with	5893
	18:14	while all these people s around you	5893
	18:23	you will be able to s the strain,	6641
	30:18	with its bronze s, for washing.	4029
	30:28	and the basin with its s.	4029
	31: 9	the basin with its s.	4029
	33:21	a place near me where you may s on a rock.	5893
	35:16	the bronze basin with its s;	4029
	38: 8	the bronze basin and its bronze s from	4029
	39:39	the basin with its s;	4029
	40:11	the basin and its s and consecrate them.	4029
Lev	8:11	and all its utensils and the basin with its s,	4029
	26:37	not be able to s before your enemies.	9538
Nu	5:16	" 'The priest shall bring her and have her s	6641
	5:18	After the priest has had the woman s before	6641
	5:30	to have her s before the LORD and is	6641
	8:13	Have the Levites s in front of Aaron	6641
	11:16	that they may s there with you.	3656
	11:24	of their elders and had them s around	6641
	16: 9	and to s before the community and minister	6641
	27:19	Have him s before Eleazar the priest and	6641
	27:21	He is to s before Eleazar the priest,	6641
	27:22	and had him s before Eleazar the priest and	6641
	30: 4	by which she obligated herself will s.	7756
	30: 5	by which she obligated herself will s;	7756
	30: 7	by which she obligated herself will s.	7756
	30:11	by which she obligated herself will s.	7756
	30:12	or pledges that came from her lips will s.	7756
Dt	9: 2	No one will be able to s up against you;	3656
	9: 2	"Who can s up against the Anakites?"	3656
	10: 8	to s before the LORD to minister and	6641
	11:25	No man will be able to s against you.	3656
	18: 5	of all your tribes to s and minister in	6641
	19:16	If a malicious witness takes the s to	928+7756
	19:17	the two men involved in the dispute must s	6641
	27:12	these tribes shall s on Mount Gerizim	6641
	27:13	And these tribes shall s on Mount Ebal	6641
Jos	1: 5	to s up against you all the days of your life.	3656
	3: 8	the Jordan's waters, go and s in the river.' "	6641
	3:13	will be cut off and s up in a heap.	6641
	7:10	The LORD said to Joshua, "S up!	7756
	7:12	the Israelites cannot s against their enemies;	7756
	7:13	You cannot s against your enemies	7756
	10:12	"O sun, s still over Gibeon, O moon,	1957
	20: 4	he is to s in the entrance of the city gate	6641
Jdg	4:20	"S in the doorway of the tent," he told her.	6641
1Sa	6:20	"Who can s in the presence of the LORD,	6641
	12: 3	Here I s. Testify against me in the presence	NIH
	12: 7	s here, because I am going to confront you	3656
	12:16	"Now then, s still and see this great thing	3656
	14:40	"You s over there; I and Jonathan	2118
	14:40	I and Jonathan my son will s over here."	2118
	17:16	and evening and took his s.	3656
	19: 3	I will go out and s with my father in	6641
2Sa	1: 9	he said to me, 'S over me and kill me!	6641
	2:25	a group and took their s on top of a hill.	6641
	15: 2	He would get up early and s by the side of	6641
	18:30	The king said, "S aside and wait here."	6015
	22:34	he enables me to s on the heights.	6641
	23:12	But Shammah took his s in the middle of	3656
1Ki	7:30	Each s had four bronze wheels	4807
	7:31	inside of the s there was an opening that	2084S
	7:32	axles of the wheels were attached to the s.	4807
	7:34	Each s had four handles,	4807
	7:34	one on each corner, projecting from the s.	4807
	7:35	of the s there was a circular band half	4807
	7:35	and panels were attached to the top of the s.	4807
	10: 8	who continually s before you	6641
	19:11	and s on the mountain in the presence of	6641
2Ki	5:11	that he would surely come out to me and s	6641
1Ch	5:11	they took their s in the middle of the field.	3656
	23:30	They were also to s every morning to thank	6641
2Ch	9: 7	officials, who continually s before you	6641
	20: 9	we will s in your presence	6641
	20:17	s firm and see the deliverance	6641
	29:11	the LORD has chosen you to s before him	6641
	35: 5	"S in the holy place with a group of Levites	6641
Ezr	9:15	of it not one of us can s in your presence."	6641
	10:13	so we cannot s outside.	6641
Ne	9: 5	"S up and praise the LORD your God,	7756
Est	6:13	you cannot s against him—	3523+4202
	9: 2	No one could s against them,	6641
Job	11:15	you will s firm and without fear.	2118
	19:25	and that in the end he will s upon the earth.	7756
	21:16	I s aloof from the counsel of the wicked.	8178
	22:18	I s aloof from the counsel of the wicked.	8178
	30:20	I s up, but you merely look at me.	6641
	30:28	I s up in the assembly and cry for help.	7756
	32:16	now that they s there with no reply?	6641
	38:14	its features s out like those of a garment.	3656
	39:24	he cannot s still when the trumpet sounds.	586
	40:12	crush the wicked where they s.	9393
	41:10	Who then is able to s against me?	3656
Ps	1: 1	in the counsel of the wicked or s in the way	6641
	1: 5	the wicked will not s in the judgment,	7756
	2: 2	The kings of the earth take their s and	3656
	5: 5	The arrogant cannot s in your presence;	3656
	10: 1	O LORD, do you s far off?	6641
	18:33	he enables me to s on the heights.	6641
	20: 8	but we rise up and s firm.	6386
	24: 3	Who may s in his holy place?	7756
	26:12	My feet s on level ground;	6641
	30: 7	you made my mountain s firm;	6641
	33:11	But the plans of the LORD s firm forever,	6641
	40: 2	on a rock and gave me a firm place to s.	892
	76: 7	Who can s before you when you are angry?	6641

Ps	78:13	*he* **made** the water s **firm**	5893
	93: 5	Your statutes s **firm;**	586+4394
	94:16	Who *will* **take** a s for me	3656
	101: 7	no one who speaks falsely *will* s	3922
	109: 6	*let* an accuser s at his right hand.	6641
	119:120	*I* s **in awe** of your laws.	3707
	122: 5	There the thrones for judgment s,	3782
	127: 1	the watchmen s **guard** in vain.	9193
	130: 3	O Lord, who *could* s?	6641
Pr	8: 2	where the paths meet, *she* **takes** *her* s;	5893
	10:25	but the righteous s **firm** forever.	3572
	27: 4	but who *can* s before jealousy?	6641
Ecc	5: 7	Therefore s **in awe** *of* God.	3707
	8: 3	*Do* not s **up** for a bad cause,	6641
Isa	7: 9	If you do not s **firm** in your **faith,**	586
	7: 9	*you* **will** not s at all.' "	586
	8:10	propose your plan, but *it will* not s,	7756
	11:10	of Jesse *will* s as a banner for the peoples;	6641
	14:24	and as I have purposed, so it *will* s.	7756
	21: 8	my lord, I s on the watchtower;	6641
	28:18	your agreement with the grave *will* not s.	7756
	29:23	and will s **in awe** *of the* God of Israel.	6907
	44:11	all come together and **take** *their* s.	6641
	46:10	I say: My purpose *will* s,	7756
	48:13	I summon them, they *all* s **up** together.	6641
	60:11	Your gates *will* always s **open,**	AIT
Jer	1:17	S **up** and say to them whatever I command	7756
	1:18	a bronze wall to s against the whole land—	NIH
	6:16	"S at the crossroads and look;	6641
	7: 2	"S at the gate of the LORD's house	6641
	7:10	then come and s before me in this house,	6641
	14: 6	Wild donkeys s on the barren heights	6641
	15: 1	if Moses and Samuel *were to* s before me,	6641
	17:19	"Go and s at the gate of the people,	6641
	17:19	s also at all the other gates of Jerusalem.	NIH
	26: 2	S in the courtyard of the LORD's house	6641
	30:18	and the palace *will* s in its proper place.	3782
	33:18	to have a man to s before me continually	NIH
	44:28	in Egypt will know whose word *will* s—	7756
	44:29	of harm against you *will* **surely** s.'	7756+7756
	46:15	cannot s, for the LORD will push them down.	6641
	46:21	*they* **will** not s *their* **ground,**	6641
	48:19	S by the road and watch,	6641
	48:45	of Heshbon the fugitives s helpless,	6641
	49:19	And what shepherd *can* s against me?"	6641
	50:44	And what shepherd *can* s against me?"	6641
	51:29	the LORD's purposes against Babylon s—	7756
Eze	2: 1	s **up** on your feet and I will speak to you."	6641
	13: 5	the house of Israel so that *it will* s **firm** in	6641
	22:30	and s before me in the gap on behalf of	6641
	27:29	the mariners and all the seamen *will* s on	6641
	44:11	and sacrifices for the people and s before	6641
	44:15	*they are to* s before me to offer sacrifices	6641
	46: 2	through the portico of the gateway and s by	6641
	47:10	Fishermen *will* s along the shore;	6641
Da	8: 4	No animal *could* s against him,	6641
	8: 7	The ram was powerless to s against him,	6641
	8:25	and **take** *his* s against the Prince of princes.	6641
	10:11	and s **up,** for I have now been	6584+6641+6642
	11: 1	I **took** my s to support and protect him.)	6641
	11:15	will not have the strength to s.	6641
	11:16	no *one* will be able to s against him;	6641
	11:25	*be able to* s because of the plots devised	6641
Am	2:15	The archer *will* not s *his* **ground,**	6641
	5:21	*I* cannot s your assemblies.	8193
Mic	5: 4	*He will* s and shepherd his flock in	6641
	6: 1	Listen to what the LORD says: "S **up,**	7756
Hab	2: 1	*I will* s at my watch and station myself on	6641
	3: 2	*I* s **in awe** of your deeds, O LORD.	3707
Zep	3: 8	"for the day I *will* s **up** to testify,	7756
Zec	14: 4	On that day his feet *will* s on the Mount	6641
Mal	3: 2	Who *can* s when he appears?	6641
Mt	4: 5	and *had* him s on the highest point of	2705
	5:15	Instead they put it on its s,	3393
	12:25	household divided against itself *will* not s.	2705
	12:26	How then *can* his kingdom s?	2705
	12:41	men of Nineveh *will* s **up** at the judgment	482
	12:46	a little child and *had* him s among them.	2705
Mk	3: 3	"S **up** in front of everyone."	1586
	3:24	divided against itself, that kingdom cannot s	2705
	3:25	divided against itself, that house cannot s.	2705
	3:26	he cannot s; his end has come.	2705
	4:21	Instead, don't you put it on its s?	3393
	9:36	a little child and *had* him s among them.	2705
	11:25	And when *you* s praying,	2705
	13: 9	account of me *you will* s before governors	2705
Lk	1:19	I s in the presence of God,	4225
	4: 9	and *had* him s on the highest point of	2705
	6: 8	"Get up and s in front of everyone."	2705
	8:16	Instead, he puts it on a s,	3393
	9:47	took a little child and *had* him s beside him.	2705
	11:18	against himself, how *can* his kingdom s?	2705
	11:32	men of Nineveh *will* s **up** at the judgment	482
	11:33	Instead he puts it on its s,	3393
	13:25	*you will* s outside knocking and pleading,	2705
	21:28	s **up** and lift up your heads,	376
	21:36	that *you may be able to* s before the Son	2705
Jn	8: 3	*They* **made** her s before the group	2705
	8:16	I s with the Father, who sent me.	NIG
Ac	1:11	"why *do you* s here looking into the sky?	2705
	4:26	The kings of the earth **take** *their* s and	4225
	5:20	"Go, s in the temple courts," he said,	2705
	6:10	but they could not s **up against** his wisdom	468
	10:26	"S **up,**" he said, "I am only a man myself."	482
	14:10	"S **up** on your feet!"	482+3981
	22:30	he brought Paul and *had* him s before them.	2705
	23: 6	I s **on trial** because of my hope in	3212

Ac	25: 9	to Jerusalem and s **trial** before me there	3212
	25:20	to go to Jerusalem and s **trial** there	3212
	26: 2	to s before you today as I make my defense	NIG
	26:16	'Now get up and s on your feet.	2705
	26:22	and so *I* s here and testify to small	2705
	27:24	You must s **trial before** Caesar;	4225
Ro	5: 2	by faith into this grace in which *we* **now** s.	2705
	9:11	that God's purpose in election *might* s:	3531
	11:20	because of unbelief, and you s by faith.	2705
	14: 4	And *he will* s, for the Lord is able to make	2705
	14: 4	for the Lord is able *to* **make** him s.	2705
1Co	10:13	*we will* all s **before** God's judgment seat.	4225
	10:13	a way out so that *you can* s **up under** it.	5722
	15: 1	and on which *you have* **taken** your s.	2705
	15:58	Be on your guard; s **firm.**	1181+1612
	16:13	Be on your guard; s **firm** in the faith;	2705
2Co	1:21	God who **makes** both us and you s **firm**	1011
	1:24	because it is by faith you s **firm.**	2705
	2: 9	if *you would* s the test and be obedient	1509
Gal	5: 1	S **firm,** then, and do not let yourselves	2705
Eph	6:11	of God so that *you can* **take** your s against	2705
	6:13	you may be able to s **your ground,**	468
	6:13	and after you have done everything, *to* s.	2705
	6:14	S **firm** then, with the belt of truth buckled	2705
Php	1:27	I will know that *you* s **firm** in one spirit,	2705
	4: 1	that is how *you should* s **firm** in the Lord,	2705
Col	4:12	that *you may* s **firm** in all the will of God,	2705
1Th	3: 8	So when we *could* s it no longer,	5095
	3: 5	For this reason, *when I could* s it no longer,	5095
2Th	2:15	s **firm** and hold to the teachings we passed	4500
Jas	2: 3	"You s **there**" or "Sit on the floor	2705
	5: 8	You too, be patient and s **firm,**	2840+3836+5114
1Pe	5:12	the true grace of God. S **fast** in it.	2705
Rev	3:20	*I* s at the door and knock.	2705
	6:17	their wrath has come, and who can s?"	2705
	8: 2	I saw the seven angels who s before God,	2705
	11: 4	the two lampstands that s before the Lord	2705
	18:10	*they will* s far off and cry: "Woe!	2705
	18:15	gained their wealth from her *will* s far off,	2705
	18:17	their living from the sea, *will* s far off.	2705

STANDARD (16) [STANDARDS]

Nu	1:52	each man in his own camp under his own s.	1840
	2: 2	under his s with the banners of his family."	1840
	2: 3	of Judah are to encamp under their s.	1840
	2:10	of the camp of Reuben under their s.	1840
	2:17	each in his own place under his s.	1840
	2:18	of the camp of Ephraim under their s.	1840
	2:25	of the camp of Dan, under their s.	1840
	10:14	the camp of Judah went first, under their s.	1840
	10:18	of Reuben went next, under their s.	1840
	10:22	of Ephraim went next, under their s.	1840
	10:25	of the camp of Dan set out, under their s.	1840
2Sa	14:26	two hundred shekels by the royal s.	74
2Ch	3: 3	(using the cubit of the old s).	4500
Isa	31: 9	the **battle** s their commanders will panic,"	5812
Jer	4:21	How long must I see the **battle** s and hear	5812
Eze	45:11	the homer is to be the s **measure** *for* both.	5504

STANDARDBEARER (KJV) See SICK
MAN (Isa 10:18)

STANDARDS (12) [STANDARD]

Lev	19:35	not use dishonest s when **measuring** length,	5477
Nu	2:31	They will set out last, under their s.	1840
	2:34	is the way they encamped under their s,	1840
Ps	74: 4	they set up their s as signs.	253
Eze	5: 7	not even conformed to the s *of* the nations	5477
	7:27	and by their own s I will judge them.	5477
	11:12	but have conformed to the s *of* the nations	5477
	23:24	they will punish you according to their s.	5477
Jn	8:15	You judge by **human** s;	3836+4922
1Co	1:26	Not many of you were wise **by human** s;	2848
	3:18	of you thinks he is wise **by the** s of this age,	NIG
2Co	10: 2	that we live **by the** s of this world.	2848

STANDING (154) [STAND]

Ge	18: 2	looked up and saw three men s nearby.	5893
	18:22	Abraham remained s before the LORD.	6641
	24:13	See, *I am* s beside this spring,	5893
	24:30	the man and found *him* s by the camels near	6641
	24:31	"Why *are you* s out here?	6641
	24:43	See, *I am* s beside this spring;	5893
	41: 1	*He was* s by the Nile,	6641
	41:17	"In my dream *I was* s on the bank of	6641
Ex	3: 5	the place where *you are* s is holy ground."	6641
	22: 6	so that it burns shocks of grain or s **grain** or	7850
	26:32	of acacia wood overlaid with gold and s	NIH
	33:10	the people saw the pillar of cloud s at	6641
Nu	16:27	and Abiram had come out and *were* s	5893
	22:23	the angel of the LORD s in the road with	5893
	22:31	and he saw the angel of the LORD s in	5893
	22:34	I did not realize *you were* s in the road	5893
	23: 6	to him and found *him* s beside his offering,	5893
	23:17	to him and found *him* s beside his offering,	5893
	32:14	s in the place of your fathers and making	7756
Dt	16: 9	to put the sickle to the s **grain.**	7850
	23:25	but you must not put a sickle to his s **grain.**	7850
	29:10	All of you are s here in the presence of	5893
	29:12	You are s here in order to enter into	NIH
	29:15	who are s here with us today in	6641
Jos	4:10	the priests who carried the ark *remained* s in	6641
	5:13	a man s in front of him with a drawn sword	6641
	5:15	for the place where *you are* s is holy."	6641

Ex	8:33	were s on both sides of the ark of	6641
	20: 9	by the avenger of blood prior *to* s **trial**	6641
Jdg	9:35	of Ebed had gone out and *was* s at	6641
	15: 5	and let the foxes loose in the s **grain** *of*	7850
	15: 5	He burned up the shocks and s **grain,**	7850
Ru	2: 1	from the clan of Elimelech, a man of s,	1475+2657
	2:13	not have the s *of* one of your servant girls."	3869
	4:11	May you have s in Ephrathah and	2657
1Sa	9: 1	There was a Benjamite, a man of s,	2657
	17:26	David asked the men s near him,	6641
	19:20	with Samuel s there as their leader,	6641
	22: 6	with all his officials s around him.	5893
	22: 9	who *was* s with Saul's officials, said,	5893
2Sa	13:34	Now the man s **watch** looked up	7595
1Ki	7:25	the whole assembly of Israel *was* s there,	6641
	10:19	with a lion beside each of them.	6641
	11:28	Now Jeroboam was a man of s,	1475+2657
	13: 1	as Jeroboam *was* by the altar to make	6641
	13:24	both the donkey and the lion s beside it.	6641
	13:25	with the lion s beside the body,	6641
	13:28	with the donkey and the lion s beside it.	6641
	22:19	the host of heaven s around him on his right	6641
2Ki	9:17	When the lookout s on the tower	6641
	11:14	s by the pillar, as the custom was.	6641
	11:14	the Asherah pole *remained* s in Samaria.	6641
1Ch	21:15	the LORD *was* then s at the threshing floor	6641
	21:16	of the LORD s between heaven and earth,	6641
2Ch	5: 7	the whole assembly of Israel *was* s there,	6641
	7: 6	and all the Israelites *were* s.	6641
	9:18	with a lion s beside each of them.	6641
	18:18	on his throne with all the host of heaven s	6641
	23:13	s by his pillar at the entrance.	6641
Ne	8: 5	the people could see him because *he was* s	2118
	8: 7	in the Law while the people *were* s there.	6642
	9: 4	S on the stairs were the Levites—	7756
Est	5: 2	When he saw Queen Esther s in the court,	6641
	6: 5	"Haman *is* s in the court."	6641
Ps	122: 2	Our feet are s in your gates, O Jerusalem.	6641
Isa	17: 5	a reaper gathers the s **grain** and harvests	7850
	27: 9	or incense altars *will be left* s.	7756
Jer	28: 5	the priests and all the people who *were* s in	6641
	36:21	and read it to the king and all the officials s	6641
La	3:63	Sitting or s, they mock me in their songs.	7800
Eze	3:23	And the glory of the LORD *was* s there,	6641
	8:11	and Jaazaniah son of Shaphan *was* s	6641
	10: 3	Now the cherubim *were* s on the south side	6641
	40: 3	he *was* s in the gateway with a linen cord	6641
	43: 6	While the man *was* s beside me,	6641
Da	7:16	I approached one of *those* s there	10624
	8: 3	s beside the canal, and the horns were long.	6641
	8: 6	toward the two-horned ram I had seen s	6641
	8:17	he came near the **place where** I *was* s,	6642
	10: 4	as I *was* s on the bank of the great river,	NIH
	10:16	I said to the *one* s before me,	6641
Am	7: 7	The Lord *was* s by a wall	5893
	9: 1	I saw the Lord s by the altar, and he said:	5893
Zec	1: 8	*He was* s among the myrtle trees in a ravine.	6641
	1:10	man s among the myrtle trees explained,	6641
	1:11	who *was* s among the myrtle trees,	6641
	3: 1	Then he showed me Joshua the high priest s	6641
	3: 1	and Satan s at his right side to accuse him.	6641
	3: 4	The angel said to those *who were* s	6641
	3: 7	I will give you a place among these s here.	6641
	6: 5	going out from s in the presence of the Lord	3656
	14:12	Their flesh will rot while they *are still* s	6641
Mt	6: 5	for they love to pray s in the synagogues	2705
	12:47	"Your mother and brothers *are* s outside,	2705
	16:28	some who are s here will not taste death	2705
	20: 3	the third hour he went out and saw others s	2705
	20: 6	and found still others s around.	2705
	20: 6	'Why *have you been* s here all day long	2705
	24:15	"So when you see s in the holy place	2705
	26:73	those s there went up to Peter and said,	2705
	27:47	When some of those s there heard this,	2705
Mk	3:31	S outside, they sent someone in to call him.	2705
	9: 1	some who are s here will not taste death	2705
	11: 5	some people s there asked,	2705
	13:14	'the abomination that causes desolation' s	2705
	14:47	of those s **near** drew his sword and struck	4225
	14:69	she said again to those s **around,**	4225
	14:70	those s **near** said to Peter,	4225
	15:35	When some of those s **near** heard this,	4225
Lk	1:11	s at the right side of the altar of incense.	2705
	5: 1	as Jesus *was* s by the Lake of Gennesaret,	2705
	8:20	"Your mother and brothers *are* s outside,	2705
	9:27	some who are s here will not taste death	2705
	9:32	they saw his glory and the two men s **with**	5319
	19:24	"Then he said *to* those s **by,**	4225
	21:19	By s **firm** you will gain life.	5705
	23:10	and the teachers of the law *were* s there,	2705
Jn	8: 9	with the woman *still* s there.	1639
	11:42	for the benefit of the people s **here,**	4325
	18: 5	the traitor *was* s there with them.)	2705
	18:18	Peter also *was* s with them,	2705
	19:26	and the disciple whom he loved s **nearby,**	4225
	20:14	she turned around and saw Jesus s there,	2705
Ac	4:14	the man who had been healed s there	2705
	5:23	with the guards s at the doors;	2705
	5:25	in jail are in the temple courts teaching	2705
	7:33	the place where *you are* s is holy ground.	2705
	7:55	and Jesus s at the right hand of God.	2705
	7:56	the Son of Man s at the right hand of God."	2705
	13:16	S **up,** Paul motioned with his hand	482
	13:50	of **high** s and the leading men of the city.	2363
	16: 9	man of Macedonia s and begging him,	1639+2705
	22:25	Paul said to the centurion s there,	2705
	23: 2	the high priest Ananias ordered those s **near**	4225

Ac	23: 4	Those who *were* s near Paul said,	4225
	25:10	"I am now s before Caesar's court,	2705
1Co	10:12	So, if you think *you are* s firm,	2705
1Th	3: 8	since you *are* s firm in the Lord.	2705
1Ti	3:13	an excellent s and great assurance	957
Heb	9: 8	as long as the first tabernacle was still s.	5087
Jas	5: 9	The Judge *is* s at the door!	2705
1Pe	5: 9	Resist him, s firm in the faith,	5104
Rev	4: 1	before me was a door s open in heaven.	487
	5: 6	s in the center of the throne,	2705
	7: 1	After this I saw four angels s at	2705
	7: 9	s before the throne and in front of	2705
	7:11	All the angels *were* s around the throne and	2705
	10: 5	Then the angel I had seen s on the sea and	2705
	10: 8	in the hand of the angel who *is* s on the sea	2705
	14: 1	s on Mount Zion, and with him 144,000	2705
	15: 2	s beside the sea, those who had been	2705
	19:11	I saw heaven s open and there before me	487
	19:17	And I saw an angel s in the sun,	2705
	20:12	s before the throne, and books were opened.	2705

STANDS (52) [STAND]

Nu	35:12	of murder may not die before he s trial	6641
Dt	17:12	or for the priest who s ministering there to	6641
Jos	22:19	where the LORD's tabernacle s,	8905
	22:29	the altar of the LORD our God that s	NIH
Jdg	6:24	To this day it s in Ophrah of the Abiezrites.	6388
1Sa	16: 6	"Surely the LORD's anointed s here	NIH
1Ki	7:27	He also made ten **movable** s of bronze;	4807
	7:28	This is how the s were made:	4807
	7:31	The panels of the s were square, not round.	2157S
	7:37	This is the way he made the ten s.	4807
	7:38	one basin to go on each of the ten s.	4807
	7:39	He placed five of the s on the south side of	4807
	7:43	the ten s with their ten basins;	4807
2Ki	16:17	the basins from the **movable** s.	4807
	25:13	the **movable** s and the bronze Sea that were	4807
	25:16	the Sea and the **movable** s,	4807
2Ch	4:14	the s with their basins;	4807
Est	7: 9	"A gallows seventy-five feet high s	6641
Job	9:35	but as it now s with me, I cannot.	NIH
	23:13	"But he s alone, and who can oppose him?	NIH
Ps	89: 2	I will declare that your love s firm forever,	1215
	109:31	For *he* s at the right hand of the needy one,	6641
	119:89	is eternal; it s firm in the heavens.	5893
Pr	12: 7	but the house of the righteous s firm.	6641
SS	2: 9	There *he* s behind our wall,	6641
Isa	27:10	The fortified city s desolate,	NIH
	32: 8	and by noble deeds he s.	7756
	40: 8	but the word of our God s forever."	7756
	46: 7	they set it up in its place, and there *it* s.	6641
	59:14	and righteousness s at a distance;	6641
	65: 6	"See, *it* s **written** before me:	AIT
Jer	27:19	the **movable** s and the other furnishings	4807
	52:17	the **movable** s and the bronze Sea that were	4807
	52:20	and the **movable** s, which King Solomon	4807
Da	6:12	The king answered, "The decree—	10327
Mt	10:22	but he who s **firm** to the end will be saved.	5702
	13:38	good seed s **for** the sons of the kingdom.	1639
	24:13	but he who s **firm** to the end will be saved.	5702
Mk	13:13	but he who s **firm** to the end will be saved.	5702
Lk	8:14	that fell among thorns s **for** those who hear,	1639
	8:15	But the seed on good soil s **for** those with	1639
Jn	1:26	"but among you s one you do not know.	2705
	3:18	does not believe s **condemned** already	AIT
	16:11	the prince of this world *now* s **condemned**.	AIT
Ac	4:10	that this man s before you healed.	4225
Ro	14: 4	To his own master *he* s or falls.	2705
Gal	4:25	Now Hagar s **for** Mount Sinai in Arabia	1639
2Ti	2:19	God's solid foundation s firm,	2705
Heb	4: 1	the promise of entering his rest *still* s,	2901
	10:11	Day after day every priest s	2705
1Pe	1:25	but the word of the Lord s forever."	3531
Rev	19: 8	(Fine linen s **for** the righteous acts of	1639

STANDSTILL (1)

Ezr	4:24	the house of God in Jerusalem **came to a** s	10098

STAR (17) [STARGAZERS, STARRY, STARS]

Nu	24:17	A s will come out of Jacob;	3919
Isa	14:12	you have fallen from heaven, O **morning** s,	2122
Am	5:26	pedestal of your idols, the s *of* your god—	3919
Mt	2: 2	We saw his s in the east and have come	843
	2: 7	the exact time the s had appeared.	843
	2: 9	the s they had seen in the east went ahead	843
	2:10	When they saw the s, they were overjoyed.	843
Ac	7:43	of Molech and the s of your god Rephan,	849
1Co	15:41	and s differs from star in splendor.	843
	15:41	and star differs *from* s in splendor.	843
2Pe	1:19	until the day dawns and the **morning** s rises	5892
Rev	2:28	I will also give him the morning s.	843
	8:10	and a great s, blazing like a torch,	843
	8:11	the name *of* the s is Wormwood.	843
	9: 1	and I saw a s that had fallen from the sky to	843
	9: 1	The s was given the key to the shaft of	899S
	22:16	and the bright Morning S."	843

STARE (4) [STARED, STARES]

Ps	22:17	people s and gloat over me.	5564
SS	1: 6	*Do not* s at me because I am dark,	8011
Isa	14:16	Those who see you s at you,	8708
Ac	3:12	Why *do you* s at us as if by our own power	867

STARED (3) [STARE]

2Ki	8:11	He s at him **with a fixed gaze** until Hazael felt ashamed.	906+2256+6641+7156+8492
Jn	13:22	His disciples s at one another,	1063
Ac	10: 4	Cornelius s at him in fear.	867

STARES (1) [STARE]

Ps	55: 3	voice of the enemy, at the s *of* the wicked;	6821

STARGAZERS (1) [STAR]

Isa	47:13	s who make predictions month	928+2600+3919

STARRY (15) [STAR]

2Ki	17:16	They bowed down to all the s hosts,	9028
	21: 3	down to all the s hosts and worshiped them.	9028
	21: 5	he built altars to all the s hosts.	9028
	23: 4	for Baal and Asherah and all the s hosts.	9028
	23: 5	to the constellations and to all the s hosts.	9028
2Ch	33: 3	down to all the s hosts and worshiped them.	9028
	33: 5	he built altars to all the s hosts.	9028
Ne	9: 6	and all their s host,	7372
Ps	33: 6	their s host by the breath of his mouth.	7372
Isa	34: 4	the s host will fall like withered leaves from	7372
	40:26	He who brings out the s host one by one,	7372
	45:12	I marshaled their s hosts.	7372
Jer	19:13	the s hosts and poured out drink offerings	9028
Da	8:10	of the s host down to the earth and trampled	3919
Zep	1: 5	down on the roofs to worship the s host,	9028

STARS (55) [STAR]

Ge	1:16	He also made the s.	3919
	15: 5	"Look up at the heavens and count the s—	3919
	22:17	as numerous as the s *in* the sky and as	3919
	26: 4	as numerous as the s *in* the sky	3919
	37: 9	and moon and eleven s were bowing down	3919
Ex	32:13	as numerous as the s *in* the sky	3919
Dt	1:10	so that today you are as many as the s *in*	3919
	4:19	the sun, the moon and the s—	3919
	10:22	as numerous as the s *in* the sky.	3919
	17: 3	to the sun or the moon or the s *of* the sky,	7372
	28:62	as numerous as the s *in* the sky will be left	3919
Jdg	5:20	From the heavens the s fought,	3919
1Ch	27:23	to make Israel as numerous as the s *in*	3919
Ne	4:21	the first light of dawn till the s came out.	3919
	9:23	You made their sons as numerous as the s	3919
Job	3: 9	May its morning s become dark;	3919
	9: 7	he seals off the light of the s.	3919
	22:12	And see how lofty are the highest s!	3919
	25: 5	not bright and the s are not pure in his eyes,	3919
	38: 7	while the morning s sang together and all	3919
Ps	8: 3	the moon and the s, which you have set in	3919
	136: 9	the moon and s to govern the night;	3919
	147: 4	the number of the s and calls them each	3919
	148: 3	praise him, all you shining s.	3919
Ecc	12: 2	the light and the moon and the s grow dark,	3919
SS	6:10	majestic as the s in procession?	NIH
Isa	13:10	The s *of* heaven and their constellations	3919
	14:13	I will raise my throne above the s *of* God;	3919
	34: 4	the s *of* the heavens will be dissolved and	7372
Jer	8: 2	and the moon and all the s *of* the heavens,	7372
	31:35	and s to shine by night, who stirs up the sea	3919
	33:22	before me as countless as the s *of* the sky	7372
Eze	32: 7	I will cover the heavens and darken their s;	3919
Da	12: 3	like the s for ever and ever.	3919
Joel	2:10	and the s no longer shine.	3919
	3:15	and the s no longer shine.	3919
Ob	1: 4	the eagle and make your nest among the s,	3919
Na	3:16	till they are more than the s *of* the sky,	3919
Mt	24:29	the s will fall from the sky,	843
Mk	13:25	the s will fall from the sky,	843
Lk	21:25	"There will be signs in the sun, moon and s.	843
Ac	27:20	nor s appeared for many days and	843
1Co	15:41	the moon another and the s another;	843
Php	2:15	in which you shine like s in the universe	5891
Heb	11:12	the s in the sky and as countless as the sand	843
Jude	1:13	wandering s, for whom the blackest darkness	843
Rev	1:16	In his right hand he held seven s,	843
	1:20	the seven s that you saw in my right hand	843
	1:20	The seven s are the angels of the seven	843
	2: 1	the words of him who holds the seven s	843
	3: 1	the seven spirits of God and the seven s.	843
	6:13	and the s in the sky fell to earth,	843
	8:12	a third of the moon, and a third *of* the s,	843
	12: 1	under her feet and a crown *of* twelve s	843
	12: 4	His tail swept a third *of* the s out of the sky	843

START (5) [STARTED, STARTING]

Nu	34: 3	your southern boundary *will* s from	2118
1Sa	9: 5	the donkeys and *s* **worrying** about us."	AIT
1Ki	20:14	"And who *will* s the battle?"	673
Ne	2:18	They replied, "*Let us* s rebuilding."	7756
	2:20	We his servants *will* s rebuilding.	7756

STARTED (23) [START]

Ge	33:16	So that day Esau s on his way **back** to Seir.	8740
Ex	4:20	put them on a donkey and s **back** to Egypt.	8740
	22: 6	the *one who* s the fire must make restitution.	1277
Nu	11: 4	and again the Israelites s **wailing** and said,	AIT
	16:46	from the LORD; the plague *has* s."	2725
	16:47	The plague had already s among the people,	2725
	22: 3	Then the two men s **back**.	8740
	15: 2	Their southern boundary s from the bay at	2118

Jos	15: 5	The northern boundary s from the bay	4200+6991
	18: 8	the men s on their way to map out the land,	7756
Est	6:13	before whom your downfall *has* s,	2725
Jer	37:12	Jeremiah *s to* **leave** the city to go to the	AIT
Da	8: 9	which s small but grew in power to	4946
Jnh	3: 4	On the first day, Jonah s into the city.	2725
Mk	10:17	As Jesus s on his way,	1744
Lk	9:46	An argument s among the disciples as	1656
	23: 5	*He* s in Galilee and has come all	806
Jn	8: 6	But Jesus bent down and *s to* **write** on	AIT
	20: 3	Peter and the other disciple s for the tomb.	2002
Ac	8:27	So *he* s **out,** and on his way he met an	4513
	10:23	The next day Peter s out with them,	482+2002
	17: 5	formed a mob and *s a* **riot** in the city.	AIT
	21:38	"Aren't you the Egyptian who *s a* **revolt**	AIT

STARTING (4) [START]

2Ki	15:16	At that time Menahem, s **out from** Tirzah,	4946
Pr	17:14	S a quarrel is like breaching a dam;	8040
Eze	21:19	both s from the same country.	3655
Mt	27:24	but that instead an uproar *was* s,	1181

STARTLE (1) [STARTLED]

Job	18:11	Terrors s him on every side	1286

STARTLED (3) [STARTLE]

Ru	3: 8	In the middle of the night *something* s	3006
Lk	1:12	he was s and was gripped with fear.	5429
	24:37	They were s and frightened,	4765

STARVATION (2) [STARVE]

Jer	15: 2	those for s, to starvation;	8280
	15: 2	those for starvation, to s;	8280

STARVE (2) [STARVATION, STARVING]

Ex	16: 3	into this desert to s this entire assembly	8280
Jer	38: 9	where he will s to death	8280

STARVING (5) [STARVE]

Ge	42:19	and take grain back for your s households.	8282
	42:33	and take food for your s households and go.	8282
2Ki	7: 4	They know we are s;	8281
Pr	6:30	to satisfy his hunger when *he is* s.	8279
Lk	15:17	and here I *am* s **to death!**	660+3350

STATE (7) [STATED, STATEMENT, STATEMENTS]

Jos	20: 4	the city gate and s his case before the elders	1819
Job	23: 4	*I would* s my case before him	6885
	33:26	he is restored by God to his **righteous** s.	7407
Isa	14:18	the kings of the nations **lie in** s,	928+3883+8886
	43:26	s the case for your innocence.	6218
Lk	1:48	for he has been mindful of the **humble** s	5428
Ac	24:20	are here *should* s what crime they found	3306

STATED (3) [STATE]

Ac	13:34	never to decay, *is* s in these words:	3306
	13:35	So *it is* s elsewhere: "You will not let your	3306
Ro	9: 9	For this was how the promise was s:	3364

STATELY (4)

Pr	30:29	*that are* s in their stride, four that move	3512
	30:29	four that move with s **bearing:**	3512
Isa	2:16	for every trading ship and every s vessel.	2775
Zec	11: 2	the s trees are ruined!	129

STATEMENT (2) [STATE]

Ac	20:38	What grieved them most was his s	3364
	28:25	leave *after* Paul *had* **made** this final s:	3306+4839

STATEMENTS (1) [STATE]

Mk	14:56	against him, but their s did not agree.	3456

STATION (4) [STATIONED]

2Ki	11: 8	S yourselves around the king,	5938
2Ch	23: 7	The Levites *are to* s **themselves** around	5938
Jer	51:12	Reinforce the guard, s the watchmen,	7756
Hab	2: 1	at my watch and s **myself** on the ramparts;	3656

STATIONED (16) [STATION]

Jdg	20:22	where *they had* s **themselves** the first day.	6885
2Ki	3:21	who could bear arms was called up and s on	6641
	11:11	s *themselves* around the king—	6641
1Ch	9: 18	being s **at** the King's Gate on the east,	928
	9:27	They would spend the night s **around**	6017
	16:42	The sons of Jeduthun were s **at** the gate.	4200
2Ch	17: 2	*He* s troops in all the fortified cities of Judah	5989
	17:19	besides those he s in the fortified cities	5989
	23:10	*He* s all the men, each with his weapon	6641
	23:19	*He* also s doorkeepers at the gates of	6641
	29:25	*He* s the Levites in the temple of the LORD	6641
	33:14	*He* s military commanders in all	8492
Ne	4:13	Therefore *I* s some of the people behind	6641
	13:11	Then I called them together and s them	6641
	13:19	I s some of my own men at the gates so	6641
Eze	21:15	*I have* s the sword for slaughter	5989

STATUE (5)

Da	2:31	O king, and there before you stood a large s	10614
	2:31	an enormous, dazzling s,	10614
	2:32	The head of the s was made of pure gold,	10614
	2:34	It struck the s on its feet of iron and clay	10614
	2:35	that struck the s became a huge mountain	10614

STATURE (3)

1Sa	2:26	And the boy Samuel continued to grow in s	1541
SS	7: 7	Your s is like that of the palm,	7757
Lk	2:52	And Jesus grew in wisdom and s,	2461

STATUTE (3) [STATUTES]

1Sa	30:25	David made this a s and ordinance for Israel	2976
Ps	81: 5	as a s for Joseph when he went out	6343
	122: 4	according to the s given to Israel.	6343

STATUTES (39) [STATUTE]

1Ki	3: 3	the LORD by walking according to the s	2978
	3:14	And if you walk in my ways and obey my s	2976
	11:33	nor kept my s and laws as David,	2978
	11:34	who observed my commands and s.	2978
	11:38	by keeping my s and commands,	2978
Ps	19: 7	The s of the LORD are trustworthy,	6343
	78: 5	He decreed s for Jacob and established	6343
	78:56	they did not keep his s.	6343
	89:30	and do not follow my s,	5477
	93: 5	Your s stand firm;	6343
	99: 7	they kept his s and the decrees he gave them	6343
	119: 2	Blessed are they who keep his s	6343
	119:14	I rejoice in following your s as one rejoices	6343
	119:22	for I keep your s.	6343
	119:24	Your s are my delight;	6343
	119:31	I hold fast to your s, O LORD;	6343
	119:36	toward your s and not toward selfish gain.	6343
	119:46	I will speak of your s before kings and will	6343
	119:59	and have turned my steps to your s.	6343
	119:79	those who understand your s.	6343
	119:88	and I will obey the s of your mouth.	6343
	119:95	but I will ponder your s.	6343
	119:99	for I meditate on your s.	6343
	119:111	Your s are my heritage forever;	6343
	119:119	therefore I love your s.	6343
	119:125	that I may understand your s.	6343
	119:129	Your s are wonderful;	6343
	119:138	The s you have laid down are righteous;	6343
	119:144	Your s are forever right;	6343
	119:146	save me and I will keep your s.	6343
	119:152	from your s that you established them	6343
	119:157	but I have not turned from your s.	6343
	119:167	I obey your s, for I love them greatly,	6343
	119:168	I obey your precepts and your s,	6343
	132:12	and the s I teach them,	6343
Isa	24: 5	they have disobeyed the laws, violated the s	2976
Eze	20:18	the s of your fathers or keep their laws	2976
	20:25	also gave them over to s that were not good	2976
Mic	6:16	You have observed the s of Omri and all	2978

STAVES (KJV) See CLUBS, POLES, SPEAR, STAFF, STAFFS, STICKS

STAY (127) [STAYED, STAYING, STAYS]

Ge	13: 6	that they were not able to s together.	3782
	19:30	for he was afraid to s in Zoar.	3782
	22: 5	"S here with the donkey while I and	3782
	26: 3	S in this land for a while,	1591
	27:44	S with him for a while	3782
	29:19	S here with me."	3782
	30:27	found favor in your eyes, please s.	NIH
	38: 1	Judah left his brothers and went down to s	5742
	42:19	let one of your brothers s here in prison,	673
Ex	2:21	Moses agreed to s with the man,	3782
	9:28	you don't have to s any longer."	6641
	16:29	to s where he is on the seventh day;	3782
	22:30	Let them s with their mothers	2118
	24:12	up to me on the mountain and s here,	2118
	33: 9	the pillar of cloud would come down and s	6641
Lev	8:35	You must s at the entrance to the Tent	3782
	14: 8	he must s outside his tent for seven days.	3782
Nu	22:19	Now s here tonight as the others did,	3782
	23: 3	"S here beside your offering while I go	3656
	23:15	"S here beside your offering while I meet	3656
	31:19	touched anyone who was killed must s	2837
		outside the camp	
	35:25	He must s there until the death of	3782
	35:28	The accused must s in his city of refuge	3782
Dt	2:27	We will s on the main road;	2143
	3:19	your livestock (I know you have much	
		livestock) may s	3782
	5:31	But you s here with me so	6641
	23:10	he is to go outside the camp and s away.	995+4202
	24: 5	be free to s at home and bring happiness to	NIH
	24:11	S outside and let the man	6641
Jos	1:14	your children and your livestock may s in	3782
	4: 3	down at the place where you s tonight."	4328
	7: 7	to s on the other side of the Jordan!	3782
	20: 6	to s in that city until he has stood trial	3782
Jdg	5:16	Why did you s among the campfires to hear	3782
	13:15	"We would like you to s until we prepare	6806
	17: 8	that town in search of some other place to s.	1591
	17: 9	he said, "and I'm looking for a place to s."	1591
	19: 4	the girl's father, prevailed upon him to s;	NIH
	19: 6	"Please s tonight and enjoy yourself."	4328
Jdg	19: 9	S and enjoy yourself.	4328
	19:10	But, unwilling to s another night,	4328
Ru	1:16	and where you s I will stay.	4328
	1:16	and where you stay I will s.	4328
	2: 8	S here with my servant girls.	1815
	2:21	'S with my workers	1815
	3:13	S here for the night,	4328
1Sa	1:23	"S here until you have weaned him;	3782
	5: 7	of the god of Israel must not s here with us,	3782
	9:27	"but you s here awhile,	6641
	14: 9	we will s where we are and not go up	6641
	19: 2	go into hiding and s there.	2461
	22: 3	and mother come and s with you	NIH
	22: 5	"Do not s in the stronghold.	3782
	22:23	S with me; don't be afraid;	3782
2Sa	10: 5	"S at Jericho till your beards have grown,	3782
	11:12	David said to him, "S here one more day,	3782
	15:19	Go back and s with King Absalom.	3782
	19:32	He had provided for the king during his s	8859
	19:33	over with me and s with me in Jerusalem,	NIH
1Ki	17: 9	at once to Zarephath of Sidon and s there.	3782
2Ki	2: 2	Elijah said to Elisha, "S here;	3782
	2: 4	Then Elijah said to him, "S here, Elisha;	3782
	2: 6	Then Elijah said to him, "S here;	3782
	4: 8	who urged him to s for a meal.	430+4312
	4:10	he can s there whenever he comes to us."	6073
	7: 3	"Why s here until we die?	3782
	7: 4	And if we stay, we will die.	3782
	8: 1	and s for a while wherever you can,	1591
	11: 8	S close to the king wherever he goes."	2118
	14:10	Glory in your victory, but s at home!	3782
	19:27	where you s and when you come and go and	3782
1Ch	19: 5	"S at Jericho till your beards have grown,	3782
2Ch	23: 7	S close to the king wherever he goes."	2118
	25:19	But s at home!	3782
Ezr	6: 6	s away from there.	10201
Ne	4:22	s inside Jerusalem at night,	4328
	5: 2	in order for us to eat and s alive,	2649
	10:39	the gatekeepers and the singers s.	NIH
	11: 1	while the remaining nine were to s	NIH
Job	24:13	who do not know its ways or s in its paths.	3782
	39: 9	s by your manger at night?	4328
Ps	38:11	my neighbors s far away.	6641
	55: 7	I would flee far away and s in the desert;	4328
	92:14	they will s fresh and green,	2118
	119:148	My eyes s open through the watches of	7709
	127: 2	In vain you rise early and s up late,	3782
Pr	7:11	her feet never s at home;	8905
	14: 7	S away from a foolish man,	2143
	20:13	s awake and you will have food	6524+7219
Isa	5:11	who s up late at night till they are inflamed	336
	16: 4	Let the Moabite fugitives s with you;	1591
	21: 8	every night I s at my post.	5893
	37:28	where you s and when you come and go and	3782
Jer	25: 5	and you can s in the land the LORD gave	3782
	40:10	I myself will s at Mizpah to represent you	3782
	42:10	'If you s in this land, I will build you	3782+3782
	42:13	if you say, 'We will not s in this land,'	3782
	43: 4	the LORD's command to s in the land	3782
	49:30	S in deep caves, you who live in Hazor,"	3782
La	4:15	"They can s here no longer."	1591
Mic	7:18	You do not s angry forever but delight	2616
Mt	2:13	S there until I tell you,	1639
	10:11	search for some worthy person there and s	3531
	17:17	"how long shall I s with you?	1639
	26:38	S here and keep watch with me."	3531
Mk	6:10	s there until you leave that town.	3531
	9:19	"how long shall I s with you?	1639
	14:34	"S here and keep watch."	3531
Lk	9: 4	s there until you leave that town.	3531
	9:41	"how long shall I s with you and put up	1639
	10: 7	S in that house, eating and drinking	3531
	19: 5	I must s at your house today."	3531
	24:29	But they urged him strongly, "S with us,	3531
	24:29	So he went in to s with them.	3531
	24:49	but s in the city until you have been clothed	2767
Jn	4:40	they urged him to s with them,	3531
	12:46	so that no one who believes in me should s	3531
Ac	8:29	"Go to that chariot and s near it."	3140
	10:48	Then they asked Peter to s with them for	2152
	13:17	the people prosper during their s in Egypt,	4229
	16:15	said, "come and s at my house."	3531
	21:16	home of Mnason, where we were to s.	3826
	27:31	"Unless these men s with the ship,	3531
1Co	7: 8	It is good for them to s unmarried, as I am.	3531
	16: 6	Perhaps I will s with you awhile,	4169
	16: 8	But I will s on at Ephesus until Pentecost,	2152
1Ti	1: 3	s there in Ephesus so that you may	4693

STAYED (94) [STAY]

Ge	13: 6	not support them while they s together,	3782
	20: 1	For a while he s in Gerar,	1591
	21:34	And Abraham s in the land of the Philistines	1591
	22:19	And Abraham s in Beersheba.	3782
	26: 6	So Isaac s in Gerar.	3782
	29:14	After Jacob had s with him for	3782
	35:27	Hebron), where Abraham and Isaac had s.	1591
	37: 1	in the land where his father had s,	4472
	49:24	his strong arms s limber,	AIT
	50:22	Joseph s in Egypt, along with all his	3782
Ex	20:18	They s at a distance	6641
	24:18	and s on the mountain forty days	2118
Nu	9:18	As long as the cloud s over the tabernacle,	8905
	9:21	the cloud s only from evening till morning,	2118
	9:22	cloud s over the tabernacle for two days	799+8905
	11:35	the people traveled to Hazeroth and s there.	2118

STAYING (24) [STAY]

Ge	25:27	Jacob was a quiet man, s among the tents.	3782
	32: 4	'Your servant Jacob says, I have been s	1591
	36: 7	where they were s could not support them	4472
Nu	25: 1	While Israel was s in Shittim,	3782
Jdg	19:26	to the house where her master was s,	NIH
1Sa	13:16	with them were s in Gibeah in Benjamin,	3782
	14: 2	Saul was s on the outskirts of Gibeah under	3782
2Sa	11:11	"The ark and Israel and Judah are s in tents,	3782
	16: 3	Ziba said to him, "He is s in Jerusalem,	3782
	17:17	Jonathan and Ahimaaz were s at En Rogel,	6641
1Ki	17:19	to the upper room where he was s,	3782
	17:20	also upon this widow I am s with,	1591
2Ki	2:18	who was s in Jericho, he said to them,	3782
Ne	2:11	to Jerusalem, and after s there three days	2118
Mt	24:48	'My master is s away a long time,'	5988
Jn	1:38	(which means Teacher), "where are you s?"	3531
	1:39	So they went and saw where he was s,	3531
	7: 1	purposely s away from Judea	1877+4024+4344
Ac	1:13	to the room where they were s.	2910
	2: 5	Now there were s in Jerusalem	2997
	10: 6	He is s with Simon the tanner,	3826
	10:18	Simon who was known as Peter was s there.	3826
	11:11	stopped at the house where I was s.	NIG
	28:23	larger numbers to the place where he was s.	3825

Nu	20: 1	and they s at Kadesh.	3782
	22: 8	So the Moabite princes s with him.	3782
Dt	1: 6	"You have s long enough at this mountain.	3782
	1:46	And so you s in Kadesh many days—	3782
	3:29	So we s in the valley near Beth Peor.	3782
	9: 9	I s on the mountain forty days	3782
	10:10	Now I had s on the mountain forty days	6641
Jos	2: 1	of a prostitute named Rahab and s there.	8886
	2:22	into the hills and s there three days,	3782
Jdg	5:17	Gilead s beyond the Jordan.	8905
	5:17	Asher remained on the coast and s	8905
	9:41	Abimelech s in Arumah,	3782
	11:17	So Israel s at Kadesh.	3782
	15: 8	down and s in a cave in the rock of Etam.	3782
	19: 7	so he s there that night.	2256+3782+4328
	20:47	where they s four months.	3782
Ru	2:23	So Ruth s close to the servant girls of Boaz	1815
1Sa	1:23	So the woman s at home and nursed her son	3782
	19:18	he and Samuel went to Naioth and s there.	3782
	22: 4	and they s with him as long as David was in	3782
	23:14	David s in the desert strongholds and in	3782
	23:25	to the rock and s in the Desert of Maon.	3782
	25:13	while two hundred s with the supplies.	3782
	26: 3	but David s in the desert.	3782
	30: 9	Besor Ravine, where some s behind,	6641
	30:24	of the man who s with the supplies is to be	3782
2Sa	1: 1	the Amalekites and s in Ziklag two days.	3782
	13:38	went to Geshur, he s there three years.	2118
	15:29	of God back to Jerusalem and s there.	3782
	20: 2	the men of Judah s by their king all the way	1815
1Ki	2:38	And Shimei s in Jerusalem for a long time.	3782
	11:16	and all the Israelites s there for six months,	3782
	11:40	and s there until Solomon's death.	2118
	17: 5	east of the Jordan, and s there.	3782
2Ki	8: 2	and her family went away and s in the land	1591
	10:21	of Baal came; not one s away.	995+4202
	15:20	So the king of Assyria withdrew and s in	6641
	19:36	He returned to Nineveh and s there.	3782
1Ch	9:33	s in the rooms of the temple	NIH
Ne	4:18	man who sounded the trumpet s with me.	NIH
Est	7: 3	s behind to beg Queen Esther for his life.	6641
Ecc	2: 9	In all this my wisdom s with me.	6641
Isa	37:37	He returned to Nineveh and s there.	3782
Jer	40: 6	to Gedaliah son of Ahikam at Mizpah and s	3782
Mt	2:15	where he s until the death of Herod.	1639
Mk	1:45	but s outside in lonely places.	1639
Lk	1:21	and wondering why he s so long in	5988
	1:56	Mary s with Elizabeth for about three	3531
	2:43	the boy Jesus s behind in Jerusalem,	5702
	24:53	And they s continually at the temple,	1639
Jn	4:40	There they s for a few days.	3531
	4:40	and he s two days.	1695+3531
	6:22	the crowd that had s on the opposite shore	2705
	7: 9	Having said this, he s in Galilee.	3531
	10:40	in the early days. Here he s	3531
	11: 6	he s where he was two more days.	3531
	11:20	but Mary s at home.	2757
	11:54	where he s with his disciples.	3531
Ac	9:28	So Saul s with them and moved	1639
	9:43	Peter s in Joppa for some time with	3531
	12:19	from Judea to Caesarea and s there a while.	1417
	14:28	they s there a long time with the disciples.	1417
	16:12	And we s there several days.	1417
	17: 14	but Silas and Timothy s at Berea.	5702
	18: 3	he s and worked with them.	3531
	18:11	So Paul s for a year and a half,	2767
	18:18	Paul s on in Corinth for some time.	4693
	19:22	he s in the province of Asia a little longer.	2091+5989
	20: 3	where he s three months.	4472
	20: 6	Troas, where we s seven days.	1417
	21: 4	we s with them seven days.	2152
	21: 7	the brothers and s with them for a day.	3531
	21: 8	and s at the house of Philip the evangelist,	3531
	28:12	in at Syracuse and s three days.	2152
	28:30	For two whole years Paul s there in	1844
Gal	1:18	with Peter and s with him fifteen days.	2152
2Ti	4:20	Erastus s in Corinth,	3531

STAYS (8) [STAY]

Nu	14:14	that your cloud s over them,	6641
Job	39:28	He dwells on a cliff and s there **at night;**	4328
Pr	22: 5	he who guards his soul s far from them.	8178
Jer	14: 8	like a traveler *who* s **only a night?**	4328+5742
	21: 9	Whoever s in this city will die by	3782
	38: 2	'Whoever s in this city will die by	3782
1Co	7:40	she is happier if *she* s as she is—	3531
Rev	16:15	Blessed is he who s **awake**	1213

STEAD (1) [INSTEAD]

Isa	43: 3	Cush and Seba **in** your s.	9393

STEADFAST (9) [STEADFASTLY]

Ps	51:10	O God, and renew a s spirit within me.	3922
	57: 7	My heart *is* s, O God;	3922
	57: 7	my heart *is* s; I will sing and make music.	3922
	108: 1	My heart *is* s, O God,	3922
	111: 8	*They are* s for ever and ever,	6164
	112: 7	his heart *is* s, trusting in the LORD.	3922
	119: 5	my ways *were* s in obeying your decrees!	3922
Isa	26: 3	in perfect peace him whose mind *is* s,	6164
1Pe	5:10	and make you strong, firm and s.	2530

STEADFASTLY (1) [STEADFAST]

2Ch	27: 6	Jotham grew powerful because he walked s	3922

STEADILY (3) [STEADY]

Ge	8: 3	The water **receded** s from the earth.	
			2143+2256+8740+8740
Ru	2: 7	and *has* **worked** s from morning till now,	AIT
2Co	3: 7	the Israelites could not **look** s at the face	867

STEADY (4) [STEADILY]

Ge	49:24	But his bow remained s,	419
Ex	17:12	so that his hands remained s till sunset.	575
1Ch	13: 9	Uzzah reached out his hand to s the ark,	296
Isa	35: 3	s the knees that give way;	599

STEAL (25) [STEALING, STEALS, STOLE, STOLEN]

Ge	31:30	But why *did you* s my gods?"	1704
	44: 8	So why *would we* s silver or gold	1704
Ex	20:15	"You shall not s.	1704
Lev	19:11	" 'Do not s.	1704
Dt	5:19	"You shall not s.	1704
2Sa	19: 3	that day as men s in who are ashamed	1704
	19:41	s the king **away** and bring him	1704
Ps	69: 4	I am forced to restore what *I did* not s.	1608
	104:22	The sun rises, and *they* s **away;**	665
Pr	30: 9	Or I may become poor and s,	1704
Jer	7: 9	" 'Will you s and murder,	1704
	23:30	"I am against the prophets *who* s	1704
	49: 9	not s only as much as they wanted?	8845
Ob	1: 5	not s only as much as they wanted?	1704
Mt	6:19	and where thieves break in and s,	3096
	6:20	and where thieves do not break in and s.	3096
	19:18	*do not* s, do not give false testimony,	3096
	27:64	his disciples may come and s the body	3096
Mk	10:19	*do not* s, do not give false testimony,	3096
Lk	18:20	*do not* s, do not give false testimony,	3096
Jn	10:10	thief comes only to s and kill and destroy;	3096
Ro	2:21	against stealing, *do you* s?	3096
	13: 9	"Do not murder," "Do not s,"	3096
Eph	4:28	He who has been stealing *must* s no longer,	3096
Tit	2:10	and not to s from them,	3802

STEALING (3) [STEAL]

Hos	4: 2	lying and murder, s and adultery;	1704
Ro	2:21	You who preach against s, do you steal?	3096
Eph	4:28	He who *has been* s must steal no longer,	3096

STEALS (3) [STEAL]

Ex	22: 1	a man s an ox or a sheep and slaughters it	1704
Job	24:14	in the night *he* s forth like a thief.	2118
Pr	6:30	a thief if *he* s to satisfy his hunger.	1704

STEALTH (KJV) See STOLE

STEDFAST (KJV) See ENDURES, FAITHFUL, FIRM, FIRMLY, SECURE

STEEDS (3)

Jdg	5:22	galloping, galloping go his mighty s.	NIH
Jer	46: 4	Harness the horses, mount the s!	7304
	47: 3	at the sound of the hoofs of galloping s,	52

STEEL (KJV) See BRONZE

STEEP (4) [STEEPED]

Isa	7:19	in the s ravines and in the crevices in	1431
Mt	8:32	the whole herd rushed down the s **bank into**	3204
Mk	5:13	the s **bank** into the lake and were drowned.	3204
Lk	8:33	the s **bank** into the lake and was drowned.	3204

STEEPED (1) [STEEP]

Jn	9:34	"You were s in sin at birth;	3910

STEERED (1)

Jas	3: 4	*they are* s by a very small rudder wherever	3555

STEM (KJV) See STUMP

STENCH (10) [STINK]

Ge	34:30	on me by **making** me a s to the Canaanites	944
Ex	5:21	You have **made** us a s to Pharaoh	944+8194
1Sa	13: 4	Israel *has* become a s to the Philistines."	944
2Sa	10: 6	that *they had* become a s in David's nostrils,	944
	16:21	that *you have* **made yourself a** s	944
1Ch	19: 6	that *they had* become a s in David's nostrils,	944
Isa	3:24	Instead of fragrance there will be a s;	5215
	34: 3	their dead bodies will send up a s;	945
Joel	2:20	And its s will go up; its smell will rise."	945
Am	4:10	I filled your nostrils with the s	945

STEP (14) [FOOTSTEPS, OVERSTEP, STEPPED, STEPPING, STEPS]

Dt	21: 5	the sons of Levi, *shall* s **forward,**	5602
1Sa	5: 5	at Ashdod s on the threshold.	2005
	20: 3	there is only a s between me and death."	7315
1Ki	10:20	one at either end of each s.	NIH
2Ch	9:19	one at either end of each s.	NIH
Job	18: 7	The vigor of his s is weakened;	7576
	18:11	on every side and dog his *every* s.	8079
	31: 4	not see my ways and count my every s?	7576
	31:37	an account of my *every* s;	7576
	34:21	he sees their *every* s.	7576
Ps	89:51	with which they have mocked *every* s	6811
La	4:18	Men stalked us at *every* s,	7576
Eze	26:16	of the coast *will* s **down** from their thrones	3718
Gal	5:25	*let us* **keep in** s with the Spirit.	5123

STEPHANAS (3)

1Co	1:16	(Yes, I also baptized the household *of* S;	5107
	16:15	the household *of* S were the first converts	5107
	16:17	I was glad when S, Fortunatus and	5107

STEPHEN (11)

Ac	6: 5	They chose S, a man full of faith and of	5108
	6: 8	Now S, a man full of God's grace	5108
	6: 9	These men began to argue with S,	5108
	6:11	"We have heard S speak words	899S
	6:12	They seized S and brought him before	899S
	6:15	in the Sanhedrin looked intently at S,	899S
	7:55	But S, full of the Holy Spirit,	NIG
	7:59	While they were stoning him, S prayed,	NIG
	8: 2	Godly men buried S and mourned deeply	5108
	11:19	in connection with S traveled as far	5108
	22:20	when the blood of your martyr S was shed,	5108

STEPPED (14) [STEP]

Lev	9:22	and the fellowship offering, *he* s **down.**	3718
Nu	12: 5	When both of them s **forward,**	3655
Jdg	8:21	So Gideon s **forward** and killed them,	7756
	9:27	the house and s **out** to continue on his way,	3655
1Sa	17:23	s **out** from his lines	6590
2Sa	2:23	So he s **aside** and stood there.	6015
	20: 8	he s **forward,** it dropped out of its sheath.	3655
1Ki	14:17	as she s over the threshold of the house,	995
	18:36	the prophet Elijah s **forward** and prayed:	5602
Job	29: 8	the young men saw me and s **aside**	2461
Jer	26:17	of the elders of the land s **forward** and said	7756
Mt	9: 1	Jesus s into a boat, crossed over	1832
	26:50	Then the *men* s **forward,** seized Jesus	4665
Lk	8:27	*When* Jesus s ashore, he was met by	2002

STEPPING (2) [STEP]

Pr	7:22	like a deer s into a noose	NIH
Zep	1: 9	On that day I will punish all who **avoid** s	1925

STEPS (47) [STEP]

Ex	20:26	And do not go up to my altar on s,	5092
2Sa	6:13	the ark of the LORD *had* **taken** six s,	7575+7576
1Ki	10:19	The throne had six s,	5092
	10:20	Twelve lions stood on the six s,	5092
2Ki	9:13	and spread them under him on the bare s.	5092
	20: 9	Shall the shadow go forward ten s,	5092
	20: 9	or shall it go back ten s?"	5092
	20:10	for the shadow to go forward ten s,"	5092
	20:10	"Rather, have it go back ten s."	5092
	20:11	the ten s it had gone down on the stairway	5092
2Ch	9:11	The king used the algumwood to make s for	5019
	9:18	The throne had six s,	5092
	9:19	Twelve lions stood on the six s,	5092
Ne	3:15	as the s going down from the City of David.	5092
	12:37	up the s of the City of David on the ascent	5092
Job	14:16	then you will count my s but not keep track	7576
	23:11	My feet have closely followed his s;	892
	31: 7	if my s have turned from the path,	892
Ps	17: 5	My s have held to your paths;	892
	37:23	he makes his s firm;	5202
	56: 6	They conspire, they lurk, they watch my s,	6811
	74: 3	Turn your s toward these everlasting ruins,	7193
	85:13	before him and prepares the way for his s.	7193
	119:59	and have turned my s to your statutes.	8079
Pr	4:12	you walk, your s will not be hampered;	7576
	5: 5	her s lead straight to the grave.	7576
	14:15	but a prudent man gives thought to his s.	892
	16: 9	but the LORD determines his s.	7576

Pr	20:24	A man's s are directed by the LORD.	5202
Ecc	5: 1	Guard your s when you go to the house	8079
Isa	3:16	**tripping along with mincing** s,	2143+2256+3262
	38: 8	shadow cast by the sun go back the ten s	5092
	38: 8	went back the ten s it had gone down.	5092
Jer	10:23	it is not for man to direct his s.	7576
Eze	40: 6	He climbed its s and measured	5092
	40:22	Seven s led up to it,	5092
	40:26	Seven s led up to it.	5092
	40:31	and eight s led up to it.	5092
	40:34	and eight s led up to it.	5092
	40:37	and eight s led up to it.	5092
	40:40	near the s at the entrance to	6590
	40:40	on the other side of the s were two tables.	NIH
	43:17	The s of the altar face east."	5092
Hab	3: 5	pestilence followed his s.	8079
Ac	21:35	When Paul reached the s,	325
	21:40	stood on the s and motioned to the crowd.	325
1Pe	2:21	that you should follow *in* his s.	2717

STERILE (2)

Jdg	13: 2	a wife who was s and remained childless.	6829
	13: 3	"You are s and childless,	6829

STERN (4) [STERNLY, STERN-FACED, STERNNESS]

Pr	15:10	S discipline awaits him who leaves	8273
Mk	4:38	Jesus was in the s, sleeping on a cushion.	4744
Ac	27:29	they dropped four anchors from the s	4744
	27:41	the s was broken to pieces by the pounding	4744

STERN-FACED (1) [STERN, FACE]

Da	8:23	s king, a master of intrigue, will arise.	6434+7156

STERNLY (3) [STERN]

Mt	9:30	Jesus **warned** them s, "See that no one	1839
Mk	1:25	**said** Jesus s. "Come out of him!"	2203
Lk	4:35	Jesus **said** s. "Come out of him!"	2203

STERNNESS (2) [STERN]

Ro	11:22	Consider therefore the kindness and s	704
	11:22	s to those who fell, but kindness to you,	704

STEW (7)

Ge	25:29	Once when Jacob was cooking *some* s,	5686
	25:30	"Quick, let me have some of that **red** s!"	AIT
	25:34	some bread and *some* lentil s.	5686
2Ki	4:38	"Put on the large pot and cook *some* s	5686
	4:39	he cut them up into the pot of s,	5686
	4:40	The s was poured out for the men,	5686
Hag	2:12	and that fold touches some bread or s,	5686

STEWARD (9) [STEWARDS]

Ge	43:16	he said to **the** s *of* his house,	889+6584S
	43:19	So they went up to Joseph's s and spoke	
			408+889+1074+2021+6584S
	43:24	The s took the men into Joseph's house,	408S
	44: 1	Joseph gave these instructions to the s	889+6584S
	44: 4	city when Joseph said to his s,	889+1074+6584S
	44:12	Then the s proceeded to search,	NIH
2Sa	16: 1	there was Ziba, the s *of* Mephibosheth,	5853
	19:17	along with Ziba, the s *of* Saul's household,	5853
Isa	22:15	"Go, say to this s, to Shebna,	6125

STEWARDS (1) [STEWARD]

Est	1: 8	for the king instructed all the **wine** s	1074+8042

STICK (21) [STICKING, STICKS, STUCK]

2Ki	6: 6	Elisha cut a s and threw it there,	6770
Job	33:21	and his bones, once hidden, now s **out.**	9142
	38:38	and the clods of earth s **together?**	1815
Isa	28:27	and cummin with a s.	8657
	57: 4	and s **out** your tongue?	799
La	4: 8	it has become as dry as a s.	6770
Eze	3:26	*I will* **make** your tongue s to the roof	1815
	21:10	The sword despises every such s.	6770
	29: 4	**make** the fish of your streams s	1815
	37:16	take a s *of* **wood** and write on it,	6770
	37:16	Then take another s *of* **wood,**	6770
	37:16	and write on it, 'Ephraim's s,	6770
	37:17	into one s so that they will become one	6770
	37:19	I am going to take the s *of* Joseph—	6770
	37:19	and join it to Judah's s,	6770
	37:19	making them a single s *of* **wood,**	6770
Hos	4:12	and are answered by a s *of* **wood.**	5234
Am	4:11	You were like a **burning** s snatched from	202
Zec	3: 2	Is not this man a **burning** s snatched from	202
Mt	27:48	He filled it with wine vinegar, put it on a s,	2812
Mk	15:36	put it on a s, and offered it to Jesus	2812

STICKING (1) [STICK]

Eze	29: 4	with all the fish s to your scales.	1815

STICKS (8) [STICK]

1Sa	17:43	"Am I a dog, that you come at me with s?"	5234
1Ki	17:10	a widow was there gathering s.	6770
	17:12	a few to take home and make a meal	6770
Ps	22:15	and my tongue s *to* the roof of my mouth;	1815
Pr	18:24	but there is a friend *who* s closer than	1816

La	4: 4	Because of thirst the infant's tongue s to	1815
Eze	37:20	before their eyes the s you have written on	6770
Lk	10:11	of your town that s to our feet we wipe off	3140

STIFF-NECKED (19) [NECK]

Ex	32: 9	"and they are a s people.	6902+7997
	33: 3	a s people and I might destroy you on	6902+7997
	33: 5	Tell the Israelites, 'You are a s people.	6902+7997
	34: 9	Although this is a s people,	6902+7997
Dt	9: 6	for you are a s people.	6902+7997
	9:13	and they are a s people indeed!	6902+7997
	10:16	therefore, and *do not be* s any longer.	6902+7996
	31:27	I know how rebellious and s you are.	6902+7997
2Ki	17:14	they would not listen and *were as* s	6902+7996
2Ch	30: 8	*Do not be* s, as your fathers were;	6902+7996
	36:13	He *became* s and hardened his heart	6902+7996
Ne	9:16	forefathers, became arrogant and s,	6902+7996
	9:17	*They became* s and	6902+7996
	9:29	*became* s and refused to listen.	6902+7996
Pr	29: 1	A man *who remains* s	6902+7996
Jer	7:26	*They were* s and did more evil than	6902+7996
	17:23	*they were* s and would not listen or	6902+7996
	19:15	*they were* s and would not listen	6902+7996
Ac	7:51	"You s *people*, with uncircumcised hearts	5019

STIFFHEARTED (KJV) See STUBBORN

STIFLING (1)

Am	1:11	his brother with a sword, s all compassion,	8845

STILL (287) [STILLED]

Ge	9: 4	not eat meat that has its lifeblood s in it.	NIH
	11:28	**While** his father Terah was s **alive,**	6584+7156
	16:14	it is s **there,** between Kadesh and Bered.	2180
	25: 6	But while he was s living,	6388
	29: 7	"Look," he said, "the sun is s high;	6388
	29: 9	**While** he was s talking with them,	6388
	31:14	"Do we s have any share in the inheritance	6388
	34:25	while all of them were *s in pain,*	AIT
	35:16	While they were s some distance	6388
	38: 5	s **another** son and named him Shelah.	3578+6388
	43: 1	Now the famine was s severe in the land.	NIH
	43: 7	'Is your father s living?'	6388
	43:27	Is he s living?"	6388
	43:28	"Your servant our father is s alive	6388
	44:14	Joseph was s in the house when Judah	6388
	45: 3	Is my father s living?"	6388
	45:11	because five years of famine are *s to come.*	6388
	45:26	They told him, "Joseph is s alive!	6388
	45:28	My son Joseph is s alive.	6388
	46:30	I have seen for myself that you are s alive."	6388
	47:26	s *in force* today—that a fifth of the	6330
	48: 7	in the land of Canaan while we were s on	6388
Ex	4:18	in Egypt to see if any of them are s alive."	6388
	9:17	You s set yourself against my people	6388
	9:19	that has not been brought in and *is* s **out** in	5162
	9:30	that you and your officials s do **not** fear	3270
	14:14	you *need only to be* s."	3087
	15:16	By the power of your arm *they will be* as s	1957
	21:16	or s has him when he is caught must be put	NIH
	22:17	he must s **pay** the bride-price for virgins.	AIT
Lev	10: 5	s in their tunics, outside the camp,	NIH
	19:26	" 'Do not eat any meat with the blood s	NIH
	26:10	You will s be **eating** last year's harvest	AIT
	26:27	in spite of this *you* s do **not** listen to me	AIT
Nu	9:10	on a journey, *they* may s **celebrate**	AIT
	11:33	**while** the meat was s between their teeth	6388
	30: 3	"When a young woman s living in her	NIH
	30:16	a father and his young daughter s living	NIH
Dt	3:11	It is s in Rabbah of the Ammonites.)	NIH
	4: 4	to the LORD your God are s alive today.	NIH
	10: 8	as they s do today.	6330
	22:21	in Israel by being promiscuous while s	NIH
	31:27	the LORD while I am s alive and with you,	6388
Jos	5: 7	They were s uncircumcised	3954
	10:12	"O sun, **stand** s over Gibeon, O moon,	1957
	10:13	So the sun **stood** s, and the moon stopped,	1957
	13: 1	and *there are* s very large areas of land to	8636
	14:11	I am s as strong today as the day	6388
	18: 2	*there were* s seven Israelite tribes who had	3855
Jdg	7: 4	"There are s too many men.	6388
	8: 5	and I am s **pursuing** Zebah and Zalmunna,	AIT
	15:19	it is s there in Lehi.	2021+2021+2296+3427+6330
Ru	1:12	Even if I thought there was s hope for me—	NIH
1Sa	8:12	and s others to make weapons of war	NIH
	12:16	**stand** s and see this great thing	3656
	14:34	the LORD by eating meat with blood s	NIH
	16:11	"There is s the youngest,"	6388+8636
	17:57	while David s holding the Philistine's head.	NIH
	18:29	Saul became s more afraid of him,	6388
2Sa	1: 9	in the throes of death, but I'm s alive.'	3972+6388
	3:35	to eat something while it was s day;	6388
	9: 1	"Is there anyone s left of the house of Saul	6388
	9: 3	"Is there no one s left of the house of Saul	6388
	9: 3	"There is s a son of Jonathan,	6388
	12:18	"While the child was s living,	AIT
	12:22	He answered, "While the child was s alive,	6388
	13:25	Absalom urged him, *he* s **refused** to go,	AIT
	14:32	be better for me if I were s there!" '	6388
	18:14	Absalom's heart **while** Absalom was s alive	6388
	19:35	Can I s hear the voices of men	6388
	21:20	In s another battle, which took place	6388
1Ki	1:14	**While** you are s there talking to the king,	6388
	1:22	**While** she was s speaking with the king,	6388

1Ki	3: 2	were s **sacrificing** at the high places,	AIT
		and they are s there today.	6330
	11:17	But Hadad, s only a boy,	NIH
	12: 2	son of Nebat heard this (he was s in Egypt,	6388
	12:17	Rehoboam s **ruled** over them.	AIT
	20:32	The king answered, "Is he s alive?	6388
	22: 8	"There is s one man through whom	6388
2Ki	6:33	**While** he was s talking with them,	6388
	12: 6	of King Joash the priests s *had* not repaired	AIT
	17:23	they are s there.	2021+2021+2296+3427+6330
	19: 4	pray for the remnant that s **survives.**"	AIT
	25:19	Of *those* s in the city,	5162
1Ch	20: 6	In s another battle, which took place	6388
2Ch	5: 9	and they are s there today.	6330
	10:17	Rehoboam s **ruled** over them.	AIT
	14: 7	The land is s ours,	6388
	18: 7	"There is s one man through whom	6388
	20:33	and the people s had not set their hearts on	6388
	25:16	**While** he was s speaking,	AIT
	34: 3	**while** he was s young,	6388
Ezr	10: 2	in spite of this, **there** is s hope for Israel.	AIT
Ne	5: 4	S others were saying,	2256
	7: 3	While the gatekeepers *are* s **on duty,**	AIT
	8:11	saying, "**Be** s, for this is a sacred day.	2187
Est	6:14	**While** they were s talking with him,	6388
Job	1:16	**While** he was s speaking,	6388
	1:17	**While** he was s speaking,	6388
	1:18	**While** he was s speaking,	6330
	2: 3	And he s maintains his integrity,	6388
	2: 9	"Are you s holding on to your integrity?"	6388
	6:10	Then I would s have this consolation—	6388
	6:11	that *I should* s **hope?**	AIT
	8:12	**While** s growing and uncut,	6388
	9:28	I s **dread** all my sufferings,	AIT
	23:14	and many such plans he s has in store.	NIH
	24:10	they carry the sheaves, but s go hungry.	NIH
	29: 5	when the Almighty was s with me	6388
	39:24	he cannot **stand** s when the trumpet sounds.	586
Ps	17:14	You s **the hunger** *of* those you cherish;	1061+4848
	27:13	I am s confident of this:	4295
	37: 7	**Be** s before the LORD and wait patiently	1957
	39: 2	But when I was silent and s,	1875
	46:10	"*Be* s, and know that I am God;	8332
	58:11	"Surely the righteous s are rewarded;	NIH
	76: 6	both horse and chariot **lie** s.	8101
	78:30	even **while** it was s in their mouths,	6388
	83: 1	be not quiet, O God, *be* not s.	9200
	89: 9	when its waves mount up, you s them.	8656
	92:14	They will s bear fruit in old age,	6388
	139:18	When I awake, I am s with you.	6388
Pr	4: 3	I was a boy in my father's house, s tender,	NIH
	9: 9	Instruct a wise man and he will be wiser s;	6388
	31:15	She gets up while it is s dark;	6388
Ecc	2: 3	my mind s **guiding** me with wisdom.	AIT
	4: 2	are happier than the living, who are s alive.	6364
	5: 8	and over them both are others higher s.	NIH
	7:28	**while** I was s searching but not finding—	6388
	8:12	a hundred crimes and s lives a long time,	2256
Isa	5:25	not turned away, his hand is s upraised.	6388
	9:12	not turned away, his hand is s upraised.	6388
	9:17	not turned away, his hand is s upraised.	6388
	9:20	but *s be* **hungry;**	AIT
	9:21	not turned away, his hand is s upraised.	6388
	10: 4	not turned away, his hand is s upraised.	6388
	15: 9	but I will bring s **more** upon Dimon—	3578
	22: 3	while the enemy was s far away.	NIH
	37: 4	pray for the remnant that s **survives.**"	AIT
	44: 5	s **another** will write on his hand,	2256
	46:10	from ancient times, what *is* s **to come.**	4202+6913
	56: 8	"I will gather s others to them besides	AIT
	65: 8	when juice is s **found** in a cluster of grapes	AIT
	65:24	**while** they are s speaking I will hear.	6388
Jer	2:22	**stain** of your guilt is s before me,"	AIT
	5: 2	s they are swearing falsely."	4027+4200
	15: 9	Her sun will set while it is s day;	6388
	22:24	I would s pull you off.	3954
	31:20	I s remember him.	6388
	32:20	and have gained the renown that s	2021+2021+2296+3427+3869
	33: 1	**While** Jeremiah was s confined in	6388
	34: 7	of Judah that *were* s **holding out**—	AIT
	40: 7	the army officers and their men who were s	NIH
	40:13	of Kareah and all the army officers s in	NIH
	42:21	but *you have* not **obeyed** the LORD	AIT
	47: 6	Return to your scabbard; cease and **be** s.'	1957
	52:25	Of *those* s in the city,	5162
Eze	1:21	when the creatures **stood** s,	6641
	1:21	the creatures stood still, *they* also **stood** s;	6641
	1:24	they **stood** s, they lowered their wings.	6641
	10:17	the cherubim **stood** s, they also stood still;	6641
	10:17	the cherubim stood still, *they* also **stood** s;	6641
	16:28	after that, you s were not satisfied.	1685+2256
	23: 5	in prostitution while she was s mine;	NIH
	23:14	**carried** her prostitution s	3578
	33:25	with the blood s in it and look to your idols	NIH
Da	4:31	The words were s on his lips when	10531
	6:13	He s **prays** three times a day."	AIT
	9:21	**while** I was s in prayer,	6388
	11:27	an end will s come at the appointed time.	6388
	11:35	for it will s come at the appointed time.	6388
Am	4: 7	when the harvest was s three months away.	6388
	6:10	of the house and asks anyone s hiding there,	6388
Jnh	4: 2	not what I said when I was s at home?	6330
Mic	6:10	Am I s to forget, O wicked house,	6388
		your stomach will s be empty.	NIH
Hab	3:11	and moon **stood** s in the heavens at the glint	6641
Zep	3: 7	But *they were* s **eager** to act corruptly	AIT

Zec	2:13	**Be** s before the LORD, all mankind,	2187
	13: 3	And if anyone s prophesies,	6388
	14:12	while they *are* s **standing** on their feet,	AIT
Mt	5:25	Do it while you are s with him on the way,	NIG
	12:46	While Jesus was s talking to the crowd,	2285
	13: 8	S other seed fell on good soil.	1254
	13:33	He told them s another parable:	257
	15:16	"Are you s so dull?" Jesus asked them.	197
	16: 9	Do you s **not** understand?	4037
	16:14	s others, Jeremiah or one of the prophets."	2283
	17: 5	While he was s speaking,	2285
	19:20	"What do I s lack?"	2285
	20: 6	and found s **others** standing around.	AIT
	24: 6	but the end is s **to come.**	4037
	26:45	"Are you s sleeping and resting?	3370+3836
	26:47	While he was s speaking, Judas,	2285
	27:63	that **while** he was s alive that deceiver said,	2285
Mk	1:35	**while it was s dark,** Jesus got up,	1939
	1:45	the people s came to him from everywhere.	NIG
	4: 8	S other seed fell on good soil.	2779
	4:18	S others, like seed sown among thorns,	2779
	4:39	and said to the waves, "Quiet! Be s!"	5821
	4:40	Do you s have **no faith?**	4037
	5:35	While Jesus was s speaking,	2285
	6:15	And s **others** claimed, "He is a prophet,	257
	8:17	Do you s **not** see or understand?	4037
	8:21	"Do you s **not** understand?"	4037
	8:28	and s **others,** one of the prophets."	257
	12: 5	He sent s **another,** and that one they killed.	257
	13: 7	but the end is s **to come.**	4037
	14:41	"Are you s sleeping and resting?	3370+3836
	15: 5	But Jesus s made **no reply,**	4033
Lk	7:14	and those carrying it stood s.	NIG
	8: 8	S other seed fell on good soil.	2779
	8:49	While Jesus was s speaking,	2285
	9: 8	and s **others** that one of the prophets	AIT
	9:19	and s **others,** that one of the prophets	AIT
	9:61	S another said, "I will follow you, Lord;	2779
	14:20	"S another said, 'I just got married,	2779
	14:22	but there is s room.'	2285
	14:32	the other is s a long way off and will ask	2285
	15:20	"But while he was s a long way off,	2285
	18:22	he said to him, "You s lack one thing.	2285
	20:12	He sent s a third,	2779
	22:47	While he was s speaking a crowd came up,	2285
	24: 6	He is not here; he has s risen!	2285
	24:17	They stood s, their faces downcast.	NIG
	24:36	*While* they *were* s talking about this,	AIT
	24:41	And while they s did not believe it because	2285
	24:44	"This is what I told you while I was s	2285
Jn	1:48	"I saw you while you were s under	NIG
	3:11	**but** s you people do not accept our	2779
	4:51	While he was s on the way,	2453
	6:36	you have seen me **and** s you do not believe.	2779
	7:28	Then Jesus, s **teaching** in the temple courts,	AIT
	7:31	**S,** many in the crowd put their faith in him.	1254
	7:41	S others asked, "How can the Christ come from Galilee?"	1254+3836
	8: 9	with the woman s **standing** there.	AIT
	9:18	The Jews s did not believe	4036
	11:30	but was s at the place where Martha had met	2285
	12:37	they s would not believe in him.	NIG
	14:25	"All this I have spoken *while* s with you.	3531
	17:11	but they are s in the world,	NIG
	17:13	I say these things while I am s in the world,	NIG
	18:24	Then Annas sent him, s **bound,**	AIT
	20: 1	while it was s dark, Mary Magdalene went	2285
	20: 9	(They s did **not** understand from Scripture	4031
Ac	7: 2	to our father Abraham while he was s	NIG
	9: 1	Saul was s breathing out murderous threats	2285
	9:39	that Dorcas had made while she was s	NIG
	10:19	*While* Peter *was* s **thinking** about the vision,	AIT
	10:44	While Peter was s speaking these words,	2285
	27:27	fourteenth night we were s *being driven*	AIT
Ro	3: 7	why am I s condemned as a sinner?"	2285
	4:11	by faith while he was s uncircumcised.	NIG
	5: 6	when we were s powerless, Christ died for	2285
	5: 8	While we were s sinners, Christ died for us.	2285
	7: 3	*while* her husband is s **alive,**	AIT
	9:19	"Then why does God s blame us?	2285
1Co	1:12	s **another,** "I follow Christ."	1254
	3: 2	Indeed, you are s not ready.	2285+3814
	3: 3	You are s worldly.	2285
	8: 7	people are s so accustomed to idols	785+2401
	12:10	to s another the interpretation of tongues.	NIG
	15: 6	most of whom are s living,	785+2401
	15:17	you are s in your sins.	2285
2Co	2:13	I s had no peace of mind,	NIG
Gal	1:10	If I were s trying to please men,	2285
	5:11	Brothers, if I am s preaching circumcision,	2285
	5:11	why am I s being persecuted?	2285
Eph	4:26	the sun go down while you are s angry,	NIG
Php	1:30	and now hear that I s have.	NIG
Col	1:24	up in my flesh what is s lacking in regard	NIG
	2:20	why, as though *you* s **belonged** to it,	AIT
1Th	4:15	we tell you that we who *are* s **alive,**	AIT
	4:17	we who *are* s **alive** and are s with us	AIT
Heb	4: 1	the promise of entering his rest s **stands,**	AIT
	4: 6	It s remains that some will enter that rest,	NIG
	5:13	who lives on milk, being s an infant,	NIG
	7:10	Levi was s in the body of his ancestor.	2285
	9: 8	why was there s need for another priest	2285
	9: 8	**as long as** the first tabernacle was s	2285
	11: 4	And by faith he s speaks,	2285
	11:13	All these people were s living by faith	2285
	11:36	while s others were chained and put	2285
1Jn	2: 9	but hates his brother is s in the darkness.	785+2401

Rev	9:20	not killed by these plagues s did not repent	*NIG*
	14:18	S another angel, who had charge of the fire,	2779

STILLBORN (4) [BEAR]

Nu	12:12	a s **infant** coming from its mother's womb	4637
Job	3:16	not hidden in the ground like a s **child,**	5878
Ps	58: 8	like a s **child,** may they not see the sun.	851+5878
Ecc	6: 3	I say that a s **child** is better off than he.	5878

STILLED (7) [STILL]

Ps	65: 7	who s the roaring of the seas,	8656
	107:29	He s the storm to a whisper;	7756
	131: 2	But I have s and quieted my soul;	8750
Isa	16: 9	and over your harvests have been s.	5877
	24: 8	The gaiety of the tambourines is s,	8697
	25: 5	so the song of the ruthless is s.	6700
1Co	13: 8	where there are tongues, they will be s;	4264

STIMULATE (1)

2Pe	3: 1	both of them as reminders to s you to	1444

STING (3) [STINGING, STINGS]

1Co	15:55	Where, O death, is your s?"	3034
	15:56	The s of death is sin,	3034
Rev	9: 5	of the s of a scorpion when it strikes a man.	990

STINGING (1) [STING]

Eze	5:15	in anger and in wrath and with s rebuke.	2779

STINGS (1) [STING]

Rev	9:10	They had tails and s like scorpions,	3034

STINGY (2)

Pr	23: 6	Do not eat the food of a s **man,**	6524+8273
	28:22	A s man is eager to get rich and	6524+8273

STINK (3) [STENCH]

Ex	7:18	fish in the Nile will die, and the river will s;	944
	16:24	and it did not s or get maggots in it.	944
Isa	19: 6	The canals will s; the streams of Egypt will	2395

STIPULATIONS (4)

Dt	4:45	These are the s, decrees and laws	6343
	6:17	and the s and decrees he has given you.	6343
	6:20	"What is the meaning of the s,	6343
Jer	44:23	or followed his law or his decrees or his s,	6343

STIR (17) [ASTIR, STIRRED, STIRRING, STIRS]

Jdg	13:25	and the Spirit of the LORD began to s him	7192
Ne	4: 8	and fight against Jerusalem and s up trouble	6913
Ps	78:38	and did not s up his full wrath.	6424
	140: 2	in their hearts and s up war every day.	1592
Pr	29: 8	Mockers s up a city,	7032
Isa	13:17	See, I will s up against them the Medes,	6424
	19: 2	"I will s up Egyptian against Egyptian—	6056
	42:13	like a warrior he will s up his zeal;	6424
Jer	50: 9	For I will s up and bring against Babylon	6424
	51: 1	"See, I will s up the spirit of a destroyer	6424
Eze	23:22	I will s up your lovers against you,	6424
	24: 8	To s up wrath and take revenge	6590
Da	11: 2	he will s up everyone against the kingdom	6424
	11:25	a large army he will s up his strength	6424
Hos	7: 4	like an oven whose fire the baker need not s	6424
Am	6:14	"I will s up a nation against you,	7756
Php	1:17	that they can s up trouble for me while I am	1586

STIRRED (22) [STIR]

Ru	1:19	the whole town was s because of them,	2101
1Ki	14:22	s up his **jealous anger** more than their	7861
1Ch	5:26	the God of Israel s up the spirit of Pul king	6424
Ps	45: 1	My heart is s by a noble theme	8180
	107:25	and s up a tempest that lifted high	6641
Ecc	12: 5	along and desire **no longer** is s.	7296
Isa	41: 2	"Who has s up one from the east,	6424
	41:25	"I have s up one from the north,	6424
Jer	6:22	a great nation is being s up from the ends	6424
	50:41	and many kings are being s up from	6424
	51:11	LORD has s up the kings of the Medes,	6424
Eze	32:13	to be s by the foot of man or muddied by	1931
Am	8: 8	it will be s up and then sink like the river	1764
Hag	1:14	So the LORD s up the spirit of Zerubbabel	6424
Mt	21:10	the whole city was s and asked,	4940
Mk	11:11	But the chief priests s up the crowd	411
Jn	5: 7	into the pool when the water is s.	5429
Ac	6:12	So they s up the people and the elders and	5167
	13:50	s up persecution against Paul and	2074
	14: 2	But the Jews who refused to believe s up	2074
	21:27	They s up the whole crowd and seized him,	5177
2Co	9: 2	enthusiasm has most of them **to action.**	2241

STIRRING (6) [STIR]

Jdg	9:31	and are s up the city against you.	7443
Ne	13:18	Now you are s up more wrath against Israel	3578
Pr	30:33	so s up anger produces strife."	4790
Ac	17:13	agitating the crowds and s them **up.**	5429
	24: 5	s up riots among the Jews all over	3075
	24:12	or s up a crowd in the synagogues	2180+4472

STIRS (13) [STIR]

Dt	32:11	that s up its nest and hovers over its young,	6424
Job	41:31	a boiling caldron and s up the sea like a pot	8492
Ps	147:18	he s up his breezes, and the waters flow.	5959
Pr	6:14	he always s up dissension.	8938
	6:19	a man who s up dissension among brothers.	8938
	10:12	Hatred s up dissension,	6424
	15: 1	but a harsh word s up anger.	6590
	15:18	A hot-tempered man s up dissension,	1741
	16:28	A perverse man s up dissension,	8938
	28:25	A greedy man s up dissension,	1741
	29:22	An angry man s up dissension,	1741
Jer	31:35	who s up the sea so that its waves roar—	8088
Lk	23: 5	"He s up the people all over Judea	411

STOCK (2) [STOCKS]

Job	5:24	you will take s of your property	7212
Jer	2:21	like a choice vine of sound and reliable s.	2446

STOCKS (4) [STOCK]

Jer	20: 2	in the s at the Upper Gate of Benjamin at	4551
	20: 3	when Pashhur released him from the s,	4551
	29:26	like a prophet into the s and neck-irons.	4551
Ac	16:24	and fastened their feet in the s.	3833

STOIC (1)

Ac	17:18	A group of Epicurean and S philosophers	5121

STOLE (6) [STEAL]

Ge	31:19	Rachel s her father's household gods.	1704
2Sa	15: 6	and so he s the hearts of the men of Israel.	1704
	19: 3	The men s into the city that day	995+1704+4200
2Ki	11: 2	took Joash son of Ahaziah and s him **away**	1704
2Ch	22:11	took Joash son of Ahaziah and s him **away**	1704
Mt	28:13	and s him away while we were asleep.'	3096

STOLEN (16) [STEAL]

Ge	30:33	will be considered s."	1704
	31:32	Now Jacob did not know that Rachel had s	1704
	31:39	from me for whatever was s by day or night.	1704
Ex	22: 4	s animal is found alive in his possession—	1706
	22: 7	and they are s from the neighbor's house,	1704
	22:12	if the animal was s from the neighbor,	1704+1704
Lev	6: 2	to him or left in his care or s,	1610
	6: 4	he must return what he has s or taken	1608+1611
Jos	7:11	they have s, they have lied,	1704
Job	24: 2	they pasture flocks they have s.	1608
Ps	62:10	in extortion or take pride in s **goods;**	1610
Pr	9:17	"S water is sweet; food eaten in secret	1704
SS	4: 9	You have s my **heart,** my sister, my bride;	4220
	4: 9	you have s my **heart** with one glance	4220
Eze	33:15	returns what he has s, follows the decrees	1611
Hab	2: 6	to him who piles up s **goods**	2257+4200+4202

STOMACH (20) [STOMACHS]

2Sa	2:23	thrust the butt of his spear into Asahel's s,	2824
	3:27	Joab stabbed him in the s, and he died.	2824
	4: 6	and they stabbed him in the s.	2824
Job	20:14	yet his food will turn sour in his s;	5055
	20:15	God will make his s vomit them up.	1061
Pr	13:25	but the s of the wicked goes hungry.	1061
	18:20	the fruit of his mouth a man's s is filled;	1061
Jer	30: 6	with his hands on his s like a woman	2743
	51:34	and filled his s with our delicacies,	4160
Eze	3: 3	and fill your s with it."	5055
Mic	6:14	your s will still be empty.	7931
Mt	15:17	the mouth goes into the s and then out of	3120
Mk	7:19	it doesn't go into his heart but into his s,	3120
Lk	15:16	He longed to fill his s with the pods that	3120
1Co	6:13	for the s and the stomach for food"—	3120
	6:13	for the stomach and the s for food"—	3120
Php	3:19	their god is their s,	3120
1Ti	5:23	and use a little wine because of your s	5126
Rev	10: 9	It will turn your s sour,	3120
	10:10	but when I had eaten it, my s turned sour.	3120

STOMACHS (2) [STOMACH]

Eze	7:19	not satisfy their hunger or fill their s with it,	5055
Am	4: 6	"I gave you **empty** s in every city	5931+9094

STONE (186) [CAPSTONE, CORNERSTONE, CORNERSTONES, FIELDSTONES, MILLSTONE, MILLSTONES, SLINGSTONES, STONE'S, STONECUTTERS, STONED, STONEMASONS, STONES, STONING, TOMBSTONE]

Ge	11: 3	They used brick instead of s,	74
	28:18	the s he had placed under his head and set it	74
	28:22	and this s that I have set up as a pillar will	74
	29: 2	The s over the mouth of the well was large.	74
	29: 3	the s away from the well's mouth and water	74
	29: 3	the s to its place over the mouth of the well.	74
	29: 8	the s has been rolled away from the mouth	74
	29:10	over and rolled the s away from the mouth	74
	31:45	So Jacob took a s and set it up as a pillar.	74
	35:14	as a pillar at the place where God had talked	74
Ex	7:19	even in the wooden buckets and s **jars.**"	74
	8:26	detestable in their eyes, will they not s us?	6232

Ex	15: 5	they sank to the depths like a s.	74
	15:16	of your arm they will be as still as a s—	74
	17: 4	They are almost ready to s me."	6232
	17:12	a s and put it under him and he sat on it.	74
	21:18	with a s or with his fist and he does not die	74
	24: 4	and set up twelve s **pillars** representing	5167
	24:12	and I will give you the tablets of s,	74
	28:10	on one s and the remaining six on the other.	74
	31:18	tablets of s inscribed by the finger of God.	74
	34: 1	"Chisel out two s tablets like the first ones,	74
	34: 1	So Moses chiseled out two s tablets like	74
	34: 4	he carried the two s tablets in his hands.	74
Lev	20: 2	The people of the community are to s him.	74+928+2021+8083
	20:27	You are to s them;	74+928+2021+8083
	24:14	and the entire assembly is to s him.	8083
	24:16	The entire assembly must s him.	8083+8083
	26: 1	up an image or a **sacred** s for yourselves,	5167
	26: 1	not place a carved s in your land to bow	74
Nu	15:35	The whole assembly must s him outside the camp."	74+928+2021+8083
	35:17	if anyone has a s in his hand that could kill,	74
	35:23	drops a s on him that could kill him,	74
Dt	4:13	and then wrote them on two s tablets.	74
	4:28	man-made gods of wood and s,	74
	5:22	on two s tablets and gave them to me.	74
	9: 9	on the mountain to receive the tablets of s,	74
	9:10	The LORD gave me two s tablets inscribed	74
	9:11	the LORD gave me the two s tablets,	74
	10: 1	"Chisel out two s tablets like the first ones	74
	10: 3	and chiseled out two s tablets like	74
	13:10	S him to death, because he tried to turn you	6232
	16:22	and do not erect a **sacred** s,	5167
	17: 5	his town shall s him to death.	74+928+2021+6232
	19:14	Do not move your neighbor's **boundary** s	1473
	21:21	his town shall s him to death.	74+928+2021+8083
	22:21	her town shall s her to death.	74+928+2021+6232
	22:24	the gate of that town and s them to death—	6232
	27:17	man who moves his neighbor's **boundary** s.	1473
	28:36	worship other gods, gods of wood and s.	74
	28:64	worship other gods—gods of wood and s,	74
	29:17	and idols of wood and s,	74
Jos	4: 5	of you is to take up a s on his shoulder,	74
	7: 5	as the **quarries** and struck them down on	8696
	15: 6	of Beth Arabah to the S of Bohan son	74
	18:17	ran down to the S of Bohan son of Reuben.	74
	24:26	a large s and set it up there under the oak	74
	24:27	"This s will be a witness against us.	74
Jdg	9: 5	and on one s murdered his seventy brothers,	74
	9:18	murdered his seventy sons on a single s,	74
	20:16	each of whom could sling a s at a hair and	74
1Sa	7:12	a s and set it up between Mizpah and Shen.	74
	14:33	"Roll a large s over here at once."	74
	17:49	Reaching into his bag and taking out a s,	74
	17:49	The s sank into his forehead;	74
	17:50	over the Philistine with a sling and a s;	74
	20:19	and wait by the s Ezel.	74
	20:41	David got up from the south side [of the s]	*NIH*
	25:37	his heart failed him and he became like a s.	74
1Ki	1: 9	and fattened calves at the S of Zoheleth	74
	5:17	from the quarry large blocks of quality s	74
	5:17	a foundation of dressed s for the temple.	74
	5:18	of Gebal cut and prepared the timber and s	74
	6:18	Everything was cedar; no s was to be seen.	74
	6:36	of three courses of **dressed** s and one course	1607
	7: 9	were made of blocks of high-grade s cut	74
	7:12	of three courses of **dressed** s and one course	1607
	8: 9	the two s tablets that Moses had placed in it	74
	21:10	Then take him out and s him to death."	6232
2Ki	3: 2	He got rid of the **sacred** s of Baal	5167
	3:25	a s on every good field until it was covered.	74
	10:26	They brought the **sacred** s out of the temple	5167
	10:27	They demolished the **sacred** s of Baal	5167
	12:12	and dressed s for the repair of the temple of	74
	16:17	that supported it and set it on a s base.	74
	19:18	they were not gods but only wood and s,	74
	19:25	turned fortified cities into piles of s.	1643+5898
	22: 6	and dressed s to repair the temple.	74
1Ch	22: 2	to prepare dressed s for building the house	74
	22:14	too great to be weighed, and wood and s.	74
	29: 2	and all kinds of fine s and marble—	74
2Ch	2:14	bronze and iron, s and wood,	74
	34:11	and builders to purchase dressed s,	74
Ne	9:11	like a s into mighty waters.	74
Job	6:12	Do I have the strength of s?	74
	38:30	when the waters become hard as s,	74
Ps	91:12	you will not strike your foot against a s.	74
	118:22	The s the builders rejected has become	74
Pr	22:28	Do not move an ancient **boundary** s set up	1473
	23:10	Do not move an ancient **boundary** s	1473
	24:31	and the s wall was in ruins.	74
	26: 8	a s in a sling for a point of honor to	74
	26:27	if a man rolls a s, it will roll back on him.	74
	27: 3	S is heavy and sand a burden,	74
Isa	8:14	but for both houses of Israel he will be a s	74
	9:10	but we will rebuild with **dressed** s;	1607
	28:16	"See, I lay a s in Zion, a tested stone,	74
	28:16	"See, I lay a stone in Zion, a tested s,	74
	37:19	they were not gods but only wood and s,	74
	37:26	turned fortified cities into piles of s.	1643+5898
Jer	2:27	and to s, 'You gave me birth.'	74
	3: 9	and committed adultery with s and wood.	74
	5: 3	They made their faces harder than s	6152
	51:26	nor any s for a foundation,	74
	51:63	tie a s to it and throw it into the Euphrates.	74
La	3: 9	He has barred my way with **blocks** of s;	1607
Eze	3: 9	I will make your forehead like the **hardest** s	9032

Eze	11:19	remove from them their heart of s and give	74
	16:40	who will s you and hack you to pieces	74+928+2021+8083
	20:32	who serve wood and s."	74
	23:47	The mob will s them and cut them down	74+8083
	28:13	every precious s adorned you:	74
	36:26	I will remove from you your heart of s	74
	40:42	There were also four tables of dressed s for	74
	46:23	of each of the four courts was a ledge of s,	3215
Da	5: 4	of bronze, iron, wood and s,	10006
	5:23	of bronze, iron, wood and s,	10006
	6:17	A s was brought and placed over the mouth	10006
Am	5:11	though you have built s mansions,	1607
Hab	2:19	Or to lifeless s, 'Wake up!'	74
Hag	2:15	how things were before one s was laid	74
Zec	3: 9	See, the s I have set in front of Joshua!	74
	3: 9	There are seven eyes on that one s,	74
Mt	4: 6	you will not strike your foot against a s.'"	3345
	7: 9	if his son asks for bread, will give him a s?	3345
	21:42	" 'The s the builders rejected has become	3345
	21:44	He who falls on this s will be broken	3345
	23:37	you who kill the prophets and s those sent	3344
	24: 2	not one s here will be left on another;	3345
	27:60	He rolled a big s in front of the entrance to	3345
	27:66	the tomb secure by putting a seal on the s	3345
	28: 2	rolled back the s and sat on it.	3345
Mk	12:10	" 'The s the builders rejected has become	3345
	13: 2	"Not one s here will be left on another;	3345
	15:46	Then he rolled a s against the entrance of	3345
	16: 3	"Who will roll the s away from the entrance	3345
	16: 4	when they looked up, they saw that the s,	3345
Lk	4: 3	tell this s to become bread."	3345
	4:11	you will not strike your foot against a s.'"	3345
	13:34	you who kill the prophets and s those sent	3344
	19:44	They will not leave one s on another,	3345
	20: 6	'From men,' all the people will s us,	2902
	20:17	" 'The s the builders rejected has become	3345
	20:18	Everyone who falls on that s will be broken	3345
	21: 6	the time will come when not one s will	3345
	24: 2	They found the s rolled away from	3345
Jn	2: 6	Nearby stood six s water jars,	3343
	8: 5	Moses commanded us to s such women.	3342
	8: 7	let him be the first to throw a s at her."	3345
	8:59	At this, they picked up stones to s him,	965+2093
	10:31	Again the Jews picked up stones to s him,	3342
	10:32	For which of these do you s me?"	3342
	11: 8	"a short while ago the Jews tried to s you,	3342
	11:38	a cave with a s laid across the entrance.	3345
	11:39	"Take away the s," he said.	3345
	11:41	So they took away the s.	3345
	19:13	at a place known as the S Pavement (which	3346
	20: 1	the s had been removed from the entrance.	3345
Ac	4:11	He is " 'the s you builders rejected,	3345
	5:26	they feared that the people would s them.	3342
	7:58	out of the city and began to s him.	3344
	14: 5	to mistreat them and s them.	3344
Ro	9:32	They stumbled over the "stumbling s."	3345
	9:33	I lay in Zion a s that causes men to stumble	3345
2Co	3: 3	not on tablets of s but on tablets	3343
	3: 7	which was engraved in letters on s,	3345
Heb	9: 4	and the s tablets of the covenant.	4419
1Pe	2: 4	As you come to him, the living S—	3345
	2: 6	"See, I lay a s in Zion,	3345
	2: 7	Now to you who believe, this s is precious.	NIG
	2: 7	"The s the builders rejected has become	3345
	2: 8	"A s that causes men to stumble and a rock	3345
Rev	2:17	a white s with a new name written on it,	6029
	9:20	silver, bronze, s and wood—	3343
	21:19	with every kind of precious s.	3345

STONE'S (1) [STONE]

| Lk | 22:41 | He withdrew about a s throw beyond them, | 3345 |

STONECUTTERS (6) [STONE]

1Ki	5:15	and eighty thousand s in the hills,	2935
2Ki	12:12	the masons and s.	74+2935
1Ch	22: 2	and from among them he appointed s	2935
	22:15	You have many workmen: s,	2935
2Ch	2: 2	and eighty thousand as s in the hills	2935
	2:18	and 80,000 to be s in the hills,	2935

STONED (19) [STONE]

Ex	19:13	He shall surely be s or shot with	6232+6232
	21:28	the bull must be s to death,	6232+6232
	21:29	the bull must be s and the owner also must	6232
	21:32	and the bull must be s.	6232
Lev	24:23	blasphemer outside the camp and s him.	74+8083
Nu	15:36	the camp and s him to death,	74+928+2021+8083
Jos	7:25	Then all Israel s him,	74+8083
	7:25	and after they had the rest,	74+928+2021+6232
1Ki	12:18	but all Israel s him to death.	74+8083
	21:13	the city and s him to death.	74+928+2021+6232
	21:14	"Naboth has been s and is dead."	6232
	21:15	as Jezebel heard that Naboth had been s	6232
2Ch	10:18	but the Israelites s him to death.	74+8083
	24:21	by order of the king they s him to death	74+8083
Mt	21:35	they beat one, killed another, and s a third.	3344
Ac	14:19	They s Paul and dragged him outside	3342
2Co	11:25	once I was s, three times I was shipwrecked,	3342
Heb	11:37	They were s; they were sawed in two;	3342
	12:20	touches the mountain, it must be s."	3344

STONEMASONS (2) [STONE]

| 2Sa | 5:11 | cedar logs and carpenters and s, | 74+3093+7815 |
| 1Ch | 14: 1 | s and carpenters to build a palace for | 3093+7815 |

STONES (128) [STONE]

Ge	28:11	Taking one of the s there,	74
	31:46	He said to his relatives, "Gather some s."	74
	31:46	So they took s and piled them in a heap,	74
Ex	20:25	If you make an altar of s for me,	74
	20:25	do not build it with dressed s,	1607
	23:24	and break their sacred s to pieces.	5167
	25: 7	and onyx s and other gems to be mounted	74
	28: 9	"Take two onyx s and engrave on them	74
	28:11	the names of the sons of Israel on the two s	74
	28:11	Then mount the s in gold filigree settings	4392S
	28:12	the ephod as memorial s for the sons	74
	28:17	Then mount four rows of precious s on it.	74
	28:21	There are to be twelve s,	74
	31: 5	to cut and set s, to work in wood,	74
	34:13	smash their sacred s and cut	5167
	35: 9	and onyx s and other gems to be mounted	74
	35:27	The leaders brought onyx s and other gems	74
	35:33	to cut and set s, to work in wood,	74
	39: 6	The onyx s in gold filigree settings	74
	39: 7	of the ephod as memorial s for the sons	74
	39:10	They mounted four rows of precious s,	74
	39:14	There were twelve s, one for each of	74
Lev	14:40	to order that the contaminated s be torn out	74
	14:42	to take other s to replace these	74
	14:43	the house after the s have been torn out and	74
	14:45	its s, timbers and all the plaster—	74
Dt	7: 5	down their altars, smash their sacred s,	5167
	12: 3	smash their sacred s and burn their Asherah	5167
	27: 2	up some large s and coat them with plaster.	74
	27: 4	set up these s on Mount Ebal,	74
	27: 5	to the LORD your God, an altar of s.	74
	27: 8	of this law on these s you have set up."	74
Jos	4: 3	up twelve s from the middle of the Jordan	74
	4: 6	'What do these s mean?'	74
	4: 7	These s are to be a memorial to the people	74
	4: 8	They took twelve s from the middle of	74
	4: 9	up the twelve s that had been in the middle	74
	4:20	up at Gilgal the twelve s they had taken out	74
	4:21	'What do these s mean?'	74
	8:31	an altar of uncut s, on which no iron tool	74
	8:32	Joshua copied on s the law of Moses,	74
1Sa	17:40	chose five smooth s from the stream,	74
2Sa	12:30	and it was set with precious s—	74
	16: 6	and all the king's officials with s,	74
	16:13	and throwing s at him and showering him	74
1Ki	7:10	The foundations were laid with large s	74
	7:11	Above were high-grade s, cut to size,	74
	10: 2	large quantities of gold, and precious s—	74
	10:10	large quantities of spices, and precious s.	74
	10:11	of almugwood and precious s.	74
	10:27	as common in Jerusalem as s,	74
	14:23	high places, sacred s and Asherah poles	5167
	15:22	and they carried away from Ramah the s	74
	18:31	Elijah took twelve s, one for each of the	74
	18:32	With the s he built an altar in the name of	74
	18:38	the wood, the s and the soil,	74
2Ki	3:19	and ruin every good field with s."	74
	3:25	Only Kir Hareseth was left with its s	74
	17:10	They set up sacred s and Asherah poles	5167
	18: 4	smashed the sacred s and cut down	5167
	23:14	and cut down the Asherah poles	5167
1Ch	12: 2	arrows or to sling s right-handed or	74+928+2021
	20: 2	and it was set with precious s—	74
	29: 2	turquoise, s of various colors,	74
	29: 8	Any who had precious s gave them to	74
2Ch	1:15	and gold as common in Jerusalem as s,	74
	3: 6	He adorned the temple with precious s.	74
	9: 1	large quantities of gold, and precious s—	74
	9: 9	large quantities of spices, and precious s.	74
	9:10	also brought algumwood and precious s.	74
	9:27	as common in Jerusalem as s,	74
	14: 3	smashed the sacred s and cut down	5167
	16: 6	the s and timber Baasha had been using.	74
	26:15	to shoot arrows and hurl large s.	74
	31: 1	smashed the sacred s and cut down	5167
	32:27	and gold and for his precious s,	74
Ezr	5: 8	with large s and placing the timbers	10006+10146
	6: 4	with three courses of large s and	10006+10146
Ne	4: 2	the s back to life from those heaps	74
	4: 3	he would break down their wall of s!"	74
Est	1: 6	mother-of-pearl and other costly s.	6090
Job	5:23	For you will have a covenant with the s of	74
	8:17	of rocks and looks for a place among the s.	74
	14:19	as water wears away s	74
	24: 2	Men move boundary s;	1474
Ps	102:14	For her s are dear to your servants;	74
Ecc	3: 5	time to scatter s and a time to gather them,	74
	10: 9	Whoever quarries s may be injured	74
Isa	5: 2	and cleared it of s and planted it with	6232
	14:19	those who descend to the s of the pit.	74
	27: 9	the altar to be like chalk stones crushed	74
	27: 9	the altar stones to be like chalk s crushed	74
	54:11	I will build you with s of turquoise,	74
	54:12	and all your walls of precious s.	74
	57: 6	[The idols] among the smooth s of	NIH
	60:17	and iron in place of s.	74
	62:10	Remove the s.	74
Jer	43: 9	take some large s with you and bury them	74
	43:10	over these s I have buried here;	74
La	3:53	to end my life in a pit and threw s at me;	74

Eze	26:12	and throw your s, timber and rubble into	74
	27:22	of all kinds of spices and precious s,	74
	28:14	you walked among the fiery s.	74
	28:16	O guardian cherub, from among the fiery s.	74
Da	11:38	with precious s and costly gifts.	74
Hos	3: 4	without sacrifice or sacred s,	5167
	5:10	like those who move boundary s.	1473
	10: 1	his land prospered, he adorned his sacred s.	5167
	10: 2	and destroy their sacred s.	5167
	12:11	Their altars will be like piles of s on	1643
Mic	1: 6	I will pour her s into the valley	74
	5:13	and your sacred s from among you;	5167
Hab	2:11	The s of the wall will cry out,	74
Zec	5: 4	both its timbers and its s.'"	74
Mt	3: 9	I tell you that out of these s God can raise	3345
	4: 3	tell these s to become bread."	3345
Mk	5: 5	and cut himself with s.	3345
	13: 1	What massive s! What magnificent	3345
Lk	3: 8	that out of these s God can raise up children	3345
	19:40	"if they keep quiet, the s will cry out."	3345
	21: 5	the temple was adorned with beautiful s and	3345
Jn	8:59	At this, they picked up s to stone him,	3345
	10:31	Again the Jews picked up s to stone him,	3345
1Co	3:12	silver, costly s, wood, hay or straw,	3345
1Pe	2: 5	also, like living s, are being built into	3345
Rev	17: 4	glittering with gold, precious s and pearls	3345
	18:12	cargoes of gold, silver, precious s and pearls	3345
	18:16	glittering with gold, precious s and pearls!	3345

STONING (4) [STONE]

Nu	14:10	the whole assembly talked about s them.	74+928+2021+8083
1Sa	30: 6	because the men were talking of s him;	6232
Jn	10:33	"We are not s you for any of these,"	3342
Ac	7:59	While they were s him, Stephen prayed,	3344

STOOD (216) [STAND]

Ge	18: 8	While they ate, he s near them under a tree.	6641
	19:27	the place where he had s before the LORD.	6641
	28:13	There above it s the LORD, and he said:	5893
	37: 7	and s upright, while your sheaves gathered	5893
	41: 1	came up out of the Nile and s beside those	5893
Ex	2: 4	His sister s at a distance to see	3656
	9:10	So they took soot from a furnace and s	6641
	14:19	of cloud also moved from in front and s	6641
	15: 8	The surging waters s firm like a wall;	5893
	18:13	and s around him from morning	6641
	19:17	and they s at the foot of the mountain.	3656
	32:26	he s at the entrance to the camp and said,	6641
	33: 8	all the people rose and s at the entrances	5893
	33:10	they all s and worshiped,	7756
	34: 5	down in the cloud and s there with him	3656
Lev	9: 5	the entire assembly came near and s before	6641
Nu	12: 5	he s at the entrance to the Tent	6641
	12:10	there s Miriam—leprous, like snow.	NIH
	16:18	and s with Moses and Aaron at the entrance	6641
	16:48	He s between the living and the dead,	6641
	22:22	of the LORD s in the road to oppose him.	3656
	22:24	the angel of the LORD s in a narrow path	6641
	22:26	of the LORD moved on ahead and s in	6641
	27: 2	to the Tent of Meeting and s before Moses,	6641
Dt	4:10	the day you s before the LORD your God	6641
	4:11	near and s at the foot of the mountain	6641
	5: 5	that time I s between the LORD and you	6641
	31:15	the cloud s over the entrance to the Tent.	6641
Jos	3:17	of the LORD s firm on dry ground in	6641
	4: 3	from right where the priests s	3922+5163+8079
	4: 9	the ark of the covenant had s.	5163+8079
	8:33	of the people s in front of Mount Gerizim	NIH
	10:13	So the sun s still, and the moon stopped,	1957
	20: 6	to stay in that city until he has a trial before	6641
Jdg	16:25	When they s him among the pillars,	6641
	16:29	two central pillars on which the temple s.	3922
	18:16	s at the entrance to the gate.	5893
	18:17	the priest and the six hundred armed men s	5893
1Sa	1: 9	and drinking in Shiloh, Hannah s up.	7756
	1:26	the woman who s here beside you praying	5893
	3:10	The LORD came and s there,	3656
	10:23	and as he s among the people he was	3656
	12:18	So all the people s in awe of the LORD	3707+4394
	14: 5	One cliff s to the north toward Micmash,	5187
	17: 8	Goliath s and shouted to the ranks of Israel,	6641
	17:51	David ran and s over him.	6641
	26:13	and s on top of the hill some distance away;	6641
2Sa	1:10	"So I s over him and killed him,	6641
	2:15	So they s up and were counted off—	7756
	12:17	of his household s beside him to get him up	7756
	13:31	The king s up, tore his clothes and lay	7756
	13:31	all his servants s by with their clothes torn.	5893
	18: 4	So the king s beside the gate while all	6641
	18:30	So he stepped aside and s there.	6641
	20:11	of Joab's men s beside Amasa and said,	6641
	20:15	and it s against the outer fortifications,	6641
	23:10	but he s his ground and struck down	7756
1Ki	1:28	So she came into the king's presence and s	6641
	2: 7	They s by me when I fled	7928
	2:19	the king s up to meet her,	7756
	3:15	s before the ark of the Lord's covenant	6641
	3:16	Now two prostitutes came to the king and s	6641
	7:25	The Sea on twelve bulls,	6641
	8:22	Then Solomon s before the altar of	6641
	8:55	He s and blessed the whole assembly	6641
	10:20	Twelve lions s on the six steps,	6641
	19:13	and went out and s at the mouth of the cave.	6641
	20:38	and s by the road waiting for the king.	6641

1Ki	22:21	came forward, s before the LORD and said,	6641
2Ki	2: 7	of the company of the prophets went and s	6641
	2:13	from Elijah and went back and s on	6641
	4:12	So he called her, and *she* s before him.	6641
	4:15	So he called her, and *she* s in the doorway.	6641
	5:15	*He* s before him and said,	6641
	5:25	he went in and s before his master Elisha.	6641
	8: 9	He went in and s before him, and said,	6641
	10: 9	*He* s before all the people and said,	6641
	13:21	the man came to life and s up on his feet.	7756
	16:14	that s before the LORD he brought from	NIH
	18:28	the commander s and called out in Hebrew:	6641
	23: 3	The king s by the pillar and renewed	6641
2Ch	3:13	They s on their feet, facing the main hall.	6641
	4: 4	The Sea s on twelve bulls,	6641
	5:12	s on the east side of the altar,	6641
	6:12	Then Solomon s before the altar of	6641
	6:13	*He* s on the platform and then knelt down	6641
	9:19	Twelve lions s on the six steps,	6641
	13: 4	Abijah s on Mount Zemaraim,	7756
	18:20	came forward, s before the LORD and said,	6641
	20: 5	Then Jehoshaphat s up in the assembly	6641
	20:13	s there before the LORD.	6641
	20:14	as he s in the assembly.	NIH
	20:19	and Korahites s up and praised the LORD,	7756
	24: 4	As they set out, Jehoshaphat s and said,	6641
	24:20	*He* s before the people and said,	6641
	29:26	Levites s *ready* with David's instruments,	6641
	30:27	The priests and the Levites s to bless	7756
	34:31	The king s by his pillar and renewed	6641
	35:10	the priests s in their places with the Levites	6641
Ezr	10:10	Then Ezra the priest s up and said to them,	7756
Ne	4:14	*I* s up and said to the nobles,	7756
	8: 4	Ezra the scribe s on a high wooden platform	6641
	8: 4	Beside him on his right s Mattithiah,	6641
	8: 5	and as he opened it, the people all s up.	6641
	9: 2	*They* s in *their* places and confessed	6641
	9: 3	*They* s where they were and read from	7756
	12: 9	s opposite them in the services.	NIH
	12:24	who s opposite them to give praise	NIH
Est	5: 1	on her royal robes and s in the inner court	6641
	8: 4	to Esther and she arose and s before him.	6641
Job	4:15	and the hair on my body s on end.	6169
	4:16	A form s before my eyes,	NIH
Ps	33: 9	he commanded, and *it* s firm.	6641
	104:	6 the waters s above the mountains.	6641
	106:23	s in the breach before him to keep his wrath	6641
	106:30	But Phinehas s up and intervened,	6641
Isa	36:13	the commander s and called out in Hebrew,	6641
Jer	18:20	that I s before you and spoke in their behalf	6641
	19:14	and s in the court of the LORD's temple	6641
	23:18	of *them* has s in the council of the LORD	6641
	23:22	But if *they* had s in my council,	6641
Eze	1:21	when the creatures s **still,**	6641
	1:21	the creatures stood still, *they* also s **still;**	6641
	1:24	they s **still,** they lowered their wings.	6641
	1:25	above the expanse over their heads as they s	6641
	8: 3	where the idol that provokes to jealousy s.	4632
	8:11	of them s seventy elders of the house	6641
	9: 2	They came in and s beside the bronze altar.	6641
	10: 6	the man went in and s beside a wheel.	6641
	10:17	the cherubim s **still,** they also stood still;	6641
	10:17	the cherubim stood still, *they* also s **still;**	6641
	37:10	they came to life and s up on their feet—	6641
Da	2: 2	When they came in and s before the king,	6641
	2:31	and there before you s a large statue—	10624
	3: 3	and *they* s before it.	10624
	4:10	and there before me s a tree in the middle of	NIH
	7: 4	from the ground so that *it* s on two feet	10624
	7:10	ten thousand times ten thousand s before	10624
	8:15	before me s one who looked like a man.	6641
	10:11	when he said this to me, *I* s up trembling.	6641
	12: 5	looked, and there before me s two others,	6641
Ob	1:11	On the day you s aloof	6641
Hab	3: 6	*He* s, and shook the earth;	6641
	3:11	Sun and moon s **still** in the heavens at	6641
Zec	3: 3	in filthy clothes as he s before the angel.	6641
	3: 5	while the angel of the LORD's s by.	6641
Mal	2: 5	he revered me and s **in awe** of my name.	3169
Mt	12:46	his mother and brothers s outside,	2705
	13: 2	while all the people s on the shore.	2705
	26:62	Then the high priest s up and said to Jesus,	482
	27:11	Meanwhile Jesus s before the governor,	2705
Mk	5:42	Immediately the girl s up and walked	482
	9:27	lifted him to his feet, and *he* s up.	482
	14:57	some s up and gave this false testimony	482
	14:60	Then the high priest s up before them	482
	15:39	the centurion, who s **there** in front of Jesus,	4225
Lk	4:16	And he s up to read.	482
	5:25	Immediately he s up in front of them,	482
	6: 8	So he got up and s there.	482
	6:17	down with them and s on a level place.	2705
	7:14	and those carrying it s still.	2705
	7:38	and *as she* s behind him at his feet weeping,	2705
	8:55	Her spirit returned, and at once *she* s up.	482
	10:25	On one occasion an expert in the law s up	482
	17:12	They s at a distance	2705
	18:11	Pharisee s up and prayed about himself:	2705
	18:13	"But the tax collector s at a distance	2705
	19: 8	But Zacchaeus s up and said to the Lord,	2705
	22:28	You are those who *have* s by me	1373
	23:35	The people s watching,	2705
	23:49	s at a distance, watching these things.	2705
	24: 4	that gleamed like lightning s **beside** them.	2392
	24:17	*They* s still, their faces downcast.	2705
	24:36	Jesus himself s among them and said	2705
Jn	2: 6	Nearby s six stone water jars,	1639+3023

Jn	7:37	Jesus s and said in a loud voice,	2705
	11:56	and *as they* s in the temple area	2705
	18:18	and officials s around a fire they had made	2705
	18:25	As Simon Peter s warming himself,	1639+2705
	19:25	Near the cross of Jesus s his mother,	2705
	20:11	but Mary s outside the tomb crying.	2705
	20:19	Jesus came and s among them and said,	2705
	20:26	Jesus came and s among them and said,	2705
	21: 4	Early in the morning, Jesus s on the shore,	2705
Ac	1:10	two men dressed in white s **beside** them.	4225
	1:15	In those days Peter s up among	482
	2:14	Then Peter s up with the Eleven,	2705
	5:34	s up in the Sanhedrin and ordered that	482
	9: 7	men traveling with Saul s there speechless;	2705
	9:39	All the widows s **around** him,	4225
	10:30	a man in shining clothes s before me	2705
	11:28	s up and through the Spirit predicted that	482
	12: 6	and sentries s guard at the entrance.	5498
	15: 5	to the party of the Pharisees s up and said,	1985
	17:22	then s up in the meeting of the Areopagus	2705
	21:40	Paul s on the steps and motioned to	2705
	22:13	He s **beside** me and said, 'Brother Saul,	2392
	22:20	I s there giving my approval and	1639+2392
	23: 9	of the law who were Pharisees s up	482
	23:11	The following night the Lord s **near** Paul	2392
	24:20	in me *when* I s before the Sanhedrin—	2705
	24:21	unless it was this one thing I shouted *as I* s	2705
	25: 7	down from Jerusalem s **around** him,	4325
	27:21	Paul s up before them and said:	2705
	27:23	and whom I serve s **beside** me	4225
2Co	13: 7	that people will see that we have s **the test**	1511
Col	2:14	against us and that s **opposed** to us;	1639+5641
2Ti	4:17	the Lord s **at** my **side** and gave me strength,	4225
Heb	10:32	when *you* s *your* **ground** in a great contest	5702
	10:33	at other times *you* s side by side	1181
Jas	1:12	because *when he* has s the test,	1181
Rev	8: 3	came and s at the altar.	2705
	11:11	and *they* s on their feet, and terror struck	2705
	12: 4	The dragon s in front of the woman	2705
	13: 1	And the dragon s on the shore of the sea.	2705
	22: 2	On each side of the river s the tree of life,	NIG

STOOL (1) [FOOTSTOOL]

Ex	1:16	and observe them on the **delivery s,**	78

STOOP (5) [STOOPED, STOOPS]

2Sa	22:36	you s **down** to make me great.	6700
Ps	18:35	you s **down** to make me great.	6708
Ecc	12: 3	and the strong men s, when the grinders	6430
Isa	46: 2	*They* s and bow down together;	7970
Mk	1: 7	of whose sandals I am not worthy to s **down**	3252

STOOPED (1) [STOOP]

Jn	8: 8	Again *he* s **down** and wrote on the ground.	2893

STOOPS (2) [STOOP]

Ps	113: 6	who s **down** to look on the heavens and	9164
Isa	46: 1	Bel bows down, Nebo s **low;**	7970

STOP (67) [STOPPED, STOPPING, STOPS]

Ge	19:17	and don't s anywhere in the plain!	6641
Ex	9:29	The thunder *will* s and there will	2532
Nu	11:28	"Moses, my lord, s them!"	3973
Jos	10:19	But don't s! Pursue your enemies,	6641
	22:25	descendants *might cause* ours to s fearing	8697
Jdg	15: 7	I won't s until I get my revenge on you."	2532
	19:11	let's s at this city of the Jebusites	6073
1Sa	7: 8	"Do not s crying out to the LORD our God	3087
	9: 5	or my father *will* s thinking about	2532
	15:16	"S!" Samuel said to Saul.	8332
	20:38	"Hurry! Go quickly! Don't s!"	6641
2Sa	2:21	But Asahel would not s chasing him.	6073
	2:22	Abner warned Asahel, "S chasing me!	6073
	2:26	your men to s pursuing their brothers?"	8740
2Ki	3:19	s up all the springs, and ruin every good	6258
2Ch	25:16	S! Why be struck down?"	2532
	35:21	so s opposing God, who is with me,	2532
Ezr	4:21	Now issue an order to these men to s **work,**	10098
	4:23	and compelled them by force to s.	10098
	6: 8	so that the work *will* not s.	10098
Ne	5:10	But *let* the exacting of usury s!	6440
	6: 3	the work s while I leave it and go down	8697
Job	9:12	If he snatches away, who *can* s him?	8740
	13:21	and s frightening me with your terrors.	440
	37:14	s and consider God's wonders.	6641
Pr	19:27	S listening to instruction, my son,	2532
Isa	1:13	S bringing meaningless offerings!	3578+4202
	1:16	out of my sight! S doing wrong,	2532
	2:22	S **trusting** in man,	2532+4946
	28:22	Now s your mocking,	440
	30:11	and s confronting us with the Holy One	8697
	33: 1	When you s destroying,	9462
	33: 1	when you s betraying, you will be betrayed.	5801
Jer	5: 3	Who *will* s to ask how you are?	6073
	32:40	*I will* never s doing good to them,	8740
	44: 5	from their wickedness or s burning incense	1194
Eze	16:41	*I will* **put** a s *to* your prostitution,	8697
	21:21	of Babylon *will* s at the fork in the road, at	6641
	23:27	So *I will* **put** a s *to* the lewdness	8697
	45: 9	S dispossessing my people,	8123
Hos	2:11	*I will* s all her celebrations:	8697
Am	7: 5	"Sovereign LORD, I beg you, s!	2532
	7:16	and s preaching against the house of Isaac.'	4202
Na	2: 8	"S! Stop!" they cry, but no one turns back.	6641

Na	2: 8	"Stop! S!" they cry, but no one turns back.	6641
Mk	9:38	in your name and *we* told him **to** s,	3266
	9:39	"Do not s him," Jesus said.	3266
Lk	6:29	*do* not s him **from taking** your tunic.	3590
	8:52	"S wailing," Jesus said.	3590
	9:49	in your name and *we* **tried** to s him,	3266
	9:50	"Do not s him," Jesus said,	3266
Jn	5:14	S sinning or something worse may happen	3600
	6:43	"S grumbling among yourselves,"	3590
	7:24	S judging by mere appearances,"	3590
	20:27	S doubting and believe."	3590
Ac	4:17	to s this thing from spreading any further	3590
	5:39	you will not be able *to* s these men;	2907
	8:38	And he gave orders *to* s the chariot.	2705
	13:10	*Will you* never s perverting the right ways	4264
Ro	14:13	let us s passing judgment on one another.	3600
1Co	14:20	Brothers, s thinking like children.	3590
	14:30	the first speaker should s.	4967
2Co	11:10	the regions of Achaia *will* s this boasting	5852
1Ti	5:23	S drinking only water, and use a little wine	3600
2Pe	2:14	eyes full of adultery, they **never** s sinning;	188
Rev	4: 8	Day and night *they* never s saying:	398+2400
	9:20	they did not s worshiping demons,	NIG

STOPPED (78) [STOP]

Ge	8: 2	and the rain *had* s **falling** from the sky.	3973
	11: 8	and *they* s building the city.	2532
	26:15	the Philistines s **up,** filling them with earth.	6258
	26:18	the Philistines *had* s up after Abraham died,	6258
	28:11	*he* s **for the night** because the sun had set.	4328
	29:35	Then *she* s having children.	6641
	30: 9	Leah saw that *she had* s having children,	6641
	41:49	it was so much that *he* s keeping records	2532
	42:27	At **place where they** s **for the night**	4869
	43:21	But at **place where we** s **for the night**	4869
Ex	9:33	the thunder and hail s,	2532
	9:34	and hail and thunder *had* s, he sinned again:	2532
	9:48	and the plague s.	6806
Nu	16:48	and the plague had s.	6806
	16:50	for the plague *had* s.	6806
	25: 8	Then the plague against the Israelites **was** s;	6806
Jos	3:16	the water from upstream s flowing.	6641
	5:12	The manna s the day after they ate this food	8697
	10:13	So the sun stood still, and the moon s,	6641
	10:13	The sun s in the middle of the sky	6641
Jdg	19:15	There *they* s to spend the night.	6073
Ru	1:18	determined to go with her, *she* s urging her.	2532
	2:20	not s **showing** his kindness *to* the living and	6440
1Sa	6:14	and there *it* s beside a large rock.	6641
	10: 2	now your father has s **thinking** *about* them	5759
	10:13	After Saul s prophesying,	3983
	14:46	Then Saul s pursuing the Philistines,	4946+6590
2Sa	2:23	And every man s when he came to the place	6641
	18:16	and the troops s pursuing Israel,	8740
	20:12	that everyone who came up to Amasa s,	6641
	24:21	that the plague on the people *may* **be** s."	6806
	24:25	and the plague on Israel **was** s.	6806
1Ki	15:21	*he* s building Ramah and withdrew	2532
	17:17	and finally s breathing.	3855+4202
	22:33	not the king of Israel and s pursuing him.	8740
2Ki	2: 7	where Elijah and Elisha *had* s at the Jordan.	6641
	3:25	*They* s up all the springs and cut	6258
	4: 6	Then the oil s flowing.	6641
	4: 8	So whenever he came by, *he* s there to eat.	6073
	5: 9	with his horses and chariots and s at	6641
	6:23	Aram raiding Israel's territory.	3578+4202+6388
	13:18	He struck it three times and s.	6641
	18:17	and s at the aqueduct of the Upper Pool,	6641
1Ch	21:22	that the plague on the people *may* **be** s.	6806
2Ch	16: 5	*he* s building Ramah and abandoned his	2532
	18:32	*they* s pursuing him.	8740
	25:16	So the prophet s but said,	2532
Ezr	5: 5	and they *were* not s until a report could go	10098
Ne	12:39	At the Gate of the Guard *they* s.	6641
Job	4:16	*It* s, but I could not tell what it was.	6641
	32: 1	So these three men s answering Job,	8697
Ps	58: 4	like that of a cobra *that has* s its ears,	357
Isa	24: 8	the noise of the revelers has s,	8697
	36: 2	When the commander s at the aqueduct of	6641
Jer	44:18	since *we* s burning incense to the Queen	2532
	48:33	*I have* s the flow of wine from the presses;	8697
	51:30	Babylon's warriors *have* s fighting.	2532
La	5:14	the young men have s their music.	4946
Eze	10:16	from over the threshold of the temple and s	6641
	10:19	*They* s at the entrance to the east gate of	6641
	11:23	the city and s above the mountain east of it.	6641
Zec	7:11	they turned their backs and s up	3877+4946+9048
Mt	2: 9	the east went ahead of them until *it* s over	2705
	20:32	Jesus s and called them.	2705
Mk	5:29	Immediately her bleeding s and she felt	3830
	10:49	Jesus s and said, "Call him."	2705
Lk	7:45	the time I entered, *has* not s kissing my feet.	1364
	8:44	and immediately her bleeding s.	2705
	18:40	Jesus s and ordered the man to be brought	2705
	23:45	for the sun s **shining.**	1722
Ac	5:42	*they* never s teaching and proclaiming	4264
	10:17	where Simon's house was and s **at** the gate.	2392
	11:11	to me from Caesarea s at the house	2392
	20:31	that for three years I never s warning each	4264
	21:32	and his soldiers, *they* s beating Paul.	4264
Eph	1:16	*I have* not s giving thanks for you,	4264
Col	1: 9	not s praying for you and asking God	4264
1Th	2:18	did, again and again—but Satan s us.	1601
Heb	10: 2	would *they* not *have* s being offered?	4264

STOPPING (2) [STOP]
Ex	5: 5	and *you are* s them from working."	8697
Jer	41:17	s at Geruth Kimham near Bethlehem	3782

STOPS (8) [STOP]
1Ki	18:44	and go down before the rain s you.' "	6806
Job	18: 5	the flame of his fire s burning.	4202
	30:27	The churning inside me never s;	1957
	37: 7	*he* s every man from his labor.	3159
Isa	33:15	who s his ears against plots of murder	357
	44:19	No one s **to think**,	448+4213+8740
Ac	6:13	"This fellow never s speaking	4264
3Jn	1:10	*He* also s those who want to do so	3266

STORAGE (2) [STORE]
Jer	40:10	and put them in your s jars,	3998
Eze	4: 9	in a s jar and use them to make bread	3998

STORE (29) [STORAGE, STORED, STORES, STORING]
Ge	6:21	and s it *away* as food for you and for them."	665
	41:35	that are coming and s up the grain under	7392
Ex	1:11	and Rameses as s cities for Pharaoh.	5016
Dt	14:28	that year's produce and s it in your towns,	5663
1Ki	9:19	as well as all his s cities and the towns	5016
2Ch	8: 4	in the desert and all the s cities he had built	5016
	8: 6	as well as Baalath and all his s cities,	5016
	16: 4	Abel Maim and all the s cities of Naphtali.	5016
	17:12	he built forts and s cities in Judah	5016
	32:28	He also made **buildings** to s the harvest	5016
Ne	13: 5	with a large room formerly used to s	5989
Job	23:14	and many such plans he still has **in** s.	6640
Ps	17:14	and *they* s up wealth for their children.	5663
Pr	2: 1	and s **up** my commands within you,	7621
	2: 7	He holds victory **in** s for the upright,	7621
	7: 1	keep my words and s **up** my commands	7621
	10:14	Wise men s up knowledge,	7621
	30:25	yet *they* s up their food in the summer;	3922
Isa	2:12	The LORD Almighty has a day **in** s for all	6584
	10:28	*they* s supplies at Micmash.	7212
	33: 6	a rich s *of* salvation and wisdom	2890
Mic	6:14	*You* will s up but save nothing,	6047
Mt	6:19	not s up for yourselves treasures on earth,	2564
	6:20	But s up for yourselves treasures in heaven,	2564
	6:26	they do not sow or reap or s *away* in barns,	5251
Lk	12:17	I have no place *to* s my crops.'	5251
	12:18	there *I will* s all my grain and my goods.	5251
2Co	9:10	and increase your s of seed and will enlarge	NIG
2Ti	4: 8	Now *there is* **in** s for me the crown	641

STORED (19) [STORE]
Ge	41:48	of abundance in Egypt and s it in the cities.	5989
	41:49	Joseph s huge quantities of grain,	7392
2Ki	20:17	all that your fathers *have* s up until this day,	732
Ezr	6: 1	in the archives s in the treasury at Babylon.	10474
Job	15:20	the ruthless through all the years s up	7621
Ps	31:19	which *you* have s up for those who fear you,	7621
Pr	13:22	a sinner's wealth **is** s up for the righteous.	7621
SS	7:13	both new and old, that *I* have s up for you,	7621
Isa	15: 7	and s up they carry away over the Ravine of	7213
	22: 9	*you* s up water in the Lower Pool.	7695
	23:18	*they* will not **be** s up or hoarded.	732
	39: 6	all that your fathers *have* s up until this day,	732
	45: 3	riches s *in* secret places,	AIT
Hos	13:12	The guilt of Ephraim *is* s up,	7674
Mt	12:35	good things out of the good s up in him,	2565
	12:35	evil things out of the evil s up in him.	2565
Lk	6:45	things out of the good s up in his heart,	2565
	6:45	evil things out of the evil s **up** in his heart.	2565
Col	1: 5	from the hope that is s **up** for you in heaven	641

STOREHOUSE (5) [HOUSE]
Dt	28:12	the heavens, the s *of* his bounty,	238
1Ch	26:15	and the lot for the s fell to his sons.	667+1074
	26:17	on the south and two at a time at the s.	667
Hos	13:15	His s will be plundered of all its treasures.	238
Mal	3:10	Bring the whole tithe into the s,	238+1074

STOREHOUSES (12) [HOUSE]
Ge	41:56	Joseph opened the s and	889+928+2157+3972S
2Ki	20:13	showed them all that was in his s—	1074+5800
1Ch	27:25	of Adiel was in charge of the royal s.	238
	27:25	in charge of the s in the outlying districts,	238
Job	38:22	the s *of* the snow or seen the storehouses of	238
	38:22	the storehouses of the snow or seen the s *of*	238
Ps	33: 7	he puts the deep into s.	238
	135: 7	the rain and brings out the wind from his s.	238
Isa	39: 2	and showed them what was in his s—	1074+5800
Jer	10:13	the rain and brings out the wind from his s.	238
	51:16	the rain and brings out the wind from his s.	238
Joel	1:17	The s are in ruins.	238

STOREROOM (2) [ROOM]
Mt	13:52	of his s new treasures as well as old."	2565
Lk	12:24	they have no s or barn; yet God feeds them.	5421

STOREROOMS (11) [ROOM]
1Ch	28:11	its buildings, its s, its upper parts,	1711
2Ch	31:11	to prepare s in the temple of the LORD,	4384
Ne	10:37	we will bring to the s *of* the house	4384
	10:38	house of our God, to the s of the treasury.	4384
	10:39	new wine and oil to the s where the articles	4384
	12:25	who guarded the s *at* the gates.	667
	12:44	of the s for the contributions,	238+4200+5969
	12:44	into **the** s portions required by the Law	2157S
	13: 4	the priest had been put in charge of the s *of*	4384
	13:12	new wine and oil into the s.	238
	13:13	**put** Shelemiah the priest, Zadok the scribe, and a Levite named Pedaiah **in charge of the** s	238+732+6584

STORES (4) [STORE]
Job	21:19	'God s up a man's punishment for his sons.'	7621
Pr	6: 8	yet *it* s its provisions in summer	3922
	21:20	the house of the wise are s of choice food	238
Lk	12:21	be with anyone who s up things for himself	2564

STORIES (2) [STORY]
2Pe	1:16	We did not follow cleverly invented s	3680
	2: 3	exploit you *with* s they have made up.	3364

STORING (2) [STORE]
Ecc	2:26	of gathering and s up wealth to hand it over	4043
Ro	2: 5	*you are* s up wrath against yourself for	2564

STORK (6)
Lev	11:19	the s, any kind of heron, the hoopoe and	2884
Dt	14:18	the s, any kind of heron, the hoopoe and	2884
Job	39:13	with the pinions and feathers of the s.	2884
Ps	104:17	the s has its home in the pine trees.	2884
Jer	8: 7	s in the sky knows her appointed seasons,	2884
Zec	5: 9	They had wings like those of a s,	2884

STORM (34) [STORMED, STORMS, STORMY, THUNDERSTORM, WINDSTORM]
Ex	9:24	It was the worst s in all the land of Egypt	1352
Job	9:17	a s and multiply my wounds for no reason.	8554
	30:22	you toss me about in the s.	9583
	36:33	His thunder announces the coming s;	2257S
	38: 1	Then the LORD answered Job out of the s.	6194
	40: 6	Then the LORD spoke to Job out of the s:	6194
Ps	55: 8	far from the tempest and s."	6193
	83:15	and terrify them with your s.	6070
	107:29	He stilled the s to a whisper;	6194
Pr	1:27	when calamity overtakes you like a s,	8739
	10:25	When the s has swept by,	6070
Isa	4: 6	refuge and hiding place from the s and rain.	2443
	25: 4	from the s and a shade from the heat.	2443
	25: 4	the breath of the ruthless is like a s *driving*	2443
	32: 2	from the wind and a refuge from the s,	2443
Jer	11:16	But with the roar of a mighty s he will set it	2167
	23:19	the s of the LORD will burst out in wrath,	6194
	25:32	a mighty s is rising from the ends of	6193
	30:23	the s *of* the LORD will burst out in wrath,	6194
Eze	30:16	Thebes will be **taken** by s;	1324
	38: 9	you will go up, advancing like a s;	8739
Da	11:40	and the king of the North *will* s out	8548
Jnh	1: 4	a violent s arose that the ship threatened	6193
	1:12	that it is my fault that this great s has come	6193
Na	1: 3	His way is in the whirlwind and the s,	8554
	2: 4	The chariots s through the streets,	2147
Zec	10: 1	it is the LORD who makes the s **clouds**.	2613
Mt	8:24	a furious s came up on the lake,	4939
Lk	8:24	the s subsided, and all was calm.	NIG
Ac	27:15	by the s and could not head into the wind;	NIG
	27:18	took such a violent **battering from** the s	5928
	27:20	for many days and the s continued raging,	5930
Heb	12:18	to darkness, gloom and s;	2590
2Pe	2:17	without water and mists driven by a s.	3278

STORMED (2) [STORM]
Jdg	9:52	Abimelech went to the tower and s it.	4309
Hab	3:14	when his warriors s **out** to scatter us,	6192

STORMS (2) [STORM]
Isa	54:11	**lashed by** s and not comforted,	6192
Zec	9:14	he will march in the s of the south,	6194

STORMY (3) [STORM]
Ps	148: 8	s winds that do his bidding,	6194
Am	1:14	amid violent winds on a s day.	6070
Mt	16: 3	'Today it will be s,	5930

STORY (4) [STORIES]
Ge	39:17	Then she told him this s:	1821
	39:19	the s his wife told him,	1821
Mt	28:15	And this s has been widely circulated	3364
Ac	20: 9	he fell to the ground from the **third** s and	5566

STOUT (KJV) See HARSH, IMPOSING, WILLFUL PRIDE

STOUTHEARTED (1) [HEART]
Ps	138: 3	you made me bold and s.	5883+6437

STRAGGLER (1)
Isa	14:31	and there is not a s in its ranks.	969

STRAIGHT (40) [STRAIGHTEN, STRAIGHTENED]
Jos	6: 5	and the people will go up, every man s **in**."	5584
	6: 5	so every man charged s **in**,	5584
1Sa	6:12	the cows **went** s up toward Beth Shemesh,	3837
2Sa	5:23	and he answered, "*Do not* **go** s up,	6590
1Ch	14:14	and God answered him, "*Do* not go s **up**,	6590
Job	10:19	s from the womb **to** the grave!	4200
Ps	5: 8	**make** s your way before me.	3837
	27:11	in a s path because of my oppressors.	4793
	107: 7	by a s way to a city where they could settle.	3838
Pr	2:13	who leave the s paths to walk in dark ways,	3841
	3: 6	and he *will* **make** your paths s.	3837
	4:11	of wisdom and lead you along s paths.	3841
	4:25	Let your eyes look s **ahead**,	4200+5790
	5: 5	her steps **lead** s *to* the grave.	9461
	9:15	who go s *on* their way.	3837
	11: 5	of the blameless **makes** *a* s way for them,	3837
	15:21	a man of understanding **keeps** a s course.	3837
SS	7: 9	May the wine go s to my lover,	4797
Isa	40: 3	**make** s in the wilderness a highway for	3837
	45:13	*I will* make all his ways s.	3837
Jer	31:39	The measuring line will stretch from there s	5584
Eze	1: 7	Their legs were s;	3838
	1: 9	Each one went s **ahead**;	448+6298+7156
	1:12	Each one went s **ahead**.	448+6298+7156
	10:22	each marches s **ahead**.	5019
Joel	2: 8	Each plunges s **ahead**.	5019
Am	4: 3	You will each go s **out** **through** breaks in	5584
Mt	3: 3	way for the Lord, make s paths for him.' "	2318
Mk	1: 3	way for the Lord, make s paths for him.' "	2318
Lk	3: 4	way for the Lord, make s paths for him.	2318
	3: 5	The crooked roads shall become s,	2318
	22:61	The Lord turned and **looked** s at Peter.	1838
Jn	1:23	'Make s the way for the Lord.' "	2316
Ac	3: 4	Peter **looked** s at him, as did John.	867
	9:11	the house of Judas on s Street and ask for	2318
	13: 9	**looked** s at Elymas and said,	867
	16:11	From Troas *we* put out to sea and **sailed** s	2312
	21: 1	we put out to sea and **sailed** s to Cos.	2312
	23: 1	Paul **looked** s at the Sanhedrin and said,	867
2Pe	2:15	They have left the s way and wandered off	2318

STRAIGHTEN (3) [STRAIGHT]
Ecc	7:13	Who can s what he has made crooked?	9545
Lk	13:11	She was bent over and could not s **up** at all.	376
Tit	1: 5	*you might* s **out** what was left unfinished	2114

STRAIGHTENED (4) [STRAIGHT]
Ecc	1:15	What is twisted cannot **be** s;	9545
Lk	13:13	and immediately *she* s **up** and praised God.	494
Jn	8: 7	*he* s **up** and said to them,	376
	8:10	Jesus s **up** and asked her, "Woman,	376

STRAIGHTWAY (KJV) See AS SOON AS, AT ONCE, AT THAT MOMENT, HURRIED, IMMEDIATELY, RIGHT AWAY, WITHOUT DELAY

STRAIN (2) [STRAINING]
Ex	18:23	you will be able *to* **stand the** s,	6641
Mt	23:24	You s **out** a gnat but swallow a camel.	1494

STRAINING (3) [STRAIN]
Zec	6: 7	they were s to go throughout the earth.	1335
Mk	6:48	He saw the disciples s at the oars,	989
Php	3:13	Forgetting what is behind and s **toward**	2085

STRANDS (3)
Ex	39: 3	of gold and cut s to be worked into the blue,	7348
Ecc	4:12	A cord of **three** s is not quickly broken.	AIT
Eze	5: 3	But take a few s of hair and tuck them away	NIH

STRANGE (12) [ESTRANGED, STRANGER, STRANGER'S, STRANGERS]
Ex	3: 3	"I will go over and see this s sight—	1524
Pr	23:33	Your eyes will see s sights	2424
Isa	18: 2	an aggressive nation of s **speech**,	7743+7743
	18: 7	an aggressive nation of s **speech**,	7743+7743
	28:11	and s tongues God will speak to this people,	337
	28:21	to do his work, his s work,	2424
	33:19	with their s, incomprehensible tongue.	4352
Ac	17:20	You are bringing some s *ideas* to our ears,	3826
1Co	14:21	"Through **men of** s **tongues** and through	2280
Heb	13: 9	be carried away by all kinds of s teachings.	3828
1Pe	4: 4	*They* **think** it s that you do not plunge	3826
		though *something* s were happening to you.	3828

STRANGER (18) [STRANGE]
Ge	23: 4	"I am an alien and a s among you.	9369
	42: 7	**pretended to be a** s and spoke harshly	5796
Job	19:15	and my maidservants count me a s;	2424
	29:16	I took up the case of the s.	3359+4202
	31:32	but no s had to spend the night in the street,	1731
Ps	39:12	For I dwell with you as an alien, a s,	9369
	69: 8	I am a s to my brothers,	2319
	119:19	I am a s on earth;	1731
Pr	20:16	garment of one who puts up security for a s;	2424
	27:13	garment of one who puts up security for a s;	2424

Ecc	6: 2	and as enjoys them instead.	5799
Jer	14: 8	why are you like as in the land,	1731
Mt	25:35	I was as and you invited me in,	3828
	25:38	When did we see you as and invite you in,	3828
	25:43	I was as and you did not invite me in,	3828
	25:44	as or needing clothes or sick or in prison,	3828
Jn	10: 5	But they will never follow as;	259
Heb	11: 9	in the promised land like as in	259

STRANGER'S (1) [STRANGE]
Jn	10: 5	because they do not recognize as voice."	259

STRANGERS (19) [STRANGE]
Ge	15:13	that your descendants will be s in a country	1731
1Ch	16:19	few in number, few indeed, and s in it,	1591
	29:15	We are aliens and s in your sight,	9369
Ps	54: 3	S are attacking me;	2424
	105:12	few in number, few indeed, and s in it,	1591
	109:11	may s plunder the fruits of his labor.	2424
Pr	5:10	lest s feast on your wealth	2424
	5:17	never to be shared with s.	2424
Isa	1: 7	laid waste as when overthrown by s.	2424
Eze	16:32	You prefer s to your own husband!	2424
Ob	1:11	while s carried off his wealth	2424
Zec	7:14	all the nations, where they were s.	3359+4202
Ac	7: 6	'Your descendants will be s in a country	4230
Heb	11:13	that they were aliens and s on earth.	4215
	13: 2	Do not forget to entertain s,	5810
1Pe	1: 1	s in the world, scattered throughout Pontus,	4215
	1:17	live your lives as s here in reverent fear.	4229
	2:11	I urge you, as aliens and s in the world,	4215
3Jn	1: 5	even though they are s to you.	3828

STRANGLED (4) [STRANGLING]
Na	2:12	The lion killed enough for his cubs and s	2871
Ac	15:20	from the meat of s animals and from blood.	4465
	15:29	from blood, from the meat of s animals	4465
	21:25	from blood, from the meat of s animals	4465

STRANGLING (1) [STRANGLED]
Job	7:15	so that I prefer s and death,	4725

STRAP (1) [STRAPPED, STRAPS]
Ex	32:27	'Each man s a sword to his side.	8492

STRAPPED (2) [STRAP]
Jdg	3:16	which he s to his right thigh under his	2520
2Sa	20: 8	and s over it at his waist was a belt with	7537

STRAPS (1) [STRAP]
Jer	27: 2	a yoke out of s and crossbars and put it	4593

STRATEGY (3)
2Ki	18:20	You say you have s and military strength—	6783
Isa	8:10	Devise your s, but it will be thwarted;	6783
	36: 5	You say you have s and military strength—	6783

STRAW (22)
Ge	24:25	"We have plenty of s and fodder,	9320
	24:32	S and fodder were brought for the camels,	9320
Ex	5: 7	the people with s for making bricks;	9320
	5: 7	let them go and gather their own s.	9320
	5:10	'I will not give you any more s.	9320
	5:11	get your own s wherever you can find it,	9320
	5:12	over Egypt to gather stubble to use for s.	9320
	5:13	just as when you had s."	9320
	5:16	Your servants are given no s,	9320
	5:18	You will not be given any s.	9320
Jdg	19:19	We have both s and fodder for our donkeys	9320
1Ki	4:28	the proper place their quotas of barley and s	9320
Job	21:18	How often are they like s before the wind,	9320
	41:27	like s and bronze like rotten wood.	9320
	41:29	A club seems to him but a piece of s;	7990
Isa	5:24	of fire lick up s and as dry grass sinks down	7990
	11: 7	and the lion will eat s like the ox,	9320
	25:10	be trampled under him as s is trampled	5495
	33:11	You conceive chaff, you give birth to s;	7990
	65:25	and the lion will eat s like the ox,	9320
Jer	23:28	For what has s to do with grain?"	9320
1Co	3:12	silver, costly stones, wood, hay or s,	2811

STRAWED (KJV) See SCATTERED

STRAY (9) [ASTRAY, STRAYED, STRAYING, STRAYS]
Ex	22: 5	or vineyard and lets them s and they graze	8938
1Ki	22:43	in the ways of his father Asa and did not s	6073
2Ch	20:32	in the ways of his father Asa and did not s	6073
Ps	119:10	do not let me s from your commands.	8706
	119:21	and who s from your commands.	8706
	119:118	You reject all who s from your decrees,	8706
Pr	7:25	Do not let your heart turn to her ways or s	9494
	19:27	you will s from the words of knowledge.	8706
Eze	14:11	people of Israel will no longer s from me,	9494

STRAYED (6) [STRAY]
Ps	44:18	our feet had not s from your path.	5742
	119:110	but I have not s from your precepts.	9494
	119:176	I have s like a lost sheep.	9494

Jer	2: 5	that they s so far from me?	8178
	31:19	After I s, I repented;	8740
Hos	7:13	Woe to them, because they have s from me!	5610

STRAYING (1) [STRAY]
Dt	22: 1	If you see your brother's ox or sheep s,	5615

STRAYS (5) [STRAY]
Pr	21:16	A man who s from the path	9494
	27: 8	Like a bird that s from its nest is a man	5610
	27: 8	from its nest is a man who s from his home.	5610
Eze	34: 4	not brought back the s or searched for	5615
	34:16	for the lost and bring back the s.	5615

STREAKED (7)
Ge	30:35	the male goats that were s or spotted,	6819
	30:39	that were s or speckled or spotted.	6819
	30:40	the rest face the s and dark-colored animals	6819
	31: 8	if he said, 'The s ones will be your wages,'	6819
	31: 8	then all the flocks bore s young.	6819
	31:10	male goats mating with the flock were s,	6819
	31:12	the male goats mating with the flock are s,	6819

STREAM (16) [DOWNSTREAM, STREAMING, STREAMS, UPSTREAM]
Ge	32:23	After he had sent them across the s,	5707
Dt	9:21	as fine as dust and threw the dust into a s	5707
	21: 4	or planted and where there is a flowing s.	419
1Sa	17:40	chose five smooth stones from the s,	5707
2Ch	32: 4	and they blocked all the springs and the s	5707
Job	30: 6	They were forced to live in the dry s beds,	5707
	40:22	the poplars by the s surround him.	5707
	41:19	Firebrands s from his mouth;	2143
Isa	2: 2	and all nations will s to it.	5641
	30:33	like a s of burning sulfur, sets it ablaze.	5707
	32:20	sowing your seed by every s,	4784
	66:12	and the wealth of nations like a flooding s;	5707
Jer	17: 8	the water that sends out its roots by the s.	3414
	51:44	The nations will no longer s to him.	5641
Am	5:24	righteousness like a never-failing s!	5707
Mic	4: 1	and peoples will s to it.	5641

STREAMING (1) [STREAM]
SS	4:15	of flowing water s down from Lebanon.	5688

STREAMS (61) [STREAM]
Ge	2: 6	but s came up from the earth and watered	116
Ex	7:19	over the s and canals,	5643
	8: 5	with your staff over the s and canals	5643
Lev	11: 9	in the water of the seas and the s,	5707
	11:10	But all creatures in the seas or s that do	5707
Dt	8: 7	a land with s and pools of water,	5707
	10: 7	a land with s of water.	5707
2Ki	19:24	the soles of my feet I have dried up all the s	3284
Job	6:15	as undependable as intermittent s,	5707
	6:15	as the s that overflow	692+5707
	20:17	He will not enjoy the s,	7106
	29: 6	the rock poured out for me s of olive oil.	7104
	36:27	which distill as rain to the s;	116
Ps	1: 3	He is like a tree planted by s of water,	7104
	42: 1	As the deer pants for s of water,	692
	46: 4	There is a river whose s make glad the city	7104
	65: 9	The s of God are filled with water	5707
	74:15	It was you who opened up springs and s;	5707
	78:16	He brought s out of a rocky crag	5689
	78:20	water gushed out, and s flowed abundantly.	5707
	78:44	their s so they could not drink from s.	5689
	119:136	S of tears flow from my eyes,	7104
	126: 4	O Lord, like s in the Negev.	692
Pr	5:16	your s of water in the public squares?	7104
Ecc	1: 7	All s flow into the sea,	5707
	1: 7	To the place the s come from,	5707
SS	5:12	His eyes are like doves by the water s,	692
Isa	7:18	the distant s of Egypt and for bees from	3284
	11:15	up into seven s so that men can cross over	5707
	19: 6	the s of Egypt will dwindle and dry up.	3284
	30:25	s of water will flow on every high	7104
	32: 2	like s of water in the desert and the shadow	7104
	33:21	It will be like a place of broad rivers and s.	3284
	34: 9	Edom's s will be turned into pitch,	5707
	35: 6	in the wilderness and s in the desert.	5707
	37:25	the soles of my feet I have dried up all the s	3284
	43:19	a way in the desert and s in the wasteland.	5643
	43:20	because I provide water in the desert and s	5643
	44: 3	and s on the dry ground;	5689
	44: 4	like poplar trees by flowing s.	3298+4784
	44:27	'Be dry, and I will dry up your s,'	5643
	47: 2	bare your legs, and wade through the s.	5643
Jer	9:18	till our eyes overflow with tears and water s	5688
	31: 9	I will lead them beside s of water on	5707
La	3:48	S of tears flow from my eyes	7104
Eze	29: 3	you great monster lying among your s.	3284
	29: 4	the fish of your s stick to your scales.	3284
	29: 4	I will pull you out from among your s,	3284
	29: 5	you and all the fish of your s.	3284
	29:10	against you and against your s,	3284
	30:12	I will dry up the s of the Nile and sell	3284
	31: 4	their s flowed all around its base	5643
	31:15	I held back its s, and its abundant waters	5643
	32: 2	in the seas thrashing about in your s,	5643
	32: 2	with your feet and muddying the s.	5643
	32:14	and make her s flow like oil,	5643
Joel	1:20	the s of water have dried up	692

Hab	3: 8	Was your wrath against the s?	5643
Mt	7:25	The rain came down, the s rose,	4532
	7:27	The rain came down, the s rose,	4532
Jn	7:38	s of living water will flow from	4532

STREET (26) [STREETS]
Dt	32:25	In the s the sword will make them childless;	2575
Jos	2:19	the s, his blood will be on his own head;	2575
2Ch	28:24	up altars at every s corner in Jerusalem.	7157
Job	31:32	the s, for my door was always open to	2575
Ps	31:11	those who see me on the s flee from me.	2575
Pr	1:20	Wisdom calls aloud in the s,	2575
	7: 8	He was going down the s near her corner,	8798
	7:12	now in the s, now in the squares,	2575
Ecc	12: 4	the doors to the s are closed and the sound	8798
Isa	51:20	they lie at the head of every s,	2575
	51:23	like a s to be walked over."	2575
Jer	6:11	"Pour it out on the children in the s and on	2575
	37:21	of the guard and given bread from the s of	2575
La	2:19	from hunger at the head of every s.	2575
	4: 1	scattered at the head of every s.	2575
Eze	16:25	of every s you built your lofty shrines	2006
	16:31	of every s and made your lofty shrines	2006
Na	3:10	to pieces at the head of every s.	2575
Mt	6: 5	in the synagogues and on the s corners to	4423
	22: 9	Go to the s corners and invite to	3847
Mk	11: 4	They went and found a colt outside in the s,	316
Ac	9:11	to the house of Judas on Straight S and ask	4860
	12:10	When they had walked the length of one s,	4860
Rev	11: 8	Their bodies will lie in the s of the great	4423
	21:21	The great s of the city was of pure gold,	4423
	22: 2	down the middle of the great s of the city.	4423

STREETS (65) [STREET]
2Sa	1:20	proclaim it not in the s of Ashkelon,	2575
	22:43	and trampled them like mud in the s.	2575
Est	6: 9	on the horse through the city s,	8148
	6:11	led him on horseback through the city s,	8148
Ps	18:42	I poured them out like mud in the s.	2575
	55:11	threats and lies never leave its s.	8148
	144:14	no cry of distress in our s.	8148
Pr	1:21	the noisy s she cries out, in the gateways of	NIH
	5:16	Should your springs overflow in the s,	8148
	22:13	or, "I will be murdered in the s!"	8148
	26:13	a fierce lion roaming the s!"	8148
Ecc	12: 5	of heights and dangers in the s;	2006
	12: 5	and mourners go about the s.	8798
SS	3: 2	through its s and squares;	8798
Isa	5:25	and the dead bodies are like refuse in the s.	2575
	10: 6	to trample them down like mud in the s.	2575
	15: 3	In the s they wear sackcloth;	2575
	24:11	In the s they cry out for wine;	2575
	33: 7	Look, their brave men cry aloud in the s;	2575
	42: 2	or raise his voice in the s.	2575
	58:12	Restorer of S with Dwellings.	5986
	59:14	truth has stumbled in the s.	8148
Jer	5: 1	"Go up and down the s of Jerusalem,	2575
	7:17	towns of Judah and in the s of Jerusalem?	2575
	7:34	the towns of Judah and the s of Jerusalem	2575
	9:21	the children from the s and the young men	2575
	11: 6	of Judah and in the s of Jerusalem:	2575
	11:13	that shameful god Baal are as many as the s	2575
	14:16	the s of Jerusalem because of the famine	2575
	33:10	the towns of Judah and the s of Jerusalem	2575
	44: 6	the towns of Judah and the s of Jerusalem	2575
	44: 9	in the land of Judah and the s of Jerusalem?	2575
	44:17	of Judah and in the s of Jerusalem.	2575
	44:21	the s of Jerusalem by you and your fathers,	2575
	49:26	Surely, her young men will fall in the s;	8148
	50:30	Therefore, her young men will fall in the s;	8148
	51: 4	fatally wounded in her s.	2575
La	2:11	because children and infants faint in the s	8148
	2:12	as they faint like wounded men in the s of	8148
	2:21	and old lie together in the dust of the s;	2575
	4: 5	once ate delicacies are destitute in the s.	2575
	4: 8	they are not recognized in the s.	2575
	4:14	through the s like men who are blind.	2575
	4:18	so we could not walk in our s.	8148
Eze	7:19	They will throw their silver into the s,	2575
	11: 6	in this city and filled its s with the dead.	2575
	26:11	hoofs of his horses will trample all your s;	2575
	28:23	upon her and make blood flow in her s.	2575
Da	9:25	It will be rebuilt with s and a trench,	8148
Hos	7: 1	bandits rob in the s;	2575
Am	5:16	"There will be wailing in all the s and cries	2575
Mic	7:10	be trampled underfoot like mire in the s.	2575
Na	2: 4	The chariots storm through the s,	2575
Zep	3: 6	I have left their s deserted.	2575
Zec	8: 4	and women of ripe old age will sit in the s	8148
	8: 5	The city's will be filled with boys	8148
	9: 3	and gold like the dirt of the s.	2575
	10: 5	be mighty men trampling the muddy s	2575
Mt	6: 2	in the synagogues and on the s	4860
	12:19	no one will hear his voice in the s.	4423
	22:10	So the servants went out into the s	3847
Lk	10:10	go into its s and say,	4423
	13:26	and you taught in our s.'	4423
	14:21	into the s and alleys of the town and bring	4423
Ac	5:15	the s and laid them on beds and mats so that	4423

STRENGTH (183) [STRONG]
Ge	31: 6	I've worked for your father with all my s,	3946
	48: 2	Israel rallied his s and sat up on the bed.	2616
	49: 3	the first sign of my s, excelling in honor,	226
Ex	15: 2	The Lord is my s and my song;	6437

Ex	15:13	In your s you will guide them	6437
Lev	26:20	Your s will be spent in vain,	3946
Nu	14:17	"Now may the Lord's s be displayed,	3946
	23:22	they have the s of a wild ox.	9361
	24: 8	they have the s of a wild ox.	9361
Dt	4:37	of Egypt by his Presence and his great s,	3946
	6: 5	and with all your soul and with all your s.	4394
	8:17	"My power and the s of my hands have	6797
	11: 8	so that you may have the s to go in and take	2616
	21:17	That son is the first sign of his father's s.	226
	32:36	on his servants when he sees their s is gone	3338
	33:25	and your s will equal your days.	1801
	34: 7	yet his eyes were not weak nor his s	4301
Jdg	5:31	be like the sun when it rises in its s."	1476
	6:14	"Go in the s you have and save Israel out	3946
	7: 2	against me that her own s has saved her,	3338
	8:21	'As is the man, so is his s.' "	1476
	15:19	his s returned and he revived.	8120
	16: 5	into showing you the secret of his great s	3946
	16: 6	of your great s and how you can be tied up	3946
	16: 9	So the secret of his s was not discovered.	3946
	16:15	haven't told me the secret of your great s."	3946
	16:17	head were shaved, my s would leave me,	3946
	16:19	And his s left him.	3946
1Sa	2: 4	but those who stumbled are armed with s.	2657
	2: 9	"It is not by s that one prevails;	3946
	2:10	"He will give s to his king and exalt	6437
	2:31	when I will cut short your s and the strength	2432
	2:31	when I will cut short your strength and the s	2432
	23:16	and **helped** him **find** s in God.	906+2616+3338
	28:20	His s was gone, for he had eaten nothing	3946
	28:22	so you may eat and have the s to go	3946
	30: 4	until they had no s left to weep.	3946
	30: 6	But David **found** s in the LORD his God.	2616
2Sa	15:12	And so the conspiracy gained s,	579
	22:33	with s and makes my way perfect.	2657
	22:40	You armed me with s for battle;	2657
2Ki	18:20	You say you have strategy and military s—	1476
	19: 3	of birth and there is no s to deliver them.	3946
	23:25	and with all his soul and with all his s,	4394
1Ch	16:11	Look to the LORD and his s;	6437
	16:27	s and joy in his dwelling place.	6437
	16:28	ascribe to the LORD glory and s,	6437
	26: 8	with the s to do the work—	3946
	29:12	In your hands are s and power to exalt	3946
	29:12	and power to exalt and **give** s to all.	2616
2Ch	1: 9	But Abijah grew in s	2616
	23: 1	In the seventh year Jehoiada **showed** his s.	2616
	25:11	then **marshaled** his s and led his army to	2616
Ne	1:10	by your great s and your mighty hand.	3946
	4:10	"The s of the laborers is giving out,	3946
	8:10	for the joy of the LORD is your s."	5057
Job	6:11	"What s do I have, that I should still hope?	3946
	6:12	Do I have the s of stone?	3946
	9:19	If it is a matter of s, he is mighty!	3946
	12:16	To him belong s and victory;	6437
	22: 9	and broke the s of the fatherless.	2432
	30: 2	Of what use was the s of their hands to me,	3946
	39:11	Will you rely on him for his great s?	3946
	39:19	Do you give the horse his s or	1476
	39:21	He paws fiercely, rejoicing in his s,	3946
	40:16	What s he has in his loins,	3946
	41:12	his s and his graceful form.	1476
	41:22	S resides in his neck;	6437
Ps	10:10	they collapse; they fall under his s.	6786
	18: 1	I love you, O LORD, my s.	2619
	18:32	with s and makes my way perfect.	2657
	18:39	You armed me with s for battle;	2657
	21: 1	O LORD, the king rejoices in your s.	6437
	21:13	Be exalted, O LORD, in your s;	6437
	22:15	My s is dried up like a potsherd,	3946
	22:19	O my S, come quickly to help me.	394
	28: 7	The LORD is my s and my shield;	6437
	28: 8	The LORD is the s of his people,	6437
	29: 1	ascribe to the LORD glory and s.	6437
	29:11	The LORD gives to his people;	6437
	31:10	my s fails because of my affliction,	3946
	32: 4	my s was sapped as in the heat of summer.	4382
	33:16	no warrior escapes by his great s.	3946
	33:17	despite all its great s it cannot save.	2657
	38:10	My heart pounds, my s fails me;	3946
	46: 1	God is our refuge and s,	6437
	59: 9	O my S, I watch for you;	6437
	59:16	But I will sing of your s,	6437
	59:17	O my S, I sing praise to you;	6437
	65: 6	having armed yourself with s,	1476
	68:28	**show** us your s, O God,	6451
	68:35	of Israel gives power and s to his people.	9508
	71: 9	do not forsake me when my s is gone.	3946
	73:26	the s of my heart and my portion forever.	7446
	79:11	by the s of your arm preserve those	1542
		condemned to die.	
	81: 1	Sing for joy to God our s;	6437
	83: 8	Even Assyria has joined them to lend s to	2432
	84: 5	Blessed are those whose s is in you,	6437
	84: 7	They go from s to strength,	2657
	84: 7	They go from strength to s,	2657
	86:16	grant your s to your servant and save	6437
	88: 4	I am like a man without s.	384
	89:17	For you are their glory and s,	6437
	89:19	"I have bestowed s on a warrior,	6469
	90:10	or eighty, if we have the s;	1476
	93: 1	in majesty and is armed with s.	6437
	96: 6	s and glory are in his sanctuary.	6437
	96: 7	ascribe to the LORD glory and s.	6437
	102:23	In the course of my life he broke my s;	3946
	105: 4	Look to the LORD and his s;	6437

Ps	118:14	The LORD is my s and my song;	6437
	147:10	His pleasure is not in the s of the horse,	1476
Pr	5: 9	lest you give your **best** s to others	2086
	14: 4	the s of an ox comes an abundant harvest.	3946
	20:29	The glory of young men is their s,	3946
	24: 5	and a man of knowledge increases s;	3946
	24:10	how small is your s!	3946
	30:25	Ants are creatures of little s, yet they store	6434
	31: 3	do not spend your s on women,	2657
	31:25	She is clothed with s and dignity;	6437
Ecc	9:16	So I said, "Wisdom is better than s."	1476
	10:10	*more* s is needed but skill will bring success.	2657
	10:17	for s and not for drunkenness.	1476
Isa	10:13	" 'By the s of my hand I have done this,	3946
	12: 2	the LORD, is my s and my song;	6437
	28: 6	a **source of** s to those who turn back	1476
	30:15	in quietness and trust is your s,	1476
	31: 1	and in the great s of their horsemen,	6793
	33: 2	Be our s every morning,	2432
	36: 5	You say you have strategy and military s—	1476
	37: 3	of birth and there is no s to deliver them.	3946
	40:26	Because of his great power and mighty s,	3946
	40:29	He gives s to the weary and increases	3946
	40:31	in the LORD will renew their s.	3946
	41: 1	Let the nations renew their s!	3946
	44:12	He gets hungry and loses his s;	3946
	45:24	the LORD alone are righteousness and s.' "	6437
	49: 4	I have spent my s in vain and for nothing.	3946
	49: 5	of the LORD and my God has been my s—	6437
	50: 2	Do I lack the s to rescue you?	3946
	51: 9	Clothe yourself with s,	6437
	52: 1	awake, O Zion, clothe yourself with s.	6437
	57:10	You found renewal of your s,	3338
	63: 1	striding forward in the greatness of his s?	3946
Jer	9:23	of his s or the rich man boast of his riches,	1476
	16:19	O LORD, my s and my fortress,	6437
	17: 5	for his s and whose heart turns away from	2432
	51:30	Their s is exhausted;	1476
La	1:14	and the Lord has sapped my s.	3946
Eze	30: 6	of Egypt will fall and her proud s will fail.	6437
	30:18	there her proud s will come to an end.	6437
	33:28	and her proud s will come to an end,	6437
Da	2:41	yet it will have some of the s of iron in it,	10487
	10: 8	I had no s left, my face turned deadly pale	3946
	10:17	My s is gone and I can hardly breathe."	3946
	10:18	like a man touched me and **gave** me s.	2616
	10:19	my lord, since *you have* **given** me s."	2616
	11:15	even their best troops will not have the s	3946
	11:25	up his s and courage against the king of	3946
Hos	7: 9	Foreigners sap his s,	3946
	10:13	Because you have depended on your own s	2006
Am	2:14	the strong will not muster their s,	3946
	6:13	"Did we not take Karnaim by our own s?"	2620
Mic	5: 4	and shepherd his flock in the s *of*	6437
Na	2: 1	brace yourselves, marshal all your s!	3946
	2: 1	Cush and Egypt were her boundless s;	6797
Hab	1:11	guilty men, whose own s is their god."	3946
	3:19	The Sovereign LORD is my s;	2657
Mk	12:30	and with all your mind and with all your s.'	2709
	12:33	all your understanding and with all your s	2709
Lk	10:27	and with all your s and with all your mind';	2709
Ac	9:19	after taking some food, *he* **regained** his s.	1932
1Co	1:25	weakness of God is stronger than man's s.	NIG
Eph	1:19	power is like the working *of* his mighty s,	3197
Php	4:13	through him who **gives** me s.	1904
1Ti	1:12	Christ Jesus our Lord, who *has* **given** me s,	1904
2Ti	4:17	the Lord stood at my side and **gave** me s,	1904
Heb	11:34	whose weakness *was* **turned** to s;	1540
1Pe	4:11	he should do it with the s God provides,	2709
Rev	3: 8	I know that you have little s,	1539
	5:12	and wealth and wisdom and s and honor	2709
	7:12	and honor and power and s be to our God	2709
	14:10	which has been poured **full** s into the cup	204

STRENGTHEN (32) [STRONG]

Dt	3:28	and encourage and s him,	599
Jdg	16:28	O God, please s me just once more,	2616
1Ki	20:22	"S **your position** and see what must	2616
2Ki	15:19	to gain his support and s his own hold on	2616
2Ch	16: 9	to s those whose hearts are fully committed	2616
Ne	6: 9	[But I prayed,] "Now s my hands."	2616
Job	8:20	a blameless man or s the hands of evildoers.	2616
Ps	89:21	surely my arm *will* s him.	599
	119:28	s me according to your word.	7756
SS	2: 5	S me with raisins, refresh me with apples,	6164
Isa	22:10	in Jerusalem and tore down houses to s	1307
	35: 3	S the feeble hands, steady the knees	2616
	41:10	*I will* s you and help you;	599
	45: 5	*I will* s you, though you have not	273
	54: 2	lengthen your cords, s your stakes.	2616
	58:11	a sun-scorched land and *will* s your frame.	2741
Jer	23:14	*They* s the hands of evildoers.	2616
Eze	30:24	*I will* s the arms of the king of Babylon	2616
	30:25	*I will* s the arms of the king of Babylon	2616
	34:16	I will bind up the injured and s the weak,	2616
Na	3:14	Draw water for the siege, s your defenses!	2616
Zec	10: 6	"*I will* s the house of Judah and save	1504
	10:12	*I will* s them in the LORD and	1504
Lk	22:32	you have turned back, s your brothers."	5114
Ac	15:32	said much to encourage and s the brothers.	2185
Eph	3:16	out of his glorious riches *he may* s you	1443+3194
1Th	3: 2	and to encourage you in your faith,	5114
	3:13	*May he* s your hearts so that you will	5114
2Th	2:17	and s you in every good deed and word.	5114
	3: 3	and *he will* s and protect you from	5114
Heb	12:12	s your feeble arms and weak knees.	494

Rev	3: 2	S what remains and is about to die,	5114

STRENGTHENED (18) [STRONG]

2Sa	16:21	the hands of everyone with you *will be* s."	2616
1Ki	19: 8	S by that food, he traveled forty days and	3946
2Ch	11:17	He s their defenses and put commanders	2616
	11:17	*They* s the kingdom of Judah	2616
	17: 1	as king and s **himself** against Israel.	2616
Job	4: 3	how you have s feeble hands.	2616
	4: 4	*you have* s faltering knees.	599
Isa	9:11	the LORD *has* s Rezin's foes against them	8435
Eze	34: 4	not s the weak or healed the sick or bound	2616
Da	10:19	When he spoke to me, *I was* s and said,	2616
Hos	7:15	I trained them and s them,	2432+2616
Lk	22:43	from heaven appeared to him and s him.	1932
Ac	9:31	*It was* s; and encouraged by the Holy Spirit,	3868
	16: 5	So the churches *were* s in the faith	5105
Ro	4:20	but *was* s in his faith and gave glory to God,	1904
Col	1:11	*being* s with all power according	1540
	2: 7	s in the faith as you were taught,	1011
Heb	13: 9	It is good for our hearts *to be* s by grace,	1011

STRENGTHENING (7) [STRONG]

2Sa	3: 6	Abner had been s **his own position** in	2616
Ac	14:22	the disciples and encouraging them	2185
	15:41	through Syria and Cilicia, s the churches.	2185
	18:23	s all the disciples.	2185
1Co	14:26	who prophesies speaks to men for their s,	3869
	14:26	All of these must be done for the s of	3869
2Co	12:19	dear friends, is for your s.	3869

STRENGTHENS (1) [STRONG]

Ps	147:13	for *he* s the bars of your gates	2616

STRESS (2)

Jer	19: 9	during the s of the siege imposed on them	5186
Tit	3: 8	And I want you *to* s these things,	1331

STRETCH (35) [OUTSTRETCHED, STRETCHED, STRETCHES, STRETCHING]

Ex	3:20	So *I will* s out my hand and strike	8938
	7: 5	that I am the LORD when I s out my hand	5742
	7:19	'Take your staff and s out your hand over	5742
	8: 5	'S out your hand with your staff over	5742
	8:16	'S out your staff and strike the dust of	5742
	9:22	"S out your hand toward the sky so	5742
	10:12	"S out your hand over Egypt so	5742
	10:21	"S out your hand toward the sky so	5742
	14:16	and s out your hand over the sea to divide	5742
	14:26	"S out your hand over the sea so that	5742
2Ki	21:13	*I will* s out over Jerusalem the measuring	5742
Job	1:11	But s out your hand and strike everything	8938
	2: 5	But s out your hand and strike his flesh	8938
	11:13	to him and s out your hands to him,	7298
Ps	138: 7	*you* s out your hand against the anger	8938
Isa	28:20	The bed is too short *to* s out *on*,	8594
	34:11	God *will* s out over Edom the measuring	5742
	54: 2	s your tent curtains **wide**,	5742
Jer	6:12	when *I* s out my hand against those who	5742
	31:39	The measuring line *will* s from there	3655
	51:25	"*I will* s out my hand against you,	5742
Eze	6:14	And *I will* s out my hand against them	5742
	14: 9	and *I will* s out my hand against him	5742
	14:13	by being unfaithful and *I* s out my hand	5742
	25: 7	therefore *I will* s out my hand against you	5742
	25:13	*I will* s out my hand against Edom	5742
	25:16	*to* s out my hand against the Philistines,	5742
	35: 3	and *I will* s out my hand against you	5742
Zep	1: 4	"*I will* s out my hand against Judah and	5742
	2:13	*He will* s out his hand against the north	5742
Mt	12:13	he said to the man, "S out your hand."	1753
Mk	3: 5	said to the man, "S out your hand."	1753
Lk	6:10	said to the man, "S out your hand."	1753
Jn	21:18	you are old *you will* s out your hands,	1753
Ac	4:30	S out your hand to heal and perform	1753

STRETCHED (38) [STRETCH]

Ge	10:30	The region where they lived s from Mesha	2118
Ex	8: 6	So Aaron s out his hand over the waters	5742
	8:17	when Aaron s out his hand with the staff	5742
	9:15	For by now *I could have* s out my hand	8938
	9:23	When Moses s out his staff toward the sky,	5742
	10:13	So Moses s out his staff over Egypt,	5742
	10:22	So Moses s out his hand toward the sky,	5742
	14:21	Then Moses s out his hand over the sea,	5742
	14:27	Moses s out his hand over the sea,	5742
	15:12	*You* s out your right hand and	5742
2Sa	24:16	angel s out his hand to destroy Jerusalem,	8938
1Ki	13: 4	*he* s out his hand from the altar and said,	8938
	13: 4	hand *he* s out toward the man shriveled up,	8938
	17:21	Then *he* s **himself** out on the boy	4499
2Ki	4:34	As he s **himself** out upon him,	1566
	4:35	the room and then got on the bed and s **out**	1566
Job	38: 5	Who s a measuring line across it?	5742
Ps	77: 2	at night I s out untiring hands	5599
Pr	1:24	*when I* s out my hand,	5742
Isa	14:26	this is the hand s **out** over all nations.	5742
	14:27	His hand *is* s **out**, and who can turn it back?	5742
	23:11	The LORD *has* s out his hand over the sea	5742
	42: 5	he who created the heavens and s them **out**,	5742
	44:24	*who alone* s **out** the heavens,	5742

Isa	45:12	My own hands s out the heavens; 5742
	51:13	who s out the heavens and laid 5742
Jer	10:12	and s out the heavens by his understanding. 5742
	51:15	and s out the heavens by his understanding. 5742
La	2: 8	He s out a measuring line and did 5742
Eze	1:23	the expanse their wings were s out one 3838
	2: 9	I looked, and I saw a hand s out to me. 8938
	8: 3	He s out what looked like a hand 8938
	16:27	So I s out my hand against you 5742
	17: 7	where it was planted and s out its branches 8938
Zec	1:16	And the measuring line will be s out 5742
Mt	12:13	he s it out and it was completely restored, 1753
Mk	3: 5	He s it out, and his hand was completely 1753
Ac	22:25	As they s him out to flog him, 4727

STRETCHES (7) [STRETCH]

Job	9: 8	He alone s out the heavens and treads on 5742
Ps	104: 2	he s out the heavens like a tent 5742
Isa	31: 3	When the LORD s out his hand, 5742
	33:17	in his beauty and view a land that s afar. 5305
	40:22	He s out the heavens like a canopy, 5742
La	1:17	Zion s out her hands, 7298
Zec	12: 1	The LORD, who s out the heavens, 5742

STRETCHING (3) [STRETCH]

Est	1: 1	over 127 provinces s from India to Cush: AIT
	8: 9	of the 127 provinces s from India to Cush. AIT
Jer	4:31	s out her hands and saying, "Alas! 7298

STREWN (2)

1Sa	17:52	Their dead were s along the Shaaraim road 5877
2Ki	7:15	and they found the whole road s with 4849

STRICKEN (3) [STRIKE]

Isa	53: 4	yet we considered him s by God, 5595
	53: 8	for the transgression of my people he was s. 5596
Zec	14:13	men will be s by the LORD with great panic. AIT

STRICT (5) [STRICTEST, STRICTLY]

1Sa	14:28	bound the army under a s oath, 8678+8678
Mk	3:12	But he gave them s orders not to tell 4498
	5:43	He gave s orders not to let anyone know 4498
Ac	5:28	"We gave you s orders not to teach 4132+4133
1Co	9:25	in the games goes into s training. 4246

STRICTEST (1) [STRICT]

Ac	26: 5	that according to the s sect of our religion, 207

STRICTLY (2) [STRICT]

Lk	9:21	Jesus s warned them not to tell this 2203+4133
Jas	3: 1	that we who teach will be judged more s. NIG

STRIDE (1) [STRIDING, STRODE]

Pr	30:29	three things that are stately in their s, 7576

STRIDING (1) [STRIDE]

Isa	63: 1	s forward in the greatness of his strength? 7579

STRIFE (12) [STRIVE]

Ps	55: 9	for I see violence and s in the city. 8190
Pr	17: 1	a house full of feasting, with s. 8190
	18: 6	A fool's lips bring him s, 8190
	20: 3	It is to a man's honor to avoid s, 8190
	22:10	Drive out the mocker, and out goes s; 4506
	23:29	Who has s? 4506
	26:21	so is a quarrelsome man for kindling s. 8190
	30:33	so stirring up anger produces s." 8190
Isa	58: 4	Your fasting ends in quarreling and s, 5175
Hab	1: 3	there is s, and conflict abounds. 8190
Ro	1:29	They are full of envy, murder, s, 2251
1Ti	6: 4	about words that result in envy, s, 2251

STRIKE (81) [STRICKEN, STRIKES, STRIKING, STROKE, STRUCK]

Ge	3:15	crush your head, and you will s his heel." 8790
Ex	3:20	and s the Egyptians with all the wonders 5782
	5: 3	he may s us with plagues or with the sword. 7003
	7:17	in my hand I will s the water of the Nile, 5782
	8:16	'Stretch out your staff and s the dust of 5782
	12:12	through Egypt and s down every firstborn— 5782
	12:13	will touch you when I s Egypt. 5782
	12:23	the LORD goes through the land to s down 5597
	12:23	to enter your houses and s you down. 5597
	17: 6	S the rock, and water will come out of it 5782
Nu	8:19	so that no plague will s the Israelites 928+2118
	14:12	I will s them down with a plague 5782
Dt	28:22	LORD will s you with wasting disease, 5782
	33:11	s his foes till they rise no more." NIH
Jdg	6:16	and you will s down all the Midianites 5782
1Sa	17:46	and I'll s you down and cut off your head. 5782
	22:17	not willing to raise a hand to s the priests of 7003
	22:18	"You turn and s down the priests." 7003
	26: 8	I won't s him twice." 9101
	26:10	he said, "the LORD himself will s him; 5597
2Sa	1:15	of his men and said, "Go, s him down!" 7003
	2:22	Why should I s you down? 5782
	5:24	the LORD has gone out in front of you to s 5782
	13:28	'S Amnon down,' then kill him. 5782
	17: 2	I would s him with terror, 3006

2Sa	17: 2	I would s down only the king 5782
	18:11	Why didn't you s him to the ground 5782
1Ki	2:29	son of Jehoiada, "Go, s him down!" 7003
	2:31	S him down and bury him, 7003
	14:15	And the LORD will s Israel, 5782
	20:35	"S me with your weapon," 5782
	20:37	prophet found another man and said, "S me, 5782
2Ki	6:18	"S these people with blindness." 5782
	13:18	Elisha told him, "S the ground." 5782
1Ch	14:15	in front of you to s the Philistine army." 5782
2Ch	21:14	the LORD is about to s your people, 5597
Job	1:11	your hand and s everything he has, 5595
	5: 2	But stretch out your hand and s his flesh 5595
	16:10	they s my cheek in scorn and unite together 5782
	36:32	and commands it to s its mark. 7003
Ps	3: 7	S all my enemies on the jaw; 5782
	9:20	S them with terror, O LORD; 8883
	81: 2	Begin the music, the tambourine, 5989
	89:23	I will crush his foes before him and s down 5597
	91:12	you will not s your foot against a stone. 5597
	141: 5	Let a righteous man s me— 2150
Pr	11:15	to s hands in pledge is safe. 9364
Isa	11: 4	He will s the earth with the rod 5782
	13:18	Their bows will s down the young men; 8187
	19:22	The LORD will s Egypt with a plague; 5597
	19:22	he will s them and heal them. 5597
	30:31	with his scepter he will s them down. 5782
Jer	21: 6	I will s down those who live in this city— 5782
La	3:30	offer his cheek to one who would s him, 5782
Eze	5: 2	and s it with the sword all around the city. 5782
	6:11	S your hands together and stamp your feet 5782
	21:14	prophesy and s your hands together. 5782
	21:14	Let the sword s twice, even three times. 4100
	21:17	I too will s my hands together, 5782
	22:13	" 'I will surely s my hands together at 5782
	32:15	when I s down all who live there, 5782
	39: 3	Then I will s your bow from your left hand 5782
Am	9: 1	"S the tops of the pillars so that 5782
Mic	5: 1	They will s Israel's ruler on the cheek with 5782
Zec	11:17	May the sword s his arm and his right eye! 6584
	12: 4	that day I will s every horse with panic 5782
	13: 7	"S the shepherd, and the sheep will 5782
	14:12	the plague with which the LORD will s all 5597
	14:15	A similar plague will s the horses 2118
Mal	4: 6	or else I will come and s the land with 5782
Mt	4: 6	you will not s your foot against a stone.' " 4684
	26:31	" 'I will s the shepherd, and the sheep 4250
Mk	14:27	" 'I will s the shepherd, and the sheep 4250
Lk	4:11	you will not s your foot against a stone.' " 4684
	22:49	"Lord, should we s with our swords?" 4250
Jn	18:23	if I spoke the truth, why did you s me?" 1296
Ac	23: 2	near Paul to s him on the mouth. 5597
	23: 3	Then Paul said to him, "God will s you, 5597
Rev	2:23	I will s her children dead. 650
	11: 6	and to s the earth with every kind of plague 4250
	19:15	a sharp sword with which to s down 4250

STRIKER (KJV) See VIOLENT

STRIKES (16) [STRIKE]

Ex	21:12	"Anyone who s a man and kills him shall 5782
Nu	35:16	" 'If a man s someone with an iron object so 5782
	35:17	and he s someone so that he dies, 5782
Job	4: 5	it s you, and you are dismayed. 5595
Ps	29: 7	of the LORD s with flashes of lightning. 2934
Pr	11:15	in judgment s hands in pledge and puts 9546
	22:26	not be a man who s hands in pledge or puts 9546
	27:10	when disaster s you— NIH
Isa	5:25	his hand is raised and he s them down. 5782
	41: 7	the hammer spurs on him who s the anvil. 2150
Jer	11:12	not help them at all when disaster s. NIH
Eze	7: 9	that it is I the LORD who s the blow. 5782
	17:10	when the east wind s it— 5595
Mt	5:39	If someone s you on the right cheek, 4824
Lk	6:29	If someone s you on one cheek, 5597
Rev	9: 5	of the sting of a scorpion when it s a man. 4091

STRIKING (6) [STRIKE]

1Sa	14:20	s each other with their swords. 928+2118
2Sa	8:13	from s down eighteen thousand Edomites in 5782
	24:17	When David saw the angel who was s down 5782
Job	39:20	s terror with his proud snorting? NIH
Isa	58: 4	and in s each other with wicked fists. 5782
Da	8: 7	s the ram and shattering his two horns. 5782

STRING (4) [STRINGED, STRINGS, STRUNG, TEN-STRINGED]

Jdg	16: 9	as a piece of s snaps when it comes 5861+7348
2Sa	16: 1	He had a s of donkeys saddled and loaded 7538
Ps	7:12	he will bend and s his bow. 3922
Jer	51: 3	Let not the archer s his bow, 2005

STRINGED (9) [STRING]

Ps	4: T	With s instruments. 5593
	6: T	With s instruments. 5593
	54: T	With s instruments. 5593
	55: T	With s instruments. 5593
	61: T	With s instruments. 5593
	67: T	With s instruments. 5593
	76: T	With s instruments. 5593
Isa	38:20	with s instruments all the days of our lives 5593
Hab	3:19	On my s instruments. 5593

STRINGS (4) [STRING]

Ps	11: 2	they set their arrows against the s to shoot 3857
	45: 8	the music of the s makes you glad. 4944
	150: 4	praise him with the s and flute, 4944
SS	1:10	your neck with s of jewels. 3016

STRIP (19) [STRIPPED, STRIPS]

1Sa	31: 8	when the Philistines came to s the dead, 7320
2Sa	2:21	take on one of the young men and s him of 4374
	23:10	but only to s the dead. 7320
1Ch	10: 8	when the Philistines came to s the dead, 7320
Job	41:13	Who can s off his outer coat? 1655
Isa	27:10	they s its branches bare. 3983
	32:11	S off your clothes, 2256+6910+7320
	45: 1	to subdue nations before him and to s kings 7337
Jer	5:10	S off her branches, 6073
	49:10	But I will s Esau bare; 3106
Eze	16:39	and will s you in front of them, 1655+6872
	16:39	They will s you of your clothes 7320
	23:26	They will also s you of your clothes 7320
	32:15	When I make Egypt desolate and s the land 9037
Da	4:14	s off its leaves and scatter its fruit. 10499
Hos	2: 3	Otherwise I will s her naked and make her 7320
Mic	2: 8	You s off the rich robe from those who pass 7320
	3: 3	s off their skin and break their bones 7320
Na	3:16	but like locusts they s the land and 7320

STRIPE, STRIPES (KJV) See BEATINGS, BLOWS, BRUISE, FLOGGED, FLOGGING, FLOGGINGS, LASHES, WOUNDS

STRIPES (1)

Ge	30:37	and plane trees and made white s on them 7203

STRIPLING (KJV) See YOUNG MAN

STRIPPED (33) [STRIP]

Ge	37:23	they s him of his robe— 7320
Ex	9:25	in the fields and every tree. 8689
	33: 6	So the Israelites s off their ornaments 5911
Jdg	14:19	s them of their belongings 4374
1Sa	19:24	He s off his robes and also prophesied 7320
	31: 9	They cut off his head and s off his armor, 7320
2Ki	18:16	At this time Hezekiah king of Judah s off 7915
1Ch	10: 9	They s him and took his head 7320
Job	12:17	He leads counselors away s 8768
	12:19	He leads priests away s 8768
	15:33	He will be like a vine s of its unripe grapes, 2803
	19: 9	He has s me of my honor and removed 7320
	22: 6	you s men of their clothing, 7320
Isa	1: 7	your fields are being s by foreigners right 430
	20: 2	And he did so, going around s and barefoot. 6873
	20: 3	"Just as my servant Isaiah has gone s 6873
	20: 4	of Assyria will lead away s and barefoot 6873
	22: 8	the defenses of Judah are s away. 1655
	23:13	they s its fortresses bare and turned it into 6910
La	4:21	you will be drunk and s naked. 6867
Eze	12:19	for their land will be s of everything in it 9037
	17: 9	Will it not be uprooted and s of its fruit so 7878
	19:12	it was s of its fruit; 7293
	23:10	They s her naked, took away her sons and 1655
Da	5:20	he was deposed from his royal throne and s 10528
	5:21	(The other beasts had been s of their 10528
Joel	1: 7	It has s off their bark and thrown it 3106+3106
Am	7: 2	When they had s the land clean, I cried out, 430
Na	2:10	She is pillaged, plundered, s! 1191
Hab	3:13	you s him from head to foot. 6867
Mt	27:28	They s him and put a scarlet robe on him, 1694
Lk	10:30	They s him of his clothes, beat him and 1694
Ac	16:22	the magistrates ordered them to be s and beaten. 2668+3836+4351

STRIPS (6) [STRIP]

Ps	29: 9	the oaks and s the forests bare. 3106
Lk	24:12	he saw the s of linen lying by themselves, 3856
Jn	11:44	and feet wrapped with s of linen, 3024
	19:40	with the spices, in s of linen. 3856
	20: 5	the s of linen lying there but did not go in. 3856
	20: 6	He saw the s of linen lying there, 3856

STRIVE (2) [STRIFE, STRIVES, STRIVING]

Ac	24:16	So I always to keep my conscience clear 828
1Ti	4:10	(and for this we labor and s), 76

STRIVES (2) [STRIVE]

Isa	64: 7	No one calls on your name or s to lay hold 6424
Jer	15:10	with whom the whole land s and contends! 8190

STRIVING (1) [STRIVE]

Ecc	2:22	and anxious s with which he labors 4213+8301

STRODE (1) [STRIDE]

Hab	3:12	In wrath you s through the earth and 7575

STROKE (4) [STRIKE]

Job	5:20	and in battle from the s of the sword. 3338
Isa	30:32	Every s the LORD lays on them 5044
Mt	5:18	not least s of a pen, will by any means 3037
Lk	16:17	for least s of a pen to drop out of the Law. 3037

STROKES (KJV) See BEATING

STRONG (157) [STRENGTH, STRENGTHEN, STRENGTHENED, STRENGTHENING, STRENGTHENS, STRONGER, STRONGEST, STRONGLY]

Ge	30:42	to Laban and the s ones to Jacob.	8003
	49:24	his **arms** stayed limber,	2432+3338
Ex	10:19	the wind to a very s west wind,	2617
	14:21	the sea back with a s east wind and turned it	6434
Nu	13:18	and whether the people who live there are s	2617
	24:18	will be conquered, but Israel will grow s.	2657
Dt	2:10	a people s and numerous,	1524
	2:21	They were a people s and numerous,	1524
	2:36	not one town was too s for us.	8435
	3:24	your greatness and your s hand.	2617
	9:2	The people are s and tall—Anakites!	1524
	31:6	Be s and courageous.	2616
	31:7	"Be s and courageous,	2616
	31:23	"Be s and courageous,	2616
Jos	1:6	"Be s and courageous,	2616
	1:7	Be s and very courageous.	2616
	1:9	Be s and courageous.	2616
	1:18	Only be s and courageous!"	2616
	10:25	Be s and courageous.	2616
	14:11	as s today as the day Moses sent me out;	2617
	17:18	though they are s, you can drive them out."	2617
	23:6	"Be very s; be careful to obey all that	2616
Jdg	1:28	When Israel became s,	2616
	3:29	all vigorous and s; not a man escaped.	2657
	5:21	March on, my soul; be s!	6437
	9:51	Inside the city, however, was a s tower,	6437
	14:14	out of the s, something sweet."	6434
	18:26	seeing that they were too s for him,	2617
1Sa	4:9	Be s, Philistines! Be men,	2616
2Sa	2:7	Now then, be s and brave,	2616+3338
	3:39	and these sons of Zeruiah are too s for me.	7997
	10:11	"If the Arameans are too s for me,	2616
	10:11	but if the Ammonites are too s for you,	2616
	10:12	Be s and let us fight bravely for our people	2616
	13:28	Be s and brave."	2616
	22:18	from my foes, who were too s for me.	599
1Ki	2:2	"So be s, show yourself a man,	2616
	15:4	to succeed him and by **making** Jerusalem s.	6641
	20:23	That is why they were too s for us.	2616
2Ki	6:14	and chariots and a s force there.	3878
	24:16	seven thousand fighting men, s and fit for	1475
1Ch	11:10	gave his kingship to **support**	2616+6640
	19:12	"If the Arameans are too s for me,	2616
	19:12	but if the Ammonites are too s for you,	2616
	19:13	Be s and let us fight bravely for our people	2616
	22:13	Be s and courageous.	2616
	28:10	Be s and do the work."	2616
	28:20	"Be s and courageous, and do the work.	2616
		and **made** them very s.	2616
2Ch	12:1	and he had **become** s, he and all Israel	2621
	13:7	and indecisive and not s enough	2616
	15:7	But as for you, be s and do not give up,	2616
	32:7	"Be s and courageous.	2616
Ezr	9:12	that you may be s and eat the good things of	2616
Job	15:26	against him with a thick, s shield.	1461
	39:4	Their young thrive and **grow** s in the wilds;	2730
Ps	18:17	from my foes, who were too s for me.	599
	22:12	s bulls of Bashan encircle me.	52
	24:8	The LORD s and mighty,	6450
	27:14	be s and take heart and wait for the LORD.	2388
	31:2	a **fortress** to save me.	1074+5181
	31:24	Be s and take heart,	2616
	35:10	You rescue the poor from those too s	2617
	52:7	but trusted in his great wealth and grew s	6395
	61:3	a strong tower against the foe.	6437
	62:11	that you, O God, are s,	6437
	71:7	but you are my s refuge.	6437
	73:4	their bodies are healthy and s.	9447
	89:10	with your s arm you scattered your enemies.	6437
	89:13	your hand is s, your right hand exalted.	6451
	140:7	O Sovereign LORD, my s deliverer,	6437
	142:6	for they are too s for me.	599
Pr	18:10	The name of the LORD is a s tower;	6437
	18:18	and keeps s opponents apart.	6786
	23:11	for their Defender is s;	2617
	31:17	her arms are s for her tasks.	599
Ecc	9:11	or the battle to the s, nor does food come to	1475
	12:3	and the s men stoop,	2657
SS	8:6	for love is as s as death,	6434
Isa	8:11	The LORD spoke to me with his s hand	2621
	17:9	In that day their s cities,	5057
	25:3	Therefore s peoples will honor you;	6434
	26:1	We have a s city;	6434
	28:2	the Lord has one who is powerful and s.	579
	35:4	"Be s, do not fear;	2616
	41:6	the other and says to his brother, "Be s!"	2616
	53:12	and he will divide the spoils with the s,	6786
	59:10	among the s, we are like the dead.	875
Jer	4:12	a wind too s for that comes from me.	4849
	9:23	or the s **man** boast of his strength or	1475
	30:6	Then why do I see every s **man**	1505
	46:6	"The swift cannot flee nor the s escape.	1475
	50:34	Yet their Redeemer is s;	2617
Eze	3:14	with the hand of the LORD upon me.	2617
	17:9	not take a s arm or many people to pull it	1524
	19:3	and he became a s **lion.**	4097
	19:5	of her cubs and made him a s **lion.**	4097
	19:6	for he was now a s **lion.**	4097

Eze	19:11	Its branches were s, fit for a ruler's scepter.	6437
	19:12	its s branches withered	6437
	19:14	No s branch is left on it fit for	6437
	22:14	or your hands be s in the day I deal	2616
	26:11	and your s pillars will fall to the ground.	6437
	30:21	in a splint so as to **become** s enough to hold	2616
	34:16	but the sleek and the s I will destroy.	2617
Da	2:40	there will be a fourth kingdom, s as iron—	10768
	2:42	so this kingdom will be partly s	10768
	4:11	and s and its top touched the sky;	10772
	4:20	The tree you saw, which grew large and s,	10772
	4:22	You have become great and s;	10772
	8:24	He will become **very** s,	3946+6793
	10:19	Be s now; be strong."	2616
	10:19	Be strong now; be s."	2616
	11:5	"The king of the South will become s,	2616
Joel	3:10	Let the weakling say, "I am s!"	1475
Am	2:9	he was tall as the cedars and s as the oaks.	2891
	2:14	the s will not muster their strength,	2617
	5:3	"The city that marches out a thousand s	NIH
	5:3	a hundred s will have only ten left."	NIH
	8:13	s young men will faint because of thirst.	1033
Mic	4:3	and will settle disputes for s nations far	6786
	4:7	those driven away a s nation.	6786
Hag	2:4	be s, O Zerubbabel,' declares the LORD.	2616
	2:4	'Be s, O Joshua son of Jehozadak,	2616
	2:4	Be s, all you people of the land,'	2616
Zec	8:9	let your hands be s so that the temple may	2616
	8:13	Do not be afraid, but let your hands be s."	2616
	12:5	'The people of Jerusalem are s,	602
Mt	12:29	How can anyone enter a s man's house	2708
	12:29	unless he first ties up the s man?	2708
Mk	1:43	sent him away at once with a s **warning:**	1839
	3:27	no one can enter a s man's house	2708
	3:27	unless he first ties up the s man.	2708
	5:4	No one was s enough to subdue him.	2710
Lk	1:80	And the child grew and **became** s in spirit;	3194
	2:40	And the child grew and **became** s;	3194
	11:21	"When a s **man**, fully armed,	2708
	16:3	I'm not s enough to dig,	2710
Jn	6:18	A s wind was blowing and	3489
Ac	3:7	the man's feet and ankles **became** s.	5105
	3:16	whom you see and know was made s.	5105
Ro	1:11	to you some spiritual gift to **make** you s—	5114
	15:1	We who are s ought to bear with	1543
1Co	1:8	He will **keep** you s to the end,	1011
	1:27	the weak things of the world to shame the s.	2708
	4:10	We are weak, but you are s!	2708
	16:13	be men of courage; be s.	3194
2Co	12:10	For when I am weak, then I am s.	1543
	13:9	whenever we are weak but you are s;	1543
Eph	6:10	be s in the Lord and in his mighty power.	1904
1Th	2:2	tell you his gospel in spite of s opposition.	4498
2Ti	2:1	be s in the grace that is in Christ Jesus.	1904
Jas	3:4	they are so large and are driven by s winds,	5017
1Pe	5:10	will himself restore you and **make** you s,	5114
1Jn	2:14	young men, because you are s,	2708
Rev	6:13	from a fig tree when shaken by a s wind.	3489
	12:8	But he was not s enough,	2710

STRONGER (30) [STRONG]

Ge	25:23	one people will be s than the other,	599
	30:41	Whenever the s females were in heat,	8003
Nu	13:31	they are s than we are."	2617
	14:12	into a nation greater and s than they."	6786
Dt	1:28	'The people are s and taller than we are;	1524
	4:38	before you nations greater and s than you	6786
	7:1	seven nations larger and s than you—	6786
	7:17	"These nations are s than we are.	8041
	9:1	dispossess nations greater and s than you,	6786
	9:14	a nation s and more numerous than they.	6786
	11:23	dispossess nations larger and s than you.	6786
Jos	17:13	However, when the Israelites grew s,	2616
Jdg	4:24	Israelites **grew s and stronger**	2143+2256+7997
	4:24	Israelites **grew stronger and** s	2143+2256+7997
	14:18	What is s than a lion?"	6434
2Sa	1:23	they were s than lions.	1504
	3:1	David **grew s and stronger**,	2143+2256+2618
	3:1	David **grew stronger and** s,	2143+2256+2618
	13:14	and since he was s than she, he raped her.	2616
1Ki	16:22	But Omri's followers **proved** s than those	2616
	20:23	surely we will be s than they.	2616
	20:25	Then surely we will be s than they."	2616
Job	17:9	and those with clean hands will **grow** s.	601+3578
Ecc	6:10	with one who is s than he.	9544
Jer	31:11	from the hand of those s than they.	2617
Da	11:5	even s than he and will rule his own	2616
Lk	11:22	someone s attacks and overpowers him,	2708
1Co	1:25	weakness of God is s than man's strength.	2708
	10:22	Are we s than he?	2708
2Pe	2:11	although they are s and more powerful,	2709

STRONGEST (3) [STRONG]

2Sa	11:16	where he knew the s **defenders** were.	408+2657
1Ch	5:2	and though Judah was the s of his brothers	1504
Da	3:20	commanded some of the s **soldiers**	10132+10264

STRONGHOLD (31) [STRONGHOLDS]

Jdg	9:46	in the tower of Shechem went into the s of	7663
	9:49	They piled them against the s and set it	7663
1Sa	22:4	with him as long as David was in the s.	5181
	22:5	"Do not stay in the s.	5181
	24:22	but David and his men went up to the s.	5181
2Sa	5:17	about it and went down to the s.	5181
	22:3	He is my s, my refuge and my savior—	5369

2Sa	23:14	At that time David was in the s,	5181
1Ch	11:16	At that time David was in the s,	5181
	12:8	Some Gadites defected to David at his s in	5171
	12:16	from Judah also came to David in his s.	5171
Job	39:28	a rocky crag is his s.	5181
Ps	9:9	for the oppressed, a s in times of trouble.	5369
	18:2	and the horn of my salvation, my s.	5369
	27:1	The LORD is s of my life—	5057
	37:39	he is their s in time of trouble.	5057
	43:2	You are God my s.	5057
	52:7	is the man who did not make God his s	5057
	144:2	my s and my deliverer, my shield,	5369
Pr	21:22	the city of the mighty and pulls down the s	6437
Isa	25:4	the foreigners' s a city no more;	810
	31:9	Their s will fall because of terror;	6152
Jer	48:1	the s will be disgraced and shattered.	5369
	51:53	reaches the sky and fortifies her lofty s,	6437
Eze	24:21	the s in which you take pride,	6437
	24:25	son of man, on the day I take away their s,	5057
	30:15	my wrath on Pelusium, the s of Egypt,	5057
Joel	3:16	a s for the people of Israel.	5057
Am	5:9	he flashes destruction on the s and	6434
Mic	4:8	O s of the Daughter of Zion,	6755
Zec	9:3	Tyre has built herself a s;	5190

STRONGHOLDS (19) [STRONGHOLD]

Jdg	6:2	in mountain clefts, caves and s.	5171
1Sa	23:14	David stayed in the desert s and in the hills	5171
	23:19	"Is not David hiding among us in the s	5171
	23:29	up from there and lived in the s of En Gedi.	5171
2Sa	22:46	they come trembling from their s.	4995
Ps	18:45	they come trembling from their s.	4995
	89:40	through all his walls and reduced his s	4448
Isa	13:22	Hyenas will howl in her s,	528
	34:13	nettles and brambles her s.	4448
Jer	48:41	Kerioth will be captured and the s taken.	5171
	51:30	they remain in their s.	5171
La	2:2	in his wrath he has torn down the s of	4448
	2:5	up all her palaces and destroyed her s.	4448
Eze	19:7	down their s and devastated their towns.	810
	33:27	and those in s and caves will die of	5171
Am	3:11	down your s and plunder your fortresses."	6437
Mic	5:11	of your land and tear down all your s.	4448
Zep	3:6	their s are demolished.	7157
2Co	10:4	they have divine power to demolish s.	4065

STRONGLY (4) [STRONG]

Ge	19:3	But he insisted so s that they did go	4394
Lk	24:29	But they **urged** him s, "Stay with us,	4128
1Co	16:12	I urged him to go to you with the brothers.	4498
2Ti	4:15	because he s opposed our message.	3336

STRUCK (146) [STRIKE]

Ge	19:11	Then they s the men who were at the door	5782
Ex	7:20	and his officials and s the water of the Nile,	5782
	7:25	Seven days passed after the LORD s	5782
	8:17	with the staff and s the dust of the ground,	5782
	9:15	and s you and your people with a plague	5782
	9:25	Throughout Egypt hail s everything in	5782
	12:27	and spared our homes when he s down	5597
	12:29	the LORD s **down** all the	5782
	17:5	in your hand the staff with which you s	5782
	21:19	the one who s **the blow** will not	5782
	22:2	"If a thief is caught breaking in and is s so	5782
	32:35	the LORD s the people **with a plague**	5597
Nu	3:13	When I s **down** all the firstborn in Egypt,	5782
	8:17	When I s **down** all the firstborn in Egypt,	5782
	11:33	and he s them with a severe plague.	5782
	14:37	the land were s **down and died** of a plague	4637
	20:11	and s the rock twice with his staff.	5782
	21:35	So they s him **down**,	5782
	24:10	He s his hands **together** and said to him,	6215
	31:16	so that a plague s the LORD's people.	928+2118
	33:4	whom the LORD had s **down** among them;	5782
Dt	2:33	over to us and we s him **down**,	5782
	3:3	We s them **down**, leaving no survivors.	5782
Jos	7:5	as far as the stone quarries and s them **down**	5782
	10:26	Then Joshua s and killed the kings	5782
	11:17	and s them **down**,	5782
Jdg	1:4	and they s **down** ten thousand men at Bezek.	5782
	3:29	At that time they s **down**	5782
	3:31	who s **down** six hundred Philistines with	5782
	5:26	She s Sisera, she s his head,	2150
	7:13	It s the tent with such force that	5782
	9:44	upon those in the fields and s them **down**.	5782
	12:4	The Gileadites s them **down** because	5782
	14:19	s **down** thirty of their men,	5782
	15:15	he grabbed it and s **down** a thousand men.	5782
	20:35	and on that day the Israelites s **down** 25,100	8845
	20:45	the Benjamites as far as Gidom and s **down**	5782
		the gods who s the Egyptians with all kinds	5782
1Sa	6:4	same plague has s both you and your rulers.	4200
	6:9	not his hand that s us and that it happened	5595
	6:19	But God s **down** some of the men	5782
	14:15	Then panic s the whole army—	928+2118
	14:31	the Israelites had s **down** the Philistines	5782
	17:35	s it and rescued the sheep from its mouth.	5782
	17:35	I seized it by its hair, s it and killed it.	5782
	17:49	and s the Philistine on the forehead.	5782
	17:50	a sword in his hand he s **down** the Philistine	5782
	19:8	He s them with such force that they fled	5782
	22:18	Doeg the Edomite turned and s them **down**.	7003
	25:38	the LORD s Nabal and he died.	5597
2Sa	1:15	So he s him **down**, and he died.	5782
	5:25	and he s **down** the Philistines all the way	5782

2Sa	6: 7	therefore God s him **down** and he died there	5782
	8: 5	David s **down** twenty-two thousand of them	5782
	10:18	He also s **down** Shobach the commander	5782
	11:15	from him so *he will be* s **down** and die."	5782
	12: 9	*You* s Uriah the Hittite with the sword	5782
	12:15	the LORD s the child that Uriah's wife had	5597
	13:30	"Absalom *has* s **down** all the king's sons;	5782
	14: 6	One s the other and killed him.	5782
	14: 7	'Hand over the *one who* s his brother **down**,	5782
	18:15	surrounded Absalom, s and killed him.	5782
	21:12	after they s Saul **down** on Gilboa.)	5782
	21:17	*he* s the Philistine **down** and killed him.	5782
	23:10	but he stood his ground and s **down**	5782
	23:12	He defended it and s the Philistines **down**,	5782
	23:20	He s **down** two of Moab's best men.	5782
	23:21	And he s **down** a huge Egyptian.	5782
1Ki	2:25	and *he* s **down** Adonijah and he died.	7003
	2:34	of Jehoiada went up and s **down** Joab	7003
	2:46	and he went out and s Shimei **down**	7003
	11:15	*had* s **down** all the men in Edom.	5782
	15:27	and he s him **down** at Gibbethon,	5782
	16:10	Zimri came in, s him **down** and killed him	5782
	20:20	and each one s **down** his opponent.	5782
	20:37	So the man s him and wounded him.	5782+5782
2Ki	2: 8	rolled it up and s the water with it.	5782
	2:14	that had fallen from him and s the water!	5782
	2:14	When *he* s the water, it divided	5782
	6:18	So *he* s them with blindness,	5782
	13:18	*He* s it three times and stopped.	5782
	13:19	"You *should have* s the ground five	5782
1Ch	11:14	They defended it and s the Philistines **down**,	5782
	11:22	He s **down** two of Moab's best men.	5782
	11:23	And he s **down** an Egyptian who was	5782
	13:10	burned against Uzzah, and *he* s him **down**	5782
	14:16	and *they* s **down** the Philistine army,	5782
	18: 5	David s **down** twenty-two thousand of them	5782
	18:12	Abishai son of Zeruiah s **down**	5782
2Ch	13:20	And the LORD s him **down** and he died.	5597
	14:12	The LORD s **down** the Cushites before Asa	5597
	25:16	Stop! Why *be* s **down**?"	5782
Est	9: 5	The Jews s **down** all their enemies	4804+5782
Job	1:19	in from the desert and s the four corners of	5595
	19:21	have pity, for the hand of God *has* s me.	5595
Ps	60:T	and s **down** twelve thousand Edomites in	5782
	64:T	suddenly they will be s **down**.	4804
	78:20	When *he* s the rock, water gushed out,	5782
	78:51	*He* s **down** all the firstborn of Egypt,	5782
	105:33	he s **down** their vines and fig trees	5782
	105:36	He s **down** all the firstborn in their land,	5782
	135: 8	He s **down** the firstborn of Egypt,	5782
	135:10	He s **down** many nations	5782
	136:10	to *him who* s **down** the firstborn	5782
	136:17	*who* s **down** great kings,	5782
Pr	6: 1	if *you have* s hands **in pledge** for another,	9546
Isa	9:13	people have not returned to him *who* s them,	5782
	10:20	will no longer rely on *him who* s them **down**	5782
	10:26	when he s **down** Midian at the rock of Oreb;	4804
	14: 6	*which* in anger s **down** peoples	5782
	14:29	that the rod *that* s you is broken;	5782
	27: 7	*Has* [the LORD] s her as he struck	5782
	27: 7	Has [the LORD] struck her as he s **down**	4804
	27: 7	as he struck down *those who* s her?	5782
	60:10	Though in anger *I* s you,	5782
Jer	5: 3	*You* s them, but they felt no pain;	5782
	26:23	*who had* s him **down** with a sword	5782
	30:14	*I have* s you as an enemy would	5782
	41: 2	with him got up and s **down** Gedaliah son	5782
Da	2:34	It s the statue on its feet of iron and clay	10411
	2:35	that s the statue became a huge mountain	10411
Am	4: 9	"Many times *I* s your gardens	5782
	4: 9	I s them with blight and mildew.	NIH
Hag	2:17	*I* s all the work of your hands with blight,	5782
Zec	13: 8	"two-thirds *will be* s **down** and perish;	4162
Mt	26:51	and s the servant of the high priest,	4250
	26:67	s him with *their* fists.	3139
	27:30	and s him on the head again and again.	5597
Mk	12: 4	s this man **on the head**	3052
	14:47	of those standing near drew his sword and s	4091
	14:65	s him with *their* fists,	3139
	15:19	*Again and again they* s him on the head	5597
Lk	6:48	torrent s that house but could not shake it,	4703
	6:49	The moment the torrent s that house,	4703
	22:50	one of them s the servant of the high priest,	4250
Jn	18:10	drew it and s the high priest's servant,	4091
	18:22	one of the officials nearby s him **in the face**.	1443+4825
	19: 3	And *they* s him **in the face**.	1443+4825
Ac	7:11	Then a famine s all Egypt and Canaan,	2093+2262
	12: 7	He s Peter on the side and woke him up.	4250
	12:23	an angel of the Lord s him **down**,	4250
	23: 3	violate the law by commanding that I *be* s!"	5597
	27:41	But the ship s a sandbar and ran aground.	4346
2Co	4: 9	s **down**, but not destroyed.	2850
Rev	8:12	and a third of the sun *was* s,	4448
	11:11	and terror s those who saw them.	2158

STRUCTURE (7) [STRUCTURES]

1Ki	6: 5	he built a s around the building,	3666
1Ch	29: 1	this **palatial** s is not for man but for the LORD God.	1072
	29:19	to do everything to build the **palatial** s	1072
Ezr	5: 3	to rebuild this temple and restore this s?"	10082
	5: 9	to rebuild this temple and restore this s?"	10082
Eze	1:16	the appearance and s *of* the wheels;	5126
	41: 7	The s **surrounding** the temple was built	AIT

STRUCTURES (1) [STRUCTURE]

1Ki	7: 9	All **these** s, from the outside to the great	AIT

STRUGGLE (8) [STRUGGLED, STRUGGLES, STRUGGLING]

Ge	30: 8	*"I have had a great s with my sister,*	5887+7349
Jdg	12: 2	"I and my people were engaged in a great s	8190
Job	9:29	why *should I* s in vain?	3333
	41: 8	will remember the s and never do it again!	4878
Ro	15:30	**join** me in my s by praying to God for me.	5253
Eph	6:12	For our s is not against flesh and blood,	4097
Php	1:30	through the same s you saw I had,	74
Heb	12: 4	*In your* s against sin, you have not yet	497

STRUGGLED (3) [STRUGGLE]

Ge	32:28	because *you have* s with God and with men	8575
Hos	12: 3	as a man *he* s with God.	8575
	12: 4	He s with the angel and overcame him;	8575

STRUGGLES (1) [STRUGGLE]

Ps	73: 4	They have no s; their bodies are healthy and	3078

STRUGGLING (2) [STRUGGLE]

Col	1:29	To this end I labor, s with all his energy,	76
	2: 1	how much I am s for you and for those	74

STRUM (1)

Am	6: 5	*You* s **away** on your harps like David	7260

STRUNG (2) [STRING]

Isa	5:28	Their arrows are sharp, all their bows *are* s;	2005
La	2: 4	Like an enemy he *has* s his bow;	2005

STRUT (1) [STRUTTING]

Ps	12: 8	The wicked **freely** s about when what is vile	2143

STRUTTING (1) [STRUT]

Pr	30:31	a **rooster**, a he-goat, and a king	2435+5516

STUBBLE (7)

Ex	5:12	over Egypt to gather s to use for straw.	7990
	15: 7	it consumed them like s.	7990
Isa	47:14	they are like s; the fire will burn them up.	7990
Joel	2: 5	like a crackling fire consuming s,	7990
Ob	1:18	the house of Esau will be s,	7990
Na	1:10	they will be consumed like dry s.	7990
Mal	4: 1	the arrogant and every evildoer will be s,	7990

STUBBORN (15) [STUBBORN-HEARTED, STUBBORNLY, STUBBORNNESS]

Lev	26:19	I will break down your s pride and make	6437
Dt	2:30	the LORD your God *had* **made** his spirit s	7996
	21:18	a man has a s and rebellious son who does	6253
	21:20	"This son of ours *is* s and rebellious.	6253
Jdg	2:19	to give up their evil practices and s ways.	7997
Ps	78: 8	a s and rebellious generation,	6253
	81:12	to their s hearts to follow their own devices.	9244
Isa	48: 4	For I knew how s you were;	7997
Jer	5:23	these people have s and rebellious hearts;	6253
	7:24	instead, they followed the s inclinations	9244
Eze	2: 4	The people to whom I am sending you are obstinate and s.	2617+4213
Hos	4:16	The Israelites *are* s, like a stubborn heifer.	6253
	4:16	The Israelites are stubborn, like a s heifer.	6253
Mk	3: 5	deeply distressed at their s hearts,	4801
	16:14	for their lack of faith and their s **refusal**	5016

STUBBORN-HEARTED (1) [HEART, STUBBORN]

Isa	46:12	Listen to me, you s, you who are far	52+4213

STUBBORNLY (3) [STUBBORN]

Ex	13:15	When Pharaoh s **refused** to let us go,	7996
Ne	9:29	S they turned their backs on you,	6253
Zec	7:11	s they turned their backs and stopped	6253

STUBBORNNESS (9) [STUBBORN]

Dt	9:27	Overlook the s *of* this people,	8001
Jer	3:17	No longer will they follow the s *of*	9244
	9:14	they have followed the s *of* their hearts;	9244
	11: 8	they followed the s *of* their evil hearts.	9244
	13:10	the s *of* their hearts and go after other gods	9244
	16:12	See how each of you is following the s *of*	9244
	18:12	*us* will follow the s *of* his evil heart.' "	9244
	23:17	who follow the s *of* their hearts they say,	9244
Ro	2: 5	of your s and your unrepentant heart,	5018

STUBS (1)

Isa	7: 4	of these two smoldering s of firewood—	2387

STUCK (3) [STICK]

1Sa	26: 7	with his spear s in the ground near his head.	5080
Job	29:10	their tongues s to the roof of their mouths.	1815
Ac	27:41	The bow s **fast** and would not move,	2242

STUDDED (1)

SS	1:11	earrings of gold, s with silver.	5925

STUDENT (4) [STUDY]

1Ch	25: 8	Young and old alike, teacher as well as s,	9441
Mt	10:24	"A s is not above his teacher,	3412
	10:25	It is enough *for* the s to be like his teacher,	3412
Lk	6:40	A s is not above his teacher,	3412

STUDIED (1) [STUDY]

Jn	7:15	"How did this man get such learning without *having* s?"	3443

STUDY (4) [STUDENT, STUDIED]

Ezr	7:10	s and observance of the Law of the LORD,	2011
Ecc	1:13	I devoted myself to s and to explore	2011
	12:12	and much s wearies the body.	4261
Jn	5:39	*You* **diligently** s the Scriptures because	2236

STUDY (KJV) See also DO BEST

STUFF (KJV) See BAGGAGE, BELONGINGS, GOODS, POSSESSIONS, SUPPLIES, THINGS

STUMBLE (43) [STUMBLED, STUMBLES, STUMBLING]

Lev	26:37	*They will* s over one another as though	4173
Ps	9: 3	*they* s and perish before you.	4173
	27: 2	*they will* s and fall.	4173
	37:24	though *he* s, he will not fall, for the LORD	5877
	119:165	and nothing can **make** them s.	4842
Pr	3:23	and your foot *will not* s,	5597
	4:12	when you run, *you will* not s.	4173
	4:19	they do not know what *makes them* s.	4173
Isa	8:14	be a stone that **causes** men to s and a rock	5598
	8:15	Many of them *will* s; they will fall	4173
	28: 7	*they* s when rendering decisions.	7048
	31: 3	he who helps *will* s,	4173
	40:30	and young men s **and fall**;	4173+4173
	59:10	At midday *we* s as if it were twilight;	4173
	63:13	Like a horse in open country, *they did* not s;	4173
Jer	6:21	Fathers and sons alike *will* s over them;	4173
	12: 5	If you s in safe country,	1054
	13:16	before your feet s on the darkening hills.	5597
	18:15	which **made** them s in their ways and in	4173
	20:11	so my persecutors *will* s and not prevail.	4173
	31: 9	on a level path where *they will* not s,	4173
	46: 6	In the north by the River Euphrates *they* s	4173
	46:12	One warrior *will* s over another;	4173
	46:16	They *will* s repeatedly;	4173
	50:32	The arrogant one *will* s and fall	4173
Eze	7:19	for it has made them s *into* sin.	4842
Da	11:19	the fortresses of his own country but *will* s	4173
	11:35	Some of the wise *will* s,	4173
Hos	4: 5	*You* s day and night,	4173
	4: 5	and the prophets s with you.	4173
	5: 5	the Israelites, even Ephraim, s in their sin;	4173
	14: 9	but the rebellious s in them.	4173
Na	2: 5	yet *they* s on their way.	4173
Mal	2: 8	by your teaching *have* **caused** many *to* s;	4173
Jn	11: 9	A man who walks by day *will not* s,	4684
Ro	9:33	I lay in Zion a stone that **causes** men to s	4682
	11:11	*Did they* s so as to fall beyond recovery?	4760
	14:21	that causes someone else to s.	4682
1Co	10:32	*Do* **not cause** anyone to s, whether Jews,	718
Jas	3: 2	We all s in many ways.	4760
1Pe	2: 8	"A stone that **causes** men to s and a rock	4684
	2: 8	They s because they disobey the message—	4684
1Jn	2:10	and there is nothing in him to make him s.	4998

STUMBLED (8) [STUMBLE]

1Sa	2: 4	but *those who* s are armed with strength.	4173
2Sa	6: 6	because the oxen s.	9023
1Ch	13: 9	because the oxen s.	9023
Job	4: 4	Your words have supported *those who* s;	4173
Ps	35:15	But when I s, they gathered in glee;	7520
	107:12	*they* s, and there was no one to help.	4173
Isa	59:14	truth *has* s in the streets,	4173
Ro	9:32	*They* s **over** the "stumbling stone."	4684

STUMBLES (5) [STUMBLE]

Pr	24:17	when he s, do not let your heart rejoice,	4173
Isa	5:27	Not one of them grows tired or s,	4173
Hos	5: 5	Judah also s with them.	4173
Jn	11:10	It is when he walks by night that *he* s,	4684
Jas	2:10	For whoever keeps the whole law and yet s	4760

STUMBLING (15) [STUMBLE]

Lev	19:14	not curse the deaf or put a s **block** in front	4842
Ps	56:13	from death and my feet from s,	1892
	116: 8	my eyes from tears, my feet from s,	1892
Eze	3:20	and I put a s **block** before him, he will die.	4842
	14: 3	and put wicked s **blocks** before their faces	4842
	14: 4	and put a wicked s **block** before his face	4842
	14: 7	and puts a wicked s **block** before his face	4842
Na	3: 3	*people* s over the corpses—	4173
Mt	16:23	You are a s **block** to me;	4998
Ro	9:32	They stumbled over the "s stone."	4682

Ro	11: 9	a **s block** and a retribution for them.	4998
	14:13	make up your mind not to put any **s block**	4682
1Co	1:23	a **s block** to Jews and foolishness to	4998
	8: 9	of your freedom does not become a **s block**	4682
2Co	6: 3	We put no **s block** in anyone's path,	4683

STUMP (6) [STUMPS]

Job	14: 8	in the ground and its **s** die in the soil,	1614
Isa	6:13	so the holy seed will be the **s** *in* the land."	5169
	11: 1	A shoot will come up from the **s** *of* Jesse;	1614
Da	4:15	But let the **s** and its roots,	10567
	4:23	but leave the **s**, bound with iron and bronze,	10567
	4:26	The command to leave the **s** of the tree	10567

STUMPS (1) [STUMP]

Isa	6:13	and oak leave **s** when they are cut down,	5169

STUNNED (2)

Ge	45:26	Jacob *was* **s**; he did not believe them.	4213+7028
Isa	29: 9	*Be* **s** and amazed, blind yourselves and	9449

STUNTED (1)

Lev	22:23	an ox or a sheep that is deformed or **s**,	7832

STUPID (4) [STUPIDITY]

Job	18: 3	as cattle and **considered s** in your sight?	3241
Pr	12: 1	but he who hates correction is **s**.	1280
Ecc	10: 3	and shows everyone *how* **s** he is.	6119
2Ti	2:23	to do with foolish and **s** arguments,	553

STUPIDITY (1) [STUPID]

Ecc	7:25	and to understand the **s** of wickedness and	4073

STUPOR (2)

Ps	78:65	as a man *wakes from the* **s** of wine.	8130
Ro	11: 8	"God gave them a spirit *of* **s**,	2919

STURDIEST (1) [STURDY]

Ps	78:31	he put to death the **s** among them,	5458

STURDY (1) [STURDIEST]

Isa	10:16	a wasting disease upon his **s** *warriors;*	5458

SUAH (1)

1Ch	7:36	The sons of Zophah: **S,** Harnepher, Shual,	6053

SUBDIVISION (1) [DIVIDE]

2Ch	35: 5	a group of Levites for *each* **s** of the families	7107

SUBDIVISIONS (1) [DIVIDE]

2Ch	35:12	the **s** of the families of the people to offer to	5141

SUBDUE (10) [SUBDUED, SUBDUES, SUBDUING]

Ge	1:28	increase in number; fill the earth and **s** it.	3899
Nu	24:24	*they will* **s** Asshur and Eber,	6700
Dt	9: 3	he *will* **s** them before you.	4044
Jdg	16: 5	so we may tie him up and **s** him.	6700
	16:19	and so began to **s** him.	6700
1Ch	17:10	*I will* also **s** all your enemies.	4044
Ps	81:14	how quickly *would I* **s** their enemies.	4044
Isa	45: 1	to **s** nations before him and to strip kings	3718
Da	7:24	*he will* **s** three kings.	10737
Mk	5: 4	No one was strong enough *to* **s** him.	1238

SUBDUED (19) [SUBDUE]

Nu	32: 4	the LORD **s** before the people of Israel—	5782
	32:22	then when the land *is* **s** before the LORD,	3899
	32:29	then when the land *is* **s** before you,	3899
Jos	10:40	So Joshua **s** the whole region,	5782
	10:41	Joshua **s** them from Kadesh Barnea to Gaza	5782
Jdg	4:23	On that day God **s** Jabin,	4044
	8:28	Thus Midian *was* **s** before the Israelites	4044
	11:33	Thus Israel **s** Ammon.	4044
	16: 6	and how you can be tied up and **s**."	6700
1Sa	7:13	So the Philistines **were s** and did	4044
2Sa	8: 1	David defeated the Philistines and **s** them,	4044
	8:11	and gold from all the nations *he had* **s**:	3899
1Ch	18: 1	David defeated the Philistines and **s** them,	4044
2Ch	13:18	The men of Israel **were s** on that occasion,	4044
Ne	9:24	*You* **s** before them the Canaanites.	4044
Ps	47: 3	*He* **s** nations under us,	1818
Isa	10:13	like a mighty one *I* **s** their kings.	3718
	14: 6	in fury **s** nations with relentless aggression.	8097
Zec	10:11	the surging sea *will be* **s** and all the depths	5782

SUBDUES (3) [SUBDUE]

Ps	18:47	*who* **s** nations under me,	1818
	144: 2	who **s** peoples under me.	8096
Isa	41: 2	He hands nations over to him and **s** kings	8097

SUBDUING (1) [SUBDUE]

Job	41: 9	Any hope of **s** him is false;	NIH

SUBJECT (42) [SUBJECTED,

Ge	14: 4	*For* twelve years *they had been* **s to**	6268
Dt	20:11	all the people in it shall be **s to** forced labor	4200
Jdg	1:30	but they did **s** them to forced labor.	NIH
	3: 8	**to** whom the Israelites *were* **s** for eight years	6268
	3:14	The Israelites *were* **s** to Eglon king of Moab	6268
	3:30	Moab *was* **made s** to Israel,	3338+4044+9393
	9:28	Shechem, *that we should be* **s** to him?	6268
	9:38	'Who is Abimelech that *we should be* **s to**	6268
1Sa	4: 9	Be men, or *you will be* **s** to the Hebrews,	6268
	11: 1	and *we will be* **s** to you."	6268
2Sa	8: 2	So the Moabites became **s** to David	6269
	8: 6	and the Arameans became **s** to him	6269
	8:14	and all the Edomites became **s** to David.	6269
	10:19	with the Israelites and *became* **s** to them.	6268
	22:44	People I did not know *are* **s** to me,	6268
1Ch	18: 2	they became **s** to him and brought tribute.	6269
	18: 6	and the Arameans became **s** to him	6269
	18:13	and all the Edomites became **s** to David.	6269
	19:19	they made peace with David and *became* **s**	6268
	22:18	land **is s** to the LORD and to his people.	3899
2Ch	12: 8	They will, however, become **s** to him,	6269
Ne	5: 5	yet we *have* to **s** our sons and daughters	3899
Ps	18:43	people I did not know *are* **s** to me.	6268
	89:22	No enemy *will* **s** him **to tribute;**	5957
Isa	11:14	and the Ammonites will be **s** to them.	5463
Jer	27: 6	I will make even the wild animals **s** to him.	6268
Mt	5:21	and anyone who murders will be **s**	1944
	5:22	with his brother will be **s** to judgment.	1944
	9:20	then a woman *who had been* **s to**	137
Mk	5:25	woman was there who had been **s to bleeding** for twelve years.	135+1877+4868
Lk	8:43	woman was there who had been **s to bleeding** for twelve years.	135+1877+4868
Ac	17:32	"We want to hear you again on **this s**."	AIT
1Co	2:15	he himself is not **s** to any man's judgment:	5679
	14:32	The spirits of prophets *are* **s to the control**	5718
	15:28	*be made* **s** to him who put everything	5718
Gal	4: 2	He is **s** to guardians and trustees until	5679
Tit	2: 5	to be kind, and to be **s** to their husbands,	5718
	2: 9	*to be* **s** to their masters in everything,	5718
	3: 1	the people *to be* **s** to rulers and authorities,	5718
Heb	2: 8	God left nothing that is **not s** to him.	538
	2: 8	Yet at present we do not see everything **s**	5718
	5: 2	since *he himself is* **s** to weakness.	4329

SUBJECTED (7) [SUBJECT]

Jos	17:13	*they* **s** the Canaanites to forced labor	5989
Ezr	9: 7	and our kings and our priests *have been* **s**	5989
Ps	106:42	Their enemies oppressed them and **s** *them*	4044
	107:12	So he **s** them to bitter labor;	4044
Ro	8:20	For the creation *was* **s** to frustration,	5718
	8:20	but by the will of the one who **s** it,	5718
Heb	2: 5	to angels that *he has* **s** the world to come,	5718

SUBJECTING (1) [SUBJECT]

Heb	6: 6	and **s** him **to public disgrace.**	4136

SUBJECTION (KJV) See SUBMISSIVE

SUBJECTS (7) [SUBJECT]

1Sa	17: 9	we will become your **s;**	6269
	17: 9	you will become our **s** and serve us."	6269
1Ki	4:21	and *were* Solomon's **s** all his life.	6268
1Ch	21: 3	are they not all my lord's **s?**	6269
Pr	14:28	but without **s** a prince is ruined.	4211
Mt	8:12	**s** of the kingdom will be thrown outside,	5626
Lk	19:14	"But his **s** hated him and sent a delegation	4489

SUBJUGATE (1) [SUBJUGATED]

Jer	27: 7	and great kings *will* **s** him.	6268

SUBJUGATED (1) [SUBJUGATE]

1Ch	20: 4	and the Philistines *were* **s**.	4044

SUBMISSION (6) [SUBMIT]

1Ch	29:24	pledged their **s** *to* King Solomon.	9393
Da	11:43	with the Libyans and Nubians in **s**.	5202
1Co	14:34	but *must be* in **s**, as the Law says.	5718
1Ti	2:11	woman should learn in quietness and full **s**.	5717
Heb	5: 7	and he was heard because of his reverent **s**.	NIG
1Pe	3:22	authorities and powers in **s** to him.	5718

SUBMISSIVE (4) [SUBMIT]

Jas	3:17	then peace-loving, considerate, **s**,	2340
1Pe	3: 1	the same way *be* **s** to your husbands so that,	5718
	3: 5	*They were* **s** to their own husbands,	5718
	5: 5	the same way *be* **s** to those who are older.	5718

SUBMIT (24) [SUBMISSION, SUBMISSIVE, SUBMITS, SUBMITTED]

Ge	16: 9	"Go back to your mistress and **s** to her."	6700
	41:40	and all my people are *to* **s** to your orders.	5976
	49:15	to the burden and **s** to forced labor.	6268
2Ch	30: 8	as your fathers were *to* **s** to the LORD.	3338+5989
Job	22:21	"**S** to God and be at peace with him;	6122
Ps	68:31	Cush *will* **s** herself to God.	3338+8132
	81:11	Israel *would* not **s** to me.	14
Lk	10:17	even the demons **s** to us in your name."	5718
	10:20	do not rejoice that the spirits **s** to you,	5718

Ro	8: 7	*It does* not **s** to God's law,	5718
	10: 3	*they did* not **s** to God's righteousness.	5718
	13: 1	Everyone *must* **s** himself to the	5718
	13: 5	it is necessary *to* **s** to the authorities,	5718
1Co	16:16	to **s** to such as these and to everyone who	5718
Eph	5:21	**S** to one another out of reverence	5718
	5:22	Wives, **s** to your husbands as to the Lord.	NIG
	5:24	so also wives should **s** to their husbands	NIG
Col	2:20	*do you* **s** to its **rules:**	1505
	3:18	Wives, **s** to your husbands, as is fitting	5718
Heb	12: 9	How much more *should we* **s** to the Father	5718
	13:17	Obey your leaders and **s** to their authority.	5640
Jas	4: 7	**S** yourselves, then, to God.	5718
1Pe	2:13	**S** yourselves for the Lord's sake to every	5718
	2:18	Slaves, **s** yourselves to your masters	5718

SUBMITS (1) [SUBMIT]

Eph	5:24	Now as the church **s** to Christ,	5718

SUBMITTED (1) [SUBMIT]

La	5: 6	*We* **s** to Egypt and Assyria	3338+5989

SUBORDINATES (1)

1Ki	11:11	from you and give it to one of your **s**.	6269

SUBORNED (KJV) See SECRETLY PERSUADED

SUBSCRIBE (KJV) See SIGNED, WRITE

SUBSIDE (3) [SUBSIDED, SUBSIDES]

Eze	5:13	and my wrath against them *will* **s**,	5663
	16:42	Then my wrath against you *will* **s**	5663
	21:17	and my wrath *will* **s**.	5663

SUBSIDED (5) [SUBSIDE]

Jdg	8: 3	At this, their resentment against him **s**.	8332
Est	2: 1	Later when the anger of King Xerxes *had* **s**,	8896
	7:10	Then the king's fury **s**.	8896
Eze	24:13	until my wrath against you *has* **s**.	5663
Lk	8:24	the storm **s**, and all was calm.	4264

SUBSIDES (1) [SUBSIDE]

Ge	27:44	for a while until your brother's fury **s**.	8740

SUBSTANCE (1)

Da	7: 1	He wrote down the **s** of his dream.	10418+10646

SUBSTITUTE (4) [SUBSTITUTION]

Lev	27:10	He must not exchange it or **s** a good one for	4614
	27:10	if *he should* **s** one animal for another,	4614+4614
	27:10	both it and the **s** become holy.	9455
	27:33	both the animal and its **s** become holy	9455

SUBSTITUTION (2) [SUBSTITUTE]

Lev	27:33	the good from the bad or **make** any **s**.	4614
	27:33	If *he does* **make a s**,	4614+4614

SUBTIL (KJV) See CRAFTY

SUBTRACT (1)

Dt	4: 2	not add to what I command you and *do* not **s**	1757

SUBURBS (KJV) See FARM LANDS, OPEN LAND, PASTURELAND, SHORELANDS

SUBVERT (KJV) See DEPRIVE, RUINING

SUBVERTING (1)

Lk	23: 2	"We have found this man **s** our nation.	1406

SUCATHITES (1)

1Ch	2:55	the Tirathites, Shimeathites and **S**.	8460

SUCCEED (28) [SUCCEEDED, SUCCEEDS, SUCCESS, SUCCESSFUL, SUCCESSFULLY, SUCCESSIVE, SUCCESSOR, SUCCESSORS]

Lev	6:22	to **s** him as anointed priest shall prepare it.	9393
	16:32	and ordained to **s** his father as high priest is	9393
Nu	14:41	This *will* not **s!**	7503
1Sa	30: 8	overtake them and **s** in the rescue."	5911+5911
2Sa	7:12	I will raise up your offspring to **s** you,	339
1Ki	5: 1	anointed king to **s** his father David,	9393
	15: 4	to **s** him and by making Jerusalem strong.	339
	19:16	from Abel Meholah to **s** you as prophet.	9393
	22:22	"*You will* **s** in enticing him,'	3523
2Ki	3:27	firstborn son, who was to **s** him as king,	9393
1Ch	17:11	I will raise up your offspring to **s** you,	339
2Ch	13:12	the God of your fathers, *for you will* not **s**."	7503
	18:21	"*You will* **s** in enticing him,'	3523
Job	30:13	*they* **s** in destroying me—	3603

Ps	20: 4	and **make** all your plans s. 4848
	21:11	and devise wicked schemes, *they* cannot s; 3523
	37: 7	do not fret when men s in their ways, 7503
	140: 8	*do not* **let** their plans s, 7049
Pr	15:22	but with many advisers they s. 7756
	16: 3	and your plans *will* s. 3922
	21:30	no plan that can s **against** the LORD. 4200+5584
Ecc	11: 6	for you do not know which *will* s, 4178
Isa	47:12	Perhaps you will s, perhaps you will cause 3603
	48:15	and *he* will s in his mission. 7503
Jer	32: 5	against the Babylonians, *you* will not s.' " 7503
Eze	17:15	*Will he* s? Will he who does such things 7503
Da	8:24	and *will* s in whatever he does. 7503
	11:17	but his plans *will* not s or help him. 6641

SUCCEEDED (73) [SUCCEED]

Ge	36:33	Jobab son of Zerah from Bozrah s him 9393
	36:34	the land of the Temanites s him as king. 9393
	36:35	in the country of Moab, s him as king. 9393
	36:36	Samlah from Masrekah s him as king. 9393
	36:37	from Rehoboth on the river s him as king. 9393
	36:38	Baal-Hanan son of Acbor s him as king. 9393
	36:39	Hadad s him as king. 9393
Dt	10: 6	and Eleazar his son s him as priest. 9393
2Sa	10: 1	and his son Hanun s him as king. 9393
1Ki	8:20	*I have* s David my father and now I sit 7756+9393
	11:43	And Rehoboam his son s him as king. 9393
	14:20	And Nadab his son s him as king. 9393
	14:31	And Abijah his son s him as king. 9393
	15: 8	And Asa his son s him as king. 9393
	15:24	And Jehoshaphat his son s him as king. 9393
	15:28	of Asa king of Judah and s him as king. 9393
	16: 6	And Elah his son s him as king. 9393
	16:10	Then he s him as king. 9393
	16:28	And Ahab his son s him as king. 9393
	22:40	And Ahaziah his son s him as king. 9393
	22:50	And Jehoram his son s him. 9393
2Ki	1:17	Joram s him as king in the second year 9393
	8:15	Then Hazael s him as king. 9393
	8:24	And Ahaziah his son s him as king. 9393
	10:35	And Jehoahaz his son s him as king. 9393
	12:21	And Amaziah his son s him as king. 9393
	13: 9	And Jehoash his son s him as king. 9393
	13:13	and Jeroboam s him on the throne. 3782
	13:24	and Ben-Hadad his son s him as king. 9393
	14:16	And Jeroboam his son s him as king. 9393
	14:29	And Zechariah his son s him as king. 9393
	15: 7	And Jotham his son s him as king. 9393
	15:10	assassinated him and s him as king. 9393
	15:14	assassinated him and s him as king. 9393
	15:22	And Pekahiah his son s him as king. 9393
	15:25	Pekah killed Pekahiah and s him as king. 9393
	15:30	and then s him as king in the twentieth year 9393
	15:38	And Ahaz his son s him as king. 9393
	16:20	And Hezekiah his son s him as king. 9393
	19:37	And Esarhaddon his son s him as king. 9393
	20:21	And Manasseh his son s him as king. 9393
	21:18	And Amon his son s him as king. 9393
	21:26	And Josiah his son s him as king. 9393
	24: 6	And Jehoiachin his son s him as king. 9393
1Ch	1:44	Jobab son of Zerah from Bozrah s him 9393
	1:45	the land of the Temanites s him as king. 9393
	1:46	in the coutnry of Moab, s him as king. 9393
	1:47	Samlah from Masrekah s him as king. 9393
	1:48	from Rehoboth on the river s him as king. 9393
	1:49	Baal-Hanan son of Acbor s him as king. 9393
	1:50	Baal-Hanan died, Hadad s him as king. 9393
	19: 1	and his son s him as king. 9393
	27:34	Ahithophel was s *by* Jehoiada son 339
	29:28	His son Solomon s him as king. 9393
2Ch	6:10	*I have* s David my father and now I sit 7756+9393
	7:11	had s in carrying out all he had in mind 7503
	9:31	And Rehoboam his son s him as king. 9393
	12:16	And Abijah his son s him as king. 9393
	14: 1	Asa his son s him as king 9393
	17: 1	Jehoshaphat his son s him as king 9393
	21: 1	And Jehoram his son s him as king 9393
	24:27	And Amaziah his son s him as king. 9393
	26:23	And Jotham his son s him as king. 9393
	27: 9	And Ahaz his son s him as king. 9393
	28:27	And Hezekiah his son s him as king. 9393
	32:30	He is in everything he undertook. 7503
	32:33	And Manasseh his son s him as king. 9393
	33:20	And Amon his son s him as king. 9393
	36: 8	And Jehoiachin his son s him as king. 9393
Isa	37:38	And Esarhaddon his son s him as king. 9393
Jer	22:11	who s his father as king of Judah 9393
Da	11:21	be s *by* a contemptible person 4030+6584+6641
Ac	24:27	Felix *was* s by Porcius Festus, *1345+3284*

SUCCEEDS (2) [SUCCEED]

Ex	29:30	The son who s him as priest and comes to 9393
Pr	17: 8	wherever he turns, *he* s. 8505

SUCCESS (25) [SUCCEED]

Ge	24:12	of my master Abraham, **give** me s today, 7936
	24:40	with you and **make** your journey a s, 7503
	24:42	please **grant** s *to* the journey 7503
	24:56	the LORD *has* **granted** s *to* my journey. 7503
	27:20	"The LORD your God gave me s," 7936
	39: 3	with him and that the LORD gave him s 7503
	39:23	and gave him s *in* whatever he did. 7503
1Sa	18:14	In everything he did he had great s, 8505
	18:30	David **met with** more s than the rest 8505
	25:31	when the LORD *has* **brought** my master s, 3512

1Ki	22:13	the other prophets are predicting s for 3202
1Ch	12:18	S, success to you, and success to those 8934
	12:18	s to you, and success to those who help you, 8934
	12:18	and s to those who help you, 8934
	22:11	and *may you* **have** s and build the house of 7503
2Ch	18:12	the other prophets are predicting s for 3202
	26: 5	God **gave** him s. 7503
Ne	1:11	**Give** your servant s today 7503
	2:20	"The God of heaven *will* **give** us s. 7503
Job	5:12	so that their hands achieve no s. 9370
	6:13	now that s has been driven from me? 9370
Ps	118:25	O LORD, save us; O LORD, **grant** us s. 7503
Ecc	10:10	strength is needed but skill will bring s. 3862
Da	11:14	in fulfillment of the vision, but **without** s. 4173

SUCCESSFUL (8) [SUCCEED]

Ge	24:21	or not the LORD *had* **made** his journey s. 7503
Jos	1: 7	that *you may be* s wherever you go. 8505
	1: 8	Then you will be prosperous and s. 8505
Jdg	18: 5	to learn whether our journey *will be* s." 7503
1Sa	18:15	When Saul saw how s he *was*, 8505
2Ki	18: 7	*he was* s in whatever he undertook. 8505
2Ch	20:20	in his prophets and *you will be* s." 7503
Da	11:36	*be* s until the time of wrath is completed, 7503

SUCCESSFULLY (1) [SUCCEED]

1Sa	18: 5	*so* s that Saul gave him a high rank in 8505

SUCCESSIVE (2) [SUCCEED]

2Sa	21: 1	was a famine *for* three s **years**; 339+9102+9102
Eze	41: 7	all around the temple were wider **at each** s **level.** 2025+2025+4200+4200+5087+5087

SUCCESSOR (6) [SUCCEED]

1Ki	1:48	who has allowed my eyes to see a s 3782
1Ch	27: 7	his son Zebadiah was his s. 339
Ecc	2:12	What more can the king's s do than what has already been done? 132+339+995+8611
	4:15	followed the youth, the king's s. 6641+9393
	4:16	came later were not pleased with **the** s. 2257S
Da	11:20	"His s will send out a tax collector to maintain 4030+6584+6641

SUCCESSORS (1) [SUCCEED]

1Ch	3:16	The s *of* Jehoiakim: Jehoiachin his son, 1201

SUCCOUR, SUCCOURED, SUCCOURER (KJV) See HELP, HELPED, RESCUE, SUPPORT

SUCCOTH (18) [SUCCOTH BENOTH]

Ge	33:17	Jacob, however, went to S, 6111
	33:17	That is why the place is called S. 6111
Ex	12:37	Israelites journeyed from Rameses to S. 6111
	13:20	After leaving S they camped at Etham on 6111
Nu	33: 5	Israelites left Rameses and camped at S. 6111
	33: 6	They left S and camped at Etham, 6111
Jos	13:27	S and Zaphon with the rest of the realm 6111
Jdg	8: 5	He said to the men of S, 6111
	8: 6	But the officials of S said, 6111
	8: 8	but they answered as the men of S had. 6111
	8:14	a young man of S and questioned him, 6111
	8:14	of the seventy-seven officials of S, 6111
	8:15	Gideon came and said to the men of S, 6111
	8:16	the town and taught the men of S a lesson 6111
1Ki	7:46	of the Jordan between S and Zarethan. 6111
2Ch	4:17	of the Jordan between S and Zarethan. 6111
Ps	60: 6	and measure off the Valley of S. 6111
	108: 7	and measure off the Valley of S. 6111

SUCCOTH BENOTH (1) [SUCCOTH]

2Ki	17:30	The men from Babylon made S, 6112

SUCH (227)

Ge	18:25	Far be it from you to do s a thing— 3869
	20: 9	that you have brought s great guilt AIT
	34:14	They said to them, "We can't do s a thing; 2296
	39: 9	could I do s a wicked thing and sin 1524+2296
	41:19	I had never seen s ugly cows in all the land 3869
	44: 7	"Why does my lord say s things? 3869
	44:17	"Far be it from me to do s *a thing!* 2296
Ex	10:14	had there been s a plague of locusts, 4017+4027
	28: 3	in s matters that they are to make garments NIH
	32:21	that you led them into s a great sin?" AIT
Lev	6: 3	he commits any s sin that people may do— 2179
	10:19	but s things as this have happened to me. 3869
	11:34	but has water on it from s a pot is unclean, 3972
	13:45	"The person with s an infectious disease 889
	18:29	s persons must be cut off from their people. 2021+6913S
	19: 5	sacrifice it **in** s **a way that** it will be 4200
	21: 2	s **as** his mother or father, 4200
	22: 6	The one who touches **any** s **thing** will 2257S
	22:25	you must not accept s animals from 3972+4946
	22:29	sacrifice it **in** s **a way that** the LORD becomes holy. 889
	25:21	I will send you s a blessing in the sixth year NIH
	27: 9	s an animal given to the LORD becomes holy. 889
Dt	4: 8	s righteous decrees and laws **as this** 3869
	13:11	among you will do s an evil thing again. 3869

Dt	19:20	and never again will s an evil thing be done 3869
	29:18	among you that produces s bitter poison. NIH
	29:19	When s a person hears the words NIH
	33:17	S are the ten thousands of Ephraim; 2156S
	33:17	s are the thousands of Manasseh." 2156S
Jdg	7:13	with s **force** that the tent overturned 5877S
	16:16	With s nagging she prodded him day 1821S
	19:24	don't do s a disgraceful thing." 2296
	19:30	"S a thing has never been seen or done, 3869
Ru	2:10	"Why have I found s favor in your eyes NIH
1Sa	1:16	or let your mouth speak s arrogance, NIH
	2:23	he said to them, "Why do you do s things? 3869
	4: 5	all Israel raised s a great shout that NIH
	6:10	They took two s cows and hitched them to 6402S
	7:10	and **threw** them **into** s a panic that AIT
	8: 5	s as all the other nations have." 3869
	9:21	Why do you say s a thing to me?" 3869
	19: 8	He struck them with s force that they fled 1524
	24: 6	that I should do s a thing to my master, 2296
	25:17	He is s a wicked man that no one can talk NIH
	27:11	And s was his practice as long as he lived 3907
2Sa	11:11	surely as you live, I will not do s a thing!" 2296
	12: 6	because he did s a thing and had no pity." 2296
	13:12	S *a thing* should not be done in Israel! 4027
	17:15	the elders of Israel to do s and such, 2296+3869
	17:15	the elders of Israel to do such and s, 2296+3869
	17:21	Ahithophel has advised s **and such** 3970
	17:21	Ahithophel has advised **such and** s 3970
	23:17	S were the exploits of the three mighty men. 465
	23:22	S were the exploits of Benaiah son 465
	24: 3	But why does my lord the king want to do s 2296
1Ki	9: 8	the LORD done s *a thing* to this land and 3970
	14: 5	are to give her s and such an answer. 2297+3869
	14: 5	are to give her such and s an answer. 3869
2Ki	6: 8	"I will set up my camp in s and such 532+7141
	6: 8	"I will set up my camp in such and s 532+7141
	6:10	so that he was on his guard in s places. 9004S
	8:13	a mere dog, accomplish s a feat?" 2296
	18:21	S is Pharaoh king of Egypt 4027
	19: 7	to put s a spirit in him that when he hears NIH
	21:12	I am going to bring s disaster on Jerusalem NIH
	23:22	had any s Passover been observed. 3869
1Ch	11:19	S were the exploits of the three mighty men. 465
	11:24	S were the exploits of Benaiah son 465
	29:25	and bestowed on him royal splendor s as AIT
2Ch	1:12	s as no king who was before you ever had 4027
	7:21	the LORD done s **a thing** to this land and 3970
	9: 9	There had never been s spices as those 3869
	14:13	S a great number of Cushites fell NIH
	35:18	of the kings of Israel had ever celebrated s 3869
Ezr	9:14	peoples who commit s detestable practices? 465
Ne	5:13	So *may* s *a man* **be** shaken out and emptied! AIT
Est	4:14	to royal position for s a time **as this?"** 3869
	7: 4	no s distress would justify disturbing 2021
	7: 5	Where is the man who has dared to do s 4027
Job	6: 7	I refuse to touch it; s food makes me ill. 3869
	8: 2	"How long will you say s *things?* 465
	8:13	S is the destiny of all who forget God; 4027
	14: 3	Do you fix your eye on s *a one?* 2296
	15:13	and pour out s **words** from your mouth? AIT
	18:21	Surely s is the dwelling of an evil man; 465
	18:21	s is the place of one who knows not God." 2296
	20:29	S is the fate God allots the wicked, 2296
	22:13	Does he judge through s darkness? NIH
	23:14	and many s plans he still has in store. 3869
	24: 1	who know him look in vain for s days? 2257S
	31:23	fear of his splendor I could not do s things. NIH
Ps	12: 7	and protect us from s people forever. 2306
	17:14	by your hand save me from s men, NIH
	24: 6	S is the generation of those who seek him, 2296
	139: 6	S **knowledge** is too wonderful for me, AIT
Pr	1:19	S is the end of all who go after ill-gotten 4027
	29: 7	but the wicked **have** no s **concern.** AIT
Ecc	7:10	do not be surprised at s **things;** 2914S
	7:10	For it is not wise to ask s **questions.** 2296S
Isa	36: 6	S is Pharaoh king of Egypt 4027
	38:16	Lord, by s things men live; 2157S
	38:17	for my benefit that I suffered *s* **anguish.** AIT
	40:20	to **present** *s* **an offering** selects wood AIT
	65: 5	S people are smoke in my nostrils, 465
	66: 8	Who has ever heard of s a thing? 3869
	66: 8	Who has ever seen s things? 3869
Jer	5: 9	not avenge myself on s a nation **as this?** 3869
	5:29	not avenge myself on s a nation **as this?** 3869
	9: 9	not avenge myself on s a nation **as this?** 3869
	16:10	the LORD decreed s a great disaster 2296
	22: 8	'Why has the LORD done s **a thing** 3970
	32:35	that they should do a detestable thing and 2296
	40:16	"Don't do s a thing! 2296
	44: 7	Why bring s **great** disaster on yourselves AIT
La	3:36	would not the Lord see s things? NIH
Eze	1:	S were their faces. NIH
	16:16	S things should not **happen,** AIT
	17:15	Will he who does s *things* escape? 465
	18:13	*Will* s *a man* **live?** AIT
	18:14	he does not do s things: 3869
	21:10	The sword despises every s stick. NIH
	31:14	are ever to reach s a **height,** AIT
	43:12	S is the law of the temple. 2296
Da	2:10	ever asked s a thing of any magician 10180+10341
	2:15	"Why did the king issue s a **harsh** decree?" AIT
	10: 7	but s terror overwhelmed them that they fled 1524
	12: 1	be a time of distress s as has not happened 889
Hos	9: 4	S sacrifices will be to them like the bread NIH
Joel	2: 2	s as never was of old nor ever will be 4017
Am	5:13	the prudent man keeps quiet in s times, 2085
Jnh	1: 4	and s a violent storm arose that NIH

Mic	2: 7	Does he do s *things?"*	465
Mal	1: 9	With s **offerings** from your hands,	2296S
Mt	8:10	anyone in Israel with s **great** faith.	5537
	9: 8	who had given s authority to men.	5525
	13: 2	S large crowds gathered around him	NIG
	15:33	in this remote place to feed s a crowd?"	5537
	18: 7	S **things** must come, but woe to	3836+4998S
	19:14	kingdom of heaven belongs to s **as these.**"	5525
	24: 6	S things must happen, but the end is still	NIG
Mk	4:32	with s big branches that the birds of	NIG
	7: 4	s as the washing of cups,	NIG
	7:29	he told her, "For s a reply, you may go;	4047
	10:14	the kingdom of God belongs to s **as these.**	5525
	12:40	S **men** will be punished most severely."	4047
	13: 7	S things must happen, but the end is still	NIG
Lk	5: 6	they caught s a large number of fish	NIG
	7: 9	not found s great faith even in Israel."	5537
	9: 9	Who, then, is this I hear s *things* about?"	5525
	12:30	For the pagan world runs after all s *things,*	4047
	18:16	the kingdom of God belongs to s **as these.**	5525
	20:47	S *men* will be punished most severely."	4047
Jn	7:15	"How did this man get s learning	NIG
	7:32	the crowd whispering s *things* about him.	4047
	8: 5	Moses commanded us to stone s *women.*	5525
	8:40	Abraham did not do s *things.*	4047
	9:16	"How can a sinner do s miraculous signs?"	5525
	14: 9	after I have been among you s a long time?	5537
	15: 6	s branches are picked up, thrown into the	899
	16: 3	They will do s *things* because they have	4047
Ac	5: 4	What made you think of doing s a thing?	4047
	8:22	Perhaps he will forgive you for having s a	3836
	15:39	They had a sharp disagreement that	NIG
	16:24	Upon receiving s orders,	5525
	16:26	there was a violent earthquake **that**	6063
	17:30	In the past God overlooked s ignorance,	3836
	18:15	I will not be a judge of s *things."*	4047
	19:16	He gave them s a beating that they ran out	NIG
	25:20	at a loss how to investigate s *matters;*	4047
	26:28	in s a short time you can persuade me to be	NIG
	27:18	We took s a **violent** battering from	5380
Ro	1:32	that those who do s *things* deserve death,	5525
	2: 2	against those who do s *things* is based	5525
	2:29	S **a man's** praise is not from men,	4005S
	16:18	s *people* are not serving our Lord Christ,	5525
1Co	5:11	With s **a man** do not even eat.	5525
	6: 4	if you have disputes about s **matters,**	1053S
	7:15	not bound in s *circumstances;*	4047
	8: 7	to idols that when they eat s **food** they think	1628
	9:15	in the hope that you will do s **things** for me.	4048
	9:24	Run **in s a way** as to get the prize.	4048
	14: 7	s as the flute or harp,	1664
	16:16	to s **as these** and to everyone who joins in	5525
	16:18	S *men* deserve recognition.	5525
2Co	1:10	He has delivered us from s a deadly peril,	5496
	2:16	And who is equal to s a *task?*	4047
	3: 4	S confidence as this is ours through Christ	5525
	3:12	since we have s a hope, we are very bold.	5525
	7: 3	I have said before that *you* **have s a** lhrief	1639
	10:11	S *people* should realize that what we are	5496
	11:13	For s *men* are false apostles,	5525
Gal	5:23	Against s *things* there is no law.	5525
Eph	5: 5	s **a man** is an idolater—	4005
	5: 6	for because of s *things* God's wrath comes	4047
Php	3: 4	I myself have reasons for s confidence.	NIG
	3:15	mature *should* **take s a view of things.**	5858
	4: 8	or praiseworthy—think about s *things.*	4047
Col	2:18	S a person goes into great detail	NIG
	2:23	S **regulations** indeed have an appearance	4015S
	3: 8	now you must rid yourselves of all s things	NIG
1Th	4: 6	The Lord will punish men for all s **sins,**	4047S
2Th	3: 2	because we do not have the right to s help,	5525
	3:12	S *people* we command and urge in	5525
1Ti	4: 2	S teachings come through hypocritical liars,	NIG
	5:10	s as bringing up children,	NIG
	5:11	*do* **not put** them **on s a list.**	4148
Tit	3:11	be sure that s **a man** is warped and sinful,	5525
Heb	2: 3	if we ignore s a **great** salvation?	5496
	7:26	S a high priest meets our need—	5525
	8: 1	We do have s a high priest,	5525
	11:14	People who say s *things* show	5525
	12: 1	since we are surrounded by s a **great** cloud	5537
	12: 3	Consider him who endured s opposition	5525
	12:19	or to s a voice speaking words	NIG
	13:16	for *with* s sacrifices God is pleased.	5525
Jas	2:14	Can s faith save him?	3836
	3:15	S "wisdom" does not come down	4047
	4:16	All s boasting is evil.	5525
1Pe	1:18	with perishable things s as silver or gold	NIG
	2:12	Live s good lives among the pagans that,	NIG
	3: 3	s as braided hair and the wearing	NIG
2Pe	2:11	against s **beings** in the presence of the Lord.	899
1Jn	2:22	S a man is the antichrist—	4047
2Jn	1: 7	**Any** s person is the deceiver and	4047
3Jn	1: 8	to s *men* so that we may work together for	5525
Rev	18:17	In one hour s **great** wealth has been brought	5537
	18:21	"**With** s violence the great city	4048

SUCHATHITES (KJV) See SUCATHITES

SUCK (1) [SUCKLING]

Job	20:16	*He will* s the poison of serpents;	3567

SUCK, SUCKED, SUCKING (KJV) See
also FEAST, NOURISHED, NURSE,

NURSED, NURSING

SUCKLING (1) [SUCK]

1Sa	7: 9	Then Samuel took a s lamb and offered it	2692

SUCKLING, SUCKLINGS (KJV) See
also INFANT, INFANTS

SUDDEN (11) [SUDDENLY]

Lev	26:16	I will bring upon you s **terror,**	988
Dt	28:20	to s ruin because of the evil you have done	4554
Jdg	20:37	in ambush made a s dash into Gibeah,	2590
Job	9:23	When a scourge brings s death,	7328
	22:10	why s peril terrifies you,	7328
Ps	6:10	they will turn back in s disgrace.	8092
Pr	3:25	of s disaster or of the ruin that overtakes	7328
	24:22	for those two will send s destruction	7328
Isa	17:14	In the evening, s **terror!**	1166
Zep	1:18	for he will make a s end of all who live in	987
Jn	19:34	bringing a s flow of blood and water.	2317

SUDDENLY (45) [SUDDEN]

Ge	37: 7	when s my sheaf rose and stood upright,	2180
Nu	6: 9	If someone dies s in his presence,	928+7328+7353
	16:42	s the cloud covered it and the glory of	2180
	35:22	if without hostility someone s shoves	928+7353
Jos	11: 7	and his whole army came against them s at	7328
Jdg	14: 5	s a young lion came roaring toward him.	2180
2Ki	2:11	s a chariot of fire and horses of fire	
		appeared	2180
	13:21	s they saw a band of raiders;	2180
Job	1:19	when s a mighty wind swept in from	2180
	5: 3	but s his house was cursed.	7328
Ps	64: 4	they shoot at him s, without fear.	7328
	64: 7	s they will be struck down.	7328
	73:19	How s are they destroyed,	3869+8092
Pr	6:15	he will be destroyed—without remedy.	7353
	28:18	*he* whose ways are perverse will s fall.	285+928
	29: 1	after many rebukes will s be destroyed—	7353
Isa	29: 5	like blown chaff. S, in an instant,	7328
	30:13	cracked and bulging, that collapses s,	7328
	47:11	catastrophe you cannot foresee will s come	7328
	48: 3	then s I acted, and they came to pass.	7328
Jer	6:26	for s the destroyer will come upon us.	7328
	15: 8	I will bring down on them anguish	7328
	18:22	when you s bring invaders against them,	7328
	51: 8	Babylon will s fall and be broken.	7328
Da	5: 5	S the fingers of a human hand appeared	
			10191+10734
	8: 5	s a goat with a prominent horn	2180
Hab	2: 7	Will not your debtors s arise?	7353
Mal	3: 1	Then s the Lord you are seeking will come	7328
Mt	28: 9	S Jesus met them.	2627+2779
Mk	13:36	If he comes s, do not let him find you	1978
Lk	2:13	S a great company of the heavenly host	1978
	9:39	A spirit seizes him and he s screams;	1978
	24: 4	s two men in clothes that gleamed	2627
Ac	1:10	when s two men dressed in white stood	2627
	2: 2	S a sound like the blowing of a violent wind	924
	8:39	the Spirit of the Lord s **took** Philip **away,**	773
	9: 3	s a light from heaven flashed around him.	1978
	10:30	S a man in shining clothes stood before me	2627
	12: 7	S an angel of the Lord appeared and	2627
	12:10	the angel left him.	2311
	16:26	S there was such a violent earthquake that	924
	22: 6	a bright light from heaven flashed	1978
	28: 6	expected him to swell up or s fall dead,	924
1Th	5: 3	destruction will come on them s,	167

SUE (1)

Mt	5:40	And if someone wants *to* s you	3212

SUFFER (50) [LONG-SUFFERING,
SUFFERED, SUFFERING, SUFFERINGS,
SUFFERS]

Ge	4:15	*he will* s **vengeance** seven times over."	5933
Nu	14:34	*you will* s **for** your sins	5951
Dt	26: 6	the Egyptians mistreated us and **made** us s,	6700
Ezr	4:13	and the royal revenues *will* s.	10472
Job	24:11	they tread the winepresses, *yet* s **thirst.**	7532
	36:15	*those who* s he delivers in their suffering;	6714
Ps	42:10	My bones s mortal agony	928
Pr	9:12	*if you are* a mocker, you alone *will* s."	5951
	11:15	up security for another *will* **surely** s,	8273+8317
	22: 3	but the simple keep going and s for it.	6740
	27:12	but the simple keep going and s for it.	6740
Isa	47: 8	be a widow or s the loss of children.'	3359
	53:10	to crush him and **cause** him s,	2703
	54: 4	"Do not be afraid; you will not s **shame.**	1017
Jer	14:13	'You will not see the sword or s famine,	2118
		think of *how* I s reproach for your sake.	5951
Eze	23:49	*will* s the penalty for your lewdness	5989+6584
	36: 7	the nations around you will also s scorn.	5951
	36:15	and no longer *will* you s the scorn of	5951
	36:30	that *you* will no longer s disgrace among	4374
Da	6: 2	to them so that the king *might* not s **loss.**	10472
Mt	16:21	to Jerusalem and s many things at the hands	4248
	17:12	the Son of Man is going to s at their hands."	4248
Mk	8:31	that the Son of Man must s many things and	4248
	9:12	Son of Man must s much and be rejected?	4248

Lk	9:22	"The Son of Man must s many things and	4248
	17:25	But first he must s many things and	4248
	22:15	to eat this Passover with you before I s.	4248
	24:26	*to* s these things and then enter his glory?"	4248
	24:46	The Christ will s and rise from the dead on	4248
Ac	3:18	saying that his Christ *would* s.	4248
	9:16	I will show him how much he must s	4248
	17: 3	the Christ had *to* s and rise from the dead.	4248
	26:23	that the Christ would s and,	4078
1Co	3:15	If it is burned up, *he will* s **loss;**	2423
2Co	1: 6	of the same sufferings we s.	4248
Php	1:29	but also *to* s for him,	4248
1Th	5: 9	For God did not appoint us to s wrath but	NIG
Heb	9:26	*to* s many times since the creation of	4248
1Pe	1: 6	a little while you may have had to s **grief**	3382
	2:20	if *you* s for doing good and you endure it,	4248
	3:14	But even if *you should* s for what is right,	4248
	3:17	*to* s for doing good than for doing evil.	4248
	4:15	If you s, it should not be as a murderer	NIG
	4:16	However, if you s as a Christian,	NIG
	4:19	those who s according to God's will	4248
Jude	1: 7	an example of those who s the punishment	5674
Rev	2:10	not be afraid of what you are about *to* s.	4248
	2:10	*you will* s **persecution** for ten days.	2400+2568
	2:22	who commit adultery with her s intensely,	2568

SUFFERED (29) [SUFFER]

1Sa	4:17	and the army *has* s heavy losses.	928+2118
Ps	88:15	*I have* s your terrors and am in despair.	5951
	107:17	and s **affliction** because of their iniquities.	6700
	119:107	*I have* s much; preserve my life, O LORD.	6700
Isa	38:17	it was for my benefit that I s such anguish.	5352
Jer	14:17	*has* s a grievous wound, a crushing blow.	8689
	44:17	of food and were well off and s no harm.	8011
La	3:47	We *have* s terror and pitfalls,	2118+4200
Eze	36: 6	because *you have* s the scorn of the nations.	5951
Mt	27:19	for *I have* s a great deal today in a dream	4248
Mk	5:26	She had s a great deal under the care	4248
Lk	13: 2	because *they* s this way?	4248
Ac	28: 5	into the fire and s no ill effects.	4248
2Co	1: 8	the hardships we s in the province of Asia.	1181
Gal	3: 4	*Have you* s so much for nothing—	4248
Col	1:24	Now I rejoice in what was s for you,	4077
1Th	2:14	*We had* **previously** s and been insulted	4634
	2:14	You s from your own countrymen	4248
	2:14	the same things those churches s from	NIG
Heb	2: 9	with glory and honor because he s death,	4077
	2:18	Because *he* himself s when he was tempted,	4248
	5: 8	he learned obedience from what *he* s	4248
	13:12	so Jesus also s outside the city gate to make	4248
1Pe	2:21	because Christ s for you,	4248
	2:23	*when he* s, he made no threats.	4248
	4: 1	Therefore, *since* Christ s in his body,	4248
	4: 1	he who *has* s in his body is done with sin.	4248
	5:10	*after you have* s a little while,	4248
Rev	9: 5	the agony they s was like that of the sting	NIG

SUFFERING (53) [SUFFER]

Ge	16: 5	"You are responsible for the **wrong** I am s.	AIT
	41:52	has made me fruitful in the land of my s."	6715
Ex	3: 7	and I am concerned about their s.	4799
Nu	5:24	this water will enter her and cause **bitter** s.	5253
	5:27	it will go into her and cause **bitter** s;	5253
	14:33	s **for** your unfaithfulness,	5951
Dt	28:53	of the s that your enemy will inflict on you	5186
	28:55	the s your enemy will inflict on you during	5186
2Ki	13:14	Now Elisha *was* s *from* the illness	2703
	14:26	was s; there was no one to help them.	6715
Ne	9: 9	"You saw the s of our forefathers in Egypt;	6715
Job	2:13	because they saw how great his s was.	3873
	30:16	now my life ebbs away; days of s grip me.	6715
	30:27	days of s confront me.	6715
	36:15	But those who suffer he delivers in their s;	6715
Ps	22:24	For he has not despised or disdained the s	6713
	55: 3	for they bring down s upon me	224
	107:10	prisoners s in iron chains,	6715
	119:50	My comfort in my s is this:	6715
	119:153	Look upon my s and deliver me,	6715
Isa	14: 3	the day the LORD gives you relief from s	6778
	53: 3	a man of sorrows, and familiar with s.	2716
	53:11	After the s *of* his soul, he will see the light	6662
La	1:12	Is any s like my suffering that was inflicted	4799
	1:12	Is any suffering like my s that was inflicted	4799
	1:18	Listen, all you peoples; look upon my s.	4799
Joel	1:18	even the flocks of sheep are s.	870
Mt	4:24	those s severe pain, the demon-possessed,	5309
	8: 6	at home paralyzed and in terrible s."	989
	15:22	s terribly **from demon-possession.**"	1227
	17:15	"He has seizures and *is* s greatly.	4248
Mk	5:29	in her body that she was freed from her s.	3465
	5:34	Go in peace and be freed from your s."	3465
Lk	4:38	Now Simon's mother-in-law was s from	5309
	14: 2	in front of him was a man s **from dropsy.**	5622
Ac	1: 3	After his s, he showed himself to these men	4248
	5:41	counted worthy of s **disgrace** for the Name.	869
	7:11	all Egypt and Canaan, bringing great s,	2568
	28: 8	s *from* fever and dysentery.	5309
Ro	5: 3	we know that s produces perseverance.	2568
1Th	1: 6	in spite of severe s, you welcomed the	2568
2Th	1: 5	the kingdom of God, for which *you are* s.	4248
2Ti	1: 8	But **join** with me **in** s for the gospel,	5155
	1:12	That is why *I am* s as I am.	4248
	2: 9	for which *I am* s even to the point of being	2802
Heb	2:10	author of their salvation perfect through s.	4077
	10:32	in a great contest in the face *of* s.	4077

Heb	13: 3	as if you yourselves were s.	NIG
Jas	5:10	as an example of patience in the face of s,	2801
1Pe	2:19	the pain of unjust s because he is conscious	4248
	4:12	be surprised at the painful trial you s,	1181
Rev	1: 9	in the s and kingdom and patient endurance	2568
	2:22	So I will cast her on a bed of s,	3109

SUFFERINGS (14) [SUFFER]

Job	9:28	I still dread all my s,	6780
Ro	8: 5	Not only so, but we also rejoice in our s,	2568
	8:17	with Christ, if indeed we share in his s	5224
	8:18	that our present s are not worth comparing	4077
2Co	1: 5	as the s of Christ flow over into our lives,	4077
	1: 6	patient endurance of the same s we suffer.	4077
	1: 7	We know that just as you share in our s,	4077
Eph	3:13	to be discouraged because of my s for you,	2568
Php	3:10	and the fellowship of sharing in his s,	4077
2Ti	3:11	persecutions,—what kinds of things	4077
1Pe	1:11	when he predicted the s of Christ and	4077
	4:13	But rejoice that you participate in the s	4077
	5: 1	of Christ's s and one who also will share in	4077
	5: 9	undergoing the same kind of s.	4077

SUFFERS (4) [SUFFER]

Job	15:20	All his days the wicked man s torment,	2655
Pr	13:20	but a companion of fools s harm.	8317
1Co	12:26	If one part s, every part suffers with it;	4248
	12:26	If one part suffers, every part s with it;	5224

SUFFICE, SUFFICED, SUFFICETH
(KJV) See ALL WANTED, ENOUGH

SUFFICIENT (5)

Lev	25:26	and acquires means to redeem it,	1896+3869
Isa	40:16	Lebanon is not s for altar fires,	1896
2Co	2: 6	on him by the majority is s for him.	2653
	12: 9	But he said to me, "My grace is s for you,	758
Php	1:20	but will have s courage so that now	4246

SUGGEST (1) [SUGGESTED, SUGGESTION]

Ru	4: 4	to your attention and s that you buy it in	606

SUGGESTED (5) [SUGGEST]

1Ki	22:20	"One s this, and another that.	606
2Ch	18:19	"One s this, and another that.	606
Ezr	10: 5	all Israel under oath to do what had been s.	1821+2021+2021+2296
Est	2:15	who was in charge of the harem, s.	606
	6:10	and the horse and do just as you have s	1819

SUGGESTION (1) [SUGGEST]

Est	5:14	This s delighted Haman,	1821

SUIT (1) [SUITABLE]

2Ti	4: 3	Instead, to s their own desires,	2848

SUITABLE (4) [SUIT]

Ge	2:18	I will make a helper s for him."	3869+5584
	2:20	But for Adam no s helper was found.	3869+5584
Nu	32: 1	of Jazer and Gilead were s for livestock.	5226
	32: 4	are s for livestock, and your servants have	824

SUKKIIMS (KJV) See SUKKITES

SUKKITES (1)

2Ch	12: 3	S and Cushites that came with him	6113

SULFUR (15)

Ge	19:24	down burning s on Sodom and Gomorrah—	1730
Dt	29:23	be a burning waste of salt and s—	1730
Job	18:15	burning s is scattered over his dwelling.	1730
Ps	11: 6	On the wicked he will rain fiery coals and burning s;	1730
Isa	30:33	like a stream of burning s, sets it ablaze.	1730
	34: 9	her dust into burning s;	1730
Eze	38:22	of rain, hailstones and burning s on him and	1730
Lk	17:29	fire and s rained down from heaven	2520
Rev	9:17	dark blue, and yellow as s.	2523
	9:17	their mouths came fire, smoke and s.	2520
	9:18	smoke and s that came out of their mouths.	2520
	14:10	be tormented with burning s in the presence	2520
	19:20	into the fiery lake of burning s.	2520
	20:10	was thrown into the lake of burning s,	2520
	21: 8	be in the fiery lake of burning s.	2520

SULKING (1)

1Ki	21: 4	He lay on his bed s and refused	906+6015+7156

SULLEN (3)

1Ki	20:43	S and angry, the king of Israel went	6234
	21: 4	went home, s and angry because Naboth	6234
	21: 5	"Why are you so s?	6234

SUM (4) [SUMMED, SUMS]

Ps	139:17	How vast is the s of them!	8031
Mt	28:12	they gave the soldiers a large s of money,	2653

Ac	7:16	at Shechem for a certain s of money.	5507
1Co	16: 2	a s of money in keeping with his income,	2564

SUMMED (2) [SUM]

Ro	13: 9	are s up in this one rule: "Love your neighbor as yourself."	368
Gal	5:14	The entire law is s up in a single command:	4444

SUMMER (19)

Ge	8:22	cold and heat, s and winter,	7811
Jdg	3:20	in the upper room of his s palace and said,	5249
Ps	32: 4	my strength was sapped as in the heat of s.	7811
	74:17	you made both s and winter.	7811
Pr	6: 8	in s and gathers its food at harvest.	7811
	10: 5	He who gathers crops in s is a wise son,	7811
	26: 1	Like snow in s or rain in harvest,	7811
	30:25	yet they store up their food in the s;	7811
Isa	18: 6	the birds will feed on them all s,	7810
Jer	8:20	"The harvest is past, the s has ended,	7811
	40:10	harvest the wine, s fruit and oil,	7811
	40:12	an abundance of wine and s fruit.	7811
Da	2:35	like chaff on a threshing floor in the s,	10627
Am	3:15	the winter house along with the s house;	7811
Mic	7: 1	like one who gathers s fruit at the gleaning	7811
Zec	14: 8	to the western sea, in s and in winter.	7811
Mt	24:32	you know that s is near.	2550
Mk	13:28	you know that s is near.	2550
Lk	21:30	for yourselves and know that s is near.	2550

SUMMIT (4)

2Sa	15:32	When David arrived at the s,	8031
	16: 1	a short distance beyond the s,	8031
SS	4: 8	from the top of Senir, the s of Hermon,	NIH
Jer	22: 6	like the s of Lebanon,	8031

SUMMON (27) [SUMMONED, SUMMONING, SUMMONS]

Nu	22: 5	sent messengers to s Balaam son of Beor,	7924
	22:20	"Since these men have come to s you,	7924
Dt	25: 8	the elders of his town shall s him and talk	7924
	33:19	They will s peoples to the mountain	7924
2Sa	17: 5	Absalom said, "S also Hushai the Arkite,	7924
	20: 4	"S the men of Judah to come to me	2410
	20: 5	But when Amasa went to s Judah,	2410
1Ki	18:19	Now s the people from all over Israel	8938
	22:13	who had gone to s Micaiah said to him,	7924
2Ki	10:19	Now s all the prophets of Baal,	7924
2Ch	18:12	who had gone to s Micaiah said to him,	7924
Job	9:19	a matter of justice, who will s him?	3585
	13:22	Then s me and I will answer,	7924
	19:16	I s my servant, but he does not answer,	7924
Ps	68:28	S your power, O God;	7422
Isa	22:20	"In that day I will s my servant,	7924
	45: 4	I s you by name and bestow on you a title	7924
	46:11	From the east I s a bird of prey;	7924
	48:13	when I s them, they all stand up together.	7924
	55: 5	Surely you will s nations you know not,	7924
Jer	1:15	I am about to s all the peoples of the	7924
	25: 9	I will s all the peoples of the	2256+4374+8938
	50:29	"S archers against Babylon,	9048
	51:27	s against her these kingdoms;	9048
La	2:22	"As you s to a feast day,	7924
Eze	38:21	I will s a sword against Gog	7924
Joel	1:14	S the elders and all who live in the land to	665

SUMMONED (65) [SUMMON]

Ge	12:18	So Pharaoh s Abram.	7924
	20: 8	next morning Abimelech s all his officials,	7924
	26: 9	So Abimelech s Isaac and said,	7924
Ex	1:18	of Egypt s the midwives and asked them,	7924
	7:11	Pharaoh then s wise men and sorcerers,	7924
	8: 8	Pharaoh s Moses and Aaron and said,	7924
	8:25	Then Pharaoh s Moses and Aaron and said,	7924
	9:27	Pharaoh s Moses and Aaron and said,	2256+7924+8938
	10:16	Pharaoh quickly s Moses and Aaron	7924
	10:24	Then Pharaoh s Moses and said, "Go,	7924
	12:21	Then Moses s all the elders of Israel	7924
	12:31	the night Pharaoh s Moses and Aaron	7924
	19: 7	So Moses went back and s the elders of	7924
	36: 2	Then Moses s Bezalel and Oholiab	7924
Lev	9: 1	the eighth day Moses s Aaron and his sons	7924
	10: 4	Moses s Mishael and Elzaphan,	7924
Nu	12: 5	at the entrance to the Tent and s Aaron	7924
	16:12	Moses s Dathan and Abiram,	4200+7924+8938
	24:10	"I s you to curse my enemies,	7924
Dt	5: 1	Moses s all Israel and said:	7924
	29: 2	Moses s all the Israelites and said to them:	7924
	31: 7	Then Moses s Joshua and said to him in	7924
Jos	9:22	Then Joshua s the Gibeonites and said,	7924
	10:24	s all the men of Israel and said to	7924
	22: 1	Then Joshua s the Reubenites,	7924
	23: 2	s all Israel—their elders, leaders,	7924
	24: 1	He s the elders, leaders,	7924
Jdg	4:10	where he s Zebulun and Naphtali.	2410
1Sa	10:17	Samuel s the people of Israel to the LORD	7590
	13: 4	the people were s to join Saul at Gilgal.	7590
	15: 4	So Saul s the men and mustered them	9048
2Sa	9: 9	Then the king s Ziba, Saul's servant,	7924
	14:33	Then the king s Absalom,	7924
	20: 4	Then Joshua s the Gibeonites and spoke	7924
1Ki	2:42	king s Shimei and said to him,	2256+7924+8938
	8: 1	Then King Solomon s into his presence	7735
	18: 3	and Ahab had s Obadiah.	7924

1Ki	20: 7	The king of Israel s all the elders of the land	7924
	20:15	So Ahab s the young officers of	7212
2Ki	4:36	Elisha s Gehazi and said,	7924
	6:11	He s his officers and demanded of them,	7924
	9: 1	The prophet Elisha s a man from	7924
	12: 7	Therefore King Joash s Jehoiada the priest	7924
1Ch	15:11	David s Zadok and Abiathar the priests,	7924
	28: 1	s all the officials of Israel to assemble	7735
2Ch	5: 2	Solomon s to Jerusalem the elders of Israel,	7735
	24: 6	the king s Jehoiada the chief priest and said	7924
Ezr	8:16	So I s Eliezer, Ariel, Shemaiah, Elnathan,	8938
Ne	5:12	Then I s the priests and made the nobles	7924
Est	2:14	unless he was pleased with her and s her	7924
	3:12	the first month the royal secretaries were s.	7924
	4: 5	Then Esther s Hathach,	7924
	4:11	the inner court without being s the king has	7924
	5: 2	At once the royal secretaries were s—	7924
Job	9:16	Even if I s him and he responded,	7924
Isa	13: 3	I have s my warriors	7924
	43: 1	I have s you by name; you are mine.	7924
La	1:15	he has s an army against me	7924
	2:22	so you s against me terrors on every side.	NIH
Da	2: 2	So the king s the magicians, enchanters,	7924
	3: 2	He then s the satraps,	10359+10378+10714
	3:13	Nebuchadnezzar s Shadrach,	10042+10085+10378
Am	5:16	be s to weep and the mourners to wail.	7924
Jn	9:24	A second time they s the man who	5888
	18:33	s Jesus and asked him, "Are you the king	5888

SUMMONING (2) [SUMMON]

Jdg	6:34	s the Abiezrites to follow him.	2410
Mk	15:44	S the centurion, he asked him	4673

SUMMONS (5) [SUMMON]

Nu	22:37	"Did I not send you an urgent s?	7924
Ps	50: 1	and s the earth from the rising of the sun to	7924
	50: 4	He s the heavens above, and the earth,	7924
Isa	45: 3	the God of Israel, who s you by name.	7924
Na	2: 5	He s his picked troops,	2349

SUMPTUOUSLY (KJV) See LUXURY

SUMS (1) [SUM]

Mt	7:12	for this s up the Law and the Prophets.	1639

SUN (142) [SUNDOWN, SUNRISE, SUNSET, SUNSHINE]

Ge	15:12	As the s was setting, Abram fell into a deep	9087
	15:17	When the s had set and darkness had fallen,	9087
	19:23	the s had risen over the land.	9087
	28:11	for the night because the s had set.	9087
	29: 7	"Look," he said, "the s is still high;	3427
	32:31	The s rose above him as he passed Peniel,	9087
	37: 9	and this time the s and moon	9087
Ex	16:21	and when the s grew hot, it melted away.	9087
Lev	22: 7	When the s goes down, he will be clean,	9087
Dt	4:19	when you look up to the sky and see the s,	9087
	11:30	west of the road, toward the setting s,	9087
	16: 6	when the s goes down,	9087
	17: 3	to the s or the moon or the stars of the sky,	9087
	33:14	the best the s brings forth and the finest	9087
Jos	10:12	"O s, stand still over Gibeon, O moon,	9087
	10:13	So the s stood still, and the moon stopped,	9087
	10:13	The s stopped in the middle of the sky	9087
Jdg	5:31	be like the s when it rises in its strength."	9087
	5:31	s set as they neared Gibeah in Benjamin.	9087
1Sa	11: 9	'By the time the s is hot tomorrow,	9087
2Sa	2:24	and as the s was setting,	9087
	3:35	or anything else before the s sets!"	9087
1Ki	22:36	As the s was setting,	9087
2Ki	3:22	the s was shining on the water.	9087
	23: 5	to the s and moon,	9087
	23:11	the kings of Judah had dedicated to the s.	9087
	23:11	then burned the chariots dedicated to the s.	9087
Ne	7: 3	not to be opened until the s is hot.	9087
Job	9: 7	He speaks to the s and it does not shine;	3064
	30:28	I go about blackened, but not by the s;	2780
	31:26	if I have regarded the s in its radiance or	240
	37:21	Now no one can look at the s,	240
Ps	19: 4	the heavens he has pitched a tent for the s,	9087
	37: 6	the justice of your cause like the noonday s.	7416
	50: 1	the rising of the s to the place where it sets.	9087
	58: 8	may they not see the s.	9087
	72: 5	He will endure as long as the s,	9087
	72:17	may it continue as long as the s.	9087
	74:16	you established the s and moon.	9087
	84:11	For the LORD God is a s and shield;	9087
	89:36	and his throne endure before me like the s;	9087
	104:19	and the s knows when to go down.	9087
	104:22	The s rises, and they steal away;	9087
	113: 3	the rising of the s to the place where it sets,	9087
	121: 6	the s will not harm you by day,	9087
	136: 8	the s to govern the day,	9087
	148: 3	Praise him, s and moon, praise him,	9087
Ecc	1: 3	at which he toils under the s?	9087
	1: 5	The s rises and the sun sets,	9087
	1: 5	The sun rises and the s sets,	9087
	1: 9	there is nothing new under the s.	9087
	1:14	the things that are done under the s;	9087
	2:11	nothing was gained under the s.	9087
	2:17	that is done under the s was grievous to me.	9087
	2:18	the things I had toiled for under the s,	9087
	2:19	poured my effort and skill under the s.	9087

Ecc	2:20	over all my toilsome labor under the s.	9087
	2:22	with which he labors under the s?	9087
	3:16	And I saw something else under the s:	9087
	4: 1	that was taking place under the s:	9087
	4: 3	not seen the evil that is done under the s.	9087
	4: 7	I saw something meaningless under the s:	9087
	4:15	and walked under the s followed the youth,	9087
	5:13	I have seen a grievous evil under the s:	9087
	5:18	in his toilsome labor under the s during	9087
	6: 1	I have seen another evil under the s,	9087
	6: 5	it never saw the s or knew anything,	9087
	6:12	will happen under the s after he is gone?	9087
	7:11	and benefits those who see the s.	9087
	8: 9	to everything done under the s.	9087
	8:15	a man under the s than to eat and drink and	9087
	8:15	of the life God has given him under the s.	9087
	8:17	comprehend what goes on under the s.	9087
	9: 3	in everything that happens under the s:	9087
	9: 6	a part in anything that happens under the s.	9087
	9: 9	that God has given you under the s—	9087
	9: 9	and in your toilsome labor under the s.	9087
	9:11	I have seen something else under the s:	9087
	9:13	under the s this example of wisdom	9087
	10: 5	There is an evil I have seen under the s,	9087
	11: 7	and it pleases the eyes to see the s.	9087
	12: 2	before the s and the light and the moon and	9087
SS	1: 6	because I am darkened by the s.	9087
	6:10	fair as the moon, bright as the s,	2780
Isa	13:10	The rising s will be darkened and	9087
	24:23	The moon will be abashed, the s ashamed;	2780
	30:26	The moon will shine like the s,	2780
	38: 8	the s go back the ten steps it has gone down	9087
	41:25	from the rising s who calls on my name.	9087
	45: 6	so that from the rising of the s to the place	9087
	49:10	the desert heat or the s beat upon them.	9087
	59:19	and from the rising of the s,	9087
	60:19	The s will no more be your light by day,	9087
	60:20	Your s will never set again,	9087
Jer	8: 2	They will be exposed to the s and the moon	9087
	15: 9	Her s will set while it is still day;	9087
	31:35	he who appoints the s to shine by day,	9087
	43:13	of the s in Egypt he will demolish	9087
Eze	8:16	they were bowing down to the s in the east.	9087
	32: 7	I will cover the s with a cloud,	9087
Hos	6: 3	As surely as the s rises, he will appear;	8840
Joel	2:10	the s and moon are darkened,	9087
	2:31	The s will be turned to darkness and	9087
	3:15	The s and moon will be darkened,	9087
Am	8: 9	the s go down at noon and darken the earth	9087
Jnh	4: 8	When the s rose, God provided a scorching	9087
	4: 8	and the s blazed on Jonah's head so	9087
Mic	3: 6	The s will set for the prophets,	9087
Na	3:17	but when the s appears they fly away,	9087
Hab	3:11	S and moon stood still in the heavens at	9087
Mal	1:11	from the rising to the setting of the s.	9087
	4: 2	the s of righteousness will rise with healing	9087
Mt	5:45	He causes his s to rise on the evil and	2463
	13: 6	But when the s came up,	2463
	13:43	Then the righteous will shine like the s in	2463
	17: 2	His face shone like the s,	2463
	24:29	" 'the s will be darkened, and the moon will	2463
Mk	4: 6	But when the s came up,	2463
	13:24	" 'the s will be darkened, and the moon will	2463
Lk	1:78	the rising s will come to us from heaven	424
	4:40	When the s was setting,	2463
	21:25	"There will be signs in the s,	2463
	23:45	for the s stopped shining.	2463
Ac	2:20	The s will be turned to darkness and	2463
	13:11	be unable to see the light of the s."	2463
	26:13	a light from heaven, brighter than the s,	2463
	27:20	When neither s nor stars appeared	2463
1Co	15:41	The s has one kind of splendor,	2463
Eph	4:26	the s go down while you are still angry,	2463
Jas	1:11	the s rises with scorching heat and withers	2463
Rev	1:16	like the s shining in all its brilliance.	2463
	6:12	The s turned black like sackcloth made	2463
	7:16	The s will not beat upon them,	2463
	8:12	and a third of the s was struck,	2463
	9: 2	The s and sky were darkened by the smoke	2463
	10: 1	his face was like the s,	2463
	12: 1	a woman clothed with the s,	2463
	16: 8	on the s, and the sun was given power	2463
	16: 8	and the s was given power to scorch people	899S
	19:17	And I saw an angel standing in the s,	2463
	21:23	not need the s or the moon to shine on it,	2463
	22: 5	the light of a lamp or the light of the s,	2463

SUN-SCORCHED (2) [SCORCH]

| Ps | 68: 6 | but the rebellious live in a s land. | 7461 |
| Isa | 58:11 | in a s land and will strengthen your frame. | 7463 |

SUNDER (KJV) See AWAY, PIECES, SHATTERS, THROUGH

SUNDOWN (1) [SUN]

| Da | 6:14 | and made every effort until s to save him. | 10002+10436+10728 |

SUNDRY (KJV) See MANY

SUNG (3) [SING]

| Isa | 26: 1 | In that day this song will be s in the land | 8876 |
| Mt | 26:30 | When they had s a hymn, | 5630 |

| Mk | 14:26 | When they had s a hymn, | 5630 |

SUNK (3) [SINK]

Jer	38:22	Your feet are s in the mud;	3190
La	2: 9	Her gates have s into the ground;	3190
Hos	9: 9	They have s deep into corruption,	6676

SUNLIGHT (2) [LIGHT]

| Isa | 30:26 | and the s will be seven times brighter, | 240+2780 |
| | 38: 8 | s went back the ten steps it had gone down. | 9087 |

SUNRISE (13) [SUN]

Ex	22: 3	but if it happens after s,	2021+2436+9087
	27:13	On the east end, toward the s,	4667
	38:13	The east end, toward the s,	4667
Nu	2: 3	On the east, toward the s,	4667
	3:38	of the tabernacle, toward the s, in front of	4667
	21:11	desert that faces Moab toward the s.	4667+9087
	34:15	of the Jordan of Jericho, toward the s."	4667
Jos	1:15	of the Jordan toward the s."	4667+9087
	19:12	turned east from Sarid, toward the s	4667+9087
Jdg	9:33	In the morning at s, advance	2021+2436+9087
2Sa	23: 4	at s on a cloudless morning,	2436+9087
Hab	3: 4	His splendor was like the s;	240
Mk	16: 2	first day of the week, just after s	422+2463+3836

SUNSET (10) [SUN]

Ex	17:12	his hands remained steady till s.	995+2021+9087
	22:26	return it to him by s,	995+2021+9087
Dt	23:11	at s he may return to the camp.	995+2021+9087
	24:13	by s so that he may sleep in it.	995+2021+9087
	24:15	Pay him his wages each day before s,	995+2021+9087
Jos	8:29	At s, Joshua ordered them to take	995+2021+9087
	10:27	At s Joshua gave the order	995+2021+6961+9087
Jdg	14:18	Before s on the seventh day	995+2021+3064
2Ch	18:34	Then at s he died.	995+2021+6961+9087
Mk	1:32	That evening after s the people	1544+2463

SUNSHINE (2) [SUN]

| Job | 8:16 | He is like a well-watered plant in the s, | 9087 |
| Isa | 18: 4 | like shimmering heat in the s, | 240 |

SUP (KJV) See ADVANCE, EAT

SUPER-APOSTLES (2) [APOSTLE]

| 2Co | 11: 5 | I am in the least inferior to those "s." | 693+5663 |
| | 12:11 | I am not in the least inferior to the "s," | 693+5663 |

SUPERFLUITY, SUPERFLUOUS (KJV)
See DEFORMED, NO NEED, PREVALENT

SUPERIOR (7)

Da	8:25	and he will consider himself s.	1540
Ro	2:18	of what is s because you are instructed by	1422
1Co	2: 1	not come with eloquence or s wisdom	5053+5667
Heb	1: 4	So he became as much s to the angels as	3202
	1: 4	the angels as the name he has inherited is s	1427
	8: 6	But the ministry Jesus has received is as s	1427
	8: 6	covenant of which he is mediator is s to	3202

SUPERSCRIPTION (KJV) See
INSCRIPTION, WRITTEN NOTICE

SUPERSTITIONS (1)

| Isa | 2: 6 | They are full of s from the East; | NIH |

SUPERVISE (5) [SUPERVISED, SUPERVISING, SUPERVISION, SUPERVISOR, SUPERVISORS]

2Ki	12:11	to the men appointed to s the work on	6913
	22: 5	to the men appointed to s the work on	6913
1Ch	23: 4	to s the work of the temple of the LORD	5904
2Ch	34:10	to s the work on the LORD's temple.	6913
Ezr	3: 8	and older to s the building of the house of	5904

SUPERVISED (2) [SUPERVISE]

| 1Ki | 5:16 | as thirty-three hundred foremen who s | 6584 |
| 2Ch | 34:13 | the laborers and s all the workers from job | 5904 |

SUPERVISING (3) [SUPERVISE]

1Ki	9:23	550 officials s the men who did the work.	928
2Ch	8:10	two hundred and fifty officials s the men.	928
Ezr	3: 9	in s those working on the house of God.	5904

SUPERVISION (7) [SUPERVISE]

Nu	8:22	Tent of Meeting under the s of Aaron	4200+7156
1Ch	25: 2	sons of Asaph were under the s of Asaph,	3338
	25: 2	who prophesied under the king's s.	3338
	25: 3	under the s of their father Jeduthun,	3338
	25: 6	under the s of their fathers for the music of	3338
	25: 6	Jeduthun and Heman were under the s of	3338
Gal	3:25	we are no longer under the s of the law.	4080

SUPERVISOR (1) [SUPERVISE]

| Ne | 11:11 | the son of Ahitub, s in the house of God, | 5592 |

SUPERVISORS (4) [SUPERVISE]

2Ki	22: 9	and have entrusted it to the workers and s at	7212
2Ch	31:13	and Benaiah were s under Conaniah	7224
	34:17	and have entrusted it to the s and workers."	7212
Ne	3: 5	their shoulders to the work under their s.	123

SUPH (1)

| Dt | 1: 1 | opposite S, between Paran and Tophel, | 6069 |

SUPHAH (1)

| Nu | 21:14 | "…Waheb in S and the ravines, | 6071 |

SUPPER (7)

Lk	17: 8	he not rather say, 'Prepare my s,	1268+5515
	22:20	In the same way, after the s he took the cup,	1268
Jn	21:20	who leaned back against Jesus at the s	1270
1Co	11:20	it is not the Lord's S you eat,	1270
	11:25	In the same way, after s he took the cup,	1268
Rev	19: 9	to the wedding s of the Lamb!' "	1270
	19:17	gather together for the great s of God,	1270

SUPPLANT (KJV) See DECEIVER

SUPPLE (Anglicized) See LIMBER

SUPPLE (KJV) See MAKE CLEAN

SUPPLICATION (5) [SUPPLICATIONS]

1Ki	8:30	Hear the s of your servant and	9382
	8:33	praying and making s to you in this temple,	2858
2Ch	6:24	and making s before you in this temple,	2858
Ps	119:170	May my s come before you;	9382
Zec	12:10	of Jerusalem a spirit of grace and s.	9384

SUPPLICATIONS (2) [SUPPLICATION]

| 1Ki | 8:54 | all these prayers and s to the LORD, | 9382 |
| 2Ch | 6:21 | Hear the s of your servant and of your | 9384 |

SUPPLIED (14) [SUPPLY]

Nu	31: 5	were s from the clans of Israel.	5034
1Ki	4: 7	who s provisions for the king and	3920
	4:27	s provisions for King Solomon	3920
	5:10	In this way Hiram kept Solomon s with all	5989
	9:11	because Hiram had s him with all the cedar	5951
	18: 4	and had s them with food and water.)	3920
	18:13	and s them with food and water.	3920
1Ch	12:39	for their families had s provisions for them.	3922
Isa	33:16	His bread will be s, and water will not fail	5989
Jer	5: 7	I s all their needs, yet they committed	8425
Ac	20:34	these hands of mine have s my own needs	5676
1Co	16:17	they have s what was lacking from you.	405
2Co	11: 9	who came from Macedonia s what I needed.	4650
Php	4:18	I am amply s, now that I have received	4444

SUPPLIES (18) [SUPPLY]

Jos	1:11	'Get your s ready.	7476
1Sa	17:22	David left his things with the keeper of s,	3998
	25:13	while two hundred stayed with the s.	3998
	30:24	of the man who stayed with the s is to be	3998
1Ki	4: 7	Each one had to provide s for one month in	3920
1Ch	12:40	There were plentiful s of flour, fig cakes,	4407
	27:28	Joash was in charge of the s of olive oil.	238
2Ch	11:11	with s of food, olive oil and wine.	238
	17:13	and had large s in the towns of Judah.	4856
Ne	13:13	for distributing the s to their brothers.	2745
Ps	105:16	the land and destroyed all their s of food;	4751
	147: 8	he s the earth with rain and makes grass	3922
Pr	31:24	and s the merchants with sashes.	5989
Isa	3: 1	all s of food and all supplies of water,	5472
	3: 1	all supplies of food and all s of water,	5472
	10:28	they store s at Micmash.	3998
Ac	28:10	they furnished us with the s we needed.	NIG
2Co	9:10	Now he who s seed to the sower and bread	2220

SUPPLY (23) [SUPPLIED, SUPPLIES, SUPPLYING]

Ex	5: 7	"You are no longer to s the people	5989
Lev	26:26	When I cut off your s of bread,	4751
Nu	4: 9	and all its jars for the oil used to s it.	9250
Dt	15:14	S him liberally from your flock,	6735+6735
Jos	9: 5	All the bread of their food s was dry	7474
Jdg	19:20	"Let me s whatever you need.	NIH
2Sa	12:27	against Rabbah and taken its water s.	4784
1Ki	17: 9	a widow in that place to s you with food."	3920
2Ki	3: 9	and he had to s the king of Israel with	8740
Ezr	7:20	that you may have occasion to s,	10498
Ne	5:18	and every ten days an abundant s of wine	2221
Ps	78:20	Can he s meat for his people?"	3922
Isa	3: 1	to take from Jerusalem and Judah both s	5473
Eze	4:16	I will cut off the s of food in Jerusalem.	4751
	5:16	upon you and cut off your s of food.	4751
	14:13	to cut off its food s and send famine upon it	4751
	48:18	Its produce will s food for the workers	2118+4200
Na	2: 9	The s is endless, the wealth from all its	9414
Ac	12:20	on the king's country for their food s.	5555

2Co	8:14 your plenty will s what they need,	1181
	8:14 in turn their plenty will s what you need.	NIG
	9:10 for food will also s and increase your store	5961
1Th	3:10 and s what is lacking in your faith.	2936

SUPPLYING (1) [SUPPLY]

2Co	9:12 not only s the needs of God's people but is	4650

SUPPORT (24) [SUPPORTED, SUPPORTING, SUPPORTS]

Ge	13: 6 not s them while they stayed together,	5951
	36: 7 not s them both because of their livestock.	5951
Lev	25:35 and is unable to s himself among you,	3338+4572
Jdg	16:26 "Put me where I can feel the pillars that s	3922
2Sa	18: 3 It would be better now for you to give us s	6468
	22:19 but the LORD was my s.	5472
1Ki	1: 7 and they gave him their s.	339+6468
2Ki	15:19 a thousand talents of silver to gain his s	907+2118+3338
1Ch	11:10 gave his kingship strong s	2616+6640
2Ch	26:13 to s the king against his enemies.	6468
Ezr	10: 4 We will s you, so take courage and do it."	6640
Ps	18:18 but the LORD was my s.	5472
	20: 2 the sanctuary and grant you s from Zion.	6184
Pr	29:19 a fugitive till death; let no one s him.	9461
Isa	3: 1 and Judah both supply and s:	5474
	63: 5 I was appalled that no one gave s;	6164
Jer	37: 1 which has marched out to s you,	6476
Da	11: 1 I took my stand to s and protect him.)	2616
Lk	8: 3 These women were helping to s them out	1354
Ac	12:20 Having secured the s of Blastus,	4275
Ro	11:18 You do not s the root,	1002
1Co	9:12 If others have this right of s from you,	NIG
2Co	11: 8 I robbed other churches by receiving s	4072
2Ti	4:16 At my first defense, no one came to my s,	4134

SUPPORTED (11) [SUPPORT]

1Ki	16:21 half s Tibni son of Ginath for king,	339+2118
	16:21 and the other half s Omri.	339
2Ki	16:17 from the bronze bulls that s it and set it on	9393
2Ch	11:17 the kingdom of Judah and s Rehoboam son	599
Ezr	10:15 s by Meshullam and Shabbethai the Levite,	6468
Job	4: 4 Your words have s those who stumbled;	7756
Ps	89:43 of his sword and have not s him in battle.	7756
	94:18 your love, O LORD, s me.	6184
Jer	26:24 son of Shaphan s Jeremiah,	907+2118+3338
Da	11: 6 and her father and the one who s her.	2616
Col	2:19 s and held together by its ligaments,	2220

SUPPORTING (8) [SUPPORT]

2Sa	5: 9 from the s terraces inward.	4864
1Ki	7: 2 of cedar columns s trimmed cedar beams.	6584
	9:15 the s terraces, the wall of Jerusalem,	4864
	9:24 he constructed the s terraces.	4864
	11:27 the s terraces and had filled in the gap in	4864
1Ch	11: 8 from the s terraces to the surrounding wall,	4864
2Ch	32: 5 and reinforced the s terraces of the City	4864
Eph	4:16 and held together by every s ligament,	2221

SUPPORTS (8) [SUPPORT]

1Ki	7:30 and each had a basin resting on four s,	4190+7193
	7:35 The s and panels were attached to the top of	3338
	7:36 lions and palm trees on the surfaces of the s	3338
	10:12 The king used the almugwood to make s for	5026
Eze	41: 6 the temple to serve as s for the side rooms,	296
	41: 6 so that the s were not inserted into the wall	296
Da	10:21 (No one s me against them except Michael, your prince.)	2616+6640
Ro	11:18 do not support the root, but the root s you.	NIG

SUPPOSE (21) [SUPPOSED, SUPPOSEDLY, SUPPOSING]

Ex	3:13 "S I go to the Israelites and say to them,	2180
Nu	36: 3 Now s they marry men	NIH
Jdg	11: 9 "S you take me back to fight	561
Job	34:31 "S a man says to God,	3954
Eze	18: 5 "S there is a righteous man who does what	3954
	18:10 "S he has a violent son,	2256
	18:14 "But s this son has a son who sees all	2180
Mt	10:34 "Do not s that I have come to bring peace to	3787
	24:48 s that servant is wicked and says to himself,	1569
Lk	7:43 "I s the one who had the bigger debt	5696
	11: 5 he said to them, "S one of you has a friend,	5515
	12:45 But s the servant says to himself,	1569
	14:28 "S one of you wants to build a tower.	5515
	14:31 "Or s a king is about to go to war	5515
	15: 4 "S one of you has a hundred sheep	476+5515
	15: 8 "Or s a woman has ten silver coins	1569+5515
	17: 7 "S one of you had a servant plowing	5515
Jn	21:25 I s that even the whole world would	3887
Ac	2:15 These men are not drunk, as you s.	5696
Jas	2: 2 S a man comes into your meeting	1142+1569
	2:15 S a brother or sister is without clothes	1569

SUPPOSED (2) [SUPPOSE]

1Sa	20: 5 and I am s to dine with the king;	430+3782+3782
2Th	2: 2 report or letter s to have come from us,	6055

SUPPOSEDLY (1) [SUPPOSE]

Jer	23:30 prophets who steal from one another words s from me.	NIH

SUPPOSING (2) [SUPPOSE]

Jn	11:31 s she was going to the tomb to mourn there.	1506
Php	1:17 s that they can stir up trouble for me	3887

SUPPRESS (1)

Ro	1:18 of men who s the truth by their wickedness,	2988

SUPREMACY (1) [SUPREME]

Col	1:18 so that in everything he might have the s.	4750

SUPREME (5) [SUPREMACY]

2Ki	18:17 The king of Assyria sent his s commander,	9580
Pr	4: 7 Wisdom is s; therefore get wisdom.	8040
Ecc	12: 8 Since a king's word is s,	8950
Isa	20: 1 In the year that the s commander,	9580
1Pe	2:13 whether to the king, as the s authority,	5660

SUR (1)

2Ki	11: 6 at the S Gate, and a third at the gate behind	6075

SURE (62) [SURELY]

Ge	20: 7 you may be s that you and all yours will die.	3359
	24: 6 "Make s that you do take my son back	9068
	32:20 And be s to say,	2180
Ex	8:29 s that Pharaoh does not act deceitfully	AIT
	10:28 Make s you do not appear before me again!	9068
	17:14 make s that Joshua hears	265+928+8492
	23: 4 be s to take it back to him.	8740+8740
	23: 5 be s you help him with it.	6441+6441
Nu	26:55 Be s that the land is distributed by lot.	421
	28:31 Be s the animals are without defect.	NIH
	32:23 you may be s that your sin will find you out.	3359
Dt	5: 1 Learn them and be s to follow them.	9068
	6:17 Be s to keep the commands of	9068+9068
	11:32 be s that you obey all the decrees	9068
	12:23 But be s you do not eat the blood,	2616
	14:22 Be s to set aside a tenth	6923+6923
	17:15 be s to appoint over you the king	8492+8492
	21:23 Be s to bury him that same day,	7699+7699
	22: 1 be s to take it back to him.	8740+8740
	22: 7 be s to let the mother go,	8938+8938
	23:23 Whatever your lips utter you must be s	9068
	28:66 never s of your life.	586
	29:18 Make s there is no man or woman,	NIH
	29:18 make s there is no root among you	8845+8845
	31:29 you are s to become utterly corrupt	8845+8845
Jos	2:12 Give me a s sign	622
	13: 6 Be s to allocate this land to Israel for	8370
	23:13 then you may be s that the LORD	3359+3359
Jdg	15: 2 "I was so s you thoroughly hated her,"	606+606
1Sa	12:24 But be s to fear the LORD and serve	AIT
	20: 7 you can be s that he is determined	3359
	22:22 I knew he would be s to tell Saul.	5583+5583
1Ki	2:37 you can be s you will die;	3359+3359
	2:42 you can be s you will die'?	3359+3359
Ezr	7:17 With this money be s to buy bulls,	10056
Ps	19: 9 the LORD are s and altogether righteous.	622
	69:13 O God, answer me with your s salvation.	622
	132:11 a s oath that he will not revoke;	622
Pr	11:14 but many advisers make victory s.	NIH
	11:18 he who sows righteousness reaps a reward.	622
	11:21 Be s of this: The wicked will not go unpunished,	3338+3338+4200
	16: 5 Be s of this: They will not go unpunished.	3338+3338+4200
	27:23 Be s you know the condition of your flocks,	3359+3359
Isa	28:16 a precious cornerstone for a s foundation;	3569
	33: 6 He will be the s foundation for your times,	575
Jer	42:19 Be s of this: I warn you today	3359+3359
	42:22 Be s of this: you will die by the sword,	3359+3359
Eze	30: 9 Egypt's doom, for it is s to come.	2180
Mt	17:11 Jesus replied, "To be s, Elijah comes and	3525
Mk	9:12 Jesus replied, "To be s, Elijah does come	NIG
Lk	1:18 "How can I be s of this?	1182
	10:11 be s of this: The kingdom of God is near.'	1182
Ac	13:34 and blessings promised to David.'	4412
Ro	15:28 and have made s that they have received	5381
2Co	13: 4 For to be s, he was crucified in weakness,	1142
Eph	5: 5 For of this you can be s:	1182+3857
1Th	5:15 Make s that nobody pays back wrong	3972
Tit	3:11 be s that such a man is warped and sinful;	3857
Heb	6:11 in order to make your hope s	4443
	11: 1 Now faith is being s of what we hope for	5712
	11:18 We are s that we have a clear conscience	4275
2Pe	1:10 to make your calling and election s.	1010

SURELY (304) [SURE]

Ge	2:17 for when you eat of it you will s die."	4637+4637
	3: 4 "You will not s die,"	4637+4637
	6:13 I am going to destroy both them and	2180
	9: 5 And for your lifeblood I will s demand	421
	17:16 I will bless her and will s give you a son	1685
	17:20 I will s bless him;	2180
	18:10 "I will s return to you	8740+8740
	18:18 Abraham will s become a great	2118+2118
	20:11 'There is s no fear of God in this place,	8370
	22:17 I will s bless you	1385+1385
	26:11 shall s be put to death."	4637+4637
	28:16 he thought, "S the LORD is in this place,	434
	29:32 S my husband will love me now."	3954
	31:16 S all the wealth that God took away	3954
Ge	31:42 you would s have sent me away	3954+6964
	32:12 'I will s make you prosper	3512+3512
	37:33 Joseph has s been torn to pieces."	3271+3271
	42:15 As s as Pharaoh lives,	2644
	42:16 as s as Pharaoh lives,	2644
	42:21 "S we are being punished because	66
	44:28 and I said, "He has s been torn to pieces."	421
	46: 4 and I will s bring you back again.	6590+6590
	50:24 God will s come to your aid	7212+7212
	50:25 God will s come to your aid,	7212+7212
Ex	4:25 "S you are a bridegroom of blood to me,"	3954
	13:19 "God will s come to your aid,	7212+7212
	19:12 He shall s be put to death.	4637+4637
	19:13 He shall s be stoned or shot with	6232+6232
	21:12 shall s be put to death.	4637+4637
Nu	14:21 as s as I live and as surely as the glory of	2644
	14:21 as surely as I live and as s as the glory of	NIH
	14:28 'As s as I live, declares the LORD,	2644
	14:35 and I will s do these things	561+4202
	15:31 that person must s be cut off;	4162+4162
	26:65 the LORD had told those Israelites they would s die	4637+4637
	35:31 He must s be put to death.	3954
Dt	4: 6 "S this great nation is a wise	8370
	8:19 that you will s be destroyed.	6+6
	32:40 As s as I live forever,	2645
	33: 3 S it is you who love the people;	677
Jos	2:24 "The LORD has s given the whole land	3954
	10:14 S the LORD was fighting for Israel!	3954
Jdg	8:19 As s as the LORD lives,	2644
Ru	3:13 as s as the LORD lives	2644
1Sa	1:26 "As s as you live,	2644+5883
	10: 8 I will s come down to you	2180
	14:39 As s as the LORD who rescues Israel lives,	2644
	14:45 As s as the LORD lives,	2644
	15:32 thinking, "S the bitterness of death is past."	434
	16: 6 "S the LORD's anointed stands here	421
	17:55 "As s as you live,	2644
	19: 6 "As s as the LORD lives,	2644
	20: 3 as s as the LORD lives	2644
	20:12 "By the LORD, the God of Israel, I will s	3954
	20:21 as s as the LORD lives,	2644
	20:26 s he is unclean."	3954
	22:16 But the king said, "You will s die,	4637+4637
	24:20 I know that you will s be king and that	4887+4887
	25:26 as s as the LORD lives	2644
	25:34 as s as the LORD, the God of Israel, lives,	2644
	26:10 "As s as the LORD lives,"	2644
	26:16 as s as the LORD lives	2644
	26:21 S I have acted like a fool	2180
	26:24 As s as I valued your life today,	2180
	26:25 will do great things and s triumph."	3523+3523
	28: 9 "S you know what Saul has done.	2180
	28:10 "As s as the LORD lives,	2644
	29: 6 "As s as the LORD lives,	2644
2Sa	2:27 "As s as God lives,	2644
	4: 9 "As s as the LORD lives,	2644
	5:19 s hand the Philistines over	928+3338+5989+5989
	9: 7 "for I will s show you kindness for	6913+6913
	11:11 as s as you live,	2256+2644+5883
	12: 5 "As s as the LORD lives,	2644
	14:11 "As s as the LORD lives,"	2644
	14:19 "As s as you live,	2644+5883
	15:21 "As s as the LORD lives,	2644
	18: 2 "I myself will s march out with you."	3655+3655
1Ki	1:13 "S Solomon your son shall be king	3954
	1:29 "As s as the LORD lives,	2644
	1:30 I will s carry out today what I swore to you	3954
	2:24 as s as the LORD lives—	2644
	11: 2 because they will s turn your hearts	434
	17:12 "As s as the LORD your God lives,"	2644
	18:10 As s as the LORD your God lives,	2644
	18:15 I will s present myself to Ahab today."	3954
	18:27 "S he is a god!	3954
	20:23 s we will be stronger than they.	561+4202
	20:25 Then s we will be stronger than they."	561+4202
	22:14 "As s as the LORD lives,	2644
	22:32 they thought, "S this is the king of Israel."	421
2Ki	2: 2 "As s as the LORD lives	2644
	2: 4 "As s as the LORD lives	2644
	2: 6 "As s as the LORD lives	2644
	3:14 "As s as the LORD Almighty lives,	2644
	4:30 "As s as the LORD lives	2644
	5:11 "I thought that he would s come out to	3655+3655
	5:16 "As s as the LORD lives,	2644
	5:20 As s as the LORD lives,	2644
	7:12 thinking, 'They will s come out,	3954
	9:26 I will make you pay for it on this plot	561+4202
	18:30 'The LORD will s deliver us;	5911+5911
	19:11 S you have heard what the kings	2180
	20:17 The time will s come when everything	2180
	24: 3 S these things happened to Judah according	421
2Ch	18:13 "As s as the LORD lives,	2644
Ezr	7:26 law of the king must s be punished	10056
Est	6:13 you will s come to ruin!"	5877+5877
Job	2: 1 and he will s curse you to your face."	561+4202
	2: 5 and he will s curse you to your face."	561+4202
	5: 7 to trouble as s as sparks fly upward.	2256
	6: 3 It would outweigh the sand of the seas—	3954
	8:19 S its life withers away,	2176
	8:20 "S God does not reject a blameless man	2176
	11:11 S he recognizes deceitful men;	3954
	11:16 You will s forget your trouble,	3954
	13:10 He would s rebuke you	3519+3519
	13:15 I will s defend my ways to his face.	421
	14:16 S then you will count my steps but	3954
	16: 7 S, O God, you have worn me out;	421+6964

Ref	Text	Number
Job 17: 2	S mockers surround me;	561+4202
18:21	S such is the dwelling of an evil man;	421
20: 4	"S you know how it has been from of old,	2022
20:20	"S he will have no respite from his craving,	3954
22:20	'S our foes are destroyed,	561+4202
22:26	S then you will find delight in	3954
27: 2	"As s as God lives,	2644
30:24	"S no one lays a hand on a broken man	421
31:36	S I would wear it on my shoulder,	561+4202
38: 5	S you know!	3954
38:21	S you know, for you were already born!	3954
42: 3	S I spoke of things I did not understand,	4027+4200
Ps 5:12	For s, O LORD, you bless the righteous;	3954
16: 6	s I have a delightful inheritance.	677
21: 6	S you have granted him eternal blessings	3954
23: 6	S goodness and love will follow me all	421
32: 6	s when the mighty waters rise,	8370
49:15	he will s take me to himself.	3954
51: 5	S I was sinful at birth,	2176
51: 6	S you desire truth in the inner parts;	2176
52: 5	S God will bring you down	1685
54: 4	S God is my help;	2180
58:11	"S the righteous still are rewarded;	421
58:11	s there is a God who judges the earth."	421
62:12	S you will reward each person according	3954
64: 6	S the mind and heart of man are cunning.	2256
66:19	but God has s listened and heard my voice	434
68:21	S God will crush the heads of his enemies,	421
73: 1	S God is good to Israel,	421
73:13	S in vain have I kept my heart pure;	421
73:18	S you place them on slippery ground;	421
76:10	S your wrath against men brings you praise,	3954
85: 9	S his salvation is near those who fear him,	421
89:21	s my arm will strengthen him.	677
91: 3	S he will save you from the fowler's snare	3954
92: 9	For s your enemies, O LORD,	2180
92: 9	O LORD, s your enemies will perish;	2180
112: 6	S he will never be shaken;	3954
139:11	"S the darkness will hide me and	421
140:13	S the righteous will praise your name and	421
Pr 11:15	up security for another will s suffer,	8273+8317
12:14	a man is filled with good things as s as	2256
21: 5	the diligent lead to profit as s as haste leads	421
23: 5	they will s sprout wings and fly off	6913+6913
23:18	There is a s a future hope for you,	561+3954
Isa 5: 9	"S the great houses will become desolate,	561+4202
9:18	S wickedness burns like a fire;	3954
12: 2	S God is my salvation;	2180
14:24	The LORD Almighty has sworn, "S,	561+4202
25: 9	"S this is our God;	2180
36:15	'The LORD will s deliver us;	5911+5911
37:11	S you have heard what the kings	2180
38:17	S it was for my benefit that I suffered	2180
39: 6	The time will s come when everything	2180
40: 7	S the people are grass.	434
40:15	S the nations are like a drop in a bucket;	2176
41:11	"All who rage against you will s be ashamed	NIH
45:14	'S God is with you, and there is no other;	421
47:14	S they are like stubble;	2180
49:18	As s as I live,"	2644
51: 3	The LORD will s comfort Zion	3954
53: 4	S he took up our infirmities	434
55: 5	S you will summon nations you know not,	2176
56: 3	"The LORD will s exclude me	976+976
59: 1	S the arm of the LORD is not too short	2176
60: 9	S the islands look to me;	3954
63: 8	He said, "S they are my people,	421
Jer 3:23	the [idolatrous] commotion on the hills	434
3:23	s in the LORD our God is the salvation	434
4: 2	'As s as the LORD lives,'	2644
5: 2	'As s as the LORD lives,'	2644
5: 5	s they know the way of the LORD,	3954
12:16	'As s as the LORD lives'—	2644
15:11	S I will deliver you for a good purpose;	561+4202
15:11	s I will make your enemies plead with you	561+4202
16:14	'As s as the LORD lives,	2644
16:15	'As s as the LORD lives,	2644
22: 6	I will s make you like a desert,	561+4202
22:24	"As s as I live,"	2644
23: 7	'As s as the LORD lives,	2644
23: 8	'As s as the LORD lives,	2644
23:39	I will s forget you and cast you out	5960+5960
29:32	I will s punish Shemaiah the Nehelamite	2180
30:10	'I will s save you out of a distant place,	3954
31:18	"I have s heard Ephraim's moaning:	9048+9048
32:37	I will s gather them from all the lands	2180
34: 3	will s be captured and handed over	9530+9530
37: 9	'The Babylonians will s leave us.'	2143+2143+4946+6584
38:16	"As s as the LORD lives,	2644
44:26	"As s as the Sovereign LORD lives."	2644
44:29	of harm against you will s stand.'	7756+7756
46:18	"As s as I live,"	2644
46:27	I will s save you out of a distant place,	3954
49:26	S, her young men will fall in the streets;	4027+4200
51:14	I will s fill you with men,	561+3954
51:47	For the time will s come when I will punish	2180
Eze 3: 6	S if I had sent you to them,	4202
3:18	I say to a wicked man, 'You will s die,'	4637+4637
3:21	he will s live because he took warning,	2649+2649
5:11	as s as I live, declares the Sovereign LORD,	2644
7: 4	I will s repay you for your conduct and	3954
14:16	as s as I live, declares the Sovereign LORD,	2644
Eze 14:18	as s as I live, declares the Sovereign LORD,	2644
14:20	as s as I live, declares the Sovereign LORD,	2644
16:43	I will s bring down on your head	2026
16:48	As s as I live, declares the Sovereign LORD,	2644
17:16	'As s as I live, declares the Sovereign LORD,	2644
17:19	As s as I live, I will bring down on his head	2644
18: 3	As s as I live, declares the Sovereign LORD,	2644
18: 9	That man is righteous; he will s live,	2649+2649
18:13	s be put to death	4637+4637
18:17	for his father's sin; he will s live.	2649+2649
18:19	keep all my decrees, he will s live.	2649+2649
18:21	he will s live; he will not die.	2649+2649
18:28	he will s live; he will not die.	2649+2649
20: 3	As s as I live, I will not let you	2644
20:31	As s as I live, declares the Sovereign LORD,	2644
20:33	As s as I live, declares the Sovereign LORD,	2644
20:39	But afterward you will s listen to me	401+561
21: 7	It will s take place,	2118
21:13	"Testing will s come.	3954
22:13	" 'I will s strike my hands together at	2180
33: 8	'O wicked man, you will s die,'	4637+4637
33:11	'As s as I live, declares the Sovereign LORD,	2644
33:13	the righteous man that he will s live,	2649+2649
33:14	the wicked man, 'You will s die,'	4637+4637
33:15	and does no evil, he will s live;	2649+2649
33:16	what is just and right; he will s live.	2649+2649
33:24	the land has been given to us	NIH
33:27	As s as I live, those who are left	2644
33:33	"When all this comes true—and it s will—	2180
34: 8	As s as I live, declares the Sovereign LORD,	2644
35: 6	as s as I live, declares the Sovereign LORD,	2644
35:11	as s as I live, declares the Sovereign LORD,	2644
39: 8	It will s take place,	2180
Da 2:47	"S your God is the God of gods and the Lord of kings	10168+10427+10643
Hos 4:15	'As s as the LORD lives!'	2644
6: 3	As s as the sun rises, he will appear;	3869
Joel 1:12	S the joy of mankind is withered away.	3954
2:20	S he has done great things.	3954
2:21	S the LORD has done great things.	3954
Am 3: 7	S the Sovereign LORD does nothing	3954
4: 2	"The time will s come when you will	3954
5: 5	For Gilgal will s go into exile,	1655+1655
7:11	and Israel will s go into exile,	1655+1655
8:14	'As s as your god lives,	2644
8:14	'As s as the god of Beersheba lives'—	2644
9: 8	"S the eyes of the Sovereign LORD are on	2180
Mic 2:12	"I will s gather all of you, O Jacob;	665+665
2:12	I will s bring together the remnant	7695+7695
Zep 2: 9	as s as I live," declares the LORD Almighty,	2644
2: 9	"Moab will become like Sodom,	3954
3: 7	'S you will fear me and accept correction!'	421
Zec 2: 9	I will s raise my hand against them so	3954
10: 8	S I will redeem them;	3954
Mal 4: 1	"S the day is coming;	2180+3954
Mt 26:22	to say to him one after the other, "S not I,	NIG
26:25	said, "S not I, Rabbi?"	3614
26:73	"S you are one of them,	242
27:54	exclaimed, "S he was the Son of God!"	242
28:20	And s I am with you always,	2627
Mk 14:19	and one by one they said to him, "S not I?"	3614
14:70	"S you are one of them,	242
15:39	he said, "S this man was the Son of God!"	242
Lk 4:23	"S you will quote this proverb to me."	4122
13:33	for s no prophet can die outside Jerusalem!	NIG
23:47	"S this was a righteous man."	3953
Jn 3: 4	"S he cannot enter a second time	NIG
6:14	"S this is the Prophet who is to come into	242
7:40	"S this man is the Prophet."	242
18:21	S they know what I said.	3972
Ac 10:14	"S not, Lord!" Peter replied.	3592
11: 8	"I replied, 'S not, Lord,	3592
Ro 14:11	" 'As s as I live,' says the Lord,	1609+2409
1Co 9: 2	an apostle to others, s I am to you!	247+1145
9:10	he says this for us, doesn't he?	4122
15:31	I mean that, brothers—just as s as I glory	3755
2Co 1:18	But as s as God is faithful,	NIG
11:10	As s as the truth of Christ is in me,	NIG
Eph 3: 2	S you have heard about the administration of God's grace	1145+1623
4:21	S you heard of him and were taught	1145+1623
1Th 2: 9	S you remember, brothers,	1142
Heb 2: 9	For s it is not angels who helps,	1327
6:14	"I will s bless you and give you many	1623+3605

SURETY (KJV) See CERTAIN, ENSURE, GUARANTEE, GUARANTEED, PLEDGE, REALLY, SECURITY, WITHOUT DOUBT

SURF (1)
Ac 27:41	broken to pieces by the pounding of the s.	3246

SURFACE (12) [SURFACES]
Ge 1: 2	darkness was over the s of the deep,	7156
2: 6	and watered the whole s of the ground—	7156
7:18	and the ark floated on the s of the water.	7156
8: 8	to see if the water had receded from the s	7156
8: 9	because there was water over all the s of	7156
8:13	the covering from the ark and saw that the s	7156
Lev 14:37	that appear to be deeper than the s of	7156
Job 24:18	"Yet they are foam on the s of the water;	7156
38:30	when the s of the deep is frozen?	7156
Isa 28:25	When he has leveled the s,	7156
Hos 10: 7	like a twig on the s of the waters.	7156

2Co 10: 7	are looking only on the s of things.	2848+4725

SURFACES (1) [SURFACE]
1Ki 7:36	lions and palm trees on the s of the supports	4283

SURFEITING (KJV) See DISSIPATION

SURGE (2) [SURGED, SURGING]
Job 40:23	the Jordan should s against his mouth.	1631
Isa 54: 8	In a s of anger I hid my face from you for	9192

SURGED (1) [SURGE]
1Sa 17:52	Then the men of Israel and Judah s forward	7756

SURGING (7) [SURGE]
Ex 15: 8	The s waters stood firm like a wall;	5689
Ps 46: 3	and the mountains quake with their s.	1452
89: 9	You rule over the s sea;	1455
Isa 17:13	the peoples roar like the roar of s waters,	8041
Jer 46: 7	like rivers of s waters?	1723
46: 8	like rivers of s waters.	1723
Zec 10:11	the s sea will be subdued and all the depths	1644

SURLY (1)
1Sa 25: 3	a Calebite, was s and mean in his dealings.	7997

SURMISINGS (KJV) See SUSPICIONS

SURMOUNTED (1)
Eze 40:16	inside the gateway were s by	448

SURNAME (KJV) See CALLED, NAME

SURPASS (1) [ALL-SURPASSING, SURPASSED, SURPASSES, SURPASSING, SURPASSINGLY]
Pr 31:29	women do noble things, but you s them all."	6590

SURPASSED (2) [SURPASS]
Jn 1:15	'He who comes after me has s me	1181+1869
1:30	'A man who comes after me has s me	1181+1869

SURPASSES (3) [SURPASS]
Pr 8:19	what I yield s choice silver.	4946
Mt 5:20	that unless your righteousness s that of	4355+4498
Eph 3:19	and to know this love that s knowledge—	5650

SURPASSING (4) [SURPASS]
Ps 150: 2	praise him for his s greatness.	8044
2Co 3:10	now in comparison with the s glory.	5650
9:14	because of the s grace God has given you.	5650
Php 3: 8	a loss compared to the s greatness	5660

SURPASSINGLY (1) [SURPASS]
2Co 12: 7	because of these s great revelations,	5651

SURPRISE (6) [SURPRISED, SURPRISING]
Jos 10: 9	Joshua took them by s.	7328
Ps 35: 8	may ruin overtake them by s—	3359+4202
55:15	Let death take my enemies by s;	5958
Jer 51: 2	Why are you like a man taken by s,	1850
Ac 3:12	"Men of Israel, why does this s you?	2513
1Th 5: 4	not in darkness so that this day should s you	2898

SURPRISED (7) [SURPRISE]
Ecc 5: 8	do not be s at such things;	9449
Mk 15:44	Pilate was s to hear that he was already dead	2513
Lk 11:38	not first wash before the meal, was s.	2513
Jn 3: 7	You should not be s at my saying,	2513
4:27	Just then his disciples returned and were s	2513
1Pe 4:12	be s at the painful trial you are suffering,	3826
1Jn 3:13	Do not be s, my brothers,	2513

SURPRISING (1) [SURPRISE]
2Co 11:15	It is not s, then, if his servants masquerade	3489

SURRENDER (14) [SURRENDERED, SURRENDERS]
Jos 20: 5	they must not s the one accused,	928+3338+6037
Jdg 20:13	Now s those wicked men of Gibeah so	5989
1Sa 11: 3	no one comes to rescue us, we will s to you.	3655
11:10	"Tomorrow we will s to you,	3655
23:11	Will the citizens of Keilah s me to him?	6037
23:12	the citizens of Keilah and my men	6037
2Ki 7: 4	over to the camp of the Arameans and s.	5877
Ps 41: 2	he will bless him in the land and not s him	5989
Isa 54:15	whoever attacks you will s to you.	5877
Jer 38:17	'If you s to the officers of the king	3655+3655
38:18	if you will not s to the officers of the king	3655
38:21	But if you refuse to s, this is what	3655
Da 8:13	and the s of the sanctuary and of the host	5989
1Co 13: 3	to the poor and s my body to the flames,	4140

SURRENDERED (2) [SURRENDER]

2Ki	24:12	his nobles and his officials *all* s to him.	3655
Lk	23:25	and s Jesus to their will.	*4140*

SURRENDERS (2) [SURRENDER]

Jer	21: 9	whoever goes out and s to the Babylonians	5877
	50:15	*She* s, her towers fall,	3338+5989

SURROUND (21) [SURROUNDED, SURROUNDING, SURROUNDS]

Jos	7: 9	and *they will* s us and wipe out our name	6015
Job	16:13	his archers s me.	6015
	17: 2	Surely mockers s me;	6643
	40:22	the poplars by the stream s him.	6015
Ps	5:12	*you* s them *with* your favor as with	6496
	17: 9	from my mortal enemies *who* s me.	5938
	17:11	*they* now s me, with eyes alert,	6015
	22:12	Many bulls s me;	6015
	27: 6	be exalted above the enemies *who* s me;	6017
	32: 7	you will protect me from trouble and s me	6015
	40:12	For troubles without number s me;	705
	49: 5	*when* wicked deceivers s me—	6015
	88:17	All day long *they* s me like a flood;	6015
	89: 7	he is more awesome than all *who* s him.	6017
	97: 2	Clouds and thick darkness s him;	6017
	109:19	*With* vigours of hatred *they* s me;	6015
	125: 2	As the mountains s Jerusalem,	6017
	140: 9	the heads of *those who* s me be covered with	4990
Jer	4:17	*They* s her like men guarding a field,	2118+4946+6017
	12: 9	that other birds of prey s and attack?	6017
	31:22	a woman *will* s a man."	6015

SURROUNDED (28) [SURROUND]

Ge	19: 4	both young and old—s the house.	6015
Jdg	16: 2	So *they* s the place and lay in wait	6015
	19:22	of the wicked men of the city s the house.	6015
	20: 5	of Gibeah came after me and s the house,	6015
	20:43	*They* s the Benjamites,	4193
2Sa	18:15	ten of Joab's armor-bearers s Absalom,	6015
1Ki	7:12	The great courtyard was s *by* a wall	6017
2Ki	3:25	with slings s it and attacked it as well.	6015
	6:14	They went by night and s the city.	5938
	6:15	an army with horses and chariots *had* s	6015
	8:21	The Edomites s him and his chariot	6015
1Ch	29:30	and the circumstances that s him and Israel	6296
2Ch	21: 9	The Edomites s him and his chariot	6015
Ps	22:16	Dogs *have* s me; a band of evil men	6015
	118:10	All the nations s me,	6015
	118:11	*They* s me on every side,	6015
Ecc	9:14	s it and built huge siegeworks against it.	6015
La	3: 5	and s me *with* bitterness and hardship.	5938
Eze	1: 4	flashing lightning and s by brilliant light.	6017
	1:27	and brilliant light s him.	6017
	27:32	"Who was ever silenced like Tyre, s by	928+9348
	32:22	she is s *by* the graves of all her slain,	6017
Hos	11:12	Ephraim *has* s me with lies,	6015
Jnh	2: 5	waters threatened me, the deep s me;	6015
Lk	21:20	"When you see Jerusalem *being* s	3240
Jn	5: 2	and which *is* s *by* five covered colonnades,	2400
Heb	12: 1	since we are s by such a great cloud	4329
Rev	20: 9	the earth and s the camp of God's people,	3238

SURROUNDING (57) [SURROUND]

Ge	41:48	the food grown in the fields s it.	6017
Ex	38:20	and of the s courtyard were bronze.	6017
	38:31	for the s courtyard and those for its entrance	6017
	38:31	the tabernacle and those for the s courtyard.	6017
Nu	3:26	the curtain at the entrance to the courtyard s	6017
	3:37	the posts of the s courtyard with their bases,	6017
	4:26	of the courtyard s the tabernacle and altar,	6017
	4:32	the posts of the s courtyard with their bases,	6017
	21:25	Heshbon and all its s settlements.	1426
	21:32	the Israelites captured its s settlements	1426
	32:42	and its s settlements and called it Nobah	1426
Jos	15:45	Ekron, with its s settlements and villages;	1426
	15:47	its s settlements and villages;	1426
	17:11	together with their s settlements (the third	1426
	21:11	Hebron), with its s pastureland.	1426
	21:42	Each of these towns had pasturelands s it;	6017
Jdg	1:27	or Megiddo and their s settlements,	1426
	11:26	the s settlements and all the towns along	1426
1Ki	4:31	And his fame spread to all the s nations.	6017
2Ki	25: 5	though the Babylonians were s the city.	6017
1Ch	2:23	as well as Kenath with its s settlements—	1426
	4:32	Their s villages were Etam, Ain,	2958
	6:55	in Judah with its s pasturelands.	6017
	7:28	Bethel and its s villages,	1426
	8:12	and Lod with its s villages,	1426
	11: 8	from the supporting terraces to the s *wall*.	6017
	18: 1	and he took Gath and its s villages from	1426
	28:12	of the LORD and all the s rooms,	6017
2Ch	13:19	and Ephron, with their s villages.	1426
	17:10	on all the kingdoms of the lands s Judah,	6017
	28:18	Timnah and Gimzo, with their s villages.	1426
Ne	3:22	by the priests from the s region.	3971
	5:17	as those who came to us from the s nations.	6017
	6:16	all the s nations were afraid	6017
	11:25	in Kiriath Arba and its s settlements,	1426
Jer	1:15	they will come against all her s walls and	6017
	25: 9	and against all the s nations.	6017
	34: 1	against Jerusalem and all its s towns,	NIH
	49: 2	and its s villages will be set on fire.	1426

Jer	52: 7	though the Babylonians were s the city.	6017
	52:23	of pomegranates above the s network was	6017
Eze	34:26	I will bless them and the *places* s my hill.	6017
	40: 5	I saw a wall **completely** s the temple	6017+6017
	41: 7	The *structure* s the temple was built	6015
	43:12	All the s area on top of the mountain	6017+6017
Zec	7: 7	when Jerusalem and its s towns were at rest	6017
	12: 2	a cup that sends all the s peoples reeling.	6017
	12: 6	and left all the s peoples,	6017
	14:14	of all the s nations will be collected—	6017
Mt	14:35	they sent word to all the s **country.**	4369
Mk	6:36	so they can go to the s countryside	3241
Lk	4:37	about him spread throughout the s area.	4369
	7:17	throughout Judea and the s **country.**	4369
	9:12	the s villages and countryside and find food	3241
Ac	14: 6	of Lystra and Derbe and to the s **country,**	4369
Jude	1: 7	and the s towns gave themselves up	899+4309
Rev	4: 6	S the throne were twenty-four other thrones,	3239

SURROUNDS (3) [SURROUND]

Ps	32:10	but the LORD's unfailing love s the man who	6015
	89: 8	O LORD, and your faithfulness s you.	6017
	125: 2	so the LORD s his people both now	6017

SURVEY (2) [SURVEYED]

Jos	18: 4	send them out *to* **make a s** of the land	928+2143
	18: 8	"Go and **make a s** of the land and write	928+2143

SURVEYED (1) [SURVEY]

Ecc	2:11	Yet *when* I s all that my hands had done	7155

SURVIVE (16) [SURVIVED, SURVIVES, SURVIVING, SURVIVOR, SURVIVORS]

Dt	4:27	of *you will* s among the nations to which	8636
Jos	11:22	only in Gaza, Gath and Ashdod *did any* s.	8636
2Sa	1:10	that after he had fallen *he could* not s.	2649
Job	27:15	The plague will bury *those who* s with,	8586
Isa	66:19	and I will send some of those *who* s to	7128
Jer	21: 7	and the people in this city who s the plague,	8636
	31: 2	"The people *who* s the sword will find favor	8586
	42:17	not one of them will s or escape	8586
	44:14	to live in Egypt will escape or s to return to	8586
Eze	7:16	All *who* s and escape will be in	7117
Am	7: 2	How *can* Jacob s? He is so small!"	7756
	7: 5	How *can* Jacob s? He is so small!"	7756
Zec	10: 9	*They* and their children *will* s,	2649
Mt	24:22	had not been cut short, no one *would* s,	323+5392
Mk	13:20	not cut short those days, no one would s.	5392
Ac	27:34	take some food. You need it *to* s.	5401

SURVIVED (9) [SURVIVE]

Ex	14:28	Not one of them s.	8636
Nu	14:38	son of Nun and Caleb son of Jephunneh s.	2649
Dt	5:26	speaking out of fire, as we have, and s?	2649
Jos	13:12	and *had* s as one of the last of the Rephaites.	8636
1Sa	11:11	Those *who* s were scattered,	8636
Ne	1: 2	about the Jewish remnant that s the exile,	8636
	1: 3	"Those who s the exile and are back in	8636
Ps	106:11	not one of them s.	3855
La	2:22	of the LORD's anger no one escaped or s;	8586

SURVIVES (4) [SURVIVE]

2Ki	19: 4	pray for the remnant that *still* s."	5162
Isa	37: 4	pray for the remnant that *still* s."	5162
Eze	6:12	he *that* s and is spared will die of famine.	8636
1Co	3:14	If what he has built s, he will receive	3531

SURVIVING (3) [SURVIVE]

Dt	28:54	wife he loves or his s children,	889+3855+3856
Jer	29: 1	to the s elders among the exiles and to	3856
Eze	17:14	s only by keeping his treaty.	6641

SURVIVOR (5) [SURVIVE]

Jdg	12: 5	and whenever a s *of* Ephraim said,	7127
2Ki	10:11	leaving him no s.	8586
	10:14	*He* left no s.	8636
Ezr	9:14	leaving us no remnant or s?	7129
Job	18:19	no s where once he lived.	8586

SURVIVORS (41) [SURVIVE]

Nu	21:35	his whole army, leaving them no s.	8586
	24:19	of Jacob and destroy the s of the city."	8586
Dt	2:34	We left no s.	8586
	3: 3	We struck them down, leaving no s.	8586
	7:20	the s who hide from you have perished.	8636
Jos	8:22	leaving them neither s nor fugitives.	8586
	10:28	destroyed everyone in it. He left no s.	8586
	10:30	Joshua put to the sword. He left no s there.	8586
	10:33	until no s were left.	8586
	10:37	and everyone in it. They left no s.	8586
	10:39	they totally destroyed. They left no s.	8586
	10:40	together with all their kings. He left no s.	8586
	11: 8	until no s were left.	8586
	23:12	with the s *of* these nations that remain	3856
	21:17	The Benjamite s have heirs,"	7129
2Sa	21: 2	a part of Israel but were s of the Amorites.	3856
2Ki	19:31	and out of Mount Zion a **band of** s.	7129
Ezr	9: 8	of any place where s may now be living are	8636
Ps	76:10	and the s of your wrath are restrained.	8642
Isa	1: 9	the LORD Almighty had left us some s,	8586
	4: 2	the land will be the pride and glory of the s	7129

Isa	10:20	the s *of* the house of Jacob,	7129
	14:22	from Babylon her name and s,	8637
	14:30	it will slay your s.	8642
	16:14	and her s will be very few and feeble."	8637
	21:17	The s *of* the bowmen,	8637
	37:32	and out of Mount Zion a **band of** s.	7129
Jer	8: 3	all the s of this evil nation will prefer death	8642
	15: 9	the s to the sword before their enemies,"	8642
	24: 8	his officials and the s *from* Jerusalem,	8642
	41:16	the s from Mizpah whom he had recovered	8642
	47: 4	and to cut off all s who could help Tyre	8586
Eze	5:10	and will scatter all your s to the winds.	8642
	14:22	Yet there will be some s—	7129
	17:21	and the s will be scattered to the winds.	8636
Joel	2:32	among the s whom the LORD calls.	8586
Ob	1:14	over their s in the day of their trouble,	8586
	1:18	There will be no s from the house of Esau."	8586
Zep	2: 9	the s *of* my nation will inherit their land."	3856
Zec	14:16	Then the s from all the nations	3855
Rev	11:13	and the s were terrified and gave glory to	3370

SUSA (22)

Ezr	4: 9	Erech and Babylon, the Elamites **of** S,	10704
Ne	1: 1	while I was in the citadel of S,	8809
Est	1: 2	from his royal throne in the citadel of S,	8809
	1: 5	who were in the citadel of S.	8809
	2: 3	into the harem at the citadel of S.	8809
	2: 5	Now there was in the citadel of S a Jew of	8809
	2: 8	many girls were brought to the citadel of S	8809
	3:15	and the edict was issued in the citadel of S.	8809
	3:15	but the city of S was bewildered.	8809
	4: 8	which had been published in S,	8809
	4:16	gather together all the Jews who are in S,	8809
	8:14	the edict was also issued in the citadel of S.	8809
	8:15	And the city of S held a joyous celebration.	8809
	9: 6	In the citadel of S, the Jews killed and	8809
	9:11	in the citadel of S was reported to the king	8809
	9:12	the ten sons of Haman in the citadel of S.	8809
	9:13	"give the Jews in S permission	8809
	9:14	An edict was issued in S,	8809
	9:15	in S came together on the fourteenth day of	8809
	9:15	they put to death in S three hundred men,	8809
	9:18	The Jews in S, however, had assembled	8809
Da	8: 2	in the citadel of S in the province of Elam;	8809

SUSAH SEE HAZAR SUSAH

SUSANCHITES (KJV) See SUSA

SUSANNA (1)

Lk	8: 3	of Herod's household; S; and many others.	5052

SUSI (1)

Nu	13:11	(a tribe of Joseph), Gaddi son of S;	6064

SUSIM See HAZAR SUSIM

SUSPECTS (3) [SUSPICIONS]

Nu	5:14	and *he* s his wife and she is impure—	7861
	5:14	if he is jealous and s her even though she is	7861
	5:30	over a man because *he* s his wife.	7861

SUSPENDS (1)

Job	26: 7	*he* s the earth over nothing.	9434

SUSPENSE (3)

Dt	28:66	You will live *in* constant s,	9428
Jn	10:24	"How long *will you* keep us *in* s?	149+3836+6034
Ac	27:33	"you have been in constant s and have gone	4659

SUSPICIONS (1) [SUSPECTS]

1Ti	6: 4	in envy, strife, malicious talk, evil s	*5707*

SUSTAIN (10) [SUSTAINED, SUSTAINING, SUSTAINS]

Ru	4:15	He will renew your life and s you	3920
Job	36:19	or even all your mighty efforts s you	6885
Ps	41: 3	The LORD *will* s him on his sickbed	6184
	51:12	and grant me a willing spirit, *to* s me.	6164
	55:22	your cares on the LORD and he *will* s you;	3920
	89:21	My hand *will* s him;	3922
	119:116	S me according to your promise,	6164
	119:175	and *may* your laws s me.	6468
Isa	46: 4	I am he *who will* s you.	6022
	46: 4	I *will* s you and I will rescue you.	6022

SUSTAINED (4) [SUSTAIN]

Ge	27:37	and *I have* s him *with* grain and new wine.	6164
Ne	9:21	For forty years *you* s them in the desert;	3920
Isa	59:16	and his own righteousness s him.	6164
	63: 5	and my own wrath s me.	6164

SUSTAINING (1) [SUSTAIN]

Heb	1: 3	s all things by his powerful word.	5770

SUSTAINS (8) [SUSTAIN]

Ps	3: 5	I wake again, because the LORD s me.	6164
	18:35	and your right hand s me;	6184

Ps	54: 4	the Lord is the *one who* s me.	6164
	104:15	and bread *that* s his heart.	6184
	146: 9	The LORD watches over the alien and s	6386
	147: 6	The LORD s the humble but casts	6386
Pr	18:14	A man's spirit s him in sickness,	3920
Isa	50: 4	to know the word *that* s the weary.	6431

SUSTENANCE (KJV) See FOOD, LIVING THING

SWADDLED, SWADDLING, SWADDLINGBAND (KJV) See CARED FOR, WRAPPED IN CLOTHS

SWALLOW (14) [SWALLOWED, SWALLOWING, SWALLOWS]

Nu	14: 9	because we will s them **up.**	4312
	16:34	shouting, "The earth *is going to* s us too!"	1180
2Sa	20:19	you want *to* s **up** the LORD's inheritance?"	1180
	20:20	"Far be it from me *to* s **up** or destroy!"	1180
Ps	21: 9	In his wrath the LORD *will* s them **up,**	1180
	69:15	the depths s me **up** or the pit close its mouth	1180
	84: 3	and the s a nest for herself,	2000
Pr	1:12	*let's* s them alive, like the grave,	1180
	26: 2	Like a fluttering sparrow or a darting s,	2000
Isa	25: 8	he will s **up** death forever.	1180
Hos	8: 7	foreigners *would* s it **up.**	1180
Jnh	1:17	the LORD provided a great fish to s Jonah,	1180
Hab	1:13	Why are you silent while the wicked s **up**	1180
Mt	23:24	You strain out a gnat but s a camel.	2927

SWALLOWED (22) [SWALLOW]

Ge	41: 7	heads of grain s **up** the seven healthy,	1180
	41:24	heads of grain s **up** the seven good heads.	1180
Ex	7:12	But Aaron's staff s **up** their staffs.	1180
	15:12	and the earth s them.	1180
Nu	16:32	and the earth opened its mouth and s them,	1180
	26:10	The earth opened its mouth and s them	1180
Dt	11: 6	in the middle of all Israel and s them **up**	1180
2Sa	17:16	and all the people with him *will* be s **up.'** "	1180
Job	20:15	He will spit out the riches he s;	1180
	37:20	Would any man ask *to* be s **up?**	1180
Ps	35:25	or say, "We have s him **up.**"	1180
	106:17	The earth opened **up** and s Dathan;	1180
	124: 3	*they* would have s us alive;	1180
Jer	51:34	a serpent *he has* s us and filled his stomach	1180
	51:44	and make him spew out **what** he has s.	1183
La	2: 2	the Lord *has* s **up** all the dwellings of Jacob;	1180
	2: 5	Lord is like an enemy; *he has* s **up** Israel.	1180
	2: 5	*He has* s **up** all her palaces	1180
	2:16	"We have s her **up.**	1180
Hos	8: 8	Israel is s **up;** now she is among the nations	1180
1Co	15:54	"Death *has been* s **up** in victory."	2927
2Co	5: 4	so that what is mortal *may be* s **up** by life.	2927

SWALLOWING (1) [SWALLOW]

Rev	12:16	by opening its mouth and s the river that	2927

SWALLOWS (2) [SWALLOW]

Nu	16:30	and the earth opens its mouth and s them,	1180
Isa	28: 4	and takes it in his hand, *he* s it.	1180

SWAMPED (2) [SWAMPLAND, SWAMPS]

Mk	4:37	so that it *was* nearly s.	1153
Lk	8:23	so that the boat *was being* s,	5230

SWAMPLAND (1) [SWAMPED]

Isa	14:23	into a place for owls and into s;	106+4784

SWAMPS (1) [SWAMPED]

Eze	47:11	the s and marshes will not become fresh;	1289

SWARM (11) [SWARMED, SWARMING, SWARMS]

Ge	7:21	all the creatures that s over the earth,	9237
Ex	10:12	over Egypt so that locusts *will* s over	6590
Dt	1:44	a s **of bees** and beat you down from Seir all	1805
	14:19	All flying **insects that** s are unclean to you;	9238
Jdg	14: 8	In it was a s **of bees** and some honey,	6337
Isa	33: 4	like a s of locusts men pounce on it	5480
Jer	12:12	the desert destroyers *will* s, for the sword	995
	51:14	fill you with men, as with a s **of locusts,**	3540
	51:27	send up horses like a s of locusts.	6170
Joel	1: 4	What the **locust** s has left the great locusts	1612
	2:25	the other locusts and the **locust** s—	1612

SWARMED (1) [SWARM]

Ps	118:12	*They* s around me like bees,	6015

SWARMING (1) [SWARM]

Lev	11:10	whether among all the s **things** or among all	9238

SWARMS (10) [SWARM]

Ex	8:21	I will send s **of flies** on you	6856
	8:22	no s **of flies** will be there,	6856
	8:24	Dense s **of flies** poured into Pharaoh's	6856
Dt	28:42	S **of locusts** will take over all your trees	7526

Jdg	6: 5	and their tents like s *of* locusts.	1896
Ps	78:45	He sent s **of flies** that devoured them,	6856
	105:31	He spoke, and there came s **of flies,**	6856
Eze	47: 9	S of living creatures will live wherever	9237
Am	7: 1	He was preparing s **of locusts** after	1479
Na	3:17	your officials like s *of* locusts that settle in	1571

SWAN (KJV) See WHITE OWL

SWARE (KJV) See SWORE

SWAY (4) [SWAYED, SWAYING, SWAYS]

Jdg	9: 9	to **hold** s over the trees?'	5675
	9:11	to **hold** s over the trees?'	5675
	9:13	to **hold** s over the trees?'	5675
Ps	72:16	on the tops of the hills *may it* s.	8321

SWAYED (5) [SWAY]

Mt	11: 7	A reed s by the wind?	4888
	22:16	You aren't s by men, because you pay no	3508
Mk	12:14	You aren't s by men, because you pay no	3508
Lk	7:24	A reed s by the wind?	4888
2Ti	3: 6	who are loaded down with sins and *are* s	72

SWAYING (2) [SWAY]

1Ki	14:15	so that it will be like a reed s in the water.	5653
Jer	4:24	they were quaking; all the hills *were* s.	7837

SWAYS (3) [SWAY]

Job	28: 4	far from men he dangles and s.	5675
	40:17	His tail s like a cedar;	2912
Isa	24:20	*it* s like a hut in the wind;	5653

SWEAR (53) [SWEARING, SWEARS, SWORE, SWORN]

Ge	21:23	Now s to me here before God *that* you will	8678
	21:24	Abraham said, "I s it."	8678
	22:16	"I s by myself, declares the LORD,	8678
	24: 3	I **want** you *to* s by the LORD,	8678
	24:37	And my master made me s **an oath,**	8678
	25:33	But Jacob said, "S to me first."	8678
	47:31	"S to me," he said.	8678
	50: 5	'My father **made** me s **an oath**	8678
	50: 6	as *he* **made** you s *to do.*"	8678
	50:25	Joseph **made** the sons of Israel s **an oath**	8678
Ex	13:19	*had* **made** the sons of Israel s **an oath.**	8678+8678
Lev	5: 4	in any matter one might carelessly s about—	8652
	19:12	not s falsely by my name and so profane	8678
Jos	2:12	please s to me by the LORD	8678
	2:17	"This oath *you* **made** us s will not	8678
	2:20	be released from the oath *you* **made** us s."	8678
	23: 7	do not invoke the names of their gods or s	8678
Jdg	15:12	Samson said, "S to me that you won't kill	8678
1Sa	24:21	Now s to me by the LORD that you will	8678
	30:15	"S to me before God that if you don't go out,	8678
2Sa	19: 7	I s by the LORD that if you don't go out,	8678
1Ki	1:13	*did* you not s to me your servant?	8678
	1:51	'Let King Solomon s to me today	8678
	2:42	not **make** you s by the LORD and warn you,	8678
	18:10	*he* **made** them s they could not find you.	8678
	22:16	"How many times *must* I **make** you s	8678
2Ch	18:15	"How many times *must* I **make** you s	8678
Ps	24: 4	who does not lift up his soul to an idol or s	8678
	63:11	all who s by God's name will praise him,	8678
Isa	19:18	and s **allegiance** to the LORD Almighty.	8678
	45:23	by me every tongue *will* s.	8678
	65:16	he who takes an oath in the land *will* s by	8678
Jer	4: 2	just and righteous way *you* s,	8678
	12:16	the ways of my people and s by my name,	8678
	12:16	they once taught my people to s by Baal—	8678
	22: 5	I s by myself that this palace will become	8678
	44:26	'I s by my great name,' says the LORD,	8678
	44:26	or s, "As surely as the Sovereign LORD	606
	49:13	I s by myself," declares the LORD,	8678
Eze	36: 7	I s **with uplifted** hand that the nations	5951
Da	12: 7	and I heard him s by him who lives forever,	8678
Hos	4:15	And do not s, 'As surely as the LORD	8678
Am	8:14	They *who* s by the shame of Samaria,	8678
Zep	1: 5	those who bow down and s by the LORD	8678
	1: 5	by the LORD and who also s by Molech,	8678
Zec	8:17	and do not love to s falsely."	8652
Mt	5:34	But I tell you, Do not s at all:	3923
	5:36	And do not s by your head,	3923
Mk	5: 7	S to God that you won't torture me!"	3991
Heb	3:18	And to whom *did* God s that they would	3923
	6:13	there was no one greater for him *to* s by,	3923
	6:16	Men s by someone greater than themselves,	3923
Jas	5:12	*do* not s—not **by** heaven or by earth or	3923

SWEARING (1) [SWEAR]

Jer	5: 2	as the LORD lives,' still *they are* s falsely."	8678

SWEARS (15) [SWEAR]

Lev	6: 3	and lies about it, or if *he* s falsely,	8678
1Ki	8:31	to take an oath and he comes and s **the oath**	457
2Ch	6:22	to take an oath and he comes and s **the oath**	457
Zec	5: 3	everyone who s **falsely** will be banished.	8678
	5: 4	the house of him *who* s falsely by my name.	8678
Mt	23:16	You say, 'If anyone s by the temple,	3923
	23:16	but if anyone s by the gold of the temple,	3923
	23:18	You also say, 'If anyone s by the altar,	3923

Mt	23:18	but if anyone s by the gift on it,	3923
	23:20	he who s by the altar swears by it and	3923
	23:20	by the altar s by it and by everything on it.	3923
	23:21	And he who s by the temple swears by it	3923
	23:21	And he who swears by the temple s by it	3923
	23:22	And he who s by heaven swears by God's	3923
	23:22	by heaven s by God's throne and by	3923

SWEAT (2)

Ge	3:19	the s *of* your brow you will eat your food	2399
Lk	22:44	and his s was like drops of blood falling to	2629

SWEEP (22) [SWEEPING, SWEEPINGS, SWEEPS, SWEPT]

Ge	18:23	"Will you s away the righteous with	6200
	18:24	Will you really s it **away** and not spare	6200
Ps	90: 5	You s men **away** in the sleep of death;	2441
Isa	8: 8	and s on into Judah, swirling over it,	2736
	11:15	with a scorching wind *he will* s his hand	5677
	14:23	I will s her with the broom of destruction,"	3173
	28:17	hail *will* s away your refuge, the lie,	3589
	28:19	by day and by night, *it will* s **through.**"	6296
	43: 2	*they* will not s **over** you.	8851
	64: 6	and like the wind our sins s us **away.**	5951
Eze	5:17	Plague and bloodshed *will* s through you,	6296
Da	11:10	*which will* s **on** like an irresistible flood	995+995
	11:40	and s **through** them like a flood.	6296
Hos	4:19	A whirlwind *will* s them **away,**	928+4053+7674
Am	5: 9	or *he will* s **through** the house of Joseph	7502
Hab	1: 6	who s across the whole earth	2143
	1:11	Then *they* s past like the wind and go on—	2736
Zep	1: 2	"I will s everything from the face	665+6066
	1: 3	"I will s **away** both men and animals,"	6066
	1: 3	I will s **away** the birds of the air and	6066
Lk	15: 8	s the house and search carefully	4924
Rev	12:15	s her **away** with the torrent.	4472+4533

SWEEPING (1) [SWEEP]

Isa	21: 1	Like whirlwinds s through the southland,	2736

SWEEPINGS (1) [SWEEP]

Am	8: 6	selling even the s *with* the wheat.	5139

SWEEPS (7) [SWEEP]

Job	27:21	*it* s him **out** of his place.	8548
Pr	9:26	when disaster s **over** you like a whirlwind,	910
	13:23	but injustice s it **away.**	6200
Isa	28:15	When an overwhelming scourge s **by,**	6296
	28:18	When the overwhelming scourge s **by,**	6296
	40:24	and a whirlwind s them **away** like chaff.	5951
Zep	2: 2	the appointed time arrives and that day s **on**	6296

SWEET (26) [SWEETER, SWEETNESS]

Ex	15:25	and the water *became* s.	5517
Jdg	9:11	so good and s, to hold sway over the trees?'	5519
	14:14	out of the strong, *something* s."	5498
Ne	8:10	"Go and enjoy choice food and s drinks,	4941
Job	20:12	"Though evil *is* s in his mouth	5517
	21:33	The soil in the valley *is* s to him;	5517
Ps	55:14	with whom *I* once **enjoyed** s fellowship	5517
	119:103	How s *are* your words to my taste,	4914
Pr	3:24	when you lie down, your sleep *will be* s.	6844
	9:17	"Stolen water *is* s; food eaten in secret	5517
	13:19	A longing fulfilled *is* s to the soul,	6844
	16:24	s to the soul and healing to the bones.	5498
	20:17	Food gained by fraud **tastes** s to a man,	6853
	24:13	honey from the comb is s to your taste.	5498
	24:14	Know **also** that wisdom is s to your soul;	4027s
	27: 7	to the hungry even what is bitter tastes s.	5498
Ecc	5:12	The sleep of a laborer is s,	5498
	11: 7	Light is s, and it pleases the eyes to see	5498
SS	2: 3	and his fruit is s to my taste.	5498
	2:14	for your voice is s, and your face is lovely.	6853
Isa	5:20	who put bitter for s and sweet for bitter.	5498
	5:20	who put bitter for sweet and s for bitter.	5498
Jer	6:20	about incense from Sheba or s calamus	3203
Eze	3: 3	and it tasted as s as honey in my mouth.	5498
Rev	10: 9	but in your mouth it will be as s as honey."	1184
	10:10	*It* tasted as s as honey in my mouth,	1184+1639

SWEETER (3) [SWEET]

Jdg	14:18	"What is s than honey?	5498
Ps	19:10	they are s than honey, than honey from the	5498
	119:103	s than honey to my mouth!	NIH

SWEETNESS (2) [SWEET]

SS	4:11	Your lips drop s **as the honeycomb,**	5885
	5:16	His mouth is s *itself*;	4941

SWEETSMELLING (KJV) See FRAGRANT

SWELL (5) [SWELLING, SWELLS, SWOLLEN]

Nu	5:21	to waste away and your abdomen to s.	7379
	5:27	her abdomen *will* s and her thigh waste	7377
Dt	8: 4	not wear out and your feet *did* not s	1301
Isa	60: 5	your heart will throb and s **with joy;**	8143
Ac	28: 6	The people expected him to s **up**	4399

SWELLING (6) [SWELL]
Lev	13: 2	a s or a rash or a bright spot on his skin	8421
	13:10	a white s in the skin that has turned	8421
	13:10	and if there is raw flesh in the s,	8421
	13:19	a white s or reddish-white spot appears,	8421
	13:28	it is a *from* the burn,	8421
	14:56	and for a s, a rash or a bright spot,	8421

SWELLS (1) [SWELL]
Nu	5:22	so that your abdomen s and your thigh	7377

SWELTER (1)
Job	37:17	You who s in your clothes when	2768

SWEPT (32) [SWEEP]
Ge	19:15	or *you will* be s away when the city	6200
	19:17	to the mountains or *you will* be s away!”	6200
Ex	14:27	and the LORD s them into the sea.	5850
Nu	16:26	or *you will* be s away because	6200
Jdg	5:21	The river Kishon s them away,	1759
1Sa	12:25	both you and your king *will* be s away.”	6200
1Ch	21:12	of *being* s away before your enemies,	6200
Job	1:17	and s down on your camels	7320
	1:19	when suddenly a mighty wind s in from	995
	5:13	and the schemes of the wily *are* s away.	4554
	21:18	like chaff s away by a gale?	1704
	37:21	in the skies after the wind has s them clean.	6296
Ps	42: 7	all your waves and breakers *have* s over me.	6296
	58: 9	the wicked *will* be s away.	8548
	73:19	completely s away by terrors!	6200
	88:16	Your wrath *has* s over me;	6296
	124: 4	the torrent *would have* s over us,	6296
	124: 5	the raging waters *would have* s us away.	6296
	136:15	s Pharaoh and his army into the Red Sea;	5850
Pr	10:25	When the storm *has* s by,	6296
Isa	44:22	I have s away your offenses like a cloud,	4681
Da	2:35	The wind s them away without leaving	10492
	11:22	an overwhelming army *will* be s away	8851
	11:26	his army *will* be s away,	8851
Jnh	2: 3	all your waves and breakers s over me.	6296
Mic	7: 2	The godly *have been* s from the land;	6
Hab	3:10	Torrents of water s by;	6296
Mt	8:24	so that the waves s over the boat.	2821
	12:44	s clean and put in order.	4924
Lk	11:25	it finds the house s clean and put in order.	4924
Ac	27:14	the “northeaster,” s down from the island.	965
Rev	12: 4	His tail s a third of the stars out of the sky	5359

SWERVE (2) [SWERVING]
Pr	4: 5	do not forget my words or s from them.	5742
	4:27	*Do* not s *to* the right or the left;	5742

SWERVING (1) [SWERVE]
Joel	2: 7	march in line, not s *from* their course.	6293

SWIFT (16) [SWIFTER, SWIFTLY]
1Ch	12: 8	they were as s as gazelles in the mountains.	4554
Pr	1:16	*they are* s to shed blood,	4554
Ecc	9:11	The race is not to the s or the battle to	7824
Isa	18: 2	Go, s messengers, to a people tall	7824
	19: 1	on a s cloud and is coming to Egypt.	7824
	30:16	You said, ‘We will ride off on s horses.’	7824
	30:16	Therefore your pursuers *will be* s!	7837
	38:14	I cried like a s or thrush,	6101
	59: 7	*they are* s to shed innocent blood.	4554
Jer	2:23	a she-camel running here and there,	7824
	8: 7	the s and the thrush observe the time	6101
	46: 6	“The s cannot flee nor the strong escape.	7824
Da	9:21	came to me in s **flight** about the time	3616+3618
Am	2:14	The s will not escape,	7824
Ro	3:15	“Their feet are s to shed blood;	3955
2Pe	2: 1	bringing s destruction on themselves.	5442

SWIFTER (6) [SWIFT]
2Sa	1:23	*They were* s than eagles,	7837
Job	7: 6	“My days *are* s than a weaver’s shuttle,	7837
	9:25	“My days *are* s than a runner;	7837
Jer	4:13	his horses *are* s than eagles.	7837
La	4:19	Our pursuers were s than eagles in the sky;	7824
Hab	1: 8	Their horses *are* s than leopards,	7837

SWIFTLY (4) [SWIFT]
Ps	147:15	his word runs s.	4559+6330
Isa	5:26	Here they come, s and speedily!	4559
	60:22	in its time I *will* do this s.”	2590
Joel	3: 4	I will s and speedily return on your own	7824

SWIM (4) [SWIMMER, SWIMMING]
Ps	8: 8	all *that* s the paths of the seas.	6296
Isa	25:11	as a swimmer spreads out his hands to s.	8466
Eze	47: 5	and was **deep enough to** s in—	8467
Ac	27:43	He ordered those who could s	3147

SWIMMER (1) [SWIM]
Isa	25:11	as a s spreads out his hands to swim.	8466

SWIMMING (1) [SWIM]
Ac	27:42	to prevent any of them *from* s away	1713

SWINDLER (1) [SWINDLERS]
1Co	5:11	an idolater or a slanderer, a drunkard or a s.	774

SWINDLERS (2) [SWINDLER]
1Co	5:10	or the greedy and s, or idolaters.	774
	6:10	nor s will inherit the kingdom of God.	774

SWINE (KJV) See PIG

SWING (3) [SWINGS, SWUNG]
Ex	28:28	so that the breastpiece *will* not s *out* from	2322
	39:21	that the breastpiece *would* not s *out* from	2322
Joel	3:13	S the sickle, for the harvest is ripe.	8938

SWINGS (2) [SWING]
Dt	19: 5	and as he s his ax to fell a tree,	5616
Isa	10:15	Does the ax raise itself above him *who* s it,	2933

SWIRL (1) [SWIRLED, SWIRLING]
Job	37:12	At his direction they s around over the face	2200

SWIRLED (2) [SWIRL]
2Sa	22: 5	“The waves of death s about me;	705
Jnh	2: 3	and the currents s about me;	6015

SWIRLING (4) [SWIRL]
Isa	8: 8	and sweep on into Judah, s over it, passing	8851
Jer	23:19	a whirlwind s down on the heads of	2565
	30:23	a driving wind s down on the heads of	2565
Hos	13: 3	like chaff s from a threshing floor,	6192

SWOLLEN (3) [SWELL]
Lev	13:43	and if the s sore on his head	8421
Ne	9:21	not wear out nor *did* their feet *become* s.	1301
Job	6:16	by thawing ice and s with melting snow,	6623

SWOON, SWOONED (KJV) See FAINT

SWOOP (2) [SWOOPING]
Isa	11:14	*They will* s down on the slopes of Philistia	6414
Jer	49:22	An eagle will soar and s down,	1797

SWOOPING (4) [SWOOP]
Dt	28:49	like an eagle s down,	1797
Job	9:26	like eagles s down on their prey.	3216
Jer	48:40	An eagle *is* s down, spreading its wings	1797
Hab	1: 8	They fly like a vulture s to devour;	2590

SWORD (402) [SWORDS, SWORDSMEN]
Ge	3:24	a flaming s flashing back and forth to guard	2995
	27:40	by the s and you will serve your brother.	2995
	34:26	put Hamor and his son Shechem to the s	2995
	48:22	from the Amorites with my s and my bow.”	2995
Ex	5: 3	he may strike us with plagues or with the s.”	2995
	5:21	to Pharaoh and his officials and have put a s	2995
	15: 9	I will draw my s and my hand will destroy	2995
	17:13	the Amalekite army with the s.	2995
	18: 4	he saved me from the s *of* Pharaoh.”	2995
	22:24	and I will kill you with the s;	2995
	32:27	‘Each man strap a s to his side.	2995
Lev	26: 6	the s will not pass through your country.	2995
	26: 7	and they will fall by the s before you.	2995
	26: 8	your enemies will fall by the s before you.	2995
	26:25	And I will bring the s upon you to avenge	2995
	26:33	among the nations and will draw out my s	2995
	26:36	They will run as though fleeing from the s,	2995
	26:37	as though fleeing from the s,	2995
Nu	14: 3	to this land only to let us fall by the s?	2995
	14:43	not be with you and you will fall by the s.”	2995
	19:16	with a s or someone who has died	2995
	20:18	and attack you with the s.”	2995
	21:24	put him to the s and took over his land from	2995
	22:23	in the road with a drawn s in his hand,	2995
	22:29	If I had a s in my hand,	2995
	22:31	in the road with his s drawn.	2995
	31: 8	also killed Balaam son of Beor with the s.	2995
Dt	13:15	you must certainly put to the s all who live	2995
	20:13	put to the s all the men in it.	2995
	32:25	In the street the s will make them childless;	2995
	32:41	when I sharpen my flashing s	2995
	32:42	while my s devours flesh:	2995
	33:29	and helper and your glorious s.	2995
Jos	5:13	in front of him with a drawn s in his hand.	2995
	6:21	and destroyed with the s every living thing	2995
	8:24	every one of them had been put to the s,	2995
	10:28	to the s and totally destroyed everyone in it.	2995
	10:30	and everyone in it Joshua put to the s.	2995
	10:32	The city and everyone in it he put to the s,	2995
	10:35	to the s and totally destroyed everyone in it,	2995
	10:37	They took the city and put it to the s,	2995
	10:39	and put them to the s.	2995
	11:10	and put its king to the s.	2995
	11:11	Everyone in it they put to the s.	2995
	11:12	their kings and put them to the s.	2995
	11:14	the s until they completely destroyed them,	2995
	13:22	the Israelites had put to the s Balaam son	2995
	19:47	took it, put it to the s and occupied it.	2995
	24:12	You did not do it with your own s and bow.	2995
Jdg	1: 8	They put the city to the s and set it on fire.	2995

Jdg	1:25	and they put the city to the s but spared	2995
	3:16	Now Ehud had made a double-edged s	2995
	3:21	the s from his right thigh and plunged it	2995
	3:22	Ehud did not pull the s out,	2995
	4:15	and all his chariots and army by the s,	2995
	4:16	All the troops of Sisera fell by the s;	2995
	7:14	be nothing other than the s *of* Gideon son	2995
	7:20	“A s for the LORD and for Gideon!”	2995
	8:20	But Jether did not draw his s,	2995
	9:54	“Draw your s and kill me.	2995
	18:27	They attacked them with the s and burned	2995
	20:37	spread out and put the whole city to the s,	2995
	20:48	to Benjamin and put all the towns to the s,	2995
	21:10	and put to the s those living there,	2995
1Sa	13:22	not a soldier with Saul and Jonathan had a s	2995
	15: 8	all his people he totally destroyed with the s.	2995
	15:33	“As your s has made women childless,	2995
	17:39	on his s over the tunic and tried walking	2995
	17:45	against me with s and spear and javelin,	2995
	17:47	not by s or spear that the LORD saves;	2995
	17:50	a s in his hand he struck down the Philistine	2995
	17:51	of the Philistine’s s and drew it from	2995
	17:51	he killed him, he cut off his head with **the** s.	2023S
	18: 4	and even his s, his bow and his belt.	2995
	21: 8	“Don’t you have a spear or a s here?	2995
	21: 8	I haven’t brought my s or any other weapon,	2995
	21: 9	“The s *of* Goliath the Philistine,	2995
	21: 9	there is no s here but that one.”	337S
	22:10	he also gave him provisions and the s	2995
	22:13	giving him bread and a s and inquiring	2995
	22:19	He also put to the s Nob,	2995
	31: 4	“Draw your s and run me through,	2995
	31: 4	so Saul took his own s and fell on it.	2995
	31: 5	he too fell on his s and died with him.	2995
2Sa	1:12	because they had fallen by the s.	2995
	1:22	the s of Saul did not return unsatisfied.	2995
	2:26	“Must the s devour forever?	2995
	3:29	or who falls by the s or who lacks food.”	2995
	11:25	the s devours one as well as another.	2995
	12: 9	with the s and took his wife to be your own.	2995
	12: 9	with the s *of* the Ammonites.	2995
	12:10	the s will never depart from your house,	2995
	15:14	upon us and put the city to the s.”	2995
	18: 8	claimed more lives that day than the s.	2995
	21:16	and who was armed with a new [s],	NIH
	23:10	till his hand grew tired and froze to the s.	2995
	24: 9	able-bodied men who could handle a s,	2995
1Ki	1:51	not put his servant to death with the s.’ ”	2995
	2: 8	‘I will not put you to death by the s.’	2995
	2:32	and killed them with the s.	2995
	3:24	Then the king said, “Bring me a s.”	2995
	3:24	So they brought a s for the king.	2995
	19: 1	he had killed all the prophets with the s.	2995
	19:10	and put your prophets to death with the s,	2995
	19:14	and put your prophets to death with the s.	2995
	19:17	Jehu will put to death any who escape the s	2995
	19:17	to death any who escape the s *of* Jehu.	2995
2Ki	6:22	with your own s or bow?	2995
	8:12	kill their young men with the s,	2995
	10:25	So they cut them down with the s.	2995
	11:15	and put to the s anyone who follows her.”	2995
	11:20	because Athaliah had been slain with the s	2995
	19: 7	there I will have him cut down with the s.’ ”	2995
	19:37	and Sharezer cut him down with the s,	2995
1Ch	5:18	handle shield and s, and could use a bow,	2995
	10: 4	“Draw your s and run me through,	2995
	10: 4	so Saul took his own s and fell on it.	2995
	10: 5	he too fell on his s and died.	2995
	21: 5	men who could handle a s,	2995
	21:12	or three days of the s of the LORD—	2995
	21:16	with a drawn s in his hand extended	2995
	21:27	and he put his s back into its sheath.	2995
	21:30	because he was afraid of the s of the angel	2995
2Ch	20: 9	whether the s of judgment,	2995
	21: 4	to the s along with some of the princes	2995
	23:14	and put to the s anyone who follows her.”	2995
	23:21	because Athaliah had been slain with the s.	2995
	29: 9	This is why our fathers have fallen by the s	2995
	32:21	some of his sons cut him down with the s.	2995
	36:17	who killed their young men with the s in	2995
	36:20	who escaped from the s,	2995
Ezr	9: 7	and our priests have been subjected to the s	2995
Ne	4:18	of the builders wore his s at his side	2995
Est	9: 5	down all their enemies with the s,	2995
Job	1:15	They put the servants to the s,	2995
	1:17	They put the servants to the s,	2995
	5:15	the needy from the s in their mouth;	2995
	5:20	and in battle from the stroke of the s.	2995
	15:22	he is marked for the s.	2995
	19:29	you should fear the s yourselves;	2995
	19:29	for wrath will bring punishment by the s,	2995
	27:14	their fate is the s;	2995
	33:18	his life from perishing by the s.	8939
	36:12	by the s and die without knowledge.	8939
	39:22	he does not shy away from the s.	2995
	40:19	yet his Maker can approach him with his s.	2995
	41:26	The s that reaches him has no effect,	2995
Ps	7:12	If he does not relent, he will sharpen his s;	2995
	17:13	rescue me from the wicked by your s.	2995
	22:20	Deliver my life from the s,	2995
	37:14	The wicked draw the s and bend the bow	2995
	44: 3	It was not by their s that they won the land,	2995
	44: 6	my s does not bring me victory;	2995
	45: 3	Gird your s upon your side, O mighty one;	2995
	63:10	over to the s and become food for jackals.	2995
	78:62	He gave his people over to the s;	2995
	78:64	their priests were put to the s,	2995

Ps 89:43 You have turned back the edge of his s 2995
144:10 his servant David from the deadly s. 2995
149: 6 be in their mouths and a double-edged s 2995
Pr 5: 4 sharp as a double-edged s. 2995
12:18 Reckless words pierce like a s, 2995
25:18 Like a club or a s or a sharp arrow is 2995
SS 3: 8 all of them wearing the s, 2995
3: 8 each with his s at his side, 2995
Isa 1:20 you will be devoured by the s." 2995
2: 4 Nation will not take up s against nation, 2995
3:25 Your men will fall by the s, 2995
13:15 all who are caught will fall by the s. 2995
14:19 with those pierced by the s, 2995
21:15 They flee from the s, 2995
21:15 flee from the sword, from the drawn s, 2995
22: 2 Your slain were not killed by the s, 2995
27: 1 the LORD will punish with his s, 2995
27: 1 his fierce, great and powerful s, NIH
31: 8 "Assyria will fall by a s that is not of man; 2995
31: 8 a s, not of mortals, will devour them. 2995
31: 8 before the s and their young men will 2995
34: 5 My s has drunk its fill in the heavens; 2995
34: 6 The s of the LORD is bathed in blood, 2995
37: 7 there I will have him cut down with the s.' " 2995
37:38 and Sharezer cut him down with the s, 2995
41: 2 He turns them to dust with his s, 2995
49: 2 He made my mouth like a sharpened s, 2995
51:19 ruin and destruction, famine and s— 2995
65:12 for the s, and you will all bend down for 2995
66:16 For with the s and with his s 2995
Jer 2:30 Your s has devoured your prophets like 2995
4:10 when the s is at our throats." 2995
5:12 we will never see s or famine. 2995
5:17 the s they will destroy the fortified cities 2995
6:25 for the enemy has a s, 2995
9:16 with the s until I have destroyed them." 2995
11:22 Their young men will die by the s, 2995
12:12 for the s of the LORD will devour 2995
14:12 Instead, I will destroy them with the s, 2995
14:13 'You will not see the s or suffer famine. 2995
14:15 'No s or famine will touch this land. 2995
14:15 Those same prophets will perish by s 2995
14:16 of Jerusalem because of the famine and s. 2995
14:18 I see those slain by the s; 2995
15: 2 those for the s, to the sword; 2995
15: 2 those for the sword, to the s. 2995
15: 3 "the s to kill and the dogs to drag away and 2995
15: 9 the survivors to the s before their enemies," 2995
16: 4 They will perish by s and famine, 2995
18:21 hand them over to the power of the s. 2995
18:21 their young men slain by the s in battle. 2995
19: 7 fall by the s before their enemies, 2995
20: 4 fall by the s of their enemies. 2995
20: 4 away to Babylon or put them to the s. 2995
21: 7 s and famine, to Nebuchadnezzar king 2995
21: 7 He will put them to the s; 2995
21: 9 Whoever stays in this city will die by the s, 2995
24:10 I will send the s, famine and plague 2995
25:16 because of the s I will send among them." 2995
25:27 to rise no more because of the s I will send 2995
25:29 for I am calling down a s upon all who live 2995
25:31 and put the wicked to the s,' " 2995
25:38 of the s of the oppressor and because of 2995
26:23 down with a s and his body thrown into 2995
27: 8 I will punish that nation with the s, 2995
27:13 Why will you and your people die by the s, 2995
29:17 "I will send the s, famine and plague 2995
29:18 I will pursue them with the s, famine 2995
31: 2 the s will find favor in the desert; 2995
32:24 Because of the s, famine and plague, 2995
32:36 "You are saying about this city, 'By the s, 2995
33: 4 to be used against the siege ramps and the s 2995
34: 4 You will not die by the s; 2995
34:17 'freedom' to fall by the s, plague and 2995
38: 2 in this city will die by the s, famine or 2995
39:18 you will not fall by the s but will escape 2995
41: 2 the son of Shaphan, with the s, 2995
42:16 then the s you fear will overtake you there, 2995
42:17 to Egypt to settle there will die by the s, 2995
42:22 You will die by the s, famine and plague 2995
43:11 and to those destined for the sword. 2995
43:11 and the sword to those destined for the s. 2995
44:12 they will fall by the s or die from famine. 2995
44:12 they will die by s or famine. 2995
44:13 in Egypt with the s, famine and plague. 2995
44:18 been perishing by s and famine." 2995
44:27 by s and famine until they are all destroyed. 2995
44:28 Those who escape the s and return to 2995
46:10 The s will devour till it is satisfied, 2995
46:14 for the s devours those around you.' 2995
46:16 away from the s of the oppressor.' 2995
47: 6 " 'Ah, s of the LORD,' 2995
48: 2 the s will pursue you. 2995
48:10 on him who keeps his s from bloodshed! 2995
49:37 with the s until I have made an end of them. 2995
50:16 of the s of the oppressor let everyone return 2995
50:35 "A s against the Babylonians!" 2995
50:36 A s against her false prophets! 2995
50:36 A s against her warriors! 2995
50:37 A s against her horses and chariots and all 2995
50:37 A s against her treasures! 2995
51:50 You who have escaped the s, 2995
La 1:20 Outside, the s bereaves; 2995
2:21 and maidens have fallen by the s. 2995
4: 9 by the s are better off than those who die 2995
5: 9 of our lives because of the s in the desert. 2995
Eze 5: 1 take a sharp s and use it as a barber's razor 2995

Eze 5: 2 and strike it with the s all around the city. 2995
5: 2 For I will pursue them with drawn s. 2995
5:12 a third will fall by the s outside your walls; 2995
5:12 to the winds and pursue with drawn s, 2995
5:17 and I will bring the s against you. 2995
6: 3 I am about to bring a s against you, 2995
6: 8 the s when you are scattered among 2995
6:11 for they will fall by the s, 2995
6:12 and he that is near will fall by the s, 2995
7:15 the s, inside are plague and famine; 2995
7:15 those in the country will die by the s, 2995
11: 8 You fear the s, and the sword is what 2995
11: 8 and the s is what I will bring against you, 2995
11:10 You will fall by the s, 2995
12:14 and I will pursue them with drawn s. 2995
12:16 But I will spare a few of them from the s, 2995
14:17 if I bring a s against that country and say, 2995
14:17 'Let the s pass throughout the land,' 2995
14:21 s and famine and wild beasts and plague— 2995
17:21 All his fleeing troops will fall by the s, 2995
21: 3 I will draw my s from its scabbard 2995
21: 4 my s will be unsheathed against everyone 2995
21: 5 that I the LORD have drawn my s 2995
21: 9 " 'A s, a sword, sharpened and polished— 2995
21: 9 " 'A sword, a s, sharpened and polished— 2995
21:10 The s despises every such stick. NIH
21:11 " 'The s is appointed to be polished, 2995
21:13 They are thrown to the s along 2995
21:13 which the s despises, does not continue? NIH
21:14 Let the s strike twice, even three times. 2995
21:14 It is a s for slaughter— 2995
21:14 a s for great slaughter, 2995
21:15 the s for slaughter at all their gates. 2995
21:16 O s, slash to the right, then to the left, NIH
21:19 mark out two roads for the s of the king 2995
21:20 Mark out one road for the s to come 2995
21:28 " 'A s, a sword, drawn for the slaughter, 2995
21:28 " 'A sword, a s, drawn for the slaughter, 2995
21:30 Return the s to its scabbard. NIH
23:10 and daughters and killed her with the s. 2995
23:25 those of you who are left will fall by the s. 2995
24:21 behind will fall by the s. 2995
25:13 to Dedan they will fall by the s. 2995
26: 6 on the mainland will be ravaged by the s. 2995
26: 8 on the mainland with the s; 2995
26:11 he will kill your people with the s, 2995
28:23 with the s against her on every side. 2995
29: 8 a s against you and kill your men 2995
30: 4 A s will come against Egypt, 2995
30: 5 of the covenant land will fall by the s along 2995
30: 6 to Aswan they will fall by the s within her, 2995
30:17 and Bubastis will fall by the s, 2995
30:21 so as to become strong enough to hold a s. 2995
30:22 and make the s fall from his hand. 2995
30:24 of Babylon and put my s in his hand, 2995
30:25 when I put my s into the hand of the king 2995
31:17 joining those killed by the s. 2995
31:18 with those killed by the s. 2995
32:10 of you when I brandish my s before them. 2995
32:11 " 'The s of the king of Babylon will come 2995
32:20 They will fall among those killed by the s. 2995
32:20 The s is drawn; 2995
32:21 with those killed by the s.' 2995
32:22 all who have fallen by the s. 2995
32:23 are slain, fallen by the s, 2995
32:24 All of them are slain, fallen by the s. 2995
32:25 uncircumcised, killed by the s. 2995
32:26 by the s because they spread their terror in 2995
32:28 with those killed by the s. 2995
32:29 they are laid with those killed by the s, 2995
32:30 by the s and bear their shame 2995
32:31 for all his hordes that were killed by the s, 2995
32:32 with those killed by the s, 2995
33: 2 'When I bring the s against a land, 2995
33: 3 and he sees the s coming against the land 2995
33: 4 but does not take warning and the s comes 2995
33: 6 the s coming and does not blow the trumpet 2995
33: 6 the s comes and takes the life of one 2995
33:26 You rely on your s, 2995
33:27 in the ruins will fall by the s, 2995
35: 5 and delivered the Israelites over to the s at 2995
35: 8 those killed by the s will fall on your hills 2995
38:21 a s against Gog on all my mountains, 2995
38:21 Every man's s will be against his brother. 2995
39:23 and they all fell by the s. 2995
Da 11:33 the s or be burned or captured or plundered. 2995
Hos 1: 7 not by bow, s or battle, 2995
2:18 Bow and s and battle I will abolish from 2995
7:16 by the s because of their insolent words. 2995
13:16 They will fall by the s; 2995
Am 1:11 Because he pursued his brother with a s, 2995
4:10 I killed your young men with the s, 2995
7: 9 with my s I will rise against the house 2995
7:11 "'Jeroboam will die by the s, 2995
7:17 your sons and daughters will fall by the s. 2995
9: 1 those who are left I will kill with the s. 2995
9: 4 there I will command the s to slay them. 2995
9:10 among my people will die by the s, 2995
Mic 4: 3 Nation will not take up s against nation, 2995
5: 6 the land of Assyria with the s, 2995
5: 6 the land of Nimrod with drawn s. 7347
Na 2:13 and the s will devour your young lions. 2995
Zep 2:12 O Cushites, will be slain by my s." 2995
Hag 2:22 each by the s of his brother. 2995
Zec 9:13 O Greece, and make you like a warrior's s. 2995

Zec 11:17 May the s strike his arm and his right eye! 2995
13: 7 "Awake, O s, against my shepherd, 2995
Mt 10:34 I did not come to bring peace, but a s. 3479
26:51 one of Jesus' companions reached for his s, 3479
26:52 "Put your s back in its place," 3479
26:52 all who draw the s will die by the sword. 3479
26:52 all who draw the sword will die by the s. 3479
Mk 14:47 of those standing near drew his s and struck 3479
Lk 2:35 And a s will pierce your own soul too." 4855
21:24 They will fall by the s and 3479+5125
22:36 and if you don't have a s, 3479
Jn 18:10 Then Simon Peter, who had a s, 3479
18:11 Jesus commanded Peter, "Put your s away! 3479
Ac 12: 2 the brother of John, put to death with the s. 3479
16:27 he drew his s and was about to kill himself 3479
Ro 8:35 or famine or nakedness or danger or s? 3479
13: 4 for he does not bear the s for nothing. 3479
Eph 6:17 Take the helmet of salvation and the s of 3479
Heb 4:12 Sharper than any double-edged s, 3479
11:34 and escaped the edge of the s; 3479+5125
11:37 they were put to death by the s. 3479
Rev 1:16 of his mouth came a sharp double-edged s. 4855
2:12 of him who has the sharp, double-edged s. 4855
2:16 to you and will fight against them with the s 4855
6: 4 To him was given a large s. 3479
6: 8 over a fourth of the earth to kill by s, 4855
13:10 If anyone is to be killed with the s, 3479
13:10 with the s he will be killed. 3479
13:14 of the beast who was wounded by the s and 3479
19:15 of his mouth comes a sharp s with which 4855
19:21 of them were killed by the s that came out 4855

SWORDS (40) [SWORD]

Ge 34:25 took their s and attacked 2995
49: 5 their s are weapons of violence. 4839
Jos 10:11 the hailstones than were killed by the s of 2995
Jdg 7:22 the camp to turn on each other with their s. 2995
20: 2 four hundred thousand soldiers armed with s 2995
20:25 all of them armed with s. 2995
20:35 Benjamites, all armed with s. 2995
1Sa 13:19 "Otherwise the Hebrews will make s 2995
14:20 striking each other with their s. 2995
25:13 David said to his men, "Put on your s!" 2995
25:13 So they put on their s, 2995
1Ki and slashed themselves with s and spears, 2995
1Ch 21:12 with their s overtaking you, 2995
Ne 4:13 posting them by families, with their s, 2995
Ps 37:15 But their s will pierce their own hearts, 2995
55:21 yet they are drawn s. 7347
57: 4 whose tongues are sharp s. 2995
59: 7 they spew out s from their lips, 2995
64: 3 They sharpen their tongues like s 2995
76: 3 the shields and the s, the weapons of war. 2995
Pr 30:14 those whose teeth are s and whose jaws 2995
Isa 2: 4 They will beat their s into plowshares 2995
Eze 16:40 and hack you to pieces with their s. 2995
23:47 and cut them down with their s; 2995
28: 7 they will draw their s against your beauty 2995
30:11 They will draw their s against Egypt 2995
32:12 I will cause your hordes to fall by the s 2995
32:27 whose s were placed under their heads? 2995
38: 4 all of them brandishing their s. 2995
Hos 11: 6 S will flash in their cities, 2995
Joel 3:10 into s and your pruning hooks into spears. 2995
Mic 4: 3 They will beat their s into plowshares 2995
Na 3: 3 flashing s and glittering spears! 2995
Mt 26:47 With him was a large crowd armed with s 3479
26:55 that you have come out with s and clubs 3479
Mk 14:43 With him was a crowd armed with s 3479
14:48 "that you have come out with s and clubs 3479
Lk 22:38 "See, Lord, here are two s." 3479
22:49 "Lord, should we strike with our s?" 3479
22:52 that you have come with s and clubs? 3479

SWORDSMEN (5) [SWORD]

Jdg 8:10 a hundred and twenty thousand s had fallen. 408+2995+8990
20:15 Benjamites mobilized twenty-six thousand s 408+2995+8990
20:17 mustered four hundred thousand s, 408+2995+8990
20:46 that day twenty-five thousand Benjamite s fell, 408+2995+8990
2Ki 3:26 with him seven hundred s to 408+2995+8990

SWORE (60) [SWEAR]

Ge 21:31 because the two men s an oath there. 8678
24: 9 and s an oath to him concerning this matter. 8678
25:33 So he s an oath to him, 8678
26: 3 the oath I s to your father Abraham. 8678
26:31 Early the next morning the men s an oath 8678
47:31 Then Joseph s to him, 8678
Ex 6: 8 to the land I s with uplifted hand to give 5951
13: 5 the land he s to your forefathers to give you, 8678
32:13 to whom you s by your own self: 8678
Lev 6: 5 or whatever it was he s falsely about. 8678
Nu 14:16 the land I s with uplifted hand to make 5951
32:10 that day and he s this oath: 8678
Dt 1: 8 of the land that the LORD s he would give 8678
1:34 he was angry and solemnly s: 8678
1:35 the good land I s to give your forefathers, 8678
4:21 and he solemnly s that I would not cross 8678
6:10 into the land he s to your fathers, 8678
7: 8 the LORD loved you and kept the oath he s 8678
7:12 as he s to your forefathers. 8678

Dt	7:13	in the land that *he* s to your forefathers	8678
	8:18	which *he* s to your forefathers, as it is today.	8678
	9: 5	to accomplish what *he* s to your fathers,	8678
	10:11	and possess the land that *I* s to their fathers	8678
	11: 9	that the LORD s to your forefathers to give	8678
	11:21	that the LORD s to give your forefathers	8678
	26: 3	the LORD s to our forefathers to give us."	8678
	28:11	in the land *he* s to your forefathers	8678
	29:13	be your God as he promised you and as *he* s	8678
	30:20	in the land he s to give to your fathers,	8678
	31: 7	that the LORD s to their forefathers	8678
Jos	1: 6	to inherit the land *I* s to their forefathers	8678
	9:20	on us for breaking the oath *we* s to them."	8678
	14: 9	So on that day Moses s to me,	8678
Jdg	2: 1	the land that *I* s to give to your forefathers.	8678
1Sa	3:14	Therefore, *I* s to the house of Eli,	8678
	28:10	Saul s to her by the LORD.	8678
2Sa	21:17	Then David's men s to him, saying,	8678
1Ki	1:17	*you* yourself s to me your servant by	8678
	1:30	surely carry out today what *I* s to you by	8678
	2: 8	*I* s to him by the LORD:	8678
	2:23	Then King Solomon s by the LORD:	8678
1Ch	16:16	the oath he s to Isaac.	8652
Ps	89:49	which in your faithfulness *you* s to David?	NIH
	105: 9	the oath he s to Isaac.	NIH
	106:26	So he s to them with **uplifted** hand	5951
	132: 2	He s **an oath** to the LORD and made	8678
	132:11	The LORD s **an oath** to David,	8678
Isa	54: 9	when *I* s that the waters	8678
Jer	11: 5	I will fulfill the oath *I* s to your forefathers,	8678
	38:16	But King Zedekiah s *this* oath secretly	8678
Eze	20: 5	I s **with uplifted** hand to the descendants	5951
	20: 6	On that day *I* s to them	3338+5951
	20:15	**with uplifted** hand I s to them in the desert	5951
	20:23	**with uplifted** hand I s to them in the desert	5951
	47:14	Because I s **with uplifted** hand to give it	5951
Mt	26:74	down curses on himself and s to them,	3923
Mk	14:71	and *he* s to them, "I don't know this man	3923
Lk	1:73	the oath he s to our father Abraham:	3923
Heb	6:13	for him to swear by, *he* s by himself,	3923
Rev	10: 6	*he* s by him who lives for ever and ever,	3923

SWORN (31) [SWEAR]

Ge	26:28	we said, 'There ought to be a s **agreement**	460
Nu	30:13	or any s pledge to deny herself.	8652
Dt	2:14	as the LORD *had* s to them.	8678
Jos	5: 6	the LORD *had* s to them that they would	8678
	9:18	the leaders of the assembly *had* s **an oath**	8678
	21:43	the LORD gave Israel all the land *he had* s	8678
	21:44	just as *he had* s to their forefathers.	8678
Jdg	2:15	just as he *had* s to them.	8678
1Sa	20:42	for we *have* s friendship with each other in	8678
2Sa	21: 2	the Israelites *had* s to [spare] them,	8678
2Ch	15:15	because *they had* s it wholeheartedly.	8678
Ne	9:15	of the land *you had* s **with uplifted** hand	5951
Ps	89: 3	*I have* s to David my servant,	8678
	89:35	Once for all, *I have* s by my holiness—	8678
	110: 4	LORD *has* s and will not change his mind:	8678
Isa	14:24	The LORD Almighty *has* s, "Surely,	8678
	45:23	By myself *I have* s,	8678
	54: 9	So now *I have* s not to be angry with you,	8678
	62: 8	The LORD *has* s by his right hand and	8678
Jer	5: 7	Your children have forsaken me and s	8678
	32:22	You gave them this land *you had* s	8678
	51:14	The LORD Almighty *has* s by himself:	8678
Eze	20:28	into the land I *had* s to give them	906+3338+5951
	20:42	the land I *had* s **with uplifted** hand to give	5951
	21:23	to those *who have* s **allegiance** to him,	8652+8678
	44:12	therefore I *have* s **with uplifted** hand	5951
Da	9:11	the curses and s **judgments** written in	8652
Am	4: 2	Sovereign LORD *has* s by his holiness:	8678
	6: 8	The Sovereign LORD *has* s by himself—	8678
	8: 7	The LORD *has* s by the Pride of Jacob:	8678
Heb	7:21	Lord *has* s and will not change his mind:	3923

SWUNG (3) [SWING]

Eze	26: 2	and its doors *have* s **open** to me;	6015
Rev	14:16	on the cloud s his sickle over the earth,	965
	14:19	The angel s his sickle on the earth,	965

SYCAMINE (KJV) See MULBERRY

SYCAMORE-FIG (6) [FIG]

1Ki	10:27	cedar as plentiful as s **trees** in the foothills.	9204
1Ch	27:28	the olive and s **trees** in the western foothills.	9204
2Ch	1:15	cedar as plentiful as s **trees** in the foothills.	9204
	9:27	cedar as plentiful as s **trees** in the foothills.	9204
Am	7:14	and I also took care of s **trees.**	9204
Lk	19: 4	ahead and climbed a s **tree** to see him,	5191

SYCAMORE-FIGS (1) [FIG]

| Ps | 78:47 | with hail and their s with sleet. | 9204 |

SYCHAR (1)

| Jn | 4: 5 | So he came to a town in Samaria called S, | 5373 |

SYCHEM (KJV) See SHECHEM

SYCOMORE (KJV) See SYCAMORE-FIG

SYENE (KJV) See ASWAN

SYMBOL (2) [SYMBOLIC, SYMBOLIZES, SYMBOLS]

| Ex | 13:16 | on your hand and a s on your forehead that | 3213 |
| Nu | 6: 7 | s of his **separation** *to* God is on his head. | 5694 |

SYMBOLIC (1) [SYMBOL]

| Zec | 3: 8 | who are men s **of things to come:** | 4603 |

SYMBOLIZES (1) [SYMBOL]

| 1Pe | 3:21 | and this water s baptism that now saves you | 531 |

SYMBOLS (4) [SYMBOL]

Dt	6: 8	Tie them as on your hands and bind them	253
	11:18	tie them as s on your hands and bind them	253
Isa	8:18	and s in Israel from the LORD Almighty,	4603
	57: 8	your doorposts you have put your **pagan** s.	2355

SYMPATHETIC (1) [SYMPATHY]

| 1Pe | 3: 8 | *be* s, love as brothers, be compassionate | 5218 |

SYMPATHIZE (2) [SYMPATHY]

| Job | 2:11 | and met together by agreement to go and s | 5653 |
| Heb | 4:15 | a high priest who is unable *to* s with | 5217 |

SYMPATHIZED (1) [SYMPATHY]

| Heb | 10:34 | *You* s with those in prison | 5217 |

SYMPATHY (8) [SYMPATHETIC, SYMPATHIZE, SYMPATHIZED]

2Sa	10: 2	So David sent a delegation to **express** his s	5714
	10: 3	by sending men to you *to* **express** s?	5714
1Ch	19: 2	So David sent a delegation to **express** his s	5714
	19: 2	in the land of the Ammonites to **express** s	5714
	19: 3	by sending men to you *to* **express** s?	5714
Ps	69:20	I looked for s, but there was none,	5653
Jer	16: 5	do not go to mourn or **show** s,	5653
Da	1: 9	the official to show favor and s to Daniel,	8171

SYNAGOGUE (45) [SYNAGOGUES]

Mt	12: 9	he went into their s,	5252
	13:54	he began teaching the people in their s,	5252
Mk	1:21	Jesus went into the s and began to teach.	5252
	1:23	then a man in their s who was possessed by	5252
	1:29	As soon as they left the s,	5252
	3: 1	Another time he went into the s,	5252
	5:22	Then one of the s **rulers,** named Jairus,	801
	5:35	from the house of Jairus, the s **ruler.**	801
	5:36	Jesus told the s **ruler,** "Don't be afraid;	801
	5:38	to the home *of* the s **ruler,**	801
	6: 2	he began to teach in the s,	5252
Lk	4:16	and on the Sabbath day he went into the s,	5252
	4:20	The eyes of everyone in the s were fastened	5252
	4:28	in the s were furious when they heard this.	5252
	4:33	In the s there was a man possessed by	5252
	4:38	the s and went to the home of Simon.	5252
	6: 6	On another Sabbath he went into the s	5252
	7: 5	he loves our nation and has built our s."	5252
	8:41	Then a man named Jairus, a ruler of the s,	5252
	8:49	from the house of Jairus, the s **ruler.**	801
	13:14	the s **ruler** said to the people,	801
Jn	6:59	while teaching in the s in Capernaum.	5252
	9:22	was the Christ would be **put out of the** s.	697
	12:42	for fear they would be **put out of the** s;	697
	16: 2	*They will* **put** you **out of the** s;	697+4472
Ac	6: 9	the S of the Freedmen (as it was called)—	5252
	13:14	On the Sabbath they entered the s	5252
	13:15	the s **rulers** sent word to them, saying,	801
	13:42	As Paul and Barnabas were leaving the s,	5252
	14: 1	went as usual into the Jewish s.	5252
	17: 1	where there was a Jewish s.	NIG
	17: 2	As his custom was, Paul went into the s,	5252
	17:10	they went to the s.	5252
	17:17	So he reasoned in the s with the Jews and	5252
	18: 4	Every Sabbath he reasoned in the s,	5252
	18: 7	Then Paul left **the** s and went next door to	1696S
	18: 8	Crispus, the s **ruler,** and his entire	801
	18:17	on Sosthenes the s **ruler** and beat him	801
	18:19	He himself went into the s and reasoned	5252
	18:26	He began to speak boldly in the s.	5252
	19: 8	Paul entered the s and spoke boldly there	5252
	22:19	'these men know that I went from one s	5252
	26:11	I went **from one** s **to another**	2848+4246+5252
Rev	2: 9	Jews and are not, but are a s of Satan.	5252
	3: 9	I will make those who are of the s of Satan,	5252

SYNAGOGUES (23) [SYNAGOGUE]

Mt	4:23	teaching in their s, preaching the good news	5252
	6: 2	the hypocrites do in the s and on the streets,	5252
	6: 5	in the s and on the street corners to be seen	5252
	9:35	teaching in their s, preaching the good news	5252
	10:17	to the local councils and flog you in their s.	5252
	23: 6	and the most important seats in the s;	5252
	23:34	others you will flog in your s and pursue	5252
Mk	1:39	in their s and driving out demons.	5252
	12:39	in the s and the places of honor at banquets.	5252
	13: 9	to the local councils and flogged in the s.	5252
Lk	4:15	He taught in their s, and everyone praised	5252
	4:44	And he kept on preaching in the s of Judea.	5252
	11:43	in the s and greetings in the marketplaces.	5252
	12:11	"When you are brought before s,	5252
	13:10	Jesus was teaching in one *of* the s,	5252
	20:46	in the s and the places of honor at banquets.	5252
	21:12	They will deliver you to s and prisons,	5252
Jn	18:20	"I always taught in s or at the temple,	5252
Ac	9: 2	asked him for letters to the s in Damascus,	5252
	9:20	to preach in the s that Jesus is the Son	5252
	13: 5	the word of God in the Jewish s.	5252
	15:21	from the earliest times and is read in the s	5252
	24:12	stirring up a crowd in the s or anywhere else	5252

SYNTYCHE (1)

| Php | 4: 2 | with S to agree with each other in the Lord. | 5345 |

SYRACUSE (1)

| Ac | 28:12 | We put in at S and stayed there three days. | 5352 |

SYRIA (8) [SYRIAN]

Mt	4:24	News about him spread all over S,	5353
Lk	2: 2	while Quirinius was governor *of* S.)	5353
Ac	15:23	S and Cilicia: Greetings.	5353
	15:41	He went through S and Cilicia,	5353
	18:18	Then he left the brothers and sailed for S,	5353
	20: 3	as he was about to sail for S,	5353
	21: 3	we sailed on to S.	5353
Gal	1:21	Later I went to S and Cilicia.	5353

SYRIA-DAMASCUS (KJV) See ARAMEAN KINGDOM OF DAMASCUS

SYRIA-MAACHAH (KJV) See ARAM MAACAH

SYRIACK (KJV) See ARAMAIC

SYRIAN (1) [SYRIA]

| Lk | 4:27 | of them was cleansed—only Naaman the S. | 5354 |

SYRIAN PHOENICIA (1) [PHOENICIA, SYRIA]

| Mk | 7:26 | The woman was a Greek, born in S. | 5355 |

SYRIANS (KJV) See ARAMEANS

SYROPHENICIAN (KJV) See SYRIAN PHOENICIA

SYRTIS (1)

| Ac | 27:17 | would run aground on the **sandbars of** S, | 5358 |

T

TAANACH (7)

Jos	12:21	the king of T one the king of Megiddo one	9505
	17:11	Endor, T and Megiddo,	9505
	21:25	the tribe of Manasseh they received T	9505
Jdg	1:27	not drive out the people of Beth Shan or T	9505
	5:19	of Canaan fought at T by the waters	9505
1Ki	4:12	in T and Megiddo, and in all	9505
1Ch	7:29	of Manasseh were Beth Shan, T, Megiddo	9505

TAANATH SHILOH (1)

| Jos | 16: 6 | the north it curved eastward to T, | 9304 |

TABALIAH (1)

| 1Ch | 26:11 | T the third and Zechariah the fourth. | 3189 |

TABBAOTH (2)

| Ezr | 2:43 | the descendants of Ziha, Hasupha, T, | 3191 |
| Ne | 7:46 | the descendants of Ziha, Hasupha, T, | 3191 |

TABBATH (1)

| Jdg | 7:22 | as the border of Abel Meholah near T. | 3195 |

TABEEL (2)

| Ezr | 4: 7 | T and the rest of his associates wrote | 3175 |
| Isa | 7: 6 | and make the son of T king over it." | 3174 |

TABERAH (2)

| Nu | 11: 3 | So that place was called T, | 9323 |
| Dt | 9:22 | You also made the LORD angry at T, | 9323 |

TABERING (KJV) See BEAT

TABERNACLE (114) [TABERNACLES]

Ex	25: 9	Make this t and all its furnishings exactly	5438
	26: 1	"Make the t with ten curtains	5438
	26: 6	the curtains together so that the t is a unit.	5438
	26: 7	of goat hair for the tent over the t—	5438
	26:12	over is to hang down at the rear of the t.	5438
	26:13	what is left will hang over the sides of the t	5438
	26:15	of acacia wood for the t.	5438
	26:17	Make all the frames of the t in this way.	5438
	26:18	for the south side of the t	5438
	26:20	For the other side, the north side of the t,	5438
	26:22	that is, the west end of the t,	5438
	26:26	five for the frames on one side of the t,	5438
	26:27	at the far end of the t.	5438
	26:30	the t according to the plan shown you on	5438
	26:35	the t and put the lampstand opposite it on	5438
	27: 9	"Make a courtyard for the t.	5438
	27:19	articles used in the service of the t,	5438
	35:11	the t with its tent and its covering,	5438
	35:15	for the doorway at the entrance to the t;	5438
	35:18	the t and for the courtyard, and their ropes;	5438
	36: 8	the workmen made the t with ten curtains	5438
	36:13	of curtains together so that the t was a unit.	5438
	36:14	of goat hair for the tent over the t—	5438
	36:20	frames of acacia wood for the t.	5438
	36:22	They made all the frames of the t	5438
	36:23	for the south side of the t	5438
	36:25	For the other side, the north side of the t,	5438
	36:27	that is, the west end of the t,	5438
	36:28	for the corners of the t at the far end.	5438
	36:31	five for the frames on one side of the t,	5438
	36:32	at the far end of the t.	5438
	38:20	All the tent pegs of the t and of	5438
	38:21	the amounts of the materials used for the t,	5438
	38:21	the t of the Testimony,	5438
	38:31	and all the tent pegs for the t and those for	5438
	39:32	So all the work on the t,	5438
	39:33	Then they brought the t to Moses:	5438
	39:40	all the furnishings for the t,	5438
	40: 2	"Set up the t, the Tent of Meeting,	5438
	40: 5	and put the curtain at the entrance to the t.	5438
	40: 6	the entrance to the t, the Tent of Meeting;	5438
	40: 9	"Take the anointing oil and anoint the t	5438
	40:17	So the t was set up on the first day of	5438
	40:18	When Moses set up the t,	5438
	40:19	Then he spread the tent over the t and put	5438
	40:21	into the t and hung the shielding curtain	5438
	40:22	the north side of the t outside the curtain	5438
	40:24	the table on the south side of the t	5438
	40:28	up the curtain at the entrance to the t.	5438
	40:29	of burnt offering near the entrance to the t,	5438
	40:33	the courtyard around the t and altar and put	5438
	40:34	and the glory of the LORD filled the t.	5438
	40:35	and the glory of the LORD filled the t.	5438
	40:36	from above the t, they would set out;	5438
	40:38	cloud of the LORD was over the t by day,	5438
Lev	8:10	and anointed the t and everything in it,	5438
	17: 4	an offering to the LORD in front of the t	5438
Nu	1:50	to be in charge of the t of the Testimony—	5438
	1:50	to carry the t and all its furnishings;	5438
	1:51	Whenever the t is to move,	5438
	1:51	and whenever the t is to be set up,	5438
	1:53	the t of the Testimony so that wrath will	5438
	1:53	to be responsible for the care of the t of	5438
	3: 7	of Meeting by doing the work of the t.	5438
	3: 8	of the Israelites by doing the work of the t.	5438
	3:23	to camp on the west, behind the t.	5438
	3:25	for the care of the t and tent,	5438
	3:26	the courtyard surrounding the t and altar,	5438
	3:29	to camp on the south side of the t.	5438
	3:35	to camp on the north side of the t.	5438
	3:36	to take care of the frames of the t,	5438
	3:38	to camp to the east of the t,	5438
	4:16	be in charge of the entire t and everything	5438
	4:25	They are to carry the curtains of the t,	5438
	4:26	the courtyard surrounding the t and altar,	5438
	4:31	to carry the frames of the t, its crossbars,	5438
	5:17	and put some dust from the t floor into	5438
	7: 1	When Moses finished setting up the t,	5438
	7: 3	These they presented before the t.	5438
	9:15	On the day the t, the Tent of Testimony,	5438
	9:15	till morning the cloud above the t looked	5438
	9:18	As long as the cloud stayed over the t,	5438
	9:19	the cloud remained over the t a long time,	5438
	9:20	the cloud was over the t only a few days;	5438
	9:22	the cloud stayed over the t for two days or	5438
	10:11	the cloud lifted from above the t of	5438
	10:17	Then the t was taken down,	5438
	10:21	The t was to be set up before they arrived.	5438
	16: 9	the work at the LORD's t and to stand	5438
	17:13	Anyone who even comes near the t of	5438
	19:13	to purify himself defiles the LORD's t.	5438
	31:30	for the care of the LORD's t."	5438
	31:47	for the care of the LORD's t.	5438
Jos	22:19	where the LORD's t stands,	5438
	22:29	the LORD our God that stands before his t."	5438
1Ch	6:32	They ministered with music before the t,	5438
	6:48	to all the other duties of the t,	5438
	16:39	the priest and his fellow priests before the t	5438
	21:29	The t of the LORD, which Moses had made	5438
	23:26	the Levites no longer need to carry the t	5438
2Ch	1: 5	in Gibeon in front of the t of the LORD;	5438
Ps	27: 5	in the shelter of his t and set me high upon	185
	27: 6	at his t will I sacrifice with shouts of joy;	185
	78:60	He abandoned the t of Shiloh,	
Ac	7:44	the t of the Testimony with them in	5008

Ac	7:45	Having received the t,	4005s
Heb	8: 2	the true t set up by the Lord, not by man.	5008
	8: 5	when he was about to build the t:	5008
	9: 2	A t was set up.	5008
	9: 8	as long as the first t was still standing.	5008
	9:11	and more perfect t that is not man-made,	5008
	9:21	the blood both the t and everything used	5008
	13:10	who minister at the t have no right to eat.	5008
Rev	15: 5	that is, the t of the Testimony, was opened.	5008

TABERNACLES (10) [TABERNACLE]

Lev	23:34	the LORD's Feast of T begins,	6109
Dt	16:13	of T for seven days after you have gathered	6109
	16:16	the Feast of Weeks and the Feast of T.	6109
	31:10	for canceling debts, during the Feast of T,	6109
2Ch	8:13	the Feast of Weeks and the Feast of T.	6109
Ezr	3: 4	the Feast of T with the required number	6109
Zec	14:16	and to celebrate the Feast of T.	6109
	14:18	not go up to celebrate the Feast of T.	6109
	14:19	not go up to celebrate the Feast of T.	6109
Jn	7: 2	But when the Jewish Feast of T was near,	5009

TABITHA (2)

Ac	9:36	In Joppa there was a disciple named T	5412
	9:40	the dead woman, he said, "T, get up."	5412

TABLE (86) [TABLES]

Ge	43:34	were served to them from Joseph's t,	7156s
Ex	25:23	"Make a t of acacia wood—	8947
	25:26	Make four gold rings for the t	2257s
	25:27	to hold the poles used in carrying the t.	8947
	25:28	overlay them with gold and carry the t	8947
	25:30	Put the bread of the Presence on this t to	8947
	26:35	the t outside the curtain on the north side	8947
	30:27	the t and all its articles,	8947
	31: 8	the t and its articles,	8947
	35:13	the t with its poles and all its articles and	8947
	37:10	They made the t of acacia wood—	8947
	37:13	They cast four gold rings for the t	2257s
	37:14	to hold the poles used in carrying the t.	8947
	37:15	The poles for carrying the t were made	8947
	37:16	from pure gold the articles for the t—	8947
	39:36	the t with all its articles and the bread of	8947
	40: 4	Bring in the t and set out what belongs	8947
	40:22	Moses placed the t in the Tent of Meeting	8947
	40:24	of Meeting opposite the t on the south side	8947
Lev	24: 6	on the t of pure gold before the LORD.	8947
Nu	3:31	the t, the lampstand, the altars,	8947
	4: 7	the t of the Presence they are to spread	8947
Jdg	1: 7	have picked up scraps under my t.	8947
1Sa	20:29	why he has not come to the king's t."	8947
	20:34	Jonathan got up from the t in fierce anger,	8947
2Sa	9: 7	and you will always eat at my t."	8947
	9:10	will always eat at my t."	8947
	9:11	So Mephibosheth ate at David's t like one	8947
	9:13	because he always ate at the king's t,	8947
	19:28	a place among those who sat at your t.	8947
1Ki	2: 7	be among those who eat at your t.	8947
	4:27	and all who came to the king's t.	8947
	7:48	the golden t on which was the bread of	8947
	10: 5	the food on his t, the seating of his officials,	8947
	13:20	While they were sitting at the t,	8947
	18:19	of Asherah, who eat at Jezebel's t."	8947
2Ki	4:10	on the roof and put in it a bed and a t,	8947
	25:29	of his life ate regularly at the king's t.	4200+7156s
1Ch	9:32	the bread set out on the t.	5121
	23:29	the bread set out on the t,	5121
	28:16	each t for consecrated bread;	2256+8947+8947
2Ch	9: 4	the food on his t, the seating of his officials,	8947
	13:11	the bread on the ceremonially clean t	8947
	29:18	the t for setting out the consecrated bread,	8947
Ne	5:17	and fifty Jews and officials ate at my t,	8947
	10:33	for the bread set out on the t;	5121
Job	36:16	of your t laden with choice food.	8947
Ps	23: 5	You prepare a t before me in the presence	8947
	69:22	May the t set before them become a snare;	8947
	78:19	saying, "Can God spread a t in the desert?	8947
	128: 3	be like olive shoots around your t.	8947
Pr	9: 2	she has also set her t.	8947
SS	1:12	While the king was at his t,	4990
Isa	65:11	who spread a t for Fortune and fill bowls	8947
Jer	52:33	of his life ate regularly at the king's t.	4200+7156s
Eze	23:41	an elegant couch, with a t spread before it	8947
	39:20	At my t you will eat your fill of horses	8947
	41:22	"This is the t that is before the LORD."	8947
	44:16	to come near my t to minister before me	8947
Da	1: 5	of food and wine from the king's t.	5492
	11:27	will sit at the same t and lie to each other,	8947
Mal	1: 7	that the LORD's t is contemptible.	8947
	1:12	you profane it by saying of the Lord's t,	8947
Mt	15:27	the crumbs that fall from their masters' t."	5544
	26: 7	on his head as he was reclining at the t.	367
	26:20	Jesus was reclining at the t with	367
Mk	7:28	under the t eat the children's crumbs."	5544
	14: 3	reclining at the t in the home of a man	2879
	14:18	While they were reclining at the t eating,	367
Lk	7:36	the Pharisee's house and reclined at the t.	2884
	11:37	so he went in and reclined at the t.	404
	12:37	have them recline at the t and will come	369
	14: 7	guests picked the places of honor at the t,	4752
	14:15	of those at the t with him heard this,	5263
	16:21	to eat what fell from the rich man's t.	5544
	22:14	Jesus and his apostles reclined at the t.	404
	22:21	to betray me is with mine on the t.	5544
	22:27	one who is at the t or the one who serves?	367

Lk	22:27	Is it not the one who is at the t?	367
	22:30	at my t in my kingdom and sit on thrones,	5544
	24:30	When he was at the t with them,	2884
Jn	12: 2	among those reclining at the t with him.	367
Ro	11: 9	"May their t become a snare and a trap,	5544
1Co	10:21	you cannot have a part in both the Lord's t	5544
	10:21	both the Lord's table and the t of demons.	5544
Heb	9: 2	the t and the consecrated bread;	5544

TABLES (18) [TABLE]

1Ch	28:16	the weight of silver for the silver t;	8947
2Ch	4: 8	He made ten t and placed them in	8947
	4:19	the t on which was the bread of the Presence	8947
Est	9: 1	but now the t were turned and the Jews got	2200
Isa	21: 5	They set the t, they spread the rugs,	8947
	28: 8	the t are covered with vomit and there is	8947
Eze	40:39	In the portico of the gateway were two t	8947
	40:40	to the north gateway were two t,	8947
	40:40	on the other side of the steps were two t.	8947
	40:41	So there were four t on one side of	8947
	40:41	eight t in all—on which the sacrifices	8947
	40:42	There were also four t of dressed stone for	8947
	40:43	The t were for the flesh of the offerings.	8947
Mt	21:12	He overturned the t of the money changers	5544
Mk	11:15	He overturned the t of the money changers	5544
Jn	2:14	and others sitting at t exchanging money.	NIG
	2:15	the money changers and overturned their t.	5544
Ac	6: 2	of the word of God in order to wait on t.	5544

TABLET (5) [TABLETS]

Pr	3: 3	write them on the t of your heart.	4283
	7: 3	write them on the t of your heart.	4283
Isa	30: 8	Go now, write it on a t for them,	4283
Eze	4: 1	"Now, son of man, take a clay t,	4246
Lk	1:63	He asked for a writing t,	4400

TABLETS (36) [TABLET]

Ex	24:12	and I will give you the t of stone,	4283
	31:18	he gave him the two t of the Testimony,	4283
	31:18	t of stone inscribed by the finger of God.	4283
	32:15	the two t of the Testimony in his hands.	4283
	32:16	The t were the work of God;	4283
	32:16	the writing of God, engraved on the t.	4283
	32:19	his anger burned and he threw the t out	4283
	34: 1	"Chisel out two stone t like the first ones.	4283
	34: 1	on them the words that were on the first t,	4283
	34: 4	So Moses chiseled out two stone t like	4283
	34: 4	and he carried the two stone t in his hands.	4283
	34:28	on the t the words of the covenant—	4283
	34:29	down from Mount Sinai with the two t of	4283
Dt	4:13	and then wrote them on two stone t.	4283
	5:22	on two stone t and gave them to me.	4283
	9: 9	on the mountain to receive the t of stone,	4283
	9: 9	the t of the covenant that the LORD made	4283
	9:10	The LORD gave me two stone t inscribed	4283
	9:11	the LORD gave me the two stone t,	4283
	9:11	two stone tablets, the t of the covenant.	4283
	9:15	two t of the covenant were in my hands.	4283
	9:17	the two t and threw them out of my hands,	4283
	10: 1	"Chisel out two stone t like the first ones	4283
	10: 2	I will write on the t the words that were on	4283
	10: 2	the words that were on the first t,	4283
	10: 3	and chiseled out two stone t like the first	4283
	10: 3	the mountain with the two t in my hands.	4283
	10: 4	on these t what he had written before,	4283
	10: 5	down the mountain and put the t in the ark	4283
1Ki	8: 9	the two stone t that Moses had placed in it	4283
2Ch	5:10	the two t that Moses had placed in it	4283
Jer	17: 1	on the t of their hearts and on the horns	4283
Hab	2: 2	the revelation and make it plain on t so that	4283
2Co	3: 3	not on t of stone but on tablets of human	4419
	3: 3	of stone but on t of human hearts.	4419
Heb	9: 4	and the stone t of the covenant.	4419

TABOR (10) [AZNOTH TABOR, KISLOTH TABOR]

Jos	19:22	The boundary touched T,	9314
Jdg	4: 6	and Zebulun and lead the way to Mount T.	9314
	4:12	of Abinoam had gone up to Mount T,	9314
	4:14	So Barak went down Mount T,	9314
	8:18	"What kind of men did you kill at T?"	9314
1Sa	10: 3	until you reach the great tree of T.	9314
1Ch	6:77	Kartah, Rimmono and T.	9314
Ps	89:12	T and Hermon sing for joy at your name.	9314
Jer	46:18	"one will come who is like T among	9314
Hos	5: 1	a net spread out on T.	9314

TABRET, TABRETS (KJV) See TAMBOURINES

TABRIMMON (1)

1Ki	15:18	and sent them to Ben-Hadad son of T,	3193

TACHES (KJV) See CLASP

TACHMONITE (KJV) See TAHKEMONITE

TACKLE (1)

Ac	27:19	they threw the ship's t overboard	5006

TACT (1)
Da 2:14 Daniel spoke to him with wisdom and **t**. 10302

TADMOR (2)
1Ki 9:18 and **T** in the desert, within his land, 9330
2Ch 8: 4 He also built up **T** in the desert and all 9330

TAHAN (2) [TAHANITE]
Nu 26:35 through **T**, the Tahanite clan. 9380
1Ch 7:25 Resheph his son, Telah his son, **T** his son, 9380

TAHANITE (1) [TAHAN]
Nu 26:35 through Tahan, the **T** clan. 9385

TAHAPANES (KJV) See TAHPANHES

TAHASH (1)
Ge 22:24 Tebah, Gaham, **T** and Maacah. 9392

TAHATH (6)
Nu 33:26 They left Makheloth and camped at **T**. 9395
  33:27 They left **T** and camped at Terah. 9395
1Ch 6:24 **T** his son, Uriel his son, Uzziah his son 9394
  6:37 the son of **T**, the son of Assir, 9394
  7:20 Shuthelah, Bered his son, **T** his son, 9394
  7:20 Tahath his son, Eleadah his son, **T** his son, 9394

TAHKEMONITE (1)
2Sa 23: 8 Josheb-Basshebeth, a **T**, 9376

TAHPANHES (7)
Jer 2:16 and **T** have shaved the crown of your head. 9387
  43: 7 to the LORD and went as far as **T**. 9387
  43: 8 In **T** the word of the LORD came 9387
  43: 9 at the entrance to Pharaoh's palace in **T**. 9387
  44: 1 in Migdol, **T** and Memphis— 9387
  46:14 proclaim it also in Memphis and **T**: 9387
Eze 30:18 Dark will be the day at **T** when I break 9387

TAHPENES (3)
1Ki 11:19 sister of his own wife, Queen **T**, in marriage 9388
  11:20 sister of **T** bore him a son named Genubath, 9388
  11:20 whom **T** brought up in the royal palace. 9388

TAHREA (1)
1Ch 9:41 Pithon, Melech, **T** and Ahaz. 9390

TAHTIM HODSHI (1)
2Sa 24: 6 to Gilead and the region of **T**, 9398

TAIL (15) [TAILS]
Ex 4: 4 "Reach out your hand and take it by the **t**." 2387
  29:22 "Take from this ram the fat, the fat **t**, 487
Lev 3: 9 entire fat **t** cut off close to the backbone, 487
  7: 3 the fat **t** and the fat that covers 487
  8:25 He took the fat, the fat **t**, 487
  9:19 the fat **t**, the layer of fat, 487
Dt 28:13 will make you the head, not the **t**. 2387
  28:44 He will be the head, but you will be the **t**. 2387
Jdg 15: 4 and tied them **t** to tail in pairs. 2387
  15: 4 and tied them tail to **t** in pairs. 2387
Job 40:17 His **t** sways like a cedar; 2387
Isa 9:14 and **t**, both palm branch and reed in 2387
  9:15 the prophets who teach lies are the **t**. 2387
  19:15 head or **t**, palm branch or reed. 2387
Rev 12: 4 His **t** swept a third of the stars out of *4038*

TAILS (5) [TAIL]
Jdg 15: 4 He then fastened a torch to every pair of **t**, 2387
Rev 9:10 They had **t** and stings like scorpions, *4038*
  9:10 in their **t** they had power to torment people *4038*
  9:19 in their mouths and in their **t**; *4038*
  9:19 for their **t** were like snakes, *4038*

TAKE (861) [RETAKE, TAKEN, TAKES, TAKING, TOOK]
Ge 2:15 Garden of Eden to work it and **t** care of it. 9068
  3:22 be allowed to reach out his hand and **t** also 4374
  6:21 *to* **t** every kind of food that is to be eaten 4374
  7: 2 **T** with you seven of every kind of clean 4374
  12:19 **T** her and go!" 4374
  15: 7 to give you this land to **t** possession *of* it." 3769
  19:15 **T** your wife and your two daughters who 4374
  21:18 Lift the boy up and **t** him by the hand, 2616
  22: 2 Then God said, "**T** your son, your only son, 4374
  22:17 Your descendants *will* **t** possession *of* 3769
  24: 5 *Shall I then* **t** your son **back** to 8740+8740
  24: 6 that *you do* not **t** my son **back** there," 8740
  24: 8 Only *do* not **t** my son **back** there." 8740
  24:51 Here is Rebekah; **t** her and go, 4374
  27:10 Then **t** it to your father to eat, 995
  28: 2 A wife for yourself there, 4374
  28: 4 so that you *may* **t** possession *of* the land 3769
  28: 6 to Paddan Aram to **t** a wife from there, 4374
  29: 7 the sheep and **t** them **back** *to* pasture." 2143
  30:15 *Will you* **t** my son's mandrakes too?" 4374
  31:31 **t** your daughters away from me **by force**. 1608

Ge 31:32 of yours here with me; and if so, **t** it." 4374
  31:50 if *you* **t** any wives besides my daughters, 4374
  34: 9 give us your daughters and **t** our daughters 4374
  34:16 and **t** your daughters for ourselves. 4374
  34:17 we'll **t** our sister and go." 4374
  37:21 "*Let's* not **t** his life," he said. 5782
  37:22 to rescue him from them and **t** him **back** 8740
  37:25 and they were on their way to **t** them **down** 3718
  41:34 *to* **t** a **fifth** *of* the harvest of Egypt during 2821
  42:19 while the rest of you go and **t** grain **back** 995
  42:33 of your brothers here with me, and **t** food 4374
  42:36 and now *you want to* **t** Benjamin. 4374
  43:11 in your bags and **t** them **down** to the man *as* 3718
  43:12 **T** double the amount of silver with you, 4374
  43:13 **T** your brother also and go back to the man 4374
  43:16 "**T** these men to my house, 995
  43:18 and seize us as slaves and **t** our donkeys." NIH
  44:29 If *you* **t** this one from me too 4374
  45:19 **T** some carts from Egypt for your children 4374
  48:21 but God will be with you and **t** you **back** to 8740
  50:24 to your aid and **t** you **up** out of this land to 6590
Ex 2: 9 "**T** this baby and nurse him for me, 2143
  3: 5 "**T off** your sandals. 5970
  3:18 *Let us* **t** a three-day journey into 2143
  4: 4 "Reach out your hand and **t** it by the tail." 296
  4: 9 **t** some water from the Nile and pour it on 4374
  4: 9 The water *you* **t** from the river will become 4374
  4:17 But **t** this staff in your hand 4374
  5: 3 Now *let us* **t** a three-day journey into 2143
  6: 7 *I will* **t** you as my own people, 4374
  7: 9 '**T** your staff and throw it down 4374
  7:15 and **t** in your hand the staff 4374
  7:19 '**T** your staff and stretch out your hand 4374
  7:23 and *did* not **t** even this *to* heart. 8883
  8: 8 to the LORD *to* **t** the frogs **away** from me 6073
  8:27 *We must* **t** a three-day journey into 2143
  9: 8 "**T** handfuls of soot from a furnace 4374
  10:17 **t** this deadly plague **away** from me." 6073
  12: 3 of this month each man *is to* **t** a lamb 4374
  12: 5 and *you may* **t** them from the sheep or 4374
  12: 7 **T care of** them until the fourteenth day 2118+4200+5466
  12: 7 Then *they are to* **t** some of the blood 4374
  12:22 **T** a bunch of hyssop, 4374
  12:32 **T** your flocks and herds, as you have said, 4374
  12:46 none of the meat outside the house. 3655
  12:48 then *he may* **t** **part** like one born in 6913+7928
  16:16 **T** an omer for each person you have 4374
  16:32 '**T** an omer of manna and keep it for 4850
  16:33 "**T** a jar and put an omer of manna in it. 4374
  17: 5 **T** with you some of the elders of Israel 4374
  17: 5 with you some of the elders of Israel and **t** 4374
  21: 6 his master *must* **t** him before the judges. 5602
  21: 6 *He shall* **t** him to the door or the doorpost 5602
  21:14 **t** him away from my altar and put him 4374
  21:23 *you are to* **t** life for life, 5989
  22:22 not **t advantage** of a widow or an orphan. 6700
  22:26 **t** your neighbor's cloak **as a pledge**, 2471+2471
  23: 4 **be sure to** **t** it **back** to him. 8740+8740
  23:25 *I will* **t away** sickness from among you, 6073
  23:30 *to* **t** possession *of* the land. 5706
  28: 9 **T** two onyx stones and engrave on them 4374
  29: 1 **T** a young bull and two rams 4374
  29: 5 **T** the garments and dress Aaron with 4374
  29: 7 **T** the anointing oil and anoint him 4374
  29:12 **T** some of the bull's blood and put it on 4374
  29:13 Then **t** all the fat around the inner parts, 4374
  29:15 "**T** one of the rams, 4374
  29:16 Slaughter it and **t** the blood and sprinkle it 4374
  29:19 "**T** the other ram, 4374
  29:20 **t** some of its blood and put it on the lobes 4374
  29:21 And **t** some of the blood on the altar 4374
  29:22 "**T** from this ram the fat, the fat tail, 4374
  29:23 which is before the LORD, **t** a loaf, NIH
  29:25 Then **t** them from their hands 4374
  29:26 After *you* **t** the breast of the ram 4374
  29:31 "**T** the ram for the ordination and cook 4374
  30:12 "When *you* **t** a census of the Israelites 906+5951+8031
  30:23 "**T** the following fine spices: 4374
  30:34 said to Moses, "**T** fragrant spices— 4374
  32: 2 "**T off** the gold earrings that your wives, 7293
  32:24 'Whoever has any gold jewelry, **t** it **off**.' 7293
  33: 5 Now **t off** your ornaments 3718+4946+6584
  33: 7 Moses *used to* **t** a tent and pitch it outside 4374
  34: 9 **t** us as your **inheritance**." 5706
  35: 5 **t** an offering for the LORD. 4374
  40: 9 "**T** the anointing oil and anoint 4374
Lev 2: 2 and **t** it to Aaron's sons the priests. 995
  2: 2 The priest *shall* **t** a **handful** of 4850+7858+7859
  2: 8 *who shall* **t** it to the altar. 5602
  2: 9 He *shall* **t out** the memorial portion from 8123
  4: 5 Then the anointed priest *shall* **t** some of 4374
  4:12 *he must* **t** outside the camp to 3655
  4:16 *to* **t** some of the bull's blood into the Tent 995
  4:21 Then *he shall* **t** the bull outside the camp 3655
  4:25 Then the priest *shall* **t** some of the blood 4374
  4:30 Then the priest *is to* **t** some of the blood 4374
  4:34 Then the priest *shall* **t** some of the blood 4374
  5:12 who *shall* **t** a **handful** of it as 4850+7858+7859
  6:11 then *he is to* **t off** these clothes and put 7320
  6:15 The priest *is to* **t** a handful of fine flour 8123
  9: 2 "**T** a bull calf for your sin offering and 4374
  9: 3 "**T** a male goat for a sin offering, 4374
  10:12 "**T** the grain offering left over from 4374
  10:17 to you to **t away** the guilt of the community 5951
  14: 6 *He is then to* **t** the live bird and dip it, 4374

Lev 14:12 *to* **t** one of the male lambs and offer it as 4374
  14:14 *to* **t** some of the blood of the guilt offering 4374
  14:15 priest *shall* then **t** some of the log of oil, 4374
  14:21 *he must* **t** one male lamb as a guilt offering 4374
  14:24 *to* **t** the lamb for the guilt offering, 4374
  14:25 the lamb for the guilt offering and **t** some 4374
  14:42 *to* **t** other stones to replace these 4374
  14:42 to replace these and **t** new clay and plaster 4374
  14:49 To purify the house *he is to* **t** two birds 4374
  14:51 Then *he is to* **t** the cedar wood, 4374
  15:14 On the eighth day *he must* **t** two doves 4374
  15:29 On the eighth day *she must* **t** two doves 4374
  16: 5 *to* **t** two male goats for a sin offering and 4374
  16: 7 *to* **t** the two goats and present them before 4374
  16:12 *He is to* **t** a censer full of burning coals 4374
  16:12 and **t** them behind the curtain. 995
  16:14 *He is to* **t** some of the bull's blood and 4374
  16:15 and **t** its blood behind the curtain and do 995
  16:18 *He shall* **t** some of the bull's blood 4374
  16:23 to go into the Tent of Meeting and **t off** 7320
  18:18 " '*Do not* **t** your wife's sister as a rival wife 4374
  23:40 the first day *you are to* **t** choice fruit from 4374
  24: 5 "**T** fine flour and bake twelve loaves 3655
  24:14 "**T** the blasphemer outside the camp. 3655
  25:14 *do not* **t advantage of** 3561
  25:17 *Do not* **t advantage of** each other, 3561
  25:36 *Do not* **t** interest of any kind from him, 4374
  26:31 and *I will* **t** no **delight** in the pleasing aroma 8193
Nu 1: 2 "**T** a census *of* the whole Israelite 5951+8031
  1:50 *to* **t** care of it and encamp around it. 9250
  1:51 the Levites *are to* **t** it **down**, 3718
  3: 8 *They are to* **t** care of all the furnishings of 9068
  3:36 The Merarites were appointed to **t** care of 5466
  3:41 **T** the Levites for me in place of all 4374
  3:45 "**T** the Levites in place of all the firstborn 4374
  4: 2 "**T** a census *of* the Kohathite 906+5951+8031
  4: 5 Aaron and his sons are to go in and **t down** 3718
  4: 9 *to* **t** a blue cloth and cover the lampstand 4374
  4:12 *to* **t** all the articles used for ministering in 4374
  4:22 "**T** a census also *of* the Gershonites 5951+8031
  5:15 then he is to **t** his wife to the priest. 995
  5:15 also **t** an offering of a tenth of an ephah 995
  5:17 Then he *shall* **t** some holy water in 4374
  5:25 *to* **t** from her hands the grain offering 4374
  5:26 then *to* **t** a **handful** of the grain offering 7858
  6:18 *to* **t** the hair and put it in the fire that is 4374
  8: 6 "**T** the Levites from among the other 4374
  8: 8 *Have them* **t** a young bull 4374
  8: 8 *to* **t** a second young bull for a sin offering. 4374
  8:24 shall come to **t** **part** in the work at 7371+7372
  11:17 and *I will* **t** of the Spirit that is on you 724
  13:30 "We should go up and **t possession** of 3769
  16: 6 followers are to do this: **T** censers 4374
  16:17 each man *is to* **t** his censer and put incense in it— 4374
  16:37 *to* **t** the censers out of the smoldering 8123
  16:46 "**T** your censer and put incense in it, 4374
  19: 4 Then Eleazar the priest *is to* **t** some 4374
  19: 6 The priest *is to* **t** some cedar wood, 4374
  19:18 ceremonially clean *is to* **t** some hyssop, 4374
  20: 8 "**T** the staff, and you and your brother 4374
  20:25 and his son Eleazar and **t** them **up** 6590
  21: 7 that the LORD *will* **t** the snakes **away** 6073
  23:27 "Come, *let me* **t** you to another place. 4374
  25: 4 "**T** all the leaders of these people, 4374
  26: 2 "**T** a census *of* the whole 906+5951+8031
  26: 4 "**T** a census *of* the men twenty years old NIH
  27:18 "**T** Joshua son of Nun, 4374
  31: 2 "**T** **vengeance** on the Midianites *for* 5933+5935
  31:29 **T** this tribute from their half share 4374
  33:53 **T** possession *of* the land and settle in it, 3769
  35: 8 **T** **many** towns from a tribe that has many, 8049
Dt 1: 8 Go in and **t possession** *of* the land 3769
  1:21 Go up and **t possession** *of* it as the LORD, 3769
  1:22 a report about the route *we are to* **t** and 6590
  1:39 to them and they *will* **t possession** *of* it. 3769
  2:24 Begin *to* **t possession** *of* it and engage him 3769
  3: 4 not one of the sixty cities that *we did* not **t** 4374
  3:18 given you this land to **t possession** *of* it. 3769
  4: 1 and may go in and **t possession** *of* the land 3769
  4: 5 in the land you are entering to **t possession** 3769
  4:22 over and **t possession** *of* that good land. 3769
  4:34 *to* **t** for himself one nation out of another 4374
  4:39 Acknowledge and **t** to heart this day that 8740
  6:13 serve him only and **t** *your* oaths 8678
  6:18 with you and you may go in and **t over** 3769
  7: 3 or **t** their daughters for your sons, 4374
  7:11 Therefore, **t** care to follow the commands, 9068
  7:25 and *do not* **t** it for yourselves, 4374
  9: 4 to **t possession** *of* this land because 3769
  9: 5 that you are going in to **t possession** 3769
  9:23 "Go up and **t possession** *of* the land 3769
  9:28 the LORD was not able to **t** them into 995
  10:20 to him and **t** *your* oaths in his name. 8678
  11: 8 in and **t over** the land that you are crossing 3769
  11:10 The land you are entering to **t over** is not 3769
  11:11 to **t possession** of is a land of mountains 3769
  11:31 to cross the Jordan to enter and **t possession** 3769
  12:26 But **t** your consecrated things 5951
  12:32 do not add to it or **t away** from it. 1757
  14:25 and **t** the silver with you and go to 7443
  15:17 **t** an awl and push it through his ear 7443
  17: 5 **t** the man or woman who has done this evil 3655
  17: 8 **t** them to the place the LORD your God will 6590
  17:17 *He must* not **t many** wives, 8049
  18:22 the LORD *does* not **t place** or come true, 2118
  20:14 *you may* **t** these as plunder for yourselves. 1024
  21: 3 the town nearest the body *shall* **t** a heifer 4374

Dt
21:10 into your hands and *you* t captives, 8647+8660
21:11 *you may* t her as your wife. 4374
21:19 his father and mother *shall* t hold of him 9530
22: 1 be sure to t it **back** to him. 8740+8740
22: 2 t it home with you and keep it 665
22: 6 *do not* t the mother with the young. 4374
22: 7 You may t the young, 4374
22:18 the elders *shall* t the man and punish him. 4374
22:24 *you shall* t both of them to the gate of 3655
24: 6 not t a pair of millstones—not even the
    upper one—**as security for a debt,** 2471
24:14 *Do not* t advantage of a hired man 6943
24:17 or t the cloak of the widow **as a pledge.** 2471
25: 1 *to* t it to court and the judges will decide 5602
25: 5 Her husband's brother *shall* t her 995+6584
25: 9 t off one of his sandals, 2740
26: 2 t some of the firstfruits of all 4374
26: 4 The priest *shall* t the basket 4374
28:30 but another will t her and ravish her. NIH
28:42 of locusts *will* t over all your trees and 3769
30: 1 before you come upon you and *you* t them 8740
30: 5 and *you will* t possession of it. 3769
31: 3 and *you will* t possession of their land. 3769
31:26 "T this Book of the Law and place it beside 4374
32:41 *I will* t vengeance on my adversaries 5934+8740
32:43 *he will* t vengeance on his enemies 5934+8740
32:46 "T to heart all the words I have solemnly 8492

Jos
1:11 the Jordan here to go in and t possession *of* 3769
3: 6 "T up the ark of the covenant and pass on 5951
4: 3 *to* t up twelve stones from the middle of 5951
4: 5 of you *is* *to* t up a stone on his shoulder, 8123
5:15 "T off your sandals, for the place 5970
6: 6 "T up the ark of the covenant of the LORD 5951
7: 3 Send two or three thousand men *to* t it 5782
8: 1 T the whole army with you, 4374
8: 7 to rise up from ambush and t the city. 3769
8:13 had the soldiers t up *their* **positions—** 8492
8:29 Joshua ordered them *to* t his body from 3718
9:11 'T provisions for your journey;' 4374
18: 3 before you begin to t possession *of* the land 3769
23: 5 and *you will* t possession of their land, 3769

Jdg
2: 6 they went to t possession *of* the land, 3769
4: 6 t with you ten thousand men of Naphtali 4374
5: 2 "When the princes in Israel t the lead, 7276
5:12 T captive your captives, 8647
6:20 "T the meat and the unleavened bread, 4374
6:25 "T the second bull from your father's herd, 4374
7: 4 T them **down** to the water, 3718
9:15 come and t refuge in my shade; 2879
11: 9 "Suppose you t me **back** to fight 8740
11:15 Israel *did not* t the land of Moab or 4374
11:23 what right have you *to* t it **over?** 3769
11:24 not t what your god Chemosh gives you? 3769
15: 2 T her instead." 2118+4200
15:10 "We have come to t Samson **prisoner,**" 673
18: 9 Don't hesitate to go there and t it **over.** 3769
20:10 We'll t ten men out of every hundred 4374

Ru
1: 7 the road that *would* t them **back** to the land 8740
2: 2 whose wings you have come to t refuge." 2879

1Sa
1:16 *Do not* t your servant for a wicked woman; 4200+5989+7156
1:22 *I will* t him and present him before the LORD 995
2:14 and the priest *would* t for himself whatever 4374
2:16 and then t whatever you want," 4374
2:16 if you don't, I'll t it by force." 4374
2:20 to t the place of the one she prayed for 9393
6: 7 but t their calves **away** and pen them up. 8740
6: 8 T the ark of the LORD and put it on 4374
6:21 Come down and t it **up** to your place." 6590
8:11 *He will* t your sons and make them serve 4374
8:13 *He will* t your daughters to be perfumers 4374
8:14 *He will* t the best of your fields 4374
8:15 *He will* t a **tenth** *of* your grain and 6923
8:16 and donkeys *he will* t for his own use. 4374
8:17 *He will* t a **tenth** *of* your flocks, 6923
9: 3 "T one of the servants with you and go 4374
9: 6 Perhaps he will tell us what way *to* t." 2143
9: 7 We have no gift to t the man of God. 995
9: 8 of God so that he will tell us what way to t." NIH
16: 2 "T a heifer with you and say, 4374
16:23 David *would* t his harp and play. 4374
17:17 "T this ephah of roasted grain 4374
17:18 T these ten cheeses to the 995
18:25 to t **revenge** on his enemies.'" 5933
20: 1 that *he is* trying to t my life?" 1335
21: 9 If you want it, t it; 4374
23:15 that Saul had come out to t his life. 1335
24:11 but you are hunting me down to t my life. 4374
25:11 Why *should* I t my bread and water, 1335
25:29 someone is pursuing you to t your life, 1335
25:40 to you so to t you to become his wife." 4374
30:15 and *I will* t you **down** to them." 3718
30:22 each man *may* t his wife and children 5627

2Sa
2:21 t on one of the young men and strip him 296
4: 8 your enemy, who tried to t your life. 1335
6:10 to t the ark of the LORD up with him in 6073
12:11 Before your very eyes *I will* t your wives 4374
12:28 Otherwise *I will* t the city, 4334
12:28 Don't t this thing to heart." 8883
14:14 But God *does* not t **away** life; 5951
15: 5 t hold of him and kiss him. 2616
15:16 but he left ten concubines to t **care of** 9068
15:20 Go back, and t your countrymen. 8740
15:25 "T the ark of God back into the city. 8740
15:27 and Abiathar t your two sons with you. NIH
16:11 *is* trying to t my life. 1335
16:21 whom he left to t **care of** the palace. 9068

2Sa
18:19 "Let me run and t the news *to* the king that 1413
18:20 "You are not the one to t the news today," NIH
18:20 "You may t the news another time, 1413
19:18 at the ford to t the king's household **over** 6296
19:30 "Let him t everything, 4374
20: 3 the ten concubines he had left to t **care of** 9068
20: 6 T your master's men and pursue him, 4374
22: 3 my God is my rock, in whom *I* t refuge, 2879
22:31 He is a shield for all who t refuge in him. 2879
24: 1 "Go and t a **census** *of* Israel and Judah." 4948
24:10 I beg you, t **away** the guilt of your servant. 6296
24:22 my lord the king t whatever pleases him 4374

1Ki
1: 2 to attend the king and t **care of** him. 2118+6125
1:33 "T your lord's servants with you 4374
1:33 on my own mule and t him **down** to Gihon. 3718
5: 9 and you *can* t them **away.** 5951
8:31 and is required to t an **oath** and he comes 457
11:31 T ten pieces for yourself, 4374
11:34 "But *I* will not t the whole kingdom out 4374
11:35 *I will* t the kingdom from his son's hands 4374
11:37 However, as for you, *I will* t you, 4374
14: 3 T ten loaves of bread with you, 4374
17:12 a few sticks *to* t home and make a meal 995
19: 4 he said. "T my life; 4374
20:18 they have come out for peace, t them alive; 9530
20:18 they have come out for war, t them alive." 9530
21:10 Then t him **out** and stone him to death." 3655
21:15 and t possession *of* the vineyard of Naboth 3769
21:16 down to t possession of Naboth's vineyard. 3769
21:18 where he has gone to t possession of it. 3769
22:26 "T Micaiah and send him back to Amon 4374

2Ki
2: 1 *to* t Elijah up to heaven in a whirlwind, 6590
2: 3 that the LORD *is going to* t your master 4374
2: 5 that the LORD *is going to* t your master 4374
4: 1 to t my two boys as his slaves." 4374
4:29 t my staff in your hand and run. 4374
4:36 When she came, he said, "T your son." 5951
5:23 "By all means, t two talents," 4374
5:26 Is this the time to t money, 4374
7:12 and then *we will* t them alive and get into 9530
7:13 "Have some men t five of the horses 4374
8: 8 "T a gift with you and go to meet the man 4374
9: 1 t this flask of oil with you and go 995
9: 2 and t him **into** an inner room. 995
9: 3 Then t the flask and pour the oil 4374
9:34 "T **care** of that cursed woman," he said, 7212
10: 6 t the heads of your master's sons and come 4374
10:14 "T them alive!" he ordered. 9530
11: 6 who t **turns** guarding the temple— 5005
12: 7 T no more money from your treasurers, 4374
13:16 "T the bow in your hands," 8206
13:18 Then he said, "T the arrows," 4374
18:32 and t you to a land like your own, 4374
19:30 of the house of Judah will t root below NIH

1Ch
9:29 to t **care** of the furnishings and all 6584
13:13 not the ark to be with him in the City 6073
17:13 *I will* never t my love **away** from him, 6073
21: 1 and incited David to t a **census** *of* Israel. 4948
21: 8 I beg you, t **away** the guilt of your servant. 6296
21:11 This is what the LORD says: 'T your **choice:** 7691
21:23 Araunah said to David, "T it! 4374
21:24 *I will* not t for the LORD what is yours, 5951
27:23 David *did* not t the number of the men who 5951

2Ch
2:16 You *can* then t them **up** to Jerusalem. 6590
6:22 and is required to t an **oath** and he comes 457
18:25 "T Micaiah and send him back to Amon 4374
20:17 T up your **positions;** 3656
20:25 more than *they could* t **away.** 5362+5911
25:13 *to* t **part** in the war raided Judean 2143+6640
35:23 and he told his officers, "T me **away;** 6296
36: 6 with bronze shackles to t him to Babylon. 2143
36:13 had made him t an **oath** in God's name. 8678

Ezr
5:15 'T these articles and go and deposit them 10492
7:15 you are to t with you the silver and gold 10308
9:12 or t their daughters for your sons. 5951
10: 4 so t **courage** and do it." 2616

Ne
2: 6 asked me, "How long *will* your journey t, 2118
5:12 made the nobles and officials t an **oath** 8678
9:12 on the way *they were* to t. 2143
9:15 and t possession *of* the land you had sworn 3769
9:19 to shine on the way *they were* to t. 2143
10:30 around us or t their daughters for our sons. 4374
13:25 I made them t an **oath** in God's name 8678
13:25 nor *are you* t their daughters **in marriage** 5951

Est
2:13 Anything she wanted was given her to t 995

Job
1: 4 t **turns** holding feasts in their homes, 2143+3427
5:24 *you will* t **stock** *of* your property 7212
11:11 and when he sees evil, *does he* not t **note?** 1067
11:18 you will look about you and t *your* **rest** 8886
13:14 in jeopardy and t my life in my hands? 8492
13:17 let your ears t in what I say. 928
23:10 But he knows the way that I t; NIH
24: 3 t the widow's ox **in pledge.** 2471
32:22 my Maker *would* soon t me **away.** 5951
35:15 not t the least **notice** of wickedness. 3359
36: 7 He *does* not t his eyes off the righteous; 1757
37: 8 The animals t **cover;** 995+1198
38:13 that *it might* t the earth by the edges 296
38:20 *Can you* t them to their places? 4374
39:26 "*Does* the hawk t **flight** by your wisdom 87
41: 4 an agreement with you for *you to* t him 4374
42: 8 now t seven bulls and seven rams and go 4374

Ps
2: 2 The kings of the earth t *their* **stand** and 3656
2:12 Blessed are all *who* t refuge in him. 2879
5:11 But let all *who* t refuge in you be glad; 2879
7: 1 O LORD my God, *I* t refuge in you; 2879
10:14 you consider *us* to t it in hand. 5989

Ps
11: 1 In the LORD *I* t refuge. 2879
16: 1 O God, for in you *I* t refuge. 2879
16: 4 not pour out their libations of blood or t **up** 5951
17: 7 by your right hand *those who* t refuge 2879
18: 2 my God is my rock, in whom *I* t refuge. 2879
18:30 He is a shield for all who t refuge in him. 2879
25:18 and my distress and t **away** all my sins. 5951
25:20 for *I* t refuge in you. 2879
26: 9 *Do not* t **away** my soul along with sinners, 665
27:14 and t **heart** and wait for the LORD. 599+4213
31:13 against me and plot to t my life. 4374
31:19 in the sight of men on those *who* t refuge 4374
31:24 Be strong and t **heart,** 599+4222
35: 2 T **up** shield and buckler; 2616
37:40 because *they* t refuge in him. 2879
40:14 to t my life be put to shame and confusion; 6200
45: 6 Your sons *will* t the place of 2118+9393
49:15 *he will* surely t me to himself. 4374
49:17 *he will* t nothing with him when he dies, 4374
50:16 to recite my laws or t my covenant 5951
51:11 from your presence or t your Holy Spirit 4374
51:16 *you do* not t **pleasure** in burnt offerings. 8354
55:15 *Let* death t my enemies **by surprise;** 5958
56: 6 they watch my steps, eager to t my life. NIH
57: 1 *I will* t refuge in the shadow 2879
61: 4 to dwell in your tent forever and t refuge in 2879
62: 4 *they* t **delight** in lies. 8354
62:10 in extortion or t **pride** in stolen goods; 2038
64:10 in the LORD and t refuge in him; 2879
72:13 *He will* t **pity** on the weak and the needy 2571
73: 9 and their tongues t possession of the earth. 2143
73:24 and afterward *you will* t me *into* glory. 4374
74:11 It it from the folds of your garment NIH
83:12 "Let *us* t possession *of* the pasturelands 3769
89:33 but *I will* not t my love from him, 7296
94: 8 T **heed,** you senseless ones among 1067
94:16 Who *will* t a stand for me 3656
94:22 and my God the rock in whom *I* t refuge. NIH
102:24 So I said: "*Do* not t me **away,** O my God, 6590
104:29 *when you* t **away** their breath, 665
109: 8 *may* another t his place of leadership. 4374
109:12 to him or t **pity** on his fatherless children. 2858
118: 8 It is better to t refuge in the LORD than 2879
118: 9 It is better to t refuge in the LORD than 2879
119:39 T **away** the disgrace I dread, 6296
119:109 Though I *constantly* t my life in my hands, NIH
141: 4 to t **part** in wicked deeds 6618
141: 8 in you *I* t refuge— 2879
144: 2 my shield, in whom *I* t refuge, 2879

Pr
4:26 for your feet and t only ways that are firm. NIH
13:10 but wisdom is found in *those who* t **advice.** 3619
16:13 Kings t pleasure in honest lips; NIH
20:16 T the garment of one who puts up security 4374
22:23 for the LORD *will* t up their case 8189
23:11 he *will* t up their case against you. 8189
27:12 The prudent see danger and t refuge, 6259
27:13 T the garment of one who puts up security 4374
30: 5 he is a shield to those *who* t refuge in him. 2879

Ecc
4:13 who no longer knows how to t **warning.** 2302
7: 2 the living *should* t this to heart. 5989
9: 2 as it is with those *who* t oaths, 8678
9: 2 so with those who are afraid to t them. NIH

SS
1: 4 T me **away** with you—let us hurry! 5432
1: 6 and made me t **care** of the vineyards; 5757
7: 8 *I will* t hold of its fruit. 296

Isa
1:16 T your evil deeds out of my sight! 6073
2: 4 Nation *will* not t up sword against nation, 5951
3: 1 *to* t from Jerusalem and Judah both supply 6073
3: 6 t **charge** of this heap of ruins!" 3338+9393
3: 6 In that day seven women *will* t hold 2616
4: 1 T **away** our disgrace!" 665
5: 5 *I will* t away its hedge, 6073
7: 7 "'It will not t **place,** it will not happen, 7756
7:20 and *to* t off your beards also. 6200
8: 1 "T a large scroll and write on it with 4374
9:17 Therefore the Lord *will* t no **pleasure** in 8523
10:31 the people of Gebim t **cover.** 6395
14: 2 Nations *will* t them and bring them 4374
14: 4 *you will* t up this taunt against the king 5951
18: 5 down and t **away** the spreading branches. 6073
20: 2 "T off the sackcloth from your body and 7337
22:17 *to* t firm hold *of* you and hurl you 6487+6487
23:16 "T up a harp, walk through 4374
27: 6 In days to come Jacob *will* t root, 9245
31: 2 he *does* not t **back** his words. 6073
36:17 and t you to a land like your own— 4374
37:31 of the house of Judah will t root below NIH
40:24 no sooner *do they* t root in the ground, 1614+9245
42: 6 *I will* t hold of your hand. 2616
42:25 but *they did* not t it to heart. 8492
44:11 all come together and t *their* **stand;** 6641
45: 1 whose right hand *I* t hold *of* 2616
45:21 *let them* t **counsel** together. 3619
46: 8 fix it in mind, t it to heart, you rebels. 8740
47: 2 T millstones and grind flour; 4374
47: 2 t off your veil. 1655
47: 3 *I will* t vengeance; I will spare no one." 4374
48: 1 you who t oaths in the name of the LORD 8678
51:18 the sons she reared there was none *to* t her 2616
62: 4 for the LORD *will* t **delight** in you, 2911
65:19 I will rejoice over Jerusalem, and t **delight** 8464

Jer
6: 8 T **warning,** O Jerusalem, 3579
7:29 t up a lament on the barren heights; 5951
8:13 "'I will t **away** their harvest, 665
9:10 for the mountains and t up a lament NIH
13: 4 "T the belt you bought and are wearing 4374

Jer	15:15	You are long-suffering—*do* not t me **away**;	4374
	19: 1	T along some of the elders of the people	NIH
	20: 5	*They will* t it **away** as plunder	4374
	20:10	over him and t our revenge on him."	4374
	25:15	"T from my hand this cup filled with	4374
	25:28	if they refuse to t the cup from your hand	4374
	27:20	not t **away** when he carried Jehoiachin son	4374
	31: 4	Again *you will* t **up** your tambourines	6335
	31:21	T **note** of the highway,	4213+8883
	31:21	the highway, the road that you t.	2143
	32: 5	*He will* t Zedekiah to Babylon,	2143
	32:14	T these documents, both the sealed	4374
	32:24	"See how the siege ramps are built up to t	4334
	34:22	t it and burn it down.	4334
	36: 2	"T a scroll and write on it all	4374
	36:28	"T another scroll and write on it all	4374
	38:10	"T thirty men from here with you	4374
	39: 7	with bronze shackles to t him to Babylon,	995
	39:12	"T him and look after him;	4374
	39:14	to t him **back** to his home.	3655
	40:14	of Nethaniah to t your life?'	5782
	40:15	Why *should he* t your life and cause all	5782
	43: 9	t some large stones with you	4374
	43:12	and t their gods **captive**.	8647
	44:12	I *will* t away the remnant	4374
	46: 4	T your **positions** with helmets on!	3656
	46:14	'T your **positions** and get ready,	3656
	50: 9	*They will* t **up** *their* **positions** against her,	6885
	50:14	"T **up** your **positions** around Babylon,	6885
	50:15	t **vengeance** on her; do to her as she has	5933
	51:11	"Sharpen the arrows, t **up** the shields!	4848
	51:11	The LORD will t **vengeance**,	NIH
Eze	3:10	and t to heart all the words I speak to you.	4374
	4: 1	"Now, son of man, t a clay tablet,	4374
	4: 3	Then t an iron pan,	4374
	4: 9	"T wheat and barley, beans and lentils,	4374
	5: 1	t a sharp sword and use it as	4374
	5: 1	t a set of scales and divide up the hair.	4374
	5: 2	T a third and strike it with the sword all	4374
	5: 3	But t a few strands of hair	4374
	5: 4	t a few of these and throw them into	4374
	7:24	the nations to t **possession** *of* their houses;	3769
	10: 6	"T fire from among the wheels,	4374
	12: 5	t your belongings **out** through it.	3655
	16:39	of your clothes and t your fine jewelry	4374
	17: 9	not t a strong arm or many people to pull it	NIH
	17:22	I myself *will* t a shoot from the very top	4374
	18: 8	not lend at usury or t excessive interest.	4374
	18:23	*Do I* t any **pleasure in** the death of	2911+2911
	18:32	I t no **pleasure** in the death of anyone,	2911
	19: 1	"T **up** a lament concerning the princes	5951
	20:37	I will t **note** of you as you **pass**	6296
	21: 7	*It will* **surely** t **place**,	2118
	21:19	for the sword of the king of Babylon to t,	995
	21:23	of their guilt and t them **captive**.	9530
	21:26	T **off** the turban, remove the crown.	6073
	22:12	you t usury and excessive interest.	4374
	22:25	they devour people, t treasures	4374
	23:24	*they will* t **up** **positions** against you	8492
	23:25	They *will* t **away** your sons and daughters,	4374
	23:26	of your clothes and t your fine jewelry.	4374
	23:29	t **away** everything you have worked for.	4374
	23:48	that all women *may* t **warning** and	3579
	24: 5	t the pick of the flock.	4374
	24: 8	To stir up wrath and t **revenge**	5933+5934
	24:16	*about to* t **away** from you the delight	4374
	24:21	the stronghold in which you t pride,	NIH
	24:25	on the day I t **away** their stronghold,	4374
	25:14	I *will* t **vengeance** on Edom by the hand	5989
	25:17	when I t **vengeance** on them.' "	5989
	26:16	and t **off** their embroidered garments,	7320
	26:17	Then *they will* t **up** a lament	5951
	26:20	and you will not return or t your **place** in	3656
	27: 2	t **up** a lament concerning Tyre.	5951
	27:26	Your oarsmen t you **out** to the high seas.	995
	27:32	*they will* t **up** a **lament** concerning you:	7801
	28:12	t **up** a lament concerning the king of Tyre	5951
	30: 9	Anguish *will* t **hold of** them on the day	928+2118
	32: 2	t **up** a lament concerning Pharaoh king	5951
	33: 4	the trumpet but *does* not t **warning** and	2302
	33: 5	of the trumpet but *did* not t **warning**.	2302
	33:11	I t no **pleasure** in the death of the wicked,	2911
	34: 2	the shepherds of Israel who *only* t **care of**	8286
	34: 2	*Should* not shepherds t **care of** the flock?	8286
	34: 3	but *you do* not t **care of** the flock.	8286
	35:10	be ours and *we will* t **possession** *of* them,"	3769
	36:24	" 'For *I will* t you out of the nations;	4374
	37:16	t a stick of wood and write on it,	4374
	37:16	Then t another stick of wood,	4374
	37:19	*I am going to* t the stick of Joseph—	4374
	37:21	t the Israelites out of the nations	4374
	38: 7	and t **command** of them.	2118+4200+5464
	38:13	to t **away** livestock and goods and	4374
	38:14	*will you* not t **notice** of it?	3359
	39: 8	*It will* **surely** t **place**,	2118
	43:20	You are to t some of its blood and put it on	4374
	43:21	*to* t the bull for the sin offering and burn it	4374
	44:19	*they are to* t **off** the clothes they have been	7320
	45:18	*to* t a young bull without defect and purify	4374
	45:19	*to* t some of the blood of the sin offering	4374
	46:18	not t any of the inheritance of the people,	4374
Da	2:24	T me to the king,	10549
	2:45	the king what *will* t **place** in the future.	10201
	8:13	"How long will it for the vision to t	NIH
	8:14	He said to him, "It will t 2,300	NIH
	8:25	he will destroy many and t *his* **stand**	6641
	11: 7	her family line will arise to t her place.	NIH

Da	11:18	to the coastlands and *will* t many of them,	4334
	11:28	*He will* t **action** against it and then return	6913
	11:36	what has been determined *must* t place.	6913
Hos	1: 2	t to yourself an adulterous wife	4374
	2: 9	"Therefore *I will* t **away** my grain	4374
	2: 9	*I will* t **back** my wool and my linen,	5911
	2:10	no one will t her out of my hands.	5911
	4:11	*which* t away the understanding	4374
	10: 4	t false **oaths** and make agreements;	457
	14: 2	T words with you and return to the LORD.	4374
Joel	2:18	for his land and t **pity** on his people.	2798
Am	5: 1	this lament *I will* t concerning you:	5951
	5:12	the righteous and t bribes and you deprive	4374
	6:13	not t Karnaim by our own strength?"	4374
	9: 2	from there my hand *will* t them.	4374
Jnh	1: 6	Maybe he *will* t **notice** of us,	6951
	4: 3	Now, O LORD, t **away** my life,	4374
Mic	2: 9	You t **away** my blessing from their children	4374
	2: 9	and houses, and t them.	5951
	4: 3	Nation *will* not t **up** sword against nation,	5951
	5:15	I *will* t **vengeance** in anger and wrath	6913
Zep	3:17	He *will* t **great delight** in you,	928+8464+8525
Hag	1: 8	*I may* t **pleasure** in it and be honored,"	8354
	2:23	*'I will* t you, my servant Zerubbabel	4374
Zec	3: 4	"T **off** his filthy clothes."	6073
	6:10	"T [silver and gold] from the exiles Heldai,	4374
	6:11	T the silver and gold and make a crown,	4374
	8:23	and nations *will* t **firm hold** *of* one Jew	2616
	9: 4	But the Lord *will* t **away** her **possessions**	3769
	9: 7	I *will* t the blood from their mouths,	6073
	9:10	I *will* t **away** the chariots from Ephraim	4162
	11:15	"T again the equipment of a foolish	4374
	14:18	Egyptian people do not go up and t **part**,	995
	14:21	and all who come to sacrifice *will* t some	4374
Mt	1:20	not be afraid *to* t Mary home as your wife,	4161
	2:13	"t the child and his mother and escape	4161
	2:20	t the child and his mother and go to	4161
	2:20	for those who *were* **trying** to t	2426
	5:40	someone wants to sue you and t your tunic,	3284
	7: 4	'Let *me* t the **speck out** of your eye,'	1675
	7: 5	first t the plank **out** of your own eye,	1675
	8:11	t their **places at the feast** with Abraham,	369
	9: 2	"T **heart**, son; your sins are forgiven."	2510
	9: 6	"Get up, t your mat and go home."	149
	9:22	"T **heart**, daughter," he said,	2510
	10: 9	not t **along** any gold or silver or copper	3227
	10:10	t no bag for the journey, or extra tunic,	NIG
	10:38	not t his cross and follow me is not worthy	3284
	11:29	T my yoke upon you and learn from me,	149
	12:11	*will you* not t **hold of** it and lift it out?	3195
	14:27	immediately said to them: "T **courage!**	2510
	15:26	"It is not right *to* t the children's **bread**	3284
	16: 5	the disciples forgot *to* t bread.	3284
	16:24	must deny himself and t **up** his cross	149
	17:27	T the first fish you catch;	149
	17:27	T it and give it to them for my tax	3284
	18:16	t one or two others **along**,	4161
	20:14	T your pay and go.	149
	21:38	Come, let's kill him and t his **inheritance**.'	2400
	24:17	of his house go down *to* t anything out of	149
	24:20	that your flight *will* not t **place** in winter	1181
	25: 3	but *did* not t any oil with them.	3284
	25:28	" 'T the talent from him and give it to	149
	25:34	t your **inheritance**, the kingdom prepared	3099
	26:26	saying, "T and eat; this is my body."	3284
	27:65	"T a guard," Pilate answered.	2400
Mk	2: 9	or to say, 'Get up, t your mat and walk'?	149
	2:11	get up, t your mat and go home."	149
	3:21	they went to t **charge of** him, for they said,	3195
	6: 8	"T nothing for the journey except a staff—	149
	6:37	would t eight months of a man's wages!	NIG
	6:50	he spoke to them and said, "T **courage!**	2510
	7:27	"for it is not right *to* t the children's **bread**	3284
	8:34	after me, he must deny himself and t **up**	149
	9:22	t **pity** on us and help us."	5072
	13:15	down or enter the house *to* t anything out.	149
	13:18	Pray that *this* will not t **place** in winter,	1181
	14:22	and gave it to his disciples, saying, "T it;	3284
	14:36	T this cup from me.	4195
	15:23	but he *did* not t it.	3284
	15:36	Let's see if Elijah comes *to* t him **down**,"	2747
Lk	1:15	He *is* never *to* t wine or other fermented	4403
	5:18	a paralytic on a mat and tried *to* t him **into**	1662
	5:24	get up, t your mat and go home."	149
	6:42	let *me* t the **speck out** of your eye,'	1675
	6:42	first t the plank **out** of your eye,	1675
	9: 3	He told them: "T nothing for the journey—	149
	9:23	after me, he must deny himself and t **up**	149
	10: 4	*Do* not t a purse or bag or sandals;	1002
	12:19	T **life easy**; eat, drink and be merry." '	399
	13:29	t *their* **places at the feast** in the kingdom	369
	14: 8	*do* not t the place of honor,	1650+2884
	14: 9	*to* t the least important place.	2988
	14:10	when you are invited, t the lowest place	404+1650
	16: 6	"The manager told him, 'T your bill,	1312
	16: 7	'T your bill and make it eight hundred.'	1312
	19:17	t **charge of** ten cities.'	1639+2400
	19:19	'You t **charge of** five cities.'	1181+2062
	19:21	You t **out** what you did not put in	149
	19:24	'T his mina **away** from him and give it to	149
	21: 7	the sign that they are about to t place?"	1181
	21:28	When these things begin *to* t **place**,	1181
	22:17	"T this and divide it among you.	3284
	22:36	But now if you have a purse, t it,	149
	22:42	if you are willing, t this cup from me;	4195
Jn	1:22	an answer to t **back** to those who sent us.	1443
	2: 8	"Now draw some out and t it to the master	5770

Jn	6:21	they were willing *to* t him into the boat,	3284
	7: 1	the Jews there were waiting *to* t his **life.**	650
	10:17	I lay down my life—only *to* t it **up** again.	3284
	10:18	to lay it down and authority *to* t it **up**	3284
	11:39	"T **away** the stone," he said.	149
	11:44	"T **off** the grave clothes and let him go."	3395
	11:48	and then the Romans will come and t **away**	149
	11:53	from that day on they plotted to t *his* **life.**	650
	14: 3	and t you to be with me that you also may	4161
	16:15	the Spirit *will* t from what is mine	3284
	16:22	and no one will t **away** your joy.	149
	16:33	But t **heart!** I have overcome the world."	2510
	17:15	not that *you* t them out of the world but	149
	18:31	"T him yourselves and judge him	3284
	19: 6	"You t him and crucify him."	3284
	19:15	But they shouted, "T him **away!**	149
	19:15	T him **away!** Crucify him!"	149
	21:16	Jesus said, "T **care of** my sheep."	4477
Ac	1:20	" 'May another t his place of leadership.'	3284
	1:25	*to* t **over** this apostolic ministry,	3284
	4:26	The kings of the earth t *their* **stand** and	4225
	7:33	the Lord said to him, 'T **off** your sandals;	3395
	9: 2	he might *to* t them as prisoners to Jerusalem.	72
	9:21	to t them as prisoners to the chief priests?"	72
	9:34	Get up and t **care of** *your* **mat.**	4932+5143
	13:40	T **care** that what the prophets have said	1063
	15:37	wanted *to* t John, also called Mark, **with**	5221
	15:38	but Paul did not think it wise *to* t him,	5221
	16: 3	Paul wanted *to* t him along on the journey,	2002
	20:13	where we were going to t Paul **aboard.**	377
	21:24	T these men, join in their purification rites	4161
	21:37	As the soldiers were about to t Paul **into**	1652
	23:10	t him away from them **by force**	773
	23:11	near Paul and said, "T **courage!**	2510
	23:17	"T this young man to the commander;	552
	24:23	permit his friends *to* t **care of** his **needs.**	5676
	27:34	Now I urge you to t some food.	3561
Ro	2:16	This will t place on the day when God	NIG
	11:27	with them when *I* t **away** their sins."	904
	12:19	*Do* not t **revenge**, my friends,	1688+4932
1Co	4: 6	not t **pride** in one man over against another.	5881
	6: 1	t it before the ungodly *for* **judgment**	3212
	6:15	Shall I then t the members of Christ	149
	9: 5	the right to t a believing wife **along**	4310
	10:30	If I t **part** in the meal with thankfulness,	3576
2Co	5: 9	but are giving you an opportunity to t pride	NIG
	5:12	so that you can answer those who t **pride**	3016
	7: 4	I t great pride in you.	NIG
	10: 5	and *we* t **captive** every thought	170
	11:16	I repeat: Let no one t me **for** a fool.	1506+1639
	12: 8	with the Lord to t it **away** from me.	923
Gal	3:15	let *me* t **an example** from everyday life.	3306
	5:10	in the Lord that *you* will t no other **view.**	5858
	6: 4	Then he can t pride in himself,	2400
Eph	6:11	of God so that you can t your **stand** against	2705
	6:16	t **up** the shield of faith, with which you can	377
	6:17	T the helmet of salvation and the sword of	1312
Php	2:25	whom you sent to t **care** of my needs.	3313
	3:12	but I press on to t **hold** of that	2898
	3:15	mature *should* t such a view of things.	5858
	3:17	and t **note** of those who live according to	5023
1Th	4: 6	wrong his brother or t **advantage of** him.	4430
2Th	3:14	t **special note** of him.	4957
1Ti	3: 5	how *can he* t **care of** God's church?)	2150
	5:20	so that the others *may* t **warning**.	2400
	6: 7	and we can t nothing **out of** it.	1766
	6:12	T **hold** of the eternal life	2138
	6:19	*they may* t **hold** of the life that is truly life.	2138
Phm	1:13	that he could t your **place** in helping me	5642
Heb	5: 5	*did* not t upon himself the **glory**	1519
	6:18	*to* t **hold** of the hope offered to us may	3195
	9:28	so Christ was sacrificed once to t **away**	429
	10: 4	the blood of bulls and goats *to* t **away** sins.	904
	10:11	which can never t **away** sins.	4311
Jas	1: 9	in humble circumstances *ought to* t **pride**	3016
	1:10	But the one who is rich should t **pride**	NIG
	1:19	My dear brothers, t **note** of this:	3857
	3: 4	Or t ships as an example.	NIG
	5:10	t the prophets who spoke in the name of	3284
1Jn	3: 5	so that *he might* t **away** our sins.	149
2Jn	1:10	not t him into your house or welcome him.	3284
Rev	1: 1	show his servants what must soon t **place.**	1181
	1: 3	and t to **heart** what is written in it,	5498
	1:19	what is now and what will t **place** later.	1181
	3:11	so that no one will t your **crown.**	3284
	4: 1	and I will show you what must t **place**	1181
	5: 9	"You are worthy *to* t the scroll and	3284
	6: 4	Its rider was given power to t peace from	3284
	10: 8	"Go, t the scroll that lies open in the hand	3284
	10: 9	He said to me, "T it and eat it.	3284
	14:15	"T your sickle and reap,	4287
	14:18	"T your sharp sickle and gather the clusters	4287
	22: 6	the things that must soon t **place.**"	1181
	22:17	let *him* t the free gift of the water of life.	3284
	22:19	God *will* t **away from** him his share in	904

TAKEN (268) [TAKE]

Ge	2:22	woman from the rib *he had* t out of the man,	4374
	2:23	'woman,' for she *was* t out of man."	4374
	3:19	since from it *you* were t;	4374
	3:23	the ground from which *he had* been t.	4374
	12:15	and she *was* t into his palace.	4374
	14:14	that his relative *had* been t **captive**,	8647
	14:22	"I *have* **raised** my hand to the LORD, God Most High, Creator of heaven and earth, **and** *have* t **an oath**	8123

Ge	20: 3	as dead because of the woman *you have* t;	4374
	27:36	and now *he's* t my blessing!"	4374
	30:23	"God *has* t away my disgrace."	665
	31: 1	"Jacob *has* t everything our father owned	4374
	31: 9	So God *has* t away your father's livestock	5911
	31:34	Now Rachel *had* t the household gods	4374
	39: 1	Now Joseph *had been* t down to Egypt.	3718
	39: 1	from the Ishmaelites who *had* t him there.	3718
	42:24	*He had* t Simeon t from them and bound	4374
	43:18	the men were frightened when *they were* t	995
Ex	12: 4	having t into account the number	928
	22:10	or is t away while no one is looking,	8647
Lev	6: 4	what he has stolen or t by extortion,	6943+6945
	7:34	*I have* t the breast that is waved and	4374
	10:18	its blood *was* not t into the Holy Place,	995
	14:45	and t out of the town to an unclean place.	3655
	16:27	*must be* t outside the camp;	3655
	25:12	eat only *what is* t directly from the fields.	9311
Nu	3:12	"I have t the Levites from among	4374
	8:16	*I have* t them as my own in place of	4374
	8:18	And *I have* t the Levites in place of all	4374
	10:17	Then the tabernacle *was* t down,	3718
	14: 3	and children *will be* t as plunder.	2118
	14:31	for your children that you said *would be* t	2118
	16:15	not t so much as a donkey from them,	5951
	19: 3	*to be* t outside the camp and slaughtered	3655
	21:26	against the former king of Moab and *had* t	4374
	30: 9	"Any vow or **obligation** t by a widow	673
	31:53	Each soldier *had* t **plunder** for himself.	1024
	36: 3	then their inheritance *will be* t	1757
	36: 3	inheritance allotted to us *will be* t away.	1757
	36: 4	and their property *will be* t	1757
Dt	1:39	*be* t **captive**, your children who do not	1020
	3:20	and they too *have* t over the land that	3769
	11:31	*you have* t over and are living there,	3769
	17:14	and *have* t **possession** *of* it and settled in it,	3769
	17:18	t from that of the priests,	4200+4946+7156
	23:15	If a slave *has* t **refuge** with you,	5911
	26: 1	as an inheritance and *have* t **possession** *of* it	3769
	28:31	Your donkey *will be* **forcibly** t from you	1608
Jos	1:15	until they too *have* t **possession** *of* the land	3769
	2: 4	woman *had* t the two men and hidden them.	4374
	2: 6	(But she *had* t them up to the roof	6590
	4:20	up at Gilgal the twelve stones *they had* t out	4374
	7:11	*They have* t some of the devoted things;	4374
	7:16	came forward by tribes, and Judah *was* t.	4334
	7:17	came forward by families, and Zimri *was* t.	4334
	7:18	of the tribe of Judah, *was* t.	4334
	8: 8	When you *have* t the city, set it on fire.	9530
	8:12	Joshua *had* t about five thousand men	4374
	8:21	and all Israel saw that the ambush *had* t	4334
	10: 1	that Joshua *had* t Ai and totally destroyed it,	4334
	13: 1	very large areas of land to *be* t over.	3769
	13:12	Moses *had* defeated them and t over	3769
	19: 9	The inheritance of the Simeonites was t	NIH
Jdg	14: 9	not tell them that *he had* t the honey from	8098
	17: 2	of silver that *were* t from you and	4374
	19:18	No one *has* t me into his house.	665
	21: 1	The men of Israel *had* t **an oath** at Mizpah;	8678
	21: 5	For they *had* t a solemn oath	2118
	21: 7	since we *have* t **an oath** by the LORD not	8678
	21:18	since *we* Israelites *have* t **this oath**;	8678
1Sa	12: 3	Whose ox *have I* t?	4374
	12: 3	Whose donkey *have I* t?	4374
	12: 4	not t anything from anyone's hand."	4374
	14:41	And Jonathan and Saul *were* t by lot,	4334
	14:42	And Jonathan *was* t.	4334
	21: 6	by hot bread on the day it *was* t away.	4374
	30: 2	and *had* t **captive** the women	8647
	30: 3	and sons and daughters t **captive**.	8647
	30:16	the great amount of plunder *they had* t from	4374
	30:18	the Amalekites *had* t	4374
	30:19	plunder or anything else *they had* t.	4374
2Sa	2: 8	*had* t Ish-Bosheth son of Saul	4374
	3:15	and *had* her t away from her husband	4374
	6:13	the ark of the LORD *had* t six **steps**,	7575+7576
	7:15	my love *will* never *be* t away from him,	6073
	8:12	the plunder t from Hadadezer son of Rehob,	NIH
	12:13	"The LORD *has* t away your sin.	6296
	12:27	against Rabbah and t its water supply.	4334
	18:18	During his lifetime Absalom *had* t a pillar	4374
	19:24	*He had* not t **care of** his feet	6913
	19:40	the troops of Israel *had* t the king over.	4334
	19:42	*Have we* t **anything** for ourselves?"	5951+5951
	21:12	(*They had* them **secretly** from	1704
1Ki	1:46	Solomon *has* t his **seat** on the royal throne.	3782
	13:12	the man of God from Judah *had* t.	2143
	16:18	When Zimri saw that the city *was* t,	4334
	18: 4	Obadiah *had* t a hundred prophets	4374
2Ki	2: 9	what can I do for you before *I am* t	4374
	2:10	"yet if you see me when *I am* t from you,	4374
	5: 2	from Aram had gone out and *had* t **captive**	8647
	6:13	When *he had* t it, Elishah put his hands	8206
	13:25	of Hazael the towns *he had* t in battle	4374
	17:23	t from their homeland **into exile**	1655
	20:18	that will be born to you, *will be* t away,	4374
	24: 7	the king of Babylon *had* t all his territory,	4374
	25: 6	He *was* t to the king of Babylon at Riblah,	6590
1Ch	9: 1	The people of Judah *were* t **captive**	1655
	9:28	in and *when they were* t out.	3655
	18:11	and gold he *had* t from all these nations:	5951
	22:14	"I have t **great pains** to provide for	928+6715
	24: 6	one family *being* t from Eleazar and	296
	26:27	the plunder t *in* battle they dedicated for	4946
2Ch	2:17	**census** his father David *had* t;	6218+6222

2Ch	34:14	the money that *had been* t into the temple	995
Ezr	2: 1	king of Babylon *had* t **captive** to Babylon	1655
	5:14	which Nebuchadnezzar *had* t from	10485
	8:30	*be* t to the house of our God in Jerusalem.	995
	9: 2	t some of their daughters **as wives**	5951
	10:13	this matter cannot *be* t care of in a day	NIH
Ne	7: 6	of Babylon *had* t **captive** (they returned	1655
Est	1:15	of King Xerxes that the eunuchs *have* t	928+3338
	2: 6	among those t **captive** with Jehoiachin	1655
	2: 7	and Mordecai *had* t her as his own daughter	4374
	2: 8	Esther also *was* t to the king's palace	4374
	2:16	She *was* t to King Xerxes in the royal	4374
Job	1:21	and the LORD *has* t away;	4374
	28: 2	Iron is t from the earth,	4374
	33: 6	I too *have been* t from clay.	7975
	36:17	judgment and justice *have* t **hold** of you.	9461
Ps	31: 1	In you, O LORD, *I have* t **refuge**;	2879
	71: 1	In you, O LORD, *I have* t **refuge**;	2879
	78:54	to the hill country his right hand *had* t.	7864
	88: 8	*You have* t from me my closest friends	8178
	88:18	*You have* t my companions and loved ones	8178
	102:10	for you *have* t me up and thrown me aside.	5951
	119:106	*I have* t **an oath** and confirmed it,	8678
Pr	27:14	*it will be* t as a curse.	3108
Ecc	3:14	nothing can be added to it and nothing t	1757
	5: 9	The increase from the land is t by all;	NIH
	9:12	or birds *are* t in a snare,	296
SS	2: 4	*He has* t me to the banquet hall,	995
	5: 3	*I have* t **off** my robe—	7320
Isa	6: 6	which *he had* t with tongs from the altar.	4374
	6: 7	your guilt *is* t away and your sin atoned for.	6073
	14:25	His yoke *will be* t from my people,	6073
	16:10	and gladness *are* t away from the orchards;	665
	22: 3	All you who were caught *were* t **prisoner** together,	673
	23: 7	whose feet *have* t her to settle in far-off	3297
	28: 9	to *those just* t from the breast?	6972
	38:12	has been pulled down and t from me.	1655
	39: 7	who will be born to you, *will be* t away,	4374
	42: 9	See, the former things *have* t **place**,	995
	49:24	*Can* plunder *be* t from warriors,	4374
	49:25	"Yes, captives *will be* t *from* warriors,	4374
	51:22	"See, *I have* t out of your hand the cup	4374
	52: 5	my people *have been* t away for nothing,	4374
	53: 8	By oppression and judgment he *was* t away.	4374
	57: 1	devout men *are* t away,	665
	57: 1	that the righteous *are* t away to be spared	665
Jer	8:13	What I have given them *will be* t from	6296
	12: 2	and *they have* t root;	9245
	13:17	the LORD's flock *will be* t **captive**.	8647
	14: 9	Why are you like a man t **by surprise**,	1850
	27:18	the king of Judah and in Jerusalem not *be* t	995
	27:22	'They *will be* t to Babylon	995
	34:16	each of *you has* t **back** the male	8740
	38:28	This is how Jerusalem *was* t:	4334
	39:14	sent and had Jeremiah t out of the courtyard	4374
	40:10	and live in the towns *you have* t over.	9530
	41:14	All the people Ishmael *had* t **captive**	8647
	48: 7	you too *will be* t **captive**,	4334
	48:41	be captured and the strongholds t.	9530
	48:46	your sons *are* t into exile	4374
	49: 1	Why then *has* Molech t **possession** *of* Gad?	3769
	49:29	Their tents and their flocks *will be* t;	4374
	50:28	how the LORD our God has t vengeance,	NIV
	51:26	No rock *will be* t from you for	4374
	52: 9	He *was* t to the king of Babylon at Riblah,	6590
	52:30	745 Jews t **into exile** by Nebuzaradan	1655
Eze	15: 3	Is wood *ever* t from it to make anything	4374
	21:24	*you will be* t **captive**.	928+2021+4090+9530
	30:16	Thebes will be t **by storm**;	1324
	33: 5	If he *had* t **warning**,	2302
	33: 6	that man *will be* t away because of his sin,	4374
	45:15	*be* t from every flock of two hundred from	NIH
Da	4:31	Your royal authority *has been* t from you.	10528
	5: 2	that Nebuchadnezzar his father *had* t from	10485
	5: 3	in the gold goblets that *had been* t from	10485
	7:26	and his power *will be* t away	10528
Hos	9: 6	Their treasures of silver *will be* t over	3769
	10: 5	because *it is* t from them **into exile**.	1655
Am	2: 8	beside every altar on garments t **in pledge**.	2471
	2: 8	In the house of their god they drink **wine** t	AIT
	4: 2	surely come when you *will be* t away	5951
Mic	1:11	its protection *is* t from you.	4374
Na	3:10	Yet she *was* t **captive** and went into exile.	4200
Zep	3:15	The LORD *has* t away your punishment,	6073
Zec	3: 4	"See, *I have* t away your sin,	6296
	14: 2	of the people *will* not *be* t from the city.	4162
Mt	9:15	when the bridegroom *will be* t **from** them;	554
	13:12	even what he has *will be* t from him.	149
	21:43	of God *will be* t away from you and given	149
	23:30	not *have* t **part** with them in shedding	1639+3128
	24:40	one *will be* t and the other left.	4161
	24:41	one *will be* t and the other left.	4161
	25:29	even what he has *will be* t from him.	149
	26:39	if it is possible, *may* this cup *be* t from me.	4216
	26:42	if it is not possible for this cup to *be* t away	4216
	26:56	But this has all t **place** that the writings of	1181
Mk	2:20	when the bridegroom *will be* t **from** them,	554
	4:25	even what he has *will be* t from him."	149
	8: 6	*When he had* t the seven loaves	3284
	16:19	*he was* t up into heaven and he sat at	377
Lk	1:25	and t away my disgrace among	904
	2: 1	**census** *should be* t of the entire Roman	616
	5: 9	at the catch of fish *they had* t,	5197
	5:35	when the bridegroom *will be* t **from** them,	554
	8:18	even what he thinks he has *will be* t	149
	9:51	As the time approached for him to *be* t up	378

Lk	10:42	and it will not *be* t away from her."	904
	11:52	*you have* t away the key to knowledge.	149
	17:34	one *will be* t and the other left.	4161
	17:35	one *will be* t and the other left.	4161
	19:26	even what he has *will be* t away.	149
	21:24	the sword and *will be* t **as prisoners** to all	170
	24:51	he left them and *was* t up into heaven.	429
Jn	2:20	"It has t forty-six years to build this	NIG
	13:30	As soon as Judas *had* t the bread,	3284
	18:40	*had* t **part in a rebellion**.	1639+3334
	19:31	the legs broken and the bodies t down.	149
	20: 2	"They *have* t the Lord out of the tomb,	149
	20:13	"They *have* t my Lord away," she said,	149
	21: 7	(for he had t *it off*) and jumped into	1218
Ac	1: 2	until the day *he was* t up to heaven,	377
	1: 9	*he was* t up before their very eyes,	2048
	1:11	who *has been* t from you into heaven,	377
	1:22	to the time when Jesus *was* t up from us.	377
	8:33	For his life *was* t from the earth."	149
	9:39	he arrived he *was* t **upstairs** to the room.	343
	10:16	and immediately the sheet *was* t **back**	377
	18:18	at Cenchrea because of a vow he *had* t.	2400
	19:12	and aprons that had touched him *were* t to	708
	21:34	he ordered that Paul *be* t into the barracks.	72
	22:24	the commander ordered Paul to *be* t **into**	1652
	23:14	"We *have* t a **solemn oath** not	353+354
	23:21	They *have* t **an oath** not to eat or drink	354
	23:24	that he may be t safely to Governor Felix."	2097
	27:21	"Men, you should *have* t my **advice** not	4272
Ro	5:13	not t **into account** where there is no law.	1824
1Co	15: 1	and on which *you have* t your **stand**.	2705
2Co	3:14	because only in Christ *is it* t away.	2934
	3:16	turns to the Lord, the veil *is* t away.	4311
Gal	4:24	These things may be t **figuratively**,	251
Php	3:13	not consider myself yet *to have* t **hold** of	2898
Col	3: 9	*since you have* t **off** your old self	588
2Th	2: 7	to do so till he *is* t out of the way.	1181
1Ti	3:16	believed on in the world, *was* t up in glory.	377
2Ti	2:18	that the resurrection *has* already t **place**,	1181
	2:26	who *has* t them **captive** to do his will.	2436
Heb	11: 5	By faith Enoch *was* t from this life,	3572
	11: 5	because God *had* t him away.	3572
	11: 5	For before he was t, he was commended	3557
Jude	1:11	*They have* t the way of Cain;	4513
Rev	5: 8	And when *he had* t it,	3284
	11:17	because *you have* t your great power	3284
	12: 6	where she *might be* t **care of** for 1,260	5555
	12:14	where she *would be* t **care of** for a time,	5555

TAKES (72) [TAKE]

Ge	27:46	If Jacob t a wife from among the women	4374
Lev	5: 4	" 'Or if a person thoughtlessly t **an oath**	8678
	24:17	'If anyone t the **life** *of* a human being,	5782+5883
	24:18	*Anyone* who t the **life** *of* someone's	5782+5883
Nu	24:22	be destroyed when Asshur t you **captive**."	8647
	30: 2	or t **an oath** to obligate himself	8652+8678
Dt	1: 2	(It t eleven days to go from Horeb	NIH
	13: 2	of which he has spoken t **place**,	995
	17:18	When he t the throne of his kingdom,	3782+6584
	19:16	If a malicious witness t **the stand** to	928+7756
	22:13	If a man t a wife and, after lying with her,	4374
Jos	7:14	that the LORD t shall come forward clan	4334
	7:14	the LORD t shall come forward family	4334
	7:14	that the LORD t shall come forward man	4334
2Sa	15: 8	'If the LORD t me **back** *to* Jerusalem,	8740+8740
1Ki	8:46	who t them **captive** to his own land,	8647+8647
	20:11	not boast like *one who* t it **off**.' "	7337
2Ch	6:36	to the enemy, who t them **captive** to	8647+8647
Job	12:18	*He* t **off** the shackles put on by kings	7337
	12:20	the lips of trusted advisers t away	4374
	27: 8	when God t away his life?	8923
	34:25	Because he t **note** of their deeds,	5795
	38:14	The earth t **shape** like clay under a seal;	2200
Ps	5: 4	You are not a God who t **pleasure** in evil;	2913
	34: 8	blessed is the man who t **refuge** in him.	2879
	34:22	no one will be condemned who t **refuge**	2879
	57: 1	for in you my soul t **refuge**.	2879
	149: 4	For the LORD t **delight** in his people;	8354
Pr	1:19	*it* t away the lives of those who get it.	4374
	3:32	for the LORD detests a perverse man but t	NIH
	6:34	he will show no mercy when he t revenge.	NIH
	8: 2	where the paths meet, *she* t her **stand**;	5893
	10: 9	he who t **crooked** paths will be found out.	6835
	16:32	a man who controls his temper than one who t a city.	4334
	21:12	The Righteous One t **note** of the house of	8505
	22: 3	A prudent man sees danger and t **refuge**,	6259
	25:20	Like *one who* t away a garment on	6334
	31:23	he t his **seat** among the elders of the land.	3782
Ecc	5:15	*He* t nothing from his labor	5951
Isa	3:13	The LORD t his **place** in court;	5893
	21: 2	The traitor betrays, the looter t **loot**.	8720
	22: 6	Elam t up the quiver,	5951
	28: 4	as someone sees it and t it in his hand,	NIH
	41:13	who t **hold** *of* your right hand and says	2616
	44:12	The blacksmith t a tool and works with it	NIH
	44:15	some of it he t and warms himself,	4374
	65:16	he who t **an oath** in the land will swear by	8678
Jer	4:29	and archers every town t **to flight**.	1368
Eze	18:13	He lends at usury and t **excessive interest**.	4374
	18:17	and t no usury or excessive interest.	4374
	26:15	and *the* **slaughter** t **place** in you?	2222+2223
	33: 4	and the sword comes and t his **life**,	4374
	33: 6	and the sword comes and t the **life** of one	4374
Mic	2: 4	*He* t it from me! He assigns our fields	4631
Na	1: 2	the LORD t **vengeance** and is filled	5933

Na	1: 2	The LORD **t** vengeance on his foes	5933
Hab	2: 5	to himself all the nations and **t** captive all	7695
Mt	12:45	Then it goes and **t** with it	4161
Mk	4:15	and **t away** the word that was sown	149
Lk	6:29	If someone **t** your cloak,	149
	6:30	and if anyone **t** what belongs to you,	149
	8:12	then the devil comes and **t away** the word	149
	11:22	he **t away** the armor in which	149
	11:26	**t** seven other spirits more wicked than itself,	4161
Jn	1:29	who **t away** the sin of the world!	149
	10:18	No one **t** it from me, but I lay it down	149
2Co	11:20	or exploits you or **t advantage of** you	3284
Php	2:20	who **t** a genuine **interest** in your welfare.	3534
Col	2: 8	no one **t** you **captive** through hollow	1639+5194
Heb	5: 4	No one **t** this honor upon himself;	3284
	9:17	it never **t effect** while the one who made it	2710
Rev	22:19	And if anyone **t** words **away from** this book	904

TAKING (59) [TAKE]

Ge	8:20	**t** some of all the clean animals	4374
	24:10	**t** with him all kinds of good things	928+3338
	28:11	**T** one of the stones there,	4374
	28:20	over me on this journey I am **t**	2143
	31:23	**T** his relatives with him,	4374
	34:29	**t as plunder** everything in the houses.	1024
	42:38	to him on the journey you are **t**,	2143
	50: 3	**t** a **full** forty days,	4848
Ex	5: 4	why are you **t** the people **away**	7277
	22:11	by the **t** of an oath before the LORD that	NIH
	29:35	**t** seven days to ordain them.	NIH
Nu	15:18	you enter the land to which I am **t** you	995
	22: 7	**t** with them the fee for divination.	928+3338
Dt	1:25	**T** with them some of the fruit of the land,	4374
	24: 6	**t** a man's livelihood **as security.**	2471
Jos	6:18	about your own destruction by **t** any	4374
	19:47	had difficulty **t possession of** their	3655+4946
Jdg	3:28	**t possession** of the fords of the Jordan	4334
1Sa	14:32	They pounced on the plunder and, **t** sheep,	4374
	17:49	Reaching into his bag and **t** out a stone,	4374
	29: 4	by **t** the heads of our own men?	NIH
2Sa	4: 5	while he was **t** his noonday **rest.**	5435+8886
	4: 7	**T** it with them,	4374
	12: 4	but the rich man refrained from **t** one	4374
1Ki	11:18	Then **t** men from Paran with them,	4374
2Ki	5: 5	**t** with him ten talents of silver,	4374
	8: 9	**t** with him as a gift forty camel-loads of all	4374
	15:25	**T** fifty men of Gilead with him,	NIH
1Ch	2: 7	by violating the ban on **t** devoted things.	NIH
2Ch	17: 9	**t** with them the Book of the Law of	NIH
Job	5: 3	I myself have seen a fool **t root**,	9245
	5: 5	**t** it even from among thorns,	4374
Ecc	4: 1	the oppression that was **t place** under	6913
Isa	30:14	a fragment will be found for **t** coals from	3149
Eze	17: 3	**T hold** of the top of a cedar,	4374
Hos	11: 3	**t** them by the arms;	4374
Jnh	1:14	please do not let us die for **t** this man's life.	NIH
Zec	5:10	"Where are they **t** the basket?"	2143
Mt	5:25	**adversary** who is **t** you to court.	508
	14:19	**T** the five loaves and the two fish	3284
Mk	6:41	**T** the five loaves and the two fish	3284
	9:36	**T** him **in his arms,**	1878
Lk	6: 4	and **t** the consecrated bread,	3284
	6:29	do not **stop him from t** your tunic.	3266
	9:16	**T** the five loaves and the two fish	3284
	12:45	'My master is **t a long time** in coming,'	5988
	14: 4	So **t hold** of the man,	2138
	16: 3	My master is **t away** my job.	904
	19:22	**t** out what I did not put in,	149
	20:35	of **t part** in that age and in the resurrection	5593
	22:17	After **t** the cup, he gave thanks and said,	1312
Jn	16:14	He will bring glory to me by **t** from what is	3284
	19:40	**T** Jesus' body, the two of them wrapped it,	3284
Ac	3: 7	**T** him by the right hand, he helped him up,	4389
	9:19	and after **t** some food, he regained	3284
	12:25	**t** with them John, also called Mark.	5221
	15:14	by **t** from the Gentiles a people for himself.	3284
2Co	8:21	For we are **t pains** to do what is right,	4629
Php	2: 7	**t** the very nature of a servant,	3284

TALENT (14) [TALENTS]

Ex	25:39	A **t** of pure gold is to be used for	3971
	37:24	and all its accessories from one **t**	3971
	38:27	one **t** for each base.	3971
2Sa	12:30	its weight was a **t** of gold,	3971
1Ki	20:39	or you must pay a **t** of silver.'	3971
2Ki	5:22	Please give them a **t** of silver and two sets	3971
	23:33	a levy of a hundred talents of silver and a **t**	3971
1Ch	20: 2	its weight was found to be a **t** of gold,	3971
2Ch	36: 3	a levy of a hundred talents of silver and a **t**	3971
Mt	25:15	and to another one **t**,	NIG
	25:18	man who had received the one **t** went off,	NIG
	25:24	the man who had received the one **t** came.	5419
	25:25	So I was afraid and went out and hid your **t**	5419
	25:28	" 'Take the **t** from him and give it to	5419

TALENTS (49) [TALENT]

Ex	38:24	on the sanctuary was 29 **t** and 730 shekels,	3971
	38:25	in the census was 100 **t** and 1,775 shekels,	3971
	38:27	The 100 **t** of silver were used to cast	3971
	38:27	100 bases from the 100 **t**,	3971
	38:29	from the wave offering was 70 **t** and 2,400	3971
1Ki	9:14	Hiram had sent to the king 120 **t** of gold.	3971
	9:28	to Ophir and brought back 420 **t** of gold,	3971
	10:10	And she gave the king 120 **t** of gold,	3971
	10:14	that Solomon received yearly was 666 **t**,	3971

1Ki	16:24	of Samaria from Shemer for two **t** of silver	3971
2Ki	5: 5	taking with him ten **t** of silver,	3971
	5:23	"By all means, take two **t**," said Naaman.	3971
	5:23	then tied up the two **t** of silver in two bags,	3971
	15:19	a thousand **t** of silver to gain his support	3971
	18:14	of Judah three hundred **t** of silver	3971
	18:14	of silver and thirty **t** of gold.	3971
	23:33	a levy of a hundred **t** of silver and a talent	3971
1Ch	19: 6	the Ammonites sent a thousand **t** of silver	3971
	22:14	the LORD a hundred thousand **t** of gold,	3971
	22:14	a million **t** of silver,	3971
	29: 4	three thousand **t** of gold (gold of Ophir)	3971
	29: 4	and seven thousand **t** of refined silver,	3971
	29: 7	on the temple of God five thousand **t**	3971
	29: 7	ten thousand **t** of gold,	3971
	29: 7	eighteen thousand **t** of bronze and	3971
	29: 7	of bronze and a hundred thousand **t** of iron.	3971
2Ch	3: 8	the inside with six hundred **t** of fine gold.	3971
	8:18	and brought back four hundred and fifty **t**	3971
	9: 9	Then she gave the king 120 **t** of gold,	3971
	9:13	that Solomon received yearly was 666 **t**,	3971
	25: 6	from Israel for a hundred **t** of silver.	3971
	25: 9	"But what about the hundred **t** I paid	3971
	27: 5	the Ammonites paid him a hundred **t**	3971
	36: 3	a levy of a hundred **t** of silver and a talent	3971
Ezr	7:22	up to a hundred **t** of silver,	10352
	8:26	I weighed out to them 650 **t** of silver,	3971
	8:26	silver articles weighing 100 **t**,	3971
	8:26	100 **t** of gold,	3971
Est	3: 9	and I will put ten thousand **t** of silver into	3971
Mt	18:24	who owed him ten thousand **t** was brought	5419
	25:15	To one he gave five **t** of **money,**	5419
	25:15	to another two **t**, and to another one talent,	NIG
	25:16	The man who had received the five **t** went	5419
	25:17	the one with the two **t** gained two more.	NIG
	25:20	the five **t** brought the other five.	5419
	25:20	he said, 'you entrusted me with five **t**.	5419
	25:22	"The man with the two **t** also came.	5419
	25:22	he said, 'you entrusted me with two **t**;	5419
	25:28	and give it to the one who has the ten **t**.	5419

TALE (KJV) See COUNTED, FULL QUOTA, SAME NUMBER

TALEBEARER (KJV) See GOSSIP, SPREADING SLANDER

TALES (1)

1Ti	4: 7	with godless myths and **old wives' t**;	1212

TALITHA (1)

Mk	5:41	**"T** koum!" (which means, "Little girl,	5420

TALK (43) [TALKED, TALKER, TALKERS, TALKING, TALKS]

Ge	34: 6	Hamor went out to **t** with Jacob.	1819
Nu	12: 1	and Aaron began to **t** against Moses	1819
Dt	6: 7	**T** about them when you sit at home and	1819
	25: 8	elders of his town shall summon him and **t**	1819
Jdg	9:38	"Where is your **big t** now, you who said,	7023
1Sa	25:17	He is such a wicked man that no one can **t**	1819
Job	11: 3	Will your **idle t** reduce men to silence?	966
	18: 2	Be sensible, and then we can **t**.	1819
	27:12	Why then this **meaningless t**?	2038+2039
	35:16	So Job opens his mouth with **empty t**;	2039
Ps	38:12	those who would harm me **t** of my ruin;	1819
	64: 5	they **t about** hiding their snares;	6218
	69:26	For they persecute those you wound and **t**	6218
Pr	4:24	keep **corrupt t** far from your lips.	4299
	7:21	she seduced him with her smooth **t**.	8557
	12:13	An evil man is trapped by his sinful **t**,	8557
	14: 3	A fool's **t** brings a rod to his back,	7023
	14:23	but **mere t** leads only to poverty.	1821+8557
	24: 2	and their lips **t** about making trouble.	1819
Isa	58: 9	with the pointing finger and malicious **t**,	1819
Jer	3: 5	This is how you **t**,	1819
Eze	36: 3	and the **object of** people's **malicious t**	4383+6584+6590+8557
Da	10:17	How can I, your servant, **t** with you,	1819
Mt	9:32	and **could not t** was brought to Jesus.	3273
	12:22	so that he could both **t** and see.	3281
Mk	1:45	Instead he went out and began to **t** freely,	3062
	2: 7	"Why does this fellow **t** like that?	3281
	7:32	a man who was deaf and **could hardly t**,	3652
Lk	7:15	The dead man sat up and began to **t**,	3281
Jn	18:34	"or did others **t** to you about me?"	3306
Ac	28:20	I asked to see you and **t with** you.	4688
Ro	9:20	But who are you, O man, to **t** back to God?	503
	16:18	By **smooth t** and flattery they deceive	5981
1Co	4:20	For the kingdom of God is not a matter of **t**	3364
2Co	11:23	(I am out of my mind to **t** like this.)	3281
Eph	4:29	Do not let any unwholesome **t** come out	3364
	5: 4	nor **foolish t** or coarse joking,	3703
1Ti	1: 6	from these and turned to **meaningless t.**	3467
	6: 4	that result in envy, strife, **malicious t**,	1060
Tit	2: 9	to try to please their masters, not to **t** back to them,	515
1Pe	2:15	**silence** the ignorant **t** of foolish men.	5821
3Jn	1:12	to visit you and **t** with you face to face,	3281
	1:14	and we will **t** face to face.	3281

TALKED (29) [TALK]

Ge	35:13	at the place where he had **t** with him.	1819

Ge	35:14	a stone pillar at the place where God had **t**	1819
	35:15	the place where God had **t** with him Bethel.	1819
	45:15	Afterward his brothers **t** with him.	1819
Nu	3: 1	the LORD **t** with Moses on Mount Sinai.	1819
	14:10	the whole assembly **t** about stoning them.	606
Jos	22:33	And they **t** no more about going to war	606
Jdg	13:11	"Are you the one who **t** to my wife?"	1819
	14: 7	Then he went down and **t** with the woman,	1819
1Sa	9:25	Samuel **t** with Saul on the roof	1819
1Ki	10: 2	and **t** with him about all that she had	1819
2Ch	9: 1	she came to Solomon and **t** with him	1819
Jer	38:25	If the officials hear that I **t** with you,	1819
Da	1:19	The king **t** with them,	1819
Hos	12: 4	at Bethel and **t** with him there—	1819
Zec	1:13	and comforting words to the angel who **t**	1819
	4: 1	Then the angel who **t** with me returned	1819
	4: 4	I asked the angel who **t** with me.	1819
Mal	3:16	Then those who feared the LORD **t** with each	1819
Lk	20:14	saw him, they **t** the matter over.	253+1368+4639
	24:15	As they **t** and discussed these things	3917
	24:32	not our hearts burning within us while he **t**	3281
Ac	9:29	He **t** and debated with the Grecian Jews,	3281
	13:43	who **t** with them and urged them	4688
	13:45	with jealousy and **t** abusively **against**	515
	20: 9	into a deep sleep as Paul **t** on and on.	1363
	24:26	he sent for him frequently and **t** with him.	3917
1Co	13:11	When I was a child, I **t** like a child,	3281
Rev	21:15	The angel who **t** with me had a measuring	3281

TALKER (1) [TALK]

Job	11: 2	Is this **t** to be vindicated?	408+8557

TALKERS (2) [TALK]

1Ti	3:11	not **malicious t** but temperate and	1333
Tit	1:10	rebellious people, **mere t** and deceivers,	3468

TALKING (48) [TALK]

Ge	29: 9	While he was still **t** with them,	1819
Dt	11:19	**t** about them when you sit at home and	1819
Jdg	6:17	give me a sign that it is really you **t** to me.	1819
1Sa	2: 3	"Do not keep **t** so proudly	1819
	14:19	While Saul was **t** to the priest,	1819
	17:23	As he was **t** with them, Goliath,	1819
	18: 1	After David had finished **t** with Saul,	1819
	30: 6	because the men were **t** of stoning him;	606
1Ki	1:14	While you are still there **t** to the king,	1819
2Ki	2:11	As they were walking along and **t** together,	1819
	6:33	While he was still **t** to them,	1819
	8: 4	The king was **t** to Gehazi,	1819
Est	6:14	While they were still **t** with him,	1819
Job	2:10	He replied, "You are **t** like a foolish woman	1819
Eze	33:30	your countrymen are **t together** about you	1819
Zec	1: 9	The angel who was **t** with me answered,	1819
Mt	12:46	While Jesus was still **t** to the crowd,	3281
	16: 8	why are you **t** among yourselves	1368
	16:11	that I was not **t** to you about bread?	1368
	17: 3	before them Moses and Elijah, **t** with Jesus.	5196
	17:13	Then the disciples understood that he was **t**	3306
	21:45	they knew he was **t** about them.	3306
	26:70	"I don't know what you're **t about,**"	3306
Mk	7:36	the more they kept **t** about it.	3062
	8:17	"Why are you **t** about having no bread?	1368
	9: 4	Elijah and Moses, who were **t** with Jesus.	5196
	14:68	or understand what you're **t about,**"	3306
	14:71	"I don't know this man you're **t about.**"	3306
Lk	1:65	of Judea people were **t** about	1362
	9:31	in glorious splendor, **t** with Jesus.	5196
	18:34	they did not know what he was **t** about.	3306
	22:60	"Man, I don't know what you're **t about!**"	3306
	24:14	They were **t** with each other	3917
	24:36	While they were still **t** about this,	3281
Jn	4:27	and were surprised to find him **t** with	3281
	4:27	or "Why are you **t** with her?"	3281
Ac	8:34	please, who is the prophet **t** about,	3306
	10:27	**T** with him, Peter went inside and found	5326
	17:21	but **t** about and listening to the latest ideas.)	3306
	20: 7	kept on **t** until midnight.	3364
	20:11	After **t** until daylight, he left.	3917
	26:31	and while **t** with one another, they said,	3306
	28:22	that people everywhere are **t against**	515
Ro	11:13	I am **t** to you Gentiles.	3364
1Co	4:19	not only how these arrogant people are **t**,	3364
2Co	11:17	In this self-confident boasting I am not **t** as	3281
Eph	5:32	but I am **t** about Christ and the church.	3306
1Ti	1: 7	not know what they are **t** about	3306

TALKS (1) [TALK]

Pr	20:19	so avoid a **man who t** too much.	7331+8557

TALL (15) [TALLER, TALLEST]

Dt	2:10	and as **t** as the Anakites.	8123
	2:21	and as **t** as the Anakites.	8123
	9: 2	The people are strong and **t**—Anakites!	8123
1Sa	17: 4	He was over nine feet **t**.	1470
1Ch	11:23	Egyptian who was seven and a half feet **t**.	4500
Job	8:11	Can papyrus **grow t** where there is no	1448
Isa	2:13	**t** and lofty, and all the oaks of Bashan,	8123
	10:33	the **t ones** will be brought low.	1469
	18: 2	to a people **t** and smooth-skinned,	5432
	18: 7	from a people **t** and smooth-skinned, from	5432
	45:14	and those **t** Sabeans—come over	408+4500
Eze	17:24	the LORD bring down the **t** tree and make	1469
	17:24	**make** the low tree **grow t**.	1467
	31: 4	deep springs **made** it **grow t**;	8123

Am	2: 9	though he was *t* as the cedars and strong as	1470

TALLER (3) [TALL]

Dt	1:28	'The people are stronger and *t* than we are;	8123
1Sa	9: 2	a head *t* than any of the others.	1469
	10:23	among the people *he was* a head *t* than any	1467

TALLEST (2) [TALL]

2Ki	19:23	I have cut down its *t* cedars,	7757
Isa	37:24	I have cut down its *t* cedars,	7757

TALMAI (6)

Nu	13:22	Sheshai and T, the descendants of Anak,	9440
Jos	15:14	Sheshai, Ahiman and T—	9440
Jdg	1:10	and defeated Sheshai, Ahiman and T.	9440
2Sa	3: 3	of Maacah daughter of T king of Geshur;	9440
	13:37	Absalom fled and went to T son of	9440
1Ch	3: 2	of Maacah daughter of T king of Geshur;	9440

TALMON (5)

1Ch	9:17	The gatekeepers: Shallum, Akkub, T,	3236
Ezr	2:42	the descendants of Shallum, Ater, T,	3236
Ne	7:45	the descendants of Shallum, Ater, T,	3236
	11:19	Akkub, T and their associates,	3236
	12:25	Obadiah, Meshullam, T	3236

TAMAH (KJV) See TEMAH

TAMAR (26) [BAAL TAMAR, HAZAZON TAMAR]

Ge	38: 6	his firstborn, and her name was T.	9470
	38:11	Judah then said to his daughter-in-law T,	9470
	38:11	So T went to live in her father's house.	9470
	38:13	When T was told,	9470
	38:24	"Your daughter-in-law T is guilty	9470
Ru	4:12	whom T bore to Judah."	9470
2Sa	13: 1	Amnon son of David fell in love with T,	9470
	13: 2	of illness on account of his sister T,	9470
	13: 4	Amnon said to him, "I'm in love with T,	9470
	13: 5	'I would like my sister T to come	9470
	13: 6	"I would like my sister T to come	9470
	13: 7	David sent word to T at the palace:	9470
	13: 8	T went to the house of her brother Amnon.	9470
	13:10	Then Amnon said to T,	9470
	13:10	And T took the bread she had prepared	9470
	13:19	T put ashes on her head and tore	9470
	13:20	T lived in her brother Absalom's house,	9470
	13:22	because he had disgraced his sister T.	9470
	13:32	since the day Amnon raped his sister T.	9470
	14:27	The daughter's name was T.	9470
1Ch	2: 4	T, Judah's daughter-in-law,	9470
	3: 9	And T was their sister.	9470
Eze	47:18	to the eastern sea and as far as T.	9471
	47:19	"On the south side it will run from T as far	9471
	48:28	of Gad will run south from T to the waters	9471
Mt	1: 3	whose mother was T,	2500

TAMARISK (3)

Ge	21:33	Abraham planted a *t* tree in Beersheba,	869
1Sa	22: 6	was seated under the *t* tree on the hill	869
	31:13	and buried them under a *t* tree at Jabesh,	869

TAMBOURINE (5) [TAMBOURINES]

Ex	15:20	Aaron's sister, took a *t* in her hand,	9512
Job	21:12	They sing to the **music of** *t* and harp;	9512
Ps	81: 2	Begin the music, strike the *t*,	9512
	149: 3	and make music to him with *t* and harp.	9512
	150: 4	praise him with *t* and dancing,	9512

TAMBOURINES (12) [TAMBOURINE]

Ge	31:27	and singing to the **music of** *t* and harps,	9512
Ex	15:20	women followed her, with *t* and dancing.	9512
Jdg	11:34	his daughter, dancing to the sound of *t*!	9512
1Sa	10: 5	with lyres, *t*, flutes and harps being played	9512
	18: 6	with joyful songs and with *t* and lutes.	9512
2Sa	6: 5	with songs and with harps, lyres, *t*,	9512
1Ch	13: 8	with songs and with harps, lyres, *t*,	9512
Ps	68:25	with them are the maidens **playing** *t*.	9528
Isa	5:12	*t* and flutes and wine,	9512
	24: 8	The gaiety of the *t* is stilled,	9512
	30:32	be to the **music of** *t* and harps,	9512
Jer	31: 4	Again you will take up your *t* and go out	9512

TAME (1) [TAMED]

Jas	3: 8	but no man can *t* the tongue.	1238

TAMED (2) [TAME]

Jas	3: 7	reptiles and creatures of the sea *are being* t	1238
	3: 7	of the sea are being tamed and **have been** t	1238

TAMMUZ (1)

Eze	8:14	I saw women sitting there, mourning for T.	9452

TANACH (KJV) See TAANACH

TANHUMETH (2)

2Ki	25:23	Seraiah son of T the Netophathite,	9489
Jer	40: 8	the sons of Kareah, Seraiah son of T,	9489

TANNER (3)

Ac	9:43	for some time with a *t* named Simon.	*1114*
	10: 6	He is staying with Simon the *t*,	*1114*
	10:32	He is a guest in the home *of* Simon the *t*,	*1114*

TAPESTRY (1)

SS	7: 5	Your hair is like royal *t*;	763

TAPHATH (1)

1Ki	4:11	(he was married to T daughter of Solomon);	3264

TAPPUAH (6) [BETH TAPPUAH, EN TAPPUAH]

Jos	12:17	the king of T one the king of Hepher one	9517
	15:34	Zanoah, En Gannim, T, Enam,	9517
	16: 8	From T the border went west to	9517
	17: 8	(Manasseh had the land of T,	9517
	17: 8	but T itself, on the boundary of Manasseh,	9517
1Ch	2:43	Korah, T, Rekem and Shema.	9516

TAR (3)

Ge	11: 3	brick instead of stone and *t* for mortar.	2819
	14:10	the Valley of Siddim was full of *t* pits,	2819
Ex	2: 3	for him and coated it with *t* and pitch.	2819

TARAH (KJV) See TERAH

TARALAH (1)

Jos	18:27	Rekem, Irpeel, T,	9550

TARE (KJV) See CONVULSION, MAULED, TORE

TAREA (1)

1Ch	8:35	Pithon, Melech, T and Ahaz.	9308

TARES (KJV) See WEEDS

TARGET (4)

1Sa	20:20	as though I were shooting at a *t*.	4766
Job	7:20	Why have you made me your *t*?	5133
	16:12	He has made me his *t*;	4766
La	3:12	He drew his bow and made me the *t*	4766

TARPELITES (KJV) See TRIPOLIS

TARRIED, TARRIEST, TARRIETH, TARRY, TARRYING (KJV) See HALTED, LONG TIME, REST, SPEND TIME, SPENT TIME, STAYED, SUSPENSE, WAIT, WAITED

TARSHISH (19)

Ge	10: 4	Elishah, T, the Kittim and the Rodanim.	9576
1Ch	1: 7	Elishah, T, the Kittim and the Rodanim.	9576
	7:10	Ehud, Kenaanah, Zethan, T and Ahishahar.	9578
Est	1:14	Carshena, Shethar, Admatha, T, Meres,	9578
Ps	48: 7	like ships of T shattered by an east wind.	9578
	72:10	of T and of distant shores will bring tribute	9578
Isa	23: 1	Wail, O ships of T!	9576
	23: 6	Cross over to T; wail, you people	9576
	23:10	O Daughter of T, for you no longer have	9576
	23:14	Wail, you ships of T;	9576
	60: 9	in the lead are the ships of T,	9576
	66:19	to T, to the Libyans and Lydians	9576
Jer	10: 9	Hammered silver is brought from T	9576
Eze	27:12	" 'T did business with you because	9576
	27:25	ships of T serve as carriers for your wares.	9576
	38:13	Sheba and Dedan and the merchants of T	9576
Jnh	1: 3	from the LORD and headed for T.	9576
	1: 3	and sailed for T to flee from the LORD.	9576
	4: 2	That is why I was so quick to flee to T.	9576

TARSUS (5)

Ac	9:11	and ask for a **man from** T named Saul,	*5432*
	9:30	down to Caesarea and sent him off to T.	*5433*
	11:25	Then Barnabas went to T to look for Saul,	*5433*
	21:39	"I am a Jew, **from** T in Cilicia,	*5432*
	22: 3	"I am a Jew, born in T of Cilicia,	*5433*

TARTAK (1)

2Ki	17:31	the Avvites made Nibhaz and T,	9581

TARTAN (KJV) See SUPREME COMMANDER

TASK (16) [TASKS]

Ge	31:36	Jacob was angry and **took** Laban **to** t.	8189
Lev	16:21	in the care of a man **appointed for the** t.	6967
1Ch	29: 1	The *t* is great, because this palatial structure	4856
2Ch	29:34	until the *t* was finished and	4856
Ne	13:30	each to his own *t*.	4856
Ecc	2:26	but to the sinner he gives the *t* of gathering	6721

Isa	28:21	his strange work, and perform his *t*,	6275
	28:21	and perform his task, his alien *t*.	6275
Mk	13:34	each with his assigned *t*,	2240
Ac	20:24	the *t* the Lord Jesus has given me—	*1355*
	20:24	*t* of testifying to the gospel of God's grace.	NIG
Ro	15:28	So after I have completed **this** *t*	AIT
1Co	3: 5	as the Lord has assigned to each his *t*.	NIG
2Co	2:16	And who is equal to **such** a *t*?	AIT
Gal	2: 7	with the *t* of preaching the gospel to	NIG
1Ti	3: 1	on being an overseer, he desires a noble *t*.	2240

TASKMASTERS (KJV) See SLAVE MASTERS, SLAVE DRIVERS

TASKS (2) [TASK]

2Ch	31:16	the daily duties of their *various* t,	6275
Pr	31:17	her arms are strong for her *t*.	NIH

TASSEL (1) [TASSELS]

Nu	15:38	with a blue cord on each *t*.	7492

TASSELS (4) [TASSEL]

Nu	15:38	to make *t* on the corners of your garments,	7492
	15:39	You will have these *t* to look at and	7492
Dt	22:12	Make *t* on the four corners of your	1544
Mt	23: 5	and the *t* on their garments long;	*3192*

TASTE (17) [TASTED, TASTELESS, TASTES, TASTING, TASTY]

Ge	25:28	Isaac, who had a *t* *for* wild game,	7023
2Sa	3:35	with me, be it ever so severely, if *I* t bread	3247
	19:35	*Can* your servant *t* what he eats	3247
Job	27: 2	*who has* **made** me *t* **bitterness** of soul,	5352
Ps	34: 8	*T* and see that the LORD is good;	3247
	119:103	How sweet are your words to my *t*,	2674
Pr	24:13	honey from the comb is sweet to your *t*.	2674
SS	2: 3	and his fruit is sweet to my *t*.	2674
	4:16	into his garden and *t* its choice fruits.	430
Jnh	3: 7	anything; do not let them eat or drink.	3247
Mt	16:28	not *t* death before they see the Son	1174
Mk	9: 1	not *t* death before they see the kingdom	1174
Lk	9:27	not *t* death before they see the kingdom	1174
	14:24	of those men who were invited *will* get a *t*	1174
Jn	8:52	*he will* never *t* death.	1174
Col	2:21	"Do not handle! *Do not* t! Do not touch!"?	1174
Heb	2: 9	so that by the grace of God *he might* t death	1174

TASTED (11) [TASTE]

Ex	16:31	like coriander seed and *t* like wafers made	3248
Nu	11: 8	it *t* like something made with olive oil.	3248
1Sa	14:24	So none of the troops *t* food.	3247
	14:29	how my eyes brightened when *I* t a little	3247
	14:43	"*I* **merely** *t* a little honey with the end	3247+3247
Eze	3: 3	and *it* t as sweet as honey in my mouth.	2118
Jn	2: 9	and the master of the banquet *t* the water	1174
Heb	6: 4	who *have* t the heavenly gift,	1174
	6: 5	who *have* t the goodness of the word	1174
1Pe	2: 3	now that *you have* t that the Lord is good.	1174
Rev	10:10	It *t* as **sweet** as honey in my mouth,	1184+1639

TASTELESS (1) [TASTE]

Job	6: 6	Is *t* *food* eaten without salt,	9522

TASTES (5) [TASTE]

Job	12:11	not the ear test words as the tongue *t* food?	3247
	34: 3	the ear tests words as the tongue *t* food.	3247
Pr	20:17	Food gained by fraud *t* **sweet** to a man,	6853
	27: 7	to the hungry even what is bitter *t* sweet.	NIH
Jer	48:11	So she *t* as she did,	3248

TASTING (1) [TASTE]

Mt	27:34	but *after* t it, he refused to drink it.	*1174*

TASTY (6) [TASTE]

Ge	27: 4	the kind of *t* food I like and bring it to me	4761
	27: 7	and prepare me *some* t food to eat,	4761
	27: 9	I can prepare *some* t food for your father,	4761
	27:14	and she prepared *some* t food,	4761
	27:17	the *t* food and the bread she had made.	4761
	27:31	He too prepared *some* t food and brought it	4761

TATTENAI (4)

Ezr	5: 3	At that time T, governor of	10779
	5: 6	This is a copy of the letter that T,	10779
	6: 6	Now then, T, governor of Trans-Euphrates,	10779
	6:13	T, governor of Trans-Euphrates,	10779

TATTLERS (KJV) See GOSSIPS

TATTOO (1)

Lev	19:28	for the dead or put *t* marks on yourselves.	7882

TAUGHT (59) [TEACH]

Dt	4: 5	*I have* t you decrees and laws as	4340
	31:22	wrote down this song that day and *t* it *to*	4340
Jdg	8:16	and *t* the men of Succoth **a lesson**	3359
2Sa	1:18	men of Judah *be* t this lament of the bow	4340

1Ki	4:33	He also t about animals and birds, 1819
2Ki	17:28	and t them how to worship the LORD. 2118+3723
2Ch	17: 9	They t throughout Judah, 4340
	17: 9	to all the towns of Judah and t the people. 4340
Ps	71:17	Since my youth, O God, you have t me, 4340
	119:102	for you yourself have t me. 3723
Pr	4: 4	he t me and said, "Lay hold of my words 3723
	31: 1	an oracle his mother t him: 3579
SS	8: 2	to my mother's house—she who has t me. 4340
Isa	29:13	of me is made up only of rules t by men. 4340
	40:14	and who t him the right way? 4340
	40:14	that t him knowledge or showed him 4340
	50: 4	wakens my ear to listen like one being t. 4341
	54:13	All your sons will be t by the LORD, 4341
Jer	9: 5	They have t their tongues to lie; 4340
	9:14	as their fathers t them." 4340
	10: 8	they are t by worthless wooden idols. 4592
	12:16	they once t my people to swear by Baal— 4340
	32:33	though I t them again and again, 4340
Hos	11: 3	It was I who t Ephraim to walk, 8078
Mt	7:29	because he t as one who had authority, 1438+1639
	15: 9	their teachings are but rules t by men.' " NIG
Mk	1:22	he t them as one who had authority, 1438+1639
	4: 2	He t them many things by parables, 1438
	6:30	to him all they had done and t. 1438
	7: 7	their teachings are but rules t by men.' NIG
	10: 1	and as was his custom, he t them. 1438
	11:17	And as he t them, he said, "Is it not written: 1438
	12:38	As he t, Jesus said, "Watch out for 1439
Lk	1: 4	the certainty of the things you have been t. 2994
	4:15	He t in their synagogues, 1438
	5: 3	he sat down and t the people from the boat. 1438
	11: 1	just as John t his disciples." 1438
	13:26	and you t in our streets.' 1438
Jn	6:45	'They will all be t by God.' 1435
	8:28	but speak just what the Father has t me. 1438
	18:20	"I always t in synagogues or at the temple, 1438
Ac	11:26	the church and t great numbers of people. 1438
	15: 1	according to the custom t by Moses, NIG
	15:35	and many others t and preached the word 1438
	18:25	and he spoke with great fervor and t 1438
	20:20	be helpful to you but have t you publicly 1438
	28:31	of God and t about the Lord Jesus Christ. 1438
1Co	2:13	not in words t us by human wisdom but 1435
	2:13	by human wisdom but in words t by 1435
Gal	1:12	not receive it from any man, nor was I t it; 1438
Eph	4:21	Surely you heard of him and were t in him 1438
	4:22	You were t, with regard to your former way NIG
Col	2: 7	strengthened in the faith as you were t, 1438
1Th	4: 9	for you yourselves have been t by God 2531
1Ti	1:20	whom I have handed over to Satan to be t 4084
	4: 1	and follow deceiving spirits and things t 1436
Tit	1: 9	to the trustworthy message as it has been t, 1439
1Jn	2:27	just as it has t you, remain in him. 1438
Rev	2:14	who t Balak to entice the Israelites to sin 1438

TAUNT (8) [TAUNTED, TAUNTS]

Dt	32:27	but I dreaded the t of the enemy, lest 4088
1Ki	18:27	At noon Elijah began to t them. 2252
Ps	42:10	suffer mortal agony as my foes t me, 3070
	102: 8	All day long my enemies t me; 3070
Isa	14: 4	you will take up this t against the king 5442
Eze	5:15	You will be a reproach and a t, 1527
Mic	2: 4	they will t you with this mournful song: 5629
Hab	2: 6	Will not all of them t him with ridicule 5442+5951

TAUNTED (4) [TAUNT]

Jdg	8:15	about whom you t me by saying, 3070
2Sa	21:21	When he t Israel, Jonathan son of Shimeah, 3070
	23: 9	when they t the Philistines gathered 3070
1Ch	20: 7	When he t Israel, Jonathan son of Shimea, 3070

TAUNTS (6) [TAUNT]

Ps	44:16	the t of those who reproach and revile me, 7754
	89:50	I bear in my heart the t of all the nations, 8190
	89:51	t with which your enemies have mocked, NIH
	119:42	then I will answer the one who t me, 3070
Eze	36:15	No longer will I make you hear the t of 4009
Zep	2: 8	"I have heard the insults of Moab and the t 1526

TAVERNS See THREE TAVERNS

TAX (33) [TAXED, TAXES]

2Ch	24: 6	in from Judah and Jerusalem the t imposed 5368
	24: 9	to the LORD that Moses the servant 5368
Ne	5: 4	the king's t on our fields and vineyards, 4501
Da	11:20	a t collector to maintain the royal splendor. 5601
Mt	5:46	Are not even the t collectors doing that? 5467
	9: 9	Matthew sitting at the t collector's booth. 5468
	9:10	many t collectors and "sinners" came 5467
	9:11	with t collectors and 'sinners'? 5467
	10: 3	Thomas and Matthew the t collector; 5467
	11:19	a friend of t collectors and "sinners." 5467
	17:24	collectors of the two-drachma t 3284
	17:24	"Doesn't your teacher pay the temple t?" NIG
	17:27	and give it to them for my t and yours. NIG
	18:17	as you would a pagan or a t collector. 5467
	21:31	the t collectors and the prostitutes 5467
	21:32	the t collectors and the prostitutes did. 5467
	22:19	Show me the coin used for paying the t." 3056
Mk	2:14	sitting at the t collector's booth. 5468
	2:15	at Levi's house, many t collectors 5467
	2:16	with the "sinners" and t collectors, 5467
	2:16	"Why does he eat with t collectors 5467
Lk	3:12	T collectors also came to be baptized. 5467
	5:27	a t collector by the name of Levi sitting 5467
	5:27	by the name of Levi sitting at his t booth. 5468
	5:29	of t collectors and others were eating 5467
	5:30	with t collectors and 'sinners'?" 5467
	7:29	(All the people, even the t collectors, 5467
	7:34	a friend of t collectors and "sinners." ' 5467
	15: 1	Now the t collectors and "sinners." 5467
	18:10	a Pharisee and the other a t collector. 5467
	18:11	or even like this t collector. 5467
	18:13	"But the t collector stood at a distance. 5467
	19: 2	a chief t collector and was wealthy. 803

TAXED (1) [TAX]

2Ki	23:35	he t the land and exacted the silver 6885

TAXES (12) [TAX]

1Sa	17:25	exempt his father's family from t 2930+6913
Ezr	4:13	no more t, tribute or duty will be paid, 10402
	4:20	and t, tribute and duty were paid to them. 10402
	7:24	that you have no authority to impose t, 10402
Mt	17:25	the kings of the earth collect duty and t— 3056
	22:17	Is it right to pay t to Caesar or not?" 3056
Mk	12:14	Is it right to pay t to Caesar or not? 3056
Lk	20:22	Is it right for us to pay t to Caesar or not?" 5843
	23: 2	of t to Caesar and claims to be Christ, 5843
Ro	13: 6	This is also why you pay t, 5843
	13: 7	If you owe taxes; 5843
	13: 7	If you owe taxes, pay t; 5843

TAXING (KJV) See CENSUS

TEACH (123) [TAUGHT, TEACHER, TEACHERS, TEACHES, TEACHING, TEACHINGS]

Ex	4:12	I will help you speak and will t you what 3723
	4:15	of you speak and will t you what to do. 3723
	18:20	T them the decrees and laws, 2302
	33:13	me your ways so I may know you 3359
	35:34	of the tribe of Dan, the ability to t others. 3723
Lev	10:11	and you must t the Israelites all the decrees 3723
Dt	4: 1	the decrees and laws I am about to t you. 4340
	4: 9	T them to your children and 3359
	4:10	the land and may t them to their children." 3359
	4:14	to t you the decrees and laws you are 4340
	5:31	and laws you are to t them to follow in 4340
	6: 1	the LORD your God directed me to t you 4340
	8: 3	to t you that man does not live on bread 3359
	11:19	T them to your children, 4340
	17:11	Act according to the law they t you and 3723
	20:18	they will t you to follow all 4340
	31:19	down for yourselves this song and t it to 4340
Jdg	3: 2	to t warfare to the descendants of 4340
	13: 8	to t us how to bring up the boy who is to 3723
1Sa	12:23	And I will t you the way that is good 3384
	14:12	"Come up to us and we'll t you a lesson." 3359
1Ki	8:36	T them the right way to live, 3384
2Ki	17:27	to live there and t the people what the god 3723
2Ch	6:27	T them the right way to live, 3384
	15: 3	without a priest to t and without the law. 3723
	17: 7	and Micaiah to t in the towns of Judah. 4340
Ezr	7:25	you are to t any who do not know them. 10313
Job	6:24	"T me, and I will be quiet; 3723
	12: 7	"But ask the animals, and they will t you, 3723
	12: 8	or speak to the earth, and it will t you, 3723
	21:22	"Can anyone t knowledge to God, 4340
	27:11	"I will t you about the power of God; 3723
	32: 7	advanced years should t wisdom.' 3359
	33:33	be silent, and I will t you wisdom. 544
	34:32	T me what I cannot see; 3723
Ps	25: 4	O LORD, t me your paths; 4340
	25: 5	guide me in your truth and t me, 4340
	27:11	T me your way, O LORD; 3723
	32: 8	and t you in the way you should go; 4340
	34:11	I will t you the fear of the LORD. 4340
	51: 6	you t me wisdom in the inmost place. 3359
	51:13	Then I will t transgressors your ways, 4340
	78: 5	our forefathers to t their children, 3359
	86:11	T me your way, O LORD, 3723
	90:12	T us to number our days aright, 3359
	94:12	O LORD, the man you t from your law; 4340
	105:22	as he pleased and t his elders wisdom. 2681
	119:12	t me your decrees. 4340
	119:26	t me your decrees. 4340
	119:33	T me, O LORD, to follow your decrees; 3723
	119:64	t me your decrees. 4340
	119:66	t me knowledge and good judgment, 4340
	119:68	t me your decrees. 4340
	119:108	and t me your laws. 4340
	119:124	to your love and t me your decrees. 4340
	119:135	upon your servant and t me your decrees. 4340
	119:171	for you t me your decrees. 4340
	132:12	and the statutes I t them, 4340
	143:10	T me to do your will, for you are my God; 4340
Pr	9: 9	a righteous man and he will add to his 3359
	22:17	apply your heart to what I t, 1981
	22:19	to you today, even you. 3359
Isa	2: 3	He will t us his ways, 3723
	9:15	the prophets who t lies are the tail. 3384
	28: 9	"Who is it he is trying to t? 1978+3723
Jer	9:20	T your daughters how to wail; 4340
	9:20	t one another a lament. NIH
	16:21	"Therefore I will t them— 3359
Jer	16:21	this time I will t them my power 3359
	31:34	No longer will a man t his neighbor, 4340
Eze	22:26	they t that there is no difference between 3359
	44:23	They are to t my people the difference 3723
Da	1: 4	to t them the language and literature of 4340
Mic	3:11	her priests t for a price, 3723
	4: 2	He will t us his ways, 3723
Mt	5: 2	and he began to t them, saying: 1438
	11: 1	on from there to t and preach in the towns 1438
	22:16	of integrity and that you t the way of God 1438
Mk	1:21	into the synagogue and began to t. 1438
	2:13	and he began to t them. 1438
	4: 1	Again Jesus began to t by the lake. 1438
	6: 2	he began to t in the synagogue, 1438
	8:31	He then began to t them that the Son 1438
	12:14	but you t the way of God in accordance 1438
Lk	4:31	and on the Sabbath began to t the people. 1438
	11: 1	"Lord, t us to pray, 1438
	12:12	for the Holy Spirit will t you at 1438
	20:21	that you speak and t what is right, 1438
	20:21	but t the way of God in accordance with 1438
Jn	7:14	up to the temple courts and begin to t. 1438
	7:35	among the Greeks, and t the Greeks? 1438
	8: 2	and he sat down to t them. 1438
	14:26	will t you all things and will remind you 1438
Ac	1: 1	about all that Jesus began to do and to t 1438
	4:18	to speak or t at all in the name of Jesus. 1438
	5:21	and began to t the people. 1438
	5:28	"We gave you strict orders not to t 1438
	21:21	They have been informed that you t all 1438
Ro	2:21	who t others, do you not teach yourself? 1438
	2:21	who teach others, do you not t yourself? 1438
	12: 7	if it is teaching, let him t; 1436
	15: 4	in the past was written to t us, 1436
1Co	4:17	with what I t everywhere in every church. 1438
	11:14	of things t you that if a man has long hair, 1438
Col	3:16	of Christ dwell in you richly as you t 1438
1Ti	1: 3	not to t false doctrines any longer 2281
	2:12	a woman to t or to have authority over 1438
	3: 2	respectable, hospitable, able to t, 1434
	4:11	Command and t these things. 1438
	6: 2	These are the things you are to t and urge 1438
2Ti	2: 2	also be qualified to t others. 1438
	2:24	he must be kind to everyone, able to t, 1434
Tit	1:11	by teaching things they ought not to t— NIG
	2: 1	You must t what is in accord 3281
	2: 2	T the older men to be temperate, NIG
	2: 3	t the older women to be reverent in NIG
	2: 3	but to t what is good. 2815
	2: 9	T slaves to be subject to their masters NIG
	2:15	These, then, are the things you should t. 3281
Heb	5:12	to t you the elementary truths 1438
	8:11	No longer will a man t his neighbor, 1438
Jas	3: 1	that we who t will be judged more strictly. NIG
1Jn	2:27	and you do not need anyone to t you. 1438

TEACHER (68) [TEACH]

1Ch	25: 8	Young and old alike, t as well as student, 1067
Ezr	7: 6	a t well versed in the Law of Moses, 6221
	7:11	and t, a man learned in matters concerning 6221
	7:12	a t of the Law of the God of heaven, 10516
	7:21	a t of the Law of the God of heaven, 10516
Job	36:22	Who is a t like him? 4621
Ecc	1: 1	The words of the T, son of David, 7738
	1: 2	"Meaningless! Meaningless!" says the T. 7738
	1:12	I, the T, was king over Israel in Jerusalem. 7738
	7:27	says the T, "this is what I have discovered: 7738
	12: 8	"Meaningless! Meaningless!" says the T. 7738
	12: 9	Not only was the T wise, 7738
	12:10	The T searched to find just the right words, 7738
Mt	8:19	Then a t of the law came to him and said, 1208
	8:19	"T, I will follow you wherever you go." 1437
	9:11	"Why does your t eat with tax collectors 1437
	10:24	"A student is not above his t, 1437
	10:25	It is enough for the student to be like his t, 1437
	12:38	of the law said to him, "T, we want to see 1437
	13:52	every t of the law who has been instructed 1208
	17:24	"Doesn't your t pay the temple tax?" 1437
	19:16	a man came up to Jesus and asked, "T, 1437
	22:16	"T," they said, "we know you are a man 1437
	22:24	"T," they said, "Moses told us that if 1437
	22:36	"T, which is the greatest commandment in 1437
	23:10	Nor are you to be called 't,' 2762
	23:10	for you have one T, the Christ, 2762
	26:18	'The T says: My appointed time is near. 1437
Mk	4:38	"T, don't you care if we drown?" 1437
	5:35	"Why bother the t any more?" 1437
	9:17	A man in the crowd answered, "T, 1437
	9:38	"T," said John, "we saw a man driving out 1437
	10:17	"Good t," he asked, "what must I do 1437
	10:20	"T," he declared, "all these I have kept 1437
	10:35	"T," they said, "we want you to do 1437
	12:14	They came to him and said, "T, 1437
	12:19	"T," they said, "Moses wrote for us that if 1437
	12:32	"Well said, t," the man replied. 1437
	13: 1	one of his disciples said to him, "Look, T! 1437
	14:14	of the house he enters, 'The T asks: 1437
Lk	3:12	"T," they asked, "what should we do?" 1437
	6:40	A student is not above his t, 1437
	6:40	who is fully trained will be like his t. 1437
	7:40	"Tell me, t," he said. 1437
	8:49	"Don't bother the t any more." 1437
	9:38	A man in the crowd called out, "T, 1437
	10:25	"T," he asked, "what must I do 1437
	11:45	"T, when you say these things, 1437
	12:13	Someone in the crowd said to him, "T, 1437

Lk	18:18	A certain ruler asked him, "Good t,	1437
	19:39	"T, rebuke your disciples!"	1437
	20:21	So the spies questioned him: "T,	1437
	20:28	"T," they said, "Moses wrote for us that if	1437
	20:39	of the law responded, "Well said, t!"	1437
	21: 7	"T," they asked, "When will these things	1437
	22:11	to the owner of the house, 'The T asks:	1437
Jn	1:38	They said, "Rabbi" (which means T),	1437
	3: 2	we know you are a t who has come	1437
	3:10	"You are Israel's t," said Jesus,	1437
	8: 4	to Jesus, "T, this woman was caught in	1437
	11:28	"The T is here," she said,	1437
	13:13	"You call me 'T' and 'Lord,'	1437
	13:14	Now that I, your Lord and T,	1437
	20:16	"Rabboni!" (which means T).	1437
Ac	5:34	Pharisee named Gamaliel, a t of the law,	3791
Ro	2:20	a t of infants, because you have in the law	1437
1Ti	2: 7	and a t of the true faith to the Gentiles.	1437
2Ti	1:11	a herald and an apostle and a t.	1437

TEACHERS (73) [TEACH]

Ps	119:99	I have more insight than all my t,	4340
Pr	5:13	not obey my t or listen to my instructors.	4621
Isa	30:20	your t will be hidden no more;	4621
Mt	2: 4	the people's chief priests and t of the law,	1208
	5:20	that of the Pharisees and the t of the law,	1208
	7:29	and not as their t of the law.	1208
	9: 3	some of the t of the law said to themselves,	1208
	12:38	the Pharisees and t of the law said to him,	1208
	15: 1	and t of the law came to Jesus	1208
	16:21	chief priests and t of the law,	1208
	17:10	"Why then do the t of the law say	1208
	20:18	to the chief priests and the t of the law.	1208
	21:15	the chief priests and the t of the law saw	1208
	23: 2	"The t of the law and the Pharisees sit	1208
	23:13	"Woe to you, t of the law and Pharisees,	1208
	23:15	"Woe to you, t of the law and Pharisees,	1208
	23:23	"Woe to you, t of the law and Pharisees,	1208
	23:25	"Woe to you, t of the law and Pharisees,	1208
	23:27	"Woe to you, t of the law and Pharisees,	1208
	23:29	"Woe to you, t of the law and Pharisees,	1208
	23:34	sending you prophets and wise men and t.	1208
	26:57	t of the law and the elders had assembled.	1208
	27:41	the chief priests, the t of the law and	1208
Mk	1:22	who had authority, not as the t of the law.	1208
	2: 6	Now some t of the law were sitting there,	1208
	2:16	t of the law who were Pharisees saw him eating	1208
	3:22	And the t of the law who came down	1208
	7: 1	some of the t of the law who had come	1208
	7: 5	the Pharisees and t of the law asked Jesus,	1208
	8:31	chief priests and t of the law,	1208
	9:11	"Why do the t of the law say	1208
	9:14	around them and the t of the law arguing	1208
	10:33	to the chief priests and t of the law.	1208
	11:18	and the t of the law heard this	1208
	11:27	the t of the law and the elders came	1208
	12:28	One of the t of the law came	1208
	12:35	that the t of the law say that the Christ is	1208
	12:38	"Watch out for the t of the law.	1208
	14: 1	and the t of the law were looking	1208
	14:43	the t of the law, and the elders.	1208
	14:53	elders and t of the law came together.	1208
	15: 1	the t of the law and the whole Sanhedrin,	1208
	15:31	and the t of the law mocked him	1208
Lk	2:46	sitting among the t, listening to them	1437
	5:17	Pharisees and t of the law,	3791
	5:21	and the t of the law began thinking	1208
	5:30	and the t of the law who belonged	1208
	6: 7	the t of the law were looking for a reason	1208
	9:22	chief priests and t of the law,	1208
	11:53	the Pharisees and the t of the law began	1208
	15: 2	and the t of the law muttered,	1208
	19:47	the t of the law and the leaders among	1208
	20: 1	the chief priests and the t of the law,	1208
	20:19	The t of the law and the chief priests	1208
	20:39	Some of the t of the law responded,	1208
	20:46	"Beware of the t of the law.	1208
	22: 2	and the t of the law were looking	1208
	22:66	both the chief priests and t of the law,	1208
	23:10	and the t of the law were standing there,	1208
Jn	8: 3	The t of the law and the Pharisees brought	1208
Ac	4: 5	elders and t of the law met in Jerusalem.	1208
	6:12	and the elders and the t of the law.	1208
	13: 1	at Antioch there were prophets and t:	1437
	23: 9	the t of the law who were Pharisees stood	1208
1Co	12:28	third t, then workers of miracles,	1437
	12:29	Are all prophets? Are all t?	1437
Eph	4:11	and some to be pastors and t,	1437
1Ti	2: 7	They want to be t of the law,	3791
2Ti	4: 3	of t to say what their itching ears want	1437
Heb	5:12	though by this time you ought to be t,	1437
Jas	3: 1	Not many of you should presume to be t,	1437
2Pe	2: 1	just as there will be false t among you.	6015
	2: 3	In their greed these t will exploit you	NIG

TEACHES (14) [TEACH]

Dt	33:10	He t your precepts to Jacob and your law	3723
Job	35:11	who t more to us than to the beasts of	544
Ps	25: 9	in what is right and t them his way.	4340
	94:10	Does he who t man lack knowledge?	4340
Pr	15:33	The fear of the LORD t a man wisdom,	4592
Isa	28:26	His God instructs him and t him	3723
	48:17	who t you what is best for you,	4340
Hab	2:18	Or an image that t lies?	3723

Mt	5:19	of these commandments and t others to do	1438
	5:19	and t these commands will be called great	1438
Ac	21:28	This is the man who t all men everywhere	1438
1Ti	6: 3	If anyone t false doctrines and does	2281
Tit	2:12	It t us to say "No" to ungodliness	4084
1Jn	2:27	But as his anointing t you about all things	1438

TEACHING (89) [TEACH]

Dt	32: 2	Let my t fall like rain and my words	4375
Ezr	7:10	and to t its decrees and laws in Israel.	4340
Ps	60: T	A miktam of David. For t.	4340
	78: 1	O my people, hear my t;	9368
	119:27	Let me understand the t of your precepts;	2006
Pr	1: 8	and do not forsake your mother's t.	9368
	3: 1	My son, do not forget my t,	9368
	4: 2	so do not forsake my t.	9368
	6:20	and do not forsake your mother's t.	9368
	6:23	commands are a lamp, this t is a light,	9368
	13:14	The t of the wise is a fountain of life,	9368
	22:21	t you true and reliable words,	3359
Jer	18:18	t of the law by the priest will not be lost,	9368
Eze	7:26	the t of the law by the priest will be lost,	9368
Mal	2: 6	the way and by your t have caused many	9368
Mt	4:23	t in their synagogues,	1438
	7:28	the crowds were amazed at his t,	1439
	9:35	t in their synagogues,	1438
	13:54	he began t the people in their synagogue,	1439
	16:12	the t of the Pharisees and Sadducees.	1439
	21:23	and, while he was t,	1438
	22:33	they were astonished at his t.	1439
	26:55	Every day I sat in the temple courts t,	1438
	28:20	and t them to obey everything I have	1438
Mk	1:22	The people were amazed at his t,	1439
	1:27	A new t—and with authority!	1439
	4: 2	by parables, and in his t said:	1439
	6: 6	Jesus went around t from village to village.	1438
	6:34	So he began t them many things.	1438
	9:31	because he was t his disciples.	1438
	11:18	the whole crowd was amazed at his t.	1439
	12:35	While Jesus was t in the temple courts,	1438
	14:49	t in the temple courts,	1438
Lk	4:32	They were amazed at his t,	1439
	4:36	"What is this t? With authority and power	3364
	5:17	One day as he was t,	1438
	6: 6	into the synagogue and was t.	1438
	13:10	On a Sabbath Jesus was t in one of	1438
	13:22	t as he made his way to Jerusalem.	1438
	19:47	Every day he was t at the temple.	1438
	20: 1	as he was t the people in the temple courts	1438
	21:37	Each day Jesus was t at the temple,	1438
	23: 5	up the people all over Judea by his t.	1438
Jn	6:59	while in the synagogue in Capernaum.	1438
	6:60	"This is a hard t. Who can accept it?"	3364
	7:16	Jesus answered, "My t is not my own.	1439
	7:17	he will find out whether my t comes	1439
	7:28	Then Jesus, still t in the temple courts,	1438
	8:20	while t in the temple area near the place	1438
	8:31	Jesus said, "If you hold to my t,	3364
	14:23	"If anyone loves me, he will obey my t.	3364
	14:24	not love me will not obey my t.	3364
	15:20	If they obeyed my t, they will obey yours	3364
	18:19	about his disciples and his t.	1439
Ac	2:42	They devoted themselves to the apostles' t	1439
	4: 2	because the apostles were t the people	1438
	5:25	in jail are standing in the temple courts t	1439
	5:28	"Yet you have filled Jerusalem with your t	1439
	5:42	they never stopped t and proclaiming	1438
	13:12	for he was amazed at the t about the Lord.	1439
	15: 1	down from Judea to Antioch and were t	1438
	17:19	"May we know what this new t is	1439
	18:11	t them the word of God.	1438
Ro	6:17	the form of t to which you were entrusted.	1439
	12: 7	if it is t, let him teach;	1438
	16:17	that are contrary to the t you have learned.	1439
Eph	4:14	by every wind of t and by the cunning	1436
Col	1:28	and t everyone with all wisdom,	1438
2Th	3: 6	according to the t you received from us.	4142
1Ti	4: 6	and of the good t that you have followed.	1436
	4:13	to preaching and to t.	1436
	5:17	especially those whose work is preaching and t.	1436
	6: 1	so that God's name and our t may not be	1436
	6: 3	of our Lord Jesus Christ and to godly t,	1436
2Ti	1:13	keep as the pattern of sound t,	3364
	2:17	Their t will spread like gangrene.	3364
	3:10	You, however, know all about my t,	1436
	3:16	God-breathed and is useful for t,	1436
Tit	1:11	by t things they ought not to teach—	1438
	2: 7	In your t show integrity,	1436
	2:10	so that in every way they will make the t	1436
Heb	5:13	with the t about righteousness.	3364
2Jn	1: 9	in the t of Christ does not have God;	1439
	1: 9	in the t has both the Father and the Son.	1439
	1:10	comes to you and does not bring this t,	1439
Rev	2:14	You have people there who hold to the t	1439
	2:15	also have those who hold to the t of	1438
	2:20	By her t she misleads my servants	1438
	2:24	to you who do not hold to her t and have	1439

TEACHINGS (9) [TEACH]

Pr	7: 2	guard my t as the apple of your eye.	9368
Mt	15: 9	their t are but rules taught by men.' "	1436+1438
Mk	7: 7	their t are but rules taught by men.'	1436+1438
1Co	11: 2	in everything and for holding to the t,	4142
Col	2:22	they are based on human commands and t.	1436

2Th	2:15	stand firm and hold to the t we passed on	1438
1Ti	4: 2	Such t come through hypocritical liars,	NIG
Heb	6: 1	the elementary t about Christ and go on	3364
	13: 9	be carried away by all kinds of strange t.	1439

TEAM (2) [TEAMS]

Isa	21: 9	here comes a man in a chariot with a t	7538
Mic	1:13	harness the t to the chariot.	8224

TEAMS (1) [TEAM]

Isa	21: 7	When he sees chariots with t of horses,	7538

TEAR (54) [TEARING, TEARS, TORE, TORN]

Ex	28:32	so that it will not t.	7973
	39:23	so that it would not t.	7973
Lev	1:17	He shall t it open by the wings,	9117
	10: 6	and do not t your clothes,	7268
	13:56	he is to t the contaminated part out of	7973
	21:10	his hair become unkempt or t his clothes.	7268
Jdg	6:25	T down your father's altar to Baal and cut	2238
	8: 7	I will t your flesh with desert thorns	1889
	8: 9	I will t down this tower."	5997
2Sa	3:31	"T your clothes and put on sackcloth	7973
1Ki	11:11	most certainly t the kingdom away	7973+7973
	11:12	I will t it out of the hand of your son.	7973
	11:13	I will not t the whole kingdom from him,	7973
	11:31	to t the kingdom out of Solomon's hand	7973
Job	18: 4	You who t yourself to pieces in your anger,	3271
Ps	7: 2	or they will t me like a lion and rip me	3271
	28: 5	he will t them down and never build them	2238
	50:22	or I will t you to pieces,	3271
	52: 5	He will snatch you up and t you	5815
	58: 6	t out, O LORD, the fangs of the lions!	5997
	137: 7	"T it down," they cried,	6867
	137: 7	they cried, "t it down to its foundations!"	6867
Ecc	3: 3	a time to t down and a time to build,	7287
	3: 7	a time to t and a time to mend,	7973
Isa	7: 6	let us t it apart and divide it among	7763
	22:12	to t out your hair and put on sackcloth.	7947
Jer	1:10	and kingdoms to uproot and t down,	5997
	5: 6	to t to pieces any who venture out,	3271
	24: 6	I will build them up and not t them down;	2238
	30: 8	and will t off their bonds;	5998
	31:28	over them to uproot and t down,	2238
	36:24	nor did they t their clothes.	7973
	42:10	I will build you up and not t you down;	2238
La	2: 8	The LORD determined to t down the wall	8845
Eze	13:14	I will t down the wall you have covered	2238
	13:20	and I will t them from your arms;	7973
	13:21	I will t off your veils and save my people	7973
	16:39	and they will t down your mounds	2238
	19: 3	to t the prey and he devoured men.	3271
	19: 6	to t the prey and he devoured men.	3271
	23:34	you will dash it to pieces and t your breasts.	5998
Hos	5:14	I will t them to pieces and go away;	3271
	13: 8	a wild animal will t them apart.	1324
Am	3:15	I will t down the winter house along with	5782
Mic	3: 2	who t the skin from my people and the flesh	1608
	5:11	the cities of your land and t down	2238
Na	1:13	from your neck and t your shackles away."	5998
Mt	7: 6	and then turn and t you to pieces.	4838
	9:16	away from the garment, making the t worse.	5388
Mk	2:21	pull away from the old, making the t worse.	5388
Lk	12:18	I will t down my barns and build	2747
Jn	19:24	"Let's not t it," they said to one another.	5387
Rev	7:17	And God will wipe away every t	1232
	21: 4	He will wipe every t from their eyes.	1232

TEARING (6) [TEAR]

Dt	33:20	like a lion, t at arm or head.	3271
Ps	22:13	Roaring lions t their prey open their mouths	3271
Eze	22:25	within her like a roaring lion t its prey;	3271
	22:27	within her are like wolves t their prey;	3271
Zec	11:16	of the choice sheep, t off their hoofs.	7293
2Co	13:10	for building you up, not for t you down.	2746

TEARS (45) [TEAR]

1Sa	2:33	be spared only to blind your eyes with t	NIH
2Ki	20: 5	I have heard your prayer and seen your t;	1965
Job	12:14	What he t down cannot be rebuilt;	2238
	16: 9	and t me in his anger and gnashes his teeth	3271
	16:20	as my eyes pour out t to God;	1940
	19:10	He t me down on every side till I am gone;	5997
	31:38	and all its furrows are wet with t,	1134
Ps	6: 6	with weeping and drench my couch with t.	1965
	42: 3	My t have been my food day and night,	1965
	56: 8	list my t on your scroll—	1965
	80: 5	You have fed them with the bread of t;	1965
	80: 5	you have made them drink t by	1965
	102: 9	as my food and mingle my drink with t	1140
	116: 8	my eyes from t, my feet from stumbling,	1965
	119:136	Streams of t flow from my eyes,	4784
	126: 5	Those who sow in t will reap with songs	1965
Pr	14: 1	the foolish one t hers down.	2238
	15:25	The LORD t down the proud man's house	5815
	29: 4	but one who is greedy for bribes t it down.	2238
Ecc	4: 1	I saw the t of the oppressed—	1965
Isa	16: 9	O Elealeh, I drench you with t!	1965
	25: 8	LORD will wipe away the t from all faces;	1965
	38: 5	I have heard your prayer and seen your t;	1965
Jer	9: 1	of water and my eyes a fountain of t!	1965
	9:18	with t and water streams from our eyelids.	1965

Jer 13:17 with t, because the LORD's flock will | 1965
14:17 with t night and day without ceasing; | 1965
31:16 from weeping and your eyes from t, | 1965
50: 4 the people of Judah together will go *in* t | 1134
La 1: 2 t are upon her cheeks. | 1965
1:16 and my eyes overflow with t. | 4784
2:18 let your t flow like a river day and night; | 1965
3:48 Streams of t flow from my eyes | 4784
Eze 24:16 Yet do not lament or weep or shed any t. | 1965
Mal 2:13 You flood the LORD's altar with t. | 1965
Lk 5:36 "No one t a patch from a new garment | 5387
7:38 she began to wet his feet *with* her t. | 1232
7:44 *with* her t and wiped them with her hair. | 1232
Ac 20:19 the Lord with great humility and with t, | 1232
20:31 of you night and day with t. | 1232
2Co 2: 4 and anguish of heart and with many t, | 1232
Php 3:18 before and now say again even with t, | 3081
2Ti 1: 4 Recalling your t, I long to see you, | 1232
Heb 5: 7 and petitions with loud cries and t to | 1232
12:17 though he sought the blessing with t. | 1232

TEATS (KJV) See BREASTS

TEBAH (3)
Ge 22:24 T, Gaham, Tahash and Maacah. | 3182
2Sa 8: 8 From T and Berothai, | 3183
1Ch 18: 8 From T and Cun, | 3187

TEBALIAH (KJV) See TABALIAH

TEBETH (1)
Est 2:16 in the tenth month, the month of T, | 3194

TEDIOUS (KJV) See WEARY

TEEM (2) [TEEMED, TEEMING, TEEMS]
Ge 1:20 "*Let* the water t with living creatures, | 9237+9238
Ex 8: 3 The Nile *will* t with frogs. | 9237

TEEMED (1) [TEEM]
Ps 105:30 Their land t *with* frogs, which went up into | 9237

TEEMING (1) [TEEM]
Ps 104:25 t with **creatures** beyond number— | 8254

TEEMS (1) [TEEM]
Ge 1:21 and moving thing with which the water t, | 9237

TEETH (42) [TOOTH]
Ge 49:12 his t whiter than milk. | 9094
Nu 11:33 while the meat was still between their t | 9094
Job 4:10 yet the t *of* the great lions are broken. | 9094
16: 9 and tears me in his anger and gnashes his t | 9094
19:20 I have escaped with only the skin of my t. | 9094
29:17 and snatched the victims from their t. | 9094
41:14 ringed about with his fearsome t? | 9094
Ps 3: 7 break the t *of* the wicked. | 9094
35:16 they gnashed their t at me. | 9094
37:12 the righteous and gnash their t at them; | 9094
57: 4 men whose t are spears and arrows, | 9094
58: 6 Break the t in their mouths, O God; | 9094
112:10 he will gnash his t and waste away; | 9094
124: 6 who has not let us be torn by their t. | 9094
Pr 10:26 As vinegar to the t and smoke to the eyes, | 9094
30:14 those whose t are swords | 9094
SS 4: 2 Your t are like a flock of sheep just shorn, | 9094
6: 6 Your t are like a flock of sheep coming up | 9094
7: 9 flowing gently over lips and t. | 9094
Isa 41:15 new and sharp, with **many** t. | 7092
Jer 31:29 and the children's t are set on edge.' | 9094
31:30 his own t will be set on edge. | 9094
La 2:16 they scoff and gnash their t and say, | 9094
3:16 He has broken my t with gravel; | 9094
Eze 18: 2 and the children's t are set on edge'? | 9094
Da 7: 5 it had three ribs in its mouth between its t. | 10730
7: 7 It had large iron t; | 10730
7:19 with its iron and bronze claws— | 10730
Joel 1: 6 it has the t *of* a lion, the fangs of a lioness. | 9094
Am 1: 6 with sledges having iron t, | NIH
Zec 9: 7 the forbidden food from between their t. | 9094
Mt 8:12 there will be weeping and gnashing *of* t." | 3848
13:42 there will be weeping and gnashing *of* t. | 3848
13:50 there will be weeping and gnashing *of* t. | 3848
22:13 be weeping and gnashing *of* t.' | 3848
24:51 there will be weeping and gnashing *of* t. | 3848
25:30 there will be weeping and gnashing *of* t.' | 3848
Mk 9:18 gnashes his t and becomes rigid. | 3848
Lk 13:28 be weeping there, and gnashing *of* t, | 3848
Ac 7:54 they were furious and gnashed their t | 3848
Rev 9: 8 and their t were like lions' teeth. | 3848
9: 8 and their teeth were like lions' t. | NIG

TEHAPHNEHES (KJV) See TAHPANHES

TEHINNAH (1)
1Ch 4:12 Paseah and T the father of Ir Nahash. | 9383

TEIL (KJV) See TEREBINTH

TEKEL (2)
Da 5:25 that was written: MENE, MENE, T, PARSIN | 10770
5:27 T: You have been weighed on the scales | 10770

TEKOA (13) [TEKOITE]
2Sa 14: 2 to T and had a wise woman brought | 9541
14: 4 When the woman **from** T went to the king, | 9542
14: 9 But the woman **from** T said to him, | 9542
23:26 Helez the Paltite, Ira son of Ikkesh **from** T, | 9542
1Ch 2:24 of Hezron bore him Ashhur the father of T. | 9541
4: 5 Ashhur the father of T had two wives, | 9541
11:28 Ira son of Ikkesh **from** T, | 9542
2Ch 11: 6 Bethlehem, Etam, T, | 9541
20:20 in the morning they left for the Desert of T. | 9541
Ne 3: 5 section was repaired by the **men of T,** | 9542
3:27 the **men of T** repaired another section, | 9542
Jer 6: 1 Sound the trumpet in T! | 9541
Am 1: 1 words of Amos, one of the shepherds of T | 9541

TEKOITE (1) [TEKOA]
1Ch 27: 9 was Ira the son of Ikkesh the T. | 9542

TEL ABIB (1)
Eze 3:15 I came to the exiles who lived at T | 9425

TEL ASSAR (2)
2Ki 19:12 the people of Eden who were in T? | 9431
Isa 37:12 the people of Eden who were in T? | 9431

TEL HARSHA (2) [HARSHA]
Ezr 2:59 T, Kerub, Addon and Immer, | 9426
Ne 7:61 T, Kerub, Addon and Immer, | 9426

TEL MELAH (2)
Ezr 2:59 of T, Tel Harsha, Kerub, Addon | 9427
Ne 7:61 of T, Tel Harsha, Kerub, Addon | 9427

TELAH (1)
1Ch 7:25 Resheph his son, T his son, Tahan his son, | 9436

TELAIM (1)
1Sa 15: 4 the men and mustered them at T— | 3230

TELEM (2)
Jos 15:24 Ziph, T, Bealoth, | 3234
Ezr 10:24 From the gatekeepers: Shallum, T and Uri. | 3235

TELL (576) [TELLING, TELLS, TOLD]
Ge 12:18 "Why didn't *you* t me she was your wife? | 5583
21:26 You *did* not t me, and I heard about it | 5583
22: 2 of the mountains *I will* t you *about.*" | 606
24:23 Please t me, is there room | 5583
24:30 and had heard Rebekah t what | 606+1821
24:33 "Then t us," [Laban] said. | 1819
24:49 and faithfulness to my master, t me; | 5583
24:49 t me, so I may know which way to turn." | 5583
26: 2 live in the land where *I* t you to live. | 606
27: 8 listen carefully and do what I t you: | 7422
29:15 T me what your wages should be." | 5583
31:27 Why didn't *you* t me, so I could send you | 5583
32:29 Jacob said, "Please t me your name." | 5583
37:16 *Can you* t me where they are | 5583
40: 8 T me your dreams." | 6218
41:21 no *one* could t that they had done so; | 3359
42:22 "Didn't *I* t you not to sin against the boy? | 606
45:13 T my father *about* all the honor | 5583
45:17 Pharaoh said to Joseph, "T your brothers, | 606
45:19 You are also directed to t them, 'Do this: | NIH
49: 1 around so *I can* t you what will happen | 5583
50: 4 speak to Pharaoh for me. T him, | 606
Ex 3:13 Then what *shall I* t them?" | 606
6:11 t Pharaoh king of Egypt to let | 1819
6:29 t Pharaoh king of Egypt everything I tell | 1819
6:29 king of Egypt everything I t you." | 1819
7: 2 and your brother Aaron *is to* t Pharaoh | 1819
7:19 The LORD said to Moses, "T Aaron, | 606
8: 5 Then the LORD said to Moses, "T Aaron, | 606
8:16 Then the LORD said to Moses, "T Aaron, | 606
10: 2 that *you may* t your children | 5583
11: 2 T the people that men and women | 265+928+1819
12: 3 T the whole community of Israel that on | 1819
12:27 then t them, 'It is the Passover sacrifice of | 1819
13: 8 On that day t your son, | 5583
14: 2 "T the Israelites to turn back and encamp | 1819
14:15 T the Israelites to move on. | 1819
16:12 T them, 'At twilight you will eat meat, | 1819
19: 3 and what *you are* to t the people of Israel: | 5583
19:12 around the mountain and t them, | 606
20:22 "T the Israelites: | 1819
25: 2 "T the Israelites to bring me an offering. | 1819
28: 3 T all the skilled men to whom I have given | 1819
33: 5 For the LORD had said to Moses, "T | 606
Lev 14:35 the owner of the house must go and t | 5583
16: 2 "T your brother Aaron not to come | 1819
22: 2 "T Aaron and his sons to treat with respect | 1819
Nu 6:23 "T Aaron and his sons, | 1819
9:10 "T the Israelites: 'When any of you | 1819
11:12 Why *do you* t me to carry them | 606
11:18 "T the people: 'Consecrate yourselves | 606
14:14 And *they will* t the inhabitants of this land | 606

Nu 14:28 So t them, 'As surely as I live, | 606
16:37 "T Eleazar son of Aaron, the priest, to take | 606
19: 2 T the Israelites to bring you a red heifer | 1819
22:19 find out what else the LORD *will* t me." | 1819
22:20 go with them, but do only what *I* t you." | 1819
22:35 but speak only what *I* t you." | 1819
23: 3 Whatever he reveals to me *I will* t you." | 5583
23:26 "*Did I* not t you I must do whatever | 1819
24:12 "*Did I* not t the messengers you sent me, | 1819
25:12 Therefore t him I am making my covenant | 606
Dt 1:42 But the LORD said to me, "T them, | 606
5:27 Then t us whatever the LORD tells you. | 1819
5:30 "Go, t them to return to their tents." | 606
6:21 t him: "We were slaves of Pharaoh | 606
17:11 Do not turn aside from what *they* t you, | 5583
18:18 *he will* t them everything I command him. | 1819
32: 7 Ask your father and *he will* t you, | 5583
Jos 1:11 "Go through the camp and t the people, | 7422
2:14 "If *you* don't t what we are doing, | 5583
3: 8 But if *you* t what we are doing, | 5583
3: 8 T the priests who carry the ark of | 7422
4: 3 and t them to take up twelve stones from | 7422
4: 7 t them that the flow of the Jordan | 606
4:22 t them, 'Israel crossed the Jordan on dry | 3359
6:10 do not say a word until the day I t you | 606
7:13 T them, 'Consecrate yourselves | 606
7:19 T me what you have done; | 5583
20: 2 "T the Israelites to designate the cities | 1819
Jdg 2: 3 Now therefore *I* t you that I will | 606
13:13 and he didn't t me his name. | 5583
13:10 The woman hurried *to* t her husband, | 5583
14: 9 not t them that he had taken the honey | 5583
14:12 "*Let me* t you a riddle," | 2554
14:13 If you can't t me *the* **answer,** | 5583
14:13 "T us your riddle," they said. | 2554
16: 6 "T me the secret of your great strength and | 5583
16:10 Come now, t me how you can be tied." | 5583
16:13 T me how you can be tied." | 5583
19:30 T us what to do!" | 1819
20: 3 "T us how this awful thing happened." | 1819
Ru 3: 4 He *will* t you what to do." | 606
4: 4 But if you will not, t me, so I will know. | 5583
1Sa 3:15 He was afraid *to* t Eli the vision, | 5583
6: 2 T us how we should send it back | 3359
9: 6 Perhaps *he will* t us what way to take." | 5583
9: 8 so that *he will* t us what way to take." | 5583
9:18 "*Would you* please t me where | 5583
9:19 and *will* t you all that is in your heart. | 5583
9:27 "T the servant to go on ahead of us"— | 606
10: 8 until I come to you and t you what you are | 3359
10:15 "T me what Samuel said to you." | 5583
10:16 not t his uncle what Samuel had said about | 5583
14: 1 But *he did* not t his father. | 5583
14:34 "Go out among the men and t them, | 606
14:43 "T me what you have done." | 5583
15:16 "*Let me* t you what the LORD said | 5583
15:16 "T me," Saul replied. | 1819
19: 3 about you and *will* t you what I find out." | 5583
20: 6 If your father misses me at all, t him, | 606
20: 9 to harm you, wouldn't *I* t you?" | 5583
20:10 "Who *will* t me if your father answers you | 5583
22:17 yet *they did* not t me." | 265+906+1655
22:22 I knew *he would* be sure to t Saul. | 5583+5583
23:11 O LORD, God of Israel, t your servant." | 5583
23:22 *They* t me he is very crafty. | 606
25: 8 and *they will* t you. | 5583
25:19 But *she did* not t her husband Nabal. | 5583
28:15 I have called on you to t me what to do." | 3359
2Sa 1: 4 David asked. "T me." | 5583
1:20 "T it not in Gath, | 5583
3:19 to Hebron to t David everything that Israel | 1819
7: 5 "Go and t my servant David, 'This is what | 606
7: 8 "Now then, t my servant David, | 606
12:18 David's servants were afraid to t him that | 5583
12:18 How *can we* t him the child is dead? | 606
13: 4 Won't *you* t me?" | 5583
15:35 T them anything you hear in | 5583
17:16 a message immediately and t David, 'Do | 5583
17:17 and they were to go and t King David, | 5583
18:21 "Go," Joab said, "t the king what you have seen." | 606
19:35 *Can I* t **the** difference between what is good | 3359
20:16 T Joab to come here so I can speak | 606
24:12 "Go and t David, 'This is what | 1819
1Ki 12:10 "T these people who have said to you, | 606
12:10 but make our yoke lighter'—t them, | 1819
14: 3 He *will* t you what will happen to | 5583
14: 7 t Jeroboam that this is what the LORD, | 606
18: 8 "Go t your master, 'Elijah is here.' | 606
18:11 now you t me to go to my master and say, | 606
18:12 If I go and t Ahab and he doesn't find you, | 5583
18:14 now you t me to go to my master and say, | 606
18:44 So Elijah said, "Go and t Ahab, | 606
20: 9 "T my lord the king, | 606
22:14 The king of Israel answered, "T him: | 1819
22:14 *I can* t him only what the LORD tells me." | 1819
22:16 *to* t me nothing but the truth in the name | 1819
22:18 "Didn't *I* t you that he never prophesies | 606
2Ki 1: 6 and t him, 'This is what the LORD says: | 1819
2: 9 Elijah said to Elisha, "T me, | 8626
2:18 "Didn't *I* t you not to go?" | 606
4: 2 T me, what do you have in your house?" | 5583
4:13 Elisha said to him, "T her, | 606
4:24 don't slow down for me unless *I* t you." | 606
4:28 "Didn't *I* t you, 'Don't raise my hopes'?" | 606
6:11 "*Will you* not t me which of us is on | 5583
7:12 "I will t you what the Arameans have done | 5583
8: 4 "T me *about* all the great things Elisha | 6218

2Ki	9:12	"That's not true!" they said. "T us."	5583
	9:15	of the city to go and t **the news** in Jezreel."	5583
	18:19	"T Hezekiah: " 'This is what	606
	19: 6	"T your master, 'This is what	606
	20: 5	"Go back and t Hezekiah, the leader	606
	22:15	T the man who sent you to me,	606
	22:18	T the king of Judah, who sent you	606
1Ch	16: 9	t of all his wonderful acts.	8488
	17: 4	"Go and t my servant David, 'This is what	606
	17: 7	"Now then, t my servant David,	606
	21:10	"Go and t David, 'This is what	1819
	21:18	the LORD ordered Gad to t David to go	606
2Ch	10:10	"T the people who have said to you,	606
	10:10	but make our yoke lighter'—t them,	606
	18:13	*I* can t him only what my God says."	1819
	18:15	to t me nothing but the truth in the name	1819
	18:17	"Didn't *I* t you that he never prophesies	606
	34:23	T the man who sent you to me,	606
	34:26	T the king of Judah, who sent you	606
Job	1:15	the only one who has escaped to t you!"	5583
	1:16	the only one who has escaped to t you!"	5583
	1:17	the only one who has escaped to t you!"	5583
	1:19	the only one who has escaped to t you!"	5583
	4:16	It stopped, but *I* could not t what it was.	5795
	8:10	Will they not instruct you and t you?	606
	10: 2	t me what charges you have against me.	3359
	12: 7	or the birds of the air, and *they* will t you;	5583
	15:17	*let me* t you what I have seen,	6218
	32: 6	not daring *to* t you what I know.	2555
	32:10	I too will t you what I know.	2555
	32:17	I too *will* t what I know.	2555
	33:12	"But *I* t you, in this you are not right,	6699
	33:23	to t a man what is right for him,	5583
	34:33	so t me what you know.	1819
	37:19	"T us what we should say to him;	3359
	38: 4	T me, if you understand.	5583
	38:18	T me, if you know all this.	5583
Ps	5: 6	You destroy *those who* t lies;	1819
	9: 1	*I* will t of all your wonders.	6218
	40: 5	were I to speak and t of them,	1819
	48:13	*you may* t of them to the next generation.	6218
	50:12	If I were hungry *I* *would* not t you,	606
	66:16	*let me* t you what he has done for me,	6218
	71:15	My mouth *will* t of your righteousness,	6218
	71:24	My tongue *will* t of your righteous acts	2047
	73:28	I *will* t of all your deeds.	6218
	75: 1	*men t* of your wonderful deeds.	6218
	78: 4	we will t the next generation	6218
	78: 6	and *they* in turn *would* t their children.	6218
	105: 2	t of all his wonderful acts.	8488
	107:22	Let them sacrifice thank offerings and t	6218
	142: 2	before him *I* t my trouble.	5583
	145: 4	*they will* t of your mighty acts.	5583
	145: 6	They will t of the power of your awesome	606
	145:11	*They will* t of the glory of your kingdom	606
Pr	30: 4	T me if you know!	NIH
Ecc	6:12	Who *can* t him what will happen under	5583
	8: 7	who *can* t him what is to come?	5583
	10:14	who *can* t him what will happen after him?	5583
SS	1: 7	T me, you whom I love,	5583
	5: 8	you find my lover, what *will you* t him?	5583
	5: 8	T him I am faint with love.	NIH
Isa	3:10	T the righteous it will be well with them,	606
	5: 5	Now *I will* t you what I am going to do	3359
	6: 9	He said, "Go and t this people:	606
	8:19	When *men* t you to consult mediums	606
	21:10	*I* t you what I have heard from	5583
	30:10	T us pleasant things, prophesy illusions.	1819
	36: 4	"T Hezekiah, " 'This is what the great king	606
	37: 6	"T your master, 'This is what the LORD	606
	38: 5	and t Hezekiah, 'This is what the LORD,	606
	38:19	fathers t their children about your	3359
	41:22	"Bring in [your idols] *to* t us what is going	5583
	41:22	T us what the former things were,	5583
	41:23	t us what the future holds,	5583
	41:27	I was the first to t Zion, 'Look,	NIH
	48: 6	now on *I will* t you *of* new things,	9048
	63: 7	*I will* t of the kindnesses of the LORD,	2349
Jer	4:16	"T this to the nations,	2349
	5:19	*you will* t them, 'As you have forsaken me	606
	7:27	"When *you* t them all this,	1819
	10:11	"T them this: 'These gods, who did not	10042
	11: 2	to the terms of this covenant and t them to	1819
	11: 3	T them that this is what the LORD,	606
	13:13	then t them, 'This is what the LORD says:	606
	15: 2	t them, 'This is what the LORD says:	606
	16:10	"When *you* t these people all this	5583
	19: 2	There proclaim the words *I* t you,	1819
	21: 3	But Jeremiah answered them, "T Zedekiah,	606
	21: 8	"Furthermore, t the people, 'This is what	606
	23:27	dreams *they* t one another will make my	
		people forget my name,	6218
	23:28	the prophet who has a dream t his dream,	6218
	23:32	*They* t them and lead my people astray	6218
	25:27	"Then t them, 'This is what the LORD	606
	25:28	t them, 'This is what the LORD Almighty	606
	26: 2	T them everything I command you;	1819
	27: 4	"T this to your masters:	606
	27: 9	your mediums or your sorcerers who t you,	606
	28:13	"Go and t Hananiah, 'This is what the LORD	606
	29:23	which *I did* not t them to do.	7422
	29:24	T Shemaiah the Nehelamite,	606
	33: 3	and I will answer you and t you great	5583
	34: 2	Go to Zedekiah king of Judah and t him,	606
	35:13	Go and t the men of Judah and the people	606
	36:17	Then they asked Baruch, "T us,	5583
	36:29	Also t Jehoiakim king of Judah,	606

Jer	37: 7	T the king of Judah, 'This is what the LORD	606
	38:20	"Obey the LORD by doing what I t you.	1819
	38:25	'T us what you said to the king and what	5583
	38:26	then t them, 'I was pleading with the king	606
	39:16	"Go and t Ebed-Melech the Cushite,	606
	42: 3	Pray that the LORD your God *will* t us	5583
	42: 4	*I will* t you everything the LORD says	5583
	42: 5	the LORD your God sends you to t us.	NIH
	42:20	t us everything he says and we will do it.'	5583
	42:21	in all he sent me to t you.	NIH
	43: 1	the LORD had sent him to t them—	NIH
	51:10	come, *let us* t in Zion what the LORD	6218
Eze	13:11	t those who cover it with whitewash	606
	14: 4	Therefore speak to them and t them,	606
	17: 2	set forth an allegory and t the house	5439
	24: 3	T this rebellious house a parable and say	5439
	24:19	"Won't *you* t us what these things mean	5583
	24:26	on that day a fugitive will come to t you	NIH
	33:13	If I t the righteous man that he will	606
	37:18	'Won't *you* t us what you mean by this?'	5583
	40: 4	T the house of Israel everything you see."	5583
	44: 5	and give attention to everything I t you	1819
Da	2: 2	to t him what he had dreamed.	5583
	2: 4	T your servants the dream,	10042
	2: 5	If *you do* not t me what my dream was	10313
	2: 6	But if *you* t me the dream and explain it,	10252
	2: 6	So t me the dream and interpret it for me."	10252
	2: 7	"*Let* the king t his servants the dream,	10042
	2: 9	If *you do* not t me the dream,	10313
	2: 9	You have conspired to t me misleading	10042
	2: 9	So then, t me the dream,	10042
	2:25	among the exiles from Judah who *can* t	10313
	2:26	"Are you able to t me what I saw	10313
	4: 2	to t you *about* the miraculous signs	10252
	4:18	Now, Belteshazzar, t me what it means,	10042
	5: 8	but they could not read the writing or t	10313
	5:12	and *he will* t you what the writing means."	10252
	5:15	and t me what it means,	10313
	5:16	and t me what it means,	10313
	5:17	for the king and t him what it means.	10313
	8:16	t this man **the meaning** of the vision."	1067
	8:19	*to* t you what will happen later in the time	3359
	9:23	which I have come to t you,	5583
	10:21	but first I *will* t you what is written in	5583
	11: 2	"Now then, *I* t you the truth:	5583
Joel	1: 3	T it to your children,	6218
	1: 3	and let your children t it to their children,	NIH
Jnh	1: 8	So they asked him, "T us,	5583
	4:11	a hundred and twenty thousand people who	
		cannot t their right hand	3359
Mic	1:10	T it not in Gath; weep not at all.	5583
	3:11	and her prophets t **fortunes** for money.	7876
Hag	2:21	"T Zerubbabel governor of Judah	606
Zec	1: 3	Therefore t the people:	606
	2: 4	"Run, t that young man,	1819
	6:12	T him this is what the LORD Almighty	606
	10: 2	*they* t dreams that are false,	1819
Mt	2:13	Stay there until *I* t you,	3306
	3: 9	t you out of these stones	3306
	4: 3	t these stones to become bread."	3306
	5:18	*I* t you the truth, until heaven and earth	3306
	5:20	For *I* t you that unless your righteousness	3306
	5:22	But I t you that anyone who is angry	3306
	5:26	*I* t you the truth, you will not get out	3306
	5:28	But I t you that anyone who looks at	3306
	5:32	I t you that anyone who divorces his wife,	3306
	5:34	But I t you, Do not swear at all;	3306
	5:39	But I t you, Do not resist an evil person.	3306
	5:44	But I t you: Love your enemies	3306
	6: 2	*I* t you the truth, they have received	3306
	6: 5	*I* t you the truth, they have received	3306
	6:16	*I* t you the truth, they have received	3306
	6:25	"Therefore *I* t you, do not worry	3306
	6:29	Yet *I* t you that not even Solomon	3306
	7:23	Then *I will* t them **plainly,**	3933
	8: 4	"See that *you* don't t anyone.	3306
	8: 9	I t this one, 'Go,' and he goes;	3306
	8:10	"*I* t you the truth, I have not found anyone	3306
	10:15	*I* t you the truth, it will be more bearable	3306
	10:23	*I* t you the truth, you will not finish going	3306
	10:27	What *I* t you in the dark,	3306
	10:42	*I* t you the truth, he will certainly not lose	3306
	11: 9	Yes, *I* t you, and more than a prophet.	3306
	11:11	*I* t you the truth: Among those born of	3306
	11:22	But *I* t you, it will be more bearable	3306
	11:24	But *I* t you that it will be more bearable	3306
	12: 6	*I* t you that one greater than the temple	3306
	12:16	warning them not to t who he was.	4472+5745
	12:31	And so *I* t you, every sin and blasphemy	3306
	12:36	But *I* t you that men will have	3306
	13:17	For *I* t you the truth, many prophets and	3306
	13:30	At that time *I* *will* t the harvesters:	3306
	14:28	"t me to come to you on the water."	3027
	16:18	And I t you that you are Peter,	3306
	16:20	not *to* t anyone that he was the Christ.	3306
	17: 9	"Don't t anyone what you have seen,	3306
	17:12	But *I* t you, Elijah has already come,	3306
	17:20	*I* t you the truth, if you have faith as small	3306
	18: 3	And he said: "*I* t you the truth,	3306
	18:10	For *I* t you that their angels	3306
	18:13	And if he finds it, *I* t you the truth,	3306
	18:17	t it to the church; and if he refuses	3306
	18:18	*I* t you the truth, whatever you bind on	3306
	18:19	*I* t you that if two of you on earth agree	3306
	18:22	Jesus answered, "*I* t you, not seven times,	3306
	19: 9	*I* t you that anyone who divorces his wife,	3306

Mt	19:23	"*I* t you the truth, it is hard for a rich man	3306
	19:24	Again *I* t you, it is easier for a camel	3306
	19:28	Jesus said to them, "*I* t you the truth,	3306
	21: 3	t him that the Lord needs them,	3306
	21:21	Jesus replied, "*I* t you the truth,	3306
	21:24	I *will* t you by what authority I am doing	3306
	21:27	"Neither *will I* t you by what authority	3306
	21:31	Jesus said to them, "*I* t you the truth,	3306
	21:43	"Therefore *I* t you that the kingdom	3306
	22: 3	to the banquet *to* t them to come,	2813
	22: 4	'T those who have been invited	3306
	22:17	T us then, what is your opinion?"	3306
	23: 3	and do everything *they* t you.	3306
	23:36	*I* t you the truth, all this will come upon this	3306
	23:39	For *I* t you, you will not see me again until	3306
	24: 2	"*I* t you the truth, not one stone here will be	3306
	24: 3	"T us," they said, "when will this happen,	3306
	24:34	*I* t you the truth, this generation	3306
	24:47	*I* t you the truth, he will put him in charge	3306
	25:12	"But he replied, '*I* t you the truth,	3306
	25:40	"The King will reply, '*I* t you the truth,	3306
	25:45	"He will reply, '*I* t you the truth,	3306
	26:13	*I* t you the truth, wherever this gospel is	3306
	26:18	into the city to a certain man and t him,	3306
	26:21	they were eating, he said, "*I* t you the truth,	3306
	26:29	*I* t you, I will not drink of this fruit of	3306
	26:34	*I* t you," Jesus answered,	3306
	26:63	T us if you are the Christ, the Son of God."	3306
	27:64	and t the people that he has been raised	3306
	28: 7	Then go quickly and t his disciples:	3306
	28: 8	and ran *to* t his disciples.	550
	28:10	Go and t my brothers to go to Galilee;	550
Mk	1:44	"See that *you* don't t this to anyone.	3306
	2:11	"*I* t you, get up, take your mat	3306
	3:12	not to t who he was.	4472+5745
	3:28	*I* t you the truth,	3306
	5:19	and t them how much the Lord has done	550
	5:33	So the man went away and began to t in	3062
	7:36	Jesus commanded them not to t anyone.	3306
	8:12	*I* t you the truth, all sins and blasphemies	3306
	8:30	Jesus warned them not *to* t anyone	3306
	9: 1	And he said to them, "*I* t you the truth,	3306
	9: 9	not *to* t anyone what they had seen until	1455
	9:13	But *I* t you, Elijah has come,	3306
	9:41	*I* t you the truth, anyone who gives you	3306
	10:15	*I* t you the truth, anyone who will not	3306
	10:29	"*I* t you the truth," Jesus replied,	3306
	11: 3	t him, 'The Lord needs it	3306
	11:23	*I* t you the truth, if anyone says to this	3306
	11:24	Therefore *I* t you, whatever you ask for	3306
	11:29	I *will* t you by what authority I am doing	3306
	11:30	from heaven, or from men? T me!"	646
	11:33	"Neither *will* I t you by what authority	3306
	12:43	Jesus said, "*I* t you the truth,	3306
	13: 4	"T us, when will these things happen?	3306
	13:30	*I* t you the truth, this generation	3306
	14: 9	*I* t you the truth, wherever this gospel is	3306
	14:18	he said, "*I* t you the truth,	3306
	14:25	"*I* t you the truth, I will not drink again	3306
	14:30	"*I* t you the truth," Jesus answered,	3306
	16: 7	But go, t his disciples and Peter,	3306
Lk	1:19	and to t you this **good news.**	2294
	3: 8	For *I* t you that out of these stones God can	3306
	4: 3	t this stone to become bread."	3306
	4:24	"*I* t you the truth," he continued,	3306
	5:14	Then Jesus ordered him, "Don't t anyone,	3306
	5:24	He said to the paralyzed man, "*I* t you,	3306
	6:27	"But *I* t you who hear me:	3306
	7: 8	*I* t this one, 'Go,' and he goes;	3306
	7: 9	he said, "*I* t you, I have not found such	3306
	7:26	Yes, *I* t you, and more than a prophet.	3306
	7:28	*I* t you, among those born of women	3306
	7:40	"Simon, I have something *to* t you."	3306
	7:40	"T me, teacher," he said,	—
	7:47	*I* t you, her many sins have been forgiven—	3306
	8:39	and t how much God has done for you."	1455
	8:56	not *to* t anyone what had happened.	3306
	9:21	Jesus strictly warned them not *to* t this	3306
	9:27	*I* t you the truth, some who are standing	3306
	9:44	to what I **am about to t** you:	3364+3836+4047
	10: 9	Heal the sick who are there and t them,	3306
	10:12	*I* t you, it will be more bearable on	3306
	10:24	For *I* t you that many prophets	3306
	10:40	T her to help me!"	3306
	11: 8	*I* t you, though he will not get up	3306
	11:51	*I* t you, this generation will be held	3306
	12: 4	"*I* t you, my friends, do not be afraid of	3306
	12: 5	Yes, *I* t you, fear him.	3306
	12: 8	"*I* t you, whoever acknowledges me	3306
	12:13	t my brother to divide the inheritance	3306
	12:22	"Therefore *I* t you, do not worry	3306
	12:27	Yet *I* t you, not even Solomon in all his	3306
	12:37	*I* t you the truth, he will dress himself to	3306
	12:44	*I* t you the truth, he will put him in charge	3306
	12:51	No, *I* t you, but division.	3306
	12:59	*I* t you, you will not get out until you have	3306
	13: 3	*I* t you, no!	3306
	13: 5	*I* t you, no!	3306
	13:24	because many, *I* t you, will try to enter	3306
	13:32	He replied, "Go t that fox,	3306
	13:35	*I* t you, you will not see me again	3306
	14:17	*to* t those who had been invited,	3306
	14:24	*I* t you, not one of those men	3306
	15: 7	*I* t you that in the same way there will	3306
	15:10	In the same way, *I* t you, there is rejoicing	3306
	16: 9	*I* t you, use worldly wealth to gain friends	3306
	17:23	*Men will* t you, 'There he is!'	3306

Lk	17:34	*I* t you, on that night two people will be	3306
	18: 8	*I* t you, he will see that they get justice,	3306
	18:14	"*I* t you that this man, rather than the other,	3306
	18:17	*I* t you the truth, anyone who will not	3306
	18:29	"*I* t you the truth," Jesus said to them,	3306
	19:11	he went on *to* t them a parable,	3306
	19:26	'*I* t you that to everyone who has,	3306
	19:31	t him, 'The Lord needs it.' "	3306
	19:40	"*I* t you," he replied, "if they keep quiet,	3306
	20: 2	"**T** us by what authority you are doing	
		these things,"	3306
	20: 3	"I will also ask you a question. **T** me,	3306
	20: 8	"Neither *will* I t you by what authority	3306
	20: 9	He went on *to* t the people this parable:	3306
	21: 3	"*I* t you the truth," he said,	3306
	21:32	"*I* t you the truth,	3306
	22:16	For *I* t you, this generation	3306
	22:18	For *I* t you I will not drink again of	3306
	22:34	Jesus answered, "*I* t you, Peter,	3306
	22:37	*I* t you that this must be fulfilled in me.	3306
	22:67	"If you are the Christ," they said, "**t** us."	3306
	22:67	Jesus answered, "If *I* t you,	3306
	23:43	Jesus answered, "*I* t you the truth,	3306
Jn	1:41	to find his brother Simon and t him,	3306
	1:51	He then added, "*I* t you the truth,	3306
	3: 3	In reply Jesus declared, "*I* t you the truth,	3306
	3: 5	Jesus answered, "*I* t you the truth,	3306
	3: 8	but *you* cannot t where it comes from or	3857
	3:11	*I* t you the truth, we speak of what we know	3306
	4:35	*I* t you, open your eyes and look at	3306
	5:19	"*I* t you the truth, the Son can do nothing by	3306
	5:24	"*I* t you the truth, whoever hears my word	3306
	5:25	*I* t you the truth, a time is coming	3306
	6:26	Jesus answered, "*I* t you the truth,	3306
	6:32	Jesus said to them, "*I* t you the truth,	3306
	6:47	*I* t you the truth, he who believes has	3306
	6:53	Jesus said to them, "*I* t you the truth,	3306
	8:26	and what I have heard from him *I* t	3281
	8:34	Jesus replied, "*I* t you the truth,	3306
	8:45	I t the truth, you do not believe me!	3306
	8:51	*I* t you the truth, if anyone keeps my word,	3306
	8:58	"*I* t you the truth," Jesus answered,	3306
	9:36	"T me so that I may believe in him."	NIG
	10: 1	"*I* t you the truth, the man who does not	3306
	10: 7	Jesus said again, "*I* t you the truth,	3306
	10:24	If you are the Christ, t us plainly."	3306
	10:25	Jesus answered, "*I* did t you,	3306
	11:11	he went on *to* t them, "Our friend Lazarus	3306
	11:40	"*Did I* not t you that if you believed,	3306
	12:22	Philip went *to* t Andrew;	3306
	12:24	*I* t you the truth, unless a kernel of wheat	3306
	13:16	*I* t you the truth, no servant is greater than	3306
	13:20	*I* t you the truth, whoever accepts anyone	3306
	13:21	"*I* t you the truth, one of you is going to	3306
	13:33	and just as I told the Jews, so *I* t you now:	3306
	13:38	*I* t you the truth, before the rooster crows,	3306
	14:12	*I* t you the truth, anyone who has faith in me	3306
	16: 4	*I* did not t you this at first because I was	3306
	16: 7	But I t you the truth: It is for your good	3306
	16:13	and he will t you what is yet to come.	334
	16:20	*I* t you the truth, you will weep	3306
	16:23	*I* t you the truth, my Father will give you	3306
	16:25	but *will* t you plainly about my Father.	550
	20:15	t me where you have put him,	3306
	20:17	Go instead to my brothers and t them,	3306
	21:18	*I* t you the truth, when you were younger	3306
Ac	2:29	*I* can t you confidently that the patriarch	3306
	5: 8	Peter asked her, "**T** me, is this the price	3306
	5:20	"and t the people the full message	3281
	8:34	The eunuch asked Philip, "**T** me, please,	NIG
	10:33	the Lord has commanded you to t us."	NIG
	12:17	"**T** James and the brothers **about** this,"	550
	13:32	"*We* t you **the good news:**	2294
	21:23	so do what *we* t you.	3306
	22:27	"**T** me, are you a Roman citizen?"	3306
	23:17	he has something *to* t him."	550
	23:18	because he has something *to* t you."	3281
	23:19	"What is it you want *to* t me?"	550
	23:22	and cautioned him, "Don't t anyone	1718
Ro	15: 8	For *I* t you that Christ has become	3306
1Co	12: 3	Therefore *I* t you that no one who is	1192
	15:51	Listen, *I* t you a mystery:	3306
2Co	6: 2	**I** t you, now is the time of God's favor,	2627
	12: 4	things that man is not permitted *to* t.	3281
Gal	4:21	T me, you who want to be under the law,	3306
	5: 2	Paul, t you that if you let yourselves be	
Eph	4:17	So *I* t you this, and insist on it in the Lord,	3306
	6:21	*will* t you everything, so that you also may	1192
Col	2: 4	*I* t you this so that no one may deceive you	3306
	4: 7	Tychicus *will* t you all the news	1192
	4: 9	They *will* t you everything	1192
	4:17	T Archippus: "See to it that you complete	3306
1Th	1: 9	They t how you turned to God from idols	NIG
	2: 2	of our God we dared *to* t you his gospel	3281
	3: 4	*we* t you that we who are still alive,	3306
2Th	2: 5	with you *I* used *to* t you these things?	3306
Heb	11:32	I do not have time *to* t about Gideon,	1455
3Jn	1: 3	and t **about** your faithfulness to the truth	3455
Rev	2:10	**I** t **you,** the devil will put some of you	2627

TELLING (36) [TELL]

Ge	31:20	by not t him he was running away.	5583
	42:16	be tested to see if you are t the truth.	NIH
	43: 6	"Why did you bring this trouble on me by t	5583
Ex	33:12	"You *have been* t me, 'Lead these people,'	606
Jdg	7:13	Gideon arrived just as a man *was* t a friend	6218

2Ki	8: 5	Just as Gehazi was t the king	6218
Ne	6:19	and then t him what I said.	3655
Ps	26: 7	proclaiming aloud your praise and t	6218
Jer	14:13	the prophets *keep* t them,	606
	26: 8	But as soon as Jeremiah finished t all	1819
	38: 1	of Malkijah heard what Jeremiah *was* t all	1819
	43: 1	When Jeremiah finished t the people all	1819
Eze	20:49	'Isn't he *just* t parables?' "	5439
Mt	16:12	not t them to guard against the yeast used	3306
	28:13	t them, "You are to say, 'His disciples came	3306
Mk	14:13	So he sent two of his disciples, t them,	3306
Lk	12:41	"Lord, *are you* t this parable to us,	3306
Jn	8:27	not understand that *he was* t them **about**	3306
	8:38	*I am* t you what I have seen in	3281
	8:46	If *I am* t the truth, why don't you believe	3306
	10: 6	not understand what he was t them.	3281
	13:19	"*I am* t you now before it happens,	3306
	13:29	some thought Jesus *was* t him	3306
Ac	10:36	t **the good news** of peace through Jesus	2294
	11: 7	Then I heard a voice t me, 'Get up, Peter.	3306
	11:19	t the message only to Jews.	3281
	11:20	t them **the good news** about the Lord Jesus.	2294
	14:15	t you to turn from these worthless things to	NIG
	15:12	and Paul t **about** the miraculous signs	2007
	15:20	t them to abstain from food polluted	NIG
	16:17	who *are* t you the way to be saved."	2859
	21:21	t them not to circumcise their children	3306
2Co	9: 2	t them that since last year you in Achaia	NIG
Gal	4:16	become your enemy *by* t you the **truth?**	238
1Th	3: 4	*we kept* t you that we would be persecuted.	4625
1Ti	2: 7	*I am* t the truth, I am not lying—	3306

TELLS (17) [TELL]

Ge	21:12	Listen to whatever Sarah t you,	606
	41:55	"Go to Joseph and do what *he* t you."	606
Dt	5:27	tell us whatever the Lord our God t you.	1819
1Sa	22: 8	No *one* t me when my son makes	265+906+1655
	22: 8	None of you is concerned about me or t me	
			265+906+1655
1Ki	22:14	I can tell him only what the Lord t me."	606
2Ki	5:13	How much more, then, when *he* t you,	606
	6:12	t the king of Israel the very words	5583
Job	36: 9	*he* t them what they have done—	5583
Pr	12: 7	but a false witness t lies.	NIH
Da	5: 7	and t me what it means will be clothed	10252
Am	5:10	in court and despise *him who* t the truth.	1819
Mt	24:26	"So if anyone t you, 'There he is,	3306
Mk	13:34	and t the one at the door to keep watch.	1948
Jn	2: 5	"Do whatever *he* t you."	3306
	19:35	He knows that *he* t the truth,	3306
Ac	3:22	you must listen to everything *he* t you.	3281

TEMA (5)

Ge	25:15	Hadad, **T,** Jetur, Naphish and Kedemah.	9401
1Ch	1:30	Mishma, Dumah, Massa, Hadad, **T,**	9401
Job	6:19	The caravans of **T** look for water,	9401
Isa	21:14	you who live in **T,** bring food	824+9401
Jer	25:23	**T,** Buz and all who are in distant places;	9401

TEMAH (2)

Ezr	2:53	Barkos, Sisera, **T,**	9457
Ne	7:55	Barkos, Sisera, **T,**	9457

TEMAN (11) [TEMANITE, TEMANITES]

Ge	36:11	**T,** Omar, Zepho, Gatam and Kenaz.	9403
	36:15	Chiefs **T,** Omar, Zepho, Kenaz,	9403
	36:42	Kenaz, **T,** Mibzar,	9403
1Ch	1:36	**T,** Omar, Zepho, Gatam and Kenaz;	9403
	1:53	Kenaz, **T,** Mibzar,	9403
Jer	49: 7	"Is there no longer wisdom in **T?**	9403
	49:20	against those who live in **T:**	9403
Eze	25:13	and from **T** to Dedan they will fall by	9403
Am	1:12	I will send fire upon **T** that will consume	9403
Ob	1: 9	Your warriors, O **T,** will be terrified,	9403
Hab	3: 3	God came from **T,** the Holy One from	9403

TEMANITE (6) [TEMAN]

Job	2:11	When Job's three friends, Eliphaz the **T,**	9404
	4: 1	Then Eliphaz the **T** replied:	9404
	15: 1	Then Eliphaz the **T** replied:	9404
	22: 1	Then Eliphaz the **T** replied:	9404
	42: 7	he said to Eliphaz the **T,**	9404
	42: 9	the **T,** Bildad the Shuhite and Zophar	9404

TEMANITES (2) [TEMAN]

Ge	36:34	the land of the **T** succeeded him as king.	9404
1Ch	1:45	the land of the **T** succeeded him as king.	9404

TEMENI (1)

1Ch	4: 6	Hepher, **T** and Haahashtari.	9405

TEMPER (2) [EVEN-TEMPERED, HOT-TEMPERED, ILL-TEMPERED, QUICK-TEMPERED]

1Sa	20: 7	But if *he* **loses** his **t,** you can be sure	3013+3013
Pr	16:32	a man who controls his t than one who takes	8120

TEMPERANCE (KJV) See
SELF-CONTROL

TEMPERATE (3)

1Ti	3: 2	t, self-controlled, respectable, hospitable,	3767
	3:11	not malicious talkers but t and trustworthy	3767
Tit	2: 2	Teach the older men to be t,	3767

TEMPERED (KJV) See COMBINED, MIXED

TEMPEST (7)

Job	27:20	a t snatches him away in the night.	6070
	37: 9	The t comes out from its chamber,	6070
Ps	50: 3	and around him a t **rages.**	4394+8548
	55: 8	far from my t and storm."	6185+8120
	83:15	with your t and terrify them	6193
	107:25	and stirred up a t that lifted high	6194+8120
Isa	29: 6	and t and flames of a devouring fire.	6194

TEMPLE (683) [TEMPLES]

Jdg	4:21	the peg through his t into the ground,	8377
	4:22	with the tent peg through his t—	8377
	5:26	she shattered and pierced his t.	8377
	9: 4	of silver from the t of Baal-Berith.	1074
	9:27	they held a festival in the t *of* their god.	1074
	9:46	into the stronghold of the t of El-Berith.	1074
	16:26	the pillars that support the t,	1074
	16:27	the t was crowded with men and women;	1074
	16:29	the two central pillars on which the t stood.	1074
	16:30	and down came the t on the rulers and all	1074
1Sa	1: 9	a chair by the doorpost of the Lord's t.	2121
	3: 3	Samuel was lying down in the t of the Lord	2121
	5: 2	Then they carried the ark into Dagon's t	1074
	5: 5	nor any others who enter Dagon's t	1074
	31: 9	the Philistines to proclaim the news in the t	1074
	31:10	They put his armor in the t of the Ashtoreths	1074
2Sa	22: 7	From his t he heard my voice;	2121
1Ki	3: 1	building his palace and the t of the Lord,	1074
	3: 2	a t had not yet been built for the Name of	1074
	5: 3	a t for the Name of the Lord his God	1074
	5: 5	a t for the Name of the Lord my God,	1074
	5: 5	on the throne in your place will build the t	1074
	5:17	a foundation of dressed stone for the t.	1074
	5:18	and stone for the building of the t.	1074
	6: 1	he began to build the t of the Lord.	1074
	6: 2	The t that King Solomon built for the Name	1074
	6: 3	the main hall of the t extended the width of	1074
	6: 3	of the temple extended the width of the t,	1074
	6: 3	from the front of the t.	1074
	6: 4	made narrow clerestory windows in the t.	1074
	6: 6	the t so that nothing would be inserted into	1074
	6: 6	be inserted into the t walls.	1074
	6: 7	In building the t, only blocks dressed at	1074
	6: 7	at the t site while it was being built.	1074
	6: 8	on the south side of the t;	1074
	6: 9	So he built the t and completed it,	1074
	6:10	And he built the side rooms all along the t.	1074
	6:10	and they were attached to the t by beams	1074
	6:12	"As for this t you are building,	1074
	6:14	So Solomon built the t and completed it.	1074
	6:15	paneling them from the floor of the t to	1074
	6:15	and covered the floor of the t with planks	1074
	6:16	of the t with cedar boards from floor	1074
	6:16	from floor to ceiling to form within the t	1074
	6:18	The inside of the t was cedar,	1074
	6:19	within the t to set the ark of the covenant	1074
	6:21	Solomon covered the inside of the t	1074
	6:27	inside the innermost room of the t,	1074
	6:29	On the walls all around the t,	1074
	6:30	of both the inner and outer rooms of the t	1074
	6:37	of the t of the Lord was laid in	1074
	6:38	the t was finished in all its details	1074
	7:12	the inner courtyard of the t of the Lord	1074
	7:21	the pillars at the portico of the t.	2121
	7:39	of the stands on the south side of the t	1074
	7:39	at the southeast corner of the t.	1074
	7:40	for King Solomon in the t of the Lord:	1074
	7:45	for King Solomon for the t *of* the Lord	1074
	7:48	that were in the Lord's t:	1074
	7:50	also for the doors of the main hall of the t.	1074
	7:51	the work King Solomon had done for the t	1074
	7:51	in the treasuries of the Lord's t.	1074
	8: 6	to its place in the inner sanctuary of the t,	1074
	8:10	the cloud filled the t *of* the Lord.	1074
	8:11	for the glory of the Lord filled his t.	1074
	8:13	I have indeed built a magnificent t for you,	1074
	8:16	a city in any tribe of Israel to have a t built	1074
	8:17	to build a t for the Name of the Lord,	1074
	8:18	'Because it was in your heart to build a t	1074
	8:19	you are not the one to build the t,	1074
	8:19	the one who will build the t for my Name.'	1074
	8:20	the Lord promised, and I have built the t	1074
	8:27	How much less this t I have built!	1074
	8:29	May your eyes be open toward this t night	1074
	8:31	the oath before your altar in this t,	1074
	8:33	and making supplication to you in this t,	1074
	8:38	and spreading out his hands toward this t—	1074
	8:42	when he comes and prays toward this t,	1074
	8:44	and the t I have built for your Name,	1074
	8:48	and the t I have built for your Name;	1074
	8:63	and all the Israelites dedicated the t	1074
	8:64	of the courtyard in front of the t *of*	1074
	9: 1	When Solomon had finished building the t	1074
	9: 3	I have consecrated this t,	1074
	9: 7	and will reject this t I have consecrated	1074
	9: 8	And though this t is now imposing,	1074
	9: 8	a thing to this land and to this t?'	1074

1Ki	9:10	the t *of* the LORD and the royal palace—	1074
	9:15	to build the LORD's t, his own palace,	1074
	9:25	and so fulfilled the t obligations.	1074
	10: 5	and the burnt offerings he made at the t *of*	1074
	10:12	the almugwood to make supports for the t	1074
	12:27	up to offer sacrifices at the t *of* the LORD	1074
	14:26	of the t *of* the LORD and the treasures of	1074
	14:28	the king went to the LORD's t,	1074
	15:15	into the t *of* the LORD the silver and gold	1074
	15:18	of the LORD's t and of his own palace.	1074
	16:32	He set up an altar for Baal in the t *of* Baal	1074
2Ki	5:18	When my master enters the t *of* Rimmon,	1074
	5:18	when I bow down in the t *of* Rimmon,	1074
	10:21	the t *of* Baal until it was full from one end	1074
	10:23	son of Recab went into the t *of* Baal.	1074
	10:25	and then entered the inner shrine of the t	1074
	10:26	They brought the sacred stone out of the t	1074
	10:27	of Baal and tore down the t *of* Baal,	1074
	11: 3	He remained hidden with his nurse at the t	1074
	11: 4	and had them brought to him at the t *of*	1074
	11: 4	with them and put them under oath at the t	1074
	11: 6	who take turns guarding the t—	1074
	11: 7	to guard the t for the king.	1074
	11:10	to King David and that were in the t *of*	1074
	11:11	near the altar and the t,	1074
	11:11	the south side to the north side of the t.	1074
	11:13	to the people at the t *of* the LORD.	1074
	11:15	not be put to death in the t *of* the LORD."	1074
	11:18	the people of the land went to the t *of* Baal	1074
	11:18	the priest posted guards at the t *of*	1074
	11:19	down from the t *of* the LORD and went	1074
	12: 4	that is brought as sacred offerings to the t	1074
	12: 4	and the money brought voluntarily to the t.	1074
	12: 5	repair whatever damage is found in the t."	1074
	12: 6	the priests still had not repaired the t.	1074
	12: 7	the damage done to the t?	1074
	12: 7	but hand it over for repairing the t."	1074
	12: 8	that they would not repair the t themselves.	1074
	12: 9	on the right side as one enters the t *of*	1074
	12: 9	that was brought to the t *of* the LORD.	1074
	12:10	the money that had been brought into the t	1074
	12:11	to supervise the work on the t.	1074
	12:11	those who worked on the t *of* the LORD—	1074
	12:12	and dressed stone for the repair of the t *of*	1074
	12:12	the other expenses of restoring the t.	1074
	12:13	The money brought into the t was	1074
	12:13	of gold or silver for the t *of* the LORD;	1074
	12:14	who used it to repair the t.	1074
	12:16	and sin offerings was not brought into the t	1074
	12:18	the treasuries of the t *of* the LORD and of	1074
	14:14	the t *of* the LORD and in the treasuries of	1074
	15:35	Jotham rebuilt the Upper Gate of the t *of*	1074
	16: 8	the t *of* the LORD and in the treasuries of	1074
	16:14	from the front of the t—	1074
	16:14	the new altar and the t *of* the LORD—	1074
	16:14	that had been built at the t and removed	1074
	16:18	the royal entryway outside the t *of*	1074
	18:15	the t *of* the LORD and in the treasuries of	1074
	18:16	and doorposts of the t *of* the LORD,	2121
	19: 1	and put on sackcloth and went into the t *of*	1074
	19:14	up to the t *of* the LORD and spread it out	1074
	19:37	while he was worshiping in the t	1074
	20: 5	now you will go up to the t *of* the LORD.	1074
	20: 8	and that I will go up to the t *of* the LORD	1074
	21: 4	He built altars in the t *of* the LORD,	1074
	21: 5	In both courts of the t *of* the LORD,	1074
	21: 7	and put it in the t,	1074
	21: 7	"In this t and in Jerusalem,	1074
	22: 3	to the t *of* the LORD.	1074
	22: 4	the money that has been brought into the t	1074
	22: 5	to supervise the work on the t.	1074
	22: 5	the workers who repair the t *of* the LORD—	1074
	22: 6	and dressed stone to repair the t.	1074
	22: 8	"I have found the Book of the Law in the t	1074
	22: 9	the money that was in the t *of* the LORD	1074
	22: 9	to the workers and supervisors at the t."	1074
	23: 2	the t *of* the LORD with the men of Judah,	1074
	23: 2	which had been found in the t *of*	1074
	23: 4	and the doorkeepers to remove from the t	2121
	23: 6	the Asherah pole from the t *of* the LORD	1074
	23: 7	which were in the t *of* the LORD and	1074
	23:11	He removed from the entrance to the t *of*	1074
	23:12	in the two courts of the t *of* the LORD.	1074
	23:24	the priest had discovered in the t *of*	1074
	23:27	and this t, about which I said,	1074
	24:13	the treasures from the t *of* the LORD and	1074
	24:13	of Israel had made for the t *of* the LORD.	2121
	25: 9	He set fire to the t *of* the LORD,	1074
	25:13	and the bronze Sea that were at the t *of*	1074
	25:14	the bronze articles used in the t service.	NIH
	25:16	which Solomon made for the t *of*	1074
1Ch	6:10	in the t Solomon built in Jerusalem),	1074
	6:32	until Solomon built the t *of* the LORD	1074
	9: 2	priests, Levites and t **servants.**	5987
	9:28	of the articles used in the t service;	NIH
	9:33	of the t and were exempt from other duties	NIH
	10:10	the t *of* their gods and hung up his head in	1074
	10:10	of their gods and hung up his head in the t	1074
	22:14	to provide for the t *of* the LORD	1074
	22:19	into the t that will be built for the Name of	1074
	23: 4	of the t and six thousand are to	1074
	23:24	or more who served in the t *of* the LORD.	1074
	23:28	in the service of the t *of* the LORD:	1074
	23:32	for the service of the t *of* the LORD.	1074
	24:19	of ministering when they entered the t *of*	1074
	25: 6	of their fathers for the music of the t *of*	1074
	26:12	for ministering in the t *of* the LORD,	1074
1Ch	26:22	of the treasuries of the t *of* the LORD.	1074
	26:27	for the repair of the t *of* the LORD.	1074
	26:29	from the t, as officials and judges	NIH
	28:10	for the LORD has chosen you to build a t	1074
	28:11	the plans for the portico of the t,	NIH
	28:12	the courts of the t *of* the LORD and all	1074
	28:12	for the treasuries of the t *of* God and for	1074
	28:13	the work of serving in the t *of* the LORD,	1074
	28:20	until all the work for the service of the t *of*	1074
	28:21	for all the work on the t *of* God,	1074
	29: 2	I have provided for the t *of* my God—	1074
	29: 3	in my devotion to the t *of* my God I	1074
	29: 3	and silver for the t *of* my God, over and	1074
	29: 3	I have provided for this holy t;	1074
	29: 7	on the t *of* God five thousand talents	1074
	29: 8	to the treasury of the t *of* the LORD in	1074
	29:16	that we have provided for building you a t	1074
2Ch	2: 1	to build a t for the Name of the LORD	1074
	2: 4	Now I am about to build a t for the Name	1074
	2: 5	"The t I am going to build will be great,	1074
	2: 6	But who is able to build a t for him,	1074
	2: 6	Who then am I to build a t for him,	1074
	2: 9	the t I build must be large and magnificent.	1074
	2:12	a t for the LORD and a palace for himself.	1074
	3: 1	to build the t *of* the LORD in Jerusalem	1074
	3: 3	the t *of* God was sixty cubits long	1074
	3: 4	at the front of the t was twenty cubits long	NIH
	3: 6	He adorned the t with precious stones.	1074
	3: 7	walls and doors of the t with gold,	1074
	3: 8	to the width of the t—	1074
	3:11	and touched the t wall,	1074
	3:12	and touched the other t wall,	1074
	3:15	In the front of the t he made two pillars,	1074
	3:17	He erected the pillars in the front of the t,	2121
	4: 7	for them and placed them in the t,	2121
	4: 8	and placed them in the t,	2121
	4:11	for King Solomon in the t *of* God:	1074
	4:16	for King Solomon for the t *of* the LORD	1074
	4:19	the furnishings that were in God's t:	1074
	4:22	and the gold doors of the t.	1074
	5: 1	the work Solomon had done for the t *of*	1074
	5: 1	he placed them in the treasuries of God's t.	1074
	5: 7	to its place in the inner sanctuary of the t,	1074
	5:13	t *of* the LORD was filled with a cloud,	1074
	5:14	the glory of the LORD filled the t *of* God.	1074
	6: 2	I have built a magnificent t for you,	1074
	6: 5	a city in any tribe of Israel to have a t built	1074
	6: 7	to build a t for the Name of the LORD,	1074
	6: 8	'Because it was in your heart to build a t	1074
	6: 9	you are not the one to build the t,	1074
	6: 9	the one who will build the t for my Name.'	1074
	6:10	and I have built the t for the Name of	1074
	6:18	How much less this t I have built!	1074
	6:20	May your eyes be open toward this t day	1074
	6:22	the oath before your altar in this t,	1074
	6:24	making supplication before you in this t,	1074
	6:29	and spreading out his hands toward this t—	1074
	6:32	when he comes and prays toward this t,	1074
	6:34	and the t I have built for your Name,	1074
	6:38	toward the t I have built for your Name;	1074
	7: 1	and the glory of the LORD filled the t.	1074
	7: 2	the t *of* the LORD because the glory of	1074
	7: 3	and the glory of the LORD above the t,	1074
	7: 5	the king and all the people dedicated the t	1074
	7: 7	of the courtyard in front of the t *of*	1074
	7:11	the t *of* the LORD and the royal palace,	1074
	7:11	the t *of* the LORD and in his own palace,	1074
	7:12	for myself as a t *for* sacrifices.	1074
	7:16	I have chosen and consecrated this t so	1074
	7:20	and will reject this t I have consecrated	1074
	7:21	And though this t is now so imposing,	1074
	7:21	a thing to this land and to this t?'	1074
	8: 1	of the t *of* the LORD and his own palace,	1074
	8:16	from the day the foundation of the t *of*	1074
	8:16	So the t *of* the LORD was finished.	1074
	9: 4	and the burnt offerings he made at the t *of*	1074
	9:11	to make steps for the t *of* the LORD and	1074
	12: 9	of the t *of* the LORD and the treasures of	1074
	12:11	the king went to the LORD's t,	1074
	15: 8	in front of the portico of the LORD's t.	NIH
	15:18	into the t *of* God the silver and gold and	1074
	16: 2	of the LORD's t and of his own palace	1074
	20: 5	and Jerusalem at the t *of* the LORD in	1074
	20: 9	we will stand in your presence before this t	1074
	20:28	and went to the t *of* the LORD with harps	1074
	22:12	with them at the t *of* God for six years	1074
	23: 3	a covenant with the king at the t *of* God.	1074
	23: 5	be in the courtyards of the t *of* the LORD.	1074
	23: 6	the t *of* the LORD except the priests	1074
	23: 7	Anyone who enters the t must be put	1074
	23: 9	to King David and that were in the t	1074
	23:10	near the altar and the t,	1074
	23:10	the south side to the north side of the t.	1074
	23:12	she went to them at the t *of* the LORD.	1074
	23:14	"Do not put her to death at the t *of*	1074
	23:17	All the people went to the t *of* Baal	1074
	23:18	Then Jehoiada placed the oversight of the t	1074
	23:18	in the t, to present the burnt offerings of	1074
	23:19	of the LORD's t so that no one who was	1074
	23:20	the king down from the t *of* the LORD.	1074
	24: 4	to restore the t *of* the LORD.	1074
	24: 5	to repair the t *of* your God.	1074
	24: 7	into the t *of* God and had used	1074
	24: 8	at the gate of the t *of* the LORD.	1074
	24:12	the work required for the t *of* the LORD.	1074
	24:12	and carpenters to restore the LORD's t,	1074
	24:12	workers in iron and bronze to repair the t.	1074
2Ch	24:13	They rebuilt the t *of* God according to	1074
	24:14	made articles for the LORD's t:	1074
	24:14	presented continually in the t *of* the LORD.	1074
	24:16	had done in Israel for God and his t.	1074
	24:18	They abandoned the t *of* the LORD,	1074
	24:21	in the courtyard of the LORD's t.	1074
	24:27	the t *of* God are written in the annotations	1074
	25:24	and silver and all the articles found in the t	1074
	26:16	the t *of* the LORD to burn incense on	2121
	26:19	before the incense altar in the LORD's t,	1074
	26:21	and excluded from the t *of* the LORD.	1074
	27: 2	but unlike him he did not enter the t *of*	2121
	27: 3	Jotham rebuilt the Upper Gate of the t *of*	1074
	28:21	Ahaz took some of the things from the t *of*	1074
	28:24	from the t *of* God and took them away.	1074
	28:24	He shut the doors of the LORD's t	1074
	29: 3	he opened the doors of the t *of* the LORD	1074
	29: 5	now and consecrate the t *of* the LORD,	1074
	29:15	they went in to purify the t *of* the LORD,	1074
	29:16	of the LORD's t everything unclean	1074
	29:16	that they found in the t *of* the LORD.	2121
	29:17	For eight more days they consecrated the t	1074
	29:18	"We have purified the entire t *of* the LORD	1074
	29:20	and went up to the t *of* the LORD.	1074
	29:25	in the t *of* the LORD with cymbals, harps	1074
	29:31	and thank offerings to the t *of* the LORD.	1074
	29:35	of the t *of* the LORD was reestablished.	1074
	30: 1	to the t *of* the LORD in Jerusalem	1074
	30:15	and brought burnt offerings to the t *of*	1074
	31:11	to prepare storerooms in the t *of* the LORD,	1074
	31:13	and Azariah the official in charge of the t	1074
	31:16	all who would enter the t *of* the LORD	1074
	31:21	of God's t and in obedience to the law and	1074
	32:21	And when he went into the t *of* his god,	1074
	33: 4	He built altars in the t *of* the LORD,	1074
	33: 5	In both courts of the t *of* the LORD,	1074
	33: 7	and put it in God's t,	1074
	33: 7	"In this t and in Jerusalem,	1074
	33:15	from the t *of* the LORD, as well as all	1074
	33:15	as all the altars he had built on the t hill	1074
	34: 8	to purify the land and the t,	1074
	34: 8	to repair the t *of* the LORD his God.	1074
	34: 9	the money that had been brought into the t	1074
	34:10	to supervise the work on the LORD's t.	1074
	34:10	who repaired and restored the t.	1074
	34:14	the money that had been taken into the t *of*	1074
	34:14	"I have found the Book of the Law in the t	1074
	34:17	the money that was in the t *of* the LORD	1074
	34:30	the t *of* the LORD with the men of Judah,	1074
	34:30	which had been found in the t *of* the LORD.	1074
	35: 2	in the service of the LORD's t.	1074
	35: 3	in the t that Solomon son of David king	1074
	35: 8	the administrators of God's t,	1074
	35:20	all this, when Josiah had set the t in order,	1074
	36: 7	also took to Babylon articles from the t *of*	1074
	36: 7	of the LORD and put them in his t there.	2121
	36:10	together with articles of value from the t	1074
	36:14	of the nations and defiling the t *of* the LORD,	1074
	36:18	to Babylon all the articles from the t	1074
	36:18	and the treasures of the LORD's t and	1074
	36:19	They set fire to God's t and broke down	1074
	36:23	to build a t for him at Jerusalem in Judah.	1074
Ezr	1: 2	to build a t for him at Jerusalem in Judah.	1074
	1: 3	up to Jerusalem in Judah and build the t *of*	1074
	1: 4	and with freewill offerings for the t *of* God	1074
	1: 7	the articles belonging to the t *of* the LORD,	1074
	1: 7	from Jerusalem and had placed in the t	1074
	2:42	The gatekeepers of the t:	NIH
	2:43	The t **servants:** the descendants of Ziha,	5987
	2:58	The t **servants** and the descendants of	5987
	2:70	the gatekeepers and the t **servants** settled	5987
	3: 6	the foundation of the LORD's t had not	2121
	3:10	the builders laid the foundation of the t *of*	2121
	3:12	who had seen the former t,	1074
	3:12	the foundation of this t being laid,	1074
	4: 1	the exiles were building a t for the LORD,	2121
	4: 3	"You have no part with us in building a t	1074
	5: 3	to rebuild this t and restore this structure?"	10103
	5: 8	to the t *of* the great God.	10103
	5: 9	to rebuild this t and restore this structure?"	10103
	5:11	and earth, and we are rebuilding the t	10103
	5:12	who destroyed this t and deported	10103
	5:14	the t *of* Babylon the gold and silver articles	10206
	5:14	from the t in Jerusalem and brought to	10206
	5:14	in Jerusalem and brought to the t	10206
	5:15	and deposit them in the t in Jerusalem.	10206
	6: 3	the king issued a decree concerning the t	10103
	6: 3	Let the t be rebuilt as a place to present	10103
	6: 5	the t in Jerusalem and brought to Babylon,	10206
	6: 5	are to be returned to their places in the t	10206
	6: 7	Do not interfere with the work on this t	10103
	6:12	to change this decree or to destroy this t	10103
	6:14	the t according to the command of the God	NIH
	6:15	The t was completed on the third day of	10103
	7: 7	singers, gatekeepers and t **servants,**	5987
	7:16	for the t *of* their God in Jerusalem.	10103
	7:17	the altar of the t *of* your God in Jerusalem.	10103
	7:19	to you for worship in the t *of* your God.	10103
	7:20	And anything else needed for the t	10103
	7:23	be done with diligence for the t *of* the God	10103
	7:24	t **servants** or other workers at this house	10497
	8:17	the t **servants** in Casiphia,	5987
	8:20	They also brought 220 of the t **servants**—	5987
Ne	2: 8	of the citadel by the t and for the city wall	1074
	3:26	and the t **servants** living on the hill	5987
	3:31	the t **servants** and the merchants, opposite	5987

Ne	6:10	the t, and let us close the temple doors,	2121
	6:10	and let us close the t doors,	2121
	6:11	like me go into the t to save his life?	2121
	7:46	The t servants: the descendants of Ziha,	5987
	7:60	The t servants and the descendants of	5987
	7:73	the singers and the t servants,	5987
	10:28	gatekeepers, singers, t servants	5987
	11:3	t servants and descendants of Solomon's	5987
	11:12	who carried on work for the t—	1074
	11:21	The t servants lived on the hill of Ophel,	5987
	13:5	and incense and t articles,	NIH
Ps	5:7	will I bow down toward your holy t.	2121
	11:4	The LORD is in his holy t;	2121
	18:6	From his t he heard my voice;	2121
	27:4	of the LORD and to seek him in his t.	2121
	29:9	And in his t all cry, "Glory!"	2121
	30:T	For the dedication of the t.	1074
	48:9	Within your t, O God, we meditate	2121
	65:4	of your house, of your holy t.	2121
	66:13	I will come to your t with burnt offerings	1074
	68:29	Because of your t at Jerusalem	2121
	79:1	they have defiled your holy t,	2121
	138:2	I will bow down toward your holy t	2121
Ecc	5:6	And do not protest to the [t] messenger,	NIH
Isa	2:2	the LORD's t will be established as chief	1074
	6:1	and the train of his robe filled the t.	2121
	6:4	and thresholds shook and the t was filled	1074
	15:2	Dibon goes up to its t,	1074
	37:1	and put on sackcloth and went into the t of	1074
	37:14	up to the t of the LORD and spread it out	1074
	37:38	while he was worshiping in the t	1074
	38:20	of our lives in the t of the LORD.	1074
	38:22	that I will go up to the t of the LORD?"	1074
	43:28	So I will disgrace the dignitaries of your t,	7731
	44:28	and of the t, "Let its foundations be laid." '	2121
	56:5	within my t and its walls a memorial and	1074
	60:7	and I will adorn my glorious t.	1074
	64:11	Our holy and glorious t,	1074
	66:6	hear that noise from the t!	2121
	66:20	grain offerings, to the t of the LORD	1074
Jer	7:4	"This is the t of the LORD,	2121
	7:4	the t of the LORD,	2121
	7:4	the t of the LORD!"	2121
	7:14	the t you trust in, the place I gave to you	889S
	11:15	in my t as she works out her evil schemes	1074
	19:14	the court of the LORD's t and said to all	1074
	20:1	the chief officer in the t of the LORD,	1074
	20:2	Upper Gate of Benjamin at the LORD's t.	1074
	23:11	even in my t I find their wickedness,"	1074
	24:1	of figs placed in front of the t of the LORD.	2121
	26:18	of rubble, the t hill a mound overgrown	1074
	36:5	I cannot go to the LORD's t.	1074
	36:8	at the LORD's t he read the words of	1074
	36:10	at the entrance of the New Gate of the t,	1074
	36:10	the LORD's t the words of Jeremiah from	1074
	38:14	the third entrance to the t of the LORD.	1074
	43:13	the t of the sun in Egypt he will demolish	1074
	50:28	has taken vengeance, vengeance for his t.	2121
	51:11	will take vengeance, vengeance for his t.	2121
	52:17	He set fire to the t of the LORD,	1074
	52:17	at the t of the LORD and they carried all	1074
	52:18	the bronze articles used in the t service.	NIH
	52:20	which King Solomon had made for the t	1074
Eze	8:16	and there at the entrance to the t,	2121
	8:16	the t of the LORD and their faces toward	2121
	9:3	and moved to the threshold of the t.	1074
	9:6	with the elders who were in front of the t.	1074
	9:7	the t and fill the courts with the slain.	1074
	10:3	the south side of the t when the man went	1074
	10:4	and moved to the threshold of the t.	1074
	10:4	The cloud filled the t,	1074
	10:18	of the t and stopped above the cherubim.	1074
	40:5	a wall completely surrounding the t area.	1074
	40:7	the portico facing the t was one rod deep.	1074
	40:9	The portico of the gateway faced the t.	1074
	40:45	for the priests who have charge of the t,	1074
	40:47	And the altar was in front of the t.	1074
	40:48	the portico of the t and measured the jambs	1074
	41:1	Then he measured the wall of the t;	1074
	41:5	around the t was four cubits wide.	1074
	41:6	the wall of the t to serve as supports for	1074
	41:6	not inserted into the wall of the t.	1074
	41:7	The side rooms all around the t were wider	NIH
	41:7	The structure surrounding the t was built	1074
	41:8	that the t had a raised base all around it,	1074
	41:9	between the side rooms of the t	1074
	41:10	twenty cubits wide all around the t.	1074
	41:12	The building facing the t courtyard on	NIH
	41:13	Then he measured the t;	1074
	41:13	a hundred cubits long, and the t courtyard	NIH
	41:14	The width of the t courtyard on the east,	NIH
	41:14	including the front of the t,	1074
	41:15	at the rear of the t, including its galleries	2023S
	41:19	They were carved all around the whole t.	1074
	41:26	of the t also had overhangs.	1074
	42:1	the t courtyard and opposite the outer wall	NIH
	42:10	the t courtyard and opposite the outer wall,	NIH
	42:13	and south rooms facing the t courtyard are	NIH
	42:15	the t area, he led me out by the east gate	1074
	43:4	The glory of the LORD entered the t	1074
	43:5	and the glory of the LORD filled the t.	1074
	43:6	speaking to me from inside the t.	1074
	43:10	describe the t to the people of Israel,	1074
	43:11	make known to them the design of the t—	1074
	43:12	"This is the law of the t:	1074
	43:12	Such is the law of the t.	1074
	43:21	in the designated part of the t area outside	1074
Eze	44:4	of the north gate to the front of the t.	1074
	44:4	of the LORD filling the t of the LORD,	1074
	44:5	the regulations regarding the t of the LORD.	1074
	44:5	to the entrance of the t and all the exits of	1074
	44:7	into my sanctuary, desecrating my t	1074
	44:11	of the gates of the t and serving in it;	1074
	44:14	of the t and all the work that is to be done	1074
	44:17	the gates of the inner court or inside the t.	1074
	45:5	the Levites, who serve in the t,	1074
	45:19	and put it on the doorposts of the t,	1074
	45:20	so you are to make atonement for the t.	1074
	46:24	where those who minister at the t will cook	1074
	47:1	to the entrance of the t,	1074
	47:1	under the threshold of the t toward the east	1074
	47:1	toward the east (for the t faced east).	1074
	47:1	down from under the south side of the t,	1074
	48:21	the sacred portion with the t sanctuary will	1074
Da	1:2	along with some of the articles from the t	1074
	1:2	to the t of his god in Babylonia and put in	1074
	5:2	father had taken from the t in Jerusalem	10206
	5:3	that had been taken from the t of God	10206
	5:23	You had the goblets from his t brought	10103
	9:27	[of the t] he will set up an abomination	NIH
	11:31	to desecrate the t fortress and will abolish	5219
Hos	8:14	it will not come into the t of the LORD.	1074
Joel	2:17	weep between the t porch and the altar.	395
Am	7:13	the king's sanctuary and the t of	1074
	8:3	"the songs in the t will turn to wailing.	2121
Jnh	2:4	yet I will look again toward your holy t.'	2121
	2:7	and my prayer rose to you, to your holy t.	2121
Mic	1:2	the Lord from his holy t.	2121
	1:7	all her t gifts will be burned with fire;	924
	3:12	the t hill a mound overgrown with thickets,	1074
	4:1	the LORD's t will be established as chief	1074
Na	1:14	that are in the t of your gods.	1074
Hab	2:20	But the LORD is in his holy t;	2121
Zep	1:9	who fill the t of their gods with violence	1074
Hag	2:15	stone was laid on another in the LORD's t.	2121
	2:18	the foundation of the LORD's t was laid.	2121
Zec	4:9	have laid the foundation of this t;	1074
	6:12	from his place and build the t of the LORD.	2121
	6:13	It is he who will build the t of the LORD,	2121
	6:14	of Zephaniah as a memorial in the t of	2121
	6:15	and help to build the t of the LORD,	2121
	8:9	let your hands be strong so that the t may	2121
Mal	1:10	that one of you would shut the t doors,	NIH
	3:1	Then suddenly the Lord you are seeking	2121
	3:1	will come to his t;	2121
Mt	4:5	on the highest point of the t.	2639
	12:5	on the Sabbath the priests in the t desecrate	2639
	12:6	I tell you that one greater than the t is here.	2639
	17:24	"Doesn't your teacher pay the t tax?"	NIG
	21:12	Jesus entered the t area and drove out	2639
	21:14	and the lame came to him at the t,	2639
	21:15	and the children shouting in the t area,	2639
	21:23	Jesus entered the t courts, and,	2639
	23:16	You say, 'If anyone swears by the t,	3724
	23:16	but if anyone swears by the gold of the t,	3724
	23:17	gold, or the t that makes the gold sacred?	3724
	23:21	And he who swears by the t swears by it	3724
	23:35	whom you murdered between the t and	3724
	24:1	Jesus left the t and was walking away	2639
	26:55	Every day I sat in the t courts teaching,	2639
	26:61	the t of God and rebuild it in three days.' "	3724
	27:5	Judas threw the money into the t and left.	3724
	27:40	to destroy the t and build it in three days,	3724
	27:51	that moment the curtain of the t was torn	3724
Mk	11:11	Jesus entered Jerusalem and went to the t.	2639
	11:15	Jesus entered the t area and began	2639
	11:16	to carry merchandise through the t courts.	2639
	11:27	while Jesus was walking in the t courts,	2639
	12:35	While Jesus was teaching in the t courts,	2639
	12:41	putting their money into the t treasury.	1126
	13:1	As he was leaving the t,	2639
	13:3	on the Mount of Olives opposite the t,	2639
	14:49	I was with you, teaching in the t courts,	2639
	14:58	'I will destroy this man-made t	3724
	15:29	to destroy the t and build it in three days,	3724
	15:38	the t was torn in two from top to bottom.	3724
Lk	1:9	into the t of the Lord and burn incense.	3724
	1:21	why he stayed so long in the t.	3724
	1:22	They realized he had seen a vision in the t,	3724
	2:27	he went into the t courts.	2639
	2:37	She never left the t but worshiped night	2639
	2:46	they found him in the t courts,	2639
	2:49	had him stand on the highest point of the t.	2639
	18:10	"Two men went up to the t to pray,	2639
	19:45	He entered the t area and began	2639
	19:47	Every day he was teaching at the t.	2639
	20:1	in the t courts and preaching the gospel,	2639
	21:1	putting their gifts into the t treasury.	1126
	21:5	the t was adorned with beautiful stones and	2639
	21:37	Each day Jesus was teaching at the t,	2639
	21:38	in the morning to hear him at the t.	2639
	22:4	and the officers of the t guard	5130
	22:52	the officers of the t guard, and the elders,	2639
	22:53	Every day I was with you in the t courts,	2639
	23:45	And the curtain of the t was torn in two.	3724
	24:53	And they stayed continually at the t,	2639
Jn	2:14	In the t courts he found men selling cattle,	2639
	2:15	and drove all from the t area,	2639
	2:19	Jesus answered them, "Destroy this t,	3724
	2:20	"It has taken forty-six years to build this t,	3724
	2:21	But the t he had spoken of was his body.	3724
	5:14	Later Jesus found him at the t and said	2639
	7:14	the Feast did Jesus go up to the t courts	2639
	7:28	Then Jesus, still teaching in the t courts,	2639
Jn	7:32	the Pharisees sent t guards to arrest him.	5677
	7:45	the t guards went back to the chief priests	5677
	8:2	At dawn he appeared again in the t courts,	2639
	8:20	while teaching in the t area near the place	2639
	8:59	slipping away from the t grounds.	2639
	10:23	and Jesus was in the t area walking	2639
	11:56	in the t area they asked one another,	2639
	18:20	"I always taught in synagogues or at the t,	2639
Ac	2:46	to meet together in the t courts.	2639
	3:1	and John were going up to the t at the time	2639
	3:2	to the t gate called Beautiful,	2639
	3:2	to beg from those going into the t courts.	2639
	3:8	Then he went with them into the t courts,	2639
	3:10	to sit begging at the t gate called Beautiful,	2639
	4:1	of the t guard and the Sadducees came up	2639
	5:20	"Go, stand in the t courts," he said,	2639
	5:21	At daybreak they entered the t courts,	2639
	5:24	the captain of the t guard and	2639
	5:25	in jail are standing in the t courts teaching	2639
	5:42	in the t courts and from house to house,	2639
	14:13	Zeus, whose t was just outside the city,	NIG
	19:27	that the t of the great goddess Artemis will	2639
	19:35	the city of Ephesus is the guardian of the t	3753
	21:26	to the t to give notice of the date when	2639
	21:27	the province of Asia saw Paul at the t,	2639
	21:28	into the t area and defiled this holy place."	2639
	21:29	that Paul had brought him into the t area.)	2639
	21:30	Seizing Paul, they dragged him from the t,	2639
	22:17	to Jerusalem and was praying at the t,	2639
	24:6	and even tried to desecrate the t;	2639
	24:12	not find me arguing with anyone at the t,	2639
	24:18	they found me in the t courts doing this.	2639
	25:8	against the law of the Jews or against the t	2639
	26:21	in the t courts and tried to kill me.	2639
Ro	9:4	the t worship and the promises.	3301
1Co	3:16	that you yourselves are God's t and	3724
	3:17	If anyone destroys God's t, God will	3724
	3:17	God's t is sacred, and you are that temple.	3724
	3:17	God's temple is sacred, and you are that t.	4015S
	6:19	know that your body is a t of the Holy Spirit	3724
	8:10	have this knowledge eating in an idol's t,	1627
	9:13	that those who work in the t get their food	2641
	9:13	in the temple get their food from the t,	2639
2Co	6:16	What agreement is there between the t	3724
	6:16	For we are the t of the living God.	3724
Eph	2:21	and rises to become a holy t in the Lord.	3724
2Th	2:4	so that he sets himself up in God's t,	3724
Rev	3:12	I will make a pillar in the t of my God.	3724
	7:15	and serve him day and night in his t;	3724
	11:1	and measure the t of God and the altar,	3724
	11:19	Then God's t in heaven was opened,	3724
	11:19	and within his t was seen the ark	3724
	14:15	Then another angel came out of the t	3724
	14:17	Another angel came out of the t in heaven,	3724
	15:5	After this I looked and in heaven the t,	3724
	15:6	Out of the t came the seven angels with	3724
	15:8	the t was filled with smoke from the glory	3724
	15:8	and no one could enter the t until	3724
	16:1	Then I heard a loud voice from the t saying	3724
	16:17	of the t came a loud voice from the throne,	3724
	21:22	I did not see a t in the city,	3724
	21:22	Lord God Almighty and the Lamb are its t.	3724

TEMPLES (9) [TEMPLE]

SS	4:3	Your t behind your veil are like the halves	8377
	6:7	Your t behind your veil are like the halves	8377
Jer	43:12	He will set fire to the t of the gods	1074
	43:12	he will burn their t and take their gods	4392S
	43:13	the sacred pillars and will burn down the t	1074
Joel	3:5	and carried off my finest treasures to your t.	2121
Ac	17:24	and does not live in t built by hands.	3724
	19:37	though they have neither robbed t	2645
Ro	2:22	You who abhor idols, do you rob t?	2644

TEMPORAL (KJV) See TEMPORARY

TEMPORARY (7)

Ex	12:45	a t resident and a hired worker may not eat	9369
Lev	25:6	the hired worker and t resident who live	9369
	25:35	as you would an alien or a t resident,	9369
	25:40	be treated as a hired worker or a t resident	9369
	25:45	also buy some of the t residents living	9369
	25:47	or a t resident among you becomes rich	9369
2Co	4:18	For what is seen is t, but what is unseen	4672

TEMPT (2) [TEMPTATION, TEMPTED, TEMPTER, TEMPTING]

| 1Co | 7:5 | so that Satan will not t you because of your | 4279 |
| Jas | 1:13 | be tempted by evil, nor does he t anyone; | 4279 |

TEMPTATION (8) [TEMPT]

Mt	6:13	And lead us not into t, but deliver us from	4280
	26:41	and pray so that you will not fall into t.	4280
Mk	14:38	and pray so that you will not fall into t.	4280
Lk	11:4	And lead us not into t.' "	4280
	22:40	"Pray that you will not fall into t."	4280
	22:46	up and pray so that you will not fall into t."	4280
1Co	10:13	No t has seized you except what is common	4280
1Ti	6:9	People who want to get rich fall into t and	4280

TEMPTED (13) [TEMPT]

| Mt | 4:1 | the Spirit into the desert to be t by the devil. | 4279 |
| Mk | 1:13 | in the desert forty days, being t by Satan. | 4279 |

Lk	4: 2	where for forty days he was t by the devil.	4279
1Co	10:13	not let you be t beyond what you can bear.	4279
	10:13	But when you are t, he will also provide a way out	3836+4280+5250
Gal	6: 1	But watch yourself, or you also may be t.	4279
1Th	3: 5	in some way the tempter might have t you	4279
Heb	2:18	Because he himself suffered when he was t,	4279
	2:18	he is able to help those who are being t.	4279
	4:15	we have one who has been t in every way,	4279
Jas	1:13	When t, no one should say, "God is	4279
	1:13	For God cannot be t by evil, nor does he	585
	1:14	but each one is t when, by his own evil	4279

TEMPTER (2) [TEMPT]

Mt	4: 3	The t came to him and said,	4279
1Th	3: 5	in some way the t might have tempted you	4279

TEMPTING (2) [TEMPT]

Lk	4:13	When the devil had finished all this t,	4280
Jas	1:13	tempted, no one should say, "God is t me."	4279

TEN (199) [ONE-TENTH, TENS, TENTH, TITHE, TITHES, TWO-TENTHS]

Ge	16: 3	Abram had been living in Canaan t years,	6924
	18:32	What if only t can be found there?"	6927
	18:32	He answered, "For the sake of t,	6927
	24:10	the servant took t of his master's camels	6927
	24:22	and two gold bracelets weighing t shekels.	6927
	24:55	"Let the girl remain with us t days or so;	6917
	31: 7	by changing my wages t times.	6930
	31:41	and you changed my wages t times.	6930
	32:15	forty cows and t bulls,	6927
	32:15	and t male donkeys.	6927
	42: 3	Then t of Joseph's brothers went down	6927
	45:23	t donkeys loaded with the best things	6927
	45:23	and t female donkeys loaded with grain	6924
	50:22	He lived a hundred and t years	6924
	50:26	Joseph died at the age of a hundred and t.	6924
Ex	26: 1	with t curtains of finely twisted linen	6924
	26:16	Each frame is to be t cubits long and	6924
	27:12	with t posts and ten bases.	6927
	27:12	with ten posts and t bases.	6924
	34:28	the T Commandments.	6930
	36: 8	with t curtains of finely twisted linen	6924
	36:21	Each frame was t cubits long and a cubit	6924
	38:12	with t posts and ten bases.	6927
	38:12	with ten posts and t bases,	6927
Lev	26: 8	a hundred of you will chase t thousand,	8047
	26:26	t women will be able to bake your bread	6924
	27: 5	and of a female at t shekels.	6930
	27: 7	and of a female at t shekels.	6927
Nu	7:14	one gold dish weighing t shekels, filled	6927
	7:20	one gold dish weighing t shekels, filled	6927
	7:26	one gold dish weighing t shekels, filled	6927
	7:32	one gold dish weighing t shekels, filled	6927
	7:38	one gold dish weighing t shekels, filled	6927
	7:44	one gold dish weighing t shekels, filled	6927
	7:50	one gold dish weighing t shekels, filled	6927
	7:56	one gold dish weighing t shekels, filled	6927
	7:62	one gold dish weighing t shekels, filled	6927
	7:68	one gold dish weighing t shekels, filled	6927
	7:74	one gold dish weighing t shekels, filled	6927
	7:80	one gold dish weighing t shekels, filled	6927
	7:86	with incense weighed t shekels each,	6927
	11:19	or two days, or five, t or twenty days,	6927
	11:32	No one gathered less than t homers.	6927
	14:22	and tested me t times—	6924
	29:23	" 'On the fourth day prepare t bulls,	6927
Dt	4:13	his covenant, the T Commandments.	6930
	10: 4	the T Commandments he had proclaimed	6930
	32:30	or two put t thousand to flight,	8047
	33:17	Such are the t thousands of Ephraim;	8047
Jos	15:57	t towns and their villages.	6924
	17: 5	Manasseh's share consisted of t tracts	6927
	21: 5	Kohath's descendants were allotted t towns	6924
	21:26	All these t towns and their pasturelands	6924
	22:14	With him they sent t of the chief men,	6927
	24:29	died at the age of a hundred and t.	6924
Jdg	1: 4	and they struck down t thousand men	6930
	2: 8	died at the age of a hundred and t.	6924
	3:29	about t thousand Moabites, all vigorous	6930
	4: 6	take with you t thousand men of Naphtali	6930
	4:10	T thousand men followed him,	6930
	4:14	followed by t thousand men.	6930
	6:27	So Gideon took t of his servants and did as	6930
	7: 3	while t thousand remained.	6930
	12:11	Elon the Zebulunite led Israel t years.	6924
	17:10	and I'll give you t shekels of silver a year,	6930
	20:10	We'll take t men out of every hundred	6924
	20:10	and a thousand from t thousand,	8047
	20:34	Then t thousand of Israel's finest men	6930
Ru	1: 4	After they had lived there about t years,	6924
	2: 1	Boaz took t of the elders of that town	6927
1Sa	1: 8	Don't I mean more to you than t sons?"	6924
	15: 4	and t thousand men from Judah.	6930
	17:17	of roasted grain and these t loaves of bread	6927
	17:18	along these t cheeses to the commander	6930
	25: 5	So he sent t young men and said to him,	6930
	25:38	About t days later, the LORD struck Nabal	6930
2Sa	15:16	but he left t concubines to take care of	6924
	18: 3	but you are worth t thousand of us.	6927
	18:11	to give you t shekels of silver and	6927
	18:15	And t of Joab's armor-bearers surrounded Absalom,	6927

2Sa	19:43	"We have t shares in the king;	6924
	20: 3	the t concubines he had left to take care of	6924
1Ki	4:23	t head of stall-fed cattle,	6927
	5:14	to Lebanon in shifts of t thousand a month,	6930
	6: 3	and projected t cubits from the front of	6924
	6:23	cherubim of olive wood, each t cubits high.	6924
	6:24	t cubits from wing tip to wing tip.	6924
	6:25	The second cherub also measured t cubits,	6924
	6:26	The height of each cherub was t cubits.	6924
	7:10	some measuring t cubits and some eight.	6924
	7:23	measuring t cubits from rim to rim	6924
	7:24	gourds encircled it—t to a cubit.	6924
	7:27	He also made t movable stands of bronze;	6924
	7:37	This is the way he made the t stands.	6924
	7:38	He then made t bronze basins;	6927
	7:38	one basin to go on each of the t stands.	6924
	7:43	the t stands with their ten basins;	6924
	7:43	the ten stands with their t basins;	6927
	11:31	"Take t pieces for yourself,	6927
	11:31	of Solomon's hand and give you t tribes.	6924
	11:35	from his son's hands and give you t tribes.	6930
	14: 3	Take t loaves of bread with you,	6927
2Ki	5: 5	taking with him t talents of silver,	6924
	5: 5	six thousand shekels of gold and t sets	6924
	13: 7	t chariots and ten thousand foot soldiers,	6924
	13: 7	ten chariots and t thousand foot soldiers,	6930
	14: 7	the one who defeated t thousand Edomites	6930
	15:17	and he reigned in Samaria t years.	6924
	20: 9	Shall the shadow go forward t steps,	6924
	20: 9	or shall it go back t steps?"	6924
	20:10	for the shadow to go forward t steps,"	6924
	20:10	"Rather, have it go back t steps.	6924
	20:11	the shadow go back the t steps it had gone	6924
	24:14	and artisans—a total of t thousand.	6930
	25:25	came with t men and assassinated Gedaliah	6924
1Ch	6:61	Kohath's descendants were allotted t towns	6924
	29: 7	and t thousand darics of gold,	8052
	29: 7	t thousand talents of silver,	6930
2Ch	4: 1	twenty cubits wide and t cubits high.	6924
	4: 2	measuring t cubits from rim to rim	6924
	4: 3	figures of bulls encircled it—t to a cubit.	6924
	4: 6	He then made t basins for washing	6927
	4: 7	He made t gold lampstands according to	6924
	4: 8	He made t tables and placed them in	6927
	14: 1	the country was at peace for t years.	6924
	25:11	where he killed t thousand men of Seir.	6924
	25:12	also captured t thousand men alive,	6930
	27: 5	t thousand cors of wheat	6924
	27: 5	of wheat and t thousand cors of barley.	6930
	30:24	with a thousand bulls and t thousand sheep	6930
	36: 9	in Jerusalem three months and t days.	6924
Ezr	8:24	Hashabiah and t of their brothers,	6927
Ne	4:12	near them came and told us t times over,	6924
	5:18	and every t days an abundant supply	6930
	11: 1	to bring one out of every t to live	6927
Est	3: 9	and I will put t thousand talents of silver	6930
	9:10	the t sons of Haman son of Hammedatha,	6930
	9:12	the t sons of Haman in the citadel of Susa.	6930
	9:13	let Haman's t sons be hanged on gallows."	6930
	9:14	and they hanged the t sons of Haman.	6930
Job	19: 3	T times now you have reproached me;	6924
Ps	91: 7	t thousand at your right hand,	8047
Ecc	7:19	Wisdom makes one wise man more powerful than t rulers	6927
SS	5:10	outstanding among t thousand.	8047
Isa	38: 8	by the sun go back the t steps it has gone	6924
	38: 8	the t steps it had gone down.	6924
Jer	41: 1	with t men to Gedaliah son of Ahikam	6927
	41: 2	and the t men who were with him got up	6930
	41: 8	t of them said to Ishmael, "Don't kill us!	6927
	42: 7	T days later the word of the LORD came	6930
Eze	40:11	it was t cubits and its length was thirteen	6924
	41: 2	The entrance was t cubits wide,	6924
	42: 4	an inner passageway t cubits wide and	6924
	45:14	from each cor (which consists of t baths	6930
	45:14	for t baths are equivalent to a homer).	6930
Da	1:12	"Please test your servants for t days:	6927
	1:14	to this and tested them for t days.	6927
	1:15	the end of the t days they looked healthier	6927
	1:20	he found them t times better than all	6924
	7: 7	the former beasts, and it had t horns.	10573
	7:10	t thousand times ten thousand stood	10649
	7:10	ten thousand times t thousand	10649
	7:20	to know about the t horns on its head and	10573
	7:24	The t horns are ten kings who will come	10573
	7:24	The ten horns are t kings who will come	10573
	8: 3	a hundred strong will have only t left."	6927
Am	5: 3	If t men are left in one family,	6927
Mic	6: 7	with t thousand rivers of oil?	8047
Hag	2:16	of twenty measures, there were only t.	6927
Zec	8:23	"In those days t men from all languages	6927
Mt	18:24	owed him t thousand talents was brought	3691
	20:24	When the t heard about this,	1274
	25: 1	be like t virgins who took their lamps	1274
	25:28	and give it to the one who has the t talents.	1274
Mk	10:41	When the t heard about this,	1274
Lk	14:31	with t thousand men to oppose the one	1274
	15: 8	a woman has t silver coins and loses one.	1274
	17:12	t men who had leprosy met him.	1274
	17:17	Jesus asked, "Were not all t cleansed?	1274
	19:13	So he called t of his servants	1274
	19:13	of his servants and gave them t minas.	1274
	19:16	'Sir, your mina has earned t more.'	1274
	19:17	take charge of t cities.'	1274
	19:24	and give it to the one who has t minas.'	1274
	19:25	" 'Sir,' they said, 'he already has t!'	1274
Ac	25: 6	After spending eight or t days with them,	1274

1Co	4:15	though you have t thousand guardians	3692
	14:19	to instruct others than t thousand words in	3692
Rev	2:10	and you will suffer persecution for t days.	1274
	5:11	and ten thousand times t thousand.	3689
	5:11	and ten thousand times t thousand.	3689
	12: 3	and t horns and seven crowns on his heads.	1274
	13: 1	He had t horns and seven heads,	1274
	13: 1	with t crowns on his horns,	1274
	17: 3	and had seven heads and t horns.	1274
	17: 7	which has the seven heads and t horns.	1274
	17:12	The t horns you saw are ten kings who have	1274
	17:12	The ten horns you saw are t kings who have	1274
	17:16	The beast and the t horns you saw will hate	1274

TEN-ACRE (1) [ACRE]

Isa	5:10	A t vineyard will produce only a bath	6930+7538

TEN-STRINGED (3) [STRING]

Ps	33: 2	make music to him on the t lyre.	6917
	92: 3	to the music of the t lyre and the melody of	6917
	144: 9	on the t lyre I will make music to you,	6917

TENANTS (16)

Lev	25:23	and you are but aliens and my t.	9369
Job	31:39	or broken the spirit of its t,	1251
SS	8:11	he let out his vineyard to t.	5757
Mt	21:34	he sent his servants to the t	1177
	21:35	"The t seized his servants;	1177
	21:36	and he treated them the same way.	NIG
	21:38	"But when the t saw the son,	1177
	21:40	what will he do to those t?"	1177
	21:41	"and he will rent the vineyard to other t,	1177
Mk	12: 2	the t to collect from them some of the fruit.	1177
	12: 7	the t said to one another, 'This is the heir.	1177
	12: 9	He will come and kill those t and give	1177
Lk	20:10	At harvest time he sent a servant to the t	1177
	20:10	But the t beat him and sent him away	1177
	20:14	the t saw him, they talked the matter over.	1177
	20:16	He will come and kill those t and give	1177

TEND (12) [TENDED, TENDING, TENDS]

Ge	30:36	Jacob continued to t the rest of Laban's	8286
	46:32	are shepherds; they t livestock,	408+2118+5238
Lev	24: 3	Aaron is to t the lamps before the LORD	6885
1Sa	17:15	and forth from Saul to t his father's sheep	8286
SS	8:12	two hundred are for those who t its fruit.	5757
Jer	23: 2	says to the shepherds who t my people:	8286
	23: 4	place shepherds over them who will t them,	8286
Eze	34:14	I will t them in a good pasture,	8286
	34:15	I myself will t my sheep	8286
	34:23	my servant David, and he will t them;	8286
	34:23	he will t them and be their shepherd.	8286
Jnh	4:10	though you did not t it or make it grow.	6661

TENDED (3) [TEND]

Ge	46:34	'Your servants have t livestock	408+2118+5238
Lev	24: 4	before the LORD must be t continually.	6885
Hos	12:12	and to pay for her he t sheep.	9068

TENDER (12) [TENDERLY, TENDERNESS]

Ge	18: 7	t calf and gave it to a servant,	8205
	33:13	"My lord knows that the children are t and	8205
Dt	32: 2	like abundant rain on t plants.	6912
2Ki	19:26	like t green shoots,	3764
Pr	4: 3	I was a boy in my father's house, still t,	8205
Isa	37:27	like t green shoots,	3764
	47: 1	No more will you be called t or delicate.	8205
	53: 2	He grew up before him like a t shoot,	3437
Eze	17:22	a t sprig from its topmost shoots	8205
Mt	24:32	as its twigs get t and its leaves come out,	559
Mk	13:28	as its twigs get t and its leaves come out,	559
Lk	1:78	because of the t mercy of our God,	1799+5073

TENDERHEARTED (KJV) See COMPASSIONATE, INDECISIVE

TENDERLY (3) [TENDER]

Ge	34: 3	he loved the girl and spoke t to her.	4213+6584
Isa	40: 2	Speak t to Jerusalem,	4213+6584
Hos	2:14	lead her into the desert and speak t	4213+6584

TENDERNESS (2) [TENDER]

Isa	63:15	Your t and compassion are withheld	2162+5055
Php	2: 1	if any t and compassion,	5073

TENDING (11) [TEND]

Ge	30:31	go on t your flocks and watching over them:	8286
	37: 2	was t the flocks with his brothers,	8286
Ex	3: 1	Now Moses was t the flock of Jethro	8286
1Sa	16:11	Jesse answered, "but he is t the sheep."	8286
Ps	78:71	from t the sheep he brought him to be	339
Jer	6: 3	each t his own portion."	8286
Eze	34:10	I will remove them from t the flock so that	8286
Am	7:15	But the LORD took me from t the flock	8286
Mt	8:33	Those t the pigs ran off, went into the town	1081
Mk	5:14	Those t the pigs ran off and reported this in	1081
Lk	8:34	those t the pigs saw what had happened,	1081

TENDON (2) [TENDONS]
Ge 32:32 Israelites do not eat the t attached to   1630+5962
     32:32 of Jacob's hip was touched near the t.   1630+5962

TENDONS (2) [TENDON]
Eze 37: 6 I will attach t to you and make flesh come   1630
     37: 8 and t and flesh appeared on them   1630

TENDS (4) [TEND]
Ex 30: 7 every morning when he t the lamps.   3512
Pr 27:18 He who t a fig tree will eat its fruit,   5915
Isa 40:11 He t his flock like a shepherd;   8286
1Co 9: 7 Who t a flock and does not drink of   4477

TENONS (KJV) See PROJECTIONS

TENS (10) [TEN]
Ex 18:21 thousands, hundreds, fifties and t.   6930
     18:25 thousands, hundreds, fifties and t.   6930
Dt 1:15 of fifties and of t and as tribal officials.   6930
1Sa 18: 7 and David his t of thousands."   8047
     18: 8 credited David with t of thousands,"   8047
     21:11 and David his t of thousands'?"   8047
     29: 5 and David his t of thousands'?"   8047
Ps 3: 6 I will not fear the t of thousands drawn up   8047
     68:17 of God are t of thousands and thousands   8052
     144:13 by t of thousands in our fields;   8045

TENT (286) [TENTMAKER, TENTS]
Ge 9:21 and lay uncovered inside his t.   185
     12: 8 the hills east of Bethel and pitched his t,   185
     13: 3 and Ai where his t had been earlier   185
     18: 1 while he was sitting at the entrance to his t   185
     18: 2 of his t to meet them and bowed low to   185
     18: 6 So Abraham hurried into the t to Sarah.   185
     18: 9 "There, in the t," he said.   185
     18:10 Sarah was listening at the entrance to the t,   185
     24:67 brought her into the t of his mother Sarah,   185
     26:25 There he pitched his t,   185
     31:25 Jacob had pitched his t in the hill country   185
     31:33 into Jacob's t and into Leah's tent and into   185
     31:33 into Jacob's tent and into Leah's t and into   185
     31:33 and into the t of the two maidservants,   185
     31:33 After he came out of Leah's t,   185
     31:33 he entered Rachel's t.   185
     31:34 Laban searched through everything in the t   185
     33:19 the plot of ground where he pitched his t.   185
     35:21 Israel moved on again and pitched his t   185
Ex 16:16 for each person you have in your t.' "   185
     18: 7 and then went into the t.   185
     26: 7 of goat hair for the t over the tabernacle—   185
     26: 9 curtain double at the front of the t.   185
     26:11 the loops to fasten the t together as a unit.   185
     26:12 for the additional length of the t curtains,   185
     26:13 The t curtains will be a cubit longer on   185
     26:14 for the t a covering of ram skins dyed red,   185
     26:36 the entrance to the t make a curtain of blue,   185
     27:19 the t pegs for it and those for the courtyard,   3845
     27:21 In the T of Meeting, outside the curtain   185
     28:43 the T of Meeting or approach the altar   185
     29: 4 and his sons to the entrance to the T   185
     29:10 the bull to the front of the T of Meeting,   185
     29:11 at the entrance to the T of Meeting.   185
     29:30 and comes to the T of Meeting to minister   185
     29:32 At the entrance to the T of Meeting   185
     29:42 at the entrance to the T of Meeting before   185
     29:44 "So I will consecrate the T of Meeting and   185
     30:16 for the service of the T of Meeting.   185
     30:18 between the T of Meeting and the altar,   185
     30:20 Whenever they enter the T of Meeting,   185
     30:26 Then use it to anoint the T of Meeting,   185
     30:36 of the Testimony in the T of Meeting,   185
     31: 7 the T of Meeting, the ark of the Testimony   185
     31: 7 and all the other furnishings of the t—   185
     33: 7 to take a t and pitch it outside   185
     33: 7 calling it the "t of meeting."   185
     33: 7 to the t of meeting outside the camp.   185
     33: 8 And whenever Moses went out to the t,   185
     33: 8 watching Moses until he entered the t.   185
     33: 9 As Moses went into the t,   185
     33:10 of cloud standing at the entrance to the t,   185
     33:10 each at the entrance to his t.   185
     33:11 Joshua son of Nun did not leave the t.   185
     35:11 the tabernacle with its t and its covering,   185
     35:18 the t pegs for the tabernacle and for   3845
     35:21 the LORD for the work on the T of Meeting,   185
     36:14 of goat hair for the t over the tabernacle—   185
     36:18 to fasten the t together as a unit.   185
     36:19 for the t a covering of ram skins dyed red,   185
     36:37 to the t they made a curtain of blue, purple   185
     38: 8 at the entrance to the T of Meeting.   185
     38:20 All the t pegs of the tabernacle and of   3845
     38:30 to make the bases for the entrance to the T   185
     38:31 and those for its entrance and all the t pegs   3845
     39:32 the T of Meeting, was completed.   185
     39:33 the t and all its furnishings, its clasps,   185
     39:38 and the curtain for the entrance to the t;   185
     39:40 the ropes and t pegs for the courtyard,   3845
     39:40 all the furnishings for the tabernacle, the T   185
     40: 2 the tabernacle, the T of Meeting,   185
     40: 6 the tabernacle, the T of Meeting;   185
     40: 7 place the basin between the T of Meeting   185
     40:12 and his sons to the entrance to the T   185

Ex 40:19 Then he spread the t over the tabernacle   185
     40:19 and put the covering over the t,   185
     40:22 Moses placed the table in the T of Meeting   185
     40:24 the lampstand in the T of Meeting opposite   185
     40:26 in the T of Meeting in front of the curtain   185
     40:29 the tabernacle, the T of Meeting,   185
     40:30 the basin between the T of Meeting and   185
     40:32 They washed whenever they entered the T   185
     40:34 Then the cloud covered the T of Meeting,   185
     40:35 Moses could not enter the T of Meeting   185
Lev 1: 1 and spoke to him from the T of Meeting.   185
     1: 3 He must present it at the entrance to the T   185
     1: 5 the altar on all sides at the entrance to the T   185
     3: 2 and slaughter it at the entrance to the T   185
     3: 8 and slaughter it in front of the T   185
     3:13 on its head and slaughter it in front of the T   185
     4: 4 the bull at the entrance to the T of Meeting   185
     4: 5 of the bull's blood and carry it into the T   185
     4: 7 before the LORD in the T of Meeting.   185
     4: 7 of burnt offering at the entrance to the T   185
     4:14 as a sin offering and present it before the T   185
     4:16 to take some of the bull's blood into the T   185
     4:18 the altar that is before the LORD in the T   185
     4:18 of burnt offering at the entrance to the T   185
     6:16 they are to eat it in the courtyard of the T   185
     6:26 in the courtyard of the T of Meeting.   185
     6:30 into the T of Meeting to make atonement   185
     8: 3 the entire assembly at the entrance to the T   185
     8: 4 at the entrance to the T of Meeting.   185
     8:31 to the T of Meeting and eat it there with   185
     8:33 not leave the entrance to the T of Meeting   185
     8:35 at the entrance to the T of Meeting day   185
     9: 5 to the front of the T of Meeting,   185
     9:23 Moses and Aaron then went into the T   185
     10: 7 not leave the entrance to the T of Meeting   185
     10: 9 into the T of Meeting,   185
     12: 6 to the T of Meeting a year-old lamb for   185
     14: 8 he must stay outside his t for seven days.   185
     14:11 before the LORD at the entrance to the T   185
     14:23 at the entrance to the T of Meeting,   185
     15:14 before the LORD to the entrance to the T   185
     15:29 at the entrance to the T of Meeting.   185
     16: 7 before the LORD at the entrance to the T   185
     16:16 He is to do the same for the T of Meeting,   185
     16:17 No one is to be in the T of Meeting from   185
     16:20 the T of Meeting and the altar,   185
     16:23 "Then Aaron is to go into the T of Meeting   185
     16:33 for the T of Meeting and the altar,   185
     17: 4 of bringing it to the entrance to the T   185
     17: 5 to the T of Meeting and sacrifice them   185
     17: 6 the entrance to the T of Meeting and burn   185
     17: 9 to the T of Meeting to sacrifice it to   185
     19:21 to the T of Meeting for a guilt offering to   185
     24: 3 of the Testimony in the T of Meeting,   185
Nu 1: 1 to Moses in the T of Meeting in the Desert   185
     2: 2 "The Israelites to camp around the T   185
     2:17 Then the T of Meeting and the camp of   185
     3: 7 the whole community at the T of Meeting   185
     3: 8 of all the furnishings of the T of Meeting   185
     3:25 At the T of Meeting the Gershonites were   185
     3:25 for the care of the tabernacle and t,   185
     3:25 at the entrance to the T of Meeting,   185
     3:37 their bases, t pegs and ropes.   3845
     3:38 in front of the T of Meeting.   185
     4: 3 to serve in the work in the T of Meeting.   185
     4: 4 "This is the work of the Kohathites in the T   185
     4:15 to carry those things that are in the T   185
     4:23 to serve in the work at the T of Meeting.   185
     4:25 the tabernacle, the T of Meeting,   185
     4:25 for the entrance to the T of Meeting,   185
     4:28 the service of the Gershonite clans at the T   185
     4:30 to serve in the work at the T of Meeting.   185
     4:31 as they perform service at the T   185
     4:32 t pegs, ropes, all their equipment   3845
     4:33 of the Merarite clans as they work at the T   185
     4:35 to serve in the work in the T of Meeting,   185
     4:37 in the Kohathite clans who served in the T   185
     4:39 to serve in the work at the T of Meeting,   185
     4:41 in the Gershonite clans who served at the T   185
     4:43 to serve in the work at the T of Meeting,   185
     4:47 of serving and carrying the T of Meeting   185
     6:10 at the entrance to the T of Meeting.   185
     6:13 He is to be brought to the entrance to the T   185
     6:18 at the entrance to the T of Meeting,   185
     7: 5 that they may be used in the work at the T   185
     7:89 When Moses entered the T of Meeting   185
     8: 9 the Levites to the front of the T of Meeting   185
     8:15 they are to come to do their work at the T   185
     8:19 T of Meeting on behalf of the Israelites   185
     8:22 to do their work at the T of Meeting under   185
     8:24 in the work at the T of Meeting,   185
     8:26 in performing their duties at the T   185
     9:15 the T of the Testimony, was set up,   185
     9:17 from above the T, the Israelites set out;   185
     10: 3 at the entrance to his t.   185
     11:10 each at the entrance to his t.   185
     11:16 Have them come to the T of Meeting,   185
     11:24 and had them stand around the T.   185
     11:26 but did not go out to the T.   185
     12: 4 "Come out to the T of Meeting,   185
     12: 5 to the T and summoned Aaron and Miriam.   185
     12:10 When the cloud lifted from above the T,   185
     14:10 the glory of the LORD appeared at the T   185
     16:18 at the entrance to the T of Meeting,   185
     16:19 at the entrance to the T of Meeting,   185
     16:42 and turned toward the T of Meeting,   185
     16:43 and Aaron went to the front of the T   185

Lev 16:50 at the entrance to the T of Meeting,   185
     17: 4 Place them in the T of Meeting in front of   185
     17: 7 the staffs before the LORD in the T   185
     17: 8 The next day Moses entered the T   185
     18: 2 and your sons minister before the T of   185
     18: 3 and are to perform all the duties of the T   185
     18: 4 and be responsible for the care of the T   185
     18: 4 all the work at the T—   185
     18: 6 to the LORD to do the work at the T   185
     18:21 for the work they do while serving at the T   185
     18:22 on the Israelites must not go near the T   185
     18:23 the Levites who are to do the work at the T   185
     18:31 for it is your wages for your work at the T   185
     19: 4 toward the front of the T of Meeting.   185
     19:14 that applies when a person dies in a t: 185
     19:14 the t and anyone who is in it will   185
     19:18 dip it in the water and sprinkle the t and all   185
     20: 6 from the assembly to the entrance to the T   185
     25: 6 at the entrance to the T of Meeting.   185
     25: 8 and followed the Israelite into the t.   7688
     27: 2 the entrance to the T of Meeting and stood   185
     31:54 into the T of Meeting as a memorial for   185
Dt 31:14 Call Joshua and present yourselves at the T   185
     31:14 and presented themselves at the T   185
     31:15 the LORD appeared at the T in a pillar   185
     31:15 the cloud stood over the entrance to the T.   185
Jos 7:21 They are hidden in the ground inside my t,   185
     7:22 and they ran to the t, and there it was,   185
     7:22 hidden in his t, with the silver underneath.   185
     7:23 They took the things from the t,   185
     7:24 his t and all that he had,   185
     18: 1 and set up the T of Meeting there.   185
     19:51 of the LORD at the entrance to the T   185
Jdg 4:11 and pitched his t by the great tree   185
     4:17 however, fled on foot to the t of Jael,   185
     4:18 So he entered her t, and she put a covering   185
     4:20 "Stand in the doorway of the t," he told her.   185
     4:21 up a t peg and a hammer and went quietly   185
     4:22 with the t peg through his temple—   3845
     5:26 Her hand reached for the t peg,   3845
     7:13 It struck the t with such force that   185
     7:13 that the t overturned and collapsed."   185
1Sa 2:22 at the entrance to the T of Meeting.   185
     4:10 and every man fled to his t.   185
     17:54 the Philistine's weapons in his own t.   185
2Sa 6:17 inside the t that David had pitched for it,   185
     7: 2 while the ark of God remains in a t."   3749
     7: 6 to place with a t as my dwelling.   185
     16:22 they pitched a t for Absalom on the roof,   185
     20: 1 Every man to his t, O Israel!"   185
1Ki 1:39 from the sacred t and anointed Solomon.   185
     2:28 to the t of the LORD and took hold of   185
     2:29 that Joab had fled to the t of the LORD   185
     2:30 So Benaiah entered the t of the LORD   185
     8: 4 the LORD and the T of Meeting and all   185
2Ki 7: 8 and entered another t and took some things   185
1Ch 6:32 the tabernacle, the T of Meeting,   185
     9:19 for guarding the thresholds of the T just   185
     9:21 the gatekeeper at the entrance to the T   185
     9:23 the house called the T.   185
     15: 1 a place for the ark of God and pitched a t   185
     16: 1 inside the t that David had pitched for it,   185
     17: 1 of the covenant of the LORD is under a t."   3749
     17: 5 I have moved from one t site to another,   185
     23:32 responsibilities for the T of Meeting,   185
2Ch 1: 3 for God's T of Meeting was there,   185
     1: 4 he had pitched a t for it in Jerusalem.   185
     1: 6 the bronze altar before the LORD in the T   185
     1:13 from before the T of Meeting.   185
     5: 5 up the ark and the T of Meeting and all   185
     24: 6 and by the assembly of Israel for the T of   185
Job 4:21 Are not the cords of their t pulled up,   3857
     5:24 You will know that your t is secure;   185
     11:14 and allow no evil to dwell in your t,   185
     18: 6 The light in his t becomes dark;   185
     18:14 from the security of his t and marched off   185
     18:15 Fire resides in his t;   185
     19:12 against me and encamp around my t.   185
     20:26 and devour what is left in his t.   185
     22:23 If you remove wickedness far from your t   185
Ps 19: 4 the heavens he has pitched a t for the sun,   185
     52: 5 snatch you up and tear you from your t;   185
     61: 4 to dwell in your t forever and take refuge   185
     76: 2 His t is in Salem, his dwelling place in Zion.   6108
     78:60 the t he had set up among men.   185
     91:10 no disaster will come near your t.   185
     104: 2 he stretches out the heavens like a t   3749
Pr 14:11 but the t of the upright will flourish.   185
SS 1: 5 like the t curtains of Solomon.   3749
Isa 13:20 no Arab will pitch his t there,   182
     33:20 a t that will not be moved;   185
     38:12 a shepherd's t my house has been pulled   185
     40:22 and spreads them out like a t to live in.   185
     54: 2 "Enlarge the place of your t,   185
     54: 2 stretch your t curtains wide,   5438
Jer 10:20 My t is destroyed;   185
     10:20 now to pitch my t or to set up my shelter.   185
La 2: 4 like fire on the t of the Daughter of Zion.   185
Am 9:11 "In that day I will restore David's fallen t.   6109
Zec 10: 4 From Judah will come the cornerstone,
         from him the t peg,   3845
Ac 15:16 and rebuild David's fallen t.   5008
2Co 5: 1 that if the earthly t we live in is destroyed,   5011
     5: 4 For while we are in this t,   5008
2Pe 1:13 as long as I live in the t of this body,   5013
Rev 7:15 and he who sits on the throne will spread
         his t over them.   5012

TENT-DWELLING (1) [DWELL]
Jdg 5:24 most blessed of t women. 185+928+2021

TENTH (68) [TEN]
Ge	8: 5	continued to recede until the t month, 6920
	8: 5	and on the first day of the t month the tops 6920
	14:20	Then Abram gave him a t of everything. 5130
	28:22	that you give me I will give you a t." 6923+6923
Ex	12: 3	that on the t day of this month each man is 6917
	16:36	(An omer is one t of an ephah.) 6920
	29:40	With the first lamb offer a t of an ephah 6928
Lev	5:11	for his sin a t of an ephah of fine flour for 6920
	6:20	a t of an ephah of fine flour as 6920
	14:21	a t of an ephah of fine flour mixed with oil 6928
	16:29	On the t day of the seventh month 6917
	23:27	"The t day of this seventh month is 6917
	25: 9	on the t day of the seventh month; 6917
	27:32	every t animal that passes under 6920
Nu	5:15	also take an offering of a t of an ephah 6920
	7:66	On the t day Ahiezer son of Ammishaddai, 6920
	15: 4	of a t of an ephah of fine flour mixed with 6928
	18:26	as your inheritance, you must present a t of 5130
	28: 5	of a t of an ephah of fine flour mixed with 6920
	28:13	a t of an ephah of fine flour mixed with oil. 6928
	29: 7	" 'On the t day of this seventh month hold 6917
Dt	14:22	Be sure to set aside a t of all that 6923+6923
	23: 2	even down to the t generation. 6920
	23: 3	even down to the t generation. 6920
	26:12	you have finished setting aside a t 5130+6923
Jos	4:19	the t day of the first month the people went 6917
1Sa	8:15	He will take a t of your grain and 6923
	8:17	He will take a t of your flocks, 6923
2Ki	25: 1	on the t day of the tenth month, 6917
	25: 1	on the tenth day of the t month, 6920
1Ch	12:13	Jeremiah the t and Macbannai 6920
	24:11	the ninth to Jeshua, the t to Shecaniah, 6920
	25:17	the t to Shimei, his sons and relatives, 12 6920
	27:13	The t, for the tenth month, 6920
	27:13	The tenth, for the t month, 6920
Ezr	10:16	of the t month they sat down to investigate 6920
Ne	10:38	the Levites are to bring a t of the tithes up 5130
Est	2:16	in the royal residence in the t month, 6920
Isa	6:13	And though a t remains in the land, 6920
Jer	32: 1	the LORD in the t year of Zedekiah king 6920
	39: 1	in the t month, Nebuchadnezzar king of 6920
	52: 4	on the t day of the tenth month, 6917
	52: 4	on the tenth day of the t month, 6920
	52:12	On the t day of the fifth month, 6917
Eze	20: 1	in the fifth month on the t day, 6917
	24: 1	in the t month on the tenth day, 6920
	24: 1	in the tenth month on the t day, 6917
	29: 1	In the t year, in the tenth month on 6920
	29: 1	in the t month on the twelfth day, 6920
	33:21	in the t month on the fifth day, 6920
	40: 1	on the t of the month, in the fourteenth 6917
	45:11	a t of a homer and the ephah a tenth of 5130
	45:11	of a homer and the ephah a t of a homer; 6920
	45:14	a t of a bath from each cor (which consists 5130
Zec	8:19	seventh and t months will become joyful 6920
Mt	23:23	You give a t of your spices— 620
Lk	11:42	because you give God a t of your mint, 620
	18:12	I fast twice a week and give a t of 620
Jn	1:39	It was about the t hour. 1281
Heb	7: 2	and Abraham gave him a t of everything. 1281
	7: 4	Even the patriarch Abraham gave him a t 1281
	7: 5	to collect a t from the people— 620+2400
	7: 6	yet he collected a t from Abraham 1282
	7: 8	the t is collected by men who die; 1281
	7: 9	that Levi, who collects the t, 1281
	7: 9	paid the t through Abraham. 1282
Rev	11:13	a severe earthquake and a t of the city 1281
	21:20	the t chrysoprase, the eleventh jacinth, 1281

TENTMAKER (1) [TENT]
Ac 18: 3 and because he was a t as they were, 5010

TENTS (58) [TENT]
Ge	4:20	of those who live in t and raise livestock. 185
	9:27	may Japheth live in the t of Shem, 185
	13: 5	also had flocks and herds and t. 185
	13:12	of the plain and pitched his t near Sodom. 182
	13:18	So Abram moved his t and went to live 182
	25:27	a quiet man, staying among the t. 185
Ex	33: 8	and stood at the entrances to their t, 185
Nu	1:52	The Israelites are to set up their t 2837
	1:53	are to set up their t around the tabernacle 2837
	16:24	'Move away from the t of Korah, 5438
	16:26	from the t of these wicked men! 185
	16:27	So they moved away from the t of Korah, 5438
	16:27	and little ones at the entrances with their t. 185
	24: 5	"How beautiful are your t, 185
Dt	1:27	You grumbled in your t and said, 185
	5:30	"Go, tell them to return to their t. 185
	11: 6	their t and every living thing that belonged 185
	16: 7	Then in the morning return to your t. 185
	33:18	and you, Issachar, in your t. 185
Jdg	6: 5	with their livestock and their t like swarms 185
	7: 8	the rest of the Israelites to their t but kept 185
2Sa	11:11	ark and Israel and Judah are staying in t. 6109
1Ki	12:16	To your t, O Israel! 185
	20:12	and the kings were drinking in their t, 6109
	20:16	with him were in their t getting drunk. 6109
2Ki	7: 7	and fled in the dusk and abandoned their t 185
	7: 8	of the camp and entered one of the t. 185

2Ki	7:10	and the t left just as they were."	185
2Ch	10:16	To your t, O Israel!	185
Job	8:22	and the t of the wicked will be no more."	185
	12: 6	The t of marauders are undisturbed,	185
	15:34	the t of those who love bribes.	185
	21:28	the t where wicked men lived?'	185
Ps	78:28	inside their camp, all around their t.	5438
	78:51	the firstfruits of manhood in the t of Ham.	185
	78:67	Then he rejected the t of Joseph,	185
	83: 6	the t of Edom and the Ishmaelites,	185
	84:10	the house of my God than dwell in the t of	185
	106:25	They grumbled in their t and did not obey	185
	118:15	Shouts of joy and victory resound in the t	185
	120: 5	that I live among the t of Kedar!	185
SS	1: 5	dark like the t of Kedar,	185
	1: 8	and graze your young goats by the t of	5438
Jer	4:20	In an instant my t are destroyed,	185
	6: 3	they will pitch their t around her,	185
	30:18	" 'I will restore the fortunes of Jacob's t	185
	35: 7	but must always live in t.	185
	35:10	We have lived in t and have fully obeyed	185
	37:10	and only wounded men were left in their t,	185
	49:29	Their t and their flocks will be taken;	185
Eze	25: 4	set up their camps and pitch their t among	5438
Da	11:45	He will pitch his royal t between the seas	185
Hos	9: 6	and thorns will overrun their t.	185
	12: 9	I will make you live in t again,	185
Hab	3: 7	I saw the t of Cushan in distress,	185
Mal	2:12	may the LORD cut him off from the t of Jacob	185
Heb	11: 9	he lived in t, as did Isaac and Jacob,	5008

TERAH (13)
Ge	11:24	he became the father of T.	9561
	11:25	And after he became the father of T,	9561
	11:26	After T had lived 70 years,	9561
	11:27	This is the account of T.	9561
	11:27	T became the father of Abram,	9561
	11:28	While his father T was still alive,	9561
	11:31	T took his son Abram,	9561
	11:32	T lived 205 years, and he died in Haran.	9561
Nu	33:27	They left Tahath and camped at T.	9562
	33:28	They left T and camped at Mithcah.	9562
Jos	24: 2	'Long ago your forefathers, including T	9561
1Ch	1:26	Serug, Nahor, T	9561
Lk	3:34	the son of Abraham, the son of T,	2508

TEREBINTH (2)
Isa 6:13 But as the t and oak leave stumps 461
Hos 4:13 poplar and t, where the shade is pleasant. 461

TERESH (2)
Est 2:21 at the king's gate, Bigthana and T, two of 9575
6: 2 that Mordecai had exposed Bigthana and T, 9575

TERMS (14)
Ge	23:16	Abraham agreed to Ephron's t	AIT
Dt	29: 1	These are the t of the covenant	1821
	29: 9	Carefully follow the t of this covenant,	1821
1Sa	11: 4	of Saul and reported these t to the people,	1821
1Ki	5: 1	because he had always been on friendly t	170
Job	34:33	Should God then reward you on your t 4946+6640
Jer	11: 2	"Listen to the t of this covenant and	1821
	11: 3	'Cursed is the man who does not obey the t	1821
	11: 4	the t I commanded your forefathers	889S
	11: 6	to the t of this covenant and follow them.	1821
	32:11	the sealed copy containing the t and	5184
	34:18	the t of the covenant they made before me,	1821
Lk	14:32	a long way off and will ask for t of peace.	3836
Ro	6:19	I put this in human t because you are 474+3306

TERRACES (8)
2Sa	5: 9	from the supporting t inward.	4864
1Ki	9:15	the supporting t, the wall of Jerusalem,	4864
	9:24	he constructed the supporting t.	4864
	11:27	the supporting t and had filled in the gap	4864
1Ch	11: 8	the supporting t to the surrounding wall,	4864
2Ch	32: 5	and reinforced the supporting t of the City	4864
Job	24:11	They crush olives among the t;	8805
Jer	31:40	the t out to the Kidron Valley on the east	8727

TERRESTRIAL (KJV) See EARTHLY

TERRIBLE (11) [TERROR]
Ex	9: 3	will bring a t plague on your livestock 3878+4394
Nu	20: 5	bring us up out of Egypt to this t place?	8273
Dt	6:22	signs and wonders—great and t—	8273
Ne	13:27	that you too are doing all this t wickedness	1524
Jer	4: 6	from the north, even t destruction."	1524
	6: 1	looms out of the north, even t destruction.	1524
	21: 6	and they will die of a t plague.	1524
	26:19	about to bring a t disaster on ourselves!"	1524
Mt	8: 6	at home paralyzed and in t suffering."	1267
2Ti	3: 1	There will be t times in the last days.	5901
Rev	16:21	because the plague was so t.	3489

TERRIBLY (1) [TERROR]
Mt 15:22 My daughter is suffering t from 2809

TERRIFIED (51) [TERROR]
Ge 45: 3 because they were t at his presence. 987

Ex	14:10	They were t and cried out to the LORD. 3707+4394
	15:15	The chiefs of Edom will be t,	987
Nu	22: 3	and Moab was t because there were	1593
Dt	1:29	Then I said to you, "Do not be t;	6907
	7:21	Do not be t by them,	6907
	20: 3	not be t or give way to panic before them.	2905
	31: 6	Do not be afraid or t because of them,	6907
Jos	1: 9	Do not be t; do not be discouraged,	6907
Jdg	20:41	and the men of Benjamin were t,	987
1Sa	17:11	all the Israelites were dismayed and t. 3707+4394
	31: 4	his armor-bearer was t and would not 3707+4394
2Ki	10: 4	But they were t and said, 3707+4394
1Ch	10: 4	his armor-bearer was t and would not 3707+4394
Est	7: 6	Haman was t before the king and queen.	1286
Job	21: 6	When I think about this, I am t,	987
	23:15	That is why I am t before him;	987
	23:16	the Almighty has t me.	987
	41:25	When he rises up, the mighty are t;	1593
Ps	90: 7	by your anger and t by your indignation.	987
	104:29	When you hide your face, they are t;	987
Isa	19:17	to whom Judah is mentioned will be t,	7064
	33:14	The sinners in Zion are t;	7064
	51: 7	Do not fear the reproach of men or be t	3169
Jer	1:17	Do not be t by them,	3169
	10: 2	the ways of the nations or be t by signs in	3169
	10: 2	though the nations are t by them.	3169
	17:18	let them be t, but keep me from terror.	3169
	23: 4	and they will no longer be afraid or t,	3169
	46: 5	They are t, they are retreating,	3146
	51:32	the marshes set on fire, and the soldiers t."	987
Eze	2: 6	not be afraid of what they say or t by them,	3169
	3: 9	Do not be afraid of them or t by them,	3169
	19: 7	and all who were in it were t by his roaring.	9037
	26:18	in the sea are t at your collapse.'	987
Da	4: 5	that passed through my mind t me.	10097
	4:19	and his thoughts t him.	10097
	5: 9	even more t and his face grew more pale.	10097
	8:17	I was t and fell prostrate.	1286
Ob	1: 9	Your warriors, O Teman, will be t,	3169
Jnh	1:10	This t them and they asked, 1524+3707+3711
Mt	14:26	saw him walking on the lake, they were t,	5429
	17: 6	they fell facedown to the ground, t. 5379+5828
	27:54	they were t, and exclaimed, 5379+5828
Mk	4:41	They were t and asked each other, 3489+5828+5832
	6:50	because they all saw him and were t.	5429
Lk	2: 9	glory of the Lord shone around them and they were t. 3489+5828+5832
Jn	6:19	walking on the water, and they were t.	5828
Rev	11:13	and the survivors were t and gave glory to	1873
	18:10	T at her torment, they will stand far off	5832
	18:15	will stand far off, t at her torment. 1328+5832

TERRIFIES (2) [TERROR]
Job 22:10 why sudden peril t you, 987
Ps 2: 5 in his anger and t them in his wrath, 987

TERRIFY (9) [TERROR]
2Ch	32:18	to t them and make them afraid in order	3707
Job	7:14	then you frighten me with dreams and t me	1286
	13:11	Would not his splendor t you?	1286
	33:16	in their ears and t them with warnings,	3169
Ps	10:18	who is of the earth, may t no more.	6907
	83:15	your tempest and t them with your storm.	987
Jer	1:17	or I will t you before them.	3169
Hab	2:17	your destruction of animals will t you.	3169
Zec	1:21	to t them and throw down these horns of	3006

TERRIFYING (4) [TERROR]
Job	15:21	T sounds fill his ears;	7065
Da	7: 7	t and frightening and very powerful.	10167
	7:19	the others and most t, with its iron teeth	10167
Heb	12:21	The sight was so t that Moses said,	5829

TERRITORIES (5) [TERRITORY]
Ge	10: 5	the maritime peoples spread out into their t	824
	10:20	in their t and nations.	824
	10:31	in their t and nations.	824
Jos	19:51	These are the t that Eleazar the priest,	5709
1Ch	13: 2	to the rest of our brothers throughout the t	824

TERRITORY (97) [TERRITORIES]
Ge	9:27	May God extend the t of Japheth;	7332
	14: 7	and they conquered the whole t of the	8441
	48: 6	in the t they inherit they will be reckoned	5709
Ex	34:24	before you and enlarge your t,	1473
Nu	20:16	a town on the edge of your t.	1473
	20:17	until we have passed through your t."	1473
	20:21	to let them go through their t,	1473
	21:13	in the desert extending into Amorite t.	1473
	21:22	until we have passed through your t."	1473
	21:23	not let Israel pass through his t.	1473
	22:36	the Arnon border, at the edge of his t.	1473
	32:33	the whole land with its cities and the t	1473
Dt	1: 5	East of the Jordan in the t of Moab,	824
	2: 4	the t of your brothers the descendants	1473
	3: 8	of the Amorites the t east of the Jordan,	824
	3:12	the Reubenites and the Gadites the t north	889S
	3:16	and the Gadites I gave the t extending	NIH
	11:24	Your t will extend from the desert	1473
	11:30	in the t of those Canaanites living in	824
	12:20	the LORD your God has enlarged your t	1473
	19: 8	If the LORD your God enlarges your t,	1473
	34: 2	the t of Ephraim and Manasseh,	824

Jos	1: 4	Your t will extend from the desert	1473
	11:22	No Anakites were left in Israelite t;	824
	12: 1	whose t they took over east of the Jordan,	824
	12: 4	And the t of Og king of Bashan,	1473
	13: 3	of Egypt to the t of Ekron on the north, all	1473
	13: 3	(the t of the five Philistine rulers in Gaza,	NIH
	13:11	the t of the people of Geshur and Maacah,	1473
	13:16	The t from Aroer on the rim of	1473
	13:25	The t of Jazer, all the towns of Gilead	1473
	13:26	and from Mahanaim to the t of Debir,	1473
	13:27	the t up to the end of the Sea	1473
	13:30	The t extending from Mahanaim	1473
	15: 1	extended down to the t of Edom,	1473
	16: 2	over to the t of the Arkites in Ataroth,	1473
	16: 3	the t of the Japhletites as far as the region	1473
	16: 5	This was the t of Ephraim, clan by clan:	1473
	17: 7	The t of Manasseh extended from Asher	1473
	17:10	The t of Manasseh reached the sea	1473
	18: 5	Judah is to remain in its t on the south and	1473
	18: 5	the south and the house of Joseph in its t	1473
	18:11	Their allotted t lay between the tribes	1473
	19: 1	Their inheritance lay within the t of Judah.	5709
	19: 9	inheritance within the t of Judah.	5709
	19:12	to the t of Kisloth Tabor and went on	1473
	19:18	Their t included: Jezreel,	1473
	19:25	Their t included: Helkath,	1473
	19:41	the t of their inheritance included:	1473
	19:47	had difficulty taking possession of their t,	1473
	21:41	the t held by the Israelites were forty-eight	299
Jdg	1: 3	"Come up with us into the t allotted	1598
	1:18	each city with its t.	1473
	11:18	They did not enter the t of Moab,	1473
	11:20	did not trust Israel to pass through his t.	1473
1Sa	6: 1	in Philistine seven months,	8441
	6: 9	If it goes up to its own t,	1473
	7:13	and did not invade Israelite t again.	1473
	7:14	and Israel delivered the **neighboring** t from	1473
	9: 4	When he passed through the t of Benjamin,	824
	27: 7	in Philistine t a year and four months.	8441
	27:11	as long as he lived in Philistine t.	8441
	30:14	and the t belonging to Judah and the Negev	889S
1Ki	9:19	and throughout all the t he ruled.	824
		from leaving or entering the t of Asa king	NIH
2Ki	6:23	from Aram stopped raiding Israel's t.	824
	10:32	the Israelites throughout their t	1473
	18: 8	as far as Gaza and its t.	1473
	24: 7	the king of Babylon had taken all his t,	889S
1Ch	4:10	that you would bless me and enlarge my t!	1473
	6:54	of their settlements **allotted** as their t	1473
	6:66	as their t towns from the tribe of Ephraim.	1473
2Ch	8: 6	and throughout all the t he ruled.	824
	16: 1	from leaving or entering the t of Asa king	NIH
	20:10	whose t you would not allow Israel	889S
	34:33	from all the t belonging to the Israelites,	824
Jer	1: 1	one of the priests at Anathoth in the t	824
	17:26	from the t of Benjamin and	824
	32: 8	'Buy my field at Anathoth in the t	824
	32:44	sealed and witnessed in the t of Benjamin,	824
	33:13	in the t of Benjamin, in the villages	824
	37:12	to leave the city to go to the t of Benjamin	824
Eze	16:27	against you and reduced your t;	2976
	48: 1	it will border the t of Dan from east	1473
	48: 3	it will border the t of Asher from east	1473
	48: 4	it will border the t of Naphtali from east	1473
	48: 5	it will border the t of Manasseh from east	1473
	48: 6	it will border the t of Ephraim from east	1473
	48: 7	it will border the t of Reuben from east	1473
	48: 8	the t of Judah from east to west will be	1473
	48:12	bordering the t of the Levites.	1473
	48:13	"Alongside the t of the priests,	1473
	48:24	it will border the t of Benjamin from east	1473
	48:25	it will border the t of Simeon from east	1473
	48:26	it will border the t of Issachar from east	1473
	48:27	it will border the t of Zebulun from east	1473
2Co	10:16	work already done in another man's t.	2834

TERROR (74) [TERRIBLE, TERRIBLY, TERRIFIED, TERRIFIES, TERRIFY, TERRIFYING, TERRORISTS, TERRORS]

Ge	35: 5	and the t of God fell upon the towns all	3150
Ex	15:16	terror and dread will fall upon them.	399
	23:27	"I will send my t ahead of you and throw	399
Lev	26:16	I will bring upon you **sudden t**,	988
Dt	2:25	the t and fear of you on all the nations	7065
	11:25	the t and fear of you on the whole land,	7065
	26: 8	with great t and with miraculous signs	4616
	28:67	the t that will fill your hearts and the sights	7065
	32:25	in their homes t will reign.	399
1Sa	11: 7	the t of the LORD fell on the people,	7065
	28: 5	he was afraid; t **filled** his heart.	3006+4394
2Sa	17: 2	I would **strike** him **with t**,	3006
2Ch	14:14	the t of the LORD had fallen upon them.	7065
Job	9:34	so that his t would frighten me no more.	399
	15:24	Distress and anguish **fill** him **with t**;	1286
	39:20	striking t with his proud snorting?	399
Ps	9:20	Strike them with t, O LORD;	4616
	31:13	there is t on every side;	4471
	48: 5	and were astounded; they fled in t.	987
	78:33	their days in futility and their years in t.	988
	91: 5	You will not fear the t of night,	7065
Pr	21:15	to the righteous but t to evildoers.	4745
Isa	13: 8	T will **seize** them, pain and anguish	987
	17:14	In the evening, **sudden t**!	1166
	19:17	land of Judah will bring t to the Egyptians;	2505
	21: 1	from the desert, from a land of t.	3707

Isa	22: 5	of tumult and trampling and t in the Valley	4428
	24:17	T and pit and snare await you,	7065
	24:18	Whoever flees at the sound of t will fall	7065
	28:19	of this message will bring sheer t.	2317
	31: 9	Their stronghold will fall because of t;	4471
	33:18	In your thoughts you will ponder the former:	399
	44:11	they will be **brought down to** t and infamy.	7064
	47:12	perhaps you will **cause** t.	6907
	51:13	that you live in constant t every day	7064
	54:14	T will be far removed;	4745
Jer	6:25	and there is t on every side.	4471
	8:15	for a time of healing but there was only t.	1287
	14:19	for a time of healing but there is only t.	1287
	15: 8	down on them anguish and t.	988
	17:17	Do not be a t to me;	4745
	17:18	let them be terrified, but keep me from t.	3169
	20: 4	a t to yourself and to all your friends;	4471
	20:10	I hear many whispering, "T on every side!	4471
	30: 5	Cries of fear are heard—t, not peace.	7065
	32:21	and an outstretched arm and with great t.	4616
	46: 5	and there is t on every side,"	4471
	48:43	T and pit and snare await you,	7065
	48:44	"Whoever flees from the t will fall into	7065
	49: 5	I will bring t on you from all those	7065
	49:16	The t you inspire and the pride	9526
	49:29	Men will shout to them, 'T on every side!'	4471
	50: 2	put to shame, Marduk **filled with** t.	3169
	50: 2	put to shame and her idols **filled with** t.'	3169
	50:36	They will be **filled with** t.	3169
	50:38	idols that will go mad with t.	399
La	3:47	We have suffered t and pitfalls,	7065
Eze	7:18	on sackcloth and be clothed with t.	7146
	7:25	When t comes, they will seek peace,	7888
	23:46	a mob against them and give them over to t	2400
	26:16	Clothed with t, they will sit on the ground,	3010
	26:17	you put your t on all who lived there.	3154
	32:23	All who had spread t in the land of	3154
	32:24	All who had spread t in the land of	3154
	32:25	their t had spread in the land of the living,	3154
	32:26	by the sword because they spread their t in	3154
	32:27	the t of these warriors had stalked through	3154
	32:30	the slain in disgrace despite the t caused	3154
	32:32	I had him spread t in the land of the living,	3154
Da	10: 7	not see it, but such t overwhelmed them	3010
Am	5:19	the evil day and bring near a reign of t.	2805
Lk	21:26	Men will faint from t,	5832
Ro	13: 3	rulers **hold** no t for those who do right,	1639+5832
Rev	11:11	and t struck those who saw them.	3489+5832

TERRORISTS (1) [TERROR]

Ac	21:38	a revolt and led four thousand t	467+3836+4974

TERRORS (14) [TERROR]

Job	6: 4	God's t are marshaled against me.	1243
	13:21	and stop frightening me with your t.	399
	18:11	T startle him on every side	1166
	18:14	of his tent and marched off to the king of t.	1166
	20:25	T will come over him;	399
	24:17	they make friends with the t of darkness.	1166
	27:20	T overtake him like a flood;	1166
	30:15	T overwhelm me; my dignity is driven away	1166
Ps	55: 4	the t of death assail me.	399
	73:19	completely swept away by t!	1166
	88:15	I have suffered your t and am in despair.	399
	88:16	your t have destroyed me.	1243
SS	3: 8	prepared for the t of the night.	7065
La	2:22	so you summoned against me t	4471

TERTIUS (1)

Ro	16:22	I, T, who wrote down this letter,	5470

TERTULLUS (2)

Ac	24: 1	of the elders and a lawyer named T,	5472
	24: 2	T presented his case before Felix:	5472

TEST (56) [TESTED, TESTER, TESTING, TESTINGS, TESTS]

Ex	16: 4	In this way I will t them	5814
	17: 2	Why do you **put** the LORD **to the t?**"	5814
	20:20	God has come to t you,	5814
Dt	6:16	Do not t the LORD your God as you did	5814
	8: 2	and to t you in order to know what was	5814
	8:16	to t you so that in the end it might go well	5814
Jdg	2:22	to t Israel and see whether they will keep	5814
	3: 1	to t all those Israelites who had	5814
	3: 4	They were left to t the Israelites	5814
	6:39	Allow me one more t with the fleece.	5814
1Ki	10: 1	she came to t him with hard questions.	5814
1Ch	29:17	that you t the heart and are pleased	1043
2Ch	9: 1	to Jerusalem to t him with hard questions.	5814
	32:31	to t him and to know everything that was	5814
Job	7:18	and t him every moment?	1043
	12:11	the ear t words as the tongue tastes food?	1043
Ps	17: 3	though you try me, you will find nothing;	7671
	26: 2	T me, O LORD, and try me,	1043
	78:18	They willfully **put** God to the t	5814
	78:41	Again and again, they **put** God **to the t**;	5814
	78:56	But they **put** God **to the t**	5814
	106:14	they **put** God **to the t**	5814
	139:23	t me and know my anxious thoughts.	1043
Ecc	2: 1	I will t you with pleasure	5814
Isa	7:12	I will not **put** the LORD **to the t**."	5814

Jer	6:27	that you may observe and t their ways.	1043
	9: 7	"See, I will refine and t them,	1043
	11:20	you who judge righteously and t the heart	1043
	12: 3	you see me and t my thoughts about you.	1043
La	3:40	Let us examine our ways and t them,	2983
Da	1:12	"Please t your servants for ten days:	5814
Zec	13: 9	I will refine them like silver and t them	1043
Mal	3:10	T me in this," says the LORD Almighty,	1043
Mt	4: 7	'Do not **put** the Lord your God **to the t.'** "	1733
	19: 3	Some Pharisees came to him to t him.	4279
Mk	8:11	To t him, they asked him for a sign	4279
Lk	4:12	'Do not **put** the Lord your God **to the t.'** "	1733
	10:25	an expert in the law stood up to t Jesus.	1733
Jn	6: 6	He asked this only to t him.	4279
Ac	5: 9	could you agree to t the Spirit of the Lord?	4279
	15:10	why do you try to t God by putting on	4279
Ro	12: 2	to t and approve what God's will is—	1507
1Co	3:13	fire will t the quality of each man's work.	1507
	9: 9	We should not t the Lord,	1733
2Co	2: 9	if you **would stand the** t and be obedient	1509
	8: 8	but I want to t the sincerity of your love	1507
	13: 5	whether you are in the faith; t yourselves.	1507
	13: 5	unless, of course, you **fail the t?**	99+1639
	13: 6	discover that we have not **failed the t.**	99+1639
	13: 7	see that we have **stood** the t but	1511
Gal	6: 4	Each one should t his own actions.	1507
1Th	5:21	t everything. Hold on to the good.	1507
Jas	1:12	because when he has stood the t,	1511
1Jn	4: 1	but t the spirits to see whether they are	1507
Rev	2:10	will put some of you in prison to t you,	4279
	3:10	upon the whole world to t those who live	4279

TESTATOR (KJV) See ONE WHO MADE IT

TESTED (29) [TEST]

Ge	22: 1	Some time later God t Abraham.	5814
	42:15	And this is how you will be t:	1043
	42:16	in prison, so that your words may be t to see	1043
Ex	15:25	and there he t them.	5814
	17: 7	the Israelites quarreled and because they t	5814
Nu	14:22	who disobeyed and t me ten times—	5814
Dt	33: 8	You t him at Massah,	5814
Job	23:10	when he has t me, I will come forth as gold.	1043
	28:27	he confirmed it and t it.	2983
	34:36	that Job might be t to the utmost	1043
Ps	66:10	For you, O God, t us;	1043
	81: 7	I t you at the waters of Meribah.	1043
	95: 9	where your fathers t and tried me,	5814
	119:140	Your promises have been thoroughly t,	7671
Pr	27:21	but man is t by the praise he receives.	NIH
Ecc	7:23	All this I t by wisdom and I said,	5814
Isa	28:16	"See, I lay a stone in Zion, a t stone,	1046
	48:10	I have t you in the furnace of affliction.	1047
Da	1:14	he agreed to this and t them for ten days.	5814
Mt	16: 1	and Sadducees came to Jesus and t him	4279
	22:35	t him with this question:	4279
Mk	10: 2	Some Pharisees came and t him by asking,	4279
Lk	11:16	Others t him by asking for a sign	4279
Ac	20:19	although I was severely t by the plots of	4279
Ro	16:10	Greet Apelles, **t and approved** in Christ.	1511
1Ti	3:10	They must first be t;	1507
Heb	3: 9	where your fathers t and tried me and	4279
	11:17	By faith Abraham, when God t him,	4279
Rev	2: 2	you have t those who claim to be apostles	4279

TESTER (1) [TEST]

Jer	6:27	a t of metals and my people the ore,	1031

TESTICLES (2)

Lev	21:20	or running sores or damaged t.	863
	22:24	the LORD an animal whose t are bruised,	NIH

TESTIFIED (14) [TESTIFY]

2Sa	1:16	Your own mouth t against you	6699
2Ch	24:19	and though they t against them,	6386
Mk	14:56	Many t **falsely** against him,	6018
Jn	3:26	the one you t about—	3455
	5:33	"You have sent to John and he has t to	3455
	5:37	And the Father who sent me has himself t	3455
	13:21	Jesus was troubled in spirit and t,	3455
Ac	6:13	They produced false witnesses, who t,	3306
	8:25	When they had t and proclaimed the word of	1371
	13:22	He t concerning him:	3455
	23:11	As you have t about me in Jerusalem,	1371
1Co	15:15	for we have t about God that he raised	3455
Heb	2: 4	God also t to it by signs,	5296
	2: 6	But there is a place where someone has t:	1371

TESTIFIES (17) [TESTIFY]

Job	16: 8	my gauntness rises up and t against me.	6699
Isa	3: 9	The look on their faces t against them;	6699
Hos	5: 5	Israel's arrogance t against them,	6699
	7:10	Israel's arrogance t against him,	6699
Jn	1:15	John t concerning him.	3455
	3:32	He t to what he has seen and heard,	3455
	5:32	There is another who t in my favor,	3455
	5:36	that the Father has sent me.	3455
	8:18	I am one who t for myself;	3455
	19:35	and he t so that you also may believe.	NIG
	21:24	This is the disciple who t to these things	3455
Ro	8:16	The Spirit himself t **with** our spirit	5210
2Co	1:12	Our conscience t that we have conducted	3457
Heb	10:15	The Holy Spirit also t to us **about** this.	3455

1Jn	5: 6	And it is the Spirit who t,	3455
Rev	1: 2	who t to everything he saw—	3455
	22:20	He who t to these things says, "Yes,	3455

TESTIFY (47) [TESTIFIED, TESTIFIES, TESTIFYING, TESTIMONY]

Ge	30:33	my honesty will t for me in the future,	6699
Lev	5: 1	to t regarding something he has seen	6332
Dt	8:19	I t against you today that you will surely	6386
	31:21	this song will t against them,	4200+6332+6699
	31:28	call heaven and earth to t against them.	6386
1Sa	12: 3	T against me in the presence of the LORD	6699
1Ki	21:10	and have them t that he has cursed	6386
Job	15: 6	your own lips t against you.	6699
Ps	50: 7	O Israel, and I will t against you:	6386
Pr	24:28	Do not t against your neighbor without cause,	2118+6332
	29:24	he is put under oath and dare not t.	5583
Isa	59:12	and our sins t against us.	6699
Jer	14: 7	Although our sins t against us, O LORD,	6699
Am	3:13	"Hear this and t against the house	6386
Zep	3: 8	"for the day I will stand up to t.	6332
Mal	3: 5	I will be quick to t against sorcerers,	6332
Mt	23:31	So you t against yourselves that you are	3455
Lk	11:48	So you t that you approve of what	1639+3459
Jn	1: 7	as a witness to t concerning that light,	3455
	1:34	have seen and I t that this is the Son of God.	3455
	3:11	and we t to what we have seen,	3455
	3:28	You yourselves can t that I said,	3455
	5:31	I t about myself, my testimony is not valid.	3455
	5:39	These are the Scriptures that t about me,	3455
	7: 7	because I t that what it does is evil.	3455
	8:14	"Even if I t on my own behalf,	3455
	15:26	from the Father, he will t about me.	3455
	15:27	And you also must t,	3455
	18:23	Jesus replied, "t as to what is wrong.	3455
	18:37	I came into the world, to t to the truth.	3455
Ac	4:33	power the apostles continued to t to	625+3457
	10:42	to preach to the people and to t that he is	1371
	10:43	All the prophets t about him	3455
	22: 5	the high priest and all the Council can t.	3455
	23:11	so you must also t in Rome."	3455
	26: 5	have known me for a long time and can t,	3455
	26:22	and so I stand here and t to small and great	3455
Ro	3:21	to which the Law and the Prophets t.	3455
	10: 2	For I can t about them that they are zealous	3455
2Co	8: 3	For I t that as much as they were	3455
Gal	4:15	I can t that, if you could have done so,	3459
Php	1: 8	God can t how I long for all of you with	3459
2Ti	1: 8	So do not be ashamed to t about our Lord,	3457
Jas	5: 3	Their corrosion will t against you	1639+3457
1Jn	1: 2	we have seen it and t to it,	3455
	4:14	and t that the Father has sent his Son to be	3455
	5: 7	For there are three that t:	3455

TESTIFYING (5) [TESTIFY]

Ac	18: 5	t to the Jews that Jesus was the Christ.	1371
	20:24	the task of t to the gospel of God's grace.	1371
1Ti	6:13	who while t before Pontius Pilate made	3455
Heb	3: 5	t to what would be said in the future.	1650+3457
1Pe	5:12	and t that this is the true grace of God.	2148

TESTIMONY (113) [TESTIFY]

Ex	16:34	Aaron put the manna in front of the T,	6343
	20:16	not give false t against your neighbor.	6332
	23: 2	When you give t in a lawsuit,	6699
	25:16	put in the ark the T, which I will give you.	6343
	25:21	on top of the ark and put in the ark the T,	6343
	25:22	that are over the ark of the T,	6343
	26:33	the clasps and place the ark of the T behind	6343
	26:34	Put the atonement cover on the ark of the T	6343
	27:21	outside the curtain that is in front of the T,	6343
	30: 6	the curtain that is before the ark of the T—	6343
	30: 6	the atonement cover that is over the T—	6343
	30:26	the Tent of Meeting, the ark of the T,	6343
	30:36	of it to powder and place it in front of the T	6343
	31: 7	the ark of the T with the atonement cover	6343
	31:18	he gave him the two tablets of the T,	6343
	32:15	the mountain with the two tablets of the T	6343
	34:29	with the two tablets of the T in his hands,	6343
	38:21	the tabernacle, the tabernacle of the T,	6343
	39:35	the ark of the T with its poles and	6343
	40: 3	the ark of the T in it and shield the ark with	6343
	40: 5	of the T and put the curtain at the entrance	6343
	40:20	He took the T and placed it in the ark,	6343
	40:21	and shielded the ark of the T,	6343
Lev	16:13	the atonement cover above the T,	6343
	24: 3	the curtain of the T in the Tent of Meeting,	6343
Nu	1:50	to be in charge of the tabernacle of the T—	6343
	1:53	the tabernacle of the T so that wrath will	6343
	1:53	for the care of the tabernacle of the T."	6343
	4: 5	and cover the ark of the T with it.	6343
	7:89	the atonement cover on the ark of the T.	6343
	9:15	the Tent of the T, was set up,	6343
	10:11	from above the tabernacle of the T.	6343
	17: 4	in the Tent of Meeting in front of the T,	6343
	17: 7	before the LORD in the Tent of the T.	6343
	17: 8	of the T and saw that Aaron's staff	6343
	17:10	"Put back Aaron's staff in front of the T,	6343
	18: 2	before the Tent of the T.	6343
	35:30	be put to death as a murderer only on the t	7023
	35:30	But no one is to be put to death on the t	6699
Dt	5:20	not give false t against your neighbor.	6332
	17: 6	the t of two or three witnesses a man shall	7023

Dt	17: 6	no one shall be put to death on the t of only	7023
	19:15	A matter must be established by the t of two	7023
	19:18	giving false t against his brother,	6699
Jos	4:16	of the T to come up out of the Jordan."	6343
2Ch	24: 6	of Israel for the Tent of the T?"	6343
Pr	12:17	A truthful witness gives honest t,	5583
	25:18	a sharp arrow is the man who gives false t	6332
Isa	8:16	Bind up the t and seal up the law	9496
	8:20	To the law and to the t!	9496
	29:21	with false t deprive the innocent of justice.	NIH
Mt	8: 4	the gift Moses commanded, as a t to them."	3457
	15:19	adultery, sexual immorality, theft, false t,	6019
	18:16	by the t of two or three witnesses.'	5125
	19:18	do not steal, do not give false t,	6018
	24:14	in the whole world as a t to all nations,	3457
	26:62	t that these men are bringing against you?"	2909
	27:13	t they are bringing against you?"	2909
Mk	1:44	for your cleansing, as a t to them."	3457
	6:11	when you leave, as a t against them."	3457
	10:19	do not give false t, do not defraud,	6018
	14:57	Then some stood up and gave this false t	6018
	14:59	Yet even then their t did not agree.	3456
	14:60	What is this t that these men are bringing against you?"	2909
Lk	5:14	for your cleansing, as a t to them."	3457
	9: 5	you leave their town, as a t against them."	3457
	18:20	do not steal, do not give false t,	6018
	22:71	"Why do we need any more t?	3456
Jn	1:19	Now this was John's t when the Jews	3456
	1:32	Then John gave this t: "I saw the Spirit	3455
	2:25	He did not need man's t about man,	3455
	3:11	but still you people do not accept our t.	3456
	3:32	but no one accepts his t.	3456
	4:39	in him because of the woman's t,	3455
	5:31	"If I testify about myself, my t is not valid.	3456
	5:32	and I know that his t about me is valid.	3455+3456+4005
	5:34	Not that I accept human t;	3456
	5:36	"I have t weightier than that of John.	3456
	8:13	as your own witness; your t is not valid."	3456
	8:14	my t is valid, for I know where I came from	3456
	8:17	In your own Law it is written that the t	3456
	19:35	The man who saw it has given t,	3455
	19:35	and his t is true.	3456
	21:24	We know that his t is true.	3456
Ac	7:44	the tabernacle of the T with them in	3457
	14:17	Yet he has not left himself without t:	282
	22:18	they will not accept your t about me.'	3456
1Co	1: 6	our t about Christ was confirmed in you.	3457
	2: 1	as I proclaimed to you the t about God.	3456
2Co	13: 1	"Every matter must be established by the t	5125
2Th	1:10	because you believed our t to you.	3457
1Ti	2: 6	the t given in its proper time.	3457
Tit	1:13	This t is true.	3456
Heb	10:28	died without mercy on the t of two or three	3459
1Jn	5: 9	We accept man's t, but God's testimony	3456
	5: 9	but God's t is greater because it is	3456
	5: 9	because it is the t of God,	3456
	5:10	in the Son of God has this t in his heart.	3456
	5:10	the t God has given about his Son.	3456
	5:11	this is the t: God has given us eternal life,	3456
3Jn	1:12	and you know that our t is true.	3456
Rev	1: 2	the word of God and the t of Jesus Christ.	3456
	1: 9	of the word of God and the t of Jesus.	3456
	6: 9	of God and the t they had maintained.	3456
	11: 7	Now when they have finished their t,	3456
	12:11	of the Lamb and by the word of their t;	3456
	12:17	and hold to the t of Jesus.	3456
	15: 5	the tabernacle of the T, was opened.	3457
	17: 6	the blood of those who bore t to Jesus.	3459
	19:10	and with your brothers who hold to the t	3456
	19:10	For the t of Jesus is the spirit of prophecy."	3456
	20: 4	of their t for Jesus and because of the word	3456
	22:16	have sent my angel to give you this t for	3455

TESTING (5) [TEST]

Dt	13: 3	The LORD your God is t you to find out	5814
Eze	21:13	" 'T will surely come.	1043
Lk	8:13	but in the time of t they fall away.	4280
Heb	3: 8	during the time of t in the desert,	4280
Jas	1: 3	the t of your faith develops perseverance.	1510

TESTINGS (1) [TEST]

Dt	4:34	by t, by miraculous signs and wonders,	4999

TESTS (4) [TEST]

Job	34: 3	the ear t words as the tongue tastes food.	1043
Pr	17: 3	but the LORD t the heart.	1043
Ecc	3:18	God t them so that they may see that	1405
1Th	2: 4	but God, who t our hearts.	1507

TETHER (1) [TETHERED]

Ge	49:11	He will t his donkey to a vine,	673

TETHERED (1) [TETHER]

2Ki	7:10	only t horses and donkeys,	673

TETRARCH (7)

Mt	14: 1	At that time Herod the t heard the reports	5490
Lk	3: 1	Herod t of Galilee, his brother Philip	5489
	3: 1	of Galilee, his brother Philip t of Iturea	5489
	3: 1	and Lysanias t of Abilene—	5489
	3:19	when John rebuked Herod the t because	5490

Lk	9: 7	Now Herod the t heard about all that was going on.	5490
Ac	13: 1	up with Herod the t) and Saul.	5490

TEXT (4)

Est	3:14	of the t of the edict was to be issued as law	4181
	4: 8	of the t of the edict for their annihilation,	4181
	8:13	of the t of the edict was to be issued as law	4181
Jer	29: 1	This is the t of the letter that the prophet	1821

THADDAEUS (2)

Mt	10: 3	James son of Alphaeus, and T;	2497
Mk	3:18	Thomas, James son of Alphaeus, T,	2497

THAHASH (KJV) See TAHASH

THAMAH (KJV) See TEMAH

THAMAR (KJV) See TAMAR

THAN (535)

Ge	3: 1	Now the serpent was more crafty t any of	4946
	4:13	"My punishment is more t I can bear.	4946
	7:20	to a depth of more t twenty feet.	4946
	18:28	number of the righteous is five less t	2893
	19: 9	We'll treat you worse t them."	4946
	25:23	one people will be stronger t the other,	4946
	27:12	a curse on myself rather t a blessing."	2256+4202
	28:17	This is none other t the house of God;	561+3954
	29:19	that I give her to you t to some other man.	4946
	29:30	and he loved Rachel more t Leah.	4946
	37: 3	Now Israel loved Joseph more t any	4946
	37: 4	that their father loved him more t any	4946
	38:26	"She is more righteous t I,	4946
	39: 9	No one is greater in this house t I am.	4946
	41:40	to the throne will I be greater t you."	4946
	48:19	his younger brother will be greater t he,	4946
	49:12	His eyes will be darker t wine,	4946
	49:12	his teeth whiter t milk.	4946
	49:26	Your father's blessings are greater t	6584
	49:26	t the bounty of the age-old hills.	NIH
Ex	11: 6	worse t there has ever been or ever will	AIT
	14:12	for us to serve the Egyptians t to die in	4946
	18:11	that the LORD is greater t all other gods,	4946
	22:20	"Whoever sacrifices to any god other t the LORD must be destroyed.	963+1194+4200
	30:15	not to give more t a half shekel and	4946
	30:33	puts it on anyone other t a priest	2424
	36: 5	"The people are bringing more t enough	4946
	36: 7	what they already had was more t enough	AIT
Lev	13: 3	and the sore appears to be more t skin deep,	4946
	13: 4	to be more t skin deep and the hair in it has	4946
	13:20	and if it appears to be more t skin deep and	4946
	13:21	and it is not more t skin deep and has faded,	4946
	13:25	and it appears to be more t skin deep,	4946
	13:26	in the spot and if it is not more t skin deep	4946
	13:30	and if it appears to be more t skin deep and	4946
	13:31	it does not seem to be more t skin deep	4946
	13:32	not appear to be more t skin deep,	4946
	13:34	and appears to be no more t skin deep,	4946
	14:37	that appear to be deeper t the surface of	4946
	15:25	at a time other t her monthly period or has	4202
	22:12	daughter marries anyone other t a priest,	2424
Nu	5:20	with a man other t your husband"—	1187+4946
	11:32	No one gathered less t ten homers.	5070
	12: 3	more humble t anyone else on the face of	4946
	13:31	they are stronger t we are."	4946
	14:12	into a nation greater and stronger t they."	4946
	22:15	more numerous and more distinguished t	4946
	24: 7	"Their king will be greater t Agag;	4946
Dt	1:28	people are stronger and taller t we are;	4946
	3:11	and was more t thirteen feet long	564+9596
	4:38	and stronger t you and to bring you	4946
	7: 1	seven nations larger and stronger t you—	4946
	7: 7	you were more numerous t other peoples,	4946
	7:14	be blessed more t any other people;	4946
	7:17	"These nations are stronger t we are.	4946
	9: 1	nations greater and stronger t you,	4946
	9:14	nation stronger and more numerous t they."	4946
	11:23	nations larger and stronger t you.	4946
	17:20	not consider himself better t his brothers	4946
	20: 1	and chariots and an army greater t yours,	4946
	25: 3	he must not give him more t forty lashes.	AIT
	25: 3	If he is flogged more t that,	6584
	30: 5	prosperous and numerous t your fathers.	4946
Jos	4:18	No sooner had they set their feet on the dry ground t the waters	3869
	10: 2	it was larger t Ai,	4946
	10:11	the hailstones t were killed by the swords	4946
	19: 9	Judah's portion was more t they needed.	4946
	22:19	other t the altar of the LORD our God.	1187+4946
	22:29	other t the altar of the LORD	963+4200+4946
Jdg	2:19	to ways even more corrupt t those	4946
	6:27	he did it at night rather t in the daytime.	4946
	7:12	Their camels could no more be counted t	3869
	7:14	be nothing other t the sword of Gideon son	561
	8: 2	the gleanings of Ephraim's grapes better t	4946
	8:33	No sooner had Gideon died t	889+3869
	11:25	Are you better t Balak son of Zippor,	4946
	14:18	"What is sweeter t honey?	4946
	14:18	What is stronger t a lion?"	4946
	16:30	he killed many more when he died t	4946
	18:19	priest rather t just one man's household?"	196

Ru	1:13	It is more bitter for me t for you,	4946

Ru 1:13 It is more bitter for me t for you, 4946
3:10 "This kindness is greater t I. 4946
3:12 there is a kinsman-redeemer nearer t I. 4946
4:15 and who is better to you t seven sons, 4946
1Sa 1: 8 Don't I mean more to you t ten sons?" 4946
2:29 Why do you honor your sons more t me 4946
9: 2 a head taller t any of the others. 4946
10:23 the people he was a head taller t any of 4946
15:22 To obey is better t sacrifice, 4946
15:22 and to heed is better t the fat of rams. 4946
15:28 one of your neighbors—to one better t you. 4946
18:25 other price for the bride t 3954
18:30 David met with more success t the rest 4946
24:17 "You are more righteous t I," he said. 4946
29: 4 better could he regain his master's favor t 4202
2Sa 1:23 They were swifter t eagles, 4946
1:23 they were stronger t lions. 4946
1:26 more wonderful t that of women. 4946
6:21 who chose me rather t your father 4946
6:22 I will become even more undignified t this, 4946
13:14 and since he was stronger t she, 4946
13:15 he hated her more t he had loved her. 4946
13:16 greater wrong t what you have already done 4946
17:14 "The advice of Hushai the Arkite is better t 4946
18: 8 and the forest claimed more lives that day t 4946
19: 7 for you t all the calamities that have come 4946
19:43 we have a greater claim on David t you 4946
19:43 of Judah responded even more harshly t 4946
20: 5 he took longer t the time the king had set 4946
20: 6 will do us more harm t Absalom did. 4946
23:19 not held in greater honor t the Three? 4946
23:23 He was held in greater honor t any of 4946
1Ki 1:37 to make his throne even greater t 4946
1:47 'May your God make Solomon's name more famous t yours 4946
1:47 and his throne greater t yours!' 4946
2:32 were better men and more upright t he. 4946
4:30 Solomon's wisdom was greater t 4946
4:30 and greater t all the wisdom of Egypt. 4946
4:31 He was wiser t any other man, 4946
4:31 wiser t Heman, Calcol and Darda, NIH
10:23 in riches and wisdom t all the other kings 4946
12:10 My little finger is thicker t my father's waist 4946
14: 9 You have done more evil t all who lived 4946
14:22 jealous anger more t their fathers had done. 4946
16:22 Omri's followers proved stronger t those AIT
16:25 of the LORD and sinned more t all those 4946
16:30 more evil in the eyes of the LORD t 4946
16:33 to anger t did all the kings of Israel 4946
19: 4 I am no better t my ancestors." 4946
20:23 surely we will be stronger t they. 4946
20:25 Then surely we will be stronger t they." 4946
2Ki 5:12 better t any of the waters of Israel? 4946
6:16 with us are more t those who are 4946
21: 9 so that they did more evil t the nations 4946
21:11 He has done more evil t 4946
25:16 was more t could be weighed. 4202
25:28 gave him a seat of honor higher t 4946+6584
1Ch 4:9 Jabez was more honorable t his brothers. 4946
11:25 He was held in greater honor t any of 4946
22: 3 and more bronze t could be weighed. 401
22: 4 also provided more cedar logs t could 401+4200
24: 4 among Eleazar's descendants t among 4946
2Ch 2: 5 because our God is greater t all other gods. 4946
9:12 gave her more t she had brought 963+4200+4946
9:22 in riches and wisdom t all the other kings 4946
10:10 My little finger is thicker t my father's waist 4946
11:21 of Absalom more t any of his other wives 4946
17: 4 and followed his commands rather t 2256+4202
20:25 more t they could take away. AIT
21:13 men who were better t you. 4946
25: 9 "The LORD can give you much more t that." 4946
29:34 more conscientious in consecrating themselves the priests 4946
32: 7 there is a greater power with us t with him. 4946
33: 9 so that they did more evil t the nations 4946
Ezr 9: 6 because our sins are higher t our heads 2025+4200+5087+8049
9:13 punished us less t our sins have deserved 4946
Ne 7: 2 and feared God more t most men do. 4946
Est 1:19 to someone else who is better t she. 4946
2:15 she asked for nothing other t what 561+3954
2:17 Now the king was attracted to Esther more t 4946
2:17 his favor and approval more t any of 4946
3: 1 a seat of honor higher t that of all the other nobles. 4946+6584
6: 6 the king would rather honor t me?" 3463+4946
Job 3:21 who search for it more t for hidden treasure, 4946
4:17 'Can a mortal be more righteous t God? 4946
4:17 Can a man be more pure t his Maker? 4946
4:19 are crushed more readily t a moth! 4200+7156
7: 6 "My days are swifter t a weaver's shuttle, 4974
7:15 rather t this body of mine. 4946
8:12 they wither more quickly t grass. 4200+7156
9:25 "My days are swifter t a runner; 4974
11: 8 They are higher t the heavens— AIT
11: 8 They are deeper t the depths of the grave— 4946
11: 9 Their measure is longer t the earth 4974
11: 9 the earth and wider t the sea. 4974
11:12 a witless man can no more become wise t 2256
11:17 Life will be brighter t noonday, 4946
15:10 men even older t your father. 4946
23:12 words of his mouth more t my daily bread. 4946
30: 1 "But now they mock me, men younger t I, 4946
32: 2 for justifying himself rather t God. 4946
32: 4 to Job because they were older t he. 4946
33:12 for God is greater t man. 4946

Job 35:11 who teaches more to us t to the beasts of 4946
35:11 the beasts of the earth and makes us wiser t 4946
42:12 the latter part of Job's life more t the first. 4946
Ps 4: 7 You have filled my heart with greater joy t 4946
8: 5 a little lower t the heavenly beings 4946
19:10 They are more precious t gold, 4946
19:10 t much pure gold; 4946
19:10 they are sweeter t honey, 4946
19:10 t honey from the comb. NIH
37:16 Better the little that the righteous have t 4946
40:12 They are more t the hairs of my head, 4946
51: 7 wash me, and I will be whiter t snow. 4946
52: 3 You love evil rather t good, 4946
52: 3 falsehood rather t speaking the truth. 4946
55:21 his words are more soothing t oil, 4946
61: 2 lead me to the rock that is higher t I. 4946
63: 3 Because your love is better t life, 4946
69:31 This will please the LORD more t an ox, 4946
69:31 more t a bull with its horns and hoofs. NIH
76: 4 more majestic t mountains rich with game. 4946
78:29 for till they had more t enough, 4394
84:10 in your courts t a thousand elsewhere; 4946
84:10 the house of my God t dwell in the tents of 4946
87: 2 of Zion more t all the dwellings of Jacob. 4946
89: 7 he is more awesome t all who surround him. 6584
93: 4 Mightier t the thunder of the great waters, 4946
93: 4 mightier t the breakers of the sea— NIH
108: 4 your love, higher t the heavens; 4946+6584
118: 8 It is better to take refuge in the LORD t 4946
118: 9 It is better to take refuge in the LORD t 4946
119:72 from your mouth is more precious to me t 4946
119:98 Your commands make me wiser t my enemies, 4946
119:99 I have more insight t all my teachers, 4946
119:100 I have more understanding t the elders, 4946
119:103 sweeter t honey to my mouth! 4946
119:127 I love your commands more t gold, 4946
119:127 more t pure gold, 4946
130: 6 waits for the Lord more t watchmen wait 4946
130: 6 more t watchmen wait for the morning. NIH
135: 5 that our Lord is greater t all gods. 4946
Pr 3:14 for she is more profitable t silver 4946
3:14 and yields better returns t gold. 4946
3:15 She is more precious t rubies; 4946
5: 3 and her speech is smoother t oil; 4946
8:10 knowledge rather t choice gold, 4946
8:11 for wisdom is more precious t rubies, 4946
8:19 My fruit is better t fine gold; 4946
12: 9 a nobody and yet have a servant t pretend 4946
15:16 of the LORD t great wealth with turmoil. 4946
15:17 a meal of vegetables where there is love t 4946
16: 8 a little with righteousness t much gain 4946
16:16 How much better to get wisdom t gold, 4946
16:16 to choose understanding rather t silver! 4946
16:19 among the oppressed t to share plunder 4946
16:32 Better a patient man t a warrior, 4946
16:32 a man who controls his temper t one who 4946
17: 1 Better a dry crust with peace and quiet t 4946
17:10 of discernment more t a hundred lashes 4946
17:12 Better to meet a bear robbed of her cubs t 440
18:19 An offended brother is more unyielding t 4946
18:24 but there is a friend who sticks closer t 4946
19: 1 a poor man whose walk is blameless t 4946
19:22 better to be poor t a liar. 4946
21: 3 and just is more acceptable to the LORD t 4946
21: 9 Better to live on a corner of the roof t share 4946
21:19 to live in a desert t with a quarrelsome 4946
22: 1 good name is more desirable t great riches; 4946
22: 1 to be esteemed is better t silver or gold. 4946
25: 7 t for him to humiliate you before 4946
25:24 Better to live on a corner of the roof t share 4946
26:12 There is more hope for a fool t 4946
26:16 seven men who answer discreetly. 4946
27: 3 but provocation by a fool is heavier t both. 4946
27: 5 Better is open rebuke t hidden love. 4946
27:10 a neighbor nearby t a brother far away. 4946
28: 6 a poor man whose walk is blameless t 4946
28:23 in the end gain more favor t he who has 4946
29:20 There is more hope for a fool t for him. 4946
31:10 She is worth far more t rubies. 4946
Ecc 1: 8 are wearisome, more t one can say. 4202
1:16 in wisdom more t anyone who has ruled 6584
2: 7 also owned more herds and flocks t anyone 4946
2: 9 by far t anyone in Jerusalem before me. 4946
2:12 What more can the king's successor do t what has already been done? NIH
2:13 I saw that wisdom is better t folly, 4946
2:13 just as light is better t darkness. 4946
2:24 A man can do nothing better t to eat 8611
3:12 that there is nothing better for men t to 561+3954
3:22 that there is nothing better for a man t 889+4946
4: 2 are happier t the living, who are still alive. 4946
4: 3 better t both is he who has not yet been, 4946
4: 6 with tranquillity t two handfuls with toil 4946
4: 9 Two are better t one, 4946
4:13 Better a poor but wise youth t an old 4946
5: 1 near to listen rather t to offer the sacrifice 4946
5: 5 It is better not to vow t to make a vow and 4946
6: 3 I say that a stillborn child is better off t he. 4946
6: 9 the eye sees t the roving of the appetite. 4946
6:10 with one who is stronger t he. 4946
7: 1 A good name is better t fine perfume, 4946
7: 1 the day of death better t the day of birth. 4946
7: 2 of mourning t to go to a house of feasting, 4946
7: 3 Sorrow is better t laughter, 4946

Ecc 7: 5 a wise man's rebuke t to listen to the song 4946
7: 8 end of a matter is better t its beginning, 4946
7: 8 and patience is better t pride. 4946
7:10 "Why were the old days better t these?" 4946
7:19 Wisdom makes one wise man more powerful t ten rulers 4946
7:26 I find more bitter t death the woman who is 4946
8:15 a man under the sun t eat and drink 561+3954
9: 4 even a live dog is better off t a dead lion! 4946
9:16 So I said, "Wisdom is better t strength." 4946
9:17 words of the wise are more to be heeded t 4946
9:18 Wisdom is better t weapons of war, 4946
SS 1: 2 for your love is more delightful t wine. 4946
1: 4 we will praise your love more t wine. 4946
4:10 much more pleasing is your love t 4946
4:10 the fragrance of your perfume t any spice! 4946
5: 9 How is your beloved better t others, 4946
5: 9 How is your beloved better t others, 4946
Isa 1:11 "I have more t enough of burnt offerings, 8425
5: 4 for my vineyard t I have done for it? 2256+4202
13:12 I will make man scarcer t pure gold, 4946
13:12 more rare t the gold of Ophir. 4946
32:10 In little more t a year you who feel 3427+6584
40:17 by him as worthless and less t nothing. 4946
40:24 t the blows on them and they wither, 1685+2256
41:24 But you are less t nothing 4946
54: 1 children of the desolate woman t of her who 4946
55: 9 "As the heavens are higher t the earth, 4946
55: 9 so are my ways higher t your ways 4946
55: 9 and my thoughts t your thoughts. 4946
56: 5 and a name better t sons and daughters; 4946
66: 8 no sooner is Zion in labor t she gives birth 1685
Jer 3:11 "Faithless Israel is more righteous t unfaithful Judah. 4946
4:13 his horses are swifter t eagles. 4946
5: 3 They made their faces harder t stone 4946
7:26 and did more evil t their forefathers.' 4946
15: 8 I will make their widows more numerous t 4946
16:12 you have behaved more wickedly t your fathers. 4946
31:11 from the hand of those stronger t they. 4946
46:23 They are more numerous t locusts, 4946
52:20 was more t could be weighed. 4202
52:32 and gave him a seat of honor higher t those 4200
La 3: 2 walk in darkness rather t light; 4202
4: 6 The punishment of my people is greater t 4946
4: 7 Their princes were brighter t snow 4946
4: 7 and whiter t milk, 4946
4: 7 their bodies more ruddy t rubies, 4946
4: 8 But now they are blacker t soot; 4946
4: 9 by the sword are better off t those who die 4946
4:19 Our pursuers were swifter t eagles in 4946
Eze 3: 9 like the hardest stone, harder t flint. 4946
5: 6 against my laws and decrees more t 4946
5: 7 You have been more unruly t the nations 4946
8:15 that are even more detestable t this." 4946
15: 2 of a vine better t that of a branch on any of 4946
16:47 you soon became more depraved t they. 4946
16:51 You have done more detestable things t they 4946
16:52 Because your sins were more vile t theirs, 4946
16:52 they appear more righteous t you. 4946
16:61 both those who are older t you 4946
23:11 and prostitution she was more depraved t her sister. 4946
28: 3 Are you wiser t Daniel? 4946
31: 5 So it towered higher t all the trees of 4946
32:19 'Are you more favored t others? 4946
33:32 to them you are nothing more t one who sings love songs 3869
34: 8 for themselves rather t for my flock, 4202
36:11 and will make you prosper more t before. 4946
42: 5 more space from them t from the rooms 4946
42: 6 so they were smaller in floor space t those 4946
Da 1:10 Why should he see you looking worse t 4946
1:15 and better nourished t any of 4946
1:20 he found them ten times better t all 6584
2:30 I have greater wisdom t other living men, 10427
2:43 any more t iron mixes with clay. 10168+10195+10341
3:19 furnace heated seven times hotter t usual 10542
3:28 to give up their lives rather t serve 10379
4:36 and became even greater t before. NIH
7:20 that looked more imposing t the others and 10427
8: 3 the horns was longer t the other but grew 4946
11: 2 who will be far richer t all the others. 4946
11: 5 commanders will become even stronger t he 6584
11:13 muster another army, larger t the first; 4946
Hos 2: 7 for then I was better off t now.' 4946
6: 6 acknowledgment of God rather t burnt 4946
Am 6: 2 Are they better off t your two kingdoms? 4946
6: 2 Is their land larger t yours? 4946
Jnh 1:13 for the sea grew even wilder t before. NIH
4: 3 for it is better for me to die t to live." 4946
4: 8 "It would be better for me to die t to live." 4946
4:11 But Nineveh has more t a hundred and 4946
Mic 7: 4 the most upright worse t a thorn hedge. 4946
Na 3: 8 Are you better t Thebes, 4946
3: 8 till they are more t the stars of the sky, 4946
Hab 1: 8 Their horses are swifter t leopards, 4946
1: 8 fiercer t wolves at dusk. 4946
1:13 up those more righteous t themselves? 4946
Hag 2: 9 be greater t the glory of the former house,' 4946
Zec 12: 7 not be greater t that of Judah. 6584
Mt 3:11 me will come one who is more powerful t I, AIT
5:29 for you to lose one part of your body t NIG
5:30 of your body t for your whole body to go NIG
5:47 what are you doing more t others? NIG

Mt	6:25	Is not life *more* important *t* food,	AIT
	6:25	and the body more important *t* clothes?	NIG
	6:26	Are you not much more valuable *t* they?	899
	10:15	and Gomorrah on the day of judgment *t* for	2445
	10:31	you *are* worth more *t* many sparrows.	1422
	10:37	or mother more *t* me is not worthy of me;	5642
	10:37	or daughter more *t* me is not worthy of me;	5642
	11: 9	Yes, I tell you, and more *t* a prophet.	4358
	11:11	not risen anyone greater *t* John the Baptist;	3505
	11:11	in the kingdom of heaven is greater *t* he.	3505
	11:22	and Sidon on the day of judgment *t* for you.	2445
	11:24	Sodom on the day of judgment *t* for you."	2445
	12: 6	that one greater *t* the temple is here.	3505
	12:12	much more valuable is a man *t* a sheep!	AIT
	12:41	and now *one* greater *t* Jonah is here.	AIT
	12:42	and now *one* greater *t* Solomon is here.	AIT
	12:45	seven other spirits more wicked *t* itself,	4505
	12:45	the final condition of that man is worse *t*	5937
	18: 8	or crippled *t* to have two hands or two feet	2445
	18: 9	with one eye *t* to have two eyes and	2445
	18:13	he is happier about that one sheep *t* about	2445
	19:24	through the eye of a needle *t* for a rich man	2445
	21:36	more *t* the first time,	2062
	26:53	my disposal *more t* twelve legions of angels?	AIT
	27:64	This last deception will be worse *t*	5937
Mk	1: 7	After me will come one more powerful *t* I,	2708
	9: 3	whiter *t* anyone in the world could bleach	NIG
	9:43	to enter life maimed *t* with two hands to go	2445
	9:45	to enter life crippled *t* to have two feet and	2445
	9:47	to enter the kingdom of God with one eye *t*	2445
	10:25	through the eye of a needle *t* for a rich man	2445
	12:31	There is no commandment greater *t* these."	3505
	12:33	is more important *t* all burnt offerings	4358
	12:43	widow has put *more* into the treasury *t*	AIT
	14: 5	It could have been sold for more *t*	2062
Lk	3:13	"Don't collect any *more t* you are required	AIT
	3:16	But one more powerful *t* I will come,	2708
	7:26	Yes, I tell you, and more *t* a prophet.	4358
	7:28	of women there is no one greater *t* John;	3505
	7:28	in the kingdom of God is greater *t* he."	3505
	8: 8	a hundred times more *t* was sown."	NIG
	10:12	be more bearable on that day for Sodom *t*	2445
	10:14	for Tyre and Sidon at the judgment *t*	2445
	11:26	seven other spirits more wicked *t* itself,	4505
	11:26	the final condition of that man is worse *t*	5937
	11:31	and now *one* greater *t* Solomon is here.	AIT
	11:32	and now *one* greater *t* Jonah is here.	AIT
	12: 7	*you are* worth more *t* many sparrows.	1422
	12:23	Life is more *t* food,	AIT
	12:23	and the body more *t* clothes.	NIG
	12:24	how much more valuable you are *t* birds!	3437
	13: 2	these Galileans were worse sinners *t* all	4123
	13: 4	do you think they were more guilty *t* all	4123
	14: 8	a person more distinguished *t* you	1952
	15: 7	more rejoicing in heaven over one sinner who repents *t* over	2445
	16: 8	shrewd in dealing with their own kind *t*	AIT
	16:17	and earth to disappear *t* for the least stroke	2445
	17: 2	a millstone tied around his neck *t* for him	2445
	18:14	"I tell you that this man, rather *t* the other,	4123
	18:25	through the eye of a needle *t* for a rich man	2445
	21: 3	"this poor widow has put in more *t* all	AIT
Jn	1:50	You shall see greater *things t* that."	3505
	4: 1	and baptizing more disciples *t* John,	2445
	4:12	Are you greater *t* our father Jacob,	3505
	5:20	even greater things *t* these.	3505
	5:36	"I have testimony weightier *t* that of John.	3505
	7:31	he do more miraculous signs *t* this man?"	AIT
	8:53	Are you greater *t* our father Abraham?	3505
	10:29	who has given them to me, is greater *t* all;	3505
	11:18	Bethany was less *t* two miles from	NIG
	11:50	people *t* that the whole nation perish."	2779+3590
	12:43	from men more *t* praise from God.	2472
	13:16	no servant is greater *t* his master,	3505
	13:16	nor is a messenger greater *t* the one who	3505
	14:12	He will do even greater things *t* these,	3505
	14:28	for the Father is greater *t* I.	3505
	15:13	Greater love has no one *t* this, that he lay	3505
	15:20	'No servant is greater *t* his master.'	3505
	16:12	to say to you, more *t* you can now bear.	NIG
	17:14	world *any* more *t* I am of the world.	2777+4024
	21:15	do you truly love me more *t* these?"	AIT
Ac	4:19	in God's sight to obey you rather *t* God.	2445
	5:29	"We must obey God rather *t* men!	2445
	17:11	Bereans were of more noble character *t*	2302
	20:35	'It is more blessed to give *t* to receive.' "	2445
	23:13	More *t* forty men were involved	4498
	23:21	because more *t* forty of them are waiting	4498
	24:11	that no more *t* twelve days ago I went up	4498
	26:13	light from heaven, brighter *t* the sun,	3288+5642
Ro	1:25	served created things rather *t* the Creator—	4123
	8:34	more *t* that, who was raised to life—	3437
	8:37	in all these things *we are* more *t* conquerors through him	5664
	12: 3	of yourself more highly *t* you ought,	4123
	13:11	because our salvation is nearer now *t*	2445
	14: 5	One man considers one day more sacred *t* another;	4123
1Co	1:25	foolishness of God is wiser *t* man's wisdom,	AIT
	1:25	weakness of God is stronger *t* man's strength.	AIT
	3:11	For no one can lay any foundation other *t*	4123
	7: 9	it is better to marry *t* to burn with passion.	AIT
	9:12	anything rather *t* hinder the gospel	2671+3590
	9:15	I would rather die *t* have anyone deprive me	2445
	10:22	Are we stronger *t* he?	2708
	11:17	for your meetings do more harm *t* good.	NIG

1Co	14: 5	He who prophesies is greater *t* one who speaks in tongues,	2445
	14:18	that I speak in tongues more *t* all of you.	2445
	14:19	to instruct others *t* ten thousand words in	2445
	15: 6	to more *t* five hundred of the brothers at	2062
	15:10	No, I worked harder *t* all of them—	4358
	15:15	More *t* that, we are then found to	2779
	15:19	we are to be pitied more *t* all men.	1795
2Co	5:12	in what is seen rather *t* in what is in	2779+3590
	7: 7	so that my joy was greater *t* ever.	3437
	10: 8	building you up rather *t* pulling you	2779+4024
	11: 4	a Jesus other *t* the Jesus we preached,	257
	12: 6	no one will think more of me *t* is warranted	AIT
Gal	1: 8	from heaven should preach a gospel other *t*	4123
	1: 9	to you a gospel other *t* what you accepted,	4123
	4:27	children of the desolate woman *t* of	2445+3437
Eph	3: 8	I am less *t* the least of all God's people,	AIT
	3:20	to do immeasurably more *t* all we ask	5642
	4:10	the very one who ascended higher *t* all	AIT
Php	2: 3	in humility consider others better *t* yourselves.	5660
Col	2: 8	of this world rather *t* on Christ.	2779+4024
1Ti	1: 4	These promote controversies rather *t* God's work—	2445
	5: 8	the faith and is worse *t* an unbeliever.	5937
2Ti	3: 4	lovers of pleasure rather *t* lovers of God—	2445
Phm	1:16	but better *t* a slave, as a dear brother.	5642
	1:21	knowing that you will do even more *t* I ask.	5642
Heb	2: 7	You made him a little lower *t* the angels;	4123
	2: 9	who was made a little lower *t* the angels,	4123
	3: 3	worthy of greater honor *t* Moses,	4123
	3: 3	the builder of a house has greater honor *t*	AIT
	4:12	Sharper *t* any double-edged sword,	5642
	6:16	by *someone* greater *t* themselves,	3505+3836
	9:23	with better sacrifices *t* these.	AIT
	11: 4	Abel offered God a better sacrifice *t* Cain	4123
	11:25	with the people of God rather *t* to enjoy	2445
	11:26	of Christ as *of* greater value *t* the treasures	3505
	12:24	that speaks a better word *t* the blood	4123
1Pe	1: 7	your faith—of greater worth *t* gold,	AIT
	3:17	to suffer for doing good *t* for doing evil.	2445
2Pe	2:20	they are worse off at the end *t*	5937
	2:21	*t* to have known it and then to turn their	2445
1Jn	3:20	For God is greater *t* our hearts,	3505
	4: 4	because the one who is in you is greater *t*	2445
3Jn	1: 4	I have no greater joy *t* to hear	3504
Rev	2:19	and that you are now doing more *t* you did	AIT

THANK (34) [THANKED, THANKFUL, THANKFULNESS, THANKING, THANKS, THANKSGIVING]

Lev	7:12	with this *t* offering he is to offer cakes	9343
	22:29	"When you sacrifice a *t* offering to	9343
Dt	24:13	Then *he will t* you, and it will be regarded	1385
1Ch	23:30	They were also to stand every morning to *t*	3344
2Ch	29:31	Come and bring sacrifices and *t* offerings	9343
	29:31	assembly brought sacrifices and *t* offerings,	9343
	29:31	fellowship offerings and *t* offerings on it,	9343
Ps	50:14	Sacrifice *t* offerings to God,	9343
	50:23	He who sacrifices *t* offerings honors me,	9343
	56:12	I will present my *t* offerings to you.	9343
	107:22	Let them sacrifice *t* offerings and tell	9343
	116:17	a *t* offering to you and call on the name of	9343
Jer	17:26	and *t* offerings to the house of the LORD.	9343
	33:11	of those who bring *t* offerings to the house	9343
Da	2:23	I *t* and praise you, O God of my fathers:	10312
Am	4: 5	Burn leavened bread as a *t* offering	9343
Lk	17: 9	Would *he t* the servant because he did	2400+5921
	18:11	*t* you that I am not like other men—	2373
Jn	11:41	"Father, *I t* you that you have heard me.	2373
Ro	1: 8	*t* my God through Jesus Christ for all	2373
1Co	1: 4	*I* always *t* God for you because	2373
	10:30	because of something I *t* God for?	2373
	14:18	*I t* God that I speak in tongues more than all	2373
2Co	8:16	I *t* God, who put into the heart of Titus	5921
Php	1: 3	*I t* my God every time I remember you.	2373
Col	1: 3	*We* always *t* God, the Father of our Lord	2373
1Th	1: 2	*We* always *t* God for all of you,	2373
	2:13	And we also *t* God continually because,	2373
	3: 9	How can we *t* God enough for you	2374
2Th	1: 3	We ought always *to t* God for you,	2373
	2:13	But we ought always *to t* God for you,	2373
1Ti	1:12	*I t* Christ Jesus our Lord,	2400+5921
2Ti	1: 3	*I t* God, whom I serve,	2400+5921
Phm	1: 4	*I* always *t* my God as I remember you	2373

THANKED (2) [THANK]

Lk	17:16	He threw himself at Jesus' feet and *t* him—	2373
Ac	28:15	At the sight of these men Paul *t* God	2373

THANKFUL (4) [THANK]

1Co	1:14	*I am t* that I did not baptize any of you	2373
Col	3:15	you were called to peace. And be *t*.	2375
	4: 2	to prayer, being watchful and *t*.	2374
Heb	12:28	*let us be t*, and so worship God	2400+5921

THANKFULNESS (3) [THANK]

Lev	7:12	" 'If he offers it as an expression of *t*,	9343
1Co	10:30	If I take part in the meal *with t*,	5921
Col	2: 7	as you were taught, and overflowing with *t*.	2374

THANKING (1) [THANK]

1Ch	25: 3	using the harp in *t* and praising the LORD.	3344

THANKS (81) [THANK]

1Ch	16: 4	to give *t*, and to praise the LORD,	3344
	16: 7	his associates *this* psalm of *t* to the LORD.	3344
	16: 8	Give *t* to the LORD, call on his name;	3344
	16:34	Give *t* to the LORD, for he is good;	3344
	16:35	that *we may* give *t* to your holy name,	3344
	16:41	and designated by name to give *t*	3344
	29:13	Now, our God, we give you *t*,	3344
2Ch	5:13	to give praise and *t* to the LORD.	3344
	7: 3	they worshiped and gave *t* to the LORD,	3344
	7: 6	and which were used when he gave *t*,	2146
	20:21	"Give *t* to the LORD, for his love endures	3344
	31: 2	to give *t* and to sing praises at the gates of	3344
Ne	12:31	I also assigned two large choirs to give *t*.	9343
	12:40	The two choirs that gave *t*	9343
Ps	7:17	*I will* give *t* to the LORD because	3344
	28: 7	for joy and *I will* give *t* to him in song.	3344
	30:12	*I will* give you *t* forever.	3344
	35:18	*I will* give you *t* in the great assembly;	3344
	75: 1	*We* give *t* to you, O God, we give *t*,	3344
	75: 1	We give thanks to you, O God, we give *t*,	3344
	100: T	A psalm. For giving *t*.	9343
	100: 4	give *t* to him and praise his name.	3344
	105: 1	Give *t* to the LORD, call on his name;	3344
	106: 1	Give *t* to the LORD, for he is good;	3344
	106:47	that *we may* give *t* to your holy name	3344
	107: 1	Give *t* to the LORD, for he is good;	3344
	107: 8	*Let them* give *t* to the LORD	3344
	107:15	*Let them* give *t* to the LORD	3344
	107:21	*Let them* give *t* to the LORD	3344
	107:31	*Let them* give *t* to the LORD	3344
	118: 1	Give *t* to the LORD, for he is good;	3344
	118:19	I will enter and give *t* to the LORD.	3344
	118:21	*I will* give you *t*, for you answered me;	3344
	118:28	You are my God, and *I will* give you *t*;	3344
	118:29	Give *t* to the LORD, for he is good;	3344
	119:62	to give you *t* for your righteous laws.	3344
	136: 1	Give *t* to the LORD, for he is good.	3344
	136: 2	Give *t* to the God of gods.	3344
	136: 3	Give *t* to the Lord of lords:	3344
	136:26	Give *t* to the God of heaven.	3344
Isa	12: 4	"Give *t* to the LORD, call on his name;	3344
Jer	33:11	saying, "Give *t* to the LORD Almighty,	3344
Da	6:10	and prayed, giving *t* to his God,	10312
Mt	14:19	he gave *t* and broke the loaves.	2328
	15:36	and *when* he had given *t*,	2373
	26:26	Jesus took bread, gave *t* and broke it,	2328
	26:27	gave *t* and offered it to them, saying,	2373
Mk	6:41	he gave *t* and broke the loaves.	2328
	8: 6	the seven loaves and given *t*,	2328
	8: 7	he gave *t* for them also and told	2373
	14:22	Jesus took bread, gave *t* and broke it,	2328
	14:23	gave *t* and offered it to them,	2373
Lk	2:38	*she* gave *t* to God and spoke about	469
	9:16	he gave *t* and broke them.	2328
	22:17	After taking the cup, *he* gave *t* and said,	2373
	22:19	he took bread, gave *t* and broke it,	2373
	24:30	he took bread, gave *t*, broke it	2328
Jn	6:11	Jesus then took the loaves, gave *t*,	2373
	6:11	the bread *after* the Lord *had* given *t*.	2373
Ac	27:35	and gave *t* to God in front of them all.	2373
Ro	1:21	neither glorified as God nor gave *t* to him,	2373
	6:17	But *t* be to God that,	5921
	7:25	*T* be to God—through Jesus Christ	5921
	14: 6	eats to the Lord, for *he* gives *t* to God;	2373
	14: 6	does so to the Lord and gives *t* to God.	2373
1Co	10:16	for which *we* give *t* a participation in	2328
	11:24	and *when* he had given *t*, he broke it	2373
	14:17	You *may be* giving *t* well enough,	2373
	15:57	But *t* be to God!	5921
2Co	1:11	Then many *will* give *t* on our behalf for	2373
	2:14	But *t* be to God, who always leads us in	5921
	9:12	also overflowing in many expressions of *t*	2374
	9:15	*T* be to God for his indescribable gift!	5921
Eph	1:16	I have not stopped giving *t* for you,	2373
	5:20	always giving *t* to God the Father	2373
Col	1:12	giving *t* to the Father, who has qualified you	2373
	3:17	giving *t* to God the Father through him.	2373
1Th	5:18	give *t* in all circumstances,	2373
Rev	4: 9	honor and *t* to him who sits on the throne	2374
	7:12	and *t* and honor and power and strength be	2374
	11:17	"We give *t* to you, Lord God Almighty,	2373

THANKSGIVING (25) [THANK]

Lev	7:13	of *t* he is to present an offering with cakes	9343
	7:15	of *t* must be eaten on the day it is offered;	9343
Ezr	3:11	With praise and *t* they sang to the LORD:	3344
Ne	11:17	the director *who* led in *t* and prayer;	3344+9378
	12: 8	was in charge of the songs of *t*.	2117
	12:24	stood opposite them to give praise and *t*,	3344
	12:27	the dedication with songs of *t* and with	9343
	12:46	and for the songs of praise and *t* to God.	3344
Ps	42: 4	the house of God, with shouts of joy and *t*	9343
	69:30	in song and glorify him with *t*.	9343
	95: 2	with *t* and extol him with music and song.	9343
	100: 4	Enter his gates with *t* and his courts	9343
	147: 7	Sing to the LORD with *t*;	9343
Isa	51: 3	*t* and the sound of singing.	9343
Jer	30:19	From them will come songs of *t*	9343
Jnh	2: 9	I, with a song of *t*, will sacrifice to you.	9343
1Co	10:16	not the cup *of t* for which we give thanks	2330
2Co	4:15	and more people may cause *t* to overflow	2374
	9:11	us your generosity will result in *t* to God.	2374
Eph	5: 4	which are out of place, but rather *t*.	2374

Php	4: 6	with t, present your requests to God.	2374
1Ti	2: 1	intercession and t be made for everyone—	2374
	4: 3	with t by those who believe and who know	2374
	4: 4	nothing is to be rejected if it is received with t,	2374

THANKWORTHY (KJV) See
COMMENDABLE

THARA (KJV) See TERAH

THARSHISH (KJV) See TRADING,
TARSHISH

THAT (5758) [THAT'S] See Index of Articles
Etc.

THAT'S (10) [BE, THAT]
Ge	42:21	t why this distress has come upon us."	4027+6584
Ex	5:17	Pharaoh said, "Lazy, t what you are—	NIH
	10:11	since t what you have been asking for."	2023
1Ki	1:45	T the noise you hear.	2085
2Ki	3:23	"T blood!" they said. "Those kings must	2296
	9:12	"T not true!"	NIH
Est	5:12	"And t not all," Haman added.	NIH
Jer	37:14	"T not true!"	NIH
Mt	27: 4	"T your responsibility."	3972+5148
Ac	24:25	"T enough for now!	NIG

THAWING (1)
Job	6:16	by t ice and swollen with melting snow,	NIH

THE (55728) See Index of Articles Etc.

THEATER (2)
Ac	19:29	and rushed as one man into the t.	2519
	19:31	begging him not to venture into the t.	2519

THEBES (5)
Jer	46:25	to bring punishment on Amon god of T,	5530
Eze	30:14	to Zoan and inflict punishment on T.	5530
	30:15	and cut off the hordes of T.	5530
	30:16	T will be taken by storm;	5530
Na	3: 8	Are you better than T, situated on the Nile,	5531

THEBEZ (2)
Jdg	9:50	Next Abimelech went to T and besieged it	9324
2Sa	11:21	so that he died in T?	9324

THEFT (3) [THIEF]
Ex	22: 3	he must be sold to pay for his t.	1706
Mt	15:19	murder, adultery, sexual immorality, t,	3113
Mk	7:21	come evil thoughts, sexual immorality, t,	3113

THEFTS (1) [THIEF]
Rev	9:21	their sexual immorality or their t.	3092

THEIR (3701) [THEY] See Index of Articles
Etc.

THEIRS (21) [THEY] See Index of Articles
Etc.

THELASAR (KJV) See TEL ASSAR

THEM (5162) [THEY] See Index of Articles
Etc.

THEME (3)
Ps	22:25	the t of my praise in the great assembly;	9335
	45: 1	a noble t as I recite my verses for the king;	1821
	119:54	the t of my song wherever I lodge.	2369

THEMSELVES (236) [SELF, THEY] See
Index of Articles Etc.

THEN (2931) See Index of Articles Etc.

THEOPHILUS (2)
Lk	1: 3	orderly account for you, most excellent T,	2541
Ac	1: 1	In my former book, T, I wrote about all	2541

THERE (1873) [THERE'S] See Index of
Articles Etc.

THERE'S (1) [BE, THERE]
2Ki	4:25	T the Shunammite!	2137

THEREFORE (446)
Ge	32:32	T to this day the Israelites do not eat	4027+6584

Ex	6: 6	"T, say to the Israelites:	4027+4200
	9:18	T, at this time tomorrow I will send	2180
	20:11	T the LORD blessed the Sabbath day	4027+6584
Lev	11:45	t be holy, because I am holy.	2256
	17:12	T I say to the Israelites,	4027+6584
	20:25	" 'You must t make a distinction	2256
Nu	11:34	T the place was named Kibroth Hattaavah,	2256
	25:12	T tell him I am making my covenant	4027+4200
Dt	4:15	T watch yourselves very carefully,	2256
	5:15	T the LORD your God has commanded	4027+6584
	7: 9	Know t that the LORD your God is God;	2256
	7:11	T, take care to follow the commands,	2256
	10:16	Circumcise your hearts, t,	2256
	11: 8	Observe t all the commands I am giving you	2256
	15:11	T I command you to be openhanded	4027+6584
	28:48	t in hunger and thirst, in nakedness	2256
	29:19	he invokes a blessing on himself and t	NIH
	29:27	T the LORD's anger burned	2256
	32:52	T, you will see the land only from	3954
Jos	7:26	T that place has been called the Valley	4027+6584
Jdg	1:17	T it was called Hormah.	2256
	2: 3	Now t I tell you that I will not drive them	2256
	2:20	T the LORD was very angry with Israel	2256
1Sa	2:30	"T the LORD, the God of Israel,	4027+4200
	3:14	T, I swore to the house of Eli,	4027+4200
	14:38	Saul t said, "Come here,	2256
	25: 8	T be favorable toward my young men,	2256
2Sa	6: 7	t God struck him down and he died there	2256
	12:10	Now, t, the sword will never depart	2256
	22:50	T I will praise you, O LORD,	4027+6584
1Ki	5: 5	t, to build a temple for the Name of	2256
	13:22	T your body will not be buried in the tomb	NIH
	20:42	T it is your life for his life,	2256
	22:19	"T hear the word of the LORD:	2256
2Ki	1: 4	T this is what the LORD says:	4027+4200
	1: 6	T you will not leave the bed	4027+4200
	12: 7	T King Joash summoned Jehoiada	2256
	17: 4	T Shalmaneser seized him and put him	2256
	17:20	T the LORD rejected all the people	2256
	19: 4	T pray for the remnant that still survives."	2256
	19:32	"T this is what the LORD says	4027+4200
	21:12	T this is what the LORD,	4027+4200
	22:20	T I will gather you to your fathers,	4027+4200
1Ch	22: 5	T I will make preparations for it."	5528
2Ch	1:12	t wisdom and knowledge will be given you.	NIH
	2: 7	t, a man skilled to work in gold and silver,	6964
	12: 5	t, I now abandon you to Shishak.' "	2256
	18:18	"T hear the word of the LORD:	4027+4200
	24: 6	T the king summoned Jehoiada	2256
	28: 5	T the LORD his God handed him over to	2256
	29: 8	T, the anger of the LORD has fallen	2256
	32:25	t the LORD's wrath was on him and	2256
	32:26	t the LORD's wrath did not come	2256
Ezr	9:12	T, do not give your daughters in marriage	6964
Ne	4:13	T I stationed some of the people behind	2256
	6: 6	and t you are building the wall.	4027+6584
	7:65	The governor, t, ordered them not	2256
	9:17	T you did not desert them,	2256
	9:32	"Now t, O our God, the great,	2256
	13:15	T I warned them against selling food on	2256
Est	1:19	"T, if it pleases the king,	NIH
	3: 4	T they told Haman about it	2256
	9:26	(T these days were called Purim,	4027+6584
Job	7:11	"T I will not keep silent;	1685
	10: 1	t I will give free rein to my complaint	NIH
	17: 4	t you will not let them triumph.	4027+6584
	32:10	"T I say: Listen to me;	4027+4200
	37:24	T, men revere him, for does he	4027+4200
	42: 6	T I despise myself and repent in dust	4027+6584
Ps	1: 5	T the wicked will not stand in	4027+6584
	2:10	T, you kings, be wise;	6964
	16: 9	T my heart is glad and my tongue	4027+4200
	18:49	T I will praise you among the nations,	4027+6584
	25: 8	t he instructs sinners in his ways.	4027+6584
	32: 6	T let everyone who is godly pray to	2296+6584
	42: 6	t I will remember you from the land of	4027+6584
	45: 7	t God, your God, has set you	4027+6584
	45:17	t the nations will praise you for ever	4027+6584
	46: 2	T we will not fear,	4027+6584
	73: 6	T pride is their necklace;	4027+4200
	73:10	T their people turn to them and drink	4027+4200
	106:40	T the LORD was angry with his people	2256
	110: 7	t he will lift up his head.	4027+6584
	116:10	I believed; t I said, "I am greatly afflicted."	3954
	119:104	t I hate every wrong path.	4027+6584
	119:119	t I love your statutes.	4027+4200
	119:129	statutes are wonderful; t I obey them.	4027+6584
	130: 4	t you are feared.	5100
Pr	4: 7	Wisdom is supreme; t get wisdom.	NIH
	6:15	T disaster will overtake him	4027+6584
Ecc	5: 7	T stand in awe of God.	3954
	7:14	T, a man cannot discover	1826+6584+8611
Isa	1:24	T the Lord, the LORD Almighty,	4027+4200
	3:17	T the Lord will bring sores on the heads of	2256
	5:13	T my people will go into exile	4027+4200
	5:14	T the grave enlarges its appetite	4027+4200
	5:24	T, as tongues of fire lick up straw and	4027+4200
	5:25	T the LORD's anger burns	4027+4200
	7:14	T the Lord himself will give you a sign:	4027+4200
	8: 7	t the Lord is about to bring against	4027+4200
	9:17	T the Lord will take no pleasure in	4027+6584
	10:16	T, the Lord, the LORD Almighty,	4027+4200
	10:24	T, this is what the Lord,	4027+4200
	13:13	T I will make the heavens tremble;	4027+6584
	15: 4	T the armed men of Moab cry out,	4027+4200
	16: 7	T the Moabites wail,	4027+4200

Isa	17:10	T, though you set out the finest plants	4027+6584
	22: 4	T I said, "Turn away from me;	4027+6584
	24: 6	T a curse consumes the earth;	4027+6584
	24: 6	T earth's inhabitants are burned up,	4027+6584
	24:15	T in the east give glory to the LORD;	4027+6584
	25: 3	T strong peoples will honor you;	4027+6584
	28:14	T hear the word of the LORD,	4027+4200
	29:14	T once more I will astound these	4027+4200
	29:22	T this is what the LORD,	4027+4200
	30: 7	T I call her Rahab the Do-Nothing.	4027+4200
	30:12	T, this is what the Holy One of Israel	4027+4200
	30:16	T you will flee!	4027+6584
	30:16	T your pursuers will be swift!	4027+4200
	37: 4	T pray for the remnant that still survives."	2256
	37:33	"T this is what the LORD says	4027+4200
	48: 5	T I told you these things long ago;	2256
	50: 7	T have I set my face like flint,	4027+6584
	51:21	T hear this, you afflicted one,	4027+4200
	52: 6	T my people will know my name;	4027+4200
	52: 6	t in that day they will know	4027+4200
	53:12	T I will give him a portion among	4027+4200
	65:13	T this is what the Sovereign LORD	4027+4200
Jer	2: 9	"T I bring charges against you again,"	4027+4200
	3: 3	T the showers have been withheld,	2256
	4:28	T the earth will mourn and	2296+6584
	5: 6	T a lion from the forest will attack	4027+6584
	5:14	T this is what the LORD God	4027+4200
	6:18	T hear, O nations;	4027+4200
	6:21	T this is what the LORD says:	4027+4200
	7:14	T, what I did to Shiloh I will now do to	2256
	7:20	" 'T this is what the Sovereign LORD	4027+4200
	7:28	T say to them,	2256
	8:10	T I will give their wives to other men	4027+4200
	9: 7	T this is what the LORD Almighty	4027+4200
	9:15	T, this is what the LORD Almighty,	4027+4200
	11:11	T this is what the LORD says:	4027+4200
	11:21	T this is what the LORD says about	4027+4200
	11:22	t this is what the LORD Almighty says:	4027+4200
	12: 8	She roars at me; t I hate her.	4027+6584
	14:15	T, this is what the LORD says about	4027+4200
	14:22	T our hope is in you,	2256
	15:19	T this is what the LORD says:	4027+4200
	16:21	"T I will teach them—	2256
	18:11	"Now t say to the people of Judah	2256
	18:13	T this is what the LORD says:	4027+4200
	22:18	T this is what the LORD says	4027+4200
	23: 2	T this is what the LORD,	4027+4200
	23:12	"T their path will become slippery;	4027+4200
	23:15	T, this is what the LORD Almighty	4027+4200
	23:30	"T," declares the LORD,	4027+4200
	23:39	T, I will surely forget you and	4027+4200
	25: 8	T the LORD Almighty says this:	4027+4200
	27:15	T, I will banish you and you will perish,	5100
	28:16	T, this is what the LORD says:	4027+4200
	29:20	T, hear the word of the LORD,	2256
	29:28	T build houses and settle down;	NIH
	31:20	T my heart yearns for him;	4027+6584
	32:28	T, this is what the LORD says:	4027+4200
	34:17	"T, this is what the LORD says:	4027+4200
	35:17	"T, this is what the LORD God	4027+4200
	35:19	T, this is what the LORD Almighty,	4027+4200
	36:30	T, this is what the LORD says	4027+4200
	44: 6	T, my fierce anger was poured out;	2256
	44:11	"T, this is what the LORD Almighty,	4027+4200
	48:31	T I wail over Moab, for all Moab I cry	4027+6584
	49:20	T, hear what the LORD has planned	4027+4200
	50:18	T this is what the LORD Almighty,	4027+4200
	50:30	T, her young men will fall in the	4027+4200
	50:45	T, hear what the LORD has planned	4027+4200
	51: 7	t they have now gone mad.	4027+6584
	51:36	T, this is what the LORD says:	4027+4200
La	3:21	this I call to mind and t I have hope:	4027+6584
	3:24	t I will wait for him."	4027+6584
Eze	5: 7	"T this is what the Sovereign LORD	4027+4200
	5: 8	"T this is what the Sovereign LORD	4027+4200
	5:10	T in your midst fathers will eat their children,	4027+4200
	5:11	T as surely as I live,	4027+4200
	7:20	T I will turn these into an unclean	4027+6584
	8:18	T I will deal with them in anger;	1685+2256
	11: 4	T prophesy against them;	4027+4200
	11: 7	"T this is what the Sovereign LORD	4027+4200
	11:16	"T say: 'This is what the Sovereign	4027+4200
	11:17	"T say: 'This is what the Sovereign	4027+4200
	12: 3	"T, son of man, pack your belongings	2256
	12:28	T say to them, 'This is what	4027+4200
	13: 8	" 'T this is what the Sovereign LORD	4027+4200
	13:11	t tell those who cover it with whitewash	NIH
	13:13	" 'T this is what the Sovereign LORD	4027+4200
	13:20	" 'T this is what the Sovereign LORD	4027+4200
	13:23	t you will no longer see false visions	4027+4200
	14: 4	T speak to them and tell them,	4027+4200
	14: 6	"T say to the house of Israel,	4027+4200
	15: 6	"T this is what the Sovereign LORD	4027+4200
	16:35	"T, you prostitute, hear the word of	4027+4200
	16:37	t I am going to gather all your lovers,	4027+4200
	16:50	T I did away with them as you have seen.	2256
	17:19	" 'T this is what the Sovereign LORD	4027+4200
	18:30	"T, O house of Israel, I will judge you,	4027+4200
	20:10	T I led them out of Egypt	2256
	20:27	"T, son of man, speak to the people	4027+4200
	20:30	"T say to the house of Israel:	4027+4200
	21: 6	"T groan, son of man!	2256
	21:12	T beat your breast.	4027+4200
	21:24	"T this is what the Sovereign LORD	4027+4200
	22: 4	T I will make you an object of scorn	4027+6584
	22:19	T this is what the Sovereign LORD	4027+4200

Eze	23: 9	"T I handed her over to her lovers,	4027+4200
	23:22	"T, Oholibah, this is what	4027+4200
	23:35	"T this is what the Sovereign LORD	4027+4200
	24: 9	" 'T this is what the Sovereign LORD	4027+4200
	25: 4	t I am going to give you to the people	4027+4200
	25: 7	t I will stretch out my hand against you	4027+4200
	25: 9	t I will expose the flank of Moab,	4027+4200
	25:13	t this is what the Sovereign LORD	4027+4200
	25:16	t this is what the Sovereign LORD	4027+4200
	26: 3	"T this is what the Sovereign LORD	4027+4200
	28: 6	" 'T this is what the Sovereign LORD	4027+4200
	29: 8	" 'T this is what the Sovereign LORD	4027+4200
	29:10	t I am against you and	4027+4200
	29:19	T this is what the Sovereign LORD	4027+4200
	30:22	T this is what the Sovereign LORD	4027+4200
	31:10	"T this is what the Sovereign LORD	4027+4200
	31:14	T no other trees by the waters are ever	5100
	33:12	"T, son of man, say to your countrymen,	2256
	33:25	T say to them, 'This is what	4027+4200
	34: 7	" 'T, you shepherds, hear the word of	4027+4200
	34: 9	t, O shepherds, hear the word of	4027+4200
	34:20	" 'T this is what the Sovereign LORD	4027+4200
	35: 6	t as surely as I live,	
	35:11	t as surely as I live,	
	36: 3	T prophesy and say, 'This is what	4027+4200
	36: 4	t, O mountains of Israel, hear the word	4027+4200
	36: 6	T prophesy concerning the land of Israel	4027+4200
	36: 7	T this is what the Sovereign LORD	4027+4200
	36:14	t you will no longer devour men	4027+4200
	36:22	"T say to the house of Israel,	4027+4200
	37:12	T prophesy and say to them:	4027+4200
	38:14	"T, son of man, prophesy and say	4027+4200
	39:25	"T this is what the Sovereign LORD	4027+4200
	44:12	t I have sworn with uplifted hand	4027+6584
Da	3: 7	T, as soon as they heard	10180+10353+10619
	3:29	T I decree that the people of any nation	10221
	4:27	T, O king, be pleased to accept my advice:	10385
	5:24	T he sent the hand that wrote	10008+10089
	9:11	"T the curses and sworn judgments written	2256
	9:23	T, consider the message and understand	2256
Hos	2: 6	T I will block her path with thornbushes;	4027+4200
	2: 9	"T I will take away my grain	4027+4200
	2:14	"T I am now going to allure her;	4027+4200
	4:13	T your daughters turn to prostitution	4027+6584
	6: 5	T I cut you in pieces with my prophets	4027+6584
	10: 4	t lawsuits spring up like poisonous weeds	2256
	13: 3	T they will be like the morning mist,	4027+4200
Am	3: 2	t I will punish you for all your sins."	4027+6584
	3:11	T this is what the Sovereign LORD	4027+4200
	4:12	"T this is what I will do to you, Israel,	4027+4200
	5:11	T, though you have built stone mansions,	3610+4027+4200
	5:13	T the prudent man keeps quiet	4027+4200
	5:16	T this is what the Lord,	4027+4200
	5:27	T I will send you into exile	2256
	6: 7	T you will be among the first to go	4027+4200
	7:17	"T this is what the LORD says:	4027+4200
Mic	1: 6	"T I will make Samaria a heap of rubble,	2256
	1:14	T you will give parting gifts	4027+4200
	2: 3	T, the LORD says:	4027+4200
	2: 5	T you will have no one	4027+4200
	3: 6	T night will come over you,	4027+4200
	3:12	T because of you,	4027+4200
	5: 3	T Israel will be abandoned until	4027+4200
	6:13	T, I have begun to destroy you,	1685+2256
	6:16	T I will give you over to ruin	5100
Hab	1: 4	T the law is paralyzed,	4027+6584
	1:16	T he sacrifices to his net and	4027+6584
Zep	2: 9	T, as surely as I live,"	4027+4200
	3: 8	T wait for me," declares the LORD,	4027+4200
Hag	1:10	T, because of you the heavens have withheld their dew	4027+6584
Zec	1: 3	T tell the people:	2256
	1:16	"T, this is what the LORD says:	4027+4200
	8:19	T love truth and peace."	2256
	10: 2	T the people wander like sheep	4027+6584
Mt	5:23	T, if you are offering your gift at the altar	4036
	5:48	t, as your heavenly Father is perfect.	4036
	6:25	"T I tell you, do not worry about your life,	1328+4047
	6:34	T do not worry about tomorrow,	4036
	7:24	"T everyone who hears these words	4036
	9:38	Ask the Lord of the harvest, t,	4036
	10:16	T be as shrewd as snakes and as innocent	4036
	12:12	T it is lawful to do good on the Sabbath.	6063
	13:52	T every teacher of the law	1328+4047
	18: 4	T, whoever humbles himself	4036
	18:23	"T, the kingdom of heaven is like	1328+4047
	19: 6	T what God has joined together,	4036
	21:40	"T, when the owner of the vineyard comes,	4036
	21:43	"T I tell you that the kingdom of God	1328+4047
	23:20	T, he who swears by the altar swears by it	4036
	23:34	T I am sending you prophets and wise	1328+4047
	24:42	"T keep watch, because you do not know	4036
	25:13	"T keep watch, because you do not know	4036
	28:19	T go and make disciples of all nations,	4036
Mk	10: 9	T what God has joined together,	4036
	11:24	T I tell you, whatever you ask for	1328+4047
	13:35	"T keep watch because you do not know	4036
Lk	1: 3	T, since I myself have carefully investigated everything	NIG
	7:47	T, I tell you, her many sins have been forgiven—	4005+5920
	8:18	T consider carefully how you listen.	4036
	10: 2	Ask the Lord of the harvest, t,	4036

Lk	11:36	T, if your whole body is full of light,	4036
	11:50	T this generation will be held responsible	2671
	12:22	"T I tell you, do not worry about your life,	1328+4047
	23:16	T, I will punish him and then release him."	4036
	23:22	T I will have him punished and	4036
Jn	7: 6	T Jesus told them, "The right time	4036
	9:15	T the Pharisees also asked him	4036
	10: 7	T Jesus said again, "I tell you the truth,	4036
	11:45	T many of the Jews who had come	4036
	11:54	T Jesus no longer moved about publicly	4036
	19:11	T the one who handed me over	1328+4047
	19:32	The soldiers t came and broke the legs of	4036
Ac	1:21	T it is necessary to choose one of	4036
	2:26	T my heart is glad and my tongue	1328+4047
	2:36	"T let all Israel be assured of this:	4036
	5:38	T, in the present case I advise you:	2779
	7:43	T I will send you into exile'	2779
	13:38	"T, my brothers, I want you to know that	4036
	15:19	"It is my judgment, t,	1475
	15:27	T we are sending Judas and Silas	4036
	17:29	"T since we are God's offspring,	4036
	19:36	T, since these facts are undeniable,	4036
	20:26	T, I declare to you today that I am innocent	1484
	25:26	T I have brought him before all of you,	1475
	26: 3	T, I beg you to listen to me patiently.	1475
	28:28	"T I want you to know	4036
Ro	1:24	T God gave them over in the sinful desires	1475
	2: 1	You, t, have no excuse,	1475
	3:20	T no one will be declared righteous	1484
	4:16	T, the promise comes by faith,	1328+4047
	5: 1	T, since we have been justified	4036
	5:12	T, just as sin entered the world	1328+4047
	6: 4	We were t buried with him	4036
	6:12	T do not let sin reign in your mortal body	4036
	8: 1	T, there is now no condemnation	726
	8:12	T, brothers, we have an obligation—	726+4036
	9:16	t, depend on man's desire or effort,	726+4036
	9:18	T God has mercy on whom he wants	726+4036
	11:22	Consider t the kindness and sternness	4036
	12: 1	T, I urge you, brothers,	4036
	13: 5	T, it is necessary to submit to the authorities	1475
	13:10	T love is the fulfillment of the law.	4036
	14:13	T let us stop passing judgment	4036
	14:19	Let us t make every effort to do	726+4036
	15: 9	T I will praise you among the Gentiles	1328+4047
	15:17	T I glory in Christ Jesus in my service	4036
1Co	1: 7	T you do not lack any spiritual gift	6063
	1:31	T, as it is written:	2671
	4: 5	T judge nothing before the appointed time;	6063
	4:16	T I urge you to imitate me.	6063
	5: 8	T let us keep the Festival,	6063
	6: 4	T, if you have disputes about such matters,	4036
	6:20	T honor God with your body.	1314
	8:13	T, if what I eat causes my brother to fall	1478
	9:26	T I do not run like a man running aimlessly;	5523
	10:14	T, my dear friends, flee from idolatry.	1478
	11:27	T, whoever eats the bread or drinks the cup	6063
	12: 3	T I tell you that no one who is speaking by	1475
	14:39	T, my brothers, be eager to prophesy,	6063
	15:58	T, my dear brothers, stand firm.	6063
2Co	2: 8	I urge you, t, to reaffirm your love for him.	1475
	3:12	T, since we have such a hope,	4036
	4: 1	T, since through God's mercy we have this ministry,	1328+4047
	4:13	It is written: "I believed; t I have spoken."	1475
	4:13	of faith we also believe and t speak,	4036
	4:16	T we do not lose heart.	1475
	5: 6	T we are always confident and know that	4036
	5:14	and t all died.	726
	5:17	T, if anyone is in Christ,	6063
	5:20	We are t Christ's ambassadors,	4036
	6:17	"T come out from them and be separate,	1475
	8:24	T show these men the proof of your love	4036
	12: 9	T I will boast all the more gladly	4036
Gal	3:21	t, opposed to the promises of God?	4036
	4:31	T, brothers, we are not children of	1475
	6:10	T, as we have opportunity,	726+4036
Eph	2:11	T, remember that formerly you who are Gentiles by birth	1475
	3:13	t, not to be discouraged because	1475
	4:25	T each of you must put off falsehood	1475
	5: 1	Be imitators of God, t,	4036
	5: 7	T do not be partners with them.	4036
	5:17	T do not be foolish,	1328+4047
	6:13	T put on the full armor of God,	1328+4047
Php	2: 9	T God exalted him to the highest place	1475
	2:12	T, my dear friends, as you have always	6063
	2:23	t, to send him as soon as I see how things	4036
	2:28	T I am all the more eager to send him,	4036
	4: 1	T, my brothers, you whom I love and long	6063
Col	2:16	T do not let anyone judge you	4036
	3: 5	t, whatever belongs to your earthly nature:	4036
	3:12	T, as God's chosen people,	4036
1Th	1: 8	T we do not need to say anything about it,	6063
	3: 7	T, brothers, in all our distress	1328+4047
	4: 8	T, he who rejects this instruction does	5521
	4:18	T encourage each other with these words.	6063
	5:11	T encourage one another	1475
2Th	1: 4	T, among God's churches we boast	6063
2Ti	2:10	T I endure everything for the sake of	1328+4047
Tit	1:13	T, rebuke them sharply,	162+1328+4005
Phm	1: 8	T, although in Christ I could be bold	1475
Heb	1: 9	t God, your God, has set you	1328+4047
	2: 1	We must pay more careful attention, t,	1328+4047
	3: 1	T, holy brothers, who share in	3854
	4: 1	T, since the promise of entering his rest,	4036

Heb	4: 7	T God again set a certain day,	NIG
	4:11	t, make every effort to enter that rest,	4036
	4:14	T, since we have a great high priest,	4036
	6: 1	T let us leave the elementary teachings	1475
	7:25	T he is able to save completely	3854
	10: 5	T, when Christ came into the world,	1475
	10:19	T, brothers, since we have confidence	4036
	11:16	T God is not ashamed to be called their	1475
	12: 1	T, since we are surrounded by such	5521
	12:12	T, strengthen your feeble arms	1475
	12:28	T, since we are receiving a kingdom	1475
	13:15	t, let us continually offer to God a sacrifice	4036
Jas	1:21	T, get rid of all moral filth and the evil	1475
	5:16	T confess your sins to each other and pray	4036
1Pe	1:13	T, prepare your minds for action;	1475
	2: 1	T, rid yourselves of all malice	4036
	4: 1	T, since Christ suffered in his body,	4036
	4: 7	T be clear minded and self-controlled so	4036
	5: 6	Humble yourselves, t,	4036
2Pe	1:10	T, my brothers, be all the more eager	1475
	3:17	T, dear friends, since you already know this,	4036
1Jn	4: 5	They are from the world and t speak	1328+4047
3Jn	1: 8	We ought t to show hospitality	4036
Rev	1:19	"Write, t, what you have seen,	4036
	2:16	Repent t! Otherwise, I will soon come	4036
	3: 3	t, what you have received and heard;	4036
	7:15	T, "they are before the throne of God	1328+4047
	12:12	T rejoice, you heavens and you who	1328+4047
	18: 8	T in one day her plagues will overtake	1328+4047

THESE (1120) [THIS] See Index of Articles Etc.

THESSALONIANS (3) [THESSALONICA]

Ac	17:11	of more noble character than the T,	1877+2553
1Th	1: 1	the church of the T in God the Father and	2552
2Th	1: 1	the church of the T in God our Father and	2552

THESSALONICA (6) [THESSALONIANS]

Ac	17: 1	they came to T, where there was a Jewish	2553
	17:13	in T learned that Paul was preaching	2553
	20: 4	Aristarchus and Secundus from T,	2552
	27: 2	Aristarchus, a Macedonian from T,	2552
Php	4:16	for even when I was in T,	2553
2Ti	4:10	has deserted me and has gone to T.	2553

THEUDAS (1)

Ac	5:36	Some time ago T appeared,	2554

THEY (6563) [THEIR, THEIRS, THEM, THEMSELVES] See Index of Articles Etc.

THICK (28) [THICKER, THICKNESS]

Ge	15:12	a t and dreadful darkness came over him.	1524
Ex	19:16	with a t cloud over the mountain,	3878
	20:21	while Moses approached the t darkness	6906
Jdg	7:12	settled in the valley, t as locusts.	8044
2Sa	18: 9	and as the mule went under the t branches	8449
1Ki	20:39	"Your servant went into the t of the battle,	7931
2Ki	8:15	But the next day he took a t cloth,	4802
Job	3: 6	That night—may t darkness seize it;	694
	15:26	defiantly charging against him with a t,	6295
	22:14	T clouds veil him,	6265
	23:17	by the t darkness that covers my face.	694
	38: 9	and wrapped it in t darkness,	6906
Ps	97: 2	Clouds and t darkness surround him;	6906
Isa	60: 2	the earth and t darkness is over the peoples,	6906
Jer	13:16	to t darkness and change it to deep gloom.	7516
	51:58	"Babylon's t wall will be leveled	8146
	52:21	each was four fingers t, and hollow.	6295
Eze	19:11	It towered high above the t foliage,	6291
	31: 3	its top above the t foliage.	6291
	31:10	lifting its top above the t foliage,	6291
	31:14	lifting their tops above the t foliage.	6291
	40: 5	it was one measuring rod t	8145
	40: 7	between the alcoves were five cubits t.	NIH
	40: 9	and its jambs were two cubits t.	NIH
	41: 5	the wall of the temple; it was six cubits t,	NIH
	41: 9	of the side rooms was five cubits t.	8145
	41:12	of the building was five cubits t all around,	8145
Rev	21:17	its wall and it was 144 cubits t,	NIG

THICKER (2) [THICK]

1Ki	12:10	'My little finger is t than my father's waist.	6286
2Ch	10:10	'My little finger is t than my father's waist.	6286

THICKET (6) [THICKETS]

Ge	22:13	Abraham looked up and there in a t he saw	6019
Job	38:40	in their dens or lie in wait in a t?	6109
Ps	74: 5	like men wielding axes to cut through a t	6020
Hos	2:12	I will make them a t,	6019
Am	3: 4	a lion roar in the t when he has no prey?	3623
Zec	11: 3	the lush t of the Jordan is ruined!	1454

THICKETS (11) [THICKET]

1Sa	13: 6	they hid in caves and t, among the rocks,	2560
Isa	9:18	it sets the forest t ablaze,	6019
	10:34	He will cut down the forest t with an ax;	6019
	17: 9	will be like places abandoned to t	3091
	21:13	who camp in the t of Arabia,	3623

Jer	4:29	Some go into the t;	6266
	12: 5	how will you manage in the t by	1454
	26:18	the temple hill a mound overgrown with t.'	3623
	49:19	"Like a lion coming up from Jordan's t to	1454
	50:44	Like a lion coming up from Jordan's t to	1454
Mic	3:12	the temple hill a mound overgrown with t.	3623

THICKNESS (2) [THICK]

1Ki	7:26	It was a handbreadth in t,	6295
2Ch	4: 5	It was a handbreadth in t,	6295

THIEF (23) [THEFT, THEFTS, THIEVES]

Ex	22: 2	"If a t is caught breaking in and is struck	1705
	22: 3	"A t must certainly make restitution,	NIH
	22: 7	the t, if he is caught, must pay back	1705
	22: 8	But if the t is not found,	1705
Job	24:14	in the night he steals forth like a t.	1705
Ps	50:18	When you see a t, you join with him;	1705
Pr	6:30	a t if he steals to satisfy his hunger	1705
	29:24	The accomplice of a t is his own enemy;	1705
Jer	2:26	"As a t is disgraced when he is caught,	1705
Zec	5: 3	every t will be banished,	1704
	5: 4	and it will enter the house of the t and	1705
Mt	24:43	at what time of night the t was coming,	3095
Lk	12:33	no t comes near and no moth destroys.	3095
	12:39	at what hour the t was coming,	3095
Jn	10: 1	by some other way, is a t and a robber.	3095
	10:10	t comes only to steal and kill and destroy;	3095
	12: 6	about the poor but because he was a t;	3095
1Th	5: 2	of the Lord will come like a t in the night.	3095
	5: 4	that this day should surprise you like a t.	3095
1Pe	4:15	not be as a murderer or t or any other kind	3095
2Pe	3:10	But the day of the Lord will come like a t.	3095
Rev	3: 3	if you do not wake up, I will come like a t,	3095
	16:15	"Behold, I come like a t!	3095

THIEVES (11) [THIEF]

Job	30: 5	shouted at as if they were t.	1705
Isa	1:23	Your rulers are rebels, companions of t;	1705
Jer	48:27	Was she caught among t,	1705
	49: 9	If t came during the night,	1705
Hos	7: 1	They practice deceit, t break into houses,	1705
Joel	2: 9	like t they enter through the windows.	1705
Ob	1: 5	"If t came to you, if robbers in the night—	1705
Mt	6:19	and where t break in and steal.	3095
	6:20	and where t do not break in and steal.	3095
Jn	10: 8	All who ever came before me were t.	3095
1Co	6:10	nor t nor the greedy nor drunkards	3095

THIGH (22) [THIGHS]

Ge	24: 2	"Put your hand under my t."	3751
	24: 9	the t of his master Abraham and swore	3751
	47:29	put your hand under my t and promise	3751
Ex	28:42	reaching from the waist to the t.	3751
	29:22	kidneys with the fat on them, and the right t.	8797
	29:27	the breast that was waved and the t	8797
Lev	7:32	the right t of your fellowship offerings to	8797
	7:33	the right t as his share.	8797
	7:34	the t that is presented and have given them	8797
	8:25	both kidneys and their fat and the right t.	8797
	8:26	on the fat portions and on the right t.	8797
	9:21	Aaron waved the breasts and the right t	8797
	10:14	the breast that was waved and the t	8797
	10:15	The t that was presented and the breast	8797
Nu	5:21	and denounce you when he causes your t	3751
	5:22	and your t wastes away."	3751
	5:27	and her t waste away,	3751
	6:20	with the breast that was waved and the t	8797
	18:18	the wave offering and the right t are yours.	8797
Jdg	3:16	he strapped to his right t under his clothing,	3751
	3:21	the sword from his right t and plunged it	3751
Rev	19:16	and on his t he has this name written:	3611

THIGHS (2) [THIGH]

Job	40:17	the sinews of his t are close-knit.	7066
Da	2:32	its belly and t of bronze,	10334

THIMNATHAH (KJV) See TIMNAH

THIN (8)

Ge	41: 6	t and scorched by the east wind.	1987
	41: 7	The t heads of grain swallowed up	1987
	41:23	and t and scorched by the east wind.	1987
	41:24	The t heads of grain swallowed up	1987
Ex	16:14	t flakes like frost on the ground appeared	1987
	39: 3	They hammered out t sheets of gold	7063
Lev	13:30	and the hair in it is yellow and t,	1987
Ps	109:24	my body is t and gaunt.	3950

THING (148) [SOMETHING, THINGS]

Ge	1:21	and moving t with which the water teems,	5883
	7:16	and female of every living t,	1414
	7:21	Every living t that moved on the earth	1414
	7:23	Every living t on the face of the earth	3685
	18:25	Far be it from you to do such a t—	1821
	19: 7	Don't do this wicked t.	8317
	30:31	"But if you will do this one t for me,	1821
	31:28	You have done a foolish t.	AIT
	32:19	the same t to Esau when you meet him.	1821
	34: 2	a disgraceful t in Israel by lying	5576
	34: 7	t that should not be done.	AIT
	34:14	They said to them, "We can't do such a t;	1821

Ge	39: 9	How then could I do such a wicked t	8288
	44: 5	This is a wicked t you have done.' "	AIT
	44:17	"Far be it from me to do such a t!	AIT
Ex	33:17	"I will do the very t you have asked,	1821
Lev	7:21	or any unclean, detestable t—	AIT
	11:46	every living t that moves in the water	5883
	22: 5	or if he touches any crawling t	9238
	22: 6	The one who touches any such t will	2257S
Dt	7:26	not bring a detestable t into your house	9359
	9:21	Also I took that sinful t of yours,	2633
	11: 6	and every living t that belonged to them.	3685
	13:11	among you will do such an evil t again	1821
	13:14	that this detestable t has been done	9359
	14: 3	Do not eat any detestable t.	9359
	17: 4	that this detestable t has been done	9359
	19:20	and never again will such an evil t be done	1821
	22:21	She has done a disgraceful t in Israel	5576
	27:15	a t detestable to the LORD,	9359
	28:25	a t of horror to all the kingdoms on earth.	2400
	28:37	a t of horror and an object of scorn	9014
Jos	6:21	with the sword every living t in it—	889S
	7:15	and has done a disgraceful t in Israel!' "	5576
Jdg	6: 4	and did not spare a living t for Israel,	4695
	13:19	the LORD did an amazing t while Manoah	AIT
	19:23	don't do this disgraceful t.	5576
	19:24	don't do such a disgraceful t."	1821
	19:30	"Such a t has never been seen or done,	2296S
	20: 6	"Tell us how this awful t happened."	8288
1Sa	9:21	Why do you say such a t to me?"	1821
	12:16	stand still and see this great t the LORD	1821
	12:17	an evil t you did in the eyes of the LORD	8288
	24: 6	a t to my master, the LORD's anointed,	1821
	25:30	for my master every good t he promised	3208
	27: 1	The best t I can do is to escape to the land	AIT
2Sa	3:13	But I demand one t of you:	1821
	7:21	you have done this great t and	1525
	11:11	surely as you live, I will not do such a t!"	1821
	11:27	t David had done displeased the LORD.	1821
	12: 6	because he did such a t and had no pity.	1821
	12:12	but I will do this t in broad daylight	1821
	13:12	Such a t should not be done in Israel!	AIT
	13:12	Don't do this wicked t.	5576
	13:20	Don't take this t to heart."	1821
	14:13	then have you devised a t like this against	NIH
	24: 3	the king want to do such a t?"	1821
	24:10	I have done a very foolish t."	6118
1Ki	9: 8	the LORD done such a t to this land and	AIT
	12:30	And this t became a sin;	1821
	22:12	other prophets were prophesying the same t.	AIT
2Ki	2:10	"You have asked a difficult t,"	AIT
	3:18	This is an easy t in the eyes of the LORD;	AIT
	5:13	prophet had told you to do some great t,	1821
	5:16	whom I serve, I will not accept a t."	NIH
	5:18	forgive your servant for this one t:	1821
1Ch	17:19	you have done this great t	1525
	21: 8	I have done a very foolish t."	6118
2Ch	7:21	the LORD done such a t to this land and	3970
	16: 9	You have done a foolish t,	6118
	18:11	other prophets were prophesying the same t.	AIT
Ezr	10:13	because we have sinned greatly in this t.	1821
Ne	13: 7	about the evil t Eliashib had done	8288
	13:17	"What is this wicked t you are doing—	1821
Est	7: 5	the man who has dared to do such a t?"	1821
	8: 5	with favor and thinks it the right t to do,	1821
Job	28:21	from the eyes of every living t,	2645
	39: 8	for his pasture and searches for any green t.	3728
Ps	16: 2	apart from you I have no good t."	3208
	27: 4	One t I ask of the LORD,	AIT
	34:10	those who seek the LORD lack no good t.	AIT
	62:11	One t God has spoken,	AIT
	84:11	no good t does he withhold from those	AIT
	101: 3	I will set before my eyes no vile t.	1821
	105:35	they ate up every green t in their land,	6912
	145:16	and satisfy the desires of every living t.	AIT
Ecc	7:11	is a good t and benefits those who see	AIT
	7:27	"Adding one t to another to discover	AIT
	12:14	including every hidden t,	AIT
Isa	43:19	See, I am doing a new t!	AIT
	44:19	a detestable t from what is left?	9359
	44:20	"Is not this t in my right hand a lie?"	NIH
	49: 6	"It is too small a t for you to	AIT
	52:11	Touch no unclean t!	AIT
	64: 4	Who has ever heard of such a t?	2296S
Jer	5:30	"A horrible and shocking t has happened in	9136
	18:13	A most horrible t has been done	9137
	22: 8	'Why has the LORD done such a t	3970
	23:13	of Samaria I saw this repulsive t:	9524
	31:22	The LORD will create a new t on earth—	AIT
	32:35	that they should do such a detestable t	9359
	40:16	"Don't do such a t!	1821
	44: 4	'Do not do this detestable t that I hate!'	1821
La	1:17	Jerusalem has become an unclean t.	5614
Eze	7:19	and their gold will be an unclean t.	5614
	7:20	I will turn these into an unclean t for them.	5614
Da	2:10	has ever asked such a t of any magician	10418
Hos	6:10	I have seen a horrible t in the house	9137
	8: 8	she is among the nations like a worthless t.	3998
	9:10	and became as vile as the t they loved.	171
Mal	2:11	A detestable t has been committed	9359
	2:13	Another t you do:	2296S
Mt	19:16	what good t must I do to get eternal life?"	AIT
	20: 5	and the ninth hour and did the same t.	6058
	21:30	to the other son and said the same t.	6058
	26:10	She has done a beautiful t to me.	2240
	26:44	prayed the third time, saying the same t.	3364
Mk	10:21	"One t you lack," he said.	AIT

Mk	14: 6	She has done a beautiful t to me.	2240
	14:39	he went away and prayed the same t.	3364
Lk	2:15	"Let's go to Bethlehem and see this t	4839
	10:42	but only one t is needed.	AIT
	12:26	Since you cannot do this very little t,	AIT
	18:22	he said to him, "You still lack one t.	AIT
Jn	1:41	The first t Andrew did was to find his	AIT
	9:25	One t I do know. I was blind but now I see!"	AIT
Ac	4:17	to stop this t from spreading any further	NIG
	9:21	What made you think of doing such a t?	4547
	19:32	Some were shouting one t, some another.	5516
	21:34	the crowd shouted one t and some another,	AIT
	24:21	unless it was this one t I shouted as I stood	AIT
Ro	4: 6	David says the same t when he speaks	2749+2779
	7:37	this man also does the right t.	2822
1Co	9: 8	Doesn't the Law say the same t?	NIG
2Co	6:17	Touch no unclean t, and I will receive you."	NIG
Gal	2:10	the very t I was eager to do.	899+4047
	3: 2	I would like to learn just one t from you:	AIT
	5: 6	The only t that counts is faith expressing itself through love.	NIG
Php	1:18	The important t is that in every way,	4440
	3:13	But one t I do: Forgetting what is behind	AIT
Phm	1: 6	of every good t we have in Christ.	AIT
	1: 6	and one t more: Prepare a guest room	275
Heb	10:29	who has treated as an unholy t the blood	AIT
	10:31	It is a dreadful t to fall into the hands of	AIT
2Pe	2:16	But do not forget this one t, dear friends:	AIT
Rev	3:17	I have acquired wealth and do not need a t.'	4029
	16: 3	and every living t in the sea died.	6034

THINGS (598) [THING]

Ge	20: 9	You have done t to me that should not	5126
	24:10	taking with him all kinds of good t	3206
	24:28	told her mother's household about these t.	1821
	29:13	and there Jacob told him all these t.	1821
	41:13	And t turned out exactly	AIT
	44: 7	"Why does my lord say such t?	1821
	44:15	find t out by divination?"	5727+5727
	45:23	ten donkeys loaded with the best t	3206
Ex	7:11	the Egyptian magicians also did the same t	AIT
	7:22	But the Egyptian magicians did the same t	AIT
	8: 7	But the magicians did the same t	AIT
	18: 9	the good t the LORD had done for Israel	3208
	21:11	not provide her with these three t,	AIT
	35: 1	the t the LORD has commanded you	1821
Lev	2: 8	Bring the grain offering made of these t to	AIT
	5:15	in regard to any of the LORD's holy t,	7731
	5:16	failed to do in regard to the holy t,	7731
	6: 7	of these t he did that made him guilty."	3972S
	9: 5	They took the t Moses commanded	889
	10:19	but such t as this have happened to me.	AIT
	11:10	among all the swarming t or among all	9238
	15:10	and whoever touches any of the t	AIT
	15:10	up those t must wash his clothes and bathe	4392S
	15:31	separate from t that make them unclean,	3240
	18:26	not do any of these detestable t,	9359
	18:27	for all these t were done by the people	9359S
	18:29	who does any of these detestable t—	9359
	20:23	they did all these t, I abhorred them.	AIT
	26:23	of these t you do not accept my correction	AIT
Nu	4: 4	the care of the most holy t.	7731+7731
	4:15	not touch the holy t or they will die.	7731
	4:15	The Kohathites are to carry those t that are	7731
	4:19	near the most holy t, do this for them:	7731+7731
	4:20	not go in to look at the holy t,	7731
	4:26	to do all that needs to be done with these t.	2157S
	4:32	each man the specific t he is to carry.	3998+5466
	7: 9	to carry on their shoulders the holy t,	AIT
	10:21	the Kohathites set out, carrying the holy t.	5219
	10:29	the LORD has promised good t to Israel."	AIT
	10:32	we will share with you whatever good t	2085S
	14:28	I will do to you the very t I heard you say:	889+3869+4027
	14:35	and I will surely do these t to this whole	AIT
	15:13	who is native-born must do these t	AIT
	16:28	the LORD has sent me to do all these t	5126
Dt	4: 9	the t your eyes have seen or let them slip	1821
	4:19	and worshiping t the LORD your God has	4392S
	4:30	in distress and all these t have happened	1821
	4:34	the t the LORD your God did for you	889
	4:35	You were shown these t so	NIH
	6:11	with all kinds of good t you did	3206
	11: 3	and the t he did in the heart of Egypt, both	5126
	11: 7	that saw all these great t the LORD has done.	5126
	12:26	But take your consecrated t and	7731
	12:31	all kinds of detestable t the LORD hates.	9359
	13:17	None of those condemned t is to be found	3051
	18:12	Anyone who does these t is detestable to	AIT
	20:18	to follow all the detestable t they do	9359
	25:16	your God detests anyone who does these t,	AIT
	26:11	the good t the LORD your God has given	AIT
	29:29	The secret t belong to the LORD our God,	AIT
	29:29	but the t revealed belong to us and	AIT
Jos	3: 5	for tomorrow the LORD will do amazing t	AIT
	6:18	But keep away from the devoted t;	3051
	7: 1	unfaithfully in regard to the devoted t;	3051
	7:11	They have taken some of the devoted t;	3051
	7:15	He who is caught with the devoted t shall	3051
	7:23	They took the t from the tent,	4392S
	9: 1	of the Jordan heard about these t	NIH
	22:20	the devoted t, did not wrath come upon	3051
	24:26	And Joshua recorded these t in the Book of	1821
	24:29	After these t, Joshua son of Nun,	1821
Jdg	2: 4	the angel of the LORD had spoken these t	1821
	2: 7	the great t the LORD had done for Israel.	5126

Jdg	8:35	for all the **good** t he had done for them.	3208
	13:23	nor shown us all **these** t or told us this."	AIT
	18: 8	**"How** did you **find** t?"	4537
1Sa	2:23	he said to them, "Why do you do such t?	1821
	12:24	what **great** t *he has* done for you.	1540
	16: 7	not look at the t man looks at.	889
	17:22	David left his t with the keeper of supplies,	3998
	18:26	When the attendants told David these **t,**	1821
	21: 5	The men's t are holy even on missions	3998
	25:37	his wife told him all these **t,**	1821
	26:25	*you will* do great t and surely triumph.	6913+6913
2Sa	7:28	and you have promised these **good** t	3208
1Ki	2:15	But t changed, and the kingdom has gone	AIT
	7:47	Solomon left all these t unweighed,	3998
	7:51	t his father David had **dedicated**—	7731
	8:66	joyful and glad in heart for all the **good** t	3208
	10: 7	But I did not believe these t until I came	1821
	16: 7	provoking him to anger by the t he **did**	3338+5126
	16:27	what he did and the t he achieved,	1476S
	18:36	and have done all these t at your command.	1821
	22:45	the t he achieved and his military exploits,	1476S
2Ki	5:24	the t from the servants and put them away	NIH
	7: 8	and took some t from it and hid them also.	NIH
	8: 4	about all the **great** t Elisha has done."	AIT
	9:11	the man and the **sort of t** he says,"	8490
	17: 9	The Israelites secretly did t against	1821
	17:11	They did wicked t that provoked the LORD	1821
	17:15	the t the LORD had forbidden them to do.	NIH
	18:27	to say these t, and not to the men sitting on	1821
	23:16	by the man of God who foretold these t.	1821
	23:17	the altar of Bethel the very t you have done	1821
	23:24	the other **detestable** t seen in Judah	9199
	24: 3	Surely *these* t happened to Judah according	AIT
1Ch	2: 7	by violating the ban on taking **devoted** t.	3051
	17:26	You have promised these **good** t	3208
	23:13	to consecrate the **most holy** t,	7731+7731
	23:28	of all **sacred** t and the performance	7731
	26:20	and the treasuries for the **dedicated** t.	7731
	26:26	of all the treasuries for the t dedicated	7731S
	26:28	the other **dedicated** t were in the care	AIT
	28:12	and for the treasuries for the **dedicated** t	7731
	29:12	you are the ruler of **all** t.	AIT
	29:17	All **these** t I have given willingly and	AIT
2Ch	4: 6	In them the t to be *used for* the burnt	5126
	4:18	All these t that Solomon made amounted	3998
	5: 1	t his father David had **dedicated**—	7731
	7:10	the **good** t the LORD had done for David	3208
	27: 7	all his wars and the other t he **did,**	2006
	28:21	Ahaz **took some of t** from the temple	2745
	31: 6	and a tithe of the **holy** t dedicated to	7731
	31:12	a Levite, was in charge of these **t,**	AIT
	36: 8	Jehoiakim's reign, the **detestable** t he did	9359
Ezr	7: 1	After these **t,** during the reign of	1821
	9: 1	After these t had been done,	1821
	9:12	and eat the **good** t *of* the land and leave it	3206
Ne	1: 4	When I heard these **t,** I sat down and wept.	1821
	4:14	After I **looked** t over,	8011
	9:25	of houses filled with all kinds of **good** t,	3206
	9:36	and the other **good** t it **produces**	3206
	13:18	Didn't your forefathers do *the* **same** t,	AIT
Job	8: 2	"How long will you say **such** t?"	AIT
	12: 3	Who does not know all **these** t?	AIT
	12:22	He reveals the **deep** t of darkness	AIT
	13:20	"Only grant me these **two** t, O God,	AIT
	13:26	For you write down **bitter** t against me	5353
	16: 2	"I have heard **many** t like these;	AIT
	22:18	he who filled their houses with **good** t,	AIT
	28:11	and brings **hidden** t to light.	9502
	31:23	fear of his splendor I could not do such t.	NIH
	33:29	"God does all **these** t to a man—	AIT
	37: 5	he does **great** t beyond our understanding.	AIT
	42: 2	"I know that you can do **all** t;	AIT
	42: 3	Surely I spoke of t I did not understand,	NIH
	42: 3	t too **wonderful** for me to know.	AIT
	42: 7	After the LORD had said these t to Job,	1821
Ps	15: 5	He who does **these** t will never be shaken.	AIT
	35:11	they question me on t I know nothing about.	889
	40: 5	The t you **planned** for us	4742
	42: 4	**These** t I remember as I pour out my soul:	AIT
	50:21	**These** t you have done and I kept silent;	AIT
	62:11	God has spoken, two t have I heard:	2306
	65: 4	with the **good** t *of* your house,	3206
	71:19	O God, you who have done **great** t.	AIT
	78: 2	I will utter **hidden** t, things from of old—	2648
	78: 2	I will utter hidden things, t from of old—	NIH
	87: 3	**Glorious** t are said of you, O city of God:	AIT
	98: 1	for he has done **marvelous** t;	AIT
	103: 5	with **good** t so that your youth is renewed	AIT
	104:25	**living** t both large and small.	2651
	104:28	they are satisfied with **good** t.	AIT
	106:21	who had done **great** t in Egypt,	AIT
	107: 9	and fills the hungry with **good** t.	AIT
	107:43	let him heed **these** t and consider	AIT
	118:15	LORD's right hand has done **mighty t!**	2657
	118:16	The LORD's right hand has done **mighty t!"**	2657
	119:18	Open my eyes that I may see **wonderful** t	AIT
	119:37	Turn my eyes away from **worthless** t;	8736
	119:91	for **all** t serve you.	AIT
	126: 2	"The LORD has done **great** t for them."	AIT
	126: 3	The LORD has done **great** t for us,	AIT
	131: 1	with great matters or t too **wonderful**	AIT
	138: 2	above **all** t your name and your word.	AIT
Pr	1:13	we will get all sorts of **valuable** t	2104+3701
	6:16	There are six t the LORD **hates,**	2179S
	8: 6	Listen, for I have **worthy** t to say;	5592
	12:14	fruit of his lips a man is filled with **good** t	AIT
	13: 2	the fruit of his lips a man enjoys **good** t,	AIT

Pr	14:17	A quick-tempered man does **foolish** t,	AIT
	23:33	and your mind imagine **confusing** t.	9337
	30: 7	**"Two** t I ask of you, O LORD;	AIT
	30:15	"There are three t that are never satisfied,	2179S
	30:18	"There are three t that are too amazing	2156S
	30:21	"Under three t the earth trembles,	AIT
	30:24	"Four t on earth are **small,**	2156S
	30:29	"There are three t that are stately	2156S
	31:29	"Many women do **noble** t,	AIT
Ecc	1: 8	All t are wearisome, more than one can say.	1821
	1:14	I have seen all the t that are done under	5126
	2:18	I hated all the t I had toiled for under	6662S
	5: 8	do not be surprised at **such** t;	2914S
	7:25	to search out wisdom and the **scheme of** t	3113
	7:27	to another to discover the **scheme of** t—	3113
	8: 1	Who knows the explanation of t?	1821
	11: 5	the work of God, the Maker of **all** t.	AIT
	11: 9	that for all **these** t God will bring you	AIT
Isa	12: 5	for he has done **glorious** t;	1455
	25: 1	in perfect faithfulness you have done **marvelous** t,	7099
	25: 1	t **planned** long ago.	AIT
	29:16	You turn t upside down,	NIH
	30:10	Tell us **pleasant** t, prophesy illusions.	AIT
	36:12	to say these t, and not to the men sitting on	AIT
	38:16	Lord, by **such** t men live;	2157S
	41:22	Tell us what the **former** t were,	AIT
	41:22	Or declare to us the t *to* come,	AIT
	42: 9	See, the **former** t have taken place,	AIT
	42: 9	and **new** t I declare;	AIT
	42:16	These are the t I will do;	1821
	42:20	You have seen **many** t,	AIT
	43: 9	and proclaimed to us the **former** t?	AIT
	43:18	"Forget the **former** t;	AIT
	44: 9	and the t they **treasure** are worthless.	AIT
	44:21	"Remember **these** t, O Jacob,	AIT
	44:24	I am the LORD, who has made **all** t,	AIT
	45: 7	I, the LORD, do all these t.	AIT
	45:11	Concerning t *to* come, do you question	910
	46: 9	Remember the **former** t, those of long ago;	AIT
	47: 7	But you did not consider **these** t or reflect	AIT
	48: 3	I foretold the **former** t long ago,	AIT
	48: 5	Therefore I told you these t long ago;	NIH
	48: 6	You have heard these t; look at them all.	NIH
	48: 6	"From now on I will tell you of **new** t,	AIT
	48: 6	of **hidden** t unknown to you.	AIT
	48:14	Which of [the idols] has foretold these t?	AIT
	57: 6	In the light of **these** t, should I relent?	AIT
	59: 3	and your tongue mutters **wicked** t.	AIT
	63: 7	the many **good** t he has done for the house	3206
	64: 3	you did **awesome** t that we did not expect,	AIT
	65:17	The **former** t will not be remembered,	AIT
	66: 2	Has not my hand made all **these** t,	AIT
	66: 8	Who has ever seen such t?	465S
	66:17	of pigs and rats and other **abominable** t—	9211
Jer	7:10	safe to do all these **detestable** t?	9359
	7:13	While you were doing all these **t,**	5126
	10:16	for he is the Maker of **all** t,	AIT
	17: 9	The heart is deceitful above **all** t and	AIT
	20: 1	heard Jeremiah prophesying these **t,**	1821
	25:13	that land all the t I have spoken against it,	1821
	26:10	the officials of Judah heard these **t,**	1821
	26:12	and this city all the t you have heard.	1821
	26:20	he prophesied the same t against this city	1821
	27:21	says about the t that are left in the house of	3998
	29:23	For they have done **outrageous** t in Israel;	5576
	29:32	the **good** t I will do for my people,	AIT
	30:15	and many sins I have done **these** t to you.	AIT
	33: 3	and **unsearchable** t you do not know.'	AIT
	33: 9	on earth that hear of all the **good** t I do	3208
	35: 7	you must never have any of these t,	NIH
	38: 4	by the t he is saying to them.	1821
	44:22	and the **detestable** t you did,	9359
	45: 5	Should you then seek **great** t for yourself?	AIT
	51:19	for he is the Maker of **all** t,	AIT
La	3:36	would not the Lord see such t?	NIH
	3:38	that both calamities and **good** t come?	AIT
	5:17	because of **these** t our eyes grow dim	AIT
Eze	3:20	The **righteous** t he did will not be	7407
	8: 6	the utterly **detestable** t the house	9359
	8: 6	t far more detestable for me from my sanctuary?	NIH
	8: 6	t *that* are even more **detestable."**	9359
	8: 9	and **detestable** t they are doing here.	9359
	8:10	over the walls all kinds of **crawling** t	8254
	8:13	t *that* are even more **detestable."**	9359
	8:15	t *that* are even more **detestable**	9359
	8:17	to do the **detestable** t they are doing here?	9359
	9: 4	over all the **detestable** t that are done	9359
	12: 7	During the day I brought out my t packed	3998
	12:12	among them will put his t on his shoulder	NIH
	15: 3	they make pegs from it to hang t on?	3972+3998
	16: 5	to do any of these t for you.	AIT
	16:16	*Such t should* not **happen,**	AIT
	16:30	when you do all these **t,**	AIT
	16:43	but enraged me with all these **t,**	AIT
	16:50	They were haughty and did **detestable** t	9359
	16:51	You have done more **detestable** t than they,	9359
	16:51	by all these t you have done.	9359S
	17:12	'Do you not know what **these** t mean?'	AIT
	17:15	Will he who does **such** t escape?	AIT
	17:18	his hand in pledge and yet did all **these** t,	AIT
	18:10	or does any of these **other** t	AIT
	18:12	He does **detestable** t.	9359
	18:13	he has done all these **detestable** t,	9359
	18:14	he does not do such t:	2177
	18:22	of the **righteous** t he has done, he will live.	7407
	18:24	does the same **detestable** t the wicked man	9359

Eze	18:24	None of the **righteous** t he has done will	7407
	22: 8	You have despised my **holy** t	7731
	22:25	and **precious** t and make many widows	3702
	22:26	to my law and profane my **holy** t;	7731
	23:27	You will not look on **these** t with longing	AIT
	24:19	"Won't you tell us what **these** t have to do	AIT
	33:13	none of the **righteous** t he has done	7407
	33:26	rely on your sword, you do **detestable** t,	9359
	33:29	of all the **detestable** t they have done.'	9359
	35:12	the **contemptible** t you have said against	5542
	36:22	that I am going to do these **t,**	NIH
	44: 8	your duty in regard to my **holy** t,	7731
	44:13	as priests or come near any of my **holy** t	7731
Da	2: 9	to tell me misleading and wicked **t,**	10418
	2:22	He reveals deep and **hidden** t;	AIT
	2:29	O king, your mind turned to t to come,	10408
	2:40	and as iron breaks t to pieces,	NIH
	7:16	and gave me the interpretation of these **t:**	10418
	11:36	above every god and will say **unheard-of** t	AIT
	12: 6	be before these **astonishing** t are fulfilled?"	7099
	12: 7	all these t will be completed."	AIT
Hos	8:12	I wrote for them the **many** t of my law,	AIT
	14: 9	He will realize these t.	AIT
Joel	2:20	Surely he has done **great** t.	AIT
	2:21	Surely the LORD has done **great** t.	AIT
Am	9:12	declares the LORD, who will do **these** t.	AIT
Mic	2: 6	"Do not prophesy about **these** t;	AIT
	2: 7	Does he do **such** t?"	AIT
Hag	2:13	with a dead body touches one of **these** t,	AIT
	2:15	how t were before one stone was laid	NIH
Zec	3: 8	who are men **symbolic of** t to come:	4603
	4:10	"Who despises the day of **small** t?"	AIT
	8:12	I will give all **these** t as an inheritance to	AIT
	8:16	These are the t you are to do:	1821
Mal	3:13	"You *have* said harsh t against me,"	AIT
	4: 3	of your feet on the day when I do these **t,"**	NIH
Mt	6:32	For the pagans run after all **these** t,	AIT
	6:33	and all **these** t will be given to you as well.	AIT
	7:28	When Jesus had finished saying these **t,**	AIT
	11:25	because you have hidden **these** t from	AIT
	11:27	**"All** t have been committed to me	AIT
	12:35	The good man brings **good** t out of	AIT
	12:35	and the evil man brings **evil** t out of	AIT
	13: 3	he told them **many** t in parables, saying:	AIT
	13:34	Jesus spoke all **these** t to the crowd	AIT
	13:35	I will utter t **hidden** since the creation of	AIT
	13:51	"Have you understood all **these** t?"	AIT
	13:56	Where then did this man get all **these** t?"	AIT
	15:18	But the t that come out of the mouth come	AIT
	16:21	and suffer **many** t at the hands of the elders,	AIT
	16:23	you do not have in mind **the** t of God,	AIT
	16:23	but the t of men."	AIT
	17:11	Elijah comes and will restore **all** t.	AIT
	18: 7	because of t that cause people to sin!	4998
	18: 7	**Such** t must come, but woe to	3836+4998S
	19: 1	When Jesus had finished saying these **t,**	AIT
	19:26	but with God **all** t are possible."	AIT
	19:28	"I tell you the truth, at the renewal of all **t,**	NIG
	21:15	of the law saw the **wonderful** t he did and	AIT
	21:23	"By what authority are you doing **these** t?"	AIT
	21:24	by what authority I am doing **these** t.	AIT
	21:27	by what authority I am doing **these** t."	AIT
	24: 2	"Do you see all **these** t?"	AIT
	24: 6	Such t must happen, but the end is still	NIG
	24:33	Even so, when you see all **these** t,	AIT
	24:34	until all **these** t have happened.	AIT
	25:21	You have been faithful with a **few** t;	AIT
	25:21	I will put you in charge of **many** t.	AIT
	25:23	You have been faithful with a **few** t;	AIT
	25:23	I will put you in charge of **many** t.	AIT
	26: 1	When Jesus had finished saying all **these** t,	AIT
Mk	2: 8	"Why are you thinking **these** t?	AIT
	4: 2	He taught them **many** t by parables,	AIT
	4:19	and the desires for **other** t come in and choke	AIT
	6: 2	"Where did this man get **these** t?"	AIT
	6:34	So he began teaching them **many** t.	AIT
	7:13	And you do **many** t like that."	AIT
	8:31	that the Son of Man must suffer **many** t and	AIT
	8:33	"You do not have in mind **the** t of God,	AIT
	8:33	but **the** t of men."	AIT
	9:12	Elijah does come first, and restores **all** t.	AIT
	10:27	**all** t are possible with God."	AIT
	11:28	"By what authority are you doing **these** t?"	AIT
	11:29	by what authority I am doing **these** t.	AIT
	11:33	by what authority I am doing **these** t."	AIT
	13: 4	when will **these** t happen?	AIT
	13: 7	Such t must happen, but the end is still	NIG
	13:29	Even so, when you see **these** t happening,	AIT
	13:30	until all **these** t have happened.	AIT
	14:16	and found t just as Jesus had told them.	NIG
	15: 3	The chief priests accused him of **many** t.	AIT
	15: 4	See **how many** t they are accusing you of."	AIT
Lk	1: 1	an account of the t that have been **fulfilled**	4547
	1: 4	the certainty of the t you have been taught.	3364
	1:49	the Mighty One has done **great** t for me—	AIT
	1:53	He has filled the hungry *with* **good** t	AIT
	2:19	But Mary treasured up all **these** t	4839
	2:20	for **all** t they had heard and seen,	AIT
	2:51	his mother treasured all these t in her heart.	4839
	3:19	and all the other **evil** t he had done,	AIT
	5:22	"Why are you thinking **these** t	NIG
	5:26	"We have seen **remarkable** t today."	AIT
	6:45	The good man brings **good** t out of	NIG
	6:45	and the evil man brings evil t out of	NIG
	7:18	John's disciples told him about all **these** t.	AIT
	9: 9	Who, then, is this I hear **such** t about?"	AIT

Column 1

Lk	9:22	"The Son of Man must suffer **many** *t* and	AIT
	9:52	a Samaritan village to get *t* ready for him;	NIG
	10:21	because you have hidden **these** *t* from	AIT
	10:22	**"All** *t* have been committed to me	AIT
	10:41	"you are worried and upset about **many** *t*,	AIT
	11:27	As Jesus was saying **these** *t*,	AIT
	11:45	when you say **these** *t*, you insult us also."	AIT
	12:19	"You have plenty of **good** *t* laid up	AIT
	12:21	be with anyone who stores up *t* for himself	NIG
	12:30	For the pagan world runs after all **such** *t*,	AIT
	12:31	and **these** *t* will be given to you as well.	AIT
	12:48	and does *t* **deserving** punishment will	AIT
	13:17	with all the **wonderful** *t* he was doing.	AIT
	16:25	in your lifetime you received your **good** *t*,	AIT
	16:25	while Lazarus received **bad** *t*,	AIT
	17: 1	"*T* **that** cause people to sin are bound	3836
	17:25	But first he must suffer **many** *t* and	AIT
	20: 2	by what authority you are doing **these** *t*,"	AIT
	20: 8	by what authority I am doing **these** *t*."	AIT
	21: 7	they asked, "when will **these** *t* happen?	AIT
	21: 9	**These** *t* must happen first,	AIT
	21:28	When **these** *t* begin to take place,	AIT
	21:31	Even so, when you see **these** *t* happening,	AIT
	21:32	until **all** **these** *t* have happened.	AIT
	22:13	and found *t* just as Jesus had told them.	NIG
	22:65	they said **many other** insulting *t* to him.	AIT
	23:31	For if men do **these** *t* when the tree is green,	AIT
	23:49	stood at a distance, watching **these** *t*.	AIT
	24: 9	they told all **these** *t* to the Eleven and to all	AIT
	24:15	and discussed **these** *t* with each other,	NIG
	24:18	not know the *t* that have happened there	AIT
	24:19	**"What** *t*?" he asked. **"About** Jesus	AIT
	24:26	Did not the Christ have to suffer **these** *t* and	AIT
	24:48	You are witnesses **of these** *t*.	AIT
Jn	1: 3	Through him **all** *t* were made;	AIT
	1:50	You shall see **greater** *t* than that."	AIT
	3:10	"and do you not understand **these** *t*?	AIT
	3:12	to you of **earthly** *t* and you do not believe;	2103
	3:12	will you believe if I speak of **heavenly** *t*?	2230
	5:16	Jesus was doing **these** *t* on the Sabbath.	AIT
	5:20	he will show him even **greater** *t* than these.	2240
	7: 4	Since you are doing **these** *t*,	AIT
	7:32	the crowd whispering **such** *t* about him.	AIT
	8:39	"then you would do the *t* Abraham did.	2240
	8:40	Abraham did not do **such** *t*.	AIT
	8:41	You are doing the *t* your own father does."	2240
	12:16	that **these** *t* had been written about him and	AIT
	12:16	about him and that they had done **these** *t*	AIT
	13: 3	the Father had put **all** *t* under his power,	AIT
	13:17	Now that you know **these** *t*,	AIT
	14:12	He will do even greater *t* than **these**,	AIT
	14:26	will teach you **all** *t* and will remind you	AIT
	16: 3	They will do **such** *t* because they have	AIT
	16: 6	Because I have said **these** *t*,	AIT
	16:30	Now we can see that you know **all** *t* and	AIT
	16:33	"I have told you **these** *t*,	AIT
	17:13	I say **these** *t* while I am still in the world,	AIT
	19:36	**These** *t* happened so that the scripture	AIT
	20:18	she told them that he had said **these** *t* to her.	AIT
	21:17	He said, "Lord, you know **all** *t*;	AIT
	21:24	This is the disciple who testifies to **these** *t*	AIT
	21:25	Jesus did many **other** *t* as well.	AIT
Ac	5:32	We are witnesses of these *t*,	4839
	7:50	Has not my hand made all **these** *t*?'	AIT
	13:42	about these *t* on the next Sabbath.	4839
	14:15	telling you to turn from these **worthless** *t*	AIT
	15:17	says the Lord, who does **these** *t*'	AIT
	15:29	You will do well to avoid **these** *t*.	AIT
	18:15	I will not be a judge of **such** *t*."	AIT
	24: 9	asserting that **these** *t* were true.	AIT
	26:26	The king is familiar with **these** *t*,	AIT
Ro	1:25	and served **created** *t* rather than the Creator	3232
	1:32	that those who do **such** *t* deserve death,	AIT
	1:32	they not only continue to do **these** very *t* but	AIT
	2: 1	you who pass judgment do the **same** *t*.	AIT
	2: 2	against those who do **such** *t* is based	AIT
	2: 3	judgment on them and yet do the **same** *t*,	AIT
	2:14	do by nature *t* required by the law,	3836
	4:17	to the dead and calls *t* **that** are not as	3836
	6:21	from the *t* you are now ashamed of?	AIT
	6:21	**Those** *t* result in death!	AIT
	8:28	And we know that in **all** *t* God works for	AIT
	8:32	graciously give us **all** *t*?	AIT
	8:37	in all **these** *t* we are more than conquerors	AIT
	10: 5	"The man who does **these** *t* will live	AIT
	11:36	and through him and to him are **all** *t*.	3836+4246
	14:22	So whatever you believe about these *t* keep	NIG
1Co	1:27	But God chose the **foolish** *t* of the world	AIT
	1:27	God chose the **weak** *t* of the world to shame	AIT
	1:28	He chose the **lowly** *t* of this world and	AIT
	1:28	things of this world and the **despised** *t*—	AIT
	1:28	and the *t* that are not—	AIT
	1:28	to nullify the *t* that are,	AIT
	2:10	The Spirit searches **all** *t*,	AIT
	2:10	even the **deep** *t* of God.	AIT
	2:14	not accept the *t* that come from the Spirit	AIT
	2:15	about **all** *t*, but he himself is not subject	AIT
	3: 7	but only God, who makes *t* grow.	NIG
	3:21	no more boasting about men! **All** *t* are yours,	AIT
	4: 1	as those entrusted with the **secret** *t* of God.	AIT
	4: 6	I have applied **these** *t* to myself and Apollos	AIT
	6: 3	How much more the *t* **of this life!**	AIT
	7:31	those who use the *t* of the world,	NIG
	8: 6	from whom **all** *t* came and	3836+4246
	8: 6	through whom **all** *t* came and	AIT
	9:15	in the hope that you will do **such** *t* for me.	4048
	9:22	I have become **all** *t* to all men so that	AIT

Column 2

1Co	10: 6	Now **these** *t* occurred as examples	AIT
	10: 6	from setting our hearts on **evil** *t*	AIT
	10:11	**These** *t* happened to them as examples	AIT
	11:14	Does not the very nature of *t* teach you that	NIG
	14: 7	in the case of **lifeless** *t* that make sounds,	AIT
2Co	5:10	for the *t* done while in the body,	AIT
	9: 8	so that in **all** *t* at all times,	AIT
	10: 7	You are looking only on the surface of *t*.	NIG
	11:12	with us in the *t* they boast about.	AIT
	11:30	of the *t* that show my weakness.	AIT
	12: 4	He heard **inexpressible** *t*,	AIT
	12: 4	*t* that man is not permitted to tell.	4839
	12:12	The *t* that mark an apostle—	AIT
	12:19	This is why I write **these** *t*	AIT
Gal	3:12	man who does **these** *t* will live by them."	AIT
	4:24	**These** *t* may be taken figuratively,	AIT
	5:23	Against **such** *t* there is no law.	AIT
	6: 6	in the word must share all **good** *t* with his	AIT
Eph	1:10	to bring **all** *t* in heaven and on earth	3836+4246
	1:22	And God placed **all** *t* under his feet	AIT
	3: 9	hidden in God, who **created all** *t*.	3836+4246
	4:15	we will in **all** *t* grow up into him who is	AIT
	5: 6	for because of **such** *t* God's wrath comes	AIT
Php	2:23	to send him as soon as I see how *t* go	3836
	3: 1	It is no trouble for me to write the **same** *t*,	899
	3: 8	for whose sake I have lost **all** *t*.	AIT
	3:15	mature **should** take such a **view** of *t*.	5858
	3:19	Their mind is on **earthly** *t*.	2103
	4: 8	think about **such** *t*.	AIT
Col	1:16	For by him **all** *t* were created:	3836+4246
	1:16	*t* in heaven and on earth,	NIG
	1:16	**all** *t* were created by him and for him.	AIT
	1:17	He is before **all** *t*, and in him all things	AIT
	1:17	and in him **all** *t* hold together.	3836+4246
	1:20	to reconcile to himself **all** *t*,	3836+4246
	1:20	whether *t* on earth or things in heaven,	3836
	1:20	whether things on earth or *t* in heaven,	3836
	2:17	These are a shadow of the *t* that were	AIT
	3: 1	set your hearts on *t* above,	3836
	3: 2	Set your minds on *t* above,	3836
	3: 2	on things above, not on **earthly** *t*.	3836
	3: 8	rid yourselves of **all such** *t* as these:	AIT
1Th	2:14	the **same** *t* those churches suffered from	AIT
2Th	2: 5	with you I used to tell you **these** *t*?	AIT
	3: 4	and will continue to do the *t* we command.	4005
1Ti	4: 1	and follow deceiving spirits and *t* **taught**	1436
	4: 6	If you point **these** *t* out to the brothers,	AIT
	4: 8	but godliness has value for **all** *t*,	AIT
	4:11	Command and teach **these** *t*.	AIT
	5:13	and busybodies, saying *t* they ought not to.	3836
	6: 2	**These** are the *t* you are to teach and urge	AIT
2Ti	2: 2	And the *t* you have heard me say in	AIT
	2:14	Keep reminding them of **these** *t*.	AIT
	3:11	**what kinds of** *t* happened to me in Antioch,	AIT
Tit	1:11	by teaching *t* they ought not to teach—	4005
	1:15	To the **pure, all** *t* are pure,	AIT
	2:15	**These,** then, are the *t* you should teach.	AIT
	3: 5	not because of **righteous** *t* we had done,	2240
	3: 8	And I want you to stress **these** *t*,	AIT
	3: 8	**These** *t* are excellent and profitable	AIT
Heb	1: 2	whom he appointed heir **of all** *t*,	AIT
	1: 3	sustaining **all** *t* by his powerful word.	3836+4246
	6: 9	we are confident of **better** *t* in your case—	AIT
	6: 9	*t* that accompany salvation.	NIG
	6:18	by two unchangeable *t* in which it is	4547
	7:13	He of whom **these** *t* are said belonged to	AIT
	9: 5	But we cannot discuss **these** *t* in detail now.	AIT
	9:11	of the **good** *t* that are already here,	AIT
	9:23	for the copies of the **heavenly** *t*	1877+3836+4041
	9:23	but the **heavenly** *t* themselves	AIT
	10: 1	a shadow of the **good** *t* that are coming—	AIT
	11: 7	when warned about *t* not yet seen,	3836
	11:13	They did not receive the *t* promised;	3836
	11:14	People who say **such** *t* show that they are	AIT
	12:27	what can be shaken—that is, **created** *t*—	4472
1Pe	1:12	of the *t* that have now been told you	AIT
	1:12	Even angels long to look into **these** *t*.	AIT
	1:18	not with **perishable** *t* such as silver or gold	AIT
	4: 7	The end of **all** *t* is near.	AIT
	4:11	so that in **all** *t* God may be praised	AIT
2Pe	1:10	For if you do **these** *t*, you will never fall,	AIT
	1:12	So I will always remind you of **these** *t*,	AIT
	1:15	be able to remember **these** *t*.	AIT
	3:16	His letters contain **some** *t* that are hard	AIT
1Jn	2:26	I am writing **these** *t* to you about those who	AIT
	2:27	as his anointing teaches you about **all** *t*	AIT
	5:13	I write **these** *t* to you who believe in	AIT
Jude	1:10	and **what** *t* they do understand by instinct,	AIT
	1:10	**these** are the very *t* that destroy them.	NIG
Rev	2: 5	Repent and do the *t* you did at first.	2240
	2:14	Nevertheless, I have a **few** *t* against you:	AIT
	4:11	for you created **all** *t*, and by your will	3836+4246
	17: 4	filled with **abominable** *t* and the filth	AIT
	18:15	The merchants who sold **these** *t*	AIT
	21: 4	for the old order of *t* has passed away."	NIG
	22: 6	the *t* that must soon take place."	AIT
	22: 8	John, am the one who heard and saw **these** *t*.	AIT
	22:20	He who testifies to **these** *t* says, "Yes,	AIT

THINK (87) [AFORETHOUGHT, THINKING, THINKS, THOUGHT, THOUGHTLESSLY, THOUGHTS]

Ge	16: 6	"Do with her whatever you *t* best."	928+6524
Ex	14: 3	Pharaoh **will** *t*, 'The Israelites are wandering	606
Jdg	9:17	and to *t* that my father fought for you,	NIH

Column 3

Jdg	10:15	Do with us whatever you *t* best,	928+6524
	19:30	*T* about it! Consider it!	4013+4200+8492
1Sa	18:23	"Do you *t* it is a small matter to become	928+6524
	25:17	Now *t* it over and see what you can do,	3359
2Sa	10: 3	"Do you *t* David is honoring your father	928+6524
	13:32	"My lord **should** not *t* that they killed all	606
	24:13	*t* it over and decide how I should answer	3359
1Ki	20:28	'Because the Arameans *t* the LORD is	606
2Ki	9: 5	you do whatever you *t* best."	928+6524
1Ch	19: 3	Do you *t* David is honoring your father	928+6524
Est	4:13	"Do not *t* that because you are in	1948
Job	4: 3	*T* how you have instructed many,	2180
	7: 4	I lie down I *t*, 'How long before I get up?'	606
	7:13	When I *t* my bed will comfort me	606
	21: 6	When I *t* **about** this, I am terrified;	2349
	23:15	**when** I *t* of all this, I fear him.	1067
	35: 2	"Do you *t* this is just?	3108
	41:32	one **would** *t* the deep had white hair.	3108
Ps	35:25	Do not **let them** *t*, "Aha,	606+928+4213
	40:17	I am poor and needy; **may** the Lord *t* of me.	3108
	63: 6	I *t* of you through the watches of the night.	2047
	144: 3	the son of man that **you** *t* of him?	3108
Isa	29:15	who do their work in darkness and *t*,	606
	44:19	No one **stops** to *t*,	448+4213+8740
Jer	15:15	of how I suffer reproach for your sake.	3359
	23:27	They *t* the dreams they tell one another will	
		make my people forget my name,	3108
	26:14	whatever you *t* is good and right.	928+6524
	44:21	*t* **about** the incense burned in	4213+6584+6590
	51:50	and *t* **on** Jerusalem."	4222+6584+6590
Eze	28: 2	though **you** *t* you are as wise as a god.	4213+5989
	28: 6	"Because you *t* you are **wise**,	AIT
Zep	1:12	who *t*, 'The LORD will do nothing,	606+928+4222
Zec	7:10	In your hearts **do not** *t* evil of each other.'	3108
	11:12	I told them, "If you *t* best,	928+6524
Mt	3: 9	And **do not** *t* you can say to yourselves,	1506
	5:17	not *t* that I have come to abolish the Law	3787
	6: 7	for **they** *t* they will be heard because	1506
	17:25	"What do you *t*, Simon?"	1506
	18:12	"What do you *t*? If a man owns a hundred	1506
	21:28	"What do you *t*? There was a man who had	1506
	22:42	"What do you *t* about the Christ?	1506
	26:53	Do you *t* I cannot call on my Father,	1506
	26:66	What do you *t*?"	1506
Mk	14:64	heard the blasphemy. **What** do you *t*?"	5743
Lk	10:36	of these three **do** you *t* was a neighbor to	1506
	12:51	Do you *t* I came to bring peace on earth?	1506
	13: 2	Jesus answered, "Do you *t* that these	1506
	13: 4	**do** you *t* they were more guilty than all	1506
Jn	5:39	study the Scriptures because you *t* that	1506
	5:45	do not *t* I will accuse you before the Father.	1506
	8:53	**Who** do you *t* you are?"	4472+4932+5515
	11:56	"What do you *t*? Isn't he coming	1506
	16: 2	anyone who kills you **will** *t* he is offering	1506
Ac	5: 4	What **made** you *t* of doing such a thing?	
			1877+2840+3836+5502
	11:17	who was I to *t* that I could oppose God?"	NIG
	13:25	'Who **do** you *t* I am?	5706
	15:38	but Paul **did** not *t* it **wise** to take him,	546
	17:29	we should not *t* that the divine being is	3787
	25:27	For I *t* it is unreasonable to send on	1506
	26:28	"Do you *t* that in such a short time	NIG
Ro	1:28	not *t* it **worthwhile** to retain the knowledge	1507
	2: 3	do **you** *t* you will escape God's judgment?	3357
	12: 3	Do not *t* of yourself more **highly** than	5672
	12: 3	but rather *t* of yourself with sober judgment,	5858
	13:14	not *t* **about** how to gratify the desires	4472+4630
1Co	1:26	*t* of what you were when you were called.	1063
	7:26	I *t* that it is good for you to remain	3787
	7:40	and I *t* that I too have the Spirit of God.	1506
	8: 7	to idols that when they eat such food they *t*	NIG
	10:12	So, **if** you're are standing firm,	1506
	12:23	parts that **we** *t* are less honorable we treat	1506
2Co	10: 2	toward some people who *t* that we live by	3357
	11: 5	But **I** do not *t* I am in the least inferior	3357
	12: 6	so no one **will** *t* more of me than is	3357
Php	2:25	But **I** *t* it is necessary to send back	2451
	3:15	And if **on** some point **you** *t* differently,	5858
	4: 8	or praiseworthy—*t* **about** such things.	3357
1Ti	6: 5	who *t* **that** godliness is a means to financial	3787
Heb	7: 4	Just *t* how great he was:	2555
	10:29	How much more severely **do** you *t*	1506
Jas	1: 7	not *t* he will receive anything from	3887
	4: 5	Or **do** you *t* Scripture says without reason	1506
1Pe	4: 4	**They** *t* it **strange** that you do not plunge	3826
2Pe	1:13	I *t* it is right to refresh your memory	2451

THINKING (33) [THINK]

Ex	2:14	**Are** you *t* of killing me as you killed	606
Dt	1:41	*t* it **easy** to go up into the hill country.	2103
1Sa	9: 5	or my father will stop *t* about the donkeys	NIH
	10: 2	now your father **has stopped** *t* **about** them	5759
	15:32	Agag came to him confidently, *t*,	606
2Ki	7:12	*t*, 'They will surely come out,	606
2Ch	13: 7	*t* to conquer them for himself.	606
Ne	6: 9	They were all trying to frighten us, *t*,	606
Job	1: 5	*t*, "Perhaps my children have sinned	606
	21:27	"I know full well **what** you are *t*	4742
Pr	23: 7	for he is the kind of **man who** is **always** *t*	9132
Jer	37: 9	Do not deceive yourselves, *t*,	606
Da	7: 8	"While I was *t* about the horns,	10683
	8: 5	As I was *t* about this, suddenly a goat	1067
Mk	2: 6	the law were sitting there, *t* to themselves,	1368
	2: 8	in his spirit that this was what **they were** *t*	1368
	2: 8	"Why **are you** *t* these things?	1368
Lk	2:44	*T* he was in their company, they traveled on	3787

Lk	5:21	and the teachers of the law began t	1368
	5:22	Jesus knew what they were t and asked,	1369
	5:22	"Why are you t these things in your hearts?	1368
	6: 8	But Jesus knew what they were t and said	1369
	24:37	and frightened, t they saw a ghost.	1506
Jn	20:15	T he was the gardener, she said, "Sir,	1506
Ac	10:19	While Peter was still t about the vision,	1445
	14:19	dragged him outside the city, t he was dead.	3787
Ro	1:21	but their t became futile and their foolish	1369
1Co	14:20	Brothers, stop t like children.	1181+3836+5856
	14:20	but in your t be adults.	5856
2Co	12:19	Have you been t all along that we have been	1506
Eph	4:17	as the Gentiles do, in the futility of their t.	3808
Heb	11:15	If they had been t of the country	3648
2Pe	3: 1	to stimulate you to wholesome t.	1379

THINKS (11) [THINK]

Dt	29:19	and therefore t, "I will be safe,	606+928+4222
2Sa	16: 3	"He is staying in Jerusalem, because he t,	606
Est	8: 5	with favor and t it the right thing to do,	4178
Job	24:15	he t, 'No eye will see me,'	606
Lk	8:18	what he t he has will be taken from him."	1506
1Co	8:2	of you t he is wise by the standards	1506
	7:36	If anyone t he is acting improperly toward	3787
	8: 2	The man who t he knows something does	1506
	14:37	If anybody t he is a prophet	1506
Gal	6: 3	If anyone t he is something	1506
Php	3: 4	If anyone else t he has reasons to put	1506

THIRD (181) [THREE]

Ge	1:13	and there was morning—the t day.	8958
	2:14	The name of the t river is the Tigris.	8958
	22: 4	On the t day Abraham looked up and saw	8958
	31:22	On the t day Laban was told	8958
	32:19	the t and all the others who followed	8958
	40:20	Now the t day was Pharaoh's birthday,	8958
	42:18	On the t day, Joseph said to them,	8958
	50:23	the t generation of Ephraim's children.	9000
Ex	19: 1	the t month after the Israelites left Egypt—	8958
	19:11	and be ready by the t day,	8958
	19:15	"Prepare yourselves for the t day.	8993
	19:16	the morning of the t day there was thunder	8958
	20: 5	of the fathers to the t and fourth generation	9000
	25:35	and a t bud under the third pair—	NIH
	25:35	and a third bud under the t pair—	NIH
	28:19	in the t row a jacinth, an agate and	8958
	34: 7	the fathers to the t and fourth generation."	9000
	37:21	and a t bud under the third pair—	NIH
	37:21	and a third bud under the t pair—	NIH
	39:12	in the t row a jacinth, an agate and	8958
Lev	7:17	of the sacrifice left over till the t day must	8958
	7:18	fellowship offering is eaten on the t day,	8958
	19: 6	over until the t day must be burned up.	8958
	19: 7	If any of it is eaten on the t day,	8958
Nu	2:24	They will set out t.	8958
	7:24	On the t day, Eliab son of Helon,	8958
	14:18	the fathers to the t and fourth generation.'	9000
	15: 6	of an ephah of fine flour mixed with a t of	8958
	15: 7	and a t of a hin of wine as a drink offering.	8958
	19:12	on the t day and on the seventh day;	8958
	19:12	But if he does not purify himself on the t	8958
	19:19	to sprinkle the unclean person on the t	8958
	28:14	with the ram, a t of a hin;	8958
	29:20	" 'On the t day prepare eleven bulls,	8958
	31:19	the t and seventh days you must purify	8958
Dt	5: 9	of the fathers to the t and fourth generation	9000
	23: 8	The t generation of children born	8958
	26:12	a tenth of all your produce in the t year,	8958
Jos	9:17	the Israelites set out and on the t day came	8958
	17:11	with their surrounding settlements (the t in	8993
	19:10	The t lot came up for Zebulun,	8958
Jdg	20:30	up against the Benjamites on the t day	8958
1Sa	3: 8	The LORD called Samuel a t time,	8958
	13:18	the t toward the borderland overlooking	285S
	13:21	and a t of a shekel for sharpening forks	8993
	17:13	the second, Abinadab; and the t,	8958
	19:21	Saul sent men a t time,	8958
	30: 1	and his men reached Ziklag on the t day.	8958
2Sa	1: 2	the t day a man arrived from Saul's camp,	8958
	3: 3	the t, Absalom the son of Maacah daughter	8958
	8: 2	and the t length was allowed to live.	4850S
	18: 2	a t under the command of Joab,	8958
	18: 2	a third under the command of Joab, a t	8958
	18: 2	and a t under Ittai the Gittite.	8958
1Ki	3:18	The t day after my child was born,	8958
	6: 6	and the t floor seven.	8958
	6: 8	to the middle level and from there to the t.	8958
	15:28	in the t year of Asa king of Judah,	8993
	15:33	In the t year of Asa king of Judah,	8993
	18: 1	After a long time, in the t year,	8958
	18:34	"Do it a t time," he ordered,	8992
	18:34	and they did it the t time.	8992
	22: 2	the t year Jehoshaphat king of Judah went	8958
2Ki	1:13	the king sent a t captain with his fifty men.	8958
	1:13	This t captain went up and fell	8958
	11: 5	a t of you guarding the royal palace,	8958
	11: 6	a t at the Sur Gate, and a third at the gate	8958
	11: 6	and a t at the gate behind the guard,	8958
	18: 1	In the t year of Hoshea son of Elah king	8993
	19:29	But in the t year sow and reap,	8958
	20: 5	On the t day from now you will go up to	8958
	20: 8	up to the temple of the LORD on the t day	8958
1Ch	2:13	the second son was Abinadab, the t Shimea,	8958
	3: 2	the t, Absalom the son of Maacah daughter	8958

1Ch	3:15	Jehoiakim the second son, Zedekiah the t,	8958
	8: 1	Ashbel the second son, Aharah the t,	8958
	8:39	Jeush the second son and Eliphelet the t.	8958
	12: 9	the second in command, Eliab the t,	8958
	23:19	Jahaziel the t and Jekameam the fourth.	8958
	24: 8	the t to Harim, the fourth to Seorim,	8958
	24:23	Jahaziel the t and Jekameam the fourth.	8958
	25:10	the t to Zaccur, his sons and relatives, 12	8958
	26: 2	Zebadiah the t, Jathniel the fourth,	8958
	26: 4	Jehozabad the second, Joah the t,	8958
	26:11	Tabaliah the t and Zechariah the fourth.	8958
	27: 5	The t army commander,	8958
	27: 5	third army commander, for the t month,	8958
2Ch	15:10	in the t month of the fifteenth year	8958
	17: 7	In the t year of his reign he sent	8993
	23: 4	A t of you priests and Levites	8958
	23: 5	a t of you at the royal palace and a third at	8958
	23: 5	a third of you at the royal palace and a t at	8958
	27: 5	also in the second and t years.	8958
	31: 7	They began doing this in the t month	8958
Ezr	6:15	The temple was completed on the t day of	10760
Ne	10:32	a t of a shekel each year for the service of	8993
Est	1: 3	in the t year of his reign he gave a banquet	8993
	5: 1	On the t day Esther put on her royal robes	8958
	8: 9	on the twenty-third day of the t month,	8958
Job	42:14	and the t Keren-Happuch.	8958
Isa	19:24	In that day Israel will be the t,	8958
	37:30	But in the t year sow and reap,	8958
Jer	38:14	the t entrance to the temple of the LORD.	8958
Eze	5: 2	burn a t of the hair with fire inside the city.	8958
	5: 2	a t and strike it with the sword all around	8958
	5: 2	And scatter a t to the wind.	8958
	5:12	A t of your people will die of the plague	8958
	5:12	a t will fall by the sword outside your walls;	8958
	5:12	a t I will scatter to the winds and pursue	8958
	10:14	the t the face of a lion,	8958
	31: 1	in the t month on the first day,	8958
	42: 6	The rooms on the t floor had no pillars,	8992
	46:14	with a t of a hin of oil to moisten the flour.	8958
Da	1: 1	In the t year of the reign of Jehoiakim king	8993
	2:39	Next, a t kingdom, one of bronze,	10759
	5: 7	made the t highest ruler in the kingdom."	10761
	5:16	made the t highest ruler in the kingdom.	10761
	5:29	and he was proclaimed the t highest ruler	10761
	8: 1	In the t year of King Belshazzar's reign,	8993
	10: 1	In the t year of Cyrus king of Persia,	8993
Hos	6: 2	on the t day he will restore us,	8958
Zec	6: 3	the t white, and the fourth dappled—	8958
	13: 9	This t I will bring into the fire;	8958
Mt	16:21	and that he must be killed and on the t day	5569
	17:23	and on the t day he will be raised to life."	5569
	20: 3	"About the t hour he went out	5569
	20:19	On the t day he will be raised to life!"	5569
	21:35	killed another, and stoned a t.	NIG
	22:26	to the second and t brother,	5569
	26:44	and prayed the t time,	1666+5569
	27:64	the tomb to be made secure until the t day.	5569
Mk	12:21	It was the same with the t.	5569
	14:41	Returning the t time, he said to them,	5568
	15:25	It was the t hour when they crucified him.	5569
Lk	9:22	be killed and on the t day be raised to life."	5569
	12:38	even if he comes in the second or t watch	5569
	13:32	and on the t day I will reach my goal.'	5569
	18:33	On the t day he will rise again."	5569
	20:12	He sent still a t, and they wounded him	5569
	20:31	and then the t married her,	5569
	23:22	For the t time he spoke to them: "Why?	5568
	24: 7	and on the t day be raised again.' "	5569
	24:21	it is the t day since all this took place.	5569
	24:46	and rise from the dead on the t day,	5569
Jn	2: 1	On the t day a wedding took place at Cana	5569
	21:14	the t time Jesus appeared to his disciples	5568
	21:17	The t time he said to him,	5568
	21:17	because Jesus asked him the t time,	5568
Ac	10:40	from the dead on the t day and caused him	5569
	20: 9	the ground from the t story and was picked	5566
	27:19	On the t day, they threw the ship's tackle	5569
1Co	12:28	t teachers, then workers of miracles,	5568
	15: 4	that he was raised on the t day according to	5569
2Co	12: 2	who fourteen years ago was caught up to	
		the t heaven.	5569
	12:14	Now I am ready to visit you for the t time,	5568
	13: 1	This will be my t visit to you.	5568
Rev	4: 7	the t had a face like a man,	5569
	6: 5	When the Lamb opened the t seal,	5569
	6: 5	I heard the t living creature say, "Come!"	5569
	8: 7	A t of the earth was burned up,	5569
	8: 7	A t of the trees were burned up,	5569
	8: 8	A t of the sea turned into blood,	5569
	8: 9	a t of the living creatures in the sea died,	5569
	8: 9	and a t of the ships were destroyed.	5569
	8:10	The t angel sounded his trumpet,	5569
	8:10	fell from the sky on a t of the rivers and on	5569
	8:11	A t of the waters turned bitter,	5569
	8:12	and a t of the sun was struck,	5569
	8:12	a t of the moon, and a third of the stars,	5569
	8:12	a third of the moon, and a t of the stars,	5569
	8:12	so that a t of them turned dark.	5569
	8:12	A t of the day was without light,	5569
	8:12	and also a t of the night.	NIG
	9:15	and year were released to kill a t	5569
	9:18	A t of mankind was killed by	5569
	11:14	the t woe is coming soon.	
	12: 4	His tail swept a t of the stars out of the sky	5569
	14: 9	A t angel followed them and said in	5569
	16: 4	The t angel poured out his bowl on	5569
	21:19	the second sapphire, the t chalcedony,	5569

THIRDS (1) [THREE]

1Sa	13:21	The price was two t of a shekel for	7088

THIRST (24) [THIRSTS, THIRSTY]

Ex	17: 3	and our children and livestock die of t?"	7533
Dt	28:48	therefore in hunger and t,	7533
Jdg	15:18	Must I now die of t and fall into the hands	7533
2Ch	32:11	to let you die of hunger and t?	7533
Ne	9:15	and in their t you brought them water from	7533
	9:20	and you gave them water for their t.	7533
Job	24:11	they tread the winepresses, yet suffer t.	7532
Ps	69:21	in my food and gave me vinegar for my t.	7533
	104:11	the wild donkeys quench their t.	7533
Isa	5:13	and their masses will be parched with t.	7533
	29: 8	he awakens faint, with his t unquenched.	5883
	41:17	their tongues are parched with t.	7533
	48:21	not t when he led them through the deserts;	7532
	49:10	They will neither hunger nor t,	7532
	50: 2	their fish rot for lack of water and die of t.	7533
Jer	46:10	till it has quenched its t with blood.	8115
La	4: 4	Because of t the infant's tongue sticks to	7533
Hos	2: 3	and slay her with t.	7533
Am	8:11	not a famine of food or a t for water,	7533
	8:13	strong young men will faint because of t.	7533
Mt	5: 6	Blessed are those who hunger and t for	1498
Jn	4:14	the water I give him will never t.	1498
2Co	11:27	and t and have often gone without food;	1499
Rev	7:16	will they hunger; never again will they t.	1498

THIRSTS (3) [THIRST]

Ps	42: 2	My soul t for God, for the living God.	7532
	63: 1	my soul t for you, my body longs for you,	7532
	143: 6	my soul t for you like a parched land.	NIH

THIRSTY (33) [THIRST]

Ex	17: 3	But the people were t for water there,	7532
Dt	8:15	that t and waterless land,	7536
Jdg	4:19	"I'm t," he said.	7532
	15:18	Because he was very t,	7532
Ru	2: 9	And whenever you are t,	7532
2Sa	17:29	and tired and t in the desert."	7534
Job	5: 5	and the t pant after his wealth.	7534
Ps	107: 5	They were hungry and t,	7534
	107: 9	for he satisfies the t and fills the	5883+8799
	107:33	flowing springs into t ground,	7536
Pr	25:21	if he is t, give him water to drink.	7532
Isa	21:14	bring water for the t;	7534
	29: 8	as when a t man dreams that he is drinking,	7534
	32: 2	and the shadow of a great rock in a t land.	6546
	32: 6	and from the t he withholds water.	7534
	35: 7	the t ground bubbling springs.	7536
	44: 3	For I will pour water on the t land,	7534
	55: 1	"Come, all you who are t,	7534
	65:13	my servants will drink, but you will go t;	7532
Eze	19:13	in the desert, in a dry and t land.	7533
Mt	25:35	I was t and you gave me something	1498
	25:37	or t and give you something to drink?	1498
	25:42	I was t and you gave me nothing to drink,	1498
	25:44	or t or a stranger or needing clothes or sick	1498
Jn	4:13	who drinks this water will be t again,	1498
	4:15	give me this water so that I won't get t	1498
	6:35	he who believes in me will never be t.	1498
	7:37	"If anyone is t, let him come to me and	1498
	19:28	Jesus said, "I am t."	1498
Ro	12:20	If he is t, give him something to drink.	1498
1Co	4:11	To this very hour we go hungry and t,	1498
Rev	21: 6	To him who is t I will give to drink	1498
	22:17	Whoever is t, let him come;	1498

THIRTEEN (13) [THIRTEENTH, 13]

Ge	17:25	and his son Ishmael was t;	6926+8993
Nu	29:13	a burnt offering of t young bulls,	6925+8993
	29:14	of the t bulls prepare a grain offering	6925+8993
Dt	3:11	of iron and was more than t feet long	564+9596
Jos	19: 6	t towns and their villages;	6926+8993
	21: 4	the priest were allotted t towns	6925+8993
	21: 6	of Gershon were allotted t towns from	6926+8993
	21:19	t, together with their pasturelands.	6926+8993
	21:33	towns of the Gershonite clans were t,	6926+8993
1Ki	7: 1	It took Solomon t years, however,	6926+8993
1Ch	6:60	Kohathite clans, were t in all.	6926+8993
	6:62	were allotted t towns from the tribes	6926+8993
Eze	40:11	and its length was t cubits.	6926+8993

THIRTEENTH (11) [THIRTEEN]

Ge	14: 4	but in the t year they rebelled.	6926+8993
1Ch	24:13	the t to Huppah,	6925+8993
	25:20	the t to Shubael, his sons and relatives,	6925+8993
Est	3:12	Then on the t day of the first month	6925+8993
	3:13	the t day of the twelfth month,	6925+8993
	8:12	was the t day of the twelfth month,	6925+8993
	9: 1	On the t day of the twelfth month,	6925+8993
	9:17	happened on the t day of the month,	6925+8993
	9:18	had assembled on the t and fourteenth,	6925+8993
Jer	1: 2	the LORD came to him in the t year of	6926+8993
	25: 3	from the t year of Josiah son of Amon	6926+8993

THIRTIETH (1) [THIRTY]

Eze	1: 1	In the t year, in the fourth month on the	8993

THIRTY (95) [THIRTIETH, 30]

Ge	18:30	What if only t can be found there?"	8993

Ge	18:30	"I will not do it if I find t there."	8993
	32:15	t female camels with their young,	8993
	41:46	Joseph was t years old when he entered	8993
	47: 9	of my pilgrimage are a hundred and t.	8993
Ex	21:32	the owner must pay t shekels of silver to	8993
	26: 8	t cubits long and four cubits wide.	8993
	36:15	t cubits long and four cubits wide.	8993
Lev	27: 4	set her value at t shekels.	8993
Nu	4: 3	Count all the men from t to fifty years	8993
	4:23	Count all the men from t to fifty years	8993
	4:30	Count all the men from t to fifty years	8993
	4:35	from t to fifty years of age who came	8993
	4:39	from t to fifty years of age who came	8993
	4:43	from t to fifty years of age who came	8993
	4:47	from t to fifty years of age who came to do	8993
	7:13	plate weighing a hundred and t shekels,	8993
	7:19	plate weighing a hundred and t shekels,	8993
	7:25	plate weighing a hundred and t shekels,	8993
	7:31	plate weighing a hundred and t shekels,	8993
	7:37	plate weighing a hundred and t shekels,	8993
	7:43	plate weighing a hundred and t shekels,	8993
	7:49	plate weighing a hundred and t shekels,	8993
	7:55	plate weighing a hundred and t shekels,	8993
	7:61	plate weighing a hundred and t shekels,	8993
	7:67	plate weighing a hundred and t shekels,	8993
	7:73	plate weighing a hundred and t shekels,	8993
	7:79	plate weighing a hundred and t shekels,	8993
	7:85	plate weighed a hundred and t shekels,	8993
	20:29	house of Israel mourned for him t days.	8993
Dt	34: 8	for Moses in the plains of Moab t days,	8993
Jos	8: 3	He chose t thousand of his best fighting	8993
Jdg	10: 4	He had t sons, who rode thirty donkeys.	8993
	10: 4	He had thirty sons, who rode t donkeys.	8993
	10: 4	They controlled t towns in Gilead,	8993
	12: 9	He had t sons and thirty daughters.	8993
	12: 9	He had thirty sons and t daughters.	8993
	12: 9	for his sons he brought in t young women	8993
	12:14	He had forty sons and t grandsons,	8993
	14:11	he was given t companions.	8993
	14:12	I will give you t linen garments	8993
	14:12	linen garments and t sets of clothes.	8993
	14:13	you must give me t linen garments	8993
	14:13	linen garments and t sets of clothes."	8993
	14:19	struck down t of their men,	8993
	20:31	that about t men fell in the open field and	8993
	20:39	casualties on the men of Israel (about t).	8993
1Sa	4:10	Israel lost t thousand foot soldiers.	8993
	9:22	who were invited—about t in number.	8993
	11: 8	and the men of Judah t thousand.	8993
	13: 1	Saul was [t] years old when he became king	8993
2Sa	5: 4	David was t years old when he became king	8993
	6: 1	chosen men, t thousand in all.	8993
	23:13	of the t chief men came down to David at	8993
	23:23	in greater honor than any of the T,	8993
	23:24	Among the T were:	8993
1Ki	4:22	Solomon's daily provisions were t cors	8993
	5:13	from all Israel—t thousand men.	8993
	6: 2	twenty wide and t high.	8993
	7: 2	fifty wide and t high,	8993
	7: 6	a colonnade fifty cubits long and t wide.	8993
	7:23	a line of t cubits to measure around it.	8993
2Ki	18:14	of silver and t talents of gold.	8993
1Ch	11:15	Three of the t chiefs came down to David	8993
	11:25	in greater honor than any of the T,	8993
	11:42	and the t with him,	8993
	12: 4	a mighty man among the T,	8993
	12: 4	who was a leader of the T;	8993
	12:18	Spirit came upon Amasai, chief of the T,	8993
	23: 3	The Levites t years old or more	8993
	27: 6	a mighty man among the T and was over	8993
	27: 6	among the Thirty and was over the T.	8993
2Ch	4: 2	a line of t cubits to measure around it.	8993
	24:15	and he died at the age of a hundred and t.	8993
	35: 7	a total of t thousand sheep and goats for	8993
Est	4:11	But t days have passed since I was called	8993
Pr	22:20	Have I not written t sayings for you,	8993
Jer	38:10	"Take t men from here with you	8993
Eze	40:17	there were t rooms along the pavement.	8993
	41: 6	one above another, t on each level.	8993
	46:22	forty cubits long and t cubits wide;	8993
Da	6: 7	to any god or man during the next t days,	10762
	6:12	during the next t days anyone who prays	10762
Zec	5: 2	a flying scroll, t feet long	564+928+2021+6929
	11:12	So they paid me t pieces of silver.	8993
	11:13	the t pieces of silver and threw them into	8993
Mt	13: 8	sixty or t times what was sown.	5558
	13:23	sixty or t times what was sown."	5558
	26:15	they counted out for him t silver coins.	5558
	27: 3	the t silver coins to the chief priests and	5558
	27: 9	"They took the t silver coins,	5558
Mk	4: 8	grew and produced a crop, multiplying t,	5558
	4:20	t, sixty or even a hundred times what was sown."	5558
Lk	3:23	Now Jesus himself was about t years old	5558
Jn	2: 6	from twenty to t gallons.	1545+2445+3583+5552

THIRTY-EIGHT (3) [THIRTY-EIGHTH]

Dt	2:14	T years passed from the time	2256+8993+9046
1Ch	23: 3	number of men was t thousand.	2256+8993+9046
Jn	5: 5	had been an invalid for t years.	2779+3893+5558

THIRTY-EIGHTH (2) [THIRTY-EIGHT]

1Ki	16:29	the t year of Asa king of Judah,	2256+8993+9046
2Ki	15: 8	t year of Azariah king of Judah,	2256+8993+9046

THIRTY-FIFTH (1) [THIRTY-FIVE]

2Ch	15:19	was no more war until the t year	2256+2822+8993

THIRTY-FIRST (1)

1Ki	16:23	the t year of Asa king of Judah,	285+2256+8993

THIRTY-FIVE (3) [THIRTY-FIFTH, 35]

1Ki	22:42	Jehoshaphat was t years old	2256+2822+8993
2Ch	3:15	were t cubits long, each with	2256+2822+8993
	20:31	He was t years old when he	2256+2822+8993

THIRTY-NINTH (3)

2Ki	15:13	t year of Uzziah king of Judah,	2256+8993+9596
	15:17	t year of Azariah king of Judah,	2256+8993+9596
2Ch	16:12	In the t year of his reign Asa	2256+8993+9596

THIRTY-ONE (3)

Jos	12:24	t kings in all.	285+2256+8993
2Ki	22: 1	he reigned in Jerusalem t years.	285+2256+8993
2Ch	34: 1	he reigned in Jerusalem t years.	285+2256+8993

THIRTY-SECOND (2)

Ne	5:14	until his t year—twelve years—	2256+8993+9109
	13: 6	for in the t year of Artaxerxes	2256+8993+9109

THIRTY-SEVEN (2) [THIRTY-SEVENTH]

Ge	25:17	Ishmael lived a hundred and t years	2256+8679+8993
2Sa	23:39	There were t in all.	2256+8679+8993

THIRTY-SEVENTH (3) [THIRTY-SEVEN]

2Ki	13:10	t year of Joash king of Judah,	2256+8679+8993
	25:27	t year of the exile of Jehoiachin	2256+8679+8993
Jer	52:31	t year of the exile of Jehoiachin	2256+8679+8993

THIRTY-SIX (2) [THIRTY-SIXTH]

Jos	7: 5	who killed about t of them.	2256+8993+9252
2Ch	2: 2	and t hundred as foremen over them.	547+2256+4395+9252

THIRTY-SIXTH (1) [THIRTY-SIX]

2Ch	16: 1	In the t year of Asa's reign	2256+8993+9252

THIRTY-THREE (7)

Ge	46:15	These sons and daughters of his were t in all.	2256+8993+8993
Lev	12: 4	must wait t days to be purified	2256+8993+8993
2Sa	5: 5	over all Israel and Judah t years.	2256+8993+8993
1Ki	2:11	seven years in Hebron and t in Jerusalem.	2256+8993+8993
	5:16	t hundred foremen who supervised the project	547+2256+4395+8993+8993
1Ch	3: 4	David reigned in Jerusalem t years,	2256+8993+8993
	29:27	seven in Hebron and t in Jerusalem.	2256+8993+8993

THIRTY-TWO (6) [32]

1Ki	20: 1	Accompanied by t kings with	2256+8993+9109
	22:31	his t chariot commanders,	2256+8993+9109
2Ki	8:17	He was t years old when he	2256+8993+9109
1Ch	19: 7	They hired t thousand chariots	2256+8993+9109
2Ch	21: 5	Jehoram was t years old	2256+8993+9109
	21:20	Jehoram was t years old	2256+8993+9109

THIS (3712) [THESE] See Index of Articles Etc.

THISTLE (4) [THISTLES]

2Ki	14: 9	"A t in Lebanon sent a message to a cedar	2560
	14: 9	along and trampled the t underfoot.	2560
2Ch	25:18	"A t in Lebanon sent a message to a cedar	2560
	25:18	along and trampled the t underfoot.	2560

THISTLES (4) [THISTLE]

Ge	3:18	It will produce thorns and t for you,	1998
Hos	10: 8	and t will grow up and cover their altars.	1998
Mt	7:16	grapes from thornbushes, or figs from t?	5560
Heb	6: 8	that produces thorns and t is worthless	5560

THOMAS (11)

Mt	10: 3	T and Matthew the tax collector;	2605
Mk	3:18	T, James son of Alphaeus, Thaddaeus,	2605
Lk	6:15	T, James son of Alphaeus,	2605
Jn	11:16	Then T (called Didymus) said to the rest of	2605
	14: 5	T said to him, "Lord, we don't know where	2605
	20:24	Now T (called Didymus), one of the Twelve	2605
	20:26	and T was with them.	2605
	20:27	Then he said to T, "Put your finger here;	2605
	20:28	T said to him, "My Lord and my God!"	2605
	21: 2	T (called Didymus), Nathanael from Cana	2605
Ac	1:13	Philip and T, Bartholomew and Matthew;	2605

THONG (2) [THONGS]

Ge	14:23	not even a thread or the t of a sandal,	8579
Isa	5:27	not a sandal t is broken.	8579

THONGS (6) [THONG]

Jdg	16: 7	with seven fresh t that have not been dried,	3857
	16: 8	of the Philistines brought her seven fresh t	3857
	16: 9	But he snapped the t as easily as a piece	3857
Mk	1: 7	the t of whose sandals I am not worthy	2666
Lk	3:16	the t of whose sandals I am not worthy	2666
Jn	1:27	the t of whose sandals I am not worthy	2666

THORN (2) [THORNBUSH, THORNBUSHES, THORNS]

Mic	7: 4	the most upright worse than a t hedge.	5004
2Co	12: 7	there was given me a t in my flesh,	5022

THORNBUSH (5) [THORN]

Jdg	9:14	"Finally all the trees said to the t,	353
	9:15	"The t said to the trees, 'If you really want	353
	9:15	then let fire come out of the t and consume	353
Pr	26: 9	Like a t in a drunkard's hand is a proverb	2560
Isa	55:13	Instead of the t will grow the pine tree,	5848

THORNBUSHES (6) [THORN]

Ex	22: 6	"If a fire breaks out and spreads into t so	7764
Isa	7:19	on all the t and at all the water holes.	5848
	33:12	like cut t they will be set ablaze."	7764
Hos	2: 6	Therefore I will block her path with t;	6106
Mt	7:16	Do people pick grapes from t,	180
Lk	6:44	People do not pick figs from t,	180

THORNS (43) [THORN]

Ge	3:18	It will produce t and thistles for you,	7764
Nu	33:55	barbs in your eyes and t in your sides.	7564
Jos	23:13	whips on your backs and t in your eyes,	7564
Jdg	2: 3	be [t] in your sides and their gods will be	NIH
	8: 7	I will tear your flesh with desert t	7764
	8:16	by punishing them with desert t and briers.	7764
2Sa	23: 6	But evil men are all to be cast aside like t,	7764
	23: 7	Whoever touches t uses a tool of iron or	2157S
Job	5: 5	taking it even from among t,	7553
Ps	58: 9	Before your pots can feel [the heat of] the t	353
	118:12	but they died out as quickly as burning t;	7764
Pr	15:19	The way of the sluggard is blocked with t,	2537
	22: 5	In the paths of the wicked lie t and snares,	7553
	24:31	t had come up everywhere,	7853
Ecc	7: 6	Like the crackling of t under the pot,	6106
SS	2: 2	among t is my darling among the maidens.	2560
Isa	5: 6	and briers and t will grow there.	8885
	7:23	there will be only briers and t.	8885
	7:24	the land will be covered with briers and t.	8885
	7:25	for fear of the briers and t;	8885
	9:18	it consumes briers and t,	8885
	10:17	a single day it will burn and consume his t	8885
	27: 4	and t confronting me!	8885
	32:13	a land overgrown with t and briers—	7764
	34:13	T will overrun her citadels,	6106
Jer	4: 3	and do not sow among t.	7764
	12:13	They will sow wheat but reap t;	7764
Eze	2: 6	though briers and t are all around you	6141
	28:24	who are painful briers and sharp t.	7764
Hos	9: 6	and t will overrun their tents.	2560
	10: 8	T and thistles will grow up	6106
Na	1:10	They will be entangled among t and drunk	6106
Mt	13: 7	Other seed fell among t,	180
	13:22	that fell among the t is the man who hears	180
	27:29	then twisted together a crown of t and set it	180
Mk	4: 7	Other seed fell among t,	180
	4:18	Still others, like seed sown among t,	180
	15:17	then twisted together a crown of t and set it	181
Lk	8: 7	Other seed fell among t,	180
	8:14	that fell among t stands for those who hear,	180
Jn	19: 2	The soldiers twisted together a crown of t	180
	19: 5	the crown of t and the purple robe,	181
Heb	6: 8	that produces t and thistles is worthless	180

THOROUGH (3) [THOROUGHLY]

Dt	19:18	The judges must make a t investigation,	3512
Ac	12:19	Herod had a t search made for him	2118
	18:24	with a t knowledge of the Scriptures.	1543

THOROUGHLY (11) [THOROUGH]

Ge	11: 3	make bricks and bake them t."	4200+8596+8599
Dt	13:14	must inquire, probe and investigate it t.	3512
	17: 4	then you must investigate it t.	3512
Jdg	15: 7	"I was so sure you t hated her,"	8533+8533
Ps	119:140	Your promises have been t tested,	4394
Isa	1:25	I will t purge away your dross and remove	1342+2021+3869+7671
	24:19	split asunder, the earth is t shaken.	4572+4572
Jer	6: 9	glean the remnant of Israel as t	6618+6618
	20:11	They will fail and be t disgraced;	4394
Ac	22: 3	Under Gamaliel I was t trained in the law of our fathers	205+2848
2Ti	3:17	so that the man of God may be t equipped	787

THOSE (1368) [THAT] See Index of Articles Etc.

THOUGH (329) [ALTHOUGH]

Ge	8:21	even t every inclination of his heart is evil	3954
	18:27	t I am nothing but dust and ashes,	2256
	20:12	daughter of my father t not of my mother;	421

Ge 28:19 t the city used to be called Luz. 219
31:50 even t no one is with us, NIH
38:14 t Shelah had now **grown up,** AIT
39:10 And t she spoke to Joseph day after day, 3869
42:30 to us and treated us as t we were spying on 3869
44:18 t you are equal to Pharaoh himself. 3954
48:14 t he was the younger, 2256
48:14 even t Manasseh was the firstborn. 3954
Ex 3: 2 that t the bush was on fire it did 2180
7: 3 and t I multiply my miraculous signs 2256
13:17 t that was shorter. 3954
Lev 4:13 even t the community is unaware of 2256
5: 2 even t he is unaware of it, 2256
5: 3 even t he is unaware of it, 2256
5: 4 even t he is unaware of it, 2256
5:17 even t he does not know it, 2256
11: 4 The camel, t it chews the cud, 3954
11: 5 The coney, t it chews the cud, 3954
11: 6 The rabbit, t it chews the cud, 3954
11: 7 t it has a split hoof completely divided, 3954
13:55 even t it has not spread, it is unclean. 2256
26:36 They will run as t fleeing from the sword, NIH
26:36 even t no one is pursuing them. 2256
26:37 They will stumble over one another as t 3869
26:37 even t no one is pursuing them. 2256
Nu 5:14 or if he is jealous and suspects her even t 2256
14:44 t neither Moses nor the ark of the LORD's 2256
Dt 18: 8 even t he has received money from 963+4200
19: 6 and kill him even t he is not deserving 2256
22:27 and t the betrothed girl screamed, NIH
29:19 even t I persist in going my own way." 3954
Jos 17:18 t the Canaanites have iron chariots and 3954
17:18 the Canaanites have iron chariots and t 3954
22:17 even t a plague fell on the community of 2256
Jdg 13:16 "Even t you detain me, 561
18:29 t the city used to be called Laish. 219
Ru 2:13 t I do not have the standing of one 2256
1Sa 12:12 t the LORD your God was your king. 2256
15:35 t Samuel mourned for him. 3954
20:20 as t I were shooting at a target. NIH
25:29 Even t someone is pursuing you 2256
2Sa 3:27 as t to speak with him privately. NIH
3:39 And today, t I am the anointed king, 2256
16: 6 t all the troops and the special guard were 2256
19:14 over the hearts of all the men of Judah as t 3869
23:19 even t he was not included among them. 2256
1Ki 2:28 who had conspired with Adonijah t not 2256
9: 8 And t this temple is now imposing, 2256
12:31 even t they were not Levites. 889
2Ki 4:39 t no one knew what they were. 3954
5:16 And even t Naaman urged him, he refused. 2256
17:12 t the LORD had said, 889
18:24 even t you are depending on Egypt 2256
25: 4 t the Babylonians were surrounding 2256
1Ch 5: 2 and t Judah was the strongest 3954
11:21 t he was not included among them. 3954
17:17 on me as t I were the most exalted of men, 3869
2Ch 7:14 And t this temple is now so imposing, 889
16:12 T his disease was severe, 6330
24:19 and t they testified against them, 2256
Ezr 3: 6 t the foundation of the LORD's temple 2256
9: 9 T we are slaves, 3954
9:15 t because of it not one of us can stand 3954
Ne 5: 5 as our countrymen and t our sons are NIH
6: 1 t up to that time I had not set the doors in 1685
Est 4:16 even t it is against the law. 889
Job 2: 3 t you incited me against him to ruin him 2256
6:14 even t he forsakes the fear of the Almighty. 2256
9: 3 T one wished to dispute with him, 561
9:15 T I were innocent, I could not answer him; 561
10: 7 t you know that I am not guilty and 6584
12: 4 t I called upon God and he answered— NIH
12: 4 t righteous and blameless! NIH
13:15 T he slay me, yet will I hope in him; 2176
15:27 "T his face is covered with fat 3954
19: 7 "T I cry, 'I've been wronged!' 2176
19: 7 t I call for help, there is no justice. NIH
19:16 t I beg him with my own mouth. NIH
20: 6 T his pride reaches to the heavens 561
20:12 "T evil is sweet in his mouth 561
20:13 t he cannot bear to let it go and keeps it NIH
20:24 T he flees from an iron weapon, NIH
22: 8 t you were a powerful man, owning land— 2256
24:22 t they become established, 2256
27:16 T he heaps up silver like dust and clothes 561
33:14 t man may not perceive it. NIH
40:23 he is secure, t the Jordan should surge 3954
Ps 17: 3 T you probe my heart and examine me NIH
17: 3 t you test me, you will find nothing; NIH
21:11 T they plot evil against you 3954
23: 4 Even t I walk through the valley of 2256
25:11 forgive my iniquity, t it is great. 3954
27: 3 T an army besiege me, 561
27: 3 t war break out against me, 561
27:10 T my father and mother forsake me, 3954
31:12 I am forgotten by them as t I were dead; 3869
35:14 I went about mourning as t for my friend 3869
35:14 I bowed my head in grief as t weeping 3869
37:10 t you look for them, they will not be found. 2256
37:24 t he stumble, he will not fall, 3954
37:36 t I looked for him, he could not be found. 2256
44:17 t we had not forgotten you or been false 2256
46: 2 t the earth give way and the mountains fall 928
46: 3 t its waters roar and foam and NIH
49:11 t they had named lands after themselves. NIH
49:18 T while he lived he counted himself blessed 3954
55:18 even t many oppose me. 3954

Ps 62:10 t your riches increase, 3954
71:15 t I know not its measure. 3954
71:20 T you have made me see troubles, 889
77:19 t your footprints were not seen. 2256
78: 9 The men of Ephraim, t armed with bows, NIH
90: 6 in the morning it springs up new, 2256
92: 7 that t the wicked spring up like grass 928
95: 9 t they had seen what I did. 1685
99: 8 t you punished their misdeeds. 1685
119:23 T rulers sit together and slander me, 1685
119:61 T the wicked bind me with ropes, NIH
119:69 T the arrogant have smeared me with lies, NIH
119:83 T I am like a wineskin in the smoke, 3954
119:109 T I constantly take my life in my hands, NIH
119:141 T I am lowly and despised, NIH
138: 6 T the LORD is on high, 3954
138: 7 T I walk in the midst of trouble, 561
Pr 4: 7 T it cost all you have, get understanding. 2256
6:31 t it costs him all the wealth of his house. NIH
19: 7 T he pursues them with pleading, NIH
24:16 for t a righteous man falls seven times, AIT
26:25 T his speech is charming, 3954
27:22 T you grind a fool in a mortar, 561
28: 1 The wicked man flees t no one pursues, NIH
29:19 t he understands, he will not respond. 3954
Ecc 4:12 T one may be overpowered, 561
6: 5 T it never saw the sun or knew anything, 1685
8: 6 t a man's misery weighs heavily upon him. 3954
Isa 1:18 "T your sins are like scarlet, 561
1:18 t they are red as crimson, 561
6:13 And t a tenth remains in the land, 2256
10:22 T your people, O Israel, 561+3954
17:10 t you set out the finest plants AIT
17:11 t on the day you set them out, NIH
26:10 T grace is shown to the wicked, NIH
28:28 T he drives the wheels of his threshing cart 2256
30: 4 T they have officials in Zoan 3954
31: 4 and t a whole band of shepherds is called 889
32:19 T hail flattens the forest and 2256
36: 9 even t you are depending on Egypt 2256
40:15 the islands as t they were fine dust. 3869
41:12 T you search for your enemies, NIH
45: 4 t you do not acknowledge me. 2256
45: 5 t you have not acknowledged me, 2256
46: 7 T one cries out to it, it does not answer; 677
48:10 See, I have refined you, t not as silver; 2256
49:15 T she may forget, I will not forget you! 1685
49:19 "T you were ruined and made desolate 3954
53: 9 t he had done no violence, 6584
53:10 t the LORD makes his life a guilt offering, 561
54:10 T the mountains be shaken and the hills 3954
60:10 T in anger I struck you, 3954
63:16 t Abraham does not know us 3954
Jer 2:34 t you did not catch them breaking in. NIH
4:27 t I will not destroy it completely. 2256
6:14 They dress the wound of my people as t 6584
8:11 They dress the wound of my people as t 6584
10: 2 t the nations are terrified by them. 3954
12: 6 t they speak well of you. 3954
14:12 t they offer burnt offerings 3954
22: 6 "T you are like Gilead to me, NIH
23:38 even t I told you that you must not claim, 2256
25: 4 And t the LORD has sent all his servants 2256
26: 5 (t you have not listened), 2256
29:31 even t I did not send him, 2256
30:11 'T I completely destroy all the nations 3954
31:20 T I often speak against him, 3954
31:32 t I was a husband to them," 2256
32:25 And t the city will be handed over to 2256
32:33 t I taught them again and again, 2256
32:35 t I never commanded, 889
36:25 Even t Elnathan, Delaiah 2256
42: 2 For as you now see, t we were once many, NIH
46:23 declares the LORD, "dense t it be. 3954
46:28 'T I completely destroy all the nations 3954
49:16 T you build your nest as high as 3954
51: 5 t their land is full of guilt before 3954
52: 7 t the Babylonians were surrounding 2256
La 3:32 T he brings grief, 561+3954
Eze 2: 6 t briers and thorns are all around you 3954
2: 6 t they are a rebellious house. 3954
3: 9 t they are a rebellious house." 3954
3:26 t they are a rebellious house. 3954
7:14 T they blow the trumpet NIH
12: 3 t they are a rebellious house. 3954
13: 7 t I have not spoken? 2256
18:11 (t the father has done none of them): 2256
18:14 and t he sees them, 2256
28: 2 t you think you are as wise as a god. 2256
32:27 t the terror of these warriors had stalked 3954
35:10 even t I the LORD was there, 2256
39:28 t I sent them into exile among the nations, 928
Da 9: 9 t you knew all this. 10168+10353+10619
9: 9 even t we have rebelled against him; 3954
11:33 t for a time they will fall by the sword or 2256
Hos 3: 1 t she is loved by another and is NIH
3: 1 t they turn to other gods and love 2256
4:15 "T you commit adultery, O Israel, 561
8:11 "T Ephraim built many altars 3954
13:15 even t he thrives among his brothers. 3954
Am 2: 9 t he was tall as the cedars and strong as 889
5:11 t you have built stone mansions, NIH
5:11 t you have planted lush vineyards, NIH
5:19 be as t a man fled from a lion only to 889+3869
5:19 as t he entered his house NIH
5:22 Even t you bring me burnt offerings 561
5:22 T you bring choice fellowship offerings, 2256

Am 9: 2 T they dig down to the depths of the grave, 561
9: 2 T they climb up to the heavens, 561
9: 3 T they hide themselves on the top 561
9: 3 T they hide from me at the bottom of 561
9: 4 T they are driven into exile 561
Ob 1: 4 T you soar like the eagle 561
Jnh 4:10 t you did not tend it or make it grow. 889
Mic 5: 2 t you are small among the clans of Judah, NIH
7: 8 T I have fallen, I will rise. 3954
7: 8 T I sit in darkness, 3954
Na 2: 2 t destroyers have laid them waste 3954
Hab 2: 3 T it linger, wait for it; 561
3:14 gloating as t about to devour 4017
3:17 T the fig tree does not bud 3954
3:17 t the olive crop fails and NIH
3:17 t there are no sheep in the pen and no cattle NIH
Zec 9: 2 t they are very skillful. 3954
10: 6 They will be as t I had not rejected them, 889
10: 9 T I scatter them among the peoples, 2256
Mal 1: 4 "T we have **been crushed,** AIT
2:12 even t he brings offerings to the LORD 2256
2:14 t she is your partner, 2256
Mt 7:11 If you, then, t you **are** evil, AIT
13:13 "T seeing, they do not see; AIT
13:13 t hearing, they do not hear or understand. AIT
13:32 T it is the smallest of all your seeds, 3525
26:60 t many false witnesses **came forward.** AIT
Mk 4:27 t he does not know how. NIG
Lk 8:10 so that, " 't seeing, they may not see; AIT
8:10 t hearing, they may not understand.' AIT
8:29 and t he was chained hand and foot NIG
11: 8 T he will not get up and give him 1623+2779
11:13 If you then, t you **are** evil, AIT
18: 4 'Even t I don't fear God or care about men, 1623
Jn 1:10 and t the world was made through him, 2779
2: 9 t the servants who had drawn 1254
6:71 who, t one of the Twelve, 1639
7:22 t **actually** it did not come from Moses, 4022
8:55 T you do not know him, I know him. 2779
10:38 But if I do it, even t you do not believe me, 1569
10:41 "T John never performed a miraculous sign, 3525
11:25 who believes in me will live, even t he dies; 1569
13:10 And you are clean, t not every one of you." 247
16:25 "T I have been speaking figuratively, NIG
17:25 t the world does not know you, 2779
20:26 T the doors were locked, AIT
Ac 3:13 t he had **decided** to let him go. AIT
5:13 even t they were highly regarded by 247
7: 5 t at that time Abraham **had** no child. AIT
13:28 T they **found** no proper ground for a death AIT
16:37 even t we **are** Roman citizens, AIT
17:27 t he is not far from each one of us. 1145+2779
18:25 t he knew only the baptism of John. AIT
19:37 t they have neither **robbed temples** nor AIT
28: 4 for t he **escaped** from the sea, AIT
Ro 2:14 t they do not **have** AIT
2:25 as t you had not been circumcised. NIG
2:26 be regarded as t they were circumcised? NIG
2:27 even t you have the written code NIG
4:17 and calls things that are not as t they **were.** AIT
5: 7 for a righteous man, t for 1142
6:17 t you used to be slaves to sin, NIG
7: 3 even t she **marries** another man. AIT
9: 6 It is not as t God's word had failed. 4022
9:27 "T the number of the Israelites be like 1569
11:17 t a **wild olive shoot,** AIT
1Co 4: 7 why do you boast as t you did not? 6055
4:15 **Even** t you have ten thousand guardians in 1142+1569
Christ,
5: 3 **Even** t I am not physically present, 1142+3525
9: 2 **Even** t I may not be an apostle to others, 1623
9:19 T I **am** free and belong to no man, AIT
9:20 the law (t I myself **am** not under the law), AIT
9:21 the law (t I **am** not free from God's law AIT
11: 5 it is **just** as t her head were shaved. 899+1651+2779+3836
12:12 t it is made up of many parts; 2779
12:12 and t all its parts **are** many, 2779
15: 6 t some have fallen asleep. 1254
2Co 2: 6 because of its glory, **fading** t it was, AIT
4:16 T outwardly we are wasting away, 1623+2779
5:16 T we once regarded Christ in this way, 1623+2779
5:20 as t God were making his appeal 6055
7: 8 T I did regret it— 1623+2779
7:12 So even t I wrote to you, 1623
8: 9 that t he **was** rich, yet for your sakes AIT
10: 3 For t we **live** in the world, AIT
12:11 even t I am nothing. 1623
13: 7 but that you will do what is right even t NIG
Gal 2: 3 even t he **was** a Greek. AIT
4:14 **Even** t my illness was a trial to you, 2779
Php 3: 4 t I myself have reasons for such confidence. 2788
Col 2: 5 For t I am absent from you in body, 1623
2:20 why, **as** t you still belonged to it, 6055
1Ti 1:13 *Even* t I *was* once a blasphemer and AIT
Heb 5:12 by this time *you* **ought** to be teachers, 1623
6: 7 **Even** t we speak like this, dear friends, 1623
7: 5 **even** t their brothers are descended 2788
11: 4 by faith he still speaks, even t he is **dead.** AIT
11: 8 t he **did** not **know** where he was AIT
11:11 even t he was past age— 2779
11:18 even t God had said to him, NIG
12:17 t he sought the blessing with tears. 2788
1Pe 1: 6 t now for a little while you may have had 1623
1: 7 which perishes even t **refined** by fire— AIT
1: 8 T you **have** not **seen** him, you love him; AIT
1: 8 t you do not **see** him now, you believe in him AIT

1Pe	2:12	*t* they **accuse** you of doing wrong,	AIT
	4:12	as *t* something strange were happening	6055
2Pe	1:12	of these things, even *t* you know them	2788
3Jn	1: 5	even *t* they are strangers to you.	2779
Jude	1: 5	**T** you already **know** all this,	3857
Rev	1:17	When I saw him, I fell at his feet **as** *t* dead.	6055
	3: 9	who claim to be Jews *t* they are not,	2779

THOUGHT (94) [THINK]

Ge	18:12	So Sarah laughed to herself *as she t,*	606
	19:14	But his sons-in-law *t* he was joking.	928+6524
	21:16	for *she t,* "I cannot watch the boy die."	606
	26: 7	He *t,* "The men of this place might kill me	NIH
	26: 9	I *t* I might lose my life on account of her."	606
	27:42	with the *t* of killing you.	NIH
	28:16	When Jacob awoke from his sleep, *he t,*	606
	31:31	I *t* you would take your daughters away	606
	32: 8	*He t,* "If Esau comes and attacks	606
	32:20	For he *t,* "I will pacify him	606
	38:11	For *he t,* "He may die too,	606
	38:15	Judah saw her, *he t* she was a prostitute,	3108
	43:18	*They t,* "We were brought here because of	606
Ex	2:14	Then Moses was afraid and *t,*	606
	3: 3	So Moses *t,* "I will go over and see	606
Dt	15: 9	Be careful not to harbor this wicked *t:*	1821
Jdg	16:20	He awoke from his sleep and *t,*	606
Ru	1:12	Even if *I t* there was still hope for me—	606
	4: 4	I *t* I should bring the matter	606
1Sa	1:13	Eli *t* she was drunk	3108
	13:12	I *t,* 'Now the Philistines will come down	606
	16: 6	Samuel saw Eliab and *t,*	606
	18: 8	*he t,* "but me with only thousands.	606
	18:21	"I will give her to him," *he t,*	606
	20:26	Saul said nothing that day, for *he t,*	606
	27: 1	But David *t* to himself, "One of these days	606
	27:11	for *he t,* "They might inform on us and say,	606
2Sa	4:10	and *t* he was bringing good news,	928+6524
	5: 6	They *t,* "David cannot get in here."	606
	10: 2	David *t,* "I will show kindness	606
	12:18	for *they t,* "While the child was still living,	606
	12:22	I *t,* 'Who knows?	606
	14:15	Your servant *t,* 'I will speak to the king;	606
	18:18	to himself, for *he t,* "I have no son to carry	606
1Ki	12:26	Jeroboam *t* to himself, "The kingdom will	606
	18:27	Perhaps *he is* **deep in** *t,* or busy,	8488
	22:32	they *t,* "Surely this is the king of Israel."	606
2Ki	5:11	"*I t* that he would surely come out	448+606+3276
	20:19	For he *t,* "Will there not be peace	606
1Ch	19: 2	David *t,* "I will show kindness	606
2Ch	18:31	they *t,* "This is the king of Israel."	606
	28:23	for *he t,* "Since the gods of the kings	606
Est	6: 6	Now Haman *t* to himself, "Who is there	606
Job	29:18	"*I t,* 'I will die in my own house,	606
	32: 7	*I t,* 'Age should speak,'	606
Ps	50:21	*you t* I was altogether like you.	1948
	77: 5	*I t about* the former days,	3108
	77:10	Then *I t,* "To this I will appeal:	606
	106: 7	*they* **gave** no *t to* your miracles;	8505
	109:16	For he never *t* of doing a kindness,	2349
Pr	5: 6	She **gives** no *t to* the way of life;	7143
	14: 8	of the prudent is *to* **give** *t to* their ways,	1067
	14:15	but a prudent man **gives** *t to* his steps.	1067
	17:28	Even a fool **is** *t* wise if he keeps silent,	3108
	21:29	but an upright man **gives** *t to* his ways.	1067
Ecc	1:16	I *t* to myself, "Look, I have grown and	1819
	2: 1	I *t* in my heart, "Come now, I will test you	606
	2:15	Then I *t* in my heart, "The fate of the fool	606
	3:17	I *t* in my heart, "God will bring to judgment	606
	3:18	I also *t,* "As for men, God tests them	606
Isa	29:16	as *if* the potter **were** *t* to be like the clay!	3108
	39: 8	For he *t,* "There will be peace and security	606
	65:20	at a hundred will be *t* a mere youth;	NIH
Jer	3: 7	I *t* that after she had done all this she would	606
	3:19	*I t* you would call me 'Father' and	606
	5: 4	I *t,* "These are only the poor;	606
La	3:54	and *I t* I was about to be cut off.	606
	4:20	*We t* that under his shadow we would live	606
Hag	1: 5	"**Give careful** *t* to your ways.	4222+8492
	1: 7	"**Give careful** *t* to your ways.	4222+8492
	2:15	" '**Now give careful** *t* to this	4222+8492
	2:18	**give careful** *t* to the day when	4222+8492
	2:18	temple was laid. **Give careful** *t:*	4222+8492
Mk	5:28	because *she t,* "If I just touch his clothes,	3306
	6:49	saw him walking on the lake, *they* he was a ghost.	1506
Lk	3:23	He was the son, so *it was t,* of Joseph,	3787
	12:17	*He t* to himself, 'What shall I do?	1368
	19:11	near Jerusalem and the people *t* that	1506
Jn	8:56	Your father Abraham rejoiced at the *t*	NIG
	11:13	but his disciples *t* he meant natural sleep.	1506
	13:29	some *t* Jesus was telling him to buy	1506
Ac	7:25	Moses *t* **that** his own people would realize	3787
	8:20	with you, because *you t* you could buy	3787
	8:22	for having such a *t* in your heart.	2154
	12: 9	*he t* he was seeing a vision.	1506
	16:27	and was about to kill himself *because he t*	3787
	27:13	*they t* they had obtained what they wanted;	1506
1Co	1:10	be perfectly united in mind and *t.*	1191
	13:11	I *t* like a child, I reasoned like a child.	5858
2Co	9: 5	So *I t* it necessary to urge the brothers	2451
	10: 5	and we take captive every *t*	3784
1Th	2:17	for a short time (in person, not *in t*),	2840
	3: 1	*we t* it best to be left by ourselves	2305
Heb	12:10	Our fathers disciplined us for a little while as they *t* best;	1506

THOUGHTLESSLY (1) [THINK]

Lev	5: 4	if a person *t* takes an oath	928+1051+4200+8557

THOUGHTS (47) [THINK]

Ge	6: 5	the *t of* his heart was only evil all the time.	4742
1Ch	28: 9	and understands every motive behind the *t.*	4742
Job	20: 2	"My **troubled** *t* prompt me to answer	8546
Ps	10: 4	in all his *t* there is no room for God.	4659
	13: 2	must I wrestle with my *t*	928+5883+6783
	55: 2	My *t* trouble me and I am distraught	8490
	92: 5	O Lord, how profound your *t!*	4742
	94:11	The Lord knows the *t of* man;	4742
	139: 2	you perceive my *t* from afar.	8277
	139:17	How precious to me are your *t,* O God!	8277
	139:23	test me and know my **anxious** *t.*	8595
Pr	1:23	to you and made my *t* known to you.	1821
	15:26	The Lord detests the *t of* the wicked,	4742
Ecc	2:12	Then I turned my *t* to consider wisdom,	NIH
	10:20	Do not revile the king even in your *t,*	4529
Isa	33:18	In your *t* you will ponder the former terror:	4213
	55: 7	and the evil man his *t.*	4742
	55: 8	"For my *t* are not your thoughts,	4742
	55: 8	"For my thoughts are not your *t,*	4742
	55: 9	and my *t* than your thoughts.	4742
	55: 9	and my thoughts than your *t.*	4742
	59: 7	Their *t* are evil thoughts;	4742
	59: 7	Their thoughts are evil *t;*	4742
Jer	4:14	How long will you harbor wicked *t?*	4742
	12: 3	you see me and test my *t* about you.	4213
Eze	38:10	On that day *t* will come into your mind	1821
Da	4:19	and his *t* terrified him.	10669
	7:28	I, Daniel, was deeply troubled by my *t,*	10669
Am	4:13	creates the wind, and reveals his *t* to man,	8465
Mic	4:12	But they do not know the *t* of the Lord;	4742
Mt	9: 4	Knowing their *t,* Jesus said,	1927
	9: 4	"Why *do you* **entertain** evil *t*	1926
	12:25	Jesus knew their *t* and said to them,	1927
	15:19	For out of the heart come evil *t,* murder,	1369
Mk	7:21	come evil *t,* sexual immorality, theft,	1369
Lk	1:51	who are proud *in* their inmost *t.*	1379
	2:35	that the *t* of many hearts will be revealed.	1369
	9:47	Jesus, knowing their *t,* took a little child	1369
	11:17	Jesus knew their *t* and said to them:	1378
Ro	2:15	and their *t* now accusing,	3361
1Co	2:11	among men **knows** the *t* of a man except	3857
	2:11	In the same way no one **knows** the *t*	1182
	3:20	that the *t* of the wise are futile."	1369
Eph	2: 3	and following its desires and *t.*	1379
Heb	3: 1	**fix** *your t* on Jesus, the apostle and high	2917
	4:12	it judges the *t* and attitudes of the heart.	1927
Jas	2: 4	and become judges *with* evil *t?*	1369

THOUSAND (272) [THOUSANDS, 1000]

Ge	20:16	"I am giving your brother a *t* shekels	547
Ex	12:37	There were about six hundred *t* men	547
	20: 6	to a *t* [generations] of those who love me	547
	32:28	that day about three *t* of the people died.	547
Lev	26: 8	and a hundred of you will chase **ten** *t,*	8047
Nu	7:85	dishes weighed *two t* four hundred shekels,	547
	11:21	"Here I am among six hundred *t* men	547
	31: 4	into battle a *t* men from each of the tribes	547
	31: 5	So twelve *t* men armed for battle,	547
	31: 5	a *t* from each tribe,	547
	31: 6	a *t* from each tribe,	547
	35: 5	measure **three** *t* **feet** on the east side,	547+564
	35: 5	*three t* on the south side,	547
	35: 5	*three t* on the west and three thousand on	547
	35: 5	three thousand on the west and *three t* on	547
Dt	1:11	a *t* times and bless you as he has promised!	547
	5:10	to a *t* [generations] of those who love me	547
	7: 9	to a *t* generations of those who love him	547
	32:30	How could one man chase a *t,*	547
	32:30	or two put **ten** *t* to flight,	8047
Jos	3: 4	of about a *t* yards between you and the ark;	547
	4:13	about forty *t* armed for battle crossed over	547
	7: 3	Send *two* or three *t* men to take it and do	547
	7: 4	So about three *t* men went up;	547
	8: 3	He chose thirty *t* of his best fighting men	547
	8:12	about five *t* men and set them in ambush	547
	8:25	Twelve *t* men and women fell that day—	547
	23:10	One of *you* routs a *t,*	547
Jdg	1: 4	and they struck down ten *t* men at Bezek.	547
	3:29	down about ten *t* Moabites, all vigorous	547
	4: 6	'Go, take with you ten *t* men of Naphtali	547
	4:10	Ten *t* men followed him,	547
	4:14	followed by ten *t* men.	547
	5: 8	or spear was seen among forty *t* in Israel.	547
	7: 3	So twenty-two *t* men left,	547
	7: 3	while ten *t* remained.	547
	8:10	of about fifteen *t* men, all that were left of	547
	8:10	and twenty *t* swordsmen had fallen.	547
	9:49	about a *t* men and women, also died.	547
	12: 6	Forty-two *t* Ephraimites were killed at	547
	15:11	Then three *t* men from Judah went down to	547
	15:15	he grabbed it and struck down a *t* men.	547
	15:16	a donkey's jawbone I have killed a *t* men."	547
	16:27	and on the roof were about three *t* men	547
	20: 2	four hundred *t* soldiers armed with swords.	547
	20:10	and a hundred from a *t,*	547
	20:10	and a *t* from ten thousand,	547
	20:10	and a thousand from **ten** *t,*	8047
	20:15	mobilized twenty-six *t* swordsmen	547
	20:17	mustered four hundred *t* swordsmen,	547
	20:21	and cut down twenty-two *t* Israelites on	547
	20:25	they cut down another eighteen *t* Israelites,	547

Jdg	20:34	Then ten *t* of Israel's finest men made	547
	20:44	Eighteen *t* Benjamites fell,	547
	20:45	the Israelites cut down five *t* men along	547
	20:45	as Gidom and struck down *two* more.	547
	20:46	twenty-five *t* Benjamite swordsmen fell,	547
	21:10	So the assembly sent twelve *t* fighting men	547
1Sa	4: 2	about four *t* of them on the battlefield.	547
	4:10	Israel lost thirty *t* foot soldiers.	547
	11: 8	the men of Israel numbered three hundred *t*	547
	11: 8	and the men of Judah thirty *t.*	547
	13: 2	Saul chose three *t* men from Israel;	547
	13: 2	*two t* were with him at Micmash and in	547
	13: 2	in the hill country of Bethel, and a *t* were	547
	13: 5	with three *t* chariots,	547
	13: 5	six *t* charioteers, and soldiers as numerous	547
	15: 4	two hundred *t* foot soldiers	547
	15: 4	and ten *t* men from Judah.	547
	17: 5	of bronze weighing five *t* shekels;	547
	18:13	and gave him command over a *t men,*	547
	24: 2	So Saul took three *t* chosen men	547
	25: 2	He had a *t* goats and three thousand sheep,	547
	25: 2	He had a thousand goats and three *t* sheep,	547
	26: 2	with his three *t* chosen men of Israel,	547
2Sa	6: 1	chosen men, thirty *t* in all.	547
	8: 4	David captured a *t* of his chariots,	547
	8: 4	of his chariots, seven *t* charioteers	547
	8: 4	and twenty *t* foot soldiers.	547
	8: 5	David struck down twenty-two *t* of them.	547
	8:13	from striking down eighteen *t* Edomites in	547
	10: 6	they hired twenty *t* Aramean foot soldiers	547
	10: 6	well as the king of Maacah with a *t* men,	547
	10: 6	and also twelve *t* men from Tob.	547
	10:18	and forty *t of* their foot soldiers.	547
	17: 1	"I would choose twelve *t* men	547
	18: 3	but you are worth ten *t* of us.	547
	18: 7	that day were great—twenty *t* men.	547
	18:12	"Even if a *t* shekels were weighed out	547
	19:17	With him were a *t* Benjamites,	547
	24: 9	In Israel there were eight hundred *t* able-bodied men who could handle	547
	24: 9	and in Judah five hundred *t.*	547
	24:15	and seventy *t* of the people from Dan	547
1Ki	3: 4	and Solomon offered a *t* burnt offerings on	547
	4:26	Solomon had four *t* stalls	547
	4:26	and twelve *t* horses.	547
	4:32	He spoke three *t* proverbs	547
	4:32	and his songs numbered a *t* and five.	547
	5:11	and Solomon gave Hiram twenty *t* cors	547
	5:11	to twenty *t* baths of pressed olive oil.	547
	5:13	from all Israel—thirty *t* men.	547
	5:14	to Lebanon in shifts of ten *t* a month,	547
	5:15	Solomon had seventy *t* carriers	547
	5:15	and eighty *t* stonecutters in the hills,	547
	7:26	It held *two t* baths.	547
	8:63	twenty-two *t* cattle and a hundred	547
	8:63	a hundred and twenty *t* sheep and goats.	547
	10:26	and twelve *t* horses,	547
	12:21	a hundred and eighty *t* fighting men—	547
	19:18	Yet I reserve seven *t* in Israel—	547
	20:29	a hundred *t* casualties on the Aramean	547
	20:30	where the wall collapsed on twenty-seven *t*	547
2Ki	3: 4	with a hundred *t* lambs and with the wool	547
	3: 4	and with the wool of a hundred *t* rams.	547
	5: 5	six *t* shekels of gold and ten *t* sets	547
	13: 7	ten chariots and ten *t* foot soldiers,	547
	14: 7	the one who defeated ten *t* Edomites in	547
	15:19	and Menahem gave him a *t* talents of silver	547
	18:23	I will give you *two t* horses—	547
	19:35	to death a hundred and eighty-five *t* men in	547
	24:14	and artisans—a total of ten *t.*	547
	24:16	the entire force of seven *t* fighting men,	547
	24:16	and a *t* craftsmen and artisans.	547
1Ch	5:21	of the Hagrites—fifty *t* camels,	547
	5:21	two hundred fifty *t* sheep	547
	5:21	and *two t* donkeys.	547
	5:21	also took one hundred *t* people captive,	547
	12:14	and the greatest for a *t.*	547
	12:20	leaders of **units of a** *t* in Manasseh.	547
	15:25	of **units of a** *t* went to bring up the ark of	547
	16:15	the word he commanded, for a *t* generations,	547
	18: 4	David captured a *t* of his chariots,	547
	18: 4	of his chariots, seven *t* charioteers	547
	18: 4	and twenty *t* foot soldiers.	547
	18: 5	David struck down twenty-two *t* of them.	547
	18:12	down eighteen *t* Edomites in the Valley	547
	19: 6	Hanun and the Ammonites sent a *t* talents	547
	19: 7	They hired thirty-two *t* chariots	547
	19:18	and David killed seven *t* of their charioteers	547
	19:18	and forty *t of* their foot soldiers.	547
	21: 5	In all Israel there were one million one hundred *t* men who could handle	547
	21: 5	including four hundred and seventy *t*	547
	21:14	and seventy *t* men of Israel fell dead.	547
	22:14	of the Lord a hundred *t* talents of gold,	547
	23: 3	the total number of men was thirty-eight *t.*	547
	23: 4	twenty-four *t* are to supervise the work of	547
	23: 4	of the temple of the Lord and six *t* are to	547
	23: 5	Four *t* are to be gatekeepers	547
	23: 5	to be gatekeepers and four *t* are to praise	547
	29: 4	three *t* talents of gold (gold of Ophir)	547
	29: 4	and seven *t* talents of refined silver,	547
	29: 4	on the temple of God five *t* talents	547
	29: 7	and **ten** *t* darics of gold,	8052
	29: 7	ten *t* talents of silver,	547
	29: 7	**eighteen** *t* talents of bronze	547+2256+8052+9046
	29: 7	of bronze and a hundred *t* talents of iron.	547
	29:21	a *t* bulls, a thousand rams and	547

1Ch	29:21	a t rams and a thousand male lambs,	547
	29:21	a thousand rams and a t male lambs,	547
2Ch	1: 6	of Meeting and offered a t burnt offerings	547
	1:14	and twelve t horses,	547
	2: 2	He conscripted seventy t men as carriers	547
	2: 2	as carriers and eighty t as stonecutters in	547
	2:10	twenty t cors of ground wheat,	547
	2:10	twenty t cors of barley,	547
	2:10	twenty t baths of wine	547
	2:10	of wine and twenty t baths of olive oil."	547
	4: 5	It held three t baths.	547
	7: 5	a sacrifice of twenty-two t head of cattle	547
	7: 5	of cattle and a hundred and twenty t sheep	547
	9:25	Solomon had four t stalls for horses	547
	9:25	and twelve t horses,	547
	11: 1	a hundred and eighty t fighting men—	547
	12: 3	and sixty t horsemen and	547
	13: 3	of four hundred t able fighting men,	547
	13: 3	with eight hundred t able troops.	547
	13:17	so that there were five hundred t casualties	547
	14: 8	Asa had an army of three hundred t men	547
	14: 8	two hundred and eighty t from Benjamin,	547
	15:11	of cattle and seven t sheep and goats from	547
	17:11	seven t seven hundred rams	547
	17:11	and seven t seven hundred goats.	547
	25: 5	that there were three hundred t men ready	547
	25: 6	a hundred t fighting men from Israel for	547
	25:11	where he killed ten t men of Seir.	547
	25:12	of Judah also captured ten t men alive,	547
	25:13	They killed three t people	547
	27: 5	ten t cors of wheat and ten thousand cors	547
	27: 5	ten thousand cors of wheat and ten t cors	547
	28: 6	a hundred and twenty t soldiers in Judah—	547
	28: 8	from their kinsmen two hundred t wives,	547
	29:33	to six hundred bulls and three t sheep	547
	30:24	Hezekiah king of Judah provided a t bulls	547
	30:24	a thousand bulls and seven t sheep	547
	30:24	a t bulls and ten thousand sheep and goats.	547
	30:24	a thousand bulls and ten t sheep and goats.	547
	35: 7	a total of thirty t sheep and goats for	547
	35: 7	and also three t cattle—	547
	35: 9	provided five t Passover offerings	547
Est	3: 9	and I will put ten t talents of silver into	547
	9:16	They killed seventy-five t of them but did	547
Job	1: 3	and he owned seven t sheep,	547
	1: 3	three t camels, five hundred yoke of oxen	547
	9: 3	not answer him one time out of a t.	547
	33:23	as a mediator, one out of a t,	547
	42:12	He had fourteen t sheep,	547
	42:12	six t camels, a thousand yoke of oxen and	547
	42:12	a yoke of oxen and a thousand donkeys.	547
	42:12	a thousand yoke of oxen and a t donkeys.	547
Ps	50:10	and the cattle on a t hills.	547
	60:T	and struck down twelve t Edomites in	547
	84:10	in your courts than a t elsewhere;	547
	90: 4	For a t years in your sight are like a day	547
	91: 7	A t may fall at your side,	547
	91: 7	ten t at your right hand,	8047
	105: 8	the word he commanded, for a t generations,	547
Ecc	6: 6	if he lives a t years twice over but fails	547
	7:28	I found one [upright] man among a t,	547
SS	4: 4	on it hang a t shields,	547
	5:10	outstanding among ten t.	8047
	8:11	Each was to bring for its fruit a t shekels	547
	8:12	the t shekels are for you, O Solomon,	547
Isa	7:23	a t vines worth a thousand silver shekels,	547
	7:23	a thousand vines worth a t silver shekels.	547
	30:17	A t will flee at the threat of one;	547
	36: 8	I will give you two t horses—	547
	37:36	to death a hundred and eighty-five t men in	547
	60:22	The least of you will become a t,	547
Eze	47: 3	he measured off a t cubits and then led me	547
	47: 4	He measured off another t cubits	547
	47: 4	He measured off another t and led me	547
	47: 5	He measured off another t,	547
Da	5: 1	a t of his nobles and drank wine with them.	10038
	7:10	ten t times ten thousand stood before him.	10649
	7:10	ten thousand times ten t. stood before him.	10649
Am	5: 3	"The city that marches out a t strong	547
Jnh	4:11	a hundred and twenty t people who cannot tell their right hand	6926+8052+9109
Mic	6: 7	with ten t rivers of oil?	8047
Mt	14:21	of those who ate was about five t men,	4295
	15:38	The number of those who ate was four t,	5483
	16: 9	the five loaves for the five t,	4295
	16:10	Or the seven loaves for the four t,	5483
	18:24	who owed him ten t talents was brought	3691
Mk	5:13	The herd, about two t in number,	1493
	6:44	of the men who had eaten was five t.	4295
	8: 9	About four t men were present.	5483
	8:19	I broke the five loaves for the five t,	4295
	8:20	I broke the seven loaves for the four t,	5483
Lk	9:14	(About five t men were there.)	4295
	14:31	with ten t men to oppose the one coming	5942
	14:31	against him with twenty t?	5942
	16: 7	" 'A t bushels of wheat,' he replied.	1669+3174
Jn	6:10	the men sat down, about five t of them.	4295
Ac	2:41	about three t were added to their number	5567
	4: 4	the number of men grew to about five t.	5942
	19:19	the total came to fifty t drachmas.	3689+4297
	21:38	a revolt and led four t terrorists out into	5483
Ro	11: 4	for myself seven t who have not bowed	2233
1Co	4:15	though you have ten t guardians in Christ,	3692
	10: 8	and in one day twenty-three t of them died.	5942
	14:19	to instruct others than ten t words in	3692
2Pe	3: 8	With the Lord a day is like a t years,	5943
	3: 8	and a t years are like a day.	5943

Rev	5:11	and ten t times ten thousand.	3689
	5:11	and ten thousand times ten t.	3689
	11:13	Seven t people were killed in	5942
	20: 2	or Satan, and bound him for a t years.	5943
	20: 3	until the t years were ended.	5943
	20: 4	to life and reigned with Christ a t years.	5943
	20: 5	to life until the t years were ended.)	5943
	20: 6	and will reign with him for a t years.	5943
	20: 7	When the t years are over,	5943

THOUSANDS (53) [THOUSAND]

Ge	24:60	may you increase to t upon thousands;	547
	24:60	may you increase to thousands upon t;	8047
Ex	18:21	and appoint them as officials over t,	547
	18:25	officials over t, hundreds, fifties and tens.	547
	34: 7	maintaining love to t, and forgiving	547
Nu	10:36	O LORD, to the countless t of Israel."	547
	31:14	the commanders of t and commanders	547
	31:48	the commanders of t and commanders	547
	31:52	All the gold from the commanders of t	547
	31:54	the commanders of t and commanders	547
Dt	1:15	as commanders of t, of hundreds,	547
	33:17	Such are the ten t of Ephraim;	8047
	33:17	such are the t of Manasseh."	547
1Sa	8:12	Some he will assign to be commanders of t	547
	18: 7	"Saul has slain his t,	547
	18: 7	and David his tens of t."	8047
	18: 8	"They have credited David with tens of t,"	8047
	18: 8	he thought, "but me with only t.	547
	21:11	" 'Saul has slain his t,	547
	21:11	and David his tens of t'?"	8047
	22: 7	of you commanders of t and commanders	547
	29: 2	with their units of hundreds and t,	547
	29: 5	" 'Saul has slain his t,	547
	29: 5	and David his tens of t'?"	8047
2Sa	18: 1	and appointed over them commanders of t	547
	18: 4	in units of hundreds and of t.	547
1Ch	13: 1	the commanders of t and commanders	547
	26:26	of families who were the commanders of t	547
	27: 1	heads of families, commanders of t	547
	28: 1	the commanders of t and commanders	547
	29: 6	the commanders of t and commanders	547
2Ch	1: 2	to the commanders of t and commanders	547
	25: 5	to commanders of t and commanders	547
Ps	3: 6	not fear the tens of t drawn up against me	8047
	68:17	chariots of God are tens of t and thousands	8052
	68:17	are tens of thousands and t of thousands;	547
	68:17	tens of thousands and thousands of t;	9099
	119:72	to me than t of pieces of silver and gold.	547
	144:13	Our sheep will increase by t,	545
	144:13	by tens of t in our fields;	8045
Jer	32:18	to t but bring the punishment for	547
Da	7:10	T upon thousands attended him;	10038
	7:10	Thousands upon t attended him;	10038
	11:12	with pride and will slaughter many t,	8052
Mic	6: 7	Will the LORD be pleased with t of rams,	547
Lk	12: 1	when a crowd of many t had gathered,	3689
Ac	21:20	how many t of Jews have believed,	3689
Heb	12:22	You have come to t upon thousands	3689
	12:22	You have come to thousands upon t	3689
Jude	1:14	the Lord is coming with t upon thousands	3689
	1:14	the Lord is coming with thousands upon t	3689
Rev	5:11	many angels, numbering t upon thousands,	5942
	5:11	many angels, numbering thousands upon t,	5942

THRASHING (2)

| Job | 41:25 | they retreat before his t. | 8691 |
| Eze | 32: 2 | you are like a monster in the seas t about | 1631 |

THREAD (3) [THREADS]

Ge	14:23	not even a t or the thong of a sandal,	2562
	38:28	so the midwife took a scarlet t and tied it	9106
	38:30	who had the scarlet t on his wrist,	9106

THREADS (1) [THREAD]

| Jdg | 16:12 | the ropes off his arms as if they were t. | 2562 |

THREAT (6) [THREATEN, THREATENED, THREATS]

Ezr	4:22	Why let this t grow,	10244
Ne	4: 9	a guard day and night to meet this t.	2157S
Ps	64: 1	protect my life from the t of the enemy.	7065
Pr	13: 8	but a poor man hears no t.	1722
Isa	7	A thousand will flee at the t of one;	1722
	30:17	at the t of five you will all flee away,	1722

THREATEN (3) [THREAT]

Ps	73: 8	in their arrogance they t oppression.	1819
Eze	6:10	I did not t in vain to bring this calamity	1819
Eph	6: 9	Do not t them, since you know that	581

THREATENED (6) [THREAT]

Ex	32:14	not bring on his people the disaster he had t.	1819
Jos	23:15	will bring on you all the evil he has t,	1821
Jer	27:13	with which the LORD has t any nation	1819
Jnh	1: 4	a violent storm arose that the ship t	3108
	2: 5	The engulfing waters t me,	5883+6330
	3:10	bring upon them the destruction he had t.	1819

THREATS (8) [THREAT]

| Ps | 10: 7 | His mouth is full of curses and lies and t; | 9412 |

Ps	55:11	t and lies never leave its streets.	9412
Jer	44:29	'so that you will know that my t of harm	1821
Zep	2: 8	who insulted my people and made t	1540
Ac	4:21	After further t they let them go.	4653
	4:29	consider their t and enable your servants	581
	9: 1	Saul was still breathing out murderous t	581
1Pe	2:23	when he suffered, he made no t.	580

THREE (393) [THIRD, THIRDS, THREE TAVERNS, THREE-DAY, THREE-PRONGED, THREE-TENTHS, THREE-YEAR-OLD, TWO-THIRDS]

Ge	6:10	Noah had t sons: Shem, Ham and Japheth.	8993
	7:13	with his wife and the wives of his t sons,	8993
	9:19	These were the t sons of Noah,	8993
	15: 9	a goat and a ram, each t years old,	8992
	18: 2	looked up and saw t men standing nearby.	8993
	18: 6	"get t seahs of fine flour and knead it	8993
	29: 2	with t flocks of sheep lying near it because	8993
	29:34	because I have borne him t sons."	8993
	34:25	T days later, while all of them were still	8958
	38:24	About t months later Judah was told,	8993
	40:10	and on the vine were t branches.	8993
	40:12	"The t branches are three days.	8993
	40:12	"The three branches are t days.	8993
	40:13	Within t days Pharaoh will lift	8993
	40:16	On my head were t baskets of bread.	8993
	40:18	"The t baskets are three days.	8993
	40:18	"The three baskets are t days.	8993
	40:19	Within t days Pharaoh will lift off your head	8993
	42:17	And he put them all in custody for t days.	8993
	45:22	but to Benjamin he gave t hundred shekels	8993
Ex	2: 2	she hid him for t months.	8993
	10:22	total darkness covered all Egypt for t days.	8993
	10:23	or leave his place for t days.	8993
	15:22	For t days they traveled in the desert	8993
	21:11	not provide her with these t things,	8993
	23:14	"T times a year you are to celebrate	8993
	23:17	"T times a year all the men are to appear	8993
	25:32	t on one side and three on the other.	8993
	25:32	three on one side and t on the other.	8993
	25:33	T cups shaped like almond flowers	8993
	25:33	t on the next branch,	8993
	27: 1	an altar of acacia wood, t cubits high;	8993
	27:14	with t posts and three bases,	8993
	27:14	with three posts and t bases,	8993
	27:15	with t posts and three bases.	8993
	27:15	with three posts and t bases.	8993
	32:28	about t thousand of the people died.	8993
	34:23	T times a year all your men are to appear	8993
	34:24	up t times each year to appear before	8993
	37:18	t on one side and three on the other.	8993
	37:18	three on one side and t on the other.	8993
	37:19	T cups shaped like almond flowers	8993
	37:19	t on the next branch and the same	8993
	38: 1	of acacia wood, t cubits high;	8993
	38:14	with t posts and three bases,	8993
	38:14	with three posts and t bases,	8993
	38:15	with t posts and three bases.	8993
	38:15	with three posts and t bases.	8993
Lev	19:23	For t years you are to consider it forbidden;	8993
	25:21	that the land will yield enough for t years.	8993
	27: 6	and that of a female at t shekels of silver.	8993
Nu	10:33	of the LORD and traveled for t days.	8993
	10:33	during those t days to find them a place	8993
	11:31	the camp to about t feet above the ground,	564
	12: 4	to the Tent of Meeting, all t of you."	8993
	12: 4	So the t of them came out.	8993
	22:28	to you to make you beat me these t times?"	8993
	22:32	"Why have you beaten your donkey these t times?	8993
	22:33	and turned away from me these t times.	8993
	24:10	but you have blessed them these t times.	8993
	33: 8	and when they had traveled for t days in	8993
	35: 5	measure t thousand feet on the east side,	547+564
	35: 5	t thousand on the south side,	AIT
	35: 5	t thousand on the west and three thousand	AIT
	35: 5	three thousand on the west and t thousand	AIT
	35:14	Give t on this side of the Jordan and three	8993
	35:14	and t in Canaan as cities of refuge.	8993
Dt	4:41	Moses set aside t cities east of the Jordan,	8993
	14:28	At the end of every t years,	8993
	16:16	T times a year all your men must appear	8993
	17: 6	or t witnesses a man shall be put to death,	8993
	19: 2	for yourselves t cities centrally located in	8993
	19: 3	Build roads to them and divide into t parts	8992
	19: 7	to set aside for yourselves t cities.	8993
	19: 9	then you are to set aside t more cities.	8993
	19:15	by the testimony of two or t witnesses.	8993
Jos	1:11	T days from now you will cross	8993
	2:16	Hide yourselves there t days	8993
	2:22	into the hills and stayed there t days,	8993
	3: 2	After t days the officers went throughout	8993
	7: 3	Send two or t thousand men to take it	8993
	7: 4	So about t thousand men went up;	8993
	9:16	T days after they made the treaty with	8993
	15:14	From Hebron Caleb drove out the t Anakites—	8993
	18: 4	Appoint t men from each tribe.	8993
	21:32	with their pasturelands—t towns.	8993
Jdg	1:20	who drove from it the t sons of Anak.	8993
	7: 6	T hundred men lapped with their hands	8993
	7: 7	"With the t hundred men that lapped	8993
	7: 8	to their tents but kept the t hundred.	8993
	7:16	the t hundred men into three companies,	8993

Ref		Text	Strong's
Jdg	7:16	the three hundred men into t companies,	8993
	7:20	The t companies blew the trumpets	8993
	7:22	When the t hundred trumpets sounded,	8993
	8: 4	Gideon and his t hundred men,	8993
	9:22	Abimelech had governed Israel t years,	8993
	9:43	into t companies and set an ambush in	8993
	11:26	t hundred years Israel occupied Heshbon,	8993
	14:14	For t days they could not give the answer.	8993
	15: 4	So he went out and caught t hundred foxes	8993
	15:11	Then t thousand men from Judah went	8993
	16:27	and on the roof were about t thousand men	8993
	19: 4	so he remained with him t days,	8993
1Sa	2:21	and gave birth to t sons and two daughters.	8993
	9:20	As for the donkeys you lost t days ago,	8993
	10: 3	T men going up to God	8993
	10: 3	One will be carrying t young goats,	8993
	10: 3	another t loaves of bread,	8993
	11: 8	of Israel numbered t hundred thousand and	8993
	11:11	Saul separated his men into t divisions;	8993
	13: 2	Saul chose t thousand men from Israel;	8993
	13: 5	with t thousand chariots,	8993
	13:17	from the Philistine camp in t detachments.	8993
	17:13	Jesse's t oldest sons had followed Saul to	8993
	17:14	The t oldest followed Saul,	8993
	20:20	I will shoot t arrows to the side of it,	8993
	20:41	and bowed down before Jonathan t times,	8993
	24: 2	So Saul took t thousand chosen men	8993
	25: 2	a thousand goats and t thousand sheep,	8993
	26: 2	with his t thousand chosen men of Israel,	8993
	30:12	or drunk any water for t days	8993
	30:12	for three days and t nights.	8993
	30:13	when I became ill t days ago.	8993
	31: 6	and his t sons and his armor-bearer	8993
	31: 8	and his t sons fallen on Mount Gilboa.	8993
2Sa	2:18	The t sons of Zeruiah were there:	8993
	2:31	But David's men had killed t hundred	8993
	6:11	of Obed-Edom the Gittite for t months,	8993
	13:38	he stayed there t years.	8993
	14:27	T sons and a daughter were born	8993
	18:14	So he took t javelins in his hand	8993
	20: 4	of Judah to come to me within t days,	8993
	21: 1	there was a famine for t successive years;	8993
	21:16	spearhead weighed t hundred shekels	8993
	23: 8	a Tahkemonite, was chief of the T;	8998
	23: 9	As one of the t mighty men,	8993
	23:13	t of the thirty chief men came down	8993
	23:16	So the t mighty men broke through	8993
	23:17	the exploits of the t mighty men.	8993
	23:18	of Joab son of Zeruiah was chief of the T.	8998
	23:18	He raised his spear against t hundred men,	8993
	23:18	and so he became as famous as the T.	8993
	23:19	not held in greater honor than the T?	8998
	23:22	he too was as famous as the t mighty men.	8993
	23:23	but he was not included among the t mighty men.	8993
	24:12	I am giving you t options.	8993
	24:13	upon you t years of famine in your land?	8993
	24:13	Or t months of fleeing from your enemies	8993
	24:13	Or t days of plague in your land?	8993
1Ki	2:39	But t years later, two of Shimei's slaves	8993
	4:32	He spoke t thousand proverbs	8993
	6:36	the inner courtyard of t courses	8993
	7: 4	Its windows were placed high in sets of t,	8993
	7: 5	they were in the front part in sets of t,	8993
	7:12	by a wall of t courses of dressed stone	8993
	7:25	Sea stood on twelve bulls, t facing north,	8993
	7:25	three facing north, t facing west,	8993
	7:25	t facing south and three facing east.	8993
	7:25	three facing south and t facing east.	8993
	7:27	four wide and t high.	8993
	9:25	T times a year Solomon sacrificed burnt offerings	8993
	10:17	He also made t hundred small shields	8993
	10:17	with t minas of gold in each shield.	8993
	10:22	Once every t years it returned,	8993
	11: 3	of royal birth and t hundred concubines,	8993
	12: 5	"Go away for t days and then come back	8993
	12:12	T days later Jeroboam and all	8958
	12:12	"Come back to me in t days."	8958
	15: 2	and he reigned in Jerusalem t years.	8993
	17:21	on the boy t times and cried to the LORD,	8993
	22: 1	For t years there was no war	8993
2Ki	2:17	who searched for t days but did	8993
	3:10	the LORD called us t kings together only	8993
	3:13	the LORD who called us t kings together	8993
	9:32	Two or t eunuchs looked down at him.	8993
	11: 5	the t companies that are going on duty on	NIH
	13:18	He struck it t times and stopped.	8993
	13:19	But now you will defeat it only t times."	8993
	13:25	T times Jehoash defeated him,	8993
	17: 5	and laid siege to it for t years.	8993
	18:10	At the end of t years the Assyrians took it.	8993
	18:14	of Judah t hundred talents of silver	8993
	23:31	and he reigned in Jerusalem t months.	8993
	24: 1	Jehoiakim became his vassal for t years.	8993
	24: 8	and he reigned in Jerusalem t months.	8993
	25:18	in rank and the t doorkeepers.	8993
1Ch	2: 3	These t were born to him by	8993
	2:16	Zeruiah's t sons were Abishai,	8993
	3:23	and Azrikam—t in all.	8993
	7: 6	T sons of Benjamin:	8993
	10: 6	So Saul and his t sons died,	8993
	11:11	he raised his spear against t hundred men,	8993
	11:12	one of the t mighty men.	8993
	11:15	T of the thirty chiefs came down to David	8993
	11:18	So the T broke through the Philistine lines,	8993
	11:19	the exploits of the t mighty men.	8993
	11:20	the brother of Joab was chief of the T.	8993
1Ch	11:20	He raised his spear against t hundred men,	8993
	11:20	and so he became as famous as the T.	8993
	11:21	above the T and became their commander,	8993
	11:24	he too was as famous as the t mighty men.	8993
	11:25	but he was not included among the T.	8993
	12:39	The men spent t days there with David,	8993
	13:14	of Obed-Edom in his house for t months,	8993
	21:10	I am giving you t options.	8993
	21:12	t years of famine, three months	8993
	21:12	t months of being swept away	8993
	21:12	or t days of the sword of the LORD—	8993
	23: 8	and Joel—t in all.	8993
	23: 9	and Haran—t in all.	8993
	23:23	and Jerimoth—t in all.	8993
	25: 5	God gave Heman fourteen sons and t daughters.	8993
	29: 4	t thousand talents of gold (gold of Ophir)	8993
2Ch	4: 4	Sea stood on twelve bulls, t facing north,	8993
	4: 4	three facing north, t facing west,	8993
	4: 4	t facing south and three facing east.	8993
	4: 4	three facing south and t facing east.	8993
	4: 5	It held t thousand baths.	8993
	6:13	five cubits wide and t cubits high,	8993
	8:13	New Moons and the t annual feasts—	8993
	9:16	He also made t hundred small shields	8993
	9:16	with t hundred bekas of gold	8993
	9:21	Once every t years it returned,	8993
	10: 5	"Come back to me in t days."	8993
	10:12	T days later Jeroboam and all	8958
	10:12	"Come back to me in t days."	8958
	11:17	Rehoboam son of Solomon t years,	8993
	13: 2	and he reigned in Jerusalem t years.	8993
	14: 8	of t hundred thousand men from Judah,	8993
	14: 9	with a vast army and t hundred chariots,	8993
	20:25	so much plunder that it took t days	8993
	25: 5	there were t hundred thousand men ready	8993
	25:13	They killed t thousand people	8993
	29:33	to six hundred bulls and t thousand sheep	8993
	31:16	they distributed to the males t years old	8993
	35: 7	and also t thousand cattle—	8993
	35: 8	and t hundred cattle.	8993
	36: 2	and he reigned in Jerusalem t months.	8993
	36: 9	and he reigned in Jerusalem t months	8993
Ezr	6: 4	with t courses of large stones and one	10760
	8:15	and we camped there t days.	8993
	8:32	where we rested t days.	8993
	10: 8	within t days would forfeit all his property,	8993
	10: 9	Within the t days, all the men of Judah	8993
Ne	2:11	and after staying there t days	8993
Est	4:16	Do not eat or drink for t days, night or day.	8993
	9:15	they put to death in Susa t hundred men,	8993
Job	1: 2	He had seven sons and t daughters,	8993
	1: 3	t thousand camels, five hundred yoke	8993
	1: 4	and they would invite their t sisters to eat	8993
	1:17	"The Chaldeans formed t raiding parties	8993
	2:11	When Job's t friends, Eliphaz the Temanite,	8993
	32: 1	So these t men stopped answering Job,	8993
	32: 3	He was also angry with the t friends,	8993
	32: 5	that the t men had nothing more to say,	8993
	33:29	to a man—twice, even t times—	8993
	42:13	he also had seven sons and t daughters.	8993
Pr	30:15	"There are t things that are never satisfied,	8993
	30:18	"There are t things that are too amazing	8993
	30:21	"Under things the earth trembles,	8993
	30:29	"There are t things that are stately	8993
Ecc	4:12	A cord of t strands is not quickly broken.	8992
Isa	16:14	But now the LORD says: "Within t years,	8993
	17: 6	or t olives on the topmost branches,	8993
	20: 3	stripped and barefoot for t years,	8993
Jer	36:23	Whenever Jehudi had read t or four columns	8993
	52:24	next in rank and the t doorkeepers.	8993
Eze	14:14	even if these t men—Noah, Daniel and Job	8993
	14:16	even if these t men were in it,	8993
	14:18	even if these t men were in it,	8993
	21:14	Let the sword strike twice, even t times.	8958
	40:10	the east gate were t alcoves on each side;	8993
	40:10	t he had the same measurements,	8993
	40:21	Its alcoves—t on each side—	8993
	40:48	and its projecting walls were t cubits wide	8993
	41: 6	The side rooms were on t levels,	8993
	41:16	and galleries around the t of them—	8993
	41:22	There was a wooden altar t cubits high	8993
	42: 3	gallery faced gallery at the t levels.	8958
	48:31	The t gates on the north side will be	8993
	48:32	which is 4,500 cubits long, will be t gates:	8993
	48:33	measures 4,500 cubits, will be t gates:	8993
	48:34	which is 4,500 cubits long, will be t gates:	8993
Da	1: 5	They were to be trained for t years,	8993
	3:23	and these t men, firmly tied, fell into	10760
	3:24	"Weren't there t men that we tied up	10760
	6: 2	with t administrators over them,	10760
	6:10	T times a day he got down on his knees	10760
	6:13	He still prays t times a day."	10760
	7: 5	it had t ribs in its mouth between its teeth.	10760
	7: 8	and t of the first horns were uprooted	10760
	7:20	before which t of them fell—	10760
	7:24	he will subdue t kings.	10760
	10: 2	Daniel, mourned for t weeks.	8993
	10: 3	at all until the t weeks were over.	8993
	11: 2	T more kings will appear in Persia,	8993
Am	1: 3	"For t sins of Damascus, even for four,	8993
	1: 6	"For t sins of Gaza, even for four,	8993
	1: 9	"For t sins of Tyre, even for four,	8993
	1:11	"For t sins of Edom, even for four,	8993
	1:13	"For t sins of Ammon, even for four,	8993
	2: 1	"For t sins of Moab, even for four,	8993
	2: 4	"For t sins of Judah, even for four,	8993
Am	2: 6	"For t sins of Israel, even for four,	8993
	4: 4	your tithes every t years.	8993
	4: 7	when the harvest was still t months away.	8993
Jnh	1:17	inside the fish t days and three nights.	8993
	1:17	inside the fish three days and t nights.	8993
	3: 3	a visit required t days.	8993
Zec	11: 8	In one month I got rid of the t shepherds.	8993
Mt	12:40	For as Jonah was t days and three nights in	5552
	12:40	For as Jonah was three days and t nights	5552
	12:40	Son of Man will be t days and three nights	5552
	12:40	Son of Man will be three days and t nights	5552
	15:32	with me t days and have nothing to eat.	5552
	17: 4	If you wish, I will put up t shelters—	5552
	18:16	by the testimony of two or t witnesses.	5552
	18:20	where two or t come together in my name,	5552
	26:34	you will disown me t times."	5565
	26:61	the temple of God and rebuild it in t days.' "	5565
	26:75	you will disown me t times."	5565
	27:40	to destroy the temple and build it in t days,	5552
	27:63	'After t days I will rise again.'	5552
Mk	8: 2	with me t days and have nothing to eat.	5552
	8:31	be killed and after t days rise again.	5552
	9: 5	Let us put up t shelters—	5552
	9:31	and after t days he will rise."	5552
	10:34	T days later he will rise."	5552
	14:30	rooster crows twice you yourself will disown me t times."	5565
	14:58	and in t days will build another,	5552
	14:72	crows twice you will disown me t times."	5565
	15:29	to destroy the temple and build it in t days,	5552
Lk	1:56	about t months and then returned home.	5552
	2:46	After t days they found him in	5552
	4:25	the sky was shut for t and a half years	5552
	9:33	Let us put up t shelters—	5552
	10:36	of these t do you think was a neighbor to	5552
	11: 5	'Friend, lend me t loaves of bread,	5552
	12:52	t against two and two against three.	5552
	12:52	three against two and two against t.	5552
	13: 7	'For t years now I've been coming to look	5552
	22:34	you will deny t times that you know me."	5565
	22:61	you will disown me t times."	5565
Jn	2:19	and I will raise it again in t days."	5552
	2:20	and you are going to raise it in t days?"	5552
	6:19	they had rowed t or three and a half miles,	1633+2445+4297+5084+5558
	6:19	they had rowed three or t and a half miles,	1633+2445+4297+5084+5558
	13:38	you will disown me t times!	5565
Ac	2:41	and about t thousand were added	5567
	3: 1	time of prayer—at t in the afternoon.	1888
	5: 7	About t hours later his wife came in,	5552
	7:20	For t months he was cared for	5552
	9: 9	For t days he was blind,	5552
	10: 3	at about t in the afternoon he had a vision.	1888+2465+3836+6052
	10:16	This happened t times,	5565
	10:19	"Simon, t men are looking for you.	5552
	10:30	praying at this hour, at t in the afternoon.	1888
	11:10	This happened t times,	5565
	11:11	"Right then t men who had been sent to me	5552
	17: 2	on t Sabbath days he reasoned with them	5552
	19: 8	and spoke boldly there for t months,	5552
	20: 3	where he stayed t months.	5552
	20:31	for t years I never stopped warning each	5562
	25: 1	T days after arriving in the province,	5552
	28: 7	and for t days entertained us hospitably.	5552
	28:11	After t months we put out to sea in a ship	5552
	28:12	in at Syracuse and stayed there t days.	5552
	28:17	T days later he called together the leaders	5552
1Co	13:13	now these t remain: faith, hope and love.	5552
	14:27	two—or at the most t—should speak,	5552
	14:29	Two or t prophets should speak,	5552
2Co	11:25	T times I was beaten with rods,	5565
	11:25	t times I was shipwrecked,	5565
	12: 8	T times I pleaded with the Lord	5565
	13: 1	by the testimony of two or t witnesses."	5552
Gal	1:18	Then after t years, I went up to Jerusalem	5552
1Ti	5:19	unless it is brought by two or t witnesses.	5552
Heb	10:28	on the testimony of two or t witnesses.	5552
	11:23	for t months after he was born,	5564
Jas	5:17	not rain on the land for t and a half years.	5552
1Jn	5: 7	For there are t that testify:	5552
	5: 8	and the t are in agreement.	5552
Rev	6: 6	and t quarts of barley for a day's wages,	5552
	8:13	about to be sounded by the other t angels!"	5552
	9:18	of mankind was killed by the t plagues	5552
	11: 9	For t and a half days men from every	5552
	11:11	after the t and a half days a breath of life	5552
	16:13	I saw t evil spirits that looked like frogs;	5552
	16:19	The great city split into t parts,	5552
	21:13	There were t gates on the east,	5552
	21:13	t on the north, three on the south	5552
	21:13	t on the south and three on the west.	5552
	21:13	three on the south and t on the west.	5552

THREE TAVERNS (1) [THREE]

| Ac | 28:15 | Forum of Appius and the T to meet us. | 5553 |

THREE-DAY (4) [DAY, THREE]

Ge	30:36	he put a t journey between himself	3427+8993
Ex	3:18	Let us take a t journey into the desert	3427+8993
	5: 3	let us take a t journey into the desert	3427+8993
	8:27	We must take a t journey into the desert	3427+8993

THREE-PRONGED (1) [THREE]
1Sa	2:13	of the priest would come with a t fork	8993+9094

THREE-TENTHS (8) [TEN, THREE]
Lev	14:10	with t of an ephah of fine flour mixed	6928+8993
Nu	15: 9	offering of t of an ephah of fine flour	6928+8993
	28:12	offering of t of an ephah of fine flour	6928+8993
	28:20	offering of t of an ephah of fine flour	6928+8993
	28:28	offering of t of an ephah of fine flour	6928+8993
	29: 3	offering of t of an ephah of fine flour	6928+8993
	29: 9	offering of t of an ephah of fine flour	6928+8993
	29:14	offering of t of an ephah of fine flour	6928+8993

THREE-YEAR-OLD (1) [THREE, YEAR]
1Sa	1:24	young as he was, along with a t bull,	8992

THREESCORE (KJV) See SIXTY

THRESH (4) [THRESHED, THRESHER, THRESHES, THRESHING]
Isa	27:12	In that day the LORD will t from	2468
	41:15	You will t the mountains and crush them,	1889
Hos	10:11	Ephraim is a trained heifer that loves to t;	1889
Mic	4:13	"Rise and t, O Daughter of Zion,	1889

THRESHED (4) [THRESH]
Ru	2:17	Then she t the barley she had gathered,	2468
Isa	28:27	Caraway is not t with a sledge,	1889
Am	1: 3	she t Gilead with sledges having iron teeth.	1889
Hab	3:12	the earth and in anger you t the nations.	1889

THRESHER (1) [THRESH]
1Co	9:10	the plowman plows and the t threshes,	262

THRESHES (1) [THRESH]
1Co	9:10	the plowman plows and the thresher t,	NIG

THRESHING (51) [THRESH]
Ge	50:10	When they reached the t floor of Atad,	1755
	50:11	the mourning at the t floor of Atad,	1755
Lev	26: 5	Your t will continue until grape harvest	1912
Nu	15:20	as an offering from the t floor.	1755
	18:27	to you as grain from the t floor or juice	1755
	18:30	to you as the product of the t floor or	1755
Dt	15:14	your t floor and your winepress.	1755
	16:13	of your t floor and your winepress.	1755
Jdg	6:11	where his son Gideon was t wheat in	2468
	6:37	I will place a wool fleece on the t floor.	1755
Ru	3: 2	be winnowing barley on the t floor.	1755
	3: 3	Then go down to the t floor,	1755
	3: 6	So she went down to the t floor	1755
	3:14	that a woman came to the t floor."	1755
1Sa	23: 1	and are looting the t floors,"	1755
2Sa	6: 6	When they came to the t floor of Nacon,	1755
	24:16	at the t floor of Araunah the Jebusite.	1755
	24:18	to the LORD on the t floor of Araunah	1755
	24:21	"To buy your t floor," David answered,	1755
	24:22	and here are t sledges and ox yokes for	4617
	24:24	So David bought the t floor and the oxen	1755
1Ki	22:10	at the t floor by the entrance of the gate	1755
2Ki	6:27	can I get help for you? From the t floor?	1755
	13: 7	and made them like the dust at t time.	1889
1Ch	13: 9	When they came to the t floor of Kidon,	1755
	21:15	then standing at the t floor of Araunah	1755
	21:18	to the LORD on the t floor of Araunah	1755
	21:20	While Araunah was t wheat,	1889
	21:21	the t floor and bowed down before David	1755
	21:22	of your t floor so I can build an altar to	1755
	21:23	the t sledges for the wood,	4617
	21:28	on the t floor of Araunah the Jebusite.	1755
2Ch	3: 1	on the t floor of Araunah the Jebusite.	1755
	18: 9	at the t floor by the entrance to the gate	1755
Job	39:12	and gather it to your t floor?	1755
	41:30	leaving a trail in the mud like a sledge.	3023
Pr	20:26	he drives the t wheel over them.	AIT
Isa	21:10	O my people, crushed on the t floor,	1755
	28:28	so one does not go on t for it.	1889+1889
	28:28	Though he drives the wheels of his t cart	6322
	41:15	"See, I will make you into a t sledge,	4617
Jer	50:11	a heifer t grain and neigh like stallions,	1889
	51:33	like a t floor at the time it is trampled;	1755
Da	2:35	like chaff on a t floor in the summer.	10010
Hos	9: 1	wages of a prostitute at every t floor.	1755+1841
	9: 2	T floors and winepresses will not feed	1755
	13: 3	like chaff swirling from a t floor,	1755
Joel	2:24	The t floors will be filled with grain;	1755
Mic	4:12	like sheaves to the t floor.	1755
Mt	3:12	and he will clear his t floor,	272
Lk	3:17	in his hand to clear his t floor and	272

THRESHOLD (15) [THRESHOLDS]
Jdg	19:27	with her hands on the t.	6197
1Sa	5: 4	broken off and were lying on the t;	5159
	5: 5	Dagon's temple at Ashdod step on the t.	5159
1Ki	14:17	as she stepped over the t of the house,	6197
Eze	9: 3	and moved to the t of the temple.	5159
	10: 4	above the cherubim and moved to the t of	5159
	10:18	over the t of the temple and stopped above	5159
	40: 6	He climbed its steps and measured the t	6197
	40: 7	the t of the gate next to the portico facing	6197

THREW (70) [THROW]
Ge	33: 4	he t his arms around his neck	5877+6584
	37:24	they took him and t him into the cistern.	8959
	44:14	and they t themselves to the ground	5877
	45:14	Then he t his arms around	5877+6584+7418
	46:29	he t his arms around his father	5877+6584+7418
	50: 1	Joseph himself upon his father and wept	5877
	50:18	and t themselves down before him.	5877
Ex	4: 3	Moses t it on the ground and it became	8959
	7:10	Aaron t his staff down in front of Pharaoh	8959
	7:12	Each one t down his staff and it became	8959
	14:24	the Egyptian army and t it into confusion.	2169
	15: 7	the greatness of your majesty you t down	2238
	15:25	He t it into the water,	8959
	32:19	his anger burned and he t the tablets out	8959
	32:24	and I t it into the fire,	8959
Dt	9:17	the two tablets and t them out of my hands,	8959
	9:21	as fine as dust and t the dust into a stream	8959
Jos	10:10	The LORD t them into confusion	2169
	10:27	from the trees and t them into the cave	8959
Jdg	8:25	each man t a ring from his plunder onto it.	8959
	14:16	Then Samson's wife t herself on him,	NIH
	15:17	he t away the jawbone;	8959
1Sa	7:10	and t them into such a panic that	2169
2Sa	18:17	t him into a big pit in the forest and piled	8959
	20:12	from the road into a field and t a garment	8959
	20:22	the head of Sheba son of Bicri and t it	8959
1Ki	19:19	up to him and t his cloak around him.	8959
2Ki	2:21	and t the salt into it, saying, "This is what	8959
	3:25	and each man t a stone on every good field	8959
	6: 6	Elisha cut a stick and t it there,	9023
	9:33	So they t her down,	8959
	10:25	The guards and officers t the bodies out	8959
	13:21	they t the man's body into Elisha's tomb.	8959
	23:12	smashed them to pieces and t the rubble	8959
2Ch	25:12	took them to the top of a cliff and t them	8959
	30:14	and t them into the Kidron Valley.	8959
	33:15	and he t them out of the city.	8959
Ne	13: 8	and t all Tobiah's household goods out of	8959
Jer	36:23	a scribe's knife and t them into the firepot,	8959
	41: 7	with him slaughtered them and t them into	NIH
	41: 9	Now the cistern where he t all the bodies	8959
La	3:53	to end my life in a pit and t stones at me;	3343
Eze	28:17	So I t you to the earth;	8959
Da	3:24	that we tied up and t into the fire?"	10667
	6:16	and they brought Daniel and t him into	10667
	8:10	t some of the starry host down to the earth	5877
Jnh	1: 5	And they t the cargo into the sea to lighten	3214
	1:15	Then they took Jonah and t him overboard,	3214
Zec	11:13	the thirty pieces of silver and t them into	8959
Mt	13:48	the good fish in baskets, but t the bad away.	965
	21:39	So they took him and t him out of	1675
	27: 5	Judas t the money into the temple and left.	4849
Mk	9:20	immediately the boy into a convulsion.	5360
	11: 7	the colt to Jesus and t their cloaks over it,	2095
	12: 8	and t him out of the vineyard.	1675
	12:41	Many rich people t in large amounts.	965
Lk	4:35	the demon t the man down before them all	4849
	9:42	the demon t him to the ground	4838
	15:20	t his arms around him	2093+2158+3836+5549
	17:16	t himself at Jesus' feet	2093+4406+4725
	19:35	t their cloaks on the colt and put Jesus	2166
	20:12	and they wounded him and t him out.	1675
	20:15	So they t him out of the vineyard	1675
Jn	9:34	And they t him out.	1675
Ac	16:37	and t us into prison.	965
	20:10	went down, t himself on the young man	2158
	27:19	they t the ship's tackle overboard	4849
Rev	18:19	and t dust on their heads, and with	965
	18:21	the size of a large millstone and t it into	965
	20: 3	He t him into the Abyss,	965

THRICE (KJV) See THREE TIMES

THRIVE (11) [THRIVES, THRIVING]
Dt	31:20	and when they eat their fill and t,	2014
Job	8:11	Can reeds t without water?	8436
	39: 4	Their young t and grow strong in	8049
Ps	72:16	let it t like the grass of the field.	6424
Pr	11:28	but the righteous will t like a green leaf.	7255
	28:28	when the wicked perish, the righteous t.	8049
	29: 2	When the righteous t, the people rejoice;	8049
	29:16	When the wicked t, so does sin,	8049
Eze	17: 9	what the Sovereign LORD says: Will it t?	7503
	17:10	Even if it is transplanted, will it t?	7503
Zec	9:17	Grain will make the young men t,	5649

THRIVES (1) [THRIVE]
Hos	13:15	even though he t among his brothers,	7229

THRIVING (1) [THRIVE]
Jer	11:16	a t olive tree with fruit beautiful in form.	8316

THROAT (4) [THROATS]
Ps	5: 9	Their t is an open grave;	1744
	69: 3	calling for help; my t is parched.	1744
Pr	23: 2	and put a knife to your t if you are given	4350
Jer	2:25	until your feet are bare and your t is dry.	1744

THROATS (3) [THROAT]
Ps	115: 7	nor can they utter a sound with their t.	1744
Jer	4:10	when the sword is at our t."	5883
Ro	3:13	"Their t are open graves;	3296

THROB (1)
Isa	60: 5	your heart will t and swell with joy;	7064

THROES (1)
2Sa	1: 9	I am in the t of death, but I'm still alive.'	8688

THRONE (170) [DETHRONED, ENTHRONED, ENTHRONES, THRONES]
Ge	41:40	to the t will I be greater than you."	4058
Ex	11: 5	Pharaoh, who sits on the t,	4058
	12:29	Pharaoh, who sat on the t,	4058
Dt	17:18	For hands were lifted up to the t of	4058
	17:18	When he takes the t of his kingdom,	4058
1Sa	2: 8	with princes and has them inherit a t	4058
2Sa	3:10	of Saul and establish David's t over Israel	4058
	7:13	establish the t of his kingdom forever.	4058
	7:16	your t will be established forever.' "	4058
	14: 9	and let the king and his t be without guilt."	4058
1Ki	1:13	and he will sit on my t"?	4058
	1:17	and he will sit on my t.'	4058
	1:20	from you who will sit on the t of my lord	4058
	1:24	and that he will sit on your t?	4058
	1:27	on the t of my lord the king after him?"	4058
	1:30	and he will sit on my t in my place."	4058
	1:35	and he is to come and sit on my t and reign	4058
	1:37	to make his t even greater than the throne	4058
	1:37	to make his throne even greater than the t	4058
	1:46	Solomon has taken his seat on the royal t.	4058
	1:47	and his t greater than yours!'	4058
	1:48	to see a successor on my t today.' "	4058
	2: 4	you will never fail to have a man on the t	4058
	2:12	Solomon sat on the t of his father David,	4058
	2:19	bowed down to her and sat down on his t.	4058
	2:19	He had a t brought for the king's mother,	4058
	2:24	the t of my father David and has founded	4058
	2:33	his descendants, his house and his t,	4058
	2:45	and David's t will remain secure before	4058
	3: 6	a son to sit on his t this very day.	4058
	5: 5	on the t in your place will build the temple	4058
	7: 7	He built the t hall, the Hall of Justice,	4058
	8:20	and now I sit on the t of Israel,	4058
	8:25	a man to sit before me on the t of Israel,	4058
	9: 5	I will establish your royal t over Israel	4058
	9: 5	to have a man on the t of Israel.'	4058
	10: 9	in you and placed you on the t of Israel.	4058
	10:18	the king made a great t inlaid with ivory	4058
	10:19	The t had six steps,	4058
	16:11	to reign and was seated on the t,	4058
	22:19	the LORD sitting on his t with all the host	4058
2Ki	10: 3	and set him on his father's t.	4058
	10:30	on the t of Israel to the fourth generation."	4058
	11:19	The king then took his place on the royal t,	4058
	13:13	and Jeroboam succeeded him on the t.	4058
	15:12	on the t of Israel to the fourth generation."	4058
1Ch	17:12	and I will establish his t forever.	4058
	17:14	his t will be established forever.' "	4058
	22:10	the t of his kingdom over Israel forever.'	4058
	28: 5	on the t of the kingdom of the LORD	4058
	29:23	So Solomon sat on the t of the LORD	4058
2Ch	6:10	and now I sit on the t of Israel,	4058
	6:16	a man to sit before me on the t of Israel,	4058
	7:18	I will establish your royal t,	4058
	9: 8	and placed you on his t as king to rule for	4058
	9:17	the king made a great t inlaid with ivory	4058
	9:18	The t had six steps,	4058
	18:18	the LORD sitting on his t with all the host	4058
	23:20	and seated the king on the royal t,	4058
Est	2:21	from royal t in the citadel of Susa,	4058
	5: 1	The king was sitting on his royal t in	4058
Ps	9: 4	you have sat on your t,	4058
	9: 7	he has established his t for judgment.	4058
	11: 4	the LORD is on his heavenly t.	4058
	45: 6	Your t, O God, will last for ever and ever;	4058
	47: 8	God is seated on his holy t.	4058
	89: 4	make your t firm through all generations.'	4058
	89:14	and justice are the foundation of your t;	4058
	89:29	his t as long as the heavens endure.	4058
	89:36	and his t endure before me like the sun;	4058
	89:44	to his splendor and cast his t to the ground.	4058
	93: 2	Your t was established long ago;	4058
	94:20	Can a corrupt t be allied with you—	4058
	97: 2	and justice are the foundation of his t.	4058
	103:19	LORD has established his t in heaven,	4058
	123: 1	to you whose t is in heaven.	3782
	132:11	your own descendants I will place on your t	4058
	132:12	then their sons will sit on your t for ever	4058
Pr	16:12	for a t is established through righteousness.	4058
	20: 8	When a king sits on his t to judge,	4058
	20:28	through love his t is made secure.	4058

Pr	25: 5	and his t will be established through	4058
	29:14	his t will always be secure.	4058
Isa	6: 1	I saw the Lord seated on a t,	4058
	9: 7	on David's t and over his kingdom,	4058
	14:13	I will raise my t above the stars of God;	4058
	16: 5	In love a t will be established;	4058
	47: 1	sit on the ground without a t,	4058
	63:15	from heaven and see from your **lofty** t,	2292
	66: 1	"Heaven is my t, and the earth is my	4058
Jer	3:17	they will call Jerusalem The T of the LORD	4058
	13:13	including the kings who sit on David's t,	4058
	14:21	do not dishonor your glorious t.	4058
	17:12	A glorious t, exalted from the beginning,	4058
	17:25	then kings who sit on David's t	4058
	22: 2	O king of Judah, you who sit on David's t—	4058
	22: 4	then kings who sit on David's t will come	4058
	22:30	none will sit of the t of David or rule	4058
	29:16	about the king who sits on David's t	4058
	33:17	a man to sit on the t of the house of Israel,	4058
	33:21	a descendant to reign on his t.	4058
	36:30	He will have no one to sit on the t	4058
	43:10	of Babylon, and I will set his t	4058
	49:38	I will set my t in Elam	4058
La	5:19	your t endures from generation	4058
Eze	1:26	over their heads was what looked like a t	4058
	1:26	and high above on the t was a figure like	4058
	10: 1	a t of sapphire above the expanse that was	4058
	17:16	the king who **put** him **on** the t,	4887
	28: 2	on the t of a god in the heart of the seas."	4632
	43: 7	"Son of man, this is the place of my t and	4058
Da	4:36	and I was restored to my t and became	10424
	5:20	from his royal t and stripped of his glory.	10372
	7: 9	His t was flaming with fire,	10372
Jnh	3: 6	he rose from his t, took off his royal robes,	4058
Zec	6:13	with majesty and will sit and rule on his t.	4058
	6:13	And he will be a priest on his t.	4058
Mt	5:34	either by heaven, for it is God's t;	2585
	19:28	when the Son of Man sits on his glorious t,	2585
	23:22	by God's t and by the one who sits on it.	2585
	25:31	he will sit on his t in heavenly glory.	2585
Lk	1:32	The Lord God will give him the t	2585
Ac	2:30	would place one of his descendants on his t.	2585
	7:49	"'Heaven is my t, and the earth is my	2585
	12:21	sat on his t and delivered a public address	1037
Heb	1: 8	But about the Son he says, "Your t,	2585
	4:16	Let us then approach the t of grace	2585
	8: 1	who sat down at the right hand of the t of	2585
	12: 2	sat down at the right hand of the t of God.	2585
Rev	1: 4	and from the seven spirits before his t,	2585
	2:13	where Satan has his t.	2585
	3:21	I will give the right to sit with me on my t,	2585
	3:21	and sat down with my Father on his t.	2585
	4: 2	a t in heaven with someone sitting on it.	2585
	4: 3	resembling an emerald, encircled the t.	2585
	4: 4	the t were twenty-four other thrones,	2585
	4: 5	From the t came flashes of lightning,	2585
	4: 5	Before the t, seven lamps were blazing,	2585
	4: 6	t there was what looked like a sea of glass,	2585
	4: 6	In the center, around the t,	2585
	4: 9	honor and thanks to him who sits on the t	2585
	4:10	down before him who sits on the t,	2585
	4:10	They lay their crowns before the t and say:	2585
	5: 1	on the t a scroll with writing on both sides	2585
	5: 6	standing in the center of the t,	2585
	5: 7	the right hand of him who sat on the t.	2585
	5:11	the t and the living creatures and	2585
	5:13	"To him who sits on the t and to the Lamb	2585
	6:16	the face of him who sits on the t and from	2585
	7: 9	before the t and in front of the Lamb.	2585
	7:10	who sits on the t, and to the Lamb."	2585
	7:11	the angels were standing around the t and	2585
	7:11	They fell down on their faces before the t	2585
	7:15	the t of God and serve him day and night	2585
	7:15	and he who sits on the t will spread his tent	2585
	7:17	the center of the t will be their shepherd;	2585
	8: 3	on the golden altar before the t.	2585
	12: 5	child was snatched up to God and to his t.	2585
	13: 2	and his t and great authority.	2585
	14: 3	And they sang a new song before the t and	2585
	16:10	poured out his bowl on the t of the beast,	2585
	16:17	of the temple came a loud voice from the t,	2585
	19: 4	worshiped God, who was seated on the t.	2585
	19: 5	Then a voice came from the t, saying:	2585
	20:11	a great white t and him who was seated	2585
	20:12	great and small, standing before the t,	2585
	21: 3	And I heard a loud voice from the t saying,	2585
	21: 5	He who was seated on the t said,	2585
	22: 1	flowing from the t of God and of the Lamb	2585
	22: 3	The t of God and of the Lamb will be in	2585

THRONES (17) [THRONE]

1Ki	22:10	on their t at the threshing floor by	4058
2Ch	18: 9	on their t at the threshing floor by	4058
Ps	122: 5	There the t for judgment stand,	4058
	122: 5	the t of the house of David.	4058
Isa	14: 9	it makes them rise from their t—	4058
Jer	1:15	"Their kings will come and set up their t in	4058
	13:18	"Come down from **your** t,	3782
Eze	26:16	down from their t and lay aside their robes	4058
Da	7: 9	"As I looked, "t were set in place,	10372
Hag	2:22	I will overturn royal t and shatter	4058
Mt	19:28	also sit on twelve t,	2585
Lk	1:52	down rulers from their t but has lifted up	2585
	22:30	at my table in my kingdom and sit on t,	2585
Col	1:16	and invisible, whether t or powers or rulers	2585
Rev	4: 4	the throne were twenty-four other t,	2585
	11:16	who were seated on their t before God,	2585
	20: 4	I saw t on which were seated those who	2585

THRONG (10) [THRONGED, THRONGS]

Job	21:33	and a countless t goes before him.	NIH
Ps	42: 4	and thanksgiving among the festive t.	2162
	55:14	as we walked with the t at the house	8094
	68:27	there the **great** t of Judah's princes,	8086
	109:30	in the **great** t I will praise him.	AIT
Pr	7:26	her slain are a mighty t.	3972
Jer	31: 8	a great t will return.	7736
Eze	23:24	and wagons and with a t of people;	7736
	32: 3	a great t of people I will cast my net	7736
Mic	2:12	the place will t with people.	2101

THRONGED (1) [THRONG]

Jer	5: 7	adultery and t to the houses of prostitutes.	1518

THRONGS (1) [THRONG]

Ps	35:18	among t of people I will praise you.	6786

THROUGH (740) [THROUGHOUT]

Ge	2:11	it **winds** t the entire land of Havilah,	6015
	2:13	it **winds** t the entire land of Cush.	6015
	3:17	t painful toil you will eat of it all the days	928
	12: 3	all peoples on earth will be blessed t you."	928
	12: 6	Abram traveled t the land as far as the site	928
	13:17	walk t the length and breadth of the land,	4200
	16: 2	perhaps I can build a family t her."	4946
	18:18	all nations on earth will be blessed t him.	928
	19:32	and preserve our family line t our father."	4946
	19:34	we can preserve our family line t our father.	4946
	21:12	because it is t Isaac that your offspring will	928
	22:18	t your offspring all nations will be blessed,	928
	26: 4	t your offspring all nations will be blessed,	928
	28:14	All peoples on earth will be blessed t you	928
	30: 3	that she can bear children for me and that t	4946
	30:32	Let me go t all your flocks today	928
	31:34	Laban **searched** t everything in the tent	5491
	31:37	Now that *you have* **searched** t all my goods,	5491
	47:17	And he brought them t that year with food	928
Ex	9:35	just as the LORD had said t Moses.	928+3338
	12:12	"On that same night I will pass t Egypt	928
	12:15	the first day t the seventh must be cut off	6330
	12:23	When the LORD **goes** t the land to strike	6296
	13:17	God did not lead them on the **road** t	AIT
	14: 4	But I will gain glory for myself t Pharaoh	928
	14:16	the water so that the Israelites can go t	928+9348
	14:17	And I will gain glory t Pharaoh	928
	14:17	t his chariots and his horsemen.	928
	14:18	that I am the LORD when I gain glory t	928
	14:22	Israelites went t the sea on dry ground,	928+9348
	14:29	Israelites went t the sea on dry ground,	928+9348
	15:19	walked t the sea on dry ground.	928+9348
	19:21	the people so *they* do not **force** *their* **way** t	2238
	19:24	and the people *must* not **force** *their* **way** t	2238
	32:27	Go back and forth t the camp from one end	928
	35:29	the LORD t Moses had commanded	928+3338
Lev	8:36	the LORD commanded t Moses.	928+3338
	10:11	the decrees the LORD has given them t	928+3338
	22: 8	and so become unclean t it.	928
	26: 6	and the sword will not pass t your country.	928
	26:46	himself and the Israelites t Moses.	928+3338
Nu	4:37	to the LORD's command t Moses.	928+3338
	4:45	to the LORD's command t Moses.	928+3338
	4:49	At the LORD's command t Moses,	928+3338
	9:23	accordance with his command t Moses.	928+3338
	10:13	at the LORD's command t Moses?	928+3338
	12: 2	"Has the LORD spoken only t Moses?"	928
	12: 2	"Hasn't he also spoken t us?"	928
	13:17	up t the Negev and on into the hill country.	928
	13:22	up t the Negev and came to Hebron,	928
	14: 7	"The land we passed t and explored	928
	15:23	of the LORD's commands to you t him,	928+3338
	15:23	and continuing t the generations to come—	4200
	16:40	as the LORD directed him t Moses.	928+3338
	20:17	Please let us pass t your country.	928
	20:17	We will not go t any field or vineyard,	928
	20:17	the right or to the left until *we have* **passed** t	6296
	20:18	"You may not pass t here;	928
	20:19	*We* only *want to* **pass** t on foot—	6296
	20:20	they answered: "You may not pass t."	6296
	20:21	Since Edom refused to let them go t	928
	21:22	"Let us pass t your country.	928
	21:22	the king's highway until *we have* **passed** t	6296
	21:23	But Sihon would not let Israel pass t	928
	25: 8	*He* drove the spear t both of them—	1991
	25: 8	the Israelite and into the woman's body.	NIH
	26: 5	t Hanoch, the Hanochite clan;	NIH
	26: 5	t Pallu, the Palluite clan;	4200
	26: 6	t Hezron, the Hezronite clan;	4200
	26: 6	t Carmi, the Carmite clan.	4200
	26:12	t Nemuel, the Nemuelite clan;	4200
	26:12	t Jamin, the Jaminite clan;	4200
	26:12	t Jakin, the Jakinite clan;	4200
	26:13	t Zerah, the Zerahite clan;	4200
	26:13	t Shaul, the Shaulite clan.	4200
	26:15	t Zephon, the Zephonite clan;	4200
	26:15	t Haggi, the Haggite clan;	4200
	26:15	t Shuni, the Shunite clan;	4200
	26:16	t Ozni, the Oznite clan;	4200
	26:16	t Eri, the Erite clan;	4200
	26:17	t Arodi, the Arodite clan;	4200
	26:17	t Areli, the Arelite clan.	4200
Nu	26:20	t Shelah, the Shelanite clan;	4200
	26:20	t Perez, the Perezite clan;	4200
	26:20	t Zerah, the Zerahite clan.	4200
	26:21	t Hezron, the Hezronite clan;	4200
	26:21	t Hamul, the Hamulite clan.	4200
	26:23	t Tola, the Tolaite clan;	NIH
	26:23	t Puah, the Puite clan;	4200
	26:24	t Jashub, the Jashubite clan;	4200
	26:24	t Shimron, the Shimronite clan.	4200
	26:26	t Sered, the Seredite clan;	4200
	26:26	t Elon, the Elonite clan;	4200
	26:26	t Jahleel, the Jahleelite clan.	4200
	26:28	The descendants of Joseph by their clans t	NIH
	26:29	t Makir, the Makirite clan (Makir was	4200
	26:29	t Gilead, the Gileadite clan.	4200
	26:30	t Iezer, the Iezerite clan;	NIH
	26:30	t Helek, the Helekite clan;	4200
	26:31	t Asriel, the Asrielite clan;	NIH
	26:31	t Shechem, the Shechemite clan;	4200
	26:32	t Shemida, the Shemidaite clan;	NIH
	26:32	t Hepher, the Hepherite clan.	NIH
	26:35	t Shuthelah, the Shuthelahite clan;	4200
	26:35	t Beker, the Bekerite clan;	4200
	26:35	t Tahan, the Tahanite clan.	4200
	26:36	t Eran, the Eranite clan.	4200
	26:38	t Bela, the Belaite clan;	4200
	26:38	t Ashbel, the Ashbelite clan;	4200
	26:38	t Ahiram, the Ahiramite clan;	4200
	26:39	t Shupham, the Shuphamite clan;	4200
	26:39	t Hupham, the Huphamite clan.	4200
	26:40	of Bela t Ard and Naaman were:	NIH
	26:40	t Ard, the Ardite clan;	4200
	26:40	t Naaman, the Naamite clan.	4200
	26:42	t Shuham, the Shuhamite clan.	4200
	26:44	t Imnah, the Imnite clan;	4200
	26:44	t Ishvi, the Ishvite clan;	4200
	26:44	t Beriah, the Beriite clan;	4200
	26:45	and t the descendants of Beriah:	4200
	26:45	t Heber, the Heberite clan;	4200
	26:45	t Malkiel, the Malkielite clan.	4200
	26:48	t Jahzeel, the Jahzeelite clan;	4200
	26:48	t Guni, the Gunite clan;	4200
	26:49	t Jezer, the Jezerite clan;	4200
	26:49	t Shillem, the Shillemite clan.	4200
	26:57	t Gershon, the Gershonite clan;	4200
	26:57	t Kohath, the Kohathite clan;	4200
	26:57	t Merari, the Merarite clan.	4200
	27:23	as the LORD instructed t Moses.	928+3338
	31:23	that can withstand fire must be put t the fire,	928
	31:23	must be put t that water.	928
	33: 8	left Pi Hahiroth and passed t the sea	928+9348
	36:13	and regulations the LORD gave t Moses	928+3338
Dt	1:19	went toward the hill country of the Amorites t all that vast	AIT
	2: 4	to pass t the territory of your brothers	928
	2: 7	He has watched over your **journey** t	AIT
	2:27	"Let us pass t your country.	928
	2:28	Only *let us* **pass** t on foot—	6296
	2:30	of Heshbon refused to let us pass t.	928
	8:15	He led you t the vast and dreadful desert,	928
	15:17	then take an awl and push it t his ear lobe	928
	29: 5	the forty years that I led you t the desert,	928
	29:16	and how we passed t the countries on	928+7931
Jos	1:11	"Go t the camp and tell the people,	928+7931
	2:15	she let them down by a rope t the window,	1237
	2:18	in the window t which you let us down,	928
	14: 2	as the LORD had commanded t Moses.	928+3338
	16: 1	from there t the desert into the hill country	NIH
	18: 9	So the men left and went t the land.	928
	19:34	The boundary **ran** west t Aznoth Tabor	AIT
	20: 2	as I instructed you t Moses,	928+3338
	21: 2	"The LORD commanded t Moses	928+3338
	21: 8	as the LORD had commanded t Moses.	928+3338
	22: 9	the command of the LORD t Moses.	928+3338
	24:17	all the nations t which we traveled.	928+7931
Jdg	3: 4	which he had given their forefathers t	928+3338
	4:21	drove the peg t his temple into the ground,	928
	4:22	there lay Sisera with the tent peg t his temple	928
	5:28	"T the window peered Sisera's mother;	1237
	9:54	So his servant **ran** him t, and he died.	1991
	11:16	Israel went t the desert to the Red Sea and	928
	11:17	'Give us permission to go t your country,'	928
	11:18	"Next they traveled t the desert,	928
	11:19	'Let us pass t your country	928
	11:20	did not trust Israel to pass t his territory.	928
	11:29	**passed** t Mizpah of Gilead,	6296
Ru	4:12	T the offspring the LORD gives you	4946
1Sa	3:21	and there he revealed himself to Samuel t	928
	9: 4	So he passed t the hill country of Ephraim	928
	9: 4	of Ephraim and t the area around Shalisha,	928
	9: 4	Then he passed t the territory of Benjamin,	928
	19:12	So Michal let David down t a window,	1237
	28:17	The LORD has done what he predicted t	928+3338
	31: 4	"Draw your sword and **run** me t	1991
	31: 4	and **run** me t and abuse me."	1991
	31:12	all their valiant men journeyed t the night	3972
2Sa	2:23	and the spear came out t his back.	4946
	2:29	that night Abner and his men marched t	928
	2:29	**continued** t the whole Bithron and came	AIT
	12:25	he sent word t Nathan the prophet	928+3338
	20:14	Sheba passed t all the tribes of Israel	928
	20:14	and t the entire region of the Berites,	NIH
	23: 2	"The Spirit of the LORD spoke t me;	928
	23:16	So the three mighty men broke t	928
	24: 5	and then went t Gad and on to Jazer.	NIH
	24: 8	After they had gone t the entire land,	928
	24:19	as the LORD had commanded t Gad.	1821+3869

Ref	Text	Num
1Ki 6:12	I will fulfill t you the promise I gave	907
8:53	as you declared t your servant Moses	928+3338
8:56	of all the good promises he gave t	928+3338
12:15	to Jeroboam son of Nebat t Ahijah	928+3338
14:18	as the LORD had said t his servant	928+3338
15:29	of the LORD given t his servant Ahijah	928+3338
16:7	of the LORD came t the prophet Jehu	928+3338
16:12	of the LORD spoken against Baasha t	928+3338
18:5	"Go t the land to all the springs	928
22:8	"There is still one man t whom we can	907+4946
22:28	the LORD has not spoken t me."	928
22:36	a cry spread t the army;	928
2Ki 1:2	Now Ahaziah had fallen t the lattice	1237
3:8	"T the Desert of Edom," he answered.	2006
3:11	we may inquire of the LORD t him?"	907+4946
3:26	to break t to the king of Edom,	1324
5:1	because t him the LORD had given victory	928
8:8	Consult the LORD t him;	907+4946
8:21	but he rose up and broke t by night;	5782
9:36	the word of the LORD that he spoke t	928+3338
10:10	The LORD has done what he promised t	928+3338
10:33	from Aroer by the Arnon Gorge t Gilead	2256
14:25	spoken t his servant Jonah son of	928+3338
17:13	The LORD warned Israel and Judah t	928+3338
17:13	that I delivered to you t my servants	928+3338
17:23	as he had warned t all his servants	928+3338
21:10	The LORD said t his servants	928+3338
25:4	Then the city wall was broken t,	1324
25:4	and the whole army fled at night t the gate	2006
1Ch 7:14	Asriel was his descendant t his Aramean	AIT
10:4	"Draw your sword and run me t,	1991
11:3	as the LORD had promised t Samuel.	928+3338
11:18	So the Three broke t the Philistine lines,	928
25:5	They were given him t the promises	928
26:12	the gatekeepers, their chief men,	4200
26:21	who were Gershonites t Ladan	4200
26:25	His relatives t Eliezer:	4200
2Ch 10:15	to Jeroboam son of Nebat t Ahijah	928+3338
12:7	wrath will not be poured out on Jerusalem t Shishak.	928+3338
18:7	"There is still one man t whom we can	907+4946
18:27	the LORD has not spoken t me."	928
21:9	but he rose up and broke t by night.	5782
22:7	T Ahaziah's visit to Joram,	NIH
23:20	went into the palace t the Upper Gate	928+9348
29:25	this was commanded by the LORD t	928+3338
32:4	the springs and the stream that flowed t	928+9348
33:8	decrees and ordinances given t Moses."	928+3338
34:14	the LORD that had been given t Moses.	928+3338
35:6	doing what the LORD commanded t	928+3338
36:15	to them t his messengers again and	928+3338
Ezr 2:6	of Pahath-Moab (t the line of Jeshua	4200
2:16	of Ater (t Hezekiah) 98	4200
2:36	the descendants of Jedaiah (t the family	4200
2:40	the descendants of Jeshua and Kadmiel (t	4200
9:11	you gave t your servants the prophets	928+3338
Ne 2:13	By night I went out t the Valley Gate	928
2:14	not enough room for my mount to get t;	6296
2:15	and reentered t the Valley Gate.	928
7:11	of Pahath-Moab (t the line of Jeshua	4200
7:21	of Ater (t Hezekiah) 98	4200
7:39	the descendants of Jedaiah (t the family	4200
7:43	of Jeshua (t Kadmiel through the line	4200
7:43	of Jeshua (through Kadmiel t the line	4200
8:14	the LORD had commanded t Moses.	928+3338
9:11	so that they passed t it on dry ground,	928+9348
9:14	decrees and laws t your servant Moses.	928+3338
9:30	By your Spirit you admonished them t	928+3338
10:29	the Law of God given t Moses	928+3338
Est 6:9	and lead him on the horse t the city streets,	928
6:11	and led him on horseback t the city streets,	928
Job 1:7	"From roaming the earth and going back	928
2:2	"From roaming t the earth and going back	928
12:24	he sends them wandering t a trackless waste.	928
15:20	the ruthless t all the years stored up for him.	NIH
22:13	Does he judge t such darkness?	1237
22:30	who will be delivered t the cleanness	928
28:10	He tunnels t the rock;	928
29:3	and by his light I walked t darkness!	AIT
30:14	They advance as t a gaping breach;	AIT
37:11	he scatters his lightning t them.	AIT
41:2	a cord in his nose or pierce his jaw with	928
Ps 21:5	T the victories you gave, his glory is great;	928
21:7	t the unfailing love of the Most High	928
23:4	I walk t the valley of the shadow of death,	928
32:3	my bones wasted away t my groaning	928
33:11	the purposes of his heart t all generations.	4200
44:5	T you we push back our enemies;	928
44:5	t your name we trample our foes.	928
45:17	I will perpetuate your memory t all	928
63:6	I think of you t the watches of the night.	928
66:6	they passed t the waters on foot—	928
66:12	we went t fire and water,	928
68:7	O God, when you marched t the wasteland,	928
72:5	as long as the moon, t all generations.	1887+1887
72:17	All nations will be blessed t him,	928
74:5	like men wielding axes to cut t a thicket	928
77:19	Your path led t the sea,	928
77:19	your way t the mighty waters,	928
78:13	He divided the sea and led them t;	6296
78:52	he led them like sheep t the desert.	928
84:6	As they pass t the Valley of Baca,	928
85:5	Will you prolong your anger t	4200
89:1	I will make your faithfulness known t all	4200
89:4	make your throne firm t all generations.'	4200
89:24	and t my name his horn will be exalted.	928
89:40	You have broken t all his walls	7287

Ref	Text	Num
Ps 100:5	his faithfulness continues t all generations.	6330
102:12	your renown endures t all generations.	4200
102:24	your years go on t all generations.	928
106:9	he led them t the depths as through	928
106:9	he led them through the depths as t	NIH
107:16	down gates of bronze and cuts t bars	1548
107:17	Some became fools t their rebellious ways	4946
118:20	This is the gate of the LORD t which	928
119:29	be gracious to me t your law.	NIH
119:90	Your faithfulness continues t all generations	4200
119:148	My eyes stay open t the watches of	AIT
135:13	your renown, O LORD, t all generations.	4200
136:14	and brought Israel t the midst of it,	928
136:16	to him who led his people t the desert,	928
145:13	your dominion endures t all generations.	928
Pr 7:6	At the window of my house I looked out t	1237
9:11	For t me your days will be many,	928
11:9	but t knowledge the righteous escape.	928
11:11	T the blessing of the upright	928
12:3	A man cannot be established t wickedness,	928
16:6	T love and faithfulness sin is atoned for;	928
16:6	t the fear of the LORD a man avoids evil.	928
16:12	for a throne is established t righteousness.	928
20:28	t love his throne is made secure.	928
24:3	and t understanding it is established;	928
24:4	t knowledge its rooms are filled with rare	928
25:5	throne will be established t righteousness.	928
25:15	T patience a ruler can be persuaded,	928
28:11	a poor man who has discernment sees t him.	2983
Ecc 5:14	or wealth lost t some misfortune,	928
6:12	the few and meaningless days he passes t	6913
10:8	whoever breaks t a wall may be bitten by	7287
12:3	those looking t the windows grow dim;	928
SS 2:9	gazing t the windows,	4946
2:9	peering t the lattice.	4946
3:2	t its streets and squares;	928
5:4	My lover thrust his hand t the latch-opening	4946
Isa 8:8	passing t it and reaching up to the neck.	6296
8:21	they will roam t the land;	928
10:28	They enter Aiath; they pass t Migron;	928
13:15	Whoever is captured will be thrust t;	1991
13:20	be inhabited or lived in t all generations;	6330
20:2	at the same time the LORD spoke t Isaiah	928+3338
21:1	Like whirlwinds sweeping t the southland,	928
23:16	walk t the city, O prostitute forgotten;	6015
28:19	by day and by night, it will sweep t."	6296
30:6	T a land of hardship and distress,	928
34:10	no one will ever pass t it again.	928
38:10	the prime of my life must I go t the gates	928
41:4	Who has done this and carried it t,	6913
43:2	you pass t the waters, I will be with you;	928
43:2	and when you pass t the rivers,	928
43:2	you walk t the fire, you will not be burned;	1198
43:16	he who made a way t the sea,	928
43:16	a path t the mighty waters,	928
45:2	down gates of bronze and cut t bars	1548
47:2	bare your legs, and wade t the streams.	6296
48:21	not thirst when he led them t the deserts;	928
51:8	my salvation t all generations."	4200
51:9	pierced that monster t?	2726
60:15	with no one traveling t,	6296
62:10	Pass t, pass through the gates!	6296
62:10	Pass through, pass t the gates!	6296
63:11	where is he who brought them t the sea,	4946
63:13	who led them t the depths?	928
Jer 1:3	and t the reign of Jehoiakim son of Josiah	928
2:2	you loved me and followed me t the desert,	928
2:2	t a land not sown.	928
2:6	and led us t the barren wilderness,	928
2:6	t a land of deserts and rifts,	928
5:1	search t her squares.	928
5:10	"Go t her vineyards and ravage them,	928
7:2	all you people of Judah who come t	928
9:21	Death has climbed in t our windows	928
17:4	T your own fault you will lose	928
17:19	t which the kings of Judah go in and out;	928
17:20	in Jerusalem who come t these gates.	928
17:21	on the Sabbath day or bring it t the gates	928
17:24	and bring no load t the gates of this city on	928
17:25	David's throne will come t the gates	928
17:27	as you come t the gates of Jerusalem	928
22:2	your officials and your people who come t	928
22:4	on David's throne will come t the gates	928
23:27	just as their fathers forgot my name t	928
27:3	and Sidon t the envoys who have come	928+3338
37:2	to the words the LORD had spoken t	928+3338
39:2	the city wall was broken t.	1324
39:4	t the gate between the two walls,	928
39:11	orders about Jeremiah t Nebuzaradan	928+3338
39:16	about to fulfill my words against this city t	4200
50:1	the LORD spoke t Jeremiah the prophet	928+3338
51:43	t which no man travels.	928
52:7	Then the city wall was broken t,	1324
52:7	at night t the gate between the two walls	2006
La 3:44	with a cloud so that no prayer can get t.	6296
Eze 5:17	Now they grope t the streets	928
5:17	Plague and bloodshed will sweep t you,	928
9:5	"Follow him t the city and kill,	928
11:5	but I know what is going t your mind.	5091
12:5	dig t the wall and take your belongings out	928
12:5	the wall and take your belongings out t	928
12:7	Then in the evening I dug t the wall	928
12:12	hole will be dug in the wall for him to go t.	928
12:15	among the nations and scatter them t	928
14:15	"Or if I send wild beasts t that country	928
14:15	so that no one can pass t it because of	6296
14:19	and pour out my wrath upon it t bloodshed,	928

Ref	Text	Num
Eze 20:23	among the nations and scatter them t	928
20:26	I let them become defiled t their gifts—	928
22:15	the nations and scatter you t the countries;	928
26:10	a city whose walls have been broken t.	1324
28:16	T your widespread trade you were filled	928
29:11	No foot of man or animal will pass t it;	928
29:12	among the nations and scatter them t	928
30:23	among the nations and scatter them t	928
30:26	among the nations and scatter them t	928
32:27	of these warriors had stalked t the land of	928
36:19	and they were scattered t the countries;	928
36:23	I show myself holy t you before their eyes.	928
36:34	in the sight of all who pass t it.	6296
38:16	when I show myself holy t you	928
39:15	As they go t the land and one of them sees	928
39:27	I will show myself holy t them in the sight	928
40:28	Then he brought me into the inner court t	928
41:7	up from the lowest floor to the top floor t	4200
43:4	of the LORD entered the temple t	2006
44:2	no one may enter t it.	928
44:2	the God of Israel, has entered t it.	2006
45:20	for anyone who sins unintentionally or t	4946
46:2	to enter from the outside t the portico of	2006
46:8	he is to go in t the portico of the gateway,	2006
46:9	to return t the gate by which he entered,	2006
46:19	Then the man brought me t the entrance at	928
47:2	he then brought me out t the north gate	2006
47:3	a thousand cubits and then led me t water	928
47:4	and led me t water that was knee-deep.	928
47:4	and led me t water that was up to	6296
Da 2:28	Your dream and the visions that passed t	AIT
2:30	and that you may understand what went t	NIH
4:5	the images and visions that passed t	AIT
7:1	and visions passed t his mind	AIT
7:15	and the visions that passed t	AIT
9:10	kept the laws he gave us t his servants	928+3338
11:21	and he will seize it t intrigue.	928
11:40	He will invade many countries and sweep t	6296
Hos 1:2	When the LORD began to speak t Hosea,	928
12:10	many visions and told parables t them."	928+3338
13:3	like smoke escaping t a window.	4946
Joel 2:8	They plunge t defenses	1237
2:9	like thieves they enter t the windows.	1237
3:20	be inhabited forever and Jerusalem t	4200
Am 4:3	You will each go straight out t breaks in	5584
5:6	or he will sweep t the house of Joseph like	7502
5:17	for I will pass t your midst,"	928
8:11	"when I will send a famine t the land—	928
Ob 1:13	not march t the gates of my people in	928
Mic 2:13	they will break t the gate and go out.	6296
2:13	Their king will pass t before them,	6296
5:5	and marches t our fortresses,	928
Na 2:4	The chariots storm t the streets,	928
2:4	rushing back and forth t the squares.	928
Hab 3:12	In wrath you strode t the earth and	7575
Zep 2:14	Their calls will echo t the windows,	928
3:6	streets deserted, with no one passing t.	6296
Hag 1:1	of the LORD came t the prophet Haggai	928+3338
1:3	of the LORD came t the prophet Haggai:	928+3338
1:3	of the LORD came t the prophet Haggai:	928+3338
Zec 7:7	the words the LORD proclaimed t the	928+3338
7:12	by his Spirit t the earlier prophets.	928+3338
10:11	They will pass t the sea of trouble;	928
Mal 1:1	word of the LORD to Israel t Malachi.	928+3338
Mt 1:18	to be with child t the Holy Spirit.	1666
1:22	to fulfill what the Lord had said t the	1328
2:15	so was fulfilled what the Lord had said t	1328
2:17	Then what was said t the prophet Jeremiah	1328
2:23	was fulfilled what was said t the prophets:	1328
3:3	This is he who was spoken of t the prophet	1328
4:14	to fulfill what was said t the prophet Isaiah:	1328
7:13	"Enter t the narrow gate.	1328
7:13	and many enter t it.	1328
8:17	This was to fulfill what was spoken t the	1328
9:26	News of this spread t all that region.	1650
9:35	Jesus went t all the towns and villages,	4310
10:20	the Spirit of your Father speaking t you.	1877
10:23	not finish going t the cities of Israel before	NIG
12:1	At that time Jesus went t the grainfields on	1328
12:17	This was to fulfill what was spoken t the	1328
12:43	it goes t arid places seeking rest and does	1451
13:33	until it worked all t the dough."	2435
13:35	So was fulfilled what was spoken t the	1328
18:7	but woe to the man t whom they come!	1328
19:24	a camel to go t the eye of a needle than for	1451
21:4	to fulfill what was spoken t the prophet:	1328
24:15	spoken of t the prophet Daniel—	1328
Mk 2:4	after digging t it, lowered the mat	2021
2:23	One Sabbath Jesus was going t	1328
7:31	the vicinity of Tyre and went t Sidon,	1328
9:30	They left that place and passed t Galilee.	1328
10:25	a camel to go t the eye of a needle than for	1451
11:16	to carry merchandise t the temple courts.	1328
Lk 1:70	(as he said t his holy prophets of long ago),	1328
1:77	of salvation t the forgiveness of their sins,	1877
4:14	about him spread t the whole countryside.	2848
4:30	But he walked right t the crowd and went	1451
5:19	and lowered him on his mat t the tiles into	1328
6:1	One Sabbath Jesus was going t	1388
10:21	full of joy t the Holy Spirit, said,	1877
11:24	it goes t arid places seeking rest and does	1451
13:21	until it worked all t the dough."	2435
13:22	Then Jesus went t the towns and villages,	1388
13:24	"Make every effort to enter t the narrow	1328
17:1	but woe to that person t whom they come.	1328
18:25	a camel to go t the eye of a needle than for	1328
19:1	Jesus entered Jericho and was passing t.	1451

Lk	20:23	He **saw** t their duplicity and said to them,	2917
Jn	1: 3	T him all things were made;	1328
	1: 7	so that t him all men might believe.	1328
	1:10	and though the world was made t him,	1328
	1:17	For the law was given t Moses;	1328
	1:17	grace and truth came t Jesus Christ.	1328
	3:17	but to save the world t him.	1328
	3:21	that what he has done has been done t	1877
	4: 4	Now he had *to go* t Samaria.	1451
	7:14	Not until **halfway** t the Feast did Jesus go	3548
	10: 9	whoever enters t me will be saved.	1328
	11: 4	so that God's Son may be glorified t it."	1328
	14: 6	No one comes to the Father except t me.	1328
	17:10	And glory has come to me t them.	1877
	17:20	also for those who will believe in me t	1328
Ac	1: 2	after giving instructions t the Holy Spirit to	1328
	1:16	the Holy Spirit spoke long ago t the mouth	1328
	2:22	which God did among you t him,	1328
	3:16	It is Jesus' name and the faith that comes t	1328
	3:18	how God fulfilled what he had foretold t	1328
	3:21	he promised long ago t his holy prophets.	1328
	3:25	'T your offspring all peoples on earth will	1877
	4:25	the Holy Spirit t the **mouth** of your servant,	AIT
	4:30	signs and wonders t the name of your holy	1328
	7:35	t the angel who appeared to him	5250+5931
	7:53	into effect t angels but have not obeyed it."	1650
	9:25	and lowered him in a basket t an opening	1328
	10:36	the good news of peace t Jesus Christ,	1328
	10:43	in him receives forgiveness of sins t	1328
	11:14	He will bring you a message t which you	1877
	11:28	stood up and t the Spirit predicted that	1328
	12:10	opened for them by itself, and *they* **went** t it.	2002
	13: 6	*They* **traveled** the whole island	1451
	13:38	to know that t Jesus the forgiveness	1328
	13:39	T him everyone who believes is justified	1877
	13:49	of the Lord spread t the whole region.	1328
	14:22	"We must **go** t many hardships to enter	1328
	14:24	*After* **going** t Pisidia,	1451
	14:27	and reported all that God had done t them	3552
	15: 3	as they **traveled** t Phoenicia and Samaria,	1451
	15: 4	reported everything God had done t them.	3552
	15:11	We believe it is t the grace of our Lord	1328
	15:12	God had done among the Gentiles t them.	1328
	15:41	*He* **went** t Syria and Cilicia,	1451
	17: 1	*When they had* **passed** t Amphipolis	1476
	19: 1	Paul **took the road** t the interior and arrived	1451
	19:11	God did extraordinary miracles t Paul,	1328
	19:21	**passing** t Macedonia and Achaia.	1451
	20: 2	*He* **traveled** t that area,	1451
	20: 3	he decided to go back t Macedonia.	1451
	21: 4	T the Spirit they urged Paul not to go on	1328
	21:19	among the Gentiles t his ministry.	1328
	28:25	the truth to your forefathers when he said t	1328
Ro	1: 2	the gospel he promised beforehand t his	1328
	1: 4	and who t the Spirit of holiness	2848
	1: 5	T him and for his name's sake,	1328
	1: 8	I thank my God t Jesus Christ for all	1328
	2:16	when God will judge men's secrets t	1328
	3:20	t the law we become conscious of sin.	1328
	3:22	This righteousness from God comes t faith	1328
	3:24	by his grace t the redemption that came	1328
	3:25	atonement, t faith in his blood.	1328
	3:30	and the uncircumcised t that same faith.	1328
	4:13	It was not t law that Abraham	1328
	4:13	but t the righteousness that comes by faith.	1328
	4:20	Yet he did not waver t **unbelief** regarding	AIT
	5: 1	since we have been justified t faith,	1666
	5: 1	with God t our Lord Jesus Christ,	1328
	5: 2	t whom we have gained access by faith	1328
	5: 9	be saved from God's wrath t him!	1328
	5:10	we were reconciled to him t the death	1328
	5:10	shall we be saved t his life!	1877
	5:11	also rejoice in God t our Lord Jesus Christ,	1328
	5:11	t whom we have now received	
		reconciliation.	1328
	5:12	just as sin entered the world t one man,	1328
	5:12	and death t sin, and in this way death came	1328
	5:17	death reigned t that one man,	1328
	5:17	of the gift of righteousness reign in life t	1328
	5:19	as t the disobedience of the one man	1328
	5:19	so also t the obedience of the one man	1328
	5:21	so also grace might reign t righteousness	1328
	5:21	to bring eternal life t Jesus Christ our Lord.	1328
	6: 4	with him t baptism into death in order that,	1328
	6: 4	just as Christ was raised from the dead t	1328
	7: 4	also died to the law t the body of Christ,	1328
	7: 7	not have known what sin was except t	1328
	7:11	and t the commandment put me to death.	1328
	7:13	it produced death in me t what was good,	1328
	7:13	so that t the commandment sin might	1328
	7:25	Thanks be to God—t Jesus Christ our Lord!	1328
	8: 2	because t Christ Jesus the law of the Spirit	1877
	8:11	also give life to your mortal bodies t	1328
	8:37	in all these things we are more than	
		conquerors t him who loved us.	1328
	9: 7	"It is t Isaac that your offspring will	1877
	10:17	the message is heard t the word of Christ.	1328
	11:36	and t him and to him are all things.	1328
	15: 4	so that t endurance and the encouragement	1328
	15:18	except what Christ has accomplished t me	1328
	15:19	and miracles, t the power of the Spirit.	1877
	15:24	*while* **passing** t and to have you assist me	1388
	16:26	and made known t the prophetic writings	1328
	16:27	to the only wise God be glory forever t	1328
1Co	1:21	For since in the wisdom of God the world t	1328
	1:21	God was pleased t the foolishness of what	1328
	3: 5	servants, t whom you came to believe—	1328

1Co	3:15	but only as one escaping t the flames.	1328
	4:15	for in Christ Jesus I became your father t	1328
	5: 6	Don't you know that a little yeast **works** t	2435
	7:14	unbelieving husband has been sanctified t	1877
	7:14	the unbelieving wife has been sanctified t	1877
	8: 6	and there is but one Lord, Jesus Christ, t	1328
	8: 6	whom all things came and t whom we live.	1328
	10: 1	the cloud and that *they* all **passed** t the sea.	1451
	12: 8	To one there is given t the Spirit	1328
	14:21	"T men of strange tongues and through	1877
	14:21	and t the lips of foreigners I will speak to	1877
	15:21	For since death came t a man,	1328
	15:21	the resurrection of the dead comes also t	1328
	15:57	the victory t our Lord Jesus Christ.	1328
	16: 5	After *I* **go** t Macedonia,	1451
	16: 5	for *I will be* **going** t Macedonia.	1451
2Co	1: 5	so also t Christ our comfort overflows.	1328
	1:20	And so t him the "Amen" is spoken by us	1328
	2:14	and t us spreads everywhere the fragrance	1328
	3: 4	Such confidence as this is ours t Christ	1328
	4: 1	since t God's mercy we have this ministry,	NIG
	5:18	to himself t Christ and gave us the ministry	1328
	5:20	though God were making his appeal t us.	1328
	6: 8	t glory and dishonor, bad report	1328
	8: 9	that you t his **poverty** might become rich.	AIT
	9:11	and t us your generosity will result	1328
	11:33	window in the wall and **slipped** t his hands.	1767
	12:17	Did I exploit you t any of the men I sent	1328
	13: 3	that Christ is speaking t me.	1877
Gal	2:19	For t the law I died to the law so	1328
	2:21	if righteousness could be gained t the law,	1328
	3: 8	"All nations *will be* **blessed** t you."	1922
	3:14	might come to the Gentiles t Christ Jesus,	1877
	3:18	but God in his grace gave it to Abraham t	1328
	3:19	The law was put into effect t angels by	1328
	3:22	being given t faith in Jesus Christ,	1666
	3:26	You are all sons of God t faith	1328
	5: 5	But by faith we eagerly await t the **Spirit**	AIT
	5: 6	that counts is faith expressing itself t love.	1328
	5: 9	"A little yeast **works** t the whole batch	2435
	6:14	t which the world has been crucified to me,	1328
Eph	1: 5	as his sons t Jesus Christ, in accordance	1328
	1: 7	In him we have redemption t his blood,	1328
	2: 8	it is by grace you have been saved, t faith—	1328
	2:13	brought near t the blood of Christ.	1877
	2:16	to reconcile both of them to God t the cross,	1328
	2:18	For t him we both have access to the Father	1328
	3: 6	This mystery is that t the gospel	1328
	3: 7	of God's grace given me t the working	2848
	3:10	His intent was that now, t the church,	1328
	3:12	and t faith in him we may approach God	1328
	3:16	with power t his Spirit in your inner being,	1328
	3:17	that Christ may dwell in your hearts t faith.	1328
	4: 3	the unity of the Spirit t the bond of peace.	1877
	4: 6	who is over all and t all and in all.	1328
	5:26	cleansing her by the washing with water t	1877
Php	1:11	with the fruit of righteousness that comes t	1328
	1:19	that t your prayers and the help given by	1328
	1:26	so that t my being with you again your joy	1328
	1:30	**since** you are **going** t the same struggle	2400
	3: 9	but that which is t faith in Christ—	1328
	4:13	I can do everything t him who gives me	1877
Col	1: 9	to fill you with the knowledge of his will t	1877
	1:20	and t him to reconcile to himself all things,	1328
	1:20	by making peace t his blood,	1328
	1:22	by Christ's physical body t death	1328
	2: 8	to it that no one takes you captive t hollow	1328
	2:12	in baptism and raised with him t your faith	1328
	2:17	giving thanks to God the Father t him.	1328
1Th	5: 9	to suffer wrath but to receive salvation t	1328
	5:23	sanctify you t **and through.**	3911
	5:23	sanctify you **through and t.**	3911
2Th	2:13	God chose you to be saved t the sanctifying	1877
	2:13	work of the Spirit and t belief in the truth.	NIG
	2:14	He called you t this t our gospel,	1328
1Ti	2:15	But women will be saved t childbearing—	1328
	4: 2	Such teachings come t hypocritical liars,	1877
	4:14	which was given you t a prophetic message	1328
2Ti	1: 6	in you t the laying on of my hands.	1328
	1:10	now been revealed t the appearing	1328
	1:10	and immortality to light t the gospel.	1328
	3:15	to make you wise for salvation t faith	1328
	4:17	so that t me the message might	1328
Tit	1: 3	to light t the preaching entrusted to me by	1877
	3: 5	He saved us t the washing of rebirth	1328
	3: 6	on us generously t Jesus Christ our Savior,	1328
Heb	1: 1	In the past God spoke to our forefathers t	1877
	1: 2	and t whom he made the universe.	1328
	2:10	for whom and t whom everything exists,	1328
	2:10	author of their salvation perfect t suffering.	1328
	4: 7	when a long time later he spoke t David,	1877
	4:14	great high priest *who has* **gone** t the heavens	1451
	6:12	but to imitate those who t faith	1328
	7: 9	paid the tenth t Abraham,	1328
	7:11	If perfection could have been attained t	1328
	7:19	those who come to God t him,	1328
	9:11	he went t the greater and more perfect	1328
	9:14	Christ, who t the eternal Spirit offered	1328
	10:10	we have been made holy t the sacrifice of	1328
	10:20	and living way opened for us t the curtain,	1328
	11:18	"It is t Isaac that your offspring will	1877
	11:29	By faith the people **passed** t the Red Sea as	1329
	11:33	who t faith conquered kingdoms,	1328
	13:12	to make the people holy t his own blood.	1328
	13:15	T Jesus, therefore, let us continually offer	1328
	13:20	who t the blood of the eternal covenant	1877
	13:21	t Jesus Christ, to whom be glory for ever	1328

Jas	1:18	He chose to give us birth t the **word**	AIT
1Pe	1: 2	t the sanctifying work of the Spirit,	1877
	1: 3	into a living hope t the resurrection	1328
	1: 5	who t faith are shielded by God's power	1328
	1:21	T him you believe in God,	1328
	1:23	t the living and enduring word of God.	1328
	2: 5	acceptable to God t Jesus Christ.	1328
	3:19	t whom also he went and preached to	1877
	3:20	eight in all, *were* **saved** t water,	1407
	4:11	so that in all things God may be praised t	1328
2Pe	1: 1	To those who t the righteousness	1877
	1: 2	in abundance t the knowledge of God and	1877
	1: 3	for life and godliness t our knowledge	1328
	1: 4	T these he has given us his very great	1328
	1: 4	so that t them you may participate in	1328
	3: 2	by our Lord and Savior t your **apostles.**	AIT
1Jn	4: 9	into the world that we might live t him.	1328
Jude	1:25	t Jesus Christ our Lord, before all ages,	1328
Rev	18:19	on the sea became rich t her wealth!	1666
	22:14	of life and may go t the gates into the city.	NIG

THROUGHLY (KJV) See ALL, PERFECTLY, REALLY, THOROUGHLY, VIGOROUSLY

THROUGHOUT (134) [THROUGH]

Ge	7: 3	various kinds alive t the earth.	3972+6584+7156
	41:29	great abundance are coming t the land	928+3972
	41:45	And Joseph went t the land of Egypt.	6584
	41:46	from Pharaoh's presence and traveled t	928+3972
	41:56	for the famine was severe t Egypt.	928
Ex	8:16	and t the land of Egypt	928+3972
	8:17	dust t the land of Egypt became gnats.	928+3972
	8:24	t Egypt the land was ruined by the flies.	928+3972
	9: 9	on men and animals t the land."	928+3972
	9:25	T Egypt hail struck everything in	928+3972
	11: 4	'About midnight I will go t Egypt.	928+9348
	11: 6	There will be loud wailing t Egypt—	928+3972
	14:20	*T* the **night** the cloud brought darkness to	AIT
	36: 6	and *they* **sent** this word t the camp:	6296
Lev	6: 9	is to remain on the altar hearth t the night,	3972
	25: 9	Day of Atonement sound the trumpet t	928+3972
	25:10	the fiftieth year and proclaim liberty t	928
	25:24	The country that you hold as	928+3972
Nu	6: 6	T the period of his separation to the LORD	3972
	6: 8	T the period of his separation	3972
	15:21	T the generations to come you are	4200
	15:38	'T the generations to come you are	4200
	35:29	for you t the generations to come,	4200
Dt	28:40	You will have olive trees t your country	928+3972
	28:52	They will lay siege to all the cities t	928+3972
	28:52	They will besiege all the cities t the land	928+3972
Jos	3: 2	After three days the officers went t	928+7931
	6:27	and his fame spread t the land.	928+3972
	24: 3	the land beyond the River and led him t	928+3972
	24:31	served the LORD t the lifetime of Joshua	3972
Jdg	2: 7	served the LORD t the lifetime of Joshua	3972
	6:35	He sent messengers t Manasseh,	928+3972
	7:22	men t the camp to turn on each other	928+3972
	7:24	sent messengers t the hill country	928+3972
	19:25	they raped her and abused her t the night,	3972
	20:12	Israel sent men t the tribe of Benjamin,	928+3972
Ru	4:14	May he become famous t Israel!	928
1Sa	7:13	T Samuel's lifetime, the hand of	3972
	11: 3	we can send messengers t Israel;	928+1473+3972
	11: 7	the pieces by messengers t Israel,	928+1473+3972
	13: 3	the trumpet blown t the land and said,	928+3972
	31: 9	and they sent messengers t the land of	928+6017
2Sa	8:14	He put garrisons t Edom,	928+3972
	15:10	Then Absalom sent secret messengers t	928+3972
	19: 9	T the tribes of Israel,	3972
	19:11	to his palace, since what is being said t	3972
	24: 2	"Go t the tribes of Israel from Dan	928+3972
1Ki	1: 3	Then they searched t Israel for	928+1473+3972
	9:19	in Lebanon and t all the territory he ruled.	928
	15: 6	between Rehoboam and Jeroboam t	3972
	15:16	between Asa and Baasha king of Israel t	3972
	15:32	between Asa and Baasha king of Israel t	3972
	18:20	So Ahab sent word t all Israel	928
2Ki	10:21	Then he sent word t Israel,	928+3972
	10:32	Hazael overpowered the Israelites t	928+3972
	13:22	Hazael king of Aram oppressed Israel t	3972
	23:22	nor t the days of the kings of Israel and	3972
1Ch	5:10	of the Hagrites t the entire region east	6584
	10: 9	and sent messengers t the land of	928+6017
	13: 2	the rest of our brothers t the territories	928+3972
	14:17	So David's fame spread t every land,	928
	21: 4	and went t Israel and then came back	928+3972
	27: 1	that were on duty month by month t	3972+4200
2Ch	8: 6	in Lebanon and t all the territory he ruled.	928
	11:13	and Levites from all their districts t	928+3972
	11:23	dispersing some of his sons t the	3972+4200
	16: 9	the eyes of the LORD range t the earth	928+3972
	17: 9	They taught t Judah, taking with them	928
	17:19	in the fortified cities t Judah.	928+3972
	23: 2	*They* **went** t Judah and gathered the Levites	6015
	30: 5	They decided to send a proclamation t	928+3972
	30: 6	couriers went t Israel and Judah	928+3972
	31: 1	and the altars t Judah and Benjamin	3972+4946
	31:20	This is what Hezekiah did t Judah,	928+3972
	34: 7	and cut to pieces all the incense altars t	928+3972
	36:22	to make a proclamation t his realm and	928+3972
Ezr	1: 1	to make a proclamation t his realm and	928+3972
	10: 7	then issued t Judah and Jerusalem for all	928
Ne	8:15	and spread it t their towns and	928+3972

Column 1

Est	1:20	Then when the king's edict is proclaimed t	928
	2:18	He proclaimed a holiday t the provinces	4200
	3: 6	the Jews, t the whole kingdom of Xerxes.	928
	9: 4	his reputation spread t the provinces,	928+3972
	9:20	Jews t the provinces of King Xerxes.	928+3972
	10: 1	King Xerxes imposed tribute t the empire,	6584
Job	1:10	his flocks and herds are spread t the land.	928
Ps	45:16	you will make them princes t the land.	928+3972
	72:16	Let grain abound t the land;	928
	90: 1	you have been our dwelling place t all	928
	105:31	and gnats t their country.	928+3972
	105:32	with lightning t their land;	928
	106:27	the nations and scatter them t the lands.	928
Jer	4: 5	'Sound the trumpet t the land!'	928
	15:13	because of all your sins t your country.	928+3972
	17: 3	because of sin t your country.	928+3972
	23:15	of Jerusalem ungodliness has spread t	3972+4200
	45: 4	and uproot what I have planted, t the land.	3972
	51:52	and t her land the wounded will groan.	928
Eze	9: 4	"Go t the city of Jerusalem and put	928+9348
	9: 7	they went out and began killing t the city.	928
	14:17	'Let the sword pass t the land,'	928
	30:13	and I will spread fear t the land.	928
	39:14	Some will go t the land and,	928
Da	6: 1	to appoint 120 satraps to rule t	10089+10353
	6:25	men of every language t the land:	10089+10353
Zec	1:10	the LORD has sent to go t the earth."	928
	1:11	"We have gone t the earth and found	928
	4:10	which range t the earth.)	928+3972
	5: 6	the iniquity of the people t the land."	928+3972
	6: 7	they were straining to go t the earth.	928
	6: 7	And he said, "Go t the earth!"	928
	6: 7	So they went t the earth.	928
Mt	4:23	Jesus went t Galilee,	1877+3910
	26:13	wherever this gospel is preached t	1877+3910
Mk	1:39	So he traveled t Galilee,	1650+3910
	6:55	*They* ran t that whole region and carried	4366
	14: 9	the gospel is preached t the world,	1650+3910
Lk	1:65	and t the hill country	1877+3910
	4:25	there was a severe famine t the land.	2093+4246
	4:37	spread t the surrounding area.	1650+4246
	7:17	This news about Jesus spread t Judea	1877+3910
Ac	8: 1	and all except the apostles were scattered t	2848
	9:31	Then the church t Judea,	2848+3910
	10:37	You know what has happened t Judea,	2848+3910
	11: 1	The apostles and the brothers t Judea heard	2848
	16: 6	and his companions **traveled** t the region	1451
	18:23	**traveled** from place to place t the region	1451
	19:27	who is worshiped t the province of Asia	3910
2Co	1: 1	together with all the saints t Achaia:	1877+3910
Eph	3:21	be glory in the church and in Christ Jesus t	1650
Php	1:13	it has become clear t the whole palace guard	1877
1Th	4:10	do love all the brothers t Macedonia.	1877+3910
1Pe	1: 1	strangers in the world, **scattered** t Pontus,	1402
	5: 9	because you know that your brothers t	1877

THROW (70) [THREW, THROWING, THROWN, THROWS]

Ge	27:40	t this yoke from **off** your neck."	7293
	37:20	and t him into one of these cisterns and say	8959
	37:22	T him into this cistern here in the desert,	8959
Ex	1:22	"Every boy that is born *you must* t into	8959
	4: 3	The LORD said, "T it on the ground."	8959
	7: 9	and t it **down** before Pharaoh,'	8959
	22:31	torn by wild beasts; t it to the dogs.	8959
	23:27	and t into confusion every nation you	2169
Lev	1:16	with its contents and t it to the east side of	8959
Nu	19: 6	hyssop and scarlet wool and t them onto	8959
Jos	8:29	to take his body from the tree and t it **down**	8959
	24:14	T away the gods your forefathers worshiped	6073
	24:23	"t away the foreign gods that are among	6073
2Sa	11:21	a woman t an upper millstone on him from	8959
2Ki	9:25	up and t him on the field that belonged	8959
	9:26	pick him up and t him on that plot,	8959
	9:33	"T her **down**!" Jehu said.	9023
Job	18: 7	his own schemes t him **down**.	8959
	30:11	*they* t **off** restraint in my presence.	8938
Ps	2: 3	they say, "and t **off** their fetters."	8959
	17:11	with eyes alert, to t me to the ground.	5742
	50:18	you t in your lot with adulterers.	NIH
	62: 3	*Would* all of you t him **down**—	8357
Pr	1:14	t in your lot with us, and we will share	5877
Ecc	3: 6	a time to keep and a time to t **away**,	8959
Isa	2:20	In that day men *will* t **away** to the rodents	8959
	19: 8	*those who* t nets on the waters will pine	7298
	22:18	like a ball and t you into a large country.	NIH
	28: 2	*he will* t it forcefully to the ground.	5663
	30:22	*you will* t them **away** like a menstrual cloth	2430
Jer	7:29	Cut off your hair and t it **away**;	8959
	16:13	So I *will* t you out of this land into	3214
	22: 7	up your fine cedar beams and t them into	5877
	51:63	tie a stone to it and t it into the Euphrates.	8959
Eze	5: 4	take a few of these and t them into the fire	8959
	7:19	*They will* t their silver into the streets,	8959
	26:12	and t your stones, timber and rubble	8492
	32: 4	*I will* t you on the land and hurl you on	5759
Da	3:20	Meshach and Abednego and t them into	10667
Hos	7:16	*I will* t my net over them;	7298
	8: 5	T out your calf-idol, O Samaria!	2396
Jnh	1:12	"Pick me up and t me into the sea,"	3214
Zec	11: 1	to terrify them and t **down** these horns of	3343
	11:13	LORD said to me, "T it to the potter"—	8959
Mal	3:10	not t **open** the floodgates of heaven	7337
Mt	4: 6	he said, "t yourself down.	965
	5:29	causes you to sin, gouge it out and t it **away**.	965
	5:30	causes you to sin, cut it off and t it **away**.	965

Column 2

Mt	7: 6	*do* not t your pearls to pigs.	965
	13:42	*They will* t them into the fiery furnace,	965
	13:50	and t them into the fiery furnace,	965
	17:27	go to the lake and t out your line.	965
	18: 8	causes you to sin cut it off and t it **away**.	965
	18: 9	causes you to sin, gouge it out and t it **away**.	965
	21:21	'Go, t yourself into the sea,'	965
	22:13	'Tie him hand and foot, and t him **outside**,	1675
	25:30	And t that worthless servant outside,	1675
Mk	11:23	'Go, t yourself into the sea,'	965
Lk	4: 9	he said, "t yourself down from here.	965
	4:29	in order to t him **down the cliff.**	2889
	12: 5	has power *to* t you into hell.	1833
	12:58	and the officer t you into prison.	965
	22:41	about a stone's t beyond them,	1074
Jn	8: 7	*let him* be the first *to* t a stone at her."	965
	21: 6	"T your net on the right side of the boat	965
Ac	7:19	*to* t out their newborn babies so	1704
	27:18	they began to t **the cargo overboard.**	1678
Heb	10:35	So *do* not t **away** your confidence;	610
	12: 1	*let us* t **off** everything that hinders and	700
Rev	18:19	*They will* t dust on their heads,	965

THROWING (11) [THROW]

Dt	7:23	t them **into** great **confusion**	2169+4539
1Sa	5: 9	t it into a great panic.	NIH
2Sa	16:13	and t stones at him and showering him	6232
Ezr	10: 1	and t himself **down** before the house	5877
Mk	10:50	T his cloak **aside**, he jumped to his feet	610
Ac	16:20	and *are* t our city **into an uproar**	1752
	22: 4	arresting both men and women and t them	4140
	22:23	and t **off** their cloaks and flinging dust	4849
	27:38	they lightened the ship *by* t the grain into	1675
Gal	1: 7	some people are t you **into confusion**	5429
	5:10	one who *is* t you **into confusion** will pay	5429

THROWN (76) [THROW]

Lev	4:12	**where** the ashes are t, and burn it	9162
	14:40	the contaminated stones be torn out and t	8959
2Sa	20:21	"His head *will* be t to you from the wall."	8959
1Ki	13:24	and his body was t **down** on the road,	8959
	13:25	by saw the body t **down** there,	8959
	13:28	and found the body t **down** on the road,	8959
2Ki	7: 8	and equipment the Arameans had t **away**	8959
	19:18	*They have* t their gods into the fire	5989
Ne	4: 5	for *they have* t insults in the face of	4087
Job	16:11	over to evil men and t me into the clutches	3740
Ps	36:12	t **down**, not able to rise!	1890
	102:10	*for you have* taken me up and t me **aside.**	8959
	140:10	*may* they be t into the fire, into miry pits,	5877
	141: 6	their rulers *will* be t **down** from the cliffs,	9023
Isa	34: 3	Their slain *will* be t out,	8959
	37:19	*They have* t their gods into the fire	5989
Jer	14:16	be t out into the streets of Jerusalem	8959
	22:19	and t outside the gates of Jerusalem."	8959
	26:23	a sword and his body t into the burial place	8959
	31:40	where dead bodies and ashes are t,	NIH
	36:30	be t out and exposed to the heat by day	8959
	38: 9	*They have* t him into a cistern,	8959
	51:34	*he has* t us **into confusion**,	2169
Eze	11: 7	The bodies you *have* t there are the meat	8492
	15: 4	And after *it is* t on the fire as fuel and	5989
	16: 5	Rather, *you* were t out into the open field,	8959
	19:12	it was uprooted in fury and t to the ground.	8959
	21:12	*They* are t to the sword along	4489
Da	3: 6	down and worship *will* immediately be t	10667
	3:11	not fall down and worship will be t into	10667
	3:15	*you will* be t immediately into	10667
	3:17	If we are t into the blazing furnace,	NIH
	3:21	were bound and t into the blazing furnace,	10667
	6: 7	O king, *shall* be t into the lions' den.	10667
	6:12	O king, *would* be t into the lions' den?"	10667
	6:24	brought in and t into the lions' den,	10667
	7:11	its body destroyed and t into the blazing	10314
	8:12	and truth *was* t to the ground.	8959
Joel	1: 7	It has stripped off their bark and t it **away**,	8959
Na	2: 6	The river gates *are* t **open** and	7337
Mt	3:10	be cut down and t into the fire.	965
	5:13	except *to* be t out and trampled by men.	965
	5:25	and *you may* be t into prison.	965
	5:29	than for your whole body to be t into hell.	965
	6:30	which is here today and tomorrow *is* t into	965
	7:19	not bear good fruit is cut down and t into	965
	8:12	subjects of the kingdom will be t **outside**,	1675
	18: 8	or two feet and *be* t into eternal fire.	965
	18: 9	to have two eyes and *be* t into the fire	965
	18:30	*he* went off and *had* the man t into prison	965
	24: 2	every one *will be* t **down**."	2907
Mk	9:22	"*It has* often t him into fire or water	965
	9:42	*be* t into the sea with a large millstone tied	965
	9:45	to have two feet and *be* t into hell.	965
	9:47	to have two eyes and *be* t into hell,	965
	13: 2	every one *will be* t **down**."	2907
Lk	3: 9	be cut down and t into the fire."	965
	12:28	and tomorrow *is* t into the fire,	965
	13:28	but you yourselves t out.	1675
	14:35	nor for the manure pile; it *is* t out.	1675
	17: 2	be better for him *to* be t into the sea with	4849
	21: 6	every one of them *will be* t **down**."	2907
	23:19	(Barabbas had been t into prison for	965
	23:25	He released the man who *had* been t	965
Jn	9:35	Jesus heard that *they* had t him out,	1675
	15: 6	like a branch that is t **away** and withers;	965
	15: 6	branch that is t into the fire and burned.	965
Ac	16:23	they *were* t into prison,	965

Column 3

Ac	17: 8	and the city officials *were* t **into turmoil.**	5429
Rev	8: 8	huge mountain, all ablaze, *was* t into the sea.	965
	18:21	the great city of Babylon *will be* t **down**,	965
	19:20	of them *were* t **alive** into the fiery lake	965
	20:10	*was* t into the lake of burning sulfur,	965
	20:10	the beast and the false prophet had been t.	NIG
	20:14	Then death and Hades *were* t into the lake	965
	20:15	he *was* t into the lake of fire.	965

THROWS (6) [THROW]

Nu	35:20	or t something at him intentionally so	8959
	35:22	or t something at him unintentionally	8959
Job	30:19	*He* t me into the mud,	3721
	41:18	His snorting t out flashes *of* light;	2145
Mk	9:18	it t him **to the ground.**	4838
Lk	9:39	it t him **into convulsions**	5057

THRUSH (2)

| Isa | 38:14 | I cried like a swift or t, | 6315 |
| Jer | 8: 7 | the t observe the time of their migration. | 6315 |

THRUST (15) [THRUSTING]

Dt	29:28	and t them into another land,	8959
1Sa	26: 8	to the ground with one t of my spear;	7193
2Sa	2:16	and t his dagger into his opponent's side,	NIH
	2:23	so Abner t the butt of his spear	5782
1Ki	14: 9	to anger and t me behind your back.	8959
2Ki	9:24	until *he* t them from his presence.	8959
	24:20	and in the end he t them from his presence.	8959
Job	18: 8	His feet t *him* into a net and he wanders	8938
	24: 4	*They* t the needy from the path	5742
SS	5: 4	My lover t his hand through	8938
Isa	8:22	and *they will* be t into utter darkness.	5615
	13:15	Whoever is captured *will* be t **through**;	1991
Jer	7:15	I *will* t you from my presence,	8959
	23:39	and t you out of my presence.	8959
Eze	23:35	Since you have forgotten me and t me	8959

THRUSTING (1) [THRUST]

| Dt | 6:19 | t out all your enemies before you, | 2074 |

THUMB (5) [THUMBS]

Lev	8:23	the t *of* his right hand and on the big toe	991
	14:14	the t *of* his right hand and on the big toe	991
	14:17	the t *of* his right hand and on the big toe	991
	14:25	the t *of* his right hand and on the big toe	991
	14:28	be cleansed, on the t *of* his right hand and	991

THUMBS (4) [THUMB]

Ex	29:20	on the t *of* their right hands,	991
Lev	8:24	on the t *of* their right hands and on	991
Jdg	1: 6	and cut off his t and big toes.	984+3338
	1: 7	"Seventy kings with their t and big toes	984+3338

THUMMIM (5)

Ex	28:30	put the Urim and the T in the breastpiece,	9460
Lev	8: 8	and put the Urim and T in the breastpiece.	9460
Dt	33: 8	"Your T and Urim belong to the man	9460
Ezr	2:63	a priest ministering with the Urim and T.	9460
Ne	7:65	a priest ministering with the Urim and T.	9460

THUNDER (30) [THUNDERED, THUNDERING, THUNDERS]

Ex	9:23	the LORD sent t and hail,	7754
	9:28	for we have had enough t and hail.	7754
	9:29	t will stop and there will be no more hail,	7754
	9:33	the t and hail stopped,	7754
	9:34	that the rain and hail and t had stopped,	7754
	19:16	On the morning of the third day there was t	7754
	20:18	the t and lightning and heard the trumpet	7754
1Sa	2:10	*He will* t against them from heaven;	8306
	7:10	that day the LORD thundered with loud t	7754
	12:17	I will call upon the LORD to send t	7754
	12:18	that same day the LORD sent t and rain.	7754
Job	26:14	then can understand the t *of* his power?"	8308
	36:33	His t announces the coming storm;	8275
	40: 9	and *can* your voice t like his?	8306
Ps	77:17	the skies resounded with t;	7754
	77:18	Your t was heard in the whirlwind,	8308
	93: 4	Mightier than the t *of* the great waters,	7754
	104: 7	at the sound of your t they took to flight;	8308
Isa	29: 6	the LORD Almighty will come with t	8306
	33: 3	At the t *of* your voice, the peoples flee;	2162
Jer	25:30	*he will* t from his holy dwelling	5989+7754
Joel	3:16	The LORD will roar from Zion and t	5989+7754
Mk	3:17	Boanerges, which means Sons *of* T);	1103
Rev	4: 5	lightning, rumblings and **peals of** t,	1103
	6: 1	four living creatures say in a voice like t,	1103
	8: 5	and there came **peals of** t, rumblings,	1103
	11:19	lightning, rumblings, **peals of** t,	1103
	14: 2	and like a loud **peal of** t.	1103
	16:18	**peals of** t and a severe earthquake.	1103
	19: 6	of rushing waters and like loud peals *of* t,	1103

THUNDERCLOUD (1) [CLOUD]

| Ps | 81: 7 | I answered you out of a t; | 6260+8308 |

THUNDERED (5) [THUNDER]

| Jdg | 5:22 | Then t the horses' hoofs— | 2150 |
| 1Sa | 7:10 | that day the LORD t with loud thunder | 8306 |

2Sa	22:14	The LORD t from heaven;	8306
Ps	18:13	The LORD t from heaven;	8306
Jn	12:29	that was there and heard it said it had t;	1103

THUNDERING (1) [THUNDER]

Rev	9: 9	and the sound of their wings was like the t	5889

THUNDERS (13) [THUNDER]

Job	36:29	how he t from his pavilion?	9583
	37: 4	he t with his majestic voice.	8306
	37: 5	God's voice t in marvelous ways;	8306
Ps	29: 3	the God of glory t, the LORD thunders over	8306
	29: 3	the LORD t over the mighty waters.	NIH
	68:33	who t with mighty voice.	928+5989+7754
Jer	10:13	he t, the waters in the heavens roar;	5989+7754
	51:16	he t, the waters in the heavens roar;	5989+7754
Joel	2:11	The LORD t at the head of his army;	5989+7754
Am	1: 2	"The LORD roars from Zion and t	5989+7754
Rev	10: 3	the voices of the seven t spoke.	1103
	10: 4	the seven t spoke, I was about to write;	1103
	10: 4	"Seal up what the seven t have said and do	1103

THUNDERSTORM (3) [STORM]

Job	28:26	decree for the rain and a path for the t,	2613+7754
	38:25	torrents of rain, and a path for the t,	2613+7754
Isa	30:30	with cloudburst, t and hail.	2443

THUS (32)

Ge	2: 1	T the heavens and the earth were completed	2256
	19:25	T he overthrew those cities and	2256
	30:40	T he made separate flocks for himself	2256
	41:43	T he put him in charge of the whole land	2256
Ex	28:30	T Aaron will always bear the means	2256
Lev	6: 4	when he t sins and becomes guilty,	NIH
Nu	4:49	T they were counted,	2256
	6: 9	t defiling the hair he has dedicated,	2256
Jdg	8:28	T Midian was subdued before the Israelites	2256
	9:56	T God repaid the wickedness	2256
	11:33	T Israel subdued Ammon.	2256
	16:30	T he killed many more when he died than	2256
1Sa	7:12	"T far has the LORD helped us."	2178+6330
2Ki	23: 3	and all his soul, t confirming the words of	4200
Ezr	4:24	T the work on the house of God	10008+10089
Ps	73:15	If I had said, "I will speak t,"	4017
	78:54	T he brought them to the border	2256
	128: 4	T is the man blessed who fears the LORD.	4027
Pr	2:20	T you will walk in the ways of good men	5100
SS	8:10	T I have become in his eyes	255
Eze	43:26	t they will dedicate it.	2256
Hos	10:15	T will it happen to you, O Bethel,	3970
Mt	1:17	T there were fourteen generations in all	4036
	7:20	T, by their fruit you will recognize them	726+1145
	15: 6	T you nullify the word of God for the sake	2779
Mk	7:13	T you nullify the word of God	NIG
Jn	2:11	He t revealed his glory,	2779
	4:37	T the saying 'One sows and another	1877+4047
	7:43	T the people were divided because	4036
Gal	3:17	and t do away with the promise.	1650+3836
Eph	2:15	new man out of the two, t making peace,	NIG
1Ti	5:12	T they bring judgment on themselves,	NIG

THWART (1) [THWARTED, THWARTS]

Isa	14:27	Almighty has purposed, and who can t him?	7296

THWARTED (2) [THWART]

Job	42: 2	no plan of yours can be t.	1307
Isa	8:10	Devise your strategy, but it will be t;	7296

THWARTS (3) [THWART]

Job	5:12	He t the plans of the crafty,	7296
Ps	33:10	he t the purposes of the peoples.	5648
Pr	10: 3	but he t the craving of the wicked.	2074

THYATIRA (4)

Ac	16:14	a dealer in purple cloth from the city of T,	2587
Rev	1:11	to Ephesus, Smyrna, Pergamum, T, Sardis,	2587
	2:18	"To the angel of the church in T write:	2587
	2:24	Now I say to the rest of you in T,	2587

THYINE (KJV) See CITRON

TIARAS (1)

Isa	3:23	and the linen garments and t and shawls.	7566

TIBERIAS (3) [GALILEE]

Jn	6: 1	the Sea of Galilee (that is, the Sea of T),	5500
	6:23	Then some boats from T landed near	5500
	21: 1	to his disciples, by the Sea of T.	5500

TIBERIUS (1)

Lk	3: 1	the fifteenth year of the reign of T Caesar—	5501

TIBNI (3)

1Ki	16:21	half supported T son of Ginath for king,	9321
	16:22	stronger than those of T son of Ginath.	9321
	16:22	So T died and Omri became king.	9321

TIDAL (2)

Ge	14: 1	king of Elam and T king of Goiim	9331
	14: 9	T king of Goiim, Amraphel king of Shinar	9331

TIDINGS (4)

Isa	40: 9	You who bring good t to Zion,	1413
	40: 9	You who bring good t to Jerusalem,	1413
	41:27	I gave to Jerusalem a messenger of good t.	1413
	52: 7	who bring good t, who proclaim salvation,	1413

TIDY UP (Anglicized) See TAKE CARE

TIE (15) [TIED, TIES, TYING]

Ex	29: 9	Then t sashes on Aaron and his sons.	2520
Lev	16: 4	t the linen sash around	2520
Dt	6: 8	T them as symbols on your hands	8003
	11:18	t them as symbols on your hands	8003
Jdg	15:12	"We've come to t you up and hand you	673
	15:13	"We will only t you up and hand you	673+673
	16: 5	so we may t him up and subdue him.	673
Job	41: 1	with a fishhook or t down his tongue with	9205
Jer	51:63	this scroll, t a stone to it and throw it into	8003
Eze	3:25	you, son of man, they will t with ropes;	5989+6584
	4: 8	I will t you up with ropes so	5989
Da	3:20	of the strongest soldiers in his army to t up	10366
Mt	13:30	and t them in bundles to be burned;	1313
	22:13	'T him hand and foot,	1313
	23: 4	They t up heavy loads and put them	1297

TIED (25) [TIE]

Ge	38:28	so the midwife took a scarlet thread and t it	8003
Ex	28:28	The rings of the breastpiece are to be t to	8220
	39:21	They t the rings of the breastpiece to	8220
Lev	8: 7	t the sash around him,	2520
	8: 7	He also t the ephod to him	2520
	8:13	t sashes around them and put headbands	2520
Jos	2:18	you have t this scarlet cord in the window.	8003
	2:21	And she t the scarlet cord in the window.	8003
Jdg	15: 4	and t them tail to tail in pairs.	7155
	16: 6	and how you can be t up and subdued."	673
	16: 8	and she t him with them.	673
	16:10	Come now, tell me how you can be t."	673
	16:12	So Delilah took new ropes and t him	673
	16:13	Tell me how you can be t."	673
2Ki	5:23	t up the two talents of silver in two bags,	7443
Ps	109:19	like a belt t forever around him.	2520
Da	3:23	firmly t, fell into the blazing furnace.	10366
	3:24	"Weren't there three men that we t up	10366
Mt	21: 2	and at once you will find a donkey t there,	1313
Mk	9:42	into the sea with a large millstone t around	4329
	11: 2	you will find a colt t there,	1313
	11: 4	a colt outside in the street, t at a doorway.	1313
Lk	17: 2	a millstone t around his neck than for him	4329
	19:30	you will find a colt t there,	1313
Ac	21:11	t his own hands and feet with it and said,	1313

TIES (6) [TIE]

Jdg	16: 7	"If anyone t me with seven fresh thongs	673
	16:11	"If anyone t me securely with new ropes	673+673
Job	12:18	and t a loincloth around their waist.	673
Hos	11: 4	cords of human kindness, with t of love;	6310
Mt	12:29	unless he first t up the strong man?	1313
Mk	3:27	unless he first t up the strong man.	1313

TIGHT (1) [TIGHTEN, TIGHTENED, TIGHTFISTED, TIGHTLY]

Jas	1:26	and yet does not keep a t rein on his tongue	5902

TIGHTEN (1) [TIGHT]

Jdg	16:13	and t it with the pin, I'll become as weak as	9546

TIGHTENED (1) [TIGHT]

Jdg	16:14	and t it with the pin.	9546

TIGHTFISTED (1) [FIST, TIGHT]

Dt	15: 7	or t toward your poor brother.	906+3338+7890

TIGHTLY (5) [TIGHT]

Jos	6: 1	Now Jericho was t shut up	2256+6037+6037
Job	41:15	has rows of shields t sealed together;	7639
	41:23	The folds of his flesh are t joined;	1815
Isa	22:18	He will roll you up t like a ball	7571+7571+7572
Eze	27:24	with cords twisted and t knotted.	775

TIGLATH-PILESER (6) [PUL]

2Ki	15:29	T king of Assyria came and took Ijon,	9325
	16: 7	Ahaz sent messengers to say to T king	9325
	16:10	to Damascus to meet T king of Assyria.	9325
1Ch	5: 6	whom T king of Assyria took into exile.	9433
	5:26	(that is, T king of Assyria), who took	9433
2Ch	28:20	T king of Assyria came to him,	9433

TIGRIS (2)

Ge	2:14	The name of the third river is the T;	2538
Da	10: 4	on the bank of the great river, the T,	2538

TIKVAH (2)

2Ki	22:14	who was the wife of Shallum son of T,	9537

Ezr	10:15	son of Asahel and Jahzeiah son of T,	9537

TIKVATH (KJV) See TOKHATH

TILES (1)

Lk	5:19	through the t into the middle of the crowd,	3041

TILGATHPILNESER (KJV) See TIGLATH-PILESER

TILL (137)

Ge	32: 4	with Laban and have remained there t now.	6330
	32:24	and a man wrestled with him t daybreak.	6330
Ex	9:18	from the day it was founded t now.	6330
	10: 6	the day they settled in this land t now.' "	6330
	12:10	Do not leave any of it t morning;	6330
	12:10	if some is left t morning, you must burn it.	6330
	17:12	so that his hands remained steady t sunset.	6330
	18:13	and they stood around him from morning t	6330
	18:14	around you from morning t evening?"	6330
	27:21	the LORD from evening t morning.	6330
	29:34	or any bread is left over t morning,	6330
Lev	6: 9	on the altar hearth throughout the night, t	6330
	7:15	he must leave none of it t morning.	6330
	7:17	the sacrifice left over t the third day must	928
	11:24	will be unclean t evening.	6330
	11:25	and he will be unclean t evening.	6330
	11:27	will be unclean t evening.	6330
	11:28	and he will be unclean t evening.	6330
	11:31	when they are dead will be unclean t	6330
	11:32	Put it in water; it will be unclean t evening,	6330
	11:39	the carcass will be unclean t evening.	6330
	11:40	and he will be unclean t evening.	6330
	11:40	and he will be unclean t evening.	6330
	14:46	while it is closed up will be unclean t	6330
	15: 5	and he will be unclean t evening.	6330
	15: 6	and he will be unclean t evening.	6330
	15: 7	and he will be unclean t evening.	6330
	15: 8	and he will be unclean t evening.	6330
	15:10	that were under him will be unclean t	6330
	15:10	and he will be unclean t evening.	6330
	15:11	and he will be unclean t evening.	6330
	15:16	and he will be unclean t evening.	6330
	15:17	and it will be unclean t evening.	6330
	15:18	and they will be unclean t evening.	6330
	15:19	will be unclean t evening.	6330
	15:21	and he will be unclean t evening.	6330
	15:22	and he will be unclean t evening.	6330
	15:23	he will be unclean t evening.	6330
	15:27	and he will be unclean t evening.	6330
	17:15	he will be ceremonially unclean t evening;	6330
	22: 6	will be unclean t evening.	6330
	22:30	leave none of it t morning.	6330
	24: 3	the LORD from evening t morning,	6330
Nu	9:12	not leave any of it t morning or break any	6330
	9:15	From evening t morning the cloud above	6330
	9:21	the cloud stayed only from evening t	6330
	12:15	not move on t she was brought back.	6330
	19: 7	he will be ceremonially unclean t evening.	6330
	19: 8	and he too will be unclean t evening.	6330
	19:10	and he too will be unclean t evening.	6330
	19:21	the water of cleansing will be unclean t	6330
	19:22	anyone who touches it becomes unclean t	6330
	23:24	not rest t he devours his prey and drinks	6330
Dt	33:11	strike his foes t they rise no more."	4946
Jos	7: 6	remaining there t evening.	6330
	10:13	t the nation avenged itself on its enemies,	6330
Jdg	19: 8	"Refresh yourself. Wait t afternoon!"	6330
Ru	1: 7	has worked steadily from morning t now,	6330
1Sa	1: 7	her rival provoked her t she wept	2256
	14:36	the Philistines by night and plunder them t	6330
2Sa	1:12	and wept and fasted t evening for Saul	6330
	10: 5	"Stay at Jericho t your beards have grown,	6330
	19: 7	upon you from your youth t now."	6330
	20: 3	They were kept in confinement t the day	6330
	21:10	of the harvest t the rain poured down from	6330
	22:38	I did not turn back t they were destroyed.	6330
	23:10	the Philistines t his hand grew tired	3954+6330
1Ki	18:26	on the name of Baal from morning t noon.	6330
1Ch	19: 5	at Jericho t your beards have grown,	889+6330
Ne	4: 6	the wall t all of it reached half its height,	2256
	4:21	the first light of dawn t the stars came out.	6330
	8: 3	He read it aloud from daybreak t noon	6330
Job	7: 4	The night drags on, and I toss t dawn.	6330
	14: 6	t he has put in his time like a hired man.	6330
	14:12	t the heavens are no more,	6330
	14:13	and conceal me t your anger has passed!	6330
	19:10	He tears me down on every side t	2256
	27: 5	t I die, I will not deny my integrity.	6330
	39: 2	Do you count the months t they bear?	NIH
	39:10	Will he t the valleys behind you?	8440
Ps	18:37	I did not turn back t they were destroyed.	6330
	59:13	consume them t they are no more.	2256
	71:18	t I declare your power to the next generation	6330
	72: 7	prosperity will abound t the moon is no	6330
	73:17	t I entered the sanctuary of God;	6330
	78:29	They ate t they had more than enough,	2256
	84: 7	t each appears before God in Zion.	NIH
	94:13	t a pit is dug for the wicked.	6330
	105:19	t what he foretold came to pass,	6330+6961
	105:19	t the word of the LORD proved him true.	NIH
	123: 2	t he shows us his mercy.	6330+8611
	132: 5	t I find a place for the LORD,	6330
Pr	4:16	For they cannot sleep t they do evil;	561+4202

Pr	4:16	of slumber t they make someone fall.	561+4202
	4:18	shining ever brighter t the full light of day.	6330
	7:18	Come, let's drink deep of love t morning;	6330
	7:20	with money and will not be home t	4200
	7:23	t an arrow pierces his liver,	6330
	18:17	t another comes forward and questions him.	2256
	28:17	by the guilt of murder will be a fugitive t	6330
SS	4:3	I held him and would not let him go t	6330+8611
Isa	5:8	to field t no space is left and you live alone	6330
	5:11	at night t they *are* **inflamed** *with* wine.	AIT
	22:14	"T your dying *day* this sin will not	6330
	23:10	T your land as along the Nile,	6268
	30:17	t you are left like a flagstaff on a	561+6330
	32:15	t the Spirit is poured upon us from on high,	6330
	38:13	I waited patiently t dawn,	6330
	42:4	or be discouraged t he establishes justice	6330
	62:1	t her righteousness shines out like the dawn,	6330
	62:7	give him no rest t he establishes Jerusalem	6330
Jer	3:25	from our youth t this day we have	6330
	9:18	and wail over us t our eyes overflow	2256
	27:11	that nation remain in its own land *to* t it	6268
	36:2	to you in the reign of Josiah t now.	6330
	46:10	The sword will devour t it is satisfied,	2256
	46:10	t it has quenched its thirst with blood.	2256
	47:6	'how long t you rest?	4202
	52:11	put him in prison t the day of his death.	6330
	52:34	t the day of his death.	6330
Eze	24:11	the empty pot on the coals t it becomes hot	5100
	28:15	from the day you were created t	6330
	39:19	you will eat fat t you are glutted	4200
	39:19	and drink blood t you are drunk.	4200
Da	4:16	t seven times pass by for him.	10221
	12:13	"As for you, go your way t the end.	4200
Hos	7:4	from the kneading of the dough t it rises.	6330
Am	1:8	t the last of the Philistines is dead,"	2256
Na	3:16	t they are more than the stars of the sky,	NIH
Hab	2:15	from the wineskin t they are drunk,	677+2256
Mt	12:20	t he leads justice to victory.	323+2401
Jn	2:10	but you have saved the best t now."	2401
Ac	28:23	From morning t evening he explained	2401
1Co	4:5	wait t the Lord comes.	2401
1Th	4:15	who are left t the coming of the Lord,	1650
2Th	2:7	now holds it back will continue to do so t	2401
Heb	3:14	to share in Christ if we hold firmly t	3588

TILLAGE (KJV) See FARMED, FIELD, WORK

TILLED, TILLER, TILLEST, TILLETH (KJV) See CULTIVATED, PLOWED, WORK, WORKED, WORKS

TILON (1)
1Ch	4:20	Amnon, Rinnah, Ben-Hanan and **T**.	9400

TILTING (1)
Jer	1:13	a boiling pot, t **away from** the north,"	4946+7156

TIMAEUS (1) [BARTIMEAUS]
Mk	10:46	Bartimaeus (that is, the Son *of* T),	5505

TIMBER (12) [TIMBERS]
1Ki	5:6	that we have no one so skilled in felling t	6770
	5:18	men of Gebal cut and prepared the t and	6770
	15:22	stones and t Baasha had been using there.	6770
2Ki	12:12	They purchased t and dressed stone for	6770
	22:6	Also have them purchase t and dressed	6770
2Ch	2:8	that your men are skilled in cutting t there.	6770
	2:10	the woodsmen who cut the t,	6770
	16:6	the stones and t Baasha had been using.	6770
	34:11	and t for joists and beams for the buildings	6770
Ne	2:8	so he will give me t to make beams for	6770
Eze	26:12	your stones, t and rubble into the sea.	6770
Hag	1:8	Go up into the mountains and bring down t	6770

TIMBER (Anglicized) See also LUMBER

TIMBERS (5) [TIMBER]
Lev	14:45	its stones, t and all the plaster—	6770
Ezr	5:8	with large stones and placing the t in	10058
	6:4	of large stones and one of t.	10058
Eze	27:5	They made all your t of pine trees	4283
Zec	5:4	both its t and its stones.'"	6770

TIMBREL (KJV) See TAMBOURINE

TIME (771) [TIMELY, TIMES]
Ge	4:3	In the course of t Cain brought some of	3427
	4:26	**At that** t men began to call on the name of	255
	6:5	of his heart was only evil all the t.	3427
	6:9	blameless among the **people of** his t,	1887
	8:12	but this t it did not return to him.	NIH
	10:25	because in his t the earth was divided;	3427
	12:6	**At that** t the Canaanites were in the land.	255
	13:7	also living in the land at that t.	255
	14:1	At *this* t Amraphel king of Shinar,	3427
	17:21	Sarah will bear to you by this t next year."	4595
	18:10	surely return to you about this t next year,	6961
	18:14	return to you at the appointed t next year	6961

Ge	19:23	**By the** t Lot reached Zoar,	2256
	21:2	at the very t God had promised him.	4595
	21:22	At that t Abimelech and Phicol	6961
	21:34	in the land of the Philistines *for* a long t.	3427
	22:1	**Some** t later God tested Abraham.	339+465+1821+2021+2021
	22:15	called to Abraham from heaven a **second** t	9108
	22:20	**Some** t later Abraham was told,	339+465+1821+2021+2021
	24:11	the t the women go out to draw water.	6961
	25:24	When the t came for her to give birth,	6961
	26:1	besides the earlier famine of Abraham's t—	3427
	26:8	When Isaac had been there a long t,	3427
	26:15	that his father's servants had dug in the t	3427
	26:18	the wells that had been dug in the t	3427
	29:7	it is not t for the flocks to be gathered.	6961
	29:21	My t is completed,	3427
	29:35	"This t I will praise the LORD."	7193
	30:20	This t my husband will treat me	7193
	30:21	**Some** t later she gave birth to a daughter	339
	34:19	**lost** no t in doing what they said,	336
	37:9	and this t the sun and moon	NIH
	38:1	At that t, Judah left his brothers and went	6961
	38:12	After a long t Judah's wife,	3427
	38:27	When the t came *for* her to give birth,	6961
	39:5	the t he put him in charge of his household	255
	40:1	**Some** t later, the cupbearer and the baker	339+465+1821+2021+2021
	40:4	After they had been in custody for **some** t,	3427
	43:18	that was put back into our sacks the **first** t.	9378
	43:20	down here the **first** t to buy food.	9378
	46:29	around his father and wept *for* **a long** t.	6388
	47:29	When the t drew near *for* Israel to die,	3427
	48:1	**Some** t later Joseph was told, "Your father is ill."	339+465+1821+2021+2021
	50:3	for that was the t *required for* embalming.	3427
Ex	4:26	(**At that** t she said "bridegroom of blood,"	255
	8:9	leave to you the honor of **setting the** t	4200+5503
	8:32	But this t also Pharaoh hardened his heart	7193
	9:5	The LORD set a t and said,	4595
	9:14	or this t I will send the full force	7193
	9:18	at this t tomorrow I will send	6961
	9:27	"This t I have sinned," he said to them.	7193
	12:39	and *did* not **have** t to prepare food	3523+4538
	12:40	the **length of** t the Israelite people lived	4632
	13:10	at the **appointed** t year after year.	4595
	21:19	the injured man for the **loss of** his t	8700
	23:15	at the **appointed** t *in* the month of Abib,	4595
	30:12	a ransom for his life **at the** t he is counted.	928
	32:34	when the t comes for me to punish,	3427
	34:18	at the **appointed** t *in* the month of Abib,	4595
Lev	14:2	at the t *of* his ceremonial cleansing,	3427
	15:25	at a t other than her monthly period or has	6961
	16:17	the Tent of Meeting **from the** t Aaron goes	928
	19:10	**go over** your vineyard **a second** t	6618
	25:29	**During that** t he may redeem it.	3427
	25:50	to count the t from the year he sold himself	NIH
	26:34	the t *that* it lies desolate and you are in	3427
	26:35	All the t that it lies desolate.	3427
Nu	3:1	of the family of Aaron and Moses at the t	3427
	9:2	celebrate the Passover at the **appointed** t.	4595
	9:3	Celebrate it at the **appointed** t.	4595
	9:7	the other Israelites at the **appointed** t?"	4595
	9:13	the LORD's offering at the **appointed** t.	4595
	9:19	remained over the tabernacle a long t,	3427
	10:13	They set out, this **first** t,	AIT
	14:15	If you put these people to death all at **one** t,	285
	14:19	from the t they left Egypt until now."	NIH
	22:4	who was king of Moab at that t,	6961
	28:2	that you present to me at the **appointed** t	4595
	30:15	he nullifies them **some** t **after** he hears	339
Dt	1:9	At that t I said to you,	6961
	1:16	And I charged your judges at that t:	6961
	1:18	that I told you everything you were to do.	6961
	1:46	all the t you spent there.	3427
	2:1	*For* a long t we made our way around	3427
	2:14	from the t we left Kadesh Barnea	3427
	2:34	At that t we took all his towns	6961
	3:4	At that t we took all his cities.	6961
	3:8	So at that t we took from these two kings	6961
	3:12	Of the land that we took over at that t,	6961
	3:18	I commanded you at that t:	6961
	3:21	At that t I commanded Joshua:	6961
	3:23	At that t I pleaded with the LORD:	6961
	4:14	And the LORD directed me at that t	6961
	4:25	**lived** in the land a **long** t—	3823
	4:32	long before your t, from	NIH
	4:40	that the LORD your God gives you *for* all t.	3427
	5:5	that I stood between the LORD and you	6961
	9:20	but at that t I prayed for Aaron too.	6961
	10:1	At that t the LORD said to me,	6961
	10:8	that the LORD set apart the tribe of Levi	6961
	10:10	as I did the first t,	3427
	10:10	the LORD listened to me at this t also.	7193
	15:2	the LORD's **t for canceling debts**	9024
	16:3	of your life you may remember the t	3427
	16:9	from the t you begin to put the sickle to	NIH
	17:9	and to the judge who is in office at that t.	6961
	17:20	and his descendants will reign a long t	3427
	19:17	and the judges who are in office at the t.	6961
	20:19	When you lay siege to a city *for* a long t,	3427
	24:20	not **go over the branches** a second t.	339+6994
	26:3	and say to the priest in office at the t,	3427
	28:47	and gladly in the t of prosperity.	NIH
	32:35	In **due** t their foot will slip;	6961
	34:8	the t *of* weeping and mourning was over.	3427
Jos	2:5	when it was t to close the city gate,	NIH

Jos	5:2	At that t the LORD said to Joshua,	6961
	6:9	**All this** t the trumpets were sounding.	2143
	6:16	The seventh t around,	7193
	6:26	that t Joshua pronounced this solemn oath:	6961
	11:6	because by this t tomorrow I will hand all	6961
	11:10	At that t Joshua turned back	6961
	11:18	against all these kings *for* a long t.	3427
	11:21	At that t Joshua went and destroyed	6961
	14:10	for forty-five years since the t he said this	255
	20:6	of the high priest who is serving at that t.	3427
	22:3	*For* a long t now—	3427
	23:1	After a long t had passed and	3427
	24:7	Then you lived in the desert *for* a long t.	3427
Jdg	3:29	At that t they struck down about	6961
	4:4	was leading Israel at that t.	6961
	6:39	This t make the fleece dry and the ground	NIH
	10:1	**After the** t of Abimelech a man	339
	11:4	**Some** t later, when the Ammonites	3427+4946
	11:26	Why didn't you retake them during that t?	6961
	12:6	Forty-two thousand Ephraimites were killed at that t.	6961
	14:4	for at that t they were ruling over Israel.)	6961
	14:8	**Some** t later, when he went back	3427+4946
	15:1	Later on, at the t *of* wheat harvest,	3427
	15:3	"This t I have a right to get even with	7193
	16:4	**Some** t later, he fell in love with a	339+4027
	16:15	This is the third t you have made a fool	7193
	18:30	the tribe of Dan until the t *of* the captivity	3427
	18:31	all the t the house of God was in Shiloh.	3427
	20:25	This t, when the Benjamites came out	3427
	21:14	So the Benjamites returned at that t	6961
	21:24	At that t the Israelites left that place	6961
1Sa	1:20	So in the course of t Hannah conceived	3427
	2:31	The t is coming when I will cut short	3427
	3:8	The LORD called Samuel a **third** t,	AIT
	3:12	At that t I will carry out against Eli	3427
	4:19	pregnant and **near the** t of delivery.	3528
	7:2	It was a long t, twenty years in all,	3427
	9:13	you should find him about this t."	3427
	9:16	"About this t tomorrow I will send you	6961
	9:24	from the t I said, 'I have invited guests.'"	NIH
	11:9	'**By the** t the sun is hot tomorrow,	3869
	13:8	He waited seven days, the t **set** by Samuel;	4595
	13:11	and that you did not come at the **set t**,	3427+4595
	13:13	your kingdom over Israel for **all** t.	6409
	14:18	(At that t it was with the Israelites.)	3427
	14:35	it *was* the **first** t he had done this.	2725
	17:12	in Saul's t he was old and well advanced	3427
	18:9	that t on Saul kept a jealous eye on David.	3427
	18:19	So when the t came *for* Merab,	6961
	18:26	So before the **allotted** t elapsed,	3427
	19:21	Saul sent men a **third** t,	AIT
	20:12	I will surely sound out my father by this t	6961
	22:15	*Was* that day the **first** t I inquired of God	2725
	25:7	"'Now I hear that *it is* **sheep-shearing t.**	1605
	25:7	the whole t they were at Carmel nothing	3427
	25:8	since we come at a festive t.	3427
	25:15	and the whole t we were out in the fields	3427
	25:16	the t we were herding our sheep near them.	3427
	25:18	Abigail **lost** no t.	4554
	26:10	either his t will come and he will die,	3427
2Sa	2:1	**In the course of** t, David inquired of	339+4027
	2:11	The length of t David was king in Hebron	3427
	3:1	and the house of David lasted a **long** t.	801
	3:17	"For some t you have wanted to make David your king.	1685+1685+8997+9453
	7:11	since the t I appointed leaders	3427
	8:1	**In the course of** t, David defeated	339+4027
	10:1	**In the course of** t, the king of	339+4027
	11:1	at the t *when* kings go off to war,	6961
	11:27	After the t **of mourning** was over,	65
	13:1	**In the course of** t, Amnon son of David	339+4027
	14:26	from t to time when it became too heavy	3427
	14:26	to t when it became too heavy for him—	3427
	14:29	he sent a second t, but he refused to come.	6388
	15:1	**In the course of** t, Absalom	339+4027+4946
	17:7	Ahithophel has given is not good this t.	7193
	18:20	"You may take the news another t,	3427
	20:5	he took longer than the t the king had set	4595
	21:18	**In the course of** t, there was another	339+4027
	21:18	**At that** t Sibbecai the Hushathite killed	255
	23:13	During **harvest** t, three of the thirty chief	7907
	23:14	**At that** t David was in the stronghold,	255
	24:15	until the end of the t designated,	6961
1Ki	2:1	When the t drew near for David to die,	3427
	2:38	Shimei stayed in Jerusalem *for* a long t.	3427
	2:42	**At that** t you said to me,	2256
	8:2	to King Solomon at the t of the festival in	928
	8:40	so that they will fear you all the t they live	3427
	8:61	obey his commands, as at this t."	3427
	8:65	So Solomon observed the festival at that t,	6961
	9:2	the LORD appeared to him a **second** t,	9108
	11:29	About that t Jeroboam was going out	6961
	14:1	that t Abijah son of Jeroboam became ill,	6961
	16:9	Elah was in Tirzah at the t,	NIH
	16:34	In Ahab's t, Hiel of Bethel rebuilt Jericho	3427
	17:7	**Some** t later the brook dried up	3427
	17:17	**Some** t later the son of the woman who owned the house	339+465+1821+2021+2021
	18:1	After a long t, in the third year,	3427
	18:29	prophesying **until** the t for the evening	6330
	18:34	"**Do it** a third t," he ordered.	8992
	18:34	and *they* did *it* the third t.	8992
	18:36	**At the** t of sacrifice, the prophet Elijah	928
	18:44	The seventh t the servant reported,	NIH
	19:2	by this t tomorrow I do not make your life	6961
	19:7	a **second** t and touched him and said,	9108

1Ki	20: 6	But about this t tomorrow I am going	6961
	20: 9	servant will do all you demanded the **first** *t*,	AIT
	21: 1	**Some t later** there was an incident involving a vineyard	339+465+1821+2021+2021
	22:49	**At that t** Ahaziah son of Ahab said	255
2Ki	3: 6	at that t King Joram set out from Samaria	3427
	3:20	about the t for offering the sacrifice.	NIH
	4:16	"About this t next year," Elisha said,	4595
	4:17	about that same t she gave birth to a son,	4595
	5:26	Is this the t to take money,	6961
	6:10	**T and again** Elisha warned the king,	285+2256+4202+4202+9109
	6:24	**Some t later**, Ben-Hadad king of Aram	339+4027
	7: 1	About this t tomorrow, a seah of flour	6961
	7:18	"About this t tomorrow, a seah of flour	6961
	8:20	In the t of Jehoram, Edom rebelled	3427
	8:22	Libnah revolted at the same **t**.	6961
	10: 6	to me in Jezreel by this t tomorrow."	6961
	10:36	The t that Jehu reigned over Israel	3427
	12:17	**About this t** Hazael king of Aram went up	255
	13: 3	*for* a long t he kept them under the power	3427
	13: 7	and made them like the dust at **threshing t**.	1889
	15:16	**At that t** Menahem, starting out from Tirzah	255
	15:29	In the t of Pekah king of Israel,	3427
	16: 6	that t, Rezin king of Aram recovered Elath	6961
	18: 4	for up to that t the Israelites had been	3427
	18:16	At this t Hezekiah king of Judah	6961
	20:12	At that t Merodach-Baladan son of	6961
	20:17	The t will surely come when everything	3427
	24:10	that t the officers of Nebuchadnezzar king	6961
1Ch	1:19	because in his t the earth was divided;	3427
	9:18	on the east, up to **the present t**	2178
	9:25	in their villages had to come from t to time	6961
	9:25	in their villages had to come from time to t	6961
	11:16	**At that t** David was in the stronghold,	255
	15:13	did not bring it up the **first** *t* that	AIT
	17:10	since the t I appointed leaders over my	3427
	18: 1	**In the course of t**, David defeated	339+4027
	19: 1	**In the course of t**, Nahash king of	339+4027
	20: 1	at the t *when* kings go off to war,	6961
	20: 4	**In the course of t**, war broke out	339+4027
	20: 4	**At that t** Sibbecai the Hushathite killed	255
	21:28	At that t, when David saw that the LORD	6961
	21:29	and the altar of burnt offering were at that t	6961
	26:17	and **two at a t** at the storehouse.	9109+9109
	28: 7	as is being done at this t.'	3427
	29:22	Solomon son of David as king a **second t**,	9108
2Ch	5: 3	to the king **at the t** of the festival in	928
	6:31	and walk in your ways all the t they live in	3427
	7: 8	So Solomon observed the festival at that t	6961
	11:17	of David and Solomon during **this t**.	8993+9102S
	13:20	Jeroboam did not regain power during the t	3427
	15: 3	a long t Israel was without the true God,	3427
	15:11	At that t they sacrificed to the LORD	3427
	16: 7	that Hanani the seer came to Asa king	6961
	16:10	At the same t Asa brutally oppressed some	6961
	21: 8	In the t of Jehoram, Edom rebelled	3427
	21:10	Libnah revolted at the same **t**,	6961
	21:19	**In the course of t**,	3427+3427+4200+4946
	24: 4	**Some t later** Joash decided to restore	339+4027
	25:27	From the t that Amaziah turned away	6961
	28:16	At that t King Ahaz sent to the king	6961
	28:22	In his t of trouble King Ahaz became	6961
	30: 3	not been able to celebrate it at the regular t	6961
	35:16	So at that t the entire service of the LORD	3427
	35:17	celebrated the Passover at that t and	6961
	35:21	It is not you I am attacking **at this t**,	2021+3427
	36:21	all the t of its desolation it rested,	3427
Ezr	4: 2	since the t of Esarhaddon king of Assyria,	3427
	5: 3	At that t Tattenai, governor of	10232
	8:34	the entire weight was recorded at that t.	6961
	9:12	a treaty of friendship with them at **any t**,	6409
	10:14	a foreign woman come at a set t,	6961
Ne	2: 6	It pleased the king to send me; so I set a t.	2375
	4:22	At that t I also said to the people,	6961
	6: 1	that I had not set the doors in the gates—	6961
	6: 4	and each t I gave them the same answer.	NIH
	6: 5	Then, the fifth t, Sanballat sent his aide	7193
	9:28	in your compassion you delivered them t **after time.**	6961+8041
	9:28	in your compassion you delivered them **time after t.**	6961+8041
	12:23	among the descendants of Levi up to the t	3427
	12:44	that men were appointed to be in charge	3427
	13: 6	**Some t** later I asked his permission	3427
	13:21	From that t on they no longer came on	6961
Est	1: 1	what happened during the t of Xerxes,	3427
	1: 2	At that t King Xerxes reigned	3427
	2:19	the virgins were assembled a **second t**,	9108
	2:21	During the t Mordecai was sitting at	3427
	4:14	For if you remain silent at this t,	6961
	4:14	to royal position for such a t as this?"	6961
	8:16	For the Jews it was a t of happiness and joy	245
	9:22	as the t when the Jews got relief	3427
	9:27	the way prescribed and at the t **appointed.**	2375
Job	9: 3	not answer him **one** *t* out of a thousand.	AIT
	14: 6	till he has put in his t like a hired man.	3427
	14:13	If only you would set me a t and	2976
	15:32	Before his t he will be paid in full,	3427
	22:16	They were carried off before their t,	6961
	39: 2	Do you know the t they give birth?	6961
Ps	21: 9	the t of your appearing	6961
	37:39	he is their stronghold in t of trouble.	6961
	51: 5	sinful from the t my mother conceived me.	NIH
	69:13	O LORD, in the t of your favor;	6961
	75: 2	You say, "I choose the **appointed t;**	4595
	77: 8	Has his promise failed for **all t**?	1887+1887+2256

Ps	78:38	**T after time** he restrained his anger	8049
	78:38	**Time after t** he restrained his anger	8049
	102:13	for it is t to show favor to her;	6961
	102:13	the **appointed t** has come.	4595
	104:27	to give them their food at the **proper t**.	6961
	119:126	It is t for you to act, O LORD.	6961
	145:15	you give them their food at the **proper t**.	6961
Pr	20: 4	so at **harvest** t he looks but finds nothing.	7907
	25:13	Like the coolness of snow at harvest t is	3427
Ecc	1:10	it was here **before** our t.	4200+4946+7156
	3: 1	There is a t for everything,	2375
	3: 2	a t to be born and a time to die,	6961
	3: 2	a time to be born and a t to die,	6961
	3: 2	a t to plant and a time to uproot,	6961
	3: 2	a time to plant and a t to uproot,	6961
	3: 3	a t to kill and a time to heal,	6961
	3: 3	a time to kill and a t to heal,	6961
	3: 3	a t to tear down and a time to build,	6961
	3: 3	a time to tear down and a t to build,	6961
	3: 4	a t to weep and a time to laugh,	6961
	3: 4	a time to weep and a t to laugh,	6961
	3: 4	a t to mourn and a time to dance,	6961
	3: 4	a time to mourn and a t to dance,	6961
	3: 5	a t to scatter stones and a time	6961
	3: 5	to scatter stones and a t to gather them,	6961
	3: 5	a t to embrace and a time to refrain,	6961
	3: 5	a time to embrace and a t to refrain,	6961
	3: 6	a t to search and a time to give up,	6961
	3: 6	a time to search and a t to give up,	6961
	3: 6	a t to keep and a time to throw away,	6961
	3: 6	a time to keep and a t to throw away,	6961
	3: 7	a t to tear and a time to mend,	6961
	3: 7	a time to tear and a t to mend,	6961
	3: 7	a t to be silent and a time to speak,	6961
	3: 7	a time to be silent and a t to speak,	6961
	3: 8	a t to love and a time to hate,	6961
	3: 8	a time to love and a t to hate,	6961
	3: 8	a t *for* war and a time for peace.	6961
	3: 8	a time for war and a t *for* peace.	6961
	3:11	He has made everything beautiful in its **t**.	6961
	3:17	for there will be a t for every activity,	6961
	3:17	a t for every deed."	NIH
	7:17	why die before your t?	6961
	8: 5	and the wise heart will know the proper t	6961
	8: 6	a proper t and procedure for every matter,	6961
	8: 8	As no one is discharged in t **of war,**	4878
	8: 9	There is a t when a man lords it over others	6961
	8:12	a hundred crimes and still **lives a long t**,	799
	9:11	but t and chance happen to them all.	6961
	10:17	and whose princes eat at a *proper t*—	6961
Isa	7:17	on the house of your father a t unlike any	3427
	9: 7	and righteousness from **that t on**	6964
	11:11	a **second t** to reclaim the remnant that is left	9108
	13:22	Her t is at hand,	6961
	18: 7	At that t gifts will be brought to the LORD	6961
	20: 2	that t the LORD spoke through Isaiah son	6961
	23:15	At that t Tyre will be forgotten	3427
	29:17	**In a very short t**,	4663+5071+6388
	33: 2	our salvation in t of distress.	6961
	39: 1	At that t Merodach-Baladan son	6961
	39: 6	The t will surely come when everything	3427
	42:14	"For a **long t** I have kept silent,	6409
	42:23	to this or pay close attention in **t to come?**	294
	48:16	at the t it happens, I am there."	6961
	49: 8	"In the t of my favor I will answer you,	6961
	59:21	of their descendants from **this t on**	6964
	60:22	in its t I will do this swiftly."	6961
Jer	2:24	at **mating** t who will find her.	2544
	3:17	that t they will call Jerusalem The Throne	6961
	4:11	At that t this people and Jerusalem will	6961
	7:25	From the t your forefathers left Egypt until	3427
	8: 1	" 'At that t, declares the LORD,	6961
	8: 7	the thrush observe the t of their migration.	6961
	8:15	for a t of healing but there was only terror.	6961
	11: 7	From the t I brought your forefathers up	3427
	11:14	not listen when they call to me in the t	6961
	11:18	**at that** t he showed me what they were doing.	255
	13: 3	word of the LORD came to me a **second t:**	9108
	14:19	for a t of healing but there is only terror.	6961
	16:19	my refuge in t of distress,	3427
	16:21	this t I will teach them my power	7193
	18: 2	If at any t I announce that a nation	8092
	18: 9	if at another t I announce that a nation	8092
	18:23	deal with them in the t of your anger.	6961
	25:33	At that t those slain by the LORD will	3427
	25:34	For your t to be slaughtered has come;	3427
	27: 7	and his son and his grandson until the t	6961
	29:28	It will be a **long t**.	801
	30: 7	It will be a t of trouble for Jacob,	6961
	31: 1	"At that t," declares the LORD,	6961
	31:31	"The t is coming," declares the LORD,	3427
	31:33	with the house of Israel after that t,"	6961
	32:14	in a clay jar so they will last a long t.	3427
	33: 1	of the LORD came to him a **second t:**	9108
	33:15	" 'In those days and at that t I will make	6961
	33:20	no longer come at their **appointed t**,	6961
	35: 7	Then you will live a long t in the land	3427
	36: 2	the t I began speaking to you in the reign	3427
	36: 9	a t of **fasting** before the LORD	7427
	37:16	where he remained a long t.	3427
	39:10	at that t he gave them vineyards and fields.	6961
	39:16	At that t they will be fulfilled	3427
	44:17	**At that t** we had plenty of food	2256
	46:21	the t *for* them to be punished.	6961
	49: 8	disaster on Esau *at* the t I punish him.	6961

Jer	50: 4	"In those days, at that t,"	6961
	50:20	In those days, at that **t,"**	6961
	50:27	the t *for* them to be punished.	6961
	50:31	the t *for* you to be punished.	6961
	51: 6	It is t *for* the LORD's vengeance;	6961
	51:13	the t *for* you to be cut off.	564
	51:33	like a threshing floor at the t it is trampled;	6961
	51:33	the t to harvest her will soon come."	6961
	51:47	the t will surely come when I will punish	3427
Eze	4: 6	lie down again, **this** t on your right side,	9108
	7: 7	The t has come, the day is near;	6961
	7:12	The t has come, the day has arrived.	6961
	11: 3	'Will it not soon be t to build houses?	NIH
	21:25	of Israel, whose day has come, whose t	6961
	21:29	to be slain, whose day has come, whose t	6961
	23:38	At that same t they defiled my sanctuary	3427
	24:14	The t has come for me to act.	NIH
	24:27	At that t your mouth will be opened;	3427
	30: 3	day of clouds, a t of doom *for* the nations.	6961
	35: 5	over to the sword at the t of their calamity,	6961
	35: 5	the t their punishment reached its climax,	6961
	38:17	At that t they prophesied for years	3427
	38:19	at that t there shall be a great earthquake in	3427
	48:35	the name of the city from that t on will be:	3427
Da	1:18	of the t set by the king to bring them in,	3427
	2: 8	"I am certain that you are trying to gain t,	10530
	2:16	Daniel went in to the king and asked for t,	10232
	2:35	the gold were broken to pieces at the **same** *t*	AIT
	2:44	"In the t of those kings,	10317
	3: 8	At this t some astrologers came forward	10232
	4:34	Belteshazzar) was greatly perplexed for a t,	10734
	4:34	At the end of that t, I, Nebuchadnezzar,	10317
	4:36	At the same t that my sanity was restored,	10232
	5:11	In the t of your father he was found	10317
	7:12	but were allowed to live for a **period of t.)**	10221+10232+10530
	7:22	t came when they possessed the kingdom.	10232
	7:25	be handed over to him for a t, times and	10530
	7:25	over to him for a time, times and half a	10530
	8:17	that the vision concerns the t *of* the end."	6961
	8:19	tell you what will happen **later in** the t	344+928
	8:19	vision concerns the **appointed** t *of* the end.	4595
	9:21	came to me in swift flight about the t *of*	6961
	10: 2	At that t I, Daniel, mourned for three weeks.	3427
	10:14	for the vision concerns a t yet to come."	3427
	11:24	but only for a t.	6961
	11:27	an end will still come at the **appointed t**.	4595
	11:29	"At the **appointed t** he will invade	4595
	11:29	but this t the outcome will be different	340
	11:33	*a* t they will fall by the sword or be burned	3427
	11:35	and made spotless until the t *of* the end,	6961
	11:35	for it will still come at the **appointed t**.	4595
	11:36	until the t of wrath is completed,	NIH
	11:40	"At the t *of* the end the king of the South	6961
	12: 1	"At that t Michael, the great prince	6961
	12: 1	be a t of distress such as has not happened	6961
	12: 1	But at that t your people—	6961
	12: 4	and seal the words of the scroll until the t	6961
	12: 7	"It will be for a t, times and half a time.	4595
	12: 7	"It will be for a time, times and half a t.	NIH
	12: 9	up and sealed until the t of the end.	6961
	12:11	the t *that* the daily sacrifice is abolished	6961
Hos	10:12	for it is t to seek the LORD,	6961
	13:13	when the t arrives, he does not come	6961
Joel	3: 1	"In those days and at that t,	6961
Am	4: 2	"The t will surely come when you will	3427
	8: 2	"The t **is ripe** for my people Israel;	995+7891
	8:10	I will make **that** t like mourning for	2023S
Jnh	3: 1	of the LORD came to Jonah a **second t:**	9108
Mic	2: 3	for it will be a t of calamity.	6961
	3: 4	At that t he will hide his face from them	6961
	5: 3	be abandoned until the t when she who is	6961
	7: 4	Now is the t of their confusion.	NIH
Na	1: 9	trouble will not come a **second t**.	7193
Hab	2: 3	For the revelation awaits an **appointed t;**	4595
	3: 2	in our t make them known;	9102
Zep	1:12	that I will search Jerusalem with lamps	6961
	2: 2	the **appointed t** arrives and that day sweeps	2976
	3:19	At that t I will deal with all who oppressed	6961
	3:20	At that t I will gather you;	6961
	3:20	at that t I will bring you home.	6961
Hag	1: 2	"These people say, 'The t has not yet come	6961
	1: 4	"Is it a t for you yourselves to be living	6961
	2:20	the LORD came to Haggai a **second t** on	9108
Zec	8: 6	to the remnant of this people at that t,	3427
	8:10	Before that t there were no wages for man	3427
Mal	3: 7	Ever since the t of your forefathers	3427
Mt	1:11	of Jeconiah and his brothers **at the t** of	2093
	2: 1	during the t of King Herod,	2465
	2: 7	and found out from them the exact t	5989
	2:16	with the t he had learned from the Magi.	5989
	4:17	From that t on Jesus began to preach,	5538
	7: 4	the t there is a plank in your own eye?	NIG
	8:29	to torture us before the appointed t?"	2789
	9:15	The t will come when the bridegroom will	2465
	10:19	At that t you will be given what to say,	6052
	11:25	At that t Jesus said, "I praise you, Father,	2789
	12: 1	that t Jesus went through the grainfields on	2789
	13:21	he has no root, he lasts **only a short t**.	4672
	13:30	At that t I will tell the harvesters:	2789
	14: 1	that t Herod the tetrarch heard the reports	2789
	16:21	From **that** t on Jesus began to explain	5538
	18: 1	At that t the disciples came to Jesus	6052
	21:34	When the harvest t approached,	2789
	21:36	other servants to them, more than the first t,	NIG
	21:41	his share of the crop at harvest t."	2789
	24:10	**At that t** many will turn away from	5538

Mt 24:23 **At that t** if anyone says to you, 'Look, 5538
24:25 See, *I have* **told** you **ahead of t**. 4625
24:30 "**At that t** the sign of the Son of Man 5538
24:43 of the house had known *at* what **t of night** 5871
24:45 to give them their food at **the proper t?** 2789
24:48 'My master *is* **staying away a long t**,' 5988
25: 1 "**At that t** the kingdom of heaven will be 5538
25: 5 The bridegroom *was* **a long t in coming**, 5988
25:19 "After a long t the master of those servants 5989
26:18 My appointed t is near. 2789
26:42 He went away a **second t** and prayed, 1311+1666+4099
26:44 once more and prayed the **third t**, 1666+5569
26:55 At that t Jesus said to the crowd, 6052
27:16 they had a notorious prisoner, 5538
Mk 1: 9 that t Jesus came from Nazareth in Galilee 2465
1:15 "The t has come," he said. 2789
2:20 the t will come when the bridegroom will 2465
3: 1 **Another t** he went into the synagogue, 4099
4:17 they have no root, they last **only a short t**. 4672
6:21 Finally the opportune t came. 2465
6:35 **By this t** it was late in the day, 2453
12: 2 *At* harvest t he sent a servant to the tenants 2789
13:11 Just say whatever is given you at the **t**, 6052
13:21 **At that t** if anyone says to you, 'Look, 5538
13:23 *I have* **told** you everything **ahead of t**. 4625
13:26 "**At that t** men will see the Son of Man 5538
13:33 You do not know when that t will come. 2789
14: 7 and you can help them **any t** you want. 4020
14:41 Returning the **third t**, he said to them, 5568
14:72 the rooster crowed the **second t**. 1311+1666
Lk 1: 5 In the t of Herod king of Judea there was 2465
1:10 *when* the t for the burning of incense came, 6052
1:20 which will come true at their **proper t.**" 2789
1:23 When his t of service was completed, 2465
1:39 that t Mary got ready and hurried to a town 2465
1:57 When it was t for Elizabeth to have her 5989
2: 6 the t came for the baby to be born, 2465
2:21 when *it was* t to circumcise him, 4398
2:22 When the t of their purification according 2465
4:13 he left him until an **opportune t**. 2789
4:25 many widows in Israel in Elijah's **t**, 2465
4:27 with leprosy **in the t of** Elisha the prophet, 2093
5:35 the t will come when the bridegroom will 2465
7:21 very t Jesus cured many who had diseases, 6052
7:45 but this woman, **from the t** I entered, 608+4005
8:13 but in the t of testing they fall away. 2789
8:27 *For* a long t this man had not worn clothes 5989
9:36 told no one at that t what they had seen. 2465
9:51 As the t approached for him to be taken up 2465
10:21 At that t Jesus, full of joy through the Holy 6052
12:12 teach you at that t what you should say." 6052
12:42 their food allowance at **the proper t?** 2789
12:45 'My master *is* **taking a long t in coming**,' 5988
12:56 how to interpret this present **t?** 2789
13: 1 some present at that t who told Jesus about 2789
13:31 At that t some Pharisees came to Jesus 6052
14:17 *At* the t of the banquet he sent his servant 6052
16:16 Since that t, the good news of the kingdom 1181+1254
16:22 "**The t** came **when** the beggar died 1181+1254
17:22 "The t is coming when you will long to 2465
18: 4 "For **some t** he refused. 5989
19:44 you did not recognize the t of God's coming 2789
20: 9 and went away *for* a long **t**. 5989
20:10 *At* harvest t he sent a servant to the tenants 2789
21: 6 the t will come when not one stone will 2465
21: 8 claiming, 'I am he,' and, 'The t is near.' 2789
21:22 the t of punishment in fulfillment of all 2465
21:27 **At that t** they will see the Son of Man 5538
23: 7 who was also in Jerusalem at that t. 2465
23: 8 a long t he had been wanting to see him. 5989
23:22 *For* the **third t** he spoke to them: "Why? 5568
23:29 For the t will come when you will say, 2465
Jn 2: 4 "My t has not yet come." 6052
2:13 it was almost t for the Jewish Passover, 1584
3: 4 a **second t** into his mother's womb to 1309
3:22 where *he* **spent some t** with them, 1417
4:21 a t is coming when you will worship 6052
4:23 Yet a t is coming and has now come when 6052
4:52 as to the t when his son got better, 6052
4:53 the father realized that this was the exact t 6052
5: 1 **Some t later**, Jesus went up to Jerusalem 3552+4047
5: 6 he had been in this condition *for* a long **t**, 5989
5:25 a t is coming and has now come when 6052
5:28 for a t is coming when all who are 6052
5:35 and you chose for a t to enjoy his light. 6052
6: 1 **Some t after** this, Jesus crossed to the far 3552
6:66 From this t many of his disciples turned *NIG*
7: 6 "The **right t** for me has not yet come; 2789
7: 6 for you any t is right. 2789
7: 8 for me the **right t** has not yet come." 2789
7:30 because his t had not yet come. 6052
7:33 "I am with you for only a short **t**, 5989
7:39 **Up to that t** the Spirit had **not** been given, 4037
8: 9 began to go away **one at a t**, 1651+1651+2848
8:20 because his t had not yet come. 6052
9:24 **A second t** they summoned the man 1311+1666
11:39 "**by this t** there is a bad odor, 2453
11:55 it was almost t for the Jewish Passover, 1584
12:31 Now is the t for judgment on this world; *NIG*
12:42 **Yet at the same t** many even among 3940
13: 1 the t had come for him to leave this world 6052
14: 9 I have been among you such a long **t?** 5989
16: 2 in fact, a t is coming when anyone who kills 6052
16: 4 that when the t comes you will remember 6052
16:21 to a child has pain because her t has come; 6052

Jn 16:22 Now **is your t** of grief, 2400+3383
16:25 a t is coming when I will no longer use this 6052
16:32 "But a t is coming, and has come, 6052
17: 1 "Father, the t has come. 6052
18:39 to release to you one prisoner **at the t of** 1877
19:27 From that t on, this disciple took her 6052
21:14 the **third t** Jesus appeared to his disciples 5568
21:17 The **third t** he said to him, "Simon 5568
21:17 because Jesus asked him the **third t**, 5568
Ac 1: 6 you at this t going to restore the kingdom 5989
1:21 the men who have been with us the whole t 5989
1:22 to the t when Jesus was taken up from us. 2465
3: 1 up to the temple at the t of prayer— 6052
3:21 the t comes for God to restore everything, 5989
4:34 For from t to time those who owned lands *NIG*
4:34 For from time to t those who owned lands *NIG*
5:36 **Some t ago** Theudas appeared, claiming to
be somebody, 2465+3836+4047+4574
7: 5 though at that t Abraham had no child. *NIG*
7:17 "As the t drew near for God 5989
7:20 "At that t Moses was born, 2789
7:41 **That was the t** they made an idol in the
form of a calf. 1697+1877+2465+3836
7:45 It remained in the land until the t of David, 2465
8: 9 Now **for some t** a man named Simon 4732
8:11 because he had amazed them *for* a long **t** 5989
9:31 Galilee and Samaria enjoyed a t of peace. *NIG*
9:37 About that t she became sick and died, 2465
9:43 *for* some t with a tanner named Simon. 2465
10:15 voice spoke to him a **second t**, 1311+1666+4099
11: 9 voice spoke from heaven a **second t**, 1311+1666
11:27 During this t some prophets came down 2465
12: 1 It was about this t that King Herod 2465
13:11 for a t you will be unable to see the light of 2789
13:20 until the t of Samuel the prophet. *NIG*
14: 3 and Barnabas spent considerable t there, 5989
14:28 And they stayed there **a long t** 3900+4024+5989
15: 7 you know that **some t ago** God 608+792+2465
15:33 After spending some t there, 5989
15:36 Some t later Paul said to Barnabas, 2465
17:21 **spent** *their* t doing nothing but talking about 2320
18:18 Paul stayed on in Corinth *for* some **t**. 2465
18:20 When they asked him *to* **spend** more t with
them, 2093+3531+5989
18:23 After spending some t in Antioch, 5989
19:23 About that t there arose a great disturbance 2789
20:16 to avoid **spending** t in the province of Asia, 1181+5990
20:18 "You know how I lived the whole t I was 5989
21: 5 But when our t was up, we left 2465
21:38 the desert **some t ago?**" 2465+3836+4047+4574
24:26 **At the same t** he was hoping that Paul 275
26: 5 They have known me **for a long t** 540
26:11 **Many a t** I went from one synagogue 4490
26:28 in such a **short t** you can persuade me to be 3900
26:29 Paul replied, "**Short t** or long— 1877+3900
27: 9 Much t had been lost, 5989
27:21 the men had gone a **long t** without food, 4498
27:28 A short t later they took soundings again *NIG*
27:40 in the sea and **at the same t** untied the ropes 275
28: 6 but after waiting **a long t** and seeing 2093+4498
Ro 3:26 to demonstrate his justice at the present **t**, 2789
5: 6 You see, **at just the right t**, 2789+2848
5:14 from the t of Adam to the time of Moses, *NIG*
5:14 from the t of Adam to the time of Moses, *NIG*
6:21 What benefit did you reap **at that t** from 5538
8:22 of childbirth right up to the **present t**. 3814
9: 9 "At the appointed t I will return, 2789
11: 5 at the present t there is a remnant chosen 2789
11:30 Just as you who were **at one** t disobedient 4537
13: 6 *who* **give** *their* **full** t to governing. 4674
13:11 And do this, understanding the **present t**. 2789
1Co 7: 2 God destined for our glory before t began. 172
4: 5 judge nothing before the appointed **t**; 2789
4: 5 **At that** t each will receive his praise 5538
7: 5 by mutual consent and for a t, 2789
7:29 What I mean, brothers, is that the t is short. 2789
14:27 should speak, **one at a t**, 324+3538
15: 6 five hundred of the brothers **at the same t**, 2384
16: 7 I hope *to* **spend** some t with you, 2152+5989
2Co 6: 2 he says, "*In* the t of my favor I heard you, 2789
6: 2 I tell you, now is the t of God's favor, 2789
8:14 **At the present** t your plenty will supply
what they need, 2789
12:14 Now I am ready to visit you *for* the **third t**, 5568
13: 1 when I am with you the **second t**. 1309
Gal 2: 1 again to Jerusalem, this t with Barnabas. *NIG*
4: 2 and trustees until the t **set** by his father. 4607
4: 4 But when the t had fully come, 5989
4:29 **At that** t the son born in the ordinary way 5538
6: 9 the proper t we will reap a harvest if we do 2789
Eph 1:10 All of us also lived among them **at one t**, 4537
2:12 remember that *at* that t you were separate 2789
Php 1: 3 I thank my God every t I remember you, *NIG*
1:17 we were torn away from you for a short t 2789
2Th 2: 6 so that he may be revealed at the proper t. 2789
1Ti 2: 6 the testimony given in its proper t. 2789
6:15 which God will bring about in his own t— 2789
2Ti 1: 9 Christ Jesus before the **beginning of t**, 173+5989
4: 3 For the t will come when men will not put 2789
4: 6 and the t has come for my departure. 2789
Tit 1: 2 promised before the **beginning of t**, 173+5989
3: 3 **At one** t we too were foolish, disobedient, 4537
3:10 and then warn him a **second t**. *AIT*
Heb 3: 8 during the t of testing in the desert, 2465
4: 7 a long t later he spoke through David, 5989
4:16 and find grace to help us in our **t of need**. 2322

Heb 5:12 though by this t you ought to be teachers, 5989
8: 8 "The t is coming, declares the Lord, 2465
8:10 with the house of Israel after that **t**, 2465
9: 9 This is an illustration for the present **t**, 2789
9:10 external regulations applying until the t of 2789
9:28 and he will appear a **second t**, 1311+1666
10:12 this priest had offered **for all** t one sacrifice 1457+1650+3836
10:13 **Since that** t he waits for his enemies 3370+3836
10:16 covenant I will make with them after that **t**, 2465
11:25 to enjoy the pleasures of sin *for* **a short t**, 4672
11:32 I do not have t to tell about Gideon, Barak, 5989
12:11 No discipline seems pleasant at the **t**, 4205
12:26 **At that** t his voice shook the earth, 5538
1Pe 1: 5 that is ready to be revealed in the last **t**. 2789
1:11 the t and circumstances to which the Spirit 2789
4: 3 For you have spent enough t in the past 5989
4:17 For it is t for judgment to begin with 2789
5: 6 that he may lift you up in **due t**. 2789
2Pe 3: 6 also the world **of that** t was deluged 5538
Rev 1: 3 because the t is near. 2789
2:21 I have given her t to repent 5989
3: 3 not know at what t I will come to you. 6052
11: 6 not rain *during* the t they are prophesying; 2465
11:18 The t has come for judging the dead, 2789
12:12 because he knows that his t is short." 2789
12:14 where she would be taken care of *for* a **t**, 2789
12:14 for a **time, times** and half a **t**, 2789
14:15 because the t to reap has come, 6052
20: 3 After that, he must be set free *for* a short **t**. 5989
22:10 because the t is near. 2789

TIMELY (1) [TIME]

Pr 15:23 an apt reply—and how good is a t word! 928+6961

TIMES (183) [TIME]

Ge 4:15 he will suffer vengeance **seven t over**." *AIT*
4:24 If Cain is avenged **seven t**, *AIT*
4:24 then Lamech **seventy-seven t**." *AIT*
27:36 He has deceived me these *two* **t**: 7193
31: 7 by changing my wages ten **t**. 4951
31:41 and you changed my wages ten **t**. 4951
33: 3 and bowed down to the ground seven t 7193
43:34 Benjamin's portion was five t as much 3338
Ex 18:22 as judges for the people at all **t**, 6961
18:26 as judges for the people at all **t**. 6961
23:14 "Three t a year you are to celebrate 8079
23:17 "Three t a year all the men are to appear 7193
25:30 on this table to be before me **at all t**. 9458
34:23 Three t a year all your men are to appear 7193
34:24 when you go up three t each year to appear 7193
Lev 4: 6 the blood and sprinkle some of it seven **t** 7193
4:17 the LORD seven t in front of the curtain. 7193
8:11 some of the oil on the altar seven **t**, 7193
14: 7 Seven t he shall sprinkle the one to 7193
14:16 some of it before the LORD seven **t**. 7193
14:27 from his palm seven t before the LORD. 7193
14:51 and sprinkle the house seven **t**. 7193
16:14 of it with his finger seven t before 7193
16:19 of the blood on it with his finger seven **t** 7193
23: 4 to proclaim at their **appointed t**: 4595
25: 8 sabbaths of years—seven t seven years— 7193
26:18 punish you for your sins **seven t over**. *AIT*
26:21 I will multiply your afflictions **seven t** *AIT*
26:24 afflict you for your sins **seven t over**. *AIT*
26:28 punish you for your sins **seven t over**. *AIT*
Nu 10:10 Also at your t *of* rejoicing— 3427
14:22 but who disobeyed me and tested me ten t— 7193
19: 4 on his finger and sprinkle it seven t toward 7193
22:28 to you to make you beat me these three **t?"** 8079
22:32 "Why have you beaten your donkey these
three **t?** 8079
22:33 and turned away from me these three **t**. 8079
24: 1 he did not resort to sorcery as at other **t**, 928+7193+7193
24:10 but you have blessed them these three **t**. 7193
Dt 1:11 increase you a thousand t and bless you 7193
16:16 Three t a year all your men must appear 7193
Jos 6: 4 march around the city seven **t**, 7193
6:15 and marched around the city seven t in 7193
6:15 on that day they circled the city seven **t**. 7193
Ru 4: 7 (Now in **earlier** t in Israel, 7156
1Sa 3:10 calling as at the other **t**, "Samuel! 7193
20:41 and bowed down before Jonathan three **t**, 7193
27: 8 (From **ancient** t these peoples had lived in 6409
2Sa 12: 6 He must pay for that lamb **four t over**. *AIT*
24: 3 multiply the troops a hundred **t over**, 7193
1Ki 9:25 Three t a year Solomon sacrificed burnt
offerings 7193
17:21 on the boy three t and cried to the LORD, 7193
18:43 Seven t Elijah said, "Go back." 7193
22:16 "How many t must I make you swear 7193
2Ki 4:35 The boy sneezed seven t and opened his 7193
5:10 "Go, wash yourself seven t in the Jordan, 7193
5:14 and dipped himself in the Jordan seven **t**, 7193
13:18 He struck it three t and stopped. 7193
13:19 should have struck the ground five or six **t**; 7193
13:19 But now you will defeat it only three **t**." 7193
13:25 Three t Jehoash defeated him, 7193
1Ch 4:22 (These records are **from ancient** t.) 6972
9:20 **In earlier** t Phinehas son of Eleazar 4200+7156
12:32 who understood the t and knew what Israel 6961
18:11 multiply his troops a hundred **t over**. 7193
2Ch 18:15 "How many t must I make you swear 7193
Ezr 4:15 a place of rebellion from ancient **t**. 10317

Ne	4:12	near them came and told us ten t over,	7193
	6: 4	Four t they sent me the same message,	7193
	10:34	of our God at set t each year a contribution	6961
	13:31	for contributions of wood at designated t,	6961
Est	1:13	with the wise men who understood the t	6961
	9:31	days of Purim at their designated t,	2375
	9:31	and their descendants in regard to their t	1821
Job	19: 3	Ten t now you have reproached me;	7193
	24: 1	the Almighty not set t for judgment?	6961
	27:10	Will he call upon God at all t?	6961
	33:29	to a man—twice, even three t—	AIT
	38:23	which I reserve for t of trouble,	6961
Ps	9: 9	a stronghold in t of trouble,	6961
	10: 1	Why do you hide yourself in t of trouble?	6961
	12: 6	in a furnace of clay, purified seven t.	AIT
	31:15	My t are in your hands;	6961
	34: 1	I will extol the LORD at all t;	6961
	37:19	In t of disaster they will not wither;	6961
	41: 1	the LORD delivers him in t of trouble.	3427
	59:16	my refuge in t of trouble.	3427
	60: 3	You have shown your people desperate t;	7997
	62: 8	Trust in him at all t, O people;	6961
	79:12	into the laps of our neighbors seven t	AIT
	106:43	Many t he delivered them,	7193
	119:20	with longing for your laws at all t.	6961
	119:164	Seven t a day I praise you	AIT
Pr	17:17	A friend loves at all t,	6961
	24:10	If you falter in t of trouble,	3427
	24:16	for though a righteous man falls seven t,	AIT
	25:19	a lame foot is reliance on the unfaithful in t	3427
Ecc	7:14	When t are good, be happy;	3427
	7:14	but when t are bad, consider:	3427
	7:22	many t you yourself have cursed others.	7193
	9:12	by evil t that fall unexpectedly upon them.	6961
Isa	30:26	and the sunlight will be seven t brighter,	AIT
	33: 6	He will be the sure foundation for your t,	6961
	46:10	from ancient t, what is still to come.	7710
	64: 4	Since ancient t no one has heard,	6409
Jer	14: 8	O Hope of Israel, its Savior in t of distress,	6961
	15:11	in t of disaster and times of distress.	6961
	15:11	in times of disaster and t of distress.	6961
	21: 2	perform wonders for us as in t past	3869+3972
	28: 8	From early t the prophets who preceded	6409
	46:26	Egypt will be inhabited as in t past,"	3427
Eze	4:10	and eat it at set t.	4946+6330+6961+6961
	4:11	water and drink it at set t.	4946+6330+6961+6961
	21:14	Let the sword strike twice, even three t.	AIT
Da	1:20	he found them ten t better than all	3338
	2:21	He changes t and seasons;	10530
	3:19	the furnace heated seven t hotter than usual	10248
	4:16	till seven t pass by for him.	10530
	4:23	until seven t pass by for him.'	10530
	4:25	Seven t will pass by for you	10530
	4:32	Seven t will pass by for you	10530
	6:10	Three t a day he got down on his knees	10232
	6:13	He still prays three t a day."	10232
	7:10	ten thousand t ten thousand stood	AIT
	7:25	and try to change the set t and the laws.	10232
	7:25	for a time, t and half a time.	10530
	9:25	but in t of trouble.	6961
	11:14	"In those t many will rise against the king	6961
	12: 7	"It will be for a time, t and half a time.	4595
Am	4: 9	"Many t I struck your gardens	8049
	5:13	the prudent man keeps quiet in such t,	6961
	5:13	in such times, for the t are evil.	6961
Mic	5: 2	from of old, from ancient t."	3427
Na	1: 7	The LORD is good, a refuge in t of trouble.	3427
Mt	13: 8	hundred, sixty or thirty t what was sown.	AIT
	13:23	hundred, sixty or thirty t what was sown."	AIT
	16: 3	but you cannot interpret the signs of the t.	2789
	18:21	how many t shall I forgive my brother	4529
	18:21	Up to seven t?"	2232
	18:22	Jesus answered, "I tell you, not seven t,	2232
	18:22	not seven times, but seventy-seven t.	1574+2231
	19:29	for my sake will receive a hundred t as	1671
	26:34	you will disown me three t."	5565
	26:75	you will disown me three t."	5565
Mk	4: 8	thirty, sixty or even a hundred t."	AIT
	4:20	thirty, sixty or even a hundred t	AIT
	10:30	will fail to receive a hundred t as much	1671
	14:30	you yourself will disown me three t."	5565
	14:72	crows twice you will disown me three t."	5565
Lk	8: 4	a hundred t more than was sown."	1671
	8:29	Many t it had seized him,	5989
	17: 4	If he sins against you seven t in a day,	2232
	17: 4	and seven t comes back to you and says,	2232
	18:30	to receive many t as much in this age and,	4491
	19: 8	I will pay back four t the amount."	5486
	21:24	be trampled on by the Gentiles until the t	2789
	22:34	you will deny three t that you know me."	5565
	22:61	you will disown me three t."	5565
Jn	13:38	you will disown me three t!	5565
Ac	1: 7	to know the t or dates the Father has set	5989
	3:19	t of refreshing may come from the Lord,	2789
	10:16	This happened three t,	5565
	11:10	This happened three t,	5565
	15:21	in every city from the earliest t and is read	1155
	17:26	and he determined the t set for them and	2789
Ro	1:10	in my prayers at all t;	4121
	1:13	that I planned many t to come to you	4490
2Co	9: 8	so that in all things at all t,	4121
	11:24	Five t I received from the Jews the forty	4294
	11:25	Three t I was beaten with rods,	5565
	11:25	three t I was shipwrecked,	5565
	12: 8	Three t I pleaded with the Lord	5565
Eph	1:10	the t will have reached their fulfillment—	2789
1Th	5: 1	about t and dates we do not need to write	5989
2Th	3:16	Lord of peace himself give you peace at all t	AIT
1Ti	4: 1	that in later t some will abandon the faith	2789
2Ti	3: 1	There will be terrible t in the last days.	2789
Heb	1: 1	through the prophets at many t and	4495
	9:26	to suffer many t since the creation of	4490
	10:33	at other t you stood side by side	1254+4047
1Pe	1:20	was revealed in these last t for your sake.	5989
Jude	1:18	"In the last t there will be scoffers	5989
Rev	5:11	and ten thousand t ten thousand.	NIG
	12:14	for a time, t and half a time,	2789

TIMID (2) [TIMIDITY]

2Co	10: 1	who am "t" when face to face with you,	5424
1Th	5:14	warn those who are idle, encourage the t,	3901

TIMIDITY (1) [TIMID]

2Ti	1: 7	For God did not give us a spirit of t,	1261

TIMNA (6)

Ge	36:12	Eliphaz also had a concubine named T,	9465
	36:22	T was Lotan's sister.	9465
	36:40	to their clans and regions: T,	9465
1Ch	1:36	Gatam and Kenaz; by T:	9465
	1:39	T was Lotan's sister.	9465
	1:51	The chiefs of Edom were: T, Alvah,	9465

TIMNAH (11) [TIMNITE'S]

Ge	38:12	he went up to T,	9463
	38:13	"Your father-in-law is on his way to T	9463
	38:14	which is on the road to T.	9463
Jos	15:10	down to Beth Shemesh and crossed to T.	9463
	15:57	Gibeah and T—ten towns and their villages.	9463
	19:43	Elon, T, Ekron,	9463
Jdg	14: 1	Samson went down to T and saw there	9463
	14: 2	"I have seen a Philistine woman in T;	9463
	14: 5	to T together with his father and mother.	9463
	14: 5	As they approached the vineyards of T,	9463
2Ch	28:18	as well as Soco, T and Gimzo,	9463

TIMNATH HERES (1) [HERES]

Jdg	2: 9	at T in the hill country of Ephraim,	9466

TIMNATH SERAH (2) [SERAH]

Jos	19:50	T in the hill country of Ephraim.	9467
	24:30	T in the hill country of Ephraim.	9467

TIMNITE'S (1) [TIMNAH]

Jdg	15: 6	they were told, "Samson, the T son-in-law,	9464

TIMON (1)

Ac	6: 5	also Philip, Procorus, Nicanor, T,	5511

TIMOTHEUS (KJV) See TIMOTHY

TIMOTHY (25)

Ac	16: 1	where a disciple named T lived,	5510
	17:14	but Silas and T stayed at Berea.	5510
	17:15	then left with instructions for Silas and T	5510
	18: 5	When Silas and T came from Macedonia,	5510
	19:22	He sent two of his helpers, T and Erastus,	5510
	20: 4	Gaius from Derbe, T also,	5510
Ro	16:21	T, my fellow worker, sends his greetings	5510
1Co	4:17	For this reason I am sending to you T,	5510
	16:10	If T comes, see to it that he has nothing to	5510
2Co	1: 1	and T our brother, To the church of God	5510
	1:19	among you by me and Silas and T,	5510
Php	1: 1	Paul and T, servants of Christ Jesus,	5510
	2:19	in the Lord Jesus to send T to you soon,	5510
	2:22	But you know that T has proved himself,	899S
Col	1: 1	and T our brother,	5510
1Th	1: 1	and T, To the church of the Thessalonians	5510
	3: 2	We sent T, who is our brother	5510
	3: 6	But T has just now come to us from you	5510
2Th	1: 1	and T, To the church of the Thessalonians	5510
1Ti	1: 2	To T my true son in the faith:	5510
	1:18	T, my son, I give you this instruction	5510
	6:20	T, guard what has been entrusted	5510
2Ti	1: 2	To T, my dear son: Grace, mercy and peace	5510
Phm	1: 1	and T our brother,	5510
Heb	13:23	that our brother T has been released.	5510

TIN (4)

Nu	31:22	Gold, silver, bronze, iron, t, lead	974
Eze	22:18	all of them are the copper, t,	974
	22:20	lead and t into a furnace to melt it with	974
	27:12	iron, t and lead for your merchandise.	974

TINDER (1)

Isa	1:31	The mighty man will become t and his work	5861

TINGLE (3)

1Sa	3:11	the ears of everyone who hears of it t.	7509
2Ki	21:12	the ears of everyone who hears of it will t.	7509
Jer	19: 3	make the ears of everyone who hears of it t.	7509

TINKLING (KJV) See CLANGING

TIP (7)

Jdg	6:21	With the t of the staff that was in his hand,	7895
1Ki	6:24	ten cubits from wing t to wing tip.	7896
	6:24	ten cubits from wing tip to wing t.	7896
Est	5: 2	So Esther approached and touched the t of	8031
Job	33: 2	words are on the t of my tongue.	928+2674+4383
	38:37	Who can t over the water jars of the heavens	8886
Lk	16:24	and send Lazarus to dip the t of his finger	216

TIPHSAH (3)

1Ki	4:24	from T to Gaza, and had peace on all sides.	9527
2Ki	15:16	attacked T and everyone in the city	9527
	15:16	He sacked T and ripped open all	NIH

TIRAS (2)

Ge	10: 2	Madai, Javan, Tubal, Meshech and T.	9410
1Ch	1: 5	Madai, Javan, Tubal, Meshech and T.	9410

TIRATHITES (1)

1Ch	2:55	the T, Shimeathites and Sucathites.	9571

TIRE (2) [TIRED]

Jer	2:24	that pursue her need not t themselves;	3615
2Th	3:13	brothers, never t of doing what is right.	1591

TIRED (8) [TIRE]

Ex	17:12	When Moses' hands grew t,	3878
Jdg	16:16	after day until he was t to death.	7918
2Sa	17:29	"The people have become hungry and t	6546
	23:10	the Philistines till his hand grew t and froze	3333
Isa	5:27	Not one of them grows t or stumbles,	6546
	40:28	He will not grow t or weary,	3615
	40:30	Even youths grow t and weary,	3615
Jn	4: 6	and Jesus, t as he was from the journey,	3159

TIRES (KJV) See NECKLACES, TURBANS

TIRHAKAH (2)

2Ki	19: 9	Now Sennacherib received a report that T,	9555
Isa	37: 9	Now Sennacherib received a report that T,	9555

TIRHANAH (1)

1Ch	2:48	Maacah was the mother of Sheber and T.	9563

TIRIA (1)

1Ch	4:16	Ziph, Ziphah, T and Asarel.	9409

TIRSHATHA (KJV) See GOVERNOR

TIRZAH (18)

Nu	26:33	Noah, Hoglah, Milcah and T.)	9573
	27: 1	Noah, Hoglah, Milcah and T.	9573
	36:11	Mahlah, T, Hoglah, Milcah and Noah—	9573
Jos	12:24	the king of T one thirty-one kings in all.	9574
	17: 3	Noah, Hoglah, Milcah and T.	9573
1Ki	14:17	got up and left and went to T.	9573
	15:21	stopped building Ramah and withdrew to T.	9574
	15:33	of Ahijah became king of all Israel in T,	9574
	16: 6	with his fathers and was buried in T.	9574
	16: 8	and he reigned in T two years.	9574
	16: 9	Elah was in T at the time,	9574
	16: 9	the man in charge of the palace at T.	9574
	16:15	Zimri reigned in T seven days.	9574
	16:17	from Gibbethon and laid siege to T.	9574
	16:23	reigned twelve years, six of them in T.	9574
2Ki	15:14	Then Menahem son of Gadi went from T	9574
	15:16	Menahem, starting out from T, attacked	9574
SS	6: 4	You are beautiful, my darling, as T,	9574

TISHBE (1) [TISHBITE]

1Ki	17: 1	Now Elijah the Tishbite, from T in Gilead,	9586

TISHBITE (6) [TISHBE]

1Ki	17: 1	Now Elijah the T, from Tishbe in Gilead,	9585
	21:17	word of the LORD came to Elijah the T:	9585
	21:28	word of the LORD came to Elijah the T:	9585
2Ki	1: 3	angel of the LORD said to Elijah the T,	9585
	1: 8	The king said, "That was Elijah the T."	9585
	9:36	through his servant Elijah the T:	9585

TITHE (15) [TEN]

Lev	27:30	"'A t of everything from the land,	5130
	27:31	If a man redeems any of his t,	5130
	27:32	The entire t of the herd and flock—	5130
Nu	18:26	the t I give you as your inheritance,	5130
	18:26	a tenth of that t as the LORD's offering.	5130
Dt	12:17	You must not eat in your own towns the t	5130
	14:23	Eat the t of your grain, new wine and oil,	5130
	14:24	and cannot carry your t (because the place	2257S
	14:25	then exchange your t for silver,	NIH
	26:12	in the third year, the year of the t,	5130
2Ch	31: 5	brought a great amount, a t of everything.	5130
	31: 6	a t of their herds and flocks and a tithe of	5130
	31: 6	a tithe of their herds and flocks and a t of	5130
Ne	10:37	And we will bring a t of our crops to	5130
Mal	3:10	Bring the whole t into the storehouse,	5130

TITHES (16) [TEN]

Nu	18:21	the t in Israel as their inheritance in return	5130
	18:24	to the Levites as their inheritance the t that	5130
	18:28	the LORD from all the t you receive from	5130
	18:28	From these t you must give the LORD's	5647S
Dt	12: 6	and sacrifices, your t and special gifts,	5130
	12:11	and sacrifices, your t and special gifts,	5130
	14:28	the t of that year's produce and store it	5130
2Ch	31:12	the contributions, t and dedicated gifts.	5130
Ne	10:37	for it is the Levites who collect the t	6923
	10:38	the Levites when they receive the t,	6923
	10:38	a tenth of the t up to the house of our God,	5130
	12:44	for the contributions, firstfruits and t.	5130
	13: 5	and also the t of grain, new wine and oil	5130
	13:12	All Judah brought the t of grain,	5130
Am	4: 4	your t every three years.	5130
Mal	3: 8	'How do we rob you?' "In t and offerings.	5130

TITIUS (1) [JUSTUS]

Ac	18: 7	went next door to the house of T Justus,	5517

TITLE (3)

Isa	45: 4	and bestow on you a t of honor,	4033
Eph	1:21	and every t that can be given,	3950+3951
Rev	17: 5	This t was written on her forehead:	3950

TITTLE (KJV) See SMALLEST STROKE

TITUS (14)

2Co	2:13	because I did not find my brother T there.	5519
	7: 6	comforted us by the coming of T,	5519
	7:13	delighted to see how happy T was,	5519
	7:14	so our boasting about you to T has proved	5519
	8: 6	So we urged T, since he had earlier made a	5519
	8:16	into the heart of T the same concern I have	5519
	8:17	For T not only welcomed our appeal,	NIG
	8:23	for T, he is my partner and fellow worker	5519
	12:18	I urged T to go to you	5519
	12:18	T did not exploit you, did he?	5519
Gal	2: 1	I took T along also.	5519
	2: 3	Yet not even T, who was with me,	5519
2Ti	4:10	and T to Dalmatia.	5519
Tit	1: 4	To T, my true son in our common faith:	5519

TIZITE (1)

1Ch	11:45	Jediael son of Shimri, his brother Joha the T,	9407

TO (20933) [TOWARD] See Index of Articles Etc.

TO AND FRO (Anglicized) See BACK AND FORTH

TOAH (1)

1Ch	6:34	the son of Eliel, the son of T,	9346

TOB (4)

Jdg	11: 3	and settled in the land of T,	3204
	11: 5	to get Jephthah from the land of T.	3204
2Sa	10: 6	and also twelve thousand men from T.	3204
	10: 8	men of T and Maacah were by themselves	3204

TOB-ADONIJAH (1)

2Ch	17: 8	Jehonathan, Adonijah, Tobijah and T—	3207

TOBIAH (14) [TOBIAH'S]

Ezr	2:60	T and Nekoda 652	3209
Ne	2:10	When Sanballat the Horonite and T	3209
	2:19	The Ammonite official and Geshem	3209
	4: 3	T the Ammonite, who was at his side, said,	3209
	4: 7	But when Sanballat, T, the Arabs,	3209
	6: 1	When word came to Sanballat, T,	3209
	6:12	because T and Sanballat had hired him.	3209
	6:14	Remember T and Sanballat, O my God,	3209
	6:17	of Judah were sending many letters to T,	3209
	6:17	and replies from T kept coming to them.	3209
	6:19	And T sent letters to intimidate me.	3209
	7:62	T and Nekoda 642	3209
	13: 4	He was closely associated with T,	3209
	13: 7	in providing T a room in the courts of	3209

TOBIAH'S (1) [TOBIAH]

Ne	13: 8	and threw all T household goods out of	3209

TOBIJAH (3)

2Ch	17: 8	Adonijah, T and Tob-Adonijah—	3210
Zec	6:10	from the exiles Heldai, T and Jedaiah,	3209
	6:14	The crown will be given to Heldai, T,	3209

TOCHEN (KJV) See TOKEN

TODAY (212) [TODAY'S]

Ge	4:14	T you are driving me from the land,	2021+3427
	19:37	he is the father of the Moabites of t.	2021+3427
	19:38	he is the father of the Ammonites of t.	2021+3427
	21:26	and I heard about it only t."	2021+3427
	24:12	give me success t,	2021+3427
	24:42	"When I came to the spring t, I said,	2021+3427
	30:32	go through all your flocks t and	2021+3427
	31:43	what can I do t about these daughters	2021+3427
	31:48	a witness between you and me t."	2021+3427
	40: 7	"Why are your faces so sad t?"	2021+3427
	41: 9	T I am reminded of my shortcomings.	2021+3427
	47:23	that I have bought you and your land t	2021+3427
	47:26	still in force t—	2021+2021+2296+3427
Ex	2:18	"Why have you returned so early t?"	2021+3427
	5:14	you quota of bricks yesterday or t,	2021+3427
	13: 4	T, in the month of Abib,	2021+3427
	14:13	deliverance the LORD will bring you t.	2021+3427
	14:13	The Egyptians you see t you will never see again.	2021+3427
	16:25	"Eat it t," Moses said,	2021+3427
	16:25	"because t is a Sabbath to the LORD.	2021+3427
	16:25	You will not find any of it on the ground t.	2021+3427
	19:10	to the people and consecrate them t	2021+3427
	32:29	You have been set apart to the LORD t,	2021+3427
	34:11	Obey what I command you t.	2021+3427
Lev	8:34	What has been done t was commanded by the LORD	2021+2021+2296+3427
	9: 4	For t the LORD will appear to you.' "	2021+3427
	10:19	"T they sacrificed their sin offering	2021+3427
	10:19	if I had eaten the sin offering t?"	2021+3427
Dt	1:10	so that t you are as many as the stars in heaven	2021+3427
	2:18	"T you are to pass by the region of Moab	2021+3427
	4: 4	to the LORD your God are still alive t.	2021+3427
	4: 8	of laws I am setting before you t?	2021+3427
	4:38	your inheritance, as it is t.	2021+2021+2296+3427
	4:40	commands, which I am giving you t,	2021+3427
	5: 1	and laws I declare in your hearing t.	2021+3427
	5: 3	with all of us who are alive here t.	2021+3427
	5:24	T we have seen that a man can live even if God speaks	2021+2021+2296+3427
	6: 6	I give you t are to be upon your hearts.	2021+3427
	6:24	kept alive, as is the case t.	2021+2021+2296+3427
	7:11	decrees and laws I give you t.	2021+3427
	8: 1	every command I am giving you t,	2021+3427
	8:18	he swore to your forefathers, as it is t.	2021+2021+2296+3427
	8:19	I testify against you t that you will	2021+3427
	9: 3	be assured t that the LORD your God is	2021+3427
	10: 8	as they still do t.	2021+2021+2296+3427
	10:13	I am giving you t for your own good?	2021+3427
	10:15	above all the nations, as it is t.	2021+2021+2296+3427
	11: 2	Remember t that your children were not the ones who saw	2021+3427
	11: 8	the commands I am giving you t,	2021+3427
	11:13	the commands I am giving you t—	2021+3427
	11:26	I am setting before you t a blessing	2021+3427
	11:27	that I am giving you t;	2021+3427
	11:28	from the way that I command you t	2021+3427
	11:32	and laws I am setting before you t	2021+3427
	12: 8	You are not to do as we do here t,	2021+3427
	13:18	that I am giving you t	2021+3427
	15: 5	to follow all these commands I am giving you t,	2021+3427
	15:15	I give you this command t.	2021+3427
	19: 9	you carefully follow all these laws I command you t,	2021+3427
	20: 3	O Israel, t you are going into battle	2021+3427
	26: 3	"I declare t to the LORD your God	2021+3427
	27: 1	commands that I give you t.	2021+3427
	27: 4	as I command you t,	2021+3427
	27:10	and decrees that I give you t."	2021+3427
	28: 1	follow all his commands I give you t,	2021+3427
	28:14	any of the commands I give you t,	2021+3427
	28:15	and decrees I am giving you t,	2021+3427
	29:10	you are standing t in the presence of	2021+3427
	29:15	who are standing here with us t in	2021+3427
	29:15	but also with those who are not here t.	2021+3427
	29:18	among you t whose heart turns away	2021+3427
	30: 2	to everything I command you t,	2021+3427
	30: 8	follow all his commands I am giving you t.	2021+3427
	30:11	Now what I am commanding you t is	2021+3427
	30:15	I set before you t life and prosperity,	2021+3427
	30:16	For I command you t to love the LORD	2021+3427
Jos	3: 7	"T I will begin to exalt you in the eyes of all Israel,	2021+2021+2296+3427
	5: 9	"T I have rolled away the reproach	2021+3427
	7:25	The LORD will bring trouble on you t."	2021+2021+2296+3427
	14:10	So here I am t, eighty-five years old!	2021+3427
	14:11	strong t as the day Moses sent me out;	2021+3427
	22:18	" 'If you rebel against the LORD t,	2021+3427
	22:29	and turn away from him t by building	2021+3427
	22:31	"T we know that the LORD is with us,	2021+3427
Jdg	9:18	(but t you have revolted against my	2021+3427
	9:19	in good faith toward Jerub-Baal and his family t,	2021+2021+2296+3427
	12: 3	why have you come up t to fight me?"	2021+2021+2296+3427
	21: 3	one tribe be missing from Israel t?"	2021+3427
	21: 6	"One tribe is cut off from Israel,"	2021+3427
Ru	2:19	"Where did you glean t?	2021+3427
	2:19	of the man I worked with t is Boaz,"	2021+3427
	3:18	not rest until the matter is settled t."	2021+3427
	4: 9	"T you are witnesses that I have bought from Naomi	2021+3427
	4:10	T you are witnesses!"	2021+3427
1Sa	4: 3	the LORD bring defeat upon us t before	2021+3427
	9: 9	prophet of t used to be called a seer.)	2021+3427
	9:12	he has just come to our town t,	2021+3427
	9:19	for t you are to eat with me,	2021+3427
	10: 2	When you leave me t,	2021+3427
	11:13	Saul said, "No one shall be put to death t,	2021+2021+2296+3427
	14:28	'Cursed be any man who eats food t!'	2021+3427
	14:30	if the men had eaten t some of	2021+3427
	14:38	let us find out what sin has been committed t,	2021+3427
	14:45	for he did this t with God's help."	2021+2021+2296+3427
	15:28	torn the kingdom of Israel from you t	2021+3427
	17:46	T I will give the carcasses	2021+2021+2296+3427
	20:27	either yesterday or t?"	2021+3427
	21: 5	How much more so t!"	2021+3427
	22: 8	to lie in wait for me, as he does t."	2021+2021+2296+3427
	22:13	and lies in wait for me, as he does t?"	2021+2021+2296+3427
	24:19	for the way you treated me t.	2021+2021+2296+3427
	25:32	who has sent you t to meet me.	2021+2021+2296+3427
	26: 8	"T God has delivered your enemy	2021+3427
	26:21	Because you considered my life precious t,	2021+2021+2296+3427
	26:23	delivered you into my hands t,	2021+3427
	26:24	as I valued your life t,	2021+2021+2296+3427
	27:10	"Where did you go raiding t?"	2021+3427
	28:18	the LORD has done this to you t.	2021+2021+2296+3427
2Sa	3:39	And t, though I am the anointed king,	2021+3427
	6:20	"How the king of Israel has distinguished himself t,	2021+3427
	14:22	"T your servant knows that	2021+3427
	15:20	t shall I make you wander about	2021+3427
	16: 3	'T the house of Israel will give me	2021+3427
	16:12	repay me with good for the cursing I am receiving t."	2021+2021+2296+3427
	18:20	"You are not the one to take the news t,"	2021+2021+2296+3427
	18:20	but you must not do so t,	2021+2021+2296+3427
	18:31	The LORD has delivered you t	2021+3427
	19: 5	"T you have humiliated all your men,	2021+3427
	19: 6	You have made it clear t that	2021+3427
	19: 6	be pleased if Absalom were alive t	2021+3427
	19:20	but t I have come here as the first of	2021+3427
	19:22	anyone be put to death in Israel t?	2021+3427
	19:22	not know that t I am king over Israel?"	2021+3427
1Ki	1:25	T he has gone down and sacrificed	2021+3427
	1:30	I will surely carry out t what I swore to you	2021+2021+2296+3427
	1:48	to see a successor on my throne t.' "	2021+3427
	1:51	to me t that he will not put his servant	2021+3427
	2:24	Adonijah shall be put to death t!"	2021+3427
	5: 7	"Praise be to the LORD t,	2021+3427
	8: 8	and they are still there t.	2021+2021+2296+3427
	8:24	fulfilled it—as it is t.	2021+2021+2296+3427
	12: 7	"If t you will be a servant to these people	2021+3427
	18:15	I will surely present myself to Ahab t.	2021+3427
	18:36	let it be known t that you are God in Israel	2021+3427
	20:13	I will give it into your hand t,	2021+3427
2Ki	2: 3	to take your master from you t?"	2021+3427
	2: 5	to take your master from you t?"	2021+3427
	4:23	"Why go to him t?"	2021+3427
	6:28	Give up your son so we may eat him t,	2021+3427
	6:31	of Shaphat remains on his shoulders t!	2021+3427
1Ch	29: 5	who is willing to consecrate himself t	2021+3427
2Ch	5: 9	and they are still there t.	2021+2021+2296+3427
	6:15	fulfilled it—as it is t.	2021+2021+2296+3427
Ezr	9: 7	foreign kings, as it is t.	2021+2021+2296+3427
Ne	1:11	Give your servant success t	2021+3427
	9:32	the days of the kings of Assyria until t.	2021+2021+2296+3427
	9:36	"But see, we are slaves t,	2021+3427
Est	5: 4	come t to a banquet I have prepared	2021+3427
Job	23: 2	"Even t my complaint is bitter;	2021+3427
Ps	2: 7	t I have become your Father.	2021+3427
	95: 7	T, if you hear his voice,	2021+3427
Pr	7:14	t I fulfilled my vows.	2021+3427
	22:19	I teach you t, even you.	2021+3427
Isa	38:19	they praise you, as I am doing t;	2021+3427
	48: 7	you have not heard of them before t.	3427
	56:12	And tomorrow will be like t,	2296+3427
	58: 4	as you do t and expect your voice to	2021+3427
Jer	1:10	t I appoint you over nations and kingdoms	2021+2021+2296+3427
	1:18	T I have made you a fortified city,	2021+3427
	11: 5	the land you possess t."	2021+2021+2296+3427
	11: 7	up from Egypt until t,	2021+2021+2296+3427
	25:18	and cursing, as they are t;	2021+2021+2296+3427
	40: 4	But I am freeing you from the chains	2021+3427
	42:19	Be sure of this: I warn you t	2021+3427
	42:21	I have told you t, but you still have	2021+3427
	44: 2	T they lie deserted and in ruins	2021+2021+2296+3427
	44: 6	desolate ruins they are t.	2021+2021+2296+3427
	44:22	a desolate waste without inhabitants, as it is t.	2021+2021+2296+3427
Mt	6:11	Give us t our daily bread.	4958
	6:30	which is here t and tomorrow is thrown	4958
	16: 3	'T it will be stormy,'	4958
	21:28	'Son, go and work t in the vineyard.'	4958
	27:19	for I have suffered a great deal t in a dream	4958

Mk	14:30	"I tell you the truth," Jesus answered, "t— 4958
Lk	2:11	T in the town of David a Savior has been 4958
	4:21	T this scripture is fulfilled in your hearing." 4958
	5:26	"We have seen remarkable things t." 4958
	12:28	the grass of the field, which is here t, 4958
	13:32	'I will drive out demons and heal people t 4958
	13:33	I must keep going t and tomorrow and 4958
	19: 5	I must stay at your house t." 4958
	19: 9	"T salvation has come to this house, 4958
	22:34	Peter, before the rooster crows t, 4958
	22:61	"Before the rooster crows t, 4958
	23:43	t you will be with me in paradise." 4958
Ac	4: 9	to account t for an act of kindness shown 4958
	13:33	t I have become your Father.' 4958
	20:26	I declare to you t that I am innocent of the blood 1877+2465+3836+4958
	22: 3	as zealous for God as any of you are t. 4958
	24:21	of the dead that I am on trial before you t.' " 4958
	26: 2	to stand before you t as I make my defense 4958
	26: 6	that I am on trial. NIG
	26:29	listening to me t may become what I am, 4958
Heb	1: 5	t I have become your Father"? 4958
	3: 7	So, as the Holy Spirit says: "T, if you hear 4958
	3:13	as long as it is called T, 4958
	3:15	As has just been said: "T, if you hear 4958
	4: 7	God again set a certain day, calling it T, 4958
	4: 7	"T, if you hear his voice, 4958
	5: 5	t I have become your Father." 4958
	13: 8	Jesus Christ is the same yesterday and t 4958
Jas	4:13	"T or tomorrow we will go to this or 4958

TODAY'S (1) [TODAY]
Ac 19:40   with rioting because of t events.   4958

TOE (5) [TOES]
Lev	8:23	the thumb of his right hand and on the big t 991
	14:14	the thumb of his right hand and on the big t 991
	14:17	the thumb of his right hand and on the big t 991
	14:25	the thumb of his right hand and on the big t 991
	14:28	the thumb of his right hand and on the big t 991

TOES (8) [TOE]
Ex	29:20	and on the big t of their right feet. 991
Lev	8:24	of their right hands and on the big t 991
Jdg	1: 6	and cut off his thumbs and big t 8079
	1: 7	and big t cut off have picked up scraps 8079
2Sa	21:20	on each hand and six t on each foot— 720
1Ch	20: 6	on each hand and six t on each foot NIH
Da	2:41	and t were partly of baked clay and partly 10064
	2:42	As the t were partly iron and partly 10064+10655

TOGARMAH (2) [BETH TOGARMAH]
Ge 10: 3   Ashkenaz, Riphath and T.   9328
1Ch 1: 6   Ashkenaz, Riphath and T.   9328

TOGETHER (390) [ALTOGETHER]
Ge	3: 7	so they sewed fig leaves t 9529
	7:13	t with his wife and the wives 2256
	8:18	t with his sons and his wife 2256
	11:31	and they set out from Ur of the Chaldeans 907
	13: 6	not support them while they stayed t, 3481
	13: 6	so great that they were not able to stay t. 3481
	14:16	t with the women and the other 1685+2256
	22: 6	As the two of them went on t, 3481
	22: 8	And the two of them went on t. 3481
	22:19	and they set off t for Beersheba. 3481
	29:22	So Laban brought t all the people of 665
	36: 7	too great for them to remain t; 3481
	50:14	Joseph returned to Egypt, t with his 2256
Ex	4:29	Moses and Aaron brought t all the elders 665
	18: 5	t with Moses' sons and wife, 2256
	19: 8	The people all responded t, 3481
	26: 3	Join five of the curtains t, 295+448+851
	26: 6	use them to fasten the curtains t so 295+448+851
	26: 9	Join five of the curtains t 2489
	26:11	in the loops to fasten the tent t as a unit. 2489
	36:10	They joined five of the curtains t 285+285+448
	36:13	to fasten the two sets of curtains t 285+285+448
	36:18	to fasten the tent t as a unit. 2489
Lev	2: 2	t with all the incense, 6584
	2:16	t with all the incense, 6584
	6:15	t with all the incense on the grain offering, 2256
	7:30	he is to bring the fat, t with the breast, 6584
	9: 4	t with a grain offering mixed with oil. 2256
	14: 6	t with the cedar wood, 2256
	14:20	t with the grain offering, 2256
	14:21	t with a tenth of an ephah 2256
	14:24	t with the log of oil, 2256
	14:31	t with the grain offering. 6584
	23:13	t with its grain offering of two-tenths of 2256
	23:18	t with their grain offerings 2256
	23:20	t with the bread of the firstfruits. 6584
Nu	1:18	called the whole community t 7735
	4: 9	t with its lamps, 2256
	6:15	t with their grain offerings 2256
	6:17	t with its grain offering and drink offering, 2256
	6:20	the priest, t with the breast that was waved 6584
	7:87	t with their grain offering. 2256
	9:11	with unleavened bread and bitter herbs. 6584
	10: 2	use them for calling the community t 5246
	11:24	He brought t seventy of their elders 665
	14:35	which has banded t against me. 3585
	16:11	and all your followers have banded t. 3585
	20: 8	your brother Aaron gather the assembly t. 7735

Nu	20:10	He and Aaron gathered the assembly t 7735
	21:16	"Gather the people t and 665
	21:35	t with his sons and his whole army, 2256
	24:10	He struck his hands t and said to him, 6215
	27: 3	who banded t against the LORD, 3585
	28: 5	t with a grain offering of a tenth of 2256
	28: 9	t with its drink offering and a grain offering 2256
	28:31	Prepare these t with their drink offerings, 2256
	35: 7	forty-eight towns, t with their pasturelands. 2256
Dt	2:33	t with his sons and his whole army. 2256
	3:12	hill country of Gilead, t with its towns. 2256
	22:10	not plow with an ox and a donkey yoked t 3481
	22:11	clothes of wool and linen woven t. 3481
	25: 5	If brothers are living t and one 3481
	29:11	t with your children and your wives, NIH
Jos	4: 4	So Joshua called t the twelve men 7924
	7:24	Then Joshua, t with all Israel, 6640
	9: 2	they came t to make war against Joshua and Israel. 3481+7695
	10:37	put it to the sword, t with its king, 2256
	10:40	the mountain slopes, t with all their kings. 2256
	11: 5	and made camp t at the Waters of Merom, 3481
	15:46	vicinity of Ashdod, t with their villages; 2256
	17:11	t with their surrounding settlements 2256
	21:16	t with their pasturelands—nine towns 2256
	21:18	t with their pasturelands—four towns 2256
	21:19	were thirteen, t with their pasturelands. 2256
	21:22	t with their pasturelands—four towns 2256
	21:24	t with their pasturelands—four towns 2256
	21:25	t with their pasturelands—two towns 2256
	21:27	t with their pasturelands—two towns 2256
	21:29	t with their pasturelands—four towns 2256
	21:31	t with their pasturelands—four towns 2256
	21:32	t with their pasturelands—three towns 2256
	21:33	were thirteen, t with their pasturelands. 2256
	21:35	t with their pasturelands—four towns 2256
	21:37	t with their pasturelands—four towns 2256
	21:39	t with their pasturelands—four towns in all. 2256
	21:41	forty-eight in all, t with their pasturelands. 2256
Jdg	4:13	Sisera gathered t his nine hundred iron chariots 2410
	6:16	strike down all the Midianites." 285+408+3869
	12: 4	Jephthah then called t the men of Gilead 7695
	13:19	t with the grain offering, 2256
	14: 5	to Timnah t with his father and mother. 2256
	15: 5	t with the vineyards and olive groves. 2256+6330
	16: 3	t with the two posts, and tore them loose, 2256
	18:22	near Micah were called t and overtook 2410
	19: 6	two of them sat down to eat and drink. 3481
	19: 8	So the two of them ate t. NIH
	20:11	So all the men of Israel got t and united 665
	20:14	From their towns they came t at Gibeah 665
Ru	1: 1	t with his wife and two sons, 2256
	4:11	who t built up the house of Israel. 9109
1Sa	5: 8	So they called t all the rulers of 665+2256+8938
	5:11	So they called t all the rulers of 665+2256+8938
	6:15	t with the chest containing the gold objects, 2256
	8: 4	of Israel gathered t and came to Samuel 7695
	9:26	he and Samuel went outside t. 9109
	11:11	so that no two of them were left t. 3481
	14:32	and ate them, t with the blood. 6584
	20:11	So they went there t. 9109
	20:41	Then they kissed each other and wept t— 408+907+2084+8276
	31: 6	and his armor-bearer and all his men died t 3481
2Sa	2:12	t with the men of Ish-Bosheth son of Saul, 2256
	2:16	and they fell down t. 3481
	6: 1	David again brought t out of Israel 665
	19:41	across the Jordan, t with all his men?" 6640
	20:14	who gathered t and followed him. 7735
	21: 8	t with the five sons of Saul's daughter 2256
	21: 9	All seven of them fell t; 3480
	23:11	the Philistines banded t at 665+2021+2653+4200
1Ki	8: 2	the men of Israel came t to King Solomon 7735
	22: 6	the king of Israel brought t the prophets— 7695
2Ki	2:11	As they were walking along and talking t, AIT
	3:10	the LORD called us three kings t 7924
	3:13	the LORD who called us three kings t 7924
	9: 5	he found the army officers sitting t. NIH
	9:25	Remember how you and I were riding t 7538
	10:18	Jehu brought t all the people t 7695
	11:19	t they brought the king down AIT
	23: 1	the king called t all the elders of Judah 665+2256+8938
	25:26	t with the army officers, 2256
1Ch	6:33	the men who served, t with their sons: 2256
	6:59	Beth Shemesh, t with their pasturelands. 2256
	6:60	and Anathoth, t with their pasturelands. 2256
	6:69	Gath Rimmon, t with their pasturelands. 2256
	6:70	and Bileam, t with their pasturelands. 2256
	6:71	also Ashtaroth, t with their pasturelands; 2256
	6:73	and Anem, t with their pasturelands; 2256
	6:75	and Rehob, t with their pasturelands; 2256
	6:76	and Kiriathaim, t with their pasturelands; 2256
	6:77	and Tabor, t with their pasturelands; 2256
	6:79	and Mephaath, t with their pasturelands; 2256
	6:81	and Jazer, t with their pasturelands. 2256
	7:29	Megiddo and Dor, t with their villages. 2256
	10: 6	and all his house died t. 3481
	11: 1	All Israel came t to David at Hebron 7695
	11:10	they, t with all Israel, 6640
	12:34	1,000 officers, t with 37,000 men 6640
	15: 4	He called t the descendants of Aaron 665
	23: 2	He also gathered t all the leaders of Israel, 665
	25: 1	David, t with the commanders of the army, 6640
	28: 1	t with the palace officials, 6640
	29:21	t with their drink offerings, 2256

1Ch	29:30	t with the details of his reign and power, 6640
2Ch	3:15	which [t] were thirty-five cubits long, NIH
	5: 3	And all the men of Israel came t to the king 7735
	18: 5	the king of Israel brought t the prophets 7695
	20: 4	The people of Judah came t to seek help 7695
	21:17	t with his sons and wives. 1685+2256
	24: 5	He called t the priests and Levites 7695
	25: 5	Amaziah called the people of Judah t 7695
	25:24	t with the palace treasures and the hostages, 2256
	28:24	Ahaz gathered t the furnishings from 665
	29:20	Hezekiah gathered the city officials t 665
	29:35	t with the fat of the fellowship offerings 928
	34:29	the king called t all the elders of Judah 665+2256+8938
	36:10	t with articles of value from the temple of 6640
Ezr	3: 9	joined t in supervising those 285+3869+6641
	4: 9	t with the rest of their associates— 10221
	6:21	t with all who had separated themselves 2256
	7:16	t with all the silver and gold 10221
	7:17	t with their grain offerings 10221
	8:19	t with Jeshaiah from the descendants 907
	8:24	of the leading priests, t with Sherebiah, 4200
Ne	4: 8	They all plotted t to come and fight 3481
	5: 7	So I called t a large meeting to deal 5989
	6: 2	"Come, let us meet t in one of the villages 3481
	6: 7	so come, let us confer t." 3481
	9: 1	the Israelites gathered t, fasting and 665
	10:28	of the Law of God, t with their wives NIH
	12: 8	Mattaniah, who, t with his associates, 2256
	12:28	The singers also were brought t from 665
	12:38	t with half the people— 2256
	12:40	so did I, t with half the officials, 6640
	13:11	Then I called them t and stationed them 7695
	13:15	t with wine, grapes, figs and all other 677+2256
Est	4:16	gather t all the Jews who are in Susa, 4043
	5: 4	replied Esther, "let the king, t with Haman, 2256
	5:10	Calling t his friends and Zeresh, 995+2256+8938
	9:15	in Susa came t on the fourteenth day of 7735
	10: 2	t with a full account of the greatness 2256
Job	2:11	from their homes and met t by agreement 3481
	10:11	and knit me t with bones and sinews? 6115
	16:10	strike my cheek in scorn and unite t against 3480
	17:16	Will we descend t into the dust?" 3480
	34: 4	let us learn t what is good. 1068
	34:15	all mankind would perish t 3480
	38: 7	while the morning stars sang t and all 3480
	38:38	and the clods of earth stick t? 1815
	40:13	Bury them all in the dust t; 3480
	41:15	of shields tightly sealed t; 2597+6037
	41:17	they cling t and cannot be parted. 4334
Ps	2: 2	the rulers gather t against the LORD and 3480
	14: 3	they have t become corrupt; 3481
	34: 3	let us exalt his name t. 3481
	41: 7	All my enemies whisper t against me; 3480
	48: 4	when they advanced t, 3481
	53: 3	they have t become corrupt; 3481
	62: 9	t they are only a breath. 3480
	71:10	those who wait to kill me conspire t. 3481
	83: 5	With one mind they plot t; 3481
	85:10	Love and faithfulness meet t; 7008
	94:21	They band t against the righteous 1518
	98: 8	let the mountains sing t for joy; 3480
	119:23	Though rulers sit t and slander me, AIT
	122: 3	like a city that is closely compacted t. 3481
	133: 1	when brothers live t in unity! 3480
	139:13	you knit me t in my mother's womb. 6115
	139:15	I was woven t in the depths of the earth, 8387
Pr	30:27	yet they advance t in ranks; 3972
Ecc	4:11	if two lie down t, they will keep warm. AIT
Isa	1:18	"Come now, let us reason t," 3519
	1:31	both will burn t, with no one to quench 3481
	9:21	t they will turn against Judah. 3481
	11: 6	the calf and the lion and the yearling t; 3481
	11: 7	their young will lie down t, 3481
	11:14	t they will plunder the people to the east. 3481
	13: 4	like nations massing t! 665
	16: 7	they wail t for Moab. 3972
	19:23	Egyptians and Assyrians will worship t. 907
	22: 3	All your leaders have fled t; 3480
	22: 3	you who were caught were taken prisoner t, 3480
	24:22	They will be herded t like prisoners 665+669
	31: 3	both will perish t. 3481
	31: 4	band of shepherds is called t against him, 7924
	34:16	and his Spirit will gather them t. 7695
	40: 5	and all mankind t will see it. 3481
	41: 1	let us meet t at the place of judgment. 3481
	41:19	the fir and the cypress t, 3481
	43: 9	All the nations gather t and 3481
	43:17	the army and reinforcements t, 3481
	43:26	let us argue the matter t; 3480
	44:11	Let them all come t and take their stand, 7695
	45:16	they will go off into disgrace t. 3481
	45:20	"Gather t and come; 7695
	45:21	let them take counsel t. 3481
	46: 2	They stoop and bow down t; 3481
	48:13	when I summon them, they all stand up t. 3481
	48:14	"Come t, all of you, and listen: 7695
	52: 8	t they shout for joy. 3481
	52: 9	Burst into songs of joy t, 3481
	60:13	the pine, the fir and the cypress t, 3481
	65:25	The wolf and the lamb will feed t, 285+3869
	66:17	they will meet their end t," 3481
Jer	3:18	and t they will come from a northern land 3481
	4: 5	Cry aloud and say: 'Gather t! 665
	6:11	and on the young men gathered t; 3481
	6:12	t with their fields and their wives, 3481

Jer	8:14	"Why are we sitting here? **Gather t!**	665
	17: 3	t with your high places,	NIH
	31:24	People will live t in Judah	3481
	41: 1	While they were eating t there,	3481
	42: 8	So **he called** t Johanan son of Kareah	7924
	46:12	both will fall down t."	3481
	46:21	They too will turn and flee t,	3481
	48: 7	t with his priests and officials.	3481
	49: 3	t with his priests and officials.	NIH
	50: 4	of Israel and the people of Judah t will go	3481
La	1:14	by his hands *they were* **woven** t.	8571
	2: 8	t they wasted away.	3481
	2:21	and old **lie** t in the dust of the streets;	AIT
Eze	6:11	**Strike** your hands t and stamp your feet	5782
	21:14	prophesy and strike your **hands** t.	448+4090+4090
	21:17	I too will strike my **hands** t,	448+4090+4090
	22:13	" '*I will* surely **strike** my hands t at	5782
	33:30	your countrymen *are* **talking** t about you	1819
	37: 7	a rattling sound, and the bones **came** t,	7928
	37:17	Join them t into one stick so	285+285+448
	39:17	'Assemble and come t from all around to	665
Da	5: 6	was so frightened that his knees knocked t	
			10154+10154+10378
	11: 6	t with her royal escort and her father and	2256
Hos	7:12	I hear them **flocking** t, I will catch them.	6337
	7:14	*They* **gather** t for grain and new wine	1591
	8:10	*I will* now **gather** them t.	7695
Joel	2:16	**bring** the elders, gather the children,	7695
Am	1:15	he and his officials t," says the LORD.	3481
	3: 3	Do two walk t unless they have agreed	3481
Mic	2:12	*I will* **surely bring** the remnant	7695+7695
	2:12	I will bring them t like sheep in a pen,	3480
	7: 3	*they all* **conspire** t.	AIT
Zep	2: 1	**Gather** t, gather together, O shameful	8006
	2: 1	Gather together, **gather** t, O shameful	8006
Zec	7: 2	t with their men, to entreat the LORD.	2256
	10: 5	**T** they will be like mighty men trampling	3481
Mt	1:18	but before they **came** t,	5302
	2: 4	*When he had* **called** t all the people's	5251
	13:30	Let both **grow** t until the harvest.	5277
	17:22	*When they* **came** t in Galilee,	3481
	18:20	two or three **come** t in my name,	1639+5251
	19: 6	Therefore what God *has* **joined** t,	5183
	20:25	Jesus **called** them t and said,	4673
	22:34	the Pharisees **got** t.	5251
	22:41	*While* the Pharisees *were* **gathered** t,	5251
	23:37	have longed to **gather** your children t,	2190
	27:29	then **twisted** t a crown of thorns and set it	4428
Mk	10: 9	Therefore what God *has* **joined** t,	5183
	10:42	Jesus **called** them t and said,	4673
	10:46	t with a large crowd, were leaving the city,	2779
	14:53	elders and teachers of the law **came** t.	5302
	15:16	and **called** t the whole company	5157
	15:17	then **twisted** t a crown of thorns and set it	4428
Lk	6:38	pressed down, **shaken** t and running over,	4888
	9: 1	When Jesus *had* **called** the Twelve t,	5157
	13:34	have longed to **gather** your children t,	2190
	15: 6	**calls** his friends and neighbors t	5157
	15: 9	**calls** her friends and neighbors t	5157
	15:13	the younger son **got** t all he had,	5251
	17:35	Two women will be grinding grain t;	
			899+2093+3836
	20: 1	t with the elders, came up to him.	5250
	22:55	of the courtyard and *had* **sat down** t,	5154
	22:66	**met** t, and Jesus was led before them.	5251
	23:13	Pilate **called** t the chief priests,	5157
	24:17	What are you discussing t as you walk	253+4639
	24:33	and those with them, **assembled** t	125
Jn	4:36	the sower and the reaper may be glad t.	3938
	11:52	to **bring** them t and make them one.	5251
	18:20	at the temple, where all the Jews **come** t.	5302
	19: 2	The soldiers **twisted** t a crown of thorns	4428
	20:19	when the disciples were t,	3963
	21: 2	and two other disciples were t.	3938
Ac	1: 6	So *when* they **met** t, they asked him, "Lord,	5302
	1:14	They all joined t constantly in prayer,	3924
	2: 1	they were all t in one place.	3938
	2: 6	a crowd **came** t in bewilderment,	5302
	2:44	All the believers were t and had	899+2093+3836
	2:46	Every day they continued to meet t in	3924
	2:46	They broke bread in their homes and ate t	3561
	4:15	the Sanhedrin and then conferred t.	253+4639
	4:24	they raised their voices t in prayer to God.	3924
	4:26	rulers gather t against the Lord	899+2093+3836
	4:27	Indeed Herod and Pontius Pilate **met** t with	5251
	5: 1	Ananias, t with his wife Sapphira,	5250
	5:12	And all the believers used to meet t	3924
	5:21	*they* **called** t the Sanhedrin—	5157
	6: 2	the Twelve **gathered** all the disciples t	4673
	10:24	and *had* **called** t his relatives	5157
	12:20	*they* now **joined** t and sought an audience	3924
	14: 5	Gentiles and Jews, t with their leaders,	5250
	14:27	they **gathered** the church t and reported all	5251
	15:30	where *they* **gathered** the church t	5251
	19:19	**brought** their scrolls t and burned them	5237
	19:25	He **called** them t, along with the workmen	5255
	20: 7	On the first day of the week we **came** t	5251
	27:17	**passed** ropes **under** the ship itself **to hold**	
		it t.	5690
	28:17	Three days later he **called** t the leaders	5157
Ro	3:12	they have t become worthless;	275
	15:32	t with you *be* **refreshed.**	5265
1Co	1: 2	t with all those everywhere who call on	5250
	7: 5	Then **come** t again so that	1639+1639+2093+3836
	11:18	I hear that *when* you **come** t as a church,	5302
	11:20	*When* you **come** t, it is not the Lord's Supper	5302
	11:33	then, my brothers, *when* you **come** t to eat,	5302

1Co	11:34	*you* **meet** t it may not result in judgment.	5302
	14:23	So if the whole church **comes** t and	
		everyone speaks	899+2093+3836+5302
	14:26	When you **come** t, everyone has a hymn,	5302
2Co	1: 1	t with all the saints throughout Achaia:	5250
	6:14	Do not be **yoked** t with unbelievers.	2282
Eph	1:10	**bring** all things in heaven and on earth t	
		under one head,	368
	2:21	the whole building is **joined** t and rises	5274
	2:22	And in him you too *are being* **built** t	5325
	3: 6	the gospel the Gentiles are **heirs** t with	5169
	3: 6	**members** t of one body, and sharers	5362
	3: 6	and **sharers** t in the promise in Christ Jesus.	5212
	3:18	may have power, t with all the saints,	5250
	4:16	and **held** t by every supporting ligament,	5204
Php	1: 1	t with the overseers and deacons:	5250
Col	1:17	and in him all things **hold** t.	5319
	2:19	and **held** t by its ligaments and sinews,	5204
	3:14	**binds** them all t in perfect unity.	1639+5278
1Th	4:17	and are left will be caught up t with them	275
	5:10	awake or asleep, we may live t with him.	275
Heb	9:19	he took the blood of calves, t with water,	3552
	10:25	Let us not give up **meeting** t,	2191
	11:40	t with us would they be made perfect.	3590+6006
Jas	2:22	his faith and his actions *were* **working** t,	5300
1Pe	5:13	She who is in Babylon, **chosen** t with you,	5293
3Jn	1: 8	so that *we may* **work** t for the truth.	1181+5301
Rev	8: 4	t *with* the **prayers** of the saints,	AIT
	16:16	Then *they* **gathered** the kings t to the place	5251
	19:17	**gather** t for the great supper of God,	5251
	19:19	and their armies **gathered** t to make war	5251

TOHU (1)
1Sa	1: 1	the son of Elihu, the son of **T**,	9375

TOIL (14) [TOILED, TOILING, TOILS, TOILSOME]
Ge	3:17	through **painful** t you will eat of it all	6779
	5:29	and **painful** t of our hands caused by	6779
	31:42	But God has seen my hardship and the t	3330
Dt	26: 7	and saw our misery, our t and oppression.	6662
Jos	24:13	on which *you did* not t and cities you did	3333
Pr	5:10	and your t enrich another man's house.	6776
Ecc	2:22	a man get for all the t and anxious striving	6662
	3: 9	What does the worker gain from his t?	6665
	3:13	and find satisfaction in all his t—	6662
	4: 6	with tranquillity than two handfuls with t	6662
	4: 8	There was no end to his t,	6662
Isa	65:23	not t in vain or bear children doomed	3333
La	5:13	Young men *at* the millstones;	5951
1Th	2: 9	brothers, our t and hardship;	3160

TOILED (6) [TOIL]
Job	20:18	**What** he t for he must give back uneaten;	3334
Ps	105:44	they fell heir to **what** others had t **for**—	6662
Ecc	2:11	that my hands had done and what *I had* t	6661
	2:18	I hated all the things I had t **for** under	6665
Isa	62: 8	the new wine for which *you have* t;	3333
2Co	11:27	I have labored, t and have often gone	3677

TOILING (3) [TOIL]
Ps	127: 2	and stay up late, t for food to eat—	6776
Ecc	4: 8	"For whom am I t," he asked,	6665
2Th	3: 8	and t so that we would not be a burden	3677

TOILS (2) [TOIL]
Ecc	1: 3	all his labor at which *he* t under the sun?	6661
	5:16	since *he* t for the wind?	6661

TOILSOME (3) [TOIL]
Ecc	2:20	to despair over all my t labor under	6662
	5:18	and to find satisfaction in his t labor under	6662
	9: 9	in life and in your t labor under the sun.	6665

TOKEN (1)
1Ch	4:32	Ain, Rimmon, **T** and Ashan—	9421

TOKHATH (1)
2Ch	34:22	who was the wife of Shallum son of **T**,	9534

TOLA (6) [TOLAITE]
Ge	46:13	**T**, Puah, Jashub and Shimron.	9356
Nu	26:23	through **T**, the Tolaite clan;	9356
Jdg	10: 1	**T** son of Puah, the son of Dodo,	9356
1Ch	7: 1	**T**, Puah, Jashub and Shimron—four in all.	9356
	7: 2	The sons of **T**:	9356
	7: 2	the descendants of **T** listed as fighting men	9356

TOLAD (1)
1Ch	4:29	Bilhah, Ezem, **T**,	9351

TOLAITE (1) [TOLA]
Nu	26:23	through Tola, the **T** clan;	9358

TOLD (451) [TELL]
Ge	3:11	he said, "Who t you that you were naked?	5583
	9:22	and t his two brothers outside.	5583
	12: 4	So Abram left, as the LORD *had* t him;	1819
	16: 9	Then the angel of the LORD t her,	606

Ge	17:23	and circumcised them, as God t him.	1819
	20: 8	he t them all that had happened,	265+928+1819
	22: 3	for the place God *had* t him about.	606
	22: 9	When they reached the place God *had* t him	606
	22:20	Some time later Abraham **was** t,	5583
	24:28	The girl ran and t her mother's household	5583
	24:33	until *I have* t *you* what I have to say."	1819
	24:66	Then the servant t Isaac all he had done.	6218
	26:32	That day Isaac's servants came and t him	5583
	27:19	I have done as *you* t me.	1819
	27:42	Rebekah **was** t what her older son Esau had	
		said,	5583
	29:12	He **had** t Rachel that he was a relative	5583
	29:12	So she ran and t her father.	5583
	29:13	and there Jacob t him all these things.	6218
	31:16	So do whatever God *has* t you."	606
	31:22	On the third day Laban **was** t	5583
	37: 5	and when *he* t it to his brothers,	5583
	37: 9	and *he* t it to his brothers.	6218
	37:10	When *he* t his father as well as his brothers,	5583
	38:13	When Tamar **was** t, "Your father-in-law	5583
	38:24	About three months later Judah **was** t,	5583
	39: 8	"With me in charge," *he* t her,	606
	39:17	Then *she* t him this story:	1819
	39:19	the story his wife t him,	1819
	40: 9	So the chief cupbearer t Joseph his dream.	6218
	41: 8	Pharaoh t them his dreams,	6218
	41:12	*We* t him our dreams,	6218
	41:24	*I* t this to the magicians,	606
	41:55	Then Pharaoh t all the Egyptians,	606
	42:29	*they* t him all that had happened to them.	5583
	43:17	The man did as Joseph t him and took	606
	43:27	"How is your aged father *you* t me *about?*	606
	43:29	the one *you* t me *about?*"	606
	44:23	But *you* t your servants,	606
	44:24	*we* t him what my lord had said.	5583
	45:26	*They* t him, "Joseph is still alive!"	5583
	45:27	*they* t him everything Joseph had said	1819
	47: 1	Joseph went and t Pharaoh,	5583
	48: 1	Some time later Joseph *was* t,	606
	48: 2	When Jacob *was* t, "Your son Joseph	5583
Ex	1:17	not do what the king of Egypt *had* t them	1819
	4:23	and *I* t you, 'Let my son go,	606
	4:28	Then Moses t Aaron everything	5583
	4:30	and Aaron t them everything	1819
	5:16	yet we *are* t, 'Make bricks!'	606
	5:19	in trouble *when* they *were* t,	606
	14: 5	of Egypt **was** t that the people had fled,	5583
	16: 9	Then Moses t Aaron, "Say to the entire	606
	16:17	The Israelites did as they were t;	NIH
	18: 8	Moses t his father-in-law *about* everything	6218
	19: 9	Then Moses t the LORD what the people	5583
	19:25	went down to the people and t them.	606
	24: 3	and t the people all the LORD's words	6218
	32:24	So *I* t them, 'Whoever has any gold	606
	34:34	And when he came out and t	1819
Lev	21:24	So Moses t this to Aaron and his sons and	1819
Nu	4:49	each was assigned his work and what	NIH
	9: 4	So Moses t the Israelites to celebrate	1819
	11:24	and t the people what the LORD had said.	1819
	11:27	A young man ran and t Moses,	5583
	22: 7	*they* t him what Balak had said.	1819
	26:65	LORD *had* t those Israelites they would	606
	29:40	Moses t the Israelites all that the LORD	606
Dt	1:18	at that time *I* t you everything you were	7422
	1:21	the God of your fathers, t you.	1819
	1:43	So *I* t you, but you would not listen.	1819
	9:12	Then the LORD t me, "Go down from here	606
	10: 9	as the LORD your God t them.)	1819
	17:16	for the LORD *has* t you,	606
	32:48	On that same day the LORD t Moses,	1819
Jos	2: 2	The king of Jericho **was** t, "Look!	606
	2:23	to Joshua son of Nun and t him everything	6218
	3: 5	Joshua t the people, "Consecrate yourselves,	606
	4: 8	as the LORD *had* t Joshua:	1819
	7: 2	of Bethel, and t them, "Go up and spy out	606
	9:24	"Your servants **were clearly** t how	5583+5583
	10:17	When Joshua *was* t that the five kings	5583
Jdg	4:12	When *they* t Sisera that Barak son	5583
	4:20	"Stand in the doorway of the tent," *he* t her.	606
	6:13	that our fathers t us *about* when they said,	6218
	6:27	and did as the LORD t him.	1819
	6:29	*they were* t, "Gideon son of Joash did it."	606
	7: 5	There the LORD t him,	606
	7:17	"Watch me," *he* t them.	606
	8:23	But Gideon t them, "I will not rule over you,	606
	9: 7	When Jotham *was* t about this,	5583
	13: 6	the woman went to her husband and t him,	606
	13:13	"Your wife must do all that *I have* t her.	606
	13:23	all these things or now t us this."	9048
	14: 6	But *he* t neither his father	5583
	14:16	but *you* haven't t me *the* **answer.**"	5583
	14:17	So on the seventh day he finally t her,	5583
	15: 6	*they were* t, "Samson, the Timnite's	606
	16: 2	people of Gaza *were* t, "Samson is here!"	606
	16:15	a fool of me and haven't t me the secret	5583
	16:17	So *he* t her everything.	5583
	16:18	Delilah saw that *he had* t her everything,	5583
	16:18	*he has* t me everything."	5583
	18: 2	*They* t them, "Go, explore the land."	606
	18: 4	*He* t them what Micah had done for him,	606
Ru	1:20	"Don't call me Naomi," *she* t them.	606
	2: 9	*I have* t the men not to touch you.	7422
	2:11	"I've **been** t all about what you have done	
			5583+5583
	2:19	Then Ruth t her mother-in-law *about*	5583

Ru 3: 6 and did everything her mother-in-law t her 7422
3:16 *she* t her everything Boaz had done for her 5583
1Sa 1:23 Elkanah her husband t her. 606
3: 9 So Eli t Samuel, "Go and lie down, 606
3:13 For *I* t him that I would judge his family 5583
3:17 if you hide from me anything he t you." 1819
3:18 So Samuel t him everything, 5583
4:13 the town and t what had happened, 5583
4:16 He t Eli, "I have just come from 606
8: 7 And the LORD t him: "Listen to all that 606
8:10 Samuel t all the words of the LORD to 606
9:23 the one *I* t you to lay aside." 606
11: 9 *They* t the messengers who had come, 606
14:28 Then one of the soldiers t him, 6699
14:43 So Jonathan t him, "I merely tasted 5583
15:12 but he was t, "Saul has gone to Carmel. 5583
17:27 and t him, "This is what will be done for 606
18:20 and when *they* t Saul *about* it, 5583
18:24 Saul's servants t him what David had said, 5583
18:26 When the attendants t David these things, 5583
19: 1 Saul t his son Jonathan and all 1819
19: 7 So Jonathan called David and t him 5583
19:15 the men back to see David and t them, 606
19:17 Michal t him, "He said to me, 606
19:18 at Ramah and t him all that Saul had done 5583
19:21 Saul was t *about* it, and he sent more men, 5583
21: 2 *I have* t them to meet me at a certain place. 3359
22:21 He t David that Saul had killed the priests 5583
23: 1 When David was t, "Look, 5583
23: 7 Saul was t that David had gone to Keilah, 5583
23:13 When Saul was t that David had escaped 5583
23:25 and when David was t *about* it, 5583
24: 1 from pursuing the Philistines, he *was* t, 5583
24:18 now t me *of* the good you did to me; 5583
25:14 One of the servants t Nabal's wife Abigail: 5583
25:19 Then *she* t her servants, "Go on ahead; 606
25:36 So *she* t him nothing until daybreak. 5583
25:37 his wife t him all these things, 5583
27: 4 Saul was t that David had fled to Gath, 5583
28:21 in my hands and did what *you* t me to do. 1819

2Sa 2: 4 When David *was* t that it was the men 5583
3:23 he *was* t that Abner son of Ner had come to 5583
4:10 when a *man* t me, 'Saul is dead,' 5583
6:12 Now King David *was* t, "The LORD has 5583
10: 5 When David *was* t *about* this, 5583
10:17 When David *was* t of this, he gathered all 5583
11:10 When David *was* t, "Uriah did not go home, 5583
11:22 *he* t David everything Joab had sent him 5583
11:25 David t the messenger, "Say this to Joab: 606
13:34 The watchman went and t the king, 5583
14:33 So Joab went to the king and t him this. 5583
15:13 A messenger came and t David, 606
15:31 Now David had been t, "Ahithophel 5583
16:11 let him curse, for the LORD has t him to. 606
17:15 Hushai t Zadok and Abiathar, the priests, 606
17:18 But a young man saw them and t Absalom. 5583
18: 2 The king t the troops, 606
18:10 When one of the men saw this, *he* t Joab, 5583
18:11 Joab said to the man who *had* t him this, 5583
18:20 to take the news today," Joab t him. 606
19: 1 Joab was t, "The king is weeping 5583
19: 8 When the men *were* t, 5583
21:11 David *was* t what Aiah's daughter Rizpah, 5583

1Ki 1:23 And *they* t the king, "Nathan the prophet 5583
1:51 Then Solomon was t, "Adonijah is afraid 5583
2:29 King Solomon was t that Joab had fled to 5583
2:39 king of Gath, and Shimei was t, 5583
2:41 When Solomon was t that Shimei had gone 5583
5: 5 as the LORD t my father David, 1819
10: 7 Indeed, not even half was t me; 5583
11: 2 about which the LORD *had* t the Israelites, 606
13:11 whose sons came and t him all that 6218
13:11 *They* also t their father what he had said to 6218
13:17 I have been t by the word of the LORD: 1821
13:22 and drank water in the place where *he* t you 1819
14: 2 the one *who* t me I would be king 1819
14: 5 But the LORD *had* t Ahijah, 606
17: 5 So he did what the LORD had t him. 1821
17:15 She went away and did as Elijah had t her. 1821
18:16 So Obadiah went to meet Ahab and t him, 5583
18:43 look toward the sea," *he* t his servant. 606
19: 1 Ahab t Jezebel everything Elijah had done 5583
20:28 up and t the king of Israel, "This is what 606
22:34 The king t his chariot driver, 606

2Ki 1: 7 who came to meet you and t you this?" 1819
1:16 *He* t the king, "This is what the LORD says: 1819
4: 7 She went and t the man of God, 5583
4:17 just as Elisha *had* t her. 1819
4:19 His father t a servant, "Carry him to 606
4:27 from me and *has* not t me why." 5583
4:31 went back to meet Elisha and t him, 5583
5: 4 Naaman went to his master and t him what 5583
5:13 prophet *had* t you to do some great thing, 1819
5:14 as the man of God *had* t him, 1821
6:19 Elisha t them, "This is not the road 606
7:10 the city gatekeepers and t them, "We went 5583
8: 6 asked the woman about it, and *she* t him. 6218
8: 7 When the king *was* t, "The man of God 5583
8:14 "*He* t me that you would certainly recover." 606
9:12 Jehu said, "Here is what *he* t me: 606
9:36 They went back and t Jehu, who said, 5583
10: 8 When the messenger arrived, *he* t Jehu, 5583
13:18 Elisha t him, "Strike the ground." 606
18:25 The LORD *himself* t me to march against 606
18:37 t him what the field commander had said. 5583
19: 3 *They* t him, "This is what Hezekiah says: 606

1Ch 15:16 David t the leaders of the Levites 606

1Ch 19: 5 someone came and t David about the men, 5583
19:17 When David *was* t of this, 5583
2Ch 9: 6 the greatness of your wisdom *was* t me; 5583
18:33 The king t the chariot driver, 606
19: 6 *He* t them, "Consider carefully what you do, 606
20: 2 Some men came and t Jehoshaphat, 5583
33:16 and t Judah to serve the LORD, 606
35:21 God *has* t me to hurry; 606
35:23 and he t his officers, "Take me away; 606
Ezr 5:15 and t him, 'Take these articles and go 10042
8:17 *I* t them what to say to Iddo 928+7023+8492
8:22 because *we had* t the king, 606
Ne 2:12 *I* had not t anyone what my God had put 5583
2:18 *I* also t them *about* the gracious hand 5583
4:12 near them came and t us ten times over, 606
5: 7 *I* t them, "You are exacting usury 606
8: 1 *They* t Ezra the scribe to bring out 606
9:15 *you* t them to go in and take possession of 606
9:23 the land that *you* t their fathers to enter 606
Est 2:20 and nationality just as Mordecai *had* t her 7422
2:22 about the plot and t Queen Esther, 5583
3: 4 Therefore *they* t Haman *about* it 5583
3: 4 for *he had* t them he was a Jew. 5583
4: 4 Esther's maids and eunuchs came and t her 5583
4: 7 Mordecai t him everything 5583
4: 8 and he t him to urge her to go into NIH
6:13 and t Zeresh his wife and all his friends 6218
6:13 For Esther *had* t how he was related to her. 5583
Job 37:20 *Should* he be t that I want to speak? 6218
42: 9 did what the LORD t them; 1819
Ps 22:30 future generations *will* be t about 6218
44: 1 our fathers *have* t us what you did 6218
52: T The Edomite had gone to Saul and t him: 6218
78: 3 what our fathers *have* t us. 6218
Isa 7: 2 Now the house of David *was* t, 5583
28:22 the LORD Almighty, *has* t me of 907+4946+9048
36:10 The LORD *himself* t me to march against 606
36:22 him what the field commander had said. 5583
37: 3 *They* t him, "This is what Hezekiah says: 606
40:21 *Has* it not *been* t you from the beginning? 5583
41:26 Who t *of* this from the beginning, 5583
41:26 No *one* t of this, no one foretold it, 5583
48: 5 Therefore *I* t you these things long ago; 5583
48:15 For what they *were* not t, they will see, 6218
Jer 4:11 this people and Jerusalem *will* be t, 606
13: 5 as the LORD t me. 7422
13: 6 "Go now to Perath and get the belt *I* t you 7422
23:38 even though *I* t you that you must not claim, 606+4200+8938
26:18 *He* t all the people of Judah, 606
34: 6 the prophet t all this to Zedekiah king 1819
36: 5 Then Jeremiah t Baruch, "I am restricted; 7422
36: 8 Jeremiah the prophet t him to do; 7422
36:13 Micaiah t them everything he had heard 5583
38:27 and *he* t them everything the king had 5583
42:19 the LORD *has* t you, 'Do not go to Egypt.' 1819
42:21 *I have* t you today, but you still have not 5583
45: 1 the prophet Baruch son of Neriah in 1819
Eze 11: 5 came upon me, and *he* t me to say: 606
11:25 and *I* t the exiles everything 1819
Da 1:10 but the official t Daniel, "I am afraid 606
4: 7 *I* t them the dream, 560
4: 8 Daniel came into my presence and *I* t him 10042
7: 1 It *was* t, 'Get up and eat your fill of flesh!' 10042
7:16 So he t me and gave me the interpretation 10042
Hos 3: 3 Then *I* t her, "You are to live with me 606
12:10 gave them many visions and t *parables* 1948
Jnh 1:10 because he *had already* t them so.) 5583
Hab 1: 5 would not believe, even if *you were* t. 6218
Zec 1: 7 *I* t them, "If you think it best, 606
13: 3 because *you have* t lies in the LORD's name. 1819
Mt 8:22 But Jesus t him, "Follow me, 3306
9: 9 "Follow me," *he* t him, 3306
12:47 Someone t him, "Your mother 3306
13: 3 *he* t them many things in parables, saying: 3281
13:24 Jesus t them another parable: 3306+4192
13:31 *He* t them another parable: 3306+4192
13:33 *He* t them still another parable: 3281
14:12 Then *they* went and t Jesus. 550
15:35 *He* t the crowd to sit down on the ground. 4133
18:31 and went and t their master everything 1397
20: 4 *He* t them, 'You also go and work 3306
20:31 The crowd rebuked them and t them to NIG
22:13 "Then the king t the attendants, 3306
22:24 "Moses t us that if a man dies without 3306
24:25 See, *I have* t you *ahead of time.* 4625
26:13 what she has done *will* also be t, 3281
26:31 Then Jesus t them, "This very night 3306
28: 7 Now *I have* t you." 3306
28:16 the mountain where Jesus *had* t them to go. 5435
Mk 1:30 and they t Jesus about her. 3306
2:14 "Follow me," Jesus t him, 3306
3: 9 Because of the crowd *he* t his disciples 3306
3:32 and they t him, "Your mother and brothers 3306
4:11 *He* t them, "The secret of the kingdom 3306
5:16 Those who had seen it t the people 1455
5:16 and t about the pigs as well. NIG
5:33 trembling with fear, t him the whole truth. 3306
5:36 Jesus t the synagogue ruler, 3306
5:43 and t them to give her something to eat. 3306
7:27 the children eat all they want," *he* t her, 3306
7:29 *he* t her, "For such a reply, you may go; 3306
8: 6 *He* t the crowd to sit down on the ground. 4133
8: 7 and t the disciples to distribute them. 3306
9:38 in your name and *we* t him *to stop,* 3266
10:32 and t them what was going to happen 3306
10:48 Many rebuked him and t him to be quiet, NIG

Mk 11: 6 They answered as Jesus *had* t them to, 3306
13:23 t you everything *ahead of time.* 4625
14: 9 what she has done *will* also be t, 3281
14:16 and found things just as Jesus *had* t them. 3306
14:27 "You will all fall away," Jesus t them, 3306
16: 7 There you will see him, just as *he* t you.' " 3306
16:10 She went and t those who had been 3306
Lk 2:15 which the Lord has t us *about.*" 1192
2:17 the word *concerning* what had been t them 3281
2:20 which were just as they *had been* t. 3281
3:13 "Don't collect any more than you are required to," he t them. 3306
5:36 *He* t them this parable: 3306
6:39 *He* also t them this parable: 3306
7:18 John's disciples t him about all these things. 550
8: 4 from town after town, *he* t this parable: 3306
8:20 Someone t him, "Your mother 550
8:36 Those who had seen it t the people how 550
8:39 So the man went away and t all over town 3062
8:47 *she* t why she had touched him and 550
8:55 Jesus t them to give her something to eat. 1411
9: 3 *He* t them: "Take nothing for the journey 3306
9:36 t no one at that time what they had seen. 550
10: 2 *He* t them, "The harvest is plentiful, 3306
10:37 Jesus t him, "Go and do likewise." 3306
12:16 And *he* t them this parable: 3306
13: 1 at that time *who* t Jesus about 550
13: 6 Then *he* t this parable: 3306
14: 7 *he* t them this parable: 3306
14:23 "Then the master t his servant, 3306
15: 3 Then Jesus t them this parable: 3306
16: 1 Jesus t his disciples: "There was a rich man 3306
16: 6 "The manager t him, 'Take your bill 3306
16: 7 "*He* t him, 'Take your bill 3306
17: 9 because he did what *he was* t *to do?* 1411
17:10 you have done everything you *were* t *to do,* 1411
18: 1 Then Jesus t his disciples a parable 3306
18: 9 Jesus t this parable: 3306
18:31 Jesus took the Twelve aside and t them, 3306
18:37 *They* t him, "Jesus of Nazareth 550
18:39 the way rebuked him and t him to be quiet, NIG
19:32 and found it just as *he had* t them. 3306
21:29 *He* t them this parable: 3306
22:13 and found things just as Jesus *had* t them. 3306
24: 6 Remember how he t you, 3281
24: 9 *they* t all these things to the Eleven and 550
24:10 others with them who t this to the apostles. 3306
24:23 They came and t us that they had seen 3306
24:35 the two t what had happened on the way, 2007
24:44 "This is what *I* t you while I was still 3281
24:46 *He* t them, "This is what is written: 3306
Jn 1:33 who sent me to baptize with water t me, 3306
1:45 Philip found Nathanael and t him, 3306
1:50 "You believe because *I* t you I saw you 3306
2: 8 Then *he* t them, "Now draw some out 3306
4:16 *He* t her, "Go, call your husband 3306
4:29 see a man who t me everything I ever did. 3306
4:39 "*He* t me everything I ever did." 3306
4:48 Jesus t him, "you will never believe." 3306
5:12 "Who is this fellow who t you to pick it up 3306
5:15 The man went away and t the Jews 334
6:36 But as *I* t you, you have seen me 3306
6:65 "This is why *I* t you that no one can come 3306
7: 6 Therefore Jesus t them, "The right time 3306
8:24 I t you that you would die in your sins; 3306
8:40 a man who *has* t you the truth that I heard 3281
9: 7 he t him, "wash in the Pool of Siloam" 3306
9:11 *He* t me to go to Siloam and wash. 3306
9:27 "*I have* t you already and you did 3306
11:14 So then he t them plainly, 3306
11:27 "Yes, Lord," *she* t him, 3306
11:46 and t them what Jesus had done. 3306
12:22 Andrew and Philip in turn t Jesus. 3306
12:35 Then Jesus t them, "You are going to have 3306
12:50 what the Father *has* t me to say." 3306
13:27 about to do, do quickly," Jesus t him, 3306
13:33 and just as *I* t the Jews, so I tell you now: 3306
14: 2 if it were not so, I would *have* t you. 3306
14:29 *I have* t you now before it happens, 3306
15:11 *I have* t you this so that my joy may be 3281
16: 1 "All this *I have* t you so that you will 3281
16: 4 *I have* t you this, so that when the time 3281
16:33 "*I have* t you these things, 3281
18: 8 "*I* t you that I am he," Jesus answered. 3306
20:18 And she t them that he had said these things NIG
20:25 So the other disciples t him, 3306
20:29 Then Jesus t him, "Because you have seen 3306
21: 3 Simon Peter t them, and they said, 3306
Ac 5:21 the temple courts, *as they had been* t, 201
7:13 Joseph t his brothers *who he was,* 341
7:37 "This is that Moses who t the Israelites, 3306
7:40 *They* t Aaron, 'Make us gods who will go 3306
8:29 The Spirit t Philip, "Go to that chariot 3306
8:35 t him **the good news about** Jesus. 2294
9: 6 and you *will be* t what you must do." 3281
9:11 The Lord t him, "Go to the house of Judas NIG
9:27 *He* t them how Saul on his journey 1455
10: 8 He t them everything that had happened 2007
10:13 a voice t him, "Get up, Peter, 899+1181+4639
10:22 A holy angel t *him* to have you come 5976
11:12 The Spirit t me to have no hesitation 3306
11:13 He t us how he had seen an angel appear 550
12: 8 and follow me," the angel t him. 3306
12:15 "You're out of your mind," they t her, 3306
13:41 would never believe, even if someone t you. 1687
15: 3 they t how the Gentiles had been converted. 1687
16:36 The jailer t Paul, "The magistrates have 550

Ac	19: 4	*He* t the people to believe in the one	3306
	22:10	*be* t all that you have been assigned to do.'	3281
	23:16	he went into the barracks and t Paul.	550
	25:16	"I t them that it is not the Roman custom	646
	27:25	in God that it will happen just as *he* t me.	3281
Ro	9:12	she *was* t, "The older will serve	3306
	15:21	"Those who *were* not t about him will see,	334
1Co	10:28	both for the sake of the man who t you and	3606
	16: 1	Do what *I* t the Galatian churches to do.	1411
2Co	7: 7	*He* t us about your longing for me,	334
Php	3:18	as *I* have often t you before and	3306
Col	1: 8	who also t us of your love in the Spirit.	1317
1Th	3: 6	He has t us that you always have	NIG
	4: 6	as *we* have **already** t you and warned you.	4625
	4:11	work with your hands, just as *we* t you,	4133
1Pe	1:12	of the things that *have* now *been* t you	334
2Pe	1:16	when *we* t you **about** the power	1192
3Jn	1: 6	They have t the church **about** your love.	3455
Rev	6:11	and they *were* t to wait a little longer,	3306
	9: 4	They *were* not to harm the grass of	3306
	10:11	Then I *was* t, "You must prophesy again	3306
	11: 1	a reed like a measuring rod and *was* t,	3306
	22:10	Then *he* t me, "Do not seal up the words	3306

TOLERANCE (1) [TOLERATE]

| Ro | 2: 4 | the riches *of* his kindness, t and patience, | 496 |

TOLERATE (6) [TOLERANCE, TOLERATED]

Est	3: 8	not in the king's best interest to t them.	5663
Hab	1: 3	Why *do you* t wrong?	5564
	1:13	you cannot t wrong.	5564
	1:13	Why then *do you* t the treacherous?	5564
Rev	2: 2	I know that you cannot t wicked men,	1002
	2:20	*You* t that woman Jezebel,	918

TOLERATED (1) [TOLERATE]

| Est | 3: 4 | whether Mordecai's behavior *would be* t, | 6641 |

TOLL (KJV) See TAXES

TOMB (64) [TOMBS]

Ge	23: 6	None of us will refuse you his t	7700
	35:20	Over her t Jacob set up a pillar,	7690
	35:20	and to this day that pillar marks Rachel's t.	7690
	50: 5	bury me in the t I dug for myself in	7700
Jdg	8:32	and was buried in the t *of* his father Joash	7700
	16:31	and Eshtaol in the t *of* Manoah his father.	7700
1Sa	10: 2	you will meet two men near Rachel's t,	7690
2Sa	2:32	and buried him in his father's t	7700
	3:32	and the king wept aloud at Abner's t.	7700
	4:12	of Ish-Bosheth and buried it in Abner's t	7700
	17:23	So he died and was buried in his father's t.	7700
	19:37	that I may die in my own town near the t	7700
	21:14	of Saul and his son Jonathan in the t	7700
1Ki	13:22	not be buried in the t *of* your fathers.' "	7700
	13:30	Then he laid the body in his own t,	7700
2Ki	9:28	and buried him with his fathers in his t in	7690
	13:21	they threw the man's body into Elisha's t.	7700
	23:17	the t *of* the man of God who came	7700
	23:30	to Jerusalem and buried him in his own t.	7690
2Ch	16:14	in the t that he had cut out for himself in	7700
Job	21:32	and watch is kept over his t.	1539
Isa	14:18	lie in state, each in his own t.	1074
	14:19	But you are cast out of your t like	7700
Mt	27:60	in his own new t that he had cut out of	3646
	27:60	a big stone in front of the entrance *to* the t	3646
	27:61	Mary were sitting there opposite the t.	5439
	27:64	the t to be made secure until the third day.	5439
	27:65	make the t as secure as you know how."	NIG
	27:66	and made the t secure by putting a seal on	5439
	28: 1	and the other Mary went to look at the t.	5439
	28: 2	going to the t, rolled back the stone	NIG
	28: 8	So the women hurried away from the t,	3646
Mk	6:29	and took his body and laid it in a t.	3646
	15:46	and placed it in a t cut out of rock.	3646
	15:46	a stone against the entrance of the t.	3646
	16: 2	they were on their way to the t	3646
	16: 3	from the entrance of the t?"	3646
	16: 5	As they entered the t,	3646
	16: 8	the women went out and fled from the t.	3646
Lk	23:53	in linen cloth and placed it in a t cut in	3645
	23:55	and saw the t and how his body was laid	3645
	24: 1	and went to the t.	3645
	24: 2	the stone rolled away from the t,	3646
	24: 9	When they came back from the t,	3646
	24:12	Peter, however, got up and ran to the t.	3646
	24:22	They went to the t early this morning	3646
	24:24	of our companions went to the t	3646
Jn	11:17	that Lazarus had already been in the t	3646
	11:31	supposing she was going to the t	3646
	11:38	once more deeply moved, came to the t.	3646
	12:17	when he called Lazarus from the t	3646
	19:41	and in the garden a new t,	3646
	19:42	of Preparation and since the t was nearby,	3646
	20: 1	Mary Magdalene went to the t and saw	3646
	20: 2	"They have taken the Lord out of the t	3646
	20: 3	and the other disciple started for the t.	3646
	20: 4	and reached the t first.	3646
	20: 6	arrived and went into the t.	3646
	20: 8	who had reached the t first,	3646
	20:11	but Mary stood outside the t crying.	3646
	20:11	she bent over to look into the t	3646

Ac	2:29	and his t is here to this day.	3645
	7:16	in the t that Abraham had bought from	3645
	13:29	down from the tree and laid in a t.	3646

TOMBS (20) [TOMB]

Ge	23: 6	Bury your dead in the choicest of our t.	7700
2Ki	23:16	he saw the t that were there on the hillside,	7700
2Ch	21:20	but not in the t *of* the kings.	7700
	24:25	but not in the t *of* the kings.	7700
	28:27	but he was not placed in the t *of* the kings	7700
	32:33	where the t *of* David's descendants are.	7700
	35:24	He was buried in the t *of* his fathers,	7700
Ne	3:16	made repairs up to a point opposite the t	7700
Ps	49:11	Their t will remain their houses forever,	7700
Mt	8:28	men coming from the t met him.	3646
	23:27	You are like whitewashed t,	5439
	23:29	You build t for the prophets and decorate	5439
	27:52	The t broke open and the bodies	3646
	27:53	They came out of the t,	3646
Mk	5: 2	an evil spirit came from the t to meet him.	3646
	5: 3	This man lived in the t,	3645
	5: 5	the t and in the hills he would cry out	3645
Lk	8:27	but had lived in the t.	3645
	11:47	because you build t for the prophets,	3646
	11:48	and you build their t.	NIG

TOMBSTONE (1) [STONE]

| 2Ki | 23:17 | The king asked, "What is that t I see?" | 7483 |

TOMORROW (58)

Ex	8:10	"T," Pharaoh said.	4737
	8:23	This miraculous sign will occur t.' "	4737
	8:29	and t the flies will leave Pharaoh	4737
	9: 5	"T the LORD will do this in the land."	4737
	9:18	at this time t I will send the worst hailstorm	4737
	10: 4	I will bring locusts into your country t.	4737
	16:23	'T is to be a day of rest,	4737
	17: 9	T I will stand on top of the hill with	4737
	19:10	and consecrate them today and t.	4737
	32: 5	"T there will be a festival to the LORD."	4737
Nu	11:18	in preparation for t,	4737
	14:25	turn back t and set out toward the desert	4737
	16: 7	and t put fire and incense in them before	4737
	16:16	to appear before the LORD t—	4737
Jos	3: 5	for t the LORD will do amazing things	4737
	7:13	in preparation for t;	4737
	11: 6	by this time t I will hand all of them over	4737
	22:18	he will be angry with the whole	4737
Jdg	19: 9	Early t morning you can get up and be	4737
	20:28	for t I will give them into your hands."	4737
1Sa	9:16	"About this time t I will send you a man	4737
	11: 9	'By the time the sun is hot t,	4737
	11:10	"T we will surrender to you,	4737
	19: 2	Be on your guard t morning;	2021S
	19:11	t you'll be killed."	4737
	20: 5	"Look, t is the New Moon festival,	4737
	20: 5	until the evening of the **day after t.**	8958
	20:12	by this time the day after t!	4737
	20:18	"T is the New Moon festival.	4737
	20:19	The **day after t,** toward evening,	8992
2Sa	11:12	and t I will send you back."	4737
1Ki	19: 2	if by this time t I do not make your life like	4737
	20: 6	But about this time t I am going	4737
2Ki	6:28	and t we'll eat my son.'	4737
	7: 1	About this time t, a seah of flour will sell	4737
	7:18	"About this time t, a seah of flour will sell	4737
	10: 6	and come to me in Jezreel by this time t."	4737
2Ch	20:17	T march down against them.	4737
	20:17	Go out to face them t,	4737
Est	5: 8	let the king and Haman come t to	4737
	5:12	along with the king t.	4737
	9:13	to carry out this day's edict t also,	4737
Pr	3:28	"Come back later; I'll give it t"—	4737
	27: 1	Do not boast about t,	3427+4737
Isa	22:13	you say, "for t we die!"	4737
	56:12	t will be like today, or even far better."	4737
Mt	6:30	which is here today and t is thrown into	892
	6:34	Therefore do not worry about t,	892+3836
	6:34	for t will worry about itself.	892+3836
Lk	12:28	and t is thrown into the fire,	892
	13:32	and heal people today and t,	892
	13:33	I must keep going today and t and	892
Ac	23:20	to bring Paul before the Sanhedrin t on	892
	23:22	He replied, "T you will hear him."	892
1Co	15:32	"Let us eat and drink, for t we die."	892
Jas	4:13	"Today or t we will go to this or that city,	892
	4:14	you do not even know what will happen t.	892+3836

TONE (1)

| Gal | 4:20 | could be with you now and change my t, | 5889 |

TONGS (3)

1Ki	7:49	the gold floral work and lamps and t;	4920
2Ch	4:21	and lamps and t (they were solid gold);	4920
Isa	6: 6	which he had taken with t from the altar.	4920

TONGUE (93) [TONGUES]

Ex	4:10	I am slow of speech and t."	4383
2Sa	23: 2	his word was on my t.	4383
Est	1:22	in each people's t that every man should	4383
Job	5:21	be protected from the lash of the t,	4383
	12:11	not the ear test words as the t tastes food?	2674
	15: 5	you adopt the t *of* the crafty.	4383
	20:12	in his mouth and he hides it under his t,	4383
	27: 4	and my t will utter no deceit.	4383
	33: 2	my words are **on the tip of** my t.	928+2674+4383
	34: 3	For the ear tests words as the t tastes food.	2674
	41: 1	a fishhook or tie down his t with a rope?	4383
Ps	5: 9	with their t they speak deceit.	4383
	10: 7	trouble and evil are under his t.	4383
	12: 3	all flattering lips and every boastful t	4383
	15: 3	and has no slander on his t,	4383
	16: 9	my heart is glad and my t rejoices;	3883
	22:15	and my t sticks to the roof of my mouth;	4383
	34:13	keep your t from evil and your lips	4383
	35:28	My t will speak of your righteousness and	4383
	37:30	and his t speaks what is just.	4383
	39: 1	"I will watch my ways and keep my t	4383
	39: 3	then I spoke with my t:	4383
	45: 1	my t is the pen of a skillful writer.	4383
	50:19	mouth for evil and harness your t to deceit.	4383
	51:14	and my t will sing of your righteousness.	4383
	52: 2	Your t plots destruction;	4383
	52: 4	O you deceitful t!	4383
	66:17	his praise was on my t!	4383
	71:24	My t will tell of your righteous acts	4383
	114: 1	house of Jacob from a people of **foreign** t,	4357
	119:172	May my t sing of your word,	4383
	120: 3	and what more besides, O deceitful t?	4383
	137: 6	May my t cling to the roof of my mouth	4383
	139: 4	a word is on my t you know it completely,	4383
Pr	6:17	a lying t, hands that shed innocent blood,	4383
	6:24	from the smooth t *of* the wayward wife.	8557
	10:19	but he who holds his t is wise.	4383
	10:20	The t *of* the righteous is choice silver,	4383
	10:31	but a perverse t will be cut out.	4383
	11:12	but a man of understanding **holds** *his* t.	3087
	12:18	but the t of the wise brings healing.	4383
	12:19	but a lying t lasts only a moment.	4383
	15: 2	The t *of* the wise commends knowledge,	4383
	15: 4	The t that brings healing is a tree of life,	4383
	15: 4	but a deceitful t crushes the spirit.	2023S
	16: 1	from the LORD comes *the* reply *of* the t.	4383
	17: 4	a liar pays attention to a malicious t.	4383
	17:20	he whose t is deceitful falls into trouble.	4383
	17:28	and discerning if he holds his t.	8557
	18:21	The t has the power of life and death,	4383
	21: 6	fortune made by a lying t is a fleeting vapor	4383
	21:23	and his t keeps himself from calamity.	4383
	25:15	and a gentle t can break a bone.	4383
	25:23	so a sly t brings angry looks.	4383
	26:28	A lying t hates those it hurts,	4383
	28:23	more favor than he who has a flattering t	4383
	31:26	and faithful instruction is on her t.	4383
SS	4:11	milk and honey are under your t.	4383
Isa	30:27	and his t is a consuming fire.	4383
	32: 4	the stammering t will be fluent and clear.	4383
	33:19	with their strange, incomprehensible t.	4383
	35: 6	and the mute t shout for joy.	4383
	45:23	by me every t will swear.	4383
	50: 4	an instructed t, to know the word	4383
	54:17	you will refute every t that accuses you.	4383
	57: 4	and stick out your t?	4383
	59: 3	and your t mutters wicked things.	4383
Jer	9: 3	"They make ready their t like a bow,	4383
	9: 8	Their t is a deadly arrow;	4383
La	4: 4	Because of thirst the infant's t sticks to	4383
Eze	3:26	I will make your t stick to the roof	4383
Mk	7:33	Then he spit and touched the man's t.	1185
	7:35	his t was loosened and he began to speak	1185
Lk	1:64	and his t was loosed,	1185
	16:24	the tip of his finger in water and cool my t,	1185
Ac	2:26	my heart is glad and my t rejoices;	1185
Ro	14:11	every t will confess to God.' "	1185
1Co	14: 2	*in* a t does not speak to men but to God.	1185
	14: 4	He who speaks *in* a t edifies himself,	1185
	14: 9	you speak intelligible words with your t,	1185
	14:13	who speaks *in* a t should pray that he may	1185
	14:14	For if I pray *in* a t, my spirit prays,	1185
	14:19	words to instruct others than ten thousand words in a t.	1185
	14:26	a revelation, a t or an interpretation.	1185
	14:27	If anyone speaks *in* a t, two—	1185
Php	2:11	every t confess that Jesus Christ is Lord,	1185
Jas	1:26	and yet does not keep a tight rein on his t,	1185
	3: 5	Likewise the t is a small part of the body,	1185
	3: 6	The t also is a fire,	1185
	3: 8	but no man can tame the t.	1185
	3: 9	With **the** t we praise our Lord and Father,	899S
1Pe	3:10	and see good days must keep his t	1185
1Jn	3:18	not love *with* words or t but with actions	1185

TONGUES (45) [TONGUE]

Jdg	7: 5	who lap the water with their t like a dog	4383
Job	29:10	their t stuck to the roof of their mouths.	4383
Ps	12: 4	"We will triumph with our t;	4383
	31:20	you keep them safe from accusing t.	4383
	57: 4	whose t are sharp swords.	4383
	64: 3	They sharpen their t like swords.	4383
	64: 8	He will turn their own t against them	4383
	68:23	while the t *of* your dogs have their share."	4383
	73: 9	and their t take possession of the earth.	4383
	78:36	lying to him with their t;	4383
	109: 2	they have spoken against me with lying t.	4383
	120: 2	from lying lips and deceitful t.	4383
	126: 2	our t with songs of joy.	4383
	140: 3	They make their t as sharp as a serpent's;	4383

Isa	5:24	as t of fire lick up straw and	4383
	28:11	and strange t God will speak to this people,	4383
	41:17	their t are parched with thirst.	4383
	66:18	about to come and gather all nations and t,	4383
Jer	9: 5	They have taught their t to lie;	4383
	18:18	with our t and pay no attention	4383
	23:31	against the prophets who wag their own t	4383
Mic	6:12	and their t speak deceitfully.	4383
Zec	14:12	and their t will rot in their mouths.	4383
Mk	16:17	they will speak in new t;	1185
Ac	2: 3	be t of fire that separated and came to rest	1185
	2: 4	in other t as the Spirit enabled them.	1185
	2:11	the wonders of God in our own t!"	1185
	10:46	For they heard them speaking in t	1185
	19: 6	and they spoke in t and prophesied.	1185
Ro	3:13	their t practice deceit."	1185
1Co	12:10	**speaking in** different kinds of t,	1185
	12:10	and to still another the interpretation of t.	1185
	12:28	*those* **speaking in** different kinds of t.	1185
	12:30	Do all speak in t?	1185
	13: 1	If I speak in the t of men and of angels,	1185
	13: 8	where there are t, they will be stilled;	1185
	14: 5	like every one of you to speak in t,	1185
	14: 5	one who speaks in t, unless he interprets,	1185
	14: 6	brothers, if I come to you and speak in t,	1185
	14:18	I thank God that I speak in t more than all	1185
	14:21	"Through **men of strange** t and through	2280
	14:22	T, then, are a sign, not for believers but	1185
	14:23	and everyone speaks in t,	1185
	14:39	and do not forbid speaking in t.	1185
Rev	16:10	Men gnawed their t in agony	1185

TONIGHT (13)

Ge	19: 5	are the men who came to you t?	2021+4326
	19:34	Let's get him to drink wine again t,	2021+4326
	30:15	"he can sleep with you t in return	2021+4326
Nu	22:19	Now stay here t as the others did,	2021+4326
Jos	2: 2	Israelites have come here t to spy out	2021+4326
	4: 3	down at the place where you stay t."	2021+4326
Jdg	19: 6	"Please **stay** t and enjoy yourself."	4328
Ru	1:12	even if I had a husband t and then	2021+4326
	3: 2	T he will be winnowing barley on	2021+4326
1Sa	19:11	"If you don't run for your life t,	2021+4326
2Sa	17: 1	and set out t in pursuit of David.	2021+4326
Mk	14:30	Jesus answered, "today—yes, t	3816+3836+4047
Ac	23:23	spearmen to go to Caesarea at nine t.	3816

TOO (258)

Ge	9: 5	**And** from each man, t,	2256
	16:10	that they will be t numerous to count."	4946
	18:14	Is anything t hard for the LORD?	4946
	19:21	"Very well, I will grant this request t;	1685
	24:14	'Drink, and I'll water your camels t'—	1685
	24:19	"I'll draw water for your camels too	1685
	24:44	and I'll draw water for your camels t,"	1685
	24:46	'Drink, and I'll water your camels t.'	1685
	26:16	you have become t powerful for us.	4394
	27:31	He t prepared some tasty food	1685
	27:34	to his father, "Bless me—me t,	1685
	27:38	Bless me t, my father!"	1685
	29:33	he gave me this one t."	1685
	30: 3	for me and that through her I t can build	1685
	30:15	Will you take my son's mandrakes t?"	1685
	31:25	Laban and his relatives camped there t.	NIH
	33: 7	**and** they t bowed down.	2256
	36: 7	Their possessions were t great for them	4946
	38:11	For he thought, "He may die t,	1685
	40:16	he said to Joseph, "I t had a dream:	677
	44:29	from me t and harm comes to him,	1685
	47:20	because the famine *was* t severe for them.	AIT
	48:11	God has allowed me to see your children t."	1685
	48:19	He t will become a people,	1685
	48:19	and he t will become great.	1685
Ex	1: 9	Israelites have become **much t numerous**	
		for us.	2256+6786+8041
	10:26	Our livestock t must go with us;	1685
	12: 4	If any household is t small for a whole lamb	4946
	16:18	he who gathered much *did* not **have t much,**	6369
	16:18	he who gathered little not **have t little.**	2893
	18:18	The work is t heavy for you;	4946
	23:29	and the wild animals t numerous for you.	6584
Lev	25: 4	If anyone making the vow is t poor to pay	4946
Nu	11:14	the burden is t heavy for me.	4946
	11:23	"Is the LORD's arm t short?	7918
	16: 3	"You have **gone t far!**	8041
	16: 7	You Levites have **gone t far!"**	8041
	16:10	now you are trying to get the priesthood t.	1685
	16:34	"The earth is going to swallow us t!"	7153
	19: 8	**and** he t will be unclean till evening.	2256
	19:10	**and** he t will be unclean till evening.	2256
	22: 6	because they are t powerful for me.	4946
	24:24	but they t will come to ruin."	1685
	27:13	you t will be gathered to your people,	1685
Dt	1: 9	"You *are* t **heavy a burden** for me **to**	
		carry alone.	3523+4202+5951
	1:17	Bring me any case t hard for you,	4946
	2:11	they t were considered Rephaites,	677
	2:20	t was considered a land of the Rephaites,	677
	2:36	not one town was t strong for us.	4946
	3:20	and they t have taken over the land that	1685
	9:20	but at that time I prayed for Aaron t.	1685
	12:21	to put his Name *is* t far away from you,	AIT
	14:24	But if that place is t distant	4946
	17: 8	that are t difficult for you to judge—	4946
	19: 6	overtake him if the distance *is* t great,	AIT

Dt	20: 8	not become disheartened t."	3869
	30:11	not t difficult for you or	4946
Jos	1:15	and until they t have taken possession of	1685
	17:15	if the hill country of Ephraim *is* t **small**	AIT
	24:18	We t will serve the LORD,	1685
Jdg	1:33	**but** the Naphtalites t lived among	2256
	1:35	they t were pressed into forced labor.	2256
	3:31	He t saved Israel.	1685
	6:35	so that they t went up to meet them.	NIH
	7: 2	"You have t many men for me	4946
	7: 4	"There are still t many men.	NIH
	9:19	and may you be his, t!	1685
	14: 9	he gave them some, **and** they t ate it.	2256
	18:26	seeing that they were t strong for him,	4946
Ru	1:12	I am t old to have another husband.	4946
1Sa	19:21	and they prophesied t.	1685
	22:17	because they t have sided with David.	1685
	30:10	for two hundred men were t exhausted	4946
	30:21	two hundred men who had been t exhausted	4946
	31: 5	he t fell on his sword and died with him.	1685
2Sa	2: 6	and I t will show you the same favor	1685
	3:39	these sons of Zeruiah are t strong for me.	4946
	10:11	"If the Arameans are t strong for me,	4946
	10:11	but if the Ammonites are t strong for you,	4946
	12: 8	And if all this had been t little,	5071
	13:36	The king, t, and all his servants wept	1685+2256
	14:26	to time when it became t heavy for him—	6584
	15:24	t, and all the Levites who were with him	1685
	15:30	the people with him covered their heads t	2256
	18:26	"He must be bringing good news, t."	1685
	22:18	from my foes, who were t strong for me.	4946
	23:22	he t was as famous as the three mighty men.	2256
1Ki	3: 8	t numerous to count or number.	4946
	8:64	before the LORD was t small to hold	4946
	10: 3	nothing was t hard for the king to explain	1685
	12:28	"It is t much for you to go up to Jerusalem.	4946
	13:18	"I t am a prophet, as you are.	1685
	19: 7	for the journey is t much for you."	4946
	19:10	and now they are trying to kill me t."	NIH
	19:14	and now they are trying to kill me t."	NIH
	20:23	That is why they were t strong for us.	4946
2Ki	2:17	But they persisted until he was t ashamed	NIH
	5:20	"My master *was* t easy on Naaman,	3104
	6: 1	where we meet with you is t small for us.	4946
	9:27	Jehu chased him, shouting, "Kill him t!"	1685
1Ch	8:32	They t lived near their relatives	677+2256
	9:38	They t lived near their relatives	677+2256
	10: 5	he t fell on his sword and died.	1685
	11:24	he t was as famous as the three mighty men.	2256
	19:12	"If the Arameans are t strong for me,	4946
	19:12	but if the Ammonites are t strong for you,	4946
	19:15	they t fled before his brother Abishai	1685
	22:14	of bronze and iron t great to be weighed,	401
2Ch	9: 2	nothing was t hard for him to explain	4946
	22: 3	He t walked in the ways of the house	1685
	29:34	were t **few** to skin all the burnt offerings;	5071
Ezr	9: 6	"O my God, I am t **ashamed** and disgraced	AIT
	10: 1	They t wept bitterly.	3954
Ne	6: 9	"Their hands will get t weak for the work,	4946
	13:27	you t are doing all this terrible wickedness	2256
Job	5:21	Now you t have proved to be of no help;	3954
	32:10	I t will tell you what I know.	677
	32:17	I t will have my say;	677
	32:17	I t will tell what I know.	677
	33: 6	I t have been taken from clay.	1685
	42: 3	things t wonderful for me to know.	4946
Ps	18:17	from my foes, who were t strong for me.	4946
	35:10	You rescue the poor from those t strong	4946
	36: 2	in his own eyes he **flatters** himself *t much*	AIT
	38: 4	like a burden t heavy to bear.	4946
	40: 5	they would be t many to declare.	4946
	77: 4	I was t troubled to speak.	4202
	87: 4	Philistia t, and Tyre, along with Cush—	2180
	89: 5	O LORD, your faithfulness t,	677
	105:24	he made them t numerous for their foes,	4946
	120: 6	T long have I lived	8041
	131: 1	with great matters or things t wonderful	4946
	139: 6	Such knowledge is t wonderful for me,	4946
	139: 6	t lofty for me to attain.	NIH
	142: 6	for they are t strong for me.	4946
Pr	20:19	so avoid a *man* who **talks** t much.	7331+8557
	21:13	he t will cry out and not be answered.	4946
	23:20	Do not join *those who* **drink** t much wine	6010
	24: 7	Wisdom *is* t **high** for a fool;	AIT
	25:16	t much of it, and you will vomit.	8425
	25:17	t much of you, and he will hate you.	8425
	25:27	It is not good to eat t much honey,	8049
	26:15	*he is* t **lazy** to bring it back to his mouth.	AIT
	30: 9	*I may* **have** t much and disown you and say,	8425
	30:18	"There are three things that are t amazing	4946
Ecc	1:17	t, is a chasing after the wind.	1685
	2:15	I said in my heart, "This t is meaningless."	1685
	2:16	Like the fool, the wise man t must die!	375
	2:19	This t is meaningless.	1685
	2:21	This t is meaningless and	1685
	2:23	This t is meaningless.	1685
	2:24	This t, I see, is from the hand of God,	1685
	2:26	This t is meaningless,	1685
	4: 4	This t is meaningless,	1685
	4: 8	This t is meaningless—	1685
	4:16	This t is meaningless,	1685
	5:10	This t is meaningless.	1685
	5:16	This t is a grievous evil:	1685+2256
	6: 9	This t is meaningless,	1685
	7: 6	This t is meaningless.	1685+2256
	8:10	Then t, I saw the wicked buried—	4027
	8:10	This t is meaningless.	1685

Ecc	8:14	This t, I say, is meaningless.	1685
Isa	7: 8	be t shattered to be a people.	4946
	28:20	The bed is t short to stretch out on,	4946
	28:20	the blanket t **narrow** to wrap around you.	AIT
	31: 2	Yet he t is wise and can bring disaster;	1685
	38:16	**and** my spirit finds life in them t.	2256
	40:20	A *man* t poor to present such	6123
	49: 6	"It is t small a thing for you to	4946
	49:19	now you will be t small for your people,	4946
	49:20	'This place is t small for us;	NIH
	50: 2	Was my arm t short to ransom you?	4946
	59: 1	arm of the LORD is not t short to save,	4946
	59: 1	nor his ear t dull to hear.	4946
	63: 9	In all their distress he t was distressed,	NIH
	65: 5	for I am t **sacred** for you!'	AIT
Jer	4:12	a wind t strong for that comes from me.	4946
	5: 5	**But** with one accord they t had broken off	421
	25:26	the king of Sheshach will drink it t.	NIH
	29: 6	in marriage, so that they t may have sons	NIH
	29: 7	because if it prospers, you t will prosper."	NIH
	32:17	Nothing is t hard for you.	4946
	32:27	Is anything t hard for me?	4946
	46:21	They t will turn and flee together,	1685
	48: 2	You t, O Madmen, will be silenced;	1685
	48: 7	you t will be taken captive,	1685
	49:11	Your widows t can trust in me."	2256
Eze	16:28	in prostitution with the Assyrians t,	2256
	21:17	I t will strike my hands together,	1685+2256
	23:12	She lusted after the Assyrians—	NIH
	23:13	I saw that she defiled herself;	NIH
	24: 9	I, t, will pile the wood high.	1685
	31:18	t, will be brought down with the trees	NIH
	32:28	"You t, O Pharaoh, will be broken	2256
Da	2:11	What the king asks is t **difficult.**	10330
	4: 9	and no mystery is t **difficult** for you.	AIT
Am	6: 9	they t will die.	2256
Na	3:11	You t will become drunk;	1685
Hab	1:13	Your eyes are t pure to look on evil;	4946
Zep	2:12	"You t, O Cushites, will be slain	1685
Zec	9: 2	and upon Hamath t,	1685
	9: 5	Gaza will writhe in agony, **and** Ekron t,	2256
	14:14	Judah t will fight at Jerusalem.	1685
Mt	4: 8	so that I t may go and worship him."	2779
	7: 1	"Do not judge, or you t will be judged.	NIG
Mk	12:22	Last of all, the woman died t.	2779
Lk	2:35	And a sword will pierce your own soul t."	2779
	3:21	Jesus was baptized t.	2779
	13: 3	But unless you repent, you t will all perish.	3931
	13: 5	unless you repent, you t will all perish."	6058
	19: 9	because this man, t, is a son of Abraham.	2779
	20:32	Finally, the woman died t.	2779
Jn	2:10	after the guests have **had** t much to drink;	3499
	5:17	**and** I, t, am working."	2779
	6:67	"You do not want to leave t, do you?"	2779
	7:52	They replied, "Are you from Galilee, t?	2779
	9:27	Do you want to become his disciples, t?"	2779
	9:40	Are we blind t?"	2779
	10:16	They t will listen to my voice,	2779
	14:21	**and** I t will love him and show myself	2779
		that they t may be truly sanctified.	2779
Ac	2:13	"They have **had** t much wine."	1639+3551
	5:37	He t was killed,	2779
	14:15	We t are only men, human like you.	2779
	17:13	they went there t, agitating the crowds	2779
	26: 9	"I t was convinced that I ought to do all	4036
Ro	3:29	Is he not the God of Gentiles t?	2779
	3:29	God of Gentiles too? Yes, of Gentiles t,	2779
	6: 4	we t may live a new life.	2779
	11: 5	So t, at the present time there is	2779
	11:31	so they t have now become disobedient	2779
	11:31	in order that they t may now receive mercy	2779
	16:13	who has been a mother to me, t.	2779
1Co	7:40	and I think that I t have the Spirit of God.	2779
	9:11	is it t much if we reap a material harvest	NIG
	10:21	of the Lord and the cup of demons t;	NIG
2Co	1: 5	not to **put it** t severely.	2096
	8:15	who gathered much *did* not **have t much,**	4429
	8:15	who gathered little *did* not **have t little."**	1782
	10:14	*We are* not **going** t far in our boasting,	5657
	11:18	I t will boast.	2779
	11:21	To my shame I admit that we were t weak	NIG
Gal	2:16	So we, t, have put our faith in Christ Jesus	2779
Eph	2:22	And in him you t are being built together	2779
Php	2:18	you t should be glad and rejoice with me.	2779
	3:15	that t God will make clear to you.	2779
Col	4: 3	And pray for us t,	2779
1Ti	5: 7	Give the people these instructions, t,	2779
2Ti	2:10	that they t may obtain the salvation that is	2779
	4:15	You t should be on your guard	2779
Tit	3: 3	At one time we t were foolish, disobedient,	2779
Heb	2:14	he t shared in their humanity so that	4181
Jas	5: 8	You t, be patient and stand firm,	2779
2Pe	2:12	and like beasts they t will perish.	2779
Rev	14:10	t, will drink of the wine of God's fury,	2779
	14:17	**and** he t had a sharp sickle.	2779

TOOK (668) [TAKE]

Ge	2:15	The LORD God t the man and put him in	4374
	2:21	*he* t one of the man's ribs and closed up	4374
	3: 6	*she* t some and ate it.	4374
	5:24	he was no more, because God t him **away.**	4374
	8: 9	He reached out his hand and t the dove	4374
	9:23	and Japheth t a garment and laid it	4374
	11:31	Terah t his son Abram,	4374
	12: 5	He t his wife Sarai, his nephew Lot,	4374

Ge	12:19	so that *I* t her to be my wife?	4374
	15: 5	*He* t him outside and said,	3655
	16: 3	Sarai his wife t her Egyptian maidservant	4374
	17:23	that very day Abraham t his son Ishmael	4374
	20: 2	king of Gerar sent for Sarah and t her.	4374
	21:14	the next morning Abraham t some food	4374
	22: 3	*He* t with him two of his servants	4374
	22: 6	Abraham t the wood for the burnt offering	4374
	22:10	Then he reached out his hand and t	4374
	22:13	over and t the ram and sacrificed it as	4374
	24:10	the servant t ten of his master's camels	4374
	24:22	the man t out a gold nose ring weighing	4374
	24:61	So the servant t Rebekah and left.	4374
	24:65	So *she* t her veil and covered herself.	4374
	25: 1	Abraham t another wife,	4374
	27:15	Then Rebekah t the best clothes	4374
	27:35	came deceitfully and t your blessing."	4374
	27:36	*He* t my birthright,	4374
	28:18	Early the next morning Jacob t	4374
	29:23	he t his daughter Leah and gave her	4374
	30: 9	*she* t her maidservant Zilpah and gave her	4374
	30:15	that you t **away** my husband?	4374
	30:37	however, t fresh-cut branches from poplar,	4374
	31:16	that God t **away** from our father belongs	5911
	31:36	Jacob was angry and t Laban **to task.**	8189
	31:45	So Jacob t a stone and set it up as a pillar.	4374
	31:46	So *they* t stones and piled them in a heap,	4374
	31:53	So Jacob t an oath in the name of the Fear	8678
	32:22	Jacob got up and t his two wives,	4374
	34: 2	saw her, *he* t her and violated her.	4374
	34:25	t their swords and attacked	4374
	34:26	and t Dinah from Shechem's house	4374
	36: 2	Esau t his wives from the women	4374
	36: 6	Esau t his wives and sons and daughters	4374
	37:24	*they* t him and threw him into the cistern.	4374
	37:28	the Ishmaelites, *who* t him to Egypt.	995
	37:32	t the ornamented robe **back**	995+2256+8938
	38:14	*she* t off her widow's clothes,	6073
	38:19	*she* t off her veil and put	6073
	38:28	so the midwife t a scarlet thread and tied it	4374
	39: 7	after a while his master's wife t **notice**	5951+6524
	39:20	Joseph's master t him and put him in prison,	4374
	40:11	and *I* t the grapes, squeezed them into	4374
	41:42	Then Pharaoh t his signet ring	6073
	43:15	the men t the gifts and double the amount	4374
	43:17	The man did as Joseph told him and t	995
	43:24	The steward t the men into Joseph's house,	995
	46: 5	and Israel's sons t their father Jacob	5951
	46: 6	*They* also t with them their livestock and	4374
	46: 7	*He* t with him to Egypt his sons	995
	48: 1	So he t his two sons Manasseh	4374
	48:13	And Joseph t both of them,	4374
	48:17	so he t **hold** of his father's hand to move it	9461
	48:22	the ridge of land *I* t from the Amorites	4374
Ex	2: 5	So the woman t the baby and nursed him.	4374
	2:10	*she* t him to Pharaoh's daughter	995
	4: 4	and t **hold** of the snake and it turned back	2616
	4: 6	and when *he* t it **out**, it was leprous,	3655
	4: 7	and when *he* t it **out**, it was restored,	3655
	4:20	So Moses t his wife and sons,	4374
	4:20	And he t the staff of God in his hand.	4374
	4:25	But Zipporah t a flint knife,	4374
	9:10	So *they* t soot from a furnace and stood	4374
	12:34	So the people t their dough before	5951
	13:19	Moses t the bones of Joseph with him	4374
	14: 6	and t his army with him.	4374
	14: 7	*He* t six hundred of the best chariots,	4374
	15:20	Aaron's sister, t a tambourine in her hand,	4374
	17:12	*they* t a stone and put it under him	4374
	18:13	The next day Moses t *his* seat to serve	3782
	24: 6	Moses t half of the blood and put it	4374
	24: 7	Then *he* t the Book of the Covenant	4374
	24: 8	Moses then t the blood,	4374
	32: 3	So all the people t **off** their earrings	7293
	32: 4	*He* t what they handed him and made it into	4374
	32:20	And *he* t the calf they had made	4374
	40:20	*He* t the Testimony and placed it in the ark,	4374
Lev	8:10	Then Moses t the anointing oil	4374
	8:15	Moses slaughtered the bull and t some of	4374
	8:16	also t all the fat around the inner parts,	4374
	8:23	the ram and t some of its blood and put it	4374
	8:25	*He* t the fat, the fat tail,	4374
	8:26	he t a cake of bread, and one made with oil,	4374
	8:28	Then Moses t them from their hands	4374
	8:29	He also t the breast—	4374
	8:30	Then Moses t some of the anointing oil	4374
	9: 5	*They* t the things Moses commanded to	4374
	9:15	*He* t the goat for the people's sin offering	4374
	9:17	t a **handful** of it and burned it	4090+4848
	10: 1	and Abihu t their censers, put fire in them	4374
	24:23	and *they* t the blasphemer outside	3655
Nu	1:17	Aaron t these men whose names had been given,	4374
	7: 6	So Moses t the carts and oxen	4374
	11:25	and *he* t of the Spirit that was on him	724
	15:36	So the assembly t him outside the camp	3655
	16:18	So each man t his censer,	4374
	17: 9	and each man t his own staff.	4374
	20: 9	So Moses t the staff from	4374
	21:24	put him to the sword and t **over** his land	3769
	21:35	And *they* t **possession** of his land.	3769
	22:41	The next morning Balak t Balaam up	4374
	23:14	So *he* t him *to* the field of Zophim on	4374
	23:28	And Balak t Balaam *to* the top of Peor,	4374
	25: 7	left the assembly, t a spear in his hand	4374
	27:22	*He* t Joshua and had him stand	4374
	31: 6	t with him articles from the sanctuary	928+3338

Nu	31: 9	t all the Midianite herds, flocks and goods **as plunder.**	1024
	31:11	*They* t all the plunder and spoils,	4374
	31:27	the soldiers who t **part** in the battle	3655+4200
	31:32	the spoils that the soldiers t was 675,000	1024
Dt	1:15	So *I* t the leading men of your tribes,	4374
	2:34	At that time *we* t all his towns	4334
	3: 4	At that time *we* t all his cities.	4334
	3: 8	So at that time *we* t from these two kings	4374
	3:12	We t all the towns on the plateau,	NIH
	3:12	Of the land that *we* t **over** at that time,	3769
	3:14	t the whole region of Argob as far as	4374
	4:20	the LORD t you and brought you out of	4374
	4:47	*They* t **possession** *of* his land and the land	3769
	9:17	So *I* t the two tablets and threw them out	9530
	9:21	Also *I* t that sinful thing of yours,	4374
	29: 8	*We* t their land and gave it as	4374
	32:37	are their gods, the rock *they* t **refuge** in,	2879
Jos	3: 6	So *they* t it **up** and went ahead of them.	5951
	4: 8	*They* t twelve stones from the middle of	5951
	6:12	and the priests t **up** the ark of the LORD.	5951
	6:20	and *they* t the city.	4334
	7: 1	of the tribe of Judah, t some of them.	4374
	7:17	and *he* t the Zerahites.	4334
	7:21	I coveted them and t them.	4374
	7:23	*They* t the things from the tent,	4374
	7:24	t Achan son of Zerah, the silver, the robe,	4374
	8:23	But *they* t the king of Ai alive	9530
	10: 5	up with all their troops and t **up** positions	2837
	10: 9	Joshua t them by surprise.	448+995
	10:27	the order and *they* t them **down** from	3718
	10:28	That day Joshua t Makkedah.	4334
	10:31	he t **up** positions against it and attacked it.	2837
	10:32	and Joshua t it on the second day.	4334
	10:34	*they* t **up** positions against it	2837
	10:37	*They* t the city and put it to the sword,	4334
	10:39	*They* t the city, its king and its villages,	4334
	11:12	Joshua t all these royal cities	4334
	11:16	So Joshua t this entire land:	4374
	11:19	*who* t them all in battle.	4374
	11:23	So Joshua t the entire land,	4374
	12: 1	and whose territory *they* t **over** east of	3769
	15:17	Othniel son of Kenaz, Caleb's brother, t it;	4334
	19:47	so they went up and attacked Leshem, t it,	4334
	21:43	and *they* t **possession** of it and settled there.	3769
	24: 3	But *I* t your father Abraham from the land	4374
	24: 8	and *you* t **possession** of their land.	3769
	24:26	Then *he* t a large stone and set it up there	4374
Jdg	1: 8	of Judah attacked Jerusalem also and t it.	4334
	1:13	Caleb's younger brother, t it;	4334
	1:18	The men of Judah also t Gaza,	4334
	1:19	*They* t **possession** of the hill country,	3769
	3: 6	t their daughters **in marriage**	851+4200+4374
	3:13	and *they* t **possession** of the City of Palms.	3769
	3:25	*they* t a key and unlocked them.	4374
	5: 6	travelers t to winding paths.	2143
	6:27	So Gideon t ten of his servants and did as	4374
	7: 5	So Gideon t the men **down** to the water.	3718
	7: 8	*who* t **over** the provisions and trumpets of	4374
	7:24	and *they* t the waters of the Jordan as far	4334
	8:16	*He* t the elders of the town and taught	4374
	8:21	and killed them, and t the ornaments	4374
	9:34	and t up **concealed positions**	741
	9:43	So *he* t his men, divided them into three	4374
	9:48	He t an ax and cut off some branches,	4374
	11:13	they t **away** my land from the Arnon to	4374
	11:21	Israel t **over** all the land of the Amorites	3769
	12: 3	*I* t my life in my hands and crossed over	8492
	13:19	Then Manoah t a young goat,	4374
	15: 1	Samson t a young goat and went	928
	16: 3	up and t **hold** of the doors of the city gate,	296
	16:12	So Delilah t new ropes and tied him	4374
	16:13	Delilah t the seven braids of his head,	NIH
	16:21	gouged out his eyes and t him **down**	3718
	17: 2	I have that silver with me; *I* t it."	4374
	17: 4	and she t two hundred shekels of silver	4374
	18:17	inside and t the carved image,	4374
	18:18	into Micah's house and t the carved image,	4374
	18:20	*He* t the ephod, the other household gods	4374
	18:24	He replied, "You t the gods I made,	4374
	18:27	Then they t what Micah had made,	4374
	19: 1	of Ephraim t a concubine from Bethlehem	4374
	19: 3	*She* t him **into** her father's house,	995
	19:15	no one t them into his home for the night.	665
	19:21	So *he* t him into his house	995
	19:25	So the man t his concubine	2616
	19:29	*he* t a knife and cut up his concubine,	4374
	20: 2	of Israel t *their* places in the assembly of	3656
	20: 6	*I* t my concubine, cut her into pieces	296
	20:20	the Benjamites and t **up** battle positions	6885
	20:22	and again t **up** *their* positions	6885
	20:30	on the third day and t **up** positions	6885
	20:33	from their places and t **up** positions	6885
	21:12	and *they* t them to the camp at Shiloh	995
Ru	2:19	Blessed be the *man who t* **notice** of you!"	5795
	4: 2	Boaz t ten of the elders of the town	4374
	4: 7	one party t **off** his sandal and gave it to	8990
	4:13	So Boaz t Ruth and she became his wife.	4374
	4:16	Then Naomi t the child,	4374
1Sa	1:24	*she* t the boy with her, young as he was,	6590
	2:19	a little robe and t it to him when she went	6590
	5: 1	*they* t it from Ebenezer to Ashdod.	995
	5: 3	*They* t Dagon and put him back	4374
	6:10	*They* t two such cows and hitched them to	4374
	6:15	The Levites t **down** the ark of the LORD,	3718
	7: 1	of Kiriath Jearim came and t **up** the ark of	6590
	7: 1	*They* t it to Abinadab's house on the hill	995

1Sa	7: 9	Then Samuel t a suckling lamb	4374
	7:12	Then Samuel t a stone and set it up	4374
	9:24	the cook t **up** the leg with what was on it	8123
	10: 1	Then Samuel t a flask of oil and poured it	4374
	11: 7	*He* t a pair of oxen, cut them into pieces,	4374
	14:30	of the plunder *they* t from their enemies.	5162
	14:52	he t him **into his service.**	665
	15: 8	*He* t Agag king of the Amalekites alive,	9530
	15:21	The soldiers t sheep and cattle from	4374
	16:13	So Samuel t the horn of oil	4374
	16:20	So Jesse t a donkey loaded with bread,	4374
	17:16	and evening and t *his* **stand.**	3656
	17:39	So he t them **off.**	6073
	17:40	Then *he* t his staff in his hand,	4374
	17:51	*He* t **hold** of the Philistine's sword	4374
	17:54	David t the Philistine's head and brought it	4374
	17:57	Abner t him and brought him before Saul,	4374
	18: 4	Jonathan t **off** the robe he was wearing	7320
	19: 5	*He* t his life in his hands when he killed	8492
	19: 6	Saul listened to Jonathan and t *this* **oath:**	8678
	19:13	Michal t an idol and laid it on the bed,	4374
	20: 3	But David t an oath and said,	8678
	21:12	David t these words to heart	8492
	24: 2	So Saul t three thousand chosen men	4374
	25:18	*She* t two hundred loaves of bread,	4374
	26:12	So David t the spear and water jug	4374
	27: 9	but t sheep and cattle, donkeys and camels,	4374
	28:21	*I* t my life in my hands	8492
	28:24	*She* t some flour,	4374
	30:20	He t all the flocks and herds,	4374
	31: 4	so Saul t his own sword and fell on it.	4374
	31:12	*They* t **down** the bodies of Saul and his sons	4374
	31:13	Then *they* t their bones and buried them	4374
2Sa	1:10	And *I* t the crown that was on his head	4374
	1:11	the men with him t **hold** of their clothes	2616
	1:17	David t **up** this **lament** concerning Saul and his son Jonathan,	7801+7806
	2: 3	David also t the men who were with him,	6590
	2:25	a group and *their* **stand** on top of a hill.	6641
	2:32	*They* t Asahel and buried him	5951
	3:27	Joab t him **aside** into the gateway,	5742
	3:35	but David t an oath, saying,	8678
	3:36	All the people t **note** and were pleased;	5795
	4:12	But *they* t the head of Ish-Bosheth	4374
	5: 9	David then t **up** residence in the fortress	3782
	5:13	David t more concubines and wives	4374
	6: 6	Uzzah reached out and t **hold** of the ark	296
	6:10	he t it **aside** *to* the house of Obed-Edom	5742
	7: 8	I t you from the pasture and	4374
	7:15	as *I* t it **away** from Saul,	6073
	8: 1	and he t Metheg Ammah from the control	4374
	8: 7	David t the gold shields that belonged to	4374
	8: 8	King David t a great quantity of bronze.	4374
	12: 4	he t the ewe lamb that belonged to	4374
	12: 9	the Hittite with the sword and t his wife to	4374
	12:10	because you despised me and t the wife	4374
	12:30	*He* t the crown from the head	4374
	12:30	t a great quantity of plunder **from**	3655
	13: 8	*She* t some dough, kneaded it,	4374
	13: 9	she t the pan and served him the bread,	4374
	13:10	And Tamar t the bread she had prepared	4374
	13:11	But when *she* t it to him to eat,	5602
	15:29	t the ark of God **back** to Jerusalem	8740
	17:19	His wife t a covering and spread it out over	4374
	18: 6	the battle t **place** in the forest of Ephraim.	2118
	18:14	So *he* t three javelins in his hand	4374
	18:17	*They* t Absalom, threw him into a big pit in	4374
	19: 8	king got up and t *his* **seat** in the gateway.	3782
	20: 3	he t the ten concubines he had left	4374
	20: 5	he t **longer** than the time the king had set	336
	20: 9	Then Joab t Amasa by the beard	296
	21: 8	But the king t Armoni and Mephibosheth,	4374
	21:10	of Aiah t sackcloth and spread it out	4374
	21:12	he went and t the bones of Saul	4374
	21:20	*which* t **place** at Gath,	2118
	22:17	down from on high and t **hold** *of* me;	4374
	23:12	But Shammah t *his* **stand** in the middle of	3656
1Ki	1: 4	she t **care** of the king and	2118+6125
	1:29	The king then t an oath:	8678
	1:39	Zadok the priest t the horn of oil from	4374
	1:50	went and t **hold** of the horns of the altar.	2616
	2:28	of the LORD and t **hold** of the horns of	2616
	3:20	up in the middle of the night and t my son	4374
	7: 1	It t Solomon thirteen years, however,	NIH
	7:23	It t a line of thirty cubits to measure	NIH
	8: 3	the priests t **up** the ark,	5951
	8:48	of their enemies who t them **captive,**	8647
	11:24	where they settled and t **control.**	4887
	11:30	and Ahijah t **hold** of the new cloak	9530
	13:10	So *he* t another road and did not return by	2143
	14:26	*He* t everything, including all	4374
	15:18	then t all the silver and gold that was left	4374
	17:19	*He* t him from her arms,	4374
	18:26	*they* t the bull given them and prepared it.	4374
	18:31	Elijah t twelve stones,	4374
	19:21	*He* t his yoke of oxen	4374
	20: 9	and the answer **back** to Ben-Hadad.	8740
	20:33	The men t *this* **as a good sign**	5727
	20:34	the cities my father t from your father,"	4374
	21:13	So *they* t him outside the city	3655
2Ki	2: 8	Elijah t his cloak, rolled it up	4374
	2:12	he t **hold** of his own clothes	2616
	2:14	Then *he* t the cloak that had fallen	4374
	3:26	*he* t with him seven hundred swordsmen	4374
	3:27	Then he t his firstborn son,	4374
	4:27	*she* t **hold** of his feet.	2616
	4:37	Then *she* t her son and went out.	5951

2Ki	5: 6	that *he* t to the king of Israel read;	995
	5:24	*he* t the things from the servants	4374
	6: 7	Then the man reached out his hand and t it.	4374
	7: 8	and entered another tent and t some things	5951
	8:15	But the next day *he* t a thick cloth,	4374
	9:13	and t their cloaks and spread them	4374
	9:28	His servants t him **by chariot** to Jerusalem	8206
	10: 7	these men the princes and slaughtered	4374
	10:14	So *they* t them alive and slaughtered them	9530
	11: 2	t Joash son of Ahaziah and stole him away	4374
	11: 9	Each one t his men—	4374
	11:19	*He* t with him the commanders	4374
	11:19	king then t *his* **place** on the royal throne,	3782
	12: 9	Jehoiada the priest t a chest and bored	4374
	12:18	of Judah t all the sacred objects dedicated	4374
	13:18	"Take the arrows," and the king t them.	4374
	14:14	*He* t all the gold and silver and all	4374
	14:14	He also t hostages and returned to Samaria.	NIH
	14:21	Then all the people of Judah t Azariah,	4374
	15:29	of Assyria came and t Ijon,	4374
	15:29	He t Gilead and Galilee,	NIH
	16: 8	And Ahaz t the silver and gold found in	4374
	16:17	King Ahaz t away the side panels	7915
	16:18	*He* t away the Sabbath canopy	6015
	17: 7	*All this* t **place** because	2118
	17:24	*They* t **over** Samaria and lived in its towns.	3769
	17:27	"Have one of the priests *you* t **captive**	AIT
	18:10	At the end of three years the Assyrians t it.	4334
	21: 7	He t the carved Asherah pole he had made	NIH
	22:20	So *they* t her answer **back** *to* the king.	8740
	23: 4	and t the ashes to Bethel.	5951
	23: 6	*He* t the Asherah pole from the temple of	3655
	23:30	And the people of the land t Jehoahaz son	4374
	23:34	*he* t Jehoahaz and carried him off to Egypt,	4374
	24:12	*he* t Jehoiachin **prisoner.**	4374
	24:13	and t **away** all the gold articles	7915
	24:15	Nebuchadnezzar t Jehoiachin **captive**	1655
	24:15	*He* also t from Jerusalem to Babylon	1583+2143
	25: 7	bound him with bronze shackles and t him	995
	25:14	*They* also t **away** the pots, shovels,	4374
	25:15	of the imperial guard t **away** the censers	4374
	25:18	of the guard t **as prisoners** Seraiah	4374
	25:19	*he* t the officer in charge of the fighting men	4374
	25:19	also t the secretary who was chief officer	NIH
	25:20	Nebuzaradan the commander t them all	4374
	25:24	Gedaliah t **an oath** to reassure them	8678
1Ch	5: 6	king of Assyria t **into exile.**	1655
	5:21	t one hundred thousand people captive,	NIH
	5:26	t the Reubenites, the Gadites and the half-tribe of Manasseh **into exile.**	1655
	5:26	*He* t them to Halah, Habor,	995
	7:15	Makir t a wife from among the Huppites	3947
	9:30	the priests t **care of mixing** the spices.	5351+8379
	10: 4	so Saul t his own sword and fell on it.	4374
	10: 9	They stripped him and t his head	5951
	10:12	all their valiant men went and t the bodies	5951
	11: 7	David then t **up residence** in the fortress,	3782
	11:14	But *they* t *their* **stand** in the middle of	3656
	13:13	*he* t it aside to the house of Obed-Edom	5742
	14: 3	In Jerusalem David t more wives	4374
	17: 7	I t you from the pasture and	4374
	17:13	as *I* t it **away** from your predecessor.	6073
	18: 1	and *he* t Gath and its surrounding villages	4374
	18: 7	David t the gold shields carried by	4374
	18: 8	David t a great quantity of bronze,	4374
	20: 2	David t the crown from the head	4374
	20: 2	t a great quantity of plunder **from**	3655
	20: 6	*which* t **place** at Gath,	2118
	27:32	of Hacmoni t **care of** the king's sons.	6640
2Ch	2:17	Solomon t **a census** *of* all the aliens	6218
	4: 2	It t a line of thirty cubits to measure	NIH
	5: 4	the Levites t **up** the ark,	5951
	7: 6	The priests t their positions,	6641
	11:23	and t many wives for them.	8626
	12: 9	*He* t everything, including	4374
	13:19	Abijah pursued Jeroboam and t from him	4334
	14:10	and *they* t **up** battle **positions** in the Valley	6885
	15: 8	of Oded the prophet, *he* t **courage.**	2616
	15:14	*They* t **an oath** to the LORD.	8678
	16: 2	Asa then t the silver and gold **out**	3655
	20:25	so much plunder that it t three days	NIH
	22:11	t Joash son of Ahaziah and stole him away	4374
	23: 8	Each one t his men—	4374
	23:20	*He* t with him the commanders	4374
	25:12	t them to the top of a cliff and threw them	995
	25:24	He t all the gold and silver and all	NIH
	26: 1	Then all the people of Judah t Uzziah,	4374
	28: 5	t many of his people **as prisoners**	8647+8664
	28: 8	The Israelites t **captive**	8647
	28: 8	*They* also t a great deal of plunder,	1024
	28:15	The men designated by name t the prisoners	2616
	28:15	So *they* t **back** to their fellow	995
	28:21	Ahaz t **some of the things** from the temple	2745
	28:24	from the temple of God and t them **away.**	7915
	29:16	The Levites t it and carried it out to	7691
	29:22	and the priests t the blood and sprinkled it	7691
	30:16	Then *they* t up their regular positions	6584+6641
	32:22	*He* t **care of** them on every side.	5633
	33: 7	He t the carved image he had made	NIH
	33:11	who t Manasseh **prisoner.**	4334
	33:11	bound him with bronze shackles and t him	2143
	34:16	Then Shaphan t the book to the king	995
	34:28	So *they* t her answer **back** *to* the king.	8740
	35:24	So they t him out of his chariot,	6296
	36: 1	And the people of the land t Jehoahaz son	4374
	36: 4	But Neco t Eliakim's brother Jehoahaz	4374
	36: 7	Nebuchadnezzar also t to Babylon articles	995

Ezr	3:10	t their **places** to praise the LORD,	6641
	6: 5	which Nebuchadnezzar t from the temple	10485
	7:28	I t **courage** and gathered leading men	2616
	10: 5	And *they* t **the oath.**	8678
Ne	2: 1	*I* t the wine and gave it to the king.	5951
	4:23	nor the guards with me t **off** our clothes;	7320
	5:15	on the people and t forty shekels of silver	4374
	9:22	*They* t **over** the country of Sihon king	3769
	9:24	Their sons went in and t **possession** *of*	3769
	9:25	*they* t **possession** of houses filled	3769
	12:40	then t *their* **places** in the house of God;	6641
Est	3:10	So the king t his signet ring from his finger	6073
	8: 2	The king t **off** his signet ring,	6073
	9:27	the Jews t it upon themselves to establish	7691
Job	2: 8	Then Job t a piece of broken pottery	4374
	29: 7	the city and t my seat in the public square,	3922
	29:16	*I* t **up** the case of the stranger.	2983
Ps	18:16	He reached down from on high and t **hold**	4374
	78:70	He chose David his servant and t him from	4374
	80: 9	and *it* t **root** and filled the land.	9245+9247
	104: 7	the sound of your thunder *they* t to **flight;**	2905
	106:44	But he t **note** of their distress	8011
Pr	7:13	*She* t hold of him and kissed him and with	2616
	7:20	*He* t his purse filled with money and will	4374
Ecc	2:10	My heart *t* **delight** in all my work,	AIT
	8: 2	I say, because you t an oath before God.	NIH
SS	5: 7	*they* t away my cloak,	5951
Isa	33:18	Where is the *one who* t **the revenue?**	9202
	41: 9	*I* t you from the ends of the earth,	2616
	43:14	in the ships in which they t pride.	NIH
	44:14	or perhaps t a cypress or oak.	4374
	53: 4	Surely he t **up** our infirmities	5951
Jer	13: 7	to Perath and dug up the belt and t it from	4374
	25:17	So *I* t the cup from the LORD's hand	4374
	26:10	and t *their* **places** at the entrance of	3782
	26:23	They brought Uriah out of Egypt and t him	995
	28: 3	of Babylon removed from here and t	995
	28:10	Then the prophet Hananiah t the yoke off	4374
	31:32	with their forefathers when *I* t them by	2616
	32:11	*I* t the deed of purchase—	4374
	32:23	They came in and t **possession** of it,	3769
	34:11	and t **back** the slaves they had freed	8740
	36:32	So Jeremiah t another scroll and gave it to	4374
	38: 6	So *they* t Jeremiah and put him into	4374
	38:11	So Ebed-Melech t the men with him	4374
	38:11	*He* t some old rags and worn-out clothes	4374
	39: 3	of the king of Babylon came and t **seats** in	3782
	39: 5	and t him to Nebuchadnezzar king	6590
	40: 9	t **an oath** to reassure them and their men.	8678
	41:10	Ishmael son of Nethaniah t them **captive**	8647
	41:12	*they* t all their men and went	4374
	52:11	bound him with bronze shackles and t him	995
	52:18	*They* also t **away** the pots, shovels,	4374
	52:19	of the imperial guard t **away** the basins,	4374
	52:24	of the guard t **as prisoners** Seraiah	4374
	52:25	*he* t the officer in charge of the fighting men	4374
	52:25	also t the secretary who was chief officer	NIH
	52:26	Nebuzaradan the commander t them all	4374
La	3:58	O Lord, *you* t **up** my case;	8189
Eze	3:14	The Spirit then lifted me up and t me **away,**	4374
	3:21	he will surely live because *he* t **warning,**	2302
	8: 3	a hand and t me by the hair of my head.	4374
	8: 3	and in visions of God *he* t me to Jerusalem,	995
	10: 7	*He* t **up** some of it and put it into the hands	5951
	10: 7	*who* t it and went out.	4374
	12: 7	*I* t my belongings **out** at dusk,	3655
	16:16	*You* t some of your garments	4374
	16:17	*You* also t the fine jewelry I gave you,	4374
	16:18	And *you* t your embroidered clothes to put	4374
	16:20	" 'And *you* t your sons and daughters	4374
	17: 5	" '*He* t some of the seed of your land	4374
	17:13	Then *he* t a member of the royal family	4374
	18: 7	but returns **what** he t **in pledge**	2481
	18:12	He does not return **what** he t **in pledge.**	2478
	19: 5	*she* t another of her cubs and made him	4374
	23:10	t **away** her sons and daughters	4374
	25:12	Because Edom t **revenge** on the house	5933+5934
	25:15	t **revenge** with malice in their hearts,	5933+5934
	27: 5	*they* t a cedar from Lebanon to make	4374
	33:15	gives back **what** he t **in pledge for a loan,**	2478
	40: 1	the LORD was upon me and *he* t me there.	995
	40: 2	In visions of God *he* t me to the land	995
	40: 3	*He* t me there, and I saw a man	995
	42: 5	the galleries t more **space** from them than	430
Da	1:16	So the guard t **away** their choice food and	5951
	2:25	Arioch t Daniel to the king at once	10549
	3:22	of the fire killed the soldiers who t **up**	10513
	5:31	and Darius the Mede t **over** the kingdom,	10618
	7: 9	and the Ancient of Days t *his* **seat.**	10338
	8:11	*it* t **away** the daily sacrifice from him,	8123
	11: 1	I t my **stand** to support and protect him.)	6641
Hos	13:11	and in my wrath *I* t him **away.**	4374
Joel	3: 5	For *you* t my silver and my gold	4374
Am	1: 6	because *they* t **captive** whole communities	1655
	7:14	and I also t **care of** sycamore-fig trees.	1179
	7:15	the LORD t me from tending the flock	4374
Jnh	1: 5	they t Jonah and threw him overboard,	5951
	3: 6	rose from his throne, t **off** his royal robes,	6296
Zec	11: 7	Then *I* t two staffs and called one Favor	4374
	11:10	*I* t my staff called Favor and broke it,	4374
	11:13	So *I* t the thirty pieces of silver	4374
Mt	1:22	All this t **place** to fulfill what the Lord	1181
	1:24	and t Mary home as his wife.	4161
	2:14	t the child and his mother during the night	4161
	2:21	t the child and his mother and went to	4161
	4: 5	Then the devil t him to the holy city	4161
	4: 8	the devil t him to a very high mountain	4161

Mt	8:17	"He t **up** our infirmities	3284
	9:25	he went in and t the girl by the hand,	3195
	13:31	which a man t and planted in his field.	3284
	13:33	a woman t and mixed into a large amount	3284
	13:57	And *they* t **offense** at him.	4997
	14:12	John's disciples came and t his body	149
	15:36	Then *he* t the seven loaves and the fish,	3284
	16:22	Peter t him **aside** and began to rebuke him.	4689
	17: 1	After six days Jesus t **with** him Peter,	4161
	18:27	The servant's master t **pity** on him,	5072
	20:17	*he* t the twelve disciples aside and said	4161
	21: 4	This t **place** to fulfill what was spoken	1181
	21:39	So they t him and threw him out of	3284
	24:39	until the flood came and t them all **away.**	149
	25: 1	be like ten virgins who t their lamps	3284
	25: 3	The foolish ones t their lamps but did	3284
	25: 4	t oil in jars along with their lamps.	3284
	26:26	While they were eating, Jesus t bread,	3284
	26:27	Then he t the cup, gave thanks and	3284
	26:37	t Peter and the two sons of Zebedee **along**	4161
	26:57	Those who had arrested Jesus t him	552
	27: 9	"They t the thirty silver coins,	3284
	27:24	he t water and washed his hands in front of	3284
	27:27	Then the governor's soldiers t Jesus into	4161
	27:30	and t the staff and struck him on	3284
	27:31	*they* t **off** the robe and put his own clothes	1694
	27:59	Joseph t the body, wrapped it in a clean	3284
	28:15	So the soldiers t the money and did	3284
Mk	1:31	t her hand and helped her up.	3195
	2:12	t his mat and walked out in full view	149
	4:36	*they* t him **along,** just as he was,	4161
	5:40	*he* t the child's father and mother and	4161
	5:41	He t her by the hand and said to her,	3195
	6: 3	And *they* t **offense** at him.	4997
	6:29	John's disciples came and t his body	149
	7:33	he t him aside, **away from** the crowd,	655
	8:23	He t the blind man by the hand	2138
	8:32	Peter t him **aside** and began to rebuke him.	4689
	9: 2	Jesus t Peter, James and John **with** him	4161
	9:27	But Jesus t him by the hand and lifted him	3195
	9:36	He t a little child and had him stand	3284
	10:16	And he t the children in his **arms,**	1878
	10:32	Again he t the Twelve **aside**	4161
	12: 8	So they t him and killed him,	3284
	14:22	While they were eating, Jesus t bread,	3284
	14:23	Then he t the cup, gave thanks and	3284
	14:33	He t Peter, James and John along with him,	4161
	14:53	*They* t Jesus to the high priest,	552
	14:65	And the guards t him and beat him.	3284
	15:20	*they* t **off** the purple robe	1694
	15:46	t **down** the body, wrapped it in the linen,	2747
Lk	2: 2	that t place while Quirinius was governor	NIG
	2:22	Joseph and Mary t him to Jerusalem	343
	2:28	Simeon t him in his arms and praised God,	1312
	4:29	and t him to the brow of the hill on which	72
	5:25	t what he had been lying on and went home	149
	8:54	But he t her by the hand and said,	3195
	9:10	Then *he* t them with him	4161
	9:28	after Jesus said this, *he* t Peter, John	4161
	9:47	t a little child and had him stand	2138
	10:33	and when he saw him, *he* t **pity** on him.	5072
	10:34	t him to an inn and took care of him.	72
	10:34	took him to an inn and t **care of** him.	2150
	10:35	The next day he t **out** two silver coins	1675
	13: 7	the man who t **care of the vineyard,**	307
	13:19	which a man t and planted in his garden.	3284
	13:21	a woman t and mixed into a large amount	3284
	18:31	Jesus t the Twelve **aside** and told them,	4161
	22:19	And he t bread, gave thanks and broke it,	3284
	22:20	after the supper he t the cup, saying,	NIG
	22:54	and t him **into** the house of the high priest.	1652
	23:48	to witness this sight saw what t **place,**	1181
	23:53	Then he t it **down,** wrapped it in a linen	2747
	24: 1	the *women* t the spices they had prepared	5770
	24:21	it is the third day since all this t **place.**	1181
	24:30	he t bread, gave thanks,	3284
	24:43	and he t it and ate it in their presence.	3284
Jn	2: 1	the third day a wedding t **place** at Cana	1181
	4:50	The man t Jesus at his **word**	3364+4409
	5: 9	on which this t place was a Sabbath,	NIG
	6:11	Jesus then t the loaves, gave thanks,	3284
	11:41	So *they* t **away** the stone.	149
	12: 3	Then Mary t about a pint of pure nard,	3284
	12:13	t palm branches and went out	3284
	13: 4	t **off** his outer clothing,	5502
	13:27	As soon as Judas t the bread,	NIG
	19: 1	Then Pilate t Jesus and had him flogged.	3284
	19:16	So the soldiers t **charge** of Jesus.	4161
	19:23	*they* t his clothes, dividing them into four	3284
	19:27	this disciple t her into his home.	3284
	19:38	he came and t the body **away.**	149
	21:13	t the bread and gave it to them,	3284
Ac	4:13	and *they* t **note** that these men had been	2105
	7:21	Pharaoh's daughter t him and brought him	359
	7:45	with them when they t the land from	2959
	8:39	Spirit of the Lord **suddenly** t Philip **away,**	773
	9:25	But his followers t him by night	3284
	9:27	But Barnabas t him and brought him to	2138
	9:30	*they* t him **down** to Caesarea	2864
	9:41	t her by the hand and helped her	1443
	13:20	All this t about 450 years.	NIG
	13:29	they t him **down** from the tree and laid him	2747
	15:39	Barnabas t Mark and sailed for Cyprus,	4161
	16:33	the jailer t them and washed their wounds;	4161
	17:19	Then they t him and brought him to	2138
	19: 1	Paul t **the road through** the interior	1451
	19: 9	*He* t the disciples with him	928

Ac	20:12	The *people* t the young man home alive	72
	20:14	we t him **aboard** and went on to Mitylene.	377
	21:11	Coming over to us, *he* t Paul's belt,	149
	21:26	The next day Paul t the men	4161
	21:32	at once t some officers and soldiers and ran	4161
	23:18	So he t him to the commander.	72+4161
	23:19	The commander t the young man by	2138
	23:31	Paul t him during the night	377
	27:18	t such a violent **battering from the storm**	5928
	27:28	They t **soundings** and found that	1075
	27:28	A short time later they t **soundings** again	1075
	27:35	he t some bread and gave thanks to God	3284
1Co	11:23	on the night he was betrayed, t bread,	3284
	11:25	In the same way, after supper he t the cup,	NIG
Gal	2: 1	I t Titus **along** also.	5221
Php	3:12	that for which Christ Jesus t **hold of** me.	2898
Col	2:14	he t it **away**, nailing it to the cross.	149
Heb	9: 8	when I t them by the hand to lead them out	2138
	9:19	he t the blood of calves,	3284
Rev	5: 7	and t the scroll from the right hand	3284
	8: 5	Then the angel t the censer,	3284
	10:10	I t the little scroll from the angel's hand	3284

TOOL (9) [TOOLS]

Ex	20:25	for you will defile it if you use a t on it.	2995
	32: 4	the shape of a calf, fashioning it with a t.	3032
Dt	27: 5	Do not use any **iron** t upon them.	1366
Jos	8:31	on which no **iron** t had been used.	1366
2Sa	23: 7	Whoever touches thorns uses a t **of iron** or	1366
1Ki	6: 7	chisel or any other iron t was heard at	3998
Job	19:24	they were inscribed with an iron t on lead,	6485
Isa	44:12	The blacksmith takes a t and works with it	5108
Jer	17: 1	"Judah's sin is engraved with an iron t,	6485

TOOLS (1) [TOOL]

Ge	4:22	who forged all kinds of t out of bronze	3086

TOOTH (11) [TEETH]

Ex	21:24	t for tooth, hand for hand, foot for foot,	9094
	21:24	tooth for t, hand for hand, foot for foot,	9094
	21:27	And if he knocks out the t of a manservant	9094
	21:27	the servant go free to compensate for the t.	9094
Lev	24:20	eye for eye, t for tooth.	9094
	24:20	eye for eye, tooth for t.	9094
Dt	19:21	life for life, eye for eye, t for tooth,	9094
	19:21	life for life, eye for eye, tooth for t,	9094
Pr	25:19	Like a bad t or a lame foot is reliance on	9094
Mt	5:38	'Eye for eye, and t for tooth.'	3848
	5:38	'Eye for eye, and tooth for t.'	3848

TOP (91) [TOPMOST, TOPS]

Ge	6:16	ark to within 18 inches of the t.	2025+4200+5087
	22: 9	on the altar, on t of the wood.	5087
	28:12	with its t reaching to heaven,	8031
	28:18	and set it up as a pillar and poured oil on t	8031
	40:17	the t basket were all kinds of baked goods	6609
	47:31	and Israel worshiped as he leaned on the t	8031
Ex	12:22	and put some of the blood on the t and on	5485
	12:23	he will see the blood on the t and sides of	5485
	17: 9	Tomorrow I will stand on t of the hill with	8031
	17:10	Aaron and Hur went to the t of the hill.	8031
	19:20	the t of Mount Sinai and called Moses to	8031
	19:20	and called Moses to the t of the mountain.	8031
	24:17	like a consuming fire on t of the mountain.	8031
	25:21	the cover on t of the ark	2025+4200+4946+5087
	26:24	the bottom all the way to the t, and fitted	8031
	30: 3	the t and all the sides and the horns	1511
	34: 2	Present yourself to me there on t of	8031
	36:29	the bottom all the way to the t and fitted	8031
	37:26	They overlaid the t and all the sides and	1511
Lev	3: 5	the altar on t of the burnt offering that is	6584
	4:35	the priest shall burn it on the altar **on** t of	6584
	5:12	on the altar **on** t of the offerings made to	6584
	8:28	on the altar **on** t of the burnt offering as	6584
	9:14	and burned them **on** t of the burnt offering	6584
	14:17	**on** t of the blood of the guilt offering.	6584
Nu	20:28	Aaron died there on t of the mountain.	8031
	21:20	in Moab where the t of Pisgah overlooks	8031
	23:14	to the field of Zophim on the t of Pisgah,	8031
	23:28	And Balak took Balaam to the t of Peor,	8031
Dt	3:27	to the t of Pisgah and look west and north	2025+5087
	28:13	you will always be at the t,	8031
	28:35	the soles of your feet to the t of your **head**.	7721
	34: 1	from the plains of Moab to the t of Pisgah,	8031
Jos	15: 8	the t of the hill west of the Hinnom Valley	8031
Jdg	6:26	of altar to the LORD your God on the t	8031
	9: 7	up on the t of Mount Gerizim and shouted	8031
	16: 3	to his shoulders and carried them to the t	8031
1Sa	26:13	over to the other side and stood on t of	8031
	28:12	she cried out at the t of her voice and said	1524
2Sa	2:25	a group and took their stand on t of a hill.	8031
	14:25	From the t of his **head** to the sole	7721
1Ki	7:17	the capitals on t of the pillars,	8031
	7:18	to decorate the capitals on t of the pillars.	8031
	7:19	on t of the pillars in the portico were in	8031
	7:22	The capitals on t were in the shape	8031
	7:25	Sea rested on t of them,	2025+4200+4946+5087
	7:35	At the t of the stand there was	8031
	7:35	panels were attached to the t of the stand.	8031
	7:41	the two bowl-shaped capitals on t of	8031
	7:41	the two bowl-shaped capitals on t of	8031
	7:42	decorating the bowl-shaped capitals on t	7156
	10:19	and its back had a rounded t.	8031
	18:42	but Elijah climbed to the t of Carmel.	8031

2Ki	1: 9	who was sitting on the t of a hill,	8031
	25:17	The bronze capital **on** t of one pillar	6584
2Ch	3:15	with a capital on t measuring five cubits.	8031
	3:16	and put them on t of the pillars.	8031
	4: 4	Sea rested on t of them,	2025+4200+4946+5087
	4:12	the two bowl-shaped capitals on t of	8031
	4:12	the two bowl-shaped capitals on t of	8031
	4:13	decorating the bowl-shaped capitals on t	7156
	25:12	to the t of a cliff and threw them down so	8031
Ne	12:31	the leaders of Judah go up on t of the wall.	6584
	12:31	to proceed on t of the wall to the right,	6584
	12:38	I followed them on t of the wall,	6584
Job	2: 7	the soles of his feet to the t of his **head**.	7721
Pr	23:34	lying on t of the rigging.	8031
SS	4: 8	from the t of Senir, the summit of Hermon,	8031
Isa	1: 6	the t of your **head** there is no soundness—	AIT
Jer	52:22	The bronze capital **on** t of one pillar	6584
Eze	17: 3	Taking hold of the t of a cedar,	7550
	17:22	I myself will take a shoot from the **very** t	8123
	31: 3	its t above the thick foliage,	7550
	31:10	lifting its t above the thick foliage,	7550
	40:13	the gateway from the t **of the** *rear* **wall**	1511
	40:13	of one alcove to the t of the opposite one;	1511
	41: 7	to the t *floor* through the middle floor.	6609
	43:12	on t of the mountain will be most holy.	8031
Da	4:11	and strong and its t touched the sky;	10660
	4:20	with its t touching the sky,"	10660
Am	1: 2	and the t of Carmel withers."	8031
	9: 3	Though they hide themselves on the t	8031
Zec	4: 2	a solid gold lampstand with a bowl at the t	8031
Mt	27:51	curtain of the temple was torn in two from t	540
Mk	5: 7	He shouted **at the** t of his voice,	3489
	15:38	curtain of the temple was torn in two from t	540
Lk	4:33	cried out **at the** t of his **voice**,	3489+5889
	8:28	**shouting at the** t of *his* **voice**,	3306+3489+5889
Jn	19:23	woven in one piece from t to bottom.	540
Ac	7:57	yelling **at the** t of their **voices**,	3489+5889
Heb	11:21	worshiped as he leaned on the t of his staff.	216

TOPAZ (5)

Ex	28:17	a ruby, a t and a beryl;	7077
	39:10	a ruby, a t and a beryl;	7077
Job	28:19	The t of Cush cannot compare with it;	7077
Eze	28:13	ruby, t and emerald, chrysolite,	7077
Rev	21:20	the ninth t, the tenth chrysoprase,	5535

TOPHEL (1)

Dt	1: 1	opposite Suph, between Paran and T,	9523

TOPHETH (10)

2Ki	23:10	He desecrated T, which was in the Valley	9532
Isa	30:33	T has long been prepared;	9533
Jer	7:31	They have built the high places of T in	9532
	7:32	when people will no longer call it T or	9532
	7:32	the dead in T until there is no more room.	9532
	19: 6	people will no longer call this place T	9532
	19:11	the dead in T until there is no more room.	9532
	19:12	will make this city like T.	9532
	19:13	of Judah will be defiled like this place, T—	9532
	19:14	Jeremiah then returned from T,	9532

TOPMOST (3) [TOP, MOST]

Isa	17: 6	or three olives on the t branches,	8031
Eze	17: 4	he broke off its t shoot and carried it away	8031
	17:22	a tender sprig from its t shoots and plant it	8031

TOPPLE (3)

Ps	62: 4	to t him from his lofty place;	5615
Isa	40:20	to set up an idol *that will* not t.	4572
	41: 7	He nails down the idol so *it will* not t.	4572

TOPS (14) [TOP]

Ge	8: 5	on the first day of the tenth month the t *of*	8031
Ex	12: 7	of the blood and put it on the sides and t of	5485
	36:38	the t of the posts and their bands with gold	8031
	38:17	and their t were overlaid with silver;	8031
	38:19	and their t were overlaid with silver.	8031
	38:28	to overlay the t of the posts,	8031
Jdg	9:36	people are coming down from the t of	8031
2Sa	5:24	as you hear the sound of marching in the t	8031
1Ki	7:16	of cast bronze to set on the t of the pillars;	8031
1Ch	14:15	as you hear the sound of marching in the t	8031
Ps	72:16	on the t of the hills may it sway.	8031
Isa	14:14	I will ascend above the t of the clouds;	1195
Eze	31:14	lifting their t above the thick foliage.	7550
Am	9: 1	"Strike the t **of the pillars** so that	4117

TORCH (5) [TORCHES]

Ge	15:17	a blazing t appeared and passed between	4365
Jdg	15: 4	He then fastened a t to every pair of tails,	4365
Isa	62: 1	her salvation like a blazing t.	4365
Zec	12: 6	like a flaming t among sheaves,	4365
Rev	8:10	and a great star, blazing like a t,	3286

TORCHES (9) [TORCH]

Jdg	7:16	in the hands of all of them, with t inside.	4365
	7:20	in their left hands and holding	4365
	15: 5	lit the t and let the foxes loose in	4365
Isa	50:11	and provide yourselves with **flaming** t,	2338
	50:11	and of the t you have set ablaze.	2338
Eze	1:13	like burning coals of fire or like t.	4365
Da	10: 6	his eyes like flaming t,	4365

Na	2: 4	They look like **flaming** t;	4365
Jn	18: 3	They were carrying t, lanterns and weapons.	5749

TORE (44) [TEAR]

Ge	37:29	that Joseph was not there, *he* t his clothes.	7973
	37:34	Then Jacob t his clothes,	7973
	44:13	At this, *they* t their clothes.	7973
Nu	14: 6	explored the land, t their clothes	7973
Jos	7: 6	Then Joshua t his clothes	7973
Jdg	11:35	he t his clothes and cried, "Oh!	7973
	14: 6	that *he* t the lion **apart** with his bare hands	9117
	16: 3	and t them **loose**, bar and all.	5825
1Sa	15:27	caught hold of the hem of his robe, and *it* t.	7973
2Sa	1:11	took hold of their clothes and t them.	7973
	13:19	Tamar put ashes on her head and t	7973
	13:31	t his clothes and lay down on the ground;	7973
1Ki	11:30	of the new cloak he was wearing and t it	7973
	14: 8	t the kingdom **away** from the house	7973
	19:11	powerful wind t the mountains **apart**	7293
	21:27	*he* t his clothes, put on sackcloth and	7973
2Ki	2:12	took hold of his own clothes and t them **apart**.	4200+7973+7974+9109
	5: 7	*he* t his robes and said, "Am I God?	7973
	6:30	heard the woman's words, *he* t his robes.	7973
	10:27	of Baal and t down the temple of Baal,	5997
	11:14	Then Athaliah t her robes and called out,	7973
	11:18	to the temple of Baal and t it **down**.	5997
	17:21	*he* t Israel **away** from the house of David,	7973
	19: 1	*he* t his clothes and put on sackcloth	7973
	22:11	of the Book of the Law, *he* t his robes.	7973
	22:19	*you* t your robes and wept in my presence,	7973
	23: 7	*He* also t **down** the quarters of	5997
2Ch	23:13	Then Athaliah t her robes and shouted,	7973
	23:17	to the temple of Baal and t it **down**.	5997
	34: 7	he t **down** the altars and the Asherah poles	5997
	34:19	the words of the Law, *he* t his robes.	7973
	34:27	and t your robes and wept in my presence,	7973
Ezr	9: 3	When I heard this, *I* t my tunic and cloak,	7973
Est	4: 1	*he* t his clothes, put on sackcloth and ashes,	7973
Job	1:20	up and t his robe and shaved his head.	7973
	2:12	and *they* t their robes and sprinkled dust	7973
Isa	22:10	and t **down** houses to strengthen the wall.	5997
	37: 1	*he* t his clothes and put on sackcloth	7973
Jer	2:20	and t **off** your bonds;	5998
Eze	29: 7	and *you* t **open** their shoulders;	1324
Mt	26:65	Then the high priest t his clothes and said,	1396
Mk	5: 4	but he t the chains **apart** and broke	1400
	14:63	The high priest t his clothes.	1396
Ac	14:14	they t their clothes and rushed out into	1396

TORMENT (13) [TORMENTED, TORMENTING, TORMENTORS]

Job	13:25	*Will you* t a windblown leaf?	6907
	15:20	All his days the wicked man **suffers** t,	2655
	19: 2	"How long *will you* t me and crush me	3324
Isa	50:11	You will lie down in t.	5107
La	1:20	I *am* in t within,	2813
	2:11	I *am* in t within,	2813
Lk	16:23	In hell, where he was in t,	992
	16:28	they will not also come to this place *of* t.'	992
2Co	12: 7	a messenger of Satan, to t me.	3139
Rev	9: 5	in their tails they had power *to* t people	92
	14:11	the smoke of their t rises for ever and ever.	990
	18:10	Terrified *at* her t, they will stand far off	990
	18:15	will stand far off, terrified *at* her t.	990

TORMENTED (7) [TORMENT]

1Sa	16:14	and an evil spirit from the LORD t him.	1286
Pr	28:17	A man t by the guilt of murder will be	6943
Ac	5:16	bringing their sick and *those* t	4061
2Pe	2: 8	*was* t in his righteous soul by	989
Rev	11:10	these two prophets *had* t those who live	989
	14:10	*be* t with burning sulfur in the presence of	989
	20:10	*They will be* t day and night for ever	989

TORMENTING (1) [TORMENT]

1Sa	16:15	"See, an evil spirit from God *is* t you.	1286

TORMENTORS (2) [TORMENT]

Ps	137: 3	our t demanded songs of joy;	9354
Isa	51:23	I will put it into the hands of your t,	3324

TORN (56) [TEAR]

Ge	31:39	did not bring you **animals** t by wild beasts;	3274
	37:33	Joseph *has* **surely** been t to pieces."	3271+3271
	44:28	*"He has* surely been t to pieces."	3271+3271
Ex	22:13	was t to pieces by a wild animal,	3271+3271
	22:13	not be required to pay for the t animal.	NIH
	22:31	the meat of an **animal** t by wild **beasts**;	3274
Lev	7:24	or t **by wild animals** may be used	3274
	13:45	an infectious disease must wear t clothes,	7268
	14:40	that the contaminated stones *be* t **out**	2740
	14:43	the house after the stones *have been* t **out**	2740
	14:45	It *must be* t **down**—	5997
	17:15	t **by wild animals** must wash his clothes,	3274
	22: 8	anything found dead or t **by wild animals**,	3274
	22:24	are bruised, crushed, t or cut.	5998
Jdg	14: 6	with his bare hands *as he might have* t	9117
1Sa	4:12	his clothes t and dust on his head.	7973
	15:28	"The LORD *has* t the kingdom of Israel	7973
	28:17	The LORD *has* t the kingdom out	7973
2Sa	1: 2	with his clothes t and with dust on his head.	7973
	13:31	his servants stood by with their clothes t.	7973

2Sa	15:32	his robe t and dust on his head.	7973
2Ki	5: 8	that the king of Israel had t his robes,	7973
	5: 8	"Why have you t your robes?	7973
	18:37	went to Hezekiah, with their clothes t,	7973
2Ch	34: 4	the altars of the Baals were t down;	5997
Ezr	9: 5	with my tunic and cloak t,	7973
Job	8:18	But when it is t from its spot,	1180
	18:14	He is t from the security of his tent	5998
Ps	60: 2	You have shaken the land and t it open;	7204
	124: 6	who has not let us be t by their teeth.	3272
Pr	2:22	and the unfaithful will be t from it.	5815
Isa	36:22	went to Hezekiah, with their clothes t,	7973
Jer	13:22	that your skirts have been t off	1655
	13:22	uprooted, t down and destroyed,	5997
	18: 7	t down and destroyed,	5997
	33: 4	of Judah that have been t down to be used	5997
	41: 5	t their clothes and cut themselves came	7973
	50:15	her towers fall, her walls are t down.	2238
La	2: 5	broken off the yoke and t off the bonds.	5998
Eze	4:14	anything found dead or t by wild animals.	3274
	30: 4	and her foundations t down.	2238
	44:31	found dead or t by wild animals.	3274
Da	7: 4	until its wings were t off and it was lifted	10440
Hos	6: 1	He has t us to pieces but he will heal us;	3271
Mt	27:51	the temple was t in two from top to bottom.	5387
Mk	1:10	he saw heaven t open and	5387
	15:38	the temple was t in two from top to bottom.	5387
Lk	5:36	If he does, he will have t the new garment,	5387
	23:45	And the curtain of the temple was t in two.	5387
Jn	21:11	but even with so many the net was not t.	5387
Ac	21: 1	After we had t ourselves away from them,	685
	23:10	afraid Paul would be t to pieces by them.	1400
Ro	11: 3	they have killed your prophets and t down	2940
Gal	4:15	you would have t out your eyes	2021
Php	1:23	I am t between the two:	5309
1Th	2:17	when we were t away from you for a short	682

TORRENT (6) [TORRENTS]

Ps	124: 4	the t would have swept over us,	5707
Isa	30:28	His breath is like a rushing t,	5707
Jer	47: 2	they will become an overflowing t.	5707
Lk	6:48	t struck that house but could not shake it,	4532
	6:49	The moment the t struck that house,	4532
Rev	12:15	and sweep her away with the t.	4472+4533

TORRENTS (8) [TORRENT]

2Sa	22: 5	the t of destruction overwhelmed me.	5707
Job	14:19	and t wash away the soil,	6207
	38:25	Who cuts a channel for the t of rain,	8852
Ps	18: 4	the t of destruction overwhelmed me.	5707
Eze	13:11	Rain will come in t,	8851
	13:13	t of rain will fall with destructive fury.	8851
	38:22	I will pour down t of rain,	8851
Hab	3:10	T of water swept by;	2443

TORTOISE (KJV) See GREAT LIZARD

TORTURE (5) [TORTURED]

Mt	8:29	"Have you come here to t us before	989
Mk	5: 7	Swear to God that you won't t me!"	989
Lk	8:28	I beg you, don't t me!"	989
Rev	9: 5	but only to t them for five months.	989
	18: 7	Give her as much t and grief as the glory	990

TORTURED (2) [TORTURE]

Mt	18:34	turned him over to the jailers to be t,	991
Heb	11:35	Others were t and refused to be released,	5594

TOSS (7) [TOSSED, TOSSES, TOSSING]

Ex	9: 8	and have Moses t it into the air in	2450
Job	7: 4	The night drags on, and I t till dawn.	5611+8425
	30:22	you t me about in the storm.	4570
Ps	60: 8	upon Edom I t my sandal;	8959
	108: 9	upon Edom I t my sandal;	8959
Mt	15:26	the children's bread and t it to their dogs.	965
Mk	7:27	the children's bread and t it to their dogs."	965

TOSSED (3) [TOSS]

Ex	9:10	Moses t it into the air,	2450
Eph	4:14	be infants, t back and forth by the waves,	3115
Jas	1: 6	a wave of the sea, blown and t by the wind.	4847

TOSSES (2) [TOSS]

2Ki	19:21	The Daughter of Jerusalem t her head	5675
Isa	37:22	The Daughter of Jerusalem t her head	5675

TOSSING (2) [TOSS]

Isa	57:20	But the wicked are like the t sea,	1764
Lk	21:25	and perplexity at the roaring and t of	4893

TOTAL (24) [TOTALED, TOTALLY]

Ex	10:22	and t darkness covered all Egypt for three days.	696+3125
	38:24	The t amount of the gold from the wave	3972
	38:26	twenty years old or more, a t of 603,550	4200
Nu	1:46	The t number was 603,550.	3972
	3:39	The t number of Levites counted at	3972
	3:43	The t number of firstborn males a month old	3972
	4:37	This was the t of all those in the Kohathite	7212
	4:41	This was the t of those in the	3972+7212

Nu	4:45	the t of those in the Merarite clans.	7212
	7:87	The t number of animals for the burnt	3972
	7:88	The t number of animals for the sacrifice	3972
	26:51	The t number of the men of Israel	465S
Jos	14:20	a t of twenty-nine towns and their villages.	3972
1Sa	14:20	found the Philistines in t confusion,	1524+4394
2Ki	24:14	and artisans—a t of ten thousand.	NIH
1Ch	23: 3	were counted, and the t number of men	1653
2Ch	3:11	The t wingspan of the cherubim	802+4053
	26:12	The t number of family leaders over	3972
	35: 7	a t of thirty thousand sheep and	3972+4200+5031
Ne	7:72	The t given by the rest of the people	889S
Job	20:26	t darkness lies in wait for his treasures.	3972
Jer	52:23	the t number of pomegranates above	3972
Eze	48:13	Its t length will be 25,000 cubits	3972
Ac	19:19	the t came to fifty thousand drachmas.	NIG

TOTALED (2) [TOTAL]

Ne	11: 6	who lived in Jerusalem t 468 able men.	3972
	11:18	The Levites in the holy city t 284.	3972

TOTALLY (25) [TOTAL]

Nu	16:30	if the LORD brings about something t new,	1375
	21: 2	we will t destroy their cities."	3049
Dt	7: 2	then you must destroy them t.	3049+3049
Jos	10: 1	that Joshua had taken Ai and t destroyed it,	3049
	10:28	to the sword and t destroyed everyone in it.	3049
	10:35	to the sword and t destroyed everyone in it,	3049
	10:37	they t destroyed it and everyone in it.	3049
	10:39	Everyone in it they t destroyed.	3049
	10:40	He t destroyed all who breathed,	3049
	11:11	They t destroyed them,	3049
	11:12	He t destroyed them,	3049
	11:20	so that he might destroy them t,	3049
	11:21	Joshua t destroyed them and their towns.	3049
Jdg	1:17	and they t destroyed the city.	3049
1Sa	15: 3	the Amalekites and t destroy everything	3049
	15: 8	his people he t destroyed with the sword.	3049
	15: 9	and weak they t destroyed.	3049
	15:15	but we t destroyed the rest."	3049
2Ch	12:12	and he was not t destroyed.	3986
Isa	2:18	and the idols will t disappear.	4003
	24: 3	laid waste and t plundered.	1024+1024
	34: 2	He will t destroy them,	3049
	34: 5	the people I have t destroyed.	3051
Am	9: 8	yet I will not t destroy the house of Jacob,"	9012+9012
Zec	11:17	his right eye t blinded!"	3908+3908

TOTTER (1) [TOTTERING]

Jer	10: 4	with hammer and nails so it will not t.	7048

TOTTERING (1) [TOTTER]

Ps	62: 3	this leaning wall, this t fence?	1890

TOU (4)

2Sa	8: 9	When T king of Hamath heard	9497
	8:10	who had been at war with T.	9497
1Ch	18: 9	When T king of Hamath heard	9495
	18:10	who had been at war with T.	9495

TOUCH (40) [TOUCHED, TOUCHES, TOUCHING]

Ge	3: 3	and you must not t it, or you will die.'"	5595
	20: 6	That is why I did not let you t her.	5595
	27:21	"Come near so I can t you, my son,	4630
Ex	12:13	No destructive plague will t you	928+2118
	19:12	not go up the mountain or t the foot of it.	5595
Lev	11: 8	not eat their meat or t their carcasses;	5595
	11: 8	not t anything sacred or go to the sanctuary	5595
Nu	4:15	not t the holy things or they will die.	5595
	16:26	Do not t anything belonging to them,	5595
Dt	14: 8	not to eat their meat or t their carcasses.	5595
	28:56	that she would not venture to t the ground	3657
Jos	9:19	and we cannot t them now.	5595
Ru	2: 9	I have told the men not to t you.	5595
1Sa	24:12	but my hand will not t you.	928+2118
	24:13	so my hand will not t you."	928+2118
2Sa	21:10	of the air t them by day or the wild animals	5663
1Ch	16:22	"Do not t my anointed ones;	5595
Job	6: 7	I refuse to t it; such food makes me ill.	5595
Ps	105:15	"Do not t my anointed ones;	5595
	144: 5	t the mountains, so that they smoke.	5595
Isa	28:15	scourge sweeps by, it cannot t us,	995
	52:11	T no unclean thing!	5595
Jer	13: 1	but do not let it t water."	928+995
	14:15	'No sword or famine will t this land.'	928+2118
La	4:14	that no one dares to t their garments.	5595
	4:15	"Away! Away! Don't t us!"	5595
Eze	9: 6	but do not t anyone who has the mark.	5602
Mt	9:21	She said to herself, "If I only t his cloak,	721
	14:36	to let the sick just t the edge of his cloak,	721
Mk	3:10	with diseases were pushing forward to t him.	721
	5:28	"If I just t his clothes, I will be healed."	721
	6:56	to let them even t the edge of his cloak,	721
	8:22	a blind man and begged Jesus to t him.	721
	10:13	to Jesus to have him t them,	721
Lk	6:19	and the people all tried to t him,	721
	18:15	bringing babies to Jesus to have him t them.	721
	24:39	T me and see; a ghost does not have flesh	6027
2Co	6:17	no unclean thing, and I will receive you."	721
Col	2:21	"Do not handle! Do not taste! Do not t!"?	2566
Heb	11:28	the destroyer of the firstborn would not t	2566

TOUCHED (59) [TOUCH]

Ge	27:22	his father Isaac, who t him and said,	5491
	32:25	he t the socket of Jacob's hip so	5595
	32:32	socket of Jacob's hip was t near the tendon.	5595
Ex	4:25	son's foreskin and t [Moses'] feet with it.	5595
Nu	19:18	He must also sprinkle anyone who has t	5595
	31:19	anyone who has been killed must stay outside	5595
Jos	3:15	the Jordan and their feet t the water's edge,	3188
	16: 7	t Jericho and came out at the Jordan.	7003
	19:11	to Maralah, t Dabbesheth, and extended to	7003
	19:22	The boundary t Tabor.	7003
	19:26	the boundary t Carmel and Shihor Libnath,	7003
	19:27	t Zebulun and the Valley of Iphtah El,	7003
	19:34	It t Zebulun on the south,	7003
Jdg	6:21	the angel of the LORD t the meat and	5595
1Sa	10:26	by valiant men whose hearts God had t.	5595
1Ki	6:27	The wing of one cherub t one wall,	5595
	6:27	the wing of the other t the other wall,	5595
	6:27	and their wings t each other in the middle	5595
	19: 5	All at once an angel t him and said,	5595
	19: 7	a second time and t him and said,	5595
2Ki	13:21	When the body t Elisha's bones,	5595
2Ch	3:11	the first cherub was five cubits long and t	5595
	3:11	t the wing of the other cherub.	5595
	3:12	and t the other temple wall,	5595
	3:12	t the wing of the first cherub.	1816
Est	5: 2	So Esther approached and t the tip of	5595
Isa	6: 7	With it he t my mouth and said, "See,	5595
	6: 7	"See, this has t your lips;	5595
Jer	1: 9	and t my mouth and said to me,	5595
Eze	1: 9	and their wings t one another.	2489
Da	4:11	The tree grew large and strong and its top t	10413
	8:18	Then he t me and raised me to my feet.	5595
	10: 3	no meat or wine t my lips;	448+995
	10:10	A hand t me and set me trembling	5595
	10:16	Then one who looked like a man t my lips,	5595
	10:18	Again the one who looked like a man t me	5595
Mt	8: 3	Jesus reached out his hand and t the man.	721
	8:15	He t her hand and the fever left her,	721
	9:20	for twelve years came up behind him and t	721
	9:29	Then he t their eyes and said,	721
	14:36	and all who t him were healed.	721
	17: 7	But Jesus came and t them.	721
	20:34	had compassion on them and t their eyes.	721
Mk	1:41	Jesus reached out his hand and t the man.	721
	5:27	behind him in the crowd and t his cloak,	721
	5:30	"Who t my clothes?"	721
	5:31	"and yet you can ask, 'Who t me?'"	721
	6:56	and all who t him were healed.	721
	7:33	Then he spit and t the man's tongue.	721
Lk	5:13	Jesus reached out his hand and t the man.	721
	7:14	Then he went up and t the coffin,	721
	8:44	up behind him and t the edge of his cloak,	721
	8:45	"Who t me?" Jesus asked.	721
	8:46	But Jesus said, "Someone t me;	721
	8:47	she told why she had t him and	721
	22:51	And he t the man's ear and healed him.	721
Ac	19:12	and aprons that had t him	608+3836+5999
Heb	12:18	that can be t and that is burning with fire;	6027
1Jn	1: 1	we have looked at and our hands have t—	6027

TOUCHES (47) [TOUCH]

Ge	27:12	What if my father t me?	5491
Ex	19:12	Whoever t the mountain shall surely be put	5595
	29:37	and whatever t it will be holy.	5595
	30:29	and whatever t them will be holy.	5595
Lev	5: 2	person t anything ceremonially unclean—	5595
	5: 3	"'Or if he t human uncleanness—	5595
	6:18	Whatever t them will become holy.'"	5595
	6:27	Whatever t any of the flesh will become	5595
	7:19	that t anything ceremonially unclean must	5595
	7:21	If anyone t something unclean—	5595
	11:24	whoever t their carcasses will be unclean	5595
	11:26	whoever t [the carcass of] any of them will	5595
	11:27	whoever t their carcasses will be unclean	5595
	11:31	Whoever t them when they are dead will	5595
	11:36	but anyone who t one of these carcasses	5595
	11:39	anyone who t the carcass will be unclean	5595
	15: 5	Anyone who t his bed must wash his clothes	5595
	15: 7	"'Whoever t the man who has	5595
	15:10	and whoever t any of the things that were	5595
	15:11	a discharge t without rinsing his hands	5595
	15:12	"'A clay pot that the man t must	5595
	15:19	and anyone who t her will be unclean	5595
	15:21	Whoever t her bed must wash his clothes	5595
	15:22	Whoever t anything she sits	5595
	15:23	when anyone t it, he will be unclean	5595
	15:24	with her and her monthly flow t him,	2118+6584
	15:27	Whoever t them will be unclean;	5595
	22: 4	also be unclean if he t something defiled	5595
	22: 5	or if he t any crawling thing	5595
	22: 6	The one who t any such thing will	5595
Nu	19:11	"Whoever t the dead body of anyone will	5595
	19:13	Whoever t the dead body of anyone	5595
	19:16	open who t someone who has been killed	5595
	19:16	or anyone who t a human bone or a grave,	NIH
	19:21	and anyone who t the water	5595
	19:22	that an unclean person t becomes unclean,	5595
	19:22	and anyone who t it becomes unclean	5595
2Sa	23: 7	Whoever t thorns uses a tool of iron or	5595
Ps	104:32	who t the mountains, and they smoke,	5595
Pr	6:29	no one who t her will go unpunished.	5595
Am	9: 5	he who t the earth and it melts,	5595
Hag	2:12	and that fold t some bread or stew,	5595

Hag	2:13	with a dead body t one of these things,	5595
Zec	2: 8	whoever t you touches the apple of his eye	5595
	2: 8	whoever touches you t the apple of his eye	5595
Heb	12:20	"If even an animal t the mountain,	2566

TOUCHING (4) [TOUCH]

Eze	1:11	one t the wing of another creature on	2489
Da	4:20	with its top t the sky,	10413
	8: 5	the whole earth without t the ground.	5595
Lk	7:39	he would know who *is* t him	721

TOW (KJV) See STRING, TINDER, WICK

TOWARD (229) [TO]

Ge	10:19	reached from Sidon t Gerar	995+2025+3870
	10:19	and then t Sodom, Gomorrah,	995+2025+3870
	10:30	they lived stretched from Mesha t	995+2025+3870
	12: 8	From there he went on t the hills east	2025
	12: 9	Abram set out and continued t the Negev.	2025
	13:10	like the land of Egypt, t Zoar.	995+3870
	13:11	the whole plain of the Jordan and set out t	4946
	16:12	will live in hostility t all his brothers."	6584+7156
	18:16	they looked down t Sodom,	6584+7156
	18:22	The men turned away and went t Sodom,	2025
	19:28	looked down t Sodom and Gomorrah,	6584+7156
	19:28	t all the land of the plain,	6584+7156
	24:11	it was t evening, the time the women go out	4200
	25:18	the border of Egypt, as you go t Asshur.	2025
	25:18	*they* lived in hostility t all their brothers.	5877+6584+7156
	31: 2	And Jacob noticed that Laban's attitude t	6640
	31: 5	"I see that your father's attitude t me is	448
	34:21	"These men are friendly t us," they said.	907
	48:13	Ephraim on his right t Israel's left hand	4946
	48:13	on his left t Israel's right hand,	4946
	49:13	his border will extend t Sidon.	6584
Ex	3:21	Egyptians favorably disposed t	928+2834+6524
	9:22	"Stretch out your hand t the sky so	6584
	9:23	Moses stretched out his staff t the sky,	6584
	9:33	He spread out his hands t the LORD;	448
	10:21	"Stretch out your hand t the sky so	6584
	10:22	So Moses stretched out his hand t the sky,	6584
	11: 3	Egyptians favorably disposed t	928+2834+6524
	12:36	Egyptians favorably disposed t	928+2834+6524
	13:18	led the people around *by* the desert road t	AIT
	14:27	The Egyptians were fleeing t it,	7925
	16:10	they looked t the desert,	448
	25:20	face each other, looking t the cover.	448
	27:13	On the east end, t the sunrise,	2025
	37: 9	faced each other, looking t the cover.	448
	38:13	The east end, t the sunrise,	2025
Lev	9:22	Then Aaron lifted his hands t the people	448
	26:21	" 'If you remain hostile t me and refuse	6640
	26:23	but continue to be hostile t me,	6640
	26:24	be hostile t you and will afflict you	6640
	26:27	not listen to me but continue to be hostile t	6640
	26:28	then in my anger I will be hostile t you,	6640
	26:40	against me and their hostility t me,	6640
	26:41	which made me hostile t them so	6640
Nu	2: 3	On the east, t the sunrise,	2025
	3:38	of the tabernacle, t the sunrise, in front of	2025
	6:26	the LORD turn his face t you and give you	448
	12:10	Aaron turned t her and saw that she had	448
	13:21	from the Desert of Zin as far as Rehob, t	NIH
	14:25	and set out t the desert along the route to	AIT
	14:40	Early the next morning they went up t	448
	14:44	in their presumption they went up t	448
	16:42	to Moses and Aaron and turned t the Tent	448
	19: 4	and sprinkle it seven times t the front	448+5790
	21:11	in the desert that faces Moab t the sunrise.	4946
	21:33	and went up along the road t Bashan,	AIT
	24: 1	but turned his face t the desert.	AIT
	34:15	on the east side of the Jordan of Jericho, t	2025
Dt	1:19	and went t the hill country of the Amorites	2006
	1:40	turn around and set out t the desert along	2025
	2: 1	and set out t the desert along the route to	2025
	3: 1	and went up along the road t Bashan,	AIT
	11:30	west of the road, t the setting sun,	NIH
	15: 7	do not be hardhearted or tightfisted t	4946
	15: 9	near," so that you do not show ill will t	928
	15:11	be openhanded t your brothers and toward	4200
	15:11	be openhanded toward your brothers and t	4200
	32: 5	They have acted corruptly t him;	4200
Jos	1:15	the LORD gave you east of the Jordan t	NIH
	8:15	and they fled t the desert.	2006
	8:18	"Hold out t Ai the javelin that is	448
	8:18	So Joshua held out his javelin t Ai.	448
	8:20	for the Israelites who *had been* fleeing t	AIT
	11:17	from Mount Halak, which *rises* t Seir,	AIT
	12: 7	which rises t Seir (their lands Joshua gave	2025
	15: 9	From the hilltop the boundary headed t	448
	15: 9	of Mount Ephron and went down t Baalah	AIT
	15:11	of Ekron, turned t Shikkeron, passed along	2025
	15:21	the Negev t the boundary of Edom were:	448
	19:12	It turned east from Sarid t the sunrise to	AIT
	19:13	it came out at Rimmon and turned t Neah.	AIT
	19:27	*It* then turned east t Beth Dagon,	AIT
	19:29	The boundary then turned back t Ramah	AIT
	19:29	turned t Hosah and came out at the sea in	AIT
	22:31	because you have not acted unfaithfully t	928
Jdg	7:22	The army fled to Beth Shittah t Zererah	2006
	9:17	and in good faith t Jerub-Baal	6640
	13:20	As the flame blazed up from the altar t	2025
	14: 5	suddenly a young lion came roaring t him.	7925
	15:14	the Philistines came t him shouting.	7925

Jdg	16:29	Then Samson reached t the two central	4369
	19:10	the man left and went t Jebus (that is,	5790+6330
	20:45	As they turned and fled t the desert to	2025
1Sa	6: 9	to its own territory, t Beth Shemesh, then	NIH
	6:12	cows went straight up t Beth Shemesh,	2006+6584
	9:14	coming t them on his way up to	7925
	13:17	One turned t Ophrah in the vicinity	448+2006
	13:18	another t Beth Horon,	2006
	13:18	and the third t the borderland overlooking	2006
	14: 5	One cliff stood to the north t Micmash,	4578
	14: 5	the other to the south t Geba.	4578
	14: 8	over t the men and let them see us.	448
	17:48	David ran quickly t the battle line	AIT
	20:12	If he is favorably disposed t you,	448
	20:19	The day after tomorrow, t evening,	3718+4394
	25: 8	Therefore *be* favorable t my young men,	928+2834+5162+6524
	25:20	there were David and his men descending t	7925
2Sa	15: 6	in this way t all the Israelites who came to	4200
	15:23	people moved on t the desert.	2006+6584+7156
	20:17	He went t her, and she asked,	448
	24: 6	and on to Dan Jaan and around t Sidon.	448
	24: 7	Then *they* went t the fortress of Tyre	AIT
	24:20	and saw the king and his men coming t	6584
1Ki	7:25	and their hindquarters were t the center.	2025
	8:22	spread out his hands t heaven	AIT
	8:29	May your eyes be open t this temple night	448
	8:29	the prayer your servant prays t this place.	448
	8:30	and of your people Israel when they pray t	448
	8:35	and when they pray t this place	448
	8:38	and spreading out his hands t this temple—	448
	8:42	when he comes and prays t this temple,	448
	8:44	the LORD t the city you have chosen and	2006
	8:48	to you t the land you gave their fathers,	2006
	8:48	t the city you have chosen and	NIH
	8:54	with his hands spread out t heaven.	AIT
	11:25	So Rezon ruled in Aram and was hostile t	928
	13: 4	But the hand he stretched out t	6584
	18:43	"Go and look t the sea,"	2006
2Ki	5:21	When Naaman saw him running t him,	339
	6:18	As the enemy came down t him,	448
	10:12	Jehu then set out and went t Samaria.	AIT
	25: 4	They fled t the Arabah,	2006
1Ch	29: 7	They gave the work on the temple	4200
2Ch	4: 4	and their hindquarters were t the center.	2025
	6:13	of Israel and spread out his hands t heaven.	2025
	6:20	May your eyes be open t this temple day	448
	6:20	the prayer your servant prays t this place.	448
	6:21	and of your people Israel when they pray t	448
	6:26	and when they pray t this place	448
	6:29	and spreading out his hands t this temple—	448
	6:32	when he comes and prays t this temple,	448
	6:34	to you t this city you have chosen and	2006
	6:38	and pray t the land you gave their fathers,	2006
	6:38	t the city you have chosen and toward	NIH
	6:38	toward the city you have chosen and t	4200
	20:24	that overlooks the desert and looked t	448
Ezr	2:68	of the families gave freewill offerings t	4200
	8:15	I assembled them at the canal that flows t	448
Ne	1: 7	We have acted very wickedly t you.	2006
	2:13	the Valley Gate t the Jackal Well	448+7156
	2:14	Then I moved on t the Fountain Gate and	448
	3:26	a point opposite the Water Gate t the east	4200
	12:31	t the Dung Gate.	4200
Job	10:17	against me and increase your anger t me;	6643
	39:26	by your wisdom and spread his wings t	4200
Ps	5: 7	in reverence will I bow down t your holy	448
	28: 2	I lift up my hands t your Most Holy Place.	448
	74: 3	Turn your steps t these everlasting ruins,	4200
	85: 4	and put away your displeasure t us.	6640
	86:13	For great is your love t me;	6584
	117: 2	For great is his love t us,	6584
	119:36	Turn my heart t your statutes and not	448
	119:36	toward your statutes and not t selfish gain.	448
	119:80	May my heart be blameless t your decrees,	928
	138: 2	I will bow down t your holy temple	448
	145:13	and loving t all he has made.	928
	145:17	and loving t all he has made.	928
Pr	24:11	hold back those staggering t slaughter.	4200
SS	7: 4	the tower of Lebanon looking t Damascus.	7156
Isa	8:22	Then they will look t the earth	448
	11:13	nor Judah hostile t Ephraim.	AIT
	16: 8	which once reached Jazer and spread t	AIT
Jer	3:12	Go, proclaim this message t the north:	2025
	4:11	in the desert blows t my people, but not	2006
	39: 4	and headed t the Arabah.	2006
	50: 5	the way to Zion and turn their faces t it.	2178
	52: 7	They fled t the Arabah,	2006
Eze	1:23	expanse their wings were stretched out one t	448
	4: 3	and the city and turn your face t it.	448
	4: 7	Turn your face t the siege of Jerusalem and	448
	8: 5	"Son of man, look t the north."	2006
	8:16	With their backs t the temple of	448
	8:16	the temple of the LORD and their faces t	2025
	17: 6	Its branches turned t him,	448
	17: 7	The vine now sent out its roots t him from	6584
	20:46	set your face t the south;	2006
	39:11	in the valley of those who travel east t	AIT
	39:26	and all the unfaithfulness they showed t	928
	41:19	of a man t the palm tree on one side and	448
	41:19	and the face of a lion t the palm tree on	448
	47: 1	under the threshold of the temple t the east	2025
	47: 8	"This water flows t the eastern region	448
Da	3:19	and his attitude t them changed.	10542
	4:34	Nebuchadnezzar, raised my eyes t heaven,	10378
	6:10	where the windows opened t Jerusalem.	10458
	8: 4	I watched the ram as he charged t the west	2025

Da	8: 6	He came t the two-horned ram I had seen	6330
	8: 8	in its place four prominent horns grew up t	4200
	8: 9	in power to the south and to the east and t	448
	10:15	I bowed with my face t the ground	2025
	11: 4	up and parceled out t the four winds	4200
	11:19	he will turn back t the fortresses	4200
	12: 7	lifted his right hand and his left hand t	448
Am	4: 3	and you will be cast out t Harmon,"	2025
Jnh	2: 4	yet I will look again t your holy temple.'	448
Zec	6: 6	The one with the black horses is going t	448
	6: 6	the one with the white horses t the west,	448
	6: 6	one with the dappled horses t the south."	448
	6: 8	Then he called to me, "Look, those going t	448
Mt	14:29	walked on the water and came t Jesus.	4639
Lk	7:44	he turned t the woman and said to Simon,	4639
	12:21	up things for himself but is not rich t	1650
Jn	1:29	The next day John saw Jesus coming t him	4639
	4:30	of the town and made their way t him.	4639
	6: 5	up and saw a great crowd coming t him,	4639
	17: 1	he looked t heaven and prayed:	1650
	20:16	She turned t him and cried out in Aramaic,	5138
Ac	9:40	Turning t the dead woman, he said,	4639
Ro	2: 4	God's kindness leads you t repentance?	1650
1Co	7:36	If anyone thinks he is acting improperly t	2093
2Co	10: 2	be t some people who think that we live by	2093
Php	3:13	Forgetting what is behind and straining t	2085
	3:14	I press on t the goal to win the prize	2848
Col	4: 5	Be wise in the way you act t outsiders;	4639
Tit	3: 2	and to show true humility t all men.	4639
Heb	10:24	how we may spur one another on t love	NIG
Jas	4: 4	with the world is hatred t God?	AIT
1Pe	3:21	but the pledge of a good conscience t God.	1650
	5: 5	yourselves with humility t one another,	AIT

TOWEL (2)

Jn	13: 4	and wrapped a t around his waist.	3317
	13: 5	drying them *with* the t that was wrapped	3317

TOWER (31) [TOWERED, TOWERING, TOWERS, WATCHTOWER, WATCHTOWERS]

Ge	11: 4	with a t that reaches to the heavens,	4463
	11: 5	and the t that the men were building.	4463
Jdg	8: 9	I will tear down this t."	4463
	8:17	also pulled down the t of Peniel and killed	4463
	9:46	the t of Shechem went into the stronghold	4463
	9:49	So all the people in the t of Shechem,	4463
	9:51	Inside the city, however, was a strong t,	4463
	9:51	in and climbed up on the t roof.	4463
	9:52	Abimelech went to the t and stormed it.	4463
	9:52	But as he approached the entrance to the t	4463
2Ki	9:17	When the lookout standing on the t	4463
Ne	3: 1	building as far as the T of the Hundred,	4463
	3: 1	and as far as the T of Hananel.	4463
	3:11	and the T of the Ovens.	4463
	3:25	the t projecting from the upper palace near	4463
	3:26	toward the east and the projecting t.	4463
	3:27	the great projecting t to the wall of Ophel.	4463
	12:38	past the T of the Ovens to the Broad Wall,	4463
	12:39	the T of Hananel and the Tower of the	4463
	12:39	Hananel and the T of the Hundred,	4463
Ps	61: 3	a strong t against the foe.	4463
Pr	18:10	The name of the LORD is a strong t;	4463
SS	4: 4	Your neck is like the t of David,	4463
	7: 4	Your neck is like an ivory t.	4463
	7: 4	Your nose is like the t of Lebanon looking	4463
Isa		for every lofty t and every fortified wall,	4463
Jer	31:38	be rebuilt for me from the T of Hananel to	4463
Eze		the waters *are ever* to proudly on high,	1467
Zec	14:10	the T of Hananel to the royal winepresses.	4463
Lk	13: 4	Or those eighteen who died when the t	4788
	14:28	"Suppose one of you wants to build a t.	4788

TOWERED (4) [TOWER]

Eze	19:11	*It* t high above the thick foliage,	1467
	31: 3	it t on high, its top above the thick foliage.	1468
	31: 5	So *it* t higher than all the trees of the field;	1467
	31:10	Because *it* t on high, lifting its top above	1467

TOWERING (1) [TOWER]

Isa	2:14	the t mountains and all the high hills,	8123

TOWERS (19) [TOWER]

2Ch	14: 7	"and put walls around them, with t,	4463
	26: 9	Uzziah built t in Jerusalem at the Corner	4463
	26:10	He also built t in the desert	4463
	26:15	for use on the t and on the corner defenses	4463
	27: 4	and forts and t in the wooded areas.	4463
	32: 5	of the wall and building t on it.	4463
Ps	48:12	go around her, count her t,	4463
SS	8: 9	we will build t of silver on her.	3227
	8:10	I am a wall, and my breasts are like t.	4463
Isa	23:13	they raised up their siege t,	1032
	29: 3	with t and set up my siege works	5164
	30:25	the day of great slaughter, when the t fall,	4463
	33:18	Where is the officer in charge of the t?"	4463
Jer	50:15	She surrenders, her t fall,	859
La	4:17	from our t we watched for a nation	7610
Eze	26: 4	the walls of Tyre and pull down her t;	4463
	26: 9	against your walls and demolish your t	4463
	27:11	men of Gammad were in your t.	4463
Zep	1:16	the fortified cities and against the corner t.	1469

TOWING (1)

Jn	21: 8	followed in the boat, t the net full of fish,	5359

TOWN (177) [HOMETOWN, TOWNS, TOWNSMEN, TOWNSPEOPLE]

Ge	19:20	Look, here is a t near enough to run to,	6551
	19:21	I will not overthrow the t you speak of.	6551
	19:22	(That is why the t was called Zoar.)	6551
	24:10	and made his way to the t of Nahor.	6551
	24:11	down near the well outside the t;	6551
	26:33	the name of the t has been Beersheba.	6551
Lev	14:40	into an unclean place outside the t.	6551
	14:41	into an unclean place outside the t.	6551
	14:45	and taken out of the t to an unclean place.	6551
	14:53	in the open fields outside the t.	6551
	25:33	that is, a house sold in any t they hold—	6551
Nu	20:16	a t on the edge of your territory.	6551
	22:36	he went out to meet him at the Moabite t.	6551
	35: 4	fifteen hundred feet from the t wall.	6551
	35: 5	Outside the t, measure three thousand feet	6551
	35: 5	with the t in the center.	6551
Dt	2:36	and from the t in the gorge,	6551
	2:36	not one t was too strong for us.	7953
	13:13	and have led the people of their t astray,	6551
	13:15	to the sword all who live in that t.	6551
	13:16	of the t into the middle of the public square	2023S
	13:16	the public square and completely burn the t	6551
	16: 5	in any t the LORD your God gives you	9133
	16:18	for each of your tribes in every t	9133
	19:12	the elders of his t shall send for him,	6551
	21: 3	of the t nearest the body shall take a heifer	6551
	21: 6	Then all the elders of the t nearest	6551
	21:19	to the elders at the gate of his t.	6551
	21:21	the men of his t shall stone him to death.	6551
	22:15	that she was a virgin to the t elders at	6551
	22:17	the cloth before the elders of the t,	6551
	22:21	and there the men of her t shall stone her	6551
	22:23	in a t a virgin pledged to be married	6551
	22:24	the gate of that t and stone them to death—	6551
	22:24	because she was in a t and did not scream	6551
	23:16	and in whatever t he chooses.	9133
	25: 7	she shall go to the elders at the t gate	9133
	25: 8	of his t shall summon him and talk to him.	6551
Jos	3:16	a t called Adam in the vicinity of Zarethan,	6551
	13: 9	and from the t in the middle of the gorge,	6551
	13:16	and from the t in the middle of the gorge,	6551
	18: 9	t by town, in seven parts,	NIH
	18: 9	town by t, in seven parts,	6551
	18:14	Kiriath Jearim), a t of the people of Judah.	6551
	19:50	They gave him the t he asked for—	6551
	19:50	And he built up the t and settled there.	6551
	20: 6	in the t from which he fled."	6551
Jdg	6:27	of his family and the men of the t,	6551
	6:28	the morning when the men of the t got up,	6551
	6:30	The men of the t demanded of Joash,	6551
	8:14	officials of Succoth, the elders of the t.	2023S
	8:16	of the t and taught the men of Succoth	6551
	8:17	of Peniel and killed the men of the t.	6551
	8:27	which he placed in Ophrah, his t.	6551
	12: 7	and was buried in a t in Gilead.	6551
	14:18	on the seventh day the men of the t said	6551
	17: 8	that t in search of some other place to stay.	6551
Ru	1:19	the whole t was stirred because of them,	6551
	2:18	She carried it back to t,	6551
	3:15	Then he went back to t.	6551
	4: 1	Meanwhile Boaz went up to the t gate	9133
	4: 2	Boaz took ten of the elders of the t	6551
	4:10	his family or from the t records.	5226+9133
1Sa	1: 3	Year after year this man went up from his t	6551
	4:13	the t and told what had happened,	6551
	4:13	the whole t sent up a cry.	6551
	8:22	"Everyone go back to his t."	6551
	9: 6	"Look, in this t there is a man of God;	6551
	9:10	So they set out for the t where the man	6551
	9:11	As they were going up the hill to the t,	6551
	9:12	he has just come to our t today,	6551
	9:13	As soon as you enter the t,	6551
	9:14	They went up to the t,	6551
	9:25	down from the high place to the t,	6551
	9:27	they were going down to the edge of the t,	6551
	10: 5	As you approach the t,	6551
	16: 4	of the t trembled when they met him.	6551
	20:29	in the t and my brother has ordered me to	6551
	20:40	"Go, carry them back to t."	6551
	20:42	and Jonathan went back to t.	6551
	22:19	put to the sword Nob, the t of the priests,	6551
	23: 7	by entering a t with gates and bars."	6551
	23:10	to Keilah and destroy the t on account	6551
	28: 3	and buried him in his own t of Ramah.	6551
2Sa	12: 1	"There were two men in a certain t,	6551
	15: 2	"What t are you from?"	6551
	19:37	that I may die in my own t near the tomb	6551
	24: 5	south of the t in the gorge,	6551
1Ki	15:27	at Gibbethon, a Philistine t, while Nadab	NIH
	16:15	near Gibbethon, a Philistine t.	889S
	17:10	When he came to the t gate,	6551
	22:36	"Every man to his t;	6551
2Ki	2:19	"Look, our lord, this t is well situated,	6551
	2:23	some youths came out of the t and jeered	6551
	3:19	every fortified city and every major t.	6551
2Ch	14: 5	and incense altars in every t in Judah,	6551
	20: 4	indeed, they came from every t in Judah	6551
	28:25	In every t in Judah he built high places	6551
	30:10	from t to town in Ephraim and Manasseh,	6551
	30:10	from town to t in Ephraim and Manasseh,	6551

Ezr	2: 1	to Jerusalem and Judah, each to his own t,	6551
	10:14	the elders and judges of each t,	2256+6551+6551
Ne	7: 6	to Jerusalem and Judah, each to his own t,	6551
Job	39: 7	He laughs at the commotion in the t;	7953
Ecc	10:15	he does not know the way to t.	6551
Isa	22: 2	O t full of commotion,	6551
	25: 2	the fortified t a ruin,	7953
Jer	3:14	one from a t and two from a clan—	6551
	4:29	of horsemen and archers every t takes	6551
	48: 8	The destroyer will come against every t,	6551
	48: 8	and not a t will escape.	6551
	49:25	the t in which I delight?	7953
Eze	39:16	(Also a t called Hamonah will be there.)	6551
Am	4: 6	in every city and lack of bread in every t,	5226
	4: 7	I sent rain on one t, but withheld it from	6551
	4: 8	People staggered from t to town for water	6551
	4: 8	People staggered from town to t for water	6551
	5: 3	the t that marches out a hundred strong	NIH
Mic	1:14	The t of Aczib will prove deceptive to	1074
Hab	2:12	bloodshed and establishes a t by crime!	7953
Mt	2:23	he went and lived in a t called Nazareth.	4484
	8:33	went into the t and reported all this,	4484
	8:34	Then the whole t went out to meet Jesus.	4484
	9: 1	crossed over and came to his own t.	4484
	10: 5	not go among the Gentiles or enter any t of	4484
	10:11	"Whatever t or village you enter,	4484
	10:14	when you leave that home or t.	4484
	10:15	on the day of judgment than for that t.	4484
	23:34	in your synagogues and pursue from t	4484
	23:34	and pursue from town to t.	4484
Mk	1:33	The whole t gathered at the door,	4484
	1:45	Jesus could no longer enter a t openly	4484
	5:14	and reported this in the t and countryside,	4484
	6:10	stay there until you leave that t.	NIG
Lk	1:26	the angel Gabriel to Nazareth, a t in Galilee,	4484
	1:39	that time Mary got ready and hurried to a t	4484
	2: 3	And everyone went to his own t to register.	4484
	2: 4	from the t of Nazareth in Galilee to Judea,	4484
	2: 4	to Bethlehem the t of David,	4484
	2:11	in the t of David a Savior has been born	4484
	2:39	they returned to Galilee to their own t	4484
	4:29	They got up, drove him out of the t,	4484
	4:29	of the hill on which the t was built,	4484
	4:31	he went down to Capernaum, a t in Galilee,	4484
	7:11	Jesus went to a t called Nain,	4484
	7:12	As he approached the t gate,	4484
	7:12	And a large crowd from the t was with her.	4484
	7:37	in that t learned that Jesus was eating at	4484
	8: 1	Jesus traveled about from one t and village	4484
	8: 4	and people were coming to Jesus from t	4484
	8: 4	coming to Jesus from town after t,	2848
	8:27	met by a demon-possessed man from the t.	4484
	8:34	and reported this in the t and countryside,	4484
	8:39	over t how much Jesus had done for him.	4484
	9: 4	stay there until you leave that t.	1696S
	9: 5	dust off your feet when you leave their t,	4484
	9:10	by themselves to a t called Bethsaida,	4484
	10: 1	of him to every t and place where he was	4484
	10: 8	"When you enter a t and are welcomed,	4484
	10:10	when you enter a t and are not welcomed,	4484
	10:11	of your t that sticks to our feet we wipe off	4484
	10:12	on that day for Sodom than for that t.	4484
	14:21	the streets and alleys of the t and bring in	4484
	18: 2	"In a certain t there was a judge	4484
	18: 3	a widow in that t who kept coming to him	4484
	23:51	He came from the Judean t of Arimathea	4484
Jn	1:44	was from the t of Bethsaida.	4484
	4: 5	So he came to a t in Samaria called Sychar,	4484
	4: 8	disciples had gone into the t to buy food.)	4484
	4:28	the woman went back to the t and said to	4484
	4:30	They came out of the t and made their way	4484
	4:39	the Samaritans from that t believed in him	4484
	7:42	from Bethlehem, the t where David lived?"	3267
Ac	16: 4	As they traveled from t to town,	3836+4484
	16: 4	As they traveled from town to t,	3836+4484
	27: 8	Fair Havens, near the t of Lasea.	4484
Tit	1: 5	and appoint elders in every t,	4484

TOWNCLERK (KJV) See CITY CLERK

TOWNS (299) [TOWN]

Ge	35: 5	terror of God fell upon the t all around them	6551
Lev	25:32	to redeem their houses in the Levitical t,	6551
	25:33	the Jubilee, because the houses in the t of	6551
	25:34	the pastureland belonging to their t must	6551
Nu	13:19	What kind of t do they live in?	6551
	21: 3	They completely destroyed them and their t;	6551
	31:10	the t where the Midianites had settled,	6551
	35: 2	the Levites t to live in from the inheritance	6551
	35: 2	And give them pastureland around the t.	6551
	35: 3	Then they will have t to live in	6551
	35: 4	"The pasturelands around the t	6551
	35: 5	as pastureland for the t.	6551
	35: 6	of the t you give the Levites will be cities	6551
	35: 6	In addition, give them forty-two other t.	6551
	35: 7	you must give the Levites forty-eight t,	6551
	35: 8	The t you give the Levites from the land	6551
	35: 8	Take many t from a tribe that has many,	6551
	35:11	select some t to be your cities of refuge,	6551
	35:13	These six t you give will be your cities	6551
	35:15	These six t will be a place of refuge	6551
Dt	1:22	we are to take and the t we will come to."	6551
	2:34	At that time we took all his t	6551
	2:35	from the t we had captured we carried off	6551
	2:37	nor that around the t in the hills.	6551

Dt	3:10	We took all the t on the plateau,	6551
	3:10	and Edrei, t of Og's kingdom in Bashan.	6551
	3:12	hill country of Gilead, together with its t.	6551
	3:19	in the t I have given you,	6551
	12:12	and the Levites from your t,	9133
	12:15	of your t and eat as much of the meat	9133
	12:17	not eat in your own t the tithe of your grain	9133
	12:18	and the Levites from your t—	9133
	12:21	and in your own t you may eat as much	9133
	13:12	of the t the LORD your God is giving you	6551
	14:21	to an alien living in any of your t,	9133
	14:27	do not neglect the Levites living in your t,	9133
	14:28	that year's produce and store it in your t,	9133
	14:29	the widows who live in your t may come	9133
	15: 7	among your brothers in any of the t of	9133
	15:22	You are to eat it in your own t.	9133
	16:11	the Levites in your t, and the aliens,	9133
	16:14	and the widows who live in your t.	9133
	17: 2	or woman living among you in one of the t	9133
	18: 6	from one of your t anywhere in Israel	9133
	19: 1	and settled in their t and houses,	6551
	21: 2	from the body to the neighboring t.	6551
	24:14	or an alien living in one of your t.	9133
	26:12	that they may eat in your t and be satisfied.	9133
	31:12	and the aliens living in your t—	9133
Jos	11:21	Joshua totally destroyed them and their t.	6551
	13:10	all the t of Sihon king of the Amorites,	6551
	13:17	to Heshbon and all its t on the plateau,	6551
	13:21	the t on the plateau and the entire realm	6551
	13:23	These t and their villages were	6551
	13:25	all the t of Gilead and half the Ammonite	6551
	13:28	These t and their villages were	6551
	13:30	the settlements of Jair in Bashan, sixty t,	6551
	14: 4	of the land but only t to live in.	6551
	15: 9	at the t of Mount Ephron and went down	6551
	15:21	The southernmost t of the tribe of Judah in	6551
	15:32	a total of twenty-nine t and their villages.	6551
	15:36	fourteen t and their villages.	6551
	15:41	sixteen t and their villages.	6551
	15:44	nine t and their villages.	6551
	15:51	eleven t and their villages.	6551
	15:54	nine t and their villages.	6551
	15:57	ten t and their villages.	6551
	15:59	six t and their villages.	6551
	15:60	two t and their villages.	6551
	15:62	six t and their villages.	6551
	16: 9	It also included all the t and their villages	6551
	17: 9	There were t belonging to Ephraim lying	6551
	17: 9	belonging to Ephraim lying among the t	6551
	17:12	Manassites not able to occupy these t,	6551
	18:24	twelve t and their villages.	6551
	18:28	fourteen t and their villages.	6551
	19: 6	thirteen t and their villages;	6551
	19: 7	four t and their villages—	6551
	19: 8	and all the villages around these t as far	6551
	19:15	There were twelve t and their villages.	6551
	19:16	These t and their villages were	6551
	19:22	There were sixteen t and their villages.	6551
	19:23	These t and their villages were	6551
	19:30	There were twenty-two t and their villages.	6551
	19:31	These t and their villages were	6551
	19:38	There were nineteen t and their villages.	6551
	19:39	These t and their villages were	6551
	19:48	These t and their villages were	6551
	21: 2	through Moses that you give us t to live in,	6551
	21: 3	the following t and pasturelands out	6551
	21: 4	of Aaron the priest were allotted thirteen t	6551
	21: 5	of Kohath's descendants were allotted ten t	6551
	21: 6	of Gershon were allotted thirteen t from	6551
	21: 7	received twelve t from the tribes	6551
	21: 8	the Israelites allotted to the Levites these t	6551
	21: 9	and Simeon they allotted the following t	6551
	21:10	(these t were assigned to the descendants	NIH
	21:16	nine t from these two tribes.	6551
	21:18	with their pasturelands—four t.	6551
	21:19	All the t for the priests,	6551
	21:20	of the Levites were allotted t from the tribe	6551
	21:22	with their pasturelands—four t.	6551
	21:24	with their pasturelands—four t.	6551
	21:25	with their pasturelands—two t.	6551
	21:26	All these ten t and their pasturelands	6551
	21:27	with their pasturelands—two t;	6551
	21:29	with their pasturelands—four t;	6551
	21:31	with their pasturelands—four t;	6551
	21:32	with their pasturelands—three t.	6551
	21:33	the t of the Gershonite clans were thirteen,	6551
	21:35	with their pasturelands—four t;	6551
	21:37	with their pasturelands—four t;	6551
	21:39	with their pasturelands—four t in all.	6551
	21:40	All the t allotted to the Merarite clans,	6551
	21:41	The t of the Levites in the territory held by	6551
	21:42	Each of these t had pasturelands	6551+6551
	21:42	this was true for all these t.	6551
Jdg	10: 4	They controlled thirty t in Gilead,	6551
	11:26	the surrounding settlements and all the t	6551
	11:33	He devastated twenty t from Aroer to	6551
	20:14	From their t they came together at Gibeah	6551
	20:15	twenty-six thousand swordsmen from their t	6551
	20:42	of Israel who came out of the t cut them	6551
	20:48	to Benjamin and put all the t to the sword,	6551
	20:48	All the t they came across they set on fire.	6551
	21:23	and rebuilt the t and settled in them.	6551
1Sa	6:18	to the number of Philistine t belonging to	6551
	6:18	the fortified t with their country villages.	6551
	7:14	The t from Ekron to Gath were	6551
	18: 6	from all the t of Israel to meet King Saul	6551
	27: 5	be assigned to me in one of the country t,	6551

1Sa	30:29	the t of the Jerahmeelites and the Kenites;	6551
	31: 7	they abandoned their t and fled.	6551
2Sa	2: 1	"Shall I go up to one of the t of Judah?"	6551
	2: 3	and they settled in Hebron and its t.	6551
	8: 8	t that belonged to Hadadezer,	6551
	12:31	He did this to all the Ammonite t.	6551
	24: 7	and all the t of the Hivites and Canaanites.	6551
1Ki	9:11	King Solomon gave twenty t in Galilee	6551
	9:12	to see the t that Solomon had given him,	6551
	9:13	of t are these you have given me,	6551
	9:19	the t for his chariots and for his horses—	6551
	12:17	for the Israelites who were living in the t	6551
	13:32	the t of Samaria will certainly come true."	6551
	15:20	the commanders of his forces against the t	6551
2Ki	3:25	They destroyed the t,	6551
	13:25	of Hazael the t he had taken in battle	6551
	13:25	and so he recovered the Israelite t.	6551
	17: 6	the Habor River and in the t of the Medes.	6551
	17: 9	built themselves high places in all their t.	6551
	17:24	in the t of Samaria to replace the Israelites.	6551
	17:24	They took over Samaria and lived in its t.	6551
	17:26	the t of Samaria do not know what the god	6551
	17:29	in the several t where they settled,	6551
	18:11	on the Habor River and in t of the Medes.	6551
	23: 5	to burn incense on the high places of the t	6551
	23: 8	Josiah brought all the priests from the t	6551
	23:19	that the kings of Israel had built in the t	6551
1Ch	2:22	who controlled twenty-three t in Gilead.	6551
	2:23	with its surrounding settlements—sixty t.)	6551
	4:31	These were their t until the reign of David.	6551
	4:32	Token and Ashan—five t—	6551
	4:33	and all the villages around these t as far	6551
	6:60	These t, which were distributed among	6551
	6:61	of Kohath's descendants were allotted ten t	6551
	6:62	were allotted thirteen t from the tribes	6551
	6:63	were allotted twelve t from the tribes	6551
	6:64	the Levites these t and their pasturelands.	6551
	6:65	they allotted the previously named t	6551
	6:66	as their territory t from the tribe of Ephraim.	6551
	7:29	of Joseph son of Israel lived in these t.	NIH
	9: 2	in their own t were some Israelites,	6551
	10: 7	they abandoned their t and fled.	6551
	13: 2	and Levites who are with them in their t	6551
	18: 8	t that belonged to Hadadezer,	6551
	19: 7	the Ammonites were mustered from their t	6551
	20: 3	David did this to all the Ammonite t.	6551
	27:25	in the t, the villages and the watchtowers.	6551
2Ch	10:17	for the Israelites who were living in the t	6551
	11: 5	in Jerusalem and built up t for defense	6551
	13:19	and took from him the t of Bethel,	6551
	14: 7	"Let us build up these t," he said to Judah,	6551
	15: 8	and from the t he had captured in the hills	6551
	16: 4	the commanders of his forces against the t	6551
	17: 2	and put garrisons in Judah and in the t	6551
	17: 7	and Micaiah to teach in the t of Judah.	6551
	17: 9	to all the t of Judah and taught the people.	6551
	17:13	and had large supplies in the t of Judah.	6551
	23: 2	of Israelite families from all the t.	6551
	24: 5	"Go to the t of Judah and collect	6551
	25:13	in the war raided Judean t from Samaria	6551
	26: 6	then rebuilt t near Ashdod and elsewhere	6551
	27: 4	He built t in the Judean hills and forts	6551
	28:18	the Philistines had raided t in the foothills	6551
	31: 1	went out to the t of Judah,	6551
	31: 1	to their own t and to their own property.	6551
	31: 6	and Judah who lived in the t of Judah	6551
	31:15	assisted him faithfully in the t of the priests,	6551
	31:19	who lived on the farm lands around their t	6551
	31:19	around their towns or in any other t,	6551
	34: 6	In the t of Manasseh, Ephraim and Simeon,	6551
Ezr	2:59	The following came up from the t	NIH
	2:70	the temple servants settled in their own t,	6551
	2:70	the rest of the Israelites settled in their t.	6551
	3: 1	and the Israelites had settled in their t,	6551
	10:14	Then let everyone in our t who has married	6551
Ne	7:61	The following came up from the t	NIH
	7:73	rest of the Israelites, settled in their own t.	6551
	7:73	and the Israelites had settled in their t,	6551
	8:15	throughout their t and in Jerusalem:	6551
	10:37	the tithes in all the t where we work.	6551
	11: 1	remaining nine to stay in their own t.	6551
	11: 1	of Solomon's servants lived in the t	6551
	11: 3	each on his own property in the various t,	6551
	11:20	were in all the t of Judah,	6551
	12:44	the t they were to bring into the storerooms	6551
Job	15:28	he will inhabit ruined t and houses	6551
Isa	40: 9	say to the t of Judah, "Here is your God!"	6551
	42:11	Let the desert and its t raise their voices;	6551
	44:26	'It shall be inhabited,' of the t of Judah,	6551
Jer	1:15	and against all the t of Judah.	6551
	2:15	his t are burned and deserted.	6551
	2:28	For you have as many gods as you have t,	6551
	4: 7	Your t will lie in ruins without inhabitant.	6551
	4:26	all its t lay in ruins before the LORD,	6551
	4:29	All the t are deserted; no one lives in them.	6551
	5: 6	a leopard will lie in wait near their t to tear	6551
	7:17	Do you not see what they are doing in the t	6551
	7:34	the t of Judah and the streets of Jerusalem,	6551
	9:11	the t of Judah so no one can live there."	6551
	10:22	It will make the t of Judah desolate,	6551
	11: 6	"Proclaim all these words in the t of Judah	6551
	11:12	The t of Judah and the people	6551
	11:13	You have as many gods as you have t,	6551
	17:26	People will come from the t of Judah and	6551
	20:16	the t the LORD overthrew without pity.	6551
	22: 6	surely make you like a desert, like t	6551
	25:18	and the t of Judah, its kings and officials,	6551

Jer	26: 2	of the t of Judah who come to worship in	6551
	31:21	Return, O Virgin Israel, return to your t.	6551
	31:23	in its t will once again use these words:	6551
	31:24	will live together in Judah and all its t—	6551
	32:44	in the t of Judah and in the towns of	6551
	32:44	of Judah and in the t of the hill country,	6551
	33:10	the t of Judah and the streets of Jerusalem	6551
	33:12	in all its t there will again be pastures	6551
	33:13	In the t of the hill country,	6551
	33:13	the villages around Jerusalem and in the t	6551
	34: 1	against Jerusalem and all its surrounding t,	6551
	34:22	the t of Judah so no one can live there."	6551
	36: 6	of Judah who come in from their t.	6551
	36: 9	and those who had come from the t	6551
	40: 5	king of Babylon has appointed over the t	6551
	40:10	and live in the t you have taken over.	6551
	44: 2	on Jerusalem and on all the t of Judah.	6551
	44: 6	the t of Judah and the streets of Jerusalem	6551
	44:17	and our officials did in the t of Judah and	6551
	44:21	and think about the incense burned in the t	6551
	47: 2	the t and those who live in them.	6551
	48: 9	her t will become desolate,	6551
	48:15	Moab will be destroyed and her t invaded;	6551
	48:24	to all the t of Moab, far and near.	6551
	48:28	Abandon your t and dwell among	6551
	49: 1	Why do his people live in its t?	6551
	49:13	and all its t will be in ruins forever."	6551
	49:18	along with their neighboring t,"	NIH
	50:32	a fire in her t that will consume all who are	6551
	50:40	along with their neighboring t," declares	NIH
	51:43	Her t will be desolate,	6551
La	5:11	and virgins in the t of Judah.	6551
Eze	6: 6	the t will be laid waste and	6551
	12:20	The inhabited t will be laid waste and	6551
	19: 7	and devastated their t.	6551
	25: 9	beginning at its frontier t—	6551
	35: 4	I will turn your t into ruins and you will	6551
	35: 9	your t will not be inhabited.	6551
	36: 4	and the deserted t that have been plundered	6551
	36:10	The t will be inhabited and	6551
	36:33	I will resettle your t,	6551
	39: 9	in the t of Israel will go out and use	6551
	45: 5	as their possession for t to live in.	6551
Hos	8:14	Judah has fortified many t.	6551
	13:10	Where are your rulers in all your t,	6551
Ob	1:20	in Sepharad will possess the t of the Negev.	6551
Zec	1:12	from Jerusalem and from the t of Judah,	6551
	1:17	'My t will again overflow with prosperity,	6551
	7: 7	when Jerusalem and its surrounding t were	6551
Mt	9:35	Jesus went through all the t and villages,	4484
	11: 1	on from there to teach and preach in the t	4484
	14:13	crowds followed him on foot from the t.	4484
Mk	6:33	and ran on foot from all the t and got there	4484
	6:56	into villages, t or countryside—	4484
Lk	4:43	of the kingdom of God to the other t also,	4484
	5:12	While Jesus was in one of the t,	4484
	13:22	Then Jesus went through the t and villages,	4484
Ac	5:16	also from the t around Jerusalem,	4484
	8:40	in all the t until he reached Caesarea.	4484
	15:36	the brothers in all the t where we preached	4484
Jude	1: 7	and the surrounding t gave themselves up	4484

TOWNSMEN (2) [TOWN]

Ge	34:20	of their city to speak to their fellow t.	408+6551
Ru	3:11	All my fellow t know that you are	6639+9133

TOWNSPEOPLE (1) [TOWN]

Ge	24:13	the daughters of the t are coming out	408+6551

TRACE (2) [TRACED, TRACING]

Da	2:35	wind swept them away without leaving a t.	10087
Heb	7: 6	however, did not t his descent from Levi,	1156

TRACED (1) [TRACE]

Ro	9: 5	and from them is t the human ancestry	NIG

TRACHONITIS (KJV) See TRACONITIS

TRACING (1) [TRACE]

Ro	11:33	and his paths beyond t out!	453

TRACK (2) [TRACKED, TRACKLESS, TRACKS]

1Sa	23:23	in the area, I will t him down among all	2924
Job	14:16	but not keep t of my sin.	9068

TRACKED (1) [TRACK]

Ps	17:11	They have t me down, they now surround me	892

TRACKLESS (2) [TRACK]

Job	12:24	them wandering through a t waste.	2006+4202
Ps	107:40	made them wander in a t waste.	2006+4202

TRACKS (1) [TRACK]

SS	1: 8	follow the sheep	6811

TRACONITIS (1)

Lk	3: 1	his brother Philip tetrarch of Iturea and T,	5551

TRACT (1) [TRACTS]

Jos	24:32	were buried at Shechem in the t of land	2754

TRACTS (1) [TRACT]

Jos	17: 5	consisted of ten t of land besides Gilead	824

TRADE (11) [TRADED, TRADERS, TRADES, TRADING]

Ge	34:10	Live in it, t in it,	6086
	34:21	"Let them live in our land and t in it;	6086
	42:34	and you can t in the land.' "	6086
2Ch	9:16	and were not able to set sail to t.	9576
Isa	23:17	as a prostitute and will ply her t with all	2388
Eze	27: 9	and their sailors came alongside to t	6842
	28:16	Through your widespread t you were filled	8219
	28:18	sins and dishonest t you have desecrated your sanctuaries.	8219
Zep	1:11	all who t with silver will be ruined.	5744
Ac	19:27	not only that our t will lose its good name,	3538
Rev	18:22	No workman of any t will ever be found	5492

TRADED (8) [TRADE]

Eze	27:13	" 'Greece, Tubal and Meshech t with you;	8217
	27:15	" 'The men of Rhodes t with you,	8217
	27:17	" 'Judah and Israel t with you;	8217
	27:20	" 'Dedan t in saddle blankets with you.	8217
	27:22	" 'The merchants of Sheba and Raamah t	8217
	27:23	Asshur and Kilmad t with you.	8217
	27:24	In your marketplace they t with you	8217
Joel	3: 3	for my people and t boys for prostitutes;	5989

TRADERS (6) [TRADE]

1Ki	10:15	and t and from all the Arabian kings and	8217
2Ch	9:14	revenues brought in by merchants and t.	6086
Job	41: 6	Will t barter for him?	2493
Isa	23: 8	whose t are renowned in the earth?	4048
Eze	17: 4	where he planted it in a city of t.	8217
1Ti	1:10	for slave t and liars and perjurers—	435

TRADES (1) [TRADE]

Ac	19:25	along with the workmen in related t,	5525S

TRADING (8) [TRADE]

1Ki	10:22	The king had a fleet of t ships at sea	639+9576
	22:48	fleet of t ships to go to Ophir for gold,	641+9576
2Ch	9:21	a fleet of t ships manned by Hiram's men.	641+2143+9576
	20:36	construct a fleet of t ships.	641+2143+4200+9576
Job	20:18	he will not enjoy the profit from his t.	9455
Pr	31:18	She sees that her t is profitable,	6087
Isa	2:16	for every t ship and every stately vessel.	641+9576
Eze	28: 5	in t you have increased your wealth,	8219

TRADITION (8) [TRADITIONS]

2Ch	35:25	a t in Israel and are written in the Laments.	2976
Mt	15: 2	"Why do your disciples break the t of	4142
	15: 3	of God for the sake of your t?	4142
	15: 6	the word of God for the sake of your t.	4142
Mk	7: 3	holding to the t of the elders.	4142
	7: 5	according to the t of the elders instead	4142
	7:13	by your t that you have handed down.	4142
Col	2: 8	on human t and the basic principles	4142

TRADITIONS (5) [TRADITION]

Mic	6:16	and you have followed their t.	4600
Mk	7: 4	And they observe many other t,	4161
	7: 8	of God and are holding on to the t of men."	4142
	7: 9	of God in order to observe your own t!	4142
Gal	1:14	extremely zealous for the t of my fathers.	4142

TRAFFICK, TRAFFICKERS (KJV) See MERCHANTS, TRADE, TRADERS, TRADING

TRAFFICKED (1)

Isa	47:15	these you have labored with and t with	6086

TRAGEDY (1)

1Ki	17:20	have you brought t also upon this widow	8317

TRAIL (2)

Job	41:30	leaving a t in the mud like a threshing	8331
1Ti	5:24	the sins of others t behind them.	2051

TRAIN (8) [TRAINED, TRAINING, TRAINS, WELL-TRAINED]

Ps	68:18	you led captives in your t;	8647
Pr	22: 6	T a child in the way he should go,	2852
Isa	2: 4	nor will they t for war anymore.	4340
	6: 1	and the t of his robe filled the temple.	8767
Mic	4: 3	nor will they t for war anymore.	4340
Eph	4: 8	led captives in his t and gave gifts to	168+169
1Ti	4: 7	rather, t yourself to be godly.	1214
Tit	2: 4	Then they can t the younger women	5405

TRAINED (13) [TRAIN]

Ge	14:14	the 318 **men** born in his household	2849
1Ch	5:18	and who were t for battle.	4340
	25: 7	all of them t and skilled in music for	4340
2Ch	2:14	He is t to work in gold and silver,	3359
	26:13	an army of 307,500 men t for war,	6913
Da	1: 5	They were to be t for three years,	1540
Hos	7:15	I t them and strengthened them,	3579
	10:11	Ephraim is a t heifer that loves to thresh;	4340
Lk	6:40	but everyone who is **fully** t will be	2936
Ac	22: 3	Under Gamaliel I was thoroughly t in	4084
2Co	11: 6	I may **not** be a t speaker,	2626
Heb	5:14	who by constant use have t themselves	1214
	12:11	and peace for those who have been t by it.	1214

TRAINING (4) [TRAIN]

1Co	9:25	competes in the games **goes into** strict t.	1603
Eph	6: 4	bring them up in the t and instruction of	4082
1Ti	4: 8	For physical t is of some value,	1215
2Ti	3:16	rebuking, correcting and t in righteousness,	4082

TRAINS (3) [TRAIN]

2Sa	22:35	He t my hands for battle;	4340
Ps	18:34	He t my hands for battle;	4340
	144: 1	who t my hands for war,	4340

TRAITOR (5) [TREASON]

2Ki	17: 4	of Assyria discovered that Hoshea was a t,	8004
Isa	21: 2	The t betrays, the looter takes loot.	953
	33: 1	Woe to you, O you who have not been	953
Lk	6:16	and Judas Iscariot, who became a t.	4595
Jn	18: 5	Judas the t was standing there with them.)	4140

TRAITORS (2) [TREASON]

Ps	59: 5	show no mercy to wicked t.	953
Mic	2: 4	He assigns our fields to t.' "	8745

TRAMPLE (21) [TRAMPLED, TRAMPLING]

Dt	33:29	and you will **t down** their high places."	2005
Job	39:15	that some wild animal may t them.	1889
Ps	7: 5	let him t my life to the ground	8252
	44: 5	through your name we t our foes.	1008
	60:12	and he will t down our enemies.	1008
	91:13	you will t the great lion and the serpent.	8252
	108:13	and he will t **down** our enemies.	1008
Isa	10: 6	to t them **down** like mud in the streets.	5330+8492
	14:25	on my mountains I will t him **down.**	1008
	26: 6	Feet t it **down**—the feet of the oppressed,	8252
Jer	12:10	and t **down** my field;	1008
Eze	26:11	hoofs of his horses will t all your streets;	8252
	34:18	Must you also t the rest of your pasture	8252
Joel	3:13	t the grapes, for the winepress is full and	8097
Am	2: 7	They t on the heads of the poor as upon	8635
	5:11	You t on the poor and force him	1424
	8: 4	you who t the needy and do away with	8635
Mal	4: 3	Then you will t **down** the wicked;	6748
Mt	7: 6	If you do, they may t them under their feet,	2922
Lk	10:19	I have given you authority to t on snakes	4251
Rev	11: 2	They will t **on** the holy city for 42 months.	4251

TRAMPLED (32) [TRAMPLE]

2Sa	22:43	and t them like mud in the streets.	8392
2Ki	7:17	and the people t him in the gateway,	8252
	7:20	for the people t him in the gateway,	8252
	9:33	and the horses as they t her **underfoot.**	8252
	14: 9	and t the thistle **underfoot.**	8252
2Ch	25:18	and t the thistle **underfoot.**	8252
Isa	5: 5	I will break down its wall, and it will be t.	5330
	14:19	Like a corpse t **underfoot,**	1008
	16: 8	the nations have t **down** the choicest vines,	2150
	25:10	but Moab will be t under him	1889
	25:10	be trampled under him as straw is t **down** in	1889
	28: 3	will be t underfoot.	8252
	63: 3	I t them in my anger and trod them down	2005
	63: 6	I t the nations in my anger;	1008
	63:18	our enemies have t **down** your sanctuary.	1008
Jer	51:33	like a threshing floor at the time it is t;	2005
La	1:15	the Lord has t the Virgin Daughter	2005
	3:16	he has t me in the dust.	4115
Eze	34:19	my flock feed on **what** you have t	5330+8079
Da	7: 7	and t underfoot whatever was left.	10672
	7:19	and t underfoot whatever was left.	10672
	8: 7	the goat knocked him to the ground and t	8252
	8:10	of the starry host down to the earth and t	8252
	8:13	and of the host that will be t **underfoot?"**	5330
Hos	5:11	Ephraim is oppressed, t in judgment,	8368
Mic	7:10	even now she will be t **underfoot** like mire	5330
Hab	3:15	You t the sea with your horses,	2005
Mt	5:13	except to be thrown out and t by men.	2922
Lk	8: 5	it was t **on,** and the birds of the air ate it up.	2922
	21:24	Jerusalem will be t **on** by the Gentiles until	4251
Heb	10:29	who has t the Son of God **under foot,**	2922
Rev	14:20	They were t in the winepress outside	4251

TRAMPLING (5) [TRAMPLE]

Isa	1:12	asked this of you, this t of my courts?	8252
	22: 5	and t and terror in the Valley of Vision,	4431
Da	7:23	t it **down** and crushing it.	10165
Zec	10: 5	Together they will be like mighty men t	1008
Lk	12: 1	so that they were t **on** one another,	2922

TRANCE (3)

Ac	10:10	he **fell into** a t.	1181+1749+2093
	11: 5	and in a t I saw a vision.	1749
	22:17	and was praying at the temple, I fell into a t	1749

TRANQUILLITY (1)

Ecc	4: 6	handful with t than two handfuls with toil	5739

TRANS-EUPHRATES (17) [EUPHRATES]

Ezr	4:10	Samaria and elsewhere in T.	10191+10468+10526
	4:11	your servants, the men of T:	10191+10468+10526
	4:16	you will be left with nothing in T.	10002+10468+10526
	4:17	Samaria and elsewhere in T:	10191+10468+10526
	4:20	over the whole of T,	10191+10468+10526
	5: 3	At that time Tattenai, governor of T,	10191+10468+10526
	5: 6	that Tattenai, governor of T,	10191+10468+10526
	5: 6	the officials of T, sent to King Darius.	10191+10468+10526
	6: 6	Tattenai, governor of T,	10191+10468+10526
	6: 8	from the revenues of T,	10191+10468+10526
	6:13	Tattenai, governor of T,	10191+10468+10526
	7:21	order all the treasurers of T	10191+10468+10526
	7:25	to administer justice to all the people of T—	10191+10468+10526
	8:36	and to the governors of T,	2021+5643+6298
Ne	2: 7	letters to the governors of T,	2021+5643+6298
	2: 9	to the governors of T and gave them the king's letters.	2021+5643+6298
	3: 7	under the authority of the governor of T.	2021+5643+6298

TRANSACTION (1) [TRANSACTIONS]

Jer	32:25	with silver and **have the t witnessed.'**	6332+6386

TRANSACTIONS (1) [TRANSACTION]

Ru	4: 7	This was the **method of legalizing t**	9496

TRANSCENDS (1)

Php	4: 7	peace of God, which t all understanding,	5660

TRANSFER (2) [TRANSFERRED]

Ru	4: 7	redemption and t **of property**	1821+3972+9455
2Sa	3:10	and t the kingdom from the house of Saul	6296

TRANSFERRED (1) [TRANSFER]

Ac	25: 3	to **have** Paul t to Jerusalem,	3569

TRANSFIGURED (2)

Mt	17: 2	There he was t before them.	3565
Mk	9: 2	There he was t before them.	3565

TRANSFORM (1) [TRANSFORMED]

Php	3:21	will t our lowly bodies so that they will	3571

TRANSFORMED (3) [TRANSFORM]

Job	38: 5	is t below as by fire;	2200
Ro	12: 2	but be t by the renewing of your mind.	3565
2Co	3:18	are being t into his likeness	3565

TRANSGRESSED (1) [TRANSGRESSION]

Da	9:11	All Israel has t your law and turned away,	6296

TRANSGRESSION (11)
[TRANSGRESSED, TRANSGRESSIONS, TRANSGRESSORS]

Ps	19:13	will I be blameless, innocent of great t.	7322
Isa	53: 8	for the t of my people he was stricken.	7322
Da	9:24	and your holy city to finish t,	7322
Mic	1: 5	All this is because of Jacob's t,	7322
	1: 5	What is Jacob's t? Is it not Samaria?	7322
	3: 8	to declare to Jacob his t, to Israel his sin.	7322
	6: 7	Shall I offer my firstborn for my t,	7322
	7:18	the t of the remnant of his inheritance?	7322
Ro	4:15	And where there is no law there is no t.	4126
	11:11	Rather, because of their t, salvation has	4183
	11:12	But if their t means riches for the world,	4183

TRANSGRESSIONS (15)
[TRANSGRESSION]

Ps	32: 1	Blessed is he whose t are forgiven,	7322
	32: 5	"I will confess my t to the LORD"—	7322
	39: 8	Save me from all my t;	7322
	51: 1	to your great compassion blot out my	7322
	51: 3	For I know my t,	7322
	65: 3	you forgave our t.	7322
	103:12	so far has he removed our t from us.	7322
Isa	43:25	"I, even I, am he who blots out your t,	7322
	50: 1	of your t your mother was sent away.	7322
	53: 5	But he was pierced for our t,	7322
Mic	1:13	for the t of Israel were found in you.	7322
Ro	4: 7	"Blessed are they whose t are forgiven,	490
Gal	3:19	It was added because of t until the Seed	4126
Eph	2: 1	you were dead in your t and sins,	4183
	2: 5	with Christ even when we were dead in t—	4183

TRANSGRESSORS (4)
[TRANSGRESSION]

Ps	51:13	Then I will teach t your ways,	7321
Isa	53:12	and was numbered with the t.	7321
	53:12	and made intercession for the t.	7321
Lk	22:37	'And he was numbered with the t';	491

TRANSLATE (KJV) See TRANSFER

TRANSLATED (3)

Ezr	4:18	The letter you sent us has been read and t	10597
Jn	1:42	called Cephas" (which, when t, is Peter).	2257
Ac	9:36	named Tabitha (which, when t, is Dorcas),	1450

TRANSLATION (KJV) See TAKEN

TRANSPARENT (1)

Rev	21:21	of the city was of pure gold, like t glass.	1420

TRANSPLANTED (1) [PLANT]

Eze	17:10	Even if it is t, will it thrive?	9278

TRANSPORT (1)

Ge	46: 5	in the carts that Pharaoh had sent to t him.	5951

TRAP (25) [TRAPPED, TRAPS]

1Sa	28: 9	Why have you **set** a t for my life to bring	5943
Job	18: 9	A t seizes him by the heel;	7062
	18:10	a t lies in his path.	4892
	40:24	or t him and pierce his nose?	4613
Ps	31: 4	Free me from the t that is set for me,	8407
	69:22	may it become retribution and a t.	4613
Pr	20:25	a t for a man to dedicate something rashly	4613
	28:10	along an evil path will fall into his own t,	8819
Ecc	7:26	a t and whose hands are chains.	3052
Isa	8:14	the people of Jerusalem he will be a t and	7062
Jer	5:26	but in his heart he sets a t for him.	744
	50:24	I set a t for you, O Babylon,	3704
Am	3: 5	Does a bird fall into a t on the ground	7062
	3: 5	Does a t spring up from the earth	7062
Ob	1: 7	those who eat your bread will set a t	4650
Mt	22:15	and laid plans to t him in his words.	4074
	22:18	why are you **trying to t** me?	4279
Mk	12:15	"Why are you **trying to t** me?"	4279
Lk	11:26	unable to t him in what he had said there	2138
	21:34	will close on you unexpectedly like a t.	4075
Jn	8: 6	They were using this question as a t,	4279
Ro	11: 9	"May their table become a snare and a t,	2560
1Ti	3: 7	not fall into disgrace and into the devil's t.	4075
	6: 9	to get rich fall into temptation and a t and	4075
2Ti	2:26	to their senses and escape from the t of	4075

TRAPPED (8) [TRAP]

Pr	6: 2	if you have **been** t by what you said,	3704
	11: 6	but the unfaithful are t by evil desires.	4334
	12:13	An evil man is t by his sinful talk,	4613
Ecc	9:12	or birds are taken in a snare, so men are t	3704
Isa	42:22	of them t in pits or hidden away in prisons.	7072
Jer	8: 9	they will be dismayed and t.	4334
Eze	19: 4	and he was t in their pit.	9530
	19: 8	and he was t in their pit.	9530

TRAPS (6) [TRAP]

Jos	23:13	they will become snares and t for you,	4613
Ps	38:12	Those who seek my life set their t,	5943
	140: 5	the cords of their net and have set t for me	4613
	141: 9	from the t set by evildoers.	4613
Jer	5:26	and like those who set t to catch men.	5422
La	4:20	our very life breath, was caught in their t.	8827

TRAVAIL, TRAVAILED, TRAVAILEST, TRAVAILETH (KJV) See BIRTH, BURDEN, BUSINESS, HARDSHIP, HARDSHIPS, LABOR, MISFORTUNE, PAIN, PAINS, SUFFERING, TASK, TOIL

TRAVEL (9) [TRAVELED, TRAVELER, TRAVELERS, TRAVELING, TRAVELS]

Ex	13:21	so that they could t by day or night.	2143
Nu	20:17	We will t along the king's highway and	2143
	21:22	We will t along the king's highway	2143
2Ch	15: 5	In those days it was not safe to t about,	995+2256+3655
Job	21:29	you never questioned those who t?	2006+6296
Pr	4:15	Avoid it, do not t on it;	6296
Eze	39:11	in the valley of those who t east toward	6296
Mt	23:15	You t over land and sea to win a single convert,	4310
Rev	18:17	"Every sea captain, and all who t **by ship,**	4434

TRAVELED (36) [TRAVEL]

Ge	12: 6	Abram t through the land as far as the site	6296
	41:46	Pharaoh's presence and throughout Egypt.	
Ex	15:22	For three days they t in the desert	2143
Nu	10:12	t **from place to place** until the cloud came	5023
	10:33	mountain of the LORD and t for three days.	2006

Nu	11:35	the people t to Hazeroth and stayed there.	5825
	21: 4	They t from Mount Hor along the route to	5825
	22: 1	Then the Israelites t to the plains of Moab	5825
	33: 8	they had t for three days in the Desert	2006+2143
Dt	2: 8	and t along the desert road of Moab.	6296
	10: 6	(The Israelites t from the wells of	5825
	10: 7	From there they t to Gudgodah and on	5825
Jos	24:17	among all the nations through which we t.	6296
Jdg	11:18	"Next they t through the desert,	2143
2Sa	4: 7	they t all night by way of the Arabah.	2143
1Ki	19: 8	he t forty days and forty nights	2143
2Ki	5:19	After Naaman had t some distance,	2143
Isa	41: 3	by a path his feet have not t before.	995
Mk	1:39	So he t throughout Galilee.	2262
Lk	2:44	they t on for a day.	2262
	8: 1	Jesus t about from one town and village	1476
	10:33	But a Samaritan, as he t, came where	3841
	17:11	Jesus t along the border between Samaria	1451
Ac	8:36	As they t along the road,	4513
	8:40	however, appeared at Azotus and t about,	1451
	9:32	As Peter t about the country,	1328+1451+4246
	11:19	t as far as Phoenicia, Cyprus and Antioch,	1451
	13: 6	They t through the whole island	1451
	13:31	by those who had t with him from Galilee	5262
	15: 3	as they t through Phoenicia and Samaria,	1451
	16: 4	As they t from town to town,	1388
	16: 6	Paul and his companions t throughout	1451
	16:12	From there we t to Philippi,	NIG
	18:23	t from place to place throughout	1451
	20: 2	He t through that area,	1451
	28:15	and they t as far as the Forum of Appius	2262

TRAVELER (5) [TRAVEL]

Jdg	19:17	he looked and saw the t in the city square,	782
2Sa	12: 4	"Now a t came to the rich man,	2144
	12: 4	to prepare a meal for the t who had come	782
Job	31:32	for my door was always open to the t—	782
Jer	14: 8	like a t who stays only a night?	782

TRAVELERS (4) [TRAVEL]

Jdg	5: 6	t took to winding paths.	2143+5986
Isa	33: 8	no t are on the roads.	6296
Jer	9: 2	in the desert a lodging place for t,	782
Eze	39:11	It will block the way of t,	6296

TRAVELING (8) [TRAVEL]

Ex	14:19	who had been t in front of Israel's army,	2143
	17: 1	t from place to place as the LORD	5023
1Ki	18:27	Perhaps he is deep in thought, or busy, or t.	2006
Job	6:19	the t merchants of Sheba look in hope.	2142
Isa	60:15	with no one t through,	6296
Lk	14:25	Large crowds were t with Jesus,	5233
Ac	9: 7	The men t with Saul stood there speechless;	5321
	19:29	Paul's t companions from Macedonia,	5292

TRAVELS (4) [TRAVEL]

Ex	40:36	In all the t of the Israelites,	5023
	40:38	of all the house of Israel during all their t.	5023
Jer	2: 6	a land where no one t and no one lives?'	6296
	51:43	through which no man t.	6296

TRAVERSING (KJV) See RUNNING

TRAYS (3)

Ex	25:38	Its wick trimmers and t are to be	4746
	37:23	as well as its wick trimmers and t,	4746
Nu	4: 9	its wick trimmers and t,	4746

TREACHEROUS (7) [TREASON]

Ps	25: 3	be put to shame who are t without excuse.	953
Isa	24:16	Woe to me! The t betray!	953
	24:16	With treachery the t betray!"	953
	48: 8	Well do I know how t you are;	953+953
Hab	1:13	Why then do you tolerate the t?	953
Zep	3: 4	Her prophets are arrogant; they are t men.	956
2Ti	3: 4	t, rash, conceited, lovers of pleasure	4595

TREACHEROUSLY (2) [TREASON]

Jdg	9:23	Shechem, who acted t against Abimelech.	953
Ac	7:19	He dealt t with our people and oppressed	2947

TREACHERY (4) [TREASON]

Lev	26:40	their t against me and their hostility	5085+5086
2Ki	9:23	calling out to Ahaziah, "T, Ahaziah!"	5327
Isa	24:16	With t the treacherous betray!"	954
	59:13	rebellion and t against the LORD,	3950

TREAD (5) [TREADING, TREADS, TROD, TRODDEN]

Job	24:11	they t the winepresses, yet suffer thirst.	2005
Ps	91:13	You will t upon the lion and the cobra;	2005
Jer	25:30	He will shout like those who t the grapes,	2005
Mic	7:19	you will t our sins underfoot.	3899
Na	3:14	Work the clay, t the mortar,	8252

TREADING (7) [TREAD]

Dt	25: 4	an ox while it is t out the grain.	1889
Ne	13:15	in Judah t winepresses on the Sabbath	2005
Isa	41:25	as if he were a potter t the clay.	8252

Isa	63: 2	like those of one t the winepress?	2005
Am	9:13	and the planter by the one t grapes.	2005
1Co	9: 9	an ox while it is t out the grain."	262
1Ti	5:18	the ox while it is t out the grain,"	262

TREADS (7) [TREAD]

Job	9: 8	He alone stretches out the heavens and t on	2005
Isa	16:10	no one t out wine at the presses,	2005
	41:25	He t on rulers as if they were mortar,	995
Jer	48:33	no one t them with shouts of joy.	2005
Am	4:13	and t the high places of the earth—	2005
Mic	1: 3	he comes down and t the high places of	2005
Rev	19:15	He t the winepress of the fury of the wrath	4251

TREASON (4) [TRAITOR, TRAITORS, TREACHEROUS, TREACHEROUSLY, TREACHERY]

2Ki	11:14	Athaliah tore her robes and called out, "T!	8004
	11:14	and called out, "Treason! T!"	8004
2Ch	23:13	Athaliah tore her robes and shouted, "T!	8004
	23:13	and shouted, "Treason! T!"	8004

TREASURE (18) [TREASURED, TREASURER, TREASURERS, TREASURES, TREASURIES, TREASURY]

Ge	43:23	has given you t in your sacks;	4759
Job	3:21	who search for it more than for hidden t,	4759
	20:20	he cannot save himself by his t.	2773
Pr	2: 4	for silver and search for it as for hidden t,	4759
	15: 6	house of the righteous contains great t,	2890
Ecc	2: 8	and the t of kings and provinces.	6035
Isa	33: 6	the fear of the LORD is the key to this t.	238
	44: 9	and the things they t are worthless.	2773
Da	1: 2	in Babylonia and put in the t house	238
Mt	6:21	your t is, there your heart will be also.	2565
	13:44	"The kingdom of heaven is like t hidden in	2565
	19:21	and you will have t in heaven.	2565
Mk	10:21	and you will have t in heaven.	2565
Lk	12:33	a t in heaven that will not be exhausted,	2565
	12:34	your t is, there your heart will be also.	2565
	18:22	and you will have t in heaven.	2565
2Co	4: 7	But we have this t in jars of clay to show	2565
1Ti	6:19	In this way they will lay up t	631

TREASURED (11) [TREASURE]

Ex	19: 5	of all nations you will be my t possession.	6035
Dt	7: 6	the earth to be his people, his t possession.	6035
	14: 2	chosen you to be his t possession.	6035
	26:18	his t possession as he promised,	6035
Job	23:12	I have t the words of his mouth more than	7621
Ps	135: 4	Israel to be his t possession.	6035
Isa	64:11	and all that we t lies in ruins.	4718
Eze	7:22	and they will desecrate my t place;	7621
Mal	3:17	the day when I make up my t possession.	6035
Lk	2:19	But Mary t up all these things	5337
	2:51	his mother t all these things in her heart.	1413

TREASURER (1) [TREASURE]

Ezr	1: 8	had them brought by Mithredath the t,	1601

TREASURERS (5) [TREASURE]

2Ki	12: 5	receive the money from one of the t,	4837
	12: 7	Take no more money from your t,	4837
Ezr	7:21	the t of Trans-Euphrates to provide	10139
Da	3: 2	prefects, governors, advisers, t, judges,	10133
	3: 3	prefects, governors, advisers, t, judges,	10133

TREASURES (44) [TREASURE]

Dt	33:19	on the t hidden in the sand."	3243+8561
1Ki	14:26	the t of the temple of the LORD and	238
	14:26	the LORD and the t of the royal palace.	238
2Ki	20:13	and everything found among his t.	238
	20:15	"There is nothing among my t that I did	238
	24:13	the t from the temple of the LORD and	238
1Ch	29: 3	now give my personal t of gold and silver	6035
2Ch	12: 9	the t of the temple of the LORD and	238
	12: 9	the LORD and the t of the royal palace.	238
	25:24	together with the palace and the hostages,	238
	36:18	and the t of the LORD's temple,	238
	36:18	the LORD's temple and the t of the king	238
Job	20:26	total darkness lies in wait for his t.	7621
	28:10	his eyes see all its t.	3702
Pr	10: 2	Ill-gotten t are of no value,	238
	24: 4	its rooms are filled with rare and beautiful t.	2104
Isa	2: 7	there is no end to his t.	238
	10:13	I plundered their t;	6965
	30: 6	their t on the humps of camels,	238
	39: 2	and everything found among his t.	238
	39: 4	"There is nothing among my t that I did	238
	45: 3	I will give you the t of darkness,	238
Jer	15:13	Your wealth and your t I will give	238
	17: 3	and all your t I will give away as plunder,	238
	20: 5	all its valuables and all the t of the kings	238
	50:37	A sword against her t!	238
	51:13	who live by many waters and are rich in t,	238
La	1: 7	the t that were hers in days of old.	4719
	1:10	The enemy laid hands on all her t;	4718
	1:11	they barter their t for food	4718
Eze	22:25	they devour people, take t and precious	2890
Da	11:43	the t of gold and silver and all the riches	4819
Hos	9: 6	Their t of silver will be taken over	4718

Hos	13:15	will be plundered of all its t.	2775+3998
Joel	3: 5	and carried off my finest t to your temples.	4718
Ob	1: 6	will be ransacked, his hidden t pillaged!	5208
Mic	6:10	your ill-gotten t and the short ephah,	238
Na	2: 9	the wealth from all its t!	2775+3998
Mt	2:11	Then they opened their t and presented him	2565
	6:19	"Do not store up for yourselves t on earth,	2565
	6:20	But store up for yourselves t in heaven,	2565
	13:52	of his storeroom new t as well as old."	NIG
Col	2: 3	in whom are hidden all the t of wisdom	2565
Heb	11:26	as of greater value than the t of Egypt,	2565

TREASURIES (20) [TREASURE]

1Ki	7:51	in the t of the LORD's temple.	238
	15:18	the silver and gold that was left in the t of	238
2Ki	12:18	in the t of the temple of the LORD and of	238
	14:14	in the temple of the LORD and in the t of	238
	16: 8	the LORD and in the t of the royal palace	238
	18:15	in the temple of the LORD and in the t of	238
1Ch	9:26	with the responsibility for the rooms and t	238
	26:20	in charge of the t of the house of God and	238
	26:20	the treasuries of the house of God and the t	238
	26:22	They were in charge of the t of the temple	238
	26:24	was the officer in charge of the t.	238
	26:26	and his relatives were in charge of all the t	238
	28:12	for the t of the temple of God and for	238
	28:12	of the temple of God and for the t for	238
2Ch	5: 1	he placed them in the t of God's temple.	238
	8:15	including that of the t.	238
	16: 2	then took the silver and gold out of the t of	238
	32:27	and he made t for his silver and gold and	238
Pr	8:21	and making their t full.	238
Eze	28: 4	and amassed gold and silver in your t.	238

TREASURY (19) [TREASURE]

Jos	6:19	sacred to the LORD and must go into his t."	238
	6:24	the articles of bronze and iron into the t of	238
1Ch	29: 8	gave them to the t of the temple of the LORD	238
Ezr	2:69	gave to the t of the work this amount:	10148
	6: 1	in the archives stored in the t at Babylon.	10148
	6: 4	The costs are to be paid by the royal t.	10103
	6: 8	to be fully paid out of the royal t,	10103
	7:20	you may provide from the royal t.	10103+10148
Ne	7:70	The governor gave to the t 1,000 drachmas	238
	7:71	the heads of the families gave to the t for	238
	10:38	to the storerooms of the t.	238+1074
Est	3: 9	of silver into the royal t for the men	1709
	4: 7	the royal t for the destruction of the Jews.	1709
Jer	38:11	with him and went to a room under the t in	238
Mt	27: 6	"It is against the law to put this into the t,	3168
Mk	12:41	putting their money into the temple t.	1126
	12:43	poor widow has put more into the t than all	1126
Lk	21: 1	the rich putting their gifts into the temple t.	1126
Ac	8:27	an important official in charge of all the t	1125

TREAT (31) [TREATED, TREATING, TREATMENT, TREATMENTS, TREATS]

Ge	19: 9	We'll t you worse than them."	8317
	30:20	This time my husband will t me with honor	2290
Lev	22: 2	"Tell Aaron and his sons to t with respect	5692
Nu	10:29	Come with us and we will t you well,	3512
	11:15	If this is how you are going to t me,	6913
	14:11	will these people t me with contempt?	5540
	25:17	"T the Midianites as enemies and kill them,	7675
Dt	20:15	how you are to t all the cities that are at	6913
	21:14	You must not sell her or t her as a slave,	6683
Jos	2:14	we will t you kindly and faithfully when	6913
2Sa	19:43	So why do you t us with contempt?	7837
Job	6:26	t the words of a despairing man as wind?	NIH
Ps	103:10	not t us as our sins deserve or repay us	6913
Jer	3:19	" 'How gladly would I t you like sons	8883
	29:22	'The LORD t you like Zedekiah	8492
	34:18	I will t like the calf they cut in two and	5989
Eze	15: 6	so will I t the people living in Jerusalem.	5989
	35:11	I will t you in accordance with the anger	6913
	35:15	that is how I will t you.	6913
Da	1:13	and t your servants in accordance	6913
Hos	11: 8	How can I t you like Admah?	5989
Na	3: 6	I will t you with contempt and make you	5571
Mt	18:17	the church, t him as you would a pagan or	1639
	18:35	how my heavenly Father will t each	4472
Jn	15:21	They will t you this way because	1650+4472
1Co	12:23	that we think are less honorable we t with	4363
Gal	4:14	you did not t me with contempt or scorn.	2024
Eph	6: 9	masters, t your slaves in the same way.	4472
1Th	5:20	do not t prophecies with contempt.	2024
1Ti	5: 1	T younger men as brothers,	NIG
1Pe	3: 7	t them with respect as the weaker partner	671

TREATED (38) [TREAT]

Ge	12:13	so that I will be t well for your sake and	3512
	12:16	He t Abram well for her sake,	3512
	26:29	but always t you well and sent you away	6913
	34:31	"Should he have t our sister like a	6913
	39:19	saying, "This is how your slave t me,"	6913
	42:30	to us and t us as though we were spying on	5989
Ex	5:15	"Why have you t your servants this way?	6913
	1:14	to those who had t Israel arrogantly."	2326
Lev	19:34	The alien living with you must be t as one	2118
	25:40	He is to be t as a hired worker or	6913
	25:53	to be t as a man hired from year to	2118+6640
Nu	14:23	No one who has t me with contempt will	5540
		ever see it.	
	16:30	these men have t the LORD with contempt."	5540

Nu	25:18	because they t you **as enemies**	7675
Jdg	1:24	and *we will see that* you *are* t well."	6913
	8: 1	"Why **have** you t us like this?	6913
	9:16	and if *you* **have** t him as he deserves—	6913
1Sa	2:14	how *they* t all the Israelites who came	6913
	6: 6	When *he* t them **harshly,**	6618
	24:17	"You **have** t me well,	1694
	24:17	but I **have** t you badly.	1694
	24:19	for the way *you* t me today.	6913
1Ki	1:21	I and my son Solomon *will* **be** t as criminals	2118
1Ch	24:31	the oldest brother were t **the same as**	4200+6645
Ne	9:10	how **arrogantly** the Egyptians t them.	2326
La	2:20	Whom **have** you **ever** t like this?	6618
Eze	22: 7	t father and mother **with contempt;**	7837
Mt	21:36	and the tenants t them the same way.	4472
Mk	12: 4	on the head and t him **shamefully.**	870
Lk	6:23	"Son, why **have** you t us like this?	4472
	6:23	For that is how their fathers t the prophets.	4472
	6:26	how their fathers t the false prophets.	4472
	20:11	that one also they beat and t **shamefully.**	869
1Co	4:11	*we are* **brutally** t, we are homeless.	3139
	12:23	the parts that are unpresentable *are* t **with**	2400
Heb	10:29	**who** *has* t as an unholy thing the blood of	2451
	10:33	by side *with* those who *were* so t.	418
Rev	18:20	God has judged her for the **way** she t you.'	3210S

TREATING (6) [TREAT]

Ge	18:25	t the righteous and the wicked alike.	2118
	50:17	and the wrongs *they* **committed** *in* t you	AIT
Lev	22: 9	t them **with contempt.**	2725
1Sa	2:17	t the LORD's offering **with contempt.**	5540
	25:39	against Nabal for t me with contempt.	NIH
Heb	12: 7	God *is* t you as sons.	4712

TREATISE   (KJV) See BOOK

TREATMENT (4) [TREAT]

1Sa	20:34	grieved at his father's **shameful** t *of* David.	4007
Isa	66: 4	so I also will choose **harsh** t *for* them	9500
1Co	12:24	our presentable parts need no **special** t.	5507
Col	2:23	false humility and their **harsh** t of the body,	910

TREATMENTS (3) [TREAT]

Est	2: 3	and let **beauty** t be given to them.	9475
	2: 9	with her **beauty** t and special food.	9475
	2:12	of **beauty** t prescribed for the women,	5299

TREATS (4) [TREAT]

Dt	24: 7	and t him **as a slave** or sells him,	6683
Job	39:16	*She* t her young **harshly,**	7996
	41:27	Iron *he* t like straw and bronze like rotten	3108
Pr	27:11	answer *anyone who* t me **with contempt.**	3070

TREATY (31)

Ge	21:27	and the two men made a t.	1382
	21:32	After the t had been made at Beersheba,	1382
	26:28	Let us make a t with you	1382
Ex	34:12	to make a t with those who live in the land	1382
	34:15	to make a t with those who live in the land;	1382
Dt	7: 2	Make no t with them,	1382
	23: 6	not seek a t of **friendship** *with* them as long as you live.	2256+3208+8934
Jos	9: 6	make a t with us."	1382
	9: 7	How then can we make a t with you?"	1382
	9:11	"We are your servants; make a t with us."	1382
	9:15	Then Joshua made a t of peace with them	1382
	9:16	after they made the t with the Gibeonites.	1382
	10: 1	Gibeon *had* **made a** t **of peace** with Israel	8966
	11:19	not one city **made a** t **of peace** with the	8966
1Sa	11: 1	"Make a t with us, and we will be subject	1382
	11: 2	"*I will* **make a** t with you only on the	4162
1Ki	5:12	and the two of them made a t.	1382
	15:19	"Let there be a t between you and me,"	1382
	15:19	Now break your t with Baasha king	1382
	20:34	"On the basis of a t I will set you free."	1382
	20:34	So he made a t with him, and let him go.	1382
2Ch	16: 3	"Let there be a t between me and you	1382
	16: 3	Now break your t with Baasha king	1382
Ezr	9:12	Do not seek a t **of friendship** *with* them at any time,	2256+3208+8934
Isa	33: 8	The t is broken, its witnesses are despised.	1382
Eze	17:13	a member of the royal family and made a t	1382
	17:14	surviving only by keeping his t.	1382
	17:15	Will he break the t and yet escape?	1382
	17:18	oath he despised and whose t he broke.	1382
Hos	12: 1	He makes a t with Assyria and sends	1382
Am	1: 9	disregarding a t *of* brotherhood,	1382

TREE (180) [TREES]

Ge	1:29	of the whole earth and every t that has fruit	6770
	2: 9	the garden were the t *of* life and the tree of	6770
	2: 9	the garden were the tree of life and the t *of*	6770
	2:16	"You are free to eat from any t *in*	6770
	2:17	the t *of* the knowledge of good and evil,	6770
	3: 1	not eat from any t *in* the garden'?"	6770
	3: 3	'You must not eat from the fruit of the t that is *in*	6770
	3: 6	of the t was good for food and pleasing to	6770
	3:11	from the t that I commanded you not	6770
	3:12	she gave me some fruit from the t,	6770
	3:17	from the t about which I commanded you,	6770
	3:22	and take also from the t *of* life and eat,	6770
	3:24	and forth to guard the way to the t *of* life.	6770

Ge	12: 6	as far as the site of the **great** t *of* Moreh	471
	18: 4	wash your feet and rest under this t.	6770
	18: 8	he stood near them under a t.	6770
	21:33	Abraham planted a **tamarisk** t in Beersheba.	869
	40:19	lift off your head and hang you on a t.	6770
Ex	9:25	in the fields and stripped every t.	6770
	10: 5	including every t that is growing	6770
	10:15	Nothing green remained on t or plant in all	6770
Lev	19:23	the land and plant any kind of fruit t,	6770
Dt	12: 2	the hills and under every spreading t where	6770
	19: 5	and as he swings his ax to fell a t,	6770
	21:22	to death and his body is hung on a t,	6770
	21:23	not leave his body on the t overnight.	6770
	21:23	who is hung on a t is under God's curse.	NIH
	22: 6	either in a t or on the ground,	6770
Jos	8:29	the king of Ai on a t and left there	6770
	8:29	the t and throw it down at the entrance of	6770
	19:33	and the **large** t in Zaanannim,	471
Jdg	4:11	by the **great** t in Zaanannim near Kedesh.	471
	9: 6	and Beth Millo gathered beside the **great** t	471
	9: 8	They said to the **olive** t, 'Be our king.'	2339
	9: 9	"But the **olive** t answered,	2339
	9:10	"Next, the trees said to the **fig** t,	9300
	9:11	"But the **fig** t replied,	9300
	9:37	from the direction of the soothsayers' t."	471
1Sa	10: 3	on from there until you reach the **great** t	471
	14: 2	under a **pomegranate** t in Migron.	8232
	22: 6	was seated under the **tamarisk** t on the hill	869
	31:13	and buried them under a **tamarisk** t	869
2Sa	18: 9	Absalom's head got caught in the t.	461
	18:10	"I just saw Absalom hanging in an **oak** t."	461
	18:14	while Absalom was still alive in the **oak** t.	461
1Ki	4:25	each man under his own vine and **fig** t.	9300
	13:14	He found him sitting under an **oak** t	461
	14:23	every high hill and under every spreading t.	6770
	19: 4	He came to a **broom** t, sat down under it	8413
	19: 5	he lay down under the t and fell asleep.	8413
2Ki	3:19	You will cut down every good t,	6770
	3:25	the springs and cut down every good t.	6770
	6: 5	As one of them was cutting down a t,	7771
	16: 4	the hilltops and under every spreading t.	6770
	17:10	every high hill and under every spreading t.	6770
	18:31	of you will eat from his own vine and **fig** t	9300
1Ch	10:12	their bones under the **great** t in Jabesh,	461
2Ch	3: 5	**palm** t and chain **designs.**	9474
Ne	10:35	of our crops and of every fruit t.	6770
Job	14: 7	"At least there is hope for a t:	6770
	15:33	like an **olive** t shedding its blossoms.	2339
	19:10	he uproots my hope like a t.	6770
	24:20	but are broken like a t.	6770
	30: 4	and their food was the root of the **broom** t.	8413
Ps	1: 3	He is like a t planted by streams of water,	6770
	37:35	and ruthless man flourishing like a **green** t	8316
	52: 8	like an **olive** t flourishing in the house	2339
	92:12	The righteous will flourish like a **palm** t,	9469
	120: 4	with burning coals of the **broom** t.	8413
Pr	3:18	She is a t *of* life to those who embrace her;	6770
	11:30	The fruit of the righteous is a t *of* life,	6770
	13:12	but a longing fulfilled is a t *of* life.	6770
	15: 4	tongue that brings healing is a t *of* life,	6770
	27:18	He who tends a **fig** t will eat its fruit,	9300
Ecc	11: 3	a t falls to the south or to the north,	6770
	12: 5	when the **almond** t blossoms and	9196
SS	2: 3	Like an **apple** t among the trees of	9515
	2:13	The **fig** t forms its early fruit;	9300
	4:14	with every kind of incense t,	6770
	7: 8	I said, "I will climb the **palm** t;	9469
	8: 5	Under the **apple** t I roused you;	9515
Isa	17: 6	as when an **olive** t is beaten,	2339
	24:13	as when an **olive** t is beaten,	2339
	34: 4	like shriveled figs from the **fig** t.	9300
	36:16	of you will eat from his own vine and **fig** t	9300
	55:13	of the thornbush will grow the **pine** t,	1360
	56: 3	"I am only a dry t."	6770
	57: 5	the oaks and under every spreading t;	6770
	65:22	For as the days of a t,	6770
Jer	1:11	"I see the branch of an **almond** t," I replied.	9196
	2:20	and under every spreading t you lay down	6770
	3: 6	and under every spreading t and has	6770
	3:13	to foreign gods under every spreading t,	6770
	8:13	There will be no figs on the t,	9300
	10: 3	they cut a t out of the forest,	6770
	11:16	The LORD called you a thriving **olive** t	2339
	11:19	saying, "Let us destroy the t and its fruit;	6770
	11:19	He will be a t planted by the water	6770
Eze	6:13	under every spreading t and every leafy oak	6770
	17:24	the LORD bring down the tall t and make	6770
	17:24	the tall tree and make the low t grow tall.	6770
	17:24	the green t and make the dry tree flourish.	6770
	17:24	the green tree and make the dry t flourish.	6770
	20:28	and they saw any high hill or any leafy t,	6770
	31: 8	no t in the garden of God could match	6770
	31:13	the birds of the air settled on the fallen t,	NIH
	40:22	its portico and its **palm** t decorations had	9474
	40:26	it had **palm** t decorations on the faces of	9474
	41:19	toward the **palm** t on one side and the face	9474
	41:19	and the face of a lion toward the **palm** t on	9474
	41:19	and there before me stood a t in the middle	10027
Da	4:10	The t grew large and strong and its top	10027
	4:11	'Cut down the t and trim off its branches;	10027
	4:20	The t you saw, which grew large and	10027
	4:22	O king, are **that** t!	10200S
	4:23	'Cut down the t and destroy it,	10027
	4:26	The command to leave the stump of the t	10027
Hos	9:10	like seeing the early fruit on the **fig** t.	9300
	14: 6	His splendor will be like an **olive** t,	2339

Hos	14: 8	I am like a green **pine** t;	1360
Joel	1:12	vine is dried up and the **fig** t is withered;	9300
	1:12	pomegranate, the palm and the **apple** t—	9515
	2:22	the **fig** t and the vine yield their riches.	9300
Mic	4: 4	and under his own **fig** t,	9300
Hab	3:17	Though the **fig** t does not bud	9300
Hag	2:19	Until now, the vine and the **fig** t,	9300
	2:19	the pomegranate and the olive t have	6770
Zec	3:10	to sit under his vine and **fig** t,'	9300
	11: 2	Wail, O **pine** t, for the cedar has fallen;	1360
Mt	3:10	and every t that does not produce good fruit	1285
	7:17	Likewise every good t bears good fruit,	1285
	7:17	but a bad t bears bad fruit.	1285
	7:18	A good t cannot bear bad fruit,	1285
	7:18	and a bad t cannot bear good fruit.	1285
	7:19	Every t that does not bear good fruit is cut	1285
	12:33	"Make a t good and its fruit will be good,	1285
	12:33	or make a t bad and its fruit will be bad,	1285
	12:33	for a t is recognized by its fruit.	1285
	13:32	largest of garden plants and becomes a t,	1285
	21:19	Seeing a **fig** t by the road,	5190
	21:19	Immediately the t withered.	5190
	21:20	"How did the **fig** t wither so quickly?"	5190
	21:21	can you do what was done *to* the **fig** t,	5190
	24:32	"Now learn this lesson from the **fig** t:	5190
Mk	11:13	Seeing in the distance a **fig** t in leaf,	5190
	11:14	Then he said *to* the t, "May no one ever	899S
	11:20	they saw the **fig** t withered from the roots.	5190
	11:21	The **fig** t you cursed has withered!"	5190
	13:28	"Now learn this lesson from the **fig** t:	5190
Lk	3: 9	and every t that does not produce good fruit	1285
	6:43	"No good t bears bad fruit,	1285
	6:43	nor does a bad t bear good fruit.	1285
	6:44	Each t is recognized by its own fruit.	1285
	13: 6	"A man had a **fig** t,	5190
	13: 7	on this **fig** t and haven't found any.	5190
	13:19	It grew and became a t,	1285
	17: 6	you can say *to* this **mulberry** t,	5189
	19: 4	and climbed a **sycamore-fig** t to see him,	5191
	21:29	"Look at the **fig** t and all the trees.	5190
	23:31	if men do these things when the t is green,	3833
Jn	1:48	under the **fig** t before Philip called you."	5190
	1:50	because I told you I saw you under the **fig** t.	5190
Ac	5:30	whom you had killed by hanging him on a t.	3833
	10:39	They killed him by hanging him on a t,	3833
	13:29	down from the t and laid him in a tomb.	3833
Ro	11:24	you were cut out of an **olive** t *that is* wild	66
	11:24	were grafted into a **cultivated olive** t,	2814
	11:24	be grafted into their own **olive** t!	1777
Gal	3:13	"Cursed is everyone who is hung on a t."	3833
Jas	3:12	My brothers, can a **fig** t bear olives,	5190
1Pe	2:24	bore our sins in his body on the t,	3833
Rev	2: 7	I will give the right to eat from the t of life,	3833
	6:13	*from* a **fig** t when shaken by a strong wind.	899S
	7: 1	on the land or on the sea or on any t.	1285
	9: 4	the grass of the earth or any plant or t,	1285
	22: 2	On each side of the river stood the t of life,	3833
	22: 2	And the leaves of the t are for the healing	3833
	22:14	that they may have the right to the t of life	3833
	22:19	from him his share in the t of life and in	3833

TREES (137) [TREE]

Ge	1:11	and t on the land that bear fruit with seed	6770
	1:12	and bearing fruit with seed in it according	6770
	2: 9	of t grow out of the ground—	6770
	2: 9	t that were pleasing to the eye and good	NIH
	3: 2	"We may eat fruit from the t in the garden,	6770
	3: 8	from the LORD God among the t *of*	6770
	13:18	and went to live near the **great** t *of* Mamre	471
	14:13	near the **great** t *of* Mamre the Amorite,	471
	18: 1	the **great** t *of* Mamre while he was sitting	471
	23:17	all the t within the borders of the field—	6770
	30:37	and **plane** t and made white stripes	6895
Ex	10:15	in the fields and the fruit on the t.	6770
	15:27	twelve springs and seventy **palm** t,	9469
Lev	23:40	to take choice fruit from the t,	6770
	26: 4	the ground will yield its crops and the t *of*	6770
	26:20	nor will the t *of* the land yield their fruit.	6770
	27:30	from the soil or fruit from the t, belongs to	6770
Nu	13:20	Are there t on it or not?	6770
	33: 9	twelve springs and seventy **palm** t,	9469
Dt	8: 8	vines and **fig** t, pomegranates,	9300
	11:30	near the **great** t *of* Moreh.	471
	20:19	not destroy its t by putting an ax to them,	6770
	20:19	Are the t of the field people,	6770
	20:20	down t that you know are not fruit trees	6770
	20:20	that you know are not fruit t and use them	6770
	24:20	When you beat the **olives from** your t,	2339
	28:40	You will have **olive** t throughout your	2339
	28:42	Swarms of locusts will take over all your t	6770
Jos	10:26	the kings and hung them on five t,	6770
	10:26	and they were left hanging on the t	6770
	10:26	from the t and threw them into the cave	6770
Jdg	9: 8	One day the t went out to anoint a king	6770
	9: 9	to hold sway over the t?'	6770
	9:10	"Next, the t said to the fig tree,	6770
	9:11	to hold sway over the t?'	6770
	9:12	t said to the vine, 'Come and be our king.'	6770
	9:13	to hold sway over the t?'	6770
	9:14	"Finally all the t said to the thornbush,	6770
	9:15	"The thornbush said to the t,	6770
2Sa	5:23	and attack them in front of the **balsam** t.	1132
	5:24	of marching in the tops of the **balsam** t,	1132
1Ki	6:29	**palm** t and open flowers,	9474
	6:32	**palm** t and open flowers,	9474
	6:32	the cherubim and **palm** t with beaten gold.	9474

1Ki	6:35	palm t and open flowers on them	9474

```
1Ki   6:35  palm t and open flowers on them               9474
      7:36  and palm t on the surfaces of the supports    9474
     10:27  and cedar as plentiful as sycamore-fig t in    9204
2Ki   6: 4  to the Jordan and began to cut down t.         6770
     18:32  a land of olive t and honey.             2339+3658
1Ch  14:14  and attack them in front of the balsam t.      1132
     14:15  of marching in the tops of the balsam t,       1132
     16:33  Then the t of the forest will sing             6770
     27:28  in charge of the olive and sycamore-fig t in   9204
2Ch   1:15  and cedar as plentiful as sycamore-fig t in    9204
      9:27  and cedar as plentiful as sycamore-fig t in    9204
Ne    8:15  and wild olive t, and branches from            6770
      8:15  palms and shade t, to make booths"—            6770
      9:25  olive groves and fruit t in abundance.         6770
     10:37  of the fruit of all our t and of our new wine  6770
Ps   74: 5  to cut through a thicket of t.                 6770
     96:12  all the t of the forest will sing for joy;     6770
    104:16  The t of the LORD are well watered,            6770
    104:17  the stork has its home in the pine t.          1360
    105:33  down their vines and fig t and shattered       9300
    105:33  and shattered the t of their country.          6770
    148: 9  and all hills, fruit t and all cedars,         6770
Ecc   2: 5  and parks and planted all kinds of fruit t     6770
      2: 6  to water groves of flourishing t.              6770
SS    2: 3  the t of the forest is my lover among          6770
      6:11  I went down to the grove of nut t to look       100
Isa   7: 2  the t of the forest are shaken by the wind.    6770
      9:10  the fig t have been felled,                    9204
     10:19  And the remaining t of his forests will be     6770
     10:33  the lofty t will be felled,              7757+8123
     14: 8  the pine t and the cedars of Lebanon exult     1360
     44: 4  like poplar t by flowing streams.             6857
     44:14  He let it grow among the t of the forest,      6770
     44:23  you mountains, you forests and all your t,     6770
     55:12  all the t of the field will clap their hands.  6770
Jer   5:17  devour your vines and fig t.                   9300
      6: 6  "Cut down the t and build siege ramps          6785
      7:20  on this place, on man and beast, on the t of   6770
     17: 2  and Asherah poles beside the spreading t       6770
     46:22  like men who cut down t.                       6770
Eze  15: 2  of a branch on any of the t in the forest?     6770
     15: 6  the vine among the t of the forest as fuel     6770
     17:24  All the t of the field will know that I        6770
     20:47  and it will consume all your t,                6770
     27: 5  They made all your timbers of pine t           1360
     31: 4  and sent their channels to all the t of        6770
     31: 5  So it towered higher than all the t of         6770
     31: 8  nor could the pine t equal its boughs,         1360
     31: 8  the plane t compare with its branches—         6895
     31: 9  the envy of all the t of Eden in the garden    6770
     31:14  Therefore no other t by the waters are ever    6770
     31:14  No other t so well-watered are ever            NIH
     31:15  and all the t of the field withered away.      6770
     31:16  Then all the t of Eden,                        6770
     31:16  all the t that were well-watered,              NIH
     31:18  of the t of Eden can be compared with you      6770
     31:18  will be brought down with the t of Eden to     6770
     34:27  The t of the field will yield their fruit and  6770
     36:30  the fruit of the t and the crops of the field, 6770
     40:16  walls were decorated with palm t.             9474
     40:31  palm t decorated its jambs,                   9474
     40:34  palm t decorated the jambs on either side,    9474
     40:37  palm t decorated the jambs on either side,    9474
     41:18  were carved cherubim and palm t.              9474
     41:18  Palm t alternated with cherubim.              9474
     41:20  and palm t were carved on the wall of         9474
     41:25  and palm t like those carved on the walls,    9474
     41:26  with palm t carved on each side.              9474
     47: 7  I saw a great number of t on each side of      6770
     47:12  Fruit t of all kinds will grow on both banks   6770
Hos   2:12  I will ruin her vines and her fig t,           9300
Joel  1: 7  laid waste my vines and ruined my fig t.       9300
      1:12  all the t of the field—are dried up.           6770
      1:19  flames have burned up all the t of the field.  6770
      2:22  The t are bearing their fruit;                 6770
Am    4: 9  Locusts devoured your fig and olive t,         2339
      7:14  and I also took care of sycamore-fig t.        9204
Na    3:12  like fig t with their first ripe fruit;        9300
Zec   1: 8  He was standing among the myrtle t in          2072
      1:10  among the myrtle t explained,                  2072
      1:11  who was standing among the myrtle t,           2072
      4: 3  Also there are two olive t by it,              2339
      4:11  "What are these two olive t on the right       2339
     11: 2  the stately t are ruined!                      NIH
Mt    3:10  The ax is already at the root of the t,        1285
     21: 8  from the t and spread them on the road.        1285
Mk    8:24  they look like t walking around."              1285
Lk    3: 9  The ax is already at the root of the t,        1285
     21:29  "Look at the fig tree and all the t.           1285
Jude  1:12  autumn t, without fruit and uprooted—          1285
Rev   7: 1  the t until we put a seal on the foreheads of  1285
      8: 7  a third of the t were burned up,               1285
     11: 4  the two olive t and the two lampstands         1777
```

TREMBLE (39) [TREMBLED, TREMBLES, TREMBLING]

```
Ex   15:14  The nations will hear and t;                   8074
Dt    2:25  They will hear reports of you and will t       8074
1Ch  16:30  T before him, all the earth!                   2655
Job   9: 6  from its place and makes its pillars t         7145
Ps   96: 9  t before him, all the earth.                   2655
     99: 1  The LORD reigns, let the nations t;            8074
    114: 7  T, O earth, at the presence of the Lord,       2655
Ecc  12: 3  of the house t, and the strong men stoop,      2316
Isa  13:13  Therefore I will make the heavens t;           8074
     14:16  who shook the earth and made kingdoms t,       8321
     19: 1  The idols of Egypt t before him,               5675
     21: 4  My heart falters, fear makes me t;             1286
     23:11  over the sea and made its kingdoms t.          8074
     32:10  a year you who feel secure will t;             8074
     32:11  T, you complacent women;                       3006
     41: 5  the ends of the earth t.                       3006
     44: 8  Do not t, do not be afraid.                    7064
     64: 1  that the mountains would t before you!         2362
     66: 5  you who t at his word:                         3007
Jer   5:22  "Should you not t in my presence?              2655
     23: 9  heart is broken within me; all my bones t.     8173
     33: 9  and will t at the abundant prosperity          8074
     49:21  At the sound of their fall the earth will t;   8321
     50:46  of Babylon's capture the earth will t;         8321
Eze   7:27  the hands of the people of the land will t.     987
     12:18  t as you eat your food,                        8323
     26:10  Your walls will t at the noise of the war      8321
     26:15  the coastlands t at the sound of your fall,    8321
     26:18  the coastlands t on the day of your fall;      3006
     31:16  I made the nations t at the sound of its fall  8321
     32:10  of them will t every moment for his life.      3006
     38:20  the face of the earth will t at my presence.   8321
Joel  2: 1  Let all who live in the land t,                8074
      3:16  the earth and the sky will t.                  8321
Am    3: 6  do not the people t?                           3006
      8: 8  "Will not the land t for this,                 8074
Na    2:10  Hearts melt, knees give way, bodies t,         2714
Hab   2: 7  Will they not wake up and make you t?          2316
      3: 6  he looked, and made the nations t.             6001
```

TREMBLED (16) [TREMBLE]

```
Ge   27:33  Isaac t violently     1524+3006+3010+4394+6330
Ex   19:16  Everyone in the camp t.                        3006
     19:18  the whole mountain t violently,                3006
     20:18  saw the mountain in smoke, they t with fear.   5675
1Sa  16: 4  of the town t when they met him.               3006
     21: 1  Ahimelech t when he met him, and asked,        3006
2Sa  22: 8  "The earth t and quaked,                       1723
     22: 8  they t because he was angry.                   1723
Ezr   9: 4  everyone who t at the words of the God of      3007
Ps   18: 7  The earth t and quaked,                        1723
     18: 7  they t because he was angry.                   1723
     77:18  the earth t and quaked.                        8074
Isa  64: 3  and the mountains t before you.                2362
Hos  13: 1  When Ephraim spoke, men t;                     8417
Hab   3:16  decay crept into my bones, and my legs t.      8074
Ac    7:32  Moses t with fear and did not dare to look.
                                                      1181+1958
```

TREMBLES (13) [TREMBLE]

```
Jdg   7: 3  'Anyone who t with fear may turn back          3007
Ps   97: 4  the earth sees and t.                          2655
    104:32  and it t, who touches the mountains,           8283
    119:120 My flesh t in fear of you;                     6169
    119:161 but my heart t at your word.                   7064
Pr   30:21  "Under three things the earth t,               8074
Isa  10:29  Ramah t; Gibeah of Saul flees.                 3006
     66: 2  and contrite in spirit, and t at my word.      3007
Jer   8:16  of their stallions the whole land t.           8321
     10:10  When he is angry, the earth t;                 8321
     51:29  The land t and writhes,                        8321
Joel  2:10  Before them the earth shakes, the sky t,       8321
Na    1: 5  The earth t at his presence,                   5951
```

TREMBLING (25) [TREMBLE]

```
Ge   42:28  and they turned to each other t and said,      3006
Ex   15:15  the leaders of Moab will be seized with t,     8284
2Sa  22:46  they come t from their strongholds.            3004
Job   4:14  fear and t seized me and made all my bones     8285
     21: 6  I am terrified; t seizes my body.              7146
Ps    2:11  the LORD with fear and rejoice with t.         8285
     18:45  they come t from their strongholds.            3004
     48: 6  T seized them there,                           8285
     55: 5  Fear and t have beset me;                      8284
Isa  33:14  t grips the godless:                           8285
Eze  26:16  t every moment, appalled at you.               3006
Da   10:10  and set me t on my hands and knees.            5675
     10:11  And when he said this to me, I stood up t.     8283
Hos   3: 5  They will come t to the LORD and               7064
     11:10  his children will come t from the west.        3006
     11:11  They will come t like birds from Egypt,        3006
Mic   7:17  They will come t out of their dens;            8074
Mk    5:33  came and fell at his feet and, t with fear,    5554
     16: 8  T and bewildered, the women went out and
            fled from the tomb.                 899+2400+5571
Lk    8:47  came t and fell at his feet.                   5554
Ac   16:29  and fell t before Paul and Silas.       1181+1958
1Co   2: 3  in weakness and fear, and with much t.         5571
2Co   7:15  receiving him with fear and t.                 5571
Php   2:12  to work out your salvation with fear and t,    5571
Heb  12:21  that Moses said, "I am t with fear."           1958
```

TREMENDOUS (1)

```
Rev  16:18  has been on earth, so t was the quake.   3489+5496
```

TRENCH (4)

```
1Ki  18:32  and he dug a t around it large enough          9498
     18:35  down around the altar and even filled the t.   9498
     18:38  and also licked up the water in the t.         9498
Da    9:25  It will be rebuilt with streets and a t,       3022
```

TRESPASS (5) [TRESPASSES]

```
Ro    5:15  But the gift is not like the t.                4183
      5:15  if the many died by the t of the one man,      4183
      5:17  For if, by the t of the one man,               4183
      5:18  as the result of one t was condemnation        4183
      5:20  so that the t might increase.                  4183
```

TRESPASSES (1) [TRESPASS]

```
Ro    5:16  but the gift followed many t and brought       4183
```

TRESSES (1)

```
SS    7: 5  the king is held captive by its t.             8111
```

TRIAL (19) [TRIALS]

```
Nu   35:12  of murder may not die before he stands t       5477
Jos  20: 6  He is to stay in that city until he has stood t 5477
     20: 9  by the avenger of blood prior to standing t    6641
Ps   37:33  be condemned when brought to t.                9149
Mk   13:11  Whenever you are arrested and brought to t,      72
Ac   12: 4  to bring him out for public t after            NIG
     12: 6  before Herod was to bring him to t,            NIG
     16:37  "They beat us publicly without a t,             185
     23: 6  I stand on trial because of my hope in         3212
     24:21  the dead that I am on t before you today.' "   3212
     25: 9  to Jerusalem and stand t before me there       3212
     25:20  to go to Jerusalem and stand t there           3212
     26: 6  that I am on t today,                     2705+3212
     27:24  You must stand t before Caesar;                4225
2Co   8: 2  Out of the most severe t,                1509+2568
Gal   4:14  Even though my illness was a t to you,         4280
Jas   1:12  the man who perseveres under t,                4280
1Pe   4:12  at the painful t you are suffering,            4280
Rev   3:10  the hour of t that is going to come upon       4280
```

TRIALS (8) [TRIAL]

```
Dt    7:19  You saw with your own eyes the great t,        4999
     29: 3  With your own eyes you saw those great t,      4999
Lk   22:28  those who have stood by me in my t.            4280
1Th   3: 3  that no one would be unsettled by these t.     2568
2Th   1: 4  the persecutions and t you are enduring,       2568
Jas   1: 2  whenever you face t of many kinds,             4280
1Pe   1: 6  have had to suffer grief in all kinds of t.    4280
2Pe   2: 9  Lord knows how to rescue godly men from t      4280
```

TRIBAL (18) [TRIBE]

```
Ge   25:16  the names of the twelve t rulers according      569
Nu    4:18  the Kohathite t clans are not cut off from     8657
      7: 2  heads of families who were the t leaders       4751
     25:15  Zur, a t chief of a Midianite family.           569
     36: 4  from the t inheritance of our forefathers."    4751
     36: 6  as long as they marry within the t clan        4751
     36: 7  the t land inherited from his forefathers.     4751
     36: 8  must marry someone in her father's t clan,     4751
Dt    1:15  of fifties and of tens and as t officials.     8657
Jos  11:23  to Israel according to their t divisions.      8657
     12: 7  of Israel according to their t divisions—      4713
     14: 1  the heads of the t clans of Israel allotted    4751
     18:10  the Israelites according to their t divisions. 4713
     19:51  the heads of the t clans of Israel assigned    4751
     21: 1  the heads of the other t families of Israel    4751
Eze  45: 7  parallel to one of the t portions.             NIH
     48: 8  to west will equal one of the t portions;      NIH
     48:21  of the t portions will belong to the prince,   NIH
```

TRIBE (206) [HALF-TRIBE, TRIBAL, TRIBES]

```
Ex   31: 2  the son of Hur, of the t of Judah,             4751
     31: 6  of the t of Dan, to help him.                  4751
     35:30  the son of Hur, of the t of Judah,             4751
     35:34  of the t of Dan, the ability to teach others.  4751
     38:22  the son of Hur, of the t of Judah,             4751
     38:23  of the t of Dan—a craftsman                    4751
Nu    1: 4  One man from each t,                           4751
      1:21  number from the t of Reuben was 46,500.        4751
      1:23  number from the t of Simeon was 59,300.        4751
      1:25  The number from the t of Gad was 45,650.       4751
      1:27  number from the t of Judah was 74,600.         4751
      1:29  number from the t of Issachar was 54,400.      4751
      1:31  number from the t of Zebulun was 57,400.       4751
      1:33  number from the t of Ephraim was 40,500.       4751
      1:35  from the t of Manasseh was 32,200.             4751
      1:37  from the t of Benjamin was 35,400.             4751
      1:39  The number from the t of Dan was 62,700.       4751
      1:41  number from the t of Asher was 41,500.         4751
      1:43  number from the t of Naphtali was 53,400.      4751
      1:47  The families of the t of Levi, however,        4751
      1:49  the t of Levi or include them in the census    4751
      2: 5  The t of Issachar will camp next to them.      4751
      2: 7  The t of Zebulun will be next.                 4751
      2:12  The t of Simeon will camp next to them.        4751
      2:14  The t of Gad will be next.                     4751
      2:20  The t of Manasseh will be next to them.        4751
      2:22  The t of Benjamin will be next.                4751
      2:27  The t of Asher will camp next to them.         4751
      2:29  The t of Naphtali will be next.                4751
      3: 6  the t of Levi and present them to Aaron        4751
      7:12  of Amminadab of the t of Judah.                4751
     10:15  over the division of the t of Issachar,        4751
     10:16  of Helon was over the division of the t        4751
     10:19  over the division of the t of Simeon,          4751
     10:20  of Deuel was over the division of the t        4751
     10:23  of Pedahzur was over the division of the t     4751
     10:24  of Gideoni was over the division of the t      4751
     10:26  of Ocran was over the division of the t        4751
     10:27  over the division of the t of Naphtali.        4751
```

Nu 13: 2 From each ancestral t send one — 4751
   13: 4 from the t of Reuben, Shamma son of — 4751
   13: 5 from the t of Simeon, Shaphat son of Hori; — 4751
   13: 6 the t of Judah, Caleb son of Jephunneh; — 4751
   13: 7 from the t of Issachar, Igal son of Joseph; — 4751
   13: 8 the t of Ephraim, Hoshea son of Nun; — 4751
   13: 9 the t of Benjamin, Palti son of Raphu; — 4751
   13:10 the t of Zebulun, Gaddiel son of Sodi; — 4751
   13:11 from the t of Manasseh (a tribe of Joseph), — 4751
   13:11 from the tribe of Manasseh (a t of Joseph), — 4751
   13:12 the t of Dan, Ammiel son of Gemalli; — 4751
   13:13 the t of Asher, Sethur son of Michael; — 4751
   13:14 the t of Naphtali, Nahbi son of Vophsi; — 4751
   13:15 from the t of Gad, Geuel son of Maki. — 4751
   17: 3 for the head of each ancestral t. — 1074
   18: 2 from your ancestral t to join you — 8657
   24: 2 and saw Israel encamped t by tribe, — NIH
   24: 2 and saw Israel encamped tribe by t, — 8657
   26:55 according to the names for its ancestral t. — 4751
   31: 5 a thousand from each t, — 4751
   31: 6 a thousand from each t, — 4751
   34:14 because the families of the t of Reuben, — 4751
   34:14 the t of Gad and the half-tribe — 4751
   34:18 And appoint one leader from each t — 4751
   34:19 from the t of Judah; — 4751
   34:20 from the t of Simeon; — 4751
   34:21 from the t of Benjamin; — 4751
   34:22 the leader from the t of Dan; — 4751
   34:23 from the t of Manasseh son of Joseph; — 4751
   34:24 from the t of Ephraim son of Joseph; — 4751
   34:25 the leader from the t of Zebulun; — 4751
   34:26 the leader from the t of Issachar; — 4751
   34:27 the leader from the t of Asher; — 4751
   34:28 the leader from the t of Naphtali." — 4751
   35: 8 in proportion to the inheritance of each t: — 2257S
   35: 8 Take many towns from a t that has many, — 2257S
   36: 3 and added to that of the t they marry into. — 4751
   36: 4 to that of the t into which they marry, — 4751
   36: 5 "What the t of the descendants — 4751
   36: 7 No inheritance in Israel is to pass from t — 4751
   36: 7 in Israel is to pass from tribe to t, — 4751
   36: 8 in any Israelite t must marry someone — 4751
   36: 9 No inheritance may pass from t to tribe, — 4751
   36: 9 No inheritance may pass from tribe to t, — 4751
   36: 9 for each Israelite t is to keep — 4751
   36:12 in their father's clan and t. — 4751
Dt 1:23 one man from each t. — 8657
   3:13 I gave to the half t of Manasseh. — 8657
   10: 8 that time the LORD set apart the t of Levi — 8657
   18: 1 indeed the whole t of Levi— — 8657
   29:18 man or woman, clan or t among you today — 8657
Jos 3:12 one from each t. — 8657
   4: 2 one from each t, — 8657
   4: 4 one from each t, — 8657
   7: 1 of the t of Judah, took some of them. — 4751
   7:14 present yourselves t by tribe. — NIH
   7:14 present yourselves tribe by t. — 8657
   7:14 The t that the LORD takes shall come — 8657
   7:18 the son of Zerah, of the t of Judah, — 4751
   13: 7 among the nine tribes and half of the t — 8657
   13:14 to the t of Levi he gave no inheritance, — 8657
   13:15 This is what Moses had given to the t — 4751
   13:24 This is what Moses had given to the t — 4751
   13:33 But to the t of Levi, Moses had given no — 8657
   15: 1 The allotment for the t of Judah, — 4751
   15:20 This is the inheritance of the t of Judah, — 4751
   15:21 The southernmost towns of the t of Judah — 4751
   16: 8 the inheritance of the t of the Ephraimites, — 4751
   17: 1 the t of Manasseh as Joseph's firstborn, — 4751
   17: 6 so the t of **Manasseh** received an inheritance — 4985
   18: 4 Appoint three men from each t. — 8657
   18:11 The lot came up for the t of Benjamin, — 4751
   18:21 The t of Benjamin, clan by clan, — 4751
   19: 1 The second lot came out for the t — 4751
   19: 8 the inheritance of the t of the Simeonites, — 4751
   19:23 the inheritance of the t of Issachar, — 4751
   19:24 The fifth lot came out for the t of Asher, — 4751
   19:31 the inheritance of the t of Asher, — 4751
   19:39 the inheritance of the t of Naphtali, — 4751
   19:40 The seventh lot came out for the t of Dan, — 4751
   19:48 the inheritance of the t of Dan, — 4751
   20: 8 in the desert on the plateau in the t of — 4751
   20: 8 Ramoth in Gilead in the t of Gad, — 4751
   20: 8 and Golan in Bashan in the t of Manasseh. — 4751
   21:17 the t of Benjamin they gave them Gibeon, — 4751
   21:20 the Levites were allotted towns from the t — 4751
   21:23 from the t of Dan they received Eltekeh, — 4751
   21:25 from the t of Manasseh they received Taanach — 4751
   21:28 from the t of Issachar, Kishion, Daberath, — 4751
   21:30 from the t of Asher, Mishal, Abdon, — 4751
   21:32 the t of Naphtali, Kedesh in Galilee (a city — 4751
   21:34 from the t of Zebulun, Jokneam, Kartah, — 4751
   21:36 from the t of Reuben, Bezer, Jahaz, — 4751
   21:38 from the t of Gad, Ramoth in Gilead — 4751
   22: 7 the other half of the t Joshua gave land on — 2257S
Jdg 18: 1 the t of the Danites was seeking a place — 8657
   18:19 Isn't it better that you serve a t and clan — 8657
   18:30 the t of Dan until the time of the captivity — 8657
   20:12 of Israel sent men throughout the t — 8657
   21: 3 Why should one t be missing — 8657
   21: 6 "Today one t is cut off from Israel," — 8657
   21:17 "so that a t of Israel will not be wiped out. — 8657
1Sa 9:21 a Benjamite, from the smallest t of Israel, — 8657
   9:21 of all the clans of the t of Benjamin? — 8657
   10:20 the t of Benjamin was chosen. — 8657
   10:21 he brought forward the t of Benjamin, — 8657
2Sa 4: 2 the Beerothite from the t of Benjamin— — 1201

1Ki 7:14 the t of Naphtali and whose father was — 4751
   8:16 not chosen a city in any t of Israel to have — 8657
   11:13 but will give him one t for the sake of David — 8657
   11:32 he will have one t. — 8657
   11:36 I will give one t to his son so that David — 8657
   12:20 the t of Judah remained loyal to the house — 8657
   12:21 the whole house of Judah and the t — 8657
2Ki 17:18 Only the t of Judah was left, — 8657
1Ch 6:60 the t of Benjamin they were given Gibeon, — 4751
   6:61 from the clans of half the t of Manasseh, — 4751
   6:62 from the part of the t of Manasseh that is — 4751
   6:66 as their territory towns from the t — 4751
   6:70 the t of Manasseh the Israelites gave Aner — 4751
   6:72 the t of Issachar they received Kedesh, — 4751
   6:74 from the t of Asher they received Mashal, — 4751
   6:76 the t of Naphtali they received Kedesh — 4751
   6:77 the t of Zebulun they received Jokneam, — 4751
   6:78 the t of Reuben across the Jordan east — 4751
   6:80 from the t of Gad they received Ramoth — 4751
   12: 2 kinsmen of Saul from the **t of Benjamin**): — 1228
   12:31 men of half the t of Manasseh, designated — 4751
   23:14 of God were counted as part of the t — 8657
   27:20 over half the t of Manasseh: — 8657
2Ch 6: 5 not chosen a city in any t of Israel to have — 8657
   11:16 from every t of Israel who set their hearts — 8657
   19:11 the leader of the t of Judah, — 1074
Est 2: 5 of Susa a Jew of the **t of Benjamin,** — 408+3549
Job 30:12 On my right the t attacks; — 7259
Ps 68:27 There is the little **t of Benjamin,** — 1228
   74: 2 the t of your inheritance, — 8657
   78:67 he did not choose the t of Ephraim; — 8657
   78:68 but he chose the t of Judah, — 8657
Jer 10:16 including Israel, the t of his inheritance— — 8657
   51:19 including the t of his inheritance— — 8657
Eze 47:23 In whatever t the alien settles, — 8657
Lk 2:36 the daughter of Phanuel, of the t of Asher. — 5876
Ac 13:21 Saul son of Kish, of the t of Benjamin, — 5876
Ro 11: 1 of Abraham, *from* the t of Benjamin. — 5876
Php 3: 5 of the people of Israel, of the t of Benjamin, — 5876
Heb 7:13 things are said belonged to a different t, — 5876
   7:13 and no one from **that** t has ever served at — 4005S
   7:14 to that t Moses said nothing about priests. — 5876
Rev 5: 5 See, the Lion of the t of Judah, — 5876
   5: 9 from every t and language and people — 5876
   7: 5 From the t of Judah 12,000 were sealed, — 5876
   7: 5 were sealed, from the t of Reuben 12,000, — 5876
   7: 5 from Gad 12,000, — 5876
   7: 6 from the t of Asher 12,000, — 5876
   7: 6 from the t of Naphtali 12,000, — 5876
   7: 6 from the t of Manasseh 12,000, — 5876
   7: 7 from the t of Simeon 12,000, — 5876
   7: 7 from the t of Levi 12,000, — 5876
   7: 7 from the t of Issachar 12,000, — 5876
   7: 8 from the t of Zebulun 12,000, — 5876
   7: 8 from the t of Joseph 12,000, — 5876
   7: 8 from the t of Benjamin 12,000. — 5876
   7: 9 from every nation, t, people and language, — 5876
   11: 9 and a half days men from every people, t, — 5876
   13: 7 And he was given authority over every t, — 5876
   14: 6 to every nation, t, language and people. — 5876

TRIBES (109) [TRIBE]

Ge 49:16 for his people as one of the t of Israel. — 8657
   49:28 All these are the twelve t of Israel, — 8657
Ex 24: 4 representing the twelve t of Israel. — 8657
   28:21 a seal with the name of one of the twelve t. — 8657
   39:14 a seal with the name of one of the twelve t. — 8657
Nu 1:16 the leaders of their ancestral t. — 4751
   10: 5 the t camping on the east are to set out. — 4722
   17: 2 from the leader of each of their ancestral t. — 1074
   17: 6 for the leader of each of their ancestral t, — 1074
   30: 1 Moses said to the heads of the t of Israel: — 4751
   31: 4 a thousand men from each of the t — 4751
   32:28 and to the family heads of the t of Israel, — 4751
   33:54 Distribute it according to your ancestral t. — 4751
   34:13 that it be given to the nine and a half t, — 4751
   34:15 and a half t have received their inheritance — 4751
   36: 3 they marry men from other Israelite t; — 8657
Dt 1:13 and respected men from each of your t, — 8657
   1:15 So I took the leading men of your t, — 8657
   5:23 of your t and your elders came to me. — 8657
   12: 5 among all your t to put his Name there — 8657
   12:14 the LORD will choose in one of your t, — 8657
   16:18 for each of your t in every town — 8657
   18: 5 and their descendants out of all your t — 8657
   27:12 these t shall stand on Mount Gerizim — NIH
   27:13 And these t shall stand on Mount Ebal — NIH
   29:21 from all the t of Israel for disaster, — 8657
   31:28 Assemble before me all the elders of your t — 8657
   33: 5 along with the t of Israel. — 8657
Jos 3:12 choose twelve men from the t of Israel, — 8657
   4: 5 to the number of the t of the Israelites, — 8657
   4: 8 to the number of the t of the Israelites, as — 8657
   7:16 Joshua had Israel come forward by t, — 8657
   12: 7 an inheritance to the t of Israel according — 8657
   13: 7 an inheritance among the nine t and half of — 8657
   14: 2 assigned by lot to the nine-and-a-half t, — 4751
   14: 3 the two-and-a-half t their inheritance east — 4751
   14: 4 for the sons of Joseph had become two t— — 4751
   18: 2 there were still seven Israelite t who had — 8657
   18:11 Their allotted territory lay between the t — 1201
   21: 4 thirteen towns from the t of Judah, — 4751
   21: 5 from the clans of the t of Ephraim, — 4751
   21: 6 from the clans of the t of Issachar, — 4751
   21: 7 received twelve towns from the t of Reuben, — 4751
   21: 9 the t of Judah and Simeon they allotted — 4751

Jos 21:16 nine towns from these two t. — 8657
   22:14 one for each of the t of Israel, — 4751
   23: 4 as an inheritance for your t all the land of — 8657
   24: 1 Then Joshua assembled all the t of Israel — 8657
Jdg 18: 1 into an inheritance among the t Israel. — 8657
   20: 2 of the t of Israel took their places in — 8657
   20:10 of every hundred from all the t of Israel, — 8657
   20:12 The t of Israel sent men throughout — 8657
   21: 5 the t of Israel has failed to assemble before — 8657
   21: 8 of the t of Israel failed to assemble before — 8657
   21:15 LORD had made a gap in the t of Israel. — 8657
   21:24 and went home to their t and clans, — 8657
1Sa 2:28 I chose your father out of all the t of Israel — 8657
   10:19 before the LORD by your t and clans." — 8657
   10:20 Samuel brought all the t of Israel near, — 8657
   15:17 not become the head of the t of Israel? — 8657
2Sa 5: 1 All the t of Israel came to David at Hebron — 8657
   15: 2 "Your servant is from one of the t — 8657
   15:10 throughout the t of Israel to say, — 8657
   19: 9 Throughout the t of Israel, — 8657
   20:14 the t of Israel to Abel Beth Maacah and — 8657
   24: 2 "Go throughout the t of Israel from Dan — 8657
1Ki 8: 1 the t and the chiefs of the Israelite families, — 4751
   11:31 of Solomon's hand and give you ten t. — 8657
   11:32 which I have chosen out of all the t — 8657
   11:35 from his son's hands and give you ten t. — 8657
   14:21 the t of Israel in which to put his Name. — 8657
   18:31 for each of the t descended from Jacob, — 8657
2Ki 21: 7 which I have chosen out of all the t — 8657
1Ch 6:62 were allotted thirteen towns from the t — 4751
   6:63 were allotted twelve towns from the t — 4751
   6:65 From the t of Judah, — 4751
   27:16 The officers over the t of Israel: — 8657
   27:22 These were the officers over the t — 8657
   28: 1 the officers over the t, — 8657
   29: 6 the officers of the t of Israel, — 8657
2Ch 5: 2 the t and the chiefs of the Israelite families, — 4751
   12:13 the t of Israel in which to put his Name. — 8657
   33: 7 which I have chosen out of all the t — 8657
Ezr 6:17 one for each of the t of Israel. — 10694
Ps 72: 9 The **desert** t will bow before him — 7470
   78:55 he settled the t of Israel in their homes. — 8657
   105:37 and from among their t no one faltered. — 8657
   122: 4 That is where the t go up, — 8657
   122: 4 the t of the LORD, — 8657
Isa 49: 6 to be my servant to restore the t of Jacob — 8657
   63:17 the t that are your inheritance. — 8657
Eze 37:19 and of the Israelite t associated with him, — 8657
   45: 8 to possess the land according to their t. — 8657
   47:13 for an inheritance among the twelve t — 8657
   47:21 among yourselves according to the t — 8657
   47:22 to be allotted an inheritance among the t — 8657
   48: 1 "These are the t, listed by name: — 8657
   48:19 from all the t of Israel. — 8657
   48:23 "As for the rest of the t: — 8657
   48:29 to allot as an inheritance to the t of Israel, — 8657
   48:31 the city will be named after the t of Israel. — 8657
Hos 5: 9 the t of Israel I proclaim what is certain. — 8657
Zec 9: 1 and all the t of Israel are on the LORD— — 8657
Mt 19:28 judging the twelve t of Israel. — 5876
Lk 22:30 judging the twelve t of Israel. — 5876
Ac 26: 7 the promise our **twelve** t are hoping to see — 1559
Jas 1: 1 the twelve t scattered among the nations: — 5876
Rev 7: 4 144,000 from all the t of Israel. — 5876
   21:12 the names of the twelve t of Israel. — 5876

TRIBULATION (1)

Rev 7:14 they who have come out of the great t; — 2568

TRIBUTARIES, TRIBUTARY (KJV) See FORCED LABOR, FORCED LABORERS, SLAVE

TRIBUTE (27)

Nu 31:28 set apart as t for the LORD one out of every — 4830
   31:29 Take this t from their half share and give it — NIH
   31:37 of which the t for the LORD was 675; — 4830
   31:38 of which the t for the LORD was 72; — 4830
   31:39 of which the t for the LORD was 61; — 4830
   31:40 of which the t for the LORD was 32. — 4830
   31:41 Moses gave the t to Eleazar the priest as — 4830
Jdg 3:15 sent him with t to Eglon king of Moab. — 4966
   3:17 He presented the t to Eglon king of Moab, — 4966
   3:18 After Ehud had presented the t, — 4966
2Sa 8: 2 became subject to David and brought t. — 4966
   8: 6 became subject to him and brought t. — 4966
1Ki 4:21 These countries brought t — 4966
2Ki 9: 1 Shalmaneser's vassal and had paid him t. — 4966
   17: 4 he no longer paid t to the king of Assyria, — 4966
1Ch 18: 2 they became subject to him and brought t. — 4966
   18: 6 became subject to him and brought t. — 4966
2Ch 17:11 as t, and the Arabs brought him flocks: — 5362
   26: 8 The Ammonites brought t to Uzziah, — 4966
Ezr 4:13 no more taxes, t or duty will be paid, — 10107
   4:20 and taxes, t and duty were paid to them. — 10107
   7:24 t or duty on any of the priests, Levites, — 10107
Est 10: 1 King Xerxes imposed t throughout — 4989
Ps 72:10 and of distant shores will bring t to him; — 4966
   89:22 No enemy *will* **subject** him to t; — 5957
Isa 16: 1 Send lambs as t to the ruler of the land, — NIH
Hos 10: 6 be carried to Assyria as t for the great king. — 4966

TRICK (1) [TRICKERY, TRICKING]
1Th 2: 3 nor are we trying to t you.   *1515*

TRICKERY (2) [TRICK]
Ac 13:10 You are full of all kinds of deceit and t.   *4816*
2Co 12:16 crafty fellow that I am, I caught you *by* t!   *1515*

TRICKING (1) [TRICK]
Ge 27:12 *to be* t him and would bring down a curse   *9506*

TRICKLETH (KJV) See FLOW

TRIED (44) [TRY]
Ge 37:21 *he t to* rescue him from their hands.   AIT
Ex   2:15 Pharaoh heard of this, *he* t to kill Moses,   *1335*
     8:18 when the magicians t to produce gnats   4027+6913
Dt   4:34 *Has* any god *ever* t to take for himself   *5814*
   13: 5 *he has* t to turn you from the way   AIT
   13:10 because *he* t to turn you away from   *1335*
1Sa 18:11 on his sword over the tunic and t walking   *3283*
   19:10 Saul t to pin him to the wall with his spear,   *1335*
2Sa 4: 2 *your enemy, who* t *to take* your life.   *1335*
   21: 2 in his zeal for Israel and Judah *had* t   *1335*
1Ki 11:40 Solomon t to kill Jeroboam,   *1335*
Ps 73:16 When *I* t to understand all this,   *3108*
   95: 9 where your fathers tested and t me,   *1043*
  109: 7 When he *is* t, let him be found guilty,   *9149*
Ecc 2: 3 *I* t cheering myself with wine,   928+4213+9365
La 3:53 *They* t *to* end my life in a pit   AIT
Eze 24:13 Because *I* t to cleanse you   AIT
Da   6: 4 the satraps t to find grounds for charges   10114
Mt   3:14 But John t to deter him, saying,   AIT
Lk   4:42 *they* t to keep him from leaving them.   AIT
   5:18 and t to take him into the house to lay him   *2426*
   6:19 and the people all t to touch him,   *2426*
   9: 9 And *he* t to see him.   *2426*
   9:49 in your name and *we* t to stop him,   AIT
Jn   5:18 For this reason the Jews t all the harder   *2426*
   7:30 At this *they* t to seize him,   *2426*
  10:39 Again *they* t to seize him,   *2426*
  11: 8 "a short while ago the Jews t to stone you,   *2426*
  19:12 From then on, Pilate t to set Jesus free,   *2426*
Ac   7:26 *He t to* reconcile them by saying, 'Men,   AIT
   9:26 *he* t to join the disciples,   *4279*
   9:29 but they t to kill him.   *2217*
  13: 8 and t to turn the proconsul from the faith.   *2426*
  16: 7 *they* t to enter Bithynia,   *4279*
  19:13 around driving out evil spirits t to invoke   *2217*
  24: 6 and even t to desecrate the temple;   *4279*
  25:10 where I ought *to be* t.   *3212*
  26:11 and *I* t to force them to blaspheme.   AIT
  26:21 in the temple courts and t to kill me.   *4281*
  28:23 and *t to* convince them about Jesus from   AIT
Gal 1:13 the church of God and *t to* destroy it.   AIT
   1:23 the faith *he* once t to destroy."   *4514*
Heb 3: 9 where your fathers tested and t me and   *1508*
  11:29 when Egyptians *t to do* so, they were drowned.   3284+4278

TRIES (3) [TRY]
Job 34: 9 a man nothing when he *t to* please God.'   AIT
Lk 17:33 Whoever t to keep his life will lose it,   *2426*
Rev 11: 5 If anyone t to harm them, fire comes from   *2527*

TRIFLING (1)
Ne 9:32 *do not let* all this hardship *seem* t   *5070*

TRIM (2) [TRIMMED, TRIMMERS]
Dt 21:12 and have her shave her head, t her nails   *6913*
Da   4:14 'Cut down the tree and t off its branches;   10635

TRIMMED (7) [TRIM]
2Sa 19:24 not taken care of his feet or t his mustache   *6913*
1Ki 6:36 and one course of t cedar beams,   *4164*
   7: 2 of cedar columns supporting t cedar beams.   *4164*
   7: 9 of high-grade stone cut to size and t with   *1760*
   7:12 and one course of t cedar beams,   *4164*
Eze 44:20 keep *the* hair of their heads t.   4080+4080
Mt 25: 7 all the virgins woke up and t their lamps.   *3175*

TRIMMERS (8) [TRIM]
Ex 25:38 Its wick t and trays are to be of pure gold.   *4920*
  37:23 as well as its wick t and trays, of pure gold.   *4920*
Nu   4: 9 together with its lamps, its wick t and trays,   *4920*
1Ki 7:50 wick t, sprinkling bowls,   *4662*
2Ki 12:13 wick t, sprinkling bowls,   *4662*
  25:14 also took away the pots, shovels, wick t   *4662*
2Ch 4:22 the pure gold wick t, sprinkling bowls,   *4662*
Jer 52:18 shovels, wick t, sprinkling bowls,   *4662*

TRIP (1) [TRIPPING]
Ps 140: 4 men of violence who plan to t my feet.   *1890*

TRIPOLIS (1)
Ezr 4: 9 judges and officials over the men from T,   10305

TRIPPING (1) [TRIP]
Isa 3:16 t along with mincing steps,   2143+2256+3262

TRIUMPH (22) [TRIUMPHAL, TRIUMPHANT, TRIUMPHED, TRIUMPHING, TRIUMPHS]
Jdg 8: 9 "When I return in t, I will tear down this   8934
  11:31 of my house to meet me when I return in t   8934
1Sa 26:25 you will do great things and surely t."   3523+3523
Job 17: 4 therefore *you* will not let them t.   8123
Ps   9:19 Arise, O LORD, *let* not man t;   6451
  12: 4 "We will t with our tongues;   1504
  13: 2 How long *will* my enemy t over me?   8123
  25: 2 nor *let* my enemies t over me.   6636
  41:11 for my enemy *does* not t over me.   8131
  54: 7 and my eyes have looked in t on my foes.   NIH
  60: 6 *"In* t I will parcel out Shechem   6600
  60: 8 over Philistia *I* shout in t."   8131
  108: 7 *"In* t I will parcel out Shechem   6600
  108: 9 over Philistia *I* shout in t."   8131
  112: 8 in the end he will look in t on his foes.   NIH
  118: 7 I will look in t on my enemies.   NIH
Pr 28:12 the righteous t, there is great elation;   6636
Isa 13: 3 those who rejoice in my t.   1452
  42:13 the battle cry and *will* t over his enemies.   1504
Jer 9: 3 it is not by truth that *they* t in the land.   1504
  51:14 and *they* will shout in t over you.   2116+6702
Mic 5: 9 be lifted up in t over your enemies,   NIH

TRIUMPHAL (2) [TRIUMPH]
Isa 60:11 their kings led in t procession.   5627
2Co 2:14 God, who always leads us in t procession   2581

TRIUMPHANT (1) [TRIUMPH]
Da 11:12 yet *he will* not *remain* t.   6451

TRIUMPHED (4) [TRIUMPH]
Dt 32:27 'Our hand *has* t; the LORD has not done   8123
1Sa 17:50 So David t over the Philistine with a sling   2616
La 1: 9 on my affliction, for the enemy *has* t."   1540
Rev 5: 5 the Root of David, *has* t.   3771

TRIUMPHING (1) [TRIUMPH]
Col 2:15 spectacle of them, t over them by the cross.   2581

TRIUMPHS (1) [TRIUMPH]
Jas 2:13 Mercy t over judgment!   2878

TRIVIAL (3)
1Ki 16:31 not only considered *it* t to commit the sins   7837
Eze 8:17 *Is it a* t *matter* for the house of Judah   7837
1Co 6: 2 are you not competent to judge t cases?   1788

TROAS (6)
Ac 16: 8 they passed by Mysia and went down to T.   5590
  16:11 From T we put out to sea   5590
  20: 5 on ahead and waited for us at T.   5590
  20: 6 and five days later joined the others at T,   5590
2Co 2:12 Now when I went to T to preach the gospel   5590
2Ti 4:13 bring the cloak that I left with Carpus at T,   5590

TROD (2) [TREAD]
Job 22:15 to the old path that evil men *have* t?   2005
Isa 63: 3 in my anger and t them down in my wrath;   8252

TRODDEN (2) [TREAD]
Jdg 9:27 and gathered the grapes and t them,   2005
Isa 63: 3 *I have* t the winepress alone;   2005

TRODE, TRODDEN (KJV) See also OVERRAN, TRAMPLED

TROOP (2) [TROOPS]
2Sa 22:30 With your help I can advance against a t;   1522
Ps 18:29 With your help I can advance against a t;   1522

TROOPS (68) [TROOP]
Ex 14: 9 and chariots, horsemen and t—   2657
Jos 10: 5 They moved up with all their t and took   4722
  11: 4 with all their t and a large number   4722
Jdg 4: 7 and his t to the Kishon River and give him   2162
  4:16 All the t *of* Sisera fell by the sword;   4722
  8: 5 "Give my t some bread;   6639
  8: 6 Why should we give bread to your t?"   7372
  9:34 So Abimelech and all his t set out by night   6639
1Sa 13: 7 all the t with him were quaking with fear.   6639
  14:24 So none of the t tasted food.   6639
  18:13 and David led the t in their campaigns.   6639
2Sa 10: 9 so he selected some of the best *t in* Israel   AIT
  10:13 Then Joab and the t with him advanced   6639
  12:28 of the t and besiege the city and capture it.   6639
  16: 6 though all the t and the special guard were   6639
  17: 8 he will not spend the night with the t.   6639
  17: 9 If he should attack your t first,   2157S
  17: 9 among the t who follow Absalom.'   6639
  18: 2 David sent the t out—   6639
  18: 2 The king told the t,   6639
  18: 5 And all the t heard the king giving orders   6639
  18:16 and the t stopped pursuing Israel,   6639
  19: 2 because on that day the t heard it said,   6639
  19:40 All the t *of* Judah and half the troops   6639

2Sa 19:40 of Judah and half the t *of* Israel had taken   6639
  20:12 man saw that all the t came to a halt there.   6639
  20:15 the t with Joab came and besieged Sheba   6639
  23:10 The t returned to Eleazar,   6639
  23:11 Israel's t fled from them.   6639
  24: 3 "May the LORD your God multiply the t   6639
2Ki 9:17 in Jezreel saw Jehu's t approaching,   9180
  9:17 he called out, "I see *some* t coming."   9180
  11:15 who were in charge of the t,   2657
1Ch 11:13 the t fled from the Philistines.   6639
  19: 7 as well as the king of Maacah with his t,   6639
  19:10 so he selected some of the best *t* in Israel   AIT
  19:14 Then Joab and the t with him advanced   6639
  21: 2 to Joab and the commanders of the t,   6639
  21: 3 "May the LORD multiply his t a hundred   6639
2Ch 12: 3 and the innumerable t of Libyans,   6639
  13: 3 with eight hundred thousand able t.   1475+2657
  13:13 Jeroboam had sent t around to the rear,   4422
  17: 2 He stationed t in all the fortified cities   2657
  23:14 who were in charge of the t,   2657
  25: 7 these t *from* Israel must not march   7372
  25: 9 hundred talents I paid for these Israelite t?"   1522
  25:10 So Amaziah dismissed the t who had come   1522
  25:13 the t that Amaziah had sent back and   1201+1522
Job 19:12 His t advance in force;   1522
  29:25 I dwelt as a king among his t;   1522
Ps 110: 3 Your t will be willing on your day of battle.   6639
SS 6: 4 majestic as t with banners.   1839
Eze 12:14 his staff and all his t—   111
  17:21 All his fleeing t will fall by the sword,   111
  38: 6 with all its t, and Beth Togarmah from   111
  38: 6 from the far north with all its t—   111
  38: 9 You and all your t and the many nations   111
  38:22 on his t and on the many nations with him.   111
  39: 4 and all your t and the nations with you.   111
Da 11:15 even their best t will not have the strength   6639
Mic 5: 1 Marshal *your* t, O city of troops,   1518
  5: 1 Marshal your troops, O city of t,   1522
Na 2: 5 He summons his picked t,   129
  3:13 Look at your t—they are all women!   6639
Ac 21:31 reached the commander *of the* Roman t   5061
  23:10 the t to go down and take him away   5128
  23:27 but I came with my t and rescued him,   5128
Rev 9:16 *of* the mounted t was two hundred million.   5128

TROPHIMUS (3)
Ac 20: 4 Tychicus and T from the province of Asia.   5576
  21:29 (They had previously seen T the Ephesian   5576
2Ti 4:20 and I left T sick in Miletus.   5576

TROUBLE (131) [TROUBLED, TROUBLEMAKER, TROUBLEMAKERS, TROUBLER, TROUBLES, TROUBLESOME, TROUBLING]
Ge 34:30 "You have brought t on me by making me   6579
  41:51 because God has made me forget all my t   6662
  43: 6 "Why *did you* bring *this* t on me   8317
Ex 5:19 they were in t when they were told,   8273
  5:22 why *have you* brought t upon this people?   8317
  5:23 he has brought t upon this people,   8317
Nu 11:11 "Why *have you* brought *this* t   8317
  33:55 They *will give you* t in the land   7675
Jos 6:18 of Israel liable to destruction and bring t   6579
  7:25 "Why *have you* brought *this* t *on* us?   6579
  7:25 The LORD *will* bring t *on* you today."   6579
Jdg 10:14 Let them save you when you are in t!"   7650
  11: 7 you come to me now, when you're in t?"   7639
1Sa 4: 7 "We're in t! Nothing like this has happened   208
  14:29 "My father *has* made t *for* the country.   6579
  20:19 the place where this t began,   5126
  26:24 and deliver me from all t."   7650
2Sa 4: 9 who has delivered me out of all t,   7650
1Ki 1:29 who has delivered me out of every t,   7650
  11:25 adding to the t caused by Hadad.   8288
  18:18 *I have* not made t *for* Israel,"   6579
  20: 7 "See how this man is looking for t!   8288
2Ki 4:13 *'You have* gone to all this t   3006+3010
  14:10 for t and cause your own downfall and that   8288
1Ch 2: 7 who brought t *on* Israel by violating   6579
2Ch 25:19 for t and cause your own downfall and that   8288
  28:20 but *he* gave him t instead of help.   7674
  28:22 In his time of t King Ahaz became   7674
Ne 1: 3 in the province are in great t and disgrace.   8288
  2:17 I said to them, "You see the t we are in: 8288
  4: 8 against Jerusalem and stir up t against it.   9360
Job 2:10 we accept good from God, and not t?"   8273
  3:10 of the womb on me to hide t from my eyes.   6662
  4: 5 t comes to you, and you are discouraged;   NIH
  4: 8 and those who sow t reap it.   6662
  5: 6 nor does t sprout from the ground.   6662
  5: 7 to t as surely as sparks fly upward.   6662
  11:16 You will surely forget your t,   6662
  14: 1 of woman is of few days and full of t.   8075
  15:35 They conceive t and give birth to evil;   6662
  19:28 since the root of the t lies in him,'   1821
  30:25 Have I not wept for *those in* t?   3427+7997
  31:29 or gloated over the t that came to him—   8273
  38:23 which I reserve for times of t,   7639
  42:11 the LORD had brought upon him.   8288
Ps 7:14 with evil and conceives t gives birth   6662
  7:16 The t *causes* recoils on himself;   6662
  9: 9 a stronghold in times of t.   1314
  10: 1 Why do you hide yourself in times of t?   1314
  10: 6 I'll always be happy and never have t."   8273

Ps	10: 7	t and evil are under his tongue.	6662
	10:14	But you, O God, do see t and grief;	6662
	22:11	for t is near and there is no one to help.	7650
	27: 5	of t he will keep me safe in his dwelling;	8288
	32: 7	from t and surround me with songs	7639
	37:39	he is their stronghold in time of t.	7650
	41: 1	the LORD delivers him in times of t.	8288
	46: 1	an ever-present help in t.	7650
	50:15	and call upon me in the day of t;	7650
	55: 2	My thoughts t me and I am distraught	8113
	59:16	my refuge in times of t.	7639
	66:14	and my mouth spoke when I was in t.	7639
	69:17	answer me quickly, for I am in t.	7639
	86: 7	In the day of my t I will call to you,	7650
	88: 3	For my soul is full of t and my life draws	8288
	90:10	yet their span is but t and sorrow,	6662
	90:15	for as many years as we have seen t.	8288
	91:15	I will be with him in t,	7650
	94:13	you grant him relief from days of t,	8273
	106:32	and t came to Moses because of them;	8317
	107: 6	they cried out to the LORD in their t,	7639
	107:13	Then they cried to the LORD in their t,	7639
	107:19	Then they cried to the LORD in their t,	7639
	107:28	they cried out to the LORD in their t,	7639
	116: 3	I was overcome by t and sorrow.	7650
	119:143	T and distress have come upon me,	7639
	138: 7	Though I walk in the midst of t,	7650
	140: 9	with the t their lips have caused.	6662
	142: 2	before him I tell my t.	7650
	143:11	in your righteousness, bring me out of t.	7650
Pr	1:27	when distress and t overwhelm you.	7442
	10:22	and he adds no t to it.	6776
	11: 8	The righteous man is rescued from t,	7650
	11:17	but a cruel man brings t on himself.	6579
	11:29	He who brings t on his family will inherit	6579
	12:13	but a righteous man escapes t.	7650
	12:21	but the wicked have their fill of t.	8273
	13:17	A wicked messenger falls into t,	8273
	15: 6	the income of the wicked brings them t.	6579
	15:27	A greedy man brings t to his family,	6579
	17:20	he whose tongue is deceitful falls into t.	8288
	19:23	Then one rests content, untouched by t.	8273
	22: 8	He who sows wickedness reaps t,	224
	24: 2	and their lips talk about making t.	6662
	24:10	If you falter in times of t,	7650
	25:19	on the unfaithful in times of t.	7650
	28:14	but he who hardens his heart falls into t.	8288
Ecc	12: 1	the days of t come and the years approach	8288
Isa	59: 4	they conceive t and give birth to evil.	6662
Jer	2:27	yet when they are in t, they say,	8288
	2:28	if they can save you when you are in t!	8288
	20:18	to see t and sorrow and to end my days	6662
	30: 7	It will be a time of t for Jacob,	7650
Eze	32: 9	I will t the hearts of many peoples	4087
Da	9:25	with streets and a trench, but in times of t.	7441
Ob	1:12	nor boast so much in the day of their t.	7650
	1:14	over their survivors in the day of their t.	7650
Jnh	1: 8	who is responsible for making all this t	8288
Na	1: 7	The LORD is good, a refuge in times of t.	7650
	1: 9	t will not come a second time.	7650
Zep	1:15	a day of t and ruin,	8739
Zec	10:11	They will pass through the sea of t;	7650
Mt	6:34	Each day has enough t of its own.	2798
	13:21	When t or persecution comes because of	2568
	28:14	we will satisfy him and keep you out of t."	291
Mk	4:17	When t or persecution comes because of	2568
Lk	7: 6	"Lord, don't t yourself,	5035
Jn	16:33	In this world you will have t.	2568
Ac	17: 6	"These men who have caused t all over	415
Ro	2: 9	There will be t and distress for every human	2568
	8:35	Shall t or hardship or persecution	2568
1Co	7:21	Don't let it t you—although if you can gain	3508
2Co	1: 4	so that we can comfort those in any t with	2568
Gal	6:17	Finally, let no one cause me t,	3160
Php	1:17	that they can stir up t for me while I am	2568
	3: 1	It is no t for me to write the same things	3891
2Th	1: 6	He will pay back t to those who trouble you	2568
	1: 6	He will pay back trouble to those who t you	2567
1Ti	5:10	helping those in t and devoting herself	2567
Heb	12:15	and that no bitter root grows up to cause t	1943
Jas	5:13	Is any one of you in t?	2802

TROUBLED (24) [TROUBLE]

Ge	41: 8	In the morning his mind was t,	7192
Nu	11:10	angry and Moses was t.	928+6524+8273
1Sa	1:15	"I am a woman who is deeply t.	7997+8120
	15:11	Samuel was t, and he cried out to	3013
Job	20: 2	"My t thoughts prompt me to answer	8546
Ps	38:18	I confess my iniquity; I am t by my sin.	1793
	77: 4	I was too t to speak.	7192
Isa	38:14	I am t; O Lord, come to my aid!"	6946
Jer	49:23	t like the restless sea.	3523+4202+9200
Da	2: 1	his mind was t and he could not sleep.	7192
	7:15	"I, Daniel, was t in spirit,	10369
	7:28	I, Daniel, was deeply t by my thoughts,	10097
Mt	26:37	and he began to be sorrowful and t.	86
Mk	14:33	and he began to be deeply distressed and t.	86
Lk	1:29	Mary was greatly t at his words	1410
	6:18	Those t by evil spirits were cured.	1943
	24:38	He said to them, "Why are you t,	5429
Jn	11:33	he was deeply moved in spirit and t.	5429
	12:27	"Now my heart is t, and what shall I say?	5429
	13:21	Jesus was t in spirit and testified,	5429
	14: 1	"Do not let your hearts be t.	5429
	14:27	Do not let your hearts be t and do not	5429
Ac	16:18	Finally Paul became so t that he turned	1387

2Th	1: 7	and give relief to you who are t, and to us	2567

TROUBLEMAKER (2) [TROUBLE]

2Sa	20: 1	Now a t named Sheba son of Bicri,	408+1175
Ac	24: 5	"We have found this man to be a t,	3369

TROUBLEMAKERS (2) [TROUBLE]

1Sa	10:27	But some t said, "How can this fellow	1175+1201
	30:22	and t among David's followers said,	1175

TROUBLER (1) [TROUBLE]

1Ki	18:17	"Is that you, you t of Israel?"	6579

TROUBLES (21) [TROUBLE]

Job	2:11	about all the t that had come upon him,	8288
Ps	25:17	The t of my heart have multiplied;	7650
	25:22	Redeem Israel, O God, from all their t!	7650
	34: 6	he saved him out of all his t.	7650
	34:17	he delivers them from all their t.	7650
	34:19	A righteous man may have many t,	8288
	40:12	For t without number surround me;	8288
	54: 7	For he has delivered me from all my t,	7650
	71:20	Though you have made me see t,	7650
Ecc	11:10	from your heart and cast off the t	8288
Isa	22: 1	What t you now, that you have all gone up	4200
	46: 7	it cannot save him from his t.	7650
	65:16	For the past t will be forgotten and hidden	7650
Da	2: 3	"I have had a dream that t me and I want	7192
Ac	7:10	and rescued him from all his t.	2568
1Co	7:28	But those who marry will face many t	2568
2Co	1: 4	who comforts us in all our t,	2568
	4:17	and momentary t are achieving for us	2568
	6: 4	in t, hardships and distresses;	2568
	7: 4	in all our t my joy knows no bounds.	2568
Php	4:14	Yet it was good of you to share in my t.	2568

TROUBLESOME (1) [TROUBLE]

Ezr	4:15	a rebellious city, t to kings and provinces,	10472

TROUBLING (4) [TROUBLE]

2Sa	14: 5	The king asked her, "What is t you?"	4537
2Ch	15: 6	God was t them with every kind of distress.	2169
Est	4: 5	to find out what was t Mordecai and why.	NIH
Ac	15:24	t your minds by what they said.	412

TROUGH (3) [TROUGHS]

Ge	24:20	So she quickly emptied her jar into the t,	9216
Dt	28: 5	Your basket and your kneading t will	5400
	28:17	Your basket and your kneading t will	5400

TROUGHS (5) [TROUGH]

Ge	30:38	peeled branches in all the watering t,	8110+9216
	30:41	the branches in the t in front of the animals	8110
Ex	2:16	and they came to draw water and fill the t	8110
	8: 3	and into your ovens and kneading t.	5400
	12:34	on their shoulders in kneading t wrapped	5400

TROUSERS (1)

Da	3:21	So these men, wearing their robes, t,	10582

TRUCEBREAKERS (KJV) See
UNFORGIVING

TRUDGE (1)

Isa	45:14	they will t behind you, coming over to you	2143

TRUE (117) [TRUTH]

Nu	11:23	or not what I say will come t for you."	7936
	12: 7	But this is not t of my servant Moses;	4027
Dt	13:14	And if it is t and it has been proved	622
	17: 4	If it is t and it has been proved	622
	18:22	not take place or come t, that is a message	995
	22:20	the charge is t and no proof of the girl's	622
Jos	7:20	Achan replied, "It is t!	593
	21:42	this was t for all these towns.	4027
	23:15	promise of the LORD your God has come t,	995
Jdg	13:17	when your word comes t?"	995
Ru	3:12	Although it is t that I am near of kin,	597
1Sa	9: 6	and everything he says comes t.	995+995
1Ki	8:26	your servant David my father come t.	586
	10: 6	and your wisdom is t.	622
	13:32	of Samaria will certainly come t."	2118+2118
2Ki	9:12	"That's not t!" they said.	9214
	19:17	"It is t, O LORD, that the Assyrian kings	597
2Ch	6:17	you promised your servant David come t.	586
	9: 5	and your wisdom is t.	622
	15: 3	a long time Israel was without the t God,	622
Ne	6: 6	and Geshem says it is t—	NIH
Est	2:23	report was investigated and found to be t,	5162
Job	5:27	"We have examined this, and it is t.	4027
	9: 2	I know that this is t.	4027
	11: 6	for t wisdom has two sides.	9370
	19: 4	If it is t that I have gone astray,	597
Ps	33: 4	For the word of the LORD is right and t;	3838
	105:19	till the word of the LORD proved him t.	7671
	119:142	righteousness is everlasting and your law is t.	622
	119:151	O LORD, and all your commands are t.	622
Ps	119:160	All your words are t;	622
	144:15	Blessed are the people of whom this is t;	3970

Pr	8: 7	My mouth speaks what is t,	622
	22:21	teaching you t and reliable words,	7999
Ecc	12:10	and what he wrote was upright and t.	622
Isa	37:18	"It is t, O LORD, that the Assyrian kings	597
	43: 9	so that others may hear and say, "It is t."	622
Jer	10:10	But the LORD is the t God;	622
	28:17	the LORD only if his prediction comes t."	995
	37:14	"That's not t!" Jeremiah said.	9214
	40:16	you are saying about Ishmael is not t."	9214
	42: 5	a t and faithful witness against us if we do	622
	50: 7	sinned against the LORD, their t pasture,	7406
Eze	16:45	You are a t daughter of your mother,	NIH
	16:45	and you are a t sister of your sisters,	NIH
	33:33	"When all this comes t—and it surely will	995
Da	2:45	The dream is t and the interpretation	10327
	3:14	said to them, "Is it t, Shadrach,	10190+10609
	7:16	and asked him the t meaning of all this.	10327
	7:19	to know the t meaning of the fourth beast,	10326
	8:26	and mornings that has been given you is t,	622
	10: 1	Its message was t and it concerned	622
Am	2:11	Is this not t, people of Israel?"	677
	7: 7	by a wall that had been built t to plumb,	643
Mic	7:20	You will be t to Jacob,	622
Zec	7: 9	'Administer t justice; show mercy and	622
	8:16	Speak the truth to each other, and render t	622
Mal	2: 6	T instruction was in his mouth	622
Lk	1: 20	which will come t at their proper time."	4444
	16:11	who will trust you with t riches?	240
	24:34	and saying, "It is t! The Lord has risen	3953
Jn	1: 9	The t light that gives light to every man	240
	1:47	he said of him, "Here is a t Israelite,	242
	4:18	What you have just said is quite t."	239
	4:23	the t worshipers will worship the Father	240
	4:37	'One sows and another reaps' is t.	240
	6:32	who gives you the t bread from heaven.	240
	7:28	but he who sent me is t.	240
	10:41	all that John said about this man was t."	239
	15: 1	"I am the t vine, and my Father is the	240
	17: 3	that they may know you, the only t God,	240
	19:35	and his testimony is t.	240
	21:24	We know that his testimony is t.	239
Ac	7: 1	"Are these charges t?"	4048
	10:34	"I now realize how t it is that God does	237+2093
	11:23	to remain t to the Lord with all their hearts.	4606
	14:22	and encouraging them to remain t to	1844
	17:11	to see if what Paul said was t.	4048
	24: 9	asserting that these things were t.	4048
	25:11	against me by these Jews are not t,	NIG
	26:25	"What I am saying is t and reasonable.	237
Ro	3: 4	Let God be t, and every man a liar.	239
1Co	15:54	then the saying that is written will come t:	1181
2Co	7:14	just as everything we said to you was t,	237+1877
	7:14	about you to Titus has proved to be t	237
Eph	4:24	like God in t righteousness and holiness.	237
Php	1:15	It is t that some preach Christ out of envy	NIG
	1:18	whether from false motives or t,	237
	4: 8	Finally, brothers, whatever is t,	239
1Th	1: 9	from idols to serve the living and t God,	240
1Ti	1: 2	To Timothy my t son in the faith:	1188
	2: 7	and a teacher of the t faith to the Gentiles.	237
Tit	1: 4	my t son in our common faith:	1188
	1:13	This testimony is t.	239
	3: 2	and to show t humility toward all men.	4559
Heb	8: 2	the t tabernacle set up by the Lord,	240
	9:24	that was only a copy of the t one;	240
	12: 8	illegitimate children and not t sons.	NIG
1Pe	5:12	and testifying that this is the t grace	239
2Pe	2:10	This is especially t of those who follow	NIG
	2:22	Of them the proverbs are t:	239
1Jn	2: 8	and the t light is already shining.	240
	5:20	so that we may know him who is t.	240
	5:20	And we are in him who is t—	240
	5:20	He is the t God and eternal life.	240
3Jn	1:12	and you know that our testimony is t.	239
Rev	2:13	Yet you remain t to my name.	3195
	3: 7	the words of him who is holy and t,	240
	3:14	the faithful and t witness,	240
	6:10	"How long, Sovereign Lord, holy and t,	240
	15: 3	Just and t are your ways, King of the ages.	240
	16: 7	t and just are your judgments."	240
	19: 2	for t and just are his judgments,	240
	19: 9	he added, "These are the t words of God."	240
	19:11	whose rider is called Faithful and T.	240
	21: 5	for these words are trustworthy and t."	240
	22: 6	"These words are trustworthy and t.	240

TRULY (11) [TRUTH]

Ps	116:16	O LORD, t I am your servant;	3954
Pr	11:19	The t righteous man attains life,	4026
Isa	10:20	will t rely on the LORD, the Holy One	622+928
	45:15	T you are a God who hides himself,	434
Jer	28: 9	as one t sent by the LORD only if	622+928
Mt	14:33	saying, "T you are the Son of God."	242
Jn	17:19	that they too may be t sanctified.	237+1877
	21:15	do you t love me more than these?"	26
	21:16	"Simon son of John, do you t love me?"	26
1Ti	6:19	they may take hold of the life that is t life.	3953
1Jn	2: 5	God's love is t made complete in him.	242

TRUMP (KJV) See TRUMPET

TRUMPET (66) [TRUMPETERS, TRUMPETS]

Ex	19:16	over the mountain, and a very loud t blast.	8795

Ex	19:19	the sound of the t grew louder and louder.	8795
	20:18	the thunder and lightning and heard the t	8795
Lev	23:24	a sacred assembly commemorated with t blasts.	9558
	25: 9	the t sounded everywhere on the tenth day	8795+9558
	25: 9	on the Day of Atonement sound the t	8795
Nu	10: 5	When a t blast is sounded,	9558
Jos	6:16	when the priests sounded the t blast,	8795
	6:20	and at the sound of the t,	8795
Jdg	3:27	he blew a t in the hill country of Ephraim,	8795
	6:34	and he blew a t, summoning the Abiezrites	8795
1Sa	13: 3	the t blown throughout the land and said,	8795
2Sa	2:28	So Joab blew the t, and all the men came	8795
	18:16	Then Joab sounded the t,	8795
	20: 1	He sounded the t and shouted,	8795
	20:22	So he sounded the t, and his men dispersed	8795
1Ki	1:34	Blow the t and shout,	8795
	1:39	the t and all the people shouted,	8795
	1:41	On hearing the sound of the t, Joab asked,	8795
2Ki	9:13	Then they blew the t and shouted,	8795
Ne	4:18	the man who sounded the t stayed with me.	8795
	4:20	Wherever you hear the sound of the t,	8795
Job	39:24	he cannot stand still when the t sounds.	8795
	39:25	At the blast of the t he snorts, 'Aha!'	8795
Ps	150: 3	Praise him with the sounding of the t,	8795
Isa	18: 3	and when a t sounds, you will hear it.	8795
	27:13	And in that day a great t will sound.	8795
	58: 1	Raise your voice like a t.	8795
Jer	4: 5	'Sound the t throughout the land!'	8795
	4:19	For I have heard the sound of the t;	8795
	4:21	and hear the sound of the t?	8795
	6: 1	Sound the t in Tekoa!	8795
	6:17	'Listen to the sound of the t!'	8795
	42:14	where we will not see war or hear the t or	8795
	51:27	Blow the t among the nations!	8795
Eze	7:14	they blow the t and get everything ready,	9540
	33: 3	against the land and blows the t to warn	8795
	33: 4	the t but does not take warning and	8795
	33: 5	the sound of the t but did not take warning,	8795
	33: 5	and does not blow the t to warn the people	8795
Hos	5: 8	"Sound the t in Gibeah,	8795
	8: 1	"Put the t to your lips!	8795
Joel	2: 1	Blow the t in Zion; sound the alarm	8795
	2:15	Blow the t in Zion, declare a holy fast,	8795
Am	2: 2	amid war cries and the blast of the t.	8795
	3: 6	When a t sounds in a city,	8795
Zep	1:16	a day of t and battle cry against	8795
Zec	9:14	The Sovereign LORD will sound the t;	8795
Mt	24:31	he will send his angels with a loud t call,	4894
1Co	14: 8	Again, if the t does not sound a clear call,	4894
	15:52	in the twinkling of an eye, at the last t.	4894
	15:52	For the t will sound, the dead will be raised	4895
1Th	4:16	the archangel and with the t call of God,	4894
Heb	12:19	a t blast or to such a voice speaking words	4894
Rev	1:10	I heard behind me a loud voice like a t,	4894
	4: 1	speaking to me like a t said,	4894
	8: 7	The first angel sounded his t,	4895
	8: 8	The second angel sounded his t,	4895
	8:10	The third angel sounded his t,	4895
	8:12	The fourth angel sounded his t,	4895
	8:13	because of the t blasts about to be sounded	4894
	9: 1	The fifth angel sounded his t,	4895
	9:13	The sixth angel sounded his t,	4895
	9:14	It said to the sixth angel who had the t,	4894
	10: 7	the seventh angel is about to sound his t,	4895
	11:15	The seventh angel sounded his t,	4895

TRUMPETERS (5) [TRUMPET]

2Ki	11:14	The officers and the t were beside the king,	2956
2Ch	5:13	The t and singers joined in unison,	2955
	23:13	The officers and the t were beside the king,	2956
	29:28	while the singers sang and the t played,	2956
Rev	18:22	harpists and musicians, flute players and t,	4896

TRUMPETS (53) [TRUMPET]

Nu	10: 2	"Make two t of hammered silver,	2956
	10: 7	To gather the assembly, blow the t,	9546
	10: 8	the priests, are to blow the t.	2956
	10: 9	sound a blast on the t.	2956
	10:10	to sound the t over your burnt offerings	2956
	29: 1	It is a day for you to sound the t.	9558
	31: 6	from the sanctuary and the t for signaling.	2956
Jos	6: 4	Have seven priests carry t of rams' horns	8795
	6: 4	with the priests blowing the t,	8795
	6: 5	hear them sound a long blast on the t,	3413+7967
	6: 6	and have seven priests carry t in front	3413+8795
	6: 8	the seven priests carrying the seven	3413+8795
	6: 8	blowing their t, and the ark of the LORD's	8795
	6: 9	ahead of the priests who blew the t,	8795
	6: 9	All this time the t were sounding.	8795
	6:13	the seven t went forward,	3413+8795
	6:13	the ark of the LORD and blowing the t.	8795
	6:13	while the t kept sounding.	8795
	6:20	When the t sounded, the people shouted,	8795
Jdg	7:16	over the provisions and t of the others.	8795
	7:16	he placed t and empty jars in the hands	8795
	7:18	I and all who are with me blow our t,	8795
	7:19	They blew their t and broke the jars	8795
	7:20	The three companies blew the t	8795
	7:20	in their right hands the t they were to blow,	8795
	7:22	When the three hundred t sounded,	8795
2Sa	6:15	the LORD with shouts and the sound of t.	8795
	15:10	"As soon as you hear the sound of the t,	8795
2Ki	11:14	of the land were rejoicing and blowing t.	2956

2Ki	12:13	t or any other articles of gold or silver for	2956
1Ch	13: 8	lyres, tambourines, cymbals and t.	2956
	15:24	the priests were to blow t before the ark	2956
	15:28	with the sounding of rams' horns and t,	2956
	16: 6	to blow the t regularly before the ark of	2956
	16:42	of the t and cymbals and for the playing of	2956
2Ch	5:12	accompanied by 120 priests sounding t.	2956
	5:13	Accompanied by t, cymbals and other	2956
	7: 6	the priests blew their t, and all the	2955
	13:12	with their t will sound the battle cry	2956
	13:14	The priests blew their t	2956
	15:14	with shouting and with t and horns.	2956
	20:28	of the LORD with harps and lutes and t.	2956
	23:13	of the land were rejoicing and blowing	2956
	29:26	and the priests with their t.	2956
	29:27	by t and the instruments of David king	2956
Ezr	3:10	the priests in their vestments and with t,	2956
Ne	12:35	as well as some priests with t,	2956
	12:41	Zechariah and Hananiah with their t—	2956
Ps	47: 5	the LORD amid the sounding of t.	8795
	98: 6	with t and the blast of the ram's horn—	2956
Mt	6: 2	do not announce it with t,	4895
Rev	8: 2	and to them were given seven	4894
	8: 6	the seven t prepared to sound them.	4894

TRUST (89) [ENTRUST, ENTRUSTED, TRUSTED, TRUSTEES, TRUSTFULLY, TRUSTING, TRUSTS, TRUSTWORTHY]

Ex	14:31	feared the LORD and put their t in him	586
	19: 9	with you and will always put their t	586
Nu	20:12	not t in me enough to honor me as holy in	586
Dt	1:32	you did not t in the LORD your God,	586
	9:23	You did not t him or obey him.	586
	28:52	fortified walls in which you t fall down.	1053
Jdg	11:20	did not t Israel to pass through his territory.	586
2Ki	17:14	who did not t in the LORD their God.	586
	18:30	Do not let Hezekiah persuade you to t	1053
1Ch	9:22	to their positions of t by David and Samuel	575
Job	4:18	If God places no t in his servants,	586
	15:15	If God places no t in his holy ones,	586
	31:24	"If I have put my t in gold or said	4073
	39:12	Can you t him to bring in your grain	586
Ps	4: 5	Offer right sacrifices and t in the LORD.	1053
	9:10	Those who know your name will t in you,	1053
	13: 5	But I t in your unfailing love;	1053
	20: 7	Some t in chariots and some in horses,	NIH
	20: 7	we t in the name of the LORD our God.	2349
	22: 4	In you our fathers put their t;	1053
	22: 9	you made me t in you even at my mother's	1053
	25: 2	in you I t, O my God.	1053
	31: 6	I t in the LORD.	1053
	31:14	But I t in you, O LORD;	1053
	33:21	for we t in his holy name.	1053
	37: 3	T in the LORD and do good;	1053
	37: 5	t in him and he will do this:	1053
	40: 3	Many will see and fear and put their t in	1053
	40: 4	the man who makes the LORD his t,	4440
	44: 6	I do not t in my bow,	1053
	49: 6	those who t in their wealth and boast	1053
	49:13	the fate of those who t in themselves,	4073
	52: 8	I t in God's unfailing love for ever	1053
	55:23	But as for me, I t in you.	1053
	56: 3	When I am afraid, I will t in you.	1053
	56: 4	In God, whose word I praise, in God I t;	1053
	56:11	in God I t; I will not be afraid.	1053
	62: 8	T in him at all times, O people;	1053
	62:10	Do not t in extortion or take pride	1053
	78: 7	Then they would put their t in God	4073
	78:22	not believe in God or t in his deliverance.	1053
	91: 2	my fortress, my God, in whom I t."	1053
	115: 8	and so will all who t in them.	1053
	115: 9	O house of Israel, t in the LORD—	1053
	115:10	O house of Aaron, t in the LORD—	1053
	115:11	You who fear him, t in the LORD—	1053
	118: 8	to take refuge in the LORD than to t	1053
	118: 9	to take refuge in the LORD than to t	1053
	119:42	for I t in your word.	1053
	125: 1	Those who t in the LORD are	1053
	135:18	and so will all who t in them.	1053
	143: 8	for I have put my t in you.	1053
	146: 3	Do not put your t in princes,	1053
Pr	3: 5	T in the LORD with all your heart	1053
	21:22	pulls down the stronghold in which they t.	4440
	22:19	So that your t may be in the LORD,	4440
Isa	8:17	I will put my t in him.	7747
	12: 2	I will t and not be afraid.	1053
	26: 4	T in the LORD forever, for the LORD,	1053
	30:15	in quietness and t is your strength,	1057
	31: 1	who t in the multitude of their chariots and	1053
	36:15	Do not let Hezekiah persuade you to t	1053
	42:17	But those who t in idols, who say to images,	1053
	50:10	t in the name of the LORD and rely	1053
Jer	2:37	for the LORD has rejected those you t;	4440
	5:17	the fortified cities in which you t.	1053
	7: 4	Do not t in deceptive words and say,	1053
	7:14	the temple you t in, the place I gave you	1053
	9: 4	do not t your brothers.	586
	12: 6	Do not t them, though they speak well of	586
	28:15	have persuaded this nation to t in lies.	1053
	39:18	because you t in me,	1053
	48: 7	Since you t in your deeds and riches,	1053
	49: 4	you t in your riches and say,	1053
	49:11	Your widows too can t in me."	1053
Mic	7: 5	Do not t a neighbor;	586
Na	1: 7	He cares for those who t in him,	2879

Zep	3: 2	She does not t in the LORD,	1053
	3:12	who t in the name of the LORD.	2879
Lk	16:11	who will t you with true riches?	4409
Jn	12:36	Put your t in the light while you have it,	4409
	14: 1	T in God; trust also in me.	4409
	14: 1	Trust in God; t also in me.	4409
Ac	14:23	in whom they had put their t.	4409
Ro	15:13	with all joy and peace as you t in him,	4409
1Co	9:17	those who have been given a t must prove	3874
	9:17	I am simply discharging the t committed	3873
2Co	13: 6	And I t that you will discover	1827
Heb	2:13	And again, "I will put my t in him."	1639+4275

TRUSTED (27) [TRUST]

1Sa	27:12	Achish t David and said to himself,	586
2Ki	18: 5	Hezekiah t in the LORD, the God of Israel.	1053
1Ch	5:20	their prayers, because they t in him.	1053
Job	12:20	He silences the lips of t advisers	586
Ps	5: 9	Not a word from their mouth can be t;	3922
	22: 4	they t and you delivered them.	1053
	22: 5	in you they t and were not disappointed.	1053
	26: 1	I have t in the LORD without wavering.	1053
	41: 9	Even my close friend, whom I t,	1053
	52: 7	but t in his great wealth and grew strong	1053
Pr	27: 6	Wounds from a friend can be t,	586
Isa	20: 5	Those who t in Cush and boasted	4438
	25: 9	we t in him, and he saved us.	7747
	25: 9	This is the LORD, we t in him;	7747
	47:10	You have t in your wickedness	1053
Jer	13:25	you have forgotten me and t in false gods.	1053
	38:22	those t friends of yours.	408+8934
	48:13	was ashamed when they t in Bethel	4440
Eze	16:15	"'But you t in your beauty	1053
Da	3:28	They t in him and defied	10665
	6:23	because he had t in his God.	10041
Lk	11:22	he takes away the armor in which the man t	4275
	16:10	"Whoever can be t with very little can also	4412
	16:10	with very little can also be t with much,	4412
Ac	12:20	t personal servant of the king,	2093+3131+3836
Tit	2:10	but to show that they can be fully t,	4411
	3: 8	so that those who have t in God may	4409

TRUSTEES (1) [TRUST]

Gal	4: 2	He is subject to guardians and t until	3874

TRUSTFULLY (1) [TRUST]

Pr	3:29	your neighbor, who lives t near you.	1055+4200

TRUSTING (4) [TRUST]

Job	15:31	not deceive himself by t what is worthless,	586
Ps	112: 7	his heart is steadfast, t in the LORD.	1053
Isa	2:22	Stop t in man, who has but a breath	2532+4946
Jer	7: 8	But look, you are t in deceptive words	1053

TRUSTS (24) [TRUST]

Job	8:14	What he t in is fragile;	4073
Ps	21: 7	For the king t in the LORD;	1053
	22: 8	"He t in the LORD; let the LORD rescue him."	1670
	28: 7	my heart t in him, and I am helped.	1053
	32:10	love surrounds the man who t in him.	1053
	84:12	blessed is the man who t in you.	1053
	86: 2	save your servant who t in you.	1053
Pr	11:28	Whoever t in his riches will fall,	1053
	16:20	and blessed is he who t in the LORD.	1053
	28:25	but he who t in the LORD will prosper.	1053
	28:26	He who t in himself is a fool,	1053
	29:25	but whoever t in the LORD is kept safe.	1053
Isa	26: 3	mind is steadfast, because he t in you.	1053
	28:16	the one who t will never be dismayed.	586
Jer	17: 5	"Cursed is the one who t in man,	1053
	17: 7	blessed is the man who t in the LORD,	1053
Eze	33:13	but then he t in his righteousness	1053
Hab	2:13	For he who makes it t in his own creation;	1053
Mt	27:43	He t in God. Let God rescue him now	4275
Ro	4: 5	but t God who justifies the wicked,	4409
	9:33	and the one who t in him will never be put	4409
	10:11	"Anyone who t in him will never be put	4409
1Co	13: 7	It always protects, always t, always hopes,	4409
1Pe	2: 6	and the one who t in him will never be put	4409

TRUSTWORTHY (25) [TRUST]

Ex	18:21	t men who hate dishonest gain—	622
2Sa	7:28	Your words are t, and you have promised	622
Ne	13:13	because these men were considered t.	586
Ps	19: 7	The statutes of the LORD are t,	586
	111: 7	all his precepts are t.	586
	119:86	All your commands are t;	575
	119:138	are righteous; they are fully t.	575
Pr	11:13	but a t man keeps a secret.	586+8120
	13:17	but a t envoy brings healing.	574
	25:13	of snow at harvest time is a t messenger	586
Da	2:45	dream is true and the interpretation is t."	10041
	6: 4	because he was t and neither corrupt	10041
Lk	16:11	not been t in handling worldly wealth,	4412
	16:12	not been t with someone else's property,	4412
	19:17	'Because you have been t in a very small	4412
1Co	7:25	as one who by the Lord's mercy is t.	4412
1Ti	1:15	a t saying that deserves full acceptance:	4412
	3: 1	Here is a t saying: If anyone sets his heart	4412
	3:11	not malicious talkers but temperate and t	4412
	4: 9	a t saying that deserves full acceptance	4412
2Ti	2:11	Here is a t saying: If we died with him	4412
Tit	1: 9	to the t message as it has been taught,	4412

Tit	3: 8	This is a t saying. And I want you to stress	4412
Rev	21: 5	for these words are t and true."	4412
	22: 6	"These words are t and true.	4412

TRUTH (224) [TRUE, TRULY, TRUTHFUL, TRUTHFULLY, TRUTHFULNESS, TRUTHS]

Ge	42:16	be tested to see if you are telling the t.	622
1Ki	17:24	of the LORD from your mouth is the t."	622
	22:16	to tell me nothing but the t in the name of	622
2Ch	18:15	to tell me nothing but the t in the name of	622
Ps	15: 2	who speaks the t from his heart	622
	25: 5	guide me in your t and teach me,	622
	26: 3	and I walk continually in your t.	622
	31: 5	redeem me, O LORD, the God of t.	622
	40:10	I do not conceal your love and your t from	622
	40:11	and your t always protect me.	622
	43: 3	Send forth your light and your t,	622
	45: 4	in behalf of t, humility and righteousness;	622
	51: 6	Surely you desire t in the inner parts;	622
	52: 3	falsehood rather than speaking the t.	7406
	86:11	O LORD, and I will walk in your t;	622
	96:13	in righteousness and the peoples in his t.	575
	119:30	I have chosen the way of t;	575
	119:43	not snatch the word of t from my mouth,	622
	145:18	to all who call on him in t.	622
Pr	16:13	they value a man who speaks the t.	3838
	23:23	Buy the t and do not sell it;	622
Isa	45:19	I, the LORD, speak the t;	7406
	48: 1	but not in t or righteousness—	622
	59:14	t has stumbled in the streets,	622
	59:15	T is nowhere to be found,	622
	65:16	in the land will do so by the God of t;	589
	65:16	in the land will swear by the God of t.	589
Jer	5: 1	who deals honestly and seeks the t,	575
	5: 3	O LORD, do not your eyes look for t?	575
	7:28	T has perished; it has vanished from	575
	9: 3	it is not by t that they triumph in the land.	575
	9: 5	and no one speaks the t.	622
	26:15	for in t the LORD has sent me to you	622
Da	8:12	and t was thrown to the ground.	622
	9:13	and giving attention to your t.	622
	10:21	what is written in the Book of T.	622
	11: 2	"Now then, I tell you the t:	622
Am	5:10	in court and despise him who tells the t.	9459
Zec	8: 3	Jerusalem will be called the City of T,	622
	8:16	Speak the t to each other,	622
	8:19	Therefore love t and peace."	622
Mt	5:18	I tell you the t, until heaven and earth	297
	5:26	I tell you the t, you will not get out	297
	6: 2	I tell you the t, they have received their	297
	6: 5	I tell you the t, they have received their	297
	6:16	I tell you the t, they have received their	297
	8:10	"I tell you the t, I have not found anyone	297
	10:15	I tell you the t, it will be more bearable	297
	10:23	I tell you the t, you will not finish going	297
	10:42	I tell you the t, he will certainly not lose his	297
	11:11	I tell you the t: Among those born of women	297
	13:17	For I tell you the t, many prophets and	297
	16:28	I tell you the t, some who are standing here	297
	17:20	I tell you the t, if you have faith	297
	18: 3	And he said: "I tell you the t,	297
	18:13	And if he finds it, I tell you the t,	297
	18:18	"I tell you the t, whatever you bind on earth	297
	19:23	Jesus said to his disciples, "I tell you the t,	297
	19:28	Jesus said to them, "I tell you the t,	297
	21:21	Jesus replied, "I tell you the t,	297
	21:31	Jesus said to them, "I tell you the t,	297
	22:16	the way of God in accordance with the t.	237
	23:36	I tell you the t, all this will come	297
	24: 2	"I tell you the t, not one stone here will be	297
	24:34	I tell you the t, this generation will	297
	24:47	I tell you the t, he will put him in charge	297
	25:12	"But he replied, 'I tell you the t,	297
	25:40	"The King will reply, 'I tell you the t,	297
	25:45	"He will reply, 'I tell you the t,	297
	26:13	I tell you the t, wherever this gospel	297
	26:21	they were eating, he said, "I tell you the t,	297
	26:34	"I tell you the t," Jesus answered,	297
Mk	3:28	I tell you the t, all the sins and blasphemies	297
	5:33	trembling with fear, told him the whole t.	237
	8:12	I tell you the t, no sign will be given to it."	297
	9: 1	And he said to them, "I tell you the t,	297
	9:41	I tell you the t, anyone who gives you a cup	297
	10:15	I tell you the t, anyone who will not receive	297
	10:29	"I tell you the t," Jesus replied,	297
	11:23	"I tell you the t, if anyone says to this	297
	12:14	the way of God in accordance with the t.	237
	12:43	Jesus said, "I tell you the t,	297
	13:30	I tell you the t, this generation will	297
	14: 9	I tell you the t, wherever this gospel	297
	14:18	he said, "I tell you the t,	297
	14:25	I tell you the t, I will not drink again	297
	14:30	"I tell you the t," Jesus answered, "today—	297
Lk	4:24	"I tell you the t," he continued,	297
	9:27	I tell you the t, some who are standing here	242
	12:37	I tell you the t, he will dress himself to serve	297
	12:44	I tell you the t, he will put him in charge	242
	18:17	I tell you the t, anyone who will not receive	297
	18:29	"I tell you the t," Jesus said to them,	297
	20:21	the way of God in accordance with the t.	237
	21: 3	"I tell you the t," he said,	242
	21:32	"I tell you the t, this generation	242
	23:43	Jesus answered him, "I tell you the t,	297
Jn	1:14	who came from the Father, full of grace and t	237
	1:17	grace and t came through Jesus Christ.	237
	1:51	He then added, "I tell you the t,	297

Jn	3: 3	In reply Jesus declared, "I tell you the t,	297
	3: 5	Jesus answered, "I tell you the t,	297
	3:11	I tell you the t, we speak of what we know, and testify to what we have seen,	297
	3:21	whoever lives by the t comes into the light,	237
	4:23	will worship the Father in spirit and t,	237
	4:24	must worship in spirit and in t."	237
	5:19	"I tell you the t, the Son can do nothing	297
	5:24	"I tell you the t, whoever hears my word	297
	5:25	I tell you the t, a time is coming	297
	5:33	to John and he has testified to the t.	237
	6:26	Jesus answered, "I tell you the t,	297
	6:32	Jesus said to them, "I tell you the t,	297
	6:47	I tell you the t, he who believes has eternal	297
	6:53	Jesus said to them, "I tell you the t,	297
	7:18	of the one who sent him is a man of t;	239
	8:32	Then you will know the t, and the truth	237
	8:32	and the t will set you free."	237
	8:34	Jesus replied, "I tell you the t,	297
	8:40	a man who has told you the t that I heard	237
	8:44	not holding to the t, for there is no truth in	237
	8:44	for there is no t in him.	237
	8:45	because I tell the t, you do not believe me!	237
	8:46	If I am telling the t, why don't you believe	237
	8:51	I tell you the t, if anyone keeps my word,	297
	8:58	"I tell you the t," Jesus answered,	297
	10: 1	"I tell you the t, the man who does not enter	297
	10: 7	Jesus said again, "I tell you the t,	297
	12:24	I tell you the t, unless a kernel of wheat falls	297
	13:16	I tell you the t, no servant is greater than	297
	13:20	I tell you the t, whoever accepts anyone	297
	13:21	"I tell you the t, one of you is going to betray	297
	13:38	I tell you the t, before the rooster crows,	297
	14: 6	"I am the way and the t and the life.	237
	14:12	I tell you the t, anyone who has faith in me	297
	14:17	the Spirit of t. The world cannot accept him,	237
	15:26	Spirit of t who goes out from the Father,	237
	16: 7	But I tell you the t: It is for your good	237
	16:13	But when he, the Spirit of t, comes,	237
	16:13	comes, he will guide you into all t.	237
	16:20	I tell you the t, you will weep	297
	16:23	I tell you the t, my Father will give you	297
	17:17	Sanctify them by the t; your word is truth.	237
	17:17	Sanctify them by the truth; your word is t.	237
	18:23	if you spoke the t, why did you strike me?"	2822
	18:37	I came into the world, to testify to the t.	237
	18:37	Everyone on the side of t listens to me."	237
	18:38	"What is t?" Pilate asked.	237
	19:35	He knows that he tells the t,	239
	21:18	I tell you the t, when you were younger	297
Ac	20:30	men will arise and distort the t	1406+3281
	21:24	Then everybody will know there is no t	4029
	21:34	not get at the t because of the uproar,	855+1182
	24: 8	you will be able to learn the t	2105
	28:25	"The Holy Spirit spoke the t to your	2822
Ro	1:18	and wickedness of men who suppress the t	237
	1:25	They exchanged the t of God for a lie,	237
	2: 2	judgment against those who do such things is based on t.	237
	2: 8	and who reject the t and follow evil,	237
	2:20	the embodiment of knowledge and t—	237
	9: 1	I speak the t in Christ—	237
	15: 8	a servant of the Jews on behalf of God's t,	237
1Co	5: 8	the bread of sincerity and t.	237
	13: 6	not delight in evil but rejoices with the t.	237
2Co	5: 8	the t plainly we commend ourselves	237
	11:10	As surely as the t of Christ is in me,	237
	12: 6	because I would be speaking the t.	237
	13: 8	For we cannot do anything against the t,	237
	13: 8	but only for the t.	237
Gal	2: 5	the t of the gospel might remain with you.	237
	2:14	that they were not acting in line with the t	237
	4:16	become your enemy by telling you the t?	238
	5: 7	on you and kept you from obeying the t?	237
Eph	1:13	in Christ when you heard the word of t,	237
	4:15	Instead, speaking the t in love,	238
	4:21	in accordance with the t that is in Jesus.	237
	5: 9	in all goodness, righteousness and t)	237
	6:14	the belt of t buckled around your waist,	237
Col	1: 5	about in the word of t,	237
	1: 6	and understood God's grace in all its t.	237
2Th	2:10	because they refused to love the t and so	237
	2:12	be condemned who have not believed the t	237
	2:13	of the Spirit and through belief in the t.	237
1Ti	2: 4	and to come to a knowledge of the t.	237
	2: 7	I am telling the t, I am not lying—	237
	3:15	the pillar and foundation of the t.	237
	4: 3	by those who believe and who know the t.	237
	6: 5	of the t and who think that godliness is	237
2Ti	2:15	and who correctly handles the word of t.	237
	2:18	who have wandered away from the t.	237
	2:25	leading them to a knowledge of the t,	237
	3: 7	but never able to acknowledge the t.	237
	3: 8	so also these men oppose the t—	237
	4: 4	They will turn their ears away from the t	237
Tit	1: 1	of God's elect and the knowledge of the t	237
	1: 1	to the commands of those who reject the t.	237
Heb	10:26	keep on sinning after we have received the knowledge of the t,	237
Jas	1:18	to give us birth through the word of t,	237
	3:14	not boast about it or deny the t.	237+2848+6017
	5:19	if one of you should wander from the t	237
1Pe	1:22	obeying the t so that you have sincere love	237
2Pe	1:12	and are firmly established in the t you	237
	2: 2	and will bring the way of t into disrepute.	237
1Jn	1: 6	we lie and do not live by the t.	237
	1: 8	we deceive ourselves and the t is not in us.	237

1Jn	2: 4	is a liar, and the t is not in him.	237
	2: 8	its t is seen in him and you,	239
	2:20	and all of you know the t.	NIG
	2:21	write to you because you do not know the t,	237
	2:21	and because no lie comes from the t.	237
	3:18	or tongue but with actions and in t.	237
	3:19	how we know that we belong to the t,	237
	4: 6	the Spirit of t and the spirit of falsehood.	237
	5: 6	because the Spirit is the t.	237
2Jn	1: 1	whom I love in the t—	237
	1: 1	not I only, but also all who know the t—	237
	1: 2	because of the t, which lives in us and will	237
	1: 3	will be with us in t and love.	237
	1: 4	of your children walking in the t,	237
3Jn	1: 1	whom I love in the t.	237
	1: 3	tell about your faithfulness to the t and	237
	1: 3	and how you continue to walk in the t.	237
	1: 4	that my children are walking in the t.	237
	1: 8	so that we may work together for the t.	237
	1:12	and even by the t itself.	237

TRUTHFUL (8) [TRUTH]

Pr	12:17	A t witness gives honest testimony,	575
	12:19	T lips endure forever,	622
	12:22	but he delights in men who are t.	575
	14: 5	A t witness does not deceive,	574
	14:25	A t witness saves lives,	622
Jer	4: 2	if in a t, just and righteous way you swear,	622
Jn	3:33	has accepted it has certified that God is t.	239
2Co	6: 7	in t speech and in the power of God;	237

TRUTHFULLY (1) [TRUTH]

Eph	4:25	of you must put off falsehood and speak t	237

TRUTHFULNESS (1) [TRUTH]

Ro	3: 7	"If my falsehood enhances God's t and	237

TRUTHS (4) [TRUTH]

1Co	2:13	expressing spiritual t in spiritual words.	NIG
1Ti	3: 9	They must keep hold of the deep t of	3696
	4: 6	the t of the faith and of the good teaching	3364
Heb	5:12	the elementary t of God's word	794+3836+5122

TRY (23) [TRIED, TRIES, TRYING]

Nu	20:18	if you t, we will march out and attack you	NIH
Jdg	19:13	let's t to reach Gibeah or Ramah	AIT
Ru	3: 1	should I not t to find a home for you,	1335
1Sa	26:21	I will not t to harm you again.	AIT
Job	17:10	"But come on, all of you, t again!	8740
Ps	26: 2	Test me, O LORD, and t me,	5814
Isa	7:13	Is it not enough to t the patience of men?	4206
	7:13	Will you t the patience of my God also?	4206
	22: 4	Do not t to console me over the destruction	237
Eze	7:26	They will t to get a vision from the prophet;	1335
Da	7:25	the Most High and oppress his saints and t	10503
	11:26	king's provisions will t to destroy him;	AIT
Zec	12: 3	All who t to move it will injure themselves.	AIT
Mal	1: 8	T offering them to your governor!	AIT
Lk	12:58	t hard to be reconciled to him on the way,	1443+2238
	13:24	will t to enter and will not be able to.	2426
	14:19	and I'm on my way to t them out.	1507
Ac	15:10	why do you t to test God by putting on	AIT
1Co	10:33	as I t to please everybody in every way.	743
	14:12	t to excel in gifts that build up the church.	2426
2Co	5:11	to fear the Lord, we t to persuade men.	AIT
1Th	5:15	but always t to be kind to each other and	1503
Tit	2: 9	to t to please them, not to talk back to them,	NIG

TRYING (41) [TRY]

Nu	16:10	now you are t to get the priesthood too.	1335
Jdg	6:31	Are you t to save him?	AIT
1Sa	20: 1	that he is t to take my life?"	1335
2Sa	14:16	the hand of the man who is t to cut off	AIT
	16:11	my own flesh, is t to take my life.	1335
	20:19	You are t to destroy a city that is a mother	1335
1Ki	19:10	and now they are t to kill me too."	1335
	19:14	and now they are t to kill me too.	1335
2Ki	5: 7	he is t to pick a quarrel with me!"	628
Ne	6: 9	They were all t to frighten us, thinking,	AIT
	6:14	prophets who have been t to intimidate me.	AIT
Isa	28: 9	"Who is it he is t to teach?	AIT
Da	2: 8	"I am certain that you are t to gain time,	AIT
	8:15	watching the vision and t to understand it.	1335
Mt	2:20	for those who were t to take the child's	2426
	22:18	why are you t to trap me?	4279
	23:13	nor will you let those enter who are t to.	NIG
Mk	12:15	"Why are you t to trap me?"	4279
Lk	19:47	and the leaders among the people were t	2426
Jn	5: 7	While I am t to get in,	AIT
	7:19	Why are you t to kill me?"	2426
	7:20	"Who is t to kill you?"	2426
	7:25	"Isn't this the man they are t to kill?	2426
Ac	17:18	"What is this babbler t to say?"	2527
	18: 4	t to persuade Jews and Greeks.	4275
	21:31	While they were t to kill him,	AIT
Ro	11: 3	and they are t to kill me"?	2426+3836+6034
1Co	10:22	Are we t to arouse the Lord's jealousy?	AIT
2Co	3: 1	not to commend ourselves again,	AIT
	10: 9	not want to seem to be t to frighten you	NIG
Gal	1: 7	and are t to pervert the gospel of Christ.	2527
	1:10	Am I now t to win the approval of men,	4275
	1:10	Or am I t to please men?	2426

Gal	1:10	If I were still t to please men,	743
	3:3	are you now t to attain your goal by human	AIT
	5:4	You who are t to be justified by law	AIT
	6:12	are t to compel you to be circumcised.	AIT
1Th	2:3	nor are we t to trick you.	NIG
	2:4	We are not t to please men but God,	743
1Pe	1:11	t to find out the time and circumstances	2236
1Jn	2:26	those who are t to lead you astray.	AIT

TRYPHENA (1)
| Ro | 16:12 | Greet T and Tryphosa, those women who | 5586 |

TRYPHOSA (1)
| Ro | 16:12 | Greet Tryphena and T, those women who | 5589 |

TUBAL (8)
Ge	10:2	Gomer, Magog, Madai, Javan, T,	9317
1Ch	1:5	Gomer, Magog, Madai, Javan, T,	9317
Isa	66:19	and Lydians (famous as archers), to T	9317
Eze	27:13	" 'Greece, T and Meshech traded with you;	9317
	32:26	"Meshech and T are there,	9317
	38:2	the chief prince of Meshech and T;	9317
	38:3	O Gog, chief prince of Meshech and T.	9317
	39:1	O Gog, chief prince of Meshech and T.	9317

TUBAL-CAIN (1) [TUBAL-CAIN'S]
| Ge | 4:22 | Zillah also had a son, T, | 9340 |

TUBAL-CAIN'S (1) [TUBAL-CAIN]
| Ge | 4:22 | T sister was Naamah. | 9340 |

TUBES (1)
| Job | 40:18 | His bones are t of bronze, | 692 |

TUCK (3) [TUCKED, TUCKING]
2Ki	4:29	"T your cloak into your belt,	2520+5516
	9:1	T your cloak into your belt,	2520+5516
Eze	5:3	a few strands of hair and t them away in	7443

TUCKED (1) [TUCK]
| Ex | 12:11 | with your cloak t into your belt, | 2520+5516 |

TUCKING (1) [TUCK]
| 1Ki | 18:46 | t his cloak into his belt, he ran ahead | 5516+9113 |

TUMBLES (1) [TUMBLING]
| Ge | 49:17 | the horse's heels so that its rider t backward. | 5877 |

TUMBLEWEED (2) [WEED]
| Ps | 83:13 | Make them like t, O my God, | 1650 |
| Isa | 17:13 | like chaff on the hills, like t before a gale. | 1650 |

TUMBLING (1) [TUMBLES]
| Jdg | 7:13 | "A round loaf of barley bread came t into | 2200 |

TUMORS (8)
Dt	28:27	with the boils of Egypt and with t,	6754
1Sa	5:6	upon them and afflicted them with t.	6754
	5:9	both young and old, with an outbreak of t.	6754
	5:12	who did not die were afflicted with t,	6754
	6:4	"Five gold t and five gold rats,	6754
	6:5	of the rats that are destroying	6754
	6:11	the gold rats and the models of the t.	3224
	6:17	These are the gold t the Philistines sent as	3224

TUMULT (6)
1Sa	14:19	the t in the Philistine camp increased more	2162
Isa	22:2	O city of t and revelry?	2159
	22:5	of t and trampling and terror in the Valley	4539
Jer	25:31	The t will resound to the ends of the earth,	8623
Eze	1:24	like the t of an army.	2167+7754
Am	2:2	in great t amid war cries and the blast of	8623

TUNE (13) [TUNED]
Ps	9:T	To [the t of] "The Death of the Son."	NIH
	22:T	To [the t of] "The Doe of the Morning."	NIH
	45:T	To [the t of] "Lilies."	NIH
	56:T	To [the t of] "A Dove on Distant Oaks."	NIH
	57:T	[To the t of] "Do Not Destroy."	NIH
	58:T	[To the t of] "Do Not Destroy."	NIH
	58:5	that will not heed the t of the charmer,	7754
	59:T	[To the t of] "Do Not Destroy."	NIH
	60:T	To [the t of] "The Lily of the Covenant."	NIH
	69:T	To [the t of] "Lilies."	NIH
	75:T	[To the t of] "Do Not Destroy."	NIH
	80:T	To [the t of] "The Lilies of the Covenant."	NIH
1Co	14:7	will anyone know what t is being played	NIG

TUNED (1) [TUNE]
| Job | 30:31 | My harp is t to mourning, | 4200 |

TUNIC (16) [TUNICS]
Ex	28:4	a breastpiece, an ephod, a robe, a woven t,	4189
	28:39	the t of fine linen and make the turban	4189
	29:5	the garments and dress Aaron with the t,	4189
Lev	8:7	He put the t on Aaron,	4189
Lev	16:4	He is to put on the sacred linen t,	4189
1Sa	17:38	Then Saul dressed David in his own t.	4496
	17:39	on his sword over the t and tried walking	4496
	18:4	along with his t, and even his sword,	4496
2Sa	20:8	Joab was wearing his military t,	4230+4496
Ezr	9:3	When I heard this, I tore my t and cloak,	955
	9:5	with my t and cloak torn,	955
Mt	5:40	someone wants to sue you and take your t,	5945
	10:10	or extra t, or sandals or a staff;	5945
Mk	6:9	Wear sandals but not an extra t.	5945
Lk	6:29	do not stop him from taking your t.	5945
	9:3	no bag, no bread, no money, no extra t.	5945

TUNICS (7) [TUNIC]
Ex	28:40	Make t, sashes and headbands	4189
	29:8	Bring his sons and dress them in t	4189
	39:27	they made t of fine linen	4189
	40:14	Bring his sons and dress them in t	4189
Lev	8:13	put t on them,	4189
	10:5	they came and carried them, still in their t,	4189
Lk	3:11	"The man with two t should share	5945

TUNNEL (1) [TUNNELS]
| 2Ki | 20:20 | and the t by which he brought water into | 9498 |

TUNNELS (1) [TUNNEL]
| Job | 28:10 | He t through the rock; | 1324+3284 |

TURBAN (15) [TURBANS]
Ex	28:4	a robe, a woven tunic, a t and a sash.	5200
	28:37	Fasten a blue cord to it to attach it to the t;	5200
	28:37	it is to be on the front of the t.	5200
	28:39	of fine linen and make the t of fine linen.	5200
	29:6	Put the t on his head and attach	5200
	29:6	and attach the sacred diadem to the t.	5200
	39:28	and the t of fine linen,	5200
	39:31	a blue cord to it to attach to the t,	5200
Lev	8:9	Then he placed the t on Aaron's head	5200
	8:9	around him and put on the linen t.	5200
Job	29:14	justice was my robe and my t.	7565
Eze	21:26	Take off the t, remove the crown.	7565
	24:17	Keep your t fastened and your sandals	6996
Zec	3:5	Then I said, "Put a clean t on his head."	7565
	3:5	a clean t on his head and clothed him,	7565

TURBANS (4) [TURBAN]
Eze	23:15	around their waists and flowing t	3178
	24:23	You will keep your t on your heads	6996
	44:18	They are to wear linen t on their heads	6996
Da	3:21	trousers, t and other clothes,	10368

TURBULENT (1)
| Ge | 49:4 | T as the waters, you will no longer excel, | 7070 |

TURMOIL (8)
2Ch	15:5	the inhabitants of the lands were in great t.	4539
Job	3:17	There the wicked cease from t,	8075
	3:26	I have no rest, but only t."	8075
Ps	65:7	and the t of the nations.	2162
Pr	15:16	than great wealth with t.	4539
Isa	14:3	from suffering and t and cruel bondage,	8075
Eze	22:5	O infamous city, full of t.	4539
Ac	17:8	and the city officials were thrown into t.	5429

TURN (327) [TURNED, TURNING, TURNS]
Ge	19:2	"please t aside to your servant's house.	6073
	24:49	tell me, so I may know which way to t."	7155
	37:30	Where can I t now?"	995
Ex	7:19	and they will t to blood.	2118
	14:2	"Tell the Israelites to t back and encamp	8740
	23:27	make all your enemies t their backs	448+5989
	32:8	to t away from what I commanded them	6073
	32:12	T from your fierce anger.	8740
	34:22	Feast of Ingathering at the t of the year.	9543
Lev	15:3	Should the raw flesh change and t white,	2200
	19:4	not t to idols or make gods of cast metal	7155
	19:29	or the land will t to prostitution and	2388
	19:31	not t to mediums or seek out spiritists,	7155
	26:31	I will t your cities into ruins	5989
Nu	6:26	the LORD t his face toward you	5951
	14:25	t back tomorrow and set out toward	7155
	20:17	the king's highway and not t to the right	5742
	21:22	not t aside into any field or vineyard,	5742
	22:26	where there was no room to t,	5742
	24:1	that the LORD's fierce anger may t away	8740
	27:7	their father's inheritance over to them.	6296
	27:8	t his inheritance over to his daughter.	6296
	32:15	If you t away from following him,	8740
	34:5	where it will t, join the Wadi of Egypt	6015
Dt	1:40	t around and set out toward the desert	7155
	2:3	this hill country long enough; now t north.	7155
	2:27	we will not t aside to the right or to	6073
	5:32	do not t aside into the right or to the left.	6073
	7:4	for they will t your sons away from	6073
	11:16	to t away and worship other gods and bow	6073
	11:28	the LORD your God and t from the way	6073
	13:5	he has tried to t you from the way	5615
	13:10	to t you away from the LORD your God,	5615
	13:17	the LORD will t from his fierce anger;	8740
	17:11	Do not t aside from what they tell you,	6073
	17:20	and t from the law to the right or to	6073
	23:14	among you anything indecent and t away	8740
Dt	28:14	Do not t aside from any of the commands	6073
	28:24	t the rain of your country into dust	5989
	30:10	of the Law and t to the LORD your God	8740
	31:20	they will t to other gods	7155
	31:29	to t from the way I have commanded you.	6073
Jos	1:7	do not t from it to the right or to the left,	6073
	7:12	they t their backs and run	7155
	22:16	How could you t away from the LORD	8740
	22:23	If we have built our own altar to t away	8740
	22:29	and t away from him today by building	8740
	23:12	"But if you t away and ally yourselves	8740+8740
	24:20	he will t and bring disaster on you	8740
Jdg	1:3	We in t will go with you into yours."	1685
	7:3	'Anyone who trembles with fear may t back	8740
	7:22	caused the men throughout the camp to t	8492
	14:17	She in t explained the riddle to her people.	2256
	20:39	then the men of Israel would t in the battle.	2200
Ru	1:16	"Don't urge me to leave you or to t back	8740
1Sa	6:12	they did not t to the right or to the left.	6073
	12:20	yet do not t away from the LORD,	6073
	12:21	Do not t away after useless idols.	6073
	22:17	"T and kill the priests of the LORD,	6015
	22:18	"You t and strike down the priests."	6015
	29:4	or he will t against us during the fighting.	2118+4200+8477
	29:7	T back and go in peace;	8740
2Sa	2:21	"T aside to the right or to the left;	5742
	2:21	the bow of Jonathan did not t back,	6047
	14:19	no one can t to the right or to the left;	3554
	15:31	t Ahithophel's counsel into foolishness."	6118
	22:37	so that my ankles do not t.	5048
	22:38	I did not t back till they were destroyed.	8740
	22:41	You made my enemies t their backs	5989
1Ki	8:33	they t back to you and confess your name,	8740
	8:35	and confess their name and t from their sin	8740
	8:48	and if they t back to you with all their heart	8740
	8:58	May he t our hearts to him,	5742
	9:6	if you or your sons t away from me	8740+8740
	11:2	because they will surely t your hearts	5742
	12:15	for this t of events was from the LORD,	6016
	13:16	"I cannot t back and go with you,	8740
	17:3	t eastward and hide in the Kerith Ravine,	7155
2Ki	9:23	he did not t away from them.	6073
	10:29	not t away from the sins of Jeroboam	6073
	10:31	not t away from the sins of Jeroboam,	6073
	13:2	and he did not t away from them.	6073
	13:6	But they did not t away from the sins of	6073
	13:11	the LORD and did not t away from any of	6073
	14:24	the LORD and did not t away from any of	6073
	15:9	not t away from the sins of Jeroboam son	6073
	15:18	not t away from the sins of Jeroboam son	6073
	15:24	not t away from the sins of Jeroboam son	6073
	15:28	not t away from the sins of Jeroboam son	6073
	17:13	"T from your evil ways.	8740
	17:22	of Jeroboam and did not t away from them	6073
	23:26	not t away from the heat of his fierce anger,	6073
1Ch	12:23	to t Saul's kingdom over to him,	6015
2Ch	6:24	when they t back and confess your name,	8740
	6:26	and confess their name and t from their sin	8740
	6:38	and if they t back to you with all their heart	8740
	7:14	and pray and seek my face and t	8740
	7:19	"But if you t away and forsake the decrees	8740
	10:15	for this t of events was from God,	5813
	24:23	At the t of the year, the army of Aram	9543
	29:10	that his fierce anger will t away from us.	8740
	30:8	that his fierce anger will t away from you.	8740
	30:9	not t his face from you if you return	6073
	35:22	however, would not t away from him,	6015+7156
	36:13	and hardened his heart and would not t to	8740
Ne	4:4	T their insults back on their own heads.	8740
	4:12	"Wherever you t, they will attack us."	8740
	9:26	in order to t them back to you;	8740
	9:35	not serve you or t from their evil ways.	8740
Est	2:12	a girl's t came to go in to King Xerxes,	9366
	2:15	When the t came for Esther	9366
	2:22	who in t reported it to the king,	2256
Job	3:1	That day—may it t to darkness;	2118
	5:1	To which of the holy ones will you t?	7155
	6:18	Caravans t aside from their routes;	4369
	10:8	Will you now t and destroy me?	6017
	10:9	Will you now t me to dust again?	8740
	10:20	T away from me so I can have	8883
	13:9	Would it t out well if he examined you?	NIH
	13:16	Indeed, this will t out for my deliverance,	NIH
	17:12	These men t night into day;	8492
	20:14	yet his food will t sour in his stomach;	2200
	30:21	You t on me ruthlessly;	2200
	33:17	to t man from wrongdoing and keep him	6073
	33:30	to t back his soul from the pit,	8740
	36:18	do not let a large bribe t you aside.	5742
Ps	4:2	O men, will you t my glory into shame?	4200
	6:4	T, O LORD, and deliver me;	8740
	6:10	they will t back in sudden disgrace.	8740
	9:3	My enemies t back;	8740
	18:36	so that my ankles do not t.	5048
	18:37	I did not t back till they were destroyed.	8740
	18:40	You made my enemies t their backs	5989
	21:12	for you will make them t their backs	8883
	22:27	the ends of the earth will remember and t	8740
	25:16	T to me and be gracious to me,	7155
	27:9	do not t your servant away in anger;	5742
	27:12	Do not t me over to the desire of my foes,	5989
	28:1	do not t a deaf ear to me.	3087
	31:2	T your ear to me,	5742
	34:14	T from evil and do good;	6073
	37:8	Refrain from anger and t from wrath;	6440
	37:27	T from evil and do good;	6073

Ps	40: 4	to *those who* **t** aside *to* false gods.	8454
	49: 4	*I will* **t** my ear to a proverb;	5742
	51:13	and sinners *will* **t back** to you.	8740
	56: 9	Then my enemies *will* **t back** when I call	8740
	64: 8	He will **t** their own tongues against them	NIH
	69:16	in your great mercy **t** to me.	7155
	70: 3	**t back** because of their shame.	8740
	71: 2	**t** your ear to me and save me.	5742
	73:10	Therefore their people **t** to them and drink	8740
	74: 3	**T** your steps toward these everlasting ruins,	8123
	78: 6	and they **in t** would tell their children.	7756
	80:18	Then *we will* not **t away** from you;	6047
	81:14	and **t** my hand against their foes!	8740
	86:16	**T** to me and have mercy on me;	7155
	88: 2	**t** your ear to my cry.	5742
	90: 3	*You* **t** men **back** to dust, saying,	8740
	102: 2	**T** your ear to me; when I call,	5742
	119:36	**T** my heart toward your statutes and not	5742
	119:37	**T** my eyes **away** from worthless things;	6296
	119:51	but *I* do not **t** from your law.	5742
	119:79	*May* those who fear you **t** to me,	8740
	119:132	**T** to me and have mercy on me,	7155
	125: 5	But those *who* **t** to crooked ways	5742
Pr	1:26	I **in t** will laugh at your disaster;	1685
	4:15	**t** from it and go on your way.	8474
	5: 7	*do not* **t** aside from what I say.	6073
	7:25	not *let* your heart **t** to her ways or stray	8474
	22: 6	and when he is old *he will* not **t** from it.	6073
	24:18	and disapprove and **t** his wrath **away**	8740
	29: 8	but wise men **t away** anger.	8740
SS	2:17	the shadows flee, **t**, my lover, and be like	6015
	6: 1	Which *way did* your lover **t**,	7155
	6: 5	**T** your eyes from me; they overwhelm me.	6015
Isa	1:25	*I will* **t** my hand against you;	8740
	3:12	*they* **t** you *from* the path.	1182
	6:10	with their hearts, and **t** and be healed."	8740
	9:21	together they will **t** against Judah.	NIH
	14:23	"*I will* **t** her into a place for owls and	8492
	14:27	and who *can* **t** it **back**?	8740
	17: 7	and **t** their eyes to the Holy One of Israel.	8011
	19:22	*They will* **t** to the LORD,	8740
	22: 4	Therefore I said, "**T away** from me;	9120
	28: 6	of strength to *those who* **t back** the battle at	8740
	29:16	You **t** things **upside down**,	2201
	30:21	*Whether* you **t to the right** or to the left,	3554
	41:18	*I will* **t** the desert into pools of water,	8492
	42:15	*I will* **t** rivers into islands and dry up	8492
	42:16	*I will* **t** the darkness into light	8492
	45:22	"**T** to me and be saved,	7155
	49:11	*I will* **t** all my mountains into roads,	8492
	50: 2	*I* **t** rivers **into** a desert;	8492
	55: 7	*Let* him **t** to the LORD,	8740
	56:11	they all **t** to their own way,	7155
	58: 7	*to* **t away** from your own flesh and blood?	6623
Jer	2:21	then *did you* **t** against me **into** a corrupt,	2200
	3:19	and not **t away** from following me.	8740
	4:28	I have decided and *will* not **t back**."	8740
	6: 8	or I *will* **t away** from you	3697
	8: 5	Why does Jerusalem always **t away**?	5412
	12:10	*they* will **t** my pleasant field into	5989
	13:16	but *he will* **t** it to thick darkness	8492
	15:19	*Let* this people **t** to you,	8740
	15:19	but you *must* not **t** to them.	8740
	17:13	*Those who* **t away** *from* you will be written	6073
	18:11	So **t** from your evil ways, each one of you,	8740
	18:20	in their behalf to **t** your wrath **away**	8740
	21: 4	I *am about to* **t against** you the weapons	6015
	23:20	The anger of the LORD *will* not **t back**	8740
	25: 5	They said, "**T** now, each of you,	8740
	26: 3	Perhaps they will listen and each *will* **t**	8740
	30:24	not **t back** until he fully accomplishes	8740
	31:13	*I will* **t** their mourning into gladness;	2200
	31:39	to the hill of Gareb and then **t** to Goah.	6015
	32:40	so that they *will* never **t away** from me.	6073
	35:15	*of you* must **t** from your wicked ways	8740
	36: 3	each *of them* will **t** from his wicked way;	8740
	36: 7	and each will **t** from his wicked ways,	8740
	44: 5	they did not **t** from their wickedness	8740
	46:21	They too *will* **t** and flee together,	7155
	47: 3	Fathers *will* not **t to** help their children;	8740
	49: 8	**T** and flee, hide in deep caves,	7155
	50: 5	the way to Zion and **t** their faces toward it.	NIH
Eze	1: 9	*they did* not **t** as they moved.	6015
	1:17	not **t** about as the creatures went.	6015
	3:19	and *he does* not **t** from his wickedness or	6015
	4: 3	between you and the city and **t** your face	3922
	4: 7	**T** your face toward the siege of Jerusalem	3922
	4: 8	so that you cannot **t** from one side to	2200
	7:20	Therefore *I will* **t** these into an unclean	5989
	10:11	*I will* **t** my face away from them,	6015
	10:11	not **t** about as the cherubim went.	6015
	13:22	the wicked not *to* **t** from their evil ways	8740
	14: 6	**T** from your idols and renounce all your	8740
	16:42	and my jealous anger *will* **t away**	6073
	18:23	not pleased when they **t** from their ways	8740
	18:30	**T away** from all your offenses;	8740
	23:24	*I will* **t** you **over** to them for punishment,	5989
	25: 5	*I will* **t** Rabbah into a pasture for camels	5989
	33: 9	to **t** from his ways and he does not do so,	8740
	33:11	rather that they **t** from their ways and live.	8740
	33:11	from their ways and live. **T**!	8740
	33:11	**T** from your evil ways!	8740
	35: 4	*I will* **t** your towns **into** ruins	8492
	38: 4	*I will* **t** you **around**, put hooks in your jaws	8740
	38:12	and **t** my hand against the resettled ruins	8740
	39: 2	*I will* **t** you **around** and drag you along.	8740
Da	9:16	**t away** your anger and your wrath	8740

Da	11:18	Then *he will* **t** his attention to	8740
	11:18	and *will* **t** his insolence **back** upon him.	8740
	11:19	*he will* **t back** toward the fortresses	8740
	11:30	Then *he will* **t back** and vent his fury	8740
Hos	2: 3	**t** her into a parched land,	8883
	3: 1	though they **t** to other gods and love	7155
	4:13	Therefore your daughters **t to** prostitution	2388
	4:14	when *they* **t to** prostitution,	2388
	7:14	and new wine but **t away** from me.	6073
	7:16	*They* do not **t** to the Most High;	8740
	9:12	Woe to them when I **t away** from them!	8740
	11: 7	My people are determined to **t** from me.	5412
	11: 9	nor *will I* **t** and devastate Ephraim.	8740
Joel	2:14	*He may* **t** and have pity and leave behind	8740
Am	1: 3	*I will* not **t back** [my wrath].	8740
	1: 6	*I will* not **t back** [my wrath].	8740
	1: 8	*I will* **t** my hand against Ekron,	8740
	1: 9	*I will* not **t back** [my wrath].	8740
	1:11	*I will* not **t back** [my wrath].	8740
	1:13	*I will* not **t back** [my wrath].	8740
	2: 1	*I will* not **t back** [my wrath].	8740
	2: 4	*I will* not **t back** [my wrath].	8740
	2: 6	*I will* not **t back** [my wrath].	8740
	5: 7	*You who* **t** justice into bitterness	2200
	8: 3	songs in the temple *will* **t to** wailing.	3536
	8:10	*I will* **t** your religious feasts into mourning	2200
Jnh	3: 9	with compassion **t** from his fierce anger so	7064
Mic	7:17	*they* will **t in fear** to the LORD our God	7064
Hab	2:16	Now it is your **t**! Drink and be exposed!	NIH
Zep	1: 6	those *who* **t back** from following the LORD	6047
Hag	2:17	mildew and hail, yet you did not **t** to me,'	NIH
Zec	1: 4	'**T** from your evil ways and your evil	8740
	13: 7	*I will* **t** my hand against the little ones.	8740
Mal	4: 6	He will **t** the hearts of the fathers	8740
Mt	5:39	the right cheek, **t** to him the other also.	5138
	5:42	and *do not* **t away from** the one who wants	695
	7: 6	and then **t** and tear you to pieces.	5138
	10:35	*to* **t** " 'a man against his father, a daughter	1495
	13:15	understand with their hearts and **t**,	2188
	15:36	and they in **t** to the people.	NIG
	20:19	and *will* **t** him **over** to the Gentiles to	4140
	24:10	that time many *will* **t away** from the faith	4997
Mk	4:12	otherwise they *might* **t** and be forgiven!' "	2188
Lk	1:17	**t** the hearts of the fathers **to** their children	2188
	6:29	on one cheek, **t** to him the other also.	4218
	12:58	and the judge **t** you **over** to the officer,	4140
Jn	2:16	**t** my Father's house **into** a market!"	4472
	12:22	Andrew and Philip **in t** told Jesus.	2779
	12:40	nor understand with their hearts, nor **t**—	5138
	16:20	but your grief *will* **t** to joy.	1181
Ac	3:19	Repent, then, and **t** to God,	2188
	6: 3	*We will* **t** this responsibility **over to** them	2770
	13: 8	and tried to **t** the proconsul from the faith.	1406
	13:46	*we* now **t** to the Gentiles.	5138
	14:15	**t** from these worthless things **to** the living	2188
	20:21	*they* must **t** to God in repentance	3567
	21:21	among the Gentiles **to t away from** Moses,	686
	26:18	and **t** them from darkness to light,	2188
	26:20	I preached that they should repent and **t** to	2188
	28:27	understand with their hearts and **t**,	2188
Ro	11:26	*he will* **t** godlessness **away** from Jacob.	695
1Co	14:31	For you can all prophesy **in t** so	1651+2848
	15:23	But each in his own **t**:	5413
2Co	7: 5	but we were harassed at every **t**—	NIG
	8:14	**in t** their plenty will supply what you need.	2779
Php	1:19	to me *will* **t out** for my deliverance.	1650
Col	4:16	that you **in t** read the letter from Laodicea.	2779
1Ti	6:20	**T away from** godless chatter and	1762
2Ti	2:19	The Lord *must* **t away** from wickedness."	923
	4: 4	*They will* **t** their ears **away from** the truth	695
	4: 4	from the truth and **t aside** to myths.	1762
Heb	12:25	*if* we **t away from** him who warns us	695
Jas	3: 3	we can **t** the whole animal.	3555
1Pe	3:11	*He must* **t** from evil and do good;	1712
2Pe	2:21	to have known it and then to **t their backs**	5715
Rev	10: 9	*It will* **t** your stomach **sour**,	4393
	11: 6	*to* **t** the waters into blood and to strike	5138

TURN, TURNED (Anglicized) See also HAND, HANDED

TURNED (262) [TURN]

Ge	9:23	Their faces were **t the other way** so	345
	14: 7	*they* **t back** and went to En Mishpat (that is,	8740
	18:22	The men **t away** and went toward Sodom,	7155
	41:13	And *things* **t** out exactly as he interpreted	2118
	42:24	*He* **t away** from them and began to weep,	6015
	42:24	but then **t back** and spoke to them again.	8740
	42:28	and *they* **t** to each other **trembling**	AIT
Ex	4: 4	of the snake and *it* **t back into** a staff	2118+4200
	7:23	Instead, he **t** and went into his palace,	7155
	10: 6	Then Moses **t** and left Pharaoh.	7155
	14:21	a strong east wind and **t** it into dry land.	8492
	32:15	Moses **t** and went down the mountain with	7155
Lev	13: 3	the sore *has* **t** white and the sore appears to	2200
	13: 4	and the hair in it *has* not **t** white,	2200
	13:10	in the skin that *has* **t** the hair white and	2200
	13:13	Since it *has* all **t** white, he is clean.	2200
	13:17	and if the sores *have* **t** white,	2200
	13:20	and the hair in it *has* **t** white,	2200
	13:25	and if the hair in it *has* **t** white,	2200
Nu	12:10	Aaron **t** toward her and saw	7155
	14:43	Because *you have* **t away** from the LORD,	8740
	16:42	to Moses and Aaron and **t** toward the Tent	7155
	20:21	Israel **t away** from them.	5742

Nu	21:33	Then *they* **t** and went up along the road	7155
	22:23	she **t** off the road into a field.	5742
	22:33	and **t away** from me these three times.	5742
	22:33	If *she had* not **t away**,	5742
	24: 1	but **t** his face toward the desert.	8883
	25:11	*has* **t** my anger **away** from the Israelites;	8740
	33: 7	They left Etham, **t back** to Pi Hahiroth,	8740
Dt	1:45	your weeping and **t a deaf ear** to you.	263+4202
	2: 1	Then *we* **t back** and set out toward	7155
	2: 8	*We* **t** from the Arabah road,	7155
	3: 1	Next *we* **t** and went up along the road	7155
	9:12	*They have* **t away** quickly from what	6073
	9:15	So *I* **t** and went down from the mountain	7155
	9:16	*You had* **t aside** quickly from the way that	6073
	23: 5	to Balaam but **t** the curse into a blessing	2200
	26:13	*I have* not **t aside** from your commands	6296
Jos	7:26	Then the LORD **t** from his fierce anger.	8740
	8:20	the desert *had* **t back** against their pursuers.	2200
	8:21	**t around** and attacked the men of Ai.	8740
	10:38	with him **t around** and attacked Debir.	8740
	11:10	that time Joshua **t back** and captured Hazor	8740
	15: 7	the Valley of Achor and **t** north to Gilgal,	7155
	15:11	of Ekron, **t** toward Shikkeron, passed	9305
	18:14	on the south the boundary **t** south along	9305
	19:12	*It* **t** east from Sarid toward the sunrise to	8740
	19:13	it came out at Rimmon and **t** toward Neah.	9305
	19:27	It then **t** east *toward* Beth Dagon,	8740
	19:29	The boundary then **t back** *toward* Ramah	8740
	19:29	**t** toward Hosah and came out at the sea in	8740
Jdg	2:17	*they* quickly **t** from the way	6073
	3:19	At the idols near Gilgal *he* himself **t back**	8740
	6:14	The LORD **t** to him and said,	7155
	14: 8	he **t aside** to look at the lion's carcass.	6073
	18: 3	so *they* **t in** there and asked him,	6073
	18:15	So *they* **t in** there and went to the house of	6073
	18:21	*they* **t away** and left.	7155
	18:23	the Danites **t** and said to Micah,	6015+7156
	18:26	**t around** and went back home.	7155
	20:40	the Benjamites **t** and saw the smoke of	6015
	20:41	Then the men of Israel **t on** them,	2200
	20:45	As *they* **t** and fled toward the desert to	7155
	20:47	But six hundred men **t** and fled into	7155
Ru	2: 3	As it **t** out, she found herself working	5247+7936
	3: 8	and *he* **t** and discovered a woman lying	4369
	3: 8	*They* **t aside** after dishonest gain	5742
1Sa	8: 3	to whom is all the desire of Israel **t**,	4200
	10: 9	As Saul **t** to leave Samuel,	7155+8900
	11: 7	and *they* **t out** as one man.	3655
	13:17	One **t** toward Ophrah in the vicinity	7155
	14:47	Wherever *he* **t**, he inflicted punishment	7155
	15:11	because *he has* **t away** from me and has	7155
	15:12	up a monument in his own honor and *has* **t**	6015
	15:27	As Samuel **t** to leave,	6015
	17:30	then **t away** to someone else and brought	6015
	17:35	When *it* **t** on me, I seized it by its hair,	7756
	17:51	that their hero was dead, *they* **t** and **ran**.	5674
	22:18	Doeg the Edomite **t** and struck them down.	6015
	25:12	David's men **t around** and went back.	2200
	28:15	and God *has* **t away** from me.	6073
	28:16	now that the LORD *has* **t away** from you	6073
2Sa	1: 7	When *he* **t around** and saw me,	7155
	19: 2	victory that day *was* **t into** mourning,	2118+4200
	22:23	*I have* not **t away** from his decrees.	6073
1Ki	6:34	each having two leaves *that* **t in sockets**.	1664
	8:14	the king **t around** and blessed them.	6015
	11: 4	his wives **t** his heart after other gods,	5742
	11: 9	with Solomon because his heart *had* **t away**	5742
	22:32	So *they* **t** to attack him,	6073
2Ki	2:24	*He* **t around**, looked at them and called	7155
	4:35	Elisha **t away** and walked back and forth in	8740
	5:12	So *he* **t** and went off in a rage.	7155
	9:23	Joram **t about** and fled,	2200+3338
	12:17	Then he **t** to attack Jerusalem.	7156+8492
	19:25	you *have* **t** fortified cities **into** piles of stone.	8615
	20: 2	Hezekiah **t** his face to the wall and prayed	6015
	23:25	like him who **t** to the LORD as he did—	8740
1Ch	10:14	and **t** the kingdom **over** to David son	6015
	21:20	he **t** and saw the angel.	8740
2Ch	6: 3	the king **t around** and blessed them.	6015
	11: 4	of the LORD and **t back** from marching	8740
	12:12	the LORD's anger **t** from him,	8740
	13:14	Judah **t** and saw that they were being	7155
	15: 4	But in their distress *they* **t** to the LORD,	8740
	18:31	So *they* **t** to attack him,	6015
	19: 4	of Ephraim and **t** them **back** to the LORD,	8740
	20:10	so *they* **t away** from them and did not	6073
	25:27	that Amaziah **t away** from following	6073
	29: 6	*They* **t** their faces **away** from the LORD's	6015
	29: 6	and **t** their backs on him.	5989
Ezr	10:14	of our God in this matter *is* **t away**	8740
Ne	2:15	*I* **t back** and reentered through	8740
	9:29	Stubbornly *they* **t** their backs on you,	5989
	13: 2	however, *t* the curse into a blessing.)	2200
Est	9: 1	but now **the tables were t** and the Jews got	2200
	9:22	the month when their sorrow **was t into** joy	2200
Job	6:14	God *has* **t** me **over** to evil men	6037
	16:19	those I love *have* **t** against me.	2200
	31: 7	if my steps *have* **t** from the path,	5742
	34:27	because *they* **t** from following him	6073
Ps	14: 3	All *have* **t aside**,	6073
	18:22	*I have* not **t away** from his decrees.	6073
	22:14	My heart *has* **t** to wax;	2118
	30:11	*You* **t** my wailing into dancing;	2118
	35: 4	*may* those who plot my ruin *be* **t back**	6047
	40: 1	he **t** to me and heard my cry.	5742
	40:14	*may* all who desire my ruin *be* **t back**	6047
	44:18	Our hearts *had* not **t back**;	6047

Ps	53: 3	Everyone *has* **t** away,	6047
	66: 6	He **t** the sea into dry land,	2200
	70: 2	*may* all who desire my ruin **be t** back	6047
	78: 9	**t** back on the day of battle;	2200
	78:30	before *they* **t** from the food they craved,	2319
	78:34	*they* eagerly **t** to him **again.**	8740
	78:44	He **t** their rivers to blood;	2200
	85: 3	You set aside all your wrath and **t**	8740
	89:43	*You have* **t** back the edge of his sword	8740
	105:25	whose hearts he **t** to hate his people,	2200
	105:29	He **t** their waters into blood,	2200
	105:32	He **t** their rain **into** hail,	5989
	107:33	He **t** rivers into a desert,	8492
	107:35	He **t** the desert into pools of water and	8492
	114: 3	The sea looked and fled, the Jordan **t** back;	6015
	114: 5	that you fled, O Jordan, *that you* **t** back,	6015
	114: 8	who **t** the rock **into** a pool,	2200
	116: 2	Because he **t** his ear to me,	5742
	119:59	and *have* **t** my steps to your statutes.	8740
	119:157	but *I have* not **t** from your statutes.	5742
	129: 5	*May* all who hate Zion **be t** back in shame.	6047
Ecc	2:12	Then I **t** my thoughts to consider wisdom,	7155
	7:25	So I **t** my mind to understand,	6015
Isa	1: 4	the Holy One of Israel and **t** *their* backs	2319
	5:25	Yet for all this, his anger *is* not **t** away,	8740
	7:25	become **places where** cattle are **t** loose	5448
	9:12	Yet for all this, his anger *is* not **t** away,	8740
	9:17	Yet for all this, his anger *is* not **t** away,	8740
	9:21	Yet for all this, his anger *is* not **t** away,	8740
	10: 4	Yet for all this, his anger *is* not **t** away,	8740
	12: 1	your anger *has* **t** away and	8740
	23:13	they stripped its fortresses bare and **t** it into	8492
	29:17	*will* not Lebanon **be t** into a fertile field	8740
	34: 9	Edom's streams *will* **be t** into pitch,	2200
	37:26	to pass, that you *have* **t** fortified cities **into**	8615
	38: 2	Hezekiah **t** his face to the wall and prayed	6015
	42:17	*will* **be t** back in utter shame.	6047
	53: 6	each of *us has* **t** to his own way;	7155
	59: 8	*They have* **t** them *into* **crooked** roads;	6835
	63:10	So he **t** and **became** their enemy	2200
Jer	2:27	*They have* **t** their backs to me and	7155
	4: 8	of the LORD *has* not **t** away from us.	8740
	5:23	*they have* **t** aside and gone away.	6073
	6:12	Their houses *will* **be t** over to others,	6015
	8: 5	Why have these people **t** away?	8740
	23:22	to my people and *would have* **t** them	8740
	30: 6	every face **t** deathly pale?	2200
	32:33	*They* **t** their backs to me and	7155
	34:16	*you have* **t** around and profaned my name;	8740
	39:14	*They* **t** him **over** to Gedaliah son	5989
	40: 5	However, before Jeremiah **t** to go,	8740
	41:14	at Mizpah **t** and went over to Johanan son	6015
	49:24	*she has* **t** to flee and panic has gripped her;	7155
La	1:13	He spread a net for my feet and **t** me back.	8740
	3: 3	*he has* **t** his hand against me again	2200
	4: 6	in a moment without a hand **t** to help her.	2565
	5: 2	Our inheritance *has* **been t** over to aliens,	2200
	5:15	our dancing *has* **t** to mourning.	2200
Eze	6: 9	which *have* **t** away from me,	6073
	17: 6	Its branches **t** toward him,	7155
	21:16	then to the left, wherever your blade *is* **t.**	3585
	23:17	she **t** away from them **in disgust.**	3697
	23:18	I **t** away from her **in disgust,**	3697
	23:18	just as I *had* **t** away from her sister.	5936
	23:22	those you **t** away from **in disgust,**	5936
	23:28	to those you **t** away from **in disgust.**	5936
	42:19	Then he **t** to the west side and measured;	6015
Da	2: 5	into pieces and your houses **t into** piles	10682
	2:29	O king, your mind **t** *to* come,	10513
	3:29	be cut into pieces and their houses **be t into**	10702
	5: 6	His face **t** pale and he was so frightened	10731
	7:28	and my face **t** pale,	10731
	9: 3	So I **t** to the Lord God and pleaded	5989+7156
	9: 5	we *have* **t** away from your commands	6073
	9:11	Israel has transgressed your law and **t** away,	6073
	10: 8	my face **t** deathly pale and I was helpless.	2200
Hos	5: 3	*you have* now **t** to **prostitution;**	2388
	5:13	then Ephraim **t** to Assyria,	2143
	7: 8	Ephraim is a flat cake not **t** over.	2200
	14: 4	for my anger *has* **t** away from them.	2200
Joel	2:31	The sun *will* **be t** to darkness and	2200
Am	6:12	But *you have* **t** justice into poison and	2200
Jnh	3:10	and how *they* **t** from their evil ways,	8740
Zep	3:15	he has **t** back your enemy.	7155
Hag	1: 9	but see, it **t** out to be little.	NIH
Zec	7:11	stubbornly *they* **t** their backs and stopped	5989
	8:10	for I *had* **t** every man against his neighbor.	8938
Mal	1: 3	I *have* **t** his mountains **into** a wasteland	8492
	2: 6	and **t** many from sin.	8740
	3: 7	But *you have* **t** from the way and	6073
	3: 7	of your forefathers *you have* **t** away	6073
Mt	9:22	Jesus **t** and saw her.	5138
	16:23	Jesus **t** and said to Peter, "Get behind me,	5138
	18:34	In anger his master **t** him **over** to	4140
Mk	5:30	He **t** around in the crowd and asked,	2188
	8:33	*when* Jesus **t** and looked at his disciples,	2188
Lk	7:44	he **t** toward the woman and said to Simon,	5138
	9:55	But Jesus **t** and rebuked them,	5138
	10:23	he **t** to his disciples and said privately,	5138
	22:32	you *have* **t** back, strengthen your brothers."	2188
	22:61	The Lord **t** and looked straight at Peter.	5138
	23:28	Jesus **t** and said to them,	5138
Jn	2: 9	the water *that had* **been t** into wine.	1181
	4:46	where *he had* **t** the water **into** wine.	4472
	6:66	From this time many of his disciples **t** back	599+1650+3836+3958
	9:17	Finally *they* **t** again to the blind man,	3306

Jn	20:14	*she* **t** around and saw Jesus standing there,	1650+3836+3958+5138
	20:16	She **t** toward him and cried out	5138
	21:20	Peter **t** and saw that the disciple whom Jesus	2188
Ac	2:20	*be* **t** to darkness and the moon to blood	3570
	7:39	they rejected him and in their hearts **t** back	5138
	7:42	But God **t** away and gave them over to	5138
	9:35	and Sharon saw him and **t** to the Lord.	2188
	11:21	a great number of people believed and **t** to	2188
	16:18	so troubled that he **t** around and said to	2188
	18:17	Then they all **t** on Sosthenes	2138
Ro	3:12	All *have* **t** away, they have together become	1712
1Th	1: 9	They tell how *you* **t** to God from idols	2188
	3: 4	And *it* **t** **out** that way, as you well know.	1181
1Ti	1: 6	from these and **t** to meaningless talk.	846
	5:15	in fact already **t** away to follow Satan.	1762
Heb	8: 9	and I **t** away from them, declares the Lord.	288
	11:34	whose weakness *was* **t** to strength;	1540
Rev	1:12	I **t** around to see the voice	2188
	1:12	*when* I **t** I saw seven golden lampstands,	2188
	6:12	The sun **t** black like sackcloth made	1181
	6:12	the whole moon **t** blood red,	1181
	8: 8	A third of the sea **t into** blood,	1181
	8:11	A third of the waters **t** bitter,	1181+1650
	8:12	so that a third of them **t** **dark.**	5029
	10:10	but when I had eaten it, my stomach **t** sour.	4393
	16: 3	*it* **t into** blood like that of a dead man,	1181

TURNING (33) [TURN]

Nu	31:16	and were the means of **t** the Israelites **away**	5086
Dt	31:18	of all their wickedness *in* **t** to other gods.	7155
Jos	22:18	And *are* you now **t** away from the LORD?	8740
	23: 6	without **t** aside to the right or to the left.	6073
Jdg	8:20	**T** to Jether, his oldest son, he said,	NIH
	11: 8	"Nevertheless, *we are* **t** to you now;	8740
2Sa	2:19	**t** neither to the right nor to the left	5742
	22:22	I have not done evil by **t** *from* my God.	4946
1Ki	18:37	and that you *are* **t** their hearts back again."	6015
2Ki	21:13	wiping it and **t** it upside down.	2200
	22: 2	not **t** aside *to* the right *or to* the left.	6073
2Ch	34: 2	not **t** aside *to* the right *or to* the left.	6073
Job	23:11	I have kept to his way without **t** aside.	5742
	36:21	Beware of **t** to evil,	7155
Ps	18:21	I have not done evil by **t** *from* my God.	4946
Pr	2: 2	**t** your ear to wisdom and	7992
	13:14	a man from the snares of death.	6073
	13:19	but fools detest **t** from evil.	6073
	14:27	a man from the snares of death.	6073
Isa	59:13	**t** our backs *on* our God,	6047
Eze	1:12	they would go, without **t** as they went.	6015
	10:11	without **t** as they went.	6015
	29:16	a reminder of their sin in **t** to her for help.	7155
Da	9:13	of the LORD our God by **t** from our sins	8740
Hos	7:11	now calling to Egypt, now **t** to Assyria,	2143
Lk	7: 9	and **t** to the crowd following him, he said,	5138
	14:25	and **t** to them he said:	5138
Jn	1:38	**T** around, Jesus saw them following	5138
Ac	3:26	**t** each of you *from* your wicked ways."	695
	9:40	**T** toward the dead woman, he said,	2188
	15:19	for the Gentiles who *are* **t** to God.	2188
Gal	1: 6	of Christ and are **t** to a different gospel—	NIG
	4: 9	how is it that *you* **t** back **to** those weak	2188

TURNS (40) [TURN]

Lev	20: 6	the person who **t** to mediums and spiritists	7155
Dt	29:18	among you today whose heart **t** away from	7155
	30:17	your heart **t** away and you are not obedient,	7155
2Sa	22:29	the LORD **t** my darkness **into light.**	5585
2Ki	11: 6	who **take t** guarding the temple—	5005
Job	1: 4	to **take t** holding feasts in their homes,	2143+3427
	23: 9	when *he* **t** *to* the south, I catch no glimpse	6493
Ps	18:28	my God **t** my darkness **into light.**	5585
Pr	15: 1	A gentle answer **t** away wrath,	8740
	17: 8	wherever *he* **t,** he succeeds.	7155
	26:14	As a door **t** on its hinges,	6015
	26:14	so a sluggard **t** on his bed.	NIH
	28: 9	If *anyone* **t** a deaf ear to the law,	6073
Ecc	1: 6	wind blows to the south and **t** to the north;	6015
	7: 7	Extortion **t** a wise man **into a fool,**	2147
Isa	24:11	all joy **t to gloom,**	6845
	41: 2	*He* **t** them to dust *with* his sword,	5989
	44:25	of the wise and **t** it **into nonsense,**	6118
Jer	8: 4	When *a man* **t** away, does he not return?	8740
	17: 5	and whose heart **t** away from the LORD.	6073
	23:14	so that no one **t** from his wickedness.	8740
	48:39	How Moab **t** *her* back in shame!	7155
La	1: 8	she herself groans and **t** away.	8740
Eze	3:20	a righteous man **t** from his righteousness	8740
	18:21	"But if a wicked man **t** away from all	8740
	18:24	if a righteous man **t** from his righteousness	8740
	18:26	If a righteous man **t** from his righteousness	8740
	18:27	But if a wicked man **t** away from	8740
	18:28	and **t** away from them, he will surely live;	8740
	33:12	not cause him to fall when he **t** from it.	8740
	33:14	but *he* then **t** away from his sin	8740
	33:18	If a righteous man **t** from his righteousness	8740
	33:19	a wicked man **t** away from his wickedness	8740
Joel	2: 6	every face **t** pale.	6999+7695
Am	4:13	*he who* **t** dawn **to** darkness,	6913
	5: 8	*who* **t** blackness into dawn and darkens day	2200
Na	2: 8	they cry, but no one **t** back.	7155
2Co	3:16	But whenever *anyone* **t** to the Lord,	2188
Heb	3:12	unbelieving heart that **t** away from	923
Jas	5:20	Whoever **t** a sinner from the error of his way	2188

TURQUOISE (6)

Ex	28:18	in the second row a **t,** a sapphire and	5876
	39:11	in the second row a **t,** a sapphire and	5876
1Ch	29: 2	as well as onyx for the settings, **t,**	7037
Isa	54:11	I will build you with stones of **t,**	7037
Eze	27:16	they exchanged **t,** purple fabric,	5876
	28:13	onyx and jasper, sapphire, **t** and beryl.	5876

TURTLE, TURTLEDOVE, TURTLES
(KJV) See DOVE, DOVES

TUSKS (1)

| Eze | 27:15 | they paid you with ivory **t** and ebony. | 7967 |

TUTORS (KJV) See GUARDIANS

TWAIN (KJV) See TWO

TWELFTH (23) [TWELVE]

Nu	7:78	On the **t** day Ahira son of Enan,	6925+9109
1Ki	19:19	and he himself was driving the **t** pair.	6925+9109
2Ki	8:25	In the **t** year of Joram son of Ahab	6926+9109
	17: 1	In the **t** year of Ahaz king of Judah,	6926+9109
	25:27	the twenty-seventh day of the **t** month.	6926+9109
1Ch	24:12	eleventh to Eliashib, the **t** to Jakim,	6925+9109
	25:19	the **t** to Hashabiah,	6925+9109
	27:15	The **t,** for the twelfth month,	6925+9109
	27:15	The twelfth, for the **t** month,	6925+9109
2Ch	34: 3	In his **t** year he began to purge Judah	6926+9109
Ezr	8:31	the **t** day of the first month we set out	6925+9109
Est	3: 7	In the **t** year of King Xerxes,	6926+9109
	3: 7	fell on the **t** month, the month of Adar.	6925+9109
	3:13	the thirteenth day of the **t** month,	6925+9109
	8:12	the thirteenth day of the **t** month,	6925+9109
	9: 1	On the thirteenth day of the **t** month,	6925+9109
Jer	52:31	on the twenty-fifth day of the **t** month.	6925+9109
Eze	29: 1	in the tenth month on the **t** day,	6925+9109
	32: 1	In the **t** year, in the twelfth month on	6926+9109
	32: 1	in the **t** month on the first day,	6925+9109
	32:17	In the **t** year, on the fifteenth day of	6926+9109
	33:21	In the **t** year of our exile,	6926+9109
Rev	21:20	the eleventh jacinth, and the **t** amethyst.	1558

TWELVE (146) [TWELFTH, 12, 12,000, 144,000]

Ge	14: 4	For **t** years they had been subject	6926+9109
	17:20	He will be the father of **t** rulers,	6925+9109
	25:16	the names of the **t** tribal rulers	6925+9109
	35:22	Jacob had **t** sons:	6925+9109
	42:13	"Your servants were **t** brothers,	6925+9109
	42:32	We were **t** brothers, sons of one father.	6925+9109
	49:28	All these are the **t** tribes of Israel,	6925+9109
Ex	15:27	where there were **t** springs and	6926+9109
	24: 4	and set up **t** stone pillars representing	6926+9109
	24: 4	the **t** tribes of Israel.	6925+9109
	28:21	There are to be **t** stones,	6925+9109
	28:21	with the name of one of the **t** tribes.	6925+9109
	39:14	There were **t** stones,	6926+9109
	39:14	with the name of one of the **t** tribes.	6925+9109
Lev	24: 5	"Take fine flour and bake **t** loaves	6926+9109
Nu	1:44	by Moses and Aaron and the **t** leaders	6926+9109
	7: 3	six covered carts and **t** oxen—	6925+9109
	7:84	when it was anointed: **t** silver plates,	6926+9109
	7:84	**t** silver sprinkling bowls	6926+9109
	7:84	and **t** gold dishes.	6926+9109
	7:86	The **t** gold dishes filled with incense	6926+9109
	7:87	burnt offering came to **t** young bulls,	6926+9109
	7:87	**t** rams and twelve male lambs a year	6925+9109
	7:87	rams and **t** male lambs a year old,	6925+9109
	7:87	**T** male goats were used for	6925+9109
	17: 2	Israelites and get **t** staffs from them,	6925+9109
	17: 6	and their leaders gave him **t** staffs,	6925+9109
	29:17	the second day prepare **t** young bulls,	6925+9109
	31: 5	So **t** thousand men armed for battle,	6925+9109
	33: 9	where there were **t** springs and	6926+9109
Dt	1:23	so I selected **t** of you,	6925+9109
Jos	3:12	choose **t** men from the tribes of Israel,	6925+9109
	4: 2	Choose **t** men from among the people,	6925+9109
	4: 3	take up **t** stones from the middle of the Jordan	6926+9109
	4: 4	the **t** men he had appointed from	6925+9109
	4: 8	They took **t** stones from the middle of	6926+9109
	4: 9	the **t** stones that had been in the	6926+9109
	4:20	at Gilgal the **t** stones they had taken	6926+9109
	8:25	**T** thousand men and women fell that day—	6926+9109
	18:24	**t** towns and their villages.	6926+9109
	19:15	There were **t** towns and their villages.	6926+9109
	21: 7	**t** towns from the tribes of Reuben,	6926+9109
	21:40	were the rest of the Levites, were **t.**	6926+9109
Jdg	19:29	limb by limb, into **t** parts and sent	6926+9109
	21:10	assembly sent **t** thousand fighting men	6926+9109
2Sa	2:15	**t** men for Benjamin and Ish-Bosheth	6925+9109
	2:15	son of Saul, and **t** for David.	6925+9109
	10: 6	and also **t** thousand men from Tob.	6925+9109
	17: 1	"I would choose **t** thousand men	6925+9109
1Ki	4: 7	had **t** district governors over all Israel,	6925+9109
	4:26	and **t** thousand horses.	6925+9109
	7:15	each eighteen cubits high and **t** cubits	6926+9109
	7:25	The Sea stood on **t** bulls,	6925+9109
	7:44	the Sea and the **t** bulls under it;	6925+9109
	10:20	**T** lions stood on the six steps,	6925+9109

1Ki	10:26	and t thousand horses,	6925+9109
	11:30	and tore it into t pieces.	6925+9109
	16:23	king of Israel, and he reigned t years,	6926+9109
	18:31	Elijah took t stones,	6926+9109
	19:19	He was plowing with t yoke of oxen,	6925+9109
2Ki	3: 1	king of Judah, and he reigned t years.	6926+9109
	21: 1	Manasseh was t years old when	6926+9109
1Ch	6:63	were allotted t towns from the tribes	6926+9109
2Ch	1:14	and t thousand horses,	6925+9109
	4: 4	The Sea stood on t bulls,	6925+9109
	4:15	the Sea and the t bulls under it;	6925+9109
	9:19	T lions stood on the six steps,	6925+9109
	9:25	and t thousand horses,	6925+9109
	12: 3	With t hundred chariots	547+2256+4395
	33: 1	Manasseh was t years old when	6926+9109
Ezr	6:17	offering for all Israel, t male goats,	10573+10775
	8:24	Then I set apart t of the leading priests,	6925+9109
	8:35	t bulls for all Israel, ninety-six rams,	6925+9109
	8:35	as a sin offering, t male goats.	6925+9109
Ne	5:14	until his thirty-second year—t years	6926+9109
Est	2:12	she had to complete t months	6926+9109
Ps	60: T	and struck down t thousand Edomites	6925+9109
Jer	52:20	the Sea and the t bronze bulls under it,	6925+9109
	52:21	and t cubits in circumference;	6926+9109
Eze	40:49	and t cubits from front to back.	6926+9109
	43:16	t cubits long and twelve cubits wide.	6926+9109
	43:16	twelve cubits long and t cubits wide;	6926+9109
	47:13	inheritance among the t tribes of Israel,	6925+9109
Da	4:29	T months later, as the king was	10573+10775
Mt	9:20	subject to bleeding for t years came up	1557
	10: 1	He called his t disciples to him	1557
	10: 2	These are the names of the t apostles:	1557
	10: 5	These t Jesus sent out with	1557
	11: 1	Jesus had finished instructing his t disciples,	1557
	14:20	and the disciples picked up t basketfuls	1557
	19:28	have followed me will also sit on t thrones,	1557
	19:28	judging the t tribes of Israel.	1557
	20:17	the t disciples aside and said to them,	1557
	26:14	Then one of the T—the one called Judas	1557
	26:20	Jesus was reclining at the table with the T.	1557
	26:47	Judas, one of the T, arrived.	1557
	26:53	at my disposal more than t legions	1557
Mk	3:14	He appointed t—designating them apostles	1557
	3:16	These are the t he appointed:	1557
	4:10	the T and the others around him asked him	1557
	5:25	had been subject to bleeding for t years	1557
	5:42	and walked around (she was t years old).	1557
	6: 7	Calling the T to him, he sent them out	1557
	6:43	up t basketfuls of broken pieces of bread	1557
	8:19	"T," they replied.	1557
	9:35	Sitting down, Jesus called the T and said,	1557
	10:32	the T aside and told them what was going	1557
	11:11	he went out to Bethany with the T.	1557
	14:10	Then Judas Iscariot, one of the T,	1557
	14:17	Jesus arrived with the T.	1557
	14:20	"It is one of the T," he replied,	1557
	14:43	Judas, one of the T, appeared.	1557
Lk	2:42	When he was t years old, they went up	1557
	6:13	he called his disciples to him and chose t	1557
	8: 1	The T were with him,	1557
	8:42	a girl of about t, was dying.	1557
	8:43	had been subject to bleeding for t years,	1557
	9: 1	When Jesus had called the T together,	1557
	9:12	the afternoon the T came to him and said,	1557
	9:17	and the disciples picked up t basketfuls	1557
	18:31	Jesus took the T aside and told them,	1557
	22: 3	Judas, called Iscariot, one of the T.	1557
	22:30	judging the t tribes of Israel.	1557
	22:47	Judas, one of the T, was leading them.	1557
Jn	6:13	So they gathered them and filled t baskets	1557
	6:67	Jesus asked the T.	1557
	6:70	"Have I not chosen you, the T?	1557
	6:71	though one of the T, was later to betray him	1557
	11: 9	"Are there not t hours of daylight?	1557
	20:24	Thomas (called Didymus), one of the T,	1557
Ac	6: 2	So the T gathered all the disciples together	1557
	7: 8	Jacob became the father of the t patriarchs.	1557
	19: 7	There were about t men in all.	1557
	24:11	that no more than t days ago I went up	1557
	26: 7	This is the promise our t tribes are hoping	1559
1Co	15: 5	he appeared to Peter, and then to the T.	1557
Jas	1: 1	the t tribes scattered among the nations:	1557
Rev	12: 1	moon under her feet and a crown of t stars	1557
	21:12	It had a great, high wall with t gates,	1557
	21:12	and with t angels at the gates.	1557
	21:12	the names of the t tribes of Israel.	1557
	21:14	The wall of the city had t foundations,	1557
	21:14	on them were the names of the t apostles	1557
	21:21	The t gates were twelve pearls,	1557
	21:21	The twelve gates were t pearls,	1557
	22: 2	bearing t crops of fruit,	1557

TWENTIETH (9) [TWENTY]

Nu	10:11	On the t day of the second month of	6929
1Ki	15: 9	In the t year of Jeroboam king of Israel,	6929
2Ki	15:30	then succeeded him as king in the t year	6929
1Ch	24:16	nineteenth to Pethahiah, the t to Jehezkel,	6929
	25:27	the t to Eliathah, his sons and relatives,	6929
Ezr	10: 9	And on the t day of the ninth month,	6929
Ne	1: 1	In the month of Kislev in the t year,	6929
	2: 1	of Nisan in the t year of King Artaxerxes,	6929
	5:14	from the t year of King Artaxerxes,	6929

TWENTY (125) [TWENTIETH, 20]

Ge	6: 3	his days will be a hundred and t years."	6929
Ge	7:20	to a depth of more than t feet.	564+2822+6926
	18:31	what if only t can be found there?"	6929
	18:31	He said, "For the sake of t, I will not	6929
	31:38	"I have been with you for t years now.	6929
	31:41	for the t years I was in your household.	6929
	32:14	female goats and t male goats,	6929
	32:14	two hundred ewes and t rams,	6929
	32:15	t female donkeys and ten male donkeys.	6929
	37:28	for t shekels of silver to the Ishmaelites,	6929
Ex	26:18	Make t frames for the south side of	6929
	26:20	of the tabernacle, make t frames	6929
	27:10	with t posts and twenty bronze bases and	6929
	27:10	with twenty posts and t bronze bases and	6929
	27:11	with t posts and twenty bronze bases and	6929
	27:11	with twenty posts and t bronze bases and	6929
	27:16	provide a curtain t cubits long, of blue,	6929
	30:13	sanctuary shekel, which weighs t gerahs.	6929
	30:14	those t years old or more,	6929
	36:23	They made t frames for the south side	6929
	36:25	side of the tabernacle, they made t frames	6929
	38:10	with t posts and twenty bronze bases,	6929
	38:10	with twenty posts and t bronze bases,	6929
	38:11	also a hundred cubits long and had t posts	6929
	38:11	and had twenty posts and t bronze bases,	6929
	38:18	It was t cubits long and,	6929
	38:26	t years old or more, a total of 603,550	6929
Lev	27: 3	of a male between the ages of t and sixty	6929
	27: 5	a person between the ages of five and t,	6929
	27: 5	at t shekels and of a female at ten shekels.	6929
	27:25	t gerahs to the shekel.	6929
Nu	1: 3	in Israel t years old or more who are able	6929
	1:18	and the men t years old or more were listed	6929
	1:20	the men t years old or more who were able	6929
	1:22	the men t years old or more who were able	6929
	1:24	the men t years old or more who were able	6929
	1:26	the men t years old or more who were able	6929
	1:28	the men t years old or more who were able	6929
	1:30	the men t years old or more who were able	6929
	1:32	the men t years old or more who were able	6929
	1:34	the men t years old or more who were able	6929
	1:36	the men t years old or more who were able	6929
	1:38	the men t years old or more who were able	6929
	1:40	the men t years old or more who were able	6929
	1:42	the men t years old or more who were able	6929
	1:45	All the Israelites t years old	6929
	3:47	sanctuary shekel, which weighs t gerahs.	6929
	7:86	dishes weighed a hundred and t shekels.	6929
	11:19	or two days, or five, ten or t days,	6929
	14:29	every one of you t years old of more	6929
	18:16	sanctuary shekel, which weighs t gerahs.	6929
	26: 2	all those t years old or more who are able	6929
	26: 4	a census of the men t years old or more,	6929
	32:11	of the men t years old or more who came	6929
Dt	31: 2	and t years old and I am no longer able	6929
	34: 7	a hundred and t years old when he died,	6929
Jdg	4: 3	cruelly oppressed the Israelites for t years,	6929
	8:10	and t thousand swordsmen had fallen.	6929
	11:33	He devastated t towns from Aroer to	6929
	15:20	Samson led Israel for t years in the days of	6929
	16:31	He had led Israel t years.	6929
1Sa	7: 2	It was a long time, t years in all,	6929
	14:14	and his armor-bearer killed some t men in	6929
2Sa	3:20	When Abner, who had t men with him,	6929
	8: 4	and t thousand foot soldiers.	6929
	9:10	(Now Ziba had fifteen sons and t servants.)	6929
	10: 6	they hired t thousand Aramean foot soldiers	6929
	18: 7	that day were great—t thousand men.	6929
	19:17	and his fifteen sons and t servants.	6929
	24: 8	at the end of nine months and t days.	6929
1Ki	4:23	t of pasture-fed cattle and a hundred sheep	6929
	5:11	and Solomon gave Hiram t thousand cors	6929
	5:11	thousand baths of pressed olive oil.	6929
	6: 2	t wide and thirty high.	6929
	6: 3	width of the temple, that is t cubits,	6929
	6:16	He partitioned off t cubits at the rear of	6929
	6:20	The inner sanctuary was t cubits long,	6929
	6:20	t wide and twenty high.	6929
	6:20	twenty wide and t high.	6929
	8:63	a hundred and t thousand sheep and goats.	6929
	9:10	At the end of t years, during which Solomon	6929
	9:11	King Solomon gave t towns in Galilee	6929
2Ki	4:42	of God t loaves of barley bread baked from	6929
	15:27	and he reigned t years.	6929
	16: 2	Ahaz was t years old when he became king,	6929
1Ch	18: 4	and t thousand foot soldiers.	6929
	23:24	the workers t years old or more who served	6929
	23:27	from those t years old or more.	6929
	27:23	not take the number of the men t years old	6929
2Ch	2:10	t thousand cors of ground wheat,	6929
	2:10	t thousand cors of barley,	6929
	2:10	t thousand baths of wine	6929
	2:10	of wine and t thousand baths of olive oil."	6929
	3: 3	and t cubits wide (using the cubit of	6929
	3: 4	at the front of the temple was t cubits long	6929
	3: 4	the width of the building and t cubits high.	6929
	3: 8	t cubits long and twenty cubits wide.	6929
	3: 8	twenty cubits long and t cubits wide.	6929
	3:11	of the cherubim was t cubits.	6929
	3:13	wings of these cherubim extended t cubits.	6929
	4: 1	He made a bronze altar t cubits long,	6929
	4: 1	t cubits wide and ten cubits high.	6929
	7: 5	a hundred and t thousand sheep and goats.	6929
	8: 1	At the end of t years, during which Solomon	6929
	25: 5	He then mustered those t years old or more	6929
	28: 1	Ahaz was t years old when he became king,	6929
	28: 6	and t thousand soldiers in Judah—	6929
	31:17	and likewise to the Levites t years old	6929
Ezr	3: 8	appointing Levites t years of age and older	6929
Eze	4:10	Weigh out t shekels of food to eat each day	6929
	40:49	The portico was t cubits wide,	6929
	41: 2	it was forty cubits long and t cubits wide.	6929
	41: 4	of the inner sanctuary; it was t cubits,	6929
	41: 4	and its width was t cubits across the end of	6929
	41:10	was t cubits wide all around the temple.	6929
	42: 3	in the section t cubits from the inner court	6929
	45:12	The shekel is to consist of t gerahs.	6929
	45:12	T shekels plus twenty-five shekels plus fifteen shekels equal one mina.	6929
Jnh	4:11	a hundred and t thousand people who cannot tell their right hand	6926+8052+9109
Hag	2:16	anyone came to a heap of t measures,	6929
	2:16	to draw fifty measures, there were only t.	6929
Lk	14:31	one coming against him with t thousand?	1633
Jn	2: 6	each holding from t to thirty gallons.	1545+2445+3583+5552
Ac	1:15	(a group numbering about a hundred and t)	1633
	27:28	water was a hundred and t feet deep.	1633+3976

TWENTY-EIGHT (4) [28]

Ex	26: 2	t cubits long and four cubits	2256+6929+9046
	36: 9	t cubits long and four cubits	2256+6929+9046
2Ki	10:36	Israel in Samaria was t years.	2256+6929+9046
2Ch	11:21	t sons and sixty daughters.	2256+6929+9046

TWENTY-FIFTH (3) [TWENTY-FIVE]

Ne	6:15	So the wall was completed on the t of Elul,	2256+2822+6929
Jer	52:31	freed him from prison on the t day of the twelfth month.	2256+2822+6929
Eze	40: 1	In the t year of our exile,	2256+2822+6929

TWENTY-FIRST (4) [TWENTY-ONE]

Ex	12:18	until the evening of the t day.	285+2256+6929
1Ch	24:17	the t to Jakin, the twenty-second	285+2256+6929
	25:28	the t to Hothir, his sons and	285+2256+6929
Hag	2: 1	the t day of the seventh month,	285+2256+6929

TWENTY-FIVE (23) [TWENTY-FIFTH]

Nu	8:24	Men t years old or more shall	2256+2822+6929
Jdg	20:46	On that day t thousand Benjamite swordsmen fell,	2256+2822+6929
1Ki	22:42	he reigned in Jerusalem t years.	2256+2822+6929
2Ki	14: 2	He was t years old when he	2256+2822+6929
	15:33	He was t years old when he	2256+2822+6929
	18: 2	He was t years old when he	2256+2822+6929
	23:36	Jehoiakim was t years old when	2256+2822+6929
2Ch	20:31	he reigned in Jerusalem t years.	2256+2822+6929
	25: 1	Amaziah was t years old when	2256+2822+6929
	27: 1	Jotham was t years old when	2256+2822+6929
	27: 8	He was t years old when he	2256+2822+6929
	29: 1	Hezekiah was t years old when	2256+2822+6929
	36: 5	Jehoiakim was t years old when	2256+2822+6929
Eze	8:16	were about t men.	2256+2822+6929
	11: 1	entrance to the gate were t men,	2256+2822+6929
	40:21	the distance was t cubits	2256+2822+6929
	40:21	cubits long and t cubits wide.	2256+2822+6929
	40:25	cubits long and t cubits wide.	2256+2822+6929
	40:29	cubits long and t cubits wide.	2256+2822+6929
	40:30	inner court were t cubits wide	2256+2822+6929
	40:33	cubits long and t cubits wide.	2256+2822+6929
	40:36	cubits long and t cubits wide.	2256+2822+6929
	45:12	Twenty shekels plus t shekels plus fifteen shekels equal one mina.	2256+2822+6929

TWENTY-FOUR (11) [TWENTY-FOURTH]

Nu	7:88	the fellowship offering came to t oxen,	752+2256+6929
2Sa	21:20	six toes on each foot—t in all.	752+2256+6929
1Ki	15:33	and he reigned t years.	752+2256+6929
1Ch	20: 6	six toes on each foot—t in all.	752+2256+6929
	23: 4	t thousand are to supervise the	752+2256+6929
Rev	4: 4	the throne were t other thrones,	1633+5475
	4: 4	and seated on them were t elders.	1633+5475
	4:10	the t elders fall down before him	1633+5475
	5: 8	the t elders fell down before the Lamb.	1633+5475
	11:16	And the t elders, who were seated	1633+5475
	19: 4	The t elders and the four living	1633+5475

TWENTY-FOURTH (9) [TWENTY-FOUR]

1Ch	24:18	and the t to Maaziah.	752+2256+6929
	25:31	the t to Romamti-Ezer,	752+2256+6929
Ne	9: 1	On the t day of the same month,	752+2256+6929
Da	10: 4	On the t day of the first month,	752+2256+6929
Hag	1:15	on the t day of the sixth month in	752+2256+6929
	2:10	On the t day of the ninth month,	752+2256+6929
	2:18	from this t day of the ninth month,	752+2256+6929
	2:20	a second time on the t day of the	752+2256+6929
Zec	1: 7	the t day of the eleventh month,	752+2256+6929

TWENTY-NINE (5) [29]

Jos	15:32	of t towns and their villages.	2256+6929+9596
2Ki	14: 2	he reigned in Jerusalem t years.	2256+6929+9596
	18: 2	he reigned in Jerusalem t years.	2256+6929+9596
2Ch	25: 1	he reigned in Jerusalem t years.	2256+6929+9596
	29: 1	he reigned in Jerusalem t years.	2256+6929+9596

TWENTY-ONE (4) [TWENTY-FIRST]

2Ki	24:18	Zedekiah was t years old when	285+2256+6929
2Ch	36:11	Zedekiah was t years old when	285+2256+6929

Jer 52: 1 Zedekiah was t years old when 285+2256+6929
Da 10:13 the prince of the Persian kingdom resisted
me t days. 285+2256+6929

TWENTY-SECOND (2) [TWENTY-TWO]
1Ch 24:17 to Jakin, the t to Gamul, 2256+6929+9109
25:29 the t to Giddalti, his sons and 2256+6929+9109

TWENTY-SEVEN (4) [TWENTY-SEVENTH]
Ge 23: 1 to be a hundred and t years old. 2256+6929+8679
1Ki 20:30 the wall collapsed on t thousand 2256+6929+8679
2Ki 25:17 Each pillar was t feet high. 564+6926+9046
1Ch 26:32 Jeriah had t hundred relatives, 547+2256+4395+8679

TWENTY-SEVENTH (6) [TWENTY-SEVEN]
Ge 8:14 the t day of the second month 2256+6929+8679
1Ki 16:10 killed him in the t year of Asa 2256+6929+8679
16:15 In the t year of Asa king of 2256+6929+8679
2Ki 15: 1 In the t year of Jeroboam king 2256+6929+8679
25:27 the t day of the twelfth month. 2256+6929+8679
Eze 29:17 In the t year, in the first month 2256+6929+8679

TWENTY-SIX (2) [TWENTY-SIXTH]
Jdg 20:15 Benjamites mobilized t thousand
swordsmen 2256+6929+9252
2Ch 35: 8 gave the priests t hundred Passover
offerings 547+2256+4395+9252

TWENTY-SIXTH (1) [TWENTY-SIX]
1Ki 16: 8 the t year of Asa king of Judah, 2256+6929+9252

TWENTY-THIRD (7) [TWENTY-THREE]
2Ki 12: 6 But by the t year of King Joash 2256+6929+8993
13: 1 In the t year of Joash son of 2256+6929+8993
1Ch 24:18 the t to Delaiah and 2256+6929+8993
25:30 the t to Mahazioth, 2256+6929+8993
2Ch 7:10 the t day of the seventh month 2256+6929+8993
Est 8: 9 on the t day of the third month, 2256+6929+8993
Jer 52:30 in his t year, 745 Jews taken 2256+6929+8993

TWENTY-THREE (7) [TWENTY-THIRD]
Nu 33:39 Aaron was a hundred and t years old when
he died 2256+6929+8993
Jdg 10: 2 He led Israel t years; 2256+6929+8993
2Ki 23:31 Jehoahaz was t years old when 2256+6929+8993
1Ch 2:22 controlled t towns in Gilead. 2256+6929+8993
2Ch 36: 2 Jehoahaz was t years old when 2256+6929+8993
Jer 35: 3 For t years—from the thirteenth 2256+6929+8993
1Co 10: 8 in one day t thousand of them died. 1633+5552

TWENTY-TWO (15) [TWENTY-SECOND, 22]
Jos 19:30 were t towns and their villages. 2256+6929+9109
Jdg 7: 3 So t thousand men left, 2256+6929+9109
10: 3 who led Israel t years. 2256+6929+9109
20:21 cut down t thousand Israelites 2256+6929+9109
2Sa 8: 5 David struck down t thousand 2256+6929+9109
1Ki 8:63 t thousand cattle and 2256+6929+9109
14:20 He reigned for t years and 2256+6929+9109
16:29 in Samaria over Israel t years. 2256+6929+9109
2Ki 8:26 Ahaziah was t years old when 2256+6929+9109
21:19 Amon was t years old when 2256+6929+9109
1Ch 18: 5 David struck down t thousand 2256+6929+9109
2Ch 7: 5 of t thousand head of cattle and 2256+6929+9109
13:21 fourteen wives and had t sons 2256+6929+9109
22: 2 Ahaziah was t years old when 2256+6929+9109
33:21 Amon was t years old when 2256+6929+9109

TWICE (21) [TWO]
Ge 43:10 we could have gone and returned t." 7193
Ex 16: 5 and that is to be t as much as they gather on 5467
16:22 On the sixth day, they gathered t as much— 5467
Nu 20:11 and struck the rock t with his staff. 7193
Dt 15:18 worth t as much as that of a hired hand. 5467
1Sa 18:11 But David eluded him t. 7193
26: 8 I won't strike him t." 9101
1Ki 11: 9 who had appeared to him t. 7193
Ne 13:20 or t the merchants and sellers of all kinds 9109
Job 33:29 "God does all these things to a man—t, 7193
40: 5 t, but I will say no more." 9109
42:10 and gave him t as much as he had before. 5467
Ecc 6: 6 if he lives a thousand years t over but fails 7193
Eze 21:14 Let the sword strike t, even three times. 4100
Zec 9:12 now I announce that I will restore t as much 5467
Mt 26:34 you make him t as much a son of hell 1486
Mk 14:30 rooster crows t you yourself will disown
me three times." 1489
14:72 rooster crows t you will disown me three
times." 1489
Lk 18:12 I fast t a week and give a tenth of all I get.' 1489
2Co 1:15 so that you might benefit t. 1311
Jude 1:12 without fruit and uprooted—t dead. 1489

TWIG (1) [TWIGS]
Hos 10: 7 and its king will float away like a t on 7913

TWIGS (4) [TWIG]
Isa 27:11 When its t are dry, they are broken off 7908

Isa 64: 2 fire sets t ablaze and causes water to boil, 2173
Mt 24:32 as its t get tender and its leaves come out, 3080
Mk 13:28 as its t get tender and its leaves come out, 3080

TWILIGHT (14) [LIGHT]
Ex 12: 6 Israel must slaughter them at t. 1068+2021+6847
16:12 'At t you will eat meat, 1068+2021+6847
29:39 the morning and the other at t. 1068+2021+6847
29:41 Sacrifice the other lamb at t 1068+2021+6847
30: 8 when he lights the lamps at t 1068+2021+6847
Lev 23: 5 LORD's Passover begins at t 1068+2021+6847
Nu 9: 3 at t on the fourteenth day of this month, 1068+2021+6847
9: 5 and they did so in the Desert of Sinai at t 1068+2021+6847
9:11 of the second month at t. 1068+2021+6847
28: 4 the morning and the other at t, 1068+2021+6847
28: 8 Prepare the second lamb at t, 1068+2021+6847
Pr 7: 9 at t, as the day was fading, as the dark 5974
Isa 21: 4 the t I longed for has become a horror 5974
59:10 At midday we stumble as if it were t; 5974

TWIN (6) [TWINS]
Ge 25:24 there were t boys in her womb. 9339
38:27 there were t boys in her womb. 9339
SS 4: 2 Each has its t; not one of them is alone. 9298
4: 5 like t fawns of a gazelle that browse 9339
6: 6 Each has its t, not one of them is alone. 9298
Ac 28:11 figurehead of the t gods Castor and Pollux. 1483

TWINED (KJV) See TWISTED

TWINKLING (1)
1Co 15:52 in the t of an eye, at the last trumpet. 4846

TWINS (2) [TWIN]
SS 7: 3 breasts are like two fawns, t of a gazelle. 9339
Ro 9:11 Yet, before the t were born or had done NIG

TWIST (1) [TWISTED, TWISTING, TWISTS]
Ps 56: 5 All day long they t my words; 6772

TWISTED (26) [TWIST]
Ex 26: 1 with ten curtains of finely t linen 8813
26:31 purple and scarlet yarn and finely t linen, 8813
26:36 and scarlet yarn and finely t linen— 8813
27: 9 and is to have curtains of finely t linen, 8813
27:16 and scarlet yarn and finely t linen— 8813
27:18 of finely t linen five cubits high, 8813
28: 6 and scarlet yarn, and of finely t linen— 8813
28: 8 and scarlet yarn, and with finely t linen. 8813
28:15 and scarlet yarn, and of finely t linen. 8813
36: 8 with ten curtains of finely t linen 8813
36:35 purple and scarlet yarn and finely t linen, 8813
36:37 and scarlet yarn and finely t linen. 8813
38: 9 and had curtains of finely t linen. 8813
38:16 the courtyard were of finely t linen. 8813
38:18 and scarlet yarn and finely t linen— 8813
39: 2 and scarlet yarn, and of finely t linen. 8813
39: 5 and scarlet yarn, and with finely t linen. 8813
39: 8 and scarlet yarn, and of finely t linen. 8813
39:24 and scarlet yarn and finely t linen around 8813
39:28 and the undergarments of finely t linen. 8813
39:29 The sash was of finely t linen and blue, 8813
Ecc 1:15 What is t cannot be straightened; 6430
Eze 27:24 and multicolored rugs with cords t 2502
Mt 27:29 then together a crown of thorns and set it 4428
Mk 15:17 then together a crown of thorns and set it 4428
Jn 19: 2 The soldiers t together a crown of thorns 4428

TWISTING (1) [TWIST]
Pr 30:33 and as t the nose produces blood, 4790

TWISTS (3) [TWIST]
Ex 23: 8 a bribe blinds those who see and t the words 6156
Dt 16:19 a bribe blinds the eyes of the wise and t the 6156
Ps 29: 9 The voice of the LORD t the oaks 2655

TWO (621) [SECOND, TWICE,
TWO-AND-A-HALF, TWO-DRACHMA,
TWO-HORNED, TWO-TENTHS,
TWO-THIRDS]
Ge 1:16 God made t great lights— 9109
4:19 Lamech married t women, 9109
6:19 into the ark t of all living creatures, 9109
6:20 T of every kind of bird, 9109
7: 2 and t of every kind of unclean animal, 9109
9:22 and told his t brothers outside. 9109
10:25 T sons were born to Eber: 9109
11:10 T years after the flood, AIT
13:11 The t men parted company; NIH
15:10 cut them in t and arranged the halves 9348
19: 1 The t angels arrived at Sodom in 9109
19: 8 I have t daughters who have never slept 9109
19:12 The t men said to Lot, NIH
19:15 and your t daughters who are here 9109
19:16 the hands of his wife and of his t daughters 9109
19:30 and his t daughters left Zoar and settled in 9109
19:30 He and his t daughters lived in a cave. 9109

Ge 21:27 and the t men made a treaty. 9109
21:31 because the t men swore an oath there. 9109
22: 3 He took with him t of his servants 9109
22: 6 As the t of them went on together, 9109
22: 8 And the t of them went on together. 9109
24:22 and t gold bracelets weighing ten shekels. 9109
25:23 "T nations are in your womb, 9109
25:23 and t peoples from within you will 9109
27: 9 and bring me t choice young goats, 9109
27:36 He has deceived me these t times: AIT
29:16 Now Laban had t daughters; 9109
31:33 and into the tent of the t maidservants, 9109
31:37 and let them judge between the t of us. 9109
31:41 for you fourteen years for your t daughters 9109
32: 7 with him into t groups, 9109
32:10 but now I have become t groups. 9109
32:14 t hundred female goats and twenty male AIT
32:14 t hundred ewes and twenty rams, AIT
32:22 up and took his t wives, 9109
32:22 his t maidservants and his eleven sons 9109
33: 1 Rachel and the t maidservants. 9109
34:25 t of Jacob's sons, Simeon and Levi, 9109
40: 2 Pharaoh was angry with his t officials, 9109
40: 5 each of the t men— 9109
41: 1 When t full years had passed, AIT
41:32 to Pharaoh in t forms is that AIT
41:50 t sons were born to Joseph 9109
44:27 'You know that my wife bore me t sons. 9109
45: 6 For t years now there has been famine in AIT
46:27 the t sons who had been born to Joseph 9109
48: 1 So he took his t sons Manasseh 9109
48: 5 your t sons born to you in Egypt 9109
49:14 lying down between t saddlebags. 5478
Ex 2:13 and saw t Hebrews fighting. 9109
4: 9 if they do not believe these t signs or listen 9109
16:22 t omers for each person— 9109
16:29 the sixth day he gives you bread for t days. AIT
18: 3 and her t sons. 9109
18: 6 to you with your wife and her t sons." 9109
21:21 if the slave gets up after a day or t, 3427S
25:10 t and a half cubits long, AIT
25:12 with t rings on one side and two rings on 9109
25:12 with two rings on one side and t rings on 9109
25:17 t and a half cubits long, AIT
25:18 And make t cherubim out of hammered gold 9109
25:19 of one piece with the cover, at the t ends. 9109
25:22 the cover between the t cherubim that are 9109
25:23 t cubits long, a cubit wide and a cubit and AIT
26:17 with t projections set parallel to each other. 9109
26:19 t bases for each frame, 9109
26:21 t under each frame. 9109
26:23 and make t frames for the corners at 9109
26:24 At these t corners they must be double 9109
26:25 t under each frame. 9109
27: 7 be on t sides of the altar when it is carried. 9109
28: 7 to have t shoulder pieces attached to two 9109
28: 7 to have two shoulder pieces attached to t 9109
28: 9 "Take t onyx stones and engrave on them 9109
28:11 of the sons of Israel on the t stones the way 9109
28:14 and t braided chains of pure gold, 9109
28:23 Make t gold rings for it and fasten them 9109
28:23 for it and fasten them to t corners of 9109
28:24 the t gold chains to the rings at the corners 9109
28:25 of the chains to the t settings, 9109
28:26 Make t gold rings and attach them to 9109
28:26 the other t corners of the breastpiece on the 9109
28:27 Make t more gold rings and attach them to 9109
29: 1 a young bull and t rams without defect. 9109
29: 3 along with the bull and the t rams. 9109
29:38 regularly each day: t lambs a year old. 9109
30: 2 a cubit wide, and t cubits high— AIT
30: 4 Make t gold rings for the altar below 9109
30: 4 t on opposite sides—to hold the poles 9109
31:18 he gave him the t tablets of the Testimony, 9109
32:15 the t tablets of the Testimony in his hands. 9109
34: 1 "Chisel out t stone tablets like the first ones 9109
34: 4 So Moses chiseled out t stone tablets like 9109
34: 4 he carried the t stone tablets in his hands. 9109
34:29 the t tablets of the Testimony in his hands, 9109
36:13 to fasten the t sets of curtains together so AIT
36:22 with t projections set parallel to each other. 9109
36:24 t bases for each frame, 9109
36:26 t under each frame. 9109
36:28 and t frames were made for the corners of 9109
36:29 At these t corners the frames were double 9109
36:30 t under each frame. 9109
37: 1 t and a half cubits long, AIT
37: 3 with t rings on one side and two rings on 9109
37: 3 with two rings on one side and t rings on 9109
37: 6 t and a half cubits long AIT
37: 7 Then he made t cherubim out 9109
37: 8 the t ends he made them of one piece with 9109
37:10 t cubits long, a cubit wide, AIT
37:25 a cubit wide, and t cubits high— AIT
37:27 They made t gold rings below 9109
37:27 t on opposite sides—to hold the poles 9109
39: 4 which were attached to t of its corners, 9109
39:16 They made t gold filigree settings 9109
39:16 gold filigree settings and t gold rings, 9109
39:16 and fastened the rings to t of the corners of 9109
39:17 They fastened the t gold chains to the rings 9109
39:18 of the chains to the t settings, 9109
39:19 They made t gold rings and attached them 9109
39:19 the other t corners of the breastpiece on the 9109
39:20 Then they made t more gold rings 9109
Lev 5: 7 he is to bring t doves or two young pigeons 9109
5: 7 he is to bring two doves or t young pigeons 9109

Lev	5:11	If, however, he cannot afford t doves	9109
	5:11	or t young pigeons,	9109
	8: 2	the t rams and and the basket containing	9109
	12: 5	for t weeks the woman will be unclean,	AIT
	12: 8	to bring t doves or two young pigeons,	9109
	12: 8	to bring two doves or t young pigeons,	9109
	14: 4	the priest shall order that t live clean birds	9109
	14:10	the eighth day he must bring t male lambs	9109
	14:22	and t doves or two young pigeons,	9109
	14:22	and two doves or t young pigeons,	9109
	14:49	To purify the house he is to take t birds	9109
	15:14	On the eighth day he must take t doves	9109
	15:14	or t young pigeons and come before	9109
	15:29	On the eighth day she must take t doves	9109
	15:29	or t young pigeons and bring them to	9109
	16: 1	the death of the t sons of Aaron who died	9109
	16: 5	to take t male goats for a sin offering and	9109
	16: 7	to take the t goats and present them before	9109
	16: 8	He is to cast lots for the t goats—	9109
	16:12	and t handfuls of finely ground	2908+4850
	19:19	not plant your field with t kinds of seed.	3977
	19:19	" 'Do not wear clothing woven of t kinds	3977
	23:17	bring t loaves made of two-tenths of	9109
	23:18	one young bull and t rams.	9109
	23:19	for a sin offering and t lambs,	9109
	23:20	to wave the t lambs before the LORD as	9109
	24: 6	Set them in t rows, six in each row,	9109
Nu	6:10	on the eighth day he must bring t doves	9109
	6:10	or t young pigeons to the priest at	9109
	7: 3	from each leader and a cart from every t.	9109
	7: 7	He gave t carts and four oxen to	9109
	7:17	and t oxen, five rams, five male goats	9109
	7:23	and t oxen, five rams, five male goats	9109
	7:29	and t oxen, five rams, five male goats	9109
	7:35	and t oxen, five rams, five male goats	9109
	7:41	and t oxen, five rams, five male goats	9109
	7:47	and t oxen, five rams, five male goats	9109
	7:53	and t oxen, five rams, five male goats	9109
	7:59	and t oxen, five rams, five male goats	9109
	7:65	and t oxen, five rams, five male goats	9109
	7:71	and t oxen, five rams, five male goats	9109
	7:77	and t oxen, five rams, five male goats	9109
	7:83	and t oxen, five rams, five male goats	9109
	7:85	the silver dishes weighed t thousand four hundred shekels,	AIT
	7:89	to him from between the t cherubim above	9109
	9:22	over the tabernacle for t days or a month or	AIT
	10: 2	"Make t trumpets of hammered silver,	9109
	11:19	or t days, or five, ten or twenty days,	AIT
	11:26	However, t men, whose names were Eldad	9109
	13:23	T of them carried it on a pole	9109
	22:22	and his t servants were with him.	9109
	22:24	in a narrow path between t vineyards,	2021S
	23: 2	the t of them offered a bull	1189+1192+2256S
	28: 3	t lambs a year old without defect,	9109
	28: 9	make an offering of t lambs a year old	9109
	28:11	a burnt offering of t young bulls,	9109
	28:19	a burnt offering of t young bulls,	9109
	28:27	Present a burnt offering of t young bulls,	9109
	29:13	t rams and fourteen male lambs a year old,	9109
	29:14	with each of the t rams, two-tenths;	9109
	29:17	t rams and fourteen male lambs a year old,	9109
	29:20	t rams and fourteen male lambs a year old,	9109
	29:23	t rams and fourteen male lambs a year old,	9109
	29:26	t rams and fourteen male lambs a year old,	9109
	29:29	t rams and fourteen male lambs a year old,	9109
	29:32	t rams and fourteen male lambs a year old,	9109
	34:15	These t and a half tribes have received their inheritance on the east	9109
Dt	3: 8	So at that time we took from these t kings	9109
	3:21	LORD your God has done to these t kings	9109
	4:13	and then wrote them on t stone tablets.	9109
	4:47	the t Amorite kings east of the Jordan.	9109
	5:22	on t stone tablets and gave them to me.	9109
	9:10	The LORD gave me t stone tablets inscribed	9109
	9:11	the LORD gave me the t stone tablets,	9109
	9:15	t tablets of the covenant were in my hands.	9109
	9:17	So I took the t tablets and threw them out	9109
	10: 1	"Chisel out t stone tablets like the first ones	9109
	10: 3	and chiseled out t stone tablets like	9109
	10: 3	up on the mountain with the t tablets	9109
	14: 6	a split hoof divided in t and that chews	9109
	17: 6	of t or three witnesses a man shall be put	9109
	19:15	by the testimony of t or three witnesses.	9109
	19:17	the t men involved in the dispute	9109
	21:15	If a man has t wives, and he loves one	9109
	22: 9	not plant t kinds of seed in your vineyard;	3977
	25:11	If t men are fighting and the wife of one	278+408+2256+3481
	25:13	Do not have t differing weights	74+74+2256
	25:14	Do not have t differing measures	406+406+2256
	32:30	or t put ten thousand to flight,	9109
Jos	2: 1	of Nun secretly sent t spies from Shittim.	9109
	2: 4	But the woman had taken the t men	9109
	2:10	the t kings of the Amorites east of	9109
	2:23	Then the t men started back.	9109
	6:22	Joshua said to the t men who had spied out	9109
	7: 3	Send t or three thousand men to take it	AIT
	7:21	t hundred shekels of silver and a wedge	AIT
	9:10	to the t kings of the Amorites east of	9109
	14: 4	the sons of Joseph had become t tribes—	9109
	15:60	and Rabbah — t towns and their villages.	9109
	21:16	nine towns from these t tribes.	9109
	21:25	with their pasturelands—t towns.	9109
	21:27	with their pasturelands—t towns;	9109
	24:12	also the t Amorite kings.	9109
Jdg	5:30	a girl or t for each man,	8169S

Jdg	7:25	also captured t of the Midianite leaders,	9109
	8:12	the t kings of Midian, fled,	9109
	9:44	Then t companies rushed upon those in	9109
	11:37	"Give me t months to roam the hills	9109
	11:38	And he let her go for t months.	9109
	11:39	After the t months, she returned	9109
	15:13	with t new ropes and led him up from	9109
	16: 3	together with the t posts,	9109
	16:28	on the Philistines for my t eyes."	9109
	16:29	toward the t central pillars on which	9109
	17: 4	and she took t hundred shekels of silver	AIT
	19: 3	He had with him his servant and t donkeys.	7538
	19: 6	So the t of them sat down to eat	9109
	19: 8	So the t of them ate together.	9109
	19:10	with his t saddled donkeys	7538
	20:45	and struck down t thousand more.	AIT
Ru	1: 1	together with his wife and t sons,	9109
	1: 2	and the names of his t sons were Mahlon	9109
	1: 3	died, and she was left with her t sons.	9109
	1: 5	and Naomi was left without her t sons	9109
	1: 7	With her t daughters-in-law she left	9109
	1: 8	Then Naomi said to her t daughters-in-law,	9109
	1:19	So the t women went on until they came	9109
1Sa	1: 2	He had t wives; one was called Hannah	9109
	1: 3	the t sons of Eli, were priests of the LORD	9109
	2:21	to three sons and t daughters.	9109
	2:34	" 'And what happens to your t sons,	9109
	4: 4	And Eli's t sons, Hophni and Phinehas,	9109
	4:11	and Eli's t sons, Hophni and Phinehas,	9109
	4:17	Also your t sons, Hophni and Phinehas,	9109
	6: 7	with t cows that have calved	9109
	6:10	They took t such cows and hitched them to	9109
	10: 2	you will meet t men near Rachel's tomb,	9109
	10: 4	They will greet you and offer you t loaves	9109
	11:11	so that no t of them were left together.	9109
	13: 2	t thousand were with him at Micmash and	AIT
	13:21	was t thirds of a shekel for sharpening	7088
	15: 4	t hundred thousand foot soldiers	AIT
	18:27	and killed t hundred Philistines.	AIT
	23:18	The t of them made a covenant before	9109
	25:13	while t hundred stayed with the supplies.	AIT
	25:18	She took t hundred loaves of bread,	AIT
	25:18	t skins of wine, five dressed sheep,	9109
	25:18	and t hundred cakes of pressed figs,	AIT
	27: 3	and David had his t wives:	9109
	28: 8	at night he and t men went to the woman.	9109
	30: 5	David's t wives had been captured—	9109
	30:10	for t hundred men were too exhausted	AIT
	30:12	part of a cake of pressed figs and t cakes	AIT
	30:18	Amalekites had taken, including his t wives.	9109
	30:21	t hundred men who had been too exhausted	AIT
2Sa	1: 1	the Amalekites and stayed in Ziklag t days.	9109
	2: 2	So David went up there with his t wives,	9109
	2:10	and he reigned t years.	9109
	4: 2	Saul's son had t men who were leaders	9109
	8: 2	Every t lengths of them were put to death,	9109
	12: 1	"There were t men in a certain town,	9109
	13:23	T years later, when Absalom's sheepshearers	AIT
	14: 6	I your servant had t sons.	9109
	14:26	and its weight was t hundred shekels by	AIT
	14:28	Absalom lived t years in Jerusalem	AIT
	15:11	T hundred men from Jerusalem	AIT
	15:27	and Abiathar take your t sons with you.	9109
	15:36	Their t sons, Ahimaaz son of Zadok	9109
	16: 1	and loaded with t hundred loaves of bread,	AIT
	17:18	So the t of them left quickly and went to	9109
	17:21	he climbed out of the well and went	NIH
	21: 8	the t sons of Aiah's daughter Rizpah,	9109
	23:20	He struck down t of Moab's best men.	9109
1Ki	2: 5	to the t commanders of Israel's armies,	9109
	2:32	of my father David he attacked t men	9109
	2:39	t of Shimei's slaves ran off to Achish son	9109
	3:16	Now t prostitutes came to the king	9109
	3:18	was no one in the house but the t of us.	9109
	3:25	the living child in t and give half to one	9109
	3:26	Cut him in t!"	1615
	5:12	and the t of them made a treaty.	9109
	5:14	in Lebanon and t months at home.	9109
	6:25	for the t cherubim were identical in size	9109
	6:32	t olive wood doors he carved cherubim,	9109
	6:34	He also made t pine doors,	9109
	6:34	each having t leaves that turned in sockets.	9109
	7:15	He cast t bronze pillars,	9109
	7:16	also made t capitals of cast bronze to set	9109
	7:18	in t rows encircling each network	9109
	7:20	were the t hundred pomegranates	AIT
	7:24	in t rows in one piece with the Sea.	9109
	7:26	It held t thousand baths.	AIT
	7:41	the t pillars; the two bowl-shaped capitals	9109
	7:41	the t bowl-shaped capitals on top of	9109
	7:41	the t sets of network decorating	9109
	7:41	the t bowl-shaped capitals on top of	9109
	7:42	for the t sets of network (two rows	9109
	7:42	of network (t rows of pomegranates	9109
	8: 9	the t stone tablets that Moses had placed	9109
	9:10	Solomon built these t buildings—	9109
	10:16	Solomon made t hundred large shields	AIT
	11:29	The t of them were alone out in	9109
	12:28	the king made t golden calves.	9109
	15:25	and he reigned over Israel t years.	AIT
	16: 8	and he reigned in Tirzah t years.	AIT
	16:21	people of Israel were split into t factions;	2942
	16:24	for t talents of silver and built a city on	AIT
	18: 4	and hidden them in t caves.	NIH
	18:13	hundred of the LORD's prophets in t caves,	NIH
	18:21	"How long will you waver between t opinions?"	9109

1Ki	18:23	Get t bulls for us.	9109
	18:32	around it large enough to hold t seahs	AIT
	20:27	like t small flocks of goats,	9109
	21:10	But seat t scoundrels opposite him	9109
	21:13	Then t scoundrels came	9109
	22:51	and he reigned over Israel t years.	AIT
2Ki	1:14	the first t captains and all their men.	9109
	2: 6	So the t of them walked on.	9109
	2: 8	the t of them crossed over on dry ground.	9109
	2:11	of fire appeared and separated the t	9109
	2:24	Then t bears came out of the woods	9109
	4: 1	to take my t boys as his slaves."	9109
	4:33	on the t of them and prayed to the LORD.	9109
	5:22	'T young men from the company of	9109
	5:22	a talent of silver and t sets of clothing.' "	9109
	5:23	"By all means, take t talents,"	AIT
	5:23	tied up the t talents of silver in two bags,	AIT
	5:23	tied up the two talents of silver in t bags,	9109
	5:23	with t sets of clothing.	9109
	5:23	He gave them to t of his servants,	9109
	7: 1	a shekel and t seahs of barley for a shekel at	AIT
	7:14	they selected t chariots with their horses,	9109
	7:16	and t seahs of barley sold for a shekel,	AIT
	7:18	a shekel and t seahs of barley for a shekel at	AIT
	9:32	T or three eunuchs looked down at him.	9109
	10: 4	"If t kings could not resist him,	AIT
	10: 8	in t piles at the entrance of the city gate	9109
	11: 7	and you who are in the other t companies	AIT
	15:23	and he reigned t years.	AIT
	17:16	and made for themselves t idols cast in	9109
	18:23	I will give you t thousand horses—	AIT
	21:19	and he reigned in Jerusalem t years.	9109
	23:12	in the t courts of the temple of the LORD.	9109
	25: 4	through the gate between the t walls near	AIT
	25:16	The bronze from the t pillars,	9109
1Ch	1:19	T sons were born to Eber:	9109
	4: 5	Ashhur the father of Tekoa had t wives,	9109
	5:21	t hundred fifty thousand sheep	AIT
	5:21	and t thousand donkeys.	AIT
	11:22	He struck down t of Moab's best men.	9109
	26:17	and t at a time at the storehouse.	9109+9109
	26:18	there were four at the road and t at	9109
2Ch	3:15	In the front of the temple he made t pillars,	9109
	4: 3	The bulls were cast in t rows in one piece	9109
	4:12	the t pillars; the two bowl-shaped capitals	9109
	4:12	the t bowl-shaped capitals on top of	9109
	4:12	the t sets of network decorating	9109
	4:12	the t bowl-shaped capitals on top of	9109
	4:13	for the t sets of network (two rows	9109
	4:13	of network (t rows of pomegranates	9109
	5:10	the t tablets that Moses had placed in it	9109
	8:10	t hundred and fifty officials supervising	AIT
	9:15	Solomon made t hundred large shields	AIT
	14: 8	and t hundred and eighty thousand	AIT
	24: 3	Jehoiada chose t wives for him,	9109
	28: 8	their kinsmen t hundred thousand wives,	AIT
	29:32	hundred rams and t hundred male lambs—	AIT
	33:21	and he reigned in Jerusalem t years.	AIT
Ezr	6:17	t hundred rams, four hundred male lambs	AIT
	8:27	and t fine articles of polished bronze,	AIT
	10:13	be taken care of in a day or t,	9109
Ne	11:16	t of the heads of the Levites,	NIH
	12:31	also assigned t large choirs to give thanks.	9109
	12:40	The t choirs that gave thanks	9109
Est	2:21	t of the king's officers who guarded	9109
	2:23	the t officials were hanged on a gallows.	9109
	6: 2	t of the king's officers who guarded	9109
	9:27	without fail observe these t days every year,	9109
Job	11: 6	for true wisdom has t sides.	4101
	13:20	"Only grant me these t things, O God,	9109
	42: 7	"I am angry with you and your t friends,	9109
Ps	62:11	t things have I heard:	9109
Pr	24:22	for those t will send sudden destruction	9109
	30: 7	"T things I ask of you, O LORD;	9109
	30:15	"The leech has t daughters. 'Give! Give!'	9109
Ecc	4: 6	with tranquillity than t handfuls with toil	AIT
	4: 9	T are better than one,	9109
	4:11	I lie down together, they will keep warm.	9109
	4:12	t can defend themselves.	9109
SS	4: 5	Your t breasts are like two fawns,	9109
	4: 5	Your two breasts are like t fawns,	9109
	7: 3	Your breasts are like t fawns,	9109
	7: 7	t hundred are for those who tend its fruit.	AIT
Isa	6: 2	With t wings they covered their faces,	9109
	6: 2	with t they covered their feet,	9109
	6: 2	and with t they were flying.	9109
	7: 4	of these t smoldering stubs of firewood—	9109
	7:16	of the t kings you dread will be laid waste.	9109
	7:21	a young cow and t goats.	9109
	17: 6	leaving t or three olives on	9109
	22:11	You built a reservoir between the t walls	AIT
	36: 8	I will give you t thousand horses—	AIT
Jer	2:13	"My people have committed t sins:	9109
	3:14	one from a town and t from a clan—	9109
	24: 1	the LORD showed me t baskets	9109
	28: 3	Within t years I will bring back	AIT
	28:11	the neck of all the nations within t years.' "	AIT
	33:24	the t kingdoms he chose'?	9109
	34:18	like the calf they cut in t and then walked	9109
	39: 4	through the gate between the t walls,	AIT
	52: 7	through the gate between the t walls near	AIT
	52:20	The bronze from the t pillars,	9109
Eze	1:11	each had t wings,	9109
	1:11	t wings covering its body.	9109
	1:23	and each had t wings covering its body.	9109
	21:19	mark out t roads for the sword of the king	9109
	21:21	at the junction of the t roads,	9109

Eze 23: 2	there were t women, daughters of the same	9109
35:10	"These t nations and countries will be ours	9109
37:22	and they will never again be t nations or	9109
37:22	or be divided into t kingdoms.	9109
40: 9	and its jambs were t cubits thick.	9109
40:39	In the portico of the gateway were t tables	9109
40:40	to the north gateway were t tables,	9109
40:40	on the other side of the steps were t tables.	9109
40:44	within the inner court, were t rooms,	9109
41: 3	each was t cubits wide.	9109
41:18	Each cherub had t faces:	9109
41:22	and t cubits square;	9109
41:24	Each door had t leaves—	9109
41:24	t hinged leaves for each door.	9109
43:14	up to the lower ledge it is t cubits high and	9109
45:15	be taken from every flock of t hundred	AIT
47:13	with t portions for Joseph.	AIT
Da 7: 4	from the ground so that it stood on t feet	AIT
8: 3	before me was a ram with t horns,	AIT
8: 7	striking the ram and shattering his t horns.	9109
11:27	The t kings, with their hearts bent on evil,	9109
12: 5	looked, and there before me stood t others,	9109
Hos 6: 2	After t days he will revive us;	AIT
Am 1: 1	what he saw concerning Israel t years	AIT
3: 3	Do t walk together unless they have agreed	9109
3:12	the lion's mouth only t leg bones or a piece	9109
6: 2	Are they better off than your t kingdoms?	465ˢ
Zec 4: 3	Also there are t olive trees by it,	9109
4:11	"What are these t olive trees on the right	9109
4:12	"What are these t olive branches beside	9109
4:12	the t gold pipes that pour out golden oil?"	9109
4:14	"These are the t who are anointed to serve	9109
5: 9	and there before me were t women,	9109
6: 1	from between t mountains—	9109
6:13	And there will be harmony between the t.'	9109
11: 7	Then I took t staffs and called one Favor	9109
14: 4	and the Mount of Olives will be split in t	2942
Mt 2:16	and its vicinity who were t years old and	1453
4:18	he saw t brothers, Simon called Peter	1545
4:21	he saw t other brothers, James son of	1545
5:41	to go one mile, go with him t miles.	1545
6:24	"No one can serve t masters.	1545
8:28	t demon-possessed men coming from	1545
9:27	t blind men followed him, calling out,	1545
10:29	Are not t sparrows sold for a penny?	1545
14:17	five loaves of bread and t fish,"	1545
14:19	the five loaves and the t fish and looking	1545
18: 8	or crippled than to have t hands or two feet	1545
18: 8	or crippled than to have two hands or t feet	1545
18: 9	to have t eyes and be thrown into the fire	1545
18:15	just between the t of you.	899+2779+5148
18:16	take one or t others along,	1545
18:16	by the testimony of t or three witnesses.'	1545
18:19	I tell you that if t of you on earth agree	1545
18:20	t or three come together in my name,	1545
19: 5	and the t will become one flesh'?	1545
19: 6	So they are no longer t, but one.	1545
20:21	that one of these t sons of mine may sit	1545
20:24	they were indignant with the t brothers.	1545
20:30	T blind men were sitting by the roadside,	1545
21: 1	Jesus sent t disciples,	1545
21:28	There was a man who had t sons.	1545
21:31	of the t did what his father wanted?"	1545
22:40	hang on these t commandments."	1545
24:40	T men will be in the field; one will be taken	1545
24:41	T women will be grinding with a hand mill;	1545
25:15	to another t talents,	1545
25:17	the one with the t talents gained two more.	1545
25:17	the one with the two talents gained t more.	1545
25:22	"The man with the t talents also came.	1545
25:22	he said, 'you entrusted me with t talents;	1545
25:22	see, I have gained t more.'	1545
26: 2	the Passover is t days away—	1545
26:37	and the t sons of Zebedee along with him,	1545
26:60	Finally t came forward	1545
27:21	of the t do you want me to release to you?"	1545
27:38	T robbers were crucified with him,	1545
27:51	the curtain of the temple was torn in t	1545
Mk 5:13	The herd, about t thousand in number,	1493
6: 7	he sent them out t by two	1545+1545
6: 7	two by t and gave them authority	1545+1545
6:38	they said, "Five—and t fish."	1545
6:41	the five loaves and the t fish and looking	1545
6:41	He also divided the t fish among them all.	1545
9:43	to enter life maimed than with t hands	1545
9:45	to enter life crippled than to have t feet and	1545
9:47	of God with one eye than to have t eyes	1545
10: 8	and the t will become one flesh.'	1545
10: 8	So they are no longer t, but one.	1545
11: 1	Jesus sent t of his disciples,	1545
12:42	and put in t very small copper coins,	1545
14: 1	Feast of Unleavened Bread were only t	
	days away,	1545
14:13	So he sent t of his disciples, telling them,	1545
15:27	They crucified t robbers with him,	1545
15:38	The curtain of the temple was torn in t	1545
16:12	to t of them while they were walking in	1545
Lk 2:24	"a pair of doves or t young pigeons."	1545
3:11	The man with t tunics should share	1545
5: 2	he saw at the water's edge t boats,	1545
7:18	Calling t of them,	1545
7:41	"T men owed money to a certain	1545
9:13	only five loaves of bread and t fish—	1545
9:16	the five loaves and the t fish and looking	1545
9:30	T men, Moses and Elijah,	1545
9:32	they saw his glory and the t men standing	1545
10: 1	sent them t by two ahead of him	324+1545+1545

Lk 10: 1	sent them two by t ahead of him	324+1545+1545
10:35	The next day he took out t silver coins	1545
12: 6	Are not five sparrows sold for t pennies?	1545
12:52	three against t and two against three.	1545
12:52	three against two and t against three.	1545
15:11	"There was a man who had t sons.	1545
16:13	"No servant can serve t masters.	1545
17:34	on that night t people will be in one bed;	1545
17:35	T women will be grinding grain together;	1545
18:10	"T men went up to the temple to pray,	1545
19:29	he sent t of his disciples, saying to them,	1545
21: 2	widow put in t very small copper coins.	1545
22:38	"See, Lord, here are t swords."	1545
23:32	T other men, both criminals,	1545
23:45	And the curtain of the temple was torn in t.	3545
24: 4	suddenly t men in clothes that gleamed	1545
24:13	Now that same day t of them were going to	1545
24:35	the t told what had happened on the way,	899ˢ
Jn 1:35	The next day John was there again with t	1545
1:37	When the t disciples heard him say this,	1545
1:40	of the t who heard what John had said	1545
4:40	and he stayed t days.	1545
4:43	After the t days he left for Galilee.	1545
6: 9	five small barley loaves and t small fish,	1545
8:17	that the testimony of t men is valid.	1545
11: 6	he stayed where he was t more days.	1545
11:18	Bethany was less than t miles from	1278+5084
19:18	crucified him, and with him t others—	1545
19:40	the t of them wrapped it, with the spices,	NIG
20:12	and saw t angels in white,	1545
21: 2	and t other disciples were together.	1545
Ac 1:10	when suddenly t men dressed	1545
1:23	So they proposed t men:	1545
1:24	Show us which of these t you have chosen	1545
7:26	upon t Israelites who were fighting.	899ˢ
7:29	he settled as a foreigner and had t sons.	1545
9:38	they sent t men to him and urged him,	1545
10: 7	Cornelius called t of his servants and	1545
12: 6	Peter was sleeping between t soldiers,	1545
12: 6	bound with t chains, and sentries stood	1545
13: 4	The t then, sent on their way	NIG
15:22	t men who were leaders among the brothers.	AIT
19:10	This went on for t years,	1545
19:22	He sent t of his helpers,	1545
19:34	in unison for about t hours.	1545
21:33	and ordered him to be bound with t chains.	1545
23:23	Then he called t of his centurions	1545
23:23	a detachment of t hundred soldiers,	1357
23:23	seventy horsemen and t hundred spearmen,	1357
24:27	When t years had passed,	1454
28:30	For t whole years Paul stayed there	1454
1Co 6:16	it is said, "The t will become one flesh."	1545
14:27	If anyone speaks in a tongue, t—	1545
14:29	T or three prophets should speak,	1545
2Co 13: 1	by the testimony of t or three witnesses."	1545
Gal 4:22	For it is written that Abraham had t sons,	1545
4:24	for the women represent t covenants.	1545
Eph 2:14	who has made the t one and has destroyed	317
2:15	in himself one new man out of the t,	1545
5:31	and the t will become one flesh."	1545
Php 1:23	I am torn between the t:	1545
1Ti 5:19	unless it is brought by t or three witnesses.	1545
Heb 6:18	by t unchangeable things	1545
10:28	on the testimony of t or three witnesses.	1545
11:37	They were stoned; they were sawed in t;	4569
Rev 9:12	t other woes are yet to come.	1545
9:16	troops was t hundred million.	1490+3689
11: 3	And I will give power to my t witnesses,	1545
11: 4	the t olive trees and the two lampstands	1545
11: 4	the t lampstands that stand before the Lord	1545
11:10	these t prophets had tormented those who	
	live on the earth.	1545
12:14	the woman was given the t wings of	1545
13:11	He had t horns like a lamb,	1545
19:20	The t of them were thrown alive into the	1545

TWO-AND-A-HALF (1) [HALF, TWO]

Jos 14: 3	the t tribes their inheritance east of the	
	Jordan	2256+2942+9109

TWO-DRACHMA (1) [DRACHMAS, TWO]

Mt 17:24	the collectors of the t tax came to Peter	1440

TWO-EDGED (KJV) See DOUBLE-EDGED

TWO-HORNED (2) [HORN, TWO]

Da 8: 6	the t ram I had seen standing	1251+2021+7967
8:20	t ram that you saw represents	1251+2021+7967

TWO-TENTHS (11) [TEN, TWO]

Lev 23:13	with its grain offering of t of an ephah	6928+9109
23:17	bring two loaves made of t of an ephah	6928+9109
24: 5	using t of an ephah for each loaf.	6928+9109
Nu 15: 6	a grain offering of t of an ephah	6928+9109
28: 9	and a grain offering of t of an ephah	6928+9109
28:12	and a grain offering of t of an ephah	6928+9109
28:20	with the ram, t;	6928+9109
28:28	with the ram, t;	6928+9109
29: 3	with the ram, t;	6928+9109
29: 9	with the ram, t;	6928+9109
29:14	with each of the two rams, t;	6928+9109

TWO-THIRDS (1) [THREE, TWO]

Zec 13: 8	"t will be struck down and perish;	7023+9109

TYCHICUS (5)

Ac 20: 4	and T and Trophimus from the province	5608
Eph 6:21	T, the dear brother and faithful servant in	5608
Col 4: 7	T will tell you all the news about me.	5608
2Ti 4:12	I sent T to Ephesus.	5608
Tit 3:12	As soon as I send Artemas or T to you,	5608

TYING (1) [TIE]

Pr 26: 8	Like t a stone in a sling is the giving of	
	honor to a fool.	7674

TYPE (2)

1Ch 12:33	with every t of weapon, to help David	AIT
12:37	armed with every t of weapon—120,000.	AIT

TYRANNICAL (1) [TYRANNY]

Pr 28:16	A t ruler lacks judgment,	5131+8041

TYRANNUS (1)

Ac 19: 9	discussions daily in the lecture hall of T.	5598

TYRANNY (1) [TYRANNICAL]

Isa 54:14	T will be far from you;	6945

TYRE (60) [TYRIANS]

Jos 19:29	and went to the fortified city of T,	7450
2Sa 5:11	Hiram king of T sent messengers to David,	7450
24: 7	toward the fortress of T and all the towns	7450
1Ki 5: 1	When Hiram king of T heard that Solomon	7450
7:13	Solomon sent to T and brought Huram,	7450
7:14	a man of T and a craftsman in bronze.	7660
9:11	towns in Galilee to Hiram king of T,	7450
9:12	when Hiram went from T to see the towns	7450
1Ch 14: 1	Hiram king of T sent messengers to David,	7450
2Ch 2: 3	sent this message to Hiram king of T:	7450
2:11	of T replied by letter to Solomon:	7450
2:14	from Dan and whose father was from T.	7660
Ezr 3: 7	and oil to the people of Sidon and T,	7660
Ne 13:16	Men from T who lived in Jerusalem	7660
Ps 45:12	The Daughter of T will come with a gift,	7450
83: 7	Philistia, with the people of T.	7450
87: 4	Philistia too, and T, along with Cush—	7450
Isa 23: 1	An oracle concerning T:	7450
23: 1	For T is destroyed and left without house	NIH
23: 3	harvest of the Nile was the revenue of T,	2023ˢ
23: 5	be in anguish at the report from T.	7450
23: 8	Who planned this against T,	7450
23:15	At that time T will be forgotten	7450
23:15	to T as in the song of the prostitute:	7450
23:17	the Lord will deal with T.	7450
Jer 25:22	all the kings of T and Sidon;	7450
27: 3	T and Sidon through the envoys	7450
47: 4	to cut off all survivors who could help T	7450
Eze 26: 2	because T has said of Jerusalem, 'Aha!	7450
26: 3	I am against you, O T;	7450
26: 4	They will destroy the walls of T and pull	7450
26: 7	to bring against T Nebuchadnezzar king	7450
26:15	the Sovereign Lord says to T:	7450
27: 2	take up a lament concerning T.	7450
27: 3	Say to T, situated at the gateway to the sea,	7450
27: 3	" 'You say, O T, "I am perfect in beauty."	7450
27: 8	your skilled men, O T, were aboard	7450
27:32	"Who was ever silenced like T,	7450
28: 2	"Son of man, say to the ruler of T,	7450
28:12	take up a lament concerning the king of T	7450
29:18	in a hard campaign against T;	7450
29:18	from the campaign he led against T.	7450
Hos 9:13	I have seen Ephraim, like T,	7450
Joel 3: 4	O T and Sidon and all you regions	7450
Am 1: 9	"For three sins of T, even for four,	7450
1:10	of T that will consume her fortresses."	7450
Zec 9: 2	which borders on it, and upon T and Sidon,	7450
9: 3	T has built herself a stronghold,	7450
Mt 11:21	in you had been performed in T and Sidon,	5602
11:22	it will be more bearable for T and Sidon on	5602
15:21	Jesus withdrew to the region of T	5602
Mk 3: 8	the regions across the Jordan and around T	5602
7:24	that place and went to the vicinity of T.	5602
7:31	Then Jesus left the vicinity of T and went	5602
Lk 6:17	and from the coast of T and Sidon,	5602
10:13	in you had been performed in T and Sidon,	5602
10:14	for T and Sidon at the judgment than	5602
Ac 12:20	with the people of T and Sidon;	5601
21: 3	We landed at T, where our ship was to	5602
21: 7	We continued our voyage from T	5602

TYRIANS (1) [TYRE]

1Ch 22: 4	and T had brought large numbers of them	7660

TYRUS (KJV) See TYRE

U

UCAL (1)
Pr 30: 1 man declared to Ithiel, to Ithiel and to U: 432

UEL (1)
Ezr 10:34 of Bani: Maadai, Amram, U,   198

UGLY (8)
Ge	41: 3	seven other cows, **u** and gaunt,	5260+8273
	41: 4	the cows that were **u** and gaunt ate up	5260+8273
	41:19	scrawny and very **u** and lean.	8273+9307
	41:19	I had never seen such **u** cows in all the land	8278
	41:20	**u** cows ate up the seven fat cows that came	8273
	41:21	they looked just as **u** as before.	8273
	41:27	The seven lean, **u** cows that came up	8273
Rev	16: 2	and **u** and painful sores broke out on	2805

ULAI (2)
Da	8: 2	in the vision I was beside the **U** Canal.	217
	8:16	I heard a man's voice from the **U** calling,	217

ULAM (4)
1Ch	7:16	and his sons were **U** and Rakem.	220
	7:17	The son of **U**: Bedan.	220
	8:39	**U** his firstborn, Jeush the second son	220
	8:40	of **U** were brave warriors who could handle	220

ULLA (1)
1Ch 7:39 The sons of **U**: Arah, Hanniel and Rizia.   6587

UMMAH (1)
Jos 19:30 **U**, Aphek and Rehob.   6646

UNABLE (12)
Lev	25:35	*is* **u** *to support* himself among you,	3338+4572
Jdg	1:19	but they were **u** to drive the people from	4202
Isa	46: 2	**u** to rescue the burden,	3523+4202
Eze	3:26	you will be silent and **u** to rebuke them,	4202
	17:14	would be brought low, **u** to rise again,	1194
Da	6: 4	but *they were* **u** to do so.	10321+10379
Lk	1:22	signs to them but remained **u to speak.**	3273
	20:26	*They were* **u** to trap him in what he	2710+4024
Jn	8:43	Because *you are* **u** to hear what I say.	1538+4024
	21: 6	*they were* **u** to haul the net in because	2710+4033
Ac	13:11	*you will* **be u** to see the light of the sun	1063+3590
Heb	4:15	we do not have a high priest *who is* **u**	1538+3590

UNADVISEDLY (KJV) See RASH

UNAFRAID (1)
Ps 78:53 He guided them safely, so *they were* **u**   4202+7064

UNANSWERED (2)
Job	11: 2	*"Are* all these words *to go* **u?**	4202+6699
Ps	35:13	When my prayers **returned** to me,	2668+8740

UNAPPROACHABLE (1)
1Ti 6:16 alone is immortal and who lives in **u** light,   717

UNASHAMED (1)
1Jn 2:28 and **u** before him at his coming.   159+3590

UNAUTHORIZED (4)
Lev	10: 1	and they offered **u** fire before the LORD,	2424
	22:13	No **u person**, however, may eat any of it.	2424
Nu	3: 4	when they made an offering with **u** fire	2424
	26:61	an offering before the LORD with **u** fire.)	2424

UNAWARE (9)
Lev	4:13	though the community *is* **u** *of* the matter,	4946+6524+6623
	5: 2	even though he *is* **u** of *it,*	4946+6623
	5: 3	even though he *is* **u** of *it,*	4946+6623
	5: 4	even though he *is* **u** of *it,*	4946+6623
Ps	35:15	against me when *I was* **u**.	3359+4202
Pr	28:22	and *is* **u** that poverty awaits him.	3359+4202
Lk	2:43	but they *were* **u** of *it.*	1182+4202
Ro	1:13	I do not want you *to be* **u**, brothers,	51
2Co	2:11	For *we are* not **u** of his schemes.	51

UNAWARES (KJV) See ACCIDENTALLY, DECEIVED, SECRETLY, UNINTENTIONALLY, WITHOUT KNOWING

UNBELIEF (6) [UNBELIEVER, UNBELIEVERS, UNBELIEVING]
Mk 9:24 "I do believe; help me overcome my **u!**"   602

Ro	4:20	not waver *through* **u** regarding the promise	602
	11:20	But they were broken off *because of* **u**,	602
	11:23	And if they do not persist in **u**,	602
1Ti	1:13	because I acted in ignorance and **u**.	602
Heb	3:19	were not able to enter, because of their **u**.	602

UNBELIEVER (5) [UNBELIEF]
1Co	7:15	But if the **u** leaves, let him do so.	603
	10:27	If some **u** invites you to a meal	603
	14:24	But if an **u** or someone who does not	603
2Co	6:15	a believer have in common with an **u?**	603
1Ti	5: 8	the faith and is worse than an **u**.	603

UNBELIEVERS (8) [UNBELIEF]
Lk	12:46	to pieces and assign him a place with the **u**.	603
Ro	15:31	that I may be rescued from the **u** in Judea	578
1Co	6: 6	and this in front of **u!**	603
	14:22	then, are a sign, not for believers but *for* **u**;	603
	14:22	however, is for believers, not *for* **u**.	603
	14:23	who do not understand or some **u** come in,	603
2Co	4: 4	god of this age has blinded the minds *of* **u**,	603
	6:14	Do not be yoked together *with* **u**.	603

UNBELIEVING (7) [UNBELIEF]
Mt	17:17	"O **u** and perverse generation,"	603
Mk	9:19	"O **u** generation," Jesus replied,	603
Lk	9:41	"O **u** and perverse generation,"	603
1Co	7:14	For the **u** husband has been sanctified	603
	7:14	and the **u** wife has been sanctified through	603
Heb	3:12	**u** heart that turns away from the living God.	602
Rev	21: 8	But the cowardly, the **u**, the vile,	603

UNBLAMEABLE (KJV) See BLAMELESS, WITHOUT BLEMISH

UNBLEMISHED (1)
Heb 9:14 through the eternal Spirit offered himself **u**   320

UNBORN (1) [BEAR]
Ps 22:31 proclaim his righteousness to a people **yet u**   3528

UNBOUND (1)
Da 3:25 walking around in the fire, **u** and unharmed, 10742

UNCEASING (2) [UNCEASINGLY]
Isa	14: 6	struck down peoples with **u** blows,	1194+6239
Ro	9: 2	I have great sorrow and **u** anguish in my	89

UNCEASINGLY (1) [UNCEASING]
La 3:49 My eyes will flow **u**, without relief,   1949+4202

UNCERTAIN (1)
1Ti 6:17 which is so **u**, but to put their hope in God,   84

UNCHANGEABLE (1) [UNCHANGED]
Heb 6:18 by two **u** things in which it is impossible   292

UNCHANGED (5) [UNCHANGEABLE, UNCHANGING]
Lev	13: 5	the sore *is* **u** and has not spread in the skin,	6641
	13:23	But if the spot *is* **u** and has not spread,	6641+9393
	13:28	spot *is* **u** and has not spread in the skin	6641+9393
	13:37	If, however, in his judgment it *is* **u**	6641
Jer	48:11	tastes as she did, and her aroma *is* **u**.	4202+4614

UNCHANGING (1) [UNCHANGED]
Heb 6:17 Because God wanted to make the **u** nature   292

UNCHECKED (1)
Am 1:11 continually and his fury **flamed u**,   5905+9068

UNCIRCUMCISED (38) [UNCIRCUMCISION]
Ge	17:14	Any **u** male, who has not been circumcised	6888
Ex	12:48	No **u** *male* may eat of it.	6888
Lev	26:41	then when their **u** hearts are humbled	6888
Jos	5: 7	They were still **u** because they had	6888
Jdg	14: 3	Must you go to the **u** Philistines to get	6888
	15:18	of thirst and fall into the hands of the **u?"**	6888
1Sa	14: 6	over to the outpost of those **u** *fellows*.	6888
	17:26	Who is this **u** Philistine that he should defy	6888
	17:36	this **u** Philistine will be like one of them,	6888
	31: 4	or these **u** *fellows* will come and run me	6888
2Sa	1:20	lest the daughters of the **u** rejoice.	6888
1Ch	10: 4	or these **u** *fellows* will come and abuse me."	6888
Isa	52: 1	The **u** and defiled will not enter you again.	6888
Jer	9:26	For all these nations are really **u**,	6888
	9:26	the whole house of Israel is **u** *in* heart."	6888
Eze	28:10	You will die the death of the **u** at the hands	6888
	31:18	you will lie among the **u**,	6888
	32:19	Go down and be laid among the **u**.'	6888
	32:21	down and they lie with the **u**,	6888
	32:24	the living went down **u** to the earth below.	6888
	32:25	All of them are **u**, killed by the sword.	6888
	32:26	All of them are **u**, killed by the sword	6888
	32:27	with the other **u** warriors who have fallen,	6888

Eze	32:28	will be broken and will lie among the **u**,	6888
	32:29	They lie with the **u**,	6888
	32:30	They lie **u** with those killed by the sword	6888
	32:32	and all his hordes will be laid among the **u**,	6888
	44: 7	you brought foreigners **u** *in* heart and flesh	6888
	44: 9	No foreigner **u** in heart and flesh is to enter	6888
Ac	7:51	stiff-necked people, with **u** hearts and ears!	598
	11: 3	the house of **u** men and ate with them."	213+2400
Ro	3:30	the circumcised by faith and the **u** through	213
	4: 9	only for the circumcised, or also for the **u?**	213
	4:11	that he had by faith while he was still **u**.	213
1Co	7:18	He should not **become u**.	2177
	7:18	*Was* a man **u** when he was called?	213+1877
Eph	2:11	and called "**u**" by those who call themselves	213
Col	3:11	circumcised or **u**, barbarian, Scythian,	213

UNCIRCUMCISION (4) [UNCIRCUMCISED]
1Co	7:19	Circumcision is nothing and **u** is nothing.	213
Gal	5: 6	neither circumcision nor **u** has any value.	213
	6:15	Neither circumcision nor **u** means anything;	213
Col	2:13	and *in* the **u** of your sinful nature,	213

UNCLE (12) [UNCLE'S]
Lev	10: 4	sons of Aaron's **u** Uzziel, and said to them,	1856
	20:20	he has dishonored his **u**.	1856
	25:49	An **u** or a cousin or any blood relative	1856
1Sa	10:14	Now Saul's **u** asked him and his servant,	1856
	10:15	Saul's **u** said, "Tell me what Samuel said	1856
	10:16	not tell his **u** what Samuel had said about	1856
	14:50	and Ner was Saul's **u**.	1856
2Ki	24:17	He made Mattaniah, Jehoiachin's **u**, king	1856
1Ch	27:32	Jonathan, David's **u**, was a counselor,	1856
2Ch	36:10	and he made Jehoiachin's **u**, Zedekiah,	278
Est	2:15	had adopted, the daughter of his **u** Abihail	1856
Jer	32: 7	of Shallum your **u** is going to come to you	1856

UNCLE'S (1) [UNCLE]
Ge 29:10 of the well and watered his **u** sheep.   278+562

UNCLEAN (209) [UNCLEANNESS]
Ge	7: 2	and two of every kind of **u** animal,	3196+4202
	7: 8	Pairs of clean and **u** animals,	401+3196
Lev	5: 2	person touches anything **ceremonially u—**	3238
	5: 2	of **u** wild animals or of unclean livestock or	3238
	5: 2	of unclean wild animals or of **u** livestock or	3238
	5: 2	or of unclean livestock or of **u** creatures	3238
	5: 2	he *has become* **u** and is guilty.	3237
	5: 3	anything *that would make* him **u—**	3237
	7:19	touches anything **ceremonially u** must	3238
	7:20	But if anyone who is **u** eats any meat of	3240
	7:21	If anyone touches something **u—**	3238
	7:21	whether human uncleanness or an **u** animal	3238
	7:21	or an unclean animal or any **u**, detestable	3238
	10:10	the common, between the **u** and the clean,	3238
	11: 4	it is **ceremonially u** for you.	3238
	11: 5	not have a split hoof; it is **u** for you.	3238
	11: 6	not have a split hoof; it is **u** for you.	3238
	11: 7	does not chew the cud; it is **u** for you.	3238
	11: 8	they are **u** for you.	3238
	11:24	" 'You will **make yourselves u** by these;	3237
	11:24	whoever touches their carcasses *will be* **u**	3237
	11:25	and *he will be* **u** till evening.	3237
	11:26	or that does not chew the cud is **u** for you;	3238
	11:26	[the carcass of] any of them *will be* **u**.	3237
	11:27	those that walk on their paws are **u** for you;	3238
	11:27	whoever touches their carcasses *will be* **u**	3237
	11:28	and *he will be* **u** till evening.	3237
	11:28	They are **u** for you.	3238
	11:29	these are **u** for you: the weasel, the rat,	3238
	11:31	these are **u** for you.	3238
	11:31	when they are dead *will be* **u** till evening.	3237
	11:32	that article, whatever its use, *will be* **u**,	3237
	11:32	Put it in water; *it will be* **u** till evening,	3237
	11:33	everything in it *will be* **u**,	3237
	11:34	but has water on it from such a pot *is* **u**,	3237
	11:34	any liquid that could be drunk *from it is* **u**.	3237
	11:35	of their carcasses falls on *becomes* **u**;	3237
	11:35	They are **u**, and you are to regard them	3238
	11:35	and you are to regard them as **u**.	3238
	11:36	who touches one of these carcasses *is* **u**.	3237
	11:38	it is **u** for you.	3237
	11:39	anyone who touches the carcass *will be* **u**	3237
	11:40	and *he will be* **u** till evening.	3237
	11:40	and *he will be* **u** till evening.	3237
	11:43	*Do* not **make yourselves u** by means of	3237
	11:43	by means of them or **be made u** by them.	3237
	11:44	*Do* not **make** yourselves **u** by any creature	3237
	11:47	You must distinguish between the **u** and	3238
	12: 2	**be ceremonially u** for seven days,	3238
	12: 2	just as *she is* **u** during her monthly period.	3237
	12: 5	for two weeks the woman *will be* **u**,	3237
	13: 3	**pronounce** him **ceremonially u**.	3237
	13: 8	he *shall* **pronounce** him **u**;	3237
	13:11	and the priest *shall* **pronounce** him **u**;	3237
	13:11	in isolation, because he is already **u**.	3238
	13:14	raw flesh appears on him, *he will be* **u**.	3237
	13:15	he *shall* **pronounce** him **u**;	3237
	13:15	raw flesh is **u**; he has an infectious disease.	3238
	13:20	the priest *shall* **pronounce** him **u**;	3237
	13:22	the priest *shall* **pronounce** him **u**;	3237
	13:25	The priest *shall* **pronounce** him **u**;	3237
	13:27	the priest *shall* **pronounce** him **u**;	3237
	13:30	the priest *shall* **pronounce** that person **u**;	3237

Lev	13:36	to look for yellow hair; the person is **u**.	3238
	13:44	the man is diseased and is **u**.	3238
	13:44	The priest *shall* **pronounce** him **u**	3237+3237
	13:45	the lower part of his face and cry out, '**U**!	3238
	13:45	and cry out, 'Unclean! **U**!'	3238
	13:46	As long as he has the infection he **remains u**.	3237+3238
	13:51	a destructive mildew; the article is **u**.	3238
	13:55	even though it has not spread, it is **u**.	3238
	13:59	for pronouncing them clean or **u**.	3237
	14:36	in the house *will be* **pronounced u**.	3237
	14:40	and thrown into an **u** place outside	3238
	14:41	into an **u** place outside the town.	3238
	14:44	a destructive mildew; the house is **u**.	3238
	14:45	and taken out of the town to an **u** place.	3238
	14:46	while it is closed up **u** till evening.	3237
	14:57	to determine when something is clean or **u**.	3238
	15: 2	a bodily discharge, the discharge is **u**.	3238
	15: 3	it will make him **u**.	3240
	15: 4	the man with a discharge lies on *will be* **u**,	3237
	15: 4	and anything he sits on *will be* **u**.	3237
	15: 5	and *he will be* **u** till evening.	3237
	15: 6	and *he will be* **u** till evening.	3237
	15: 7	and *he will be* **u** till evening.	3237
	15: 8	and *he will be* **u** till evening.	3237
	15: 9	the man sits on when riding *will be* **u**,	3237
	15:10	of the things that were under him *will be* **u**	3237
	15:10	and *he will be* **u** till evening.	3237
	15:11	and *he will be* **u** till evening.	3237
	15:16	and *he will be* **u** till evening.	3237
	15:17	and *it will be* **u** till evening.	3237
	15:18	and *they will be* **u** till evening.	3237
	15:19	and anyone who touches her *will be* **u**	3237
	15:20	on during her period *will be* **u**,	3237
	15:20	and anything she sits on *will be* **u**.	3237
	15:21	and *he will be* **u** till evening.	3237
	15:22	and *he will be* **u** till evening.	3237
	15:23	*he will be* **u** till evening.	3237
	15:24	*he will be* **u** for seven days;	3237
	15:24	any bed he lies on *will be* **u**.	3237
	15:25	be **u** as long as she has the discharge,	3238
	15:26	on while her discharge continues will be **u**,	3240
	15:26	and anything she sits on will be **u**;	3238
	15:27	Whoever touches them *will be* **u**;	3237
	15:27	and *he will be* **u** till evening.	3237
	15:31	separate from **things that make** them **u**,	3240
	15:32	*anyone made* **u** by an emission of semen,	3237
	15:33	with a **woman who** is **ceremonially u**.	3238
	17:15	he will be **ceremonially u** till evening;	3237
	20:25	a distinction between clean and **u** animals	3238
	20:25	and unclean animals and between **u**	3238
	20:25	those which I have set apart as **u** for you.	3237
	21: 1	*must* not **make himself ceremonially u**	3237
	21: 3	for her *he may* **make himself u**.	3237
	21: 4	not **make himself u** for people related to him	3237
	21:11	*He must* not **make himself u**,	3237
	22: 3	of your descendants is **ceremonially u** and	3240
	22: 4	also be **u** if he touches something defiled	NIH
	22: 5	any crawling thing that *makes* him **u**,	3237
	22: 5	or any person who *makes* him **u**,	3237
	22: 6	any such thing *will be* **u** till evening.	3237
	22: 8	and so **become u** through it.	3237
	27:11	a **ceremonially u** animal—	3238
	27:27	If it is one of the **u** animals,	3238
Nu	5: 2	or who is **ceremonially u** because of	3238
	6: 7	*must* not **make himself ceremonially u**	3237
	9: 6	because they were **ceremonially u**	3238
	9: 7	"We have become **u** because of	3238
	9:10	of you or your descendants are **u** because of	3238
	18:15	and every firstborn male of **u** animals.	3238
	19: 7	he **will be ceremonially u** till evening.	3237
	19: 8	and *he too will be* **u** till evening.	3237
	19:10	and *he too will be* **u** till evening.	3237
	19:11	of anyone *will be* **u** for seven days.	3237
	19:13	he is **u**; his uncleanness remains on him.	3238
	19:14	the tent and anyone who is in it *will be* **u**	3238
	19:15	without a lid fastened on it will be **u**.	3238
	19:16	*will be* **u** for seven days.	3237
	19:17	"For the **u** *person*, put some ashes from	3238
	19:19	the **u** *person* on the third and seventh days,	3238
	19:20	a person who *is* **u** does not purify himself,	3237
	19:20	not been sprinkled on him, and he is **u**.	3238
	19:21	of cleansing *will be* **u** till evening.	3237
	19:22	that an **u** *person* touches becomes unclean,	3237
	19:22	that an unclean person touches *becomes* **u**,	3237
	19:22	and anyone who touches it *becomes* **u**	3237
Dt	12:15	**ceremonially u** and the clean may eat.	3238
	12:22	the **ceremonially u** and the clean may eat.	3238
	14: 7	they are **ceremonially u** for you.	3238
	14: 8	pig is also **u**; although it has a split hoof,	3238
	14:10	you may not eat it; for it is **u**.	3238
	14:19	All flying insects that swarm are **u** to you;	3238
	15:22	**ceremonially u** and the clean may eat it,	3238
	23:10	If one of your men is **u** because of	3196+4202
	26:14	nor have I removed any of it while I was **u**,	3238
Jdg	13: 4	and that you do not eat anything **u**,	3238
	13: 7	do not eat anything **u**,	3240
	13:14	nor eat anything **u**.	3240
1Sa	20:26	to David to make him **ceremonially u**	1194+3196
	20:26	ceremonially **unclean**—surely he is.	3196+4202
2Ch	23:19	no one who in any way **u** might enter.	3238
	29:16	of the LORD's temple everything **u**	3238
Ezr	2:62	so were excluded from the priesthood *as* **u**.	1458
	6:21	the **u practices** *of* their Gentile neighbors.	3240
Ne	7:64	so were excluded from the priesthood *as* **u**.	1458
Ecc	9: 2	the good and the bad, the clean and the **u**,	3238

Isa	6: 5	For I am a man of **u** lips,	3238
	6: 5	and I live among a people of **u** lips,	3238
	35: 8	The **u** will not journey on it;	3238
	52:11	Touch no **u** *thing*!	3238
	64: 6	All of us have become like one *who* is **u**,	3238
	65: 4	and whose pots hold broth of **u** **meat**;	7002
Jer	13:27	How long *will you be* **u**?"	3197+4202
La	1: 8	and so has become **u**.	5765
	1:17	Jerusalem has become an **u thing**	5614
	4:15	"Go away! You are **u**!"	3238
Eze	4:14	No **u** meat has ever entered my mouth."	7002
	7:19	and their gold will be an **u thing**.	5614
	7:20	Therefore I will turn these into an **u thing**	5614
	22:10	when they are **ceremonially u**.	3238
	22:26	that there is no difference between the **u**	3238
	44:23	to distinguish between the **u** and the clean.	3238
Hos	9: 3	Ephraim will return to Egypt and eat **u** food	3237
	9: 4	all who eat them *will be* **u**.	3237
Mt	15:11	into a man's mouth *does not* **make** him '**u**,'	3124
	15:11	that *is* **what makes** him '**u**.'"	3124
	15:18	and these **make** a man '**u**.'	3124
	15:20	These are what **make** a man '**u**';	3124
	15:20	unwashed hands does not **make** him '**u**.'"	3124
	23:27	of dead men's bones and everything **u**.	174
Mk	7: 2	eating food *with* hands that were "**u**,"	3123
	7: 5	of eating their food *with* '**u**' hands?"	3123
	7:15	a man can **make** him '**u**' by going into him.	3124
	7:15	of a man that **makes** him '**u**.'"	3124
	7:18	a man from the outside can **make** him '**u**'?	3124
	7:20	of a man is what **makes** him '**u**.'	3124
	7:23	from inside and **make** a man '**u**.'"	3124
Ac	10:14	"I have never eaten anything impure or **u**."	176
	10:28	that I should not call any man impure or **u**.	176
	11: 8	or **u** has ever entered my mouth.'	176
Ro	14:14	I am fully convinced that no food is **u**	3123
	14:14	But if anyone regards something as **u**,	3123
	14:14	then for him it is **u**.	3123
1Co	7:14	Otherwise your children would be **u**,	176
2Co	6:17	Touch no **u** *thing*, and I will receive you."	176
Heb	9:13	who *are* **ceremonially u** sanctify them	3124
Rev	18: 2	a haunt *for* every **u** and detestable bird.	176

UNCLEANNESS (18) [UNCLEAN]

Lev	5: 3	"'Or if he touches human **u**—	3240
	7:21	whether human **u** or an unclean animal	3240
	14:19	for the one to be cleansed from his **u**.	3240
	15: 3	how his discharge will bring about **u**:	3240
	15:30	the LORD for the **u** of her discharge.	3240
	15:31	in their **u** for defiling my dwelling place,	3240
	16:16	for the Most Holy Place because of the **u**	3240
	16:16	among them in the midst of their **u**.	3240
	16:19	to consecrate it from the **u** of the Israelites.	3240
	18:19	to have sexual relations during the **u**	3240
	22: 5	whatever the **u** may be.	3240
Nu	19:13	his **u** remains on him.	3240
2Sa	11: 4	(She had purified herself from her **u**.)	3240
Eze	22:15	and I will put an end to your **u**.	3240
	36:17	like a **woman's monthly u** in my sight.	2021+3240+5614
	36:29	I will save you from all your **u**.	3240
	39:24	according to their **u** and their offenses,	3240
Jn	18:28	and to avoid **ceremonial u** the Jews did	3620

UNCLOTHED (1)

2Co	5: 4	because we do not wish *to be* **u** but to	1694

UNCOMELY (KJV) See IMPROPERLY, UNPRESENTABLE

UNCONCERNED (1)

Eze	16:49	were arrogant, overfed and **u**;	8932+9200

UNCONDEMNED (KJV) See HASN'T BEEN FOUND GUILTY, WITHOUT A TRIAL

UNCORRUPTIBLE (KJV) See IMMORTAL

UNCOVER (2) [UNCOVERED, UNCOVERS]

Ru	3: 4	Then go and **u** his feet and lie down.	1655
Jer	49:10	*I will* **u** his hiding places,	1655

UNCOVERED (12) [UNCOVER]

Ge	9:21	he became drunk and *lay* **u** inside his tent.	1655
	44:16	God *has* **u** your servants' guilt.	5162
Lev	20:18	and she *has* also **u** it.	1655
Ru	3: 7	approached quietly, **u** his feet and lay down.	1655
Job	26: 6	before God; Destruction lies **u**.	401+4064
Isa	47: 3	be exposed and your shame is **u**.	8011
	57: 8	Forsaking me, *you* **u** your bed,	1655
Eze	16:57	before your wickedness was **u**.	1655
Hab	3: 9	*You* **u** your bow, you called for many	6423+6880
1Co	11: 5	*with* her head **u** dishonors her head—	184
	11:13	a woman to pray to God with her head **u**?	184
Heb	4:13	Everything is **u** and laid bare before the	1218

UNCOVERS (2) [UNCOVER]

Ex	21:33	"If a man **u** a pit or digs one and fails	7337
Isa	22: 6	charioteers and horses; Kir **u** the shield.	6867

UNCTION (KJV) See ANOINTING

UNCUT (2)

Jos	8:31	the Law of Moses—an altar of **u** stones,	8969
Job	8:12	While still growing and **u**,	4202+7786

UNDEFILED (KJV) See BLAMELESS, FAULTLESS, FLAWLESS, PERFECT, PURE, NEVER SPOIL

UNDENIABLE (1)

Ac	19:36	Therefore, since these facts are **u**,	394

UNDEPENDABLE (1)

Job	6:15	brothers are as **u** as intermittent streams,	953

UNDER (370)

Ge	1: 7	and separated the water **u** the expanse	4946+9393
	1: 9	"Let the water **u** the sky be gathered	4946+9393
	4:11	Now you *are* **u** a curse and driven from	826
	6:17	earth to destroy all life **u** the heavens,	4946+9393
	7:19	and all the high mountains **u**	9393
	17:18	Ishmael might live **u** your **blessing!**"	4200+7156
	18: 4	then you may all wash your feet and rest **u**	9393
	18: 8	While they ate, he stood near them **u** a tree.	9393
	19: 8	for they have come **u** the protection	928
	21:15	she put the boy **u** one of the bushes.	9393
	24: 2	"Put your hand **u** my thigh.	9393
	24: 9	So the servant put his hand **u** the thigh	9393
	28:11	he put it **u** his **head** and lay down to sleep.	5265
	28:18	the stone he had placed **u** his **head** and set it	5265
	30:29	how your livestock has fared **u** my **care**.	907
	35: 4	Jacob buried them **u** the oak at Shechem.	9393
	35: 8	and was buried **u** the oak below Bethel.	9393
	39:23	The warden paid no attention to anything **u**	928
	41:35	that are coming and store up the grain **u**	9393
	47:29	put your hand **u** my thigh and promise	9393
	48: 6	be reckoned **u** the names of their brothers.	6584
Ex	6: 6	the LORD, and I will bring you out from **u**	9393
	6: 7	who brought you out from **u** the yoke of	9393
	17:12	a stone and put it **u** him and he sat on it.	9393
	17:14	the memory of Amalek from **u** heaven."	9393
	23: 5	of someone who hates you fallen down **u**	9393
	24:10	**U** his feet was something like a pavement	9393
	25:35	be **u** the first pair of branches extending	9393
	25:35	a second bud **u** the second pair,	9393
	25:35	and a third bud **u** the third pair—	9393
	26:19	and make forty silver bases to go **u** them—	9393
	26:19	one **u** each projection.	4200
	26:21	and forty silver bases—two **u** each frame.	9393
	26:25	two **u** each frame.	9393
	27: 5	Put it **u** the ledge of the altar so	9393
	36:24	and made forty silver bases to go **u** them—	9393
	36:24	one **u** each projection.	4200
	36:26	and forty silver bases—two **u** each frame.	9393
	36:30	two **u** each frame.	9393
	37:21	One bud was **u** the first pair	9393
	37:21	a second bud **u** the second pair—	9393
	37:21	and a third bud **u** the third pair—	9393
	38: 4	to be **u** its ledge, halfway up the altar.	9393
	38:21	the Levites **u** the direction of Ithamar son	928
Lev	15:10	the things that were **u** him will be unclean	9393
	27:32	that passes **u** the shepherd's rod—	9393
Nu	1:52	in his own camp **u** his own standard.	6584
	2: 2	each man **u** his standard with the banners	6584
	2: 3	of Judah are to encamp **u** their standard.	NIH
	2:10	be the divisions of the camp of Reuben **u**	NIH
	2:17	each in his own place **u** his standard.	4200
	2:18	be the divisions of the camp of Ephraim **u**	NIH
	2:25	be the divisions of the camp of Dan, **u**	NIH
	2:31	They will set out last, **u** their standards.	4200
	2:34	is the way they encamped **u** their standards,	4200
	4:27	is to be done **u** the direction of Aaron	6584
	4:28	be **u** the direction of Ithamar son of Aaron,	928
	4:33	of Meeting **u** the direction of Ithamar son	928
	5:19	priest *shall* **put** the woman **u** oath	8678
	5:21	to put the woman **u** this curse of the oath—	928
	6:18	and put it in the fire that is **u** the sacrifice of	9393
	7: 8	They were all **u** the direction	928
	8:22	the Tent of Meeting **u** the **supervision**	4200+7156
	10:14	of Judah went first, **u** their standard.	4200
	10:18	of Reuben went next, **u** their standard.	4200
	10:22	of Ephraim went next, **u** their standard.	4200
	10:25	the divisions of the camp of Dan set out, **u**	4200
	16:31	the ground **u** them split apart	9393
	19: 2	and that *has* never **been u** a yoke.	6584+6590
	22:27	she lay down **u** Balaam,	9393
	30:10	a vow or obligates herself by a pledge **u**	928
	31:49	"Your servants have counted the soldiers **u**	928
	33: 1	by divisions **u** the leadership of Moses	928
Dt	2:25	and fear of you on all the nations **u** heaven.	9393
	4:19	to all the nations **u** heaven.	9393
	7:24	and you will wipe out their names from **u**	9393
	9:14	and blot out their name from **u** heaven	9393
	12: 2	and on the hills and **u** every spreading tree	9393
	21:23	who is hung on a tree is **u** God's **curse**.	AIT
	25:19	the memory of Amalek from **u** heaven.	9393
	29:20	the LORD will blot out his name from **u**	9393
	30: 4	to the **most distant land** **u** the heavens,	AIT
Jos	2: 6	up to the roof and hidden them **u** the stalks	928
	9:23	You *are* now **u** a curse:	826
	18: 1	country **was brought u** their **control**,	3899
	24:26	a large stone and set it up there **u** the oak	9393
Jdg	1: 7	and big toes cut off have picked up scraps **u**	9393
	2:18	they groaned **u** those who oppressed	4946+7156

Jdg	3:16	which he strapped to his right thigh **u**	4946+9393
	4: 5	She held court **u** the Palm of Deborah	9393
	6:11	of the LORD came and sat down **u** the oak	9393
	6:19	and offered them to him **u** the oak.	9393
	9:29	If only this people were **u** my command!	928
	9:31	**U cover** he sent messengers to Abimelech,	928+9564
Ru	2:12	**u** whose wings you have come to take	9393
1Sa	2:11	the boy ministered before the LORD **u**	907+7156
	2:27	when they were in Egypt **u** Pharaoh?	1074+4200
	3: 1	ministered before the LORD **u** Eli.	4200+7156
	14: 2	of Gibeah **u** a pomegranate tree in Migron.	9393
	14:24	**bound** the people **u an oath,**	457
	14:28	**bound** the army **u a strict oath,**	8678+8678
	22: 6	was seated **u** the tamarisk tree on the hill	9393
	31:13	and buried them **u** a tamarisk tree at Jabesh,	9393
2Sa	10:10	He put the rest of the men **u** the command	928
	11:16	So while Joab *had* the city **u** siege,	9068
	18: 2	a third **u** the command of Joab,	928
	18: 2	under the command of Joab, a third	928+3338
	18: 2	and a third **u** Ittai the Gittite.	928+3338
	18: 9	and as the mule went **u** the thick branches	9393
	20: 3	the palace and put them in a house **u guard.**	5466
	20: 7	warriors went out **u** the command of	339
	22:10	dark clouds were **u** his feet.	9393
	22:48	who puts the nations **u** me,	9393
1Ki	4:25	each man **u** his own vine and fig tree.	9393
	5: 3	until the LORD put his enemies **u** his feet.	9393
	7:32	The four wheels were **u** the panels,	4946+9393
	7:44	the Sea and the twelve bulls **u** it;	9393
	13:14	He found him sitting **u** an oak tree	9393
	14:23	and Asherah poles on every high hill and **u**	9393
	19: 4	sat down **u** it and prayed that he might die.	9393
	19: 5	Then he lay down **u** the tree and fell asleep.	9393
2Ki	9:13	and spread them **u** him on the bare steps.	9393
	11: 4	a covenant with them and **put** them **u oath**	8678
	13: 3	for a long time he kept them **u** the power	928
	14:27	the name of Israel from **u** heaven,	9393
	16: 4	on the hilltops and **u** every spreading tree.	9393
	17: 7	from **u** the power of Pharaoh king of Egypt.	9393
	17:10	and Asherah poles on every high hill and **u**	9393
	25: 2	The city was kept **u** siege until	928
	25:10	**u** the commander of the imperial guard,	889
1Ch	10:12	Then they buried their bones **u** the great tree	9393
	12:32	with all their relatives **u** their command;	6584
	17: 1	of the covenant of the LORD is **u** a tent."	9393
	19:11	He put the rest of the men **u** the command	928
	23:24	as they were registered **u** their names	928
	23:32	**u** their brothers the descendants of Aaron,	NIH
	25: 2	of Asaph were **u** the supervision of Asaph,	6584
	25: 2	who prophesied **u** the king's supervision.	6584
	25: 3	**u** the supervision of their father Jeduthun,	6584
	25: 6	All these men were **u** the supervision	6584
	25: 6	and Heman were **u** the supervision of	6584
2Ch	4:15	the Sea and the twelve bulls **u** it;	9393
	14: 5	and the kingdom was at peace **u** him.	4200+7156
	17: 5	The LORD established the kingdom **u**	928
	24:13	and the repairs progressed **u** them.	928+3338
	26:11	the secretary and Maaseiah the officer **u**	6584
	26:13	**U** their command was an army of 307,500	6584
	28: 4	on the hilltops and **u** every spreading tree.	9393
	31:13	Benaiah were supervisors **u** Conaniah	3338+4946
	32:10	that you remain in Jerusalem **u** siege?	928
	34: 4	**U** his **direction** the altars of the Baals	4200+7156
Ezr	4:14	*we are* **u obligation** *to* the palace	10419+10420
	5: 8	and is making rapid progress **u**	10089
	5:16	to the present *it has been* **u construction**	10111
	6:14	the Jews continued to build and prosper **u**	10089
	10: 5	**put** the leading priests and Levites and all	
		Israel **u oath**	8678
Ne	3: 5	not put their shoulders to the **work** *u*	AIT
	3: 7	places **u** the authority of the governor	4200
	3:17	the repairs were made by the Levites **u**	NIH
	3:18	by their countrymen **u** Binnui son	NIH
	6:18	many in Judah were **u oath** to him,	1251+8652
	11:23	The singers were **u** the king's orders,	6584
	12:42	The choirs sang **u** the direction	NIH
Est	2: 3	Let them be placed **u** the care of Hegai,	448
	2: 8	to the citadel of Susa and put **u** the care	448
Job	7:12	that you put me **u guard?**	5464+6584
	20:12	in his mouth and he hides it **u** his tongue,	9393
	26: 8	yet the clouds do not burst **u** their weight.	9393
	28:24	the earth and sees everything **u** the heavens.	9393
	35: 9	"Men cry out **u** a load of oppression;	4946
	37:17	when the land lies hushed **u** the south wind,	4946
	38:14	The earth takes shape like **clay** *u* a seal;	AIT
	40:21	**U** the lotus plants he lies,	9393
	41:11	Everything **u** heaven belongs to me.	9393
Ps	8: 6	you put everything **u** his feet:	9393
	10: 7	trouble and evil are **u** his tongue.	9393
	10:10	they fall **u** his strength.	928
	18: 9	dark clouds were **u** his feet.	9393
	18:47	who subdues nations **u** me,	9393
	47: 3	He subdued nations **u** us,	9393
	47: 3	nations under us, peoples **u** our feet.	9393
	56:12	I am **u** vows to you, O God;	6584
	90: 9	All our days pass away **u** your wrath;	928
	91: 4	and **u** his wings you will find refuge;	9393
	95: 7	the flock **u** his **care.**	3338
	144: 2	who subdues peoples **u** me.	9393
Pr	22:14	*he who is* **u** the LORD's **wrath** will fall	2404
	22:27	your very bed will be snatched from **u** you.	9393
	29:11	but a wise man keeps himself **u control.**	294+928
	29:24	*he is* **put u oath** and dare not testify.	460+9048
	30:21	"**U** three things the earth trembles,	9393
	30:21	**u** four it cannot bear up:	9393
Ecc	1: 3	all his labor at which he toils **u** the sun?	9393

Ecc	1: 9	there is nothing new **u** the sun.	9393
	1:13	explore by wisdom all that is done **u** the sun	9393
	1:14	I have seen all the things that are done **u**	9393
	2: 3	to see what was worthwhile for men to do **u**	9393
	2:11	nothing was gained **u** the sun.	9393
	2:17	that is done **u** the sun was grievous to me.	9393
	2:18	I hated all the things I had toiled for **u** the	9393
	2:19	and skill **u** the sun.	9393
	2:20	to despair over all my toilsome labor **u**	9393
	2:22	and anxious striving with which he labors **u**	9393
	3: 1	and a season for every activity **u** heaven:	9393
	3:16	And I saw something else **u** the sun:	9393
	4: 1	the oppression that was taking place **u**	9393
	4: 3	who has not seen the evil that is done **u**	9393
	4: 7	Again I saw something meaningless **u**	9393
	4:15	and walked **u** the sun followed the youth,	9393
	5:13	I have seen a grievous evil **u** the sun:	9393
	5:18	to find satisfaction in his toilsome labor **u**	9393
	6: 1	I have seen another evil **u** the sun,	9393
	6:12	Who can tell him what will happen **u**	9393
	7: 6	Like the crackling of thorns **u** the pot,	9393
	8: 9	as I applied my mind to everything done **u**	9393
	8:15	a man **u** the sun than to eat and drink and	9393
	8:15	the days of the life God has given him **u**	9393
	8:17	No one can comprehend what goes on **u**	9393
	9: 3	This is the evil in everything that happens **u**	9393
	9: 6	a part in anything that happens **u** the sun.	9393
	9: 9	that God has given you **u** the sun—	9393
	9: 9	in life and in your toilsome labor **u** the sun.	9393
	9:11	I have seen something else **u** the sun:	9393
	9:13	also saw **u** the sun this example of wisdom	9393
	10: 5	There is an evil I have seen **u** the sun,	9393
SS	2: 6	His left arm is **u** my head,	9393
	4:11	milk and honey are **u** your tongue.	9393
	8: 3	His left arm is **u** my head	9393
	8: 5	**U** the apple tree I roused you;	9393
Isa	1: 8	like a city **u** siege.	7443
	10:16	**u** his pomp a fire will be kindled like	9393
	25:10	be trampled **u** him as straw is trampled	9393
	34:15	for her young **u** the shadow of her wings;	928
	57: 5	among the oaks and **u** every spreading tree;	9393
	57: 5	in the ravines and **u** the overhanging crags.	9393
Jer	2:20	and **u** every spreading tree you lay down as	9393
	3: 6	She has gone up on every high hill and **u**	9393
	3:13	to foreign gods **u** every spreading tree,	9393
	7:29	and abandoned this **generation** *that is* **u**	AIT
	10:11	from the earth and from **u** the heavens.' "	10757
	10:17	you who live **u** siege.	928
	27: 8	of Babylon or bow its neck **u** his yoke,	928
	27:11	if any nation will bow its neck **u** the yoke	928
	27:12	"Bow your neck **u** the yoke of the king	928
	33:13	flocks will again pass **u** the hand of the one	6584
	38:11	with him and went to a room **u** the treasury	9393
	38:12	"Put these old rags and worn-out clothes **u**	9393
	52: 5	The city was kept **u** siege until	928
	52:14	The whole Babylonian army **u** the	907
	52:20	the Sea and the twelve bronze bulls **u** it,	9393
La	3:66	and destroy them from **u** the heavens of	9393
	4:20	that **u** his shadow we would live among	928
	5:13	boys stagger **u** loads of wood.	928
Eze	1: 8	**U** their wings on their four sides	4946+9393
	1:23	**U** the expanse their wings were stretched	9393
	4: 3	It will be **u** siege, and you shall besiege it.	928
	6:13	**u** every spreading tree and every leafy oak	9393
	10: 8	(**U** the wings of the cherubim could	9393
	10:21	and their wings was what looked like	9393
	17: 6	but its roots remained **u** it.	9393
	17:13	made a treaty with him, putting him **u** oath.	928
	20:37	I will take note of you as you pass **u**	9393
	31: 6	all the beasts of the field gave birth **u**	9393
	31:12	the nations of the earth came out from **u**	AIT
	32:27	whose swords were placed **u** their heads?	9393
	46:23	with places for fire built all around **u**	4946+9393
	47: 1	from **u** the threshold of the temple toward	9393
	47: 1	down from **u** the south side of the temple,	9393
Da	4:12	**U** it the beasts of the field found shelter,	10757
	4:14	Let the animals flee from **u** it and the birds	10757
	7:27	of the kingdoms **u** the whole heaven will	10757
	9:12	**U** the whole heaven nothing has ever been	9393
Hos	4:13	**u** oak, poplar and terebinth,	9393
	8:10	to waste away **u** the oppression of	4946
Mic	4: 4	Every man will sit **u** his own vine and	9393
	4: 4	under his own vine and **u** his own fig tree,	9393
Zec	3:10	of you will invite his neighbor to sit **u**	9393
Mal	1: 4	a people always **u** the **wrath** of the LORD.	2404
	3: 9	You are **u** a curse—the whole nation	928
Mt	2:16	vicinity who were two years old and **u,**	3006
	5:15	Neither do people light a lamp and put it **u**	5679
	7: 6	you do, they may trample them **u** their feet,	1877
	8: 8	not deserve to have you come **u** my roof.	5679
	8: 9	For I myself am a man **u** authority,	5679
	8: 9	a man under authority, with soldiers **u** me.	5679
	22:44	at my right hand until I put your enemies **u**	5691
	23:37	as a hen gathers her chicks **u** her wings,	5679
	26:63	"*I charge* you **u oath** by the living God:	2019
Mk	4:21	"Do you bring in a lamp to put it **u** a bowl	5679
	5:26	She had suffered a great deal **u** the care	5679
	7:28	"but even the dogs **u** the table eat	5691
	12:36	at my right hand until I put your enemies **u**	5691
	14:44	arrest him and lead him away **u guard.**"	857
Lk	7: 6	not deserve to have you come **u** my roof.	5679
	7: 8	For I myself am a man **u** authority,	5679
	7: 8	a man under authority, with soldiers **u** me.	5679
	8:16	hides it in a jar or puts it **u** a bed.	5691
	8:29	chained hand and foot and **kept u guard,**	5875
	11:33	where it will be hidden, or **u** a bowl.	5679

Lk	13:34	as a hen gathers her chicks **u** her wings,	5679
	23: 7	that Jesus was **u** Herod's jurisdiction,	1666
	23:40	"since you are **u** the same sentence?	1877
Jn	1:48	"I saw you while you were still **u**	5679
	1:50	because I told you I saw you **u** the fig tree.	5691
	13: 3	Father had put all things **u** his **power,**	1650+5931
Ac	2: 5	from every nation **u** heaven.	5679
	4:12	for there is no other name **u** heaven given	5679
	7:45	our fathers **u** Joshua brought it with them	3552
	10:38	and healing all who *were* **u** the **power** of	2872
	22: 3	**U** Gamaliel I was thoroughly trained in the	
		law of our fathers	3836+4123+4546
	23:35	Paul *be* kept **u** guard in Herod's palace.	5875
	24: 2	"We have enjoyed a long period of peace **u**	1328
	24:23	the centurion *to* keep Paul **u** guard but	5498
	27:17	*they* passed ropes **u** the ship itself **to hold**	
		it **together.**	5690
Ro	2:12	and all who sin **u** the law will be judged by	1877
	3: 9	that Jews and Gentiles alike are all **u** sin.	5679
	3:19	it says to those who are **u** the law,	1877
	4:10	**U** what circumstances was it credited?	4802
	6:14	because you are not **u** law, but under grace.	5679
	6:14	because you are not under law, but **u** grace.	5679
	6:15	because we are not **u** law but under grace?	5679
	6:15	because we are not under law but **u** grace?	5679
1Co	7:37	*who* **is u** no compulsion but has control	2400
	9:20	To those **u** the law I became like one under	5679
	9:20	To those under the law I became like one **u**	5679
	9:20	the law (though I myself am not **u** the law),	5679
	9:20	so as to win those **u** the law.	5679
	9:21	from God's law but am **u** Christ's **law),**	1937
	10: 1	that our forefathers were all **u** the cloud and	5679
	10:13	a way out so that you can **stand up u** it.	5722
	11:31	we would not **come u** judgment.	3212
	15:25	until he has put all his enemies **u** his feet.	5679
	15:27	For *he* "has **put** everything **u** his feet."	5718
	15:27	that "everything" *has* been **put u** him,	5718
	15:27	who **put** everything **u** Christ.	5718
	15:28	to him who **put** everything **u** him,	5718
2Co	1: 8	*We were* **u** great **pressure,**	976
	9: 7	not reluctantly or **u** compulsion,	1666
	11:12	to **cut** the ground **from u** those who want	1716
	11:32	the governor **u** King Aretas had the city of	AIT
Gal	3:10	All who rely on observing the law are **u**	5679
	3:25	we are no longer **u** the supervision of	5679
	4: 3	we were in slavery **u** the basic principles of	5679
	4: 4	born of a woman, born **u** law,	5679
	4: 5	to redeem those **u** law,	5679
	4:21	Tell me, you who want to be **u** the law,	5679
	5:18	you are led by the Spirit, you are not **u** law.	5679
Eph	1:10	**bring** all things in heaven and on earth	
		together u one head,	368
	1:22	And God **placed** all things **u** his feet	5718
Php	2:10	in heaven and on earth and **u** the **earth,**	2973
	3:21	**bring** everything **u** his **control,**	5718
Col	1:23	to every creature **u** heaven,	5679
1Ti	3: 6	and fall **u** the same judgment as the devil.	1650
	6: 1	All who are **u** the yoke of slavery	5679
Heb	2: 8	and **put** everything **u** his feet."	5718
	2: 8	In **putting** everything **u** him,	5718
	9:15	to set them free from the sins committed **u**	2093
	10:29	**trampled** the Son of God **u** foot,	2922
Jas	1:12	the man who perseveres **u** trial,	AIT
1Pe	2:19	*man* bears up **u** the pain of unjust suffering	5722
	5: 2	that is **u** your care, serving as overseers—	1877
	5: 6	therefore, **u** God's mighty hand,	5679
1Jn	5:19	and that the whole world *is* **u** the **control**	3023
Rev	4: 8	with eyes all around, even **u** his wings.	2277
	5: 3	on earth or **u** the earth could open the scroll	5691
	5:13	and on earth and **u** the earth and on the sea,	5691
	6: 9	I saw **u** the altar the souls of those who	5691
	12: 1	with the sun, with the moon **u** her feet and	5691

UNDERFOOT (11) [FOOT]

2Ki	9:33	and the horses as *they* **trampled** her **u.**	8252
	14: 9	and **trampled** the thistle **u.**	8252
2Ch	25:18	and **trampled** the thistle **u.**	8252
Isa	14:19	Like a corpse **trampled u,**	1008
	28: 3	will be trampled **u.**	928+8079
La	3:34	To crush **u** all prisoners in the land,	8079+9393
Da	7: 7	and trampled **u** whatever was left.	10089+10655
	7:19	and trampled **u** whatever was left.	10089+10655
	8:13	and of the host that will be **trampled u?**"	5330
Mic	7:10	even now she will be **trampled u** like mire	5330
	7:19	*you will* **tread** our sins **u** and hurl all our	3899

UNDERGARMENT (1) [GARMENT]

Jn	19:23	one for each of them, with the **u** remaining.	5945

UNDERGARMENTS (5) [GARMENT]

Ex	28:42	"Make linen **u** as a covering for the body,	4829
	39:28	and the **u** of finely twisted linen.	965+4829
Lev	6:10	with linen **u** next to his body,	4829
	16: 4	with linen **u** next to his body;	4829
Eze	44:18	and linen **u** around their waists.	4829

UNDERGIRDING (KJV) See UNDER THE SHIP

UNDERGO (2) [UNDERGOES, UNDERGOING]

Ge	17:11	You *are to* **u** circumcision,	906+1414+4576+6889

Lk 12:50 But I have a **baptism** to u,   966+967

UNDERGOES (1) [UNDERGO]
Heb 12: 8 (and everyone u discipline),   1181+3581

UNDERGOING (1) [UNDERGO]
1Pe 5: 9 the world *are* u the same kind of sufferings.   2200

UNDERGROWTH (2) [GROWTH]
Job 30: 7 among the bushes and huddled in the u.   3017
Isa 17: 9 be like places abandoned to thickets and u.   580

UNDERLINGS (2)
2Ki 19: 6 those words with which the u *of* the king   5853
Isa 37: 6 those words with which the u *of* the king   5853

UNDERMINE (1)
Job 15: 4 But you even u piety and hinder devotion   7296

UNDERNEATH (4) [BENEATH]
Dt 33:27 and u are the everlasting arms.   4946+9393
Jos 7:21 inside my tent, with the silver u."   9393
    7:22 hidden in his tent, with the silver u   9393
2Ki 6:30 there, u, he had sackcloth on his body.   1074+4946

UNDERSETTERS (KJV) See HANDLES, SUPPORTS

UNDERSIDES (1)
Job 41:30 His u are jagged potsherds,   9393

UNDERSTAND (124) [UNDERSTANDING, UNDERSTANDS, UNDERSTOOD]
Ge 11: 7 so *they* will not u each other."   9048
  42:23 not realize that Joseph *could* u them,   9048
Dt 9: 6 U, then, that it is not because of your   3359
  28:49 a nation whose language *you* will not u,   9048
  32:29 If only they were wise and *would* u this   8505
1Sa 24:11 Now u and recognize that I am not guilty   1067
  28: 1 "You **must** u that you and your men   3359+3359
2Ki 18:26 to your servants in Aramaic, since we u it.   9048
Ne 8: 2 and women and all who were able to u.   9048
  8: 3 women and others *who could* u.   1067
  8: 8 the people *could* u what was being read.   1067
  10:28 and daughters who are able to u—   1067
Job 26:14 Who *then can* u the thunder of his power?"   1067
  32: 9 not only the aged *who* u what is right.   1067
  36:29 Who can u how he spreads out the clouds,   1067
  38: 4 Tell me, if you u.   1069+3359
  42: 3 Surely I spoke of things I did not u,   1067
Ps 14: 2 of men to see if there are *any* who u,   8505
  53: 2 of men to see if there are *any* who u,   8505
  73:16 When I tried to u all this,   3359
  81: 5 where we heard a language *we did* not u.   3359
  82: 5 "They know nothing, *they* u nothing.   1067
  92: 6 man does not know, fools *do* not u,   1067
  119:27 Let me u the teaching of your precepts;   1067
  119:79 *those who* u your statutes.   3359
  119:125 that *I may* u your statutes.   3359
Pr 2: 5 then *you will* u the fear of the LORD   1067
  2: 9 Then *you will* u what is right and just   1067
  20:24 How *then can* u his own way?   1067
  28: 5 Evil men *do* not u justice,   1067
  28: 5 but those who seek the LORD u it fully.   1067
  30:18 four *that I do* not u: 3359
Ecc 7:25 So I turned my mind to u,   3359
  7:25 the scheme of things and to u the stupidity   3359
  11: 5 so you cannot u the work of God,   3359
Isa 1: 3 my people *do* not u."   1067
  6:10 u with their hearts, and turn, and be healed."   1067
  32: 4 The mind of the rash will know and u,   1067
  36:11 to your servants in Aramaic, since we u it.   9048
  41:20 may see and know, may consider and u,   8505
  42:25 yet *they did* not u;   3359
  43:10 that you may know and believe me and u   1067
  44:18 They know nothing, *they* u nothing;   1067
  44:18 and their minds closed so they cannot u.   8505
  52:15 and what they have not heard, *they* will u.   1067
Jer 5:15 whose speech *you do* not u.   9048
  9:12 What man is wise enough to u this?   1067
  15:15 You, O LORD; remember me and care for   3359
  17: 9 and beyound cure. Who *can* u it?   3359
  23:20 In days to come *you will* u it *clearly*.   1067+1069
  30:24 In days to come *you will* u this.   1067
  31:19 after I *came* to u, I beat my breast.   3359
Eze 3: 6 whose words *you* cannot u.   9048
  12: 3 Perhaps *they* will u,   8011
Da 1: 4 well informed, **quick to** u,   1067+4529
  1:17 And Daniel *could* u visions and dreams   1067
  2:30 and that *you may* u what went through   10313
  5:23 which cannot see or hear or u.   10313
  8:15 was watching the vision and trying to u it,   1069
  8:17 "u that the vision concerns the time of   1067
  9:23 consider the message and u the vision: 1067
  9:25 "Know and u this: 8505
  12: 8 I heard, but *I did* not u.   1067
  12:10 None of the wicked will u,   1067
  12:10 but those who are wise *will* u.   1067
Hos 14: 9 Who is discerning? *He* will u them.   3359
Mic 4:12 *they do* not u his plan,   1067

Mt 13:13 though hearing, *they do* not hear or u.   5317
  13:15 u with their hearts and turn,   5317
  13:19 about the kingdom and *does* not u it,   5317
  15:10 the crowd to him and said, "Listen and u.   5317
  16: 9 *Do you* still not u?   3783
  16:11 How is it *you* don't u that I was not talking   3783
  24:15 the prophet Daniel—*let the reader* u—   3783
  24:43 But u this: If the owner of the house   1182
Mk 4:13 "Don't *you* u this parable?   3857
  4:13 How then *will you* u any parable?   1182
  4:33 as much as they could u.   201
  7:14 "Listen to me, everyone, and u this.   5317
  8:17 Do you still not see or u?   5317
  8:21 He said to them, "Do you still not u?"   5317
  9:32 But they *did* not u what he meant   51
  13:14 it does not belong—*let the reader* u—   3783
  14:68 "I don't know or u what you're talking   2179
Lk 2:50 they *did* not u what he was saying to them.   5317
  8:10 though hearing, *they may* not u.'   5317
  9:45 But they *did* not u what this meant.   51
  12:39 But u this: If the owner of the house   1182
  18:34 The disciples *did not* u any of this.   5317
  24:45 *so they could* u the Scriptures.   5317
Jn 3:10 said Jesus, "and *do you* not u these things?   1182
  8:27 *They* did not u that he was telling them   1182
  10: 6 but they *did* not u what he was telling them.   1182
  10:38 that you may know and u that the Father is   1182
  12:16 At first his disciples *did* not u all this.   1182
  12:40 nor u with their hearts, nor turn—   3783
  13: 7 but later *you will* u."   1182
  13:12 "Do you u what I have done for you?"   1182
  16:18 *We don't* u what he is saying."   3857
  20: 9 not u from Scripture that Jesus had to rise   3857
Ac 8:30 "Do you u what you are reading?"   1182
  22: 9 not u the voice of him who was speaking   201
  28:27 u with their hearts and turn,   5317
Ro 7:15 I *do* not u what I do.   1182
  10:19 Again I ask: Did Israel not u?   1182
  15:21 and those who have not heard *will* u."   5317
1Co 2:14 that *we may* u what God has freely given us.   3857
  2:14 and he cannot u them,   1182
  14:16 among **those who** do not u say "Amen"   2626
  14:23 **some** who do not u or some unbelievers   2626
  14:24 or **someone** who does not u come in   2626
2Co 1:13 not write you anything you cannot read or u.   2105
  1:14 *you will* **come to** u fully that you can boast   2105
Gal 3: 7 U, then, that those who believe are children   1182
Eph 3: 4 *to* u my insight into the mystery of Christ,   3783
  5:17 but u what the Lord's will is.   5317
Heb 11: 3 By faith *we* u that the universe was formed   3783
2Pe 1:20 you must u that no prophecy of Scripture   1182
  2:12 men blaspheme in matters *they do* not u.   51
  3: 3 *you must* u that in the last days scoffers will   1182
  3: 9 in keeping his promise, as some u slowness.   2451
  3:16 contain some things that are **hard to** u,   1554
Jude 1:10 against whatever *they do* not u;   3857
  1:10 and what things *they do* u by instinct,   2179

UNDERSTANDING (115) [UNDERSTAND]
Dt 1:13 u and respected men from each of your   1067
  4: 6 for this will show your wisdom and u to   1069
  4: 6 this great nation is a wise and u people."   1067
  32:21 angry by a nation that has **no** u.   5572
Jdg 13:18 you ask my name? It is **beyond** u."   7100
1Ki 4:29 a breadth of u as measureless as the sand   4213
1Ch 22:12 May the LORD give you discretion and u   8505
  28:19 *he* gave me u *in* all the details of the plan."   8505
2Ch 30:22 who **showed** good u of the service of   8505+8507
Job 8:10 not bring forth words from their u?   4213
  12:12 Does not long life bring u?   9312
  12:13 counsel and u,   9312
  17: 4 You have closed their minds to u;   8507
  20: 3 and my u inspires me to reply.   1069
  28:12 Where does u dwell?   1069
  28:20 Where does u dwell?   1069
  28:28 that is wisdom, and to shun evil is u.' "   1069
  32: 8 breath of the Almighty, *that gives* him u.   1067
  34:10 "So listen to me, you men of u.   4222
  34:16 "If you have u, hear this;   1069
  34:34 "Men of u declare, wise men who hear me   4222
  36:26 How great is God—beyond *our* u!   3359
  37: 5 he does great things beyond *our* u.   3359
  38:36 with wisdom or gave u to the mind?   1069
Ps 32: 9 *which have* no u but must be controlled   1067
  49: 3 the utterance from my heart will give u.   9312
  49:20 A man who has riches without u is like   1067
  111:10 all who follow his precepts have good u.   8507
  119:34 Give me u, and I will keep your law   1067
  119:73 give me u to learn your commands.   1067
  119:100 I **have** more u than the elders,   1067
  119:104 I gain u from your precepts;   1067
  119:130 *it gives* u *to* the simple.   1067
  119:144 give me u that I may live.   1067
  119:169 give me u according to your word.   1067
  136: 5 who by his u made the heavens,   9312
  147: 5 his u has no limit.   9312
Pr 1: 2 for u words of insight;   1067
  1: 6 for u proverbs and parables,   1067
  2: 2 to wisdom and applying your heart to u,   9312
  2: 3 you call out for insight and cry aloud for u,   9312
  2: 6 from his mouth come knowledge and u.   9312
  2:11 and u will guard you.   9312
  3: 5 and lean not on your own u;   1069
  3:13 the man who gains u,   9312
  3:19 by u he set the heavens in place;   9312
  4: 1 pay attention and gain u.   1069

Pr 4: 5 Get wisdom, get u; do not forget my words   1069
  4: 7 Though it cost all you have, get u.   1069
  7: 4 and call u your kinsman;   1069
  8: 1 Does not u raise her voice?   9312
  8: 5 you who are foolish, gain u.   4213
  8:14 I have u and power.   1069
  9: 6 walk in the way of u.   1069
  9:10 and knowledge of the Holy One is u.   1069
  10:23 but a man of u delights in wisdom   9312
  11:12 but a man of u holds his tongue.   9312
  13:15 Good u wins favor,   8507
  14:29 A patient man has great u,   9312
  15:21 but a man of u keeps a straight course.   9312
  15:32 but whoever heeds correction gains u.   4213
  16:16 to choose u rather than silver!   1069
  16:22 U is a fountain of life to those who have it,   8507
  17:27 and a man of u is even-tempered.   9312
  18: 2 in u but delights in airing his own opinions.   9312
  19: 8 he who cherishes u prospers.   9312
  20: 5 but a man of u draws them out.   9312
  21:16 A man who strays from the path of u comes   8505
  23:23 get wisdom, discipline and u.   1069
  24: 3 and through u it is established;   9312
  28: 2 a man of u and knowledge maintains order.   1067
  30: 2 I do not have a man's u.   1069
Ecc 1:17 Then I applied myself to the u *of* wisdom,   3359
Isa 5:13 my people will go into exile for lack of u;   1981
  6: 9 " 'Be ever hearing, but never u;   1067
  10:13 and by my wisdom, because *I* **have** u.   1067
  11: 2 the Spirit of wisdom and of u,   1069
  27:11 For this is a people without u;   1069
  28:19 The u of this message will bring sheer terror   1067
  29:24 who are wayward in spirit will gain u;   1069
  40:14 or showed him the path of u?   9312
  40:28 and his u no one can fathom.   9312
  44:19 no one has the knowledge or u to say,   9312
  56:11 They are shepherds *who* lack u;   3359
Jer 3:15 who will lead you with knowledge and u.   8505
  4:22 senseless children; they **have** no u.   1067
  10:12 and stretched out the heavens by his u.   9312
  51:15 and stretched out the heavens by his u.   9312
Eze 28: 4 and u you have gained wealth for yourself   9312
Da 1:17 and u of all kinds of literature and learning.   8505
  1:20 In every matter of wisdom and u   1069
  5:12 to have a keen mind and knowledge and u,   10684
  8:27 appalled by the vision; it was beyond u.   1067
  9:22 I have now come to give you insight and u.   1069
  10: 1 The u *of* the message came to him in   1067
  10:12 that you set your mind to **gain** u and   1067
Hos 4:11 old wine and new, which take away the u   4213
  4:14 a people without u will come to ruin!   1067
Ob 1: 8 men of u in the mountains of Esau?   9312
Mt 13:14 " 'You will be ever hearing but never u;   5317
Mk 4:12 and ever hearing but never u;   5317
  12:33 with all your u and with all your strength,   5304
Lk 2:47 was amazed at his u and his answers.   5304
Ac 28:26 "You will be ever hearing but never u;   5317
Ro 10:19 make you angry by a nation that has **no** u."   852
  13:11 And do this, u the present time.   3857
2Co 6: 6 in purity, u, patience and kindness;   1194
Eph 1: 8 he lavished on us with all wisdom and u.   5860
  4:18 They are darkened in their u and separated   1379
Php 4: 7 the peace of God, which transcends all u,   3808
Col 1: 9 through all spiritual wisdom and u.   5304
  2: 2 the full riches of complete u,   5304
Phm 1: 6 a **full** u of every good thing we have   2106
Jas 3:13 Who is wise and u among you?   2184
1Jn 5:20 of God has come and has given us u,   1379

UNDERSTANDS (10) [UNDERSTAND]
Dt 29: 4 the LORD has not given you a mind that u   3359
1Ch 28: 9 and u every motive behind the thoughts.   1067
Job 28:23 God u the way to it and he alone knows   1067
Pr 29:19 though *he* u, he will not respond.   1067
Isa 57: 1 devout men are taken away, and no *one* u   1067
Jer 9:24 that *he* u and knows me,   8505
Mt 13:23 the man who hears the word and u it.   5317
Ro 3:11 no one who u, no one who seeks God.   5317
1Co 14: 2 Indeed, no one u him; he utters mysteries   201
1Ti 6: 4 he is conceited and u nothing.   2179

UNDERSTOOD (19) [UNDERSTAND]
1Ch 12:32 *who* u the times and knew what Israel   1069+3359
Ne 8:12 because *they* now u the words   1067
Est 1:13 he spoke with the wise men *who* u the times   3359
Job 13: 1 my ears have heard and u.   1067
Ps 73:17 then *I* u their final destiny.   1067
Isa 40:13 Who *has* u the mind of the LORD,   9419
  40:21 not u since the earth was founded?   1067
  48: 8 You have neither heard nor u;   3359
Da 9: 2 I, Daniel, u from the Scriptures,   1067
Mt 13:51 "Have you u all these things?"   5317
  16:12 Then *they* u that he was not telling them   5317
  17:13 the disciples u that he was talking to them   5317
Mk 6:52 for *they had* not u about the loaves;   5317
Jn 1: 5 but the darkness *has* not u it.   2898
  13:28 but no one at the meal u why Jesus said this   1182
Ro 1:20 *being* u from what has been made,   3783
1Co 13:11 None of the rulers of this age u it,   1182
2Co 1:14 as *you have* u us in part,   2105
Col 1: 6 the day you heard it and u God's grace   2105

UNDERTAKEN (3) [UNDERTOOK]
1Ki 7:40 So Huram finished all the work he had u   6913
2Ch 4:11 So Huram finished the work he had u   6913

Lk 1: 1 Many *have* u to draw up an account of 2217

UNDERTAKES (1) [UNDERTOOK]
Jos 6:26 the man who u to rebuild this city, Jericho: 7756

UNDERTOOK (4) [UNDERTAKEN, UNDERTAKES]
2Ki 18: 7 he was successful in whatever *he* u. 3655
2Ch 31:21 that *he* u in the service of God's temple and 2725
   32:30 He succeeded in everything *he* u. 5126
Ecc 2: 4 *I* u great projects: I built houses for myself 1540

UNDESERVED (1)
Pr 26: 2 an u curse does not come to rest. 2855

UNDESIRABLE (1)
Jos 24:15 But if serving the LORD seems u to you, 8273

UNDETECTED (1)
Nu 5:13 from her husband and her impurity *is* u 6259

UNDIGNIFIED (1)
2Sa 6:22 *I will* become even more u than this, 7837

UNDISCIPLINED (1)
Pr 9:13 she is u and without knowledge, 7346

UNDISTURBED (2)
Job 12: 6 The tents of marauders *are* u, 8922
Isa 32:18 in secure homes, in u places of rest. 8633

UNDIVIDED (4)
1Ch 12:33 to help David with u loyalty—50,000 2256+4202+4213+4213
Ps 86:11 give me an u heart, that I may fear your 3479
Eze 11:19 an u heart and put a new spirit in them; 285
1Co 7:35 in a right way in u devotion to the Lord. 597

UNDOING (2) [UNDONE]
2Ch 22: 4 they became his advisers, to his u. 5422
Pr 18: 7 A fool's mouth is his u, 4745

UNDONE (2) [UNDOING]
Jos 11:15 *he* left nothing u of all that the LORD 6073
Lk 11:42 the latter without leaving the former u. 4205

UNDOUBTEDLY (1)
1Co 14:10 U there are all sorts of languages in 1623+5593

UNDRESSED (KJV) See UNTENDED

UNDULY (1)
Pr 11:24 withholds u, but comes to poverty. 3841+4946

UNDYING (1)
Eph 6:24 love our Lord Jesus Christ with an u love. 914

UNEATEN (1)
Job 20:18 he toiled for he must give back u; 1180+4202

UNENDING (1)
Jer 15:18 Why is my pain u and my wound grievous 5905

UNEQUALED (2)
Mt 24:21 great distress, u from the beginning of the world 1181+3888+4024
Mk 13:19 be days of distress u from the beginning, 1181+3888+4024+5525

UNEXPECTEDLY (2)
Ecc 9:12 so men are trapped by evil times that fall u 7328
Lk 21:34 and that day will close on you u like a trap. 167

UNFADING (1)
1Pe 3: 4 the u beauty of a gentle and quiet spirit, 915

UNFAILING (35)
Ex 15:13 "In your u love you will lead the people 2876
1Sa 20:14 But show me u kindness *like that of* 2876
2Sa 22:51 he shows u kindness to his anointed, 2876
Ps 6: 4 save me because of your u love. 2876
   13: 5 But I trust in your u love; 2876
   18:50 he shows u kindness to his anointed, 2876
   21: 7 the u love *of* the Most High he will not 2876
   31:16 save me in your u love. 2876
   32:10 but the LORD's u love surrounds 2876
   33: 5 the earth is full of his u love. 2876
   33:18 on those whose hope is in his u love, 2876
   33:22 May your u love rest upon us, O LORD, 2876
   36: 7 How priceless is your u love! 2876
   44:26 redeem us because of your u love. 2876
   48: 9 O God, we meditate on your u love. 2876
   51: 1 O God, according to your u love; 2876

Ps 52: 8 I trust in God's u love for ever and ever. 2876
   77: 8 Has his u love vanished forever? 2876
   85: 7 Show us your u love, O LORD, 2876
   90:14 in the morning with your u love, 2876
   107: 8 for his u love and his wonderful deeds 2876
   107:15 for his u love and his wonderful deeds 2876
   107:21 for his u love and his wonderful deeds 2876
   107:31 for his u love and his wonderful deeds 2876
   119:41 May your u love come to me, O LORD, 2876
   119:76 May your u love be my comfort, 2876
   130: 7 for with the LORD is u love and 2876
   143: 8 the morning bring me word of your u love, 2876
   143:12 In your u love, silence my enemies; 2876
   147:11 who put their hope in his u love. 2876
Pr 19:22 What a man desires is u love; 2876
   20: 6 Many a man claims to have u love, 2876
Isa 54:10 yet my u love for you will not be shaken 2876
La 3:32 so great is his u love. 2876
Hos 10:12 reap the fruit of u love, 2876

UNFAIR (1)
Mt 20:13 'Friend, *I am* not *being* u *to* you. 92

UNFAITHFUL (50) [UNFAITHFULLY, UNFAITHFULNESS]
Lev 6: 2 "If anyone sins and *is* u to the LORD 5085+5086
Nu 5: 6 in any way and so *is* u to the LORD, 5085+5086
   5:12 man's wife goes astray and *is* u to him 5085+5086
   5:27 If she has defiled herself and *been* u 5085+5086
Dt 32:20 perverse generation, children who are u. 574+4202
Jdg 19: 2 But she *was* u to him. 2388
1Ch 5:25 But *they were* u to the God of their fathers 5085
   10:13 Saul died because he was u to the LORD; 5085+5086
2Ch 12: 2 Because *they had been* u to the LORD, 5085
   26:16 *He was* u to the LORD his God, 5085
   26:18 Leave the sanctuary, for *you have been* u; 5085
   28:19 and *had been* most u to the LORD. 5085+5086
   28:22 Ahaz became even more u to the LORD. 5085
   29: 6 Our fathers *were* u; they did evil 5085
   30: 7 who *were* u to the LORD, 5085
   36:14 and the people *became* more and more u, 5085+5086+8049
Ezr 10: 2 "We *have been* u to our God by marrying 5085
   10:10 You *have been* u; you have married foreign 5085
Ne 1: 8 saying, 'If you *are* u, I will scatter you 5085
   13:27 and *are being* u to our God by marrying 5085
Job 31:28 for I would have been u to God on high. 3950
Ps 73:27 you destroy all *who are* u to you. 2388
Pr 2:22 and the u will be torn from it. 953
   11: 3 but the u are destroyed by their duplicity. 953
   11: 6 but the u are trapped by evil desires. 953
   13: 2 but the u have a craving for violence. 953
   13:15 but the way of the u is hard. 953
   21:18 and the u for the upright. 953
   22:12 but he frustrates the words of the u. 953
   23:28 and multiplies the u among men. 953
   25:19 or a lame foot is reliance on the u in times 953
Jer 3: 7 and her u sister Judah saw it. 957
   3: 8 her u sister Judah had no fear; 953
   3:10 her u sister Judah did not return to me 957
   3:11 "Faithless Israel is more righteous than u Judah. 953
   3:20 But like a woman u to her husband, 953
   3:20 so *you have been* u to me, 953
   5:11 the house of Judah have been utterly u 953+953
   9: 2 they are all adulterers, a crowd of u *people.* 953
   31:22 How long will you wander, O u daughter? 8745
   49: 4 O u daughter, you trust in your riches 8745
Eze 14:13 if a country sins against me by *being* u 5085+5086
   15: 8 desolate because *they have been* u, 5085+5086
   17:20 upon him there because *he was* u to me. 5085
   39:23 because *they were* u to me. 5085
Hos 2: 5 Their mother *has been* u and has conceived 2388
   4:12 *they are* u to their God. 2388
   5: 7 *They are* u to the LORD; 953
   6: 7 *they were* u to me there. 953
   9: 1 For *you have been* u to your God; 2388

UNFAITHFULLY (3) [UNFAITHFUL]
Jos 7: 1 But the Israelites acted u in regard to 5085+5086
   22:20 *When* Achan son of Zerah acted u 5085+5086
   22:31 because *you have* not acted u toward 5085

UNFAITHFULNESS (14) [UNFAITHFUL]
Nu 14:33 for forty years, suffering for your u, 2394
1Ch 9: 1 captive to Babylon because of their u. 5086
2Ch 29:19 articles that King Ahaz removed in his u 5086
   33:19 as well as all his sins and u, 5086
Ezr 9: 2 and officials have led the way in this u." 5086
   9: 4 around me because of this u *of* the exiles. 5086
   10: 6 because he continued to mourn over the u 5086
Eze 18:24 Because of the u he *is* guilty *of* 5085+5086
   39:26 and all the u *they* showed toward me 5085+5086
Da 9: 7 scattered us because of our u. 5085+5086
Hos 1: 2 an adulterous wife and children of u, 2393
   1: 2 the adulterous look from her face and the u 5538
Mt 5:32 divorces his wife, except for marital u, 4518
   19: 9 divorces his wife, except for marital u, 4518

UNFAMILIAR (1)
Isa 42:16 along u paths I will guide them; 3359+4202

UNFANNED (1)
Job 20:26 A fire u will consume him and devour 4202+5870

UNFAVORABLE (1)
Jer 42: 6 Whether it is favorable or u, we will obey 8273

UNFEELING (1)
Ps 119:70 Their hearts *are* callous and u, 3263

UNFEIGNED (KJV) See SINCERE

UNFILLED (1)
Jer 14: 3 They return with their jars u; 8200

UNFINISHED (1)
Tit 1: 5 you might straighten out what was left u NIG

UNFIT (1)
Tit 1:16 disobedient and u for doing anything good. 99

UNFOLDING (1)
Ps 119:130 The u *of* your words gives light; 7340

UNFORGIVING (1)
2Ti 3: 3 u, slanderous, without self-control, brutal, 836

UNFORMED (1)
Ps 139:16 your eyes saw my u body. 1677

UNFRIENDLY (1)
Pr 18: 1 An u *man* pursues selfish ends; 7233

UNFRUITFUL (3)
Mt 13:22 deceitfulness of wealth choke it, making it u. 182
Mk 4:19 come in and choke the word, making it u. 182
1Co 14:14 my spirit prays, but my mind is u. 182

UNFULFILLED (1)
Eze 19: 5 " 'When she saw *her* hope u, 3498

UNFURLED (1)
Ps 60: 4 you have raised a banner to be u against 5824

UNGIRDED (KJV) See UNLOADED

UNGODLINESS (3) [UNGODLY]
Isa 32: 6 He practices u and spreads error concerning 2869
Jer 23:15 the prophets of Jerusalem u has spread 2870
Tit 2:12 to say "No" to u and worldly passions, 813

UNGODLY (18) [UNGODLINESS]
Job 17: 8 the innocent are aroused against the u. 2868
Ps 35:16 Like the u they maliciously mocked; 2868
   43: 1 plead my cause against an u nation; 2883+4202
Pr 11:31 how much more the u and the sinner! 8401
Isa 9:17 for everyone is u and wicked, 2868
Ro 5: 6 still powerless, Christ died for the u. 815
1Co 6: 1 before the u for judgment instead of before 96
1Ti 1: 9 the u and sinful, the unholy and irreligious; 815
2Ti 2:16 in it will become more and more u. 813
1Pe 4:18 what will become of the u and the sinner?" 815
2Pe 2: 5 when he brought the flood on its u people, 815
   2: 6 of what is going to happen to the u; 815
   3: 7 day of judgment and destruction *of* u men. 815
Jude 1:15 the u of all the ungodly acts they have done 815
   1:15 the ungodly of all the u acts they have done 813
   1:15 *they have* done in the u way, 814
   1:15 the harsh words u sinners have spoken 815
   1:18 there will be scoffers who will follow their own u desires." 813

UNGRATEFUL (2)
Lk 6:35 because he is kind to the u and wicked. 940
2Ti 3: 2 abusive, disobedient to their parents, u, 940

UNHARMED (4)
1Sa 24:19 does he let him get away u? 3208
2Sa 17: 3 all the people will be u." 8934
Ps 55:18 He ransoms me u from the battle waged 928+8934
Da 3:25 in the fire, unbound and u, 10029+10244+10379

UNHEALTHY (1)
1Ti 6: 4 an u interest in controversies and quarrels 3796

UNHEARD-OF (2)
Eze 7: 5 An u disaster is coming. 285
Da 11:36 above every god and will say u things 7098

UNHOLY (3)
1Ti 1: 9 the ungodly and sinful, the u and irreligious; 495
2Ti 3: 2 disobedient to their parents, ungrateful, u, 495
Heb 10:29 who has treated as an u *thing* the blood of 3123

UNICORN, UNICORNS (KJV) See WILD OX, WILD OXEN

UNIMPRESSIVE (1)
2Co 10:10 in person he is **u** and his speaking amounts   822

UNINFORMED (1)
2Co 1: 8 We do not want you *to be* **u**, brothers,   51

UNINTENTIONAL (1)
[UNINTENTIONALLY]
Nu 15:26 all the people were involved in the **u wrong.** 8705

UNINTENTIONALLY (17)
[UNINTENTIONAL]
Lev	4: 2	'When anyone sins **u** and does	928+8705
	4:13	" 'If the whole Israelite community **sins u**	8706
	4:22	leader sins **u** and does what is forbidden	928+8705
	4:27	" 'If a member of the community sins **u**	928+8705
	5:15	sins **u** in regard to any of the LORD's	928+8705
	5:18	for the **wrong** *he has* **committed u,**	8704+8705
Nu	15:22	" 'Now if *you* **u** fail to keep any of these	8706
	15:24	and if this is done **u** without	4200+8705
	15:27	" 'But if just one person sins **u,**	928+8705
	15:28	for the one who erred by sinning **u,**	928+8705
	15:29	the same law applies to everyone *who* **sins u,**	928+6913+8705
	35:22	or throws something at him **u**	928+4202+7402
Dt	4:42	if *he had* **u** killed his neighbor	928+1172+1981
	19: 4	one who kills his neighbor **u,**	928+1172+1981
Jos	20: 3	kills a person accidentally and **u**	928+1172+1981
	20: 5	because he killed his neighbor **u**	928+1172+1981
Eze	45:20	for anyone *who* **sins u** or through ignorance;	8706

UNION (3) [UNITE]
Zec	11: 7	and called one Favor and the other **U,**	2482
	11:14	Then I broke my second staff called **U,**	2482
Mt	1:25	But *he had* no **u** with her until she gave birth to a son.	1182

UNIQUE (2)
SS	6: 9	is **u,** the only daughter of her mother,	285
Zec	14: 7	It will be a **u** day, without daytime or	285

UNISON (2) [UNITE]
2Ch	5:13	The trumpeters and singers joined in **u,**	285+3869
Ac	19:34	they all shouted in **u** for about two hours:	1651

UNIT (6) [UNITS]
Ex	26: 6	so that the tabernacle is a **u.**	285
	26:11	the loops to fasten the tent together as a **u.**	285
	36:13	so that the tabernacle was a **u.**	285
	36:18	to fasten the tent together as a **u.**	285
1Sa	17:18	to the commander of their **u.**	548
1Co	12:12	The body is a **u,** though it is made up of	1651

UNITE (4) [REUNITED, UNION, UNISON, UNITED, UNITES, UNITY]
1Ch	12:17	I *am ready* to have you **u** with me.	2118+3480+4200+4222
Job	16:10	in scorn and **u** together against me.	4848
Isa	14: 1	Aliens will join them and **u** with the house	6202
1Co	6:15	take the members of Christ and **u** them with a prostitute?	3517+4472

UNITED (12) [UNITE]
Ge	2:24	and mother and *be* **u** to his wife,	1815
Jdg	20:11	So all the men of Israel got together and **u**	2492
Da	2:43	be a mixture and will not remain **u,**	10158+10180+10180+10554
Mt	19: 5	and mother and *be* **u** to his wife,	3140
Mk	10: 7	and mother and *be* **u** to his wife,	4681
Ac	18:12	a **u** attack on Paul and brought him	3924
Ro	6: 5	If we have been **u** with him like this	5242
	6: 5	also be **u** with him in his resurrection.	NIG
1Co	1:10	you may be **perfectly u** in mind	899+2936+3836
Eph	5:31	and mother and *be* **u** to his wife,	4681
Php	2: 1	encouragement from being **u with** Christ,	1877
Col	2: 2	be encouraged in heart and **u** in love,	5204

UNITES (2) [UNITE]
1Co	6:16	Do you not know that he who **u** *himself*	3140
	6:17	But he who **u** *himself* with the Lord is one	3140

UNITS (13) [UNIT]
Nu	10:25	Finally, as the rear guard for all the **u,**	4722
	31:48	officers who were over the **u** *of* the army—	548
1Sa	29: 2	with their **u of hundreds** and thousands,	4395
2Sa	18: 4	the men marched out in **u of hundreds** and	4395
2Ki	11: 4	for the commanders of **u of a hundred,**	4395
	11: 9	the commanders of **u of a hundred** did just	4395
	11:15	the commanders of **u of a hundred,**	4395
1Ch	12:20	leaders of **u of a thousand** in Manasseh.	547
	15:25	of **u of a thousand** went to bring up the ark	547
2Ch	17:14	From Judah, commanders of **u of 1,000:**	547
	23: 1	with the commanders of **u of a hundred:**	4395
	23: 9	of **u of a hundred** the spears and the large	4395
	23:14	of **u of a hundred,** who were in charge of	4395

UNITY (7) [UNITE]
2Ch	30:12	of God was on the people to give them **u**	285
Ps	133: 1	when brothers live **together in u!**	3480
Jn	17:23	May they be brought to complete **u** to let	1651
Ro	15: 5	give you a **spirit of u** among	899+3836+5858
Eph	4: 3	to keep the **u** of the Spirit through the bond	1942
	4:13	until we all reach **u** in the faith and in	1942
Col	3:14	which binds them all together in perfect **u.**	NIG

UNIVERSE (5)
1Co	4: 9	have been made a spectacle *to* the whole **u,**	3180
Eph	4:10	in order to fill the **whole u.**	4246
Php	2:15	in which you shine like stars in the **u**	3180
Heb	1: 2	and through whom he made the **u.**	172
	11: 3	that the **u** was formed at God's command,	172

UNJUST (19) [UNJUSTLY]
Job	6:29	Relent, do not be **u;**	6406
	27: 7	my adversaries like the **u!**	6405
Ps	82: 2	the **u** and show partiality to the wicked?	6404
Isa	10: 1	Woe to those who make **u** laws,	224
Jer	17:11	the man who gains riches by **u** means.	4202+5477
Eze	18:25	Hear, O house of Israel: *Is* my way **u?**	4202+9419
	18:25	Is it not your ways *that are* **u?**	4202+9419
	18:29	*Are* my ways **u,** O house of Israel?	4202+9419
	18:29	Is it not your ways *that are* **u?**	4202+9419
	22:12	and excessive interest and **make u gain**	1298
	22:13	at the **u gain** you have made and at	1299
	22:27	and kill people to **make u gain.**	1298+1299
	33:31	but their hearts are greedy for **u gain.**	1299
Hab	2: 9	Woe to him who builds his realm by **u** gain	8273
Lk	18: 6	Lord said, "Listen to what the **u** judge says.	94
Ro	3: 5	That God is **u** in bringing his wrath on us?	96
	9:14	Is God **u?** Not at all!	94
Heb	6:10	God is not **u;** he will not forget your work	96
1Pe	2:19	a man bears up under the pain *of* **u** suffering	96

UNJUSTLY (1) [UNJUST]
Jer 23:10 an evil course and use their power **u.**   4026+4202

UNKEMPT (3)
Lev	10: 6	"*Do* not *let* your hair *become* **u,**	7277
	13:45	must wear torn clothes, let his hair be **u,**	7277
	21:10	*must* not *let* his hair *become* **u** or tear his	7277

UNKNOWN (7)
Dt	28:36	to a nation **u** to you or to your fathers.	3359+4202
Isa	48: 6	of hidden things **u** *to you.*	3359+4202
Da	11:38	a god **u** *to* his fathers he will honor	3359+4202
Ac	17:23	with this inscription: TO AN **U** GOD.	58
	17:23	Now what you worship *as something* **u**	51
2Co	6: 9	known, yet regarded as **u;**	51
Gal	1:22	I was personally **u** to the churches of Judea	51

UNLADE (KJV) See UNLOAD

UNLAWFUL (4)
Mt	12: 2	Your disciples are doing what is **u** on	2003+4024
Mk	2:24	why are they doing what *is* **u** on	2003+4024
Lk	6: 2	"Why are you doing what *is* **u** on	2003+4024
Ac	16:21	advocating customs **u** for us Romans	2003+4024

UNLEARNED (KJV) See IGNORANT, NOT UNDERSTAND, STUPID, UNSCHOOLED

UNLEASH (3) [UNLEASHED, UNLEASHES]
Job	40:11	**U** the fury of your wrath,	7046
Eze	7: 3	now upon you and *I will* **u** my anger	8938
	13:13	In my wrath *I will* **u** a violent wind,	1324

UNLEASHED (2) [UNLEASH]
Ex	15: 7	*You* **u** your burning anger;	8938
Ps	78:49	He **u** against them his hot anger, his wrath,	8938

UNLEASHES (1) [UNLEASH]
Job 37: 3 He **u** his lightning beneath the whole heaven 9223

UNLEAVENED (29)
Ex	12:17	"Celebrate the **Feast of U Bread,**	5174
	12:20	Wherever you live, you must eat **u bread."**	5174
	12:39	they baked cakes of **u bread.**	5174
	13: 7	Eat **u bread** during those seven days;	5174
	23:15	"Celebrate the **Feast of U Bread;**	5174
	34:18	"Celebrate the Feast of **U Bread.**	5174
Lev	23: 6	the LORD's **Feast of U Bread** begins;	5174
Nu	6:17	He is to present the basket of **u bread** and	5174
	9:11	together with **u bread** and bitter herbs.	5174
Dt	16: 3	but for seven days eat **u bread,**	5174
	16: 8	For six days eat **u bread** and on	5174
	16:16	at the Feast of **U Bread,** the Feast of Weeks	5174
Jos	5:11	**u bread** and roasted grain.	5174
Jdg	6:20	"Take the meat and the **u bread,**	5174
	6:21	meat and the **u bread.**	5174
2Ki	23: 9	they ate **u bread** with their fellow priests.	5174
1Ch	23:29	the **u** wafers, the baking and the mixing,	5174
2Ch	8:13	the Feast of **U Bread,** the Feast of Weeks	5174
	30:13	the Feast of **U Bread** in the second month.	5174
	30:21	the Feast of **U Bread** for seven days	5174
	35:17	the Feast of **U Bread** for seven days.	5174
Ezr	6:22	with joy the Feast of **U Bread,**	5174
Mt	26:17	On the first day of the **Feast of U Bread,**	109
Mk	14: 1	**Feast of U Bread** were only two days away,	109
	14:12	On the first day of the **Feast of U Bread,**	109
Lk	22: 1	Now the Feast *of* **U Bread,**	109
	22: 7	Then came the day *of* **U Bread** on which	109
Ac	12: 3	during the **Feast of U Bread.**	109
	20: 6	Philippi after the **Feast of U Bread,**	109+2465

UNLESS (64)
Ge	32:26	"I will not let you go **u** you bless me."	561+3954
	42:15	you will not leave this place **u** your	561+3954
	43: 3	not see my face again **u** your brother is	1194
	43: 5	not see my face again **u** your brother is	1194
	44:23	'**U** your youngest brother comes down	561+4202
	44:26	the man's face **u** our youngest brother is	4202
Ex	3:19	that the king of Egypt will not let you go **u**	4202
	33:16	with your people **u** you go with us?	2022+4202
Lev	22: 6	not eat any of the sacred offerings **u**	561+3954
Dt	32:30	**u** their Rock had sold them,	561+3954+4202
	32:30	**u** the LORD had given them up?	NIH
Jos	2:18	**u,** when we enter the land,	2180
	2:18	**u** you have brought your father and mother,	NIH
	7:12	not be with you anymore **u** you destroy	561+4202
2Sa	3:13	Do not come into my presence **u** you bring Michal	561+3954+4200+7156
2Ki	4:24	don't slow down for me **u** I tell you."	561+3954
Est	2:14	not return to the king **u** he was pleased	561+3954
Ps	94:17	**U** the LORD had given me help,	4295
	127: 1	**U** the LORD builds the house,	561+4202
	127: 1	**U** the LORD watches over the city,	561+4202
Isa	1: 9	**U** the LORD Almighty had left us some survivors,	4295
La	5:22	**u** you have utterly rejected us and	561+3954
Da	6: 5	against this man Daniel **u** it has something	10386
Am	3: 3	two walk together **u** they have agreed	561+1194
Mt	5:20	that **u** your righteousness surpasses	1569+3590
	12:29	carry off his possessions **u** he first ties	1569+3590
	18: 3	**u** you change and become like little	1569+3590
	18:35	of you **u** you forgive your brother	1569+3590
	26:42	for this cup to be taken away **u** I drink	1569+3590
Mk	3:27	carry off his possessions **u** he first ties	1569+3590
	7: 3	Pharisees and all the Jews do not eat **u**	1569+3590
	7: 4	from the marketplace they do not eat **u**	1569+3590
Lk	9:13	**u** we go and buy food for all this	1623+3614
	13: 3	**u** you repent, you too will all perish.	1569+3590
	13: 5	**u** you repent, you too will all perish."	1569+3590
Jn	3: 3	kingdom of God **u** he is born again."	1569+3590
	3: 5	of God **u** he is born of water and	1569+3590
	4:48	"**U** you people see miraculous signs	1569+3590
	6:44	**u** the Father who sent me draws him,	1569+3590
	6:53	**u** you eat the flesh of the Son of Man	1569+3590
	6:65	**u** the Father has enabled him."	1569+3590
	10:37	**u** I do what my Father does.	1623+4024
	12:24	**u** a kernel of wheat falls to the ground	1569+3590
	13: 8	Jesus answered, "**U** I wash you,	1569+3590
	15: 4	bear fruit **u** you remain in me.	1569+3590
	16: 7	**U** I go away, the Counselor will not	1569+3590
	20:25	"**U** I see the nail marks in his hands	1569+3590
Ac	8:31	"**u** someone explains it to me?"	1569+3590
	15: 1	"**U** you are circumcised,	1569+3590
	24:21	**u** it was this one thing I shouted as I stood	2445
	27:31	"**U** these men stay with the ship,	1569+3590
Ro	9:29	"**U** the Lord Almighty had left us descendants,	1623+3590
	10:15	how can they preach **u** they are sent?	1569+3590
1Co	14: 5	**u** he interprets, so that the church may be edified.	1623+1760+3590
	14: 6	**u** I bring you some revelation or	1569+3590
	14: 7	**u** there is a distinction in the notes?	1569+3590
	14: 9	**U** you speak intelligible words	1569+3590
	15:36	What you sow does not come to life **u**	1569+3590
2Co	13: 5	**u,** of course, you fail the test?	1623+3614
1Ti	5: 9	on the list of widows **u** she is over sixty,	NIG
	5:19	an accusation against an elder **u**	1623+1760+4200
2Ti	2: 5	**u** he competes according to the rules.	1569+3590
Rev	2:22	**u** they repent of her ways.	1569+3590
	13:17	could buy or sell **u** he had the mark,	1623+3590

UNLIKE (9)
Jdg	2:17	**U** their fathers, they quickly turned from the way	4027+4202+6913
2Ki	16: 2	**U** David his father, he did not do	3869+4202
2Ch	27: 2	but **u** him he did not enter the temple of	NIH
	28: 1	**U** David his father, he did not do	3869+4202
	33:23	But **u** his father Manasseh,	3869+4202
Isa	7:17	on the house of your father a time **u** any	4202
Eze	16:31	you were **u** a prostitute, because you	3869+4202
2Co	2:17	**U** so many, we do not peddle the word	4024+6055
Heb	7:27	**U** the other high priests, he does not need	6061

UNLIMITED (1)
1Ti 1:16 Christ Jesus might display his **u** patience as   570

UNLOAD (1) [UNLOADED]
Ac 21: 3 where our ship was to **u** its cargo.   711

UNLOADED (1) [UNLOAD]
Ge 24:32 and the camels *were* **u.**   7337

UNLOCKED (1)
Jdg 3:25 they took a key and **u** them.   7337

UNLOOSE (KJV) See UNTIE

UNLOVED (2)
Dt 21:17 He must acknowledge the son of his **u** wife   8533
Pr 30:23 an **u** woman who is married,   8533

UNMARKED (1)
Lk 11:44 because you are like **u** graves,   83

UNMARRIED (10)
Lev 21: 3 or an **u** sister who is dependent on him   1435
Ru 1:13 *Would you* **remain u** for them?   408+1194+4200+4200+6328
Eze 44:25 brother or **u** sister,   408+2118+4200+4202
Ac 21: 9 He had four **u** daughters who prophesied.   4221
1Co 7: 8 Now *to* the **u** and the widows I say: 23
   7: 8 It is good for them to stay **u**, as I am.   NIG
   7:11 she must remain **u** or else be reconciled   23
   7:27 *Are you* **u**? Do not look for a   608+1222+3395
   7:32 An **u** man is concerned about the Lord's   23
   7:34 An **u** woman or virgin is concerned about   23

UNMINDFUL (1)
Job 39:15 **u** that a foot may crush them,   8894

UNMOVEABLE (KJV) See NOT MOVE, NOTHING MOVE

UNNATURAL (1)
Ro 1:26 Even their women exchanged natural relations for **u** ones.   3836+4123+5882

UNNI (3)
1Ch 15:18 Zechariah, Jaaziel, Shemiramoth, Jehiel, U,   6716
   15:20 Aziel, Shemiramoth, Jehiel, U, Eliab,   6716
Ne 12: 9 Bakbukiah and U, their associates,   6716

UNNOTICED (3)
1Sa 24: 4 David crept up **u** and cut off a   928+2021+4319
Job 4:20 **u**, they perish forever.   1172+4946+8492
Lk 8:47 the woman, seeing that *she could* not go **u**,   3291

UNOCCUPIED (1)
Mt 12:44 When it arrives, it finds the house **u**,   5390

UNPERFECT (KJV) See UNFORMED

UNPLOWED (3)
Ex 23:11 during the seventh year *let* the land lie **u**   9023
Jer 4: 3 "Break up your **u** ground and do not sow   5776
Hos 10:12 and break up your **u** ground;   5776

UNPREPARED (1)
2Co 9: 4 Macedonians come with me and find you **u**,   564

UNPRESENTABLE (1)
1Co 12:23 that are **u** are treated with special modesty,   860

UNPRODUCTIVE (4)
2Ki 2:19 but the water is bad and the land *is* **u**."   8897
   2:21 will it cause death or **make** the land **u**.'"   8897
Tit 3:14 for daily necessities and not live **u** lives.   182
2Pe 1: 8 being ineffective and **u** in your knowledge   182

UNPROFITABLE (2)
Isa 30: 6 the humps of camels, to that **u** nation,   3603+4202
Tit 3: 9 because these are **u** and useless.   543

UNPROTECTED (2)
Ge 42: 9 You have come to see where our land is **u**."   6872
   42:12 You have come to see where our land is **u**."   6872

UNPUNISHED (19)
Ex 34: 7 Yet *he does* not **leave the guilty u**;   5927+5927
Nu 14:18 Yet *he does* not **leave the guilty u**;   5927+5927
Job 10:14 and *would* not **let** my offense go **u**.   5927
Pr 6:29 no one who touches her *will* go **u**.   5927
   11:21 Be sure of this: The wicked *will* not go **u**,   5927
   16: 5 Be sure of this: *They will* not go **u**.   5927
   17: 5 whoever gloats over disaster *will* not go **u**.   5927
   19: 5 A false witness *will* not go **u**,   5927
   19: 9 A false witness *will* not go **u**,   5927
   28:20 but one eager to get rich *will* not go **u**.   5927
Jer 25:29 and *will* you indeed go **u**?   5927+5927
   25:29 *You will* not go **u**,   5927
   30:11 *I will* not let you go entirely **u**.'   5927+5927
   46:28 *I will* not let you go entirely **u**."   5927+5927
   49:12 why *should* you go **u**?   5927+5927
   49:12 *You will* not go **u**, but must drink it.   5927
Na 1: 3 the LORD *will* not **leave the guilty u**.   5927+5927
Zec 11: 5 Their buyers slaughter them and *go* **u**.   870+4202
Ro 3:25 **left** the sins committed beforehand **u**—   4217

UNQUENCHABLE (3) [UNQUENCHED]
Jer 17:27 then I will kindle an **u** fire in the gates   3882+4202
Mt 3:12 and burning up the chaff *with* **u** fire."   812
Lk 3:17 but he will burn up the chaff *with* **u** fire."   812

UNQUENCHED (1) [UNQUENCHABLE]
Isa 29: 8 but he awakens faint, with his thirst **u**.   8799

UNREASONABLE (1) [UNREASONING]
Ac 25:27 For I think it is **u** to send on a prisoner   263

UNREASONING (1) [UNREASONABLE]
Jude 1:10 by instinct, like **u** animals—   263

UNREBUKEABLE (KJV) See BLAME

UNRELENTING (1)
Job 6:10 this consolation—my joy in **u** pain—   2798+4202

UNRELIABLE (1)
Ps 78:57 disloyal and faithless, as **u** as a faulty bow.   2200

UNREPENTANT (1)
Ro 2: 5 of your stubbornness and your **u** heart,   295

UNREPROVEABLE (KJV) See FREE FROM ACCUSATION

UNREST (2)
Jer 50:34 but **u** to those who live in Babylon.   8074
Am 3: 9 the great **u** within her and the oppression   4539

UNRIGHTEOUS (4) [UNRIGHTEOUSNESS]
Zep 3: 5 yet the **u** know no shame.   6405
Mt 5:45 and sends rain on the righteous and the **u**.   96
1Pe 3:18 Christ died for sins once for all, the righteous for the **u**,   96
2Pe 2: 9 and to hold the **u** for the day of judgment,   96

UNRIGHTEOUSNESS (3) [UNRIGHTEOUS]
Jer 22:13 "Woe to him who builds his palace by **u**,   4202+7406
Ro 3: 5 But if our **u** brings out God's righteousness   94
1Jn 1: 9 forgive us our sins and purify us from all **u**.   94

UNRIPE (1)
Job 15:33 be like a vine stripped of its **u** grapes,   1235

UNROLLED (1) [UNROLLING]
Eze 2:10 which *he* **u** before me.   7298

UNROLLING (1) [UNROLLED]
Lk 4:17 **U** it, he found the place where it is written: 408

UNRULY (3)
Jer 31:18 'You disciplined me like an **u** calf,   4202+4340
Eze 5: 7 You *have been* more **u** than the nations   2171
Hos 11:12 And Judah *is* **u** against God,   8113

UNSANDALED (1)
Dt 25:10 in Israel as The Family of the U.   2740+5837

UNSATIABLE (KJV) See INSATIABLE

UNSATISFIED (1)
2Sa 1:22 the sword of Saul did not return **u**.   8200

UNSAVOURY (KJV) See SHREWD, TASTELESS

UNSCALABLE (1)
Pr 18:11 they imagine it an **u** wall.   8435

UNSCATHED (3)
Job 9: 4 Who has resisted him and *come out* **u**?   8966
Isa 41: 3 He pursues them and moves on **u**,   8934
Jer 43:12 around himself and depart from there **u**.   928+8934

UNSCHOOLED (1)
Ac 4:13 Peter and John and realized that they were **u**,   63

UNSEALED (3)
Ne 6: 5 and in his hand was an **u** letter   7337
Jer 32:11 as well as the **u** *copy*—   1655
   32:14 both the sealed and **u** copies of the deed   1655

UNSEARCHABLE (4)
Pr 25: 3 so the hearts of kings are **u**.   401+2984

Jer 33: 3 and tell you great and **u** *things* you do   1290
Ro 11:33 How **u** his judgments,   451
Eph 3: 8 preach to the Gentiles the **u** riches of Christ,   453

UNSEEMLY (KJV) See INDECENT, RUDE

UNSEEN (4)
Mt 6: 6 pray to your Father, who is **u**.   1877+3220+3836
   6:18 only to your Father, who is **u**;   1877+3224+3836
2Co 4:18 not on what is seen, but on what *is* **u**.   1063+3590
   4:18 but what *is* **u** is eternal.   1063+3590

UNSETTLED (2)
1Th 3: 3 so that no one *would be* **u** by these trials.   4883
2Th 2: 2 not *to become* easily **u** or alarmed   4888

UNSHARPENED (1)
Ecc 10:10 If the ax is dull and its edge **u**,   4202+7837

UNSHEATHED (1)
Eze 21: 4 my sword *will be* **u** against   3655+4946+9509

UNSHOD (KJV) See BARE

UNSHRUNK (2)
Mt 9:16 a patch *of* **u** cloth on an old garment,   47
Mk 2:21 a patch *of* **u** cloth on an old garment,   47

UNSKILFUL (KJV) See NOT ACQUAINTED

UNSPEAKABLE (KJV) See INDESCRIBABLE, INEXPRESSIBLE

UNSPIRITUAL (3)
Ro 7:14 but I am **u**, sold as a slave to sin.   4921
Col 2:18 his **u** mind puffs him up with idle notions.   4922
Jas 3:15 but is earthly, **u**, of the devil.   6035

UNSPOTTED (KJV) See FROM BEING POLLUTED

UNSTABLE (3)
Jas 1: 8 he is a double-minded man, **u** in all he does.   190
2Pe 2:14 never stop sinning; they seduce the **u**;   844+6034
   3:16 which ignorant and **u** people distort,   844

UNSTOPPED (1)
Isa 35: 5 blind be opened and the ears of the deaf **u**.   7337

UNSTRUNG (1)
Job 30:11 that God *has* **u** my bow and afflicted me,   7337

UNSUCCESSFUL (1)
Dt 28:29 *You will be* **u** in everything you do;   4202+7503

UNSUITABLE (1) [UNSUITED]
Ac 27:12 Since the harbor was **u** to winter in,   460

UNSUITED (1) [UNSUITABLE]
Pr 17: 7 Arrogant lips are **u** to a fool—   4202+5534

UNSUSPECTING (6)
Ge 34:25 took their swords and attacked the **u** city,   1055
Jdg 8:11 and Jogbehah and fell upon the **u** army.   1055
   18: 7 like the Sidonians, and secure.   9200
   18:10 an **u** people and a spacious land   1053
   18:27 against a peaceful and **u** people.   1053
Eze 38:11 I will attack a peaceful and **u** people—   1055+4200

UNSWERVING (1) [UNSWERVINGLY]
1Ch 28: 7 if *he is* **u** in carrying out my commands   2616

UNSWERVINGLY (1) [UNSWERVING]
Heb 10:23 Let us hold **u** to the hope we profess,   195

UNTAKEN (KJV) See NOT REMOVED

UNTENDED (2)
Lev 25: 5 or harvest the grapes of your **u** vines.   5687
   25:11 of itself or harvest the **u** vines.   5687

UNTHANKFUL (KJV) See UNGRATEFUL

UNTHINKABLE (1)
Job 34:12 It is **u** that God would do wrong,   597+4202

UNTIE (9) [UNTIED, UNTYING]
Isa 58: 6 the chains of injustice and **u** the cords of   6002
Mt 21: 2 **U** them and bring them to me.   3395
Mk 1: 7 not worthy *to* stoop down and **u**.   3395
   11: 2 **U** it and bring it here.   3395

Lk	3:16	of whose sandals I am not worthy *to* u.	3395
	13:15	of you on the Sabbath u his ox or donkey	3395
	19:30	U it and bring it here.	3395
Jn	1:27	of whose sandals I am not worthy *to* u."	3395
Ac	13:25	whose sandals I am not worthy *to* u.'	3395

UNTIED (3) [UNTIE]

Job	39: 5	Who u his ropes?	7337
Mk	11: 4	tied at a doorway. As *they* u it,	3395
Ac	27:40	same time u the ropes that held the rudders.	479

UNTIL (414)

Ge	3:19	sweat of your brow you will eat your food u	6330
	8: 5	The waters continued to recede u	6330
	8: 7	and forth u the water had dried up from	6330
	13: 3	the Negev he went from place to place u	6330
	19:22	I cannot do anything u you reach it."	6330
	24:19	u they have finished drinking.	561+6330
	24:33	"I will not eat u I have told you what	561+6330
	26:13	and his wealth continued to grow u	3954+6330
	27:44	a while u your brother's fury subsides.	889+6330
	28: 3	and increase your numbers u you become	2256
	28:15	I will not leave you u I have done	889+6330
	29: 8	"u all the flocks are gathered and	889+6330
	33:14	u I come to my lord in Seir."	889+6330
	34: 5	so he kept quiet about it u they came home.	6330
	38:11	"Live as a widow in your father's house u	6330
	38:17	"Will you give me something as a pledge u	6330
	39:16	beside her u his master came home.	6330
	49:10	u he comes to whom it belongs and	3954+6330
Ex	7:16	But u now you have not listened.	6330
	10:15	They covered all the ground u it was black.	2256
	10:26	and u we get there we will not know	6330
	12: 6	of them u the fourteenth day of the month,	6330
	12:18	from the evening of the fourteenth day u	6330
	12:22	of you shall go out the door of his house u	6330
	15:16	u your people pass by, O LORD,	6330
	15:16	u the people you bought pass by.	6330
	16:19	"No one is to keep any of it u morning."	6330
	16:20	they kept part of it u morning,	6330
	16:23	Save whatever is left and keep it u	6330
	16:24	So they saved it u morning,	6330
	16:35	u they came to a land that was settled;	6330
	16:35	they ate manna u they reached the border	6330
	23:18	of my festival offerings must not be kept u	6330
	23:30	u you have increased enough	889+6330
	24:14	"Wait here for us u we come back	889+6330
	33: 8	watching Moses u he entered the tent.	6330
	33:22	in the rock and cover you with my hand u	6330
	34:25	from the Passover Feast remain u morning.	4200
	34:34	he removed the veil u he came out.	6330
	34:35	over his face u he went in to speak with	6330
	40:37	u the day it lifted.	6330
Lev	8:33	to the Tent of Meeting for seven days, u	6330
	12: 4	or go to the sanctuary u the days	6330
	16:17	in the Most Holy Place u he comes out,	6330
	19: 6	over u the third day must be burned up.	6330
	22: 4	he may not eat the sacred offerings u	889+6330
	23:14	u the very day you bring this offering	6330
	23:32	the evening of the ninth day of the month u	6330
	24:12	in custody u the will of the LORD should	4200
	25:22	and will continue to eat from it u	6330
	25:28	in the possession of the buyer u the Year	6330
	25:40	he is to work for you u the Year of Jubilee.	6330
	25:52	a few years remain u the Year of Jubilee,	6330
	26: 5	threshing *will* **continue** u grape harvest	5952
	26: 5	the grape harvest *will* **continue** u planting,	5952
	27:18	that remain u the next Year of Jubilee,	6330
Nu	6: 5	be holy u the period of his separation to	6330
	9: 8	"Wait u I find out what the LORD	2256
	10:12	from place to place u the cloud came to rest	2256
	11:20	u it comes out of your nostrils	889+6330
	14:19	from the time they left Egypt u now."	6330
	14:33	u the last of your bodies lies in the desert.	6330
	20:17	the right or to the left u we have passed	889+6330
	21:22	the king's highway u we have passed	889+6330
	32:13	u the whole generation of those who	6330
	32:17	u we have brought them to their	561+889+6330
	32:18	We will not return to our homes u	6330
	32:21	the LORD u he has driven his enemies out	6330
	35:25	He must stay there u the death of the high	6330
	35:28	of refuge u the death of the high priest;	6330
Dt	1:31	all the way you went u you reached	6330
	2:14	from the time we left Kadesh Barnea u	889+6330
	2:15	The LORD's hand was against them u	6330
	2:29	u we cross the Jordan into the land	889+6330
	3:20	u the LORD gives rest to your brothers	889+6330
	7:20	among them u even the survivors who hide	6330
	7:23	into great confusion u they are destroyed.	6330
	9: 7	the day you left Egypt u you arrived here.	6330
	11: 5	in the desert u you arrived at this place,	6330
	16: 4	on the evening of the first day remain u	4200
	20:20	to build siege works u the city at war	6330
	22: 2	with you and keep it u he comes looking	6330
	28:20	u you are destroyed and come to sudden	6330
	28:21	with diseases u he has destroyed you from	6330
	28:22	which will plague you u you perish.	6330
	28:24	down from the skies u you are destroyed.	6330
	28:45	They will pursue you and overtake you u	6330
	28:48	He will put an iron yoke on your neck u	6330
	28:51	the crops of your land u you are destroyed.	6330
	28:51	or lambs of your flocks u you are ruined.	6330
	28:52	to all the cities throughout your land u	6330
	28:61	u you are destroyed.	6330
	34: 8	u the time of weeping	2256

Jos	1:15	u the LORD gives them rest,	889+6330
	1:15	and u they too have taken possession of	NIH
	2:16	Hide yourselves there three days u	6330
	2:22	u the pursuers had searched all along	6330
	3:17	by u the whole nation had completed	889+6330
	4:10	in the middle of the Jordan u everything	6330
	4:23	before you u you had crossed over.	6330
	4:23	the Red Sea when he dried it up before us u	6330
	5: 1	before the Israelites u we had crossed over,	6330
	5: 6	about in the desert forty years u all	6330
	5: 8	they remained where they were in camp u	6330
	6:10	not say a word u the day I tell you to shout.	6330
	7:13	You cannot stand against your enemies u	6330
	8: 6	They will pursue us u we have lured them	6330
	8:26	the hand that held out his javelin u	889+6330
	8:29	of Ai on a tree and left him there u evening.	6330
	10:26	and they were left hanging on the trees u	6330
	10:33	u no survivors were left.	6330
	11: 8	u no survivors were left.	6330
	11:14	but all the people they put to the sword u	6330
	20: 6	He is to stay in that city u he has stood trial	6330
	20: 6	before the assembly and u the death of	6330
	23: 8	as you have u now.	6330
	23:13	u you perish from this good land,	6330
	23:15	u he has destroyed you	6330
Jdg	3:11	u Othniel son of Kenaz died.	2256
	4:24	Canaanite king, u they destroyed him.	889+6330
	5: 7	Village life in Israel ceased, ceased u	6330+8611
	6:18	Please do not go away u I come back	6330
	6:18	the LORD said, "I will wait u you return."	6330
	9:45	against the city u he had captured it	2256
	13: 7	of God from birth u the day of his death.' "	6330
	13:15	to stay u we prepare a young goat for you."	2256
	15: 7	I **won't** stop u I get my revenge on you.	561+3954
	16: 3	But Samson lay there only u the middle of	6330
	16:13	Delilah then said to Samson, "U now,	6330
	16:16	after day u he was tired to death.	2256
	18:30	the tribe of Dan u the time of the captivity	6330
	19:26	down at the door and lay there u daylight.	6330
	20:23	up and wept before the LORD u evening,	6330
	20:26	They fasted that day u evening	6330
	21: 2	where they sat before God u evening,	6330
Ru	1:13	would you wait u they grew up?	889+6330
	1:19	So the two women went on u they came	6330
	2:17	So Ruth gleaned in the field u evening.	6330
	2:21	'Stay with my workers u they finish	561+6330
	2:23	to the servant girls of Boaz to glean u	6330
	3: 3	but don't let him know you are there u	6330
	3:13	Lie here u morning."	6330
	3:14	So she lay at his feet u morning,	6330
	3:18	u you find out what happens.	889+6330
	3:18	not rest u the matter is settled today."	561+3954
1Sa	1:23	"Stay here u you have weaned him;	6330
	1:23	and nursed her son u she had weaned him.	6330
	3:15	down u morning and then opened the doors	6330
	8: 8	the day I brought them up out of Egypt u	6330
	9:13	The people will not begin eating u	6330
	10: 3	on from there u you reach the great tree	2256
	10: 8	but you must wait seven days u I come	6330
	11:11	and slaughtered them u the heat of the day.	6330
	12: 2	I have been your leader from my youth u	6330
	14: 9	'Wait there u we come to you,'	6330
	15:18	on them u you have wiped them out.'	6330
	15:35	U the day Samuel died,	6330
	16:11	we will not sit down u he arrives."	6330
	19:23	along prophesying u he came to Naioth.	6330
	20: 5	and hide in the field u the evening of	6330
	22: 3	and mother come and stay with you u	889+6330
	25:36	So she told him nothing u daybreak.	6330
	29: 3	and from the day he left Saul u now,	6330
	29: 6	From the day you came to me u now,	6330
	29: 8	from the day I came to you u now?	6330
	30: 4	So David and his men wept aloud u	889+6330
	30:17	David fought them from dusk u the evening	6330
2Sa	2:27	the pursuit of their brothers u morning."	4946
	15:24	and Abiathar offered sacrifices u all	6330
	15:28	at the fords in the desert u word comes	6330
	17:13	we will drag it down to the valley u not	889+6330
	19:24	the king left u the day he returned safely.	6330
	24:15	on Israel from that morning u **the end of**	6330
1Ki	3: 1	of David u he finished building his palace	6330
	5: 3	for the Name of the LORD his God u	6330
	10: 7	I did not believe these things u I came	889+6330
	11:16	u they had destroyed all the men in Edom.	6330
	11:40	and stayed there u Solomon's death.	6330
	14:10	as one burns dung, u it is all gone.	6330
	17:14	not run dry u the day the LORD gives rain	6330
	18:28	as was their custom, u their blood flowed.	6330
	18:29	u **the time for** the evening sacrifice.	6330
	19: 8	he traveled forty days and forty nights u	6330
	22:11	'With these you will gore the Arameans u	6330
	22:27	and give him nothing but bread and water u	6330
2Ki	2:17	But they persisted u he was too ashamed	6330
	3:24	the Israelites rose up and fought them u	2256
	3:25	on every good field u it was covered.	2256
	4:20	the boy sat on her lap u noon,	6330
	7: 3	"Why stay here u we die?	6330
	7: 9	If we wait u daylight,	6330
	8: 6	from the day she left the country u now."	6330
	8:11	with a fixed gaze u Hazael felt ashamed.	6330
	10: 8	at the entrance of the city gate u morning.	6330
	10:21	They crowded into the temple of Baal u	2256
	15: 5	the king with leprosy u the day he died,	6330
	17:18	u the LORD removed them from his presence.	889+6330
	17:23	u the LORD removed them from his	889+6330
	18:32	u I come and take you to a land	6330
	20:17	that your fathers have stored up u this day,	6330

2Ki	21:15	came out of Egypt u this day."	6330
	25: 2	The city was kept under siege u	6330
1Ch	4:31	These were their towns u the reign	6330
	5:22	And they occupied the land u the exile.	6330
	6:32	u Solomon built the temple of the LORD	6330
	12:22	u he had a great army,	6330
	12:29	remained loyal to Saul's house u then;	6330
	28:20	or forsake you u all the work for the service	6330
2Ch	9: 6	But I did not believe what they said u	889+6330
	15:19	There was no more war u	6330
	18:10	'With these you will gore the Arameans u	6330
	18:26	and give him nothing but bread and water u	6330
	18:34	up in his chariot facing the Arameans u	6330
	21:15	u the disease causes your bowels	6330
	24:10	dropping them into the chest u it was full.	6330
	26:15	for he was greatly helped u he became	3954+6330
	26:21	King Uzziah had leprosy u the day he died.	6330
	29:28	All this continued u the sacrifice of	6330
	29:34	so their kinsmen the Levites helped them u	6330
	29:34	and u other priests had been consecrated,	6330
	35:14	the burnt offerings and the fat portions u	6330
	36:16	and scoffed at his prophets u the wrath of	6330
	36:20	and his sons u the kingdom of Persia came	6330
	36:21	all the time of its desolation it rested, u	6330
Ezr	2:63	not to eat any of the most sacred food u	6330
	4:21	that this city will not be rebuilt u I so order.	10527
	4:24	to a standstill u the second year of the reign	10527
	5: 5	not stopped u a report could go to Darius	10527
	8:29	Guard them carefully u you weigh them out	6330
	9: 4	I sat there appalled u the evening sacrifice.	6330
	10:14	u the fierce anger of our God	6330
Ne	2: 7	they will provide me safe-conduct u	889+6330
	5:14	u his thirty-second year—	6330
	7: 3	gates of Jerusalem are not to be opened u	6330
	7:65	of the most sacred food u there should be	6330
	8:17	the days of Joshua son of Nun u that day,	6330
	9:32	the days of the kings of Assyria u today,	6330
	13:19	and not opened u the Sabbath was over.	6330
Ps	57: 1	u the disaster has passed.	6330
	104:23	to his labor u evening.	6330
	110: 1	at my right hand u I make your enemies	6330
SS	2: 7	or awaken love u it so desires.	6330+8611
	2:17	U the day breaks and the shadows flee,	6330+8611
	3: 5	or awaken love u it so desires.	6330+8611
	4: 6	U the day breaks and the shadows flee,	6330+8611
	8: 4	or awaken love u it so desires.	6330+8611
Isa	6:11	"U the cities lie ruined and	561+889+6330
	6:11	u the houses are left deserted and	2256
	6:12	u the LORD has sent everyone far away	2256
	26:20	for a little while u his wrath has passed by.	6330
	36:17	u I come and take you to a land	6330
	39: 6	that your fathers have stored up this day,	6330
Jer	2:25	Do not run u your feet are bare	4946
	7:25	From the time your forefathers left Egypt u	6330
	7:32	for they will bury the dead in Topheth u	4946
	9:16	with the sword u I have destroyed them."	6330
	11: 7	up from Egypt u today,	6330
	19:11	They will bury the dead in Topheth u	4946
	23:20	not turn back u he fully accomplishes	6330
	24:10	against them u they are destroyed from	6330
	25: 3	of Amon king of Judah u this very day—	6330
	27: 7	and his son and his grandson u the time	6330
	27: 8	u I destroy it by his hand.	6330
	27:22	and there they will remain u the day I come	6330
	30:24	not turn back u he fully accomplishes	6330
	32: 5	where he will remain u I deal with him,	6330
	32:31	From the day it was built u now,	6330
	36:23	u the entire scroll was burned in the fire.	6330
	37:21	from the street of the bakers each day u all	6330
	38:28	in the courtyard of the guard u	6330
	44:27	in Egypt will perish by sword and famine u	6330
	49:37	the sword u I have made an end of them.	6330
	52: 5	The city was kept under siege u	6330
La	3:50	u the LORD looks down from heaven	6330
Eze	4: 8	to the other u you have finished the days	6330
	4:14	From my youth u I have never eaten	6330
	21:27	It will not be restored u he comes	6330
	24:13	you will not be clean again u my wrath	6330
	34:21	the weak sheep with your horns u	889+6330
	39:15	beside it u the gravediggers have buried it	6330
	42:14	not to go into the outer court u they leave	2256
	46: 2	but the gate will not be shut u evening.	6330
	46:17	the servant may keep it u the year	6330
Da	1:21	And Daniel remained there u the first year	6330
	4:22	your greatness has grown u it reaches	10221
	4:23	u seven times pass by for him."	10168+10527
	4:25	by for you u you acknowledge that	10168+10527
	4:32	by for you u you acknowledge that	10168+10527
	4:33	u his hair grew like the feathers	10168+10527
	5:21	u he acknowledged that the Most	10168+10527
	6:14	to rescue Daniel and made every effort u	10527
	7: 4	I watched u its wings were torn off	10168+10527
	7:11	I kept looking u the beast was slain	10168+10527
	7:22	u the Ancient of Days came	10168+10527
	8:10	It grew u it reached the host of the heavens,	6330
	9:25	and rebuild Jerusalem u the Anointed One,	6330
	9:26	War will continue u the end,	6330
	9:27	u the end that is decreed is poured out	6330
	10: 3	at all u the three weeks were over.	6330
	11:35	and made spotless u the time of the end,	6330
	11:36	He will be successful u the time	6330
	12: 1	from the beginning of nations u then.	6330
	12: 4	close up and seal the words of the scroll u	6330
	12: 9	the words are closed up and sealed u	6330
Hos	5:15	to my place u they admit their guilt.	889+6330

Hos	10:12	**u** he comes and showers righteousness	6330
Joel	2:26	You will have plenty to eat, **u** you are full,	2256
Mic	5: 3	be abandoned **u** the time when she who is	6330
	7: 9	**u** he pleads my case	889+6330
Hag	2:19	U now, the vine and the fig tree,	6330
Mt	1:25	with her **u** she gave birth to a son,	2401+4005
	2: 9	in the east went ahead of them **u** it stopped	2401
	2:13	Stay there **u** I tell you,	323+2401
	2:15	where he stayed **u** the death of Herod.	2401
	5:18	**u** heaven and earth disappear,	323+2401
	5:18	by any means disappear from the Law **u**	323+2401
	5:26	get out **u** you have paid the last penny.	323+2401
	10:11	and stay at his house **u** you leave.	323+2401
	11:12	From the days of John the Baptist **u** now,	2401
	11:13	the Prophets and the Law prophesied **u**	2401
	13:30	Let both grow together **u** the harvest.	2401
	13:33	**u** it worked all through the dough."	2401+4005
	17: 9	**u** the Son of Man has been raised from	2401+4005
	18:30	the man thrown into prison **u** he could pay	2401
	18:34	**u** he should pay back all he owed.	2401+4005
	22:44	at my right hand **u** I put your enemies	323+2401
	23:39	you will not see me again **u** you say,	2401
	24:21	from the beginning of the world **u** now—	2401
	24:34	not pass away **u** all these things	323+2401
	24:39	about what would happen **u** the flood came	2401
	26:29	on **u** that day when I drink it anew with you	2401
	27:45	From the sixth hour **u** the ninth hour	2401
	27:64	the tomb to be made secure **u** the third day.	2401
Mk	6:10	stay there **u** you leave that town.	323+2401
	9: 9	**u** the Son of Man had risen	1623+3590+4020
	12:36	my right hand **u** I put your enemies	323+2401
	13:19	**u** now—and never to be equaled again.	2401
	13:30	not pass away **u** all these things	3588+4005
	14:25	of the vine **u** that day when I drink it anew	2401
	15:33	over the whole land **u** the ninth hour.	2401
Lk	1:20	not able to speak **u** the day this happens,	948
	1:80	the desert **u** he appeared publicly to Israel.	2401
	2:37	then was a widow **u** she was eighty-four.	2401
	4:13	he left him **u** an opportune time.	948
	9: 4	stay there **u** you leave that town.	NIG
	12:50	how distressed I am **u** it is completed!	2401+4015
	12:59	not get out **u** you have paid the last penny."	2401
	13:21	**u** it worked all through the dough."	2401+4005
	13:35	you will not see me again **u** you say,	2401
	15: 4	and go after the lost sheep **u** he finds it?	2401
	15: 8	and search carefully **u** she finds it?	2401+4005
	16:16	and the Prophets were proclaimed **u** John.	3588
	19:13	he said, '**u** I come back.'	1877+4005
	20:43	I make your enemies a footstool	2401
	21:24	trampled on by the Gentiles **u** the times	948+4005
	21:32	not pass away **u** all these things	323+2401
	22:16	not eat it again **u** it finds fulfillment	2401+4005
	22:18	the vine **u** the kingdom of God comes.	2401+4005
	23:44	and darkness came over the whole land **u**	2401
	24:49	**u** you have been clothed with power	2401+4005
Jn	7:14	Not **u** halfway through the Feast	1254+2453
	8: 9	the older ones first, **u** only Jesus was left,	2779
	9:18	had received his sight **u** they sent for	2401+4015
	16:24	U now you have not asked for anything	2401
	21:22	"If I want him to remain alive **u** I return,	2401
	21:23	"If I want him to remain alive **u** I return,	2401
Ac	1: 2	**u** the day he was taken up to heaven,	948
	2:35	**u** I make your enemies a footstool	323+2401
	3:21	in heaven **u** the time comes for God	948
	4: 3	they put them in jail **u** the next day.	1650
	7:45	It remained in the land **u** the time of David,	2401
	8:40	in all the towns **u** he reached Caesarea.	2401
	13: 6	They traveled the whole island **u**	948
	13:20	God gave them judges **u** the time	2401
	20: 7	kept on talking **u** midnight.	3588
	20:11	After talking **u** daylight, he left.	948
	22:22	The crowd listened to Paul **u** he said this.	948
	23:12	to eat or drink **u** they had killed Paul.	2401+4005
	23:14	to eat anything **u** we have killed Paul.	2401+4005
	23:21	to eat or drink **u** they have killed him.	2401+4005
	25:21	I ordered him held **u** I could send him	2401+4005
Ro	1:13	(but have been prevented from doing so **u**	948
	11:25	has experienced a hardening in part **u**	948+4005
1Co	11:26	proclaim the Lord's death **u** he comes.	948+4005
	15:25	For he must reign **u** he has put all	948+4005
	16: 8	But I will stay on at Ephesus **u** Pentecost,	2401
Gal	3:19	was added because of transgressions **u**	948+4005
	3:23	locked up **u** faith should be revealed.	1650
	4: 2	He is subject to guardians and trustees **u**	948
	4:19	pains of childbirth **u** Christ is formed	3588+4005
Eph	1:14	a deposit guaranteeing our inheritance **u**	1650
	4:13	**u** we all reach unity in the faith and in	3588
Php	1: 5	in the gospel from the first day **u** now,	948
	1: 6	on to completion by the day of Christ Jesus.	948
	1:10	be pure and blameless **u** the day of Christ,	1650
2Th	2: 3	**u** the rebellion occurs and	1569+3590+4754
1Ti	4:13	U I come, devote yourself to the public	2401
	6:14	without spot or blame **u** the appearing	3588
2Ti	1:17	he searched hard for me **u** he found me.	2779
Heb	1:13	at my right hand **u** I make your enemies	323+2401
	9:10	regulations applying **u** the time of the new	3588
Jas	5: 7	then, brothers, **u** the Lord's coming.	2401
1Pe	1: 5	by God's power until the coming of	1650
2Pe	1:19	the day dawns and the morning star	2401+4005
Rev	2:25	hold on to what you have **u** I come	323+948+4005
	6:10	**u** you judge the inhabitants of the earth and avenge our blood?"	3212+4024
	6:11	**u** the number of their fellow servants	2401
	7: 3	the trees **u** we put a seal on the foreheads of	948
	15: 8	and no one could enter the temple **u**	948
	17:17	**u** God's words are fulfilled.	948
	20: 3	from deceiving the nations anymore **u**	948

Rev	20: 5	(The rest of the dead did not come to life **u**	948

UNTIMELY (KJV) See LATE, STILLBORN

UNTIRING (1)

Ps	77: 2	at night I stretched out **u** hands	4202+7028

UNTO (2)

Isa	53:12	because he poured out his life **u** death,	4200
Ac	11:18	even the Gentiles repentance **u** life."	1650

UNTOUCHED (1)

Pr	19:23	Then one rests content, **u** by trouble.	1153+7212

UNTOWARD (KJV) See CORRUPT

UNTRAVELED (1)

Jer	9:10	They are desolate and **u**,	408+1172+4946+6296

UNTRUE (1)

Jos	24:27	It will be a witness against you if you are **u**	3950

UNTYING (4) [UNTIE]

Mk	11: 5	"What are you doing, **u** that colt?"	3395
Lk	19:31	If anyone asks you, 'Why are you **u** it?'	3395
	19:33	As they were **u** the colt,	3395
	19:33	"Why are you **u** the colt?"	3395

UNUSED (1)

Ex	23:11	seventh year let the land lie unplowed and **u**	5759

UNUSUAL (2)

Ac	28: 2	The islanders showed us **u** kindness.	4024+5593
	28: 6	a long time and seeing nothing **u** happen	876

UNVEILED (1)

2Co	3:18	who with **u** faces all reflect the Lord's glory,	365

UNWALLED (3)

Nu	13:19	Are they **u** or fortified?	4722
Dt	3: 5	and there were also a great many **u** villages.	7253
Eze	38:11	"I will invade a land of **u** villages;	7253

UNWASHED (2)

Mt	15:20	but eating with **u** hands does not make him	481
Mk	7: 2	with hands that were "unclean," that is, **u**.	481

UNWEIGHED (1)

1Ki	7:47	Solomon left all these things **u**,	5663

UNWHOLESOME (1)

Eph	4:29	not let any **u** talk come out of your mouths,	4911

UNWILLING (9)

Ge	24: 5	If the woman is **u** to come back with me	14+4202
	24: 8	If the woman is **u** to come back with you,	14+4202
Dt	1:26	But you were **u** to go up;	14+4202
Jdg	19:10	But, **u** to stay another night,	14+4202
1Sa	15: 9	These they were **u** to destroy completely,	14+4202
2Ki	13:23	To this day he has been **u** to destroy	14+4202
Isa	30: 9	children **u** to listen to the LORD's	14+4202
1Co	16:12	He was quite **u** to go now,	2525+4024
Rev	2:21	repent of her immorality, but she is **u**.	2527+4024

UNWISE (2)

Dt	32: 6	O foolish and **u** people?	2682+4202
Eph	5:15	how you live—not as **u** but as wise,	831

UNWORTHY (4)

Ge	32:10	I am **u** of all the kindness	7781
Job	40: 4	"I am **u**—how can I reply to you?	7837
Lk	17:10	should say, 'We are **u** servants;	945
1Co	11:27	of the Lord in an **u** manner will be guilty	397

UNYIELDING (5)

Ex	7:14	"Pharaoh's heart is **u**; he refuses	3878
	9: 7	Yet his heart was **u** and he would not let	3877
Pr	18:19	An offended brother is more **u** than	NIH
SS	8: 6	its jealousy **u** as the grave.	7997
Eze	3: 8	But I will make you as **u** and hardened	2617+7156

UP (1905) [UPPER, UPWARD]

Ge	2: 5	and no plant of the field had yet sprung **u**,	7541
	2: 6	but streams came **u** from the earth	6590
	2:21	he took one of the man's ribs and closed **u**	6037
	8: 7	until the water had dried **u** from the earth.	3312
	8:13	the water had dried **u** from the earth.	2990
	13: 1	So Abram went **u** from Egypt to the Negev,	6590
	13:10	Lot looked **u** and saw that the whole plain	5951
	13:14	"Lift **u** your eyes from where you are	5951
	14: 8	and drew **u** their battle lines	6885
	15: 5	"Look **u** at the heavens and count	5564
	17:22	God went **u** from him.	6590
	18: 2	Abraham looked **u** and saw three men	5951

Ge	18:16	When the men got **u** to leave,	7756
	18:27	Then Abraham spoke **u** again:	6699
	19: 1	he got **u** to meet them and bowed down	7756
	19:27	Early the next morning Abraham got **u**	8899
	19:33	of it when she lay down or when she got **u**.	7756
	19:35	of it when she lay down or when she got **u**.	7756
	20:18	the LORD had closed **u** every womb	6806+6808
	21:18	Lift the boy **u** and take him by the hand,	5951
	21:20	God was with the boy as he grew **u**.	1540
	22: 3	Early the next morning Abraham got **u**	8899
	22: 4	the third day Abraham looked **u** and saw	5951
	22: 7	Isaac spoke **u** and said	606
	22:13	Abraham looked **u** and there in	5951
	24:16	filled her jar and came **u** again.	6590
	24:54	When they got **u** the next morning, he said,	7756
	24:63	and as he looked **u**,	5951
	24:64	Rebekah also looked **u** and saw Isaac.	5951
	25:27	The boys grew **u**,	1540
	25:34	He ate and drank, and then got **u** and left.	7756
	26:15	the Philistines stopped **u**,	6258
	26:18	which the Philistines had stopped **u**	6258
	26:23	From there he went **u** to Beersheba.	6590
	27:19	Please sit **u** and eat some of my game so	7756
	27:31	"My father, sit **u** and eat some of my game,	7756
	28:18	and set it **u** as a pillar and poured oil on top	8492
	28:22	and this stone that I have set **u** as	8492
	31:10	a dream in which I looked **u** and saw that	5951
	31:12	'Look **u** and see that all the male goats	5951
	31:15	but he has used **u** what was paid for us.	430+430
	31:23	and caught **u** with him in the hill country	1815
	31:35	that I cannot stand **u** in your presence;	7756
	31:45	Jacob took a stone and set it **u** as a pillar.	8123
	31:51	and here is this pillar I have set **u**	3721
	32:22	That night Jacob got **u** and took his	7756
	33: 1	Jacob looked **u** and there was Esau,	5951
	33: 5	Then Esau looked **u** and saw the women	5951
	33:20	There he set **u** an altar.	5893
	35: 1	"Go **u** to Bethel and settle there,	6590
	35: 3	Then come, let us go **u** to Bethel.	6590
	35:13	Then God went **u** from him at the place	6590
	35:14	Jacob set **u** a stone pillar at the place	5893
	35:20	Over her tomb Jacob set **u** a pillar,	5893
	37:25	they looked **u** and saw a caravan	5951
	37:26	if we kill our brother and cover **u**	4059
	37:28	his brothers pulled Joseph **u** out of	6590
	38:11	until my son Shelah grows **u**."	1540
	38:12	he went **u** to Timnah.	6590
	38:14	though Shelah had now grown **u**,	1540
	40:13	Within three days Pharaoh will lift **u**	5951
	40:20	He lifted **u** the heads of	5951
	41: 2	out of the river there came **u** seven cows,	6590
	41: 3	came **u** out of the Nile and stood	6590
	41: 4	the cows that were ugly and gaunt ate **u**	430
	41: 4	Then Pharaoh woke **u**.	3699
	41: 7	of grain swallowed **u** the seven healthy,	1180
	41: 7	Then Pharaoh woke **u**; it had been a dream.	3699
	41:18	out of the river there came **u** seven cows,	6590
	41:19	After them, seven other cows came **u**—	6590
	41:20	ugly cows ate **u** the seven fat cows	430
	41:20	up the seven fat cows that came **u** first.	NIH
	41:21	Then I woke **u**.	3699
	41:24	The thin heads of grain swallowed **u**	1180
	41:27	that came **u** afterward are seven years, and	6590
	41:35	that are coming and store **u** the grain under	7392
	41:49	Joseph stored **u** huge quantities of grain,	7392
	43:19	So they went **u** to Joseph's steward	5602
	44: 4	and when you catch **u** with them,	5952
	44: 6	When he caught **u** with them,	5952
	44:18	Then Judah went **u** to him and said:	5602
	44:30	whose life is closely bound **u** with	8003
	45:25	So they went **u** out of Egypt and came	6590
	46:31	"I will go **u** and speak to Pharaoh	6590
	47:15	Our money is used **u**."	699
	48: 2	Israel rallied his strength and sat **u** on	3782
	49: 4	for you went **u** onto your father's bed,	6590
	49:33	he drew his feet **u** into the bed,	665
	50: 5	Now let me go **u** and bury my father;	6590
	50: 6	Pharaoh said, "Go **u** and bury your father,	6590
	50: 7	So Joseph went **u** to bury his father.	6590
	50: 9	and horsemen also went **u** with him.	6590
	50:24	surely come to your aid and take you **u** out	6590
	50:25	and then you must carry my bones **u**	6590
Ex	2:11	One day, after Moses had grown **u**,	1540
	2:17	but Moses got **u** and came to their rescue	7756
	2:23	for help because of their slavery went **u**	6590
	3: 2	the bush was on fire it did not burn **u**.	430
	3: 3	why the bush does not burn **u**."	1277
	3: 8	of the Egyptians and to bring them **u** out of	6590
	3:17	to bring you **u** out of your misery in Egypt	6590
	7:12	But Aaron's staff swallowed **u** their staffs.	1180
	8: 3	They will come **u** into your palace	6590
	8: 4	The frogs will go **u** on you	6590
	8: 5	make frogs come **u** on the land of Egypt.' "	6590
	8: 6	and the frogs came **u** and covered the land.	6590
	8: 7	made frogs come **u** on the land of Egypt.	6590
	8:20	"Get **u** early in the morning	8899
	9:13	"Get **u** early in the morning,	8899
	9:16	I have raised you **u** for this very purpose,	6641
	10:19	which caught **u** the locusts and carried them	5951
	12:30	the Egyptians got **u** during the night,	7756
	12:31	Moses and Aaron said, "U!	7756
	12:38	Many other people went **u** with them,	6590
	13:18	The Israelites went **u** out of Egypt armed	6590
	13:19	then you must carry my bones **u** with you	6590
	14:10	the Israelites looked **u**,	5951
	15: 8	of your nostrils the waters piled **u**.	6890
	17: 3	"Why did you bring us **u** out of Egypt	6590

Ex
17:11 As long as Moses **held u** his hands, — 8123
17:12 Aaron and Hur **held** his hands **u**— — 9461
17:16 "For hands were lifted **u** to the throne of — NIH
19: 3 Then Moses **went u** to God, — 6590
19:12 that you do not **go u** the mountain or touch — 6590
19:13 a long blast may **go u** to the mountain." — 6590
19:18 The smoke **billowed u** from it like smoke — 6590
19:20 So Moses **went u** — 6590
19:23 "The people cannot **come u** Mount Sinai. — 6590
19:24 "Go down and **bring** Aaron **u** with you. — 6590
19:24 not force their way through to **come u** to — 6590
20:26 And do not **go u** to my altar on steps, — 6590
21:19 if the other **gets u** and walks around outside — 7756
21:21 not to be punished if the slave **gets u** after — 6641
21:29 but has not **kept** it **penned u** and it kills — 9068
21:36 yet the owner did not **keep** it **penned u,** — 9068
24: 1 he said to Moses, "**Come u** to the LORD, — 6590
24: 2 And the people may not **come u** with him." — 6590
24: 4 He **got u** early the next morning and built — 8899
24: 4 and **set u** twelve stone pillars representing — NIH
24: 9 and the seventy elders of Israel **went u** — 6590
24:12 "**Come u** to me on the mountain — 6590
24:13 and Moses **went u** on the mountain of God. — 6590
24:15 When Moses **went u** on the mountain, — 6590
24:18 the cloud as he **went u** on the mountain. — 6590
25:37 "Then make its seven lamps and **set them u** — 6590
26:30 "**Set u** the tabernacle according to — 7756
27: 5 the ledge of the altar so that it is halfway **u** — 6330
29:34 over till morning, **burn** it **u.** — 836+928+2021+8596
32: 1 for this fellow Moses who **brought** us **u** out of Egypt — 6590
32: 4 O Israel, who **brought** you **u** out of Egypt." — 6590
32: 6 down to eat and drink and **got u** to indulge — 7756
32: 7 whom you **brought u** out of Egypt, — 6590
32: 8 O Israel, who **brought** you **u** out of Egypt.' — 6590
32:23 for this fellow Moses who **brought** us **u** out — 6590
32:30 But now I will **go u** to the LORD; — 6590
33: 1 and the people you **brought u** out of Egypt, — 6590
33: 1 and **go u** to the land I promised on oath — 6590
33: 3 **Go u** to the land flowing with milk — NIH
33:15 do not **send** us **u** from here. — 6590
34: 2 and then **come u** on Mount Sinai. — 6590
34: 4 the first ones and **went u** Mount Sinai early — 6590
34:24 when you **go u** three times each year — 6590
38: 4 to be under its ledge, halfway **u** the altar. — 6330
40: 2 "**Set u** the tabernacle, — 7756
40: 4 bring in the lampstand and **set u** its lamps. — 8492
40: 8 **Set u** the courtyard around it and put — 8492
40:17 So the tabernacle was **set u** on the first day — 7756
40:18 When Moses **set u** the tabernacle, — 7756
40:18 inserted the crossbars and **set u** the posts. — 7756
40:25 and **set u** the lamps before the LORD. — 6590
40:28 Then he **put u** the curtain at the entrance to — 8492
40:33 Then Moses **set u** the courtyard around — 7756
40:33 around the tabernacle and altar and **put u** — 5989

Lev
5: 1 because he does not **speak u** when he hears — 5583
7:17 third day must be **burned u.** — 836+928+2021+8596
7:19 it must be **burned u.** — 836+928+2021+8596
8:17 and its offal he **burned u** — 836+928+2021+8596
8:32 **burn u** the rest of the meat — 836+928+2021+8596
9:11 and the hide he **burned u** — 836+928+2021+8596
10:16 and found that it had been **burned u,** — 8596
11:25 Whoever **picks u** one of their carcasses — 5951
11:28 Anyone who **picks u** their carcasses — 5951
11:35 an oven or cooking pot must be **broken u.** — 5997
11:40 Anyone who **picks u** the carcass — 5951
11:45 I am the LORD who **brought** you **u** out — 6590
He must **burn u** the clothing, — 8596
13:52 article must be **burned u.** — 836+928+2021+8596
14:38 of the house and **close** it **u** for seven days. — 6037
14:46 into the house while it is **closed u** will — 6037
15:10 whoever **picks u** those things must wash — 5951
16:27 offal are to be **burned u.** — 836+928+2021+8596
19: 6 third day must be **burned u.** — 8596
19:10 over your vineyard a second time or **pick u** — 4377
21: 8 because they **offer u** the food of your God. — 7928
23:16 Count off fifty days **u** to the day after — 6330
25:50 from the year he sold himself **u** to the Year — 6330
26: 1 " 'Do not make idols or **set u** an image or — 7756
27:23 the priest will determine its value **u** to — 6330

Nu
1:51 the tabernacle is to be **set u,** — 2837
1:52 The Israelites are to **set u** their **tents** — 2837
1:53 to **set u** their **tents** around the tabernacle of — 2837
7: 1 When Moses finished **setting u** — 7756
8: 2 'When you **set u** the seven lamps, — 6590
8: 3 he **set u** the lamps so that they faced — 6590
9:15 the Tent of the Testimony, was **set u,** — 7756
10:21 to be **set u** before they arrived. — 7756
10:35 Moses said, "**Rise u,** O LORD! — 7756
11:28 **spoke u** and said, "Moses, my lord, — 6699
13:17 "**Go u** through the Negev and on into — 6590
13:21 So they **went u** and explored the land from — 6590
13:22 They **went u** through the Negev and came — 6590
13:30 "We should **go u** and take possession — 6590+6590
13:31 But the men who had **gone u** with him said, — 5927
14: 9 because we will **swallow** them **u.** — 4312
14:13 **brought** these people **u** from among them. — 6590
14:40 Early the next morning they **went u** toward — 6590
14:40 "We will **go u** to the place — 6590
14:42 Do not **go u,** because the LORD is not with — 6590
14:44 in their presumption they **went u** toward — 6590
16: 2 and **rose u** against Moses. — 7756
16:13 Isn't it enough that you have **brought** us **u** — 6590
16:25 Moses **got u** and went to Dathan — 7756
16:39 by those who had been **burned u,** — 8596
19: 9 "A man who is clean shall **gather u** — 665
19:10 The man who **gathers u** the ashes of — 665
20: 5 Why did you **bring** us **u** out of Egypt — 6590

Nu
20:25 and his son Eleazar and **take** them **u** — 6590
20:27 They **went u** Mount Hor in the sight of — 6590
21: 5 "Why have you **brought** us **u** out of Egypt — 6590
21: 8 "Make a snake and **put** it **u** on a pole; — 8492
21: 9 So Moses made a bronze snake and **put it u** — 8492
21:17 Israel sang this song: "**Spring u,** O well! — 6590
21:29 He has **given u** his sons as fugitives — 5989
21:33 Then they turned and **went u** along the road — 6590
22: 4 "This horde is going to **lick u** everything — 4308
22: 4 as an ox **licks u** the grass of the field." — 4308
22:13 The next morning Balaam **got u** and said — 7756
22:21 Balaam **got u** in the morning, — 7756
22:41 The next morning Balak **took** Balaam **u** — 6590
24:25 Then Balaam **got u** and returned home — 7756
27:12 "**Go u** this mountain in the Abarim range — 6590
32: 9 After they **went u** to the Valley of Eshcol — 6590
32:11 or more who **came u** out of Egypt will see — 6590
32:16 Then they **came u** to him and said, — 5602
32:34 The Gadites **built u** Dibon, Ataroth, — 1215
33:38 the priest **went u** Mount Hor. — 6590

Dt
1:21 **Go u** and take possession of it as — 6590
1:24 They left and **went u** into the hill country, — 6590
1:26 But you were unwilling to **go u;** — 6590
1:28 the cities are large, with walls **u** to the sky. — 928
1:41 We will **go u** and fight, — 6590
1:41 to **go u** into the hill country. — 6590
1:42 "Tell them, 'Do not **go u** and fight, — 6590
1:43 and in your arrogance you **marched u** into — 6590
2: 8 which comes **u** from Elath — NIH
2:13 "Now **get u** and cross the Zered Valley." — 7756
3: 1 and **went u** along the road toward Bashan, — 6590
3:27 **Go u** to the top of Pisgah and look west — 6590
4:19 when you look **u** to the sky and see the sun,) — 5951
5: 5 of the fire and did not **go u** the mountain.) — 6590
6: 7 when you lie down and when you **get u.** — 7756
7:24 No one will be able to **stand u** against you; — 3656
9: 1 with large cities that have walls **u** to — 928
9: 2 "Who can **stand u** against the Anakites?" — 3656
9: 9 When I **went u** on the mountain to receive — 6590
9:23 "**Go u** and take possession of the land — 6590
10: 1 like the first ones and **come u** to me on — 6590
10: 3 and I **went u** on the mountain with — 6590
11: 6 of all Israel and **swallowed** them **u** — 1180
11:19 when you lie down and when you **get u.** — 7756
16:21 not **set u** any wooden Asherah pole beside — 5749
18:15 The LORD your God will **raise u** for you — 7756
18:18 I will **raise u** for them a prophet like you — 7756
19:14 move your neighbor's boundary stone **set u** — 1487
20: 1 who **brought** you **u** out of Egypt, — 6590
20:10 When you **march u** to attack a city, — 7928
23:13 and **cover u** your excrement. — 2256+4059+8740
25: 9 his brother's widow shall **go u** to him in — 5602
25: 9 not **build u** his brother's family line." — 1215
27: 2 **set u** some large stones and coat them — 7756
27: 4 **set u** these stones on Mount Ebal, — 7756
27: 8 of this law on these stones you have set **u.**" — NIH
27:15 and **sets** it **u** in secret." — 8492
28: 7 that the enemies who **rise u** against you will — 7756
30:12 It is not **u** in heaven, — NIH
32: 8 he **set u** boundaries for the peoples — 5893
32:11 like an eagle that **stirs u** its nest and hovers — 6424
32:30 unless the LORD had **given** them **u?** — 6037
32:38 Let them **rise u** to help you! — 7756
32:49 "**Go u** into the Abarim Range — 6590
33:11 the loins of those who **rise u** against him; — 7756

Jos
1: 5 be able to **stand u** against you all the days — 3656
2: 5 You may **catch u** with them." — 5952
2: 6 (But she had **taken** them **u** to the roof — 6590
2: 8 she **went u** on the roof — 6590
2:10 the LORD **dried u** the water of the Red Sea — 3312
3: 6 "**Take u** the ark of the covenant and pass on — 5951
3: 6 So they **took** it **u** and went ahead of them. — 5951
3:13 be cut off and **stand u** in a heap." — 6641
3:16 It **piled u** in a heap a great distance away, — 7756
4: 3 to **take u** twelve stones from the middle of — 5951
4: 5 of you is to **take u** a stone on his shoulder, — 8123
4: 9 Joshua **set u** the twelve stones — 7756
4:16 the Testimony to **come u** out of the Jordan." — 6590
4:17 "**Come u** out of the Jordan." — 6590
4:18 the priests **came u** out of the river carrying — 6590
4:19 of the first month the people **went u** from — 6590
4:20 And Joshua **set u** at Gilgal — 7756
4:23 For the LORD your God **dried u** the Jordan — 3312
4:23 to the Red Sea when he **dried** it **u** before us — 3312
5: 1 the coast heard how the LORD had **dried u** — 3312
5: 7 So he **raised u** their sons in their place, — 7756
5:13 he looked **u** and saw a man standing — 5951
5:13 Joshua **went u** to him and asked, — 2143
6: 1 Now Jericho was tightly shut **u** — 2256+6037+6037
6: 5 and the people will **go u,** — 6590
6: 6 "**Take u** the ark of the covenant of — 5951
6:12 Joshua **got u** early the next morning and — 8899
6:12 the priests **took u** the ark of the LORD. — 5951
6:15 they **got u** at daybreak and marched — 8899
6:26 at the cost of his youngest will he **set u** — 5893
7: 2 "**Go u** and spy out the region." — 6590
7: 2 So the men **went u** and spied out Ai. — 6590
7: 3 the people will have to **go u** against Ai. — 6590
7: 4 So about three thousand men **went u;** — 6590
7:10 The LORD said to Joshua, "**Stand u!** — 7756
7:26 Over Achan they **heaped u** a large pile — 7756
8: 1 and **go u** and attack Ai. — 6590
8: 7 to **rise u** from ambush and take the city. — 7756
8:11 **marched u** and approached the city, — 6590
8:11 They **set u** camp north of Ai, — 2837
8:13 had the soldiers **take u** their **positions**— — 8492
8:21 and that smoke was **going u** from the city, — 6590

Jos
10: 4 "**Come u** and help me attack Gibeon," — 6590
10: 5 They **moved u** with all their troops and took — 6590
10: 5 up with all their troops and **took u positions** — 2837
10: 6 **Come u** to us quickly and save us! — 6590
10: 7 So Joshua **marched u** from Gilgal — 6590
10:10 Israel pursued them along the road **going u** — 5090
10:18 "Roll large rocks **u** to the mouth of — 448
10:31 he **took u positions** against it — 2837
10:33 of Gezer had **come u** to help Lachish, — 6590
10:33 they **took u positions** against it — 2837
10:36 Then Joshua and all Israel with him **went u** — 6590
11:11 he **burned u** Hazor itself. — 836+928+2021+8596
13:27 the territory **u** to the end of the Sea — 6330
14: 8 but my brothers who **went u** with me made — 6590
15: 3 past Hezron **u** to Addar and curved around — 6590
15: 6 **went u** to Beth Hoglah and continued north — 6590
15: 7 The boundary then **went u** to Debir from — 6590
15: 8 Then it **ran u** the Valley of Ben Hinnom — 6590
16: 1 and **went u** from there through the desert — 6590
16: 1 **go u** into the forest and clear land — 6590
18: 1 of the Israelites gathered at Shiloh and **set u** — 8905
18:11 The lot **came u** for the tribe of Benjamin, — 6590
19:10 The third lot **came u** for Zebulun, — 6590
19:12 and went on to Daberath and **u** to Japhia. — 6590
19:47 so they **went u** and attacked Leshem, — 6590
19:50 And he **built u** the town and settled there. — 1215
22:17 **U** to this very day we have not cleansed — 6330
24:17 **brought** us and our fathers **u** out of Egypt, — 6590
24:25 at Shechem he **drew u** for them decrees — 8492
24:26 Then he took a large stone and **set** it **u** there — 7756
24:32 the Israelites had **brought u** from Egypt, — 6590

Jdg
1: 1 be the first to **go u** and fight for us against — 6590
1: 3 "**Come u** with us into the territory allotted — 6590
1: 7 and big toes cut off have **picked u** scraps — 4377
1:16 **went u** from the City of Palms with the men — 6590
2: 1 the LORD **went u** from Gilgal to Bokim — 6590
2: 1 "I **brought** you **u** out of Egypt and led you — 6590
2:10 another generation **grew u,** — 7756
2:16 Then the LORD **raised u** judges, — 7756
2:18 Whenever the LORD **raised u** a judge — 7756
2:19 They refused to **give u** their evil practices — 5877
3: 9 he **raised u** for them a deliverer, — 7756
4:12 of Abinoam had **gone u** to Mount Tabor, — 6590
4:19 gave him a drink, and **covered** him **u.** — 4059
4:21 **picked u** a tent peg and a hammer — 4374
5:12 '**Wake u,** wake up, Deborah! — 6424
5:12 'Wake up, **wake u,** Deborah! — 6424
5:12 **Wake u,** wake up, break out in song! — 6424
5:12 Wake up, **wake u,** break out in song! — 6424
6: 5 They **came u** with their livestock — 6590
6: 8 I **brought** you **u** out of Egypt, — 6590
6:13 not the LORD **bring** us **u** out of Egypt?' — 6590
6:28 when the men of the town **got u,** — 8899
6:35 so that they too **went u** to meet them. — 6590
7: 9 "**Get u,** go down against the camp, — 7756
7:15 the camp of Israel and called out, "**Get u!** — 7756
8: 4 exhausted yet keeping **u** the **pursuit,** — AIT
8: 8 From there he **went u** to Peniel and made — 6590
8:11 Gideon **went u** by the route of — 6590
8:33 They **set u** Baal-Berith as their god — 8492
9: 7 he **climbed u** on the top of Mount Gerizim — 2143
9: 9 'Should I **give u** my oil, — 2532
9:11 fig tree replied, 'Should I **give u** my fruit, — 2532
9:13 'Should I **give u** my wine, — 2532
9:31 and are **stirring u** the city against you. — 7443
9:34 **took u** concealed positions — 741
9:37 But Gaal **spoke u** again: — 1819
9:48 he and all his men **went u** Mount Zalmon. — 6590
9:51 They locked themselves in and **climbed u** — 6590
11: 2 and when they were **grown u,** — 1540
11:13 "When Israel **came u** out of Egypt, — 6590
11:16 But when they **came u** out of Egypt, — 6590
12: 3 why have you **come u** today to fight me?" — 6590
13: 8 how to **bring u** the boy who is to be born." — 6913
13:11 Manoah **got u** and followed his wife. — 7756
13:20 As the flame **blazed u** from the altar — 6590
14:19 he **went u** to his father's house. — 6590
15: 5 He **burned u** the shocks and standing grain, — 1277
15: 6 So the Philistines **went u** and burned her — 6590
15: 9 The Philistines **went u** and camped — 6590
15:12 "We've come to **tie** you **u** and hand you — 673
15:13 "We will only **tie** you **u** and hand you — 673+673
15:13 with two new ropes and **led** him **u** from — 6590
15:19 God **opened u** the hollow place in Lehi, — 1324
16: 3 Then he **got u** and took hold of the doors of — 7756
16: 5 so we may **tie** him **u** and subdue him. — 673
16: 6 and how you can be **tied u** and subdued." — 673
16:14 from his sleep and **pulled u** the pin and — 5825
18:12 On their way they **set u** camp — 2837
18:30 the Danites **set u** for themselves the idols, — 7756
19: 5 On the fourth day they **got u** early — 8899
19: 7 And when the man **got u** to go, — 7756
19: 9 **got u** to leave, his father-in-law, — 7756
19: 9 **Early** tomorrow **morning** you can **get u** — 8899
19:27 When her master **got u** in the morning — 7756
19:28 He said to her, "**Get u;** let's go." — 7756
19:29 he took a knife and **cut u** his concubine, — 5983
19:30 the day the Israelites **came u** out of Egypt. — 6590
20: 3 that the Israelites had **gone u** to Mizpah.) — 6590
20: 7 **speak u** and give your verdict. — 1821
20:18 We'll **go u** against it as the lot directs. — NIH
20:18 The Israelites **went u** to Bethel — 6590
20:19 The next morning the Israelites **got u** — 7756
20:20 and **took u battle positions** — 6885
20:22 and again **took u** their **positions** — 6885
20:23 The Israelites **went u** and wept before — 6590
20:23 "Shall we **go u** again to battle against — 5602

Jdg	20:23	"Go u against them."	6590
	20:26	all the people, went u to Bethel,	6590
	20:28	"Shall we go u again to battle	3655
	20:30	They went u against the Benjamites on	6590
	20:30	on the third day and took u positions	6885
	20:33	from their places and took u positions	6885
	20:38	with the ambush that they should send u	6590
	20:40	the smoke of the whole city going u into	6590
Ru	1:13	would you wait until they grew u?	1540
	2: 2	and pick u the leftover grain behind anyone	4377
	2:15	As she got u to glean,	7756
	2:16	and leave them for her to pick u,	4377
	3:14	got u before anyone could be recognized;	7756
	4: 1	Meanwhile Boaz went u to the town gate	6590
	4:11	who together built u the house of Israel.	1215
1Sa	1: 3	after year this man went u from his town	6590
	1: 7	Whenever Hannah went u to the house of	6590
	1: 9	and drinking in Shiloh, Hannah stood u.	7756
	1:21	the man Elkanah went u with all his family	6590
	2: 6	he brings down to the grave and raises u.	6590
	2:14	for himself whatever the fork brought u.	6590
	2:16	"Let the fat be burned u first,	7787+7787
	2:19	when she went u with her husband to offer	6590
	2:21	the boy Samuel grew u in the presence of	1540
	2:28	to go u to my altar, to burn incense,	6590
	2:35	I will raise u for myself a faithful priest,	7756
	3: 6	Samuel got u and went to Eli and said,	7756
	3: 8	and Samuel got u and went to Eli and said,	7756
	3:19	The LORD was with Samuel as he grew u,	1540
	4:13	the whole town sent u a cry.	2410
	5:12	and the outcry of the city went u to heaven.	6590
	6: 7	take their calves away and pen them u.	1074+2025
	6: 9	If it goes u to its own territory,	6590
	6:10	and penned u their calves.	928+1074+2021+3973
	6:12	Then the cows went straight u	AIT
	6:13	and when they looked u and saw the ark,	5951
	6:14	The people chopped u the wood of the cart	1324
	6:20	To whom will the ark go u from here?"	6590
	6:21	Come down and take it u to your place."	6590
	7: 1	the men of Kiriath Jearim came and took u	6590
	7: 7	of the Philistines came u to attack them.	6590
	7: 9	and offered it u as a whole burnt offering	6590
	7:12	and set it u between Mizpah and Shen.	8492
	8: 8	the day I brought them u out of Egypt,	6590
	9:11	As they were going u the hill to the town,	6590
	9:13	before he goes u to the high place to eat.	6590
	9:13	those who are invited will eat. Go u now;	6590
	9:14	They went u to the town,	6590
	9:14	coming toward them on his way u to	6590
	9:19	"Go u ahead of me to the high place,	6590
	9:24	the cook took the leg with what was on it	8123
	10: 3	Three men going u to God	6590
	10:18	'I brought Israel u out of Egypt,	6590
	11: 1	Nahash the Ammonite went u	6590
	12: 6	brought your forefathers u	6590
	13: 5	They went u and camped at Micmash,	6590
	13: 9	And Saul offered u the burnt offering.	6590
	13:15	Then Samuel left Gilgal and went u	6590
	14: 9	we will stay where we are and not go u	6590
	14:10	But if they say, 'Come u to us,'	6590
	14:10	'Come up to us,' we will climb u,	6590
	14:12	"Come u to us and we'll teach you	6590
	14:12	"Climb u after me;	6590
	14:13	Jonathan climbed u, using his hands	6590
	14:21	the Philistines and had gone u with them	6590
	15: 2	when they waylaid them as they came u	6590
	15: 6	to all the Israelites when they came u out	6590
	15:12	Early in the morning Samuel got u	8899
	15:12	There he has set u a monument	5893
	15:34	Saul went u to his home in Gibeah of Saul.	6590
	17: 2	drew u their battle line to meet	6885
	17: 8	"Why do you come out and line u	6885
	17:20	loaded u and set out, as Jesse had directed.	5951
	17:21	Israel and the Philistines were drawing u	6885
	17:30	and brought u the same matter,	606
	19:15	"Bring him u to me in his bed so	6590
	20:30	Saul's anger flared u at Jonathan	3013
	20:34	Jonathan got u from the table	7756
	20:38	The boy picked u the arrow and returned	4377
	20:41	David got u from the south side	7756
	23: 8	Saul called u all his forces for battle,	9048
	23:19	The Ziphites went u to Saul at Gibeah	6590
	23:29	And David went u from there and lived in	6590
	24: 4	Then David crept u unnoticed and cut off	7756
	24:22	and his men went u to the stronghold.	6590
	25: 5	"Go u to Nabal at Carmel and greet him	6590
	25:13	About four hundred men went u	6590
	26:12	nor did anyone wake u.	7810
	27: 1	Then Saul will give u searching	3286
	27: 8	Now David and his men went u and raided	6590
	28: 4	and came and set u camp at Shunem,	2837
	28: 4	the Israelites and set u camp at Gilboa.	2837
	28: 8	"and bring u for me the one I name."	6590
	28:11	"Whom shall I bring u for you?"	6590
	28:11	"Bring u Samuel," he said.	6590
	28:13	"I see a spirit coming u out of the ground."	6590
	28:14	"An old man wearing a robe is coming u,"	6590
	28:15	disturbed me by bringing me u?"	6590
	28:23	He got u from the ground and sat on	7756
	28:25	That same night they got u and left.	7756
	29: 9	'He must not go u with us into battle.'	6590
	29:10	Now get u early,	8899
	29:11	and his men got u early in the morning	8899
	29:11	and the Philistines went u to Jezreel.	6590
2Sa	1:17	David took u this lament concerning Saul and his son Jonathan,	7801+7806
	2: 1	"Shall I go u to one of the towns	6590

2Sa	2: 1	The LORD said, "Go u."	6590
	2: 2	So David went u there with his two wives,	6590
	2:14	the young men get u and fight hand to hand	7756
	2:15	So they stood u and were counted off—	7756
	2:23	But Asahel refused to give u the pursuit;	6073
	4: 4	His nurse picked him u and fled,	5951
	5: 9	David built u the area around it,	3782
	5: 9	He built u the area around it,	1215
	5:17	they went u in full force to search for him,	6590
	5:22	the Philistines came u and spread out in	6590
	5:23	and he answered, "Do not go straight u,	6590
	6: 2	from Baalah of Judah to bring u from there	6590
	6:12	So David went down and brought u the ark	6590
	6:15	the entire house of Israel brought u the ark	6590
	7: 6	brought the Israelites u out of Egypt	6590
	7:12	I will raise u your offspring	7756
	10: 8	The Ammonites came out and drew u	6885
	11: 2	One evening David got u from his bed	7756
	11:20	the king's anger may flare u,	6590
	12: 3	and it grew u with him and his children.	1540
	12:17	beside him to get him u from the ground,	7756
	12:20	Then David got u from the ground.	7756
	12:21	you get u and eat!"	7756
	13:15	Amnon said to her, "Get u and get out!"	7756
	13:29	Then all the king's sons got u,	7756
	13:31	The king stood u, tore his clothes and lay	7756
	13:34	Now the man standing watch looked u	5951
	14: 7	Now the whole clan has risen u	7756
	15: 2	He would get u early and stand by	8899
	15:30	David continued up the Mount of Olives,	6590
	15:30	and were weeping as they went u.	6590
	17:16	with him will be swallowed u."	1180
	17:17	and piled u a large heap of rocks over him.	5893
	18:24	the watchman went u to the roof of	2143
	18:28	He has delivered u the men who	6037
	18:31	from all who rose u against you."	7756
	18:32	the king and all who rise u to harm you be	7756
	18:33	He went u to the room over the gateway	6590
	19: 8	So the king got u and took his seat in	7756
	19:34	I should go u to Jerusalem with the king?	6590
	20:12	that everyone who came u to	6584
	20:15	They built a siege ramp u to the city,	448
	20:19	to swallow u the LORD's inheritance?"	1180
	20:20	be it from me to swallow u or destroy!	1180
	20:21	has lifted u his hand against the king,	5951
	21:13	and exposed were gathered u.	665
	23: 7	they are burned u where they lie."	836+928+2021+8596+8596
	24:11	Before David got u the next morning,	7756
	24:18	"Go u and build an altar to the LORD on	6590
	24:19	So David went u, as the LORD had	6590
	24:22	whatever pleases him and offer it u.	6590
1Ki	1:35	Then you are to go u with him,	6590
	1:40	And all the people went u after him,	6590
	1:45	From there they have gone u cheering,	6590
	2:19	the king stood u to meet her,	6590
	2:34	of Jehoiada went u and struck down Joab	6590
	3:20	So she got u in the middle of the night	7756
	3:21	I got u to nurse my son—	7756
	6: 8	a stairway led u to the middle level and	6590
	8: 1	to bring u the ark of the LORD's covenant	6590
	8: 3	the priests took u the ark,	5951
	8: 4	and they brought u the ark of the LORD	6590
	8: 4	The priests and Levites carried them u,	6590
	8:35	the heavens are shut u and there is no rain	6806
	9:17	He built u Lower Beth Horon,	NIH
	9:24	After Pharaoh's daughter had come u from	6590
	11:14	Then the LORD raised u against Solomon	7756
	11:15	who had gone u to bury the dead,	6590
	11:20	whom Tahpenes brought u in	1694
	11:23	And God raised u against Solomon	7756
	12: 8	the young men who had grown u with him	1540
	12:10	The young men who had grown u	1540
	12:24	Do not go u to fight against your brothers,	6590
	12:25	From there he went out and built u Peniel.	1215
	12:27	If these people go u to offer sacrifices at	6590
	12:28	"It is too much for you to go u	6590
	12:28	O Israel, who brought you u out of Egypt."	6590
	12:29	One he set u in Bethel,	8492
	12:33	the festival for the Israelites and went u to	6590
	13: 4	toward the man shriveled u,	3312
	13:29	the prophet picked u the body of the man	5951
	14: 7	'I raised you u from among the people	8123
	14:10	I will burn u the house of Jeroboam	1277
	14:14	"The LORD will raise u for himself	7756
	14:16	And he will give Israel u because of	5989
	14:17	Then Jeroboam's wife got u and left	7756
	14:22	stirred u his jealous anger more than	7861
	14:23	They also set u for themselves high places,	1215
	15: 4	a lamp in Jerusalem by raising u a son	7756
	15:17	Baasha king of Israel went u against Judah	6590
	15:22	With them King Asa built u Geba	1215
	16: 2	"I lifted you u from the dust	8123
	16:32	He set u an altar for Baal in the temple	7756
	16:34	and he set u its gates at the cost	5893
	17: 7	Some time later the brook dried u	3312
	17:14	be used u and the jug of oil will not run dry	3983
	17:16	was not used u and the jug of oil	3983
	17:23	Elijah picked u the child and carried him	4374
	18:38	fell and burned u the sacrifice,	430
	18:38	and also licked u the water in the trench.	4308
	18:43	And he went u and looked.	6590
	18:44	'Hitch u your chariot and go down before	673
	19: 7	"Get u and eat,"	7756
	19: 7	"Get u and eat,	7756
	19: 8	So he got u and ate and drank.	7756
	19:19	Elijah went u to him and threw his cloak	6296

1Ki	20: 1	he went u and besieged Samaria	6590
	20:26	and went u to Aphek to fight against Israel.	6590
	20:28	of God came u and told the king of Israel,	5602
	20:33	as a good sign and were quick to pick u	2715
	20:33	Ahab had him come u into his chariot.	6590
	20:34	"You may set u your own market areas	8492
	21: 7	Get u and eat! Cheer up.	7756
	21: 7	Get up and eat! Cheer u.	3512+4213
	21:15	"Get u and take possession of the vineyard	7756
	21:16	he got u and went down to take possession	7756
	21:19	where dogs licked u Naboth's blood,	4379
	21:19	dogs will lick u your blood—	4379
	22:24	of Kenaanah went u and slapped Micaiah in	5602
	22:29	and Jehoshaphat king of Judah went u	6590
	22:35	the king was propped u in his chariot	6641
	22:38	and the dogs licked u his blood,	4379
2Ki	1: 3	"Go u and meet the messengers of the king	6590
	1: 9	The captain went u to Elijah,	6590
	1:13	This third captain went u and fell	6590
	1:15	So Elijah got u and went down with him to	7756
	2: 1	to take Elijah u to heaven in a whirlwind,	6590
	2: 5	at Jericho went u to Elisha and asked him,	5602
	2: 8	rolled it u and struck the water with it.	1676
	2:11	Elijah went u to heaven in a whirlwind.	6590
	2:13	He picked u the cloak that had fallen	8123
	2:16	of the LORD has picked him u and set him	5951
	2:23	From there Elisha went u to Bethel.	6590
	2:23	"Go on u, you baldhead!"	6590
	2:23	"Go on u, you baldhead!"	6590
	3:19	stop u all the springs, and ruin every good	6258
	3:21	who could bear arms was called u	7590
	3:22	When they got u early in the morning,	8899
	3:24	the Israelites rose u and fought them	7756
	3:25	They stopped u all the springs and cut	6258
	4:11	he went u to his room and lay down there.	6073
	4:20	After the servant had lifted him u	5951
	4:21	She went u and laid him on the bed of	6590
	4:30	So he got u and followed her.	7756
	4:39	he cut them u into the pot of stew,	7114
	5:23	tied u the two talents of silver in two bags,	7443
	6: 8	"I will set u my camp in such and such	9381
	6:15	of the man of God got u and went out early	7756
	6:24	and marched u and laid siege to Samaria.	6590
	6:28	'Give u your son so we may eat him today,	5989
	6:29	'Give u your son so we may eat him,'	5989
	7: 5	At dusk they got u and went to the camp of	7756
	7: 7	So they got u and fled in the dusk	7756
	7:12	The king got u in the night and said	7756
	8: 7	"The man of God has come all the way u	6330
	8:20	and set u its own king.	4887+4889
	8:21	but he rose u and broke through by night;	7756
	9: 6	Jehu got u and went into the house.	7756
	9:21	"Hitch u my chariot," Joram ordered.	673
	9:21	And when it was hitched u,	673
	9:25	"Pick him u and throw him on the field	5951
	9:26	then, pick him u and throw him on that plot,	5951
	9:27	he fled u the road to Beth Haggan.	5674
	9:27	in his chariot on the way u to Gur	5090
	9:32	He looked u at the window and called out,	5951
	10:15	and Jehu helped him u into the chariot.	6590
	12:17	of Aram went u and attacked Gath	6590
	13:21	the man came to life and stood u	7756
	15:14	of Gadi went from Tirzah u to Samaria	6590
	16: 5	of Remaliah king of Israel marched u	6590
	16: 7	"Come u and save me out of the hand of	6590
	16:13	He offered u his burnt offering	7787
	17: 3	Shalmaneser king of Assyria came u	6590
	17: 7	who had brought them u out of Egypt from	6590
	17:10	They set u sacred stones and Asherah poles	5893
	17:29	and set them u in the shrines the people	5663
	17:36	who brought you u out of Egypt	6590
	18: 4	for u to that time the Israelites had been	6330
	18:17	They came u to Jerusalem and stopped at	6590
	19:14	Then he went u to the temple of	6590
	19:24	With the soles of my feet I have dried u all	2990
	19:26	scorched before it grows u.	7756
	19:35	When the people got u the next morning—	8899
	20: 5	On the third day from now you will go u	6590
	20: 8	and that I will go u to the temple of	6590
	20:17	and all that your fathers have stored u	732
	22: 4	"Go u to Hilkiah the high priest	6590
	23: 2	He went u to the temple of the LORD	6590
	23:29	of Egypt went u to the Euphrates River	6590
	24:11	and Nebuchadnezzar himself came u to	995
1Ch	5: 9	To the east they occupied the land u to	6330
	5:26	So the God of Israel stirred u the spirit	6424
	9:18	u to the present time.	6330
	10:10	temple of their gods and hung u his head	9546
	11: 6	Joab son of Zeruiah went u first,	6590
	11: 7	David then took u residence in the fortress,	3782
	11: 8	He built u the city around it,	1215
	13: 6	to bring u from there the ark of God	6590
	14: 8	they went u in full force to search for him,	6590
	14:11	David and his men went u to Baal Perazim,	6590
	14:14	"Do not go straight u,	6590
	15: 3	to bring u the ark of the LORD to	6590
	15:12	to consecrate yourselves and bring u	6590
	15:13	did not bring it u the first time that	NIH
	15:14	in order to bring u the ark of the LORD,	6590
	15:25	of a thousand went to bring u the ark of	6590
	15:28	So all Israel brought u the ark of	6590
	17: 5	a house from the day I brought Israel u out	6590
	17:11	I will raise u your offspring	7756
	19: 9	The Ammonites came out and drew u	6885
	21: 1	Satan rose u against Israel and incited	6641
	21:16	David looked u and saw the angel of	5951

1Ch	21:18	to go *u* and build an altar to the LORD on	6590
	21:19	So David went *u* in obedience to the word	6590
2Ch	1: 4	Now David *had* brought *u* the ark of God	6590
	1: 6	Solomon went *u* to the bronze altar before	6590
	2:16	You *can* then take them *u to* Jerusalem."	6590
	5: 2	to bring *u* the ark of the LORD's covenant	6590
	5: 4	the Levites took *u* the ark,	5951
	5: 5	and *they* brought *u* the ark and the Tent	6590
	5: 5	priests, who were Levites, carried them *u*;	6590
	6:26	the heavens *are* shut *u* and there is no rain	6806
	7:13	"When *I* shut *u* the heavens so	6806
	8: 4	also built *u* Tadmor in the desert and all	1215
	8:11	brought Pharaoh's daughter *u*	6590
	10: 8	the young men who *had* grown *u* with him	1540
	10:10	The young men who *had* grown *u*	1540
	11: 4	*Do* not go *u* to fight against your brothers.	6590
	11: 5	Rehoboam lived in Jerusalem and built *u*	1215
	13: 3	Jeroboam drew *u a* battle line	6885
	14: 6	*He* built *u* the fortified cities of Judah,	1215
	14: 7	"*Let us* build *u* these towns,"	1215
	14:10	and *they* took *u* battle positions	6885
	15: 7	as for you, be strong and *do* not give *u*,	3338+8332
	15:16	broke it *u* and burned it in	1990
	16: 1	of Asa's reign Baasha king of Israel went *u*	6590
	16: 6	With them *he* built *u* Geba and Mizpah.	1215
	18:23	of Kenaanah went *u* and slapped Micaiah in	5602
	18:28	and Jehoshaphat king of Judah went *u*	6590
	18:34	and the king of Israel propped *himself u*	6641
	20: 5	Then Jehoshaphat stood *u* in the assembly	6641
	20:16	They *will be* climbing *u* by the Pass	6590
	20:17	Take *u your* positions;	3656
	20:19	from the Kohathites and Korahites stood *u*	7756
	20:23	The men of Ammon and Moab rose *u*	6641
	21: 8	set *u* its own king.	4887+4889
	21: 9	but *he* rose *u* and broke through by night.	7756
	25:14	*He* set them *u* as his own gods,	6641
	28:14	So the soldiers gave *u* the prisoners	6440
	28:24	the doors of the LORD's temple and set *u*	6913
	29:20	and went *u to* the temple of the LORD.	6590
	30:16	*they* took *u* their regular positions	6584+6641
	33:19	where he built high places and set *u*	6641
	34:30	He went *u to* the temple of the LORD	6590
	35:20	of Egypt went *u* to fight at Carchemish on	6590
	36:17	*He* brought *u* against them the king of	6590
	36:23	his God be with him, and *let him go u*.' "	6590
Ezr	1: 3	may his God be with him, and *let him* go *u*	6590
	1: 5	to go *u* and build the house of the LORD	6590
	1:11	along when the exiles came *u* from Babylon	6590
	2: 1	the people of the province who came *u*	6590
	2:59	The following came *u* from the towns	6590
	4:12	that the Jews who came *u* to us	10513
	6:11	and *he is to be* lifted *u* and impaled on it.	10238
	7: 6	this Ezra came *u* from Babylon.	6590
	7: 7	came *u* to Jerusalem in the seventh year	6590
	7:22	*u to* a hundred talents of silver,	10527
	7:28	from Israel to go *u* with me.	6590
	8: 1	and those registered with them who came *u*	6590
	9: 6	I am too ashamed and disgraced to lift *u*	8123
	10: 4	Rise *u*; this matter is in your hands.	7756
	10: 5	So Ezra rose *u* and put the leading priests	7756
	10:10	Ezra the priest stood *u* and said to them,	7756
Ne	2:15	so *I* went *u* the valley by night,	6590
	3:16	made repairs *u* to a point opposite	6330
	3:26	on the hill of Ophel made repairs *u* to	6330
	4: 3	if even a fox climbed *u* on it,	6590
	4: 5	not cover *u* their guilt or blot out their sins	4059
	4: 8	and fight against Jerusalem and stir *u*	6913
	4:14	*I* stood *u* and said to the nobles,	7756
	6: 1	though *u* to that time I had not set a	6330
	6: 8	you *are* just making it *u* out of your head."	968
	7: 6	the people of the province who came *u*	6590
	7:61	The following came *u* from the towns	6590
	8: 2	which was made *u* of men and women	4946
	8: 5	and as he opened it, the people all stood *u*.	6641
	9: 5	"Stand *u* and praise the LORD your God,	7756
	9:18	who brought you *u* out of Egypt,'	6590
	10:38	bring a tenth of the tithes *u*	6590
	12:23	the descendants of Levi *u* to the time	6330
	12:31	had the leaders of Judah go *u*	6590
	12:37	the Fountain Gate *they* continued directly *u*	6590
	13:18	Now you *are* stirring *u* more wrath	3578
Est	2: 7	whom *he had* brought *u*	587
	2:20	when he was bringing her *u*.	594
	5: 3	Even *u* to half the kingdom,	6330
	5: 6	*u to* half the kingdom, it will be granted."	6330
	7: 2	*u to* half the kingdom, it will be granted."	6330
	7: 7	The king got *u* in a rage,	7756
	7: 9	who spoke *u* to help the king."	1819
	10: 3	and spoke *u for* the welfare of all the Jews.	1819
Job	1:16	from the sky and burned *u* the sheep and	1277
	1:20	Job got *u* and tore his robe	7756
	4:21	*Are* not the cords of their tent pulled *u*,	5825
	5:18	For he wounds, but *he* also binds *u*;	2502
	6:18	*they* go *u* into the wasteland and perish.	6590
	7: 4	'How long before *I* get *u*?'	7756
	9:35	Then *I would* speak *u* without fear of him,	1819
	11:15	then *you will* lift *u* your face	5951
	14: 2	*He* springs *u* like a flower and withers	3655
	14:17	My offenses *will be* sealed *u* in a bag;	3159
	15:16	*who* drinks *u* evil like water!	9272
	15:20	The ruthless through all the years stored *u*	7621
	16: 8	my gauntness rises *u* and testifies	7756
	17: 3	Who else *will* put *u* security *for* me?	3338+4200+9546
	18:16	His roots dry *u* below	3312
	20:15	God *will* make his stomach vomit them *u*.	3769
	20:27	the earth *will* rise *u* against him.	7756
Job	21:19	'God stores *u* a man's punishment	7621
	22:22	from his mouth and lay *u* his words	8492
	22:26	in the Almighty and *will* lift *u* your face	5951
	22:29	and you say, 'Lift them *u*!'	1575
	24:14	the murderer rises *u* and kills the poor	7756
	24:24	they are brought low and gathered *u*	7890
	26: 8	*He* wraps *u* the waters in his clouds,	7674
	26:12	By his power *he* churned *u* the sea;	8088
	27:16	Though *he* heaps *u* silver like dust	7392
	27:17	what *he* lays *u* the righteous will wear,	3922
	29:16	I took *u* the case of the stranger.	2983
	30:13	*They* break *u* my road;	5995
	30:20	*I* stand *u*, but you merely look at me.	6641
	30:22	*You* snatch me *u* and drive me before	5951
	30:28	*I* stand *u* in the assembly and cry for help.	7756
	31:40	then *let* briers come *u* instead of wheat	3655
	33:32	speak *u*, for I want you to be cleared.	1819
	34:24	the mighty and sets *u* others in their place.	6641
	35: 5	Look *u at* the heavens and see;	5564
	36:27	"*He* draws *u* the drops of water,	1758
	37:19	*we* cannot draw *u* our case because	6885
	37:20	Would any man ask *to be* swallowed *u*?	1180
	38: 8	"Who shut *u* the sea behind doors	6114
	38:33	*Can* you set *u* [God's] dominion over	8492
	39:24	In frenzied excitement *he* eats *u* the ground;	1686
	41: 6	*Will they* divide him *u* among	2936
	41:25	When *he* rises *u*, the mighty are terrified;	8420
	41:31	and stirs *u* the sea like a pot of ointment;	8492
Ps	2:12	for his wrath *can* flare *u* in a moment.	1277
	3: 1	How many rise *u* against me!	7756
	3: 3	you bestow glory on me and lift *u* my head.	8123
	3: 6	I will not fear the tens of thousands drawn *u* against me	8883
	7: 6	rise *u* against the rage of my enemies.	5951
	9:13	Have mercy and lift me *u* from the gates	8123
	10:12	Lift *u* your hand, O God.	5951
	16: 4	of blood or take *u* their names on my lips.	5951
	17:10	*They* close *u* their callous hearts,	6037
	17:13	Rise *u*, O LORD, confront them,	7756
	17:14	and store *u* wealth for their children.	5663
	20: 5	and *will* lift *u our* banners in the name	1839
	20: 8	but we rise *u* and stand firm.	7756
	21: 9	the LORD *will* swallow them *u*,	1180
	22:15	My strength *is* dried *u* like a potsherd,	3312
	24: 4	who *does not* lift *u* his soul to an idol	5951
	24: 7	Lift *u* your heads, O you gates;	5951
	24: 7	be lifted *u*, *you* ancient doors,	5951
	24: 9	Lift *u* your heads, O you gates;	5951
	24: 9	lift them *u*, *you* ancient doors,	5951
	25: 1	To you, O LORD, *I* lift *u* my soul;	5951
	27:12	for false witnesses rise *u* against me,	7756
	28: 2	as *I* lift *u* my hands	5951
	28: 5	down and never build them *u again*.	1215
	30: 3	*you* brought me *u* from the grave;	6590
	31:19	which *you have* stored *u* for those who fear	7621
	32: 5	to you and *did not* cover *u* my iniquity.	4059
	35: 2	Take *u* shield and buckler;	2616
	35:25	or say, "We have swallowed him *u*."	1180
	39: 6	he heaps *u* wealth,	7392
	41: 8	*he will* never get *u from* the place	7756
	41: 9	*has* lifted *u* his heel against me.	1540
	41:10	raise me *u*, that I may repay them.	7756
	44:11	*You* gave us *u* to be devoured like sheep	5989
	44:26	Rise *u* and help us;	7756
	51:18	build *u* the walls of Jerusalem.	1215
	52: 5	*He will* snatch you *u* and tear you	3149
	59: 1	from those who rise *u against* me.	7756
	63: 4	in your name *I will* lift *u* my hands.	5951
	66: 7	*let* not the rebellious rise *u* against him.	8123
	69: 1	for the waters have come *u* to my neck.	6330
	69:15	or the depths swallow me *u* or	1180
	71:20	of the earth *you will* bring me *u*.	6590
	73:10	to them and drink *u* waters in abundance.	5172
	74: 4	*they* set *u* their standards as signs.	8492
	74:15	It was *you who* opened *u* springs	1324
	74:15	you dried *u* the ever flowing rivers.	3312
	74:22	Rise *u*, O God, and defend your cause;	7756
	75: 4	'*Do not* lift *u* your horns.	8123
	75:10	horns of the righteous *will be* lifted *u*.	8123
	76: 9	O God, rose *u* to judge,	6965
	77:18	your lightning lit *u* the world;	239
	78:38	and *did not* stir *u* his full wrath.	6424
	78:60	the tent he had set *u* among men.	8905
	80:15	the son *you have* raised *u* for yourself.	599
	80:17	of man *you have* raised *u* for yourself.	599
	81:10	who brought you *u* out of Egypt.	6590
	82: 8	Rise *u*, O God, judge the earth,	6965
	86: 4	for to you, O Lord, *I* lift *u* my soul.	5951
	88:10	*Do* those who are dead rise *u* and praise	7756
	89: 9	when its waves mount *u*, you still them.	5951
	90: 6	though in the morning it springs *u* new,	7437
	91:12	*they will* lift you *u* in their hands,	5951
	92: 7	that though the wicked spring *u* like grass	7255
	93: 3	The seas *have* lifted *u*, O LORD,	5951
	93: 3	the seas *have* lifted *u* their voice;	5951
	93: 3	seas *have* lifted *u* their pounding waves.	5951
	94: 2	Rise *u*, O Judge of the earth;	5375
	94:16	Who *will* rise *u* for me against the wicked?	7756
	97: 3	His lightning lights *u* the world;	239
	102:10	for *you have* taken me *u* and	5375
	104:28	When you give it to them, they gather it *u*;	4377
	105:30	which went *u* into the bedrooms	NIH
	105:35	they ate *u* every green thing in their land,	430
	105:35	ate *u* the produce of their soil.	430
	106: 9	He rebuked the Red Sea, and *it* dried *u*;	2990
	106:17	The earth opened *u* and swallowed Dathan;	7337
	106:30	But Phinehas stood *u* and intervened,	6641
Ps	107:25	and stirred *u* a tempest that lifted high	6641
	107:26	*They* mounted *u* to the heavens and went	6590
	110: 6	heaping *u* the dead and crushing the rulers	4848
	110: 7	therefore *he will* lift *u* his head.	8123
	116:13	*I will* lift *u* the cup of salvation and call	5951
	118:27	join in the festal procession *u* to the horns	6330
	119:48	*I* lift *u* my hands to your commands,	5951
	121: 1	*I* lift *u* my eyes to the hills—	5951
	122: 4	That is where the tribes go *u*,	6590
	123: 1	*I* lift *u* my eyes to you,	5951
	127: 2	In vain you rise early and stay *u* late,	3782
	132:17	a horn grow for David and set *u* a lamp	6885
	134: 1	Lift *u* your hands in the sanctuary	5951
	139: 8	If *I* go *u to* the heavens, you are there;	6158
	139:21	and abhor *those who* rise *u* against you?	7756
	140: 2	in their hearts and stir *u* war every day.	1592
	141: 2	may the lifting *u of* my hands be like	5368
	141: 7	"As one plows and breaks *u* the earth,	1324
	142: 1	lift *u* my voice to the LORD for mercy.	2858
	143: 8	for to you *I* lift *u* my soul.	5951
	145:14	and lifts *u* all who are bowed down.	2422
	146: 8	the LORD lifts *u* those who are bowed	2422
	147: 2	The LORD builds *u* Jerusalem;	1215
	147: 3	brokenhearted and binds *u* their wounds.	2502
	147:18	he stirs *u* his breezes, and the waters flow.	5959
	148:14	He has raised *u* for his people a horn,	8123
Pr	2: 1	and store *u* my commands within you,	7621
	3:35	but fools he holds *u to* shame.	8123
	6: 1	*you have* put *u* security for your neighbor,	6842
	6: 9	When *will you* get *u* from your sleep?	7756
	6:14	he always stirs *u* dissension	8938
	6:19	and *a man who* stirs *u* dissension	8938
	7: 1	keep my words and store *u* my commands	7621
	10:12	Hatred stirs *u* dissension,	6424
	10:14	Wise men store *u* knowledge,	7621
	11:15	*He who* puts *u* security *for* another will	6842
	12:25	but a kind word cheers him *u*.	8523
	13:22	sinner's wealth *is* stored *u* for the righteous.	7621
	15: 1	but a harsh word stirs *u* anger.	6590
	15:18	A hot-tempered man stirs *u* dissension,	1741
	16:28	A perverse man stirs *u* dissension,	8938
	17:18	and puts *u* security for his neighbor.	6842+6859
	17:22	but a crushed spirit dries *u* the bones.	3312
	20:16	the garment of *one who* puts *u* security *for*	6842
	20:17	but he ends *u* with a mouth full of gravel.	339
	21:29	wicked man puts *u* a bold front,	928+6451+7156
	22:15	Folly *is* bound *u* in the heart of a child,	8003
	22:23	for the LORD *will* take *u* their case	8189
	22:26	in pledge or puts *u* security *for* debts;	6842
	22:28	not move an ancient boundary stone set *u*	6913
	23: 8	*You will* vomit *u* the little you have eaten	7794
	23:11	he *will* take *u* their case against you.	8189
	23:35	*will I* wake *u* so I can find another drink?"	7810
	24:31	thorns *had* come *u* everywhere,	6590
	25: 7	to say to you, "Come *u* here," than for him	6590
	27:13	the garment of *one who* puts *u* security *for*	6842
	28:25	A greedy man stirs *u* dissension,	1741
	29: 8	Mockers stir *u* a city,	7032
	29:22	An angry man stirs *u* dissension,	1741
	30: 4	Who *has* gone *u to* heaven	6590
	30: 4	Who *has* gathered *u* the wind in the hollow	665
	30: 4	Who *has* wrapped *u* the waters in his cloak?	7674
	30:21	under four it cannot bear *u*:	5951
	30:25	yet *they* store *u* their food in the summer;	3922
	30:33	so stirring *u* anger produces strife."	4790
	31: 8	"Speak *u* for those who cannot speak	7023+7337
	31: 9	Speak *u* and judge fairly;	7023+7337
	31:15	She gets *u* while it is still dark;	7756
Ecc	2:26	the task of gathering and storing *u* wealth	4043
	3: 6	a time to search and a time to give *u*,	6
	4:10	his friend *can* help him *u*.	7756
	4:10	and has no one to help him *u*!	7756
	8: 3	*Do* not stand *u* for a bad cause,	6641
	12: 4	when *men* rise *u* at the sound of birds,	7756
SS	3: 2	*I will* get *u* now and go about the city,	7756
	3: 6	Who is this coming *u* from the desert like	6590
	4: 2	coming *u* from the washing.	6590
	4:12	You are a garden locked *u*, my sister,	5835
	6: 6	of sheep coming *u* from the washing.	6590
	7:13	that *I have* stored *u* for you, my lover.	7621
	8: 5	Who is this coming *u* from	6590
Isa	1: 2	"I reared children and brought them *u*,	8123
	2: 3	*let us* go *u* to the mountain of the LORD	6590
	2: 4	not take *u* sword against nation,	5951
	3: 5	The young *will* rise *u* against the old,	8104
	5: 2	*He* dug it *u* and cleared it of stones	6466
	5:11	who stay *u* late at night	336
	5:24	of fire lick *u* straw and as dry grass sinks	430
	5:26	*He* lifts *u* a banner for the distant nations,	5951
	7: 1	of Remaliah king of Israel marched *u*	6590
	8: 8	through it and reaching *u* to the neck.	6330
	8:16	Bind *u* the testimony and seal up the law	7674
	10:15	As if a rod were to wield *him who* lifts *it u*,	8123
	10:24	who beat you with a rod and lift *u* a club	5951
	11: 1	A shoot *will* come *u* from the stump	3655
	11:15	The LORD *will* dry *u* the gulf of	2990
	11:15	*He will* break it *u* into seven streams so	5782
	11:16	as there was for Israel when they came *u*	6590
	13:17	See, *I will* stir *u* against them the Medes,	6424
	14: 3	*you will* take *u* this taunt against the king	5951
	14:22	"*I will* rise *u* against them,"	7756
	14:29	the root of that snake *will* spring *u* a viper,	3655
	15: 2	Dibon goes *u to* its temple,	6590
	15: 5	*They* go *u* the way to Luhith,	6590
	15: 6	The waters of Nimrim are dried *u* and	5457

Isa	15: 7	the wealth they have acquired and **stored u**	7213
	19: 2	"I will **stir u** Egyptian against Egyptian—	6056
	19: 5	The waters of the river will **dry u**,	5980
	19: 6	streams of Egypt will dwindle and **dry u**.	2990
	21: 5	**Get u**, you officers, oil the shields!	7756
	22: 1	that you have all **gone u** on the roofs,	6590
	22: 6	Elam **takes u** the quiver,	5951
	22: 9	you **stored u** water in the Lower Pool.	7695
	22:18	He will **roll** you u tightly like a ball	7571+7571+7572
	23: 4	I have neither reared sons nor **brought u**	8123
	23:12	"U, cross over to Cyprus;	7756
	23:13	they **raised u** their siege towers,	7756
	23:16	"**Take u** a harp, walk through	4374
	23:18	they will not be **stored u** or hoarded.	732
	24: 4	The earth **dries u** and withers,	62
	24: 6	Therefore earth's inhabitants are **burned u**,	3081
	24: 7	The new wine **dries u** and the vine withers;	62
	24:19	The earth is **broken u**,	8318+8318
	24:22	they will be **shut u** in prison and	6037
	25: 8	he will **swallow u** death forever.	1180
	26:19	**wake u** and shout for joy.	7810
	27:12	O Israelites, will be **gathered u** one by one.	4377
	28:21	The LORD will **rise u** as he did	7756
	28:24	Does he keep on **breaking u** and harrowing	7337
	29: 3	I will encircle you with towers and **set u**	7756
	29:13	of me is made u only of rules taught	AIT
	30:26	the LORD **binds u** the bruises of his people	2502
	30:28	**rising u** to the neck.	2936
	30:29	your hearts will rejoice as when people go u	2143
	31: 2	He will **rise u** against the house of	7756
	32: 7	he **makes u** evil schemes to destroy the poor	3619
	32: 9	**rise u** and listen to me;	7756
	33: 3	when you **rise u**, the nations scatter.	8129
	33:10	will I be exalted; now will I be **lifted u**.	5951
	33:20	its stakes will never be **pulled u**,	5825
	34: 3	their dead bodies will **send u** a stench;	6590
	34: 4	be dissolved and the sky **rolled u** like	1670
	35: 9	nor will any ferocious beast **get u** on it;	6590
	37:14	Then he **went u** to the temple of	6590
	37:25	With the soles of my feet I have **dried u** all	2990
	37:27	scorched before it **grows u**.	7756
	37:36	When the people **got u** the next morning—	8899
	38:12	Like a weaver I have **rolled u** my life,	7886
	38:22	"What will be the sign that I will **go u** to	6590
	39: 6	and all that your fathers have **stored u**	732
	40: 4	Every valley shall be **raised u**,	5951
	40: 9	**go u** on a high mountain.	6590
	40: 9	**lift u** your voice with a shout, lift it up,	8123
	40: 9	**lift u**, do not be afraid;	8123
	40:20	a skilled craftsman to **set u** an idol that will	3922
	41: 2	"Who has **stirred u** one from the east,	6424
	41:16	the wind will **pick them u**,	5951
	41:25	"I have **stirred u** one from the north,	6424
	42:13	like a warrior he will **stir u** his zeal;	6424
	42:15	and hills and **dry u** all their vegetation;	3312
	42:15	I will turn rivers into islands and **dry u**	3312
	43: 6	I will say to the north, '**Give them u!**'	5989
	43:19	Now it **springs u**; do you not perceive it?	7541
	44: 4	They will **spring u** like grass in a meadow,	7541
	44: 9	Those who would **speak u for** a stench	6332
	44:27	'Be dry, and I will **dry u** your streams,'	3312
	45: 8	let salvation **spring u**,	7238
	45:13	I will **raise u** Cyrus in my righteousness;	6424
	46: 7	they **set it u** in its place, and there it stands.	5663
	47: 2	**Lift u** your skirts, bare your legs,	3106
	47:14	the fire will **burn them u**.	8596
	48:13	I summon them, they all **stand u** together.	6641
	49: 7	"Kings will see you and **rise u**,	7756
	49:11	and my highways will be **raised u**,	8123
	49:18	**Lift u** your eyes and look around;	5951
	49:21	Who **brought** these u?	1540
	49:22	I will **lift u** my banner to the peoples;	8123
	50: 2	By a mere rebuke I **dry u** the sea,	2990
	50: 9	the moths will **eat them u**.	430
	51: 6	**Lift u** your eyes to the heavens,	5951
	51: 8	the moth will **eat them u** like a garment;	430
	51:10	Was it not you who **dried u** the sea,	2990
	51:15	who **churns u** the sea so that its waves roar	8088
	51:17	**Rise u**, O Jerusalem, you who have drunk	7756
	52: 2	**rise u**, sit enthroned, O Jerusalem.	7756
	52: 8	Your watchmen **lift u** their voices;	5951
	52:13	be raised and **lifted u** and highly exalted.	5951
	53: 2	He **grew u** before him like a tender shoot,	6590
	53: 4	Surely he **took u** our infirmities	5951
	57: 7	there you **went u** to offer your sacrifices.	6590
	57:14	"**Build u**, build up, prepare the road!	6148
	57:14	"Build up, **build u**, prepare the road!	6148
	57:20	whose waves **cast u** mire and mud.	1764
	58:12	and will **raise u** the age-old foundations;	7756
	60: 4	"**Lift u** your eyes and look about you:	5951
	61: 1	He has sent me to **bind u** the brokenhearted,	2502
	61:11	**makes** the sprout **come u**	3655
	61:11	**make** righteousness and praise **spring u**	7541
	62:10	**Build u**, build up the highway!	6148
	62:10	Build up, **build u** the highway!	6148
	63: 9	he **lifted** them u and carried them all	5747
	64: 6	we all **shrivel u** like a leaf,	5570
	66: 9	"Do I **close u** the womb when I bring	6806
Jer	1:15	and set u their thrones in the entrance of	5989
	1:17	**Stand u** and say to them	7756
	2: 6	who **brought** us u out of Egypt and led us	6590
	3: 2	"Look u to the barren heights and see.	5951
	3: 6	She has **gone u** on every high hill and	2143
	4: 3	"**Break u** your unplowed ground and do	5774
	4:29	some **climb u** among the rocks.	6590

Jer	5: 1	"**Go u and down** the streets of Jerusalem,	8763
	6:22	a great nation is being **stirred u** from	6424
	7:29	**take u** a lament on the barren heights,	5951
	7:30	They have **set u** their detestable idols in	8492
	8: 2	They will not be **gathered u** or buried,	665
	8: 4	men fall down, do they not **get u?**	7756
	9:10	for the mountains and take u a lament	NIH
	10:17	**Gather u** your belongings to leave the land,	665
	10:20	now to pitch my tent or to **set u** my shelter.	7756
	11: 7	**brought** your forefathers u from Egypt	6590
	11:13	the altars you have **set u** to burn incense to	8492
	13: 7	to Perath and **dug u** the belt and took it	2916
	13:19	The cities in the Negev will be **shut u**,	6037
	13:20	**Lift u** your eyes and see	5951
	13:26	I will **pull u** your skirts over your face	3106
	14: 2	and a cry **goes u** from Jerusalem.	6590
	16:14	**brought** the Israelites u out of Egypt,'	6590
	16:15	**brought** the Israelites u out of the land	6590
	18: 9	that a nation or kingdom is to be **built u**	1215
	18:15	in bypaths and on roads not **built u**.	6148
	20: 9	a fire **shut u** in my bones.	6806
	22: 7	and they will **cut u** your fine cedar beams	4162
	22:20	"**Go u** to Lebanon and cry out,	6590
	23: 5	I will **raise u** to David a righteous Branch,	7756
	23: 7	**brought** the Israelites u out of Egypt,'	6590
	23: 8	**brought** the descendants of Israel u	6590
	24: 6	I will **build them u** and	1215
	25:33	not be mourned or **gathered u** or buried,	665
	26:10	they **went u** from the royal palace to	6590
	29:15	"The LORD has **raised u** prophets for us	7756
	30: 9	whom I will **raise u** for them.	7756
	31: 4	I will **build** you u again and you will	1215
	31: 4	Again you will **take u** your tambourines	6335
	31: 6	'Come, let us **go u** to Zion,	6590
	31:21	"**Set u** road signs; put up guideposts.	5893
	31:21	"Set up road signs; **put u** guideposts.	8492
	31:35	who **stirs u** the sea so that its waves roar—	8088
	32:24	how the siege ramps are **built u** to take	995
	32:34	They **set u** their abominable idols in	8492
	36:28	which Jehoiakim king of Judah **burned u**.	8596
	38:13	and they **pulled** him u with the ropes	5432
	41: 2	and the ten men who were with him **got u**	7756
	41:12	They **caught u** with him near the great pool	5162
	42:10	I will **build** you u and	1215
	46:11	"**Go u** to Gilead and get balm,	6590
	46:16	They will say, '**Get u**,	7756
	48: 5	They **go u** the way to Luhith,	6590
	48:18	for he who destroys Moab will **come u**	6590
	48:34	for even the waters of Nimrim are **dried u**.	5457
	49:14	**Rise u** for battle!"	7756
	49:19	a lion **coming u** from Jordan's thickets to	6590
	50: 2	**lift u** a banner and proclaim it;	5951
	50: 9	For I will **stir u** and bring against Babylon	6424
	50: 9	They will **take u** their positions	6885
	50:14	"**Take u** your positions around Babylon,	6885
	50:26	pile her u like heaps of grain.	6148
	50:32	and fall and no one will **help** her u;	7756
	50:38	They will **dry u**.	3312
	50:41	and many kings are being **stirred u** from	6424
	50:44	Like a lion **coming u** from Jordan's thickets	6590
	51: 1	"See, I will **stir u** the spirit of a destroyer	6424
	51:11	"Sharpen the arrows, **take u** the shields!	4848
	51:11	The LORD has **stirred u** the kings of	6424
	51:12	**Lift u** a banner against the walls	5951
	51:27	"**Lift u** a banner in the land!	5951
	51:27	**send u** horses like a swarm of locusts.	6590
	51:36	I will **dry u** her sea	2990
	52:17	The Babylonians **broke u** the bronze pillars,	8689
La	2: 2	the Lord has **swallowed u** all the dwellings	1180
	2: 5	he has **swallowed u** Israel.	1180
	2: 5	He has **swallowed u** all her palaces	1180
	2:16	"We have **swallowed** her u.	1180
	2:19	**Lift u** your hands to him for the lives	5951
	3:41	Let us **lift u** our hearts and our hands	5951
	3:58	O Lord, you **took u** my case;	8189
	5:12	Princes have been hung u by their hands;	9434
Eze	1:27	what appeared to be his waist u	2025+4200+5087
	2: 1	**stand u** on your feet and I will speak	6641
	3:12	Then the Spirit **lifted me u**,	5951
	3:14	Spirit then **lifted** me u and took me away,	5951
	3:22	"**Get u** and go out to the plain,	7756
	3:23	So I **got u** and went out to the plain.	7756
	4: 2	build a ramp **u to** it,	6584
	4: 2	against it, build a ramp up to it, **set u** camps	5989
	4: 8	I will **tie** you u with ropes so	5989
	4: 8	take a set of scales and **divide u** the hair.	2745
	5: 4	the fire and **burn** them u.	836+928+2021+8596
	8: 2	from there u his appearance was	2025+4200+5087
	8: 3	The Spirit **lifted** me u between earth	5951
	9: 3	of Israel **went u** from above the cherubim,	6590
	10: 7	He **took u** some of the fire and put it into	5951
	11: 1	the Spirit **lifted** me u and brought me to	5951
	11:23	of the LORD **went u** from within the city	6590
	11:24	The Spirit **lifted** me u and brought me to	5951
	11:24	Then the vision I had seen **went u** from me,	6590
	13: 5	You have not **gone u** to the breaks in	6590
	14: 3	these men have **set u** idols in their hearts	6590
	14: 4	When any Israelite **sets u** idols in his heart	6590
	14: 7	from me and **sets u** idols in his heart	6590
	16: 7	You **grew u** and developed and became	8049
	17: 9	a strong arm or many people to **pull** it u	5428
	17:24	I **dry u** the green tree and make	3312
	19: 1	"**Take u** a lament concerning the princes	5951
	19: 3	She **brought u** one of her cubs,	6590
	21:22	where he is to **set u** battering rams,	8492
	22:30	for a man among them who would **build u**	1553
	23: 8	not **give u** the prostitution she began	6440

Eze	23:22	I will **stir u** your lovers against you,	6424
	23:24	they will take **u** positions against you	8492
	24: 8	To **stir u** wrath and take revenge	6590
	25: 4	They will **set u** their camps	3782
	26: 3	like the sea **casting u** its waves.	6590
	26: 8	he will **set u** siege works against you,	5989
	26: 8	a ramp **u to** your walls and raise his shields	6584
	26:17	Then they will **take u** a lament	5951
	27: 2	**take u** a lament concerning Tyre.	5951
	27:32	they will **take u** a lament concerning you:	7801
	28:12	**take u** a lament concerning the king of Tyre	5951
	29: 5	and not be gathered or **picked u**.	7695
	30:12	I will **dry u** the streams of the Nile	3000+5989
	30:21	It has not been **bound u** for healing or put	2502
	32: 2	**take u** a lament concerning Pharaoh king	5951
	32: 3	and they will **haul** you u in my net.	6590
	34: 4	or healed the sick or **bound u** the injured.	2502
	34:16	I will **bind u** the injured and strengthen	2502
	37:10	to life and **stood u** on their feet—	6641
	37:11	'Our bones are **dried u**	3312
	37:12	to open your graves and **bring you u**	6590
	37:13	when I open your graves and **bring you u**	6590
	38: 9	and the many nations with you will **go u**,	6590
	39: 9	the weapons for fuel and **burn them u**—	5956
	39:15	he will **set u** a marker beside it until	1215
	40:14	The measurement was u to the portico	448
	40:22	Seven steps **led u** to it,	6590
	40:26	Seven steps **led u** to it,	6590
	40:31	and eight steps **led u** to it.	6590
	40:34	and eight steps **led u** to it.	6590
	40:37	and eight steps **led u** to it.	6590
	41: 7	A stairway **went u** from the lowest floor to	6590
	41:16	The floor, the wall **u to** the windows,	6330
	43: 5	the Spirit **lifted** me u and brought me into	5951
	43:14	From the gutter on the ground **u to**	6330
	43:14	and from the smaller ledge u to	6330
	45: 9	Give u your violence and oppression	6073
	47: 4	and led me through water that was u to	AIT
Da	2:21	he **sets u** kings and deposes them.	10624
	2:44	the God of heaven will **set u** a kingdom	10624
	3: 1	set it u on the plain of Dura in	10624
	3: 2	to the dedication of the image he had **set u**.	10624
	3: 3	that King Nebuchadnezzar had **set u**,	10624
	3: 5	that King Nebuchadnezzar has **set u**,	10624
	3: 7	gold that King Nebuchadnezzar had **set u**.	10624
	3:12	the image of gold you have **set u**."	10624
	3:14	the image of gold I have **set u?**	10624
	3:18	the image of gold you have **set u**."	10624
	3:20	of the strongest soldiers in his army to **tie u**	10366
	3:22	of the fire killed the soldiers who **took u**	10513
	3:24	"Weren't there three men that we **tied u**	10366
	3:28	to give u their lives rather than serve	10314
	5:23	you have **set yourself u** against the Lord	10659
	6:19	king **got u** and hurried to the lions' den.	10513
	7: 2	the four winds of heaven **churning u**	10137
	7: 3	**came u** out of the sea.	10513
	7: 5	It was **raised u** on one of its sides,	10624
	7: 5	'**Get u** and eat your fill of flesh!'	10624
	7: 5	a little one, which **came u** among them;	10513
	7:20	and about the other horn that **came u**,	10513
	8: 3	I looked **u**, and there before me was a ram	5951
	8: 3	the other but **grew u** later.	6590
	8: 8	in its place four prominent horns **grew u**	6590
	8:11	set itself u to be as great as the Prince	1540
	8:26	but **seal u** the vision,	6258
	8:27	Then I **got u** and went about	7756
	9:24	to **seal u** vision and prophecy and to anoint	3159
	9:27	[of the temple] he will set u an abomination	NIH
	10: 5	I looked u and there before me was	5951
	10:11	to speak to you, and **stand u**,	6584+6641+6642
	10:11	he said this to me, I **stood u** trembling.	6641
	11: 2	he will **stir u** everyone against	6424
	11: 4	his empire will be **broken u**	8689
	11:15	and **build u** siege ramps and will capture	9161
	11:25	a large army he will **stir u** his strength	6424
	11:31	"His armed forces will **rise u** to desecrate	6641
	11:31	Then they will **set u** the abomination	5989
	12: 4	**close u** and seal the words of the scroll	6258
	12: 9	because the words are **closed u** and sealed	6258
	12:11	that causes desolation is **set u**,	5989
Hos	1:11	and will **come u** out of the land,	6590
	2:15	as in the day she **came u** out of Egypt.	6590
	4:15	do not go u to Beth Aven.	6590
	6: 1	he has injured us but he will **bind u**	2502
	8: 4	They **set u** kings without my consent;	4887
	8: 7	foreigners would **swallow** it u.	1180
	8: 8	Israel is **swallowed u**;	1180
	8: 9	For they have **gone u** to Assyria like	6590
	10: 4	therefore lawsuits **spring u**	7255
	10: 8	Thorns and thistles will **grow u**	6590
	10:11	and Jacob must **break u** the ground.	8440
	10:12	and **break u** your unplowed ground;	5774
	11: 8	"How can I give you u, Ephraim?	5989
	12:13	a prophet to **bring** Israel u from Egypt,	6590
	13:12	The guilt of Ephraim is **stored u**,	7674
	13:15	his spring will fail and his well **dry u**.	2990
Joel	1: 5	**Wake u**, you drunkards, and weep!	7810
	1:10	fields are ruined, the ground is **dried u**;	62
	1:10	the new wine is **dried u**, the oil fails.	3312
	1:12	vine is **dried u** and the fig tree is withered;	3312
	1:12	of the field—are **dried u**.	3312
	1:17	for the grain has **dried u**.	3312
	1:19	the open pastures and flames have **burned u**	4265
	1:20	of water have **dried u** and fire has devoured	3312
	2: 5	like a mighty army **drawn u for** battle.	6885
	2:20	its stench will go u; its smell will rise."	6590
	3: 2	among the nations and **divided u** my land.	2745

Am	1: 2	the pastures of the shepherds **dry u,**	62
	2:10	"**I brought** you **u** out of Egypt,	6590
	2:11	*I* also **raised u** prophets from	7756
	3: 1	the whole family *I* **brought u** out of Egypt:	6590
	3: 5	*Does* a trap **spring u** from the earth	6590
	4: 7	another had none and **dried u.**	3312
	5: 1	this lament I **take** concerning you:	5951
	5: 2	with no **one** to **lift** her **u.**"	7756
	5:26	*You* have **lifted u** the shrine of your king,	5951
	6: 8	*I* will **deliver u** the city and everything	6037
	6:14	"I *will* **stir u** a nation against you,	7756
	7: 1	and just as the second crop *was* **coming u.**	6590
	7: 4	it **dried u** the great deep and devoured	430
	7:17	be measured and **divided u,**	2745
	8: 8	it will be **stirred u** and then sink like	1764
	9: 2	Though *they* **climb u** *to* the heavens,	6590
	9: 7	"*Did I* not bring Israel **u** from Egypt,	6590
Ob	1:21	Deliverers *will* **go u** on Mount Zion	6590
Jnh	1: 2	its wickedness *has* **come u** before me."	6590
	1: 4	that the ship threatened to **break u.**	8689
	1: 6	**Get u** and call on your god!	7756
	1:12	"**Pick me u** and throw me into the sea,"	5951
	2: 6	But *you* **brought** my life **u** from the pit,	6590
	3: 8	*Let* them **give u** their evil ways	4946+8740
	4: 6	**made** it **grow u** over Jonah to give shade	6590
	4:10	*It* **sprang u** overnight and died overnight.	2118
Mic	2: 4	my people's possession *is* **divided u.**	4614
	2: 8	Lately my people *have* **risen u** like	7756
	2:10	**Get u,** go away!	7756
	2:13	One who breaks open the way *will* **go u**	6590
	3: 3	who **chop** them **u** like meat for the pan,	7298
	4: 2	*let us* **go u** to the mountain of	6590
	4: 3	not **take u** sword against nation,	5951
	5: 9	be **lifted u** in triumph over your enemies,	8123
	6: 1	Listen to what the LORD says: "**Stand u,**	7756
	6: 4	*I* **brought** you **u** out of Egypt	6590
	6:14	*You* will **store u** but save nothing,	6047
	7: 6	a daughter **rises u** against her mother,	7756
Na	1: 4	He rebukes the sea and **dries** it **u;**	3312
	2:13	"*I* will **burn u** your chariots in smoke,	1277
Hab	1: 6	*I am* **raising u** the Babylonians,	7756
	1:13	while the wicked **swallow u** those more	1180
	1:15	**pulls** all of them **u** with hooks,	6590
	1:15	he **gathers** them **u** in his dragnet;	665
	2: 4	"See, he is **puffed u;**	6752
	2: 6	" 'Woe to him *who* **piles u** stolen goods	8049
	2: 7	not **wake u** and make you tremble?	3699
	2:19	Or to lifeless stone, '**Wake u!**	6424
Zep	1:10	"a cry will **go u** from the Fish Gate,	NIH
	3: 8	"for the day I *will* **stand u** to testify.	7756
Hag	1: 8	**Go u** *into* the mountains and bring	6590
	1:14	So the LORD **stirred u** the spirit	6424
Zec	1:18	Then I looked **u**—	5951
	1:21	of the nations who **lifted u** their horns	5951
	2: 1	Then I looked **u**—	5951
	5: 5	"**Look u** and see what this is	5951
	5: 9	Then I looked **u**—	5951
	5: 9	and *they* **lifted u** the basket	5951
	6: 1	I looked **u** again—	5951
	7:11	and **stopped u** their ears.	3877+4946+9048
	9: 3	she has **heaped u** silver like dust,	7392
	10:11	and all the depths of the Nile will **dry u.**	3312
	11:16	For I *am going to* **raise u** a shepherd over	7756
	14:10	But Jerusalem *will be* **raised u** and remain	8027
	14:16	that have attacked Jerusalem *will* **go u**	6590
	14:17	not **go u** to Jerusalem to worship the King,	6590
	14:18	If the Egyptian people *do not* **go u**	6590
	14:18	on the nations that *do not* **go u** to celebrate	6590
	14:19	the nations that *do not* **go u** to celebrate	6590
Mal	3:17	when I **make u** my treasured possession.	6913
Mt	1:24	**When** Joseph **woke u,**	1586
	2:13	"**Get u,**" he said, "take the child	1586
	2:14	So he **got u,** took the child and his mother	1586
	2:20	"**Get u,** take the child and his mother	1586
	2:21	So he **got u,** took the child and his mother	1586
	3: 9	of these stones God can **raise u** children	1586
	3:12	into the barn and **burning u** the chaff	2876
	3:16	he **went u** out of the water.	326
	4: 6	and *they* will **lift** you **u** in their hands,	149
	5: 1	he **went u** on a mountainside and sat down.	326
	6:19	"*Do* not **store u** for yourselves treasures	2564
	6:20	**store u** for yourselves treasures in heaven,	2564
	7:12	for this **sums u** the Law and the Prophets.	1639
	8:15	and *she* **got u** and began to wait on him.	1586
	8:17	"He **took u** our infirmities	3284
	8:24	a furious storm **came u** on the lake,	1181
	8:26	Then he **got u** and rebuked the winds and	1586
	9: 5	or to say, '**Get u** and walk'?	1586
	9: 6	Then he said to the paralytic, "**Get u,**	1586
	9: 7	And the man **got u** and went home.	1586
	9: 9	and Matthew **got u** and followed him.	482
	9:19	Jesus **got u** and went with him,	1586
	9:20	for twelve years **came u** behind him	4665
	9:25	took the girl by the hand, and *she* **got u.**	1586
	11:23	*will* you be **lifted u** to the skies?	5738
	12:29	unless *he* first **ties u** the strong man?	1313
	12:35	good things out of the good **stored u** in him,	2565
	12:35	evil things out of the evil **stored u** in him,	2565
	12:41	of Nineveh *will* **stand u** at the judgment	482
	13: 4	and the birds came and **ate** it **u.**	2983
	13: 5	*It* **sprang u** quickly,	1984
	13: 6	But *when* the sun **came u,**	422
	13: 7	which **grew u** and choked the plants.	326
	13:28	to go and **pull** them **u?**"	5198
	13:29	*you may* **root u** the wheat with them.	1748
	13:40	"As the weeds *are* **pulled u** and burned in	5198
	13:48	the fishermen **pulled** it **u** on the shore.	328

Mt	14:19	and the two fish and **looking u** to heaven,	329
	14:20	and the disciples **picked u** twelve basketfuls	149
	14:23	*he* **went u** on a mountainside by himself	326
	15:13	*will be* **pulled u** by the roots.	1748
	15:29	he **went u** on a mountainside and sat down.	326
	15:37	the disciples **picked u** seven basketfuls	149
	16:24	he must deny himself and **take u** his cross	149
	17: 1	**led** them **u** a high mountain by themselves.	429
	17: 4	If you wish, *I* will **put u** three shelters—	4472
	17: 7	"**Get u,**" he said.	1586
	17: 8	*When they* **looked u,**	2048+3836+4057
	17:17	How long *shall I* **put u with** you?	462
	18:21	**U** to seven times?"	2401
	19:16	Now a man **came u** to Jesus and asked,	4665
	20:17	Now *as Jesus was* **going u** to Jerusalem,	326
	20:18	"*We are going u* to Jerusalem,	326
	21:19	he **went u** to it but found nothing	2093
	23: 4	They **tie u** heavy loads and put them	1297
	23:32	**Fill u,** then, the measure of the sin	4444
	24: 1	when his disciples **came u** to him	4665
	24:38	**u** to the day Noah entered the ark;	948
	25: 7	the virgins **woke u** and trimmed their lamps.	1586
	26:58	**right u** to the courtyard of the high priest,	2401
	26:62	the high priest **stood u** and said to Jesus,	482
	26:73	those standing there **went u** to Peter	4665
	27: 6	The chief priests **picked u** the coins	3284
	27:35	they **divided u** his clothes by casting lots.	1374
	27:50	*he* **gave u** his spirit.	918
Mk	1:10	As Jesus *was* **coming u** out of the water,	326
	1:31	took her hand and **helped** her **u.**	1586
	1:35	while it was still dark, Jesus **got u,**	482
	2: 9	or to say, '**Get u,** take your mat and walk'?	1586
	2:11	**get u,** take your mat and go home."	1586
	2:12	*He* **got u,** took his mat and walked out	1586
	2:14	and Levi **got u** and followed him.	482
	3: 3	"**Stand u** in front of everyone."	1586
	3:13	Jesus **went u** on a mountainside and called	326
	3:27	unless *he* first **ties u** the strong man.	1313
	4: 4	and the birds came and **ate** it **u.**	2983
	4: 5	*It* **sprang u** quickly,	1984
	4: 6	But when the sun **came u,**	422
	4: 7	which **grew u** and choked the plants,	326
	4: 8	It **came u,** grew and produced a crop,	326
	4:27	Night and day, whether he sleeps or **gets u,**	1586
	4:37	A furious squall **came u,**	1181
	4:39	*He* **got u,** rebuked the wind and said	1444
	5:27	she **came u** behind him in the crowd	NIG
	5:41	"Little girl, I say to you, **get u!**").	1586
	5:42	Immediately the girl **stood u** and walked	482
	6:23	**u** to half my kingdom."	2401
	6:41	and the two fish and **looking u** to heaven,	329
	6:43	and the disciples **picked u** twelve basketfuls	149
	6:46	*he* **went u** on a mountainside to pray.	599
	7:34	He **looked u** to heaven and with	329
	8: 8	the disciples **picked u** seven basketfuls	149
	8:19	many basketfuls of pieces *did you* **pick u?**"	149
	8:20	many basketfuls of pieces *did you* **pick u?**"	149
	8:24	He **looked u** and said, "I see people;	329
	8:34	after me, he must deny himself and **take u**	149
	9: 2	with him and led them **u** a high mountain,	1650
	9: 5	*Let us* **put u** three shelters—	4472
	9:19	How long *shall I* **put u with** you?	462
	9:27	and *he* **stood u.**	482
	10:17	a man **ran u** to him and fell on his knees	4708
	10:32	**were** on their way *up* to Jerusalem,	326+1639
	10:33	"*We are* **going u** to Jerusalem," he said,	326
	10:49	So they called to the blind man, "**Cheer u!**	2510
	14:57	Then some **stood u** and gave this false	482
	14:60	Then the high priest **stood u** before them	482
	15: 8	The crowd **came u** and asked Pilate to do	326
	15:11	But the chief priests **stirred u** the crowd	411
	15:24	**Dividing u** his clothes,	1374
	15:41	Many other women who *had* **come u** with	5262
	16: 4	But *when they* **looked u,**	329
	16:18	*they* will **pick u** snakes with their hands;	149
	16:19	*he* was **taken u** into heaven and he sat at	377
Lk	1: 1	to **draw u** an account of the things	421
	1:52	from their thrones but *has* **lifted u**	5738
	1:60	but his mother **spoke u** and said,	646
	1:69	*He has* **raised u** a horn of salvation for us in	1586
	2: 4	also **went u** from the town of Nazareth	326
	2:19	But Mary **treasured u** all these things	5337
	2:38	**Coming u** to them at that very moment,	2392
	2:42	they **went u** to the Feast,	326
	3: 8	of these stones God can **raise u** children	1586
	3:17	but *he will* **burn u** the chaff	2876
	3:20	He locked John **u** in prison.	NIG
	4: 5	The devil **led** him **u** to a high place	343
	4:11	*they* will **lift** you **u** in their hands,	149
	4:16	where he had been **brought u,**	5555
	4:16	And he **stood u** to read.	482
	4:20	Then he **rolled u** the scroll,	4771
	4:29	They **got u,** drove him out of the town,	482
	4:39	She **got u** at once and began to wait	482
	5:11	So they **pulled** their boats **u** on shore,	2864
	5:19	*they* **went u** on the roof and lowered him	326
	5:23	or to say, '**Get u** and walk'?	1586
	5:24	**get u,** take your mat and go home."	1586
	5:25	Immediately he **stood u** in front of them,	482
	5:28	and Levi **got u,** left everything and followed	482
	6: 8	"**Get u** and stand in front of everyone."	1586
	6: 8	So *he* **got u** and stood there.	2705
	6:45	out of the good **stored u** in his heart,	2565
	6:45	out of the evil **stored u** in his heart.	2565
	7:14	Then he **went u** and touched the coffin,	4665
	7:14	He said, "Young man, I say to you, **get u!**"	1586
	7:15	The dead man **sat u** and began to talk,	361

Lk	8: 5	and the birds of the air **ate** it **u.**	2983
	8: 6	Some fell on rock, and *when* it **came u,**	5886
	8: 7	which **grew u** with it and choked the plants.	5243
	8: 8	*It* **came u** and yielded a crop,	5886
	8:24	He **got u** and rebuked the wind and	1444
	8:44	She **came u** behind him and touched	4665
	8:54	by the hand and said, "My child, **get u!**"	1586
	8:55	Her spirit returned, and at once *she* **stood u.**	482
	9:16	and the two fish and **looking u** to heaven,	329
	9:17	and the disciples **picked u** twelve basketfuls	149
	9:23	after me, he must deny himself and **take u**	149
	9:28	John and James with him and **went u** onto	326
	9:33	*Let us* **put u** three shelters—	4472
	9:41	with you and **put u with** you?	462
	9:51	the time approached for him to be **taken u**	482
	10:15	*will* you be **lifted u** to the skies?	5738
	10:25	an expert in the law **stood u** to test Jesus.	482
	11: 7	I can't **get u** and give you anything."	482
	11: 8	though he will not **get u** and give him	482
	11: 8	because of the man's boldness he will **get u**	1586
	11:22	the man trusted and **divides u** the spoils.	1344
	11:32	of Nineveh *will* **stand u** at the judgment	482
	12:19	"You have plenty of good things **laid u**	3023
	12:21	with anyone who **stores u** things for himself	2564
	13: 7	Why *should it* **use u** the soil?'	2934
	13:11	over and could not **straighten u** at all.	376
	13:13	and immediately *she* **straightened u**	494
	13:25	the owner of the house **gets u** and closes	1586
	14:10	'Friend, move **u** to a better place.'	542
	14:33	not **give u** everything he has cannot	698
	15:20	So he **got u** and went to his father.	1586
	16:23	he **looked u** and saw Abraham	2048+3836+4057
	17:24	and **lights u** the sky from one end to	3290
	17:27	marrying and being given in marriage **u** to	948
	18: 1	they should always pray and not **give u.**	1591
	18:10	"Two men **went u** to the temple to pray,	326
	18:11	Pharisee **stood u** and prayed to himself:	2705
	18:13	He would not even **look u** to heaven,	2048+3836+4057
	18:31	"*We are* **going u** to Jerusalem,	326
	19: 5	*he* **looked u** and said to him, "Zacchaeus,	329
	19: 8	Zacchaeus **stood u** and said to the Lord,	2705
	19:28	he went on ahead, **going u** to Jerusalem.	326
	20: 1	together with the elders, **came u** to him.	2392
	21: 1	As he **looked u,** Jesus saw the rich	329
	21:14	**make u** your **mind** not to	1877+2840+3836+5502
	21:28	**stand u** and lift up your heads,	376
	21:28	stand up and **lift u** your heads,	2048
	22:46	"**Get u** and pray so that you will not fall	482
	22:47	he was still speaking a crowd **came u,**	NIG
	23: 5	"He **stirs u** the people all over Judea	411
	23:34	they **divided u** his clothes by casting lots.	1374
	23:36	The soldiers also **came u** and mocked him.	4665
	24:12	Peter, however, **got u** and ran to the tomb.	482
	24:15	Jesus himself **came u** and walked along	1581
	24:33	They **got u** and returned at once	482
	24:50	he **lifted u** his hands and blessed them.	2048
	24:51	he left them and *was* **taken u** into heaven.	429
Jn	2:13	Jesus **went u** to Jerusalem.	326
	3:14	as Moses **lifted u** the snake in the desert,	5738
	3:14	so the Son of Man must be **lifted u,**	5738
	4:14	in him a spring of water **welling u**	256
	5: 1	Jesus **went u** to Jerusalem for a feast of	326
	5: 8	Then Jesus said to him, "**Get u!**	1586
	5: 8	**Pick u** your mat and walk."	149
	5: 9	*he* **picked u** his mat and walked.	149
	5:11	'**Pick u** your mat and walk.' "	149
	5:12	to **pick** it **u** and walk?"	149
	6: 3	Then Jesus **went u** on a mountainside	456
	6: 5	*When* Jesus **looked u** and saw	2048+3836+4057
	6: 8	Andrew, Simon Peter's brother, **spoke u,**	NIG
	6:39	but **raise** them **u** at the last day.	482
	6:40	and I *will* **raise** him **u** at the last day."	482
	6:44	and I *will* **raise** him **u** at the last day.	482
	6:54	and I *will* **raise** him **u** at the last day.	482
	7: 8	I *am* not yet **going u** to this Feast,	326
	7:14	the Feast *did* Jesus **go u** to the temple courts	326
	7:39	**U** to that time the Spirit had **not** been given	4037
	8: 7	*he* **straightened u** and said to them,	376
	8:10	Jesus **straightened u** and asked her,	376
	8:28	"When *you have* **lifted u** the Son of Man,	5738
	8:59	At this, *they* **picked u** stones to stone him,	149
	10:17	lay down my life—only *to* **take** it **u** again.	3284
	10:18	to lay it down and authority *to* **take** it **u**	3284
	10:31	the Jews **picked u** stones to stone him,	1002
	11:11	but I am going there to **wake** him **u.**"	2030
	11:29	*she* **got u** quickly and went to him.	1586
	11:31	how quickly she **got u** and went out,	482
	11:41	Then Jesus **looked u** and said, "Father,	539
	11:49	who was high priest that year, **spoke u,**	3306
	11:55	many **went u** from the country to Jerusalem	326
	12:20	among those who **went u** to worship at	326
	12:32	But I, when *I am* **lifted u** from the earth,	5738
	12:34	The crowd **spoke u,**	646
	12:34	'The Son of Man must be **lifted u'?**	5738
	13: 4	so *he* **got u** from the meal,	1586
	13:18	'He who shares my bread *has* **lifted u**	2048
	15: 6	such branches *are* **picked u,**	5251
	19: 3	and went **u** to him again and again,	4639
	19:30	*he* bowed his head and **gave u** his spirit.	4140
Ac	20: 7	The cloth *was* **folded u** by itself,	1962
	1: 2	until the day *he was* **taken u** to heaven,	377
	1: 9	*he was* **taken u** before their very eyes,	2048
	1:10	They were looking intently **u** into the sky	NIG
	1:15	In those days Peter **stood u** among	482
	1:22	the time when Jesus *was* **taken u** from us.	377
	2:14	Then Peter **stood u** with the Eleven,	2705

Ac	3: 1	One day Peter and John *were* **going** u to	326
	3: 7	by the right hand, *he* **helped** him u,	1586
	3:22	'The Lord your God *will* **raise** u for you	482
	3:26	*When* God **raised** u his servant,	482
	4: 1	the Sadducees **came** u to Peter and John	2392
	5: 6	**wrapped** u his body,	5366
	5:34	**stood** u in the Sanhedrin and ordered that	482
	6:10	but they could not **stand** u against	468
	6:12	So *they* **stirred** u the people and the elders	5167
	7:21	and **brought** him u as her own son.	427
	7:43	*You have* **lifted** u the shrine of Molech	377
	7:55	looked u to heaven and saw the glory	NIG
	8:30	Then Philip **ran** u to the chariot and heard	4708
	8:31	So he invited Philip *to* **come** u and sit	326
	8:39	When *they* **came** u out of the water,	326
	9: 6	"Now **get** u and go into the city,	482
	9: 8	Saul **got** u from the ground,	1586
	9:18	He **got** u and was baptized,	482
	9:34	**Get** u and take care of your mat."	482
	9:34	Immediately Aeneas **got** u.	482
	9:40	he said, "Tabitha, **get** u."	482
	9:40	and seeing Peter *she* **sat** u.	361
	10: 4	*have* **come** u as a memorial offering	326
	10: 9	Peter **went** u on the roof to pray.	326
	10:13	Then a voice told him, "**Get** u, Peter.	482
	10:20	So **get** u and go downstairs.	482
	10:26	But Peter **made** him **get** u.	1586
	10:26	"**Stand** u," he said, "I am only	482
	11: 2	So when Peter **went** u to Jerusalem,	326
	11: 7	I heard a voice telling me, '**Get** u, Peter.	482
	11:10	then *it was* all **pulled** u to heaven again.	413
	11:28	**stood** u and through the Spirit predicted	482
	12: 7	*He* struck Peter on the side and **woke** him u.	1586
	12: 7	"Quick, **get** u!" he said,	482
	13: 1	Manaen (who had been **brought** u with	5343
	13:16	**Standing** u, Paul motioned with his hand	482
	13:33	their children, *by* **raising** u Jesus.	482
	13:50	**stirred** u persecution **against** Paul and	2074
	14: 2	the Jews who refused to believe **stirred** u	2074
	14:10	"**Stand** u on your feet!"	482+3981
	14:10	the **man** **jumped** u and began to walk.	256
	14:20	he **got** u and went back into the city.	482
	15: 2	*to* **go** u to Jerusalem to see the apostles	326
	15: 5	the party of the Pharisees **stood** u and said,	1985
	15: 7	Peter **got** u and addressed them:	482
	15:13	When they finished, James **spoke** u:	646
	16:18	*She* **kept** this u for many days.	4472
	16:27	The jailer **woke** u, and when he saw	1181+2031
	17: 5	so *they* **rounded** u some bad characters	4689
	17:13	agitating the crowds and **stirring** them u.	5429
	17:22	Paul then **stood** u in the meeting of	2705
	18:22	he **went** u and greeted the church and	326
	19:39	If there is anything further *you* **want** to	
		bring u,	2118
	20: 9	from the third story and *was* **picked** u dead.	149
	20:32	which can **build** you u and give you	3868
	21: 5	But when our time **was** u,	1992
	21:12	with Paul not *to* **go** u to Jerusalem.	326
	21:14	*we* **gave** u and said,	2483
	21:15	*we* got ready and **went** u to Jerusalem.	326
	21:27	*They* **stirred** u the whole crowd	5177
	21:33	but **brought** u in this city.	427
	22: 3	but **brought** u in this city.	427
	22:10	" '**Get** u,' the Lord said,	482
	22:16	u, be baptized and wash your sins away,	482
	23: 9	of the law who were Pharisees **stood** u	482
	24: 5	**stirring** u riots among the Jews all over	3075
	24:11	that no more than twelve days ago *I* **went** u	326
	24:12	**stirring** u a crowd in the synagogues	2180+4472
	25: 1	Festus **went** u from Caesarea to Jerusalem,	326
	25: 9	"Are you willing to **go** u to Jerusalem	326
	25:18	*When* his accusers **got** u to speak,	2705
	26:16	'Now **get** u and stand on your feet.	482
	27:20	we finally **gave** u all hope of being saved.	4311
	27:21	Paul **stood** u before them and said:	2705
	27:22	But now I urge you *to* **keep** u your **courage**,	2313
	27:25	So **keep** u your **courage**, men,	2313
	28: 6	The people expected him to **swell** u	4399
	28:13	The next day the south wind **came** u,	2104
Ro	2: 5	*you are* **storing** u wrath against yourself	2564
	8:22	of childbirth right u to the present time.	948
	8:32	but **gave** him u for us all—	4140
	9:17	"I **raised** you u for this very purpose,	1995
	9:17	(that is, *to* **bring** Christ u from the dead?)	343
	13: 9	*are* **summed** u in this one rule:	368
	13:11	for you to **wake** u from your slumber,	1586
	14:13	**make** u *your* **mind** not to put any stumbling	3212
	15: 2	for his good, to **build** him u.	3869
	15:12	"The Root of Jesse will spring u,	NIG
1Co	3:15	If it *is* **burned** u, he will suffer loss;	2876
	4:13	U to this moment we have become	2401
	7:37	and *who has* **made** u his mind not to marry	3212
	8: 1	Knowledge **puffs** u, but love builds up.	5881
	8: 1	Knowledge puffs up, but **builds** u.	3868
	9:12	*we* **put** u with anything rather than hinder	5095
	10: 7	down to eat and drink and **got** u to indulge	482
	10:13	a way out so that you can **stand** u **under** it.	5722
	12:12	though *it is* **made** u of many parts;	2400
	12:14	Now the body is not made u of one part but	NIG
	14:12	try to excel in gifts that **build** u the church.	3869
	15:54	"Death has been **swallowed** u in victory."	2927
	16: 2	in keeping with his income, saving *it* u, so	3869
2Co	2: 1	So *I* **made** u my **mind** that I would	3212
	5: 4	what is mortal *may be* **swallowed** u by life.	2927
	8: 2	and their extreme poverty **welled** u	4355
	10: 5	*that* **sets** *itself* u against the knowledge	2048
	10: 8	for **building** you u rather than pulling you	3869

2Co	11: 1	I hope *you will* **put** u with a little of my	462
	11: 4	*you* **put** u with it easily enough.	462
	11:19	You gladly **put** u with fools since you are	462
	11:20	even **put** u with anyone who enslaves you	462
	12: 2	*who* fourteen years ago *was* **caught** u	773
	12: 4	*was* **caught** u to paradise.	773
	12:14	not have *to* **save** u for their parents,	2564
	13:10	the Lord gave me for **building** you u,	3869
Gal	1:11	not something that **man** made u.	476+2848
	1:17	nor *did I* **go** u to Jerusalem	456
	1:18	I **went** u to Jerusalem to get acquainted	456
	2: 1	Fourteen years later *I* **went** u again	326
	3:23	**locked** u until faith should be revealed.	5168
	5:14	The entire law *is* **summed** u in a single	4444
	6: 9	a harvest *if we do* not **give** u.	1725
Eph	2: 6	And God **raised** us u with Christ	5283
	4:12	so that the body of Christ may be **built** u	3869
	4:15	in all things **grow** u into him who is	889
	4:16	grows and **builds** itself u in love,	3869
	4:29	for **building** others u according	3869
	5: 2	as Christ loved us **and** gave himself u for us	2779
	5:14	This is why it is said: "**Wake** u, O sleeper,	1586
	5:25	the church and **gave** himself u for her	4140
	6: 4	**bring** them u in the training and instruction	1763
	6:16	**take** u the shield of faith,	377
Php	1:17	supposing that they can **stir** u trouble	1586
	2:30	to **make** u for the help you could	405
	3:16	Only let us **live** u to what we have already	5123
Col	1: 5	the hope that is **stored** u for you in heaven	641
	1:24	and I **fill** u in my flesh what is still lacking	499
	2: 7	rooted and **built** u in him,	2224
	2:18	and his unspiritual mind **puffs** him u	5881
1Th	2:16	nor *did we* **put** u on a mask to **cover** u greed	4733
	2:16	**heap** u their sins **to the limit.**	405
	4:17	and are left *will be* **caught** u together	773
	5:11	and **build** each other u,	3868
2Th	2: 4	so that he **sets** *himself* u in God's temple,	2767
1Ti	2: 8	I want men everywhere to **lift** u holy hands	2048
	3:16	*was* **taken** u in glory.	377
	4: 6	**brought** u in the truths of the faith and of	1957
	5:10	such as **bringing** u children,	5452
	6:19	In this way *they* will **lay** u treasure	631
2Ti	4: 3	when *men* will not **put** u with	462
Heb	1:12	You will **roll** them u like a robe;	1813
	5: 7	he **offered** u prayers and petitions	4712
	8: 2	the true tabernacle **set** u by the Lord,	4381
	9: 2	A tabernacle *was* **set** u.	2941
	10:25	*Let us* not **give** u meeting together,	1593
	11:24	By faith Moses, *when he had* **grown** u	1181+3489
	12:15	that no bitter root grows u to cause trouble	539
Jas	4:10	and *he will* **lift** you u.	5738
	5:15	the Lord *will* **raise** him u.	1586
1Pe	2: 2	that by it *you may* **grow** u in your salvation,	889
	2:19	if a **man** bears u **under** the pain	5722
	5: 6	that *he may* **lift** you u in due time.	5738
2Pe	2: 3	*with* stories they have **made** u.	4422
Jude	1: 7	**gave** themselves u to sexual immorality	1745
	1:13	waves of the sea, **foaming** u their shame;	2072
	1:20	**build** yourselves u in your most holy faith	2224
Rev	3: 2	**Wake** u! Strengthen what remains	1181+1213
	3: 3	But if *you* do not **wake** u,	1213
	4: 1	to me like a trumpet said, "**Come** u here,	326
	6:14	The sky receded like a scroll, **rolling** u,	1813
	7: 2	I saw another angel **coming** u from the east,	326
	8: 4	**went** u before God from the angel's hand.	326
	8: 7	A third of the earth *was* **burned** u,	2876
	8: 7	a third of the trees *were* **burned** u,	2876
	8: 7	and all the green grass *was* **burned** u.	2876
	10: 4	"**Seal** u what the seven thunders have said	5381
	11: 6	These men have power to shut u the sky so	NIG
	11: 7	the beast that **comes** u from the Abyss	326
	11:12	from heaven saying to them, "**Come** u	326
	11:12	And they **went** u to heaven in a cloud,	326
	12: 5	And her child *was* **snatched** u to God and	773
	13:14	He ordered them *to* **set** u an image	4472
	16:12	its water *was* **dried** u to prepare the way	3830
	17: 8	and will **come** u out of the Abyss and go	326
	18: 5	for her sins *are* **piled** u to heaven,	3140
	18:21	a mighty angel **picked** u a boulder the size	149
	19: 3	The smoke from her **goes** u for ever	326
	20:13	The sea **gave** u the dead that were in it,	1443
	20:13	and death and Hades **gave** u the dead	1443
	22:10	"*Do* not **seal** u the words of the prophecy	5381

UPBRAID, UPBRAIDED, UPBRAIDETH
(KJV) See DENOUNCED, FINDING FAULT, REBUKED, TAUNTED

UPHARSIN (KJV) See PARSIN

UPHAZ (1)
Jer	10: 9	from Tarshish and gold from U.	233

UPHELD (4) [UPHOLD]
1Sa	25:39	who *has* u my cause against Nabal	8189
2Ch	20:20	the LORD your God and *you will* **be** u;	586
Ps	9: 4	For *you have* u my right and my cause;	6913
Isa	46: 3	whom I *have* u since you were conceived,	6673

UPHOLD (16) [UPHELD, UPHOLDING, UPHOLDS]
Dt	27:26	"Cursed is the man *who does* not u	7756

Dt	32:51	because *you did* not u my **holiness** among	7727
1Sa	24:15	May he consider my cause and u it;	8189
1Ki	8:45	and their plea, and u their cause.	6913
	8:49	and their plea, and u their cause.	6913
	8:59	that he *may* u the cause of his servant and	6913
2Ch	6:35	and their plea, and u their cause.	6913
	6:39	and their pleas, and u their cause.	6913
	9: 8	for Israel and his desire to u them forever,	6641
Ps	41:12	In my integrity *you* u me and set me	9461
	119:117	U me, and I will be delivered;	6184
Isa	34: 8	a year of retribution, to u Zion's **cause.**	8189
	41:10	I *will* u you with my righteous right hand.	9461
	42: 1	"Here is my servant, whom *I* u,	9461
La	3:59	U my cause!	9149
Ro	3:31	Not at all! Rather, *we* u the law.	2705

UPHOLDING (1) [UPHOLD]
Isa	9: 7	and u it with justice and righteousness from	6184

UPHOLDS (6) [UPHOLD]
Ps	37:17	but the LORD u the righteous.	6164
	37:24	for the LORD u him *with* his hand.	6164
	63: 8	your right hand u me.	9461
	140:12	for the poor and u the cause of the needy.	NIH
	145:14	The LORD u all those who fall and lifts	6164
	146: 7	*He* u the cause of the oppressed	6913

UPHOLSTERED (1)
SS	3:10	Its seat was u with purple, its interior	NIH

UPLIFTED (13) [LIFT]
Ex	6: 8	to the land I swore with u hand to give	5951
Nu	14:30	the land I swore with u hand to make your	5951
Ne	9:15	of the land *you had* sworn with u hand	5951
Ps	106:26	swore to them with u hand that he would	5951
Isa	19:16	the u hand that the LORD Almighty raises	9485
Eze	20: 5	the day I chose Israel, I swore with u hand	5951
	20: 5	*With* u hand I said to them, "I am the LORD	5951
	20:15	with u hand I swore to them in the desert	5951
	20:23	with u hand I swore to them in the desert	5951
	20:42	the land I *had* sworn with u hand to give	5951
	36: 7	I swear with u hand that the nations	5951
	44:12	therefore I *have* sworn with u hand	5951
	47:14	Because I swore with u hand to give it	5951

UPON (351) See Index of Articles Etc.

UPPER (45) [UP]
Ge	6:16	make lower, middle and u decks.	8958
Dt	24: 6	not even the u one—as security for a debt,	8207
Jos	15:19	So Caleb gave her the u and lower springs.	6606
	16: 5	in the east to U Beth Horon	6609
Jdg	1:15	Caleb gave her the u and lower springs.	6606
	3:20	the u room *of* his summer palace and said,	6608
	3:23	of the u room behind him and locked them.	6608
	3:24	and found the doors of the u room locked.	6608
	9:53	a woman dropped an u millstone on his	8207
2Sa	11:21	a woman throw an u millstone on him from	8207
1Ki	17:19	to the u room where he was staying,	6608
2Ki	1: 2	through the lattice of his u room in Samaria	6608
	15:35	rebuilt the U Gate of the temple of	6608
	18:17	and stopped at the aqueduct of the U Pool,	6609
	23:12	on the roof near the u room *of* Ahaz,	6608
1Ch	7: 24	who built Lower and U Beth Horon as well	6609
	26:16	and the Shalleketh Gate on the u road fell	6590
	28:11	its buildings, its storerooms, its u **parts,**	6608
2Ch	3: 9	He also overlaid the u **parts** with gold.	6608
	8: 5	He rebuilt U Beth Horon	6609
	23:20	through the U Gate and seated the king on	6609
	27: 3	Jotham rebuilt the U Gate of the temple of	6609
	32:30	It was Hezekiah who blocked the u outlet	6609
Ne	3:25	the tower projecting from the u palace near	6608
Est	9: 1	and the Jews **got the** u **hand**	8948
Ps	104: 3	beams of his u chambers on their waters.	6608
	104:13	the mountains from his u **chambers;**	6608
Isa	7: 3	at the end of the aqueduct of the U Pool,	6609
	11:11	from U Egypt, from Cush, from Elam,	7356
	36: 2	at the aqueduct of the U Pool,	6609
Jer	20: 2	in the stocks at the U Gate of Benjamin at	6609
	22:13	his u rooms by injustice,	6608
	22:14	a great palace with spacious u rooms.'	6608
	36:10	in the u courtyard at the entrance of the	6608
	44: 1	and Memphis—and in U Egypt:	824+7356
	44:15	all the people living in Lower and U Egypt,	7356
Eze	9: 2	from the direction of the u gate,	6608
	29:14	captivity and return them to U Egypt,	824+7356
	30:14	I will lay waste U Egypt,	7356
	42: 5	Now the u rooms were narrower,	6609
	43:17	The u ledge also is square,	NIH
	43:20	on the four corners of the u ledge and all	NIH
	45:19	the u ledge of the altar and on the gateposts	NIH
Mk	14:15	He will show you a large u room,	333
Lk	22:12	He will show you a large u room,	333

UPPERMOST (KJV) See HONOR, MOST IMPORTANT, TOP, TOPMOST

UPRAISED (6) [RISE]
Job	38:15	and their u arm is broken.	8123
Isa	5:25	anger is not turned away, his hand *is* still u.	5742
	9:12	anger is not turned away, his hand *is* still u.	5742

Isa	9:17	anger is not turned away, his hand *is* still **u.**	5742
	9:21	anger is not turned away, his hand *is* still **u.**	5742
	10: 4	anger is not turned away, his hand *is* still **u.**	5742

UPRIGHT (67) [UPRIGHTLY, UPRIGHTNESS, UPRIGHTS]

Ge	37: 7	when suddenly my sheaf rose and **stood u,**	5893
Ex	26:15	"Make **u** frames of acacia wood for	6641
	36:20	They made **u** frames of acacia wood for	6641
Dt	32: 4	God who does no wrong, and just is he.	7404
1Ki	2:32	were better men and more **u** than he.	7404
	3: 6	to you and righteous and **u** *in* heart.	3842
Job	1: 1	This man was blameless and **u;**	3838
	1: 8	he is blameless and **u,**	3838
	2: 3	he is blameless and **u,**	3838
	4: 7	Where were the **u** ever destroyed?	3838
	8: 6	if you are pure and **u,**	3838
	17: 8	**U** men are appalled at this;	3838
	23: 7	an **u** man could present his case before him,	3838
	33: 3	My words come from an **u** heart;	3841
Ps	7:10	who saves the **u** *in* heart.	3838
	11: 2	to shoot from the shadows at the **u** *in* heart.	3838
	11: 7	**u** men will see his face.	3838
	25: 8	Good and **u** is the LORD;	3838
	32:11	sing, all you *who* are **u** *in* heart!	3838
	33: 1	it is fitting for the **u** to praise him.	3838
	36:10	your righteousness to the **u** *in* heart.	3838
	37:14	to slay *those* whose ways are **u.**	3838
	37:37	Consider the blameless, observe the **u;**	3838
	49:14	The **u** will rule over them in the morning;	3838
	64:10	let all the **u** *in* heart praise him!	3838
	92:15	"The LORD is **u;**	3838
	94:15	and all the **u** *in* heart will follow it.	3838
	97:11	the righteous and joy on the **u** *in* heart.	3838
	107:42	The **u** see and rejoice,	3838
	111: 1	with all my heart in the council of the **u** and	3838
	112: 2	the generation of the **u** will be blessed.	3838
	112: 4	Even in darkness light dawns for the **u,**	3838
	119: 7	an **u** heart as I learn your righteous laws.	3841
	125: 4	to *those* who are **u** in heart.	3838
	140:13	and the **u** will live before you.	3838
Pr	2: 7	He holds victory in store for the **u,**	3838
	2:21	For the **u** will live in the land,	3838
	3:32	but takes the **u** into his confidence.	3838
	11: 3	The integrity of the **u** guides them,	3838
	11: 6	The righteousness of the **u** delivers them,	3838
	11:11	the blessing of the **u** a city is exalted,	3838
	12: 6	but the speech of the **u** rescues them.	3838
	14: 2	He whose walk is **u** fears the LORD,	3841
	14: 9	but goodwill is found among the **u.**	3838
	14:11	but the tent of the **u** will flourish.	3838
	15: 8	but the prayer of the **u** pleases him.	3838
	15:19	but the path of the **u** is a highway.	3838
	16:17	The highway of the **u** avoids evil;	3838
	21: 8	but the conduct of the innocent is **u.**	2341
	21:18	and the unfaithful for the **u.**	3838
	21:29	but an **u** man gives thought to his ways.	3838
	28:10	the **u** along an evil path will fall	3838
	29:10	a man of integrity and seek to kill the **u.**	3838
	29:27	the wicked detest the **u.**	2006+3838
Ecc	7:28	I found one [**u**] man among a thousand,	NIH
	7:28	but not one [**u**] woman among them all.	NIH
	7:29	God made mankind **u,** but men have gone	3838
	12:10	and what he wrote was **u** and true.	3841
Isa	26: 7	The path of the righteous is level; O **u** One,	3838
Mic	7: 2	do good to him whose ways are **u?**	3838
	7: 2	not one **u** man remains.	3838
	7: 4	the most **u** worse than a thorn hedge.	3838
Hab	2: 4	"See, he is puffed up; his desires *are* not **u**	3837
Lk	1: 6	Both of them were **u** in the sight of God,	1465
	23:50	member of the Council, a good and **u** man,	1465
Tit	1: 8	who is self-controlled, **u,** holy and	1465
	2:12	**u** and godly *lives* in this present age,	1469

UPRIGHTLY (3) [UPRIGHT]

Ps	58: 1	Do you judge **u** among men?	4797
	75: 2	it is I who judge **u,**	4797
Isa	57: 2	Those who walk **u** enter into peace;	5791

UPRIGHTNESS (5) [UPRIGHT]

1Ki	9: 4	before me in integrity of heart and **u,**	3841
Ps	25:21	May integrity and **u** protect me,	3841
	111: 8	done in faithfulness and **u.**	3838
Isa	26:10	even in a land of **u** they go on doing evil	5791
Mal	2: 6	He walked with me in peace and **u,**	4793

UPRIGHTS (3) [UPRIGHT]

1Ki	7:28	They had side panels attached to **u.**	8918
	7:29	On the panels between the **u** were lions,	8918
	7:29	and on the **u** as well.	8918

UPRISING (1) [RISE]

| Mk | 15: 7 | who had committed murder in the **u.** | 5087 |

UPROAR (15)

1Sa	4: 6	Hearing the **u,** the Philistines asked,	7754+9558
	4:14	"What is the meaning of this **u?"**	2162+7754
Ps	46: 6	Nations *are* in **u,** kingdoms fall;	2159
	74:23	the **u** of your enemies,	8623
Isa	13: 4	Listen, an **u** among the kingdoms,	8623
	17:12	Oh, the **u** of the peoples—	8623
	25: 5	You silence the **u** of foreigners;	8623
	66: 6	Hear that **u** from the city,	8623

Mt	27:24	but that instead an **u** was starting,	2573
Ac	16:20	and *are* **throwing** our city **into an u**	1752
	19:29	Soon the whole city *was* in an **u.**	4398+5180
	20: 1	When the **u** had ended,	2573
	21:31	the whole city of Jerusalem *was* in an **u.**	5177
	21:34	not get at the truth because of the **u,**	2573
	23: 9	There was a great **u,**	3199

UPROOT (14) [UPROOTED, UPROOTS]

1Ki	14:15	He will **u** Israel from this good land	6004
2Ch	7:20	then I will **u** Israel from my land,	6004
Ps	52: 5	he will **u** you from the land of the living.	9245
Ecc	3: 2	a time to plant and a time to **u,**	6827
Jer	1:10	over nations and kingdoms to **u** and tear	6004
	12:14	I will **u** them from their land	6004
	12:14	from their lands and I will **u** the house	6004
	12:15	But after I **u** them, I will again have	6004
	12:17	I will **completely u** and destroy it,"	6004+6004
	24: 6	I will plant them and not **u** them.	6004
	31:28	as I watched over them to **u** and tear down,	6004
	42:10	I will plant you and not **u** you,	6004
	45: 4	and **u** what I have planted,	6004
Mic	5:14	I will **u** from among you your Asherah	6004

UPROOTED (17) [UPROOT]

Dt	28:63	*You* will be **u** from the land	5815
	29:28	and in great wrath the LORD **u** them	6004
Job	31: 8	and *may* my crops be **u.**	9245
	31:12	*it would* have **u** my harvest.	9245
Ps	9: 6	you have **u** their cities;	6004
Pr	10:30	The righteous *will* never be **u,**	4572
	12: 3	but the righteous cannot be **u.**	4572+9247
Jer	18: 7	that a nation or kingdom *is to be* **u,**	6004
	31:40	city will never again be **u** or demolished."	6004
Eze	17: 9	Will it not *be* **u** and stripped of its fruit	5998+9247
	19:12	it was **u** in fury and thrown to the ground.	6004
Da	7: 8	and three of the first horns were **u** before it.	10566
	11: 4	his empire *will* be **u** and given to others.	6004
Am	9:15	*to be* **u** from the land I have given them,"	6004
Zep	2: 4	Ashdod will be emptied and Ekron **u.**	6827
Lk	17: 6	'*Be* **u** and planted in the sea,'	1748
Jude	1:12	autumn trees, without fruit and **u**—	1748

UPROOTS (1) [UPROOT]

| Job | 19:10 | he **u** my hope like a tree. | 5825 |

UPSET (2)

| 2Sa | 11:25 | 'Don't *let* this **u** you; | 928+6524+8317 |
| Lk | 10:41 | "you are worried and **u** about many things, | 2571 |

UPSIDE (2)

| 2Ki | 21:13 | wiping it and turning it **u** down. | 6584+7156 |
| Isa | 29:16 | You **turn** things **u** down, | 2201 |

UPSTAIRS (6) [STAIRS]

Da	6:10	to his **u** room where the windows opened	10547
Ac	1:13	they went **u** to the **room**	5673
	9:37	and placed in an **u** room.	5673
	9:39	he arrived he *was* **taken u** to the room.	343
	20: 8	in the **u** room where we were meeting.	5673
	20:11	*he* went **u** again and broke bread and ate.	326

UPSTREAM (1) [STREAM]

| Jos | 3:16 | water from **u** stopped flowing. | 2025+4200+5087 |

UPWARD (11) [UP]

Ex	25:20	to have their wings spread **u,**	2025+4200+5087
	37: 9	The cherubim had their wings spread **u,**	2025+4200+5087
Job	5: 7	to trouble as surely as sparks fly **u.**	1467
Pr	15:24	path of life leads **u** for the wise	2025+4200+5087
Ecc	3:21	Who knows if the spirit of man rises **u** and	2025+4200+5087
Isa	8:21	become enraged and, looking **u,**	2025+4200+5087
	9:18	so that *it* **rolls u** in a column of smoke.	60
Eze	1:11	wings were spread out **u;**	2025+4200+4946+5087
	10:15	Then the cherubim **rose u.**	8250
	41: 7	rooms widened as one went **u.**	2025+4200+5087
	43:15	and four horns **project u** from the hearth.	2025+4200+5087

UR (5)

Ge	11:28	Haran died in **U** *of* the Chaldeans,	243
	11:31	from **U** *of* the Chaldeans to go to Canaan.	243
	15: 7	of **U** *of* the Chaldeans to give you this land	243
1Ch	11:35	Eliphal son of **U,**	244
Ne	9: 7	and brought him out of **U** *of* the Chaldeans	243

URBANE (KJV) See URBANUS

URBANUS (1)

| Ro | 16: 9 | Greet **U,** our fellow worker in Christ, | 4042 |

URGE (23) [URGED, URGENT, URGENTLY, URGING]

Ru	1:16	"Don't **u** me to leave you or to turn back	7003
Est	4: 8	to **u** her to go into the king's presence	7422
Ac	27:22	But now I **u** you to keep up your courage,	4147
	27:34	Now I **u** you to take some food.	4151

Ro	12: 1	Therefore, *I* **u** you, brothers,	4151
	15:30	I **u** you, brothers, by our Lord Jesus Christ	4151
	16:17	I **u** you, brothers, to watch out	4151
1Co	4:16	Therefore I **u** you to imitate me.	4151
	16:15	the service of the saints. I **u** you, brothers,	4151
2Co	2: 8	I **u** you, therefore, to reaffirm your love	4151
	6: 1	As God's fellow workers we **u** you not	4151
	9: 5	So I thought it necessary *to* **u** the brothers	4151
Eph	4: 1	I **u** you to live a life worthy of the calling	4151
1Th	4: 1	and **u** you in the Lord Jesus to do this more	4151
	4:10	we **u** you, brothers, to do so more and more.	4151
	5:14	And we **u** you, brothers, warn those who	4151
2Th	3:12	and **u** in the Lord Jesus Christ to settle	4151
1Ti	2: 1	I **u,** then, first of all, that requests, prayers,	4151
	6: 2	These are the things *you are* to teach and **u**	4151
Heb	13:19	I particularly **u** you to pray so that I may	4151
	13:22	I **u** you to bear with my word	4151
1Pe	2:11	Dear friends, I **u** you, as aliens and strangers	4151
Jude	1: 3	to write and **u** you to contend for the faith	4151

URGED (27) [URGE]

Ge	19:15	With the coming of dawn, the angels **u** Lot,	237
Ex	12:33	The Egyptians **u** the people to hurry	2616
Jos	15:18	she **u** him to ask her father for a field.	6077
Jdg	1:14	she **u** him to ask her father for a field.	6077
1Sa	24:10	Some **u** me to kill you, but I spared you;	606
2Sa	3:35	and **u** David **to eat** something	1356
	13:25	Although Absalom **u** him, he still refused	7287
	13:27	But Absalom **u** him, so he sent with him	7287
1Ki	21:25	**u** on by Jezebel his wife.	6077
2Ki	4: 8	who **u** him to stay for a meal.	2616
	5:16	even though Naaman **u** him, he refused.	7210
	5:23	He **u** Gehazi to accept them,	7287
2Ch	18: 2	for him and the people with him and **u** him	6077
Jer	36:25	Delaiah and Gemariah **u** the king not	7003
Da	2:18	He **u** them to plead for mercy from the God	NIH
Mt	15:23	So his disciples came to him and **u** him,	2263
Lk	24:29	But *they* **u** him **strongly,** "Stay with us,	4128
Jn	4:31	Meanwhile his disciples **u** him, "Rabbi,	2263
	4:40	*they* **u** him to stay with them,	2263
Ac	9:38	they sent two men to him and **u** him,	4151
	13:43	and **u** them to continue in the grace of God.	4275
	21: 4	Through the Spirit they **u** Paul not to go on	3306
	27:33	Just before dawn Paul **u** them all to eat.	4151
1Co	16:12	I strongly **u** him to go to you with	4151
2Co	8: 6	So we **u** Titus, since he had earlier made	4151
	12:18	I **u** Titus to go to you and I sent	4151
1Ti	1: 3	As I **u** you when I went into Macedonia,	4151

URGENT (3) [URGE]

Nu	22:37	"Did I not **send** you an **u** summons?	8938+8938
1Sa	21: 8	because the king's business was **u."**	5722
Da	3:22	so **u** and the furnace so hot that the flames	10280

URGENTLY (3) [URGE]

Jnh	3: 8	Let everyone call **u** on God.	928+2622
Ac	25: 3	*They* **u** requested Festus, as a favor to	160+4151
2Co	8: 4	they **u** pleaded with us for the privilege of sharing in this service	3552+4155+4498

URGING (3) [URGE]

Ru	1:18	determined to go with her, she stopped **u** her.	1819
1Sa	28:23	But his men joined the woman *in* **u** him,	7287
1Th	2:12	comforting and **u** you to live lives worthy	3458

URI (8)

Ex	31: 2	I have chosen Bezalel son of **U,**	247
	35:30	the LORD has chosen Bezalel son of **U,**	247
	38:22	(Bezalel son of **U,** the son of Hur,	247
1Ki	4:19	Geber son of **U**—in Gilead	788
1Ch	2:20	Hur was the father of **U,**	247
	2:20	and **U** the father of Bezalel.	247
2Ch	1: 5	But the bronze altar that Bezalel son of **U,**	247
Ezr	10:24	Shallum, Telem and **U.**	247

URIAH (33) [URIAH'S]

2Sa	11: 3	the daughter of Eliam and the wife of **U**	249
	11: 6	"Send me **U** the Hittite."	249
	11: 7	When **U** came to him,	249
	11: 8	Then David said to **U,** "Go down to your	249
	11: 8	So **U** left the palace,	249
	11: 9	But **U** slept at the entrance to the palace	249
	11:10	David was told, "**U** did not go home,"	249
	11:11	**U** said to David, "The ark and Israel	249
	11:12	So **U** remained in Jerusalem that day and	249
	11:13	the evening **U** went out to sleep on his mat	NIH
	11:14	a letter to Joab and sent it with **U.**	249
	11:15	"Put **U** in the front line where	249
	11:16	he put **U** at a place where he knew	249
	11:17	moreover, **U** the Hittite died.	249
	11:21	'Also, your servant **U** the Hittite is dead.'"	249
	11:24	your servant **U** the Hittite is dead."	249
	12: 9	You struck down **U** the Hittite with	249
	12:10	the wife of **U** the Hittite to be your own.'	249
	23:39	**U** the Hittite.	249
1Ki	15: 5	except in the case of **U** the Hittite.	249
2Ki	16:10	He saw an altar in Damascus and sent to **U**	249
	16:11	So **U** the priest built an altar in accordance	249
	16:15	King Ahaz then gave these orders to **U**	249
	16:16	And **U** the priest did just as King Ahaz	249
1Ch	11:41	**U** the Hittite, Zabad son of Ahlai,	249
Ezr	8:33	into the hands of Meremoth son of **U,**	249
Ne	3: 4	Meremoth son of **U,** the son of Hakkoz,	249

Ne	3:21	Next to him, Meremoth son of U,	249
	8: 4	Shema, Anaiah, U, Hilkiah and Maaseiah;	249
Isa	8: 2	in U the priest and Zechariah son	249
Jer	26:20	(Now U son of Shemaiah from Kiriath	250
	26:21	But U heard of it and fled in fear to Egypt.	250
	26:23	They brought U out of Egypt and took him	250

URIAH'S (3) [URIAH]

2Sa	11:26	U wife heard that her husband was dead,	249
	12:15	the child that U wife had borne to David,	249
Mt	1: 6	Solomon, whose mother had been U wife,	4043

URIAS, URIJAH (KJV) See URIAH

URIEL (4)

1Ch	6:24	U his son, Uzziah his son	248
	15: 5	U the leader and 120 relatives;	248
	15:11	and U, Asaiah, Joel, Shemaiah,	248
2Ch	13: 2	a daughter of U of Gibeah.	248

URIM (7)

Ex	28:30	the U and the Thummim in the breastpiece.	242
Lev	8: 8	the U and Thummim in the breastpiece.	242
Nu	27:21	by inquiring of the U before the LORD.	242
Dt	33: 8	and U belong to the man you favored.	242
1Sa	28: 6	not answer him by dreams or U or prophets.	242
Ezr	2:63	priest ministering with the U and Thummim.	242
Ne	7:65	priest ministering with the U and Thummim.	242

URINE (2)

2Ki	18:27	eat their own filth and drink their own u?"	8875
Isa	36:12	eat their own filth and drink their own u?"	8875

US (1431) [WE] See Index of Articles Etc.

USE (86) [USED, USEFUL, USELESS, USES, USING]

Ex	5:12	over Egypt to gather stubble to u for straw.	NIH
	10:26	We have to u some of them in worshiping	4374
	10:26	not know what we are to u to worship	AIT
	20:25	for you will defile it if you u a tool on it.	5677
	26: 6	and u them to fasten the curtains together	928
	28: 5	Have them u gold, and blue,	4374
	30:16	from the Israelites and u it for the service	5989
	30:26	Then u it to anoint the Tent of Meeting,	928
Lev	11:32	article, whatever its u, will be unclean,	4856+6913
	13:51	whatever its u, it is a destructive mildew;	6913
	19:35	" 'Do not u dishonest standards	6913
	19:36	U honest scales and honest weights,	2118+4200
Nu	3:26	and everything related to their u.	6275
	3:31	and everything related to their u.	6275
	3:36	and everything related to their u,	6275
	4:32	and everything related to their u.	6275
	8:12	u the one for a sin offering to the LORD	6913
	10: 2	and u them for calling the community	6913
	19: 9	be kept by the Israelite community for u in	5466
Dt	14:26	U the silver to buy whatever you like:	AIT
	20:14	And you may u the plunder	430
	20:20	and u them to build siege works until	AIT
	27: 5	Do not u any iron tool upon them.	5677
	28:40	but you will not u the oil,	6057
Jdg	2:22	I will u them to test Israel	928
	18:31	to u the idols Micah had made,	8492
	19:24	and you can u them and do	6700
1Sa	8:16	donkeys he will take for his own u.	4856+6913
2Sa	5: 8	the Jebusites will have to u the water shaft	928
	14: 2	and don't u any cosmetic lotions.	6057
1Ki	21: 2	"Let me have your vineyard to u for	2118
2Ki	16:15	But I will u the bronze altar	2118+4200
	23:10	so no one could u it to sacrifice his son	AIT
1Ch	5:18	who could u a bow,	2005
	28:15	according to the u of each lampstand;	6275
2Ch	26:15	by skillful men for u on the towers and on	2118
Job	19: 5	above me and u my humiliation against me,	3519S
	30: 2	Of what u was the strength of their hands	4200+4537
Ps	50:19	You u your mouth for evil	8938
	102: 8	against me u my name as a curse.	928+8678
	125: 3	righteous might u their hands to do evil.	8938
Pr	17:16	Of what u is money in the hand of a fool,	2296+4200+4537
	24:28	or u your lips to deceive.	928
Isa	7:20	that day the Lord will u a razor hired from	928
Jer	2:22	with soda and u an abundance of soap,	8049
	2:25	But you said, 'It's no u!	3286
	18:12	But they will reply, 'It's no u.	3286
	23:10	an evil course and u their power unjustly.	NIH
	29:22	In Babylon will u this curse:	4374
	31:23	in its towns will once again u these words:	606
Eze	4: 9	in a storage jar and u them to make bread	6913
	5: 1	a sharp sword and u it as a barber's razor	4374
	23:43	let them u her as a prostitute,	2388+9373
	39: 9	and u the weapons for fuel	1277
	39: 9	seven years they will u them for fuel.	836+1277
	39:10	they will u the weapons for fuel.	836+1277
	45:10	You are to u accurate scales,	2118
	45:16	in this special gift u to u of the prince	4200
	48:15	will be for the common u of the city,	2687
Am	2: 7	Father and son u the same girl and	448+2143
	6: 6	by the bowlful and u the finest lotions,	5417
Mic	6:15	you will press olives but not u the oil	6057
Mt	7: 2	and with the measure you u,	3582S

Mt	27: 7	to u the money to buy the potter's field as	NIG
Mk	4:24	"With the measure you u,	3582S
	4:30	or what parable shall we u to describe it?"	5502
Lk	6:38	For with the measure you u,	3582S
	13: 7	Why should it u up the soil?'	2934
	16: 9	u worldly wealth to gain friends	NIG
Jn	16:25	no longer u this kind of language	3281
Ac	5:26	They did not u force,	1040+3552
Ro	9:21	noble purposes and some for common u?	NIG
	12: 6	let him u it in proportion to his faith.	NIG
1Co	7:31	those who u the things of the world,	5968
	9:12	But we did not u this right.	5968
	9:18	so not make u of my rights in preaching it.	2974
2Co	4: 2	we do not u deception,	1877+4111+4344
	13:10	not have to be harsh in my u of authority—	5968
Gal	5:13	But do not u your freedom to indulge	NIG
	6:11	See what large letters I u as I write to you	NIG
Col	2:22	These are all destined to perish with u,	712
1Ti	5:23	and u a little wine because of your stomach	5968
Heb	5:14	who by constant u have trained themselves	2011
1Pe	2:16	do not u your freedom as a cover-up for evil	AIT
	4:10	Each one should u whatever gift he has received to serve others,	NIG
2Jn	1:12	but I do not want to u paper and ink.	1328

USED (115) [USE]

Ge	11: 3	They u brick instead of stone,	2118
	28:19	the city u to be called Luz.	2021+4200+8037
	31:15	but he has u up what was paid for us.	430+430
	40:13	just as you u to do when you were	8037
	41:36	to be u during the seven years of famine	NIH
	47:15	Our money is u up."	699
Ex	1:14	the Egyptians u them ruthlessly.	6268
	25:27	to the rim to hold the poles u in carrying	AIT
	25:39	of pure gold is to be u for the lampstand	6913
	27:19	All the other articles u in the service of	AIT
	30: 4	to hold the poles u to carry it.	928
	33: 7	Now Moses u to take a tent and pitch it	AIT
	36:13	and u them to fasten the two sets	928
	37:14	to the rim to hold the poles u in carrying	NIH
	37:27	to hold the poles u to carry it.	928
	38:21	These are the amounts of the materials u	NIH
	38:24	of the gold from the wave offering u for all	6913
	38:27	The 100 talents of silver were u to cast	2118
	38:28	They u the 1,775 shekels to make the hooks	6913
	38:30	They u it to make the bases for the entrance	928
	40:31	and Moses and Aaron and his sons u it	4946
Lev	7:24	or torn by wild animals may be u	6913
	16:10	to be u for making atonement by sending it	6584
	18: 3	as they do in Egypt, where you u to live,	AIT
Nu	3:31	of the sanctuary u in ministering,	928
	4: 9	and all its jars for the oil u to supply it.	928
	4:12	to take all the articles u for ministering in	928
	4:14	the utensils u for ministering at the altar,	928
	4:26	and all the equipment u in its service.	AIT
	6: 5	of separation no razor may be u on his head.	6296
	7: 5	that they may be u in the work at the Tent	6268
	7:87	Twelve male goats were u for	4200
Dt	2:10	(The Emites u to live there—	4200+7156
	2:12	Horites u to live in Seir,	4200+7156
	2:20	Rephaites, u to live there;	4200+7156
	3:13	u to be known as a land of the Rephaites.	AIT
Jos	8:31	on which no iron tool had been u.	5677
	14:15	(Hebron u to be called Kiriath Arba	4200+7156
Jdg	9: 4	and Abimelech u it to hire reckless	928
	13: 5	No razor may be u on his head,	6590
	16:11	new ropes that have never been u,	4856+6913
	16:17	"No razor has ever been u on my head,"	6590
	18:29	the city u to be called Laish.	2021+4200+8037
1Sa	1:11	and no razor will ever be u on his head."	6590
	9: 9	prophet of today u to be called a seer.)	4200+7156
	17:39	because he was not u to them.	5814
	17:39	"because I am not u to them."	5814
2Sa	14:26	he u to cut his hair from time to time	2118
	15:32	where people u to worship God,	AIT
	20:18	continued, "Long ago they u to say,	1819+1819
1Ki	6: 7	only blocks dressed at the quarry were u,	1215
	10:12	The king u the almugwood to make	6913
	17:14	be u up and the jug of oil will not run dry	3983
	17:16	For the jar of flour was not u up and the jug	3983
2Ki	3:11	He u to pour water on the hands	AIT
	10:27	and people have u it for a latrine to this day.	8492
	12: 5	be u to repair whatever damage is found	AIT
	12:14	who u it to repair the temple.	928
	13:20	Now Moabite raiders u to enter	AIT
	21:13	the measuring line u against Samaria and	AIT
	21:13	and the plumb line u against the house	AIT
	25:14	the bronze articles u in the temple service.	928
1Ch	9:28	of them were in charge of the articles u	AIT
	18: 8	which Solomon u to make the bronze Sea,	928
	23:26	the tabernacle or any of the articles u in	4200
	28:13	for all the articles to be u in its service.	AIT
	28:14	the gold articles u for various kinds	AIT
	28:14	of silver for all the silver articles to be u	AIT
2Ch	3: 6	And the gold he u was gold of Parvaim.	NIH
	4: 6	In them the things to be u for	AIT
	4: 6	but the Sea was to be u by the priests	4200
	7: 6	for praising the LORD and which were u	928+3338
	9:11	The king u the algumwood to make	6913
	24: 7	of God and had u even its sacred objects for	6913
Ne	13: 5	with a large room formerly u to store	2118
Job	1: 4	His sons u to take turns holding feasts	AIT
Ps	42: 4	how I u to go with the multitude,	AIT
Ecc	8:10	those who u to come and go from	AIT
Isa	1:21	righteous u to dwell in her—	AIT
	9: 5	Every warrior's boot u in battle	NIH

Isa	44:19	"Half of it I u for fuel;	836+1198+8596
Jer	23:38	You u the words, 'This is the oracle of	606
	33: 4	be u against the siege ramps and the sword	NIH
	52:18	the bronze articles u in the temple service.	928
	52:19	and bowls u for drink offerings—	4984
Eze	7:20	and u it to make their detestable idols	928
	16:15	in your beauty and u your fame to become	6584
	19:14	This is a lament and is to be u as a lament."	4200
	45:15	These will be u for the grain offerings,	NIH
Da	10: 3	and I u no lotions at all until	6057+6057
Hos	2: 8	silver and gold—which they u for Baal.	6913
	12:13	The LORD u a prophet to bring Israel up	928
Am	9:11	and build it as it u to be,	3427+6409
Mic	1: 7	as wages of prostitutes they will again be u.	8740
Zec	9:15	be full like a bowl u for sprinkling	928
Mt	16:12	not telling them to guard against the yeast u	NIG
	22:19	Show me the coin u for paying the tax."	NIG
	27:10	and they u them to buy the potter's field,	NIG
Jn	2: 6	kind u by the Jews for ceremonial washing,	NIG
	5: 3	a great number of disabled people u to lie—	AIT
	9: 8	the same man who u to sit and beg?"	AIT
	10: 6	Jesus u this figure of speech,	3306
	12: 6	u to help himself to what was put into it.	AIT
Ac	3:10	as the same man who u to sit begging at	AIT
	5:12	And all the believers u to meet together	AIT
Ro	6:17	though you u to be slaves to sin,	AIT
	6:19	as you u to offer the parts of your body	AIT
1Co	9:15	But I have not u any of these rights.	5968
Gal	2:12	he u to eat with the Gentiles.	AIT
Eph	2: 2	in which you u to live when you followed	4537
Col	3: 7	You u to walk in these ways,	4537
1Th	2: 5	You know we never u flattery,	1181
2Th	2: 5	with you I u to tell you these things?	AIT
Heb	9:21	both the tabernacle and everything u	NIG
1Pe	3: 5	u to make themselves beautiful.	AIT

USEFUL (9) [USE]

Eze	15: 3	wood taken from it to make anything u?	4856
	15: 4	is it then u for anything?	7503
	15: 5	not u for anything when it was whole,	6913
	15: 5	into something u when the fire has burned	4856
Eph	4:28	doing something u with his own hands,	19
2Ti	2:21	u to the Master and prepared to do any good	2378
	3:16	All Scripture is God-breathed and is u	6068
Phm	1:11	he has become u both to you and to me.	2378
Heb	6: 7	on it and that produces a crop u to those	2310

USELESS (17) [USE]

1Sa	12:21	Do not turn away after u idols.	9332
	12:21	nor can they rescue you, because they are u.	9332
	25:21	David had just said, "It's been u	2021+4200+9214
Job	15: 3	Would he argue with u words,	4202+6122
Pr	1:17	How u to spread a net in full view of all	2855
Isa	30: 5	shame because of a people u to them,	3603+4202
	30: 7	Egypt, whose help is utterly u.	2039+2256+8198
	59: 6	Their cobwebs are u for clothing;	4202
Jer	13: 7	now it was ruined and completely u.	4202+7503
	13:10	like this belt—completely u!	4202+7503
Mal	1:10	that you would not light u fires on my altar!	2855
1Co	15:14	our preaching is u and so is your faith.	3031
1Th	3: 5	and our efforts might have been u.	3031
Tit	3: 9	because these are unprofitable and u.	3469
Phm	1:11	Formerly he was u to you, but now	947
Heb	7:18	is set aside because it was weak and u	543
Jas	2:20	evidence that faith without deeds is u?	734

USES (8) [USE]

Ge	44: 5	from and also u for divination?	5727+5727
1Sa	23:23	the hiding places he u and come back to me	2461S
2Sa	23: 7	Whoever touches thorns u a tool of iron or	4848
Pr	17:27	man of knowledge u words with restraint,	3104
Isa	10:15	or the saw boast against him who u it?	5677
Eze	22: 6	of Israel who are in you u his power	4202
Hos	12: 7	The merchant u dishonest scales;	928+3338
1Ti	1: 8	that the law is good if one u it properly.	5968

USHERS (1)

Pr	18:16	for the giver and u him into the presence of	5697

USING (18) [USE]

Ge	42:23	since he was u an interpreter.	1068
Lev	24: 5	u two-tenths of an ephah for each loaf.	2118
Jdg	6:26	U the wood of the Asherah pole	928
1Sa	14:13	Jonathan climbed up, u his hands and feet,	6584
1Ki	15:22	and timber Baasha had been u there,	1215S
1Ch	25: 3	of their father Jeduthun, who prophesied, u	928
2Ch	3: 3	and twenty cubits wide (u the cubit of	928
	16: 6	the stones and timber Baasha had been u.	1215S
Isa	22: 3	they have been captured without u	AIT
Jer	21: 1	that are in your hands, which you are u	928
Eze	4:12	u human excrement for fuel."	928
Mt	13:34	he did not say anything to them without u	NIG
Mk	4:34	He did not say anything to them without u	NIG
Jn	8: 6	They were u this question as a trap,	NIG
Ac	7:25	that God was u him to rescue them,	1328+5931
Ro	3: 5	(I am u a human argument.)	3306
1Co	3:12	If any man builds on this foundation u gold,	NIG
Rev	21:17	which the angel was u.	NIG

USUAL (7) [USUALLY]

1Sa	3: 2	was lying down in his u place.	NIH
	17:23	from his lines and shouted his u defiance,	3869
	21: 5	as u whenever I set out.	3869+8997+9453

2Sa	7:19	Is this your **u way of dealing** *with* man,	9368
Da	3:19	furnace heated seven times hotter than **u**	10255
Lk	22:39	Jesus went out **as u** to the	1621+2848+3836
Ac	14: 1	At Iconium Paul and Barnabas went **as u**	
		into the Jewish synagogue.	899+2848+3836

USUALLY (5) [USUAL]

Nu	16:29	experience only **what u happens** *to* men,	7213
1Sa	18:10	David was playing the harp, **as he u** did.	
			928+3427+3427+3869
	23:22	Find out where David **u goes**	AIT
Eze	33:31	My people come to you, **as they u** do,	3869
Mk	15: 8	asked Pilate to do for them what he **u** did.	NIG

USURER (KJV) See MONEYLENDER

USURP [AUTHORITY] (KJV) See HAVE [AUTHORITY]

USURY (8)

Ne	5: 7	"You are exacting **u** from your own	5391
	5:10	But let the **exacting of u** stop!	5391
	5:11	and also *the* **u** you *are* **charging** them—	5957
Ps	15: 5	who lends his money without **u** and does	5968
Eze	18: 8	not lend at **u** or take excessive interest.	5968
	18:13	He lends at **u** and takes excessive interest.	5968
	18:17	and takes no **u** or excessive interest,	5968
	22:12	you take **u** and excessive interest	5968

UTENSILS (13)

Ex	27: 3	Make all its **u** of bronze—	3998
	30:28	the altar of burnt offering and all its **u,**	3998
	31: 9	of burnt offering and all its **u;**	3998
	35:16	its poles and all its **u;**	3998
	38: 3	They made all its **u** *of* bronze—	3998
	38:30	with its bronze grating and all its **u,**	3998
	39:39	its poles and all its **u;**	3998
	40:10	the altar of burnt offering and all its **u;**	3998
Lev	8:11	- and all its **u** and the basin with its stand,	3998
Nu	4:14	to place on it all the **u** used for ministering	3998
	7: 1	and consecrated the altar and all its **u.**	3998
2Ch	29:18	the altar of burnt offering with all its **u,**	3998
Eze	40:42	On them were placed the **u** for slaughtering	3998

UTHAI (2)

1Ch	9: 4	**U** son of Ammihud,	6433
Ezr	8:14	**U** and Zaccur, and with them 70 men.	6433

UTMOST (5)

2Ki	19:23	the **u heights** *of* Lebanon.	3752
Job	34:36	to the **u** for answering like a wicked man!	5905
Ps	48: 2	Like the **u heights** *of* Zaphon is Mount Zion	3752
Isa	14:13	on the **u heights** *of* the sacred mountain.	3752
	37:24	the **u heights** *of* Lebanon.	3752

UTTER (19) [UTTERANCE, UTTERED, UTTERING, UTTERLY, UTTERS]

Nu	30: 6	after she makes a vow or after her lips **u**	NIH
Dt	23:23	Whatever your lips **u** you must be sure	4604
Jdg	17: 2	and about which I heard you **u a curse**—	457
2Sa	12:14	*you have* **made** the enemies of the LORD	
		show u contempt,	5540+5540
Job	26: 4	Who has helped *you* **u** these words?	5583
	27: 4	and my tongue *will* **u** no deceit.	2047
Ps	31:11	I am the **u** contempt of my neighbors;	4394
	59:12	For the curses and lies *they* **u,**	6218
	78: 2	I will **u** hidden things,	5580
	115: 7	nor *can they* **u a sound** with their throats.	2047
Pr	5:14	I have come to the brink of **u** ruin in	3972
Ecc	5: 2	do not be hasty in your heart to **u** anything	3655
Isa	8:22	and they will be thrust into **u darkness.**	696
	42:17	will be turned back in **u shame.**	1017+1425
Jer	15:19	if *you* **u** worthy, not worthless, words,	3655
Eze	13: 9	and **u** lying **divinations.**	7876
	14: 9	if the prophet is enticed *to* **u** a prophecy,	1819
Mt	13:35	*I will* **u** things hidden since the creation	2243
Rev	13: 5	a mouth *to* **u** proud words and blasphemies	3281

UTTERANCE (1) [UTTER]

Ps	49: 3	the **u** *from* my heart will give understanding	2050

UTTERED (11) [UTTER]

Nu	23: 7	Then Balaam **u** his oracle:	606+2256+5951
	23:18	Then *he* **u** his oracle:	606+2256+5951
	24: 3	and *he* **u** his oracle:	606+2256+5951
	24:15	Then *he* **u** his oracle:	606+2256+5951
	24:20	Then Balaam saw Amalek and **u** his oracle:	
			606+2256+5951
	24:21	Then he saw the Kenites and **u** his oracle:	
			606+2256+5951
	24:23	Then *he* **u** his oracle:	606+2256+5951
Jos	10:21	and no one **u a word** against the Israelites.	
			906+3076+4383
Ps	89:34	or alter **what** my lips have **u.**	4604
Isa	45:23	my mouth *has* **u** in all integrity a word	3655+4946
Eze	13: 7	and **u** lying divinations when you say,	606

UTTERING (1) [UTTER]

Isa	59:13	**u** lies our hearts have conceived.	2047

UTTERLY (20) [UTTER]

Dt	7:26	**U abhor** and detest it,	9210+9210
	31:29	**sure to become u corrupt**	8845+8845
Ps	38: 8	I am feeble and **u** crushed;	4394+6330
	119: 8	do not **u** forsake me.	4394+6330
Ecc	1: 2	says the Teacher. **"U meaningless!**	2039+2039
SS	8: 7	it *would be* **u** scorned.	996+996
Isa	6:12	and the land is **u** forsaken.	8041
	30: 7	whose help is **u useless.**	2039+2256+8198
	41:24	and your works are **u** worthless;	4946
	60:12	it *will be* **u ruined.**	2990+2990
Jer	5:11	house of Judah *have been* **u unfaithful**	953+953
La	5:22	unless *you have* **u rejected** us	4415+4415
Eze	8: 6	the **u** detestable things the house of Israel	1524
	20:13	and they **u** desecrated my Sabbaths.	4394
Ob	1: 2	you will be **u** despised.	4394
Mic	2: 4	'*We are* **u ruined;**	8720+8720
Hab	1: 5	and watch—and *be* **u amazed.**	9449+9449
Zep	2:13	leaving Nineveh **u desolate** and dry as	9039
Ac	2: 7	**U amazed,** they asked:	2014+2513
Ro	7:13	commandment sin might become **u** sinful.	5651

UTTERMOST (KJV) See COMPLETELY, DISTANT, EDGE, EDGES, EXTREME, FAR, FARTHEST, MOUTH, OUTER, SOUTHERNMOST, TIP, WESTERN

UTTERS (2) [UTTER]

Ps	37:30	The mouth of the righteous man **u** wisdom,	2047
1Co	14: 2	he **u** mysteries with his spirit.	3281

UZ (8)

Ge	10:23	**U,** Hul, Gether and Meshech.	6419
	22:21	**U** the firstborn, Buz his brother, Kemuel	6419
	36:28	The sons of Dishan: **U** and Aran.	6419
1Ch	1:17	**U,** Hul, Gether and Meshech.	6419
	1:42	The sons of Dishan: **U** and Aran.	6419
Job	1: 1	In the land of **U** there lived a man	6420
Jer	25:20	all the kings of **U;**	824+6420
La	4:21	you who live in the land of **U.**	6420

UZAI (1)

Ne	3:25	and Palal son of **U** worked opposite	206

UZAL (3)

Ge	10:27	Hadoram, **U,** Diklah,	207
1Ch	1:21	Hadoram, **U,** Diklah,	207
Eze	27:19	from **U** bought your merchandise;	207

UZZA (5)

2Ki	21:18	in his palace garden, the garden of **U.**	6438
	21:26	in his grave in the garden of **U.**	6438
1Ch	8: 7	and who was the father of **U** and Ahihud.	6438
Ezr	2:49	**U,** Paseah, Besai,	6438
Ne	7:51	Gazzam, **U,** Paseah,	6438

UZZAH (9)

2Sa	6: 3	**U** and Ahio, sons of Abinadab,	6438
	6: 6	**U** reached out and took hold of the ark,	6438
	6: 7	against **U** because of his irreverent act;	6446
	6: 8	LORD's wrath had broken out against **U,**	6446
1Ch	6:29	Libni his son, Shimei his son, **U** his son,	6446
	13: 7	with **U** and Ahio guiding it.	6438
	13: 9	**U** reached out his hand to steady the ark,	6438
	13:10	The LORD's anger burned against **U,**	6438
	13:11	LORD's wrath had broken out against **U,**	6438

UZZEN SHEERAH (1)

1Ch	7:24	and Upper Beth Horon as well as **U.**	267

UZZI (12)

1Ch	6: 5	Bukki the father of **U,**	6454
	6: 6	**U** the father of Zerahiah,	6454
	6:51	Bukki his son, **U** his son, Zerahiah his son,	6454
	7: 2	The sons of Tola: **U,** Rephaiah, Jeriel,	6454
	7: 3	The son of **U:** Izrahiah.	6454
	7: 7	The sons of Bela: Ezbon, **U,** Uzziel,	6454
	9: 8	Elah son of **U,** the son of Micri;	6454
Ezr	7: 4	the son of **U,** the son of Bukki,	6454
Ne	11:22	of the Levites in Jerusalem was **U** son	6454
	11:22	**U** was one of Asaph's descendants,	NIH
	12:19	of Joiarib's, Mattenai; of Jedaiah's, **U;**	6454
	12:42	**U,** Jehohanan, Malkijah, Elam and Ezer.	6454

UZZIA (1)

1Ch	11:44	**U** the Ashterathite, Shama and Jeiel	6455

UZZIAH (28) [AZARIAH, UZZIAH'S]

2Ki	15:13	in the thirty-ninth year of **U** king of Judah,	6459
	15:30	in the twentieth year of Jotham son of **U.**	6459
	15:32	Jotham son of **U** king of Judah began	6460
	15:34	just as his father **U** had done.	6460
1Ch	6:24	Uriel his son, **U** his son and Shaul his son.	6459
	27:25	of **U** was in charge of the storehouses in	6460
2Ch	26: 1	Then all the people of Judah took **U,**	6460
	26: 3	**U** was sixteen years old when	6460
	26: 8	The Ammonites brought tribute to **U,**	6460
	26: 9	**U** built towers in Jerusalem at	6460
	26:11	**U** had a well-trained army,	6460
	26:14	**U** provided shields, spears, helmets,	6460
	26:16	But after **U** became powerful, his pride led	2257S
	26:18	**U,** to burn incense to the LORD.	6460
	26:19	**U,** who had a censer in his hand ready	6460
	26:21	King **U** had leprosy until the day he died.	6460
	26:23	**U** rested with his fathers and was buried	6460
	27: 2	just as his father **U** had done,	6459
Ezr	10:21	Maaseiah, Elijah, Shemaiah, Jehiel and **U.**	6459
Ne	11: 4	Athaiah son of **U,** the son of Zechariah,	6459
Isa	1: 1	of Amoz saw during the reigns of **U,**	6460
	6: 1	In the year that King **U** died,	6460
	7: 1	When Ahaz son of Jotham, the son of **U,**	6460
Hos	1: 1	of **U,** Jotham, Ahaz and Hezekiah, kings	6459
Am	1: 1	the earthquake, when **U** was king of Judah	6459
Zec	14: 5	from the earthquake in the days of **U** king	6459
Mt	1: 8	Jehoram the father of **U,**	3852
	1: 9	**U** the father of Jotham,	3852

UZZIAH'S (1) [UZZIAH]

2Ch	26:22	The other events of **U** reign,	6460

UZZIEL (16) [UZZIELITES]

Ex	6:18	Kohath were Amram, Izhar, Hebron and **U.**	6457
	6:22	The sons of **U** were Mishael,	6457
Lev	10: 4	sons of Aaron's uncle **U,** and said to them,	6457
Nu	3:19	Amram, Izhar, Hebron and **U.**	6457
	3:30	The Kohathite clans was Elizaphan son of **U.**	6457
1Ch	4:42	Neariah, Rephaiah and **U,** the sons of Ishi.	6457
	6: 2	Amram, Izhar, Hebron and **U.**	6457
	6:18	Amram, Izhar, Hebron and **U.**	6457
	7: 7	The sons of Bela: Ezbon, Uzzi, **U,**	6457
	15:10	from the descendants of **U,**	6457
	23:12	Amram, Izhar, Hebron and **U**—four in all.	6457
	23:20	The sons of **U:** Micah the first	6457
	24:24	The son of **U:** Micah;	6457
	25: 4	Bukkiah, Mattaniah, **U,**	6457
2Ch	29:14	of Jeduthun, Shemaiah and **U.**	6457
Ne	3: 8	**U** son of Harhaiah, one of the goldsmiths,	6457

UZZIELITES (2) [UZZIEL]

Nu	3:27	Izharites, Hebronites and **U;**	6458
1Ch	26:23	the Izharites, the Hebronites and the **U:**	6458

V

VAGABOND, VAGABONDS (KJV) See WANDERER, WANDERING BEGGARS

VAIL, VAILS (KJV) See VEIL, VEILS

VAIN (33)

Lev	26:16	You will plant seed in **v,**	4200+8198
	26:20	Your strength will be spent in **v,**	4200+8198S
Job	9: 9	for daylight in **v** and not see the first rays	401
	9:29	why should I struggle in **v?**	2039
	24: 1	Why must those who know him look in **v**	4202
	39:16	she cares not that her labor was in **v,**	4200+8198
Ps	2: 1	and the peoples plot in **v?**	8198
	33:17	A horse is a **v hope** for deliverance	9214
	39: 6	He bustles about, but only in **v;**	2039
	73:13	Surely in **v** have I kept my heart pure;	8198
	73:13	in **v** have I washed my hands in innocence.	NIH
	119:118	for their deceitfulness is in **v.**	9214
	127: 1	Unless the LORD builds the house, its	
		builders labor in **v.**	8736
	127: 1	the watchmen stand guard in **v.**	8736
	127: 2	In **v** you rise early and stay up late,	8736
Isa	45:19	to Jacob's descendants, 'Seek me in **v.**'	9332
	49: 4	I have spent my strength in **v** and	2039
	65:23	not toil in **v** or bear children doomed	4200+8198
Jer	2:30	"In **v** I punished your people;	2021+4200+8736
	4:30	You adorn yourself in **v.**	2021+4200+8736
	6:29	but the refining goes on in **v;**	2021+4200+8736
	46:11	But you multiply remedies in **v;**	2021+4200+8736
La	4:17	our eyes failed, looking in **v** for help;	2039
Eze	6:10	not threaten in **v** to bring this calamity	448+2855
Zec	10: 2	they give comfort in **v.**	2039
Mt	15: 9	They worship me in **v;**	3472
Mk	7: 7	They worship me in **v;**	3472
Ac	4:25	the nations rage and the peoples plot in **v?**	3031
1Co	15: 2	Otherwise, you have believed in **v.**	1632
	15:58	that your labor in the Lord is not in **v.**	3031
2Co	6: 1	not to receive God's grace in **v.**	3031
Gal	2: 2	that I was running or had run my race in **v.**	3031
Php	2: 3	of selfish ambition or **v conceit,**	3029

VAIZATHA (1)

Est	9: 9	Parmashta, Arisai, Aridai and **V,**	2262

VALE (KJV) See FOOTHILLS, VALLEY

VALIANT (11) [VALIANTLY]

Jdg	20:44	all of them **v fighters.**	408+2657
	20:46	all of them **v fighters.**	408+2657
1Sa	10:26	by **v** *men* whose hearts God had touched.	2657
	31:12	all their **v** men journeyed through the night	2657
2Sa	23:20	was a **v fighter** from Kabzeel,	408+1201+2657
2Ki	5: 1	He was a **v soldier,** but he had leprosy.	1475+2657
1Ch	10:12	all their **v** men went and took the bodies	2657
	11:22	was a **v fighter** from Kabzeel,	408+1201+2657
2Ch	17:17	From Benjamin: Eliada, a **v soldier,**	1475+2657
Ps	76: 5	**V men** lie plundered,	52+4213
Jer	48:14	'We are warriors, men **v** in battle'?	2657

VALIANTLY (1) [VALIANT]

1Sa	14:48	He fought **v** and defeated the Amalekites,	2657

VALID (6)

2Sa	15: 3	"Look, your claims are **v** and proper,	3202
Jn	5:31	my testimony is not **v.**	239
	5:32	I know that his testimony about me is **v.**	239
	8:13	as your own witness; your testimony is not **v.**	239
	8:14	my testimony is **v,** for I know where I came	239
	8:17	that the testimony of two men is **v.**	239

VALLEY (146) [VALLEYS]

Ge	14: 3	All these latter kings joined forces in the **V**	6677
	14: 8	up their battle lines in the **V** *of* Siddim	6677
	14:10	Now the **V** *of* Siddim was full of tar pits,	6677
	14:17	came out to meet him in the **V** *of* Shaveh	6677
	14:17	Valley of Shaveh (that is, the King's **V**).	6677
	26:17	in the **V** *of* Gerar and settled there.	5707
	26:19	in the **v** and discovered a well	5707
	37:14	he sent him off from the **V** *of* Hebron.	6677
Nu	13:23	When they reached the **V** *of* Eshcol,	5707
	13:24	the **V** *of* Eshcol because of the cluster	5707
	21:12	on and camped in the Zered **V.**	5707
	21:20	and from Bamoth to the **v** in Moab where	1628
	32: 9	up to the **V** *of* Eshcol and viewed the land,	5707
Dt	1:24	came to the **V** *of* Eshcol and explored it.	5707
	2:13	"Now get up and cross the Zered **V.**"	5707
	2:13	So we crossed the **v.**	5707
	2:14	until we crossed the Zered **V.**	5707
	3:29	So we stayed in the **v** near Beth Peor.	1628
	4:46	in the **v** near Beth Peor east of the Jordan,	1628
	21: 4	to a **v** that has not been plowed or planted	5707
	21: 4	in the **v** they are to break the heifer's neck.	5707
	21: 6	the heifer whose neck was broken in the **v,**	5707
	34: 3	the whole region from the **V** *of* Jericho,	1326
	34: 6	in the **v** opposite Beth Peor,	1628
Jos	7:24	to the **V** *of* Achor.	6677
	7:26	Therefore that place has been called the **V**	6677
	8:11	with the **v** between them and the city.	1628
	8:13	That night Joshua went into the **v.**	6677
	10:12	O moon, over the **V** *of* Aijalon."	6677
	11: 8	and to the **V** *of* Mizpah on the east,	1326
	11:17	the **V** *of* Lebanon below Mount Hermon.	1326
	12: 7	in the **V** *of* Lebanon to Mount Halak,	1326
	13:19	Sibmah, Zereth Shahar on the hill in the **v,**	6677
	13:27	and in the **v,** Beth Haram, Beth Nimrah,	6677
	15: 7	the **V** *of* Achor and turned north to Gilgal,	6677
	15: 8	Then it ran up the **V** *of* Ben Hinnom along	1628
	15: 8	to the top of the hill west of the Hinnom **V**	1628
	15: 8	at the northern end of the **V** *of* Rephaim,	6677
	17:16	and its settlements and those in the **V**	6677
	18:16	of the hill facing the **V** *of* Ben Hinnom,	1628
	18:16	north of the **V** *of* Rephaim.	6677
	18:16	the Hinnom **V** along the southern slope of the	1628
	19:14	and ended at the **V** *of* Iphtah El.	1628
	19:27	touched Zebulun and the **V** *of* Iphtah El,	1628
Jdg	5:15	rushing after him into the **v.**	6677
	6:33	the Jordan and camped in the **V** *of* Jezreel.	6677
	7: 1	of Midian was north of them in the **v** near	6677
	7: 8	camp of Midian lay below him in the **v.**	6677
	7:12	other eastern peoples had settled in the **v,**	6677
	16: 4	in the **V** *of* Sorek whose name was Delilah.	5707
	18:28	The city was in a **v** near Beth Rehob.	6677
1Sa	6:13	in the **v,** and when they looked up and saw	6677
	13:18	toward the borderland overlooking the **V**	1628
	17: 2	the **V** *of* Elah and drew up their battle line	6677
	17: 3	with the **v** between them.	6677
	17:19	with Saul and all the men of Israel in the **V**	6677
	21: 9	whom you killed in the **V** *of* Elah, is here;	6677
2Sa	5:18	and spread out in the **V** *of* Rephaim;	6677
	5:22	up and spread out in the **V** *of* Rephaim;	6677
	8:13	eighteen thousand Edomites in the **V** *of* Salt.	1628
	15:23	The king also crossed the Kidron **V,**	5707
	17:13	and we will drag it down to the **v** until not	5707
	18:18	in the King's **V** as a monument to himself,	6677
	23:13	of Philistines was encamped in the **V**	6677
1Ki	2:37	The day you leave and cross the Kidron **V,**	5707
	15:13	down and burned it in the Kidron **V.**	5707
	18:40	to the Kishon **V** and slaughtered there.	5707
2Ki	2:16	down on some mountain or in some **v.**"	1628
	3:16	Make this **v** full of ditches.	5707
	3:17	yet this **v** will be filled with water,	5707
	14: 7	the **V** *of* Salt and captured Sela in battle,	1628
	23: 4	the Kidron **V** and took the ashes to Bethel.	NIH
	23: 6	to the Kidron **V** outside Jerusalem	5707
	23:10	which was in the **V** *of* Ben Hinnom,	1628
	23:12	and threw the rubble into the Kidron **V.**	5707
1Ch	4:39	the **v** in search of pasture for their flocks.	1628
	10: 7	When all the Israelites in the **v** saw that	6677
	11:15	of Philistines was encamped in the **V**	6677

1Ch	14: 9	come and raided the **V** *of* Rephaim;	6677
	14:13	Once more the Philistines raided the **v;**	6677
	18:12	eighteen thousand Edomites in the **V** *of* Salt.	1628
2Ch	14:10	up battle positions in the **V** *of* Zephathah	1628
	15:16	broke it up and burned it in the Kidron **V.**	5707
	20:26	On the fourth day they assembled in the **V**	6677
	20:26	This is why it is called the **V** *of* Beracah	6677
	25:11	and led his army to the **V** *of* Salt,	1628
	26: 9	at the **V** Gate and at the angle of the wall,	1628
	28: 3	burned sacrifices in the **V** *of* Ben Hinnom	1628
	29:16	and carried it out to the Kidron **V.**	5707
	30:14	and threw them into the Kidron **V.**	5707
	33: 6	He sacrificed his sons in the fire in the **V**	1628
	33:14	west of the Gihon spring in the **v,**	5707
Ne	2:13	through the **V** Gate toward the Jackal Well	1628
	2:15	so I went up the **v** by night,	5707
	2:15	and reentered through the **V** Gate.	1628
	3:13	The **V** Gate was repaired by Hanun and	1628
	11:30	from Beersheba to the **V** *of* Hinnom.	1628
	11:35	and in the **V** *of* the Craftsmen.	1628
Job	21:33	The soil in the **v** is sweet to him;	5707
Ps	23: 4	though I walk through the **V** *of* the shadow	1628
	60: T	twelve thousand Edomites in the **V** *of* Salt.	1628
	60: 6	and measure off the **V** *of* Succoth.	6677
	84: 6	As they pass through the **V** *of* Baca,	6677
	108: 7	and measure off the **V** *of* Succoth.	6677
Pr	30:17	will be pecked out by the ravens of the **v,**	5707
SS	6:11	to look at the new growth in the **v,**	5707
Isa	17: 5	when a man gleans heads of grain in the **V**	6677
	22: 1	An oracle concerning the **V** *of* Vision:	1628
	22: 5	of tumult and trampling and terror in the **V**	1628
	28: 1	set on the head of a fertile **v—**	1628
	28: 4	set on the head of a fertile **v,**	1628
	28:21	he will rouse himself as in the **V**	1628
	40: 4	Every **v** shall be raised up,	1628
	65:10	the **V** *of* Achor a resting place for herds,	6677
Jer	2:23	See how you behaved in the **v;**	1628
	7:31	in the **V** *of* Ben Hinnom to burn their sons	1628
	7:32	Topheth or the **V** *of* Ben Hinnom,	1628
	7:32	Ben Hinnom, but the **V** *of* Slaughter,	1628
	19: 2	and go out to the **V** *of* Ben Hinnom,	1628
	19: 6	Topheth or the **V** *of* Ben Hinnom,	1628
	19: 6	Ben Hinnom, but the **V** *of* Slaughter.	1628
	21:13	above this **v** on the rocky plateau, declares	6677
	31:40	The whole **v** *where* dead bodies	6677
	31:40	the terraces out to the Kidron **V** on the east	5707
	32:35	They built high places for Baal in the **V**	1628
	48: 8	The **v** will be ruined and	6677
Eze	37: 1	and set me in the middle of a **v;**	1326
	37: 2	a great many bones on the floor of the **v,**	1326
	39:11	in the **v** *of* those who travel east toward	1628
	39:11	So it will be called the **V** *of* Hamon Gog.	1628
	39:15	the gravediggers have buried it in the **V**	1628
Hos	1: 5	that day I will break Israel's bow in the **V**	6677
	2:15	will make the **V** *of* Achor a door of hope.	6677
Joel	3: 2	down to the **V** *of* Jehoshaphat.	6677
	3:12	let them advance into the **V** *of* Jehoshaphat,	6677
	3:14	multitudes in the **v** *of* decision!	6677
	3:14	day of the LORD is near in the **v** *of* decision.	6677
	3:18	of the LORD's house and will water the **v**	5707
Am	1: 5	in the **V** *of* Aven and the one who holds	1326
	6:14	the way from Lebo Hamath to the **v** *of*	5707
Mic	1: 6	into the **v** and lay bare her foundations.	1628
Zec	14: 4	forming a great **v,** with half of the mountain	1628
	14: 5	You will flee by my mountain **v,**	1628
Lk	3: 5	Every **v** shall be filled in,	5754
Jn	18: 1	and crossed the Kidron **V.**	5929

VALLEYS (26) [VALLEY]

Nu	14:25	and Canaanites are living in the **v,**	6677
	24: 6	"Like **v** they spread out,	5707
Dt	8: 7	with springs flowing in the **v** and hills;	1326
	11:11	a land of mountains and **v** that drinks rain	1326
2Sa	22:16	The **v** *of* the sea were exposed and	692
1Ki	18: 5	through the land to all the springs and **v.**	5707
	20:28	a god of the hills and not a god of the **v,**	6677
1Ch	12:15	put to flight everyone living in the **v,**	6677
	27:29	in charge of the herds in the **v.**	6677
Job	30:10	Will he till the **v** behind you?	6677
Ps	18:15	The **v** *of* the sea were exposed and	692
	65:13	with flocks and the **v** are mantled	6677
	104: 8	they went down into the **v,**	1326
SS	2: 1	I am a rose of Sharon, a lily of the **v.**	6677
Isa	7:19	Your choicest **v** are full of chariots,	6677
	41:18	and springs within the **v.**	1326
Jer	49: 4	Why do you boast of your **v,**	6677
	49: 4	boast of your **v** so fruitful?	6677
Eze	6: 3	mountains and hills, to the ravines and **v:**	1628
	7:16	moaning like doves of the **v,**	1516
	31:12	on the mountains and in all the **v;**	1628
	32: 5	and fill the **v** with your remains.	1628
	35: 8	and in your **v** and in all your ravines.	1516
	36: 4	mountains and hills, to the ravines and **v,**	1628
	36: 6	mountains and hills, to the ravines and **v,**	1516
Mic	1: 4	and the **v** split apart, like wax before	6677

VALOUR (KJV) See ABLE, BRAVE, CAPABLE, FIGHTERS, FIGHTING MEN, STANDING, STRONG, VALIANT, WARRIOR

VALUABLE (8) [VALUE]

2Ch	32:23	for the LORD and **v gifts** for Hezekiah king	4458
Ezr	1: 6	and with **v gifts,** in addition to all the	4458

Pr	1:13	we will get all sorts of **v** things	2104+3701
Da	11: 8	their metal images and their **v** articles	2775
Mt	6:26	*Are* you not much **more v than** they?	1422
Lk	12:24	And how much more **v** you *are* than birds!	1422
Jas	5: 7	to yield its **v** crop and how patient he is for	5508

VALUABLES (2) [VALUE]

2Ch	32:27	spices, shields and all kinds of **v.**	2775
Jer	20: 5	all its **v** and all the treasures of the kings	3702

VALUE (58) [VALUABLE, VALUABLES, VALUED, VALUES]

Lev	5:15	one without defect and of the **proper v**	6886
	5:16	add a fifth of the **v** to that and give it all to	2257S
	5:18	one without defect and of the **proper v.**	6886
	6: 5	of the **v** to it and give it all to the owner on	2257S
	6: 6	one without defect and of the **proper v.**	6886
	22:14	the offering and add a fifth of the **v** to it.	2257S
	25:27	he is to **determine** the **v** for the years	3108
	27: 3	the **v** *of* a male between the ages of twenty	6886
	27: 4	set her **v** at thirty shekels.	6886
	27: 5	set the **v** *of* a male at twenty shekels and	6886
	27: 6	the **v** *of* a male at five shekels of silver and	6886
	27: 7	set the **v** *of* a male at fifteen shekels and of	6886
	27: 8	who *will* **set** *the* **v** for him according	6885
	27:12	Whatever **v** the priest then sets,	6886
	27:13	he must add a fifth to its **v.**	6886
	27:14	Whatever **v** the priest then **sets,**	6885
	27:15	he must add a fifth to its **v,**	4084+6886
	27:16	its **v** is to be set according to the amount	6886
	27:17	the **v** that has been set remains.	6886
	27:18	the priest will determine the **v** according to	4084
	27:18	and its **set v** will be reduced.	6886
	27:19	he must add a fifth to its **v,**	4084+6886
	27:23	the priest will determine its **v** up to	4831+6886
	27:23	and the man must pay its **v** on that day	6886
	27:25	Every **v** is to be set according to	6886
	27:27	he may buy it back at its **set v,**	6886
	27:27	adding a fifth of the **v** to it.	2257S
	27:27	it is to be sold at its **set v.**	6886
	27:31	he must add a fifth of the **v** to it.	2257S
1Sa	26:24	so *may* the LORD **v** my life and	928+1540+6524
1Ki	10:21	silver was considered of **little v**	4202+4399
	20: 6	They will seize everything you **v**	4718+6524
2Ch	9:20	because silver was considered of **little v**	4399
	20:25	and clothing and also articles of **v—**	2776
	21: 3	of silver and gold and **articles of v,**	4458
	36:10	together with articles of **v** *from* the temple	2775
	36:19	and destroyed everything of **v** there.	4718
Job	15: 3	with speeches that **have no v?**	3603
Pr	10: 2	Ill-gotten treasures *are* of no **v,**	3603
	10:20	the heart of the wicked is **of little v.**	3869+5071
	16:13	*they* **v** a man who speaks the truth.	170
	31:11	in her and lacks nothing of **v.**	8965
Eze	7:11	no wealth, nothing of **v.**	5625
Hab	2:18	**"Of** what **v** *is* an idol,	3603
Mt	13:46	When he found one of **great v,**	4501
Ac	19:19	When they calculated the **v** of the scrolls,	5507
Ro	2:25	Circumcision *has* **v** if you observe the law,	6067
	3: 1	or what **v** is there in circumcision?	6066
	3: 3	faith *has* **no v** and the promise is worthless,	3033
Gal	5: 2	Christ *will be of* no **v** to you at all.	6067
	5: 6	circumcision nor uncircumcision *has* any **v.**	2710
Col	2:23	but they lack any **v** in restraining sensual	5507
1Ti	4: 8	For physical training is of some **v,**	6068
	4: 8	but godliness has **v** for all things,	6068
2Ti	2:14	it is of no **v,** and only ruins those who	5978
Heb	4: 2	message they heard *was of* no **v** to them,	6067
	11:26	as *of* greater **v** than the treasures of Egypt,	4458
	13: 9	which *are* of no **v** to those who eat them.	6067

VALUED (4) [VALUE]

1Sa	26:24	As surely as I **v** your life today,	928+1540+6524
Ezr	8:27	20 bowls of gold **v** *at* 1,000 darics,	4200
Lk	7: 2	servant, whom his master **v highly,**	1639+1952
	16:15	is **highly v** among men is detestable	3836+5734

VALUES (1) [VALUE]

Lev	27: 2	persons to the LORD by giving **equivalent v,**	6886

VANIAH (1)

Ezr	10:36	**V,** Meremoth, Eliashib,	2264

VANISH (14) [VANISHED, VANISHES]

Job	6:17	and in the heat **v** from their channels.	1980
Ps	37:20	*they* will **v**—vanish like smoke.	3983
	37:20	they will vanish—**v** like smoke.	3983
	58: 7	*Let them* **v** like water that flows away;	4416
	102: 3	For my days **v** like smoke;	3983
	104:35	But *may* sinners **v** from the earth and	9462
Isa	11:13	Ephraim's jealousy *will* **v,**	6073
	16: 4	the aggressor *will* **v** from the land.	9462
	29:14	the intelligence of the intelligent *will* **v.**"	6259
	29:20	The ruthless *will* **v,** the mockers will	699
	34:12	all her princes will **v away.**	700
	51: 6	the heavens *will* **v** like smoke,	4872
Jer	18:14	of Lebanon *ever* **v** from its rocky slopes?	6440
	31:36	"Only if these decrees **v** from my sight,"	4631

VANISHED (5) [VANISH]

Ps	12: 1	the faithful *have* **v** from among men.	7182

Ps	77: 8	*Has* his unfailing love *v* forever?	699
Ecc	9: 6	and their jealousy *have* long since *v*;	6
Jer	7:28	*it has v* from their lips.	4162
Rev	18:14	All your riches and splendor *have v*,	660

VANISHES (3) [VANISH]

Job	7: 9	As a cloud *v* and is gone,	3983
	30:15	my safety *v* like a cloud.	6296
Jas	4:14	that appears for a little while and then *v*.	906

VANITIES, VANITY (KJV) See BREATH, DECEIT, DELUSIONS, DESTRUCTION, DISHONEST, EMPTY, EVIL, FALSE, FALSEHOOD, FALSELY, FLEETING, FRUSTRATION, FUTILE, FUTILITY, LIES, MEANINGLESS, NO MEANING, WORTHLESS IDOLS

VAPOR (1)

Pr	21: 6	by a lying tongue is a fleeting *v* and	2039

VAPOUR (KJV) See MIST

VARIABLENESS (KJV) See CHANGE

VARIANCE (KJV) See AGAINST, DISCORD

VARIED (1) [VARIOUS]

Eze	17: 3	and full plumage *of v* colors came	8391

VARIOUS (25) [VARIED]

Ge	1:11	according to their *v* **kinds."**	4786
	7: 3	to keep their *v* **kinds** alive throughout	2446
Jdg	2:12	They followed and worshiped *v* gods of	337
1Ch	18: 8	the pillars and *v* bronze articles.	NIH
	28:14	be used in *v* **kinds of service,**	2256+6275+6275
	28:14	be used in *v* **kinds of service;**	2256+6275+6275
	29: 2	turquoise, stones of *v* **colors,**	8391
2Ch	8:14	by divisions for the *v* **gates,**	2256+9133+9133
	16:14	with spices and *v* blended perfumes,	2385
	31:16	to perform the daily duties of their *v* **tasks,**	AIT
	32:28	and he made stalls for *v* kinds of cattle,	3972
Ne	11: 3	each on his own property in the *v* **towns,**	AIT
Est	3:12	governors of the *v* **provinces**	2256+4519+4519
	3:12	and the nobles of the *v* **peoples.**	2256+6639+6639
Eze	13:18	and make veils of *v* lengths for their heads	3972
Mt	4:24	to him all who were ill *with v* diseases,	4476
	24: 7	be famines and earthquakes **in** *v* places.	2848
Mk	1:34	Jesus healed many who had *v* diseases,	4476
	13: 8	There will be earthquakes in *v* places,	2848
Lk	4:40	to Jesus all who had *v* **kinds** of sickness,	4476
	21:11	famines and pestilences **in** *v* places.	2848
Heb	1: 1	the prophets at many times and **in** *v* **ways,**	4502
	2: 4	by signs, wonders and *v* miracles.	4476
	9:10	and drink and *v* ceremonial washings—	1427
1Pe	4:10	administering God's grace in its *v* forms.	4476

VASHNI (KJV) See SECOND

VASHTI (10)

Est	1: 9	Queen *V* also gave a banquet for the women	2267
	1:11	to bring before him Queen **V,**	2267
	1:12	Queen *V* refused to come.	2267
	1:15	what must be done to Queen **V?"**	2267
	1:16	"Queen *V* has done wrong,	2267
	1:17	'King Xerxes commanded Queen *V* to	2267
	1:19	that *V* is never again to enter the presence	2267
	2: 1	he remembered *V* and what she had done	2267
	2: 4	pleases the king be queen instead of **V."**	2267
	2:17	and made her queen instead of **V.**	2267

VASSAL (3) [VASSALS]

2Ki	16: 7	"I am your servant and *v*.	1201
	17: 3	Hoshea, who had been Shalmaneser's *v*	6269
	24: 1	Jehoiakim became his *v* for three years.	6269

VASSALS (2) [VASSAL]

2Sa	10:19	the kings who were *v of* Hadadezer saw	6269
1Ch	19:19	When the *v of* Hadadezer saw that	6269

VAST (25)

Ge	2: 1	were completed in all their *v* **array.**	7372
Dt	1:19	through all that *v* and dreadful desert	1524
	2: 7	over your journey through this *v* desert.	1524
	8:15	through the *v* and dreadful desert,	1524
1Ki	8:65	a *v* assembly, people from Lebo Hamath to	1524
	20:13	'Do you see this *v* army?	1524
	20:28	I will deliver this *v* army into your hands,	1524
2Ch	7: 8	*v* assembly, people from Lebo Hamath	1524+4394
	13: 8	You are indeed a *v* army and have	8041
	14: 9	a *v* army and three hundred chariots,	547+547
	14:11	we have come against this *v* **army.**	2162
	20: 2	"A *v* army is coming against you	8041
	20:12	For we have no power to face this *v* army	8041
	20:15	or discouraged because of this *v* army.	8041
	20:24	the desert and looked toward the *v* **army,**	2162

2Ch	32: 7	of the king of Assyria and the *v* army	3972
Est	1: 4	a full 180 days he displayed the *v* wealth	3883
	1:20	throughout all his *v* realm,	8041
	5:11	Haman boasted to them about his *v* wealth,	3883
Job	9: 4	His wisdom is profound, his power is *v*.	579
	38:18	Have you comprehended the *v* **expanses** *of*	8144
Ps	104:25	There is the sea, *v* and spacious,	1524
	139:17	How *v* *is* the sum of them!	6793
Eze	26:19	over you and its *v* waters cover you,	8041
	37:10	up on their feet—a *v* army.	1524+4394+4394

VAT (1) [VATS]

Hag	2:16	went to a **wine** *v* to draw fifty measures,	3676

VATS (5) [VAT]

Ex	22:29	from your granaries or your *v*.	1964
1Ch	27:27	produce of the vineyards for the wine *v*.	238
Pr	3:10	and your *v* will brim over with new wine.	3676
Joel	2:24	the *v* will overflow with new wine and oil.	3676
	3:13	the winepress is full and the *v* overflow—	3676

VAULTED (2) [VAULT]

Job	22:14	as he goes about in the *v* heavens.'	2553
Jer	37:16	Jeremiah was put into a *v* cell in	2844

VAULTS (1) [VAULTED]

Dt	32:34	kept this in reserve and sealed it in my *v*?	238

VAUNT, VAUNTETH (KJV) See BOAST

VAUNTS (1)

Job	15:25	at God and **himself** against the Almighty,	1504

VEGETABLE (2) [VEGETABLES]

Dt	11:10	and irrigated it by foot as in a *v* garden.	3763
1Ki	21: 2	your vineyard to use for a *v* garden,	3763

VEGETABLES (4) [VEGETABLE]

Pr	15:17	Better a meal of *v* where there is love than	3763
Da	1:12	Give us nothing but *v* to eat and water	2447
	1:16	they were to drink and gave them *v* instead.	2448
Ro	14: 2	whose faith is weak, eats only *v*.	3303

VEGETATION (6)

Ge	1:11	Then God said, "Let the land produce *v*	2013
	1:12	The land produced *v*:	2013
	1:25	and also the *v* in the land.	7542
Dt	29:23	nothing sprouting, no *v* growing on it.	6912
Isa	15: 6	the *v* is gone and nothing green is left.	2013
	42:15	and hills and dry up all their *v*;	6912

VEHEMENT (KJV) See LONGING, MIGHTY, SCORCHING

VEHEMENTLY (1)

Lk	23:10	teachers of the law were standing there, *v* accusing him.	2364

VEIL (16) [VEILED, VEILS]

Ge	24:65	So she took her *v* and covered herself.	7581
	38:14	with a *v* to disguise herself,	7581
	38:19	she took off her *v* and put	7581
Ex	34:33	he put a *v* over his face.	5003
	34:34	he removed the *v* until he came out.	5003
	34:35	the *v* back over his face until he went in	5003
Job	22:14	Thick clouds *v* him,	6260
SS	4: 1	Your eyes behind your *v* are doves.	7539
	4: 3	Your temples behind your *v* are like	7539
	6: 7	Your temples behind your *v* are like	7539
Isa	47: 2	take off your *v*.	7539
La	3:65	Put a *v over* their hearts,	4485
2Co	3:13	who would put a *v* over his face to keep	2820
	3:14	for to this day the same *v* remains when	2820
	3:15	when Moses is read, a *v* covers their hearts.	2820
	3:16	turns to the Lord, the *v* is taken away.	2820

VEILED (3) [VEIL]

SS	1: 7	Why should I be like a *v* **woman** beside	6486
2Co	4: 3	And even if our gospel is *v*,	2821
	4: 3	it is *v* to those who are perishing.	2821

VEILS (3) [VEIL]

Isa	3:19	the earrings and bracelets and *v*,	8304
Eze	13:18	and make *v* of various lengths	5029
	13:21	I will tear off your *v* and save my people	5029

VEIN (KJV) See MINE

VENGEANCE (33) [AVENGE, AVENGED, AVENGER, AVENGES, AVENGING, REVENGE]

Ge	4:15	he will suffer *v* seven times over."	5933
Nu	31: 2	"Take *v* on the Midianites **for**	5933+5935
	31: 3	and to carry out the LORD's *v* on them.	5935
Dt	32:41	*I will take v* on my adversaries	5934+8740
	32:43	*he will take v* on his enemies	5934+8740

Ps	149: 7	to inflict *v* on the nations and punishment	5935
Isa	34: 8	For the LORD has a day of *v*,	5934
	35: 4	your God will come, he will come with *v*;	5934
	47: 3	I will take *v*; I will spare no one."	5934
	59:17	on the garments of *v* and wrapped himself	5934
	61: 2	of the LORD's favor and the day of *v*	5934
	63: 4	For the day of *v* was in my heart,	5934
Jer	11:20	let me see your *v* upon them,	5935
	20:12	let me see your *v* upon them,	5935
	46:10	a day of *v*, for vengeance on his foes.	5935
	46:10	a day of vengeance, for *v* on his foes.	5933
	50:15	Since this is the *v of* the LORD,	5935
	50:15	**take** *v* on her; do to her as she has done	5933
	50:28	how the LORD our God has taken *v*,	5935
	50:28	God has taken vengeance, *v for* his temple.	5935
	51: 6	It is time for the LORD's *v*;	5935
	51:11	The LORD will take *v*,	5935
	51:11	LORD will take vengeance, *v for* his temple.	5935
La	3:60	You have seen the depth of their *v*,	5935
Eze	16:38	upon you the **blood** *v of* my wrath	1947
	25:14	I will take *v* on Edom by the hand	5935
	25:14	they will know my *v*, declares the Sovereign	5935
	25:15	the Philistines acted in *v* and took revenge	5935
	25:17	I will carry out great *v* on them	5935
	25:17	when I take *v* on them.' "	5935
Mic	5:15	I will take *v* in anger and wrath upon	5934
Na	1: 2	the LORD **takes** *v* and is filled with wrath.	5933
	1: 2	The LORD **takes** *v* on his foes	5933

VENISON (KJV) See GAME, WILD GAME

VENOM (5) [VENOMOUS]

Dt	32:24	the *v* of vipers that glide in the dust.	2779
	32:33	Their wine is the *v of* serpents,	2779
Job	20:14	it will become the *v of* serpents	5355
Ps	58: 4	Their *v* is like the venom of a snake,	2779
	58: 4	Their venom is like the *v of* a snake,	2779

VENOMOUS (4) [VENOM]

Nu	21: 6	the LORD sent *v* snakes among them;	8597
Dt	8:15	with its *v* snakes and scorpions.	8597
Isa	14:29	its fruit will be a darting, *v* **serpent.**	8597
Jer	8:17	"See, I will send *v* **snakes** among you,	5729

VENT (5)

Job	15:13	so that *you v* your rage against God	8740
	20:23	God *will v* his burning anger against him	8938
Pr	29:11	A fool **gives** full *v* to his anger,	3655
La	4:11	LORD *has* **given** full *v* to his wrath;	3983
Da	11:30	and *his* **fury** against the holy covenant.	2404

VENTURE (4) [VENTURES]

Dt	28:56	that *she would* not *v* to touch the ground	5814
Jer	5: 6	to tear to pieces any who *v* **out,**	3655
Ac	19:31	sent him a message begging him not *to v*	1443
Ro	15:18	*I will* not *v* to speak of anything except	5528

VENTURES (1) [VENTURE]

Job	4: 2	"If *someone v* a word with you,	5814

VERDANT (1)

SS	1:16	And our bed is *v*.	8316

VERDICT (6)

Dt	17: 9	of them and they will give you the *v*.	1821+5477
Jdg	20: 7	speak up and give your *v*."	6783
1Ki	3:28	all Israel heard the *v* the king had given,	5477
2Ch	19: 6	is with you whenever you give a *v*.	1821+5477
Da	4:17	the holy ones declare the *v*,	10690
Jn	3:19	This is the *v*: Light has come into the world,	3213

VERIFIED (1) [VERIFY]

Ge	42:20	that your words *may* **be** *v* and that you may	586

VERIFY (1) [VERIFIED]

Ac	24:11	You can easily *v* that no more than twelve	2105

VERILY (KJV) See TRUTH

VERITY (KJV) See FAITHFUL

VERMILION (KJV) See RED

VERSED (1)

Ezr	7: 6	a teacher **well** *v* in the Law of Moses,	4542

VERSES (1)

Ps	45: 1	a noble theme as I recite my *v* for the king;	5126

VERY (297)

Ge	1:31	God saw all that he had made, and it was *v* good.	4394
	4: 5	So Cain was *v* angry,	4394
	7:13	On that *v* day Noah and his sons, Shem,	6795
	12:14	that she was a *v* beautiful woman.	4394
	13: 2	Abram had become *v* wealthy in livestock	4394
	15: 1	I am your shield, your *v* great reward."	4394

Ge	17: 6	I will make you v fruitful;	928+4394+4394
	17:23	that v day Abraham took his son Ishmael	6795
	18: 5	"V well," they answered, "do as you say."	4027
	19:20	Let me flee to it—it is v small, isn't it?	AIT
	19:21	He said to him, "V well,	2180
	20: 8	they were v much afraid.	4394
	21: 2	at the v time God had promised him.	NIH
	24:16	The girl was v beautiful, a virgin,	4394
	26:13	to grow until he became v wealthy.	4394
	30:15	"V well," Rachel said,	4027+4200
	37:13	"V well," he replied.	2180
	41:19	scrawny and v ugly and lean.	4394
	44:10	"V well, then," he said,	1685
	50: 9	It was a v large company.	4394
Ex	8:28	but you must not go v far.	8178+8178
	9:16	I have raised you up for this v purpose,	2296
	10:19	the wind to a v strong west wind,	4394
	12:17	because it was on this v day	6795
	12:41	At the end of the 430 years, to the v day,	6795
	12:51	And on that v day the LORD brought	6795
	19: 1	the Israelites left Egypt—on the v day—	2296
	19:16	and a loud trumpet blast.	4394
	33:17	"I will do the v thing you have asked,	2296
Lev	19: 9	do not reap to the v edges of your field	3983
	23:14	until the v day you bring this offering	6795
	23:22	do not reap to the v edges of your field	3983
Nu	12: 3	(Now Moses was a v humble man,	4394
	13:28	and the cities are fortified and v large.	4394
	14:28	you the v things I heard you say:	889+3869+4027
	16:15	Then Moses became v angry and said to	4394
	22:22	But God was v angry when he went,	678+3013
	32: 1	who had v large herds and flocks,	4394+6786
Dt	1:30	did for your in Egypt, before your v eyes,	NIH
	2: 4	They will be afraid of you, but be v careful.	4394
	2:25	This v day I will begin to put the terror	2296
	4:11	while it blazed with fire to the v heavens,	4213
	4:15	Therefore watch yourselves v carefully,	4394
	4:34	for you in Egypt before your v eyes?	NIH
	13: 6	If your v own brother,	278+562+1201+3870
	24: 8	In cases of leprous diseases be v careful	4394
	27: 8	And you shall write v clearly all the words	3512
	30:14	No, the word is v near you;	4394
Jos	1: 7	Be strong and v courageous.	4394
	5:11	The day after the Passover, that v day,	6795
	8: 4	Don't go v far from it.	4394
	9: 9	a v distant country because of the fame of	4394
	9:13	worn out by the v long journey."	4394
	10: 2	and his people were v much alarmed at this,	4394
	13: 1	the LORD said to him, "You are v old,	928+995+2021+2416+3427
	13: 1	and there are still v large areas of land to	4394
	17:17	"You are numerous and v powerful.	1524
	22: 3	For a long time now—to this v day—	2296
	22: 5	But be v careful to keep the commandment	4394
	22:17	Up to this v day we have not cleansed	2296
	23: 6	"Be v strong; be careful to obey	4394
	23:11	be v careful to love the LORD your God.	4394
Jdg	2:20	LORD was v angry with Israel and said,	678+3013
	3:17	Eglon king of Moab, who was a v fat man.	4394
	4: 9	"V well," Deborah said, "I will go	2143+2143
	5:18	The people of Zebulun risked their v lives;	NIH
	9:30	he was v angry.	678+3013
	13: 6	like an angel of God, v awesome.	4394
	15:18	Because he was v thirsty,	4394
	18: 9	We have seen that the land is v good.	4394
Ru	1:20	the Almighty has made my life v bitter.	4394
1Sa	2:17	This sin of the young men was v great in	4394
	2:22	Now Eli, who was v old,	4394
	4:10	The slaughter was v great;	4394
	4:16	I fled from it this v day."	2021
	5:11	God's hand was v heavy upon it.	4394
	16:21	Saul liked him v much,	4394
	18: 8	Saul was v angry; this refrain galled him.	4394
	19: 1	But Jonathan was v fond of David	4394
	20: 3	"Your father knows v well	3359+3359
	20: 7	If he says, 'V well,'	3202
	21:12	and was v much afraid of Achish king	4394
	23:22	They tell me he is v crafty,	6891+6891
	25: 2	property there at Carmel, was v wealthy.	4394
	25:15	Yet these men were v good to us.	4394
	25:36	He was in high spirits and v drunk.	4394+6330
	28: 2	Achish replied, "V well,	4027+4200
2Sa	1:26	you were v dear to me.	4394
	2:17	The battle that day was v fierce,	4394+6330
	3: 8	Abner was v angry because	4394
	3: 8	This v day I am loyal to the house	2021
	7:24	as your v own forever,	3870+4200
	11: 2	The woman was v beautiful,	4394
	12: 2	a v large number of sheep and cattle,	4394
	12:11	Before your v eyes I will take your wives	NIH
	13: 3	Jonadab was a v shrewd man.	4394
	13:36	too, and all his servants wept v bitterly.	4394
	14:21	The king said to Joab, "V well,	2180+5528
	19:32	Now Barzillai was a v old man,	4394
	19:32	for he was a v wealthy man.	4394
	24:10	I have done a v foolish thing."	4394
1Ki	1: 4	The girl was v beautiful;	4394+6330
	1: 6	also v handsome and was born next	4394
	2:18	"V well," Bathsheba replied,	3202
	3: 6	a son to sit on his throne this v day.	2296
	4:29	gave Solomon wisdom and v great insight,	4394
	10: 2	at Jerusalem with a v great caravan—	4394
	16:16	over Israel that v day there in the camp.	2085
	19:10	"I have been v zealous for the LORD	7861+7861
	19:14	"I have been v zealous for the LORD	7861+7861
2Ki	6:12	the v words you speak in your bedroom."	NIH
	17:18	So the LORD was v angry with Israel	4394

2Ki	23:17	of Bethel the v things you have done to it."	465
1Ch	17:22	You made your people Israel your v own forever,	3870+4200
	21: 8	I have done a v foolish thing."	4394
	21:13	for his mercy is v great;	4394
	23:17	of Rehabiah were v numerous.	2025+4200+5087
	26: 6	because they were v capable men.	1475+2657
2Ch	9: 1	Arriving with a v great caravan—	4394
	11:12	and made them v strong.	2221+4394
	20:19	God of Israel, with v loud voice.	2025+4200+5087
	21:15	will be v ill with a lingering disease of	8041
	26: 8	because he had become v powerful.	2025+4200+5087+6330
	30:13	A v large crowd of people assembled	4394
	32:27	Hezekiah had v great riches and honor,	4394
	32:29	for God had given him v great riches.	4394
Ne	1: 7	We have acted v wickedly toward you	2472+2472
	2: 2	I was v much afraid.	4394
	2:10	they were v much disturbed	8288+8317
	4: 7	they were v angry.	4394
	5: 6	and these charges, I was v angry.	4394
	8:17	And their joy was v great.	4394
Est	1:18	This v day the Persian and Median women	2296
Job	1:12	The LORD said to Satan, "V well, then,	2180
	2: 6	The LORD said to Satan, "V well, then,	2180
	10: 1	"I loathe my v life;	NIH
	32: 2	became v angry with Job for	678+3013
	33: 8	I heard the v words—	7754
	33:20	so that his v being finds food repulsive	2652
Ps	37:32	for the righteous, seeking their v lives;	NIH
	38: 6	I am bowed down and brought v low;	4394+6330
	75: 8	of the earth drink it down to its v dregs.	NIH
	77:16	the v depths were convulsed,	677
	78:21	the LORD heard them, he was v angry;	6297
	78:59	When God heard them, he was v angry;	6297
	78:62	he was v angry with his inheritance.	6297
	89:38	you have been v angry with your anointed	6297
	102:14	her v dust moves them to pity.	NIH
	104: 1	O LORD my God, you are v great;	4394
	105:24	The LORD made his people v fruitful;	4394
	119:112	set on keeping your decrees to the v end.	4200+6409+6813
	146: 4	on that v day their plans come to nothing.	2085
Pr	6:26	and the adulteress preys upon your v life.	3701
	22:27	your v bed will be snatched from under you.	NIH
Isa	10:25	V soon my anger against you will end	4663+5071+6388
	16:14	her survivors will be v few and feeble.	4663+5071
	24: 6	and v few are left.	632+4663
	25:12	down to the ground, to the v dust.	NIH
	28:11	V well then, with foreign lips	3954
	29:17	In a v short time, will not	4663+5071+6388
	47: 6	Even on the aged you laid a v heavy yoke.	4394
	65: 3	to my v face, offering sacrifices in gardens	NIH
Jer	20:15	who made him v glad, saying,	8523+8523
	24: 2	One basket had v good figs,	4394
	24: 2	the other basket had v poor figs,	4394
	24: 3	"The good ones are v good,	4394
	25: 3	of Amon king of Judah until this v day—	2296
	27:16	not listen to the prophets who say, 'V soon	4559
	28:16	This v year you are going to die,	NIH
	29:21	put them to death before your v eyes.	NIH
	44:28	of Judah from Egypt will be v few.	5031+5493
La	4:20	The LORD's anointed, our v life breath,	NIH
Eze	2: 3	in revolt against me to this v day.	6795
	4:15	"V well," he said, "I will let you bake your	8011
	16:13	You became v beautiful and rose	928+4394+4394
	16:34	You are the v opposite, for you give	2201
	17:22	I myself will take a shoot from the v top	8123
	23:39	On the v day they sacrificed their children	2085
	24: 2	record this date, this v date,	6795
	24: 2	has laid siege to Jerusalem this v day.	6795
	25:12	the house of Judah and became v guilty	870+870
	37: 2	bones that were v dry.	4394
	40: 1	on that v day the hand of the LORD was	6795
	40: 2	of Israel and set me on a v high mountain,	4394
Da	3:15	and worship the image I made, v good.	NIH
	5:30	That v night Belshazzar, king of the	NIH
	7: 7	terrifying and frightening and v powerful.	10339
	8: 8	The goat became v great,	4394+6330
	8:24	He will become v strong,	3946+6793
	11:25	with a large and v powerful army,	4394+6330
Hos	12: 8	Ephraim boasts, "I am v rich;	421
Joel	1:16	the food been cut off before our v eyes—	NIH
Am	7:10	a conspiracy against you in the v heart	NIH
Jnh	2: 3	into the v heart of the seas,	NIH
	3: 3	Now Nineveh was a v important city—	466+4200
	4: 6	and Jonah was v happy about the vine.	1524
Mic	1: 9	It has reached the v gate of my people,	NIH
Zep	3:20	restore your fortunes before your v eyes,"	NIH
Zec	1: 2	"The LORD was v angry with your forefathers.	7911+7912
	1:14	'I am v jealous for Jerusalem and Zion,	1524
	1:15	but I am v angry with the nations	1524
	7:12	So the LORD Almighty was v angry.	1524
	8: 2	"I am v jealous for Zion;	1524
	9: 2	though they are v skillful.	4394
Mt	4: 8	the devil took him to a v high mountain	3336
	8:13	And his servant was healed at that v hour.	1697
	10:30	the v hairs of your head are all numbered.	NIH
	15:28	her daughter was healed from that v hour.	NIH
	21: 8	A v large crowd spread their cloaks on	AIT
	26: 7	an alabaster jar of v expensive perfume,	988
	26:22	They were v sad and began to say	5379
	26:31	"This v night you will all fall away	4047
	26:34	"this v night, before the rooster crows,	4047
	28:15	among the Jews to this v day.	2465+4958

Mt	28:20	with you always, to the v end of the age."	5333
Mk	1:35	V early in the morning,	3336
	6:35	they said, "and it's already v late.	4498+6052
	9:35	he must be the v last, and the servant of all."	4246
	12:42	and put in two v small copper coins,	NIG
	14: 3	an alabaster jar of v expensive perfume,	4500
	15: 1	V early in the morning,	2317+4745
	16: 2	V early on the first day of the week,	3336
	16: 4	they saw that the stone, which was v large,	5379
Lk	2:36	She was v old; she had lived with her	4498
	2:38	Coming up to them at that v moment,	899
	7:21	At that v time Jesus cured many	NIG
	9:25	and yet lose or forfeit his v self?	NIG
	9:32	Peter and his companions were v sleepy	976+5678
	12: 7	the v hairs of your head are all numbered.	NIG
	12:20	This v night your life will be demanded	4047
	12:26	Since you cannot do this v little thing,	1788
	16:10	trusted with v little can also be trusted	1788
	16:10	dishonest with v little will also be dishonest	1788
	18:23	When he heard this, he became v sad,	4337
	19:17	have been trustworthy in a v small matter,	1788
	21: 2	widow put in two v small copper coins.	1788
	24: 1	v early in the morning,	960+3986
Jn	5:17	is always at his work to this v day,	785
	5:36	the v work that the Father has given me	NIG
	10:36	the Father set apart as his v own and sent	NIG
	12:27	for this v reason I came to this hour.	1328+4047
	12:48	that v word which I spoke will condemn him at the last day.	1697
Ac	1: 9	he was taken up before their v eyes,	899+1063
	8:35	that v passage of Scripture and told him	NIG
	15: 3	This news made all the brothers v glad.	3489
	17:22	that in every way you are v religious.	1273
	22: 2	they became v quiet.	3437
	22:13	at that v moment I was able to see him.	899
	25:10	as you yourself know v well.	2822
	26:22	But I have had God's help to this v day,	4047
	27:14	Before v long, a wind of	3552+4024+4498
Ro	1:32	they not only continue to do these v things	NIG
	3: 2	they have been entrusted with the v words	NIG
	5: 7	V rarely will anyone die for a righteous	3660
	7:10	that the v commandment that was intended	NIG
	9:17	"I raised you up for this v purpose,	899
	9:26	in the v place where it was said to them,	NIG
	11: 8	that they could not hear, to this v day.	2465+4958
	14: 9	For this v reason, Christ died and	1650+4047
	16: 6	Greet Mary, who worked v hard for you.	4498
	16:12	another woman who has worked v hard in	4498
1Co	4: 3	I care v little if I am judged by you or by any human court;	1639+1650+1788
	4:11	To this v hour we go hungry and thirsty,	785
	4:19	But I will come to you v soon,	5441
	6: 7	The v fact that you have lawsuits	NIG
	11:14	not the v nature of things teach you that if	899
2Co	3:12	since we have such a hope, we are v bold.	4498
	5: 5	for this v purpose and has given us	899
	12:15	So I will v gladly spend for you everything	4047
Gal	2:10	the v thing I was eager to do.	899+4047
	3: 1	Before your v eyes Jesus Christ was clearly portrayed as crucified.	NIG
Eph	4:10	He who descended is the v one who ascended higher than all	899
	5:15	Be v careful, then, how you live—	209
	6:22	I am sending him to you for this v purpose,	899
Php	2: 6	Who, being in v nature God,	NIG
	2: 7	taking the v nature of a servant,	209
1Th	5: 2	for you know v well that the day of the Lord	209
1Ti	1:16	for that v reason I was shown mercy	1328+4047
2Ti	1:18	You know v well in how many ways	1019
	2: 9	But they will not get v far	2093+4498+4621
Tit	2:14	for himself a people that are his v own,	4342
Phm	1:12	I am sending him—who is my v heart—	5073
	1:16	He is v dear to me but even dearer to you,	3436
	1:19	to mention that you owe me your v self.	4932
Heb	6:11	to show this same diligence to the v end,	NIG
	6:17	of his purpose v clear to the heirs	4358
	10:37	For in just a v little while,	2285+4012+4012
Jas	3: 4	a v small rudder wherever the pilot wants	1788
1Pe	4:11	as one speaking the v words of God.	NIG
2Pe	1: 4	Through these he has given us his v great	3492
	1: 5	For this v reason, make every effort to	899+4047
Jude	1: 3	although I was v eager to write to you	4246
	1: 8	In the v same way, these dreamers pollute	3530
	1:10	these are the v things that destroy them.	NIG
Rev	9:15	ready for this v hour and day and month	NIG
	11:13	that v hour there was a severe earthquake	NIG
	21:11	like that of a v precious jewel.	5508

VESSEL (1) [VESSELS]

Isa 2:16 for every trading ship and every stately v. 8500

VESSELS (3) [VESSEL]

Isa 22:24 all its lesser v, from the bowls to all the jars. 3998
52:11 you who carry the v of the LORD. 3998
66:20 of the LORD in ceremonially clean v. 3998

VESTMENTS (1) [VESTMENT]

Ezr 3:10 the priests in their v and with trumpets, 4252

VESTRY (KJV) See WARDROBE

VESTURE (KJV) See CLOAK, CLOTHING, ROBE

VETERAN (1)
Eze 27: 9   V craftsmen of Gebal were on board   2418

VEX, VEXATION, VEXED (KJV) See
AFFLICTED, CHASING, CONFUSION, ENEMIES, ENEMY, FRUSTRATED, HOSTILE, MISTREAT, MISTREATED, PERSECUTE, PUNISHMENT, RIVAL, SHATTERED, TERRIFIES, TIRED, TORMENT, TREMBLE, TROUBLE, TROUBLING

VEXED (2)
Ps 78:41   they v the Holy One of Israel.   9345
   112:10   The wicked man will see and be v,   4087

VIAL, VIALS (KJV) See FLASK, BOWL, BOWLS

VICINITY (14)
Dt 11:30   in the Arabah in the v of Gilgal.   4578
Jos   3:16   a town called Adam in the v of Zarethan,   7396
   15:46   all that were in the v of Ashdod,   3338
Jdg 11:33   from Aroer to the v of Minnith,   995+3870+6330
   20:43   and easily overran them in the v of Gibeah   5790
1Sa   5: 6   upon the people of Ashdod and its v;   1473
   7:17   One turned toward Ophrah in the v   824
2Ki 15:16   and everyone in the city and its v,   1473
Mt   2:16   and its v who were two years old and   3990
   15:22   A Canaanite woman from that v came   3990
   15:39   the boat and went to the v of Magadan.   3990
Mk   7:24   Jesus left that place and went to the v of   3990
   7:31   Then Jesus left the v of Tyre and went   3990
Lk 24:50   he had led them out to the v of Bethany,   4639

VICIOUSLY (1)
Jdg 15: 8   He attacked them v and slaughtered many   3751+5782+6584+8797

VICTIM (2) [VICTIMS]
Ps 10:14   The v commits himself to you;   2724
Hab   2: 7   Then you will become their v.   5468

VICTIMS (10) [VICTIM]
Nu 23:24   and drinks the blood of his v."   2728
   31: 8   Among their v were Evi, Rekem, Zur,   2728
Job 29:17   and snatched the v from their teeth.   3272
Ps 10: 8   watching in secret for his v.   2724
   10:10   His v are crushed, they collapse;   2724
Pr   7:26   Many are the v she has brought down;   2728
Eze 34:29   and they will no longer be v of famine in   665
Da   7: 7   it crushed and devoured its v   NIH
   7:19   the beast that crushed and devoured its v   NIH
Na   3: 1   full of plunder, never without v!   3272

VICTOR'S (1) [VICTORY]
2Ti   2: 5   not receive the v crown unless he competes   5110

VICTORIES (5) [VICTORY]
2Sa 22:51   He gives his king great v;   3802
Ps 18:50   He gives his king great v;   3802
   21: 1   How great is his joy in the v you give!   3802
   21: 5   Through the v you gave, his glory is great;   3802
   44: 4   who decrees v for Jacob.   3802

VICTORIOUS (9) [VICTORY]
1Ki 22:12   "Attack Ramoth Gilead and be v,"   7503
   22:15   "Attack and be v," he answered,   7503
2Ch 13:18   men of Judah were v because they relied on   599
   18:11   "Attack Ramoth Gilead and be v,"   7503
   18:14   "Attack and be v," he answered,   7503
Ps 20: 5   when you are v and will lift up our banners   3802
Da 11: 7   he will fight against them and be v.   2616
Hab   3: 8   with your horses and your v chariots?   3802
Rev 15: 2   those who had been v over the beast   3771

VICTORIOUSLY (1) [VICTORY]
Ps 45: 4   In your majesty ride forth v in behalf   7503

VICTORY (40) [VICTOR'S, VICTORIES, VICTORIOUS, VICTORIOUSLY]
Ex 32:18   Moses replied: "It is not the sound of v,   1476
Dt 20: 4   against your enemies to give you v."   3828
Jos 10:10   who defeated them in a great v at Gibeon.   4804
Jdg 12: 3   LORD gave me the v over them.   928+3338+5989
   15:18   "You have given your servant this great v   9591
1Sa 14:23   the LORD won a great v for all Israel,   9591
2Sa   8: 6   The LORD gave David v wherever he went.   3828
   8:10   to greet him and congratulate him on his v   5782
   8:14   The LORD gave David v wherever he went.   3828
   19: 2   the whole army the v that day was turned   9591
   22:36   You give me your shield of v,   3829
   23:10   The LORD brought about a great v   9591
   23:12   and the LORD brought about a great v.   9591
2Ki   5: 1   through him the LORD had given v   9591

2Ki 13:17   "The LORD's arrow of v,   9591
   13:17   the arrow of v over Aram!"   9591
   14:10   Glory in your v, but stay at home!   NIH
1Ch 17:14   the LORD brought about a great v.   3828+9591
   18: 6   LORD gave David v everywhere he went.   3828
   18:10   to greet him and congratulate him on his v   5782
   18:13   LORD gave David v everywhere he went.   3828
Job 12:16   To him belong strength and v;   9370
Ps 18:35   You give me your shield of v,   3829
   44: 3   nor did their arm bring them v;   3828
   44: 6   my sword does not bring me v;   3828
   44: 7   but you give us v over our enemies,   3828
   60:12   With God we will gain the v,   2657
   108:13   With God we will gain the v,   2657
   118:15   and v resound in the tents of the righteous.   3802
   129: 2   but they have not gained the v over me.   3523
   144:10   to the One who gives v to kings,   9591
Pr   2: 7   He holds v in store for the upright,   9370
   11:14   but many advisers make v sure.   9591
   21:31   but v rests with the LORD.   9591
   24: 6   and for v many advisers.   9591
Mt 12:20   till he leads justice to v.   3777
1Co 15:54   "Death has been swallowed up in v."   3777
   15:55   "Where, O death, is your v?   3777
   15:57   the v through our Lord Jesus Christ.   3777
1Jn   5: 4   This is the v that has overcome the world,   3772

VICTUAL, VICTUALS (KJV) See FOOD, PROVISIONS

VIEW (18) [VIEWED, VIEWPOINT, VIEWS]
Nu 23: 9   from the heights I v them.   8800
   33: 3   They marched out boldly in full v of all   6524
Dt 32:49   across from Jericho, and v Canaan,   8011
Ne   9:38   "In v of all this, we are making a binding   928
Ps 48:13   v her citadels, that you may tell of them to   7170
   68:24   Your procession has come into v, O God,   8011
Pr   1:17   to spread a net in full v of all the birds!   6524
   5:21   man's ways are in full v of the LORD,   5790+6524
   17:24   A discerning man keeps wisdom in v,   907+7156
Isa 33:17   the king in his beauty and v a land   8011
Mk   2:12   took his mat and walked out in full v of   1869
Ro   1:12   I urge you, brothers, in v of God's mercy,   1328
1Co   9: 8   merely from a human point of v?   476+2848
2Co   5:16   no one from a worldly point of v.   2848+4922
Gal   5:10   in the Lord that you will take no other v.   5858
Php   3:15   mature should take such a v of things.   5858
2Ti   4: 1   and in v of his appearing and his kingdom,   NIG
Rev 13:13   down from heaven to earth in full v of men.   1967

VIEWED (2) [VIEW]
Nu 32: 9   up to the Valley of Eshcol and v the land,   8011
Ps 102:19   from heaven he v the earth,   5564

VIEWPOINT (1) [VIEW]
1Jn   4: 5   and therefore speak from the v of the world,   NIG

VIEWS (2) [VIEW]
Job 28:24   for he v the ends of the earth   5564
Ac 28:22   But we want to hear what your v are,   5858

VIGIL (3)
Ex 12:42   Because the LORD kept v that night   9081
   12:42   on this night all the Israelites are to keep v   9081
Isa 65: 4   and spend their nights keeping secret v;   5915

VIGILANT (KJV) See ALERT, TEMPERATE

VIGOR (7) [VIGOROUS, VIGOROUSLY]
Job   5:26   You will come to the grave in full v,   3995
   18: 7   The v of his step is weakened;   226
   20:11   The youthful v that fills his bones will lie   6596
   21:23   One man dies in full v,   6795
   30: 2   since their v had gone from them?   3995
Pr 31: 3   your v on those who ruin kings.   2006
Ecc 11:10   for youth and v are meaningless.   8841

VIGOROUS (4) [VIGOR]
Ex   1:19   are v and give birth before the midwives   2650
Jos 14:11   as v to go out to battle now as I was then.   3946
Jdg   3:29   all v and strong; not a man escaped.   9045
Ps 38:19   Many are those who are my v enemies;   2645

VIGOROUSLY (4) [VIGOR]
Pr 31:17   She sets about her work v;   928+6437
Jer 50:34   He will v defend their cause so   8189+8189
Ac 18:28   For he v refuted the Jews in public debate,   2364
   23: 9   Pharisees stood up and argued v.   1372

VILE (26) [VILENESS, VILEST]
Jdg 19:23   "No, my friends, don't be so v.   8317
2Ki 23:13   Ashtoreth the v goddess of the Sidonians,   9199
   23:13   for Chemosh the v god of Moab,   9199
Est   7: 6   and enemy is this v Haman."   8273
Job 15:16   how much less man, who is v and corrupt,   9493
   14: 1   They are corrupt, their deeds are v;   9493
   15: 4   a v man but honors those who fear   4415
   41: 8   "A v disease has beset him;   1175

Ps 53: 1   They are corrupt, and their ways are v;   9493
   101: 3   I will set before my eyes no v thing.   1175
Jer 16:18   with the lifeless forms of their v images   9199
Eze   5:11   with all your v images and detestable   9199
   7:20   to make their detestable idols and v images.   9199
   11:18   return to it and remove all its v images   9199
   11:21   to their v images and detestable idols,   9199
   16:52   Because your sins were more v than theirs,   9493
   20: 7   of the v images you had set your eyes on,   9199
   20: 8   of the v images they had set their eyes on,   9199
   20:30   and lust after their v images?   9199
   37:23   and v images or with any of their offenses,   9199
Hos   9:10   to that shameful idol and became as v as   9199
Na   1:14   I will prepare your grave, for you are v."   7837
Rev 21: 8   But the cowardly, the unbelieving, the v,   1009
   22:11   let him who is v continue to be vile;   4865
   22:11   let him who is vile continue to be v;   4862

VILENESS (2) [VILE]
Jdg 20:10   for all this v done in Israel."   5576
Isa   9:17   ungodly and wicked, every mouth speaks v.   5576

VILEST (2) [VILE]
1Ki 21:26   He behaved in the v manner by   4394+9493
Hos   1: 2   the land is guilty of the v adultery   2388+2388

VILLAGE (22) [VILLAGES]
Jdg   5: 7   V life in Israel ceased, ceased until I,   7251
Mt 10:11   "Whatever town or v you enter,   3267
   21: 2   "Go to the v ahead of you,   3267
Mk   6: 6   around teaching from v to village.   3241+3267
   6: 6   around teaching from village to v.   3241+3267
   8:23   by the hand and led him outside the v.   3267
   8:26   saying, "Don't go into the v."   3267
   11: 2   "Go to the v ahead of you,   3267
Lk   5:17   who had come from every v of Galilee and   3267
   8: 1   Jesus traveled about from one town and v   3267
   9: 6   out and went from v to village,   2848+3267+3836
   9: 6   out and went from village to v,   2848+3267+3836
   9:52   a Samaritan v to get things ready for him;   3267
   9:56   and they went to another v.   3267
   10:38   came to a v where a woman named Martha   3267
   17:12   As he was going into a v,   3267
   19:30   "Go to the v ahead of you,   3267
   24:13   of them were going to a v called Emmaus,   3267
   24:28   the v to which they were going,   3267
Jn 11: 1   the v of Mary and her sister Martha.   3267
   11:30   Now Jesus had not yet entered the v,   3267
   11:54   near the desert, to a v called Ephraim,   4484

VILLAGES (87) [VILLAGE]
Lev 25:31   in v without walls around them are to   2958
Dt   2:23   the Avvites who lived in v as far as Gaza,   2958
   3: 5   there were also a great many unwalled v.   6551
Jos 10:37   its v and everyone in it.   6551
   10:39   They took the city, its king and its v,   6551
   13:23   and their v were the inheritance of   2958
   13:28   and their v were the inheritance of   2958
   15:32   a total of twenty-nine towns and their v.   2958
   15:36   fourteen towns and their v.   2958
   15:41   sixteen towns and their v.   2958
   15:44   nine towns and their v.   2958
   15:45   with its surrounding settlements and v;   2958
   15:46   together with their v;   2958
   15:47   its surrounding settlements and v;   2958
   15:47   and Gaza, its settlements and v,   2958
   15:51   eleven towns and their v.   2958
   15:54   nine towns and their v.   2958
   15:57   ten towns and their v.   2958
   15:59   six towns and their v.   2958
   15:60   two towns and their v.   2958
   15:62   six towns and their v.   2958
   16: 9   It also included all the towns and their v   2958
   18:24   twelve towns and their v.   2958
   18:28   fourteen towns and their v.   2958
   19: 6   thirteen towns and their v;   2958
   19: 7   four towns and their v—   2958
   19: 8   and all the v around these towns as far   2958
   19:15   There were twelve towns and their v.   2958
   19:16   and their v were the inheritance   2958
   19:22   There were sixteen towns and their v.   2958
   19:23   and their v were the inheritance of the tribe   2958
   19:30   There were twenty-two towns and their v.   2958
   19:31   and their v were the inheritance of the tribe   2958
   19:38   There were nineteen towns and their v.   2958
   19:39   and their v were the inheritance of the tribe   2958
   19:48   and their v were the inheritance of the tribe   2958
   21:12   and v around the city they had given   2958
1Sa   6:18   the fortified towns with their country v.   4108
1Ch   4:32   Their surrounding v were Etam, Ain,   2958
   4:33   the v around these towns as far as Baalath.   2958
   5:16   in Bashan and its outlying v,   1426
   6:56   the fields and v around the city were given   2958
   7:28   included Bethel and its surrounding v,   1426
   7:28   Gezer and its v to the west,   1426
   7:28   and Shechem and its v all the way   1426
   7:28   the way to Ayyah and its v.   1426
   7:29   Megiddo and Dor, together with their v.   1426
   8:12   and Lod with its surrounding v),   1426
   9:16   who lived in the v of the Netophathites.   2958
   9:22   registered by genealogy in their v.   2958
   9:25   in their v had to come from time to time   2958
   18: 1   and its surrounding v from the control of   1426
   27:25   in the towns, the v and the watchtowers.   4107

2Ch	8: 2	the v that Hiram had given him,	6551
	13:19	with their **surrounding** v.	1426
	14:14	They destroyed all the v around Gerar,	6551
	14:14	They plundered all these v,	6551
	28:18	and Gimzo, with their **surrounding** v.	1426
	32:29	He built v and acquired great numbers	6551
Ne	6: 2	"Come, let us meet together in one of the v	4099
	11:25	As for the v with their fields,	2958
	11:25	in Jekabzeel and its v,	2958
	11:30	Adullam and their v,	2958
	12:28	from the v of the Netophathites,	2958
	12:29	for the singers had built v for themselves	2958
Est	9:19	why rural Jews—those living in v—	6551+7252
Ps	10: 8	He lies in wait near the v;	2958
	48:11	the v of Judah are glad because	1426
	97: 8	and rejoices and the v of Judah are glad	1426
SS	7:11	let us spend the night in the v.	4107
Jer	17:26	of Judah and the v around Jerusalem,	NIH
	19:15	the v around it every disaster I pronounced	6551
	32:44	in the v around Jerusalem, in the towns of	NIH
	33:13	in the v around Jerusalem and in the towns	NIH
	49: 2	and its **surrounding** v will be set on fire.	1426
Eze	30:18	and her v will go into captivity.	1426
	38:11	"I will invade a land of **unwalled** v;	7253
	38:13	of Tarshish and all her v will say to you,	4099
Mt	9:35	Jesus went through all the towns and v,	3267
	14:15	to the v and buy themselves some food."	3267
Mk	1:38	to the nearby v—so I can preach there also.	3268
	6:36	and v and buy themselves something	3267
	6:56	into v, towns or countryside—	3267
	8:27	Jesus and his disciples went on to the v	3267
Lk	9:12	to the surrounding v and countryside	3267
	13:22	Then Jesus went through the towns and v,	3267
Ac	8:25	preaching the gospel in many Samaritan v.	3267

VILLAIN (1)

Pr	6:12	A scoundrel and v, who goes about with	224

VINDICATE (6) [VINDICATED, VINDICATES, VINDICATION]

1Sa	24:15	may he v me by delivering me from your	9149
Ps	26: 1	V me, O LORD, for I have led a blameless	9149
	35:24	V me in your righteousness,	9149
	43: 1	V me, O God, and plead my cause against	9149
	54: 1	v me by your might.	1906
	135:14	For the LORD *will* v his people	1906

VINDICATED (6) [VINDICATE]

Ge	20:16	*you* **are** completely v."	3519
	30: 6	Then Rachel said, "God has v me;	1906
Job	11: 2	*Is* this talker *to be* v?	7405
	13:18	I have prepared my case, I know I *will be* v.	7405
Jer	51:10	" 'The LORD *has* v us;	3655+7407
1Ti	3:16	He appeared in a body, *was* v by the Spirit,	1467

VINDICATES (1) [VINDICATE]

Isa	50: 8	*He who* v me is near.	7405

VINDICATION (4) [VINDICATE]

Ps	17: 2	May my v come from you;	5477
	24: 5	from the LORD and v from God his Savior.	7407
	35:27	May those who delight in my v shout	7406
Isa	54:17	and this is their v from me,"	7407

VINE (53) [VINES, VINEYARD, VINEYARDS, VINTAGE]

Ge	40: 9	"In my dream I saw a v in front of me,	1728
	40:10	and on the v were three branches.	1728
	49:11	He will tether his donkey to a v,	1728
	49:22	"Joseph is a **fruitful** v,	1201+7238
	49:22	a **fruitful** v near a spring,	1201+7238
Dt	32:32	Their v comes from the vine of Sodom and	1728
	32:32	from the v of Sodom and from the fields	1728
Jdg	9:12	"Then the trees said to the v,	1728
	9:13	"But the v answered,	1728
1Ki	4:25	each man under his own v and fig tree.	1728
2Ki	4:39	to gather herbs and found a wild v.	1728
	18:31	of you will eat from his own v and fig tree	1728
Job	15:33	be like a v stripped of its unripe grapes,	1728
Ps	80: 8	You brought a v out of Egypt;	1728
	80:14	Watch over this v,	1728
	80:16	Your v is cut down, it is burned with fire;	NIH
	128: 3	be like a fruitful v within your house;	1728
SS	7: 8	your breasts like the clusters of the v,	1728
Isa	24: 7	The new wine dries up and the v withers;	1728
	34: 4	like withered leaves from the v,	1728
	36:16	of you will eat from his own v and fig tree	1728
Jer	2:21	like a **choice** v of sound and reliable stock.	8603
	2:21	against me into a corrupt, wild v?	1728
	6: 9	the remnant of Israel as thoroughly as a v;	1728
	8:13	There will be no grapes on the v.	1728
Eze	15: 2	how is the wood of a v better than that	1728
	15: 6	As I have given the wood of the v among	1728
	17: 6	and became a low, spreading v.	1728
	17: 6	So it became a v and produced branches	1728
	17: 7	The v now sent out its roots toward him	1728
	17: 8	bear fruit and become a splendid v.'	1728
	19:10	a v in your vineyard planted by the water;	1728
Hos	10: 1	Israel was a spreading v;	1728
	14: 7	He will blossom like a v,	1728
Joel	1:11	Despair, you farmers, wail, you **v growers;**	4144
	1:12	v is dried up and the fig tree is withered;	1728

Joel	2:22	the fig tree and the v yield their riches.	1728
Jnh	4: 6	a v and made it grow up over Jonah	7813
	4: 6	and Jonah was very happy about the v.	7813
	4: 7	which chewed the v so that it withered.	7813
	4: 9	a right to be angry about the v?"	7813
	4:10	"You have been concerned about this v,	7813
Mic	4: 4	Every man will sit under his own v and	1728
Hag	2:19	Until now, the v and the fig tree,	1728
Zec	3:10	to sit under his v and fig tree,'	1728
	8:12	the v will yield its fruit,	1728
Mt	26:29	not drink of this fruit *of* the v from now on	306
Mk	14:25	*of* the v until that day when I drink it anew	306
Lk	22:18	*of* the v until the kingdom of God comes."	306
Jn	15: 1	"I am the true v, and my Father is the	306
	15: 4	bear fruit by itself; it must remain in the v.	306
	15: 5	"I am the v; you are the branches.	306
Rev	14:18	the clusters of grapes *from* the earth's v,	306

VINEDRESSERS (KJV) See VINE GROWERS, WORK THE VINEYARDS

VINEGAR (9)

Nu	6: 3	and must not drink v *made from* wine or	2810
Ru	2:14	Have some bread and dip it in the **wine**."	2810
Ps	69:21	They put gall in my food and gave me v	2810
Pr	10:26	As v to the teeth and smoke to the eyes,	2810
	25:20	or like v poured on soda,	2810
Mt	27:48	He filled it *with* **wine**, put it on a stick,	3954
Mk	15:36	One man ran, filled a sponge *with* **wine** v,	3954
Lk	23:36	They offered him **wine** v	3954
Jn	19:29	A jar *of* **wine** v was there,	3954

VINES (23) [VINE]

Lev	25: 5	or harvest the grapes of your **untended** v.	5687
	25:11	of itself or harvest the **untended** v.	5687
Dt	8: 8	v and fig trees, pomegranates,	1728
	24:21	*do not* go over the v again.	339+6618
Ps	78:47	He destroyed their v with hail	1728
	105:33	down their v and fig trees and shattered	1728
SS	2:13	the blossoming v spread their fragrance.	1728
	6:11	to see if the v had budded or	1728
	7:12	the vineyards to see if the v have budded,	1728
Isa	5: 2	of stones and planted it with the **choicest** v.	8603
	7:23	where there were a thousand v worth	1728
	16: 8	of Heshbon wither, the v of Sibmah also.	1728
	16: 8	nations have trampled down the **choicest** v,	8602
	16: 9	as Jazer weeps, for the v of Sibmah.	1728
	17:10	the finest plants and plant imported v,	2367
	32:12	for the pleasant fields, for the fruitful v	1728
Jer	5:17	devour your v and fig trees.	1728
	48:32	as Jazer weeps, O v of Sibmah.	1728
Hos	2:12	I will ruin her v and her fig trees,	1728
Joel	1: 7	It has laid waste my v and ruined my fig	1728
Na	2: 2	and have ruined their v.	2367
Hab	3:17	not bud and there are no grapes on the v,	1728
Mal	3:11	the v in your fields will not cast their fruit,"	1728

VINEYARD (69) [VINE]

Ge	9:20	a man of the soil, proceeded to plant a v.	4142
Ex	22: 5	a man grazes his livestock in a field or v	4142
	22: 5	from the best of his own field or,	4142
	23:11	the same with your v and your olive grove.	4142
Lev	19:10	not go over your v a second time or pick	4142
Nu	20:17	We will not go through any field or v,	4142
	21:22	We will not turn aside into any field or v,	4142
Dt	20: 6	Has anyone planted a v and not begun	4142
	22: 9	Do not plant two kinds of seed in your v;	4142
	22: 9	but also the fruit of the v will be defiled.	4142
	23:24	If you enter your neighbor's v,	4142
	24:21	When you harvest the grapes in your v,	4142
	28:30	You will plant a v, but you will not even	4142
1Ki	21: 1	a v belonging to Naboth the Jezreelite.	4142
	21: 1	**The** v was in Jezreel, close to the palace	889S
	21: 2	"Let me have your v to use for	4142
	21: 2	In exchange I will give you a better v or,	4142
	21: 6	'Sell me your v; or if you prefer,	4142
	21: 6	I will give you another v in its place.'	4142
	21: 6	But he said, 'I will not give you my v.' "	4142
	21: 7	I'll get you the v of Naboth the Jezreelite."	4142
	21:15	up and take possession of the v of Naboth	4142
	21:16	down to take possession of Naboth's v.	4142
	21:18	He is now in Naboth's v,	4142
Pr	24:30	past the v of the man who lacks judgment;	4142
	31:16	out of her earnings she plants a v.	4142
SS	1: 6	my own v I have neglected.	4142
	8:11	Solomon had a v in Baal Hamon;	4142
	8:11	he let out his v to tenants.	4142
	8:12	But my own v is mine to give;	4142
Isa	1: 8	Daughter of Zion is left like a shelter in a v,	4142
	3:14	"It is you who have ruined my v;	4142
	5: 1	for the one I love a song about his v:	4142
	5: 1	My loved one had a v on a fertile hillside.	4142
	5: 3	judge between me and my v.	4142
	5: 4	for my v than I have done for it?	4142
	5: 5	what I am going to do to my v:	4142
	5: 7	v of the LORD Almighty is the house of Israel,	4142
	5:10	A ten-acre v will produce only a bath	4142
	27: 2	In that day—"Sing about a fruitful v:	4142
Jer	12:10	Many shepherds will ruin my v	4142
Eze	19:10	like a vine in your v planted by the water;	4142
Mic	7: 1	summer fruit at the gleaning of the v;	1292
Mt	20: 1	the morning to hire men to work in his v.	308
	20: 2	for the day and sent them into his v.	308

Mt	20: 4	'You also go and work in my v,	308
	20: 7	'You also go and work in my v.'	308
	20: 8	the owner *of* the v said to his foreman,	308
	21:28	'Son, go and work today in the v.'	308
	21:33	There was a landowner who planted a v.	308
	21:33	Then he rented **the** v to some farmers	899S
	21:39	and threw him out of the v and killed him.	308
	21:40	when the owner *of* the v comes,	308
	21:41	"and he will rent the v to other tenants,	308
Mk	12: 1	"A man planted a v.	308
	12: 1	Then he rented **the** v to some farmers	899S
	12: 2	from them some of the fruit of the v.	308
	12: 8	and threw him out of the v.	308
	12: 9	"What then will the owner *of* the v do?	308
	12: 9	and kill those tenants and give the v	308
Lk	13: 6	"A man had a fig tree, planted in his v,	308
	13: 7	he said to the man who **took care of** the v,	307
	20: 9	this parable: "A man planted a v,	308
	20:10	would give him some of the fruit of the v.	308
	20:13	the owner *of* the v said, 'What shall I do?	308
	20:15	So they threw him out *of* the v	308
	20:15	then will the owner *of* the v do to them?	308
	20:16	and kill those tenants and give the v	308
1Co	9: 7	a v and does not eat of its grapes?	308

VINEYARDS (54) [VINE]

Lev	25: 3	and for six years prune your v	4142
	25: 4	Do not sow your fields or prune your v,	4142
Nu	16:14	or given us an inheritance of fields and v.	4142
	22:24	in a narrow path between two v,	4142
Dt	6:11	and v and olive groves you did not plant—	4142
	28:39	You will plant v and cultivate them	4142
Jos	24:13	in them and eat from v and olive groves	4142
Jdg	14: 5	As they approached the v of Timnah,	4142
	15: 5	together with the v and olive groves.	4142
	21:20	saying, "Go and hide in the v	4142
	21:21	then rush from the v and each of you seize	4142
1Sa	8:14	He will take the best of your fields and v	4142
	22: 7	of Jesse give all of you fields and v?	4142
2Ki	5:26	or to accept clothes, olive groves, v,	4142
	18:32	a land of bread and v, a land of olive trees	4142
	19:29	plant v and eat their fruit.	4142
	25:12	the poorest people of the land to **work** *the* v	4144
1Ch	27:27	the Ramathite was in charge of the v.	4142
	27:27	of the produce of the v for the wine vats.	4142
2Ch	26:10	**working** his **fields and** v in the hills	4144
Ne	5: 3	our v and our homes to get grain during	4142
	5: 4	to pay the king's tax on our fields and v.	4142
	5: 5	because our fields and our v belong to	4142
	5:11	v, olive groves and houses,	4142
	9:25	of good things, wells already dug, v,	4142
Job	24: 6	the fields and glean in the v *of* the wicked.	4142
	24:18	so that no one goes to the v.	4142
Ps	107:37	They sowed fields and planted v	4142
Ecc	2: 4	I built houses for myself and planted v.	4142
SS	1: 6	with me and made me take care of the v;	4142
	1:14	of henna blossoms from the v *of* En Gedi.	4142
	2:15	the little foxes that ruin the v,	4142
	2:15	our v that are in bloom.	4142
	7:12	to the v to see if the vines have budded,	4142
Isa	16:10	no one sings or shouts in the v;	4142
	36:17	and new wine, a land of bread and v.	4142
	37:30	plant v and eat their fruit.	4142
	61: 5	foreigners will work your fields and v	4144
	65:21	they will plant v and eat their fruit.	4142
Jer	5:10	"Go through her v and ravage them,	9224
	31: 5	Again you will plant v on the hills	4142
	32:15	Houses, fields and v will again be bought	4142
	35: 7	sow seed or plant v;	4142
	35: 9	or built houses to live in or had v,	4142
	39:10	and at that time he gave them v and fields.	4142
	52:16	the poorest people of the land to **work** the v	4144
Eze	28:26	and will build houses and plant v;	4142
Hos	2:15	There I will give her back her v,	4142
Am	4: 9	"Many times I struck your gardens and v,	4142
	5:11	though you have planted lush v,	4142
	5:17	There will be wailing in all the v,	4142
	9:14	They will plant v and drink their wine;	4142
Mic	1: 6	a place for planting v.	4142
Zep	1:13	they will plant v but not drink the wine.	4142

VINTAGE (1) [VINE]

1Sa	8:15	and of your v and give it to his officials	4142

VIOL, VIOLS (KJV) See HARPS

VIOLATE (6) [VIOLATED, VIOLATES, VIOLATING, VIOLATION]

Lev	26:15	and so v my covenant,	7296
Jos	23:16	If you v the covenant of the LORD your God	6296
Ps	89:31	if *they* v my decrees and fail to keep my	2725
	89:34	*I will* not v my covenant or alter what	2725
Eze	22:10	in you are *those who* v **women** during their	6700
Ac	23: 3	yet you yourself v **the law** by commanding	4174

VIOLATED (12) [VIOLATE]

Ge	34: 2	saw her, he took her and v her.	2256+6700+8886
Dt	22:24	the man because *he* v another man's wife.	6700
	22:29	He must marry the girl, for *he has* v her.	6700
Jos	7:11	Israel has sinned; *they have* v my covenant,	6296
	7:15	*He has* v the covenant of the LORD	6296
Jdg	2:20	"Because this nation *has* v the covenant	6296
1Sa	15:24	*I* v the LORD's command	6296

2Ki 18:12 but *had* v his covenant—all that Moses 6296
Isa 24: 5 the laws, v the statutes and broken 2736
Jer 34:18 The men who *have* v my covenant 6296
Da 11:32 With flattery he will corrupt *those who have* v the covenant, 8399
Mal 2: 8 *you have* v the covenant with Levi," 8845

VIOLATES (2) [VIOLATE]
Ps 55:20 attacks his friends; *he* v his covenant. 2725
Eze 22:11 and another v his sister, his own father's 6700

VIOLATING (1) [VIOLATE]
1Ch 2: 7 who brought trouble on Israel *by* v the ban 5085

VIOLATION (3) [VIOLATE]
Lev 5:15 "When a person **commits a** v 5085+5086
Dt 17: 2 the LORD your God in v of his covenant, 6296
Heb 2: 2 by angels was binding, and every v 4126

VIOLENCE (53) [VIOLENT]
Ge 6:11 in God's sight and was full of v. 2805
6:13 the earth is filled with v because of them. 2805
49: 5 their swords are weapons of v. 2805
1Ch 12:17 when my hands are free from v, 2805
Job 16:17 yet my hands have been free of v 2805
Ps 7: 9 to an end the v *of* the wicked and make 8273
7:16 his v comes down on his own head. 2805
11: 5 and those who love v his soul hates. 2805
27:12 rise up against me, breathing out v. 2805
55: 9 for I see v and strife in the city. 2805
58: 2 and your hands mete out v on the earth. 2805
72:14 He will rescue them from oppression and v, 2805
73: 6 they clothe themselves with v. 2805
74:20 haunts of v fill the dark places of the land. 2805
140: 1 protect me from men of v, 2805
140: 4 from men of v who plan to trip my feet. 2805
140:11 may disaster hunt down men of v. 2805
Pr 4:17 bread of wickedness and drink the wine of v 2805
10: 6 v overwhelms the mouth of the wicked. 2805
10:11 v overwhelms the mouth of the wicked. 2805
13: 2 but the unfaithful have a craving for v. 2805
21: 7 The v of the wicked will drag them away, 8719
24: 2 for their hearts plot v, and their lips talk 8719
26: 6 Like cutting off one's feet or drinking v is 2805
Isa 42:25 his burning anger, the v of war. 6449
53: 9 though he had done no v, 2805
59: 6 and acts of v are in their hands. 2805
60:18 No longer will v be heard in your land, 2805
Jer 6: 7 V and destruction resound in her; 2805
20: 8 I cry out proclaiming v and destruction. 2805
22: 3 Do no wrong or v *to* the alien, 2803
51:35 the v done to our flesh be upon Babylon," 2805
51:46 of v in the land and of ruler against ruler. 2805
Eze 7:11 V has grown into a rod to punish 2805
7:23 full of bloodshed and the city is full of v. 2805
8:17 Must they also fill the land with v 2805
12:19 in it because of the v *of* all who live there. 2805
22:26 Her priests **do** v to my law 2803
28:16 Through your widespread trade you were filled with v, 2805
45: 9 Give up your v and oppression 2805
Hos 12: 1 and multiplies lies and v. 8719
Joel 3:19 because of v *done to* the people of Judah, 2805
Ob 1:10 of the v *against* your brother Jacob, 2805
Jnh 3: 8 give up their evil ways and their v. 2805
Hab 1: 2 Or cry out to you, "V!" 2805
1: 3 Destruction and v are before me; 2805
1: 9 they all come bent on v. 2805
2:17 The v you have done to Lebanon 2805
Zep 1: 9 the temple of their gods with v and deceit. 2805
3: 4 Her priests profane the sanctuary and **do** v 2803
Mal 2:16 a man's covering himself with v as well as 2805
Ac 21:35 the v of the mob was so great he had to 1040
Rev 18:21 "With such v the great city of Babylon will 3996

VIOLENT (23) [VIOLENCE, VIOLENTLY]
2Sa 22: 3 from v *men* you save me. 2805
22:49 from v men you rescued me. 2805
Ps 17: 4 I have kept myself from the ways of the v. 7265
18:48 from v men you rescued me. 2805
Pr 3:31 Do not envy a v man or choose any 2805
16:29 A v man entices his neighbor 2805
Eze 13:11 and v **winds** will burst forth. 6194+8120
13:13 In my wrath I will unleash a v **wind,** 6194+8120
18:10 "Suppose he has a v son, 2728
28: 8 and you will die a v death in the heart of 2728
Da 11:14 v men *among* your own people will rebel 7265
Am 1:14 amid v **winds** on a stormy day. 6193
Jnh 1: 4 a v storm arose that the ship threatened 1524
Mic 6:12 Her rich men *are* v; 2805+4848
Mt 8:28 They were so v that no one could pass 3336+4848
28: 2 There was a v earthquake, 3489
Ac 2: 2 the blowing of a v wind came from heaven 1042
16:26 Suddenly there was such a v earthquake, 3489
23:10 The dispute became so v that 4498
27:18 We took such a v battering from the storm 5380
1Ti 1:13 a blasphemer and a persecutor and a v **man,** 5616
3: 3 not but gentle, not quarrelsome, 4438
Tit 1: 7 not v, not pursuing dishonest gain. 4438

VIOLENTLY (4) [VIOLENT]
Ge 27:33 Isaac **trembled** v 1524+3006+3010+4394+6330
Ex 19:18 the whole mountain trembled v, 4394

Mk 1:26 The evil spirit **shook** the man v and came 5057
9:26 shrieked, convulsed him v and came out. 4498

VIPER (4) [VIPER'S, VIPERS]
Ge 49:17 a v along the path, that bites the horse's 9159
Pr 23:32 like a snake and poisons like a v. 7626
Isa 14:29 the root of that snake will spring up a v, 7625
Ac 28: 3 a v, driven out by the heat, 2399

VIPER'S (1) [VIPER]
Isa 11: 8 young child put his hand into the v nest. 7626

VIPERS (9) [VIPER]
Dt 32:24 the venom of v that glide in the dust. NIH
Ps 140: 3 the poison of v is on their lips. 6582
Isa 59: 5 the eggs of v and spin a spider's web. 7626
Jer 8:17 v that cannot be charmed, 7626
Mt 3: 7 "You brood *of* v! Who warned you to flee 2399
12:34 You brood *of* v, how can you who are evil 2399
23:33 You brood *of* v! How will you escape 2399
Lk 3: 7 "You brood *of* v! Who warned you to flee 2399
Ro 3:13 "The poison *of* v is on their lips." 835

VIRGIN (41) [VIRGIN'S, VIRGINITY, VIRGINS]
Ge 24:16 The girl was very beautiful, a v; 1435
Ex 22:16 "If a man seduces a v who is not pledged 1435
Lev 21:13 'The woman he marries must **be a** v. 928+1436
21:14 but only a v from his own people, 1435
Dt 22:15 mother shall bring **proof that** she was **a** v 1436
22:17 'I did not find your daughter **to be a** v.' 1436
22:19 because this man has given an Israelite v 1435
22:23 a v pledged to be married and he sleeps 1435
22:28 a v who is not pledged to be married 1435
Jdg 11:39 And she *was a* v. 408+3359+4202
19:24 Look, here is my v daughter, 1435
21:11 every woman *who is* **not a** v." 2351+3359+5435
2Sa 13: 2 his sister Tamar, for she was a v, 1435
13:18 the kind of garment the v daughters of 1435
1Ki 1: 2 a young v to attend the king and take care 1435
2Ki 19:21 " 'The V Daughter of Zion despises you 1435
Ps 45:14 her v companions follow her 1435
Isa 7:14 The v will be with child and will give birth 6625
23:12 O V Daughter of Sidon, now crushed! 1435
37:22 "The V Daughter of Zion despises 1435
47: 1 sit in the dust, V Daughter of Babylon; 1435
Jer 14:17 for my v daughter—my people— 1435
18:13 A most horrible thing has been done by V Israel. 1435
31: 4 and you will be rebuilt, O V Israel. 1435
31:21 Return, O V Israel, return to your towns. 1435
46:11 O V Daughter of Egypt. 1435
La 1:15 the Lord has trampled the V Daughter 1435
2:13 O V Daughter of Zion? 1435
Eze 23: 3 and their v bosoms caressed. 1436
23: 8 slept with her, caressed her v bosom 1435
Joel 1: 8 a v in sackcloth grieving for the husband 1435
Am 5: 2 "Fallen is V Israel, never to rise again, 1435
Mt 1:23 "The v will be with child and will give birth 4221
Lk 1:27 to a v pledged to be married to a man 4221
1:34 Mary asked the angel, "since I am a v?" NIG
1Co 7:28 and if a v marries, she has not sinned. 4221
7:34 or v is concerned about the Lord's affairs; 4221
7:36 toward the v he is engaged to, 4221
7:37 made up his mind not to marry the v— 4221
7:38 So then, he who marries the v does right, 4221
2Co 11: 2 that I might present you as a pure v to him. 4221

VIRGIN'S (1) [VIRGIN]
Lk 1:27 The v name was Mary. 4221

VIRGINITY (3) [VIRGIN]
Dt 22:14 I did not find **proof of** her v," 1436
22:17 But here is **proof of** my daughter's v." 1436
22:20 and no **proof of** the girl's v can be found, 1436

VIRGINS (11) [VIRGIN]
Ex 22:17 he must still pay the bride-price for v. 1435
Est 2: 2 be made for beautiful young v for the king. 1435
2:17 and approval more than any of the other v. 1435
2:19 When the v were assembled a second time, 1435
SS 6: 8 and v beyond number; 6625
La 5:11 and v in the towns of Judah. 1435
Eze 44:22 they may marry only v of Israelite descent 1435
Mt 25: 1 be like ten v who took their lamps 4221
25: 7 all the v woke up and trimmed their lamps. 4221
25:10 The v who were ready went in with him to NIG
1Co 7:25 Now about v: I have no command from the 4221

VIRTUE (KJV) See EXCELLENT, GOODNESS, POWER

VIRTUES (1)
Col 3:14 And over all these v put on love, NIG

VISAGE (KJV) See APPEARANCE, ATTITUDE

VISIBLE (8)
Ge 8: 5 the tops of the mountains *became* v. 8011
Da 4:11 it was v to the ends of the earth. 10257
4:20 touching the sky, v to the whole earth, 10257
Mt 24:27 as lightning that comes from the east *is* v 5743
Eph 5:13 everything exposed by the light *becomes* v, 5746
5:14 for it is light that **makes** everything v. 5746
Col 1:16 v and invisible, whether thrones or powers 3971
Heb 11: 3 was not made out of what was v. 5743

VISION (70) [VISIONS]
Ge 15: 1 word of the LORD came to Abram in a v: 4690
46: 2 And God spoke to Israel in a v *at* night 5261
Nu 24: 4 who sees a v *from* the Almighty, 4690
24:16 who sees a v *from* the Almighty, 4690
1Sa 3:15 He was afraid to tell Eli the v, 5261
2Ch 32:32 and his acts of devotion are written in the v 2606
Job 20: 8 banished like a v *of* the night. 2612
33:15 In a dream, in a v *of* the night, 2612
Ps 89:19 Once you spoke in a v, 2606
Isa 1: 1 The v concerning Judah and Jerusalem 2606
21: 2 A dire v has been shown to me: 2607
22: 1 An oracle concerning the Valley of V: 2612
22: 5 terror in the Valley of V, 2612
29: 7 with a v *in* the night— 2606
29:11 For you this whole v is nothing 2607
Eze 7:13 the v concerning the whole crowd will not 2606
7:26 They will try to get a v from the prophet; 2606
8: 4 as in the v I had seen in the plain. 5260
11:24 to the exiles in Babylonia in the v given by 5260
11:24 Then the v I had seen went up from me, 5260
12:22 'The days go by and every v comes 2606
12:23 'The days are near when every v will 2606
12:27 'The v he sees is for many years from now, 2606
43: 3 The v I saw was like the vision I had seen 5260
43: 3 The vision I saw was like the v I had seen 5260
Da 2:19 the mystery was revealed to Daniel in a v. 10256
2:45 *the* v of the rock cut out of a mountain, but 10255
7: 2 Daniel said: "In my v at night I looked, 10256
7: 7 "After that, in my v *at* night I looked, 10256
7:13 "In my v *at* night I looked, 10256
8: 1 I, Daniel, had a v, after the one that 2606
8: 2 In my v I saw myself in the citadel of Susa 2606
8: 2 in the v I was beside the Ulai Canal. 2606
8:13 "How long will it take for the v to be 2606
8:13 the v concerning the daily sacrifice, NIH
8:15 watching the v and trying to understand it, 2606
8:16 tell this man the meaning of the v." 5260
8:17 "understand that the v concerns the time of 2606
8:19 v concerns the appointed time of the end. NIH
8:26 "The v *of* the evenings and mornings 5260
8:26 but seal up the v, for it concerns the 2606
8:27 I was appalled by the v; 5260
9:21 the man I had seen in the earlier v, 2606
9:23 the message and understand the v: 2606
9:24 to seal up v and prophecy and to anoint 2606
10: 1 of the message came to him in a v. 5260
10: 7 I, Daniel, was the only one who saw the v; 5261
10: 8 So I was left alone, gazing at this great v; 5261
10:14 for the v concerns a time yet to come." 2606
10:16 overcome with anguish because of the v, 5261
11:14 people will rebel in fulfillment of the v, 2606
Ob 1: 1 The v *of* Obadiah. 2606
Mic 1: 1 the v he **saw** concerning Samaria and 2600
Na 1: 1 The book of the v *of* Nahum the Elkoshite. 2606
Zec 2: 8 During the night *I had a* v— 8011
13: 4 prophet will be ashamed of his prophetic v. 2612
Lk 1:22 They realized he had seen a v in 3965
24:23 and told us that they had seen a v of angels, 3965
Ac 9:10 The Lord called to him in a v, "Ananias!" 3969
9:12 In a v he has seen a man named Ananias 3969
10: 3 at about three in the afternoon he had a v, 3969
10:17 wondering about the meaning of the v, 3969+3972
10:19 While Peter was still thinking about the v, 3969
11: 5 and in a trance I saw a v. 3969
12: 9 he thought he was seeing a v. 3969
16: 9 Paul **had** a v of a man of Macedonia 3969+3972
16:10 After Paul had seen the v, 3969
18: 9 One night the Lord spoke to Paul in a v: 3969
26:19 not disobedient to the v from heaven. 3965
Rev 9:17 The horses and riders I saw in my v looked 3970

VISIONS (37) [VISION]
Nu 12: 6 I reveal myself to him in v, 5261
1Sa 3: 1 there were not many v, 2606
2Ch 9:29 the Shilonite in the v *of* Iddo the seer 2608
Job 7:14 with dreams and terrify me with v, 2612
Isa 28: 7 they stagger when **seeing** v, 8015
30:10 They say to the seers, "See no *more* v!" 8011
30:10 and to the prophets, "Give us no *more* 2600
Jer 14:14 They are prophesying to you false v, 2606
23:16 They speak v *from* their own minds, 2606
La 2: 9 and her prophets no longer find v from 2606
2: 9 *The* v of your prophets have failed 2606
Eze 1: 1 heavens were opened and I saw v *of* God. 5261
8: 3 and in v *of* God he took me to Jerusalem, 5261
12:24 no more false v or flattering divinations 2606
13: 6 *Their* v *are* false and their divinations a lie. 2600
13: 7 Have you not seen false v and uttered 4690
13: 8 Because of your false words and lying v, 2600
13: 9 be against the prophets who **see** false v 2600
13:16 Jerusalem and **saw** v *of* peace for her 2600+2606
13:23 therefore *you* will no longer **see** false v 2600
21:29 Despite false v concerning you 2600
22:28 for them by false v and lying divinations. 2600

Eze	40: 2	In v of God he took me to the land of Israel	5261
	43: 3	and like the v I had seen by the Kebar River,	5261
Da	1:17	And Daniel could understand v and dreams	2606
	2:28	and the v that passed through your mind	10256
	4: 5	and v that passed through my mind	10256
	4:10	the v I saw while lying in my bed:	10256
	4:13	"In the v I saw while lying in my bed,	10256
	7: 1	and v passed through his mind	10256
	7:15	and the v that passed through my mind	10256
Hos	12:10	gave them many v and told parables	2606
Joel	2:28	your young men will see v.	2612
Mic	3: 6	night will come over you, without v,	2606
Zec	10: 2	diviners see v that lie;	2600
Ac	2:17	your young men will see v,	3970
2Co	12: 1	go on to v and revelations from the Lord.	3965

VISIT (26) [VISITED, VISITOR, VISITORS, VISITS]

Ge	34: 1	went out to v the women of the land.	8011
Jdg	15: 1	a young goat and went to v his wife.	7212
2Ch	18: 2	Some years later he went down to v Ahab	NIH
	22: 7	Through Ahaziah's v to Joram,	995
Jnh	3: 3	a v required three days.	4544
Mt	25:36	I was in prison and you came to v me.'	NIG
	25:39	or in prison and go to v you?'	NIG
Jn	11:45	many of the Jews who had come to v Mary,	NIG
Ac	7:12	he sent our fathers on their first v.	NIG
	7:13	On their second v, Joseph told his brothers	AIT
	7:23	he decided to v his fellow Israelites.	2170
	9:32	he went to v the saints in Lydda.	NIG
	10:28	a Jew to associate with a Gentile or v him.	4665
	15:36	"Let us go back and v the brothers in all	2170
	19:21	he said, "I must v Rome also."	3972
Ro	15:24	I hope to v you while passing through and	2517
	15:28	I will go to Spain and v you on the way.	1328
1Co	16: 7	now and make only a passing v;	NIG
2Co	1:15	I planned to v you first so	2262
	1:16	I planned to v on my way to Macedonia	1451
	2: 1	that I would not make another painful v	2262
	9: 5	urge the brothers to v you in advance	1650+4601
	12:14	I am ready to v you for the third time,	2262
	13: 1	This will be my third v to you.	2262
1Th	2: 1	that our v to you was not a failure.	1658
2Jn	1:12	to v you and talk with you face to face,	1181

VISITATION (KJV) See PUNISH, JUDGMENT

VISITED (2) [VISIT]

Jn	4:46	Once more he v Cana in Galilee,	1650+2262
	19:39	man who earlier had v Jesus at night.	2262+4639

VISITOR (1) [VISIT]

Lk	24:18	"Are you only a v to Jerusalem and	4228

VISITORS (1) [VISIT]

Ac	2:10	parts of Libya near Cyrene; v from Rome	2111

VISITS (2) [VISIT]

Mic	7: 4	watchmen has come, the day God v you.	7213
1Pe	2:12	and glorify God on the day he v us.	2175

VOCATION (KJV) See CALLING

VOICE (198) [VOICES]

Ge	27:22	"The v is the voice of Jacob,	7754
	27:22	"The voice is the v of Jacob,	7754
Ex	15:26	"If you listen carefully to the v of the LORD	7754
	19:19	and the v of God answered him.	7754
	24: 3	they responded with one v,	7754
Nu	7:89	he heard the v speaking to him from	7754
Dt	4:12	but saw no form; there was only a v.	7754
	4:33	the v of God speaking out of fire,	7754
	4:36	From heaven he made you hear his v	7754
	5:22	a loud v to your whole assembly there on	7754
	5:23	When you heard the v out of the darkness,	7754
	5:24	and we have heard his v from the fire.	7754
	5:25	the v of the LORD our God any longer.	7754
	5:26	For what mortal man has ever heard the v	7754
	18:16	not hear the v of the LORD our God	7754
	26: 7	LORD heard our v and saw our misery.	7754
	27:14	to all the people of Israel in a loud v:	7754
	30:20	listen to his v, and hold fast to him.	7754
Jdg	5:11	the v of the singers at the watering places.	7754
	18: 3	they recognized the v of the young Levite;	7754
1Sa	1:13	and her lips were moving but her v was	7754
	15:22	and sacrifices as much as in obeying the v	7754
	24:16	"Is that your v, David my son?"	7754
	26:17	Saul recognized David's v and said,	7754
	26:17	"Is that your v, David my son?"	7754
	28:12	she cried out at the top of her v and said	7754
2Sa	22: 7	From his temple he heard my v;	7754
	22:14	the v of the Most High resounded.	7754
1Ki	8:55	the whole assembly of Israel in a loud v,	7754
	19:13	Then a v said to him, "What are you doing	7754
2Ki	19:22	Against whom have you raised your v	7754
2Ch	5:13	and singers joined in unison, as with one v,	7754
	20:19	the God of Israel, with very loud v.	7754
Ezr	3:12	whole assembly responded with a loud v:	7754
Job	4:16	and I heard a hushed v:	7754
	37: 2	Listen to the roar of his v,	7754
Job	37: 4	he thunders with his majestic v.	7754
	37: 4	his v resounds, he holds nothing back.	7754
	37: 5	God's v thunders in marvelous ways;	7754
	38:34	"Can you raise your v to the clouds	7754
	40: 9	and can your v thunder like his?	7754
Ps	5: 3	In the morning, O LORD, you hear my v;	7754
	18: 6	From his temple he heard my v;	7754
	18:13	the v of the Most High resounded.	7754
	19: 3	or language where their v is not heard.	7754
	19: 4	Their v goes out into all the earth,	7754
	27: 7	Hear my v when I call, O LORD;	7754
	29: 3	The v of the LORD is over the waters;	7754
	29: 4	The v of the LORD is powerful;	7754
	29: 4	the v of the LORD is majestic.	7754
	29: 5	The v of the LORD breaks the cedars;	7754
	29: 7	The v of the LORD strikes with flashes	7754
	29: 8	The v of the LORD shakes the desert;	7754
	29: 9	The v of the LORD twists the oaks	7754
	46: 6	he lifts his v, the earth melts.	7754
	55: 3	at the v of the enemy, at the stares of	7754
	55:17	and he hears my v.	7754
	64: 1	Hear me, O God, as I v my complaint;	7754
	66:19	surely listened and heard my v in prayer.	7754
	68:33	who thunders with mighty v.	7754
	93: 3	O LORD, the seas have lifted up their v;	7754
	95: 7	Today, if you hear his v,	7754
	116: 1	I love the LORD, for he heard my v;	7754
	119:149	Hear my v in accordance with your love;	7754
	130: 2	O Lord, hear my v.	7754
	141: 1	Hear my v when I call to you.	7754
	142: 1	I lift up my v to the LORD for mercy.	7754
Pr	1:20	she raises her v in the public squares;	7754
	8: 1	Does not understanding raise her v?	7754
	8: 4	I raise my v to all mankind.	7754
SS	2:14	show me your face, let me hear your v;	7754
	2:14	for your v is sweet, and your face is lovely.	7754
	8:13	let me hear your v!	7754
Isa	6: 8	Then I heard the v of the Lord saying,	7754
	28:23	Listen and hear my v;	7754
	29: 4	Your v will come ghostlike from the earth;	7754
	30:21	your ears will hear a v behind you, saying,	1821
	30:30	will cause men to hear his majestic v	7754
	30:31	The v of the LORD will shatter Assyria;	7754
	33: 3	At the thunder of your v, the peoples flee;	7754
	37:23	Against whom have you raised your v	7754
	40: 3	A v of one calling: "In the desert prepare	7754
	40: 6	A v says, "Cry out."	7754
	40: 9	lift up your v with a shout, lift it up,	7754
	42: 2	or raise his v in the streets.	7754
	58: 1	Raise your v like a trumpet.	7754
	58: 4	and expect your v to be heard on high.	7754
Jer	4:15	A v is announcing from Dan,	7754
	22:20	let your v be heard in Bashan,	7754
	31:15	"A v is heard in Ramah, mourning and	7754
	31:16	"Restrain your v from weeping	7754
Eze	1:24	like the v of the Almighty,	7754
	1:25	Then there came a v from above	7754
	1:28	and I heard the v of one speaking.	7754
	9: 1	Then I heard him call out in a loud v,	7754
	10: 5	the v of God Almighty when he speaks.	7754
	11:13	I fell facedown and cried out in a loud v,	7754
	27:30	They will raise their v and cry bitterly	7754
	33:32	a beautiful v and plays an instrument well,	7754
	43: 2	His v was like the roar of rushing waters,	7754
Da	4:14	He called in a **loud** v:	AIT
	4:31	on his lips when a v came from heaven,	10631
	6:20	he called to Daniel in an anguished v,	10631
	8:16	I heard a man's v from the Ulai calling,	7754
	10: 6	and his v like the sound of a multitude,	1821
Hag	1:12	the v of the LORD their God and	7754
Mt	2:18	"A v is heard in Ramah, Rachel weeping	5889
	3: 3	"A v of one calling in the desert,	5889
	3:17	And a v from heaven said,	5889
	12:19	no one will hear his v in the streets.	5889
	17: 5	and a v from the cloud said,	5889
	27:46	the ninth hour Jesus cried out in a loud v,	5889
	27:50	Jesus had cried out again in a loud v,	5889
Mk	1: 3	"a v of one calling in the desert,	5889
	1:11	And a v came from heaven:	5889
	5: 7	He shouted at the top of his v,	5889
	9: 7	and a v came from the cloud:	5889
	15:34	the ninth hour Jesus cried out in a loud v,	5889
Lk	1:42	In a loud v she exclaimed:	3199
	3: 4	"A v of one calling in the desert,	5889
	3:22	And a v came from heaven:	5889
	4:33	cried out at the top of his v,	3489+5889
	8:28	shouting at the top of his v,	3306+3489+5889
	9:35	A v came from the cloud, saying,	5889
	9:36	When the v had spoken,	5889
	17:13	and called out in a loud v,	149+5889
	17:15	came back, praising God in a loud v.	5889
	23:18	With one v they cried out,	4101
	23:46	Jesus called out with a loud v, "Father,	5889
Jn	1:23	"I am the v of one calling in the desert,	5889
	3:29	of joy when he hears the bridegroom's v.	5889
	5:25	now come when the dead will hear the v of	5889
	5:28	who are in their graves will hear his v	5889
	5:37	You have never heard his v nor seen his	5889
	7:37	Jesus stood and said in a loud v,	3189
	10: 3	and the sheep listen to his v.	5889
	10: 4	sheep follow him because they know his v.	5889
	10: 5	they do not recognize a stranger's v."	5889
	10:16	They too will listen to my v,	5889
	10:27	My sheep listen to my v; I know them,	5889
	11:43	Jesus called in a loud v, "Lazarus,	5889
	12:28	Then a v came from heaven,	5889
	12:30	Jesus said, "This v was for your benefit,	5889
Ac	2:14	raised his v and addressed the crowd:	5889
	7:31	to look more closely, he heard the Lord's v:	5889
	9: 4	to the ground and heard a v say to him,	5889
	10:13	Then a v told him, "Get up, Peter.	5889
	10:15	The v spoke to him a second time,	5889
	11: 7	Then I heard a v telling me, 'Get up, Peter.	5889
	11: 9	"The v spoke from heaven a second time,	5889
	12:14	When she recognized Peter's v,	5889
	12:22	They shouted, "This is the v of a god,	5889
	22: 7	to the ground and heard a v say to me,	5889
	22: 9	the v of him who was speaking to me.	5889
	26:14	and I heard a v saying to me in Aramaic,	5889
Ro	10:18	"Their v has gone out into all the earth,	5782
1Th	4:16	with the v of the archangel and with	5889
Heb	3: 7	"Today, if you hear his v,	5889
	3:15	"Today, if you hear his v,	5889
	4: 7	"Today, if you hear his v,	5889
	12:19	or to such a v speaking words	5889
	12:26	At that time his v shook the earth,	5889
2Pe	1:17	the Father when the v came to him from	5889
	1:18	We ourselves heard this v that came	5889
	2:16	who spoke with a man's v and restrained	5889
Rev	1:10	I heard behind me a loud v like a trumpet,	5889
	1:12	around to see the v that was speaking	5889
	1:15	his v was like the sound of rushing waters.	5889
	3:20	If anyone hears my v and opens the door,	5889
	4: 1	And the v I had first heard speaking to me	5889
	5: 2	a mighty angel proclaiming in a loud v,	5889
	5:11	I looked and heard the v of many angels,	5889
	5:12	In a loud v they sang: "Worthy is the Lamb	5889
	6: 1	of the four living creatures say in a v	5889
	6: 6	Then I heard what sounded like a v among	5889
	6: 7	the v of the fourth living creature say,	5889
	6:10	They called out in a loud v, "How long,	5889
	7: 2	He called out in a loud v to	5889
	7:10	And they cried out in a loud v:	5889
	8:13	in midair call out in a loud v:	5889
	9:13	and I heard a v coming from the horns of	5889
	10: 4	but I heard a v from heaven say,	5889
	10: 8	the v that I had heard from heaven spoke	5889
	11:12	a loud v from heaven saying to them,	5889
	12:10	Then I heard a loud v in heaven say:	5889
	14: 7	He said in a loud v, "Fear God	5889
	14: 9	and said in a loud v: "If anyone worships	5889
	14:13	Then I heard a v from heaven say, "Write:	5889
	14:15	in a loud v to him who was sitting on	5889
	14:18	came from the altar and called in a loud v	5889
	16: 1	a loud v from the temple saying to	5889
	16:17	the temple came a loud v from the throne,	5889
	18: 2	With a mighty v he shouted: "Fallen!	5889
	18: 4	Then I heard another v from heaven say:	5889
	18:23	The v of bridegroom and bride will never	5889
	19: 5	Then a v came from the throne, saying,	5889
	19:17	who cried in a loud v to all the birds flying	5889
	21: 3	I heard a loud v from the throne saying,	5889

VOICES (26) [VOICE]

Nu	14: 1	the people of the community raised their v	7754
Jos	6:10	do not raise your v, do not say a word	7754
Jdg	21: 2	raising their v and weeping bitterly.	7754
2Sa	19:35	the v of men and women singers?	7754
2Ch	5:13	they raised their v in praise to the LORD	7754
Ne	9: 4	with loud v to the LORD their God.	7754
Job	29:10	the v of the nobles were hushed,	7754
Isa	6: 4	At the sound of their v the doorposts	7924
	15: 4	their v are heard all the way to Jahaz.	7754
	24:14	They raise their v, they shout for joy;	7754
	42:11	Let the desert and its towns raise their v;	NIH
	52: 8	Your watchmen lift up their v;	7754
Jer	7:34	the v of bride and bridegroom in the towns	7754
	16: 9	the sounds of joy and gladness and to the v	7754
	25:10	the v of bride and bridegroom,	7754
	33:11	the v of bride and bridegroom,	7754
	33:11	the v of those who bring thank offerings to	7754
	51:55	the roar of their v will resound.	7754
Da	5:10	hearing the v of the king and his nobles,	10418
Na	2:13	The v of your messengers will no longer	7754
Lk	19:37	to praise God in loud v for all the miracles	5889
Ac	4:24	they raised their v together in prayer	5889
	7:57	yelling at the top of their v,	3489+5889
	22:22	Then they raised their v and shouted,	5889
Rev	10: 3	the v of the seven thunders spoke.	5889
	11:15	and there were loud v in heaven,	5889

VOID (KJV) See BROKEN, CLEAR, EMPTY, LACKED, LACKING, LACKS, NO VALUE, NULLIFIES, NULLIFY, PLUNDERED, RENOUNCED, WITHOUT

VOLUME (KJV) See SCROLL

VOLUNTARILY (4) [VOLUNTEERS]

2Ki	12: 4	and the money brought v to the temple.	408+4213+6584+6590
2Ch	35: 8	officials also contributed v to the people and	5607
1Co	9:17	If I preach v, I have a reward;	1776
	9:17	if not v, I am simply discharging the trust	220

VOLUNTEERED (3) [VOLUNTEERS]

1Ch	12:38	All these were fighting men who v to serve	6370
2Ch	17:16	who v himself for the service of the LORD,	5605
Ne	11: 2	The people commended all the men who v	5605

VOLUNTEERS (1) [VOLUNTARILY, VOLUNTEERED]

Jdg	5: 9	with the **willing** v among the people.	5605

VOMIT (11) [VOMITED]

Lev	18:28	it *will* v you **out** as it vomited out	7794
	20:22	I am bringing to live *may* not v you **out.**	7794
Job	20:15	God *will* **make** his stomach v them **up.**	3769
Pr	23: 8	*You will* **v up** the little you have eaten	7794
	25:16	too much of it, and *you will* **v.**	7794
	26:11	As a dog returns to its v,	7683
Isa	19:14	as a drunkard staggers around in his v.	7795
	28: 8	All the tables are covered with v and	7795
Jer	25:27	Drink, get drunk and v,	7794
	48:26	Let Moab wallow in her v;	7795
2Pe	2:22	"A dog returns to its v," and,	2000

VOMITED (3) [VOMIT]

Lev	18:25	and the land **v out** its inhabitants.	7794
	18:28	as *it* **v out** the nations that were before you.	7794
Jnh	2:10	and *it* v Jonah onto dry land.	7794

VOPHSI (1)

Nu	13:14	from the tribe of Naphtali, Nahbi son of **V;**	2265

VOTE (1)

Ac	26:10	I cast my v against them.	6029

VOUCH (1)

Col	4:13	*I* v for him that he is working hard for you	3455

VOW (42) [VOWED, VOWS]

Ge	28:20	Then Jacob **made a v,** saying,	5623+5624
	31:13	and where *you* **made a v** to me.	5623+5624
Lev	7:16	the result of a v or is a freewill offering,	5624
	22:18	either to fulfill a v or as a freewill offering,	5624
	22:21	to the LORD to **fulfill a special** v or	5624+7098
	22:23	it will not be accepted in fulfillment of a **v.**	5624
	27: 2	'If anyone **makes a special** v	5624+7098
	27: 8	If anyone making the **v** is too poor to pay	NIH
	27: 8	to what the *man* **making** *the* v can afford.	5623
Nu	6: 2	or woman *wants* to **make a special** v,	5623+7098
	6: 2	to make a special vow, a v *of* separation to	5624
	6: 5	of his v *of* separation no razor may be used	5624
	6:21	He must fulfill the *v he has* **made,**	5623+5624
	15: 8	for a **special** v or a fellowship offering	5624+7098
	21: 2	Then Israel **made** *this* v to the LORD:	5623+5624
	29:39	to *what* you v and your freewill offerings,	5624
	30: 2	a man **makes a** v to the LORD or takes	5623+5624
	30: 3	in her father's house **makes a** v	5623+5624
	30: 4	and her father hears about her v or pledge	5624
	30: 6	after she makes a v or after her lips utter	5624
	30: 8	the **v** that obligates her or the rash promise	5624
	30: 9	"Any v or obligation taken by a widow	5624
	30:10	A woman living with her husband **makes a v**	5623
	30:13	may confirm or nullify any v she makes	5624
Dt	23:18	house of the LORD your God to pay any **v,**	5624
	23:21	If *you* **make a v** to the LORD your God	5623+5624
	23:22	But if you refrain from **making a v,**	5623
	23:23	because *you* **made** *your* v freely to the LORD	5623
Jdg	11:30	And Jephthah **made a v** to the LORD:	5623+5624
	11:35	because I *have* **made a** v to the LORD	7023+7198
1Sa	1:11	And *she* **made a** v, saying,	5623+5624
	1:21	sacrifice to the LORD and to fulfill his **v,**	5624
2Sa	15: 7	and fulfill a v *I* **made** to the LORD.	5624
	15: 8	*I* **made** *this* v: 'If the LORD takes me	5623+5624
Ps	132: 2	and **made a** v to the Mighty One of Jacob:	5623
Ecc	5: 4	When *you* **make a** v to God,	5623+5624
	5: 4	He has no pleasure in fools; fulfill *your* **v.**	5623
	5: 5	It is better not *to* v than to make a vow and	5623
	5: 5	than *to* **make a** v and not fulfill it.	5623
	5: 6	**"My** v was a mistake."	2085S
Ac	18:18	at Cenchrea because of a v he had taken.	2376
	21:23	four men with us who have made a **v.**	2376

VOWED (9) [VOW]

Lev	23:38	whatever you have v and all the freewill	5624
	27: 9	" 'If what he v is an animal	NIH
	27:11	If what he v is a ceremonially unclean	NIH
Dt	12: 6	*what* you have v to give and your freewill	5624
	12:11	all the choice possessions you have v	5623+5624
	12:17	or whatever you *have* v to give,	5623+5624
	12:26	and whatever things by which she	5624
Jdg	11:39	father and he did to her as he *had* **v.**	5623+5624
Jnh	2: 9	What *I* have **v** I will make good.	5623

VOWS (30) [VOW]

Nu	6:21	the law of the Nazirite who v his offering	5623
	15: 3	for **special** v or freewill offerings	5624+7098
	30: 4	then all her v and every pledge by which	5624
	30: 5	none of her v or the pledges by which she	5624
	30: 7	then her v or the pledges by which	5624
	30:11	then all her v or the pledges by which she	5624
	30:12	then none of the v or pledges that came	5624
	30:14	then he confirms all her v or the pledges	5624
2Ki	12: 4	the money received from **personal** v	5883+6886
Job	22:27	and you will fulfill your v.	5624
Ps	22:25	before those who fear you will I fulfill my **v.**	5624
	50:14	fulfill your v to the Most High,	5624
	56:12	I am under v *to* you, O God;	5624
	61: 5	For you have heard my **v,** O God;	5624

Ps	61: 8	to your name and fulfill my v day after day.	5624
	65: 1	to you our v will be fulfilled.	5624
	66:13	v my lips promised and my mouth spoke	889S
	66:14	v my lips promised and my mouth spoke	889S
	76:11	**Make** v to the LORD your God and fulfill	5623
	116:14	I will fulfill my v to the LORD.	5624
	116:18	I will fulfill my v to the LORD.	5624
Pr	7:14	today I fulfilled my v.	5624
	20:25	rashly and only later to consider his v.	5624
	31: 2	O son of my womb, O son of my v,	5624
Isa	19:21	*they will* **make** v to the LORD	5623+5624
Jer	44:25	'We will certainly carry out the v *we* made	5623+5624
	44:25	do what you promised! Keep your v!	5624
Jnh	1:16	sacrifice to the LORD and **made** v to	5623+5624
Na	1:15	O Judah, and fulfill your v.	5624
Mal	1:14	acceptable male in his flock and **v** to give it,	5623

VOYAGE (2)

Ac	21: 7	We continued our v from Tyre and landed	4452
	27:10	I can see that our v is going to be disastrous	4452

VULGAR (1)

2Sa	6:20	of his servants as any v *fellow* would!"	8199

VULTURE (6) [VULTURES]

Lev	11:13	the eagle, the v, the black vulture,	7272
	11:13	the eagle, the vulture, the **black** v,	6465
Dt	14:12	the eagle, the v, the black vulture,	7272
	14:12	the eagle, the vulture, the **black** v,	6465
Mic	1:16	make yourselves as bald as the v,	5979
Hab	1: 8	They fly like a v swooping to devour;	5979

VULTURES (4) [VULTURE]

Job	15:23	He wanders about—food for v;	370
Pr	30:17	will be eaten by the v.	1201+5979
Mt	24:28	there is a carcass, there the v will gather.	108
Lk	17:37	there is a dead body, there the v will gather."	108

W

WADE (1)

Isa	47: 2	bare your legs, and **w through** the streams.	6296

WADI (9)

Nu	34: 5	join the **W** *of* Egypt and end at the Sea.	5707
Jos	15: 4	along to Azmon and joined the **W** *of* Egypt,	5707
	15:47	and villages, as far as the **W** *of* Egypt and	5707
1Ki	8:65	from Lebo Hamath to the **W** *of* Egypt.	5707
2Ki	24: 7	the **W** *of* Egypt to the Euphrates River.	5707
2Ch	7: 8	from Lebo Hamath to the **W** *of* Egypt.	5707
Isa	27:12	the flowing Euphrates to the **W** *of* Egypt,	5707
Eze	47:19	along the **W** [of Egypt] to the Great Sea.	5711
	48:28	along the **W** [of Egypt] to the Great Sea.	5711

WAFER (3) [WAFERS]

Ex	29:23	and a cake made with oil, and a **w.**	8386
Lev	8:26	and one made with oil, and a **w;**	8386
Nu	6:19	and a cake and a **w** from the basket,	8386

WAFERS (6) [WAFER]

Ex	16:31	like coriander seed and tasted like **w** made	7613
	29: 2	cakes mixed with oil, and **w** spread with oil.	8386
Lev	2: 4	**w** *made* without yeast and spread with oil.	8386
	7:12	**w** made without yeast and spread with oil,	8386
Nu	6:15	flour mixed with oil, and **w** spread with oil.	8386
1Ch	23:29	for the grain offerings, the unleavened **w,**	8386

WAG (1)

Jer	23:31	the prophets who **w** their own tongues and	4374

WAGE (7) [WAGED, WAGES, WAGING]

Jos	11:20	to **w war** *against* Israel,	7925
Pr	20:18	if *you* **w war,** obtain guidance.	6913
Isa	19:10	and all the **w** earners will be sick at heart.	8512
	41:12	Those who **w war** against you will be	NIH
Da	11:25	The king of the South *will* **w war** with a large and	1741+2021+4200+4878
Mic	3: 5	prepare to **w war** against him.	NIH
2Co	10: 3	we *do* not **w war** as the world does.	5129

WAGED (5) [WAGE]

Jos	11:18	Joshua **w** war against all these kings for	6913
1Ki	5: 3	**w against** my father David **from all sides,**	6015
1Ch	5:19	During Saul's reign *they* **w** war	6913
	5:19	*They* **w** war against the Hagrites, Jetur,	6913
Ps	55:18	He ransoms me unharmed from the battle **w**	NIH

WAGES (35) [WAGE]

Ge	29:15	Tell me what your **w** should be."	5382

Ge	30:28	He added, "Name your **w,**	8510
	30:32	They will be my **w.**	8510
	30:33	you check on the **w** you *have* **paid** me.	8510
	31: 7	by changing my **w** ten times.	5382
	31: 8	he said, 'The speckled ones will be your **w,'**	8510
	31: 8	he said, 'The streaked ones will be your **w,'**	8510
	31:41	and you changed my **w** ten times.	5382
Lev	19:13	hold back the **w** *of* a hired man overnight.	7190
Nu	18:31	for it is your **w** for your work at the Tent	8510
Dt	24:15	Pay him his **w** each day before sunset,	8510
1Ki	5: 6	*for* your men whatever **w** you set.	8510
Job	7: 2	or a hired man waiting eagerly for his **w,**	7189
Pr	10:16	The **w** *of* the righteous bring them life,	7190
	11:18	The wicked man earns deceptive **w,**	7190
Hos	9: 1	you love the **w** *of a prostitute*	924
Mic	1: 7	Since she gathered her gifts from the **w**	924
	1: 7	as the **w** *of prostitutes* they will again be used	924
Hag	1: 6	You **earn** w, only to put them in a purse with holes in it."	8509+8509
Zec	8:10	that time there were no **w** *for* man or beast.	8510
Mal	3: 5	who defraud laborers of their **w,**	8510
Mt	20: 8	'Call the workers and pay them their **w,**	3635
Mk	6:37	take **eight months of a man's w!**	1324+1357
	14: 5	have been sold for more than a year's **w**	NIG
Lk	10: 7	for the worker deserves his **w.**	3635
Jn	4:36	Even now the reaper draws his **w,**	3635
	6: 7	**"Eight months'** w would not buy	1324+1357
	12: 5	the money given to the poor? It was **worth a year's w."**	1324+5559
Ro	4: 4	his **w** are not credited to him as a gift,	3635
	6:23	For the **w** of sin is death, but the gift of God	4072
1Ti	5:18	and "The worker deserves his **w."**	3635
Jas	5: 4	The **w** you failed to pay the workmen	3635
2Pe	2:15	who loved the **w** of wickedness.	3635
Rev	6: 6	saying, "A quart of wheat for **a day's w,**	1324
	6: 6	and three quarts of barley for **a day's w,**	1324

WAGGING (KJV) See SHAKING

WAGING (4) [WAGE]

Jdg	11:27	but you are doing me wrong by **w** war	4309
Pr	24: 6	for **w** war you need guidance.	6913
Da	7:21	this horn *was* **w** war against the saints	10522
Ro	7:23	**w** war **against** the law of my mind	529

WAGON (KJV) See CART

WAGONS (3)

Isa	66:20	on horses, in chariots and **w,**	7369
Eze	23:24	chariots and **w** and with a throng of people;	1649
	26:10	**w** and chariots when he enters your gates	1649

WAHEB (1)

Nu	21:14	"...**W** in Suphah and the ravines,	2259

WAIL (40) [WAILED, WAILING, WAILS]

Isa	13: 6	**W,** for the day of the LORD is near;	3536
	14:31	**W,** O gate! Howl, O city!	3536
	15: 3	and in the public squares they all **w,**	3536
	16: 7	Therefore the Moabites **w,**	3536
	16: 7	they **w** together for Moab.	3536
	22:12	called you on that day to weep and to **w,**	5027
	23: 1	**W,** O ships of Tarshish!	3536
	23: 6	**w,** you people of the island.	3536
	23:14	**W,** *you* ships of Tarshish;	3536
	65:14	from anguish of heart and **w** in brokenness	3536
Jer	4: 8	So put on sackcloth, lament and **w,**	3536
	9:10	and **w** for the mountains and take up	5631
	9:18	Let them come quickly and **w** over us	5631+5951
	9:20	Teach your daughters how to **w;**	5631
	14: 2	*they* **w** for the land,	7722
	25:34	Weep and **w,** you shepherds;	2410
	47: 2	all who dwell in the land *will* **w**	3536
	48:20	**W** and cry out!	3536
	48:31	Therefore *I* **w** over Moab,	3536
	48:39	How *they* **w!** How Moab turns her back	3536
	49: 3	**"W,** O Heshbon, for Ai is destroyed!	3536
	51: 8	**W** over her! Get balm for her pain;	3536
Eze	21:12	Cry out and **w,** son of man,	3536
	27:32	As they **w** and mourn over you,	5760
	30: 2	" **'W** and say, "Alas for that day!"**	3536
	32:18	**w** for the hordes of Egypt and consign to	5629
Hos	7:14	not cry out to me from their hearts but **w**	3536
Joel	1: 5	**W,** all you drinkers of wine;	3536
	1: 5	**w** because of the new wine,	NIH
	1:11	Despair, you farmers, **w,** you vine growers;	3536
	1:13	**w,** you who minister before the altar.	3536
Am	5:16	to weep and the mourners to **w.**	5027
Mic	1: 8	Because of this I will weep and **w;**	3536
Zep	1:11	**W,** you who live in the market district;	3536
Zec	11: 2	**W,** O pine tree, for the cedar has fallen;	3536
	11: 2	**W,** oaks of Bashan;	3536
	11: 3	Listen to the **w** of the shepherds,	3538
Mal	2:13	and **w** because he no longer pays attention	651
Jas	4: 9	Grieve, mourn and **w.**	3081
	5: 1	and **w** because of the misery that is coming	3909

WAILED (3) [WAIL]

Nu	11:18	The LORD heard you when *you* **w,**	1134
	11:20	who is among you, and *have* **w** before him,	1134
Lk	23:27	women who mourned and **w** *for* him.	2577

WAILING (24) [WAIL]

Ex	11: 6	There will be loud **w** throughout Egypt—	7591
	12:30	and there was loud **w** in Egypt,	7591
Nu	11: 4	and again the Israelites *started* **w** and said,	1134
	11:10	Moses heard the people of every family **w**,	1134
	11:13	*They keep* **w** to me, 'Give us meat to eat!'	1134
2Sa	13:36	the king's sons came in, **w** loudly.	1134
Est	4: 1	**w** loudly and bitterly.	2410+2411
	4: 3	with fasting, weeping and **w**.	5027
Job	30:31	and my flute to the sound of **w**.	1134
Ps	30:11	You turned my **w** into dancing;	5027
Isa	15: 8	their **w** reaches as far as Eglaim,	3538
Jer	6:26	mourn with bitter **w** as for an only son,	5027
	9:17	Call for the **w** *women* to come;	7801
	9:19	The sound of **w** is heard from Zion:	5631
	20:16	May he hear **w** in the morning,	2411
	25:36	the **w** *of* the leaders of the flock,	3538
Am	5:16	"There will be **w** in all the streets and cries	5027
	5:17	There will be **w** in all the vineyards,	5027
	8: 3	"the songs in the temple *will* **turn to w**.	3536
Zep	1:10	**w** from the New Quarter,	3538
Mk	5:38	with people crying and **w** loudly.	226
	5:39	"Why all this commotion and **w**?	3081
Lk	8:52	all the people *were* **w** and mourning for her.	3081
	8:52	"Stop **w**," Jesus said.	3081

WAILS (1) [WAIL]

Isa	15: 2	Moab **w** over Nebo and Medeba.	3536

WAIST (24) [WAISTS]

Ex	28:42	reaching from the **w** to the thigh.	5516
2Sa	20: 8	and strapped over it at his **w** was a belt with	5516
1Ki	2: 5	that blood stained the belt around his **w** and	5516
	12:10	'My little finger is thicker than my father's **w**.	5516
2Ki	1: 8	and with a leather belt around his **w**."	5516
2Ch	10:10	'My little finger is thicker than my father's **w**.	5516
Job	12:18	by kings and ties a loincloth around their **w**.	5516
	15:27	with fat and his **w** bulges with flesh,	4072
SS	7: 2	Your **w** is a mound of wheat encircled	1061
Isa	5:27	not a belt is loosened at the **w**,	2743
	11: 5	and faithfulness the sash around his **w**.	2743
Jer	13: 1	a linen belt and put it around your **w**,	5516
	13: 2	and put it around my **w**.	5516
	13: 4	and are wearing around your **w**,	5516
	13:11	For as a belt is bound around a man's **w**,	5516
	48:37	and every **w** is covered with sackcloth.	5516
Eze	1:27	his **w** up he looked like glowing metal,	5516
	8: 2	to be his **w** down he was like fire,	5516
	47: 4	through water that was up to the **w**.	5516
Da	10: 5	with a belt of the finest gold around his **w**.	5516
Mt	3: 4	and he had a leather belt around his **w**,	4019
Mk	1: 6	with a leather belt around his **w**,	4019
Jn	13: 4	**wrapped** a towel **around** his **w**.	1346
Eph	6:14	the belt of truth **buckled around** your **w**,	4322

WAISTBAND (8)

Ex	28: 8	Its skillfully woven **w** is to be like it—	3109
	28:27	to the seam just above the **w** *of* the ephod.	3109
	28:28	connecting it to the **w**,	3109
	29: 5	the ephod on him by its skillfully woven **w**.	3109
	39: 5	Its skillfully woven **w** was like it—	3109
	39:20	to the seam just above the **w** *of* the ephod.	3109
	39:21	to the **w** so that the breastpiece would	3109
Lev	8: 7	ephod to him by its **skillfully woven w**;	3109

WAISTS (5) [WAIST]

1Ki	20:31	around our **w** and ropes around our heads.	5516
	20:32	Wearing sackcloth around their **w** and ropes	5516
Isa	32:11	put sackcloth around your **w**.	2743
Eze	23:15	belts around their **w** and flowing turbans	5516
	44:18	and linen undergarments around their **w**.	5516

WAIT (92) [AWAIT, AWAITS, WAITED, WAITING, WAITS]

Ex	7:15	**W** on the bank of the Nile to meet him,	5893
	24:14	"**W** here for us until we come back to you.	3782
Lev	12: 4	Then the woman *must* **w** thirty-three days	3782
	12: 5	*she must* **w** sixty-six days to be purified	3782
Nu	9: 8	"**W** until I find out what the LORD	6641
Dt	19:11	if a man hates his neighbor and **lies in w**	741
Jos	8: 9	of ambush and **lay in w** between Bethel	3782
	18: 3	"How long *will* you **w** before you begin	8332
Jdg	6:18	LORD said, "I *will* **w** until you return."	3782
	9:32	and your men should come and **lie in w** in	741
	16: 2	So they surrounded the place and **lay in w**	741
	19: 8	**W** till afternoon!"	4538
Ru	1:13	*would* you **w** until they grew up?	8432
	3:18	Then Naomi said, "**W**, my daughter,	3782
1Sa	15:28	but *you must* **w** seven days until I come	3498
	14: 9	'**W** there until we come to you,'	1957
	20:19	and **w** by the stone Ezel.	3782
	22: 8	incited my servant to **lie in w** for me,	741
	22:13	against me and **lies in w** for me,	741
2Sa	15:28	I *will* **w** at the fords in the desert	4538
	18:14	"I'm not *going to* **w** like this for you."	3498
	18:30	The king said, "Stand aside and **w** here."	3656
2Ki	6:33	Why *should* I **w** for the LORD any longer?"	3498
	7: 9	If *we* **w** until daylight,	2675
Job	3: 9	*may it* **w** for daylight in vain and not see	7747
	14:14	the days of my hard service I *will* **w** for	3498
	20:26	total darkness **lies in w** for his treasures.	3243
	32:16	*Must* I **w**, now that they are silent,	3498
	35:14	before him and *you must* **w** for him,	2565
	38:40	when they crouch in their dens or lie in **w** in	743
Ps	5: 3	requests before you and **w in expectation.**	7595
	10: 8	He lies in **w** near the villages;	4422
	10: 9	He lies in **w** like a lion in cover;	741
	10: 9	he lies in **w** to catch the helpless;	741
	27:14	**W** for the LORD;	7747
	27:14	and take heart and **w** for the LORD.	7747
	33:20	We **w in hope** for the LORD;	2675
	37: 7	Be still before the LORD and **w patiently**	2565
	37:32	The wicked **lie in w** for the righteous,	7595
	37:34	**W** for the LORD and keep his way.	7747
	38:15	*I* **w** for you, O LORD;	3498
	59: 3	See how they **lie in w** for me!	741
	71:10	*those who* **w** to kill me conspire	5883+9068
	106:13	and *did* not **w** for his counsel.	2675
	119:84	**How long must** *your servant* **w**?	3427+3869+4537
	119:166	*I* **w** for your salvation, O LORD,	8432
	130: 5	*I* **w** for the LORD, my soul waits,	7747
	130: 6	waits for the Lord more than watchmen **w**	NIH
	130: 6	more than watchmen **w** for the morning.	NIH
Pr	1:11	*let's* **lie in w** for someone's blood;	741
	1:18	These men **lie in w** for their own blood;	741
	12: 6	words of the wicked **lie in w** *for* blood,	741
	20:22	**W** for the LORD, and he will deliver you.	7747
	23:28	Like a bandit she **lies in w**,	741
	24:15	*Do* not **lie in w** like an outlaw against	741
Isa	8:17	I will **w** for the LORD,	2675
	26: 8	the way of your laws, *we* **w** for you;	7747
	30:18	Blessed are all *who* **w** for him!	2675
	51: 5	The islands will look to me and **w in hope**	3498
	64: 4	who acts on behalf of *those who* **w** for him.	2675
Jer	5: 6	a leopard *will* **lie in w** near their towns	9193
	5:26	are wicked men *who* **lie in w**	8800
La	3:10	Like a bear **lying in w**,	741
	3:24	therefore I *will* **w** for him."	3498
	3:26	to **w** quietly for the salvation of the LORD.	3497
	4:19	and **lay in w** for us in the desert.	741
Eze	44:26	After he is cleansed, *he must* **w** seven days.	6218
Hos	12: 6	and **w** for your God always.	7747
Ob	1:14	*You should* not **w** at the crossroads to cut	6641
Mic	5: 7	not **w** for man or linger for mankind.	7747
	7: 2	All men **lie in w** to shed blood;	741
	7: 7	*I* **w** for God my Savior;	3498
Hab	2: 3	Though it linger, **w** for it;	2675
	3:16	I *will* **w patiently** for the day of calamity	5663
Zep	3: 8	Therefore **w** for me," declares the LORD,	2675
Mt	8:15	and she got up and *began to* **w** on him.	1354
Mk	1:31	The fever left her and *she began to* **w on**	1354
Lk	4:39	*She* got up at once and *began to* **w on** them.	1354
	12:37	at the table and *will* come and **w** on them.	1354
	17: 8	get yourself ready and **w** on me while I eat	1354
Jn	18:16	but Peter **had to** **w** outside at the door.	2705
Ac	1: 4	but **w** for the gift my Father promised,	4338
	6: 2	of the word of God *in order to* **w** on tables.	1354
Ro	8:23	*as we* **w eagerly** for our adoption as sons,	587
	8:25	we do not yet have, *we* **w** for it patiently.	587
1Co	1: 7	*as you* **eagerly w** for our Lord Jesus Christ	587
	4: 5	**w** till the Lord comes.	NIG
	11:33	come together to eat, **w for** each other.	1683
1Th	1:10	and *to* **w** for his Son from heaven,	388
Tit	2:13	*while we* **w** for the blessed hope—	4657
Jude	1:21	in God's love *as* you **w** for the mercy	4657
Rev	6:11	and they were told to **w** a little longer,	399

WAITED (16) [WAIT]

Ge	8:10	*He* **w** seven more days and again sent out	3498
	8:12	*He* **w** seven more days and sent	3498
Jdg	3:25	*They* **w** to the point of embarrassment,	3498
	3:26	While they **w**, Ehud got away.	4538
1Sa	13: 8	*He* **w** seven days, the time set by Samuel;	3498
	25: 9	Then *they* **w**.	5663
1Ki	1: 4	she took care of the king and **w** on him;	9250
Job	29:23	*They* **w** for me as for showers and drank	3498
	32: 4	Now Elihu *had* **w** before speaking to Job	2675
	32:11	I **w** while you spoke,	3498
Ps	40: 1	I **w patiently** for the LORD;	7747+7747
Isa	38:13	I **w patiently** till dawn,	8750
La	2:16	This is the day *we have* **w** for;	7747
Jnh	4: 5	and **w** to see what would happen to the city.	6330
Ac	20: 5	These men went on ahead and **w for** us	3531
1Pe	3:20	when God **w** patiently in the days of Noah	587

WAITING (26) [WAIT]

Ex	5:20	they found Moses and Aaron **w** to meet	5893
2Sa	16: 1	steward of Mephibosheth, **w** to meet him.	NIH
1Ki	20:38	**stood** by the road **w** for the king.	6641
Job	7: 2	or a hired man **w eagerly** *for* his wages.	7747
	29:21	in **silence** *for* my counsel.	1957
Ps	119:95	The wicked *are* **w** to destroy me,	7747
Pr	8:34	at my doors, **w** *at* my doorway.	9068
Jer	3: 2	By the roadside *you* **sat w** for lovers,	3782
	20:10	All my friends *are* **w** for me to slip, saying,	9068
Mic	1:12	**w** for relief, because disaster has come from	NIH
Mk	15:43	who was himself **w** for the kingdom	4657
Lk	1:21	the people were **w** for Zechariah	4659
	2:25	*He was* **w** for the consolation of Israel,	4657
	3:15	The people *were* **w expectantly**	4659
	11:54	**w** to catch him in something he might say.	1910
	12:36	like men **w** for their master to return from	4657
	23:51	and he *was* **w** for the kingdom of God.	4657
Jn	5: 3	from Judea because the Jews there were **w**	2426
Ac	17:16	*While* Paul was **w** for them in Athens,	1683
	22:16	And now *what are you* **w** for?	3516

Ac	23:21	forty of them *are* **w** in ambush for him.	1910
	23:21	**w** for your consent to their request."	4657
	28: 6	but *after* **w** a long time and seeing nothing	4659
1Co	11:21	ahead without **w** for anybody else.	NIG
Heb	6:15	And so *after* **w patiently**,	3428
	9:28	to bring salvation *to* those who *are* **w for**	587

WAITS (7) [WAIT]

Ps	130: 5	I wait for the LORD, my soul **w**,	7747
	130: 6	My soul **w** for the Lord more than	NIH
Da	12:12	Blessed is the *one who* **w for** and reaches	2675
Jn	3:29	The friend who attends the bridegroom **w**	2705
Ro	8:19	The creation **w** in eager expectation for	587
Heb	10:13	Since that time **w** for his enemies to	1683
Jas	5: 7	See how the farmer **w** for the land	1683

WAKE (17) [AWAKE, AWAKEN, AWAKENED, AWAKENS, AWAKES, AWOKE, WAKENED, WAKENS, WAKES, WOKE]

Jdg	5:12	'**W up**, wake up, Deborah!	6424
	5:12	'Wake up, **w up**, Deborah!	6424
	5:12	**W up**, wake up, break out in song!	6424
	5:12	Wake up, **w up**, break out in song!	6424
1Sa	26:12	nor *did anyone* **w** up.	7810
Job	41:32	Behind him he leaves a glistening **w**;	5985
Ps	3: 5	*I* **w** again, because the LORD sustains me.	7810
Pr	23:35	*will I* **w up** so I can find another drink?"	7810
Isa	26:19	**w up** and shout for joy.	7810
Joel	1: 5	**W up**, you drunkards, and weep!	7810
Hab	2: 7	*Will they* not **w up** and make you tremble?	3699
	2:19	Or to lifeless stone, '**W up!**	6424
Jn	11:11	but I am going there to **w** him **up**."	2030
Ro	13:11	for you *to* **w up** from your slumber,	1586
Eph	5:14	This is why it is said: "**W up**, O sleeper,	1586
Rev	3: 2	**W up!** Strengthen what remains	1181+1213
	3: 3	But if *you do* not **w up**,	1213

WAKENED (2) [WAKE]

Zec	4: 1	who talked with me returned and **w** me,	6424
	4: 1	as a man *is* **w** from his sleep.	6424

WAKENS (2) [WAKE]

Isa	50: 4	*He* **w** me morning by morning,	6424
	50: 4	**w** my ear to listen like one being taught.	6424

WAKES (1) [WAKE]

Ps	78:65	as a man **w** *from* *the* stupor of wine.	8130

WALK (137) [WALKED, WALKING, WALKS]

Ge	13:17	**w** through the length and breadth of the land	2143
	17: 1	**w** before me and be blameless.	2143
Ex	17: 5	"**W on** ahead of the people.	6296
Lev	11:20	" 'All flying insects that **w** on all fours are	2143
	11:21	some winged creatures that **w** on all fours	2143
	11:27	Of all the animals that **w** on all fours,	2143
	11:27	*that* **w** on their paws are unclean for you;	2143
	26:12	I *will* **w** among you and be your God,	2143
	26:13	the bars of your yoke and **enabled** you to **w**	2143
Nu	11:31	as far as a day's **w** in any direction.	2006
Dt	5:33	**W** in all the way that the LORD your God	2143
	6: 7	at home and when you **w** along the road,	2143
	10:12	to **w** in all his ways, to love him,	2143
	11:19	at home and when you **w** along the road,	2143
	11:22	the LORD your God, to **w** in all his ways,	2143
	19: 9	the LORD your God and to **w** always	2143
	26:17	and that you *will* **w** in his ways,	2143
	28: 9	of the LORD your God and **w** in his ways.	2143
	30:16	love the LORD your God, to **w** in his ways,	2143
Jos	22: 5	to **w** in all his ways, to obey his commands,	2143
Jdg	2:22	and **w** in it as their forefathers did."	2143
	5:10	and *you who* **w** along the road,	2143
1Sa	8: 3	But his sons *did* not **w** in his ways.	2143
	8: 5	and your sons *do* not **w** in your ways;	2143
2Sa	3:31	and put on sackcloth and **w** in mourning	6199
1Ki	2: 3	**W** in his ways, and keep his decrees	2143
	2: 4	how they live, and if they **w** faithfully	2143
	3:14	if *you* **w** in my ways and obey my statutes	2143
	8:25	to **w** before me as you have done.'	2143
	8:58	to **w** in all his ways and to keep	2143
	9: 4	if *you* **w** before me in integrity of heart	2143
	11:38	If *you do* whatever I command you and **w**	2143
2Ki	21:22	and *did* not **w** in the way of the LORD.	2143
2Ch	6:16	in all they do to **w** before me according	2143
	6:31	and **w** in your ways all the time they live in	2143
	7:17	*you* **w** before me as David your father did,	2143
Ne	5: 9	Shouldn't *you* **w** in the fear of our God	2143
Ps	1: 1	not **w** in the counsel of the wicked or stand	2143
	15: 2	*He whose* **w** is blameless	2143
	23: 4	Even though I **w** through the valley of	2143
	26: 3	and I **w continually** in your truth.	2143
	48:12	**W about** Zion, go around her,	6015
	56:13	that I *may* **w** before God in the light of life.	2143
	82: 5	*They* **w about** in darkness;	2143
	84:11	from *those whose* **w** is blameless.	2143
	86:11	O LORD, and I *will* **w** in your truth;	2143
	89:15	*who* **w** in the light of your presence,	2143
	101: 2	I *will* **w** in my house with blameless heart.	2143
	101: 6	*he whose* **w** is blameless will	928+2006+2143
	115: 7	but cannot feel, feet, but *they* cannot **w**;	2143
	116: 9	that I *may* **w** before the LORD in the land	2143
	119: 1	who **w** according to the law of the LORD.	2143

Ps	119: 3	They do nothing wrong; *they* w in his ways.	2143
	119:45	*I will* w about in freedom,	2143
	128: 1	who fear the LORD, who w in his ways.	2143
	138: 7	Though *I* w in the midst of trouble,	2143
	142: 3	where *I* w men have hidden a snare for me.	2143
Pr	2: 7	he is a shield to *those whose* w is blameless,	2143
	2:13	leave the straight paths to w in dark ways,	2143
	2:20	Thus *you will* w in the ways of good men	2143
	4:12	you w, your steps will not be hampered;	2143
	4:14	of the wicked or w in the way of evil men.	886
	6:22	When you w, they will guide you;	2143
	6:28	Can a man w on hot coals without	2143
	8:20	*I* w in the way of righteousness,	2143
	9: 6	w in the way of understanding.	886
	14: 2	*He* whose w is upright fears the LORD,	2143
	19: 1	a poor man whose w is blameless than	2143
	28: 6	a poor man *whose* w is blameless than	2143
	28:18	*He whose* w is blameless is kept safe,	2143
Isa	2: 3	so that *we may* w in his paths."	2143
	2: 5	*let us* w in the light of the LORD.	2143
	23:16	w through the city, O prostitute forgotten,	6015
	30:21	"This is the way; w in it."	2143
	35: 8	it will be for those *who* w in that Way;	2143
	35: 9	But only the redeemed *will* w there,	2143
	38:15	*I will* w humbly all my years because	1844
	40:31	*they will* w and not be faint.	2143
	42: 5	and life to those *who* w on it:	2143
	43: 2	When you w through the fire,	2143
	50:11	w in the light of your fires and of	2143
	51:23	'Fall prostrate that *we may* w over you.'	6296
	57: 2	*Those who* w uprightly enter into peace;	2143
	59: 9	for brightness, but *we* w in deep shadows.	2143
	65: 2	who w *in* ways not good,	2143
Jer	6:16	ask where the good way is, and w in it,	2143
	6:16	But you said, '*We will* not w in it.'	2143
	6:25	not go out to the fields or w on the roads,	2143
	7:23	W in all the ways I command you,	2143
	10: 5	they must be carried because *they* cannot w.	7575
	18:15	They *made* them w in bypaths and on roads	2143
La	3: 2	He has driven me away and *made* me w	2143
	4:18	so we *could* not w in our streets.	2143
Eze	36:12	*I will* **cause** people, my people Israel, to w	2143
Da	4:37	those *who* w in pride he is able to humble.	10207
Hos	11: 3	It was I *who* **taught** Ephraim to w,	8078
	14: 9	the righteous w in them, but the rebellious	2143
Am	3: 3	*Do* two w together unless they have agreed	2143
Mic	2: 3	*You will* no longer w proudly,	2143
	4: 2	so that *we may* w in his paths."	2143
	4: 5	the nations *may* w in the name of their gods;	2143
	4: 5	we *will* w in the name of the LORD	2143
	6: 8	and to love mercy and *to* w humbly	2143
Zep	1:17	the people and *they will* w like blind men,	2143
Zec	3: 7	'If *you will* w in my ways	2143
	10:12	in the LORD and in his name *they will* w,"	2143
Mt	9: 5	or to say, 'Get up and w'?	4344
	11: 5	The blind receive sight, the lame w,	4344
Mk	2: 9	or to say, 'Get up, take your mat and w'?	4344
	12:38	They like *to* w **around** in flowing robes and	4344
Lk	5:23	or to say, 'Get up and w'?	4344
	7:22	The blind receive sight, the lame w,	4344
	11:44	which men w over without knowing it."	4344
	20:46	like *to* w **around** in flowing robes and love	4344
	24:17	you discussing together *as you* w **along**?"	4344
Jn	5: 8	Pick up your mat and w."	4344
	5:11	'Pick up your mat and w.' "	4344
	5:12	to pick it up and w?"	4344
	8:12	follows me *will* never w in darkness,	4344
	12:35	W while you have the light,	4344
Ac	1:12	a **Sabbath** day's w **from** the city. 1584+2400+3847+4879	
	3: 6	In the name of Jesus Christ of Nazareth, w."	4344
	3: 8	He jumped to his feet and *began to* w.	4344
	3:12	or godliness we had made this man w?	4344
	14:10	At that, the *man* jumped up and *began to* w.	4344
Ro	4:12	not only are circumcised but who also w in	5123
2Co	6:16	"I will live with them and w **among** them,	1853
Col	3: 7	You used to w in these ways,	4344
1Jn	1: 6	fellowship with him yet w in the darkness,	4344
	1: 7	But if *we* w in the light, as he is in the light,	4344
	2: 6	claims to live in him must w as Jesus did.	4344
2Jn	1: 6	that *we* w in obedience to his commands.	4344
	1: 6	his command is that *you* w in love.	4344
3Jn	1: 3	to the truth and how you *continue to* w in	4344
Rev	3: 4	*They will* w with me, dressed in white,	4344
	9:20	idols that cannot see or hear or w.	4344
	21:24	The nations *will* w by its light,	4344

WALKED (60) [WALK]

Ge	5:22	Enoch w with God 300 years	2143
	5:24	Enoch w with God; then he was no more,	2143
	6: 9	and he w with God.	2143
	9:23	then *they* w *in* backward	2143
	18:16	and Abraham w **along** with them	2143
	24:40	'The LORD, before whom *I have* w,	2143
	48:15	my fathers Abraham and Isaac w,	2143
Ex	15:19	Israelites w through the sea on dry ground.	2143
Jos	14: 9	'The land on which your feet *have* w will	2005
Jdg	2:17	from the way in which their fathers *had* w,	2143
1Sa	19:23	and *he* w **along** prophesying until	2143+2143
2Sa	3:31	King David *himself* w behind the bier.	2143
	11: 2	up from his bed and w **around** on the roof	2143
1Ki	11:33	and *have* not w in my ways,	2143
	16: 2	but *you* w in the ways of Jeroboam	2143
	16:26	*He* w in all the ways of Jeroboam son	2143
	22:43	In everything *he* w in the ways of his father	2143
	22:52	because *he* w in the ways of his father	2143

2Ki	2: 6	So the two of them w on.	2143
	4:35	Elisha turned away and w back and forth in	2143
	8:18	*He* w in the ways of the kings of Israel,	2143
	8:27	*He* w in the ways of the house of Ahab	2143
	16: 3	*He* w in the ways of the kings of Israel and	2143
	20: 3	how *I have* w before you faithfully and	2143
	21:21	*He* w in all the ways of his father;	2143
	22: 2	and w in all the ways of his father David,	2143
2Ch	17: 3	because in his early years *he* w in the ways	2143
	20:32	*He* w in the ways of his father Asa and did	2143
	21: 6	*He* w in the ways of the kings of Israel,	2143
	21:12	'*You have* not w in the ways of your father	2143
	21:13	But *you have* w in the ways of the kings	2143
	22: 3	He too w in the ways of the house of Ahab,	2143
	27: 6	because he w steadfastly before the LORD	2006
	28: 2	*He* w in the ways of the kings of Israel and	2143
	34: 2	in the eyes of the LORD and w in the ways	2143
Est	6: 1	Every day he w **back and forth** near	2143
Job	29: 3	and by his light *I* w through darkness!	2143
	31: 5	"If *I have* w in falsehood	2143
	38:16	of the sea or w in the recesses of the deep?	2143
Ps	55:14	*as we* w with the throng at the house	2143
Ecc	4:15	and w under the sun followed the youth,	2143
Isa	38: 3	how *I have* w before you faithfully and	2143
	51:23	like a street to *be* w over."	6296
Jer	34:18	like the calf they cut in two and then w	6296
	34:19	who w between the pieces of the calf,	6296
Eze	16:47	*You* not only w in their ways	2143
	28:14	*you* w among the fiery stones.	2143
Mal	2: 6	*He* w with me in peace and uprightness,	2143
Mt	14:29	the water and came toward Jesus.	4344
Mk	1:16	As Jesus w **beside** the Sea of Galilee,	4135
	2:12	took his mat and w **out** in full view	2002
	2:14	As he w **along**, he saw Levi son of	4135
	2:23	and as his disciples w **along**,	3847+4472
	5:42	and w around (she was twelve years old).	4043
Lk	4:30	But he w **right through** the crowd and went	1451
	24:15	Jesus himself came up and w **along** with	5233
Jn	5: 9	he picked up his mat and w.	4344
Ac	2:10	When *they had* w the length of one street,	4601
	14: 8	who was lame from birth and *had* never w.	4344
	17:23	For *as I* w around and looked carefully	1451

WALKING (36) [WALK]

Ge	3: 8	the sound of the LORD God *as he was* w in	2143
Ex	2: 5	her attendants *were* w along the river bank.	2143
Dt	8: 6	w in his ways and revering him.	2143
1Sa	17:39	over the tunic and tried w **around**,	2143
2Sa	6: 4	and Ahio *was* w in front of it.	2143
1Ki	3: 3	the LORD by w according to the statutes	2143
	15:26	w in the ways of his father and in his sin,	2143
	15:34	w in the ways of Jeroboam and in his sin,	2143
	16:19	in the eyes of the LORD and w in the ways	2143
	18: 7	As Obadiah was w **along**, Elijah met him. 928+2006+2021	
2Ki	2:11	were w **along** and talking *together*,	2143+2143
	2:23	As he *was* w along the road,	6590
2Ch	11:17	w in the ways of David and Solomon	2143
Pr	7: 8	w **along** *in* the direction of her house	7575
Isa	3:16	w **along** with outstretched necks,	2143
	9: 2	The people in darkness have seen	2143
	26: 8	Yes, LORD, w in the way of your laws,	NIH
Da	3:25	I see four men w **around** in the fire,	10207
	4:29	as the king was w on the roof of the royal	10207
Mt	4:18	*As* Jesus *was* w beside the Sea of Galilee,	4344
	14:25	Jesus went out to them, w on the lake.	4344
	14:26	When the disciples saw him w on the lake,	4344
	15:31	the lame and the blind seeing,	4344
	24: 1	and was w **away** when his disciples came	4513
Mk	6:48	he went out to them, w on the lake.	4344
	6:49	but when they saw him w on the lake,	4344
	8:24	they look like trees w **around**."	4344
	11:27	and *while* Jesus *was* w in the temple courts,	4344
	16:12	of them *while they were* w in the country.	4344
Lk	9:57	*As they were* w along the road,	4513
Jn	6:19	w on the water; and they were terrified.	4344
	10:23	the temple area w in Solomon's Colonnade.	4344
Ac	3: 8	w and jumping, and praising God.	4344
	3: 9	all the people saw him w and praising God,	4344
2Jn	1: 4	to find some of your children w in the truth,	4344
3Jn	1: 4	to hear that my children *are* w in the truth.	4344

WALKS (15) [WALK]

Ex	21:19	if the other gets up and w **around** outside	2143
Lev	11:42	whether it moves on its belly or w	2143
Pr	10: 9	The man of integrity w securely,	2143
	13:20	*He who* w with the wise grows wise,	2143
	28:26	but *he who* w in wisdom is kept safe.	2143
Ecc	2:14	while the fool w in the darkness;	2143
	10: 3	Even as he w along the road,	2143
Isa	33:15	*He who* w righteously	2143
	50:10	Let *him who* w in the dark,	2143
	59: 8	no one *who* w in them will know peace.	2005
Jn	11: 9	A man who w by day will not stumble,	4344
	11:10	It is when he w by night that he stumbles,	4344
	12:35	The man who w in the dark does not know	4344
1Jn	2:11	the darkness and w **around** in the darkness;	4344
Rev	2: 1	and w among the seven golden lampstands:	4344

WALL (169) [WALLED, WALLS]

Ge	49:22	whose branches climb over a w.	8803
Ex	14:22	a w of water on their right and on their left.	2570
	14:29	a w of water on their right and on their left.	2570
	15: 8	The surging waters stood firm like a w;	5603
Lev	11:30	the w **lizard**, the skink and the chameleon.	4321

Lev	14:37	to be deeper than the surface of the w,	7815
Nu	22:25	she pressed close to the w,	7815
	35: 4	fifteen hundred feet from the town w.	7815
Jos	2:15	house she lived in was part of the city w.	2570
	6: 5	then the w *of* the city will collapse and	2570
	6:20	a loud shout, the w collapsed;	2570
1Sa	18:11	saying to himself, "I'll pin David to the w."	7815
	19:10	Saul tried to pin him to the w with his spear,	7815
	19:10	as Saul drove the spear into the w.	7815
	20:25	He sat in his customary place by the w,	7815
	25:16	Night and day they were a w around us all	2570
	31:10	and fastened his body to the w	2570
	31:12	the bodies of Saul and his sons from the w	2570
2Sa	11:20	know they would shoot arrows from the w?	2570
	11:21	an upper millstone on him from the w,	2570
	11:21	Why did you get so close to the w?'	2570
	11:24	at your servants from the w,	2570
	18:24	up to the roof of the gateway by the w,	2570
	20:15	they were battering the w to bring it down,	2570
	20:21	His head will be thrown to you from the w."	2570
	22:30	with my God I can scale a w.	8803
1Ki	3: 1	and the w around Jerusalem.	2570
	6:27	The wing of one cherub touched one w,	7815
	6:27	the wing of the other touched the other w,	7815
	7:12	The great courtyard was surrounded by a w	NIH
	9:15	the supporting terraces, the w of Jerusalem,	2570
	11:27	and had filled in the **gap in the** w of the city	7288
	20:30	the w collapsed on twenty-seven thousand	2570
	21:23	'Dogs will devour Jezebel by the w	2658
2Ki	3:27	and offered him as a sacrifice on the **city w.**	2570
	6:26	the king of Israel was passing by on the w,	2570
	6:30	As he went along the w, the people looked,	2570
	9:33	of her blood spattered the w and the horses	7815
	14:13	the w of Jerusalem from the Ephraim Gate	2570
	18:26	in the hearing of the people on the w."	2570
	18:27	and not to the men sitting on the w—	2570
	20: 2	to the w and prayed to the LORD,	7815
	25: 4	Then the city w was broken through,	NIH
1Ch	11: 8	terraces to the **surrounding** w,	AIT
2Ch	3:11	and touched the temple w,	7815
	3:12	and touched the other temple w,	7815
	25:23	the w of Jerusalem from the Ephraim Gate	2570
	26: 9	the Valley Gate and at the **angle of the** w,	5243
	27: 3	and did extensive work on the w *at* the hill	2570
	32: 5	sections of the w and built up the towers on.	2570
	32: 5	He built another w outside that one	2570
	32:18	the people of Jerusalem who were on the w,	2570
	33:14	Afterward he rebuilt the outer w of the City	2570
	36:19	to God's temple and broke down the w	2570
Ezr	9: 9	a w **of protection** in Judah and Jerusalem.	1555
Ne	1: 3	The w *of* Jerusalem is broken down,	2570
	2: 8	the citadel by the temple and for the city w	2570
	2:15	up the valley by night, examining the w.	2570
	2:17	Come, let us rebuild the w *of* Jerusalem,	2570
	3: 8	as far as the Broad W.	2570
	3:13	also repaired five hundred yards of the w	2570
	3:15	also repaired the w *of* the Pool of Siloam,	2570
	3:27	from the great projecting tower to the w	2570
	4: 1	that we were rebuilding the w,	2570
	4: 2	*Will they* **restore** their w?	6441
	4: 3	he would break down their w *of* stones!"	2570
	4: 6	the w till all of it reached half its height,	2570
	4:10	that we cannot rebuild the w."	2570
	4:13	the people behind the lowest points of the w	2570
	4:15	we all returned to the w,	2570
	4:17	who were building the w.	2570
	4:19	from each other along the w.	2570
	5:16	I devoted myself to the work on this w	2570
	6: 1	of our enemies that I had rebuilt the w and	2570
	6: 6	and therefore you are building the w.	2570
	6:15	So the w was completed on the twenty-fifth	2570
	7: 1	After the w had been rebuilt and I had set	2570
	12:27	At the dedication of the w *of* Jerusalem,	2570
	12:30	purified the people, the gates and the w.	2570
	12:31	the leaders of Judah go up on top of the w.	2570
	12:31	to proceed on top of the w to the right,	2570
	12:37	the w and passed above the house of David	2570
	12:38	I followed them on top of the w,	2570
	12:38	the Tower of the Ovens to the Broad W,	2570
	13:21	"Why do you spend the night by the w?	2570
Ps	18:29	with my God I can scale a w.	8803
	62: 3	this leaning w, this tottering fence?	7815
	78:13	he made the water stand firm like a w.	5603
Pr	18:11	they imagine it an unscalable w.	2570
	24:31	and the stone w was in ruins.	1555
Ecc	10: 8	whoever breaks through a w may be bitten	1555
SS	2: 9	There he stands behind our w,	4185
	8: 9	If she is a w, we will build towers of silver	2570
	8:10	I am a w, and my breasts are like towers.	2570
Isa	2:15	for every lofty tower and every fortified w,	2570
	5: 5	I will break down its w,	1555
	22:10	and tore down houses to strengthen the w.	2570
	25: 4	like a storm driving against a w	7815
	30:13	this sin will become for you like a high w,	2570
	36:11	in the hearing of the people on the w."	2570
	36:12	and not to the men sitting on the w—	2570
	38: 2	to the w and prayed to the LORD,	7815
	59:10	Like the blind we grope along the w,	7815
Jer	1:18	an iron pillar and a bronze w to stand	2570
	15:20	I will make you a w to this people,	2570
	15:20	a fortified w of bronze;	NIH
	21: 4	who are outside the w besieging you.	2570
	39: 2	the city w was broken through.	NIH
	51:44	And the w of Babylon will fall.	2570
	51:58	"Babylon's thick w will be leveled	2570
	51:58	Then the city w was broken through,	NIH
La	2: 8	The LORD determined to tear down the w	2570

La	2:18	O **w** of the Daughter of Zion,	2570
Eze	4: 3	as an iron **w** between you and the city	7815
	8: 7	I looked, and I saw a hole in the **w.**	7815
	8: 8	"Son of man, now dig into the **w.**"	7815
	8: 8	I dug into the **w** and saw a doorway there.	7815
	12: 5	through the **w** and take your belongings out	7815
	12: 7	Then in the evening I dug through the **w**	7815
	12:12	and a hole will be dug in the **w** for him	7815
	13: 5	You have not gone up to the breaks in the **w**	1555
	13:10	and because, when a **flimsy w** is built,	2666
	13:12	When the **w** collapses,	7815
	13:14	I will tear down the **w** you have covered	7815
	13:15	So I will spend my wrath against the **w** and	7815
	13:15	"The **w** is gone and so are those who	7815
	22:30	up the **w** and stand before me in the gap	1555
	23:14	She saw men portrayed on a **w,**	7815
	38:20	the cliffs will crumble and every **w** will fall	2570
	40: 5	I saw a **w** completely surrounding	2570
	40: 5	He measured the	1230
	40:12	of each alcove was a **w** one cubit high,	1473
	40:13	from the **top of the** *rear* **w**	1511
	40:40	the outside **w** of the portico of the gateway,	4190
	40:43	were attached to the **w** all around.	1074
	41: 5	Then he measured the **w** of the temple;	7815
	41: 6	the **w** of the temple to serve as supports for	7815
	41: 6	the supports were not inserted into the **w** of	7815
	41: 9	The outer **w** of the side rooms	1555
	41:12	The **w** of the building was five cubits thick	7815
	41:16	The floor, the **w** up to the windows,	NIH
	41:20	and palm trees were carved on the **w** of	7815
	42: 1	and opposite the **outer w** on the north side.	1230
	42: 7	There was an outer **w** parallel to the rooms	1555
	42:10	along the length of the **w** of the outer court,	1555
	42:10	and opposite the **outer w,**	1230
	42:12	to the corresponding **w** extending eastward,	1556
	42:20	It had a **w** around it,	2570
	43: 8	with only a **w** between me and them,	7815
Da	5: 5	and wrote on the plaster of the **w,**	10376
Hos	2: 6	*I will* **w** her **in** so that she cannot find	1553+1555
Joel	2: 9	they run along the **w.**	2570
Am	4: 3	straight out through **breaks in the w,**	7288
	5:19	and rested his hand on the **w** only to have	7815
	7: 7	by a **w** that had been built true to plumb,	2570
Na	2: 5	They dash to the **city w;**	2570
	3: 8	The river was her defense, the waters her **w.**	2570
Hab	2:11	The stones of the **w** will cry out,	7815
Zec	2: 5	And I myself will be a **w** of fire around it,'	2570
Mt	21:33	He put a **w** around it,	5850
Mk	12: 1	He put a **w** around it,	5850
Ac	9:25	in a basket through an opening in the **w,**	5446
	23: 3	"God will strike you, *you* whitewashed **w!**	5526
2Co	11:33	in the **w** and slipped through his hands.	5446
Eph	2:14	the **dividing w** of hostility,	3546
Rev	21:12	It had a great, high **w** with twelve gates,	5446
	21:14	The **w** of the city had twelve foundations,	5446
	21:17	He measured its **w** and it was 144 cubits	5446
	21:18	The **w** was made of jasper,	5446

WALLED (4) [WALL]

Lev	25:29	" 'If a man sells a house in a **w** city,	2570
	25:30	the house in the **w** city shall belong	
		permanently to the buyer	2257+2570+4200
1Ki	4:13	Argob in Bashan and its sixty large **w** cities	2570
La	3: 7	*He has* **w** me in so I cannot escape;	1553

WALLOW (1) [WALLOWING]

Jer	48:26	*Let* Moab **w** in her vomit;	6216

WALLOWING (2) [WALLOW]

2Sa	20:12	Amasa **lay w** in his blood in the middle of	1670
2Pe	2:22	"A sow that is washed goes back to her **w** in	3243

WALLS (98) [WALL]

Lev	14:37	He is to examine the mildew on the **w,**	7815
	14:39	If the mildew has spread on the **w,**	7815
	14:41	the inside of the house scraped and	NIH
	25:31	houses in villages without **w** around them	2570
Nu	22:24	two vineyards, with **w** on both sides.	1555
Dt	1:28	the cities are large, with **w** up to the sky.	1290
	3: 5	All these cities were fortified with high **w**	2570
	9: 1	with large cities that have **w** up to the sky.	1290
	28:52	until the high fortified **w** in which you trust	2570
1Ki	4:33	to the hyssop that grows out of **w.**	7815
	6: 5	Against the **w** of the main hall	7815
	6: 6	be inserted into the temple **w.**	7815
	6:15	He lined its interior **w** with cedar boards,	7815
	6:29	On the **w** all around the temple,	7815
2Ki	25: 4	at night through the gate between the *two* **w**	2570
	25:10	broke down the **w** around Jerusalem.	2570
1Ch	29: 4	for the overlaying of the **w** of the buildings,	7815
2Ch	3: 7	**w** and doors of the temple with gold,	7815
	3: 7	and he carved cherubim on the **w.**	7815
	8: 5	with **w** and with gates and bars,	2570
	14: 7	he said to Judah, "and put **w** around them,	2570
	26: 6	the Philistines and broke down the **w**	2570
Ezr	4:12	They are restoring the **w** and repairing	10703
	4:13	if this city is built and its **w** are restored,	10703
	4:16	if this city is built and its **w** are restored,	10703
	5: 8	and placing the timbers in the **w.**	10376
Ne	2:13	examining the **w** of Jerusalem,	2570
	4: 7	the repairs to Jerusalem's **w** had gone ahead	2570
Ps	51:18	build up the **w** of Jerusalem.	2570
	55:10	Day and night they prowl about on its **w;**	2570
	80:12	Why have you broken down its **w** so	1555

Ps	89:40	You have broken through all his **w**	1556
	122: 7	May there be peace within your **w**	2658
	144:14	There will be no **breaching of w,**	7288
Pr	25:28	Like a city whose **w** are broken down is	2570
SS	5: 7	those watchmen of the **w!**	2570
Isa	22: 5	a day of battering down **w** and of crying out	7815
	22:11	You built a reservoir between the *two* **w** for	2570
	25:12	He will bring down your high fortified **w**	2570
	26: 1	God makes salvation its **w** and ramparts.	2570
	49:16	your **w** are ever before me.	2570
	54:12	and all your **w** of precious stones.	1473
	56: 5	within my temple and its **w** a memorial and	2570
	58:12	**Repairer of** Broken **W,**	1553
	60:10	"Foreigners will rebuild your **w,**	2570
	60:18	but you will call your **w** Salvation	2570
	62: 6	I have posted watchmen on your **w,**	2570
Jer	1:15	against all her surrounding **w** and against all	2570
	39: 4	through the gate between the *two* **w,**	2570
	39: 8	and broke down the **w** of Jerusalem.	2570
	49: 3	rush here and there inside the the **w,**	1555
	49:27	"I will set fire to the **w** of Damascus;	2570
	50:15	her towers fall, her **w** are torn down.	2570
	51:12	Lift up a banner against the **w** *of* Babylon!	2570
	52: 7	at night through the gate between the *two* **w**	2570
	52:14	of the imperial guard broke down all the **w**	2570
La	2: 7	over to the enemy the **w** *of* her palaces;	2570
	2: 8	He made ramparts and **w** lament;	2570
Eze	5:12	by the sword **outside** your **w;**	6017
	8:10	and I saw portrayed all over the **w** all kinds	7815
	26: 4	They will destroy the **w** *of* Tyre and pull	2570
	26: 8	to your **w** and raise his shields against you.	NIH
	26: 9	against your **w** and demolish your towers	2570
	26:10	Your **w** will tremble at the noise of	2570
	26:10	a city whose **w** have been broken through.	NIH
	26:12	down your **w** and demolish your fine houses	2570
	27:10	and helmets on your **w,**	NIH
	27:11	Men of Arvad and Helech manned your **w**	2570
	27:11	They hung their shields around your **w;**	2570
	33:30	by the **w** and at the doors of the houses,	7815
	38:11	of them living without **w** and without gates	2570
	40: 7	and the projecting **w** between	NIH
	40:10	of the **projecting w** on each side had	382
	40:14	the faces of the **projecting w** all around the	382
	40:16	The alcoves and the **projecting w** inside	382
	40:16	of the **projecting w** were decorated	382
	40:21	its **projecting w** and its portico had	382
	40:26	the faces of the **projecting w** on each side.	382
	40:29	its **projecting w** and its portico had	382
	40:33	its **projecting w** and its portico had	382
	40:36	its **projecting w** and its portico,	382
	40:48	and its **projecting w** were three cubits wide	4190
	41: 2	and the **projecting w** on each side	4190
	41: 3	and the **projecting w** on each side	NIH
	41:13	with its **w** were also a hundred cubits long.	7815
	41:17	and on the **w** at regular intervals all around	7815
	41:25	and palm trees like those carved on the **w,**	7815
Joel	2: 7	they scale **w** like soldiers.	2570
Am	1: 7	I will send fire upon the **w** *of* Gaza	2570
	1:10	I will send fire upon the **w** *of* Tyre	2570
	1:14	I will set fire to the **w** *of* Rabbah	2570
Mic	7:11	The day for building your **w** will come,	1556
Na	3:17	like swarms of locusts that settle in the **w** on	1556
Zec	2: 4	'Jerusalem will be a **city w** without	7252
Lk	19:44	you and the children within your **w.**	NIG
Heb	11:30	By faith the **w** of Jericho fell,	5446
Rev	21:15	to measure the city, its gates and its **w.**	5446
	21:19	the city **w** were decorated with every kind	5446

WANDER (17) [WANDERED, WANDERER, WANDERERS, WANDERING, WANDERS]

Ge	20:13	And when God **had** me **w** from my father's	9494
Nu	32:13	he **made** them **w** in the desert forty years,	5675
2Sa	15:20	today *shall I* **make** you **w** about with us,	5675
2Ki	21: 8	I will not again **make** the feet of the	
		Israelites **w** from the land	5653
Job	38:41	when its young cry out to God and **w about**	9494
Ps	59:11	In your might **make** them **w** about,	5675
	59:15	They **w about** for food and howl if	5675
	107:40	**made** them **w** in a trackless waste.	9494
Pr	17:24	but a fool's eyes **w** to the ends of the earth.	NIH
Isa	63:17	*do you* **make** us **w** from your ways	9494
Jer	14:10	"They greatly love to **w;**	5675
	31:22	How long *will you* **w,**	2811
La	4:15	When they flee and **w** about,	5675
Am	8:12	from sea to sea and **w** from north to east,	8763
Zec	10: 2	*the people* **w** like sheep oppressed for lack	5825
Mt	18:13	about the ninety-nine that *did* not **w off.**	4414
Jas	5:19	if one of you *should* **w** from the truth	4414

WANDERED (14) [WANDER]

Ge	21:14	She went on her way and **w** in the desert	9494
1Ch	16:20	*they* **w** from nation to nation,	2143
Ps	105:13	*they* **w** from nation to nation,	2143
	107: 4	*Some* **w** in desert wastelands,	9494
Jer	50: 6	over mountain and hill	2143
Eze	34: 6	My sheep **w** over all the mountains and	8706
	44:10	when Israel went astray and who **w** from me	9494
Mt	18:12	and go to look for the one that **w off?**	4414
1Ti	1: 6	Some *have* **w away from** these and turned	1762
	6:10	eager for money, *have* **w from** the faith	675
	6:21	and in so doing *have* **w from** the faith.	846
2Ti	2:18	who *have* **w away from** the truth.	846
Heb	11:38	*They* **w** in deserts and mountains,	NIH
2Pe	2:15	and **w off** to follow the way of Balaam son	4414

WANDERER (3) [WANDER]

Ge	4:12	You will be a restless **w** on the earth."	5653
	4:14	I will be a restless **w** on the earth,	5653
Isa	58: 7	and to provide the poor **w** with shelter—	5291

WANDERERS (1) [WANDER]

Hos	9:17	they will be **w** among the nations.	5610

WANDERING (10) [WANDER]

Ge	37:15	a man found him **w around** in the fields	9494
Ex	14: 3	**w around** the land **in confusion,**	1003
	23: 4	across your enemy's ox or donkey **w off,**	9494
Dt	26: 5	"My father *was* a **w** Aramean,	6
Job	12:24	*he* **sends** them **w** through a trackless waste.	9494
Ps	109:10	*May* his children *be* **w** beggars;	5675
La	1: 7	her affliction in Jerusalem remembers	5291
	3:19	I remember my affliction and my **w,**	5291
Hos	8: 9	up to Assyria like a wild donkey **w alone.**	969
Jude	1:13	**w** stars, for whom the blackest darkness	4417

WANDERS (3) [WANDER]

Job	15:23	He **w about**—food for vultures;	5610
	18: 8	His feet thrust him into a net and *he* **w** into	2143
Mt	18:12	and one of them **w away,**	4414

WANE (1)

Isa	60:20	and your moon *will* **w** no more;	665

WANT (175) [WANTED, WANTING, WANTS]

Ge	24: 3	*I* **w** you to swear by the LORD,	8678
	29:21	and *I* **w** to **lie with** her."	AIT
	42:36	and now *you* **w** to **take** Benjamin.	AIT
Ex	16: 8	**all** the bread you **w** in the morning,	8425
	16:23	So bake what *you* **w** to **bake**	AIT
	16:23	to bake and boil what *you* **w** to **boil.**	AIT
	21: 5	and children and *do* not **w** to **go** free,'	AIT
Lev	26: 5	you will eat **all** the food you **w**	8427
Nu	16:13	And now *you* also **w** to **lord** it over us?	AIT
	20:19	We only **w** to **pass through** on foot—	AIT
Dt	12:15	and eat as much of the meat as you **w,**	205
	12:20	then you may eat as much of it as you **w.**	205
	12:21	you may eat as much of them as you **w.**	205
	15:16	"I *do* not **w** to **leave** you,"	AIT
	23:24	you may eat **all** the grapes you **w,**	8427
	25: 7	man *does* not **w** to marry his brother's wife,	2911
	25: 7	"I *do* not **w** to marry her,"	2911
Jdg	9:15	you really **w** to **anoint** me king over you,	AIT
1Sa	2:16	and then take whatever you **w,"**	203
	8:19	"We **w** a king over us.	2118S
	12:12	'No, we **w** a king to rule over us'—	NIH
	20: 4	"Whatever you **w** me to do, I'll do for you."	606
	If you **w** it, take it;		4374
2Sa	14:32	Now then, *I* **w** to **see** the king's face,	AIT
	18:22	"My son, why *do you* **w** to **go?**	AIT
	18:23	He said, "Come what may, *I* **w** to **run.**"	AIT
	20:19	Why *do you* **w** to **swallow up**	AIT
	21: 4	"What *do you* **w** me to do for you?"	606
	24: 3	But why *does* my lord the king **w** to do such	2911
1Ki	1:16	"What is it you **w?"**	4200
	3: 5	"Ask for whatever you **w** me to give you."	NIH
	5: 8	and will do all you **w** in providing the cedar	2914
	11:22	"What have you lacked here that you **w**	1335
1Ch	21: 3	Why *does* my lord **w** to do this?	1335
2Ch	1: 7	"Ask for whatever you **w** me to give you."	NIH
Ne	2: 4	The king said to me, "What is it you **w?"**	1335
Job	24:16	*they* **w** nothing **to do with** the light.	3359
	30: 3	Haggard from **w** and hunger,	2895
	33:32	speak up, for *I* **w** you to be cleared.	2911
	37:20	Should he be told that *I* **w** to **speak?**	AIT
Ps	23: 1	The LORD is my shepherd, *I* shall not be	
		in **w.**	2893
	71:13	may *those who* **w** to harm me be covered	1335
Jer	40: 4	but if you do **not w** to, then don't come.	
			928+6524+8273
	42:22	and plague in the place *where you* **w** to go	2911
Eze	20:32	" 'You say, "We **w** to be like the nations,	AIT
	36:32	*I* **w** you to **know** that I am not doing this	AIT
Da	2: 3	a dream that troubles me and *I* **w**	NIH
	3:18	But even if he does not, we **w** you to **know,**	AIT
Mt	1:19	did not **w** to expose her to public disgrace	2527
	8:29	**"What do** you **w** with us,	2779+5515
	12:38	we **w** to see a miraculous sign from you."	2527
	13:28	'*Do you* **w** us to go and pull them up?'	2527
	15:32	I *do* not **w** to send them away hungry,	2527
	19:17	If *you* **w** to enter life,	2527
	19:21	Jesus answered, "If *you* **w** to be perfect, go,	2527
	20:14	*I* **w** to give the man who was hired last	2527
	20:15	to do what *I* **w** with my own money?	2527
	20:21	"What is it you **w?"**	2527
	20:32	"What *do you* **w** me to do for you?"	2527
	20:33	"Lord," they answered, "we **w** our sight."	2671
	26:17	"Where *do you* **w** us to make preparations	2527
	27:17	"Which one *do you* **w** me to release to you:	2527
	27:21	of the two *do you* **w** me to release to you?"	2527
Mk	1:24	**"What do** you **w** with us, Jesus	2779+5515
	5: 7	**"What do** you **w** with me, Jesus,	2779+5515
	6:22	"Ask me for anything you **w,**	2527
	6:25	"I **w** you to give me right now the head	2527
	6:26	he *did* not **w** to refuse her.	2527
	7:24	a house and *did* not **w** anyone to know it;	2527
	7:27	"First let the children **eat all they w,"**	5963
	9:30	not **w** anyone to know where they were,	2527
	10:35	"we **w** you to do for us whatever we ask."	2527

Mk	10:36	"What *do you* w me to do for you?"	2527
	10:51	"What *do you* w me to do for you?"	2527
	10:51	The blind man said, "Rabbi, I w to see."	2671
	14: 7	and you can help them any time *you* w.	2527
	14:12	"Where *do you* w us to go	2527
	15: 9	*"Do you* w me to release to you the king of	2527
Lk	4: 6	and I can give it to anyone *I* w to.	2527
	4:34	**What do** you w with us, Jesus	2779+5515
	8:28	**"What do** you w with me, Jesus,	2779+5515
	9:54	*do you* w us to call fire down from heaven	2527
	16:26	those who w to go from here to you cannot,	2527
	18:41	"What *do you* w me to do for you?"	2527
	18:41	"Lord, I w to see," he replied.	2671
	19:14	*'We* don't w this man to be our king.'	2527
	19:27	of mine who *did* not w me to be king	2527
	22: 9	"Where *do you* w us to prepare for it?"	2527
Jn	1:38	"What *do you* w?"	2426
	4:27	But no one asked, "What *do you* w?"	2426
	5: 6	he asked him, *"Do you* w to get well?"	2527
	6:67	"You *do* not w to leave too, do you?"	2527
	8:44	and *you* w to carry out your father's desire.	2527
	9:27	Why *do you* w to hear it again?	2527
	9:27	*Do you* w to become his disciples, too?"	2527
	17:24	*I* w those you have given me to be with me	2527
	18: 4	"Who is it *you* w?"	2426
	18: 7	Again he asked them, "Who is it *you* w?"	2426
	18:39	*Do you* w me to release 'the king of	1089
	19:31	Because the Jews did not w the bodies left	NIG
	21:18	and lead you where *you do* not w to go."	2527
	21:22	"If *I* w him to remain alive until I return,	2527
	21:23	"If *I* w him to remain alive until I return,	2527
Ac	7:26	why do you w to hurt each other?"	NIG
	7:28	*Do you* w to kill me as you killed	2527
	13:22	he will do everything I w him to do.'	2525
	13:38	*I* w you to know that through Jesus	1639
	16:37	now *do they* w to **get rid of** us quietly?	AIT
	17:20	and *we* w to know what they mean."	1089
	17:32	*"We* w to **hear** you again on this subject."	AIT
	19:39	there is anything further *you* w **to bring up,**	2118
	23:19	"What is it *you* w to tell me?"	2400
	28:22	But *we* w to hear what your views are,	546
	28:28	"Therefore *I* w **you to know** that God's	AIT
Ro	1:13	*I do* not w you to be unaware, brothers,	2527
	7:15	For what *I* w to do I do not do,	2527
	7:16	And if I do what *I do* not w to do,	2527
	7:19	For what I do is not the good *I* w to do;	2527
	7:19	no, the evil *I do* not w to do—	2527
	7:20	Now if I do what *I do* not w to do,	2527
	7:21	I w to do good, evil is right there with me.	2527
	11:25	not w you to be ignorant of this mystery,	2527
	13: 3	*Do you* w to be free from fear of the one	2527
	16:19	but *I* w you to be wise about what is good,	2527
1Co	4: 8	Already *you* **have all you** w!	1639+3170
	7:28	and I w to spare you this.	NIG
	10: 1	*I do* not w you to be ignorant of the fact,	2527
	10:20	to w to be participants with demons.	2527
	10:27	invites you to a meal and *you* w to go,	2527
	11: 3	Now *I* w you to realize that the head	2527
	12: 1	brothers, *I do* not w you to be ignorant.	2527
	14:35	If *they* w to inquire about something,	2527
	15: 1	*I* w to **remind** you of the gospel I preached	AIT
	16: 7	*I do* not w to see you now and make only	2527
2Co	1: 8	*We do* not w you to be uninformed,	2527
	8: 1	*we* w **you to know** about the grace that God	AIT
	8: 8	but *I* w *to* **test** the sincerity of your love	AIT
	8:20	*We* w *to* **avoid** any criticism of the way we	AIT
	10: 9	not w to seem to be trying to frighten you	2671
	10:16	not w *to* **boast about** work already done	AIT
	11:12	from under those who w an opportunity to	2527
	12:14	what *I* w is not your possessions but you.	2426
	12:20	when I come I may not find you as *I* w you	2527
	12:20	and you may not find me as *you* w me	2527
Gal	1:11	*I* w you *to* **know,** brothers, that the gospel	AIT
	4:17	What *they* w is to alienate you [from us],	2527
	4:21	Tell me, you who w to be under the law,	2527
	5:17	so that you do not do what *you* w.	2527
	6:12	Those who w to make a good impression	2527
	6:13	yet *they* w you to be circumcised	2527
Php	1:12	Now *I* w you to know, brothers,	1089
	3:10	I w to **know** Christ and the power of his	AIT
	4:12	whether living in plenty or **in** w.	5728
Col	2: 1	*I* w you to know how much I am struggling	2527
1Th	4:13	we do not w you to be ignorant	2527
1Ti	1: 7	They w to be teachers of the law,	2527
	2: 8	I w men everywhere to lift up holy hands	1089
	2: 9	I also w women to dress modestly,	NIG
	5:11	their dedication to Christ, *they* w to marry.	2527
	6: 9	People who w to get rich fall into temptation	1089
2Ti	4: 3	to say **what** their itching ears w **to hear.**	198
Tit	3: 8	And *I* w you to stress these things,	1089
Phm	1:14	not w to do anything without your consent,	2527
Heb	6:11	*We* w each of you to show this same	2121
	6:12	We do not w you to become lazy,	2671
	13:23	*I* w *you to* **know** that our brother Timothy	AIT
Jas	2:20	*do you* w evidence that faith without deeds	2527
	4: 2	*You* w something but don't get it.	2121
	4: 2	but you cannot have what you w.	NIG
2Pe	3: 2	I w you **to recall** the words spoken in the	AIT
2Jn	1:12	but *I do* not w to use paper and ink.	1089
3Jn	1:10	He also stops those who w to do so	1089
	1:13	*I do* not w to do you with pen and ink,	1089
Jude	1: 5	*I* w to remind you that the Lord delivered	AIT
Rev	11: 6	every kind of plague as often as *they* w.	2527

WANTED (53) [WANT]

Ex	4:19	men who w **to kill** you are dead."	906+1335+5883

Ex	16: 3	and ate **all** the food we w,	8427
Ru	2:14	She ate **all** *she* w and had some left over.	8425
2Sa	3:17	For some time *you have* w to make David your king.	1335+4200
	3:19	house of Benjamin w **to do.**	928+3202+6524
1Ki	5:10	with all the cedar and pine logs he w,	2914
	9:11	with all the cedar and pine and gold he w.	2914
	13:33	Anyone *who* w to become a priest	2913
Est	2:13	Anything *she* w was given her to take	606
Ps	35:25	"Aha, **just what** we w!"	5883
	71:24	for *those who* w to harm me have been put	1335
Ecc	2: 3	*I* w *to* **see** what was worthwhile for men	AIT
Jer	49: 9	they not steal only **as much as** they w?	1896
Da	5:19	Those he w to put to death,	10605
	5:19	those *he* w to spare, he spared;	10605
	5:19	those *he* w to promote, he promoted;	10605
	5:19	and those *he* w to humble, he humbled.	10605
	7:19	"Then *I* w to know the true meaning of	10605
	7:20	I *also* w to know about the ten horns	NIH
Ob	1: 5	they not steal only **as much as** they w?	1896
Jnh	4: 8	He w to die, and said,	906+5883+8626
Mt	14: 5	Herod w to kill John,	2527
	18:23	the kingdom of heaven is like a king who w	2527
	21:31	"Which of the two did what his father w?"	2525
Mk	3:13	and called to him those he w,	2527
	6:19	a grudge against John and w to kill him.	2527
Lk	10:24	and kings w to see what you see but did	2527
	10:29	But he w to justify himself,	2527
	19: 3	*He* w to see who Jesus was,	2426
Jn	6:11	to those who were seated as much as *they* w.	2527
	7:44	Some w to seize him,	2527
	16:19	Jesus saw that they w to ask him about this,	2527
	18:28	w *to be able to* **eat** the Passover.	AIT
	21:18	and went where *you* w;	2527
Ac	5:33	were furious and w to put them to death.	1089
	10:10	He became hungry and w something to eat,	2527
	13: 7	for Barnabas and Saul because he w to hear	2118
	14:13	to the city gates because *he* and the crowd w	2527
	15:37	Barnabas w to take John, also called Mark,	1089
	16: 3	Paul w to take him along on the journey,	2527
	18:27	When Apollos w to go to Achaia,	1089
	19:30	Paul w to appear before the crowd,	1089
	22:30	*since* the commander w to find out	1089
	23:28	*I* w to know why they were accusing him,	1089
	24:27	Felix w to grant a favor to the Jews,	1089
	27:13	they thought they had obtained what they w;	4606
	27:38	When *they had* **eaten as much as** *they* w,	3170
	27:43	But the centurion w to spare Paul's life	1089
	28:18	They examined me and w to release me,	1089
1Co	12:18	every one of them, just as *he* w them to be.	2527
1Th	2:18	For *we* w to come to you—	2527
Heb	6:17	Because God w to make the unchanging	1089
	12:17	*when* he w to inherit this blessing,	2527

WANTING (10) [WANT]

Da	5:27	been weighed on the scales and found w.	10276
Mt	12:46	stood outside, w to speak to him.	2426
	12:47	standing outside, w to speak to you."	2426
Mk	15:15	W to satisfy the crowd, Pilate released	1089
Lk	8:20	standing outside, w to see you."	2527
	23: 8	for a long time he had been w to see him.	2527
	23:20	W to release Jesus, Pilate appealed to them	2527
Ac	23:15	the pretext of w more accurate information	3516
	23:20	the pretext of w more accurate information	3516
2Pe	3: 9	patient with you, not w anyone to perish,	1089

WANTON (2)

Isa	47: 8	"Now then, listen, you w *creature,*	6349
Na	3: 4	all because of the w **lust** *of* a harlot,	2393

WANTS (36) [WANT]

Ge	19: 9	now he w to **play the judge!**	AIT
	43:18	He w to attack us and overpower us	NIH
Ex	12:48	who w to **celebrate** the LORD's Passover	AIT
Nu	6: 2	w to **make a special vow,**	AIT
	9:14	who w to **celebrate** the LORD's Passover	AIT
Ru	3:13	and in the morning if he w **to redeem,** good;	AIT
1Sa	18:25	'The king w no other price for	2914
Jer	22:28	broken pot, an object no one w?	2914
	48:38	like a jar that no one w,"	2914
Eze	46: 7	the lambs as much as he w **to give,**	3338+5952
Mt	5:40	someone to sue you and take your tunic,	2527
	5:42	and do not turn away from the one who w	2527
	16:25	For whoever w to save his life will lose it,	2527
	20:26	whoever w to become great among you	2527
	20:27	whoever w to be first must be your slave—	2527
	27:43	Let God rescue him now if *he* w him,	2527
Mk	8:35	For whoever w to save his life will lose it,	2527
	9:35	"If anyone w to be first, he must be	2527
	10:43	whoever w to become great among you	2527
	10:44	whoever w to be first must be slave of all.	2527
Lk	5:39	no one after drinking old wine w the new,	2527
	9:24	For whoever w to save his life will lose it,	2527
	12:47	not do what his master w will be beaten	2525
	13:31	Herod w to kill you."	2527
	14:28	"Suppose one of you w to build a tower.	2527
Jn	7: 4	No one who w to become a public figure	2426
Ro	9:18	Therefore God has mercy on whom *he* w	2527
	9:18	and he hardens whom *he* w to harden.	2527
1Co	7:36	he should do as he w.	2527
	11:16	If anyone w to be contentious about this,	1506
1Ti	2: 4	who w all men to be saved and to come to	2527
2Ti	2: 4	he w to please his commanding officer,	2671
	3:12	everyone who w to live a godly life	2527
Jas	3: 4	by a very small rudder wherever the pilot w	1089

1Pe	5: 2	you are willing, as God w you to be;	NIG
Rev	11: 5	how anyone who w to harm them must die.	2527

WAR (134) [WARFARE, WARRIOR, WARRIOR'S, WARRIORS, WARS]

Ge	14: 2	**went to** w *against* Bera king of	4878+6913
	31:26	carried off my daughters like captives in w.	2995
Ex	1:10	if w breaks out, will join our enemies,	4878
	13:17	For God said, "If they face w,	4878
	17:16	at w against the Amalekites from generation	4878
	32:17	"There is the sound of w in the camp."	4878
Nu	31: 3	to w against the Midianites and to carry out	7372
	32: 6	"Shall your countrymen go to w	4878
Dt	2: 5	*Do* not **provoke** them to w,	1741
	2: 9	the Moabites or provoke them to w,	4878
	2:19	do not harass them or **provoke** them **to** w,	1741
	4:34	by miraculous signs and wonders, by w,	4878
	20: 1	to w against your enemies and see horses	4878
	20:20	to build siege works until the city at w	4878+6913
	21:10	When you go to w against your enemies	4878
	24: 5	not be sent to w or have any other duty laid	7372
Jos	4:13	the LORD to the plains of Jericho for w.	4878
	6:10	"Do not **give a** w cry,	8131
	9: 2	came together to **make** w against Joshua	4309
	11:18	Joshua waged w against all these kings for	4878
	11:20	to wage w against Israel,	4878
	11:23	Then the land had rest from w.	4878
	14:15	Then the land had rest from w.	4878
	22:12	of Israel gathered at Shiloh to go to w	7372
	22:33	about going to w against them to devastate	7372
Jdg	3:10	he became Israel's judge and went to w.	4878
	5: 8	chose new gods, w came to the city gates,	4311
	11: 4	when the Ammonites **made** w on Israel,	4309
	11:27	but you are doing me wrong by **waging** w	4309
	21:22	we did not get wives for them during the w,	4878
1Sa	8:12	to make weapons of w and equipment	4878
	14:52	All the days of Saul there was bitter w with	4878
	15:18	**make** w on them until you have wiped them	4309
	17: 1	the Philistines gathered their forces for w	4878
	17:13	oldest sons had followed Saul to the w:	4878
	17:20	to its battle positions, shouting the w **cry.**	4878
	19: 8	Once more w broke out,	4878
2Sa	1:27	The weapons of w have perished!"	4878
	3: 1	The w between the house of Saul and	4878
	3: 6	During the w between the house of Saul and	4878
	8:10	who had been **at** w **with** Tou.	408+4878
	11: 1	at the time when kings **go off** to w,	3655
	11: 7	the soldiers were and how the w was going.	4878
1Ki	8:44	your people go to w against their enemies,	4878
	12:21	to **make** w against the house of Israel and	4309
	15: 6	There was w between Rehoboam and	4878
	15: 7	There was w between Abijah and Jeroboam.	4878
	15:16	There was w between Asa and Baasha king	4878
	15:32	There was w between Asa and Baasha king	4878
	20:18	if they have come out for w,	4878
	22: 1	For three years there was no w	4878
	22: 6	"Shall I go to w against Ramoth Gilead,	4878
	22:15	shall we go to w against Ramoth Gilead,	4878
2Ki	6: 8	the king of Aram was **at** w with Israel.	4309
	8:28	Ahaziah went with Joram son of Ahab to w	4878
	13:12	including *his* w against Amaziah king	4309
	14:15	including *his* w against Amaziah king	4309
	24:16	fighting men, strong and fit for w,	4878
1Ch	5:10	During Saul's reign they waged w against	4878
	5:19	They waged w against the Hagrites, Jetur,	4878
	7:11	fighting men ready to go out to w.	4878
	18:10	who had been **at** w **with** Tou.	408+4878
	20: 1	at the time when kings **go off** to w,	NIH
	20: 4	w broke out with the Philistines, at Gezer.	4878
2Ch	6:34	your people go to w against their enemies,	4878
	11: 1	to **make** w against Israel and to regain	4309
	13: 2	There was w between Abijah and Jeroboam.	4878
	14: 6	at w with him during those years,	4878
	15:19	There was no more w until the thirty-fifth	4878
	16: 9	and from now on you will be at w."	4878
	17:10	that *they* did not **make** w with Jehoshaphat.	4309
	18: 3	we will join you in the w."	4878
	18: 5	"Shall we go to w against Ramoth Gilead,	4878
	18:14	shall we go to w against Ramoth Gilead,	4878
	20: 1	with some of the Meunites came to make w	4878
	22: 5	with Joram son of Ahab king of Israel to w	4878
	25:13	in the w raided Judean towns from Samaria	4309
	26: 6	*to* w against the Philistines and broke down	4309
	26:13	an army of 307,500 men trained for w,	4878
	27: 5	Jotham **made** w on the king of the	4309
	28:12	those who were arriving from the w.	7372
	32: 2	that he intended to make w on Jerusalem,	4878
	35:21	but the house with which I am **at** w."	4878
Job	38:23	for days of w and battle?	7930
Ps	27: 3	though w break out against me,	7930
	55:21	yet w is *in* his heart;	7930
	68:30	Scatter the nations who delight in w.	7930
	76: 3	and the swords, the weapons of w.	4878
	120: 7	but when I speak, they are for w.	4878
	140: 2	in their hearts and stir up w every day.	4878
	144: 1	who trains my hands for w,	7930
Pr	20:18	if you wage w, obtain guidance.	4878
	24: 6	for waging w you need guidance,	4878
Ecc	3: 8	a time for w and a time for peace.	4878
	8: 8	As no one is discharged in **time of** w,	4878
	9:18	Wisdom is better than weapons of w,	7930
Isa	2: 4	nor will they train for w anymore.	4878
	8: 9	**Raise the** w **cry,** *you* nations,	8131
	13: 4	Almighty is mustering an army for w.	4878
	41:12	Those who wage w *against* you will be	4878
	42:25	his burning anger, the violence of w.	4878

Jer	4:16	raising a **w cry** against the cities of Judah.	7754
	21: 4	about to turn against you the weapons of **w**	4878
	28: 8	and me have prophesied **w,**	4878
	42:14	where we will not see **w** or hear the trumpet	4878
	51:20	"You are my **w club,**	5151
Eze	17:17	be of no help to him in **w,**	4878
	26:10	at the noise of the **w horses,**	7304
	27:14	**w horses** and mules for your merchandise.	7304
	32:27	down to the grave with their weapons of **w,**	4878
	38: 8	a land that has recovered from **w,**	2995
	39: 9	the **w clubs** and spears.	3338+5234
Da	7:21	this horn was waging **w** against the saints	10639
	9:26	**W** will continue until the end,	
	10: 1	and it concerned a great **w.**	7372
	11:10	His sons *will* **prepare for w** and assemble	1741
	11:25	The king of the South *will* **wage w** with a large and	1741+2021+4200+4878
Hos	10: 9	Did not **w** overtake the evildoers in Gibeah?	4878
Joel	3: 9	among the nations: Prepare for **w!**	4878
Am	1:14	will consume her fortresses amid **w cries**	9558
	2: 2	in great tumult amid **w cries** and the blast of	9558
Mic	3: 5	they prepare to wage **w** against him.	4878
	4: 3	nor will they train for **w** anymore.	4878
Lk	14:31	"Or suppose a king is about *to* go to **w**	4483+5202
Ro	7:23	**waging w against** the law of my mind	529
2Co	10: 3	*we do* not **wage w** as the world does.	5129
1Pe	2:11	sinful desires, which **w** against your soul.	5129
Rev	12: 7	And there was **w** in heaven.	4483
	12:17	the woman and went off to make **w** against	4483
	13: 4	Who can **make w** against him?"	4482
	13: 7	He was given power to make **w** against	4483
	17:14	They *will* **make w** against the Lamb,	4482
	19:11	With justice he judges and **makes w.**	4482
	19:19	to make **w** against the rider on the horse	4483

WAR-HORSES (2) [HORSE]

Hos	14: 3	we will not mount **w.**	6061
Zec	9:10	from Ephraim and the **w** from Jerusalem,	6061

WARD (3)

2Sa	5: 6	even the blind and the lame *can* **w** you **off.**"	6073
Isa	47:11	that you cannot **w off with a ransom;**	4105
La	2:14	not expose your sin to **w off** your captivity.	8740

WARDEN (3)

Ge	39:21	him favor in the eyes of the prison **w.**	8569
	39:22	the **w** put Joseph in charge of all those held	8569
	39:23	The **w** paid no attention to anything	8569

WARDER (Anglicized) See WARDEN

WARDROBE (3)

2Ki	10:22	And Jehu said to the keeper of the **w,**	4921
	22:14	the son of Harhas, keeper of the **w.**	955
2Ch	34:22	the son of Hasrah, keeper of the **w.**	955

WARES (9)

2Ki	8: 9	a gift forty camel-loads of all the **finest w**	3206
Eze	27: 9	came alongside to trade for your **w.**	5114
	27:13	and articles of bronze for your **w.**	5114
	27:17	honey, oil and balm for your **w.**	5114
	27:19	cassia and calamus for your **w.**	5114
	27:25	of Tarshish serve as carriers for your **w.**	5114
	27:27	Your wealth, merchandise and **w,**	5114
	27:33	and your **w** you enriched the kings of	5114
	27:34	your **w** and all your company have gone	5114

WARFARE (4) [WAR]

Jdg	3: 2	to teach **w** to the descendants of	4878
1Ki	14:30	There was continual **w** between Rehoboam	4878
2Ch	12:15	There was continual **w** *between* Rehoboam	4878
Isa	27: 8	By **w** and exile you contend with her—	6009

WARM (12) [LUKEWARM, WARMED, WARMING, WARMLY, WARMS]

Jos	9:12	of ours was **w** when we packed it at home	2768
1Ki	1: 1	not *keep* **w** even when they put covers	2801
	1: 2	so that our lord the king *may* keep **w.**"	2801
2Ki	4:34	the boy's body grew **w.**	2801
Job	39:14	on the ground and *lets* them **w** in the sand,	2801
Ecc	4:11	if two lie down together, they will *keep* **w.**	2801
	4:11	But how *can* one *keep* **w** alone?	2801
Isa	44:16	*I am* **w;** I see the fire."	2801
	47:14	Here are no coals to **w** anyone;	2801
Hag	1: 6	You put on clothes, but *are* not **w.**	2801
Jn	18:18	around a fire they had made *to* keep **w,**"	2548
Jas	2:16	I wish you well; *keep* **w** and well fed,"	2548

WARMED (1) [WARM]

Mk	14:54	There he sat with the guards and **w** *himself*	2548

WARMING (4) [WARM]

Job	31:20	for **w** him with the fleece from my sheep,	2801
Mk	14:67	When she saw Peter **w** *himself,*	2548
Jn	18:18	also was standing with them, **w** *himself.*	2548
	18:25	As Simon Peter stood **w** *himself,*	2548

WARMLY (2) [WARM]

Ac	21:17	at Jerusalem, the brothers received us **w.**	830

1Co	16:19	Aquila and Priscilla greet you **w** in the Lord,	4498

WARMS (2) [WARM]

Isa	44:15	some of it he takes and **w** *himself,*	2801
	44:16	He also **w** *himself* and says, "Ah!	2801

WARN (24) [WARNED, WARNING, WARNINGS, WARNS]

Ex	19:21	"Go down and **w** the people so they do	6386
Nu	24:14	*let me* **w** you of what this people will do	3619
1Sa	8: 9	but **w** them solemnly;	6386+6386
1Ki	2:42	make you swear by the LORD and **w** you,	6386
2Ch	19:10	*to* **w** them not to sin against the LORD;	2302
Ps	81: 8	O my people, and *I will* **w** you—	6386
Jer	42:19	Be sure of this: *I* **w** you today	6386
Eze	3:18	not **w** him or speak out to dissuade him	2302
	3:19	But if you *do* **w** the wicked man and he does	2302
	3:20	*you did* not **w** him, he will die for his sin.	2302
	3:21	But if you *do* **w** the righteous man not to sin	2302
	33: 3	and blows the trumpet *to* **w** the people	2302
	33: 6	not blow the trumpet *to* **w** the people and	2302
	33: 9	But if you *do* **w** the wicked man to turn	2302
Lk	16:28	*Let him* **w** them, so that they will not	1371
Ac	4:17	we must **w** these men to speak no longer	580
1Co	4:14	but *to* **w** you, as my dear children.	3805
Gal	5: 2	*I* **w** you, as I did before,	4625
1Th	5:14	we urge you, brothers, **w** those who are idle,	3805
2Th	3:15	as an enemy, but **w** him as a brother.	3805
2Ti	2:14	**W** them before God against quarreling	1371
Tit	3:10	**W** a divisive person once,	3804
	3:10	and then **w** him a second time.	*NIG*
Rev	22:18	I **w** everyone who hears the words of	3455

WARNED (36) [WARN]

Ge	43: 3	"The man **w** us solemnly,	6386+6386
Ex	19:23	because *you* yourself **w** us,	6386
	21:29	habit of goring and the owner *has been* **w**	6386
Nu	16:26	*He w* the assembly, "Move back from	1819
1Sa	19: 2	and **w** him, "My father Saul is looking for	5583
	19:11	But Michal, David's wife, **w** him,	5583
2Sa	2:22	Again Abner **w** Asahel, "Stop chasing me!	606
1Ki	13:26	as the word of the LORD *had* **w** him."	1819
2Ki	6:10	Time and again Elisha **w** the king,	2302
	17:13	The LORD **w** Israel and Judah through all	6386
	17:23	as *he had* **w** through all his servants	1819
Ne	9:29	"You **w** them to return to your law,	6386
	13:15	I **w** them *against* selling food on that day.	6386
	13:21	But I **w** them and said,	6386
Ps	2:10	be **w,** you rulers of the earth.	3579
	19:11	By them *is* your servant **w;**	2302
Ecc	12:12	Be **w,** my son, *of* anything in addition	2302
Jer	11: 7	I **w** them again and again, saying,	6386+6386
	18: 8	and if that nation *I* **w** repents of its evil,	1819
	22:21	I **w** you when you felt secure, but you said,	1819
Mt	2:12	And *having been* **w** in a dream not	5976
	2:22	*Having been* **w** in a dream,	5976
	3: 7	Who **w** you to flee from the coming wrath?	5683
	9:30	Jesus **w** them sternly, "See that no one	1839
	16:20	Then *he* **w** his disciples not to tell anyone	2203
Mk	8:15	"Be careful," Jesus **w** them.	1403
	8:30	Jesus **w** them not to tell anyone about him.	2203
Lk	3: 7	Who **w** you to flee from the coming wrath?	5683
	9:21	Jesus strictly **w** them not to tell this	2203+4133
Jn	16: 4	time comes you will remember that I **w** you.	3306
Ac	2:40	With many other words *he* **w** them;	1371
	27: 9	So Paul **w** them,	4147
1Th	4: 6	as we have already told you and **w** you.	1371
Heb	11: 7	This is why Moses *was* **w** when he was	5976
	11: 7	*when* **w** about things not yet seen,	5976
	12:25	when they refused him who **w** them	5976

WARNING (20) [WARN]

Nu	26:10	And they served as a **w sign.**	5812
2Ki	10:24	had posted eighty men outside with *this* **w:**	606
Ecc	4:13	who no longer knows how to *take* **w.**	2302
Isa	8:11	**w** me not to follow the way of this people.	3579
Jer	6: 8	Take **w,** O Jerusalem, or I will turn away	3579
	6:10	To whom can I speak and *give* **w?**	6386
Eze	3:17	the word I speak and *give* them **w** from me.	2302
	3:21	he will surely live because *he* took **w,**	2302
	5:15	a **w** and an object of horror to the nations	4592
	23:48	all women *may* take **w** and not imitate you.	3579
	33: 4	but *does* not take **w** and the sword comes	2302
	33: 5	the sound of the trumpet but *did* not take **w,**	2302
	33: 5	If *he had* taken **w,** he would have saved	2302
	33: 7	the word I speak and *give* them **w** from me.	2302
Mt	8:24	*Without* **w,** a furious storm came up on	2627
	12:16	**w** them not to tell who he was.	2203
Mk	1:43	sent him away at once *with* a **strong w:**	1839
Ac	20:31	that for three years I never stopped **w** each	3805
2Co	13: 2	already gave you a **w** when I was with you	4625
1Ti	5:20	so that the others may take **w.**	5832

WARNINGS (4) [WARN]

2Ki	17:15	and the **w** he had given them.	6343+6386
Ne	9:34	commands or the **w** you gave them.	6343+6386
Job	33:16	in their ears and terrify them with **w,**	4592
1Co	10:11	as examples and were written down as **w**	3804

WARNS (2) [WARN]

Ac	20:23	that in every city the Holy Spirit **w** me	1371
Heb	12:25	if we turn away from him who **w** us	*NIG*

WARP (KJV) See WOVEN

WARPED (3)

Dt	32: 5	but a **w** and crooked generation.	6836
Pr	12: 8	but *men with* **w** minds are despised.	6390
Tit	3:11	be sure that such a man *is* **w** and sinful;	1750

WARRANTED (1)

2Co	12: 6	so no one will think more of me than is **w**	*NIG*

WARRIOR (21) [WAR]

Ge	10: 8	who grew to be a **mighty w** on the earth.	1475
Ex	15: 3	The LORD is a **w;** the LORD is his name.	408+4878
Jdg	6:12	"The LORD is with you, **mighty w.**"	1475
	11: 1	Jephthah the Gileadite was a **mighty w.**	1475+2657
1Sa	16:18	He is a brave man and a **w.**	408+4878
1Ch	1:10	who grew to be a **mighty w** on earth.	1475
	12:28	a **brave** young **w,** with 22 officers	1475+2657
	28: 3	you are a **w** and have shed blood.'	408+4878
2Ch	28: 7	Zicri, an Ephraimite **w,** killed Maaseiah	1475
Job	16:14	he rushes at me like a **w.**	1475
Ps	33:16	no **w** escapes by his great strength.	1475
	89:19	"I have bestowed strength on a **w;**	1475
	127: 4	of a **w** are sons born in one's youth.	1475
Pr	16:32	Better a patient man than a **w,**	1475
Isa	3: 2	the hero and **w,** the judge and prophet,	408+4878
	42:13	like a **w** he will stir up his zeal;	408+4878
Jer	14: 9	like a **w** powerless to save?	1475
	20:11	But the LORD is with me like a mighty **w;**	6883
	46:12	*One* will stumble over another;	1475
Am	2:14	and the **w** will not save his life.	1475
Zep	1:14	the shouting of the **w** there.	1475

WARRIOR'S (4) [WAR]

2Sa	18:11	give you ten shekels of silver and a **w belt.**"	2514
Ps	120: 4	He will punish you with a **w** sharp arrows,	1475
Isa	9: 5	Every **w** boot used in battle	6008
Zec	9:13	O Greece, and make you like a **w sword.**	1475

WARRIORS (47) [WAR]

Jdg	5:11	the righteous acts of his **w** in Israel.	7251
	18: 2	So the Danites sent five **w** from Zorah	1201+2657
1Sa	2: 4	"The bows of the **w** are broken,	1475
2Sa	20: 7	Pelethites and all the **mighty w** went out	1475
1Ch	5:24	They were brave **w,** famous men,	1475
	7:40	**brave w** and outstanding leaders.	1475+2657
	8:40	The sons of Ulam were **brave w** who	1475+2657
	12: 1	among the **w** who helped him in battle;	1475
	12: 8	They were **brave w,**	1475+2657
	12:21	for all of them were **brave w,**	1475+2657
	12:25	men of Simeon, **w** ready for battle—	1475+2657
	12:30	**brave w,** famous in their own clans—	1475+2657
	28: 1	the mighty men and all the **brave w.**	1475
Ps	76: 5	not one of the **w** can lift his hands.	408+2657
SS	3: 7	escorted by sixty **w,** the noblest of Israel,	1475
	4: 4	all of them shields of **w.**	1475
Isa	3:25	men will fall by the sword, your **w** in battle.	1476
	10:16	a wasting disease upon his **sturdy w;**	*AIT*
	13: 3	I have summoned my **w**	1475
	21:17	the **w** *of* Kedar, will be few."	1475
	49:24	Can plunder be taken from **w,**	1475
	49:25	"Yes, captives will be taken from **w,**	1475
Jer	5:16	all of them are **mighty w.**	1475
	46: 5	they are retreating, their **w** are defeated.	1475
	46: 9	O charioteers! March on, O **w**—	1475
	46:15	Why will your **w** be laid low?	52
	48:14	"How can you say, 'We are **w,**	1475
	48:41	the hearts of Moab's **w** will be like the heart	1475
	49:22	the hearts of Edom's **w** will be like the heart	1475
	50: 9	Their arrows will be like skilled **w** who do	1475
	50:36	A sword against her **w!**	1475
	51:30	Babylon's **w** have stopped fighting;	1475
	51:56	her **w** will be captured,	1475
	51:57	her governors, officers and **w** as well;	1475
La	1:15	Lord has rejected all the **w** in my midst;	52
Eze	23: 5	after her lovers, the Assyrians—**w**	7940
	23:12	governors and commanders, **w** in full dress,	7940
	32:27	the other uncircumcised **w** who have fallen,	1475
	32:27	of these **w** had stalked through the land of	1475
Hos	10:13	on your own strength and on your many **w,**	1475
Joel	2: 7	They charge like **w;** they scale walls	1475
	3: 9	Prepare for war! Rouse the **w!**	1475
	3:11	Bring down your **w,** O LORD!	1475
Am	2:16	the bravest **w** will flee naked on that day,"	1475
Ob	1: 9	Your **w,** O Teman, will be terrified,	1475
Na	2: 3	the **w** are clad in scarlet;	408+2657
Hab	3:14	when his **w** stormed out to scatter us,	7250

WARS (12) [WAR]

Nu	21:14	the Book of the **W** *of* the LORD says:	4878
Jdg	3: 1	not experienced any of the **w** in Canaan	4878
1Ki	5: 3	"You know that because of the **w** waged	4878
	14:19	Jeroboam's reign, *his* and how he ruled,	4309
1Ch	22: 8	shed much blood and have fought many **w.**	4878
2Ch	27: 7	including all his **w** and the other things	4878
Ps	46: 9	He makes **w** cease to the ends of the earth;	4878
Mt	24: 6	You will hear of **w** and rumors of wars,	4483
	24: 6	You will hear of wars and rumors *of* **w,**	4483
Mk	13: 7	When you hear of **w** and rumors of wars,	4483
	13: 7	When you hear of wars and rumors *of* **w,**	4483
Lk	21: 9	When you hear *of* **w** and revolutions,	4483

WARTS (1)
Lev 22:22   or **anything with** w or festering   3301

WAS (4158) [BE] See Index of Articles Etc.

WASH (79) [WASHED, WASHERMAN'S, WASHING, WASHINGS, WHITEWASH, WHITEWASHED]
Ge 18: 4   and then *you may all* w your feet and rest   8175
  19: 2   *You can* w your feet and spend the night and   8175
  24:32   water for him and his men to w their feet.   8175
  43:24   *to* w their feet and provided fodder   8175
  49:11   he will w his garments in wine,   3891
Ex 19:10   *Have them* w their clothes   3891
  29: 4   the Tent of Meeting and w them with water.   8175
  29:17   the ram into pieces and w the inner parts   8175
  30:19   and his sons *are to* w their hands and feet   8175
  30:20   they shall w with water so that they will   8175
  30:21   they shall w their hands and feet so   8175
  40:12   the Tent of Meeting and w them with water.   8175
  40:31   and his sons used it *to* w their hands   8175
Lev 1: 9   *to* w the inner parts and the legs with water,   8175
  1:13   *to* w the inner parts and the legs with water,   8175
  6:27   you must w it in a holy place.   3891
  11:25   of their carcasses *must* w his clothes,   3891
  11:28   up their carcasses *must* w his clothes,   3891
  11:40   of the carcass *must* w his clothes,   3891
  11:40   up the carcass *must* w his clothes,   3891
  13: 6   The man *must* w his clothes.   3891
  13:34   He must w his clothes, and he will be clean.   3891
  14: 8   to be cleansed *must* w his clothes,   3891
  14: 9   He must w his clothes and bathe himself   3891
  14:47   or eats in the house *must* w his clothes.   3891
  15: 5   who touches his bed *must* w his clothes   3891
  15: 6   with a discharge sat on *must* w his clothes   3891
  15: 7   a discharge *must* w his clothes and bathe   3891
  15: 8   that person *must* w his clothes and bathe   3891
  15:10   those things *must* w his clothes   3891
  15:11   with water *must* w his clothes and bathe   3891
  15:13   he must w his clothes and bathe himself   3891
  15:21   Whoever touches her bed *must* w his clothes   3891
  15:22   on *must* w his clothes and bathe   3891
  15:27   he must w his clothes and bathe with water,   3891
  16:26   the goat as a scapegoat *must* w his clothes   3891
  16:28   The man who burns them *must* w his clothes   3891
  17:15   or torn by wild animals *must* w his clothes   3891
  17:16   he does not w his clothes and bathe himself,   3891
Nu 5:23   and then w them **off** into the bitter water.   4681
  8: 7   and w their clothes, and so purify   3891
  19: 7   the priest *must* w his clothes   3891
  19: 8   also w his clothes and bathe with water,   3891
  19:10   of the heifer *must* also w his clothes,   3891
  19:19   person being cleansed *must* w his clothes   3891
  19:21   of cleansing *must* also w his clothes,   3891
  31:24   the seventh day w your clothes and you will   3891
Dt 21: 6   nearest the body *shall* w their hands over   8175
  23:11   as evening approaches he is to w himself,   8175
Ru 3: 3   W and perfume yourself,   8175
1Sa 25:41   and w the feet of my master's servants."   8175
2Sa 11: 8   "Go down to your house and w your feet."   8175
2Ki 5:10   "Go, w *yourself* seven times in the Jordan,   8175
  5:12   Couldn't *I* w in them and be cleansed?"   8175
  5:13   when he tells you, 'W and be cleansed'!"   8175
Job 14:19   and torrents w away the soil,   8851
Ps 26: 6   I w my hands in innocence,   8175
  51: 2   W away all my iniquity and cleanse me   3891
  51: 7   w me, and I will be whiter than snow.   3891
SS 8: 7   rivers cannot w it *away.*   8851
Isa 1:16   w and make yourselves clean.   8175
  4: 4   The Lord *will* w away the filth of   8175
Jer 2:22   Although *you* w yourself with soda   3891
  4:14   w the evil from your heart and be saved.   3891
Mt 6:17   put oil on your head and w your face,   3782
  15: 2   They don't w their hands before they eat!"   3782
Mk 7: 3   they do not eat unless *they* w.   966
Lk 11:38   that Jesus *did* not first w before the meal,   966
Jn 9: 7   "w in the Pool of Siloam"   3782
  9:11   He told me to go to Siloam and w.   3782
  13: 5   a basin and began to w his disciples' feet,   3782
  13: 6   "Lord, *are* you *going to* w my feet?"   3782
  13: 8   said Peter, "you *shall* never w my feet."   3782
  13: 8   Jesus answered, "Unless *I* w you,   3782
  13:10   a bath needs only to w his feet;   3782
  13:14   you also should w one another's feet.   3782
Ac 22:16   Get up, be baptized and w your sins *away,*   666
Jas 4: 8   W your hands, you sinners,   2751
Rev 22:14   "Blessed are those who w their robes,   4459

WASHBASIN (2)
Ps 60: 8   Moab is my w, upon Edom I toss   6105+8176
  108: 9   Moab is my w, upon Edom I toss   6105+8176

WASHED (36) [WASH]
Ge 43:31   After *he had* w his face, he came out and,   8175
Ex 19:14   and *they* w their clothes.   3891
  40:32   *They* w whenever they entered the Tent   8175
Lev 8: 6   and his sons forward and w them   8175
  8:21   *He* w the inner parts and the legs with water   8175
  9:14   *He* w the inner parts and the legs and   8175
  13:54   that the contaminated article *be* w.   3891
  13:55   After the affected article *has been* w,   3891
  13:56   after the article *has been* w,   3891
  13:58   that *has been* w and is rid of the mildew,   3891

Lev 13:58   *must* be w again, and it will be clean."   3891
  15:17   that has semen on it *must* be w with water,   3891
Nu 8:21   purified themselves and w their clothes.   3891
Jdg 19:21   After *they had* w their feet,   8175
2Sa 12:20   After *he had* w, put on lotions   8851
  19:24   or w his clothes from the day the king left   3891
1Ki 22:38   *They* w the chariot at a pool in Samaria   8851
Job 9:30   if *I* w *myself* with soap and w my hands   8175
  22:16   their foundations w away by a flood.   3668
Ps 73:13   in vain *have I* w my hands in innocence.   8175
SS 5: 3   *I have* w my feet—must I soil them again?   8175
  5:12   w in milk, mounted like jewels.   8175
Eze 16: 4   nor *were* you w with water   8175
  16: 9   " 'I bathed you with water and w the blood   8851
  40:38   where the burnt offerings were w.   1866
Mt 27:24   he took water and w his hands in front of   672
Jn 9: 7   man went and w, and came home seeing.   3782
  9:11   So *I* went and w, and then I could see."   3782
  9:15   the man replied, "and *I* w, and now I see."   3782
  13:14   I, your Lord and Teacher, *have* w your feet,   3782
Ac 9:37   and her body *was* w and placed in   3374
  16:33   the jailer took them and w their wounds;   3374
1Co 6:11   But *you were* w, you were sanctified,   666
Heb 10:22   a guilty conscience and *having* our bodies w   3374
2Pe 2:22   that *is* w goes back to her wallowing in   3374
Rev 7:14   they *have* w their robes and made them   4459

WASHERMAN'S (3) [WASH]
2Ki 18:17   on the road to the W Field.   3891
Isa 7: 3   on the road to the W Field   3891
  36: 2   on the road to the W Field,   3891

WASHING (16) [WASH]
Ex 30:18   with its bronze stand, for w.   8175
  40:30   and the altar and put water in it for w,   8175
2Ch 4: 6   then made ten basins for w and placed five   8175
  4: 6   the Sea was to be used by the priests for w.   8175
Job 9:30   with soap and my hands with w **soda,**   1342
SS 4: 2   sheep just shorn, coming up from the w.   8177
  6: 6   like a flock of sheep coming up from the w.   8177
Mk 7: 3   *give* their hands a ceremonial w,   3782
  7: 4   such as the w of cups, pitchers and kettles.)   968
Lk 5: 2   the fishermen, who *were* w their nets.   4459
Jn 2: 6   kind used by the Jews for ceremonial w,   2752
  3:25   over the matter of ceremonial w.   2752
  13:12   When he had finished w their feet,   3782
Eph 5:26   cleansing her *by* the w with water through   3373
1Ti 5:10   showing hospitality, w the feet of the saints,   3782
Tit 3: 5   through the w of rebirth and renewal by   3373

WASHINGS (1) [WASH]
Heb 9:10   food and drink and various ceremonial w—   968

WASHPOT (KJV) See WASHBASIN

WASN'T (4) [BE, NOT]
Ge 30:15   But she said to her, "W it enough   5071
1Ki 3:21   I saw that it w the son I had borne."   2118+4202
Jn 12: 5   "Why this perfume sold and   4024
Ac 5: 4   it was sold, w the money at your disposal?   5639

WASTE (73) [WASTED, WASTES, WASTING]
Lev 26:31   into ruins and lay w your sanctuaries,   9037
  26:32   I *will* lay w the land,   9037
  26:33   Your land will be laid w,   9039
  26:39   Those of you who are left *will* w away in   5245
  26:39   of their fathers' sins *they* will w away.   5245
Nu 5:21   *to* w away and your abdomen to swell.   5877
  5:27   and her thigh w away,   5877
Dt 29:23   The whole land will be a **burning** w *of* salt   8599
  32:10   in a barren and howling w.   3810
Jdg 16:24   the one who laid w our land   2990
2Ki 19:17   Assyrian kings *have* laid w these nations   2990
  22:19   they would become accursed and laid w,   9014
1Ch 20: 1   He laid w the land of the Ammonites   8845
Job 12:24   them wandering through a trackless w.   9332
Ps 107:34   and fruitful land into a **salt** w,   4877
  107:40   made them wander in a trackless w.   9332
  112:10   he will gnash his teeth and w away;   5022
Isa 1: 7   laid w as when overthrown by strangers.   9039
  6:13   it will again be laid w.   1278
  7:16   of the two kings you dread *will* be laid w.   6440
  17: 4   the fat of his body *will* w away.   8135
  24: 1   the LORD *is* going to lay w the earth   1327
  24: 3   The earth *will* be completely laid w   1327+1327
  24:16   But I said, "I w away, I waste away!   8140
  24:16   But I said, "I waste away, I w away!   8140
  37:18   Assyrian kings *have* laid w all these peoples   2990
  42:15   *I will* lay w the mountains and hills   2990
  49:17   *those who* laid *you* w depart   2238+2256+2990
  49:19   and made desolate and your land laid w,   2233
  64: 7   and **made** us w away because of our sins.   4570
Jer 2:15   They have laid w his land;   9014
  4: 7   He has left his place to lay w your land.   9014
  9:11   and I will lay w the towns of Judah   9039
  9:12   Why has the land been ruined and laid w   5898
  12:11   the whole land *will* be laid w   9037
  18:16   Their land will be laid w   9014
  25:37   The peaceful meadows *will* be laid w   1959
  32:43   It is a **desolate** w, without men or animals,   9039
  33:10   It is a **desolate** w, without men or   2992
  34:22   And I will lay w the towns of Judah   9039

Jer 44:22   and a desolate w without inhabitants,   9014
  46:19   for Memphis will be laid w and lie in ruins   9014
  48: 9   Put salt on Moab, for *she will* be laid w;   5898+5898
  50: 3   the north will attack her and lay w her land.   9014
  51:29   to lay w the land of Babylon so   9014
La 2: 6   He has laid w his dwelling like a garden;   2803
  4: 9   *they* w away for lack of food from the field.   2307
Eze 4:17   at the sight of each other and *will* w away   5245
  6: 6   be laid w and the high places demolished,   2990
  6: 6   your altars *will* be laid w and devastated,   2990
  6:14   a desolate w from the desert to Diblah—   5457
  24:23   The inhabited towns *will* be laid w and   2990
  24:23   but *will* w away because of your sins   5245
  25: 3   over the land of Israel when *it* was laid w   9037
  25:13   I will lay it w, and from Teman to Dedan   2999
  29:10   the land of Egypt a ruin and a desolate w   2997
  30:12   by the hand of foreigners *I will* lay w   9037
  30:14   *I will* lay w Upper Egypt,   9037
  33:28   I will make the land a desolate w,   5457
  33:29   when I have made the land a desolate w   5457
  35: 3   against you and make you a desolate w.   5457
  35: 7   I will make Mount Seir a desolate w   9039
  35:12   *"They have been* laid w   9037
  36:35   "This land that *was* laid w has become like   9037
Hos 4: 3   and all who live in it w away;   581
  5: 9   be laid w on the day of reckoning.   9014
  6: 8   to w away under the oppression of   5071
Joel 1: 7   It has laid w my vines and ruined   9014
  2: 3   a desert w—nothing escapes them.   9039
  3:19   Egypt will be desolate, Edom a desert w,   9039
Na 2: 2   though destroyers *have* laid them w   1327
Mt 26: 8   "Why this w?" they asked.   724
Mk 14: 4   "Why this w of perfume?   724+1181

WASTED (7) [WASTE]
Ge 47:13   and Canaan w away because of the famine.   3532
Ps 32: 3   my bones w away through my groaning   1162
  106:43   on rebellion and *they* w away in their sin.   4812
Pr 5: 9   and *will have* w your compliments.   8845
La 2: 8   together *they* w away.   581
Jn 6:12   Let nothing *be* w."   660
Gal 4:11   that somehow I have w my efforts on you.   1632

WASTELAND (21) [LAND]
Nu 21:20   where the top of Pisgah overlooks the w.   3810
  23:28   to the top of Peor, overlooking the w.   3810
2Sa 2:24   near Giah on the way to the w *of* Gibeon.   4497
Job 6:18   they go up into the w and perish.   9332
  24: 5   the w provides food for their children.   6858
  38:27   a desolate w and make it sprout with grass?   5409
  39: 6   I gave him the w as his home,   6858
Ps 68: 7   O God, when you marched through the w,   3810
  78:40   in the desert and grieved him in the w!   3810
  106:14   in the w they put God to the test.   3810
Isa 5: 6   I will make it a w, neither pruned nor   1429
  32:14   and watchtower will become a w forever,   5118
  41:19   I will set pines in the w,   6858
  43:19   a way in the desert and streams in the w.   3810
  43:20   in the desert and streams in the w,   3810
Jer 2:10   turn my pleasant field into a desolate w.   4497
  12:11   It will be made a w,   9039
  25:11   a desolate w, and these nations will serve   9014
Eze 29: 9   Egypt will become a desolate w.   2999
Zep 2: 9   a place of weeds and salt pits, a w forever.   9039
Mal 1: 3   and I have turned his mountains into a w   9039

WASTELANDS (4) [LAND]
Job 30: 3   they roamed the parched land in desolate w   5409
Ps 107: 4   Some wandered in desert w,   3810
Isa 51: 3   her w like the garden of the LORD.   6858
Jer 17: 6   He will be like a bush in the w;   6858

WASTES (5) [WASTE]
Nu 5:22   and your thigh w away."   5877
Job 13:28   "So man w away like something rotten.   1162
  33:21   His flesh w away to nothing, and his bones,   3983
Isa 10:18   as *when* a sick man w away.   5022
  33: 9   The land mourns and w away,   581

WASTING (8) [WASTE]
Lev 26:16   upon you sudden terror, w diseases   8831
Dt 28:22   The LORD will strike you with w **disease,**   8831
  32:24   I will send w famine against them,   4642
Ps 106:15   but sent a w disease upon them   8137
Isa 10:16   a w disease upon his sturdy warriors;   8137
Eze 33:10   and we *are* w away because of them.   5245
Lk 16: 1   was accused of w his possessions.   1399
2Co 4:16   Though outwardly we *are* w away,   1425

WATCH (88) [WATCHED, WATCHER, WATCHES, WATCHFUL, WATCHING, WATCHMAN, WATCHMEN]
Ge 21:16   for she thought, "I cannot w the boy die."   8011
  28:15   and *will* w over you wherever you go,   9068
  28:20   "If God will be with me and *will* w **over**   9068
  31:49   *May* the LORD keep w between you and me   7595
Ex 12:42   During **last w of** the night   874+1332
Dt 4: 9   and w yourselves closely so that you do   9068
  4:15   Therefore w yourselves very **carefully,**   9068
Jdg 7:17   "W me," he told them. "Follow my lead.   8011
  7:19   the camp at the beginning of the middle w,   874

Jdg	21:21	and w. When the girls of Shiloh come out	8011
Ru	2: 9	W the field where the men are harvesting,	
			928+6524
1Sa	11:11	during the last w of the night	874+1332+2021
	17:28	you came down only to w the battle."	8011
	19:11	Saul sent men to David's house to w it and	9068
2Sa	13: 5	in my sight so I may w her and then eat it	8011
	13:34	Now the man standing w looked up	7595
1Ki	1:52	'If your descendants w how they live,	9068
2Ch	23: 4	on the Sabbath are to keep w at the doors,	8788
Ne	11:19	who kept w at the gates—172 men.	9068
Job	13:27	you keep close w on all my paths	9068
	21:32	and w is kept over his tomb.	9193
	33:11	he keeps close w on all my paths.'	9068
	39: 1	Do you w when the doe bears her fawn?	9068
Ps	32: 8	I will counsel you and w over you.	6524
	39: 1	"I will w my ways and keep my tongue	9068
	56: 6	They conspire, they lurk, they w my steps,	9068
	59: 7	in to w David's house in order to kill him.	9068
	59: 9	O my Strength, I w for you;	9068
	66: 7	his eyes w the nations—	7595
	80:14	W over this vine,	7212
	90: 4	or like a w in the night.	874
	121: 7	he will w over your life;	9068
	121: 8	the LORD will w over your coming	9068
	141: 3	keep w over the door of my lips.	5917
Pr	4: 6	love her, and she will w over you.	5915
	6:22	when you sleep, they will w over you;	9068
	15: 3	keeping w on the wicked and the good.	7595
	22:12	eyes of the LORD keep w over knowledge,	5915
Isa	27: 3	w over it; I water it continually.	5915
Jer	24: 6	My eyes will w over them for their good,	
			6584+8492
	31:10	and will w over his flock like a shepherd.'	9068
	31:28	I will w over them to build and to plant,"	9193
	48:19	Stand by the road and w,	7595
Eze	12: 3	as they w, set out and go from	4200+6524
	12: 4	During the daytime, while they w,	4200+6524
	12: 5	While they w, dig through the wall	4200+6524
Da	7:11	to w because of the boastful words	10255
Mic	7: 7	But as for me, I w in hope for the LORD,	7595
Na	2: 1	Guard the fortress, w the road,	7595
Hab	1: 5	"Look at the nations and w—	5564
	2: 1	at my w and station myself on the ramparts;	5466
Zec	9: 8	for now I am keeping w.	928+6524+8011
Mt	7:15	"W out for false prophets.	4668
	14:25	the fourth w of the night Jesus went out	5871
	24: 4	"W out that no one deceives you.	1063
	24:42	"Therefore keep w, because you do	1213
	24:43	the thief was coming, he would have kept w	1213
	25:13	"Therefore keep w, because you do	1213
	26:38	Stay here and keep w with me."	1213
	26:40	"Could you men not keep w with me	1213
	26:41	"W and pray so that you will not fall	1213
	27:36	sitting down, they kept w over him there.	5498
Mk	6:48	About the fourth w of the night he went out	5871
	8:15	"W out for the yeast of the Pharisees and	1063
	12:38	"W out for the teachers of the law.	1063
	13: 5	"W out that no one deceives you.	1063
	13:34	and tells the one at the door to keep w.	1213
	13:35	Therefore keep w because you do not know	1213
	13:37	What I say to you, I say to everyone: 'W!' "	1213
	14:34	"Stay here and keep w."	1213
	14:37	Could you not keep w for one hour?	1213
	14:38	W and pray so that you will not fall	1213
Lk	2: 8	keeping w over their flocks at night.	5871+5875
	12:15	Then he said to them, "W out!	3972
	12:38	in the second or third w of the night.	5871
	17: 3	So w yourselves.	4668
	20:20	Keeping a close w on him, they sent spies,	4190
	21: 8	"W out that you are not deceived.	1063
	21:36	Be always on the w, and pray that	70
Ac	9:24	Day and night they kept close w on	4190
	20:28	Keep w over yourselves and all the flock	4668
Ro	16:17	w for those who cause divisions	5023
Gal	5:15	w out or you will be destroyed	1063
	6: 1	w yourself, or you also may be tempted.	5023
Php	3: 2	W out for those dogs, those men who	1063
1Ti	4:16	W your life and doctrine closely.	2091
Heb	13:17	They keep w over you as men who must	
		give an account.	70
2Jn	1: 8	W out that you do not lose what	1063+4932

WATCHED (31) [WATCH]

Ge	24:21	the man w her closely to learn whether or	8617
Ex	2:11	to where his own people were and w them	8011
	3:16	I have w over you and have seen	7212+7212
Dt	2: 7	He has w over your journey	3359
	33: 9	but he w over your word	9068
Jos	4:11	to the other side while the people w.	4200+7156
Jdg	13:19	while Manoah and his wife w:	8011
1Sa	17:55	As Saul w David going out to meet	8011
2Sa	6:16	Michal daughter of Saul w from a window.	9207
1Ch	15:29	Michal daughter of Saul w from a window.	9207
Job	10:12	and in your providence w my spirit.	9068
	29: 2	for the days when God w over me,	9068
Jer	31:28	as I w over them to uproot and tear down,	9193
La	4:17	from our towers we w for a nation that could	7595
Eze	10: 2	And as I w, he went in.	4200+6524
	10:19	I w, the cherubim spread their wings	4200+6524
	12: 7	on my shoulders while they w.	4200+6524
Da	5: 5	The king w the hand as it wrote.	10255
	7: 4	I w until its wings were torn off	10255
	7:21	As I w, this horn was waging war against	10255
	8: 4	I w the ram as he charged toward the west	8011
Mt	26:16	From then on Judas w for an opportunity	2426

Mk	3: 2	they w him closely to see if he would heal	4190
	12:41	and w the crowd putting their money into	2555
	14:11	he w for an opportunity to hand him over.	2426
Lk	6: 7	they w him closely to see if he would heal	4190
	14: 1	he was being carefully w.	4190
	22: 6	and w for an opportunity to hand Jesus	2426
Rev	6: 1	I w as the Lamb opened the first of the	3972
	6:12	I w as he opened the sixth seal.	3972
	8:13	As I w, I heard an eagle that was flying	3972

WATCHER (1) [WATCH]

Job	7:20	what have I done to you, O w of men?	5915

WATCHES (16) [WATCH]

Nu	19: 5	While he w, the heifer is to be burned—	6524
Job	24:15	The eye of the adulterer w for dusk;	9068
Ps	1: 6	LORD w over the way of the righteous,	3359
	33:14	from his dwelling place he w all who live	8708
	63: 6	I think of you through the w of the night.	874
	119:148	through the w of the night,	874
	121: 3	he who w over you will not slumber;	9068
	121: 4	he who w over Israel will neither slumber	9068
	121: 5	The LORD w over you—	9068
	127: 1	Unless the LORD w over the city,	9068
	145:20	The LORD w over all who love him,	9068
	146: 9	The LORD w over the alien and sustains	9068
Pr	31:27	She w over the affairs of her household	7595
Ecc	11: 4	Whoever w the wind will not plant;	9068
La	2:19	as the w of the night begin;	874
	4:16	he no longer w over them.	5564

WATCHFUL (2) [WATCH]

Zec	12: 4	"I will keep a w eye over the house	7219
Col	4: 2	Devote yourselves to prayer, being w and	1213

WATCHING (29) [WATCH]

Ge	30:31	I will go on tending your flocks and w over	9068
Ex	33: 8	w Moses until he entered the tent.	5564
Dt	28:32	and you will wear out your eyes w	8011
Jdg	16:27	men and women w Samson perform.	8011
1Sa	4:13	w, because his heart feared for the ark of	7595
	6: 9	but keep w it. If it goes up to its own	8011
	25:21	all my w over this fellow's property in	9068
2Ki	2:15	prophets from Jericho, who were w, said,	8011
Ezr	5: 5	The eye of their God was w over the elders	NIH
Job	10:14	If I sinned, you would be w me	9068
Ps	10: 8	w in secret for his victims.	6524
Pr	8:34	listens to me, w daily at my doors,	9193
Jer	1:12	for I am w to see that my word is fulfilled."	9193
	7:11	But I have been w!	8011
	19:10	the jar while those who go with you are w,	6524
	43: 9	"While the Jews are w, take some large	6524
	44:27	I am w over them for harm, not for good;	9193
Eze	12: 4	Then in the evening, while they are w,	4200+6524
	12: 6	they are w and carry them out at dusk.	4200+6524
	28:18	the ground in the sight of all who were w.	8011
Da	2:34	While you were w, a rock was cut out,	10255
	8:15	was w the vision and trying to understand it,	8011
Zec	11:11	of the flock who were w me knew it was	9068
Mt	27:55	Many women were there, w from a distance.	2555
Mk	15:40	Some women were w from a distance.	2555
Lk	12:37	those servants whose master finds them w	1213
	23:35	The people stood w, and the rulers even	2555
	23:49	stood at a distance, w these things.	3972
Jn	7:11	Now at the Feast the Jews were w for him	2426

WATCHMAN (16) [WATCH]

2Sa	13:34	The w went and told the king,	7595
	18:24	the w went up to the roof of the gateway by	7595
	18:25	The w called out to the king and reported it.	7595
	18:26	Then the w saw another man running,	7595
	18:27	The w said, "It seems to me that the first	7595
Job	27:18	like a hut made by a w.	5915
Isa	21:11	Someone calls to me from Seir, "W,	9068
	21:11	W, what is left of the night?"	9068
	21:12	The w replies, "Morning is coming,	9068
Eze	3:17	I have made you a w for the house of Israel;	7595
	33: 2	of their men and make him their w,	7595
	33: 6	if the w sees the sword coming and does	7595
	33: 6	I will hold the w accountable for his blood.'	7595
	33: 7	I have made you a w for the house of Israel;	7595
Hos	9: 8	along with my God, is the w over Ephraim,	7595
Jn	10: 3	The w opens the gate for him,	2601

WATCHMEN (13) [WATCH]

Ps	127: 1	the w stand guard in vain.	9068
	130: 6	more than w wait for the morning,	9068
	130: 6	more than w wait for the morning.	9068
SS	3: 3	The w found me as they made their rounds	9068
	5: 7	The w found me as they made their rounds	9068
	5: 7	those w of the walls!	9068
Isa	52: 8	Your w lift up their voices;	7595
	56:10	Israel's w are blind,	7595
	62: 6	I have posted w on your walls, O Jerusalem;	9068
Jer	6:17	I appointed w over you and said,	7595
	31: 6	when w cry out on the hills of Ephraim,	5915
	51:12	Reinforce the guard, station the w,	9068
Mic	7: 4	The day of your w has come,	7595

WATCHTOWER (8) [TOWER]

2Ki	17: 9	From w to fortified city they built	4463+5915
	18: 8	From w to fortified city, he defeated	4463+5915

Isa	5: 2	He built a w in it and cut out a winepress	4463
	21: 8	"Day after day, my lord, I stand on the w;	5205
	32:14	and w will become a wasteland forever,	1044
Mic	4: 8	As for you, O w of the flock,	4463
Mt	21:33	dug a winepress in it and built a w.	4788
Mk	12: 1	dug a pit for the winepress and built a w.	4788

WATCHTOWERS (1) [TOWER]

1Ch	27:25	in the towns, the villages and the w.	4463

WATER (482) [WATER'S, WATERCOURSE, WATERED, WATERFALLS, WATERING, WATERLESS, WATERS, WATERY, WELL-WATERED]

Ge	1: 6	the waters to separate w from water."	4784
	1: 6	the waters to separate water from w."	4784
	1: 7	and separated the w under the expanse from	4784
	1: 7	the water under the expanse from the w	4784
	1: 9	"Let the w under the sky be gathered	4784
	1:20	"Let the w teem with living creatures,	4784
	1:21	and moving thing with which the w teems,	4784
	1:22	and increase in number and fill the w in	4784
	7:18	and the ark floated on the surface of the w.	4784
	8: 3	The w receded steadily from the earth.	4784
	8: 3	the hundred and fifty days the w had gone	4784
	8: 7	until the w had dried up from the earth.	4784
	8: 8	to see if the w had receded from the surface	4784
	8: 9	because there was w all the surface of	4784
	8:11	Then Noah knew that the w had receded	4784
	8:13	the w had dried up from the earth.	4784
	18: 4	Let a little w be brought,	4784
	21:14	and a skin of w and gave them to Hagar.	4784
	21:15	When the w in the skin was gone,	4784
	21:19	and she saw a well of w.	4784
	21:19	and filled the skin with w and gave the boy	4784
	21:25	of w that Abimelech's servants had seized.	4784
	24:11	the time the women go out to draw w.	8612
	24:13	the townspeople are coming out to draw w.	8612
	24:14	'Drink, and I'll w your camels too'—	9197
	24:17	"Please give me a little w from your jar."	4784
	24:19	she said, "I'll draw w for your camels too,	8612
	24:20	ran back to the well to draw more w,	8612
	24:32	w for him and his men to wash their feet.	4784
	24:43	if a maiden comes out to draw w and I say	8612
	24:43	to her, "Please let me drink a little w"	4784
	24:44	and I'll draw w for your camels too,"	8612
	24:45	She went down to the spring and drew w,	8612
	26:19	and discovered a well of fresh w there.	4784
	26:20	"The w is ours!"	4784
	26:32	They said, "We've found w!"	4784
	29: 3	from the well's mouth and w the sheep.	9197
	29: 7	W the sheep and take them back	9197
	29: 8	then we will w the sheep.	9197
	37:24	the cistern was empty; there was no w in it.	4784
	43:24	gave them w to wash their feet	4784
Ex	2:10	saying, "I drew him out of the w."	4784
	2:16	and they came to draw w and fill	1926
	2:16	and fill the troughs to w their father's flock.	9197
	2:19	drew w for us and watered the flock."	1926+1926
	4: 9	take some w from the Nile and pour it on	4784
	4: 9	The w you take from the river will become	4784
	7:15	in the morning as he goes out to the w.	4784
	7:17	in my hand I will strike the w of the Nile,	4784
	7:18	not be able to drink its w.' "	4784
	7:20	and his officials and struck the w of	4784
	7:20	and all the w was changed into blood.	4784
	7:21	that the Egyptians could not drink its w.	4784
	7:24	along the Nile to get drinking w,	4784
	7:24	they could not drink the w of the river.	4784
	8:20	and confront Pharaoh as he goes to the w	4784
	12: 9	Do not eat the meat raw or cooked in w,	4784
	14:16	to divide the w so that the Israelites can go	2084 S
	14:22	a wall of w on their right and on their left.	4784
	14:28	The w flowed back and covered the chariots	4784
	14:29	a wall of w on their right and on their left.	4784
	15:22	in the desert without finding w.	4784
	15:23	not drink its w because it was bitter.	4784
	15:25	He threw it into the w,	4784
	15:25	and the w became sweet.	4784
	15:27	and they camped there near the w.	4784
	17: 1	but there was no w for the people to drink.	4784
	17: 2	"Give us w to drink."	4784
	17: 3	But the people were thirsty for w there,	4784
	17: 6	and w will come out of it for the people	4784
	23:25	and his blessing will be on your food and w.	4784
	29: 4	the Tent of Meeting and wash them with w.	4784
	30:18	and the altar, and put w in it.	4784
	30:19	to wash their hands and feet with w from it.	NIH
	30:20	they shall wash with w so that they will	4784
	32:20	to powder, scattered it on the w and made	4784
	34:28	without eating bread or drinking w.	4784
	40: 7	the Tent of Meeting and the altar and put w	4784
	40:12	the Tent of Meeting and wash them with w.	4784
	40:30	the Tent of Meeting and the altar and put w	4784
Lev	1: 9	to wash the inner parts and the legs with w,	4784
	1:13	to wash the inner parts and the legs with w,	4784
	6:28	the pot is to be scoured and rinsed with w.	4784
	8: 6	and washed them with w.	4784
	8:21	the legs with w and burned the whole ram	4784
	11: 9	the creatures living in the w of the seas and	4784
	11:10	among all the other living creatures in the w	4784
	11:12	the w that does not have fins and scales	4784
	11:32	Put it in w; it will be unclean till evening,	4784

Lev	11:34	Any food that could be eaten but has **w** on it	4784
	11:36	or a cistern for collecting **w** remains clean,	4784
	11:38	But if **w** has been put on the seed and	4784
	11:46	the **w** and every creature that moves about	4784
	14: 5	that one of the birds be killed over fresh **w**	4784
	14: 6	of the bird that was killed over the fresh **w**.	4784
	14: 8	shave off all his hair and bathe with **w**;	4784
	14: 9	and bathe himself with **w**,	4784
	14:50	He shall kill one of the birds over fresh **w** in	4784
	14:51	the blood of the dead bird and the fresh **w**,	4784
	14:52	the fresh **w**, the live bird, the cedar wood,	4784
	15: 5	must wash his clothes and bathe with **w**,	4784
	15: 6	must wash his clothes and bathe with **w**,	4784
	15: 7	must wash his clothes and bathe with **w**,	4784
	15: 8	must wash his clothes and bathe with **w**,	4784
	15:10	must wash his clothes and bathe with **w**,	4784
	15:11	with **w** must wash his clothes and bathe	4784
	15:11	must wash his clothes and bathe with **w**,	4784
	15:12	any wooden article is to be rinsed with **w**.	4784
	15:13	and bathe himself with fresh **w**,	4784
	15:16	he must bathe his whole body with **w**,	4784
	15:17	on it must be washed with **w**,	4784
	15:18	both must bathe with **w**,	4784
	15:21	must wash his clothes and bathe with **w**,	4784
	15:22	must wash his clothes and bathe with **w**,	4784
	15:27	he must wash his clothes and bathe with **w**,	4784
	16: 4	so he must bathe himself with **w**	4784
	16:24	He shall bathe himself with **w** in	4784
	16:26	and bathe himself with **w**;	4784
	16:28	and bathe himself with **w**;	4784
	17:15	must wash his clothes and bathe with **w**,	4784
	22: 6	unless he has bathed himself with **w**.	4784
Nu	5:17	Then he shall take some holy **w** in a clay jar	4784
	5:17	from the tabernacle floor into the **w**.	4784
	5:18	while he himself holds the bitter **w**	4784
	5:19	may this bitter **w** that brings a curse	4784
	5:22	May this **w** that brings a curse enter	4784
	5:23	and then wash them off into the bitter **w**.	4784
	5:24	He shall have the woman drink the bitter **w**	4784
	5:24	and this **w** will enter her	4784
	5:26	he is to have the woman drink the **w**.	4784
	5:27	when she is made to drink the **w** that brings	4784
	8: 7	Sprinkle the **w** *of* cleansing on them;	4784
	19: 7	and bathe himself with **w**.	4784
	19: 8	also wash his clothes and bathe with **w**,	4784
	19: 9	by the Israelite community for use in the **w**	4784
	19:12	He must purify himself with the **w** on	NIH
	19:13	the **w** of cleansing has not been sprinkled	4784
	19:17	into a jar and pour fresh **w** over them.	4784
	19:18	dip it in the **w** and sprinkle the tent and all	4784
	19:19	must wash his clothes and bathe with **w**,	4784
	19:20	The **w** *of* cleansing has not been sprinkled	4784
	19:21	"The man who sprinkles the **w**	4784
	19:21	the **w** *of* cleansing will be unclean	4784
	20: 2	Now there was no **w** for the community,	4784
	20: 5	And there is no **w** to drink!"	4784
	20: 8	before their eyes and it will pour out its **w**.	4784
	20: 8	You will bring **w** out of the rock for	4784
	20:10	must we bring you **w** out of this rock?"	4784
	20:11	**W** gushed out, and the community	4784
	20:17	or drink **w** *from* any well.	4784
	20:19	if we or our livestock drink any of your **w**,	4784
	21: 5	There is no **w**!	4784
	21:16	the people together and I will give them **w**."	4784
	21:22	or drink **w** *from* any well.	4784
	24: 7	**W** will flow from their buckets;	4784
	24: 7	their seed will have abundant **w**.	4784
	31:23	also be purified with the **w** *of* cleansing.	4784
	31:23	withstand fire must be put through that **w**.	4784
	33:14	where there was no **w** for the people	4784
Dt	2: 6	for the food you eat and the **w** you drink.' "	4784
	2:28	to eat and **w** to drink for their price in silver.	4784
	8: 7	a land with streams and pools of **w**,	4784
	8:15	He brought you **w** out of hard rock.	4784
	9: 9	I ate no bread and drank no **w**.	4784
	9:18	I ate no bread and drank no **w**,	4784
	10: 7	a land with streams of **w**.	4784
	12:16	pour it out on the ground like **w**.	4784
	12:24	pour it out on the ground like **w**.	4784
	14: 9	Of all the creatures living in the **w**,	4784
	15:23	pour it out on the ground like **w**.	4784
	23: 4	to meet you with bread and **w** on your way	4784
	29:11	who chop your wood and carry your **w**.	4784
Jos	2:10	the LORD dried up the **w** *of* the Red Sea	4784
	3:16	the **w** from upstream stopped flowing.	4784
	3:16	while the **w** flowing down to the Sea of	NIH
	7: 5	of the people melted and became like **w**.	4784
	9:21	but let them be woodcutters and **w** carriers	4784
	9:23	as woodcutters and **w** carriers for the house	4784
	9:27	the Gibeonites woodcutters and **w** carriers	4784
	15:19	give me also springs of **w**."	4784
Jdg	1:15	give me also springs of **w**."	4784
	4:19	"Please give me some **w**."	4784
	5: 4	the clouds poured down **w**.	4784
	5:25	He asked for **w**, and she gave him milk;	4784
	6:38	wrung out the dew—a bowlful of **w**.	4784
	7: 4	Take them down to the **w**,	4784
	7: 5	So Gideon took the men down to the **w**.	4784
	7: 5	the **w** with their tongues like a dog	4784
	15:19	and **w** came out of it.	4784
Ru	2: 9	a drink from the **w** jars the men have filled."	NIH
1Sa	7: 6	they drew **w** and poured it out before	4784
	9:11	they met some girls coming out to draw **w**,	4784
	25:11	Why should I take my bread and **w**,	4784
	26:11	the spear and **w** jug that are near his head,	4784
	26:12	the spear and **w** jug near Saul's head,	4784
	26:16	Where are the king's spear and **w** jug	4784

1Sa	30:11	They gave him **w** to drink and food to eat—	4784
	30:12	not eaten any food or drunk *any* **w**	4784
2Sa	5: 8	the Jebusites will have to use the **w shaft**	7562
	12:27	against Rabbah and taken its **w supply.**	4784
	14:14	Like **w** spilled on the ground,	4784
	23:15	David longed for **w** and said, "Oh,	NIH
	23:15	that someone would get me a drink of **w**	4784
	23:16	drew **w** from the well near the gate	4784
1Ki	13: 8	nor would I eat bread or drink **w** here.	4784
	13: 9	not eat bread or drink **w** or return by	4784
	13:16	nor can I eat bread or drink **w** with you	4784
	13:17	not eat bread or drink **w** there or return by	4784
	13:18	so that he may eat bread and drink **w**.' "	4784
	13:22	and drank **w** in the place where he told you	4784
	14:15	that it will be like a reed swaying in the **w**.	4784
	17:10	a little **w** in a jar so I may have a drink?"	4784
	18: 4	and had supplied them with food and **w**.)	4784
	18:13	and supplied them with food and **w**.	4784
	18:33	"Fill four large jars with **w** and pour it on	4784
	18:35	The **w** ran down around the altar and	4784
	18:38	and also licked up the **w** in the trench.	4784
	19: 6	bread baked over hot coals, and a jar of **w**.	4784
	22:27	but bread and **w** until I return safely.' "	4784
2Ki	2: 8	rolled it up and struck the **w** with it.	4784
	2: 8	The **w** divided to the right and to the left,	NIH
	2:14	that had fallen from him and struck the **w**	4784
	2:14	When he struck the **w**, it divided	4784
	2:19	the **w** is bad and the land is unproductive."	4784
	2:21	'I have healed this **w**.	4784
	2:22	the **w** has remained wholesome to this day,	4784
	3: 9	the army had no more **w** for themselves or	4784
	3:11	He used to pour **w** on the hands of Elijah."	4784
	3:17	yet this valley will be filled with **w**,	4784
	3:20	**w** flowing from the direction of Edom!	4784
	3:20	And the land was filled with **w**.	4784
	3:22	the sun was shining on the **w**.	4784
	3:22	the **w** looked red—like blood.	4784
	6: 5	the iron axhead fell into the **w**.	4784
	6:22	and **w** before them so that they may eat	4784
	8:15	in **w** and spread it over the king's face,	4784
	18:31	from his own vine and fig tree and drink **w**	4784
	19:24	in foreign lands and drunk the **w** there.	4784
	20:20	and the tunnel by which he brought in	4784
1Ch	10: 6	he ate no food and drank no **w**,	4784
	11:17	David longed for **w** and said, "Oh,	NIH
	11:17	that someone would get me a drink of **w**	4784
	11:18	drew **w** from the well near the gate	4784
2Ch	18:26	but bread and **w** until I return safely.' "	4784
	32: 3	and military staff about blocking off the **w**	4784
	32: 4	of Assyria come and find plenty of **w**?"	4784
	32:30	Gihon spring and channeled **the** **w** down	4392S
Ezr	10: 6	he ate no food and drank no **w**,	4784
Ne	3:26	a point opposite the **W** Gate toward the east	4784
	4:23	even when he went for **w**.	4784
	8: 1	as one man in the square before the **W** Gate.	4784
	8: 3	as he faced the square before the **W** Gate in	4784
	8:16	and in the square by the **W** Gate and the one	4784
	9:15	and in their thirst you brought them from	4784
	9:20	and you gave them **w** for their thirst.	4784
	12:37	above the square of David to the **W** Gate on	4784
	13: 2	and **w** but had hired Balaam to call a curse	4784
Job	3:24	my groans pour out like **w**.	4784
	5:10	he sends **w** upon the countryside.	4784
	6:19	The caravans of Tema look for **w**,	4564S
	8:11	Can reeds thrive without **w**?	4784
	14: 9	of **w** it will bud and put forth shoots like	4784
	14:11	As **w** disappears from the sea or	4784
	14:19	as **w** wears away stones and torrents wash	4784
	15:16	who drinks up evil like **w**!	4784
	22: 7	You gave no **w** to the weary	4784
	22:11	and why a flood of **w** covers you.	4784
	24:18	"Yet they are foam on the surface of the **w**;	4784
	29:19	My roots will reach to the **w**,	4784
	34: 7	who drinks scorn like **w**?	4784
	36:27	"He draws up the drops of **w**,	4784
	37:13	or to **w** his earth and show his love.	NIH
	38:26	to **w** a land where no man lives,	4763
	38:34	and cover yourself with a flood of **w**?	4784
	38:37	Who can tip over the **w** jars *of* the heavens	5574
Ps	1: 3	He is like a tree planted by streams of **w**,	4784
	22:14	I am poured out like **w**,	4784
	42: 1	As the deer pants for streams of **w**,	4784
	58: 7	Let them vanish like **w** that flows away;	4784
	63: 1	in a dry and weary land where there is no **w**.	4784
	65: 9	You care for the land and **w** it;	8796
	65: 9	with **w** to provide the people with grain,	4784
	66:12	we went through fire and **w**,	4784
	77:17	The clouds poured down **w**,	4784
	78:13	he made the **w** stand firm like a wall.	4784
	78:15	the desert and **gave** them **w** as abundant as	9197
	78:16	of a rocky crag and made **w** flow down	4784
	78:20	When he struck the rock, **w** gushed out,	4784
	79: 3	They have poured out blood like **w** all	4784
	104:10	He makes springs pour **w** into the ravines;	NIH
	104:11	*They* give **w** *to* all the beasts of the field;	9197
	105:41	He opened the rock, and **w** gushed out;	4784
	107:35	He turned the desert into pools of **w** and	4784
	109:18	it entered into his body like **w**,	4784
	114: 8	the hard rock into springs of **w**.	4784
Pr	5:15	Drink **w** from your own cistern.	4784
	5:15	**running** **w** from your own well.	5689
	5:16	your streams of **w** in the public squares?	4784
	8:24	there were no springs abounding with **w**;	4784
	9:17	"Stolen **w** is sweet; food eaten in secret	4784
	25:21	if he is thirsty, give him **w** to drink.	4784
	25:25	Like cold **w** to a weary soul is good news	4784
	27:19	As **w** reflects a face, so a man's heart	4784
	30:16	which is never satisfied with **w**, and fire,	4784

Ecc	2: 6	to **w** groves of flourishing trees.	9197
	11: 3	If clouds are full of **w**, they pour rain	NIH
SS	4:15	a well of flowing **w** streaming down	4784
	5:12	His eyes are like doves by the **w** streams,	4784
Isa	1:22	your choice wine is diluted with **w**.	4784
	1:30	like a garden without **w**.	4784
	3: 1	all supplies of food and all supplies of **w**,	4784
	7:19	the thornbushes and at all the **w** holes.	5635
	12: 3	With joy you will draw **w** from the wells	4784
	18: 2	by sea in papyrus boats over the **w**.	4784
	19: 8	who throw nets on the **w** will pine away.	4784
	21:14	bring **w** for the thirsty,	4784
	22: 9	you stored up **w** *in* the Lower Pool.	4784
	22:11	a reservoir between the two walls for the **w**	4784
	27: 3	I **w** it continually.	9197
	28:17	and **w** will overflow your hiding place.	4784
	30:14	a hearth or scooping **w** out of a cistern."	4784
	30:20	and the **w** *of* affliction, your teachers will	4784
	30:25	of **w** will flow on every high mountain	4784
	32: 2	of **w** in the desert and the shadow of	4784
	32: 6	and from the thirsty **w** he withholds.	5482
	33:16	and **w** will not fail him.	4784
	35: 6	**W** will gush forth in the wilderness	4784
	36:16	from his own vine and fig tree and drink **w**	4784
	37:25	in foreign lands and drunk the **w** there.	4784
	41:17	"The poor and needy search for **w**,	4784
	41:18	I will turn the desert into pools of **w**,	4784
	43:20	because I provide **w** in the desert	4784
	44: 3	For I will pour **w** on the thirsty land,	4784
	44:12	he drinks no **w** and grows faint.	4784
	48:21	he made **w** flow for them from the rock;	4784
	48:21	he split the rock and **w** gushed out.	4784
	49:10	and lead them beside springs of **w**.	4784
	50: 2	their fish rot for lack of **w** and die of thirst.	4784
	64: 2	fire sets twigs ablaze and causes **w** to boil,	4784
Jer	2:13	have forsaken me, the spring of living **w**,	4784
	2:13	broken cisterns that cannot hold **w**.	4784
	2:18	Now why go to Egypt to drink **w** *from*	4784
	2:18	And why go to Assyria to drink **w** *from*	4784
	6: 7	As a well pours out its **w**,	4784
	8:14	to perish and given us poisoned **w** to drink,	4784
	9: 1	a **spring of** **w** and my eyes a fountain	4784
	9:15	and drink poisoned **w**,	4784
	9:18	with tears and **w** streams from our eyelids.	4784
	13: 1	but do not let it touch **w**."	4784
	14: 3	The nobles send their servants for **w**;	4784
	14: 3	they go to the cisterns but find no **w**.	4784
	17: 8	the **w** that sends out its roots by the stream.	4784
	17:13	forsaken the LORD, the spring of living **w**.	4784
	23:15	and drink poisoned **w**,	4784
	31: 9	I will lead them beside streams of **w** on	4784
	38: 6	it had no **w** in it, only mud,	4784
La	2:19	pour out your heart like **w** in the presence of	4784
	5: 4	We must buy the **w** we drink;	4784
Eze	4:11	Also measure out a sixth of a hin of **w**	4784
	4:16	and in anxiety and drink rationed **w** in despair,	4784
	4:17	for food and **w** will be scarce.	4784
	7:17	and every knee will become as weak as **w**.	4784
	12:18	and shudder in fear as you drink your **w**.	4784
	12:19	in anxiety and drink their **w** in despair,	4784
	16: 4	nor were you washed with **w**	4784
	16: 9	with **w** and washed the blood from you	4784
	17: 5	He planted it like a willow by abundant **w**,	4784
	17: 7	and stretched out its branches to him for **w**.	9197
	17: 8	in good soil by abundant **w** so	4784
	19:10	a vine in your vineyard planted by the **w**;	4784
	19:10	and full of branches because of abundant **w**.	4784
	21: 7	and every knee become as weak as **w**.'	4784
	24: 3	put it on and pour **w** into it.	4784
	32: 2	about in your streams, churning the **w**	4784
	34:18	Is it not enough for you to drink clear **w**?	4784
	36:25	I will sprinkle clean **w** on you,	4784
	47: 1	and I saw **w** coming out from under	4784
	47: 1	The **w** was coming down from under	4784
	47: 2	and the **w** was flowing from the south side.	4784
	47: 3	then led me through **w** that was ankle-deep.	4784
	47: 4	and led me through **w** that was knee-deep.	4784
	47: 4	and led me through **w** that was *up to*	4784
	47: 5	the **w** had risen and was deep enough	4784
	47: 8	"This **w** flows toward the eastern region	4784
	47: 8	into the Sea, the **w** there becomes fresh.	4784
	47: 9	because this **w** flows there and makes	4784
	47: 9	and makes the salt **w** fresh;	NIH
	47:12	the **w** from the sanctuary flows to them.	4784
Da	1:12	Give us nothing but vegetables to eat and **w**	4784
Hos	2: 5	who give me my food and my **w**,	4784
	5:10	on them like a flood of **w**.	4784
	6: 3	like the spring rains *that* **w** the earth."	3722
Joel	1:20	of **w** have dried up and fire has devoured	4784
	3:18	all the ravines of Judah will run with **w**.	4784
	3:18	the LORD's house and *will* **w** the valley	9197
Am	4: 8	People staggered from town to town for **w**	4784
	8:11	not a famine of food or a thirst for **w**,	4784
Mic	1: 4	like **w** rushing down a slope.	4784
Na	2: 8	and its **w** is draining away.	4784
	3: 8	situated on the Nile, with **w** around her?	4784
	3:14	Draw **w** *for* the siege,	4784
Hab	3:15	Torrents of **w** swept by;	4784
Zec	14: 8	On that day living **w** will flow out	4784
Mt	3:11	"I baptize you with **w** for repentance.	5623
	3:16	he went up out *of* the **w**.	5623
	8:32	into the lake and died in the **w**.	5623
	10:42	**gives** even a cup of cold **w** to one of these	4540
	14:28	"tell me to come to you on the **w**."	5623
	14:29	walked on the **w** and came toward Jesus.	5623
	17:15	He often falls into the fire or into the **w**.	5623
	27:24	he took **w** and washed his hands in front of	5623

Mk	1: 8	I baptize you *with* w,	5623
	1:10	As Jesus was coming up out *of* the w,	5623
	9:22	"It has often thrown him into fire or w	5623
	9:41	a cup of w in my name because you belong	5623
	14:13	a man carrying a jar *of* w will meet you.	5623
Lk	3:16	"I baptize *with* w,	5623
	5: 4	he said to Simon, "Put out into deep w,	NIG
	7:44	You did not give me any w for my feet,	5623
	8:25	He commands even the winds and the w,	5623
	13:15	from the stall and lead it out *to* give it w?	4540
	16:24	of his finger *in* w and cool my tongue,	5623
	22:10	a man carrying a jar *of* w will meet you.	5623
Jn	1:26	"I baptize with w," John replied,	5623
	1:31	but the reason I came baptizing with w was	5623
	1:33	to baptize with w told me,	5623
	2: 6	Nearby stood six stone w **jars**,	5620
	2: 7	"Fill the jars *with* w";	5623
	2: 9	and the master of the banquet tasted the w	5623
	2: 9	the servants who had drawn the w knew.	5623
	3: 5	of God unless he is born of w and the Spirit.	5623
	3:23	because there was plenty of w.	5623
	4: 7	When a Samaritan woman came to draw w,	5623
	4:10	and he would have given you living w."	5623
	4:11	Where can you get this living w?	5623
	4:13	"Everyone who drinks this w will	5623
	4:14	the w I give him will never thirst.	5623
	4:14	the w I give him will become in him	5623
	4:14	a spring *of* w welling up to eternal life."	5623
	4:15	give me this w so that I won't get thirsty	5623
	4:15	and have to keep coming here *to* **draw w**."	533
	4:28	Then, leaving her w **jar**,	5620
	4:46	where he had turned the w into wine.	5623
	5: 7	into the pool when the w is stirred.	5623
	6:19	walking on the w; and they were terrified.	2498
	7:38	streams *of* living w will flow from within him."	5623
	13: 5	he poured w into a basin and began to wash	5623
	19:34	bringing a sudden flow of blood and w.	5623
	21: 7	and jumped into the w.	2498
Ac	1: 5	For John baptized *with* w,	5623
	8:36	they came to some w and the eunuch said,	5623
	8:36	and the eunuch said, "Look, here is w.	5623
	8:38	down into the w and Philip baptized him.	5623
	8:39	When they came up out of the w,	5623
	10:47	these people from being baptized with w?	5623
	11:16	'John baptized *with* w,	5623
	27:28	the w was a hundred and twenty feet deep.	NIG
Eph	5:26	by the washing *with* w through the word,	5623
1Ti	5:23	Stop **drinking only** w, and use a little wine	5621
Heb	9:19	together with w, scarlet wool and branches	5623
	10:22	and having our bodies washed *with* pure w.	5623
Jas	3:11	Can both **fresh** w and salt water flow from	1184
	3:11	Can both fresh water and **salt** w flow from	4395
	3:12	Neither can a salt spring produce fresh w.	5623
1Pe	3:20	eight in all, were saved through w,	5623
	3:21	this w symbolizes baptism that now saves	NIG
2Pe	2:17	These men are springs **without** w	536
	3: 5	the earth was formed out of w and by water.	5623
	3: 5	the earth was formed out of water and by w.	5623
1Jn	5: 6	This is the one who came by w and blood—	5623
	5: 6	He did not come by w only,	5623
	5: 6	but by w and blood.	5623
	5: 8	the Spirit, the w and the blood;	5623
Rev	7:17	he will lead them to springs of living w.	5623
	8:10	a third of the rivers and on the springs *of* w	5623
	12:15	Then from his mouth the serpent spewed w	5623
	14: 7	the earth, the sea and the springs *of* **w**."	5623
	16: 4	on the rivers and springs *of* w,	5623
	16:12	and its w was dried up to prepare the way	5623
	21: 6	without cost from the spring of the w of life.	5623
	22: 1	angel showed me the river *of* the w of life,	5623
	22:17	let him take the free gift *of* the w of life.	5623

WATER'S (3) [WATER]

Jos	3:15	and their feet touched the w edge,	4784
Mk	4: 1	along the shore at the w **edge**.	2498
Lk	5: 2	he saw at the w edge two boats,	3349

WATERCOURSE (1) [WATER]

| Pr | 21: 1 | directs it like a w wherever he pleases. | 4784+7104 |

WATERED (10) [WATER]

Ge	2: 6	up from the earth and w the whole surface	9197
	13:10	the whole plain of the Jordan *was* **well** w,	5482
	24:46	So I drank, and *she* w the camels also.	9197
	29: 2	because the flocks *were* w from that well.	9197
	29:10	of the well and w his uncle's sheep.	9197
Ex	2:17	came to their rescue and w their flock.	9197
	2:19	He even drew water for us and w the flock."	9197
Dt	29:19	This will bring disaster on the w **land**	8116
Ps	104:16	The trees of the LORD are **well** w,	8425
1Co	3: 6	I planted the seed, Apollos w it,	4540

WATERFALLS (1) [WATER]

| Ps | 42: 7 | Deep calls to deep in the roar of your w; | 7562 |

WATERFLOOD (KJV) See FLOODWATERS

WATERING (5) [WATER]

Ge	2:10	A river w the garden flowed from Eden;	9197
	30:38	the peeled branches in all the w troughs,	4784
Jdg	5:11	the voice of the singers at the w **places**.	5393
Ps	72: 6	like showers w the earth.	2449
Isa	55:10	to it without w the earth and making it bud	8115

WATERLESS (2) [WATER]

| Dt | 8:15 | that thirsty and w land, | 401+4784 |
| Zec | 9:11 | I will free your prisoners from the w pit. | 401+4784 |

WATERPOT, WATERPOTS (KJV) See JARS, WATER JAR

WATERS (165) [WATER]

Ge	1: 2	the Spirit of God was hovering over the w.	4784
	1: 6	an expanse between the w to separate water	4784
	1:10	and the gathered he called "seas."	4784
	7: 7	the ark to escape the w of the flood.	4784
	7:17	as he increased they lifted the ark high	4784
	7:18	The w rose and increased greatly on	4784
	7:20	The w rose and covered the mountains to	4784
	7:24	The w flooded the earth for a hundred	4784
	8: 1	a wind over the earth, and the w receded.	4784
	8: 5	The w continued to recede until	4784
	9:11	Never again will all life be cut off by the w	4784
	9:15	the w become a flood to destroy all life.	4784
	49: 4	Turbulent as the w, you will no longer excel	4784
Ex	7:19	and stretch out your hand over the w	4784
	8: 6	So Aaron stretched out his hand over the w	4784
	14:21	the w were divided,	4784
	14:26	the sea so that the w may flow back over	4784
	15: 5	The **deep** w have covered them;	9333
	15: 8	By the blast of your nostrils the w piled up.	4784
	15: 8	The surging w stood firm like a wall;	NIH
	15: 8	the **deep** w congealed in the heart of the sea.	9333
	15:10	They sank like lead in the mighty w.	4784
	15:19	the LORD brought the w of the sea back	4784
	20: 4	or on the earth beneath or in the w below.	4784
Nu	20:13	These were the w of Meribah,	4784
	20:24	against my command at the w *of* Meribah.	4784
	24: 6	like cedars beside the w.	4784
	27:14	for when the community rebelled at the w	4784
	27:14	(These were the w *of* Meribah Kadesh,	4784
Dt	4:18	along the ground or any fish in the w below.	4784
	5: 8	or on the earth beneath or in the w below.	4784
	11: 4	how he overwhelmed them with the w of	4784
	32:51	of the Israelites at the w *of* Meribah Kadesh	4784
	33: 8	you contended with him at the w	4784
	33:13	above and with the **deep** w that lie below;	9333
Jos	3: 8	the edge of the Jordan's w, go and stand	4784
	3:13	its w flowing downstream will be cut off	4784
	4: 7	the w of the Jordan were cut off.	4784
	4:18	the w of the Jordan returned to their place	4784
	11: 5	made camp together at the **W** *of* Merom	4784
	11: 7	against them suddenly at the **W** *of* Merom	4784
	15: 7	along to the w *of* En Shemesh and came out	4784
	15: 9	toward the spring of the w *of* Nephtoah,	4784
	16: 1	east of the w *of* Jericho,	4784
	18:15	at the spring of the w *of* Nephtoah.	4784
Jdg	5:19	of Canaan fought at Taanach by the w	4784
	7:24	down against the Midianites and seize the w	4784
	7:24	the w of the Jordan as far as Beth Barah.	4784
2Sa	5:20	"As w break out, the LORD has broken out	4784
	22:17	he drew me out of deep w.	4784
2Ki	5:12	better than any of the w *of* Israel?	4784
1Ch	14:11	"As w break out, God has broken out	4784
Ne	9:11	like a stone into mighty w.	4784
Job	11:16	recalling it only as w gone by.	4784
	12:15	If he holds back the w, there is drought;	4784
	20:28	rushing w on the day of God's wrath.	NIH
	26: 5	those beneath the w and all that live	4784
	26: 8	He wraps up the w in his clouds,	4784
	26:10	of the w for a boundary between light	4784
	28:25	of the wind and measured out the w,	4784
	37:10	and the broad w become frozen.	4784
	38:30	when the w become hard as stone,	4784
Ps	18:16	he drew me out of deep w.	4784
	23: 2	he leads me beside quiet w,	4784
	24: 2	upon the seas and established it upon the w.	5643
	29: 3	The voice of the LORD is over the w;	4784
	29: 3	the LORD thunders over the mighty w.	4784
	32: 6	the mighty w rise, they will not reach him.	4784
	33: 7	He gathers the w of the sea into jars;	4784
	46: 3	though its w roar and foam and	4784
	66: 6	they passed through the w on foot—	5643
	69: 1	O God, for the w have come up to my neck.	4784
	69: 2	I have come into the deep w;	4784
	69:14	from those who hate me, from the deep w.	4784
	73:10	to them and drink up w *in* abundance.	4784
	74:13	the heads of the monster in the w.	4784
	77:16	The w saw you, O God, the waters saw you	4784
	77:16	O God, the w saw you and writhed;	4784
	77:19	your way through the mighty w,	4784
	81: 7	I tested you at the w *of* Meribah.	4784
	93: 4	Mightier than the thunder of the great w,	4784
	104: 3	the beams of his upper chambers on their w.	4784
	104: 6	the w stood above the mountains.	4784
	104: 7	But at your rebuke the w fled,	NIH
	104:12	The birds of the air nest by **the** w;	2157
	104:13	*He* w the mountains	9197
	105:29	He turned their w into blood,	4784
	106:11	The w covered their adversaries,	4784
	106:32	the w *of* Meribah they angered the LORD,	4784
	107:23	they were merchants on the mighty w	4784
	124: 5	the raging w would have swept us away.	4784
	136: 6	who spread out the earth upon the w,	4784
	144: 7	and rescue me from the mighty w,	4784

Ps	147:18	he stirs up his breezes, and the w flow.	4784
	148: 4	you highest heavens and you w above	4784
Pr	8:29	so the w would not overstep his command,	4784
	18: 4	The words of a man's mouth are deep w,	4784
	20: 5	The purposes of a man's heart are deep w,	4784
		Who has wrapped up the w in his cloak?	4784
Ecc	11: 1	Cast your bread upon the w,	4784
SS	8: 7	Many w cannot quench love;	4784
Isa	8: 6	the gently flowing w *of* Shiloah	4784
	10:26	and he will raise his staff over the w,	3542
	11: 9	the knowledge of the LORD as the w cover	4784
	15: 6	The w *of* Nimrim are dried up and	4784
	15: 9	Dimon's w are full of blood,	4784
	17:12	they roar like the roaring of great w!	4784
	17:13	the peoples roar like the roar of surging w,	4784
	19: 5	The w of the river will dry up,	4784
	23: 3	the great w came the grain of the Shihor;	4784
	40:12	Who has measured the w in the hollow	4784
	43: 2	you pass through the w, I will be with you;	4784
	43:16	a path through the mighty w,	4784
	51:10	the w *of* the great deep,	4784
	54: 9	that the w *of* Noah would never again cover	4784
	55: 1	all you who are thirsty, come to the w;	4784
	58:11	like a spring whose w never fail.	4784
	63:12	who divided the w before them,	4784
Jer	10:13	he thunders, the w in the heavens roar;	4784
	18:14	Do its cool w from distant sources ever	4784
	46: 7	like rivers of surging w?	4784
	46: 8	like rivers of surging w.	4784
	47: 2	"See how the w are rising in the north;	4784
	48:34	for even the w *of* Nimrim are dried up.	4784
	50:38	A drought on her w!	4784
	51:13	You who live by many w and are rich	4784
	51:16	he thunders, the w in the heavens roar;	4784
	51:55	Waves [of enemies] will rage like great w;	4784
La	3:54	the w closed over my head,	4784
Eze	1:24	like the roar of rushing w,	4784
	26:19	over you and its vast w cover you,	4784
	27:34	by the sea in the depths of the w;	4784
	31: 4	The w nourished it,	4784
	31: 5	spreading because of abundant w.	4784
	31: 7	for its roots went down to abundant w.	4784
	31:14	by the w are ever to tower proudly on high,	4784
	31:15	and its abundant w were restrained.	4784
	32:13	beside abundant w no longer to be stirred	4784
	32:14	Then I will let her w settle	4784
	43: 2	His voice was like the roar of rushing w,	4784
	47:19	as far as the w of Meribah Kadesh,	4784
	48:28	of Gad will run south from Tamar to the w	4784
Da	12: 6	who was above the w of the river,	4784
	12: 7	who was above the w of the river,	4784
Hos	10: 7	like a twig on the surface of the w.	4784
Am	5: 8	the w of the sea and pours them out over	4784
	9: 6	the w of the sea and pours them out over	4784
Jnh	2: 5	The engulfing w threatened me,	4784
Na	1: 8	The river was her defense, the w her wall.	4784
Hab	2:14	glory of the LORD, as the w cover the sea.	4784
	3:15	with your horses, churning the great w.	4784
Lk	8:24	up and rebuked the wind and the raging w;	5623
Jn	6:18	and the w grew rough.	2498
1Co	3: 8	he who plants nor he who w is anything,	4540
	3: 8	and the man who w have one purpose,	4540
2Pe	3: 6	By **these** w also the world of that time	4005S
Rev	1:15	his voice was like the sound *of* rushing w.	5623
	8:11	A third of the w turned bitter.	5623
	8:11	from the w that had become bitter.	5623
	11: 6	the w into blood and to strike the earth	5623
	14: 2	from heaven like the roar *of* rushing w and	5623
	16: 5	I heard the angel in charge of the w say:	5623
	17: 1	the great prostitute, who sits on many w.	5623
	17:15	Then the angel said to me, "The w you saw,	5623
	19: 6	of rushing w and like loud peals of thunder,	5623

WATERSPOUTS (KJV) See WATERFALLS

WATERY (1) [WATER]

| Isa | 44:27 | who says to the w **deep**, 'Be dry, | 7425 |

WAVE (37) [WAVED, WAVES, WAVY]

Ex	29:24	the hands of Aaron and his sons and w them	5677
	29:24	before the LORD as a w **offering**.	9485
	29:26	w it before the LORD as a wave offering,	5677
	29:26	wave it before the LORD as a w **offering**,	9485
	35:22	as a w **offering** to the LORD.	9485
	38:24	of the gold from the w **offering** used for all	9485
	38:29	w **offering** was 70 talents and 2,400	9485
Lev	7:30	with the breast, and w the breast before	5677
	7:30	before the LORD as a w **offering**.	9485
	8:27	before the LORD as a w **offering**,	9485
	8:29	before the LORD as a w **offering**,	9485
	9:21	before the LORD as a w **offering**.	9485
	10:15	before the LORD as a w **offering**.	9485
	14:12	*he shall* w them before the LORD as	5677
	14:12	before the LORD as a w **offering**.	9485
	14:24	and w them before the LORD as	5677
	14:24	before the LORD as a w **offering**.	9485
	23:11	*to* w the sheaf before the LORD so it will	5677
	23:11	the priest *is to* w it on the day after	5677
	23:12	On the day you w the sheaf,	5677
	23:15	the sheaf of the w **offering**.	9485
	23:17	as a w **offering** of firstfruits to the LORD.	9485
	23:20	*to* w the two lambs before the LORD	5677
	23:20	before the LORD as a w **offering**,	9485
Nu	5:25	w it before the LORD and bring it to	5677
	6:20	The priest *shall* then w them before	5677

Nu	6:20	before the LORD as a w offering;	9485
	8:11	before the LORD as a w offering from	9485
	8:13	and then present them as a w offering to	9485
	8:15	and presented them as a w offering,	9485
	8:21	Then Aaron presented them as a w offering	9485
	18:11	from the gifts of all the w offerings of	9485
	18:18	the w offering and the right thigh are yours.	9485
2Ki	5:11	w his hand over the spot and cure me	5677
Job	10:17	your forces come against me w upon wave.	2722
	10:17	your forces come against me wave upon me	2722
Jas	1:6	he who doubts is like a w of the sea,	3114

WAVED (10) [WAVE]

Ex	29:27	the breast that was w and the thigh	5677+9485
Lev	7:34	the breast that is w and the thigh	9485
	8:27	the hands of Aaron and his sons and w them	5677
	8:29	w it before the LORD as a wave offering,	5677
	9:21	Aaron w the breasts and the right thigh	5677
	10:14	that was w and the thigh that was presented	9485
	10:15	the breast that was w must be brought with	9485
	10:15	be w before the LORD as a wave offering.	5677
	14:21	a guilt offering to be w to make atonement	9485
Nu	6:20	that was w and the thigh that was presented.	9485

WAVER (2) [WAVERING]

1Ki	18:21	How long will you w between two opinions?	7174
Ro	4:20	Yet he did not w through unbelief regarding	*1359*

WAVERING (1) [WAVER]

Ps	26:1	I have trusted in the LORD without w.	5048

WAVES (29) [WAVE]

2Sa	22:5	"The w of death swirled about me;	5403
Job	9:8	the heavens and treads on the w of the sea.	1195
	38:11	here is where your proud w halt'?	1644
Ps	42:7	all your w and breakers have swept	5403
	65:7	the roaring of their w,	1644
	88:7	you have overwhelmed me with all your w.	5403
	89:9	when its w mount up, you still them.	1644
	93:3	the seas have lifted up their pounding w.	1922
	107:25	up a tempest that lifted high the w.	1644
	107:29	the w of the sea were hushed.	1644
Isa	48:18	your righteousness like the w of the sea.	1644
	51:15	who churns up the sea so that its w roar—	1644
	57:20	whose w cast up mire and mud.	4784
Jer	5:22	The w may roll, but they cannot prevail;	1644
	31:35	who stirs up the sea so that its w roar—	1644
	51:42	its roaring w will cover her.	1644
	51:55	W [of enemies] will rage like great waters;	1644
Eze	26:3	like the sea casting up its w.	1644
Jnh	2:3	all your w and breakers swept over me.	1644
Hab	3:10	the deep roared and lifted its w on high.	3338
Mt	8:24	so that the w swept over the boat.	3246
	8:26	he got up and rebuked the winds and the w,	2498
	8:27	Even the winds and the w obey him!"	2498
	14:24	by the because the wind was against it.	3246
Mk	4:37	and the w broke over the boat,	3246
	4:39	rebuked the wind and said to the w,	2498
	4:41	Even the wind and the w obey him!"	2498
Eph	4:14	tossed back and forth by the w,	3115
Jude	1:13	They are wild w of the sea,	3246

WAVY (1) [WAVE]

SS	5:11	his hair is w and black as a raven.	9446

WAX (4)

Ps	22:14	My heart has turned to w;	1880
	68:2	as w melts before the fire,	1880
	97:5	mountains melt like w before the LORD,	1880
Mic	1:4	like w before the fire,	1880

WAY (595) [AWAY, WAYS]

Ge	3:24	and forth to guard the w to the tree of life.	2006
	9:23	Their faces were turned the other w so	345
	12:20	and they sent him on his w,	906+8938
	18:5	can be refreshed and then go on your w—	6296
	18:16	with them to see them on their w.	8938
	18:19	the w of the LORD by doing what is right	2006
	19:2	then go on your w early in the morning."	2006
	19:9	"Get out of our w," they replied.	2134
	21:14	She went on her w and wandered in	2143
	24:1	and the LORD had blessed him in every w.	3972
	24:10	for Aram Naharaim and made his w to	2143
	24:49	if not, tell me, so I may know which w to turn."	196+3545+6584+6584+8520
	24:50	we can say nothing to you one w or	8273S
	24:54	"Send me on my w to my master."	8938
	24:56	Send me on my w so I may go	8938
	24:59	they sent their sister Rebekah on her w,	8938
	26:31	Then Isaac sent them on their w,	8938
	27:9	just the w he likes it.	889+3869
	27:14	just the w his father liked it.	889+3869
	28:5	Then Isaac sent Jacob on his w,	8938
	30:25	"Send me on my w so I can go back	8938
	30:26	and I will be on my w.	2143
	30:43	In this w the man grew exceedingly prosperous	2256
	32:1	Jacob also went on his w,	2006
	33:12	"Let us be on our w,"	2143+2256+5825
	33:16	that day Esau started on his w back to Seir.	2006
	35:19	and was buried on the w to Ephrath (that is,	2006
	37:25	and they were on their w to take them down	2143
Ge	38:13	"Your father-in-law is on his w to Timnah	6590
	41:43	and men shouted before him, "Make w!"	91
	44:3	the men were sent on their w	8938
	45:24	"Don't quarrel on the w!"	2006
	48:7	of Canaan while we were still on the w,	2006
Ex	2:12	Glancing this w and that and seeing no one,	AIT
	3:9	the w the Egyptians are oppressing them.	4316S
	4:14	He is already on his w to meet you,	3655
	4:24	At a lodging place on the w,	2006
	5:15	Why have you treated your servants this w?	3907
	13:21	in a pillar of cloud to guide them on their w	2006
	16:4	In this w I will test them	5100
	18:8	the w and how the LORD had saved them.	2006
	18:20	the w to live and the duties they are	2006
	18:27	sent his father-in-law on his w,	8938
	19:21	not force their w through to see the LORD	2238
	19:24	the people must not force their w through	2238
	23:20	ahead of you to guard you along the w and	2006
	23:28	and Hittites out of your w.	4200+4946+7156
	26:17	the frames of the tabernacle in this w.	4027
	26:24	the bottom all the w to the top, and fitted	6584
	28:11	of the sons of Israel on the two stones the w	5126
	29:9	In this w you shall ordain Aaron	2256
	33:3	and I might destroy you on the w."	2006
	36:22	the frames of the tabernacle in this w.	4027
	36:29	the bottom all the w to the top and fitted	448
Lev	4:20	In this w the priest will make atonement	2256
	4:26	In this w the priest will make atonement for	2256
	4:31	In this w the priest will make atonement	2256
	4:35	In this w the priest will make atonement	2256
	5:5	he must confess in what w he has sinned	AIT
	5:10	in the prescribed w and make atonement	5477
	5:13	In this w the priest will make atonement	2256
	5:18	In this w the priest will make atonement	2256
	6:7	In this w the priest will make atonement	2256
	9:16	and offered it in the prescribed w.	5477
	12:8	In this w the priest will make atonement	2256
	14:31	In this w the priest will make atonement	2256
	14:53	In this w he will make atonement for	2256
	15:15	In this w he will make atonement before	2256
	15:30	In this w he will make atonement for her	2256
	16:16	In this w he will make atonement for	2256
	17:8	sacrifice it in such a w that it will be	4200
	19:25	In this w your harvest will be increased.	4200
	22:29	sacrifice it in such a w that it will be	4200
Nu	2:34	that is the w they encamped	4027
	2:34	and that is the w they set out,	4027
	5:6	in any w and so is unfaithful to the LORD,	AIT
	8:14	In this w you are to set the Levites apart	2256
	14:45	and beat them down all the w to Hormah.	6330
	15:13	native-born must do these things in this w	3970
	18:28	In this w you also will present an offering	4027
	21:4	But the people grew impatient on the w;	2006
	21:30	Heshbon is destroyed all the w to Dibon.	6330
	24:25	and Balak went his own w.	2006
	28:24	In this w prepare the food for	3869
Dt	1:31	all the w you went until you reached	2006
	1:33	and to show you the w you should go.	2006
	1:44	and beat you down from Seir all the w to	6330
	2:1	For a long time we made our w around	6015
	2:3	"You have made your w around	6015
	4:7	near them the w the LORD our God is	3869
	5:33	Walk in all the w that the LORD your God	2006
	8:2	how the LORD your God led you all the w	2006
	9:16	the w that the LORD had commanded you.	2006
	10:11	"and lead the people on their w,	5023
	11:28	the LORD your God and turn from the w	2006
	12:4	the LORD your God in their w.	4027
	12:31	the LORD your God in their w,	4027
	13:5	he has tried to turn you from the w	2006
	16:17	a gift in proportion to the w	889S
	17:16	"You are not to go back that w again."	2006
	20:3	be terrified or give w to panic before them.	6907
	23:4	to meet you with bread and water on your w	2006
	24:9	your God did to Miriam along the w	2006
	25:17	along the w when you came out of Egypt.	2006
	29:16	through the countries we came in here.	2006
	29:19	persist in going my own w."	4213+9244
	31:29	to turn from the w I have commanded you.	2006
	32:6	Is this the w you repay the LORD,	AIT
Jos	2:5	I don't know which w they went.	625+2025
	2:16	and then go on your w."	2006
	3:4	Then you will know which w to go,	2006
	5:4	since you have never been this w before.	2006
	5:4	in the desert on the w after leaving Egypt.	2006
	5:7	not been circumcised on the w.	2006
	9:22	'We live a long w from you,'	4394+8158
	10:10	and cut them down all the w to Azekah	6330
	11:8	pursued them all the w to Greater Sidon,	6330
	18:8	As the men started on their w to map out	2143
	23:5	The LORD your God himself will drive them out of your w.	7156
	23:14	"Now I am about to go the w of all	2006
Jdg	2:17	the w in which their fathers had walked,	2006
	2:17	w of obedience to the LORD's commands.	NIH
	2:22	and see whether they will keep the w of	2006
	3:18	he sent on their w the men	8938
	4:6	of Naphtali and Zebulun and lead the w	5432
	4:9	because of the w you are going about this,	2006
	6:4	the land and ruined the crops all the w to	6330
	9:40	all the w to the entrance to the gate.	6330
	11:13	all the w to the Jordan.	6330
	17:8	On his w he came to Micah's house in	2006+6913
	17:9	they lived a long w from the Sidonians	8158
	18:12	On their w they set up camp	6590
	18:26	So the Danites went their w, and Micah,	2006
	18:28	to rescue them because they lived a long w	8158
Jdg	19:9	get up and be on your w home."	2006
	19:18	"We are on our w from Bethlehem in Judah	6296
	19:27	and stepped out to continue on his w,	2006
	20:36	men of Israel had given w before Benjamin,	5226
1Sa	1:18	Then she went her w and ate something,	2006
	6:6	so they could go on their w?	2143
	6:8	Send it on its w.	2143
	6:12	keeping on the road and lowing all the w;	2143+2143
	7:11	along the w to a point below Beth Car.	NIH
	9:6	Perhaps he will tell us what w to take."	2006
	9:8	so that he will tell us what w to take."	2006
	9:14	toward them on his w up to the high place.	6590
	9:26	and I will send you on your w."	8938
	12:23	I will teach you the w that is good and right.	2006
	15:7	all the w from Havilah to Shur,	995
	16:1	Fill your horn with oil and be on your w;	2143
	19:24	He lay that w all that day and night.	6873S
	24:3	He came to the sheep pens along the w;	2006
	24:7	And Saul left the cave and went his w.	2006
	24:19	for the w you treated me today.	889S
	24:25	So David went on his w,	2006
	28:22	and have the strength to go on your w."	2006
	30:2	carried them off as they went on their w.	2006
2Sa	2:24	on the w to the wasteland of Gibeon.	2006
	3:16	weeping behind her all the w to Bahurim.	2143
	4:7	they traveled all night by w of the Arabah.	2006
	5:25	all the w from Gibeon to Gezer.	995+6330
	7:19	Is this your usual w of dealing with man,	9368
	12:21	"Why are you acting this w?	1821
	13:30	While they were on their w,	2006
	15:6	in this w toward all the Israelites who came	1821
	18:23	by w of the plain and outran the Cushite.	2006
	19:31	to send him on his w from there.	8938
	19:36	why should the king reward me in this w?	1692S
	20:2	by their king all the w from the Jordan	4946
	22:31	"As for God, his w is perfect;	2006
	22:33	with strength and makes my w perfect.	2006
1Ki	2:2	"I am about to go the w of all the earth,"	2006
	5:10	In this w Hiram kept Solomon supplied	2256
	6:33	In the same w he made four-sided jambs	4027
	7:37	This is the w he made the ten stands.	3869
	8:23	your servants who continue wholeheartedly in your w.	4200+7156
	8:36	Teach them the right w to live,	2006
	11:29	the prophet of Shiloh met him on the w,	2006
	13:9	or return by the w you came.'"	2006
	13:10	not return by the w he had come to Bethel.	2006
	13:12	"Which w did he go?"	2006
	13:17	or return by the w you came.'"	2006
	13:24	As he went on his w,	2143
	18:46	he ran ahead of Ahab all the w to Jezreel.	995+3870+6330
	19:15	"Go back the w you came,	2006
	22:24	"Which w did the spirit from the LORD	361+2296
2Ki	2:23	and Elisha were on their w from Gilgal.	2143
	3:22	To the Moabites across the w,	4946+5584
	4:9	that this man who often comes our w is	NIH
	8:7	"The man of God has come all the w up	6330
	9:15	Jehu said, "If this is the w you feel,	NIH
	9:27	in his chariot on the w up to Gur	5090
	10:15	who was on his w to meet him.	AIT
	11:19	entering by w of the gate of the guards.	2006
	19:28	I will make you return by the w you came.'	2006
	19:33	By the w that he came he will return;	2006
	21:22	and did not walk in the w of the LORD.	2006
1Ch	7:28	and Shechem and its villages all the w to	6330
	14:16	all the w from Gibeon to	6330
	15:13	about how to do it in the prescribed w."	5477
	23:31	and in the w prescribed for them.	5477
2Ch	6:14	your servants who continue wholeheartedly in your w.	4200+7156
	6:27	Teach them the right w to live,	2006
	18:23	"Which w did the spirit from the LORD go	361+2006+2021+2296
	23:19	who was in any w unclean might enter.	1821
	29:25	and lyres in the w prescribed by David	5184
Ezr	7:27	of the LORD in Jerusalem in this w	3869
	8:31	from enemies and bandits along the w.	2006
	9:2	and officials have led the w	2118+3338+8037
Ne	5:13	"In this w may God shake out of his house	3970
	9:12	of fire to give them light on the w they were	2006
	9:19	by night to shine on the w they were to take.	2006
	11:30	all the w from Beersheba to the Valley	6330
Est	1:8	was allowed to drink in his own w,	9276
	1:18	to all the king's nobles in the same w.	NIH
	3:6	for a w to destroy all Mordecai's people,	NIH
	9:27	in the w prescribed and at the time	3869
Job	3:23	to a man whose w is hidden,	2006
	8:15	He leans on his web, but it gives w;	4202+6641
	19:8	He has blocked my w so I cannot pass;	784
	22:21	in this w prosperity will come to you.	NIH
	23:10	But he knows the w that I take;	2006
	23:11	I have kept to his w without turning aside.	2006
	28:23	the w to it and he alone knows	2006
	29:25	the w for them and sat as their chief;	2006
	32:3	because they had found no w to refute Job,	5101
	33:14	For God does speak—now one w,	285+928
	36:31	This is the w he governs the nations	928+4392
	38:19	"What is the w to the abode of light?	2006
	38:24	What is the w to the place where	2006
	38:35	the lightning bolts on their w?	2143
Ps	1:1	or stand in the w of sinners or sit in the seat	2006
	1:6	LORD watches over the w of the righteous,	2006
	1:6	but the w of the wicked will perish.	2006
	2:12	be angry and you be destroyed in your w,	2006
	5:8	make straight your w before me.	2006

Ref	Text	Strong's
Ps 18:30	As for God, his w is perfect;	2006
18:32	with strength and makes my w perfect.	2006
25: 9	in what is right and teaches them his w.	2006
25:12	He will instruct him in the w chosen	2006
27:11	Teach me your w, O LORD;	2006
32: 8	and teach you in the w you should go;	2006
37: 5	Commit your w to the LORD;	2006
37:23	If the LORD delights in a man's w,	2006
37:34	Wait for the LORD and keep his w.	2006
46: 2	the earth give w and the mountains fall into	4614
50:23	the w so that I may show him the salvation	2006
77:19	your w through the mighty waters,	8666
85:13	before him and prepares the w for his steps.	2006
86:11	Teach me your w, O LORD,	2006
107: 4	finding no w to a city	2006
107: 7	He led them by a straight w to a city	2006
109:24	My knees give w from fasting;	4173
110: 7	He will drink from a brook beside the w;	2006
119: 9	How can a young man keep his w pure?	784
119:30	I have chosen the w of truth;	2006
139:24	See if there is any offensive w in me,	2006
139:24	and lead me in the w everlasting.	2006
142: 3	it is you who know my w.	5986
143: 8	Show me the w I should go,	2006
Pr 2: 8	and protects the w of his faithful ones.	2006
3:23	Then you will go on your w in safety,	2006
4:11	I guide you in the w of wisdom and	2006
4:14	of the wicked or walk in the w of evil men.	2006
4:15	turn from it and **go on** your w.	6296
4:19	the w of the wicked is like deep darkness;	2006
5: 6	She gives no thought to the w of life;	784
6:23	corrections of discipline are the w to life,	2006
8: 2	On the heights along the w,	2006
8:20	I walk in the w of righteousness,	784
9: 6	walk in the w of understanding.	2006
9:15	who go straight on their w.	784
10:17	He who heeds discipline shows the w	784
10:29	The w of the LORD is a refuge for	2006
11: 5	the blameless makes a straight w for them,	2006
12:15	The w of a fool seems right to him,	2006
12:26	but the w of the wicked leads them astray.	2006
12:28	In the w of righteousness there is life;	784
13:15	but the w of the unfaithful is hard.	2006
14:12	There is a w that seems right to a man,	2006
15: 9	The LORD detests the w of the wicked	2006
15:19	w of the sluggard is blocked with thorns,	2006
16:17	he who guards his w guards his life.	2006
16:25	There is a w that seems right to a man,	2006
18:16	A gift **opens the** w for the giver	8143
19: 2	nor to be hasty and **miss the** w.	2627
20:24	then can anyone understand his own w?	2006
21: 8	The w of the guilty is devious,	2006
22: 6	a child **in the** w he **should go,**	2006+6584+7023
25:26	a righteous man *who* **gives** w to the wicked.	4572
30:19	the w of an eagle in the sky,	2006
30:19	the w of a snake on a rock,	2006
30:19	the w of a ship on the high seas,	2006
30:19	and the w of a man with a maiden.	2006
30:20	"This is the w of an adulteress:	2006
Ecc 10:15	he does not know the w to town.	2143
SS 6: 1	**Which** w did your lover turn,	625+2025
Isa 8:11	not to follow the w of this people.	2006
9: 1	*by the* w *of* the sea, along the Jordan—	2006
15: 4	their voices are heard **all the** w to Jahaz.	6330
15: 5	They go up the w *to* Luhith,	5090
22:25	peg driven into the firm place *will* **give** w;	4631
26: 7	you make the w *of* the righteous smooth.	5047
26: 8	LORD, walking in the w *of* your laws,	784
28:26	and teaches him the **right** w.	5477
30:11	Leave this w, get off this path,	2006
30:21	saying, "This is the w; walk in it."	2006
35: 3	steady the knees *that* **give** w,	4173
35: 8	it will be called the **W** of Holiness.	2006
35: 8	it will be for those who walk in that **W;**	2006
37:29	I will make you return by the w you came.	2006
37:34	By the w that he came he will return;	2006
40: 3	"In the desert prepare the w for the LORD;	2006
40:14	and who taught him the right w?	784
40:27	O Israel, "My w is hidden from the LORD;	2006
43:16	he who made a w through the sea,	2006
43:19	I am making a w in the desert and streams	2006
48:17	who directs you in the w you should go.	2006
51: 5	my salvation **is on the** w,	3655
53: 6	each of us has turned to his own w;	2006
55: 7	Let the wicked forsake his w and	2006
56:11	they all turn to their own w,	2006
57:14	the obstacles out of the w of my people."	2006
58:13	if you honor it by not going your own w	2006
59: 8	The w of peace they do not know;	2006
59:10	**feeling** *our* w like men without eyes.	1779
62:10	Prepare the w for the people.	2006
Jer 2:17	when he led you in the w?	2006
4: 2	just and **righteous** w you swear,	AIT
5: 4	for they do not know the w of the LORD,	2006
5: 5	surely they know the w *of* the LORD,	2006
5:31	and my people love it **this** w.	4027
6:16	ask where the good w is, and walk in it,	2006
12: 1	Why does the w *of* the wicked prosper?	2006
13: 9	**In the same** w I will ruin the pride of Judah	3970
21: 8	See, I am setting before you the w of life	2006
21: 8	before you the way of life and the w	2006
22:21	This has been your w from your youth;	2006
26: 3	and each will turn from his evil w.	2006
28:11	'In the same w will I break the yoke of	3970
28:11	At this, the prophet Jeremiah went on his w.	2006
36: 3	each of them will turn from his wicked w;	2006
39: 4	the city at night *by* w *of* the king's garden,	2006
Jer 41:17	near Bethlehem *on their* w to Egypt	2143
48: 5	They go up the w *to* Luhith,	5090
50: 5	the w to Zion and turn their faces toward it.	2006
La 2:15	All who pass your w clap their hands	2006
3: 9	He has barred my w with blocks of stone;	2006
Eze 4:13	"**In this** w the people will eat defiled food	3970
18:25	you say, 'The w of the Lord is not just.'	2006
18:25	Hear, O house of Israel: Is my w unjust?	2006
18:29	'The w of the Lord is not just.'	2006
20:30	the w your fathers did and lust after	2006
23:13	both of them went the same w.	2006
23:31	You have gone the w of your sister;	2006
32: 9	with your flowing blood **all the w to**	448
33:17	'The w of the Lord is not just.'	2006
33:17	But it is their w that is not just.	2006
33:20	you say, 'The w of the Lord is not just.'	2006
39:11	It *will* **block the** w of travelers,	2888
44: 3	to enter by w of the portico of the gateway	2006
44: 3	of the gateway and go out the same w."	2006
44: 4	the man brought me *by* w *of* the north gate	2006
46: 8	and he is to come out the same w.	2006
Da 1: 8	for permission not to defile himself this w.	NIH
3:29	for no other god can save **in this** w."	10341
5: 6	and his legs **gave** w.	10742
12: 9	He replied, "**Go** *your* w, Daniel,	2143
12:13	"As for you, **go** *your* w till the end.	2143
Hos 2: 6	in so that she cannot find her w.	5986
Am 6:14	the w from Lebo Hamath to the valley of	NIH
Mic 2:13	One who breaks open the w will go up	NIH
Na 1: 3	His w is in the whirlwind and the storm,	2006
2: 5	yet they stumble on their w.	2142
2:10	Hearts melt, knees **give** w, bodies tremble,	7211
Mal 2: 8	But you have turned from the w and	2006
3: 1	who will prepare the w before me.	2006
Mt 2: 9	*they* **went on** *their* w,	4513
3: 3	'Prepare the w for the Lord,	3847
4:15	the w to the sea, along the Jordan,	3847
5:12	**in the same** w they persecuted the prophets	4048
5:16	**In the same** w, let your light shine before	4048
5:25	Do it while you are still with him on the w,	3847
7: 2	For in the same w you judge others,	3210S
8:28	so violent that no one could pass that w.	3847
11:10	who will prepare your w before you.'	3847
15:32	or they may collapse on the w."	3847
17:12	**In the same** w the Son of Man is	2779+4048
18:14	**In the same** w your Father in heaven is	4048
19: 8	But it was not **this** w from the beginning.	4048
19:12	eunuchs because they were born **that** w;	4048
19:12	others *were* **made that** w by men;	2335+2336S
21:18	*as he was* **on** *his* w **back** to the city,	2056
21:32	to you to show you the w of righteousness,	3847
21:36	and the tenants treated them **the same** w.	6058
21:46	*They* **looked for a** w to arrest him,	2426
22:16	of integrity and that you teach the w of God	3847
23:28	**In the same** w, on the outside you appear	4048
25:10	*while they were* **on their** w to buy the oil,	599
26: 4	to arrest Jesus in some **sly** w and kill him.	1515
26:54	that say it must happen **in this** w?"	4048
27:41	**In the same** w the chief priests,	3931
27:44	**In the same** w the robbers who were	899
28:11	*While* the women *were* **on their** w,	4513
Mk 1: 2	ahead of you, who will prepare your w"—	3847
1: 3	'Prepare the w for the Lord,	3847
7: 9	a fine w of setting aside the commands	2822
8: 3	home hungry, they will collapse on the w,	3847
8:27	On the w he asked them,	3847
9:34	on the w they had argued about who was	3847
10:17	As Jesus started on his w,	3847
10:32	They were on their w up to Jerusalem,	3847
10:32	with Jesus leading the w,	NIG
11:18	and began looking for a w to kill him,	4802
12:12	Then they **looked for a** w to arrest him	2426
12:14	the w of God in accordance with the truth.	3847
14: 1	for **some** sly w to arrest Jesus and kill him.	4802
15:21	was passing by on his w in from	2262
15:31	**In the same** w the chief priests	3931
16: 2	*they were* **on their** w to the tomb	2262
Lk 1:76	on before the Lord to prepare the w for him,	3847
3: 4	'Prepare the w for the Lord,	3847
4:30	through the crowd and **went on** *his* w.	4513
5:19	When they could not find **a** w to do this	4481
7:27	who will prepare your w before you.'	3847
7:29	acknowledged that God's w was right,	NIG
8:14	**on** *their* w they are choked by life's worries,	4513
8:42	As Jesus *was* **on** *his* w,	5632
10:38	As Jesus and his disciples *were* **on** *their* w,	4513
12:58	try hard to be reconciled to him on the w,	3847
13: 2	because they suffered this w?	NIG
13:22	teaching as he made his w to Jerusalem.	4512
14:19	and I'm **on** *my* w to try them out.	4513
14:32	the other is still a **long** w off and will ask	4522
14:33	**In the same** w, any of you who does not	4048
15: 7	I tell you that **in the same** w there will	4048
15:10	**In the same** w, I tell you, there is rejoicing	4048
15:20	"But while he was still a **long** w off,	3426
16:16	and everyone *is* **forcing** his w into it.	1041
17:11	Now on his w to Jerusalem,	4513
18:39	Those who **led the** w rebuked him	4575
19: 4	since Jesus was coming that w.	NIG
19:48	Yet they could not find **any** w to do it,	3836+5515
20:19	chief priests **looked for a** w to arrest him	2426
20:21	but teach the w of God in accordance with	3847
20:31	and **in the same** w the seven died,	6058
22:20	looking for **some** w to get rid of Jesus,	3836+4802
22:20	**In the same** w, after supper he took the cup,	6058
23: 5	in Galilee and has come all the w here."	NIG
23:26	*who was* **on** *his* w in from the country,	2262
Lk 24:35	the two told what had happened on the w,	3847
Jn 1:23	'Make straight the w for the Lord.'"	3847
4:30	and **made their** w toward him.	2262
4:51	*While* he *was* still **on** the w,	2849
7:46	"No one ever spoke **the** w this man does,"	4048
10: 1	but climbs in by some **other** w,	249
12:12	for the Feast heard that Jesus *was* **on his** w	2262
14: 4	the w to the place where I am going."	3847
14: 5	so how can we know the w?"	3847
14: 6	"I am the w and the truth and the life.	3847
15:21	They will treat you this w because	NIG
18:22	"Is **this the** w you answer the high priest?"	3847
21: 1	It happened **this w:**	4048
Ac 1:11	will come back **in the same** w you have	4005+5573
	seen him go into heaven."	
7: 6	God spoke to him **in this w:**	4048
8:27	and on his w he met an Ethiopian eunuch,	NIG
8:28	and **on** *his* w home was sitting	5715
8:39	but went *on* his w rejoicing.	3847
9: 2	he found any there who belonged to the **W,**	3847
13: 4	**sent on** *their* w by the Holy Spirit,	1734
14:16	he let all nations go their own w.	3847
15: 3	The church **sent** *them* **on** *their* w,	4636
16:17	who are telling you the w to be saved."	3847
17:22	I see that in **every** w you are very religious.	AIT
18:25	He had been instructed in the w of the Lord,	3847
18:26	to their home and explained to him the w	3847
19: 9	to believe and publicly maligned the **W.**	3847
19:20	**In this** w the word of the Lord spread	4048
19:23	a great disturbance about the **W.**	3847
21: 5	*we* left and **continued on** *our* w.	4513
21:11	'In this w the Jews of Jerusalem will bind	4048
22: 4	the followers of this **W** to their death,	3847
24: 3	Everywhere and in **every** w,	AIT
24:14	of our fathers as a follower of the **W,**	3847
24:22	Felix, who was well acquainted with the **W,**	3847
25: 3	an ambush to kill him along the w.	3847
26: 4	the w I have **lived** ever since I was a child,	1052
27:15	so we **gave** w to it and were driven along.	2113
27:44	**In this** w everyone reached land in safety.	4048
Ro 1:10	by God's will the w **may be opened** for me	2338
1:27	**In the same** w the men also abandoned	3931
3: 2	Much in **every** w!	5573
3: 2	and the w of peace they do not know."	3847
5:12	and **in this** w death came to all men,	4048
6:11	**In the same** w, count yourselves dead to sin	4048
7: 6	from the law so that we serve in the **new** w	2786
7: 6	and not in the **old** w of the written code.	4095
8:26	**In the same** w, the Spirit helps us	6058
10: 5	Moses describes in this w the righteousness	NIG
14:13	or obstacle in your brother's w.	NIG
14:18	in this *w* is pleasing to God and approved	AIT
15:19	from Jerusalem **all the** w around to Illyricum	3588
15:25	*I am* **on** *my* w to Jerusalem in the service of	4513
15:28	go to Spain and **visit** you **on the** w.	1328
16: 2	in the Lord **in a** w **worthy** of the saints and	547
16:17	and put obstacles in your w that are	AIT
1Co 1: 5	in him you have been enriched in **every** *w*—	AIT
2:11	**In the same** w no one knows the thoughts	2779+4048
	of God except the Spirit of God.	
4:17	He will remind you of my w of life	3847
7: 4	**In the same** w, the husband's body does not	3931
7:35	a right *w* in undivided devotion to the Lord.	AIT
8:12	you sin against your brothers **in this** w	4048
9:14	**In the same** w, the Lord has commanded	4048
9:24	Run **in such a** w as to get the prize.	4048
10:13	also provide a w **out** so that you can stand	1676
10:33	as I try to please everybody in **every** w.	AIT
11:25	**In the same** w, after supper he took the cup,	6058
12:31	now I will show you the most excellent w.	3847
14: 1	Follow the w of love and eagerly desire	NIG
14:40	be done in a fitting and **orderly** w.	2848+5423
16:11	**Send** him on his w in peace	4636
2Co 1:16	planned to **visit** you on *my* w to Macedonia	1451
1:16	to **have you send** me on my w to Judea.	4636
5:16	we once regarded Christ **in this** w,	2848+4922S
6: 4	of God we commend ourselves in **every** *w:*	AIT
7: 9	and so were **not** harmed in **any** w by us	3594
8:20	of the w we administer this liberal gift.	NIG
9:11	be made rich in **every** w so that you can	AIT
11: 6	made this perfectly clear to you in **every** w.	AIT
11: 9	from being a burden to you in **any** *w,*	AIT
11:18	many are boasting **in the** w the world **does,**	2848
Gal 1:13	heard of my previous w of life in Judaism,	419
4:23	was born **in the ordinary** w;	2848+4922
4:29	the son born **in the ordinary** w	2848+4922
5:12	go the whole w and emasculate themselves!	NIG
6: 2	**in this** w you will fulfill the law of Christ.	4048
Eph 1:23	of him who fills everything in **every** *w.*	AIT
4:20	did not come to know Christ that w.	4048
4: 4	with regard to your former w of life,	419
5:28	**In this same** w, husbands ought to	2779+4048
6: 9	masters, treat your slaves in the **same** w.	899
Php 1: 7	It is right for me to feel **this** w about all	4047
1:18	The important thing is that *in* **every** w,	5573
1:20	I eagerly expect and hope that I will in **no** w	4029
1:28	in **any** w by those who oppose you.	3594
Col 1:10	of the Lord and may please him in **every** *w:*	AIT
4: 5	Be wise in the w you act toward outsiders;	NIG
1Th 2:16	**In this** w they always heap up their sins to	3836
3: 4	And it turned out that w, as you well know.	2777
3: 5	I was afraid that **in some** w the tempter	4803
3:11	and our Lord Jesus clear the w for us	3847
4: 4	to control his own body in a w that is holy	NIG
2Th 2: 3	Don't let anyone deceive you in **any** w,	
		2848+3594+5573
2: 7	to do so till he is taken out of the w.	3545

2Th	3:16	give you peace at all times and in every **w**.	5573
1Ti	3:11	**In the same w**, their wives are to be	6058
	5:25	**In the same w**, good deeds are obvious,	6058
	6:19	In this **w** they will lay up treasure	NIG
2Ti	3: 6	the kind who **worm** *their* w into homes	1905
	3:10	know all about my teaching, my **w of life**,	73
Tit	2: 3	to be reverent in the **w** they **live**,	2949
	2:10	that in **every** *w* they will make the teaching	AIT
	3:13	to **help** Zenas the lawyer and Apollos **on** *their* **w**	4636
Heb	2:17	to be made like his brothers in **every w**,	AIT
	4:15	tempted in **every** *w*, just as we are—	AIT
	9: 8	that the **w** into the Most Holy Place had not	3847
	9:21	**In the same w**, he sprinkled with blood	3931
	9:25	the **w** the high priest enters the Most Holy	6061
	10:20	a new and living **w** opened for us through	3847
	13: 7	of their **w of life** and imitate their faith.	419
	13:18	and desire to live honorably in **every** *w*.	AIT
Jas	1:11	**In the same w**, the rich man will fade away	4048
	2:17	**In the same w**, faith by itself,	4048
	2:25	**In the same w**, was not even Rahab	3931
	5:20	the error of his **w** will save him from death	3847
1Pe	1:18	the empty **w of life** handed down to you	419
	3: 1	Wives, **in the same w** be submissive	3931
	3: 5	For **this is the w** the holy women of the	4048
	3: 6	if you do what is right and do not **give w**	4766
	3: 7	Husbands, **in the same w** be considerate	3931
	5: 5	Young men, **in the same w** be submissive	3931
2Pe	2: 2	and will bring the **w** of truth into disrepute.	3847
	2:15	the straight **w** and wandered off to follow	3847
	2:15	to follow the **w** of Balaam son of Beor,	3847
	2:21	not to have known the **w** of righteousness,	3847
1Jn	3:11	everything will be destroyed in this **w**,	3847
	3:16	He writes **the same w** in all his letters,	2779+6055
1Jn	4:17	In this **w**, love is made complete among us	AIT
3Jn	1: 6	**send** them **on their w** in a manner worthy	4636
Jude	1: 7	In a similar **w**, Sodom and Gomorrah	5573
	1: 8	**In the very same w**, these dreamers pollute	3931
	1:11	They have taken the **w** of Cain;	3847
	1:15	acts *they have* **done in the ungodly w**,	814
Rev	16:12	to prepare the **w** for the kings from the East.	3847
	18:20	judged her for the **w** she **treated** you.' "	3210S

WAYFARING (KJV) See TRAVELER, WALK

WAYLAID (1) [WAYLAY]

1Sa	15: 2	when *they* **w** them as they came up from Egypt.	928+2006+2021+8492

WAYLAY (2) [WAYLAID]

Pr	1:11	*let's* **w** some harmless soul;	7621
	1:18	*they* **w** only themselves!	7621

WAYMARKS (KJV) See ROAD SIGNS

WAYS (229) [WAY]

Ge	6:12	the people on earth had corrupted their **w**.	2006
Ex	33:13	teach me your **w** so I may know you	2006
Lev	5: 5	" 'When anyone is guilty in any of **these** *w*,	AIT
	18:24	not defile yourselves in any of **these** *w*,	AIT
	25:54	if he is not redeemed in any of **these** *w*,	AIT
Dt	8: 6	walking in his **w** and revering him.	2006
	10:12	to walk in all his **w**, to love him,	2006
	11:22	the LORD your God, to walk in all his **w**	2006
	18: 9	do not learn to imitate the **detestable w** of	9359
	19: 9	and to walk always in his **w**—	2006
	26:17	and that you will walk in his **w**,	2006
	28: 9	of the LORD your God and walk in his **w**.	2006
	30:16	love the LORD your God, to walk in his **w**,	2006
	32: 4	his works are perfect, and all his **w** are just.	2006
Jos	22: 5	to walk in all his **w**, to obey his commands,	2006
Jdg	2: 19	to **w** even more corrupt than those	NIH
	2:19	up their evil practices and stubborn **w**.	2006
1Sa	8: 3	But his sons did not walk in his **w**.	2006
	8: 5	and your sons do not walk in your **w**;	2006
2Sa	14:14	he devises **w** so that a banished person may	4742
	22:22	For I have kept the **w** of the LORD;	2006
1Ki	2: 3	Walk in his **w**, and keep his decrees	2006
	3:14	if you walk in my **w** and obey my statutes	2006
	8:58	in all his **w** and to keep the commands,	2006
	11:33	and have not walked in my **w**,	2006
	11:38	in my **w** and do what is right in my eyes	2006
	13:33	this, Jeroboam did not change his evil **w**,	2006
	15:26	walking in the **w** of his father and in his sin,	2006
	15:34	in the **w** of Jeroboam and in his sin,	2006
	16: 2	but you walked in the **w** of Jeroboam	2006
	16:19	and walking in the **w** of Jeroboam and in	2006
	16:26	in all the **w** of Jeroboam son of Nebat and	2006
	22:43	in the **w** of his father Asa and did not stray	2006
	22:52	because he walked in the **w** of his father	2006
	22:52	and mother and in the **w** of Jeroboam	2006
2Ki	8:18	He walked in the **w** of the kings of Israel,	2006
	8:27	the **w** of the house of Ahab and did evil in	2006
	16: 3	He walked in the **w** of the kings of Israel	2006
	16: 3	following the **detestable w** of the nations	9359
	17:13	"Turn from your evil **w**.	2006
	21:21	He walked in all the **w** of his father;	2006
	22: 2	and walked in all the **w** of his father David,	2006
2Ch	6:31	and turn from their wicked **w**,	2006
	7:14	walking in the **w** of David and Solomon	2006
	11:17	walking in the **w** of David and	2006
	17: 3	in the **w** his father David had followed.	2006
	17: 6	His heart was devoted to the **w** of	2006
	20:32	in the **w** of his father Asa and did not stray	2006

2Ch	21: 6	He walked in the **w** of the kings of Israel,	2006
	21:12	in the **w** of your father Jehoshaphat or	2006
	21:13	But you have walked in the **w** of the kings	2006
	22: 3	He too walked in the **w** of the house	2006
	28: 2	He walked in the **w** of the kings of Israel	2006
	28: 3	following the **detestable w** of the nations	9359
	28:26	The other events of his reign and all his **w**,	2006
	34: 2	the eyes of the LORD and walked in the **w**	2006
Ne	9:35	not serve you or turn from their evil **w**.	5095
Est	5:11	and all **the w** the king had honored him and	889S
Job	4: 6	and your blameless **w** your hope?	2006
	13:15	I will surely defend my **w** to his face.	2006
	17: 9	the righteous will hold to their **w**,	2006
	21:14	We have no desire to know your **w**.	2006
	21: 9	if your **w** were blameless?	2006
	22:28	and light will shine on your **w**.	2006
	24:13	who do not know its **w** or stay in its paths.	2006
	24:23	but his eyes are on their **w**.	2006
	27:11	**the w** of the Almighty I will not conceal.	889S
	31: 4	not see my **w** and count my every step?	2006
	34:21	"His eyes are on the **w** of men;	2006
	34:27	and had no regard for any of his **w**.	2006
	36:23	Who has prescribed his **w** for him,	2006
	37: 5	God's voice thunders *in* **marvelous** *w*;	AIT
Ps	10: 5	His **w** are always prosperous;	2006
	17: 4	I have kept myself from the **w** of the violent.	784
	18:21	For I have kept the **w** of the LORD;	2006
	25: 4	Show me your **w**, O LORD,	784
	25: 7	of my youth and my **rebellious** *w*;	AIT
	25: 8	therefore he instructs sinners in his **w**.	2006
	25:10	the **w** of the LORD are loving and faithful	784
	37: 7	do not fret when men succeed in their **w**,	2006
	37:14	to slay those whose **w** are upright.	2006
	39: 1	"I will watch my **w** and keep my tongue	2006
	51:13	Then I will teach transgressors your **w**,	2006
	53: 1	They are corrupt, and their **w** are vile;	6404
	55:19	men who never change their **w**	NIH
	67: 2	that your **w** may be known on earth,	2006
	77:13	Your **w**, O God, are holy.	2006
	81:13	if Israel would follow my **w**,	2006
	91:11	concerning you to guard you in all your **w**;	2006
	95:10	and they have not known my **w**."	2006
	103: 7	He made known his **w** to Moses,	2006
	107:17	became fools through their rebellious **w**	2006
	119: 1	Blessed are they whose **w** are blameless,	2006
	119: 3	They do nothing wrong; they walk in his **w**.	2006
	119: 5	that my **w** were steadfast in obeying	2006
	119:15	on your precepts and consider your **w**.	784
	119:26	I recounted my **w** and you answered me;	2006
	119:29	Keep me from deceitful **w**;	2006
	119:59	I have considered my **w**	2006
	119:168	for all my **w** are known to you.	2006
	125: 5	those who turn to **crooked w** the LORD	6824
	128: 1	who fear the LORD, who walk in his **w**.	2006
	138: 5	May they sing of the **w** of the LORD,	2006
	139: 3	you are familiar with all my **w**.	2006
	145:17	The LORD is righteous in all his **w**	2006
	146: 9	but he frustrates the **w** of the wicked.	2006
Pr	1:22	"How long will you simple ones love your **simple w**?	7344
	1:31	They will eat the fruit of their **w** and	2006
	2:12	Wisdom will save you from the **w**	2006
	2:13	the straight paths to walk in dark **w**,	2006
	2:15	and who are devious in their **w**.	5047
	2:20	Thus you will walk in the **w** of good men	2006
	3: 6	in all your **w** acknowledge him,	2006
	3:17	Her **w** are pleasant **w**,	2006
	3:17	Her ways are pleasant,	2006
	3:31	a violent man or choose any of his **w**,	2006
	4:26	for your feet and take only **w** that are firm.	2006
	5:21	a man's **w** are in full view of the LORD,	2006
	6: 6	consider its **w** and be wise!	2006
	7:25	Do not let your heart turn to her **w** or stray	2006
	8:32	blessed are those who keep my **w**.	2006
	9: 6	Leave your **simple w** and you will live;	7344
	11:20	in those whose **w** are blameless.	2006
	14: 2	but he whose **w** are devious despises him.	2006
	14: 8	of the prudent is to give thought to their **w**,	2006
	14:14	faithless will be fully repaid for their **w**,	2006
	16: 2	All a man's **w** seem innocent to him,	2006
	16: 7	a man's **w** are pleasing to the LORD,	2006
	19:16	he who is contemptuous of his **w** will die.	2006
	21: 2	All a man's **w** seem right to him,	2006
	21:29	but an upright man gives thought to his **w**.	2006
	22:25	or you may learn his **w**	784
	23:26	and let your eyes keep to my **w**,	2006
	28: 6	a rich man whose **w** are perverse.	2006
	28:18	he whose **w** are perverse will suddenly fall.	2006
Ecc	11: 9	Follow the **w** of your heart	2006
Isa	2: 3	He will teach us his **w**,	2006
	42:16	the blind by **w** they have not known,	2006
	42:24	For they would not follow his **w**;	2006
	45:13	I will make all his **w** straight.	2006
	55: 8	neither are your **w** my ways,	2006
	55: 8	neither are your ways my **w**,"	2006
	55: 9	so are my **w** higher than your ways	2006
	55: 9	so are my ways higher than your **w**	2006
	57:10	You were wearied by all your **w**,	2006
	57:17	yet he kept on in his willful **w**.	2006
	57:18	I have seen his **w**, but I will heal him;	2006
	58: 2	they seem eager to know my **w**,	2006
	59: 7	ruin and destruction mark their **w**.	5019
	63:17	from your **w** and harden our hearts so we do	2006
	64: 5	who gladly do right, who remember your **w**.	2006
	65: 2	who walk in **w** not good,	2006
	66: 3	They have chosen their own **w**,	2006
Jer	2:33	the worst of women can learn from your **w**.	2006

Jer	2:36	you go about so much, changing your **w**?	2006
	3:21	because they have perverted their **w**	2006
	6:27	that you may observe and test their **w**.	2006
	7: 3	Reform your **w** and your actions,	2006
	7: 5	If you really change your **w**	2006
	7:23	Walk in all the **w** I command you,	2006
	10: 2	not learn the **w** of the nations or be terrified	2006
	12:16	the **w** of my people and swear by my name,	2006
	15: 7	for they have not changed their **w**.	2006
	16:17	My eyes are on all their **w**;	2006
	18:11	So turn from your evil **w**, each one of you,	2006
	18:11	and reform your **w** and your actions.'	2006
	18:15	which made them stumble in their **w** and in	2006
	23:22	from their evil **w** and from their evil deeds.	2006
	25: 5	from your evil **w** and your evil practices,	2006
	26:13	Now reform your **w** and your actions	2006
	32:19	Your eyes are open to all the **w** of men;	2006
	35:15	"Each of you must turn from your wicked **w**	2006
	36: 7	and each will turn from his wicked **w**,	2006
La	3:40	Let us examine our **w** and test them,	2006
Eze	3:18	or speak out to dissuade him from his evil **w**	2006
	3:19	or from his evil **w**, he will die for his sin;	2006
	13:22	the wicked not to turn from their evil **w** and	2006
	16:47	You not only walked in their **w**	2006
	16:47	in all your **w** you soon became more depraved than they.	2006
	16:61	Then you will remember your **w** and	2006
	18:23	not pleased when they turn from their **w**	2006
	18:25	Is it not your **w** that are unjust?	2006
	18:29	Are my **w** unjust, O house of Israel?	2006
	18:29	Is it not your **w** that are unjust?	2006
	18:30	each one according to his **w**,	2006
	20:44	to your evil **w** and your corrupt practices,	2006
	28:15	in your **w** from the day you were created	2006
	33: 8	not speak out to dissuade him from his **w**,	2006
	33: 9	to turn from his **w** and he does not do so,	2006
	33:11	rather that they turn from their **w** and live.	2006
	33:11	Turn from your evil **w**!	2006
	33:20	each of you according to his own **w**."	2006
	36:31	Then you will remember your evil **w**	2006
Da	4:37	and all his **w** are just.	10068
	5:23	in his hand your life and all your **w**.	10068
Hos	4: 9	for their **w** and repay them for their deeds.	2006
	4:18	their rulers dearly love **shameful w**.	7830
	12: 2	according to his **w** and repay him according	2006
	14: 9	The **w** of the LORD are right;	2006
Jnh	3: 8	give up their evil **w** and their violence.	2006
	3:10	and how they turned from their evil **w**,	2006
Mic	2: 7	to *him whose* **w** are upright?	2143
	4: 2	He will teach us his **w**,	2006
Hab	3: 6	His **w** are eternal.	2142
Hag	1: 5	"Give careful thought to your **w**.	2006
	1: 7	"Give careful thought to your **w**.	2006
Zec	1: 4	from your evil **w** and your evil practices.'	2006
	1: 6	to us what our **w** and practices deserve,	2006
	3: 7	in my **w** and keep my requirements,	2006
Mal	2: 9	because you have not followed my **w**	2006
Lk	3: 5	the rough **w** smooth.	3847
Ac	3:26	by turning each of you from your **wicked w**.	4504
	13:10	Will you never stop perverting the right **w**	3847
	18:13	the people to worship God in **w** contrary to	NIG
	28:10	in **many** *w* and when we were ready to sail,	AIT
Ro	1:30	they invent **w** of doing evil;	NIG
	3:16	ruin and misery mark their **w**,	3847
1Co	13:11	I became a man, I put **childish** *w* behind me.	AIT
2Co	4: 2	we have renounced secret and shameful **w**;	NIG
	8:22	to us in **many** *w* that he is zealous,	AIT
Eph	2: 2	when you followed the **w** of this world and	172
Col	3: 7	You used to walk in **these** *w*,	AIT
2Ti	1:18	in **how many** *w* he helped me in Ephesus.	AIT
Heb	1: 1	at many times and **in various w**,	4502
	3:10	and they have not known my **w**.'	3847
Jas	1: 8	We all stumble in **many** *w*.	AIT
2Pe	2: 2	Many will follow their **shameful** *w*	AIT
Rev	2:22	unless they repent of her **w**.	2240
	15: 3	Just and true are your **w**, King of the ages.	3847

WAYSIDE (KJV) See ALONG MY PATH, SIDE OF ROAD

WAYWARD (8) [WAYWARDNESS]

Ps	58: 3	from the womb *they are* **w** and speak lies.	9494
Pr	2:16	from the **w** wife with her seductive words,	5799
	6:24	from the smooth tongue of the **w** *wife*.	5799
	7: 5	from the **w** *wife* with her seductive words.	5799
	20:16	hold it in pledge if he does it for a **w** *woman*.	5799
	23:27	for a prostitute is a deep pit and a **w** *wife* is	5799
	27:13	hold it in pledge if he does it for a **w** *woman*.	5799
Isa	29:24	*who are* **w** in spirit will gain understanding;	9494

WAYWARDNESS (2) [WAYWARD]

Pr	1:32	For the **w** of the simple will kill them,	5412
Hos	14: 4	"I will heal their **w** and love them freely,	5412

WE (1884) [OUR, OURS, OURSELVES, US, WE'LL, WE'RE, WE'VE] See Index of Articles Etc.

WE'LL (13) [BE, WE]

Ge	19: 9	**W** **treat** you **worse** than them."	AIT
	34:16	**W** **settle** among you and become one people	AIT

Ge	34:17	*w* **take** our sister and go."	AIT
	37:20	Then *w* **see** what comes of his dreams."	AIT
Jdg	8:25	*"W* be **glad to give** them."	AIT
	16: 2	saying, "At dawn *w* **kill** him."	AIT
	20: 9	But now this is what *w* **do** to Gibeah:	AIT
	20: 9	*W* go up against it as the lot directs.	NIH
	20:10	*W* **take** ten men out of every hundred	AIT
1Sa	14:12	"Come up to us and *w* **teach** you a lesson."	AIT
2Ki	6:28	and tomorrow *w* **eat** my son."	AIT
	7: 4	If we say, *'W* **go into** the city'—	AIT
Jn	21: 3	and they said, *"W* **go with** you."	1609

WE'RE (6) [BE, WE]

Ge	29: 4	*"W* from Haran," they replied.	636
Jdg	12: 1	*W* going to **burn down** your house	AIT
1Sa	4: 7	*"W* in trouble! Nothing like this has	5646
2Ki	7: 9	they said to each other, *"W* not doing right.	636
Mt	8:25	"Lord, save us! *W* going to **drown**!"	AIT
Lk	8:24	"Master, Master, *w* going to **drown**!"	AIT

WE'VE (3) [HAS, WE]

Ge	26:32	They said, *"W* **found** water!"	AIT
Jdg	15:12	*"W* **come** to tie you up and hand you over to	AIT
Lk	5: 5	*w* worked hard all night and haven't **caught**	AIT

WEAK (65) [WEAKENED, WEAKENING, WEAKER, WEAKEST, WEAKLING, WEAKNESS, WEAKNESSES]

Ge	27: 1	When Isaac was old and his eyes *were so* **w**	3908
	29:17	Leah had **w** eyes, but Rachel was lovely	8205
	30:42	but if the animals *were* **w**,	6494
	30:42	So the **w** animals went to Laban and	6488
Nu	13:18	the people who live there are strong or **w**,	8333
Dt	34: 7	his eyes *were* not **w** nor his strength gone.	3908
Jdg	16: 7	I'll become as **w** as any other man."	2703
	16:11	I'll become as **w** as any other man."	2703
	16:13	I'll become as **w** as any other man."	2703
	16:17	I would become as **w** as any other man."	2703
1Sa	3: 2	whose eyes were becoming *so* **w**	3910
	15: 9	and **w** they totally destroyed.	5022
2Sa	3:39	though I am the anointed king, I am **w**,	8205
	17: 2	I would attack him while he is weary and **w**.	3338+8333
2Ch	28:15	All *those who were* **w** they put on donkeys.	4173
Ne	6: 9	"Their hands *will get* too **w** for the work,	8332
Ps	6: 7	My eyes **grow w** with sorrow;	6949
	10: 2	the wicked man hunts down the **w**,	6714
	12: 5	the oppression of the **w** and the groaning of	6714
	31: 9	my eyes **grow w** with sorrow,	6949
	31:10	and my bones **grow w**,	6949
	34:10	The lions *may* **grow w** and hungry,	8133
	41: 1	Blessed is he who has regard for the **w**;	1924
	72:13	on the **w** and the needy and save the needy	1924
	82: 3	Defend the cause of the **w** and fatherless;	1924
	82: 4	Rescue the **w** and needy;	1924
Isa	14:10	"You also *have become* as **w**, as we are;	2703
	38:14	My eyes **grew w** as I looked to the heavens.	1937
	40:29	and increases the power of the **w**.	226+401
Eze	7:17	and every knee *will become as* **w as** water.	2143
	21: 7	and every knee *become as* **w as** water.'	2143
	29:15	*I will* **make** it *so* **w** that it will never again	5070
	34: 4	You have not strengthened the **w** or healed	2703
	34:16	up the injured and strengthen the **w**,	2703
	34:21	butting all the **w** sheep with your horns	2703
Mt	26:41	The spirit is willing, but the body is **w**."	822
Mk	14:38	The spirit is willing, but the body is **w**.	822
Ac	20:35	of hard work we must help the **w**,	820
Ro	6:19	I put this in human terms because you are **w**	819
	14: 1	Accept him whose faith is **w**,	820
	14: 2	whose faith is **w**, eats only vegetables.	820
	15: 1	to bear with the failings *of* the **w** and not	105
1Co	1:27	God chose the **w** *things* of the world	822
	4:10	We are **w**, but you are strong!	822
	8: 7	and since their conscience is **w**, it is defiled.	822
	8: 9	not become a stumbling block *to* the **w**.	822
	8:10	with a **w** conscience sees you who have this knowledge eating	822
	8:11	So this **w** brother, for whom Christ died,	820
	8:12	in this way and wound their **w** conscience,	820
	9:22	*To* the **w** I became weak, to win the weak.	822
	9:22	To the weak I became **w**, to win the weak.	822
	9:22	To the weak I became weak, to win the **w**.	822
	11:30	That is why many among you are **w**	822
2Co	11:21	To my shame I admit that we were too **w**	820
	11:29	Who is **w**, and I do not feel weak?	820
	11:29	Who is weak, and I *do* not **feel w**?	820
	12:10	For when *I am* **w**, then I am strong.	820
	13: 3	He *is* not **w** in dealing with you,	820
	13: 4	Likewise, *we are* **w** in him,	820
	13: 9	We are glad whenever we *are* **w**	820
Gal	4: 9	to those **w** and miserable principles?	822
1Th	5:14	help the **w**, be patient with everyone.	822
Heb	7:18	because it was **w** and useless	822
	7:28	as high priests men who are **w**;	819
	12:12	strengthen your feeble arms and **w** knees.	4168

WEAK-WILLED (2) [WILL]

Eze	16:30	'How **w** you are, declares the Sovereign	581+4226
2Ti	3: 6	into homes and gain control over **w** women,	1220

WEAKENED (2) [WEAK]

Job	18: 7	The vigor of his step *is* **w**;	7674
Ro	8: 3	in that *it was* **w** by the sinful nature,	820

WEAKENING (1) [WEAK]

Ro	4:19	Without **w** in his faith, he faced the fact	820

WEAKER (4) [WEAK]

2Sa	3: 1	while the house of Saul grew **w and weaker**.	1924+2143+2256
	3: 1	while the house of Saul grew **weaker and w**.	1924+2143+2256
1Co	12:22	body that seem to be **w** are indispensable,	822
1Pe	3: 7	and treat them with respect as the **w** partner	822

WEAKEST (1) [WEAK]

Jdg	6:15	My clan is the **w** in Manasseh,	1924

WEAKLING (1) [WEAK]

Joel	3:10	Let the **w** say, "I am strong!"	2766

WEAKNESS (10) [WEAK]

La	1: 6	in **w** they have fled before the pursuer.	3946+4202
Ro	8:26	the Spirit helps us *in our* **w**.	819
1Co	1:25	**w** of God is stronger than man's strength.	822
	2: 3	I came to you in **w** and fear,	819
	15:43	it is sown in **w**, it is raised in power;	819
2Co	11:30	I will boast of the things that show my **w**.	819
	12: 9	for my power is made perfect in **w**."	819
	13: 4	For to be sure, he was crucified in **w**,	819
Heb	5: 2	since he himself is subject to **w**.	819
	11:34	whose **w** was turned to strength;	819

WEAKNESSES (4) [WEAK]

2Co	12: 5	not boast about myself, except about my **w**.	819
	12: 9	I will boast all the more gladly about my **w**,	819
	12:10	is why, for Christ's sake, I delight in **w**,	819
Heb	4:15	who is unable to sympathize with our **w**,	819

WEALTH (117) [WEALTHY]

Ge	26:13	and his **w** continued to grow until	1541
	31: 1	and has gained all this **w**	3883
	31:16	Surely all the **w** that God took away	6948
	34:29	They carried off all their **w**	2657
Dt	8:17	of my hands have produced this **w** for me."	2657
	8:18	the ability to produce **w**,	2657
Jos	22: 8	"Return to your homes with your great **w**—	5794
1Sa	2: 7	The LORD sends poverty and **w**;	6947
	17:25	The king *will* **give** great **w** *to*	6947+6948
1Ki	3:11	and not for long life or **w** for yourself,	6948
	10: 7	in wisdom and **w** you have far exceeded	3202
1Ch	29:12	**W** and honor come from you;	6948
	29:28	having enjoyed long life, **w** and honor.	6948
2Ch	1:11	and you have not asked for **w**,	6948
	1:12	And I will also give you **w**,	6948
	17: 5	so that he had great **w** and honor.	6948
	18: 1	Now Jehoshaphat had great **w** and honor,	6948
Est	1: 4	the vast **w** *of* his kingdom and the splendor	6948
	5:11	Haman boasted to them about his vast **w**,	6948
Job	5: 5	and the thirsty pant after his **w**.	2657
	6:22	pay a ransom for me from your **w**,	3946
	15:29	He will no longer be rich and his **w** will	2657
	20:10	his own hands must give back his **w**.	226
	22:20	and fire devours their **w**.'	3856
	31:25	if I have rejoiced over my great **w**,	2657
	36:19	Would your **w** or even all your mighty	8782
Ps	17:14	and they store up **w** for their children.	3856
	37:16	the little that the righteous have than the **w**	2162
	39: 6	*he* **heaps up w**, not knowing who will get it.	7392
	39:11	you consume their **w** like a moth—	2773
	45:12	men of **w** will seek your favor.	6938
	49: 6	in their **w** and boast of their great riches?	2657
	49:10	the senseless alike perish and leave their **w**	2657
	52: 7	but trusted in his great **w** and grew strong	6948
	73:12	always carefree, they increase in **w**.	2657
	112: 3	**W** and riches are in his house,	2104
Pr	3: 9	Honor the LORD with your **w**,	2104
	5:10	lest strangers feast on your **w**	3946
	6:31	though it costs him all the **w** *of* his house.	2104
	8:18	enduring **w** and prosperity.	2104
	8:21	bestowing **w** *on* those who love me	3780
	10: 4	but diligent hands **bring w**.	6947
	10:15	The **w** *of* the rich is their fortified city,	2104
	10:22	The blessing of the LORD **brings w**,	6947
	11: 4	**W** is worthless in the day of wrath,	2104
	11:16	but ruthless men gain only **w**.	6948
	13: 7	another pretends to be poor, yet has great **w**.	2104
	13:22	a sinner's **w** is stored up for the righteous.	2657
	14:24	The **w** of the wise is their crown,	6948
	15:16	of the LORD than great **w** with turmoil.	238
	18:11	The **w** *of* the rich is their fortified city;	2104
	19: 4	**W** brings many friends,	2104
	19:14	Houses and **w** are inherited from parents,	2104
	22: 4	of the LORD bring **w** and honor and life.	6948
	22:16	to increase his **w** and he who gives gifts to	NIH
	28: 8	who increases his **w** by exorbitant interest	2104
	29: 3	a companion of prostitutes squanders his **w**.	2104
Ecc	2:26	of gathering and **storing up w** to hand it	4043
	4: 8	yet his eyes were not content with his **w**.	6948
	5:10	whoever loves **w** is never satisfied	2162
	5:13	**w** hoarded to the harm of its owner,	6948
	5:14	or **w** lost through some misfortune,	6948
	5:19	God gives any man **w** and possessions,	6948
	6: 2	God gives a man **w**,	6948
	9:11	or **w** to the brilliant or favor to the learned;	6948
SS	8: 7	If one were to give all the **w** *of* his house	2104

Isa	8: 4	the **w** of Damascus and the plunder	2657
	10:14	my hand reached for the **w** *of* the nations;	2657
	15: 7	So the **w** they have acquired and stored	3860
	60: 5	the **w** *on* the seas will be brought to you,	2162
	60:11	men may bring you the **w** *of* the nations—	2657
	61: 6	You will feed on the **w** *of* nations,	2657
	66:12	and the **w** of nations like a flooding stream;	3883
Jer	15:13	Your **w** and your treasures I will give	2657
	17: 3	and your **w** and all your treasures I will give	2657
	20: 5	I will hand over to their enemies all the **w**	2890
	48:36	The **w** they acquired is gone.	3860
Eze	7:11	no **w**, nothing of value.	2155
	16:36	Because you poured out your **w**	5733
	26:12	They will plunder your **w**	2657
	27:12	with you because of your great **w** *of* goods;	2104
	27:18	and great **w** *of* goods,	2104
	27:27	Your **w**, merchandise and wares,	2104
	27:33	with your great **w** and your wares	2104
	28: 4	and understanding you have gained **w**	2657
	28: 5	in trading you have increased your **w**,	2657
	28: 5	of your **w** your heart has grown proud.	2657
	29:19	and he will carry off its **w**.	2162
	30: 4	her **w** will be carried away	2162
Da	11: 2	When he has gained power by his **w**,	6948
	11:24	loot and **w** among his followers.	8214
	11:28	to his own country with great **w**,	8214
Hos	12: 8	With all my **w** they will not find	3330
Ob	1:11	while strangers carried off his **w**	2657
	1:13	nor seize their **w** in the day of their disaster.	2657
Mic	1:14	their **w** to the Lord of all the earth.	2657
Na	2: 9	the **w** from all its treasures!	3883
Zep	1:13	Their **w** will be plundered,	2657
Zec	14:14	The **w** of all the surrounding nations will	2657
Mt	13:22	and the deceitfulness *of* **w** choke it,	4458
	19:22	he went away sad, because he had great **w**.	3228
Mk	4:19	*of* **w** and the desires for other things come	4458
	10:22	He went away sad, because he had great **w**.	3228
	12:44	They all gave out *of* their **w**;	4355
Lk	15:13	and there squandered his **w** in wild living.	4045
	16: 9	use worldly **w** to gain friends	3440
	16:11	not been trustworthy in handling worldly **w**,	3440
	18:23	because he was a *man of* great **w**.	4454
	21: 4	these people gave their gifts out of their **w**;	4355
1Ti	6:17	not to be arrogant nor to put their hope in **w**,	4458
Jas	5: 2	Your **w** has rotted, and moths have eaten	4458
	5: 3	*You have* **hoarded w** in the last days.	2564
Rev	3:17	*I have* **acquired w** and do not need a thing.'	4456
	5:12	and **w** and wisdom and strength and honor	4456
	18:15	and **gained** their **w** from her	4456
	18:17	In one hour such great **w** has been brought	4458
	18:19	on the sea became rich through her **w**!	5509

WEALTHY (10) [WEALTH]

Ge	13: 2	Abram *had become* very **w** in livestock and	3877
	24:35	and *he has become*	1540
	26:13	to grow until *he became* very **w**.	1540
1Sa	25: 2	had property there at Carmel, was very **w**.	1524
2Sa	19:32	for he was a very **w** man.	1524
2Ki	15:20	Every **w** man had to contribute fifty shekels	2657
Job	27:19	He lies down **w**, but will do so no more;	6938
Hos	12: 8	"I am very rich; I have become **w**.	226
Hab	2: 6	up stolen goods and **makes** himself **w**	3877
Lk	19: 2	he was a chief tax collector and was **w**.	4454

WEANED (10)

Ge	21: 8	The child grew and was **w**,	1694
	21: 8	and on the day Isaac *was* **w** Abraham held	1694
1Sa	1:22	"After the boy is **w**,	1694
	1:23	"Stay here until you *have* **w** him;	1694
	1:23	and nursed her son until she *had* **w** him.	1694
	1:24	After he *was* **w**, she took the boy with her,	1694
Ps	131: 2	like a **w** *child* with its mother,	1694
	131: 2	like a **w** *child* is my soul within me.	1694
Isa	28: 9	To *children* **w** from their milk,	1694
Hos	1: 8	After *she had* **w** Lo-Ruhamah,	1694

WEAPON (15) [WEAPONS]

1Sa	21: 8	I haven't brought my sword or any *other* **w**,	3998
1Ki	20:35	"Strike me with your **w**,"	NIH
2Ki	11: 8	each man with his **w** in his hand.	3998
	11:11	The guards, each with his **w** in his hand,	3998
1Ch	12:33	with every type of **w**, to help David	3998+4878
	12:37	armed with every type of **w**—	3998+4878+7372
2Ch	23:10	each with his **w** in his hand,	8939
Ne	4:17	with one hand and held a **w** in the other,	8939
	4:23	had his **w**, even when he went for water.	8939
Job	20:24	Though he flees from an iron **w**,	5977
Isa	54:16	into flame and forges a **w** fit for its work.	3998
	54:17	no **w** forged against you will prevail,	3998
Jer	51:20	"You are my war club, my **w** *for* battle—	3998
Eze	9: 1	each with a **w** in his hand."	3998+5424
	9: 2	each with a deadly **w** in his hand.	3998

WEAPONS (30) [WEAPON]

Ge	27: 3	Now then, get your **w**—	3998
	49:15	their swords are **w** of violence.	3998
Dt	1:41	So every one of you put on his **w**,	3998+4878
1Sa	8:12	to make **w** of war and equipment	3998
	17:54	he put the Philistine's **w** in his own tent.	3998
	20:40	Jonathan gave his **w** to the boy and said,	3998
2Sa	1:27	The **w** *of* war have perished!"	3998
	2:21	of the young men and strip him of his **w**."	2723
1Ki	10:25	robes, **w** and spices, and horses and mules.	5977
2Ki	10: 2	chariots and horses, fortified city and **w**,	5977

2Ch	9:24	w and spices, and horses and mules.	5977
	23: 7	each man with his w in his hand.	3998
	32: 5	also made large numbers of w and shields.	8939
Ps	7:13	He has prepared his deadly w;	3998
	76: 3	the shields and the swords, the w of war.	NIH
Ecc	9:18	Wisdom is better than w of war,	3998
Isa	13: 5	the LORD and the w of his wrath—	3998
	22: 8	And you looked in that day to the w in	5977
Jer	21: 4	I am about to turn against you the w of war	3998
	22: 7	each man with his w,	3998
	50:25	and brought out the w of his wrath,	3998
Eze	23:24	They will come against you with w,	2210
	26: 9	and demolish your towers with his w.	2995
	32:27	who went down to the grave with their w	3998
	39: 9	the towns of Israel will go out and use the w	5977
	39:10	because they will use the w for fuel.	5977
Jn	18: 3	They were carrying torches, lanterns and w.	3960
2Co	6: 7	with w of righteousness in the right hand	3960
	10: 4	The w we **fight with** are not the	3836+3960+5127
	10: 4	we fight with are not the w of the world.	NIG

WEAR (45) [WEARING, WEARS, WORE, WORN, WORN-OUT]

Ge	28:20	give me food to eat and clothes to w	4252
Ex	18:18	*will* only w *yourselves* out.	5570+5570
	28:35	Aaron *must* w it when he ministers.	2118+6584
	28:43	sons *must* w them whenever they enter	2118+6584
	29:30	in the Holy Place *is to* w them seven days.	4252
Lev	13:45	an infectious disease *must* w torn clothes,	2118
	19:19	" '*Do* not w clothing woven of two kinds	6590
	21:10	on his head and who has been ordained to w	4252
Dt	8: 4	not w *out* and your feet did not swell	1162
	22: 5	A woman *must* not w men's clothing,	2118+6584
	22: 5	nor a man w women's clothing,	4252
	22:11	*Do* not w **clothes** of wool and linen woven	4252
	22:12	on the four corners of the cloak *you* w.	4059
	28:32	and you *will* w *out* your eyes watching	3983
	29: 5	your clothes *did* not w *out,*	1162
Jdg	8:24	custom of the Ishmaelites to w gold earrings	4200
1Sa	2:28	and to w an ephod in my presence.	5951
1Ki	22:30	but you w your royal robes."	4252
2Ch	18:29	but you w your royal robes."	4252
Ne	9:21	their clothes *did* not w *out*	1162
Job	27:17	what he lays up the righteous *will* w,	4252
	31:36	Surely I *would* w it on my shoulder.	5951
Ps	102:26	they *will* all w out like a garment.	1162
Pr	23: 4	*Do* not w *yourself* out to get rich;	3333
Isa	15: 3	In the streets *they* w sackcloth;	2520
	49:18	"*you will* w them all as ornaments;	4252
	50: 9	They *will* all w **out** like a garment;	1162
	51: 6	like smoke, the earth *will* w **out** like	1162
Jer	12:13	*they will* w **themselves** out	2703
Eze	44:17	*they are to* w linen clothes;	4252
	44:17	they *must* not w any woolen garment	6584+6590
	44:18	*They are to* w linen turbans on their heads	2118
	44:18	not w anything that makes them perspire.	2520
Am	8:10	**make** all of you w sackcloth	5516+6584+6590
Mt	6:25	or about your body, what *you will* w.	1907
	6:31	or '*What shall* we w?'	4314
	11: 8	who w fine clothes are in kings' palaces.	5841
Mk	6: 9	W sandals but not an extra tunic.	5686
Lk	7:25	those who w expensive clothes and indulge	1877
	12:22	or about your body, what *you will* w.	1907
	12:33	purses for yourselves *that will* not w **out,**	4096
	18: 5	so that *she* won't eventually w me **out**	5724
Heb	1:11	*they will* all w out like a garment.	4096
Rev	3:18	and white clothes to w, so you can cover	4314
	19: 8	bright and clean, was given her to w."	4314

WEARIED (6) [WEARY]

Isa	43:22	*you have* not w *yourselves* for me,	3333
	43:23	nor w you with demands for incense.	3333
	43:24	with your sins and w me with your offenses.	3333
	57:10	*You were* w by all your ways,	3333
Mal	2:17	*You have* w the LORD with your words.	3333
	2:17	"How *have* we w him?"	3333

WEARIES (2) [WEARY]

Ecc	10:15	A fool's work w him;	3333
	12:12	and much study w the body.	3331

WEARING (32) [WEAR]

Ge	37:23	the richly ornamented robe he was w—	6584
Ex	32: 2	your sons and your daughters are w,	265+928
Dt	21:13	the clothes she was w when captured.	6584
Ru	3:15	the shawl you are w and hold it out."	6584
1Sa	2:18	before the LORD—a boy w a linen ephod.	2520
	14: 3	Ahijah, *who was* w an ephod.	5951
	18: 4	the robe he was w and gave it to David,	6584
	28:14	"An old man w a robe is coming up,"	6486
2Sa	6:14	David, w a linen ephod, danced before	2520
	13:18	She was w a richly ornamented robe,	6584
	13:19	and tore the ornamented robe she was w.	6584
	20: 8	Joab *was* w his military tunic,	2520
1Ki	11:29	met him on the way, w a new cloak.	4059
	11:30	of the new cloak he was w and tore it	6584
	20:32	W sackcloth around their waists and ropes	2520
2Ki	19: 2	and the leading priests, *all* w sackcloth,	4059
Ne	9: 1	fasting and w sackcloth and having dust	928
Est	1:11	Queen Vashti, w her royal crown,	928
	8:15	the king's presence w royal garments	928
SS	3: 8	all of them w the sword,	296
	3:11	and look at King Solomon w the crown,	928
Isa	37: 2	and the leading priests, *all* w sackcloth,	4059

Jer	13: 4	"Take the belt you bought and are w	
		around your waist,	6584
Da	3:21	So these men, w their robes, trousers,	10089
	3:21	who was not w wedding clothes.	1907
Mt	22:11	w nothing but a linen garment,	1218+2093+4314
Mk	14:51	w nothing but a linen garment,	1218+2093+4314
Jn	19: 5	When Jesus came out w the crown of thorns	5841
Ac	12:21	Herod, w his royal robes, sat on his throne	1907
Jas	2: 2	comes into your meeting w a gold ring	5993
	2: 3	special attention to the man w fine clothes	5841
1Pe	3: 3	and the w of gold jewelry and fine clothes.	4324
Rev	7: 9	*They were* w white robes	4314

WEARISOME (1) [WEARY]

Ecc	1: 8	All things are w, more than one can say.	3335

WEARS (3) [WEAR]

Job	14:19	as water w away stones and torrents wash	8835
Ps	119:139	My zeal w me **out,** for my enemies ignore	7551
Isa	16:12	at her high place, *she* only w **herself** out;	4206

WEARY (29) [WEARIED, WEARIES, WEARISOME]

Dt	25:18	When you were w and worn out,	6546
	28:65	an anxious mind, eyes w **with longing,**	4001
Jos	7: 3	to take it and *do* not w all the people,	3333
2Sa	17: 2	I would attack him while he is w and weak.	3335
Job	3:17	and there the w are at rest.	3329+3946
	22: 7	You gave no water to the w and	6546
	31:16	or *let* the eyes of the widow grow w,	3983
Ps	63: 1	in a dry and w land where there is no water.	6546
	68: 9	you refreshed your w inheritance.	4206
	119:28	My soul *is* w with sorrow;	1941
Pr	25:25	to a w soul is good news from a distant land.	6546
Isa	1:14	I *am* w of bearing them.	4206
	28:12	"This is the resting place, let the w rest";	6546
	40:28	He will not grow tired or w,	3333
	40:29	He gives strength to the w and	3617
	40:30	Even youths grow tired and w,	3333
	40:31	they will run and not *grow* w,	3333
	46: 1	are burdensome, a burden for the w.	6546
	50: 4	to know the word that sustains the w.	3617
Jer	9: 5	*they* w **themselves** with sinning.	4206
	20: 9	I *am* w of holding it in; indeed, I cannot.	4206
	31:25	I will refresh the w and satisfy	5883+6546
La	5: 5	*we are* w and find no rest.	3333
Zec	11: 8	and I grew w of them	7918
Mt	11:28	"Come to me, all you who *are* w and	3159
Ac	24: 4	But in order not to w you further,	1601
Gal	6: 9	*Let us* not **become** w in doing good,	1591
Heb	12: 3	so that *you will* not **grow** w and lose heart.	2827
Rev	2: 3	for my name, and *have* not **grown** w.	3159

WEASEL (1)

Lev	11:29	the w, the rat, any kind of great lizard,	2700

WEATHER (1)

Mt	16: 2	'It will be **fair** w, for the sky is red,'	2304

WEAVE (2) [INTERWOVEN, WEAVER, WEAVER'S, WEAVERS, WEAVING, WOVE, WOVEN]

Ex	28:39	"W the tunic of fine linen and make	8687
Jdg	16:13	"If *you* w the seven braids of my head into	755

WEAVER (3) [WEAVE]

Ex	39:22	entirely of blue cloth—the work of a w—	755
	39:27	tunics of fine linen—the work of a w—	755
Isa	38:12	Like a w I have rolled up my life,	755

WEAVER'S (5) [WEAVE]

1Sa	17: 7	His spear shaft was like a w rod,	755
2Sa	21:19	who had a spear with a shaft like a w rod.	755
1Ch	11:23	the Egyptian had a spear like a w rod	755
	20: 5	who had a spear with a shaft like a w rod.	755
Job	7: 6	"My days are swifter than a w **shuttle,**	756

WEAVERS (2) [WEAVE]

Ex	35:35	and scarlet yarn and fine linen, and w—	755
Isa	19: 9	the w of fine linen will lose hope.	755

WEAVING (1) [WEAVE]

2Ki	23: 7	and where women *did* w for Asherah.	755+1428

WEB (3) [COBWEBS]

Job	8:14	what he relies on is a spider's w.	1074
	8:15	He leans on his w, but it gives way;	1074
Isa	59: 5	the eggs of vipers and spin a spider's w.	7770

WEDDING (19)

Jdg	14:20	friend who *had* **attended** him at his w.	8287
1Ki	9:16	and then gave it as a w **gift** to his daughter,	8933
Ps	45: T	A maskil. A w song.	3353
	78:63	and their maidens *had* no w **songs;**	2146
SS	3:11	crowned him on the day of his w,	3164
	3:11	a bride w her **ornaments?**	8005
Mt	22: 2	like a king who prepared a w **banquet**	1141
	22: 4	Come to the w **banquet.'**	1141
	22: 8	'The w **banquet** is ready,	1141

Mt	22:10	and the w **hall** was filled with guests.	1141
	22:11	a man there who was not wearing w clothes.	1141
	22:12	how did you get in here without w clothes?'	1141
	25:10	went in with him to the w **banquet.**	1141
Lk	12:36	for their master to return from a w **banquet,**	1141
	14: 8	"When someone invites you to a w **feast,**	1141
Jn	2: 1	On the third day a w took place at Cana	1141
	2: 2	had also been invited to the w.	1141
Rev	19: 7	For the w of the Lamb has come,	1141
	19: 9	Blessed are those who are invited to the w	
		supper of the Lamb!	1141

WEDGE (2)

Jos	7:21	and a w *of* gold weighing fifty shekels,	4383
	7:24	the gold w, his sons and daughters,	4383

[BREAK] WEDLOCK (KJV) See COMMIT ADULTERY

WEED (1) [SEAWEED, TUMBLEWEED, WEEDS]

Mt	13:41	and *they will* w out of his kingdom	5198

WEEDS (12) [WEED]

Job	31:40	instead of wheat and w instead of barley."	947
Pr	24:31	the ground was covered with w,	3017
Hos	10: 4	up like **poisonous** w in a plowed field.	8032
Zep	2: 9	place of w and salt pits, a wasteland forever.	3017
Mt	13:25	his enemy came and sowed w among	2429
	13:26	then the w also appeared.	2429
	13:27	Where then did the w come from?'	2429
	13:29	'because while you are pulling the w,	2429
	13:30	the w and tie them in bundles to be burned;	2429
	13:36	to us the parable *of* the w in the field."	2429
	13:38	The w are the sons of the evil one,	2429
	13:40	the w are pulled up and burned in the fire,	2429

WEEK (14) [WEEKS]

Ge	29:27	Finish this daughter's **bridal** w;	8651
	29:28	He finished the w *with* Leah,	8651
Mt	28: 1	at dawn on the first day *of* the w,	4879
Mk	16: 2	Very early on the first day *of* the w,	4879
	16: 9	Jesus rose early on the first **day of the w,**	4879
Lk	18:12	I fast twice a w and give a tenth of all I get.'	4879
	24: 1	On the first day *of* the w,	4879
Jn	19:14	the day of Preparation of Passover W,	NIG
	20: 1	Early on the first day *of* the w,	4879
	20:19	On the evening of that first day *of* the w,	4879
	20:26	A w later his disciples were in	2465+3552+3893
Ac	20: 7	On the first day *of* the w we came together	4879
	28:14	to spend a w with them.	2231+2465
1Co	16: 2	On the first day *of* every w,	4879

WEEKS (11) [WEEK]

Ex	34:22	the Feast of W with the firstfruits of	8651
Lev	12: 5	*for two* w the woman will be unclean,	8651
	23:15	count off seven full w.	8701
Nu	28:26	of new grain during the **Feast of W,**	8651
Dt	16: 9	Count off seven w from the time you begin	8651
	16:10	the Feast of W to the LORD your God	8651
	16:16	Feast of Unleavened Bread, the Feast of W	8651
2Ch	8:13	Feast of Unleavened Bread, the Feast of W	8651
Jer	5:24	who assures us of the regular w of harvest.'	8651
Da	10: 2	I, Daniel, mourned *for* three w.	3427+8651
	10: 3	at all until the three w were over.	3427+8651

WEEP (48) [WEEPING, WEEPS, WEPT]

Ge	23: 2	to mourn for Sarah and to w *over* her.	1134
	29:11	Jacob kissed Rachel and *began to* w aloud.	1134
	42:24	He turned away from them and *began to* w,	1134
	43:30	and looked for a place to w.	1134
Jdg	11:37	to roam the hills and w with my friends,	1134
1Sa	30: 4	until they had no strength left to w.	1134
2Sa	1:24	"O daughters of Israel, w for Saul,	1134
2Ki	8:11	Then the man of God *began to* w.	1134
Ne	8: 9	Do not mourn or w."	1134
Job	2:12	*they began to* w aloud,	1134
	27:15	and their widows *will* not w *for* them.	1134
Ps	69:10	When *I* w and fast, I must endure scorn;	1134
	78:64	and their widows *could* not w.	1134
Ecc	3: 4	a time to w and a time to laugh,	1134
Isa	15: 2	to its high places to w;	1140
	16: 9	So *I* w, as Jazer weeps.	1134
	22: 4	"Turn away from me; let me w bitterly.	1140
	22:12	called you on that day to w and to wail,	1140
	30:19	*you will* w no **more.**	1134+1134
	33: 7	the envoys of peace w bitterly.	1134
Jer	9: 1	*I would* w day and night *for* the slain	1134
	9:10	*I will* w and wail for the mountains	1140+5951
	13:17	*I will* w in secret because of your pride;	1134
	13:17	my eyes *will* w bitterly,	1963+1963
	22:10	not w *for* the dead [king] or mourn his loss;	1134
	22:10	w **bitterly** for him who is exiled,	1134+1134
	25:34	W and wail, you shepherds;	3536
	48:32	*I* w for you, as Jazer weeps.	1134
La	1:16	"This is why I w and my eyes overflow	1134
Eze	24:16	Yet do not lament or w or shed any tears.	1134
	24:23	not mourn or w but will waste away	1134
	24:23	*They will* w over you with anguish of soul	1134
Joel	1: 5	Wake up, you drunkards, and w!	1134
	2:17	w between the temple porch and the altar.	1134
Am	5:16	The farmers will be summoned to w and	65

Mic	1: 8	Because of this *I* will w and wail;	6199
	1:10	Tell it not in Gath; w not **at all.**	1134+1134
Mal	2:13	*You* w and wail because he no longer	1140
Lk	6:21	Blessed are you who w now,	3081
	6:25	for *you will* mourn and w.	3081
	23:28	"Daughters of Jerusalem, *do not* w for me;	3081
	23:28	w for yourselves and for your children.	3081
Jn	16:20	you *will* w and mourn while the world	3081
Jas	5: 1	w and wail because of the misery	3081
Rev	5: 5	one of the elders said to me, "*Do not* w!	3081
	18: 9	*they will* w and mourn over her.	3081
	18:11	of the earth *will* w and mourn over her	3081
	18:15	*They will* w and mourn	3081

WEEPING (56) [WEEP]

Ge	45:14	and Benjamin embraced him, w.	1134
Nu	25: 6	of Israel while they *were* w at the entrance	1134
Dt	1:45	to your w and turned a deaf ear to you.	7754
	34: 8	until the time of w and mourning was over.	1140
Jdg	20:26	and there they sat w before the LORD.	1134
	21: 2	raising their voices and w bitterly.	1134+1140
1Sa	1: 8	"Hannah, why *are you* w?	1134
	11: 5	Why *are they* w?"	1134
2Sa	3:16	w behind her all the way to Bahurim.	1134
	13:19	and went away, w **aloud** as she went.	2410
	15:30	up the Mount of Olives, w as he went;	1134
	15:30	and *were* w as they went up.	1134
	19: 1	"The king *is* w and mourning	1134
2Ki	8:12	"Why *is* my lord w?"	1134
Ezr	3:13	of the shouts of joy from the sound of w,	1140
	10: 1	w and throwing himself down before	1134
Ne	8: 9	the people *had been* w as they listened to	1134
Est	4: 3	with fasting, w and wailing.	1140
	8: 3	falling at his feet and w.	1134
Job	16:16	My face is red with w,	1140
Ps	6: 6	all night long I flood my bed with w	NIH
	6: 8	for the LORD has heard my w.	1140
	30: 5	w may remain for a night,	1140
	35:14	I bowed my head in grief as though w	63
	39:12	be not deaf to my w.	1965
	126: 6	He who goes out w, carrying seed to sow,	1134
Isa	15: 3	they all wail, prostrate with w.	1140
	15: 5	They go up the way to Luhith, w as they go;	1140
	65:19	the sound of w and of crying will be heard	1140
Jer	3:21	the w and pleading of the people of Israel,	1140
	31: 9	They will come with w;	1140
	31:15	heard in Ramah, mourning and great w,	1140
	31:15	Rachel w for her children and refusing to	1134
	31:16	"Restrain your voice from w and your eyes	1140
	41: 6	from Mizpah to meet them, w as he went.	1134
	48: 5	way to Luhith, w **bitterly** as they go;	1140+1134
La	2:11	My eyes fail from w,	1965
Joel	2:12	with fasting and w and mourning."	1140
Am	8:10	into mourning and all your singing into w.	7806
Zec	12:11	that day the w in Jerusalem will be great,	5027
	12:11	like the w *of* Hadad Rimmon in the plain	5027
Mt	2:18	heard in Ramah, and great mourning,	3088
	2:18	Rachel w **for** her children and refusing to	3081
	8:12	there will be w and gnashing of teeth."	3088
	13:42	where there will be w and gnashing of teeth.	3088
	13:50	where there will be w and gnashing of teeth.	3088
	22:13	where there will be w and gnashing of teeth.	3088
	24:51	where there will be w and gnashing of teeth.	3088
	25:30	where there will be w and gnashing of teeth.	3088
Mk	16:10	with him and who were mourning and w.	3081
Lk	7:38	and as she stood behind him at his feet w,	3081
	13:28	"There will be w there, and gnashing	3088+3836
Jn	11:33	When Jesus saw her w,	3081
	11:33	Jews who had come along with her also w,	3081
Ac	21:13	*are you* w and breaking my heart?	3081+4472
Rev	18:19	and *with* w and mourning cry out: " 'Woe!	3081

WEEPS (3) [WEEP]

Isa	16: 9	So I weep, as Jazer w,	1140
Jer	48:32	I weep for you, as Jazer w,	1140
La	1: 2	**Bitterly** *she* w at night,	1134+1134

WEIGH (7) [OUTWEIGH, OUTWEIGHS, WEIGHED, WEIGHING, WEIGHS, WEIGHT, WEIGHTIER, WEIGHTS, WEIGHTY]

2Sa	14:26	he would w it, and its weight was	9202
Ezr	8:29	Guard them carefully until *you* w them **out**	9202
Job	31: 6	let God w me in honest scales	9202
Isa	46: 5	from their bags and w **out** silver on scales;	9202
Eze	4:10	**W out** twenty shekels of food to eat each	5484
	33:10	"Our offenses and sins w us **down,**	6584
1Co	14:29	others *should* w **carefully** what is said.	1359

WEIGHED (31) [WEIGH]

Ge	23:16	and w **out** for him the price he had named	9202
Nu	7:85	Each silver plate w a hundred and thirty	NIH
	7:85	silver dishes w two thousand four hundred	NIH
	7:86	filled with incense w ten shekels each,	NIH
	7:86	the gold dishes w a hundred and twenty	NIH
	31:52	as a gift to the LORD w 16,750 shekels.	2118
1Sa	2: 3	and by him deeds **are** w.	9419
	17: 7	and its iron point w six hundred shekels.	NIH
2Sa	18:12	"Even if a thousand shekels *were* w **out**	9202
	21:16	bronze spearhead w three hundred shekels	5486
2Ki	25:16	was more than could be w.	5486
1Ch	22: 3	and more bronze than could be w.	5486
	22:14	of bronze and iron too great to be w,	5486

2Ch	3: 9	The gold nails w fifty shekels.	5486
Ezr	8:25	and *I* w out to them the offering of silver	9202
	8:26	*I* w out to them 650 talents of silver,	9202
	8:30	and sacred articles that had been w **out** to	5486
	8:33	*we* w out the silver and gold and	9202
Job	6: 2	"If only my anguish *could* be w	9202+9202
	28:15	nor *can* its price **be** w in silver.	9202
Ps	62: 9	if w on a balance, they are nothing;	6590
Pr	16: 2	but motives are w *by* the LORD.	9419
Isa	40:12	or w the mountains on the scales and	9202
Jer	6:11	and the old, *those* w **down** with years.	4849
	32: 9	and w **out** for him seventeen shekels	9202
	32:10	and w **out** the silver on the scales.	9202
	52:20	was more than could be w.	5486
La	3: 7	he has w me **down** with chains.	3877
Da	5:27	*You have* **been** w on the scales	10769
Lk	21:34	or your hearts *will be* w **down** with	976
Ac	27:13	so they w **anchor** and sailed along the shore	149

WEIGHING (42) [WEIGH]

Ge	24:22	the man took out a gold nose ring w a beka	5486
	24:22	a beka and two gold bracelets w ten shekels.	5486
Nu	3:50	of the Israelites he collected silver w 1,365	NIH
	7:13	silver plate w a hundred and thirty shekels	5486
	7:13	silver sprinkling bowl w seventy shekels,	NIH
	7:14	one gold dish w ten shekels, filled with	NIH
	7:19	silver plate w a hundred and thirty shekels	5486
	7:19	silver sprinkling bowl w seventy shekels,	NIH
	7:20	one gold dish w ten shekels, filled with	NIH
	7:25	silver plate w a hundred and thirty shekels	5486
	7:25	silver sprinkling bowl w seventy shekels,	NIH
	7:26	one gold dish w ten shekels, filled with	NIH
	7:31	silver plate w a hundred and thirty shekels	5486
	7:31	silver sprinkling bowl w seventy shekels,	NIH
	7:32	one gold dish w ten shekels, filled with	NIH
	7:37	silver plate w a hundred and thirty shekels	5486
	7:37	silver sprinkling bowl w seventy shekels,	NIH
	7:38	one gold dish w ten shekels, filled with	NIH
	7:43	silver plate w a hundred and thirty shekels	5486
	7:43	silver sprinkling bowl w seventy shekels,	NIH
	7:44	one gold dish w ten shekels, filled with	NIH
	7:49	silver plate w a hundred and thirty shekels	5486
	7:49	silver sprinkling bowl w seventy shekels,	NIH
	7:50	one gold dish w ten shekels, filled with	NIH
	7:55	silver plate w a hundred and thirty shekels	5486
	7:55	silver sprinkling bowl w seventy shekels,	NIH
	7:56	one gold dish w ten shekels, filled with	NIH
	7:61	silver plate w a hundred and thirty shekels	5486
	7:61	silver sprinkling bowl w seventy shekels,	NIH
	7:62	one gold dish w ten shekels, filled with	NIH
	7:67	silver plate w a hundred and thirty shekels	5486
	7:67	silver sprinkling bowl w seventy shekels,	NIH
	7:68	one gold dish w ten shekels, filled with	NIH
	7:73	silver plate w a hundred and thirty shekels	5486
	7:73	silver sprinkling bowl w seventy shekels,	NIH
	7:74	one gold dish w ten shekels, filled with	NIH
	7:79	silver plate w a hundred and thirty shekels	5486
	7:79	silver sprinkling bowl w seventy shekels,	NIH
	7:80	one gold dish w ten shekels, filled with	NIH
Jos	7:21	and a wedge of gold w fifty shekels.	5486
1Sa	17: 5	armor of bronze w five thousand shekels;	5486
Ezr	8:26	silver articles w 100 talents,	NIH

WEIGHS (10) [WEIGH]

Ex	30:13	sanctuary shekel, which w twenty gerahs.	9203
Nu	3:47	sanctuary shekel, which w twenty gerahs.	NIH
	18:16	sanctuary shekel, which w twenty gerahs.	NIH
Pr	12:25	An anxious heart w a man **down,**	8817
	15:28	The heart of the righteous w its answers,	2047
	21: 2	but the LORD w the heart.	9419
	24:12	does not he *who* w the heart perceive it?	9419
Ecc	6: 1	and it w **heavily** on men:	8041
	8: 6	a man's misery w **heavily** upon him.	8041
Isa	40:15	*he* w the islands as though they were	5747

WEIGHT (27) [WEIGH]

Ge	23:16	**according to the** w **current** among the	6296
	43:21	the **exact** w—in the mouth of his sack.	5486
Lev	19:35	when measuring length, w or quantity.	5486
	26:26	and they will dole out the bread by w.	5486
Jdg	8:26	The w *of* the gold rings he asked for came	5486
2Sa	12:30	its w was a talent of gold,	5486
	14:26	and its w was two hundred shekels by	NIH
1Ki	7:47	the w of the bronze was not determined.	5486
	10:14	The w *of* the gold that Solomon received	5486
1Ch	20: 2	its w was found to be a talent of gold,	5486
	28:14	the w of gold for all the gold articles to	5486
	28:14	and the w of silver for all the silver articles	5486
	28:15	the w of gold for the gold lampstands	5486
	28:15	the w *for* each lampstand and its lamps;	5486
	28:15	and the w of silver for each silver lampstand	5486
	28:16	the w of gold for each table	5486
	28:16	the w of silver for the silver tables;	NIH
	28:17	the w of pure gold for the forks,	5486
	28:17	the w of gold for each gold dish;	5486
	28:17	and the w of silver for each silver dish;	5486
	28:18	and the w of the refined gold for the altar	5486
2Ch	4:18	The w of the bronze was not determined.	5486
	9:13	The w *of* the gold that Solomon received	5486
Ezr	8:34	accounted for by number and w,	5486
	8:34	and the entire w was recorded at that time.	5486
Job	26: 8	yet the clouds do not burst under their w.	NIH
La	4: 2	sons of Zion, once **worth their** w in gold,	6131

WEIGHTIER (1) [WEIGH]

Jn	5:36	"I have testimony w **than** that of John.	3505

WEIGHTS (8) [WEIGH]

Lev	19:36	Use honest scales and honest w,	74
Dt	25:13	Do not have **two differing** w in your bag—	74+74+2256
	25:15	You must have accurate and honest w	74
Pr	11: 1	but accurate w are his delight.	74
	16:11	all the w *in* the bag are of his making.	74
	20:10	**Differing** w and differing measures	74+74+2256
	20:23	The LORD detests **differing** w,	74+74+2256
Mic	6:11	with a bag of false w?	74

WEIGHTY (1) [WEIGH]

2Co	10:10	some say, "His letters are w and forceful,	987

WELCOME (15) [WELCOMED, WELCOMES]

Jdg	19:20	"You are w at my house," the old man said.	8934
Mt	10:14	If anyone *will* not w you or listen	1312
Mk	6:11	if any place *will* not w you or listen to you,	1312
	9:37	and whoever welcomes me *does* not w me	1312
Lk	9: 5	If people *do* not w you,	1312
	9:53	but the *people* there *did* not w him,	1312
	16: 4	*people will* w me into their houses.'	1312
Ac	18:27	and wrote to the disciples there *to* w him.	622
Php	2:29	**W** him in the Lord with great joy,	4657
Col	4:10	if he comes to you, w him.)	1312
Phm	1:17	w him as you would welcome me.	4689
	1:17	welcome him as you would w me.	NIG
2Pe	1:11	and you will receive a rich w **into**	1658
2Jn	1:10	not take him into your house or w him.	3306+5897
3Jn	1:10	he refuses to w the brothers.	2110

WELCOMED (19) [WELCOME]

Jdg	19: 3	her father saw him, he gladly w him.	7925
Ps	21: 3	*You* w him *with* rich blessings and placed	7709
Lk	8:40	Now when Jesus returned, a crowd w him,	622
	9:11	He w them and spoke to them about	622
	10: 8	"When you enter a town and *are* w,	1312
	10:10	But when you enter a town and *are* not w,	1312
	16: 9	you *will be* w into eternal dwellings.	1312
	19: 6	So he came down at once and w him gladly.	5685
Jn	4:45	arrived in Galilee, the Galileans w him.	1312
Ac	15: 4	*they were* w by the church and the apostles	4138
	17: 7	and Jason *has* w them **into** *his* **house.**	5685
	28: 2	a fire and w us all because it was raining	4689
	28: 7	He w us to his home and	346
	28:30	in his own rented house and w all who came	622
2Co	8:17	For Titus not only w our appeal,	1312
Gal	4:14	you w me as if I were an angel of God,	1312
1Th	1: 6	*you* w the message with the joy given by	1312
Heb	11:13	*they* only saw them and w them from	832
	11:31	*because she* w the spies,	1312+1645+3552

WELCOMES (11) [WELCOME]

Mt	18: 5	"And whoever w a little child like this	1312
	18: 5	a little child like this in my name w me.	1312
Mk	9:37	"Whoever w one of these little children	1312
	9:37	of these little children in my name w me;	1312
	9:37	and whoever w me does not welcome me	1312
Lk	9:48	"Whoever w this little child in my name	1312
	9:48	child in my name w me;	1312
	9:48	and whoever w me welcomes the one who	1312
	9:48	welcomes me w the one who sent me.	1312
	15: 2	"This man w sinners and eats with them."	4657
2Jn	1:11	who w him shares in his wicked work.	3306+5897

WELDING (1)

Isa	41: 7	He says of the w, "It is good."	1817

WELFARE (3)

Ne	2:10	had come to promote the w of the Israelites.	3208
Est	10: 3	and spoke up for the w of all the Jews.	8934
Php	2:20	who takes a genuine interest in your w.	NIG

WELL (302) [WELL'S, WELLED, WELLING, WELLS]

Ge	12:13	so that I *will be* **treated** w for your sake	3512
	12:16	*He* **treated** Abram w for her sake,	3512
	13:10	plain of the Jordan *was* w **watered,**	5482
	14: 7	**as** w **as** the Amorites who were living	1685+2256
	16:14	the w was called Beer Lahai Roi,	931
	18: 5	"**Very w,**" they answered, "do as you say."	4027
	18:11	and Sarah were already old and w **advanced**	995
	19:21	He said to him, "**Very w,**	2180
	21:19	Then God opened her eyes and she saw a w	931
	21:25	complained to Abimelech about a w *of* water	931
	21:30	from my hand as a witness that I dug this w.	931
	24: 1	Abraham was now old and w **advanced**	995
	24:11	had the camels kneel down near the w	931+4784
	24:20	ran back to the w to draw more water,	931
	24:23	**as** w **as** room for you to spend the night."	1685
	26:10	**might** w **have** slept with your wife,	3869+5071
	26:19	and discovered a w *of* fresh water there.	931
	26:20	So he named the w Esek,	931
	26:21	Then they dug another w,	931
	26:22	He moved on from there and dug another w,	931
	26:25	and there his servants dug a w.	931

Ge	26:29	but always treated you w and sent you away	3202
	26:32	and told him about the w they had dug.	931
	29: 2	There he saw a w in the field,	931
	29: 2	the flocks were watered from that w.	931
	29: 2	over the mouth of the w was large.	931
	29: 3	to its place over the mouth of the w.	931
	29: 6	Then Jacob asked them, "Is he w?"	8934
	29: 8	rolled away from the mouth of the w.	931
	29:10	the stone away from the mouth of the w	931
	30:15	"Very w," Rachel said, "he can sleep	4027+4200
	32: 7	and the flocks and herds and camels as w.	2256
	36: 6	as w as his livestock and all his other	2256
	37:10	When he told his father as w as his brothers,	2256
	37:13	"Very w," he replied,	2180
	37:14	"Go and see if all is w with your brothers	8934
	40:14	But when all goes w with you,	3512
	43:28	Your servant our father is still alive and w."	8934
	44:10	"Very w," he said,	1685
	47:19	we and our land as w?	1685
Ex	2:15	in Midian, where he sat down by a w.	931
	4:14	I know he can speak w.	1819+1819
	4:18	Jethro said, "Go, and I wish you w."	4200+8934
	11: 5	and all the firstborn of the cattle as w.	2256
	12:29	and the firstborn of all the livestock as w.	2256
	12:38	as w as large droves of livestock,	2256
	23:12	and the alien as w,	2256
	25:29	as w as its pitchers and bowls for	2256
	37:23	as w as its wick trimmers and trays,	2256
Lev	4:11	as w as the head and legs,	6584
	21:22	as w as the holy food;	2256
	25: 7	as w as for your livestock and	2256
Nu	3:37	as w as the posts of	2256
	4:32	as w as the posts of	2256
	10:29	Come with us and we will treat you w,	3512
	20:17	or drink water from any w.	931
	21:16	the w where the LORD said to Moses,	931
	21:17	Israel sang this song: "Spring up, O w!	931
	21:18	the w that the princes dug, that the nobles of	931
	21:22	or drink water from any w.	931
	22:38	"W, I have come to you now,"	2180
	31:10	as w as all their camps.	2256
	31:20	Purify every garment as w as	2256
	32:38	as w as Nebo and Baal Meon	2256
Dt	4:40	that it may go w with you and your children	3512
	5:16	that you may live long and that it may go w	3512
	5:29	so that it might go w with them	3512
	6: 3	and be careful to obey so that it may go w	3512
	6:18	that it may go w with you and you may go	3512
	7:18	remember w what the LORD your God did	2349+2349
		to Pharaoh	
	8:16	to test you so that in the end it might go w	3512
	12:25	that it may go w with you and your children	3512
	12:28	so that it may always go w with you	3512
	15:16	and your family and is w off with you,	3201
	19:13	so that it may go w with you.	3201
	22: 7	so that it may go w with you.	3512
	29:19	on the watered land as w as the dry.	907
Jos	13: 1	Joshua was old and w advanced in years,	995
	17:18	but the forested hill country as w.	3954
	23: 1	by then old and w advanced in years,	995
	23: 2	"I am old and w advanced in years.	995
Jdg	1:24	and we will see that you are treated w."	2876
	4: 9	"Very w," Deborah said, "I will go	2143+2143
Ru	3: 1	where you will be w provided for?	3512
1Sa	16:17	"Find someone who plays w and bring him	3512
	16:18	He speaks w and is a fine-looking man.	1067
	17:12	in Saul's time he was old and w advanced	995
	18: 5	and Saul's officers as w.	1685
	18:30	and his name became w known.	3700+4394
	19: 4	Jonathan spoke w of David to Saul	3202
	20: 3	"Your father knows very w	3359+3359
	20: 7	If he says, 'Very w,'	3202
	24:17	"You have treated me w,	3208
	24:19	May the LORD reward you w for the way	3208
	28: 2	Achish replied, "Very w,	4027+4200
2Sa	3:26	they brought him back from the w of Sirah.	1014
	10: 6	as w as the king of Maacah with	2256
	11:25	sword devours one as w as another.	2256+3869
	14: 7	then we will get rid of the heir as w.'	1685
	14:21	said to Joab, "Very w, I will do it.	2180+5528
	17:18	He had a w in his courtyard.	931
	17:19	and spread it out over the opening of the w	931
	17:21	of the w and went to inform King David.	931
	18:28	Ahimaaz called out to the king, "All is w!"	8934
	23:15	from the w near the gate of Bethlehem!"	1014
	23:16	from the w near the gate of Bethlehem	1014
1Ki	1: 1	When King David was old and w advanced	995
	2:18	"Very w," Bathsheba replied,	3202
	2:22	as w request the kingdom for him—	AIT
	4:13	as w as the district of Argob in Bashan	NIH
	4:23	as w as deer, gazelles, roebucks	963+4200+4946
	5:16	as w as thirty-three hundred foremen who	
		supervised the project	963+4200+4946
	7:29	and on the uprights as w.	4027
	8:18	you did w to have this in your heart.	3201
	9:19	as w as all his store cities and the towns	2256
	11:28	Solomon saw how w the young man did	3954
2Ki	2:19	"Look, our lord, this town is w situated,	3202
	3:25	and attacked it as w.	2256
	4:14	"W, she has no son and her husband is old."	66
	10:11	as w as all his chief men,	2256
	10:14	and slaughtered them by the w	1014
	10:30	"Because you have done w	3201
	17: 8	as w as the practices that the kings	2256
	25:24	and it will go w with you."	3512
1Ch	2:23	as w as Kenath with its surrounding	NIH
	7:24	Upper Beth Horon as w as Uzzen Sheerah.	2256

1Ch	9:29	as w as the flour and wine, and the oil,	2256
	11:17	from the w near the gate of Bethlehem!"	1014
	11:18	from the w near the gate of Bethlehem	1014
	19: 6	as w as the king of Maacah with his troops,	2256
	22:15	stonecutters, masons and carpenters, as w as	2256
	23: 2	as w as the priests and Levites.	2256
	25: 8	teacher as w as student.	6640
	28:13	as w as for all the articles to be used	2256
	29: 2	as w as onyx for the settings, turquoise,	2256
	29:24	as w as all of King David's sons,	1685+2256
2Ch	6: 8	you did w to have this in your heart.	3201
	8: 6	as w as Baalath and all his store cities,	2256
	9: 3	as w as the palace he had built,	2256
	19:11	may the LORD be with those who do w."	3202
	21: 3	as w as fortified cities in Judah,	6640
	28:18	Aijalon and Gederoth, as w as Soco,	2256
	33:15	as w as all the altars he had built on	2256
	33:19	as w as all his sins and unfaithfulness,	2256
Ezr	3: 5	as w as those brought as freewill offerings	2256
	7: 6	a teacher w versed in the Law of Moses,	4542
	7:16	as w as the freewill offerings of the people	10554
	8:28	"You as w as these articles are consecrated	2256
Ne	2:13	the Valley Gate toward the Jackal W and	6524
	5:17	as w as those who came to us from	2256
	12:22	as w as those of the priests,	2256
	12:35	as w as some priests with trumpets,	2256
	12:41	as w as the priests—	2256
	13: 5	as w as the contributions for the priests.	2256
Job	1:12	The LORD said to Satan, "Very w, then,	2180
	2: 6	The LORD said to Satan, "Very w, then,	2180
	12: 3	But I have a mind as w as you;	4017
	13: 9	Would it turn out w if he examined you?	3202
	15:21	when all seems w, marauders attack him.	8934
	16:12	All was w with me, but he shattered me;	8929
	21:24	his body w nourished,	2692+4848
	21:27	I know full w what you are thinking,	2176
	29:11	Whoever heard me spoke w of me,	887
Ps	48:13	consider w her ramparts,	4213+8883
	104:16	The trees of the LORD are w watered,	8425
	109:21	deal w with me for your name's sake;	NIH
	139:14	I know that full w.	4394
	141: 6	that my words were w spoken.	5838
Pr	4:13	guard it w, for it is your life.	5915
	5: 1	listen w to my words of insight,	265+5742
	5:15	running water from your own w.	931
	23: 1	note w what is before you,	1067+1067
	23:27	and a wayward wife is a narrow w.	931
	24:25	But it will go w with those who convict	5838
	25:26	Like a muddied spring or a polluted w is	5227
Ecc	2: 8	and a harem as w—	NIH
	7:14	God has made the one as w as the other.	4200+6645
	8:13	it will not go w with them,	3202
	11: 6	or whether both will do equally w.	3202
	12: 6	or the wheel broken at the w,	1014
SS	4:15	a w of flowing water streaming down	931
Isa	3:10	Tell the righteous it will be w with them,	3202
	5: 2	and cut out a winepress as w.	1685
	23:16	play the harp w, sing many a song,	3512
	28:11	W do I know how treacherous you are;	3954
	48: 8	with foreign lips and	3954
Jer	6: 7	As a w pours out its water,	931
	7:23	that it may go w with you.	3512
	12: 6	though they speak w of you.	3208
	12:16	if they learn w the ways of my people	4340+4340
	22:15	so all went w with him.	3202
	22:16	and so all went w.	3202
	31:13	young men and old as w.	3481
	32:11	as w as the unsealed copy—	2256
	38: 4	left in this city, as w as all the people,	2256
	38:20	Then it will go w with you,	3512
	40: 9	and it will go w with you.	3512
	41: 3	as w as the Babylonian soldiers who were	2256
	42: 6	so that it will go w with us,	3512
	44:17	and were w off and suffered no harm.	3202
	50:33	and the people of Judah as w.	3481
	51:57	her governors, officers and warriors as w;	2256
La	3:20	I w remember them,	2349+2349
Eze	3:20	"Very w," he said, "I will let you bake	8011
	16:37	those you loved as w as those you hated.	6584
	18: 4	the father as w as the son—	3869
	24:10	Cook the meat w, mixing in the spices;	9462
	24:25	and their sons and daughters as w—	2256
	30:22	the good arm as w as the broken one,	2256
	33:32	a beautiful voice and plays an instrument w,	3512
	40:19	a hundred cubits on the east side as w as on	2256
	41:16	as w as the thresholds and	NIH
	45: 4	a place for their houses as w as a holy place	2256
Da	1: 4	w informed, quick to understand,	1981+3359
Hos	13:15	his spring will fail and his w dry up.	5078
Jnh	4:11	and many cattle as w.	2256
Zec	8:12	"The seed will grow w,	8934
	12: 2	will be besieged as w as Jerusalem.	1685+2256
Mal	2:16	with violence as w as with his garment,"	NIH
Mt	3:17	whom I love; with him I am w pleased."	2305
	5:40	let him have your cloak as w.	2779
	6:33	all these things will be given to you as w.	NIG
	13:52	of his storeroom new treasures as w as old."	2779
	15:31	the mute speaking, the crippled made w,	5618
	17: 5	whom I love; with him I am w pleased."	2305
	25:21	"His master replied, 'W done,	2292
	25:23	"His master replied, 'W done,	2292
	25:27	W then, you should have put my money	4036
Mk	1:11	whom I love; with you I am w pleased."	2305
	5:16	and told about the pigs as w.	NIG
	6:14	for Jesus' name had become w known.	5745
	7:37	"He has done everything w," they said.	2822

Mk	8: 7	They had a few small fish as w;	2779
	12:32	"W said, teacher," the man replied.	2822
	16:18	hands on sick people, and they will get w."	2822
Lk	1: 7	and they were both w along in years.	4581
	1:18	I am an old man and my wife is w along	4581
	3:22	whom I love; with you I am w pleased."	2305
	4:22	All spoke w of him and were amazed at	3455
	6:25	Woe to you who are w fed now,	1855
	6:26	Woe to you when all men speak w of you,	2822
	6:48	could not shake it, because it was w built.	2822
	7:10	to the house and found the servant w.	5617
	12:31	and these things will be given to you as w.	NIG
	14: 5	an ox that falls into a w on the Sabbath day,	5853
	17:19	your faith has made you w."	5392
	19:17	" 'W done, my good servant!'	2301
	20:39	the teachers of the law responded, "W said,	2822
Jn	3:26	w, he is baptizing, and everyone is going	3972
	4: 6	Jacob's w was there, and Jesus,	4380
	4: 6	from the journey, sat down by the w.	4380
	4:11	nothing to draw with and the w is deep.	5853
	4:12	gave us the w and drank from it himself,	5853
	5: 6	he asked him, "Do you want to get w?"	5618
	5:11	"The man who made me w said to me,	5618
	5:14	"See, you are w again.	5618
	5:15	that it was Jesus who had made him w.	5618
	12:10	priests made plans to kill Lazarus as w,	2779
	13: 9	but my hands and my head as w!"	2779
	14: 7	you would know my Father as w.	2779
	15:23	He who hates me hates my Father as w.	2779
	20: 7	as w as the burial cloth that had been	2779
	21:25	Jesus did many other things as w.	NIG
Ac	6: 9	Jews of Cyrene and Alexandria as w as	2779
	10:12	as w as reptiles of the earth and birds of	2779
	10:28	"You are w aware that it is against our law	2179
	15:29	You will do w to avoid these things.	2292
	16: 2	at Lystra and Iconium spoke w of him.	3455
	17:17	as w as in the marketplace day by day	2779
	24:22	Felix, who was w acquainted with the Way,	209
	25:10	as you yourself know very w.	2822
	26: 3	so because you are w acquainted with all	1195
		as to angels as w as to men.	2779
1Co	14:17	You may be giving thanks w enough,	2822
2Co	7:14	to Titus has proved to be true as w.	NIG
	12:15	and expend myself as w.	2779
Eph	6: 3	"that it may go w with you and	2292
Php	4:12	whether w fed or hungry,	5963
1Th	2: 8	the gospel of God but our lives as w,	2779
	3: 3	You know quite w that we were destined	NIG
	3: 4	And it turned out that way, as you w know.	NIG
	5: 2	you know very w that the day of the Lord	209
2Th	1: 7	to you who are troubled, and to us as w.	NIG
1Ti	3: 4	He must manage his own family w and	2822
	3:12	manage his children and his household w.	2822
	3:13	Those who have served w gain	2822
	5:10	and is w known for her good deeds,	3455
	5:17	of the church w are worthy of double honor,	2822
2Ti	1:18	You know very w in in how many ways	1019
Heb	5: 3	own sins, as w as for the sins of the people.	2777
	11: 4	when God spoke w of his offerings.	3455
Jas	2:16	"Go, I wish you w;	1645+1877+5632
	2:16	I wish you well; keep warm and w fed,"	5963
	5:15	offered in faith will make the sick person w	5392
2Pe	1:17	whom I love; with him I am w pleased."	2305
	1:19	and you will do w to pay attention to it,	2822
1Jn	3:17	the father loves his child as w.	2779
3Jn	1: 2	and that all may go w with you,	2338
	1: 2	even as your soul is getting along w.	2338
	1: 6	You will do w to send them on their way in	2822
	1:12	Demetrius is w spoken of by everyone—	3455
	1:12	We also speak w of him,	3455

WELL'S (1) [WELL]

Ge 29: 3 the stone away from the w mouth and water   931

WELL-BEING (4)

Ezr	6:10	and pray for the w of the king and his sons.	10261
Ps	35:27	who delights in the w of his servant."	8934
	119:122	Ensure your servant's w;	3202
Jer	14:11	"Do not pray for the w of this people.	3208

WELL-BUILT (1) [BUILD]

Ge 39: 6 Now Joseph was w and handsome,   3637+9307

WELL-DRESSED (1) [DRESS]

Isa 3:24 instead of w hair, baldness;   5126+5250

WELL-FED (1) [FEED]

Jer 5: 8 They are w, lusty stallions, each neighing   8889

WELL-KNEADED (1) [KNEAD]

Lev 7:12 cakes of fine flour w and mixed with oil.   8057

WELL-KNOWN (1) [KNOW]

Nu 16: 2 250 Israelite men, w community leaders 408+9005

WELL-MIXED (1) [MIX]

Lev 6:21 bring it w and present the grain offering   8057

WELL-NOURISHED (1) [NOURISH]

Ne 9:25 They ate to the full and were w;   9042

WELL-NURTURED (1) [NURTURED]
Ps 144:12 our sons in their youth will be like w plants, 1540

WELL-TO-DO (1)
2Ki 4: 8 And a w woman was there, who urged him 1524

WELL-TRAINED (1) [TRAIN]
2Ch 26:11 Uzziah had a w army, ready to go out 4878+6913

WELL-WATERED (6) [WATER]
Job 8:16 He is like a w plant in the sunshine, 8183
Isa 58:11 You will be like a w garden, 8116
Jer 31:12 They will be like a w garden, 8116
Eze 31:14 No other trees so w are ever to reach 4784+9272
31:16 all the trees that were w, 4784+9272
45:15 of two hundred from the w pastures 5482

WELLBELOVED (KJV) See DEAR
FRIEND, LOVE, LOVED ONE

WELLED (1) [WELL]
2Co 8: 2 extreme poverty w up in rich generosity. 4355

WELLING (1) [WELL]
Jn 4:14 a spring of water w up to eternal life." 256

WELLPLEASING (KJV) See PLEASING

WELLS (8) [WELL]
Ge 26:15 the w that his father's servants had dug 931
26:18 Isaac reopened the w that had been dug 931+4784
Dt 6:11 w you did not dig, and vineyards 1014
10: 6 from the w of the Jaakanites to Moserah. 931
2Ki 19:24 I have dug w in foreign lands and drunk 7769
Ne 9:25 w already dug, vineyards, olive groves 1014
Isa 12: 3 With joy you will draw water from the w of salvation. 5078
37:25 I have dug w in foreign lands and drunk 7769

WELLSPRING (1) [SPRING]
Pr 4:23 guard your heart, for it is the w of life. 9362

WELTS (1)
Isa 1: 6 only wounds and w and open sores, 2467

WEN (KJV) See WARTS

WENCH (KJV) See SERVANT GIRL

WENT (1232) [GO]
Ge 4:16 So Cain w out from the LORD's presence 3655
6: 4 the sons of God w to the daughters of men 995
10:11 From that land he w to Assyria, 3655
12: 4 and Lot w with him. 2143
12: 8 From there he w on toward the hills east 6980
12:10 and Abram w down to Egypt to live there 3718
13: 1 So Abram w up from Egypt to the Negev, 6590
13: 1 and Lot w with him, NIH
13: 3 From the Negev he w from place to place 2143
13:18 and w to live near the great trees of Mamre 995
14: 2 w to war against Bera king of Sodom, 4878+6913
14: 5 with him w out and defeated the Rephaites 995
14: 7 Then they turned back and w to En Mishpat 995
14:11 then they w away. 2143
14:14 in his household and w in pursuit as far 8103
14:24 that belongs to the men who w with me— 2143
17:22 God w up from him. 6590
18:22 The men turned away and w toward Sodom, 2143
19: 6 Lot w outside to meet them and shut 3655
19:14 So Lot w out and spoke to his sons-in-law, 3655
19:33 the older daughter w in and lay with him. 995
19:35 The younger daughter w and lay with him. 7756
21:14 She w on her way and wandered 2143
21:16 Then she w off and sat down nearby, 2143
21:19 So she w and filled the skin with water 2143
22: 6 As the two of them w on together, 2143
22: 8 And the two of them w on together. 2143
22:13 He w over and took the ram 2143
23: 2 and Abraham w to mourn for Sarah and 995
24:16 She w down to the spring, 3718
24:30 he w out to the man 995
24:32 So the man w to the house, 995
24:45 She w down to the spring and drew water, 3718
24:61 and mounted their camels and w back with 2143
24:63 He w out to the field one evening 3655
25:22 So she w to inquire of the LORD. 2143
26: 1 Isaac w to Abimelech king of the Philistines 2143
26:23 From there he w up to Beersheba. 6590
27:14 So he w and got them and brought them 2143
27:18 He w to his father and said, "My father." 995
27:22 Jacob w close to his father Isaac, 5602
27:27 So he w to him and kissed him. 5602
28: 5 and he w to Paddan Aram, 2143
28: 9 so he w to Ishmael and married Mahalath, 2143
29:10 he w over and rolled the stone away from 5602
30:14 Reuben w out into the fields 2143
30:16 Leah w out to meet him. 3655
30:42 So the weak animals w to Laban and 2118

Ge 31:33 So Laban w into Jacob's tent and 995
32: 1 Jacob also w on his way, 2143
32: 6 they said, "We w to your brother Esau, 995
32:21 So Jacob's gifts w on ahead of him, 6296
33: 3 He himself w on ahead and bowed down to 6296
33:17 Jacob, however, w to Succoth, 5825
34: 1 w out to visit the women of the land. 3655
34: 6 Then Shechem's father Hamor w out 3655
34:20 So Hamor and his son Shechem w to 995
34:24 the men who w out of the city gate agreed 3655
35:13 Then God w up from him at the place 6590
35:22 Reuben w in and slept with his father's 2143
37:17 So Joseph w after his brothers 2143
37:30 He w back to his brothers and said, 8740
38: 1 Judah left his brothers and w down to stay 3718
38:11 So Tamar w to live in her father's house. 2143
38:12 he w up to Timnah, 6590
38:12 his friend Hirah the Adullamite w with him. NIH
38:16 he w over to her by the roadside and said, 5742
38:22 So he w back to Judah and said, 8740
39:11 One day he w into the house to attend 995
41:45 And Joseph w throughout the land of Egypt. 3655
41:46 And Joseph w out from Pharaoh's presence 3655
42: 3 of Joseph's brothers w down to buy grain 3718
42: 5 So Israel's sons were among those who w 995
43:19 So they w up to Joseph's steward and spoke 5602
43:30 He w into his private room and wept there. 995
44:18 Then Judah w up to him and said: 5602
44:24 When we w back to your servant my father, 6590
44:28 One of them w away from me, and I said, 3655
45:25 So they w up out of Egypt and came 6590
46: 6 and Jacob and all his offspring w to Egypt. 995
46: 8 (Jacob and his descendants) who w to Egypt: 995
46:26 All those who w to Egypt with Jacob— 995
46:27 which w to Egypt, were seventy in all. 995
46:29 and w to Goshen to meet his father Israel. 6590
47: 1 Joseph w and told Pharaoh, 995
47:10 Then Jacob blessed Pharaoh and w out 3655
49: 4 for you w up onto your father's bed, 6590
50: 7 So Joseph w up to bury his father. 6590
50: 9 Chariots and horsemen also w up with him. 6590
Ex 1: 1 of Israel who w to Egypt with Jacob, each 995
2: 5 Pharaoh's daughter w down to the Nile 3718
2: 8 the girl w and got the baby's mother. 2143
2:11 he w out to where his own people were 3655
2:13 The next day he w out and saw 3655
2:15 but Moses fled from Pharaoh and w to live NIH
2:23 cry for help because of their slavery w up 6590
4:18 Then Moses w back to Jethro 2143
5: 1 Afterward Moses and Aaron w to Pharaoh 995
5:10 the foremen w out and said to the people, 3655
5:15 Then the Israelite foremen w and appealed 995
5:23 Ever since I w to Pharaoh to speak 995
7:10 and Aaron w to Pharaoh and did just as 995
7:23 Instead, he turned and w into his palace, 995
9:33 Moses left Pharaoh and w out of the city. NIH
10: 3 So Moses and Aaron w to Pharaoh and said 995
12:38 Many other people w up with them, 6590
13:18 The Israelites w up out of Egypt armed 6590
13:21 By day the LORD w ahead of them in 2143
14:19 withdrew and w behind them. 2143
14:20 so neither w near the other all night long. 7928
14:22 Israelites w through the sea on dry ground, 995
14:27 and at daybreak the sea w back to its place. 8740
14:29 Israelites w through the sea on dry ground, 2143
15:19 chariots and horsemen w into the sea, 995
15:22 the Red Sea and they w into the Desert 3655
16:27 some of the people w out on the seventh day 3655
17:10 Aaron and Hur w to the top of the hill. 6590
18: 7 So Moses w out to meet his father-in-law 3655
18: 7 They greeted each other and then w into 995
19: 3 Then Moses w up to God, 6590
19: 7 So Moses w back and summoned the elders 995
19:20 the top of the mountain. So Moses w up 6590
19:25 Moses w down to the people and told them. 3718
24: 3 When Moses w and told the people all 995
24: 9 and the seventy elders of Israel w up 6590
24:13 and Moses w up on the mountain of God. 6590
24:15 When Moses w up on the mountain, 6590
24:18 Moses entered the cloud as he w on up 6590
32:15 Moses turned and w down the mountain 3718
32:31 So Moses w back to the LORD and said, 8740
33: 8 And whenever Moses w out to the tent, 3655
33: 9 As Moses w into the tent, 995
34: 4 the first ones and w up Mount Sinai early in 6590
34: 5 over his face until he w in to speak with 995
Lev 9:23 and Aaron then w into the Tent of Meeting. 995
24:10 and an Egyptian father w out among 3655
Nu 10:14 The divisions of the camp of Judah w first, 5825
10:18 divisions of the camp of Reuben w next, 5825
10:22 divisions of the camp of Ephraim w next, 5825
10:33 the covenant of the LORD w before them 5825
11: 8 The people w around gathering it, 8763
11:24 So Moses w out and told the people what 3655
11:31 Now a wind w out from the LORD 5825
11:32 and all the next day the people w out 7756
13:21 So they w up and explored the land from 6590
13:22 They w up through the Negev and came 6590
13:27 "We w into the land to which you sent us, 995
14:24 I will bring him into the land he w to, 995
14:38 Of the men who w to explore the land, 2143
14:40 Early the next morning they w up toward 6590
14:44 in their presumption they w up toward 6590
16:25 Moses got up and w to Dathan and Abiram, 2143
16:33 They w down alive into the grave, 3718
16:43 Then Moses and Aaron w to the front of 995
20: 6 Moses and Aaron w from the assembly to 995

Nu 20:15 Our forefathers w down into Egypt, 3718
20:27 They w up Mount Hor in the sight of 6590
21:18 Then they w from the desert to Mattanah, NIH
21:28 "Fire w out from Heshbon, 3655
21:33 Then they turned and w up along the road 6590
22:21 saddled his donkey and w with the princes 2143
22:22 But God was very angry when he w, 2143
22:35 So Balaam w with the princes of Balak. 2143
22:36 he w out to meet him at the Moabite town 3655
22:39 Balaam w with Balak to Kiriath Huzoth, 2143
23: 3 Then he w off to a barren height. 2143
23: 6 So he w back to him and found him 8740
23:17 So he w to him and found him standing 995
24:25 and Balak w his own way. 2143
31:13 of the community w to meet them outside 3655
31:48 and commanders of hundreds—w to Moses 7928
32: 9 After they w up to the Valley of Eshcol 6590
32:39 of Makir son of Manasseh w to Gilead, 2143
33: 9 They left Marah and w to Elim, 995
33:38 the priest w up Mount Hor, 6590
Dt 1:19 from Horeb and w toward the hill country 2143
1:24 They left and w up into the hill country, 6590
1:31 all the way you w until you reached this 2143
1:33 who w ahead of you on your journey, 2143
2: 8 So we w on past our brothers 6296
3: 1 and w up along the road toward Bashan, 6590
9: 9 When I w up on the mountain to receive 6590
9:15 So I turned and w down from the mountain 3718
10: 3 and I w up on the mountain with the two 6590
10:22 Your forefathers who w down AIT
26: 5 he w down into Egypt with a few people 3718
29:26 They w off and worshiped other gods 2143
31: 1 Then Moses w out and spoke these words 2143
Jos 2: 1 So they w and entered the house of 2143
2: 5 I don't know which way they w. 2143
2: 8 she w up on the roof 6590
2:22 they w into the hills and stayed there 995
2:23 They w down out of the hills, 3718
3: 1 the Israelites set out from Shittim and w to 995
3: 2 After three days the officers w throughout 6296
3: 6 So they took it up and w ahead of them. 2143
3:14 the ark of the covenant w ahead of them. NIH
4:19 of the first month the people w up from 6590
5:13 Joshua w up to him and asked, 2143
6: 1 No one w out and no one came in. 3655
6: 8 w forward, blowing their trumpets, 6296
6:13 carrying the seven trumpets w forward, 2143
6:13 The armed men w ahead of them and 2143
6:23 the spying w in and brought out Rahab, 995
7: 2 So the men w up and spied out Ai. 6590
7: 4 So about three thousand men w up; 6590
8: 9 and they w to the place of ambush and lay 2143
8:13 That night Joshua w into the valley. 2143
8:17 the city open and w in pursuit of Israel. 8103
9: 4 They w as a delegation whose donkeys 2143
9: 6 Then they w to Joshua in the camp at Gilgal 2143
10:36 Then Joshua and all Israel with him w up 6590
11:21 At that time Joshua w and destroyed 995
14: 8 but my brothers who w up with me made 6590
15: 3 continued on to Zin and w over to the south 6590
15: 6 w up to Beth Hoglah and continued north 6590
15: 7 The boundary then w up to Debir from 6590
15: 9 Mount Ephron and w down toward Baalah 9305
15:11 It w to the northern slope of Ekron, 3655
16: 1 and w up from there through the desert into 6590
16: 2 It w on from Bethel (that is, Luz), 3655
16: 5 of their inheritance w from Ataroth Addar 2118
16: 7 Then it w down from Janoah to Ataroth 3718
16: 8 the border w west to the Kanah Ravine 2143
17: 4 They w to Eleazar the priest, 7928
18: 9 So the men left and w through the land. 6296
18:13 and w down to Ataroth Addar on the hill 3718
18:16 The boundary w down to the foot of 3718
18:17 It then curved north, w to En Shemesh, 3655
18:19 then w to the northern slope of Beth Hoglah 6296
19:10 The boundary of their inheritance w as far 2118
19:12 of Kisloth Tabor and w on to Daberath and 3655
19:14 There the boundary w around on the north 6015
19:27 and w north to Beth Emek and Neiel, NIH
19:28 It w to Abdon, Rehob, Hammon and Kanah, NIH
19:29 then turned back toward Ramah and w to NIH
19:33 Their boundary w from Heleph and 2118
19:47 so they w up and attacked Leshem, took it, 6590
22: 6 and they w to their homes. 2143
22:15 When they w to Gilead— 995
24: 4 but Jacob and his sons w down to Egypt. 3718
Jdg 1: 3 So the Simeonites w with them. 2143
1: 9 the men of Judah w down to fight against 3718
1:16 w up from the City of Palms with the men 6590
1:17 Then the men of Judah w with 2143
1:26 He then w to the land of the Hittites, 2143
2: 1 The angel of the LORD w up from Gilgal 6590
2: 6 they w to take possession of the land, 2143
3:10 Whenever Israel w out to fight, 3655
3:10 that he became Israel's judge and w to war. 3655
3:23 Then Ehud w out to the porch; 3655
3:27 Israelites w down with him from the hills, 3718
4: 9 So Deborah w with Barak to Kedesh, 2143
4:10 and Deborah also w with him. 6590
4:14 So Barak w down Mount Tabor, 3718
4:18 Jael w out to meet Sisera and said to him, 3655
4:21 up a tent peg and a hammer and w quietly 995
4:22 and Jael w out to meet him. 3655
4:22 So he w in with her, and there lay Sisera 995
5: 4 "O LORD, when you w out from Seir, 3655
5:11 "Then the people of the LORD w down to 3718
6:19 Gideon w in, prepared a young goat, 995

Jdg	6:35	so that *they* too w up to meet them.	6590
	7:11	So he and Purah his servant w down to	3718
	8: 1	Why didn't you call us when *you* w	2143
	8: 8	From there he w up to Peniel and made	6590
	8:11	Gideon w by the route of the nomads	6590
	8:29	Jerub-Baal son of Joash w back home	2143
	9: 1	of Jerub-Baal w to his mother's brothers	2143
	9: 5	He w to his father's home in Ophrah and	995
	9: 8	the trees w out to anoint a king	2143+2143
	9:42	The next day the people of Shechem w out	3655
	9:46	the tower of Shechem w into the stronghold	995
	9:48	he and all his men w up Mount Zalmon.	6590
	9:50	Next Abimelech w to Thebez	2143
	9:52	Abimelech w to the tower and stormed it.	995
	9:55	that Abimelech was dead, they w home.	2143
	11: 5	the elders of Gilead w to get Jephthah from	2143
	11:11	So Jephthah w with the elders of Gilead,	2143
	11:16	Israel w through the desert to the Red Sea	2143
	11:32	Jephthah w over to fight the Ammonites,	6296
	11:38	She and the girls w into the hills and wept	2143
	13: 6	the woman w to her husband and told him,	995
	14: 1	Samson w down to Timnah and saw there	3718
	14: 5	Samson w down to Timnah together	3718
	14: 7	he w down and talked with the woman,	3718
	14: 8	when he w back to marry her.	8740
	14: 9	with his hands and ate as he w along.	2143+2143
	14:10	Now his father w down to see the woman.	3718
	14:19	He w down to Ashkelon,	3718
	14:19	he w up to his father's house.	6590
	15: 1	a young goat and w to visit his wife.	AIT
	15: 4	So he w out and caught three hundred foxes	2143
	15: 6	So the Philistines w up and burned her	6590
	15: 8	Then he w down and stayed in a cave in	3718
	15: 9	The Philistines w up and camped in Judah,	6590
	15:11	from Judah w down to the cave in the rock	3718
	16: 1	One day Samson w to Gaza,	2143
	16: 1	*He* w in to spend the night with her.	448+995
	16: 5	The rulers of the Philistines w to her	6590
	16:31	and his father's whole family w down	3718
	18:13	From there *they* w on to the hill country	6296
	18:15	So they turned in there and w to the house	995
	18:17	The five men who had spied out the land w	995
	18:18	When these men w into Micah's house	995
	18:20	and the carved image and w along with	995
	18:24	and my priest, and w away.	2143
	18:26	So the Danites w their way, and Micah,	2143
	18:26	turned around and w back home.	8740
	18:27	and his priest, and w on to Laish,	995
	19: 2	and w back to her father's house	NIH
	19: 3	her husband w to her to persuade her	2143
	19:10	the man left and w toward Jebus (that is,	995
	19:14	So *they* w on, and the sun set	6296
	19:15	*They* w and sat in the city square,	995
	19:23	The owner of the house w outside and said	3655
	19:27	At daybreak the woman w back to	995
	20:18	The Israelites w up to Bethel and inquired	6590
	20:20	of Israel w out to fight the Benjamites	3655
	20:23	The Israelites w up and wept before	6590
	20:26	the Israelites, all the people, w up to Bethel,	6590
	20:30	They w up against the Benjamites on	6590
	20:48	of Israel w back to Benjamin and put all	8740
	21: 2	The people w to Bethel,	995
	21:24	the Israelites left that place and w home	3655
Ru	1: 1	w to live for a while in the country	2143
	1: 2	And *they* w to Moab and lived there.	995
	1:19	So the two women w on until they came	2143
	1:21	I w away full, but the LORD has brought me	2143
	2: 3	So *she* w out and began to glean in	2143
	2: 7	*She* w into the field and has worked	995
	3: 6	So she w down to the threshing floor	3718
	3: 7	he w over to lie down at the far end of	995
	3:15	Then *he* w back to town.	995
	4: 1	Meanwhile Boaz w up to the town gate	6590
	4: 1	So he w over and sat down.	6073
	4:13	Then *he* w to her, and the LORD enabled her	995
1Sa	1: 3	Year after year this man w up from his town	6590
	1: 7	This w on year after year.	6913
	1: 7	Whenever Hannah w up to the house of	6590
	1:18	Then she w her way and ate something,	2143
	1:19	the LORD and then w back to their home	995
	1:21	the man Elkanah w up with all his family	6590
	2:11	Then Elkanah w home to Ramah,	2143
	2:19	when she w up with her husband to offer	6590
	3: 5	So he w and lay down.	2143
	3: 6	And Samuel got up and w to Eli and said,	2143
	3: 8	and Samuel got up and w to Eli and said,	2143
	3: 9	So Samuel w and lay down in his place.	2143
	4: 1	Now the Israelites w out to fight against	3655
	4:12	A Benjamite ran from the battle line and w	995
	4:19	she w into labor and gave birth,	4156
	5:12	and the outcry of the city w up to heaven.	6590
	6:12	cows w straight up toward Beth Shemesh,	3837
	7:16	to year he w on a circuit from Bethel	2143
	7:17	But he always w back to Ramah,	9588
	9: 4	*They* w on into the district of Shaalim,	6296
	9: 9	if a man w to inquire of God, he would say,	2143
	9:14	*They* w up to the town.	6590
	9:26	he and Samuel w outside together.	3655
	10:13	he w to the high place.	995
	10:14	we w to Samuel."	2143
	10:26	Saul also w to his home in Gibeah,	2143
	11: 1	Nahash the Ammonite w and besieged	6590
	11: 9	When the messengers w and reported this to	995
	11:15	the people w to Gilgal and confirmed Saul	2143
	13: 5	So Saul w and camped at Micmash,	6590
	13:10	and Saul w out to greet him.	3655
	13:15	Then Samuel left Gilgal and w up to Gibeah	6590

1Sa	13:17	Raiding parties w out from the Philistine	3655
	13:20	So all Israel w down to the Philistines	3718
	14:20	Then Saul and all his men assembled and w	995
	14:21	up with them to their camp w over to	2118+6017
	14:26	When they w into the woods,	995
	15: 5	Saul w to the city of Amalek and set an	995
	15:12	Samuel got up and w to meet Saul,	7925
	15:20	"I w on the mission the LORD assigned me.	2143
	15:31	So Samuel w back with Saul,	8740
	15:34	Saul w up to his home in Gibeah of Saul.	6590
	16:13	Samuel then w to Ramah.	2143
	17: 7	His shield bearer w ahead of him.	2143
	17:15	but David w back and forth from Saul	2143
	17:35	I w after it, struck it and rescued the sheep	3655
	18:27	David and his men w and killed	2143
	19: 8	and David w out and fought the Philistines.	3655
	19:18	he w to Samuel at Ramah and told him all	995
	19:18	and Samuel w to Naioth and stayed there.	2143
	19:22	for Ramah and w to the great cistern	995
	19:23	So Saul w to Naioth at Ramah.	2143
	20: 1	from Naioth at Ramah and w to Jonathan	995
	20:11	So *they* w together.	3655
	20:35	In the morning Jonathan w out to the field	3655
	20:42	and Jonathan w back to the town.	995
	21: 1	David w to Nob, to Ahimelech the priest.	995
	21:10	from Saul and w to Achish king of Gath.	995
	22: 1	*they* w down to him there.	3718
	22: 3	From there David w to Mizpah in Moab	2143
	22: 5	So David left and w to the forest of Hereth.	995
	23: 5	So David and his men w to Keilah,	2143
	23:16	And Saul's son Jonathan w to David	2143
	23:18	Then Jonathan w home,	2143
	23:19	The Ziphites w up to Saul at Gibeah	6590
	23:24	So they set out and w to Ziph ahead of Saul.	2143
	23:25	he w down to the rock and stayed in	3718
	23:25	w into the Desert of Maon in pursuit	8103
	23:28	of David and w to meet the Philistines.	2143
	23:29	And David w up from there and lived in	6590
	24: 3	and Saul w in to relieve himself.	995
	24: 7	And Saul left the cave and w his way.	2143
	24: 8	Then David w out of the cave	3655
	24:22	and his men w up to the stronghold.	6590
	25:12	David's men turned around and w back.	8740
	25:13	About four hundred men w up with David,	6590
	25:36	When Abigail w to Nabal,	995
	25:40	His servants w to Carmel and said	995
	25:42	w with David's messengers	2143
	26: 1	The Ziphites w to Saul at Gibeah and said,	995
	26: 2	So Saul w down to the Desert of Ziph,	3718
	26: 5	and w to the place where Saul had camped.	995
	26: 7	David and Abishai w to the army by night,	995
	26:25	So David w on his way,	2143
	27: 2	and w over to Achish son of Maoch king	6296
	27: 8	and his men w up and raided the Geshurites,	6590
	28: 8	at night he and two men w to the woman.	995
	29:11	and the Philistines w up to Jezreel.	6590
	30: 2	but carried them off as *they* w on their way.	2143
	30:24	to be the same as that of him *who* w down	3718
	31:12	from the wall of Beth Shan and w to Jabesh,	2143
2Sa	2: 2	So David w up there with his two wives,	6590
	2: 2	left Mahanaim and w to Gibeon.	NIH
	2:13	Joab son of Zeruiah and David's men w out	3655
	3:16	Her husband, however, w with her,	2143
	3:16	So he w back.	8740
	3:19	Then he w to Hebron to tell David	2143
	3:21	David sent Abner away, and *he* w in peace.	2143
	3:24	So Joab w to the king and said,	995
	4: 6	They w into the inner part of the house as if	995
	5:17	they w up in full force to search for him,	6590
	5:17	but David heard about it and w down to	3718
	5:20	So David w to Baal Perazim,	995
	6:12	So David w down and brought up the ark	2143
	6:19	And all the people w to their homes.	2143
	7:18	King David w in and sat before the LORD,	995
	7:23	the one nation on earth that God w out	2143
	8: 3	when he w to restore his control along	2143
	8: 6	LORD gave David victory wherever *he* w.	2143
	8:14	LORD gave David victory wherever *he* w.	2143
	10:14	fled before Abishai and w inside the city.	995
	10:16	*they* w to Helam, with Shobach	995
	10:17	crossed the Jordan and w to Helam.	995
	11: 4	Then *she* w back home.	8740
	11:13	the evening Uriah w out to sleep on his mat	3655
	12:16	He fasted and w into his house and spent	995
	12:20	*he* w into the house of the LORD	995
	12:20	Then *he* w to his own house,	995
	12:24	and *he* w to her and lay with her.	995
	12:29	So David mustered the entire army and w	2143
	13: 8	So Tamar w to the house of her brother	2143
	13:19	She put her hand on her head and w away,	2143
	13:19	weeping aloud *as she* w.	2143
	13:24	Absalom w to the king and said,	995
	13:34	The watchman w and told the king,	995
	13:37	Absalom fled and w to Talmai son	2143
	13:38	After Absalom fled and w to Geshur,	2143
	14: 4	When the woman from Tekoa w to the king,	995
	14:23	Then Joab w to Geshur	2143
	14:24	So Absalom w to his own house and did	6015
	14:33	So Joab w to the king and told him this.	995
	15: 9	So he w to Hebron.	2143
	15:11	invited as guests and w quite innocently,	2143
	15:30	the Mount of Olives, weeping as *he* w;	995
	15:30	and were weeping as *they* w up.	6590
	16:13	cursing as he w and throwing stones at him	2143
	16:16	w to Absalom and said to him,	995
	17:18	left quickly and w to the house of a man	995
	17:21	out of the well and w to inform King David.	2143

2Sa	17:24	David w to Mahanaim,	995
	18: 9	and *as* the mule w under the thick branches	995
	18:24	the watchman w up to the roof of	2143
	18:33	*He* w up to the room over the gateway	6590
	18:33	As he w, he said: "O my son Absalom!	2143
	19: 5	Joab w into the house to the king and said,	995
	19:15	the king returned and w as far as the Jordan.	995
	19:24	also w down to meet the king.	3718
	20: 5	But when Amasa w to summon Judah,	2143
	20: 7	and all the mighty warriors w out under	3655
	20:13	all the men w on with Joab	6296
	20:17	*He* w toward her, and she asked,	7928
	20:22	Then the woman w to all the people	995
	20:22	And Joab w back to the king in Jerusalem.	8740
	21:12	he w and took the bones of Saul	2143
	21:15	David w down with his men to fight against	3718
	23:17	"Is it not the blood of men who w at the risk	2143
	23:20	He also w down into a pit on a snowy day	3718
	23:21	Benaiah w against him with a club.	3718
	24: 5	and then w through Gad and on to Jazer.	NIH
	24: 6	*They* w to Gilead and the region	995
	24: 7	Then *they* w toward the fortress of Tyre	995
	24: 7	*they* w on to Beersheba in the Negev	3655
	24:13	So Gad w to David and said to him,	995
	24:18	that day Gad w to David and said to him,	995
	24:19	David w up, as the LORD had commanded	6590
1Ki	1:15	So Bathsheba w to see the aged king	995
	1:23	So *he* w before the king and bowed	995
	1:38	and the Pelethites w down and put Solomon	3718
	1:40	And all the people w up after him,	6590
	1:50	w and took hold of the horns of the altar.	2143
	2: 8	down bitter curses on me the day I w	2143
	2:13	w to Bathsheba, Solomon's mother.	995
	2:19	When Bathsheba w to King Solomon	995
	2:34	So Benaiah son of Jehoiada w up and struck	6590
	2:40	he saddled his donkey and w to Achish	2143
	2:40	So Shimei w away and brought	2143
	2:46	and he w out and struck Shimei down	3655
	3: 4	The king w to Gibeon to offer sacrifices,	2143
	8:66	They blessed the king and then w home,	2143
	9:12	when Hiram w from Tyre to see the towns	3655
	10:16	six hundred bekas of gold w	6590
	11:18	They set out from Midian and w to Paran.	995
	11:18	*they* w to Egypt, to Pharaoh king of Egypt,	995
	11:24	the rebels w to Damascus,	2143
	12: 1	Rehoboam w to Shechem,	2143
	12: 3	and he and the whole assembly of Israel w	995
	12:16	So the people w away.	2143
	12:16	So the Israelites w home.	2143
	12:24	the word of the LORD and w home again,	2143
	12:25	From there *he* w out and built up Peniel.	3655
	12:30	the people w even as far as Dan to worship	2143
	12:33	the festival for the Israelites and w up to	6590
	13:24	As *he* w on his way,	2143
	13:25	and *they* w and reported it in the city where	995
	13:28	Then he w out and found the body thrown	2143
	14: 4	So Jeroboam's wife did what he said and w	2143
	14:17	Then Jeroboam's wife got up and left and w	995
	14:28	the king w to the LORD's temple,	995
	15:17	Baasha king of Israel w up against Judah	6590
	16:18	w into the citadel of the royal palace	995
	17: 5	*He* w to the Kerith Ravine,	2143
	17:10	So he w to Zarephath.	2143
	17:15	*She* w away and did as Elijah had told her.	2143
	18: 2	So Elijah w to present himself to Ahab.	2143
	18:16	So Obadiah w to meet Ahab and told him,	2143
	18:16	and Ahab w to meet Elijah.	2143
	18:21	Elijah w before the people and said,	5602
	18:42	So Ahab w off to eat and drink,	6590
	18:43	And he w up and looked.	6590
	19: 4	he himself w a day's journey into the desert.	2143
	19: 9	There he w into a cave and spent the night.	995
	19:13	he pulled his cloak over his face and w out	3655
	19:19	So Elijah w from there and found Elisha	2143
	19:19	Elijah w up to him and threw his cloak	6296
	19:21	So Elisha left him and w back.	8740
	20: 1	he w up and besieged Samaria	6590
	20:17	of the provincial commanders w out first.	3655
	20:26	and w up to Aphek to fight against Israel.	6590
	20:32	*they* w to the king of Israel and said,	995
	20:36	And after the man w away,	2143
	20:38	the prophet w and stood by the road waiting	2143
	20:39	"Your servant w into the thick of the battle,	3655
	20:43	king of Israel w to his palace in Samaria.	2143
	21: 4	So Ahab w home, sullen and angry	995
	21:16	he got up and w down to take possession	3718
	21:27	He lay in sackcloth and w around meekly.	1980
	22: 2	of Judah w down to see the king of Israel.	3718
	22:24	of Kenaanah w up and slapped Micaiah in	5602
	22:24	the LORD go when he w from me to speak	NIH
	22:29	and Jehoshaphat king of Judah w up	6590
	22:30	the king of Israel disguised himself and w	995
2Ki	1: 4	So Elijah w.	
	1: 9	The captain w up to Elijah,	6590
	1:13	This third captain w up and fell on his knees	6590
	1:15	So Elijah got up and w down with him to	3718
	2: 2	So *they* w down to Bethel.	3718
	2: 4	So *they* w to Jericho.	995
	2: 5	at Jericho w up to Elisha and asked him,	5602
	2: 7	Fifty men of the company of the prophets w	2143
	2:11	and Elijah w up to heaven in a whirlwind.	6590
	2:13	that had fallen from Elijah and w back	8740
	2:15	and *they* w to meet him and bowed to	995
	2:21	Then he w out to the spring and threw	3655
	2:23	From there Elisha w up to Bethel.	6590
	2:25	And he w on to Mount Carmel and	2143

2Ki	3:12	and the king of Edom w down to him.	3718
	4: 7	*She* w and told the man of God, and he said,	995
	4: 8	One day Elisha w to Shunem.	6296
	4:11	*he* w up to his room and lay down there.	6073
	4:18	and one day *he* w out to his father,	3655
	4:21	*She* w up and laid him on the bed of	6590
	4:21	then shut the door and w out.	3655
	4:31	Gehazi w on ahead and laid the staff on	6296
	4:31	*Gehazi* w back to meet Elisha and told him,	8740
	4:33	*He* w in, shut the door on the two of them	995
	4:37	Then she took her son and w out.	3655
	4:39	of them w out into the fields to gather herbs	3655
	5: 4	Naaman w to his master and told him what	995
	5: 9	So Naaman w with his horses and chariots	995
	5:11	But Naaman w away angry and said,	2143
	5:12	So he turned and w off in a rage.	2143
	5:13	Naaman's servants w to him and said,	5602
	5:14	So *he* w down and dipped himself in	3718
	5:15	Then Naaman and all his attendants w back	8740
	5:25	he w in and stood before his master Elisha.	995
	5:27	Then Gehazi w from Elisha's presence	3655
	6: 4	And *he* w with them.	2143
	6: 4	*They* w to the Jordan and began to cut	995
	6:14	*They* w by night and surrounded the city.	995
	6:15	of the man of God got up and w out early	3655
	6:30	As he w along the wall, the people looked,	6296
	7: 5	At dusk they got up and w to the camp of	995
	7: 8	gold and clothes, and w off and hid them.	2143
	7:10	So *they* w and called out to the city	995
	7:10	"We w into the Aramean camp and not	995
	7:16	the people w out and plundered the camp	3655
	8: 2	She and her family w away and stayed in	2143
	8: 3	the land of the Philistines and w to the king	3655
	8: 7	Elisha w to Damascus,	995
	8: 9	Hazael w to meet Elisha,	2143
	8: 9	*He* w in and stood before him, and said,	995
	8:21	So Jehoram w to Zair with all his chariots.	6296
	8:28	Ahaziah w with Joram son of Ahab to war	2143
	8:29	king of Judah w down to Jezreel to see	3718
	9: 4	the prophet, w to Ramoth Gilead.	2143
	9: 6	Jehu got up and w into the house.	995
	9:11	When Jehu w out to his fellow officers,	3655
	9:30	Then Jehu w to Jezreel.	995
	9:34	Jehu w in and ate and drank.	995
	9:35	But when *they* w out to bury her,	2143
	9:36	*They* w back and told Jehu, who said,	8740
	10: 9	The next morning Jehu w out.	3655
	10:12	Jehu then set out and w toward Samaria.	2143
	10:23	of Recab w into the temple of Baal.	995
	10:24	So *they* w in to make sacrifices	995
	11:13	*she* w to the people at the temple of	995
	11:18	All the people of the land w to the temple	995
	11:19	from the temple of the LORD and w into	995
	12:17	About this time Hazael king of Aram w up	6590
	13:14	Jehoash king of Israel w down to see him	3718
	14:13	Then Jehoash w to Jerusalem and broke	995
	15:14	Then Menahem son of Gadi w from Tirzah	995
	16:10	Then King Ahaz w to Damascus	2143
	18:18	and Joah son of Asaph the recorder w out	3655
	18:37	and Joah son of Asaph the recorder w	995
	19: 1	and put on sackcloth and w into the temple	995
	19:14	Then he w up to the temple of the LORD	6590
	19:35	That night the angel of the LORD w out	3655
	20: 1	of Amoz w to him and said, "This is what	995
	20:14	Then Isaiah the prophet w to King Hezekiah	995
	22: 9	Then Shaphan the secretary w to the king	995
	22:14	Shaphan and Asaiah w to speak to	2143
	23: 2	He w up to the temple of the LORD with	6590
	23:20	Then *he* w back to Jerusalem.	8740
	23:29	of Egypt w up to the Euphrates River	6590
	25:21	So Judah w into captivity,	1655
1Ch	4:39	and *they* w to the outskirts of Gedor to	2143
	7:21	when *they* w down to seize their livestock.	3718
	10:12	all their valiant men w and took the bodies	7756
	11: 6	Joab son of Zeruiah w up first,	6590
	11:19	the blood of these men who w at the risk	NIH
	11:22	He also w down into a pit on a snowy day	3718
	11:23	Benaiah w against him with a club.	3718
	12:17	David w out to meet them and said to them,	3655
	12:19	of Manasseh defected to David when he w	995
	12:20	When David w to Ziklag,	2143
	13: 6	and all the Israelites with him w to Baalah	6590
	14: 8	*they* w up in full force to search for him,	6590
	14: 8	but David heard about it and w out	3655
	14:11	David and *his men* w up to Baal Perazim,	6590
	15:25	of units of a thousand w to bring up the ark	2143
	17:16	King David w in and sat before the LORD,	995
	17:21	the one nation on earth whose God w out	2143
	18: 3	when he w to establish his control along	2143
	18: 6	LORD gave David victory everywhere he w.	2143
	18:13	LORD gave David victory everywhere *he* w	2143
	19:15	before his brother Abishai and w inside	995
	19:15	So Joab w back to Jerusalem.	995
	20: 1	of the Ammonites and w to Rabbah	995
	21: 4	and w throughout Israel and then came back	2143
	21:11	So Gad w to David and said to him,	995
	21:19	So David w up in obedience to the word	6590
2Ch	1: 3	and the whole assembly w to the high place	2143
	1: 6	Solomon w up to the bronze altar before	6590
	1:13	Then Solomon w to Jerusalem from	995
	8: 3	then w to Hamath Zobah and captured it.	2143
	8:17	Then Solomon w to Ezion Geber and Elath	2143
	9:15	six hundred bekas of hammered gold w	6590
	10: 1	Rehoboam w to Shechem,	2143
	10: 3	and all Israel w to Rehoboam and said	995
	10: 5	So the people w away.	2143
	10:16	So all the Israelites w home.	2143

2Ch	12:11	the king w to the LORD's temple,	995
	12:11	the guards w with him, bearing the shields,	995
	13: 3	Abijah w into battle with a force	673
	14:10	Asa w out to meet him,	3655
	15: 2	*He* w out to meet Asa and said to him,	3655
	16: 1	of Asa's reign Baasha king of Israel w up	6590
	17: 9	*they* w around to all the towns of Judah	6015
	18: 2	Some years later *he* w down to visit Ahab	3718
	18:23	of Kenaanah w up and slapped Micaiah	5602
	18:23	the LORD go when he w from me to speak	NIH
	18:28	and Jehoshaphat king of Judah w up	6590
	18:29	the king of Israel disguised himself and w	995
	19: 2	w out to meet him and said to the king,	3655
	19: 4	and *he* w out again among the people	3655
	20:21	the splendor of his holiness as they w out	3655
	20:25	and his men w to carry off their plunder,	995
	20:28	*They* entered Jerusalem and w to the temple	995
	21: 9	So Jehoram w there with his officers	6296
	22: 5	He also followed their counsel when he w	2143
	22: 6	king of Judah w down to Jezreel to see	3718
	22: 7	*he* w out with Joram to meet Jehu son	3655
	22: 9	He then w in search of Ahaziah,	1335
	23: 2	*They* w throughout Judah and gathered	6015
	23:12	*she* w to them at the temple of the LORD.	995
	23:17	All the people w to the temple of Baal	995
	23:20	*They* w into the palace through	995
	26: 6	*He* w to war against the Philistines	3655
	28: 9	and he w out to meet the army	3655
	29:15	*they* w in to purify the temple of the LORD,	995
	29:16	The priests w into the sanctuary of the LORD	995
	29:18	*they* w in to King Hezekiah and reported:	995
	29:20	and w up to the temple of the LORD.	6590
	30: 6	couriers w throughout Israel and Judah	2143
	30:10	The couriers w from town to town	6296
	30:11	and Zebulun humbled themselves and w	995
	31: 1	the Israelites who were there w out to	3655
	31: 5	As soon as the order w out,	7287
	32:21	And when *he* w into the temple of his god,	995
	34: 7	Then *he* w back to Jerusalem.	8740
	34: 9	*They* w to Hilkiah the high priest	995
	34:22	the king had sent with him w to speak to	2143
	34:30	He w up to the temple of the LORD with	6590
	35:20	of Egypt w up to fight at Carchemish on	6590
	35:22	but w to fight him on the plain of Megiddo.	995
Ezr	4:23	*they* w immediately to the Jews	10016
	5: 3	and Shethar-Bozenai and their associates w	10085
	5: 8	The king should know that *we* w to	10016
	10: 6	of God and w to the room of Jehohanan son	2143
Ne	2: 9	So *I* w to the governors of Trans-Euphrates	995
	2:11	*I* w to Jerusalem, and after staying there	995
	2:13	By night *I* w out through the Valley Gate	3655
	2:15	so *I* w up the valley by night,	6590
	3: 1	and his fellow priests w to work and rebuilt	7756
	4:23	even when he w for water.	NIH
	6:10	One day I w to the house of Shemaiah son	995
	8:12	Then all the people w away to eat and drink	2143
	8:16	So the people w out and brought back	3655
	9:24	Their sons w in and took possession of	995
Est	3:15	the couriers w out, and the edict was issued	3655
	4: 1	and w out into the city,	3655
	4: 2	But he w only as far as the king's gate,	995
	4: 6	So Hathach w out to Mordecai in	3655
	4: 9	Hathach w back and reported	995
	4:17	So Mordecai w away and carried out all	6296
	5: 5	So the king and Haman w to the banquet	995
	5: 9	Haman w out that day happy and	3655
	5:10	Haman restrained himself and w home.	995
	7: 1	and Haman w to dine with Queen Esther,	995
	7: 7	and w out into the palace garden.	NIH
	8:17	wherever the edict of the king w,	5595
Job	1:12	Then Satan w out from the presence of	3655
	2: 7	So Satan w out from the presence of	3655
	29: 7	"When I w to the gate of the city	3655
Ps	35:14	*I* w about mourning as though	2143
	66:12	we w through fire and water,	995
	68: 7	When you w out before your people,	3655
	81: 5	for Joseph when he w out against Egypt,	3655
	104: 8	*they* w down into the valleys,	3718
	105:30	which w up into the bedrooms	NIH
	107:23	*Others* w out on the sea in ships;	3718
	107:26	up to the heavens and w down to the depths;	3718
	119:67	Before I was afflicted I w astray,	8704
Pr	24:30	I w past the field of the sluggard,	6296
SS	6:11	*I* w down to the grove of nut trees to look at	3718
Isa	8: 3	Then *I* w to the prophetess,	7928
	16: 8	Their shoots spread out and w as far as	6296
	36: 3	and Joah son of Asaph the recorder w out	3655
	36:22	and Joah son of Asaph the recorder w to	995
	37: 1	and put on sackcloth and w into the temple	995
	37:14	Then he w up to the temple of the LORD	6590
	37:36	the angel of the LORD w out and put	3655
	38: 1	of Amoz w to him and said, "This is what	995
	38: 8	So the sunlight w back the ten steps	8740
	39: 3	Then Isaiah the prophet w to King Hezekiah	995
	52: 4	"At first my people w down to Egypt	3718
	57: 7	there *you* w up to offer your sacrifices.	6590
	57: 9	*You* w to Molech with olive oil	8801
Jer	1: 3	when the people of Jerusalem w into exile.	1655
	3: 8	she also w out and committed adultery.	2143
	7:24	*They* w backward and not forward.	2118
	13: 5	So *I* w and hid it at Perath,	2143
	13: 7	So *I* w to Perath and dug up the belt	2143
	18: 3	So *I* w down to the potter's house,	3718
	22:16	and so all w well.	NIH
	22:16	and so all w well.	NIH
	26:10	*they* w up from the royal palace *to*	6590
	28: 4	and all the other exiles from Judah who w	995

Jer	28:11	At this, the prophet Jeremiah w on his way.	2143
	35: 3	So *I* w to get Jaazaniah son of Jeremiah,	AIT
	36:12	*he* w down to the secretary's room in	3718
	36:14	So Baruch son of Neriah w with	995
	36:20	*they* w to the king in the courtyard	995
	38: 8	Ebed-Melech w out of the palace and said	3655
	38:11	the men with him and w to a room under	995
	40: 6	So Jeremiah w to Gedaliah son of Ahikam	995
	41: 6	of Nethaniah w out from Mizpah	3655
	41: 6	to meet them, weeping *as he* w.	2143+2143
	41: 7	When they w into the city,	995
	41:12	and w to fight Ishmael son of Nethaniah.	2143
	41:14	and w over to Johanan son of Kareah.	2143
	41:17	And *they* w on, stopping at Geruth Kimham	2143
	43: 7	in disobedience to the LORD and w to	995
	51:59	when he w to Babylon with Zedekiah king	2143
	52:27	So Judah w into captivity,	1655
Eze	1: 9	Each one w straight ahead;	2143
	1:12	Each one w straight ahead.	2143
	1:12	they would go, without turning as they w.	2143
	1:17	not turn about as the creatures w.	2143
	3:14	and *I* w in bitterness and in the anger	2143
	3:23	So I got up and w out to the plain.	3655
	8:10	So *I* w in and looked,	995
	9: 3	of Israel w up from above the cherubim,	6590
	9: 7	So *they* w out and began killing throughout	3655
	10: 2	And as I watched, he w in.	995
	10: 3	of the temple when the man w in,	995
	10: 6	the man w in and stood beside a wheel.	995
	10: 7	who took it and w out.	3655
	10:11	not turn about as the cherubim w.	2143
	10:11	The cherubim w in whatever direction	2143
	10:11	without turning as they w.	2143
	10:19	and as they w, the wheels went with them.	3655
	10:19	and as they went, the wheels w with them.	NIH
	10:22	Each one w straight ahead.	2143
	11:23	The glory of the LORD w up from within	6590
	11:24	Then the vision I had seen w up from me,	6590
	17:12	'The king of Babylon w to Jerusalem	995
	23:13	both of them w the same way.	NIH
	25: 3	the people of Judah when *they* w into exile,	2143
	27:33	When your merchandise w out on the seas,	3655
	31: 7	for its roots w down to abundant waters.	2118
	32:24	w down uncircumcised to the earth	3718
	32:27	who w down *to* the grave	3718
	32:30	*they* w down with the slain in disgrace	3718
	36:20	And wherever *they* w among the nations	995
	39:23	that the people of Israel w into exile	1655
	40: 6	Then he w to the gate facing east.	995
	41: 3	Then he w into the inner sanctuary	995
	41: 7	so that the rooms widened as one w upward.	NIH
	41: 7	A stairway w up from the lowest floor to	6590
	44:10	" 'The Levites who w far from me	8178
	44:10	when Israel w astray and who wandered	9494
	44:15	the Israelites w astray from me, are to come	9494
	47: 3	the man w eastward with a measuring line	3655
	48:11	when the Israelites w astray.	9494
Da	2:16	Daniel w in *to* the king and asked for time,	10549
	2:24	Then Daniel w to Arioch,	10549
	2:30	and that you may understand what w	NIH
	6: 6	and the satraps w as a group to the king	10656
	6:10	he w home to his upstairs room where	10549
	6:11	Then these men w as a group	10656
	6:12	So *they* w to the king and spoke to him	10638
	6:15	the men w as a group to the king and said	10656
	8:27	I got up and w about the king's business.	6913
Hos	2:13	and w after her lovers, but me she forgot,"	2143
	11: 2	the further they w from me.	2143
Jnh	1: 3	*He* w down to Joppa,	3718
	1: 3	*he* w aboard and sailed for Tarshish	928+3718
	1: 6	The captain w to him and said,	7928
	3: 3	the word of the LORD w to Nineveh.	2143
	4: 5	Jonah w out and sat down at a place east of	3655
Na	2:11	where the lion and lioness w, and the cubs,	2143
	3:10	Yet she was taken captive and w into exile.	2143
Hab	3: 5	Plague w before him;	2143
Hag	2:16	*When anyone* w to a wine vat	995
Zec	6: 7	When the powerful horses w out,	3655
	6: 7	So *they* w throughout the earth.	2143
Mt	2: 9	on their way,	4513
	2: 9	the star they had seen in the east w ahead of	4575
	2:21	and his mother and w to the land of Israel.	1656
	2:23	he w and lived in a town called Nazareth.	2262
	3: 5	People w out to him from Jerusalem	1744
	3:16	he w up out of the water.	326
	4:13	he w and lived in Capernaum,	2262
	4:23	Jesus w throughout Galilee,	4310
	5: 1	he w up on a mountainside and sat down.	326
	8:25	The disciples w and woke him, saying,	4665
	8:32	So they came out and w into the pigs,	599
	8:33	w into the town and reported all this,	599
	8:34	Then the whole town w out to meet Jesus.	2002
	9: 7	And the man got up and w home.	599
	9: 9	*As Jesus* w on from there,	4135
	9:19	Jesus got up and w with him,	199
	9:25	he w in and took the girl by the hand,	1656
	9:27	*As Jesus* w on from there,	4135
	9:31	But they w out and spread the news	2002
	9:35	Jesus w through all the towns and villages,	4310
	11: 1	*he* w on from there to teach and preach in	3553
	12: 1	that time Jesus w through the grainfields on	4513
	12: 9	he w into their synagogue,	2262
	12:14	But the Pharisees w out and plotted	2002
	12:15	That same day Jesus w out of the house	2002
	13: 3	"A farmer w out to sow his seed.	2002
	13:25	sowed weeds among the wheat, and w away.	599
	13:36	Then *he* left the crowd and w into the house.	2262

Mt	13:44	in his joy **w** and sold all he had and bought	5632

Mt 13:44 in his joy **w** and sold all he had and bought 5632
13:46 he **w** away and sold everything he had 599
14:12 Then they **w** and told Jesus. 2262
14:23 *he* **w** up on a mountainside by himself 326
14:25 the fourth watch of the night Jesus **w** out 599
15:29 Jesus left there and **w** along the Sea 2262
15:29 he **w** up on a mountainside and sat down. 326
15:39 the boat and **w** to the vicinity of Magadan. 2262
16: 4 Jesus then left them and **w** away. 599
16: 5 *When they* **w** across the lake, 2262
18:28 "But *when* that servant **w** out, 2002
18:30 he **w** off and had the man thrown 599
18:31 and **w** and told their master everything 2262
19: 1 he left Galilee and **w** into the region 2262
19:15 *he* **w** on from there. 4513
19:22 he **w** away sad, because he had great wealth. 599
20: 1 like a landowner who **w** out early in 2002
20: 3 "About the third hour he **w** out 2002
20: 5 So they **w**. 599
20: 5 "He **w** out again about the sixth hour and 2002
20: 6 About the eleventh hour he **w** out 2002
21: 6 The disciples **w** and did as Jesus had 4513
21: 9 The crowds that **w** ahead of him and those 4575
21:17 And he left them and **w** out of the city 2002
21:19 *he* **w** up to it but found nothing 2262
21:28 He **w** to the first and said, 'Son, 4665
21:29 but later he changed his mind and **w**. 599
21:30 "Then the father **w** to the other son and said 4665
21:33 and **w** away on a journey. 623
22: 5 "But *they* paid no attention and **w** off— 599
22:10 So the servants **w** out into the streets 2002
22:15 The Pharisees **w** out and laid plans 4513
22:22 So *they* left him and **w** away. 599
25: 1 and **w** out to meet the bridegroom. 2002
25:10 The virgins who were ready **w** in with him 1656
25:15 Then he **w** on *his* journey. 623
25:16 the five talents **w** at once and put his money 4513
25:18 man who had received the one talent **w** off, 599
25:25 and **w** out and hid your talent in the ground. 599
26:14 Judas Iscariot—**w** to the chief priests 4513
26:30 they **w** out to the Mount of Olives. 2002
26:36 Then Jesus **w** with his disciples to 2262
26:42 He **w** away a second time and prayed, 599
26:44 So he left them and **w** away once more 599
26:71 Then *he* **w** out to the gateway, 2002
26:73 those standing there **w** up to Peter and said, 4665
26:75 And *he* **w** outside and wept bitterly. 2002
27: 5 Then he **w** away and hanged himself. 599
27:53 and after Jesus' resurrection *they* **w** into 1656
27:60 of the entrance to the tomb and **w** away. 599
27:62 chief priests and the Pharisees **w** to Pilate. 5251
27:66 So they **w** and made the tomb secure 4513
28: 1 and the other Mary **w** to look at the tomb. 2262
28:11 of the guards **w** into the city and reported to 2262
28:16 Then the eleven disciples **w** to Galilee, 4513
Mk 1: 5 the people of Jerusalem **w** out to him. 1744
1:14 Jesus **w** into Galilee, 2262
1:21 They **w** to Capernaum, 1660
1:21 Jesus **w** into the synagogue and began 1656
1:29 *they* **w** with James and John to the home 2262
1:31 So *he* **w** to her, took her hand and 4665
1:35 left the house and **w** off to a solitary place, 599
1:36 Simon and his companions **w** to look for AIT
1:45 Instead he **w** out and began to talk freely, 2002
2:13 Once again Jesus **w** out beside the lake. 2002
3: 1 Another time *he* **w** into the synagogue, 1656
3: 6 Then the Pharisees **w** out and began to plot 2002
3:13 Jesus **w** up on a mountainside and called 326
3:21 *they* **w** to take charge of him, for they said, 2002
4: 3 "Listen! A farmer **w** out to sow his seed. 2002
5: 1 They **w** across the lake to the region of 2262
5:13 evil spirits came out and **w** into the pigs. 1656
5:14 the *people* **w** out to see what had happened. 2262
5:20 So the *man* **w** away and began to tell in 599
5:24 So Jesus **w** with him. 599
5:39 He **w** in and said to them, 1656
5:40 and **w** in where the child was. 1660
6: 1 Jesus left there and **w** to his hometown, 2262
6: 6 Then Jesus **w** around teaching from village 4310
6:12 They **w** out and preached 2002
6:24 She **w** out and said to her mother, 2002
6:27 The man **w**, beheaded John in the prison, 599
6:32 So *they* **w** away by themselves in a boat to 599
6:46 *he* **w** up on a mountainside to pray. 599
6:48 the fourth watch of the night *he* **w** out 2262
6:56 And wherever *he* **w**—into villages, 1660
7:20 He **w** on: "What comes out of a 3306
7:24 Jesus left that place and **w** to the vicinity 599
7:30 She **w** home and found her child lying on 599
7:31 Then Jesus left the vicinity of Tyre and **w** 2262
8:10 he got into the boat with his disciples and **w** 2262
8:27 Jesus and his disciples **w** on to the villages 2002
10: 1 and **w** into the region of Judea and across 2262
10:22 *He* **w** away sad, because he had great wealth. 599
11: 4 *They* **w** and found a colt outside in 599
11: 9 Those who **w** ahead and those who followed 4575
11:11 Jesus entered Jerusalem and **w** to the temple. NIG
11:11 *he* **w** out to Bethany with the Twelve. 2002
11:13 *he* **w** to find out if it had any fruit. 2262
11:19 When evening came, *they* **w** out of the city. 1744
11:20 In the morning, *as they* **w** along, 4182
12: 1 and **w** away on a journey. 623
12:12 so *they* left him and **w** away. 599
14:10 **w** to the chief priests to betray Jesus 599
14:16 **w** into the city and found things just 2262
14:26 *they* **w** out to the Mount of Olives. 2002
14:32 They **w** to a place called Gethsemane, 2262

Mk 14:39 Once more he **w** away and prayed 599
14:68 he said, and **w** out into the entryway. 2002+2032
15:43 **w** boldly to Pilate and asked for Jesus' body 1656
16: 8 the women **w** out and fled from the tomb. 2002
16:10 She **w** and told those who had been 4513
16:10 disciples **w** out and preached everywhere, 2002
Lk 1:28 The angel **w** to her and said, "Greetings, 1656
2: 3 everyone **w** to his own town to register. 4513
2: 4 also **w** up from the town of Nazareth 326
2: 5 He **w** there to register with Mary, NIG
2:27 *he* **w** into the temple courts. 2262
2:41 Every year his parents **w** to Jerusalem for 4513
2:42 they **w** up to the Feast, 326
2:45 *they* **w** back to Jerusalem to look for him. 5715
2:51 Then he **w** down to Nazareth with them 2849
3: 3 *He* **w** into all the country around the Jordan, 2262
4:16 *He* **w** to Nazareth, 2262
4:16 the Sabbath day he **w** into the synagogue, 1656
4:30 through the crowd and **w** on his way. 4513
4:31 Then he **w** down to Capernaum, 2982
4:38 Jesus left the synagogue and **w** to the home 1656
4:42 At daybreak Jesus **w** out to a solitary place. 4513
5:19 *they* **w** up on the roof and lowered him 326
5:25 on and **w** home praising God. 599
5:27 Jesus **w** out and saw a tax collector by 2002
6: 6 On another Sabbath he **w** into the synagogue 1656
6:12 of those days Jesus **w** out to a mountainside 2002
6:17 He **w** down with them and stood on 2849
7: 6 So Jesus **w** with them. 4513
7:11 Jesus **w** to a town called Nain, 4513
7:11 and a large crowd **w** along with him. 5233
7:13 *his* **heart** **w** out to her and he said, 5072
7:14 Then he **w** up and touched the coffin, 4665
7:36 so he **w** to the Pharisee's house and reclined 1656
8: 5 "A farmer **w** out to sow his seed. 2002
8:24 The disciples **w** and woke him, saying, 4665
8:33 came out of the man, *they* **w** into the pigs, 1656
8:35 the *people* **w** out to see what had happened. 2002
8:39 So the man **w** away and told all over town 599
9: 6 *they* set out and **w** from village to village, 1451
9:28 with him and **w** up onto a mountain to pray. 326
9:52 who **w** into a Samaritan village 1656+4513
9:56 and *they* **w** to another village. 4513
10:30 beat him and **w** away, 599
10:34 *He* **w** to him and bandaged his wounds, 4665
11:37 so he **w** in and reclined at the table. 1656
13: 6 and *he* **w** to look for fruit on it, 2262
13:22 Jesus **w** through the towns and villages, 1388
14: 1 when Jesus **w** to eat in the house of 2262
15:15 So he **w** and hired himself out to a citizen of 4513
15:20 So he got up and **w** to his father. 2262
15:28 So his father **w** out and pleaded with him. 2002
17:14 And as they **w**, they were cleansed. 5632
18:10 "Two men **w** up to the temple to pray, 326
18:14 **w** home justified before God. 2849
19:11 he **w** on to tell them a parable, 4707
19:12 "A man of noble birth **w** to a distant country 4513
19:28 After Jesus had said this, *he* **w** on ahead, 4513
19:32 Those who were sent ahead **w** 599
19:36 *As* he **w** along, people spread their cloaks 4513
20: 9 *He* **w** on to tell the people this parable: 806
20: 9 some farmers and **w** away for a long time. 623
21:37 each evening he **w** out to spend the night 2002
22: 4 And Judas **w** to the chief priests and 4665
22:39 Jesus **w** out as usual to the Mount 2002+4513
22:45 When he rose from prayer and **w** back to 2262
22:62 And he **w** outside and wept bitterly. 2002
23:48 *they* beat their breasts and **w** away. 5715
23:56 Then they **w** home and prepared spices AIT
24: 1 the spices they had prepared and **w** to 2262
24:12 and *he* **w** away, wondering to himself 599
24:22 They **w** to the tomb early this morning 1181
24:24 Then some of our companions **w** to 599
24:29 So *he* **w** in to stay with them. 1656
Jn 1:39 So *they* **w** and saw where he was staying, 2262
2:12 After this *he* **w** down to Capernaum 2849
2:13 Jesus **w** up to Jerusalem. 326
3:22 Jesus and his disciples **w** out into 2262
4: 3 he left Judea and **w** back once more 599
4:28 the woman **w** back to the town and said to 599
4:47 *he* **w** to him and begged him to come 599
5: 1 Jesus **w** up to Jerusalem for a feast of 326
5:15 The man **w** away and told the Jews 599
6: 3 Then Jesus **w** up on a mountainside and sat 456
6:16 his disciples **w** down to the lake, 2849
6:24 they got into the boats and **w** to Capernaum 2262
6:65 *He* **w** on to *say*, "This is why I told you AIT
7: 1 After this, Jesus **w** around in Galilee, 4344
7:10 his brothers had left for the Feast, he **w** also, 326
7:45 temple guards **w** back to the chief priests 2262
7:53 Then each **w** to his own home. 4513
8: 1 But Jesus **w** to the Mount of Olives. 4513
9: 1 *As he* **w** along, he saw a man blind 4135
9: 7 man **w** and washed, and came home seeing. 599
9:11 So *I* **w** and washed, and then I could see." 599
10:40 Then Jesus **w** back across the Jordan to 599
11:11 After he had said this, he **w** on to tell them, NIG
11:20 *she* **w** out to meet him, 5636
11:28 she **w** back and called her sister Mary aside. 599
11:29 she got up quickly and **w** to him. 2262
11:31 noticed how quickly she got up and **w** out, 2002
11:46 But some of them **w** to the Pharisees 599
11:55 many **w** up from the country to Jerusalem 326
12:13 They took palm branches and **w** out 2002
12:18 this miraculous sign, **w** out to meet him. 5636
12:20 who **w** up to worship at the Feast. 326
12:22 Philip **w** to tell Andrew; 2262

Jn 13:30 as Judas had taken the bread, *he* **w** out. 2002
18: 1 and he and his disciples **w** into it. 1656
18: 4 **w** out and asked them, 2002
18:15 *he* **w** with Jesus into the high priest's 5291
18:33 Pilate then **w** back inside the palace, 1656
18:38 With this *he* **w** out again to the Jews 2002
19: 3 and **w** up to him *again and again*, 2262
19: 9 and *he* **w** back inside the palace. 1656
19:17 *he* **w** to the place of the Skull 2002
20: 1 Mary Magdalene **w** to the tomb and saw 2262
20: 6 arrived and **w** into the tomb. 1656
20: 8 reached the tomb first, also **w** inside. 1656
20:10 Then the disciples **w** back to their homes, 599
20:18 Mary Magdalene **w** to the disciples with 2262
21: 3 So *they* **w** out and got into the boat, 2002
21:18 and **w** where you wanted; 4344
Ac 1:13 *they* **w** upstairs to the room 326
1:21 the whole time the Lord Jesus **w** in and out 1656
3: 8 Then *he* **w** with them into the temple courts, 1656
4:23 Peter and John **w** back to their own people 2262
5:22 So they **w** back and reported, 418
5:26 the captain **w** with his officers and brought 599
7:15 Then Jacob **w** down to Egypt, 2849
7:24 so he **w** to *his* defense and avenged him 310
7:31 *As* he **w** over to look more closely, 4665
8: 4 the word wherever *they* **w**. 1451
8: 5 Philip **w** down to a city in Samaria 2982
8:38 Then both Philip and the eunuch **w** down 2849
8:39 but **w** on his way rejoicing. 4513
9: 1 *He* **w** to the high priest 4665
9:17 Then Ananias **w** to the house and entered it. 599
9:32 he **w** to visit the saints in Lydda. 2982
9:39 Peter **w** with them, and when he arrived 5302
10: 9 Peter **w** up on the roof to pray. 326
10:21 Peter **w** down and said to the men, 2849
10:23 some of the brothers from Joppa **w** along. 5302
10:27 Peter **w** inside and found a large gathering 1656
10:38 and how he **w** around doing good 1451
11: 2 So when Peter **w** up to Jerusalem, 326
11: 3 You **w** into the house of uncircumcised men 1656
11:12 These six brothers also **w** with me, 2262
11:20 **w** to Antioch and began to speak to Greeks 2262
11:25 Then Barnabas **w** to Tarsus to look for Saul, 2002
12:10 and *they* **w** through it. 2002
12:12 he **w** to the house of Mary the mother 2262
12:19 Then Herod **w** from Judea to Caesarea 2982
13: 4 **w** down to Seleucia and sailed from there 2982
13:14 Perga they **w** on to Pisidian Antioch, 1451+4134
13:51 in protest against them and **w** to Iconium. 2262
14: 1 **w** as usual *into* the Jewish synagogue. 1656
14:20 he got up and **w** back into the city. 1656
14:25 *they* **w** down to Attalia. 2849
15:24 We have heard that some **w** out from us 2002
15:30 The men were sent off and **w** down 2982
15:41 *He* **w** through Syria and Cilicia, 1451
16: 8 they passed by Mysia and **w** down to Troas. 2849
16:13 On the Sabbath *we* **w** outside the city gate to 2002
16:40 *they* **w** to Lydia's house, 1656
17: 2 Paul **w** into the synagogue, 1656
17:10 they **w** to the Jewish synagogue. 583
17:13 *he* **w** there too, agitating the crowds 2262
18: 1 this, Paul left Athens and **w** to Corinth. 2262
18: 2 Paul **w** to see them, 4665
18: 7 Paul left the synagogue and **w** next door to 1656
18:19 *He* himself **w** into the synagogue 1656
18:22 he **w** up and greeted the church and 326
18:22 up and greeted the church and then **w** down 2849
19:10 This **w** on for two years, 1181
19:13 Some Jews who **w** around driving out 4320
20: 5 These men **w** on ahead and waited for us 4601
20:10 Paul **w** down, threw himself on 2849
20:11 *he* **w** upstairs again and broke bread and 326
20:13 We **w** on ahead to the ship and sailed 4601
20:14 *we* took him aboard and **w** on to Mitylene. 2262
21: 1 The next day *we* **w** to Rhodes and 2262
21: 2 **w** on board and set sail. 2094
21: 6 *we* **w** aboard the ship, 326
21:15 *we* got ready and **w** up to Jerusalem. 326
21:18 The next day Paul and the rest of us **w** 1655
21:26 Then *he* **w** to the temple to give notice of 1655
22: 5 and **w** there to bring these people 4513
22:19 that I **w** from one synagogue to another 1639
22:26 *he* **w** to the commander and reported it. 4665
22:27 The commander **w** to Paul and asked, 4665
23:14 They **w** to the chief priests and elders 4665
23:16 he **w** into the barracks and told Paul. 1656
24: 1 the high priest Ananias **w** down to Caesarea 2849
24:11 that no more than twelve days ago *I* **w** up 326
25: 1 Festus **w** up from Caesarea to Jerusalem, 326
25: 6 *he* **w** down to Caesarea, 2849
25:15 *When* I **w** to Jerusalem, 1181
26:11 a time I **w** from one synagogue to another NIG
26:11 I even **w** to foreign cities to persecute them. NIG
28: 8 Paul **w** in to see him and, after prayer, 1656
2Co 2:12 Now *when* I **w** to Troas to preach the gospel 2262
2:13 So I said good-by to them and **w** on 2002
Gal 1:17 but I **w** immediately into Arabia 599
1:18 *I* **w** up to Jerusalem to get acquainted 456
1:21 Later *I* **w** to Syria and Cilicia. 2262
2: 1 Fourteen years later *I* **w** up again 326
2: 2 *I* **w** in response to a revelation and set 326
1Ti 1: 3 As I urged you *when* I **w** into Macedonia, 4513
Heb 6:20 who **w** before us, has entered on our behalf. 4596
9:11 he **w** through the greater and more perfect NIG
11: 8 obeyed and **w**, even though he did not know 2002
11:37 *They* **w** about in sheepskins and goatskins, 4320
1Pe 3:19 through whom also he **w** and preached to 4513

1Jn	2:19	*They* w out from us, but they did not	2002
3Jn	1: 7	for the sake of the Name that *they* w out,	2002
Rev	8: 4	w up before God from the angel's hand.	326
	10: 9	So *I* w to the angel and asked him	599
	11:12	And *they* w up to heaven in a cloud,	326
	12:17	the woman and w off to make war against	599
	16: 2	The first angel w and poured out his bowl	599

WEPT (53) [WEEP]

Ge	27:38	Then Esau w aloud.	1134
	33: 4	and kissed him. And *they* w.	1134
	37:35	So his father w for him.	1134
	43:30	He went into his private room and w there.	1134
	45: 2	And he w so loudly	906+928+1140+5989+7754
	45:14	around his brother Benjamin and w,	1134
	45:15	he kissed all his brothers and w over them.	1134
	46:29	he threw his arms around his father and w	1134
	50: 1	Joseph threw himself upon his father and w	1134
	50:17	When their message came to him, Joseph w.	1134
Nu	14: 1	community raised their voices and w aloud.	1134
Dt	1:45	You came back and w before the LORD,	1134
Jdg	2: 4	the people w aloud,	1134
	11:38	She and the girls went into the hills and w	1134
	20:23	up and w before the LORD until evening,	1134
Ru	1: 9	Then she kissed them and *they* w aloud	1134
	1:14	At this *they* w again.	1134
1Sa	1: 7	her rival provoked her till *she* w and	1134
	1:10	Hannah w much and prayed to	1134+1134
	11: 4	they all w aloud.	1134
	20:41	they kissed each other and w together—	1134
	20:41	but David the most.	NIH
	24:16	And he w aloud.	1134
	30: 4	So David and his men w aloud	1134
2Sa	1:12	They mourned and w and fasted till evening	1134
	3:32	and the king w aloud at Abner's tomb.	1134
	3:32	All the people w also.	1134
	3:34	And all the people w over him again.	1134
	12:21	While the child was alive, you fasted and w,	1134
	12:22	I fasted and w.	1134
	13:36	and all his servants w very bitterly.	1134+1140
	15:23	The whole countryside w aloud as all	1134
	18:33	up to the room over the gateway and w.	1134
2Ki	13:14	of Israel went down to see him and w	1134
	20: 3	And Hezekiah w bitterly.	1134+1140
	22:19	you tore your robes and w in my presence,	1134
2Ch	34:27	and tore your robes and w in my presence,	1134
Ezr	3:12	w aloud when they saw the foundation	1134
	10: 1	They too w bitterly.	1134+1135+2221
Ne	1: 4	I sat down and w.	1134
Job	30:25	*Have I* not w for those in trouble?	1134
Ps	137: 1	By the rivers of Babylon we sat and w	1134
Isa	38: 3	And Hezekiah w bitterly.	1134+1140
Hos	12: 4	*he* w and begged for his favor.	1134
Mt	26:75	And he went outside and w bitterly.	3081
Mk	14:72	And he broke down and w.	3081
Lk	19:41	and saw the city, *he* w over it	3081
	22:62	And he went outside and w bitterly.	3081
Jn	11:35	Jesus w.	1233
	20:11	As *she* w, she bent over to look into	3081
Ac	20:37	*They* all w as they embraced	1181+2653+3088
Rev	5: 4	I w and wept because no one	3081+4498
	5: 4	I wept and w because no one	3081+4498

WERE (2530) [BE] See Index of Articles Etc.

WEREN'T (1) [BE, NOT]

Da	3:24	"W there three men that we tied up	10379

WEST (96) [NORTHWEST, SOUTHWEST, WESTERN, WESTWARD]

Ge	12: 8	with Bethel on the w and Ai on the east.	3542
	13:14	and look north and south, east and w.	2025+3542
	28:14	you will spread out to the w and to the east,	3542
Ex	10:19	the wind to a very strong w wind,	3542
	26:22	that is, the w end of the tabernacle,	2025+3542
	26:27	and five for the frames on the w,	3542
	27:12	"The w end of the courtyard shall	3542
	36:27	that is, the w end of the tabernacle,	2025+3542
	36:32	and five for the frames on the w,	3542
	38:12	The w end was fifty cubits wide	3542
Nu	2:18	On the w will be the divisions of the camp	3542
	3:23	Gershonite clans were to camp on the w,	3542
	34: 6	This will be your boundary on the w.	3542
	35: 5	three thousand on the w and three thousand	3542
Dt	3:27	top of Pisgah and look w and north	2025+3542
	11:30	w of the road, toward the setting sun,	339
Jos	1: 4	to the Great Sea on the w.	2021+4427+9087
	5: 1	all the Amorite kings w of the Jordan	2025+3542
	8: 9	to the w of Ai—	3542
	8:12	to the w of the city.	3542
	8:13	of the city and the ambush to the w of it.	3542
	9: 1	all the kings w of the Jordan heard	928+6298
	11: 2	and in Naphoth Dor on the w;	3542
	11: 3	to the Canaanites in the east and w;	3542
	12: 7	on the w side of the Jordan, from Baal Gad	3542
	15: 8	top of the hill w of the Hinnom Valley	2025+3542
	15:46	w of Ekron, all that were in the vicinity	3542
	16: 8	border went w to the Kanah Ravine	2025+3542
	18:12	slope of Jericho and headed w	2025+3542
	18:15	at the outskirts of Kiriath Jearim on the w,	3542
	19:11	Going w it ran to Maralah,	2025+3542
	19:26	On the w the boundary touched Carmel	3542
	19:34	The boundary ran w through Aznoth	2025+3542
	19:34	Asher on the w and the Jordan on the east.	3542

Jos	22: 7	gave land on the w side of the Jordan	2025+3542
	23: 4	the Jordan and the Great Sea in the w.	4427+9087
Jdg	18:12	This is why the place w of Kiriath Jearim	339
	20:33	of its place on the w of Gibeah.	3542
2Sa	13:34	and saw many people on the road w of him,	339
1Ki	4:24	For he ruled over all the kingdoms w of	6298
	7:25	three facing north, three facing w,	2025+3542
1Ch	7:28	Gezer and its villages to the w,	5115
	9:24	four sides: east, w, north and south.	2025+3542
	12:15	to the east and to the w.	5115
	26:16	for the W Gate and the Shalleketh Gate on	5115
	26:18	As for the court to the w,	5115
	26:30	Israel w of the Jordan for all the work	4946+6298
2Ch	4: 4	three facing north, three facing w,	2025+3542
	32:30	and channeled the water down to the w side	5115
	33:14	w of the Gihon spring in the valley,	2025+5115
Job	20:20	*Men of the w* are appalled at his fate;	340
	23: 8	if I go to the w, I do not find him.	294
Ps	75: 6	the east or the w or from the desert can exalt	5115
	103:12	as far as the east is from the w,	5115
	107: 3	from east and w, from north and south.	5115
Isa	9:12	the w have devoured Israel	294
	11:14	down on the slopes of Philistia to the w;	3542
	24:14	the w they acclaim the LORD's majesty.	3542
	43: 5	from the east and gather you from the w,	5115
	49:12	some from the north, some from the w,	3542
	59:19	From the w, men will fear the name of	5115
Eze	41:12	on the w side was seventy cubits wide.	3542
	42:19	Then he turned to the w side and measured;	3542
	45: 7	the w side and eastward from the east side,	3542
	47:20	"On the w side, the Great Sea will be the	3542
	47:20	This will be the w boundary.	3542
	48: 1	from the east side to the w *side*.	3542
	48: 2	the territory of Dan from east to w.	2025+3542
	48: 3	the territory of Asher from east to w.	2025+3542
	48: 4	territory of Naphtali from east to w.	2025+3542
	48: 5	territory of Manasseh from east to w.	2025+3542
	48: 6	territory of Ephraim from east to w.	2025+3542
	48: 7	the territory of Reuben from east to w.	2025+3542
	48: 8	the territory of Judah from east to w.	2025+3542
	48: 8	its length from east to w will equal	2025+3542
	48:10	10,000 cubits wide on the w *side*,	3542
	48:16	and the w side 4,500 cubits.	2025+3542
	48:17	and 250 cubits on the w.	3542
	48:18	and 10,000 cubits on the w *side*.	3542
	48:23	from the east side to the w side.	3542
	48:24	territory of Benjamin from east to w.	2025+3542
	48:25	territory of Simeon from east to w.	2025+3542
	48:26	territory of Issachar from east to w.	2025+3542
	48:27	territory of Zebulun from east to w.	2025+3542
	48:34	"On the w side, which is 4,500 cubits long,	3542
Da	8: 4	toward the w and the north and the south.	3542
	8: 5	between his eyes came from the w,	5115
Hos	11:10	his children will come trembling from the w	3542
Zec	6: 6	the one with the white horses toward the w,	339
	8: 7	the countries of the east and the w,	4427+9087
	14: 4	be split in two from east to w,	3542
Mt	8:11	from the east and the w,	1553
	24:27	from the east is visible even in the w,	1553
Lk	12:54	"When you see a cloud rising in the w,	1553
	13:29	People will come from east and w and north	1553
Rev	21:13	three on the south and three on the w.	1553

WESTERN (26) [WEST]

Nu	34: 6	" 'Your w boundary will be the coast of	3542
Dt	1: 7	in the mountains, in the w foothills,	9169
	3:17	Its w border was the Jordan	2025+4667[S]
	11:24	and from the Euphrates River to the w sea.	340
	34: 2	all the land of Judah as far as the w sea,	340
Jos	9: 1	the w foothills, and along the entire coast	9169
	10:40	the w foothills and the mountain slopes,	9169
	11: 2	in the w foothills and in Naphoth Dor on	9169
	11:16	whole region of Goshen, the w foothills,	9169
	12: 8	the w foothills, the Arabah,	9169
	15:12	The w boundary is the coastline of	3542
	15:33	In the w foothills: Eshtaol, Zorah,	9169
	18:14	the boundary turned south along the w side	3542
	18:14	This was the w side.	3542
Jdg	1: 9	the Negev and the w foothills.	9169
1Ch	27:28	and sycamore-fig trees in the w foothills.	9169
Jer	17:26	of Benjamin and the w foothills,	9169
	32:44	of the w foothills and of the Negev,	9169
	33:13	of the w foothills and of the Negev,	9169
Eze	45: 7	the w to the eastern border parallel to one of	3542
	46:19	and showed me a place at the w end.	2025+3542
	48:21	25,000 cubits to the w border.	2025+3542
Da	11:30	Ships of the w coastlands will oppose him,	4183
Joel	2:20	and those in the rear into the w sea.	340
Zec	7: 7	and the w foothills were settled?' "	9169
	14: 8	half to the eastern sea and half to the w sea,	340

WESTWARD (4) [WEST]

Jos	15:10	curved w from Baalah to Mount Seir,	2025+3542
	16: 3	descended w to the territory of	2025+3542
Eze	45: 7	It will extend w from the west side	2025+3542
	48:21	and w from the 25,000 cubits to	2025+3542

WET (3)

Job	31:38	and all its furrows *are* w with tears,	1134
Lk	7:38	she began *to* w his feet with her tears.	1101
	7:44	but she w my feet with her tears	1101

WHALE, WHALE'S, WHALES (KJV)
See CREATURES, HUGE FISH, MONSTER

WHAT (2501) [SOMEWHAT, WHAT'S, WHATEVER]

Ge	2:19	to the man to see w he would name them;	4537
	3:13	"W is this you have done?"	4537
	4: 7	If *you* do w is right,	3512
	4: 7	But if *you do* not do w is right,	3512
	4:10	The LORD said, "W have you done?	4537
	9:24	and found out w his youngest son had done	889
	12:11	"I know w a beautiful woman you are.	3954
	12:18	"W have you done to me?"	4537
	14:24	but w my men have eaten and the share	889
	15: 2	w can you give me since I remain childless	4537
	16: 2	Abram agreed to w Sarai *said*.	7754
	18:17	"Shall I hide from Abraham w I am about	889
	18:19	of the LORD by doing w is right and just,	AIT
	18:19	for Abraham w he has promised him."	889
	18:21	down and see if w they have *done* is as bad	AIT
	18:24	W if there are fifty righteous people in	218
	18:28	w if the number of the righteous is five less	218
	18:29	"W if only forty are found there?"	218
	18:30	"W if only thirty can be found there?"	218
	18:31	w if only twenty can be found there?"	218
	18:32	"W if only ten can be found there?"	218
	19: 8	and you can do w you like with them.	3869
	20: 9	"W have you done to us?	4537
	20:10	"W was your reason for doing this?"	4537
	21: 1	LORD did for Sarah w he had promised.	889+3869
	21:17	"W is the matter, Hagar?	3871+4200+4537
	21:29	"W is the meaning of these seven ewe	2179+4537
	23:15	but w is that between me and you?	4537
	24: 5	"W if the woman is unwilling to come back	218
	24:30	and had heard Rebekah tell w the man said	3907
	24:33	until I have told you w I *have to say*."	1821
	24:39	'W if the woman will not come back	218
	24:52	When Abraham's servant heard w they *said*,	1821
	25:32	"W good is the birthright to me?"	4200+4537
	26:10	"W is this you have done to us?	4537
	27: 8	my son, listen carefully and do w I tell you:	889
	27:12	W if my father touches me?	218
	27:13	Just do w I say; go and get them for me."	928
	27:37	So w can I possibly do for you, my son?"	4537
	27:42	w her older son Esau had *said*,	1821
	27:43	Now then, my son, do w I *say*:	7754
	27:45	with you and forgets w you did to him,	889
	28:15	until I have done w I have promised you."	889
	29:15	Tell me w your wages should be."	4537
	29:25	"W is this you have done to me?	4537
	30:11	Then Leah said, "W good fortune!"	928
	30:31	"W shall I give you?"	4537
	31: 1	from w belonged to our father."	889
	31: 2	attitude toward him was not w it had been.	3869
	31: 5	attitude toward me is not w it was before,	3869
	31:15	but he has used up w we have *paid for* us.	4084
	31:26	Laban said to Jacob, "W have you done?	4537
	31:36	"W is my crime?"	4537
	31:36	"W sin have I committed	4537
	31:37	w have you found that belongs	4537
	31:43	Yet w can I do today about these daughters	4537
	32: 4	This is w you are to say to my master Esau:	3907
	32:13	w he had with him he selected a gift	995+2021[S]
	32:27	The man asked him, "W is your name?"	4537
	33: 8	"W do you mean by all these droves I met?"	4769
	33: 9	Keep w you have for yourself."	889
	34: 7	as soon as they heard w had happened.	NIH
	34:19	lost no time in doing w they said,	2021[S]
	37: 8	because of his dream and w he had *said*.	1821
	37:10	"W is this dream you had?	4537
	37:15	"W are you looking for?"	4537
	37:20	Then we'll see w comes of his dreams."	4537
	37:26	"W will we gain if we kill our brother	4537
	38:10	W he did was wicked in the LORD's sight	889
	38:16	w will you give me to sleep with you?"	4537
	38:18	He said, "W pledge should I give you?"	4537
	38:23	Then Judah said, "Let her keep w she has,	NIH
	40:12	"This is w it *means*," Joseph said to him.	AIT
	40:18	"This is w it *means*," Joseph said.	AIT
	41:25	God has revealed to Pharaoh w he is about	889
	41:28	God has shown Pharaoh w he is about	889
	41:55	"Go to Joseph and do w he tells you."	889
	42:28	"W is this that God has done to us?"	4537
	44:15	"W is this you have done?	4537
	44:16	"W can we say to my lord?"	4537
	44:16	"W can we say?	4537
	44:24	we told him w my lord had *said*.	1821
	45: 9	'This is w your God says:	3907
	45:23	And this is w he sent to his father:	3869
	46:33	'W is your occupation?'	4537
	47: 3	"W is your occupation?"	4537
	49: 1	around so I can tell you w will happen	889
	49:28	and this is w their father said to them.	889
	50:15	"W if Joseph holds a grudge against us	4273
	50:17	'This is w you are to say to Joseph:	3907
	50:20	to accomplish w is now being done,	889
Ex	1:17	did not do w the king of Egypt had told	889+3869
	2: 4	at a distance to see w would happen to him.	4537
	2:14	"W I did must have become known."	1821+2021[S]
	3:13	and they ask me, 'W is his name?'	4537
	3:13	then w shall I tell them?"	4537
	3:14	This is w you are to say to the Israelites:	3907
	4: 1	over you and have seen w has been done	2021
	4: 1	"W if they do not believe me or listen	2176
	4: 2	"W is that in your hand?"	4537
	4:12	I will help you speak and will teach you w	889
	4:14	"W about your brother, Aaron	2022+4202
	4:15	of you speak and will teach you w to do.	889
	4:22	say to Pharaoh, 'This is w the LORD says:	3907

Ex	5: 1	"This is **w** the LORD, the God of Israel,	3907
	5:10	"This is **w** Pharaoh says:	3907
	5:17	Pharaoh said, "Lazy, that's **w** you are—	NIH
	6: 1	"Now you will see **w** I will do to Pharaoh:	889
	7:17	This is **w** the LORD says:	3907
	8: 1	'This is **w** the LORD says:	3907
	8:13	And the LORD did **w** Moses asked.	3869
	8:20	'This is **w** the LORD says:	3907
	8:31	and the LORD did **w** Moses asked:	3869
	9: 1	This is **w** the LORD, the God of the Hebrews	3907
	9:13	This is **w** the LORD, the God of the Hebrews	3907
	10: 3	This is **w** the LORD, the God of the Hebrews	3907
	10: 5	They will devour **w** little you have left after	2021
	10:11	since that's **w** you have been asking for."	AIT
	10:26	not know **w** we are to use to worship	4537
	11: 4	So Moses said, "This is **w** the LORD says:	3907
	12: 4	of lamb needed in accordance with **w** each	AIT
	12:26	'**W** does this ceremony mean to you'	4537
	12:28	The Israelites did just **w**	889+3869+4027
	12:36	**gave them w they asked for;**	8626
	12:50	All the Israelites did just **w**	889+3869+4027
	13: 8	'I do this because of **w** the LORD did	2296
	13:14	'**W** does this mean?'	4537
	14: 5	"**W** have we done?	4537
	14:11	**W** have you done to us by bringing us out	4537
	15:24	saying, "**W** are we to drink?"	4537
	15:26	of the LORD your God and do **w** is right	2021
	16: 5	to prepare **w** they bring in.	889
	16:15	they said to each other, "**W** is it?"	4943
	16:15	For they did not know **w** it was.	4537
	16:16	This is **w** the LORD has commanded:	1821+2021S
	16:23	"This is **w** the LORD commanded:	889
	16:23	So bake **w** you want to bake	889
	16:23	to bake and boil **w** you want to boil.	889
	16:32	"This is **w** the LORD has commanded:	1821+2021S
	17: 4	"**W** am I to do with these people?	4537
	18:14	"**W** is this you are doing for the people?	4537
	18:17	"**W** you are doing is not good.	1821+2021S
	19: 3	"This is **w** you are to say to the house	3907
	19: 3	to say to the house of Jacob and **w** you are	NIH
	19: 4	'You yourselves have seen **w** I did to Egypt,	889
	19: 9	told the LORD **w** the people had said.	1821
	22:27	**W** else will he sleep in?	4537
	23:11	the wild animals may eat **w** they leave.	AIT
	23:21	Pay attention to him and listen to **w** he says.	7754
	23:22	If you listen carefully to **w** he says	7754
	26:13	**w** is left will hang over the sides of	2021
	29: 1	This is **w** you are to do to consecrate	1821+2021S
	29:38	"This is **w** you are to offer on	889
	32: 1	we don't know **w** has happened to him."	4537
	32: 4	He took **w** they handed him and made it	NIH
	32: 8	to turn away from **w** I commanded	2006+2021S
	32:21	"**W** did these people do to you,	4537
	32:23	we don't know **w** has happened to him.'	4537
	32:27	Then he said to them, "This is **w** the LORD,	3907
	32:31	**w** a great sin these people have committed!	NIH
	32:35	of **w** they did with the calf Aaron had made.	889
	33: 5	and I will decide **w** to do with you.' "	4537
	33:16	**W** else will distinguish me and your people	NIH
	34:11	Obey **w** I command you today.	889
	34:34	the Israelites **w** he had been commanded,	889
	35: 4	"This is **w** the LORD has commanded:	1821+2021S
	35: 5	From **w** you have, take an offering	NIH
	35:25	and brought **w** she had spun—	4757
	36: 7	**w** they already had was more than enough	2021+4856S
	40: 4	Bring in the table and set out **w** belongs	6886
Lev	3:14	From **w** he offers he is to make this offering	5647
	4: 2	and does **w** is forbidden in any of	889
	4:13	and does **w** is forbidden in any of	889
	4:22	and does **w** is forbidden in any of	889
	4:27	and does **w** is forbidden in any of	889
	5: 5	he must confess in **w** way he has sinned	889
	5:16	for **w** he has failed to do in regard to	889
	5:17	a person sins and does **w** is forbidden in any	889
	6: 4	he must return **w** he has stolen or taken	889
	6: 4	or **w** was entrusted to him,	889
	8: 5	"This is **w** the LORD has commanded to	1821S
	8:34	**W** has been done today was commanded by the LORD	889+3869
	8:35	and do **w** the LORD requires, so you will	5466
	8:35	for that is **w** I have been commanded."	4027
	9: 6	"This is **w** the LORD has commanded	1821+2021S
	10: 3	"This is **w** the LORD spoke of	889
	17: 2	'This is **w** the LORD has commanded:	1821+2021S
	19: 8	because he has desecrated **w** is holy to	7731
	20:12	**W** they have done is a perversion;	NIH
	20:13	both of them have done **w** is detestable.	9359
	25: 5	Do not reap **w** grows of itself or harvest	6206
	25:11	not sow and do not reap **w** grows of itself	6206
	25:12	eat only **w** is taken directly from the fields.	9311
	25:16	because he is really selling you is	NIH
	25:20	"**W** will we eat in the seventh year if we do	4537
	25:25	redeem **w** his countryman has sold.	4928
	25:28	**w** he sold will remain in the possession of	4928
	27: 8	to the man making the vow can afford.	889
	27: 9	" 'If **w** he vowed is an animal	NIH
	27:11	If **w** he vowed is a ceremonially unclean	NIH
	27:12	that is **w** it will be.	AIT
Nu	4:19	and **w** he is to carry.	5362
	4:49	and **w** to carry.	5362
	5:10	but **w** he gives to the priest will belong to	889
	9: 8	until I find out **w** the LORD commands	4537
	11:11	**W** have I done to displease you	4200+4537
	11:23	or not **w** I say will come true for you."	AIT
	11:24	told the people **w** the LORD had said.	1821
	13:18	See **w** the land is like	4537

Nu	13:19	**W** kind of land do they live in?	4537
	13:19	**W** kind of towns do they live in?	4537
	14:34	**know w it is like** to have me against you.'	3359
	15:34	it was not clear **w** should be done to him.	4537
	16:29	and experience only **w** usually happens	7213
	20:14	"This is **w** your brother Israel says:	3907
	21:34	Do to him **w** you did to Sihon king of	889+3869
	22: 7	they told him **w** Balak had said.	1821
	22:16	"This is **w** Balak son of Zippor says:	3907
	22:19	and I will find out **w** else	4537
	22:20	but do only **w** I tell you."	1821+2021S
	22:28	"**W** have I done to you	4537
	22:35	but speak only **w** I tell you."	1821+2021S
	22:38	I must speak only **w** God puts	1821+2021S
	23:11	"**W** have you done to me?	4537
	23:12	not speak **w** the LORD puts in my mouth?"	889
	23:17	Balak asked him, "**W** did the LORD say?"	4537
	23:23	'See **w** God has done!'	4537
	24:13	and I must say only **w** the LORD says'?	889
	24:14	let me warn you of **w** this people will do	889
	26:55	**W** each group inherits will be according to	NIH
	27: 7	"**W** Zelophehad's daughters are saying	AIT
	29:39	to **w** you vow and your freewill offerings,	AIT
	30: 1	"This is **w** the LORD commands:	1821+2021S
	31:16	from the LORD in **w** happened at Peor,	1821
	32: 8	This is **w** your fathers did when I sent them	3907
	32:24	but do **w** you have promised."	2021
	32:31	"Your servants will do **w** the LORD has said.	4027
	33:56	I will do to you **w** I plan to do to them.	889+3869
	36: 5	"**W** the tribe of the descendants	NIH
	36: 6	This is **w** the LORD commands	1821+2021S
Dt	1:14	"**W** you propose to do is good."	1821+2021S
	1:34	When the LORD heard **w** you said,	1821+7754
	3: 2	Do to him **w** you did to Sihon king of	889+3869
	3:24	For **w** god is there in heaven or	4769
	4: 2	Do not add to **w** I command you	1821+2021S
	4: 3	with your own eyes **w** the LORD did	889
	4: 7	**W** other nation is so great as	4769
	4: 8	And **w** other nation is so great as	4769
	5:26	For **w** mortal man has ever heard the voice	4769
	5:28	"I have heard **w** this people said	1821+7754S
	5:32	So be careful to do **w** the LORD	889+3869
	6:18	Do **w** is right and good in the LORD's	2021S
	6:20	"**W** is the meaning of the stipulations,	4537
	7: 5	This is **w** you are to do to them:	3907
	7:18	remember well **w** the LORD your God did	889
	8: 2	and to test you in order to know **w** was	889
	9: 5	to accomplish **w** he swore	1821+2021S
	9:12	from **w** I commanded them	2006+2021S
	9:18	doing **w** was evil in the LORD's sight and	2021S
	10: 4	on these tablets **w** he had written before,	3869
	10:12	**w** does the LORD your God ask of you but	4537
	11: 4	**w** he did to the Egyptian army,	889
	11: 5	not your children who saw **w** he did for you	889
	11: 6	and **w** he did to Dathan and Abiram,	889
	12: 6	**w** you have vowed to give	AIT
	12:25	because you will be doing **w** is right in	2021
	12:28	be doing **w** is good and right in the eyes of	2021
	13:18	and doing **w** is right in his eyes.	2021
	17:11	Do not turn aside from **w** they tell you,	1821+2021S
	18:16	For this is **w** you asked of the LORD	889
	18:17	"**W** they say is good.	889
	18:22	If a prophet proclaims in the name of	889
	21: 9	since you have done **w** is right in the eyes	2021
	24: 8	You must follow carefully **w** I have commanded them.	889+3869
	24: 9	Remember **w** the LORD your God did	889
	24:10	**w** he is offering as a pledge.	AIT
	24:20	Leave **w** remains for the alien,	NIH
	24:21	Leave **w** remains for the alien,	NIH
	25: 9	"This is **w** is done to the man who will	3970
	25:17	Remember **w** the Amalekites did to you	889
	28:33	that you do not know will eat **w** your land	NIH
	30:11	Now **w** I am commanding you today is not too difficult	2021+2021+2296+5184S
	31: 4	And the LORD will do to them **w** he did	889+3869
	31:21	I know **w** they are disposed to do,	889
	31:29	**w** your hands have made."	5126
	32:20	he said, "and see **w** their end will be;	4537
	32:21	They made me jealous by **w** is no god	NIH
	32:29	and discern **w** their end will be!	NIH
	34: 9	the Israelites listened to him and did **w**	889+3869
Jos	2:10	and **w** you did to Sihon and Og,	889
	2:14	"If you don't tell **w** we are doing,	2296
	2:20	But if you tell **w** we are doing,	2296
	4: 6	'**W** do these stones mean?'	4537
	4:21	"**W** do these stones mean?	4537
	4:23	to the Jordan just **w** he had done to	889+3869
	5:14	"**W** message does my Lord have	4537
	7: 8	O Lord, **w** can I say,	4537
	7: 9	**W** then will you do for your own great name?"	
	7:10	**W** are you doing down on your face?	4200+4537
	7:13	this is **w** the LORD, the God of Israel, says:	3907
	7:19	Tell me **w** you have done;	4537
	7:20	This is **w** I have done:	3869
	8: 8	Do **w** the LORD has commanded.	3869
	8:31	according to **w** is written in the Book of	2021
	9: 3	people of Gibeon heard **w** Joshua had done	889
	9:20	This is **w** we will do to them:	NIH
	9:27	And that is **w** they are to this day.	NIH
	10:25	This is **w** the LORD will do to all	3970
	13:15	This is **w** Moses had given to the tribe	NIH
	13:24	This is **w** Moses had given to the tribe	NIH
	13:29	This is **w** Moses had given to the half-tribe	NIH
	14: 6	You know **w** the LORD said to Moses	1821+2021S

Jos	15:18	Caleb asked her, "**W** can I do for you?"	4537
	22:24	'**W** do you have to do with the LORD,	4537
	22:30	heard **w** Reuben, Gad and Manasseh	1821+2021S
	24: 2	"This is **w** the LORD, the God of Israel,	3907
	24: 5	I afflicted the Egyptians by **w** I did there,	889
	24: 7	You saw with your own eyes **w** I did to	889
Jdg	1: 7	God has paid me back for **w** I did to them."	889+3869+4027
	1:14	Caleb asked her, "**W** can I do for you?"	4537
	2:10	LORD nor **w** he had done for Israel.	2021+5126S
	6: 8	"This is **w** the LORD, the God of Israel,	3907
	6:38	And that is **w** happened.	AIT
	7:11	and listen to **w** they are saying.	4537
	8: 2	"**W** have I accomplished compared to you?	4537
	8: 3	**W** was I able to do compared to you?"	4537
	8:18	"**W** kind of men did you kill at Tabor?"	407
	9:30	**w** Gaal son of Ebed said,	1821
	9:48	Do **w** you have seen me do!"	4537
	11:12	"**W** do you have against us	4537
	11:15	"This is **w** Jephthah says:	3907
	11:23	**w** right have you to take it over?	NIH
	11:24	not take **w** your god Chemosh gives you?	889
	13:12	**w** is to be the rule for the boy's life	4537
	13:17	"**W** is your name,	4769
	14: 6	nor his mother **w** he had done.	889
	14:18	"**W** is sweeter than honey?	4537
	14:18	**W** is stronger than a lion?"	4537
	15:11	**W** have you done to us?"	4537
	15:11	did to them **w** they did to me."	889+3869+4027
	18: 3	**W** are you doing in this place?	4537
	18: 4	He told them **w** Micah had done for him,	2256+2296+2297+3869+3869
	18:14	Now you know **w** to do."	4537
	18:18	the priest said to them, "**W** are you doing?"	4537
	18:24	**W** else do I have?	4537
	18:27	Then they took **w** Micah had made,	889
	19:30	Tell us **w** to do!"	NIH
	20: 9	But now this is **w** we'll do to Gibeah:	1821+2021S
	20:10	it can give them **w** they deserve for	3869
	20:12	"**W** about this awful crime	4537
	21:11	"This is **w** you are to do," they said.	1821+2021S
	21:23	So that is **w** the Benjamites did.	4027
Ru	2:11	"I've been told all about **w** you have done	889
	2:12	the LORD repay you for **w** you have done.	7189
	2:18	also brought out and gave her **w** she had left	889
	3: 4	He will tell you **w** to do."	889
	3:18	my daughter, until you find out **w** happens.	375
1Sa	2: 3	of Israel grant you **w** you have asked	8924S
	1:23	"Do **w** seems best to you,"	2021
	1:27	LORD has granted me **w** I asked of him.	8629S
	2:27	"This is **w** the LORD says:	3907
	2:34	" 'And **w** happens to your two sons,	889
	2:35	who will do according to **w** is in my heart	889
	3:17	"**W** was it he said to you?"	4537
	3:18	let him do **w** is good in his eyes."	2021
	4:13	the town and told **w** had happened,	NIH
	4:14	"**W** is the meaning of this uproar?"	4537
	4:16	Eli asked, "**W** happened, my son?"	4537
	5: 7	the men of Ashdod saw **w** was happening,	3954
	5: 8	"**W** shall we do with the ark of the god	4537
	6: 2	"**W** shall we do with the ark of the LORD?	4537
	6: 4	"**W** guilt offering should we send to him?"	4537
	8: 9	**w** the king who will reign over them will do."	5477S
	8:11	**w** the king who will reign over you will do:	5477S
	9: 6	Perhaps he will tell us **w** way to take."	889
	9: 7	"If we go, **w** can we give the man?	4537
	9: 7	**W** do we have?"	4537
	9: 8	so that he will tell us **w** way to take."	5646S
	9:24	with **w** was on it and set it in front of Saul.	2021
	9:24	"Here is **w** has been kept for you.	2021
	10: 2	"**W** shall I do about my son?"	4537
	10: 8	until I come to you and tell you **w** you are	889
	10:11	"**W** is this that has happened to the son	4537
	10:15	"Tell me **w** Samuel said to you."	4537
	10:16	not tell his uncle **w** Samuel had said about	1821S
	10:18	"This is **w** the LORD, the God of Israel,	3907
	11: 5	he asked, "**W** is wrong with the people?"	4537
	11: 5	**w** the men of Jabesh had said.	1821
	11: 7	"This is **w** will be done to the oxen	3907
	12:17	And you will realize **w** an evil thing you did	8041
	12:24	consider **w** great things he has done for you.	889
	13:11	"**W** have you done?"	4537
	14:38	find out **w** sin has been committed	928+4537
	14:40	"Do **w** seems best to you," the men replied.	2021
	14:43	"Tell me **w** you have done."	4537
	15: 2	This is **w** the LORD Almighty says:	3907
	15: 2	'I will punish the Amalekites for **w** they did	889
	15:14	"**W** then is this bleating of sheep	4537
	15:14	**W** is this lowing of cattle that I hear?"	NIH
	15:16	"Let me tell you **w** the LORD said	889
	15:21	the best of **w** was devoted to God,	2021
	16: 3	and I will show you **w** to do.	889
	16: 4	Samuel did **w** the LORD said.	889
	17:26	"**W** will be done for the man who	4537
	17:27	to him **w** they had been saying	3869
	17:27	"This is **w** will be done for the man who	3907
	17:29	"Now **w** have I done?"	4537
	17:31	**W** David said was overheard and	1821+2021S
	18: 8	**W** more can he get but the kingdom?"	NIH
	18:18	is my family or my father's clan in Israel,	4769
	18:24	Saul's servants told him **w** David had said,	465+1821+2021+2021S
	19: 3	about you and will tell you **w** I find out.	4537
	19: 4	**w** he has done has benefited you greatly.	5126
	20: 1	"**W** have I done?	4537
	20: 1	**W** is my crime?	4537

1235   NIV EXHAUSTIVE CONCORDANCE   WHAT – WHAT

1Sa 20:32	W has he done?"	4537
21: 3	Now then, w do you have on hand?	4537
22: 3	with you until I learn w God will do	4537
25:17	Now think it over and see w you can do,	4537
25:24	w your servant has to say.	1821
25:35	from her hand w she had brought him	889
26:16	W you have done is not good.	
		1821+2021+2021+2296S
26:18	W have I done,	4537
26:18	and w wrong am I guilty of?	4537
27:11	'This is w David did.' "	3907
28: 2	for yourself w your servant can do."	889
28: 9	"Surely you know w Saul has done.	889
28:13	W do you see?"	4537
28:14	"W does he look like?"	4537
28:15	So I have called on you to tell me w to do."	4537
28:17	The LORD has done w he predicted	889+3869
28:21	in my hands and did w you told me to do.	1821S
29: 3	"W about these Hebrews?"	4537
29: 8	"But w have I done?"	4537
29: 8	"W have you found against your servant	4537
30:23	not do that with w the LORD has given us.	889
30:24	Who will listen to w you say?	1821
31:11	the people of Jabesh Gilead heard of w	889
2Sa 1: 4	"W happened?" David asked.	4537
1: 7	and I said, "W can I do?"	2180
3: 8	of w Ish-Bosheth said and he answered,	1821
3: 9	for David w the LORD promised him	889+3869
3:24	"W have you done?	4537
7: 5	'This is w the LORD says:	3907
7: 8	'This is w the LORD Almighty says:	3907
7:18	O Sovereign LORD, and w is my family,	4769
7:20	"W more can David say to you?	4537
8:15	doing w was just and right	NIH
9: 8	"W is your servant,	4537
10:12	The LORD will do w is good in his sight."	2021
12: 7	'This is w the LORD, the God of Israel,	3907
12: 9	the LORD by doing w is evil in his eyes?	2021
12:11	'This is w the LORD says:	3907
13:13	W about me?	2256
13:13	And w about you?	2256
13:16	greater wrong than w you have already done	337S
13:29	to Amnon as Absalom had ordered.	889+3869
14: 5	The king asked her, "W is troubling you?"	4537
14:15	perhaps he will do w his servant asks.	1821
14:18	the answer to w I am going to ask you."	889
15: 2	"W town are you from?"	361
16:10	"W do you and I have in common,	4537
16:20	W should we do?"	4537
17: 5	so we can hear w he has to say."	4537
17: 6	Should we do w he says?	1821
18:11	"W! You saw him?	2180
18:21	"Go, tell the king w you have seen."	889
18:22	again said to Joab, "Come w may,	2118+4537
18:23	said, "Come w may, I want to run."	2118+4537
18:29	your servant, but I don't know w it was."	4537
19:11	to his palace, since w is being said	1821
19:22	"W do you and I have in common,	4537
19:28	So w right do I have to make any more	4537
19:35	Can I tell the difference between w is good	NIH
19:35	between what is good and w is not?	NIH
19:35	Can your servant taste w he eats and drinks?	889
20:17	w your servant has to say."	1821
21: 3	"W shall I do for you?	4537
21: 4	"W do you want me to do for you?"	4537
21:11	David was told w Aiah's daughter Rizpah,	889
24:10	"I have sinned greatly in w I have done.	889
24:12	'This is w the LORD says:	3907
24:17	W have they done?	4537
1Ki 1:14	I will come in and confirm w you have said.	1821
1:16	"W is it you want?"	4537
1:30	surely carry out today w I swore to you	889+3869
2: 3	w the LORD your God requires:	5466
2: 5	"Now you yourself know w Joab son	889
2: 5	w he did to the two commanders	889
2: 9	you will know w to do to him.	889
2:38	"W you say is good.	1821
2:42	'W you say is good.	1821
3:12	I will do w you have asked.	3869
3:13	I will give you w you have not asked for—	889
8:15	his own hand has fulfilled w he promised	889
8:32	down on his own head w he has done.	2006
9:13	"W kind of towns are these you have given	4537
10:13	besides w he had given her out of his royal	889
11:22	"W have you lacked here that you want	4537
11:31	for this is w the LORD, the God of Israel,	3907
11:33	nor done w is right in my eyes,	2021
11:38	in my ways and do w is right in my eyes	2021
12: 9	He asked them, "W is your advice?	4537
12:16	"W share do we have in David,	4537
12:16	w part in Jesse's son?	NIH
12:24	'This is w the LORD says:	3907
13: 2	This is w the LORD says:	3907
13: 4	When King Jeroboam heard w the man	1821S
13:11	also told their father w he had said to	1821+2021S
13:21	'This is w the LORD says:	3907
14: 3	He will tell you w will happen to the boy."	4537
14: 4	So Jeroboam's wife did w he said and went	4027
14: 7	Go, tell Jeroboam that this is w the LORD,	3907
14: 8	doing only w was right in my eyes.	2021
14:14	This is the day! W? Yes, even now.	4537
15: 5	For David had done w was right in the eyes	2021
15:11	Asa did w was right in the eyes of the LORD	2021
16: 5	w he did and his achievements,	889
16:27	and the things he achieved,	889
17: 5	So he did w the LORD had told him.	3869
17:13	for me from w you have and bring it to me,	9004S

1Ki 17:14	this is w the LORD, the God of Israel, says:	3907
17:18	"W do you have against me, man of God?	4537
18: 9	"W have I done wrong," asked Obadiah,	4537
18:13	w I did while Jezebel was killing	889
18:24	all the people said, "W you say is good."	2021
19: 9	W are you doing here, Elijah?	3870+4200+4537
19:13	a voice said to him, "W are you doing here,	
		3870+4200+4537
19:20	"W have I done to you?"	4537
20: 2	saying, "This is w Ben-Hadad says:	3907
20: 5	'This is w Ben-Hadad says:	3907
20:13	'This is w the LORD says:	3907
20:14	'This is w the LORD says:	3907
20:22	"Strengthen your position and see w must	889
20:28	'This is w the LORD says:	3907
20:42	'This is w the LORD says:	3907
21:19	Say to him, 'This is w the LORD says:	3907
21:19	say to him, 'This is w the LORD says:	3907
22:11	'This is w the LORD says:	3907
22:14	I can tell him only w the LORD tells me."	889
22:22	" 'By w means?'	928+4537
22:27	'This is w the king says:	3907
22:43	he did w was right in the eyes of	2021
2Ki 1: 4	Therefore this is w the LORD says:	3907
1: 6	'This is w the LORD says:	3907
1: 7	"W kind of man was it who came	4537
1:11	"Man of God, this is w the king says,	3907
1:16	'This is w the LORD says:	3907
1:18	events of Ahaziah's reign, and w he did,	889
2: 9	w can I do for you before I am taken	4537
2:21	saying, "This is w the LORD says:	3907
3: 8	"By w route shall we attack?"	361+2296
3:10	"W!" exclaimed the king of Israel.	177
3:13	"W do we have to do with each other?	4537
3:16	'This is w the LORD says:	3907
3:17	For this is w the LORD says:	3907
4: 2	Tell me, w do you have in your house?"	4537
4: 7	You and your sons can live on w is left."	2021
4:13	Now w can be done for you?	4537
4:14	"W can be done for her?"	4537
4:39	though no one knew w they were.	NIH
4:43	"How can I set this before a hundred men?"	NIH
5: 4	and told him w the girl from Israel had said.	
		2256+2296+2296+3869+3869
5:20	by not accepting from him w he brought.	889
6:15	"Oh, my lord, w shall we do?"	377
7: 1	This is w the LORD says:	3907
7:12	"I will tell you w the Arameans have done	889
7:13	let us send them to find out w happened."	NIH
7:14	"Go and find out w has happened."	NIH
7:20	And that is exactly w happened to him,	AIT
8:14	"W did Elisha say to you?"	4537
9: 3	'This is w the LORD says:	3907
9: 6	"This is w the LORD, the God of Israel,	3907
9:12	Jehu said, "Here is w he told me:	
		2256+2296+2296+3869+3869
9:12	'This is w the LORD says:	3907
9:18	'This is w the king says:	3907
9:18	"W do you have to do with peace?"	4537
9:19	'This is w the king says:	3907
9:19	"W do you have to do with peace?	4537
9:27	of Judah saw w had happened,	NIH
10:10	The LORD has done w he announced	889
10:30	in accomplishing w is right in my eyes	2021
11: 5	saying, "This is w you are to do:	1821+2021S
12: 2	Joash did w was right in the eyes of	2021
14: 3	He did w was right in the eyes of	2021
14: 6	in accordance with w is written in the Book	2021
14:15	w he did and his achievements,	889
15: 3	He did w was right in the eyes of the LORD,	2021
15:34	He did w was right in the eyes of the LORD,	2021
15:36	events of Jotham's reign, and w he did,	889
16: 2	he did not do w was right in the eyes of	2021
16:19	events of the reign of Ahaz, and w he did,	889
17:26	w the god of that country requires.	5477
17:26	the people do not know w he requires."	5477
17:27	w the god of the land requires."	5477
18: 3	He did w was right in the eyes of the LORD,	2021
18:19	" 'This is the great king,	NIH
18:19	On w are you basing this confidence	4537
18:29	This is w the king says:	3907
18:31	This is w the king of Assyria says:	3907
18:37	w the field commander had said.	1821
19: 3	They told him, "This is w Hezekiah says:	3907
19: 6	'This is w the LORD says:	3907
19: 6	Do not be afraid of w you have heard—	889
19:11	Surely you have heard w the kings	889
19:20	"This is w the LORD, the God of Israel,	3907
19:29	"This year you will eat w grows by itself,	6206
19:29	and the second year w springs from that.	6084
19:32	"Therefore this is w the LORD says	3907
20: 1	"This is w the LORD says:	3907
20: 3	and have done w is good in your eyes."	2021
20: 5	'This is w the LORD,	3907
20: 8	"W will be the sign that the LORD will heal	4537
20: 9	the LORD will do w he has promised:	1821+2021S
20:14	"W did those men say,	4537
20:15	"W did they see in your palace?"	4537
21:12	Therefore this is w the LORD,	3907
21:25	other events of Amon's reign, and w he did,	889
22: 2	He did w was right in the eyes of	2021
22:13	and for all Judah about w is written	1821
22:15	She said to them, "This is w the LORD,	3907
22:16	'This is w the LORD says:	3907
22:18	'This is w the LORD, the God of Israel,	3907
22:19	when you heard w I have spoken	889
23:17	"W is that tombstone I see?"	4537

1Ch 12:32	the times and knew w Israel should do—	4537
16: 8	among the nations w he has done.	6613
17: 4	'This is w the LORD says:	3907
17: 7	'This is w the LORD Almighty says:	3907
17:16	O LORD God, and w is my family,	4769
17:18	"W more can David say to you	4537
18:14	doing w was just and right	AIT
19:13	The LORD will do w is good in his sight."	2021
21:10	'This is w the LORD says:	3907
21:11	'This is w the LORD says:	3907
21:17	W have they done?	4537
21:24	I will not take for the LORD w is yours,	889
29:14	and we have given you only w comes	NIH
2Ch 6: 4	with his hands has fulfilled w he promised	889
6:23	down on his own head w he has done.	2006
8:14	because this was w David the man	4027
9: 6	not believe w they said until I came and saw	1821
10: 9	He asked them, "W is your advice?	4537
10:16	"W share do we have in David,	4537
10:16	w part in Jesse's son?	NIH
11: 4	'This is w the LORD says:	3907
12: 5	'This is w the LORD says,	3907
13: 9	a priest of w are not gods.	NIH
13:22	he did and what he said,	2006
13:22	what he did and w he said,	1821
14: 2	Asa did w was good and right in the eyes of	2021
18:10	and he declared, "This is w the LORD says:	3907
18:13	I can tell him only w my God says."	889
18:20	" 'By w means?'	928+4537
18:26	'This is w the king says:	3907
19: 6	"Consider carefully w you do,	4537
20:12	We do not know w to do,	4537
20:15	This is w the LORD says to you:	3907
20:32	he did w was right in the eyes of	2021
20:37	the LORD will destroy w you have made."	5126
21:12	'This is w the LORD,	3907
23: 4	Now this is w you are to do:	1821+2021S
23: 6	guard w the LORD has assigned to them.	AIT
24: 2	Joash did w was right in the eyes of the	
	LORD	2021
24:20	"This is w God says:	3907
25: 2	He did w was right in the eyes of	2021
25: 4	but acted in accordance with w is written in	2021
25: 9	"But w about the hundred talents I paid	4537
26: 4	He did w was right in the eyes of the LORD,	2021
27: 2	He did w was right in the eyes of the LORD,	2021
28: 1	he did not do w was right in the eyes of	2021
29: 2	He did w was right in the eyes of the LORD,	2021
29:36	at w God had brought about for his people,	2021
30: 5	according to w was written.	2021
30:12	w the king and his officials had ordered,	5184
30:18	contrary to w was written.	2021
31:20	This is w Hezekiah did throughout Judah,	3869
31:20	doing w was good and right and faithful	2021
32: 8	w Hezekiah the king of Judah said.	1821
32:10	This is w Sennacherib king of Assyria says:	3907
32:10	On w are you basing your confidence,	4537
32:13	not know w I and my fathers have done	4537
34: 2	He did w was right in the eyes of	2021
34:21	and Judah about w is written in this book	1821
34:23	She said to them, "This is w the LORD,	3907
34:24	'This is w the LORD says:	3907
34:26	'This is w the LORD, the God of Israel,	3907
34:27	before God when you heard w he spoke	1821
35: 6	doing w the LORD commanded	3869
35:21	"W quarrel is there between you and me,	4537
35:22	He would not listen to w Neco had said	1821
35:26	to w is written in the Law of the LORD—	2021
36:23	"This is w Cyrus king of Persia says:	3907
Ezr 1: 2	"This is w Cyrus king of Persia says:	3907
3: 2	in accordance with w is written in the Law	2021
3: 4	Then in accordance with w is written,	2021
5: 4	"W are the names of the men constructing	10426
6: 8	I hereby decree w you are to do	10378+10408
6:18	to w is written in the Book of Moses.	10375
8:17	I told them w to say to Iddo	1821S
9:10	now, O our God, w can we say after this?	4537
9:13	"W has happened to us is a result	3972S
9:13	under oath to do w he has been suggested.	3869
Ne 2: 4	king said to me, "W is it you want?"	4537+6584
2:12	I had not told anyone w my God had put	4537
2:16	where I had gone or w I was doing,	4537
2:18	upon me and w the king had said to me.	1821S
2:19	"W is this you are doing?"	4537
4: 2	he said, "W are those feeble Jews doing?	4537
4: 3	said, "W they are building—	889
5: 9	"W you are doing is not right.	1821+2021S
5:12	an oath to do w they had promised.	3869
6: 8	"Nothing like w you are saying is	
	happening;	465+1821+2021+2021S
6:14	O my God, because of w they have done;	465
6:19	and then telling him w I said.	1821
7: 5	This is w I found written there:	NIH
8: 8	people could understand w was being read.	2021
9:28	they again did w was evil in your sight.	NIH
13:14	not blot out w I have so faithfully done for	889
13:17	"W is this wicked thing you are doing—	4537
Est 1: 1	This is w happened during the time	AIT
1: 8	to serve each man w he wished.	3869
1:15	w must be done to Queen Vashti?"	4537
2: 1	he remembered Vashti and w she had done	889
2: 1	and w he had decreed about her.	889
2:11	how Esther was and w was happening	4537
2:15	she asked for nothing other than w Hegai,	889
4: 5	to find out w was troubling Mordecai	4537
4: 9	and reported to Esther w Mordecai had said.	1821
5: 3	the king asked, "W is it, Queen Esther?	4537

Est
5: 3 W is your request? — 4537
5: 5 "so that we may do w Esther asks." — 1821
5: 6 "Now w is your petition? — 4537
5: 6 And w is your request? — 4537
6: 3 "W honor and recognition has Mordecai received for this?" — 4537
6: 6 "W should be done for the man — 4537
6: 9 'This is w is done for the man — 3970
6:11 "This is w is done for the man — 3970
7: 2 "Queen Esther, w is your petition? — 4537
7: 2 w is your request? — 4537
9: 5 and they did w they pleased — 3869
9:12 W have they done in the rest of — 4537
9:12 Now w is your petition? — 4537
9:12 W is your request? — 4537
9:23 doing w Mordecai had written to them. — 889
9:26 in this letter and because of w they had seen — 4537
9:26 of what they had seen and w had happened — 4537

Job
2:10 In all this, Job did not sin in w he said. — 8557
3:25 W I feared has come upon me; — 7065S
3:25 w I dreaded has happened to me. — 889
4:16 It stopped, but I could not tell w it was. — 5260S
6: 8 that God would grant w I hope for, — AIT
6:11 "W strength do I have, — 4537
6:11 W prospects, that I should be patient? — 4537
6:25 But w do your arguments prove? — 4537
6:26 Do you mean to correct w I say, — 4863
7:17 "W is man that you make so much of him, — 4537
7:20 If I have sinned, w have I done to you, — 4537
8: 3 Does the Almighty pervert w is right? — AIT
8: 8 w their fathers learned, — 2984
8:14 W he trusts in is fragile; — 889
8:14 w he relies on is a spider's web. — 4440
9:12 Who can say to him, 'W are you doing?' — 4537
10: 2 but tell me w charges you have against me. — 4537
10:13 "But this is w you concealed in your heart, — NIH
11: 8 w can you do? — 4537
11: 8 w can you know? — 4537
12:14 W he tears down cannot be rebuilt; — NIH
13: 2 W you know, I also know; — 3869
13:13 then let come to me w may. — 4537
13:17 let your ears take in w I say. — 289
14: 4 Who can bring w is pure from the impure? — AIT
15: 9 W do you know that we do not know? — 4537
15: 9 W insights do you have that we do — NIH
15:14 "W is man, that he could be pure, — 4537
15:17 let me tell you w I have seen, — 2296
15:18 w wise men have declared, — 889
15:31 by trusting w is worthless, — 2021
16: 3 W ails you that you keep on arguing? — 4537
20:18 W he toiled for he must give back uneaten; — 3334
20:26 and devour w is left in his tent. — AIT
21:15 W would we gain by praying to him?' — 4537
21:21 For w does he care about the family — 4537
21:27 "I know full well w you are thinking, — 4742
21:31 Who repays him for w he has done? — 2085
22: 3 W pleasure would it give the Almighty — NIH
22: 3 W would he gain if your ways were blameless? — NIH
22:13 Yet you say, 'W does God know? — 4537
22:17 W can the Almighty do to us?' — 4537
22:28 W you decide on will be done, — 608S
23: 5 I would find out w he would answer me, — 4863S
23: 5 and consider w he would say. — 4537
26: 3 W advice you have offered to one — 4537
26: 3 W great insight you have displayed! — NIH
27: 8 w hope has the godless when he is cut off, — 4537
27:17 w he lays up the righteous will wear, — NIH
30: 2 Of w use was the strength of their hands — 4200+4537
31: 2 For w is man's lot from God above, — 4537
31: 8 then may others eat w I have sown, — NIH
31:14 w will I do when God confronts me? — 4537
31:14 W will I answer when called to account? — 4537
32: 6 not daring to tell you w I know. — 1976
32: 9 the aged who understand w is right. — AIT
32:10 I too will tell you w I know. — 1976
32:17 I too will tell w I know. — 1976
33: 3 my lips sincerely speak w I know. — 1981
33:23 to tell a man w is right for him, — AIT
33:27 'I sinned, and perverted w was right, — AIT
33:27 but I did not get w I deserved. — 8750
34: 4 Let us discern for ourselves w is right; — AIT
34: 4 let us learn together w is good. — 4537
34: 7 W man is like Job, who drinks scorn — 4769
34:11 He repays a man for w he has done; — 7189
34:11 brings upon him w his conduct deserves. — 3869
34:16 listen to w I say. — 7754S
34:32 Teach me w I cannot see; — NIH
34:33 so tell me w you know. — 4537
35: 3 Yet you ask him, 'W profit is it to me, — 4537
35: 3 and w do I gain by not sinning? — 4537
35: 6 your sins are many, w does that do to him? — 4537
35: 7 If you are righteous, w do you give to him, — 4537
35: 7 or w does he receive from your hand? — 4537
36: 9 he tells them w they have done— — 7189
37:19 "Tell us w we should say to him; — 4537
38: 6 On w were its footings set, — 4537
38:19 "W is the way to the abode of light? — 361+2296
38:24 W is the way to the place where — 361+2296
40:16 W strength he has in his loins, — 2180
40:16 w power in the muscles of his belly! — NIH
42: 7 you have not spoken of me w is right, — AIT
42: 8 You have not spoken of me w is right, — AIT
42: 9 did w the LORD told them; — 889+3869

Ps
8: 4 w is man that you are mindful of him, — 4537
9:11 proclaim among the nations w he has done. — 6613
11: 3 w can the righteous do?" — 4537
12: 8 when w is vile is honored among men. — AIT
15: 2 and who does w is righteous, — AIT
17: 2 may your eyes see w is right. — AIT
24: 4 to an idol or swear by w is false. — AIT
25: 9 in w is right and teaches them his way. — 2021
27: 4 this is w I seek: that I may dwell in the — NIH
28: 4 upon them w their hands have done — 5126
28: 4 and bring back upon them w they deserve. — 1691
28: 5 w his hands have done, — 5126
30: 9 "W gain is there in my destruction, — 4537
35:25 "Aha, just w we wanted!" — 5883
36: 4 and does not reject w is wrong. — AIT
37:30 and his tongue speaks w is just. — AIT
38:20 when I pursue w is good. — AIT
39: 7 "But now, Lord, w do I look for? — 4537
44: 1 our fathers have told us w you did — 7189S
50:16 "W right have you to recite my laws — 3870+4200+4537
51: 4 have I sinned and done w is evil — 2021
52: 9 for w you have done; — AIT
56: 4 W can mortal man do to me? — 4537
56:11 W can man do to me? — 4537
59: 7 See w they spew from their mouths— — NIH
62:12 according to w he has done. — 5126
64: 9 and ponder w he has done. — 5126
66: 5 Come and see w God has done, — 5149
66:16 let me tell you w he has done for me. — 889
69: 4 I am forced to restore w I did not steal. — 889
73:12 This is w the wicked are like— — NIH
77:13 W god is so great as our God? — 4769
78: 3 w we have heard and known, — 889
78: 3 w our fathers have told us. — NIH
78:11 They forgot w he had done, — 6613
78:29 for he had given them w they craved. — 9294
85: 8 I will listen to w God the LORD will say; — 4537
85:12 The LORD will indeed give w is good, — 2021
89:34 w my lips have uttered. — 4604
89:47 For w futility you have created all men! — 4537
89:48 W man can live and not see death, — 4769
94: 2 pay back to the proud w they deserve. — 1691
95: 9 though they had seen w I did. — 7189
99: 4 in Jacob you have done w is just and right. — AIT
105: 1 among the nations w he has done. — 6613
105:19 till w he foretold came to pass, — 1821
105:44 w others had toiled for— — 6662
106: 3 who constantly do w is right. — AIT
106:13 But they soon forgot w he had done and did — 5126
106:15 So he gave them w they asked for, — 8629
106:39 They defiled themselves by w they did; — 5126
118: 6 W can man do to me? — 4537
118:17 w the LORD has done. — 5126
119:68 You are good, and w you do is good; — AIT
119:121 I have done w is righteous and just; — AIT
120: 3 W will he do to you, — 4537
120: 3 and w more besides, O deceitful tongue? — 4537
137: 7 w the Edomites did on the day Jerusalem — NIH
137: 8 for w you have done to us— — 1691S
141: 4 Let not my heart be drawn to w is evil, — 1821S
143: 5 w your hands have done. — 5126
144: 3 O LORD, w is man that you care for him, — 4537

Pr
1: 3 doing w is right and just and fair; — AIT
2: 9 Then you will understand w is right and just — AIT
4:10 Listen, my son, accept w I say, — 609
4:19 do not know w makes them stumble. — 928+4537
4:20 My son, pay attention to w I say; — 1821
5: 7 do not turn aside from w I say. — 609+7023
6: 2 if you have been trapped by w you said, — 609+7023
7:24 pay attention to w I say. — 609+7023
8: 6 I open my lips to speak w is right. — AIT
8: 7 My mouth speaks w is true, — AIT
8:19 w I yield surpasses choice silver. — AIT
10:24 W the wicked dreads will overtake him; — AIT
10:24 w the righteous desire will be granted. — AIT
10:32 lips of the righteous know w is fitting, — AIT
10:32 the mouth of the wicked only w is perverse. — AIT
13: 5 The righteous hate w is false, — 1821S
14:22 But those who plan w is good find love — AIT
17:16 Of w use is money in the hand of a fool, — 2296+4200+4537
18:22 a wife finds w is good and receives favor — AIT
19:17 and he will reward him for w he has done. — 1691
19:22 W a man desires is unfailing love; — AIT
21: 3 To do w is right and just is more acceptable — AIT
21: 7 for they refuse to do w is right. — AIT
22:17 apply your heart to w I teach, — 1981
23: 1 note well w is before you, — 889
23:16 when your lips speak w is right. — AIT
24:12 according to w he has done? — 7189
24:22 who knows w calamities they can bring? — NIH
24:29 I'll pay that man back for w he did." — 3869
24:32 to w I observed and learned a lesson — NIH
24:32 and learned a lesson from w I saw: — NIH
25: 7 W you have seen with your eyes — 889
25: 8 for w will you do in the end — 4537
27: 1 you do not know w a day may bring forth. — 4537
27: 7 to the hungry even w is bitter tastes sweet. — AIT
30: 4 W is his name, and the name of his son? — 4537
31: 5 lest they drink and forget w the law decrees, — NIH

Ecc
1: 3 W does man gain from all his labor — 4537
1: 9 W has been will be again, — 4537
1: 9 w has been done will be done again; — 4537
1:13 W a heavy burden God has laid on men! — 2085
1:15 W is twisted cannot be straightened; — AIT
1:15 w is lacking cannot be counted. — AIT
2: 1 with pleasure to find out w is good." — AIT
2: 2 And w does pleasure accomplish?" — 4537
2: 3 to see w was worthwhile for men — 361+2296
2:11 that my hands had done and w I had toiled — 6662S
2:12 W more can the king's successor do — 3954+4537
2:12 successor do than w has already been done? — 889
2:15 W then do I gain by being wise?" — 4200+4537
2:22 W does a man get for all the toil — 4537
3: 9 W does the worker gain from his toil? — 4537
3:11 they cannot fathom w God has done — 2021+5126S
3:15 and w will be has been before; — 889
3:22 For who can bring him to see w will happen — 4537
5: 6 be angry at w you say and destroy the work — 7754
5:11 And w benefit are they to the owner except — 4537
5:16 so he departs, and w does he gain, — 4537
6: 8 W advantage has a wise man over a fool? — 4537
6: 8 W does a poor man gain by knowing how — 4537
6: 9 Better the eye sees than the roving of — 5260
6:10 and w man is has been known; — 889
6:12 For who knows w is good for a man in life, — 4537
6:12 Who can tell him w will happen under — 4537
7:13 Consider w God has done: — 5126
7:13 Who can straighten w he has made crooked? — 889
7:20 on earth who does w is right and never sins. — AIT
7:27 "this is w I have discovered: — NIH
8: 4 who can say to him, "W are you doing?" — 4537
8: 7 who can tell him w is to come? — 889+3869
8:14 righteous men who get w the wicked deserve, — 3869+5126
8:14 wicked men who get w the righteous deserve. — 3869+5126
8:17 No one can comprehend w goes on — 2021+5126S
9: 1 the wise and w they do are in God's hands, — 6271
9: 7 for it is now that God favors w you do. — 5126
10:14 No one knows w is coming— — 4537
10:14 who can tell him w will happen after him? — 889
10:20 a bird on the wing may report w you say. — 1821
11: 2 for you do not know w disaster may come — 4537
12:10 and w he wrote was upright and true. — 1821S

SS
5: 8 if you find my lover, w will you tell him? — 4537
5: 8 W shall we do for our sister for the day — 4537

Isa
1:11 sacrifices—w are they to me?" — 4200+4537
2: 1 This is w Isaiah son of Amoz saw — 889
2: 8 to w their fingers have made. — 889
2:22 Of w account is he? — 4537
3:11 w their hands have done. — 1691
3:15 W do you mean by crushing my people — 4537
5: 4 W more could have been done — 4537
5: 5 Now I will tell you w I am going to do — 889
7: 7 Yet this is w the Sovereign LORD says: — 3907
8:12 do not fear w they fear, and do not dread it. — AIT
10: 3 W will you do on the day of reckoning, — 4537
10: 7 But this is not w he intends, — 4027
10: 7 this is not w he has in mind. — 4027
10:24 Therefore, this is w the Lord, — 3907
11: 3 He will not judge by w he sees with his eyes — 5260
11: 3 or decide by w he hears with his ears; — 5461
12: 4 among the nations w he has done, — 6613
14:32 W answer shall be given to the envoys of — 4537
18: 4 This is w the LORD says to me: — 3907
19:12 Let them show you and make known w — 4537
19:17 of w the LORD Almighty is planning — 889
20: 6 'See w has happened to those we relied on, — 3907
21: 3 I am staggered by w I hear, — AIT
21: 3 I am bewildered by w I see. — AIT
21: 6 This is w the Lord says to me: — 3907
21: 6 a lookout and have him report w he sees. — 889
21:10 I tell you w I have heard from — 889
21:11 "Watchman, w is left of the night? — 4537
21:11 Watchman, w is left of the night?" — 4537
21:16 This is w the Lord says to me: — 3907
22: 1 W troubles you now, — 4537
22:15 This is w the Lord, the LORD Almighty, — 3907
22:16 W are you doing here — 3870+4200+4537
22:22 w he opens no one can shut, — NIH
22:22 and w he shuts no one can open. — NIH
28:16 So this is w the Sovereign LORD says: — 3907
28:23 pay attention and hear w I say. — 614
29:16 Shall w is formed say to him who formed it, — AIT
29:22 Therefore this is w the LORD, — 3907
30:10 "Give us no more visions of w is right! — AIT
30:12 this is w the Holy One of Israel says: — 3907
30:15 This is w the Sovereign LORD, — 3907
31: 4 This is w the LORD says to me: — 3907
32: 9 hear w I have to say! — 614
33:13 You who are far away, hear w I have done; — 889
33:15 and speaks w is right, who rejects gain — AIT
36: 4 "Tell Hezekiah, " 'This is w the great king, — 3907
36: 4 On w are you basing this confidence — 4537
36:14 This is w the king says: — 3907
36:16 This is w the king of Assyria says: — 3907
36:22 told him w the field commander had said. — 1821
37: 3 They told him, "This is w Hezekiah says: — 3907
37: 6 'This is w the LORD says: — 3907
37: 6 Do not be afraid of w you have heard — 889
37:11 Surely you have heard w the kings — 889
37:21 "This is w the LORD, the God of Israel, — 3907
37:30 "This year you will eat w grows by itself, — 6206
37:30 and the second year w springs from that. — 8826
37:33 "Therefore this is w the LORD says — 3907
38: 1 'This is w the LORD says: — 3907
38: 3 and have done w is good in your eyes." — 2021
38: 5 'This is w the LORD, — 3907
38: 7 that the LORD will do w he has promised: — 1821+2021+2021+2296S
38:15 But w can I say? — 4537
38:22 "W will be the sign that I will go up to — 4537
39: 2 the envoys gladly and showed them w was — NIH
39: 3 "W did those men say, — 4537

Isa 39: 4	"**W** did they see in your palace?"	4537
40: 6	And I said, "**W** shall I cry?"	4537
40:18	**W** image will you compare him to?	4537
41:22	to tell us **w** is going to happen.	889
41:22	Tell us **w** the former things were,	4537
41:23	tell us **w** the future holds,	2021
42: 5	**This is w** God the LORD says—	3907
43: 1	But now, **this is w** the LORD says—	3907
43:14	**This is w** the LORD says—	3907
43:16	**This is w** the LORD says—	3907
44: 2	**This is w** the LORD says—	3907
44: 6	"**This is w** the LORD says—	3907
44: 7	and lay out before me **w** has **happened**	2023S
44: 7	and **w** is yet to **come**—	AIT
44: 7	yes, let him foretell **w** will come.	889
44:19	a detestable thing from **w** is **left**?	AIT
44:24	"**This is w** the LORD says:	3907
45: 1	"**This is w** the LORD says to his anointed,	3907
45: 9	'**W** are you making?'	4537
45:10	'**W** have you begotten?'	4537
45:10	'**W** have you brought to birth?'	4537
45:11	"**This is w** the LORD says—	3907
45:14	**This is w** the LORD says:	3907
45:18	For **this is w** the LORD says—	3907
45:19	I declare **w** is **right**.	AIT
45:21	Declare **w** is to be, present it—	NIH
46:10	from ancient times, **w** is still to come.	889
46:11	**W** I have said, that will I bring about;	NIH
46:11	**w** I have planned, that will I do.	NIH
47: 7	or reflect on **w** **might happen**.	344
47:13	let them save you from **w** is coming	889
48:17	**This is w** the LORD says—	3907
48:17	who teaches you **w** *is* **best** for you,	AIT
49: 4	Yet **w** is **due** me is in the LORD's hand,	AIT
49: 7	**This is w** the LORD says:	3907
49: 8	**This is w** the LORD says:	3907
49:22	**This is w** the Sovereign LORD says:	3907
49:25	But **this is w** the LORD says:	3907
50: 1	**This is w** the LORD says:	3907
50:11	**This is w** you shall receive from my hand:	2296
51: 7	"Hear me, you who know **w** is **right**,	AIT
51:22	**This is w** your Sovereign LORD says,	3907
52: 3	For **this is w** the LORD says:	3907
52: 4	For **this is w** the Sovereign LORD says:	3907
52: 5	"And now **w** do I have here?"	4537
52:15	For **w** they were not told, they will see,	889
52:15	they will see, and **w** they have not heard,	889
55: 2	Why spend money on **w** is not **bread**,	AIT
55: 2	and your labor on **w** does not **satisfy**?	AIT
55: 2	Listen, listen to me, and eat **w** is **good**,	AIT
55:11	to me empty, but will accomplish **w** I desire	889
56: 1	**This is w** the LORD says:	3907
56: 1	"Maintain justice and do **w** is **right**,	AIT
56: 4	For **this is w** the LORD says:	3907
56: 4	who choose **w** pleases me and hold fast	889
57:15	For **this is w** the high and lofty One says—	3907
58: 2	as if they were a nation that does **w** is **right**	AIT
58: 5	Is that **w** you call a fast,	NIH
59: 6	with **w** they **make**.	5126
59:18	According to **w** they have **done,**	1692
65: 8	**This is w** the LORD says:	3907
65:12	in my sight and chose **w** displeases me."	889
65:13	Therefore **this is w** the Sovereign LORD says	3907
65:18	and rejoice forever in **w** I will create,	889
66: 1	**This is w** the LORD says:	3907
66: 4	and will bring upon them **w** they **dread**.	AIT
66: 4	in my sight and chose **w** displeases me."	889
66:12	For **this is w** the LORD says:	3907
Jer 1:11	"**W** do you see, Jeremiah?"	4537
1:13	"**W** do you see?"	4537
1:16	worshiping **w** their hands have **made**.	5126
2: 5	**This is w** the LORD says:	3907
2: 5	"**W** fault did your fathers find in me,	4537
2:23	consider **w** you have done.	4537
3: 6	"Have you seen **w** faithless Israel has done?	889
4: 3	**This is w** the LORD says to the men	3907
4:27	**This is w** the LORD says:	3907
4:30	**W** are you doing, O devastated one?	4537
5:13	so let **w** they say be done to them."	NIH
5:14	Therefore **this is w**	3907
5:31	But **w** will you do in the end?	4537
6: 6	**This is w** the LORD Almighty says:	3907
6: 9	**This is w** the LORD Almighty says:	3907
6:16	**This is w** the LORD says:	3907
6:18	O witnesses, **w** will happen to them.	889
6:20	**W** do I care about	2296+3276+4200+4200+4537
6:21	Therefore **this is w** the LORD says:	3907
6:22	**This is w** the LORD says:	3907
7: 3	**This is w** the LORD Almighty says,	3907
7:12	and see **w** I did to it because of	889
7:14	**w** I did to Shiloh I will now do to	889+3869
7:17	not see **w** they are doing in the towns	4537
7:20	"'Therefore **this is w** the Sovereign LORD	3907
7:21	"'**This is w** the LORD Almighty,	3907
8: 4	"Say to them, '**This is w** the LORD says:	3907
8: 6	but they do not say **w** is **right**.	AIT
8: 6	saying, "**W** have I done?"	4537
8: 9	**w** kind *of* wisdom do they have?	4537
8:13	**W** I have given them will be taken	NIH
9: 7	Therefore **this is w** the LORD Almighty says	3907
9: 7	and test them, for **w** **else** can I do because	375
9:12	**W** man is wise enough to understand this?	4769
9:15	Therefore, **this is w** the LORD Almighty says,	3907
9:17	**This is w** the LORD Almighty says:	3907
9:22	Say, "**This is w** the LORD declares:	3907
9:23	**This is w** the LORD says to you,	3907
10: 1	Hear **w** the LORD says to you,	1821+2021S
Jer 10: 2	**This is w** the LORD says:	3907
10: 9	**W** the craftsman and goldsmith have **made**	5126
10:18	For **this is w** the LORD says:	3907
11: 3	Tell them that **this is w** the LORD,	3907
11:11	Therefore **this is w** the LORD says:	3907
11:15	"**W** is my beloved **doing** in my temple	4200+4537
11:18	that time he showed me **w** they were **doing**.	5095
11:21	"Therefore **this is w** the LORD says about	3907
11:22	therefore **this is w** the LORD Almighty says:	3907
12: 4	"He will not see **w** **happens** *to* us."	344
12:14	**This is w** the LORD says:	3907
13: 1	**This is w** the LORD said to me:	3907
13: 9	'**This is w** the LORD says:	3907
13:12	'**This is w** the LORD, the God of Israel,	3907
13:13	then tell them, '**This is w** the LORD says:	3907
13:21	**W** will you say when [the LORD] sets	4537
14:10	**This is w** the LORD says about this people:	3907
14:15	**this is w** the LORD says about	3907
15: 2	tell them, '**This is w** the LORD says:	3907
15: 4	of the earth because of **w** Manasseh son	889
15:19	Therefore **this is w** the LORD says:	3907
16: 3	For **this is w** the LORD says about the sons	3907
16: 5	For **this is w** the LORD says:	3907
16: 9	For **this is w** the LORD Almighty says:	3907
16:10	**W** wrong have we done?	4537
16:10	**W** sin have we committed against	4537
17: 5	**This is w** the LORD says:	3907
17:10	according to **w** his deeds **deserve**."	7262
17:16	**W** **passes** my lips is open before you.	4604
17:19	**This is w** the LORD said to me:	3907
17:21	**This is w** the LORD says:	3907
18:11	'**This is w** the LORD says: Look!	3907
18:13	Therefore **this is w** the LORD says:	3907
18:19	**w** my accusers are **saying**!	7754
19: 1	**This is w** the LORD says:	3907
19: 3	**This is w** the LORD Almighty,	3907
19:11	'**This is w** the LORD Almighty says:	3907
19:12	**This is w** I will do to this place and	4027
19:15	"**This is w** the LORD Almighty, the God	3907
20: 4	For **this is w** the LORD says:	3907
21: 4	'**This is w** the LORD, the God	3907
21: 8	tell the people, '**This is w** the LORD says:	3907
21:12	**this is w** the LORD says:	3907
22: 1	**This is w** the LORD says:	3907
22: 3	**This is w** the LORD says:	3907
22: 3	Do **w** is **just** and right.	AIT
22: 6	For **this is w** the LORD says about	3907
22:11	For **this is w** the LORD says	3907
22:15	He did **w** was **right** and just,	AIT
22:16	Is that not **w** it means to know me?"	NIH
22:18	Therefore **this is w** the LORD says	3907
22:30	**This is w** the LORD says:	3907
23: 2	Therefore **this is w** the LORD,	3907
23: 5	and do **w** is **just** and right in the land.	AIT
23:15	**this is w** the LORD Almighty says	3907
23:16	**This is w** the LORD Almighty says	3907
23:16	not listen to **w** the prophets are prophesying	1821S
23:25	"I have heard **w** the prophets say	889
23:28	For **w** has straw to do with grain?"	4537
23:33	ask you, '**W** is the oracle of the LORD?'	4537
23:33	say to them, '**W** oracle?'	4537
23:35	**This is w** each of you keeps on saying	3907
23:35	'**W** is the LORD's answer?'	4537
23:35	or '**W** has the LORD spoken?'	4537
23:37	**This is w** you keep saying to a prophet:	3907
23:37	'**W** is the LORD's answer to you?'	4537
23:37	or '**W** has the LORD spoken?'	4537
23:38	**this is w** the LORD says:	3907
24: 3	Then the LORD asked me, "**W** do you see,	4537
24: 5	"**This is w** the LORD, the God	3907
25: 6	**w** your hands have **made**.	5126
25: 7	**w** your hands have **made,**	5126
25:15	is **w** the LORD, the God of Israel,	3907
25:27	tell them, '**This is w** the LORD Almighty,	3907
25:28	'**This is w** the LORD Almighty says:	3907
25:32	**This is w** the LORD Almighty says: "Look!	3907
26: 2	'**This is w** the LORD says:	3907
26: 4	Say to them, '**This is w** the LORD says:	3907
26:18	'**This is w** the LORD Almighty says:	3907
27: 2	**This is w** the LORD said to me:	3907
27: 4	'**This is w** the LORD Almighty,	3907
27:16	'**This is w** the LORD says:	3907
27:19	For **this is w** the LORD Almighty says	3907
27:21	**this is w** the LORD Almighty,	3907
28: 2	'**This is w** the LORD Almighty, the God	3907
28: 7	listen to **w** I have to say	1821+2021+2021+2296S
28:11	"**This is w** the LORD says:	3907
28:13	'**This is w** the LORD says:	3907
28:14	**This is w** the LORD Almighty,	3907
28:16	Therefore, **this is w** the LORD says:	3907
29: 4	**This is w** the LORD Almighty, the God	3907
29: 5	plant gardens and eat **w** they **produce**.	AIT
29: 8	Yes, **this is w** the LORD Almighty,	3907
29:10	**This is w** the LORD says:	3907
29:16	but **this is w** the LORD says about	3907
29:17	**This is w** the LORD Almighty says:	3907
29:21	**This is w** the LORD Almighty says:	3907
29:25	"**This is w** the LORD Almighty, the God	3907
29:28	plant gardens and eat **w** they **produce**.' "	AIT
29:31	'**This is w** the LORD says about Shemaiah	3907
29:32	**this is w** the LORD says:	3907
30: 2	'**This is w** the LORD, the God of Israel,	3907
30: 5	"**This is w** the LORD says:	3907
30:12	"**This is w** the LORD says:	3907
30:18	"**This is w** the LORD says:	3907
31: 2	**This is w** the LORD says:	3907
31: 7	**This is w** the LORD says:	3907
Jer 31:15	**This is w** the LORD says:	3907
31:16	**This is w** the LORD says:	3907
31:23	**This is w** the LORD Almighty,	3907
31:35	**This is w** the LORD says:	3907
31:37	**This is w** the LORD says:	3907
32: 3	You say, '**This is w** the LORD says:	3907
32:14	'**This is w** the LORD Almighty, the God	3907
32:15	For **this is w** the LORD Almighty says:	3907
32:23	they did not do **w** you commanded them	3972S
32:24	**W** you said has happened, as you now see.	889
32:28	Therefore, **this is w** the LORD says:	3907
32:30	**w** their hands have **made,**	5126
32:36	but **this is w** the LORD, the God of Israel,	3907
32:42	"**This is w** the LORD says:	3907
33: 2	"**This is w** the LORD says, he who made	3907
33: 4	For **this is w** the LORD, the God of Israel,	3907
33:10	"**This is w** the LORD says:	3907
33:12	"**This is w** the LORD Almighty says:	3907
33:15	he will do **w** is **just** and right in the land.	AIT
33:17	For **this is w** the LORD says:	3907
33:20	"**This is w** the LORD says:	3907
33:25	**This is w** the LORD says:	3907
34: 2	"**This is w** the LORD, the God	3907
34: 2	'**This is w** the LORD says:	3907
34: 4	**This is w** the LORD says concerning you:	3907
34:13	"**This is w** the LORD, the God	3907
34:15	Recently you repented and did **w** is **right**	AIT
34:17	"Therefore, **this is w** the LORD says:	3907
35:13	"**This is w** the LORD Almighty, the God	3907
35:17	**this is w** the LORD God Almighty,	3907
35:18	"**This is w** the LORD Almighty,	3907
35:19	Therefore, **this is w** the LORD Almighty,	3907
36:29	'**This is w** the LORD says:	3907
36:30	**this is w** the LORD says	3907
37: 7	"**This is w** the LORD, the God	3907
37: 9	"**This is w** the LORD says:	3907
37:18	"**W** crime have I committed against you	4537
38: 1	heard **w** Jeremiah was telling all	1821+2021S
38: 2	"**This is w** the LORD says:	3907
38: 3	And **this is w** the LORD says:	3907
38:17	"**This is w** the LORD God Almighty,	3907
38:20	"Obey the LORD by doing **w** I tell you.	889
38:21	is **w** the LORD has revealed to me:	1821+2021S
38:25	'Tell us **w** you said to the king and what	4537
38:25	'Tell us what you said to the king and **w**	4537
39:16	'**This is w** the LORD Almighty,	3907
40:16	**W** you *are* **saying** about Ishmael is not true."	AIT
42: 3	we should go and **w** we should do."	1821+2021S
42: 9	He said to them, "**This is w** the LORD,	3907
42:15	**This is w** the LORD Almighty,	3907
42:18	**This is w** the LORD Almighty,	3907
43:10	'**This is w** the LORD Almighty says:	3907
44: 2	"**This is w** the LORD Almighty, the God	3907
44: 7	"Now **this is w** the LORD God Almighty,	3907
44: 8	to anger with **w** your hands have **made,**	5126
44:11	"Therefore, **this is w** the LORD Almighty,	3907
44:25	**This is w** the LORD Almighty,	3907
44:25	shown by your actions **w** you promised	NIH
44:25	"Go ahead then, do **w** you **promised!**	5624
44:30	**This is w** the LORD says:	3907
45: 1	**This is w** Jeremiah the prophet told Baruch	1821S
45: 2	"**This is w** the LORD, the God	3907
45: 4	'**This is w** the LORD says:	3907
45: 4	I will overthrow **w** I have built	889
45: 4	and uproot **w** I have planted,	889
46: 5	**W** do I see? They are terrified,	4508
47: 2	**This is w** the LORD says:	3907
48: 1	**This is w** the LORD Almighty,	3907
48:19	ask them, '**W** has happened?'	4537
48:40	**This is w** the LORD says: "Look!	3907
49: 1	**This is w** the LORD says:	3907
49: 7	**This is w** the LORD Almighty says:	3907
49:12	**This is w** the LORD says:	3907
49:19	And **w** shepherd can stand against me?"	4769
49:20	hear **w** the LORD has planned	889
49:20	**w** he has purposed against those who live	889
49:28	**This is w** the LORD says:	3907
49:35	**This is w** the LORD Almighty says:	3907
50:18	Therefore **this is w** the LORD Almighty,	3907
50:33	**This is w** the LORD Almighty says:	3907
50:44	And **w** shepherd can stand against me?	2296+4769
50:45	hear **w** the LORD has planned	889
50:45	**w** he has purposed against the land of	889
51: 1	**This is w** the LORD says:	3907
51: 6	he will pay her **w** she **deserves.**	1691
51:10	tell in Zion **w** the LORD our God has **done.'**	5126
51:33	**This is w** the LORD Almighty,	3907
51:36	Therefore, **this is w** the LORD says:	3907
51:41	**W** a horror Babylon will be among	375
51:44	make him spew out **w** he has **swallowed.**	1183
51:58	**This is w** the LORD Almighty says:	3907
La 1:21	they rejoice at **w** you have done.	NIH
2:13	**W** can I say for you?	4537
2:13	With **w** can I compare you,	4537
2:13	To **w** can I liken you,	4537
2:17	The LORD has done **w** he planned	889
3:17	I have forgotten **w** prosperity is.	NIH
3:51	**W** I see brings grief to my soul because	6524
3:62	**w** my enemies **whisper** and mutter	AIT
3:64	Pay them back **w** they **deserve**, O LORD,	1691
3:64	for **w** their hands have **done.**	5126
5: 1	O LORD, **w** has happened to us;	4537
Eze 1: 5	and in the fire was **w** **looked like**	AIT
1:22	of the living creatures was **w** **looked like**	AIT
1:26	over their heads was **w** looked like a throne	NIH
1:27	I saw that from **w** **appeared** to be his waist	AIT
2: 4	'**This is w** the Sovereign LORD says.'	3907

Eze	2: 6	be afraid of **w** they **say** or terrified by them,	1821
	2: 8	you, son of man, listen to **w** I say to you.	889
	2: 8	open your mouth and eat **w** I give you."	889
	3: 1	eat **w** is before you, eat this scroll;	889
	3:11	'This is **w** the Sovereign LORD says,'	3907
	3:27	'This is **w** the Sovereign LORD says.'	3907
	5: 5	"This is **w** the Sovereign LORD says:	3907
	5: 7	"Therefore **this is w** the Sovereign LORD	3907
	5: 8	"Therefore **this is w** the Sovereign LORD	3907
	5: 9	I will do to you **w** I have never done	889+4017
	6: 3	**This is w** the Sovereign LORD says to	3907
	6: 6	and **w** you have **made** wiped out.	5126
	6:11	" 'This is **w** the Sovereign LORD says:	3907
	7: 2	**this is w** the Sovereign LORD says to	3907
	7: 5	"This is **w** the Sovereign LORD says:	3907
	8: 2	From **w appeared** to be his waist	AIT
	8: 3	He stretched out **w looked like** a hand	AIT
	8: 6	do you see **w** they are doing—	4537
	8:12	have you seen **w** the elders of the house	889
	9:10	on their own heads **w** they have **done."**	2006
	10: 8	be seen **w looked like** the hands of a man.)	AIT
	10:21	and under their wings was **w looked like**	AIT
	11: 5	"This is **w** the LORD says:	3907
	11: 5	That is **w** you are saying, O house of Israel,	4027
	11: 5	but I know **w** is **going through** your mind.	5091
	11: 7	"Therefore **this is w** the Sovereign LORD	3907
	11: 8	and the sword is **w** I will bring against you,	NIH
	11:16	'This is **w** the Sovereign LORD says:	3907
	11:17	'This is **w** the Sovereign LORD says:	3907
	11:21	down on their own heads **w** they have **done**,	2006
	12: 9	'**W** are you doing?'	4537
	12:10	'This is **w** the Sovereign LORD says	3907
	12:19	'This is **w** the Sovereign LORD says	3907
	12:22	**w** is this proverb you have in the land	4537
	12:23	'This is **w** the Sovereign LORD says:	3907
	12:25	But I the LORD will speak **w** I will,	889
	12:28	'This is **w** the Sovereign LORD says:	3907
	13: 3	**This is w** the Sovereign LORD says:	3907
	13: 8	" 'Therefore **this is w** the Sovereign LORD	3907
	13:13	" 'Therefore **this is w** the Sovereign LORD	3907
	13:18	" 'Therefore **this is w** the Sovereign LORD	3907
	13:20	" 'Therefore **this is w** the Sovereign LORD	3907
	14: 4	'This is **w** the Sovereign LORD says:	3907
	14: 6	'This is **w** the Sovereign LORD says:	3907
	14:21	"For **this is w** the Sovereign LORD says:	3907
	15: 6	"Therefore **this is w** the Sovereign LORD	3907
	16: 3	**This is w** the Sovereign LORD says	3907
	16:19	*That is w* **happened**,	AIT
	16:36	**This is w** the Sovereign LORD says:	3907
	16:43	down on your head **w** you have **done**,	2006
	16:48	and her daughters never did **w** you	889+3869
	16:55	will return to **w** they were **before;**	AIT
	16:55	will return to **w** you were **before.**	AIT
	16:59	" 'This is **w** the Sovereign LORD says:	3907
	17: 3	'This is **w** the Sovereign LORD says:	3907
	17: 9	'This is **w** the Sovereign LORD says:	3907
	17:12	'Do you not know **w** these things **mean?'**	4537
	17:19	" 'Therefore **this is w** the Sovereign LORD	3907
	17:22	" 'This is **w** the Sovereign LORD says:	3907
	18: 2	"**W do you** people **mean**	4013+4200+4537
	18: 5	a righteous man who does **w** is **just**	AIT
	18: 7	but returns **w** he **took in pledge**	2481
	18:12	does not return **w** he **took in pledge.**	2478
	18:18	robbed his brother and did **w** was wrong	889
	18:19	Since the son has done **w** is **just** and right,	AIT
	18:21	and keeps all my decrees and does **w** is **just**	AIT
	18:27	and does **w** is **just** and right,	AIT
	19: 2	" '**W** a lioness was your mother among	4537
	20: 3	'This is **w** the Sovereign LORD says:	3907
	20: 5	'This is **w** the Sovereign LORD says:	3907
	20: 9	the sake of my name I did **w** would keep it	NIH
	20:14	the sake of my name I did **w** would keep it	NIH
	20:22	the sake of my name I did **w** would keep it	NIH
	20:27	'This is **w** the Sovereign LORD says:	3907
	20:29	**W** is this high place you go to?' "	4537
	20:30	'This is **w** the Sovereign LORD says:	3907
	20:32	But **w** you have in mind will never happen.	2021
	20:39	**this is w** the Sovereign LORD says:	3907
	20:47	**This is w** the Sovereign LORD says:	3907
	21: 3	'This is **w** the LORD says:	3907
	21: 9	prophesy and say, 'This is **w** the Lord says:	3907
	21:13	And **w** if the scepter [of Judah],	4537
	21:24	"Therefore **this is w** the Sovereign LORD	3907
	21:26	**this is w** the Sovereign LORD says:	3907
	21:28	'This is **w** the Sovereign LORD says about	3907
	22: 3	'This is **w** the Sovereign LORD says:	3907
	22:19	Therefore **this is w** the Sovereign LORD	3907
	22:28	'This is **w** the Sovereign LORD says'—	3907
	23:22	**this is w** the Sovereign LORD says:	3907
	23:28	"For **this is w** the Sovereign LORD says:	3907
	23:32	"This is **w** the Sovereign LORD says:	3907
	23:35	"Therefore **this is w** the Sovereign LORD	3907
	23:39	That is **w** they did in my house.	3907
	23:46	"This is **w** the Sovereign LORD says:	3907
	24: 3	'This is **w** the Sovereign LORD says:	3907
	24: 6	" 'For **this is w** the Sovereign LORD says:	3907
	24: 9	" 'Therefore **this is w** the Sovereign LORD	3907
	24:19	"Won't you tell us **w** these things have	4537
	24:21	'This is **w** the Sovereign LORD says:	3907
	25: 3	**This is w** the Sovereign LORD says:	3907
	25: 6	For **this is w** the Sovereign LORD says:	3907
	25: 8	"This is **w** the Sovereign LORD says:	3907
	25:12	"This is **w** the Sovereign LORD says:	3907
	25:13	therefore **this is w** the Sovereign LORD says:	3907
	25:15	"This is **w** the Sovereign LORD says:	3907
	25:16	therefore **this is w** the Sovereign LORD says:	3907
	26: 3	therefore **this is w** the Sovereign LORD says:	3907

Eze	26: 7	"For **this is w** the Sovereign LORD says:	3907
	26:15	"This is **w** the Sovereign LORD says	3907
	26:19	"This is **w** the Sovereign LORD says:	3907
	27: 3	'This is **w** the Sovereign LORD says:	3907
	28: 2	'This is **w** the Sovereign LORD says:	3907
	28: 6	" 'Therefore **this is w** the Sovereign LORD	3907
	28:12	'This is **w** the Sovereign LORD says:	3907
	28:22	'This is **w** the Sovereign LORD says:	3907
	28:25	" 'This is **w** the Sovereign LORD says:	3907
	29: 3	'This is **w** the Sovereign LORD says:	3907
	29: 8	" 'Therefore **this is w** the Sovereign LORD	3907
	29:13	" 'Yet **this is w** the Sovereign LORD says:	3907
	29:19	Therefore **this is w** the Sovereign LORD	3907
	30: 2	'This is **w** the Sovereign LORD says:	3907
	30: 6	" 'This is **w** the LORD says:	3907
	30:10	" 'This is **w** the Sovereign LORD says:	3907
	30:13	" 'This is **w** the Sovereign LORD says:	3907
	30:22	Therefore **this is w** the Sovereign LORD	3907
	31:10	" 'Therefore **this is w** the Sovereign LORD	3907
	31:15	" 'This is **w** the Sovereign LORD says:	3907
	32: 3	" 'This is **w** the Sovereign LORD says:	3907
	32:11	" 'For **this is w** the Sovereign LORD says:	3907
	33:10	'This is **w** you are saying:	4027
	33:14	from his sin and does **w** is **just** and right—	AIT
	33:15	**w** he **took in pledge** for a loan,	2478
	33:15	returns **w** he has **stolen,**	1611
	33:16	He has done **w** is **just** and right;	AIT
	33:19	from his wickedness and does **w** is **just**	AIT
	33:25	'This is **w** the Sovereign LORD says:	3907
	33:27	'This is **w** the Sovereign LORD says:	3907
	34: 2	'This is **w** the Sovereign LORD says:	3907
	34:10	**This is w** the Sovereign LORD says:	3907
	34:11	" 'For **this is w** the Sovereign LORD says:	3907
	34:17	**this is w** the Sovereign LORD says:	3907
	34:19	flock feed on **w** you have **trampled**	5330+8079
	34:19	and drink **w** you have **muddied**	5343
	34:20	" 'Therefore **this is w** the Sovereign LORD	3907
	35: 3	'This is **w** the Sovereign LORD says:	3907
	35:14	**This is w** the Sovereign LORD says:	3907
	36: 2	**This is w** the Sovereign LORD says:	3907
	36: 3	**This is w** the Sovereign LORD says:	3907
	36: 4	**This is w** the Sovereign LORD says to	3907
	36: 5	**this is w** the Sovereign LORD says:	3907
	36: 6	**This is w** the Sovereign LORD says:	3907
	36: 7	Therefore **this is w** the Sovereign LORD	3907
	36:13	" 'This is **w** the Sovereign LORD says:	3907
	36:22	**This is w** the Sovereign LORD says:	3907
	36:33	" 'This is **w** the Sovereign LORD says:	3907
	36:36	the LORD have rebuilt **w** was destroyed	2021
	36:36	and have replanted **w** was desolate.	2021
	36:37	"This is **w** the Sovereign LORD says:	3907
	37: 5	**This is w** the Sovereign LORD says	3907
	37: 9	'This is **w** the Sovereign LORD says:	3907
	37:12	'This is **w** the Sovereign LORD says:	3907
	37:18	'Won't you tell us **w** you mean by this?'	4537
	37:19	'This is **w** the Sovereign LORD says:	3907
	37:21	'This is **w** the Sovereign LORD says:	3907
	38: 3	" 'This is **w** the Sovereign LORD says:	3907
	38:10	" 'This is **w** the Sovereign LORD says:	3907
	38:14	'This is **w** the Sovereign LORD says:	3907
	38:17	" 'This is **w** the Sovereign LORD says:	3907
	38:18	*This is w* **will happen** in that day:	AIT
	39: 1	'This is **w** the Sovereign LORD says:	3907
	39:17	**this is w** the Sovereign LORD says:	3907
	39:25	"Therefore **this is w** the Sovereign LORD	3907
	42:15	When he had finished measuring **w** was	NIH
	43:18	**this is w** the Sovereign LORD says:	3907
	44: 6	'This is **w** the Sovereign LORD says:	3907
	44: 9	'This is **w** the Sovereign LORD says:	3907
	45: 9	" 'This is **w** the Sovereign LORD says:	3907
	45: 9	and oppression and do **w** is **just** and right.	AIT
	45:18	" 'This is **w** the Sovereign LORD says:	3907
	46: 1	" 'This is **w** the Sovereign LORD says:	3907
	46:16	" 'This is **w** the Sovereign LORD says:	3907
	47:13	**This is w** the Sovereign LORD says:	3907
	48:18	**W** remains of the area,	2021
	48:21	"**W** remains on both sides of the area	2021
Da	1:13	in accordance with **w** you see."	889
	2: 2	to tell him **w** he had **dreamed.**	AIT
	2: 3	and I want to **know w** it **means."**	3359
	2: 5	"This is **w** I have firmly decided:	NIH
	2: 5	not tell me **w** my dream was and interpret it,	NIH
	2: 8	that this is **w** I have firmly decided:	NIH
	2:10	a man on earth who can do **w** the king **asks!**	10418S
	2:11	**W** the king asks is too difficult.	10002+10418S
	2:22	he knows **w** lies in darkness,	10408
	2:23	you have made known to me **w** we asked	10168
	2:25	who can tell the king **w** his dream **means."**	AIT
	2:26	"Are you able to tell me **w** I saw	10168
	2:28	He has shown King Nebuchadnezzar **w** will	10408
	2:29	revealer of mysteries showed you **w** is	10408
		going to happen.	
	2:30	and that you may understand **w** went	NIH
	2:45	the king **w** will take place in the future.	10408
	3: 4	"This is **w** you are commanded to do,	NIH
	3:15	Then **w** god will be able to rescue you	10426
	4:18	Now, Belteshazzar, tell me **w** it **means,**	AIT
	4:27	Renounce your sins by doing **w** is **right,**	AIT
	4:31	"This is **w** is decreed for you,	NIH
	4:33	Immediately **w** had been **said**	10418
	4:35	**W** have you done?"	10408
	5: 7	and tells me **w** it **means** will be clothed	AIT
	5: 8	the writing or tell the king **w** it **meant.**	AIT
	5:12	and he will tell you **w** the writing **means."**	AIT
	5:15	to read this writing and tell me **w** it **means,**	AIT
	5:16	and tell me **w** it **means,**	AIT

Da	5:17	for the king and tell him **w** it **means.**	AIT
	5:26	"This is **w** these **words** mean:	AIT
	8:19	"I am going to tell you **w** will happen later	889
	9:12	like **w** has been done to Jerusalem.	889
	10:14	to you **w** will happen to your people in	889
	10:21	but first I will tell you **w** is written in	2021
	11:24	and will achieve **w** neither his fathers	889
	11:29	be different from **w** it was before.	NIH
	11:36	for **w has been determined** must take place.	AIT
	12: 8	**w** will the outcome of all this be?"	4537
Hos	5: 9	the tribes of Israel I proclaim **w** is **certain.**	AIT
	6: 4	"**W** can I do with you, Ephraim?	4537
	6: 4	**W** can I do with you, Judah?	4537
	8: 3	But Israel has rejected **w** is good;	NIH
	9: 5	**W** will you do on the day of your appointed	4537
	9:14	**w** will you give them?	4537
	10: 3	if we had a king, **w** could he do for us?"	4537
	14: 3	to **w** our own hands have **made,**	5126
	14: 8	O Ephraim, **w** more have I to do with idols?	4537
Joel	1: 4	**W** the locust swarm has **left**	AIT
	1: 4	**w** the great locusts have **left**	AIT
	1: 4	**w** the young locusts have **left**	AIT
	3: 4	"Now **w** have you against me,	4537
	3: 4	on your own heads **w** you have **done.**	1691
	3: 7	on your own heads **w** you have **done.**	1691
Am	1: 1	**w** he saw concerning Israel two years	889
	1: 3	**This is w** the LORD says:	3907
	1: 6	**This is w** the LORD says:	3907
	1: 9	**This is w** the LORD says:	3907
	1:11	**This is w** the LORD says:	3907
	1:13	**This is w** the LORD says:	3907
	2: 1	**This is w** the LORD says:	3907
	2: 4	**This is w** the LORD says:	3907
	2: 6	**This is w** the LORD says:	3907
	3:11	Therefore **this is w** the Sovereign LORD	3907
	3:12	**This is w** the LORD says:	3907
	4: 5	you Israelites, for **this is w** you love to do,"	4027
	4:12	"Therefore **this is w** I will do to you, Israel,	3907
	5: 3	**This is w** the Sovereign LORD says:	3907
	5: 4	**This is w** the LORD says to the house	3907
	5:16	Therefore **this is w** the Lord,	3907
	7: 1	**This is w** the Sovereign LORD showed me:	3907
	7: 4	**This is w** the Sovereign LORD showed me:	3907
	7: 7	**This is w** he showed me:	3907
	7: 8	LORD asked me, "**W** do you see, Amos?"	4537
	7:11	For **this is w** Amos is saying:	3907
	7:17	"Therefore **this is w** the LORD says:	3907
	8: 1	**This is w** the Sovereign LORD showed me:	3907
	8: 2	"**W** do you see, Amos?"	4537
Ob	1: 1	**This is w** the Sovereign LORD says	3907
	1: 5	Oh, **w** a disaster awaits you—	375
Jnh	1: 8	**W** do you do? Where do you come from?	4537
	1: 8	**W** is your country?	4537
	1: 8	From **w** people are you?"	2296
	1:10	"**W** have you done?"	4537
	1:11	"**W** should we do to you to make the sea	4537
	2: 9	**W** I have vowed I will make good.	889
	3:10	When God saw **w** they **did** and	5126
	4: 2	is this not **w** I **said** when I was still at home?	1821
	4: 5	and waited to see **w** would happen to	4537
Mic	1: 5	**W** is Jacob's transgression?	4769
	1: 5	**W** is Judah's high place?	4769
	3: 5	**This is w** the LORD says:	3907
	6: 1	Listen to **w** the LORD says:	889
	6: 1	let the hills hear **w** you **have to say.**	7754
	6: 3	"My people, **w** have I done to you?	4537
	6: 5	remember **w** Balak king of Moab counseled	4537
	6: 5	of Moab counseled and **w** Balaam son	4537
	6: 6	With **w** shall I come before the LORD	4537
	6: 8	He has showed you, O man, **w** is good.	4537
	6: 8	And **w** does the LORD require of you?	4537
	6:14	because **w** you save I will give to the sword.	889
	7: 1	**W** misery is mine!	518
	7: 3	the powerful dictate **w** they desire—	NIH
Na	1:12	**This is w** the LORD says:	3907
Hab	2: 1	I will look to see **w** he will say to me,	4537
	2: 1	**w** answer I am to give to this complaint.	4537
	2:18	"Of **w** value is an idol,	4537
Zep	2: 3	you who do **w** he commands.	889
	2:10	This is **w** they will get in return	NIH
	2:15	**W** a ruin she has become,	375
Hag	1: 2	"This is **w** the LORD Almighty says:	3907
	1: 5	Now **this is w** the LORD Almighty says:	3907
	1: 7	"This is **w** the LORD Almighty says:	3907
	1: 9	**W** you brought home, I blew away.	NIH
	2: 5	'This is **w** I covenanted with you	889
	2: 6	"This is **w** the LORD Almighty says:	3907
	2:11	"This is **w** the LORD Almighty says:	3907
	2:11	'Ask the priests **w** the law says:	NIH
Zec	1: 3	**This is w** the LORD Almighty says:	3907
	1: 4	**This is w** the LORD Almighty says:	3907
	1: 6	**w** our ways and practices **deserve,**	3869
	1: 9	I asked, "**W** are these, my lord?"	4537
	1: 9	"I will show you **w** they are."	4537
	1:14	**This is w** the LORD Almighty says:	3907
	1:16	"Therefore, **this is w** the LORD says:	3907
	1:17	**This is w** the LORD Almighty says:	3907
	1:19	to me, "**W** are these?"	4537
	1:21	I asked, "**W** are these coming to do?"	4537
	2: 8	For **this is w** the LORD Almighty says:	3907
	3: 7	"This is **w** the LORD Almighty says:	3907
	4: 2	He asked me, "**W** do you **see?"**	4537
	4: 4	"**W** are these, my lord?"	4537
	4: 5	"Do you not know **w** these are?"	4537
	4: 7	"**W** are you, O mighty mountain?	4769
	4:11	"**W** are these two olive trees on the right	4537
	4:12	"**W** are these two olive branches beside	4537

Zec	4:13	He replied, "Do you not know w these are?"	4537
	5: 2	He asked me, "W do you see?"	4537
	5: 3	for according to w it says on one side,	NIH
	5: 3	and according to w it says on the other,	NIH
	5: 5	up and see w this is that is appearing."	4537
	5: 6	I asked, "W is it?"	4537
	6: 4	"W are these, my lord?"	4537
	6:12	Tell him this is w the LORD Almighty says:	3907
	7: 9	'This is w the LORD Almighty says:	3907
	8: 2	This is w the LORD Almighty says:	3907
	8: 3	This is w the LORD says:	3907
	8: 4	This is w the LORD Almighty says:	3907
	8: 6	This is w the LORD Almighty says:	3907
	8: 7	This is w the LORD Almighty says:	3907
	8: 9	This is w the LORD Almighty says:	3907
	8:14	This is w the LORD Almighty says:	3907
	8:19	This is w the LORD Almighty says:	3907
	8:20	This is w the LORD Almighty says:	3907
	8:23	This is w the LORD Almighty says:	3907
	11: 4	This is w the LORD my God says:	3907
	13: 6	'W are these wounds on your body?'	4537
Mal	1: 4	But this is w the LORD Almighty says:	3907
	1:13	And you say, 'W a burden!'	4537
	3:13	you ask, 'W have we said against you?'	4537
	3:14	W did we gain by carrying out his	4537
Mt	1:20	because w is conceived in her is from	3836
	1:22	to fulfill w the Lord had said through	3836
	1:24	he did w the angel of the Lord had	6055
	2: 5	"for this is w the prophet has written:	4048
	2:15	so was fulfilled w the Lord had said through	3836
	2:17	Then w was said through the prophet	3836
	2:23	So was fulfilled w was said through	3836
	4:14	to fulfill w was said through	3836
	5:46	w reward will you get?	5515
	5:47	w are you doing more than others?	5515
	6: 3	know w your right hand is doing,	5515
	6: 4	your Father, who sees w is done in secret,	NIG
	6: 6	your Father, who sees w is done in secret,	NIG
	6: 8	for your Father knows w you need	4005
	6:18	your Father, who sees w is done in secret,	NIG
	6:25	w you will eat or drink;	5515
	6:25	or about your body, w you will wear.	5515
	6:31	So do not worry, saying, 'W shall we eat?'	5515
	6:31	or 'W shall we drink?'	5515
	6:31	or 'W shall we wear?'	5515
	7: 6	"Do not give dogs w is sacred;	3836
	7:12	do to others w you would have them do to you,	1569+4012
	8:17	This was to fulfill w was spoken through	3836
	8:27	"W kind of man is this?	5515
	8:29	"W do you want with us,	2779+5515
	8:33	including w had happened to	3836
	9:13	But go and learn w this means:	3836
	10:19	not worry about w to say or how to say it.	5515
	10:19	At that time you will be given w to say,	5515
	10:27	W I tell you in the dark,	4005
	10:27	w is whispered in your ear,	4005
	11: 2	John heard in prison w Christ was doing,	3836
	11: 4	"Go back and report to John w you hear	4005
	11: 7	"W did you go out into the desert to see?	5515
	11: 8	If not, w did you go out to see?	5515
	11: 9	Then w did you go out to see?	5515
	11:16	"To w can I compare this generation?	5515
	12: 2	Your disciples are doing w is unlawful on	4005
	12: 3	"Haven't you read w David did when he	5515
	12: 7	If you had known w these words mean,	5515
	12:17	This was to fulfill w was spoken through	3836
	13: 8	a hundred, sixty or thirty times w was sown.	NIG
	13:12	even w he has will be taken from him.	4005
	13:17	and righteous men longed to see w you see	4005
	13:17	and to hear w you hear but did not hear it.	4005
	13:18	then to w the parable of the sower means:	NIG
	13:19	and snatches away w was sown in his heart.	3836
	13:23	sixty or thirty times w was sown."	NIG
	13:35	So was fulfilled w was spoken through	3836
	14:13	When Jesus heard w had happened,	NIG
	15:11	W goes into a man's mouth does	3836
	15:11	but w comes out of his mouth,	3836
	15:11	that is w makes him 'unclean.'	3124
	15:20	These are w make a man 'unclean';	3836
	16:15	"But w about you?"	NIG
	16:26	W good will it be for a man if he gains	5515
	16:26	w can a man give in exchange for his soul?	5515
	16:27	according to w he has done.	3836
	17: 9	"Don't tell anyone w you have seen,	3836
	17:25	"W do you think, Simon?"	5515
	18:12	"W do you think?	5515
	18:28	'Pay back w you owe me!'	1623+5516
	18:31	the other servants saw w had happened,	3836
	19: 6	Therefore w God has joined together,	4005
	19:16	w good thing must I do to get eternal life?"	5515
	19:17	"Why do you ask me about w is good?"	3836
	19:20	"W do I still lack?"	5515
	19:27	W then will there be for us?"	5515
	20:15	to do w I want with my own money?	4005
	20:21	"W is it you want?"	5515
	20:22	"You don't know w you are asking,"	5515
	20:32	"W do you want me to do for you?"	5515
	21: 4	to fulfill w was spoken through the prophet:	3836
	21:16	"Do you hear w these children are saying?"	5515
	21:21	only can you do w was done to the fig tree,	3836
	21:23	By w authority are you doing these things?"	4481
	21:24	by w authority I am doing these things.	4481
	21:27	by w authority I am doing these things.	4481
	21:28	"W do you think?	5515
	21:31	"Which of the two did w his father wanted?"	NIG
	21:40	w will he do to those tenants?"	5515
Mt	22:17	Tell us then, w is your opinion?	5515
	22:21	"Give to Caesar w is Caesar's,	3836
	22:21	and to God w is God's."	3836
	22:31	have you not read w God said to you,	3306+3836S
	22:42	"W do you think about the Christ?	5515
	23: 3	But do not do w they do,	NIG
	23: 3	for they do not practice w they preach.	NIG
	24: 3	and w will be the sign of your coming and	5515
	24:39	about w would happen until the flood came	NIG
	24:42	not know on w day your Lord will come.	4481
	24:43	of the house had known at w time of night	4481
	25:25	See, here is w belongs to you.'	3836
	25:29	even w he has will be taken from him.	4005
	26:13	w she has done will also be told,	4005
	26:15	"W are you willing to give me if I hand him	5515
	26:50	replied, "Friend, do w you came for."	2093+4005
	26:62	W is this testimony that these men	5515
	26:66	W do you think?"	5515
	26:70	"I don't know w you're talking about,"	5515
	27: 4	"W is that to us?"	5515
	27: 9	Then w was spoken by Jeremiah	3836
	27:22	"W shall I do, then, with Jesus	5515
	27:23	W crime has he committed?"	5515
Mk	1:24	"W do you want with us, Jesus	2779+5515
	1:27	that they asked each other, "W is this?	5515
	2: 8	that this was w they were thinking	NIG
	2:24	why are they doing w is unlawful on	4005
	2:25	"Have you never read w David did when he	5515
	4:20	sixty or even a hundred times w was sown."	NIG
	4:24	"Consider carefully w you hear,"	4005
	4:25	even w he has will be taken from him."	4005
	4:26	"This is w the kingdom of God is like.	4048
	4:30	"W shall we say the kingdom of God is	4802
	4:30	w parable shall we use to describe it?	1877+5515
	5: 7	"W do you want with me, Jesus,	2779+5515
	5: 9	Then Jesus asked him, "W is your name?"	5515
	5:14	the people went out to see w had happened.	5515
	5:16	told the people w had happened to	4802
	5:33	woman, knowing w had happened to her,	4005
	5:36	Ignoring w they said, Jesus told	3364+3836S
	6:24	"W shall I ask for?"	5515
	7:15	it is w comes out of a man that makes him	3836
	7:20	"W comes out of a man is what makes	3836
	7:20	of a man is w makes him 'unclean.'	NIG
	8:29	"But w about you?"	NIG
	8:36	W good is it for a man to gain the whole	5515
	8:37	w can a man give in exchange for his soul?	5515
	9: 6	(He did not know w to say,	5515
	9: 9	to tell anyone w they had seen until the Son	4005
	9:10	discussing w "rising from the dead" meant.	NIG
	9:16	"W are you arguing with them about?"	5515
	9:32	not understand w he meant and were afraid	NIG
	9:33	"W were you arguing about on the road?"	5515
	10: 3	"W did Moses command you?" he replied.	5515
	10: 9	Therefore w God has joined together,	4005
	10:17	"w must I do to inherit eternal life?"	5515
	10:32	and told them w was going to happen	3836
	10:36	"W do you want me to do for you?"	5515
	10:38	"You don't know w you are asking,"	5515
	10:51	"W do you want me to do for you?"	5515
	11: 5	"W are you doing, untying that colt?"	5515
	11:23	but believes that w he says will happen,	4005
	11:28	By w authority are you doing these things?"	4481
	11:29	by w authority I am doing these things.	4481
	11:33	by w authority I am doing these things."	4481
	12: 9	"W then will the owner of the vineyard do?	5515
	12:17	"Give to Caesar w is Caesar's and	3836
	12:17	and to God w is God's."	3836
	13: 1	W massive stones!	4534
	13: 1	W magnificent buildings!"	4534
	13: 4	and w will be the sign that they are all	5515
	13:11	do not worry beforehand about w to say.	NIG
	13:37	W I say to you, I say to everyone:	4005
	14: 8	She did w she could.	4005
	14: 9	w she has done will also be told,	4005
	14:36	Yet not w I will, but what you will."	5515
	14:36	Yet not what I will, but w you will."	5515
	14:40	They did not know w to say to him.	5515
	14:60	W is this testimony that these men	5515
	14:64	W do you think?"	5515
	14:68	or understand w you're talking about,"	5515
	15: 8	to do for them w he usually did.	NIG
	15:12	"W shall I do, then, with the one you call	5515
	15:14	W crime has he committed?"	5515
	15:24	they cast lots to see w each would get.	5515
Lk	1:29	at his words and wondered w kind of	4534
	1:45	Blessed is she who has believed that w	3836
	1:62	to find out w he would like to name	5515
	1:66	asking, "W then is this child going to be?"	5515
	2:17	the word concerning w had been told them	3836
	2:18	and all who heard it were amazed at w	3836
	2:24	to offer a sacrifice in keeping with w is said	3836
	2:27	for him w the custom of the Law required,	NIG
	2:33	and mother marveled at w was said	3836
	2:50	not understand w he was saying to them.	4005
	3:10	"W should we do then?" the crowd asked.	5515
	3:12	"Teacher," they asked, "w should we do?"	5515
	3:14	"And w should we do?"	5515
	4:23	Do here in your hometown w we have heard	4012
	4:34	W do you want with us, Jesus	2779+5515
	4:36	"W is this teaching?	5515
	5:22	Jesus knew w they were thinking and asked,	NIG
	5:25	took w he had been lying on	4005
	6: 2	"Why are you doing w is unlawful on	4005
	6: 3	"Have you never read w David did when he	4005
	6: 4	he ate w is lawful only for priests to eat.	4005
	6: 8	But Jesus knew w they were thinking	3836
Lk	6:11	to discuss with one another w they might do	5515
	6:30	and if anyone takes w belongs to you,	3836
	6:32	w credit is that to you?	4481
	6:33	w credit is that to you?	4481
	6:34	w credit is that to you?	4481
	6:46	'Lord, Lord,' and do not do w I say?	4005
	6:47	I will show you w he is like who comes	5515
	7:22	to John w you have seen and heard:	4005
	7:24	"W did you go out into the desert to see?	5515
	7:25	If not, w did you go out to see?	5515
	7:26	But w did you go out to see?	5515
	7:31	"To w, then, can I compare the people	5515
	7:31	W are they like?	5515
	7:39	and w kind of woman she is—	4534
	8: 9	disciples asked him w this parable meant.	5515
	8:18	he thinks he has will be taken from him."	4005
	8:28	"W do you want with me, Jesus,	2779+5515
	8:30	Jesus asked him, "W is your name?"	5515
	8:34	the pigs saw w had happened,	3836
	8:35	the people went out to see w had happened.	3836
	8:56	not to tell anyone w had happened.	3836
	9:10	they reported to Jesus w they had done.	4012
	9:20	"But w about you?"	NIG
	9:25	W good is it for a man to gain the whole	5515
	9:33	(He did not know w he was saying.)	4005
	9:36	told no one at that time w they had seen.	4005
	9:44	"Listen carefully to w I am about	NIG
	9:45	But they did not understand w this meant.	3836
	10: 8	eat w is set before you.	3836
	10:23	"Blessed are the eyes that see w you see.	4005
	10:24	and kings wanted to see w you see but did	4005
	10:24	and to hear w you hear but did not hear it."	4005
	10:25	"w must I do to inherit eternal life?"	5515
	10:26	W is written in the Law?"	5515
	10:39	at the Lord's feet listening to w he said.	3836
	10:42	Mary has chosen w is better,	3535S
	11:41	But give w is inside [the dish] to the poor,	3836
	11:48	that you approve of w your forefathers did;	NIG
	12: 3	W you have said in the dark will be heard in	4012
	12: 3	w you have whispered in the ear in	4005
	12:11	defend yourselves or w you will say,	5515
	12:12	at that time w you should say."	4005
	12:17	He thought to himself, 'W shall I do?	5515
	12:18	"Then he said, 'This is w I'll do.	NIG
	12:20	Then who will get w you have prepared	4005
	12:22	not worry about your life, w you will eat;	4005
	12:22	or about your body, w you will wear.	5515
	12:29	And do not set your heart on w you will eat	4005
	12:39	of the house had known at w hour	4481
	12:47	not do w his master wants will be beaten	NIG
	12:57	judge for yourselves w is right?	3836
	13:16	free on the Sabbath day from w bound her?"	3836
	13:18	"W is the kingdom of God like?	5515
	13:18	W shall I compare it to?	5515
	13:20	"W shall I compare the kingdom	5515
	14:22	'w you ordered has been done,	NIG
	15:26	and asked him w was going on.	323+4047+5515
	16: 2	'W is this I hear about you?	5515
	16: 3	'W shall I do now?	5515
	16: 4	I know w I'll do so that,	5515
	16:15	W is highly valued among men is detestable	4022
	16:21	to eat w fell from the rich man's table.	3836
	17: 9	the servant because he did w he was told	3836
	18: 6	"Listen to w the unjust judge says.	5515
	18:18	w must I do to inherit eternal life?"	5515
	18:27	"W is impossible with men is possible	3836
	18:34	they did not know w he was talking about.	3836
	18:36	he asked w was happening.	5515
	18:41	"W do you want me to do for you?"	5515
	19:10	to seek and to save w was lost."	3836
	19:15	in order to find out w they had gained	5515
	19:21	You take out w you did not put in	4005
	19:21	not put in and reap w you did not sow.'	4005
	19:22	taking out w I did not put in,	4005
	19:22	and reaping w I did not sow?	4005
	19:26	even w he has will be taken away.	4005
	19:42	on this day w would bring you peace—	3836
	20: 2	by w authority you are doing these things,"	4481
	20: 8	by w authority I am doing these things.	4481
	20:13	owner of the vineyard said, 'W shall I do?	5515
	20:15	"W then will the owner of the vineyard do	5515
	20:17	w is the meaning of that which is written:	5515
	20:21	that you speak and teach w is right,	3987
	20:25	"Then give to Caesar w is Caesar's,	3836
	20:25	and to God w is God's."	3836
	20:26	to trap him in w he had said there in public.	4839
	21: 6	for w you see here, the time will come when	4005
	21: 7	And w will be the sign that they are about	5515
	21:26	apprehensive of w is coming on the world,	3836
	22:37	w is written about me is reaching its fulfillment."	3836
	22:49	When Jesus' followers saw w was going	3836
	22:60	I don't know w you're talking about!"	4005
	23: 8	From w he had heard about him,	3836
	23:22	W crime has this man committed?	5515
	23:31	w will happen when it is dry?"	5515
	23:34	for they do not know w they are doing."	5515
	23:41	for we are getting w our deeds deserve.	4005
	23:47	The centurion, seeing w had happened,	3836
	23:48	to witness this sight saw w took place,	3836
	24:12	wondering to himself w had happened.	3836
	24:17	"W are you discussing together	5515
	24:19	"W things?" he asked. "About Jesus	4481
	24:21	And w is more, it is the third day	247+1145+2779+4047+4246+5250
	24:27	he explained to them w was said in all	1450
	24:35	the two told w had happened on the way,	3836

Lk	24:44	"This is w I told you while I was still	4005
	24:46	He told them, "This is w is written:	4048
	24:49	to send you w my Father has promised;	3836
Jn	1:22	W do you say about yourself?"	5515
	1:38	"W do you want?"	5515
	1:40	of the two who heard w John had said	NIG
	2:18	"W miraculous sign can you show us	5515
	2:22	his disciples recalled w he had said.	4047
	2:25	for he knew w was in a man.	5515
	3:11	I tell you the truth, we speak of w we know,	4005
	3:11	and we testify to w we have seen,	4005
	3:21	that w he has done has been done	3836
	3:27	"A man can receive only w is given him	4005
	3:32	He testifies to w he has seen and heard,	4005
	4:18	W you have just said is quite true."	4047
	4:22	You Samaritans worship w you do	4005
	4:22	we worship w we do know,	4005
	4:27	But no one asked, "W do you want?"	5515
	4:38	to reap w you have not worked for.	4005
	4:42	because of w you said;	NIG
	5:19	can do only w he sees his Father doing,	323+5516
	5:47	But since you do not believe w he wrote,	3836
	5:47	how are you going to believe w I say?"	3836
	6:6	for he already had in mind w he was going	5515
	6:28	"W must we do to do	5515
	6:30	"W miraculous sign then will you give	5515
	6:30	W will you do?	5515
	6:62	W if you see the Son of Man ascend to	NIG
	7:7	because I testify that w it does is evil.	3836
	7:36	W did he mean when he said,	5515
	7:51	to find out w he is doing?"	5515
	8:5	Now w do you say?"	5515
	8:25	Just w I have been claiming all along,"	4005+5516
	8:26	w I have heard from him I tell the world."	4005
	8:28	but speak just w the Father has taught me.	NIG
	8:29	for I always do w pleases him."	3836
	8:38	I am telling you w I have seen in	4005
	8:38	you do w you have heard from your father."	4005
	8:43	Because you are unable to hear w I say.	NIG
	8:47	He who belongs to God hears w God says.	3836
	9:17	"W have you to say about him?	5515
	9:26	Then they asked him, "W did he do to you?	5515
	9:40	with him heard him say this and asked, "W?	NIG
	10:6	not understand w he was telling them.	4005
	10:36	w about the one whom the Father set apart	4005
	10:37	unless I do w my Father does.	2240+3836S
	11:45	and had seen w Jesus did,	4005
	11:46	and told them what Jesus had done.	4005
	11:47	"W are we accomplishing?"	5515
	11:56	"W do you think?	5515
	12:6	he used to help himself to w was put into it.	3836
	12:27	my heart is troubled, and w shall I say?	5515
	12:49	the Father who sent me commanded me w	5515
	12:50	So whatever I say is just w	2777
	13:7	"You do not realize now w I am doing,	4005
	13:12	"Do you understand w I have done	5515
	13:13	and rightly so, for that is w I am.	NIG
	13:27	"W you are about to do, do quickly,"	4005
	13:29	to buy w was needed for the Feast,	4005
	14:12	in me will do w I have been doing.	4005
	14:15	love me, you will obey w I command.	NIG
	14:31	I do exactly w my Father has commanded me.	2777
	15:14	You are my friends if you do w I command.	4005
	15:24	not done among them w no one else did,	4005
	15:25	this is to fulfill w is written in their Law:	3836
	16:13	he will speak only w he hears,	4012
	16:13	and he will tell you w is yet to come.	3836
	16:14	from w is mine and making it known	3836
	16:15	from w is mine and make it known to you.	3836
	16:17	"W does he mean by saying,	5515
	16:18	"W does he mean by 'a little while'?	4036+5515
	16:18	We don't understand w he is saying."	5515
	16:19	Are you asking one another w I meant	4047+4309
	18:21	Surely they know w I said."	4005
	18:23	Jesus replied, "testify as to w is wrong.	3836
	18:29	"W charges are you bringing	5515
	18:35	W is it you have done?"	5515
	18:38	"W is truth?" Pilate asked.	5515
	19:22	Pilate answered, "W I have written,	4005
	19:24	So this is w the soldiers did.	NIG
	21:21	he asked, "Lord, w about him?"	5515
	21:22	w is that to you?	5515
	21:23	w is that to you?"	5515
Ac	2:3	They saw w seemed to be tongues of fire	6059
	2:12	"W does this mean?"	5515
	2:14	listen carefully to w I say.	3836
	2:16	this is w was spoken by the prophet Joel:	3836
	2:31	Seeing w was ahead, he spoke of the	4632
	2:33	and has poured out w you now see and hear.	4005
	2:37	"Brothers, w shall we do?"	5515
	3:6	but w I have I give you.	4005
	3:10	and amazement at w had happened to him.	3836
	3:18	how God fulfilled w he had foretold	4005
	4:7	w power or what name did you do	4481
	4:7	or w name did you do this?"	4481
	4:16	"W are we going to do with these men?"	5515
	4:20	about w we have seen and heard."	4005
	4:21	for w had happened.	3836
	4:28	They did w your power	4012
	5:4	W made you think of doing such a thing?	5515
	5:5	fear seized all who heard w had happened.	NIG
	5:7	not knowing w had happened.	3836
	5:24	wondering w would come of this.	5515
	5:35	of Israel, consider carefully w you intend	5515
	7:40	we don't know w has happened to him!'	NIG
	7:41	in honor of w their hands had made.	NIG

Ac	7:42	This agrees with w is written in the book	AIT
	7:49	W kind of house will you build for me?	4481
	8:6	they all paid close attention to w he said.	AIT
	8:30	"Do you understand w you are reading?"	4005
	9:6	and you will be told w you must do."	4005+5515
	10:1	in w was known as the Italian Regiment.	3836
	10:4	"W is it, Lord?" he asked.	5515
	10:22	so that he could hear w you have to say."	NIG
	10:35	and do w is right.	1466
	10:37	You know w has happened	3836
	11:16	Then I remembered w the Lord had said:	3364
	12:9	but he had no idea that w	3836
	12:18	the soldiers as to w had become of Peter.	5515
	13:8	that is w his name means) opposed them	NIG
	13:12	When the proconsul saw w had happened,	4005
	13:32	W God promised our fathers	3836
	13:40	that w the prophets have said does	3836
	13:45	against w Paul was saying.	3836
	13:47	For this is w the Lord has commanded us:	4048
	14:11	When the crowd saw w Paul had done,	4005
	15:24	troubling your minds by w they said.	3364
	15:27	by word of mouth w we are writing.	899+3836S
	16:30	"Sirs, w must I do to be saved?"	5515
	17:11	to see if w Paul said was so.	4047S
	17:18	"W is this babbler trying to say?"	5515
	17:19	"May we know w this new teaching is	5515
	17:20	and we want to know w they mean."	5515
	17:23	Now w you worship as something unknown	4005
	19:3	"Then w baptism did you receive?"	1650+5515
	20:22	not knowing w will happen to me there.	3836
	20:38	W grieved them most was his statement	NIG
	21:19	and reported in detail w God had done	4005
	21:22	W shall we do?	1639+4036+5515
	21:23	so do w we tell you.	4005
	21:33	he asked who he was and w he had done.	5515
	22:10	"'W shall I do, Lord?'	4005
	22:15	to all men of w you have seen and heard.	4005
	22:16	And now w are you waiting for?	5515
	22:26	"W are you going to do?	5515
	23:9	"W if a spirit or an angel has spoken	1623
	23:19	"W is it you want to tell me?"	5515
	23:34	and asked w province he was from.	4481
	24:20	are here should state w crime they found	5515
	26:6	in w God has promised our fathers that I am	NIG
	26:10	And that is just w I did in Jerusalem.	4005
	26:16	and as a witness of w you have seen of me	4005
	26:16	of me and w I will show you.	4005
	26:22	I am saying nothing beyond w the prophets	4005
	26:25	"W I am saying is true and reasonable.	247
	26:29	to me today may become w I am,	3961+5525
	27:11	instead of listening to w Paul said,	3836
	27:13	thought they had obtained w they wanted;	NIG
	28:22	But we want to hear w your views are,	4005
	28:24	Some were convinced by w he said,	3836
Ro	1:19	since w may be known about God is plain	3836
	1:20	being understood from w has been made,	3836
	1:28	to do w ought not to be done.	3836
	2:6	to each person according to w he has done."	3836
	2:18	of w is superior because you are instructed	3836
	3:1	W advantage, then, is there in being a Jew,	5515
	3:1	or w value is there in circumcision?	5515
	3:3	W if some did not have faith?	5515
	3:5	w shall we say? That God is unjust in	5515
	3:9	W shall we conclude then?	5515
	3:27	On w principle? On that of observing	4481
	4:1	W then shall we say that Abraham,	5515
	4:3	W does the Scripture say?	5515
	4:10	Under w circumstances was it credited?	4802
	4:21	to do w he had promised.	4005
	6:1	W shall we say, then?	5515
	6:15	W then? Shall we sin because we are not	5515
	6:21	W benefit did you reap at that time from	4005
	7:6	But now, by dying to w once bound us,	4005
	7:7	W shall we say, then? Is the law sin?	5515
	7:7	not have known w sin was except through	281
	7:7	not have known w coveting really was if	2123
	7:13	in me through w was good,	3836
	7:15	I do not understand w I do.	4005
	7:15	For w I want to do I do not do,	4005
	7:15	but w I hate I do.	4005
	7:16	And if I do w I do not want to do,	3836
	7:18	For I have the desire to do w is good,	NIG
	7:19	For w I do is not the good I want to do;	4005
	7:20	Now if I do w I do not want to do,	4005
	7:24	W a wretched man I am!	NIG
	8:3	For w the law was powerless to do in	NIG
	8:5	the sinful nature have their minds set on w	3836
	8:5	with the Spirit have their minds set on w	3836
	8:24	Who hopes for w he already has?	4005
	8:25	But if we hope for w we do not yet have,	4005
	8:26	We do not know w we ought to pray for,	5515
	8:31	W, then, shall we say in response to this?	5515
	8:34	W then shall we say? Is God unjust?	5515
	9:14	W then shall we say? Is God unjust?	5515
	9:20	"Shall w is formed say to him who formed	3836
	9:22	W if God, choosing to show his wrath	NIG
	9:23	W if he did this to make the riches	NIG
	9:30	W then shall we say?	5515
	10:8	But w does it say? "The word is near you;	5515
	11:2	Don't you know w the Scripture says in	5515
	11:4	And w was God's answer to him?	5515
	11:7	W then? What Israel sought so earnestly	5515
	11:7	W Israel sought so earnestly it did	4005
	11:15	will their acceptance be but life from	5515
	12:2	to test and approve w God's will is—	5515
	12:9	Hate w is evil; cling to w is good.	3836
	12:9	Hate what is evil; cling to w is good.	3836
	12:17	to do w is right in the eyes of everybody.	NIG

Ro	13:2	against w God has instituted,	3836
	13:3	do w is right and he will commend you.	3836
	13:7	Give everyone w you owe him:	3836
	14:15	brother is distressed because of w you eat,	1109
	14:16	not allow w you consider good to be spoken	3836
	14:19	therefore make every effort to do w leads	3836
	14:22	not condemn himself by w he approves.	4005
	15:18	anything except w Christ has accomplished	4005
	15:18	the Gentiles to obey God by w I have said	NIG
	16:19	but I want you to be wise about w is good,	3836
	16:19	and innocent about w is evil.	3836
1Co	1:12	W I mean is this: One of you says,	NIG
	1:21	through the foolishness of w was preached	3060
	1:26	think of w you were when you were called.	NIG
	2:9	no mind has conceived w God has prepared	4005
	2:12	may understand w God has freely given us.	3836
	2:13	This is w we speak,	4005
	3:5	W, after all, is Apollos?	5515
	3:5	And w is Paul? Only servants,	5515
	3:13	his work will be shown for w it is,	NIG
	3:14	If w he has built survives,	2240+3836+5516S
	4:5	He will bring to light w is hidden	3836
	4:6	"Do not go beyond w is written.	4005
	4:7	W do you have that you did not receive?	5515
	4:17	with w I teach everywhere in every church.	NIG
	4:19	but w power they have.	3836
	4:21	W do you prefer? Shall I come to you with	5515
	5:12	W business is it of mine to judge	1609+5515
	6:11	And that is w some of you were.	NIG
	7:19	Keeping God's commands is w counts.	NIG
	7:29	W I mean, brothers, is that the time is short.	4047
	8:10	be emboldened to eat w has been sacrificed	3836
	8:13	if w I eat causes my brother to fall into sin,	1109
	9:13	the altar share in w is offered on the altar?	NIG
	9:18	W then is my reward?	5515
	10:13	No temptation has seized you except w is	NIG
	10:13	common to man.	
	10:13	be tempted beyond w you can bear.	4005
	10:15	judge for yourselves w I say.	4005
	11:22	W shall I say to you?	5515
	11:23	from the Lord w I also passed on to you:	4005
	14:6	w good will I be to you,	5515
	14:7	will anyone know w tune is being played	3836
	14:9	how will anyone know w you are saying?	3836
	14:11	the meaning of w someone is saying,	3836
	14:13	that he may interpret w he says.	NIG
	14:16	So w shall I do? I will pray with my spirit,	5515
	14:16	since he does not know w you are saying?	5515
	14:26	W then shall we say, brothers?	5515
	14:29	the others should weigh carefully w is said.	NIG
	14:37	let him acknowledge that w I am writing	4005
	15:3	For w I received I passed on to you as	4005
	15:10	But by the grace of God I am w I am,	4005
	15:11	then, it was I or they, this is w we preach,	4048
	15:11	and this is w you believed.	4048
	15:29	w will those do who are baptized for	5515
	15:32	for merely human reasons, w have I gained?	5515
	15:35	With w kind of body will they come?"	4481
	15:36	W you sow does not come to life	4005
	16:1	Do w I told the Galatian churches to do.	6061
	16:17	they have supplied w was lacking from you.	3836
2Co	1:22	guaranteeing w is to come.	NIG
	2:10	And I have forgiven—	4005
	3:10	For w was glorious has no glory now	3836
	3:11	And if w was fading away came with glory,	3836
	4:18	So we fix our eyes not on w is seen,	3836
	4:18	but on w is unseen.	3836
	4:18	For w is seen is temporary,	3836
	4:18	but w is unseen is eternal.	3836
	5:4	w is mortal may be swallowed up by life.	3836
	5:5	guaranteeing w is to come.	NIG
	5:10	that each one may receive w is due him for	3836
	5:11	then, we know w it is to fear the Lord,	NIG
	5:11	W we are is plain to God,	AIT
	5:12	in w is seen rather than in what is in	NIG
	5:12	in what is seen rather than in w is in	NIG
	6:14	For w do righteousness and wickedness	5515
	6:14	w fellowship can light have with darkness?	5515
	6:15	W harmony is there between Christ	5515
	6:15	W does a believer have in common with	5515
	6:16	W agreement is there between the temple	5515
	7:11	See w this godly sorrow has produced	4531
	7:11	w earnestness, what eagerness	NIG
	7:11	w eagerness to clear yourselves,	NIG
	7:11	w indignation, what alarm, what longing,	NIG
	7:11	what indignation, w alarm, what longing,	NIG
	7:11	what indignation, what alarm, w concern,	NIG
	7:11	what alarm, what longing, w concern,	NIG
	7:11	w readiness to see justice done.	NIG
	8:10	And here is my advice about w is best	NIG
	8:12	is acceptable according to w one has,	1569+4005
	8:12	not according to w he does not have.	4005
	8:14	your plenty will supply w they need,	NIG
	8:14	in turn their plenty will supply w you need.	NIG
	8:19	W is more, he was chosen by the churches	247+1254+2779+3667+4024
	8:21	For we are taking pains to do w is right,	NIG
	9:7	Each man should give w he has decided	2777
	10:11	Such people should realize that w we are	3888
	11:9	from Macedonia supplied w I needed.	3836
	11:12	And I will keep on doing w I am doing	NIG
	11:15	Their end will be w their actions deserve.	AIT
	11:21	W anyone else dares to boast about—	NIG
	12:6	of me than is warranted by w I do or say.	4005
	12:14	w I want is not your possessions but you.	NIG
	13:7	the test but that you will do w is right even	3836
Gal	1:9	to you a gospel other than w you accepted,	4005

Gal	1:20	that w I am writing you is no lie.	4005
	2:18	If I rebuild w I destroyed,	4005
	3: 2	or by believing w you **heard?**	198
	3: 5	or because you believe w you **heard?**	198
	3:17	W I mean is this: The law,	NIG
	3:19	W, then, was the purpose of the law?	5515
	3:22	so that w was promised,	3836
	4: 1	W I am saying is that as long as the heir is	NIG
	4:15	W has happened to all your joy?	4544
	4:17	W they want is to alienate you [from us],	NIG
	4:21	are you not aware of w the law says?	NIG
	4:30	But w does the Scripture say?	5515
	5:17	For the sinful nature desires w is contrary to	NIG
	5:17	the Spirit w is contrary to the sinful nature.	NIG
	5:17	so that you do not do w you want.	1569+4005
	6: 7	A man reaps w he sows.	1569+4005
	6:11	See w **large** letters I use as I write to you	4383
	6:15	w counts is a new creation.	NIG
Eph	4: 9	(W does "he ascended" mean except that he	5515
	4:29	but only w is helpful for building others up	5516
	5:10	and find out w pleases the Lord.	5515
	5:12	to mention w the disobedient do in secret.	NIG
	5:17	but understand w the Lord's will is.	5515
	6:21	also may know how I am and w I am doing.	5515
Php	1:10	be able to discern w is best and	1422+3836
	1:12	that w **has happened to** me has really served to advance the gospel.	2848+3836
	1:18	But w **does it matter?**	1142+5515
	1:19	w has happened to me will turn out	4047
	1:22	Yet w shall I choose?	5515
	3: 8	W **is more,** I consider everything	247+3529
	3:13	Forgetting w is behind and straining	NIG
	3:13	behind and straining toward w is ahead,	NIG
	3:16	up to w we have already attained.	4005
	4:12	I know w it is to be in need,	NIG
	4:12	and I know w it is to have plenty.	NIG
	4:17	but I am looking for w may be credited	3836
Col	1:24	Now I rejoice in w was suffered for you,	3836
	1:24	up in my flesh w is still **lacking** in regard	5729
	2:16	not let anyone judge you by w you eat	NIG
	2:18	into great detail about w he has seen,	4005
	4: 1	provide your slaves with w is right and fair,	3836
1Th	1: 9	for they themselves report w **kind of**	3961
	2:19	For w is our hope, our joy,	5515
	3:10	and supply w is lacking in your faith.	3836
	4: 2	For you know w instructions we gave you	5515
2Th	2: 6	And now you know w is holding him back,	3836
	3:13	you, brothers, never tire of **doing w is right.**	2818
1Ti	1: 7	but they do not know w they are talking	4005
	1: 7	about or w they so confidently affirm.	5515
	6:20	w **has been entrusted to** your care.	4146
	6:20	of w is falsely called knowledge,	3836
2Ti	1:12	that he is able to guard w I have entrusted	3836
	1:13	W you heard from me, keep as the pattern	4005
	2: 7	Reflect on w I am saying,	4005
	3:11	w **kinds of** things happened to me	3888
	3:14	continue in w you have learned	4005
	4: 3	to say w their itching ears want to hear.	198
	4:14	The Lord will repay him for w he has done.	3836
Tit	1: 5	might straighten out w was left unfinished	3836
	1: 8	hospitable, **one who loves w is good,**	5787
	2: 1	You must teach w is in accord	4005
	2: 3	but to **teach w is good.**	2815
	2: 7	an example by doing w is good.	NIG
	2:14	eager to do w is good.	NIG
	3: 8	to devote themselves to doing w is good.	NIG
	3:14	to devote themselves to doing w is good,	NIG
Phm	1: 8	order you to do w **you ought to do,**	465+3836
Heb	2: 1	therefore, to w we have heard,	3836
	2: 6	"W is man that you are mindful of him,	5515
	2: 6	testifying to w would it be in the future.	3836
	3: 5	and for forty years saw w I did.	NIG
	5: 8	he learned obedience from w he suffered	4005
	6:12	patience inherit w **has been promised.**	2039+3836
	6:15	Abraham received w **was promised.**	2039+3836
	6:16	the oath confirms w is said and puts an end	NIG
	6:17	the heirs of w **was promised,**	2039+3836
	7:15	And w we have said is even more clear	NIG
	8: 1	The point of w we are saying is this:	3836
	8: 5	a copy and shadow of w is in heaven.	3836
	8:13	w is obsolete and aging will soon disappear.	3836
	10:36	you will receive w he has promised.	3836
	11: 1	Now faith is being sure of w we **hope for**	AIT
	11: 1	hope for and certain of w we do not see.	4547
	11: 2	This is w the ancients were commended for.	NIG
	11: 3	so that w is seen was not made out	3836
	11: 3	not made out of w was visible.	NIG
	11:32	And w more shall I say?	5515
	11:33	and gained w **was promised;**	2039
	11:39	none of them received w **had been promised.**	2039+3836
	12: 7	For w son is not disciplined by his father?	5515
	12:20	they could not bear w was commanded:	3836
	12:27	the removing of w can be shaken—	3836
	12:27	so that w cannot be shaken may remain.	3836
	13: 5	of money and be content **with** w you have,	3836
	13: 6	W can man do to me?"	5515
	13:21	and may he work in us w is pleasing to him,	3836
Jas	1:22	Do w it says.	NIG
	1:23	to the word but does not do w it says is like	4047
	1:24	and immediately forgets w he looks like.	3961
	1:25	not forgetting w **he has heard,** but doing it	AIT
	1:25	he will be blessed in w he does.	3836
	2:14	W good is it, my brothers,	5515
	2:16	about his physical needs, w good is it?	5515
	2:18	and I will show you my faith by w I do.	NIG
	2:21	for w **he did** when he offered his son Isaac	2240

Jas	2:22	his faith was made complete by w **he did.**	2240
	2:24	that a person is justified by w **he does** and	2240
	2:25	for w **she did** when she gave lodging to	2240
	3: 2	If anyone is never at fault in w he **says,**	3364
	3: 5	Consider w **a great** forest is set on fire by	2462
	4: 1	W causes fights and quarrels among you?	4470
	4: 2	but you cannot have w you want.	NIG
	4: 3	that you may spend w you get	NIG
	4:14	not even know w **will happen**	3836+4481
	4:14	W is your life? You are a mist	NIG
	5:11	of Job's perseverance and have seen w	NIG
1Pe	2: 8	which is also w they were destined for.	4005
	3: 6	You are her daughters if you **do w is right**	16
	3:14	But even if you should suffer for w **is right,**	1466
	3:14	"Do not fear w they fear;	3836
	4: 3	in the past doing w pagans choose to do—	NIG
	4:17	and if it begins with us, w will the outcome	5515
	4:18	w will become of the ungodly and	4544
2Pe	2: 6	w is **going to happen to** the ungodly;	AIT
	3:11	w **kind of** people ought you to be?	4534
1Jn	1: 3	We proclaim to you w we have seen	4005
	2: 4	but does not do w he commands is a liar,	3836
	2:16	the boasting of w **he has and does—**	1050
	2:24	See that w you have heard from the	4005
	2:25	this is w he promised us—even eternal life.	4005
	2:29	everyone who does w **is right** has been born	1466
	3: 1	And that is w we are!	NIG
	3: 2	w we will be has not yet been made known.	5515
	3: 7	He who does w **is right** is righteous,	1466
	3: 8	He who does w **is sinful** is of the devil,	281
	3:10	Anyone who does not do w **is right** is not	1466
	3:16	This is how we know w love is:	NIG
	3:22	and do w pleases him.	3836
	5:15	we know that we have w we asked of him.	4005
2Jn	1: 8	that you do not lose w you have worked for,	4005
3Jn	1: 5	you are faithful in w you are doing for	4005
	1:10	I will call attention to w he is doing,	4005
	1:11	do not imitate w is evil but what is good.	3836
	1:11	do not imitate what is evil but w is good.	3836
	1:11	Anyone who **does w is good** is from God.	16
	1:11	who **does w is evil** has not seen God.	2803
Jude	1:10	w things they do understand by instinct,	4012
	1:17	remember w the apostles of our Lord	NIG
Rev	1: 1	show his servants w must soon take place.	4005
	1: 3	and take to heart w is written in it,	3836
	1:11	"Write on a scroll w you see and send it to	4005
	1:19	"Write, therefore, w you have seen,	4005
	1:19	w is now and what will take place later.	4005
	1:19	what is now and w will take place later.	4005
	2:10	let him hear w the Spirit says to	5515
	2:10	not be afraid of w you are about to suffer.	4005
	2:11	him hear w the Spirit says to the churches.	5515
	2:17	him hear w the Spirit says to the churches.	5515
	2:25	Only hold on to w you have until I come.	4005
	2:29	him hear w the Spirit says to the churches.	5515
	3: 2	Strengthen w remains and is about to die,	3836
	3: 3	therefore, w you have received and heard;	4802
	3: 3	not know at w time I will come to you.	4481
	3: 6	him hear w the Spirit says to the churches.	5515
	3: 7	W he opens no one can shut,	NIG
	3: 7	and w he shuts no one can open.	NIG
	3:11	Hold on to w you have,	4005
	3:13	him hear w the Spirit says to the churches.	5515
	3:22	him hear w the Spirit says to the churches.	5515
	4: 1	and I will show you w must take place	4005
	4: 6	Also before the throne there was w looked	NIG
	6: 6	Then I heard w sounded like a voice among	NIG
	10: 4	up w the seven thunders have said and do	4005
	15: 2	And I saw w looked like a sea	NIG
	16:11	they refused to repent of w they had done.	3836
	18: 6	pay her back double for w she has done.	3836
	19: 1	After this I heard w **sounded like** the roar of	6055
	19: 6	I heard w sounded like a great multitude,	NIG
	20:12	according to w they had done as recorded in	3836
	20:13	according to w he had done.	3836
	21:27	nor will anyone who does w **is shameful**	1007
	22:12	to everyone according to w he has done.	3836

WHAT'S (6) [WHAT]

Jdg	18:23	**"W the matter** with you	4537
	18:24	**'W the matter** with you?'"	4537
1Sa	4: 6	"W all this shouting in the Hebrew camp?"	4537
1Ki	1:41	**"W the meaning of** all the noise in the city?	4508
2Ki	6:28	Then he asked her, **"W the matter?"**	4537
Mk	6: 2	"W this wisdom that has been given him,	5515

WHATEVER (182) [WHAT]

Ge	2:19	w the man called each living creature,	889+3972
	16: 6	"Do with her w you think best."	2021
	21:12	Listen to w Sarah tells you,	889+3972
	31:16	So do w God has told you."	889+3972
	31:39	from me for w **was stolen** by day or night.	AIT
	34:11	and I will give you w you ask.	889
	34:12	and I'll pay w you ask me.	889+3869
	39:23	and gave him success in w he did.	889
Ex	16:23	Save w is left and keep it until morning.' "	3972
	21:22	fined w the woman's husband demands	889+3869
	21:30	by paying w is demanded.	889+3869+3972
	27:19	w their function, including all the tent pegs	3972
	28:38	w their gifts may be.	3972
	29:37	and w touches it will be holy.	3972
	30:29	and w touches them will be holy.	3972
Lev	6: 5	or w it was he swore falsely about.	889+3972
	6:18	W touches them will become holy.' "	889+3972
	6:27	W touches any of the flesh will become	889+3972

Lev	11:32	that article, w its use, will be unclean,	889
	13:51	w its use, it is a destructive mildew;	889+3972
	13:57	w has the mildew must be burned with fire.	889
	16:16	w their sins have been.	3972
	22: 5	w the uncleanness may be.	3972
	23:38	to your gifts and w you have vowed and all	3972
	24:19	w he has done must be done to him:	889+3869+4027
	25: 6	W the land yields during the sabbath year	NIH
	25: 7	W the land produces may be eaten.	3972
	27:12	W value the priest then sets,	3869
	27:14	W value the priest then sets,	889+3869
Nu	6:21	in addition to w **else** he can afford.	889
	10:32	we will share with you w good things	889
	18:11	w is **set aside** from the gifts of all	AIT
	18:19	W is set aside from the holy offerings	3972
	22:17	and do w you say.	889+3972
	23: 3	W he reveals to me I will tell you."	1821+4537
	23:26	tell you I must do w the LORD says?"	889+3972
	31:23	And w cannot withstand fire must be	889+3972
	33:54	W falls to them by lot will be theirs.	889
Dt	5:27	tell us w the LORD our God tells you.	889+3972
	12:17	or w you have vowed to give,	3972
	12:26	and w you have vowed to give,	889
	14:26	Use the silver to buy w you like:	889+3972
	15: 8	and freely lend him w he needs.	1896
	23:16	and in w town he chooses.	285S
	23:23	W your lips utter you must be sure to	889+3869
Jos	1:16	W you have commanded us we will do,	889+3972
	1:18	w you may command them,	889+3972
	7:12	unless you destroy w among you is devoted	2021
	9:25	Do to us w seems good and right to you."	3869
Jdg	9:33	do w your hand finds to do."	889+3869
	10:15	Do with us w you think best,	3869+3972
	11:24	w the LORD our God has given us,	889+3972
	11:31	w comes out of the door of my house	2021+3655S
	18:10	a land that lacks **nothing w."**	401+1821+3972
	19:20	"Let me supply w you need.	3972
	19:24	and do to them w you wish.	2021
Ru	3: 5	"I will do w you say," Ruth answered.	889+3972
1Sa	2:14	and the priest would take for himself w	889+3972
	2:16	and then take w you want,"	889+3869
	10: 7	do w your hand finds to do,	889
	11:10	can do to us w seems good to you."	3869+3972
	14:36	"Do w seems best to you," they replied.	3972
	18: 5	W Saul sent him to do,	889+928+3972
	20: 4	"W you want me to do, I'll do for you."	4537
	21: 3	or w you can find."	2021
	25: 8	and your son David w you can find	889
2Sa	3:21	"W you have in mind, go ahead and do	889+3972
	9:11	"Your servant will do w my lord the king commands	889+3869+3972+4027
	15:15	"Your servants are ready to do w our lord the king chooses."	889+3869+3972
	15:26	let him do to me w seems good to him."	889+3869
	18: 4	"I will do w seems best to you."	889
	19:18	over and to do w he wished.	2021
	19:27	so do w pleases you.	2021
	19:37	Do for him w pleases you."	889
	19:38	and I will do for him w pleases you.	2021
	24:22	the king take w pleases him and offer it up.	2021
1Ki	3: 5	"Ask for w you want me to give you."	4537
	5: 6	for your men w wages you set.	889+3869+3972
	8:37	w disaster or disease may come,	3972
	8:43	do w the foreigner asks of you,	889+3869+3972
	9:19	w he desired to build in Jerusalem,	889
	11:38	If you do w I command you and walk	889+3972
	21: 2	if you prefer, I will pay you w it is **worth."**	AIT
2Ki	10: 5	you do w you think best."	2021
	12: 5	repair w damage is found in the temple.	889+3972
	18: 7	he was successful in w he undertook.	889+3972
	18:14	and I will pay w you demand of me."	889
1Ch	17: 2	"W you have in mind, do it,	889+3972
	21:23	Let my lord the king do w pleases him.	2021
2Ch	1: 7	"Ask for w you want me to give you."	4537
	6:28	w disaster or disease may come,	3972
	6:33	do w the foreigner asks of you,	889+3869+3972
	8: 6	w he desired to build in Jerusalem,	3972
Ezr	6: 9	W is needed—young bulls,	10408
	7:18	then do w seems best with the rest	10168+10408
	7:21	to provide with diligence w Ezra	10168+10353
	7:23	W the God of heaven has prescribed,	10168+10353
Job	23:13	He does w he pleases.	NIH
	37:12	the whole earth to do w he commands	889+3972
Ps	1: 3	W he does prospers.	889+3972
	115: 3	he does w pleases him.	889+3972
	135: 6	The LORD does w pleases him,	889+3972
Pr	16: 3	Commit to the LORD w you **do,**	5126
Ecc	3:15	W is has already been,	4537
	6:10	W exists has already been named,	4537
	7:24	W wisdom may be, it is far off	4537
	8: 3	for he will do w he pleases.	3972
	9:10	W your hand finds to do,	889+3972
	11: 9	the ways of your heart and w your eyes **see,**	AIT
		and say w I command you.	889+3972
Jer	1: 7	up and say to them w I command you.	889+3972
	1:17	with me w you think is good and right.	3869
	26:14	do with me w you think is good and right.	3869
	39:12	but do for him w he asks."	889+3869+4027
Eze	10:11	The cherubim went in w direction	889
	12:25	you rebellious house, I will fulfill w I **say,**	AIT
	12:28	w I say will be fulfilled,	889
	47:23	In w tribe the alien settles,	2021
Da	7: 7	and trampled underfoot w was **left.**	AIT
	7:19	and trampled underfoot w was **left.**	AIT
	8:24	and will succeed in w he does.	NIH
Na	1: 9	W they plot against the LORD	4537
Hag	1:11	the oil and w the ground produces,	889

Hag	2:14	'W they do and whatever they offer there is	3972
	2:14	and w they offer there is defiled.	889
Mt	10:11	'W town or village you enter,	323+1650+4005
	14:7	with an oath to give her w she asked.	1569+4005
	15:5	'W help you might otherwise have	1569+4005
	15:17	that w enters the mouth goes into	3836+4246
	16:19	w you bind on earth will be bound	1569+4005
	16:19	w you loose on earth will be loosed	1569+4005
	18:18	w you bind on earth will be bound	1569+4005
	18:18	w you loose on earth will be loosed	1569+4005
	20:4	and I will pay you w is right.'	1569+4005
	21:22	will receive w you ask for in prayer."	4012+4246
	25:40	w you did for one of the least	2093+4012
	25:45	w you did not do for one of the least	2093+4012
Mk	4:22	For w is hidden is meant to be disclosed,	1569
	4:22	and w is concealed is meant to	NIG
	6:23	"W you ask I will give you,	1569+4005+5516
	7:11	'W help you might otherwise have	1569+4005
	10:35	"we want you to do for us w we ask."	1569+4005
	11:24	w you ask for in prayer,	4012+4246
	13:11	Just say w is given you at the time,	1569+4005
Lk	9:4	W house you enter,	323+1650+4005
		eating and drinking w they give you,	3836
Jn	2:5	"Do w he tells you."	323+4005+5516
	5:19	w the Father does the Son also does.	4005
	11:22	even now God will give you w you ask.	323+4012
	12:50	So w I say is just what the Father	4005
	14:13	And I will do w you ask in my name,	323+4005
	15:7	ask w you wish, and it will be given	1569+4005
	15:16	the Father will give you w you ask in my name.	4005+5516
	16:23	my Father will give you w you ask in my name.	323+5516
Ac	18:17	But Gallio showed no concern w.	4029
Ro	2:1	for at w point you judge the other,	4005
	3:19	Now we know that w the law says,	4005
	13:9	w other commandment there may be,	1623+5516
	14:22	So w you believe about these things keep	4005
1Co	10:27	eat w is put before you without raising	4246
	10:31	So whether you eat or drink or w you do,	5516
Gal	2:6	w they were makes no difference to me;	3961
Eph	6:8	reward everyone for w good he does,	1569+4005
Php	1:27	W happens, conduct yourselves in	3668
	3:7	But w was to my profit I now consider loss	4015
	4:8	Finally, brothers, w is true,	4012
	4:8	brothers, whatever is true, w is noble,	4012
	4:8	whatever is noble, w is right,	4012
	4:8	w is pure, whatever is lovely,	4012
	4:8	w is lovely, whatever is admirable—	4012
	4:8	whatever is lovely, w is admirable—	4012
	4:9	W you have learned or received or heard	4005
	4:11	to be content w the circumstances.	4005
Col	3:5	therefore, w belongs to your earthly nature:	NIG
	3:13	forgive w grievances you may have	1569+5516
	3:17	w you do, whether in word or deed,	1569+5516
	3:23	W you do, work at it with all your heart,	1569+4005
1Ti	1:10	w else is contrary to the sound doctrine	1623+5516
Tit	3:1	to be obedient, to be ready to do w is good,	4246
1Pe	4:10	Each one should use w gift he has received	NIG
2Pe	2:19	for a man is a slave to w has mastered him.	4005
1Jn	5:15	that he hears us—w we ask—	1569+4005
Jude	1:10	against w they do not understand;	4012

WHEAT (46)

Ge	30:14	During w harvest, Reuben went out into	2636
Ex	9:32	The w and spelt, however, were not	2636
	29:2	And from fine w flour, without yeast,	2636
	34:22	with the firstfruits of the w harvest,	2636
Dt	8:8	a land with w and barley, vines	2636
	32:14	of Bashan and the finest kernels of w.	2636
Jdg	6:11	where his son Gideon was threshing w in	2636
	15:1	Later on, at the time of w harvest,	2636
Ru	2:23	the barley and w harvests were finished.	2636
1Sa	6:13	of Beth Shemesh were harvesting their w in	2636
	12:17	Is it not w harvest now?	2636
2Sa	4:6	of the house as if to get some w,	2636
	17:28	They also brought w and barley,	2636
1Ki	5:11	of w as food for his household,	2636
1Ch	21:20	While Araunah was threshing w,	2636
	21:23	and the w for the grain offering.	2636
2Ch	2:10	twenty thousand cors of ground w,	2636
	2:15	"Now let my lord send his servants the w	2636
	27:5	of w and ten thousand cors of barley.	2636
Ezr	6:9	and w, salt, wine and oil,	10272
	7:22	a hundred cors of w,	10272
Job	31:40	then let briers come up instead of w	2636
Ps	81:16	But you would be fed with the finest of w;	2636
	147:14	and satisfies you with the finest of w.	2636
SS	7:2	Your waist is a mound of w encircled	2636
Isa	28:25	Does he not plant w in its place,	2636
Jer	12:13	They will sow w but reap thorns;	2636
	41:8	We have w and barley, oil and honey,	2636
Eze	4:9	"Take w and barley, beans and lentils,	2636
	27:17	they exchanged w from Minnith	2636
	45:13	an ephah from each homer of w and a sixth	2636
Joel	1:11	grieve for the w and the barley,	2636
Am	8:5	Sabbath be ended that we may market w?"	1339
	8:5	selling even the sweepings with the w.	1339
Mt	3:12	gathering his w into the barn and burning	4992
	13:25	and sowed weeds among the w,	4992
	13:26	When the w sprouted and formed heads,	5965
	13:29	you may root up the w with them.	4992
	13:30	the w and bring it into my barn.'"	4992
Lk	3:17	and to gather the w into his barn,	4992
	16:7	"'A thousand bushels of w,' he replied.	4992
Lk	22:31	Simon, Satan has asked to sift you as w.	4992
Jn	12:24	a kernel of w falls to the ground and dies,	4992
1Co	15:37	perhaps w or of something else.	4992
Rev	6:6	saying, "A quart of w for a day's wages,	4992
	18:13	of wine and olive oil, of fine flour and w;	4992

WHEEL (12) [WHEELS]

1Ki	7:32	The diameter of each w was a cubit and	236
	22:34	"W around and get me out of the	2200+3338
2Ch	18:33	"W around and get me out of the	2200+3338
Pr	20:26	he drives the threshing w over them.	236
Ecc	12:6	or the w broken at the well,	1649
Jer	18:3	and I saw him working at the w.	78
Eze	1:15	a w on the ground beside each creature	236
	1:16	to be made like a w intersecting a wheel.	236
	1:16	to be made like a wheel intersecting a w.	236
	10:6	the man went in and stood beside a w.	236
	10:10	each was like a w intersecting a wheel.	236
	10:10	each was like a wheel intersecting a w.	236

WHEELS (32) [WHEEL]

Ex	14:25	He made the w of their chariots come off so	236
1Ki	7:30	Each stand had four bronze w	236
	7:32	The four w were under the panels,	236
	7:32	axles of the w were attached to the stand.	236
	7:33	The w were made like chariot wheels;	236
	7:33	The wheels were made like chariot w;	236
Isa	5:28	their **chariot** w like a whirlwind.	1649
	28:28	the w of his threshing cart over it,	1651
Jer	47:3	and the rumble of their w.	1649
Eze	1:16	the appearance and structure of the w:	236
	1:17	w did not turn about as the creatures went.	NIH
	1:19	the w beside them moved;	236
	1:19	from the ground, the w also rose.	236
	1:20	and the w would rise along with them,	236
	1:20	spirit of the living creatures was in the w.	236
	1:21	the w rose along with them,	236
	1:21	spirit of the living creatures was in the w.	236
	3:13	against each other and the sound of the w.	236
	10:2	"Go in among the w beneath the cherubim.	1649
	10:6	"Take fire from among the w,	1649
	10:9	and I saw beside the cherubim four w,	236
	10:9	the w sparkled like chrysolite.	236
	10:11	w did not turn about as the cherubim went.	NIH
	10:12	as were their four w.	236
	10:13	the w being called "the whirling wheels."	236
	10:13	the wheels being called "the **whirling w.**"	1649
	10:16	the w beside them moved;	236
	10:16	the w did not leave their side.	236
	10:19	and as they went, the w went with them.	236
	11:22	Then the cherubim, with the w beside them,	236
Da	7:9	and its w were all ablaze.	10143
Na	3:2	The crack of whips, the clatter of w,	236

WHELP, WHELPS (KJV) See CUB, CUBS

WHEN (2816) [WHENEVER] See Index of Articles Etc.

WHENCE (KJV) See WHERE, WHICH

WHENEVER (72) [WHEN]

Ge	9:14	W I bring clouds over the earth and	928
	9:16	W the rainbow appears in the clouds,	2256
	30:33	w you check on the wages you have paid me	3954
	30:41	W the stronger females were in heat,	928+3972
	38:9	so w he lay with his brother's wife,	561
Ex	17:11	but w he lowered his hands,	889+3869
	18:16	W they have a dispute, it is brought to me,	3954
	28:29	"W Aaron enters the Holy Place,	928
	28:30	over Aaron's heart w he enters the presence	928
	28:43	and his sons must wear them w they enter	928
	30:20	W they enter the Tent of Meeting,	928
	33:8	And w Moses went out to the tent,	3869
	33:10	W the people saw the pillar of cloud	2256
	34:34	But w he entered the LORD's presence	928
	40:32	They washed w they entered the Tent	928
	40:36	w the cloud lifted from above the tabernacle	928
Lev	10:9	or other fermented drink w you go into	928
	13:14	But w raw flesh appears on him,	928+3427
	16:2	not to come w he chooses into	928+3972+6961
Nu	1:51	W the tabernacle is to move,	928
	1:51	and the tabernacle is to be set up,	928
	9:17	W the cloud lifted from above the	4200+7023
	9:21	w the cloud lifted, they set out.	2256
	10:35	W the ark set out, Moses said, "Rise up,	928
	10:36	W it came to rest, he said, "Return,	928
	15:14	w an alien or anyone else living	3954
Dt	4:7	the LORD our God is near us w we pray	928+3972
Jdg	2:15	W Israel went out to fight,	889+928+3972
	2:18	W the LORD raised up a judge for them,	3954
	6:3	W the Israelites planted their crops,	561
	12:5	and w a survivor of Ephraim said,	3954
Ru	2:9	And w you are **thirsty**,	AIT
1Sa	1:4	W the day came for Elkanah to sacrifice,	2256
	1:7	W Hannah went up to the house of	1896+4946
	2:13	the people that w anyone offered a sacrifice	NIH
	14:52	and w Saul saw a mighty or brave man,	2256
	16:23	W the spirit from God came upon Saul,	928
	21:5	as usual w I set out.	928
	23:20	come down w it pleases you to do so,	3972
	27:9	W David attacked an area,	2256
2Sa	14:26	W he cut the hair of his head—	928
2Sa	15:2	W anyone came with a complaint to	2256
	15:5	w anyone approached him to bow down	928
1Ki	8:52	may you listen to them w they cry out	928+3972
	14:28	W the king went to the LORD's temple,	1896+4946
	18:10	And w a nation or kingdom claimed you	NIH
2Ki	4:8	So w he came by, he stopped there	1896+4946
	4:10	Then he can stay there w he comes to us."	928
	4:10	they saw that there was a large amount	928
1Ch	23:31	and w burnt offerings were presented	3972+4200
2Ch	12:11	W the king went to the LORD's temple,	1896+4946
	19:6	w is with you w you give a verdict.	928
	24:11	W the chest was brought in	928+6961
Ps	41:9	W one comes to see me, he speaks falsely,	561
	78:34	W God slew them, they would seek him;	561
Jer	20:8	W I speak, I cry out proclaiming violence	1896+3954+4946
	36:23	W Jehudi had read three or four columns of	3869
	48:27	in scorn w you speak of	1896+4946
Hos	6:11	"W I would restore the fortunes of my	928
	7:1	w I would heal Israel,	3869
Mk	4:20	W the evil spirits saw him, they fell down	4020
	6:10	W you enter a house, stay there until	1569+3963
	9:18	W it seizes him, it throws him to	1569+3963
	13:11	W you are arrested and brought to trial,	4020
1Co	11:25	do this, w you drink it,	1569+4006
	11:26	For w you eat this bread and drink	1569+4006
2Co	3:16	But w anyone turns to the Lord,	1569+2471
	13:9	We are glad w we are weak	4020
Eph	6:19	Pray also for me, that w I open my mouth,	NIG
Jas	1:2	w you face trials of many kinds,	4020
1Jn	3:20	w our hearts condemn us.	1569
Rev	4:9	the living creatures give glory,	4020

WHERE (697) [ELSEWHERE, SOMEWHERE, WHEREVER]

Ge	2:11	the entire land of Havilah, w there is gold.	9004
	3:9	But the LORD God called to the man, "W	361
	4:9	"W is your brother Abel?"	361
	10:11	Nineveh, Rehoboth Ir,	NIH
	10:30	The **region** w they lived stretched	4632
	13:3	to the place between Bethel and Ai w	9004
	13:4	and w he had first built an altar.	9004
	13:14	from w you are and look north	2021+5226S
	13:18	w he built an altar to the LORD.	9004
	16:8	servant of Sarai, w have you come from,	361
	16:8	and w are you going?"	625+2025
	17:8	w you are now an alien,	824S
	18:9	"W is your wife Sarah?"	372
	19:5	"W are the men who came to you tonight?"	372
	19:27	the place w he had stood before the LORD.	9004
	19:29	the catastrophe that overthrew the cities w	889
	21:23	and the country w you are living as an alien	889
	22:7	"but w is the lamb for the burnt offering?"	372
	26:2	live in the land w I tell you to live.	889
	28:4	that you may take possession of the land w	AIT
	29:4	"My brothers, w are you from?"	402
	31:4	to come out to the fields w his flocks were.	NIH
	31:13	w you anointed a pillar and	9004
	31:13	a pillar and w you made a vow to me.	9004
	32:17	and w are you going,	625+2025
	33:17	w he built a place for himself	NIH
	33:19	the plot of ground w he pitched his tent.	9004
	34:27	upon the dead bodies and looted the city w	889
	35:3	w I will build an altar to God,	9004
	35:13	Then God went up from him at the place w	889
	35:14	a stone pillar at the place w God had talked	889
	35:15	Jacob called the place w God had talked	9004
	35:27	Hebron), w Abraham and Isaac had stayed.	9004
	36:7	the **land** w they were staying could	AIT
	37:1	in the **land** w his father had stayed,	AIT
	37:16	Can you tell me w they are	407
	37:30	W can I turn now?"	625+2025
	38:21	"W is the shrine prostitute who was beside	372
	39:20	and put him in prison, the place w	889
	40:3	in the same prison w Joseph was confined.	9004
	42:7	"W do you come from?"	402
	42:9	to see w our land is unprotected."	NIH
	42:12	to see w our land is unprotected."	NIH
	42:27	At the **place w they stopped for the night**	4869
	43:21	at the **place w we stopped for the night**	4869
	47:30	of Egypt and bury me w they are buried."	928
Ex	2:11	he went out to w his own people were	AIT
	2:15	in Midian, w he sat down by a well.	NIH
	2:20	"And w is he?" he asked his daughters.	361
	3:5	for the place w you are standing is holy	889
	6:4	Canaan, w they **lived** as aliens.	4472
	8:21	and even the ground w they are.	889
	8:22	land of Goshen, w my people live;	889
	9:26	land of Goshen, w the Israelites were.	889
	10:23	in the **places** w they **lived.**	4632
	12:7	and tops of the doorframes of the houses w	889
	12:13	be a sign for you on the houses w you are;	9004
	15:27	w there were twelve springs and seventy	9004
	16:29	to stay w he is on the seventh day;	9393
	18:5	w he was camped near the mountain	9004
	20:21	the thick darkness w God was.	9004
	25:26	four corners, w the four legs are.	889
	30:6	Testimony—w I will meet with you.	2025+9004
	30:36	of Meeting—w I will meet with you.	2025+9004
	33:21	a place near me w you may stand on a rock.	NIH
	34:12	a treaty with those who live in the land w	889
	37:13	four corners, w the four legs are.	889
Lev	1:16	side of the altar, w the ashes are.	5226S
	4:12	w the ashes are **thrown,**	9162
	4:24	the place w the burnt offering is slaughtered	889
	4:33	for a sin offering at the place w	889

Ex	7: 2	to be slaughtered in the place **w**	889
	13:19	and in the place **w** the boil was,	NIH
	13:20	that has broken out **w** the boil was.	928
	14:13	the lamb in the holy place **w** the sin offering	889
	18: 3	**w** you used to live,	889
	18: 3	**w** I am bringing you.	2025+9004
	20:22	the land **w** I am bringing you to live	2025+9004
	21:11	not enter a place **w** there is a dead body.	NIH
Nu	5: 3	**w** I dwell among them."	889
	10:31	You know **w** we should camp in the desert,	NIH
	11:13	**W** can I get meat for all these people?	402+4946
	13:22	**w** Ahiman, Sheshai and Talmai,	9004
	17: 4	**w** I meet with you.	2025+9004
	18: 4	and no one else may come near **w** you are.	NIH
	20:13	**w** the Israelites quarreled with the LORD	889
	20:13	and **w** he showed himself holy among them.	NIH
	21:16	the well **w** the LORD said to Moses,	889
	21:20	and from Bamoth to the valley in Moab **w**	NIH
	22:26	a narrow place **w** there was no room to turn,	889
	23: 7	to another place **w** you can see them;	889
	31:10	the towns **w** the Midianites had settled,	928
	33: 9	**w** there were twelve springs	396+928S
	33:14	**w** there was no water for the people	9004
	33:38	**w** he died on the first day of the fifth month	9004
	33:55	They will give you trouble in the land **w**	9004
	34: 5	**w** it will turn, join the Wadi of Egypt	6801S
	35:33	" 'Do not pollute the land **w** you are.	889
	35:34	the land **w** you live and where I dwell,	889
	35:34	Do not defile the land where you live and **w**	889
Dt	1:28	**W** can we go?	625+2025
	3:21	the same to all the kingdoms over there **w**	889
	8: 9	a land **w** bread will not be scarce	889
	8: 9	a land **w** the rocks are iron	889
	11:10	**w** you planted your seed and irrigated it	889
	11:24	Every place **w** you set your foot will	889
	12: 2	the hills and under every spreading tree **w**	9004
	12:21	If the place **w** the LORD your God chooses	889
	14:24	the place **w** the LORD will choose	9004
	18: 6	of your towns anywhere in Israel **w**	9004
	21: 4	or planted and **w** there is a flowing stream.	NIH
	23:12	camp **w** you can go to relieve yourself.	2025+9004
	28:37	the nations the LORD will drive you.	2025+9004
	30: 3	gather you again from all the nations **w**	2025+9004
	31:14	**w** I will commission him."	NIH
	32:37	He will say: "Now **w** are their gods,	361
	33:28	**w** the heavens drop dew.	NIH
	34: 6	but to this day no one knows **w** his grave is.	NIH
Jos	1: 3	I will give you every place **w**	889
	2: 4	but I did not know **w** they had come from.	402
	3: 1	**w** they camped before crossing over.	9004
	4: 3	of the Jordan from **right w** the priests stood	2296
	4: 3	with you and put them down at the place **w**	889
	4: 8	**w** they put them down.	9004
	4: 9	the spot **w** the priests who carried the ark of	NIH
	5: 8	they remained **w** they were in camp	9393
	5:15	for the place **w** you are standing is holy."	889
	8:24	and in the desert **w** they had chased them,	889
	9: 8	"Who are you and **w** do you come from?"	402
	10:27	the trees and threw them into the cave **w**	9004
	22:19	**w** the LORD's tabernacle stands,	9004
	22:33	to devastate the country **w** the Reubenites	889
Jdg	1:26	**w** he built a city and called it Luz,	889
	4:10	**w** he summoned Zebulun and	2025+7730S
	5:27	**w** he sank, there he fell—dead.	889+928
	6:11	**w** his son Gideon was threshing wheat in	NIH
	6:13	**W** are all his wonders	372
	9:38	Zebul said to him, "**W** is your big talk now,	372
	11: 3	**w** a group of adventurers gathered	NIH
	13: 6	I didn't ask him **w** he came from,	361
	16: 1	**w** he saw a prostitute.	9004
	16:26	"Put me **w** I can feel the pillars that support	NIH
	17: 9	Micah asked him, "**W** are you from?"	402
	18: 1	a place of their own **w** they might settle,	NIH
	18: 2	**w** they spent the night.	9004
	18: 7	they saw that the people were living	NIH
	19:17	the old man asked, "**W** are you going?	625+2025
	19:17	**W** did you come from?"	402
	19:18	in the hill country of Ephraim **w** I live.	4946+9004
	19:26	to the house **w** her master was staying,	9004
	20:22	again took up their positions **w**	928+2021+5226S
	20:47	**w** they stayed four months.	928+6152+8234S
	21: 2	**w** they sat before God until evening,	9004
Ru	1: 7	the place **w** she had been living and	2025+9004
	1:16	**W** you go I will go,	889
	1:16	and **w** you stay I will stay.	889
	1:17	**W** you die I will die,	889
	2: 9	Watch the field **w** the men are harvesting,	889
	2:19	"**W** did you glean today?	407
	2:19	**W** did you work?	625+2025
	3: 1	**w** you will be well provided for?	889
	3: 4	note the place **w** he is lying.	9004
1Sa	1: 3	at Shiloh, **w** Hophni and Phinehas,	9004
	3: 3	**w** the ark of God was.	9004
	3:17	**w** his home was,	9004
	9:10	So they set out for the town **w** the man	9004
	9:18	"Would you please tell me **w**	361+2296
	10: 5	**w** there is a Philistine outpost.	889
	10:14	"**W** have you been?"	625
	14: 9	we will stay **w** we are and not go up	9393
	19: 3	and stand with my father in the field **w**	9004
	19:22	And he asked, "**W** are Samuel and David?"	407
	20:19	go to the place **w** you hid	9004
	20:37	to the place **w** Jonathan's arrow had fallen,	889
	23:22	Find out **w** David usually goes	5226S
	25:11	give it to men coming from who knows **w**?"	361
	26: 5	Then David set out and went to the place **w**	9004
	26: 5	He saw **w** Saul and Abner son of Ner,	2021+5226S

1Sa	26:16	**W** are the king's spear and water jug	361
	27:10	"**W** did you go raiding today?"	625
	30: 9	**w** some stayed behind,	2256
	30:13	and **w** do you come from?"	361
	30:31	and to those in all the other places **w** David	9004
	31:12	**w** they burned them.	9004
2Sa	1: 3	"**W** have you come from?"	361
	1:13	"**W** are you from?"	361
	2: 1	David asked, "**W** shall I go?"	625+2025
	2:23	to the place **w** Asahel had fallen and died.	9004
	9: 4	"**W** is he?"	407
	11:15	in the front line **w** the fighting is fiercest.	NIH
	11:16	he put Uriah at a place **w** he knew	9004
	13:13	**W** could I get rid of my disgrace?	625+2025
	15:20	when I **do not know w** I am going?	889+2143+2143+6584
	15:32	**w** people used to worship God,	9004
	16: 3	"**W** is your master's grandson?"	372
	17:20	"**W** are Ahimaaz and Jonathan?"	372
	19:17	rushed to the Jordan, **w** the king was.	4200+7156S
	21:12	**w** the Philistines had hung them	9004
	23: 7	they are burned up **w** they lie."	928
	23:11	the Philistines banded together at a place **w**	9004
1Ki	1:15	to see the aged king in his room, **w** Abishag	NIH
	7: 7	The Hall of Justice, **w** he was to judge,	9004
	8: 9	**w** the LORD made a covenant with	889
	8:47	the land **w** they are held captive, and repent	9004
	8:54	**w** he had been kneeling	9004
	11:24	**w** they settled and took control.	928+2023S
	11:36	the city **w** I chose to put my Name	9004
	12: 2	**w** he had fled from King Solomon),	889
	13:22	and drank water in the place **w** he told you	889
	13:25	and they went and reported it in the city **w**	889
	13:31	in the grave **w** the man of God is buried;	889
	17:19	to the upper room **w** he was staying,	9004
	18:10	not a nation or kingdom **w** my master has	9004
	18:12	I don't know **w** the Spirit of the LORD	889
	20:30	**w** the wall collapsed	NIH
	21:18	**w** he has gone to take possession of it.	9004
	21:19	the place **w** dogs licked up Naboth's blood,	889
	22:38	a pool in Samaria (**w** the prostitutes bathed),	9004
2Ki	2: 7	the place **w** Elijah and Elisha had stopped at	NIH
	2:14	"**W** now is the LORD, the God of Elijah?"	372
	5:25	"**W** have you been, Gehazi?"	402+4946
	6: 1	the place **w** we meet with you is too small	9004
	6: 2	**w** each of us can get a pole;	4946+9004
	6: 6	The man of God asked, "**W** did it fall?"	625+2025
	6:13	"Go, find out **w** he is," the king ordered,	378
	6:27	**w** can I get help for you?"	402+4946
	11:16	as she reached the **place w** the horses enter	AIT
	14: 6	of Moses the LORD commanded:	889
	17:29	in the several towns **w** they settled,	9004
	18:34	**W** are the gods of Hamath and Arpad?	372
	18:34	**W** are the gods of Sepharvaim,	372
	19:13	**W** is the king of Hamath, the king of Arpad,	361
	19:27	" 'But I know **w** you **stay** and	AIT
	20:14	and **w** did they come from?"	402
	23: 7	of the LORD and **w** women did weaving	9004
	23: 8	**w** the priests had burned incense.	2025+9004
	25: 6	**w** sentence was pronounced on him.	NIH
1Ch	3: 4	**w** he reigned seven years and six months.	9004
	5:26	**w** they are to this day.	NIH
	11:13	At a place **w** there was a field full of barley,	NIH
2Ch	3: 1	Mount Moriah, **w** the LORD had appeared	889
	5:10	**w** the LORD made a covenant with	889
	6:37	the land **w** they are held captive, and repent	9004
	6:38	and soul in the land of their captivity **w**	889
	10: 2	**w** he had fled from King Solomon),	889
	20:26	**w** they praised the LORD.	9004
	25: 4	**w** the LORD commanded:	889
	25:11	**w** he killed ten thousand men of Seir.	NIH
	32:33	and was buried on the **hill w** the tombs	AIT
	33:19	and the sites **w** he built high places and set	889
	35:24	and brought him to Jerusalem, **w** he died.	NIH
Ezr	1: 4	the people of any place **w** survivors may	9004
	8:32	**w** we rested three days.	9004
Ne	2: 3	when the city **w** my fathers are buried lies	1074S
	2: 5	the city in Judah **w** my fathers are buried so	NIH
	2:16	officials did not know **w** I had gone or	625+2025
	9: 3	They stood **w** they were and read	6584+6642S
	10:37	the tithes in all the towns **w** we work.	AIT
	10:39	and oil to the storerooms **w** the articles for	9004
	10:39	the articles for the sanctuary are kept and **w**	NIH
	12:27	from **w** they **lived** and were brought	5226
Est	7: 5	**W** is the man who has dared to do such	361+2296
	7: 8	on the couch **w** Esther was reclining.	889
Job	1: 7	"**W** have you come from?"	402
	2: 2	"**W** have you come from?"	361
	4: 7	**W** were the upright ever destroyed?	407
	6:24	show me **w** I have been wrong.	4537
	8:11	Can papyrus grow tall **w** there is no marsh?	928
	10:22	**w** even the light is like darkness."	NIH
	15:28	and houses **w** no one lives,	4200+4564S
	17:15	**w** then is my hope?	372
	18:19	no survivor **w** once he lived.	928
	20: 7	those who have seen him will say, '**W**	361
	21:28	You say, '**W** now is the great man's house,	372
	21:28	the tents **w** wicked men lived?'	NIH
	23: 3	If only I knew **w** to find him;	NIH
	28: 1	"There is a mine for silver and a place **w**	NIH
	28: 4	Far from **w** people dwell he cuts a shaft,	6640
	28:12	"But **w** can wisdom be found?	402+4946
	28:12	**W** does understanding dwell?	361+2296
	28:20	"**W** then does wisdom come from?	402
	28:20	**W** does understanding dwell?	361+2296
	28:23	to it and he alone knows **w** it **dwells,**	5226
	34:22	no deep shadow, **w** evildoers can hide.	9004

Job	34:26	punishes them for their wickedness **w**	928+5226S
	35:10	But no one says, '**W** is God my Maker,	372
	38: 4	"**W** were you when I laid	407
	38:11	here is **w** your proud waves halt'?	NIH
	38:19	And **w** does darkness reside?	361+2296
	38:24	to the place **w** the lightning is dispersed,	NIH
	38:24	the place **w** the east winds are scattered over	NIH
	38:26	to water a land **w** no man lives,	NIH
	39:30	and **w** the slain are, there is he."	889+928
	40:12	crush the wicked **w** they **stand.**	9393
Ps	19: 3	or language **w** their voice is not heard.	NIH
	26: 8	I love the house **w** you **live,** O LORD,	5061
	26: 8	O LORD, the place **w** your glory **dwells.**	5438
	41: 8	he will never get up from the place **w**	889
	42: 3	"**W** is your God?"	372
	42:10	"**W** is your God?"	372
	43: 3	to the **place w** you **dwell.**	5438
	46: 4	**w** the Most High **dwells.**	5438
	50: 1	the rising of the sun to the **place w** it **sets.**	4427
	53: 5	**w** there was nothing to dread.	NIH
	63: 1	in a dry and weary land **w** there is no water.	NIH
	65: 8	**w** morning **dawns** and evening fades	4604
	68:16	at the mountain **w** God chooses to reign,	NIH
	68:16	**w** the LORD himself will dwell forever?	NIH
	69: 2	**w** there is no foothold.	NIH
	74: 2	Mount Zion, **w** you dwelt.	928+2257S
	74: 4	Your foes roared in the **place w** you **met**	4595
	74: 8	**place w** God was **worshiped**	4595
	79:10	"**W** is their God?"	372
	81: 5	**w** we heard a language we did	NIH
	84: 3	**w** she may have her young—	889
	89:49	**w** is your former great love,	372
	95: 9	**w** your fathers tested and tried me,	889
	107: 4	to a city **w** they could **settle.**	4632
	107: 7	a straight way to a city **w** they could **settle.**	4632
	107:36	and they founded a city **w** they could **settle.**	4632
	113: 3	the rising of the sun to the **place w** it **sets,**	4427
	115: 2	Why do the nations say, "**W** is their God?"	372
	121: 1	**w** does my help come from?	402
	122: 4	That is **w** the tribes go up,	9004
	139: 7	**W** can I go from your Spirit?	625+2025
	139: 7	**W** can I flee from your presence?	625+2025
	142: 3	the path **w** I walk men have hidden a snare	2306
Pr	8: 2	**w** the paths meet, she takes her stand;	NIH
	14: 4	**W** there are no oxen, the manger is empty,	928
	15:17	a meal of vegetables **w** there is love than	9004
	29:18	**W** there is no revelation,	928
	31:23	**w** he takes his seat among the elders of	928
Ecc	1: 5	and hurries back to **w** it rises.	5226S
	8:10	and receive praise in the city **w**	889
	9:10	for in the grave, **w** you are going,	2025+9004
	11: 3	in the place **w** it falls, there will it lie.	8611
SS	1: 7	**w** you graze your flock and	377
	1: 7	and **w** you rest your sheep at midday.	377
	6: 1	**W** has your lover gone,	625+2025
Isa	7:23	in every place **w** there were	9004
	7:25	**places w** cattle are **turned loose**	5448
	7:25	and **w** sheep **run.**	5330
	10: 3	**W** will you leave your riches?	625+2025
	19:12	**W** are your wise men now?	361
	29: 1	Ariel, Ariel, the **city w** David settled!	AIT
	33:18	"**W** is that chief officer?	372
	33:18	**W** is the one who took the revenue?	372
	33:18	**W** is the officer in charge of the towers?"	372
	35: 7	In the haunts **w** jackals once **lay,**	8070
	36:19	**W** are the gods of Hamath and Arpad?	372
	36:19	**W** are the gods of Sepharvaim?	372
	37:13	**W** is the king of Hamath, the king of Arpad,	372
	37:28	"But I know **w** you **stay** and	AIT
	39: 3	and **w** did they come from?"	402
	42:11	let the settlements **w** Kedar lives rejoice.	NIH
	49:21	**w** have they come **from?' "**	407
	50: 1	"**W** is your mother's certificate of divorce	361+2296
	51:13	For **w** is the wrath of the oppressor?	372
	63:11	**w** is he who brought them through the sea,	372
	63:11	**W** is he who set his Holy Spirit	372
	63:15	**W** are your zeal and your might?	372
	64:11	**w** our fathers praised you,	889
	66: 1	**W** is the house you will build for me?	361+2296
	66: 1	**W** will my resting place be?	361+2296
Jer	2: 6	They did not ask, '**W** is the LORD,	372
	2: 6	a land **w** no one travels and no one lives?'	9004
	2: 8	The priests did not ask, '**W** is the LORD?'	372
	2:28	**W** then are the gods you made	372
	3: 2	Is there **any place w** you have	407
	6:16	ask **w** the good way is, and walk in it,	361+2296
	7:12	the place in Shiloh **w** I first made a dwelling	9004
	13: 7	from the place **w** I had hidden it,	2025+9004
	13:20	**W** is the flock that was entrusted to you,	372
	15: 2	And if they ask you, '**W** shall we go?'	625+2025
	16: 5	not enter a **house w** there is a funeral meal;	AIT
	16: 8	"And do not enter a **house w** there is feasting	AIT
	16:15	north and out of all the countries **w**	2025+9004
	17: 6	in a salt land **w** no one lives.	NIH
	17:15	"**W** is the word of the LORD?	372
	19:13	all the houses **w** they burned incense on	889
	19:14	**w** the LORD had sent him to prophesy,	9004
	22:12	in the place **w** they have led him captive;	9004
	22:26	**w** neither of you was born,	9004
	23: 3	of all the countries **w** I have driven them	9004
	23: 3	**w** they will be fruitful and increase	NIH
	23: 8	of the north and out of all the countries **w**	9004
	29:14	and places **w** I have banished you."	9004
	29:18	among all the nations **w** I drive them.	9004
	31: 9	on a level path **w** they will not stumble	928+2023S
	31:40	The whole **valley w** dead bodies and	AIT

Jer	32: 5	w he will remain until I deal with him, 9004
	32:29	with the houses w the people provoked me 889
	32:37	surely gather them from all the lands w 9004
	34:16	and female slaves you had set free to go w NIH
	35: 7	Then you will live a long time in the land w 9004
	36:12	w all the officials were sitting: 9004
	36:19	Don't let anyone know w you are." 407
	37:16	w he remained a long time. 9004
	37:17	w he asked him privately, NIH
	37:19	W are your prophets who prophesied 372
	38: 9	w he will starve to death 9393
	39: 5	w he pronounced sentence on him. NIH
	40:12	the countries w they had been scattered. 9004
	41: 9	Now the cistern w he threw all the bodies of 9004
	42: 3	that the LORD your God will tell us w 2006+2021^S
	42:14	w we will not see war or hear the trumpet or 889
	42:22	the sword, famine and plague in the place w 9004
	43: 5	in the land of Judah from all the nations w 9004
	44: 8	w you have come to live? 9004
	49:36	not be a nation w Elam's exiles do not go. 9004
	51:37	a place w no one lives. NIH
	51:43	and desert land, a land w no one lives, 928+2177^S
	52: 9	w he pronounced sentence on him. NIH
	52:11	w he put him in prison till the day NIH
La	3: 1	"W is bread and wine?" 372
Eze	3:15	And there, w they were living, AIT
	4:13	among the nations w I will drive them." 9004
	6: 9	Then in the nations w they have been 9004
	6:13	places w they offered fragrant incense 9004
	8: 3	w the idol that provokes to jealousy stood. 9004
	9: 3	w it had been, 889
	11:16	for them in the countries w they have gone.' 9004
	11:17	and bring you back from the countries w 889
	12: 3	and go from w you are to another place. 5226^S
	12:16	so that in the nations w they go 9004
	13:12	"W is the whitewash you covered it with?" 372
	16:16	w you carried on your prostitution. 2157+6584^S
	17: 4	w he planted it in a city of traders. NIH
	17: 7	toward him from the plot w it was planted AIT
	17:10	wither away in the plot w it grew?' " AIT
	20:34	the countries w you have been scattered— 889
	20:38	of the land w they are living, AIT
	20:41	the countries w you have been scattered, 889
	21:19	Make a signpost w the road branches off to 928
	21:22	w he is to set up battering rams, NIH
	21:30	In the place w you were created, 889
	24: 7	w the dust would cover it. NIH
	28:25	the nations w they have been scattered, 889
	29:13	the nations w they were scattered. 2025+9004
	34:12	from all the places w they were scattered on 9004
	36:21	Israel profaned among the nations w 2025+9004
	36:22	among the nations w they have gone. 9004
	37:21	I will take the Israelites out of the nations w 9004
	37:25	the land w your fathers lived. 889
	40:38	the burnt offerings were washed. 9004
	42:13	w the priests who approach 9004
	43: 7	This is w I will live among 9004
	44:19	into the outer court w 2021+2021+2667+2958^S
	46:20	"This is the place w the priests will cook 9004
	46:24	the kitchens w those who minister at 9004
	47: 8	w it enters the Sea. NIH
	47: 9	the river flows everything will live. 2025+9004
Da	6:10	to his upstairs room w the windows opened NIH
	8:17	near the place w I was standing, 6642
	9: 7	in all the countries w you have scattered us 9004
Hos	1:10	In the place w it was said to them, 889
	4:13	w the shade is pleasant. 3954
	13:10	W is your king, that he may save you? 180+686
	13:10	W are your rulers in all your towns, NIH
	13:14	W, O death, are your plagues? 180
	13:14	W, O grave, is your destruction? 180
Joel	2:17	'W is their God?' " 372
Am	3: 5	Does a bird fall into a trap on the ground w 2256
Jnh	1: 3	w he found a ship bound for that port. NIH
	1: 5	w he lay down and fell into a deep sleep. NIH
	1: 8	W do you come from? 402
Mic	7:10	"W is the LORD your God?" 361
Na	2:11	W now is the lions' den, 372
	2:11	the place w they fed their young, 5337
	2:11	w the lion and lioness went, and the cubs, 9004
	3: 7	W can I find anyone to comfort you?" 402+4946
	3:17	and no one knows w. 361+5226
Hab	3: 4	w his power was hidden. 9004
Zep	2: 6	w the Kerethites dwell, AIT
	3:19	and honor in every land w they were put AIT
Zec	1: 5	W are your forefathers now? 372
	2: 2	I asked, "W are you going?" 625+2025
	5:10	"W are they taking the basket?" 625+2025
	8:23	w they were strangers. 889
Mal	1: 6	If I am a father, w is the honor due me? 372
	1: 6	If I am a master, w is the respect due me?" 372
	2:17	with them" or "W is the God of justice?" 372
Mt	2: 2	"W is the one who has been born king of 4544
	2: 4	asked them w the Christ was to be born. 4544
	2: 9	of them until it stopped over the place w 4023
	2:15	w he stayed until the death of Herod. 1695
	3: 7	the Pharisees and Sadducees coming to w 2093
	6:19	w moth and rust destroy, 3963
	6:19	and w thieves break in and steal. 3963
	6:20	w moth and rust do not destroy, 3963
	6:20	and w thieves do not break in and steal. 3963
	6:21	For w your treasure is, 3963
	8:12	w there will be weeping and gnashing 1695
	13: 5	w it did not have much soil. 3963
	13: 8	w it produced a crop— NIG
	13:27	W then did the weeds come from?' 4470
	13:42	w there will be weeping and gnashing 1695

Mt	13:50	w there will be weeping and gnashing 1695
	13:54	"W did this man get this wisdom 4470
	13:56	W then did this man get all these things?" 4470
	15:33	"W could we get enough bread 4470
	18:20	w two or three come together in my name, 4023
	21:17	w he spent the night. 1695
	21:25	w did it come from? 4470
	22:13	w there will be weeping and gnashing 1695
	24:51	w there will be weeping and gnashing 1695
	25:24	harvesting w you have not sown 3963
	25:24	where you have not sown and gathering w 3854
	25:26	that I harvest w I have not sown and gather 3963
	25:26	where I have not sown and gather w I have 3854
	25:30	w there will be weeping and gnashing 1695
	26:17	"W do you want us to make preparations 4544
	26:57	the teachers of the law and 3963
	26:71	w another girl saw him and said to NIG
	28: 6	Come and see the place w he lay. 3963
	28:16	the mountain w Jesus had told them to go. 4023
Mk	1:35	house and went off to a solitary place, w 1695
	4: 5	w it did not have much soil. 3963
	4:15	w the word is sown. 3963
	5:40	and went in w the child was. 3963
	6: 2	"W did this man get these things?" 4470
	8: 4	His disciples answered, "But w 4470
	9: 2	w they were all alone. NIG
	9:30	not want anyone to know w they were, NIG
	9:43	w the fire never goes out. 3963
	9:48	w " 'their worm does not die, 3963
	12:41	place w the offerings were put 1126
	13:14	that causes desolation' standing w it does 3963
	14:12	"W do you want us to go 4544
	14:14	W is my guest room, 4544
	14:14	Where is my guest room, w I may eat 3963
	15:47	the mother of Joses saw w he was laid. 4544
	16: 6	See the place w they laid him. 3963
Lk	1:40	w she entered Zechariah's home 2779
	4: 2	w for forty days he was tempted by NIG
	4:16	w he had been brought up, 4023
	4:17	he found the place w it is written: 4023
	4:42	w they came to w he was, 2401
	8:25	"W is your faith?" 4544
	10: 1	of him to every town and place w he was 4023
	10:33	as he traveled, came w the man was; 2848
	10:38	he came to a village w a woman 1254
	11:33	and puts it in a place w it will be hidden, NIG
	12:33	w no thief comes near 3963
	12:34	For w your treasure is, 3963
	13:25	'I don't know you or w you come from.' 4470
	13:27	'I don't know you or w you come from.' 4470
	16:23	In hell, w he was in torment, NIG
	17:17	W are the other nine? 4544
	17:37	"W, Lord?" they asked. 4544
	17:37	He replied, "W there is a dead body, 3963
	19:37	near the place w the road goes down 2853
	20: 7	"We don't know w it was from." 4470
	22: 9	"W do you want us to prepare for it?" 4544
	22:11	W is the guest room, 4544
	22:11	the guest room, w I may eat the Passover 3963
Jn	1:28	w John was baptizing. 3963
	1:38	"w are you staying?" 4544
	1:39	So they went and saw w he was staying, 4544
	2: 9	w it had come from, 4470
	3: 8	but you cannot tell w it comes from or 4470
	3: 8	where it comes from or w it is going. 4544
	3:22	w he spent some time with them, 1695
	4:11	W can you get this living water? 4470
	4:20	that the place w we must worship is 3963
	4:46	w he had turned the water into wine. 3963
	6: 5	"W shall we buy bread for these people 4470
	6:17	w they got into a boat and set off across 2779
	6:21	the shore w they were heading. 1650+4005
	6:23	the place w the people had eaten the bread 3963
	6:62	What if you see the Son of Man ascend to w 3963
	7:11	"W is that man?" 4544
	7:27	But we know w this man is from; 4470
	7:27	no one will know w he is from." 4470
	7:28	you know me, and you know w I am from. 4470
	7:34	and w I am, you cannot come. 3963
	7:35	"W does this man intend to go 4544
	7:35	Will he go w our people live scattered 1650
	7:36	but you will not find me,' and 'W I am, 3963
	7:42	the town w David lived?" 3963
	8: 2	w all the people gathered around him, 2779
	8:10	up and asked her, "Woman, w are they? 4544
	8:14	for I know w I came from and 4470
	8:14	where I came from and w I am going. 4544
	8:14	But you have no idea w I come from or 4470
	8:14	where I come from or w I am going. 4544
	8:19	Then they asked him, "W is your father?" 4544
	8:20	place w the offerings were put. 1126
	8:21	W I go, you cannot come.' 3963
	8:22	Is that why he says, 'W I go, 3963
	9:12	"W is this man?" 4544
	9:29	we don't even know w he comes from." 4470
	9:30	You don't know w he comes from, 4470
	10:40	to the place w John had been baptizing in 3963
	11: 6	stayed w he was two more days. 1877+4005+5536
	11:30	was still at the place w Martha had met him. 3963
	11:32	When Mary reached the place w Jesus was 3963
	11:34	"W have you laid him?" 4544
	11:54	he stayed with his disciples. 1695
	11:57	that if anyone found out w Jesus was, 4544
	12: 1	Jesus arrived at Bethany, w Lazarus lived, 3963
	12:26	and w I am, my servant also will be. 3963
	12:35	in the dark does not know w he is going. 4544
	13:33	W I am going, you cannot come. 3963

Jn	13:36	"Lord, w are you going?" 4544
	13:36	Jesus replied, "W I am going, 3963
	14: 3	to be with me that you also may be w I am. 3963
	14: 4	the way to the place w I am going." 3963
	14: 5	"Lord, we don't know w you are going, 4544
	16: 5	'W are you going?' 4544
	16:10	w you can see me no longer; 2779
	17:24	given me to be with me w I am, 3963
	18:20	w all the Jews come together. 3963
	19: 9	"W do you come from?" 4544
	19:20	for the place w Jesus was crucified was near 3963
	19:41	At the place w Jesus was crucified, 3963
	20: 2	and we don't know w they have put him!" 4544
	20:12	seated w Jesus' body had been, 3963
	20:13	"and I don't know w they have put him." 4544
	20:13	tell me w you have put him, 4544
	20:25	put my finger w the nails were, 1650+3836+5596^S
	21:18	and went w you wanted; 3963
	21:18	and lead you w you do not want to go." 3963
Ac	1:13	to the room w they were staying. 3825
	1:25	which Judas left to go w he belongs." 1650+5536
	2: 2	from heaven and filled the whole house w 4023
	3: 2	w he was put every day to beg NIG
	4:31	w they were meeting was shaken. 1877+4005
	7: 4	God sent him to this land w you are 1650+4005
	7:15	w he and our fathers died. 2779
	7:29	w he settled as a foreigner 4023
	7:33	the place w you are standing is holy 2093+4005
	7:49	Or w will my resting place be? 5515
	10:17	the men sent by Cornelius found out w NIG
	11: 5	and it came down to w I was. 948
	11:11	stopped at the house w I was staying. 1877+4005
	12:12	w many people had gathered 4023
	13:13	w John left them to return to Jerusalem. 1254
	14: 7	w they continued to preach the good news. 1695
	14:26	w they had been committed to the grace 3854
	15:30	w they gathered the church together 2779
	15:35	w they and many others taught NIG
	15:36	in all the towns w we preached 1877+4005
	16: 1	w a disciple named Timothy lived, 2779
	16:13	w we expected to find a place of prayer. 4023
	16:40	w they met with the brothers NIG
	17: 1	w there was a Jewish synagogue. 3963
	17:19	w they said to him, NIG
	17:26	and the exact places w they should live. NIG
	18:19	w Paul left Priscilla and Aquila. 1695
	20: 3	w he stayed three months. NIG
	20: 6	w we stayed seven days. 3963
	20: 8	in the upstairs room w we were meeting. 4023
	20:13	we were going to take Paul aboard. 1696
	21: 3	w our ship was to unload its cargo. 1698
	21: 7	w we greeted the brothers and stayed NIG
	21:16	w we were to stay. 4005+4123
	25: 2	w the chief priests and Jewish leaders NIG
	25:10	w I ought to be tried. 4023
	27:39	w they decided to run the ship aground 1650+4005
	28:23	to the place w he was staying. 3825
Ro	3:27	W, then, is boasting? It is excluded. 4544
	4:15	w there is no law there is no transgression. 4023
	5:20	But w sin increased, grace increased 4023
	9:26	that in the very place w it was said to them, 4023
	15:20	the gospel w Christ was not known, 3963
1Co	1:20	W is the wise man? 4544
	1:20	W is the scholar? 4544
	1:20	W is the philosopher of this age? 4544
	12:17	w would the sense of hearing be? 4544
	12:17	w would the sense of smell be? 4544
	12:19	w would the body be? 4544
	13: 8	But w there are prophecies, they will cease; 1664
	13: 8	w there are tongues, they will be stilled; 1664
	13: 8	w there is knowledge, it will pass away. 1664
	15:55	"W, O death, is your victory? 4544
	15:55	W, O death, is your sting?" 4544
2Co	3:17	and w the Spirit of the Lord is, 4023
Col	3: 1	w Christ is seated at the right hand of God. 4023
Heb	2: 6	there is a place w someone has testified: 4543
	3: 9	w your fathers tested and tried me and 4023
	6:20	w Jesus, who went before us, has entered 3963
	10:18	And w these have been forgiven, 3963
	11: 8	though he did not know w he was going. 4544
Jas	3: 4	For w you have envy and selfish ambition, 3963
2Pe	3: 4	"W is this 'coming' he promised? 4544
1Jn	2:11	he does not know w he is going, 4544
Rev	2:13	I know w you live— 4544
	2:13	w Satan has his throne. 3963
	2:13	in your city—w Satan lives. 3963
	7:13	w did they come from?" 4470
	11: 8	w also their Lord was crucified. 3963
	12: 6	w she might be taken care of for 1,260 days. 3963
	12:14	w she would be taken care of for a time, 3963
	17:15	"The waters you saw, w the prostitute sits, 4023
	18:19	w all who had ships on the sea 1877+4005
	20:10	w the beast and the false prophet 3963

WHEREVER (68) [WHERE]

Ge	20:15	live w you like." 928
	28:15	and will watch over you w you go, 889+928+3972
	30:30	LORD has blessed you w I have been. 4200+8079
	35: 3	with me w I have gone." 889+928+2006+2021
Ex	5:11	get your own straw w you can find it, 889+4946
	12:20	you live, you must eat unleavened 928+3972
	20:24	W I cause my name to be honored, 889+928+2021+3972+5226
Lev	3:17	for the generations to come, w you live: 928+3972
	7:26	And w you live, you must not eat 928+3972
	23: 3	w you live, it is a Sabbath to the LORD. 928+3972

Lev	23:14	for the generations to come, w you live.	928+3972
	23:17	From w you **live,**	AIT
	23:21	for the generations to come, w you live.	928+3972
	23:31	for the generations to come, w you live.	928+3972
Nu	9:17	w the cloud settled, the Israelites encamped.	889+928+5226
	35:29	the generations to come, w you live.	928+3972
Dt	11:25	of you on the whole land, w you go.	889
	21:14	let her go w she wishes.	4200
	23:16	Let him live among you w he likes and	889+928+2021+5226
	30:1	and you take them to heart w	889+2025+9004
Jos	1:7	you may be successful w you go.	889+928+3972
	1:9	be with you w you go."	889+928+3972
	1:16	and w you send us we will go.	448+889+3972
1Sa	14:47	W he turned, he inflicted punishment	889+928+3972
2Sa	7:7	W I have moved with all the Israelites,	889+928+3972
	7:9	I have been with you w you have gone,	889+928+3972
	8:6	The LORD gave David victory w he went.	889+928+3972
	8:14	The LORD gave David victory w he went.	889+928+3972
	15:21	w my lord the king may be,	889+928+5226
	17:12	we will attack him w he may be found,	285+889+928+2021+5226
1Ki	2:3	in all you do and w you go,	889+3972+9004
	8:44	w you send them,	889+928+2006+2021
2Ki	8:1	and stay for a while w you can,	889+928
	11:8	Stay close to the king w he **goes.**"	928+3972+995+2256+3655
1Ch	17:6	W I have moved with all the Israelites,	889+928+3972
	17:8	I have been with you w you have gone,	889+928+3972
2Ch	6:34	w you send them,	889+928+2006+2021
	23:7	Stay close to the flowing w he **goes.**"	928+928+995+2256+3655
Ne	4:12	"W you turn, they will attack us."	2021+3972+4946+5226
	4:20	W you hear the sound of the trumpet,	889+928+5226
Est	8:17	w the edict of the king went,	889+5226S
Ps	119:54	the theme of my song w I lodge.	928
Pr	17:8	w he turns, he succeeds.	448+889+3972
	21:1	he directs it like a watercourse w he pleases.	889+3972+6584
Jer	8:3	W I banish them,	928+2021+3972+5226
	24:9	w I banish them.	889+928+2021+3972+5226
	40:4	lies before you; go w you please."	2025+9004
	45:5	but w you go I will let you escape	889+2021+3972+5226+6584
Eze	1:12	W the spirit would go, they would go,	2025+9004
	1:20	W the spirit would go, they would go,	9004
	6:6	W you live, the towns will be laid waste	928+3972
	6:14	to Diblah—w they live.	928+3972
	21:16	then to the left, w your blade is turned.	625+2025
	36:20	And w they went among	889
	47:9	living creatures will live w	448+889+3972
Da	2:38	W they live, he has made you ruler over them all.	10089+10168+10353
Mt	8:19	"Teacher, I will follow you w you go."	1569+3963
	24:28	W there is a carcass,	1569+3963
	26:13	w this gospel is preached throughout	1569+3963
Mk	6:55	the sick on mats to w they heard he was.	3963
	6:56	And w he went—into villages,	323+3963
	14:9	w the gospel is preached throughout	1569+3963
Lk	9:57	"I will follow you w you go."	1569+3963
Jn	3:8	The wind blows w it pleases.	3963
Ac	8:4	preached the word w they went.	NIG
1Co	16:6	can help me on my journey, w I go.	1569+4023
Jas	3:4	a very small rudder w the pilot wants to go.	3963
Rev	14:4	They follow the Lamb w he goes.	323+3963

WHET (KJV) See SHARPEN

WHETHER (120)

Ge	17:13	W born in your household or	AIT
	24:21	the man watched her closely to learn w or	2022
	27:21	to know w you really are my son Esau	2022
	31:32	see for yourself w there is anything	4537
	37:32	Examine it to see w it is your son's	561+4202
	42:33	how I will know w you are honest men:	3954
Ex	12:19	w he is an alien or native-born.	928
	13:2	w man or animal."	928
	16:4	see w they will follow my instructions.	561+2022+4202
	19:13	W man or animal,	561
	22:4	W ox or donkey or sheep—	4946
	22:8	to determine w he has laid his hands on	561+4202
	34:19	w from herd or flock.	NIH
Lev	3:1	w male or female,	561
	5:2	w the carcasses of unclean wild animals or	196
	5:4	w good or evil—	196
	7:10	w mixed with oil or	2256
	7:21	w human uncleanness or	196
	11:10	w among all the swarming things or	2256
	11:32	w it is made of wood, cloth, hide or	196
	11:42	w it moves on its belly or	2256
	13:55	w the mildew has affected one side or	196
	15:3	W it continues flowing from his body or	196
	15:23	W it is the bed or anything she was sitting	561
	16:29	w native-born or an alien living	2256

Lev	17:15	" 'Anyone, w native-born or alien,	928
	18:9	w she was born in the same home or	196
	24:16	W an alien or native-born,	3869
	27:26	w an ox or a sheep, it is the LORD's.	561
	27:28	w man or animal or family land—	4946
	27:30	w grain from the soil or fruit from the trees,	4946
Nu	3:13	w man or animal.	4946
	4:27	w carrying or doing other work,	4200
	8:17	w man or animal, is mine.	928
	9:21	W by day or by night,	196
	9:22	W the cloud stayed over the tabernacle	196
	11:23	now see w or not what I say will come true	2022
	13:18	and w the people who live there are strong	2022
	15:3	w burnt offerings or sacrifices,	196
	15:14	w he is a native-born Israelite or	2256
	15:30	w native-born or alien,	2256
	18:9	w grain or sin or guilt offerings,	2256
	31:28	w persons, cattle, donkeys, sheep or goats.	4946
	31:30	select one out of every fifty, w persons,	4946
Dt	1:16	w the case is between brother Israelites or	2256
	4:16	w formed like a man or	196
	8:2	w or not you would keep his commands.	2022
	13:3	to find out w you love him	2022
	13:7	the peoples around you, w near or far,	196
	17:8	w bloodshed, lawsuits or assaults—	1068
	23:19	w on money or food or anything else	NIH
	24:14	w he is a brother Israelite or	196
Jos	24:14	the gods your forefathers served beyond	561
Jdg	2:22	to test Israel and see w they will keep	2022
	3:4	the Israelites to see w they would obey	2022
	18:5	to learn w our journey will be successful."	2022
Ru	3:10	after the younger men, w rich or poor.	561
1Sa	14:6	w by many or by few."	196
2Sa	15:21	w it means life or death,	561
1Ki	16:11	w relative or friend.	2256
2Ki	7:4	w slave or free, was suffering;	700+2256
2Ch	15:13	were to be put to death, w small or great,	4946
	19:10	w bloodshed or other concerns of the law,	1068
	20:9	w the sword of judgment, or	2256
Est	3:4	to see w Mordecai's behavior would	2022
Ps	58:9	w he green or dry—	4017
Pr	20:11	by w his conduct is pure and right.	561
Ecc	2:19	And who knows w he will be a wise man or	2022
	5:12	w he eats little or much,	561
	9:1	no man knows w love or hate awaits him.	1685
	11:3	W a tree falls to the south or to the north,	561
	11:6	which will succeed, w this or that,	2022
	11:6	or w both will do equally well.	561
	12:14	w it is good or evil.	561
Isa	7:11	w in the deepest depths or	196
	30:21	W you turn to the right or to the left,	3954
	41:23	Do something, w good or bad,	677
Jer	24:8	w they remain in this land or live in Egypt.	2256
	42:6	W it is favorable or unfavorable,	561
Eze	2:5	And w they listen or fail to listen—	561
	2:7	w they listen or fail to listen,	561
	3:11	w they listen or fail to listen."	561
	46:12	w a burnt offering or fellowship offerings	196
Mk	4:27	Night and day, w he sleeps or gets up,	2779
	13:35	w in the evening, or at midnight,	2445
Lk	14:31	not first sit down and consider w he is able	1623
Jn	7:17	he will find out w my teaching comes	4538
	7:17	from God or w I speak on my own.	NIG
	9:25	"W he is a sinner or not,	1623
Ac	4:19	for yourselves w it is right in God's sight	1623
	9:2	belonged to the Way, w men or women,	5445
Ro	6:16	w you are slaves to sin,	2486
	14:8	So, w we live or die, we belong to the Lord.	1569
1Co	3:22	w Paul or Apollos or Cephas or the world	1664
	7:16	wife, w you will save your husband?	1623
	7:16	husband, w you will save your wife?	1623
	8:5	w in heaven or on earth	1664
	10:31	So w you eat or drink or whatever you do,	1664
	10:32	Do not cause anyone to stumble, w Jews,	2779
	12:13	w Jews or Greeks, slave or free—	1664
	12:13	w, then, it was I or they,	1664
2Co	5:9	w we are at home in the body or away	1664
	5:10	done while in the body, w good or bad.	1664
	12:2	W it was in the body or out of the body I do	1664
	12:3	w in the body or apart from the body I do	1664
	13:5	Examine yourselves to see w you are in	1623
Eph	6:8	w he is slave or free.	1664
Php	1:7	for w I am in chains or defending	NIG
	1:18	w from false motives or true,	1664
	1:20	w by life or by death.	1664
	1:27	w I come and see you or only hear	1664
	4:12	w well fed or hungry,	2779
	4:12	w living in plenty or in want.	2779
Col	1:16	w thrones or powers or rulers or authorities;	1664
	1:20	w things on earth or things in heaven,	1664
	3:17	And whatever you do, w in word or deed,	NIG
1Th	5:10	w we are awake or asleep,	1664
2Th	2:15	w by word of mouth or by letter.	1664
1Pe	2:13	w to the king, as the supreme authority,	1664
1Jn	4:1	test the spirits to see w they are from God,	1623

WHICH (707) [WHAT] See Index of Articles Etc.

WHILE (428) [AWHILE, MEANWHILE]

Ge	2:21	and w he was sleeping,	2256
	4:8	And w they were in the field,	928
	11:28	W his father Terah was **still alive,**	6584+7156
	12:10	live there for a w because the famine	1591
	13:6	not support them w they stayed together,	4200

Ge	13:12	w Lot lived among the cities of the plain	2256
	18:1	to Abraham near the great trees of Mamre w	2256
	18:8	W they ate, he stood near them under a tree.	2256
	20:1	For a w he stayed in Gerar,	1591
	21:21	W he was living in the Desert of Paran,	2256
	22:5	the donkey w I and the boy go over there.	2256
	25:6	But w he was still living,	928
	25:27	w Jacob was a quiet man,	2256
	26:3	**Stay in this land for a w,**	1591
	27:44	Stay with him **for a w**	285+3427
	29:9	W he was **still** talking with them,	6388
	30:36	w Jacob continued to tend the rest	2256
	33:14	w I move along slowly at the pace of	2256
	34:25	w all of them were still in pain,	928
	35:16	W they were still some distance	2256
	35:22	W Israel was living in that region,	928
	36:24	in the desert w he was grazing the donkeys	928
	37:7	w your sheaves gathered around mine	2256
	39:7	and **after a w** his master's wife took notice	339+465+1821+2021
	39:20	**But w** Joseph was there in the prison,	2256
	42:19	w the rest of you go and take grain back	2256
	48:7	in the land of Canaan w we were still on	928
Ex	16:10	W Aaron was speaking to the whole	3869
	18:14	w all these people stand around you	2256
	20:21	w Moses approached the thick darkness	2256
	22:10	w no one is **looking,**	AIT
	22:14	w the owner is **not**	AIT
	33:9	w the LORD spoke with Moses.	2256
Lev	14:46	house w it is closed up will be unclean	3427+3972
	15:26	w her discharge **continues**	3427+3972
	18:18	and have sexual relations with her w	928
	25:22	W you plant during the eighth year,	928
	26:43	and will enjoy its sabbaths w it lies desolate	928
Nu	5:18	w he himself holds the bitter water	2256
	5:19	and become impure w **married to**	9393
	5:20	But if you have gone astray w **married to**	9393
	5:29	and defiles herself w **married to**	9393
	11:33	w the meat was still between their teeth	6388
	15:32	W the Israelites were in the desert,	2256
	18:21	in return for the work they do w serving at	NIH
	19:5	W he watches, the heifer is to be burned—	4200
	23:3	"Stay here beside your offering w I go	2256
	23:15	"Stay here beside your offering w I meet	2256
	25:1	W Israel was staying in Shittim,	2256
	25:6	and the whole assembly of Israel w	2256
	32:6	"Shall your countrymen go to war w	2256
Dt	4:11	near and stood at the foot of the mountain w	2256
	5:23	w the mountain was ablaze with fire,	2256
	9:15	from the mountain w it was ablaze with fire.	2256
	22:21	in Israel by being promiscuous w still	NIH
	25:4	Do not muzzle an ox w it is treading out	928
	26:14	I have not eaten any of the sacred portion w	928
	26:14	nor have I removed any of it w	928
	31:27	the LORD w I am still alive and with you,	928
	32:42	w my sword devours flesh:	2256
Jos	3:16	w the water flowing down to the Sea of	2256
	3:17	w all Israel passed by until	2256
	4:11	and the priests came to the other side w	NIH
	5:10	w camped at Gilgal on the plains of Jericho,	AIT
	6:13	w the trumpets kept sounding.	2256
	9:22	w actually you live near us?	2256
	14:10	w Israel moved about in the desert.	889
Jdg	3:20	then approached him w he was sitting alone	2256
	3:26	W they waited, Ehud got away.	6330
	4:21	and a hammer and went quietly to him w	2256
	7:3	w ten thousand remained.	2256
	7:21	W each man held his position around	2256
	9:27	W they were eating and drinking,	2256
	13:9	to the woman w she was out in the field;	2256
	13:19	the LORD did an amazing thing w Manoah	2256
	13:25	the Spirit of the LORD began to stir him w	NIH
	16:13	So w he was **sleeping,**	AIT
	16:25	W they were in high spirits, they shouted,	3869
	16:30	when he died than w he lived.	928
	18:17	and the cast idol w the priest and	2256
	19:22	W they were **enjoying** themselves,	AIT
	20:32	W the Benjamites were saying,	2256
	21:23	W the girls were dancing,	4946
Ru	1:1	to **live for a w** in the country of Moab.	1591
1Sa	2:13	a sacrifice and w the meat was being boiled,	3869
	7:10	W Samuel was sacrificing	2256
	13:16	w the Philistines camped at Micmash.	2256
	14:19	W Saul was talking to the priest,	6330
	18:10	w David was playing the harp,	2256
	19:9	W David was playing the harp,	2256
	21:13	and w he was in their hands he acted like	NIH
	23:15	W David was at Horesh in the Desert	2256
	25:4	W David was in the desert,	2256
	25:13	w two hundred stayed with the supplies.	2256
	28:4	w Saul gathered all the Israelites and set	2256
2Sa	3:1	w the house of Saul grew weaker	2256
	3:35	and urged David to eat something w	928
	4:5	the day w he was taking his noonday rest.	2256
	4:7	into the house w he was lying on the bed	2256
	5:2	In the past, w Saul was king over us,	928
	6:15	w he and the entire house of Israel brought	2256
	7:2	w the ark of God remains in a tent."	2256
	10:8	w the Arameans of Zobah and Rehob and	2256
	11:16	So w Joab had the city under siege,	928
	12:18	"W the child was still living,	928
	12:21	W the child was alive, you fasted and wept,	6388
	12:22	He answered, "W the child was still alive,	928
	13:30	W they were on their way,	2256
	15:8	W your servant was living at Geshur	2256
	15:12	W Absalom was offering sacrifices,	928
	16:13	along the road w Shimei was going along	2256

2Sa	17: 2	I would attack him w he is weary and weak.	2256
	18: 4	the gate w all the men marched out in units	2256
	18: 9	w the mule he was riding kept on going.	2256
	18:14	w Absalom was still alive	6388
	18:24	W David was sitting between the inner	2256
	20: 8	W they were at the great rock in Gibeon,	NIH
	20:15	W they were battering the wall to bring it	2256
	23:13	w a band of Philistines was encamped in	2256
	24:13	from your enemies w they pursue you?	2256
1Ki	1:14	W you are still there talking to the king,	6388
	1:22	W she was still speaking with the king,	6388
	3:17	I had a baby w she was there with me.	NIH
	3:20	the night and took my son from my side w	2256
	3:23	w that one says, 'No! Your son is dead	2256
	6: 7	at the temple site w it was being built.	928
	6:27	w the wing of the other touched	2256
	8:14	W the whole assembly of Israel was	2256
	11:21	W he was in Egypt,	2256
	13:20	W they were sitting at the table,	2256
	15:27	w Nadab and all Israel were besieging it.	2256
	18: 4	W Jezebel was killing off the LORD's	928
	18:13	what I did w Jezebel was killing	928
	19: 4	w he himself went a day's journey into	2256
	20:12	Ben-Hadad heard this message w he and	3869
	20:16	They set out at noon w Ben-Hadad and	2256
	20:27	w the Arameans covered the countryside.	2256
	20:40	W your servant was busy here and there,	2256
2Ki	3:15	W the harpist was playing,	3869
	4:38	W the company of the prophets was	2256
	6:33	W he was still talking to them,	6388
	8: 1	and stay for a w wherever you can,	1591
	11: 3	at the temple of the LORD for six years w	2256
	13:21	w some Israelites were burying	AIT
	17:41	Even w these people were worshiping	2256
	19:37	w he was worshiping in the temple	AIT
	23:29	W Josiah was king,	928+3427
	24:11	to the city w his officers were besieging it.	2256
1Ch	11: 2	In the past, even w Saul was king,	928
	11: 8	w Joab restored the rest of the city.	2256
	11:15	w a band of Philistines was encamped in	2256
	12: 1	w he was banished from the presence	6388
	17: 1	w the ark of the covenant of the LORD is	2256
	19: 7	w the Ammonites were mustered	2256
	19: 9	w the kings who had come were	2256
	21:20	W Araunah was threshing wheat,	2256
2Ch	3:11	w its other wing, also five cubits long,	2256
	6: 3	W the whole assembly of Israel was	2256
	13:13	so that w he was in front of Judah	AIT
	22: 8	W Jehu was executing judgment on	3869
	22: 9	and his men captured him w he was hiding	2256
	22:12	for six years w Athaliah ruled the land.	2256
	25:16	W he was still speaking,	928
	26:19	W he was raging at the priests	928
	28:18	w the Philistines had raided towns in	2256
	29:19	in his unfaithfulness w he was king.	928
	29:28	w the singers sang and	2256
	30:21	w the Levites and priests sang to	2256
	34: 3	w he was still young,	6388
	34:14	W they were bringing out the money	928
	35:11	w the Levites skinned the animals.	2256
Ezr	3:12	w many others shouted for joy.	2256
	10: 1	W Ezra was praying and confessing,	3869
	10: 6	W he was there, he ate no food	NIH
Ne	1: 1	w I was in the citadel of Susa,	2256
	4:16	w the other half were equipped with spears,	2256
	6: 3	the work stop w I leave it and go down	889+3869
	7: 3	W the gatekeepers are still on duty,	6330
	8: 7	the Law w the people were standing there.	2256
	9:33	you have acted faithfully, w we did wrong.	2256
	9:35	Even w they were in their kingdom,	NIH
	11: 1	w the remaining nine were to stay	2256
	11: 4	w other people from both Judah	2256
	11: 6	But w all this was going on,	928
Est	6:14	W they were still talking with him,	6388
	7: 8	even molest the queen w she is with me in	NIH
Job	1:16	W he was still speaking,	6388
	1:17	W he was still speaking,	6388
	1:18	W he was still speaking,	6330
	8:12	W still growing and uncut,	6388
	10: 3	w you smile on the schemes of the wicked?	2256
	21: 3	Bear with me w I speak,	5071
	24:24	For a little w they are exalted,	5071
	32:11	I waited w you spoke,	4200
	32:11	w you were searching for words,	6330
	38: 7	w the morning stars sang together and all	928
Ps	32: 6	to you w you may be found;	4200+6961
	37:10	A little w, and the wicked will	5071+6388
	41: 6	w his heart gathers slander;	AIT
	42: 3	w men say to me all day long,	928
	49:18	w he lived he counted himself blessed—	928
	51: 4	w the mouths of liars will be silenced.	3954
	68:13	Even w you sleep among the campfires,	561
	68:23	in the blood of your foes, w the tongues	NIH
	78:30	even w it was still in their mouths,	6388
	137: 1	of the LORD w in a foreign land?	NIH
	141:10	w I pass by in safety.	6330
Pr	31:15	She gets up w it is still dark;	928
Ecc	2:14	w the fool walks in the darkness;	2256
	3:12	for men than to be happy and do good w	928
	7:28	w I was still searching but not finding—	6388
	9: 3	and there is madness in their hearts w	928
	10: 6	w the rich occupy the low ones.	2256
	10: 7	w princes go on foot like slaves.	2256
	11: 9	Be happy, young man, w you are young,	2789
SS	1:12	W the king was at his table,	6330+8611
Isa	22: 3	having fled w the enemy was still far away.	NIH
	26:20	a little w until his wrath has passed by.	5071+8092
Isa	37:38	w he was worshiping in the temple	AIT
	55: 6	Seek the LORD w he may be found;	928
	55: 6	call on him w he is near.	928
	63:18	For a little w your people possessed	5203
	65:24	w they are still speaking I will hear.	6388
Jer	7:13	W you were doing all these things,	3610
	15: 9	Her sun will set w it is still day;	928
	19:10	"Then break the jar w those who go	4200
	33: 1	W Jeremiah was still confined	6388
	34: 1	W Nebuchadnezzar king of Babylon	2256
	34: 7	w the army of the king of Babylon	2256
	36: 4	and w Jeremiah dictated all the words	NIH
	38: 7	W the king was sitting in	2256
	39:15	W Jeremiah had been confined in	928
	41: 1	W they were eating together there,	2256
	43: 9	"W the Jews are watching,	4200
	51:39	But w they are aroused,	928
La	1:19	and my elders perished in the city w	3954
	3:27	for a man to bear the yoke w he is young.	928
Eze	1: 1	w I was among the exiles by	2256
	8: 1	w I was sitting in my house and the elders	AIT
	9: 8	W they were killing and I was left alone,	3869
	10:19	W I watched, the cherubim spread their wings	NIH
	11:16	yet for a little w I have been a sanctuary	5071
	12: 4	During the daytime, w they watch,	NIH
	12: 4	Then in the evening, w they are watching,	NIH
	12: 7	W they watch, dig through the wall	NIH
	12: 7	carrying them on my shoulders w	NIH
	23: 5	in prostitution w she was still mine;	NIH
	35:14	W the whole earth rejoices.	3869
	42: 8	W the row of rooms on the side next to	3954
	43: 6	W the man was standing beside me,	2256
	44: 4	desecrating my temple w you offered me	928
	44:17	not wear any woolen garment w ministering	928
Da	2:34	W you were watching, a rock	10168+10527
	2:49	w Daniel himself remained at	10221
	4:10	the visions I saw w lying in my bed:	NIH
	4:13	"In the visions I saw w lying in my bed,	NIH
	4:23	w its roots remain in the ground.	NIH
	5: 2	W Belshazzar was drinking his wine,	10089
	7: 8	"W I was thinking about the horns,	AIT
	8:15	W I, Daniel, was watching the vision	928
	8:18	W he was speaking to me,	928
	9:20	W I was speaking and praying,	6388
	9:21	w I was still in prayer,	6388
	10:15	W he was saying this to me,	928
Ob	1:11	On the day you stood aloof w	928+3427
Hab	1:13	Why are you silent w the wicked swallow	928
Hag	1: 4	w this house remains a ruin?"	2256
	1: 9	w each of you is busy with his own house.	2256
	2: 6	'In a little w I will once more shake	5071
Zec	3: 5	w the angel of the LORD stood by.	2256
	14:12	Their flesh will rot w they are still standing	2256
Mt	5:25	Do it w you are still with him	2401+4015
	9:10	W Jesus was having dinner	AIT
	9:15	mourn w he is still with them?	2093+4012
	9:18	W he was saying this,	AIT
	9:32	W they were going out,	AIT
	12:46	W Jesus was still talking	AIT
	13: 2	w all the people stood on the shore.	2779
	13:25	w everyone was sleeping,	AIT
	13:29	'because w you are pulling the weeds,	AIT
	14:22	w he dismissed the crowd.	2401+4005
	15: 8	W he was still speaking,	AIT
	21: 8	w others cut branches from the trees	1254
	21:23	and, w he was teaching,	AIT
	22:41	W the Pharisees were gathered together,	AIT
	25:10	w they were on their way	AIT
	26: 6	W Jesus was in Bethany in the home of	AIT
	26:21	And w they were eating, he said,	AIT
	26:26	W they were eating, Jesus took bread,	AIT
	26:36	"Sit here w I go over there and pray."	2401+4005
	26:47	W he was still speaking,	AIT
	26:73	After a little w, those standing there	AIT
	27:19	W Pilate was sitting on the judge's seat,	AIT
	27:63	"we remember that w he was still alive	2285
	28:11	W the women were on their way,	AIT
	28:13	and stole him away w we were asleep.'	AIT
Mk	1:35	w it was still dark, Jesus got up,	1939
	2:15	W Jesus was having dinner at Levi's house,	NIG
	2:19	bridegroom fast w he is with them?	1877+4005
	4: 1	w all the people were along the shore at	2779
	5:21	a large crowd gathered around him w	2779
	5:35	W Jesus was still speaking,	AIT
	6:45	w he dismissed the crowd.	2401
	10:32	w those who followed were afraid.	1254
	11: 8	w others spread branches they had cut in	1254
	11:27	w Jesus was walking in the temple courts,	AIT
	12:35	W Jesus was teaching in the temple courts,	AIT
	14: 3	W he was in Bethany,	AIT
	14:18	W they were reclining at the table eating,	AIT
	14:22	W they were eating, Jesus took bread,	AIT
	14:32	"Sit here w I pray."	2401
	14:66	W Peter was below in the courtyard,	AIT
	14:70	After a little w, those standing near	AIT
	16:12	of them w they were walking in the country.	AIT
Lk	2: 2	w Quirinius was governor	AIT
	2: 6	W they were there,	1639+1877+3836
	2:43	w his parents were returning home,	1877
	5:12	W Jesus was in one of the towns,	1877
	5:34	bridegroom fast w he is with them?	1877+4005
	8: 4	W a large crowd was gathering	AIT
	8:13	They believe for a w,	2789
	8:49	W Jesus was still speaking,	AIT
	9:34	W he was speaking,	AIT
	9:42	w the boy was coming,	AIT
Lk	9:43	W everyone was marveling	AIT
	14:32	he will send a delegation w the other is still	AIT
	15:20	"But w he was still a long way off,	AIT
	16:25	w Lazarus received bad things,	2779
	17: 8	get yourself ready and wait on me w I eat	2401
	19:11	W they were listening	AIT
	20:45	W all the people were listening,	AIT
	22:47	W he was still speaking,	AIT
	24: 4	W they were wondering about this,	1877+3836
	24: 6	w he was still with you in Galilee:	AIT
	24:32	not our hearts burning within us w he talked	6055
	24:36	W they were still talking about	AIT
	24:41	w they still did not believe	AIT
	24:44	"This is what I told you w I was still	AIT
	24:51	W he was blessing them,	1877+3836
Jn	1:48	"I saw you w you were still under	AIT
	2:23	Now w he was in Jerusalem at	6055
	4:51	W he was still on the way,	AIT
	5: 7	W I am trying to get in,	1877+4005
	6:59	He said this w teaching in the synagogue	AIT
	8:20	He spoke these words w teaching in	AIT
	9: 5	W I am in the world,	4020
	11: 8	"a short w ago the Jews tried to stone you,	3814
	12: 1	w Lazarus was among those reclining at	1254
	12:25	w the man who hates his life	2779
	12:35	to have the light just a little w longer.	5989
	12:35	Walk w you have the light,	6055
	12:36	Put your trust in the light w you have it,	6055
	14:25	"All this I have spoken w still with you.	AIT
	15: 2	in me that bears no fruit, w every branch	2779
	16:16	"In a little w you will see me no more,	3625
	16:16	then after a little w you will see me."	3625
	16:17	'In a little w you will see me no more,	3625
	16:17	then after a little w you will see me,'	3625
	16:18	"What does he mean by 'a little w'?	3625
	16:19	'In a little w you will see me no more,	3625
	16:19	then after a little w you will see me'?	3625
	16:20	and mourn w the world rejoices.	1254
	17:12	W I was with them,	4021
	17:13	I say these things w I am still in the world,	NIG
	20: 1	w it was still dark,	AIT
Ac	1: 4	w he was eating with them,	AIT
	3:11	W the beggar held on to	AIT
	4: 1	John w they were speaking to the people.	AIT
	5:34	the men be put outside for a little w.	1099
	7: 2	to our father Abraham w he was still	AIT
	7:59	W they were stoning him, Stephen prayed,	AIT
	9:39	that Dorcas had made w she was still	AIT
	10:10	w the meal was being prepared,	AIT
	10:17	W Peter was wondering about the meaning	6055
	10:19	W Peter was still thinking	AIT
	10:44	W Peter was still speaking	AIT
	12:19	to Caesarea and stayed there a w.	1417
	13: 2	W they were worshiping the Lord and	AIT
	17:16	W Paul was waiting for them	AIT
	18:12	W Gallio was proconsul of Achaia,	AIT
	19: 1	W Apollos was at Corinth,	1877+3836
	19:22	w he stayed in the province of Asia	NIG
	21:31	W they were trying to kill him,	AIT
	23:32	w they returned to the barracks.	NIG
	26:31	and w talking with one another, they said,	AIT
Ro	4:11	he had by faith w he was still uncircumcised	1877
	5: 8	W we were still sinners, Christ died for us.	AIT
	7: 3	w her husband is still alive,	AIT
	15:24	I hope to visit you w passing through and	AIT
	15:24	after I have enjoyed your company for a w.	3538
1Co	2: 2	For I resolved to know nothing w I was with you except	NIG
	9: 9	an ox w it is treading out the grain."	AIT
	12:24	w our presentable parts need no special treatment.	1254
	14:24	in w everybody is prophesying,	1254
	16:10	that he has nothing to fear w he is with you,	NIG
2Co	3:13	w the radiance was fading away.	AIT
	5: 4	For w we are in this tent,	AIT
	5:10	for the things done w in the body,	NIG
	7: 8	but only for a little w—	6052
	8:13	be relieved w you are hard pressed,	NIG
	13: 2	I now repeat it w absent:	AIT
Gal	2:17	"If, w we seek to be justified in Christ,	AIT
Eph	4:26	Do not let the sun go down w you are still angry,	NIG
Php	1:17	that they can stir up trouble for me w I am	NIG
1Th	5: 3	W people are saying, "Peace and safety,"	4020
1Ti	5: 6	for pleasure is dead even w she lives.	AIT
	5:18	w it is treading out the grain,"	AIT
	6:13	and of Christ Jesus, who w testifying	AIT
2Ti	3:13	w evil men and impostors will go from bad	NIG
Tit	2:13	w we wait for the blessed hope—	AIT
Phm	1:10	who became my son w I am in chains.	1877
	1:13	in helping me w I am in chains for	1877
	1:15	was separated from you for a little w	4639+6052
Heb	9:17	it never takes effect w who made is living.	2465
	10:37	For in just a very little w,	2285+4012+4012
	11:36	w still others were chained and put	NIG
	12:10	Our fathers disciplined us for a little w	2465
Jas	1:11	the rich man will fade away even w he goes	1877
	4:14	You are a mist that appears for a little w	3900
1Pe	1: 6	for a little w you may have had to suffer	3900
	3:20	w the ark was being built.	AIT
	5:10	after you have suffered a little w,	3900
2Pe	2: 9	w continuing their punishment.	AIT
	2:13	reveling in their pleasures w they feast with	AIT
	2:19	w they themselves are slaves of depravity—	AIT
Rev	11:12	w their enemies looked on.	2779
	17:10	he must remain for a little w.	3900

WHIP (4) [WHIPS]
Pr	26: 3	A **w** for the horse, a halter for the donkey,	8765
Isa	10:26	with a **w**, as when he struck down Midian at	8765
Jn	2:15	So he made a **w** out of cords,	5848
1Co	4:21	Shall I come to you with a **w**,	4811

WHIPS (6) [WHIP]
Jos	23:13	**w** on your backs and thorns in your eyes,	8849
1Ki	12:14	My father scourged you with **w**;	8765
	12:14	My father scourged you with **w**;	8765
2Ch	10:14	My father scourged you with **w**;	8765
	10:14	My father scourged you with **w**;	8765
Na	3: 2	The crack of **w**, the clatter of wheels,	8765

WHIRLING (1)
Eze	10:13	the wheels being called "the **w** wheels."	1649

WHIRLWIND (13) [WIND]
2Ki	2: 1	about to take Elijah up to heaven in a **w**,	6194
	2:11	and Elijah went up to heaven in a **w**.	6194
Ps	77:18	Your thunder was heard in the **w**,	1649
Pr	1:27	when disaster sweeps over you like a **w**,	6070
Isa	5:28	their chariot wheels like a **w**.	6070
	40:24	and a **w** sweeps them away like chaff.	6194
	66:15	and his chariots are like a **w**;	6070
Jer	4:13	his chariots come like a **w**,	6070
	23:19	a **w** swirling down on the heads of	6193
Hos	4:19	A **w** will sweep them away,	8120
	8: 7	"They sow the wind and reap the **w**.	6070
Na	1: 3	His way is in the **w** and the storm,	6070
Zec	7:14	*'I* scattered them **with a w** among the	6192

WHIRLWINDS (1) [WIND]
Isa	21: 1	Like **w** sweeping through the southland,	6070

WHIRRING (1)
Isa	18: 1	Woe to the land of **w** wings along the rivers	7527

WHISPER (9) [WHISPERED, WHISPERING]
1Ki	19:12	And after the fire came a gentle **w**.	1960+7754
Job	4:12	my ears caught a **w** of it.	9066
	26:14	how faint the **w** we hear of him!	1821
Ps	41: 7	All my enemies **w** together against me;	4317
	107:29	He stilled the storm to a **w**;	1960
Isa	8:19	and spiritists, who **w** and mutter,	7627
	26:16	*they could* barely **w** a prayer.	4318+7440
	29: 4	out of the dust your speech *will* **w**.	7627
La	3:62	*what* my enemies **w** and mutter against me	8557

WHISPERED (2) [WHISPER]
Mt	10:27	what *is* **w** in your ear,	201^S
Lk	12: 3	and what *you have* **w** in the ear in	3281

WHISPERING (4) [WHISPER]
2Sa	12:19	that his servants *were* **w among themselves**	4317
Jer	20:10	I hear many **w**, "Terror on every side!	1804
Jn	7:12	Among the crowds there was widespread **w**	1198
	7:32	the crowd **w** such things about him.	1197

WHISTLE (1) [WHISTLES, WHISTLING]
Isa	7:18	that day the LORD *will* **w** for flies from	9239

WHISTLES (1) [WHISTLE]
Isa	5:26	he **w** for those at the ends of the earth.	9239

WHISTLING (1) [WHISTLE]
Jdg	5:16	the campfires to hear the **w** *for* the flocks?	9241

WHIT (KJV) See ALL, EVERY, EVERYTHING, IN THE LEAST

WHITE (61) [REDDISH-WHITE, WHITER]
Ge	30:35	or spotted female goats (all that had **w**	4237
	30:37	and plane trees and made **w** stripes on them	4237
	30:37	the bark and exposing the **w** inner *wood* of	4237
Ex	16:31	It was **w** like coriander seed and tasted	4237
Lev	11:18	the **w** owl, the desert owl, the osprey,	9492
	13: 3	and if the hair in the sore has turned **w** and	4237
	13: 4	the spot on his skin is **w** but does not appear	4237
	13: 4	and the hair in it has not turned **w**,	4237
	13:10	a **w** swelling in the skin that has turned	4237
	13:10	in the skin that has turned the hair **w** and	4237
	13:13	Since it has all turned **w**, he is clean.	4237
	13:16	Should the raw flesh change and turn **w**,	4237
	13:17	and if the sores have turned **w**,	4237
	13:19	a **w** swelling or reddish-white spot appears,	4237
	13:20	and the hair in it has turned **w**,	4237
	13:21	there is no **w** hair in it and it is	4237
	13:24	and a reddish-white or **w** spot appears in	4237
	13:25	and if the hair in it has turned **w**,	4237
	13:26	the priest examines it and there is no **w** hair	4237
	13:38	a man or woman has **w** spots on the skin,	4237
	13:39	and if the spots are dull **w**,	4237
Dt	14:16	the little owl, the great owl, the **w** owl,	9492
Jdg	5:10	"You who ride on **w** donkeys,	7467
2Ki	5:27	and he was leprous, as **w** as snow.	NIH
Est	1: 6	garden had hangings of **w** and blue linen,	2580
	1: 6	with cords of **w linen** and purple material	1009
	8:15	royal garments of blue and **w**,	2580
Job	6: 6	or is there flavor in the **w** *of* an egg?	8202
	41:32	one would think the deep had **w hair**.	8484
Ecc	9: 8	Always be clothed in **w**,	4237
Isa	1:18	*they shall be* as **w** as snow;	4235
Da	7: 9	His clothing was as **w** as snow;	10254
	7: 9	the hair of his head was **w** like wool.	10490
Joel	1: 7	**leaving** their branches **w**.	4235
Zec	1: 8	Behind him were red, brown and **w** horses.	4237
	6: 3	the third **w**, and the fourth dappled—	4237
	6: 6	the one with the **w** horses toward the west,	4237
Mt	5:36	you cannot make even one hair **w** or black.	3328
	17: 2	and his clothes became as **w** as the light.	3328
	28: 3	and his clothes were **w** as snow.	3328
Mk	9: 3	His clothes became dazzling **w**,	3328+3336
	16: 5	a young man dressed in a **w** robe sitting on	3328
Jn	20:12	and saw two angels in **w**,	3328
Ac	1:10	when suddenly two men dressed in **w** stood	3328
Rev	1:14	His head and hair were **w** like wool,	3328
	1:14	white like wool, as **w** as snow,	3328
	2:17	a **w** stone with a new name written on it,	3328
	3: 4	They will walk with me, dressed in **w**,	3328
	3: 5	overcomes will, like them, be dressed in **w**.	3328
	3:18	and **w** clothes to wear, so you can cover	3328
	4: 4	in **w** and had crowns of gold on their heads.	3328
	6: 2	and there before me was a **w** horse!	3328
	6:11	Then each of them was given a **w** robe	3328
	7: 9	They were wearing **w** robes	3328
	7:13	"These in **w** robes—who are they,	3328
	7:14	and **made** them **w** in the blood of the Lamb.	3326
	14:14	and there before me was a **w** cloud,	3328
	19:11	and there before me was a **w** horse,	3328
	19:14	riding on **w** horses and dressed in fine linen,	3328
	19:14	on white horses and dressed in fine linen, **w**	3328
	20:11	a great **w** throne and him who was seated	3328

WHITER (4) [WHITE]
Ge	49:12	his teeth **w** than milk.	4237
Ps	51: 7	wash me, and *I will be* **w** than snow.	4235
La	4: 7	brighter than snow and **w** than milk,	7458
Mk	9: 3	**w** than anyone in the world could bleach	NIG

WHITEWASH (6) [WASH]
Eze	13:10	they cover it with **w**,	9521
	13:11	therefore tell those who cover it with **w**	9521
	13:12	"Where is the **w** you covered it with?"	3225
	13:14	the wall you have covered with **w**	9521
	13:15	and against those who covered it with **w**.	9521
	22:28	Her prophets **w** these deeds for them	3212+9521

WHITEWASHED (3) [WASH]
Eze	13:15	"The wall is gone and so are those *who* **w** it,	3212
Mt	23:27	You are like **w** tombs,	3154
Ac	23: 3	"God will strike you, you **w** wall!	3154

WHITHER (KJV) See WHERE, WHICH

WHITHERSOEVER (KJV) See EVERYWHERE, WHENEVER, WHEREVER

WHO (5081) [WHOEVER, WHOM, WHOSE]
See Index of Articles Etc.

WHOEVER (191) [WHO]
Ge	4:14	and **w** finds me will kill me."	3972
	9: 6	"**W** sheds the blood of man,	AIT
	12: 3	and **w** curses you I will curse;	AIT
	44:10	**W** is found to have it will become my slave;	889
Ex	12:15	for **w** eats anything with yeast in it from	3972
	12:19	And **w** eats anything with yeast in it must	3972
	19:12	**W** touches the mountain shall surely be put	3972
	22:20	"**W** sacrifices to any god other than	AIT
	30:33	**W** makes perfume like it	408+889
	30:33	like it and **w** puts it on anyone other than	889
	30:38	**W** makes any like it	408+889
	31:14	does any work on that day must	3972
	31:15	**W** does any work on the Sabbath day must	3972
	32:24	So I told them, '**W** has any gold jewelry,	4769
	32:26	"**W** is for the LORD, come to me."	4769
	32:33	"**W** has sinned against me I will blot out	4769
	35: 2	**W** does any work on it must be put to death.	3972
Lev	11:24	**w** touches their carcasses will be unclean	3972
	11:25	**W** picks up one of their carcasses	3972
	11:26	**w** touches [the carcass of] any of them will	3972
	11:27	**w** touches their carcasses will be unclean	3972
	11:31	**W** touches them when they are dead will	3972
	15: 6	**W** sits on anything that the man with	2021
	15: 7	" '**W** touches the man who has	2021
	15:10	and **w** touches any of the things that were	3972
	15:10	**w** picks up those things must wash	2021
	15:21	**W** touches her bed must wash his clothes	3972
	15:22	**W** touches anything she sits	3972
	15:27	**W** touches them will be unclean;	3972
	19: 8	**W** eats it will be held responsible	AIT
	24:21	*W* kills an animal must make restitution,	AIT
	24:21	but **w** kills a man must be put to death.	AIT
Nu	19:12	"**W** touches the dead body of anyone will	2021
	19:13	**W** touches the dead body of anyone	3972
Jos	1:18	**W** rebels against your word and	408+889+3972
Jdg	6:31	**W** fights for him shall be put to death	889
Jdg	10:18	"**W** will launch the attack against	408+2021+4769
2Sa	17: 9	**w** hears about it will say,	2021
	20:11	"**W** favors Joab, and whoever is for	889+4769
	20:11	favors Joab, and **w** is for David,	889+4769
	23: 7	**W** touches thorns uses a tool of iron or	408
1Ch	11: 6	"**W** leads the attack on the Jebusites	3972
2Ch	13: 9	**W** comes to consecrate himself with	3972
Ezr	7:26	**W** does not obey the law of your God	10168+10353
Job	29:11	**W** heard me spoke well of me,	265^S
Ps	34:12	**W** of you loves life and desires	408+2021+4769
	101: 5	**W** slanders his neighbor in secret,	AIT
	101: 5	**w** has haughty eyes and a proud heart,	NIH
	107:43	**W** is wise, let him heed these things	4769
Pr	1:33	but **w** listens to me will live in safety and	AIT
	6:32	**w** does so destroys himself.	2085
	8:35	For **w** finds me finds life and receives favor	AIT
	8:36	But **w** fails to find me harms himself;	AIT
	9: 7	"**W** corrects a mocker invites insult;	AIT
	9: 7	**w** rebukes a wicked man incurs abuse.	AIT
	10:17	but **w** ignores correction leads others astray.	AIT
	10:18	and **w** spreads slander is a fool.	AIT
	11:15	but **w** refuses to strike hands in pledge	AIT
	11:28	**W** trusts in his riches will fall,	AIT
	12: 1	**W** loves discipline loves knowledge,	AIT
	13:18	but **w** heeds correction is honored.	AIT
	14:31	but **w** *is* kind *to* the needy honors God.	AIT
	15: 5	but **w** heeds correction shows prudence.	AIT
	15:32	but **w** heeds correction gains understanding.	AIT
	16:20	**W** gives heed to instruction prospers,	AIT
	17: 5	**w** gloats over disaster will not go unpunished	AIT
	17: 9	**w** repeats the matter separates close friends.	AIT
	20: 1	**w** is led astray by them is not wise.	3972
	21:17	**w** loves wine and oil will never be rich.	AIT
	21:28	**w** listens to him will be destroyed forever.	408
	24:24	**W** says to the guilty, "You are innocent"—	AIT
	28:13	**w** confesses and renounces them finds mercy	AIT
	29: 5	**W** flatters his neighbor is spreading a net	1505^S
	29:25	but **w** trusts in the LORD is kept safe.	AIT
Ecc	5:10	**W** loves money never has money enough;	AIT
	5:10	**w** loves wealth is never satisfied	4769
	8: 5	**W** obeys his command will come	AIT
	10: 8	**W** digs a pit may fall into it;	AIT
	10: 8	**w** breaks through a wall may be bitten by	AIT
	10: 9	**W** quarries stones may be injured by them;	AIT
	10: 9	**w** splits logs may be endangered by them.	AIT
	11: 4	**W** watches the wind will not plant;	AIT
	11: 4	**w** looks at the clouds will not reap.	AIT
Isa	13:15	**W** is captured will be thrust through;	3972
	24:18	**W** flees at the sound of terror will fall into	2021
	24:18	**w** climbs out of the pit will be caught in	2021
	54:15	**w** attacks you will surrender to you.	4769
	59: 5	**W** eats their eggs will die,	2021
	59:15	and **w** shuns evil becomes a prey.	AIT
	65:16	**W** invokes a blessing in the land will do so	889
	66: 3	But **w** sacrifices a bull is like one who kills	AIT
	66: 3	and **w** offers a lamb,	AIT
	66: 3	**w** makes a grain **offering**	AIT
	66: 3	and **w** burns memorial incense,	AIT
Jer	21: 9	**W** stays in this city will die by the sword,	2021
	21: 9	But **w** goes out and surrenders to	2021
	31:30	**w** eats sour grapes—	132+2021+3972
	38: 2	'**W** stays in this city will die by the sword,	2021
	38: 2	**w** goes over to the Babylonians will live.	2021
	48:44	"**W** flees from the terror will fall into a pit,	2021
	48:44	**w** climbs out of the pit will be caught in	2021
Eze	3:27	**W** will listen let him listen,	2021
	3:27	and **w** will refuse let him refuse;	2021
	46: 9	**w** enters by the north gate to worship is	2021
	46: 9	and **w** enters by the south gate is to go out	2021
Da	3: 6	**W** does not fall down and worship	10168+10426
	3:11	**w** does not fall down and worship	10168+10426
	5: 7	"**W** reads this writing	10050+10168+10353
Zec	2: 8	for **w** touches you touches the apple	2021^S
Mal	2:12	As for the man who does this, **w** he may be,	2256+6424+6699
Mt	5:19	but **w** practices and teaches these	323+4005
	10:32	"**W** acknowledges me before men,	4015+4246
	10:33	But **w** disowns me before men,	323+4015
	10:39	**W** finds his life will lose it,	3836
	10:39	and **w** loses his life for my sake will find it.	3836
	12:50	For **w** does the will of my Father	323+4005
	13:12	**W** has will be given more,	4015
	13:12	**W** does not have, even what he has	4015
	16:25	**w** wants to save his life will lose it,	1569+4005
	16:25	but **w** loses his life for me will find it.	323+4005
	18: 4	**w** humbles himself like this child is	4015
	18: 5	And **w** welcomes a little child like this	1569+4005
	20:26	**w** wants to become great among you	1569+4005
	20:27	**w** wants to be first must be your slave	323+4005
	23:12	For **w** exalts himself will be humbled,	4015
	23:12	and **w** humbles himself will be exalted.	4015
	25:29	**W** does not have, even what he has	3836
Mk	3:29	**w** blasphemes against the Holy Spirit	323+4005
	3:35	**W** does God's will is my brother and	4005
	4:25	**W** has will be given more;	4005
	4:25	**w** does not have, even what he has	4005
	8:35	**w** wants to save his life will lose it,	1569+4005
	8:35	but **w** loses his life for me and for	323+4005
	9:37	**W** welcomes one of these little children	323+4005
	9:37	**w** welcomes me does not welcome me	323+4005
	9:40	for **w** is not against us is for us.	4005
	10:43	**w** wants to become great among you	323+4005
	10:44	and **w** wants to be first must be slave of all.	323+4005
	16:16	**W** believes and is baptized will be saved,	3836
	16:16	but **w** does not believe will be condemned.	3836

Lk 8:18 W has will be given more; 323+4005
8:18 w does not have, even what he thinks 323+4005
9:24 For w wants to save his life will lose it, 323+4005
9:24 and w loses his life for me will save it. 323+4005
9:48 "W welcomes this little child 1569+4005
9:48 and w welcomes me welcomes 323+4005
9:50 "for w is not against you is for you." 4005
12:8 w acknowledges me before men, 323+4005
16:10 "W can be trusted with very little can also 3836
16:10 and w is dishonest with very little will also 3836
17:33 W tries to keep his life will lose it, 1569+4005
17:33 and w loses his life will preserve it. 4005
Jn 3:16 that w believes in him shall not perish 3836+4246
3:18 W believes in him is not condemned, 3836
3:18 but w does not believe stands condemned 3836
3:21 w lives by the truth comes into the light, 3836
3:36 W believes in the Son has eternal life, 3836
3:36 but w rejects the Son will not see life, 3836
4:14 but w drinks the water I give him will never thirst. 323+4005
5:24 w hears my word and believes him who 3836
6:37 and w comes to me I will never drive away. 3836
6:54 W eats my flesh and drinks my blood 3836
6:56 W eats my flesh and drinks my blood 3836
7:38 W believes in me, as the Scripture has said, 3836
8:12 W follows me will never walk in darkness, 3836
10:9 w enters through me will be saved. 1569+5516
11:26 w lives and believes in me will never die. 3836+4246
12:26 W serves me must follow me; 1569+5516
13:20 w accepts anyone I send accepts me; 323+3836
13:20 w accepts the one who sent me." 3836
14:21 W has my commands and obeys them, 3836
1Co 11:27 w eats the bread or drinks the cup of 323+4005
2Co 9:6 W sows sparingly will also reap sparingly, 3836
9:6 and w sows generously will also reap 3836
Gal 5:10 will pay the penalty, w he may be. 1569+4015
Jas 2:10 For w keeps the whole law and yet stumbles 4015
5:20 W turns a sinner from the error of his way 3836
1Pe 3:10 "W would love life and see good days 3836
1Jn 2:6 W claims to live in him must walk as Jesus 3836
2:10 W loves his brother lives in the light, 3836
2:11 But w hates his brother is in the darkness 3836
2:23 w acknowledges the Son has the Father 3836
4:6 and w knows God listens to us; 3836
4:6 but w is not from God does not listen to us. 4005
4:8 W does not love does not know God, 3836
4:16 W lives in love lives in God, 3836
4:21 W loves God must also love his brother. 3836
2Jn 1:9 w continues in the teaching has both 3836
Rev 22:17 W is thirsty, let him come; 3836
22:17 and w wishes, let him take the free gift of 3836

WHOLE (393) [WHOLLY, WHOLEHEARTED, WHOLEHEARTEDLY]

Ge 1:29 of the w earth and every tree that has fruit 3972
2:6 up from the earth and watered the w surface 3972
7:1 "Go into the ark, you and your w family, 3972
11:1 Now the w world had one language and 3972
11:4 be scattered over the face of the w earth." 3972
11:9 the language of the w world. 3972
11:9 over the face of the w earth. 3972
13:9 Is not the w land before you? 3972
13:10 the w plain of the Jordan was well watered, 3972
13:11 the w plain of the Jordan and set out toward 3972
14:7 and they conquered the w territory of 3972
17:8 The w land of Canaan, 3972
18:26 I will spare the w place for their sake." 3972
18:28 Will you destroy the w city because 3972
25:25 and his w body was like a hairy garment; 3972
29:14 with him for a w month, 2544+3427
41:41 "I hereby put you in charge of the w land 3972
41:43 Thus he put him in charge of the w land 3972
41:54 but in the w land of Egypt there was food. 3972
41:56 the famine had spread over the w country, 3972
47:13 no food, however, in the w region 3972
Ex 8:2 I will plague your w country with frogs. 3972
9:9 It will become fine dust over the w land 3972
12:3 Tell the w community of Israel that on 3972
12:4 If any household is too small for a w lamb, AIT
12:47 w community of Israel must celebrate it. 3972
16:1 The w Israelite community set out 3972
16:2 the w community grumbled against Moses 3972
16:10 to the w Israelite community, 3972
17:1 The w Israelite community set out from 3972
19:5 Although the w earth is mine, 3972
19:18 the w mountain trembled violently, 3972
22:6 of grain or standing grain or the w field, AIT
35:1 Moses assembled the w Israelite community 3972
35:4 Moses said to the w Israelite community, 3972
35:20 Then the w Israelite community withdrew 3972
Lev 4:13 w Israelite community sins unintentionally 3972
8:21 the w ram on the altar as a burnt offering, 3972
10:6 be angry with the w community. 3972
13:13 and if the disease has covered his w body, 3972
15:16 he must bathe his w body with water, 3972
16:17 his household and the w community 3972
Nu 1:2 of the w Israelite community by their clans 3972
1:18 and they called the w community together 3972
1:53 for the w community at the Tent of Meeting 3972
8:7 then have them shave their w bodies 3972
8:9 and assemble the w Israelite community. 3972
8:20 Aaron and the Israelite community did 3972
10:3 the w community is to assemble before you 3972
11:20 but for a w month—until it comes out of 3427
11:21 give them meat to eat for a w month!' 3427

Nu 13:26 and the w Israelite community at Kadesh in 3972
13:26 the w assembly and showed them the fruit 3972
14:2 and the w assembly said to them, 3972
14:5 of the w Israelite assembly gathered there. 3972
14:10 the w assembly talked about stoning them. 3972
14:21 as the glory of the LORD fills the w earth, 3972
14:35 to this w wicked community, 3972
14:36 the w community grumble against him 3972
15:24 the w community is to offer a young bull 3972
15:25 for the w Israelite community, 3972
15:26 The w Israelite community and 3972
15:33 to Moses and Aaron and the w assembly, 3972
15:35 The w assembly must stone him outside 3972
16:3 The w community is holy, 3972
16:41 the w Israelite community grumbled 3972
20:1 the w Israelite community arrived at 3972
20:22 The w Israelite community set out 3972
20:27 in the sight of the w community. 3972
20:29 w community learned that Aaron had died, 3972
21:33 and his w army marched out to meet them 3972
21:34 with his w army and his land. 3972
21:35 together with his sons and his w army, 3972
25:6 of Moses and the w assembly of Israel 3972
26:2 of the w Israelite community by families— 3972
27:2 the leaders and the w assembly, and said, 3972
27:20 so the w Israelite community will obey him. 3972
27:22 the priest and the w assembly. 3972
32:13 w generation of those who had done evil 3972
32:33 the w land with its cities and the territory NIH
33:33 together with his sons and his w army. 3972
Dt 2:33 with his w army marched out to meet us 3972
3:1 over to you with his w army and his land. 3972
3:2 the w region of Argob, 3972
3:4 (The w region of Argob in Bashan used to 3972
3:13 (The w region of Argob as far the greater 3972
3:14 in a loud voice to your w assembly there on 3972
5:22 and Pharaoh and his w household. 3972
6:22 king of Egypt and to his w country; 3972
11:3 the terror and fear of you on the w land, 3972
11:25 and all its plunder as a w burnt offering to 4003
13:16 indeed the w tribe of Levi— 3972
18:1 and gives you the w land he promised them, 3972
19:8 The w land will be a burning waste of salt 3972
29:23 in the hearing of the w assembly of Israel: 3972
31:30 and burnt offerings on your altar. 4003
33:10 There the LORD showed him the w land— 3972
34:1 and the w region from the Valley of Jericho 3971
34:3 and to all his officials and to his w land." 3972
34:11 they have come to spy out the w land." 3972
Jos 2:3 "The LORD has surely given the w land 3972
2:24 the w nation had completed the crossing 3972
3:17 When the w nation had finished crossing 3972
4:1 after the w nation had been circumcised, 3972
5:8 they burned the w city and everything in it, NIH
6:24 Take the w army with you, 3972
8:1 and the w army moved out to attack Ai. 3972
8:3 that Joshua did not read to the w assembly 3972
8:35 The w assembly grumbled against 3972
9:18 the w land and to wipe out all its inhabitants 3972
9:24 The w army then returned safely to Joshua 3972
10:21 So Joshua subdued the w region, 3972
10:40 and from the w region of Goshen to Gibeon. 3972
10:41 and his w army came against them suddenly 3972
11:7 all the Negev, the w region of Goshen, 3972
11:16 and included the w plateau of Medeba as far 3972
13:9 the w kingdom of Og in Bashan, 3972
13:12 and the w plateau past Medeba 3972
13:16 The w assembly of the Israelites gathered 3972
18:1 the w assembly of Israel gathered at Shiloh 3972
22:12 "The w assembly of the LORD says: 3972
22:16 be angry with the w community of Israel. 3972
22:18 did not wrath come upon the w community 3972
22:20 After that w generation had been gathered 3972
Jdg 1:25 but spared the man and his w family. 3972
2:10 After that w generation had been gathered 3972
7:14 and the w camp into his hands." 3972
9:29 'Call out your w army!' " 8049
14:17 She cried the w seven days of the feast. NIH
16:31 and his father's w family went down 3972
20:37 spread out and put the w city to the sword. 3972
20:40 and saw the smoke of the w city going up 4003
21:13 Then the w assembly sent an offer of peace 3972
Ru 1:19 the w town was stirred because of them, 3972
1Sa 1:28 For his w life he will be given over to 3972
4:13 the w town sent up a cry. 3972
7:3 And Samuel said to the w house of Israel, 3972
7:9 and offered it up as a w burnt offering to 4003
13:19 a blacksmith could be found in the w land 3972
14:15 Then panic struck the w army— 3972
17:46 the w world will know that there is a God 3972
19:7 and told him the w conversation. 3972
20:6 sacrifice is being made there for his w clan.' 3972
22:11 of Ahitub and his father's w family, 3972
22:15 knows nothing at all about this w affair." 3972
22:16 you and your father's w family, 3972
22:22 for the death of your father's w family. 3972
25:7 and the w time they were at Carmel nothing 3972
25:15 and the w time we were out in the fields 3972
25:17 over our master and his w household. 3972
2Sa 2:29 continued through the w Bithron and came 3972
3:19 and the w house of Benjamin wanted to do. 3972
6:5 and the w house of Israel were celebrating 3972
6:19 to each person in the w crowd of Israelites, 3972
11:1 the king's men and the w Israelite army. 3972
14:7 the w clan has risen up against your servant; 3972
15:23 The w countryside wept aloud as all 3972
18:8 battle spread out over the w countryside, 3972
19:2 the w army the victory that day was turned 3972

2Sa 19:20 the first of the w house of Joseph to come 3972
1Ki 6:22 So he overlaid the w interior with gold. 3972
8:14 the w assembly of Israel was standing there, 3972
8:22 of the LORD in front of the w assembly 3972
8:55 the w assembly of Israel in a loud voice, 3972
10:24 The w world sought audience with Solomon 3972
11:13 Yet I will not tear the w kingdom from him, 3972
11:28 he put him in charge of the w labor force of 3972
11:34 "'But I will not take the w kingdom out 3972
12:3 the w assembly of Israel went to Rehoboam 3972
12:21 he mustered the w house of Judah and 3972
12:23 to the w house of Judah and Benjamin, 3972
15:29 he killed Jeroboam's w family. 3972
16:11 he killed off Baasha's w family. 3972
16:12 So Zimri destroyed the w family of Baasha, 3972
2Ki 7:15 and they found the w road strewn with 3972
9:8 The w house of Ahab will perish. 3972
11:1 to destroy the w royal family. 3972
21:8 and will keep the w Law 3972
25:1 against Jerusalem with his w army. 3972
25:4 the w army fled at night through the gate 3972
25:10 The w Babylonian army, 3972
1Ch 11:10 to extend it over the w land, as 3776S
13:2 He then said to the w assembly of Israel, 3972
13:4 The w assembly agreed to do this, 3972
28:4 chose me from my w family to be king 3972
29:1 Then King David said to the w assembly: 3972
29:10 in the presence of the w assembly, 3972
29:20 Then David said to the w assembly, 3972
2Ch 6:3 and the w assembly went to the high place 3972
6:3 the w assembly of Israel was standing there, 3972
6:12 of the LORD in front of the w assembly 3972
6:13 and then knelt down before the w assembly 3972
15:8 the w land of Judah and Benjamin and from 3972
22:10 she proceeded to destroy the w royal family 3972
23:3 The w assembly made a covenant with 3972
29:28 The w assembly bowed in worship, 3972
30:2 and the w assembly in Jerusalem decided 3972
30:4 both to the king and to the w assembly. 3972
30:23 The w assembly then agreed to celebrate 3972
31:18 and daughters of the w community listed 3972
Ezr 2:64 The w company numbered 42,360, 3972
4:20 over the w of Trans-Euphrates, 10353
10:12 The w assembly responded with 3972
10:14 Let our officials act for the w assembly. 3972
Ne 5:13 At this the w assembly said, "Amen," 3972
7:66 The w company numbered 42,360, 3972
8:17 The w company that had returned 3972
Est 8:17 throughout the w kingdom of Xerxes. 3972
Job 17:7 my w frame is but a shadow. 3972
34:13 Who put him in charge of the w world? 3972
37:3 the w heaven and sends it to the ends of 3972
37:12 around over the face of the w earth 824+9315
Ps 35:10 My w being will exclaim, "Who is like you, 3972
48:2 the joy of the w earth. 3972
51:19 w burnt offerings to delight you; 4003
72:19 may the w earth be filled with his glory. 3972
110:6 and crushing the rulers of the w earth. 8041
Pr 1:12 and w, like those who go down to the pit; 9459
4:22 and health to a man's w body. 3972
5:14 the brink of utter ruin in the midst of the w assembly." 2256+6337+7736
8:31 rejoicing in his w world and 824+9315
Ecc 12:13 for this is the w [duty] of man. 3972
Isa 1:5 Your w head is injured, 3972
1:5 your w heart afflicted. 3972
6:3 the w earth is full of his glory." 3972
10:23 the destruction decreed upon the w land. 3972
13:5 to destroy the w country. 3972
14:26 This is the plan determined for the w world; 3972
28:22 the destruction decreed against the w land. 3972
29:11 For you this w vision is nothing 3972
31:4 a w band of shepherds is called together 4850
Jer 1:18 a bronze wall to stand against the w land— 3972
4:20 the w land lies in ruins. 3972
4:27 "The w land will be ruined, 3972
8:16 of their stallions the w land trembles. 3972
9:26 even the w house of Israel is uncircumcised 3972
12:11 the w land will be laid waste 3972
13:11 the w house of Israel and the w house 3972
13:11 of Israel and the w house of Judah to me,' 3972
15:10 with whom the w land strives and contends! 3972
25:11 This w country will become a desolate 3972
31:40 The w valley where dead bodies 3972
35:3 the w family of the Recabites. 3972
39:1 with his w army and laid siege to it. 3972
40:4 Look, the w country lies before you; 3972
44:28 the w remnant of Judah who came to live 3972
50:23 and shattered is the hammer of the w earth! 3972
51:7 she made the w earth drunk. 3972
51:25 you who destroy the w earth," 3972
51:41 the boast of the w earth seized! 3972
51:47 her w land will be disgraced 3972
52:4 against Jerusalem with his w army. 3972
52:7 and the w army fled. 3972
52:7 The w Babylonian army under 3972
La 2:15 the joy of the w earth?" 3972
Eze 3:7 w house of Israel is hardened and obstinate. 3972
5:4 A fire will spread from there to the w house 3972
7:12 for wrath is upon the w crowd. 3972
7:13 the vision concerning the w crowd will not 3972
7:14 my wrath is upon the w crowd. 3972
11:15 and the w house of Israel— 3972
12:10 and the w house of Israel who are there.' 3972
15:5 not useful for anything when it was w, 9459
32:22 "Assyria is there with her w army; 3972
34:6 They were scattered over the w earth, 3972

Eze	35:14	w earth rejoices, I will make you desolate.	3972
	36:10	even the w house of Israel.	3972
	37:11	these bones are the w house of Israel.	3972
	38: 4	and bring you out with your w army.	3972
	41:19	They were carved all around the w temple.	3972
	43:11	its w design and all its regulations and laws.	3972
	45: 6	it will belong to the w house of Israel.	3972
Da	1:20	and enchanters in his w kingdom.	3972
	2:35	a huge mountain and filled the w earth.	10353
	2:39	one of bronze, will rule over the w earth.	10353
	4:20	visible to the w earth,	10353
	6: 3	to set him over the w kingdom.	10353
	7:23	and will devour the w earth,	10353
	7:27	under the w heaven will be handed over to	10353
	8: 5	the w earth without touching the ground.	3972
	9:12	the w heaven nothing has ever been done	3972
Am	1: 6	Because she took captive w communities	8969
	1: 9	Because she sold w communities	8969
	3: 1	the w family I brought up out of Egypt:	3972
	8: 8	The w land will rise like the Nile;	3972
	9: 5	the w land rises like the Nile,	3972
Hab	1: 6	across the w earth to seize dwelling places	5303
Zep	1:18	In the fire of his jealousy the w world will	3972
	3: 8	The w world will be consumed by the fire	3972
Hag	1:12	and the w remnant of the people obeyed	3972
	1:14	the spirit of the w remnant of the people.	3972
Zec	1:11	and found the w world at rest and in peace."	3972
	5: 3	the curse that is going out over the w land;	3972
	6: 5	in the presence of the Lord of the w world.	3972
	13: 8	In the w land," declares the LORD,	3972
	14: 9	The LORD will be king over the w earth.	3972
	14:10	The w land, from Geba to Rimmon,	3972
Mal	3: 9	the w nation of you—	3972
	3:10	Bring the w tithe into the storehouse,	3972
Mt	3: 5	and all Judea and the w region of	4246
	5:29	for your w body to be thrown into hell.	3910
	5:30	of your body than for your w body to go	3910
	6:22	your w body will be full of light.	3910
	6:23	your w body will be full of darkness.	3910
	8:32	the w herd rushed down the steep bank into	4246
	8:34	Then the w town went out to meet Jesus.	4246
	16:26	be for a man if he gains the w world,	3910
	21:10	the w city was stirred and asked,	4246
	24:14	in the w world as a testimony to all nations,	3910
	26:59	and the w Sanhedrin were looking	3910
	27:27	the Praetorium and gathered the w company	3910
Mk	1: 5	The w Judean countryside and all	3910
	1:28	spread quickly over the w region	3910+4116
	1:33	The w town gathered at the door,	3910
	5:33	trembling with fear, told him the w truth.	4246
	6:55	that w region and carried the sick on mats	3910
	8:36	for a man to gain the w world,	3910
	11:18	the w crowd was amazed at his teaching.	4246
	14:55	the w Sanhedrin were looking for evidence	3910
	15: 1	the teachers of the law and the w Sanhedrin,	3910
	15:16	and called together the w company	3910
	15:33	over the w land until the ninth hour.	3910
Lk	4:14	through the w countryside.	3910
	9:25	for a man to gain the w world,	3910
	11:34	your w body also is full of light.	3910
	11:36	Therefore, if your w body is full of light,	3910
	15:14	there was a severe famine in that w country,	2848
	19:37	the w crowd of disciples began joyfully	570
	21:35	on the face of the w earth.	4246
	23: 1	w assembly rose and led him off to Pilate.	570
	23:44	and darkness came over the w land until	3910
Jn	7:23	for healing the w man on the Sabbath?	3910
	11:50	the people than that the w nation perish."	NIG
	12:19	Look how the w world has gone after him!"	NIG
	13:10	his w body is clean.	3910
	21:25	that even the w world would not have room	899
Ac	1:21	the men who have been with us the w time	4246
	2: 2	the w house where they were sitting.	3910
	5:11	the w church and all who heard	3910
	6: 5	This proposal pleased the w group.	4246
	6: 5	for his father Jacob and his w family,	4246
	11:26	So for a w year Barnabas and Saul met with	3910
	13: 6	the w island until they came to Paphos.	3910
	13:44	the next Sabbath almost the w city gathered	4246
	13:49	of the Lord spread through the w region.	3910
	15:12	The w assembly became silent	4246
	15:22	the apostles and elders, with the w church,	3910
	16:34	believe in God—he and his w family.	4109
	17:26	that they should inhabit the w earth;	4246
	19:26	and in practically the w province of Asia.	4246
	19:29	Soon the w city was in an uproar.	NIG
	20:18	"You know how I lived the w time I was	4246
	20:27	not hesitated to proclaim to you the w will	4246
	21:27	stirred up the w crowd and seized him,	4246
	21:30	The w city was aroused,	3910
	21:31	the w city of Jerusalem was in an uproar.	3910
	25:24	the w Jewish community has petitioned me	570
	28:30	For two w years Paul stayed there	3910
Ro	1: 9	whom I serve with my w heart in preaching	NIG
	3:19	and the w world held accountable to God.	4246
	8:22	that the w creation has been groaning as in	4246
	11:16	then the w batch is holy;	NIG
	16:23	and the w church here enjoy,	3910
1Co	4: 9	a spectacle to the w universe,	NIG
	5: 6	that a little yeast works through the w batch	3910
	12:17	If the w body were an eye,	3910
	12:17	If the w body were an ear,	3910
	14:23	So if the w church comes together	3910
Gal	3:22	the Scripture declares that the w world is	4246
	4: 1	who owns the w estate.	4246
	5: 3	that he is obligated to obey the w law.	3910
	5: 9	"A little yeast works through the w batch	3910

Gal	5:12	go the w way and emasculate themselves!	NIG
Eph	2:21	the w building is joined together and rises	4246
	3:15	from whom his w family in heaven and	4246
	4:10	in order to fill the w universe.)	4246
	4:13	to the w measure of the fullness of Christ.	NIG
	4:16	From him the w body, joined and held	4246
Php	1:13	the w palace guard and to everyone else	3910
Col	2:19	from whom the w body, supported and held	4246
1Th	5:23	May your w spirit, soul and body	3908
Tit	1:11	because they are ruining w households	3910
Jas	2:10	For whoever keeps the w law	3910
	3: 2	able to keep his w body in check.	3910
	3: 3	we can turn the w animal.	3910
	3: 6	It corrupts the w person,	3910
	3: 6	for w course of his life on fire,	NIG
1Jn	2: 2	for ours but also for the sins of the w world.	3910
	5:19	w world is under the control of the evil one.	3910
Rev	6:12	upon the w world to test those who live on	3910
	6:12	the w moon turned blood red,	3910
	12: 9	or Satan, who leads the w world astray.	3910
	13: 3	The w world was astonished and followed	3910
	16:14	and they go out to the kings of the w world,	3910

WHOLEHEARTED (4) [HEART, WHOLE]

2Ki	20: 3	you faithfully and with w devotion	4222+8969
1Ch	28: 9	w devotion and with a willing mind,	4213+8969
	29:19	give my son Solomon with w devotion	4222+8969
Isa	38: 3	you faithfully and with w devotion	4213+8969

WHOLEHEARTEDLY (16) [HEART, WHOLE]

Nu	14:24	a different spirit and follows me w,	4848
	32:11	'Because they have not followed me w,	4848
	32:12	for they followed the LORD w.'	4848
Dt	1:36	because he followed the LORD w."	4848
Jos	14: 8	however, followed the LORD my God w.'	4848
	14: 9	you have followed the LORD my God w.'	4848
	14:14	followed the LORD, the God of Israel, w.	4848
1Ki	8:23	your servants who continue w	928+3972+4213
1Ch	29: 9	given freely and w to the LORD.	928+4213+8969
2Ch	6:14	your servants who continue w	928+3972+4213
	15:15	oath because they had sworn it w.	928+3972+4222
	19: 9	"You must serve faithfully and w	928+4222+8969
	25: 2	the eyes of the LORD, but not w.	928+4222+8969
	31:21	he sought his God and worked w.	928+3972+4222
Ro	6:17	you w obeyed the form of teaching	1666+2840
Eph	6: 7	Serve w, as if you were serving the Lord,	2334+3552

WHOLESOME (2)

2Ki	2:22	And the water has remained w to this day,	8324
2Pe	3: 1	as reminders to stimulate you to w thinking.	1637

WHOLLY (3) [WHOLE]

Nu	3: 9	who are to be given w to him.	5989+5989
	8:16	Israelites who are to be given w to me.	5989+5989
1Ti	4:15	in these matters; give yourself w to them,	3509

WHOM (394) [WHO] See Index of Articles Etc.

WHOMSOEVER (KJV) See ANY, ANYONE, EVERYONE, ONE, WHATEVER, WHOEVER, WHOM

WHORE, WHORE'S, WHORES (KJV) See PROMISCUOUS, PROSTITUTE, PROSTITUTES, PROSTITUTION, UNFAITHFUL

WHOREDOM (KJV) See UNFAITHFULNESS, ADULTERY, PROSTITUTION

WHOREMONGER, WHOREMONGERS (KJV) See IMMORAL, SEXUALLY IMMORAL

WHOSO, WHOSOEVER (KJV) See ANYONE, MAN, WHO, WHOEVER

WHOSE (278) [WHO] See Index of Articles Etc.

WHY (550)

Ge	4: 6	LORD said to Cain, "W are you angry?	4200+4537
	4: 6	W is your face downcast?	4200+4537
	10: 9	that is w it is said, "Like Nimrod,	4027+6584
	11: 9	That is w it was called Babel—	4027+6584
	12:18	"W didn't you tell me she was your wife?	4200+4537
	12:19	W did you say, 'She is my sister,'	4200+4537
	16:14	That is w the well was called Beer Lahai Roi;	4027+6584

Ge	18:13	"W did Sarah laugh and say,	4200+4537
	19:22	(That is w the town was called Zoar.)	4027+6584
	20: 6	W I did not let you touch her.	4027+6584
	24:31	"W are you standing out here?	4200+4537
	25:22	and she said, "W is this happening to me?"	561+4027+4200+4537
	25:30	(That is w he was also called Edom.)	4027+6584
	26: 9	W did you say, 'She is my sister'?"	375
	26:27	Isaac asked them, "W have you come to me	4508
	27:45	W should I lose both of you in one day?"	4200+4537
	29:25	W have you deceived me?"	4200+4537
	31:27	W did you run off secretly and	4200+4537
	31:27	W didn't you tell me,	NIH
	31:30	But w did you steal my gods?"	4200+4537
	31:48	That is w it was called Galeed.	4027+6584
	32:29	he replied, "W do you ask my name?"	4200+4537
	33:15	"But w do that?"	4200+4537
	33:17	That is w the place is called Succoth.	4027+6584
	40: 7	"W are your faces so sad today?"	4508
	42: 1	"W do you just keep looking	4200+4537
	42:21	that's w this distress has come upon us."	4027+6584
	43: 6	"W did you bring this trouble on me	4200+4537
	44: 4	'W have you repaid good with evil?	4200+4537
	44: 7	"W does my lord say such things?	4200+4537
	44: 8	So w would we steal silver or gold	375
	47:15	W should we die before your eyes?	4200+4537
	47:19	W should we perish before your eyes	4200+4537
	47:22	That is w they did not sell their land.	4027+6584
	50:11	That is w that place near	4027+6584
Ex	1:18	"W have you done this?	4508
	1:18	W have you let the boys live?"	NIH
	2:13	"W are you hitting your fellow Hebrew?"	4200+4537
	2:18	"W have you returned so early today?"	4508
	2:20	"W did you leave him?	4200+4537
	3: 3	w the bush does not burn up."	4508
	5: 4	w are you taking the people away	4200+4537
	5: 8	lazy; that is w they are crying out,	4027+6584
	5:14	"W didn't you meet your quota	4508
	5:15	"W have you treated your servants this way?	4200+4537
	5:17	That is w you keep saying,	4027+6584
	5:22	w have you brought trouble	4200+4537
	5:22	Is this w you sent me?	4200+4537
	6:12	w would Pharaoh listen to me,	375
	6:30	w would Pharaoh listen to me?"	375
	13:15	This is w I sacrifice to the LORD	4027+6584
	14:15	"W are you crying out to me?	4537
	15:23	(That is w the place is called Marah.)	4027+6584
	16:29	that is w on sixth day he gives you	4027+6584
	17: 2	Moses replied, "W do you quarrel with me?	4537
	17: 2	W do you put the LORD to the test?"	4537
	17: 3	"W did you bring us up out of Egypt	4200+4537
	18:14	W do you alone sit as judge,	4508
	32:11	"w should your anger burn	4200+4537
	32:12	W should the Egyptians say,	4200+4537
Lev	10:17	"W didn't you eat the sin offering in	4508
	17:14	That is w I have said to the Israelites,	2256
Nu	9: 7	w should we be kept from presenting	4200+4537
	11:11	"W have you brought this trouble	4200+4537
	11:12	W do you tell me to carry them in my arms,	3954
	11:20	saying, "W did we ever leave Egypt?"	4200+4537
	12: 8	W then were you not afraid to speak	4508
	14: 3	W is the LORD bringing us to this land	4200+4537
	14:41	"W are you disobeying the LORD's	4200+4537
	16: 3	W then do you set yourselves above	4508
	18:24	That is w I said concerning them:	4027+6584
	20: 4	W did you bring the LORD's	4200+4537
	20: 5	W did you bring us up out of Egypt	4200+4537
	21: 5	"W have you brought us up out of Egypt to this terrible place?	4200+4537
	21:14	That is w the Book of the Wars of	4027+6584
	21:27	That is w the poets say:	4027+6584
	22:32	"W have you beaten your donkey	4537+6584
	22:37	W didn't you come to me?	4200+4537
	27: 4	W should our father's name disappear	4200+4537
	32: 7	W do you discourage the Israelites	4200+4537
Dt	5:25	But now, w should we die?	4200+4537
	10: 9	That is w the Levites have no share	4027+6584
	15:15	That is w I give you this command	4027+6584
	19: 7	This is w I command you to set aside	4027+6584
	24:18	That is w I command you to do this.	4027+6584
	24:22	That is w I command you to do this.	4027+6584
	29:24	W has the LORD done this to this land?	4537+6584
	29:24	W this fierce, burning anger?"	4537
Jos	5: 4	Now this is w he did so:	1821
	7: 7	w did you ever bring this people	4200+4537
	7:12	That is w the Israelites cannot stand	2256
	7:25	"W have you brought this trouble on us?	4537
	9:22	"W did you deceive us by saying,	4200+4537
	9:24	and that is w we did this.	2256
	17:14	"W have you given us only one allotment	4508
	22:26	"That is w we said, 'Let us get ready	2256
Jdg	2: 2	W have you done this?	4537
	5:16	W did you stay among the campfires	4200+4537
	5:17	And Dan, w did he linger by the ships?	4200+4537
	5:28	'W is his chariot so long in coming?	4508
	5:28	W is the clatter of his chariots delayed?'	4508
	6:13	w has all this happened to us?	4200+4537
	8: 1	"W have you treated us like this?	4537
	8: 1	W didn't you call us when you went	NIH
	8: 6	W should we give bread to your troops?"	3954
	8:15	W should we give bread to your exhausted	3954
	9:28	W should we serve Abimelech?"	4508
	11: 7	W do you come to me now,	4508

Jdg 11:26 W didn't you retake them during that time? 4508
12: 1 "W did you go to fight the Ammonites 4508
12: 3 w have you come up today to fight me?" 4200+4537
13:18 He replied, "W do you ask my name? 4200+4537
14:16 "so w should I explain it to you?" AIT
15:10 "W have you come to fight us?" 4200+4537
18: 3 W are you here?" 4537
18:12 This is w the place west 4027+6584
21: 3 cried, "w has this happened to Israel? 4200+4537
21: 3 W should one tribe be missing NIH
Ru 1:11 W would you come with me? 4200+4537
1:21 W call me Naomi? 4508
2:10 "W have I found such favor in your eyes 4508
1Sa 1: 8 "Hannah, w are you weeping? 4200+4537
1: 8 W don't you eat? 4200+4537
1: 8 W are you downhearted? 4200+4537
2:23 to them, "W do you do such things? 4200+4537
2:29 W do you scorn my sacrifice and 4200+4537
2:29 W do you honor your sons more than me NIH
4: 3 "W did the LORD bring defeat 4200+4537
5: 5 That is w to this day neither 4027+6584
6: 3 know w his hand has not been lifted 4200+4537
6: 6 W do you harden your hearts as 4200+4537
9:21 W do you say such a thing to me?" 4200+4537
11: 5 W are they weeping?" 3954
14:28 That is w the men are faint." 2256
15:19 W did you not obey the LORD? 4200+4537
15:19 W did you pounce on the plunder NIH
17: 8 "W do you come out and line up 4200+4537
17:28 "W have you come down here? 4200+4537
19: 5 W then would you do wrong to 4200+4537
19:17 "W did you deceive me like this 4200+4537
19:17 W should I kill you?' " 4200+4537
19:24 This is w people say, 4027+6584
20: 2 W would he hide this from me? 4508
20: 8 W hand me over to your father?" 4200+4537
20:27 "W hasn't the son of Jesse come to 4508
20:29 That is w he has not come to 4027+6584
20:32 "W should he be put to death? 4200+4537
21: 1 and asked, "W are you alone? 4508
21: 1 W is no one with you?" NIH
21:14 W bring him to me? 4200+4537
22: 8 Is that w you have all conspired 3954
22:13 "W have you conspired against me, 4200+4537
23:28 That is w they call this place Sela 4027+6584
    Hammahlekoth.
24: 9 "W do you listen when men say, 4200+4537
25:11 W should I take my bread and water, NIH
26:15 W didn't you guard your lord 4200+4537
26:18 "W is my lord pursuing his servant? 4200+4537
27: 5 W should your servant live in the 4200+4537
28: 9 W have you set a trap for my life 4200+4537
28:12 W have you deceived me? 4200+4537
28:15 "W have you disturbed me 4200+4537
28:16 Samuel said, "W do you consult me, 4200+4537
29: 8 W can't I go and fight against the enemies 3954
2Sa 1:14 W were you not afraid to lift your hand 375
2:22 W should I strike you down? 4200+4537
3: 7 "W did you sleep with my father's 4508
3:24 W did you let him go? 4200+4537
5: 8 That is w they say, 4027+6584
7: 7 "W have you not built me a house 4200+4537
11:10 W didn't you go home?" 4508
11:20 'W did you get so close to the city to fight? 4508
11:21 W did you get so close to the wall?' 4200+4537
12: 9 W did you despise the word of the LORD 4508
12:21 "W are you acting this way? 4537
12:23 now that he is dead, w should I fast? 4200+4537
13: 4 He asked Amnon, "W do you, 4508
13:26 "W should he go with you?" 4200+4537
14:13 "W then have you devised a thing 4200+4537
14:31 "W have your servants set my field 4200+4537
14:32 W have I come from Geshur? 4200+4537
15:19 "W should you come along with us? 4200+4537
16: 2 "W have you brought these?" 4537
16: 9 W should this dead dog curse my lord 4200+4537
16:10 who can ask, 'W do you do this?' " 4508
18:11 W didn't you go with your friend? 4200+4537
18:11 W didn't you strike him to the ground 4508
18:22 "My son, w do you want to go? 4200+4537
19:10 So w do you say nothing about 4200+4537
19:11 'W should you be the last to bring 4200+4537
19:12 w should you be the last to bring back 4200+4537
19:25 "W didn't you go with me, 4200+4537
19:29 The king said to him, "W say more? 4200+4537
19:35 W should your servant be an added 4200+4537
19:36 w should the king reward me 4200+4537
19:41 "W did our brothers, the men of Judah, 4508
19:42 W are you angry about it? 4200+4537
19:43 So w do you treat us with contempt? 4508
20:19 W do you want to swallow up 4508
24: 3 But w does my lord the king want 4200+4537
24:21 "W has my lord the king come 4508
1Ki 1: 6 "W do you behave as you do?" 4508
1:13 W then has Adonijah become king?' 4508
2:22 "W do you request Abishag 4200+4537
2:43 W then did you not keep your oath to 4508
9: 8 'W has the LORD done such a thing 4537+6584
9: 9 that is w the LORD brought all this disaster
    on them.' " 4027+6584
14: 6 W this pretense? 4508
20:23 That is w they were too strong for us. 4027+6584
21: 5 "W are you so sullen? 4537
21: 5 W won't you eat?" NIH
2Ki 1: 5 he asked them, "W have you come back?" 4537
4:23 "W go to him today?" 4508

2Ki 4:27 from me and has not told me w." NIH
5: 7 W does this fellow send someone to me to 3954
5: 8 "W have you torn your robes? 4200+4537
6:33 W should I wait for the LORD 4537
7: 3 "W stay here until we die? 4537
8:12 "W is my lord weeping?" 4508
9:11 W did this madman come to you?" 4508
12: 7 "W aren't you repairing the damage done to 4508
14:10 W ask for trouble 4200+4537
1Ch 17: 6 "W have you not built me a house 4200+4537
21: 3 W does my lord want to do this? 4200+4537
21: 3 W should he bring guilt on Israel?" 4200+4537
2Ch 7:21 'W has the LORD done such a thing 928+4537
7:22 that is w he brought all this disaster 4027+6584
20:26 This is w it is called the Valley of Beracah
    4027+6584
24: 6 "W haven't you required the Levites 4508
24:20 'W do you disobey the LORD's 4200+4537
25:15 "W do you consult this people's gods, 4200+4537
25:16 W be struck down?" 4200+4537
25:19 W ask for trouble 4200+4537
29: 9 This is w our fathers have fallen by 2180
29: 9 and w our sons and daughters and 2296+6584
32: 4 W should the kings of Assyria come 4200+4537
Ezr 4:15 That is w this city was destroyed. 10180+10542
4:22 W let this threat grow, 10378+10408
7:23 W should there be wrath against 10378+10408
Ne 2: 2 "W does your face look so sad 4508
2: 3 W should my face not look sad when 4508
6: 3 W should the work stop while I leave 4200+4537
3:11 "W is the house of God neglected?" 4508
13:21 "W do you spend the night by the wall? 4508
Est 3: 3 "W do you disobey the king's command?" 4508
4: 5 what was troubling Mordecai and w. 4537+6584
9:19 That is w rural Jews— 4027+6584
Job 3:11 "W did I not perish at birth, 4200+4537
3:12 W were there knees to receive me 4508
3:16 Or w was I not hidden in the ground like NIH
3:20 "W is light given to those in misery, 4200+4537
3:23 W is life given to a man whose way NIH
7:20 W have you made me your target? 4200+4537
7:21 W do not pardon my offenses 4537
9:22 It is all the same; that is w I say, 4027+6584
9:29 w should I struggle in vain? 4537
10:18 "W then did you bring me out of the womb?
    4200+4537
13:14 W do I put myself in jeopardy 4537+6584
13:24 W do you hide your face 4200+4537
15:12 W has your heart carried you away, 4537
15:12 and w do your eyes flash, 4537
18: 3 W are we regarded as cattle 4508
19:22 W do you pursue me as God does? 4200+4537
21: 4 W should I not be impatient? 4508
21: 7 W do the wicked live on, 4508
22:10 That is w snares are all around you, 4027+6584
22:10 w sudden peril terrifies you, NIH
22:11 w it is so dark you cannot see, NIH
22:11 and w a flood of water covers you. NIH
23:15 That is w I am terrified before him; 4027+6584
24: 1 "W does the Almighty not set times 4508
24: 1 W must those who know him look in vain NIH
27:12 W then this meaningless talk? 4200+4537
32: 6 that is w I was fearful, 4027+6584
33:13 W do you complain to him 4508
Ps 2: 1 W do the nations conspire and 4200+4537
10: 1 W, O LORD, do you stand far off? 4200+4537
10: 1 W do you hide yourself in times AIT
10:13 W does the wicked man revile God? 4537+6584
10:13 W does he say to himself, NIH
22: 1 my God, w have you forsaken me? 4200+4537
22: 1 W are you so far from saving me, NIH
42: 5 W are you downcast, O my soul? 4537
42: 5 W so disturbed within me? NIH
42: 9 "W have you forgotten me? 4200+4537
42: 9 W must I go about mourning, 4200+4537
42:11 W are you downcast, O my soul? 4537
42:11 W so disturbed within me? 4537
43: 2 W have you rejected me? 4537
43: 2 W must I go about mourning, 928+4537
43: 5 W are you downcast, O my soul? 4537
43: 5 W so disturbed within me? 4537
44:23 W do you sleep? 4200+4537
44:24 W do you hide your face 4200+4537
49: 5 W should I fear when evil days come, 4200+4537
52: 1 W do you boast of evil, you mighty man? 4537
52: 1 W do you boast all day long, NIH
68:16 W gaze in envy, O rugged mountains, 4200+4537
74: 1 W have you rejected us forever, 4200+4537
74: 1 W does your anger smolder against NIH
74:11 W do you hold back your hand, 4200+4537
79:10 W should the nations say, 4200+4537
80:12 W have you broken down its walls so 4200+4537
88:14 W, O LORD, do you reject me 4200+4537
114: 5 W was it, O sea, that you fled, O Jordan, 4537
115: 2 W do the nations say, 4200+4537
Pr 5:20 W be captivated, my son, by an adulteress?
    4200+4537
5:20 W embrace the bosom of another man's NIH
Ecc 4: 8 w am I depriving myself of enjoyment?" NIH
5: 6 W should God be angry at 4200+4537
7:10 "W were the old days better than these?" 4537
7:16 be overwise—w destroy yourself? 4200+4537
7:17 w die before your time? 4200+4537
SS 1: 7 W should I be like a veiled 4200+4537+8611
6:13 W would you gaze on the Shulammite as 4537
Isa 1: 5 W should you be beaten anymore? 4200+6584
1: 5 W do you persist in rebellion? NIH

Isa 5: 4 w did it yield only bad? 4508
8:19 W consult the dead on behalf of the living? NIH
40:27 W do you say, O Jacob, and complain, 4200+4537
50: 2 When I came, w was there no one? 4508
50: 2 I called, w was there no one to answer? NIH
55: 2 W spend money on what is not bread, 4200+4537
58: 3 'W have we fasted,' they say, 4200+4537
58: 3 W have we humbled ourselves, NIH
63: 2 W are your garments red, 4508
63:17 W, O LORD, do you make us wander 4200+4537
Jer 2:14 W then has he become plunder? 4508
2:18 Now w go to Egypt to drink water from 4537
2:18 And w go to Assyria to drink water from 4537
2:29 "W do you bring charges against me? 4200+4537
2:31 W do my people say, 'We are free to roam; 4508
2:36 W do you go about so much, 4508
4:30 W dress yourself in scarlet and put 3954
4:30 W shade your eyes with paint? 4537
5: 7 "W should I forgive you? 361+2296+4200
5:19 'W has the LORD our God done all this 4537+9393
8: 5 When have these people turned away? 4508
8: 5 W does Jerusalem always turn away? NIH
8:14 "W are we sitting here? 4537+6584
8:19 "W have they provoked me to anger 4508
8:22 W then is there no healing for the wound 4508
9:12 W has the land been ruined and 4537+6584
12: 1 W does the way of the wicked prosper? 4508
12: 1 W do all the faithless live at ease? NIH
13:22 "W has this happened to me?"— 4508
14: 8 w are you like a stranger in the land, 4200+4537
14: 9 W are you like a man taken by surprise,
    4200+4537
14:19 W have you afflicted us so that we cannot 4508
15:18 W is my pain unending 4200+4537
16:10 'W has the LORD decreed such 4537+6584
20:18 W did I ever come out of the womb 4200+4537
22: 8 'W has the LORD done such a thing 4537+6584
22:28 W will he and his children be hurled out, 4508
26: 9 W do you prophesy in the LORD's name 4508
27:13 W will you and your people die by 4200+4537
27:17 W should this city become a ruin? 4200+4537
29:27 w have you not reprimanded Jeremiah 4200+4537
30: 6 Then w do I see every strong man 4508
30:15 W do you cry out over your wound, 4537
32: 3 saying, "W do you prophesy as you do? 4508
36:29 that scroll and said, "W did you write on it 4508
40:15 W should he take your life and 4200+4537
44: 7 W bring such great disaster on 4200+4537
44: 8 W provoke me to anger NIH
46:15 W will your warriors be laid low? 4508
49: 1 W then has Molech taken possession 4508
49: 1 W do his people live in its towns? NIH
49: 4 W do you boast of your valleys, 4537
49:12 w should you go unpunished? NIH
49:25 W has the city of renown 375
La 1:16 "This is w I weep and my eyes 465+4537
3:39 W should any living man complain 4537
5:20 W do you always forget us? 4200+4537
5:20 W do you forsake us so long? NIH
Eze 18:19 'W does the son not share the guilt 4508
18:31 W will you die, O house of Israel? 4200+4537
21: 7 they ask you, 'W are you groaning?' 4537+6584
33:11 W will you die, O house of Israel?" 4200+4537
40: 4 for that is w you have been brought here. 5100
Da 1:10 W should he see you looking worse 4200+4537
2:15 "W did the king issue such a harsh decree?"
    10408+10542
10:20 "Do you know w I have come to you? 4200+4537
10:20 W should they say among the peoples, 4200+4537
Joel 2:17 W should they say among the peoples, 4200+4537
Am 5:18 W do you long for the day of the LORD?
    4200+4537
Jnh 4: 2 That is w I was so quick to flee 4027+6584
Mic 4: 9 W do you now cry aloud— 4200+4537
Hab 1: 3 W do you make me look at injustice? 4200+4537
1: 3 W do you tolerate wrong? NIH
1:13 W then do you tolerate the treacherous?
    4200+4537
1:13 W are you silent while the wicked swallow NIH
Hag 1: 9 you brought home, I blew away. W?" 3610+4537
Mal 2:10 W do we profane the covenant 4508
2:14 You ask, "W?" 4537+6584
2:15 And w one? 4537
Mt 6:28 "And w do you worry about clothes? 5515
7: 3 "W do you look at the speck of sawdust 5515
8:26 "You of little faith, w are you so afraid?" 5515
9: 4 "W do you entertain evil thoughts 2672
9:11 "W does your teacher eat with tax collectors
    1328+5515
13:10 "W do you speak to the people 1328+5515
13:13 This is w I speak to them in parables: 1328+4047
14: 2 That is w miraculous powers are at work
    1328+4047
14:31 he said, "w did you doubt?" 1650+5515
15: 2 "W do your disciples break the tradition of
    the elders? 1328+5515
15: 3 "And w do you break the command of God
    1328+5515
16: 8 w are you talking among yourselves 5515
17:10 "W then do the teachers of the law say 5515
17:19 "W couldn't we drive it out? 1328+5515
19: 7 "W then," they asked, "did Moses
    command 5515
19:17 W do you ask me about what is good?" 5515
20: 6 'W have you been standing here all day 5515
21:25 'Then w didn't you believe him?' 1328+5515
22:18 w are you trying to trap me? 5515
26: 8 "W this waste?" 1650+5515

Mt	26:10	"W are you bothering this woman?	5515
	26:65	W do we need any more witnesses?	5515
	27: 8	That is w it has been called the Field	1475
	27:23	"W? What crime has he committed?"	1142
	27:46	my God, w have you forsaken me?"	2672
Mk	1:38	That is w I have come."	1650+4047
	2: 7	"W does this fellow talk like that?	5515
	2: 8	"W are you thinking these things?	5515
	2:16	"W does he eat with tax collectors	4022
	2:24	w are they doing what is unlawful on	5515
	4:40	"W are you so afraid?	5515
	5:35	"W bother the teacher any more?"	5515
	5:39	"W all this commotion and wailing?	5515
	6:14	and that is w miraculous powers are	1328+4047
	7: 5	"W don't your disciples live according to the tradition of the elders	1328+5515
	8:12	"W does this generation ask for	5515
	8:17	"W are you talking about having no bread?	5515
	9:11	"W do the teachers of the law say	NIG
	9:12	When is it written that the Son of Man	4802
	9:28	"W couldn't we drive it out?"	NIG
	10:18	"W do you call me good?"	5515
	11: 3	If anyone asks you, 'W are you doing this?'	5515
	11:31	'Then w didn't you believe him?'	1328+5515
	12:15	"W are you trying to trap me?"	5515
	14: 4	"W this waste of perfume?	1650+5515
	14: 6	"W are you bothering her?	5515
	14:63	"W do we need any more witnesses?"	5515
	15:14	"W? What crime has he committed?"	1142
	15:34	my God, w have you forsaken me?"	1650+5515
Lk	1:21	for Zechariah and wondering w he stayed	2513
	1:43	But w am I so favored,	4470
	2:48	"Son, w have you treated us like this?	5515
	2:49	"W were you searching for me?"	4022+5515
	4:43	because that is w I was sent."	2093+4047
	5:22	"W are you thinking these things	5515
	5:30	"W do you eat and drink with tax collectors	1328+5515
	6: 2	"W are you doing what is unlawful on	5515
	6:41	"W do you look at the speck of sawdust	5515
	6:46	"W do you call me, 'Lord, Lord,'	5515
	7: 7	That is w I did not even consider myself	1475
	8:47	she told w she had touched him	162+1328+4005
	12:26	w do you worry about the rest?	5515
	12:57	"W don't you judge for yourselves	5515
	13: 7	W should it use up the soil?'	2672
	18:19	"W do you call me good?"	5515
	19:23	W then didn't you put my money	1328+5515
	19:31	asks you, 'W are you untying it?'	1328+5515
	19:33	"W are you untying the colt?"	5515
	20: 5	will ask, 'W didn't you believe him?'	1328+5515
	22:46	"W are you sleeping?"	5515
	22:71	"W do we need any more testimony?"	5515
	23:22	For the third time he spoke to them: "W?	1142
	24: 5	"W do you look for the living among	5515
	24:38	He said to them, "W are you troubled,	5515
	24:38	and w do doubts rise in your minds?	1328+5515
Jn	1:25	"W then do you baptize if you are not	5515
	2: 4	"Dear woman, w do you involve me?"	2779+5515
	4:27	or "W are you talking with her?"	5515
	6:65	"This is w I told you that no one can	1328+4047
	7:19	"W are you trying to kill me?"	5515
	7:23	w are you angry with me for healing	NIG
	7:45	"W didn't you bring him in?"	1328+5515
	8:22	Is that w he says, 'Where I go,	4022
	8:43	W is my language not clear to you?	1328+5515
	8:46	w don't you believe me?	1328+5515
	9:23	That was w his parents said,	1328+4047
	9:27	W do you want to hear it again?	5515
	10:20	W listen to him?"	5515
	10:36	W then do you accuse me of blasphemy	NIG
	12: 5	"W wasn't this perfume sold and	1328+5515
	13:11	that was w he said not every one was clean.	1328+4047
	13:28	at the meal understood w Jesus said this	5515
	13:37	"Lord, w can't I follow you now?	1328+5515
	14:22	w do you intend to show yourself to us and	5515
	15:19	That is w the world hates you.	1328+4047
	16:15	That is w I said the Spirit will take	1328+4047
	18:21	W question me?	5515
	18:23	if I spoke the truth, w did you strike me?"	5515
	20:13	"Woman, w are you crying?"	5515
	20:15	"Woman," he said, "w are you crying?	5515
Ac	1:11	"w do you stand here looking into the sky?	5515
	3:12	"Men of Israel, w does this surprise you?	5515
	3:12	w do you stare at us as if by our own power	5515
	4:25	" 'W do the nations rage and	2672
	7:26	w do you want to hurt each other?'	2672
	8:36	W shouldn't I be baptized?"	5515
	9: 4	"Saul, Saul, w do you persecute me?"	5515
	10:21	W have you come?"	5515
	10:29	May I ask w you sent for me?"	3364+5515
	14:15	w are you doing this?	5515
	15:10	w do you try to test God by putting on	1915+5515
	19:32	not even know w they were there.	1915+5515
	21:13	"W are you weeping	5515
	22: 7	W do you persecute me?'	5515
	22:24	w the people were shouting	162+1328+4005
	22:30	find out exactly w Paul was being accused	5515
	23:28	know w they were accusing him,	162+1328+4005
	26: 8	Why should any of you consider it incredible	5515
	26:14	'Saul, Saul, w do you persecute me?"	5515
	26:21	That is w the Jews seized me in	1915
Ro	1:15	That is w I am so eager to preach the gospel	4048
	3: 7	w am I still condemned as a sinner?"	5515
	3: 8	W not say—as we are being slanderously	NIG
	4:22	This is w "it was credited to him	1475

Ro	9:19	"Then w does God still blame us?	5515
	9:20	"W did you make me like this?' "	5515
	9:32	W not? Because they pursued it	1328+5515
	13: 6	This is also w you pay taxes,	1328+4047
	14:10	You, then, w do you judge your brother?	5515
	14:10	Or w do you look down on your brother?	5515
	15:22	This is w I have often been hindered	1475
1Co	4: 7	w do you boast as though you did not?	5515
	6: 7	W not rather be wronged?	1328+5515
	6: 7	W not rather be cheated?	1328+5515
	10:29	For w should my freedom be judged	2672
	10:30	w am I denounced because of something	5515
	11:30	That is w many among you are weak	1328+4047
	15:29	w are people baptized for them?	5515
	15:30	us, do we endanger ourselves every hour?	5515
2Co	11:11	W? Because I do not love you?	1328+5515
	12:10	That is w, for Christ's sake,	1475
	13:10	This is w I write these things	1328+4047
Gal	5:11	w am I still being persecuted?	5515
Eph	4: 8	This is w it says: "When he ascended	1475
	5:14	This is w it is said: "Wake up, O sleeper,	1475
Col	2:20	w, as though you still belonged to it,	5515
2Ti	1:12	That is w I am suffering as I am.	162+1328+4005
Heb	3:10	That is w I was angry with that generation,	1475
	5: 3	This is w he has to offer sacrifices	899+1328
	7:11	w was there still need for another priest	5515
	8: 5	This is w Moses was warned when he was	2777
	9:18	This is w even the first covenant was not	3854
Jas	4: 6	That is w Scripture says: "God opposes	1475
1Jn	3:12	And w did he murder him?	5515+5920
Rev	17: 7	said to me: "W are you astonished?	1328+5515

WICK (11)

Ex	25:38	Its w trimmers and trays are to be	4920
	37:23	as well as its w trimmers and trays,	4920
Nu	4: 9	its w trimmers and trays,	4920
1Ki	7:50	w trimmers, sprinkling bowls,	4662
2Ki	12:13	w trimmers, sprinkling bowls,	4662
2Ch	4:22	the pots, shovels, w trimmers, dishes and	4662
	4:22	the pure gold w trimmers,	4662
Isa	42: 3	and a smoldering w he will not snuff out.	7325
	43:17	extinguished, snuffed out like a w:	7325
Jer	52:18	shovels, w trimmers, sprinkling bowls,	4662
Mt	12:20	and a smoldering w he will not snuff out,	3351

WICKED (363) [OVERWICKED, WICKEDLY, WICKEDNESS]

Ge	13:13	of Sodom were w and were sinning greatly	8273
	18:23	sweep away the righteous with the w?	8401
	18:25	to kill the righteous with the w,	8401
	18:25	treating the righteous and the w alike.	8401
	19: 7	Don't do this w thing.	8317
	38: 7	was w in the LORD's sight;	8273
	38:10	What he did was w in the LORD's sight;	8317
	39: 9	How could I do such a w thing and sin	8288
	44: 5	This is a w thing you have done.' "	8317
Ex	23: 1	a w man by being a malicious witness.	8401
Lev	20:14	both a woman and her mother, it is w.	2365
Nu	14:27	"How long will this w community grumble	8273
	14:35	to this whole w community,	8273
	16:26	"Move back from the tents of these w men!	8401
Dt	13:13	that w men have arisen among you	1175+1201
	15: 9	Be careful not to harbor this w thought:	1175
Jdg	19:22	the w men of the city surrounded	1175+1201
	20:13	Now surrender w men of Gibeah	1175+1201
1Sa	1:16	Do not take your servant for a w woman;	1175
	2: 9	but the w will be silenced in darkness.	8401
	2:12	Eli's sons were w men;	1175
	2:23	the people about these w deeds of yours.	8273
	15:18	and completely destroy those w people,	2629
	17:28	and how w your heart is;	8278
	25:17	He is such a w man that no one can talk	1175
	25:25	pay no attention to that w man Nabal.	1175
2Sa	3:34	You fell as one falls before w men."	6406
	4:11	when w men have killed an innocent man	8401
	7:10	w people will not oppress them anymore,	6406
	13:12	Don't do this w thing.	5576
	13:13	You would be like one of the w fools	5572
2Ki	17:11	They did w things that provoked	8273
1Ch	2: 3	was w in the LORD's sight;	8273
	17: 9	w people will not oppress them anymore,	6406
2Ch	7:14	and turn from their w ways,	8273
	19: 2	the w and love those who hate the LORD?	8401
	24: 7	of that w woman Athaliah had broken into	5360
Ezr	4:12	rebuilding that rebellious and w city.	10090
Ne	13:17	"What is this w thing you are doing—	8273
Job	3:17	There the w cease from turmoil,	8401
	8:22	and the tents of the w will be no more.'	8401
	9:22	'He destroys both the blameless and the w.'	8401
	9:24	When a land falls into the hands of the w,	8401
	10: 3	while you smile on the schemes of the w?	8401
	11:20	But the eyes of the w will fail,	8401
	15:20	All his days the w man suffers torment,	8401
	16:11	and thrown me into the clutches of the w.	8401
	18: 5	"The lamp of the w is snuffed out;	8401
	20: 5	that the mirth of the w is brief,	8401
	20:29	Such is the fate God allots to the w,	8401
	21: 7	Why do the w live on,	8401
	21:16	so I stand aloof from the counsel of the w.	8401
	21:17	how often is the lamp of the w snuffed out?	8401
	21:28	the tents where w men lived?'	8401
	22:18	so I stand aloof from the counsel of the w.	8401
	24: 6	and glean in the vineyards of the w.	8401
	27: 7	"May my enemies be like the w,	8401

Job	27:13	"Here is the fate God allots to the w,	8401
	29:17	the fangs of the w and snatched the victims	6405
	31: 3	Is it not ruin for the w,	6405
	34: 8	he associates with w men.	8400
	34:18	and to nobles, 'You are w,'	8401
	34:36	to the utmost for answering like a w man!	224
	35:12	because of the arrogance of the w.	8273
	36: 6	He does not keep the w alive but gives	8401
	36:17	you are laden with the judgment due the w;	8401
	38:13	the earth by the edges and shake the w out	8401
	38:15	The w are denied their light,	8401
	40:12	crush the w where they stand.	8401
Ps	1: 1	of the w or stand in the way of sinners or sit	8401
	1: 4	Not so the w! They are like chaff	8401
	1: 5	the w will not stand in the judgment,	8401
	1: 6	but the way of the w will perish.	8401
	3: 7	break the teeth of the w.	8401
	5: 4	with you the w cannot dwell.	8273
	7: 9	to an end the violence of the w and make	8401
	9: 5	the nations and destroyed the w,	8401
	9:16	the w are ensnared by the work	8401
	9:17	The w return to the grave,	8401
	10: 2	In his arrogance the w man hunts down	8401
	10: 4	In his pride the w does not seek him;	8401
	10:13	Why does the w man revile God?	8401
	10:15	Break the arm of the w and evil man;	8401
	11: 2	For look, the w bend their bows;	8401
	11: 5	but the w and those who love violence	8401
	11: 6	On the w he will rain fiery coals	8401
	12: 8	The w freely strut about	8401
	17: 9	from the w who assail me,	8401
	17:13	rescue me from the w by your sword.	8401
	21:11	and devise w schemes, they cannot succeed;	4659
	26: 5	of evildoers and refuse to sit with the w.	8401
	26:10	in whose hands are w schemes,	2365
	28: 3	Do not drag me away with the w,	8401
	31:17	but let the w be put to shame and lie silent	8401
	32:10	Many are the woes of the w,	8401
	34:21	Evil will slay the w;	8401
	36: 1	concerning the sinfulness of the w:	8401
	36: 3	The words of his mouth are w and deceitful;	224
	36:11	nor the hand of the w drive me away.	8401
	37: 7	when they carry out their w schemes.	4659
	37:10	A little while, and the w will be no more;	8401
	37:12	The w plot against the righteous	8401
	37:13	but the Lord laughs at the w,	2257S
	37:14	The w draw the sword and bend the bow	8401
	37:16	the wealth of many w;	8401
	37:17	for the power of the w will be broken,	8401
	37:20	But the w will perish:	8401
	37:21	The w borrow and do not repay,	8401
	37:28	but the offspring of the w will be cut off;	8401
	37:32	The w lie in wait for the righteous,	8401
	37:34	when the w are cut off, you will see it.	8401
	37:35	a w and ruthless man flourishing like	8401
	37:38	the future of the w will be cut off.	8401
	37:40	he delivers them from the w	8401
	39: 1	a muzzle on my mouth as long as the w are	8401
	43: 1	rescue me from deceitful and w men.	6406
	49:16	when w deceivers surround me—	6411
	50:16	But to the w, God says:	8401
	55: 3	at the stares of the w,	8401
	55: 9	Confuse the w, O Lord,	NIH
	55:23	down the w into the pit of corruption;	4392S
	58: 3	Even from birth the w go astray;	8401
	58: 9	the w will be swept away.	5647S
	58:10	they bathe their feet in the blood of the w.	8401
	59: 5	show no mercy to w traitors.	224
	64: 2	Hide me from the conspiracy of the w,	8317
	68: 2	may the w perish before God.	8401
	71: 4	O my God, from the hand of the w,	8401
	73: 3	when I saw the prosperity of the w.	8401
	73:12	This is what the w are like—	8401
	75: 4	and to the w, 'Do not lift up your horns.	8401
	75: 8	and all the w of the earth drink it down	8401
	75:10	I will cut off the horns of all the w,	8401
	82: 2	the unjust and show partiality to the w?	8401
	82: 4	deliver them from the hand of the w.	8401
	84:10	of my God than dwell in the tents of the w.	8400
	89:22	no w man will oppress him.	6406
	91: 8	and see the punishment of the w.	8401
	92: 7	that though the w spring up like grass	8401
	92:11	my ears have heard the rout of my w foes.	8317
	94: 3	How long will the w, O LORD,	8401
	94: 3	O LORD, how long will the w be jubilant?	8401
	94:13	till a pit is dug for the w,	8401
	94:16	Who will rise up for me against the w?	8317
	97:10	and delivers them from the hand of the w.	8401
	101: 8	Every morning I will put to silence all the w	8401
	104:35	from the earth and the w be no more.	8401
	106:18	a flame consumed the w.	8401
	106:29	the LORD to anger by their w deeds,	5095
	107:42	but all the w shut their mouths.	6406
	109: 2	for w and deceitful men have opened their mouths against me;	8401
	112:10	The w man will see and be vexed,	8401
	112:10	the longings of the w will come to nothing.	8401
	119:53	Indignation grips me because of the w,	8401
	119:61	Though the w bind me with ropes,	8401
	119:95	The w are waiting to destroy me,	8401
	119:110	The w have set a snare for me,	8401
	119:119	the w of the earth you discard like dross;	8401
	119:150	Those who devise w schemes are near,	2365
	119:155	Salvation is far from the w,	8401
	125: 3	the w will not remain over the land allotted	8400
	129: 4	he has cut me free from the cords of the w.	8401
	139:19	If only you would slay the w, O God!	8401

Ps	140: 4	Keep me, O LORD, from the hands of the **w**;	8401
	140: 8	do not grant the **w** their desires, O LORD;	8401
	141: 4	in **w** deeds with men who are evildoers;	8400
	141: 6	and the **w** will learn that my words were	NIH
	141:10	Let the **w** fall into their own nets,	8401
	145:20	but all the **w** he will destroy.	8401
	146: 9	but he frustrates the ways of the **w**.	8401
	147: 6	the humble but casts the **w** to the ground.	8401
Pr	2:12	will save you from the ways of **w** men,	8273
	2:22	but the **w** will be cut off from the land,	8401
	3:25	or of the ruin that overtakes the **w**,	8401
	3:33	LORD's curse is on the house of the **w**,	8401
	4:14	Do not set foot on the path of the **w** or walk	8401
	4:19	But the way of the **w** is like deep darkness;	8401
	5:22	The evil deeds of a **w** man ensnare him;	8401
	6:18	a heart that devises **w** schemes,	224
	9: 7	whoever rebukes a **w** man incurs abuse.	8401
	10: 3	but he thwarts the craving of the **w**.	8401
	10: 6	violence overwhelms the mouth of the **w**.	8401
	10: 7	but the name of the **w** will rot.	8401
	10:11	violence overwhelms the mouth of the **w**.	8401
	10:16	income of the **w** brings them punishment.	8401
	10:20	but the heart of the **w** is of little value.	8401
	10:24	What the **w** dreads will overtake him;	8401
	10:25	the storm has swept by, the **w** are gone,	8401
	10:27	but the years of the **w** are cut short.	8401
	10:28	but the hopes of the **w** come to nothing.	8401
	10:30	but the **w** will not remain in the land.	8401
	10:32	the mouth of the **w** only what is perverse.	8401
	11: 5	but the **w** are brought down by their own	8401
	11: 7	When a **w** man dies, his hope perishes;	8401
	11: 8	and it comes on the **w** instead.	8401
	11:10	when the **w** perish, there are shouts of joy.	8401
	11:11	but by the mouth of the **w** it is destroyed.	8401
	11:18	The **w** man earns deceptive wages,	8401
	11:21	The **w** will not go unpunished.	8273
	11:23	but the hope of the **w** only in wrath.	8401
	12: 5	but the advice of the **w** is deceitful.	8401
	12: 6	The words of the **w** lie in wait for blood,	8401
	12: 7	**W** men are overthrown and are no more,	8401
	12:10	but the kindest acts of the **w** are cruel.	8401
	12:12	The **w** desire the plunder of evil men,	8401
	12:21	but the **w** have their fill of trouble.	8401
	12:26	but the way of the **w** leads them astray.	8401
	13: 5	but the **w** bring shame and disgrace.	8401
	13: 9	but the lamp of the **w** is snuffed out.	8401
	13:17	A **w** messenger falls into trouble,	8401
	13:25	but the stomach of the **w** goes hungry.	8401
	14:11	The house of the **w** will be destroyed,	8401
	14:19	and the **w** at the gates of the righteous.	8401
	14:32	calamity comes, the **w** are brought down,	8401
	15: 3	keeping watch on the **w** and the good.	8273
	15: 6	the income of the **w** brings them trouble.	8401
	15: 8	The LORD detests the sacrifice of the **w**,	8401
	15: 9	The LORD detests the way of the **w**	8401
	15:26	The LORD detests the thoughts of the **w**,	8273
	15:28	but the mouth of the **w** gushes evil.	8401
	15:29	The LORD is far from the **w** but he hears	8401
	16: 4	even the **w** for a day of disaster.	8401
	17: 4	A **w** man listens to evil lips;	8317
	17:23	A **w** man accepts a bribe in secret to pervert	8401
	18: 5	be partial to the **w** or to deprive the innocent	8401
	19:28	and the mouth of the **w** gulps down evil.	8401
	20:26	A wise king winnows out the **w**;	8401
	21: 4	a proud heart, the lamp of the **w**, are sin!	8401
	21: 7	The violence of the **w** will drag them away,	8401
	21:10	The **w** man craves evil;	8401
	21:12	of the house of the **w** and brings the wicked	8401
	21:12	of the house of the wicked and brings the **w**	8401
	21:18	The **w** become a ransom for the righteous,	8401
	21:27	The sacrifice of the **w** is detestable—	8401
	21:29	A **w** man puts up a bold front,	8401
	22: 5	In the paths of the **w** lie thorns and snares,	6836
	24: 1	Do not envy **w** men,	8288
	24:16	but the **w** are brought down by calamity.	8401
	24:19	because of evil men or be envious of the **w**,	8401
	24:20	and the lamp of the **w** will be snuffed out.	8401
	25: 5	remove the **w** from the king's presence,	8401
	25:26	a righteous man who gives way to the **w**.	8401
	28: 1	The **w** man flees though no one pursues,	8401
	28: 4	Those who forsake the law praise the **w**,	8401
	28:12	the **w** rise to power, men go into hiding.	8401
	28:15	or a charging bear is a **w** man ruling over	8401
	28:28	the **w** rise to power, people go into hiding;	8401
	28:28	but when **the w** perish, the righteous thrive.	4392S
	29: 2	when the **w** rule, the people groan.	8401
	29: 7	but the **w** have no such concern.	8401
	29:12	all his officials become **w**.	8401
	29:16	When the **w** thrive, so does sin,	8401
	29:27	the **w** detest the upright.	8401
Ecc	3:17	to judgment both the righteous and the **w**,	8401
	7:15	and a **w** man living long in his wickedness.	8401
	8:10	Then too, I saw the **w** buried—	8401
	8:12	a **w** man commits a hundred crimes	2627
	8:13	Yet because the **w** do not fear God,	8401
	8:14	righteous men who get what the **w** deserve,	8401
	8:14	**w** men who get what the righteous deserve.	8401
	9: 2	common destiny—the righteous and the **w**,	8401
	10:13	at the end they are **w** madness—	8273
Isa	3:11	Woe to the **w**! Disaster is upon them!	8401
	9:17	for everyone is ungodly and **w**,	8317
	11: 4	the breath of his lips he will slay the **w**.	8401
	13:11	the **w** for their sins.	8401
	14: 5	The LORD has broken the rod of the **w**,	8401
	14:20	of the **w** will never be mentioned again.	8317
	26:10	Though grace is shown to the **w**,	8401
	31: 2	He will rise up against the house of the **w**,	8317

Isa	32: 7	The scoundrel's methods are **w**,	8273
	35: 8	**w** fools will not go about on it.	211
	48:22	says the LORD, "for the **w**."	8401
	53: 9	He was assigned a grave with the **w**,	8401
	55: 7	Let the **w** forsake his way and	8401
	57:20	But the **w** are like the tossing sea,	8401
	57:21	says my God, "for the **w**."	8401
	58: 4	and in striking each other with **w** fists.	8400
	59: 3	and your tongue mutters **w** *things*.	6406
Jer	4:14	How long will you harbor **w** thoughts?	224
	5:26	"Among my people are **w** men who lie	8401
	6:29	the **w** are not purged out.	8273
	12: 1	Why does the way of the **w** prosper?	8401
	12: 4	Because those who live in it are **w**,	8288
	12:14	"As for all my **w** neighbors who seize	8273
	13:10	These **w** people, who refuse to listen	8273
	15:21	"I will save you from the hands of the **w**	8273
	20:13	of the needy from the hands of the **w**.	8317
	23:19	down on the heads of the **w**.	8401
	25:31	on all mankind and put the **w** to the sword,'	8401
	30:23	down on the heads of the **w**.	8401
	35:15	from your **w** ways and reform your actions;	8288
	36: 3	each of them will turn from his **w** way;	8401
	36: 7	and each will turn from his **w** ways,	8288
	44:22	could no longer endure your **w** actions	8278
Eze	3:18	When I say to a **w** *man*,	8401
	3:18	that **w** man will die for his sin,	8401
	3:19	But if you do warn the **w** man and he does	8401
	6:11	because of all the **w** and detestable practices	8288
	7:21	as plunder to foreigners and as loot to the **w**	8401
	7:24	I will bring the *most* **w** of the nations	8273
	8: 9	"Go in and see the **w** and detestable things	8273
	11: 2	and giving **w** advice in this city.	8273
	13:22	the **w** not to turn from their evil ways and	8401
	14: 3	in their hearts and put **w** stumbling blocks	6411
	14: 4	in his heart and puts a **w** stumbling block	6411
	14: 7	in his heart and puts a **w** stumbling block	6411
	18:20	and the wickedness of the **w** will be charged	8401
	18:21	"But if a **w** man turns away from all	8401
	18:23	I take any pleasure in the death of the **w**?	8401
	18:24	the same detestable things the **w** man does,	8401
	18:27	But if a **w** man turns away from	8401
	21: 3	from you both the righteous and the **w**.	8401
	21: 4	to cut off the righteous and the **w**,	8401
	21:25	" 'O profane and **w** prince of Israel,	8401
	21:29	it will be laid on the necks of the **w** who are	8401
	33: 8	When I say to the **w**, 'O wicked man,	8401
	33: 8	When I say to the wicked, 'O **w** *man*,	8401
	33: 8	that **w** man will die for his sin,	8401
	33: 9	warn the **w** man to turn from his ways	8401
	33:11	I take no pleasure in the death of the **w**,	8401
	33:12	of the **w** man will not cause him to fall	8401
	33:14	And if I say to the **w** *man*,	8401
	33:19	if a **w** *man* turns away from his wickedness	8401
	36:31	remember your evil ways and **w** deeds,	3202+4202
Da	2: 9	to tell me misleading and **w** things,	10705
	8:23	when rebels have become completely **w**,	NIH
	9: 5	*We have been* **w** and have rebelled;	8399
	12:10	but the **w** will continue to be wicked.	8401
	12:10	but the wicked *will continue to be* **w**.	8399
	12:10	None of the **w** will understand,	8401
Hos	6: 8	Gilead is a city of **w** men,	224
	12:11	Is Gilead **w**? Its people are worthless!	224
Mic	6:10	Am I still to forget, O **w** house,	8401
Na	1:15	No more will the **w** invade you;	1175
Hab	1: 4	The **w** hem in the righteous,	8401
	1:13	Why are you silent while the **w** swallow	8401
	1:15	The **w** foe pulls all of them up with hooks,	NIH
Zep	1: 3	The **w** will have only heaps of rubble	8401
Mal	1: 3	They will be called the **W** Land,	8402
	3:18	between the righteous and the **w**,	8401
	4: 3	Then you will trample down the **w**;	8401
Mt	12:39	"A **w** and adulterous generation asks for	4505
	12:45	seven other spirits **more w than** itself,	4505
	12:45	is how it will be *with* this **w** generation."	4505
	13:49	The angels will come and separate the **w**	4505
	16: 4	A **w** and adulterous generation looks for	4505
	18:32	'You **w** servant,' he said,	4505
	24:48	But suppose that servant is **w** and says	2805
	25:26	"His master replied, '*You* **w**, lazy servant!	4505
Lk	6:35	because he is kind to the ungrateful and **w**.	4505
	11:26	takes seven other spirits **more w than** itself,	4505
	11:29	Jesus said, "This is a **w** generation.	4505
	19:22	by your own words, *you* **w** servant!	4505
Ac	2:23	and you, with the help of **w** men,	491
	3:26	by turning each of you from your **w ways**."	4504
	24:15	*of* both the righteous and the **w**.	96
Ro	4: 5	not work but trusts God who justifies the **w**,	815
1Co	5:13	"Expel the **w** man from among you."	4505
	6: 9	Do you not know that the **w** will not inherit	96
2Th	3: 2	And pray that we may be delivered from **w**	876
2Jn	1:11	who welcomes him shares in his **w** work.	4505
Rev	2: 2	I know that you cannot tolerate **w** men,	2805

WICKEDLY (7) [WICKED]

1Ki	8:47	we have done wrong, *we have* **acted w**';	8399
2Ch	6:37	we have done wrong and **acted w**';	8399
Ne	1: 7	*We have* **acted very w** toward you.	2472+2472
Job	13: 7	Will you speak **w** on God's behalf?	6406
Ps	106: 6	we have done wrong, and **acted w**.	8399
Jer	16:12	you have behaved more **w** than your fathers.	8317
	38: 9	these men *have* **acted w** in all they have	8317

WICKEDNESS (112) [WICKED]

Ge	6: 5	The LORD saw how great man's **w** on	8288

Ex	34: 7	and forgiving **w**, rebellion and sin.	6411
	34: 9	forgive our **w** and our sin, and take us as	6411
Lev	16:21	of the live goat and confess over it all the **w**	6411
	18:17	they are her close relatives. That is **w**.	2365
	19:29	to prostitution and be filled with **w**.	2365
	20:14	so that no **w** will be among you.	2365
Dt	9: 4	on account of the **w** of these nations that	8402
	9: 5	but on account of the **w** of these nations,	8402
	9:27	their **w** and their sin.	8400
Jdg	31:18	on that day because of all their **w** in turning	8288
	9:56	the **w** that Abimelech had done to his father	8288
	9:57	the men of Shechem pay for all their **w**.	8288
2Ch	20:35	Israel, who *was* **guilty of w**.	8399
	28:19	for he had **promoted w** in Judah	7277
Ne	9: 2	and confessed their sins and the **w**	6411
	13:27	that you too are doing all this terrible **w**	8288
Job	6:30	Is there any **w** on my lips?	6406
	22: 5	Is not your **w** great?	8288
	22:23	If you remove **w** far from your tent	6406
	27: 4	my lips will not speak **w**,	6406
	34:26	for their **w** where everyone can see them,	8401
	35: 8	Your **w** affects only a man like yourself,	8400
	35:15	and he does not take the least notice of **w**.	7317
Ps	10:15	call him to account for his **w** that would not	8400
	45: 7	You love righteousness and hate **w**;	8400
	92:15	he is my Rock, and there is no **w** in him."	6406
	94:23	for their sins and destroy them for their **w**;	8288
	107:34	because of the **w** of those who lived there.	8288
Pr	4:17	They eat the bread of **w** and drink the wine	8400
	8: 7	for my lips detest **w**.	8402
	11: 5	wicked are brought down by their own **w**.	8402
	12: 3	A man cannot be established through **w**,	8400
	13: 6	but **w** overthrows the sinner.	8402
	18: 3	When **w** comes, so does contempt,	8401
	22: 8	He who sows **w** reaps trouble,	6406
	26:26	but his **w** will be exposed in the assembly.	8288
Ecc	3:16	**w** was there, in the place of justice—	8400
	3:16	in the place of justice—**w** was there.	8400
	7:15	and a wicked man living long in his **w**.	8288
	7:25	the stupidity of **w** and the madness of folly.	8400
	8: 8	so **w** will not release those who practice it.	8401
Isa	5:18	and **w** as with cart ropes,	10258
	9:18	Surely **w** burns like a fire;	8402
	47:10	You have trusted in your **w** and have said,	8288
Jer	1:16	because of their **w** in forsaking me,	8288
	2:19	Your **w** will punish you;	8288
	3: 2	the land with your prostitution and **w**.	8288
	6: 7	so she pours out her **w**.	8288
	7:12	to it because of the **w** of my people Israel.	8288
	8: 6	No one repents of his **w**, saying,	8288
	11:15	you engage in your **w**, then you rejoice."	8288
	14:10	now remember their **w** and punish them	6411
	14:20	we acknowledge our **w** and the guilt	8400
	16:18	I will repay them double for their **w**	6411
	22:22	and disgraced because of all your **w**.	8288
	23:11	even in my temple I find their **w**,"	8288
	23:14	so that no one turns from his **w**.	8288
	31:34	"For I will forgive their **w**	6411
	33: 5	from this city because of all its **w**.	8288
	36: 3	then I will forgive their **w** and their sin."	6411
	36:31	and his attendants for their **w**;	6411
	44: 5	from their **w** or stop burning incense	8288
	44: 9	the **w** committed *by* your fathers and by	8288
	44: 9	and the **w** committed *by* you and your wives	8288
La	1:22	"Let all their **w** come before you;	8288
	4:22	he will punish your sin and expose your **w**.	2633
Eze	3:19	not turn from his **w** or from his evil ways,	8400
	5: 6	in her **w** she has rebelled against my laws	8402
	7:11	Violence has grown into a rod to punish **w**;	8400
	16:23	In addition to all your other **w**,	8288
	16:57	before your **w** was uncovered.	8288
	18:20	and the **w** of the wicked will be charged	8402
	18:27	from the **w** he has committed	6411
	28:15	the day you were created till **w** was found	6406
	31:11	for him to deal with according to its **w**.	8400
	33:12	the **w** of the wicked man will not cause him	8402
	33:19	And if a wicked man turns away from his **w**	8402
Da	4:27	and your **w** by being kind to the oppressed.	10532
	9:24	to put an end to sin, to atone for **w**,	6411
Hos	4: 8	on the sins of my people and relish their **w**.	6411
	7: 3	"They delight the king with their **w**,	8288
	8:13	Now he will remember their **w**	6411
	9: 9	God will remember their **w** and punish them	6411
	9:15	of all their **w** in Gilgal, I hated them there.	8288
	10: 8	The high places of **w** will be destroyed—	224
	10:13	But you have planted **w**,	8402
	10:15	O Bethel, because your **w** is great.	8288+8288
Joel	3:13	so great is their **w**!"	8288
Jnh	1: 2	because its **w** has come up before me."	8288
Mic	3:10	and Jerusalem with **w**.	6406
Na	1:11	against the LORD and counsels **w**.	1175
Hab	1:13	You crushed the leader of the land of **w**,	8401
Zec	5: 8	He said, "This is **w**,"	8402
Mt	23:28	the inside you are full of hypocrisy and **w**.	490
	24:12	Because of the increase of **w**,	490
Lk	11:39	but inside you are full of greed and **w**.	4504
Ac	1:18	(With the reward he got *for* his **w**,	94
	8:22	Repent of this **w** and pray to the Lord.	2798
Ro	1:18	the godlessness and **w** of men who suppress	94
	1:18	of men who suppress the truth by their **w**,	94
	1:29	have become filled with every kind of **w**,	94
	6:13	*of* **w**, but rather offer yourselves to God,	94
	6:19	and *to* **ever-increasing w**,	490+490+1650+3836
1Co	5: 8	the old yeast, the yeast *of* malice and **w**,	4504
2Co	6:14	For what do righteousness and **w** have	490
2Th	2:12	the truth but have delighted *in* **w**.	94
2Ti	2:19	name of the Lord must turn away from **w**."	94

Tit	2:14	for us to redeem us from all **w** and to purify	490
Heb	1: 9	You have loved righteousness and hated **w**;	490
	8:12	For I will forgive their **w** and will remember	94
2Pe	2:15	son of Beor, who loved the wages *of* **w**.	94

WIDE (105) [WIDELY, WIDENED, WIDER, WIDTH]

Ge	6:15	75 feet **w** and 45 feet high.	8145
Ex	25:10	a cubit and a half **w**,	8145
	25:17	a half cubits long and a cubit and a half **w**.	8145
	25:23	a cubit **w** and a cubit and a half high.	8145
	25:25	make a rim around it a **handbreadth** *w*	AIT
	26: 2	twenty-eight cubits long and four cubits	8145
	26: 8	thirty cubits long and four cubits **w**.	8145
	26:16	be ten cubits long and a cubit and a half **w**,	8145
	27: 1	five cubits long and five cubits **w**.	8145
	27:12	of the courtyard shall be fifty cubits **w**	8145
	27:13	the courtyard shall also be fifty cubits **w**.	8145
	27:18	be a hundred cubits long and fifty cubits **w**,	8145
	28:16	be square—a span long and a span **w**—	**8145**
	30: 2	a cubit long and a cubit **w**,	8145
	36: 9	twenty-eight cubits long and four cubits **w**.	8145
	36:15	thirty cubits long and four cubits **w**.	8145
	36:21	and a cubit and a half **w**,	8145
	37: 1	a cubit and a half **w**,	8145
	37: 6	a half cubits long and a cubit and a half **w**.	8145
	37:10	two cubits long, a cubit **w**,	8145
	37:12	a handbreadth **w** and put a gold molding on	NIH
	37:25	It was square, a cubit long and a cubit **w**,	8145
	38: 1	five cubits long and five cubits **w**.	8145
	38:12	The west end was fifty cubits **w**	NIH
	38:13	toward the sunrise, was also fifty cubits **w**.	NIH
	39: 9	It was square—a span long and a span **w**—	8145
Dt	3:11	thirteen feet long and six feet **w**.	8145
1Sa	26:13	there was a **w** space between them.	8041
1Ki	6: 2	twenty **w** and thirty high.	8145
	6: 6	The lowest floor was five cubits **w**,	8145
	6:20	twenty **w** and twenty high.	8145
	7: 2	fifty **w** and thirty high,	8145
	7: 6	a colonnade fifty cubits long and thirty **w**.	8145
	7:27	four **w** and three high.	8145
1Ch	13: 2	let us send word **far and w** to the rest	7287
2Ch	3: 3	and twenty cubits **w** (using the cubit of	8145
	3: 8	twenty cubits long and twenty cubits **w**.	8145
	3: 11	twenty cubits **w** and ten cubits high.	8145
	6:13	five cubits **w** and three cubits high,	8145
	26:15	fame spread **far and w**, 4200+4946+6330+8158	
Ezr	6: 3	to be ninety feet high and ninety feet **w**,	10603
Ps	22:13	Roaring lions tearing their prey **open** their mouths **w** against me.	7198
	81:10	**Open w** your mouth and I will fill it.	8143
Isa	18: 2	people feared **far and w**, 2085+2134+2256+4946	
	18: 7	people feared **far and w**, 2085+2134+2256+4946	
	30:33	Its fire pit has been made deep and **w**,	8145
	45: 8	*Let* the earth **open w**, let salvation spring up	7337
	54: 2	**stretch** your tent curtains, **w**,	5742
	57: 8	you climbed into it and **opened** it **w**;	8143
La	2:16	All your enemies **open** their mouths **w**	7198
	3:46	our enemies *have* **opened** their mouths **w**	7198
Eze	40: 7	one rod long and one rod **w**,	8145
	40:18	the sides of the gateways and was as **w**	NIH
	40:21	and twenty-five cubits **w**.	8145
	40:25	and twenty-five cubits **w**.	8145
	40:29	and twenty-five cubits **w**.	8145
	40:30	the inner court were twenty-five cubits **w**	802
	40:33	and twenty-five cubits **w**.	8145
	40:36	and twenty-five cubits **w**.	8145
	40:42	a cubit and a half **w** and a cubit high.	8145
	40:47	hundred cubits long and a hundred cubits **w**.	8145
	40:48	they were five cubits **w** on either side.	NIH
	40:48	and its projecting walls were three cubits **w**	NIH
	40:49	The portico was twenty cubits **w**,	802
	41: 2	The entrance was ten cubits **w**,	8145
	41: 2	on each side of it were five cubits **w**.	NIH
	41: 2	and twenty cubits **w**.	8145
	41: 3	each was two cubits **w**.	NIH
	41: 3	The entrance was six cubits **w**,	NIH
	41: 3	on each side of it were seven cubits **w**.	8145
	41: 5	around the temple was four cubits **w**.	8145
	41:10	the [priests'] rooms was twenty cubits **w** all	8145
	41:11	the open area was five cubits **w** all around.	8145
	41:12	on the west side was seventy cubits **w**,	8145
	42: 2	a hundred cubits long and fifty cubits **w**.	8145
	42: 4	an inner passageway ten cubits **w** and	8145
	42:20	and five hundred cubits **w**,	8145
	43:13	Its gutter is a cubit deep and a cubit **w**,	8145
	43:14	and a cubit **w**.	8145
	43:14	and a cubit **w**.	8145
	43:16	twelve cubits long and twelve cubits **w**,	8145
	43:17	fourteen cubits long and fourteen cubits **w**,	8145
	45: 1	25,000 cubits long and 20,000 cubits **w**;	8145
	45: 3	cubits long and 10,000 cubits **w**.	8145
	45: 5	10,000 cubits **w** will belong to the Levites,	8145
	45: 6	5,000 cubits **w** and 25,000 cubits long,	8145
	46:22	forty cubits long and thirty cubits **w**;	8145
	48: 8	It will be 25,000 cubits **w**,	8145
	48: 9	cubits long and 10,000 cubits **w**.	8145
	48:10	10,000 cubits **w** on the west side,	8145
	48:10	10,000 cubits **w** on the east side and	8145
	48:13	25,000 cubits long and 10,000 cubits **w**.	8145
	48:15	5,000 cubits **w** and 25,000 cubits long,	8145
Da	3: 1	ninety feet high and nine feet **w**,	10603
Mic	4: 3	for strong nations **far and w**.	6330+8158
Na	3:13	your land *are* **w** open to your enemies;	7337+7337
Zec	2: 2	to find out how **w** and how long it is."	
	5: 2	thirty feet long and fifteen feet **w**."	8145

WIDELY (3) [WIDE]

Ne	4:19	and we are **w** separated from each other	8158
Mt	28:15	And this story *has* been **w** circulated	1424
Ac	19:20	In this way the word of the Lord **spread w**	889

WIDENED (1) [WIDE]

Eze	41: 7	so that the rooms **w** as one went upward.	8145

WIDENESS (KJV) See WIDE

WIDER (2) [WIDE]

Job	11: 9	longer than the earth and **w** than the sea.	8146
Eze	41: 7	the temple *were* **w** at each successive level.	8143

WIDESPREAD (2) [SPREAD]

Eze	28:16	your **w** trade you were filled with violence,	8044
Jn	7:12	Among the crowds there was **w** whispering	4498

WIDOW (58) [WIDOW'S, WIDOWHOOD, WIDOWS, WIDOWS']

Ge	38:11	"Live *as* a **w** in your father's house	530
Ex	22:22	"Do not take advantage of a **w** or an orphan.	530
Lev	21:14	He must not marry a **w**, a divorced woman,	530
	22:13	But if a priest's daughter becomes a **w**	530
Nu	30: 9	by a **w** or divorced woman will be binding	530
Dt	10:18	the cause of the fatherless and the **w**,	530
	24:17	or take the cloak of the **w** as a pledge.	530
	24:19	the alien, the fatherless and the **w**,	530
	24:20	the alien, the fatherless and the **w**.	530
	24:21	the alien, the fatherless and the **w**.	530
	25: 5	**w** must not marry outside the family.	851+4637
	25: 9	his **brother's w** shall go up to him in	3304
	26:12	the alien, the fatherless and the **w**,	530
	26:13	the alien, the fatherless and the **w**,	530
	27:19	the alien, the fatherless or the **w**."	530
Ru	4: 5	you acquire the dead man's **w**,	851
	4:10	the Moabitess, Mahlon's **w**, as my wife,	851
1Sa	27: 3	and Abigail of Carmel, the **w** *of* Nabal.	851
	30: 5	Abigail, the **w** *of* Nabal of Carmel.	851
2Sa	2: 2	Abigail, the **w** *of* Nabal of Carmel.	851
	3: 3	Kileab the son of Abigail the **w** *of* Nabal	851
	14: 5	She said, "I am indeed a **w**;	530
1Ki	7:14	whose mother was a **w** from the tribe	530
	11:26	and his mother was a **w** named Zeruah.	530
	17: 9	a **w** in that place to supply you with food."	530
	17:10	a **w** was there gathering sticks.	530
	17:20	also upon this **w** I am staying with,	530
Job	24:21	and to the **w** show no kindness.	530
	31:16	or let the eyes of the **w** grow weary,	530
	31:18	and from my birth I guided the **w**—	5626S
Ps	94: 6	They slay the **w** and the alien;	530
	109: 9	be fatherless and his wife a **w**.	530
	146: 9	and sustains the fatherless and the **w**,	530
Isa	1:17	plead the case of the **w**.	530
	47: 8	be a **w** or suffer the loss of children.'	530
Jer	7: 6	or the **w** and do not shed innocent blood	530
	22: 3	to the alien, the fatherless or the **w**,	530
La	1: 1	How like a **w** is she,	530
Eze	22: 7	and mistreated the fatherless and the **w**.	530
Zec	7:10	Do not oppress the **w** or the fatherless,	530
Mt	22:24	the **w** and have children for him.	899+1222
Mk	12:19	the **w** and have children for his brother.	1222
	12:21	The second one married **the w**,	899S
	12:42	But a poor **w** came and put in two	5939
	12:43	this poor **w** has put more into the treasury	5939
Lk	2:37	and then was a **w** until she was eighty-four.	5939
	4:26	but to a **w** in Zarephath	1222+5939
	7:12	the only son of his mother, and she was a **w**.	5939
	18: 3	a **w** in that town who kept coming to him	5939
	18: 5	yet because this **w** keeps bothering me,	5939
	20:28	the **w** and have children for his brother.	1222
	21: 2	He also saw a poor **w** put in two	5939
	21: 3	"this poor **w** has put in more than all	5939
1Ti	5: 4	But if a **w** has children or grandchildren,	5939
	5: 5	The **w** who is really in need	5939
	5: 6	the **w** who lives for pleasure is dead even	NIG
	5: 9	No **w** may be put on the list of widows	5939
Rev	18: 7	I am not a **w**, and I will never mourn.'	5939

WIDOW'S (6) [WIDOW]

Ge	38:14	she took off her **w** clothes,	531
	38:19	and put on her **w** clothes again.	531
Job	24: 3	the orphan's donkey and take the **w** ox	530
	29:13	I made the **w** heart sing.	530
Pr	15:25	but he keeps the **w** boundaries intact.	530
Isa	1:23	the **w** case does not come before them.	530

WIDOWHOOD (2) [WIDOW]

Isa	47: 9	loss of children and **w**.	529
	54: 4	remember no more the reproach of your **w**.	531

WIDOWS (31) [WIDOW]

Ex	22:24	your wives will become **w** and your children	530

Mt	7:13	For **w** is the gate and broad is the road	4426
	23: 5	*They* **make** their phylacteries **w**	4425
2Co	6:11	and **opened w** our hearts to you.	4425
	6:13	**open w** *your* hearts also.	4425
Eph	3:18	how **w** and long and high and deep is	4424
Rev	21:16	like a square, as long as it was **w**.	4424
	21:16	and as **w** and high as it is long.	4424

WIDOWS' (2) [WIDOW]

Mk	12:40	They devour **w'** houses and for a show	5939
Lk	20:47	They devour **w'** houses and for a show	5939

WIDTH (11) [WIDE]

1Ki	6: 3	of the temple extended the **w** *of* the temple,	8145
2Ch	3: 4	across the **w** *of* the building	8145
	3: 8	corresponding to the **w** *of* the temple—	8145
Eze	40:11	Then he measured the **w** *of* the entrance to	8145
	40:20	the length and **w** *of* the gate facing north,	8145
	40:48	The **w** *of* the entrance was fourteen cubits	8145
	41: 1	**w** *of* the jambs was six cubits on each side.	8145
	41: 4	and its **w** was twenty cubits across the end	8145
	41:14	The **w** *of* the temple courtyard on the east,	8145
	42:11	they had the same length and **w**,	8145
	48:13	25,000 cubits and its **w** 10,000 cubits.	8145

WIELD (1) [WIELDING]

Isa	10:15	As if a rod *were* to **w** him who lifts it up,	5677

WIELDING (1) [WIELD]

Ps	74: 5	behaved like *men* **w** axes 995+2025+4200+5087	

WIFE (333) [WIFE'S, WIVES, WIVES']

Ge	2:24	and mother and be united to his **w**,	851
	2:25	The man and his **w** were both naked,	851
	3: 8	Then the man and his **w** heard the sound of	851
	3:17	"Because you listened to your **w** and ate	851
	3:20	Adam named his **w** Eve,	851
	3:21	for Adam and his **w** and clothed them.	851
	4: 1	Adam lay with his **w** Eve,	851
	4:17	Cain lay with his **w**,	851
	4:25	Adam lay with his **w** again,	851
	6:18	and your **w** and your sons' wives with you.	851
	7: 7	and his **w** and his sons' wives entered	851
	7:13	with his **w** and the wives of his three sons,	851
	8:16	and your **w** and your sons and their wives.	851
	8:18	with his sons and his **w** and his sons' wives.	851
	11:29	The name of Abram's **w** was Sarai,	851
	11:29	and the name of Nahor's **w** was Milcah;	851
	11:31	Sarai, the **w** *of* his son Abram,	851
	12: 5	He took his **w** Sarai, his nephew Lot,	851
	12:11	he said to his **w** Sarai,	851
	12:12	they will say, 'This is his **w**.'	851
	12:17	because of Abram's **w** Sarai.	851
	12:18	"Why didn't you tell me she was your **w**?	851
	12:19	so that I took her to be my **w**?	851
	12:19	Now then, here is your **w**.	851
	12:20	with his **w** and everything he had.	851
	13: 1	with his **w** and everything he had,	851
	16: 1	Now Sarai, Abram's **w**, had borne him no	851
	16: 3	Sarai his **w** took her Egyptian maidservant	851
	16: 3	and gave her to her husband to be his **w**.	851
	17:15	"As for Sarai your **w**,	851
	17:19	"Yes, but your **w** Sarah will bear you a son,	851
	18: 9	"Where is your **w** Sarah?"	851
	18:10	and Sarah your **w** will have a son."	851
	19:15	your **w** and your two daughters who are	851
	19:16	the hands of his **w** and of his two daughters	851
	19:26	But Lot's **w** looked back,	851
	20: 2	and there Abraham said of his **w** Sarah,	851
	20: 7	Now return the man's **w**,	851
	20:11	and they will kill me because of my **w**.'	851
	20:12	and she became my **w**.	851
	20:14	and he returned Sarah his **w** to him.	851
	20:18	Abimelech, his **w** and his slave girls	851
	20:18	because of Abraham's **w** Sarah.	851
	21:21	his mother got a **w** for him from Egypt.	851
	23: 3	Then Abraham rose from beside his **dead w**	AIT
	23:19	Afterward Abraham buried his **w** Sarah in	851
	24: 3	not get a **w** for my son from the daughters	851
	24: 4	my own relatives and get a **w** for my son	851
	24: 7	that you can get a **w** for my son from there.	851

Ge	24:15	the w of Abraham's brother Nahor.	851
	24:36	My master's w Sarah has borne him a son	851
	24:37	not get a w for my son from the daughters	851
	24:38	and get a w for my son.'	851
	24:40	a w for my son from my own clan and	851
	24:51	let her become the w of your master's son,	851
	24:67	So she became his w, and he loved her;	851
	25: 1	Abraham took another w,	851
	25:10	Abraham was buried with his w Sarah.	851
	25:21	prayed to the LORD on behalf of his w,	851
	25:21	and his w Rebekah became pregnant.	851
	26: 7	men of that place asked him about his w,	851
	26: 7	he was afraid to say, "She is my w."	851
	26: 8	and saw Isaac caressing his w Rebekah.	851
	26: 9	"She is really your w!	851
	26:10	the men might well have slept with your w,	851
	26:11	or his w shall surely be put to death."	851
	27:46	If Jacob takes a w from among the women	851
	28: 2	Take a w for yourself there,	851
	28: 6	to Paddan Aram to take a w from there,	851
	29:21	Then Jacob said to Laban, "Give me my w.	851
	29:28	gave him his daughter Rachel to be his w.	851
	30: 4	So she gave him her servant Bilhah as a w.	851
	30: 9	and gave her to Jacob as a w.	851
	34: 4	"Get me this girl as my w."	851
	34: 8	Please give her to him as his w.	851
	34:12	Only give me the girl as my w."	851
	36:10	Eliphaz, the son of Esau's w Adah,	851
	36:10	and Reuel, the son of Esau's w Basemath.	851
	36:12	These were grandsons of Esau's w Adah.	851
	36:13	grandson's of Esau's w Basemath.	851
	36:14	The sons of Esau's w Oholibamah daughter	851
	36:17	they were grandsons of Esau's w Basemath.	851
	36:18	The sons of Esau's w Oholibamah:	851
	36:18	from Esau's w Oholibamah daughter	851
	38: 6	Judah got a w for Er, his firstborn,	851
	38: 8	with your brother's w and fulfill your duty	851
	38: 9	so whenever he lay with his brother's w,	851
	38:12	After a long time Judah's w,	851
	38:14	she had not been given to him as his w.	851
	39: 7	a while his master's w took notice of Joseph	851
	39: 9	because you are his w.	851
	39:19	his master heard the story his w told him,	851
	41:45	of Potiphera, priest of On, to be his w.	851
	44:27	'You know that my w bore me two sons.	851
	46:19	The sons of Jacob's w Rachel:	851
	49:31	and his w Sarah were buried,	851
	49:31	there Isaac and his w Rebekah were buried,	851
Ex	4:20	So Moses took his w and sons,	851
	18: 2	After Moses had sent away his w Zipporah,	851
	18: 5	together with Moses' sons and w,	851
	18: 6	to you with your w and her two sons."	851
	20:17	You shall not covet your neighbor's w,	851
	21: 3	but if he has a w when he comes,	851
	21: 4	a w and she bears him sons or daughters,	851
	21: 5	'I love my master and my w and children	851
	22:16	and she shall be his w.	851
Lev	18: 8	sexual relations with your father's w;	851
	18:11	with the daughter of your father's w,	851
	18:14	by approaching his w to have sexual relations	851
	18:15	She is your son's w;	851
	18:16	sexual relations with your brother's w;	851
	18:18	not take your wife's sister as a **rival** w	7675
	18:18	with her while **your** w is living.	2023S
	18:20	sexual relations with your neighbor's w	851
	20:10	commits adultery with another man's w	851
	20:10	with the w of his neighbor—	851
	20:11	" 'If a man sleeps with his father's w,	851
	20:21	" 'If a man marries his brother's w,	851
Nu	5:12	'If a man's w goes astray and is unfaithful	851
	5:14	and he suspects his w and she is impure—	851
	5:15	then he is to take his w to the priest.	851
	5:30	over a man because he suspects his w.	851
	12: 1	against Moses because of his Cushite w,	851
	26:59	the name of Amram's w was Jochebed,	851
	30:16	relationships between a man and his w,	851
Dt	5:21	"You shall not covet your neighbor's w.	851
	13: 6	or your son or daughter, or the w you love,	851
	21:11	you may take her as your w.	851
	21:13	and be her husband and she shall be your w.	851
	21:15	but the firstborn is the son of the w he does	NIH
	21:16	of the firstborn to the son of the w he loves	NIH
	21:16	the son of the w he does not love.	NIH
	21:17	the son of his unloved w as the firstborn	NIH
	22:13	If a man takes a w and, after lying with her,	851
	22:19	She shall continue to be his w;	851
	22:22	found sleeping with another man's w,	851+1249
	22:24	because he violated another man's w.	851
	22:30	A man is not to marry his father's w;	851
	24: 2	and she becomes the w of another man,	NIH
	24: 5	bring happiness to the w he has married.	851
	25: 7	does not want to marry his **brother's** w,	3304
	25:11	If two men are fighting and the w of one	851
	27:20	the man who sleeps with his father's w,	851
	28:54	or the w he loves or his surviving children,	851
Jdg	4: 4	Deborah, a prophetess, the w of Lappidoth,	851
	4:17	the w of Heber the Kenite,	851
	4:21	But Jael, Heber's w, picked up a tent peg	851
	5:24	the w of Heber the Kenite.	851
	11: 2	Gilead's w also bore him sons,	851
	13: 2	a w who was sterile and remained childless.	851
	13:11	Manoah got up and followed his w.	851
	13:11	"Are you the one who talked to my w?"	851
	13:13	"Your w must do all that I have told her.	851
	13:19	while Manoah and his w watched:	851
	13:20	and his w fell with their faces to the ground.	851
	13:21	show himself again to Manoah and his w,	851

Jdg	13:22	"We are doomed to die!" he said to his w.	851
	13:23	But his w answered,	851
	14: 2	now get her for me as my w."	851
	14: 3	the uncircumcised Philistines to get a w?"	851
	14:15	On the fourth day, they said to Samson's w,	851
	14:16	Then Samson's w threw herself on him,	851
	14:20	And Samson's w was given to	851
	15: 1	a young goat and went to visit his w.	851
	15: 6	because his w was given to his friend."	851
	21:18	be anyone who gives a w to a Benjamite.'	851
	21:21	of you seize a w from the girls of Shiloh	851
	21:23	and carried her off to be his w.	851
Ru	1: 1	together with his w and two sons,	851
	4:10	the Moabitess, Mahlon's widow, as my w,	851
	4:13	So Boaz took Ruth and she became his w.	851
1Sa	1: 2	to his w Peninnah and to all her sons	851
	1:19	Elkanah lay with Hannah his w,	851
	2:20	Eli would bless Elkanah and his w, saying,	851
	4:19	His daughter-in-law, the w of Phinehas,	851
	19:11	But Michal, David's w, warned him,	851
	25:14	One of the servants told Nabal's w Abigail:	851
	25:37	his w told him all these things,	851
	25:39	asking her to **become** his w.	851+4200+4374
	25:40	to you to take you to become his w."	851
	25:42	with David's messengers and became his w.	851
	25:44	David's w, to Paltiel son of Laish,	851
	30:22	each man may take his w and children	851
2Sa	3: 5	Ithream the son of David's w Eglah.	851
	3:14	demanding, "Give me my w Michal,	851
	11: 3	the daughter of Eliam and the w of Uriah	851
	11:11	to eat and drink and lie with my w?	851
	11:26	Uriah's w heard that her husband was dead,	851
	11:27	and she became his w and bore him a son.	851
	12: 9	the Hittite with the sword and took his w to	851
	12:10	the w of Uriah the Hittite to be your own.'	851
	12:15	the child that Uriah's w had borne to David,	851
	12:24	Then David comforted his w Bathsheba,	851
	17:19	His w took a covering and spread it out over	851
1Ki	2:17	Abishag the Shunammite as my w."	851
	9:16	wedding gift to his daughter, Solomon's w.	851
	11:19	that he gave him a sister of his own w,	851
	14: 2	and Jeroboam said to his w,	851
	14: 2	be recognized as the w of Jeroboam.	851
	14: 4	So Jeroboam's w did what he said and went	851
	14: 5	"Jeroboam's w is coming to ask you	851
	14: 6	he said, "Come in, w of Jeroboam.	851
	14:17	Then Jeroboam's w got up and left	851
	21: 5	His w Jezebel came in and asked him,	851
	21: 7	Jezebel his w said, "Is this how you act	851
	21:25	urged on by Jezebel his w.	851
2Ki	4: 1	The w of a man from the company of	851
	5: 2	and she served Naaman's w.	851
	22:14	who was the w of Shallum son of Tikvah,	851
1Ch	2:18	of Hezron had children by his w Azubah	851
	2:24	the w of Hezron bore him Ashhur the father	851
	2:26	Jerahmeel had another w,	851
	2:29	Abishur's w was named Abihail,	851
	3: 3	and the sixth, Ithream, by his w Eglah.	851
	4:18	(His Judean w gave birth to Jered the father	851
	4:19	The sons of Hodiah's w,	851
	7:15	Makir took a w from among the Huppites	851
	7:16	Makir's w Maacah gave birth to a son	851
	7:23	Then he lay with his w again,	851
	8: 9	By his w Hodesh he had Jobab, Zibia,	851
2Ch	8:11	"My w must not live in the palace	851
	22:11	the daughter of King Jehoram and w of	851
	34:22	who was the w of Shallum son of Tokhath,	851
Est	5:10	his friends and Zeresh, his w,	851
	5:14	His w Zeresh and all his friends said to him,	851
	6:13	and told Zeresh his w and all his friends	851
	6:13	His advisers and his w Zeresh said to him,	851
Job	2: 9	His w said to him, "Are you still holding on	851
	19:17	My breath is offensive to my w;	851
	31:10	then may my w grind another man's grain,	851
Ps	109: 9	May his children be fatherless and his w	851
	128: 3	Your w will be like a fruitful vine	851
Pr	2:16	the **wayward** w with her seductive words,	AIT
	5:18	and may you rejoice in the w of your youth.	AIT
	5:20	the bosom of **another** man's w?	AIT
	6:24	from the smooth tongue of the **wayward** w.	AIT
	6:29	So is he who sleeps with another man's w;	AIT
	7: 5	the **wayward** w with her seductive words.	AIT
	12: 4	A w of noble character is her husband's	
		crown,	851
	12: 4	a disgraceful w is like decay in his bones.	NIH
	18:22	a w finds what is good and receives favor	851
	19:13	a quarrelsome w is like a constant dripping.	851
	19:14	but a prudent w is from the LORD.	851
	21: 9	a house with a quarrelsome w.	851
	21:19	with a quarrelsome and ill-tempered w.	851
	23:27	and a **wayward** w is a narrow well.	AIT
	25:24	a house with a quarrelsome w.	851
	27:15	A quarrelsome w is like a constant dripping	851
	31:10	A w of noble character who can find?	851
Ecc	9: 9	Enjoy life with your w, whom you love,	851
Isa	54: 6	as if you were a w deserted and distressed	851
	54: 6	a w who married young, only to be rejected,	851
Jer	3: 1	"If a man divorces his w and she leaves him	851
	5: 8	each neighing for another man's w.	851
	6:11	both husband and w will be caught in it,	851
Eze	16:32	" 'You adulterous w! You prefer strangers	851
	18: 6	He does not defile his neighbor's w or lie	851
	18:11	He defiles his neighbor's w.	851
	18:15	He does not defile his neighbor's w,	851
	22:11	a detestable offense with his neighbor's w,	851
	24:18	and in the evening my w died.	851
	33:26	and each of you defiles his neighbor's w.	851

Hos	1: 2	to yourself an adulterous w and children	851
	2: 2	rebuke her, for she is not my w,	851
	3: 1	"Go, show your love to your w again,	851
	12:12	Israel served to get a w,	851
Am	7:17	" 'Your w will become a prostitute in	851
Mal	2:14	between you and the w of your youth,	851
	2:14	the w of your marriage covenant.	851
	2:15	do not break faith with the w of your youth.	851
Mt	1: 6	whose mother had been Uriah's w,	3836
	1:20	not be afraid to take Mary home as your w,	1222
	1:24	and took Mary home as his w.	1222
	5:31	'Anyone who divorces his w must give her	1222
	5:32	I tell you that anyone who divorces his w,	1222
	14: 3	Herodias, his brother Philip's w,	1222
	18:25	that he and his w and his children and all	1222
	19: 3	to divorce his w for any and every reason?"	1222
	19: 5	and mother and be united to his w,	1222
	19: 7	"did Moses command that a man give his w	NIG
	19: 9	I tell you that anyone who divorces his w,	1222
	19:10	the situation between a husband and w,	1222
	22:25	he left his w to his brother.	1222
	22:28	whose w will she be of the seven,	1222
	27:19	his w sent him this message:	1222
Mk	6:17	Herodias, his brother Philip's w,	1222
	6:18	not lawful for you to have your brother's w."	1222
	10: 2	"Is it lawful for a man to divorce his w?"	1222
	10: 7	and mother and be united to his w,	1222
	10:11	"Anyone who divorces his w	1222
	12:19	that if a man's brother dies and leaves a w	1222
	12:23	At the resurrection whose w will she be,	1222
Lk	1: 5	his w Elizabeth was also a descendant	1222
	1:13	Your w Elizabeth will bear you a son,	1222
	1:18	I am an old man and my w is well along	1222
	1:24	After this his w Elizabeth became pregnant	1222
	3:19	because of Herodias, his brother's w,	1222
	8: 3	Joanna the w of Cuza, the manager	1222
	14:26	his w and children, the brothers	1222
	16:18	"Anyone who divorces his w	1222
	17:32	Remember Lot's w!	1222
	18:29	"no one who has left home or w or brothers	1222
	20:28	if a man's brother dies and **leaves** a w	1222+2400
	20:33	at the resurrection whose w will she be,	1222
Jn	19:25	his mother's sister, Mary the w of Clopas,	3836
Ac	5: 1	Ananias, together with his w Sapphira,	1222
	5: 7	About three hours later his w came in,	1222
	18: 2	from Italy with his w Priscilla,	1222
	24:24	Felix came with his w Drusilla,	1222
1Co	5: 1	A man has his father's w.	1222
	7: 2	each man should have his own w,	1222
	7: 3	should fulfill his marital duty to his w,	1222
	7: 3	and likewise the w to her husband.	1222
	7: 4	not belong to him alone but also to his w.	1222
	7:10	A w must not separate from her husband.	1222
	7:11	And a husband must not divorce his w.	1222
	7:12	If any brother has a w who is not a believer	1222
	7:14	For the unbelieving husband has been	
		sanctified through his w,	1222
	7:14	and the unbelieving w has been sanctified	1222
	7:16	How do you know, w,	1222
	7:16	husband, whether you will save your w?	1222
	7:27	Do not look for a w.	1222
	7:33	how he can please his w—	1222
	9: 5	the right to take a **believing** w along	80+1222
Eph	5:23	the husband is the head of the w as Christ is	1222
	5:28	He who loves his w loves himself.	1222
	5:31	and mother and be united to his w,	1222
	5:33	also must love his w as he loves himself,	1222
	5:33	and the w must respect her husband.	1222
1Ti	3: 2	the husband of but one w, temperate,	1222
	3:12	A deacon must be the husband of but one w	1222
Tit	1: 6	blameless, the husband of but one w,	1222
Rev	21: 9	the bride, the w of the Lamb."	1222

WIFE'S (11) [WIFE]

Ge	36:39	and his w name was Mehetabel daughter	851
Lev	18:18	" 'Do not take your w sister as a rival wife	851
Jdg	15: 1	He said, "I'm going to my w room."	851
Ru	1: 2	Elimelech, his w name Naomi,	851
1Sa	14:50	His w name was Ahinoam daughter	851
	25: 3	and his w name was Abigail.	851
1Ch	1:50	and his w name was Mehetabel daughter	851
	8:29	His w name was Maacah,	851
	9:35	His w name was Maacah,	851
Ac	5: 2	With his w full knowledge he kept back part	1222
1Co	7: 4	The w body does not belong to her alone	1222

WILD (98) [WILDER, WILDERNESS, WILDS]

Ge	1:24	and w animals, each according to its kind."	824
	1:25	the w animals according to their kinds,	824
	3: 1	the w animals the LORD God had made.	8441
	3:14	the livestock and all the w animals!	8441
	7:14	with them every w animal according	2651
	7:21	birds, livestock, w **animals**,	2651
	8: 1	the w **animals** and the livestock that were	2651
	9:10	the livestock and all the w animals,	824
	16:12	He will be a w **donkey** of a man;	7230
	25:28	Isaac, who had a taste for w **game**,	7473
	27: 3	to the open country to hunt some w **game**	7473
	31:39	not bring you **animals torn by** w **beasts**;	3274
Ex	22:13	it **was torn to pieces by** a w animal,	3271+3271
	22:31	of an animal torn by w beasts;	928+2021+8441
	23:11	the w animals may eat what they leave.	8441
	23:29	and the w animals too numerous for you.	8441
	32:25	Moses saw that the people were **running** w	7277
Lev	5: 2	whether the carcasses of unclean w **animals**	2651

Lev	7:24	or **torn by w** animals may be used	3274
	17:15	or **torn by w** animals must wash his clothes	3274
	22: 8	found dead or **torn by w** animals,	3274
	25: 7	as for your livestock and the **w** animals	2651
	26:22	I will send **w** animals against you,	8441
Nu	23:22	they have the strength of a **w** ox.	8028
	24: 8	they have the strength of a **w** ox.	8028
Dt	7:22	or the **w** animals will multiply around you.	8441
	14: 5	the gazelle, the roe deer, the **w** goat,	735
	32:24	against them the fangs of **w** beasts,	989
	33:17	his horns are the horns of a **w** ox.	8028
1Sa	24: 2	his men near the Crags of the **W Goats.**	3604
2Sa	2:18	Asahel was as fleet-footed as a **w** gazelle.	928+2021+8441
	17: 8	as a **w** bear robbed of her cubs.	928+2021+8441
	21:10	the air touch them by day or the **w** animals	8441
2Ki	4:39	to gather herbs and found a **w** vine.	8441
	14: 9	Then a **w** beast in Lebanon came along	8441
2Ch	25:18	Then a **w** beast in Lebanon came along	8441
Ne	8:15	and **w** olive trees, and from myrtles, palms	9043
Job	5:23	the **w** animals will be at peace with you.	8441
	6: 5	Does a **w** donkey bray when it has grass,	7230
	11:12	a **w** donkey's colt can be born a man.	7230
	24: 5	Like **w** donkeys in the desert,	7230
	39: 5	"Who let the **w** donkey go free?	7230
	39: 9	"Will the **w** ox consent to serve you?	8028
	39:15	that some **w** animal may trample them.	8441
	40:20	and all the **w** animals play nearby.	8441
Ps	22:21	save me from the horns of the **w** oxen.	8028
	29: 6	Sirion like a young **w** ox.	8028
	74:19	over the life of your dove to **w** beasts;	2651
	92:10	exalted my horn like that of a **w** ox;	8028
	104:11	the **w** donkeys quench their thirst.	7230
	104:18	The high mountains belong to the **w** goats;	3604
	148:10	**w** animals and all cattle,	2651
Isa	13:21	and there the **w** goats will leap about.	8538
	18: 6	of prey and to the **w** animals;	824
	18: 6	the **w** animals all winter.	824
	34: 7	And the **w** oxen will fall with them,	8028
	34:14	and **w** goats will bleat to each other;	8538
	43:20	The **w** animals honor me,	8441
Jer	2:21	against me into a corrupt, **w** vine?	5799
	2:24	a **w** donkey accustomed to the desert,	7241
	12: 9	Go and gather all the **w** beasts;	8441
	14: 6	**W** donkeys stand on the barren heights	7230
	27: 6	I will make even the **w** animals subject	8441
	28:14	give him control over the **w** animals.' "	8441
Eze	14: 5	found dead or **torn by w** animals.	3274
	5:17	I will send famine and **w** beasts against you,	8273
	14:15	"Or if I send **w** beasts through that country	8273
	14:21	and famine and **w** beasts and plague—	8273
	33:27	the country I will give to the **w** animals to	2651
	34: 5	they became food for all the **w** animals.	8441
	34: 8	and has become food for all the **w** animals,	8441
	34:25	the land of **w** beasts so that they may live in	8273
	34:28	nor will **w** animals devour them.	824
	39: 4	of carrion birds and to the **w** animals.	8441
	39:17	to every kind of bird and all the **w** animals:	8441
	44:31	found dead or **torn by w** animals.	3274
Da	4:23	let him live like the **w** animals,	10119
	4:25	and will live with the **w** animals;	10119
	4:32	and will live with the **w** animals;	10119
	5:21	the **w** donkeys and ate grass like cattle;	10570
Hos	2:12	and **w** animals will devour them.	8441
	8: 9	like a **w** donkey wandering alone.	7230
	13: 8	a **w** animal will tear them apart.	8441
Joel	1:20	Even the **w** animals pant for you;	8441
	2:22	Be not afraid, O **w** animals,	8442
Zep	2:15	a lair for **w** beasts!	2651
Mt	3: 4	His food was locusts and **w** honey.	67
Mk	1: 6	and he ate locusts and **w** honey.	67
	1:13	He was with the **w** animals,	2563
Lk	15:13	and there squandered his wealth in **w** living.	862
Ac	11: 6	**w** beasts, reptiles, and birds of the air.	2563
Ro	11:17	and you, though a **w** olive shoot,	66
	11:24	olive tree that is **w**	66
1Co	15:32	If **I fought w** beasts in Ephesus	2562
Tit	1: 6	and are not open to the charge of being **w**	861
Jas	1:10	because he will pass away like a **w** flower.	5965
Jude	1:13	They are **w** waves of the sea,	67
Rev	6: 8	and by the **w** beasts of the earth.	2563

WILDER (1) [WILD]

Jnh	1:13	sea grew even **w** than before.	2143+2256+6192

WILDERNESS (5) [WILD]

Isa	35: 1	the **w** will rejoice and blossom.	6858
	35: 6	Water will gush forth in the **w** and streams	4497
	40: 3	make straight in the **w** a highway	6858
Jer	2: 6	of Egypt and led us through the **barren w,**	4497
	50:12	a **w,** a dry land, a desert.	4497

WILDS (1) [WILD]

Job	39: 4	and grow strong in the **w;**	1340

WILL (166 of 10192) [FREEWILL, WEAK-WILLED, WILLFUL, WILLFULLY, WILLING, WILLINGLY, WILLINGNESS, WILLS, WON'T] See Index of Articles Etc. for an Exhaustive Listing (See Introduction, page xi)

Ge	15: 2	the one who **w** inherit my estate	1201+5479

Ge	23:13	"Listen to me, if you **w.**	4273
	24:42	God of my master Abraham, if you **w,**	3780
	24:49	if you **w** show kindness and faithfulness	3780
	27:33	and indeed **he w** be blessed!"	2118
	27:46	my **life w** not be worth living."	2644+4200+4537
	43: 4	If you **w** send our brother along with us,	3780
	43: 5	But if you **w** not send him,	401
	45: 6	the next five years **there w** not be plowing	401
Ex	9: 9	and festering boils **w** break out on men	2118
	18:15	the people come to me to **seek** God's **w**	2011
Lev	24:12	until the **w** of the LORD should be made clear to them.	6584+7023
	25:46	*You can* **w** them to your children	5706
Dt	10:10	*It was* not his **w** to destroy you.	14
	11:17	and he will shut the heavens so that *it* **w**	2118
	15: 9	*do* not **show ill w** toward your needy brother	6524+8317
	25: 7	*He* **w** not fulfill the duty of a brother-in-law	14
	28:26	**there w** be no one to frighten them away.	401
	28:34	The sights you see **w** drive you mad.	2118
	28:66	You **w** live in constant suspense,	2118
	33:21	he carried out the LORD's **righteous w,**	7407
Jdg	6:36	"If you **w** save Israel by my hand	3780
Ru	4:15	*He* **w** renew your life and sustain you	2118
1Sa	2:25	for *it was* the LORD's **w** to put them	2911
	23:11	And the LORD said, *"He* **w."**	3718S
	23:12	And the LORD said, *"They* **w."**	6037S
2Sa	5:24	because **that w** mean the LORD has gone	255
	7:21	sake of your word and according to your **w,**	4213
	7:21	or none of us **w** escape from Absalom.	2118
2Ki	6: 3	"I **w,**" Elisha replied.	2143S
1Ch	13: 2	if it is the **w** of the LORD our God,	4946
	14:15	**because that w** mean God has gone out	3954
	17:19	of your servant and according to your **w,**	4213
Ezr	4:16	you **w** be left with nothing	10029+10378
	7:18	in accordance with the **w** of your God.	10668
	10:11	the God of your fathers, and do his **w.**	8356
Job	5: 1	"Call **if you w,** but who will answer you?	5528
Ps	40: 8	I desire to do your **w,** O my God;	8356
	103:21	you his servants who do his **w.**	8356
	143:10	Teach me to do your **w,**	8356
	144:14	**There w** be no breaching of walls,	401
Isa	5:24	so their roots **w** decay and their flowers	2118
	8: 8	Its outspread wings **w** cover the breadth	2118
	9: 7	and peace **there w** be no end.	401
	29: 2	*she* **w** mourn and lament,	2118
	30:29	And you **w** sing as on the night you	2118
	34:12	all her princes **w** vanish away.	2118
	47:12	Perhaps *you* **w** succeed,	3523
	53:10	the LORD's **w** to crush him and cause him	2911
	53:10	the **w** of the LORD will prosper in his hand.	2914
Jer	7:33	**there w** be no one to frighten them away.	401
	8:13	**There w** be no grapes on the vine.	401
	8:13	**There w** be no figs on the tree,	401
	13:19	and **there w** be no one to open them.	401
	14:16	**There w** be no one to bury them	401
	29: 7	because if it prospers, you too **w** prosper."	2118
	30: 7	**None w** be like it.	401+4946
	31: 6	**There w** be a day when watchmen cry out	3780
	42:17	not *one* of them **w** survive or escape	2118
	44:14	in Egypt **w** escape or survive to return to	2118
	50:20	but **there w** be none,	401
	51: 2	*they* **w** oppose her on every side in the day	2118
Eze	7:25	they will seek peace, but **there w** be none.	401
	12:25	But I the LORD will speak what *I* **w,**	1819+1821S
	18:13	Will such a man live? *He* **w** not!	2649S
	33:33	When all this comes true—and *it* surely **w**—	995S
Da	11:42	Egypt **w** not escape.	2118
Mic	5:12	and you **w** no longer cast spells.	2118
Zec	2: 9	so that their slaves **w** plunder them.	2118
Mt	6:10	your **w** be done on earth as it is in heaven.	2525
	7:21	the **w** of my Father who is in heaven.	2525
	10:29	apart from the **w** of your Father.	NIG
	12:50	the **w** of my Father in heaven is my brother	2525
	21:29	" '*I w* not,' he answered,	2527
	24: 6	You **w** hear of wars and rumors of wars,	3516
	26:39	Yet not as I **w,** but as you will."	2527
	26:39	Yet not as I will, but as you."	NIG
	26:42	may your **w** be done."	2525
Mk	3:35	Whoever does God's **w** is my brother	2525
	14:36	Yet not what I **w,** but what you will."	2527
	14:36	Yet not what I will, but what you **w."**	NIG
Lk	1:33	his kingdom **w** never end."	1639
	12:47	"That servant who knows his master's **w**	2525
	22:42	yet not my **w,** but yours be done."	2525
	23:25	and surrendered Jesus *to* their **w.**	2525
Jn	1:13	nor of human decision or a husband's **w,**	2525
	4:34	"is to do the **w** of him who sent me and	2525
	6: 9	but **how far w** they go among	1639+4047+5515
	6:38	down from heaven not to do my **w** but to do	2525
	6:38	but to do the **w** of him who sent me.	2525
	6:39	And this is the **w** of him who sent me,	2525
	6:40	For my Father's **w** is that everyone who	2525
	7:17	If anyone chooses to do God's **w,**	2525
	7:35	**W** he go where our people live scattered	3516
	9:31	He listens to the godly man who does his **w.**	2525
	19:24	"Let's decide by lot who **w** get it."	1639
Ac	4:28	your power and **w** had decided beforehand	1087
	17:31	when *he* **w** judge the world with justice by	3516
	18:15	I **w** not be a judge of such things."	1089
	18:21	"I **w** come back *if it is* God's **w."**	2527
	19:27	**w** be robbed of her divine majesty.	2118
	20:27	to proclaim to you the whole **w** of God.	1087
	21:14	"The Lord's **w** be done."	2525
	22:14	of our fathers has chosen you to know his **w**	2525
	23: 3	Then Paul said to him, "God **w** strike you,	3516
	24:15	that there **w** be a resurrection of both	3516

Ro	1:10	by God's **w** the way may be opened for me	2525
	2:18	if you know his **w** and approve of what	2525
	4:24	to whom God **w** credit righteousness—	3516
	8:13	according to the sinful nature, you **w** die;	3516
	8:18	not worth comparing with the glory that **w**	3516
	8:20	but by the **w** of the one who subjected it,	NIG
	9:19	For who resists his **w?"**	1088
	12: 2	**Then** you **w** be able to test and	1650+3836
	12: 2	to test and approve what God's **w** is—	2525
	12: 2	his good, pleasing and perfect **w.**	NIG
	15:12	Isaiah says, "The Root of Jesse **w** spring up,	1639
	15:32	that by God's **w** I may come to you with joy	2525
1Co	1: 1	an apostle of Christ Jesus by the **w** of God,	2525
	7:37	but has control over his own **w,**	2525
2Co	1: 1	an apostle of Christ Jesus by the **w** of God,	2525
	8: 5	and then to us in keeping with God's **w.**	2525
Gal	1: 4	according to the **w** of our God and Father,	2525
Eph	1: 1	an apostle of Christ Jesus by the **w** of God,	2525
	1: 5	in accordance with his pleasure and **w**—	2525
	1: 9	*of* his **w** according to his good pleasure,	2525
	1:11	in conformity with the purpose *of* his **w,**	2525
	5:17	but understand what the Lord's **w** is.	2525
	6: 6	doing the **w** of God from your heart.	2525
Php	1:19	to me **w turn out** for my deliverance.	1650
	2:13	for it is God who works in you *to* **w** and	2527
Col	1: 1	an apostle of Christ Jesus by the **w** of God,	2525
	1: 9	to fill you with the knowledge *of* his **w**	2525
	4:12	that you may stand firm in all the **w** of God,	2525
1Th	4: 3	It is God's **w** that you should be sanctified:	2525
	5:18	for this is God's **w** for you in Christ Jesus.	2525
2Th	3:10	"If a man **w** not work, he shall not eat."	2527
2Ti	1: 1	an apostle of Christ Jesus by the **w** of God,	2525
	2:26	who has taken them captive to do his **w.**	2525
	4: 1	who **w** judge the living and the dead,	3516
Heb	1:14	to serve those who **w** inherit salvation?	3516
	2: 4	distributed according to his **w.**	2526
	9:16	In the case of a **w,** it is necessary	1347
	9:17	**w** is in force only when somebody has died;	1347
	10: 7	I have come to do your **w,** O God.' "	2525
	10: 9	"Here I am, I have come to do your **w."**	2525
	10:10	And by that **w,** we have been made holy	2525
	10:27	of raging fire that **w** consume the enemies	3516
	10:36	so that when you have done the **w** of God,	2525
	13:21	with everything good for doing his **w,**	2525
Jas	4:15	you ought to say, "If it is the Lord's **w,**	2527
1Pe	2:15	For it is God's **w** that by doing good	2525
	3:17	It is better, if it is God's **w,** to suffer for	2525
	4: 2	but rather *for* the **w** of God.	2525
	4:19	those who suffer according to God's **w**	2525
2Pe	1:12	So *I* **w** always remind you of these things,	3516
	1:21	For prophecy never had its origin in the **w**	2525
1Jn	2:17	man who does the **w** of God lives forever.	2525
	5:14	that if we ask anything according to his **w,**	2525
Rev	1:19	what is now and what **w** take place later.	3516
	2:10	the devil **w** put some of you in prison	2240
	2:26	To him who overcomes and does my **w** to	2525
	4:11	and by your **w** they were created	2525
	12: 5	who **w** rule all the nations with	3516
	17: 8	and **w** come up out of the Abyss and go	3516

WILLFUL (3) [WILL]

Ps	19:13	Keep your servant also from **w** sins;	2294
Isa	10:12	for the **w** pride of his heart and	1542+7262
	57:17	yet he kept on in his **w** ways.	4213

WILLFULLY (1) [WILL]

Ps	78:18	They **w** put God to the test by	928+4222

WILLING (57) [WILL]

Ge	23: 8	"If you are **w** to let me bury my dead,	5883
Ex	10:27	and *he* was not **w** to let them go.	14
	35: 5	Everyone who is **w** is to bring to	4213+5618
	35:21	and everyone who was **w**	5605+8120
	35:22	All who were **w,** men and women	4213+5618
	35:26	And all the women who *were* **w** and	4213+5951
	35:29	and women who *were* **w** brought to	4213+5605
	36: 2	who *was* **w** to come and do the work.	4213+5951
Dt	29:20	LORD *will never be* **w** to forgive him;	14
Jdg	5: 9	with the **w volunteers** among the people.	5605
Ru	3:13	But if *he is* not **w,** as surely as the LORD	2911
1Sa	22:17	not **w** to raise a hand to strike the priests of	14
2Sa	6:10	He *was* not **w** to take the ark of the LORD	14
2Ki	8:19	the LORD *was* not **w** to destroy Judah.	14
	24: 4	and the LORD *was* not **w** to forgive.	14
1Ch	19:19	not **w** to help the Ammonites anymore.	14
	28: 9	wholehearted devotion and with a **w** mind,	2913
	28:21	and every *man* skilled in any craft	5618
	29: 5	who *is* **w** to consecrate himself today to	5605
	29: 9	The people rejoiced at the **w response**	5605
2Ch	21: 7	the LORD *was* not **w** to destroy the house	14
	29:31	whose hearts were **w** brought burnt offerings	5618
Job	6: 9	that God *would be* **w** to crush me,	3283
Ps	51:12	of your salvation and grant me a **w** spirit.	5618
	110: 3	Your troops will be **w** on your day of battle.	5607
	119:108	O LORD, the **w** praise of my mouth,	5607
Pr	11:26	but blessing crowns *him who is* **w** to sell.	AIT
	19:18	*do* not **be a w** party to his death.	5883+5951
Isa	1:19	If *you are* **w** and obedient,	14
Eze	3: 6	the house of Israel *is* not **w** to listen to you	14
	3: 7	to you because they *are* not **w** to listen	14
Da	3:28	the king's command and *were* **w** *to give* up	AIT
Mt	8: 2	if *you are* **w,** you can make me clean."	2527
	8: 3	*"I am* **w,"** he said.	2527
	11:14	And if *you are* **w** to accept it,	2527
	18:14	not **w** that any of these little ones should	2525

Mt	23: 4	but they themselves *are* not w to lift a finger	2527
	23:37	but *you* were not w.	2527
	26:15	"What *are you* w to give me if I hand him	2527
	26:41	The spirit is w, but the body is weak."	4609
Mk	1:40	"If *you are* w, you can make me clean."	2527
	1:41	"*I am* w," he said.	2527
	14:38	The spirit is w, but the body is weak.	4609
Lk	5:12	if *you are* w, you can make me clean."	2527
	5:13	"*I am* w," he said.	2527
	13:34	but *you* were not w!	2527
	22:42	if *you are* w, take this cup from me;	1089
Jn	6:21	Then *they* were w to take him into the boat,	2527
Ac	25: 9	"*Are you* w to go up to Jerusalem	2527
	25:20	be w to go to Jerusalem and stand trial there	1089
	26: 5	and can testify, if *they are* w,	2527
Ro	12:16	but be w to associate with people	5270
1Co	4:19	come to you very soon, if the Lord *is* w,	2527
	7:12	a wife who is not a believer and she *is* w	5306
	7:13	a husband who is not a believer and he *is* w	5306
1Ti	6:18	and to be generous and w to share.	NIG
1Pe	5: 2	because you must, but *because* you are w,	1731

WILLINGLY (5) [WILL]

Jdg	5: 2	when the people w **offer themselves**—	5605
1Ch	29: 6	in charge of the king's work **gave** w.	5605
	29:17	All these things *have* **I given** w and	5605
	29:17	w your people who are here *have* **given**	5605
La	3:33	he does not w bring affliction or grief	4213+4946

WILLINGNESS (2) [WILL]

2Co	8:11	that your eager w to do it may be matched	2527
	8:12	For if the w is there, the gift is acceptable	4608

WILLOW (1)

Eze	17: 5	He planted it like a w by abundant water,	7628

WILLOWS (KJV) See POPLAR

WILLS (1) [WILL]

Dt	21:16	when he w his property *to* his sons,	5706

WILY (1)

Job	5:13	and the schemes of the w are swept away.	7349

WIN (14) [WINNING, WINS, WON]

Pr	3: 4	Then *you will* w favor and a good name in	5162
Jer	5:28	not plead the case of the fatherless *to* w it,	7503
Mt	23:15	over land and sea *to* w a single convert,	4472
1Co	9:19	slave to everyone, to w as many as possible.	3045
	9:20	I became like a Jew, to w the Jews.	3045
	9:20	so as to w those under the law.	3045
	9:21	so as to w those not having the law.	3045
	9:22	To the weak I became weak, to w the weak.	3045
Gal	1:10	now **trying to** w the approval of men,	4275
	4:17	Those people are zealous to w you over,	NIG
Eph	6: 6	not only to w their **favor** when their eye is	473
Php	3:14	I press on toward the goal to w the prize	NIG
Col	3:22	when their eye on you and to w their **favor**,	473
1Th	4:12	so that your daily life may **the respect**	2361

WIND (125) [WINDBLOWN, WINDING, WINDS, WINDSTORM, WOUND]

Ge	8: 1	and he sent a w over the earth,	8120
	41: 6	thin and scorched by the **east w**.	7708
	41:23	and thin and scorched by the **east w**.	7708
	41:27	heads of grain scorched by the **east w**:	7708
Ex	10:13	and the LORD made an east w blow across	8120
	10:13	By morning the w had brought the locusts;	8120
	10:19	And the LORD changed the w to	NIH
	10:19	the wind to a very strong west w,	8120
	14:21	a strong east w and turned it into dry land.	8120
Nu	11:31	Now a w went out from the LORD	8120
2Sa	22:11	he soared on the wings of the w.	8120
1Ki	18:45	the sky grew black with clouds, the w rose,	8120
	19:11	and powerful w tore the mountains apart	8120
	19:11	but the LORD was not in the w.	8120
	19:11	After the w there was an earthquake,	8120
2Ki	3:17	You will see neither w nor rain,	8120
Job	1:19	when suddenly a mighty w swept in from	8120
	6:26	treat the words of a despairing man as w?	8120
	8: 2	Your words are a blustering w.	8120
	15: 2	or fill his belly with the **hot east w**?	7708
	21:18	How often are they like straw before the w,	8120
	27:21	The **east** w carries him off, and he is gone;	7708
	28:25	When he established the force of the w	8120
	30:15	my dignity is driven away as by the w;	8120
	30:22	snatch me up and drive me before the w;	8120
	37:17	the land lies hushed under the **south** w,	1999
	37:21	the skies after the w has swept them clean.	8120
Ps	1: 4	They are like chaff that the w blows away.	8120
	11: 6	a scorching w will be their lot.	8120
	18:10	he soared on the wings of the w.	8120
	18:42	I beat them as fine as dust borne on the w;	8120
	35: 5	May they be like chaff before the w,	8120
	48: 7	of Tarshish shattered by an east w.	8120
	68: 2	As smoke is blown away by the w,	NIH
	78:26	the **east** w from the heavens and led forth	7708
	78:26	from the heavens and led forth the **south** w	9402
	83:13	O my God, like chaff before the w.	8120
	103:16	the w blows over it and it is gone,	8120
	104: 3	and rides on the wings of the w.	8120

Ps	135: 7	and brings out the w from his storehouses.	8120
Pr	11:29	trouble on his family will inherit only w,	8120
	25:14	and w without rain is a man who boasts	8120
	25:23	As a north w brings rain,	8120
	27:16	like restraining the w or grasping oil with	8120
	30: 4	Who has gathered up the w in the hollow	8120
Ecc	1: 6	w blows to the south and turns to the north;	8120
	1:14	meaningless, a chasing after the w.	8120
	1:17	too, is a chasing after the w.	8120
	2:11	meaningless, a chasing after the w;	8120
	2:17	meaningless, a chasing after the w.	8120
	2:26	meaningless, a chasing after the w.	8120
	4: 4	meaningless, a chasing after the w.	8120
	4: 6	with toil and chasing after the w.	8120
	4:16	meaningless, a chasing after the w.	8120
	5:16	since he toils for the w?	8120
	6: 9	meaningless, a chasing after the w.	8120
	8: 8	No man has power over the w to contain it;	8120
	11: 4	Whoever watches the w will not plant;	8120
	11: 5	As you do not know the path of the w,	8120
SS	4:16	Awake, **north w**, and come, south wind!	7600
	4:16	Awake, north wind, and come, **south w**!	9402
Isa	7: 2	the trees of the forest are shaken by the w.	8120
	11:15	with a scorching w he will sweep his hand	8120
	17:13	driven before the w like chaff on the hills,	8120
	24:20	it sways like a hut in the w;	NIH
	26:18	we writhed in pain, but we gave birth to w.	8120
	27: 8	as on a day the **east** w blows.	7708
	28: 2	Like a hailstorm and a destructive w,	8551
	32: 2	like a shelter from the w and a refuge from	8120
	41:16	the w will pick them up,	8120
	41:29	their images are but w and confusion.	8120
	57:13	The w will carry all of them off,	8120
	64: 6	and like the w our sins sweep us away.	8120
Jer	2:24	sniffing the w in her craving—	8120
	4:11	"A scorching w *from* the barren heights in	8120
	4:12	a w too strong for that comes from me.	8120
	5:13	The prophets are but w and the word is not	8120
	10:13	and brings out the w from his storehouses.	8120
	13:24	like chaff driven by the desert w.	8120
	18:17	Like a w *from* the east,	8120
	22:22	The w will drive all your shepherds away,	8120
	30:23	a driving w swirling down on the heads of	6193
	51:16	and brings out the w from his storehouses.	8120
Eze	5: 2	And scatter a third to the w.	8120
	13:13	In my wrath I will unleash a **violent** w	6194+8120
	17:10	when the east w strikes it—	8120
	19:12	The east w made it shrivel,	8120
	27:26	But the east w will break you to pieces in	8120
Da	2:35	The w swept them away without leaving	10658
Hos	8: 7	"They sow the w and reap the whirlwind.	8120
	12: 1	Ephraim feeds on the w;	8120
	12: 1	the **east** w all day and multiplies lies	7708
	13:15	An east w *from* the LORD will come,	8120
Am	4:13	He who forms the mountains, creates the w,	8120
Jnh	1: 4	Then the LORD sent a great w on the sea,	8120
	4: 8	God provided a scorching east w,	8120
Hab	1: 9	a **desert** w and gather prisoners like sand.	7708
	1:11	they sweep past like the w and go on—	8120
Zec	5: 9	with the w in their wings!	8120
Mt	11: 7	A reed swayed by the w?	449
	14:24	by the waves because the w was against it.	449
	14:30	But when he saw the w, he was afraid and,	449
	14:32	climbed into the boat, the w died down.	449
Mk	4:39	rebuked the w and said to the waves,	449
	4:39	w died down and it was completely calm.	449
	4:41	Even the w and the waves obey him!"	449
	6:48	because the w was against them.	449
	6:51	and the w died down.	449
Lk	7:24	A reed swayed by the w?	449
	8:24	up and rebuked the w and the raging waters;	449
	12:55	And when the south w **blows,** you say,	4463
Jn	3: 8	The w blows wherever it pleases.	4460
	6:18	A strong w was blowing and	449
Ac	2: 2	blowing *of* a violent w came from heaven	4466
	27: 7	the w did not allow us to hold our course,	449
	27:13	When a gentle **south** w began to blow,	3803
	27:14	Before very long, a w of hurricane force,	449
	27:15	by the storm and could not head into the w;	449
	27:40	Then they hoisted the foresail *to* the w	4463
	28:13	The next day the **south** w came up,	3803
Eph	4:14	blown here and there *by* every w of teaching	449
Jas	1: 6	wave of the sea, **blown** and tossed by **the w**.	448
Jude	1:12	clouds without rain, blown along by the w;	449
Rev	6:13	from a fig tree when shaken by a strong w.	449
	7: 1	the four winds of the earth to prevent any w	449

WINDBLOWN (3) [WIND, BLOW]

Lev	26:36	the sound of a w leaf will put them to flight.	5622
Job	13:25	Will you torment a w leaf?	5622
Isa	41: 2	to w chaff with his bow.	5622

WINDING (1) [WIND]

Jdg	5: 6	travelers took to w paths.	6824

WINDOW (16) [WINDOWS]

Ge	8: 6	Noah opened the w he had made *in* the ark	2707
	26: 8	of the Philistines looked down from a w	2707
Jos	2:15	she let them down by a rope through the w,	2707
	2:18	in the w through which you let us down,	2707
	2:21	And she tied the scarlet cord in the w.	2707
1Sa	—	"Through the w peered Sisera's mother;	2707
	19:12	So Michal let David down through a w,	2707
2Sa	6:16	Michal daughter of Saul watched from a w.	2707
2Ki	9:30	arranged her hair and looked out of a w.	2707

2Ki	9:32	He looked up at the w and called out,	2707
	13:17	"Open the east w," he said, and he opened	2707
1Ch	15:29	Michal daughter of Saul watched from a w.	2707
Pr	7: 6	At the w *of* my house I looked out through	2707
Hos	13: 3	like smoke escaping through a w.	748
Ac	20: 9	in a w was a young man named Eutychus,	2600
2Co	11:33	in a basket from a w in the wall and slipped	2600

WINDOWS (13) [WINDOW]

1Ki	6: 4	He made narrow clerestory w in the temple.	2707
	7: 4	Its w were **placed high** in sets of three,	9209
Ecc	12: 3	and those looking through the w grow dim;	748
SS	2: 9	gazing through the w,	2707
Jer	9:21	Death has climbed in through our w	2707
	22:14	So he makes large w in it,	2707
Eze	41:16	the narrow w and galleries around the three	2707
	41:16	The floor, the wall up to the w,	2707
	41:16	and the w were covered.	2707
	41:26	the sidewalls of the portico were narrow w	2707
Da	6:10	to his upstairs room where the w opened	10348
Joel	2: 9	like thieves they enter through the w.	2707
Zep	2:14	Their calls will echo through the w,	2707

WINDS (31) [WIND]

Ge	2:11	it w **through** the entire land of Havilah,	6015
	2:13	it w **through** the entire land of Cush.	6015
Job	37: 9	the cold from the **driving** w.	4668
	38:24	or the place where the **east** w are scattered	7708
Ps	104: 4	He makes w his messengers,	8120
	148: 8	stormy w that do his bidding,	8120
Jer	49:32	to the w those who are in distant places	8120
	49:36	I will bring against Elam the four w from	8120
	49:36	I will scatter them to the four w,	8120
Eze	5:10	and will scatter all your survivors to the w.	8120
	5:12	and a third I will scatter to the w and pursue	8120
	12:14	to the w all those around him—	8120
	13:11	and **violent** w will burst forth.	6194+8120
	17:21	and the survivors will be scattered to the w.	8120
	37: 9	Come from the four w, O breath,	8120
Da	7: 2	and there before me were the four w	10658
	8: 8	up toward the four w *of* heaven.	8120
	11: 4	up and parceled out toward the four w	8120
Am	1:14	amid **violent** w on a stormy day.	6193
Zec	2: 6	"for I have scattered you to the four w	8120
Mt	7:25	and the w blew and beat against that house;	449
	7:27	and the w blew and beat against that house,	449
	8:26	he got up and rebuked the w and the waves,	449
	8:27	Even the w and the waves obey him!"	449
	24:31	they will gather his elect from the four w,	449
Mk	13:27	and gather his elect from the four w,	449
Lk	8:25	He commands even the w and the water,	449
Ac	27: 4	of Cyprus because the w were against us.	449
Heb	1: 7	"He makes his angels w, his servants	4460
Jas	3: 4	are so large and are driven by strong w,	449
Rev	7: 1	the four w of the earth to prevent any wind	449

WINDSTORM (2) [STORM, WIND]

Isa	29: 6	with w and tempest and flames of a	6070
Eze	1: 4	I saw a w coming out of the north—	6194+8120

WINDY (KJV) See TEMPEST

WINE (234) [WINES]

Ge	9:21	When he drank some of its w,	3516
	9:24	When Noah awoke from his w	3516
	14:18	king of Salem brought out bread and w.	3516
	19:32	Let's get our father to drink w and then lie	3516
	19:33	That night they got their father to drink w,	3516
	19:34	Let's get him to drink w again tonight,	3516
	19:35	So they got their father to drink w that night	3516
	27:25	and he brought *some* w and he drank.	3516
	27:28	an abundance of grain and **new** w.	9408
	27:37	I have sustained him with grain and **new** w.	9408
	49:11	he will wash his garments in w,	3516
	49:12	His eyes will be darker than w,	3516
Ex	29:40	a quarter of a hin of w as a drink offering.	3516
Lev	10: 9	"You and your sons are not to drink w	3516
	23:13	its drink offering of a quarter of a hin of w.	3516
Nu	6: 3	from w and other fermented drink and must	3516
	6: 3	and must not drink vinegar made from w or	3516
	6:20	After that, the Nazirite may drink w.	3516
	15: 5	a quarter of a hin of w as a drink offering.	3516
	15: 7	and a third of a hin of w as a drink offering.	3516
	15:10	bring half a hin of w as a drink offering.	3516
	18:12	and all the finest **new** w and grain they give	9408
	28:14	to be a drink offering of half a hin of w;	3516
Dt	7:13	your grain, **new** w and oil,	9408
	11:14	gather in your grain, **new** w and oil.	9408
	12:17	the tithe of your grain and **new** w and oil,	9408
	14:23	Eat the tithe of your grain, **new** w and oil,	9408
	14:26	cattle, sheep, w or other fermented drink,	3516
	18: 4	firstfruits of your grain, **new** w and oil,	9408
	28:39	but you will not drink the w or gather	3516
	28:51	They will leave you no grain, **new** w or oil,	9408
	29: 6	and drank no w or other fermented drink.	3516
	32:33	Their w is the venom of serpents,	3516
	32:38	and drank the w *of* their drink offerings?	3516
	33:28	in a land of grain and **new** w,	9408
Jdg	—	the vine answered, 'Should I give up my w	9408
	13: 4	Now see to it that you drink no w	3516
	13: 7	drink no w or other fermented drink and do	3516
	13:14	nor drink any w or other fermented drink	3516
	19:19	bread and w for ourselves you servants—	3516
Ru	2:14	and dip it in the w vinegar."	2810

Ref		Text	Strong's
1Sa	1:14	Get rid of your w."	3516
	1:15	I have not been drinking w or beer;	3516
	1:24	an ephah of flour and a skin of w,	3516
	10: 3	and another a skin of w.	3516
	16:20	a skin of w and a young goat and sent them	3516
	25:18	two skins of w, five dressed sheep,	3516
2Sa	13:28	in high spirits from drinking w and I say	3516
	16: 1	a hundred cakes of figs and a skin of w.	3516
	16: 2	and the w is to refresh those who become	3516
2Ki	18:32	a land of grain and new w,	9408
1Ch	9:29	as well as the flour and w, and the oil,	3516
	12:40	raisin cakes, w, oil, cattle and sheep,	3516
	27:27	the produce of the vineyards for the w vats.	3516
2Ch	2:10	of w and twenty thousand baths	3516
	2:15	and the olive oil and w he promised.	3516
	11:11	with supplies of food, olive oil and w.	3516
	31: 5	of their grain, new w, oil and honey and all	9408
	32:28	harvest of grain, new w and oil;	9408
Ezr	6: 9	and wheat, salt, w and oil,	10271
	7:22	a hundred baths of w, a hundred baths of	10271
Ne	2: 1	when w was brought for him,	3516
	2: 1	I took the w and gave it to the king.	3516
	5:11	the money, grain, new w and oil."	9408
	5:15	from them in addition to food and w.	3516
	5:18	and every ten days an abundant supply of w	3516
	10:37	of the fruit of all our trees and of our new w	9408
	10:39	new w and oil to the storerooms where	9408
	13: 5	new w and oil prescribed for the Levites,	9408
	13:12	new w and oil into the storerooms.	9408
	13:15	together with w, grapes, figs	3516
Est	1: 7	W *was served* in goblets of gold,	9197
	1: 7	and the royal w was abundant,	3516
	1: 8	the king instructed all the w **stewards**	1074+8042
	1:10	King Xerxes was in high spirits from w,	3516
	5: 6	As they were drinking w,	3516
	7: 2	as they were drinking w on that second day,	3516
	7: 7	left his w and went out into	3516
Job	1:13	and daughters were feasting and drinking w	3516
	1:18	and daughters were feasting and drinking w	3516
	32:19	inside I am like bottled-up w,	3516
Ps	4: 7	when their grain and w abound.	9408
	60: 3	you have given us w that makes us stagger.	3516
	75: 8	a cup full of foaming w mixed with spices;	3516
	78:65	as a man wakes from the stupor of w,	3516
	104:15	w that gladdens the heart of man,	3516
Pr	3:10	and your vats will brim over with **new** w.	9408
	4:17	of wickedness and drink the w *of* violence.	3516
	9: 2	prepared her meat and mixed her w;	3516
	9: 5	eat my food and drink the w I have mixed.	3516
	20: 1	W is a mocker and beer a brawler;	3516
	21:17	whoever loves w and oil will never be rich.	3516
	23:20	Do not join those who drink too much w	3516
	23:30	Those who linger over w,	3516
	23:30	who go to sample **bowls of mixed** w.	4932
	23:31	Do not gaze at w when it is red,	3516
	31: 4	O Lemuel—not for kings to drink w,	3516
	31: 6	w to those who are in anguish!	3516
Ecc	2: 3	I tried cheering myself with w,	3516
	9: 7	and drink your w with a joyful heart,	3516
	10:19	and w makes life merry,	3516
SS	1: 2	for your love is more delightful than w.	3516
	1: 4	we will praise your love more than w.	3516
	4:10	much more pleasing is your love than w,	3516
	5: 1	I have drunk my w and my milk.	3516
	7: 2	that never lacks **blended** w.	4641
	7: 9	and your mouth like the best w.	3516
	7: 9	May the w go straight to my lover,	NIH
	8: 2	I would give you spiced w to drink,	3516
Isa	1:22	your **choice** w is diluted with water.	6011
	5:10	vineyard will produce only a bath of w,	NIH
	5:11	at night till they are inflamed with w.	3516
	5:12	tambourines and flutes and w,	3516
	5:22	Woe to those who are heroes at drinking w	3516
	16:10	no one treads out w at the presses,	3516
	22:13	eating of meat and drinking of w!	3516
	24: 7	The **new** w dries up and the vine withers;	9408
	24: 9	No longer do they drink w with a song;	3516
	24:11	In the streets they cry out for w;	3516
	25: 6	a banquet of **aged** w—the best of meats	9069
	28: 1	the pride of those laid low by w!	3516
	28: 7	also stagger from w and reel from beer:	3516
	28: 7	from beer and are befuddled with w;	3516
	29: 9	be drunk, but not from w, stagger,	3516
	36:17	a land of grain and new w,	9408
	49:26	be drunk on their own blood, as with w.	6747
	51:21	made drunk, but not with w.	3516
	55: 1	buy w and milk without money and	3516
	56:12	"Come," each one cries, "let me get w!	3516
	62: 8	the new w for which you have toiled;	9408
	65:11	and fill **bowls of mixed** w for Destiny,	4932
Jer	13:12	Every wineskin should be filled with w.'	3516
	13:12	every wineskin should be filled with w?'	3516
	23: 9	like a man overcome by w,	3516
	25:15	the w of my wrath and make all the nations	3516
	31:12	the grain, the **new** w and the oil,	9408
	35: 2	of the house of the LORD and give them w	3516
	35: 5	Then I set bowls full of w and some cups	3516
	35: 5	and said to them, "Drink *some* w."	3516
	35: 6	But they replied, "We do not drink w,	3516
	35: 6	nor your descendants must ever drink w.	3516
	35: 8	daughters have ever drunk w	3516
	35:14	to drink w and this command has been kept.	3516
	35:14	To this day they do not drink w,	NIH
	40:10	but you are to harvest the w,	3516
	40:12	And they harvested an abundance of w	3516
	48:11	like w left on its dregs,	NIH
	48:33	I have stopped the flow of w from	3516
Jer	51: 7	The nations drank her w;	3516
La	2:12	"Where is bread and w?"	3516
Eze	27:18	in w *from* Helbon and wool from Zahar.	3516
	44:21	to drink when he enters the inner court.	3516
Da	1: 5	of food and w from the king's table.	3516
	1: 8	to defile himself with the royal food and w,	3516
	1:16	and the w they were to drink	3516
	5: 1	for a thousand of his nobles and drank w	10271
	5: 2	While Belshazzar was drinking his w,	10271
	5: 4	As they drank the w, they praised the gods	10271
	5:23	and your concubines drank w from them.	10271
	10: 3	no meat or w touched my lips;	3516
Hos	2: 8	who gave her the grain, the **new** w and oil,	9408
	2: 9	and my **new** w when it is ready.	9408
	2:22	respond to the grain, the **new** w and oil,	9408
	4:11	to prostitution, to **old** w and new,	3516
	7: 5	the princes become inflamed with w,	3516
	7:14	for grain and **new** w but turn away from me.	9408
	9: 2	the **new** w will fail them.	9408
	9: 4	not pour out w **offerings** to the LORD,	3516
	14: 7	his fame will be like the w *from* Lebanon.	3516
Joel	1: 5	Wail, all you drinkers of w,	3516
	1: 5	wail because of the **new** w,	6747
	1:10	grain is destroyed, the **new** w is dried up,	9408
	2:19	"I am sending you grain, **new** w and oil,	9408
	2:24	the vats will overflow with **new** w and oil.	9408
	3: 3	they sold girls for w that they might drink.	3516
	3:18	"In that day the mountains will drip **new** w,	6747
Am	2: 8	the house of their god they drink w *taken*	3516
	2:12	the Nazirites drink w and commanded	3516
	5:11	you will not drink their w.	3516
	6: 6	You drink w by the bowlful and use	3516
	9:13	**New** w will drip from the mountains	6747
	9:14	will plant vineyards and drink their w;	3516
Mic	2:11	'I will prophesy for you plenty of w	3516
	6:15	you will crush grapes but not drink the w.	3516
Na	1:10	among thorns and drunk from their w;	6011
Hab	2: 5	indeed, he betrays him;	3516
Zep	1:12	who are like w left on its dregs, who think,	NIH
	1:13	will plant vineyards but not drink the w.	3516
Hag	1:11	on the grain, the **new** w, the oil	9408
	2:12	some w, oil or other food,	3516
	2:16	to a w **vat** to draw fifty measures,	3676
Zec	9:15	They will drink and roar as with w;	3516
	9:17	and **new** w the young women.	9408
	10: 7	and their hearts will be glad as with w.	3516
Mt	9:17	Neither do men pour new w into old	3885
	9:17	the w will run out and the wineskins will	3885
	9:17	No, they pour new w into new wineskins,	3885
	27:34	There they offered Jesus w to drink,	3885
	27:48	He filled it *with* w **vinegar**,	3954
Mk	2:22	no one pours new w into old wineskins.	3885
	2:22	If he does, the w will burst the skins,	3885
	2:22	both the w and the wineskins will be ruined.	3885
	2:22	No, he pours new w into new wineskins."	3885
	15:23	Then they offered him w mixed with myrrh,	3885
	15:36	filled a sponge *with* w **vinegar**,	3954
Lk	1:15	to take w or other fermented drink,	3885
	5:37	no one pours new w into old wineskins.	3885
	5:37	If he does, the new w will burst the skins,	3885
	5:37	**the** w will run out and the wineskins will	899S
	5:38	new w must be poured into new wineskins.	3885
	5:39	no one after drinking old w wants the new,	NIG
	7:33	nor drinking w, and you say, 'He has	3885
	10:34	bandaged his wounds, pouring on oil and w.	3885
	23:36	They offered him w **vinegar**	3954
Jn	2: 3	When the w was gone,	3885
	2: 3	"They have no more w."	3885
	2: 9	the water that had been turned into w.	3885
	2:10	the choice w first and then the cheaper wine	3885
	2:10	the choice wine first and then the cheaper w	NIG
	4:46	where he had turned the water into w.	3885
	19:29	A jar *of* w **vinegar** was there,	3954
Ac	2:13	"They have had too much w."	1183
Ro	14:21	to eat meat or drink w or to do anything else	3885
Eph	5:18	Do not get drunk *on* w,	3885
1Ti	5:23	sincere, not indulging *in* much w,	3885
	5:23	and use a little w because of your stomach	3885
Tit	2: 3	not to be slanderers or addicted *to* much w,	3885
Rev	6: 6	and do not damage the oil and the w!"	3885
	14: 8	the maddening w of her adulteries.	3885
	14:10	too, will drink of the w of God's fury,	3885
	16:19	and gave her the cup filled *with* the w of	3885
	17: 2	of the earth were intoxicated with the w	3885
	18: 3	the nations have drunk the maddening w	3885
	18:13	myrrh and frankincense, of w and olive oil,	3885

WINEBIBBER, WINEBIBBERS (KJV)
See DRUNKARD, DRUNKARDS

WINEFAT (KJV) See WINEPRESS

WINEPRESS (17) [WINEPRESSES]

Ref		Text	Strong's
Nu	18:27	the threshing floor or juice from the w.	3676
	18:30	the product of the threshing floor or the w.	3676
Dt	15:14	your threshing floor and your w.	3676
	16:13	of your threshing floor and your w.	3676
Jdg	6:11	in a w to keep it from the Midianites.	1780
	7:25	and Zeeb at the w *of* Zeeb.	3676
2Ki	6:27	From the threshing floor? From the w?"	3676
Isa	5: 2	He built a watchtower in it and cut out a w	3676
	63: 2	like those of one treading the w?	1780
	63: 3	"I have trodden the w alone;	7053
La	1:15	In his w the Lord has trampled	1780
Joel	3:13	for the w is full and the vats overflow—	1780
Mt	21:33	dug a w in it and built a watchtower.	3332
Mk	12: 1	dug a **pit for the** w and built a watchtower.	5700
Rev	14:19	into the great w of God's wrath.	3332
	14:20	They were trampled in the w outside	3332
	19:15	He treads the w of the fury of	3332+3836+3885

WINEPRESSES (4) [WINEPRESS]

Ref		Text	Strong's
Ne	13:15	In those days I saw men in Judah treading w	1780
Job	24:11	they tread the w, yet suffer thirst.	3676
Hos	9: 2	Threshing floors and w will not feed	3676
Zec	14:10	from the Tower of Hananel to the royal w.	3676

WINES (1) [WINE]

Ref		Text	Strong's
Isa	25: 6	the best of meats and the finest of w.	9069

WINESKIN (4) [WINESKINS]

Ref		Text	Strong's
Ps	119:83	Though I am like a w in the smoke,	5532
Jer	13:12	Every w should be filled with wine.'	5574
	13:12	that every w should be filled with wine?'	5574
Hab	2:15	pouring it from the w till they are drunk,	2827

WINESKINS (12) [WINESKIN]

Ref		Text	Strong's
Jos	9: 4	with worn-out sacks and old w,	3516+5532
	9:13	And these w that we filled were new,	3516+5532
Job	32:19	like new w ready to burst.	199
Mt	9:17	Neither do men pour new wine into old w,	829
	9:17	the wine will run out and the w will	829
	9:17	No, they pour new wine into new w,	829
Mk	2:22	And no one pours new wine into old w.	829
	2:22	and both the wine and the w will be ruined.	829
	2:22	No, he pours new wine into new w."	829
Lk	5:37	And no one pours new wine into old w.	829
	5:37	the wine will run out and the w will	829
	5:38	No, new wine must be poured into new w.	829

WING (16) [WINGED, WINGS, WINGSPAN]

Ref		Text	Strong's
1Ki	6:24	w of the first cherub was five cubits long,	4053
	6:24	and the other w five cubits—	4053
	6:24	ten cubits from w tip to wing tip.	4053
	6:24	ten cubits from wing tip to w tip.	4053
	6:27	The w of one cherub touched one wall,	4053
	6:27	the w of the other touched the other wall,	4053
2Ch	3:11	w of the first cherub was five cubits long	4053
	3:11	while its other w, also five cubits long,	4053
	3:11	touched the w of the other cherub.	4053
	3:12	Similarly one w of the second cherub	4053
	3:12	and its other w, also five cubits long,	4053
	3:12	touched the w of the first cherub.	4053
Ecc	10:20	and a **bird on the** w may report what you say.	1251+4053
Isa	10:14	not one flapped a w, or opened its mouth	4053
Eze	1:11	one touching the w of another creature on	NIH
Da	9:27	And on a w *[of the temple]* he will set up	4053

WINGED (4) [WING]

Ref		Text	Strong's
Ge	1:21	and every w bird according to its kind.	4053
Lev	11:21	some w creatures that walk on all fours	6416
	11:23	But all other w creatures that have four	6416
Dt	14:20	any w **creature** that is clean you may eat.	6416

WINGS (73) [WING]

Ref		Text	Strong's
Ge	7:14	according to its kind, everything with w.	4053
Ex	19: 4	on eagles' w and brought you to myself.	4053
	25:20	to have their w spread upward,	4053
	37: 9	The cherubim had their w spread upward,	4053
Lev	1:17	He shall tear it open by the w,	4053
Dt	32:11	that spreads its w to catch them	4053
Ru	2:12	under whose w you have come to take refuge."	4053
2Sa	22:11	he soared on the w of the wind.	4053
1Ki	6:27	with their w spread out,	4053
	6:27	and their w touched each other in	4053
	8: 6	and put it beneath the w of the cherubim.	4053
	8: 7	The cherubim spread their w over the place	4053
1Ch	28:18	that spread their w and shelter the ark of	NIH
2Ch	3:13	w of these cherubim extended twenty cubits.	4053
	5: 7	and put it beneath the w of the cherubim.	4053
	5: 8	The cherubim spread their w over the place	4053
Job	39:13	"The w of the ostrich flap joyfully,	4053
	39:26	by your wisdom and spread his w toward	4053
Ps	17: 8	hide me in the shadow of your w	4053
	18:10	he soared on the w of the wind.	4053
	36: 7	in the shadow of your w.	4053
	55: 6	I said, "Oh, that I had the w of a dove!	88
	57: 1	I will take refuge in the shadow of your w	4053
	61: 4	and take refuge in the shelter of your w.	4053
	63: 7	I sing in the shadow of your w.	4053
	68:13	w of *[my]* dove are sheathed with silver,	4053
	91: 4	and under his w you will find refuge;	4053
	104: 3	his chariot and rides on the w of the wind.	4053
	139: 9	If I rise on the w of the dawn,	4053
Pr	23: 5	for they will surely sprout w and fly off to	4053
Isa	6: 2	Above him were seraphs, each with six w:	4053
	6: 2	With two w they covered their faces,	NIH
	8: 8	Its outspread w will cover the breadth	4053
	18: 1	to the land of whirring w along the rivers	4053
	34:15	for her young under the shadow of her w;	NIH
	40:31	They will soar on like eagles;	88
Jer	48:40	spreading its w over Moab.	4053
	49:22	spreading its w over Bozrah.	4053
Eze	1: 6	but each of them had four faces and four w.	4053

Eze	1: 8	Under their w on their four sides they had	4053

Eze 1:8 Under their w on their four sides they had 4053
1:8 All four of them had faces and w, 4053
1:9 and their w touched one another. 4053
1:11 Their w were spread out upward; 4053
1:11 each had two w, NIH
1:11 and two w covering its body. NIH
1:23 the expanse their w were stretched out one 4053
1:23 and each had two w covering its body. NIH
1:24 I heard the sound of their w, 4053
1:24 When they stood still, they lowered their w. 4053
1:25 as they stood with lowered w. 4053
3:13 of the w of the living creatures brushing 4053
10:5 The sound of the w of the cherubim could 4053
10:8 (Under the w of the cherubim could 4053
10:12 their hands and their w, 4053
10:16 when the cherubim spread their w to rise 4053
10:16 the cherubim spread their w and rose from 4053
10:21 Each had four faces and four w, 4053
10:21 and under their w was what looked like 4053
11:22 the wheels beside them, spread their w, and 4053
17:3 A great eagle with powerful w, 4053
17:7 with powerful w and full plumage. 4053
Da 7:4 and it had the w of an eagle. 10149
7:4 until its w were torn off and it was lifted 10149
7:6 on its back it had four w like those of a bird. 10149
Zec 5:9 with the wind in their w! 4053
5:9 They had w like those of a stork, 4053
Mal 4:2 will rise with healing in its w. 4053
Mt 23:37 as a hen gathers her chicks under her w, 4763
Lk 13:34 as a hen gathers her chicks under her w, 4763
Rev 4:8 Each of the four living creatures had six w 4763
4:8 with eyes all around, even under his w. NIG
9:9 the sound of their w was like the thundering 4763
12:14 The woman was given the two w of 4763

WINGSPAN (1) [WING]
2Ch 3:11 The total w of the cherubim was twenty 802+4053

WINK (1) [WINKS]
Ps 35:19 without reason maliciously w the eye. 7975

WINKS (3) [WINK]
Pr 6:13 who w with his eye, signals with his feet 7975
10:10 He who w maliciously causes grief, 6524+7975
16:30 He who w with his eye is plotting perversity 6781

WINNING (2) [WIN]
Ex 17:11 As long as Moses held up his hands, the Israelites were w, 1504
17:11 lowered his hands, the Amalekites were w. 1504

WINNOW (4) [WINNOWING, WINNOWS]
Isa 41:16 You will w them, the wind will pick them up 2430
Jer 4:11 but not to w or cleanse; 2430
15:7 I will w them with a winnowing fork at 2430
51:2 I will send foreigners to Babylon to w her 2430

WINNOWED (KJV) See SPREAD OUT

WINNOWING (4) [WINNOW]
Ru 3:2 be w barley on the threshing floor. 2430
Jer 15:7 with a w fork at the city gates of the land. 4665
Mt 3:12 His w fork is in his hand, 4768
Lk 3:17 His w fork is in his hand 4768

WINNOWS (2) [WINNOW]
Pr 20:8 he w out all evil with his eyes. 2430
20:26 A wise king w out the wicked; 2430

WINS (2) [WIN]
Pr 11:30 and he who w souls is wise. 4374
13:15 Good understanding w favor, 5989

WINTER (16) [WINTERED]
Ge 8:22 cold and heat, summer and w, 3074
Ps 74:17 you made both summer and w. 3074
SS 2:11 The w is past; the rains are over and gone. 6255
Isa 18:6 the wild animals all w. 3069
Jer 36:22 and the king was sitting in the w apartment, 3074
Hos 6:3 he will come to us like the w rains, 1773
Am 3:15 the w house along with the summer house; 3074
Zec 14:8 in summer and in w. 3074
Mt 24:20 Pray that your flight will not take place in w 5930
Mk 13:18 Pray that this will not take place in w, 5930
Jn 10:22 Feast of Dedication at Jerusalem. It was w, 5930
Ac 27:12 Since the harbor was unsuitable to w in, 4200
27:12 hoping to reach Phoenix and w there. 4199
1Co 16:6 or even spend the w, 4199
2Ti 4:21 Do your best to get here before w. 5930
Tit 3:12 because I have decided to w there. 4199

WINTERED (1) [WINTER]
Ac 28:11 to sea in a ship that had w in the island. 4199

WIPE (14) [WIPED, WIPES, WIPING]
Ge 6:7 So the LORD said, "I will w mankind, 4681
7:4 and I will w from the face of the earth 4681
Ex 23:23 and I will w them out. 3948
32:12 and to w them off the face of the earth 3983

Dt 7:24 and you will w out their names from 6
12:3 and w out their names from those places. 6
Jos 7:9 and w out our name from the earth. 4162
9:24 to w out all its inhabitants from before you. 9012
1Sa 24:21 or w out my name from my father's family. 9012
2Ki 21:13 I will w out Jerusalem as one wipes a dish, 4681
Isa 25:8 The Sovereign LORD will w away 4681
Lk 10:11 that sticks to our feet we w off against you. 669
Rev 7:17 God will w away every tear from their eyes. 1981
21:4 He will w every tear from their eyes. 1981

WIPED (15) [WIPE]
Ge 7:23 on the face of the earth was w out; 4681
7:23 the ground and the birds of the air were w 4681
Ex 9:15 with a plague that would have w you off 3948
Jdg 21:17 "so that a tribe of Israel will not be w out. 4681
1Sa 15:18 on them until you have w them out.' 3983
Ps 119:87 They almost w me from the earth, 3983
Pr 6:33 and his shame will never be w away; 4681
Isa 26:14 you w out all memory of them. 6
Eze 6:6 and what you have made be w out. 4681
Zep 1:11 all your merchants will be w out, 1950
Lk 7:38 Then she w them with her hair, 1726
7:44 with her tears and w them with her hair. 1726
Jn 11:2 on the Lord and w his feet with her hair. 1726
12:3 on Jesus' feet and w his feet with her hair. 1726
Ac 3:19 so that your sins may be w out, 1981

WIPES (2) [WIPE]
2Ki 21:13 I will wipe out Jerusalem as one w a dish, 4681
Pr 30:20 She eats and w her mouth and says, 4681

WIPING (1) [WIPE]
2Ki 21:13 w it and turning it upside down. 4681

WISDOM (218) [WISE]
Ge 3:6 and also desirable for gaining w, 8505
Ex 28:3 skilled men to whom I have given w 2683+8120
Dt 4:6 for this will show your w and understanding 2683
34:9 son of Nun was filled with the spirit of w 2683
2Sa 14:20 My lord has w like that of an angel 2682
1Ki 2:6 Deal with him according to your w, 2683
2:9 You are a man of w; 2682
3:28 because they saw that he had w from God 2683
4:29 God gave Solomon w and very great insight 2683
4:30 Solomon's w was greater than the wisdom 2683
4:30 Solomon's wisdom was greater than the w 2683
4:30 and greater than all the w of Egypt. 2683
4:34 nations came to listen to Solomon's w, 2683
4:34 who had heard of his w. 2683
5:12 The LORD gave Solomon w, just as he 2683
10:4 queen of Sheba saw all the w of Solomon 2683
10:6 about your achievements and your w is true. 2683
10:7 in w and wealth you have far exceeded 2683
10:8 before you and hear your w! 2683
10:23 in w and than all the other kings of the earth. 2683
10:24 with Solomon to hear the w God had put 2683
11:41 all he did and the w he displayed— 2683
2Ch 1:10 Give me w and knowledge, 2683
1:11 for w and knowledge to govern my people 2683
1:12 and knowledge will be given you. 2683
9:3 the queen of Sheba saw the w of Solomon, 2683
9:5 about your achievements and your w is true. 2683
9:6 half the greatness of your w was told me; 2683
9:7 before you and hear your w! 2683
9:22 and w than all the other kings of the earth. 2683
9:23 with Solomon to hear the w God had put 2683
Ezr 7:25 in accordance with the w of your God, 10266
Job 4:21 so that they die without w?' 2683
9:4 His w is profound, his power is vast. 2682
11:6 and disclose to you the secrets of w, 2683
11:6 for true w has two sides. 9370
12:2 and w will die with you! 2683
12:12 Is not w found among the aged? 2683
12:13 "To God belong w and power; 2683
13:5 For you, that would be w. 2683
15:8 Do you limit w to yourself? 2683
26:3 advice you have offered to one without w! 2683
26:12 by his w he cut Rahab to pieces. 9312
28:12 "But where can w be found? 2683
28:18 the price of w is beyond rubies. 2683
28:20 "Where then does w come from? 2683
28:27 then he looked at w and appraised it; 2023S
28:28 is w, and to shun evil is understanding.'" 2683
32:7 advanced years should teach w.' 2683
32:13 Do not say, 'We have found w; 2683
33:33 be silent, and I will teach you w." 2683
38:36 who w or gave understanding to the mind? 2683
38:37 Who has the w to count the clouds? 2683
39:17 for God did not endow her with w 2683
39:26 "Does the hawk take flight by your w 1069
Ps 37:30 The mouth of the righteous man utters w, 2683
49:3 My mouth will speak words of w; 2684
51:6 you teach me w in the inmost place. 2683
90:12 that we may gain a heart of w. 2683
104:24 In w you made them all; 2683
105:22 as he pleased and teach his elders w. 2681
111:10 The fear of the LORD is the beginning of w; 2683
Pr 1:2 for attaining w and discipline; 2683
1:7 but fools despise w and discipline. 2683
1:20 W calls aloud in the street, 2684
2:2 to w and applying your heart 2683

Pr 2:6 For the LORD gives w, 2683
2:10 For w will enter your heart, 2683
2:12 W will save you from the ways NIH
3:13 Blessed is the man who finds w, 2683
3:19 By w the LORD laid the earth's foundations, 2683
4:5 Get w, get understanding; 2683
4:6 Do not forsake w, and she will protect you; 2023S
4:7 W is supreme; therefore get wisdom. 2683
4:7 Wisdom is supreme; therefore get w. 2683
4:11 I guide you in the way of w and lead you 2683
5:1 My son, pay attention to my w, 2683
7:4 Say to w, "You are my sister," 2683
8:1 Does not w call out? 2683
8:11 for w is more precious than rubies, 2683
8:12 "I, w, dwell together with prudence; 2683
9:1 W has built her house; 2684
9:10 fear of the LORD is the beginning of w, 2683
9:12 If you are wise, your w will reward you; 2681
10:13 W is found on the lips of the discerning, 2683
10:23 but a man of understanding delights in w. 2683
10:31 The mouth of the righteous brings forth w, 2683
11:2 but with humility comes w. 2683
12:8 A man is praised according to his w, 8507
13:10 but w is found in those who take advice. 2683
14:6 The mocker seeks w and finds none, 2683
14:8 The w of the prudent is to give thought 2683
14:33 W reposes in the heart of the discerning and 2683
15:33 The fear of the LORD teaches a man w, 2683
16:16 How much better to get w than gold, 2683
17:16 since he has no desire to get w? 2683
17:24 A discerning man keeps w in view, 2683
18:4 but the fountain of w is a bubbling brook. 2683
19:8 He who gets w loves his own soul; 4213
19:11 A man's w gives him patience; 8507
21:11 a mocker is punished, the simple gain w; 2681
21:30 There is no w, no insight, 2683
23:4 have the w to show restraint. 1069
23:9 for he will scorn the w of your words. 8507
23:23 get w, discipline and understanding. 2683
24:3 By w a house is built, 2683
24:7 W is too high for a fool; 2684
24:14 Know also that w is sweet to your soul; 2683
28:26 but he who walks in w is kept safe. 2683
29:3 A man who loves w brings joy to his father, 2683
29:15 The rod of correction imparts w, 2683
30:3 I have not learned w, 2683
31:26 She speaks with w, and faithful instruction 2683
Ecc 1:13 to study and to explore by w all that is done 2683
1:16 in w more than anyone who has ruled 2683
1:16 I have experienced much of w 2683
1:17 I applied myself to the understanding of w, 2683
1:18 For with much w comes much sorrow; 2683
2:3 my mind still guiding me with w. 2683
2:9 In all this my w stayed with me. 2683
2:12 Then I turned my thoughts to consider w, 2683
2:13 I saw that w is better than folly, 2683
2:21 For a man may do his work with w, 2683
2:26 To the man who pleases him, God gives w, 2683
7:11 W, like an inheritance, is a good thing 2683
7:12 W is a shelter as money is a shelter, 2683
7:12 that w preserves the life of its possessor. 2683
7:19 W makes one wise man more powerful than ten rulers 2683
7:23 All this I tested by w and I said, 2683
7:24 Whatever w may be, it is far off 8611S
7:25 to search out w and the scheme of things 2683
8:1 W brightens a man's face 2683
8:16 When I applied my mind to know w and 2683
9:10 nor planning nor knowledge nor w. 2683
9:13 I also saw under the sun this example of w 2683
9:15 and he saved the city by his w. 2683
9:16 So I said, "W is better than strength." 2683
9:16 But the poor man's w is despised, 2683
9:18 W is better than weapons of war, 2683
10:1 so a little folly outweighs w and honor. 2683
Isa 10:13 of my hand I have done this, and by my w, 2683
11:2 the Spirit of w and of understanding, 2683
28:29 wonderful in counsel and magnificent in w. 9370
29:14 the w of the wise will perish, 2683
33:6 of salvation and w and knowledge; 2683
47:10 Your w and knowledge mislead you 2683
Jer 8:9 what kind of w do they have? 2683
9:23 "Let not the wise man boast of his w or 2683
10:12 by his w and stretched out the heavens 2683
49:7 "Is there no longer w in Teman? 2683
49:7 Has their w decayed? 2683
51:15 by his w and stretched out the heavens 2683
Eze 28:4 By your w and understanding you have gained wealth 2683
28:7 their swords against your beauty and w 2683
28:12 full of w and perfect in beauty. 2683
28:17 and you corrupted your w because 2683
Da 1:20 In every matter of w and understanding 2683
2:14 Daniel spoke to him with w and tact. 10539
2:20 w and power are his. 10266
2:21 He gives w to the wise and knowledge to 10266
2:23 You have given me w and power, 10266
2:30 I have greater w than other living men, 10266
5:11 and intelligence and w like that of the gods. 10266
5:11 insight, intelligence and outstanding w. 10266
Hos 13:13 but he is a child without w; 2682
Mic 6:9 and to fear your name is w— 9370
Mt 11:19 But w is proved right by her actions." 5053
12:42 ends of the earth to listen to Solomon's w, 5053
13:54 "Where did this man get this w 5053
Mk 6:2 "What's this w that has been given him, 5053
Lk 1:17 the disobedient to the w of the righteous— 5860

Lk	2:40	he was filled *with* w,	5053
	2:52	And Jesus grew *in* w and stature,	5053
	7:35	But w is proved right by all her children."	5053
	11:31	ends of the earth to listen to Solomon's w,	5053
	11:49	Because of this, God in his w said,	5053
	21:15	For I will give you words and w that none	5053
Ac	6: 3	known to be full of the Spirit and w.	5053
	6:10	but they could not stand up against his w or	5053
	7:10	He gave Joseph w and enabled him to gain	5053
	7:22	educated in all the w of the Egyptians	5053
Ro	11:33	the riches *of* the w and knowledge of God!	5053
1Co	1:17	not with words *of* human w,	5053
	1:19	"I will destroy the w of the wise;	5053
	1:20	not God made foolish the w of the world?	5053
	1:21	For since in the w of God the world	5053
	1:21	the world through its w did not know him,	5053
	1:22	and Greeks look for w,	5053
	1:24	Christ the power of God and the w of God.	5053
	1:25	foolishness of God is wiser than man's w,	NIG
	1:30	who has become for us w from God—	5053
	2: 1	I did not come with eloquence or	
		superior w	5053+5667
	2: 5	that your faith might not rest on men's w,	5053
	2: 6	speak a message of w among the mature,	5053
	2: 6	the w of this age or of the rulers of this age,	5053
	2: 7	No, we speak of God's secret w,	5053
	2: 7	secret wisdom, a w that has been hidden	NIG
	2:13	not in words taught us *by* human w but	5053
	3:19	For the w of this world is foolishness	5053
	12: 8	through the Spirit the message *of* w,	5053
2Co	1:12	so not according to worldly w but according	5053
Eph	1: 8	on us with all w and understanding.	5053
	1:17	the Spirit *of* w and revelation,	5053
	3:10	the manifold w of God should	5053
Col	1: 9	through all spiritual w and understanding.	5053
	1:28	and teaching everyone with all w,	5053
	2: 3	in whom are hidden all the treasures *of* w	5053
	2:23	indeed have an appearance *of* w,	5053
	3:16	and admonish one another with all w,	5053
Jas	1: 5	If any of you lacks w, he should ask God,	5053
	3:13	in the humility that comes *from* w.	5053
	3:15	Such **"w"** does not come down from heaven	5053
	3:17	But the w that comes from heaven is first	5053
2Pe	3:15	with the w that God gave him.	5053
Rev	5:12	and wealth and w and strength and honor	5053
	7:12	and thanks and honor and power	5053
	13:18	This calls for w.	5053
	17: 9	"This calls for a mind with w.	5053

WISE (186) [OVERWISE, WISELY, WISDOM, WISER, WISEST]

Ge	41: 8	so he sent for all the magicians and w *men*	2682
	41:33	for a discerning w man and put him	2682
	41:39	there is no one so discerning and w as you.	2682
Ex	7:11	then summoned w *men* and sorcerers, and	2682
Dt	1:13	Choose *some* w, understanding	2682
	1:15	w and respected men, and appointed them	2682
	4: 6	a w and understanding people."	2682
	16:19	the w and twists the words of the righteous.	2682
	32:29	If only *they were* w and would understand	2681
2Sa	14: 2	a w woman brought from there.	2682
	20:16	a w woman called from the city,	2682
	20:22	to all the people with her **advice**,	2683
1Ki	3:12	I will give you a w and discerning heart,	2682
	5: 7	a w son to rule over this great nation."	2682
1Ch	26:14	for his son Zechariah, a w counselor, and	8507
2Ch	2:12	He has given King David a w son,	2682
Est	1:13	with the w men who understood the times	2682
Job	5:13	He catches the w in their craftiness.	2682
	11:12	a witless man *can* no more **become** than	4220
	15: 2	"Would a w man answer with empty notions	2682
	15:18	what w men have declared,	2682
	17:10	I will not find a w man among you.	2682
	22: 2	Can even a *man* benefit him?	8505
	32: 9	It is not only the old *who are* w,	2681
	34: 2	"Hear my words, you w *men*;	2682
	34:34	the w men who hear me say to me,	2682
	37:24	for does he not have regard for all the w	2682
Ps	2:10	Therefore, *you* kings, *be* w;	8505
	19: 7	trustworthy, **making** w the simple.	2681
	36: 3	he has ceased to *be* w and to do good.	8505
	49:10	For all can see that w *men* die;	2682
	94: 8	you fools, when *will you* become w?	8505
	107:43	Whoever is w, let him heed these things	2682
Pr	1: 5	let the w listen and add to their learning,	2682
	1: 6	the sayings and riddles of the w.	2682
	3: 7	Do not be w in your own eyes;	2682
	3:35	The w inherit honor,	2682
	6: 6	consider its ways and *be* w!	2681
	8:33	Listen to my instruction and *be* w;	2682
	9: 8	rebuke a w *man* and he will love you.	2682
	9: 9	Instruct a w *man* and he will be wiser still;	2682
	9:12	If *you are* w, your wisdom will reward you;	2681
	10: 1	A w son brings joy to his father,	2682
	10: 5	who gathers crops in summer *is* a w son,	8505
	10: 8	The w *in* heart accept commands,	2682
	10:14	W men store up knowledge,	2682
	10:19	but he who holds his tongue *is* w.	8505
	11:29	and the fool will be servant to the w.	2682+4213
	11:30	and he who wins souls is w.	2682
	12:15	but a w *man* listens to advice.	2682
	12:18	but the tongue of the w brings healing.	2682
	13: 1	A w son heeds his father's instruction,	2682
	13:14	The teaching of the w is a fountain of life,	2682
	13:20	He who walks with the w grows wise,	2681
	13:20	He who walks with the wise *grows* w,	2681

Pr	14: 1	The w woman builds her house,	2682
	14: 3	but the lips of the w protect them.	2682
	14:16	A w *man* fears the LORD and shuns evil,	2682
	14:24	The wealth of the w is their crown,	2682
	14:35	A king delights in a w servant,	8505
	15: 2	The tongue of the w commends knowledge,	2682
	15: 7	The lips of the w spread knowledge;	2682
	15:12	he will not consult the w.	2682
	15:20	A w son brings joy to his father,	2682
	15:24	for the w to keep him from going down to	8505
	15:31	be at home among the w.	2682
	16:14	but a w man will appease it.	2682
	16:21	The w *in* heart are called discerning,	2682
	16:23	A w *man's* heart guides his mouth,	2682
	17: 2	A w servant will rule over a disgraceful son,	8505
	17:28	Even a fool is thought w if he keeps silent,	2682
	18:15	the ears of the w seek it out.	2682
	19:20	and in the end *you will be* w.	2681
	20: 1	whoever is led astray by them *is* not w.	2681
	20:26	A w king winnows out the wicked;	2682
	21:11	when a w *man* is instructed,	2682
	21:20	the house of the w are stores of choice food	2682
	21:22	A w *man* attacks the city of the mighty	2682
	22:17	and listen to the sayings of the w;	2682
	23:15	My son, if your heart is w,	2681
	23:19	Listen, my son, and *be* w,	2681
	23:24	he who has a w son delights in him.	2682
	24: 5	A w man has great power,	2682
	24:23	These also are sayings of the w:	2682
	25:12	a w *man's* rebuke to a listening ear.	2682
	26: 5	or he will be w in his own eyes.	2682
	26:12	Do you see a man w in his own eyes?	2682
	27:11	*Be* w, my son, and bring joy to my heart;	2681
	28:11	A rich man may be w in his own eyes,	2682
	29: 8	but w *men* turn away anger.	2682
	29: 9	If a w man goes to court with a fool,	2682
	29:11	but a w *man* keeps himself under control.	2682
	30:24	yet they *are* **extremely** w:	2681+2682
Ecc	2:14	The w *man* has eyes in his head,	2682
	2:15	What then do I gain *by being* w?"	2681
	2:16	For the w *man*, like the fool,	2681
	2:16	Like the fool, the w *man* too must die!	2681
	2:19	And who knows whether he will be a w *man*	2682
	4:13	Better a poor but w youth than an old	2682
	6: 8	What advantage has a w *man* over a fool?	2682
	7: 4	heart of the w is in the house of mourning,	2682
	7: 5	a w *man's* rebuke than to listen to the song	2682
	7: 7	Extortion turns a w *man* into a fool,	2682
	7:10	For it is not w to ask such questions.	2683
	7:19	Wisdom makes one w *man* more powerful	
		than ten rulers	2682
	7:23	*"I am determined to be* w"—	2681
	8: 1	Who is like the w *man*?	2682
	8: 5	and the w heart will know the proper time	2682
	8:17	Even if a w *man* claims he knows,	2682
	9: 1	the w and what they do are in God's hands,	2682
	9:11	to the w or wealth to the brilliant or favor to	2682
	9:15	there lived in that city a man poor but w,	2682
	9:17	the w are more to be heeded than the shouts	2682
	10: 2	The heart of the w inclines to the right,	2682
	10:12	Words from a w *man's* mouth are gracious,	2682
	12: 9	Not only was the Teacher w,	2682
	12:11	The words of the w are like goads,	2682
Isa	5:21	Woe to *those who are* w in their own eyes	2682
	19:11	w counselors of Pharaoh give senseless	
		advice.	2682
	19:11	"I am one of the w men,	2682
	19:12	Where are your w *men* now?	2682
	29:14	the wisdom of the w will perish,	2682
	31: 2	Yet he too is w and can bring disaster;	2682
	44:25	who overthrows the learning of the w	2682
Jer	8: 8	"How can you say, "We are w,	2682
	8: 9	The w will be put to shame;	2682
	9:12	What man is w *enough* to understand this?	2682
	9:23	"Let not the w man boast of his wisdom or	2682
	10: 7	Among all the w *men of* the nations and	2682
	18:18	nor will counsel from the w,	2682
	50:35	and against her officials and w *men*!	2682
	51:57	I will make her officials and w *men* drunk,	2682
Eze	28: 2	though you think you are w as a god.	4213
	28: 6	" 'Because you think you are w,	NIH
	28: 6	you think you are wise, as w as a god.	4213
Da	2:12	the execution of all the w *men of* Babylon.	10265
	2:13	decree was issued to put the w *men* to death	10265
	2:14	had gone out to put to death the w *men*	10265
	2:18	not be executed with the rest of the w *men*	10265
	2:21	He gives wisdom to the w and knowledge	10265
	2:24	king had appointed to execute the w *men*	10265
	2:24	"Do not execute the w *men* of Babylon.	10265
	2:27	Daniel replied, "No w *man*, enchanter,	10265
	2:48	and placed him in charge of all its w *men*.	10265
	4: 6	the w *men* of Babylon be brought before me	10265
	4:18	the w *men* in my kingdom can interpret it	10265
	5: 7	to be brought and said to these w *men*	10265
	5: 8	Then all the king's w *men* came in,	10265
	5:15	The w men and enchanters were brought	10265
	11:33	"Those *who are* w will instruct many,	8505
	11:35	Some of the w will stumble,	8505
	12: 3	Those *who are* w will shine like	8505
	12:10	but those *who are* w will understand.	8505
Hos	14: 9	Who is w? He will realize these things.	2682
Ob	1: 8	"will I not destroy the w *men* of Edom,	2682
Mt	7:24	a w man who built his house on the rock.	5861
	11:25	hidden these things from the w and learned,	5055
	23:34	prophets and w *men* and teachers.	5055
	24:45	"Who then is the faithful and w servant,	5861
	25: 2	Five of them were foolish and five were w.	5861

Mt	25: 4	The w, however, took oil in jars along	5861
	25: 8	The foolish ones said *to* the w,	5861
Lk	10:21	from the w and learned,	5055
	12:42	"Who then is the faithful and w manager,	5861
Ac	15:38	but Paul *did* not **think** it w to take him,	546
Ro	1:14	both *to* the w and the foolish.	5055
	1:22	Although they claimed to be w,	5055
	16:19	but I want you to be w about what is good,	5055
	16:27	*to* the only w God be glory forever	5055
1Co	1:19	"I will destroy the wisdom *of* the w;	5055
	1:20	Where is the w *man*?	5055
	1:26	Not many of you were w by human	
		standards;	5055
	1:27	foolish things of the world to shame the w;	5055
	2: 4	and my preaching were not with w	5053
	3:18	of you thinks he is w by the standards	5055
	3:18	become a "fool" so that he may become w.	5055
	3:19	"He catches the w in their craftiness";	5055
	3:20	that the thoughts of the w are futile."	5055
	4:10	but you are so w in Christ!	5861
	6: 5	that there is nobody among you w enough	5055
2Co	10:12	*they are* not w.	5317
	11:19	put up with fools since you are so w!	5861
Eph	5:15	how you live—not as unwise but as w,	5055
Col	4: 5	Be w in the way you act toward outsiders;	5053
2Ti	3:15	which are able *to* **make** you w for salvation	5054
Jas	3:13	Who is w and understanding among you?	5055

WISELY (4) [WISE]

2Ch	11:23	He acted w, dispersing some of his sons	1067
Isa	52:13	See, my servant *will* act w;	
Jer	23: 5	a King who will reign w and do what is just	8505
Mk	12:34	When Jesus saw that he had answered w,	3807

WISER (8) [WISE]

1Ki	4:31	He was w than any other man,	2681
		w than Heman, Calcol and Darda,	NIH
Job	35:11	and **makes** us w than the birds of the air?'	2681
Ps	119:98	commands **make** me w than my enemies,	2681
Pr	9: 9	Instruct a wise man and *he will* be w still;	2681
	26:16	The sluggard is w in his own eyes than	2682
Eze	28: 3	Are you w than Daniel?	2682
1Co	1:25	foolishness of God is w *than* man's wisdom,	5055

WISEST (1) [WISE]

Jdg	5:29	The w of her ladies answer her;	2682

WISH (22) [WISHED, WISHES, WISHING]

Ex	4:18	Jethro said, "Go, and I w you **well**."	4200+8934
Nu	11:29	I w *that* all the LORD's people were	4769+5989
Dt	14:26	other fermented drink, or anything you w.	8626
Jdg	19:24	and do to them whatever you w.	928+3202+6524
1Sa	24: 4	for you to deal with as you w.' "	928+3512+6524
1Ki	5: 9	to grant my w by providing food	2914
Ezr	7:13	*who* w to go to Jerusalem with you, may go.	10461
Job	10:18	I w I had **died** before any eye saw me.	AIT
	11: 5	**Oh, how** I w that God would speak,	4769+5989
Mt	17: 4	If *you* w, I will put up three shelters."	2527
Lk	12:49	and how I w it were already kindled!	2527
Jn	15: 7	ask whatever you w, and it will be given	2527
Ro	9: 3	For I could w that I myself were cursed	2377
1Co	4: 8	How I w that you really had become kings	4054
	7: 7	I w that all men were as I am.	2527
2Co	5: 4	because *we do* not w to be unclothed but to	2527
Gal	4: 9	*Do you* w to be enslaved by them all over	2527
	4:20	how I w I could be with you now	2527
	5:12	I w they would go the whole way	4054
Phm		I *do* w, brother, *that I may have* some **benefit**	AIT
Jas	2:16	"Go, I w you well;	1645+1877+5632
Rev	3:15	I w you were either one or the other!	4054

WISHED (6) [WISH]

2Sa	19:18	over and to do whatever he w.	928+3202+6524
Est	1: 8	to serve each man what he w.	8356
Job	9: 3	Though *one* w to dispute with him,	2911
Jer	34:16	slaves you had set free to go where they w.	5883
Mt	17:12	but have done to him everything *they* w.	2527
Mk	9:13	they have done to him everything *they* w,	2527

WISHES (9) [WISH]

Lev	27:13	If the owner w *to* **redeem** the animal,	AIT
	27:19	who dedicates the field w *to* **redeem** it,	AIT
Dt	21:14	let her go wherever she w.	5883
Da	4:17	and gives them to anyone *he* w and sets	10605
	4:25	of men and gives them to anyone *he* w.	10605
	4:32	of men and gives them to anyone *he* w."	10605
	5:21	of men and sets over them anyone *he* w.	10605
1Co	7:39	she is free to marry anyone *she* w,	2527
Rev	22:17	and whoever w, let him take the free gift of	2527

WISHING (1) [WISH]

Ac	25: 9	Festus, w to do the Jews a favor,	2527

WIST (KJV) See AWARE, IDEA, KNOW, REALIZE

WIT (KJV) See KNOW, LEARN, SEE, THAT IS

WITCH (KJV) See SORCERESS, SORCERY

WITCHCRAFT (6) [BEWITCHED]
Dt	18:10	interprets omens, **engages in** w, 4175
2Ki	9:22	and w **of** your mother Jezebel abound?" 4176
2Ch	33: 6	practiced sorcery, divination and w, 4175
Mic	5:12	I will destroy your w and you will no longer 4176
Na	3: 4	by her prostitution and peoples by her w. 4176
Gal	5:20	idolatry and w; hatred, 5758

WITH (5912) See Index of Articles Etc.

WITHDRAW (13) [WITHDRAWN, WITHDRAWS, WITHDREW]
Lev	26:25	When *you* w into your cities, 665
1Sa	14:19	So Saul said to the priest, "**W** your hand." 665
2Sa	14:15	Then from him so he will be struck down 8740
	20:21	and *I'll* w from the city." 2143
	24:16	"Enough! **W** your hand." 8332
1Ki	15:19	with Baasha king of Israel so *he will* w 6590
2Ki	18:14	"I have done wrong. **W** from me, 8740
1Ch	21:15	"Enough! **W** your hand. 8332
2Ch	16: 3	with Baasha king of Israel so *he will* w 6590
Job	13:21	**W** your hand **far** from me, 8178
Jer	21: 2	as in times past so that *he will* w from us." 6590
Eze	5:11	*I* myself *will* w *my* **favor**; 1757
Ac	4:15	So they ordered them *to* w from 599

WITHDRAWN (5) [WITHDRAW]
Jer	16: 5	because *I have* w my blessing, 665
	34:21	which has w from you. 6590
	37:11	the Babylonian army *had* w from Jerusalem 6590
La	2: 3	*He has* w his right hand 294+8740
Hos	5: 6	*he has* w *himself* from them. 2740

WITHDRAWS (1) [WITHDRAW]
2Sa	17:13	If *he* w into a city, then all Israel will bring 665

WITHDREW (30) [WITHDRAW]
Ex	14:19	w and went behind them. 5825
	35:20	Then the whole Israelite community w 3655
1Sa	14:46	and they w to their own land. 2143
1Ki	8:10	When the priests w from the Holy Place, 3655
	15:21	he stopped building Ramah and w 3782
	16:17	Then Omri and all the Israelites with him w 6590
2Ki	3:27	*they* and returned to their own land. 5825
	12:18	*who* then w from Jerusalem. 6590
	15:20	So the king of Assyria w and stayed in 8740
	19: 8	*he* w and found the king fighting 8740
	19:36	king of Assyria broke camp and w, 2143
2Ch	5:11	The priests then w from the Holy Place. 3655
	24:25	When the Arameans w, 2143+4946
	32:21	So he w to his own land in disgrace. 4946
Ezr	10: 6	Then Ezra w from before the house of God 7756
Job	34:14	If it were his intention and *he* w his spirit 665
Isa	37: 8	*he* w and found the king fighting 8740
	37:37	king of Assyria broke camp and w. 2143
Jer	37: 5	*they* w from Jerusalem. 6590
Mt	2:22	he w to the district of Galilee, 432
	12:15	Aware of this, Jesus w from that place. 432
	14:13	*he* w by boat privately to a solitary 432+1696
	15:21	Jesus w to the region of Tyre and Sidon. 432
Mk	3: 7	Jesus w with his disciples to the lake, 432
Lk	5:16	Jesus *often* w to lonely places and prayed. 1639+5723
	9:10	Then he took them with him and *they* w 5723
	22:41	He w about a stone's throw beyond them, 685
Jn	6:15	w again to a mountain by himself. 432
	11:54	Instead *he* w to a region near the desert, 599
Ac	22:29	about to question him w immediately. 923

WITHER (18) [WITHERED, WITHERS]
Job	8:12	*they* w more quickly than grass. 3312
	15:30	a flame *will* w his shoots, 3312
	18:16	dry up below and his branches w above. 4908
Ps	1: 3	fruit in season and whose leaf *does* not w 5570
	37: 2	for like the grass *they will* soon w, 4908
	37:19	In times of disaster *they will* not w; 3312
	102:11	I w away like grass. 3312
Isa	16: 8	The fields of Heshbon w, 581
	19: 6	The reeds and rushes *will* w, 7857
	40:24	than he blows on them and *they* w, 3312
Jer	8:13	and their leaves *will* w. 5570
Eze	17: 9	All its new growth *will* w. 3312
	17:10	*Will it* not w **completely** when 3312+3312
	17:10	w away in the plot where it grew?'" 3312
	47:12	Their leaves *will not* w, 5570
Na	1: 4	Bashan and Carmel w and the blossoms 581
Zec	9: 5	and Ekron too, for her hope *will* w. 3312
Mt	21:20	"How *did* the fig tree w so quickly?" 3830

WITHERED (20) [WITHER]
Ge	41:23	w and thin and scorched by the east wind. 7568
Ps	90: 6	by evening it is dry and w. 3312
	102: 4	My heart is blighted and like grass; 3312
Isa	15: 6	of Nimrim are dried up and the grass *is* w; 3312
	34: 4	the starry host will fall like w leaves from 5570
Jer	12: 4	and the grass in every field *be* w? 3312
	23:10	and the pastures in the desert *are* w. 3312
Eze	19:12	its strong branches w and fire consumed 3312
	31:15	and all the trees of the field w away. 6634
Hos	9:16	Ephraim is blighted, their root *is* w, 3312
Joel	1:12	The vine is dried up and the fig tree w; 581

Joel	1:12	Surely the joy of mankind *is* w **away**. 3312
Jnh	4: 7	which chewed the vine so that *it* w. 3312
Zec	11:17	*May* his arm *be* **completely** w, 3312+3312
Mt	13: 6	and *they* w because they had no root. 3830
	21:19	Immediately the tree w. 3830
Mk	4: 6	and *they* w because they had no root. 3830
	11:20	they saw the fig tree w from the roots. 3830
	11:21	The fig tree you cursed *has* w!" 3830
Lk	8: 6	the plants w because they had no moisture. 3830

WITHERS (14) [WITHER]
Job	8:19	Surely its life w **away**, 5376
	14: 2	He springs up like a flower and w **away**; 4908
Ps	129: 6	which w before it can grow; 3312
Isa	24: 4	The earth dries up and w, 5570
	24: 4	the world languishes and w, 5570
	24: 7	The new wine dries up and the vine w; 581
	33: 9	Lebanon is ashamed and w; 7857
	40: 7	The grass w and the flowers fall, 3312
	40: 8	The grass w and the flowers fall, 3312
Eze	17: 9	and stripped of its fruit so that *it* w? 3312
Am	1: 2	and the top of Carmel w." 3312
Jn	15: 6	like a branch that is thrown away and w; 3830
Jas	1:11	For the sun rises with scorching heat and w 3830
1Pe	1:24	the grass w and the flowers fall, 3830

WITHHELD (14) [WITHHOLD]
Ge	22:12	because *you have* not w from me your son, 3104
	22:16	you have done this and *have* not w your son, 3104
	39: 9	My master *has* nothing from me except 3104
Job	22: 7	the weary and *you* w food from the hungry, 4979
Ps	21: 2	of his heart and *have* not w the request 4979
	66:20	not rejected my prayer or w his love NIH
	77: 9	*Has he* in anger w his compassion?" 7890
Isa	63:15	Your tenderness and compassion *are* w 706
Jer	3: 3	Therefore the showers *have* **been** w, 4979
Eze	20:22	*I* w my hand, and for the sake of my name 8740
Joel	1:13	the grain offerings and drink offerings *are* w 4979
Am	4: 7	"I also w rain from you when the harvest 4979
	4: 7	but w it from another. 4202+4763S
Hag	1:10	of you the heavens *have* w their dew 3973

WITHHOLD (8) [WITHHELD, WITHHOLDING, WITHHOLDS]
Ne	9:20	not w your manna from their mouths, 4979
Ps	40:11	*Do not* w your mercy from me, O LORD; 3973
	84:11	no good thing *does he* w from those whose 4979
Pr	3:27	*Do not* w good from those who deserve it, 4979
	23:13	*Do not* w discipline from a child; 4979
Isa	10:10	and justice *from* the oppressed 1608
La	2: 8	and *did* not w his hand from destroying. 8740
Zec	1:12	how long will you w mercy from Jerusalem 4202

WITHHOLDING (2) [WITHHOLD]
2Co	6:12	We *are* not w our affection from *you*, 5102
	6:12	but *you are* w yours from us. 5102

WITHHOLDS (5) [WITHHOLD]
Dt	27:19	"Cursed is the man *who* w justice from 5742
Pr	11:24	*another* w unduly, but comes to poverty. 3104
Isa	32: 6	and *from* the thirsty he w water. 2893
Eze	18: 8	*He* w his hand from doing wrong 8740
	18:17	*He* w his hand from sin and takes no usury 8740

WITHIN (113) [IN]
Ge	6:16	and finish the ark **to** w 18 inches of the top. 448
	10: 5	into their territories by their clans w 928
	10:32	to their lines of descent, w their nations. 928
	23:17	and all the trees w the borders of the field— 928
	25:22	The babies jostled each other w her, 928+7931
	25:23	two peoples from w you will be separated; 5055
	33:18	and camped w **sight** of the city. 907+7156
	40:13	**W** three days Pharaoh will lift up 928+6388
	40:19	**W** three days Pharaoh will lift off 928+6388
Ex	3: 2	to him in flames of fire from w a bush. 9348
	3: 4	God called to him from w the bush, 9348
	13: 7	nor shall any yeast be seen anywhere w 928
	20:10	nor the alien w your gates. 928
	24:16	the LORD called to Moses from w the cloud. 9348
Nu	36: 6	as long as they marry w the tribal clan 4200
	36:12	They married w the clans of 4946
Dt	5:14	nor the alien w your gates, 928
Jos	16: 9	were set aside for the Ephraimites w 928+9348
	17:11	**W** Issachar and Asher, 928
	19: 1	Their inheritance lay w the territory 928+9348
	19: 9	Simeonites received their inheritance w 928+9348
Jdg	14:12	the answer w the seven **days** of the feast, AIT
	17: 7	who had been living w the clan of Judah, 4946
2Sa	20: 4	of Judah to come to me w three **days**, AIT
1Ki	6: 6	from floor to ceiling to form w the temple 4946
	6:19	the inner sanctuary w the temple to set 928+9348
	9:18	and Tadmor in the desert, w his land, 928
2Ki	7:11	and it was reported in the palace. 7163
Ezr	10: 8	Anyone who failed to appear w three days 4200
	10: 9	**W** the three days, all the men of Judah 4200
Job	19:27	How my heart yearns w me! 928+2668
	20:14	it will become the venom of serpents w 928+7931
	27: 3	as long as I have life w me, 928
	31:15	the same one form us both w our mothers? 928
	33: 4	and the spirit w me compels me; 1061
Ps	22:14	it has melted away w me. 928+5055+9348
	36: 1	An oracle is w my heart concerning 928+7931
	39: 3	My heart grew hot w me, 928+7931
Ps	40: 8	your law is w my heart." 928+9348
	40:12	and my heart **fails** w me. AIT
	42: 5	Why so disturbed w me? 6584
	42: 6	My soul is downcast w me; 6584
	42:11	Why so disturbed w me? 6584
	43: 5	Why so disturbed w me? 6584
	45:13	All glorious is the princess w [her chamber]; 7163
	46: 5	God is w her, she will not fall; 928+7931
	48: 9	**W** your temple, O God, we meditate 928+7931
	51:10	and renew a steadfast spirit w me. 928+7931
	55: 4	My heart is in anguish w me; 928+7931
	55:10	malice and abuse are w it. 928+7931
	94:19	When anxiety was great w me, 928+7931
	109:22	and my heart is wounded w me. 928+7931
	122: 7	be peace w your walls and security 928
	122: 7	be peace within your walls and security w 928
	122: 8	I will say, "Peace be w you." 928
	128: 3	Your wife will be like a fruitful vine w 928+3752
	131: 2	like a weaned child is my soul w me. 6584
	142: 3	When my spirit grows faint w me, 6584
	143: 4	So my spirit grows faint w me; 6584
	143: 4	my heart w me is dismayed. 928+9348
	147:13	your gates and blesses your people w 928+7931
Pr	2: 1	and store up my commands w you, 907
	4:21	keep them w your heart; 928+9348
	7: 1	and store up my commands w you. 907
Ecc	4:14	or he may have been born in poverty w 928
Isa	7: 8	**W** sixty-five years Ephraim will 928+6388
	13: 9	the land desolate and destroy the sinners w 4946
	16:14	But now the LORD says: "**W** three years, 928
	19: 1	hearts of the Egyptians melt w them. 928+7931
	21:16	"**W** one year, as a servant bound 928+6388
	41:18	and springs w the valleys. 928+9348
	56: 5	to them I will give w my temple 928
	60:18	nor ruin or destruction w your borders, 928
Jer	4:19	My heart pounds w me, 4200
	8:18	my heart is faint w me. 6584
	23: 9	My heart is broken w me; 928+7931
	28: 3	**W** two years I will bring back 928+6388
	28:11	off the neck of all the nations w two 928+6388
	51:47	and her slain will all lie fallen w her. 928+9348
La	1:20	I am in torment w, 928+7931
	2:11	I am in torment w, 5055
	3:20	and my soul is downcast w me. 6584
	4:13	shed w her the blood of the righteous. 928+7931
Eze	12	The glory of the LORD went up from w 9348
	22:25	is a conspiracy of her princes w her 928+9348
	22:25	and make many widows w her. 928+9348
	22:27	Her officials w her are 928+7931
	28:22	O Sidon, and I will gain glory w you. 928+9348
	28:22	on her and show myself holy w her. 928
	28:23	The slain will fall w her, 928+9348
	30: 6	to Aswan they will fall by the sword w her, 928
	32:21	From w the grave the mighty leaders 9348
	40:44	Outside the inner gate, w the inner court, 928
Hos	11: 8	My heart is changed w me; 6584
Am	3: 9	see the great unrest w her and 928+9348
Zep	3: 5	The LORD w her is righteous; 928+7931
	3:12	I will leave w you the meek and 928+7931
Zec	2: 5	'and I will be its glory w.' 928+9348
	12: 1	and who forms the spirit of man w him, 928+7931
Mt	6:23	If then the light w you is darkness, 1877
Mk	7:21	For **from** w, out of men's hearts, 2277
Lk	11:35	then, that the light w you is not darkness, 1877
	17:21	because the kingdom of God is w you." 1955
	19:44	you and the children w your walls. 1877
	24:32	not our hearts burning w us while he talked 1877
Jn	7:38	streams of living water will flow from w 3120
	17:13	the full measure of my joy w them. 1877
Ro	7:23	of the law of sin at work w my members. 1877
1Co	2:11	of a man except the man's spirit w him? 1877
2Co	7: 5	conflicts on the outside, fears w. 2277
Eph	3:20	according to his power that *is* at work w us, 1919
Jas	4: 1	your desires that battle w you? 1877+3517+3836
Rev	11:19	and w his temple was seen the ark 1877

WITHOUT (375)
Ge	19: 3	baking **bread** w yeast, and they ate. 5174
	24:21	**W** saying a word, the man watched her 3087
	41:44	but w your word no one will lift hand 1187
Ex	12: 5	must be year-old males w defect. 9459
	12: 8	and **bread made** w yeast. 5174
	12:15	to eat **bread made** w yeast. 5174
	12:18	to eat **bread made** w yeast, 5174
	12:30	for there was not a house w someone dead. 401
	12:39	The dough was w yeast 4202
	13: 6	For seven days eat **bread made** w yeast and 5174
	15:22	For three days they traveled in the desert w 4202
	21: 2	he shall go free, w **paying anything**. 2855
	21:11	is to go free, w **any payment** of money. 401+2855
	23:15	for seven days eat **bread made** w yeast, 5174
	29: 1	Take a young bull and two rams w defect. 9459
	29: 2	And from fine wheat flour, w yeast, 5174
	29:23	From the basket of **bread made** w yeast, 5174
	34:18	For seven days eat **bread made** w yeast, 5174
	34:28	the LORD forty days and forty nights w 4202
Lev	1: 3	he is to offer a male w **defect**. 9459
	1:10	he is to offer a male w **defect**. 9459
	2: 4	cakes made w **yeast** and mixed with oil, 5174
	2: 4	or wafers made w **yeast** and spread with oil. 5174
	2: 5	of fine flour mixed with oil, and w **yeast**. 5174
	2:11	to the LORD must be made w yeast, 4202
	3: 1	before the LORD an animal w **defect**. 9459
	3: 6	he is to offer a male or female w **defect**. 9459
	4: 3	a young bull w **defect** as a sin offering for 9459
	4:23	as his offering a male goat w **defect**. 9459

Ref		Text	Strong's
Lev	4:28	a female goat **w defect.**	9459
	4:32	he is to bring a female **w defect.**	9459
	5:15	one **w defect** and of the proper value	9459
	5:18	one **w defect** and of the proper value.	9459
	6: 6	one **w defect** and of the proper value.	9459
	6:16	but it is to be eaten **w yeast** in a holy place;	5174
	7:12	of **bread made w yeast** and mixed with oil,	5174
	7:12	wafers **made w yeast** and spread with oil,	5174
	8: 2	the basket containing **bread made w yeast,**	5174
	8:26	from the basket of **bread made w yeast,**	5174
	9: 2	both **w defect,** and present them before	9459
	9: 3	both a year old and **w defect—**	9459
	10:12	and eat it **prepared w yeast** beside the altar,	5174
	14:10	each **w defect,** along with three-tenths of	9459
	15:11	a discharge touches **w** rinsing his hands	4202
	22:19	you must present a male **w defect** from	9459
	22:21	be **w defect** or blemish to be acceptable.	9459
	23: 6	you must eat **bread made w yeast.**	5174
	23:12	to the LORD a lamb a year old **w defect,**	9459
	23:18	each a year old and **w defect,**	9459
	25:31	in villages **w** walls around them are to	401
	26:43	while it lies desolate **w** them.	4946
Nu	6:14	a year-old male lamb **w defect** for	9459
	6:14	a year-old ewe lamb **w defect** for	9459
	6:14	a ram **w defect** for a fellowship offering,	9459
	6:15	and a basket of **bread made w yeast—**	5174
	6:19	both **made w yeast.**	5174
	15:24	**w** the community **being aware**	4946+6524
	19: 2	a red heifer **w defect** or blemish and	9459
	19:15	and every open container **w** a lid fastened	401
	27:17	not be like sheep **w** a shepherd."	401
	28: 3	two lambs a year old **w defect,**	9459
	28: 9	of two lambs a year old **w defect,**	9459
	28:11	seven male lambs a year old, *all* **w defect.**	9459
	28:17	for seven days eat **bread made w yeast.**	5174
	28:19	seven male lambs a year old, *all* **w defect**	9459
	28:31	Be sure the animals are **w defect.**	9459
	29: 2	male lambs a year old, *all* **w defect.**	9459
	29: 8	male lambs a year old, *all* **w defect.**	9459
	29:13	male lambs a year old, *all* **w defect.**	9459
	29:17	male lambs a year old, *all* **w defect.**	9459
	29:20	male lambs a year old, *all* **w defect.**	9459
	29:23	male lambs a year old, *all* **w defect.**	9459
	29:26	male lambs a year old, *all* **w defect.**	9459
	29:29	male lambs a year old, *all* **w defect.**	9459
	29:32	male lambs a year old, *all* **w defect.**	9459
	29:36	male lambs a year old, *all* **w defect.**	9459
	35:22	if **w** hostility someone suddenly shoves	928+4202
	35:23	or, **w** seeing him, drops a stone on him	928+4202
	35:27	the avenger of blood may kill the accused **w**	401
Dt	4:42	he had unintentionally killed his neighbor **w**	4202
	7:14	nor any of your livestock **w young.**	6829
	15:10	to him and do so **w** a grudging heart;	4202
	19: 4	unintentionally, **w** malice aforethought.	4202
	19: 6	to his neighbor **w** malice aforethought.	4202
	25: 5	and one of them dies **w** a son,	401
	28:50	a fierce-looking nation **w** respect for the old	4202
	32:28	They are a nation **w** sense,	6
Jos	2:22	along the road and returned **w** finding them.	4202
	11:20	exterminating them **w** mercy,	1194
	20: 5	unintentionally and **w** malice aforethought.	4202
	23: 6	**w** turning aside to the right or to the left.	1194
Jdg	6:19	an ephah of flour he made **bread w yeast.**	5174
	12: 1	the Ammonites **w** calling us to go with you?	4202
Ru	1: 5	and Naomi was left **w** her two sons	4946
	4:14	not **left** you **w** a kinsman-redeemer.	8697
1Sa	9: 2	impressive young man **w equal**	401+3202+4946
	17:50	**w** a sword in his hand he struck down	401
	20: 2	great or small, **w** confiding in me.	4202
	28:24	kneaded it and baked **bread w yeast.**	5174
2Sa	3:29	*May* Joab's house never **be w**	4162+4946
	14: 9	and let the king and his throne be **w guilt."**	5929
	14:28	Absalom lived two years in Jerusalem **w**	4202
	17:16	**cross over w fail,** or the king	6296+6296
	20:10	**W** being stabbed again, Amasa died.	4202
1Ki	1:11	has become king **w** our lord David's	4202
	1:27	the king has done **w** letting his servants	4202
	2:32	because **w** the knowledge of my father	4202
	22:17	on the hills like sheep **w** a shepherd.	401
2Ki	18:25	attack and destroy this place **w** word	1187+4946
1Ch	2:30	Seled died **w** children.	4202
	2:32	Jether died **w** children.	4202
	23:22	Eleazar died **w** having sons:	4202
	29:15	on earth are like a shadow, **w** hope.	401
2Ch	15: 3	a long time Israel was **w** the true God,	4200+4200
	15: 3	**w** a priest to teach and without	4200+4200
	15: 3	a priest to teach and **w** the law.	4200+4200
	18:16	on the hills like sheep **w** a shepherd,	401
Ezr	6: 9	must be given them daily **w** fail,	10379
	7:22	baths of olive oil, and salt **w** limit.	10379
Est	4:11	in the inner court **w** being summoned	4202
	9:27	and all who join them should **w**	4202
Job	2: 3	against him to ruin him **w any reason."**	2855
	4:21	so that they die **w** wisdom?'	4202
	5: 4	crushed in court **w** a defender.	401
	6: 6	Is tasteless food eaten **w** salt,	1172+4946
	7: 6	and they come to an end **w** hope.	700+928
	8:11	Can reeds thrive **w** water?	1172
	9: 5	He moves mountains **w** their knowing it	4202
	9:25	they fly away **w** a glimpse of joy.	4202
	9:35	Then I would speak up **w** fear of him,	4202
	11:15	then you will lift up your face **w** shame;	4946
	11:15	you will stand firm and **w** fear.	4202
	16:13	**W** pity, he pierces my kidneys	4202
	23:11	I have kept to his way **w** turning aside.	4202
	26: 3	What advice you have offered to one **w**	4202
	27:22	against him **w** mercy as he flees headlong	4202
Job	30:13	**w** anyone's helping them.	4202
	31:19	or a needy man **w** a garment,	401
	31:39	if I have devoured its yield **w** payment	1172
	33: 9	'I am pure and **w** sin;	1172
	34:20	the mighty are removed **w** human hand.	4202
	34:24	**W** inquiry he shatters the mighty and sets	4202
	34:35	'Job speaks **w** knowledge;	928+4202
	35:16	**w** knowledge he multiplies words."	928+1172
	36:12	they will perish by the sword and die **w**	1172+3869
	38: 2	that darkens my counsel with words **w**	1172
	41:33	a creature **w** fear.	1172+4200
	42: 3	that obscures my counsel **w** knowledge?'	1172
Ps	7: 4	with me or **w cause** have robbed my foe—	8200
	15: 5	who lends his money **w** usury and does	928+4202
	25: 3	to shame who are treacherous **w excuse.**	8200
	26: 1	I have trusted in the LORD **w** wavering.	4202
	35: 7	for me **w cause** and without cause dug a pit	2855
	35: 7	without cause and **w cause** dug a pit for me,	2855
	35:15	They slandered me **w** ceasing.	4202
	35:19	over me who are my enemies **w cause;**	9214
	35:19	who hate me **w reason** maliciously wink	2855
	38:19	those who hate me **w reason** are numerous.	9214
	40:12	For troubles **w** number surround me;	401+6330
	49:20	A man who has riches **w** understanding is	4202
	54: 3	men **w** regard for God.	4202
	64: 4	they shoot at him suddenly, **w** fear.	4202
	69: 4	Those who hate me **w reason** outnumber	2855
	69: 4	many are my enemies **w cause,**	9214
	86:14	men **w** regard for you.	4202
	88: 4	I am like a man **w** strength.	401
	105:34	the locusts came, grasshoppers **w** number;	401
	109: 3	they attack me **w cause.**	2855
	119:51	The arrogant mock me **w restraint,**	4394+6330
	119:78	be put to shame for wronging me **w cause;**	9214
	119:86	help me, for men persecute me **w cause.**	9214
	119:161	Rulers persecute me **w cause,**	2855
Pr	1:33	and be at ease, **w** fear of harm."	4946
	6:15	will suddenly be destroyed—**w** remedy.	401
	6:28	into his lap **w** his clothes being burned?	4202
	6:28	on hot coals **w** his feet being scorched?	4202
	9:13	she is undisciplined and **w** knowledge.	1153
	14:28	but **w** subjects a prince is ruined.	700+928
	19: 2	not good to have zeal **w** knowledge,	928+4202
	20: 9	I am clean and **w** sin"?	4946
	21:26	but the righteous give **w** sparing.	4202
	24:28	not testify against your neighbor **w cause,**	2855
	25:14	and wind **w** rain is a man who boasts	401
	26:20	**W** wood a fire goes out;	700+928
	26:20	**w** gossip a quarrel dies down.	401+928
	29: 1	be destroyed—**w** remedy.	401
Ecc	2:25	for **w** him, who can eat or	2575+4946
	6: 4	It comes **w meaning,** it departs in darkness,	928+2021+2039
Isa	1:30	like a garden **w** water.	401+4200
	5: 9	the fine mansions left **w** occupants.	401+4946
	5:14	and opens its mouth **w** limit;	1172+4200
	6:11	the cities lie ruined and **w** inhabitant,	401+4946
	13:14	like sheep **w** a shepherd,	401
	22: 3	they have been captured **w** *using* the bow.	4946
	23: 1	For Tyre is destroyed and left **w** house	4946
	27:11	For this is a people **w** understanding;	4202
	28: 8	with vomit and there is not a spot **w** filth.	1172
	30: 2	who go down to Egypt **w** consulting me;	4202
	36:10	and destroy this land **w** the LORD?	1187+4946
	47: 1	sit on the ground **w** a throne,	401
	52: 3	and **w** money you will be redeemed."	928+4202
	55: 1	buy wine and milk **w** money and	928+4202
	55: 1	and milk without money and **w** cost.	928+4202
	55:10	do not return to it **w** watering the earth	561+3954
	56: 2	who keeps the Sabbath **w** desecrating it,	4946
	56: 6	all who keep the Sabbath **w** desecrating it	4946
	59:10	feeling our way like men **w** eyes.	401
Jer	2:32	Yet my people have forgotten me, days **w**	401
	4: 6	Flee for safety **w** delay!	440
	4: 7	towns will lie in ruins **w** inhabitant.	401+4946
	10:14	Everyone is senseless and **w** knowledge;	4946
	14:17	with tears night and day **w** ceasing;	440
	15:13	I will give as plunder, **w** charge,	928+4202
	20:16	like the towns the LORD overthrew **w** pity.	4202
	32:43	a desolate waste, **w** men or animals.	401+4946
	33:10	a desolate waste, **w** men or animals—	401+4946
	33:12	desolate and **w** men or animals—	401+4946
	44: 7	and so leave yourselves **w** a remnant?	1194
	44:22	and a desolate waste **w** inhabitants,	401+4946
	46: 5	They flee in haste **w** looking back,	4202
	46:19	laid waste and lie in ruins **w** inhabitant.	401+4946
	50:42	they are cruel and **w** mercy.	4202
	51:17	"Every man is senseless and **w** knowledge;	4946
La	2: 2	**W** pity the Lord has swallowed up all	4202
	2:17	He has overthrown you **w** pity.	4202
	2:21	you have slaughtered them **w** pity.	4202
	3:11	and mangled me and left me **w help.**	9037
	3:43	you have slain **w** pity.	
	3:49	My enemies will flow unceasingly, **w** relief,	401+4946
	3:52	my enemies **w cause** hunted me like a bird.	2855
	4: 6	in a moment **w** a hand turned to help her.	4202
Eze	1:12	they would go, **w** turning as they went.	4202
	9: 5	**w** showing pity or compassion.	440
	10:11	**w** turning as they went.	4202
	12:25	and it shall be fulfilled **w** delay.	4202
	14:23	that I have done nothing in it **w cause,**	2855
	24: 6	Empty it piece by piece **w** casting lots	4202
	35:13	and spoke against me **w restraint,**	6984
	38:11	all of them living **w** walls and without	401+929
	38:11	all of them living without walls and **w** gates	401
	43:22	a male goat **w defect** for a sin offering,	9459
	43:23	and a ram from the flock, both **w defect.**	9459
Eze	43:25	and a ram from the flock, *both* **w defect.**	9459
	45:18	to take a young bull **w defect** and purify	9459
	45:21	you shall eat **bread made w yeast.**	5174
	45:23	and seven rams **w defect** as a burnt offering	9459
	46: 4	be six male lambs and a ram, *all* **w defect.**	9459
	46: 6	six lambs and a ram, *all* **w defect.**	9459
	46:13	to provide a year-old lamb **w defect** for	9459
Da	1: 4	young men **w** any physical defect,	401
	2:35	The wind swept them away **w** leaving	10379
	6:18	to his palace and spent the night **w eating**	10297
	6:18	and spent the night without eating and **w**	10379
	8: 5	the whole earth **w** touching the ground.	401
	11:14	in fulfillment of the vision, but **w success.**	4173
Hos	3: 4	the Israelites will live many days **w** king	401
	3: 4	**w** sacrifice or sacred stones,	401
	3: 4	**w** ephod or idol.	401
	4:14	a people **w** understanding will come to ruin!	4202
	8: 4	They set up kings **w** my consent;	4202
	8: 4	they choose princes **w** my approval.	4202
	13:13	but he is a child **w** wisdom;	4202
Joel	1: 6	invaded my land, powerful and **w** number;	401
	2: 8	through defenses **w** breaking ranks.	4202
Am	3: 7	the Sovereign LORD does nothing **w**	561+3954
	5:20	pitch-dark, **w** a ray of brightness?	4202
Mic	2: 8	from those who pass by **w** a **care,**	1055
	3: 6	**w** visions, and darkness, without divination.	4946
	3: 6	without visions, and darkness, **w** divination.	4946
Na	3: 1	full of lies, full of plunder, never **w** victims!	4631
	3: 3	piles of dead, bodies **w** number,	401
Hab	1:17	destroying nations **w** mercy?	4202
Zec	2: 4	'Jerusalem will be a **city w walls** because	7252
	14: 7	**w** daytime or nighttime—	4202
Mt	8:24	**W warning,** a furious storm came up on	2627
	9:36	like sheep **w** a shepherd.	2400+3590
	13:34	not say anything to them **w** using a parable.	6006
	13:57	in his own house is a prophet **w honor."**	872
	22:12	in here **w** wedding clothes?'	2400+3590
	22:24	that if a man dies **w** having children,	3590
	23:23	**w** neglecting the former.	3590
Mk	1:20	**W delay** he called them,	2317
	4:34	not say anything to them **w** using a parable.	6006
	6: 4	in his own house is a prophet **w honor."**	872
	6:34	they were like sheep **w** a shepherd.	2400+3590
	12:20	The first one married and died **w** leaving	4024
Lk	1:74	and to enable us to serve him **w fear**	925
	4:35	down before them all and came out **w**	3594
	6:35	lend to them **w** expecting to get **anything**	3594
	6:49	a man who built a house on the ground **w**	6006
	11:42	the latter **w** leaving the former undone.	3590
	11:44	which men walk over **w** knowing it."	4024
	22:35	"When I sent you **w** purse, bag or sandals,	868
Jn	1: 3	**w** him nothing was made	6006
	3:34	for God gives the Spirit **w** limit.	1666+4024
	7:15	"How did this man get such learning **w**	3590
	7:51	"Does our law condemn anyone **w**	1569+3590
	8: 7	"If any one of you is **w sin,**	387
	15:25	'They hated me **w reason.'**	1562
	16:29	"Now you are speaking clearly and **w**	4029
Ac	10:29	I came **w raising any objection.**	395
	12:11	"Now I know **w a doubt** that the Lord	242
	12:14	so overjoyed she ran back **w** opening it	4024
	14:17	Yet he has not left himself **w testimony:**	282
	15:24	some went out from us **w** our authorization	4024
	16:37	"They beat us publicly **w** a trial,	185
	25:27	on a prisoner **w** specifying the charges	3590
	27:21	After the men had gone a long time **w food,**	826
	27:33	in constant suspense and have gone **w food**	827
	28:31	and **w hindrance** he preached the kingdom	219
Ro	1:20	so that men are **w excuse.**	406
	4:19	**W** weakening in his faith,	3590
	10:14	how can they hear **w** someone preaching	6006
	14: 1	**w** passing judgment on disputable matters.	1650+3590
1Co	2:14	The man **w the Spirit** does not accept	6035
	4: 8	You have become kings—and that **w** us!	6006
	5: 7	that you may be a new batch **w yeast—**	109
	5: 8	but with **bread w yeast,**	109
	10:25	Eat anything sold in the meat market **w**	3594
	10:27	eat whatever is put before you **w**	3594
	11:21	ahead **w** waiting for anybody else.	NIG
	11:29	drinks **w** recognizing the body of the Lord	3590
	14:10	yet none of them is **w meaning.**	936
	15:10	and his grace to me was not **w effect.**	3031
2Co	11:27	and **have** often **gone w sleep;**	71+1877
	11:27	and thirst and have often **gone w food;**	3763
Gal	6: 4	**w** comparing himself to somebody	2779+4024
Eph	2:12	**w** hope and without God in the world.	2400+3590
	2:12	without hope and **w God** in the world.	117
	5:27	**w** stain or wrinkle or any other blemish,	
			2400+3590
Php	1:28	**w** being frightened in any way	3590
	2:14	Do everything **w** complaining or arguing,	6006
	2:15	children of God **w fault** in a crooked	320
Col	1:22	**w blemish** and free from accusation—	320
2Th	3: 8	did we eat anyone's food **w paying for it.**	1562
1Ti	2: 8	in prayer, **w** anger or disputing.	6006
	5:21	to keep these instructions **w** partiality,	6006
	6:14	to keep this command **w spot** or blame until	834
2Ti	3: 3	**w** love, unforgiving, slanderous,	845
	3: 3	unforgiving, slanderous, **w self-control,**	203
Phm	1:14	not want to do anything **w** your consent,	6006
Heb	4:15	just as we are—yet was **w sin.**	6006
	7: 3	**W father** or mother, without genealogy,	574
	7: 3	Without father or mother, **w genealogy,**	37
	7: 3	**w** beginning of days or end of life,	3612
	7: 7	**w** doubt the lesser person is blessed by	4246+6006
	7:20	And it was not **w** an oath!	6006

Heb	7:20	Others became priests w any oath,	6006
	9: 7	and never w blood, which he offered for	6006
	9:18	the first covenant was not put into effect w	6006
	9:22	and w the shedding of blood there is no	6006
	10:28	died w mercy on the testimony of two or	6006
	11: 6	And w faith it is impossible to please God,	6006
	12:14	w holiness no one will see the Lord.	6006
	13: 2	have entertained angels w knowing it.	3291
Jas	1: 5	gives generously to all w finding fault,	2779+3590
	2:13	because judgment w mercy will be shown	447
	2:15	Suppose a brother or sister is w clothes	1218
	2:18	Show me your faith w deeds,	6006
	2:20	do you want evidence that faith w deeds	6006
	2:26	As the body w the spirit is dead,	6006
	2:26	so faith w deeds is dead.	6006
	4: 5	Or do you think Scripture says w reason	3036
1Pe	1:19	a lamb w blemish or defect.	320
	3: 1	be won over w words by the behavior	459
	4: 9	Offer hospitality to one another w grumbling	459
2Pe	2:16	by a donkey—a beast w speech—	936
	2:17	These men are springs w water	536
1Jn	1: 8	If we claim to be w sin, we deceive	281+4024
Jude	1:12	eating with you w the slightest qualm—	925
	1:12	They are clouds w rain, blown along	536
	1:12	autumn trees, w fruit and uprooted—	182
	1:24	before his glorious presence w fault and	320
Rev	8:12	A third of the day was w light,	3590+5743
	21: 6	to drink w cost from the spring of the water	1562

WITHS (KJV) See THONGS

WITHSTAND (8) [WITHSTOOD]

Nu	31:23	can w fire must be put through the fire,	928+995
	31:23	And whatever cannot w fire must be put	928+995
Jos	10: 8	Not one of them will be able to w you."	928+6641+7156
	23: 9	no one has been able to w you.	928+6641+7156
2Ch	20: 6	and no one can w you.	3656+6640
Ps	147:17	Who can w his icy blast?	4200+6641+7156
La	1:14	He has handed me over to those I cannot w.	7756
Na	1: 6	Who can w his indignation?	4200+6641+7156

WITHSTOOD (1) [WITHSTAND]

Jos	21:44	Not one of their enemies w them;	928+6641+7156

WITLESS (1) [WITS']

Job	11:12	But a w man can no more become wise than	5554

WITNESS (64) [EYEWITNESSES, WITNESSED, WITNESSES]

Ge	21:30	from my hand as a w that I dug this well."	6338
	31:44	and let it serve as a w between us."	6332
	31:48	a w between you and me today."	6332
	31:50	remember that God is a w between you	6332
	31:52	This heap is a w, and this pillar is a witness,	6332
	31:52	This heap is a witness, and this pillar is a w,	6338
Ex	23: 1	a wicked man by making a malicious w.	6332
Nu	5:13	(since there is no w against her and she has	6332
	35:30	to death on the testimony of only one w.	6332
Dt	17: 6	to death on the testimony of only one w.	6332
	19:15	One w is not enough to convict	6332
	19:16	If a malicious w takes the stand to accuse	6332
	19:18	and if the w proves to be a liar,	6332
	31:19	so that it may be a w for me against them.	6332
	31:26	There it will remain as a w against you.	6332
Jos	22:27	a w between us and you and the generations	6332
	22:28	but as a w between us and you.'	6332
	22:34	a W Between Us that the LORD is God.	6332
	24:27	"This stone will be a w against us.	6338
	24:27	It will be a w against you if you are untrue	6338
Jdg	11:10	"The LORD is our w;	1068+9048
1Sa	6:18	is a w to this day in the field of Joshua	6332
	12: 5	"The LORD is w against you,	6332
	12: 5	and also his anointed is w this day,	6332
	12: 5	"He is w," they said.	6332
	20:23	LORD is w between you and me forever."	NIH
	20:42	'The LORD is w between you and me,	NIH
Job	16: 8	and it has become a w;	6332
	16:19	my witness is in heaven; my advocate is on high.	6332
Ps	89:37	the faithful w in the sky."	6332
Pr	6:19	a false w who pours out lies and	6332
	12:17	A truthful w gives honest testimony,	NIH
	12:17	but a false w tells lies.	6332
	14: 5	A truthful w does not deceive,	6332
	14: 5	but a false w pours out lies.	6332
	14:25	A truthful w saves lives,	6332
	14:25	but a false w is deceitful.	7032
	19: 5	A false w will not go unpunished,	6332
	19: 9	A false w will not go unpunished,	6332
	19:28	A corrupt w mocks at justice,	6332
	21:28	A false w will perish,	6332
Isa	19:20	be a sign and w to the LORD Almighty in	6332
	30: 8	days to come it may be an everlasting w.	6332
	55: 4	See, I have made him a w to the peoples,	6332
Jer	29:23	I know it and am a w to it,"	6332
	42: 5	be a true and faithful w against us if we do	6332
Mic	1: 2	the Sovereign LORD may w against you,	6332
Mal	2:14	the LORD is acting as the w between you	6386
Lk	23:48	this sight saw what took place,	NIG
Jn	1: 7	as a w to testify concerning that light,	3456
	1: 8	he came only as a w to the light.	3455
	8:13	"Here you are, appearing as your own w,"	3455
	8:18	my other w is the Father, who sent me."	3455
Ac	1:22	For one of these must become a w with us	3459
	22:15	be his w to all men of what you have seen	3459
	26:16	as a w of what you have seen	3459
Ro	1: 9	is my w how constantly I remember you	3459
	2:15	their consciences also bearing w,	5210
2Co	1:23	I call God as my w that it was in order to	3459
1Th	2: 5	God is our w.	3459
1Pe	5: 1	a fellow elder, a w of Christ's sufferings	3459
Rev	1: 5	Jesus Christ, who is the faithful w,	3459
	2:13	my faithful w, who was put to death	3459
	3:14	the Amen, the faithful and true w,	3459

WITNESSED (3) [WITNESS]

Jer	32:10	I signed and sealed the deed, had it w,	6332+6386
	32:25	and have the transaction w,'"	6332+6386
	32:44	and w in the territory of Benjamin.	6332+6386

WITNESSES (48) [WITNESS]

Nu	35:30	as a murderer only on the testimony of w.	6332
Dt	4:26	I call heaven and earth as w against you	6386
	17: 6	the testimony of two or three w a man shall	6332
	17: 7	of the w must be the first in putting him	6332
	19:15	by the testimony of two or three w.	6332
	30:19	I call heaven and earth as w against you	6386
Jos	24:22	"You are w against yourselves	6332
	24:22	"Yes, we are w," they replied.	6332
Ru	4: 9	"Today you are w that I have bought	6332
	4:10	Today you are w!"	6332
	4:11	and all those at the gate said, "We are w.	6332
Job	10:17	You bring new w against me	6332
Ps	27:12	for false w rise up against me,	6332
	35:11	Ruthless w come forward;	6332
Isa	8: 2	call in Uriah the priest and Zechariah son of Jeberekiah as reliable w	6332+6386
	33: 8	The treaty is broken, its w are despised,	6332
	43: 9	bring in their w to prove they were right,	6332
	43:10	"You are my w," declares the LORD,	6332
	43:12	You are my w," declares the LORD,	6332
	44: 8	You are my w.	6332
Jer	6:18	observe, O w, what will happen to them.	6338
	32:12	of the w who had signed the deed and of all	6332
Mt	10:18	be brought before governors and kings as a	3457
	18:16	by the testimony of two or three w.'	3459
	26:60	though many false w came forward.	6019
	26:65	Why do we need any more w?	3459
Mk	13: 9	before governors and kings as w to them.	3457
	14:63	"Why do we need any more w?"	3459
Lk	21:13	This will result in your being w to them.	3457
	24:48	You are w of these things.	3459
Ac	1: 8	and you will be my w in Jerusalem,	3459
	2:32	and we are all w of the fact.	3459
	3:15	We are w of this.	3459
	5:32	We are w of these things,	3459
	6:13	They produced false w, who testified,	3459
	7:58	the w laid their clothes at the feet of	3459
	10:39	"We are w of everything he did in	3459
	10:41	but by w whom God had already chosen—	3459
	13:31	who are now his w to our people.	3459
1Co	15:15	we are then found to be false w about God,	6020
2Co	13: 1	by the testimony of two or three w."	3459
1Th	2:10	You are w, and so is God, of how holy,	3459
1Ti	5:19	unless it is brought by two or three w.	3459
	6:12	in the presence of many w.	3459
2Ti	2: 2	of many w entrust to reliable men who will	3459
Heb	10:28	on the testimony of two or three w.	NIG
	12: 1	surrounded by such a great cloud of w,	3459
Rev	11: 3	And I will give power to my two w,	3459

WITS' (1) [WITLESS]

Ps	107:27	they were at their w' end.	1182+2683+3972

WITTY (KJV) See DISCRETION

WIVES (113) [WIFE]

Ge	4:23	Lamech said to his w, "Adah and Zillah,	851
	4:23	w of Lamech, hear my words.	851
	6:18	and your wife and your sons' w with you.	851
	7: 7	and his wife and his sons' w entered the ark	851
	7:13	with his wife and the w of his three sons,	851
	8:16	and your wife and your sons and their w.	851
	8:18	with his sons and his wife and his sons' w.	851
	28: 9	in addition to the w he already had.	851
	30:26	Give me my w and children,	851
	31:17	Jacob put his children and his w on camels,	851
	31:50	or if you take any w besides my daughters,	851
	32:22	That night Jacob got up and took his two w,	851
	36: 2	Esau took his w from the women	851
	36: 6	Esau took his w and sons and daughters	851
	37: 2	his father's w, and he brought their father	851
	45:19	from Egypt for your children and your w,	851
	46: 5	and their children and their w in the carts	851
	46:26	not counting his sons' w—	851
Ex	22:24	your w will become widows	851
	32: 2	"Take off the gold earrings that your w,	851
	34:16	choose some of their daughters as w	4374
Nu	14: 3	Our w and children will be taken	851
	16:27	and were standing with their w,	851
	32:26	Our children and w, our flocks and herds	851
Dt	3:19	However, your w, your children	851
	17:17	He must not take many w,	851
	21:15	If a man has two w, and he loves one but	851
	29:11	together with your children and your w,	851
Jdg	1:14	Your w, your children and your livestock	851
	8:30	seventy sons of his own, for he had many w.	851
	12: 9	brought in thirty young women as w	995
	21: 7	can we provide w for those who are left,	851
	21:16	how shall we provide w for	851
	21:18	We can't give them our daughters as w,	851
	21:22	we did not get w for them during the war,	851
1Sa	1: 2	He had two w; one was called Hannah	851
	25:43	and they both were his w.	851
	27: 3	and David had his two w:	851
	30: 3	they found it destroyed by fire and their w	851
	30: 5	David's two w had been captured—	851
	30:18	Amalekites had taken, including his two w.	851
2Sa	2: 2	So David went up there with his two w,	851
	5:13	David took more concubines and w	851
	12: 8	and your master's w into your arms.	851
	12:11	Before your very eyes I will take your w	851
	12:11	he will lie with your w in broad daylight.	851
	19: 5	and the lives of your w and concubines.	851
1Ki	11: 3	He had seven hundred w of royal birth	851
	11: 3	and his w led him astray.	851
	11: 4	his w turned his heart after other gods,	851
	11: 8	He did the same for all his foreign w,	851
	20: 3	the best of your w and children are mine.' "	851
	20: 5	your w and your children.	851
	20: 7	When he sent for my w and my children,	851
2Ki	24:15	his w, his officials and the leading men of	851
1Ch	4: 5	Ashhur the father of Tekoa had two w,	851
	4:17	One of Mered's w gave birth to Miriam,	NIH
	7: 4	for they had many w and children.	851
	8: 8	after he had divorced his w Hushim	851
	14: 3	In Jerusalem David took more w	851
2Ch	11:21	of Absalom more than any of his other w	851
	11:21	he had eighteen and sixty concubines,	851
	11:23	and took many w for them.	851
	13:21	He married fourteen w and had	851
	20:13	with their w and children and little ones,	851
	21:14	your w and everything that is yours,	851
	21:17	together with his sons and w.	851
	24: 3	Jehoiada chose two w for him,	851
	28: 8	their kinsmen two hundred thousand w,	851
	29: 9	and daughters and our w are in captivity.	851
	31:18	They included all the little ones, the w,	851
Ezr	9: 2	taken some of their daughters as w	5951
	10:11	around you and from your foreign w."	851
	10:19	in pledge to put away their w,	851
	10:44	and some of them had children by these w.	851
Ne	4:14	your w and your homes."	851
	5: 1	the men and their w raised a great outcry	851
	10:28	of the Law of God, together with their w	851
Isa	13:16	be looted and their w ravished.	851
Jer	6:12	together with their fields and their w,	851
	8:10	Therefore I will give their w to other men	851
	14:16	be no one to bury them or their w,	851
	18:21	Let their w be made childless and widows;	851
	29: 6	find w for your sons and give your	851
	29:23	committed adultery with their neighbors' w	851
	35: 8	Neither we nor our w nor our sons	851
	38:23	"All your w and children will be brought	851
	44: 9	by you and your w in the land of Judah and	851
	44:15	that their w were burning incense	851
	44:25	You and your w have shown by your actions	851
Da	5: 2	his w and his concubines might drink	10699
	5: 3	his w and his concubines drank from them.	10699
	5:23	your w and your concubines drank wine	10699
	6:24	along with their w and children.	10493
Zec	12:12	with their w by themselves:	NIH
	12:12	the clan of the house of David and their w,	851
	12:12	the clan of the house of Nathan and their w,	851
	12:13	the clan of the house of Levi and their w,	851
	12:13	the clan of Shimei and their w,	851
	12:14	and all the rest of the clans and their w.	851
Mt	19: 8	"Moses permitted you to divorce your w	1222
Ac	21: 5	All the disciples and their w and children	1222
1Co	7:29	From now on those who have w should live	1222
Eph	5:22	W, submit to your husbands as to the Lord.	1222
	5:24	so also w should submit to their husbands	1222
	5:25	Husbands, love your w, just as Christ	1222
	5:28	to love their w as their own bodies.	1222
Col	3:18	W, submit to your husbands, as is fitting	1222
	3:19	love your w and do not be harsh with them.	1222
1Ti	3:11	their w are to be women worthy of respect,	1222
1Pe	3: 1	W, in the same way be submissive	1222
	3: 1	without words by the behavior of their w,	1222
	3: 7	be considerate as you live with your w,	1221

WIVES' (1) [WIFE]

1Ti	4: 7	with godless myths and old w' tales;	1212

WIZARD (KJV) See SPIRITIST

WOE (102) [WOES]

Nu	21:29	W to you, O Moab!	208
1Sa	4: 8	W to us! Who will deliver us	208
Job	10:15	If I am guilty—w to me!	518
Ps	120: 5	W to me that I dwell in Meshech,	210
Pr	23:29	Who has w? Who has sorrow?	208
Ecc	10:16	W to you, O land whose king was a servant	365
Isa	3: 9	W to them! They have brought disaster	208
	3:11	W to the wicked! Disaster is upon them!	208
	5: 8	W to you who add house to house	2098
	5:11	W to those who rise early in the morning	2098
	5:18	W to those who draw sin along with cords	2098
	5:20	W to those who call evil good	2098
	5:21	W to those who are wise in their own eyes	2098
	5:22	W to those who are heroes at drinking wine	2098
	6: 5	"W to me!" I cried. "I am ruined!	208

Isa 10: 1   **W** to those who make unjust laws,   2098
    10: 5   "**W** to the Assyrian, the rod of my anger,   2098
    18: 1   **W** to the land of whirring wings along   2098
    24:16   "I waste away! I waste away! **W** to me!   208
    28: 1   **W** to that wreath, the pride of Ephraim's   2098
    29: 1   **W** to you, Ariel, Ariel,   2098
    29:15   **W** to those who go to great depths   2098
    30: 1   "**W** to the obstinate children,"   2098
    31: 1   **W** to those who go down to Egypt for help,   2098
    33: 1   **W** to you, O destroyer,   2098
    33: 1   **W** to you, O traitor,   NIH
    45: 9   "**W** to him who quarrels with his Maker,   2098
    45:10   **W** to him who says to his father,   2098
Jer 4:13   **W** to us! We are ruined!   208
    10:19   **W** to me because of my injury!   208
    13:27   **W** to you, O Jerusalem!   208
    22:13   **W** to him who builds his palace   2098
    23: 1   "**W** to the shepherds who are destroying   2098
    45: 3   You said, '**W** to me!   208
    48: 1   "**W** to Nebo, for it will be ruined.   2098
    48:46   **W** to you, O Moab!   208
    50:27   **W** to them! For their day has come,   2098
La   5:16   **W** to us, for we have sinned!   208
Eze 2:10   words of lament and mourning and **w**.   2113
    13: 3   **W** to the foolish prophets who follow their   208
    13:18   **W** to the women who sew magic charms   2098
    16:23   "'**W**! Woe to you, declares the Sovereign   208
    16:23   **W** to you, declares the Sovereign Lᴏʀᴅ.   208
    24: 6   "'**W** to the city of bloodshed,   208
    24: 9   "'**W** to the city of bloodshed!   208
    34: 2   **W** to the shepherds of Israel   2098
Hos 7:13   **W** to them, because they have strayed   208
     9:12   **W** to them when I turn away from them!   208
Am   5:18   **W** to you who long for the day of   2098
     6: 1   **W** to you who are complacent in Zion,   2098
Mic 2: 1   **W** to those who plan iniquity,   2098
Na   3: 1   **W** to the city of blood, full of lies,   2098
Hab 2: 6   "**W** to him who piles up stolen goods   2098
     2: 9   "**W** to him who builds his realm   2098
     2:12   "**W** to him who builds a city with bloodshed   2098
     2:15   "**W** to him who gives drink   2098
     2:19   "**W** to him who says to wood, 'Come to life!'   2098
Zep 2: 5   **W** to you who live by the sea,   2098
     3: 1   **W** to the city of oppressors,   2098
Zec 11:17   "**W** to the worthless shepherd,   2098
Mt 11:21   "**W** to you, Korazin!   4026
    11:21   **W** to you, Bethsaida!   4026
    18: 7   "**W** to the world because of the things   4026
    18: 7   but **w** to the man through whom they come!   4026
    23:13   "**W** to you, teachers of the law   4026
    23:15   "**W** to you, teachers of the law   4026
    23:16   "**W** to you, blind guides!   4026
    23:23   "**W** to you, teachers of the law   4026
    23:25   "**W** to you, teachers of the law   4026
    23:27   "**W** to you, teachers of the law   4026
    23:29   "**W** to you, teachers of the law   4026
    26:24   **w** to that man who betrays the Son of Man!   4026
Mk 14:21   **w** to that man who betrays the Son of Man!   4026
Lk   6:24   "But **w** to you who are rich,   4026
     6:25   **W** to you who are well fed now,   4026
     6:25   **W** to you who laugh now,   4026
     6:26   **W** to you when all men speak well of you,   4026
    10:13   "**W** to you, Korazin!   4026
    10:13   **W** to you, Bethsaida!   4026
    11:42   "**W** to you Pharisees,   4026
    11:43   "**W** to you Pharisees,   4026
    11:44   "**W** to you, because you are   4026
    11:46   "And you experts in the law, **w** to you,   4026
    11:47   "**W** to you, because you build tombs for   4026
    11:52   "**W** to you experts in the law,   4026
    17: 1   **w** to that person through whom they come.   4026
    22:22   but **w** to that man who betrays him."   4026
1Co 9:16   **W** to me if I do not preach the gospel!   4026
Jude 1:11   **W** to them! They have taken the way of   4026
Rev 8:13   in a loud voice: "**W**! Woe! Woe to   4026
     8:13   in a loud voice: "Woe! **W**! Woe to   4026
     8:13   Woe! **W**! Woe to the inhabitants of the earth,   4026
     9:12   The first **w** is past;   4026
    11:14   The second **w** has passed;   4026
    11:14   the third **w** is coming soon.   4026
    12:12   But **w** to the earth and the sea,   4026
    18:10   they will stand far off and cry: "'**W**!   4026
    18:10   **W**, O great city, O Babylon, city of power!   4026
    18:16   and cry out: "'**W**! Woe, O great city,   4026
    18:16   **W**, O great city, dressed in fine linen,   4026
    18:19   cry out: "'**W**! Woe, O great city,   4026
    18:19   **W**, O great city, where all who had ships   4026

WOES (2) [WOE]

Ps 32:10   Many are the **w** of the wicked,   4799
Rev 9:12   two other **w** are yet to come.   4026

WOKE (10) [WAKE]

Ge 41: 4   Then Pharaoh **w** up;   3699
    41: 7   Then Pharaoh **w** up; it had been a dream.   3699
    41:21   Then I **w** up.   3699
Mt   1:24   When Joseph **w** up, he did what the angel   1586
     8:25   The disciples came and **w** him, saying,   1586
    25: 7   the virgins all **w** up and trimmed their lamps.   1586
Mk   4:38   The disciples **w** him and said to him,   1586
Lk   8:24   The disciples went and **w** him, saying,   1444
Ac 12: 7   He struck Peter on the side and **w** him **up**.   1586
    16:27   The jailer **w** up, and when he saw   1181+2031

WOLF (6) [WOLVES]

Ge 49:27   "Benjamin is a ravenous **w**;   2269
Isa 11: 6   The **w** will live with the lamb,   2269
    65:25   The **w** and the lamb will feed together,   2269
Jer 5: 6   a **w** from the desert will ravage them,   2269
Jn 10:12   So when he sees the **w** coming,   3380
    10:12   Then the **w** attacks the flock and scatters it.   3380

WOLVES (7) [WOLF]

Eze 22:27   within her are like **w** tearing their prey;   2269
Hab 1: 8   fiercer than **w** at dusk.   2269
Zep 3: 3   her rulers are evening **w**,   2269
Mt   7:15   but inwardly they are ferocious **w**.   3380
    10:16   I am sending you out like sheep among **w**.   3380
Lk 10: 3   I am sending you out like lambs among **w**.   3380
Ac 20:29   savage **w** will come in among you and will   3380

WOMAN (353) [WOMAN'S, WOMEN, WOMEN'S]

Ge   2:22   Then the Lᴏʀᴅ God made a **w** from   851
     2:23   she shall be called '**w**,'   851
     3: 1   He said to the **w**, "Did God really say,   851
     3: 2   The **w** said to the serpent,   851
     3: 4   the serpent said to the **w**.   851
     3: 6   the **w** saw that the fruit of the tree was good   851
     3:12   "The **w** you put here with me—   851
     3:13   Then the Lᴏʀᴅ God said to the **w**,   851
     3:13   The **w** said, "The serpent deceived me,   851
     3:15   I will put enmity between you and the **w**,   851
     3:16   To the **w** he said, "I will greatly increase   851
    12:11   "I know what a beautiful **w** you are.   851
    12:14   that she was a very beautiful **w**.   851
    20: 3   as dead because of the **w** you have taken;   851
    20: 3   she is a **married w**."   AIT
    21:10   "Get rid of that **slave w** and her son,   563
    24: 5   if the **w** is unwilling to come back with me   851
    24: 8   if the **w** is unwilling to come back with you,   851
    24:39   if the **w** will not come back with me?'   851
    28: 1   "Do not marry a Canaanite **w**.   1426
    28: 6   "Do not marry a Canaanite **w**,"   1426
    38:20   in order to get his pledge back from the **w**,   851
    46:10   Zohar and Shaul the son of a **Canaanite w**.   AIT
Ex   2: 1   of the house of Levi married a Levite **w**,   1426
     2: 9   So the **w** took the baby and nursed him.   851
     3:22   Every **w** is to ask her neighbor   851
     3:22   and any **w** living in her house for articles   AIT
     6:15   Zohar and Shaul the son of a **Canaanite w**.   AIT
    21: 4   the **w** and her children shall belong   851
    21:10   If he marries **another w**,   AIT
    21:22   "If men who are fighting hit a pregnant **w**   851
    21:28   "If a bull gores a man or a **w** to death,   851
    21:29   penned up and it kills a man or a **w**,   851
    35:25   Every skilled **w** spun with her hands   851
    36: 6   or **w** is to make anything else as an offering   851
Lev 12: 2   'A **w** who becomes pregnant and gives birth   851
    12: 4   Then the **w** must wait thirty-two days to   NIH
    12: 5   for two weeks the **w** will be unclean.   NIH
    12: 7   the regulations for the **w** who **gives birth** to AIT
    13:29   "If a man or **w** has a sore on the head or on   851
    13:38   a man or **w** has white spots on the skin,   851
    15:18   a man lies with a **w** and there is an emission   851
    15:19   "'When a **w** has her regular flow of blood,   851
    15:25   a **w** has a discharge of blood for many days   851
    15:33   **w** in her **monthly period,**   AIT
    15:33   for a man or a **w** with a discharge,   5922
    15:33   **w** who is **ceremonially unclean.**   AIT
    18:17   not have sexual relations with both a **w**   851
    18:19   not approach a **w** to have sexual relations   851
    18:22   not lie with a man as one lies with a **w**;   851
    18:23   A **w** must not present herself to an animal   851
    19:20   with a **w** who is a slave girl promised   851
    20:11   **the man and the w** must be put to death;   2157ˢ
    20:13   a man lies with a man as one lies with a **w**,   851
    20:14   a man marries both a **w** and her mother,   851
    20:16   "'If a **w** approaches an animal   851
    20:16   kill both the **w** and the animal.   851
    20:18   with a **w** during her monthly period   851
    20:27   "'A man or **w** who is a medium or spiritist   851
    21:13   "'The **w** he marries must be a virgin.   851
    21:14   He must not marry a widow, a **divorced** w,   AIT
    21:14   or a **w** defiled by prostitution.   AIT
    24:11   the Israelite **w** blasphemed the Name with   851
Nu   3:12   the first male offspring of every Israelite **w**. NIH
     5: 6   a man or **w** wrongs another in any way and   851
     5:18   After the priest has had the **w** stand before   851
     5:19   the priest shall put the **w** under oath and say   851
     5:21   the priest is to put the **w** under this curse of   851
     5:22   "Then the **w** is to say, "Amen.   851
     5:24   He shall have the **w** drink the bitter water   851
     5:26   he is to have the **w** drink the water.   851
     5:28   the **w** has not defiled herself and is free   851
     5:29   is the law of jealousy when a **w** goes astray   851
     5:31   **w** will bear the consequences of her sin.'   851
     6: 2   'If a man or **w** wants to make a special vow,   851
     8:16   first male offspring from every Israelite **w**.   8167
    25: 6   to his family a **Midianite** w right before   AIT
    25:14   who was killed with the **Midianite** w   AIT
    25:15   the name of the Midianite **w** who was put   851
    25:18   the **w** who was killed when the plague came   AIT
    30: 3   "When a young **w** still living in her father's   851
    30: 9   a widow or **divorced w** will be binding   AIT
    30:10   a **w** living with her husband makes a vow   NIH
    31:17   And kill every **w** who has slept with a man,   851
Dt   4:16   whether formed like a man or a **w**,   5922

Dt 15:12   If a fellow Hebrew, a man or a **w**,   6303ˢ
    17: 2   or **w** living among you in one of the towns   851
    17: 5   the man or **w** who has done this evil deed   851
    20: 7   Has anyone become pledged to a **w** and   851
    21:11   the captives a beautiful **w** and are attracted   851
    22: 5   A **w** must not wear men's clothing,   851
    22:14   a bad name, saying, "I married this **w**,   851
    22:22   who slept with her and the **w** must die.   851
    23:17   or **w** is to become a shrine prostitute.   1426
    24: 1   a **w** who becomes displeasing to him   851
    28:30   You will be pledged to be married to a **w**,   851
    28:56   most gentle and **sensitive** among you—   AIT
    29:18   Make sure there is no man or **w**,   851
Jos 4: 9   w had taken the two men and hidden them.   851
Jdg 4: 9   for the Lᴏʀᴅ will hand Sisera over to a **w**."   851
     9:53   a **w** dropped an upper millstone on his head   6303ˢ
     9:54   so that they can't say, 'A **w** killed him.'"   851
    11: 2   "because you are the son of another **w**."   851
    13: 6   the **w** went to her husband and told him,   851
    13: 9   and the angel of God came again to the **w**   851
    13:10   The **w** hurried to tell her husband,   851
    13:24   The **w** gave birth to a boy   851
    14: 1   and saw there a young Philistine **w**.   851
    14: 2   "I have seen a Philistine **w** in Timnah.   851
    14: 3   an acceptable **w** among your relatives or   851
    14: 7   Then he went down and talked with the **w**,   6303ˢ
    14:10   Now his father went down to see the **w**.   851
    16: 4   he fell in love with a **w** in the Valley   851
    19:26   At daybreak the **w** went back to the house   851
    20: 4   the Levite, the husband of the murdered **w**,   851
    21:11   "Kill every male and every **w** who is not   851
Ru   3: 2   "Whose **young** is that?"   5855
     3: 8   and he turned and discovered a **w** lying   851
     3:11   that you are a **w** of noble character.   851
     3:14   "Don't let it be known that a **w** came to   851
     4:11   May the Lᴏʀᴅ make the **w** who is coming   851
     4:12   the Lᴏʀᴅ gives you by this **young w**,   5855
1Sa 1:15   "I am a **w** who is deeply troubled.   851
     1:16   Do not take your servant for a wicked **w**;   1426
     1:23   So the **w** stayed at home and nursed her son   851
     1:26   the **w** who stood here beside you praying to   851
     2:20   the Lᴏʀᴅ give you children by this **w**   851
    20:30   "You son of a **perverse** and rebellious **w**!   AIT
    25: 3   She was an intelligent and beautiful **w**,   851
    27: 9   he did not leave a man or **w** alive,   851
    27:11   not leave a man or **w** alive to be brought   851
    28: 7   "Find me a **w** who is a medium,   851
    28: 8   and at night he and two men went to the **w**.   851
    28: 9   But the **w** said to him,   851
    28:11   w asked, "Whom shall I bring up for you?"   851
    28:12   When the **w** saw Samuel,   851
    28:13   The **w** said, "I see a spirit coming up out of   851
    28:21   When the **w** came to Saul and saw   851
    28:23   But his men joined the **w** in urging him,   851
    28:24   The **w** had a fattened calf at the house,   851
2Sa 3: 8   of an offense involving this **w**!   851
    11: 2   From the roof he saw a **w** bathing.   851
    11: 2   The **w** was very beautiful,   851
    11: 5   The **w** conceived and sent word to David,   851
    11:21   Didn't a **w** throw an upper millstone on him   851
    13:17   "Get this out of here and bolt the door   2296
    13:20   her brother Absalom's house, a **desolate** w.   AIT
    14: 2   and had a wise **w** brought from there.   851
    14: 2   like a **w** who has spent many days grieving   851
    14: 4   When the **w** from Tekoa went to the king,   851
    14: 8   The king said to the **w**, "Go home,   851
    14: 9   But the **w** from Tekoa said to him,   851
    14:12   Then the **w** said,   851
    14:13   "Why then have you devised   851
    14:18   Then the king said to the **w**,   851
    14:18   "Let my lord the king speak," the **w** said.   851
    14:19   The **w** answered, "As surely as you live,   851
    14:27   and she became a beautiful **w**.   851
    17:20   Absalom's men came to the **w** at the house,   851
    17:20   The **w** answered them,   851
    20:16   a wise **w** called from the city,   851
    20:21   The **w** said to Joab,   851
    20:22   Then the **w** went to all the people   851
1Ki 3:17   this **w** and I live in the same house.   851
     3:18   this **w** also had a baby.   851
     3:22   The other **w** said, "No! The living one is my   851
     3:26   The **w** whose son was alive was filled   851
     3:27   "Give the living baby to **the first w**.   2023ˢ
    17:15   for Elijah and for **the w** and her family.   2085ˢ
    17:17   of the **w** who owned the house became ill.   851
    17:24   Then the **w** said to Elijah,   851
2Ki 4: 8   And a well-to-do **w** was there,   851
     4:17   But the **w** became pregnant,   851
     6:26   a **w** cried to him, "Help me,   851
     6:28   She answered, "This **w** said to me,   851
     8: 1   to the **w** whose son he had restored to life,   851
     8: 2   The **w** proceeded to do as the man   851
     8: 5   the **w** whose son Elisha had brought back   851
     8: 5   Gehazi said, "This is the **w**,   851
     8: 6   The king asked the **w** about it,   851
     9:34   "Take care of that **cursed** w," he said,   AIT
1Ch 2: 3   three were born to him by a **Canaanite** w,   AIT
     2:16   cake of raisins to each Israelite man and **w**.   851
2Ch 15:13   whether small or great, man or **w**,   851
    24: 7   of that **wicked** w Athaliah had broken into   AIT
    24:26   son of Shimeath an **Ammonite** w,   AIT
    24:26   son of Shimrith a **Moabite** w.   AIT
    24   and spared neither young man nor **young w**,   1435
Ezr 10:14   a foreign **w** come at a set time,   851
Est 4:11   for any man or **w** who approaches the king   851
Job 2:10   "You are talking like a **foolish** w.   AIT
    14: 1   "Man born of **w** is of few days and full   851

Job	15:14	that he could be pure, or one born of **w**,	851
	24:21	They prey on the barren and **childless w**,	AIT
	25: 4	How can one born of **w** be pure?	851
	31: 9	"If my heart has been enticed by a **w**,	851
Ps	48: 6	pain like that of a **w in labor.**	AIT
	113: 9	He settles the **barren w** in her home as a happy mother	AIT
Pr	6:24	keeping you from the immoral **w**,	851
	7:10	Then out came a **w** to meet him,	851
	9:13	The **w** Folly is loud;	851
	11:16	A kindhearted **w** gains respect,	851
	11:22	a beautiful **w** who shows no discretion.	851
	14: 1	The wise **w** builds her house,	851
	20:16	in pledge if he does it for a **wayward** w.	AIT
	27:13	in pledge if he does it for a **wayward** w.	AIT
	30:23	an **unloved** w who is married,	AIT
	31:30	a **w** who fears the LORD is to be praised.	851
Ecc	7:26	I find more bitter than death the **w** who is	851
	7:28	but not one [upright] **w** among them all.	851
SS	1: 7	Why should I be like a **veiled w** beside	AIT
Isa	13: 8	they will writhe like a **w in labor.**	AIT
	21: 3	pangs seize me, like those of a **w in labor**;	AIT
	26:17	As a **w with child** and about	AIT
	42:14	But now, like a **w in childbirth**, I cry out,	AIT
	54: 1	O **barren** w, you who never bore a child;	AIT
	54: 1	of the **desolate** w than of her who has	AIT
Jer	3:20	But like a **w** unfaithful to her husband,	851
	4:31	I hear a cry as of a **w in labor**,	AIT
	6:24	pain like that of a **w in labor.**	AIT
	13:21	not pain grip you like that of a **w** in labor?	851
	22:23	pain like that of a **w in labor**!	AIT
	30: 6	on his stomach like a **w in labor**,	AIT
	31:22	a **w** will surround a man."	5922
	48:19	Ask the man fleeing and the **w escaping**,	AIT
	48:41	be like the heart of a **w** in labor.	851
	49:22	be like the heart of a **w** in labor.	851
	49:24	pain like that of a **w** in labor.	AIT
	50:43	pain like that of a **w** in labor.	AIT
	51:22	with you I shatter man and **w**,	851
Eze	5: 6	or lie with a **w** during her period.	851
	23:42	on the arms of **the w and her sister**	2177S
Hos	13:13	Pains as of a **w in childbirth** come to him,	AIT
Mic	4: 9	pain seizes you like that of a **w in labor**?	AIT
	4:10	O Daughter of Zion, like a **w in labor**,	AIT
Zec	5: 7	and there in the basket sat a **w**!	851
Mt	5:28	who looks at a **w** lustfully has already committed adultery	1222
	5:32	the **divorced** w commits adultery.	AIT
	9:20	then a **w** who had been subject to bleeding	1222
	9:22	And the **w** was healed from that moment.	1222
	13:33	that a **w** took and mixed into a large amount	1222
	15:22	A Canaanite **w** from that vicinity came	1222
	15:25	The **w** came and knelt before him.	NIG
	15:28	Jesus answered, **"W**, you have great faith!	1222
	19: 9	and marries **another** w commits adultery."	AIT
	22:27	Finally, the **w** died.	1222
	26: 7	a **w** came to him with an alabaster jar	1222
	26:10	"Why are you bothering this **w**?	1222
Mk	5:25	And a **w** was there who had been subject	1222
	5:33	Then the **w**, knowing what had happened	1222
	7:25	a **w** whose little daughter was possessed by	1222
	7:26	The **w** was a Greek,	1222
	10:11	and marries **another** w commits adultery	AIT
	12:22	Last of all, the **w** died too.	1222
	14: 3	a **w** came with an alabaster jar	1222
Lk	7:37	When a **w** who had lived a sinful life in	1222
	7:39	and what kind of **w** she is—	1222
	7:44	he turned toward the **w** and said to Simon,	1222
	7:44	"Do you see this **w**?	1222
	7:45	You did not give me a kiss, but this **w**,	AIT
	7:50	Jesus said to the **w**, "Your faith has saved	1222
	8:43	And a **w** was there who had been subject	1222
	8:47	Then the **w**, seeing that she could not go	1222
	10:38	a **w** named Martha opened her home to him.	1222
	11:27	a **w** in the crowd called out,	1222
	13:11	and a **w** was there who had been crippled by	1222
	13:12	**"W**, you are set free from your infirmity."	1222
	13:16	Then should not this **w**,	AIT
	13:21	that a **w** took and mixed into a large amount	1222
	15: 8	a **w** has ten silver coins and loses one.	1222
	16:18	and marries **another** w commits adultery.	AIT
	16:18	who marries a **divorced** w commits adultery.	AIT
	20:29	The first one **married a w** and died childless.	1222+3284
	20:32	Finally, the **w** died too.	1222
	22:57	**"W**, I don't know him," he said.	1222
Jn	2: 4	**"Dear w**, why do you involve me?"	1222
	4: 7	When a Samaritan **w** came to draw water,	1222
	4: 9	The Samaritan **w** said to him,	1222
	4: 9	"You are a Jew and I am a Samaritan **w**.	1222
	4:11	the **w** said, "you have nothing to draw with	1222
	4:15	The **w** said to him, "Sir, give me this water	1222
	4:19	the **w** said, "I can see that you are a prophet.	1222
	4:21	Jesus declared, "Believe me, **w**,	1222
	4:25	The **w** said, "I know that Messiah"	1222
	4:27	to find him talking with a **w**.	1222
	4:28	the **w** went back to the town and said to	1222
	4:42	They said to the **w**,	1222
	8: 3	and the Pharisees brought in a **w** caught	1222
	8: 4	this **w** was caught in the act of adultery.	1222
	8: 9	with the **w** still standing there.	1222
	8:10	Jesus straightened up and asked her, **"W**,	1222
	16:21	A **w** giving birth to a child has pain	1222
	19:26	he said to his mother, **"Dear w**,	1222
	20:13	They asked her, **"W**, why are you crying?"	1222
	20:15	**"W**," he said, "why are you crying?"	1222
Ac	9:40	Turning toward the **dead** w, he said,	AIT

Ac	16:14	of those listening was a **w** named Lydia,	1222
	17:34	also a **w** named Damaris,	1222
Ro	7: 2	a married **w** is bound to her husband as long	1222
	16:12	**another** w who has worked very hard in	AIT
1Co	7: 2	and **each** w her own husband.	AIT
	7:13	if a **w** has a husband who is not a believer	1222
	7:15	or **w** is not bound in such circumstances;	80
	7:34	An unmarried **w** or virgin is concerned	1222
	7:34	a **married** w is concerned about the affairs	AIT
	7:39	A **w** is bound to her husband as long as he	1222
	11: 3	and the head *of* the **w** is man,	1222
	11: 5	And every **w** who prays or prophesies	1222
	11: 6	If a **w** does not cover her head,	1222
	11: 6	if it is a disgrace *for* a **w** to have her hair cut	1222
	11: 7	but the **w** is the glory of man.	1222
	11: 8	For man did not come from **w**,	1222
	11: 8	but **w** from man;	1222
	11: 9	neither was man created for **w**,	1222
	11: 9	but **w** for man.	1222
	11:10	the **w** ought to have a sign of authority	1222
	11:11	however, **w** is not independent of man,	1222
	11:11	nor is man independent of **w**.	1222
	11:12	For as **w** came from man,	1222
	11:12	so also man is born of **w**.	1222
	11:13	Is it proper for a **w** to pray to God	1222
	11:15	but that if a **w** has long hair,	1222
	14:35	for it is disgraceful *for* a **w** to speak in	1222
Gal	4: 4	God sent his Son, born of a **w**,	1222
	4:22	one by the **slave** w and the other by	4087
	4:22	and the other by the **free** w.	AIT
	4:23	the **slave** w was born in the ordinary way;	4087
	4:23	by the **free** w was born as the result of	AIT
	4:27	For it is written: "Be glad, O **barren** w,	5096
	4:27	*of* the **desolate** w than of her who has	AIT
	4:30	"Get rid of the **slave** w and her son,	4087
	4:31	we are not children *of* the **slave** w,	4087
	4:31	but *of* the **free** w.	AIT
1Th	5: 3	as labor pains on a **pregnant** w,	1143+1877+2400
1Ti	2:11	A **w** should learn in quietness and full	1222
	2:12	not permit a **w** to teach or to have authority	1222
	2:14	it was the **w** who was deceived and became	1222
	5:16	If **any** w who is a believer has widows	AIT
Rev	2:20	You tolerate that **w** Jezebel,	1222
	12: 1	a **w** clothed with the sun,	1222
	12: 4	The dragon stood in front of the **w** who was	1222
	12: 6	The **w** fled into the desert to a place	1222
	12:13	the **w** who had given birth to the male child.	1222
	12:14	The **w** was given the two wings of a great	1222
	12:15	to overtake the **w** and sweep her away with	1222
	12:16	the earth helped the **w** by opening its mouth	1222
	12:17	at the **w** and went off to make war against	1222
	17: 3	There I saw a **w** sitting on a scarlet beast	1222
	17: 4	The **w** was dressed in purple and scarlet,	1222
	17: 6	I saw that the **w** was drunk with the blood	1222
	17: 7	I will explain to you the mystery *of* the **w**	1222
	17: 9	seven hills on which the **w** sits.	1222
	17:18	The **w** you saw is the great city that rules	1222

WOMAN'S (9) [WOMAN]

Ge	21:10	for that **slave** w son will never share in	563
Ex	21:22	be whatever the **w** husband demands	851
Nu	25: 8	through the Israelite and into the **w** body.	851
1Ki	3:19	the night this **w** son died because she lay	851
2Ki	6:30	When the king heard the **w** words,	851
Eze	36:17	Their conduct was like a **w monthly uncleanness**—	2021+3240+5614
Jn	4:39	in him because of the **w** testimony.	1222
Gal	4:30	for the **slave** w son will never share in	4087
	4:30	in the inheritance with the **free** w son."	AIT

WOMB (56) [WOMBS]

Ge	20:18	up every **w** in Abimelech's household	8167
	25:23	"Two nations are in your **w**,	1061
	25:24	there were twin boys in her **w**.	1061
	29:31	he opened her **w**, but Rachel was barren.	8167
	30:22	he listened to her and opened her **w**.	8167
	38:27	there were twin boys in her **w**.	1061
	49:25	blessings of the breast and **w**.	8167
Ex	13: 2	of every **w** among the Israelites belongs	8167
	13:12	to the LORD the first offspring of every **w**.	8167
	13:15	the first male offspring of every **w**	8167
	34:19	first offspring of every **w** belongs to me,	8167
Nu	12:12	stillborn infant from its mother's **w**	8167
	18:15	The first offspring of every **w**,	8167
Dt	7:13	He will bless the fruit of your **w**,	1061
	28: 4	The fruit of your **w** will be blessed,	1061
	28:11	in the fruit of your **w**, the young of your	1061
	28:18	The fruit of your **w** will be cursed,	1061
	28:53	you will eat the fruit of the **w**,	1061
	28:57	from her **w** and the children she bears.	1068+8079
	30: 9	of your hands and in the fruit of your **w**,	1061
1Sa	1: 5	and the LORD had closed her **w**.	8167
	1: 6	And because the LORD had closed her **w**,	8167
Job	1:21	"Naked I came from my mother's **w**,	1061
	3:10	for it did not shut the doors of the **w** on me	1061
	3:11	and die as I came from the **w**?	1061
	10:18	"Why then did you bring me out of the **w**?	8167
	10:19	or had been carried straight from the **w** to	1061
	15:35	their **w** fashions deceit."	1061
	24:20	**w** forgets them, the worm feasts on them;	8167
	31:15	not he who made me in the **w** make them?	1061
	38: 8	when it burst forth from the **w**,	8167
	38:29	From whose **w** comes the ice?	1061
Ps	22: 9	Yet you brought me out of the **w**;	1061
	22:10	from my mother's **w** you have been my God	1061

Ps	58: 3	the **w** they are wayward and speak lies.	1061
	71: 6	you brought me forth from my mother's **w**,	5055
	110: 3	the **w** *of* the dawn you will receive the dew	8167
	139:13	you knit me together in my mother's **w**.	1061
Pr	30:16	the barren **w**, land, which is never satisfied	8167
	31: 2	O son of my **w**, O son of my vows,	1061
Ecc	5:15	Naked a man comes from his mother's **w**,	1061
	11: 5	or how the body is formed in a mother's **w**,	1061
Isa	44: 2	who made you, who formed you in the **w**,	1061
	44:24	your Redeemer, who formed you in the **w**:	1061
	49: 5	the **w** to be his servant to bring Jacob back	1061
	66: 9	up the **w** when I bring to delivery?"	NIH
Jer	1: 5	"Before I formed you in the **w** I knew you,	1061
	20:17	For he did not kill me in the **w**,	8167
	20:17	her **w** enlarged forever.	8167
	20:18	of the **w** to see trouble and sorrow and	8167
Hos	12: 3	In the **w** he grasped his brother's heel;	1061
	13:13	not come to the **opening of the w**.	1201+5402
Lk	1:41	the baby leaped in her **w**,	3120
	1:44	the baby in my **w** leaped for joy.	3120
Jn	3: 4	second time into his mother's **w** to be born!	3120
Ro	4:19	and that Sarah's **w** was also dead.	3616

WOMBS (2) [WOMB]

Hos	9:14	Give them **w** that miscarry and breasts	8167
Lk	23:29	the **w** that never bore and the breasts	3120

WOMEN (228) [WOMAN]

Ge	4:19	Lamech married two **w**,	851
	14:16	together with the **w** and the other people.	851
	24:11	the time the **w** go out *to* draw water.	AIT
	27:46	with living because of these Hittite **w**;	1426
	27:46	If Jacob takes a wife from among the **w**	1426
	27:46	from Hittite **w** like these,	1426
	28: 8	the Canaanite **w** were to his father Isaac;	1426
	30:13	the **w** will call me happy."	1426
	31:43	"The **w** are my daughters,	1426
	33: 5	Esau looked up and saw the **w** and children.	851
	34: 1	went out to visit the **w** of the land.	1426
	34:29	and all their **w** and children,	851
	36: 2	Esau took his wives from the **w** *of* Canaan:	1426
Ex	1:19	the **Hebrew** w in childbirth and observe	AIT
	1:19	"**Hebrew** w are not like Egyptian women;	AIT
	1:19	"Hebrew women are not like Egyptian **w**;	851
	2: 7	the Hebrew **w** to nurse the baby for you?"	851
	10:10	along with your **w and children!**	3251
	10:24	your **w and children** may go with you;	3251
	11: 2	Tell the people that men and **w** alike are	851
	12:37	besides **w and children.**	3251
	15:20	and all the **w** followed her,	851
	35:22	All who were willing, men and **w** alike,	851
	35:26	And all the **w** who were willing and had	851
	35:29	men and **w** who were willing brought to	851
	38: 8	the **w** who **served** at the entrance to the Tent	AIT
Lev	21: 7	not marry **w** defiled by prostitution	851
	26:26	ten **w** will be able to bake your bread	851
Nu	25: 1	in sexual immorality with Moabite **w**,	1426
	31: 9	the Midianite **w** and children and took all	851
	31:15	"Have you allowed all the **w** to live?"	5922
	31:35	**w** who had never slept with a man.	851
	32:16	and cities for our **w and children.**	3251
	32:17	Meanwhile our **w and children** will live	3251
	32:24	Build cities for your **w and children**,	3251
Dt	2:34	men, **w** and children.	851
	3: 6	men, **w** and children.	851
	7:14	none of your men or **w** will be **childless**,	AIT
	20:14	As for the **w**, the children,	851
	31:12	men, **w** and children, and the aliens living	851
	32:25	Young men and **young w** will perish,	1435
Jos	6:21	men and **w**, young and old, cattle,	851
	8:25	Twelve thousand men and **w** fell that day—	851
	8:35	including the **w** and children,	851
Jdg	5:24	"Most blessed of **w** be Jael,	851
	5:24	most blessed of tent-dwelling **w**.	851
	9:49	about a thousand men and **w**, also died.	851
	9:51	to which all the men and **w**—	851
	11:40	that each year the **young w** *of* Israel go out	1426
	12: 9	for his sons he brought in thirty **young w**	1426
	16:27	the temple was crowded with men and **w**;	851
	16:27	men and **w** watching Samson perform.	851
	21:10	including the **w** and children.	851
	21:12	young **w** who had never slept with a man,	1435
	21:14	and were given the **w** *of* Jabesh Gilead	851
	21:16	"With the **w** of Benjamin destroyed,	851
Ru	1: 4	They married **Moabite** w,	AIT
	1:19	So the two **w** went on until they came	2157S
	1:19	and *the* **w** exclaimed, "Can this be Naomi?"	AIT
	4:14	The **w** said to Naomi: "Praise be to the	851
	4:17	**w living** there said, "Naomi has a son."	AIT
1Sa	2:22	the **w** who served at the entrance to the Tent	851
	4:20	As she was dying, the **w attending** her said,	AIT
	15: 3	Do not spare them; put to death men and **w**,	851
	15:33	"As your sword has made **w** childless,	851
	15:33	so will your mother be childless among **w**."	851
	18: 6	the **w** came out from all the towns of Israel	851
	21: 4	the men have kept themselves from **w**."	851
	21: 5	"Indeed **w** have been kept from us,	851
	22:19	with its men and **w**, its children and infants,	851
	30: 2	the **w** and all who were in it,	851
2Sa	1:26	more wonderful than that of **w**.	851
	6:19	crowd of Israelites, both men and **w**.	851
	19:35	the voices of men and **w** singers?	8876S
1Ki	11: 1	Solomon, however, loved many foreign **w**	851
2Ki	8:12	and rip open their **pregnant** w."	AIT
	15:16	and ripped open all the **pregnant** w.	AIT

2Ki	23: 7	and where **w** did weaving for Asherah.	851
2Ch	28:10	And now you intend to make the men and **w**	9148
	35:25	the men and **w** singers commemorate Josiah	8876[S]
Ezr	2:65	and they also had 200 men and **w** singers.	8876[S]
	10: 1	men, **w** and children—	851
	10: 2	by marrying foreign **w** from the peoples	851
	10: 3	to send away all these **w** and their children,	851
	10:10	you have married foreign **w,**	851
	10:17	the men who had married foreign **w.**	851
	10:18	the following had married foreign **w:**	851
	10:44	All these had married foreign **w,**	851
Ne	7:67	and they also had 245 men and **w** singers.	8876[S]
	8: 2	and **w** and all who were able to understand.	851
	8: 3	**w** and others who could understand.	851
	12:43	The **w** and children also rejoiced.	851
	13:23	of Judah who had married **w** from Ashdod,	851
	13:26	but even he was led into sin by foreign **w.**	851
	13:27	to our God by marrying foreign **w?**"	851
Est	1: 9	Queen Vashti also gave a banquet for the **w**	851
	1:17	conduct will become known to all the **w,**	851
	1:18	Median **w** of the **nobility** who have heard	8576
	1:20	all the **w** will respect their husbands,	851
	2: 3	who is in charge of the **w;**	851
	2:12	of beauty treatments prescribed for the **w,**	851
	2:17	to Esther more than to any of the other **w,**	851
	3:13	young and old, **w** and little children—	851
	8:11	that might attack them and their **w,**	851
Job	42:15	Nowhere in all the land were there found **w**	851
Ps	45: 9	of kings are among your **honored** **w;**	AIT
Pr	31: 3	do not spend your strength on **w,**	851
	31:29	"Many **w** do noble things,	1426
Ecc	2: 8	I acquired men and **w** singers,	8876[S]
SS	1: 8	If you do not know, most beautiful of **w,**	851
	5: 9	better than others, most beautiful of **w?**	851
	6: 1	has your lover gone, most beautiful of **w?**	851
Isa	3:12	**w** rule over them.	851
	3:16	"The **w** of Zion are haughty,	1426
	3:17	on the heads of the **w** of Zion;	1426
	4: 1	that day seven **w** will take hold of one man	851
	4: 4	The Lord will wash away the filth of the **w**	1426
	16: 2	the **w** of Moab at the fords of the Arnon.	1426
	19:16	In that day the Egyptians will be like **w.**	851
	27:11	and **w** come and make fires with them.	851
	32: 9	You **w** who are so complacent	851
	32:11	Tremble, you **complacent** **w;**	AIT
Jer	2:33	the **worst** of **w** can learn from your ways.	AIT
	7:18	and the **w** knead the dough and make cakes	851
	9:17	Call for the **wailing** **w** to come;	AIT
	9:20	Now, O **w,** hear the word of the LORD;	851
	16: 3	and about the **w** who are their mothers and	3528[S]
	31: 8	expectant mothers and **w** in **labor;**	AIT
	38:22	All the **w** left in the palace of the king	851
	38:22	Those **w** will **say** to you:	AIT
	40: 7	**w** and children who were the poorest in	851
	41:16	the soldiers, **w,** children and court officials	851
	43: 6	led away all the men, **w** and children and	851
	44: 7	by cutting off from Judah the men and **w,**	851
	44:15	along with all the **w** who were present—	851
	44:19	The **w** added, "When we burned incense to	NIH
	44:20	both men and **w,** who were answering him,	851
	44:24	the people, including the **w,** "Hear the word	851
	50:37	They will become **w.**	851
	51:30	they have become like **w.**	851
La	2:10	**young** **w** of Jerusalem have bowed their	1435
	2:20	Should **w** eat their offspring,	851
	3:51	to my soul because of all the **w** of my city.	1426
	4:10	With their own hands compassionate **w** have cooked their own children,	851
	5:11	**W** have been ravished in Zion,	851
Eze	8:14	I saw **w** sitting there, mourning for Tammuz.	851
	9: 6	young men and maidens, **w** and children,	851
	13:18	Woe to the **w** who **sew** magic charms	AIT
	16:38	the punishment of **w** who **commit adultery**	AIT
	16:41	punishment on you in the sight of many **w.**	851
	22:10	in you are *those who* **violate** **w,**	6700
	23: 2	there were two **w,** daughters of the same	851
	23:10	She became a byword among **w,**	851
	23:44	so they slept with those lewd **w,**	851
	23:45	the punishment of **w** who **commit adultery**	AIT
	23:48	all **w** may take warning and not imitate you.	851
	44:22	not marry widows or **divorced** **w;**	AIT
Da	11:37	of his fathers or for the one desired by **w,**	851
Hos	13:16	their **pregnant** **w** ripped open.	2230
Joel	2:29	Even on my servants, both men and **w,**	9148
Am	1:13	Because he ripped open the **pregnant** **w**	2226
	4: 1	you **w** who **oppress** the poor and crush	AIT
	8:13	"the lovely **young** **w** and strong young men	1435
Mic	2: 9	You drive the **w** of my people	851
Na	3:13	Look at your troops—they are all **w!**	851
Zec	5: 9	and there before me were two **w,**	851
	8: 4	and **w** of ripe old age will sit in the streets	2418[S]
	9:17	and new wine the **young.**	1435
	14: 2	the houses ransacked, and the **w** raped.	851
Mt	11:11	Among those born *of* **w** there has	1222
	14:21	besides **w** and children.	1222
	15:38	besides **w** and children.	1222
	24:19	*for* **pregnant** **w** and nursing	1143+1877+2400
	24:41	Two **w** will be **grinding** with a hand mill;	AIT
	27:55	**w** were there, watching from a distance.	1222
	28: 5	The angel said *to* the **w,** "Do not be afraid,	1222
	28: 8	So the **w** hurried away from the tomb,	NIG
	28:11	While the **w** were on their way,	899[S]
Mk	13:17	*for* **pregnant** **w** and nursing	1143+1877+2400
	15:40	Some **w** were watching from a distance.	1222
	15:41	In Galilee these **w** had followed him	AIT
	15:41	**Many other** **w** who had come up with him	AIT
	16: 8	the **w** went out and fled from the tomb.	NIG

Lk	1:42	"Blessed are you among **w,**	1222
	7:28	*of* **w** there is no one greater than John;	1222
	8: 2	and also some **w** who had been cured	1222
	8: 3	These **w** were helping to support them out	AIT
	17:35	Two **w** will be grinding grain together;	AIT
	21:23	*for* **pregnant** **w** and nursing	1143+1877+2400
	23:27	including **w** who mourned and wailed	1222
	23:29	'Blessed are the **barren** **w,**	5096
	23:49	the **w** who had followed him from Galilee,	1222
	23:55	The **w** who had come with Jesus	1222
	24: 1	the **w** **took** the spices they had prepared	AIT
	24: 5	the **w** **bowed** down with their faces to	AIT
	24:11	But they did not believe the **w,**	899[S]
	24:22	In addition, some of our **w** amazed us.	1222
	24:24	the tomb and found it just as the **w** had said,	1222
Jn	8: 5	Moses commanded us to stone **such** **w.**	AIT
Ac	1:14	with the **w** and Mary the mother of Jesus,	1222
	2:18	Even on my servants, both men and **w,**	NIG
	5:14	and **w** believed in the Lord and were added	1222
	8: 3	he dragged off men and **w** and put them	1222
	8:12	they were baptized, both men and **w.**	1222
	9: 2	belonged to the Way, whether men or **w,**	1222
	13:50	the God-fearing **w** of high standing and	1222
	16:13	to speak to the **w** who had gathered there.	1222
	17: 4	and not a few prominent **w.**	1222
	17:12	as did also a number of prominent Greek **w**	1222
	22: 4	and **w** and throwing them into prison,	1222
Ro	1:26	Even their **w** exchanged natural relations	2559
	1:27	also abandoned natural relations *with* **w**	2559
	16:12	those **w** who work hard in the Lord.	AIT
1Co	14:34	**w** should remain silent in the churches.	1222
Gal	4:24	for the **w** represent two covenants.	4047[S]
Php	4: 3	help **these** **w** who have contended at my side in the cause of the gospel,	AIT
1Ti	2: 9	I also want **w** to dress modestly,	1222
	2:10	*for* **w** who profess to worship God.	1222
	2:15	But **w** will be saved through childbearing—	NIG
	3:11	their wives are to be **w** worthy of respect,	NIG
	5: 2	**older** **w** as mothers, and younger women	AIT
	5: 2	**younger** **w** as sisters, with absolute purity.	AIT
2Ti	3: 6	and gain control over **weak-willed** **w,**	1220
Tit	2: 3	teach the **older** **w** to be reverent in	AIT
	2: 4	the **younger** **w** to love their husbands	AIT
Heb	11:35	**W** received back their dead,	1222
1Pe	3: 5	the holy **w** of the past who put their hope	1222
Rev	14: 4	not defile themselves with **w,**	1222

WOMEN'S (2) [WOMAN]

Dt	22: 5	nor a man wear **w** clothing,	851
Rev	9: 8	Their hair was like **w** hair,	1222

WOMENSERVANTS (KJV) See MAIDSERVANTS, FEMALE SLAVES

WON (11) [WIN]

Ge	30: 8	struggle with my sister, and *I have* **w.**"	3523
1Sa	19: 5	The LORD **w** a great victory for all Israel,	6913
2Sa	19:14	He **w** over the hearts of all the men of Judah	5742
Est	2: 9	pleased him and **w** his favor.	4200+5951+7156
	2:15	And Esther **w** the favor of	928+5951+6524
	2:17	*she* **w** his favor and approval	4200+5951+7156
Ps	44: 3	not by their sword that *they* **w** the land,	3769
Mt	18:15	*you* have **w** your brother **over.**	3045
Ac	14:19	and Iconium and **w** the crowd **over.**	4275
	14:21	and **w** a large number of **disciples.**	3411
1Pe	3: 1	*be* **w** **over** without words by the behavior	3045

WON'T (22) [NOT, WILL]

Ge	34:23	**W** their livestock, their property	4202
Jdg	4: 8	but if you don't go with me, I **w** go."	4202
	15: 7	I **w** stop **until** I get my revenge on you."	561+3954
	15:12	to me that you **w** kill me yourselves."	7153
	16:15	'I love you,' when you **w** confide in me?"	401
	19:12	We **w** go into an alien city,	4202
1Sa	2:15	he **w** accept boiled meat from you,	4202
	26: 8	I **w** strike him twice."	4202
2Sa	13: 4	**W** you tell me?"	4202
	15:35	**W** the priests Zadok and Abiathar be there	4202
	18: 3	they **w** care about us.	4202
	18: 3	Even if half of us die, they **w** care;	4202
1Ki	14: 2	so you **w** be recognized as the wife	4202
	21: 5	Why **w** you eat?"	401
2Ki	6: 3	"**W** you please **come** with our servants?"	AIT
Ps	10:13	"He **w** call me to account"?	4202
Eze	24:19	"**W** you tell us what these things have to do	4202
	37:18	'**W** you tell us what your people, by this?'	4202
Mk	5: 7	Swear to God that you **w** torture me!"	3590
Lk	18: 5	so that she **w** eventually wear me out	3590
Jn	4:15	give me this water so that I **w** get thirsty	3590
1Co	8:10	**w** he be emboldened to eat	4049

WONDER (12) [WONDERED, WONDERFUL, WONDERFULLY, WONDERING, WONDERS, WONDROUS]

Dt	13: 1	announces to you a miraculous sign or **w,**	4603
	13: 2	or **w** of which he has spoken takes place,	4603
	28:46	a **w** to you and your descendants forever.	4603
Job	6: 3	no **w** my words have been impetuous.	4027+6584
Ps	17: 7	**Show** the **w** of your great love,	7098
SS	1: 3	No **w** the maidens love you!	4027+6584
Isa	29:14	astound these people with **w** upon wonder;	7098
	29:14	astound these people with wonder upon **w;**	7099

Mk	9:15	*they* were **overwhelmed with** **w** and ran	1701
Ac	3:10	and they were filled *with* **w** and amazement	2502
	13:41	"Look, you scoffers, **w,** and perish,	2513
2Co	11:14	And no **w,** for Satan himself masquerades	2512

WONDERED (2) [WONDER]

Lk	1:29	and **w** what kind of greeting this might be.	1368
	1:66	Everyone who heard this **w** about it,	1877+2840+3836+5502

WONDERFUL (24) [WONDER]

2Sa	1:26	Your love for me *was* **w,**	7098
	1:26	more **w** than that of women.	NIH
1Ch	16: 9	sing praise to him; tell of all his *acts.*	7098
Job	42: 3	*things* too **w** for me to know.	7098
Ps	26: 7	and telling of all your **w** *deeds.*	7098
	31:21	for *he* showed his **w** love to me	7098
	75: 1	men tell of your **w** *deeds.*	7098
	105: 2	tell of all his **w** *acts.*	7098
	107: 8	for his unfailing love and his **w** *deeds*	7098
	107:15	for his unfailing love and his **w** *deeds*	7098
	107:21	for his unfailing love and his **w** *deeds*	7098
	107:24	his **w** *deeds* in the deep.	7098
	107:31	for his unfailing love and his **w** *deeds*	7098
	119:18	Open my eyes that I may see **w** *things*	7098
	119:129	Your statutes are **w;** therefore I obey them.	7099
	131: 1	with great matters or *things* too **w** for me.	7098
	139: 6	Such knowledge is too **w** for me,	7100
	139:14	your works **are w,** I know that full well.	7098
	145: 5	and I will meditate on your **w** *works.*	7098
Isa	9: 6	And he will be called **W** Counselor,	7099
	28:29	**w** *in* counsel and magnificent in wisdom.	7098
Mt	21:15	teachers of the law saw the **w** *things* he did	2514
Lk	13:17	delighted with all the **w** *things* he was doing	1902
1Pe	2: 9	called you out of darkness into his **w** light.	2515

WONDERFULLY (1) [WONDER]

Ps	139:14	because *I* am fearfully and **w** made;	7098

WONDERING (6) [WONDER]

Lk	1:21	and **w** why he stayed so long in the temple.	2513
	3:15	and *were* all **w** in their hearts	1368
	24: 4	While they *were* **w** about this,	679
	24:12	**w** to himself what had happened.	2513
Ac	5:24	**w** what would come of this.	NIG
	10:17	While Peter *was* **w** **about** the meaning of	1389

WONDERS (62) [WONDER]

Ex	3:20	and strike the Egyptians with all the **w**	7098
	4:21	before Pharaoh all the **w** I have given you	4603
	7: 3	my miraculous signs and **w** in Egypt,	4603
	11: 9	so that my **w** may be multiplied in Egypt."	4603
	11:10	Moses and Aaron performed all these **w**	4603
	15:11	awesome in glory, working **w?**	7099
	34:10	Before all your people I will do **w** never	7098
Dt	4:34	by testings, by miraculous signs and **w,**	4603
	6:22	the LORD sent miraculous signs and **w**—	4603
	7:19	the miraculous signs and **w,**	4603
	10:21	**awesome** **w** you saw with your own eyes.	3707
	26: 8	and with miraculous signs and **w.**	4603
	29: 3	those miraculous signs and great **w.**	4603
	34:11	who did all those miraculous signs and **w**	4603
Jdg	6:13	Where are all his **w** that our fathers told us	7098
2Sa	7:23	and **awesome** **w** by driving out nations	3707
1Ch	16:12	Remember the **w** he has done, his miracles,	7098
	17:21	and **awesome** **w** by driving out nations from	3707
Ne	9:10	You sent miraculous signs and **w**	4603
Job	5: 9	He performs **w** that cannot be fathomed,	1524
	9:10	He performs **w** that cannot be fathomed,	1524
	37:14	stop and consider God's **w.**	7098
	37:16	*those* **w** of him who is perfect in knowledge?	5140
Ps	9: 1	I will tell of all your **w.**	7098
	40: 5	O LORD my God, are the **w** you have done.	7098
	65: 5	Those living far away fear your **w;**	253
	78: 4	his power, and the **w** he has done.	7098
	78:11	the **w** he had shown them.	7098
	78:32	in spite of his **w,** they did not believe.	7098
	78:43	his **w** in the region of Zoan.	4603
	88:10	Do you show your **w** to the dead?	7099
	88:12	Are your **w** known in the place of darkness,	7099
	89: 5	The heavens praise your **w,**	7099
	105: 5	Remember the **w** he has done, his miracles,	7098
	105:27	his **w** in the land of Ham.	4603
	111: 4	He has caused his **w** to be remembered;	7098
	119:27	then I will meditate on your **w.**	7098
	135: 9	He sent his signs and **w** into your midst,	4603
	136: 4	to him who alone does great **w,**	7098
Jer	21:2	Perhaps the LORD will perform **w** for us	7098
	32:20	and **w** in Egypt and have continued them	4603
	32:21	Israel out of Egypt with signs and **w,**	4603
Da	4: 2	to tell you about the miraculous signs and **w**	10763
	4: 3	How great are his signs, how mighty his **w!**	10763
	6:27	he performs signs and **w** in the heavens	10763
Joel	2:26	your God, who has worked **w** for you;	7098
	2:30	I will show **w** in the heavens and on	4603
Mic	7:15	I will show them my **w.**"	7098
Jn	4:48	"Unless you people see miraculous signs and **w,**"	5469
Ac	2:11	we hear them declaring the **w** of God	3483
	2:19	I will show **w** in the heaven above and signs	5469
	2:22	by God to you *by* miracles, **w** and signs,	5469
	2:43	Everyone was filled with awe, and many **w**	5469
	4:30	to heal and perform miraculous signs and **w**	5469
	5:12	miraculous signs and **w** among the people.	5469

Ac   6: 8   did great **w** and miraculous signs among   5469
   7:36   and did **w** and miraculous signs in Egypt,   5469
   14: 3   to do miraculous signs and **w**.   5469
   15:12   the miraculous signs and **w** God had done   5469
2Co 12:12   mark an apostle—signs, **w** and miracles—   5469
2Th   2: 9   kinds of counterfeit miracles, signs and **w**,   5469
Heb   2: 4   God also testified to it by signs, **w** and   5469

WONDROUS (1) [WONDER]
Rev 12: 1   A great and **w** sign appeared in heaven: 4956

WONT (KJV) See CUSTOM, EXPECTED, HABIT, USUAL

WOOD (121) [BRUSHWOOD, WOODCUTTERS, WOODED, WOODEN, WOODPILE, WOODS, WOODSMAN, WOODSMEN, WOODWORK]
Ge   6:14   So make yourself an ark of cypress **w**;   6770
   22: 3   he had cut *enough of* the **w** for the burnt offering   6770
   22: 6   Abraham took the **w** for the burnt offering   6770
   22: 7   "The fire and **w** are here," Isaac said,   6770
   22: 9   an altar there and arranged the **w** on it.   6770
   22: 9   on the altar, on top of the **w**.   6770
   30:37   the bark and exposing the **white** inner **w** of   AIT
Ex   15:25   and the LORD showed him a **piece of w**   6770
   25: 5   and hides of sea cows; acacia **w**;   6770
   25:10   "Have them make a chest of acacia **w**—   6770
   25:13   of acacia **w** and overlay them with gold.   6770
   25:23   "Make a table of acacia **w**—   6770
   25:28   Make the poles of acacia **w**,   6770
   26:15   "Make upright frames of acacia **w** for   6770
   26:26   "Also make crossbars of acacia **w**—   6770
   26:32   of **acacia w** overlaid with gold and standing   8847
   26:37   and five posts of **acacia w** overlaid   8847
   27: 1   "Build an altar of acacia **w**,   6770
   27: 6   of acacia **w** for the altar and overlay them   6770
   30: 1   an altar of acacia **w** for burning incense.   6770
   30: 5   of acacia **w** and overlay them with gold.   6770
   31: 5   to cut and set stones, to work in **w**,   6770
   35: 7   and hides of sea cows; acacia **w**;   6770
   35:24   and everyone who had acacia **w** for any part   6770
   35:33   to work in **w** and to engage in all kinds   6770
   36:20   They made upright frames of acacia **w** for   6770
   36:31   They also made crossbars of acacia **w**:   6770
   36:36   They made four posts of **acacia w** for it   8847
   37: 1   Bezalel made the ark of acacia **w**—   6770
   37: 4   of acacia **w** and overlaid them with gold.   6770
   37:10   They made the table of acacia **w**—   6770
   37:15   of acacia **w** and were overlaid with gold.   6770
   37:25   the altar of incense out of acacia **w**.   6770
   37:28   of acacia **w** and overlaid them with gold.   6770
   38: 1   the altar of burnt offering of acacia **w**,   6770
   38: 6   of acacia **w** and overlaid them with bronze.   6770
Lev   1: 7   to put fire on the altar and arrange **w** on   6770
   1: 8   on the burning **w** that is on the altar.   6770
   1:12   on the burning **w** that is on the altar.   6770
   1:17   then the priest shall burn it on the **w** that is   6770
   3: 5   the burnt offering that is on the burning **w**,   6770
   4:12   and burn it in a **w** fire on the ash heap.   6770
   11:32   will be unclean, whether it is made of **w**,   6770
   14: 4   that two live clean birds and *some* cedar **w**,   6770
   14: 6   together with the cedar **w**,   6770
   14:49   to take two birds and *some* cedar **w**,   6770
   14:51   Then he is to take the cedar **w**, the hyssop,   6770
   14:52   the cedar **w**, the hyssop and the scarlet yarn.   6770
Nu   15:32   man was found gathering **w** on the Sabbath   6770
   15:33   Those who found him gathering **w** brought   6770
   19: 6   The priest is to take *some* cedar **w**,   6770
   31:20   everything made of goat hair or **w**."   6770
Dt   4:28   worship man-made gods of **w** and stone,   6770
   10: 3   So I made the ark out of acacia **w**   6770
   19: 5   into the forest with his neighbor to cut **w**,   6770
   28:36   other gods, gods of **w** and stone.   6770
   28:64   other gods—gods of **w** and stone.   6770
   29:11   in your camps who chop your **w**   6770
   29:17   and idols of **w** and stone,   6770
Jdg   6:26   the **w** of the Asherah pole that you cut   6770
1Sa   6:14   up the **w** of the cart and sacrificed the cows   6770
2Sa 24:22   and ox yokes for the **w**.   6770
1Ki   6:23   a pair of cherubim of olive **w**,   6770
   6:31   of olive **w** with five-sided jambs.   6770
   6:32   the two olive **w** doors he carved cherubim,   6770
   6:33   of olive **w** for the entrance to the main hall.   6770
   18:23   and put it on the **w** but not set fire to it.   6770
   18:23   and put it on the **w** but not set fire to it.   6770
   18:33   He arranged the **w**,   6770
   18:33   cut the bull into pieces and laid it on the **w**.   6770
   18:33   and pour it on the offering and on the **w**."   6770
   18:38   the **w**, the stones and the soil,   6770
2Ki   19:18   they were not gods but only **w** and stone,   6770
1Ch 21:23   the threshing sledges for the **w**,   6770
   22:14   and **w** and stone.   6770
   29: 2   iron for the iron and **w** for the wood,   6770
   29: 2   iron for the iron and wood for the **w**,   6770
2Ch   2:14   bronze and iron, stone and **w**,   6770
Ne   10:34   a contribution of **w** to burn on the altar of   6770
   13:31   I also made provision for contributions of **w**   6770
Job 41:27   like straw and bronze like rotten **w**.   6770
Pr   26:20   Without **w** a fire goes out;   6770
   26:21   As charcoal to embers and as **w** to fire,   6770
SS   3: 9   he made it of **w** *from* Lebanon.   6770
Isa 10:15   or a club brandish him who is not **w**!   6770

Isa 30:33   with an abundance of fire and **w**;   6770
   37:19   they were not gods but only **w** and stone,   6770
   40:20   an offering selects **w** that will not rot.   6770
   44:16   Half of **the w** he burns in the fire;   2257S
   44:19   Shall I bow down to a block of **w**?"   6770
   45:20   those who carry about idols of **w**,   6770
   60:17   Instead of **w** I will bring you bronze,   6770
Jer   2:27   They say to **w**, 'You are my father,'   6770
   3: 9   and committed adultery with stone and **w**.   6770
   5:14   a fire and these people the **w** it consumes.   6770
   7:18   The children gather **w**,   6770
La   5: 4   our **w** can be had only at a price.   6770
   5:13   boys stagger under **loads of w**.   6770
Eze 15: 2   the **w** of a vine better than that of a branch   6770
   15: 3   Is **w** ever taken from it to make anything   6770
   15: 6   As I have given the **w** of the vine among   6770
   20:32   who serve **w** and stone.   6770
   24: 5   **Pile w** beneath it *for* the bones;   1883
   24: 9   I, too, will pile the **w** high.   4509
   24:10   So heap on the **w** and kindle the fire.   6770
   27: 6   of **cypress w** from the coasts   9309
   37:16   take a **stick of w** and write on it,   6770
   37:16   Then take another **stick of w**,   6770
   37:19   making them a single **stick of w**,   6770
   39:10   not need to gather **w** from the fields or cut it   6770
   41:16   the threshold was covered with **w**.   6770
   41:22   its corners, its base and its sides were of **w**.   6770
Da   5: 4   of bronze, iron, **w** and stone.   10058
   5:23   of bronze, iron, **w** and stone.   10058
Hos   4:12   and are answered by a **stick of w**.   5234
Hab   2:19   Woe to him who says to **w**, 'Come to life!'   6770
1Co   3:12   silver, costly stones, **w**, hay or straw,   3833
2Ti   2:20   but also of **w** and clay; some are for noble   3832
Rev   9:20   silver, bronze, stone and **w**—   3832
   18:12   every sort of citron **w**,   3833
   18:12   costly **w**, bronze, iron and marble;   3833

WOODCUTTERS (3) [WOOD]
Jos   9:21   but let them be **w** and water carriers   2634+6770
   9:23   as **w** and water carriers for the house   2634+6770
   9:27   the Gibeonites **w** and water carriers   2634+6770

WOODED (1) [WOOD]
2Ch 27: 4   and forts and towers in the **w** areas.   3091

WOODEN (13) [WOOD]
Ex   7:19   even in the **w** *buckets* and stone jars."   6770
Lev 15:12   and any **w** article is to be rinsed with water.   6770
Nu   35:18   Or if anyone has a **w** object in his hand   6770
Dt   10: 1   Also make a **w** chest.   6770
   16:21   Do not set up any **w** Asherah pole beside   6770
Ne   8: 4   on a high **w** platform built for the occasion.   6770
Isa 48: 5   my **w** image and metal god ordained them.'   NIH
Jer 10: 8   they are taught by worthless **w** idols.   6770
   28:13   You have broken a **w** yoke,   6770
Eze 41:22   There was a **w** altar three cubits high   6770
   41:25   and there was a **w** overhang on the front of   6770
Hos   4:12   They consult a **w** idol and are answered by   6770
   10: 6   Israel will be ashamed of its **w idols.**   6785

WOODPILE (1) [WOOD]
Zec 12: 6   the leaders of Judah like a firepot in a **w**,   6770

WOODS (3) [WOOD]
1Sa 14:25   The entire army entered the **w**,   3623
   14:26   When they went into the **w**,   3623
2Ki   2:24   the **w** and mauled forty-two of the youths.   3623

WOODSMAN (1) [WOOD, MAN]
Isa 14: 8   no **w** comes *to* cut us down."   AIT

WOODSMEN (1) [WOOD, MAN]
2Ch   2:10   your servants, the **w** who cut the timber,   2634

WOODWORK (1) [WOOD]
Hab   2:11   and the beams of the **w** will echo it.   6770

WOOF (KJV) See KNITTED

WOOING (1)
Job 36:16   "He is **w** you from the jaws of distress to   6077

WOOL (18) [WOOLEN]
Lev 13:48   or knitted material of linen or **w**, any leather   7547
   13:52   the woven or knitted material of **w** or linen,   7547
Nu   15:12   hyssop and **scarlet w** and throw them   9106+9357
Dt   18: 4   the first **w** from *the shearing* of your sheep,   1600
   22:11   clothes of **w** and linen woven together.   7547
Jdg   6:37   a **w** fleece on the threshing floor.   7547
2Ki   3: 4   a hundred thousand lambs and with the **w** of   7547
Ps 147:16   He spreads the snow like **w** and scatters   7547
Pr 31:13   She selects **w** and flax and works   7547
Isa   1:18   they shall be like **w**.   7547
   51: 8   the worm will devour them like **w**.   7547
Eze 27:18   in wine from Helbon and **w** *from* Zahar.   7547
   34: 3   clothe yourselves with the **w** and slaughter   7547
Da   7: 9   the hair of his head was white like **w**.   10556
Hos   2: 5   my **w** and my linen, my oil and my drink.'   7547
   2: 9   I will take back my **w** and my linen,   7547
Heb   9:19   scarlet **w** and branches of hyssop,   2250

Rev   1:14   His head and hair were white like **w**,   2250

WOOLEN (3) [WOOL]
Lev 13:47   with mildew—any **w** or linen clothing,   7547
   13:59   concerning contamination by mildew in **w**   7547
Eze 44:17   not wear any **w garment** while ministering   7547

WOOLLEN (KJV) See WOOL, WOOLEN

WORD (569) [BYWORD, WORDS]
Ge 15: 1   the **w** of the LORD came to Abram in   1821
   15: 4   Then the **w** of the LORD came to him: 1821
   24:21   **Without saying a w**, the man watched her   3087
   27:45   *I'll send* **w** *for* you to come back   8938
   31: 4   So Jacob **sent w** to Rachel and   2256+7924+8938
   37: 4   hated him and could not **speak** a kind **w**   AIT
   37:14   and bring me **w** back to me."   1821
   41:44   without your **w** no one will lift hand or foot   NIH
   44:18   let your servant speak a **w** to my lord.   1821
   50:16   So *they* **sent w** to Joseph, saying,   7422
Ex   9:20   Those officials of Pharaoh who feared the **w**   1821
   9:21   the **w** of the LORD left their slaves   1821
   18: 6   Jethro *had* **sent w** to him,   606
   36: 6   and they sent this **w** throughout the camp;   7754
Nu   3:16   as he was commanded by the **w** of the LORD   7023
   3:51   as he was commanded by the **w** of the LORD   7023
   15:31   the LORD's **w** and broken his commands,   1821
   30: 2   he must not break his **w** but must do   1821
Dt   5: 5   to declare to you the **w** of the LORD,   1821
   8: 3   but on every **w** that comes from the mouth   4604
   30:14   No, the **w** is very near you;   1821
   33: 9   over your **w** and guarded your covenant.   614
Jos   1:18   Whoever rebels against your **w** and does   7023
   6:10   not say a **w** until the day I tell you to shout.   1821
   8:35   not a **w** of all that Moses had commanded   1821
   10: 6   then sent **w** to Joshua in the camp at Gilgal: 606
   10:21   no one **uttered** a **w** against the Israelites.   906+3076+4383
Jdg 11:36   "*you have* **given** your **w** to the LORD.   906+7023+7198
   12: 6   he could not pronounce the **w** correctly,   NIH
   13:17   honor you when your **w** comes true?"   1821
   16:18   she sent **w** to the rulers of the Philistines,   7924
   18:19   **Don't say a w**.   3338+6584+7023+8492
1Sa   1:23   only may the LORD make good his **w**."   1821
   3: 1   In those days the **w** of the LORD was rare;   1821
   3: 7   **w** of the LORD had not yet been revealed   1821
   3:21   revealed himself to Samuel through his **w**.   1821
   4: 1   And Samuel's **w** came to all Israel.   1821
   14:39   But not one of the men **said a w**.   6699
   15:10   Then the **w** of the LORD came to Samuel: 1821
   15:23   you have rejected the **w** of the LORD,   1821
   15:26   You have rejected the **w** of the LORD,   1821
   16:22   Then Saul **sent w** to Jesse, saying,   8938
   19:19   **W** came to Saul: 5583
   20:12   *will I* not **send** you **w** and let you know?   8938
   25:12   When they arrived, they reported every **w**.   1821
   25:39   Then David **sent w** to Abigail,   8938
2Sa   3:11   Ish-Bosheth did not dare to say another **w**   1821
   7: 4   the **w** of the LORD came to Nathan,   1821
   7:21   sake of your **w** and according to your will,   1821
   11: 5   The woman conceived and **sent w** to David,   2256+5583+8938
   11: 6   So David **sent** this **w** to Joab: 8938
   12: 9   Why did you despise the **w** of the LORD   1821
   12:25   *he* **sent w** through Nathan the prophet   8938
   13: 7   David sent **w** to Tamar at the palace: 606
   13:22   Absalom never **said a w** to Amnon.   1819
   14:12   "Let your servant speak a **w** to my lord   1821
   14:17   the **w** of my lord the king bring me rest,   1821
   14:32   "Look, *I* **sent w** to you and said,   8938
   15:28   until **w** comes from you to inform me."   1821
   19:14   *They* **sent w** to the king, "Return,   8938
   22:31   the **w** of the LORD is flawless.   614
   23: 2   his **w** was on my tongue.   4863
   24: 4   The king's **w**, however, overruled Joab   1821
   24:11   the **w** of the LORD had come to Gad   1821
1Ki   2:27   the **w** the LORD had spoken at Shiloh   1821
   5: 8   So Hiram sent **w** to Solomon: 606
   6:11   The **w** of the LORD came to Solomon: 1821
   8:26   And now, O God of Israel, let your **w**   1821
   8:56   Not one **w** has failed of all the good   1821
   12:15   to fulfill the **w** the LORD had spoken   1821
   12:22   But this **w** of God came to Shemaiah   1821
   12:24   the **w** of the LORD and went home again,   1821
   13: 1   By the **w** of the LORD a man of God came   1821
   13: 2   He cried out against the altar by the **w** of   1821
   13: 5   by the man of God by the **w** of the LORD: 1821
   13: 9   I was commanded by the **w** of the LORD: 1821
   13:17   I have been told by the **w** of the LORD: 1821
   13:18   an angel said to me by the **w** of the LORD: 1821
   13:20   the **w** of the LORD came to the old prophet   1821
   13:21   'You have defied the **w** of the LORD and   7023
   13:26   "It is the man of God who defied the **w** of   7023
   13:26   as the **w** of the LORD had warned him."   1821
   13:32   For the message he declared by the **w** of   1821
   15:29   according to the **w** of the LORD given   1821
   16: 1   Then the **w** of the LORD came to Jehu son   1821
   16: 7   the **w** of the LORD came through the prophet   1821
   16:12   the **w** of the LORD spoken against Baasha   1821
   16:34   the **w** spoken by Joshua son   1821
   17: 1   in the next few years except at my **w**."   1821
   17: 2   Then the **w** of the LORD came to Elijah: 1821
   17: 8   Then the **w** of the LORD came to him: 1821

1Ki	17:16	with the *w* *of* the LORD spoken by Elijah.	1821
	17:24	that you are a man of God and that the *w* *of*	1821
	18: 1	the *w* *of* the LORD came to Elijah:	1821
	18:20	So Ahab **sent** *w* throughout all Israel	8938
	18:31	to whom the *w* *of* the LORD had come,	1821
	19: 9	And the *w* *of* the LORD came to him:	1821
	20:33	and were quick to pick up his *w.*	2023ˢ
	20:35	By the *w* *of* the LORD one of the sons of	1821
	21:14	Then they sent to Jezebel:	606
	21:17	Then the *w* *of* the LORD came to Elijah	1821
	21:28	Then the *w* *of* the LORD came to Elijah	1821
	22:13	Let your *w* agree with theirs,	1821
	22:19	"Therefore hear the *w* *of* the LORD:	1821
	22:38	as the *w* *of* the LORD had declared.	1821
2Ki	1:17	the *w* *of* the LORD that Elijah had spoken.	1821
	2:22	according to the *w* Elisha had spoken.	1821
	3:12	"The *w* *of* the LORD is with him."	1821
	4:44	according to the *w* *of* the LORD.	1821
	6: 9	of God sent *w* to the king of Israel:	606
	7: 1	Elisha said, "Hear the *w* *of* the LORD.	1821
	9:26	in accordance with the *w* *of* the LORD."	1821
	9:36	"This is the *w* *of* the LORD that he spoke	1821
	10:10	that not a *w* the LORD has spoken against	1821
	10:17	according to the *w* *of* the LORD spoken	1821
	10:21	Then he **sent** *w* throughout Israel,	8938
	14:25	in accordance with the *w* *of* the LORD,	1821
	15:12	So the *w* *of* the LORD spoken	1821
	18:25	to attack and destroy this place without *w*	NIH
	18:28	"Hear the *w* *of* the great king,	1821
	19: 9	to Hezekiah *with this w:*	606
	19:21	This is the *w* that the LORD has spoken	1821
	20: 4	the *w* *of* the LORD came to him:	1821
	20:16	"Hear the *w* *of* the LORD:	1821
	20:19	The *w* *of* the LORD you have spoken is good	1821
	23:16	the *w* *of* the LORD proclaimed by the man	1821
	24: 2	with the *w* *of* the LORD proclaimed	1821
1Ch	10:13	he did not keep the *w* *of* the LORD and	1821
	13: 2	*let us* **send** *w* far and wide to the rest	8938
	15:15	in accordance with the *w* *of* the LORD.	1821
	16:15	the *w* he commanded,	1821
	17: 3	That night the *w* *of* God came to Nathan,	1821
	21: 4	The king's *w,* however, overruled Joab;	1821
	21:19	to the *w* that Gad had spoken in the name of	1821
	22: 8	But this *w* *of* the LORD came to me:	1821
2Ch	6:17	now, O LORD, God of Israel, let your *w*	1821
	10:15	to fulfill the *w* the LORD had spoken	1821
	11: 2	But this *w* *of* the LORD came to Shemaiah	1821
	12: 7	this *w* *of* the LORD came to Shemaiah:	1821
	18:12	Let your *w* agree with theirs,	1821
	18:18	"Therefore hear the *w* *of* the LORD:	1821
	29:15	following the *w* *of* the LORD.	1821
	30: 1	Hezekiah **sent** *w* to all Israel and Judah and	8938
	30:12	following the *w* *of* the LORD.	1821
	34:21	because our fathers have not kept the *w* *of*	1821
	36:12	who **spoke the** *w* *of* the LORD.	4946+7023
	36:15	**sent** *w* to them through his messengers	8938
	36:21	the *w* *of* the LORD spoken by Jeremiah.	1821
	36:22	the *w* *of* the LORD spoken by Jeremiah,	1821
Ezr	1: 1	the *w* *of* the LORD spoken by Jeremiah,	1821
Ne	6: 1	When *w* **came** to Sanballat, Tobiah,	9048
	8:15	and that they should proclaim this *w*	7754
Est	7: 8	As soon as the *w* left the king's mouth,	1821
	9:26	days were called Purim, from the *w* pur.)	9005
Job	2:13	No one said a *w* to him,	1821
	4: 2	"If someone ventures a *w* with you,	1821
	4:12	"A *w* was secretly brought to me,	1821
Ps	5: 9	Not a *w* from their mouth *can* **be trusted;**	AIT
	17: 4	the *w* *of* your lips I have kept myself from	1821
	18:30	the *w* *of* the LORD is flawless.	614
	33: 4	For the *w* *of* the LORD is right and true;	1821
	33: 6	By the *w* *of* the LORD were the heavens	1821
	52: 4	You love every harmful *w,*	1821
	56: 4	In God, whose *w* I praise, in God I trust;	1821
	56:10	In God, whose *w* I praise, in the LORD,	1821
	56:10	in the LORD, whose *w* I praise—	1821
	68:11	The Lord announced the *w,*	608
	103:20	who do his bidding, who obey his *w.*	1821
	105: 8	the *w* he commanded,	1821
	105:19	till the *w* *of* the LORD proved him true.	614
	107:20	He sent forth his *w* and healed them;	1821
	119: 9	By living according to your *w.*	1821
	119:11	I have hidden your *w* in my heart	614
	119:16	I will not neglect your *w.*	1821
	119:17	I will obey your *w.*	1821
	119:25	preserve my life according to your *w.*	1821
	119:28	strengthen me according to your *w.*	1821
	119:37	preserve my life according to your *w.*	1821
	119:42	for I trust in your *w.*	1821
	119:43	not snatch the *w* *of* truth from my mouth,	1821
	119:49	Remember your *w* to your servant,	1821
	119:65	to your servant according to your *w,*	1821
	119:67	but now I obey your *w.*	614
	119:74	for I have put my hope in your *w.*	1821
	119:81	but I have put my hope in your *w.*	1821
	119:89	Your *w,* O LORD, is eternal;	1821
	119:101	so that I might obey your *w.*	1821
	119:105	Your *w* is a lamp to my feet and a light	1821
	119:107	O LORD, according to your *w.*	1821
	119:114	I have put my hope in your *w.*	1821
	119:133	Direct my footsteps according to your *w;*	614
	119:147	I have put my hope in your *w.*	1821
	119:158	for they do not obey your *w.*	614
	119:161	but my heart trembles at your *w.*	1821
	119:169	give me understanding according to your *w.*	1821
	119:172	May my tongue sing of your *w,*	614
	130: 5	my soul waits, and in his *w* I put my hope.	1821
	138: 2	above all things your name and your *w.*	614

Ps	139: 4	Before a *w* is on my tongue you know it	4863
	143: 8	*Let* the morning **bring** me *w* of your	9048
	147:15	his *w* runs swiftly.	1821
	147:18	He sends his *w* and melts them;	1821
	147:19	He has revealed his *w* to Jacob,	1821
Pr	12:25	but a kind *w* cheers him up.	1821
	15: 1	but a harsh *w* stirs up anger.	1821
	15:23	and how good is a timely *w!*	1821
	25:11	A *w* aptly spoken is like apples of gold	1821
	30: 5	"Every *w* *of* God is flawless;	614
Ecc	7:21	Do not pay attention to every *w* people say,	1821
	8: 4	Since a king's *w* is supreme,	1821
Isa	1:10	Hear the *w* *of* the LORD,	1821
	2: 3	the *w* *of* the LORD from Jerusalem.	1821
	5:24	and spurned the *w* *of* the Holy One of Israel.	614
	8:20	If they do not speak according to this *w,*	1821
	16:13	the *w* the LORD has already spoken	1821
	23: 1	the land of Cyprus *w has* **come** to them.	1655
	23: 5	When *w* comes to Egypt,	9051
	24: 3	The LORD has spoken this *w.*	1821
	28:13	the *w* *of* the LORD to them will become:	1821
	28:14	Therefore hear the *w* *of* the LORD,	1821
	29:21	those who with a *w* make a man out to	1821
	37: 9	messengers to Hezekiah *with this w:*	606
	37:22	the *w* the LORD has spoken against him:	1821
	38: 4	Then the *w* *of* the LORD came to Isaiah:	1821
	39: 5	"Hear the *w* *of* the LORD Almighty:	1821
	39: 8	The *w* *of* the LORD you have spoken is good	1821
	40: 8	but the *w* *of* our God stands forever."	1821
	45:23	in all integrity a *w* that will not be revoked:	1821
	50: 4	to know the *w* that sustains the weary.	1821
	50:10	the LORD and obeys the *w* *of* his servant?	7754
	55:11	so is my *w* that goes out from my mouth:	1821
	66: 2	and trembles at my *w.*	1821
	66: 5	Hear the *w* *of* the LORD,	1821
	66: 5	you who tremble at his *w:*	1821
Jer	1: 2	The *w* *of* the LORD came to him	1821
	1: 4	The *w* *of* the LORD came to me, saying,	1821
	1:11	The *w* *of* the LORD came to me:	1821
	1:12	to see that my *w* is fulfilled."	1821
	1:13	The *w* *of* the LORD came to me again:	1821
	2: 1	The *w* *of* the LORD came to me:	1821
	2: 4	Hear the *w* *of* the LORD,	1821
	2:31	consider the *w* *of* the LORD:	1821
	5:13	The prophets are but wind and the *w* is not	1825
	6:10	The *w* *of* the LORD is offensive to them;	1821
	7: 1	This is the *w* that came to Jeremiah from	1821
	7: 2	" 'Hear the *w* *of* the LORD,	1821
	8: 9	they have rejected the *w* *of* the LORD,	1821
	9:20	Now, O women, hear the *w* *of* the LORD;	1821
	11: 1	This is the *w* that came to Jeremiah from	1821
	13: 3	*w* *of* the LORD came to me a second time:	1821
	13: 8	Then the *w* *of* the LORD came to me:	1821
	14: 1	This is the *w* *of* the LORD to Jeremiah	1821
	14:17	"Speak this *w* to them:	1821
	16: 1	Then the *w* *of* the LORD came to me:	1821
	17:15	"Where is the *w* *of* the LORD?	1821
	17:20	Say to them, 'Hear the *w* *of* the LORD,	1821
	18: 1	This is the *w* that came to Jeremiah from	1821
	18: 5	Then the *w* *of* the LORD came to me:	1821
	18:18	nor the *w* from the prophets.	1821
	19: 3	'Hear the *w* *of* the LORD,	1821
	20: 8	the *w* *of* the LORD has brought me insult	1821
	20: 9	his *w* is in my heart like a fire,	NIH
	21: 1	The *w* came to Jeremiah from the LORD	1821
	21:11	'Hear the *w* *of* the LORD,	1821
	22: 2	'Hear the *w* *of* the LORD, O king	1821
	22:29	land, land, hear the *w* *of* the LORD!	1821
	23:18	of the LORD to see or to hear his *w?*	1821
	23:18	Who has listened and heard his *w?*	1821
	23:28	the one who has my *w* speak it faithfully.	1821
	23:29	"Is not my *w* like fire,"	1821
	23:36	every man's own *w* becomes his oracle	1821
	24: 4	Then the *w* *of* the LORD came to me:	1821
	25: 1	The *w* came to Jeremiah concerning all	1821
	25: 3	the *w* *of* the LORD has come to me	1821
	26: 1	this *w* came from the LORD:	1821
	26: 2	everything I command you; do not omit a *w.*	1821
	27: 1	this *w* came to Jeremiah from the LORD:	1821
	27: 3	Then **send** *w* to the kings of Edom, Moab,	8938
	27:18	If they are prophets and have the *w* *of*	1821
	28:12	the *w* *of* the LORD came to Jeremiah:	1821
	29:20	Therefore, hear the *w* *of* the LORD,	1821
	29:30	Then the *w* *of* the LORD came to Jeremiah:	1821
	30: 1	This is the *w* that came to Jeremiah from	1821
	31:10	"Hear the *w* *of* the LORD, O nations;	1821
	32: 1	This is the *w* that came to Jeremiah from	1821
	32: 6	"The *w* *of* the LORD came to me:	1821
	32: 8	"I knew that this was the *w* *of* the LORD;	1821
	32:26	the *w* *of* the LORD came to Jeremiah:	1821
	33: 1	the *w* *of* the LORD came to him	1821
	33:19	The *w* *of* the LORD came to Jeremiah:	1821
	33:23	The *w* *of* the LORD came to Jeremiah:	1821
	34: 1	this *w* came to Jeremiah from the LORD:	1821
	34: 8	The *w* came to Jeremiah from the LORD	1821
	34:12	the *w* *of* the LORD came to Jeremiah:	1821
	35: 1	This is the *w* that came to Jeremiah from	1821
	35:12	*w* *of* the LORD came to Jeremiah, saying:	1821
	36: 1	this *w* came to Jeremiah from the LORD:	1821
	36:27	the *w* *of* the LORD came to Jeremiah:	1821
	37: 6	the *w* *of* the LORD came to Jeremiah	1821
	37:17	"Is there any *w* from the LORD?"	1821
	39:15	the *w* *of* the LORD came to him:	1821
	40: 1	The *w* came to Jeremiah from the LORD	1821
	42: 7	Ten days later the *w* *of* the LORD came	1821
	42:15	then hear the *w* *of* the LORD,	1821
	43: 8	In Tahpanhes the *w* *of* the LORD came	1821

Jer	44: 1	This *w* came to Jeremiah concerning all	1821
	44:24	"Hear the *w* *of* the LORD,	1821
	44:26	But hear the *w* *of* the LORD,	1821
	44:28	in Egypt will know whose *w* will stand—	1821
	46: 1	the *w* *of* the LORD that came to Jeremiah	1821
	47: 1	the *w* *of* the LORD that came to Jeremiah	1821
	49:34	the *w* *of* the LORD that came to Jeremiah	1821
	50: 1	the *w* the LORD spoke through Jeremiah	1821
La	2:17	he has fulfilled his *w,*	614
Eze	1: 3	*w* *of* the LORD came to Ezekiel the priest,	1821
	3:16	of seven days the *w* *of* the LORD came	1821
	3:17	the *w* I speak and give them warning	1821
	6: 1	The *w* *of* the LORD came to me:	1821
	6: 3	hear the *w* *of* the Sovereign LORD.	1821
	7: 1	The *w* *of* the LORD came to me:	1821
	9:11	the writing kit at his side brought back *w,*	1821
	11:14	The *w* *of* the LORD came to me:	1821
	12: 1	The *w* *of* the LORD came to me:	1821
	12: 8	In the morning the *w* *of* the LORD came	1821
	12:17	The *w* *of* the LORD came to me:	1821
	12:21	The *w* *of* the LORD came to me:	1821
	12:26	The *w* *of* the LORD came to me:	1821
	13: 1	The *w* *of* the LORD came to me:	1821
	13: 2	'Hear the *w* *of* the LORD!	1821
	14: 2	Then the *w* *of* the LORD came to me:	1821
	14:12	The *w* *of* the LORD came to me:	1821
	15: 1	The *w* *of* the LORD came to me:	1821
	16: 1	The *w* *of* the LORD came to me:	1821
	16:35	you prostitute, hear the *w* *of* the LORD!	1821
	17: 1	The *w* *of* the LORD came to me:	1821
	17:11	Then the *w* *of* the LORD came to me:	1821
	18: 1	The *w* *of* the LORD came to me:	1821
	20: 2	Then the *w* *of* the LORD came to me:	1821
	20:45	The *w* *of* the LORD came to me:	1821
	20:47	'Hear the *w* *of* the LORD.	1821
	21: 1	The *w* *of* the LORD came to me:	1821
	21: 8	The *w* *of* the LORD came to me:	1821
	21:18	The *w* *of* the LORD came to me:	1821
	22: 1	The *w* *of* the LORD came to me:	1821
	22:17	Then the *w* *of* the LORD came to me:	1821
	22:23	Again the *w* *of* the LORD came to me:	1821
	23: 1	The *w* *of* the LORD came to me:	1821
	24: 1	the *w* *of* the LORD came to me:	1821
	24:15	The *w* *of* the LORD came to me:	1821
	24:20	"The *w* *of* the LORD came to me:	1821
	25: 1	The *w* *of* the LORD came to me:	1821
	25: 3	'Hear the *w* *of* the Sovereign LORD.	1821
	26: 1	the *w* *of* the LORD came to me:	1821
	27: 1	The *w* *of* the LORD came to me:	1821
	28: 1	The *w* *of* the LORD came to me:	1821
	28:11	The *w* *of* the LORD came to me:	1821
	28:20	The *w* *of* the LORD came to me:	1821
	29: 1	the *w* *of* the LORD came to me:	1821
	29:17	the *w* *of* the LORD came to me:	1821
	30: 1	The *w* *of* the LORD came to me:	1821
	30:20	the *w* *of* the LORD came to me:	1821
	31: 1	The *w* *of* the LORD came to me:	1821
	32: 1	The *w* *of* the LORD came to me:	1821
	32:17	the *w* *of* the LORD came to me:	1821
	33: 1	The *w* *of* the LORD came to me:	1821
	33: 7	the *w* I speak and give them warning	1821
	33:23	Then the *w* *of* the LORD came to me:	1821
	34: 1	The *w* *of* the LORD came to me:	1821
	34: 7	you shepherds, hear the *w* *of* the LORD:	1821
	34: 9	O shepherds, hear the *w* *of* the LORD:	1821
	35: 1	The *w* *of* the LORD came to me:	1821
	36: 1	hear the *w* *of* the LORD.	1821
	36: 4	hear the *w* *of* the Sovereign LORD:	1821
	36:16	Again the *w* *of* the LORD came to me:	1821
	37: 4	'Dry bones, hear the *w* *of* the LORD!	1821
	37:15	The *w* *of* the LORD came to me:	1821
Da	9: 2	to the *w* *of* the LORD given to Jeremiah	1821
Hos	1: 1	The *w* *of* the LORD that came to Hosea	1821
	4: 1	Hear the *w* *of* the LORD, you Israelites,	1821
Joel	1: 1	The *w* *of* the LORD that came to Joel son of	1821
Am	3: 1	Hear this *w* the LORD has spoken	1821
	4: 1	Hear this *w,* you cows of Bashan	1821
	5: 1	Hear this *w,* O house of Israel,	1821
	7:16	Now then, hear the *w* *of* the LORD.	1821
	8:12	searching for the *w* *of* the LORD,	1821
Jnh	1: 1	The *w* *of* the LORD came to Jonah son of	1821
	3: 1	The *w* *of* the LORD came to Jonah	1821
	3: 3	the *w* *of* the LORD and went to Nineveh.	1821
Mic	1: 1	The *w* *of* the LORD that came to Micah	1821
	4: 2	the *w* *of* the LORD from Jerusalem.	1821
Zep	1: 1	The *w* *of* the LORD that came to Zephaniah	1821
	2: 5	the *w* *of* the LORD is against you,	1821
Hag	1: 1	the *w* *of* the LORD came through the prophet	1821
	1: 3	Then the *w* *of* the LORD came through	1821
	2: 1	the *w* *of* the LORD came through the prophet	1821
	2:10	the *w* *of* the LORD came to the prophet	1821
	2:20	the *w* *of* the LORD came to Haggai	1821
Zec	1: 1	the *w* *of* the LORD came to the prophet	1821
	1: 7	the *w* *of* the LORD came to the prophet	1821
	1:14	to me said, "Proclaim this *w:*	606
	4: 6	"This is the *w* *of* the LORD to Zerubbabel:	1821
	4: 8	Then the *w* *of* the LORD came to me:	1821
	6: 9	The *w* *of* the LORD came to me:	1821
	7: 1	the *w* *of* the LORD came to Zechariah on	1821
	7: 4	the *w* *of* the LORD Almighty came to me:	1821
	7: 8	*w* *of* the LORD came again to Zechariah:	1821
	8: 1	the *w* *of* the LORD Almighty came to me.	1821
	8:18	the *w* *of* the LORD Almighty came to me.	1821
	9: 1	The *w* *of* the LORD is against the land of	1821
	11:11	knew it was the *w* *of* the LORD.	1821
	12: 1	the *w* *of* the LORD concerning Israel.	1821

Ref		Text	Strong
Mal	1:1	w of the LORD to Israel through Malachi.	1821
Mt	4:4	but on every w that comes from the mouth	4839
	8:8	But just say the w, and my servant will be	3364
	8:16	the spirits with a w and healed all the sick.	3364
	12:32	Anyone who speaks a w against the Son	3364
	12:36	for every careless w they have spoken.	4839
	13:20	on rocky places is the man who hears the w	3364
	13:21	or persecution comes because of the w,	3364
	13:22	the thorns is the man who hears the w,	3364
	13:23	the man who hears the w and understands it.	3364
	14:35	they sent to all the surrounding country.	690
	15:6	the w of God for the sake of your tradition.	3364
	15:23	Jesus did not answer a w.	3364
	19:11	"Not everyone can accept this w,	3364
	22:46	No one could say a w in reply,	3364
	26:75	Peter remembered the w Jesus had spoken:	4839
Mk	2:2	and he preached the w to them.	3364
	4:14	The farmer sows the w.	3364
	4:15	along the path, where the w is sown.	3364
	4:15	and takes away the w that was sown	3364
	4:16	hear the w and at once receive it with joy.	3364
	4:17	or persecution comes because of the w,	3364
	4:18	like seed sown among thorns, hear the w;	3364
	4:19	for other things come in and choke the w,	3364
	4:20	hear the w, accept it, and produce a crop—	3364
	4:33	parables Jesus spoke the w to them,	3364
	7:13	the w of God by your tradition	3364
	14:72	the w Jesus had spoken to him:	4839
	16:20	with them and confirmed his w by the signs	3364
Lk	1:2	eyewitnesses and servants of the w.	3364
	2:17	the w concerning what had been told them	4839
	3:2	the w of God came to John son of Zechariah	4839
	5:1	around him and listening to the w of God,	3364
	7:7	say the w, and my servant will be healed.	3364
	8:11	The seed is the w of God.	3364
	8:12	then the devil comes and takes away the w	3364
	8:13	on the rock are the ones who receive the w	3364
	8:15	who hear the w, retain it,	3364
	8:21	and brothers are those who hear God's w	3364
	11:28	"Blessed rather are those who hear the w	3364
	12:10	And everyone who speaks a w against	3364
	22:61	the w the Lord had spoken to him:	4839
	24:19	powerful in w and deed before God and all	3364
Jn	1:1	In the beginning was the W,	3364
	1:1	and the W was with God,	3364
	1:1	and the W was God.	3364
	1:14	The W became flesh and made his dwelling	3364
	4:50	took Jesus at his w and departed.	3364+4409
	5:24	whoever hears my w and believes him who	3364
	5:38	nor does his w dwell in you,	3364
	7:26	and they are not saying a w to him.	3306+4029
	8:37	because you have no room for my w.	3364
	8:51	I tell you the truth, if anyone keeps my w,	3364
	8:52	yet you say that if anyone keeps your w,	3364
	8:55	but I do know him and keep his w.	3364
	9:7	in the Pool of Siloam" (this w means Sent).	NIG
	10:35	to whom the w of God came"	3364
	11:3	So the sisters sent w to Jesus, "Lord,	3306
	12:17	from the dead continued to spread the w.	3455
	12:38	to fulfill the w of Isaiah the prophet:	3364
	12:48	very w which I spoke will condemn him	3364
	15:3	because of the w I have spoken to you.	3364
	17:6	to me and they have obeyed your w.	3364
	17:14	I have given them your w and	3364
	17:17	Sanctify them by the truth; your w is truth.	3364
Ac	4:29	and enable your servants to speak your w	3364
	4:31	with the Holy Spirit and spoke the w	3364
	6:2	of the w of God in order to wait on tables.	3364
	6:4	to prayer and the ministry of the w."	3364
	6:7	So the w of God spread.	3364
	8:4	preached the w wherever they went.	3364
	8:14	that Samaria had accepted the w of God,	3364
	8:25	and proclaimed the w of the Lord,	3364
	11:1	the Gentiles also had received the w of God.	3364
	11:24	w of God continued to increase and spread.	3364
	13:5	the w of God in the Jewish synagogues.	3364
	13:7	and Saul because he wanted to hear the w	3364
	13:15	the synagogue rulers sent w to them, saying,	NIG
	13:44	the whole city gathered to hear the w of	3364
	13:46	"We had to speak the w of God to you first.	3364
	13:48	they were glad and honored the w of	3364
	13:49	The w of the Lord spread through	3364
	14:25	and when they had preached the w in Perga,	3364
	15:27	by w of mouth what we are writing.	3364
	15:35	and many others taught and preached the w	3364
	15:36	in all the towns where we preached the w of	3364
	16:6	by the Holy Spirit from preaching the w in	3364
	16:32	Then they spoke the w of the Lord to him	3364
	17:13	that Paul was preaching the w of God	3364
	18:11	teaching them the w of God.	3364
	19:10	in the province of Asia heard the w of	3364
	19:20	In this way the w of the Lord spread widely	3364
	20:32	"Now I commit you to God and to the w	3364
Ro	9:6	It is not as though God's w had failed.	3364
	10:8	"The w is near you; it is in your mouth,	4839
	10:8	that is, the w of faith we are proclaiming:	4839
	10:17	message is heard through the w of Christ.	4839
1Co	14:6	or prophecy or w of instruction?	NIG
	14:26	everyone has a hymn, or a w of instruction,	NIG
	14:36	Did the w of God originate with you?	3364
	15:2	you hold firmly to the w I preached to you	3364
2Co	2:17	we do not peddle the w of God for profit.	3364
	4:2	nor do we distort the w of God.	3364
Gal	6:6	in the w must share all good things with	3364
Eph	1:13	in Christ when you heard the w of truth,	3364
	5:26	by the washing with water through the w,	4839
	6:17	sword of the Spirit, which is the w of God.	4839
Php	1:14	to speak the w of God more courageously	3364
	2:16	as you hold out the w of life—	3364
Col	1:5	that you have already heard about in the w	3364
	1:25	to you the w of God in its fullness—	3364
	3:16	Let the w of Christ dwell in you richly	3364
	3:17	whatever you do, whether in w or deed,	3364
1Th	2:13	when you received the w of God,	3364
	2:13	you accepted it not as the w of men,	3364
	2:13	but as it actually is, the w of God,	3364
	4:15	According to the Lord's own w,	3364
2Th	2:15	whether by w of mouth or by letter.	3364
	2:17	in every good deed and	3364
1Ti	4:5	because it is consecrated by the w of God	3364
2Ti	2:9	But God's w is not chained.	3364
	2:15	and who correctly handles the w of truth.	3364
	4:2	Preach the W; be prepared	3364
Tit	1:3	at his appointed season he brought his w	3364
	1:9	so that no one will malign the w of God.	3364
Heb	1:3	sustaining all things by his powerful w.	4839
	4:12	For the w of God is living and active.	3364
	5:12	the elementary truths of God's w all	3364
	6:5	who have tasted the goodness of the w	4839
	12:5	that w of encouragement that addresses you	NIG
	12:19	that no further be spoken to them,	3364+4707
	12:24	that speaks a better w than the blood	NIG
	13:7	who spoke the w of God to you.	3364
	13:22	to bear with my w of exhortation,	3364
Jas	1:18	He chose to give us birth through the w	3364
	1:21	and humbly accept the w planted in you,	3364
	1:22	Do not merely listen to the w,	3364
	1:23	to the w but does not do what it says is like	3364
1Pe	1:23	through the living and enduring w of God.	3364
	1:25	but the w of the Lord stands forever."	4839
	1:25	And this is the w that was preached to you.	4839
	3:1	if any of them do not believe the w,	3364
2Pe	1:19	the w of the prophets made more certain,	3364
	3:5	by God's w the heavens existed and	3364
	3:7	By the same w the present heavens	3364
1Jn	1:1	this we proclaim concerning the W of life.	3364
	1:10	be a liar and his w has no place in our lives.	3364
	2:5	But if anyone obeys his w,	3364
	2:14	and the w of God lives in you,	3364
Rev	1:2	w of God and the testimony of Jesus Christ.	3364
	1:9	of the w of God and the testimony of Jesus.	3364
	3:8	yet you have kept my w and have	3364
	6:9	because of the w of God and	3364
	12:11	the Lamb and by the w of their testimony;	3364
	19:13	and his name is the W of God.	3364
	20:4	for Jesus and because of the w of God.	3364

WORDS (424) [WORD]

Ref		Text	Strong
Ge	4:23	wives of Lamech, hear my w.	614
	27:34	When Esau heard his father's w,	1821
	42:16	in prison, so that your w may be tested	1821
	42:20	so that your w may be verified and	1821
	44:6	he repeated these w to them.	1821
Ex	4:15	You shall speak to him and put w	1821
	19:6	the w you are to speak to the Israelites."	1821
	19:7	of the people and set before them all the w	1821
	20:1	And God spoke all these w:	1821
	23:8	and twists the w of the righteous.	1821
	24:3	the people all the LORD's w and laws,	1821
	24:8	with you in accordance with all these w."	1821
	33:4	When the people heard these distressing w,	1821
	34:1	on them the w that were on the first tablets,	1821
	34:27	"Write down these w,	1821
	34:27	for in accordance with these w I have made	1821
	34:28	on the tablets the w of the covenant—	1821
Nu	12:6	"Listen to my w:	1821
	24:4	the oracle of one who hears the w of God,	609
	24:16	the oracle of one who hears the w of God,	609
Dt	1:1	These are the w Moses spoke to all Israel in	1821
	4:10	the people before me to hear my w so	1821
	4:12	You heard the sound of w but saw no form;	1821
	4:36	and you heard his w from out of the fire.	1821
	10:2	I will write on the tablets the w that were on	1821
	11:18	Fix these w of mine in your hearts	1821
	13:3	you must not listen to the w of that prophet	1821
	16:19	the wise and twists the w of the righteous.	1821
	17:19	and follow carefully all the w of this law	1821
	18:18	I will put my w in his mouth,	1821
	18:19	not listen to my w that the prophet speaks	1821
	27:3	the w of this law when you have crossed	1821
	27:8	And you shall write very clearly all the w"	1821
	27:26	the w of this law by carrying them out."	1821
	28:58	not carefully follow all the w of this law,	1821
	29:19	a person hears the w of this oath,	1821
	29:29	that we may follow all the w of this law.	1821
	31:1	Then Moses went out and spoke these w	1821
	31:12	and follow carefully all the w of this law.	1821
	31:24	in a book the w of this law from beginning	1821
	31:28	so that I can speak these w in their hearing	1821
	31:30	so that this song from beginning to end in	1821
	32:1	hear, O earth, the w of my mouth.	609
	32:2	like rain and my w descend like dew,	614
	32:44	with Joshua son of Nun and spoke all the w	1821
	32:45	When Moses finished reciting all these w	1821
	32:46	to heart all the w I have solemnly declared	1821
	32:46	to obey carefully all the w of this law.	1821
	32:47	They are not just idle w for you—	1821
Jos	1:18	and does not obey your w,	1821
	3:9	and listen to the w of the LORD your God.	1821
	8:34	Joshua read all the w of the law—	1821
	24:27	It has heard all the w the LORD has said	609
Jdg	11:11	And he repeated all his w before	1821
	13:12	"When your w are fulfilled,	1821
1Sa	3:19	and he let none of his w fall to the ground.	1821
	8:10	Samuel told all the w of the LORD to	1821
	11:6	When Saul heard their w,	1821
	17:11	On hearing the Philistine's w,	1821
	18:23	They repeated these w to David.	1821
	21:12	David took these w to heart	1821
	24:7	With these w David rebuked his men	1821
	25:35	I have heard your w and granted your	7754
	26:19	the king listen to his servant's w.	1821
	28:20	filled with fear because of Samuel's w.	1821
2Sa	7:17	to David all the w of this entire revelation.	1821
	7:28	Your w are trustworthy,	1821
	14:3	go to the king and speak these w to him."	1821
	14:3	And Joab put the w in her mouth.	1821
	14:19	and who put all these w into the mouth	1821
	22:1	to the LORD the w of this song when	1821
	23:1	These are the last w of David:	1821
1Ki	8:59	And may these w of mine,	1821
	21:27	When Ahab heard these w,	1821
	22:28	he added, "Mark my w, all you people!"	9048
2Ki	6:12	tells the king of Israel the very w you speak	1821
	6:30	When the king heard the woman's w,	1821
	18:20	but you speak only empty w.	1821+8557
	19:4	the LORD your God will hear all the w of	1821
	19:4	for the w the LORD your God has heard.	1821
	19:6	those w with which the underlings of	1821
	19:16	to the w Sennacherib has sent to insult	1821
	22:11	the king heard the w of the Book of the Law	1821
	22:13	because our fathers have not obeyed the w	1821
	22:18	says concerning the w you heard:	1821
	23:2	in their hearing all the w of the Book of	1821
	23:3	the w of the covenant written in this book.	1821
1Ch	17:15	to David all the w of this entire revelation.	1821
2Ch	11:4	the w of the LORD and turned back	1821
	15:8	When Asa heard these w and the prophecy	1821
	18:27	he added, "Mark my w, all you people!"	9048
	29:30	the Levites to praise the LORD with the w	1821
	32:6	and encouraged them with these w	606
	33:18	to his God and the w the seers spoke to him	1821
	34:19	When the king heard the w of the Law,	1821
	34:26	says concerning the w you heard:	1821
	34:30	in their hearing all the w of the Book of	1821
	34:31	the w of the covenant written in this book.	1821
	36:16	despised his w and scoffed at his prophets	1821
Ezr	9:4	Then everyone who trembled at the w of	1821
Ne	1:1	The w of Nehemiah son of Hacaliah:	1821
	8:9	as they listened to the w of the Law.	1821
	8:13	the w that had been made known to them.	1821
	8:13	the scribe to give attention to the w of	1821
Est	4:12	Esther's w were reported to Mordecai,	1821
	9:30	w of goodwill and assurance—	1821
Job	4:4	Your w have supported those who stumbled	4863
	6:3	no wonder my w have been impetuous.	1821
	6:10	I had not denied the w of the Holy One.	609
	6:25	How painful are honest w!	609
	6:26	treat the w of a despairing man as wind?	609
	8:2	Your w are a blustering wind.	609+7023
	8:10	not bring forth w from their understanding?	4863
	9:14	How can I find w to argue with him?	1821
	11:2	"Are all these w to go unanswered?	1821
	12:11	not the ear test w as the tongue tastes food?	4863
	13:17	Listen carefully to my w;	4863
	15:3	Would he argue with useless w,	1821
	15:11	w spoken gently to you?	1821
	15:13	and pour out such w from your mouth?	4863
	19:2	and crush me with w?	4863
	19:23	"Oh, that my w were recorded,	4863
	21:2	"Listen carefully to my w;	4863
	22:22	and lay up his w in your heart.	609
	23:12	I have treasured the w of his mouth more	609
	24:25	who can prove me false and reduce my w	4863
	26:4	Who has helped you utter these w?	4863
	29:22	my w fell gently on their ears.	4863
	29:23	for me as for showers and drank in my w as	NIH
	31:40	The w of Job are ended.	1821
	32:11	while you were searching for w,	4863
	32:14	But Job has not marshaled his w against me,	4863
	32:15	no more to say; w have failed them.	4863
	32:18	For I am full of w,	4863
	33:1	"But now, Job, listen to my w;	4863
	33:2	my w are on the tip of my tongue.	1819
	33:3	My w come from an upright heart;	609
	33:8	I heard the very w—	4863
	33:13	to him that he answers none of man's w?	1821
	34:2	"Hear my w, you wise men;	4863
	34:3	For the ear tests w as the tongue tastes food.	4863
	34:35	without knowledge; his w lack insight.'	1821
	34:37	and multiplies his w against God."	609
	35:16	without knowledge he multiplies w."	4863
	36:4	Be assured that my w are not false;	4863
	38:2	that darkens my counsel with w	4863
	41:3	speak to you with gentle w?	1819
Ps	5:1	Give ear to my w, O LORD,	609
	12:6	And the w of the LORD are flawless,	614
	18:T	He sang to the LORD the w of this song	1821
	19:4	their w to the ends of the world.	4863
	19:14	May the w of my mouth and the meditation	609
	22:1	so far from the w of my groaning?	1821
	36:3	w of his mouth are wicked and deceitful;	1821
	49:3	My mouth will speak w of wisdom;	AIT
	50:17	You hate my instruction and cast my w	1821
	54:2	listen to the w of my mouth.	609
	55:21	his w are more soothing than oil,	1821
	56:5	All day long they twist my w;	1821
	59:12	sins of their mouths, for the w of their lips,	1821
	64:3	and aim their w like deadly arrows.	1821
	78:1	listen to the w of my mouth.	609

Ps	94: 4	They pour out arrogant **w**;	1819
	105:28	for had they not rebelled against his **w**?	1821
	106:33	and **rash w** came from Moses' lips.	1051
	107:11	for they had rebelled against the **w** *of* God	609
	109: 3	With **w** *of* hatred they surround me;	1821
	119:57	I have promised to obey your **w**.	1821
	119:103	How sweet are your **w** to my taste,	614
	119:130	The unfolding of your **w** gives light;	1821
	119:139	for my enemies ignore your **w**.	1821
	119:160	All your **w** are true;	1821
	138: 4	when they hear the **w** of your mouth.	609
	141: 6	that my **w** were well spoken.	609
Pr	1: 2	for understanding **w** *of* insight;	609
	2: 1	if you accept my **w** and store	609
	2:12	from men *whose* **w** are perverse,	1819
	2:16	the wayward wife with her seductive **w**,	609
	4: 4	"Lay hold of my **w** with all your heart;	1821
	4: 5	do not forget my **w** or swerve from	609+7023
	4:20	listen closely to my **w**.	609
	5: 1	listen well to my **w of insight**,	9312
	6: 2	ensnared by the **w** *of* your mouth.	609
	7: 1	keep my **w** and store up my commands	609
	7: 5	the wayward wife with her seductive **w**.	609
	7:21	With **persuasive w** she led him astray;	4375
	8: 8	All the **w** *of* my mouth are just;	609
	10:19	When **w** are many, sin is not absent,	1821
	12: 6	The **w** of the wicked lie in wait for blood,	1821
	12:18	**Reckless w** pierce like a sword,	1051
	16:21	and pleasant **w** promote instruction.	8557
	16:24	Pleasant **w** are a honeycomb,	1821
	17:27	A man of knowledge uses **w** with restraint,	609
	18: 4	The **w** *of* a man's mouth are deep waters,	1821
	18: 8	The **w** *of* a gossip are like choice morsels;	1821
	19:27	you will stray from the **w** *of* knowledge.	609
	22:12	but he frustrates the **w** *of* the unfaithful.	1821
	22:21	teaching you true and reliable **w**,	609
	23: 9	for he will scorn the wisdom of your **w**.	4863
	23:12	and your ears to **w** *of* knowledge.	609
	26:22	The **w** *of* a gossip are like choice morsels;	1821
	29:19	A servant cannot be corrected by mere **w**;	1821
	30: 6	Do not add to his **w**,	609
Ecc	1: 1	The **w** *of* the Teacher, son of David,	1821
	5: 2	so let your **w** be few.	1821
	5: 3	the speech of a fool when there are many **w**.	1821
	5: 7	and many **w** are meaningless.	1821
	6:11	The more the **w**, the less the meaning,	1821
	9:16	and his **w** are no longer heeded.	1821
	9:17	The quiet **w** *of* a wise man are more to	1821
	10:12	**W** *from* a wise man's mouth are gracious,	1821
	10:13	At the beginning his **w** are folly;	1821+7023
	10:14	and the fool multiplies **w**.	1821
	10:20	because a bird of the air may carry your **w**,	7754
	12:10	Teacher searched to find just the right **w**,	1821
	12:11	The **w** of the wise are like goads,	1821
Isa	3: 8	their **w** and deeds are against the LORD,	4383
	29:11	but **w** sealed *in* a scroll.	1821
	29:18	In that day the deaf will hear the **w** *of*	1821
	31: 2	he does not take back his **w**.	1821
	36: 5	but you speak **only empty w**.	1821+8557
	36:13	"Hear the **w** *of* the great king,	1821
	37: 4	that the LORD your God will hear the **w**	1821
	37: 4	for the **w** the LORD your God has heard.	1821
	37: 6	those **w** with which the underlings of	1821
	37:17	to all the **w** Sennacherib has sent to insult	1821
	41:26	no one heard *any* **w** *from* you.	609
	44:26	who carries out the **w** *of* his servants	1821
	51:16	I have put my **w** in your mouth	1821
	58:13	not doing as you please or speaking idle **w**,	1821
	59:21	and my **w** that I have put in your mouth will	1821
Jer	1: 1	The **w** *of* Jeremiah son of Hilkiah,	1821
	1: 9	"Now, I have put my **w** in your mouth.	1821
	5:14	"Because the people have spoken these **w**,	1821
	5:14	I will make my **w** in your mouth a fire	1821
	6:19	because they have not listened to my **w**	1821
	7: 4	Do not trust in deceptive **w** and say,	1821
	7: 8	in deceptive **w** that are worthless.	1821
	9:20	open your ears to the **w** *of* his mouth.	1821
	11: 6	"Proclaim all these **w** in the towns of Judah	1821
	11:10	who refused to listen to my **w**.	1821
	13:10	who refuse to listen to my **w**,	1821
	15:16	When your **w** came, I ate them;	1821
	15:19	if you utter worthy, not worthless, **w**,	NIH
	19: 2	There proclaim the **w** I tell you,	1821
	19:15	and would not listen to my **w**.' "	1821
	23: 9	because of the LORD and his holy **w**.	1821
	23:22	they would have proclaimed my **w**	1821
	23:30	from one another **w** supposedly *from* me.	1821
	23:36	and so you distort the **w** *of* the living God,	1821
	23:38	You used the **w**, 'This is the oracle of	1821
	25: 8	"Because you have not listened to my **w**,	1821
	25:30	"Now prophesy all these **w** against them	1821
	26: 5	if you do not listen to the **w** *of* my servants	1821
	26: 7	the people heard Jeremiah speak these **w** in	1821
	26:15	to you to speak all these **w** in your hearing."	1821
	26:21	and officials heard his **w**,	1821
	27:14	not listen to the **w** *of* the prophets who say	1821
	28: 6	the **w** you have prophesied by bringing	1821
	29:19	For they have not listened to my **w**,"	1821
	29:19	"**w** that I sent to them again and again	NIH
	30: 2	in a book all the **w** I have spoken to you.	1821
	30: 4	the **w** the LORD spoke concerning Israel	1821
	31:23	in its towns will once again use these **w**:	1821
	35:13	not learn a lesson and obey my **w**?'	1821
	36: 2	and write on it all the **w** I have spoken	1821
	36: 4	and while Jeremiah dictated all the **w**	1821
	36: 6	and read to the people from the scroll the **w**	1821
	36: 8	at the LORD's temple he read the **w** *of*	1821

Jer	36:10	at the LORD's temple the **w** *of* Jeremiah	1821
	36:11	the **w** of the LORD from the scroll,	1821
	36:16	When they heard all these **w**,	1821
	36:16	"We must report all these **w** to the king."	1821
	36:18	"he dictated all these **w** to me,	1821
	36:24	who heard all these **w** showed no fear,	1821
	36:27	the king burned the scroll containing the **w**	1821
	36:28	on it all the **w** that were on the first scroll,	1821
	36:32	Baruch wrote on it all the **w** *of* the scroll	1821
	36:32	And many similar **w** were added to them.	1821
	37: 2	of the land paid any attention to the **w**	1821
	39:16	I am about to fulfill my **w** against this city	1821
	43: 1	the **w** *of* the LORD their God—	1821
	45: 1	the **w** *of* Jeremiah was then dictating:	1821
	51:61	see that you read all these **w** aloud.	1821
	51:64	The **w** *of* Jeremiah end here.	1821
Eze	2: 6	do not be afraid of them or their **w**.	1821
	2: 7	You must speak my **w** to them,	1821
	2:10	both sides of it were written **w** *of* lament	4180
	3: 4	the house of Israel and speak my **w** to them.	1821
	3: 6	whose **w** you cannot understand.	1821
	3:10	and take to heart all the **w** I speak to you.	1821
	12:28	None of my **w** will be delayed any longer;	1821
	13: 6	yet they expect their **w** to be fulfilled.	1821
	13: 8	Because of your false **w** and lying visions,	1819
	33:31	and sit before you to listen to your **w**,	1821
	33:32	for they hear your **w** but do not put them	1821
Da	4:31	The **w** were still on his lips when	10418
	5:26	"This is *what* these **w** mean:	10418
	7:11	of the boastful the horn was speaking.	10418
	9:12	You have fulfilled the **w** spoken against us	1821
	10:11	consider carefully the **w** I am about to speak	1821
	10:12	your **w** were heard, and I have come	1821
	12: 4	up and seal the **w** of the scroll until the time	1821
	12: 9	the **w** are closed up and sealed until the time	1821
Hos	6: 5	I killed you with the **w** *of* my mouth;	609
	7:16	by the sword because of their insolent **w**.	4383
	14: 2	Take **w** with you and return to the LORD.	1821
Am	1: 1	The **w** *of* Amos, one of the shepherds	1821
	7:10	The land cannot bear all his **w**.	1821
	8:11	a famine of hearing the **w** *of* the LORD.	1821
Mic	2: 7	"Do not my **w** do good to him whose ways	1821
	7: 5	in your embrace be careful of your **w**.	7023+7339
Zec	1: 6	But did not my **w** and my decrees,	1821
	1:13	the LORD spoke kind and comforting **w** to	1821
	7: 7	Are these not the **w** the LORD proclaimed	1821
	7:12	to the **w** that the LORD Almighty had sent	1821
	8: 9	"You who now hear these **w** spoken by	1821
Mal	2:17	You have wearied the LORD with your **w**.	1821
Mt	6: 7	be heard because of their **many w**.	4494
	7:24	"Therefore everyone who hears these **w**	3364
	7:26	But everyone who hears these **w** of mine	3364
	10:14	not welcome you or listen to your **w**,	3364
	12: 7	If you had known what these **w** mean,	NIG
	12:37	For by your **w** you will be acquitted,	3364
	12:37	and by your **w** you will be condemned."	3364
	22:15	and laid plans to trap him in his **w**.	3364
	24:35	but my **w** will never pass away.	3364
Mk	8:38	If anyone is ashamed of me and my **w**	3364
	10:24	The disciples were amazed at his **w**.	3364
	12:13	to Jesus to catch him *in* his **w**.	3364
	13:31	but my **w** will never pass away.	3364
Lk	1:20	because you did not believe my **w**,	3364
	1:29	Mary was greatly troubled at his **w**	3364
	3: 4	As is written in the book *of* the **w** of Isaiah	3364
	3:18	And with many other **w** John exhorted	NIG
	4:22	and were amazed at the gracious **w**	3364
	6:47	and hears my **w** and puts them into practice.	3364
	6:49	But the one who hears my **w** and does	NIG
	7:29	when they heard Jesus' **w**,	NIG
	9:26	If anyone is ashamed of me and my **w**,	3364
	19:22	'I will judge you by your own **w**,	5125
	19:48	because all the people hung on his **w**.	NIG
	21:15	For I will give you **w** and wisdom that none	5125
	21:33	but my **w** will never pass away.	3364
	24: 8	Then they remembered his **w**.	4839
	24:11	their **w** seemed to them like nonsense.	4839
Jn	1:23	John replied in the **w** of Isaiah the prophet,	NIG
	2:22	Then they believed the Scripture and the **w**	3364
	3:34	the one whom God has sent speaks the **w**	4839
	4:41	of his **w** many more became believers.	3364
	6:63	The **w** I have spoken to you are spirit	4839
	6:68	You have the **w** of eternal life.	4839
	7:40	On hearing his **w**, some of the people said,	3364
	8:20	He spoke these **w** while teaching in	4839
	10:19	At these **w** the Jews were again divided.	3364
	12:47	for the person who hears my **w** but does	4839
	12:48	and does not accept my **w**;	4839
	14:10	The **w** I say to you are not just my own.	4839
	14:24	These **w** you hear are not my own;	3364
	15: 7	you remain in me and my **w** remain in you,	4839
	15:20	Remember the **w** I spoke to you:	3364
	17: 8	the **w** you gave me and they accepted them.	4839
	18: 9	that the **w** he had spoken would be fulfilled:	3364
	18:32	the **w** Jesus had spoken indicating the kind	3364
Ac	2:40	*With* many other **w** he warned them;	3364
	6:11	"We have heard Stephen speak **w**	4839
	7:35	Moses whom they had rejected **with the w**,	3306
	7:38	and he received living **w** to pass on to us.	3359
	10:44	While Peter was still speaking these **w**,	4839
	13:27	yet in condemning him they fulfilled the **w**	5889
	13:34	never to decay, is stated **in these w**:	4048
	14:18	Even *with* these **w**,	3306
	15:15	The **w** of the prophets are in agreement	3364
	18:15	about **w** and names and your own law—	3364
	20: 2	speaking many **w** of encouragement to	3364
	20:35	the **w** the Lord Jesus himself said:	3364

Ac	22:14	and to see the Righteous One and to hear **w**	5889
Ro	3: 2	they have been entrusted with the very **w**	3359
	4:23	The **w** "it was credited to him" were written	NIG
	8:26	for us with groans *that* **w cannot express.**	227
	9: 8	**In other w**, it is not the natural	1639+4047
	10:18	their **w** to the ends of the world."	4839
1Co	1:17	not with **w** of human wisdom,	3364
	2: 4	not with wise and persuasive **w**,	3364
	2:13	not in **w** taught us by human wisdom but	3364
	2:13	but in **w** taught by the Spirit,	NIG
	2:13	expressing spiritual truths in spiritual **w**.	NIG
	14: 9	you speak intelligible **w** with your tongue,	3364
	14:19	I would rather speak five intelligible **w** to	3364
	14:19	to instruct others than ten thousand **w** in	3364
Gal	5: 2	**Mark my w!** I, Paul, tell you	3972
Eph	5: 6	Let no one deceive you *with* empty **w**,	3364
	6:19	**w** may be given me so that I will fearlessly	3364
1Th	1: 5	our gospel came to you not simply with **w**,	3364
	4:18	encourage each other with these **w**.	3364
1Ti	6: 4	and **quarrels about w** that result in envy,	3363
2Ti	2:14	before God against **quarreling about w**;	3362
Heb	4: 4	about the seventh day **in these w**:	4048
	12:19	or to such a voice speaking **w**	4839
	12:27	The **w** "once more" indicate the removing	NIG
1Pe	3: 1	without **w** by the behavior of their wives,	3364
	4:11	he should do it as one speaking the very **w**	3359
2Pe	2:18	For *they* **mouth** empty, boastful **w**	5779
	3: 2	I want you to recall the **w** spoken in the past	4839
1Jn	3:18	not love *with* **w** or tongue but with actions	3364
Jude	1:15	the **harsh w** ungodly sinners have spoken	AIT
Rev	1: 3	the one who reads the **w** of this prophecy,	3364
	2: 1	These are the **w** of him who holds	3306
	2: 8	These are the **w** of him who is the First and	3306
	2:12	These are the **w** of him who has the sharp,	3306
	2:18	These are the **w** of the Son of God,	3306
	3: 1	the **w** of him who holds the seven spirits	3306
	3: 7	These are the **w** of him who is holy	3306
	3:14	These are the **w** of the Amen,	3306
	13: 5	a mouth to utter proud **w** and blasphemies	NIG
	17:17	until God's **w** are fulfilled.	3364
	19: 9	he added, "These are the true **w** of God."	3364
	21: 5	for these **w** are trustworthy and true."	3364
	22: 6	"These **w** are trustworthy and true.	3364
	22: 7	the **w** of the prophecy in this book."	3364
	22: 9	and of all who keep the **w** of this book.	3364
	22:10	up the **w** of the prophecy of this book,	3364
	22:18	I warn everyone who hears the **w** of	3364
	22:19	And if anyone takes **w** away from this book	3364

WORE (11) [WEAR]

Jos	9: 5	on their feet and **w** old clothes.	6584
1Sa	17: 5	and **w** a coat of scale armor of bronze	4229
	17: 6	on his legs he **w** bronze greaves,	NIH
	22:18	That day he killed eighty-five men *who* **w**	5951
2Sa	13:18	the virgin daughters of the king **w**.	4252
1Ch	15:27	David also **w** a linen ephod.	6584
Ne	4:18	of the builders **w** his sword at his side	673
Ps	109:18	*He* **w** cursing as his garment;	4252
Mk	1: 6	John **w clothing** made of camel's hair,	1639+1907
Rev	9: 7	On their heads they **w** something like crowns	NIG
	15: 6	and **w** golden sashes around their chests.	4322

WORK (394) [HARDWORKING, METALWORKER, WORKED, WORKER, WORKERS, WORKING, WORKMAN, WORKMAN'S, WORKMANSHIP, WORKMEN, WORKS]

Ge	2: 2	God had finished the **w** he had been doing;	4856
	2: 2	on the seventh day he rested from all his **w**.	4856
	2: 3	from all the **w** of creating that he had done.	4856
	2: 5	on the earth and there was no man to **w**	6268
	2:15	in the Garden of Eden to **w** it and take care	6268
	3:23	from the Garden of Eden to **w** the ground	6268
	4:12	When *you* **w** the ground,	6268
	29:15	*should* you **w** for me for nothing?	6268
	29:18	"*I'll* **w for** you seven years in return	6268
	29:27	in return for another seven years of **w**."	6275
	30:26	You know how much **w** I've done for you."	6275
Ex	1:14	in brick and mortar and with all kinds of **w**	6275
	5: 4	Get back to your **w**!"	6026
	5: 9	Make the **w** harder for the men so	6275
	5:11	but your **w** will not be reduced at all.' "	6275
	5:13	the **w** *required* of you for each day,	5126
	5:18	Now get *to* **w**.	6268
	12:16	Do no **w** at all on these days,	4856
	18:18	The **w** is too heavy for you;	1821
	20: 9	Six days you shall labor and do all your **w**,	4856
	20:10	On it you shall not do any **w**, neither you,	4856
	23:12	"Six days do your **w**,	5126
	23:12	but on the seventh day **do not w**,	8697
	26:36	the **w** *of* an embroider	5126
	27:16	the **w** *of* an embroiderer—	5126
	28: 6	the **w** *of* a skilled craftsman.	5126
	28:15	the **w** *of* a skilled craftsman.	5126
	28:39	The sash is to be the **w** *of* an embroiderer.	5126
	30:25	a fragrant blend, the **w** *of* a perfumer.	5126
	30:35	the **w** *of* a perfumer.	5126
	31: 4	to make artistic designs for **w** in gold,	6913
	31: 5	to cut and set stones, to **w** *in* wood,	3098
	31:14	whoever does any **w** on that day must	4856
	31:15	For six days, **w** is to be done,	4856
	31:15	Whoever does any **w** on the Sabbath day	4856
	31:17	on the seventh day *he* **abstained from w**	8697
	32:16	The tablets were the **w** *of* God;	5126

Ex	34:10	will see how awesome is the w that I,	5126
	35: 2	For six days, w is to be done,	4856
	35: 2	Whoever does any w on it must be put	4856
	35:21	an offering to the LORD for the w on	4856
	35:24	for any part of the w brought it.	6275
	35:29	the LORD freewill offerings for all the w	4856
	35:32	to make artistic designs for w in gold,	6913
	35:33	to w in wood and to engage in all kinds	3098
	35:35	with skill to do all kinds of w as craftsmen,	4856
	36: 1	how to carry out all the w of constructing	4856
	36: 1	the sanctuary are to do the w just as	6913
	36: 2	and who was willing to come and do the w.	4856
	36: 3	the Israelites had brought to carry out the w	4856
	36: 4	the w on the sanctuary left their work	4856
	36: 4	the work on the sanctuary left their w	4856
	36: 5	the w the LORD commanded to be done."	4856
	36: 7	more than enough to do all the w.	4856
	36:37	the w of an embroiderer;	5126
	37:29	the w of a perfumer;	5126
	38:18	the w of an embroiderer.	5126
	38:24	from the wave offering used for all the w on	4856
	39: 3	the w of a skilled craftsman.	5126
	39: 8	the w of a skilled craftsman.	5126
	39:22	the w of a weaver—	5126
	39:27	the w of a weaver—	5126
	39:29	the w of an embroiderer—	5126
	39:32	So all the w on the tabernacle,	6275
	39:42	The Israelites had done all the w just as	6275
	39:43	the w and saw that they had done it just as	4856
	40:33	And so Moses finished the w.	4856
Lev	16:29	deny yourselves and not do any w—	4856
	23: 3	'There are six days when you may w,	4856+6913
	23: 3	You are not to do any w;	4856
	23: 7	sacred assembly and do no regular w.	4856+6275
	23: 8	sacred assembly and do no regular w.	4856+6275
	23:21	sacred assembly and do no regular w.	4856+6275
	23:25	Do no regular w,	4856+6275
	23:28	Do no w on that day,	4856
	23:30	among his people anyone who does any w	4856
	23:31	You shall do no w at all.	4856
	23:35	a sacred assembly; do no regular w.	4856+6275
	23:36	closing assembly; do no regular w.	4856+6275
	25:39	do not make him a w as a slave.	6268
	25:40	he is to w for you until the Year of Jubilee.	6268
Nu	3: 7	at the Tent of Meeting by doing the w of	6275
	3: 8	of the Israelites by doing the w of	6275
	4: 3	to serve in the w in the Tent of Meeting.	4856
	4: 4	"This is the w of the Kohathites in the Tent	6275
	4:19	and assign to each man his w and what he is	6275
	4:23	serve in the w at the Tent of Meeting.	6268+6275
	4:24	of the Gershonite clans as they w	6268
	4:27	whether carrying or doing other w,	6275
	4:30	serve in the w at the Tent of Meeting.	6268+6275
	4:33	the service of the Merarite clans as they w	6275
	4:35	to serve in the w in the Tent of Meeting,	6275
	4:39	to serve in the w at the Tent of Meeting,	6275
	4:43	to serve in the w at the Tent of Meeting,	6275
	4:47	to do the w of serving and carrying the Tent	6275
	4:49	each was assigned his w and told what	6275
	7: 5	that they may be used in the w at the Tent	6275
	7: 5	to the Levites as each man's w requires."	6275
	7: 7	to the Gershonites, as their w required,	6275
	7: 8	to the Merarites, as their w required.	6275
	8:11	so that they may be ready to do the w of	6275
	8:15	they are to come to do their w at the Tent	6268
	8:19	as gifts to Aaron and his sons to do the w at	6275
	8:22	to do their w at the Tent of Meeting under	6275
	8:24	to take part in the w at the Tent of Meeting,	6275
	8:25	from their regular service and w no longer.	6268
	8:26	but they themselves must not do the w.	6275
	16: 9	and brought you near himself to do the w at	6275
	18: 4	all the w at the Tent—	6275
	18: 6	dedicated to the LORD to do the w at	6275
	18:21	in return for the w they do while serving at	6275
	18:23	to do the w at the Tent of Meeting and bear	6275
	18:31	for it is your wages for your w at the Tent	6275
	28:18	sacred assembly and do no regular w.	4856+6275
	28:25	sacred assembly and do no regular w.	4856+6275
	28:26	sacred assembly and do no regular w.	4856+6275
	29: 1	sacred assembly and do no regular w.	4856+6275
	29: 7	You must deny yourselves and do no w.	4856
	29:12	sacred assembly and do no regular w.	4856+6275
	29:35	an assembly and do no regular w.	4856+6275
Dt	2: 7	blessed you in all the w of your hands.	5126
	5:13	Six days you shall labor and do all your w,	4856
	5:14	On it you shall not do any w, neither you,	4856
	14:29	bless you in all the w of your hands.	5126+6913
	15:10	will bless you in all your w and	4856
	15:19	put the firstborn of your oxen to w,	6268
	16: 8	to the LORD your God and do no w.	4856
	16:15	in all your harvest and in all the w	5126
	20:11	be subject to forced labor and shall w for	6268
	24:19	in all the w of your hands.	5126
	27:15	the w of the craftsman's hands—	5126
	28:12	on your land in season and to bless all the w	5126
	30: 9	in all the w of your hands and in the fruit	5126
	33:11	and be pleased with the w of his hands.	7189
Jdg	13:12	to be the rule for the boy's life and w?"	5126
	19:16	came in from his w in the fields.	4856
Ru	2:19	Where did you w?	6913
2Sa	12:31	and he made them w at brickmaking.	2296
1Ki	5: 6	My men will w with yours,	2118
	7:14	and experienced in all kinds of bronze w.	4856
	7:14	to King Solomon and did all the w assigned	4856
	7:22	And so the w on the pillars was completed.	4856
	7:29	and bulls were wreaths of hammered w	5126
	7:40	the w he had undertaken for King Solomon	4856

1Ki	7:49	the gold floral w and lamps and tongs;	7258
	7:51	When all the w King Solomon had done for	4856
	9:23	supervising the men who did the w.	4856
	11:28	how well the young man did his w,	4856
2Ki	12:11	to the men appointed to supervise the w on	4856
	22: 5	to the men appointed to supervise the w on	4856
	25:12	of the land to w the vineyards and fields.	4144
1Ch	9:33	because they were responsible for the w day	4856
	22:15	as well as men skilled in every kind of w	4856
	22:16	begin the w, and the LORD be with you."	6913
	23: 4	twenty-four thousand are to supervise the w	4856
	26: 8	with the strength to do the w—	6275
	26:30	in Israel west of the Jordan for all the w of	4856
	28:10	Be strong and do the w."	6913
	28:13	and for all the w of serving in the temple of	4856
	28:20	"Be strong and courageous, and do the w.	6913
	28:20	or forsake you until all the w for the service	4856
	28:21	and Levites are ready for all the w on	6275
	28:21	in any craft will help you in all the w.	4856
	29: 2	gold for the gold w, silver for the silver,	AIT
	29: 5	for the gold w and the silver work,	AIT
	29: 5	for the gold work and the silver w,	AIT
	29: 5	for all the w to be done by the craftsmen.	4856
	29: 6	in charge of the king's w gave willingly.	4856
	29: 7	They gave toward the w on the temple	6275
2Ch	2: 7	a man skilled to w in gold and silver,	6913
	2: 7	to w in Judah and Jerusalem	NIH
	2: 8	My men will w with yours	NIH
	2:14	He is trained to w in gold and silver,	6913
	2:14	He will w with your craftsmen and	NIH
	4:11	So Huram finished the w he had undertaken	4856
	4:21	the gold floral w and lamps	7258
	5: 1	the w Solomon had done for the temple of	4856
	8: 9	not make slaves of the Israelites for his w;	4856
	8:16	All Solomon's w was carried out,	4856
	15: 7	for your w will be rewarded."	7190
	16: 5	and abandoned his w.	4856
	24:12	the men who carried out the w required for	4856
	24:13	The men in charge of the w were diligent,	4856
	27: 3	the LORD and did extensive w on the wall	1215
	29:12	Then these Levites set to w:	7756
	32:19	the w of men's hands.	5126
	34:10	to supervise the w on the LORD's temple.	4856
	34:12	The men did the w faithfully.	4856
Ezr	2:69	to the treasury for this w 61,000 drachmas	4856
	3: 8	the captivity to Jerusalem) began the w,	NIH
	4: 5	to w against them and frustrate their plans	NIH
	4:21	Now issue an order to these men to stop w,	10098
	4:24	Thus the w on the house of God	10525
	5: 2	set to w to rebuild the house	10221+10624+10742
	5: 8	The w is being carried on with diligence	10525
	6: 7	Do not interfere with the w on this temple	10525
	6: 8	so that the w will not stop.	NIH
	6:22	that he assisted them in the w on the house	4856
Ne	2:16	or any others who would be doing the w.	4856
	2:18	So they began this good w.	3208
	3: 1	and his fellow priests went to w and rebuilt	7756
	3: 5	to the w under their supervisors.	6275
	4:11	and will kill them and put an end to the w."	4856
	4:15	returned to the wall, each to his own w.	4856
	4:16	half of my men did the w,	4856
	4:17	Those who carried materials did their w	4856
	4:19	"The w is extensive and spread out,	4856
	4:21	the w with half the men holding spears,	4856
	5:16	I devoted myself to the w on this wall.	4856
	5:16	All my men were assembled there for the w;	4856
	6: 3	the w stop while I leave it and go down	4856
	6: 9	"Their hands will get too weak for the w,	4856
	6:16	that this w had been done with the help	4856
	7:70	of the families contributed to the w.	4856
	7:71	to the treasury for the w 20,000 drachmas	4856
	10:37	the tithes in all the towns where we w.	6275
	11:12	who carried on w for the temple—	4856
	11:16	of the outside w of the house of God;	4856
Job	1:10	You have blessed the w of his hands,	5126
	10: 3	to spurn the w of your hands,	3330
	23: 9	he is at w in the north, I do not see him;	6913
	34:19	for they are all the w of his hands?	5126
	36:24	Remember to extol his w,	7189
	37: 7	that all men he has made may know his w,	NIH
	39:11	Will you leave your heavy w to him?	3330
Ps	8: 3	your heavens, the w of your fingers,	5126
	9:16	the wicked are ensnared by the w	7189
	19: 1	the skies proclaim the w of his hands.	5126
	28: 4	for their deeds and their evil w;	5095
	55:11	Destructive forces are at w in the city;	NIH
	90:17	establish the w of our hands for us—	5126
	90:17	yes, establish the w of our hands.	5126
	102:25	and the heavens are the w of your hands.	5126
	104:13	the earth is satisfied by the fruit of his w.	5126
	104:23	Then man goes out to his w,	7189
Pr	12:14	surely as the w of his hands rewards him.	1691
	14:23	All hard w brings a profit,	6776
	18: 9	in his w is brother to one who destroys.	4856
	21:25	because his hands refuse to w.	6913
	22:29	Do you see a man skilled in his w?	4856
	24:27	Finish your outdoor w and	4856
	31:17	She sets about her w vigorously;	2520+5516
Ecc	2:10	My heart took delight in all my w,	6662
	2:17	because the w that is done under the sun	5126
	2:19	the w into which I have poured my effort	6662
	2:21	For a man may do his w with wisdom,	6662
	2:23	All his days his w is pain and grief;	6721
	2:24	and drink and find satisfaction in his w.	6662
	3:22	for a man than to enjoy his w,	5126
	4: 9	because they have a good return for their w:	6662
	5: 6	be angry at what you say and destroy the w	5126

Ecc	5:19	to accept his lot and be happy in his w—	6662
	8:15	Then joy will accompany him in his w all	6662
	10:15	A fool's w wearies him;	6662
	11: 5	so you cannot understand the w of God,	5126
SS	7: 1	the w of a craftsman's hands.	5126
Isa	1:31	man will become tinder and his w a spark;	7189
	2: 8	they bow down to the w of their hands,	5126
	5:12	no respect for the w of his hands.	5126
	5:19	let him hasten his w so we may see it.	5126
	10:12	When the Lord has finished all his w	5126
	17: 8	not look to the altars, the w of their hands,	5126
	19: 9	Those who w with combed flax will despair,	6268
	28:21	to do his w, his strange work,	5126
	28:21	to do his work, his strange w,	5126
	29:15	who do their w in darkness and think,	5126
	29:23	the w of my hands,	5126
	30:24	and donkeys that w the soil will eat fodder	6268
	45: 9	Does your w say, 'He has no hands'?	7189
	45:11	or give me orders about the w of my hands?	7189
	54:16	into flame and forges a weapon fit for its w.	5126
	54:16	the destroyer to w havoc;	2472
	60:21	shoot I have planted, the w of my hands,	5126
	61: 5	foreigners will w your fields	438
	64: 8	we are all the w of your hand.	5126
Jer	17:22	of your houses or do any w on the Sabbath,	4856
	17:24	the Sabbath day holy by not doing any w	4856
	22:13	making his countrymen w for nothing,	6268
	25:14	to their deeds and the w of their hands."	5126
	31:16	for your w will be rewarded,"	7190
	48:10	on him who is lax in doing the LORD's w!	4856
	50:25	for the Sovereign LORD Almighty has w	4856
	52:16	of the land to w the vineyards and fields.	4144
La	4: 2	the w of a potter's hands!	5126
Eze	27:14	of Beth Togarmah exchanged w horses,	6061
	27:16	purple fabric, embroidered w, fine linen,	8391
	27:24	embroidered w and multicolored rugs	8391
	44:14	of the temple and all the w that is to be done	6275
Hos	13: 2	all of them the w of craftsmen.	5126
Mic	5:13	you will no longer bow down to the w	5126
Na	3:14	W the clay, tread the mortar,	995
Hag	1:14	to w on the house of the LORD Almighty,	4856
	2: 4	'and w. For I am with you,'	6913
	2:17	I struck all the w of your hands with blight,	5126
Mt	14: 2	That is why miraculous powers are at w in	1919
	20: 1	to hire men to w in his vineyard.	2239
	20: 4	'You also go and w in my vineyard,	NIG
	20: 7	'You also go and w in my vineyard.'	NIG
	20:12	the burden of the w and the heat of the day.'	NIG
	20:13	Didn't you agree to w for a denarius?	NIG
	21:28	'Son, go and w today in the vineyard.'	2237
	25:16	put his money to w and gained five more.	2237
Mk	6:14	that is why miraculous powers are at w in	1919
Lk	10:40	that my sister has left me to do the w	1354
	13:14	There are six days for w.	1256+1877+2237+4005
	19:13	'Put this money to w,' he said,	4549
Jn	4:34	of him who sent me and to finish his w.	2240
	4:38	Others have done the hard w,	3159
	5:17	"My Father is always at his w to this very	2237
	5:36	For the very w that the Father has given me	2240
	6:27	Do not w for food that spoils, but for	2237
	6:29	Jesus answered, "The w of God is this:	2240
	9: 3	the w of God might be displayed in his life.	2240
	9: 4	we must do the w of him who sent me.	2240
	9: 4	Night is coming, when no one can w.	2237
	14:10	living in me, who is doing his w.	2240
	17: 4	on earth by completing the w you gave me	2240
Ac	13: 2	for the w to which I have called them."	2240
	13:25	As John was completing his w, he said:	1536
	14:26	of God for the w they had now completed.	2240
	15:38	and had not continued with them in the w.	2240
	20:35	that by this kind of hard w we must help	3159
Ro	4: 5	not w but trusts God who justifies	2237
	7: 5	by the law were at w in our bodies,	1919
	7:21	So I find this law at w:	NIG
	7:23	but I see another law at w in the members	NIG
	7:23	of the law of sin at w within my members.	1639
	14:20	Do not destroy the w of God for the sake	2240
	15:23	now that there is no more place for me to w	NIG
	16:12	those women who w hard in the Lord.	3159
1Co	3:13	his w will be shown for what it is,	2240
	3:13	fire will test the quality of each man's w.	2240
	4:12	We w hard with our own hands.	2237+3159
	9: 1	Are you not the result of my w in the Lord?	2240
	9: 6	and Barnabas who must w for a living?	2237
	9:13	Don't you know that those who w in	2237
	12:11	the w of one and the same Spirit,	1919
	12:29	Do all w miracles?	1539
	15:58	Always give yourselves fully to the w of	2240
	16: 9	a great door for effective w has opened	1921
	16:10	for he is carrying on the w of the Lord,	2240
	16:16	and to everyone who joins in the w,	5300
2Co	1:24	but we w with you for your joy,	1639+5301
	4:12	So then, death is at w in us,	1919
	4:12	but life is at w in you.	NIG
	6: 5	in hard w, sleepless nights and hunger;	3160
	8:11	Now finish the w, so that your eager	4472
	9: 8	you will abound in every good w.	2240
	10:15	beyond our limits by boasting of w done	3160
	10:16	not want to boast about w already done	2289
Gal	2: 8	at w in the ministry of Peter as an apostle	1919
	2: 8	was also at w in my ministry as an apostle	1919
	3: 5	and w miracles among you	1919
Eph	2: 2	now at w in those who are disobedient.	1919
	3:20	according to his power that is at w within	1918
	4:16	as each part does its w,	1918
	4:28	but must w, doing something useful	3159
Php	1: 6	who began a good w in you will carry it on	2240

Php	2:12	*continue to* w out your salvation	2981
	2:22	with me in the w of the gospel.	NIG
	2:30	because he almost died for the w of Christ,	2240
Col	1:10	bearing fruit in every good w.	2240
	3:23	Whatever you do, w at it with all your heart,	2237
	4:17	that you complete the w you have received	1355
1Th	1: 3	before our God and Father your w produced	2240
	2:13	which *is* at w in you who believe.	1919
	4:11	to mind your own business and *to* w	2237
	5:12	to respect those who w hard among you,	3159
	5:13	highest regard in love because of their w.	2240
2Th	2: 7	power of lawlessness *is* already at w;	1919
	2: 9	in accordance with the w of Satan displayed	1918
	2:13	through the sanctifying w of the Spirit and	NIG
	3:10	"If a man will not w, he shall not eat."	2237
1Ti	1: 4	These promote controversies rather than God's w—	3873
	5:17	especially those whose w is preaching	3159
2Ti	2:21	the Master and prepared to do any good w.	2240
	3:17	be thoroughly equipped for every good w.	2240
	4: 5	endure hardship, do the w of an evangelist,	2240
Tit	1: 7	an overseer is **entrusted with** God's w,	3874
Heb	1:10	and the heavens are the w of your hands.	2240
	4: 3	And yet his w has been finished since	2240
	4: 4	the seventh day God rested from all his w."	2240
	4:10	also rests from his own w,	2240
	6:10	he will not forget your w and	2240
	13:17	Obey them so that **their** w will be a joy,	4047S
	13:21	*and may he* w in us that is pleasing to him,	4472
Jas	1: 4	Perseverance must finish its w so	2240
1Pe	1: 2	through the sanctifying *w of the* **Spirit,**	AIT
	1:17	Father who judges each man's w impartially,	2240
1Jn	3: 8	God appeared was to destroy the devil's w.	2240
2Jn	1:11	who welcomes him shares *in* his wicked w.	2240
3Jn	1: 8	that we may w **together** for the truth.	1181+5301
Rev	2: 2	your **hard** w and your perseverance	3160
	9:20	by these plagues still did not repent of the w	2240

WORKED (44) [WORK]

Ge	4: 2	Now Abel kept flocks, and Cain w the soil.	6268
	29:30	And he w for Laban another seven years.	6268
	30:29	"You know how *I have* w for you and	6268
	31: 6	You know that *I've* w for your father	6268
	31:41	*I* w for you fourteen years	6268
Ex	1:13	and w them ruthlessly.	6268
	26: 1	with cherubim w *into* them *by* a skilled	5126
	26:31	with cherubim w into it *by* a skilled	5126
	36: 8	with cherubim w *into* them *by* a skilled	5126
	36:35	with cherubim w into it *by* a skilled	5126
	39: 3	and cut strands *to be* w into the blue, purple	6913
Dt	21: 3	that *has* never **been** w and has never worn	6268
Ru	2: 7	and *has* w steadily from morning till now,	6641
	2:19	of the man *I* w with today is Boaz,"	6913
2Ki	12:11	With it they paid those *who* w on the temple	6913
1Ch	4:23	they stayed there and w for the king.	4856
2Ch	3:14	and fine linen, with cherubim w into it.	6590
	25:20	for God so w that he might hand them over	4946
	31:21	he sought his God and w wholeheartedly.	6913
	32: 5	Then *he* w hard repairing all the broken	2616
Ne	3:25	and Palal son of Uzai w opposite the angle	NIH
	4: 6	for the people w with all their heart.	6913
	4:18	wore his sword at his side as *he* w.	1215
Est	10: 3	because *he* w for the good of his people	2011
Ps	98: 1	and his holy arm *have* w **salvation**	3828
Ecc	2: 2	to someone who *has* not w for it.	6661
Isa	59:16	so his own arm w **salvation** for him,	3828
	63: 5	so my own arm w **salvation** for me,	3828
Eze	23:29	and take away everything you have w *for.*	3330
Joel	2:26	who *has* w wonders for you;	6913
Mt	11:33	until *it* w all **through the dough."**	2435
	20:12	men who were hired last w only one hour,'	4472
Mk	16:20	and the Lord w **with** them and confirmed	5300
Lk	5: 5	"Master, we've w **hard** all night	3159
	13:21	until *it* w all **through the dough."**	2435
Jn	4:38	I sent you to reap what you *have* not w **for.**	3159
Ac	18: 3	he stayed and w with them.	2237
Ro	16: 6	Greet Mary, who w very hard for you.	3159
	16:12	another woman who *has* w very **hard** in	3159
1Co	15:10	No, *I* w harder than all of them—	3159
2Co	11:23	I have w much harder,	3160
1Th	2: 9	*we* w night and day in order not to be	2237
2Th	3: 8	On the contrary, *we* w night and day,	2237
2Jn	1: 8	that you do not lose what *you have* w **for,**	2237

WORKER (14) [WORK]

Ex	12:45	but a temporary resident and a **hired** w may	8502
Lev	22:10	nor may the guest of a priest or his **hired** w	8502
	25: 6	the **hired** w and temporary resident who	8502
	25:40	treated as a **hired** w or a temporary resident	8502
Ecc	3: 9	What does the w gain from his toil?	6913
Mt	10:10	for the w is worth his keep.	2239
Lk	10: 7	for the w deserves his wages.	2239
Ro	16: 9	Greet Urbanus, our **fellow** w in Christ,	5301
	16:21	Timothy, my **fellow** w, sends his greetings	5301
2Co	8:23	Titus, he is my partner and **fellow** w	5301
Php	2:25	my brother, **fellow** and fellow soldier,	5301
1Th	3: 2	who is our brother and God's **fellow** w	5301
1Ti	5:18	and "The w deserves his wages."	2239
Phm	1: 1	*To* Philemon our dear friend and **fellow** w,	5301

WORKERS (30) [WORK]

Ru	2:21	'Stay with my w until they finish	5853
2Ki	12:15	they gave the money to pay the w,	4856+6913
	22: 5	have these men pay the w who repair	4856+6913
	22: 9	and have entrusted it to the w	4856+6913

1Ch	4:21	clans of the linen w at Beth Ashbea,	1074+6275
	23:24	the w twenty years old or more who	4856+6913
	27:26	in charge of the field w who farmed	4856+6913
2Ch	24:12	w in iron and bronze to repair the temple.	3093
	34:10	the w who repaired and restored the temple.	6913
	34:13	supervised all the w from job to job.	4856+6913
	34:17	to the supervisors and w."	4856+6913
Ezr	7:24	temple servants or other w *at* this house	10586
Isa	19:10	The w in cloth will be dejected,	9271
	58: 3	you do as you please and exploit all your w.	6774
Jer	10: 9	blue and purple—all made by **skilled** *w.*	AIT
Eze	48:18	Its produce will supply food for the w *of*	6268
	48:19	The w *from* the city who farm it will come	6268
Mt	9:37	The harvest is plentiful but the w are few.	2239
	9:38	to send out w into his harvest field."	2239
	20: 8	'Call the w and pay them their wages,	2239
	20: 9	"The w who were hired about	NIG
Lk	10: 2	"The harvest is plentiful, but the w are few.	2239
	10: 2	to send out w into his harvest field.	2239
Ro	16: 3	and Aquila, my **fellow** w in Christ Jesus.	5301
1Co	3: 9	For we are God's **fellow** w;	5301
	12:28	third teachers, then w of **miracles,**	1539
2Co	6: 1	As God's **fellow** w we urge you not	5300
Php	4: 3	the only Jews among my **fellow** w for	5301
Col	4:11	the only Jews among my **fellow** w for	5301
Phm	1:24	Demas and Luke, my **fellow** w.	5301

WORKING (19) [WORK]

Ex	5: 5	and you are stopping them from w."	6026
	5: 9	so that *they* keep w and pay no attention	6913
	15:11	awesome in glory, w wonders?	6913
Ru	2: 3	she found herself w in a field belonging	NIH
	2:19	the one at whose place *she had been* w.	6913
2Ch	2:18	foremen over them to **keep** the people w.	6268
	26:10	He had people w his **fields and vineyards**	4144
Ezr	3: 9	in supervising *those* w on the house of God.	6213
Ne	10:31	Every seventh year we will forgo the land	NIH
Ecc	9:10	there is neither w nor planning	5126
Jer	18: 3	and I saw him w at the wheel.	4856+6913
Eze	46: 1	is to be shut on the six w days,	5126
Jn	5:17	his work to this very day, and I, too, *am* w."	2237
1Co	12: 6	There are different kinds *of* w,	1920
Eph	1:19	power is like the w of his mighty strength,	1918
	3: 7	of God's grace given me through the w	1918
Col	3:23	as w for the Lord, not for men,	NIG
	4:13	I vouch for him that *he* is w hard for you	4506
Jas	2:22	and his actions *were* w **together,**	5300

WORKMAN (2) [MAN, WORK]

2Ti	2:15	a w who does not need to be ashamed	2239
Rev	18:22	No w of any trade will ever be found	5493

WORKMAN'S (1) [MAN, WORK]

Jdg	5:26	her right hand for the w hammer.	6664

WORKMANSHIP (1) [WORK]

Eph	2:10	For we are God's w, created in Christ Jesus	4473

WORKMEN (8) [MAN, WORK]

Ex	36: 8	the w made the tabernacle with ten	4856+6913
1Ki	5:16	supervised the project and directed the w.	928+2021+4856+6913
2Ki	12:14	it was paid to the w, who used it	4856+6913
1Ch	22:15	You have many w: stonecutters,	4856+6913
Ne	4:22	as guards by night and w by day."	4856
Ac	19:25	along with the w in related trades, and said:	2239
2Co	11:13	such men are false apostles, deceitful w,	2239
Jas	5: 4	the w who mowed your fields are crying out	2239

WORKS (67) [WORK]

Dt	3:24	the deeds and **mighty** w you do?	1476
	20:20	not fruit trees and use them to build **siege** w	5189
	32: 4	He is the Rock, his w are perfect,	7189
2Ki	25: 1	the city and built **siege** w all around it.	1911
Job	26:14	And these are but the outer fringe of his w;	2006
	40:19	He ranks first among the w of God,	2006
Ps	8: 6	You made him ruler over the w *of* your	5126
	28: 5	Since they show no regard for the w *of*	7190
	46: 8	Come and see the w *of* the LORD,	5149
	64: 9	they will proclaim the w *of* God and ponder	7189
	66: 5	how awesome his w in man's behalf!	6613
	77:12	I will meditate on all your w	7189
	92: 4	I sing for joy at the w *of* your hands.	5126
	92: 5	How great are your w, O LORD,	5126
	103: 6	The LORD w righteousness and justice	6913
	103:22	all his w everywhere in his dominion.	5126
	104:24	How many are your w, O LORD!	5126
	104:31	may the LORD rejoice in his w—	5126
	107:22	and tell of his w with songs of joy.	5126
	107:24	They saw the w *of* the LORD,	5126
	111: 2	Great are the w *of* the LORD;	5126
	111: 6	the power of his w,	5126
	111: 7	The w *of* his hands are faithful and just;	5126
	138: 8	do not abandon the w *of* your hands.	5126
	139:14	your w are wonderful, I know that full well.	5126
	143: 5	I meditate on all your w	7189
	145: 4	One generation will commend your w	5126
	145: 5	and I will meditate on your **wonderful** *w.*	AIT
	145: 6	of the power of your **awesome** w,	3707
Pr	8:22	as the first of his w, before his deeds of old;	2006
	12:11	*He who* w his land will have abundant food,	6268
	16: 4	The LORD w **out** everything	7188
	16:26	The laborer's appetite w for him;	6661

Pr	26:28	and a flattering mouth w ruin.	6913
	28:19	*He who* w his land will have abundant food,	6268
	31:13	and flax and w with eager hands.	6913
	31:31	let her w bring her praise at the city gate.	5126
Isa	29: 3	and set up my **siege** w against you.	5193
	41:24	and your w are utterly worthless;	7189
	44:12	The blacksmith takes a tool and w with it in	7188
	57:12	expose your righteousness and your w,	5126
	65:22	my chosen ones will long enjoy the w	5126
Jer	11:15	in my temple *as* she w **out** her evil schemes	6913
	52: 4	the city and built **siege** w all around it.	1911
Eze	4: 2	Then lay siege to it: Erect **siege** w against it,	1911
	17:17	and **siege** w erected to destroy many lives.	1911
	21:22	to build a ramp and to erect **siege** w.	1911
	26: 8	he will set up **siege** w against you,	1911
Jn	6:28	must we do to do the w God requires?"	2240
	7:18	but he who w for the honor of the one who	2426
Ro	4: 2	If, in fact, Abraham was justified by w,	2240
	4: 4	Now *when* a man w, his wages are not	2237
	4: 6	God credits righteousness apart from w:	2240
	8:28	And we know that in all things God w for	5300
	9:12	not by w but by him who calls—	2240
	9:32	not by faith but as if it were by w.	2240
	11: 6	And if by grace, then it is no longer by w;	2240
	16:23	who is the city's **director of public** w,	3874
1Co	5: 6	Don't you know that a little yeast w through the whole batch	2435
	12: 6	but the same God w of them all in all men.	1919
Gal	5: 9	"A little yeast w **through** the whole batch	2435
Eph	1:11	*of* him who w **out** everything in conformity	1919
	2: 9	not by w, so that no one can boast.	2240
	2:10	created in Christ Jesus to do good w,	2240
	4:12	to prepare God's people for w of service,	2240
Php	2:13	for it is God who w **in** you to will and to act	1919
Col	1:29	his energy, which so powerfully w in me.	1919

WORLD (261) [WORLD'S, WORLDLY]

Ge	11: 1	Now the whole w had one language and	824
	11: 9	the language of the whole w.	824
	41:57	because the famine was severe in all the w.	824
Ex	34:10	before done in any nation in all the w.	824
1Sa	2: 8	upon them he has set the w.	9315
	17:46	the whole w will know that there is a God	824
1Ki	4:34	sent by all the kings of the w,	824
	8:53	of the w to be your own inheritance,	824
	10:24	The whole w sought audience	824
2Ki	5:15	that there is no God in all the w except	824
1Ch	16:30	The w is firmly established;	9315
2Ch	32:19	about the gods of the other peoples of the w	824
Job	18:18	into darkness and is banished from the w.	9315
	34:13	Who put him in charge of the whole w?	9315
Ps	9: 8	He will judge the w in righteousness;	9315
	17:14	of this w whose reward is in this life.	2698
	19: 4	their words to the ends of the w.	9315
	24: 1	the w, and all who live in it;	9315
	33: 8	let all the people of the w revere him.	9315
	49: 1	listen, all who live in this w,	2698
	50:12	for the w is mine, and all that is in it.	9315
	77:18	your lightning lit up the w;	9315
	89:11	you founded the w and all that is in it.	9315
	90: 2	or you brought forth the earth and the w,	9315
	93: 1	The w is firmly established;	9315
	96:10	The w is firmly established;	9315
	96:13	He will judge the w in righteousness and	9315
	97: 4	His lightning lights up the w;	9315
	98: 7	the w, and all who live in it.	9315
	98: 9	He will judge the w in righteousness and	9315
Pr	8:23	from the beginning, before the w began.	824
	8:26	or its fields or any of the dust of the w.	9315
	8:31	rejoicing in his **whole** w and delighting	824+9315
Isa	12: 5	let this be known to all the w.	824
	13:11	I will punish the w for its evil,	9315
	14: 9	all those who were leaders in the w;	824
	14:17	the man who made the w a desert,	9315
	14:26	the plan determined for the whole w;	824
	18: 3	All you people of the w,	9315
	24: 4	the w languishes and withers,	9315
	26: 9	the people of the w learn righteousness.	9315
	26:18	we have not given birth to people of the w.	9315
	27: 6	and blossom and fill all the w with fruit.	9315
	34: 1	Let the earth hear, and all that is in it, the w,	9315
	38:11	or be with those who now dwell in **this** w,	2535
	40:23	and reduces the rulers of this w to nothing.	824
Jer	10:12	he founded the w by his wisdom and	9315
	51:15	he founded the w by his wisdom and	9315
Eze	20:32	like the peoples of the w,	824
Da	4: 1	who live in all the w:	10075
Na	1: 5	the w and all who live in it.	9315
Zep	1:18	In the fire of his jealousy the whole w will	824
	3: 8	The whole w will be consumed by the fire	824
Zec	1:11	and found the whole w at rest and in peace."	824
	6: 5	in the presence of the Lord of the whole w.	824
Mt	4: 8	and showed him all the kingdoms of the w	3180
	5:14	"You are the light *of* the w.	3180
	13:35	since the creation *of* the w."	3180
	13:38	The field is the w,	3180
	16:26	if he gains the whole w, yet forfeits his soul?	3180
	18: 7	"Woe *to* the w because of the things	3180
	24:14	in the whole w as a testimony to all nations,	3876
	24:21	from the beginning of the w until now—	3180
	25:34	for you since the creation *of* the w.	3180
	26:13	the w, what she has done will also be told,	3180
Mk	8:36	to gain the whole w, yet forfeits his soul?	3180
	9: 3	than anyone in the w could bleach them.	1178
	13:19	when God created the w, until now—	3232
	14: 9	the gospel is preached throughout the w,	3180

Mk	16:15	into all the w and preach the good news	3180
Lk	2: 1	be taken of the entire **Roman** w.	3876
	4: 5	in an instant all the kingdoms of the w.	3876
	9:25	for a man to gain the whole w,	3180
	11:50	shed since the beginning of the w,	3180
	12:30	For the pagan w runs after all such things,	3180
	16: 8	For the people of this w are more shrewd	172
	21:26	apprehensive of what is coming on the w,	3876
Jn	1: 9	to every man was coming into the w.	3180
	1:10	He was in the w, and though the world was	3180
	1:10	and though the w was made through him,	3180
	1:10	the w did not recognize him.	3180
	1:29	who takes away the sin of the w!	3180
	3:16	the w that he gave his one and only Son,	3180
	3:17	For God did not send his Son into the w	3180
	3:17	the world to condemn the w,	3180
	3:17	but to save the w through him.	3180
	3:19	Light has come into the w,	3180
	4:42	that this man really is the Savior of the w."	3180
	6:14	the Prophet who is to come into the w."	3180
	6:33	down from heaven and gives life to the w."	3180
	6:51	which I will give for the life of the w."	3180
	7: 4	doing these things, show yourself to the w."	3180
	7: 7	The w cannot hate you, but it hates me	3180
	8:12	he said, "I am the light of the w.	3180
	8:23	You are of this w; I am not of this world.	3180
	8:23	You are of this world; I am not of this w.	3180
	8:26	what I have heard from him I tell the w."	3180
	9: 5	I am in the w, I am the light of the world."	3180
	9: 5	I am in the world, I am the light of the w.	3180
	9:39	"For judgment I have come into this w,	3180
	10:36	as his very own and sent into the w?	3180
	11:27	who was to come into the w."	3180
	12:19	Look how the whole w has gone after him!"	3180
	12:25	in this w will keep it for eternal life.	3180
	12:31	Now is the time for judgment on this w;	3180
	12:31	now the prince of this w will be driven out.	3180
	12:46	I have come into the w as a light,	3180
	12:47	I did not come to judge the w, but to save it.	3180
	13: 1	for him to leave this w and go to the Father.	3180
	13: 1	Having loved his own who were in the w,	3180
	14:17	The w cannot accept him,	3180
	14:19	Before long, the w will not see me anymore,	3180
	14:22	to show yourself to us and not to the w?"	3180
	14:27	I do not give to you as the w gives.	3180
	14:30	for the prince of this w is coming.	3180
	14:31	the w must learn that I love the Father and	3180
	15:18	"If the w hates you, keep in mind that	3180
	15:19	If you belonged to the w, it would love you	3180
	15:19	As it is, you do not belong to the w,	3180
	15:19	but I have chosen you out of the w.	3180
	15:19	That is why the w hates you.	3180
	16: 8	he will convict the w of guilt in regard	3180
	16:11	the prince of this w now stands condemned.	3180
	16:20	and mourn while the w rejoices.	3180
	16:21	of her joy that a child is born into the w.	3180
	16:28	I came from the Father and entered the w;	3180
	16:28	now I am leaving the w and going back to	3180
	16:33	In this w you will have trouble.	3180
	16:33	I have overcome the w."	3180
	17: 5	with you before the w began.	3180
	17: 6	to those whom you gave me out of the w.	3180
	17: 9	I am not praying for the w,	3180
	17:11	I will remain in the w no longer,	3180
	17:11	but they are still in the w,	3180
	17:13	I say these things while I am still in the w,	3180
	17:14	and the w has hated them,	3180
	17:14	for they are not of the w any more than I am	3180
	17:14	of the world any more than I am of the w.	3180
	17:15	not that you take them out of the w but	3180
	17:16	They are not of the w,	3180
	17:18	As you sent me into the w,	3180
	17:18	I have sent them into the w.	3180
	17:21	the w may believe that you have sent me.	3180
	17:23	to complete unity to let the w know	3180
	17:24	before the creation of the w.	3180
	17:25	though the w does not know you,	3180
	18:20	"I have spoken openly to the w,"	3180
	18:36	Jesus said, "My kingdom is not of this w.	3180
	18:37	and for this I came into the w,	3180
	21:25	that even the whole w would not have room	3180
Ac	11:28	would spread over the entire **Roman** w.	3876
	17: 6	over the w have now come here,	3876
	17:24	"The God who made the w and everything	3180
	17:31	a day when he will judge the w with justice	3876
	19:27	throughout the province of Asia and the w,	3876
	19:35	"Men of Ephesus, doesn't **all the w** know	476+1639+4005+5515
	24: 5	up riots among the Jews all over the w.	3876
Ro	1: 8	your faith is being reported all over the w.	3180
	1:20	since the creation of the w God's invisible	3180
	3: 6	how could God judge the w?	3180
	3:19	and the whole w held accountable to God.	3180
	4:13	the promise that he would be heir of the w,	3180
	5:12	just as sin entered the w through one man,	3180
	5:13	just as the law was given, sin was in the w.	3180
	10:18	their words to the ends of the w."	3876
	11:12	their transgression means riches for the w,	3180
	11:15	their rejection is the reconciliation of the w,	3180
	12: 2	conform any longer to the pattern of this w,	172
1Co	1:20	God made foolish the wisdom of the w?	3180
	1:21	the w through its wisdom did not know him,	3180
	1:27	But God chose the foolish things of the w	3180
	1:27	God chose the weak things of the w	3180
	1:28	He chose the lowly things of this w and	3180
	2:12	We have not received the spirit of the w but	3180
	3:19	For the wisdom of this w is foolishness	3180

1Co	3:22	whether Paul or Apollos or Cephas or the w	3180
	4:13	scum of the earth, the refuse of the w.	4246S
	5:10	the people of this w who are immoral,	3180
	5:10	In that case you would have to leave this w.	3180
	6: 2	not know that the saints will judge the w?	3180
	6: 2	And if you are to judge the w,	3180
	7:31	those who use the things of the w,	3180
	7:31	this w in its present form is passing away.	3180
	7:33	about the affairs of this w—	3180
	7:34	about the affairs of this w—	3180
	8: 4	in the w and that there is no God but one.	3180
	11:32	that we will not be condemned with the w.	3180
	14:10	there are all sorts of languages in the w,	3180
2Co	1:12	that we have conducted ourselves in the w,	3180
	5:19	that God was reconciling the w to himself	3180
	10: 2	that we live by the standards of **this** w.	4922
	10: 3	For though we live in **the** w,	4922
	10: 3	we do not wage war as **the** w does,	4922
	10: 4	with are not the weapons of the w,	4920
	11:18	many are boasting in the way the w does,	4922
Gal	3:22	the Scripture declares that the **whole** w is	4246
	4: 3	under the basic principles of the w.	3180
	6:14	which the w has been crucified to me,	3180
	6:14	crucified to me, and I to the w.	3180
Eph	1: 4	the w to be holy and blameless in his sight.	3180
	2: 2	of this w and of the ruler of the kingdom of	3180
	2:12	without hope and without God in the w.	3180
	6:12	against the **powers of** this dark w	3179
Col	1: 6	All over the w this gospel is bearing fruit	3180
	2: 8	the basic principles of this w rather than	3180
	2:20	to the basic principles of this w,	3180
1Ti	1:15	Christ Jesus came into the w to save sinners	3180
	3:16	was believed on in the w, was taken up in	3180
	6: 7	For we brought nothing into the w,	3180
	6:17	in this present w not to be arrogant nor	172
2Ti	4:10	for Demas, because he loved this w,	172
Heb	1: 6	when God brings his firstborn into the w,	3876
	2: 5	not to angels that he has subjected the w	3876
	4: 3	since the creation of the w.	3180
	9:26	since the creation of the w.	3180
	10: 5	when Christ came into the w, he said:	3180
	11: 7	the w and became heir of the righteousness	3180
	11:38	the w was not worthy of them.	3180
Jas	1:27	from being polluted by the w.	3180
	2: 5	in the eyes of the w to be rich in faith and	3180
	3: 6	a w of evil among the parts of the body.	3180
	4: 4	that friendship with the w is hatred	3180
	4: 4	to be a friend of the w becomes an enemy	3180
1Pe	1: 1	To God's elect, strangers in the w,	NIG
	1:20	He was chosen before the creation of the w,	3180
	2:11	I urge you, as aliens and strangers in the w,	NIG
	5: 9	the w are undergoing the same kind	3180
2Pe	1: 4	and escape the corruption in the w caused	3180
	2: 5	not spare the ancient w when he brought	3180
	2:20	If they have escaped the corruption of the w	3180
	3: 6	also the w of that time was deluged	3180
1Jn	2: 2	but also for the sins of the whole w.	3180
	2:15	Do not love the w or anything in the world.	3180
	2:15	Do not love the world or anything in the w.	3180
	2:15	If anyone loves the w, the love of the Father	3180
	2:16	For everything in the w—the cravings of	3180
	2:16	comes not from the Father but from the w.	3180
	2:17	The w and its desires pass away,	3180
	3: 1	The reason the w does not know us is	3180
	3:13	my brothers, if the w hates you.	3180
	4: 1	false prophets have gone out into the w.	3180
	4: 3	and even now is already in the w.	3180
	4: 4	is greater than the one who is in the w.	3180S
	4: 5	They are from the w and therefore speak	3180
	4: 5	from the viewpoint of the w,	3180
	4: 5	and the w listens to them.	3180
	4: 9	and only Son into the w that we might live	3180
	4:14	to be the Savior of the w.	3180
	4:17	because in this w we are like him.	3180
	5: 4	for everyone born of God overcomes the w.	3180
	5: 4	This is the victory that has overcome the w,	3180
	5: 5	Who is it that overcomes the w?	3180
	5:19	whole w is under the control of the evil one.	3180
2Jn	1: 7	have gone out into the w.	3180
Rev	3:10	upon the whole w to test those who live on	3876
	11:15	the w has become the kingdom of our Lord	3180
	12: 9	or Satan, who leads the whole w astray.	3876
	13: 3	The whole w was astonished and followed	1178
	13: 8	that was slain from the creation of the w.	3180
	16:14	they go out to the kings of the whole w,	3876
	17: 8	of the w will be astonished when they see	3180

WORLD'S (3) [WORLD]

La	4:12	did not believe, nor did any of the w people,	9315
Jn	11: 9	will not stumble, for he sees by this w light.	3180
Rev	18:23	Your merchants were the w great men.	1178

WORLDLY (10) [WORLD]

Lk	16: 9	use w wealth to gain friends for yourselves,	94
	16:11	not been trustworthy in handling w wealth,	96
1Co	3: 1	I could not address you as spiritual but as w	4921
	3: 3	You are still w. For since there is jealousy	4920
	3: 3	and quarreling among you, are you not w?	4920
2Co	1:12	so not according to w wisdom but according	4920
	1:17	that I make my plans in a w **manner** so	4922
	5:16	regard no one **from a w point of view.**	2848+4922
	7:10	but w sorrow brings death.	3180+3836
Tit	2:12	to say "No" to ungodliness and w passions,	3176

WORM (10) [WORMS]

Job	17:14	and to the w, 'My mother' or 'My sister,'	8231
	24:20	womb forgets them, the w feasts on them;	8231
	25: 6	a son of man, who is only a w!"	9357
Ps	22: 6	But I am a w and not a man,	9357
Isa	41:14	Do not be afraid, O w Jacob, O little Israel,	9357
	51: 8	the w will devour them like wool.	6182
	66:24	their w will not die, nor will their fire	9357
Jnh	4: 7	But at dawn the next day God provided a w,	9357
Mk	9:48	where " 'their w does not die, and the fire	5038
2Ti	3: 6	the kind who are *their* way into homes	1905

WORMS (5) [WORM]

Dt	28:39	gather the grapes, because w will eat them.	9357
Job	7: 5	My body is clothed with w and scabs,	8231
	21:26	and w cover them both.	8231
Isa	14:11	spread out beneath you and w cover you.	9357
Ac	12:23	and he was **eaten by** w and died.	5037

WORMWOOD (1)

Rev	8:11	the name of the star is W.	952

WORN (19) [WEAR]

Ge	18:12	"After I *am* w out and my master is old,	1162
Ex	35:19	the woven garments w for ministering in	NIH
	39:26	the hem of the robe to be w for ministering,	NIH
	39:41	and the woven garments w for ministering	NIH
Dt	21: 3	been worked and *has* never w a yoke	928+5432
	25:18	When you were weary and w out,	3335
Jos	9: 5	The men put w and patched sandals	1165
	9:13	And our clothes and sandals *are* w out by	1162
Jdg	8: 5	my troops some bread; they are w out,	6546
	8:26	purple garments w *by* the kings of Midian	6584
Est	6: 8	have them bring a royal robe the king *has* w	4252
Job	16: 7	Surely, O God, *you have* w me out;	4206
Ps	6: 6	*I am* w out from groaning;	3333
	69: 3	*I am* w out calling for help;	3333
Isa	47:13	counsel you have received *has only* w you out!	4206
Jer	12: 5	with men on foot and *they have* w you out,	4206
	45: 3	*I am* w out with groaning	3333
Eze	23:43	I said about the *one* w out *by* adultery,	1165
Lk	8:27	For a long time this man had not w clothes	1907

WORN-OUT (3) [WEAR]

Jos	9: 4	with w sacks and old wineskins,	1165
Jer	38:11	and w clothes from there and let them down	1170
	38:12	and w clothes under your arms to pad	NIH

WORRIED (2) [WORRY]

1Sa	10: 2	thinking about them and *is* w about you.	1793
Lk	10:41	"*you are* w and upset about many things,	3534

WORRIES (4) [WORRY]

Jer	17: 8	*It has* no w in a year of drought	1793
Mt	13:22	but the w of this life and the deceitfulness	3533
Mk	4:19	but the w of this life, the deceitfulness	3533
Lk	8:14	on their way they are choked by life's w,	3533

WORRY (13) [WORRIED, WORRIES, WORRYING]

1Sa	9:20	*do not* w about them;.	906+4213+8492
Mt	6:25	I tell you, *do not* w **about** your life,	3534
	6:28	"And why *do you* w about clothes?	3534
	6:31	So *do not* w, saying, 'What shall we eat?'	3534
	6:34	Therefore *do not* w about tomorrow,	3534
	6:34	for tomorrow *will* w about itself.	3534
	10:19	*do not* w about what to say or how to say it.	3534
Mk	13:11	*do not* w **beforehand** about what to say.	4628
Lk	12:11	*do not* w about how you will defend	3534
	12:22	*do not* w **about** your life, what you will eat;	3534
	12:26	why *do you* w about the rest?	3534
	12:29	eat or drink; *do not* w **about** it.	3577
	21:14	make up your mind not *to* w **beforehand**	4627

WORRYING (3) [WORRY]

1Sa	9: 5	about the donkeys and *start* w about us."	1793
Mt	6:27	Who of you *by* w can add a single hour	3534
Lk	12:25	Who of you *by* w can add a single hour	3534

WORSE (22) [WORST]

Ge	19: 9	*We'll treat* you w than them."	8317
Ex	11: 6	w *than* there has ever been or ever will	4017+4202
2Sa	19: 7	be w for you than all the calamities	8273
1Ki	17:17	He **grew** w and worse,	2118+2617+2716+4394
	17:17	He **grew** worse and w,	2118+2617+2716+4394
Pr	17: 7	**how much** w lying lips to a ruler!	677+3954
	19:10	**how much** w for a slave to rule over princes!	677+3954
Eze	14:21	**How much** w will it be when I send	677+3954
Da	1:10	Why should he see you **looking** w than	2407
Mic	7: 4	the most upright w than a thorn hedge.	4946
Mt	9:16	away from the garment, making the tear w.	5937
	12:45	the final condition of that man is w **than**	5937
	27:64	This last deception will be w **than** the first."	5937
Mk	2:21	pull away from the old, making the tear w.	5937
	5:26	yet instead of getting better she grew w.	5937
Lk	11:26	the final condition of that man is w **than**	5937
	13: 2	that these Galileans were w sinners than all	NIG
Jn	5:14	Stop sinning or something w may happen	5937

1Co	8:8	*we are* no w if we do not eat,	5728
1Ti	5:8	the faith and is w **than** an unbeliever.	5937
2Ti	3:13	and impostors will go **from bad to w**,	2093+3836+5937
2Pe	2:20	w **off** at the end **than** they were at the	5937

WORSHIP (158) [WORSHIPED, WORSHIPER, WORSHIPERS, WORSHIPING, WORSHIPS]

Ge	22:5	*We will* w and then we will come back	2556
Ex	3:12	*you will* w God on this mountain."	6268
	4:23	"Let my son go, so *he may* w me.	6268
	7:16	so that *they may* w me in the desert.	6268
	8:1	Let my people go, so that *they may* w me.	6268
	8:20	Let my people go, so that *they may* w me.	6268
	9:1	"Let my people go, so that *they may* w me."	6268
	9:13	Let my people go, so that *they may* w me.	6268
	10:3	"Go, w the LORD your God," he said.	6268
	10:7	so that *they may* w the LORD their God.	6268
	10:8	"Go, w the LORD your God," he said.	6268
	10:11	Have only the men go; and w the LORD,	6268
	10:24	and said, "Go, w the LORD,	6268
	10:26	not know what *we are* to use to w	6268
	12:31	Go, w the LORD as you have requested.	6268
	20:5	You shall not bow down to them or w them;	6268
	23:24	not bow down before their gods or w them	6268
	23:25	W the LORD your God,	6268
	23:33	the w *of* their gods will certainly be a snare	6268
	24:1	*You are* to w at a distance,	2556
	34:14	*Do not* w any other god, for the LORD,	2556
Dt	4:28	There *you will* w man-made gods of wood	6268
	5:9	You shall not bow down to them or w them;	6268
	8:19	and follow other gods and w and bow down	6268
	11:16	and w other gods and bow down to them.	6268
	12:2	nations you are dispossessing w their gods.	6268
	12:4	not w the LORD your God in their way.	6913
	12:31	not w the LORD your God in their way,	6913
	13:2	you have not known) "and *let us* w them,"	6268
	13:6	and w other gods" (gods that neither you	6268
	13:13	and w other gods" (gods you have not	6268
	28:36	There *you will* w other gods,	6268
	28:64	There *you will* w other gods—	6268
	29:18	the LORD our God to go and w the gods	6268
	30:17	to bow down to other gods and w them,	6268
	31:20	they will turn to other gods and w them,	6268
Jos	22:27	we will w the LORD at his sanctuary	6268+6275
Jdg	6:10	*do not* w the gods of the Amorites,	3707
1Sa	1:3	to w and sacrifice to the LORD Almighty	2556
	15:25	so that *I may* w the LORD."	2556
	15:30	so that *I may* w the LORD your God."	2556
2Sa	15:8	*I will* w the LORD in Hebron.' "	6268
	15:32	where *people used to* w God,	2556
1Ki	1:47	And the king **bowed in** w on his bed	2556
	9:6	and go off to serve other gods and w them,	2556
	12:30	people went even as far as Dan to w	4200+7156
	16:31	and began to serve Baal and w him.	2556
2Ki	10:28	So Jehu destroyed **Baal** w in Israel.	1251
	10:29	the w of the golden calves at Bethel	NIH
	17:25	*they did not* w the LORD.	3707
	17:28	and taught them how *to* w the LORD.	3707
	17:34	They neither w the LORD nor adhere to	3710
	17:35	not w any other gods or bow down to them,	3707
	17:36	is the one *you must* w.	3707
	17:37	*Do not* w other gods.	3707
	17:38	and *do not* w other gods.	3707
	17:39	Rather, w the LORD your God;	3707
	18:22	*"You must* w before this altar in Jerusalem"	2556
1Ch	16:29	w the LORD in the splendor of his holiness.	2556
2Ch	7:19	and go off to serve other gods and w them,	2556
	20:18	of Judah and Jerusalem fell down in w.	2556
	29:28	The whole assembly **bowed in** w,	2556
	32:12	*'You must* w before one altar	2556
Ezr	7:19	to you for w *in* the temple of your God.	10587
Ne	9:6	and the multitudes of heaven w you.	2556
Job	1:20	Then he fell to the ground in w	2556
Ps	22:29	All the rich of the earth will feast and w;	2556
	29:2	w the LORD in the splendor of his holiness.	2556
	86:9	the nations you have made will come and w	2556
	95:6	Come, let us bow down *in* w,	2556
	96:9	W the LORD in the splendor	2556
	97:7	All *who* w images are put to shame,	6268
	97:7	w him, all *you* gods!	2556
	99:5	the LORD our God and w at his footstool;	2556
	99:9	Exalt the LORD our God and w	2556
	100:2	W the LORD with gladness;	6268
	102:22	the kingdoms assemble to w the LORD.	2556
	132:7	*let us* w at his footstool—	2556
Isa	2:20	and idols of gold, which they made to w.	2556
	19:21	*They will* w *with* sacrifices	6268
	19:23	and Assyrians *will* w together.	6268
	27:13	in Egypt will come and w the LORD on	2556
	29:13	Their w *of* me is made up only	3707
	36:7	*"You must* w before this altar"?	2556
	46:6	and they bow down and w it.	2556
	56:6	and to w him, all who keep the Sabbath	6269
Jer	7:2	through these gates to w the LORD.	2556
	13:10	to serve and w them, will be like this belt—	2556
	23:27	fathers forgot my name through **Baal** w.	1251
	25:6	not follow other gods to serve and w them,	2556
	26:2	of the towns of Judah who come to w *in*	2556
Eze	46:2	*He is to* w at the threshold of the gateway	2556
	46:3	of the land *are to* w in the presence of	2556
	46:9	whoever enters by the north gate to w is	2556
Da	3:5	must fall down and w the image of gold	10504
	3:6	down and w will immediately be thrown	

Da	3:10	all kinds of music must fall down and w	10504
	3:11	w will be thrown into a blazing furnace.	10504
	3:12	nor w the image of gold you have set up."	10504
	3:14	or w the image of gold I have set up?	10504
	3:15	to fall down and w the image I made,	10504
	3:15	But if *you do not* w it,	10504
	3:18	or w the image of gold you have set up.	10504
	3:28	or w any god except their own God.	10504
	7:27	and all rulers *will* w and obey him.'	10586
Hos	13:1	But he became guilty of **Baal** w and died.	1251
Jnh	1:9	"I am a Hebrew and I w the LORD,	3707
Zep	1:5	**bow down** on the roofs to w the starry host,	2556
	2:11	The nations on every shore *will* w him,	2556
Zec	14:16	go up year after year to w the King,	2556
	14:17	of the earth do not go up to Jerusalem to w	2556
Mt	2:2	in the east and have come to w him."	4686
	2:8	so that I too *may* go and w him."	4686
	4:9	"if *you will* bow down and w me."	4686
	4:10	For it is written: '**W the Lord your God,**	4686
	15:9	*They* w me in vain; their teachings are but	4936
Mk	7:7	*They* w me in vain; their teachings are but	4936
Lk	4:7	So if *you* w me, it will all be yours."	4686
	4:8	'**W** the Lord your God and serve him	4686
Jn	4:20	the place where we must w is in Jerusalem."	4686
	4:21	when *you will* w the Father neither	4686
	4:22	You Samaritans w what you do not know;	4686
	4:22	we w what we do know,	4686
	4:23	now come when the true worshipers *will* w	4686
	4:24	and his worshipers must w in spirit and	4686
	12:20	among those who went up to w at the Feast.	4686
Ac	7:7	of that country and w me in this place.'	3302
	7:42	over *to* the w of the heavenly bodies.	3302
	7:43	the idols you made *to* w.	4686
	8:27	This man had gone to Jerusalem *to* w,	4686
	13:16	of Israel and you Gentiles who w God,	5828
	17:23	and looked carefully at your **objects of** w,	4934
	17:23	Now what *you* w as something unknown	2355
	18:13	"is persuading the people *to* w God in ways	4936
	24:11	I went up to Jerusalem *to* w.	4686
	24:14	I admit that *I* w the God of our fathers as	3302
Ro	9:4	the **temple** w and the promises.	3301
	12:1	this is your spiritual **act of** w.	3301
1Co	14:25	So *he will* fall down and w God,	4686
Php	3:3	we who w by the Spirit of God,	3302
Col	2:18	the w of angels disqualify you for the prize.	2579
	2:23	their **self-imposed** w, their false humility	1615
1Ti	2:10	for women who profess to w **God.**	2537
Heb	1:6	he says, *"Let all God's angels* w him."	4686
	9:1	the first covenant had regulations *for* w and	3301
	10:1	make perfect those who draw near to w,	NIG
	12:28	and so w God acceptably with reverence	3302
Rev	4:10	and w him who lives for ever and ever.	4686
	13:8	All inhabitants of the earth *will* w	4686
	13:12	and made the earth and its inhabitants w	4686
	13:15	all who **refused to** w the image to	3590+4686
	14:7	W him who made the heavens, the earth,	4686
	14:11	for those who w the beast and his image,	4686
	15:4	All nations will come and w before you,	4686
	19:10	At this I fell at his feet *to* w.	4686
	19:10	to the testimony of Jesus. **W** God!	4686
	22:8	I fell down *to* w at the feet of the angel	4686
	22:9	who keep the words of this book. **W** God!"	4686

WORSHIPED (65) [WORSHIP]

Ge	24:26	The man bowed down and w the LORD,	2556
	24:48	and I bowed down and w the LORD.	2556
	47:31	Israel w *as he* **leaned** on the top of his staff.	2556
Ex	4:31	they bowed down and w.	2556
	12:27	Then the people bowed down and w.	2556
	33:10	they all stood and w,	2556
	34:8	Moses bowed to the ground at once and w.	2556
Dt	17:3	contrary to my command *has* w other gods,	6268
	29:26	and other gods and bowed down to them,	6268
Jos	24:2	lived beyond the River and w other gods.	6268
	24:14	Throw away the gods your forefathers w	6268
Jdg	2:12	They followed and w various gods of	2556
	2:17	to other gods and w them.	6268
	7:15	the dream and its interpretation, *he* w God.	2556
1Sa	1:19	the next morning they arose and w before	2556
	1:28	And *he* w the LORD there.	2556
	15:31	and Saul w the LORD.	2556
2Sa	12:20	into the house of the LORD and w.	2556
1Ki	11:33	w Ashtoreth the goddess of the Sidonians,	2556
	18:12	Yet I your servant *have* w the LORD	3707
	22:53	and w Baal and provoked the LORD,	2556
2Ki	17:7	*They* w other gods	3707
	17:12	*They* w idols, though the LORD had said,	6268
	17:16	all the starry hosts, and *they* w Baal.	6268
	17:32	*They* w the LORD, but they also appointed	3710
	17:33	*They* w the LORD, but they also served	3710
	21:3	down to all the starry hosts and w them.	6268
	21:21	*he* w the idols his father had worshiped,	6268
	21:21	he worshiped the idols his father had w,	6268
2Ch	7:3	and *they* w and gave thanks to the LORD,	2556
	24:18	and w Asherah poles and idols.	6268
	29:29	present with him knelt down and w.	2556
	29:30	with gladness and bowed their heads and w.	2556
	33:3	down to all the starry hosts and w them.	6268
	33:22	Amon w and offered sacrifices to all	6268
Ne	9:3	Then they bowed down and w the LORD	2556
Ps	74:8	every **place where** God was w in the land.	4595
	106:19	made a calf and w an idol cast from metal.	2556
	106:36	*They* w their idols, which became a snare	6268
Jer	8:2	they have followed and consulted and w.	2556
	16:11	followed other gods and served and w them,	2556
	22:9	and *have* w and served other gods.' "	2556

Da	3:7	and men of every language fell down and w	10504
	7:14	nations and men of every language w him.	10586
Mt	2:11	and *they* bowed down and w him.	4686
	14:33	Then those who were in the boat w him,	4686
	28:9	clasped his feet and w him.	4686
	28:17	When they saw him, *they* w him;	4686
Lk	2:37	She never left the temple but w night	3302
	24:52	Then they w him and returned to Jerusalem	4686
Jn	4:20	Our fathers w on this mountain.	4686
	9:38	"Lord, I believe," and *he* w him.	4686
Ac	19:27	who *is* w throughout the province of Asia	4936
Ro	1:25	and w and served created things rather than	4933
2Th	2:4	over everything that is called God or is w,	4934
Heb	11:21	and w as he leaned on the top of his staff.	4686
Rev	5:14	"Amen," and the elders fell down and w.	4686
	7:11	on their faces before the throne and w God,	4686
	11:16	fell on their faces and w God,	4686
	13:4	*Men* w the dragon because he had given	4686
	13:4	and they also w the beast and asked,	4686
	16:2	the mark of the beast and w his image.	4686
	19:4	four living creatures fell down and w God,	4686
	19:20	the mark of the beast and w his image.	4686
	20:4	They *had* not w the beast or his image	4686

WORSHIPER (3) [WORSHIP]

Ac	16:14	who was a w of God.	4936
	18:7	the house of Titius Justus, a w of God.	4936
Heb	9:9	not able to clear the conscience of the w.	3302

WORSHIPERS (7) [WORSHIP]

Zep	3:10	From beyond the rivers of Cush my w,	6985
Lk	1:10	all the **assembled** w were praying outside.	3295+3836+4436
Jn	4:23	the true w will worship the Father in spirit	4687
	4:23	for they are the kind of w the Father seeks.	4686
	4:24	his w must worship in spirit and in truth."	4686
Heb	10:2	For the w would have been cleansed once	3302
Rev	11:1	and count the w there.	4686

WORSHIPING (19) [WORSHIP]

Ex	10:26	We have to use some of them in w	6268
Nu	25:3	So Israel **joined in** w the Baal of Peor.	7537
	25:5	*of* your men who have **joined in** w the Baal	7537
Dt	4:19	into bowing down to them and w things	6268
	12:31	because in w their gods, they do all kinds of	NIH
	20:18	detestable things they do in w their gods,	NIH
Jdg	2:19	other gods and serving and w them.	2556
	8:27	prostituted themselves *by* w it there,	339
1Ki	9:9	embraced other gods, w and serving them—	2556
2Ki	17:41	while these people were w the LORD,	3710
	19:37	*while he was* w in the temple of his god	2556
2Ch	7:22	embraced other gods, w and serving them—	2556
	28:2	and also made cast idols for w the Baals.	NIH
Ne	9:3	and *in* w the LORD their God.	2556
Isa	37:38	he *was* w in the temple of his god Nisroch,	2556
Jer	1:16	and *in* w what their hands have made.	2556
	44:3	by w other gods that neither they nor you	6268
Ac	13:2	*While they were* w the Lord and fasting,	3310
Rev	9:20	*they did* not stop w demons,	4686

WORSHIPS (4) [WORSHIP]

Isa	44:15	But he also fashions a god and w it;	2556
	44:17	he bows down to it and w.	2556
	66:3	like *one who* w an idol.	1385
Rev	14:9	"If anyone w the beast and his image	4686

WORST (6) [WORSE]

Ex	9:18	the w hailstorm that has ever fallen	3878+4394
	9:24	the w storm in all the land of Egypt	3878+4394
Ps	41:7	they imagine the w for me, saying,	8288
Jer	2:33	the w *of women* can learn from your ways.	8273
1Ti	1:15	to save sinners—of whom I am the w.	4755
	1:16	shown mercy so that in me, the w of sinners,	4755

WORTH (18) [WORTHLESS, WORTHWHILE, WORTHY]

Ge	23:15	the land is w four hundred shekels of silver,	NIH
	27:46	my **life will not be** w living."	2644+4200+4537
Dt	15:18	to you these six years has been w twice	8510
2Sa	18:3	but you are w ten thousand *of* us.	4017
1Ki	21:2	I will pay you *whatever* it is w."	4697
Job	28:13	Man does not comprehend its w;	6886
Pr	31:10	She is w far more than rubies.	4836
Isa	7:23	where there were a thousand vines w	928
La	4:2	once w **their weight** in gold,	6131
Mt	10:10	for the worker is w his keep.	545
	10:31	you are w **more than** many sparrows.	1422
Mk	12:42	w only a fraction of a penny.	NIG
Lk	12:7	*you are* w **more than** many sparrows.	1422
Jn	12:5	**the money** given to the poor? It was w **a year's wages."**	1324+5559
Ac	20:24	I consider my life as nothing to me,	5508
Ro	8:18	not w comparing with the glory that will	545
1Pe	1:7	your faith—**of greater** w *than* gold,	4501
	3:4	which is of **great** w in God's sight.	4500

WORTHIES (KJV) See PICKED TROOPS

WORTHILY (KJV) See HAVE STANDING

WORTHLESS (43) [WORTH]

Ge	41:27	so are the seven **w** heads of grain scorched	8199
Dt	32:21	and angered me with their **w idols.**	2039
1Ki	16:13	the God of Israel, to anger by their **w idols.**	2039
	16:26	the God of Israel, to anger by their **w idols.**	2039
2Ki	17:15	They followed **w idols** and	2039
	17:15	and **themselves became w.**	2038
2Ch	13: 7	Some **w** scoundrels gathered around him	8199
Job	13: 4	you are **w** physicians, all of you!	496
	15:31	not deceive himself by trusting what is **w,**	8736
	34:18	'You are **w,**' and to nobles,	1175
Ps	31: 6	I hate those who cling to **w idols;**	2039+8736
	60:11	for the help of man is **w.**	8736
	108:12	for the help of man is **w.**	8736
	119:37	Turn my eyes away from **w things;**	8736
Pr	11: 4	Wealth *is* **w** in the day of wrath,	3603+4202
Isa	40:17	by him as **w** and less than nothing.	9332
	41:24	and your works are utterly **w;**	703
	44: 9	and the things they treasure *are* **w.**	1153+3603
Jer	2: 5	They followed **w idols** and became	2039
	2: 5	and **became w** *themselves.*	2038
	2: 8	prophesied by Baal, following **w idols.**	3603+4202
	2:11	But my people have exchanged their Glory	
		for **w idols.**	3603+4202
	7: 8	in deceptive words *that are* **w.**	1194+3603
	8:19	with their **w** foreign **idols?"**	2039
	10: 3	For the customs of the peoples are **w;**	2039
	10: 8	they are taught by **w** wooden **idols.**	2039
	10:15	They are, **w,** the objects of mockery;	2039
	14:22	of the **w idols** of the nations bring rain?	2039
	15:19	if you utter worthy, not **w,** words,	2361
	16:19	**w idols** that did them no good.	2039
	18:15	they burn incense to **w idols,**	8736
	51:18	They are, **w,** the objects of mockery;	2039
La	2:14	visions of your prophets were false and **w;**	9522
Hos	8: 6	she is among the nations like a **w** thing.	401+2914
	12:11	Is Gilead wicked? Its people are **w!**	8736
Jnh	2: 8	who cling to **w idols** forfeit the grace	2039
Zec	11:17	"Woe to the **w** shepherd,	496
Mt	25:30	And throw that **w** servant outside,	945
Ac	14:15	telling you to turn from these **w** *things* to	3469
Ro	3:12	*they have* together **become w;**	946
	4:14	faith has no value and the promise *is* **w,**	2934
Heb	6: 8	that produces thorns and thistles is **w** and is	99
Jas	1:26	he deceives himself and his religion is **w.**	3469

WORTHWHILE (2) [WORTH]

Ecc	2: 3	I wanted to see what was **w** for men to do	3202
Ro	1:28	not **think it w** to retain the knowledge	1507

WORTHY (49) [WORTH]

2Sa	22: 4	I call to the Lord, *who is* **w of praise,**	2146
1Ki	1:42	A **w** man like you must be bringing good	2657
	1:52	"If he shows himself to be a **w** man,	2657
2Ki	10: 3	the best and most **of** your master's sons	3838
1Ch	16:25	great is the Lord and most **w of praise;**	2146
Job	28:18	Coral and jasper *are* not **w of mention;**	2349
Ps	18: 3	I call to the Lord, *who is* **w of praise,**	2146
	48: 1	Great is the Lord, and most **w of praise,**	2146
	96: 4	great is the Lord and most **w of praise;**	2146
	145: 3	Great is the Lord and most **w of praise;**	2146
Pr	8: 6	Listen, for I have **w things** to say;	5592
Jer	15:19	if you utter **w,** not worthless, words,	3701
Mt	10:11	search for some **w** *person* there and stay	545
	10:37	or mother more than me is not **w** of me;	545
	10:37	or daughter more than me is not **w** of me;	545
	10:38	not take his cross and follow me is not **w**	545
	26:66	"He is **w** of death," they answered.	1944
Mk	1: 7	of whose sandals I am not **w** to stoop down	2653
	14:64	They all condemned him as **w** of death.	1944
Lk	3:16	the thongs of whose sandals I am not **w**	2653
	7: 7	not even **consider** myself **w** to come to you.	546
	15:19	I am no longer **w** to be called your son;	545
	15:21	I am no longer **w** to be called your son.'	545
	20:35	those who *are* **considered w** of taking part	2921
Jn	1:27	the thongs of whose sandals I am not **w**	545
Ac	5:41	rejoicing because *they had been* **counted w**	2921
	13:25	whose sandals I am not **w** to untie.'	545
	13:46	not **consider** yourselves **w** of eternal life,	545
Ro	16: 2	in the Lord **in a way w** of the saints and	547
Eph	4: 1	a life **w** of the calling you have received.	547
Php	1:27	in a **manner w** of the gospel of Christ.	547
Col	1:10	a life **w** of the Lord and may please him	547
1Th	2:12	comforting and urging you to live lives **w**	547
2Th	1: 5	and as a result you *will be* **counted w** of	2921
	1:11	our God *may* **count** you **w** of his calling,	546
1Ti	3: 8	likewise, are to be men **w of respect,**	4948
	3:11	their wives are to be women **w of respect,**	4948
	5:17	of the church well are **w** of double honor,	546
	6: 1	of slavery should consider their masters **w**	545
Tit	2: 2	temperate, **w of respect,** self-controlled,	4948
Heb	3: 3	Jesus *has been* **found w** of greater honor	546
	11:38	the world was not **w** of them.	545
3Jn	1: 6	to send them on their way in a **manner w**	547
Rev	3: 4	dressed in white, for they are **w.**	545
	4:11	"You are **w,** our Lord and God,	545
	5: 2	"Who is **w** to break the seals and open	545
	5: 4	because no one was found who was **w**	545
	5: 9	"You are **w** to take the scroll and	545
	5:12	In a loud voice they sang: **"W** is the Lamb,	545

WOT, WOTTETH (KJV) See CONCERN, KNOW

WOULD (679) [WOULDN'T]

Ge	2:19	to the man to see what *he* **w** name them;	AIT
	3:20	she **w** become the mother of all the living.	AIT
	4:15	so that no one who found him **w** kill him.	AIT
	9:23	that *they* **w** not see their father's nakedness.	AIT
	21: 7	"Who **w** have said to Abraham	AIT
	21: 7	to Abraham that Sarah **w** nurse children?	AIT
	26:10	and *you* **w** have **brought** guilt upon us."	AIT
	27:12	*I* **w** appear to be tricking him	AIT
	27:12	and **w** bring down a curse on myself	AIT
	29: 3	the shepherds **w** roll the stone away from	AIT
	29: 3	Then *they* **w** return the stone to its place	AIT
	30:38	that they **w** be directly in front of the flocks	NIH
	30:41	Jacob **w** place the branches in the troughs	AIT
	30:41	in front of the animals so they **w** mate near	AIT
	30:42	*he* **w** not place them there.	AIT
	31:31	I thought you **w** take your daughters away	7153
	31:42	**w** surely have **sent** me away	AIT
	34:14	That **w** be a disgrace to us.	NIH
	38: 9	Onan knew that the offspring **w** not be his;	AIT
	42:21	but *we* **w** not **listen;**	AIT
	43: 7	How were we to know he **w** say,	AIT
	44: 8	So why **w** we **steal** silver or gold	AIT
	44:34	not let me see the misery that **w** come upon	AIT
Ex	2: 4	at a distance to see what **w** happen to him.	AIT
	6:12	why **w** Pharaoh **listen** to me,	AIT
	6:30	why **w** Pharaoh **listen** to me?"	AIT
	7:13	and *he* **w** not **listen** to them,	AIT
	7:22	*he* **w** not **listen** to Moses and Aaron,	AIT
	8:15	he hardened his heart and **w** not **listen**	AIT
	8:19	and *he* **w** not **listen,**	AIT
	8:26	But Moses said, "That **w** not be **right.**	AIT
	8:26	the Lord our God **w** be detestable to	NIH
	8:32	and **w** not **let** the people go.	AIT
	9: 7	and he **w** not **let** the people go.	AIT
	9:12	and *he* **w** not **listen** to Moses and Aaron,	AIT
	9:15	with a plague *that* **w** have **wiped** *you* off	AIT
	9:35	and he **w** not **let** the Israelites go,	AIT
	10:20	and *he* **w** not **let** the Israelites **go.**	AIT
	11:10	and he **w** not **let** the Israelites **go**	AIT
	14:12	It **w** have been better for us to serve	NIH
	23:29	because the land **w** become desolate and	AIT
	33: 7	Anyone inquiring of the Lord **w** go to	AIT
	33: 9	the pillar of cloud **w** come down and stay at	AIT
	33:11	The Lord **w** speak to Moses face to face,	AIT
	33:11	Then Moses **w** return to the camp,	AIT
	34:35	Moses **w** put the veil back over his face	AIT
	38: 7	into the rings so they **w** be on the sides of	NIH
	39:21	so that the breastpiece **w** not **swing** out from	AIT
	39:23	so that it **w** not **tear.**	AIT
	40:36	from above the tabernacle, *they* **w** set out;	AIT
Lev	2: 3	anything that **w** make him **unclean—**	AIT
	10:19	**W** the Lord have been **pleased**	AIT
	18: 8	that **w** dishonor your father.	NIH
	18:10	that **w** dishonor you.	NIH
	18:16	that **w** dishonor your brother.	NIH
	20:19	for *that* **w** dishonor a close relative;	NIH
	20:19	**w** be **held** responsible.	AIT
	25:35	as you **w** an alien or a temporary resident,	NIH
	26:13	of Egypt so that you **w** no longer be slaves	AIT
Nu	9:20	at the Lord's command *they* **w** encamp,	AIT
	9:20	and then at his command *they* **w** set out.	AIT
	9:22	the Israelites **w** remain in camp and	AIT
	9:22	but when it lifted, *they* **w** set out.	AIT
	11:22	**W** they have enough if flocks	AIT
	11:22	**W** they have enough if all the fish in	AIT
	11:29	that the Lord **w** put his Spirit on them!"	AIT
	12:14	*w she* not *have* **been** in disgrace	AIT
	14:31	for your children that you said **w** be taken	AIT
	16:40	*he* **w** become like Korah and his followers.	AIT
	21:23	But Sihon **w** not **let** Israel pass through	AIT
	22:29	*I* **w** kill you right now."	AIT
	22:33	*I* **w** certainly have **killed** you by now,	AIT
	22:33	but *I* **w** have **spared** her."	AIT
	24:11	**w** reward you **handsomely,**	AIT
	26:65	told those Israelites *they* **w** surely **die**	AIT
	32:16	"We **w** like to **build** pens here	AIT
Dt	1: 8	of the land that the Lord swore he **w** give	AIT
	1:39	little ones that you said **w** be taken captive,	AIT
	1:43	So I told you, but *you* **w** not **listen.**	AIT
	3:26	with me and **w** not **listen** to me.	AIT
	4:21	and he solemnly swore that I **w** not **cross**	AIT
	5:29	that their hearts **w** be **inclined** to fear me	AIT
	8: 2	whether or not you **w** keep his commands.	AIT
	9:25	the Lord had said he **w** destroy you.	AIT
	12:20	"*I* **w** like some meat,"	430S
	12:22	Eat them as you **w** gazelle or deer.	430S
	17: 1	for that **w** be detestable to him.	NIH
	23: 5	the Lord your God **w** not **listen**	14
	24: 4	That **w** be detestable in the eyes of	NIH
	24: 6	*w* be **taking** a man's livelihood **as security.**	AIT
	28:56	that **w** not **venture** to touch the ground	AIT
	32:26	I said *I* **w** scatter them	AIT
	32:29	and **w** understand this	AIT
Jos	5: 6	to them that they **w** not **see** the land	AIT
	9:27	at the place the Lord **w** choose.	AIT
	24:10	But *I* **w** not **listen** to Balaam,	14
Jdg	2:17	Yet *they* **w** not **listen** to their judges	AIT
	3: 4	the Israelites to see whether *they* **w** obey	AIT
	8:19	*I* **w** not **kill** you."	AIT
	9:29	Then *I* **w** get rid of him."	AIT
	9:29	*I* **w** say to Abimelech,	AIT
	11:17	but the king of Edom **w** not **listen.**	AIT
	11:38	and wept because she **w** never marry.	NIH
	13:15	"We **w** like you to **stay** until	AIT
	13:23	*he* **w** not *have* **accepted** a burnt offering	AIT

Jdg	14:18	*you* **w** not *have* **solved** my riddle."	AIT
	15: 1	But her father **w** not **let** him go in.	AIT
	16:17	my strength **w** leave me,	AIT
	16:17	and *I* **w** become as weak as any other man."	AIT
	19:25	But the men **w** not **listen** to him.	14
	20:13	But the Benjamites **w** not **listen**	AIT
	20:39	then the men of Israel **w** turn in the battle.	AIT
Ru	1: 7	that **w** take them **back** to the land of Judah.	AIT
	1:11	Why **w** you **come** with me?	AIT
	1:13	**w** you **wait** until they grew up?	AIT
	1:13	**W** you **remain unmarried**	AIT
1Sa	1: 4	*he* **w** give portions of the meat	AIT
	1: 7	till she wept and **w** not **eat.**	AIT
	1: 8	Elkanah her husband **w** say to her, "Hannah,	AIT
	2:13	the priest **w** come with a three-pronged fork	AIT
	2:14	*He w* **plunge** it into the pan or kettle	AIT
	2:14	and the priest **w** take for himself whatever	AIT
	2:15	the servant of the priest **w** come and say to	AIT
	2:16	the servant **w** then **answer,** "No,	AIT
	2:20	Eli **w** bless Elkanah and his wife, saying,	AIT
	2:20	Then *they* **w** go **home.**	AIT
	2:30	and your father's house **w** minister	AIT
	3:13	that I **w** judge his family forever because of	AIT
	9: 9	if a man went to inquire of God, he **w** say,	AIT
	9:18	*"W* you please **tell** me where	AIT
	13:13	he **w** have **established** your kingdom	AIT
	14:30	How much better it **w** have been if	NIH
	14:30	*W* not the slaughter of the Philistines *have*	
		been even **greater?"**	AIT
	16:23	David **w** take his harp and play.	AIT
	16:23	Then **relief w** come to Saul;	AIT
	16:23	he **w** feel **better,** and the evil spirit	AIT
	16:23	and the evil spirit **w** leave him.	AIT
	19: 5	then *w you* **do wrong** to an innocent man	AIT
	20: 2	Why **w** he **hide** this from me?	AIT
	22: 3	*"W* you **let** my father and mother **come**	AIT
	22:22	I knew *he* **w** be **sure** to tell Saul.	AIT
	25:34	belonging to Nabal **w** have **been left alive**	AIT
	26:23	but *I* **w** not lay a hand on the Lord's	14
	27:10	David **w** say, "Against the Negev of Judah"	AIT
	29: 6	and I **w** be pleased to have you serve	NIH
	31: 4	was terrified and **w** not do it;	14
2Sa	2:21	But Asahel **w** not stop chasing him.	14
	2:27	the men **w** have **continued** the pursuit	AIT
	6:20	his servants as any vulgar fellow **w!"**	1655+1655S
	11:20	Didn't you know *they* **w** shoot **arrows** from	AIT
	12: 8	**w** have **given** you **even more.**	AIT
	12:17	and *he* **w** not **eat** any food with them,	AIT
	12:18	we spoke to David but *he* **w** not **listen**	AIT
	13: 5	'**I w** like my sister Tamar to come	5528
	13: 6	"**I w** like my sister Tamar to come	5528
	13:13	*You* **w** be like one of the wicked fools	AIT
	13:16	"Sending me away **w** be a greater wrong	NIH
	13:25	*we w* only **be** a **burden** to you."	AIT
	14: 7	*They* **w** put out the only burning coal	AIT
	14:26	*he w* **weigh** it, and its weight was	AIT
	14:32	It **w** be better for me if I were still there!" '	NIH
	15: 2	He **w** get up early and stand by the side of	AIT
	15: 2	Absalom **w** call out to him,	AIT
	15: 2	*He w* **answer,** "Your servant is from one of	AIT
	15: 3	Then Absalom **w** say to him, "Look,	AIT
	15: 4	And Absalom **w** add,	AIT
	15: 4	and *I* **w** see that he gets justice."	AIT
	15: 5	Absalom **w** reach out his hand,	AIT
	17: 1	"*I* **w** choose twelve thousand men	AIT
	17: 2	*I* **w** attack him while he is weary	AIT
	17: 2	*I* **w** strike him with **terror,**	AIT
	17: 2	*I* **w** strike **down** only the king	AIT
	18: 3	It **w** be better now for you	AIT
	18:11	Then I **w** have had to give you ten shekels	NIH
	18:12	*I* **w** not **lift** my hand against the king's son.	AIT
	18:13	*you* **w** have **kept** *your* **distance**	AIT
	19: 6	I see that you **w** be pleased	NIH
	21:16	said he **w** kill David.	AIT
	23:15	"Oh, that someone **w** get me a **drink**	AIT
	23:17	And David **w** not **drink** it.	14
1Ki	6: 6	so that nothing **w** be **inserted** into the temple	AIT
	8:12	"The Lord has said that he **w** dwell in	AIT
	12: 6	**w** you **advise** me to answer these people?"	AIT
	13: 8	*I* **w** not **go** with you,	AIT
	13: 8	nor **w** *I* **eat** bread or drink water here.	AIT
	14: 2	the one who told me **w** be king	NIH
	17:10	"*W* you **bring** me a little water in a jar	AIT
2Ki	3:14	*I* **w** not **look** at you or even notice you.	AIT
	5: 3	"If only my master **w** see the prophet who is	NIH
	5: 3	*He w* **cure** him of his leprosy."	AIT
	5:11	"I thought that *he* **w** surely **come** out to me	AIT
	5:13	*w you* not *have* **done** it?	AIT
	6:22	"*W* you **kill** men you have captured	AIT
	8:14	"He told me that *you* **w** certainly **recover."**	AIT
	11:17	and the king and people that *they* **w** be	AIT
	12: 8	that *they* **w** not **collect** any more money	AIT
	12: 8	from the people and that they **w** not **repair**	AIT
	13:19	then *you* **w** have **defeated** Aram	AIT
	14:11	Amaziah, however, **w** not **listen,**	AIT
	14:27	not said he **w** blot out the name of Israel	AIT
	17:14	But *they* **w** not **listen** and were	AIT
	17:40	They **w** not **listen,** however,	AIT
	22:19	that *they* **w** become accursed and laid waste,	AIT
1Ch	4:10	*you* **w** bless me and enlarge my territory!	AIT
	9:27	They **w** spend the night stationed around	AIT
	10: 4	But his armor-bearer was terrified and **w**	14
	11:17	"Oh, that someone **w** get me a **drink**	AIT
	11:19	David **w** not **drink** it.	14
	22:11	the Lord your God, as he said you **w.**	NIH
2Ch	6: 1	"The Lord has said that he **w** dwell in	AIT
	6:20	you said you **w** put your Name there.	AIT

2Ch	10: 6	"How *w* you **advise** me to answer	AIT
	15:13	All who *w* not **seek** the LORD,	AIT
	20:10	whose territory *you w* not **allow** Israel	AIT
	23:16	that he and the people and the king *w* be	AIT
	24:11	the chief priest *w* come and empty the chest	AIT
	24:19	*they w* not **listen.**	AIT
	25:20	Amaziah, however, *w* not **listen,**	AIT
	31:16	all who *w* enter the temple of the LORD	AIT
	35:22	however, *w* not **turn away** from him,	AIT
	35:22	*He w* not **listen** to what Neco had said	AIT
	36:13	and hardened his heart and *w* not **turn** to	AIT
Ezr	3: 7	so that they *w* **bring** cedar logs by sea	AIT
	9:14	*W* you not be **angry**	AIT
	10: 8	within three days *w* **forfeit** all his property,	AIT
	10: 8	*w* himself be **expelled**	AIT
Ne	2:16	or officials or any others *who w* be **doing**	AIT
	3: 5	but their nobles *w* not **put** their shoulders to	AIT
	4: 3	he *w* **break down** their wall of stones!"	AIT
	6:13	to intimidate me so that *I w* **commit a sin**	AIT
	6:13	they *w* **give** me a bad name to discredit me.	AIT
Est	1:17	but *she w* not **come.'**	AIT
	2:13	And this is how she *w* **go** to the king:	AIT
	2:14	In the evening she *w* **go** there and in	AIT
	2:14	*She w* not **return** to the king	AIT
	3: 2	But Mordecai *w* not **kneel down**	AIT
	3: 4	whether Mordecai's behavior *w* be **tolerated,**	AIT
	3: 5	that Mordecai *w* not **kneel down**	AIT
	3:14	the people of every nationality so they *w* be	AIT
	4: 4	but *he w* not **accept** them.	AIT
	6: 6	that the king *w* **rather** honor than me?"	AIT
	7: 4	*I w* have kept **quiet,**	AIT
	7: 4	no such distress *w* **justify** disturbing	AIT
	8:13	of every nationality so that the Jews *w* be	AIT
Job	1: 4	and *they w* **invite** their three sisters to eat	AIT
	1: 5	Job *w* **send** and have them purified.	AIT
	1: 5	the morning he *w* **sacrifice** a burnt offering	AIT
	3:13	For now *I w* be **lying down** in peace;	AIT
	3:13	*I w* be **asleep** and at rest	AIT
	5: 8	"But if it were I, *I w* **appeal** to God;	AIT
	5: 8	*I w* **lay** my cause before him.	AIT
	6: 3	*It w* surely **outweigh** the sand of the seas—	AIT
	6: 8	that God *w* **grant** what I hope for,	AIT
	6: 9	that God *w* be **willing** to crush me,	AIT
	6:10	Then I *w* still **have** this consolation—	AIT
	6:27	*You w* even **cast** lots for the fatherless	AIT
	6:28	*W I* lie to your face?	AIT
	7:16	I despise my life; *I w* not **live** forever.	AIT
	9:16	I do not believe *he w* **give** me **a hearing.**	AIT
	9:17	He *w* **crush** me with a storm	AIT
	9:18	*He w* not **let** me regain my breath	AIT
	9:18	but *w* **overwhelm** me *with* misery.	AIT
	9:20	I were innocent, my mouth *w* **condemn** me;	AIT
	9:20	*it w* **pronounce** me guilty.	AIT
	9:31	*you w* **plunge** me into a slime pit so that	AIT
	9:31	so that even my clothes *w* **detest** me.	AIT
	9:34	so that his terror *w* **frighten** me no more.	AIT
	9:35	Then *I w* **speak up** without fear of him,	AIT
	10:14	*you w* be **watching** me and would	AIT
	10:14	*w* not **let** my offense go unpunished.	AIT
	11: 5	Oh, how I wish that God *w* **speak,**	AIT
	11: 5	that he *w* **open** his lips against you	AIT
	13: 5	If only *you w* be **altogether silent!**	AIT
	13: 5	For you, *that w* be wisdom.	AIT
	13: 9	*W* it turn out well if he examined you?	NIH
	13:10	*He w* **surely rebuke** you	AIT
	13:11	*W* not his splendor **terrify**	AIT
	13:11	*W* not the dread of him **fall**	AIT
	13:16	no godless man *w* **dare come** before him!	AIT
	14:13	"If only *you w* **hide** me in the grave	AIT
	14:13	If only *you w* **set** me a time and	AIT
	15: 2	"*W* a wise man **answer** with empty notions	AIT
	15: 3	*W* he **argue** with useless words,	AIT
	16: 5	But my mouth *w* **encourage** you;	AIT
	16: 5	comfort from my lips *w* **bring** you **relief.**	AIT
	19: 5	If indeed *you w* **exalt** *yourselves*	AIT
	21:15	What *w* we **gain** by praying to him?'	AIT
	21:27	the schemes by which *you w* **wrong** me.	AIT
	22: 3	What pleasure *w* it give the Almighty	NIH
	22: 3	What *w* he gain if your ways were	NIH
	23: 4	*I w* **state** my case before him	AIT
	23: 5	*I w* **find out** what he would answer me,	AIT
	23: 5	I would find out what *he w* **answer** me,	AIT
	23: 5	and consider what *he w* **say.**	AIT
	23: 6	*W he* **oppose** me with great power?	AIT
	23: 6	No, he *w* not **press charges** against me.	AIT
	23: 7	*I w* be **delivered** forever from my judge.	AIT
	30: 1	whose fathers *I w* have **disdained** to put	AIT
	31:11	*w* have been shameful, a sin to be judged.	NIH
	31:11	*it w* have **uprooted** my harvest.	NIH
	31:18	from my youth I reared him as *w* a father,	NIH
	31:28	then these also *w* be sins to be judged,	NIH
	31:28	for *I w* have been **unfaithful**	AIT
	31:34	that I kept silent and *w* not **go** outside	AIT
	31:36	Surely *I w* **wear** it on my shoulder,	AIT
	31:36	*I w* **put** it on like a crown.	AIT
	31:37	*I w* **give** him an account of my every step;	AIT
	31:37	like a prince *I w* **approach** him.)—	AIT
	32:22	my Maker *w* soon **take** me **away.**	AIT
	34:12	It is unthinkable that God *w* **do wrong,**	AIT
	34:12	that the Almighty *w* **pervert** justice.	AIT
	34:15	all mankind *w* **perish** together	AIT
	34:15	and man *w* **return** to the dust.	AIT
	35: 4	"*I w* **like** *to* reply *to* you and	AIT
	36:19	*W* your wealth or even all your mighty efforts **sustain** you	AIT
	36:19	so you *w* not be in distress?	NIH
	37:20	*W* any man **ask** to be swallowed up?	AIT
Job	40: 8	"*W you* **discredit** my justice?	AIT
	40: 8	*W you* **condemn** me to justify yourself?	AIT
	41:13	Who *w* **approach** him with a bridle?	AIT
	41:32	*one w* **think** the deep had white hair.	AIT
Ps	10:15	wickedness that *w* not be **found out.**	AIT
	14: 7	that salvation for Israel *w* come out of Zion!	NIH
	38:12	*those who w* **harm** me talk of my ruin;	2011
	39: 9	I was silent; *I w* not **open** my mouth,	AIT
	40: 5	*they w* be too **many** to declare.	AIT
	44:21	*w* not God have **discovered**	AIT
	50:12	If I were hungry *I w* not **tell** you,	AIT
	51:16	not delight in sacrifice, or *I w* **bring** it;	AIT
	53: 6	that salvation for Israel *w* come out of Zion!	NIH
	55: 6	*I w* **fly away** and be at rest—	AIT
	55: 7	*I w* **flee far away** and stay in the desert;	AIT
	55: 8	*I w* **hurry** *to* my place of shelter,	AIT
	62: 3	*W* all of you **throw** him **down**—	AIT
	66:18	the Lord *w* not have **listened;**	AIT
	73:15	*I w* have **betrayed** your children.	AIT
	78: 6	so the next generation *w* **know** them,	AIT
	78: 6	and *they w* **tell** their children.	AIT
	78: 7	Then they *w* **put** their trust in God	AIT
	78: 7	in God and *w* not **forget** his deeds	AIT
	78: 7	but *w* **keep** his commands.	AIT
	78: 8	*They w* not be like their forefathers—	AIT
	78:34	Whenever God slew them, *they w* **seek** him;	AIT
	78:36	*they w* **flatter** him with their mouths,	AIT
	81: 8	if you *w* **but listen** to me, O Israel!	AIT
	81:11	"But my people *w* not **listen** to me;	AIT
	81:11	Israel *w* not **submit** to me.	AIT
	81:13	"If my people *w but* **listen** to me,	AIT
	81:13	if Israel *w* **follow** my ways,	AIT
	81:14	how quickly *w I* **subdue** their enemies	AIT
	81:15	Those who hate the LORD *w* **cringe**	AIT
	81:15	and their punishment *w* **last** forever.	AIT
	81:16	But you *w* be **fed** with the finest of wheat;	AIT
	81:16	with honey from the rock *I w* **satisfy** you."	AIT
	84:10	*I w* **rather** be a doorkeeper in the house	1047
	94:17	*I w* soon have **dwelt** in the silence	AIT
	106:23	So he said he *w* **destroy** them—	AIT
	106:26	that he *w* **make** them **fall** in the desert,	AIT
	119: 6	Then *I w* not *be* **put to shame**	AIT
	119:92	*I w* have **perished** in my affliction.	AIT
	124: 3	*they w* have **swallowed** us alive;	AIT
	124: 4	the flood *w* have **engulfed** us,	AIT
	124: 4	the torrent *w* have **swept** over us,	AIT
	124: 5	the raging waters *w* have **swept** us **away.**	AIT
	139:18	*they w* **outnumber** the grains of sand.	AIT
	139:19	If only you *w* **slay** the wicked, O God!	AIT
Pr	1:23	*I w* have **poured out** my heart to you	AIT
	1:25	and *w* not **accept** my rebuke,	AIT
	1:30	since *they w* not **accept** my advice	AIT
	5:13	*I w* not **obey** my teachers or listen	AIT
	8:29	the waters *w* not **overstep** his command,	AIT
SS	3: 4	and *w* not **let** him go till I had brought him	AIT
	6:13	Why *w you* **gaze** on the Shulammite as on	AIT
	8: 1	Then, if I found you outside, *I w* **kiss** you,	AIT
	8: 1	I would kiss you, and no *one w* **despise** me.	AIT
	8: 2	*I w* **lead** you and bring you	AIT
	8: 2	*I w* **give** you spiced wine **to drink,**	AIT
	8: 7	*it w* be **utterly scorned.**	AIT
Isa	1: 9	we *w* have **become** like Sodom,	AIT
	1: 9	we *w* have **been** like Gomorrah.	AIT
	14:17	and *w* not *let* his captives **go**	AIT
	16:14	a servant bound by contract *w* **count** them,	NIH
	21:12	If *you w* **ask,** then ask;	AIT
	21:16	as a servant bound by contract *w* **count** it,	NIH
	27: 4	*I w* **march** against them in battle;	AIT
	27: 4	*I w* **set** them all **on fire.**	AIT
	28:12	but *they w* not **listen.**	14
	30:15	but *you w* have none of it.	14
	42:24	For *they w* not **follow** his ways;	14
	44: 9	Those who *w* speak up for them are blind;	NIH
	48:18	your peace *w* have **been** like a river,	AIT
	48:19	Your descendants *w* have **been** like the sand,	AIT
	48:19	their name *w* never **be cut off**	AIT
	54: 9	the waters of Noah *w* never again **cover**	AIT
	57:10	but you *w* not **say,** 'It is hopeless.'	AIT
	57:16	the spirit of man *w* **grow faint** before me—	AIT
	64: 1	*you w* **rend** the heavens and come down,	AIT
	64: 1	that the mountains *w* **tremble** before you!	AIT
Jer	3: 1	*W* not the land *be* **completely defiled?**	AIT
	3: 1	*w* you now **return** to me?"	AIT
	3: 7	that after she had done all this *she w* **return**	AIT
	3:19	" 'How gladly *w I* **treat** you like sons	AIT
	3:19	I thought *you w* **call** me 'Father' and	AIT
	9: 1	*I w* **weep** day and night *for* the slain	AIT
	12: 1	Yet *I w* **speak** with you about your justice:	AIT
	15: 1	my heart *w* not **go** out to this people.	NIH
	17:23	and *w* not **listen** or respond to discipline.	AIT
	19:15	and *w* not **listen** to my words.' "	AIT
	22:24	*I w* still **pull** you off.	AIT
	23:22	*they w* have **proclaimed** my words	AIT
	23:22	to my people and have **turned** them	AIT
	30:14	as an enemy *w* and punished you as would	NIH
	30:14	as an enemy would and punished you as *w*	NIH
	32:33	they *w* not **listen** or respond to discipline.	AIT
	34:10	that they *w* **free** their male and female	AIT
	36:25	he *w* not **listen** to them.	AIT
	36:29	that the king of Babylon *w* **certainly come**	AIT
	37:10	*they w* **come out** and burn this city down."	AIT
	38:15	But Irijah *w* not **listen** to him;	AIT
	38:15	*you w* not **listen** to me."	AIT
	40: 3	he has done just as he said he *w.*	AIT
	44:17	will certainly do everything we said we *w:*	NIH
	49: 9	*w* they not **leave** a few grapes?	AIT
	49: 9	*w* they not **steal** only as much as they wanted	AIT
Jer	51: 9	" 'We *w* have **healed** Babylon,	AIT
	51:60	the disasters that *w* **come** upon Babylon—	AIT
La	3:30	to one who *w* **strike** him,	AIT
	3:36	*w* not the Lord **see** such things?	AIT
	4:20	that under his shadow we *w* **live** among	AIT
Eze	1:12	Wherever the spirit *w* **go,** they would go,	AIT
	1:12	Wherever the spirit would go, they *w* **go,**	AIT
	1:17	*they w* **go** in any one of the four directions	AIT
	1:20	Wherever the spirit *w* **go,** they would go,	AIT
	1:20	Wherever the spirit would go, *they w* **go,**	AIT
	1:20	and the wheels *w* **rise** along with them,	AIT
	3: 6	they *w* have **listened** to you.	AIT
	4:12	Eat the food as you *w* a barley cake;	NIH
	10:11	*they w* **go** in any one of the four directions	AIT
	14:16	They alone *w* be **saved,**	AIT
	14:16	but the land *w* be **desolate.**	AIT
	14:18	They alone *w* be **saved.**	AIT
	14:20	They *w* **save** only themselves	AIT
	16:56	You *w* not even mention your sister Sodom	NIH
	17: 8	so that *it w* **produce** branches,	AIT
	17:14	so that the kingdom *w* be **brought low,**	AIT
	20: 6	to them that *I w* **bring** them out of Egypt	AIT
	20: 8	" 'But they rebelled against me and *w*	14
	20: 8	So I said *I w* **pour out** my wrath on them	AIT
	20: 9	the sake of my name I did what *w* keep it	NIH
	20:12	so they *w* **know** that I the LORD made them	AIT
	20:13	So I said *I w* **pour out** my wrath on them	AIT
	20:14	the sake of my name I did what *w* keep it	NIH
	20:15	to them in the desert that *I w* not **bring** them	AIT
	20:21	So I said *I w* **pour out** my wrath on them	AIT
	20:22	the sake of my name I did what *w* keep it	NIH
	20:23	to them in the desert that *I w* **disperse** them	AIT
	20:26	so *they w* **know** that I am the LORD.'	AIT
	22:30	a man among them *who w* **build up** the wall	AIT
	22:30	so *I w* not **have to destroy** it,	AIT
	24: 7	where the dust *w* **cover** it.	AIT
	24: 8	so that it *w* not **be covered.**	AIT
	24:13	to cleanse you but *you w* not be **cleansed**	AIT
	33: 5	he *w* have **saved** himself.	AIT
	38:17	for years that *I w* **bring** you against them.	AIT
Da	1:10	king *w* then have my head because of you."	NIH
	6:12	O king, *w* **be thrown** into the lions' den?"	AIT
	9: 2	of Jerusalem *w* **last** seventy years.	AIT
Hos	6:11	"Whenever I *w* **restore** the fortunes	AIT
	7: 1	whenever *I w* **heal** Israel,	AIT
	8: 7	foreigners *w* **swallow** it **up.**	AIT
Ob	1: 5	*w* they not **steal** only as much as they wanted	AIT
	1: 5	*w* they not **leave** a few grapes?	AIT
Jnh	1: 5	and waited to see what *w* **happen** to the city.	AIT
	4: 8	"It *w* be **better** for me to die than to live."	NIH
Mic	2:11	he *w* be just the prophet for this people!	AIT
Hab	1: 5	in your days that *you w* not **believe,**	AIT
Zep	3: 7	her dwelling *w* not **be cut off,**	AIT
Zec	7:12	as hard as flint and *w* not **listen** *to* the law	AIT
	7:13	so when they called, *I w* not **listen,'**	AIT
Mal	1: 8	*W* he be **pleased with** you?	AIT
	1: 8	*W* he **accept** you?"	AIT
	1:10	that one of you *w* **shut** the temple doors,	AIT
	1:10	so that *you w* not **light** useless **fires**	AIT
Mt	7:12	to others what *you w* have them do to you,	2527
	8:13	It will be done just as you believed it *w.*"	NIG
	11:21	they *w* have repented long ago in sackcloth	323
	11:23	it *w* have remained to this day.	323
	12: 7	you *w* not have condemned the innocent.	323
	13:15	and turn, and *I w* **heal** them.'	AIT
	16:24	"If anyone *w* come after me,	2527
	18: 6	it *w* be **better** for him to have	AIT
	18:17	to the church, treat him as *you w* a pagan or	NIG
	18:30	we *w* not have taken part with them	323
	24:22	no one *w* **survive,**	AIT
	24:39	about what *w* happen until the flood came	NIG
	24:43	the thief was coming, he *w* have kept watch	323
	24:43	and *w* not have let his house be broken into.	323
	25:27	when I returned I *w* have received it back	323
	26:24	*It w* be **better** for him if he had not been	AIT
	26:25	Then Judas, the one who *w* **betray** him,	AIT
	26:54	But how then *w* the Scriptures be **fulfilled**	AIT
Mk	1:34	but *he w* not **let** the demons speak	AIT
	3: 2	to see if *he w* **heal** him on the Sabbath.	AIT
	5: 5	and in the hills he *w* cry out and cut himself	1639
	6:37	*w* take eight months of a man's wages!	NIG
	8:34	"If anyone *w* come after me,	2527
	9:42	it *w* be **better** for him to be thrown into	AIT
	11:16	and *w* not **allow** anyone to carry	AIT
	13:20	no one *w* survive.	323
	14:21	It *w* be better for him if he had not been	NIG
	15:24	they cast lots to see what each *w* **get.**	AIT
Lk	1:62	to find out what he *w* like to name the child.	323
	2:26	to him by the Holy Spirit that he *w* not **die**	AIT
	4:41	and *w* not **allow** them to speak,	AIT
	6: 7	to see if *he w* **heal** on the Sabbath.	AIT
	6:31	Do to others as *you w* have them do to you.	2527
	7:39	he *w* know who is touching him	323
	9:23	"If anyone *w* come after me,	2527
	9:46	the disciples as to which of them *w* be	AIT
	10:13	they *w* have repented long ago,	323
	12:39	he *w* not have let his house be broken into.	323
	17: 2	*It w* be **better** for him to be thrown into	AIT
	17: 7	*W* he **say** to the servant when he comes in	AIT
	17: 8	*W* he not rather **say,** 'Prepare my supper,	AIT
	17: 9	*W* he **thank** the servant because he did	AIT
	17:20	when the kingdom of God *w* **come,**	AIT
	18:13	He *w* not even look up to heaven but	2527
	19:42	on this day what *w* bring you peace—	NIG
	20:10	to the tenants so *they w* **give** him some of	AIT
	22:23	which of them it might be who *w* do this.	3516

Lk	22:68	and if I asked you, *you w* not **answer.**	AIT
Jn	1:33	I *w* not *have* **known** him,	AIT
	2:24	But Jesus *w* not **entrust** himself to them,	AIT
	4:10	you *w* have asked him and	323
	4:10	and he *w* have given you living water."	323
	5:46	If you believed Moses, you *w* believe me,	323
	6:7	"Eight months' wages *w* not buy enough	NIG
	6:64	not believe and who *w* **betray** him.	AIT
	7:13	But no one *w* **say** anything publicly	AIT
	8:19	you knew me, you *w* know my Father also."	323
	8:24	I told you that *you w* **die** in your sins;	323
	8:39	"then you *w* **do** the things Abraham did.	323
	8:42	"If God were your Father, you *w* love me,	323
	8:55	If I said I did not, I *w* be a liar like you,	AIT
	9:22	the Christ *w* be put out of the synagogue.	AIT
	9:41	you *w* not be **guilty** of sin;	323
	11:21	my brother *w* not have died.	323
	11:32	my brother *w* not have died."	323
	11:40	*you w* **see** the glory of God?"	323
	11:51	that year he prophesied that Jesus *w* die for	3516
	12:21	"Sir," they said, "*we w* **like** to see Jesus."	AIT
	12:37	*they* still *w* not **believe** in him.	AIT
	12:40	nor turn—and I *w* **heal** them."	AIT
	12:42	the Pharisees *they w* not **confess** their faith	AIT
	12:42	for fear *they w* be put out of the synagogue;	AIT
	14:2	if it were not so, I *w* have told you.	323
	14:7	*you w* **know** my Father as well.	323
	14:28	you *w* be glad that I am going to the Father,	323
	15:19	it *w* love you as its own.	323
	15:22	*they w* not be **guilty** of sin.	AIT
	15:24	*they w* not be **guilty** of sin.	AIT
	17:12	so that Scripture *w* be **fulfilled.**	AIT
	18:9	the words he had spoken *w* be **fulfilled:**	AIT
	18:14	the Jews that *it w* be **good** if one man died	AIT
	18:30	"we *w* not have handed him over to you."	323
	18:32	death he was going to die *w* be **fulfilled.**	AIT
	18:36	my servants *w* **fight** to prevent my arrest by	323
	19:11	"You *w* have no power over me if it were	AIT
	19:28	and so that the Scripture *w* be **fulfilled,**	AIT
	19:36	so that the scripture *w* be **fulfilled:**	AIT
	21:19	of death by which Peter *w* **glorify** God.	AIT
	21:23	the brothers that this disciple *w* not **die.**	AIT
	21:23	But Jesus did not say that *he w* not **die;**	AIT
	21:25	world *w* not **have room for** the books	AIT
	21:25	for the books that *w* be **written.**	AIT
Ac	2:30	that he *w* place one of his descendants	NIG
	3:18	saying that his Christ *w* **suffer.**	AIT
	5:24	wondering what *w* come of this.	323
	5:26	they feared that the people *w* **stone** them.	AIT
	6:2	"*It w* not be **right** for us to neglect	AIT
	7:5	and his descendants after him *w* **possess**	AIT
	7:19	so that they *w* **die.**	AIT
	7:25	that his own people *w* **realize** that God	AIT
	11:28	that a severe famine *w* spread over	3516
	13:41	in your days that *you w* never **believe,**	AIT
	16:7	the Spirit of Jesus *w* not **allow** them to.	AIT
	17:27	that men *w* seek him and perhaps reach out	NIG
	18:14	it *w* be **reasonable** for me to listen to you.	323
	19:13	*They w* **say,** "In the name of Jesus,	AIT
	19:30	but the disciples *w* not **let** him.	AIT
	19:40	In that case *we w* not be **able** to account	AIT
	20:20	to preach anything that *w* be **helpful**	AIT
	20:38	that *they w* never see his face again.	3516
	21:14	When he *w* not be **dissuaded,**	AIT
	21:26	of purification *w* **end** and the offering would	AIT
	21:26	the **offering** *w* be **made** for each of them.	AIT
	23:10	was afraid Paul *w* be **torn to pieces**	AIT
	24:4	I *w* **request** that you be kind enough	AIT
	24:26	that Paul *w* **offer** him a bribe,	AIT
	25:20	if *he w* be **willing** to go to Jerusalem	AIT
	25:22	"I *w* **like** to hear this man myself."	AIT
	26:22	the prophets and Moses said *w* happen—	3516
	26:23	that the Christ *w* **suffer** and,	NIG
	26:23	*w* proclaim light to his own people and to	3516
	27:1	When it was decided that *we w* **sail**	AIT
	27:17	that *they w* **run aground** on the sandbars	AIT
	27:21	you *w* have spared yourselves this damage	NIG
	27:29	that *we w* be **dashed** against the rocks,	AIT
	27:41	The bow stuck fast and *w* not **move,**	810+3531
	28:24	but others *w* not **believe.**	AIT
	28:27	and turn, and I *w* **heal** them.	AIT
Ro	4:13	the promise that he *w* be **heir** of the world,	AIT
	7:7	I *w* not have **known** what sin was except	AIT
	7:7	For I *w* not have **known** what coveting really was	AIT
	9:29	we *w* have become like Sodom,	323
	9:29	we *w* have been like Gomorrah."	323
	11:6	if it were, **grace** *w* no longer be **grace.**	AIT
	15:20	so that I *w* not be **building** on someone else's	AIT
1Co	2:8	they *w* not have **crucified** the Lord of glory.	323
	5:10	In that case *you w* **have** to leave this world.	AIT
	7:14	Otherwise your children *w* be **unclean,**	AIT
	7:32	I *w* **like** you to be free from concern.	AIT
	9:15	I *w* rather **die** than have anyone deprive me	323
	11:31	we *w* not come under judgment.	323
	12:15	*w* not for that reason **cease to be** part of	AIT
	12:16	*w* not for that reason **cease to be** part of	AIT
	12:17	where *w* the sense of hearing be?	NIG
	12:17	where *w* the sense of smell be?	NIG
	12:19	where *w* the body be?	NIG
	14:5	I *w* **like** every one of you to speak	AIT
	14:5	but I *w* rather have you prophesy.	NIG
	14:19	I *w* **rather** speak five intelligible words	2527
2Co	2:1	that I *w* not make another painful visit	NIG
	2:3	that you *w* all share my joy.	NIG
	2:9	if you *w* **stand the test** and be obedient	1509
	3:13	who *w* **put** a veil over his face to keep	AIT

2Co	5:8	and *w* **prefer** to be away from the body and	AIT
	7:3	that *we w* **live** or die with you.	AIT
	9:3	you may be ready, as I said you *w* be.	NIG
	9:4	*w* be **ashamed of** having been so confident.	AIT
	10:14	as *w* be the case if we had not come to you,	NIG
	11:16	then receive me just as you *w* a **fool,**	1569
	11:17	I am not talking as the Lord *w,*	NIG
	12:6	I *w* not **be** a fool,	AIT
	12:6	because I *w* be **speaking** the truth.	AIT
Gal	1:10	I *w* not be a servant of Christ.	323
	3:2	I *w* **like** to learn just one thing from you:	AIT
	3:8	The Scripture foresaw that God *w* **justify**	AIT
	3:21	then righteousness *w* certainly have come	323
	4:15	*w* have torn out your eyes and **given**	AIT
	5:12	*w* go the whole way and **emasculate**	AIT
Eph	6:5	just as you *w* **obey** Christ.	NIG
1Th	3:3	that no one *w* be **unsettled** by these trials.	AIT
	3:4	we kept telling you that *we w* be persecuted.	3516
2Th	3:3	*w* *w* not **be** a **burden** to any of you.	AIT
1Ti	1:16	an example *for* those who *w* believe on him	3516
Phm	1:13	I *w* have **liked** to keep him with me so	AIT
	1:17	welcome him as you *w* welcome me.	NIG
Heb	3:5	to what *w* be **said** *in the future.*	AIT
	3:18	that they *w* never **enter** his rest if not	NIG
	4:8	God *w* not have **spoken** later	323
	8:4	If he were on earth, he *w* not be a priest,	323
	8:7	no place *w* have been sought for another.	323
	9:26	Then Christ *w* have **had** to suffer many times	AIT
	10:2	*w* they not have **stopped** being offered?	323
	10:2	the **worshipers** *w* have been **cleansed** once	AIT
	10:2	*w* no longer have felt **guilty** for their sins.	NIG
	11:8	to go to a place *he w* **later** receive	AIT
	11:15	they *w* have had opportunity to return.	323
	11:28	the **destroyer** of the firstborn *w* not **touch**	AIT
	11:40	together with us *w* they be **made perfect.**	5457
	13:17	for that *w* be of no advantage to you.	NIG
Jas	5:17	He prayed earnestly that *it w* not **rain,**	AIT
1Pe	1:11	Christ and the **glories** that *w* **follow.**	3552+4047
	3:10	"Whoever *w* **love life** and see good days	2527
2Pe	2:21	It *w* have been better for them not to have	1639
1Jn	2:19	they *w* have **remained** with us;	323
Rev	12:14	she *w* be **taken care of** for a time, times and	AIT

WOULDN'T (5) [NOT, WOULD]

Ge	38:26	since I *w* give her to my son Shelah."	4202
	42:22	not to sin against the boy? But you *w* listen!	4202
Nu	14:3	*W* it be better for us to go back to Egypt?"	4202
Jdg	12:3	When I saw that you *w* **help,**	401
1Sa	20:9	determined to harm you, *w* I tell you?"	4202

WOUND (21) [WIND, WINDING, WINDS, WOUNDED, WOUNDING, WOUNDS]

Ex	21:25	*w* for wound, bruise for bruise.	7206
	21:25	wound for *w,* bruise for bruise.	7206
1Ki	22:35	from his *w* ran onto the floor of the chariot,	4804
Job	34:6	his arrow inflicts an **incurable** *w.'*	631
Ps	69:26	For they persecute those *you w* and talk	5782
Jer	6:14	the *w of* my people as though it were	8691
	8:11	the *w of* my people as though it were	8691
	8:22	Why then is there no **healing for** the *w*	776
	10:19	My *w* is incurable!	4804
	14:17	has suffered a grievous *w,* a crushing blow.	8691
	15:18	and my *w* grievous and incurable?	4804
	30:12	" 'Your *w* is incurable.	8691
	30:15	Why do you cry out over your *w,*	8691
La	2:13	Your *w* is as deep as the sea.	8691
Da	6:23	no *w* was found on him,	10244
Mic	1:9	For her *w* is incurable; it has come to Judah.	4804
Na	3:19	Nothing can heal your *w;*	8691
1Co	8:12	in this way and *w* their weak conscience,	5597
Rev	13:3	of the beast seemed *to have* **had** a fatal *w,*	5377
	13:3	but the fatal *w* had been **healed.**	4435
	13:12	whose fatal *w* had been **healed.**	4435

WOUNDED (24) [WOUND]

Dt	32:39	*I have* **w** and I will heal,	4730
Jdg	9:40	and many fell *w* in the flight—	2728
1Sa	31:3	they *w* **him** critically.	2655
1Ki	20:37	So the man struck him and *w* him.	7205
	22:34	get me out of the fighting. *I've* been **w.**"	2703
2Ki	8:28	The Arameans *w* Joram;	5782
	8:29	son of Ahab because he *had been* **w.**	2703
	9:27	They *w* him in his chariot on the way up	NIH
1Ch	10:3	when the archers overtook him, they *w* him.	2655
2Ch	18:33	get me out of the fighting. *I've* been **w.**"	2703
	22:5	The Arameans *w* Joram;	5782
	22:6	son of Ahab because he *had been* **w.**	2703
	24:25	they left Joash severely *w.*	4708
	35:23	"Take me away; *I am* badly **w.**"	2703
Job	24:12	and the souls of the *w* cry out for help.	2728
Ps	109:22	and my heart *is* **w** within me.	2726
Jer	37:10	and only *w* men were left in their tents,	1991
	51:4	in Babylon, **fatally** *w* in her streets.	1991
	51:52	and throughout her land the *w* will groan.	2728
La	2:12	as they faint like *w men* in the streets of	2728
Eze	26:15	at the sound of your fall, when the *w* groan	2728
	30:24	before him like a **mortally** *w* man.	2728
Lk	20:12	and they *w* him and threw him out.	5547
Rev	13:14	in honor of the beast who *was* **w** 2400+3836+4435	

WOUNDING (1) [WOUND]

Ge	4:23	I have killed a man for *w* me,	7206

WOUNDS (27) [WOUND]

2Ki	8:29	the *w* the Arameans had inflicted on him	4804
	9:15	the *w* the Arameans had inflicted on him	4804
	18:21	a man's hand and *w* him if he leans on it!	928+995
2Ch	22:6	the *w* they had inflicted on him at Ramoth	4804
Job	5:18	For he *w,* but he also **binds up;**	3872
	9:17	a storm and multiply my *w* for no reason.	7206
Ps	38:5	My *w* fester and are loathsome because	2467
	38:11	companions avoid me because of my *w;*	5596
	147:3	the **brokenhearted** and binds up their *w.*	6780
Pr	20:30	Blows and *w* cleanse away evil,	7206
	26:10	an archer *who w* at random is he who hires	2726
	27:6	*W from* a friend can be trusted,	7206
Isa	1:6	only *w* and welts and open sores,	7206
	30:26	of his people and heals the *w* he inflicted.	4731
	36:6	a man's hand and *w* him if he leans on it!	928+995
	53:5	and by his *w* we are healed.	2467
Jer	6:7	her sickness and *w* are ever before me.	4804
	19:8	and will scoff because of all its *w.*	4804
	30:17	restore you to health and heal your *w,'*	4804
	49:17	and will scoff because of all its *w.*	4804
	50:13	be horrified and scoff because of all her *w.*	4804
Hos	6:1	he has injured us but he will bind up our *w.*	NIH
Zec	13:6	'What are these *w* on your body?'	4804
	13:6	'The *w* I was given at the house	5782
Lk	10:34	He went to him and bandaged his *w,*	5546
Ac	16:33	the jailer took them and washed their *w;*	4435
1Pe	2:24	by his *w* you have been healed.	3698

WOVE (1) [WEAVE]

Jdg	16:13	braids of his head, *w* them into the fabric	755

WOVEN (24) [WEAVE]

Ex	28:4	a breastpiece, an ephod, a robe, a *w* tunic,	9587
	28:8	Its **skillfully** *w* waistband is to be	682
	28:32	a *w* edge like a collar around this	755+5126
	29:5	on him by its skillfully *w* waistband.	NIH
	31:10	and also the *w* garments,	8573
	35:19	the *w* garments worn for ministering in	8573
	39:1	and scarlet yarn they made *w* garments	8573
	39:5	Its **skillfully** *w* waistband was like it—	682
	39:41	and the *w* garments worn for ministering in	8573
Lev	8:7	ephod to him by its **skillfully** *w* waistband;	3109
	13:48	any *w* or knitted material of linen or wool,	9274
	13:49	or leather, or *w* or knitted material,	9274
	13:51	or the *w* or knitted material, or the leather,	9274
	13:52	the *w* or knitted material of wool or linen,	9274
	13:53	or the *w* or knitted material,	9274
	13:56	or the leather, or the *w* or knitted material.	9274
	13:57	or in the *w* or knitted material,	9274
	13:58	The clothing, or the *w* or knitted material,	9274
	13:59	*w* or knitted material, or any leather article,	9274
	19:19	*w* of two kinds of **material.**	9122
Dt	22:11	of wool and linen *w* together.	9122
Ps	139:15	I *was w* **together** in the depths of the earth,	8387
La	1:14	by his hands *they were w* **together.**	8571
Jn	19:23	*w* in one piece from top to bottom.	5733

WRAP (5) [WRAPPED, WRAPS]

Nu	4:10	Then *they are to w* it and all its accessories	5989
	4:12	*w* them in a blue cloth, cover that with	5989
Isa	28:20	the blanket too narrow *to w* **around** you.	4043
Jer	43:12	so *will he w* Egypt **around himself**	6486
Ac	12:8	"*W* your cloak **around** *you* and follow me,"	4314

WRAPPED (20) [WRAP]

Ex	12:34	in kneading troughs *w* in clothing.	7674
1Sa	21:9	it *is w* in a cloth behind the ephod.	4286
Job	38:9	when I made the clouds its garment and *w* it	3157
Ps	109:19	May it be like a cloak *w* about him,	6486
	109:29	with disgrace and *w in* shame as in a cloak.	6486
Pr	30:4	Who *has w* up the waters in his cloak?	7674
Isa	59:17	the garments of vengeance and *w* himself	6486
Eze	16:4	rubbed with salt or *w* in cloths.	3156+3156
Jnh	2:5	seaweed *was w* **around** my head.	2502
Mt	27:59	*w* it in a clean linen cloth,	1962
Mk	15:46	took down the body, *w* it **in** the linen,	1912
Lk	2:7	*She w* him **in cloths** and placed him in	5058
	2:12	a baby *w* **in cloths** and lying in a manger.	5058
	23:53	*w* it in linen cloth and placed it in a tomb	1962
Jn	11:44	his hands and feet *w* with strips of linen,	1313
	13:4	*w* a towel **around** his waist.	1346
	13:5	with the towel that was *w* **around** him.	1346
	19:40	Taking Jesus' body, the two of *them w* it,	1313
	21:7	*he w* his outer garment **around** him	1346
Ac	5:6	young men came forward, *w* **up** his body,	5366

WRAPS (3) [WRAP]

Job	26:8	*He w* up the waters in his clouds,	7674
Ps	104:2	*He w* himself *in* light as with a garment,	6486
Jer	43:12	*w* his garment **around** him,	6486

WRATH (197)

Nu	1:53	of the Testimony so that *w* will not fall on	7912
	16:46	*W* has come out from the LORD;	7912
	18:5	that *w* will not fall on the Israelites again.	7912
Dt	9:8	At Horeb *you* **aroused** the LORD's *w.*	7911
	9:19	I feared the anger and *w* of the LORD,	2779
	9:19	his *w* and zeal will burn against that man.	678
	29:28	and in great *w* the LORD **uprooted** them	7912
	32:22	For a fire has been **kindled** by my *w,*	678
Jos	9:20	We will let them live, so that *w* will not fall	7912

Jos	22:20	did not w come upon the whole community	7912
1Sa	28:18	the LORD or carry out his fierce w against	678
2Sa	6: 8	because the LORD's w had broken out	7288
1Ch	13:11	because the LORD's w had broken out	7288
	27:24	W came on Israel on account of this	7912
2Ch	12: 7	My w will not be poured out on Jerusalem	2779
	19: 2	the w of the LORD is upon you.	7912
	19:10	otherwise his w will come on you	7912
	32:25	therefore the LORD's w was on him and	7912
	32:26	the LORD's w did not come upon them	7912
	36:16	and scoffed at his prophets until the w of	2779
Ezr	7:23	Why should there be w against the realm of	10634
Ne	13:18	up more w against Israel by desecrating	3019
Job	19:29	for w will bring punishment by the sword,	2779
	20:28	rushing waters on the day of God's w.	678
	21:20	let him drink of the w of the Almighty.	2779
	21:30	that he is delivered from the day of w?	6301
	40:11	Unleash the fury of your w,	678
Ps	2: 5	in his anger and terrifies them in his w,	3019
	2:12	for his w can flare up in a moment.	678
	6: 1	in your anger or discipline me in your w.	2779
	7:11	a God who expresses his w every day.	2404
	21: 9	In his w the LORD will swallow them up,	678
	37: 8	Refrain from anger and turn from w;	2779
	38: 1	in your anger or discipline me in your w.	2779
	38: 3	of your w there is no health in my body;	2405
	59:13	consume them in w, consume them till	2779
	69:24	Pour out your w on them;	2405
	76:10	your w against men brings you praise,	2779
	76:10	and the survivors of your w are restrained.	2779
	78:21	and his w rose against Israel,	678
	78:38	and did not stir up his full w.	2779
	78:49	his w, indignation and hostility—	6301
	79: 6	Pour out your w on the nations that do	2779
	85: 3	You set aside all your w and turned	6301
	88: 7	Your w lies heavily upon me;	2779
	88:16	Your w has swept over me;	3019
	89:46	How long will your w burn like fire?	2779
	90: 9	All our days pass away under your w;	6301
	90:11	For your w is as great as the fear	6301
	102:10	because of your great w,	2256+2405+7912
	106:23	stood in the breach before him to keep his w	2779
	110: 5	he will crush kings on the day of his w.	678
Pr	11: 4	Wealth is worthless in the day of w,	6301
	11:23	but the hope of the wicked only in w.	6301
	14:35	but a shameful servant incurs his w.	6301
	15: 1	A gentle answer turns away w,	2779
	16:14	A king's w is a messenger of death,	2779
	20: 2	A king's w is like the roar of a lion;	399
	21:14	bribe concealed in the cloak pacifies great w	2779
	22:14	he who is under the LORD's w will fall	2404
	24:18	and disapprove and turn his w away	2779
Isa	9:19	the w of the LORD Almighty the land will	6301
	10: 5	in whose hand is the club of my w!	2405
	10:25	against you will end and my w will	678
	13: 3	my warriors to carry out my w—	678
	13: 5	the LORD and the weapons of his w—	2405
	13: 9	a cruel day, with w and fierce anger—	6301
	13:13	the earth will shake from its place at the w	6301
	26:20	for a little while until his w has passed by.	2405
	30:27	his lips are full of w,	2405
	34: 2	his w is upon all their armies.	2779
	48: 9	For my own name's sake I delay my w;	678
	51:13	because of the w of the oppressor,	2779
	51:13	For where is the w of the oppressor?	2779
	51:17	the hand of the LORD the cup of his w,	2779
	51:20	with the w of the LORD and the rebuke	2779
	51:22	from that cup, the goblet of my w,	2779
	59:18	so will he repay w to his enemies	2779
	63: 3	in my anger and trod them down in my w;	2779
	63: 5	and my own w sustained me.	2779
	63: 6	in my w I made them drunk	2779
Jer	3: 5	Will your w continue forever?'	NIH
	4: 4	or my w will break out and burn like fire	2779
	6:11	But I am full of the w of the LORD,	2779
	7:20	and my w will be poured out on this place,	639
	7:29	this generation that is under his w.	6301
	10:10	the nations cannot endure his w.	2405
	10:25	Pour out your w on the nations that do	2779
	18:20	in their behalf to turn your w away	2779
	21: 5	a mighty arm in anger and fury and great w.	7912
	21:12	or my w will break out and burn like fire	2779
	23:19	the storm of the LORD will burst out in w,	2779
	25:15	the wine of my w and make all the nations	2779
	30:23	the storm of the LORD will burst out in w,	2779
	32:31	and w that I must remove it from my sight.	2779
	32:37	in my furious anger and great w;	7912
	33: 5	of the men I will slay in my anger and w.	2779
	36: 7	and w pronounced against this people by	2779
	42:18	'As my anger and w have been poured out	2779
	42:18	in Jerusalem, so will my w be poured out	2779
	50:25	and brought out the weapons of his w,	2405
La	2: 2	in his w he has torn down the strongholds of	6301
	2: 4	he has poured out his w like fire on the tent	2779
	3: 1	affliction by the rod of his w.	6301
	4:11	The LORD has given full vent to his w;	2779
Eze	5:13	"Then my anger will cease and my w	2779
	5:13	And when I have spent my w upon them,	2779
	5:15	in anger and in w and with stinging rebuke.	2779
	6:12	So will I spend my w upon them.	2779
	7: 8	I am about to pour out my w on you	2779
	7:12	for w is upon the whole crowd.	3019
	7:14	for my w is upon the whole crowd.	3019
	7:19	to save them in the day of the LORD's w.	2779
	9: 8	in this outpouring of your w on Jerusalem?"	2779
	13:13	In my w I will unleash a violent wind,	2779
	13:15	So I will spend my w against the wall and	2779

Eze	14:19	a plague into that land and pour out my w	2779
	16:38	upon you the blood vengeance of my w	2779
	16:42	Then my w against you will subside	2779
	20: 8	So I said I would pour out my w on them	2779
	20:13	So I said I would pour out my w on them	2779
	20:21	So I said I would pour out my w on them	2779
	20:33	an outstretched arm and with outpoured w.	2779
	20:34	an outstretched arm and with outpoured w.	2779
	21:17	and my w will subside.	2779
	21:31	I will pour out my w upon you	2405
	22:20	so will I gather you in my anger and my w	2779
	22:21	and I will blow on you with my fiery w,	6301
	22:22	that I the LORD have poured out my w	2779
	22:24	or showers in the day of w.'	2405
	22:31	So I will pour out my w on them	2405
	24: 8	up w and take revenge I put her blood on	2534
	24:13	you will not be clean again until my w	2779
	25:14	in accordance with my anger and my w;	2779
	25:17	on them and punish them in my w.	2534
	30:15	I will pour out my w on Pelusium,	2779
	36: 6	in my jealous w because you have suffered	2779
	36:18	So I poured out my w on them	2779
	38:19	In my zeal and fiery w I declare that at	6301
Da	8:19	what will happen later in the time of w,	2405
	9:16	turn away your anger and your w	2779
	11:36	until the time of w is completed.	2405
Hos	5:10	I will pour out my w on them like a flood	6301
	11: 9	I will not come in w.	6552
	13:11	and in my w I took him away.	6301
Am	1: 3	even for four, I will not turn back [my w].	5647S
	1: 9	even for four, I will not turn back [my w].	5647S
	1:11	even for four, I will not turn back [my w].	5647S
	1:13	even for four, I will not turn back [my w].	5647S
	2: 1	even for four, I will not turn back [my w].	5647S
	2: 4	even for four, I will not turn back [my w].	5647S
	2: 6	even for four, I will not turn back [my w].	5647S
Mic	5:15	I will take vengeance in anger and w upon	2779
Na	1: 2	I will bear the LORD's w,	2408
	1: 2	takes vengeance and is filled with w.	2779
	1: 2	and maintains his w against his enemies.	5757
	1: 6	His w is poured out like fire;	2779
Hab	3: 2	in w remember mercy.	8075
	3: 8	Was your w against the streams?	678
	3:12	In w you strode through the earth and	2405
Zep	1:15	That day will be a day of w,	6301
	1:18	to save them on the day of the LORD's w.	6301
	2: 2	the day of the LORD's w comes upon you.	678
	2: 3	the day of the LORD's w comes upon you.	678
	3: 8	the kingdoms and to pour out my w	2405
Mal	1: 4	a people always under the w of the LORD.	2404
Mt	3: 7	warned you to flee from the coming w?	3973
Lk	3: 7	warned you to flee from the coming w?	3973
	21:23	in the land and w against this people.	3973
Jn	3:36	for God's w remains on him."	3973
Ro	1:18	The w of God is being revealed	3973
	2: 5	you are storing up w against yourself for	3973
	2: 5	against yourself for the day of God's w,	3973
	2: 8	there will be w and anger.	3973
	3: 5	That God is unjust in bringing his w on us?	3973
	4:15	because law brings w.	3973
	5: 9	be saved from God's w through him!	3973
	9:22	to show his w and make his power known,	3973
	9:22	with great patience the objects of his w—	3973
	12:19	my friends, but leave room for God's w,	3973
	13: 4	of w to bring punishment on the wrongdoer.	3973
Eph	2: 3	we were by nature objects of w.	3973
	5: 6	for because of such things God's w comes	3973
Col	3: 6	Because of these, the w of God is coming.	3973
1Th	1:10	Jesus, who rescues us from the coming w.	3973
	2:16	The w of God has come upon them at last.	3973
	5: 9	For God did not appoint us to suffer w but	3973
Rev	6:16	on the throne and from the w of the Lamb!	3973
	6:17	For the great day of their w has come,	3973
	11:18	nations were angry; and your w has come.	3973
	14:10	poured full strength into the cup of his w.	3973
	14:19	into the great winepress of God's w.	2596
	15: 1	because with them God's w is completed.	2596
	15: 7	seven golden bowls filled with the w of God	2596
	16: 1	the seven bowls of God's w on the earth."	2596
	16:19	with the wine of the fury of his w.	3973
	19:15	He treads the winepress of the fury of the w	3973

WREATH (3) [WREATHS]

Isa	28: 1	that w, the pride of Ephraim's drunkards,	6498
	28: 3	That w, the pride of Ephraim's drunkards,	6498
	28: 5	a beautiful w for the remnant of his people.	6498

WREATHS (4) [WREATH]

1Ki	7:29	and bulls were w of hammered work.	4324
	7:30	cast with w on each side.	4324
	7:36	in every available space, with w all around.	4324
Ac	14:13	and w to the city gates because he and	5098

WRECKED (2) [SHIPWRECK, SHIPWRECKED]

1Ki	22:48	they were w at Ezion Geber.	8689
2Ch	20:37	The ships were w and were not able	8689

WRENCHED (2)

Ge	32:25	so that his hip was w as he wrestled with	3697
Eze	29: 7	you broke and their backs were w.	5048

WREST (KJV) See DENY, DISTORT,

PERVERT, TWIST

WRESTLE (1) [WRESTLED, WRESTLING]

Ps	13: 2	How long must I w with my thoughts	8883

WRESTLED (2) [WRESTLE]

Ge	32:24	and a man w with him till daybreak.	84
	32:25	so that his hip was wrenched as he w with	84

WRESTLING (1) [WRESTLE]

Col	4:12	He is always w in prayer for you,	76

WRETCHED (6) [WRETCHES]

Jdg	11:35	You have made me miserable and w,	6579
Pr	15:15	All the days of the oppressed are w,	8273
Hab	3:14	as though about to devour the w who were	6714
Mt	21:41	"He will bring those wretches to a w end,"	2809
Ro	7:24	What a w man I am!	5417
Rev	3:17	But you do not realize that you are w,	5417

WRETCHES (1) [WRETCHED]

Mt	21:41	"He will bring those w to a wretched end,"	2805

WRING (2)

Lev	1:15	w off the head and burn it on the altar;	4916
	5: 8	He is to w its head from its neck,	4916

WRINKLE (1)

Eph	5:27	without stain or w or any other blemish,	4869

WRIST (2) [WRISTS]

Ge	38:28	a scarlet thread and tied it on his w and said,	3338
	38:30	who had the scarlet thread on his w,	3338

WRISTS (3) [WRIST]

Jer	40: 4	freeing you from the chains on your w.	3338
Eze	13:18	who sew magic charms on all their w	723+3338
Ac	12: 7	he said, and the chains fell off Peter's w.	5931

WRITE (86) [WRITER, WRITES, WRITING, WRITINGS, WRITTEN, WROTE]

Ex	17:14	"W this on a scroll as something to	4180
	34: 1	and I will w on them the words that were	4180
	34:27	"W down these words,	4180
Nu	5:23	" 'The priest is to w these curses on	4180
	17: 2	W the name of each man on his staff.	4180
	17: 3	On the staff of Levi w Aaron's name,	4180
Dt	6: 9	W them on the doorframes of your houses	4180
	10: 2	I will w on the tablets the words that were	4180
	11:20	W them on the doorframes of your houses	4180
	17:18	he is to w for himself on a scroll a copy	4180
	27: 3	W on them all the words of this law	4180
	27: 8	And you shall w very clearly all the words	4180
	31:19	"Now w down for yourselves this song	4180
Jos	18: 4	a survey of the land and to w a description	4180
	18: 8	a survey of the land and w a description	4180
Ezr	5:10	so that we could w down the names	10374
Est	8: 8	Now w another decree in the king's name	4180
Job	13:26	For you w down bitter things against me	4180
Ps	87: 6	The LORD will w in the register of	6218
Pr	3: 3	w them on the tablet of your heart.	4180
	7: 3	w them on the tablet of your heart.	4180
Isa	8: 1	"Take a large scroll and w on it	4180
	10:19	be so few that a child could w them down.	4180
	30: 8	Go now, w it on a tablet for them,	4180
	44: 5	still another will w on his hand,	4180
Jer	30: 2	'W in a book all the words I have spoken	4180
	31:33	"I will put my law in their minds and w it	4180
	36: 2	and w on it all the words I have spoken	4180
	36:17	"Tell us, how did you come to w all this?	4180
	36:28	and w on it all the words that were on	4180
	36:29	that scroll and said, "Why did you w on it	4180
Eze	37:16	take a stick of wood and w on it,	4180
	37:16	and w on it, 'Ephraim's stick,	4180
	43:11	W these down before them so that they may	4180
Hab	2: 2	"W down the revelation and make it plain	4180
Mk	10: 4	"Moses permitted a man to w a certificate	1211
Lk	1: 3	to me to w an orderly account for you,	1211
Jn	8: 6	But Jesus bent down and started to w on	2863
	19:21	"Do not w 'The King of the Jews,'	1211
Ac	15:20	Instead we should w to them,	2182
	25:26	But I have nothing definite to w	1211
	25:26	investigation I may have something to w.	1211
1Co	16:21	I, Paul, w this greeting in my own hand.	NIG
2Co	1:13	not w you anything you cannot read	1211
	9: 1	to w to you about this service to the saints.	1211
		This is why I w these things	1211
Gal	6:11	See what large letters I use as I w to you	1211
Php	3: 1	It is no trouble for me to w the same things	1211
Col	4:18	I, Paul, w this greeting in my own hand.	NIG
1Th	4: 9	about brotherly love we do not need to w	1211
	5: 1	about times and dates we do not need to w	1211
2Th	3:17	I, Paul, w this greeting in my own hand,	1211
	3:17	This is how I w.	NIG
Phm	1:21	Confident of your obedience, I w to you,	1211
Heb	8:10	in their minds and w them on their hearts.	2108
	10:16	and I will w them on their minds."	2108
1Jn		We w this to make our joy complete.	1211
	2: 1	I w this to you so that you will not sin.	1211
	2:12	I w to you, dear children,	1211

1Jn	2:13	*I* **w** to you, fathers,	1211
	2:13	*I* **w** to you, young men,	1211
	2:13	*I* **w** to you, dear children,	1211
	2:14	*I* **w** to you, fathers,	1211
	2:14	*I* **w** to you, young men,	1211
	2:21	*I* do not **w** to you because you do not know	1211
	5:13	*I* **w** these things to you who believe in	1211
2Jn	1:12	I have much *to* **w** to you,	1211
3Jn	1:13	I have much *to* **w** you,	1211
Jude	1: 3	*to* **w** to you about the salvation we share,	1211
	1: 3	I felt I had *to* **w** and urge you to contend for	1211
Rev	1:11	"**W** on a scroll what you see and send it to	1211
	1:19	"**W**, therefore, what you have seen,	1211
	2: 1	"To the angel of the church in Ephesus **w:**	1211
	2: 8	"To the angel of the church in Smyrna **w:**	1211
	2:12	the angel of the church in Pergamum **w:**	1211
	2:18	"To the angel of the church in Thyatira **w:**	1211
	3: 1	"To the angel of the church in Sardis **w:**	1211
	3: 7	the angel of the church in Philadelphia **w:**	1211
	3:12	*I will* **w** on him the name of my God and	1211
	3:12	and I will also **w** on him my new name.	NIG
	3:14	"To the angel of the church in Laodicea **w:**	1211
	10: 4	the seven thunders spoke, I was about to **w;**	1211
	10: 4	and do not **w** it **down.**"	1211
	14:13	Then I heard a voice from heaven say, "**W:**	1211
	19: 9	Then the angel said to me, "**W:**	1211
	21: 5	Then he said, "**W** this **down,**	1211

WRITER (1) [WRITE]

Ps	45: 1	my tongue is the pen of a skillful **w.**	6221

WRITES (3) [WRITE]

Dt	24: 1	and *he* **w** her a certificate of divorce,	4180
	24: 3	and **w** her a certificate of divorce,	4180
2Pe	3:16	He **w** the same way in all his letters,	NIG

WRITHE (6) [WRITHED, WRITHES]

Isa	13: 8	*they will* **w** like a woman in labor.	2655
Jer	4:19	*I* **w** in pain. Oh, the agony of my heart!	2655
Eze	30:16	Pelusium *will* **w in agony.**	2655+2655
Mic	1:12	Those who live in Maroth **w in pain,**	2655
	4:10	**W** in agony, O Daughter of Zion,	2655
Zec	9: 5	Gaza *will* **w in agony,** and Ekron too,	2655+4394

WRITHED (3) [WRITHE]

Ps	77:16	O God, the waters saw you and **w;**	2655
Isa	26:18	We were with child, *we* **w in pain,**	2655
Hab	3:10	the mountains saw you and **w.**	2655

WRITHES (2) [WRITHE]

Isa	26:17	to give birth **w** and cries out in her pain,	2655
Jer	51:29	The land trembles and **w,**	2655

WRITING (35) [WRITE]

Ex	32:16	the **w** was the writing of God,	4844
	32:16	the writing was the **w** of God,	4844
Dt	31:24	After Moses finished **w** in a book the words	4180
1Ch	28:19	in **w** from the hand of the LORD on me,	4181
2Ch	36:22	throughout his realm and to put it in **w:**	4844
Ezr	1: 1	throughout his realm and to put it in **w:**	4844
Ne	9:38	**putting** it in **w,** and our leaders,	4180
Job	31:35	*let* my accuser **put** *his* indictment **in w.**	4180
Isa	38: 9	a **w** of Hezekiah king of Judah	4844
Eze	9: 2	a man clothed in linen who had a **w** kit	6221
	9: 3	the man clothed in linen who had the **w** kit	6221
	9:11	the **w** kit at his side brought back word,	7879
Da	5: 7	"Whoever reads this **w** and tells me what	10375
	5: 8	read the **w** or tell the king what it meant.	10375
	5:12	and he will tell you what the **w** means."	NIH
	5:15	to read this **w** and tell me what it means,	10375
	5:16	If you can read this **w** and tell me what	10375
	5:17	I will read the **w** for the king	10375
	6: 8	issue the decree and **put** it **in w**	10375+10673
	6: 9	So King Darius **put** the decree in **w.**	10375+10673
	6:13	O king, or to the decree *you* **put** in **w.**	10673
Lk	1:63	He asked for a **w tablet,**	4400
Ac	15:27	to confirm by word of mouth **what we are**	
		w.	899+3836ˢ
1Co	4:14	*I am* not **w** this to shame you,	1211
	5:11	now *I am* **w** you that you must not associate	1211
	9:15	And *I am* not **w** this in the hope	1211
	14:37	let him acknowledge that what *I am* **w**	1211
Gal	1:20	before God that what *I am* **w** you is no lie.	1211
1Ti	3:14	*I am* **w** you these instructions so that,	1211
Phm	1:19	I, Paul, *am* **w** this with my own hand.	1211
1Jn	2: 7	not **w** you a new command but an old one,	1211
	2: 8	Yet *I am* **w** you a new command;	1211
	2:26	*I am* **w** these things to you about those	1211
2Jn	1: 5	I am not **w** you a new command	1211
Rev	5: 1	a scroll **with** **w** on both sides and sealed	1211

WRITINGS (2) [WRITE]

Mt	26:56	the **w** of the prophets might be fulfilled."	1210
Ro	16:26	through the prophetic **w** by the command of	1210

WRITTEN (257) [WRITE]

Ge	5: 1	This is the **w** account of Adam's line.	6219
Ex	24:12	with the law and commands *I have* **w**	4180
	32:32	then blot me out of the book *you have* **w.**"	4180
Dt	10: 4	on these tablets what he had **w** before,	4844
	28:58	which *are* **w** in this book,	4180
	29:20	the curses **w** in this book will fall upon him,	4180

Dt	29:21	the curses of the covenant **w** in this Book of	4180
	29:27	so that he brought on it all the curses **w**	4180
	30:10	that *are* **w** in this Book of the Law and turn	4180
Jos	1: 8	you may be careful to do everything **w** in it.	4180
	8:31	according to what *is* **w** in the Book of	4180
	8:32	the Law of Moses, which *he* had **w.**	4180
	8:34	just as it *is* **w** in the Book of the Law.	4180
	10:13	as it *is* **w** in the Book of Jashar.	4180
	18: 6	After you *have* **w descriptions** of	4180
	23: 6	to obey all that *is* **w** in the Book of the Law	4180
2Sa	1:18	of the bow (it *is* **w** in the Book of Jashar):	4180
1Ki	2: 3	as **w** in the Law of Moses,	4180
	11:41	not **w** in the book of the annals of Solomon?	4180
	14:19	*are* **w** in the book of the annals of the kings	4180
	14:29	not **w** in the book of the annals of the kings	4180
	15: 7	not **w** in the book of the annals of the kings	4180
	15:23	not **w** in the book of the annals of the kings	4180
	15:31	not **w** in the book of the annals of the kings	4180
	16: 5	not **w** in the book of the annals of the kings	4180
	16:14	not **w** in the book of the annals of the kings	4180
	16:20	not **w** in the book of the annals of the kings	4180
	16:27	not **w** in the book of the annals of the kings	4180
	21:11	as Jezebel directed in the letters she had **w**	4180
	22:39	not **w** in the book of the annals of the kings	4180
	22:45	not **w** in the book of the annals of the kings	4180
2Ki	1:18	not **w** in the book of the annals of the kings	4180
	8:23	not **w** in the book of the annals of the kings	4180
	10:34	not **w** in the book of the annals of the kings	4180
	12:19	not **w** in the book of the annals of the kings	4180
	13: 8	not **w** in the book of the annals of the kings	4180
	13:12	not **w** in the book of the annals of the kings	4180
	14: 6	in accordance with what *is* **w** in the Book	4180
	14:15	not **w** in the book of the annals of the kings	4180
	14:18	not **w** in the book of the annals of the kings	4180
	14:28	not **w** in the book of the annals of the kings	4180
	15: 6	not **w** in the book of the annals of the kings	4180
	15:11	*are* **w** in the book of the annals of the kings	4180
	15:15	*are* **w** in the book of the annals of the kings	4180
	15:21	not **w** in the book of the annals of the kings	4180
	15:26	*are* **w** in the book of the annals of the kings	4180
	15:31	not **w** in the book of the annals of the kings	4180
	15:36	not **w** in the book of the annals of the kings	4180
	16:19	not **w** in the book of the annals of the kings	4180
	20:20	not **w** in the book of the annals of the kings	4180
	21:17	not **w** in the book of the annals of the kings	4180
	21:25	not **w** in the book of the annals of the kings	4180
	22:13	the people and for all Judah about **what** is **w**	1821
	22:13	with all that *is* **w** there concerning us."	4180
	22:16	and its people, according to everything **w**	1821
	23: 3	the words of the covenant **w** in this book.	4180
	23:21	as it *is* **w** in this Book of the Covenant."	4180
	23:24	the requirements of the law **w** in the book	4180
	23:28	not **w** in the book of the annals of the kings	4180
	24: 5	not **w** in the book of the annals of the kings	4180
1Ch	16:40	in accordance with everything **w** in the Law	4180
	29:29	*are* **w** in the records of Samuel the seer,	4180
2Ch	9:29	not **w** in the records of Nathan the prophet,	4180
	12:15	*are* they not **w** in the records of Shemaiah	4180
	13:22	*are* **w** in the annotations of the prophet Iddo.	4180
	16:11	*are* **w** in the book of the kings of Judah	4180
	20:34	*are* **w** in the annals of Jehu son of Hanani,	4180
	23:18	of the LORD as **w** in the Law of Moses,	4180
	24:27	of God *are* **w** in the annotations on the book	4180
	25: 4	in accordance with what *is* **w** in the Law, in	4180
	25:26	not **w** in the book of the kings of Judah	4180
	27: 7	*are* **w** in the book of the kings of Israel	4180
	28:26	*are* **w** in the book of the kings of Judah	4180
	30: 5	in large numbers according to what *was* **w.**	4180
	30:18	contrary to what *was* **w.**	4180
	31: 3	New Moons and appointed feasts as **w** in	4180
	32:32	and his acts of devotion *are* **w** in the vision	4180
	33:18	are **w** in the annals of the kings of Israel.	NIH
	33:19	all *are* **w** in the records of the seers.	4180
	34:21	and Judah about **what** is **w** *in* this book.	1821
	34:21	not acted in accordance with all that *is* **w**	4180
	34:24	the curses in the book that has been read	4180
	34:31	the words of the covenant **w** in this book.	4180
	35: 4	the **directions** **w** by David king of Israel and	4181
	35:12	as *is* **w** in the Book of Moses.	4180
	35:25	These became a tradition in Israel and *are* **w**	4180
	35:26	to what *is* **w** in the Law of the LORD—	4180
	35:27	*are* **w** in the book of the kings of Israel	4180
	36: 8	are **w** in the book of the kings of Israel.	4180
Ezr	3: 2	in accordance with what *is* **w** in the Law	4180
	3: 4	Then in accordance with what *is* **w,**	4180
	4: 7	The letter *was* **w** in Aramaic script and in	4180
	5: 5	a report could go to Darius and his **w reply**	10496
	6: 2	and this *was* **w** on it:	10374
	6:18	to **what** is **w** in the Book of Moses.	10375
Ne	6: 6	in which *was* **w:** "It is reported	4180
	7: 5	This is what I found **w** there:	4180
	8:14	They found **w** in the Law,	4180
	8:15	to make booths"—as it *is* **w.**	4180
	10:34	as it *is* **w** in the Law.	4180
	10:36	"As it *is* also **w** in the Law,	4180
	13: 1	and there it was found **w** that no Ammonite	4180
Est	1:19	let him issue a royal decree and *let* it be **w**	4180
	3:12	*These* were **w** in the name of King Xerxes	4180
	8: 5	*let an* **order** be **w** overruling the dispatches	4180
	8: 8	for no document **w** in the king's name	4180
	8: 9	These orders were **w** in the script	NIH
	9:23	doing what Mordecai had **w** to them.	4180
	9:25	he issued **w** orders that the evil scheme	6219
	9:26	Because of everything **w** *in* this letter and	1821
	9:32	and *it was* **w down** in the records.	4180
	10: 2	not **w** in the book of the annals of the kings	4180
Job	19:23	that *they* were **w** on a scroll,	2980

Ps	40: 7	*it is* **w** about me in the scroll.	4180
	102:18	*Let* this *be* **w** for a future generation,	4180
	139:16	for me *were* **w** in your book before one	4180
	149: 9	to carry out the sentence **w** against them.	4180
Pr	22:20	Have *I* not **w** thirty sayings for you,	4180
Isa	65: 6	"See, *it stands* **w** before me:	4180
Jer	17:13	Those who turn away from you *will* be **w**	4180
	25:13	all that *are* **w** in this book and prophesied	4180
	36:27	that Baruch had **w** at Jeremiah's dictation,	4180
	45: 1	after Baruch had **w** on a scroll	4180
	51:60	Jeremiah had **w** on a scroll *about* all	4180
Eze	2:10	of it *were* **w** words of lament and mourning	4180
	37:20	before their eyes the sticks *you* have **w** on	4180
Da	5:25	"This is the inscription that *was* **w:**	10673
	9:11	the curses and sworn judgments **w** in	4180
	9:13	Just as *it is* **w** in the Law of Moses,	4180
	10:21	but first I will tell you what *is* **w** in	8398
	12: 1	everyone whose name is found **w** in	4180
Mal	3:16	of remembrance *was* **w** in his presence	4180
Mt	2: 5	"for this is what the prophet *has* **w:**	1211
	4: 4	Jesus answered, "*It is* **w:** 'Man does not	1211
	4: 6	For *it is* **w:** " 'He will command	1211
	4: 7	Jesus answered him, "*It is* also **w:**	1211
	4:10	For *it is* **w:** 'Worship the Lord your God,	1211
	11:10	This is the one about whom *it is* **w:**	1211
	21:13	"*It is* **w,**" he said to them,	1211
	26:24	Son of Man will go just as *it is* **w** about him.	1211
	26:31	for *it is* **w:** " 'I will strike the shepherd,	1211
	27:37	Above his head they placed the **w** charge	1211
Mk	1: 2	*It is* **w** in Isaiah the prophet:	1211
	7: 6	as *it is* **w:** " 'These people honor me with	1211
	9:12	Why then *it is* **w** that the Son of Man	1211
	9:13	just as *it is* **w** about him."	1211
	11:17	as he taught them, he said, "*Is it* not **w:**	1211
	14:21	of Man will go just as *it is* **w** about him.	1211
	14:27	Jesus told them, "for *it is* **w:**	1211
	15:26	The **w** **notice** of the charge	2107
Lk	2:23	(as it *is* **w** in the Law of the Lord,	1211
	3: 4	As *is* **w** in the book of the words of Isaiah	1211
	4: 4	Jesus answered, "*It is* **w:** 'Man does not	1211
	4: 8	Jesus answered, "*It is* **w:** 'Worship the Lord	1211
	4:10	For *it is* **w:** " 'He will command	1211
	4:17	he found the place where it is **w:**	1211
	7:27	This is the one about whom *it is* **w:**	1211
	10:20	rejoice that your names *are* **w in** heaven."	1582
	10:26	"What *is* **w** in the Law?"	1211
	18:31	and everything that *is* **w** by the prophets	1211
	19:46	"*It is* **w,**" he said to them,	1211
	20:17	what is the meaning of that which *is* **w:**	1211
	21:22	in fulfillment of all that *has been* **w.**	1211
	22:37	It *is* **w:** 'And he was numbered with the	1211
	22:37	what is **w** about me is reaching its	
		fulfillment."	NIG
	23:38	There was a **w** **notice** above him,	2107
	24:44	be fulfilled that *is* **w** about me in the Law	1211
	24:46	He told them, "This is what *is* **w:**	1211
Jn	2:17	His disciples remembered that it is **w:**	1211
	6:31	as *it is* **w:** 'He gave them bread from heaven	1211
	6:45	It is **w** in the Prophets:	1211
	8:17	In your own Law it *is* **w** that	1211
	10:34	"Is it not **w** in your Law,	1211
	12:14	young donkey and sat upon it, as it is **w,**	1211
	12:16	that these things had been **w** about him and	1211
	15:25	But this is to fulfill what is **w** in their Law:	1211
	19:20	and the sign was **w** in Aramaic,	1211
	19:22	Pilate answered, "What *I have* **w,**	1211
	19:22	"What I have written, *I have* **w.**"	1211
	20:31	But these *are* **w** that you may believe	1211
	21:25	If every one of them *were* **w down,**	1211
	21:25	for the books that *would be* **w.**	1211
Ac	1:20	said Peter, "*it is* **w** in the book of Psalms,	1211
	7:42	with **what** *is* **w** in the book of the prophets:	1211
	13:29	When they had carried out all that *was* **w**	1211
	13:33	As *it is* **w** in the second Psalm:	1211
	15:15	in agreement with this, as it *is* **w:**	1211
	21:25	we *have* **w** to them our decision	2182
	23: 5	for *it is* **w:** 'Do not speak evil about	1211
	24:14	with the Law and that is **w** in the Prophets,	1211
Ro	1:17	just as *it is* **w:** "The righteous will live	1209
	2:15	that the requirements of the law are **w**	1211
	2:24	As *it is* **w:** "God's name is blasphemed	1211
	2:27	you have the **w** code and circumcision,	1207
	2:29	by the Spirit, not *by* the **w** code.	1207
	3: 4	As *it is* **w:** "So that you may be proved	1211
	3:10	As *it is* **w:** "There is no one righteous	1211
	4:17	As *it is* **w:** "I have made you a father of	1211
	4:23	The words "it was credited to him" *were* **w**	1211
	7: 6	and not in the old way of the **w** code.	1207
	8:36	As *it is* **w:** "For your sake we face death	1211
	9:13	Just as *it is* **w:** "Jacob I loved, but Esau	1211
	9:33	As *it is* **w:** "See, I lay in Zion a stone	1211
	10:15	As *it is* **w,** "How beautiful are the feet	1211
	11: 8	as *it is* **w:** "God gave them a spirit of	1211
	11:26	And so all Israel will be saved, as *it is* **w:**	1211
	12:19	for *it is* **w:** "It is mine to avenge;	1211
	14:11	It is **w:** " 'As surely as I live,"	1211
	15: 3	as *it is* **w:** "The insults of those who insult	1211
	15: 4	For everything that *was* **w in the past**	4592
	15: 4	that was written in the past was **w**	1211
	15: 9	as *it is* **w:** "Therefore I will praise you	1211
	15:15	*I have* **w** you quite boldly on some points,	1211
	15:21	Rather, as *it is* **w:** "Those who were not	1211
1Co	1:19	For *it is* **w:** "I will destroy the wisdom of	1211
	1:31	Therefore, as *it is* **w:** "Let him who boasts	1211
	2: 9	However, as *it is* **w:** "No eye has seen,	1211
	3:19	As *it is* **w:** "He catches the wise	1211
	4: 6	"Do not go beyond what *is* **w.**"	1211

1Co	5: 9	*I have* **w** you in my letter not to associate	1211
	9: 9	For *it is* **w** in the Law of Moses:	1211
	9:10	Yes, *this was* **w** for us,	1211
	10: 7	as *it is* **w**: "The people sat down to eat	1211
	10:11	as examples and *were* **w down** as warnings	1211
	14:21	In the Law *it is* **w**: "Through men of	1211
	15:45	So *it is* **w**: "The first Adam became a	1211
	15:54	then the saying that *is* **w** will come true:	1211
2Co	3: 2	**w** on our hearts, known and read by	1582
	3: 3	**w** not with ink but with the Spirit of	1582
	4:13	*It is* **w**: "I believed,"	1211
	8:15	as *it is* **w**: "He who gathered much	1211
	9: 9	As *it is* **w**: "He has scattered abroad his gifts	1211
Gal	3:10	for *it is* **w**: "Cursed is everyone who	1211
	3:10	to do everything **w** in the Book of the Law."	1211
	3:13	for *it is* **w**: "Cursed is everyone who is hung	1211
	4:22	For *it is* **w** that Abraham had two sons,	1211
	4:27	For *it is* **w**: "Be glad, O barren woman,	1211
Eph	3: 3	as *I have* **already w** briefly.	4592
Col	2:14	**w**, with its regulations, that was	5934
Heb	10: 7	*it is* **w** about me in the scroll—	1211
	12:23	whose names *are* **w** in heaven.	616
1Pe	1:16	for *it is* **w**: "Be holy, because I am holy."	1211
	5:12	*I have* **w** to you briefly,	1211
2Pe	3: 1	*I have* **w** both of them as reminders	1211
Jude	1: 4	men whose condemnation **was w** about	4592
Rev	1: 3	and take to heart what *is* **w** in it,	1211
	2:17	a white stone with a new name **w** on it,	1211
	13: 8	not *been* **w** in the book of life belonging to	1211
	14: 1	and his Father's name **w** on their foreheads.	1211
	17: 5	This title *was* **w** on her forehead:	1211
	17: 8	of the earth whose names *have* not *been* **w**	1211
	19:12	He has a name **w** on him that no one knows	1211
	19:16	and on his thigh he has this name: **w**:	1211
	20:15	If anyone's name was not found **w** in	1211
	21:12	On the gates *were* **w** the names of	2108
	21:27	but only those whose names *are* **w** in	1211

WRONG (101) [WRONGDOER, WRONGDOING, WRONGDOINGS, WRONGED, WRONGING, WRONGS]

Ge	16: 5	responsible for the **w** I am *suffering*.	2805
Ex	2:13	He asked the **one in the w**,	8401
	9:27	and I and my people are **in the w**.	8401
	23: 2	"Do not follow the crowd in *doing* **w**.	8288
Lev	5:18	**w** *he has* **committed** unintentionally, 8704+8705	
Nu	5: 7	He must make full restitution for his **w**,	871
	5: 8	to whom restitution can be made for the **w**,	871
	15:25	to the LORD for their **w** an offering made	8705
	15:26	were involved in the **unintentional w**.	8705
Dt	32: 4	A faithful God who does no **w**,	6404
Jdg	11:27	but you are doing me **w** by waging war	8288
1Sa	11: 5	and he asked, "**What is w** with the people?"	4537
	19: 4	"*Let* not the king **do w** to his servant David;	2627
	19: 5	then *would you* **do w** to an innocent man	2627
	25:39	He has kept his servant from doing **w**	8288
	26:18	and what **w** am I guilty of?	8288
2Sa	7:14	When he **does w**, I will punish him	6390
	13:16	greater **w** than what you have already done	8288
	19:19	how your servant **did w** on the day my lord	6390
	24:17	"I am the one who has sinned and **done w**.	6390
1Ki	2:44	"You know in your heart all the **w** you did	8288
	3: 9	and to distinguish between right and **w**.	8273
	8:47	*we have* **done w**, we have acted wickedly';	6390
	18: 9	"**What have** *I* **done w**," asked Obadiah,	2627
2Ki	18:14	"*I have* **done w**. Withdraw from me,	2627
1Ch	21:17	I am the one who has sinned and **done w**.	
			8317+8317
2Ch	6:37	*we have* **done w** and acted wickedly';	6390
	22: 3	for his mother encouraged him in **doing w**.	8399
Ne	9:33	you have acted faithfully, while we **did w**.	8399
Est	1:16	"Queen Vashti *has* **done w**,	6390
Job	6:24	show me where *I have* **been w**.	8706
	21:27	the schemes by which *you would* **w** me.	2803
	31: 3	disaster for those who do **w**?	224
	32:12	But not *one* of you *has* **proved** Job **w**;	3519
	34:10	from the Almighty to do **w**.	6404
	34:12	It is unthinkable that *God would* **do w**,	8399
	34:32	if I have done **w**, I will not do so again.'	6404
	36:23	or said to him, 'You have done **w**'?	6406
Ps	5: 5	you hate all who do **w**.	224
	15: 3	who does his neighbor no **w**	8288
	36: 4	and does not reject *what* is **w**.	8273
	37: 1	or be envious of those who do **w**;	6406
	59: 4	I have done no **w**, yet they are ready to	6411
	106: 6	*we have* **done w** and acted wickedly.	6390
	119: 3	They do nothing **w**; they walk in his ways.	6406
	119:104	therefore I hate every **w** path.	9214
	119:128	I hate every **w** path.	9214
Pr	2:14	in doing **w** and rejoice in the perverseness	8273
	20:22	Do not say, "I'll pay you back for this **w**!"	8273
	28:21	yet a man *will* **do w** for a piece of bread.	7321
	28:24	or mother and says, "It's not **w**"—	7322
	30:20	'I've done nothing **w**.'	224
Ecc	5: 1	who do not know that they do **w**.	8273
	8:11	the people are filled with schemes to do **w**.	8273
Isa	1:16	evil deeds out of my sight! Stop **doing w**,	8317
	7:15	when he knows enough to reject the **w**	8273
	7:16	the boy knows enough to reject the **w**	8273
Jer	16:10	What have we done?	6411
	22: 3	**Do** no **w** or violence to the alien,	3561
	51:24	in Babylonia for all the **w** they have done	8288
La	3:59	O LORD, the **w** done *to* me.	6432
Eze	18: 8	He withholds his hand from **doing w**	6404

Eze	18:18	robbed his brother and did what was **w**	3202+4202
Da	6:22	Nor have I ever done any **w** before you,	10242
	9: 5	we have sinned and **done w**.	6390
	9:15	we have sinned, *we have* **done w**.	8399
Hab	1: 3	Why do you tolerate **w**?	6662
	1:13	you cannot tolerate **w**.	6662
Zep	3: 5	LORD within her is righteous; he does no **w**.	6406
	3:13	The remnant of Israel will do no **w**;	6406
Mal	1: 8	blind animals for sacrifice, is that not **w**?	8273
	1: 8	or diseased animals, is that not **w**?	8273
Lk	23:41	But this man has done nothing **w**."	876
Jn	18:23	"If I said something," Jesus replied,	2809
	18:23	Jesus replied, "testify as to what *is* **w**.	2805
Ac	23: 9	"We find nothing **w** with this man,"	2805
	25: 5	if he has done anything **w**."	876
	25: 8	"*I have* **done** nothing **w** against the law of	279
	25:10	*I have* not **done** any **w** to the Jews,	92
Ro	13: 3	but *for* those who do **w**.	2805
	13: 4	But if you do **w**, be afraid,	2805
	13: 4	but it is **w** for a man to eat anything	2805
1Co	6: 8	Instead, *you* yourselves cheat and **do w**,	92
2Co	7:12	not on account of the one who **did** the **w** or	92
	12:13	Forgive me this **w**!	94
	13: 7	to God that you will not do anything **w**.	2805
Gal	2:11	because he was **clearly in the w**.	2861
	4:12	*You have* **done** me no **w**.	92
Col	3:25	Anyone who **does w** will be repaid	92
	3:25	will be repaid for *his* **w**,	92
1Th	4: 6	in this matter no one should **w** his brother	5648
	5:15	that nobody pays back **w** for wrong,	2805
	5:15	that nobody pays back wrong for **w**,	2805
Phm	1:18	If he has **done** you any **w** or owes you	92
Heb	8: 7	For if there had been **nothing w** with	289
Jas	4: 3	because you ask with **w** motives,	2809
1Pe	2:12	though they accuse you of **doing w**,	2804
	2:14	by him to punish *those who do* **w** and	2804
	2:20	a beating *for* **doing w** and endure it?	279
Rev	22:11	Let him who **does w** continue to do wrong;	92
	22:11	*Let* him who does wrong continue *to* **do w**;	92

WRONGDOER (1) [WRONG]

Ro	13: 4	wrath to bring punishment *on* the **w**.	2805+4556

WRONGDOING (12) [WRONG]

Lev	5:19	he has been **guilty** of **w** against the LORD 870+870	
Nu	5:31	The husband will be innocent of any **w**,	6411
1Sa	24:11	and recognize that I am not guilty of **w**	8288
	25:28	Let no **w** be found in you as long	8288
	25:39	and has brought Nabal's **w** down on his own	8288
1Ki	2:44	Now the LORD will repay you for your **w**.	8288
Job	1:22	Job did not sin by charging God with **w**.	9524
	24:12	But God charges no one with **w**.	9524
	33:17	to turn man from **w** and keep him	5126
Pr	16:12	Kings detest **w**, for a throne is	6913+8400
2Pe	2:16	he was rebuked *for* his **w** by a donkey—	4175
1Jn	5:17	All **w** is sin, and there is sin that	94

WRONGDOINGS (1) [WRONG]

Jer	5:25	Your **w** have kept these away;	6411

WRONGED (11) [WRONG]

Ge	20: 9	How have I **w** you that you have brought	2627
Nu	5: 7	to it and give it all to the person *he has* **w**.	870
	16:15	nor *have I* **w** any of them."	8317
Jdg	11:27	*I have* not **w** you, but you are doing me	2627
1Sa	19: 4	he has not **w** you, and what he has done	2627
	20: 1	How have I **w** your father,	2633
	24:11	*I have* not **w** you, but you are hunting me	2627
Job	19: 6	that God *has* **w** me and drawn his net	6430
	19: 7	"Though I cry, 'I've been **w**!'	2805
1Co	6: 7	Why not rather *be* **w**?	92
2Co	7: 2	*We have* **w** no one, we have corrupted no one	92

WRONGING (1) [WRONG]

Ps	119:78	May the arrogant be put to shame for **w** me	6430

WRONGS (10) [WRONG]

Ge	50:15	and pays us back for all the **w** we did	8288
	50:17	and the **w** they committed in treating you	2633
Nu	5: 6	man or woman **w** another in any way 2633+6913	
1Sa	24:12	the LORD **avenge** *the* **w** you have *done*	5933
1Ki	8:31	a man **w** his neighbor and is required to take	2627
2Ch	6:22	a man **w** his neighbor and is required to take	2627
Job	13:23	How many **w** and sins have I committed?	6411
Pr	10:12	but love covers over all **w**.	7322
Zep	3:11	to shame for all the **w** you *have* done to me,	7321
1Co	13: 5	it keeps no record of **w**.	2805

WROTE (59) [WRITE]

Ex	24: 4	Moses then **w** down everything the LORD	4180
	34:28	And *he* **w** on the tablets the words of	4180
Dt	4:13	and then **w** them on two stone tablets.	4180
	5:22	Then he **w** them on two stone tablets	4180
	10: 4	The LORD **w** on these tablets	4180
	31: 9	So Moses **w** down this law and gave it to	4180
	31:22	So Moses **w** down this song that day	4180
Jos	8:32	*They* **w** its **description** on a scroll,	4180
Jdg	8:14	the young man **w** down for him the names	4180
1Sa	10:25	*He* **w** them **down** on a scroll and deposited	4180
2Sa	11:14	In the morning David **w** a letter to Joab	4180
	11:15	In it *he* **w**, "Put Uriah in the front line	4180
1Ki	21: 8	So *she* **w** letters in Ahab's name,	4180

1Ki	21: 9	In those letters *she* **w**:	4180
2Ki	10: 1	So Jehu **w** letters and sent them to Samaria:	4180
	10: 6	Then Jehu **w** them a second letter, saying,	4180
	17:37	the laws and commands *he* **w** for you.	4180
2Ch	30: 1	also **w** letters to Ephraim and Manasseh,	4180
	32:17	king also **w** letters insulting the LORD,	4180
Ezr	4: 7	of his associates **w** a letter to Artaxerxes.	4180
	4: 8	the secretary **w** a letter against Jerusalem	10374
Est	3:12	*They* **w** out in the script of each province	4180
	8: 5	devised and **w** to destroy the Jews in all	4180
	8: 9	*They* **w** out all Mordecai's orders to	4180
	8:10	Mordecai **w** in the name of King Xerxes,	4180
	9:22	He **w** them to observe the days as days	NIH
	9:29	**w** with full authority to confirm	4180
Ecc	12:10	and what *he* was upright and true.	4180
Jer	36: 4	Baruch **w** them on the scroll.	4180
	36: 6	words of the LORD that *you* **w** as I dictated.	4180
	36:18	and I **w** them in ink on the scroll."	4180
	36:32	Baruch **w** on it all the words of the scroll	4180
Da	5: 5	a human hand appeared and **w** on the plaster 10374	
	5: 5	The king watched the hand as it **w**.	10374
	5:24	Therefore he sent the hand that **w**	10673
	6:25	Then King Darius **w** to all the peoples,	10374
	7: 1	*He* **w** down the substance of his dream.	10374
Hos	8:12	*I* **w** for them the many things of my law,	4180
Mk	10: 5	that Moses **w** you this law,"	1211
	12:19	"Moses **w** for us that if a man's brother dies	1211
	1:63	and to everyone's astonishment *he* **w**,	1211
Lk	20:28	"Moses **w** for us that if a man's brother dies	1211
Jn	1:45	"We have found the one Moses **w** **about** in	1211
	1:45	and about whom the prophets also **w**—	NIG
	5:46	you would believe me, for he **w** about me.	1211
	5:47	But since you do not believe what he **w**,	1207
	8: 8	Again he stooped down and **w** on	1211
	21:24	to these things and who **w** them **down**.	1211
Ac	1: 1	*I* **w** about all that Jesus began to do and	4472
	18:27	the brothers encouraged him and **w** to	1211
	23:25	*He* **w** a letter as follows:	1211
Ro	16:22	I, Tertius, who **w** down this letter,	1211
1Co	7: 1	Now for the matters *you* **w** about:	1211
2Co	2: 3	*I* **w** as I did so that when I came I should	1211
	2: 4	For I **w** you out of great distress	1211
	2: 9	The reason I **w** you was to see	1211
	7:12	So even though *I* **w** to you,	1211
2Pe	3:15	as our dear brother Paul also **w** you with	1211
3Jn	1: 9	*I* **w** to the church, but Diotrephes,	1211

WROUGHT (1)

Eze	27:19	they exchanged **w** iron, cassia and calamus	6936

WRUNG (1)

Jdg	6:38	he squeezed the fleece and **w** out the dew—	5172

X

XERXES (31)

Ezr	4: 6	At the beginning of the reign of **X**,	347
Est	1: 1	during the time of **X**, the Xerxes who ruled	347
	1: 1	the **X** who ruled over 127 provinces	347
	1: 2	At that time King **X** reigned from his royal	347
	1: 9	the women in the royal palace of King **X**.	347
	1:10	King **X** was in high spirits from wine,	347
	1:15	not obeyed the command of King **X** that	347
	1:16	the peoples of all the provinces of King **X**.	347
	1:17	'King **X** commanded Queen Vashti to	347
	1:19	never again to enter the presence of King **X**.	347
	2: 1	when the anger of King **X** had subsided,	347
	2:12	a girl's turn came to go in to King **X**,	347
	2:16	taken to King **X** in the royal residence	347
	2:21	and conspired to assassinate King **X**.	347
	3: 1	King **X** honored Haman son of Hammedatha	347
	3: 6	throughout the whole kingdom of **X**.	347
	3: 7	In the twelfth year of King **X**,	347
	3: 8	Then Haman said to King **X**,	347
	3:12	in the name of King **X** *himself* and sealed	347
	6: 2	who had conspired to assassinate King **X**.	347
	7: 5	King **X** asked Queen Esther, "Who is he?	347
	8: 1	That same day King **X** gave Queen Esther	347
	8: 7	King **X** replied to Queen Esther and	347
	8:10	Mordecai wrote in the name of King **X**,	347
	8:12	of King **X** was the thirteenth day of	347
	9: 2	in their cities in all the provinces of King **X**	347
	9:20	throughout the provinces of King **X**,	347
	9:30	in the 127 provinces of the kingdom of **X**—	347
	10: 1	King **X** imposed tribute throughout	347
	10: 3	the Jew was second in rank to King **X**,	347
Da	9: 1	In the first year of Darius son of **X** (a Mede	347

Y

YAHWEH See †LORD

YARDS (3)

Jos	3: 4	But keep a distance of about a thousand y	564
Ne	3:13	also repaired **five hundred** y of the wall	547+564
Jn	21: 8	about a **hundred** y.	1357+4388

YARN (34)

Ex	25: 4	purple and **scarlet** y and fine linen;	9106+9357
	26: 1	purple and **scarlet** y,	9106+9357
	26:31	and **scarlet** y and finely twisted linen,	9106+9357
	26:36	and **scarlet** y and finely twisted linen	9106+9357
	27:16	and **scarlet** y and finely twisted linen	9106+9357
	28: 5	purple and **scarlet** y, and fine linen.	9106+9357
	28: 6	and of blue, purple and **scarlet** y,	9106+9357
	28: 8	and with blue, purple and **scarlet** y,	9106+9357
	28:15	of blue, purple and **scarlet** y,	9106+9357
	28:33	**scarlet** y around the hem of the robe,	9106+9357
	35: 6	purple and **scarlet** y and fine linen;	9106+9357
	35:23	purple or **scarlet** y or fine linen.	9106+9357
	35:25	blue, purple or **scarlet** y or fine linen.	9106+9357
	35:35	purple and **scarlet** y and fine linen,	9106+9357
	36: 8	purple and **scarlet** y,	9106+9357
	36:35	and **scarlet** y and finely twisted linen,	9106+9357
	36:37	and **scarlet** y and finely twisted linen	9106+9357
	38:18	and **scarlet** y and finely twisted linen	9106+9357
	38:23	purple and **scarlet** y and fine linen.)	9106+9357
	39: 1	**scarlet** y they made woven garments	9106+9357
	39: 2	and of blue, purple and **scarlet** y,	9106+9357
	39: 3	purple and **scarlet** y and fine linen—	9106+9357
	39: 5	and with blue, purple and **scarlet** y,	9106+9357
	39: 8	and of blue, purple and **scarlet** y,	9106+9357
	39:24	and **scarlet** y and finely twisted linen	9106+9357
	39:29	purple and **scarlet** y—	9106+9357
Lev	14: 4	**scarlet** y and hyssop be brought for	9106+9357
	14: 6	the **scarlet** y and the hyssop,	9106+9357
	14:49	**scarlet** y and hyssop.	9106+9357
	14:51	hyssop, the **scarlet** y and the live bird,	9106+9357
	14:52	the hyssop and the **scarlet** y.	9106+9357
2Ch	2: 7	and in purple, crimson and **blue** y,	9418
	2:14	and with purple and **blue** and crimson y	9418
	3:14	**blue**, purple and crimson y	9418

YAUDI (1)

2Ki	14:28	and Hamath, which had belonged to **Y**,	3373

YEA (KJV) See YES

YEAR (350) [YEAR-OLD, YEAR'S, YEARLING, YEARLY, YEARS]

Ge	7:11	In the six hundredth y of Noah's life,	9102
	8:13	month of Noah's six hundred and first y,	9102
	14: 4	but in the thirteenth y they rebelled.	9102
	14: 5	In the fourteenth y, Kedorlaomer and	9102
	17:21	will bear to you by this time next y."	9102
	18:10	surely return to you about this time **next** y,	2645
	18:14	to you at the appointed time **next** y	2645
	26:12	and the same y reaped a hundredfold,	9102
	47:17	through that y with food in exchange	9102
	47:18	When that y was over,	9102
	47:18	they came to him the following y and said,	9102
Ex	12: 2	the first month of your y.	9102
	13:10	at the appointed time y after year.	3427
	13:10	at the appointed time year after y.	3427
	21: 2	But in the seventh y, he shall go free,	NIH
	23:11	the seventh y let the land lie unplowed	NIH
	23:14	a y you are to celebrate a festival to me.	9102
	23:16	the Feast of Ingathering at the end of the y,	9102
	23:17	"Three times a y all the men are to appear	9102
	23:29	But I will not drive them out in a single y,	9102
	29:38	regularly each day: two lambs a y old.	9102
	30:10	Once a y Aaron shall make atonement	9102
	34:22	the Feast of Ingathering at the turn of the y.	9102
	34:23	Three times a y all your men are to appear	9102
	34:24	up three times each y to appear before	9102
	40:17	of the first month in the second y.	9102
Lev	9: 3	both a y old and without defect—	9102
	14:10	and one ewe lamb a y old,	9102
	16:34	Atonement is to be made once a y for all	9102
	19:24	In the fourth y all its fruit will be holy,	9102
	19:25	But in the fifth y you may eat its fruit.	9102
	23:12	the LORD a lamb a y old and without defect,	9102
	23:18	each a y old and without defect,	9102
	23:19	each a y old, for a fellowship offering.	9102
	23:41	to the LORD for seven days each y.	9102
	25: 4	the seventh y the land is to have a sabbath	9102
	25: 5	The land is to have a y of rest.	9102
	25: 6	during the sabbath y will be food for you—	NIH
	25:10	the fiftieth y and proclaim liberty	9102
	25:11	The fiftieth y shall be a jubilee for you;	9102
	25:13	" 'In this **Y** of Jubilee everyone is to return	9102
	25:20	"What will we eat in the seventh y if we do	9102
	25:21	the sixth y that the land will yield enough	9102

Lev	25:22	While you plant during the eighth y,	9102
	25:22	until the harvest of the ninth y comes in.	9102
	25:28	in the possession of the buyer until the **Y**	9102
	25:29	he retains the right of redemption a full y	9102
	25:30	not redeemed before a full y has passed,	9102
	25:40	he is to work for you until the **Y** of Jubilee.	9102
	25:50	to count the time from the y he sold himself	9102
	25:50	from the year he sold himself up to the **Y**	9102
	25:52	a few years remain until the **Y** of Jubilee,	9102
	25:53	to be treated as a man hired from y to year;	9102
	25:53	to be treated as a man hired from year to y;	9102
	25:54	and his children are to be released in the **Y**	9102
	27:17	If he dedicates his field during the **Y**	9102
	27:18	that remain until the next **Y** of Jubilee,	9102
	27:23	determine its value up to the **Y** of Jubilee,	9102
	27:24	In the **Y** of Jubilee the field will revert to	9102
Nu	1: 1	of the second y after the Israelites came out	9102
	7:15	one ram and one male lamb a y old,	9102
	7:17	and five male lambs a y old.	9102
	7:21	one ram and one male lamb a y old,	9102
	7:23	and five male lambs a y old.	9102
	7:27	one ram and one male lamb a y old,	9102
	7:29	one ram and one male lamb a y old.	9102
	7:33	one ram and one male lamb a y old,	9102
	7:35	and five male lambs a y old.	9102
	7:39	one ram and one male lamb a y old,	9102
	7:41	and five male lambs a y old.	9102
	7:45	one ram and one male lamb a y old,	9102
	7:47	and five male lambs a y old.	9102
	7:51	one ram and one male lamb a y old,	9102
	7:53	and five male lambs a y old.	9102
	7:57	one ram and one male lamb a y old,	9102
	7:59	and five male lambs a y old.	9102
	7:63	one ram and one male lamb a y old,	9102
	7:65	and five male lambs a y old.	9102
	7:69	one ram and one male lamb a y old,	9102
	7:71	and five male lambs a y old.	9102
	7:75	one ram and one male lamb a y old,	9102
	7:77	and five male lambs a y old.	9102
	7:81	one ram and one male lamb a y old,	9102
	7:83	and five male lambs a y old.	9102
	7:87	twelve rams and twelve male lambs a y old,	9102
	7:88	and sixty male lambs a y old.	4200
	9: 1	the second y after they came out of Egypt.	9102
	9:22	a month or a y, the Israelites would remain	3427
	10:11	of the second month of the second y,	9102
	14:34	forty years—one y for each of the forty days	9102
	28: 3	two lambs a y old without defect,	9102
	28: 9	make an offering of two lambs a y old	9102
	28:11	one ram and seven male lambs a y old,	9102
	28:14	to be made at each new moon during the **y**.	9102
	28:19	one ram and seven male lambs a y old,	9102
	28:27	a y old as an aroma pleasing to the LORD.	9102
	29: 2	one ram and seven male lambs a y old,	9102
	29: 8	one ram and seven male lambs a y old,	9102
	29:13	two rams and fourteen male lambs a y old.	9102
	29:17	two rams and fourteen male lambs a y old,	9102
	29:20	two rams and fourteen male lambs a y old,	9102
	29:23	two rams and fourteen male lambs a y old,	9102
	29:26	two rams and fourteen male lambs a y old,	9102
	29:29	two rams and fourteen male lambs a y old,	9102
	29:32	two rams and fourteen male lambs a y old,	9102
	29:36	one ram and seven male lambs a y old,	9102
	33:38	of the fortieth y after the Israelites came out	3413
	36: 4	the **Y** of Jubilee for the Israelites comes,	3413
Dt	1: 3	In the fortieth y, on the first day of	9102
	11:12	on it from the beginning of the y to its end.	9102
	14:22	of all that your fields produce **each** y.	9102+9102
	15: 9	"The seventh y, the year for canceling	9102
	15: 9	the y for canceling debts, is near,'	9102
	15:12	in the seventh y you must let him go free.	9102
	15:20	**Each** y you and your family are to eat them	928+9102+9102
	16:16	Three times a y all your men must appear	9102
	24: 5	For one y he is to be free to stay at home	9102
	26:12	a tenth of all your produce in the third y,	9102
	26:12	in the third year, the y of the tithe,	9102
	31:10	in the y for canceling debts,	9102
Jos	5:12	that y they ate of the produce of Canaan.	9102
Jdg	8:28	who that y shattered and crushed them.	9102
	11:40	that **each** y the young women of Israel go	
		out for four days	2025+3427+3427+4946
	17:10	you ten shekels of silver a y,	2021+3427+4200
1Sa	1: 3	**Y** after year this man went up	3427
	1: 3	after y this man went up from his town	3427
	1: 7	This went on y after year.	9102
	1: 7	This went on year after y.	9102
	2:19	**Each** y his mother made him a little robe	
			2025+3427+3427+4946
	7:16	From y to year he went on a circuit	9102
	7:16	to y he went on a circuit from Bethel	9102
	27: 7	in Philistine territory a y and four months.	3427
	29: 3	He has already been with me for **over a** y,	
			196+2296+2296+3427+9102
1Ki	4: 7	to provide supplies for one month in the y.	9102
	5:11	Solomon continued to do this for Hiram y	9102
	5:11	to do this for Hiram year after y.	9102
	6: 1	In the four hundred and eightieth y after	9102
	6: 1	the fourth y of Solomon's reign over Israel,	9102
	6:37	of the LORD was laid in the fourth y,	9102
	6:38	In the eleventh y in the month of Bul,	9102
	9:25	a y Solomon sacrificed burnt offerings	9102
	10:25	**Y** after year, everyone who came brought	9102
	10:25	Year after y, everyone who came brought	9102
	14:25	In the fifth y of King Rehoboam,	9102
	15: 1	In the eighteenth y of the reign	9102
	15: 9	the twentieth y of Jeroboam king of Israel,	9102

1Ki	15:25	in the second y of Asa king of Judah,	9102
	15:28	in the third y of Asa king of Judah	9102
	15:33	In the third y of Asa king of Judah,	9102
	16: 8	In the twenty-sixth y of Asa king of Judah,	9102
	16:10	the twenty-seventh y of Asa king of Judah.	9102
	16:15	the twenty-seventh y of Asa king of Judah,	9102
	16:23	In the thirty-first y of Asa king of Judah,	9102
	16:29	In the thirty-eighth y of Asa king of Judah,	9102
	18: 1	After a long time, in the third y,	9102
	22: 2	the third y Jehoshaphat king of Judah went	9102
	22:41	of Asa became king of Judah in the fourth y	9102
	22:51	in the seventeenth y of Jehoshaphat king	9102
2Ki	1:17	as king in the second y of Jehoram son	9102
	3: 1	In the eighteenth y of Jehoshaphat king	9102
	4:16	"About this time **next** y," Elisha said,	2645+6961
	4:17	and the **next** y about that same time	2645+6961
	8:16	In the fifth y of Joram son of Ahab king	9102
	8:25	In the twelfth y of Joram son of Ahab king	9102
	8:26	and he reigned in Jerusalem one y.	9102
	9:29	(In the eleventh y of Joram son of Ahab,	9102
	11: 4	In the seventh y Jehoiada sent for	9102
	12: 1	In the seventh y of Jehu,	9102
	12: 6	But by the twenty-third y of King Joash	9102
	13: 1	In the twenty-third y of Joash son	9102
	13:10	the thirty-seventh y of Joash king of Judah,	9102
	14: 1	In the second y of Jehoash son of Jehoahaz	9102
	14:23	In the fifteenth y of Amaziah son of Joash	9102
	15: 1	In the twenty-seventh y of Jeroboam king	9102
	15: 8	In the thirty-eighth y of Azariah king	9102
	15:13	of Jabesh became king in the thirty-ninth y	9102
	15:17	the thirty-ninth y of Azariah king of Judah,	9102
	15:23	In the fiftieth y of Azariah king of Judah,	9102
	15:27	the fifty-second y of Azariah king of Judah,	9102
	15:30	in the twentieth y of Jotham son of Uzziah.	9102
	15:32	In the second y of Pekah son of Remaliah	9102
	16: 1	In the seventeenth y of Pekah son of	9102
	17: 1	In the twelfth y of Ahaz king of Judah,	9102
	17: 4	as he had done y by year.	9102
	17: 4	as he had done year by y.	9102
	17: 6	In the ninth y of Hoshea, the king of	9102
	18: 1	In the third y of Hoshea son of Elah king	9102
	18: 9	In King Hezekiah's fourth y,	9102
	18: 9	the seventh y of Hoshea son of Elah king	9102
	18:10	Samaria was captured in Hezekiah's sixth y,	9102
	18:10	which was the ninth y of Hoshea king	9102
	18:13	the fourteenth y of King Hezekiah's reign,	9102
	19:29	"This y you will eat what grows by itself,	9102
	19:29	and the second y what springs from that.	9102
	19:29	But in the third y sow and reap,	9102
	22: 3	In the eighteenth y of his reign,	9102
	23:23	But in the eighteenth y of King Josiah,	9102
	24:12	In the eighth y of the reign of the king	9102
	25: 1	So in the ninth y of Zedekiah's reign,	9102
	25: 2	until the eleventh y of King Zedekiah.	9102
	25: 8	in the nineteenth y of Nebuchadnezzar king	9102
	25:27	In the thirty-seventh y of the exile	9102
	25:27	in the y Evil-Merodach became king	9102
1Ch	26:31	In the fortieth y of David's reign	9102
	27: 1	on duty month by month throughout the y.	9102
2Ch	3: 2	of the second month in the fourth y	9102
	9:24	**Y** after year, everyone who came brought	9102
	9:24	Year after y, everyone who came brought	9102
	12: 2	of Egypt attacked Jerusalem in the fifth y	9102
	13: 1	the eighteenth y of the reign of Jeroboam,	9102
	15:10	in the third month of the fifteenth y	9102
	15:19	until the thirty-fifth y of Asa's reign.	9102
	16: 1	In the thirty-sixth y of Asa's reign	9102
	16:12	In the thirty-ninth y of his reign Asa	9102
	16:13	in the forty-first y of his reign Asa died	9102
	17: 7	In the third y of his reign he sent	9102
	21:19	at the end of the second y,	3427
	22: 2	and he reigned in Jerusalem one y.	9102
	23: 1	the seventh y Jehoiada showed his strength.	9102
	24:23	At the turn of the y, the army of Aram	9102
	27: 5	That y the Ammonites paid him	9102
	29: 3	In the first month of the first y of his reign,	9102
	34: 3	In the eighth y of his reign,	9102
	34: 3	In his twelfth y he began to purge Judah	9102
	34: 8	In the eighteenth y of Josiah's reign,	9102
	35:19	in the eighteenth y of Josiah's reign.	9102
	36:22	In the first y of Cyrus king of Persia,	9102
Ezr	1: 1	In the first y of Cyrus king of Persia,	9102
	3: 8	the second y after their arrival at the house	9102
	4:24	to a standstill until the second y of the reign	10732
	5:13	In the first y of Cyrus king of Babylon,	10732
	6: 3	In the first y of King Cyrus, the king issued	10732
	6:15	in the sixth y of the reign of King Darius.	10732
	7: 7	also came up to Jerusalem in the seventh y	9102
	7: 8	the fifth month of the seventh y of the king.	9102
Ne	1: 1	In the month of Kislev in the twentieth y,	9102
	2: 1	In the month of Nisan in the twentieth y	9102
	5:14	from the twentieth y of King Artaxerxes,	9102
	5:14	until his thirty-second y—	9102
	10:31	Every seventh y we will forgo working	9102
	10:32	a shekel each y for the service of the house	9102
	10:34	to the house of our God at set times **each** y	
			928+9102+9102
	10:35	of the LORD **each** y the firstfruits	928+9102+9102
	13: 6	in the thirty-second y of Artaxerxes king	9102
Est	1: 3	in the third y of his reign he gave a banquet	9102
	2:16	in the seventh y of his reign.	9102
	3: 7	In the twelfth y of King Xerxes,	9102
	9:27	without fail observe these two days every y,	9102
Job	3: 6	not be included among the days of the y nor	9102
Ps	65:11	You crown the y with your bounty,	9102
Isa	6: 1	In the y that King Uzziah died,	9102
	14:28	This oracle came in the y King Ahaz died:	9102

Isa 20: 1 In the y that the supreme commander, 9102
    21:16 "Within *one* y, as a servant bound 9102
    29: 1 Add y to year and let your cycle 9102
    29: 1 to y and let your cycle of festivals go on. 9102
    32:10 a y you who feel secure will tremble; 9102
    34: 8 a y *of* retribution, to uphold Zion's cause. 9102
    36: 1 the fourteenth y of King Hezekiah's reign, 9102
    37:30 "This y you will eat what grows by itself, 9102
    37:30 and the second y what springs from that. 9102
    37:30 But in the third y sow and reap, 9102
    61: 2 the y of the LORD's favor and the day 9102
    63: 4 and the y of my redemption has come. 9102
Jer 1: 2 in the thirteenth y of the reign of Josiah son 9102
    1: 3 down to the fifth month of the eleventh y 9102
    11:23 of Anathoth in the y *of* their punishment.' " 9102
    17: 8 a y *of* drought and never fails to bear fruit." 9102
    23:12 on them in the y they are punished," 9102
    25: 1 of Judah in the fourth y of Jehoiakim son 9102
    25: 1 the first y of Nebuchadnezzar king 9102
    25: 3 the thirteenth y of Josiah son of Amon king 9102
    28: 1 In the fifth month of that same y, 9102
    28: 1 the fourth y, early in the reign of Zedekiah 9102
    28:16 This very y you are going to die, 9102
    28:17 In the seventh month of that same y, 9102
    32: 1 the LORD in the tenth y of Zedekiah king 9102
    32: 1 the eighteenth y of Nebuchadnezzar. 9102
    34:14 'Every seventh y each of you must free any 9102
    36: 1 In the fourth y of Jehoiakim son of Josiah 9102
    36: 9 the fifth y of Jehoiakim son of Josiah king 9102
    39: 1 In the ninth y of Zedekiah king of Judah, 9102
    39: 2 the fourth month of Zedekiah's eleventh y, 9102
    45: 1 of Neriah in the fourth y of Jehoiakim son 9102
    46: 2 of Babylon in the fourth y of Jehoiakim son 9102
    48:44 upon Moab the y *of* her punishment," 9102
    51:46 one rumor comes this y, another the next, 9102
    51:59 with Zedekiah king of Judah in the fourth y 9102
    52: 4 So in the ninth y of Zedekiah's reign, 9102
    52: 5 until the eleventh y of King Zedekiah. 9102
    52:12 in the nineteenth y of Nebuchadnezzar king 9102
    52:28 in the seventh y, 3,023 Jews; 9102
    52:29 In Nebuchadnezzar's eighteenth y, 9102
    52:30 in his twenty-third y, 745 Jews taken 9102
    52:31 In the thirty-seventh y of the exile 9102
    52:31 in the y Evil-Merodach became king 9102
Eze 1: 1 In the thirtieth y, in the fourth month 9102
    1: 2 the fifth y of the exile of King Jehoiachin— 9102
    4: 6 assigned you 40 days, a day for each y. 9102
    8: 1 In the sixth y, in the sixth month 9102
    20: 1 In the seventh y, in th fifth month 9102
    24: 1 In the ninth y, in the tenth month on 9102
    26: 1 In the eleventh y, on the first day of 9102
    29: 1 In the tenth y, in the tenth month on 9102
    29:17 the twenty-seventh y, 9102
    30:20 In the eleventh y, in the first month on 9102
    31: 1 In the eleventh y, in the third month on 9102
    32: 1 In the twelfth y, in the twelfth month on 9102
    32:17 In the twelfth y, on the fifteenth day of 9102
    33:21 In them the twelfth y of our exile, 9102
    40: 1 In the twenty-fifth y of our exile, 9102
    40: 1 at the beginning of the y, 9102
    40: 1 the fourteenth y after the fall of the city— 9102
    46:17 the servant may keep it until the y 9102
Da 1: 1 In the third y of the reign of Jehoiakim king 9102
    1:21 And Daniel remained there until the first y 9102
    2: 1 In the second y of his reign, 9102
    7: 1 the first y of Belshazzar king of Babylon, 10732
    8: 1 In the third y of King Belshazzar's reign, 9102
    9: 1 the first y of Darius son of Xerxes (a Mede 9102
    9: 2 in the first y *of* his reign, 9102
    10: 1 In the third y of Cyrus king of Persia, 9102
    11: 1 And in the first y of Darius the Mede, 9102
Mic 6: 6 with burnt offerings, with calves a y old? 9102
Hag 1: 1 In the second y of King Darius, 9102
    1:15 of the sixth month in the second y 9102
    2:10 in the second y of Darius, 9102
Zec 1: 1 the eighth month of the second y of Darius, 9102
    1: 7 in the second y of Darius, 9102
    7: 1 In the fourth y of King Darius, 9102
    14:16 that have attacked Jerusalem will go up y 9102
    14:16 up year after y to worship the King, 9102
Lk 2:41 Every y his parents went to Jerusalem for 2291
    3: 1 In the fifteenth y of the reign of Tiberius 2291
    4:19 to proclaim the y of the Lord's favor." 1929
    13: 8 'leave it alone *for* one more y, 2291
    13: 9 If it bears fruit next y, fine! NIG
Jn 11:49 who was high priest that y, spoke up, 1929
    11:51 that y he prophesied that Jesus would die 1929
    18:13 Caiaphas, the high priest that y. 1929
Ac 11:26 *for* a whole y Barnabas and Saul met with 1929
    18:11 So Paul stayed *for* a y and a half, 1929
2Co 8:10 Last y you were the first not only to give 4373
    9: 2 that since *last* y you in Achaia were ready 4373
Heb 9: 7 the inner room, and that only once a y, 1929
    9:25 the Most Holy Place every y with blood 1929
    10: 1 same sacrifices repeated endlessly y **after year,** 1929+2848
    10: 1 repeated endlessly **year after y,** 1929+2848
Jas 4:13 go to this or that city, spend a y there, 1929
Rev 9:15 and day and month and y were released 1929

YEAR'S (4) [YEAR]

Lev 26:10 You will still be eating **last** y **harvest** 3823+3824
Dt 14:28 of that y produce and store it in your towns, 9102
Mk 14: 5 have been sold for more than a y wages NIG
Jn 12: 5 and **the money** given to the poor? It was **worth a** y **wages."** 1324+5559

YEAR-OLD (7) [YEAR]

Ex 12: 5 animals you choose must be y males 1201+9102
Lev 12: 6 a y lamb for a burnt offering 1201+9102
Nu 6:12 a y male lamb as a guilt offering. 1201+9102
    6:14 a y male lamb without defect for 1201+9102
    6:14 for a burnt offering, a y ewe lamb 1426+9102
    15:27 a y *female* goat for a sin offering. 1426+9102
Eze 46:13 a y lamb without defect for a burnt 1201+9102

YEARLING (1) [YEAR]

Isa 11: 6 the calf and the lion and the y together; 5309

YEARLY (3) [YEAR]

1Ki 10:14 the gold that Solomon received y was 666 talents, 285+928+9102
2Ch 9:13 the gold that Solomon received y was 666 talents, 285+928+9102
Hos 2:11 her **festivals,** her New Moons, 2504

YEARNS (4)

Job 19:27 How my heart y within me! 3983
Ps 84: 2 My soul y, even faints, for the courts of 4083
Isa 26: 9 My soul y **for** you in the night; 203
Jer 31:20 Therefore my heart y for him; 2159

YEARS (507) [YEAR]

Ge 1:14 as signs to mark seasons and days and y, 9102
    5: 3 When Adam had lived 130 y, 9102
    5: 4 Adam lived 800 y and had other sons 9102
    5: 5 Altogether, Adam lived 930 y, 9102
    5: 6 When Seth had lived 105 y, 9102
    5: 7 Seth lived 807 y and had other sons 9102
    5: 8 Altogether, Seth lived 912 y, 9102
    5: 9 When Enosh had lived 90 y, 9102
    5:10 Enosh lived 815 y and had other sons 9102
    5:11 Altogether, Enosh lived 905 y, 9102
    5:12 When Kenan had lived 70 y, 9102
    5:13 Kenan lived 840 y and had other sons 9102
    5:14 Altogether, Kenan lived 910 y, 9102
    5:15 When Mahalalel had lived 65 y, 9102
    5:16 Mahalalel lived 830 y and had other sons 9102
    5:17 Altogether, Mahalalel lived 895 y, 9102
    5:18 When Jared had lived 162 y, 9102
    5:19 Jared lived 800 y and had other sons 9102
    5:20 Altogether, Jared lived 962 y, 9102
    5:21 When Enoch had lived 65 y, 9102
    5:22 with God 300 y and had other sons 9102
    5:23 Altogether, Enoch lived 365 y, 9102
    5:25 When Methuselah had lived 187 y, 9102
    5:26 Methuselah lived 782 y and had other sons 9102
    5:27 Altogether, Methuselah lived 969 y, 9102
    5:28 Lamech had lived 182 y, he had a son. 9102
    5:30 Lamech lived 595 y and had other sons 9102
    5:31 Altogether, Lamech lived 777 y, 9102
    5:32 After Noah was 500 y old, 9102
    6: 3 his days will be a hundred and twenty y." 9102
    7: 6 Noah was six hundred y old when 9102
    9:28 After the flood Noah lived 350 y. 9102
    9:29 Altogether, Noah lived 950 y, 9102
    11:10 *Two* y after the flood, when Shem was 100 9102
    11:10 when Shem was 100 y old, 9102
    11:11 Shem lived 500 y and had other sons 9102
    11:12 When Arphaxad had lived 35 y, 9102
    11:13 Arphaxad lived 403 y and had other sons 9102
    11:14 When Shelah had lived 30 y, 9102
    11:15 Shelah lived 403 y and had other sons 9102
    11:16 When Eber had lived 34 y, 9102
    11:17 Eber lived 430 y and had other sons 9102
    11:18 When Peleg had lived 30 y, 9102
    11:19 Peleg lived 209 y and had other sons 9102
    11:20 When Reu had lived 32 y, 9102
    11:21 Reu lived 207 y and had other sons 9102
    11:22 When Serug had lived 30 y, 9102
    11:23 Serug lived 200 y and had other sons 9102
    11:24 When Nahor had lived 29 y, 9102
    11:25 Nahor lived 119 y and had other sons 9102
    11:26 After Terah had lived 70 y, 9102
    11:32 Terah lived 205 y, and he died in Haran. 9102
    12: 4 Abram was seventy-five y old when he set 9102
    14: 4 For twelve y they had been subject 9102
    15: 9 a goat and a ram, each **three** y old, 8992
    15:13 be enslaved and mistreated four hundred y. 9102
    16: 3 Abram had been living in Canaan ten y. 9102
    16:16 Abram was eighty-six y old when Hagar 9102
    17: 1 When Abram was ninety-nine y old, 9102
    17:17 a son be born to a man a hundred y old? 9102
    17:24 Abraham was ninety-nine y old 9102
    18:11 already old and well advanced in y, 3427
    21: 5 Abraham was a hundred y old 9102
    23: 1 to be a hundred and twenty-seven y *old*. 9102
    24: 1 now old and well advanced in y, 3427
    25: 7 Abraham lived a hundred and seventy-five y 9102
    25: 8 an old man and full of y; NIH
    25:17 Ishmael lived a hundred and thirty-seven y. 9102
    25:20 and Isaac was forty y old when he married 9102
    25:26 Isaac was sixty y old when Rebekah gave 9102
    26:34 When Esau was forty y old, 9102
    29:18 "I'll work for you seven y in return 9102
    29:20 So Jacob served seven y to get Rachel, 9102
    29:27 in return for another seven y *of* work." 9102
    29:30 And he worked for Laban another seven y. 9102
    31:38 "I have been with you for twenty y now. 9102
    31:41 for the twenty y I was in your household. 9102
    31:41 for you fourteen y for your two daughters 9102

Ge 31:41 two daughters and six y for your flocks, 9102
    35:28 Isaac lived a hundred and eighty y. 9102
    35:29 gathered to his people, old and full of y. 3427
    41: 1 When *two* **full** y had passed, 3427+9102
    41:26 The seven good cows are seven y, 9102
    41:26 the seven good heads of grain are seven y; 9102
    41:27 that came up afterward are seven y, and 9102
    41:27 They are seven y of famine. 9102
    41:29 Seven y of great abundance are coming 9102
    41:30 but seven y of famine will follow them. 9102
    41:34 of Egypt during the seven y of abundance. 9102
    41:35 of these good y that are coming and store 9102
    41:36 to be used during the seven y of famine 9102
    41:46 Joseph was thirty y old when he entered 9102
    41:47 During the seven y of abundance 9102
    41:48 in those seven y of abundance in Egypt 9102
    41:50 Before the y of famine came, 9102
    41:53 The seven y of abundance in Egypt came 9102
    41:54 and the seven y of famine began, 9102
    45: 6 For two y now there has been famine in 9102
    45: 6 *for* the next five y there will not be plowing 9102
    45:11 because five y of famine are still to come. 9102
    47: 9 "The y of my pilgrimage are a hundred 3427+9102
    47: 9 My y have been few and difficult, 3427+9102
    47: 9 the y of the pilgrimage of my fathers." 3427+9102
    47:28 Jacob lived in Egypt seventeen y, 9102
    47:28 and the y *of* his life were a hundred 3427+9102
    50:22 He lived a hundred and ten y 9102
Ex 6:16 Levi lived 137 y. 9102
    6:18 Kohath lived 133 y. 9102
    6:20 Amram lived 137 y. 9102
    7: 7 Moses was eighty y old and Aaron 9102
    12:40 Israelite people lived in Egypt was 430 y. 9102
    12:41 At the end of the 430 y, to the very day, 9102
    16:35 The Israelites ate manna forty y, 9102
    21: 2 he is to serve you *for* six y. 9102
    23:10 "For six y you are to sow your fields 9102
    30:14 those twenty y old or more, 9102
    38:26 twenty y old or more, a total of 603,550 9102
Lev 19:23 *For* three y you are to consider it forbidden; 9102
    25: 3 *For* six y sow your fields, 9102
    25: 3 and *for* six y prune your vineyards 9102
    25: 8 " 'Count off seven sabbaths of y— 9102
    25: 8 seven times seven y—so that the seven 9102
    25: 8 of y amount to a period of forty-nine years. 9102
    25: 8 of years amount to a period of forty-nine y. 9102
    25:15 on the basis of the number of y since 9102
    25:15 to you on the basis of the number of y *left* 9102
    25:16 When the y are many, 9102
    25:16 and when the y are few, 9102
    25:21 that the land will yield enough for three y. 9102
    25:27 he is to determine the value for the y 9102
    25:50 to a hired man for that number of y. 9102
    25:51 If many y remain, he must pay for 9102
    25:52 a few y remain until the Year of Jubilee, 9102
    26:34 the land will enjoy its sabbath y all the time NIH
    27: 6 a person between one month and five y, 9102
    27: 7 If it is a person sixty y old or more, 9102
    27:18 according to the number of y that remain 9102
Nu 1: 3 in Israel twenty y old or more who are able 9102
    1:18 the men twenty y old or more were listed 9102
    1:20 All the men twenty y old or more 9102
    1:22 All the men twenty y old or more 9102
    1:24 All the men twenty y old or more 9102
    1:26 All the men twenty y old or more 9102
    1:28 All the men twenty y old or more 9102
    1:30 All the men twenty y old or more 9102
    1:32 All the men twenty y old or more 9102
    1:34 All the men twenty y old or more 9102
    1:36 All the men twenty y old or more 9102
    1:38 All the men twenty y old or more 9102
    1:40 All the men twenty y old or more 9102
    1:42 All the men twenty y old or more 9102
    1:45 All the Israelites twenty y old or more 9102
    4: 3 Count all the men from thirty to fifty y 9102
    4:23 Count all the men from thirty to fifty y 9102
    4:30 Count all the men from thirty to fifty y 9102
    4:35 from thirty to fifty y of age who came 9102
    4:39 from thirty to fifty y of age who came 9102
    4:43 from thirty to fifty y of age who came 9102
    4:47 from thirty to fifty y of age who came to do 9102
    8:24 Men twenty-five y old or more shall come 9102
    13:22 (Hebron had been built seven y before 9102
    14:29 every one of you twenty y old or more 9102
    14:33 be shepherds here *for* forty y, 9102
    14:34 *For* forty y—one year for each of the forty 9102
    20:15 and we lived there many y. 3427
    26: 2 all those twenty y old or more who are able 9102
    26: 4 a census of the men twenty y old or more, 9102
    32:11 of the men twenty y old or more who came 9102
    32:13 he made them wander in the desert forty y, 9102
    33:39 and twenty-three y old when he died 9102
Dt 2: 7 forty y the LORD your God has been with you, 9102
    2:14 Thirty-eight y passed from the time we left 9102
    8: 2 the way in the desert these forty y, 9102
    8: 4 not swell *during* these forty y. 9102
    14:28 At the end of every three y, 9102
    15: 1 of every seven y you must cancel debts. 9102
    15:12 sells himself to you and serves you six y, 9102
    15:18 to you these six y has been worth twice 9102
    29: 5 the forty y that I led you through the desert, 9102
    30:20 he will give you **many** y in the land 802+3427
    31: 2 and twenty y old and I am no longer able 9102
    31:10 "At the end of every seven y, 9102
    34: 7 a hundred and twenty y old when he died, 9102
Jos 5: 6 moved about in the desert forty y until all 9102

Jos	13: 1	Joshua was old and well advanced in y,	3427
	14: 7	I was forty y old when Moses the servant of	9102
	14:10	he has kept me alive for forty-five y since	9102
	14:10	So here I am today, eighty-five y old!	9102
	23: 1	Joshua, by then old and well advanced in y,	3427
	23: 2	"I am old and well advanced in y.	3427
Jdg	3: 8	the Israelites were subject for eight y.	9102
	3:11	So the land had peace for forty y,	9102
	3:14	to Eglon king of Moab for eighteen y.	9102
	3:30	and the land had peace for eighty y.	9102
	4: 3	oppressed the Israelites for twenty y,	9102
	5:31	Then the land had peace forty y.	9102
	6: 1	for seven y he gave them into the hands of	9102
	6:25	your father's herd, the one seven y old.	9102
	8:28	the land enjoyed peace forty y.	9102
	9:22	Abimelech had governed Israel three y,	9102
	10: 2	He led Israel twenty-three y;	9102
	10: 3	who led Israel twenty-two y.	9102
	10: 8	For eighteen y they oppressed all	9102
	11:26	three hundred y Israel occupied Heshbon,	9102
	12: 7	Jephthah led Israel six y.	9102
	12: 9	Ibzan led Israel seven y.	9102
	12:11	Elon the Zebulunite led Israel ten y.	9102
	12:14	He led Israel eight y.	9102
	13: 1	into the hands of the Philistines for forty y.	9102
	15:20	Samson led Israel for twenty y in the days	9102
	16:31	He had led Israel twenty y.	9102
Ru	1: 4	After they had lived there about ten y,	9102
1Sa	4:15	who was ninety-eight y old	9102
	4:18	He had led Israel forty y.	9102
	7: 2	It was a long time, twenty y in all,	9102
	13: 1	Saul was [thirty] y old when he became king	9102
	13: 1	and he reigned over Israel [forty-]two y.	9102
	17:12	and well advanced in y.	NIH
2Sa	2:10	Ish-Bosheth son of Saul was forty y old	9102
	2:10	and he reigned two y.	9102
	2:11	of Judah was seven y and six months.	9102
	4: 4	was five y old when the news	9102
	5: 4	David was thirty y old when he became	9102
	5: 4	and he reigned forty y.	9102
	5: 5	In Hebron he reigned over Judah seven y	9102
	5: 5	over all Israel and Judah thirty-three y.	9102
	13:23	Two y later, when Absalom's sheepshearers	
		were at Baal Hazor	3427+9102
	13:38	he stayed there three y.	9102
	14:28	Absalom lived two y in Jerusalem	3427+9102
	15: 7	At the end of four y, Absalom said	9102
	19:32	a very old man, eighty y of age.	9102
	19:34	"How many more y will I live,	9102
	19:35	I am now eighty y old.	9102
	21: 1	a famine for three successive y;	339+9102+9102
	24:13	upon you three y of famine in your land?	9102
1Ki	1: 1	David was old and well advanced in y,	3427
	2:11	He had reigned forty y over Israel—	9102
	2:11	seven y in Hebron and thirty-three	9102
	2:39	But three y later, two of Shimei's slaves	9102
	6:38	He had spent seven y building it.	9102
	7: 1	It took Solomon thirteen y, however,	9102
	9:10	At the end of twenty y,	9102
	10:22	Once every three y it returned,	9102
	11:42	in Jerusalem over all Israel forty y.	9102
	14:20	He reigned for twenty-two y and	9102
	14:21	He was forty-one y old when he became	9102
	14:21	and he reigned seventeen y in Jerusalem,	9102
	15: 2	and he reigned in Jerusalem three y.	9102
	15:10	and he reigned in Jerusalem forty-one y.	9102
	15:25	and he reigned over Israel two y.	9102
	15:33	and he reigned twenty-four y.	9102
	16: 8	and he reigned in Tirzah two y.	9102
	16:23	and he reigned twelve y,	9102
	16:29	in Samaria over Israel twenty-two y.	9102
	17: 1	in the next few y except at my word."	9102
	22: 1	For three y there was no war	9102
	22:42	Jehoshaphat was thirty-five y old	9102
	22:42	and he reigned in Jerusalem twenty-five y.	9102
	22:51	and he reigned over Israel two y.	9102
2Ki	3: 1	and he reigned twelve y.	9102
	8: 1	a famine in the land that will last seven y."	9102
	8: 2	in the land of the Philistines seven y.	9102
	8: 3	the seven y she came back from the land of	9102
	8:17	He was thirty-two y old when he became	9102
	8:17	and he reigned in Jerusalem eight y.	9102
	8:26	Ahaziah was twenty-two y old	9102
	10:36	over Israel in Samaria was twenty-eight y.	9102
	11: 3	the LORD for six y while Athaliah ruled	9102
	11:21	Joash was seven y old when he began	9102
	12: 1	and he reigned in Jerusalem forty y.	9102
	12: 2	in the eyes of the LORD all the y Jehoiada	3427
	13: 1	and he reigned seventeen y.	9102
	13:10	and he reigned sixteen y.	9102
	14: 2	He was twenty-five y old when he became	9102
	14: 2	and he reigned in Jerusalem twenty-nine y.	9102
	14:17	for fifteen y after the death of Jehoash son	9102
	14:21	took Azariah, who was sixteen y old,	9102
	14:23	and he reigned forty-one y.	9102
	15: 2	He was sixteen y old when he became king,	9102
	15: 2	and he reigned in Jerusalem fifty-two y.	9102
	15:17	and he reigned in Samaria ten y.	9102
	15:23	and he reigned two y.	9102
	15:27	and he reigned twenty y.	9102
	15:33	He was twenty-five y old when he became	9102
	15:33	and he reigned in Jerusalem sixteen y.	9102
	16: 2	Ahaz was twenty y old when he became	9102
	16: 2	and he reigned in Jerusalem sixteen y.	9102
	17: 1	and he reigned nine y.	9102
	17: 5	and laid siege to it for three y.	9102
	18: 2	He was twenty-five y old when he became	9102

2Ki	18: 2	and he reigned in Jerusalem twenty-nine y.	9102
	18:10	At the end of three y the Assyrians took it.	9102
	20: 6	I will add fifteen y to your life.	9102
	21: 1	Manasseh was twelve y old when he became	9102
	21: 1	and he reigned in Jerusalem fifty-five y.	9102
	21:19	Amon was twenty-two y old	9102
	21:19	and he reigned in Jerusalem two y.	9102
	22: 1	Josiah was eight y old when he became	9102
	22: 1	and he reigned in Jerusalem thirty-one y.	9102
	23:31	Jehoahaz was twenty-three y old	9102
	23:36	Jehoiakim was twenty-five y old	9102
	23:36	and he reigned in Jerusalem eleven y.	9102
	24: 1	Jehoiakim became his vassal for three y.	9102
	24: 8	Jehoiachin was eighteen y old	9102
	24:18	Zedekiah was twenty-one y old	9102
	24:18	and he reigned in Jerusalem eleven y.	9102
1Ch	2:21	married her when he was sixty y old;	9102
	3: 4	where he reigned seven y and six months.	9102
	3: 4	David reigned in Jerusalem thirty-three y,	9102
	21:12	three y of famine, three months	9102
	23: 1	When David was old and full of y,	3427
	23: 3	The Levites thirty y old or more	9102
	23:24	that is, the workers twenty y old or more	9102
	23:27	from those twenty y old or more.	9102
	27:23	the number of the men twenty y old or less,	9102
	29:27	He ruled over Israel forty y—	9102
2Ch	8: 1	At the end of twenty y,	9102
	9:21	Once every three y it returned,	9102
	9:30	in Jerusalem over all Israel forty y.	9102
	11:17	Rehoboam son of Solomon three y,	9102
	12:13	He was forty-one y old when he became	9102
	12:13	and he reigned seventeen y in Jerusalem,	9102
	13: 2	and he reigned in Jerusalem three y.	9102
	14: 1	the country was at peace for ten y.	9102
	14: 6	No one was at war with him during those y,	9102
	17: 3	because in his early y he walked in	NIH
	18: 2	Some y later he went down to	4200+7891+9102
	20:31	He was thirty-five y old when he became	9102
	20:31	and he reigned in Jerusalem twenty-five y.	9102
	21: 5	Jehoram was thirty-two y old	9102
	21: 5	and he reigned in Jerusalem eight y.	9102
	21:20	Jehoram was thirty-two y old	NIH
	21:20	and he reigned in Jerusalem eight y.	9102
	22: 2	Ahaziah was twenty-two y old	9102
	22:12	with them at the temple of God for six y	9102
	24: 1	Joash was seven y old when he became	9102
	24: 1	and he reigned in Jerusalem forty y.	9102
	24: 2	the LORD all the y of Jehoiada the priest.	3427
	24:15	Now Jehoiada was old and full of y,	3427
	25: 1	Amaziah was twenty-five y old	9102
	25: 1	and he reigned in Jerusalem twenty-nine y.	9102
	25: 5	then mustered those twenty y old or more	9102
	25:25	for fifteen y after the death of Jehoash son	9102
	26: 1	who was sixteen y old,	9102
	26: 3	Uzziah was sixteen y old when he became	9102
	26: 3	and he reigned in Jerusalem fifty-two y.	9102
	27: 1	Jotham was twenty-five y old	9102
	27: 1	and he reigned in Jerusalem sixteen y.	9102
	27: 5	also in the second and third y.	9102
	27: 8	He was twenty-five y old when he became	9102
	27: 8	and he reigned in Jerusalem sixteen y.	9102
	28: 1	Ahaz was twenty y old when he became	9102
	28: 1	and he reigned in Jerusalem sixteen y.	9102
	29: 1	Hezekiah was twenty-five y old	9102
	29: 1	and he reigned in Jerusalem twenty-nine y.	9102
	31:16	they distributed to the males three y old	9102
	31:17	and likewise to the Levites twenty y old	9102
	33: 1	Manasseh was twelve y old	9102
	33: 1	and he reigned in Jerusalem fifty-five y.	9102
	33:21	Amon was twenty-two y old	9102
	33:21	and he reigned in Jerusalem two y.	9102
	34: 1	Josiah was eight y old when he became	9102
	34: 1	and he reigned in Jerusalem thirty-one y.	9102
	36: 2	Jehoahaz was twenty-three y old	9102
	36: 5	Jehoiakim was twenty-five y old	9102
	36: 5	and he reigned in Jerusalem eleven y.	9102
	36: 9	Jehoiachin was eighteen y old	9102
	36:11	Zedekiah was twenty-one y old	9102
	36:11	and he reigned in Jerusalem eleven y.	9102
	36:21	the seventy y were completed in fulfillment	9102
Ezr	3: 8	appointing Levites twenty y of age	9102
	5:11	the temple that was built many y ago,	10732
Ne	5:14	until his thirty-second year—twelve y—	9102
	9:21	For forty y you sustained them in	9102
	9:30	For many y you were patient with them.	9102
Job	10: 5	like those of a mortal or your y like those	9102
	15:20	the ruthless through all the y stored up	9102
	16:22	a few y will pass before I go on the journey	9102
	21:13	They spend their y in prosperity and go	3427
	32: 6	"I am young in y, and you are old;	3427
	32: 7	advanced y should teach wisdom.'	9102
	36:11	in prosperity and their y in contentment.	9102
	36:26	The number of his y is past finding out.	9102
	38:21	You have lived so many y!	3427
	42:16	After this, Job lived a hundred and forty y;	9102
	42:17	And so he died, old and full of y.	3427
Ps	31:10	My life is consumed by anguish and my y	9102
	39: 5	the span of my y is as nothing before you.	2698
	61: 6	his y for many generations.	9102
	77: 5	the former days, the y of long ago;	9102
	77:10	the y of the right hand of the Most High."	9102
	78:33	So he ended their days in futility and their y	9102
	90: 4	a thousand y in your sight are like a day	9102
	90: 9	we finish our y with a moan.	9102
	90:10	The length of our days is seventy y—	9102
	90:15	for as many y as we have seen trouble.	9102
	95:10	forty y I was angry with that generation;	9102

Ps	102:24	your y go on through all generations.	9102
	102:27	and your y will never end.	9102
Pr	3: 2	will prolong your life many y	2256+3427+9102
	4:10	and the y of your life will be many.	9102
	5: 9	to others and your y to one who is cruel,	9102
	9:11	and y will be added to your life.	9102
	10:27	but the y of the wicked are cut short.	9102
Ecc	6: 3	a hundred children and live many y;	9102
	6: 6	if he lives a thousand y twice over but fails	9102
	11: 8	However many y a man may live,	9102
	12: 1	and the y approach when you will say,	9102
Isa	7: 8	Within sixty-five y Ephraim will	9102
	16:14	But now the LORD says: "Within three y,	9102
	20: 3	has gone stripped and barefoot for three y,	9102
	23: 15	Tyre will be forgotten for seventy y,	9102
	23:15	But at the end of these seventy y,	9102
	23:17	At the end of seventy y,	9102
	38: 5	I will add fifteen y to your life.	9102
	38:10	and be robbed of the rest of my y?"	9102
	38:15	I will walk humbly all my y because	9102
	65:20	or an old man who does not live out his y;	3427
	65:20	and the old, those weighed down with y.	3427
Jer	6:11	and the y of her punishment	9102
	25: 3	For twenty-three y—from the thirteenth	9102
	25:11	serve the king of Babylon seventy y.	9102
	25:12	"But when the seventy y are fulfilled,	9102
	28: 3	Within two y I will bring back	3427+9102
	28:11	neck of all the nations within two y.'	3427+9102
	29:10	seventy y are completed for Babylon,	9102
	34:14	After he has served you six y,	9102
	52: 1	Zedekiah was twenty-one y old	9102
	52: 1	and he reigned in Jerusalem eleven y.	9102
Eze	4: 5	the same number of days as the y	9102
	12:27	vision he sees is for many y from now,	3427
	22: 4	and the end of your y has come.	9102
	29:11	no one will live there for forty y.	9102
	29:12	and her cities will lie desolate forty	9102
	29:13	of forty y I will gather the Egyptians from	9102
	38: 8	In future y you will invade a land	9102
	38:17	for y that I would bring you against them.	9102
	39: 9	For seven y they will use them for fuel.	9102
Da	1: 5	They were to be trained for three y,	9102
	9: 2	that the desolation of Jerusalem would last	
		seventy y.	9102
	11: 6	After some y, they will become allies.	9102
	11: 8	For some y he will leave the king of	9102
	11:13	and after several y,	2021+6961+9102
	11:20	In a few y, however, he will be destroyed,	3427
Joel	2:25	for the y the locusts have eaten—	9102
Am	1: 1	what he saw concerning Israel two y before	9102
	2:10	and I led you forty y in the desert	9102
	4: 4	your tithes every three y.	3427
	5:25	and offerings forty y in the desert,	9102
Zec	1:12	you have been angry with these seventy y?"	9102
	7: 3	as I have done for so many y?"	9102
	7: 5	and seventh months for the past seventy y,	9102
Mal	3: 4	as in days gone by, as in former y.	9102
Mt	2:16	and its vicinity who were two y old and	1453
	9:20	bleeding for twelve y came up behind him	2291
Mk	5:25	subject to bleeding for twelve y.	2291
	5:42	and walked around (she was twelve y old).	2291
Lk	1: 7	and they were both well along in y.	2465
	1:18	an old man and my wife is well along in y."	2465
	2:36	she had lived with her husband seven y	2291
	2:42	When he was twelve y old,	2291
	3:23	Now Jesus himself was about thirty y old	2291
	4:25	when the sky was shut for three and a half y	2291
	8:43	subject to bleeding for twelve y,	2291
	12:19	of good things laid up for many y.	2291
	13: 7	'For three y now I've been coming to look	2291
	13:11	crippled by a spirit for eighteen y.	2291
	13:16	Satan has kept bound for eighteen long y,	2291
	15:29	All these y I've been slaving for you	2291
Jn	2:20	"It has taken forty-six y to build this temple	2291
	5: 5	an invalid for thirty-eight y.	2291
	8:57	"You are not yet fifty y old,"	2291
Ac	4:22	miraculously healed was over forty y old.	2291
	7: 6	be enslaved and mistreated four hundred y.	2291
	7:23	"When Moses was forty y old,	5478
	7:30	"After forty y had passed,	2291
	7:36	at the Red Sea and for forty y in the desert.	2291
	7:42	and offerings forty y in the desert,	2291
	9:33	a paralytic who had been bedridden for	
		eight y.	2291
	13:18	he endured their conduct for about forty y	5478
	13:20	All this took about 450 y.	2291
	13:21	of the tribe of Benjamin, who ruled forty y.	2291
	19:10	This went on for two y,	2291
	20:31	for three y I never stopped warning each	5562
	24:10	for a number of y you have been a judge	2291
	24:17	"After an absence of several y,	2291
	24:27	When two y had passed,	1454
	28:30	For two whole y Paul stayed there	1454
Ro	4:19	since he was about a hundred y old—	1670
	15:23	I have been longing for many y to see you,	2291
1Co	7:36	and if she is getting along in y	5644
2Co	12:2	in Christ who fourteen y ago was caught up	2291
Gal	1:18	Then after three y, I went up to Jerusalem	2291
	2: 1	Fourteen y later I went up again	2291
	3:17	The law, introduced 430 y later,	2291
	4:10	and months and seasons and y!	1929
Heb	1:12	and your y will never end."	2291
	3: 9	and tried me and for forty y saw what I did.	2291
	3:17	And with whom was he angry for forty y?	2291
Jas	5:17	not rain on the land for three and a half y.	1929
2Pe	3: 8	With the Lord a day is like a thousand y,	2291
	3: 8	and a thousand y are like a day.	2291
Rev	20: 2	or Satan, and bound him for a thousand y.	2291

Rev	20: 3	until the thousand **y** were ended.	2291
	20: 4	and reigned with Christ a thousand **y**.	2291
	20: 5	to life until the thousand **y** were ended.)	2291
	20: 6	and will reign with him *for* a thousand **y**.	2291
	20: 7	When the thousand **y** are over,	2291

YEAST (58)

Ge	19: 3	baking **bread without y**, and they ate.	5174
Ex	12: 8	and **bread made without y**.	5174
	12:15	you are to eat **bread made without y**.	5174
	12:15	On the first day remove the **y** from your	8419
	12:15	whoever eats **anything with y** in it	2809
	12:18	to eat **bread made without y**,	5174
	12:19	For seven days no **y** is to be found	8419
	12:19	whoever eats **anything with y** in it	4721
	12:20	Eat nothing **made with y**.	4721
	12:34	before *the y was* **added**,	2806
	12:39	without **y** because they had been driven out	2806
	13: 3	Eat nothing **containing y**.	2809
	13: 6	For seven days eat **bread made without y**	5174
	13: 7	nothing **with y** in it is to be seen	2809
	13: 7	to be seen among you, nor shall *any* **y**	8419
	23:15	for seven days eat **bread made without y**,	5174
	23:18	along with **anything containing y**.	2809
	29: 2	And from fine wheat flour, **without y**,	5174
	29:23	From the basket of **bread made without y**,	5174
	34:18	For seven days eat **bread made without y**,	5174
	34:25	along with **anything containing y**,	2809
Lev	2: 4	cakes made **without y** and mixed with oil,	5174
	2: 4	wafers made **without y** and spread with oil.	5174
	2: 5	of fine flour mixed with oil, and **without y**,	5174
	2:11	to the LORD must be made without **y**,	2809
	2:11	to burn any **y** or honey in an offering made	8419
	6:16	it is to be eaten **without y** in a holy place;	5174
	6:17	It must not be baked with **y**;	2809
	7:12	**bread made without y** and mixed with oil,	5174
	7:12	wafers **made without y** and spread with oil,	5174
	7:13	offering with cakes of **bread made with y**.	2809
	8: 2	basket containing **bread made without y**,	5174
	8:26	from the basket of **bread made without y**,	5174
	10:12	by fire and eat it **prepared without y** beside	5174
	23: 6	you must eat **bread made without y**.	5174
	23:17	of an ephah of fine flour, baked with **y**, as	2809
Nu	6:15	and a basket of **bread made without y**—	5174
	6:19	both **made without y**.	5174
	28:17	for seven days eat **bread made without y**.	5174
Dt	16: 3	Do not eat it with **bread made with y**,	2809
	16: 4	Let no **y** be found in your possession	8419
Jdg	6:19	an ephah of flour he made **bread without y**,	5174
1Sa	28:24	kneaded it and baked **bread without y**.	5174
Eze	45:21	you shall eat **bread made without y**.	5174
Mt	13:33	like **y** that a woman took and mixed into	2434
	16: 6	on your guard against the **y** of the Pharisees	2434
	16:11	on your guard against the **y** of the Pharisees	2434
	16:12	not telling them to guard against the **y** used	2434
Mk	8:15	the **y** of the Pharisees and that of Herod.”	2434
Lk	12: 1	“Be on your guard against the **y** of	2434
	13:21	like **y** that a woman took and mixed into	2434
1Co	5: 6	a little **y** works through the whole batch	2434
	5: 7	of the old **y** that you may be a new batch	2434
	5: 7	that you may be a new batch **without y**—	109
	5: 8	let us keep the Festival, not with the old **y**,	2434
	5: 8	the **y** of malice and wickedness,	2434
	5: 8	but with **bread without y**,	109
Gal	5: 9	“A little **y** works through the whole batch	2434

YELLING (1) [YELL]

| Ac | 7:57 | **y** at the top of their voices, they all rushed | 3189 |

YELLOW (4)

Lev	13:30	in it is **y** and thin, the priest shall pronounce	7411
	13:32	there is no **y** hair in it and it does	7411
	13:36	the priest does not need to look for **y** hair;	7411
Rev	9:17	fiery red, dark blue, and **y as** sulfur.	2523

YES (97)

Ge	17:19	“**Y, but** your wife Sarah will bear you	66
	18:15	But he said, “**Y, you** did laugh.”	3954+4202
	20: 6	Then God said to him in the dream, “**Y,**	1685
	22: 7	“**Y, my son**?” Abraham replied.	2180
	27:18	“**Y, my son**,” he answered.	2180
	29: 5	“**Y, we know** him,” they answered.	NIH
	29: 6	“**Y, he is**,” they said,	8934S
Ex	2: 8	“**Y, go**,” she answered.	NIH
Jos	2: 4	She said, “**Y, the men** came to me,	4026
	24:22	“**Y, we are** witnesses,” they replied.	NIH
Jdg	5:15	**y**, Issachar was with Barak,	4027
1Sa	10:22	And the LORD said, “**Y, he has** hidden	2180
	16: 5	Samuel replied, “**Y, in** peace;	NIH
	22:12	“**Y, my lord**,” he answered.	2180
	26:17	David replied, “**Y** it is, my lord the king.”	NIH
2Sa	2:19	“**Y,**” they replied, “he is dead.”	NIH
	14:19	from anything my lord the king says. **Y,**	3954
1Ki	2:13	He answered, “**Y, peacefully**.”	NIH
	2:22	**y**, for him and for Abiathar the priest	2256
	14:14	This is the day! What? **Y**, even now.	NIH
	18: 8	“**Y**,” he replied.	638S
	20:33	“**Y, your** brother Ben-Hadad!”	NIH
	21:19	dogs will lick up your blood—**y**, yours!’ ”	1685
2Ki	2: 3	“**Y, I know**,” Elisha replied,	1685
	2: 5	“**Y, I know**,” he replied,	1685
	7:13	**y**, they will only be like all these	2180
Ps	77:11	**y**, I will remember your miracles	3954
	90:17	**y**, establish the work of our hands.	2256

Ecc	11: 2	Give portions to seven, **y** to eight,	1685+2256
Isa	26: 8	**Y, LORD**, walking in the way of your laws,	677
	27: 5	let them make peace with me, **y,**	NIH
	32:13	**y**, mourn for all houses of merriment and	3954
	43:13	**Y**, and from ancient days I am he.	NIH
	44: 7	**y**, let him foretell what will come.	2256
	48: 7	So you cannot say, ‘**Y, I knew** of them.’	2180
	48:15	I, even I, have spoken; **y**, I have called him.	677
	49:25	“**Y, captives** will be taken from warriors,	1685
	52: 6	I who foretold it. **Y, it is I**.”	2180
	57: 6	**Y**, to them you have poured out drink	1685
	63: 7	**y**, the many good things he has done for	2256
Jer	3:22	“**Y, we will** come to you,	2180
	16:20	**Y**, but they are not gods!”	NIH
	23:31	**Y,**” declares the LORD,	2180
	27:21	**y**, this is what the LORD Almighty,	3954
	29: 8	**Y**, this is what the LORD Almighty,	3954
	29:17	**y**, this is what the LORD Almighty says:	NIH
	36:18	“**Y**,” Baruch replied, “he dictated all these	NIH
	37:17	“**Y**,” Jeremiah replied, “you will be handed	3780
Da	7:18	possess it forever—**y**, for ever and ever.’	10221
Hag	2:13	“**Y**,” the priests replied,	NIH
Mal	2: 2	**Y**, I have already cursed them,	1685+2256
Mt	5:37	Simply let your ‘**Y**’ be ‘Yes,’	3721
	5:37	Simply let your ‘Yes’ be ‘**Y**,’	3721
	9:28	“**Y, Lord**,” they replied.	3721
	11: 9	**Y, I tell** you, and more than a prophet.	3721
	11:26	**Y, Father**, for this was your good pleasure.	3721
	13:51	“**Y**,” they replied.	3721
	15:27	“**Y, Lord**,” she said, “but even the dogs eat	3721
	17:25	“**Y**,” he does,” he replied.	3721
	21:16	“**Y**,” replied Jesus, “have you never read,	3721
	26:25	Jesus answered, “**Y, it is** you.”	NIG
	26:64	“**Y, it is** as you say,” Jesus replied.	NIG
	27:11	“**Y, it is** as you say,” Jesus replied.	NIG
Mk	7:28	“**Y, Lord**,” she replied,	3721
	14:30	today—**y**, tonight—before the rooster crows	NIG
	15: 2	“**Y, it is** as you say,” Jesus replied.	NIG
Lk	7:26	**Y, I tell** you, and more than a prophet.	3721
	10:21	**Y, Father**, for this was your good pleasure.	3721
	11:51	**Y, I tell** you, this generation will be held	3721
	12: 5	**Y, I tell** you, fear him.	3721
	14:26	**y**, even his own life—	2285+5445
	22:37	**Y**, what is written about me is reaching	1142
	23: 3	“**Y, it is** as you say,” Jesus replied.	NIG
Jn	5:20	**Y**, to your amazement he will show him	NIG
	7:28	cried out, “**Y**, you know me,	NIG
	11:27	“**Y, Lord**,” she told him,	3721
	21:15	“**Y, Lord**,” he said, “you know that I love	3721
	21:16	He answered, “**Y, Lord**,	3721
Ac	5: 8	“**Y**,” she said, “that is the price.”	3721
	9:10	“**Y, Lord**,” he answered.	1609+2627
	22:27	“**Y**,” he answered.	3721
Ro	3:29	the God of Gentiles too? **Y**, of Gentiles too,	3721
1Co	1:16	(**Y**, I also baptized the household	1254
	9:10	**Y**, this was written for us,	1142
2Co	1:17	**Y, yes** and “No, no”?	3721
	1:17	“Yes, **y**” and “No, no”?	3721
	1:18	our message to you is not “**Y**” and “No.”	3721
	1:19	was not “**Y**” and “No,”	3721
	1:19	but in him it has always been “**Y**.”	3721
	1:20	they are “**Y**” in Christ.	3721
Php	1:18	**Y**, and I will continue to rejoice,	247
	4: 3	**Y**, and I ask you, loyal yokefellow,	3721
Jas	5:12	Let your “**Y**” be yes, and your “No,” no,	3721
	5:12	Let your “Yes” be **y**, and your “No,” no,	3721
Rev	14:13	“**Y**,” says the Spirit, “they will rest	3721
	16: 7	And I heard the altar respond: “**Y**,	3721
	22:20	He who testifies to these things says, “**Y**,	3721

YESTERDAY (8)

Ex	5:14	meet your quota of bricks **y** or today,	9453
1Sa	20:27	come to the meal, either **y** or today?”	9453
2Sa	15:20	You came only **y**.	9453
2Ki	9:26	‘**Y** I saw the blood of Naboth and the blood	621
Job	8: 9	for we were born only **y** and know nothing,	9453
Jn	4:52	“The fever left him **y** at the seventh hour.”	2396
Ac	7:28	to kill me as you killed the Egyptian **y**?’	2396
Heb	13: 8	Jesus Christ is the same **y** and today	2396

YESTERNIGHT (KJV) See LAST NIGHT

YET (404)

Ge	2: 5	**no** shrub of the field had **y** appeared	3270
	2: 5	**no** plant of the field had **y** sprung up	3270+3972
	15:16	for the sin of the Amorites has not **y**	2178+6330
	21: 7	**Y** I have borne him a son in his old age.”	3954
	31: 7	**y** your father has cheated me	2256
	31:43	**Y** what can I do today	2256
	32:30	**and y** my life was spared.”	2256
Ex	5:16	we are told, ‘Make bricks!’	2256
	5:18	**y** you must produce your full quota	2256
	7:13	**Y** Pharaoh’s heart became hard	2256
	9: 7	**Y** his heart was unyielding and he would	2256
	10: 7	Do you **not y** realize that Egypt is ruined?”	3270
	10:23	**Y** all the Israelites had light in the places	2256
	21:36	the owner did not keep it penned up,	2256
	34: 7	**Y** he does not leave the guilty unpunished;	2256
Lev	19:20	**Y** they are not to be put to death,	NIH
	21:23	**y** because of his defect,	421
	22: 3	ceremonially unclean **and y** comes near	2256
	22:13	**y** has no children,	2256
	26:44	**Y** in spite of this, when they are in the	677+2256
Nu	11:26	the Spirit **also** rested on them,	2256
	14:18	**Y** he does not leave the guilty unpunished;	2256

Nu	24:22	**y** you Kenites will be destroyed	561+3954
Dt	1:39	your children who do not **y** know good	2021+3427
	10:15	**Y** the LORD set his affection on your	8370
	12: 9	not **y** reached the resting place and	6380+6964
	34: 7	**y** his eyes were not weak	NIH
Jos	3:15	**Y** as soon as the priests who carried	8370
	11:13	**Y** Israel did not burn any of the cities built	8370
	17:12	**Y** the Manassites were not able	2256
	18: 2	not **y received** their inheritance.	AIT
Jdg	2: 2	**Y** you have disobeyed me.	2256
	2:17	**Y** they would not listen to their judges	1685+2256
	8: 4	exhausted **y** keeping up the pursuit.	2256
	18: 1	they had not **y** come into an inheritance	2021+2021+2085+3427+6330
1Sa	3: 3	The lamp of God had **not y** gone out,	3270
	3: 7	Now Samuel did **not y** know the LORD:	3270
	3: 7	of the LORD had **not y** been revealed	3270
	10:22	“Has the man come here **y**?”	6388
	12:20	**y** do not turn away from the LORD,	421
	12:25	**Y** if you persist in doing evil,	2256
	14:26	**y** no one put his hand to his mouth,	2256
	20: 3	**y** as surely as the LORD lives and	219
	22:17	**y** they did not tell me.”	2256
	25:15	**Y** these men were very good to us.	2256
2Sa	3: 8	**Y** now you accuse me of an offense	2256
1Ki	3: 2	a temple had not **y** been built for the Name of the LORD.	2021+2021+2156+3427+6330
	8:28	**Y** give attention to your servant’s prayer	2256
	11:13	**Y** I will not tear the whole kingdom	8370
	18:12	**Y** I your servant have worshiped	2256
	19:18	**Y** I reserve seven thousand in Israel—	2256
	22: 3	that Ramoth Gilead belongs to us **and y**	2256
2Ki	2:10	“**y** if you see me when I am taken	561
	3:17	**y** this valley will be filled with water,	2256
	10:31	**Y** Jehu was not careful to keep the law of	2256
	14: 6	**Y** he did not put the sons of the assassins	2256
1Ch	5: 2	“**Y** the LORD, the God of Israel,	2256
2Ch	6:19	**Y** give attention to your servant’s prayer	2256
	13: 6	**Y** Jeroboam son of Nebat,	2256
	16: 8	**Y** when you relied on the LORD,	2256
	25: 4	**Y** he did not put their sons to death,	2256
	30:18	**y** they ate the Passover,	3954
Ezr	3: 6	the **foundation** of the LORD’s temple *had* not **y been laid.**	AIT
	5:16	under construction but is **not y** finished.”	AIT
	9:13	of our evil deeds and our great guilt, and **y**,	3954
Ne	2:16	because as **y** I had said nothing to the Jews	4027
	5: 5	**y** we have to subject our sons	2256
	7: 4	and the houses had **not y** been rebuilt.	AIT
	9:30	**Y** they paid no attention,	2256
Est	3: 4	**Y** having learned who Mordecai’s people	3954
Job	1:18	**y** another messenger came and said,	2256
	4:10	**y** the teeth of the great lions are broken.	2256
	5: 7	**Y** man is born to trouble as surely	3954
	8:21	He will **y** fill your mouth with laughter	6330
	11:13	“**Y** if you devote your heart to him	561
	13:15	Though he slay me, **y** I will hope in him;	NIH
	14: 9	**y** at the scent of water it will bud	NIH
	16: 6	“**Y** if I speak, my pain is not relieved;	561
	16:17	**y** my hands have been free of violence	6584
	19:26	in my flesh I will see God;	2256
	20:14	**y** his food will turn sour in his stomach;	NIH
	21:14	**Y** they say to God, ‘Leave us alone!	2256
	21:17	“**Y** how often is the lamp of the wicked	NIH
	22:13	**Y** you say, ‘What does God know?	2256
	22:18	**Y** it was he who filled their houses	2256
	23:17	**Y** I am not silenced by the darkness,	3954
	24:11	they tread the winepresses, **y** suffer thirst.	2256
	24:18	“**Y** they are foam on the surface of	NIH
	26: 8	**y** the clouds do not burst	2256
	30:26	**Y** when I hoped for good, evil came;	3954
	32: 3	**and y** had condemned him.	2256
	33:10	**Y** God has found fault with me;	2176
	33:23	“**Y** if there is an angel on his side as	561
	34:29	**Y** he is over man and nation alike,	2256
	35: 3	**Y** you ask him, ‘What profit is it to me,	3954
	39:18	**Y** when she spreads her feathers to run,	3869
	40:19	**y** his Maker can approach him	NIH
Ps	22: 3	**Y** you are enthroned as the Holy One;	2256
	22: 9	**Y** you brought me out of the womb;	3954
	22:31	his righteousness to a people **y unborn**—	3528
	31:22	**Y** you heard my cry for mercy	434
	35:13	**Y** when they were ill,	2256
	37:25	**y** I have never seen the righteous forsaken	2256
	40:17	**Y** I am poor and needy;	2256
	42:11	for I will **y** praise him,	6388
	42:11	for I will **y** praise him.	6388
	43: 5	for I will **y** praise him,	6388
	44:22	**Y** for your sake we face death all day long;	3954
	55:21	**y** war is in his heart;	2256
	55:21	**y** they are drawn swords.	2256
	59: 4	**y** they are ready to attack me.	NIH
	70: 5	**Y** I am poor and needy;	2256
	73:23	**Y** I am always with you;	2256
	78: 6	even the children **y** to be **born**,	AIT
	78:23	**Y** he gave a command to the skies above	2256
	78:38	**Y** he was merciful;	2256
	90:10	**y** their span is but trouble and sorrow,	2256
	102:18	that a people **not y created** may praise	1343
	106: 8	**Y** he saved them for his name’s sake,	2256
	119:151	**Y** you are near, O LORD,	NIH
	141: 5	**Y** my prayer is ever against the deeds	3954
Pr	6: 8	**y** it stores its provisions in summer	NIH
	6:31	**Y** if he is caught, he must pay sevenfold,	2256
	11:24	One man gives freely, **y** gains even more;	2256
	12: 9	a nobody **and y** have a servant than pretend	2256
	13: 7	One man pretends to be rich, **y** has nothing;	2256

Ref	Text	Num
Pr 13: 7	pretends to be poor, y has great wealth.	2256
19: 3	y his heart rages against the LORD.	2256
28:21	y a man will do wrong for a piece of bread.	2256
30:12	those who are pure in their own eyes and y	2256
30:24	y they are extremely wise:	2256
30:25	y they store up their food in the summer;	2256
30:26	y they make their home in the crags;	2256
30:27	y they advance together in ranks;	2256
30:28	y it is found in kings' palaces.	2256
Ecc 1: 7	y the sea is never full.	2256
1:11	and even those who are y to come will not	340
2:11	Y when I surveyed all that my hands	2256
2:19	Y he will have control over all the work	2256
3:11	y they cannot fathom what God has done	889+1172+4946
4: 3	better than both is he who has not y been,	6362
4: 8	y his eyes were not content with his wealth.	1685
6: 3	y no matter how long he lives,	2256
6: 7	y his appetite is never satisfied.	1685+2256
8:13	Y because the wicked do not fear God,	2256
SS 1: 5	Dark am I, y, lovely,	2256
8: 8	and her breasts are not y grown.	AIT
Isa 5:25	Y for all this, his anger is not turned away,	NIH
7: 7	Y this is what the Sovereign LORD says:	NIH
9:12	Y for all this, his anger is not turned away,	NIH
9:17	Y for all this, his anger is not turned away,	NIH
9:21	Y for all this, his anger is not turned away,	NIH
10: 4	Y for all this, his anger is not turned away,	NIH
17: 6	Y some gleanings will remain,	2256
17:11	y the harvest will be as nothing in the day	NIH
21:12	and come back y again."	NIH
23:18	Y her profit and her earnings will	2256
29: 2	Y I will besiege Ariel;	2256
30:18	Y the LORD longs to be gracious to you;	4027+4200
31: 2	Y he too is wise and can bring disaster;	2256
42:25	y they did not understand;	2256
43:22	"Y you have not called upon me, O Jacob,	2256
44: 7	and what is y to come—	AIT
49: 4	Y what is due me is in the LORD's hand,	434
49:20	during your bereavement will y say	6388
53: 4	y we considered him stricken by God,	2256
53: 7	y he did not open his mouth;	2256
53:10	Y it was the LORD's will to crush him	2256
54:10	y my unfailing love for you will not	2256
57:17	y he kept on in his willful ways.	2256
58: 3	"Y on the day of your fasting,	2176
63:10	Y they rebelled and grieved his Holy Spirit.	2256
64: 8	Y, O LORD, you are our Father.	2256+6964
65: 8	there is y some good in it,'	3954
66: 5	Y they will be put to shame.	2256
66: 8	Y no sooner is Zion in labor than	3954
Jer 2:11	(Y they are not gods at all.)	2256
2:27	y when they are in trouble, they say,	2256
2:32	Y my people have forgotten me,	2256
2:34	Y in spite of all this	3954
3: 3	Y you have the brazen look of a prostitute;	2256
3: 8	Y I saw that her unfaithful sister Judah had	2256
5: 7	y they committed adultery and thronged to	2256
5:18	"Y even in those days,"	2256
10:19	Y I said to myself, "This is my sickness,	2256
12: 1	Y I would speak with you	421
12: 3	Y you know me, O LORD;	2256
14:15	I did not send them, y they are saying,	2256
15:10	y everyone curses me.	NIH
17:23	Y they did not listen or pay attention;	2256
18:15	Y my people have forgotten me;	3954
18:20	Y they have dug a pit for me.	3954
23:21	y they have run with their message;	2256
23:21	y they have prophesied.	2256
23:31	prophets who wag their own tongues and y	2256
23:32	y I did not send or appoint them.	2256
28:15	y you have persuaded this nation to trust	2256
33:10	Y in the towns of Judah and the streets	NIH
34: 4	"'Y hear the promise of the LORD,	421
35:14	y you have not obeyed me.	2256
37: 4	for he had not y been put in prison.	AIT
48:47	"Y I will restore the fortunes of Moab	2256
49: 6	"Y afterward, I will restore the fortunes of	2256
49:39	"Y I will restore the fortunes of Elam	2256
50:34	Y their Redeemer is strong;	NIH
La 1:18	y I rebelled against his command.	3954
3:21	Y this I call to mind and	NIH
3:29	there may y be hope.	218
Eze 5: 6	Y in her wickedness she has rebelled	2256
11:16	and scattered them among the countries, y	2256
13: 6	y they expect their words to be fulfilled.	2256
14:22	Y there will be some survivors—	2256
15: 7	the fire will consume them.	AIT
16:60	Y I will remember the covenant I made	2256
17:15	Will he break the treaty and y escape?	2256
17:18	in pledge and y did all these things,	2256
18:19	"Y you ask, 'Why does the son not share	2256
18:25	"Y you say, 'The way of the Lord is	2256
18:29	Y the house of Israel says,	2256
20:13	"'Y the people of Israel rebelled	2256
20:17	Y I looked on them with pity and did	2256
20:38	y they will not enter the land of Israel.	2256
23:11	y in her lust and prostitution she was	2256
23:19	Y she became more and more promiscuous	2256
24:16	Y do not lament or weep or shed any tears.	2256
29:13	"'Y this is what the Sovereign LORD says:	3954
29:18	Y he and his army got no reward from	2256
31:18	Y you, too, will be brought down with	2256
33:17	"Y your countrymen say,	2256
33:20	Y, O house of Israel, you say,	2256
33:24	y he possessed the land.	2256

Ref	Text	Num
Eze 36:20	and y they had to leave his land.'	2256
44:14	Y I will put them in charge of the duties of	2256
Da 2:41	y it will have some of the strength of iron	10221
8:25	Y he will be destroyed,	NIH
9:13	y we have not sought the favor of the LORD	2256
9:14	y we have not obeyed him.	2256
10:14	for the vision concerns a time y to come."	6388
11:12	y he will not remain triumphant.	2256
11:20	y not in anger or in battle.	2256
11:45	Y he will come to his end,	2256
Hos 1: 7	Y I will show love to the house of Judah;	2256
1:10	"Y the Israelites will be like the sand on	2256
9: 8	y snares await him on all his paths,	NIH
Am 4: 4	go to Gilgal and sin y more.	8049
4: 6	y you have not returned to me,"	2256
4: 8	y you have not returned to me,"	2256
4: 9	y you have not returned to me,"	2256
4:10	y you have not returned to me,"	2256
4:11	y you have not returned to me,"	2256
9: 8	Y I will not totally destroy the house	700+3954
Jnh 2: 4	y I will look again toward your holy temple	421
3: 9	God may y relent and with compassion turn	NIH
Mic 3:11	Y they lean upon the LORD and say,	2256
Na 2: 5	y they stumble on their way.	NIH
3:10	Y she was taken captive and went	1685
Hab 3:16	Y I will wait patiently for the day	889
3:18	y I will rejoice in the LORD,	2256
Zep 3: 5	y the unrighteous know no shame.	2256
Hag 1: 2	not y come for the LORD's house to	AIT
2:17	mildew and hail, y you did not turn to me,'	2256
2:19	Is there y any seed left in the barn?	6388
Zec 8:20	the inhabitants of many cities will y come,	6388
10: 9	y in distant lands they will remember me.	2256
13: 8	y one-third will be left in it.	2256
Mal 1: 2	"Y I have loved Jacob,	2256
3: 8	"Will a man rob God? Y you rob me.	3954
3:13	"Y you ask, 'What have we said	2256
Mt 6:26	and y your heavenly Father feeds them.	2779
6:29	Y I tell you that not even Solomon	1254
7:25	against that house; y it did not fall,	2779
10:29	Y not one of them will fall to the ground	2779
11:11	y he who is least in the kingdom	1254
12: 5	in the temple desecrate the day and y	2779
13:32	y when it grows, it is the largest of	1254
16:26	gains the whole world, y forfeits his soul?	1254
26:39	Y not as I will, but as you will."	4440
28: 8	afraid y filled with joy,	2779
Mk 1:45	Y the people still came to him	2779
4:32	Y when planted, it grows and becomes	2779
5:26	y instead of getting better she grew worse.	247
5:31	his disciples answered, "and y you can ask,	2779
6:20	y he liked to listen to him.	2779
7:24	y he could not keep his presence secret.	2779
8:36	to gain the whole world, y forfeit his soul?	2779
14:36	Y not what I will, but what you will."	247
14:59	Y even then their testimony did not agree.	NIG
Lk 4:26	Y Elijah was not sent to any of them,	2779
4:27	y not one of them was cleansed—	2779
5:15	Y the news about him spread all the more,	1254
7:28	y the one who is least in the kingdom	1254
9:25	and y lose or forfeit his very self?	1254
10:11	Y be sure of this:	4440
11: 8	y because of the man's boldness he will get	1145
12: 6	Y not one of them is forgotten by God.	2779
12:24	no storeroom or barn; y God feeds them.	2779
12:27	Y I tell you, not even Solomon	1254
15:29	Y you never gave me even a young goat	2779
18: 5	y because this widow keeps bothering me,	1145
19:48	Y they could not find any way to do it,	2779
22:42	y not my will, but yours be done."	4440
23:53	one in which no one had y been laid.	4024+4037
Jn 1:12	Y to all who received him,	1254
2: 4	"My time has not y come."	4037
4:23	Y a time is coming and has now come	247
5:40	y you refuse to come to me to have life.	2779
5:44	y make no effort to obtain the praise	2779
6:17	and Jesus had not y joined them.	4037
6:49	the manna in the desert, y they died.	2779
6:64	Y there are some of you who do	247
6:70	Y one of you is a devil!"	2779
7: 6	"The right time for me has not y come;	4037
7: 8	I am not y going up to this Feast,	4037
7: 8	for me the right time has not y come."	4037
7:19	Y not one of you keeps the law.	2779
7:22	Y, because Moses gave you circumcision	NIG
7:30	because his time had not y come.	4037
7:39	since Jesus had not y been glorified.	4031
8:20	Y no one seized him,	2779
8:20	because his time had not y come.	4037
8:37	Y you are ready to kill me,	247
8:45	Y because I tell the truth,	1254
8:52	y you say that if anyone keeps your word,	2779
8:57	"You are not y fifty years old,"	4037
9:30	y he opened my eyes.	2779
11: 6	Y when he heard that Lazarus was sick,	4036
11: 8	and y you are going back there?"	4099
11:30	Now Jesus had not y entered the village,	4037
12:42	Y at the same time many even among	3530
15:24	and y they have hated both me	2779
16: 5	y none of you asks me,	2779
16:13	and he will tell you what is y to come.	NIG
16:32	Y I am not alone, for my Father is with me.	2779
20:17	for I have not y returned to the Father.	4037
20:29	blessed are those who have not seen and y	2779
Ac 2:34	and y he said, "'The Lord said to my Lord:	1254
5:28	"Y you have filled Jerusalem	2779
8:16	the Holy Spirit had not y come upon any	4031

Ref	Text	Num
Ac 9:22	Y Saul grew more and more powerful	1254
13:27	y in condemning him they fulfilled	2779
14:17	Y he has not left himself without testimony:	2792
23: 3	y you yourself violate the law	2779
Ro 2: 6	on them and y do the same things,	2779
2:27	not circumcised physically and y obeys	NIG
4:20	Y he did not waver through unbelief	1254
8:10	y your spirit is alive because	1254
8:25	But if we hope for what we do not y have,	NIG
9:11	Y, before the twins were born	3609
1Co 3: 2	for you were not y ready for it.	4037
8: 2	who thinks he knows something does not y	4037
8: 6	y for us there is but one God, the Father,	247
9:16	Y when I preach the gospel, I cannot boast,	1142
14:10	y none of them is without meaning.	2779
15:10	y not I, but the grace of God that was	1254
2Co 4:16	y inwardly we are being renewed day	247
6: 8	genuine, y regarded as impostors;	2779
6: 9	known, y regarded as unknown;	2779
6: 9	dying, and y we live on;	2627
6: 9	beaten, and y not killed;	2779
6:10	sorrowful, y always rejoicing;	1254
6:10	poor, y making many rich;	1254
6:10	nothing, and y possessing everything.	2779
7: 9	y now I am happy,	NIG
8: 9	y for your sakes he became poor,	NIG
12:16	Y, crafty fellow that I am,	247
13: 4	y he lives by God's power.	247
13: 4	y by God's power we will live with him	247
Gal 2: 3	Y not even Titus, who was with me,	247
2:14	y you live like a Gentile and not like a Jew.	NIG
6:13	y they want you to be circumcised	247
Php 1:22	Y what shall I choose?	2779
3:13	not consider myself y to have taken hold	NIG
4:14	Y it was good of you to share	4440
1Th 4:10	Y we urge you, brothers,	1254
2Th 3:15	Y do not regard him as an enemy,	2779
2Ti 1:12	Y I am not ashamed,	247
3:11	y the Lord rescued me from all of them.	2779
Phm 1: 9	y I appeal to you on the basis of love.	NIG
Heb 2: 8	Y at present we do not see everything	4037
4: 3	And y his work has been finished since	2792
4:15	just as we are—y was without sin.	NIG
7: 6	y he collected a tenth from Abraham	NIG
9: 8	the way into the Most Holy Place had not y	3609
11: 7	when warned about things not y seen,	3596
11:39	for their faith, y none of them received	4037
12: 4	you have not y resisted to the point	4037
Jas 1:26	If anyone considers himself religious and y	NIG
2:10	For whoever keeps the whole law and y	1254
2Pe 2:11	y even angels, although they are stronger	3963
1Jn 1: 6	If we claim to have fellowship with him y	2779
2: 8	Y I am writing you a new command;	4099
3: 2	be has not y been made known.	4037
4:20	"I love God," y hates his brother,	2779
Jude 1:10	Y these men speak abusively against	1254
Rev 2: 4	Y I hold this against you:	247
2: 9	and your poverty—y you are rich!	247
2:13	Y you remain true to my name.	2779
3: 4	Y you have a few people in Sardis who	247
3: 8	y you have kept my word and have	2779
9:12	two other woes are y to come.	3552+4047
13:14	wounded by the sword and y lived.	2779
17: 8	now is not, and y will come.	NIG
17:10	one is, the other has not y come;	4037
17:12	"The ten horns you saw are ten kings who have not y received a kingdom,	4037

YIELD (25) [YIELDED, YIELDING, YIELDS]

Ref	Text	Num
Ge 4:12	it will no longer y its crops for you.	5989
Lev 25:19	Then the land will y its fruit,	5989
25:21	that the land will y enough for three years.	6913
26: 4	the ground will y its crops and the trees of	5989
26:20	because your soil will not y its crops,	5989
26:20	nor will the trees of the land y their fruit.	5989
Dt 11:17	not rain and the ground will y no produce,	5989
13: 8	do not y to him or listen to him,	14
33:14	and the finest the moon can y;	1765
Jos 24:23	that are among you and y your hearts to	5742
2Sa 1:21	nor fields that y offerings [of grain].	AIT
Job 31:39	if I have devoured its y without payment	3946
Ps 67: 6	Then the land will y its harvest, and God,	5989
85:12	and our land will y its harvest.	5989
Pr 8:19	what I y surpasses choice silver.	9311
Isa 5: 4	why did it y only bad?	6913
48:11	I will not y my glory to another.	5989
Eze 34:27	The trees of the field will y their fruit and	5989
34:27	and the ground will y its crops;	5989
36:37	Once again I will y to the plea of	2011
Hos 8: 7	Were it to y grain,	6913
8: 7	their root is without fruit, they y no fruit.	6913
Joel 2:22	the fig tree and the vine y their riches.	5989
Zec 8:12	the vine will y its fruit,	5989
Jas 5: 7	to y its valuable crop and how patient he is	NIG

YIELDED (3) [YIELD]

Ref	Text	Num
Ps 107:37	and planted vineyards that y a fruitful	6913
Isa 5: 2	but it y only bad fruit.	6913
Lk 8: 8	It came up and y a crop,	4472

YIELDING (3) [YIELD]

Ref	Text	Num
SS 5:13	like beds of spice y perfume.	1540
Mt 13:23	He produces a crop, y a hundred,	4472
Rev 22: 2	twelve crops of fruit, y its fruit every month.	625

YIELDS (5) [YIELD]

Lev	25: 6	the land y during the sabbath year will	NIH
Ps	1: 3	which y its fruit in season	5989
Pr	3:14	and y better **returns** than gold.	9311
	14:24	but the folly of fools y folly.	NIH
Isa	55:10	that *it* y seed for the sower and bread for	5989

YOKE (61) [YOKED, YOKEFELLOW, YOKES]

Ge	27:40	you will throw his y from off your neck."	6585
Ex	6: 6	and I will bring you out from under the y	6026
	6: 7	who brought you out from under the y of	6026
Lev	26:13	the bars of your y and enabled you to walk	6585
Nu	19: 2	and that has never been under a y.	6585
Dt	21: 3	and has never worn a y	6585
	28:48	He will put an iron y on your neck	6585
1Ki	12: 4	"Your father put a heavy y *on* us,	6585
	12: 4	the harsh labor and the heavy y he put	6585
	12: 9	'Lighten the y your father put on us'?"	6585
	12:10	'Your father put a heavy y *on* us,	6585
	12:10	but make our y lighter'—	NIH
	12:11	My father laid on you a heavy y;	6585
	12:14	"My father made your y heavy;	6585
	19:19	He was plowing with twelve y **of oxen,**	7538
	19:21	He took his y of oxen	7538
2Ch	10: 4	"Your father put a heavy y *on* us,	6585
	10: 4	the harsh labor and the heavy y he put	6585
	10: 9	'Lighten the y your father put on us'?"	6585
	10:10	'Your father put a heavy y *on* us,	6585
	10:10	but make our y lighter'—	NIH
	10:11	My father laid on you a heavy y;	6585
	10:14	"My father made your y heavy;	6585
Job	1: 3	five hundred y *of* oxen	7538
	42:12	a thousand y *of* oxen and	7538
Isa	9: 4	the y *that* burdens them,	6585
	10:27	their y from your neck;	6585
	10:27	the y will be broken	6585
	14:25	His y will be taken from my people,	6585
	47: 6	Even on the aged you laid a very heavy y.	6585
	58: 6	of injustice and untie the cords of the y,	4574
	58: 6	the oppressed free and break every y?	4574
	58: 9	"If you do away with the y of oppression,	4574
Jer	2:20	"Long ago you broke off your y	6585
	5: 5	the y and torn off the bonds.	6585
	27: 2	a y *out* of straps and crossbars and put it	4593
	27: 8	of Babylon or bow its neck under his y,	6585
	27:11	the y *of* the king of Babylon and serve him,	6585
	27:12	"Bow your neck under the y *of* the king	6585
	28: 2	'I will break the y *of* the king of Babylon.	6585
	28: 4	I will break the y *of* the king of Babylon.' "	6585
	28:10	the y off the neck of the prophet Jeremiah	4574
	28:11	'In the same way will I break the y	6585
	28:12	the prophet Hananiah had broken the y off	4574
	28:13	You have broken a wooden y,	4574
	28:13	but in its place you will get a y *of* iron.	4574
	28:14	an iron y on the necks of all these nations	6585
	30: 8	'I will break the y off their necks	6585
La	1:14	"My sins have been bound into a y;	6585
	3:27	for a man to bear the y while he is young.	6585
Eze	30:18	be the day at Tahpanhes when I break the y	4574
	34:27	of their y and rescue them from the hands	6585
Hos	10:11	so I *will* put a y on her fair neck.	6296
	11: 4	I lifted the y from their neck and bent down	6585
Na	1:13	Now I will break their y from your neck	4573
Mt	11:29	Take my y upon you and learn from me,	2433
	11:30	For my y is easy and my burden is light."	2433
Lk	14:19	'I have just bought five y of oxen,	2414
Ac	15:10	by putting on the necks of the disciples a y	2433
Gal	5: 1	not let yourselves be burdened again *by* a y	2433
1Ti	6: 1	All who are under the y of slavery	2433

YOKED (4) [YOKE]

Dt	22:10	with an ox and a donkey y together.	NIH
1Sa	6: 7	have calved and *have* never been y.	6585+6590
Ps	106:28	*They* y **themselves** to the Baal of Peor	7537
2Co	6:14	Do not be y **together** with unbelievers.	2282

YOKEFELLOW (1) [YOKE]

Php	4: 3	Yes, and I ask you, loyal y,	5187

YOKES (1) [YOKE]

2Sa	24:22	and here are threshing sledges and ox y for	3998

YONDER (KJV) See OTHER, SOME DISTANCE AWAY, THERE

YOU (13727) [YOU'LL, YOU'RE, YOU'VE, YOUR, YOURS, YOURSELF, YOURSELVES] See Index of Articles Etc.

YOU'LL (1) [BE, YOU]

1Sa	19:11	run for your life tonight, tomorrow y be killed."	911

YOU'RE (9) [BE, YOU]

Jdg	4:22	"I will show you the man y looking for."	911
	11: 7	come to me now, when y in trouble?"	4013
1Sa	26:15	David said, **"Y** a man, aren't you?	911
Mt	26:70	"I don't know what y **talking about,"**	AIT
Mk	14:68	"I don't know or understand what y talking	5148
Mk	14:71	"I don't know this man y **talking about."**	AIT
Lk	22:60	I don't know what y **talking about!"**	AIT
Ac	10:21	"I'm the one y **looking for.**	AIT
	12:15	"Y out of *your* **mind,"** they told her.	AIT

YOU'VE (4) [HAVE, YOU]

Ge	31:26	"What have you done? Y **deceived** me,	AIT
	31:26	and y **carried off** my daughters	AIT
Jdg	14:16	Y given my people a riddle,	AIT
	15: 7	"Since y **acted** like this,	AIT

YOUNG (292) [YOUNGER, YOUNGEST, YOUTH, YOUTHFUL, YOUTHS]

Ge	4:23	a y man for injuring me.	3529
	15: 9	along with a dove and a y **pigeon."**	1578
	19: 4	both y and old—surrounded the house.	5853
	19:11	y and old, with blindness so that they could	7785
	27: 9	and bring me two choice y **goats,**	1531+6436
	30:39	And they **bore** y that were streaked	3528
	30:40	the y **of the flock** by themselves,	4166
	31: 8	then all the flocks gave birth to **speckled** y;	AIT
	31: 8	then all the flocks bore **streaked** y.	AIT
	32:15	thirty female camels with their y,	1201
	33:13	the ewes and cows *that are* nursing *their* y.	6402
	34:19	The y **man,** who was the most honored	5853
	37: 2	Joseph, a y **man** of seventeen,	5853
	38:17	"I'll send you a y **goat** from my flock,	1531+6436
	38:20	Judah sent the y **goat** by his friend	1531+6436
	38:23	After all, I did send her this y **goat,**	1531
	41:12	Now a y Hebrew was there with us,	5853
	44:20	there is a y son born to him in his old age.	7783
Ex	10: 9	"We will go with our y and old,	5853
	23:19	"Do not cook a y **goat** in its mother's milk.	1531
	24: 5	Then he sent y Israelite **men,**	5853
	24: 5	sacrificed y **bulls** as fellowship offerings	7228
	29: 1	Take a y bull and two rams without defect.	1201
	33:11	but his y aide Joshua son of Nun did	5853
	34:26	not cook a y **goat** in its mother's milk."	1531
Lev	1: 5	to slaughter the y bull before the LORD,	1201
	1:14	he is to offer a dove or a y **pigeon.**	1201
	4: 3	a y **bull** without defect as a sin offering for	1201
	4:14	a y **bull** as a sin offering and present it	1201
	5: 7	he is to bring two doves or two y pigeons to	1201
	5:11	cannot afford two doves or two y pigeons,	1201
	12: 6	and a y pigeon or a dove for a sin offering.	1201
	12: 8	she is to bring two doves or two y pigeons,	1201
	14:22	and two doves or two y pigeons,	1201
	14:30	the doves or the y pigeons,	1201
	15:14	or two y pigeons and come before	1201
	15:29	or two y pigeons and bring them to	1201
	16: 3	with a y bull for a sin offering and a ram	1201
	22:28	a cow or a sheep and its y on the same day.	1201
	23:18	one y bull and two rams.	1201
Nu	6:10	or two y pigeons to the priest at	1201
	7:15	one y bull, one ram and one male lamb	1201
	7:21	one y bull, one ram and one male lamb	1201
	7:27	one y bull, one ram and one male lamb	1201
	7:33	one y bull, one ram and one male lamb	1201
	7:39	one y bull, one ram and one male lamb	1201
	7:45	one y bull, one ram and one male lamb	1201
	7:51	one y bull, one ram and one male lamb	1201
	7:57	one y bull, one ram and one male lamb	1201
	7:63	one y bull, one ram and one male lamb	1201
	7:69	one y bull, one ram and one male lamb	1201
	7:75	one y bull, one ram and one male lamb	1201
	7:81	one y bull, one ram and one male lamb	1201
	7:87	the burnt offering came to twelve y **bulls,**	7228
	8: 8	a y bull with its grain offering	1201
	8: 8	to take a second y bull for a sin offering.	1201
	11:27	A y **man** ran and told Moses,	5853
	15: 8	a y **bull** as a burnt offering or sacrifice,	1201
	15:11	Each bull or ram, each lamb or y **goat,**	6436
	15:24	the whole community is to offer a y bull for	1201
	28:11	the LORD a burnt offering of two y bulls,	1201
	28:19	a burnt offering of two y bulls,	1201
	28:27	Present a burnt offering of two y bulls,	1201
	29: 2	prepare a burnt offering of one y bull,	1201
	29: 8	the LORD a burnt offering of one y bull,	1201
	29:13	a burnt offering of thirteen y bulls,	1201
	29:17	the second day prepare twelve y bulls,	1201
	30: 3	"When a y woman still living in her father's	5830
	30:16	and his y daughter still living in his house.	5830
Dt	7:14	nor any of your livestock without y.	6829
	14:21	Do not cook a y **goat** in its mother's milk.	1531
	22: 6	the mother is sitting on the y or on the eggs,	711
	22: 6	do not take the mother with the y.	1201
	22: 7	You may take the y,	1201
	28: 4	of your land and the y of your livestock—	7262
	28:11	of your womb, the y *of* your livestock and	7262
	28:50	without respect for the old or pity for the y.	5853
	28:51	They will devour the y of your livestock	7262
	30: 9	the y of your livestock and the crops	7262
	32:11	that stirs up its nest and hovers over its y,	1578
	32:25	**Y** men and young women will perish,	1033
	32:25	Young men and y women will perish,	1435
Jos	6:21	men and women, y and old, cattle,	5853
	6:23	So the y **men** who had done the spying went	5853
Jdg	6:19	Gideon went in, prepared a y **goat,**	1531+6436
	8:14	a y man of Succoth and questioned him,	5853
	8:14	the y man wrote down for him the names of	NIH
	11:40	that each year the y **women** *of* Israel go out	1426
	12: 9	for his sons he brought in thirty y **women**	1426
	13:15	until we prepare a y goat for you."	1531+6436
	13:19	Then Manoah took a y **goat,**	1531+6436
	14: 1	and saw there a y Philistine woman.	1426
Jdg	14: 5	a y **lion** came roaring toward him.	787+4097
	14: 6	as he might have torn a y **goat.**	1531
	15: 1	a y **goat** and went to visit his wife.	1531+6436
	17: 7	A y Levite from Bethlehem in Judah,	5853
	17:11	the y **man** was to him like one of his sons.	5853
	17:12	and the y **man** became his priest and	5853
	18: 3	they recognized the voice of the y Levite;	5853
	18:15	the house of the y Levite at Micah's place	5853
	19:19	your maidservant, and the y **man** with us.	5853
	21:12	in Jabesh Gilead four hundred y **women** who had never slept with a man,	5855
Ru	2: 5	"Whose y **woman** is that?"	5855
	4:12	the LORD gives you by this y **woman,**	5855
1Sa	1:24	she took the boy with her, y as he was,	5853
	2:17	This sin of the y **men** was very great in	5853
	9: 5	both y and old, with an outbreak of tumors.	7785
	9:12	an impressive y **man** without equal among	1033
	10: 3	One will be carrying three y **goats,**	1531
	14: 1	of Saul said to the y **man** bearing his armor,	5853
	14: 6	Jonathan said to his y armor-bearer,	5853
	16:20	a skin of wine and a y **goat**	1531+6436
	17:55	"Abner, whose son is that y **man?"**	5853
	17:56	"Find out whose son this y **man** is."	6624
	17:58	"Whose son are you, y **man?"**	5853
	25: 5	So he sent ten y **men** and said to them,	5853
	25: 8	Therefore be favorable toward my y **men,**	5853
	26:22	of your y **men** come over and get it.	5853
	30: 2	all who were in it, both y and old.	7785
	30:17	except four hundred y **men** who rode off	5853
	30:19	Nothing was missing: y or old, boy or girl,	7785
2Sa	1: 5	to the y **man** who brought him the report,	5853
	1: 6	the y **man** said, "and there was Saul,	5853
	1:13	David said to the y **man** who brought him	5853
	2:14	of the y **men** get up and fight hand to hand	5853
	2:21	of the y **men** and strip him of his weapons."	5853
	9:12	Mephibosheth had a y son named Mica,	7783
	14:21	Go, bring back the y **man** Absalom."	5853
	17:18	But a y **man** saw them and told Absalom.	5853
	18: 5	with the y **man** Absalom for my sake."	5853
	18:12	'Protect the y **man** Absalom for my sake.'	5853
	18:29	"Is the y **man** Absalom safe?"	5853
	18:32	"Is the y **man** Absalom safe?"	5853
	18:32	up to harm you be like that y **man."**	5853
1Ki	1: 2	a y virgin to attend the king and take care	5855
	11:28	how well the y **man** did his work,	5853
	12: 8	and consulted the y **men** who had grown up	3529
	12:10	The y **men** who had grown up	3529
	12:14	he followed the advice of the y **men**	3529
	20:14	'The y **officers** *of* the provincial	5853
	20:15	So Ahab summoned the y **officers** *of*	5853
	20:17	The y **officers** *of* the provincial	5853
	20:19	The y **officers** *of* the provincial	5853
2Ki	3:21	so every man, y **and old,**	2025+2256+5087
	5: 2	and had taken captive a y girl from Israel,	7783
	5:14	and became clean like that of a y boy.	7785
	5:22	'Two y **men** from the company of	5853
	8:12	kill their y **men** with the sword,	1033
		y **man,** the prophet, went to Ramoth Gilead.	5853
1Ch	12:28	a brave y warrior, with 22 officers	5853
	22: 5	"My son Solomon is y and inexperienced,	5853
	25: 8	**Y** and old alike, teacher as well as student,	7785
	26:13	according to their families, y and old alike.	7785
	29: 1	God has chosen, is y and inexperienced,	5853
2Ch	10: 8	and consulted the y **men** who had grown up	3529
	10:10	The y **men** who had grown up with him	3529
	10:14	he followed the advice of the y **men**	3529
	13: 7	of Solomon when he was y and indecisive	5853
	13: 9	with a y bull and seven rams may become	1201
	31:15	their divisions, old and y alike.	7783
	34: 3	while he was still y, he began to seek the	5853
	36:17	who killed their y **men** with the sword in	1033
	36:17	spared neither y **man** nor young woman,	1033
	36:17	spared neither young man nor y **woman,**	1435
Ezr	6: 9	Whatever is needed—y bulls, rams,	10120
Est	2: 2	be made for beautiful y virgins for the king.	5855
	3:13	y and old, women and little children—	5853
Job	29: 8	the y **men** saw me and stepped aside and	5853
	32: 6	"I am y in years, and you are old;	7582
	38:41	when its y cry out to God and wander about	3529
	39: 3	They crouch down and bring forth their y;	3529
	39: 4	Their y thrive and grow strong in the wilds;	1201
	39:16	She treats her y harshly,	1201
	39:30	His y **ones** feast on blood,	711
Ps	2: 9	Sirion like a y wild ox.	1201
	37:25	I was y and now I am old,	5853
	78:31	cutting down the y **men** *of* Israel.	1033
	78:63	Fire consumed their y **men,**	1033
	84: 3	where she may have her y—	711
	89:19	I have exalted a y **man** from among	1033
	119: 9	How can a y **man** keep his way pure?	5853
	147: 9	and for the y ravens when they call.	1201
	148:12	y men and maidens, old men and children.	1033
Pr	1: 4	knowledge and discretion to the y—	5853
	7: 7	I noticed among the y **men,**	1201
	20:29	The glory of y **men** is their strength,	1033
Ecc	11: 9	Be happy, y **man,** while you are young,	1033
	11: 9	Be happy, young man, while you are y,	3531
SS	1: 8	of the sheep and graze your y goats by	1537
	2: 3	of the forest is my lover among the y **men.**	1201
	2: 9	My lover is like a gazelle or a y **stag.**	385+6762
	2:17	and be like a gazelle or like a y **stag** on	385+6762
	8: 8	We have a y sister,	7783
	8:14	a y **stag** on the spice-laden mountains.	385+6762
Isa	3: 5	The y will rise up against the old,	5853
	5:29	they roar like y **lions,**	4097
	7:21	man will keep alive a y **cow** and	1330+6320
	9:17	the Lord will take no pleasure in the y **men,**	1033

Isa	11: 7	their y will lie down together,	3529
	11: 8	y child put his hand into the viper's nest.	1694
	13:18	Their bows will strike down the y men;	5853
	20: 4	y and old, with buttocks bared—	5853
	31: 8	before the sword and their y men will be put	1033
	33: 4	O nations, is harvested as by y locusts;	2885
	34:15	and care for her y under the shadow	1842
	40:11	he gently leads those that have y.	6402
	40:30	and y men stumble and fall;	1033
	54: 6	a wife who married y, only to be rejected,"	5830
	60: 6	y camels of Midian and Ephah.	1145
	62: 5	As a y man marries a maiden,	1033
Jer	6:11	and on the y men gathered together;	1033
	9:21	the children from the streets and the y men	1033
	11:22	Their y men will die by the sword,	1033
	15: 8	against the mothers of their y men;	1033
	18:21	their y men slain by the sword in battle.	1033
	31:12	the y of the flocks and herds.	1201
	31:13	y men and old as well.	1033
	48:15	her finest y will go down in	1033
	49:20	The y of the flock will be dragged away;	7582
	49:26	Surely, her y men will fall in the streets;	1033
	50:27	Kill all her y bulls!	7228
	50:30	Therefore, her y men will fall in the streets;	1033
	50:45	The y of the flock will be dragged away;	7582
	51: 3	Do not spare her y men;	1033
	51:22	with you I shatter y man and maiden,	1033
	51:38	Her people all roar like y lions,	4097
La	1:15	an army against me to crush my y men.	1033
	1:18	y men and maidens have gone into exile.	1033
	2:10	y women of Jerusalem have bowed their heads to the ground.	1435
	2:21	"Y and old lie together in the dust of	5853
	2:21	my y men and maidens have fallen by	1033
	3:27	for a man to bear the yoke while he is y.	5830
	4: 3	jackals offer their breasts to nurse their y,	1594
	5:13	Y men toil at the millstones;	1033
	5:14	the y men have stopped their music.	1033
Eze	9: 6	Slaughter old men, y men and maidens,	1033
	19: 2	among the y lions and reared her cubs.	4097
	23: 6	all of them handsome y men,	1033
	23:12	mounted horsemen, all handsome y men.	1033
	23:21	and your y breasts fondled.	5830
	23:23	the Assyrians with them, handsome y men,	1033
	30:17	The y men of Heliopolis and Bubastis	1033
	43:19	You are to give a y bull as a sin offering to	1201
	43:23	to offer a y bull and a ram from the flock,	1201
	43:25	you are also to provide a y bull and a ram	1201
	45:18	to take a y bull without defect and purify	1201
	46: 6	of the New Moon he is to offer a y bull,	1201
Da	1: 4	y men without any physical defect,	3529
	1:10	the other y men your age?	3529
	1:13	that of the y men who eat the royal food,	3529
	1:15	of the y men who ate the royal food.	3529
	1:17	To these four y men God gave knowledge	3529
Hos	14: 6	his y shoots will grow.	3438
Joel	1: 4	the y locusts have eaten;	3540
	1: 4	what the y locusts have left other locusts	3540
	2:25	the great locust and the y locust,	3540
	2:28	your y men will see visions.	1033
Am	2:11	and Nazirites from among your y men.	1033
	4:10	I killed your y men with the sword,	1033
	8:13	"In that day "the lovely y women	1435
	8:13	and strong y men will faint because	1033
Mic	5: 8	like a y lion among flocks of sheep,	4097
Na	2:11	the place where they fed their y,	4097
	2:13	and the sword will devour your y lions.	4097
Zec	2: 4	"Run, tell that y man,	5853
	9:17	Grain will make the y men thrive,	1033
	9:17	and new wine the y women.	1435
	11:16	or seek the y, or heal the injured,	5853
Mt	19:20	"All these I have kept," the y man said.	3734
	19:22	When the y man heard this,	3734
Mk	14:51	A y man, wearing nothing but a linen	3734
	16: 5	a y man dressed in a white robe sitting on	3734
Lk	2:24	"a pair of doves or two y pigeons,"	3801
	7:14	He said, "Y man, I say to you, get up!"	3734
	15:29	Yet you never gave me even a y goat	2253
Jn	12:14	Jesus found a y donkey and sat upon it,	3942
Ac	2:17	your y men will see visions.	3734
	5: 6	Then the y men came forward,	3742
	5:10	Then the y men came in and,	3734
	7:58	at the feet of a y man named Saul.	3733
	20: 9	in a window was a y man Eutychus,	3733
	20:10	went down, threw himself on the y man	899S
	20:12	The people took the y man home alive	4090
	23:17	"Take this y man to the commander,	3733
	23:18	for me and asked me to bring this y man	3734
	23:19	commander took the y man by the hand,	899S
	23:22	The commander dismissed the y man	3734
1Ti	4:12	look down on you because you are y,	3742
Tit	2: 6	encourage the y men to be self-controlled.	3742
1Pe	5: 5	Y men, in the same way be submissive	3742
1Jn	2:13	I write to you, y men,	3734
	2:14	I write to you, y men,	3734

YOUNGER (31) [YOUNG]

Ge	19:31	One day the older daughter said to the y,	7582
	19:34	the older daughter said to the y,	7582
	19:35	and the y daughter went and lay with him.	7582
	19:38	The y daughter also had a son,	7582
	25:23	and the older will serve the y."	7582
	27:15	and put them on her y son Jacob.	7783
	27:42	she sent for her y son Jacob and said	7783
	29:16	and the name of the y was Rachel.	7783
	29:18	in return for your y daughter Rachel."	7783

Ge	29:26	not our custom here to give the y daughter	7582
	29:27	then we will give you the y one also,	2296S
	48:14	on Ephraim's head, though he was the y,	7582
	48:19	his y brother will be greater than he,	7785
Jdg	1:13	Othniel son of Kenaz, Caleb's y brother,	7785
	3: 9	Othniel son of Kenaz, Caleb's y brother,	7785
	15: 2	Isn't her y sister more attractive?	7783
Ru	3:10	You have not run after the y men,	1033
1Sa	14:49	and that of the y was Michal.	7783
Job	30: 1	they mock me, men y than I,	3427+4200+7582
Eze	16:46	and your y sister, who lived to the south	7783
	16:61	and those who are y.	7783
Mk	15:40	the mother of James the y and of Joses,	3625
Lk	15:12	The y one said to his father, 'Father,	3742
	15:13	the y son got together all he had,	3742
Jn	21:18	when you were y you dressed yourself	3742
Ro	9:12	she was told, "The older will serve the y."	1781
1Ti	5: 1	Treat y men as brothers,	3742
	5: 2	and y women as sisters, with absolute purity.	3742
	5:11	y widows, do not put them on such a list.	3742
	5:14	So I counsel y widows to marry,	3742
Tit	2: 4	the y women to love their husbands	3742

YOUNGEST (22) [YOUNG]

Ge	9:24	and found out what his y son had done	7783
	42:13	The y is now with our father,	7785
	42:15	unless your y brother comes here.	7785
	42:20	But you must bring your y brother to me,	7785
	42:32	and the y is now with our father in Canaan.'	7785
	42:34	But bring your y brother to me	7785
	43:29	he asked, "Is this your y brother,	7785
	43:33	from the firstborn to the y;	7582
	44: 2	in the mouth of the y one's sack,	7785
	44:12	with the oldest and ending with the y.	7785
	44:23	your y brother comes down with you,	7785
	44:26	Only if our y brother is with us will we go.	7785
	44:26	see the man's face unless our y brother is	7785
Jos	6:26	at the cost of his y will he set up its gates."	7582
Jdg	9: 5	But Jotham, the y son of Jerub-Baal,	7785
1Sa	16:11	"There is still the y," Jesse answered,	7783
	17:14	David was the y.	7783
1Ki	16:34	up its gates at the cost of his y son Segub,	7582
1Ch	24:31	the same as those of the y.	7783
2Ch	21:17	a son was left to him except Ahaziah, the y.	7785
	22: 1	Jehoram's y son, king in his place,	7785
Lk	22:26	greatest among you should be like the y,	3742

YOUR (6631) [YOU] See Index of Articles Etc.

YOURS (86) [YOU] See Index of Articles Etc.

YOURSELF (191) [SELF, YOU] See Index of Articles Etc.

YOURSELVES (213) [SELF, YOU] See Index of Articles Etc.

YOUTH (56) [YOUNG]

Lev	22:13	to live in her father's house as in her y,	5830
Nu	11:28	who had been Moses' aide since y,	1036
1Sa	12: 2	I have been your leader from my y	5830
	17:33	and he has been a fighting man from his y."	5830
2Sa	19: 7	that have come upon you from your y	5830
1Ki	18:12	worshiped the LORD since my y.	5830
Job	13:26	and make me inherit the sins of my y.	5830
	31:18	from my y I reared him as would a father,	5830
	33:25	it is restored as in the days of his y.	6596
	36:14	They die in their y,	5854
Ps	25: 7	the sins of my y and my rebellious ways;	5830
	71: 5	my confidence since my y.	5830
	71:17	Since my y, O God, you have taught me,	5854
	88:15	From my y I have been afflicted and close	5854
	89:45	You have cut short the days of his y;	6596
	103: 5	with good things so that your y is renewed	5830
	110: 3	you will receive the dew of your y.	3531
	127: 4	of a warrior are sons born in one's y.	5830
	129: 1	They have greatly oppressed me from my y	5830
	129: 2	they have greatly oppressed me from my y,	5830
	144:12	in their y will be like well-nurtured plants,	5830
Pr	2:17	who has left the partner of her y	5830
	5:18	and may you rejoice in the wife of your y.	5830
	7: 7	a y who lacked judgment.	5853
	29:21	If a man pampers his servant from y,	5854
Ecc	4:13	Better a poor but wise y than an old but	3529
	4:14	The y may have come from prison to	NIH
	4:15	and walked under the sun followed the y,	3529
	11: 9	give you joy in the days of your y.	1035
	11:10	for y and vigor are meaningless.	3531
	12: 1	Remember your Creator in the days of your y,	1035
Isa	54: 4	the shame of your y and remember no more	6596
	65:20	dies at a hundred will be thought a mere y;	5853
Jer	2: 2	" 'I remember the devotion of your y,	5830
	3: 4	'My Father, my friend from my y,	5830
	3:24	From our y shameful gods have consumed	5830
	3:25	from our y till this day we have not obeyed	5830
	22:21	This has been your way from your y;	5830
	31:19	because I bore the disgrace of my y.	5830
	32:30	but evil in my sight from their y;	5831
	48:11	"Moab has been at rest from y,	5830
	51:22	with you I shatter old man and y,	5853

Eze	4:14	From my y until now I have never eaten	5830
	16:22	you did not remember the days of your y,	5830
	16:43	you did not remember the days of your y	5830
	16:60	I made with you in the days of your y,	5830
	23: 3	engaging in prostitution from their y.	5830
	23: 8	when during her y men slept with her,	5830
	23:19	as she recalled the days of her y,	5830
	23:21	So you longed for the lewdness of your y,	5830
Hos	2:15	There she will sing as in the days of her y,	5830
Joel	1: 8	grieving for the husband of her y.	5830
Zec	13: 5	land has been my livelihood since my y.'	5830
Mal	2:14	between you and the wife of your y,	5830
	2:15	do not break faith with the wife of your y.	5830
2Ti	2:22	Flee the evil desires of y,	3754

YOUTHFUL (1) [YOUNG]

Job	20:11	The y vigor that fills his bones will lie with	6596

YOUTHS (4) [YOUNG]

2Ki	2:23	some y came out of the town and jeered at him.	5853+7783
	2:24	of the woods and mauled forty-two of the y.	3529
Isa	3:12	Y oppress my people, women rule over	6620
	40:30	Even y grow tired and weary,	5853

Z

ZAANAIM (KJV) See ZAANANNIM

ZAANAN (1)

Mic	1:11	Those who live in Z will not come out.	7367

ZAANANNIM (2)

Jos	19:33	from Heleph his tent by the great tree in Z,	7588
Jdg	4:11	and pitched his tent by the great tree in Z	7588

ZAAVAN (2)

Ge	36:27	The sons of Ezer: Bilhan, Z and Akan.	2401
1Ch	1:42	The sons of Ezer: Bilhan, Z and Akan.	2401

ZABAD (8)

1Ch	2:36	Nathan the father of Z,	2274
	2:37	Z the father of Ephlal.	2274
	7:21	Z his son and Shuthelah his son.	2274
	11:41	Uriah the Hittite, Z son of Ahlai.	2274
2Ch	24:26	Those who conspired against him were Z,	2274
Ezr	10:27	Eliashib, Mattaniah, Jeremoth, Z and Aziza.	2274
	10:33	Mattenai, Mattattah, Z, Eliphelet, Jeremai,	2274
	10:43	Jeiel, Mattithiah, Z, Zebina, Jaddai,	2274

ZABBAI (2)

Ezr	10:28	Jehohanan, Hananiah, Z and Athlai.	2287
Ne	3:20	son of Z zealously repaired another section,	2287

ZABBUD (KJV) See ZACCUR

ZABDI (3)

1Ch	8:19	Jakim, Zicri, Z,	2275
	27:27	Z the Shiphmite was in charge of	2275
Ne	11:17	the son of Z, the son of Asaph,	2275

ZABDIEL (2)

1Ch	27: 2	was Jashobeam son of Z.	2276
Ne	11:14	Their chief officer was Z son	2276

ZABUD (1)

1Ki	4: 5	Z son of Nathan—	2280

ZABULON (KJV) See ZEBULUN

ZACCAI (2)

Ezr	2: 9	of Z 760	2347
Ne	7:14	of Z 760	2347

ZACCHAEUS (3)

Lk	19: 2	A man was there by the name of Z;	2405
	19: 5	he looked up and said to him, "Z,	2405
	19: 8	But Z stood up and said to the Lord, "Look,	2405

ZACCHUR (KJV) See ZACCUR

ZACCUR (10)

Nu	13: 4	the tribe of Reuben, Shammua son of Z;	2346
1Ch	4:26	Z his son and Shimei his son.	2346
	24:27	Beno, Shoham, Z and Ibri.	2346
	25: 2	Z, Joseph, Nethaniah and Asarelah.	2346
	25:10	the third to Z, his sons and relatives, 12	2346

Ezr	8:14	Uthai and **Z**, and with them 70 men.	2346
Ne	3: 2	and **Z** son of Imri built next to them.	2346
	10:12	**Z**, Sherebiah, Shebaniah,	2346
	12:35	the son of Micaiah, the son of **Z**,	2346
	13:13	the storerooms and made Hanan son of **Z**,	2346

ZACHARIAH, ZACHARIAS (KJV) See ZECHARIAH

ZACHER (KJV) See ZEKER

ZADOK (53) [ZADOKITES]

2Sa	8:17	**Z** son of Ahitub and Ahimelech son	7401
	15:24	**Z** was there, too, and all the Levites	7401
	15:25	Then the king said to **Z**,	7401
	15:27	The king also said to **Z** the priest,	7401
	15:29	So **Z** and Abiathar took the ark of God back	7401
	15:35	Won't the priests **Z** and Abiathar be there	7401
	15:36	Ahimaaz son of **Z** and Jonathan son	7401
	17:15	Hushai told **Z** and Abiathar, the priests,	7401
	18:19	Now Ahimaaz son of **Z** said,	7401
	18:22	Ahimaaz son of **Z** again said to Joab,	7401
	18:27	the first one runs like Ahimaaz son of **Z**."	7401
	19:11	King David sent this message to **Z**	7401
	20:25	**Z** and Abiathar were priests;	7401
1Ki	1: 8	But **Z** the priest, Benaiah son of Jehoiada,	7401
	1:26	But me your servant, and **Z** the priest,	7401
	1:32	King David said, "Call in **Z** the priest,	7401
	1:34	There have **Z** the priest and Nathan	7401
	1:38	So **Z** the priest, Nathan the prophet,	7401
	1:39	**Z** the priest took the horn of oil from	7401
	1:44	The king has sent with him **Z** the priest,	7401
	1:45	and **Z** the priest and Nathan	7401
	2:35	and replaced Abiathar with **Z** the priest.	7401
	4: 2	Azariah son of **Z**—the priest;	7401
	4: 4	**Z** and Abiathar—priests;	7401
2Ki	15:33	mother's name was Jerusha daughter of **Z**.	7401
1Ch	6: 8	Ahitub the father of **Z**,	7401
	6: 8	**Z** the father of Ahimaaz,	7401
	6:12	Ahitub the father of **Z**,	7401
	6:12	**Z** the father of Shallum,	7401
	6:53	**Z** his son and Ahimaaz his son.	7401
	9:11	the son of Meshullam, the son of **Z**,	7401
	12:28	and **Z**, a brave young warrior,	7401
	15:11	Then David summoned **Z** and Abiathar	7401
	16:39	David left **Z** the priest and his fellow priests	7401
	18:16	**Z** son of Ahitub and Ahimelech son	7401
	24: 3	of **Z** a descendant of Eleazar and Ahimelech	7401
	24: 6	**Z** the priest, Ahimelech son of Abiathar and	7401
	24:31	in the presence of King David and of **Z**,	7401
	27:17	of Kemuel; over Aaron: **Z**;	7401
	29:22	the LORD to be ruler and **Z** to be priest.	7401
2Ch	27: 1	mother's name was Jerusha daughter of **Z**.	7401
	31:10	from the family of **Z**, answered,	7401
Ezr	7: 2	the son of **Z**, the son of Ahitub,	7401
Ne	3: 4	to him **Z** son of Baana also made repairs.	7401
	3:29	Next to them, **Z** son	7401
	10:21	Meshezabel, **Z**, Jaddua,	7401
	11:11	the son of Meshullam, the son of **Z**,	7401
	13:13	I put Shelemiah the priest, **Z** the scribe,	7401
Eze	40:46	These are the sons of **Z**,	7401
	43:19	who are Levites, of the family of **Z**,	7401
	44:15	who are Levites and descendants of **Z**	7401
Mt	1:14	Azor the father of **Z**,	4882
	1:14	**Z** the father of Akim,	4882

ZADOKITES (1) [ZADOK]

Eze	48:11	the **Z**, who were faithful in serving me	1201+7401

ZAHAM (1)

2Ch	11:19	She bore him sons: Jeush, Shemariah and **Z**.	2300

ZAHAR (1)

Eze	27:18	in wine from Helbon and wool from **Z**.	7466

ZAIR (1)

2Ki	8:21	So Jehoram went to **Z** with all his chariots.	7583

ZALAPH (1)

Ne	3:30	the sixth son of **Z**, repaired another section.	7523

ZALMON (3)

Jdg	9:48	he and all his men went up Mount **Z**.	7515
2Sa	23:28	**Z** the Ahohite, Maharai the Netophathite,	7514
Ps	68:14	it was like snow fallen on **Z**.	7515

ZALMONAH (2)

Nu	33:41	They left Mount Hor and camped at **Z**.	7517
	33:42	They left **Z** and camped at Punon.	7517

ZALMUNNA (10)

Jdg	8: 5	and I am still pursuing Zebah and **Z**,	7518
	8: 6	hands of Zebah and **Z** in your possession?	7518
	8: 7	when the LORD has given Zebah and **Z**	7518
	8:10	Now Zebah and **Z** were in Karkor with	7518
	8:12	Zebah and **Z**, the two kings of Midian, fled,	7518
	8:15	"Here are Zebah and **Z**,	7518
	8:15	hands of Zebah and **Z** in your possession?	7518
	8:18	Then he asked Zebah and **Z**,	7518

Jdg	8:21	Zebah and **Z** said, "Come, do it yourself.	7518
Ps	83:11	all their princes like Zebah and **Z**,	7518

ZAMZUMMITES (1)

Dt	2:20	but the Ammonites called them **Z**.	2368

ZANOAH (5)

Jos	15:34	**Z**, En Gannim, Tappuah, Enam,	2391
	15:56	Jezreel, Jokdeam, **Z**,	2391
1Ch	4:18	and Jekuthiel the father of **Z**.)	2392
Ne	3:13	by Hanun and the residents of **Z**.	2391
	11:30	**Z**, Adullam and their villages, in Lachish	2391

ZAPHENATH-PANEAH (1)

Ge	41:45	Pharaoh gave Joseph the name **Z**	7624

ZAPHON (3)

Jos	13:27	Succoth and **Z** with the rest of the realm	7601
Jdg	12: 1	crossed over to **Z** and said to Jephthah,	7601
Ps	48: 2	Like the utmost heights of **Z** is Mount Zion,	7601

ZARA, ZARAH (KJV) See ZERAH

ZAREAH (KJV) See ZORAH

ZAREATHITES (KJV) See ZORATHITES

ZARED (KJV) See ZERED

ZAREPHATH (4)

1Ki	17: 9	"Go at once to **Z** of Sidon and stay there.	7673
	17:10	So he went to **Z**.	7673
Ob	1:20	will possess [the land] as far as **Z**;	7673
Lk	4:26	but to a widow in **Z** in the region of Sidon.	4919

ZARETHAN (4)

Jos	3:16	at a town called Adam in the vicinity of **Z**,	7681
1Ki	4:12	in all of Beth Shan next to **Z** below Jezreel,	7681
	7:46	of the Jordan between Succoth and **Z**.	7681
2Ch	4:17	of the Jordan between Succoth and **Z**.	7681

ZARETHSHAHAR (KJV) See ZERETH SHAHAR

ZARTANAH, ZARTHAN (KJV) See ZARETHAN

ZATTU (5)

Ezr	2: 8	of **Z** 945	2456
	8: 5	of the descendants of **Z**, Shecaniah son	NIH
	10:27	From the descendants of **Z**: Elioenai,	2456
Ne	7:13	of **Z** 845	2456
	10:14	Parosh, Pahath-Moab, Elam, **Z**, Bani,	2456

ZAVAN (KJV) See ZAAVAN

ZAZA (1)

1Ch	2:33	The sons of Jonathan: Peleth and **Z**.	2321

ZEAL (21) [ZEALOUS, ZEALOUSLY]

Nu	25:11	so that in my **z** I did not put an end to them.	7863
Dt	29:20	his wrath and **z** will burn against that man.	7863
2Sa	21: 2	but Saul in his **z** for Israel and Judah	7861
2Ki	10:16	with me and see my **z** for the LORD."	7863
	19:31	The **z** of the LORD Almighty will accomplish this.	7863
Ps	69: 9	for **z** for your house consumes me,	7863
	119:139	My **z** wears me out,	7863
Pr	19: 2	It is not good to have **z** without knowledge,	5883
Isa	9: 7	**z** of the LORD Almighty will accomplish this.	7863
	26:11	Let them see your **z** for your people and	7863
	37:32	The **z** of the LORD Almighty will accomplish this.	7863
	42:13	like a warrior he will stir up his **z**;	7863
	59:17	of vengeance and wrapped himself in **z** as	7863
	63:15	Where are your **z** and your might?	7863
Eze	5:13	that I the LORD have spoken in my **z**,	7863
	36: 5	In my burning **z** I have spoken against	7863
	38:19	In my **z** and fiery wrath I declare that at	7863
Jn	2:17	"**Z** for your house will consume me."	2419
Ro	10: 2	but their **z** is not based on knowledge.	NIG
	12:11	Never be lacking in **z**,	5082
Php	3: 6	as for **z**, persecuting the church;	2419

ZEALOT (4)

Mt	10: 4	Simon the **Z** and Judas Iscariot,	2831
Mk	3:18	of Alphaeus, Thaddaeus, Simon the **Z**	2831
Lk	6:15	Simon who was called the **Z**,	2421
Ac	1:13	James son of Alphaeus and Simon the **Z**,	2421

ZEALOUS (14) [ZEAL]

Nu	25:11	as **z** as I am for my honor among them,	7861+7863
	25:13	because he was **z** for the honor of his God	7861
1Ki	19:10	"I have been **very z** for the LORD God	7861+7861

1Ki	19:14	"I have been **very z** for the LORD God	7861+7861
Pr	23:17	but always be **z** for the fear of the LORD.	NIH
Eze	39:25	and I will be **z** for my holy name.	7861
Ac	21:20	and all of them are **z** for the law.	2421
	22: 3	in the law of our fathers and was just as **z**	2421
Ro	10: 2	For I can testify that they are **z**,	2419
2Co	8:22	to us in many ways that he is **z**,	5080
Gal	1:14	of my own age and was extremely **z for**	2421
	4:17	Those people are **z** to win you over,	2420
	4:17	so that you may be **z for** them.	2420
	4:18	It is fine to be **z**, provided the purpose is good,	2420

ZEALOUSLY (1) [ZEAL]

Ne	3:20	son of Zabbai **z** repaired another section,	3013

ZEBADIAH (9)

1Ch	8:15	**Z**, Arad, Eder,	2277
	8:17	**Z**, Meshullam, Hizki, Heber,	2277
	12: 7	and **Z** the sons of Jeroham from Gedor.	2277
	26: 2	**Z** the third, Jathniel the fourth,	2278
	27: 7	his son **Z** was his successor.	2277
2Ch	17: 8	Shemaiah, Nethanel, **Z**, Asahel,	2278
	19:11	and **Z** son of Ishmael,	2278
Ezr	8: 8	**Z** son of Michael, and with him 80 men;	2277
	10:20	of Immer: Hanani and **Z**.	2277

ZEBAH (10)

Jdg	8: 5	and I am still pursuing **Z** and Zalmunna	2286
	8: 6	have the hands of **Z** and Zalmunna in your possession?	2286
	8: 7	the LORD has given **Z** and Zalmunna	2286
	8:10	Now **Z** and Zalmunna were in Karkor with	2286
	8:12	**Z** and Zalmunna, the two kings of Midian,	2286
	8:15	"Here are **Z** and Zalmunna,	2286
	8:15	have the hands of **Z** and Zalmunna in your possession?	2286
	8:18	Then he asked **Z** and Zalmunna,	2286
	8:21	**Z** and Zalmunna said, "Come,	2286
Ps	83:11	all their princes like **Z** and Zalmunna,	2286

ZEBAIM (KJV) See POKERETH HAZZEBAIM

ZEBEDEE (10) [ZEBEDEE'S]

Mt	4:21	James son of **Z** and his brother John.	2411
	4:21	They were in a boat with their father **Z**,	2411
	10: 2	James son of **Z**, and his brother John;	2411
	26:37	He took Peter and the two sons of **Z** along	2411
Mk	1:19	he saw James son of **Z** and his brother John	2411
	1:20	and they left their father **Z** in the boat with	2411
	3:17	of **Z** and his brother John (to them he gave	2411
	10:35	Then James and John, the sons of **Z**,	2411
Lk	5:10	the sons of **Z**, Simon's partners.	2411
Jn	21: 2	the sons of **Z**, and two other disciples	2411

ZEBEDEE'S (2) [ZEBEDEE]

Mt	20:20	the mother of **Z** sons came to Jesus with her sons	2411
	27:56	and the mother of **Z** sons.	2411

ZEBIDAH (1)

2Ki	23:36	His mother's name was **Z** daughter of	2288

ZEBINA (1)

Ezr	10:43	Jeiel, Mattithiah, Zabad, **Z**, Jaddai,	2289

ZEBOIIM (5)

Ge	10:19	Gomorrah, Admah and **Z**, as far as Lasha.	7375
	14: 2	Shemeber king of **Z**,	7375
	14: 8	the king of **Z** and the king of Bela,	7375
Dt	29:23	Admah and **Z**, which the LORD overthrew	7375
Hos	11: 8	How can I make you like **Z**?	7375

ZEBOIM (2)

1Sa	13:18	the Valley of **Z** facing the desert.	7391
Ne	11:34	in Hadid, **Z** and Neballat,	7391

ZEBUDAH (KJV) See ZEBIDAH

ZEBUL (6)

Jdg	9:28	and isn't **Z** his deputy?	2291
	9:30	When **Z** the governor of the city heard	2291
	9:36	When Gaal saw them, he said to **Z**, "Look,	2291
	9:36	**Z** replied, "You mistake the shadows of	2291
	9:38	**Z** said to him, "Where is your big talk now,	2291
	9:41	and **Z** drove Gaal and his brothers out	2291

ZEBULONITE (KJV) See ZEBULUNITE

ZEBULUN (49) [ZEBULUNITE]

Ge	30:20	So she named him **Z**.	2282
	35:23	Simeon, Levi, Judah, Issachar and **Z**.	2282
	46:14	The sons of **Z**: Sered, Elon and Jahleel.	2282
	49:13	"**Z** will live by the seashore and become	2282
Ex	1: 3	Issachar, **Z** and Benjamin;	2282
Nu	1: 9	from **Z**, Eliab son of Helon;	2282
	1:30	From the descendants of **Z**:	2282

Nu	1:31	The number from the tribe of Z was 57,400.	2282
	2: 7	The tribe of Z will be next.	2282
	2: 7	The leader of the people of Z is Eliab son	2282
	7:24	the leader of the people of Z,	2282
	10:16	over the division of the tribe of Z.	1201+2282
	13:10	from the tribe of Z, Gaddiel son of Sodi;	2282
	26:26	The descendants of Z by their clans were:	2282
	26:27	These were the clans of Z;	2283
	34:25	the leader from the tribe of Z;	1201+2282
Dt	27:13	Reuben, Gad, Asher, Z, Dan and Naphtali.	2282
	33:18	About Z he said: "Rejoice, Zebulun,	2282
	33:18	"Rejoice, Z, in your going out, and you,	2282
Jos	19:10	The third lot came up for Z, clan by	1201+2282
	19:16	villages were the inheritance of Z,	1201+2282
	19:27	touched Z and the Valley of Iphtah El,	2282
	19:34	It touched Z on the south,	2282
	21: 7	from the tribes of Reuben, Gad and Z.	2282
	21:34	from the tribe of Z, Jokneam, Kartah,	2282
Jdg	1:30	Neither did Z drive out the Canaanites	2282
	4: 6	Z and lead the way to Mount Tabor.	1201+2282
	4:10	where he summoned Naphtali and Zebulun.	2282
	5:14	from Z those who bear a commander's staff.	2282
	5:18	The people of Z risked their very lives;	2282
	6:35	and also into Asher, Z and Naphtali,	2282
	12:12	and was buried in Aijalon in the land of Z.	2282
1Ch	2: 1	Reuben, Simeon, Levi, Judah, Issachar, Z,	2282
	6:63	from the tribes of Reuben, Gad and Z.	2282
	6:77	From the tribe of Z they received Jokneam,	2282
	12:33	men of Z, experienced soldiers prepared	2282
	12:40	Z and Naphtali came bringing food	2282
	27:19	over Z: Ishmaiah son of Obadiah;	2282
2Ch	30:10	as far as Z, but the people scorned and	2282
	30:11	Manasseh and Z humbled themselves	2282
	30:18	Issachar and Z had not purified themselves,	2282
Ps	68:27	and there the princes of Z and of Naphtali.	2282
Isa	9: 1	past he humbled the land of Z and the land	2282
Eze	48:26	"Z will have one portion;	2282
	48:27	it will border the territory of Z from east	2282
	48:33	the gate of Issachar and the gate of Z.	2282
Mt	4:13	by the lake in the area of Z and Naphtali—	2404
	4:15	"Land of Z and land of Naphtali, the way to	2404
Rev	7: 8	from the tribe of Z 12,000,	2404

ZEBULUNITE (1) [ZEBULUN]

Jdg	12:11	After him, Elon the Z led Israel ten years.	2283

ZECHARIAH (53) [ZECHARIAH'S]

2Ki	14:29	And Z his son succeeded him as king.	2357
	15: 8	Z son of Jeroboam became king of Israel	2358
	15:10	Shallum son of Jabesh conspired against Z.	2257S
	18: 2	mother's name was Abijah daughter of Z.	2357
1Ch	5: 7	Jeiel the chief, Z,	2358
	9:21	Z son of Meshelemiah was the gatekeeper at	2357
	9:37	Gedor, Ahio, Z and Mikloth.	2357
	15:18	Z, Jaaziel, Shemiramoth, Jehiel, Unni,	2358
	15:20	Z, Aziel, Shemiramoth,	2358
	15:24	Shebaniah, Joshaphat, Nethanel, Amasai, Z,	2358
	16: 5	Z second, then Jeiel, Shemiramoth, Jehiel,	2358
	24:25	from the sons of Isshiah: Z.	2358
	26: 2	Meshelemiah had sons: Z the firstborn,	2358
	26:11	Tabaliah the third and Z the fourth.	2358
	26:14	Then lots were cast for his son Z,	2358
	27:21	of Manasseh in Gilead: Iddo son of Z;	2358
2Ch	17: 7	Z, Nethanel and Micaiah to teach in	2357
	20:14	the LORD came upon Jahaziel son of Z,	2358
	21: 2	Z, Azariahu, Michael and Shephatiah.	2358
	24:20	Then the Spirit of God came upon Z son	2357
	26: 5	He sought God during the days of Z,	2358
	29: 1	mother's name was Abijah daughter of Z.	2358
	29:13	the descendants of Asaph, Z and Mattaniah;	2358
	34:12	and Z and Meshullam.	2357
	35: 8	Z and Jehiel, the administrators of God's	2358
Ezr	5: 1	Now Haggai the prophet and Z the prophet,	10230
	6:14	the preaching of Haggai the prophet and Z,	10230
	8: 3	of the descendants of Parosh, Z,	2357
	8:11	Z son of Bebai, and with him 28 men;	2357
	8:16	Jarib, Elnathan, Nathan, Z and Meshullam,	2357
	10:26	Mattaniah, Z, Jehiel, Abdi,	2357
Ne	8: 4	Hashum, Hashbaddanah, Z and Meshullam.	2357
	11: 4	Athaiah son of Uzziah, the son of Z,	2357
	11: 5	the son of Z, a descendant of Shelah.	2357
	11:12	the son of Z, the son of Pashhur,	2357
	12:16	of Iddo's, Z; of Ginnethon's, Meshullam;	2357
	12:35	and also Z son of Jonathan,	2357
	12:41	Z and Hananiah with their trumpets—	2357
Isa	8: 2	And I will call in Uriah the priest and Z son	2358
Zec	1: 1	came to the prophet Z son of Berekiah,	2357
	1: 7	word of the LORD came to the prophet Z	2357
	7: 1	the word of the LORD came to on the fourth	2357
	7: 8	the word of the LORD came again to Z:	2357
Mt	23:35	blood of righteous Abel to the blood of Z	2408
Lk	1: 5	there was a priest named Z, who belonged	2408
	1:12	When Z saw him, he was startled	2408
	1:13	the angel said to him, "Do not be afraid, Z;	2408
	1:18	Z asked the angel, "How can I be sure	2408
	1:21	for Z and wondering why he stayed so long	2408
	1:59	to name him after his father Z,	2408
	1:67	His father Z was filled with the Holy Spirit	2408
	3: 2	of God came to John son of Z in the desert.	2408
	11:51	from the blood of Abel to the blood of Z,	2408

ZECHARIAH'S (4) [ZECHARIAH]

2Ki	15:11	The other events of Z reign are written in	2357
2Ch	24:22	kindness Z father Jehoiada had shown him	2257S
Lk	1: 8	Once when Z division was on duty	899S

Lk	1:40	she entered Z home and greeted Elizabeth.	2408

ZEDAD (2)

Nu	34: 8	Then the boundary will go to Z,	7398
Eze	47:15	by the Hethlon road past Lebo Hamath to Z,	7398

ZEDEKIAH (60) [ZEDEKIAH'S]

1Ki	22:11	Z son of Kenaanah had made iron horns	7408
	22:24	Then Z son of Kenaanah went up	7409
2Ki	24:17	in his place and changed his name to Z.	7409
	24:18	Z was twenty-one years old	7409
	24:20	Z rebelled against the king of Babylon.	7409
	25: 2	until the eleventh year of King Z.	7409
	25: 7	They killed the sons of Z before his eyes.	7409
1Ch	3:15	Jehoiakim the second son, Z the third,	7409
	3:16	Jehoiachin his son, and Z.	7408
2Ch	18:10	Z son of Kenaanah had made iron horns	7408
	18:23	Then Z son of Kenaanah went up	7409
	36:10	and he made Jehoiachin's uncle, Z,	7409
	36:11	Z was twenty-one years old	7409
Ne	10: 1	the son of Hacaliah. Z,	7408
Jer	1: 3	the fifth month of the eleventh year of Z son	7409
	21: 1	when King Z sent to him Pashhur son	7409
	21: 3	But Jeremiah answered them, "Tell Z,	7409
	21: 7	I will hand over Z king of Judah,	7409
	24: 8	'so will I deal with Z king of Judah,	7409
	27: 1	the reign of Z son of Josiah king of Judah,	7409
	27: 3	to Jerusalem to Z king of Judah.	7409
	27:12	I gave the same message to Z king of Judah.	7408
	28: 1	early in the reign of Z king of Judah,	7408
	29: 3	whom Z king of Judah sent to King	7409
	29:21	says about Ahab son of Kolaiah and Z son	7409
	29:22	'The LORD treat you like Z and Ahab,	7409
	32: 1	from the LORD in the tenth year of Z king	7409
	32: 3	Z king of Judah had imprisoned him there,	7409
	32: 4	Z king of Judah will not escape out of	7409
	32: 5	He will take Z to Babylon,	7409
	34: 2	Go to Z king of Judah and tell him,	7409
	34: 4	O Z king of Judah.	7409
	34: 6	the prophet told all this to Z king of Judah,	7409
	34: 8	after King Z had made a covenant with all	7409
	34:21	"I will hand Z king of Judah and his	7409
	36:12	of Acbor, Gemariah son of Shaphan, Z son	7409
	37: 1	Z son of Josiah was made king of Judah	7408
	37: 3	King Z, however, sent Jehucal son	7409
	37:17	Then King Z sent for him	7409
	37:18	Then Jeremiah said to King Z,	7409
	37:21	King Z then gave orders for Jeremiah to	7409
	38: 5	"He is in your hands," King Z answered.	7409
	38:14	Then King Z sent for Jeremiah the prophet	7409
	38:15	Jeremiah said to Z, "If I give you an answer,	7409
	38:16	King Z swore this oath secretly to Jeremiah:	7409
	38:17	Then Jeremiah said to Z, "This is what	7409
	38:19	King Z said to Jeremiah, "I am afraid	7409
	38:24	Then Z said to Jeremiah, "Do not let anyone	7409
	39: 1	In the ninth year of Z king of Judah,	7409
	39: 4	When Z king of Judah and all the soldiers	7409
	39: 5	and overtook Z in the plains of Jericho.	7409
	39: 6	sons of Z before his eyes and also killed all	7409
	44:30	just as I handed Z king of Judah over	7409
	49:34	early in the reign of Z king of Judah:	7408
	51:59	with Z king of Judah in the fourth year	7409
	52: 1	Z was twenty-one years old	7409
	52: 3	Z rebelled against the king of Babylon.	7409
	52: 5	until the eleventh year of King Z.	7409
	52: 8	but the Babylonian army pursued King Z	7409
	52:10	of Babylon slaughtered the sons of Z	7409

ZEDEKIAH'S (5) [ZEDEKIAH]

2Ki	25: 1	So in the ninth year of Z reign,	2257S
Jer	39: 2	the fourth month of Z eleventh year,	4200+7409
	39: 7	Then he put out Z eyes and bound him	7409
	52: 4	So in the ninth year of Z reign,	2257S
	52:11	Then he put out Z eyes,	7409

ZEEB (6)

Jdg	7:25	of the Midianite leaders, Oreb and Z.	2270
	7:25	and Z at the winepress of Zeeb.	2270
	7:25	and Zeeb at the winepress of Z.	2270
	7:25	and brought the heads of Oreb and Z	2270
	8: 3	God gave Oreb and Z,	2270
Ps	83:11	Make their nobles like Oreb and Z,	2270

ZEKER (1)

1Ch	8:31	Gedor, Ahio, Z	2353

ZELA (1)

2Sa	21:14	in the tomb of Saul's father Kish, at Z	7522

ZELAH (1)

Jos	18:28	Z, Haeleph, the Jebusite city	7522

ZELEK (2)

2Sa	23:37	Z the Ammonite, Naharai the Beerothite,	7530
1Ch	11:39	Z the Ammonite, Naharai the Berothite,	7530

ZELOPHEHAD (5) [ZELOPHEHAD'S]

Nu	26:33	(Z son of Hepher had no sons;	7524
	27: 1	The daughters of Z son of Hepher,	7524
	36: 2	to give the inheritance of our brother Z	7524
Jos	17: 3	Now Z son of Hepher, the son of Gilead,	7524

1Ch	7:15	Another descendant was named Z,	7524

ZELOPHEHAD'S (4) [ZELOPHEHAD]

Nu	27: 7	"What Z daughters are saying is right.	7524
	36: 6	the LORD commands for Z daughters:	7524
	36:10	Z daughters did as the LORD commanded	7524
	36:11	Z daughters—Mahlah, Tirzah, Hoglah,	7524

ZELOTES (KJV) See ZEALOT

ZELZAH (1)

1Sa	10: 2	at Z on the border of Benjamin.	7525

ZEMARAIM (2)

Jos	18:22	Beth Arabah, Z, Bethel,	7549
2Ch	13: 4	Abijah stood on Mount Z,	7549

ZEMARITES (2)

Ge	10:18	Arvadites, Z and Hamathites.	7548
1Ch	1:16	Arvadites, Z and Hamathites.	7548

ZEMIRAH (1)

1Ch	7: 8	Z, Joash, Eliezer, Elioenai, Omri, Jeremoth,	2371

ZENAN (1)

Jos	15:37	Z, Hadashah, Migdal Gad,	7569

ZENAS (1)

Tit	3:13	Do everything you can to help Z the lawyer	2424

ZEPHANIAH (11)

2Ki	25:18	Z the priest next in rank and	7623
1Ch	6:36	the son of Azariah, the son of Z,	7622
Jer	21: 1	and the priest Z son of Maaseiah.	7622
	29:25	to Zephaniah son of Maaseiah the priest,	7622
	29:25	You said to Z,	NIH
	29:29	Z the priest, however, read the letter	7622
	37: 3	the priest Z son of Maaseiah to Jeremiah	7623
	52:24	Z the priest next in rank and	7622
Zep	1: 1	The word of the LORD that came to Z son	7622
Zec	6:10	to the house of Josiah son of Z.	7622
	6:14	Jedaiah and Hen son of Z as a memorial in	7622

ZEPHATH (1)

Jdg	1:17	and attacked the Canaanites living in Z,	7634

ZEPHATHAH (1)

2Ch	14:10	took up battle positions in the Valley of Z	7635

ZEPHO (3)

Ge	36:11	Teman, Omar, Z, Gatam and Kenaz.	7598
	36:15	Chiefs Teman, Omar, Z, Kenaz,	7598
1Ch	1:36	Teman, Omar, Z, Gatam and Kenaz;	7598

ZEPHON (2) [BAAL ZEPHON, ZEPHONITE]

Ge	46:16	The sons of Gad: Z, Haggi, Shuni, Ezbon,	7602
Nu	26:15	through Z, the Zephonite clan;	7602

ZEPHONITE (1) [ZEPHON]

Nu	26:15	through Zephon, the Z clan;	7604

ZER (1)

Jos	19:35	The fortified cities were Ziddim, Z,	7643

ZERAH (21) [ZERAHITE, ZERAHITES]

Ge	36:13	Nahath, Z, Shammah and Mizzah.	2438
	36:17	Chiefs Nahath, Z, Shammah and Mizzah.	2438
	36:33	Jobab son of Z from Bozrah succeeded him	2438
	38:30	came out and he was given the name Z.	2438
	46:12	and Z (but Er and Onan had died in the land	2438
Nu	26:13	through Z, the Zerahite clan.	2438
	26:20	through Z, the Zerahite clan.	2438
Jos	7: 1	the son of Z, of the tribe of Judah,	2438
	7:18	the son of Z, of the tribe of Judah,	2438
	7:24	took Achan son of Z, the silver, the robe,	2438
	22:20	of Z acted unfaithfully regarding	2438
1Ch	1:37	Nahath, Z, Shammah and Mizzah.	2438
	1:44	Jobab son of Z from Bozrah succeeded him	2438
	2: 4	bore him Perez and Z.	2438
	2: 6	The sons of Z: Zimri, Ethan,	2438
	4:24	Nemuel, Jamin, Jarib, Z and Shaul;	2438
	6:21	Z his son and Jeatherai his son.	2438
	6:41	the son of Z, the son of Adaiah.	2438
2Ch	14: 9	Z the Cushite marched out against them	2438
Ne	11:24	one of the descendants of Z son of Judah,	2438
Mt	1: 3	Judah the father of Perez and Z,	2406

ZERAHIAH (5)

1Ch	6: 6	Uzzi the father of Z,	2440
	6: 6	Z the father of Meraioth,	2440
	6:51	Bukki his son, Uzzi his son, Z his son,	2440
Ezr	7: 4	the son of Z, the son of Uzzi,	2440
	8: 4	Eliehoenai son of Z, and with him 200 men;	2440

ZERAHITE (4) [ZERAH]

Nu	26:13	through Zerah, the Z clan;	2439

Nu	26:20	through Zerah, the **Z** clan.	2439
1Ch	27:11	was Sibbecai the Hushathite, a **Z**.	2439
	27:13	was Maharai the Netophathite, a **Z**.	2439

ZERAHITES (3) [ZERAH]

Jos	7:17	Judah came forward, and he took the **Z**.	2439
	7:17	the clan of the **Z** come forward by families,	2439
1Ch	9: 6	Of the **Z**: Jeuel.	1201+2438

ZERED (3)

Nu	21:12	on and camped in the **Z** Valley.	2429
Dt	2:13	"Now get up and cross the **Z** Valley."	2429
	2:14	until we crossed the **Z** Valley.	2429

ZEREDAH (1)

1Ki	11:26	an Ephraimite from **Z**, and his mother was	7649

ZEREDATHAH (KJV) See ZARETHAN

ZERERAH (1)

Jdg	7:22	to Beth Shittah toward **Z** as far as the border	7678

ZERESH (4)

Est	5:10	Calling together his friends and **Z**, his wife,	2454
	5:14	His wife **Z** and all his friends said to him,	2454
	6:13	and told **Z** his wife and all his friends	2454
	6:13	His advisers and his wife **Z** said to him,	2454

ZERETH (1) [ZERETH SHAHAR]

1Ch	4: 7	The sons of Helah: **Z**, Zohar, Ethnan,	7679

ZERETH SHAHAR (1) [ZERETH]

Jos	13:19	Sibmah, **Z** on the hill in the valley,	7680

ZERI (1)

1Ch	25: 3	Gedaliah, **Z**, Jeshaiah, Shimei,	7662

ZEROR (1)

1Sa	9: 1	the son of **Z**, the son of Becorath,	7657

ZERUAH (1)

1Ki	11:26	and his mother was a widow named **Z**.	7654

ZERUBBABEL (25)

1Ch	3:19	The sons of Pedaiah: **Z** and Shimei.	2428
	3:19	The sons of **Z**: Meshullam and Hananiah,	2428
Ezr	2: 2	in company with **Z**, Jeshua, Nehemiah,	2428
	3: 2	and his fellow priests and **Z** son of Shealtiel	2428
	3: 8	**Z** son of Shealtiel, Jeshua son of Jozadak	2428
	4: 2	to **Z** and to the heads of the families	2428
	4: 3	But **Z**, Jeshua and the rest of the heads of	2428
	5: 2	Then **Z** son of Shealtiel and Jeshua son	10239
Ne	7: 7	in company with **Z**, Jeshua, Nehemiah,	2428
	12: 1	with **Z** son of Shealtiel and with Jeshua:	2428
	12:47	So in the days of **Z** and of Nehemiah,	2428
Hag	1: 1	the prophet Haggai to **Z** son of Shealtiel,	2428
	1:12	Then **Z** son of Shealtiel, Joshua son of	2428
	1:14	So the LORD stirred up the spirit of **Z** son	2428
	2: 2	"Speak to **Z** son of Shealtiel,	2428
	2: 4	now be strong, O **Z**,' declares the LORD.	2428
	2:21	"Tell **Z** governor of Judah that I will shake	2428
	2:23	my servant **Z** son of Shealtiel,'	2428
Zec	4: 6	"This is the word of the LORD to **Z**:	2428
	4: 7	Before **Z** you will become level ground.	2428
	4: 9	of **Z** have laid the foundation of this temple;	2428
	4:10	the plumb line in the hand of **Z**.	2428
Mt	1:12	Shealtiel the father of **Z**,	2431
	1:13	**Z** the father of Abiud,	2431
Lk	3:27	the son *of* **Z**, the son of Shealtiel,	2431

ZERUIAH (25) [ZERUIAH'S]

1Sa	26: 6	the Hittite and Abishai son of **Z**,	7653
2Sa	2:13	Joab son of **Z** and David's men went out	7653
	2:18	The three sons of **Z** were there:	7653
	3:39	and these sons of **Z** are too strong for me.	7653
	8:16	Joab son of **Z** was over the army;	7653
	14: 1	of **Z** knew that the king's heart longed	7653
	16: 9	Then Abishai son of **Z** said to the king,	7653
	16:10	you and I have in common, you sons of **Z**?	7653
	17:25	the daughter of Nahash and sister of **Z**	7653
	18: 2	under Joab's brother Abishai son of **Z**,	7653
	19:21	Then Abishai son of **Z** said,	7653
	19:22	you and I have in common, you sons of **Z**?	7653
	21:17	Abishai son of **Z** came to David's rescue;	7653
	23:18	the brother of Joab son of **Z** was chief of	7653
	23:37	the armor-bearer of Joab son of **Z**,	7653
1Ki	1: 7	Adonijah conferred with Joab son of **Z** and	7653
	2: 5	know what Joab son of **Z** did to me—	7653
	2:22	for Abiathar the priest and Joab son of **Z**!"	7653
1Ch	2:16	Their sisters were **Z** and Abigail.	7653
	11: 6	Joab son of **Z** went up first,	7653
	11:39	the armor-bearer of Joab son of **Z**,	7653
	18:12	Abishai son of **Z** struck down	7653
	18:15	Joab son of **Z** was over the army;	7653
	26:28	Abner son of Ner and Joab son of **Z**	7653
	27:24	Joab son of **Z** began to count the men	7653

ZERUIAH'S (1) [ZERUIAH]

1Ch	2:16	**Z** three sons were Abishai, Joab and Asahel.	7653

ZETHAM (2)

1Ch	23: 8	Jehiel the first, **Z** and Joel—three in all.	2457
	26:22	the sons of Jehieli, **Z** and his brother Joel.	2457

ZETHAN (1)

1Ch	7:10	Jeush, Benjamin, Ehud, Kenaanah, **Z**,	2340

ZETHAR (1)

Est	1:10	Harbona, Bigtha, Abagtha, **Z** and Carcas—	2458

ZEUS (2)

Ac	14:12	Barnabas they called **Z**, and Paul	2416
	14:13	The priest *of* **Z**, whose temple was	2416

ZIA (1)

1Ch	5:13	Jorai, Jacan, **Z** and Eber—seven in all.	2333

ZIBA (16) [ZIBA'S]

2Sa	9: 2	a servant of Saul's household named **Z**.	7471
	9: 2	and the king said to him, "Are you **Z**?"	7471
	9: 3	**Z** answered the king, "There is still a son	7471
	9: 4	**Z** answered, "He is at the house	7471
	9: 9	Then the king summoned **Z**, Saul's servant,	7471
	9:10	**Z** had fifteen sons and twenty servants.)	7471
	9:11	Then **Z** said to the king.	7471
	16: 1	there was **Z**, the steward of Mephibosheth,	7471
	16: 2	The king asked **Z**, "Why have you brought	7471
	16: 2	**Z** answered, "The donkeys are for	7471
	16: 3	**Z** said to him, "He is staying in Jerusalem,	7471
	16: 4	Then the king said to **Z**,	7471
	16: 4	"I humbly bow," **Z** said.	7471
	19:17	with **Z**, the steward of Saul's household,	7471
	19:26	But **Z** my servant betrayed me.	NIH
	19:29	I order you and **Z** to divide the fields."	7471

ZIBA'S (1) [ZIBA]

2Sa	9:12	the members of **Z** household were servants	7471

ZIBEON (8)

Ge	36: 2	and granddaughter of **Z** the Hivite—	7390
	36:14	and granddaughter of **Z**, whom she bore	7390
	36:20	Lotan, Shobal, **Z**, Anah,	7390
	36:24	The sons of **Z**: Aiah and Anah.	7390
	36:24	was grazing the donkeys of his father **Z**.	7390
	36:29	Lotan, Shobal, **Z**, Anah,	7390
1Ch	1:38	The sons of Seir: Lotan, Shobal, **Z**, Anah,	7390
	1:40	The sons of **Z**: Aiah and Anah.	7390

ZIBIA (1)

1Ch	8: 9	By his wife Hodesh he had Jobab, **Z**,	7384

ZIBIAH (2)

2Ki	12: 1	His mother's name was **Z**;	7385
2Ch	24: 1	His mother's name was **Z**;	7385

ZICHRI (KJV) See ZICRI

ZICRI (12)

Ex	6:21	of Izhar were Korah, Nepheg and **Z**.	2356
1Ch	8:19	Jakim, **Z**, Zabdi,	2356
	8:23	Abdon, **Z**, Hanan,	2356
	8:27	Elijah and **Z** were the sons of Jeroham.	2356
	9:15	the son of **Z**, the son of Asaph;	2356
	26:25	**Z** his son and Shelomith his son.	2356
	27:16	Eliezer son of **Z**;	2356
2Ch	17:16	Amasiah son of **Z**, who volunteered himself	2356
	23: 1	and Elishaphat son of **Z**.	2356
	28: 7	**Z**, an Ephraimite warrior, killed Maaseiah	2356
Ne	11: 9	Joel son of **Z** was their chief officer,	2356
	12:17	of Abijah's, **Z**; of Miniamin's	2356

ZIDDIM (1)

Jos	19:35	The fortified cities were **Z**, Zer, Hammath,	7403

ZIDKIJAH (KJV) See ZEDEKIAH

ZIDON, ZIDONIANS (KJV) See SIDON, SIDONIANS

ZIF (KJV) See ZIV

ZIHA (3)

Ezr	2:43	the descendants of **Z**, Hasupha, Tabbaoth,	7484
Ne	7:46	the descendants of **Z**, Hasupha, Tabbaoth,	7484
	11:21	and **Z** and Gishpa were in charge of them.	7484

ZIKLAG (15)

Jos	15:31	**Z**, Madmannah, Sansannah,	7637
	19: 5	**Z**, Beth Marcaboth, Hazar Susah,	7637
1Sa	27: 6	So on that day Achish gave him **Z**,	7637
	30: 1	and his men reached **Z** on the third day.	7637
	30: 1	the Amalekites had raided the Negev and **Z**.	7637

1Sa	30: 1	They had attacked **Z** and burned it,	7637
	30: 3	When David and his men came to **Z**,	2021+6551ˢ
	30:14	And we burned **Z**."	7637
	30:26	When David arrived in **Z**,	7637
2Sa	1: 1	the Amalekites and stayed in **Z** two days.	7637
1Ch	4:30	Bethuel, Hormah, **Z**,	7637
	12: 1	to David at **Z**, while he was banished from	7637
	12:20	When David went to **Z**,	7637
Ne	11:28	in **Z**, in Meconah and its settlements,	7637

ZILLAH (3)

Ge	4:19	one named Adah and the other **Z**.	7500
	4:22	**Z** also had a son, Tubal-Cain,	7500
	4:23	Lamech said to his wives, "Adah and **Z**,	7500

ZILLETHAI (2)

1Ch	8:20	Elienai, **Z**, Eliel,	7531
	12:20	Jediael, Michael, Jozabad, Elihu and **Z**,	7531

ZILPAH (7)

Ge	29:24	And Laban gave his servant girl **Z**	2364
	30: 9	she took her maidservant **Z** and gave her	2364
	30:10	Leah's servant **Z** bore Jacob a son.	2364
	30:12	Leah's servant **Z** bore Jacob a second son.	2364
	35:26	The sons of Leah's maidservant **Z**:	2364
	37: 2	the sons of Bilhah and the sons of **Z**,	2364
	46:18	These were the children born to Jacob by **Z**,	2364

ZILTHAI (KJV) See ZILLETHAI

ZIMMAH (3)

1Ch	6:20	Libni his son, Jehath his son, **Z** his son,	2366
	6:42	the son of **Z**, the son of Shimei,	2366
2Ch	29:12	Joah son of **Z** and Eden son of Joah;	2366

ZIMRAN (2)

Ge	25: 2	She bore him **Z**, Jokshan, Medan, Midian,	2383
1Ch	1:32	**Z**, Jokshan, Medan, Midian,	2383

ZIMRI (17) [ZIMRI'S]

Nu	25:14	the Midianite woman was **Z** son of Salu,	2381
Jos	7: 1	Achan son of Carmi, the son of **Z**,	2381
	7:17	came forward by families, and **Z** was taken.	2381
	7:18	and Achan son of Carmi, the son of **Z**,	2381
1Ki	16: 9	**Z**, one of his officials, who had command	2381
	16:10	**Z** came in, struck him down and killed him	2381
	16:12	So **Z** destroyed the whole family of Baasha,	2381
	16:15	**Z** reigned in Tirzah seven days.	2381
	16:16	in the camp heard that **Z** had plotted against	2381
	16:18	When **Z** saw that the city was taken,	2381
2Ki	9:31	she asked, "Have you come in peace, **Z**,	2381
1Ch	2: 6	**Z**, Ethan, Heman, Calcol and Darda—	2381
	8:36	Azmaveth and **Z**, and Zimri was the father	2381
	8:36	and **Z** was the father of Moza.	2381
	9:42	Azmaveth and **Z**, and Zimri was the father	2381
	9:42	and **Z** was the father of Moza.	2381
Jer	25:25	all the kings of **Z**, Elam and Media;	2382

ZIMRI'S (1) [ZIMRI]

1Ki	16:20	As for the other events of **Z** reign,	2381

ZIN (10)

Nu	13:21	and explored the land from the Desert of **Z**	7554
	20: 1	community arrived at the Desert of **Z**,	7554
	27:14	rebelled at the waters in the Desert of **Z**.	7554
	27:14	Meribah Kadesh, in the Desert of **Z**.)	7554
	33:36	camped at Kadesh, in the Desert of **Z**.	7554
	34: 3	the Desert of **Z** along the border of Edom.	7554
	34: 4	on to **Z** and go south of Kadesh Barnea.	7554
Dt	32:51	of Meribah Kadesh in the Desert of **Z** and	7554
Jos	15: 1	to the Desert of **Z** in the extreme south.	7554
	15: 3	continued on to **Z** and went over to	7554

ZION (163) [ZION'S]

2Sa	5: 7	David captured the fortress of **Z**,	7482
1Ki	8: 1	the ark of the LORD's covenant from **Z**,	7482
2Ki	19:31	"The Virgin Daughter of **Z** despises you	7482
	19:31	and out of Mount **Z** a band of survivors.	7482
1Ch	11: 5	David captured the fortress of **Z**,	7482
2Ch	5: 2	the ark of the LORD's covenant from **Z**,	7482
Ps	2: 6	"I have installed my King on **Z**,	7482
	9:11	Sing praises to the LORD, enthroned in **Z**;	7482
	9:14	praises in the gates of the Daughter of **Z**	7482
	14: 7	for Israel would come out of **Z**!	7482
	20: 2	the sanctuary and grant you support from **Z**.	7482
	48: 2	the utmost heights of Zaphon is Mount **Z**,	7482
	48:11	Mount **Z** rejoices, the villages of Judah	7482
	48:12	Walk about **Z**, go around her,	7482
	50: 2	From **Z**, perfect in beauty, God shines forth.	7482
	51:18	In your good pleasure make **Z** prosper;	7482
	53: 6	salvation for Israel would come out of **Z**!	7482
	65: 1	Praise awaits you, O God, in **Z**;	7482
	69:35	for God will save **Z** and rebuild the cities	7482
	74: 2	Mount **Z**, where you dwelt.	7482
	76: 2	His tent is in Salem, his dwelling place in **Z**.	7482
	78:68	Mount **Z**, which he loved.	7482
	84: 7	till each appears before God in **Z**.	7482
	87: 2	of **Z** more than all the dwellings of Jacob.	7482
	87: 4	and will say, 'This one was born in **Z**.' "	9004ˢ

Ps	87: 5	Indeed, of **Z** it will be said,	7482
	87: 6	"This one was born in **Z**."	9004S
	97: 8	**Z** hears and rejoices and the villages	7482
	99: 2	Great is the LORD in **Z**;	7482
	102:13	You will arise and have compassion on **Z**,	7482
	102:16	For the LORD will rebuild **Z** and appear	7482
	102:21	be declared in **Z** and his praise in Jerusalem	7482
	110: 2	The LORD will extend your mighty scepter from **Z**;	7482
	125: 1	who trust in the LORD are like Mount **Z**,	7482
	126: 1	the LORD brought back the captives to **Z**,	7482
	128: 5	the LORD bless you from **Z** all the days	7482
	129: 5	May all who hate **Z** be turned back	7482
	132:13	For the LORD has chosen **Z**,	7482
	133: 3	of Hermon were falling on Mount **Z**.	7482
	134: 3	May the LORD, the Maker of heaven and earth, bless you from **Z**.	7482
	135:21	Praise be to the LORD from **Z**,	7482
	137: 1	and wept when we remembered **Z**.	7482
	137: 3	they said, "Sing us one of the songs of **Z**!"	7482
	146:10	The LORD reigns forever, your God, O **Z**,	7482
	147:12	praise your God, O **Z**,	7482
	149: 2	let the people of **Z** be glad in their King.	7482
SS	3:11	Come out, you daughters of **Z**.	7482
Isa	1: 8	The Daughter of **Z** is left like a shelter in	7482
	1:27	**Z** will be redeemed with justice,	7482
	2: 3	The law will go out from **Z**,	7482
	3:16	"The women of **Z** are haughty,	7482
	3:17	on the heads of the women of **Z**;	7482
	3:26	The gates of **Z** will lament and mourn;	2023S
	4: 3	Those who are left in **Z**,	7482
	4: 4	the filth of the women of **Z**;	7482
	4: 5	the LORD will create over all of Mount **Z**	7482
	8:18	Almighty, who dwells on Mount **Z**.	7482
	10:12	against Mount **Z** and Jerusalem,	7482
	10:24	"O my people who live in **Z**,	7482
	10:32	at the mount of the Daughter of **Z**,	7482
	12: 6	Shout aloud and sing for joy, people of **Z**,	7482
	14:32	"The LORD has established **Z**,	7482
	16: 1	to the mount of the Daughter of **Z**.	7482
	18: 7	the gifts will be brought to Mount **Z**,	7482
	24:23	the LORD Almighty will reign on Mount **Z**	7482
	28:16	"See, I lay a stone in **Z**, a tested stone,	7482
	29: 8	of all the nations that fight against Mount **Z**.	7482
	30:19	O people of **Z**, who live in Jerusalem,	7482
	31: 4	to do battle on Mount **Z** and on its heights.	7482
	31: 9	declares the LORD, whose fire is in **Z**,	7482
	33: 5	he will fill **Z** with justice and righteousness.	7482
	33:14	The sinners in **Z** are terrified;	7482
	33:20	Look upon **Z**, the city of our festivals;	7482
	33:24	No one living in **Z** will say, "I am ill";	NIH
	35:10	They will enter **Z** with singing;	7482
	37:22	"The Virgin Daughter of **Z** despises	7482
	37:32	and out of Mount **Z** a band of survivors.	7482
	40: 9	You who bring good tidings to **Z**,	7482
	41:27	I was the first to tell **Z**, 'Look,	7482
	46:13	I will grant salvation to **Z**,	7482
	49:14	But **Z** said, "The LORD has forsaken me,	7482
	51: 3	The LORD will surely comfort **Z**	7482
	51:11	They will enter **Z** with singing;	7482
	51:16	and who say to **Z**, 'You are my people.' "	7482
	52: 1	awake, O **Z**, clothe yourself with strength.	7482
	52: 2	O captive Daughter of **Z**.	7482
	52: 7	who proclaim salvation, who say to **Z**,	7482
	52: 8	When the LORD returns to **Z**,	7482
	59:20	"The Redeemer will come to **Z**,	7482
	60:14	**Z** of the Holy One of Israel.	7482
	61: 3	and provide for those who grieve in **Z**—	7482
	62:11	"Say to the Daughter of **Z**, 'See,	7482
	64:10	even **Z** is a desert, Jerusalem a desolation.	7482
	66: 8	Yet no sooner is **Z** in labor	7482
Jer	3:14	and bring you to **Z**.	7482
	4: 6	Raise the signal to go to **Z**!	7482
	4:31	cry of the Daughter of **Z** gasping for breath,	7482
	6: 2	I will destroy the Daughter of **Z**,	7482
	6:23	to attack you, O Daughter of **Z**."	7482
	8:19	"Is the LORD not in **Z**?	7482
	9:19	The sound of wailing is heard from **Z**:	7482
	14:19	Do you despise **Z**?	7482
	26:18	" '**Z** will be plowed like a field,	7482
	30:17	**Z** for whom no one cares.'	7482
	31: 6	let us go up to **Z**, to the LORD our God.' "	7482
	31:12	and shout for joy on the heights of **Z**;	7482
	50: 5	the way to **Z** and turn their faces toward it.	7482
	50:28	and refugees from Babylon declaring in **Z**	7482
	51:10	in **Z** what the LORD our God has done.'	7482
	51:24	for all the wrong they have done in **Z**,"	7482
	51:35	say the inhabitants of **Z**.	7482
La	1: 4	The roads to **Z** mourn,	7482
	1: 6	has departed from the Daughter of **Z**	7482
	1:17	**Z** stretches out her hands,	7482
	2: 1	the Lord has covered the Daughter of **Z**	7482
	2: 4	like fire on the tent of the Daughter of **Z**.	7482
	2: 6	has made **Z** forget her appointed feasts	7482
	2: 8	down the wall around the Daughter of **Z**.	7482
	2:10	of the Daughter of **Z** sit on the ground	7482
	2:13	O Virgin Daughter of **Z**?	7482
	2:18	O wall of the Daughter of **Z**,	7482
	4: 2	How the precious sons of **Z**,	7482
	4:11	a fire in **Z** that consumed her foundations.	7482
	4:22	O Daughter of **Z**, your punishment will end;	7482
	5:11	Women have been ravished in **Z**,	7482
	5:18	for Mount **Z**, which lies desolate,	7482
Joel	2: 1	Blow the trumpet in **Z**; sound the alarm	7482
	2:15	Blow the trumpet in **Z**, declare a holy fast,	7482
	2:23	Be glad, O people of **Z**, rejoice in the LORD	7482
	2:32	for on Mount **Z** and in Jerusalem there will	7482

Joel	3:16	The LORD will roar from **Z** and thunder	7482
	3:17	the LORD your God, dwell in **Z**,	7482
	3:21	The LORD dwells in **Z**!	7482
Am	1: 2	"The LORD roars from **Z** and thunders	7482
	6: 1	Woe to you who are complacent in **Z**,	7482
Ob	1:17	But on Mount **Z** will be deliverance;	7482
	1:21	Deliverers will go up on Mount **Z** to govern	7482
Mic	1:13	the beginning of sin to the Daughter of **Z**,	7482
	3:10	who build **Z** with bloodshed,	7482
	3:12	**Z** will be plowed like a field,	7482
	4: 2	The law will go out from **Z**,	7482
	4: 7	The LORD will rule over them in Mount **Z**	7482
	4: 8	O stronghold of the Daughter of **Z**,	7482
	4:10	Writhe in agony, O Daughter of **Z**,	7482
	4:11	let our eyes gloat over **Z**!"	7482
	4:13	"Rise and thresh, O Daughter of **Z**,	7482
Zep	3:14	Sing, O Daughter of **Z**;	7482
	3:16	O **Z**; do not let your hands hang limp.	7482
Zec	1:14	'I am very jealous for Jerusalem and **Z**,	7482
	1:17	and the LORD will again comfort **Z**	7482
	2: 7	"Come, O **Z**! Escape, you who live in	7482
	2:10	"Shout and be glad, O Daughter of **Z**.	7482
	8: 2	"I am very jealous for **Z**;	7482
	8: 3	"I will return to **Z** and dwell in Jerusalem.	7482
	9: 9	Rejoice greatly, O Daughter of **Z**!	7482
	9:13	I will rouse your sons, **Z**,	7482
Mt	21: 5	"Say to the Daughter *of* **Z**,	4994
Jn	12:15	"Do not be afraid, O Daughter *of* **Z**;	4994
Ro	9:33	I lay in **Z** a stone that causes men to stumble	4994
	11:26	"The deliverer will come from **Z**;	4994
Heb	12:22	But you have come to Mount **Z**,	4994
1Pe	2: 6	"See, I lay a stone in **Z**,	4994
Rev	14: 1	was the Lamb, standing on Mount **Z**,	4994

ZION'S (2) [ZION]

Isa	34: 8	a year of retribution, to uphold **Z** cause.	7482
	62: 1	For **Z** sake I will not keep silent,	7482

ZIOR (1)

Jos	15:54	Kiriath Arba (that is, Hebron) and **Z**—	7486

ZIPH (9) [ZIPHITES]

Jos	15:24	**Z**, Telem, Bealoth,	2334
	15:55	Maon, Carmel, **Z**, Juttah,	2334
1Sa	23:14	and in the hills of the Desert of **Z**.	2334
	23:15	David was at Horesh in the Desert of **Z**	2334
	23:24	So they set out and went to **Z** ahead of Saul.	2334
	26: 2	So Saul went down to the Desert of **Z**,	2334
1Ch	2:42	his firstborn, who was the father of **Z**,	2335
	4:16	**Z**, Ziphah, Tiria and Asarel.	2335
2Ch	11: 8	Gath, Mareshah, **Z**,	2334

ZIPHAH (1)

1Ch	4:16	Ziph, **Z**, Tiria and Asarel.	2336

ZIPHITES (3) [ZIPH]

1Sa	23:19	The **Z** went up to Saul at Gibeah and said,	2337
	26: 1	The **Z** went to Saul at Gibeah and said,	2337
Ps	54: T	When the **Z** had gone to Saul and said,	2337

ZIPHRON (1)

Nu	34: 9	continue to **Z** and end at Hazar Enan.	2412

ZIPPOR (7)

Nu	22: 2	son of **Z** saw all that Israel had done to	7607
	22: 4	So Balak son of **Z**, who was king of Moab	7607
	22:10	Balaam said to God, "Balak son of **Z**,	7607
	22:16	"This is what Balak son of **Z** says:	7607
	23:18	and listen; hear me, son of **Z**.	7607
Jos	24: 9	When Balak son of **Z**, the king of Moab,	7607
Jdg	11:25	Are you better than Balak son of **Z**,	7607

ZIPPORAH (4)

Ex	2:21	who gave his daughter **Z** to Moses	7631
	2:22	**Z** gave birth to a son, and Moses named him	NIH
	4:25	But **Z** took a flint knife,	7631
	18: 2	After Moses had sent away his wife **Z**,	7631

ZITHER (4)

Da	3: 5	**z**, lyre, harp, pipes and all kinds of music,	10630
	3: 7	flute, **z**, lyre, harp and all kinds of music,	10630
	3:10	of the horn, flute, **z**, lyre, harp, pipes	10630
	3:15	lyre, harp, pipes and all kinds of music,	10630

ZITHRI (KJV) See SITHRI

ZIV (2)

1Ki	6: 1	in the month of **Z**, the second month,	2304
	6:37	in the fourth year, in the month of **Z**.	2304

ZIZ (1)

2Ch	20:16	They will be climbing up by the Pass of **Z**,	7489

ZIZA (4)

1Ch	4:37	and **Z** son of Shiphi, the son of Allon,	2330
	23:10	sons of Shimei: Jahath, **Z**, Jeush and Beriah.	2330
	23:11	Jahath was the first and **Z** the second,	2331
2Ch	11:20	Attai, **Z** and Shelomith.	2330

ZOAN (7)

Nu	13:22	(Hebron had been built seven years before **Z**	7586
Ps	78:12	in the land of Egypt, in the region of **Z**.	7586
	78:43	his wonders in the region of **Z**.	7586
Isa	19:11	The officials of **Z** are nothing but fools;	7586
	19:13	The officials of **Z** have become fools,	7586
	30: 4	in **Z** and their envoys have arrived in Hanes,	7586
Eze	30:14	to **Z** and inflict punishment on Thebes.	7586

ZOAR (10) [BELA]

Ge	13:10	like the land of Egypt, toward **Z**).	7593
	14: 2	and the king of Bela (that is, **Z**).	7593
	14: 8	the king of Bela (that is, **Z**) marched out	7593
	19:22	(That is why the town was called **Z**.)	7593
	19:23	By the time Lot reached **Z**,	7593
	19:30	Lot and his two daughters left **Z** and settled	7593
	19:30	for he was afraid to stay in **Z**.	7593
Dt	34: 3	the City of Palms, as far as **Z**.	7593
Isa	15: 5	her fugitives flee as far as **Z**,	7593
Jer	48:34	from **Z** as far as Horonaim	7593

ZOBAH (13) [ARAM ZOBAH, HAMATH ZOBAH]

1Sa	14:47	Edom, the kings of **Z**, and the Philistines.	7420
2Sa	8: 3	of **Z**, when he went to restore his control	7420
	8: 5	to help Hadadezer king of **Z**,	7420
	8:12	from Hadadezer son of Rehob, king of **Z**.	7420
	10: 6	foot soldiers from Beth Rehob and **Z**,	7419
	10: 8	the Arameans of **Z** and Rehob and the men	7419
	23:36	Igal son of Nathan from **Z**, the son of Hagri,	7420
1Ki	11:23	from his master, Hadadezer king of **Z**.	7420
	11:24	when David destroyed the forces [of **Z**];	NIH
1Ch	18: 3	David fought Hadadezer king of **Z**,	7420
	18: 5	to help Hadadezer king of **Z**,	7420
	18: 9	the entire army of Hadadezer king of **Z**,	7420
	19: 6	Aram Naharaim, Aram Maacah and **Z**.	7420

ZOHAR (5)

Ge	23: 8	to me and intercede with Ephron son of **Z**	7468
	25: 9	in the field of Ephron son of **Z**	7468
	46:10	**Z** and Shaul the son of a Canaanite woman.	7468
Ex	6:15	**Z** and Shaul the son of a Canaanite woman.	7468
1Ch	4: 7	The sons of Helah: Zereth, **Z**, Ethnan,	7468

ZOHELETH (1)

1Ki	1: 9	cattle and fattened calves at the Stone of **Z**	2325

ZOHETH (1)

1Ch	4:20	The descendants of Ishi: **Z** and Ben-Zoheth.	2311

ZOPHAH (2)

1Ch	7:35	Imna, Shelesh and Amal.	7432
	7:36	The sons of **Z**: Suah, Harnepher,	7432

ZOPHAI (1)

1Ch	6:26	Elkanah his son, **Z** his son, Nahath his son,	7433

ZOPHAR (4)

Job	2:11	Bildad the Shuhite and **Z** the Naamathite.	7436
	11: 1	Then **Z** the Naamathite replied:	7436
	20: 1	Then **Z** the Naamathite replied:	7436
	42: 9	and **Z** the Naamathite did what the LORD	7436

ZOPHIM (1)

Nu	23:14	So he took him to the field of **Z** on the top	7614

ZORAH (10)

Jos	15:33	In the western foothills: Eshtaol, **Z**, Ashnah,	7666
	19:41	**Z**, Eshtaol, Ir Shemesh,	7666
Jdg	13: 2	A certain man of **Z**, named Manoah,	7666
	13:25	in Mahaneh Dan, between **Z** and Eshtaol.	7666
	16:31	and buried him between **Z** and Eshtaol in	7666
	18: 2	So the Danites sent five warriors from **Z**	7666
	18: 8	When they returned to **Z** and Eshtaol,	7666
	18:11	armed for battle, set out from **Z** and Eshtaol.	7666
2Ch	11:10	**Z**, Aijalon and Hebron.	7666
Ne	11:29	in En Rimmon, in **Z**, in Jarmuth,	7666

ZORATHITES (2)

1Ch	2:53	From these descended the **Z** and Eshtaolites.	7670
	4: 2	These were the clans of the **Z**.	7670

ZORITES (1)

1Ch	2:54	half the Manahathites, the **Z**,	7668

ZOBEBAH (KJV) See HAZZOBEBAH

ZOREAH (KJV) See ZORAH

ZOROBABEL (KJV) See ZERUBBABEL

ZUAR (5)

Nu	1: 8	from Issachar, Nethanel son of **Z**;	7428
	2: 5	the people of Issachar is Nethanel son of **Z**.	7428
	7:18	On the second day Nethanel son of **Z**,	7428
	7:23	This was the offering of Nethanel son of **Z**.	7428

Nu 10:15   Nethanel son of Z was over the division of   7428

ZUPH (3) [ZUPHITE]
1Sa 1: 1   the son of Tohu, the son of Z,   7431
    9: 5   When they reached the district of Z,   7431
1Ch 6:35   the son of Z, the son of Elkanah,   7431

ZUPHITE (1) [ZUPH]
1Sa 1: 1   a Z from the hill country of Ephraim,   7434

ZUR (5) [BETH ZUR]
Nu 25:15   put to death was Cozbi daughter of Z,   7448
    31: 8   Among their victims were Evi, Rekem, Z,   7448
Jos 13:21   Evi, Rekem, Z, Hur and Reba—   7448
1Ch 8:30   followed by Z, Kish, Baal, Ner, Nadab,   7448
    9:36   followed by Z, Kish, Baal, Ner, Nadab,   7448

ZURIEL (1)
Nu 3:35   the families of the Merarite clans was Z son   7452

ZURISHADDAI (5)
Nu 1: 6   from Simeon, Shelumiel son of Z;   7453
    2:12   the people of Simeon is Shelumiel son of Z.   7453
    7:36   On the fifth day Shelumiel son of Z,   7453
    7:41   This was the offering of Shelumiel son of Z.   7453
    10:19   Shelumiel son of Z was over the division of   7453

ZUZIMS (KJV) See ZUZITES

ZUZITES (1)
Ge 14: 5   the Z in Ham, the Emites in Shaveh   2309

NUMERALS

12 (24) [TWELVE]
1Ch 25: 9   to Joseph, his sons and relatives, 12   6925+9109
    25: 9   he and his relatives and sons, 12   6925+9109
    25:10   to Zaccur, his sons and relatives, 12   6925+9109
    25:11   to Izri, his sons and relatives, 12   6925+9109
    25:12   Nethaniah, his sons and relatives, 12   6925+9109
    25:13   to Bukkiah, his sons and relatives, 12   6925+9109
    25:14   to Jesarelah, his sons and relatives, 12   6925+9109
    25:15   to Jeshaiah, his sons and relatives, 12   6925+9109
    25:16   Mattaniah, his sons and relatives, 12   6925+9109
    25:17   to Shimei, his sons and relatives, 12   6925+9109
    25:18   to Azarel, his sons and relatives, 12   6925+9109
    25:19   Hashabiah, his sons and relatives, 12   6925+9109
    25:20   to Shubael, his sons and relatives, 12   6925+9109
    25:21   Mattithiah, his sons and relatives, 12   6925+9109
    25:22   to Jerimoth, his sons and relatives, 12   6925+9109
    25:23   Hananiah, his sons and relatives, 12   6925+9109
    25:24   his sons and relatives, 12   6925+9109
    25:25   to Hanani, his sons and relatives, 12   6925+9109
    25:26   to Mallothi, his sons and relatives, 12   6925+9109
    25:27   to Eliathah, his sons and relatives, 12   6925+9109
    25:28   to Hothir, his sons and relatives, 12   6925+9109
    25:29   to Giddalti, his sons and relatives, 12   6925+9109
    25:30   Mahazioth, his sons and relatives, 12   6925+9109
    25:31   his sons and relatives, 12   6925+9109

13 (1) [THIRTEEN]
1Ch 26:11   and relatives of Hosah were 13 in all.   6925+8993

18 (3) [EIGHTEEN]
Ge 6:16   finish the ark to within 18 inches of the top.   564
1Ch 26: 9   who were able men—18 in all.   6925+9046
Ezr 8:18   sons and brothers, 18 men;   6925+9046

20 (2) [TWENTY]
Ezr 8:19   and his brothers and nephews, 20 men.   6929
    8:27   20 bowls of gold valued at 1,000 darics,   6929

22 (1) [TWENTY-TWO]
1Ch 12:28   with 22 officers from his family;   2256+6929+9109

28 (1) [TWENTY-EIGHT]
Ezr 8:11   of Bebai, and with him 28 men;   2256+6929+9046

29 (3) [TWENTY-NINE]
Ge 11:24   When Nahor had lived 29 years,   2256+6929+9596
Ex 38:24   on the sanctuary was 29 talents   2256+6929+9596
Ezr 1: 9   silver pans 29   2256+6929+9596

30 (5) [THIRTY]
Ge 11:14   When Shelah had lived 30 years,   8993
    11:18   When Peleg had lived 30 years,   8993
    11:22   When Serug had lived 30 years,   8993
Ezr 1: 9   gold dishes 30 silver dishes 1,000,   8993
    1:10   gold bowls 30 matching silver bowls 410   8993

32 (3) [THIRTY-TWO]
Ge 11:20   When Reu had lived 32 years,   2256+8993+9109
Nu 31:40   16,000 people, of which the tribute for the
         LORD was 32.   2256+8993+9109
1Ki 20:16   Ben-Hadad and the 32 kings   2256+8993+9109

34 (1)
Ge 11:16   When Eber had lived 34 years,   752+2256+8993

35 (1) [THIRTY-FIVE]
Ge 11:12   Arphaxad had lived 35 years,   2256+2822+8993

40 (1) [FORTY]
Eze 4: 6   I have assigned you 40 days, a day for each   752

42 (3) [FORTY-TWO]
Ezr 2:24   of Azmaveth 42   752+2256+9109
Ne 7:28   of Beth Azmaveth 42   752+2256+9109
Rev 11: 2   They will trample on the holy city for 42
         months.   1545+5477

45 (1) [FORTY-FIVE]
Ge 6:15   75 feet wide and 45 feet high.   564+8993

50 (3) [FIFTY]
Ezr 8: 6   Ebed son of Jonathan, and with him 50 men;   2822
Ne 7:70   50 bowls and 530 garments for priests.   2822
Eze 45: 2   with 50 cubits around it for open land.   2822

52 (2) [FIFTY-TWO]
Ezr 2:29   of Nebo 52   2256+2822+9109
Ne 7:33   of the other Nebo 52   2256+2822+9109

56 (1)
Ezr 2:22   of Netophah 56   2256+2822+9252

60 (1) [SIXTY]
Ezr 8:13   Jeuel and Shemaiah, and with them 60 men;   9252

61 (1)
Nu 31:39   the tribute for the LORD was 61;   285+2256+9252

62 (1) [SIXTY-TWO]
1Ch 26: 8   of Obed-Edom, 62 in all.   2256+9109+9252

65 (2) [SIXTY-FIVE]
Ge 5:15   Mahalalel had lived 65 years,   2256+2822+9252
    5:21   Enoch had lived 65 years,   2256+2822+9252

67 (1)
Ne 7:72   and 67 garments for priests.   2256+8679+9252

70 (5) [SEVENTY]
Ge 5:12   When Kenan had lived 70 years,   8679
    11:26   After Terah had lived 70 years,   8679
Ex 38:29   the wave offering was 70 talents and 2,400   8679
Ezr 8: 7   son of Athaliah, and with him 70 men;   8679
    8:14   Uthai and Zaccur, and with them 70 men.   8679

72 (1) [SEVENTY-TWO]
Nu 31:38   tribute for the LORD was 72;   2256+8679+9109

74 (2)
Ezr 2:40   through the line of Hodaviah) 74   752+2256+8679
Ne 7:43   through the line of Hodaviah) 74   752+2256+8679

75 (1) [SEVENTY-FIVE]
Ge 6:15   75 feet wide and 45 feet high.   564+2822

80 (2) [EIGHTY]
1Ch 15: 9   Eliel the leader and 80 relatives;   9046
Ezr 8: 8   and with him 80 men;   9046

90 (1) [NINETY]
Ge 5: 9   When Enosh had lived 90 years,   9596

95 (2)
Ezr 2:20   of Gibbar 95   2256+2822+9596
Ne 7:25   of Gibeon 95   2256+2822+9596

98 (2) [NINETY-EIGHT]
Ezr 2:16   of Ater (through Hezekiah) 98   2256+9046+9596
Ne 7:21   of Ater (through Hezekiah) 98   2256+9046+9596

100 (8) [HUNDRED]
Ge 11:10   when Shem was 100 years old,   4395
Ex 38:25   the census was 100 talents and   4395
    38:27   The 100 talents of silver were used to cast   4395
    38:27   100 bases from the 100 talents,   4395
    38:27   100 bases from the 100 talents,   4395
Ezr 2:69   minas of silver and 100 priestly garments.   4395
    8:26   silver articles weighing 100 talents,   4395
    8:26   100 talents of gold,   4395

105 (1)
Ge 5: 6   When Seth had lived 105 years,   2256+2822+4395

110 (1)
Ezr 8:12   and with him 110 men;   2256+4395+6927

112 (3)
1Ch 15:10   Amminadab the leader and 112 relatives.   2256+4395+6925+9109
Ezr 2:18   of Jorah 112   2256+4395+6925+9109
Ne 7:24   of Hariph 112   4395+6925+9109

119 (1)
Ge 11:25   Nahor lived 119 years   2256+4395+6926+9596

120 (6)
1Ki 9:14   Now Hiram had sent to the king 120 talents
         of gold.   2256+4395+6929
    10:10   And she gave the king 120 talents of gold,   2256+4395+6929
1Ch 15: 5   Uriel the leader and 120 relatives;   2256+4395+6929
2Ch 5:12   120 priests sounding trumpets.   2256+4395+6929
    9: 9   Then she gave the king 120 talents of gold,   2256+4395+6929
Da 6: 1   appoint 120 satraps to rule   10221+10395+10574

122 (2)
Ezr 2:27   of Micmash 122   2256+4395+6929+9109
Ne 7:31   of Micmash 122   2256+2256+4395+6929+9109

123 (2)
Ezr 2:21   men of Bethlehem 123   2256+4395+6929+8993
Ne 7:32   of Bethel and Ai 123   2256+4395+6929+8993

127 (3)
Est 1: 1   Xerxes who ruled over 127 provinces   2256+2256+4395+6929+8679
    8: 9   satraps, governors and nobles of the 127
         provinces   2256+2256+4395+6929+8679
    9:30   sent letters to all the Jews in the 127
         provinces   2256+2256+4395+6929+8679

128 (4)
Ezr 2:23   of Anathoth 128   2256+4395+6929+9046
    2:41   The singers: the descendants of Asaph 128   2256+4395+6929+9046
Ne 7:27   of Anathoth 128   2256+4395+6929+9046
    11:14   were able men—128.   2256+4395+6929+9046

130 (2)
Ge 5: 3   Adam had lived 130 years,   2256+4395+8993
1Ch 15: 7   Joel the leader and 130 relatives   2256+4395+8993

133 (1)
Ex 6:18   Kohath lived 133 years.   2256+2256+4395+8993+8993

137 (2)
Ex 6:16   Levi lived 137 years.   2256+2256+4395+8679+8993
    6:20   Amram lived 137 years.   2256+2256+4395+8679+8993

138 (1)
Ne 7:45   Hatita and Shobai 138   2256+4395+8993+9046

139 (1)
Ezr 2:42   Hatita and Shobai 139   2256+4395+8993+9596

144 (1)
Rev 21:17   and it was 144 cubits thick,   1669+5475+5477

148 (1)
Ne 7:44   The singers: the descendants of Asaph 148   752+2256+4395+9046

150 (2)
1Ch 8:40   sons and grandsons—150 in all.   2256+2822+4395
Ezr 8: 3   were registered 150 men;   2256+2822+4395

153 (1)
Jn 21:11   It was full of large fish, 153,   1669+4299+5552

156 (1)
Ezr 2:30   of Magbish 156   2256+2822+4395+9252

160 (1)
Ezr 8:10   and with him 160 men;   2256+4395+9252

162 (1)
Ge 5:18   When Jared had lived 162 years,   2256+2256+4395+9109+9252

172 (1)
Ne 11:19   at the gates—**172** men.   2256+4395+8679+9109

180 (1)
Est 1: 4   a full **180** days he displayed the vast wealth
of his kingdom   2256+4395+9046

182 (1)
Ge 5:28   Lamech had lived **182** years, he had a son.
2256+2256+4395+9046+9109

187 (1)
Ge 5:25   When Methuselah had lived **187** years,
2256+2256+4395+8679+9046

188 (1)
Ne 7:26   the men of Bethlehem and Netophah **188**
2256+4395+9046+9046

200 (5)
Ge 11:23   Serug lived **200** years and had other sons   4395
1Ch 12:32   **200** chiefs, with all their relatives   4395
15: 8   Shemaiah the leader and **200** relatives;   4395
Ezr 2:65   also had **200** men and women singers.   4395
8: 4   and with him **200** men;   4395

205 (1)
Ge 11:32   Terah lived **205** years,   2256+2822+4395

207 (1)
Ge 11:21   Reu lived **207** years   2256+4395+8679

209 (1)
Ge 11:19   Peleg lived **209** years   2256+4395+9596

212 (1)
1Ch 9:22   gatekeepers at the thresholds numbered **212**.
2256+4395+6925+9109

218 (1)
Ezr 8: 9   and with him **218** men;   2256+4395+6925+9046

220 (2)
1Ch 15: 6   Asaiah the leader and **220** relatives;
2256+4395+6929
Ezr 8:20   **220** of the temple servants—   2256+4395+6929

223 (2)
Ezr 2:19   of Hashum **223**   2256+4395+6929+8993
2:28   of Bethel and Ai **223**   2256+4395+6929+8993

232 (1)
1Ki 20:15   of the provincial commanders, **232** men.
2256+4395+8993+9109

242 (1)
Ne 11:13   heads of families—**242**   752+2256+4395+9109

245 (3)
Ezr 2:66   had 736 horses, **245** mules,   752+2256+2822+4395
Ne 7:67   and they also had **245** men and women
singers.   752+2256+2256+2822+4395
7:68   There were 736 horses, **245** mules,   NIH

250 (10)
Ex 30:23   (that is, **250** shekels)   2256+2822+4395
30:23   **250** shekels of fragrant cane,   2256+2822+4395
Nu 16: 2   were **250** Israelite men,   2256+2822+4395
16:17   **250** censers in all—   2256+2822+4395
16:35   the **250** men who were offering   2256+2822+4395
26:10   the fire devoured the **250** men.   2256+2822+4395
Eze 48:17   the city will be **250** cubits on   2256+2822+4395
48:17   **250** cubits on the south,   2256+2822+4395
48:17   **250** cubits on the east,   2256+2822+4395
48:17   and **250** cubits on the west.   2256+2822+4395

273 (1)
Nu 3:46   To redeem the **273** firstborn Israelites who
exceed   2256+2256+4395+8679+8993

276 (1)
Ac 27:37   Altogether there were **276** of us   *1357+1573+1971*

284 (1)
Ne 11:18   The Levites in the holy city totaled **284**.
752+2256+4395+9046

288 (1)
1Ch 25: 7   they numbered **288**.   2256+4395+9046+9046

300 (2)
Ge 5:22   Enoch walked with God **300** years   4395+8993
Ezr 8: 5   and with him **300** men;   4395+8993

318 (1)
Ge 14:14   the **318** trained men born in his household
2256+4395+6925+8993+9046

320 (2)
Ezr 2:32   of Harim **320**   2256+4395+6929+8993
Ne 7:35   of Harim **320**   2256+4395+6929+8993

323 (1)
Ezr 2:17   of Bezai **323**   2256+4395+6929+8993+8993

324 (1)
Ne 7:23   of Bezai **324**   752+2256+4395+6929+8993

328 (1)
Ne 7:22   of Hashum **328**   2256+4395+6929+8993+9046

345 (2)
Ezr 2:34   of Jericho **345**   752+2256+2822+4395+8993
Ne 7:36   of Jericho **345**   752+2256+2822+4395+8993

350 (1)
Ge 9:28   After the flood Noah lived **350** years.
2256+2822+4395+8993

365 (1)
Ge 5:23   Altogether, Enoch lived **365** years.
2256+2256+2822+4395+8993+9252

372 (2)
Ezr 2: 4   of Shephatiah **372**   2256+4395+8679+8993+9109
Ne 7: 9   of Shephatiah **372**   2256+4395+8679+8993+9109

390 (2)
Eze 4: 5   So for **390** days you will bear the sin of the
house of Israel.   2256+4395+8993+9596
4: 9   You are to eat it during the **390** days you lie
on your side.   2256+4395+8993+9596

392 (2)
Ezr 2:58   of the servants of Solomon **392**
2256+4395+8993+9109+9596
Ne 7:60   of the servants of Solomon **392**
2256+4395+8993+9109+9596

403 (2)
Ge 11:13   Arphaxad lived **403** years   752+2256+4395+8993
11:15   Shelah lived **403** years   752+2256+4395+8993

410 (1)
Ezr 1:10   matching silver bowls **410**   752+2256+4395+6927

420 (1)
1Ki 9:28   **420** talents of gold,   752+2256+4395+6929

430 (4)
Ge 11:17   Eber lived **430** years   752+2256+4395+8993
Ex 12:40   the Israelite people lived in Egypt was **430**
years.   752+2256+4395+8993
12:41   At the end of the **430** years, 752+2256+4395+8993
Gal 3:17   The law, introduced **430** years later,
2779+5484+5558

435 (2)
Ezr 2:67   **435** camels and   752+2256+2822+4395+8993
Ne 7:69   **435** camels and   752+2256+2822+4395+8993

450 (2)
Ge 6:15   The ark is to be **450** feet long,   564+4395+8993
Ac 13:20   All this took about **450** years.   *2779+4299+5484*

454 (1)
Ezr 2:15   of Adin **454**   752+752+2256+2822+4395

468 (1)
Ne 11: 6   totaled **468** able men. 752+2256+4395+9046+9252

500 (5)
Ge 5:32   After Noah was **500** years old,   2822+4395
11:11   Shem lived **500** years and   2822+4395
Ex 30:23   **500** shekels of liquid myrrh,   2822+4395
30:24   **500** shekels of cassia—   2822+4395
Eze 45: 2   a section **500** cubits square   2822+4395

530 (1)
Ne 7:70   **530** garments for priests.   2256+2822+4395+8993

550 (1)
1Ki 9:23   **550** officials supervising   2256+2822+2822+4395

595 (1)
Ge 5:30   Lamech lived **595** years and
2256+2256+2822+2822+4395+9596

621 (2)
Ezr 2:26   and Geba **621**   285+2256+4395+6929+9252
Ne 7:30   and Geba **621**   285+2256+4395+6929+9252

623 (1)
Ezr 2:11   of Bebai **623**   2256+4395+6929+8993+9252

628 (1)
Ne 7:16   of Bebai **628**   2256+4395+6929+9046+9252

642 (2)
Ezr 2:10   of Bani **642**   752+2256+4395+9109+9252
Ne 7:62   Nekoda **642**   752+2256+2256+4395+9109+9252

648 (1)
Ne 7:15   of Binnui **648**   752+2256+4395+9046+9252

650 (1)
Ezr 8:26   I weighed out to them **650** talents of silver,
2256+2822+4395+9252

652 (2)
Ezr 2:60   and Nekoda **652**   2256+2822+4395+9109+9252
Ne 7:10   of Arah **652**   2256+2822+4395+9109+9252

655 (1)
Ne 7:20   of Adin **655**   2256+2822+2822+4395+9252

666 (4)
1Ki 10:14   Solomon received yearly was **666** talents,
4395+9252+9252+9252
2Ch 9:13   Solomon received yearly was **666** talents,
2256+4395+9252+9252+9252
Ezr 2:13   of Adonikam **666**   2256+4395+9252+9252+9252
Rev 13:18   His number is **666**.   *1971+1980+2008*

667 (1)
Ne 7:18   of Adonikam **667**   2256+4395+8679+9252+9252

675 (1)
Nu 31:37   of which the tribute for the LORD was **675**;
2256+2822+4395+8679+9252

690 (1)
1Ch 9: 6   The people from Judah numbered **690**.
2256+4395+9252+9596

721 (1)
Ne 7:37   of Lod, Hadid and Ono **721**
285+2256+2256+6929+8679

725 (1)
Ezr 2:33   of Lod, Hadid and Ono **725**
2256+2822+4395+6929+8679

730 (1)
Ex 38:24   and **730** shekels,   2256+4395+8679+8993

736 (2)
Ezr 2:66   had **736** horses,   2256+4395+8679+8993+9252
Ne 7:68   There were **736** horses, 245 mules,   NIH

743 (2)
Ezr 2:25   Beeroth **743**   752+2256+2256+4395+8679+8993
Ne 7:29   Beeroth **743**   752+2256+4395+8679+8993

745 (1)
Jer 52:30   **745** Jews taken into exile by Nebuzaradan
752+2256+2822+4395+8679

760 (2)
Ezr 2: 9   of Zaccai **760**   2256+4395+8679+9252
Ne 7:14   of Zaccai **760**   2256+4395+8679+9252

775 (1)
Ezr 2: 5   of Arah **775**   2256+2822+4395+8679+8679

777 (1)
Ge 5:31   Altogether, Lamech lived **777** years,
2256+2256+4395+8679+8679+8679

782 (1)
Ge 5:26   Methuselah lived **782** years
2256+2256+4395+8679+9046+9109

800 (2)
Ge 5: 4   Adam lived **800** years and had other   4395+9046
5:19   Jared lived **800** years and had other   4395+9046

807 (1)
Ge 5: 7   Seth lived **807** years   2256+4395+8679+9046

815 (1)

Ge 5:10 Enosh lived **815** years and had other sons
          2256+2822+4395+6926+9046

822 (1)

Ne 11:12 who carried on work for the temple—**822**
      men;   2256+4395+6929+9046+9109

830 (1)

Ge 5:16 Mahalalel lived **830** years 2256+4395+8993+9046

832 (1)

Jer 52:29 **832** people from Jerusalem;
          2256+4395+8993+9046+9109

840 (1)

Ge 5:13 Kenan lived **840** years   752+2256+4395+9046

845 (1)

Ne 7:13 of Zattu **845**   752+2256+2822+4395+9046

895 (1)

Ge 5:17 Altogether, Mahalalel lived **895** years,
          2256+2256+2822+4395+9046+9596

905 (1)

Ge 5:11 Enosh lived **905** years,   2256+2822+4395+9596

910 (1)

Ge 5:14 Kenan lived **910** years,   2256+4395+6924+9596

912 (1)

Ge 5: 8 Altogether, Seth lived **912** years,
          2256+4395+6926+9109+9596

928 (1)

Ne 11: 8 Sallai—**928** men. 2256+4395+6929+9046+9596

930 (1)

Ge 5: 5 Adam lived **930** years,   2256+4395+8993+9596

945 (1)

Ezr 2: 8 of Zattu **945** 752+2256+2256+2822+4395+9596

950 (1)

Ge 9:29 Noah lived **950** years,   2256+2822+4395+9596

956 (1)

1Ch 9: 9 as listed in their genealogy, numbered **956**.
          2256+2256+2822+4395+9252+9596

962 (1)

Ge 5:20 Altogether, Jared lived **962** years,
          2256+2256+4395+9109+9252+9596

969 (1)

Ge 5:27 Altogether, Methuselah lived **969** years,
          2256+2256+4395+9252+9596+9596

973 (2)

Ezr 2:36 (through the family of Jeshua) **973**
          2256+4395+8679+8993+9596
Ne 7:39 (through the family of Jeshua) **973**
          2256+4395+8679+8993+9596

1,000 (6) [THOUSAND]

1Ch 12:34 men of Naphtali—**1,000** officers,   547
2Ch 17:14 From Judah, commanders of **units of 1,000:** 547
Ezr 1: 9 gold dishes 30 silver dishes **1,000**   547
    1:10 other articles **1,000**   547
    8:27 20 bowls of gold valued at **1,000**   547
Ne 7:70 The governor gave to the treasury **1,000**   547

1,017 (2)

Ezr 2:39 of Harim **1,017**   547+2256+6925+8679
Ne 7:42 of Harim **1,017**   547+6925+8679

1,052 (2)

Ezr 2:37 of Immer **1,052**   547+2256+2822+9109
Ne 7:40 of Immer **1,052**   547+2256+2822+9109

1,222 (1)

Ezr 2:12 of Azgad **1,222**   547+2256+4395+6929+9109

1,247 (2)

Ezr 2:38 of Pashhur **1,247**   547+752+2256+4395+8679
Ne 7:41 of Pashhur **1,247**   547+752+2256+4395+8679

1,254 (4)

Ezr 2: 7 of Elam **1,254**   547+752+2256+2822+4395
    2:31 the other Elam **1,254** 547+752+2256+2822+4395
Ne 7:12 of Elam **1,254**   547+752+2256+2822+4395

Ne 7:34 the other Elam **1,254** 547+752+2256+2822+4395

1,260 (2)

Rev 11: 3 and they will prophesy *for* **1,260** days,
          1357+2008+5943
    12: 6 where she might be taken care of *for* **1,260**
          1357+2008+5943

1,290 (1)

Da 12:11 there will be **1,290** days. 547+2256+4395+9596

1,335 (1)

Da 12:12 who waits for and reaches the end of the
        1,335 days. 547+2256+2822+4395+8993+8993

1,365 (1)

Nu 3:50 he collected silver weighing **1,365** shekels,
      547+2256+2256+2256+4395+8993+9252

1,600 (1)

Rev 14:20 as high as the horses' bridles for a distance
      of **1,600** stadia.   1980+5943

1,760 (1)

1Ch 9:13 who were heads of families, numbered
      1,760. 547+2256+2256+4395+8679+9252

1,775 (2)

Ex 38:25 100 talents and **1,775** shekels,
      547+2256+2256+2256+2822+4395+8679+8679
    38:28 They used the **1,775** shekels to make hooks
      547+2256+2256+2822+4395+8679+8679

2,000 (1)

Ne 7:72 **2,000** minas of silver and 67 garments   547

2,056 (1)

Ezr 2:14 of Bigvai **2,056**   547+2256+2822+9252

2,067 (1)

Ne 7:19 of Bigvai **2,067**   547+2256+8679+9252

2,172 (2)

Ezr 2: 3 the descendants of Parosh **2,172**
        547+2256+4395+8679+9109
Ne 7: 8 the descendants of Parosh **2,172**
        547+2256+4395+8679+9109

2,200 (1)

Ne 7:71 and **2,200** minas of silver.   547+2256+4395

2,300 (1)

Da 8:14 "It will take **2,300** evenings and mornings;
        547+2256+4395+8993

2,322 (1)

Ne 7:17 of Azgad **2,322**
        547+2256+4395+6929+8993+9109

2,400 (1)

Ex 38:29 the wave offering was 70 talents and **2,400**
      shekels.   547+752+2256+4395

2,600 (1)

2Ch 26:12 fighting men was **2,600.**   547+2256+4395+9252

2,630 (1)

Nu 4:40 counted by their clans and families, were
      2,630.   547+2256+2256+4395+8993+9252

2,750 (1)

Nu 4:36 counted by clans, were **2,750.**
        547+2256+2822+4395+8679

2,812 (1)

Ezr 2: 6 (through the line of Jeshua and Joab) **2,812**
      547+2256+4395+6925+9046+9109

2,818 (1)

Ne 7:11 (through the line of Jeshua and Joab) **2,818**
      547+2256+4395+6925+9046+9046

3,000 (1)

1Ch 12:29 of Benjamin, Saul's kinsmen—**3,000,**   547+8993

3,023 (1)

Jer 52:28 in the seventh year, **3,023** Jews;
      547+2256+2256+6929+8993+8993

3,200 (1)

Nu 4:44 counted by their clans, were **3,200.**
      547+2256+4395+8993

3,600 (1)

2Ch 2:18 with **3,600** foremen over them
      547+2256+4395+8993+9252

3,630 (1)

Ezr 2:35 of Senaah **3,630**
      547+2256+2256+4395+8993+8993+9252

3,700 (1)

1Ch 12:27 with **3,700** men,   547+2256+4395+8679+8993

3,930 (1)

Ne 7:38 Senaah **3,930** 547+2256+4395+8993+8993+9596

4,500 (8)

Eze 48:16 the north side **4,500** cubits,
      547+752+2256+2822+4395
    48:16 the south side **4,500** cubits,
      547+752+2256+2822+4395
    48:16 the east side **4,500** cubits,
      547+752+2256+2822+4395
    48:16 and the west side **4,500** cubits.
      547+752+2256+2822+4395
    48:30 is **4,500** cubits long, 547+752+2256+2822+4395
    48:32 "On the east side, which is **4,500** cubits long
      547+752+2256+2822+4395
    48:33 "On the south side, which measures **4,500**
      547+752+2256+2822+4395
    48:34 "On the west side, which is **4,500** cubits long
      547+752+2256+2822+4395

4,600 (2)

1Ch 12:26 men of Levi—**4,600,** 547+752+2256+4395+9252
Jer 52:30 **4,600** people in all. 547+752+2256+4395+9252

5,000 (3)

Ezr 2:69 **5,000** minas of silver and 100 priestly 547+2822
Eze 45: 6 as its property an area **5,000** cubits wide 547+2822
    48:15 "The remaining area, **5,000** cubits wide 547+2822

5,400 (1)

Ezr 1:11 **5,400** articles of gold 547+752+2256+2822+4395

6,200 (1)

Nu 3:34 were counted was **6,200.**   547+2256+4395+9252

6,720 (2)

Ezr 2:67 435 camels and **6,720** donkeys.
      547+2256+4395+6929+8679+9252
Ne 7:69 435 camels and **6,720** donkeys.
      547+2256+4395+6929+8679+9252

6,800 (1)

1Ch 12:24 of Judah, carrying shield and spear—**6,800**
      armed for battle; 547+2256+4395+9046+9252

7,000 (1)

1Ki 20:15 the rest of the Israelites, **7,000**   547+8679

7,100 (1)

1Ch 12:25 ready for battle—**7,100;** 547+2256+4395+8679

7,337 (2)

Ezr 2:65 besides their **7,337** menservants and
      547+2256+4395+8679+8679+8993+8993
Ne 7:67 besides their **7,337** menservants and
      547+2256+4395+8679+8679+8993+8993

7,500 (1)

Nu 3:22 a month old or more who were counted was
      7,500. 547+2256+2822+4395+8679

8,580 (1)

Nu 4:48 numbered **8,580.**
      547+2256+2256+2822+4395+9046+9046

8,600 (1)

Nu 3:28 the males a month old or more was **8,600.**
      547+2256+4395+9046+9252

10,000 (9)

Eze 45: 3 cubits long and **10,000** cubits wide.   547+6930
    45: 5 cubits long and **10,000** cubits wide   547+6930
    48: 9 cubits long and **10,000** cubits wide.   547+6930
    48:10 **10,000** cubits wide on the east side,   547+6930
    48:10 **10,000** cubits wide on the east side,   547+6930
    48:13 cubits long and **10,000** cubits wide.   547+6930
    48:13 cubits and its width **10,000** cubits.   547+6930
    48:18 will be **10,000** cubits on the east side   547+6930
    48:18 and **10,000** cubits on the west side   547+6930

12,000 (13)

Rev 7: 5 From the tribe of Judah **12,000**   1557+5942
    7: 5 from the tribe of Reuben **12,000,**   1557+5942
    7: 5 from the tribe of Gad **12,000,**   1557+5942

Rev 7: 6   from the tribe of Asher **12,000**,   1557+5942
    7: 6   from the tribe of Naphtali **12,000**,   1557+5942
    7: 6   from the tribe of Manasseh **12,000**,   1557+5942
    7: 7   from the tribe of Simeon **12,000**,   1557+5942
    7: 7   from the tribe of Levi **12,000**,   1557+5942
    7: 7   from the tribe of Issachar **12,000**,   1557+5942
    7: 8   from the tribe of Zebulun **12,000**,   1557+5942
    7: 8   from the tribe of Joseph **12,000**,   1557+5942
    7: 8   from the tribe of Benjamin **12,000**.   1557+5942
   21:16   and found it to be **12,000** stadia   1557+5942

14,700 (1)
Nu 16:49   But **14,700** people died from the plague,
       547+752+2256+4395+6925+8679

16,000 (2)
Nu 31:40   **16,000** people, of which the tribute for the
      LORD was 32.   547+6925+9252
   31:46   and **16,000** people.   547+6925+9252

16,750 (1)
Nu 31:52   a gift to the LORD weighed **16,750** shekels.
      547+2256+2822+4395+6925+8679+9252

17,200 (1)
1Ch 7:11   There were **17,200** fighting men ready to go
       547+2256+4395+6925+8679

18,000 (2)
1Ch 12:31   and make David king—**18,000**;   547+6925+9046
Eze 48:35   all around will be **18,000** cubits.   547+6925+9046

20,000 (3)
Ne   7:71   to the treasury for the work **20,000**   8052+9109
   7:72   by the rest of the people was **20,000**   8052+9109
Eze 45: 1   cubits long and **20,000** cubits wide;   547+6929

20,200 (1)
1Ch 7: 9   and **20,200** fighting men.   547+2256+4395+6929

20,800 (1)
1Ch 12:30   famous in their own clans—**20,800**;
       547+2256+4395+6929+9046

22,000 (1)
Nu 3:39   every male a month old or more, was
      22,000.   547+2256+6929+9109

22,034 (1)
1Ch 7: 7   Their genealogical record listed **22,034**
      547+752+2256+2256+6929+8993+9109

22,200 (1)
Nu 26:14   clans of Simeon, there were **22,200** men.
       547+2256+2256+4395+6929+9109

22,273 (1)
Nu 3:43   listed by name, was **22,273**.   547+2256+2256
       +2256+4395+6929+8679+8993+9109

22,600 (1)
1Ch 7: 2   in their genealogy numbered **22,600**.
      547+2256+2256+4395+6929+9109+9252

23,000 (1)
Nu 26:62   a month old or more numbered **23,000**.
       547+2256+6929+8993

24,000 (14)
Nu 25: 9   those who died in the plague numbered
      24,000.   547+752+2256+6929
1Ch 27: 1   Each division consisted of **24,000** men.
       547+752+2256+6929
   27: 2   **24,000** men in his division.   547+752+2256+6929
   27: 4   **24,000** men in his division.   547+752+2256+6929
   27: 5   **24,000** men in his division.   547+752+2256+6929
   27: 7   **24,000** men in his division.   547+752+2256+6929
   27: 8   **24,000** men in his division.   547+752+2256+6929
   27: 9   **24,000** men in his division.   547+752+2256+6929
   27:10   **24,000** men in his division.   547+752+2256+6929
   27:11   **24,000** men in his division.   547+752+2256+6929
   27:12   **24,000** men in his division.   547+752+2256+6929
   27:13   **24,000** men in his division.   547+752+2256+6929
   27:14   **24,000** men in his division.   547+752+2256+6929
   27:15   **24,000** men in his division.   547+752+2256+6929

25,000 (14)
Eze 45: 1   **25,000** cubits long and 20,000 cubits wide;
      547+2256+2822+6929
   45: 3   measure off a section **25,000** cubits long
      547+2256+2822+6929
   45: 5   An area **25,000** cubits long   547+2256+2822+6929
   45: 6   and **25,000** cubits long,   547+2256+2822+6929
   48: 8   It will be **25,000** cubits wide,
      547+2256+2822+6929
   48: 9   offer to the LORD will be **25,000** cubits
      547+2256+2822+6929

Eze 48:10   It will be **25,000** long on the north side,
      547+2256+2822+6929
   48:10   and **25,000** long on the south side.
      547+2256+2822+6929
   48:13   the Levites will have an allotment **25,000**
      long and   547+2256+2822+6929
   48:13   Its total length will be **25,000** cubits
      547+2256+2822+6929
   48:15   and **25,000** cubits long,   547+2256+2822+6929
   48:20   The entire portion will be a square, **25,000**
      on each side.   547+2256+2822+6929
   48:21   It will extend eastward from the **25,000**
      547+2256+2822+6929
   48:21   and westward from the **25,000** cubits
      547+2256+2822+6929

25,100 (1)
Jdg 20:35   that day the Israelites struck down **25,100**
      Benjamites,   547+2256+2256+2822+4395+6929

26,000 (1)
1Ch 7:40   as listed in their genealogy, was **26,000**.
      547+2256+6929+9252

28,600 (1)
1Ch 12:35   men of Dan, ready for battle—**28,600**;
      547+2256+2256+4395+6929+9046+9252

30,500 (2)
Nu 31:39   **30,500** donkeys,   547+2256+2822+4395+8993
   31:45   **30,500** donkeys
      547+2256+2822+4395+8993

32,000 (1)
Nu 31:35   and **32,000** women who had never slept
      with a man.   547+2256+8993+9109

32,200 (2)
Nu 1:35   from the tribe of Manasseh was **32,200**.
      547+2256+2256+4395+8993+9109
   2:21   His division numbers **32,200**.
      547+2256+2256+4395+8993+9109

32,500 (1)
Nu 26:37   those numbered were **32,500**.
      547+2256+2256+2822+4395+8993+9109

35,400 (2)
Nu 1:37   from the tribe of Benjamin was **35,400**.
      547+752+2256+2256+2822+4395+8993
   2:23   His division numbers **35,400**.
      547+752+2256+2256+2822+4395+8993

36,000 (3)
Nu 31:38   **36,000** cattle,   547+2256+8993+9252
   31:44   **36,000** cattle,   547+2256+8993+9252
1Ch 7: 4   they had **36,000** men ready for battle,
      547+2256+8993+9252

37,000 (1)
1Ch 12:34   1,000 officers, together with **37,000**
      547+2256+8679+8993

40,000 (1)
1Ch 12:36   experienced soldiers prepared for
      battle—**40,000**;   547+752

40,500 (3)
Nu 1:33   from the tribe of Ephraim was **40,500**.
      547+752+2256+2822+4395
   2:19   His division numbers **40,500**.
      547+752+2256+2822+4395
   26:18   clans of Gad; those numbered were **40,500**.
      547+752+2256+2822+4395

41,500 (2)
Nu 1:41   The number from the tribe of Asher was
      41,500.   285+547+752+2256+2822+4395
   2:28   His division numbers **41,500**.
      285+547+752+2256+2822+4395

42,360 (2)
Ezr 2:64   The whole company numbered **42,360**,
      547+752+4395+8052+8993+9252
Ne   7:66   The whole company numbered **42,360**,
      547+752+2256+4395+8052+8993+9252

43,730 (1)
Nu 26: 7   those numbered were **43,730**.   547+752+2256
      +2256+2256+4395+8679+8993+8993

44,760 (1)
1Ch 5:18   and the half-tribe of Manasseh had **44,760**
      547+752+752+2256+2256+2256+4395+8679+9252

45,400 (1)
Nu 26:50   of Naphtali; those numbered were **45,400**.
      547+752+752+2256+2256+2822+4395

45,600 (1)
Nu 26:41   of Benjamin; those numbered were **45,600**.
      547+752+2256+2256+2822+4395+9252

45,650 (2)
Nu 1:25   from the tribe of Gad was **45,650**.   547+752
      +2256+2256+2256+2822+2822+4395+9252
   2:15   His division numbers **45,650**.   547+752
      +2256+2256+2256+2256+2822+4395+9252

46,500 (2)
Nu 1:21   from the tribe of Reuben was **46,500**.
      547+752+2256+2256+2822+4395+9252
   2:11   His division numbers **46,500**.
      547+752+2256+2256+2822+4395+9252

50,000 (1)
1Ch 12:33   with undivided loyalty—**50,000**;   547+2822

52,700 (1)
Nu 26:34   those numbered were **52,700**.
      547+2256+2256+2822+4395+8679+9109

53,400 (3)
Nu 1:43   from the tribe of Naphtali was **53,400**.
      547+752+2256+2256+2822+4395+8993
   2:30   His division numbers **53,400**.
      547+752+2256+2256+2822+4395+8993
   26:47   those numbered were **53,400**.
      547+752+2256+2256+2822+4395+8993

54,400 (2)
Nu 1:29   from the tribe of Issachar was **54,400**.
      547+752+752+2256+2256+2822+4395
   2: 6   His division numbers **54,400**.
      547+752+752+2256+2256+2822+4395

57,400 (2)
Nu 1:31   from the tribe of Zebulun was **57,400**.
      547+752+2256+2256+2822+4395+8679
   2: 8   His division numbers **57,400**.
      547+752+2256+2256+2822+4395+8679

59,300 (2)
Nu 1:23   from the tribe of Simeon was **59,300**.
      547+2256+2256+2822+4395+8993+9596
   2:13   His division numbers **59,300**.
      547+2256+2256+2822+4395+8993+9596

60,500 (1)
Nu 26:27   those numbered were **60,500**.
      547+2256+2822+4395+9252

61,000 (2)
Nu 31:34   **61,000** donkeys   285+547+2256+9252
Ezr 2:69   for this work **61,000** drachmas of gold,
      547+2256+8052+9252

62,700 (2)
Nu 1:39   number from the tribe of Dan was **62,700**.
      547+2256+2256+4395+8679+9109+9252
   2:26   His division numbers **62,700**.
      547+2256+2256+4395+8679+9109+9252

64,300 (1)
Nu 26:25   those numbered were **64,300**.
      547+752+2256+2256+4395+8993+9252

64,400 (1)
Nu 26:43   and those numbered were **64,400**.
      547+752+752+2256+2256+4395+9252

70,000 (1)
2Ch 2:18   He assigned **70,000** of them   547+8679

72,000 (1)
Nu 31:33   **72,000** cattle,   547+2256+8679+9109

74,600 (2)
Nu 1:27   number from the tribe of Judah was **74,600**.
      547+752+2256+2256+4395+8679+9252
   2: 4   His division numbers **74,600**.
      547+752+2256+2256+4395+8679+9252

76,500 (1)
Nu 26:22   of Judah; those numbered were **76,500**.
      547+2256+2256+2822+4395+8679+9252

80,000 (1)
2Ch 2:18   and **80,000** to be stonecutters   547+9046

87,000 (1)

1Ch 7: 5 of Issachar, as listed in their genealogy,
were **87,000**   547+2256+8679+9046

108,100 (1)

Nu 2:24 to their divisions, number **108,100.**
     547+547+2256+2256+4395+4395+9046

120,000 (1)

1Ch 12:37 of Manasseh, armed with every type of
weapon—**120,000.**   547+2256+4395+6929

144,000 (3)

Rev 7: 4 **144,000** from all the tribes of Israel.
     1669+5475+5477+5942
14: 1 and with him **144,000** who had his name
     1669+5475+5477+5942
14: 3 could learn the song except the **144,000**
     1669+5475+5477+5942

151,450 (1)

Nu 2:16 to their divisions, number **151,450.**
     285+547+547+752+2256+2256
     +2256+2256+2822+2822+4395+4395

153,600 (1)

2Ch 2:17 and they were found to be **153,600.**
     547+547+2256+2256+2256
     +2822+4395+4395+8993+9252

157,600 (1)

Nu 2:31 to the camp of Dan number **157,600.**
     547+547+2256+2256+2256
     +2822+4395+4395+8679+9252

180,000 (1)

2Ch 17:18 with **180,000** men armed for battle.
     547+2256+4395+9046

186,400 (1)

Nu 2: 9 to their divisions, number **186,400.**
     547+547+547+752+2256
     +2256+2256+4395+4395+9046+9252

200,000 (2)

2Ch 17:16 the service of the LORD, with **200,000.**   547+4395
17:17 Eliada, a valiant soldier, with **200,000**   547+4395

280,000 (1)

2Ch 17:15 Jehohanan the commander, with **280,000;**
     547+2256+4395+9046

300,000 (1)

2Ch 17:14 Adnah the commander, with **300,000**
     547+4395+8993

307,500 (1)

2Ch 26:13 an army of **307,500**   547+547+2256+2256
     +2822+4395+4395+8679+8993

337,500 (2)

Nu 31:36 who fought in the battle was: **337,500** sheep,
     547+547+547+2256+2256+2256
     +2822+4395+4395+8679+8993+8993
31:43 the community's half—was **337,500** sheep,
     547+547+547+2256+2256
     +2822+4395+4395+8679+8993+8993

601,730 (1)

Nu 26:51 The total number of the men of Israel was
601,730.   547+547+2256+2256
     +4395+4395+8679+8993+9252

603,550 (3)

Ex 38:26 a total of **603,550** men.
     547+547+2256+2256+2256
     +2822+2822+4395+4395+8993+9252
Nu 1:46 The total number was **603,550.**
     547+547+2256+2256+2256
     +2822+2822+4395+4395+8993+9252
2:32 by their divisions, number **603,550.**
     547+547+2256+2256+2256
     +2822+2822+4395+4395+8993+9252

675,000 (1)

Nu 31:32 spoils that the soldiers took was **675,000**
sheep,   547+547+547+2256+2256
     +2822+4395+8679+9252

INDEX OF ARTICLES, CONJUNCTIONS, PARTICLES, PREPOSITIONS, AND PRONOUNS

A (9144)

Ge 2:7, 8, 10, 18, 21, 22, 24; **3:**24; **4:**1, 11, 12, 14, 15, 17, 22, 23², 25, 26; **5:**3, 28; **6:**3, 9, 16²; **7:**2², 20, 24; **8:**1, 7, 8, 11; **9:**11², 12, 15, 20², 23; **10:**8, 9²; **11:**1, 2, 4³; **12:**2², 10², 11, 14; **14:**13, 20, 23²; **15:**1, 3, 4, 9³, 12², 13, 15, 17², 18; **16:**2, 7, 11, 12², 15; **17:**5, 12, 16, 17⁴, 19, 20, 27; **18:**4, 7², 8, 10, 13, 14, 18, 25; **19:**3, 8, 20, 26, 28, 30, 37, 38; **20:**1, 3², 5, 6, 7, 16; **21:**2, 5, 7, 8, 13, 14, 16, 18, 19², 21, 25, 27, 30, 33, 34; **22:**2, 12, 13², 15, 20; **23:**1, 4², 6, 9, 20; **24:**3, 4, 7, 14², 16, 17, 18, 19, 21, 22², 29, 31, 36, 37, 38, 40², 43², 45; **25:**7, 8, 17, 25, 27³, 28; **26:**1, 3, 8², 12, 19, 25, 28², 30, 35; **27:**10², 12², 27, 34, 41, 44, 46; **28:**1, 2, 6², 11, 12², 18, 20, 22²; **29:**2, 9, 12², 14, 15, 20, 22, 32, 33, 34, 35; **30:**3, 4, 5, 6, 7, 8, 9, 10, 12, 17, 19, 20, 21, 23, 36; **31:**10, 13², 24, 28, 44², 45², 46, 48, 50, 52², 54²; **32:**13, 18, 24; **33:**17, 19; **34:**7², 14³, 30, 31; **35:**11³, 14², 20, 28; **36:**6, 12; **37:**2², 3, 4, 5, 15, 20, 22, 25, 31; **38:**1, 2, 3, 4, 6, 8, 11, 12, 14, 15, 14³, 23, 24, 25, 28; **39:**7, 9; **40:**5², 9, 15, 16², 19, 20; **41:**1, 5², 7, 11², 12², 15², 22, 33, 34, 42, 43; **42:**7; **43:**2, 11³, 12, 30; **44:**5, 15, 17, 18, 19², 20, 25, 28²; **45:**7², 10, 29; **47:**9, 22, 24, 26², 28; **48:**4, 7, 19², 49:9³, 11, 13, 14, 17², 19, 20, 21, 22⁴, 27, 30; **50:**3, 9, 10, 11, 13, 15, 22, 26²; **Ex 1:**8, 16²; **2:**1², 2³, 3, 4, 11, 15, 16, 22²; **3:**2, 8², 17, 18, 19; **4:**2, 3, 4, 20, 24, 25², **5:**1, 3, 21²; **6:**8, 15; **7:**9², 10, 12, 15; **8:**23, 27, 31; **9:**3, 4, 5, 8, 10, 15, 19, 24; **10:**7, 9, 14, 19², 26; **11:**7²; **12:**3, 4, 13, 14³, 16, 17, 22, 24, 30, 45²; **13:**3, 5, 6, 9², 13, 14, 16², 21²; **14:**21, 22, 29; **15:**3, 5, 8, 16, 20, 25³; **16:**13, 23², 25, 33, 35; **17:**12, 14; **18:**3, 12, 16; **19:**6², 9, 13², 16², 18; **20:**5, 6, 10, 18, 21, 25; **21:**2, 3, 4, 7², 9, 12, 13, 14, 18, 20², 21, 22, 26, 27, 28³, 29, 31, 32, 33², 35; **22:**1², 2, 3, 5², 6, 7, 9³, 10³, 13, 14, 16², 18, 22, 25, 26; **23:**1², 2, 3, 7, 8², 14², 17, 18, 19, 26, 29, 32, 33; **24:**1, 10, 14, 17; **25:**8, 10⁶, 11, 17³, 23⁴, 24, 25³, 31, 35², 39; **26:**1, 6, 11, 13, 14², 16², 24, 31², 36; **27:**2, 4³, 9², 11, 16, 18, 21; **28:**4⁵, 6, 11², 12, 14, 15², 16², 17³, 18², 19, 20², 21², 22, 29, 32, 32², 34², 37, 42, 43; **29:**1, 3, 9, 14, 18², 23², 24, 25, 31, 36², 38, 40², 41; **30:**2², 3, 9, 10, 12², 13, 15, 16, 18, 21, 24, 25³, 31, 35², 39; **31:**13, 15, 16, 17; **32:**4², 5, 8, 9, 10, 11, 25, 27, 30, 31, 35; **33:**3, 5², 7, 11, 21², 22; **34:**9, 10, 12², 14, 15, 20, 23, 25, 26, 27, 33; **35:**2, 3, 22; **36:**8, 13, 18, 19², 21², 29, 35, 37; **37:**1², 2, 6³, 10³, 11, 12³, 21², 25², 26, 29; **38:**2², 4², 9, 11, 18, 26, 27, 28, 29; **39:**3, 6, 8, 9², 10³, 11², 12, 13², 14, 15, 22, 23², 27, 30, 31; **40:**15; **Lev 1:**3², 9, 10², 13, 14³, 17; **2:**1, 2², 3, 4, 5, 6, 7, 9, 10, 12, 14, 15; **3:**1, 3, 6², 7, 9, 12, 16, 17; **4:**3², 10, 12², 14², 22, 23, 24, 27, 28, 32², 8², 9³, 7⁴, 9, 10, 11³, 12³, 15³, 16², 17, 18², 19; **6:**5, 6², 11, 14, 16², 29, 30, 32; **8:**21², 26², 27, 28, 29; **9:**2², 3⁶, 4³, 8, 15, 17, 21; **10:**9, 13, 14, 15; **11:**3, 4², 5, 6, 7, 26, 33, 34, 36², 37, 38; **12:**2, 5, 6⁶, 7², 8³; **13:**2⁴, 6, 10, 11, 18, 19, 23, 24², 28², 29², 38, 39, 40, 41, 42, 49, 51; **14:**5, 10², 12², 21⁴, 22², 24, 31², 34², 44, 50, 55, 56³; **15:**2, 4, 6, 7, 11, 12, 13, 15²,

16, 18², 19, 24, 25⁴, 30², 32², 33⁶; **16:**3⁴, 5³, 9, 10, 12, 21, 22, 24, 26, 29, 31², 34²; **17:**3², 7, 8, 11; **18:**17, 18, 19, 22², 23²; **19:**5², 10, 13, 14, 18, 20³, 21², 29; **20:**10, 11, 12², 13³, 14², 15, 16, 17², 18², 19, 20, 21, 24, 25, 27²; **21:**1, 2, 9², 11², 13, 14⁴, 17, 19, 21; **22:**4³, 10², 11³, 12², 13², 14², 18⁴, 19, 20, 21, 23³, 25, 27²; **23:**3³, 7, 8, 10, 12, 13³, 14, 17, 18², 19³, 20², 21², 24², 27, 31, 32, 35, 36, 39², 41², **24:**3, 7, 8, 9², 10, 11, 17, 21; **25:**2, 4⁵, 5, 8, 10, 11, 12, 21, 24, 26, 29⁴, 30, 33, 35, 37, 39, 40², 47², 49, 50, 51, 52, 53², 55², 57², 58, 59², 61², 63², 64, 65², 67², 69², 70, 71², 73², 75², 76, 77², 79², 81², 82, 83², 85, 86, 87, 88; **8:**8³, 11, 12², 13, 15, 21; **9:**6, 7, 10², 17, 19, 20, 22, 26, 27, 28, 30, 31², 33; **Nu 1:**2; **3:**15, 22, 28, 34, 39, 40², 43; **4:**2, 6, 7, 8, 9, 10², 11, 12², 13, 14, 20, 22; **5:**2², 6, 9, 12, 15³, 17, 18, 19², 21², 22, 23², 25², 27², 28, 29²; **6:**24⁴, 4, 6, 11², 12², 14⁶, 15, 17, 19³, 20², 7:3, 13², 15², 16, 17²; **8:**16, 17, 19, 23, 26; **19:**2³, 9², 10, 14², 15, 16⁴, 17, 18⁴, 20, 21; **20:**16, 20, 21; **21:**8³, 9³; **22:**5, 6, 11², 12, 17, 23², 24, 26, 29², 32²; **23:**2³, 3, 4², 5, 9, 13, 14², 16, 19², 20, 22, 24², 30²; **24:**4, 6, 8, 9², 16, 17², 19, 21, 25; **25:**6, 7, 13², 14, 15², 18², 25:6², 7, 13², 14, 15², 18², 23; **26:**11, 13, 19, 21, 23, 29; **27:**5, 28:6, 8, 9², 29:9³, 11, 12, 12², 14, 17², 18², 20, 22, 23, 30²; **31:**4, 5, 6, 16, 17, 18, 35, 52, 54; **32:**14, 41; **33:**39, 54²; **34:**7, 10, 13, 15; **35:**6, 8, 11, 12, 15, 16², 17², 18², 21, 23, 30², 31²; **32²**; **Dt 1:**9, 11, 22, 25, 31, 33, 35, 44, 45; **2:**1, 9, 10, 19, 20, 21; **3:**5, 13, 14; **4:**6, 12, 16², 24², 25², 31, 34, 42; **5:**2, 9, 10, 14, 15, 22, 24; **6:**3, 10, 15, 21; **7:**6, 8, 9, 16, 21, 26; **8:**5, 7², 8, 9²; **9:**3, 12, 13, 14, 16, 21, 26; **10:**1, 7; **11:**9, 10, 11, 12, 26²; **12:**11, 13¹, 16², 14:2, 6, 7², 8, 21², 22, 23²; **15:**3, 7, 10, 12³, 18, 21; **16:**2, 6, 10, 11, 16, 17, 19², 22; **17:**1, 2, 6, 14, 15², 18² 20; **18:**3², 6, 11, 15², 16³, 18²; **20:**5, 6, 7, 10, 15, 19²; **21:**1³, 3², 4², 11, 13, 14, 15, 17², 18² 20; **22:**5, 6², 7, 8³, 10², 14, 15, 17, 19, 21², 22³; **23:**2, 4, 5, 6, 10, 12, 13, 15, 17, 18², 20, 21, 22, 25, 24:1³, 3, 5, 6², 10², 13, 14², 17, 19, 20; **25:**1, 5², 7²; **26:**2², 5³, 8, 9, 12, 13, 14², 17, 19, 25; **28:**8, 25, 29, 30³, 32, 33, 36, 37, 46², 49² 50, 65, 68; **29:**4, 12², 19², 23; **31:**2, 15, 19, 24, 26; **32:**4, 5, 10², 20², 20, 22, 30, 52, 33:17², 20, 22, 28, 29; **34:**7; **Jos 2:**1, 9, 12, 15, 19; **3:**4², 13a, 14, 15, 4:5, 6, 7; **5:**6, 13, 14², **6:**5², 10², 20³, 7:3, 15, 21², 26; **8:**14, 17, 28², 29², 35; **9:**4², 6², 7, 9, 11, 15, 22, 23; **10:**1, 10, 13, 14³, 20, 21; **11:**4², 18, 19; **14:**7; **15:**13, 18, 19, 32²; **17:**14; **18:**4², 7, 8², 9, 14; **20:**3, 4; **21:**13, 21, 27, 32, 38; **22:**3, 8, 14, 17, 25, 27, 28, 34; **23:**1, 10; **24:**7, 9, 13², 19², 26; **Jdg 1:**14, 15, 24, 26; **2:**2, 3,

8, 18; **3:**9, 15², 16³, 17, 19, 20, 25, 27, 29; **4:**2, 4, 9, 16, 18, 19², 21²; **5:**7, 8, 14, 25, 30; **6:**4, 8, 11, 17, 19³, 26², 31, 34, 37, 38; **7:**5, 13⁴, 20; **8:**10², 14, 18, 20, 25², 27, 31, 32; **9:**8, 18, 27, 37, 44, 49, 51, 53, 54; **10:**1; **11:**1², 3, 30, 31, 35, 39; **12:**2, 5, 7; **13:**2², 3, 5, 6, 7², 15, 16, 19², 23, 24; **14:**1, 2, 3, 5, 8, 14, 18, 15², 16³, 16:1, 4², 5, 8, 15³, 16³; **17:**1, 2, 3, 4², 5, 7, 10², 14², 19² 27; **18:**1, 7, 10², 14², 19² 27, 28²; **19:**1³, 18, 24, 29, 30; **20:**10³, 16², 34, 28; **21:**1, 5, 11, 16, 17, 18², 21, 22; **Ru 1:**1³, 12; **2:**1², 3, 7, 9, 10, 11; **3:**1, 2, 8, 9, 11, 12, 14, 17; **1Sa 1:**1², 5, 9, 11², 15, 16, 20, 24²; **2:**3, 8, 13², 18², 19, 24, 25², 27, 34, 35, 36²; **3:**8, 20; **4:**5, 7, 12, 13, 20; **5:**9, 6:3, 7, 8², 14², 17, 18; **7:**2, 9², 10, 11, 12, 16, 18, 20, 22², 27; **10:**1, 3, 5², 6, 10, 12², 18, 19, 23²; **11:**1, 2, 5, 12; **12:**1, 2, 3, 12, 13, 17, 19; **13:**2, 4, 14, 19, 21³, 22²; **14:**2, 3, 4, 12, 15, 28, 29, 33, 39, 43, 45, 52; **15:**12, 18, 29; **16:**2, 12, 18⁴, 20³; **17:**4, 5², 6, 7, 8², 10, 20, 33², 34³, 38², 42, 43, 46, 49, 50², 52; **18:**3, 5, 9, 10, 13, 17, 21², 23² 25; **19:**2, 5, 13, 20, 21; **20:**3, 8, 16, 20, 21, 29, 30, 35; **21:**2², 8², 9, 13; **22:**8, 13, 17, 20; **23:**4, 7², 8, 10, 11³, 12, 13, 15, 20⁴, 21³; **24:**1, 3², 9, 10, 15; **1Ki 1:**2, 3², 42, 48, 52²; **2:**1, 2, 4, 9, 19, 24, 36, 38; **3:**2, 4, 5, 6, 7, 8², 9, 12, 14, 15², 17, 18, 24³; **4:**5, 23, 29, 32, 33²; **5:**3, 5, 7, 12, 14, 17; **6:**5, 8, 23; **7:**2, 3, 6², 8, 9, 12, 14², 17, 23, 24, 26³, 30, 31², 32², 35²; **8:**9, 12, 13², 16², 17, 18, 21, 25, 31, 38, 41, 47, 55, 63²; 65²; **9:**2, 5, 7, 8, 13, 16, 25; **10:**2, 18, 19², 22, 25, 29²; **11:**7², 17, 18, 19, 20, 24, 26, 28, 29, 36, 38; **12:**4, 7², 10, 11, 24, 30, 32, 33; **13:**1, 2, 3, 7, 11, 18, 24, 33; **14:**3, 7, 14, 15; **15:**4²², 13, 19, 27; **16:**11, 15, 24, 17:9², 10², 12², 17, 18; **18:**1, 3, 4, 10², 13, 27, 32, 34, 41, 44², 45; **19:**2, 4², 6², 7, 9, 11, 12²; **20:**10, 13, 28², 29, 33, 34², 36², 39², 42; **21:**1, 2², 9², 12², 19, 25; **22:**7, 11, 21, 22, 23, 36, 38, 47, 48; **2Ki 1:**6, 8², 9², 10, 12, 13², 2:1, 7, 9, 10, 11², 20, 24; **3:**4², 9, 15, 25, 27; **4:**1, 2, 3, 6, 8², 9, 10³, 13, 16, 17, 19, 22, 28, 38, 39, 42, 43; **5:**1², 7, 8, 9, 10, 14, 15, 16, 17, 22; **6:**2², 5, 6, 8, 14, 23, 25⁴, 26, 32; **7:**1³, 5, 6, 9, 10², 16²; **8:**1², 8, 11, 21, 24², 28², 29²; **9:**1, 5, 17, 19, 20, 30, 34; **10:**2, 6, 10, 18, 19, 27; **11:**2², 4, 5², 12²; **13:**3, 5, 15, 21² 14:9⁴, 13; **15:**5, 19; **16:**8, 10, 17², 21, 35; **18:**17, 21², 23, 32²; **19:**3, 7², 9, 20, 30, 31, 32², 35; **20:**7, 10, 12, 14; **21:**13; **22:**10; **23:**25, 30, 33³; **24:**14, 16;

25:17², 28, 30; **1Ch 1:**10; **2:**3; **4:**33; **5:**2, 6, 18; **6:**57, 67; **7:**15, 16, 23; **9:**4, 14, 31; **10:**13; **11:**3, 11, 13², 14, 15, 17, 22⁴, 23⁴; **12:**4², 14³, 20, 22, 28; **13:**7; **14:**1; **15:**1², 25, 27², 29; **16:**3³, 15, 17; **17:**1², 4, 5, 6, 9², 10, 12, 21², 25; **18:**4², 8; **19:**2, 6²; **20:**2², 5³, 6; **21:**1, 3, 5, 8, 14, 16, 24; **22:**3, 6, 7, 8, 9², 10, 14²; **24:**3², 4, 6; **26:**14, 17⁴, 24, 31; **27:**3, 6, 11, 12, 13, 18, 32²; **28:**2², 3², 9, 10²; **29:**7, 15, 16, 21³, 22, 28; **2Ch 1:**4, 6, 9, 11, 17³; **2:**1², 3, 4², 6³, 7, 12³, 13, 17; **3:**10, 15, 16; **4:**1, 2, 3, 5, 8², 5:10, 13; **6:**1, 2², 5², 7, 8, 13, 16, 22, 29, 32, 36, 37; **7:**5², 8, 12, 13, 18, 20, 21; **9:**1, 17², 18², 21, 24; **10:**4, 7, 10, 11; **11:**1; **13:**2², 3², 5, 8, 9²; **14:**9, 13; **15:**3², 12, 16; **16:**3, 8, 9, 12, 14²; **17:**17; **18:**6, 16, 21², 22², 26³, 33, 34², 36²; **20:**19, 29²; **21:**6, 7, 12, 14, 15, 17; **22:**2, 9, 11; **23:**1², 3, 4, 5², 9, 11, 14, 16; **24:**8, 9, 11², 15, 24², 26; **25:**6², 7, 10, 12, 15, 18⁴, 23; **26:**11, 13, 19, 21, 23; **27:**5; **28:**6, 8, 9², 29:10, 21, 24, 32; **30:**5, 13, 24³; **31:**5², 6², 12; **32:**4, 7, 24, 29²; **33:**11; **34:**18; **35:**5, 7, 18, 25; **36:**3³, 4, 22, 23; **Ezr 1:**1, 2; **2:**61², 63; **3:**11; **4:**1, 3, 7, 8, 11, 15³, 19³, 24; **5:**1, 6, 11, 13, 14, 17²; **6:**2, 3², 11², 12, 14, 17², 7:6, 11², 12, 21, 22⁴; **8:**10, 21², 28, 35²; **9:**8⁴, 9, 11, 12, 13²; **10:**13, 15³, 16, 19², **Ne 1:**9; **2:**6, 8, 12; **3:**9, 13, 16², 19, 26; **4:**2, 3, 4, 9, 17²; **5:**1, 7, 13, 15, 17; **6:**1, 3, 7, 11, 13²; **7:**2, 63², 65; **8:**4, 11; **9:**3, 8, 10, 11, 12², 17², 18, 29, 31, 38; **10:**29, 32², 34, 37, 38²; **11:**4, 5; **13:**2², 5, 7, 13; **Est 1:**3, 4, 5, 6, 9, 19; **2:**2, 5, 7, 12, 17, 18²; **3:**1, 4, 6, 7, 8, 9, 13, 14; **4:**8, 14; **5:**4, 14; **6:**8³; **7:**5, 7, 9; **8:**13, 15¹, 16, 9:17, 18, 19², 22; **10:**2; **Job 1:**1, 3, 5², 8, 10, 12, 14, 19; **2:**3, 4, 8, 10, 12, 13; **3:**3, 5, 16, 23; **4:**2, 12², 15, 16², 17²; **5:**19, 22, 23, 4, 23; **6:**5, 14, 22, 26; **7:**1, 2², 6, 7, 9, 20; **8:**2, 9, 14, 16, 17², 20; **9:**2, 3, 16, 17², 20, 24, 25², 31, 32; **10:**4², 5, 16, 20, 22; **11:**10, 12³, 20; **12:**3, 4², 18, 24; **13:**25, 28; **14:**2², 3, 6, 7, 9, 11, 13, 14, 17, 19²; **15:**2, 24, 26, 30, 33; **16:**8, 14, 21²; **17:**5, 6², 7, 10; **18:**8, 9², 10², **19:**10, 12, 15, 23; **20:**3, 5, 8², 24, 26, 28; **21:**11, 19, 33; **22:**2², 8, 11, 16; **24:**9, 14, 20, 23, 24; **25:**4, 6³; **26:**10; **27:**13, 18³, 20²; **28:**1², 4, 22, 26²; **29:**16, 25; **30:**8, 9, 14, 15, 24², 29³; **31:**1³, 12, 13, 18, 19², 27, 30, 36, 37; **32:**8, 33:15², 19², 23³, 24, 25, 29; **34:**6, 9, 11, 30, 31, 36; **35:**8, 9; **36:**2, 16, 18, 22; **37:**6, 18; **38:**3, 5, 14², 25², 26², 27, 28, 34, 40; **39:**7, 10, 15, 17, 19, 20, 28²; **40:**7, 17²; **41:**1², 2², 5³, 8, 11, 13; **42:**8, 11², 12², 16; **Ps 1:**3; **2:**12; **3:**T, 3; **4:**T; **5:**T, 4, 9, 12; **6:**T; **7:**T, 2, 11², 15; **8:**T, 5; **9:**T; **10:**9; **11:**1, 6; **12:**T, 6; **13:**T; **15:**T, 4, 5; **16:**T; **17:**T, 12²; **18:**19, 29², 30, 33, 34; **19:**T, 4, 5²; **20:**T; **21:**T, 3, 9; **22:**T, 6², 15, 16, 31; **23:**T, 5; **24:**T, 4; **26:**1, 11; **27:**5, 11; **28:**1, 8; **29:**T, 6²; **30:**T; **31:**T, 2, 8, 11, 21; **32:**T; **33:**3, 17²; **34:**19; **35:**7; **36:**4; **37:**10, 23, 35², 37; **38:**T², 4, 13², 14; **39:**T, 1, 5², 6, 11, 12; **40:**T, 2³, 3²; **41:**T, 8; **42:**T, 8; **44:**T, 12, 13, 14, 19, 20; **45:**T², 1², 6, 12; **46:**T, 4; **47:**T, 7; **48:**T, 6; **49:**T, 4, 7, 8, 16, 20; **50:**T, 3², 9, 10, 18; **51:**T, 10², 12, 17²; **52:**T, 1, 2; **53:**T; **54:**T, 6; **55:**T, 6, 12, 13; **56:**T²; **57:**T, 6²; **58:**T, 4², 8², 11; **59:**T; **60:**T, 4; **61:**3; **62:**T, 3, 9²; **63:**T, 1; **64:**T, 6; **65:**T²; **66:**T, 12; **67:**T²; **68:**T, 5², 6, 20; **69:**8, 22², 31; **70:**T; **71:**7; **72:**6; **73:**T, 20, 22; **74:**T, 5;

6:3, 7, 10, 13, 14; **7:**4, 8, 27; **11:**10, 12; **12:**11, 15, 16, 20, 23; **13:**8, 9, 14, 20, 21, 23; **14:**8; **15:**7; **16:**37, 62; **18:**23; **20:**5, 7, 19, 20, 26, 31, 38, 42, 44, 47; **21:**3, 4; **22:**16, 26; **23:**28, 49; **24:**16, 21, 24, 27; **25:**4, 5, 7, 11, 16, 17; **26:**3, 6, 7; **27:**3; **28:**2, 7, 9, 22²; 23, 24, 26; **29:**3, 6, 9, 10, 16, 19, 21; **30:**8, 19, 22, 25, 26; **32:**15; **33:**29; **34:**10, 27, 30, 31; **35:**3, 4, 9, 15; **36:**9, 11, 22, 23, 32, 38; **37:**6, 12, 13, 19; **38:**3, 23; **39:**1, 6, 7, 13, 17, 19, 22, 28; **40:**4; **44:**28; Da **1:**10; **2:**8; **8:**19; **10:**11, 16²; Hos **1:**9; **2:**2, 14; **5:**12; **11:**9; **12:**8, 9; **13:**4; **14:**8; Joel **2:**19, 27²; **3:**7, 10; Am **7:**8; Jnh **1:**9; **4:**9; Mic **2:**3; **3:**8; **6:**10; **7:**1; Na **2:**13; **3:**5; Hab **1:**5, 6; **2:**1; Zep **2:**15; Hag **1:**13; **2:**4; Zec **1:**14, 15; **2:**10; **3:**8; **8:**2², 21; **9:**8; **10:**6; **11:**5, 16; **12:**2; **13:**5²; Mal **1:**6²; 10, 14; Mt **3:**11, 17; **8:**3, 9; **9:**28; **10:**16; **11:**29; **16:**15; **17:**5; **18:**20; **20:**13, 15, 22; **21:**24, 27; **22:**32; **23:**34; **24:**5; **26:**18, 55, 61; **27:**24, 43; **28:**20; Mk **1:**7, 11, 41; **8:**27, 29; **10:**38, 39; **11:**29, 33; **12:**26; **13:**6; **14:**48, 62; Lk **1:**18, 19, 34, 38, 43; **3:**16, 22; **5:**8, 13; **7:**8; **9:**18, 20, 44; **10:**3; **12:**50; **15:**17, 19, 21; **16:**24; **18:**11; **19:**22; **20:**8; **21:**8; **22:**27, 33, 52, 58, 70; **24:**49; Jn **1:**20, 21, 23, 27; **3:**28²; **4:**9, 26; **5:**7, 17, 36; **6:**35, 41, 48, 51; **7:**8, 28²; 29, 33, 34, 36; **8:**12, 14², 16, 18, 21, 23², 24, 28, 38, 42, 46, 49, 50, 58; **9:**5², 9; **10:**7, 9, 11, 14, 36; **11:**11, 15, 25; **12:**26, 32; **13:**7, 13, 18, 19²; 33, 36; **14:**2, 3, 4, 6, 10, 11, 12, 20²; 28³; **15:**1, 5; **16:**5, 7, 10, 17, 26, 28, 32; **17:**9, 11, 13², 14, 16, 21, 24; **18:**5, 6, 8, 17, 25, 35, 37; **19:**4, 28; **20:**17, 21; Ac **7:**32; **9:**5; **10:**26; **13:**25³, 41; **17:**3, 23; **18:**6, 10; **20:**22, 26; **21:**13, 39; **22:**3, 8, 27; **23:**6; **24:**21; **25:**4, 10, 11; **26:**6, 15, 17, 22, 25², 26, 29; **27:**23; **28:**20; Ro **1:**14, 15, 16; **3:**5, 7; **7:**1, 14, 24, 25; **8:**38; **9:**1; **11:**1, 3, 13²; **14:**14; **15:**14, 25; **16:**19; 1Co **1:**14; **4:**3, 14, 17; **5:**3², 4, 11; **7:**7, 8, 35; **9:**1², 2, 15, 16, 17, 19, 20, 21²; **10:**30, 33; **12:**15, 16; **13:**1, 2, 12; **14:**11, 37; **15:**9, 10²; **16:**10, 11; 2Co **7:**4, 9, 16; **8:**8; **9:**3; **10:**1; **11:**2, 3, 5, 12, 17, 21, 22², 23²; 31; **12:**10², 11², 14, 16, 20, 21; **13:**10; Gal **1:**6, 10², 20; **2:**18; **4:**1, 18, 19, 20; Eph **3:**8; **5:**32; **6:**20, 21², 22; Php **1:**7, 13, 16, 17, 22, 23; **2:**17²; 24, 28; **4:**11², 17²; Col **2:**1, 5², **4:**3, 8; 1Ti **1:**15; **2:**7²; **3:**14, 15; 2Ti **1:**5, 12⁴; **2:**7, 9; **4:**6; Phm **1:**12, 13, 19; Heb **2:**13; **10:**7, 9; **12:**21; 1Pe **1:**16; 2Pe **1:**17; 1Jn **2:**7, 8, 26; **5:**16; 2Jn **1:**5; Rev **1:**8, 17, 18²; **2:**23; **3:**11, 16, 17, 20; **18:**7; **19:**10; **21:**5, 6; **22:**7, 8, 9, 12, 13, 16, 20.

AN (1185)

Ge **1:**6; **4:**3; **6:**13, 14; **8:**20; **9:**5³; **12:**7, 8; **13:**4, 18; **14:**22; **16:**1; **17:**7, 8², 13, 19; **19:**9; **20:**4; **21:**20, 23, 31; **22:**9; **23:**4; **24:**9, 37; **25:**8, 33; **26:**25, 31; **27:**2, 28; **28:**4; **31:**53; **33:**20; **35:**1, 3, 7; **39:**1; **41:**53; **42:**22, 23; **43:**16; **44:**20; **48:**4; **50:**5, 25; Ex **2:**11, 19, 22; **6:**6; **9:**19; **10:**13; **12:**19, 48; **13:**19; **16:**16, 32, 33, 36²; **17:**15; **18:**3; **20:**4, 24, 25; **21:**6, 33; **22:**1, 9, 10, 11, 14, 19, 21, 22, 31; **23:**7, 9, 20, 22; **24:**4; **25:**2, 17; **26:**36; **27:**1, 16; **28:**4, 18, 19², 20, 32, 39; **29:**18, 25, 40, 41; **30:**1, 13, 14, 20; **32:**4, 5, 8; **33:**2; **35:**5², 21, 24²; **36:**6², 37; **38:**18, 23; **39:**11, 12², 13, 23, 29, 30; Lev **1:**2², 9², 13², 17²; **2:**2², 4, 9², 11, 12, 16; **3:**1², 5², 6, 11, 16; **4:**31; **5:**4, 11²; **6:**15, 20, 21; **7:**5, 9, 12, 13, 14, 21, 24, 25²; **8:**21, 28²; **9:**4; **11:**35, 39; **13:**2, 3, 8, 9, 15, 20, 25², 27, 30², 42, 43, 45; **14:**10, 21, 32, 40, 41, 45, 54; **15:**16, 18, 32; **16:**29; **17:**3, 4, 6, 12; **18:**23²; **19:**24, 33, 36²; **20:**15, 16, 21, 24; **21:**3; **22:**4²; 18², 22, 23, 24, 27; **23:**8, 13², 16, 17, 18², 25, 27, 36; **24:**5, 7, 10², 16, 21; **25:**35, 47, 49; **26:**1; **27:**9³, 11, 26²; Nu **3:**4; **5:**2, 15²; **7:**3; **9:**14; **10:**9; **11:**12; **15:**3, 4, 6, 7, 9, 10², 12², 14³, 19, 20, 24, 25, 29; **16:**14, 21, 45; **17:**10; **18:**17³, 19, 24, 28; **19:**22; **20:**16; **22:**4, 37; **25:**6, 11; **26:**53, 61; **27:**7; **28:**2, 5, 6, 8², 9², 12², 13³, 19, 20, 24, 26, 27, 28; **29:**2, 3, 8, 9, 13², 14, 35, 36²; **30:**2; **31:**50; **34:**2, 13, 17; **35:**16; **36:**2; Dt **1:**16; **4:**16²; 23, 34; **5:**8, 15; **9:**16; **12:**10; **13:**11; **14:**21; **15:**17, 21; **16:**2, 8; **17:**1; **19:**3, 20; **20:**1, 10, 16, 19; **21:**8, 23; **22:**10, 19; **23:**7²; **24:**4, 14; **25:**4, 19; **26:**1, 8; **27:**5², 15²; 25; **28:**37, 48, 49, 65; **29:**8; **32:**11; Jos **8:**2, 4, 14, 30, 31; **9:**18; **10:**2, 9; **11:**23; **12:**7; **13:**6, 19; **14:**1, 3; **17:**4², 6, 14; **19:**49; **22:**10, 16, 19, 26, 29; **23:**4; **24:**20; Jdg **3:**31; **6:**19, 24; **8:**24, 27; **9:**23, 43, 48, 53; **11:**34; **12:**5; **13:**6, 19; **14:**3, 4; **17:**5; **18:**1, 10, 14; **19:**22; **20:**16; **22:**4, 37; **25:**6, 11; **26:**53, 61; **27:**7; Ru **2:**17; 1Sa **1:**1, 24; **2:**28, 31, 32; **4:**18; **5:**9; **7:**17; **9:**2; **12:**17; **14:**3, 14²; 24, 35; **15:**5; **16:**14, 15; **17:**12; **18:**10; **19:**5, 9, 13; **20:**3, 6, 36; **25:**3; **26:**19; **27:**9; **28:**14; **29:**3, 9; **30:**11, 13²; 2Sa **1:**8, 13²; **3:**8, 12, 13, 35; **4:**11, 12;

11:21; **14:**8, 17, 20; **15:**19; **17:**8, 25; **18:**10; **19:**27, 35; **23:**5; **24:**18, 21, 25; 1Ki **1:**29; **3:**1, 25; **6:**16; **7:**6, 31; **8:**31, 33, 36, 37; **9:**7; **11:**14, 26; **13:**1, 14, 18; **14:**5, 21, 31; **15:**22; **16:**32, 33; **18:**32; **19:**5, 11; **20:**25, 30; **21:**1; **22:**25; 2Ki **3:**11, 18; **6:**15; **8:**6; **9:**2; **10:**20; **12:**15; **16:**10, 11; **17:**16; **19:**32; **21:**3; **23:**11; **25:**8, 24; 1Ch **2:**34; **11:**23; **16:**17, 29; **21:**15, 18, 22, 26; **27:**10, 14; **28:**8; 2Ch **6:**22, 24, 27; **7:**9, 20; **12:**13; **13:**6; **14:**8; **15:**14; **18:**24; **20:**11, 35, 37; **21:**18; **24:**26; **25:**16; **26:**13; **28:**7; **29:**8; **30:**7; **32:**21; **36:**13; Ezr **4:**6, 19, 21; **6:**1; **9:**12; Ne **4:**11; **5:**12, 18; **6:**5; **8:**18, 31; **10:**29; **13:**5; Est **8:**3, 5; **9:**14; Job **3:**16; **6:**5, 6; **7:**6, 19; **15:**33; **18:**21; **19:**15, 24; **20:**16, 24; **21:**21; **22:**8; **23:**7; **28:**3; **31:**37; **33:**3, 23; **34:**6, 20; **40:**9, 15; **41:**4; **42:**15; Ps **2:**9; **5:**9; **7:**9; **24:**4; **27:**3; **36:**1; **39:**12; **43:**1; **46:**1; **48:**7; **52:**8; **55:**12; **66:**15; **69:**8, 31; **78:**55; **81:**4, 9; **83:**5; **86:**11; **89:**44; **96:**8; **102:**T, 6; **105:**10, 23; **106:**19, 20; **109:**6², 23, 25; **119:**7, 106; **132:**2, 11; **135:**12²; **136:**21, 22; **145:**13; Pr **3:**22; **4:**3; **5:**3, 20; **6:**11, 15; **7:**22, 23; **12:**13, 16, 25; **13:**22; **14:**4²; **15:**23; **16:**10; **17:**9, 11, 26; **18:**1, 11, 19; **19:**11; **20:**21; **21:**29; **22:**14, 28; **23:**5, 10; **24:**15, 26, 34; **25:**12²; **26:**2, 10, 23; **27:**6; **28:**10; **29:**6, 22, 26; **30:**1, 19, 20, 23; **31:**1; Ecc **4:**13; **7:**11; **8:**2; **10:**5; SS **2:**3; **4:**13; **7:**4; Isa **1:**30; **5:**10; **8:**1; **10:**7, 34; **13:**1, 4², 11; **14:**4; **15:**1; **16:**4, 10; **17:**1, 6; **18:**2, 7; **19:**1, 19; **21:**1², 2, 11, 13, 16; **22:**1; **23:**1, 11; **24:**13; **27:**10; **28:**15²; **29:**2, 5, 20; **30:**1, 6, 8, 13, 33; **33:**19, 23; **37:**33; **38:**12, 13; **40:**19, 20²; **44:**10, 12, 13, 15; **45:**17; **50:**4; **55:**3, 13; **56:**5; **59:**5; **61:**8; **65:**2, 16, 20²; **66:**3, 20; Jer **1:**11, 18; **2:**22; **3:**18; **4:**20; **5:**15, 16, 22; **6:**22, 26; **7:**34; **16:**9; **17:**1, 27; **18:**16; **19:**8, 25; **22:**28; **23:**10; **24:**9²; **25:**9²; 18; **26:**6; **28:**14; **29:**18; **30:**14, 17; **31:**3, 18; **32:**21, 40; **38:**7; 15, **40:**9, 12; **42:**18; **44:**8, 12, 22; **47:**2; **48:**2, 26, 35, 39², 40; **49:**13, 14, 17, 19, 22, 37; **50:**5, 9, 41, 44; **51:**12, 34, 37; La **1:**15, 17; **2:**4, 5, 7; **5:**10; Eze **1:**4, 10², 22, 24; **4:**3²; **5:**2, 15; **7:**5, 19, 20, 24; **10:**14; **11:**19; **12:**23; **14:**8; **16:**3, 10, 45, 60; **17:**2; **20:**17, 33, 34; **21:**21; **22:**4, 15; **23:**41, 48; **26:**13; **30:**10, 13, 18; **33:**28, 32; **35:**5; **37:**26; **38:**10; **42:**4, 7, 9; **45:**1, 5, 6, 10², 13², 24²; **46:**5, 11², 14; **47:**13, 22²; **48:**13, 29; Da **2:**31, 44, 46; **3:**1; **4:**3, 16, 33, 34; **5:**21, 26; **6:**7, 20; **7:**4, 14, 27²; **9:**16, 23, 24, 27²; **11:**6, 10, 17, 18, 22, 23, 27; Hos **1:**2, 4; **3:**1; **7:**4, 6, 7; **8:**1, 3; **11:**6; **13:**15; **14:**6; Joel **2:**17, 19; Am **3:**11, 12; **8:**10; Ob **1:**1; Jnh **1:**14; Mic **1:**8; **2:**8; Na **1:**1; 8², 9; **2:**1; Hab **2:**3, 18²; Zec **3:**9; **8:**12, 13, 23; **9:**8; **11:**17; **12:**3, 10; Mal **1:**1, 14; Mt **1:**20; **2:**13, 19; **5:**32, 39; **9:**16; **12:**43; **13:**12, 28; **14:**7; **22:**35; **24:**44, 50; **25:**29; **26:**7, 16, 72; **27:**24; **28:**2; Mk **1:**23; **2:**4, 21; **3:**29, 30; **5:**2; **6:**9, 23, 27; **7:**25; **14:**3, 11; Lk **1:**1, 3, 11, 18; **2:**9; **4:**5, 13, 33; **5:**36; **7:**37; **9:**46; **10:**25, 34; **11:**12, 24; **12:**14, 40, 46; **14:**5; **16:**2; **19:**43; **22:**6, 43, 59; **23:**11, 19; Jn **1:**22; **3:**25; **5:**5; **12:**3, 19; **18:**1; Ac **4:**9, 16; **5:**19; **6:**15; **7:**24, 30, 41; **8:**26, 27²; **9:**25, 37; **10:**3; **11:**13; **12:**7, 20, 23; **13:**7²; 10; **16:**20; **17:**23², 29; **19:**29; **20:**32; **21:**31; **23:**9, 12, 21; **24:**17; **25:**3, 16; **27:**6, 23, 30; **28:**7, 11; Ro **1:**1; **2:**20; **4:**4; **7:**3²; **8:**12; **11:**1, 24; **13:**4; **14:**12; **15:**16; 1Co **1:**1; **3:**10; **5:**11; **7:**32, 34; **8:**4, 7, 10; **9:**1, 2, 9; **10:**19²; **11:**27; **12:**16, 17²; **14:**24, 26; **15:**9, 52; 2Co **1:**1; **4:**17; **5:**1, 12; **6:**15; **8:**23; **11:**12, 14; **12:**12; Gal **1:**1, 8; **2:**2²; **3:**15; **4:**7, 13, 14; Eph **1:**1; **5:**5; **6:**20, 24; Php **4:**18; Col **1:**1; **2:**23; **3:**24; 2Th **3:**15; 1Ti **1:**16; **2:**7; **3:**1, 13; **4:**12; **5:**1, 8, 19²; **6:**4; 2Ti **1:**1, 11; **2:**5, 21; **4:**5; Tit **1:**1, 6, 7; **2:**7; Phm **1:**9; Heb **5:**13; **6:**16, 17, 19; **7:**16, 20, 21; **9:**1, 9; **10:**3, 14, 17; **11:**7; **12:**20; **13:**10, 14, 17; Jas **3:**4; **4:**4; **5:**10; 1Pe **1:**1, 4, 8; **2:**21; **3:**15; 2Pe **2:**6, 14; 1Jn **2:**7, 20; **4:**10; Jude **1:**7; Rev **2:**7, 11, 17, 27, 29; **3:**6, 8, 12, 22; **4:**3, 7; **8:**1, 5; **11:**19; **12:**3, 5; **13:**9, 14; **17:**11; **19:**15, 17; **20:**1.

AND (29600)

Ge **1:**1, 2², 3², 4, 5³, 6, 7², 8², 9³, 10², 11², 12², 13², 14⁴, 15², 16, 18³, 19², 20², 21⁴, 22⁴, 23², 24³, 25², 26³, 27, 28⁵, 29, 30⁴, 31³; **2:**1, 2³, 4², 5³, 6, 7², 8, 9⁴, 10, 12, 14, 15², 16, 17, 18², 19², 20, 21², 22, 23, 24³, 25²; **3:**3, 5², 6⁴, 7², 8², 10, 11, 12², 13³, 14², 15³, 16⁴, 17³, 18³, 19, 20, 21, 22, 23, 25², 26; **5:**2³, 3, 4², 5², 7, 8, 10², 11³, 13³, 14, 15, 16⁵, 18⁴, 19², 20, 22, 24², 25², 27, 28², 29, 30, 31⁴; **5:**1², 2, 3, 4, 5, 6, 7, 9, 10², 11², 13², 14², 15², 16², 17, 18², 19, 20, 21, 22, 23⁴, 24; **8:**1⁴, 2², 3, 4, 5, 7³, 9², 10, 12, 13², 16³, 17³, 18², 19², 20², 21², 22⁴; **9:**1³, 2³, 3, 5², 7², 8, 9, 10², 12³, 13², 14, 15², 16², 17, 18, 19, 21, 22, 23³, 24, 27, 29; **10:**1, 2, 3, 4, 6, 7², 10, 12, 13, 14, 15, 18, 19³, 20², 22, 23, 24, 29; 31²; **11:**1, 2, 3, 4², 6, 7², 8, 9³, 11³, 13³, 15³, 17³, 19³, 21, 22, 23³, 25³, 26, 27², 29³; 31² 32; **12:**1², 2², 3², 4, 5³, 6⁴, 7, 8³, 9, 10, 13, 14, 15², 16⁵, 17, 18, 19, 20²; **13:**1², 2², 3, 4, 5², 6³, 7², 8², 10², 11², 12, 14, 15, 16³, 17, 18, 19², 20, 21, 22²; **14:**2², 4³, 5, 6, 9³, 10², 13, 16, 17³, 18, 19²;

18², 19², 20², 21², 22⁴; **9:**1³, 2³, 3, 5², 7², 8, 9, 10², 12³, 13², 14, 15², 16², 17, 18, 19, 21, 22, 23³, 24, 27, 29; **10:**1, 2, 3, 4, 6, 7², 10, 12, 13, 14, 15, 18, 19³, 20², 22, 23, 24, 29, 31²; **11:**1, 2, 3, 4², 6, 7², 8, 9³, 11³, 13³, 15³, 17³, 19³, 21, 22, 23³, 25³, 26, 27², 29³; 31², 32; **12:**1², 2², 3², 4, 5³, 7, 8³, 9, 10, 13, 15², 16⁵, 17, 19, 20²; **13:**1², 2², 3, 4, 5², 7², 8², 10², 11², 12, 14, 15, 16³, 17, 18, 19², 20, 21, 22²; **15:**2, 3, 5², 6, 9², 10, 12², 13³, 14, 15, 17², 18, 21; **16:**3, 4, 5², 8², 9, 11, 12², 14, 15; **17:**1², 2, 3, 6, 7, 8², 9, 11², 12, 13², 14, 15, 16³, 17, 18, 19, 20³, 23², 24, 25², 27; **19:**2, 3³, 4², 5, 6², 7², 8², 10³, 11², 13², 14, 15², 16⁴, 17², 18, 19, 20³, 23², 24, 25², 26, 27², 28, 29, 30, 31³, 32², 33, 34, 35, 36, 37², 38; **20:**1², 2, 3², 4²; 5², 6, 7², 8, 9², 10², 11², 12, 13³, 14, 15², 16, 17, 18, 20, 21⁴, 22, 23; **21:**1, 5, 6, 9, 11³, 12, 18³, 19², 24⁵, 26; **21:**4³, 5³, 6, 10, 12, 14², 16, 18, 19², 20, 22², 26, 27, 28, 29³, 32, 33², 34, 35³, 36; **22:**1³, 2, 5, 6, 7, 10, 11, 13, 14, 24²; **23:**1³, 2, 3², 4², 5², 6², 7, 8, 9³, 10, 11, 13, 14², 20², 21, 22², 23², 24², 25², 26, 27², 28, 29, 31², 32²; **24:**1³, 3², 4², 5², 6², 7, 8, 9³, 10², 12, 13, 14², 16, 17, 18², 20, 22², 26, 27, 28, 29, 30², 31, 32², 33, 34, 35, 36, 37², 39, 40, 41, 42, 43, 44², 45; **30:**2², 3³, 5, 9, 10³, 11⁴, 12², 13, 14², 15, 16, 17², 18², 19², 20², 21², 22², 23, 24², 25²; **21:**1, 4, 6, 10, 12, 14⁴, 16², 17, 18², 19², 21, 23³; **1:**5²; **2:**3³, 4², 5², 6², 7, 8, 9, 10⁴, 11², 12², 13³; **3:**2², 3, 4, 5², 6, 7³, 8, 9, 10⁴, 11², 12², 13⁴; **4:**1, 2², 3, 4, 6, 7, 8², 9³; **5:**1, 2, 3, 17, 18, 20, 23, 25, 26²; **21:**1, 4, 6, 10, 23, 24²; **1:**3, 17, 18³, 19, 20, 22, 24, 26, 28, 30; **2:**1, 4, 9, 10³, 13², 15², 16², 17, 19, 20, 21, 25, 26², 27, 31, 33, 36, 37, 38², 39, 40, 41, 45, 48, 51; **2:**1, 11; 17, 19; **3:**1, 2², 4², 5², 6³, 7⁴, 8, 9², 11, 12², 13², 14, 15, 16³, 17, 19⁴, 22; **14:**2², 4⁴, 5, 6, 9³, 10², 13, 16, 17³, 18, 19²; **11:**1², 3, 7, 9², 10, 11², 12, 13, 15, 19, 25, 28, 30, 32, 33, 34, 35, 38², 40, 44, 46, 47²; **12:**2, 6, 7, 8²; **13:**1, 3², 4, 5², 6³, 8, 10², 11, 12, 13, 16, 17, 18, 19, 20², 21², 22², 24, 25², 27, 28, 31, 32, 33, 34, 35, 36, 37, 38, 40, 41, 42, 43³, 44⁴, 45, 49³; **51:**2, 5³, 6, 7², 8, 9, 10⁴, 11², 12², 13⁴, 14⁴, 16, 17, 18, 19³, 20, 21², 22², 23, 24²; **25:**26, 27⁴, 28², 29, 30; **6:**2, 3², 7, 11, 12, 15⁴;

20², 21², 22², 23³, 24², 25, 26², 27², 28², 29, 30, 31³; **15:**1², 2³, 4, 9, 10, 12, 14, 16, 17, 18, 19, 20², 21, 22², 24³, 25², 26², 27²; **16:**1², 3², 4, 5, 6, 7³, 8, 9, 10, 12, 13², 18², 20, 21, 22²; **17:**2, 3¹, 4, 5, 6, 7³, 8², 10², 12, 13, 16³, 18, 19³, 20³, 21², 23², 24, 25², 27⁴; **19:**2, 3¹, 4², 5, 6⁴, 7³, 8⁴, 9², 10², 12³, 13, 14, 15, 16⁴, 17², 18, 19³, 20³, 21³, 23, 24², 25⁴, 26²; **20:**1, 5, 6, 9, 11³, 12, 14³, 16, 18², 19², 24, 25², 26, 27, 28, 29³, 31², 33; **15:**1², 2³, 4, 9, 10, 12, 14, 16, 17, 18, 19, 20³; **21:**2³, 4, 9, 10, 12, 14, 16, 17, 18, 19, 20², 21, 22⁴, 23², 24, 28, 31, 32, 33, 37³; **17:**2³, 3¹, 4, 5, 6, 7³, 8, 9, 10², 12, 13, 16, 18², 19³, 20³, 21², 23³, 24, 25²; **18:**1³, 2, 3, 4, 5, 6, 7³, 8, 10², 12³, 13, 16³, 18, 19³, 20³, 21³, 23², 24; **13:**1, 16³, 18, 19², 21³, 23, 24², 25², 26; **2:**5², 3, 4², 5, 7, 8², 10, 11, 13³, 14, 15, 16³, 17, 18, 19²; **21:**1, 4, 6, 10, 23, 24², 25, 26, 27², 28², 29, 30; **6:**2, 3², 11, 12, 15⁵;

21³, 23, 26³, 27, 29; **22**:1, 2, 3², 4, 5⁴, 6, 8, 9⁴, 10², 11², 12, 13², 14⁴, 15, 16³, 18³, 19²; **23**:1, 2, 3, 4², 5, 6, 7, 8, 9, 10², 11², 12, 13³, 15, 19, 20, 21², 23, 24, 25, 28, 29³, 30, 31⁴, 32², **24**:1, 2³, 3, 4², 5², 6⁴, 18, 23, 26, 27, 30², 31³; **25**:1², 2, 3, 4, 5, 6², 7, 8, 9, 10, 11, 12, 13, 14, 15, 16, 17, 18, 19, 20, 21, 22, 23, 24, 25, 26, 27, 28, 29, 30, 31; **26**:3, 5, 7², 8², 9, 11², 13, 14, 15, 16², 17, 18, 19, 20, 21, 22, 23, 25, 26³, 28⁴, 29², 30², 31, 32⁴; **27**:1², 3, 5, 6, 24, 25, 28, 32, 34; **28**:1³, 2², 3, 4², 5, 6², 7, 8³, 9⁴, 10, 11, 12², 13⁴, 14, 15⁴, 17, 18², 19, 20², 21³; **29**:1, 2³, 3, 4, 5², 6², 7², 9, 11³, 12³, 13², 14², 15, 16, 17³, 18², 19³, 20², 21³, 22² 23, 24, 25, 27, 28, 29, 30⁴; **2Ch 1**:1, 2², 3², 5, 6, 7, 8, 10, 11², 12⁴, 13, 14³, 15², 16, 17³; **2**:1, 2², 4⁶, 7⁶, 8, 9, 10, 12⁴, 14¹⁰, 15³, 16², 17, 18; **3**:3, 4, 5³, 6, 7², 8, 10, 11, 12², 14², 16², 17²; **4**:1, 2, 4², 5, 6², 7², 8², 9³, 11², 15, 16, 17, 21², 22³; **5**:1³, 2, 3, 5³, 6³, 7, 8², 9, 12⁴, 13⁴, 14; **6**:3, 6, 9, 10², 12², 13⁴, 15, 17, 19², 20, 21², 22³, 23², 24³, 25³, 26⁴, 27², 29³, 30, 31, 32³, 33³, 34², 35², 36², 37², 38⁴, 39³, 40, 41², **7**:1³, 3, 4, 5, 6², 7, 8, 9, 10³, 11³, 12², 14³, 15, 16², 17³, 19⁴, 20², 21³, 22²; **8**:1, 2, 3, 4, 5, 6⁴, 7, 9², 10, 13² 14², 17, 18³; **9**:1², 4, 5, 6, 7, 8³, 9, 10², 11³, 12², 14³, 17, 18, 20, 21³, 22, 24³, 25³, 27, 28, 29, 31², 10:3³, 4², 7², 8², 12, 14, 18; **11**:1³, 3², 4, 5, 10², 11², 12³, 13, 14⁴, 15³, 17², 18, 19, 20, 21³, 23³; **12**:1², 3³, 4, 5², 6², 8, 9, 10, 11, 12, 13², 15², 16²; **13**:2², 4², 5³, 7³, 8², 9³, 10², 11³, 14², 15³, 16, 17, 18, 19², 20², 21², 22; **14**:1³, 2, 7², 8⁴, 9², 10, 12², 13³, 15²; **15**:2³, 3, 4², 6, 7³, 8³, 9³, 11², 12², 14², 15, 16, 18³; **16**:1, 2³, 3³, 4², 5, 6³, 7², 8², 9, 11, 13⁴, 14²; **17**:1², 2², 4, 5², 6, 7, 8³, 9, 11³, 12², 13, 17; **18**:1², 2³, 3, 5, 8, 9, 10, 11, 12, 14, 16, 18, 19³, 20, 21², 23, 25², 26³, 28, 29, 31, 33², 34; **19**:2³, 3, 4², 8³, 9, 10², 11³; **20**:1, 2, 3, 5, 6³, 7, 8, 9³, 10², 13², 14, 15², 16, 17³, 18², 19², 20⁴, 21², 22⁴, 23², 24², 25⁴, 27, 28³, 30, 31, 32, 33, 37; **21**:1², 2, 3², 5, 7, 8, 9³, 11³, 12², 13², 14, 16, 17², 19, 20²; **22**:2, 8², 9², 11⁴; **23**:1², 2, 4², 5, 6², 8, 9, 10³, 11², 14², 15, 16², 17³, 18, 20³, 21²; **24**:1, 3², 5³, 6³, 7, 8, 9, 10, 11³, 12⁴, 13², 14⁶, 15², 16, 17², 18³, 19, 20, 21, 22², 23³, 25², 26, 27²; **25**:1, 5³, 7, 8, 10², 11, 12, 13², 14, 15, 16, 18, 19⁴, 21, 22, 23, 24⁴, 26, 27²; **26**:1, 2, 3, 6², 7², 8, 9², 10⁴, 11, 14, 15, 16, 18², 20, 21², 23³; **27**:1, 3, 4², 5³, 7², 8, 9² **28**:1, 2, 3, 4², 5², 6, 7, 8, 9, 10³, 12², 13³, 15, 16, 17, 18, 20, 21², 22⁴, 23², 24², 25³, 26, 27, 28, 29², 30⁴, 31⁴, 32, 33², 34, 35, 36; **30**:1⁴, 2³, 3, 4, 5, 6³, 7, 9³, 10², 11², 12², 14, 15³, 17, 18, 20², 21², 22², 24⁵, 25³, 27²; **31**:1⁶, 2³, 3, 4², 5, 6², 7, 8³, 9³, 10⁴, 11, 14, 15², 16, 18², 20, 21², 23²; **32**:1, 2³, 4³, 5³, 6², 7², 8², 9², 11, 12³, 13, 15, 16, 17, 18, 20⁴, 21², 22², 23², 24², 25³, 27³, 28³, 29⁴, 30², 31⁴, 32, 33³; **33**:1, 3², 6³, 7³, 8, 9, 10, 11, 12, 13³, 14, 15³, 16³, 18, 19³, 20², 21, 22, 24, 25; **34**:1, 2, 3², 4³, 5², 6², 7², 8², 9³, 10, 11³, 12², 13³, 16, 17², 18, 20, 21³, 22, 24, 25³, 27⁵, 28², 29², 30, 31, 32, 33³; **35**:1, 2, 3, 4², 5, 6, 7, 8⁴, 9⁴, 10, 11, 13³, 14³, 15, 16, 17, 18³, 20, 21, 23, 24³, 25³, 26, 27; **36**:1²³, 2³, 4³, 5, 6, 7, 8³, 9², 10, 11, 12, 13², 14³, 15², 16², 17³, 18⁴, 19², 20², 22², 23³; Ezr 1:1, 2, 3², 4, 4⁴, 6³, 7, 11; **2**:1, 2, 6, 25, 28, 30, 33⁴, 42², 54, 57, 58, 59, 60, 61³, 62, 63, 65³, 67, 69, 70²; **3**:1, 2³, 5, 7³, 8⁴, 9², 10², 11², 12², 13; **4**:1², 3, 4, 5², 6, 7³, 8², 9³, 10⁴, 12³, 13⁴, 14, 15, 16, 17², 18, 19⁴, 20², 22³; **5**:1² 2³, 3⁴, 5, 7³, 8⁴, 9², 11³, 12, 14², 15⁴, 16; **6**:1, 2, 3², 4, 5², 6³, 7, 9², 10, 13², 14⁴, 16, 17, 18², 20³; **7**:7, 9, 10³, 11², 13, 14², 15², 16², 17³, 18², 20, 22, 23, 25³, 26, 28⁴; **8**:1, 3, 4, 5, 6, 7, 8, 9, 10, 11, 12, 13², 14², 15³, 16³, 17², 18², 19³, 20, 21², 22, 23³, 24, 25⁴, 27, 28, 29², 30², 31², 33³, 34², 35, 36; **9**:1³, 2³, 4², 5², 7⁴, 8³, 9, 11², 13, 14³, 15², 16³, 17, 18², 19², 20², 23³; Ne 1:2², 3³, 4⁵, 6³, 7, 11; **2**:1, 2, 6, 25, 28, 30, 34³, 4⁵, 6³, 7, 8, 9², 10, 11, 13², 13³, 14, 15, 16, 17², 18, 19⁴, 20², 23³; **3**:1², 3, 4, 6², 7², 8, 10, 11², 13⁴, 14, 15, 17², 18, 19³, 22²; **4**:1, 2, 3³, 4, 5², 6², 7, 9², 10², 11², 13³, 14⁴, 16, 17, 18² 20³; **7**:7, 9, 10³, 11², 13, 14², 15², 16², 17³, 18², 20, 22, 23, 25³, 26, 28⁴; **8**:1, 3, 4, 5, 6, 7, 8, 9, 10, 11, 12, 13², 14², 15³, 16³, 17², 18², 19², 20², 21², 22, 23², 24, 25⁴, 27, 28, 29², 30², 31¹, 32³, 33³; **4**:1², 7², 8², 9², 10⁴, 12³, 13⁵, 15², 17², 18²; **6**:1², 2³, 4, 5, 6, 7, 9, 10, 12, 13, 14² 16, 17, 18, 19²; **7**:1³, 2, 3², 4², 5, 6, 7, 11, 26, 29, 30, 32, 37, 43, 44; Ne 1:2², 3³, 4⁵, 6³, 7, 9², 10; **2**:1, 3, 5², 6, 8⁴, 9², 10, 11, 13², 14, 15, 17², 18, 19³; **3**:1⁴, 2, 3³, 4, 6², 8⁴, 10, 11², 13², 14, 15, 16, 17², 18, 19⁴, 20, 22², 23², 24², 25³, 26, 27, 28², 29³, 31², 32⁴, 34, 35, 36, 37, 38; **4**:1, 2², 3, 4, 5², 6, 7, 8³, 9³, 10³, 11², 12², 13³, 14⁴, 16, 17, 18³, 20, 21², 22, 23³; **5**:1, 2³, 3, 4, 5, 6, 7², 8, 10³, 11³, 12³, 13³, 15², 17²; **6**:1², 2, 4², 5, 6, 7, 9, 10, 12, 13, 14² 16, 17, 18, 19²; **7**:1³, 2, 3², 4², 5, 6, 7, 11, 26, 29, 30, 32, 37, 43, 44; Ne 1:2², 3³, 4⁵, 6³, 7, 9², 10; **2**:1, 3, 5², 6, 8⁴, 9², 10, 11, 13², 14, 15, 17², 18, 19³; **3**:1⁴, 2, 3³, 4, 6², 8⁴, 10, 11², 13², 14, 15, 16, 17², 18, 19⁴, 20, 22², 23², 24², 25³, 26, 27, 28², 29³, 31², 32⁴; **4**:1, 2², 3, 4, 5², 6, 7, 8³, 9³, 10³, 11², 12², 13³, 14⁴, 16, 17, 18³, 20, 21², 22, 23³; **5**:1, 2³, 3, 4, 5, 6, 7², 8, 10³, 11³, 12³, 13³, 15², 17²; **6**:1², 2, 4², 5, 6, 7, 9, 10, 12, 13, 14² 16, 17, 18, 19²; **7**:1³, 2, 3², 4², 5, 6, 7, 11, 26, 29, 30, 32, 37, 43, 44; **8**:2², 3, 4³, 5², 6, 7, 8, 10, 11², 13⁴, 14³, 15³, 16, 23², 24, 25², 26², 30, 31², 32², 4²; **4**:1, 2², 7², 8², 9², 10⁴, 12³, 13, 14⁶, 15, 16, 17, 18³, 19³, 22²; **5**:1, 2³, 4, 5, 6², 7², 8, 10³, 11³, 12³, 13⁵, 15², 17²; **6**:1², 2, 3, 4², 5, 6, 7, 9, 10, 12, 13, 14² 16, 17, 18, 19²; **7**:1³, 2, 3², 4², 5, 6, 7, 11, 26, 29, 30, 32, 37, 43, 44; **8**:2², 3, 4³, 5², 6, 7, 8, 10, 11², 13⁴, 14³, 15³, 16, 23², 24, 25², 26², 30, 31², 32², 4²; **10**:8, 10, 13, 27, 28³, 29⁴, 31, 33³, 34⁴, 35, 36², 37³, 38, 39³; **11**:1³, 4, 5, 8³, 9, 12, 13, 14, 16, 17³, 19, 20, 21², 25³, 27, 28, 30⁴, 31, 32, 33, 34, 35²; **12**:1², 7², 8, 9, 11, 17, 22, 24³, 25, 26³, 27³, 29³, 30², 32, 35, 36², 37,

39, 41, 42², 43², 44³, 45³, 46³, 47³; **13**:1, 2, 5⁶, 7, 8, 9², 10², 11², 12, 13², 14², 15⁴, 16², 17, 18, 19, 20, 21, 22³, 23, 24, 25³, 26, 27, 28, 29², 30², 31; Est 1:3⁴, 4², 6⁴, 7, 10, 11, 12, 13, 14⁴, 16², 17², 18², 19², 21, 22; **2**:1², 3, 4, 7³, 8³, 9⁴, 10, 11², 12², 13, 14², 15, 17³, 18³, 20, 21², 22, 23³; **3**:1, 2², 7², 8², 9, 10, 11, 12³, 13⁴, 14², 15², 17; **4**:1³, 3, 4, 7³, 8², 10, 11, 14², 15², 16², 17; **5**:1², 2, 5, 6, 7, 8³, 9², 10², 11³, 12², 14⁶; **6**:1, 2, 3, 8, 9², 10², 11², 13³, 14; **7**:1, 2, 3², 4⁴, 6², 7; **8**:1, 2, 3, 4², 5⁴, 7², 8², 9³, 10, 11³, 13, 14, 15³, 16², 17⁴; **9**:1, 3² 4², 5², 6, 9, 12³, 13, 14, 18, 19², 20, 21, 22², 24², 25², 26², 27³, 28⁴, 30², 31⁴, 32; **10**:2³, 3²; Job 1:1², 2, 3, 4², 5², 6, 7², 8², 10³, 11², 13², 14², 15³, 16⁴, 17⁴, 18³, 19³, 20²; **2**:1, 2³, 3³, 5, 7, 8, 9, 10, 11⁴, 12², 13; **3**:1, 3, 5, 9, 11, 12, 13, 14, 17, 19², 20, 22²; **4**:5², 6, 8, 10, 11, 14², 15, 16, 20; **5**:2, 5, 11, 13, 16, 20, 21, 22², 23, 24, 25, 27²; **6**:2, 9, 16, 17, 18, 21, 24, 26, 27; **7**:3, 4, 5², 6, 13, 14, 15, 18, 21; **8**:5, 6², 8, 9² 10, 12, 17, 18, 19, 21, 22; **9**:4, 5, 6, 7, 8, 9², 16, 17, 18, 19, 20, 21, 22, 27, 30; **10**:1, 6, 7, 8², 10, 11³, 12², 13, 14, 15, 16, 17, 21, 22; **11**:4, 6, 9, 10², 11, 13, 14, 15, 17, 18, 19, 20; **12**:2, 4², 6, 7², 8, 10, 13², 16², 17, 18, 19, 20, 21, 22, 23²; **13**:1, 3, 13, 14, 19, 20, 21, 22², 23², 24, 26; **14**:1, 2, 5, 6, 7, 8, 9, 10², 11, 12, 13², 15, 18², 19, 20², 22; **15**:4, 10, 13, 16, 17, 24, 25, 27, 28, 29, 30, 32, 34, 35; **16**:4, 6, 8², 7³, 8, 10, 13, 16, 18, 20²; **17**:9, 11, 14; **18**:2, 3, 8, 11, 14, 16, 18; **19**:2, 5, 6, 9, 12, 15, 20, 25, 26, 27, 29; **20**:3, 6, 12, 13, 17, 19, 23, 26; **21**:3, 5, 7, 9, 10, 12, 13, 23, 26, 32, 33; **22**:4, 7, 9², 11, 12, 19, 20, 21, 22, 24, 26, 27², 28, 29; **23**:4, 5, 7, 13, 14; **24**:3, 4, 6, 8, 12, 14, 16, 19², 21², 24², 25; **25**:2; **26**:3, 4, 5, 10, 14; **27**:1, 4, 6, 15, 9, 11, 18, 22, 23; **28**:1, 2, 4, 6, 8, 9, 11, 18, 22, 23, 24, 25, 26, 27², 28²; **29**:3, 5, 6, 7, 8², 9, 10, 11, 12, 14, 15, 17, 19, 23, 25; **30**:3, 4, 6, 7, 8, 9, 10, 13, 18, 20, 23, 27, 34², 38, 40; **32**:3, 6, 14, 15, 18, 20²; **33**:5², 9², 16, 21, 22, 24, 26², 27², 28, 31², 33; **34**:14², 15, 17, 18, 19, 20, 24, 25, 27, 29, 37³; **35**:3, 4, 5, 8, 11, 14, 15²; **36**:2, 5, 7, 10, 12², 17, 28, 31, 32; **37**:1, 3, 6, 10, 13, 14, 15, 23³; **38**:3, 7, 9, 10², 11, 13, 15, 19, 23, 25, 27, 34, 38, 39, 41; **39**:3, 4², 8, 12, 13, 14, 18, 21, 23, 25, 26, 27, 28, 30; **40**:7, 9, 10³, 12, 15, 20, 24; **41**:8, 12, 17, 21, 23, 27, 31; **42**:4², 6², 7, 8⁵, 9², 10, 11⁶, 12, 13², 14, 15, 16²; Ps 1:2², 3; **2**:1, 2³, 3, 5, 8, 11, 12; **3**:3, 4, 5, 4:1, 2, 4, 5, 7, 8; **5**:2, 3, 6; **6**:4, 6, 10; **7**:1, 2, 3, 5², 9², 12, 14, 15, 17; **8**:2³, 3, 5², 7², 8; **9**:2, 3, 4², 5², 12, 13, 14, 18; **10**:3, 5, 6, 7, 9, 11, 14, 15, 16, 17, 18; **11**:5, 6; **12**:3, 5, 6, 7; **13**:2, 3, 4; **14**:4, 7; **15**:2², 3²; **16**:5, 9; **17**:3, 6, 10, 14, 15; **18**:T, 2², 3, 7², 9, 10, 12, 14², 15, 16, 23, 31, 32, 35, 37, 40, 50; **19**:6, 9, 14²; **20**:2, 3, 4, 5, 7, 8²; **21**:2, 3, 4², 5, 6, 9, 11, 13; **22**:2, 4, 5², 6², 11, 14, 15, 16, 17, 18, 26, 27², 28, 29; **23**:4, 6², 24:1², 2, 4, 5, 8; **25**:5², 6, 7, 9, 10, 13, 16, 18², 19, 20, 21; **26**:2², 3, 5, 6, 7, 11; **27**:1², 2², 4, 5, 6, 7, 10, 14²; **28**:4², 5², 7³, 9²; **29**:1², 9², 30:1, 2, 10, 11, 12; **31**:3², 7, 9², 10³, 13, 15, 17, 18, 24; **32**:2, 4, 5², 7, 8², 9, 11; **33**:3, 4, 5, 9², 13, 19, 20; **34**:T, 2, 4, 6, 7, 8, 10, 12, 13, 14², 15, 17, 18; **35**:2², 3, 4, 5, 7, 8, 10, 11², 14, 15, 18, 21, 25, 26, 27, 28; **36**:3², 4, 5, 7, 8; **37**:3, 4² 5, 7, 8, 10, 14, 12², 14², 15, 18, 21, 25, 26, 27, 28, 29, 30, 34, 35, 36, 40²; **38**:2, 5, 6, 8, 11, 17; **39**:1, 2, 3, 4, 6, 11, 13²; **40**:1, 2², 3², 5, 6², 10², 11², 12², 13, 14, 16, 17², 41²:1, 3, 5, 6, 12, 13; **42**:2, 3, 4, 5, 7, 11; **43**:1², 3, 4, 5; **44**:2², 3, 4, 8, 9, 10, 11, 13, 15, 16, 19², 24²; **45**:2, 3, 4, 6, 7, 8², 10², 14, 15, 17; **46**:1, 2², 3, 8, 9, 10; **48**:1, 5, 14; **49**:2², 6, 9² 10, 11, 13, 14, 18; **50**:1², 3⁴, 4, 6, 7, 10, 11, 12, 15², 17, 19, 20, 21², 23; **51**:2, 3, 4², 7³, 8, 9, 10, 12, 13, 14, 15, 17; **52**:T, 5, 6, 7, 8; **53**:1, 4, 6; **54**:T, 7; **55**:2², 3, 4, 5, 6, 7, 8, 9, 10², 11, 16, 17², 19², 22, 23; **56**:13; **57**:3², 4, 7, 8; **58**:1², 2, 4, 6, 7, 10, 11, 12, 14, 15, 60:T³, 1, 2, 5, 6, 7, 10, 11, 12, 14, 15; **61**:4, 6², 7; **62**:3², 4, 5, 7, 8, 9, 10, 11³, 12²; **63**:1², 2, 4², 5, 6, 7, 8, 9³, 10³, 11, 15⁴, 17; **64**:1, 5², 6³, 7, 11², 12; **65**:3², 4², 7, 8, 9², 10, 11², 12², 14, 16, 17, 18², 19², 21², 22², 23, 25²; **66**:1², 2³, 4², 5, 9, 10, 11², 12², 13, 14, 15², 16², 17³, 18⁶, 19⁴, 20⁴, 21², 22²; **67**:1², 4², 6, 7; **68**:3², 4, 10, 11, 12, 17, 24, 27², 35; **69**:7, 9, 10, 12, 18, 20, 26, 29², 30², 32, 33, 35; **70**:2, 4, 5², **71**:2², 3, 4, 11, 13, 14, 16, 17, 18, 20, 21, 24²; **72**:4, 8, 9, 10², 11, 13², 14, 15, 17, 19; **73**:4, 8, 9, 10, 21, 22, 24, 25, 26²; **74**:6, 9, 11, 14, 15, 16², 17, 21, 22; **75**:3, 4, 8; **76**:3, 6, 8², 10, 11; **77**:2, 3², 6, 12, 15, 16, 17, 18, 20; **78**:3, 4, 5, 6, 7, 8, 10, 13, 14, 15, 16, 17, 18², 19³, 20², 21, 22², 23, 24, 25, 27³, 30, 31, 32, 33³, 35², 36, 37², 38, 39², 40, 41², 44³, 33:2, 3³, 4, 5, 6², 7, 8, 9, 10², 11³, 12, 13², 14⁴, 15², 16², 17⁴, 18, 20, 22², 23², 24², 25³, 26, 27², 28², 29², 30², 31, 32, 35², 36², 37², 38³; **38**:1² 3², 5², 6², 9, 10, 12², 13, 15, 16², 20, 21²; **39**:1², 2, 6, 7³, 8², **40**:2, 4, 5², 6², 7, 8, 10², 11, 12, 14, 17, 19³, 22², 23, 24², 26³, 27, 28, 29, 30³, 31², 41:1, 2, 3, 4², 5², 6, 7, 9, 10², 11, 12, 13, 14³, 15³, 16, 18, 19, 21, 22, 24, 43:2, 3, 4³, 5, 6², 7, 9³, 10³, 11, 12, 13, 14, 17², 19, 20², 24, 25, 28² 44:2², 3², 5², 6², 7², 8, 9, 10, 11³, 12², 13², 14, 15⁴, 16², 17², 18, 19, 23, 25², 26², 27, 28²; **45**:1, 2⁴, 4, 5, 6, 7², 11, 13, 14, 15, 16, 18², 20², 23, 24², 25²; **46**:2, 3, 4³, 6³, 7², 9², 10, 13; **47**:2², 3, 6², 8², 9², 10³, 11, 12, 15; **48**:1², 2, 3², 5, 7, 12, 13, 14², 15², 16², 20, 21; **49**:2, 6², 4, 7⁴, 8³, 9², 10, 11, 13, 15, 17, 18², 19³, 21², 22, 23, 25²; **50**:2, 3, 5, 6, 7, 10², 11², 51:1², 2³, 3², 6, 13², 14, 15², 17, 18, 19, 21², 22, 23, 26²; **52**:1, 3, 5, 9, 10, 11, 13², 14, 15²; **53**:1, 2, 3, 4², 5, 6, 7², 8², 9, 10⁴, 11², 12³, 54:2³, 4, 6, 10, 11, 12, 13, 16², 17³; **55**:1⁴, 2³, 3, 4, 5, 7, 9, 10⁵, 11, 12³, 13; **56**:1², 2, 3, 4, 5³, 6², 7², 9, 10, 12; **57**:1³, 3, 4², 5, 6, 7, 8², 9, 13³, 10³, 11, 12, 15, 18, 19², 20; **58**:1², 2³, 4³, 5², 6², 7³, 8², 9³, 10³, 11, 12, 18², 19³, 20³, 21², 22, 23, 25², 26², 27³; **3**:1² 2², 3, 6², 7, 8², 9², 13², 14², 15, 17, 18, 19², 21³, 22, 23, 24², 25²; **4**:1, 2³, 3², 4², 5³, 8², 9², 10, 11, 14, 18, 21, 23⁴, 24, 25, 26, 28³, 29, 30, 31; **5**:1³, 3, 5², 6², 7³, 10, 11, 13, 14, 15, 17⁴, 19², 20, 21, 23³, 24, 26, 27, 28², 30, 31; **6**:2, 4, 5, 6, 7, 8³, 10, 11⁴, 12, 13, 16³, 17, 19, 21², 23³, 24, 25, 26, 27, 29², 30, 31, 33³, 34⁴; **8**:1³, 2⁶, 7², 9, 10², 13, 14², 16², 17, 20, 21²; **9**:1², 2, 4, 5, 7, 10³, 11, 12², 15, 16, 18², 21², 24², 26², 10:3, 4², 6, 7², 8⁴, 9¹¹, 11, 12², 15, 16, 17², 3:2², 4, 5, 6, 8, 9, 10, 12², 13, 14, 16, 17², 18², 21, 22, 23, 24, 25³; **4**:1², 3³, 4², 5³, 8³, 9, 10, 11, 14, 18, 21, 23⁴, 24, 25, 26, 28³, 29, 30, 31; **5**:1³, 3, 5², 6², 7³, 10, 11, 13, 14, 15, 17⁴, 19², 20, 21, 23³, 24, 26, 27, 28², 30, 31; **6**:2, 4, 5, 6, 7, 8³, 10, 11⁴, 12, 13, 16³, 17, 19, 21², 23³, 24, 25, 26, 27, 29², 30, 31, 33³, 34⁴; **8**:1³, 2⁶, 7², 9, 10², 13, 14², 16², 17, 20, 21²; **9**:1², 2, 4, 5, 7, 10³, 11, 12², 15, 16, 18², 21², 24², 26²; SS 1:4, 6, 7, 8, 16; **2**:3, 4, 6, 7, 10², 11, 14, 16, 17²; **3**:2², 4, 5, 6, 11; **4**:6², 8, 10, 11, 13, 14⁴, 16²; **5**:1³, 5, 10, 11; **6**:2, 3, 8², 9²; **7**:6, 7, 9², 10, 12, 13²; **8**:1, 2, 3, 8², 9², 10, 12, 14; Isa 1:1², 2, 4, 6², 11³, 13, 14, 16, 19, 20, 23, 24, 25, 28², 31; **2**:1, 2, 3, 4², 6, 7, 9, 10, 11, 12², 13², 14, 15, 16, 17, 18, 19², 20², 21²; **3**:1³, 2³, 3², 6, 8, 14, 15, 18³, 19², 20², 21, 22², 23⁴, 26; **4**:1², 2, 3, 4², 5², 6³; **5**:2³, 3², 5², 6², 7², 8², 12⁴, 13, 14³, 15², 16², 17, 19², 20, 21², 22³, 24⁴, 25³, 26, 29, 30²; **6**:1², 2, 3, 4², 5², 7², 8, 9³, 10³, 11⁴, 12³, 13²; **7**:1, 2, 3, 4³, 5², 6³, 7, 8², 9, 11, 14², 15, 16, 17, 18², 19², 20, 21³, 23², 24; **8**:1, 2², 4, 5⁴, 7³, 8, 10¹, 12², 13, 14², 15², 16, 17, 18², 19², 20², 21⁴, 22⁴; **9**:1², 2, 3, 4², 7³, 8², 9², 11³, 12², 13², 14², 15²; **10**:1, 4, 2³, 5, 7, 8³, 9, 10, 11², 12², 13², 14, 15², 16, 18², 19, 20, 21², 25; **11**:2², 4³, 5, 6², 7, 9, 10, 12², 13, 16, 17²; **12**:2², 3, 4², 5, 6³, 7³, 8², 9⁴, 11², 12, 13, 14, 15, 16, 17, 18, 19, 20, 22², 25, 27²; **14**:2, 3, 4, 6, 9, 10, 12², 14, 15, 16², 17, 18, 20, 21; **15**:1, 2, 3⁴, 6, 7, 8, 9²; **16**:2, 3⁴, 4³, 5, 6², 8³, 9⁴, 10, 11⁴, 13², 14, 15; **17**:1², 2, 3⁴, 4, 5, 6, 7, 8, 9, 11, 13, 14², 15³, 16, 17³, 19, 20, 22², 23; **18**:2, 3, 7, 8²; **19**:1², 2, 3², 4², 7³, 8², 9², 11³, 12², 13², 14², 15²; **20**:2, 4, 5², 6, 6³, 7², 8, 9, 10², 11², 12², 18²; **21**:1, 4², 5³, 6², 7³, 8, 9, 10², 11², 15³, 16², 17³, 19, 20, 21, 22²; **23**:1, 2², 3, 4, 6, 8, 9, 10, 11, 13, 14², 15, 17, 18, 22², 23, 24, 29, 31, 32, 34, 36, 39², **24**:1², 6², 7, 8³, 9², 10³, 12³, 13, 14², 15, 16, 17⁴, 18³, 19², 20², 21, 22, 23, 24, 25, 26², 27², 28, 29, 30², 31, 34², 38²; **26**:2, 3², 4, 5², 6², 7², 8², 9, 10², 11³, 12², 13², 14², 15², 16², 17, 19², 20², 21³, 23², 24; **27**:2², 3, 4, 5⁴, 7³, 8, 10, 11²; **28**:1, 3, 4, 5, 6, 7, 8³, 10, 13, 14; **29**:1², 2², 3, 5², 6, 7², 8, 10, 11², 12², 16, 17², 18³, 19², 21³, 22², 23, 25, 26, 28², 31, 32; **30**:3², 4, 6, 8, 9, 10², 11, 14², 15, 17, 18³, 19, 20, 21, 22², 23¹, 24², 4, 5, 7, 8³, 9, 10, 11, 12⁴, 13⁴, 14, 15², 16, 18⁶, 19, 21, 22³, 23², 24²; **32**:2, 3, 4², 7², 8², 10, 11², 12³, 13², 17², 18, 19², 20⁴, 21³, 22, 23, 24, 25², 28, 30², 31, 33², 34, 35, 36, 37², 38, 39², 40, 41², 44⁴; **33**:2, 3³, 4, 5, 6³, 7, 8, 9, 10, 11³, 12, 13², 14⁴, 16, 18², 21²

19, 21³, 22, 24, 25²; **23**:1, 2, 3, 4, 9, 11, 13, 17, 18²; **24**:1², 3, 4², 5, 6, 7, 13, 17², 21, 22, 23²; **25**:1, 4, 5, 6, 9², 12; **26**:1, 5, 8, 10, 11, 14, 17², 19, 20; **27**:1, 3, 4, 6², 8, 9, 11², 12, 13²; **28**:2³, 4, 7⁴, 8, 10², 11, 12, 13⁵, 15, 17², 19², 20³, 21², 22³, 23, 25², 26, 27, 29; **29**:1, 2, 3, 6⁴, 7², 8², 9², 11³, 16, 17, 18², 20³, 21, 24²; **30**:4, 5, 6, 10, 11, 12, 13, 15², 16⁴, 17, 18, 19², 20², 23, 24, 25, 29; **42**:1, 3, 5³, 6², 7, 9, 10², 11, 12, 13, 14², 15³, 16, 18, 19, 21, 22, 24; **43**:2, 3, 4³, 5, 6², 7, 9³, 10³, 11, 12, 13, 14, 17²; **44**:2, 3² 5, 6², 7², 8, 9, 10, 11³, 12², 13², 14, 15⁴, 16², 17², 18⁴, 19⁴, 20⁴, 21², 22² 23²; Jer 1:3, 7, 8, 9², 10⁴, 15², 16, 17, 18², 19²; **2**:2³, 3, 5, 6⁴, 7³, 9², 10, 12, 13, 16, 17², 18², 19², 20², 21, 22, 23, 25², 26³, 27²; **3**:1² 2³, 3, 6², 8², 9², 13, 14², 15, 17, 18, 19² 21², 22³, 24², 25²; **4**:1, 2³, 4², 5³, 8², 9, 10, 11, 14, 18, 21, 23⁴, 24, 25, 26, 28³, 29, 30, 31; **5**:1³, 3, 5², 6², 7³, 10, 11, 13, 14, 15, 17⁴, 19², 20, 21, 23³, 24, 26, 27, 28², 30, 31; **6**:2, 4, 5, 6, 7, 8³, 10, 11⁴, 12, 13, 16³, 17, 19, 21², 23³, 24, 25, 26, 27, 29², 30, 31, 33³, 34⁴; **8**:1³, 2⁶, 7², 9, 10², 13, 14², 16², 17, 20, 21²; **9**:1², 2, 4, 5, 7, 10³, 11, 12², 15, 16, 18², 21², 24², 26²; **10**:3, 4², 6, 7², 8⁴, 9¹¹, 11, 12², 14, 16, 17, 18², 19², 20², 22, 23; **11**:2³, 4³, 5², 6, 9, 10², 12², 13⁵, 14, 15², 16, 18, 19³, 21, 22², 23³; **12**:2², 3, 4², 6², 7, 8², 9, 10, 11², 12, 14², 15², 16², 17; **13**:1², 2, 4³, 5, 6, 7³, 9, 10², 11³, 12, 13, 14, 15, 16, 18, 19, 20, 22³, 25, 27²; **14**:2, 3, 4, 6, 9, 10, 12², 14, 15, 18², 19², 20, 21; **15**:1, 2, 3⁴, 6, 7, 8, 9²; **16**:2, 3², 4³, 5⁴, 6², 8², 9⁴, 10, 11⁴, 13², 15, 16, 18², 19², 20², 21; **17**:1², 2, 3², 4, 5, 8, 9, 10, 11⁴, 14², 15², 16⁴, 17, 18⁴, 19², 20, 21, 22³; **18**:2, 3, 7, 8², 9², 10, 12², 13, 14³, 15², 16², 17³, 19, 20, 21, 22³, 23²; **19**:1³, 2, 3², 4², 7³, 8², 9², 11³, 12², 13², 14²; **20**:2, 4, 5², 6³, 7², 8, 9, 10², 11², 12², 18²; **21**:1, 4³, 5³, 6², 7³, 8, 9, 10², 11², 13², 14², 15³, 16², 17³, 19, 20, 22², 25, 26², 28; **23**:1, 2², 3, 4, 6, 8, 9, 10, 11, 13, 14², 15, 17, 18², 22², 23, 24, 29, 31, 32, 34, 36, 39²; **24**:1², 6², 7, 8³, 9², 10³, 12³, 13, 14², 15, 16, 17⁴, 18³, 19², 20², 21, 22, 23, 24, 25, 26², 27², 28, 29, 30², 31, 34², 38²; **26**:2, 3², 4, 5², 6², 7², 8², 9, 10², 11³, 12², 13², 14², 15², 16², 17, 19², 20², 21³, 23², 24; **27**:2², 3, 4, 5⁴, 7³, 8, 10, 11²; **28**:1, 3, 4, 5, 6, 7, 8³, 10, 13, 14; **29**:1², 2², 3, 5², 6, 7², 8, 10, 11², 12², 16, 17², 18³, 19², 21³, 22², 23, 25, 26, 28², 31, 32; **30**:3², 4, 6, 8, 9, 10², 11, 14², 15, 17, 18³, 19, 20, 21, 22², 23¹, 24²; **31**:1, 4², 5, 7, 8³, 9, 10, 11, 12⁴, 13⁴, 14, 15², 16, 18⁶, 19, 21, 22³, 23², 24²; **32**:2, 3, 4², 7², 8², 10, 11², 12³, 13², 17², 18, 19², 20⁴, 21³, 22, 23, 24, 25², 28, 30², 31, 33², 34, 35, 36, 37², 38, 39², 40, 41², 44⁴; **33**:2, 3³, 4, 5, 6³, 7, 8, 9, 10, 11³, 12, 13², 14⁴, 16, 18², 21²; **34**:1⁴, 2³, 3⁵, 5, 7², 9, 10⁴, 11², 15, 16², 17, 18², 19², 20, 21, 22³; **35**:2², 3², 5², 8, 10, 11, 13³, 14⁴, 15⁷, 16; **36**:2², 3, 4, 6, 7³, 9, 10, 14, 15, 16, 18, 19², 20, 21³, 22, 23, 24, 25, 26², 28, 29⁴, 30², 31⁴,

32³; **37**:4, 5, 8², 10², 13, 14, 15², 17, 21; **38**:1, 3, 6², 8, 10, 11³, 12, 13³, 14, 17², 18, 19, 20, 22, 23², 25³, 27², 28; **39**:1, 2, 3² 4², 5², 6, 7, 8², 9, 10², 12, 13, 14, 16; **40**:1, 3², 4, 5³, 6, 7⁴, 8³, 9³, 10³, 11², 12², 13, 14, 15⁴; **41**:1, 2², 5³, 7², 8³, 10, 11, 12, 13, 14, 15², 16², 17; **42**:1² 2², 3, 4, 5, 8², 10², 11², 12, 13, 14², 15, 16², 17, 18³, 20², 22; **43**:2² 4², 5, 6⁴, 7, 9, 10, 11², 12² 13, 14, 15², 17⁶, 18³, 19², 20, 21⁵, 22², 23², 25², 27, 28; **45**:3, 4; **46**:3², 5, 6, 8², 9, 11, 14³, 16, 19, 21, 25³, 26, 27²; **47**:2², 3, 4², 6, 7; **48**:1², 3, 7², 8² 11, 12², 18², 19², 20, 21, 22, 23, 24², 28, 29³, 30, 32, 33², 34², 35, 37², 38, 41, 43², 46; **49**:2², 3³, 4, 5, 8, 10², 13², 16, 17², 18, 19², 22, 23, 24², 28³, 29², 31, 32², 36, 38²; **50**:1, 2³, 3² 4, 5², 6³, 8, 9², 11², 13, 16, 18, 19³, 20, 21, 23, 24², 25, 26, 28, 32², 33, 35², 37², 39², 40, 41, 42² 43, 44²; **51**:1, 2, 5, 8, 9, 13, 14, 15, 16, 17, 21², 22², 23², 24, 25, 27, 28², 29, 31, 32, 34², 36³, 37, 39², 40, 43, 44² 46, 47, 48², 50², 51, 52, 53, 56, 57³, 58, 63, 64; **52**:1, 3², 4, 7, 8², 9, 11, 13, 15², 16², 17², 18, 19, 20², 21², 22², 24, 25², 26, 31, 32, 33; **La 1**:3, 4, 7², 8², 11, 12, 13, 14, 16, 18, 19, 20, 22; **2**:2, 5², 6², 7, 8² 9³, 10, 11, 12, 14² 15, 16², 18, 20², 21², 22; **3**:2, 3, 4², 5², 11², 12, 15, 18, 19², 20, 21, 30, 37, 38, 40², 41², 42², 43, 45, 47², 50, 53, 54, 57, 62, 65, 66; **4**:7, 12, 13, 15, 19, 21², 22; **5**:1, 3, 5, 6, 7², 8, 11, 22; **Eze 1**:1, 4², 5, 6, 7², 8, 9, 10², 13², 14, 15, 16, 17, 18², 19, 20³, 21², 23³, 24², 25, 26, 27²; **2**:1, 2², 3, 4, 6², 8, 9, 10²; **3**:1² 2, 3², 4, 5, 6, 8, 10², 11, 12, 13, 14², 15, 16, 17, 18², 19, 20³, 21², 22², 23, 24, 26, 27²; **4**:1, 2², 3, 4, 5, 6, 7, 8, 9³, 10², 11², 12², 13³, 14², 15², 16, 17²; **5**:1³, 2², 3, 4², 5, 6², 7, 8, 9, 10², 11², 12³, 13, 14, 15⁴, 16³, 17⁴; **6**:3⁴, 4², 5, 6⁴, 7, 8, 9², 10, 11⁴, 12³, 13², 14²; **7**:3² 4², 8², 9, 12, 14, 16, 17, 18, 19³, 20, 21²; **11**:1³, 2, 3, 5, 6, 7, 8, 9², 10, 12, 13, 15, 16, 17²; **12**:3², 5, 6, 10, 12², 14², 15, 16, 18, 19³, 20, 22, 23, 25, 27; **13**:3, 6, 7, 8, 9, 10², 11³, 12², 14², 15², 16², 18², 19², 20², 21², 22², 23; **14**:1, 3, 4³, 6, 7³, 8³, 9², 13⁴, 14, 15², 17², 18, 19, 20³; **15**:4³, 5, 7; **16**:3², 6², 7⁴, 8³, 9², 10², 11, 12², 13⁴, 14, 15², 17², 18³, 19, 20³, 21, 22², 23, 24², 25, 26, 27, 28, 29⁴, 36², 37², 38², 39², 40, 41², 42², 45⁴, 46, 47, 48², 49³, 50, 51, 52, 53⁴, 54, 55⁴, 57², 58, 60, 61², 62², 63²; **17**:2², 6, 7, 8, 9, 12², 13, 14, 15², 17², 18³, 19, 20³, 21, 22², 23, 24², 25, 27, 28², 30, 32, 33², 34³, 35, 37, 38, 39², 40², 41², 42², 44², 45⁴, 46, 47, 48² 49³; **21**:2³, 3², 4, 5, 6, 7³, 8, 9, 10, 11, 12², 13, 14², 15², 17; **18**:2, 5, 7, 8², 9, 11, 12², 13, 14², 15², 16², 17², 18², 19, 20³, 21², 22², 23; **19**:2³, 3², 4, 5, 6, 7², 8, 9, 10, 11, 12², 13, 14²; **20**:1, 3, 5², 6, 7², 8, 9, 10, 11, 12², 13, 14², 15², 16, 17², 19, 21², 22, 23, 24², 25, 27, 28², 30, 32, 33², 34³; **35**, 37, 38, 39², 40², 41², 43², 44², 45⁴, 46, 47, 48², 49³; **21**:2³, 3², 4, 6⁴, 7², 9, 10, 11, 12², 13, 14, 15, 17, 20³, 22, 23, 25, 26, 28⁴, 29, 31; **22**:3², 4³, 5, 7³, 8, 9, 11, 12², 13, 14, 15², 16², 17², 18, 20², 21, 22, 23³, 24³, 25², 26⁴, 27, 28, 29⁴, 30, 31; **23**:3, 4⁴, 5, 6², 7, 8, 10³, 11, 12, 15, 16², 17², 18, 19, 20, 21², 22, 23², 24², 25³, 27², 28, 29⁴, 31², 32, 34², 35, 36, 37², 38², 39², 40, 41², 42, 45³, 46, 47, 48²; **24**:3, 4, 5, 6, 7³, 8, 9, 10, 11², 12², 13⁴, 14, 16², 17⁴, 18³, 19, 20³, 22² 23²; **25**:3⁴, 4², 5², 6, 7² 8², 12², 13, 14, 15³, 16, 17², 19, 20, 21; **26**:2, 3⁴, 4, 7⁴, 8, 9, 10², 11, 12², 13, 14, 15³, 16², 17⁴, 19, 20², 21; **27**:7, 8, 9, 10², 11, 12², 13², 14, 15², 16, 17², 18², 19² 21², 22², 23³, 24², 25, 27, 28, 29⁴, 30², 31², 32, 33², 34, 35, 36; **28**:2⁴, 3, 5², 7, 8², 12, 13⁴, 16², 17, 18³, 19, 22³, 23, 24², 26², 29²; **29**:2², 3, 4, 5, 7², 8², 10³; **30**:2², 4², 5³, 6, 7, 8, 11², 12², 13², 14, 15, 17², 18, 19, 22, 23, 24², 26; **31**:2, 4, 5, 10, 12⁴, 13, 15², 16, 18²; **32**:2², 3², 4, 5, 6, 7, 10, 12, 14, 15, 16, 18², 19, 21², 23, 26, 28, 29, 30², 31², 32; **33**:2³, 3, 4², 6², 7, 10², 12, 13, 14³, 15², 16, 17², 18², 19², 20, 21, 22², 25², 26, 27² 28², 30², 31², 32; **34**:2, 3, 4², 6², 8², 10², 11, 12, 13, 14³, 15, 16, 17, 18, 19³, 21, 22², 25², 26, 27², 28, 29, 30, 31; **35**:3³, 4, 5, 6², 7², 8², 10², 11², 12, 13, 15; **36**:1, 3⁴, 4, 5², 6³, 8³, 9, 10³, 11⁴, 12, 13, 15, 17, 18², 19², 20², 24, 25², 26², 27², 28, 29², 30, 31², 32, 33, 35², 36², 37; **37**:1, 2², 3, 4², 6, 7⁴, 8², 9, 10², 11², 12², 13, 14³, 16⁴, 19², 21², 22, 23³, 24², 25³, 26², 27² 28²; **38**:2, 3², 4⁴, 5, 7², 8⁴, 9³, 10², 11², 13, 14, 15, 19, 20², 22⁴, 23²; **39**:1², 2², 3, 4³, 6², 7, 9², 10², 11, 13, 14, 15, 16, 17², 18², 19², 20², 21, 22², 23³, 25², 26, 27, 28²; **40**:1, 2, 3², 4², 5, 6², 7³, 9, 10, 11, 12, 16, 17, 18, 20², 21², 22, 23², 24, 25, 27, 28², 29², 30, 31, 32, 33², 34, 35, 36², 37, 39, 40, 41, 42⁴, 43, 44², 46, 47², 48², 49²; **41**:1, 2², 3², 4², 5, 10², 11², 12, 13², 14³, 15, 16⁴, 17², 18, 19, 20², 21², 22³, 23²; **42**:1², 2, 3, 4², 5², 7³, 9, 10, 11², 12², 15, 16, 18, 19, 20²; **43**:2³, 4, 6², 7, 9, 10², 11⁴, 13², 15², 16, 17², 18, 20², 22, 23²; **44**:1, 3, 4², 5², 7³, 9, 10, 11⁴

12, 14, 15³, 16, 18, 19², 23³, 24³, 29², 30; **45**:1, 3, 4, 5, 6, 7², 8, 9³, 10, 11², 13, 15, 17³, 18, 19², 22, 23³, 24, 25; **46**:1, 2³, 3, 4, 5, 6, 7, 8, 9, 10, 11², 12, 15², 19, 20³, 21²; **47**:1, 2³, 3, 4², 5, 8, 9, 11, 12, 16² 18³; **48**:1, 8, 9, 10, 11, 12, 13, 14, 15, 16², 17⁴, 19², 20², 21; **2:1**, 2², 3, 4, 5², 6⁴, 7, 9², 10, 11, 12, 13, 14, 15, 16², 17⁴, 19², 20², 21; **2:1**, 2², 3, 4, 5², 6⁴, 7, 9², 10, 11, 12, 13³, 14, 16, 17², 18, 20³, 21², 22², 23³, 25², 26, 27, 28, 29, 30, 31, 32, 33, 34, 35; **Da 1:1**, 3, 4², 5², 6, 7, 8², 9, 10, 11, 12, 13², 14, 15, 16², 17⁴, 19², 20², 21; **2:1**, 2², 3, 4, 5², 6⁴, 7, 9², 10, 11, 12, 13³, 14, 16, 17², 18, 20³, 21², 22², 23³, 25², 26, 27², 28², 29², **9**:3⁴, 4², 5, 6, 7², 8², 9, 11², 12, 13, 15, 16⁴, 17, 18², 19², 20³, 22², 23, 24³, 25⁴, 26², 27², 28⁴, 29²; **10**:1, 2, 3, 4⁴, 5, 6⁸, 7², 8², 10², 11, 12, 13, 14³, 15³, 16², 17, 18, 19, 20; **11**:1², 2, 3, 4, 5⁴, 6⁷, 7², 8², 10, 11, 12, 13, 15², 16³, 17, 18, 21, 22², 23³, 24⁵, 25², 26, 27², 28⁴, 29², 30³, 31², 32, 34²; **12**:1², 2³, 3, 4, 5, 6, 7⁴, 8, 9, 10², 11, 12, 13; **Hos 1:1²**, 2, 3², 4, 6, 7², 9, 11³; **2:1**, 2², 3², 5⁴, 8², 9², 12², 13², 14, 15, 18⁴, 19², 20, 21, 22³; **3:1²**, 2³, 3, 5³; **4:2³**, 3, 5, 6², 7², 8², 10², 11, 12², 13², 14³, 15, 16², 17, 18², 19, 22, 23³, 24², 25, 26, 27²; **5:4³**, 5, 6, 7, 8³, 9, 10², 11, 12, 13², 14³, 15; **6:4²**, 5, 6, 8³, 9², 10, 16²; **7:9**, 10, 12³, 14, 16²; **8:4**, 5³, 6, 8², 9, 10², 13; **9:1**, 3, 4, 5², 6², 7³, 9², 10, 11, 12³, 13⁴, 15², 16, 17², **10**:1, 2³, 3, 5², 6, 7, 8, 13²; **11**:1, 2, 4, 6, 7, 8, 12³, 16, 17², 18, 19, 20, 21, 22², 23³, 24, 25², 26, 27², 28², 29, 30³, 31, 32², 33³, 34², 35³; **4:1**, 2⁴, 3, 5², 7, 11, 12, 13, 15, 16, 19², 22², 23², 27², 28, 30, 31², 32, 34², 35³; **5:3³**, 7, 11, 12, 13, 15, 16, 19², 22², 23, 24², 25², 26, 27, 29, 30, 31, 32², 33, 34², 35²; **6:1**, 2, 3³, 4, 5, 6, 7, 11, 12, 13³, 14, 15, 17²; **7:1²**, 3, 4², 5, 6, 7, 8⁴, 9, 10², 11, 13, 14, 19², 22, 24², 25³, 27, 30³, 31², 32², 33, 34, 37; **8:1**, 2, 6³, 7, 8, 9, 10, 11, 13, 15, 16, 18², 20, 22², 23², 24, 25, 27, 28, 31⁴, 32³, 33, 34³, 35, 38², **9:1**, 2, 5, 7², 9, 14, 15, 18, 19, 20², 22, 23, 24, 25, 26, 27²; **10**:1, 3, 4, 5, 8, 11, 12², 14, 16², 17, 19, 21³, 23, 26, 27, 29, 30³, 33², 34², 35, 37, 39, 41, 42, 44, 45, 46, 48, 49, 50, 52²; **11**:1², 2, 3, 4, 6, 7, 9², 14, 15³, 16, 17, 18², 21, 23, 24, 25, 27²; **12**:1³, 3, 4, 5, 7², 8², 9², 11, 12, 13, 14, 15, 16, 17², 19², 20, 26, 28, 30³, 32, 33², 34², 35, 37², 38, 39, 41, 43², 44, 45, 46, 48, 49, 50, 52²; **13**:3, 4, 6, 7², 8², 9², 11², 13², 14, 15, 16⁴, 17², 19, 20³; **14**:1², 3, 5², 7, 11, 12, 13, 15, 16, 19², 23², 27², 29², 30, 31²; **12:1²**, 3, 4, 5, 7, 8², 9², 11, 13², 14, 15, 18², 19², 20, 22, 24², 25², 26, 27², 28, 31, 34²; **14:1²**, 3, 5², 7, 11, 12, 13, 15, 16, 19, 22², 23², 24, 26, 30², 31, 32, 33, 34, 35², 37², 38, 39, 41, 42; **20:1**, 2³, 3, 4, 5, 6, 8², 12, 13, 14, 15, 16, 17³; **21**:2, 3, 6, 7, 9, 11, 12, 13², 18³, 20², 24; **Ac 1:1**, 3, 8⁴, 9, 13⁴, 14², 15, 16, 17, 18, 20, 21, 23, 26; **2:2**, 3, 4, 9³, 10², 11², 12, 13², 14³, 17², 18³, 19², 20, 21, 22², 23², 26, 29², 30, 32, 33², 34, 36, 37², 39², 40, 41, 42², 43², 44, 45, 46²; **3:1**, 3, 7², 8², 9³, 10², 11², 13³, 14², 16², 19², 20, 21², 22², 23², 24, 25, 26²; **4:1**, 3, 7, 8², 10, 13², 14², 16², 19, 20, 23², 24, 26, 27², 28², 29³; **5:1**, 3, 7, 8², 11², 13³, 14², 16², 19, 20, 23², 24, 26, 27², 28², 29³; **5:2**, 3, 4, 5², 6², 8³, 9², 10, 11², 13, 14, 15², 16², 17, 18², 20, 21², 24², 25², 26, 28², 29, 32, 33, 34, 35, 36², 37², 40², 42²; **6:2**, 3, 4², 5², 6, 7

3, 4², 5, 10, 11², 13, 14, 15, 18, 20, 22³, 23, 25², 27, 29, 30, 31², 33², 35, 37, 38, 39, 40², 41², 42², 43, 44, 45⁴, 46, 47, 48, 49, 50²; **13**:1, 2, 4², 6, 7, 10, 12, 15³, 16, 17², 19², 20, 22, 23, 25², 26, 27, 28, 30², 32, 33, 38, 39², 40, 41², 42, 44³, 46², 47, 48, 49, 50², 54², 57²; **14**:2², 3, 6, 9, 10, 11, 12², 14², 15², 17², 19², 20, 21, 22, 26, 29²; **15**:1², 2, 4², 10², 12, 17, 18, 21, 23, 25, 26, 28, 29², 30³, 31², 32², 34, 36⁴; **15**:1², 2, 4², 10², 12, 17, 18, 21, 23, 25, 26, 28, 29², 30³, 31², 32², 34, 36⁴; **16**:2, 3, 6, 7², 10, 12, 13², 14², 16², 17, 18², 19², 21², 22, 23, 24², 27², 28³, 29, 33; **17**:3, 4², 6², 7, 8³, 11, 13, 14, 16², 18, 19, 24, 25, 27², 28³, 29³, 33, 34, 35; **18**:1, 3, 6, 7², 8, 9, 10, 11, 12, 13, 14, 16², 20, 22², 24, 30, 31², 32, 34, 39, 40, 43; **19**:1, 2, 4, 5, 6, 7², 9², 10, 11, 12, 13, 14, 15, 16, 18, 20, 21, 22, 24, 27, 29³, 32, 35, 38, 40², 41, 42, 44², 45⁴, 46², 47; **20**:1², 5, 9, 10, 11², 12², 14, 15, 16², 17, 19, 20, 21², 23, 24, 25, 26, 28², 29, 31², 34, 35, 36, 37², 40, 46³, 47; **21**:5, 7, 8, 9, 10, 11³, 12³, 15, 16², 21, 23², 24, 25³, 27, 28, 29, 30, 33, 34², 36², 37, 38; **22**:2², 4, 5, 6, 8², 11, 13, 14, 15, 17², 19³, 25, 26, 29, 30², 32, 33, 36², 37², 39, 41, 43, 44², 45, 46, 47, 50, 51², 52², 53, 54, 55, 56, 58, 61, 62², 63, 64, 65, 66², 68; **23**:1, 2², 4, 5, 10, 14², 16, 19, 22, 23, 25², 26², 27, 28², 29, 30, 34, 35, 36, 37, 39, 44², 45, 47, 48, 50², 51², 53, 54, 55², 56²; **24**:1, 7, 9, 10, 12², 15², 18, 19², 20², 21, 23, 24, 25, 26², 27, 30², 31², 32², 37, 38, 39², 40, 41², 43⁴, 44, 46, 47², 50, 51, 52, 53; **Jn 1:1²**, 4, 10, 14³, 17, 18, 19, 29, 32, 33, 34, 38, 39³, 40, 41, 42², 44, 45², 46, 51²; **2:2²**, 8, 9, 10, 11, 12², 14², 15³, 19, 20, 22, 23³; **3:2**, 5, 10, 11, 12, 16, 18, 20, 22², 23, 25, 26, 29³, 31, 32, 35; **4:1**, 3, 6, 9, 10², 11², 12², 15, 16, 18, 23², 24², 27, 28, 30, 34², 35, 36, 37, 38, 40, 41², 42, 46², 47⁴, 48, 50; **5:2**, 9, 10, 11², 12², 14, 15, 16³, 17, 19, 20, 21², 23, 24, 25, 26, 28², 29, 31², 34, 35, 36, 37², 40, 46³; **6:2**, 3, 5, 9, 10², 11², 12², 14, 15, 17², 19, 21, 22, 24, 26, 30, 33, 35, 36, 37, 39, 40², 42, 44, 45, 50, 53, 54², 55, 56², 57, 58, 63, 64², 66, 69; **7:3**, 14, 15, 21, 24, 26, 28, 29, 32, 33, 34, 35, 36, 37², 42, 45, 50, 52²; **8:2**, 3, 4, 6, 7, 8, 10, 11, 14, 21², 26, 28², 33, 38, 42, 44², 48, 49, 50, 52, 53, 55, 56, 57; **9:6**, 7², 8², 11⁴, 14, 15², 18, 20, 27, 28, 34, 35, 38, 39, 40; **10**:1², 3², 4, 8², 9², 12², 13, 14, 15², 16³, 18, 20, 23², 27, 28, 30, 35, 36, 38², 41, 42; **11**:1², 2, 5², 8, 15, 19², 21², 22, 24, 26, 30, 33, 35², 36, 37, 39, 40², 42, 44, 45, 46, 47, 48², 52², 56, 57; **12:3²**, 5, 9, 11, 13, 14, 16, 17, 22, 24, 26, 27, 28, 29, 36, 38, 40², 41, 48, 49; **13**:1, 2, 3, 4, 5, 9, 10, 11, 12, 13², 14, 20, 21, 24, 30, 31, 32, 33; **14**:3³, 6², 7, 8, 10, 11, 13, 14, 16², 17, 20², 21², 22², 23, 26, 27, 28, 31; **15**:1, 4, 5, 6², 7², 10, 11, 16², 22², 24², 27²; **16**:8², 11, 13, 14, 15, 16, 17², 19, 20, 22², 27, 28², 29, 30, 32; **17**:1, 3, 5, 6, 8², 10², 11, 12, 14, 21, 23², 24, 25², 26³; **18**:1³, 3⁴, 4, 5, 6, 7, 10, 12, 13, 14, 16, 18², 19, 20³; **Lk 1**:2, 6, 7, 8, 9, 10, 12, 13, 14², 15, 17³, 18, 19², 20², 21, 24, 25, 29, 31², 32, 33, 36, 39, 40, 41, 42, 46, 47, 55, 56, 58², 59, 60, 63, 64², 65, 67, 68, 71, 72, 74, 75, 76, 79, 80³; **2**:3, 4, 5, 7², 8, 9², 12, 13, 14², 15², 16², 17², 18, 19, 20, 21², 22, 23², 24², 25², 26, 27, 28², 29², 33, 34², 35, 37³, 38², 39, 40, 41, 42, 44; **5:1**, 2, 5, 4², 5, 7², 8, 9, 10², 11, 12², 14, 15, 16, 17⁴, 18, 19, 21, 22, 23, 24, 25, 26², 27², 28², 29², 31², 33, 34²; **6:1**, 2, 3², 4², 5², 6, 7, 8², 9, 11, 12², 13, 14, 15, 16², 17², 18², 19, 20, 21, 22², 24, 27², 29², 32², 34, 35², 36², 38²; **7:2**, 4, 5, 6², 7², 8³, 9, 10, 11², 13, 14, 15, 16, 19, 20, 21, 22², 24, 27², 29, 32², 34², 35³, 36², 37², 38, 39, 40³; **8:1²**, 2, 3, 5, 6, 7², 9, 10³, 12², 13², 14, 15², 17², 18, 19, 21², 22, 24, 25, 26, 28², 29², 30³, 31, 32², 35, 36, 37³, 38, 39², 40, 41², 42; **10:2²**, 3, 4, 7, 8, 9, 10, 11, 12, 13, 16, 17, 20, 21, 22, 23, 25², 27, 28, 29, 30², 32, 33, 35, 38³; **11:1²**, 2, 4, 7, 8², 10², 11, 13, 14, 16², 17³, 18³, 19², 21², 22, 23³, 24, 25², 26, 27², 28, 30; **12**:6, 7², 8³, 10³, 11, 12, 13, 14, 16², 17³, 18⁴, 20, 22³, 24, 25², 26, 27², 29³, 30, 32², 35³; **36²**, 38, 39, 40², 17:1, 2, 3², 4³, 5², 6, 7

41, 42², 43, 46², 47, 48, 49², 51, 52, 53²; **12**:3, 4, 10, 11, 16, 18³, 19², 23, 24, 28, 29, 30, 31, 33², 35, 36, 37², 42, 45⁴, 46², 47, 48², 49, 50, 52, 53³, 54, 55², 56, 58²; **13**:6, 7, 8², 11², 12, 13², 14, 15, 19³, 21, 24, 25², 26², 28³, 29⁴, 30, 31², 33², 34; **14**:3, 4, 6, 9, 11, 12, 14, 16, 18², 19, 21³, 25², 26⁴, 27³, 28, 29, 30², 31², 33, 34; **15**:1², 2, 4², 5, 6³, 8², 13, 14, 15, 17², 19², 20², 21, 22², 23², 24², 25, 26, 27, 28², 29, 31, 32²; **16**:2, 3, 6, 7², 10, 12, 13², 16², 18, 19², 21, 22, 23, 24², 25, 26², 27, 28², 29, 31, 32², 34, 35; **18**:1, 3, 6, 7², 8, 9, 10, 11, 12, 13, 14, 16², 20, 22², 24, 30, 31², 32, 34, 35, 36, 37²; **19**:1, 2, 3², 4, 5, 6², 7, 9, 13, 18², 19, 20², 24, 25, 26, 27², 28, 29, 30², 31², 32², 34, 35², 37, 38, 39, 41, 42; **20**:1², 3, 4, 5, 6, 8, 12, 13, 14, 15, 16², 17, 19, 20, 21², 23, 24, 25, 26, 27², 28, 29, 31²; **21**:2², 3, 6, 7, 9, 11, 12, 13², 18³, 20², 24; **Ac 1:1³**, 3, 8⁴, 9, 13⁴, 14², 15, 16, 17, 18, 20, 21, 23, 26; **2:2**, 3, 4², 9³, 10², 11², 12, 13², 14³, 17², 18³, 19², 20², 21, 22, 26, 29², 30, 32, 33², 34, 36, 37², 39², 40, 41, 42², 43², 44, 45, 46²; **3:1**, 3, 7², 8², 9³, 10², 11², 13³, 14², 16², 19², 20, 21², 22², 23², 24, 25, 26²; **4:1**, 3, 7, 8², 10, 13², 14², 16², 19, 20, 23², 24, 26, 27², 28², 29³; **5:2**, 3, 4, 5², 6², 8³, 9², 10, 11², 13, 14, 15², 16², 17, 18², 20, 21², 24², 25², 26, 28², 29, 32, 33, 34, 35, 36², 37², 40², 42²; **6:2**, 3, 4², 5², 6, 7, 8², 9², 10, 11, 12, 13, 14, 16², 17³, 18, 20, 22, 23, 24, 25; **13**:1², 2², 3, 4, 5, 9, 10, 11, 14, 15, 16², 19, 21, 24, 26, 27, 29, 31, 34, 36, 41, 42, 43², 45, 46², 48², 50³, 51, 52²; **14:1²**, 2, 3², 5, 6², 8, 10, 12², 13, 14², 15², 16, 17², 19³, 20², 22, 23, 25, 27², 28, 31, 34, 36², 37², 38², 39, 40²; **17**:1, 2, 3², 4³, 5², 6, 7

8, 9², 10, 11, 12, 13, 14, 15², 17, 18², 19, 20, 21², 22, 23, 24³, 25³, 26², 27², 28², 29, 34²; **18**:1, 3², 4, 5, 6², 7, 8³, 10², 11, 12, 15², 17, 18², 19², 22², 23², 25², 26², 27; **19**:1, 2, 6², 8, 9², 10, 12³, 15, 16², 17², 18, 19, 20, 21, 22, 25, 26⁴, 27², 28, 29², 33, 35², 36, 38²; **20**:1², 2, 4³, 5, 6, 7, 9², 10, 11², 12, 13, 14, 15², 19, 20, 21², 22, 23, 24, 28, 29, 30, 31, 32², 34, 36, 37; **21**:1², 2, 3, 5⁴, 6, 7², 8, 11³, 12, 13, 14, 15, 16², 18², 19, 20, 24, 25, 26², 27², 28⁴, 29, 30², 32³, 33³, 34², 38, 40; **22**:1, 3, 4², 5², 7, 10, 12, 13², 14², 15, 16², 17, 18, 19, 20², 22, 23², 24, 26, 27, 30³; **23**:1, 6, 7², 8, 9², 10², 11, 12, 14², 15, 16, 17, 18, 19, 22, 23², 27², 31, 33, 34; **24**:1², 2, 3, 6, 13, 14, 15², 16, 17, 19, 23, 24, 25², 26; **25**:2², 4, 5, 6², 9, 13, 15², 16, 17, 19, 20, 23³, 24², 26; **26**:1, 3², 4, 5, 6, 7, 10², 11, 12, 13, 14, 16³, 17, 18³, 20⁴, 21, 22⁴, 23, 25, 26, 30³, 31; **27**:1, 2, 3, 4, 5, 6, 7, 8, 9, 10³, 11, 12², 13, 15², 17, 20, 21², 23, 24², 28³, 29, 31, 32, 33, 35², 36, 40², 41³, 42, 43²; **28**:2², 3, 5, 6², 7, 8³, 9, 10, 11, 12, 13², 14, 15³, 17, 18, 20, 21, 23⁴, 25, 26, 27³, 28, 30, 31²; **Ro 1**:1, 4, 5², 6, 7², 10, 12, 14², 18, 20, 21, 23⁴, 25², 27², 29², 30; **2**:3, 4, 5, 7, 8³, 9, 10, 12, 15, 17, 18, 20, 27², 28, 29; **3**:4², 7, 8, 9, 14, 16, 17, 19, 21, 23, 24, 26, 30; **4**:3, 11, 12, 13, 14, 15, 16, 19, 20, 21, 22²; **5**:2, 4, 5, 12², 15, 16², 17; **6**:13, 18, 19, 22²; **7**:3, 6, 9, 11, 12², 16, 23; **8**:2, 3, 6, 9, 11, 15, 17, 21, 27, 28, 30, 34; **9**:2, 3, 4, 5, 9, 10, 15, 17, 18, 21, 22, 26, 28, 33²; **10**:1, 3, 8, 9, 10³, 12², 14², 15, 17, 20, 21; **11**:3², 4, 6, 8, 9³, 10, 12, 14, 17², 20, 22, 23, 24, 26, 27, 29, 33², 36²; **12**:1, 2, 4, 5, 14; **13**:2, 3, 9, 11, 12, 13³, 14; **14**:3, 4, 6², 7, 8, 9², 17², 18, 19, 22, 23; **15**:1, 4, 5, 6², 11², 12, 13, 14, 18, 19, 21, 23, 24, 26, 27, 28², 30, 31, 32, 33; **16**:2, 3, 7², 10, 11², 13², 14, 15³, 17, 18, 19, 21, 23², 25, 26²; **1Co 1**:1, 2², 3², 5, 10², 14, 22, 23, 24², 25, 28², 30; **2**:2, 3², 4², 7, 14; **3**:3, 4, 5, 6², 8, 11², 13², 14, 15, 19, 20, 23²; **4**:1, 5, 6, 7, 8, 11, 19, 21; **5**:1², 2, 3, 4², 5, 8², 10; **6**:2, 6, 8², 11², 13², 14, 15, 17², 19, 20, 23²; **7**:2, 3, 5, 8, 11, 12, 13², 14, 17, 19, 28², 34², 36², 37, 40; **8**:4, 5, 6³, 7, 8, 12; **9**:4, 5², 6, 7², 10, 13, 15, 18, 19, 27; **10**:1, 2, 4², 7, 8, 9, 11, 13, 16, 20, 21², 26, 27, 28; **11**:2, 3², 5, 6, 7, 10, 18, 22², 24², 26, 27, 28, 29², 30², 34²; **12**:3, 10, 11², 12, 13, 16, 21, 23², 24, 27, 28², 31; **13**:1, 2³, 3, 9, 13²; **14**:1, 3, 6, 11, 21, 23², 24, 25², 27², 28², 29, 30, 31, 34, 40², 41², 46, 48, 49, 50, 52, 53, 54, 56; **16**:3, 7, 9, 15, 16², 17, 18, 19²; **2Co 1**:1, 2³, 3, 6, 7, 10, 12², 13, 16, 21², 24, 27; **2**:4², 7, 9, 10, 12, 13, 14, 15, 16; **3**:2, 11, 17, 18; **4**:2, 3, 5, 7, 13, 14, 15, 17; **5**:4, 5, 6, 8², 11, 14, 15², 18, 19; **6**:2, 4, 5², 6², 7², 8², 9, 10, 11, 14, 15, 16², 17², 18²; **7**:1, 7, 9, 10, 14, 15², 8:1, 2, 3, 5², 7, 10, 15, 18, 19, 23², 24; **9**:2², 4, 5, 6, 8, 10³, 11, 13², 14; **10**:1², 5², 6, 10², 12; **11**:3, 4, 9³, 12, 14, 23², 25, 26, 27², 29², 31, 33; **12**:1, 3, 12, 14, 15, 16², 17, 18, 19²; **13**:6, 9, 11², 14²; **Gal 1**:1, 2, 3², 4, 5, 6, 7, 13, 14, 15, 17, 18, 21, 24; **2**:2, 4, 9³, 12, 14, 15, 16, 20²; **3**:5, 6, 8, 16³, 17, 29; **4**:2, 7, 9, 10³, 15, 18²; **5**:1, 7, 12, 15, 16, 17, 19, 20, 21³, 23, 24, 26; **6**:2, 14, 16; **Eph 1**:2², 3, 4, 5, 8, 9, 10, 16, 17, 18, 19, 20, 21³, 22²; **2**:1, 2, 3², 6², 8, 11, 12², 14, 15, 16, 17², 19, 20, 21, 22; **3**:5, 6, 8, 16³, 17, 29; **4**:2, 4, 6, 8, 11², 14², 16², 17, 18, 21, 24², 25, 27, 30, 31², 32; **5**:2², 5, 9, 10, 14, 19², 25, 27², 29, 31², 32, 33; **6**:2, 3, 4, 5², 6, 7², 8, 9², 12², 14, 15, 17², 18³, 21²; **Php 1**:1², 2², 7, 9³, 10², 11, 13, 14, 15, 18², 19, 20, 23, 25², 27, 28, 30; **2**:1, 2, 8², 9, 10³, 11, 12, 13, 15², 17², 18, 24, 25, 26, 27², 28, 29; **3**:1, 3, 9², 10², 11, 13, 15, 17, 18, 19, 20²; **4**:1², 2, 3, 4², 6, 7², 9, 12², 15, 16, 18, 19, 20²; **Col 1**:1, 2⁴, 4, 5², 6², 8, 9², 10², 11³, 13, 16³, 17², 18, 20, 21, 22², 23, 24, 26, 28; **2**:1², 2, 3, 5², 7², 8², 10², 12, 13, 14, 15², 18², 19², 22, 23; **3**:5, 8, 10, 11, 12, 13, 14, 15, 16³, 17, 19, 22³, 25; **4**:1, 2, 3, 7, 8, 9, 11, 12², 13², 14, 15², 16; **1Th 1**:1³, 3², 5, 6, 7, 8, 9, 10; **2**:2, 9², 10², 12², 13, 15³, 18, 20; **3**:2², 4, 5, 7, 10², 11², 12², 13²; **4**:1², 4, 6², 10², 11, 12, 14², 16², 17², **5**:1, 3², 5, 6, 7, 8², 10, 11, 12, 13, 14², 16², 17, 19, 23³, 24; **2Th 1**:1², 2², 3², 4², 5, 7², 8, 9², 10, 11², 12²; **2**:1, 3, 4, 6², 9², 10², 12, 13, 15², 17², 18, 24, 25, 26, 27², 28, 29, 31³, 32, 33, 34, 38; **3**:1, 11, 16, 32², 33³, 38; **30**:14, 15², 19, 32; **31**:11, 16, 32², 33³, 38; **32**:23², 31, 33³, 59; **14**:2, 13, 32, 42, 54, 57; **15**:32²; **16**:4, 27; **17**:5; **18**:17; **19**:20, 23; **20**:2, 26, 27; **21**:6, 7; **22**:7, 9, 24, 25; **23**:2², 4², 20, 21, 24, 32, 37², 38, 40, 42; **24**:9, 14, 22; **25**:15, 16⁴, 23, 31², 33, 41, 42, 44, 50, 54,

Phm 1:1², 2, 3², 5, 7, 8, 9, 11, 14, 16, 22, 24²; **Heb 1**:1, 2, 3, 5, 6, 8², 9, 10, 12; **2**:2², 4², 7, 8, 9, 10, 11, 13³, 14, 15, 17²; **3**:1, 6², 9², 10², 16, 17, 18; **4**:3, 4, 5, 6, 12⁴, 13, 16; **5**:1², 2, 6, 7³, 9, 10; **6**:1², 2, 5, 6, 7, 8², 10², 12, 14, 15, 16²; **7**:1², 2, 6, 7, 13, 14, 15, 18, 19, 20, 21, 27; **8**:2², 3, 5, 6, 8², 9, 10², 12, 13²; **9**:1, 2, 4², 7³, 9, 10², 11, 12, 13², 19³, 21, 22, 25, 27, 28; **10**:2, 4, 5, 6, 8², 10, 11², 16, 17, 18, 19, 20, 21, 22, 24², 25, 27, 29, 30, 33, 34², 37, 38, 39²; **11**:1, 4, 6², 7, 8, 9, 10, 11, 12³, 13³, 17, 18, 19, 20, 21, 22, 23, 28², 33, 34³, 35², 36², 37², 38³; **12**:1², 2², 3, 5², 6, 8², 9², 11, 12, 14, 15², 18², 24, 28²; **13**:3, 4², 5, 7, 8², 12, 16, 17, 18, 21², 24; **Jas 1**:1, 4, 5, 6², 11², 14, 15, 17, 19, 21², 22, 24², 25, 26², 27³; **2**:2², 3, 4, 5, 9, 10, 12, 15, 16, 18, 19, 22², 23², 24, 25; **3**:4, 5, 7², 9, 10, 11², 13, 14, 16², 17², 18², 19, 20; **1Pe 1**:1, 2², 3, 4, 7², 8³, 10, 11², 21³, 23, 24², 25; **2**:1², 4, 6², 8², 11, 12, 14, 18, 20², 22, 24, 25; **3**:2, 3², 4, 6², 7², 8, 10², 11², 12, 15, 19, 21, 22²; **4**:3, 4, 5, 7, 11², 14, 17, 18², 19; **5**:1, 4, 8, 10³, 11, 12, 13; **2Pe 1**:1², 2², 3², 4², 5, 6³, 7², 8, 9², 10, 11², 12, 15, 16, 17, 19³; **2**:2, 3, 5, 6², 7, 8, 9, 10², 11, 12², 13, 15, 16, 17, 18, 19, 20³, 21, 22; **3**:2², 3, 5², 6, 7, 8, 10², 11, 12², 13, 14, 16, 17, 18³; **1Jn 1**:1, 2³, 3, 5, 6, 7, 8, 9³, 10; **2**:2, 4, 6², 7, 8, 10², 11², 14², 16², 17, 18, 20, 21², 22, 24, 25, 27², 28²; **3**:1, 2, 5, 10, 14, 15², 16, 17, 18, 20³, 21, 22, 24, 25, 27², 28²; **3**:1, 2, 5, 10, 14, 15², 16, 17, 18, 20³, 22, 24, 25, 27², 28²; **3**:1, 2, 5, 10, 14, 15², 16, 17, 18, 20³, 21, 22, 24, 25, 27², 28²; **3**:2², 3, 5², 6, 7, 8, 10², 11, 12², 13, 14, 16, 17, 18³; **1Jn 1**:1², 3³, 5, 6, 7, 9², 10, 12²; **3Jn 1**:2, 3², 10, 12², 13, 14; **Jude 1**:1², 2, 3, 4², 6, 7³, 8, 10, 12, 15², 16, 19, 20, 23, 24², 25²; **Rev 1**:2, 3², 4⁴, 5³, 6², 7², 8³, 9⁴, 10, 11², 12, 13² 14², 15, 16, 17², 18⁴, 19, 20²; **2**:1, 2², 3², 5² 8², 9², 10², 14, 16, 18, 19³, 20, 22, 23² 24, 26; **3**:1, 2, 3³, 5, 7², 8, 9², 12², 14, 17², 18² 19², 20⁴, 21; **4**:1³, 2², 3², 4², 5, 6², 8³, 9³, 10³ 11⁵; **5**:1, 2², 4, 5, 6², 7, 8³, 9⁶, 10², 11⁴, 12⁶ 13⁹, 14²; **6**:2³, 4, 5, 6³, 8⁴, 9, 10², 11², 13 14², 15³, 16³, 17; **7**:2, 9², 10², 11³, 12³, 13 14³, 15³, 16, 17, 18², 19, 20, 21; **8**:2², 3, 5³, 7⁴, 8, 9, 10⁴, 11², 12², 14, 15, 16, 17² **13**:1⁴, 2³, 3, 4³, 5², 6³, 7³, 10, 12², 13², 14, 15, 16³, 14:1³, 2², 3, 4², 6², 7², 8, 9³, 10, 11³ 12, 14³, 15², 16, 17, 18², 19, 20, 15:1², 2⁴, 3⁴ 4², 5, 6, 8³, 16:2⁴, 3², 4², 5, 6², 7², 8, 9², 10, 11², 12, 13, 14, 15², 17, 18, 19², 20, 21; **17**:1, 2, 3², 4⁴, 5, 7³, 8³, 11², 13², 14³, 15, 16³, 18:1², 2², 3, 5, 7³, 8, 9, 10, 11, 12, 13³, 14, 15², 16⁴, 17², 19², 20², 21², 22², 23, 24² **19**:1², 2², 3, 4², 5, 6, 7³, 8, 9, 10, 11³, 12, 13 14², 16², 17, 18⁴, 19³, 20², 21; **20**:1², 2, 3², 4⁴ 6³, 8², 9², 10⁴, 11³, 12³, 13³, 14; **21**:1³, 3⁴, 5, 6², 7², 8, 9², 10², 11², 12³, 13, 14, 15, 16³, 17² 18, 20, 22, 23, 24, 26; **22**:1, 2, 3⁴, 5², 6, 8³, 9², 11, 12, 13³, 14, 15², 16², 17³, 19².

ARE (3890)

Ge 2:12, 16; **3**:9, 14, 19; **4**:6, 11, 14; **6**:15, 19, 21; **9**:2; **10**:20, 31, 32; **12**:11, 13; **13**:8, 14; **16**:5, 8, 11, 13; **17**:8, 10, 11, 12, 15; **18**:24, 29; **19**:5, 13, 15; **20**:3, 16²; **21**:23; **22**:7; **23**:6, 8; **24**:13, 23, 31², 47; **25**:13, 16, 23; **26**:29; **27**:21, 22, 24, 32, 41; **28**:13; **29**:4, 8, 14, 15; **31**:12, 43³, 49; **32**:4, 6, 17, 18², 19; **33**:5²; **34**:21, 22, 30; **36**:10; **37**:13, 16; **38**:25; **39**:9; **40**:7, 12, 18; **41**:25, 26², 27³, 29, 35, 40; **42**:9, 11², 14, 16³, 19, 21, 31³, 33, 34, 38; **43**:16; **44**:16, 18; **45**:11, 19; **46**:8, 30, 32, 34; **47**:1, 3, 8, 9, 30; **48**:5, 8, 9; **49**:3, 9, 26, 28; **50**:11, 17, 18; **Ex 1**:1, 19²; **2**:13, 14; **3**:5, 9, 14, 18; **4**:18, 19, 25; **5**:4, 5², 7, 8², 16³, 17, 19; **6**:5; **7**:2; **8**:21, 26; **9**:27; **10**:9, 10, 26; **11**:2; **12**:4², 7, 8, 11, 13, 14, 15, 18, 42, 43; **13**:4, 5, 12, 14²; **15**:4, 15², 16⁴, 24; **16**:4, 5, 7, 22 26; **17**:4; **18**:14, 17, 20; **19**:3², 6²; **21**:1², 22, 23, 35; **22**:7, 9, 31; **23**:10, 14, 17; **24**:1, 14; **25**:2², 15², 20², 22, 26, 27, 32, 33, 34, 38; **26**:2, 8; **27**:2, 7, 14, 15, 17, 19, 21; **28**:3, 4³, 21, 28, 34; **29**:1, 28, 32, 33², 38; **30**:14, 15² 19, 32; **31**:11, 16, 32², 43³, 59; **14**:2, 13, 32, 42, 54, 57; **15**:32²; **16**:4, 27; **17**:5; **18**:17; **19**:20, 23; **20**:2, 26, 27; **21**:6, 7; **22**:7, 9, 24, 25; **23**:2², 4², 20, 21, 24, 32, 37², 38, 40, 42; **24**:9, 14, 22; **25**:15, 16⁴, 23, 31², 33, 41, 42, 44, 50, 54,

55: **26**:3, 34, 36, 39, 41, 44, 46; **27**:34²; **Nu 1**:3², 5², 50², 51, 52, 53²; **2**:2, 3, 32; **3**:7, 8, 9², 12, 13², 40, 45; **4**:5, 6, 7, 8, 9, 10, 11, 12, 13, 14², 15³, 18, 19, 25, 26, 27, 28; **5**:10; **6**:20, 23; **8**:2, 8, 10², 14, 15, 16², 26; **9**:10²; **11**: **10**:3, 4, 5, 6, 8, 10, 29; **11**:15, 16, 27, 29; **13**:4, 16, 18, 19, 20, 28², 31², 32; **14**:14, 25, 41; **15**:21, 38; **16**:6, 10, 16, 17, 37; **17**:12², 13; **18**:1², 3², 4², 5, 9, 16, 17, 18, 23; **20**:16; **21**:29; **22**:6³, 9, 12, 34; **24**:4, 5, 16; **26**:2, 63; **27**:7; **28**:3, 31; **29**:6²; **30**:16; **31**:26, 30; **32**:4, 14, 17; **33**:1; **34**:17², 19, 29; **35**:8, 29, 33; **36**:13; **Dt 1**:1, 9, 10, 22, 28²; **2**:4, 6, 18; **3**:21, 27; **4**:4, 5, 14², 20, 22, 26, 30, 45; **5**:3, 22, 31; **6**:1², 6, 11, 25; **7**:1, 5, 6, 12, 17²; **8**:9, 10, 12, 13; **9**:1, 2, 5, 6, 13, 29; **10**:2, 5, 19²; **11**:8, 10, 11, 12, 21, 29², 30, 31²; **12**:1, 2, 5, 8, 11, 18², 29²; **14**:1, 2, 4, 7, 8, 19, 21; **15**:5, 20, 22; **17**:8, 9, 16, 18; **18**:1², 4; **19**:9, 17, 20², 3, 15², 19, 20; **20**:14², 20; **21**:14, 16³, 17; **22**:28; **23**:9, 20; **24**:8, 11, 19; **25**:1, 5, 11; **26**:18²; **27**:9; **28**:10, 20, 21, 24, 45, 51², 58, 61, 63; **29**:1, 10, 12, 15²; **30**:10, 16, 17²; **31**:13, 16, 21, 29; **32**:4², 5, 17, 20², 21, 28, 32, 37, 47²; **33**:3, 17³, 27, 29; **Jos 1**:14; **2**:9, 14, 20, 24; **3**:3²; **4**:7, 9; **5**:13, 15; **6**:17², 19; **7**:3, 10, 21; **8**:4, 6, 7; **9**:8², 11, 12, 13²; **11**:6; **12**:1, 7; **13**:1², 14; **14**:1; **15**:12; **16**:10; **17**:2, 14, 15, 17, 18; **18**:5; **19**:51; **20**:4; **22**:18; **23**:8; **24**:15, 19, 22², 23, 27², 31; **Jdg 1**:24; **3**:1; **4**:9; **5**:30; **6**:13, 23, 31²; **7**:4, 10, 11, 18; **8**:5, 15; **9**:9, 31, 36, 37; **10**:4, 14; **11**:2², 8, 25, 27; **12**:4, 5; **13**:2², 6; **15**:11; **16**:9, 12, 14, 20; **17**:9; **18**:3², 18; **19**:12, 17, 18, 20, 30; **21**:7, 11, 16, 22, 16; **Ru 2**:9², 3³, 9, 11, 15; **4**:9, 10, 11; **1Sa 1**:8²; **2**:3, 4², 8; **4**:8, 17; **6**:5, 8, 17; **7**:3; **8**:5, 7, 8; **9**:13, 19; **10**:7, 8, 11; **11**:5; **12**:2, 21; **14**:9, 11, 28, 30; **15**:17, 18, 33², 58; **19**:3, 22; **20**:2, 21², 22; **21**:1, 5²; **23**:1², 3, 27; **24**:11, 14, 17; **25**:10; **26**:11, 14, 16, 24²; **2Sa 1**:4, 5, 8, 13; **3**:25, 28, 39; **5**:1, 8, 14; **6**:2; **7**:5, 12, 22, 28²; **10**:11¹; **12**:7, 13, 21; **13**:33, 35; **14**:2; **15**:2, 3, 13, 19, 36; **16**:2², 8; **17**:8, 10, 20; **18**:3² 20; **19**:3, 12, 13², 42; **20**:9, 17, 19²; **22**:23, 28, 29, 44; **23**:1, 6², 7, 8; **24**:2, 17, 22²; **1Ki 1**:14, 20, 25, 35; **2**:9, 39; **4**:8; **5**:9; **6**:12; **8**:8, 19, 25, 35, 47, 51; **9**:13; **11**:41; **12**:28; **13**:14, 18; **14**:5, 19, 29; **15**:7, 23, 31; **16**:5, 14, 20, 27; **17**:24; **18**:9, 25, 36, 37²; **19**:9, 10, 13, 14; **20**:3², 23, 31; **21**:5; **22**:3, 4, 11, 13, 39, 45; **2Ki 1**:3, 4, 6², 16, 18; **3**:7; **4**:26; **5**:12; **6**:9², 16³, 19; **7**:9, 12, 13²; **8**:23; **9**:7; **10**:2, 5, 6, 9, 13², 15, 23, 34; **11**:5³, 7; **12**:19; **13**:8, 12, 14, 10, 15, 18, 28; **15**:6, 11, 15, 21, 26, 31, 36, 36; **16**:19; **17**:23; **26**; **18**:19, 20, 21, 22, 24, 34²; **19**:15, 19, 26²; **20**:1, 20; **21**:17, 25; **22**:7, 13; **23**:28; **24**:5; **1Ch 2**:55; **4**:22; **5**:26; **6**:17, 19, 31, 33; **11**:1; **12**:17, 18², 23; **13**:2; **14**:4; **15**:12²; **16**:14, 26, 30; **17**:4, 11, 26; **19**:12²; **21**:2, 3, 17; **22**:8, 13; **23**:4², 5²; **28**:3², 21; **29**:11, 12², 14, 15², 17²; **2Ch 1**:9; **2**:8; **5**:9; **6**:9, 16, 26, 37; **7**:14; **8**:11; **9**:29; **12**:15; **13**:8, 10, 12; **19**:6, 10; **20**:6², 10, 11, 12, 34²; **23**:4³, 5, 6², 7, 20²; **25**:19, 26; **26**:22; **27**:7; **28**:26; **29**:9, 30; **30**:6; **32**:10, 32, 33; **33**:18, 19; **34**:16; **35**:25, 27; **36**:8; **Ezr 1**:4; **2**:1; **4**:12², 13, 14², 16; **5**:4, 8, 11²; **6**:4, 5²; **7**:14, 15, 24, 25; **8**:1, 9, 6, 9, 11, 15; **10**:12, 13; **Ne 1**:3², 8, 9, 10; **2**:2, 3, 5, 17, 19²; **4**:2², 3, 4, 19; **5**:2, 3³, 7, 8, 9, 10, 11; **6**:6³, 8², 10²; **7**:3², 6; **9**:6, 7, 8, 13², 17, 31, 34, 36; **10**:28 38, 39²; **11**:3; **13**:17, 18, 25², 27²; **Est 3**:8; **4**:13, 16; **10**:2; **Job 1**:10, 19; **2**:9, 10; **3**:18, 17, 19, 22; **4**:5², 9, 11, 19², 20, 21; **5**:4, 11, 13; **6**:4², 15, 20, 21, 25; **7**:1, 6; **8**:2, 6, 9; **9**:12, 25; **10**:5, 20; **11**:2, 4, 8²; **12**:2, 5, 6², 13, 16; **13**:4², 12², 14; **14**:5, 12, 21²; **15**:7, 10, 11, 15; **16**:2²; **17**:1, 8², 11, 14; **18**:3, 20²; **19**:13; **21**:9, 18, 27; **22**:5, 10; **23**:9, 14; **24**:1, 14; **25**:2³, 5, 6; **26**:10², 13³, 14, 19; **40**:5; **13**:4, 18, 26, 34; **38**:5, 19³; **39**:1, 9; **40**:5; **45**:2; **47**:11; **42**:5, 11; **43**:2, 5; **44**:4; **45**:2; **52**:6, 8, 9, 11; **46**:4, 8, 9, 10; **14**:9; **48**:11; **49**:14; **50**:8, 11; **51**:4, 17; **52**:1; **53**:1; **54**:3; **55**:10, 11, 21²; **56**:2, 5, 8; **57**:4²; **58**:3, 10, 11; **59**:4, 9, 13, 16, 17; **62**:9⁴, 11, 12; **63**:1, 11; **64**:6; **65**:4²; **66**:3; **68**:13, 15², 17, 25²; **35; **69**:4, 19; **70**:5; **71**:3, 7, 18; **73**:1, 17, 25², 35; **69**:4, 19; **70**:5; **71**:3, 7, 18; **73**:1, 77:13, 14; **79**:4, 8; **82**:5, 6², 8; **83**:2, 18; **84**:4²; **86**:2, 5, 10², 14, 15; **87**:3, 7; **88**:5, 9, 10, 12; **89**:8, 11, 14, 15, 17, 26; **90**:2, 4,

5, 7; **92**:5, 8; **93**:2; **94**:4, 11; **95**:4, 7, 10; **96**:5, 6²; **97**:2, 7, 8, 9²; **100**:3²; **102**:11, 14, 25; **103**:11, 14², 15; **104**:1², 16, 18, 24, 28, 29, 30; **105**:7; **106**:3; **110**:4; **111**:2³, 7², 8; **112**:3; **115**:4; **116**:11; **118**:28²; **119**:1², 2, 4, 21, 24², 39, 54, 57, 68, 70, 75, 86, 95, 96, 98, 103, 111², 114, 129, 137², 138², 143, 144, 150², 151², 157, 160², 168, 172; **120**:7; **122**:2; **125**:1, 4²; **126**:3; **127**:3, 4; **128**:1; **130**:4; **131**:1; **135**:15; **139**:3, 8², 14, 17; **140**:6; **141**:4, 8; **142**:5, 6; **143**:10; **144**:4, 8², 11², 15²; **145**:14; **146**:8; **Pr 1**:16; **2**:12, 15²; **3**:16, 17²; **4**:16, 22, 26; **5**:6, 11, 21; **6**:16²; **18**, 23², 33; **7**:4, 26²; **8**:5², 8, 9², 14, 15, 18, 32²; **9**:4², 12, 16, 18²; **10**:2, 19, 25, 27; **11**:1, 3, 5, 6, 10, 20, 21; **12**:5, 7², 8, 10, 22; **13**:4, **14**:2, 4, 18, 20, 32; **15**:3, 15, 26; **16**:2, 7, 11², 21, 24; **17**:6², 7; **18**:4, 7, 8, 10, 19; **19**:1, 7, 14, 21, 29; **20**:5, 7, 15, 24, 29; **21**:4, 20; **22**:10, 22; **23**:2, 5; **24**:4, 9, 16, 23, 24; **25**:1, 3², 28; **26**:22, 23; **27**:20²; **28**:1, 6, 9, 18; **30**:11, 12², 13², 14², 15², 18², 24², 25, 26, 29²; **31**:6², 8, 17, 21; **Ecc 1**:8, 16; **4**:2³, 9; **5**:2, 3², 7, 8, 9, 10, 12³, 16, 17; **6**:7; **7**:14², 26; **8**:4, 11, 12; **9**:1, 2, 3, 10, 12³, 16, 17; **10**:6, 12, 13², 17, 18; **11**:3, 9; **12**:3, 4, 5, 11; **SS 1**:4, 10, 15², 16, 17²; **2**:11, 15; **4**:1², 2, 5, 7, 11, 12², 13, 15; **5**:12, 13², 14, 15; **6**:4, 6, 7; **7**:1, 3, 4, 6, 12; **8**:8, 10, 12; **Isa 1**:7, 11, 15, 18², 19, 23; **2**:6; **3**:8, 16; **4**:3²; **5**:7, 11, 21, 22, 25; **6**:3², 5, 13; **7**:2, 25; **8**:13³, 18, 21; **9**:15²; **16²; **10**:8; **13**:15; **14**:7, 10, 11, 15, 19, 21; **15²; **16**:2, 6, 10; **17**:14; **19**:11, 12; **22**:7², 8, 16; **23**:8²; **9**; **24**:6², 13, 18; **25**:1; **26**:8, 14; **27**:11²; **28**:7, 8; **29**:13, 24; **30**:1, 9, 17, 18, 27; **31**:3²; **32**:7, 9; **33**:8³, 13², 14; **36**:4, 5, 6, 7, 9, 19²; **37**:16, 20, 27²; **38**:1; **40**:6, 7, 15², 17², 22, 24²; **41**:9, 17, 23, 24², 27, 29²; **42**:7, 16, 17, 20; **43**:1, 4, 8², 10, 24; **46**:1¹, 12; **47**:14²; **48**:1, 7, 8; **49**:3, 16; **51**:12², 16, 20; **52**:7; **53**:5; **54**:1; **55**:1, 8², 9²; **56**:10², 11²; **57**:1², 4², 6², 20; **59**:3, 6³, 7, 10, 12²; **60**:4, 8, 9, 21; **61**:9; **63**:2, 8, 15², 16³, 17, 19; **64**:6, 8⁴, 9; **65**:5, 24; **66**:15; **Jer 2**:11, 15, 23, 25, 27², 28², 31, 3; **3**:22; **4**:13², 20, 22³, 29, 30; **5**:2, 4², 7, 8, 13, 16², 26, 27; **6**:7, 10, 13, 15, 20, 23³, 28²; **29**, 30; **7**:8², 10, 17, 19², 32²; **8**:8, 10, 12², 14, 20, 21; **9**:2, 10², 19², 25²; **26**; **10**:2, 3, 6, 8², 14, 15, 20³; 21; **11**:13, 21; **12**:1, 2, 4²; **13**:4, 20, 23; **14**:4, 8, 9², 14², 15², 16, 22; **15**:15; **16**:3², 14, 17², 20; **17**:8, 14, 17, 24; **18**:6, 19; **19**:6, 10; **20**:10; **21**:4³, 9; **22**:4, 6, 17, 20, 23; **23**:1, 5, 7, 10, 11, 12, 14, 24; **24**:3²; **8**, 10; **25**:12, 13, 18, 23; **26**:19; **27**:5, 14, 15, 16, 18, 19, 21; **28**:16; **29**:9, 10, 17, 21; **30**:3, 4, 5, 17; **31**:15, 18, 27, 29, 38, 40; **32**:19³, 24², 29, 36; **33**:10, 14, 18, 21, 24; **35**:7; **36**:7, 19; **37**:13, 19; **38**:4, 16, 22; **40**:10, 15, 16; **42**:6, 15, 17; **46**:5³, 21, 23; **47**:2; **48**:5, 12, 14, 33³, 34, 46²; **49**:2, 23², 32; **50**:7, 11, 15, 32, 33, 41, 42²; **51**:13, 17, 18, 20, 30³, 39, 46, 51, 52; **La 1**:2, 4, 5, 6, 16, 22; **2**:9, 11; **3**:22, 23, 31, 48; **4**:1, 2, 5, 8², 9, 14², 15, 16; **5**:5², 7, 12, 14, 17; **Eze 2**:4, 5, 6², 7; **3**:5, 7, 8, 9, 26, 27; **4**:4, 9; **6**:8; **7**:15; **8**:6², 9, 12, 13, 15, 17; **9**:4, 8; **11**:2³, 3, 5, 7, 15³, 21; **12**:2², 3, 4, 6, 9, 10, 23, 12, 4, 6, 15, 16, 30, 34², 45², 57, 61²; **17**:17; **18**:2, 25, 29²; **20**:38, 49; **21**:7, 12, 29; **22**:5², 6, 9², 10³, 18², 24, 27; **23**:25², 45; **26**:11, 18; **27**:25, 34, 35²; **28**:2², 3, 6, 19, 24; **30**:8; **31**:14³; **32**:2², 19, 23², 24, 25², 26, 29; **30**; **33**:10², 24², 27, 30, 31, 32; **34**:30, 31; **36**:20, 35; **37**:11³; **38**:14, 17; **39**:19²; **40**:46²; **42**:13, 14⁴; **43**:11, 13, 19², 28³; **44**:13, 15³, 16², 17, 18, 19³, 20, 23, 24³, 28, 30; **45**:1, 6, 10, 11, 13, 14, 18, 20², 21; **46**:2, 3, 13, 14, 24; **47**:13², 14, 21, 22², 23; **48**:1, 8, 9, 29, 28, 35, 37, 38; **34**, 14, 17, 23, 29, 31; **DA 2**:8, 20, 26, 28, 37, 38; **3**:4, 12, 15, 17; **4**:33, 12, 22, 35; **37**; **5**:13, 16; **7**:17, 24; **9**:7², 8, 18, 23, 24; **10**:11; **11**:33, 34; **12**:3, 6, 9, 10; **Hos 1**:9, 10; **2**:4, 23²; **3**:3; **4**:3, 4, 6, 12², 16, 18; **5**:2, 7, 10; **7**:1, 2, 4, 6, 7, 16; **8**:6; **9**:7³, 14, 15; **11**:7; **12**:11; **13**:9²; **10**, 14; **14**:9; **Joel 1**:9², 10, 12, 13, 17², 18; **2**:6, 10, 11², 22², 26; **3**:4²; **Am 5**:12; **6**:1, 2, 9; **8**:11; **9**:1, 4, 7, 8, 13; **Ob 1**:20²; **Jnh 1**:8; **4**:2; **Mic 1**:2; **2**:4, 7; **4**:11; **5**:2²; **6**:12²; **7**:3, 6; **Na 1**:3, 6, 12, 14²; **2**:3⁴; **6**:2; **3**:12, 16, 17, 18; **Hab 1**:3, 7², 8, 12, 13²; **2**:4, 8, 15; **3**:6, 17²; **Zep 1**:12²; **3**:3², 4², 6², 18; **Hag 1**:6; **Zec 1**:5, 9², 10, 19², 21²; **2**:2; **3**:8, 9; **4**:3, 4, 5, 7, 10, 11, 12, 13, 14²; **5**:10; **6**:4, 5, 15; **7**:7 **8**:16²; **9**:1, 2, 7²; **10**:2; **11**:2, 3, 9; **12**:3, 5; **13**:6, 9; **14**:12; **Mal 2**:15, 17; **3**:1, 6, 7, 9²; **Mt 1**:21; **2**:6, 18, 20; **4**:3, 6; **5**:3, 4, 5, 6, 7, 8, 9, 10², 11, 14; **6**:16; **7**:11, 15; **8**:2, 26; **9**:2, 5, 17, 37²; **10**:2, 23, 29, 30, 32²; **11**:5, 11, 28; **12**:2, 5, 34, 47, 48, 49; **13**:16, 29, 38, 39, 40; **14**:2, 33; **15**:8, 9, 14, 26, 30²; **16**, 17, 18, 23, 28; **17**:26; **19**:6, 12, 26, 30²; **20**:15, 18, 22; **21**:13, 16, 23, 26, 31; **22**:14² 16², 18, 29; **23**:4, 8², 10, 13, 15, 25, 27², 28,

Column 1

31; **24**:6, 8, 16; **25**:8, 24, 34, 41; **26**:10, 15, 45, 62², 63, 73; **27**:11, 13, 40²; **28**:5, 13; **Mk** 1:11, 24, 40; **2**:5, 8, 9, 18², 24; **3**:11, 16, 32, 33, 34; **4**:15, 40; **5**:9; **6**:14, 37; **7**:6, 7, 8, 18; **8**:17², 29; **9**:1, 16; **10**:8, 27, 31, 33, 38, 42; **11**:3, 5, 28; **12**:14², 15, 24, 27, 32, 34; **13**:4, 8, 11, 14; **14**:6, 37, 41, 60², 61, 70²; **15**:2, 4, 29; **16**:6; **Lk** 1:13, 28, 31, 42, 51; **3**:13, 22; **4**:3, 9, 34, 41; **5**:12, 20, 22, 23; **6**:2, 20², 21², 22, 24, 25, 33; **7**:19, 20, 22², 25, 31, 32, 48; **8**:12, 13, 14, 20, 21, 45; **9**:12, 27; **10**:2, 8, 9, 10, 20, 23, 41; **11**:7, 13, 21, 28, 34², 39, 44; **12**:6, 7², 11, 24, 41, 58; **13**:12, 14, 23, 30²; **14**:10; **15**:31; **16**:8², 15, 25; **17**:1, 10, 17; **18**:31; **19**:21, 31, 33; **20**:2, 6, 24, 34, 35, 36³, 38; **21**:7, 8, 21, 24; **22**:26, 28, 38, 42, 46, 48, 58, 67, 70²; **23**:3, 29, 34, 37, 40, 41²; **24**:17, 18, 25, 38, 48; **Jn** 1:21³, 22, 25, 38, 42, 49²; **2**:20; **3**:2², 10; **4**:9, 12, 17, 19, 23, 27, 35; **5**:14, 28, 39, 45, 47; **6**:12, 26, 63², 64, 69; **7**:4, 19, 20, 21, 23, 25, 26, 52; **8**:10, 13, 16, 23², 25, 31, 33, 37², 40, 41²; 43, 48, 52, 53²; 57; **9**:28², 40; **10**:16, 21, 24, 26, 30, 33, 34; **11**:8, 9, 27, 47; **12**:35; **13**:6, 10, 27, 35, 36; **14**:2, 5, 10, 24; **15**:3, 5, 6, 14; **16**:5, 6, 19, 29; **17**:9, 11², 14, 16, 21, 22; **18**:8, 17², 25², 29, 33, 37²; **19**:12; **20**:13, 15², 23², 29, 30, 31; **21**:12, 18; **Ac** 1:6; **2**:7², 15, 32, 39; **3**:15, 25; **4**:9², 16; **5**:9, 25, 28, 32; **6**:3; **7**:1, 4, 26, 33, 51; **8**:23, 30; **9**:5², 10, 19, 28, 39; **13**:10², 11, 27, 31, 33, 34; **14**:15³; **15**:1, 11², 19, 27², 29, 36; **16**:17², 20², 28, 37; **17**:7, 19, 20, 22, 28, 29; **19**:15, 26, 36, 38², 40; **20**:23, 32; **21**:13, 20, 23, 24; **22**:3, 8², 16, 26, 27; **23**:8, 15, 21²; **24**:8, 13, 19, 20; **25**:9, 11, 24; **26**:3, 5, 7², 15², 18, 24, 29; **28**:22²; **Ro** 1:6², 7, 15, 20, 29²; **3**:1, 5, 8, 13, 14, 15, 18, 19³, 26, 27²; **3**:8, 9², 13, 14, 15, 19, 24; **4**:4, 7³, 12, 14, 16²; **7**:6, 14, 15, 16², 19, 21; **8**:1, 9, 14², 16, 17², 18, 36, 37; **9**:5, 6², 7², 8², 20, 25, 26; **10**:2, 8, 10², 15², 19; **11**:3, 16, 28²; **12**:5, 13, 13, 6, 9; **14**:3; **15**:1, 14; **16**:4, 7, 11, 17, 18, 1Co 1:11, 18², 28², 30; **2**:6, 14²; **3**:2, 3³, 4, 9², 16, 17, 20, 21, 22, 23; **4**:10⁸, 11³, 12², 13, 19; **5**:2, 4, 7, 10, 12; **6**:2², 15, 18, 19²; **7**:14, 26, 27², 30, 34; **8**:5², 7, 8; **9**:1, 2; **10**:12, 13, 17², 20, 22²; **11**:18, 30, 32²; **12**:4, 5, 6, 11, 12, 20, 22, 23², 27, 29²; **13**:8²; **14**:9, 10, 12, 16², 22, 23, 32, 34², 35, 40², 48⁴; **16**:9; **2Co** 1:6², 12, 20; **2**:11, 15³, 16; **3**:1, 2, 3, 5, 13, 18; **4**:3, 8, 11², 16²; **5**:3, 4², 6³, 8, 9, 11, 12², 13², 14, 20; **6**:12², 16; **7**:12, 13; **8**:13, 18, 21, 22, 23; **10**:4, 7, 10, 11², 12, 14; **11**:1, 13, 18, 19, 22³, 23; **13**:3, 4, 5, 9³; **Gal** 1:6², 7², 22; **2**:14, 15, 17; **3**:3², 7, 9, 10, 25, 26, 28, 29; **4**:6, 7², 8, 9², 10, 17, 21, 24, 27, 28, 31; **5**:4, 17, 18², 19⁴; **6**:1, 12, 13; **Eph** 1:14²; **2**:2, 10, 11, 19, 22²; **3**:6, 13²; **4**:18, 25, 26; **5**:3, 4, 6, 8, 16, 30; **6**:22; **Php** 1:30; **3**:3, 15; **4**:3, 18, 21; **Col** 2:3, 5, 17, 22²; **3**:24; **4**:11; **1Th** 2:3, 4, 10, 14, 15, 20; **3**:8; **4**:1, 15², 17²; **5**:3, 4, 5, 6, 10, 11, 12, 14; **2Th** 1:4, 5, 7; **2**:10; **3**:4, 11³; **1Ti** 1:7, 14, 20; **3**:8, 11; **4**:12; **5**:3, 16, 17, 20, 24, 25²; **6**:1, 2⁸, 17; **2Ti** 2:13, 17, 19, 20²; **3**:6³, 8, 15; **Tit** 1:6, 10, 11, 12, 13³, 16; **2**:14, 15; **3**:8, 9; **Heb** 1:5, 10, 14; **2**:5, 6, 11², 18; **3**:6, 10; **4**:15; **5**:2², 5, 6, 11; **6**:6, 9; **7**:5, 13, 17, 21, 28; **8**:1, 4, 9, 10, 11, 13², 15, 28; **10**:1, 3, 14, 25, 39³; **11**:14; **12**:1, 8², 23, 28; **13**:3, 9, 11, 14, 18; **Jas** 2:5, 6³, 7², 8, 9, 12; **3**:4³, 7; **4**:11, 12, 14; **5**:3, 4; **1Pe** 1:5, 8, 9, 21, 24; **2**:5, 9, 10, 14, 18²; **3**:6, 12², 13, 14; **4**:6, 12, 14²; **5**:2, 5, 9, 14; **2Pe** 1:12; **2**:10, 11, 12, 13, 14, 17, 18, 19, 20²; **3**:7, 8, 13, 14, 16; **1Jn** 2:5, 14, 26; **3**:1, 2, 10²; **4**:1, 4, 5, 6, 17; **5**:3, 7, 8, 19, 20; **3Jn** 1:4, 5³; **Jude** 1:6, 10, 17; **4**:5; 11; **5**:6, 8, 9; **7**:13, 14, 15; **9**:12, 14; **11**:4, 6; **14**:4, 5, 13, 18; **15**:3², 4; **16**:5², 7, 14; **17**:7, 9, 10, 12, 15, 17; **18**:5; **19**:2, 9³, 12²; **20**:6, 7, 8; **21**:5, 22, 27; **22**:2, 6, 14, 15, 19.

Column 2

28, 39, 43, 54; **42**:7², 14, 15², 16², 30, 35; **43**:10, 11, 14, 17, 18, 29, 34²; **44**:1², 2, 3, 10, 33; **45**:21, 24; **46**:29², 34; **47**:3, 11, 19, 24², 26, 30, 31; **48**:4, 5², 7, 22; **49**:4, 6, 16, 30; **50**:6, 12, 13; **Ex** 1:11; **2**:14; **4**:16²; **5**:8, 13, 14; **6**:3, 4, 7, 8; **7**:6, 10, 13, 15, 20, 22; **8**:10, 15, 19, 20, 27, 29²; **9**:12, 35; **10**:29; **11**:5; **12**:14, 17, 24, 25, 29, 31, 32, 35, 38²; **13**:11; **14**:9, 10; **15**:16²; **16**:5², 16², 17, 18², 21²; **22**, 24, 34; **17**:1, 10, 11², 14; **18**:13, 14, 21, 22, 26; **19**:23; **21**:7², 20; **22**:13, 26, 13; **27**:8; **28**:1, 3, 4, 12², 29, 36, 41, 42; **29**:1, 24, 26, 30, 36, 40, 41, 44; **30**:23; 30; **31**:10, 11, 16; **32**:1, 13², 23, 28; **33**:9, 11; **34**:4, 9, 16, 18; **35**:19, 22, 24, 35; **36**:1, 6, 18; **37**:23²; **39**:1, 5, 7², 21, 26, 29, 31, 32, 41, 42, 43; **40**:13, 15², 16, 19, 21, 23, 25, 27, 29, 32; **Lev** 1:2; **2**:2, 9, 12², 16; **3**:5, 6, 11, 16; **4**:3, 10², 11², 14, 20, 21, 23, 26, 28, 31², 32, 35; **5**:6², 7, 10, 11, 12, 13, 15, 16, 18; **6**:6, 15, 17, 20, 21, 22; **7**:5, 12, 14, 19, 29, 30, 32, 33, 34, 35, 36; **8**:4, 9, 13, 17, 21², 27, 28, 29²; 31; **9**:7, 8, 10, 15, 18, 21²; **10**:5, 7, 14, 15², 18, 19; **11**:35; **12**:2, 5; **13**:12, 46²; **14**:12²; 21, 24, 31², 34²; **15**:25²; 26²; **16**:10², 15, 26, 32, 34; **17**:4, 5, 6; **18**:3², 18, 22, 28; **19**:18, 23, 34²; **20**:13, 24, 25; **21**:2, 8, 22²; **22**:13, 18, 21, 22, 23, 25, 27, 32; **23**:2, 12, 17, 20, 37, 41; **24**:7, 8, 20, 23; **25**:7², 24, 31, 36, 39, 40, 42, 46, 53, 55; **26**:21, 36², 37, 44; **27**:9, 11, 12, 14², 23; **Nu** 1:19, 54; **2**:17, 33; **3**:3, 4, 10, 16, 37², 42, 51; **4**:24, 27, 31, 32², 33, 49; **5**:4, 26, 6²; **6**:2, 4², 11², 12, 17, 20, 21²; **7**:3, 5, 7, 8, 13, 17, 19, 23, 25, 29, 31, 35, 37, 41, 43, 47, 49, 53, 55, 59, 61, 65, 67, 71, 73, 77, 79, 83; **8**:3, 11, 13, 15, 16, 19, 20, 22; **9**:5, 18²; **10**:25, 28; **11**:12, 16, 31²; **12**:13²; **13**:21²; **14**:3, 17, 19, 20, 21⁴, 28², 31²; **15**:2, 3, 5, 7², 8, 10, 12², 13, 14², 19, 20, 24, 36; **16**:3, 15, 31², 40, 47; **17**:10, 11; **18**:6, 7², 8, 9, 10², 11, 12, 15², 17, 18, 19, 24, 26², 27², 29, 30; **20**:9, 12, 27; **21**:24²; 26³, 29², 30²; **22**:4, 19; **23**:2, 30; **24**:1; **25**:11², 17, 18²; **26**:4, 10, 53; **27**:7, 11, 13, 14, 22, 23, 24, 27; **28**:2, 3, 6, 15, 22, 24, 28, 31, 34, 36, 38; **31**:7, 9, 10², 20², 28, 29, 31, 41², 47, 50, 52, 54; **32**:5, 25, 27, 29, 36, 38²; **34**:2, 13, 17; **35**:5, 14, 30; **36**:2, 6²; 10; **Dt** 1:7², 10², 11, 15², 19, 21, 30, 31, 40, 41; **2**:1, 5, 9, 10², 12, 14, 19, 21², 23³, 29, 30, 36²; **3**:6, 8², 10², 13, 14², 20², 6, 9², 10²; **20³**, 21, 26, 32, 33, 38, 46, 49²; **5**:12, 14, 16, 26; **6**:2³, 8, 16, 19, 24, 25; **7**:12²; **8**:5, 18; **9**:3, 21²; **10**:5, 6, 8, 9, 18, 19, 22²; **11**:4, 10, 18, 21², 25, 30; **12**:1², 8², 10, 11, 15³, 19²; **20³**, 21³, 22, 31; **13**:16, 17²; **14**:25, 26²; **15**:4, 6, 14, 18²; **16**:2², 16²; **18**:2, 14; **19**:3, 5, 8, 10, 19; **20**:14²; 16², 17²; 19, 21; **21**:11, 14, 17, 23; **22**:19²; 29²; 30²; **23**:5, 18, 23; **24**:4, 7, 8, 10, 13, 17; **25**:10, 19; **26**:1, 2, 15, 18, 19; **27**:3, 4, 28:9² 62² 63, 68; **29**:8, 13³ 19² 28; **30**:9, 19; **31**:3, 7, 13², 26; **32**:10, 31, 40², 49, 50; **34**:2²; 3², 5; **Jos** 1:3, 5, 15, 17²; **2**:7², 19, 21; **3**:7, 13²; 17²; **4**:6, 8², 10, 12²; **5**:14, 15; **6**:25; **7**:5²; **8**:2, 5, 6, 19², 27, 31, 33, 34; **9**:1², 4, 23; **10**:1, 11, 13, 28, 30, 32, 35, 37, 39, 40; **11**:4², 9, 12, 20, 23²; **12**:7; **13**:3, 4², 6², 7, 8, 9², 11², 12, 14, 25², 33; **14**:1², 5, 10, 11⁴, 12, 13, 15²; 47²; 16:3²; **17**:1, 18; **18**:8², 10², 28²; 50; **20**:2; **21**:3, 8, 12, 44; **22**:4, 28; **23**:4, 5, 8, 10, 15; **24**:6², 11, 15; **Jdg** 1:20; **2**:15, 18³, 22; **3**:20; **4**:16²; **5**:30²; **6**:26, 37; **7**:12, 13, 17, 21, 22², 24⁴; **8**:8, 12², 31, 33, 36, 39, 45³; **21**:18, 25; **Ru** 1:8, 22; **2**:3, 15; **3**:13²; **4**:10; **1Sa** 1:12, 24, 26²; **3**:10, 19, 20; **4**:2, 9, 20; **5**:10; **6**:6, 8, 12², 14, 17; **7**:9, 15; **8**:1, 5, 7, 8; **9**:11, 13², 14, 20, 27; **10**:5, 9, 23; **11**:7, 9; **12**:2², 7, 15, 23; **13**:5², 10; **14**:39²; 45²; **15**:2², 22, 23, 26, 27, 33; **16**:1; **17**:20², 23, 30, 48, 55³, 57²; **18**:1, 3, 5, 7, 10, 30²; **19**:6², 7, 10, 20²; **20**:3², 8, 13, 14², 17, 21², 31², 36; **21**:2, 5; **22**:4², 8, 13, 18²; **23**:11, 26; **24**:4, 13; **25**:20, 25, 26³, 28², 29, 34²; **26**:10², 16², 20, 24²; **27**:11²; **28**:10²; **29**:2, 6², 9², 10²; **30**:2, 11, 24; **2Sa** 2:18², 19, 24, 27²; **3**:27, 33, 34; **4**:3, 4, 6, 9²; **5**:12, 20, 24², 25; **6**:16, 20; **7**:6, 10, 15, 19, 22, 23, 24, 25; **8**:11; **10**:1, 2, 6²; **11**:11², 20²; **13**:19, 35, 36; **14**:7, 11²; **15**:3, 7, 8, 9, 11, 13, 19, 23, 24, 28, 29²; **16**:5, 6, 10, 11, 13, 19, 23, 24, 28, 29²; 31; **16**:5, 6, 10, 11, 13, 19, 23, 24, 28, 29²; 31; **16**:5, 6, 10,

Column 3

11², 14, 20, 27, 28; **17**:1, 11, 12², 13, 15; **18**:7, 10², 15, 28, 44²; **19**:16; **20**:4, 33, 34, 36², 39, 40, 45, 53; **2Ki** 1:17, 18; **2**:2³, 4³, 6², 11, 19, 23; **3**:2, 7³, 14², 25, 27²; **4**:1, 4, 17, 30², 34, 40; **5**:7, 10, 15², 16, 17, 18; **6**:5², 18², 26, 30; **7**:7, 10, 15², 16, 17, 18; **8**:2, 5, 9, 15, 16, 18, 23, 24, 27; **9**:10, 22², 31, 36; **10**:2, 5, 11², 15, 25², 34; **11**:9, 14, 16; **12**:4, 9, 19, 21; **13**:5, 8, 9, 12, 24; **14**:3, 15, 16, 18, 28, 29, 30, 31, 34, 36, 38; **16**:8, 16, 19, 20; **17**:4, 8², 11, 14² 15, 23, 31, 32, 41; **18**:3, 8²; **19**:3, 21, 37; **20**:20, 21; **21**:3, 13, 17, 18, 20; **22**:2; **23**:19, 21, 25, 27, 28, 32, 37; **24**:5, 6, 9, 13, 19; **25**:18, 23, 30²; **1Ch** 1:44, 45, 46, 47, 48, 49, 50; **2**:23²; **4**:27³, 33², 41; **5**:1, 11², 16²; **6**:10, 54, 66; **7**:2, 5, 24², 40; **8**:28; **9**:9, 19, 29², 34; **11**:3, 10, 20², 24²; **12**:8², 40², 14², 15², 16, 27², 29; **16**:17², 18; **17**:9, 13, 17², 20, 23; **18**:3², 11, 19²; **1**:7², 21:15; **22**:11, 14, 24; **24**:2, 19, 20, 21, 31²; **25**:3, 4, 8²; **26**:12, 18, 29, 31; **27**:23²; **28**:2, 4, 7, 8, 10, 13²; **29**:2², 11, 14², 15, 16, 22², 23, 24², 25, 28, 29; **2Ch** 1:9², 12, 15², 22², 3, 6; **4**:20; **5**:13; **6**:10, 15, 16, 32, 33; **7**:6, 12, 17²; **8**:5, 6, 8; **9**:3², 8, 9, 26², 27³, 29, 31; **10**:12, 17; **11**:14; **12**:1, 6, 13, 9, 10; **14**:1, 9²; **13**²; **19**:11; **20**:11, 14, 20, 22; **21**:1, 3, 6, 13, 19; **22**:4; **23**:3, 8, 15, 18²; **24**:14²; **25**:14, 26, 26:4, 5², 8², 11, 23; **27**:2, 9; **28**:5, 11, 18²; **29**:2, 8, 15, 21, 27, 33; **30**:7, 8, 10; **31**:2, 3, 5², 19; **32**:17, 19, 20, 23; **33**:14², 15², 19², 20, 22; **34**:6², 33²; **35**:10, 12, 13, 16, 18; **36**:8; **Ezr** 2:62; **3**:1, 5³, 7, 10; **4**:3, 8, 23², 5⁴; **6**:3, 9, 17; **7**:16², 8:27²; **28⁴**, 35; **9**:2, 7, 12, 15; **10**:12, 16, 19; **Ne** 1:9; **2**:16; **3**:1⁴, 8², 12, 13, 17²; **7**:3, 64; **8**:1, 3, 5, 9, 15; **9**:23², 24, 28², 37; **10**:34, 36; **11**:25; **12**:22², 24², 35², 39², 41², 45; **13**:5²; **Est** 1:21; **2**:7², 20²; **3**:11, 14; **4**:2², 14, 16; **5**:6, 13²; **6**:10²; **7**:2, 4, 8³; **8**:8, 13; **9**:19, 22²; 31²; **Job** 2:8; **3**:11; **4**:8; **5**:7², 14; **6**:15³, 26, 28; **7**:9; **9**:35; **10**:4; **11**:16; **12**:3², 5, 11; **13**:9; **14**:11, 18²; **16**:20, 21; **18**:3; **19**:15, 22; **21**:11; **22**:14; **23**:10; **24**:19; **27**:2², 3², 6², 22; **28**:5; **29**:14, 18², 23², 25², 30², 31, 32², 33², 34³; **36**:27; **37**:18, 21; **38**:30; **39**:6², 16; **41**:4, 20, 24², 42:7, 8, 10², 15²; **Ps** 1:4; **2**:9²; **11**:4, 6³; **12**:6², 7²; **16**:9³; **17**:9, 9, 15², 12³; **18**:30, 42², 44²; **22**:3; **28**:2²; **29**:10; **31**:12; **32**:4; **33**:22; **35**:14²; **39**:1³, 3, 5, 6, 12²; **40**:9², 41, 8; **42**:8; **44**:22; **45**:1²; **47**:9; **48**:8; **53**:4; **55**:14, 21, 23; **58**:8; **61**:2; **63**:4²; 5; **64**:1; **68**:2², 28; **71**:14; **72**:5⁴, 17²; **73**:2, 20², 28; **74**:4, 14; **75**:8; **77**:13; **78**:15², 55, 57², 65²; **79**:2; **80**:11²; **81**:5; **83**:4, 9², 14; **84**:6; **87**:7; **89**:29²; **90**:11², 15²; **95**:8²; **102**:8, 9; **103**:10, 11²; **104**:2, 6, 33², 34; **105**:10², 11, 17, 22, 23, 39; **106**:6, 9, 31, 34; **109**:18, 29; **113**:9; **116**:2²; **118**:12²; **119**:7, 14, 132; **123**:2²; **125**:2; **133**:3; **135**:12; **136**:21; **139**:12; **140**:3²; **141**:7; **146**:2²; **Pr** 2:4²; **3**:12; **5**:4²; **7**:2, 9²; **8**:22; **10**:26; **12**:14²; **16**:10; **17**:2; **21**:5²; **24**:8, 29; **25**:3, 23; **26**:11, 14, 21²; **27**:14, 17, 19; **28**:1²; **30**:33²; **Ecc** 2:8, 13; **3**:18, 19; **5**:3, 11, 15, 16; **7**:12, 14²; **8**:8, 9; **9**:2², 12; **10**:1, 3; **11**:5; **SS** 3:3; **4**:11; **5**:15; **6**:4³, 10³, 13; **8**:6³; **Isa** 1:7, 18³, 26²; **2**:2; **5**:2, 17, 18, 24², 29; **6**:13; **7**:2, 25; **8**:2, 13; **9**:2², 4; **10**:10, 11, 14², 15, 18, 24, 26²; **11**:9, 10, 16; **14**:2, 10, 24²; **15**:5⁴; **16**:1, 8², 9, 14; **17**:5², 12, 13; **18**:4, 5, 24, 26, 24², 13²; **25**:5, 10, 11; **26**:17; **27**:7², 8; **28**:4², 21²; **29**:7, 8; **30**:19², 29², 32, 33, 34; **31**:4²; **37**:3, 22, 38; **38**:14; **40**:13, 15², 17², 19; **41**:11, 12, 25²; **43**:14; **48**:9, 10; **49**:18³, 26; **51**:9²; **52**:14; **53**:7; **54**:6; **55**:9, 10; **57**:2; **58**:2, 3, 4, 12²; **59**:10, 17, 21; **60**:7; **61**:10², 11; **62**:5², 8; **64**:2; **65**:8, 11, 15, 22; **66**:13, 19, 20, 22²; **Jer** 1:5; **2**:2, 20, 26, 28², 36; **3**:1, 18; **4**:2², 31²; **5**:2², 9, 19, 29; **6**:7, 9², 14, 23, 26²; **7**:15; **8**:11; **9**:9, 14, 11³, 14, 15²; **12**:14, 16³; **13**:2, 5, 11, 15; **15**:13; **16**:14²; **15²**; **17**:3, 22, 27; **18**:4, 6; **19**:5, 7, 11; **20**:5, 17; **21**:2, 14; **22**:11, 24²; **23**:7, 8², 14; **25**:18; **26**:8², 14, 20; **28**:9; **29**:27; **30**:14²; **20**; **31**:9, 13, 28, 40²; **32**:3, 7, 8, 11², 14, 24, 42²; **34**:5; **36**:6, 32; **38**:4²; **16²**; **40**:3; **41**:7, 11; **42**:2, 3², 6, 9, 18; **43**:7²; **12², 44**:13, 17, 22, 23, 26², 30; **46**:18²; **48**:5, 11, 13, 32², 34², 42; **49**:9²; **16²**, 18; **50**:15, 18, 29, 33, 40, 42; **51**:9², 14, 49, 57; **52**:2, 24, 34²; **La** 1:11, 22; **2**:7², 12², 13², 19, 22; **4**:2, 8²; **5**:10, 21; **Eze** 1:9, 12, 15, 17², 25, 27², 2:2²; **3**:3², 8²; **4**:3, 5, 12; **5**:1, 11, 7:13², 17², 21², 26; **8**:2², 4²; **9**:5, 11; **10**:2, 5², 10, 11³, 12, 19; **11**:13, 15, 21; **12**:3, 6, 7, 14, 10², 16², 18²; **20²**, 21, 32, 41; **17**:7²; **20³**, 21, 31², 21², 31, 41; **21**:7², 26; **22**:20, 22; **23**:7, 16², 18, 19, 37, 43, 44; **24**:18, 22, 24, 25; **25**:4, 7,

Column 4

10; **26**:10, 20; **27**:7, 8, 9, 10, 25, 32; **28**:2², 6², 14; **29**:5, 10², 19, 20; **30**:21, 22²; **33**:11², 24, 27², 30, 31; **34**:8², 12, 17; **35**:6², 11²; **36**:11, 37², 38²; **37**:7², 10; **39**:4, 15, 18; **40**:16, 18², 19², 21, 22, 23, 24, 28, 29, 32, 33, 35, 36, 41; **42**:6, 9, 9; **43**:19, 22, 24; **44**:13, 24; **45**:1², 4², 5, 6, 22, 23, 24; **46**:5², 7³, 11², 12; **47**:3, 10, 22²; **48**:8, 11, 20, 23, 29; **Da** 2:28, 29, 30, 40², 41², 42, 43; **3**:5², 7²; **4**:5, 29, 30, 35²; **5**:4, 5; **6**:6, 10, 11, 15; **7**:1, 9³, 21; **8**:4², 5, 11², 17; **9**:13, 23²; **10**:4, 9; **11**:3, 10², 16, 36; **12**:1, 13; **Hos** 2:3², 7, 15²; **3**:1; **4**:6, 15²; **6**:3², 9; **7**:7; **8**:12²; **9**:10²; **10**:1², 6, 14; **12**:3, 9, 13³; **13**:13; **Joel** 2:2, 23, 32; **Am** 2:1, 7, 8, 9²; **13**:2; **4**:5, 10, 11; **5**:14, 19²; **7**:11; **8**:14²; **9**:7, 9, 11; **Ob** 1:5², 15, 16², 20²; **Jnh** 1:14; **4**:11; **Mic** 1:7, 16²; **3**:5, 8²; **4**:1, 8; **5**:8; **7**:7, 13, 14, 15, 20; **Hab** 2:5², 14; **3**:14; **Zep** 2:9²; **13**; **Zec** 1:6; **2**:12; **3**:3; **4**:1; **6**:14; **7**:3, 12²; **8**:8, 11, 12, 13, 14; **9**:11, 12, 13, 15, 16; **10**:6, 7, 8²; **12**:2²; **10²**; **14**:3, 5; **Mal** 1:13; **2**:12, 14, 16²; **3**:3, 4², 17; **Mt** 1:20, 24; **2**:8²; **3**:9, 16²; **4**:18; **5**:40, 48; **6**:2, 10, 12, 16, 33; **7**:29²; **8**:4, 13; **9**:9, 27; **10**:7, 12, 16, 16⁴, 18; **11**:7; **12**:13²; 40; **13**:44, 40, 52²; **14**:15; **17**:2²; 9, 20²; **18**:17, 24, 33; **19**:14, 19, 29; **20**:14, 17, 28², 29; **21**:1, 6, 18; **22**:39; **23**:15², 28, 37; **24**:3, 14, 27, 32², 37; **25**:32; **26**:2, 6, 7, 19, 24, 39², 64; **27**:7, 10, 11, 32, 57, 65²; **28**:3, 6, 15; **Mk** 1:10, 16, 22², 29², 44, 45; **2**:14, 19, 23; **4**:4, 15², 29²; **33²**, 36; **5**:16, 18; **6**:11, 54², 7:4, 6, 25²; **8**:7; **9**:3, 13, 15²; **10**:1, 14, 17, 30, 42, 45, 46; **11**:1, 2, 4, 6, 12, 17, 20; **12**:31, 33, 38; **13**:1, 3, 9, 28²; **14**:3, 16, 21, 43, 64; **15**:2, 42; **16**:5, 7, 14; **Lk** 1:2, 8, 38, 44², 55, 70; **2**:20, 23, 29; **3**:4, 8, 21; **4**:16; **5**:1, 14, 17, 6:22, 31, 36; **7**:12, 38; **8**:5, 14, 23, 42; **9**:5³, 33, 34, 46, 51, 57; **10**:27, 33, 38; **11**:1, 8², 21; **12**:31, 58; **13**:22, 34; **17**:6², 12, 14, 26; **18**:16, 30, 35; **19**:26, 29, 30, 32, 33, 36, 41; **20**:1; **21**:1, 6, 24; **22**:10, 13, 24, 27, 29, 31, 39, 60; **23**:3, 14, 15, 26; **24**:15, 17, 24, 28², 39; **Jn** 1:7, 8, 32; **3**:14, 31; **4**:6, 12, 52; **5**:21, 23, 26, 30; **6**:11², 31, 36, 57; **7**:38; **8**:6, 13, 30, 40, 54; **9**:1, 4², 29; **10**:15, 36; **11**:51, 56; **12**:6, 10, 14, 39, 46, 47; **13**:15, 27²; **30²**, 33, 34; **14**:7, 18, 27; **15**:9, 10, 12, 19²; **23**; **17**:11, 16, 18, 21, 22, 23; **18**:23, 25; **19**:6³, 13, 37; **20**:7², 11, 21; **21**:7², 25; **Ac** 1:10, 16, 23; **2**:4, 15, 22, 45; **3**:4, 10, 12, 16, 17, 21, 24²; **4**:35; **5**:15²; 21, 31; **6**:9³; **7**:7, 9, 17, 21, 28, 29, 31, 40, 44, 48; **8**:10, 12, 32, 36³; **9**:2, 3, 17, 21, 32; **10**:1, 4, 9, 12², 18, 25, 42, 47; **11**:4, 15², 17, 19²; **12**:18; **13**:5, 19, 23, 25, 33, 42; **14**:1, 9; **15**:3, 8, 11, 12, 16²; **14**:2, 13, 16³, 17²; **22²**, 25, 28; **18**:3, 14, 21; **19**:29, 40; **20**:3, 9, 37; **21**:25, 37; **22**:3², 5², 6, 23, 25; **23**:11, 25, 31²; **24**:14, 15, 21, 24, 25, 26; **26**:2, 5, 7, 13, 16², 23; **27**:16, 25, 38²; **28**:3, 15²; **Ro** 1:3, 13, 17, 21; **2**:16, 24, 25, 26; **3**:4, 7, 8, 10, 25, 26; **4**:3, 4², 5, 9, 17², 18, 19², 22; **5**:12, 14, 18, 19, 21; **6**:4, 13³, 16, 19; **7**:1², 2², 13, 14², 23², 36³; **9**:4, 6, 8, 13, 25, 29, 32, 33; **10**:11, 4, 9, 12², 18, 25, 42, 47; **11**:4, 15², 17², 12²; **12**:18; **13**:5, 19, 23, 25, 33, 42; **14**:1, 9; **15**:3, 8, 11, 12, 16²; 21; **16**:21; **1Co** 1:7, 31; **2**:1, 9; **3**:1², 5, 10, 15, 19; **4**:1², 7, 9², 14, 18; **5**:3, 7; **6**:4; **7**:6²; **8**:2, 5, 7; **9**:5, 7, 19², 20, 21, 24; **10**:6², 7², 8, 9, 10, 11³, 33; **11**:1, 2, 4, 6, 12, 17; **12**:11, 18, 20; **13**:12²; **14**:7, 33, 34; **15**:3, 8, 22, 30, 31², 34, 38, 48²; 49; **16**:10, 16; **2Co** 1:5, 7, 11, 14², 18², 22, 23; **2**:3, 5; **3**:4, 6; **4**:5², 5, 6², 20; **6**:1, 4, 8, 9, 13², 16; **7**:9, 14²; **8**:3², 5, 7, 15, 19, 23²; **9**:3, 5², 9; **10**:2³, 7, 14³, 15; **11**:2, 3, 8, 10², 13, 14, 15, 16, 17², 21; **12**:15, 16, 19, 20²; **Gal** 1:9; **2**:6, 7, 8², 3:1, 6, 14², 13, 14², 23; **5**:12, 14, 21; **6**:10, 11; **Eph** 1:5; **2**:1, 20; **3**:3, 5; **4**:1, 4, 7, 16, 17, 19, 32; **5**:1², 8, 15², 22, 23, 24, 25, 27, 28, 29, 33; **6**:5, 7, 20; **Php** 1:13, 20, 27; **2**:5, 8, 12, 16, 22, 23²; **3**:6²; **4**:15; **Col** 1:6; **2**:6², 7, 19, 20; **3**:6²; **4**:4, 10; **1Th** 2:2, 4, 6, 8, 11, 13²; **3**:4, 6, 12; **4**:1, 6, 11; **5**:3, 8², 11; **2Th** 1:5, 7; **3**:1, 13, 15²; **1Ti** 1:3, 16; **2**:6; **3**:6, 10; **4**:2; **5**:1² 2, 10, 11; **6**:19; **2Ti** 1:3², 12, 13; **2**:4, 5, 15; **3**:8; **4**:14; **Tit** 1:5, 9; **3**:12²; **Phm** 1:4, 9, 16⁴, 17; **Heb** 1:4²; **3**:2, 3, 5, 6, 7, 8, 13², 15²; **4**:2, 3, 7, 10, 15; **5**:3², 4; **6**:10, 19; **7**:16, 28; **8**:6², 9², 11, 17, 26; **10**:25²; 29; **11**:4, 5, 8, 9, 12⁸, 17, 21, 24, 26, 29; **12**:5, 6, 7, 10, 16, 17; **13**:1, 11, 17; **Jas** 1:27; **2**:1, 8, 9, 12, 23, 26; **3**:4; **4**:16; **5**:10, 11; **1Pe** 1:14, 15, 17, 18; **2**:4, 11, 13, 16²; **3**:3, 7³, 8, 14, 12, 15², 16²; **5**:1², 12; **2Pe** 1:1², 13², 14, 19, 21; **2**:1; **3**:1, 4, 9, 12, 15, 16; **1Jn** 1:7; **2**:6, 18, 27²; **3**:2, 3, 7; **4**:10; **5**:1; **8**:13; **9**:11, 17; **10**:9; **11**:6²; **12**:2, 11; **14**:4, 20; **16**:6; **17**:12; **18**:6, 7³; **20**:12; **21**:2, 11, 16⁴, 18²; **22**:1²;

AT (2217)

Ge 4:7, 26; **8:**3; **12:**6², 13:7, 18; **14:**1; **15:**5, 15; **17:**17; **18:**1, 10, 14; **19:**1, 11; **21:**2, 22, 32; **23:**2, 9, 19; **24:**29; **25:**8; **27:**43; **28:**2; **29:**34; **31:**13, 24, 40; **33:**14, 18; **35:**4, 13, 14; **37:**14; **38:**1, 5, 14, 21; **42:**1, 27; **43:**8, 13, 16, 19, 21, 25, 30, 33; **44:**4, 13; **45:**3; **46:**2; **48:**3; **49:**19, 23; **50:**11, 23, 26; **Ex** 2:4, 11; **3:**6²; **4:**24, 26, 27; **5:**11, 23; **9:**18; **11:**5, 7; **12:**6, 16, 21, 29, 41; **13:**10, 20; **14:**24, 27; **16:**12; **17:**1, 6, 8, 16; **18:**22, 26; **19:**17; **20:**18, 21; **23:**15, 16; **24:**1, 4; **25:**18, 19, 30; **26:**9, 12, 23, 24, 27, 28; **27:**2, 4; **28:**24, 25; **29:**11, 12, 32, 39, 41, 42; **30:**8, 12; **32:**19, 26; **33:**6, 8, 9, 10²; **34:**8, 18, 22; **35:**15; **36:**28, 29, 32, 33; **37:**7, 8; **38:**2, 8, 21; **39:**17, 18; **40:**5, 8, 28, 33; **Lev** 1:3, 5, 11; **3:**2; **4:**4, 7², 18², 24, 25, 29, 30, 33, 34; **5:**9; **8:**3, 4, 15, 31, 35; **9:**9; **12:**6; **14:**2, 11, 23; **15:**25, 29; **16:**7; **17:**5, 6; **19:**27; **23:**4, 5, 31; **25:**37²; **27:**3, 4, 5², 6², 7², 27²; **Nu** 3:1, 7, 25², 26, 39; **4:**14, 20, 23, 28, 30, 31, 33, 39, 41, 43, 49; **6:**10, 18; **7:**5; **8:**15, 19, 22, 24, 25, 26; **9:**2, 3², 5, 7, 11, 13, 16, 18², 20², 23²; **10:**3, 6, 10, 13; **11:**5, 9, 10; **12:**4, 5; **13:**3, 25, 26; **14:**10, 15; **15:**39; **16:**9, 18, 19, 21, 27, 34, 38, 45, 50; **17:**9; **18:**4, 6, 7, 16², 21, 23, 31; **20:**1², 16, 23, 24; **21:**8, 9, 10, 33; **22:**4, 5, 36²; **23:**25²; **24:**1, 11, 20; **25:**6; **27:**14, 21²; **28:**2, 4, 6, 7, 8, 14; **29:**39; **31:**12, 16; **33:**2, 5, 6, 8, 12, 13, 14, 16, 17, 18, 19, 20, 21, 22, 23, 24, 25, 26, 27, 28, 29, 30, 31, 32, 33, 34, 35, 36, 37, 38, 41, 42, 43, 44, 45, 46; **34:**5, 9, 12; **35:**20, 22; **36:**5; **Dt** 1:4, 6², 9, 16, 18; **2:**18, 32, 34; **3:**1, 4, 8, 12, 18, 21, 23, 27; **4:**3, 10, 11, 14, 15; **5:**2, 5; **6:**7, 16; **7:**22; **9:**8, 11, 12, 20, 22³; **10:**1, 8, 10; **11:**5, 19; **12:**14, 18; **14:**23; **28:**15; **21:**20; **16:**2, 7, 11, 14, 15, 16²; **17:**9, 10; **18:**16; **19:**17; **20:**15, 20; **21:**19; **22:**15; **23:**11; **24:**5; **25:**7; **26:**3; **28:**7, 13², 25, 29; **29:**1; **31:**10, 11, 14², 15; **32:**51; **33:**3, 8², 17, 20; **Jos** 2:5; **3:**15, 16; **4:**3, 9, 18, 19, 20, 20; **5:**2, 3, 10; **6:**15, 20, 26³; **7:**5; **8:**3, 14, 29²; **9:**6, 12, 27; **10:**2, 6, 10, 15, 16, 17, 21, 27², 37, 43; **11:**5, 7, 10, 21; **13:**21; **14:**6²; **15:**2, 4, 5, 7, 8, 9, 11; **16:**1, 3, 7, 8; **17:**7, 9; **18:**1, 8, 9, 12², 14, 15², 19²; **19:**13, 14, 22, 29, 33, 34, 51²; **20:**6; **21:**2; **22:**9, 11, 12, 24; **24:**1, 25, 29, 30, 32, 33; **Jdg** 1:4; **2:**8, 9, 23; **3:**19, 29; **4:**4, 15; **5:**11, 19, 27²; **6:**27; **7:**1, 19, 25²; **8:**3, 18, 32; **9:**6, 33, 35, 44; **10:**17; **11:**17, 20, 26; **12:**6²; **15:**14:4, 8, 20; **15:**1; **16:**2²; **18:**15, 16, 17; **19:**11, 20, 25, 26²; **20:**10, 14, 15, 16, 20, 33; **21:**1, 5, 8, 12, 13, 14, 24; **Ru** 1:14; **2:**10, 14, 19; **3:**7, 8, 14; **4:**6, 11; **1Sa** 1:3, 19, 23, 24; **2:**22; **3:**10, 12, 21; **4:**1²; **5:**5; **6:**13; **7:**2, 5, 6², 7; **8:**2, 4; **9:**12, 22; **10:**2, 3, 10, 17; **11:**8; **13:**2², 3, 4, 5, 7, 11², 12, 16, 23; **14:**16, 18, 33; **15:**4, 21, 33; **16:**4, 7⁴; **17:**1², 15, 28, 43; **19:**13, 16, 18, 19, 22²; **20:**1, 6, 20, 30, 33, 34; **21:**2, 14; **22:**6, 9, 11, 15, 17; **23:**6, 15, 16, 18, 19²; **24:**11; **25:**1, 2, 5, 7, 8, 14, 24; **26:**1; **28:**4², 8, 12, 24²; **29:**1, 2; **30:**21; **31:**13; **2Sa** 2:13, 32²; **3:**20, 21, 30, 32; **4:**8, 12; **5:**1, 3²; **7:**10; **8:**10; **9:**4, 7, 10, 11, 13; **10:**4, 5, 8; **11:**1, 9, 13, 16, 24; **12:**20, 31; **13:**7, 23; **15:**7, 8, 17, 28, 32, 37; **16:**13, 14; **17:**16, 17, 20, 21; **19:**11, 18, 28; **20:**8², 18; **21:**6, 12, 14, 18², 19, 20, 22; **22:**16², 40; **23:**4, 9, 11, 13, 14², 17; **24:**8, 16; **1Ki** 1:9, 43, 45, 49; **2:**7, 8, 19, 27, 40², 42²; **3:**2, 5, 21; **5:**14, 17; **6:**3, 7², 16; **7:**21, 35, 39; **8:**1, 2, 9, 61, 65; **9:**2, 10, 26; **10:**2, 5, 20, 22, 27²; **11:**36²; **14:**1, 6, 7; **15:**27; **16:**9², 34²; **17:**1, 9; **18:**19, 27, 36²; **19:**5, 13, 20:16, 20, 22²; **20:**9, 10, 34, 38, 44, 48, 49; **2Ki** 1:11²; **2:**3, 5, 7², 23, 24; **3:**6, 14; **4:**2, 25, 27, 37; **5:**9; **6:**8; **7:**1, 3, 5, 9, 18; **8:**3, 11, 22, 28, 29; **9:**10, 21, 32², 36, 37; **10:**8, 12, 29; **11:**3, 4², 6², 13, 18, 20; **12:**20; **13:**7, 14, 10, 11, 13; **15:**16, 25; **16:**4, 6; **18:**17, 11, 29, 32; **18:**10, 14, 16, 17²; **20:**1, 12; **22:**9; **23:**8², 9, 15, 19², 29, 33; **24:**10; **25:**4, 6, 13, 20, 21, 23, 25, 26, 29; **1Ch** 2:55; **4:**21, 23; **5:**10; **6:**39, 44; **9:**18, 21, 22; **11:**1, 3², 13², 15, 16², 19; **12:**1, 8, 23; **15:**22; **16:**39, 42; **17:**9; **18:**10, 17; **19:**4, 5, 9; **20:**1, 4², 6, 8; **21:**15, 22, 28, 29²; **23:**28, 31²; **25:**6; **26:**17², 18², 31; **28:**1; **29:**9, 28; **2Ch** 1:3, 13; **2:**4; **3:**4; **4:**10; **5:**3, 10; **7:**8, 12; **8:**1; **9:**4, 19; **12:**10; **13:**14, 15; **14:**1, 5, 6²; **15:**10, 11; **16:**7, 9, 10; **18:**8, 9, 33, 34; **20:**5, 16, 21, 30, 36; **21:**10, 19; **22:**5, 6, 12; **23:**3, 4, 5², 12, 13, 14, 19; **24:**5, 8², 15, 23; **25:**19, 21, 23; **26:**9³, 19, 20; **27:**3; **28:**4, 15, 16, 24; **29:**7, 36; **30:**3, 6; **31:**2; **32:**6, 24; **33:**17; **35:**15, 16, 17, 20, 21², 22; **36:**16, 23; **Ezr** 1:2; **2:**68; **3:**8; **4:**6; **5:**3; **6:**1, 18; **7:**24; **8:**15, 27, 34; **9:**4, 5, 7, 12; **10:**14; **Ne** 1:9; **3:**29; **4:**3, 13, 18, 22²; **5:**13, 17; **6:**10²; **7:**3, 69, 28; **10:**34; **11:**19; **12:**25, 27, 37, 39, 44; **13:**11, 19, 31; **Est** 1:2, 11; **2:**3, 19, 21; **3:**2, 3; **4:**14; **5:**5, 9,

13; **6:**10²; **8:**3, 9; **9:**27, 31; **Job** 1:13, 18, 20; **3:**11, 13, 17; **4:**9²; **5:**14, 22, 23; **6:**28, 29; **9:**13; **12:**5; **14:**7, 9; **15:**23, 25; **16:**4, 9, 10, 14; **17:**8; **18:**20; **21:**5, 23; **22:**21; **23:**9; **26:**11; **27:**10; **28:**27; **29:**24; **30:**3, 5, 20; **31:**1, 9, 22, 29; **35:**5²; **37:**1, 12, 21; **39:**7, 9, 18, 22, 25, 27, 28; **40:**11, 12, 15; **41:**29; **Ps** 2:4; **7:**4; **10:**5; **11:**2; **16:**7, 8, 11; **17:**3; **18:**15², 39; **19:**6; **21:**9, 12; **22:**9; **27:**6; **34:**1; **35:**16, 21; **37:**12, 13; **40:**15; **42:**8; **44:**14, 16; **45:**9; **46:**5; **51:**5; **52:**6; **55:**3², 6, 11, 14; **59:**6, 8², 14; **62:**8; **64:**4²; **68:**16, 29; **69:**12; **76:**6; **77:**2; **79:**12; **80:**16, 17; **81:**3, 7; **83:**9, 10; **89:**12; **91:**6, 7²; **92:**2, 4; **95:**8²; **99:**5, 9; **104:**7², 27, 32; **105:**39; **106:**19; **107:**27; **109:**6, 31; **110:**1, 5; **114:**7²; **116:**7; **119:**20, 62, 161; **121:**5; **132:**7; **141:**7; **145:**15; **Pr** 1:21, 26, 33; **5:**11; **6:**8; **7:**6, 9, 11, 12, 14, 19, 22; **8:**3, 30, 34²; **9:**14²; **12:**16; **14:**9, 19, 30; **15:**31; **16:**7; **17:**17; **19:**28; **20:**4, 21²; **23:**5, 31; **24:**7; **25:**13; **26:**10; **31:**18, 23, 25, 31; **Ecc** 1:3; **2:**23; **5:**6, 8; **10:**13², 17; **11:**4, 6; **12:**4, 6²; **SS** 1:6, 7, 12; **3:**8, 11; **5:**6; **6:**11; **7:**13; **8:**1; **Isa** 1:26; **3:**6; **5:**11, 12, 22², 26, 27, 30; **6:**4; **7:**3, 9, 19; **9:**3; **10:**26, 28, 29, 32³; **13:**8, 13, 22; **14:**7², 9, 16; **16:**2, 3, 10, 12; **18:**7; **19:**7, 10, 16, 19; **20:**2; **21:**3, 8; **30:**17²; **31:**9; **33:**3; **36:**2²; **38:**1; **39:**1; **41:**1, 12; **47:**12; **48:**6, 16; **49:**15, 23; **51:**6, 20; **52:**4, 14; **56:**1; **57:**4; **59:**10, 14; **60:**14, 16; **63:**12; **65:**20; **66:**2, 5, 11; **Jer** 1:1; **2:**11, 12, 15, 24, 33; **3:**17; **4:**10, 11, 23², 24, 29; **6:**4, 5, 15, 16; **7:**2; **8:**1, 12, 16; **10:**18; **11:**12, 18; **12:**1, 8; **13:**5; **15:**7, 8; **17:**19²; **18:**3, 7, 9; **19:**7; **20:**2², 16; **25:**20, 33; **26:**10; **28:**11; **31:**1, 26; **32:**7, 9; **33:**9, 15, 20; **36:**8, 10², 16, 22; **37:**9, 13; **38:**3, 14, 17, 14, 14, 14, 14, 14, 14, 14, 14, 14, 14, 39:**4, 5, 6, 10, 11, 12; **40:**1, 6, 8, 10, 12, 13; **41:**1, 3, 14, 17; **43:**9; **44:**17; **46:**2², 47:**3²; **48:**11, 16, 28; **49:**8, 21, 31; **50:**4, 14, 16, 20, 46; **51:**33; **52:**7, 9, 10, 17, 26, 27, 33; **La** 1:2, 5, 7², 21; **2:**3, 15², 19; **3:**53, 63; **4:**1, 18; **5:**4, 5, 9, 13; **Eze** 1:15; **3:**15, 16; **4:**10, 11, 17; **5:**16; **8:**12, 16, 17; **9:**2, 3, 6, 11; **10:**19; **11:**1, 10, 11; **12:**6, 7, 12; **14:**3; **16:**8, 25, 31; **18:**6, 8, 11, 13, 15; **21:**15, 21²; **22:**9, 13²; **23:**38; **24:**27; **25:**9; **26:**10, 15, 16, 18; **27:**3, 35, 36; **28:**10, 19; **29:**13; **30:**18; **31:**16; **32:**10; **33:**30; **35:**5; **36:**38; **38:**12, 17, 19, 20; **39:**14, 19, 20; **40:**1, 40, 44²; **41:**7, 15, 17, 21; **42:**3, 12; **43:**7, 27; **44:**17; **45:**17²; **46:**2, 3, 9, 11, 19², 24; **48:**1; **Da** 1:15, 18; **2:**16, 25, 35, 49²; **3:**8; **4:**4, 34, 36; **5:**29, 31; **6:**4, 19, 24; **7:**2, 7, 13; **8:**6, 8; **10:**2, 3, 8; **11:**27², 29, 35, 39, 40, 45; **12:**1²; **Hos** 1:4, 6; **2:**7; **5:**1; **9:**1, 7; **12:**4; **Joel** 2:1, 6, 11, 16; **3:**1; **Am** 6:2; **7:**13; **8:**9; **9:**3; **Ob** 1:14; **Jnh** 1:16; **4:**2, 5, 7; **Mic** 1:10; **2:**1, 13; **3:**4; **7:**1; **Na** 1:5; **3:**10, 13, 19; **Hab** 1:3, 5, 8, 10²; **2:**1, 5; **3:**11²; **16**; **Zep** 1:12; **2:**4; **3:**6, 19, 20²; **Zec** 1:11; **3:**1; **4:**2; **7:**7; **8:**6, 21; **11:**13; **13:**6; **14:**14; **Mal** 1:13; **4:**4; **Mt** 1:11; **3:**10, 16; **4:**20; **5:**23, 28, 34; **6:**26; **7:**3, 28; **8:**6, 11, 13, 28; **9:**3, 9, 10, 14; **10:**11, 19; **11:**25; **12:**1, 41², 42; **13:**20, 30, 40, 49, 57; **14:**1, 2, 34; **15:**30, 16:21; **17:**12; **18:**1; **19:**4, 26, 28; **20:**21³, 23; **21:**2, 14, 41; **22:**28, 30, 33, 44; **23:**6, 24, 10, 23, 30, 33, 37, 39, 43, 44, 45; **25:**1, 6, 16, 26², 7, 8, 19, 20, 49, 53²; **55:**58, 64; **27:**15, 16, 39, 51; **28:**1²; **Mk** 1:9, 12, 18, 22, 33, 43; **2:**14, 15; **3:**5², 34; **4:**1, 16; **5:**7, 22, 30, 33, 40, 42; **6:**3, 6, 14, 25, 48, 53; **7:**25, 35; **8:**33; **9:**18, 20, 50; **10:**6, 21, 22, 24, 27, 37², 40; **11:**1, 4, 11, 18; **12:**15, 17, 23, 36, 39; **13:**11, 21, 26, 29, 34, 35²; **14:**3, 18, 45, 54², 62, 65, 67; **15:**6, 29, 33, 34; **16:**18, 19, 30, 41; **Lk** 1:11, 20, 29, 39; **2:**8, 18, 33, 38, 47; **3:**9; **4:**2, 22, 32, 33, 39, 42; **5:**2, 8, 9, 27, 29; **6:**10, 20, 41; **7:**9, 21, 36, 37, 38; **8:**28², 35, 41, 47, 51, 53, 55; **9:**31, 36, 38, 39, 43²; **10:**14, 21, 39; **11:**5, 31, 32², 37; **12:**12, 37, 39, 40, 42, 46; **13:**1, 11, 29, 31; **14:**7, 14, 15², 17; **16:**14, 20; **17:**12, 16; **18:**13, 24; **19:**5, 6, 37; **22:**14, 26, 28, 30, 40, 44, 57, 14:1, 2, 34; **15:**30, 16:21; **17:**12; **18:**13, 24; **19:**5, 6, 37; **20:**21², 23; **21:**2, 14, 41; **22:**14, 3, 4, 7, 8, 12, 15, 16², 17, 19, 20; **23:**7, 35, 39, 49; **24:**30, 33, 39, 41, 53; **Jn** 1:18, 28, 42; **2:**1, 11, 14, 23; **3:**2, 7, 23; **4:**35, 45, 46, 50, 52, 53; **5:**9, 14, 17, 28; **6:**39, 40, 41, 44, 54; **7:**11, 25, 30; **8:**2, 7, 9², 52, 56, 59; **9:**28, 34; **10:**19, 22; **11:**20, 24, 30, 32, 49, 56; **12:**1, 2, 16, 20, 42, 45, 48; **13:**22², 28, 32; **14:**11; **16:**4, 31; **18:**16, 17, 20, 27; **19:**13, 19, 41; **20:**5, 12²; **14:**20; **21:**20; **Ac** 1:6; **2:**25, 34; **3:**1², 4², 10², 12; **4:**18, 35, 37; **5:**2, 4, 10², 15; **21, 23, 26; **6:**15; **7:**5, 16, 20, 31, 36, 54, 55, 56, 57²; **58; **8:**1, 18, 40; **9:**20, 38; **10:**1, 3, 4, 17, 25, 30², **11:**11, 5, 9, 11; **11:**34; **12:**5; **13:**12, 14; **14:**3²; **16:**4, 14, 18; **17:**1, 6², 7, 10, 12², 13², 17, 19; **18:**10, 13, 20, 20¹; **3², 11; **21:**8, 13², 21, 23; **22:**1, 7, 9, 17, 19,

14:27², 35; **15:**6, 29, 52; **16:**8, 16, 19; **2Co** 3:7, 13; **4:**12²; **5:**6, 8, 9; **7:**5, 11; **8:**14; **9:**8; **11:**26; **Gal** 1:7; **2:**8²; **4:**29; **5:**2; **6:**9; **Eph** 1:20; **2:**2, 3, 12; **3:**20; **Php** 1:1; **2:**10; **4:**3, 10; **Col** 1:2; **2:**1; **3:**1, 23; **4:**13, 15; **1Th** 2:13, 16; **5:**7², 23; **2Th** 1:10; **2:**6, 7; **3:**16; **2Ti** 4:13, 16, 17; **Tit** 1:3; **2:**5; **3:**3, 12; **Heb** 1:1, 3, 13; **2:**8; **3:**14; **7:**13; **8:**1, 5; **9:**26; **10:**12, 33; **11:**3; **12:**2, 11, 26; **13:**10; **Jas** 1:23, 24; **2:**10; **3:**2; **5:**9; **1Pe** 2:23; **3:**22; **4:**12; **2Pe** 2:20²; **3:**14; **1Jn** 1:1, 5; **2:**28; **3:**19; **Jude** 1:12; **Rev** 1:17; **2:**5, 11, 19; **3:**3, 9, 20; **4:**2; **7:**1, 17; **8:**3; **9:**14; **11:**13; **12:**17; **18:**10, 15; **19:**10²; **21:**12; **22:**8.

BE (5161)

Ge 1:3, 6, 9, 14, 15, 22, 28, 29; **2:**18, 23, 24; **3:**5², 16, 22; **4:**7, 12, 14²; **6:**3, 15, 20, 21; **8:**17; **9:**1, 3, 6, 7, 11², 13, 25², 26², 27; **10:**8; **11:**4, 6; **12:**2, 3, 13², 19; **13:**16; **14:**19, 20, 23; **15:**1, 3, 4, 5², 5, 13², 15; **16:**3, 10, 12²; **17:**1, 4, 5, 7, 8, 10, 11, 12, 13², 14, 15, 16, 17, 20; **18:**4, 5, 18, 25², 30², 31, 32²; **19:**15, 17, 20; **20:**7, 9; **21:**12², 17; **22:**14, 18; **23:**1; **24:**8, 14², 27, 41², 44; **25:**23²; **26:**3, 4, 11, 24, 28; **27:**12, 29³, 33, 39, 46; **28:**14², 19, 20, 21, 22; **29:**7, 15, 28, **30:**26, 32, 33, 34, 38; **31:**3, 8², 24, 29, 35; **32:**12, 20, 28; **33:**12; **34:**7, 14, 17, 22, 30; **35:**10², 11, 17; **37:**35; **38:**9; **39:**10; **41:**30, 31², 35, 36¹, 40²; **45:** **42:**7, 15, 16², 20; **43:**11, 23, 29; **44:**7, 10², 17, 18; **45:**5², 6, 10, 20; **46:**3, 34; **47:**14, 19, 25; **48:**5², 6, 16, 19, 21; **49:**7, 8, 12, 17, 19, 20, 29; **50:**19, 21; **Ex** 3:12², 15; **4:**14, 16; **5:**11, 18; **6:**7; **7:**1, 17, 18, 19; **8:**9, 10, 21, 22, 26², 29; **9:**16, 29; **10:**5, 7, 8, 10, 14, 26; **11:**6²; **12:**2, 5, 13, 19², 46; **13:**7², 9², 16; **14:**13, 14; **15:**15² 16; **16:**5, 7, 102², 23, 24, 26, 28, 29, 33, 34; **17:**14, 16; **18:**10, 19², 23; **19:**5, 6, 11, 12²; **13²; **20:**20², 23, 24, 26; **21:**6, 8, 12, 15, 16, 17, 19, 20, 21, 22, 28³, 29², 32, 34, 36²; **22:**3, 11, 13, 16², 19, 20, 24, 25, 27², 28; **23:**1, 13², 23², 24, 25, 26², 27², 28; **24:**3, 12², 15², 35²; **25:**37, 36; **28:**4², 38², 39, 43; **30:**2, 10, 12², 14², 15², 16, 17, 18, 19, 21, 29, 31, 36²; **31:**13, 14², 15², 17², 18²; **19:**2, 19:**5, 6, 11, 12², 20:20², 23, 24, 26, 25², 25, 33², 34², 35; **32:**5, 13, 22; **33:**23; **34:**2, 12, 13, 16², 17, 19, 20, 21, 26², 28; **35:**2; **36:**6; **38:**21; **39:**12; **40:**5, 13, 15; **Lev** 1:3, 4, 15; **2:**1, 5, 7, 11, 12; **4:**15, 20, 26, 31, 35; **5:**1, 3, 4, 9, 10, 13, 16, 18; **6:**7, 9, 12, 13, 16, 162², 17, 18³, 19², 23; **7:**6, 15, 162², 17, 18, 21, 27², 32, 34, 36; **8:**32; **10:**3, 6, 15³; **11:**12, 20, 24, 25, 26, 27, 28, 31, 32³, 33, 34², 35, 37, 39, 40², 41, 43, 44, 45², 47²; **12:**2, 3, 4, 5², 7, 8; **13:**2, 3, 4, 6, 7, 9, 14, 17, 20, 25, 30, 31, 32, 33, 34²; **45, 46, 52, 54, 57, 58²; **14:**4², 5, 7, 8², 9, 10²; **11², 13², 14², 15², 16, 18², 19, 21; **15:**4, 5, 6², 7, 8², 9, 10, 11², 12², 13², 14², 15, 16²; **16:**4, 16:**10², 17, 27², 29, 30²; **34²; **17:**4², 7, 9, 13, 14, 15², 16; **18:4, 5, 18, 21, 29; **19:**2, 5, 6², 7, 8², 20², 20, 23, 24, 25, 29, 31, 34², 7², 9, 10, 11², 12², 13², 14², 15, 16²; **17², 18, 19, 20, 21, 26², 27²; **21:**6², 9, 13; **22:**3, 4, 5, 6, 7, 9, 19, 20, 21, 23, 25, 27, 30, 32, 33; **23:**11, 14, 18, 21, 29, 31, 41; **24:**2, 3, 4, 7, 8, 12, 15, 16², 17, 19, 20; **25:**6, 7, 10, 11, 12, 18, 23, 28, 30, 31³, 33, 34, 38, 40, 41, 42, 50, 53, 54²; **26:**10, 12², 13, 17, 20, 22², 23, 24, 25², 26, 27, 28, 29², 32, 33; **27:**11, 12, 16, 18, 20, 25, 27, 28, 29², 32, 33, 36; **Nu** 1:50, 51², 53; **2:**7, 10, 14, 18, 20, 22, 25, 29; **3:**9, 10, 13, 38, 45; **4:**16, 26, 27, 28; **5:**8², 22, 28²; **6:**5², 21; **7:**5, 15, 16², 71, 77, 83; **8:**11, 14, 16; **9:**7, 13, 16; **10:**6, 8, 9, 10, 21, 31, 35; **11:**33; **12:**12, 14; **14:**3²; **9², 17, 33, 42, 43; **15:**10, 11, 15, 25, 26, 28, 30, 31, 34, 40, 41; **16:**7, 22, 26, 38; **17:**3, 10; **18:**3, 4, 5, 7, 9, 10², 11, 12², 13, 14, 15, 16, 19, 20, 21; **20:**24; **21:**27²; **22:**6, 11; **23:**10, 24², 25; **24:**7, 9², 18², 22; **26:**53, 55², 56; **27:**11, 13, 17, 28:7, 14², 15, 16, 17, 24, 28; **30:**9; **31:**2, 23⁴, 24; **32:**5, 15, 22², 23², 32; **33:**54, 34:**2, 6, 4, 8, 10, 18, 19; **36:**3³, 4²; **Dt** 1:17, 21², 29², 39, 42²; **2:**4², 25; **3:**2, 13, 22; **4:**9, 19, 20, 23, 26; **5:**1, 29, 32; **6:**3, 6, 12, 17, 24, 25, 26; **7:**6, 10, 14², 16, 18², 21, 24, 25, 26; **8:**1, 9, 11, 19, 20; **9:**3; **10:**16; **11:**15, 16², 21, 24, 25, 32; **12:**1, 19, 23, 25, 27, 28²; **30², 32²; **13:**5, 9, 11, 16, 17, 14:**2, 22, 29; **15:**2, 4, 7, 8, 9², 11²; **16:**4, 18, 19; **17:**1, 6², 7, 10, 12, 13², 15², 17, 19; **18:**10, 13, 20, 21², 22; **19:**10, 13, 15², 16², 17²; **18, 19, 20, 21, 26, 27²; **21:**6², 9, 13; **22:**3, 4, 5, 6, 7, 8, 12, 15, 16², 19, 26; **23:**11, 14, 18, 21, 23, 28, 30, 31², 33, 34, 40, 41, 42, 50, 53, 54; **26:**10, 12²; **13, 17, 20, 22, 23, 24, 25, 26, 28; **27:**11, 12, 16, 24, 25, 26, 27, 28, 29², 32, 33; **Nu** 1:50, 51², 53; **2:**7, 10, 14, 18, 20, 22, 25, 29; **3:**9, 10, 13, 38, 45; **4:**16, 26, 27, 28; **5:**8², 22, 28²; **6:**5², 21; **7:**5, 15, 16², 71, 77, 83; **8:**11, 14, 16; **9:**7, 13, 16; **10:**6, 8, 9, 10, 21, 31, 35; **11:**33; **12:**12, 14; **14:**3²; **9², 17, 33, 42, 43; **15:**10, 11, 15, 25, 26, 28, 30, 31, 34, 40, 41; **16:**7, 22, 26, 38; **17:**3, 10; **18:**3, 4, 5, 7, 9, 10², 11, 12², 13, 14, 15, 16, 19, 20, 21; **20:**24; **21:**27²; **22:**6, 11; **23:**10, 24², 25; **24:**7, 9², 18², 22; **26:**53, 55², 56; **27:**11, 13, 17, 28:7, 14², 15, 16, 17, 24, 28; **30:**9; **31:**2, 23⁴, 24; **32:**5, 15, 22², 23², 32; **33:**54, 34:**2, 6², 4, 8, 10, 18, 19; **36:**3³, 4²; **Ps** 2:10²; **12²; **3:**8; **4:**1, 4, 9; **5:**11; **6:**2, 10; **9:**2, 18, 19; **10:**6, 15; **11:**6; **14:**7; **15:**5; **16:**8; **17:**15; **18:**46²; **19:**13, 14; **21:**7, 13; **22:**11, 19, 26, 30; **23:**1; **24:**7; **25:**2, 3², 16, 20, 21; **26:**11; **27:**1, 3, 6, 7, 14; **28:**1, 6, 9; **30:**6, 10²; **12; **31:**1, 2, 7, 9², 17²; **18, 21, 24; **32:**6, 9², 11; **33:**9; **34:**T, 1, 20, 21, 22; **35:**4², 5, 6, 22², 26²; **36:**3; **37:**1, 7, 9, 10², 15, 17, 20, 22, 26, 28²; **33, 36, 38²; **38:**21; **39:**12; **40:**5, 13, 14, 15, 16²; **41:**13; **44:**11, 22; **45:**6; **46:**10³; **48:**3, 14; **49:**16; **50:**3; **51:**7², 19²; **53:**6; **55:**6; **56:**1, 4, 11; **57:**5², 11²; **58:**5, 7, 9² 10; **59:**12, 13; **60:**4, 5; **61:**7; **62:**2, 6; **63:**5, 9, 10, 11; **64:**7; **65:**1; **66:**8, 20; **67:**1, 2, 4; **68:**1, 3², 19, 35; **69:**6², 23², 25², 32; **70:**2², 4², **71:**1, 3, 12, 13; **72:**6, 15, 17, 18, 19², 73:**28; **74:**9; **75:**10; **76:**7, 11; **77:**2, 9; **78:**6, 8, 71; **79:**5; **80:**3, 7, 19; **81:**16; **83:**1², 4, 17; **84:**10; **85:**5; **86:**17; **87:**5; **89:**24², 37, 52; **90:**13, 14, 16; **91:**4, 15; **92:**7, 9; **93:**1; **94:**3, 15, 20; **96:**4, 10, 11, 12; **97:**1; **101:**2, 4, 6; **102:**18, 21, 26, 28; **104:**5, 34, 35; **106:**46, 48; **108:**5², 6; **109:**7, 8, 9, 10², 14², 17; **18, 20, 28, 29; **110:**3; **111:**4; **112:**2²; **6², 9, 10; **113:**2, 3; **115:**1, 8, 15; **116:**7; **118:**6, 24; **119:**4, 6, 12, 35, 38, 46, 58, 71, 76, 78, 80², 116, 117, 173; **122:**6, 7, 8; **124:**6²; **125:**1, 5; **127:**5; **128:**2, 3², 6; **129:**5, 6, 8; **130:**2; **132:**9, 18; **135:**4², 18, 21; **139:**12, 16; **140:**9, 10, 11; **141:**2², 4, 6; **143:**7; **144:**1, 12², 13, 14; **149:**2, 6; **Pr** 1:9, 31, 33; **2:**10, 22²; **3:**7, 10, 18, 22, 24²; 26; **4:**10, 12; **5:**17²; **18, 19, 20; **6:**6, 15, 33;

7:20; 8:33; 9:9, 11²; 10:7, 9, 24, 30, 31; 11:21, 25, 29; 12:3², 9²; 13:7²; 14:11, 14, 26, 33; 15:31; 16:5, 19; 17:11; 18:5; 19:2, 7, 18, 20, 22; 20:20, 21; 21:13, 17, 25, 28; 22:1, 8, 9, 13, 19, 26, 27; 23:15, 17, 18, 19, 25, 34; 24:8, 14, 19, 20; 25:5, 15; 26:4, 5, 26²; 27:6, 11, 14, 18, 23; 28:8, 11, 17, 20; 29:1, 6, 14, 19, 25; 30:17²; 28; 31:30; Ecc 1:9²; 11, 15²; 2:1, 16²; 19; 3:2, 7, 12, 14, 15, 17; 4:12; 5:2³, 6, 8, 19; 7:9, 14, 16², 17², 23, 24; 8:3, 15; 9:8, 17; 10:8, 9²; 11:6, 8, 9; 12:12; SS 1:7; 2:17; 6:8; 7:8; 8:7, 14; Isa 1:5, 18², 20, 26, 27, 28, 29²; 30; 2:2², 9, 11², 12, 17²; 3:6, 10, 11, 24; 4:1, 2³, 3, 5, 6; 5:5², 13, 15, 16, 30; 6:9², 10, 13²; 7:4²; 8²; 14, 16, 23, 24; 8:4, 9³, 10, 14³, 15², 22; 9:1, 5², 6², 7, 19²; 20²; 10:16, 19, 22, 24, 25, 27², 33²; 11:5, 9, 10, 13², 14, 16; 12:2, 5; 13:10, 15, 16², 19, 20, 22; 14:20, 24, 25, 29, 32; 16:4, 5, 14²; 17:1, 2, 3, 5, 9², 11; 18:6, 7²; 19:5, 7, 10²; 16, 17, 18, 19, 20, 23, 24, 25; 20:5; 21:7, 17; 22:14, 19, 21, 23, 25²; 23:2, 4, 5, 11, 15, 16, 18²; 24:2, 3, 13, 18, 22³, 23; 25:2, 9, 10; 26:1, 11; 27:9⁴, 12; 28:3, 4, 5, 6, 13, 16, 18², 28; 29:2, 7, 8, 9³, 16, 17, 20, 21, 22; 30:3, 5, 8, 14, 16, 18, 19, 20, 23, 26, 32; 31:8; 32:2, 3, 4, 5², 14, 17², 20; 33:1², 2², 6, 10², 12², 16², 20², 21², 23, 24; 34:3², 4, 7², 9, 10, 11, 30; 35:1, 2, 4, 5, 8³, 9², 36:15; 37:4, 6, 10, 11, 30; 38:10, 11, 22; 39:6², 7², 8; 40:4, 5, 9, 31; 41:1, 6, 10, 11², 12, 14, 23; 42:4, 6, 17; 43:2³, 5, 10; 44:2, 8, 11², 26², 27, 28²; 45:1, 14, 16, 17², 18², 21, 22, 23, 24, 25; 46:5, 13; 47:1, 3, 5, 8; 48:11, 14, 19; 49:5, 6, 8, 9, 19², 23², 24, 25, 26; 50:7²; 51:3, 7, 14, 23; 52:3, 11, 12, 13; 53:11; 54:4², 6, 9, 10⁴, 13², 14³, 15; 55:6, 12, 13²; 56:1, 5, 7², 12; 57:1, 14, 16; 58:4, 8, 11, 12; 59:15; 60:5², 7², 11, 12, 16, 18, 19³, 20, 21; 61:3, 6², 7, 9; 62:2, 3, 4²; 63:7, 8, 12, 14; 64:5, 9; 65:13, 16, 17, 18², 19, 20³, 22, 23, 25; 66:1, 5², 8², 10, 11, 12, 13, 14², 16, 21, 24²; Jer 1:8, 14, 17; 2:12, 36, 37; 3:1, 5, 12, 16³; 4:2², 9³, 11, 14, 27; 5:13; 6:6, 11, 12, 15; 7:20², 23², 33; 8:1, 2³, 9²; 12, 13³, 17; 10:2, 5, 18; 11:4², 16, 19, 23; 12:3, 4, 11², 12, 16; 13:10, 11, 12², 15, 17, 19³, 26, 27; 14:16²; 19; 15:9, 18, 19; 16:4²; 6; 17:6, 8, 11, 13², 14², 15, 17, 18², 21, 25; 18:7, 9, 16², 18, 20, 21², 22, 23; 19:8, 11, 13; 20:6, 10, 11², 14², 15, 16; 21:10; 22:9, 20, 22, 28; 23:3, 4², 6², 12, 40; 24:2, 3, 7², 8; 25:14, 33³, 34², 37; 26:9², 11, 15, 16, 18, 24; 27:16, 18, 22; 28:9; 29:14, 17, 26, 28; 30:7⁴, 10, 16², 18, 19², 20², 21², 22²; 31:1² 4, 6, 8, 12, 13, 14, 15, 16, 30, 32, 33², 36, 37², 38, 40²; 32:4, 15, 24, 25, 36, 38², 43, 44²; 33:4, 5, 9, 10, 12, 16²; 21; 34:3; 36:30; 37:17, 21; 38:3, 4, 17², 18, 20, 22, 23²; 39:16, 17; 40:9, 15; 42:5, 11², 14, 18², 19, 22; 44:28, 29; 46:15, 19, 21, 23², 24, 26, 27; 47:5, 6; 48:1³, 2⁴, 11², 13, 15, 26, 28, 41², 42, 44; 49:2, 5, 10, 13, 17, 20, 22, 26, 29², 32, 36; 50:2³, 5, 8, 9², 10, 12², 13³, 19, 20³, 27, 30, 31, 36, 37, 39, 45; 51:6, 8², 9, 13, 26², 35², 37, 44², 43, 46, 47, 56², 58, 62; 52:20; La 2:20; 3:29, 30, 54, 65; 4:21³; 5:4; Eze 1:16, 27; 2:6³; 3:9, 12, 20, 25, 26; 4:3², 17²; 5:13, 15; 6:4², 6²; 7:11, 13, 15, 16, 18³, 19², 24, 25, 26, 27; 8:2; 10:5, 8; 11:3, 11², 20³; 12:11, 12, 13, 19, 20³, 23, 24, 25, 28²; 13:6, 9², 14²; 14:10, 11², 16², 18, 21, 23², 23; 15:5; 16:13, 42, 52, 54, 61, 63; 17:9, 14, 17, 20, 21; 18:13²; 20², 22², 24, 30; 19:14, 20:19; 20:32, 47², 48; 21:4, 11², 15, 24, 26³, 27, 29², 32²; 22:14, 21, 22; 23:25, 29, 33; 24:8, 10, 11, 13², 14, 24, 27³; 25:10; 26:6, 10, 13, 14, 21³; 27:36; 28:9, 19; 29:5, 14, 15, 16²; 30:4², 7, 11, 13, 16², 18²; 31:2, 18²; 32:6, 10, 12, 13, 19, 20, 28, 31, 32; 33:4², 5, 6, 12, 13, 16, 27; 34:10, 14, 22, 23, 24², 26, 27, 28, 29; 35:4², 9, 10, 15; 36:9, 10, 11, 12, 25, 27; 38², 32, 33, 34, 38; 37:22³, 23², 24², 25, 26, 27³; 38:5, 7, 8, 9, 18, 19, 20, 21; 39:7, 11², 12, 13, 14, 16, 25; 43:10, 11, 12, 18, 22; 44:2, 14, 28²; 45:1, 2, 3, 4, 8, 11², 15², 17; 46:1², 2, 4, 5², 10, 11, 12², 15, 16, 18; 47:9, 10³, 11, 15, 18, 19, 20², 22; 48:1, 8³, 9, 10³, 11, 13, 15², 17, 18, 20, 21, 29, 30, 31², 32, 33, 34, 35²; Da 1:5; 2:18, 20, 40, 41, 42, 43, 44²; 3:6, 11³, 15, 18², 22, 25², 26, 27², 32; 4:12; 5:7³; 10, 16, 28, 29²; 6:8, 12, 13, 15, 16, 27; 7:14, 23, 25², 26, 27²; 8:11, 13², 14, 25; 9:25²; 26; 10:12, 19³; 11:2, 4², 6, 7, 11, 12, 15, 16, 19, 20, 21, 22², 25, 26, 29, 31, 33, 35, 36, 41; 12:1², 6, 7², 8, 10², 11; Hos 1:10³, 11²; 2:17; 3:3²; 4:9; 5:9, 14; 7:16; 8:5, 6; 9:1, 4³, 6, 17; 10:6³, 8, 10, 14, 15; 12:11; 13:3, 15, 16; 14:5, 6, 7; Joel 2:2, 18, 21², 22, 23, 27, 31, 32²; 3:12, 15, 16, 17, 19, 20; Am 3:12, 14, 15²; 4:2, 3; 5:5, 14, 16², 17, 18, 19, 20; 6:7; 7:9²; 17; 8:5², 8²; 9:1, 5, 8, 9, 13, 15; Ob 1:2, 6, 9², 10², 15, 16, 17², 18³, 21; Jnh 2:8; 3:4, 8; 4:4, 8, 9, 11; Mic 1:7³; 2:3, 7, 11; 3:7, 12; 4:1², 8, 4:7; 5:2, 3, 5, 7, 8, 9²; 6:7, 14²; 7:5, 8, 10², 16, 17, 20; Na 1:10², 12, 15; 2:7, 13;

Hab 1:5; 2:14, 16², 20; 3:18; Zep 1:7, 11², 13, 14, 15, 17, 18²; 2:3, 4², 5, 6, 11, 12, 14²; 3:6, 7, 8, 11², 13, 14; Hag 1:2, 4, 8, 9; 2:4³, 9; Zec 1:4, 16²; 2:4, 5², 10, 11, 13; 5:3²; 11; 6:13³, 14; 8:3², 5, 8², 9², 13³, 15; 9:4, 5, 7, 10, 15, 17; 10:5, 6, 7², 8, 10, 11²; 11:9, 17²; 12:2, 7, 8², 11; 13:1, 2, 4, 7, 8²; 14:1, 2², 4, 6, 7², 9², 10, 11³, 13, 14, 19, 20², 21²; Mal 1:4, 8, 9, 11³, 14; 2:3, 7², 9, 4, 5, 10, 12, 17; 4:1², 3; Mt 1:18², 20, 23; 2:4, 6, 18, 23; 3:10, 13, 14, 15; 4:1; 5:4, 6, 7, 9, 12, 13², 14, 19², 21, 22², 24, 25, 29, 37, 45, 48; 6:1², 2, 4, 5², 7, 8, 9, 10, 18, 21, 22, 23, 24, 33; 7:1², 2², 7², 8; 8:3, 8, 12², 13, 9:15, 17, 21, 29; 10:15, 16, 17, 18, 19, 20, 22, 25, 26³, 28², 31, 36, 11:22, 23, 24, 25, 27, 31², 32², 33², 37², 39, 40, 45; 13:12², 14², 30, 40, 42, 49, 50; 14:9, 27; 15:4, 13; 16:2, 3, 4, 6², 11, 19², 21², 26, 27; 17:4, 7, 11, 20, 22, 23; 18:6², 8, 9, 14, 16, 18², 19, 25, 26, 29, 34; 19:5, 21, 25, 27², 30²; 20:16², 18, 19², 26, 27², 28, 31; 21:13, 21, 43, 44²; 22:11, 28, 30², 45; 23:7, 8, 10, 11, 12², 26; 24:2², 3, 7, 9³, 13, 14, 19, 21², 22, 27, 29², 37, 40², 41², 43, 44, 46, 51; 25:1, 9, 14, 29², 30, 32; 26:2², 5, 13, 24, 31, 37, 39², 42, 54, 56; 27:25, 26, 58, 64²; 28:5, 10; Mk 1:25, 41; 2:20, 22; 3:14, 28, 29; 4:12², 22², 24, 25², 39; 5:23, 28, 34, 36; 6:20, 50; 7:10, 34; 8:12, 15, 31², 38; 9:5, 12¹, 31, 35², 42², 45, 47, 49, 50; 10:7, 26, 31, 33, 38, 39, 43, 44², 45, 48; 11:17, 23, 24; 12:7, 23, 25², 37, 38, 40; 13:2², 4², 7, 8, 9, 10, 13, 17², 19³, 24², 25; 14:9, 21², 27, 33, 49; 15:15; 16:6, 16²; Lk 1:13, 14, 15², 18, 20, 29, 30, 31, 32², 34, 35², 36, 48, 55, 60, 66, 68, 76; 2:1, 5, 6, 10², 12, 23, 34², 35, 49; 3:5, 7, 9, 12, 16, 17; 4:7, 35, 5:10, 13, 15, 35, 37, 38; 6:18, 21, 34, 35², 36, 37³, 38³, 40; 7:7², 8; 12², 17², 18², 50²; 9:22³, 26, 33, 44, 46, 48; 10:11, 12, 14², 15, 31, 40, 42; 11:2, 9², 10, 17, 19, 20, 30, 33, 36, 41, 50, 51; 12:1, 2², 3², 4, 7, 9, 10², 15, 19, 20, 21, 31, 32, 33, 34, 37, 38, 39, 40, 43, 47, 48³, 52, 53, 58, 59; 13:14, 16, 21, 24, 28, 29³, 30², 31, 32², 35²; 14:10, 11², 12, 14², 23, 24, 26, 27, 33, 34; 15:7, 14, 19, 21, 32; 16:2, 9, 10³, 13, 31; 17:2², 6, 24, 26², 30, 34², 35²; 18:14², 26, 31, 32, 33, 35³, 41; 19:7, 12, 16, 17², 21, 24, 26², 27, 33², 38, 40²; 20:10, 20, 28, 31; 21:13, 14², 26, 33, 34, 35; 22:5, 10, 15, 16, 24²; 23:3, 10, 24, 30, 35; 24:4, 5, 8, 15, 19, 25:6, 10, 15, 17, 20, 21, 26:28; 27:10, 17 22², 24, 29, 31; 28:4, 26²; Ro 1:1, 4, 7, 10, 12², 13, 19, 20, 26, 32; 2:5, 8, 9, 12, 13, 26; 3:4², 19, 20, 26; 4:11, 13, 16², 18; 5:9, 10, 19, 6:5, 6², 14, 17², 18², 7:1, 14, 8:11, 13², 14; 9:3², 4, 5, 11², 15; 10:2², 6, 8, 9, 11, 14; 11:6, 19, 27, 32; 12:1, 3, 15, 16, 17², 18, 19, 22, 25; 13:8; 14:5, 6, 9, 17, 20², 24², 25, 26, 31, 34, 38, 39, 40, 45; 15:9, 19, 22, 26, 28², 33³; 16:1², 7, 13², 25; Ac 1:5, 8, 16, 20², 2:3, 20, 21, 25, 36, 38; 3:13, 14, 19, 23, 25; 4:12; 5:27, 34, 36, 39; 6:2, 3; 7:6², 35, 49; 8:36; 9:6, 17; 10:23, 40, 48; 11:14, 16; 12:4, 15, 17, 19; 13:11², 39; 14:9; 15:1, 16:17, 22, 30, 31, 36; 17:17, 18; 18:6; 9², 14, 15; 19:27²; 36, 39, 40; 20:10, 20, 28, 31; 21:13, 14², 26, 33, 34, 35; 22:5, 10, 15, 16, 24²; 23:3, 10, 24, 30, 35; 24:4, 5, 8, 15, 19, 25:6, 10, 15, 17, 20, 21, 26:28; 27:10, 17, 22², 24, 29, 31; 28:4; Ro 1:1, 4, 7, 10, 12², 13, 19, 20, 26, 32; 2:5, 8, 9, 12, 13, 26; 3:4², 19, 20, 26; 4:11, 13, 16², 18; 5:9, 10, 19, 6:5, 6², 14, 17², 18², 7:1, 14, 8:11, 13², 14; 9:3², 4, 5, 11², 15; 10:2², 6, 8, 9, 11, 14; 11:6, 19, 27, 32; 12:1, 3, 15, 16, 17², 18, 19; 13:8; 14:5, 6, 9, 17, 20², 24²; 15:9, 19, 22, 26, 28², 33³; 16:1², 7, 13², 25; 1Co 1:1, 2, 7, 8, 9, 10, 19²; 2:1, 3, 13², 17²; 5:5, 6:13, 14, 16²; 7:1, 4, 5; 8:9, 12; 9:33; 12:46; 13:4, 10; Est 2:6, 8; 4:1, 8; 6:3; 7:4²; Job 6:3, 13, 20, 24, 7:3²; 10:19; 16:17; 19:7, 26; 20:4; 31:7², 9, 11, 28; 33:6; 38:17; Ps 13:6; 18:23; 22:10; 27:9; 42:3; 44:17; 45:2; 60:1; 61:1; 71:5, 24; 73:14²; 88:5; 89:38, 50; 90:1; 92:10; 116:7; 119:56, 92, 140; 124:1, 2, 7; 141:7; Pr 6:2; Ecc 1:9²; 2:12; 3:15²; 4:3, 14; 6:10²; 12:13; Isa 1:9; 5:4; 9:10; 10:22; 14:8, 11, 12; 16:9; 21:2²; 22:3, 23:4; 25:4; 27:7; 30:33³; 33:1²; 36:20; 38:12; 40:2²; 42:14, 22; 48:8, 18, 19²; 49:5; 50:5²; 52:5; 53:1; 57:11²; 60:15; 61:4; 63:19; 64:11; Jer 2:10, 31; 3:2, 3, 20; 5:11²; 7:11; 9:12²; 11:19; 13:22; 18:13²; 35:14²; 37:4; 39:15; 40:7, 12; 41:1; 42:18³; 43:5; 44:18; 48:11; 49:25; 50:6; 51:5, 51, 60; La 1:14, 20; 3:17; 5:2, 11, 12; Eze 2:3, 5; 5:7; 6:9²; 9:3; 11:16, 17; 15:8; 17:8; 18:19; 20:34, 41; 22:16; 23:17; 24:12, 18; 26:10; 28:25; 29:6; 30:21; 33:24, 33; 34:8; 35:12²; 36:4, 23; 38:8²; 40:4, 47; 44:19; Da 2:30; 4:31, 33; 5:3, 27; 6:10, 20; 7:12; 8:26; 9:5, 11, 12², 26; 10:11; 11:21, 36; 12:7; Hos 2:5; 5:1; 9:1; 14:1; Joel 1:5, 16, 17; Am 2:4; 3:5; 7:1; Ob 1:16; Jnh 2:4; 4:10; Mic 7:2; Zep 3:19; Zec 1:12; 8:13; 11:2; 13:5; Mal 1:4; 2:11; Mt 1:6; 2:2, 12, 16, 22; 4:12; 5:31; 9:20, 25; 23:37; 10:25; 11:12, 20, 21, 23, 27; 13:11, 52; 14:4; 15:32; 17:9; 19:11; 20:6, 23; 22:3, 4²; 23:35; 24:22; 25:21, 23; 26:9, 24; 27:8, 64; 28:15, 18; Mk 4:11; 5:4, 15, 18, 25; 6:2, 14, 16, 18; 8:2; 9:21; 10:40; 14:5, 21; 16:4, 10; Lk 1:1, 4, 13, 19, 48; 2:11, 17, 20, 21, 22, 26, 48; 4:6; 5:25; 7:10, 29, 30, 47²; 8:2, 10, 29, 36; 9:36; 10:13; 11:14, 50; 12:32; 14:8; 15:29, 16:11, 12; 19:11, 12; 22:22², 23:8; 12, 19; 24:49; Jn 1:3, 24; 2:2, 9; 3:21; 4:45; 5:5, 6, 10; 6:22; 7:39²; 8:25, 33; 9:13, 18, 24; 10:40; 11:13, 17, 21, 31, 32, 39; 12:16, 38; 14:9, 12; 15:27; 16:25; 17:12; 19:32, 41; 38; 21:25; 22:25; 26:6; 28:7, 12, 25, 30³, 31, 33, 38, 39, 40, 41, 43, 44², 62, 68; 29:4, 7, 15, 29; 30:17²; 32:5, 27; 33:9; 34:4, 6; Jos 1:12, 14; 2:4², 6, 20; 3:4²; 5:5, 12, 14; 6:10, 18, 24, 25; 7:1, 4; 8:9, 14, 20, 23, 27; 9:7, 8, 12, 13, 14, 18, 19, 21; 10:19, 20, 33; 11:14, 13; 13:14, 33; 14:3, 4; 16:10³; 17:8, 9, 13, 17, 18; 18:2; 19:47; 21:12; 22:3, 5, 19, 26, 28; 23:8, 12, 15; 24:3, 4, 7, 8, 10, 11, 15², 21; Jdg 1:6, 19, 25, 27, 28, 29, 30, 33, 35; 2:2, 17, 19; 3:9, 25; 4:8, 9, 16, 21; 5:19, 31; 6:10, 13², 15, 23, 37; 7:4²; 8:2, 35; 9:5, 11, 12; 14:6, 10, 19; 16:13, 9, 12, 20, 22; 19:2, 5, 10, 24, 25, 28; 20:9, 13, 22, 40, 42, 47; 21:14, 19; My 14, 16, 17, 21; 3:3, 13, 14; 4:4; 1Sa 1:2, 5, 11, 13; 2:4, 5², 9, 11, 15², 18, 25, 30³; 3:5, 16; 4:19, 20; 5:4; 6:9, 12, 19; 7:10, 17; 8:3, 6, 7, 9, 19; 9:4³, 6, 21, 27; 10:8, 14, 16, 19², 21, 27²; 11:2, 13; 12:9, 10, 11, 15, 20; 13:8, 14; 14:1, 10, 27, 36, 37, 39, 45; 15:9², 12, 14, 15, 20, 22, 26, 30, 33, 34;

BEEN (890)

Ge 2:2; 3:23; 8:2; 13:3; 14:4, 14; 16:3; 17:14; 18:8, 27, 31; 21:32; 26:8, 18, 33; 29:8; 30:30; 31:2, 5, 12, 38, 42; 32:4; 33:11; 34:5, 13, 27; 35:3; 37:3, 33; 38:14, 21, 22; 39:1, 14; 40:4; 41:7, 32; 42:28; 43:33; 44:28; 45:6; 46:27; 47:9; 48:15; Ex 3:16; 4:10; 9:19; 10:11, 14; 11:6; 12:39; 14:12, 19; 21:29; 32:8, 29; 33:12; 34:34; Lev 5:19; 8:34, 35; 10:13, 14, 19; 11:38; 13:55, 56, 58; 14:3, 43, 48; 16:16; 19:20²; 21:10, 12; 27:17; Nu 1:17; 5:13, 27; 11:28; 12:14; 13:22; 14:14; 15:28; 16:2, 39; 19:2, 13, 16, 18, 20; 22:30; 35:33; Dt 2:7; 4:32; 9:7, 24; 12:30; 13:14²; 14:24; 15:2, 18; 17:4³; 18:21; 21:3, 4; 23:1; 24:4; 30:4; 31:27; 32:22; Jos 3:4; 4:9; 5:5, 7, 8, 9; 7:7, 8, 12, 26; 8:14, 20, 24, 31; 10:14, 17, 27; 11:10; 22:22; 23:9, 14; 24:20, 33; Jdg 2:10; 9:16; 16:7, 8, 11, 13, 17²; 17:7; 19:2, 18, 30; 20:37; 21:14; Ru 1:7; 2:11, 19; 3:2; 1Sa 1:15, 16; 3:7; 4:9, 17, 19, 22; 5:4; 6:1, 3, 7; 9:20, 24; 10:2, 14, 16; 12:2; 14:21, 30², 38; 17:25, 27, 33, 34; 20:13; 21:5, 6; 22:6; 25:21, 34; 29:3, 6, 9; 30:5, 21; 2Sa 3:6; 5:17; 7:6, 9; 8:10; 10:15, 19; 12:8; 13:20, 32; 15:11, 31; 17:9, 23; 20:13; 21:5, 13; 22:24; 1Ki 3:2, 12, 15; 5:1²; 8:53, 54; 10:12, 20; 11:4; 12:19; 13:17; 14:6, 8; 15:3; 22:7; 17:9, 10, 14; 21:14, 15; 22:34; 2Ki 5:25; 8:22, 29; 9:14; 11:20; 12:10, 11; 13:7, 23; 16:18; 17:3, 28, 33; 18:4, 35; 22:4, 13; 23:22; 25:1; 1Ch 7:23; 9:19, 22; 14:2, 8; 17:8, 27; 18:10; 19:16, 19; 2Ch 6:24; 9:9, 11, 19; 10:19; 12:2; 16:6; 18:3; 21:10; 22:6, 8; 23:21; 25:24; 26:18²; 28:19; 29:34³; 30:3, 5, 26; 32:14, 15; 34:9; 14², 16, 21, 24, 30; 35:3, 18; Ezr 3:6; 4:2, 18, 19; 5:16; 8:30; 9:1, 7²; 8; 10:2, 5, 10; Ne 1:3; 2:1, 3, 13², 17; 5:5; 6:13, 14, 16; 7:1, 4, 5; 8:9, 12; 9:33; 12:46; 13:4, 10; Est 2:6, 8; 4:1, 8; 6:3; 7:4²; Job 6:3, 13, 20, 24, 7:3²; 10:19; 16:17; 19:7, 26; 20:4; 31:7², 9, 11, 28; 33:6; 38:17; Ps 13:6; 18:23; 22:10; 27:9; 42:3; 44:17; 45:2; 60:1; 61:1; 71:5, 24; 73:14²; 88:5; 89:38, 50; 90:1; 92:10; 116:7; 119:56, 92, 140; 124:1, 2, 7; 141:7; Pr 6:2; Ecc 1:9²; 2:12; 3:15²; 4:3, 14; 6:10²; 12:13; Isa 1:9; 5:4; 9:10; 10:22; 14:8, 11, 12; 16:9; 21:2²; 22:3, 23:4; 25:4; 27:7; 30:33³; 33:1²; 36:20; 38:12; 40:2²; 42:14, 22; 48:8, 18, 19²; 49:5; 50:5²; 52:5; 53:1; 57:11²; 60:15; 61:4; 63:19; 64:11; Jer 2:10, 31; 3:2, 3, 20; 5:11²; 7:11; 9:12²; 11:19; 13:22; 18:13²; 35:14²; 37:4; 39:15; 40:7, 12; 41:1; 42:18³; 43:5; 44:18; 48:11; 49:25; 50:6; 51:5, 51, 60; La 1:14, 20; 3:17; 5:2, 11, 12; Eze 2:3, 5; 5:7; 6:9²; 9:3; 11:16, 17; 15:8; 17:8; 18:19; 20:34, 41; 22:16; 23:17; 24:12, 18; 26:10; 28:25; 29:6; 30:21; 33:24, 33; 34:8; 35:12²; 36:4, 23; 38:8²; 40:4, 47; 44:19; Da 2:30; 4:31, 33; 5:3, 27; 6:10, 20; 7:12; 8:26; 9:5, 11, 12², 26; 10:11; 11:21, 36; 12:7; Hos 2:5; 5:1; 9:1; 14:1; Joel 1:5, 16, 17; Am 2:4; 3:5; 7:1; Ob 1:16; Jnh 2:4; 4:10; Mic 7:2; Zep 3:19; Zec 1:12; 8:13; 11:2; 13:5; Mal 1:4; 2:11; Mt 1:6; 2:2, 12, 16, 22; 4:12; 5:31; 9:20, 25; 23:37; 10:25; 11:12, 20, 21, 23, 27; 13:11, 52; 14:4; 15:32; 17:9; 19:11; 20:6, 23; 22:3, 4²; 23:35; 24:22; 25:21, 23; 26:9, 24; 27:8, 64; 28:15, 18; Mk 4:11; 5:4, 15, 18, 25; 6:2, 14, 16, 18; 8:2; 9:21; 10:40; 14:5, 21; 16:4, 10; Lk 1:1, 4, 13, 19, 48; 2:11, 17, 20, 21, 22, 26, 48; 4:6; 5:25; 7:10, 29, 30, 47²; 8:2, 10, 29, 36; 9:36; 10:13; 11:14, 50; 12:32; 14:8; 15:29, 16:11, 12; 19:11, 12; 22:22², 23:8; 12, 19; 24:49; Jn 1:3, 24; 2:2, 9; 3:21; 4:45; 5:5, 6, 10; 6:22; 7:39²; 8:25, 33; 9:13, 18, 24; 10:40; 11:13, 17, 21, 31, 32, 39; 12:16, 38; 14:9, 12; 15:27; 16:25; 17:12; 19:32, 41;

BUT (3983)

Ge 2:6, 17, 20; 3:3, 9; 4:4, 5, 7², 15; 6:8, 18; 8:1, 9, 12; 9:4, 23; 11:5, 31; 12:2, 17; 13:6; 14:4, 22, 24; 15:2, 4, 8, 11, 14; 16:1; 17:19, 21; 18:15, 22, 27, 30, 32; 19:3, 8, 10, 14, 18, 19, 22, 26; 20:3, 7; 21:9, 12, 26; 22:7, 11; 23:15; 24:4, 33, 38, 55, 56; 25:6, 28, 33; 26:20, 21, 29; 27:11, 22, 35, 40; 29:17, 20, 23, 31; 30:15, 27, 30, 31, 40, 42; 31:5, 15, 29, 30, 32, 33, 34, 35, 42; 32:10, 12, 21, 26, 28, 29; 33:4, 9, 13, 15; 34:8, 17, 22, 31; 35:10, 18; 37:11, 18, 22, 35; 38:7, 9, 20, 23, 29; 39:8, 12, 14, 18, 20, 40:8, 14, 17, 22; 41:8, 15, 16, 21, 24, 30, 44, 54; 42:4, 7, 13, 20, 21, 22, 24, 31, 34², 38; 43:3, 5, 21; 44:7, 17, 23, 26; 45:3, 7, 8, 22²; 46:1²; 47:24, 30; 48:14, 19, 21; 49:19, 24; 50:19, 20, 24; Ex 1:7, 12, 16, 22²; 2:3, 15, 17²; 3:11, 19; 4:9, 13, 17, 21, 23, 25; 5:4, 8, 11, 16; 6:3, 9, 12, 30; 7:3, 12, 16, 22; 8:7, 15, 18, 19, 22, 26, 28, 32; 9:4, 6, 12, 16, 21, 30; 10:8, 20, 25, 27; 11:7, 10; 12:9, 45; 13:13; 14:4, 29; 15:10, 19; 16:3, 8, 20, 26, 27; 17:1, 3, 11; 18:21, 22, 26; 19:24; 20:6, 10, 11, 19; 21:2, 3, 5, 13, 14, 18, 21, 23, 28, 29; 22:3², 8, 12, 15, 30; 23:11, 12, 29; 24:2, 11; 29:14, 33; 31:15; 32:11, 30, 32²; 33:3, 11, 12, 20, 23; 34:20, 21, 31, 34; 35:2; 40:37; Lev 2:12; 4:11; 6:16, 28, 30; 7:6, 16, 20, 24, 31; 8:17; 9:19; 10:6, 14, 19; 11:4, 10, 23, 34, 36, 38; 13:4, 7, 14, 21, 23, 26, 28, 31, 35, 42, 53, 57; 14:8, 48; 16:10; 17:16; 18:26; 19:14, 15, 18, 20, 25; 20:24; 21:14; 22:11, 13, 23, 25; 24:21; 25:4, 17, 23, 24, 28, 34, 43, 46; 27:14, 15, 27; 13:28, 31; 14:9, 10, 12, 22, 24, 32, 41; 15:27, 30; 16:10, 12, 22, 30, 42, 47, 49; 17:8; 18:3, 7, 15, 17; 19:7, 12, 20, 20:12, 16, 18; 21:4, 23, 24, 30; 22:12, 18, 20, 22, 33, 35, 38; 23:11², 13; 24:11, 10, 14, 17², 18, 20, 24; 25:9; 26:19, 61; 27:3; 30:2, 4, 5, 7, 8, 11, 12, 14; 31:18, 23; 32:17, 23, 24, 27, 30, 32; 33:55; 35:8, 22, 26, 30; Dt 1:12, 26, 38, 40, 42, 43, 45; 2:4, 11, 12, 20, 30, 35, 37; 3:7, 16, 18, 26, 28; 4:2, 4, 12, 20, 22, 26, 29; 5:3, 10, 14, 25, 31; 6:21, 23; 7:8, 10, 15, 18, 23; 8:3, 18; 9:3, 5, 19, 20, 23, 29; 10:12; 11:7, 11; 12:5, 10, 16, 23, 26, 27, 29; 14:10, 12, 20, 21, 24; 15:3, 6², 16, 23; 16:3; 17:6; 18:14, 20; 19:11; 21:15²; 22:1, 7, 9, 14, 17, 25; 23:15, 21, 22, 24, 25; 25:3; 26:6; 28:7, 12, 25, 30³, 31, 33, 38, 39, 40, 41, 43, 44², 62, 68; 29:4, 7, 15, 29; 30:17²; 32:5, 27; 33:9; 34:4, 6; Jos 1:12, 14; 2:4², 6, 20; 3:4²; 5:5, 12, 14; 6:10, 18, 24, 25; 7:1, 4; 8:9, 14, 20, 23, 27; 9:7, 8, 12, 13, 14, 18, 19, 21; 10:19, 20, 33; 11:14, 13; 13:14, 33; 14:3, 10, 15², 16, 18; 18:2; 19:47; 21:12; 22:3, 5, 19, 26, 28; 23:8, 12, 15; 24:3, 4, 7, 8, 10, 11, 15², 21; Jdg 1:6, 19, 25, 27, 28, 29, 30, 33, 35; 2:2, 17, 19; 3:9, 25; 4:8, 9, 16, 21; 5:19, 31; 6:10, 13², 15, 23, 37; 7:4²; 8:2, 35; 9:5, 11, 12; 14:6, 10, 19; 16:13, 9, 12, 20, 22; 19:2, 5, 10, 24, 25, 28; 20:9, 13, 22, 40, 42, 47; 21:14, 19; My 14, 16, 17, 21; 3:3, 13, 14; 4:4; 1Sa 1:2, 5, 11, 13; 2:4, 5², 9, 11, 15², 18, 25, 30³; 3:5, 16; 4:19, 20; 5:4; 6:9, 12, 19; 7:10, 17; 8:3, 6, 7, 9, 19; 9:4³, 6, 21, 27; 10:8, 14, 16, 19², 21, 27²; 11:2, 13; 12:9, 10, 11, 15, 20; 13:8, 14; 14:1, 10, 27, 36, 37, 39, 45; 15:9², 12, 14, 15, 20, 22, 26, 30, 33, 34;

Column 1

16:2, 7², 8, 9, 10, 11; **17:**9, 15, 34, 45; **18:**8², 11, 12, 16, 18, 23; **19:**1, 9, 10, 11, 16, 20, 23; **20:**3, 5, 7, 13, 14, 22, 25, 27, 33, 41; **21:**4, 9, 11; **22:**5, 9, 16, 17, 20; **23:**3, 14, 18; **24:**10, 11², 12, 17, 18, 22; **25:**3, 14, 19, 25, 29, 44; **26:**3, 9, 11, 23; **27:**1, 9; **28:**6, 9, 23; **29:**4, 6, 8; **30:**2, 6, 10, 22; **31:**4; **2Sa 1:**9; **2:**21, 23, 24, 31; **3:**13, 22, 26, 35; **4:**4, 12; **5:**17, 23; **6:**22; **7:**15, 22; **8:**4; **10:**11, 18; **11:**1, 9, 13, 23, 27; **12:**3, 4, 12, 14, 17, 18, 21, 23²; **13:**9, 11, 14, 16, 25, 27, 32, 37; **14:**9, 14, 24, 29²; **15:**3, 16, 21, 26, 30, 34²; **16:**10; **17:**5, 15, 18, 20; **18:**3², 12, 20, 22, 29; **19:**9, 20, 26, 28², 34, 36, 37, 43; **20:**2, 3, 5; **21:**2², 8, 17; **22:**19, 27, 28, 42²; **23:**6, 10², 12, 16, 23; **24:**3², 14, 17, 24; **1Ki 1:**4, 8, 10, 18, 19, 26, 50, 52; **2:**6, 7, 9, 15, 26, 30, 33, 36, 39, 45; **3:**7, 11, 18, 21, 22, 26; **5:**4; **8:**8, 16, 18, 19, 27, 41, 61; **9:**6, 12, 22; **10:**7; **11:**13, 17, 22, 32, 34, 39, 40; **12:**4, 8, 10, 17, 18, 22; **13:**4, 8, 18, 33; **14:**5, 8; **15:**29; **16:**2, 22, 25, 31; **17:**13; **18:**11, 18, 21², 22, 23², 25, 26, 29, 42; **19:**11², 12; **20:**6, 9, 14, 20, 23, 35; **21:**3, 6, 10, 15, 29; **22:**2, 5, 7, 8², 14, 16, 18, 27, 30, 32, 34, 48, 49; **2Ki 1:**3, 14; **2:**2, 3, 5, 17², 19; **3:**2, 5, 11, 15, 24, 25, 26; **4:**1, 6, 17, 27², 30, 31, 40, 43; **5:**1, 11, 17, 18, 26; **6:**12, 29, 32; **7:**2, 19; **8:**10, 15, 21; **9:**15, 18, 20, 27, 35; **10:**4, 9, 19; **11:**2; **12:**6, 7, 18; **13:**6, 19, 23; **14:**3, 9, 10, 19; **16:**5, 15; **17:**2, 4, 14, 32, 33, 36, 40; **18:**12, 20, 27, 36; **19:**18, 27, 29; **21:**9; **22:**7; **23:**23, 29, 34; **24:**1; **25:**5, 12; **1Ch 2:**3, 4:27; **5:**1, 25; **6:**49, 56; **9:**26, 30; **10:**4, 11:14, 18, 25; **12:**17; **14:**8, 14; **15:**2; **16:**19, 26; **17:**20; **18:**4; **19:**12, 18; **20:**1; **21:**3, 6, 13, 15, 17², 24, 30; **22:**8, 9; **23:**11, 17; **24:**2; **27:**24; **28:**3, 9; **29:**1, 14; **2Ch 1:**5, 11; **2:**6; **4:**6; **5:**9; **6:**6, 8, 9, 18, 32; **7:**19; **8:**9; **9:**6; **10:**4, 8, 10, 17, 18; **11:**2; **12:**7; **13:**9, 11, 21; **15:**2, 4, 7; **16:**12; **17:**4; **18:**4, 6, 7², 13, 15, 17, 26, 29, 31, 33; **19:**6; **20:**10, 12, 15; **21:**3, 9, 13, 20; **22:**11; **23:**6; **24:**5, 21, 22, 25; **25:**2, 4, 7, 9, 16, 18, 19, 27; **26:**16; **27:**2; **28:**9², 10, 20, 21, 23, 27; **30:**10, 18; **32:**8, 25, 31; **33:**9, 10, 17, 23; **35:**21², 22²; **36:**4, 16; **Ezr** 2:59, 62; **3:**12; **4:**3; **5:**5, 12, 16; **8:**22; **9:**8, 10; **10:**2, 13; **Ne 1:**9; **2:**2, 3, 14, 19, 20; **3:**5; **4:**7, 9, 18; **5:**5, 10, 15; **6:**2, 9, 11, 12; **7:**4, 61, 64; **9:**11, 16, 17, 26, 27, 28, 29, 31, 36; **13:**2, 6, 21, 26; **Est** 1:12, 16, 21; **2:**20, 22; **3:**2, 4, 15; **4:**2, 4, 11², 14²; **5:**9, 13; **6:**12; **7:**7; **9:**1, 10, 15, 16, 25; **Job 1:**11, 12; **2:**5, 6; **3:**26; **4:**2, 5, 16; **5:**1, 3, 8, 18²; **6:**15, 17, 25, 28; **7:**7, 8, 21; **8:**5, 9, 15²; **9:**2, 18, 35; **10:**2, 13; **11:**12, 20; **12:**3, 7; **13:**3, 14:10, 16, 18, 20, 22; **15:**4; **16:**5; **17:**7, 13; **19:**16, 20; **20:**5; **21:**16, 34; **23:**8, 10, 13; **24:**10, 12, 16, 20, 22, 23; **25:**6; **26:**14; **27:**19; **28:**12; **30:**1, 20², 28; **31:**18, 32; **32:**2, 5, 8, 12, 14; **33:**1, 8, 12, 27, 33; **34:**5, 29, 31; **35:**10; **36:**5, 6, 8, 12, 15, 17; **39:**13; **40:**5²; **41:**29; **42:**5; **Ps 1:**2, 6; **3:**3; **5:**7, 11; **9:**18, 20; **10:**14; **11:**5; **13:**5; **14:**6; **15:**4; **18:**18, 26, 27, 41²; **20:**7, 8; **22:**2, 6, 19, 24; **25:**3; **26:**11; **28:**3; **30:**5², 7; **31:**8, 14, 17, 23; **32:**9, 10; **33:**11, 18; **34:**10, 19; **35:**15, 20; **37:**9, 11, 13, 15, 17, 20, 21, 22, 28, 33, 36, 38; **39:**2, 5, 6, 7, 11; **40:**6, 16; **41:**10; **44:**7, 9, 19; **49:**12, 15; **50:**16, 21; **52:**7, 8; **55:**13, 16, 23²; **57:**6; **59:**8, 11, 16; **60:**4; **62:**4, 9²; **63:**11; **64:**7; **66:**12, 19; **68:**3, 6; **69:**13, 20²; **70:**4; **71:**7, 14; **73:**2, 25, 26, 28; **74:**12; **75:**7, 10; **78:**7, 17, 20, 30, 36, 39, 50, 52, 53, 56, 68; **81:**8, 11, 13, 16; **82:**7; **85:**8; **86:**15; **88:**13; **89:**33, 38; **90:**10; **91:**7; **92:**8; **94:**22; **96:**5; **102:**12, 26, 27; **103:**17; **104:**7, 35; **105:**12; **106:**13, 15, 30, 35, 43, 44; **107:**41, 42; **109:**4, 16, 21, 28²; **115:**1, 4, 5², 6², 7², 16; **118:**10, 11, 12, 13, 17, 18; **119:**51, 67, 70, 78, 81, 87, 95, 96, 110, 113, 143, 150, 157, 161, 163; **120:**7; **125:**1, 5; **129:**2, 4; **130:**4; **131:**2; **132:**18; **135:**16², 17; **136:**15; **138:**6; **139:**12; **141:**8; **145:**20; **146:**9; **147:**6; **Pr 1:**7, 24, 28², 33; **2:**22; **3:**1, 32, 33, 34, 35; **4:**19; **5:**4, 6; **6:**32; **8:**36; **9:**18; **10:**1, 2, 3, 4, 5, 6, 7, 8, 9, 11, 12, 13, 14, 15, 16, 17, 19, 20, 21, 23, 25, 27, 28, 29, 30, 31, 32; **11:**1, 2, 3, 4, 5, 6, 9, 11, 12, 13, 14, 15, 16, 17, 18, 19, 20, 21, 23, 24, 26, 27, 28; **12:**1, 2, 3, 4, 5, 6, 7, 8, 10, 11, 12, 13, 15, 16, 17, 18, 19, 20, 21, 23, 24, 25, 26, 27; **13:**1, 2, 3, 4, 5, 6, 8, 9, 10, 11, 12, 13, 15, 16, 17, 18, 19, 20, 21, 22, 23, 24; **14:**1, 2, 3, 4, 5, 6, 8, 9, 11, 12, 15, 16, 18, 20, 21, 22, 23, 24, 25, 28, 29, 30, 31, 32, 34, 35; **15:**1, 2, 4, 5, 6, 8, 9, 13, 14, 15, 16, 17, 18, 19, 22, 25, 26, 27, 28, 29, 30, 31, 32; **16:**1, 2, 9, 14, 22, 25, 33; **17:**3, 9, 22, 24; **18:**2, 4, 12, 14, 23, 24; **19:**4, 12, 14, 16, 21; **20:**3, 4, 5, 6, 15, 17; **21:**2, 8, 15, 20, 26, 29, 31; **22:**3, 5, 12, 13; **23:**5, 7, 17, 35²; **24:**12, 16, 25; **26:**24, 26; **27:**3, 4, 6, 7, 12, 21; **28:**1, 2, 4, 5, 7, 10, 11, 12, 16, 18, 19, 20, 25, 26, 27, 28; **29:**3, 4, 6, 7, 8, 11, 13, 16, 18, 19, 20, 23, 25, 26; **30:**8; **31:**29, 30; **Ecc 1:**4, 17; **2:**1, 14, 26; **4:**3, 10, 11, 13², 16; **5:**12; **6:**2, 6; **7:**4, 12, 14, 23, 26,

Column 2

28², 29; **9:**1, 5, 11, 15², 16, 18; **10:**2, 10, 12, 19; **11:**8, 9; **12:**4, 9; **SS 3:**1, 2; **5:**2, 6³; **6:**9; **8:**12; **Isa 1:**2, 3, 20, 21, 28; **2:**22; **3:**7; **5:**2, 7², 12, 16, 23; **6:**9²; **13:**7; **14:**12, 16; **8:**10²; **14; 9:**1, 10², 11, 13, 20²; **10:**4, 7, 20; **11:**4; **13:**21; **14:**15, 19, 30; **15:**9; **16:**6, 14; **17:**1; **19:**11; **21:**12; **22:**11, 13; **23:**15; **24:**16; **25:**10; **26:**11, 13, 18, 19; **28:**12; **29:**5, 8², 9², 11, 13; **30:**1, 3, 5, 15, 31³; **32:**8; **35:**9; **36:**5, 12; **37:**19, 28, 30; **38:**13, 15; **40:**8, 31; **41:**8, 16, 17², 24, 28, 29; **42:**14, 17, 19, 20², 25; **43:**1, 8², 24; **44:**1, 11, 15; **45:**9, 13, 17, 18, 21, 25; **47:**7; **48:**1; **49:**4, 14, 21, 25; **50:**11; **51:**2, 6, 8, 12, 21; **52:**12; **53:**5; **54:**7, 8; **55:**11; **57:**3, 10, 13, 15, 16, 18, 20; **59:**2, 9², 11²; **60:**2, 18; **62:**4, 9; **63:**5, 16, 18, 19; **64:**5; **65:**6, 11, 17²; **66:**3, 14; **Jer 1:**7, 19; **2:**7, 11, 25, 35; **3:**1, 5, 7, 10, 20; **4:**11; **5:**1, 3², 5, 10, 13, 21²; **22², 23, 31; **6:**4, 11, 16, 17, 29; **7:**8, 11, 13², 19, 23, 24, 26, 32; **8:**2, 6, 7, 15²; **9:**8, 24; **10:**10, 12, 24; **11:**8², 12, 16, 20; **12:**2, 13², 15, 17; **13:**1, 7, 11, 16; **14:**3, 13, 19²; **15:**19, 20; **16:**4, 12, 15, 16, 19, 20; **17:**7, 18², 22, 24², 27; **18:**4, 12, 23; **19:**6; **20:**3, 9, 11; **21:**3, 9; **22:**5, 11, 17, 21; **23:**8, 18, 22, 28, 36; **24:**3; **25:**3, 7, 12, 28, 33; **26:**8, 21; **27:**11; **28:**9; **29:**13; **30:**7, 11, 16, 17; **32:**4, 18, 23, 30², 36; **34:**3, 11, 16, 17²; **36:**27; **37:**13, 14, 20; **38:**2, 4, 7, 16, 18, 21, 23; **39:**5, 10, 12, 17, 18; **40:**4², 10, 14, 16; **41:**8, 15; **42:**21; **43:**3; **44:**5, 18, 26; **45:**5; **46:**10, 11, 20, 28; **47:**7; **48:**12, 30, 38; **49:**2, 10; **50:**2, 13, 19, 20², 34; **51:**9, 19, 52, 53; **52:**8, 16; **La 1:**17, 19, 21; **4:**3, 4, 8, 13, 21, 22; **Eze 1:**6; **2:**8; **3:**5, 7, 8, 19², 21, 27; **5:**3; **6:**8; **7:**25; **8:**6; **9:**6, 10; **11:**5, 7, 12, 21; **12:**2², 13, 16, 25, 28; **13:**18; **14:**16, 15, 29, 33, 43, 47, 61; **17:**6, 7, 15; **18:**7², 14, 16, 18, 21, 24, 27; **19:**12; **20:**8, 9, 13, 14, 21, 22, 24, 32, 39; **21:**23; **22:**18, 30; **23:**14, 45; **24:**13; **26:**21; **27:**26; **28:**2, 9; **29:**4, 16; **30:**24, 25; **33:**4, 5, 6², 9², 11, 13, 14, 17, 20, 24, 31², 32²; **34:**3, 8, 16; **36:**8, 22; **37:**8; **44:**12, 15, 20; **45:**8; **46:**1, 2, 9; **47:**5, 11; **Da 1:**8, 10, 12; **2:**6, 28, 30, 34, 35, 44, 45; **3:**12, 15, 18; **4:**7, 15, 18, 23; **5:**8, 15, 20, 22, 23; **6:**4; **7:**12, 18, 26, 28; **8:**3, 8, 9, 13, 14, 21, 22, 24, 32, 39, 41, 44; **9:**3, 2, 4, 15, 25, 26, 27; **9:**7, 18, 19, 24; **21:**23; **10:**7, 13, 21; **11:**5, 6, 9, 11, 14, 17, 18, 19, 24, 25, 27, 28, 29, 32, 37, 41, 44; **12:**1, 4, 8, 10²; **Hos 1:**2; **2:**7², 13; **4:**4, 10²; **5:**13; **6:**1²; **7:**2, 9², 10, 13, 14², 15; **8:**3, 12, 13, 14; **9:**10, 13; **10:**3, 13; **11:**2, 3; **12:**6, 13; **13:**1, 4², 13; **14:**9; **Joel 3:**16, 19; **Am 2:**12; **3:**8; **4:**7, 8; **5:**24; **6:**6, 12; **7:**14, 15; **8:**11, 12; **Ob 1:**6, 7, 17; **Jnh 1:**3, 5, 13, 17; **2:**6, 9; **3:**8; **4:**1, 4, 7, 9, 10, 11; **Mic 3:**4, 8; **4:**11, 12; **5:**2; **6:**14², 15²; **7:**7, 18; **Na 1:**8; **2:**8; **3:**16, 17; **Hab 1:**2²; **2:**4, 20; **Zep 1:**13²; **3:**7, 12; **Hag 1:**6², 9; **2:**4; **Zec 1:**4, 6, 15², 21; **4:**6; **7:**11; **8:**6, 11, 13; **9:**4, 8; **11:**12, 16; **12:**4, 6, 14²; **10; Mal 1:**2, 3, 4², 6, 7, 12, 14; **2:**8, 9; **3:**2, 5, 7, 8, 15; **4:**2; **Mt 1:**18, 20, 25; **2:**6, 22; **3:**7, 11, 14; **4:**4; **5:**13, 17, 19, 22², 28, 32, 33, 34, 39, 44; **6:**3, 6, 13, 15, 17, 18, 20, 23, 33; **7:**14, 15, 17, 21, 26; **8:**4, 8, 12, 22; **9:**6, 12, 13², 14, 18, 24²; **11:**19, 22, 24, 29, 30; **12:**4, 24, 28, 31, 34, 37, 44; **13:**13, 16; **14:**17², 16; **15:**5, 8, 9, 11, 14, 16, 17, 23, 25; **17:**7, 12², 16, 21, 27; **18:**6, 7, 16, 22, 28; **30; 19:**6, 8, 11, 13, 26, 30; **20:**10, 13, 23, 28; **21:**13, 15, 19, 21, 26, 29, 30, 32, 38, 44, 46; **22:**3, 5, 8, 11, 14, 18, 31, 32; **23:**3, 4, 8, 16, 18, 23, 24, 25, 27, 28, 37; **24:**6²; **25:**3, 10, 12, 46; **26:**5, 11, 24, 32, 35, 39, 41, 54, 56, 58, 60, 63, 64, 70; **27:**14, 20, 23, 24, 26, 34, 42; **28:**17, 18, 20; **3:**4, 12, 29; **4:**6, 11, 12², 17, 19, 34; **5:**4, 19, 32, 39, 40; **6:**9, 16, 19, 26, 33, 37, 49; **7:**6, 7, 11, 19, 28, 36; **8:**4, 18², 29, 33²; **9:**13, 18, 24, 27, 31, 40, 45, 48; **11:**11, 14², 16, 17², 21, 22, 23, 25, 48, 57; **14:**5, 9, 24, 27, 30; **15:**5, 8, 9, 11, 18, 20, 27; **16:**3, 4, 11, 12, 15, 17; **23:**5; **17:**7, 12², 16, 22, 28, 30; **19:**6, 8, 11, 13, 26, 30; **20:**10, 13, 23, 28; **21:**13, 15, 19, 21, 26, 29, 30, 32, 38, 44, 46; **22:**3, 5, 8, 11, 14, 18, 31, 32; **23:**3, 4, 8, 16, 18, 23, 24, 25, 27, 28, 37; **24:**6², 27, 31, 40, 45, 48; **11:**11, 13, 17, 23, 32; **12:**3, 7, 12, 14, 15, 19, 21, 27, 32, 42, 44; **13:**7, 11, 13, 20, 24, 31, 32², 34; **14:**2, 7, 21, 28, 31, 34, 38, 49, 51, 55, 56, 61, 68; **15:**5, 11, 14, 23, 31; **16:**4, 7, 13, 16; **Lk 1:**7, 13, 22, 30, 43, 52, 53, 60, 62; **2:**10, 19, 37, 43, 50, 51; **3:**16, 17, 19; **4:**26, 30, 41, 43; **5:**5, 14, 16, 21, 24, 30, 31, 32, 33, 35; **6:**8, 11, 24, 27, 35, 40, 48, 49; **7:**7, 26, 30, 33, 44, 45, 46, 47; **8:**10, 13², 14, 15, 19, 27, 38, 43, 46, 52, 54, 56; **9:**9, 11, 14, 20, 24, 32, 40, 42, 44, 45, 50, 53, 55, 61; **10:**2, 10, 14, 16, 20, 24², 29, 33, 40, 42; **11:**15, 20, 22, 29, 31, 39, 45, 48, 50, 51; **13:**3, 5, 6, 17, 25, 27, 28, 31, 33, 35; **14:**2, 7, 21, 34; **15:**7, 16², 17, 21, 22, 23, 25, 48, 57; **14:**5, 9, 24, 27, 30; **15:**5, 8, 9, 11, 18, 20, 27; **16:**3, 4, 11, 12, 15, 17; **23:**5; **17:**7, 12², 16, 22, 28, 30; **19:**6, 8, 11, 13, 26, 30; **20:**10, 13, 23, 28; **21:**13, 15, 19, 21, 26, 29, 30, 32, 38, 44, 46; **22:**3, 5, 8, 11, 14, 18, 31, 32; **23:**3, 4, 8, 16, 18, 23, 24, 25, 27, 28, 37; **24:**6², 11, 21, 24, 27, 32, 33; **Jn 1:**5, 11, 13, 18, 26, 31; **2:**10, 21, 24; **3:**6, 8, 11, 16, 17, 18, 19, 21, 24, 28, 30, 32; **4:**2, 14, 20, 27, 32; **5:**11, 18, 22, 27, 32, 36, 38, 39, 50, 58; **7:**2, 7, 10, 13, 18, 22, 27, 28, 29, 30, 34, 36, 44, 49; **8:**1, 6, 12, 14, 16, 23, 26, 28, 35, 42, 49, 50, 55, 59; **9:**3, 9, 16, 21, 25, 29, 41; **10:**1, 5, 6, 8, 18, 21, 25, 26, 32, 33, 38, 39; **11:**8, 13, 15, 20, 22, 30, 37, 39, 42, 46, 51, 52, 57; **12:**4, 6, 8, 9, 24, 32, 42, 44, 47²; **13:**7, 9, 18, 28, 36; **14:**17, 19, 22, 26, 31; **15:**16, 19, 24, 25; **16:**7², 20, 21, 22, 25, 32, 33, 38, 39; **18:**16, 18, 23, 31, 36, 39; **19:**6, 9, 12², 15², 21, 33, 38; **20:**4, 5, 11, 14, 25, 31; **21:**3, 4, 11, 18, 23; **Ac 1:**4, 5, 8; **2:**24, 30; **3:**6, 15, 18; **4:**4, 10, 14, 17, 19, 32; **5:**2, 4, 19, 29, 32, 34, 39; **6:**10; **7:**5, 7, 9, 25, 27, 39, 42, 47, 53, 55; **8:**3, 12, 39; **9:**7, 26, 27, 39, 40, 41; **11:**16; **12:**5, 9, 16, 24; **13:**8, 25, 30, 37, 50, 51; **14:**2, 19; **15:**35, 38, 40; **16:**1, 7, 28, 37; **17:**5, 6, 14, 21, 30, 34; **20:**6, 20; **21:**5, 13, 24, 22:3, 19, 23; **23:**8, 23², 28, 29, 30, 31; **25:**11, 17, 25, 26; **26:**22, 29; **27:**11, 22, 39, 41, 43; **28:**5, 6, 19, 22, 24, 26²; **Ro 1:**13, 21, 32; **2:**5, 8, 10, 13, 25, 29; **3:**5, 21, 27; **4:**2, 4, 5, 10, 11, 12, 13, 16, 20, 24; **5:**3, 8, 11, 13, 15, 16, 20; **6:**10, 11, 13, 14, 15, 17, 22, 23; **7:**2, 3, 6, 8, 9, 13, 14, 15, 17, 18, 20, 23, 25; **8:**4, 5, 6, 9, 10, 12, 13, 16, 20, 24, 31, 32; **10:**2, 6, 8, 16, 18, 21; **11:**7, 12, 15, 18, 20², 22, 28; **12:**2, 3, 11, 16, 19, 21; **13:**3, 4, 5; **14:**2, 14, 17, 20, 23, 35, 37, 38, 40, 46, 51, 57; **16:**8, 12; **2Co 1:**9², 12, 18, 19, 24; **2:**2, 4, 14; **3:**3², 5, 6², 14, 16; **4:**5, 7, 8², 9², 12, 18²; **5:**4, 12, 15; **6:**12; **7:**5, 6, 7, 8, 9, 10, 12, 14; **8:**5, 7, 8, 10, 13, 17, 21; **9:**3², 12; **10:**1, 10, 13, 17, 18; **11:**1, 3, 5, 6, 16, 17, 33; **12:**3, 5, 6, 9, 11, 14²; **13:**3, 7, 8, 9; **Gal 1:**1, 8, 15, 17; **2:**2, 4, 7, 9, 17, 23, 26, 30, 31; **5:**5, 13, 18, 22; **6:**1; **Eph 1:**21; **2:**4, 13, 19; **4:**7, 28, 29; **5:**3, 4, 8, 11, 13, 15, 17, 27, 29, 32; **6:**6, 12; **Php 1:**15, 18, 20, 24, 28, 29; **2:**3, 4, 7, 12, 17, 22, 25, 27²; **3:**7, 9, 12, 13, 20; **4:**6, 10, 17; **Col 1:**22, 26; **2:**11, 23; **3:**8, 11, 22; **1Th 1:**5; **2:**2, 4, 7, 8, 13, 17, 18; **3:**6; **4:**7, 8; **5:**4, 6, 8, 9, 15; **2Th 2:**7, 12, 13; **3:**3, 9, 15; **1Ti 1:**7, 9, 16; **2:**10, 15; **3:**2, 3, 11, 12; **4:**8, 12; **5:**1, 4, 6, 13; **6:**6, 8, 11, 17; **2Ti 1:**7, 8, 9, 10; **2:**9, 20; **3:**1, 5, 7, 9, 14; **4:**5, 8, 16, 17; **Tit 1:**6, 15, 16; **2:**3, 10; **3:**4, 5, 9; **Phm 1:**11, 14, 16²; **Heb 1:**2, 8, 11, 12; **2:**6, 9, 16; **3:**4, 6, 13; **4:**2, 15; **5:**5, 11, 14; **6:**8; **7:**8, 16, 21, 24, 28; **8:**6, 8; **9:**5, 7, 12, 23, 26, 28; **10:**3, 5, 12, 25, 27, 38, 39²; **11:**29; **12:**10, 11, 13, 22, 26²; **13:**11, 14; **Jas 1:**6, 10, 14, 23²; **2:**3, 6, 9, 11, 14, 16, 18; **3:**5, 8, 14, 15, 17; **4:**2², 6², 11, 12; **1Pe 1:**12, 15, 19, 20, 23, 25; **2:**4, 7, 9, 10², 16, 18, 20²; **3:**9, 12, 14, 16, 18, 20², 22; **4:**2, 5, 6, 13, 16; **5:**2², 3, 5; **2Pe 1:**9, 16, 21; **2:**1, 4, 5, 12, 16; **3:**5, 8, 9, 10, 13, 18; **1Jn 1:**7; **2:**1, 2, 4, 5, 8, 12; **3:**5, 17, 18; **4:**1, 3, 6, 10, 12, 18; **5:**6, 9; **2Jn 1:**1, 5, 8, 12; **3Jn 1:**9, 11, 13; **Jude 1:**5, 6, 9², 17, 20; **Rev 2:**2, 6, 9, 11, 21; **3:**1, 3, 5, 9, 17; **5:**3; **9:**4, 5, 6²; **10:**4, 7, 9, 10; **11:**2, 11; **12:**8, 12, 16; **13:**2, 3, 11; **16:**9, 11; **17:**10, 12, 14; **19:**10, 12, 20; **20:**6, 9; **21:**8, 27; **22:**9.

BY (2431)

Ge 2:2; **3:**19; **5:**29; **6:**4; **8:**13, 14; **9:**6, 11; **10:**5, 20, 31; **14:**19; **17:**16, 21; **18:**3, 19; **19:**23, 36; **21:**18, 29; **22:**13, 16; **23:**20; **24:**3, 14, 30, 31; **26:**29; **27:**40; **30:**27, 37, 40; **31:**7, 20, 31, 39², 46; **32:**16; **33:**8; **34:**7, 15, 30; **36:**40; **37:**28; **38:**16, 18, 20, 25; **39:**22; **41:**1, 6, 23, 27, 32, 36, 50; **43:**6, 32²; **44:**15; **45:**7; **46:**18, 20, 25; **48:**16; **49:**13, 17, 19; **Ex 2:**15; **3:**15; **4:**4; **5:**14; **6:**3, 17, 25, 26; **7:**11, 17, 22; **8:**7, 18, 24, 29; **9:**15; **10:**12, 13; **12:**13; **13:**3, 9, 16; **14:**2, 9, 11, 14, 16; **4:**35; **5:**12;

Column 4

6:2, 4, 17, 18; **7:**5, 24, 25, 30, 35; **8:**7, 21, 28, 34; **9:**13; **10:**6, 12, 13, 15, 17; **11:**24, 43³, 44; **13:**59; **15:**32; **16:**10²; **17:**15; **18:**5, 7, 14, 27; **19:**12, 29, 31; **20:**3, 6, 25; **21:**4, 6, 7, 9, 12, 14, 21; **22:**4²; 8, 14, 16, 22, 27, 32; **23:**8, 13, 18, 25, 27, 36², 37; **24:**7, 9; **26:**7, 8, 17, 26, 43; **27:**2; **Nu 1:**2³; 18, 18³, 20², 22², 24, 26, 28, 30, 32, 34, 36, 38, 40, 42, 44, 52; **2:**32; **3:**7, 8, 15, 16, 39, 43, 49, 51; **4:**2, 22, 29, 34, 36, 38, 40, 42, 44, 46; **5:**13, 20; **6:**11; **9:**21²; **10:**9, 34; **11:**14; **14:**3, 13, 14², 36, 42, 43; **15:**3, 10, 13, 14, 25, 28, 39; **16:**39; **17:**5; **18:**17, 32; **19:**9; **21:**9; **22:**33; **24:**2, 6; **26:**2, 3, 12, 15, 20, 23, 26, 28, 35, 37, 38, 42, 44, 48, 55, 56, 57, 63², 64; **27:**21; **28:**2, 3, 6, 8, 13, 19, 24; **29:**6, 13, 36; **30:**2, 3, 4, 5, 6, 7, 8, 9, 10, 11, 14; **31:**12; **33:**1, 2, 10, 48, 50, 54²; **34:**13; **35:**1, 33; **36:**2, 13; **Dt 1:**2, 12, 33², 42; **2:**14, 18; **3:**9, 12; **4:**31, 34⁵, 37, 46; **5:**12; **6:**2; **7:**10, 21, 22, 25; **9:**10, 26, 29; **11:**10, 28; **12:**30; **13:**1; **14:**24; **16:**1, 10; **18:**1, 21; **19:**14, 15; **20:**19; **21:**17; **22:**21; **23:**1; **24:**13; **25:**11; **27:**26; **28:**10; **31:**21, 29; **32:**19, 21³, 22, 47; **33:**24, 29; **Jos 2:**12, 15; **3:**17; **4:**10; **6:**18; **7:**4, 8, 14⁴, 15, 16, 17, 18; **9:**13, 15, 18, 19, 22; **10:**9, 11; **11:**6; **13:**14, 15, 23, 24, 28, 29, 31; **14:**2; **15:**1, 12, 20; **16:**5, 6, 8; **17:**2; **18:**9, 11, 21; **19:**1, 8, 10, 16, 17, 23, 24, 31, 32, 39, 40, 48, 51; **20:**9; **21:**1, 7, 9, 41; **22:**10, 19, 29; **23:**1, 7; **24:**5; **Jdg 2:**23; **3:**26; **4:**11, 14, 15, 16, 20, 22; **5:**17, 19; **6:**31, 36, 37; **7:**25; **8:**11, 13, 15, 16, 26, 27; **9:**5, 9, 25, 34, 56; **10:**3; **11:**27; **19:**29; **21:**7, 22; **Ru 1:**6, 22; **2:**12; **4:**12; **1Sa 1:**9; **2:**3, 9, 16, 20, 28, 29²; **3:**14; **4:**2, 13, 19; **6:**3, 9, 10, 19, 21, 26; **11:**7, 9; **12:**7, 23; **13:**8; **14:**6²; 15, 33, 34, 36, 41; **16:**9; **17:**35, 43, 47; **18:**25; **19:**5; **20:**12², 19, 25; **21:**6; **23:**7; **24:**15, 21; **25:**22, 29, 34, 42; **26:**7; **27:**1; **28:**6, 10, 15³; **29:**1; **4:**30; **3Sa 1:**2; **2:**5, 16, 17, 32; **3:**18, 29; **4:**7; **6:**2, 22; **7:**14, 23; **10:**3, 8, 15, 19; **12:**9, 14; **13:**31; **14:**26; **15:**2, 23, 34; **16:**18³; **17:**22; **18:**7, 23, 24; **19:**7²; **20:**2, 9; **21:**10²; **22:**22; **23:**1²; **1Ki 1:**6, 17, 30; **2:**7, 8², 23, 25, 27²; **4:**34; **5:**9²; **6:**10; **7:**12, 15; **9:**3, 8; **11:**25, 38; **12:**15; **13:**1², 2, 5², 9², 10, 17², 18, 25, 32; **14:**15, 22; **15:**4²; **16:**2, 7, 13, 26, 34; **17:**16, 20, 18:**24; **19:**2, 6, 8, 11; **20:**1, 35, 38, 39; **21:**23, 25, 26; **22:**10, 22; **2Ki 3:**8; **4:**8; **5:**5, 20, 23; **6:**10, 14, 26; **8:**21, 27; **9:**7, 28; **10:**6, 14, 33; **11:**13, 14, 19; **12:**6, 18; **13:**2; **14:**12, 20, 27; **16:**6, 9; **17:**4; **19:**12, 18, 23, 28, 29, 33; **20:**20; **21:**14; **22:**17; **23:**3, 5, 15, 16; **24:**2; **25:**3, 30; **1Ch 1:**36; **2:**3, 7, 18²; **3:**3, 5, 9; **4:**38, 42; **5:**7, 13, 16, 62, 63; **7:**21; **8:**9, 11, 30; **9:**22², 36; **12:**31; **13:**6; **14:**11; **15:**16; **16:**41; **17:**21; **18:**7; **19:**3, 16, 19; **21:**18; **23:**24; **24:**5, 19; **25:**1; **26:**26³, 28²; **27:**1, 34²; **28:**9; **29:**5; **2Ch 2:**11, 16; **3:**1; **4:**6; **5:**12, 13; **6:**23, 24, 29; **7:**14, 21; **8:**13, 14, 18; **9:**14, 21; **13:**5; **15:**2, 4, 6², 15; **17:**14; **18:**1, 9, 20, 20:**11, 16, 27; **21:**9; **23:**13, 24², 11, 21; **25:**22, 28; **26:**11², 15, 18, 22; **28:**15; **29:**9, 17, 25², 27; **30:**9, 16, 21; **31:**13, 17, 19; **32:**23, 31; **33:**13, 19; **34:**25, 31; **35:**4³, 15; **36:**21, 22; **Ezr 1:**1, 8; **2:**61; **3:**7², 10; **4:**23; **6:**4, 9, 22; **7:**14, 26; **8:**20, 21, 34; **9:**11²; **10:**2, 9, 15, 19, 36; **Ne 1:**10, 11; **2:**3, 8, 13², 15, 20; **3:**3, 5, 6, 7, 13, 14, 15², 17, 18, 22²; **4:**13, 22²; **6:**10, 13; **7:**5, 63, 72; **8:**16²; **9:**12², 19², 29, 30; **12:**24, 36, 44; **13:**18, 21, 26², 27; **Est 1:**8; **2:**6, 14; **3:**13, 15; **7:**9; **8:**10, 14; **9:**1, 28²; **10:**3; **Job 1:**22; **2:**11; **6:**16; **9:**11; **11:**16; **12:**18; **13:**27, 28; **15:**31; **16:**12; **18:**9; **19:**29; **20:**29; **21:**15, 18, 29; **22:**16; **23:**17²; **24:**8, 16, 22; **26:**12², 13; **27:**18; **28:**4, 5; **29:**2, 3; **30:**15, 28; **31:**7, 9, 30, 33; **33:**18, 26; **35:**2, 3; **36:**8, 12, 18; **38:**13; **39:**9, 26; **40:**22, 24; **Ps 1:**3; **5:**7; **9:**16²; **17:**4, 7, 13, 14; **18:**21; **19:**11; **22:**2², 6²; **24:**4; **31:**10²; **12; 32:**9; **33:**6², 16²; **35:**8; **38:**18; **39:**10; **42:**8, 9; **43:**2; **44:**3; **45:**1, 7, 11; **48:**7; **50:**5; **52:**7; **54:**1²; **55:**15; **56:**9; **63:**11; **65:**3, 6; **66:**7; **68:**2; **73:**5, 19, 23; **74:**13; **76:**12; **77:**20; **78:**10, 14, 18, 26; **79:**11; **80:**5, 12; **89:**17, 35, 41; **90:**4, 6, 7; **91:**5; **92:**4; **94:**20; **104:**12, 13; **106:**7, 22, 29, 32, 38, 39², 46; **107:**7, 39; **111:**2; **115:**4, 15; **116:**3; **118:**10; **119:**9, 93; **121:**6²; **124:**6; **129:**8; **134:**1; **135:**15; **136:**5; **137:**1; **141:**9, 10; **144:**13²; **147:**4; **Pr 3:**19², 20; **5:**19, 20, 23; **6:**2²; **8:**15, 16; **9:**15; **10:**25; **11:**3, 5, 6, 11; **12:**13; **13:**11; **14:**20; **16:**2, 31; **19:**7, 23; **20:**1, 11², 17, 18, 24; **21:**6; **22:**28; **24:**3, 16; **25:**1; **26:**6, 17, 26; **27:**3, 21; **28:**8, 17; **29:**4, 6, 19; **30:**27; **Ecc 1:**11, 13; **2:**9, 15; **5:**8, 9; **6:**8; **7:**23; **9:**12, 15; **10:**8, 9², 12; **12:**11; **SS 1:**6, 8; **2:**7², 3:**5², 7, 10; **5:**12; **7:**2, 4, 5; **Isa 1:**7², 20; **3:**15, 25; **4:**1, 4; **5:**16², 30; **7:**2, 25; **8:**4; **9:**1, 19; **10:**13², 22; **11:**3², 13, 15, 19; **14:**19, 30; **16:**14; **18:**2²; **19:**11, 21:**1, 3, 10; **22:**2; **24:**5; **25:**5; **26:**20; **27:**8, 9, 12; **28:**1, 15, 18², 19²; **29:**13; **30:**1; **31:**4²; **8; 32:**8, 20; **33:**4; **34:**17; **37:**12, 19, 24, 29, 30, 34; **38:**8, 16; **40:**17, 26², 27; **41:**3; **42:**16; **43:**1, 7;

44:4, 5, 24; **45:**3, 4, 17, 23²; **46:**1; **47:**13, 14; **48:**1; **49:**7; **50:**2, 4; **51:**7, 9, 18; **53:**3, 4², 5, 8, 11; **54:**11, 13; **57:**10, 17; **58:**13; **60:**19; **62:**2, 8²; **63:**14, 19; **65:**1, 16², 23; **66:**16; **Jer 1:**17; **2:**8, 14, 17, 36², 37; **3:**2; **4:**2, 10; **5:**7, 31; **9:**3, 12; **10:**2², 8, 9, 12³, 14; **11:**17, 21, 22²; **12:**5, 16²; **13:**24; **14:**9, 15, 18; **16:**4; **17:**8², 11, 24, 25, 27; **18:**13, 16, 18, 21; **19:**7, 8, 9; **20:**4; **21:**9; **22:**4, 5, 8, 13²; **23:**6, 9, 13; **24:**1; **25:**13, 14, 33; **27:**8, 13; **28:**6, 9; **29:**14, 19; **31:**32, 35²; **32:**17, 21, 29², 32, 36; **33:**10, 16; **34:**4, 17; **36:**7, 30²; **37:**1; **38:**2, 4, 6, 20, 23; **39:**4, 18; **42:**17, 22; **44:**3², 7, 9³, 12², 18, 21, 25, 26, 27; **46:**2, 6, 10, 18; **48:**19, 20; **49:**13, 17; **51:**5, 13, 14, 15³, 17; **52:**6, 30, 34; **La 1:**12, 14; **2:**21; **3:**1, 31; **4:**9; **5:**12; **Eze 1:**1, 3, 4; **2:**6; **3:**9, 23; **4:**14; **5:**12², 14; **6:**9²; **11:**12; **7:**15², 26, 27; **8:**3; **10:**15, 20, 22; **11:**10, 24; **12:**22; **13:**19; **14:**13, 14, 20; **16:**6, 8, 15, 25, 27, 51, 57, 59; **17:**5, 8, 9, 14, 15, 18, 21; **18:**2; **19:**7, 10; **20:**9, 11, 13, 21, 25, 27, 43, 47; **21:**24; **22:**3², 4, 12, 28; **23:**17, 25², 43; **24:**6, 12, 21; **25:**12, 13, 14; **26:**6, 17; **27:**32, 34; **28:**4, 5, 18; **30:**5, 6, 10, 12, 16, 17; **31:**14, 17, 18; **32:**12, 13², 20, 21, 22², 23, 24, 25, 26, 28, 29, 30², 31, 32; **33:**19, 27, 30; **34:**28; **35:**8; **36:**4, 17; **37:**1, 18; **38:**17; **39:**23; **40:**16, 38, 40, 49; **42:**12, 15, 17, 18, 19; **43:**3, 7, 8; **44:**3, 4, 19, 25, 26, 31; **45:**7, 14; **46:**2, 9³, 13, 14, 15, 16; **47:**13, 15; **48:**1, 11; **Da 1:**18; **2:**34, 45; **4:**16, 17, 23, 25, 27², 30, 32; **6:**3; **7:**28; **8:**24, 25, 27; **9:**1, 12, 13; **11:**2, 21, 33, 37; **12:**7; **Hos 1:**7³; **3:**1; **4:**12; **7:**16; **9:**6; **11:**3, 7; **12:**13; **13:**7, 16; **Am 2:**4; **4:**2; **6:**6, 8, 13; **7:**4, 7, 11, 17; **8:**7, 14; **9:**1, 4, 10, 13²; **Jnh 3:**7; **Mic 2:**5, 8; **7:**14; **Na 3:**4²; **Hab 1:**16; **2:**4, 6, 9, 12; **3:**10; **Zep 1:**5²; **2:**5, 6, 12, 15; **3:**5, 8; **Hag 2:**13, 22; **Zec 3:**5; **4:**3, 6³; **5:**4; **7:**3, 12; **8:**9, 23; **9:**4; **12:**12²; **14:**5, 13; **Mal 1:**7, 12; **2:**8, 10, 11, 17; **3:**4, 14; **Mt 2:**6, 12, 16; **3:**6, 13, 14; **4:**1², 13; **5:**13, 18, 34, 35², 36; **6:**1, 2, 5, 27; **7:**16, 20; **9:**25, 34; **11:**7, 19, 27; **12:**24, 27², 28, 33, 37²; **13:**1; **14:**8, 13, 23, 24; **15:**9, 13; **16:**1, 17²; **17:**1; **18:**16, 19; **19:**12; **20:**23, 30²; **21:**2, 19, 23, 24, 27; **22:**16, 19, 25, 27, 43, 47; **23:**13², 18³, 20³, 21³, 22³; **24:**9; **25:**34; **26:**52, 63; **27:**9²; **28:**2; **Mk 1:**5, 9, 13, 23; **2:**3; **3:**22²; **4:**1, 2, 28; **5:**15, 21², 41; **6:**1, 7, 31, 32, 35, 48; **7:**7, 13, 15, 19, 24, 39; **8:**7, 31, 35; **9:**17, 27, 29; **10:**2, 46; **11:**28, 29, 33; **12:**14, 36; **14:**19, 58, 66; **15:**21, 29; **16:**20; **Lk 1:**2, 9, 78; **2:**26, 27, 39; **3:**7; **4:**1, 2, 21, 33; **5:**1, 2, 27; **6:**18, 44; **7:**24, 29, 30, 35; **8:**14, 15, 27, 29, 54; **9:**10, 22; **10:**1, 2, 31, 32, 40²; **11:**15, 16, 18, 19², 20; **12:**6, 25; **13:**11; **16:**23; **17:**20, 25; **18:**31, 35, 36, 37; **19:**2, 22, 24; **20:**2, 8, 26; **21:**16, 19, 20, 24²; **22:**28; **23:**5, 34; **24:**12, 35; **Jn 1:**36; **2:**6; **3:**21; **4:**6; **5:**2, 19, 30, 39; **6:**13, 15², 17, 45; **7:**24, 39; **8:**15, 49; **10:**1², 2, 31; **11:**9³, 10, 39; **13:**35; **14:**21; **15:**4; **16:**14, 17, 18; **17:**4, 11, 12, 17; **18:**28, 31, 36; **19:**24, 39; **20:**7, 31; **21:**1, 19; **Ac 1:**7; **2:**16, 22², 23², 43; **3:**7, 12, 16, 26; **4:**7, 10, 12, 25; **5:**13, 15, 16, 27, 30, 34; **6:**10; **7:**19, 24, 25, 30, 34; **8:**13; **9:**8, 22, 23, 25, 31, 41; **10:**6, 11, 17, 22, 32, 39, 41³; **11:**5, 19, 30; **12:**4, 10, 23; **13:**4, 11, 31, 33, 39; **14:**3, 17; **15:**1, 4, 8, 9, 10, 14, 20, 24, 27, 33, 40; **16:**4, 6, 8, 16³, 21; **17:**17, 24, 25, 29, 31; **18:**10, 18, 28²; **20:**7, 30; **21:**11, 21; **26:**2, 16²; **22³, 23²**, 43; **3:**7, 12, 16, 26; **4:**7, 10, 12, 25; **5:**13, 15, 16, 27, 30, 34; **6:**10; **7:**19, 24, 25, 30, 34; **8:**13; **9:**8, 22, 32; **10:**6, 11, 17, 22, 32, 39, 41³; **11:**5, 19, 30; **12:**4, 10, 23; **13:**4, 17; **15:**1, 4, 8, 9, 10, 14, 20, 24, 27, 33, 40; **16:**4, 6, 8, 16³, 21; **17:**17, 24, 25, 29, 31; **18:**10, 18, 28²; **20:**7, 30; **21:**35; **22:**11, 12, 30; **23:**3, 10², 19, 27; **24:**8, 27; **25:**11; **26:**18, 20; **27:**9, 15, 38, 41; **28:**3, 16, 24; **Ro 1:**4, 7, 10, 12, 17², 18; **2:**7, 12, 14², 18, 23, 29²; **3:**20, 24², 28, 30, 31; **4:**2, 11, 13, 14, 16²; **5:**2, 5, 9, 14, 15², 17; **6:**2, 15; **7:**2, 5², 6, 8, 11, 13; **8:**3², 6, 8, 9², 13, 14, 15, 20²; **9:**12², 27, 30, 32²; **10:**5², 6, 19²; **11:**1, 5, 6², 20, 24; **12:**2, 3, 21; **13:**1; **14:**15, 18, 22; **15:**13, 16, 18, 19, 30³, 32; **16:**18, 25, 26; **1Co 1:**1, 26; **2:**10, 13²; **3:**10, 18; **4:**3²; **6:**11, 12, 14; **7:**5, 22, 25; **8:**3, 11; **9:**22; **10:**9, 10, 29; **11:**32; **12:**3², 8, 9², 13; **14:**24²; **15:**2, 10; **2Co 1:**11, 19, 20, 24; **2:**3, 6, 7; **3:**2; **4:**2, 16; **5:**1, 4, 7²; **7:**6, 7², 8, 9, 13²; **8:**8, 11, 18, 19; **9:**13; **10:**1, 2, 12, 15²; **11:**3, 7, 8; **12:**6, 11, 16; **13:**1; **Gal 1:**1³, 6, 12, 15; **2:**6, 13, 15, 16², 20; **3:**2², 3, 8, 11², 12, 13, 14, 17, 19, 21, 23, 24; **4:**2, 8, 9², 16, 22², 23², 29; **5:**1, 4, 5, 15, 16, 18, 25; **Eph 1:**1; **2:**3, 5, 8, 9, 11³, 15, 16, 18, 22; **3:**3, 5, 7; **4:**14³, 16, 22; **5:**13, 26; **Php 1:**19, 20², 23, 28²; **2:**2; **3:**3, 9, 21; **4:**6; **Col 1:**1, 16², 20, 22, 25; **2:**4, 11², 15, 16, 19; **1Th 1:**3³, 4, 6; **2:**4; **3:**1, 3; **4:**2, 9; **2Th 1:**11³; **2:**2, 8, 13, 15², 16; **1Ti 1:**1, 4, 18; **3:**16²; **4:**1, 3, 5; **6:**14, 19; **2Ti 1:**1, 8; **3:**6; **Tit 1:**3, 9, 11, 16; **2:**7; **3:**3, 5, 7; **Heb 1:**2, 3, 9; **2:**2, 3², 4, 9, 14, 15; **3:**4, 13; **4:**11³; **5:**4, 10, 12, 14; **6:**13², 16, 18; **7:**7, 8², 19; **8:**2², 4, 9; **9:**8, 12², 26; **10:**1, 10, 14, 19, 20, 33, 38; **11:**3, 4³, 5³, 8, 9, 11, 13, 17, 20, 21, 22, 23, 24, 27, 28, 29, 30, 31, 37; **12:**1, 7, 11; **13:**2, 4, 9³; **Jas 1:**6, 13, 14, 27; **2:**3, 9, 12, 17², 18, 22, 24², 3:**4², 5, 6, 7, 13², 5:**12²; **1Pe 1:**2, 5, 7, 12², 20; **2:**2, 4², 14, 15, 24; **3:**1,

18, 21; **2Pe 1:**3, 4, 20, 21; **2:**6, 7, 8, 16, 17, 18, 20; **3:**2², 5², 6, 7, 10, 12, 17; **1Jn 1:**6; **3:**24; **5:**2, 6³; **3Jn 1:**12²; 14; **Jude 1:**1², 10, 12, 23; **Rev 1:**1, 5; **2:**11, 14², 20; **4:**11; **5:**6; **6:**8²; 13; **8:**13; **9:**2, 18, 20; **10:**6; **11:**10; **12:**6, 11², 16; **13:**14; **15:**2; **16:**9; **17:**17; **18:**1, 8, 17, 23; **19:**2; **21:**17, 24.

FOR (7282)

Ge 1:29, 30; **2:**5, 9, 17, 18², 20, 23, 24; **3:**5, 6², 7, 16, 18, 19, 21; **4:**12, 23²; **6:**3, 7, 12, 13, 16, 21²; **7:**4, 17, 24; **9:**3, 5², 6, 7, 12; **11:**3, 4, 6; **12:**5, 10, 13, 16; **13:**6, 8, 11, 17; **14:**4, 21; **15:**13, 16; **16:**5, 11, 13; **17:**4, 5, 7, 9², 12, 15, 19, 20; **18:**14, 19², 24, 26, 29, 31, 32; **19:**3, 8, 16, 17, 30; **20:**1, 2, 7², 10, 18; **21:**1, 10, 16, 18, 21, 34; **22:**3², 6, 7, 8, 19; **23:**2, 4, 6, 9, 16; **24:**3, 4, 7, 10, 14, 19, 20, 23, 25, 27, 31, 32², 37, 38, 40, 44², 48, 62; **25:**24, 28; **26:**3², 16, 24², 30; **27:**1, 3, 5, 9, 13, 23, 36, 37, 41, 42, 44, 45; **28:**1, 2, 10, 11; **29:**7, 9, 14, 15², 18², 20, 25, 27, 30, 32; **30:**3, 15, 18, 26², 29, 30, 33, 33, 40; **31:**6, 12, 15, 21, 23, 32, 38, 39, 41⁴; **32:**11, 13, 20, 26; **33:**9, 10, 11, 13, 17², 19; **34:**9, 12, 16, 21; **35:**17, 18, 36², 37, 37:3, 15, 16, 28, 34, 35:8:6, 8, 9, 11, 14, 15, 27; **39:**15, 18, 22; **40:**4, 15, 17, 20; **41:**8², 12, 14, 33, 35, 36, 55, 56; **42:**2, 5, 17, 18, 19, 21, 22, 25², 27², 33; **43:**4, 9, 12, 14, 21, 24, 25, 30, 32; **44:**2, 5, 21; **45:**5, 6², 7, 11, 12, 19, 21, 23; **46:**3, 29, 30, 34; **47:**14, 16, 17², 18, 19, 20², 23², 24², 29²; **49:**1, 4, 6, 13, 16, 18, 20; **50:**3³, 4, 5, 10, 15, 20, 21; **Ex 1:**9, 11; **2:**2, 3, 6, 7, 9, 19, 23; **3:**5, 22²; **4:**16, 19; **5:**7, 9, 12, 13, 19; **8:**9³, 28; **9:**15, 16, 28; **10:**1, 11, 22, 23; **11:**2; **12:**2, 3², 4, 13, 14, 15², 16², 17, 19, 21, 24, 30, 33, 35², 36, 39, 42, 43; **13:**6, 8, 9², 17, 18; **14:**4, 12, 14, 15; **15:**1, 11, 21, 26, 27, 34, 36, 39, 42, 43; **16:**4² 9, 15, 16, 22, 29, 32, 33; **17:**1, 3, 6, 16; **18:**1², 3, 4, 8, 9, 11, 13, 14², 18, 22, 26; **19:**6, 12, 15; **20:**4, 5², 7, 11, 22, 24²; **21:**2, 6, 8, 9, 19, 23, 24⁴, 25³, 26, 27, 34, 36; **22:**1², 3, 7, 10, 13, 15, 17, 21, 27², 30; **23:**7, 8, 10, 15², 29; **24:**12, 14, 16; **25:**2, 6³, 8, 12, 22, 26, 29, 33, 39; **26:**7, 12, 14, 15, 18, 19, 20, 22, 23, 26, 27², 36, 37²; **27:**4, 6, 9, 16, 19², 20, 21; **28:**2², 3², 4, 12, 15, 21, 22, 23, 30, 32, 40, 42, 43; **29:**22, 25, 26, 28, 31, 33, 35, 36, 37², 42; **30:**1, 4, 8, 10, 12, 15, 16³, 18, 21², 31, 37; **31:**4, 10²; **32:**1, 21, 26, 29, 30, 34²; **33:**5², 20; **34:**7, 10, 14, 15, 16, 18², 27; **35:**2, 5, 8², 14², 15, 17, 18², 19³, 21³, 24, 28³, 29, 32, 36³, 37, 38; **37:**3, 15, 16², 19; **38:**4, 5, 7, 17, 18, 21, 24, 27, 28, 30², 31⁴, 39:1², 4, 7, 14, 15, 16, 24, 25, 26, 34, 39², 40³, 41³, 40:15, 30; **Lev 1:**4; **2:**11; **3:**17; **4:**3, 20², 21, 26, 28, 31, 33², 35²; **5:**6³, 7³, 8, 10², 11², 13², 16², 18²; **6:**7³, 9, 14, 18, 25; **7:**1, 8², 11, 18, 19, 24, 36, 37; **8:**2, 14, 15, 18, 22, 33², 34, 35²; **9:**2³, 3², 4², 7³, 8, 10², 11, 18; **10:**6, 7, 14, 15; **11:**4, 5, 6, 7, 9, 10, 11², 13², 15, 16, 17, 18, 19, 20, 21, 26, 28, 29, 31, 36, 50, 54, 59; **14:**2, 4, 10, 18, 19, 20, 21², 22², 23, 24, 25, 29, 32², 38, 53, 54², 57; **15:**13, 15, 24, 25, 30⁴, 31, 32², 33; **16:²**3², 5², 6, 8³, 9, 10, 11³, 15²; **16²**, 17, 18, 20, 21, 24⁴, 27, 29, 30, 33³, 34²; **17:**7², 11³; **18:**5, 21, 25, 27; **19:**4, 10, 21, 22², 23, 28, 30, 31, 34; **20:**3, 19, 25; **21:**1, 2, 3, 4, 11, 17; **22:**3, 7, 9, 14, 18, 27; **23:**6, 8, 14, 19², 20, 21, 22, 28, 31, 32, 34, 36², 37², 38, 39, 40, 41², 42; **24:**2, 3, 5, 18, 20³, 22; **25:**3², 6², 7, 9, 11², 17, 18; **6:**2, 12, 25, 31, 33; **7:**8, 17, 18, 40, 42², 50²; 51; **8:**11, 13², 15, 16, 17, 18, 19, 20, 21, 25, 28, 36, 39, 41, 42, 44, 46, 48, 51, 53, 65, 66²; **9:**4, 7, 19², 21, 24, 25; **10:**3, 9, 12², 13, 29²; **11:**7³, 8, 12, 13², 16, 31², 32, 34, 37, 38; **12:**1, 3, 5, 15, 17, 21, 24, 28, 33; **13:**6, 9, 13², 23, 29, 32, 33²; **14:**5, 9, 12, 13, 14, 18, 20, 23, 29; **15:**4, 5, 7, 23, 31; **16:**5, 14, 20, 21, 24, 27, 32; **17:**12, 13², 14, 15²; **16:**18, 10, 18, 23², 29, 31, 41; **19:**3, 7², 10, 11, 14; **20:**7², 18², 23, 25², 29, 38, 39, 42²; **21:**2; **22:**1, 6, 12, 13, 15, 23, 39, 45, 48; **2Ki 1:**13, 14, 16, 18; **2:**9, 16, 17; **3:**9², 14, 17, 19², 23, 27; **4:**7, 16², 18², 23, 27, 34; **5:**17, 18²; **6:**1, 2, 19, 23, 25², 27, 33; **7:**1², 6, 7, 16², 18², 20; **8:**1, 3, 5, 18, 19², 23, 27; **9:**2, 5, 10, 26, 34; **10:**3, 16, 19, 22², 24, 28, 30, 31, 33; **11:**3, 4, 7, 15; **12:**7, 12, 13², 19; **13:**3, 4, 4², 7, 9, 10, 11⁴, 17², 19², 23; **14:**6³, 10, 15, 17, 18², 19³, 7², 10, 11, 14, 20²; **15:**6, 21, 31, 36; **16:**6, 10, 15, 19; **17:**4, 5, 16, 32, 37; **18:**4, 18, 24, 32; **19:**4², 18, 29, 31, 34²; **20:²**6², 10, 19, 20; **21:**17, 25; **22:**7, 13³; **23:**4, 7, 13³, 28; **24:**1, 4, 5, 13, 16; **25:**3, 16, 26, 29; **1Ch 4:**23, 39, 41; **5:**18²; **6:**32, 49, 54; **7:**4², 22, 40; **9:**13, 19², 25, 26, 27, 31, 32, 33; **10:**13; **11:**13; **12:**8, 14²; **14:**1, 2, 8; **15:**1³, 3, 12, 23; **16:**1, 15, 21, 25, 26, 33³, 34, 41, 42³, 43; **17:**2, 9, 10, 12², 19, 21, 27, 27; **18:**14; **19:**5, 7, 12²; **21:**2², 3, 4, 5², 6², 7, 8, 10, 14³, 17², 18, 19, 22², 30; **22:**3, 7, 9, 14, 18, 27; **23:**6, 8, 14, 19², 20, 26, 27, 30², 31, 32²; **24:**1, 4, 5, 13, 16; **25:**3, 16, 26, 29; **26:**1, 2, 10, 12, 13³; **27:**1, 12, 13², 21², 24²; **28:**8, 21; **29:**4, 5, 7, 20², 30³, 10, 18, 33; **31:**4³, 8³, 15², 17, 21², 22; **Ecc 1:**18; **2:**3, 4, 8, 10, 16, 18, 21², 22; **25:**3:1², 8², 12, 17³, 18, 22²; **4:**8, 9; **5:**8, 14, 16, 18²; **6:**7, 12²; **7:**2, 3, 9, 10, 12; **8:**6²; 11, 15; **9:**5, 7, 9, 10; **10:**11, 17², 19²; **11:**1, 2, 6, 8, 9, 10; **12:**13, 14; **SS 1:**2; **2:**5, 14, 15; **3:**1², 2², 8, 9; **5:**4, 5, 6²; **6:**1; **7:**10, 13;

10:13, 17, 19, 21; **11:**5, 12, 15; **12:**5, 11; **14:**1, 2, 7, 10, 23, 25, 27; **15:**2, 4, 6, 9, 17²; **19:**16:2, 3, 4, 6, 8, 11, 13, 15², 18, 19, 22; **17:**1, 8, 12², 16², 18; **18:**1, 5, 14, 15, 16, 18; **19:**2, 5, 7, 11, 12, 21²; **20:**4², 11, 14², 19; **21:**5, 8², 13; **22:**2, 5, 24, 27, 29; **23:**4, 5, 7, 14, 21; **24:**5, 6, 16³, 19, 20, 21; **25:**16; **26:**27:20; **28:**26, 32, 50², 57, 65, 68; **29:**21; **30:**11, 16, 20; **31:**6, 7, 10, 19², 23, 27, 29; **32:**8, 9, 10, 20, 22, 31, 43², 47; **33:**9, 12, 21²; **34:**8, 12; **Jos 1:**9, 11, 15; **2:**8, 10, 11, 14, 15, 19; **3:**5; **4:**13²; **5:**6, 12, 13², 14, 15; **6:**3, 14, 16; **7:**3, 9, 13²; **8:**1, 2, 6, 18, 20, 22; **9:**9, 11, 10, 20; **10:**14, 19, 42; **11:**14, 18, 19, 20; **13:**6² 31²; **14:**4², 10; **15:**1, 18²; **16:**1, 9; **17:**1², 2, 12, 14, 15², 18; **18:**6, 8, 10, 11, 28; **19:**1, 10, 17, 24, 32, 40, 50; **21:**2, 4, 13, 19, 27, 29, 34, 38; **42:**2, 3, 14, 17, 19, 20, 24, 26, 28, 29, 23:3², 4, 10, 13; **24:**7², 9, 15², 25², 31, 32; **Jdg 1:**1, 7, 14², 27, 33; **2:**7, 10, 18², 20; **3:**8, 9, 11, 14, 19, 20, 28, 30; **4:**3², 6, 9, 22²; **5:**16, 25², 26², 30³; **6:**1, 2, 4, 6, 31; **7:**2, 4, 18², 20²; **8:**7, 14, 26, 30, 35²; **9:**2, 3, 8, 17, 36, 57; **10:**8, 12; **11:**18, 26, 34, 38, 40; **12:**9; **13:**1, 12; **14:**2², 3², 4, 10, 14, 15; **15:**20; **16:**2, 25, 28; **17:**3, 9; **18:**4, 11, 16, 26, 30²; **19:**15, 19², 28; **20:**10², 28; **21:**5, 6, 7, 8, 9, 14, 15, 16, 22; **Ru 1:**1, 6, 12, 13³; **2:**7, 11, 12, 16²; **22²**; **3:**1², 11, 13, 16, 18; **4:**4, 7, 15, 16; **1Sa 1:**4, 11, 16, 20, 27, 28; **2:**1, 3, 5, 8, 12, 14, 17, 20, 25³, 29, 35, 36; **3:**9, 10, 13, 14; **4:**13, 18, 22; **5:**11; **6:**2, 17; **7:**5, 8; **8:**1, 10, 12, 16, 18; **9:**3, 10, 12, 16, 19, 20; **10:**2, 7, 14, 21; **11:**13; **12:**2, 7, 8, 13, 17, 19³, 22, 23², 24; **13:**13, 17, 14:29, 45; **15:**2, 6, 23, 29, 34, 35; **16:**1, 3, 7, 11, 16, 17; **17:**9, 25; **19:**2, 5², 11, 22; **20:**4, 6, 8², 17, 26, 28, 31, 35, 42; **21:**2; **22:**3, 8, 10, 11, 13², 15², 22²; **23:**4, 7, 8, 14, 24, 25, 28; **24:**2, 4, 5, 6, 19; **25:**1, 8, 11, 21, 25, 28², 30, 33², 39; **26:**2, 20, 23; **27:**1, 4, 11; **28:**2², 8, 9², 10; **11, 20; **29:**3; **30:**10, 12², 25, 26; **2Sa 1:**12², 16, 21, 24, 26²; **2:**5, 7, 15²; **3:**9, 14, 17, 18, 20, 21, 33, 34, 39; **4:**5, 10; **5:**11, 12, 17, 18, 20, 21, 23², 27, 29; **6:**11, 17; **7:**3, 10, 11, 13, 21², 27, 29; **8:**15; **9:**1, 7, 10²; **10:**5, 11², 12, 19; **11:**4², 6, 16, 18; **13:**2², 7, 18, 37, 39; **14:**1, 2, 7, 13, 17, 25, 26, 29, 32; **15:**2, 6, 12; **16:**2, 8, 11, 22; **17:**10, 14, 17, 23, 29²; **18:**3, 5, 12, 14, 16, 18, 19, 1², 2², 7, 20, 21, 32², 33, 36, 37, 38², 42; **20:**3, 5, 11; **21:**1, 2, 3, 4, 5, 10; **22:**18, 22², 31², 32, 35, 40, 42; **23:**9, 15; **24:**12, 14, 22², 24²; **1Ki 1:**2, 3; **2:**1, 15, 18, 19², 22⁴, 23, 24, 32, 36, 38, 44; **3:**2, 3, 4, 5, 9, 10, 11², 13, 14, 24, 26; **4:**7², 24, 26, 27, 28; **5:**3, 5², 6², 7, 9, 11², 17, 18; **6:**2, 12, 25, 31, 33; **7:**8, 11, 40, 42², 45²; **50²**;

9, 10, 19, 20, 25, 26; **26:**10, 13, 14, 15², 18³, 23²; **28:**2, 11, 13, 16, 19, 23; **29:**11, 17, 18, 21³, 23, 24³, 32, 34, 36; **30:**9, 17, 18, 21, 22, 23, 24, 26, 27; **31:**3², 18, 19; **32:**1, 7, 9², 15, 23², 27², 28², 29; **34:**11², 21²; **35:**5, 6, 7², 9, 14⁴, 15, 16, 17, 24, 25; **36:**10, 23; **Ezr 1:**2, 4; **2:**62, 69; **3:**4, 5, 12; **4:**1, 3, 14; **5:**10; **6:**8, 9, 10, 11, 17³, 18, 20³, 22; **7:**6, 9, 10, 11, 16, 19, 20, 23; **8:**17, 21², 22; **9:**2, 8, 10, 12; **10:**2, 7, 14, 19; **Ne 1:**4, 6, 9; **2:**1, 8³, 12, 14, 20; **3:**17; **4:**4, 5, 6, 14, 20, 23; **5:**2, 8, 15, 16, 18, 19²; **6:**9, 18; **7:**5, 64, 70, 71, 72; **8:**1, 4, 9, 10, 11, 18; **9:**3, 10², 18, 20, 21, 30, 31; **10:**28, 30, 32², 33³, 35, 37, 39; **11:**12, 22, 25; **12:**29², 44³, 46³, 47²; **13:**5², 6, 10, 13, 14², 22, 25², 31²; **Est 1:**3, 4, 5, 8, 9, 11, 13, 17²; **2:**2², 12, 15², 18, 20; **3:**2, 4, 6, 9, 14, 4:4, 7, 8³, 11², 14³, 14³; **16²**; **5:**4, 8; **6:**3², 4, 6, 7, 9, 10, 11; **7:**4², 7, 9, 10; **8:**1, 6, 8, 10, 12, 16; **9:**19, 24², 31²; **10:**3²; **Job 1:**5, 9; **2:**4², 13; **3:**9, 10, 13, 14, 21³, 24; **4:**11; **5:**6, 18, 23; **6:**8, 19, 22, 27²; **7:**2², 8, 19, 21²; **8:**9, 17; **9:**15, 17, 21, 28; **10:**15; **11:**6; **12:**5; **13:**5, 7, 8, 16², 26; **14:**3, 7, 14, 15, 20, 22; **15:**11, 20, 22, 23, 31, 34; **16:**21; **17:**3, 5, 13, 15; **18:**4, 10, 12², 19²; **20:**18, 19, 24, 26, 29; **21:**19, 21, 31; **22:**4, 6, 25; **24:**1², 5, 8, 9, 12, 15, 24; **26:**10; **27:**8, 15; **28:**1, 3, 17, 24, 26²; **29:**2², 4, 6, 12, 21, 23², 25; **30:**12, 23, 24, 25², 26², 28; **31:**2, 3², 11, 19, 20, 23², 28, 32; **32:**2, 11, 18, 22; **33:**12, 14, 23, 24, 26, 32; **34:**3, 4, 9, 11, 19, 23, 26, 27, 30, 36, 35:9, 14; **36:**13, 20, 23; **37:**24²; **38:**7, 10, 21, 23², 25², 39, 41²; **39:**8², 11, 17; **41:**3, 4², 5, 6; **42:**3, 8², 10; **Ps 1:**6; **2:**12; **4:**T, 3, 8; **5:**T², 2², 10², 11, 12; **6:**T, 2²; **7:**T, 2, 5, 7; **8:**9; **8:**T, 4; **9:**T, 4, 5, 7, 9, 10, 12; **10:**4, 8, 15, 16; **11:**T, 2, 7; **12:**T, 1; **13:**T, 6; **14:**T, 5, 7; **16:**1, 3, 6; **17:**4, 6, 12, 14; **18:**T, 6, 17, 21, 30², 31, 34, 39, 41; **19:**T, 4; **20:**T, 5; **21:**T, 4², 7, 12; **22:**T, 11, 18, 24², 28, 31; **23:**3, 4; **24:**2; **25:**5, 6, 7, 10, 11, 12, 15, 16, 20²; **26:**1, 3; **27:**5, 12, 14²; **28:**1, 2², 4³, 5, 6²; **7, 8; **30:**T, 1, 2, 5²; **31:**T, 3, 4², 7, 9, 13, 17, 18, 19, 21, 22²; **32:**4; **33:**1, 3, 4, 9, 12, 17, 20, 21; **34:**9; **35:**7², 10, 12, 14², 23², 27; **36:**T, 2, 9; **37:**2, 7, 9, 10, 13, 17, 24, 28, 32, 34, 36, 37; **38:**2, 15, 16, 17; **39:**T², 7, 9, 11, 12²; **40:**T, 1, 12; **41:**T, 1, 4, 7, 11; **42:**T, 1², 2², 5, 11; **43:**5; **44:**T, 3, 4, 12, 19, 22; **45:**T, 1, 6, 11, 17; **46:**T; **47:**T, 4, 7, 9; **48:**14²; **49:**T, 7, 8, 10, 11, 14, 17; **50:**6, 8, 10, 12, 19; **51:**T, 3; **52:**T, 8, 9²; **53:**T, 5, 6; **54:**T, 3, 6, 7; **55:**T, 3, 9, 15, 23; **56:**T, 1, 9²; 13; **57:**T, 1, 2, 6, 10; **58:**T; **59:**T, 3, 9, 12³, 15, 16; **60:**T², 2, 4, 11; **61:**T, 3, 5, 6; **62:**T², 8; **63:**1², 10; **64:**T; **65:**T, 9², 13; **66:**T, 10, 16; **67:**T, 4²; **68:**T, 10; **69:**T, 1, 3², 7², 9², 17, 20², 21, 26, 35; **70:**T; **71:**3, 5, 10, 11, 14, 22, 23, 24; **72:**12, 14, 15; **73:**2, 3, 28; **74:**20; **75:**T, 1, 9; **76:**T; **77:**T², 1, 8; **78:**5, 20, 22, 24, 29, 50; **79:**7, 8, 9²; **80:**T, 9, 15, 17; **81:**T, 1, 4, 5; **82:**8; **84:**T, 2², 3, 11; **85:**T, 13; **86:**1, 2, 3, 4, 5, 6, 13, 14, 17; **88:**T, 3, 13; **89:**6, 12, 17, 35, 47; **90:**4, 10, 11, 14, 15², 17; **91:**11, 14; **92:**T, 4²; 9; **93:**5; **94:**13, 14, 16², 23²; **95:**1, 3, 5, 7, 10; **96:**4, 5, 12, 13; **97:**9, 10; **98:**1², 4, 6, 8, 9; **99:**9; **100:**T, 5; **102:**1, 3, 9, 10, 13, 14, 16, 18; **103:**6, 11², 14, 15; **104:**8, 14², 18, 21; **105:**8, 14, 24, 28, 42, 44; **106:**1, 8, 13, 15, 20, 31, 33, 45; **107:**1, 8², 9, 11, 15², 16, 21², 25, 31²; **108:**4, 12; **109:**T, 2, 4, 5², 16, 21, 22, 31; **110:**1; **111:**5, 8, 9; **112:**4²; **116:**1², 7, 8, 12; **117:**2; **118:**1, 19, 21, 29; **119:**20, 22, 32, 35, 39, 40, 42, 43, 44, 45, 47, 49, 62, 66, 71, 74, 77, 78, 81, 82, 85, 86, 91, 93, 94, 98, 99, 100, 102, 105, 110, 117, 118, 123², 126, 131, 136, 139, 147, 153, 155, 158, 164, 166, 167, 168, 171, 172, 173, 174, 176; **120:**7; **122:**5, 6, 8, 9; **123:**3; **125:**3; **126:**2, 3; **127:**2²; **130:**2, 5, 6³, 7; **131:**1; **132:**5², 9, 10, 12, 13², 14², 16, 17²; **133:**3; **135:**3², 4, 14; **136:**1; **137:**3², 8; **138:**2², 5, 8; **139:**T, 6², 13, 16, 22; **140:**T, 5², 6, 12; **141:**9; **142:**1, 3, 4², 6³; **143:**1, 2, 6, 9, 10, 11, 12; **144:**1², 3; **145:**1, 2, 21; **146:**10; **147:**9², 13, 20; **148:**5, 6, 13, 14; **149:**4, 5; **150:**2; **Pr 1:**2², 3, 4, 6, 11, 16, 18, 28, 32; **2:**3², 4², 6, 7, 8, 10, 18, 21; **3:**2, 14, 22, 26, 30, 32; **4:**13, 16, 22, 23, 26; **5:**3, 21, 23; **6:**1², 23, 26, 34; **7:**15; **8:**6, 7, 11, 35; **9:**11; **10:**13, 21, 29; **11:**5, 14, 15, 27; **12:**6, 10, 20; **13:**2, 13, 22²; **14:**7, 9, 14², 26, 31; **15:**22, 24; **16:**4², 6, 12, 26; **17:**3², 5, 13, 17, 18, 21², 26; **18:**16, 23; **19:**10², 17, 18, 29²; **20:**16², 22², 25; **21:**7, 18²; 26, 31; **22:**3, 9, 11, 16, 20, 23, 26; **23:**3, 5, 7, 9, 11, 17, 18, 21, 24², 26², 7, 13, 14, 16, 20, 22, 29; **25:**4, 7², 8, 26, 27; **27:**1, 12, 13², 21², 24²; **28:**8, 21; **29:**4, 5, 7, 20², 30³, 10, 18, 33; **31:**4³, 8³, 15², 17, 21², 22; **Ecc 1:**18; **2:**3, 4, 8, 10, 16, 18, 21², 22; **25:**3:1², 8², 12, 17³, 18, 22²; **4:**8, 9; **5:**8, 14, 16, 18²; **6:**7, 12²; **7:**2, 3, 9, 10, 12; **8:**6²; 11, 15; **9:**5, 7, 9, 10; **10:**11, 17², 19²; **11:**1, 2, 6, 8, 9, 10; **12:**13, 14; **SS 1:**2; **2:**5, 14, 15; **3:**1², 2², 8, 9; **5:**4, 5, 6²; **6:**1; **7:**10, 13;

8:6, 7, 8³, 11, 12²; **Isa 1:**2, 20; **2:**4², 12², 13, 14, 15, 16; **3:**10, 11; **5:**1, 2, 4³, 7², 12², 13, 20⁴, 23, 24, 25, 26²; **6:**5, 7, 8, 11; **7:**8, 11, 18², 24, 25²; **8:**2, 9², 10, 14², 17; **9:**1, 4, 5², 6, 12, 17², 19, 21; **10:**3, 4, 12, 13, 14; **11:**4, 9, 10, 12, 16²; **12:**5, 6²; **13:**4, 6, 11², 17; **14:**20, 21, 23, 26, 27; **16:**7², 9, 10, 11²; **17:**8; **18:**5; **20:**3, 6; **21:**4, 14²; **22:**11², 13, 14, 16, 23; **23:**1, 4, 10, 13, 15, 18²; **24:**2¹², 11, 14, 23; **25:**1, 4³, 6; **26:**4, 8, 9², 11², 12², 15, 19, 20, 21; **27:**5, 9, 11; **28:**5, 10, 15, 16, 24; **29:**11, 20; **30:**2², 8², 11, 14, 18², 19, 23, 33; **31:**1, 7; **32:**6, 12², 13³, 14; **33:**2, 5, 6, 22; **34:**6, 8, 13², 14, 15, 16; **35:**2, 6, 8; **36:**9; **37:**4², 19, 30, 32, 35²; **38:**17, 18²; **39:**8; **40:**2², 3², 5, 10, 16², 19², 20; **41:**10², 12, 13, 14, 17; **42:**6², 11, 14, 21, 24; **43:**1, 3², 4², 5, 7, 14, 21, 22, 23², 24, 25, 26²; **44:**3, 9, 15, 19, 21, 22, 23³; **45:**4, 13, 18, 22; **46:**1; **47:**15; **48:**4, 9², 11², 17, 21, 22; **49:**4, 5, 6², 8, 13², 19, 20; **50:**2; **51:**5, 8, 13, 15; **52:**3², 4, 5², 8, 9, 12, 15; **53:**5², 8², 12²; **54:**1, 3, 5, 7, 8, 10, 16; **55:**5, 7, 8, 10², 11, 13²; **56:**1, 4, 7²; **57:**13, 15, 16, 21; **58:**2³, 5³, 9; **59:**3, 4, 6, 9², 11², 12, 16, 19, 21; **60:**1, 9, 12, 19, 21; **61:**1², 3², 4, 8, 10, 11; **62:**1², 4, 8², 10²; **63:**4, 5, 7³, 12, 14, 17, 18; **64:**3, 4, 7, 9; **65:**1, 5², 7, 10³, 11³, 12², 16, 18, 22, 23; **66:**1, 4², 10, 11, 12, 16; **Jer 1:**8, 12, 19; **2:**11, 19, 28², 37; **3:**2, 12, 14, 22; **4:**6², 8, 12, 19, 31; **5:**3, 4, 6, 8, 9, 10, 22, 29; **6:**1², 4, 13, 25, 26²; **7:**7, 12, 16³, 18, 22, 29, 32, 33, 34; **8:**8, 10, 14, 15², 22²; **9:**1, 2², 4, 7, 8, 9, 10, 17², 24, 26; **10:**3, 16, 18, 23, 25; **11:**14², 17, 18, 20; **12:**3, 12, 14; **13:**11², 15, 16, 18, 25; **14:**2, 3, 6, 7², 10, 11, 17, 19², 21, 22; **15:**2⁴, 5, 7, 11, 14, 15², 16, 20; **16:**3, 4, 5, 6, 7², 9, 13, 15, 16, 18²; **17:**4, 5, 14, 18:10, 11, 18, 20, 22²; **19:**4; **20:**3, 4, 10, 12, 17; **21:**2², 22:4, 6, 10², 11, 13², 18², 20, 30; **23:**2, 28, 24:6, 7; **25:**3, 5, 12, 29, 31, 34, 36; **26:**14, 15; **27:**4, 7, 14, 19, 22; **28:**4; **29:**6, 7, 10, 11², 15, 19, 23, 32; **30:**7, 9, 13², 14, 17, 21; **31:**7², 11, 12, 15, 16, 24, 30, 34, 38; **32:**8, 9, 15, 17, 18, 27, 35, 39, 43, 44; **33:**4, 9², 11², 12, 17, 26; **34:**8, 17², 20; **36:**7, 9, 31; **37:**3, 4, 17, 21; **38:**14, 19, 27; **39:**12; **40:**2; **42:**2², 6, 10, 11, 14, 20; **43:**10, 11³; **44:**27³; **45:**5², 46:3, 10², 11, 14, 15, 19², 21², 28; **47:**4; **48:**1, 6, 9, 17, 18, 20, 26, 31², 32, 34, 36², 38, 44, 45; **49:**3², 8, 14, 19, 23; **50:**7, 9, 14, 20³, 24, 25², 27², 28, 29², 31², 38, 44; **51:**5, 6², 8, 9, 11, 13, 19, 20, 24, 26³, 27, 28, 29, 39, 45, 47, 48²; 51, 56, 58²; **52:**6, 19, 20, 33; **La 1:**4, 8, 9, 11³, 13, 17, 19, 20; **2:**5, 13, 16, 19, 20, 22; **3:**8, 12, 22, 24, 26, 27, 28, 31, 33, 39, 56, 64; **4:**4, 9, 17²; **18, 19; **5:**16, 18; **Eze 2:**5, 7; **3:**7, 15, 17, 18², 19, 20²; **4:**4, 5, 6, 9, 12, 17²; **5:**2; **6:**8, 9², 11; **7:**3, 4, 8, 12, 13, 14, 19, 20, 26; **8:**14, 17; **10:**10; **11:**11, 12, 16², 21; **12:**2, 3, 4, 6, 7, 12, 13, 19, 24, 25, 27; **13:**5, 16, 18, 19; **14:**5, 21, 23; **15:**4, 5, 6; **16:**5³, 8, 17, 19, 24, 33, 34², 52², 63²; **17:**7, 20; **18:**4, 7², 16², 17, 18, 26, 32; **19:**6, 8, 11², 14; **20:**6, 9, 11, 14, 16, 22, 39, 40, 43, 44; **21:**10, 11, 12, 14²; 15², 19, 20, 21, 22, 28, 32²; **22:**28, 30; **23:**9, 21, 24, 28, 29, 32, 37², 40², 43, 49; **24:**5, 6², 7, 14, 17; **25:**5², 6; **26:**5², 7, 14; **27:**5, 9, 12, 13, 14, 16, 19, 21, 22, 25; **28:**4, 14; **29:**3, 6, 11, 16², 19, 20²; 21; **30:**2, 3², 9, 11, 14²; 15; **32:**10, 11, 16, 18, 25, 27, 31; **33:**6, 7, 8², 9, 13, 15, 18, 30, 31, 32; **34:**4, 5, 6, 8⁴, 10², 11², 16, 17, 18², 29²; **36:**5, 8², 9, 20, 21, 22², 24, 29, 31, 32², 37, 38; **37:**23; **38:**17; **39:**5, 9³, 10, 12, 17, 19, 23, 25, 28, 29; **40:**4, 7, 42², 43, 45, 46; **41:**6, 24; **42:**5, 7, 13, 14²; **43:**7, 18, 20, 21, 22, 25²; 26², 44:11, 24, 27; **45:**2², 4³, 5, 11, 14, 15², 16, 17, 20², 22², 23, 24³, 25; **46:**5, 11, 12, 13, 15, 23; **47:**1, 10, 11, 12², 13², 22²; **48:**10, 11, 15³, 17, 18, 23; **Da 1:**4, 5, 8, 12, 14; **2:**6, 9², 13, 16², 18, 20, 24, 30, 40, 47; **3:**3, 29; **4:**2, 6, 7, 9², 12, 16, 18², 19, 21², 23, 25, 30, 31, 32, 36; **5:**1, 7, 12, 17²; **6:**4, 5, 11, 26; **7:**12, 18, 25; **8:**13, 26, 27; **9:**14, 15, 17, 19, 20, 23, 24², 27; **10:**2, 11, 14; **11:**8, 10, 13, 34, 40²; **12:**3, 7, 12, 13; **Hos 1:**4, 6, 9, 11; **2:**2, 7², 8, 13, 18, 23; **3:**2, 4; **4:**4, 7, 9²; **5:**13, 14; **6:**6, 9, 11; **7:**10, 14, 16; **8:**4, 9, 11², 12; **9:**1, 4, 9, 10:1, 3, 5, 6, 10, 12²; **11:**9; **12:**4, 6, 12, 13, 14; **13:**2, 5; **14:**3, 4, 8; **Joel 1:**5, 8, 11, 13, 15²; 17, 19, 20; **2:**1, 5, 13, 14, 18, 22, 23, 25, 26, 32; **3:**2, 3³, 4, 5, 9, 12, 13², 14, 16²; **Am 1:**3², 6², 9², 11², 13²; **2:**1², 4², 6³; **3:**2, 14; **4:**5, 8; **5:**3, 5, 8, 12, 13, 14, 17, 18²; **6:**11, 14; **7:**4, 11; **8:**2, 6, 8, 10, 11, 12; **9:**4², 6, 9; **Ob 1:**1, 7, 11, 15; **Jnh 1:**3³, 7, 8², 11, 13, 14³; **2:**2², 4³, 6, 8; **Mic 1:**6, 9, 12, 13, 16²; **2:**3, 10, 11²; **3:**3², 5, 6, 8, 11³; **4:**3², 4, 5, 8, 10, 13; **5:**1, 2, 4, 7²; **6:**2; **7:**6, 7³, 11²; **Na 1:**7, 14; **2:**12²; **3:**7, 10, 14, 19; **Hab 1:**2, 5, 16; **2:**3², 8, 13², 14, 17, 18; **3:**9, 16, 19; **Zep 1:**7, 18; **2:**6, 7, 10², 15; **3:**3, 8², 11, 18; **Hag 1:**2, 4, 11; **2:**4, 23; **Zec 1:**14²; **2:**6, 8², 10; **5:**3, 11; **7:**3, 5², 6; **8:**2², 9, 10², 19; **9:**1, 5, 8, 11, 15;

10:1, 2, 3², 6, 8, 10; **11:**2, 4, 6, 7, 16²; **12:**3, 10⁴; **14:**5; **Mal 1:**6², 8, 14; **2:**1, 5, 7, 12; **3:**2, 5, 10, 12; **4:**2, 4; **Mt 2:**5, 6, 8, 13², 14, 18, 20; **3:**2, 3² 9, 11, 15; **4:**6, 10, 17, 18; **5:**3, 4, 5, 6², 7, 8, 9, 10, 12, 13, 20², 30², 32, 34, 35², 36, 38², 44; **6:**5, 7, 8, 14, 16, 19, 20, 21, 32, 34; **7:**2, 8, 9, 10, 12, 13, 15; **8:**5, 9; **9:**13, 16, 20; **10:**10², 11, 15², 20, 25, 29, 35, 39; **11:**13, 17, 18, 22², 24², 26, 29³, 30; **12:**4², 8, 10, 33, 34, 36, 37, 39, 40, 41, 42, 50; **13:**15, 17, 38, 45; **14:**4², 6; **15:**3, 4, 6, 19, 23, 32; **16:**2, 3, 4, 9, 10, 17², 25², 26², 27; **17:**4², 20, 27; **18:**6, 8, 9, 10, 12, 19², 20; **19:**3², 5, 9, 12, 13², 14, 23, 24², 27, 29; **20:**1, 2, 13, 23², 28, 32; **21:**22, 26, 32, 46; **22:**2, 14, 19, 24, 43; **23:**3, 5, 8, 9, 10, 12, 29; **24:**5, 19, 21, 22, 24, 27, 38, 46; **25:**9², 11, 29, 34, 35, 40², 41, 42, 45²; **26:**12, 15, 16, 17, 24, 28², 31, 40, 42, 50, 52, 59, 73; **27:**4, 7, 18, 19, 20, 43, 55, 58, 64; **28:**2, 5², Mk 1:**3² 4, 16, 36, 37, 44; **2:**15, 26, 27²; **3:**2, 9, 10, 21, 32; **4:**19 22; **5:**4, 8, 9, 19, 20, 25; **6:**8, 14, 17, 18² 21, 22, 24, 26; **7:**10, 12, 19, 11, 27, 29; **8:**2, 7, 11, 12, 14, 15, 19, 20, 35³, 36, 37; **9:**5⁴, 23, 40² 42, 43, 45, 47; **10:**2, 7, 14, 20, 23, 25², 29, 30, 40², 45²; 51; **11:**13, 17, 18², 23, 24, 32; **12:**1, 12, 19², 38, 40; **13:**11, 17, 20, 22, 24; **14:**1, 5, 8, 11, 12, 15, 21, 24, 27, 36, 37, 55, 70; **15:**8, 41, 43²; **16:**6, 14; **Lk 1:**3, 10, 15, 17, 21, 22, 24, 25, 37, 44, 48, 49², 56, 57, 63, 66, 69, 76²; **2:**6, 7, 10, 20, 25, 27, 30, 32², 41, 44², 45, 48, 49³; 3:3, 4², 8², 4:2, 6, 10, 18², 25, 42; **5:**4, 9, 14, 17, 29, 39, 46; **6:**4, 7, 20, 21², 23², 24, 25², 30, 34, 42², 45; **7:**6, 8, 30, 32, 33, 34, 45, 47; **8:**13, 14, 15, 17, 27, 29, 33, 43, 48², 52, 53, 62; **10:**7, 12², 13, 14², 21, 24, 35; **11:**4, 10, 15, 24, 25, 26, 37; **12:**6, 12, 19, 20, 21, 30, 32, 33, 34, 35, 36², 37, 38, 43, 57; **13:**6, 7², 8, 11, 14, 16, 25, 33; **14:**8, 11, 14, 18², 28; **15:**13, 20, 24, 29, 30; **16:**8, 9, 17², 28; **17:**2², 24, 31; **18:**4, 7, 14, 16, 24, 25², 29², 30; **19:**10, 15, 26, 37; **20:**9, 19, 22, 28², 36, 37, 38, 43, 47; **21:**6, 8, 9, 16, 18, 19, 20, 22, 23, 26, 30, 35; **22:**2, 6, 8, 9, 16, 18, 42, 43, 45; **23:**4, 8, 14, 15, 19², 22², 25², 27, 28³, 29, 31, 34, 41, 45, 51, 52; **24:**5, 29; **Jn 1:**17, 23, 43; **2:**6, 12, 13, 17, 24, 25²; **3:**2, 16, 17, 20, 29, 34², 36; **4:**9², 10, 22, 23, 35, 36, 38, 42, 43, 45; **5:**1, 5, 6, 13, 18, 20, 21, 26, 28, 30, 34, 36, 41, 44², 45, 46, 47; **6:**5, 6, 7, 17, 26, 27², 33, 38, 44, 50, 51, 55, 63, 64; **7:**5, 6, 8, 10, 11, 18, 22, 23, 28, 35, 36, 38; **8:**6, 14, 18, 21, 29, 37, 42², 44², 50; **9:**16, 18, 21, 22, 29, 39; **10:**3, 7, 11, 13, 15, 25, 32, 33², 39, 40; **11:**4, 8, 17, 18², 19, 21, 31, 32, 41, 47, 48, 49; **12:**1², 3, 5, 13, 21, 27, 28, 31, 32, 34², 36, 41², 42, 47, 48, 49², 50; **13:**1, 2, 3, 16, 18, 19, 21², 26; **14:**3, 10², 16, 26, 28, 31; **15:**4, 18, 19, 20², 21², 22², 24, 25, 27; **16:**22², 27, 28³, 29, 31, 33², 34, 41, 45, 51, 52; **17:**7, 13, 20, 25, 26; **18:**1², 5, 13, 16, 19, 27, 31; **21:**7, 13, 20, 25, 26; **22:**3, 16, 25, 28; **23:**5, 18, 21², 24, 27, 29², 26; **25:**3, 21, 27; **26:**1, 5, 14, 29; **27:**1, 2, 3, 6, 7, 20, 25, 29, 33, 40; **28:**4, 7, 20, 22, 27, 30; **Ro 1:**1, 5, 8, 10, 17, 20, 21, 23, 24, 27²; **2:**1, 4, 5, 8, 9³, 10², 11, 13, 14, 19²; **3:**23, 28; **4:**9², 14, 23, 24², 25²; **5:**6, 7², 8², 10, 13, 15, 18, 19², 21; **6:**6, 9, 10, 14, 22, 23; **7:**1, 2, 5², 7, 8, 11, 15, 18, 19, 22; **8:**1, 3, 13, 15, 19, 20, 23, 24², 25², 26², 27, 28, 29, 31, 32, 36, 38; **9:**3², 5, 6², 7, 18, 21², 22, 23, 28; **10:**1, 3², 5, 13, 16, 20; **11:**4, 9, 10, 14, 18², 20, 22², 23²; 24, 26²; 30, 31², 33, 34, 35², 36; **12:**1, 9, 17², 20²; **13:**1, 3², 4², 5², 6², 7, 10, 11, 12; **14:**4, 10, 11, 14², 15², 18, 19, 20², 23³; **15:**3, 9, 15, 16², 18, 19³, 21, 24³, 28; **16:**4, 17, 18², 19, 22; **1Co 1:**4, 5, 7, 13, 17, 18, 19, 21, 22, 25, 30; **2:**2, 7, 8, 9, 11, 14, 16; **3:**2², 5, 6², 7, 9, 13, 15, 19, 3:23, 28², 41; **4:**6, 7, 9, 15, 17, 20; **5:**7, 6:1, 12², 13⁵, 15, 19, 20; **7:**5, 7, 1², 15¹, 19²; **8:**5, 6², 10, 11, 9:2, 6, 9, 10², 15, 16, 23, 27; **10:**1, 4, 11, 15, 16, 17, 26, 28², 29, 30, 31, 33; **11:**2², 6, 8, 9, 11², 12², 15, 17², 21², 22, 23, 24, 25, 26, 29, 33, 34; **12:**7, 13, 15, 18², 19², 21²; **13:**3, 4, 5, 6, 9, 10, 11, 12², 13; **14:**19², 21, 24², 35, 36, 37; **15:**3, 6², 12, 13, 16, 17, 20, 21, 22, 23, 25², 27, 29, 31², 35², 36, 37, 41, 42, 43², 45, 47, 51, 52; **16:**2, 6, 7, 18²; **2Co 1:**2, 4, 5, 7, 8², 10, 11, 14, 16, 18; **2:**2, 3, 5, 6², 7², 16²; **3:**5, 7², 11, 14, 16, 17, 18; **4:**2², 3, 6, 10, 11, 13², 14, 17³, 18²; **5:**2, 7, 8, 11, 14, 16², 17², 18², 20²; **6:**1, 7², 8³, 9², 13, 14, 17², 18⁴; **7:**1, 9², 13; **8:**2, 7, 10, 15, 19, 10:6²; **11:**2, 3, 9, 15, 18³, 12², 16², 19², 10²; 14²; **12:**6, 11, 13, 14, 15, 20; **13:**12², 10, 14²; **Gal 1:**4, 5, 13, 14; **2:**2, 5, 6, 8, 19²; 20, 21²; **3:**4², 10, 13², 18, 21, 27, 28; **4:**11, 12, 17², 19, 22, 24, 25, 27, 30; **5:**1, 5, 6, 17; **6:**5, 9, 12, 17; **Eph 1:**4, 12, 15², 16, 19, 22; **2:**1, 4, 8, 10², 14, 18; **3:**1², 2, 9, 13, 14, 21; **4:**1, 10, 11, 16, 17², 20; **5:**2, 3, 5, 6, 8, 9, 12, 14, 20, 21, 23, 25, 29, 30; **5:**2, 3, 5, 6, 8, 12, 18, 19, 20, 22; **Php 1:**4, 7³, 8, 13, 16, 17, 19², 21, 22, 24, 25, 27, 29²; **2:**13, 16, 21², 26², 30²; **3:**1², 2, 3, 4, 6², 7, 8, 12, 14, 18; **4:**1, 10, 11, 16, 17², 20; **Col 1:**3, 4, 5, 9², 13, 16², 19, 24², 26; **2:**1³, 5, 8, 9, 11, 12, 13³, 20, 22, 23², 25; **4:**3³, 8, 11, 12, 13³; **1Th 1:**2, 4, 5, 9, 10; **2:**3, 6, 7, 11, 14, 17, 18, 19, 3:3, 5, 8², 9, 11, 12², 4:2, 6, 7, 9, 16; **5:**2, 7, 9, 10, 15, 18²; 25; **2Th 1:**3², 5, 11; **2:**3, 7, 11, 13; **3:**1, 2, 7, 8, 9, 10, 16; **1Ti 1:**9⁴, 10³, 16², 17; **2:**1, 2, 5, 6, 7, 10, 13; **4:**4, 8³, 10, 12; **5:**4², 5, 6, 8², 10², 11², 14, 18; **6:**2, 7, 10², 17², 19²; **2Ti 1:**6, 7, 8, 12, 17; **2:**7, 9, 10, 13, 20², 21; **3:**14, 15, 16, 17; **4:**3, 6², 8², 10, 14, 18; **Tit 1:**1, 10, 11, 16; **2:**11, 13, 14²; **3:**8, 14; **Phm 1:**5, 10, 13, 15², 22; **Heb 1:**3, 5, 8, 13; **2:**2, 6, 9, 10, 16, 17²; **3:**4, 9, 17; **4:**2, 4, 8, 9, 10, 12, 15; **5:**1, 3², 9, 14; **6:**4, 7, 13, 18, 19; **7:**11², 12, 14, 17, 19, 25, 27², 28; **8:**3, 4, 7²; **9:**1, 7², 9, 12, 15, 23, 24², 26, 28; **10:**1, 2³, 4, 5, 10, 14, 16, 22, 23², 26, 30, 37; **11:**1, 2, 5, 10, 14, 16, 23, 25, 26, 30, 37, 40; **12:**1, 2, 7, 9, 10², 11, 13, 16, 29; **13:**2, 4, 9, 14², 16, 17, 18, 21², 22; **Jas 1:**11, 13, 20²; 3, 10, 11, 21, 25; **3:**16; **4:**14; **5:**7², 16, 17; **1Pe 1:**2, 4, 6, 9, 13, 16, 19, 20, 23; **2:**2, 6, 8, 13, 15, 16, 19, 20², 21, 24, 25; **3:**5, 10, 12, 14, 15, 17², 18⁴; **4:**2², 3, 6, 11, 14, 17³, 18; **5:**2, 7, 8, 11; **2Pe 1:**3, 5, 8, 10, 17, 21; **2:**4², 8, 9, 12, 14, 17², 18, 19, 21; **3:**7²; **1Jn 2:**2³, 16, 19, 27; **3:**2, 16², 20; **4:**7, 10, 16, 20; **5:**3, 4, 7; **2Jn 1:**8; **3Jn 1:**5, 7, 8; **Jude 1:**3³, 4², 6, 11, 13, 16, 21; **Rev 1:**6, 18; **2:**3, 10; **3:**2, 4; **4:**9, 10, 11; **5:**9, 13; **6:**6²; **7:**12, 17; **8:**1; **9:**5, 7, 10, 15, 19; **10:**6; **11:**2, 3, 9, 15, 18³; **12:**6², 10, 14²; **13:**5, 10; **14:**4, 11³, 12, 13, 15, 20; **15:**4², 7; **16:**6, 12, 14, 17², 19², 3, 6, 7, 8, 10, 17; **20:**2, 3, 4, 6, 8, 10, 11; **21:**1, 2, 4, 5, 23, 25; **22:**2, 5², 16.

FROM (5013)

Ge 1:4, 6, 7, 14, 18; **2:**2, 3, 6, 7, 10², 16, 17, 22; **3:**1, 2, 3, 8, 11², 12, 17, 19, 22, 23²; **4:**4, 10, 11, 14², 16; **6:**7; **7:**4², 23; **8:**2, 3, 7, 8, 10, 11, 13², 21; **9:**5², 19, 24; **10:**5, 11, 14, 19, 30, 32; **11:**8, 9, 31; **12:**4, 8; **13:**1, 3², 14²; **14:**17; **15:**4, 18; **16:**2, 6, 8²; **17:**6, 12, 14, 16, 22, 27; **18:**2, 17, 25²; **19:**4, 24, 28²; **20:**1, 6, 13; **21:**17, 21, 28, 30; **22:**11, 12, 15; **23:**3; **24:**3, 5, 7, 8, 10, 17, 37, 40², 41², 43, 46, 50, 62, 64; **25:**6, 10, 18, 23; **26:**8, 16, 17, 22, 23, 26; **27:**30, 39², 40, 45, 46²; **28:**2, 6, 16; **29:**2, 3, 4², 8, 10; **30:**2, 16, 32, 37; **31:**1, 16, 31, 38, 39, 40, 49; **32:**11, 13; **33:**10, 18, 19; **34:**7, 26; **35:**1, 7, 9, 11², 13, 16²; **36:**2, 6, 16, 17, 18, 33, 34, 36, 37, 40²; **37:**14, 17, 21, 22, 25; **38:**9, 11²; **39:**1, 11; **40:**36; **39:**1, 9, 10, 17, 28, 29; **45:**19; **46:**34; **47:**1, 10, 18, 21, 22²; **48:**7², 12, 16, 17², 22; **49:**9, 10², 30, 32; **50:**13, 25; **Ex 2:**15, 19; **3:**2, 4, 8, 15; **4:**3, 9²; **5:**4, 5; **6:**6²; **7:**8; **8:**9, 8, 10, 18; **10:**6, 17; **11:**1, 5; **12:**5, 15³, 18, 19, 29, 37, 39, 39; **13:**19; **14:**19, 24, 25, 30; **15:**22; **16:**1, 4; **17:**1², 14, 16; **18:**4, 9, 10², 13, 14, 21, 25; **19:**2, 3, 15, 18²; **20:**20, 22; **21:**14; **22:**5, 7, 12, 14, 29; **23:**11, 16, 21²; **24:**16; **25:**2, 3, 32, 33, 35; **26:**24, 28, 33²; **27:**21; **28:**1, 28, 42; **29:**2, 22, 23, 25, 28², 40; **30:**16, 19, 33, 38; **31:**14, 17; **32:**1, 8, 12, 27; **33:**15, 16; **34:**19, 25, 29; **35:**5, 20; **36:**3, 6, 29, 33; **37:**16, 18, 19, 21; **40:**7, 14, 17, 21, 22, 25; **38:**8, 24, 25, 26, 27, 29; **39:**1, 21; **40:**36; **Lev 1:**1, 2, 3, 10²; **2:**9; **3:**1, 3, 6, 9, 14; **4:**8, 10, 19, 31, 35; **5:**6, 8, 15, 18; **6:**9, 10², 20, 22, 25²; **7:**6, 20, 21, 25², 27, 34²; **8:**26, 28, 30, 31; **9:**10, 24; **10:**2, 4, 12; **11:**34²; **12:**4, 5, 7; **13:**12, 23, 28², 41; **14:**19, 27; **15:**4, 8, 16, 24, 30; **16:**1, 4; **17:**1², 14, 16; **18:**4, 9, 10², 13, 14, 21, 25; **19:**2, 3, 15, 18²; **20:**20, 22; **21:**14; **22:**5, 7, 12, 14, 29; **23:**11, 16, 21²; **24:**16; **25:**3, 22, 33, 35; **26:**24, 28, 33²; **27:**21; **28:**1, 28, 42; **29:**2, 22, 23, 25, 28², 40; **30:**16, 19, 33, 38; **31:**14, 17; **32:**1, 8, 12, 27; **33:**15, 16; **34:**19, 25, 29; **35:**5, 20, 30, 36, 37; **36:**16, 18, 19, 21; **37:**16, 18, 19, 21; **40:**36; **Nu 1:**4, 5, 6, 7, 8, 9, 10³, 11, 12, 13, 14, 15, 16, 20, 21, 22, 23, 24, 25, 26, 27, 28, 29, 30, 31, 32, 33, 34, 35, 38, 39, 40, 41, 42, 43; **2:**2; **3:**12, 49, 50; **4:**3, 13, 18, 23, 30, 35, 39, 43, 47; **5:**2, 3, 17, 25, 28; **6:**3³, 4; **7:**3², 13; **8:**7, 8, 14, 16², 24; **10:**11, 13, 17, 22, 33², 34; **11:**1, 3, 31¹, 35; **12:**10, 12²; **13:**2², 3, 4, 5, 6, **15:**12, 13, 19, 22, 22; **16:**26, 27, 34; **17:**1, 4, 6, 13, 19, 24; **18:**19, 26, 31, 44; **19:**16, 19; **20:**17, 24, 34, 41; **21:**21; **22:**3, 24², 35, 43; **2Ki 1:**2, 10², 12², 14; **2:**1, 3, 5, 9, 10, 13, 14, 15, 23, 25; **3:**3, 6, 20; **4:**1, 27, 42²; **5:**2², 4, 15, 20², 21², 22², 24, 26, 27, 33; **7:**8; **8:**3, 6², 8, 9, 29; **9:**1, 2, 8, 15, 10:21, 29, 31, 33; **11:**2², 11, 19; **12:**1, 4, 5, 7, 8, 15, 16, 18; **13:**2, 5, 6, 11, 14, 22, 23, 25²; **14:**2, 13, 24, 28²; **15:**2, 5, 6, 14, 16, 18, 20, 24, 28; **16:**11, 12, 14², 17²; **17:**7, 9, 13, 18, 20, 21², 22, 23², 27, 28, 30, 35, 38², 39; **18:**8, 14², 23, 24, 44, 46, 49²; **23:**4, 11, 15, 16, 17, 20, 21, 24, 30, 34; **24:**2, 13², 15²; **1Ki 1:**20, 39, 45, 53; **2:**7, 8, 15, 27, 40, 41; **3:**20; **4:**12, 21, 24, 25, 33; **5:**3, 9, 13, 17; **6:**3, 8, 15, 16, 24; **7:**7, 9², 14, 23, 34², 8:1², 10, 30, 53, 54, 39, 40, 41, 43, 45, 49, 53, 54, 65; **9:**6, 7, 12, 20, 24; **10:**11², 15², 28³, 29; **11:**2, 9, 11, 13, 14, 18²; 23, 26, 35; **12:**2², 15, 25, 31; **13:**1, 4, 12, 14, 20, 21, 26, 33, 34; **14:**7, 8, 10, 11, 15; **15:**12, 13, 17, 19, 24; **16:**1, 7², 12², 17², 20, 21², 23², 27, 28, 30, 33; **18:**8, 14², 29; **19:**14, 19; **20:**5, 6, 8, 14³; **21:**8, 15, 16, 19; **22:**1, 4, 10; **23:**2, 4, 6, 8², 12, 16, 17, 18, 26, 27, 30, 31, 33, 35, 36; **24:**3, 7², 8, 13², 15, 18, 20; **25:**5, 16, 21, 26, 27; **1Ch 1:**12, 44, 45, 47, 48; **2:**53, 55; **4:**10², 22; **5:**2, 8, 23; **6:**33, 44, 54, 60, 61, 62², 63, 65, 66, 70, 71, 72, 74, 76, 77, 78, 80; **7:**15, 9³; **8:**7, 13², 28², 31, 32; **12:**1, 2, 7, 16, 17, 28, 37, 40; **13:**5², 6, 7; **14:**16; **15:**5, 6, 7², 8, 10, 17², 25; **16:**20²; 35, 36; **17:**5³, 7², 8, 13², 21², 18:1, 8, 11; **19:**6, 7, 16; **20:**2²; 6; **21:**12, 26; **22:**2, 9; **23:**27; **24:**4², 6²,

Column 1

20², 21, 22², 24, 25, 27, 28, 29; **25:**2, 3, 4; **26:**1, 23, 29², 30; **27:**15; **28:**4³, 19; **29:**10, 12, 14², 16, 29; **2Ch 1:**4, 13², 16³, 17; **2:**8, 14², 16; **4:**2; **5:**2, 9³, 11; **6:**21, 23, 25, 26, 27, 30, 32, 33, 35, 39; **7:**1, 8, 14², 20; **8:**7, 11, 15, 16; **9:**10, 26, 28², 29; **10:**2², 15; **11:**4, 13, 16; **12:**3, 12, 15; **13:**19; **14:**8²; **15:**8², 9², 11, 16, 17; **16:**1, 3, 6, 7, 9, 11, 12²; **17:**6, 14, 17; **18:**23², 31; **19:**4, 10; **20:**2², 4², 10³, 19, 23², 32, 34; **21:**12; **22:**6, 11²; **23:**2, 10, 20; **24:**1, 5, 6; **25:**1, 6, 7, 10, 13, 14, 15, 23, 26, 27²; **26:**3, 21, 22; **28:**8, 12, 15, 21³, 24, 26; **29:**5, 6, 10, 12³, 13², 16²; **30:**5, 6³, 8, 9, 10, 18, 25²; **31:**3, 10; **32:**3, 8, 11, 13, 14², 15², 17², 22², 23; **33:**15; **34:**9²; **35:**7, 22, 27; **36:**7, 10, 18, 20; **Ezr 1:**7, 11; **2:**1, 59², 61, 62; **3:**7, 8, 13; **4:**9, 11, 12, 15; **5:**14³, 16; **6:**5, 6, 8, 11, 21²; **7:**6, 9, 16, 20, 28; **8:**1, 18, 19, 22, 31², 35; **9:**1, 3, 5, 7, 11; **10:**2, 6, 8, 11², 14, 16, 18, 19, 20, 21, 22, 24², 25, 26, 27, 28, 29, 30, 31, 33, 34, 38, 43; **Ne 1:**2, 9; **3:**7, 15, 19, 20, 21, 22, 24, 25, 27; **4:**2, 5, 6, 16, 19, 21; **5:**7, 12, 14, 15, 17; **6:**17; **7:**6, 61², 63, 64; **8:**3, 8, 15², 17², 18²; **9:**2, 3, 5, 13, 15², 20, 27, 28, 32, 35; **10:**28, 31, 38; **11:**4², 7, 10, 15, 30, 31; **12:**27, 28², 29², 44; **13:**3, 16, 21, 23, 28; **Est 1:**1, 2, 5, 7, 10, 20, 26; **2:**3, 3:8, 10; **4:**14; **7:**8; **8:**2, 9; **9:**16, 22, 26; **Job 1:**7², 12, 16, 19, 21; **2:**2²; **7:**10, 11, 12; **3:**10, 11, 17, 19; **4:**2; **5:**4, 5, 6², 15², 19, 20², 21; **6:**13, 17, 18, 22, 23²; **7:**19; **8:**10, 18, 19; **9:**6, 34; **10:**7, 19, 20; **13:**20, 21; **14:**4, 6, 11, 12, 18; **15:**13, 18; **16:**5; **18:**4, 14, 17, 18²; **19:**9, 13²; **20:**4, 18, 20, 24; **21:**9, 16, 30²; **22:**6, 7, 18, 22, 23; **23:**7, 12², 24:4, 9, 12; **26:**4; **27:**13, 22; **28:**2², 4², 5, 6, 20, 21²; **29:**9, 17; **30:**2, 3, 5; **31:**2², 7, 18², 20, 22, 23; **33:**3, 6, 9, 17², 18², 24, 28, 30; **34:**10², 27, 30²; **35:**7, 9; **36:**3, 16², 20, 25, 29; **37:**1, 2, 7, 9², **38:**8, 29², **39:**22, 25, 29²; **41:**19, 20², 21; **Ps 3:**T, 4, 8; **4:**1; **5:**9; **6:**5, 6, 8; **7:**1, 7; **8:**2; **9:**13; **10:**5, 8, 16; **11:**2; **12:**1, 5, 7; **13:**1; **14:**2; **15:**2; **16:**2; **17:**1, 2, 4, 7, 9², 13, 14²; **18:**T², 3, 6, 8², 13, 15, 16, 17², 21, 22, 23, 43, 45, 48²; **19:**5, 6, 10, 13; **20:**2², 6; **21:**10²; **22:**1², 10², 19; **24:**5²; **25:**6, 15, 17, 22; **27:**9; **30:**3²; **31:**4, 11, 15², 20², 22; **32:**7; **33:**13, 14, 19; **34:**4, 13², 14, 16, 17, 19; **35:**10², 17², 22²; **36:**8; **37:**8², 27, 39, 40; **38:**9, 10, 21; **39:**1, 8, 10, 13; **40:**10, 11; **41:**3, 8, 13; **42:**6²; **43:**1; **44:**12, 18; **45:**8; **49:**3, 14, 15; **50:**1, 2, 9²; **51:**2, 5, 9, 11², 14; **52:**5²; **53:**2; **54:**7; **55:**8, 12, 18; **56:**13²; **57:**T, 3; **58:**3²; **59:**1², 2²; **60:**6; **61:**2²; **62:**1, 4, 5; **64:**1, 2², 4; **66:**9, 20; **68:**10, 17, 18², 20², 22², 31; **69:**5, 14³, 17; **71:**4², 6², 12, 20; **72:**8², 13, 14, 15; **73:**5, 7, 27; **74:**11, 12; **75:**6²; **76:**8; **77:**4; **78:**2, 4, 14, 26, 30, 42, 44, 50, 65², 70, 71; **79:**13; **80:**13, 14, 18; **81:**6², 16; **82:**4; **84:**7, 11; **85:**3, 11²; **86:**13; **88:**5, 8, 14, 15, 18; **89:**19, 33, 48; **90:**2; **91:**3²; **93:**2; **94:**12, 13; **97:**10; **99:**7; **101:**4, 8; **102:**2, 19; **103:**4, 12², 17; **104:**13, 14, 21, 35; **105:**13², 37; **106:**10², 19, 23, 33, 47, 48; **107:**2, 3³, 6, 13, 19, 20; **108:**7; **109:**10, 13, 15, 17, 24, 31; **110:**2, 3, 7; **113:**3, 7²; **114:**1; **116:**8³, 16; **118:**26; **119:**10, 13, 19, 21, 22, 29, 37, 43, 51, 72, 87, 101, 102, 104, 110, 115, 118, 134, 136, 150, 152, 155, 157; **120:**2²; **121:**1, 2, 7; **123:**4²; **127:**3²; **128:**5; **129:**1, 2, 4; **130:**8; **134:**3; **135:**7², 21; **136:**11, 24; **138:**6; **139:**2, 7², 15, 19; **140:**1, 4²; **141:**6, 9²; **142:**6, 7; **143:**7, 9; **144:**7³, 10, 11; **148:**1, 7; **Pr 2:**6, 12², 16², 22²; **3:**26, 27; **4:**5, 15, 24², 27; **5:**7, 8, 15²; **6:**5², 9, 24²; **7:**5², 16; **8:**23², 35; **9:**3; **10:**2; **11:**4, 7, 8; **12:**2, 14; **13:**2, 14, 19; **14:**4, 7, 27; **15:**24, 29; **16:**1, 11, 33; **18:**20²; **19:**14², 27; **21:**10, 16, 22; **22:**5, 6, 15, 27; **23:**13, 14; **24:**13, 18, 32; **25:**4, 5, 25; **27:**6, 8²; **25, 29:**21, 26, 30:**8, 14²; **31:**14; **Ecc 1:**3, 7; **2:**24; **3:**9, 11, 14, 20; **4:**4, 14; **5:**9², 15²; **8:**10; **10:**5, 12; **11:**10; **12:**7; **SS 1:**14; **3:**6², 9; **4:**1, 2, 8³, 15; **6:**5²; **6:**8; **Isa 1:**6, 15, 19, 24; **2:**3², 6, 10, 19, 21; **3:**1, 12, 14; **4:**4, 6²; **6:**6; **7:**17, 18², 20; **8:**17, 18; **9:**7, 12²; **10:**2, 3³; **11:**1², 11², 18², 16; **12:**3; **13:**5² 6, 13; **14:**3, 9, 12, 22, 25², 29, 31; **16:**1, 2, 4², 5, 10; **17:**3²; **18:**4, 7; **19:**23; **20:**2²; **21:**1², 10², 11, 15⁴; **22:**4, 19², 24; **23:**1, 5; **24:**11, 14, 16; **25:**4², 8²; **27:**12; **28:**7⁴, 9²; **29:**4², 9², 13, 15; **30:**14, 23, 27²; **31:**1; **32:**2²; 6, 15; **33:**15²; **34:**4²; 6, 10, 17; **36:**2, 16², 18, 19, 20²; **37:**14, 20, 30, 38, 16, 17²; **39:**3²; **40:**2, 11, 27; **41:**2, 4, 9², 25², 26²; **42:**7², 10, 11; **43:**5², 6², 11, 13; **44:**6, 17, 19; **45:**5, 6, 19, 20, 21²; **46:**6, 7², 10², 12², 17; **47:**13, 14; **48:**1, 6, 8², 9, 16, 19, 20, 21; **49:**1, 12⁴, 17, 21, 24², 25²; **50:**6, 11; **51:**1², 4, 17, 22; **52:**2, 11²; **53:**3, 8; **54:**8, 14, 17; **55:**10, 11; **56:**2, 3; **57:**1; **58:**7; **13²; **59:**2², 9, 19²; **21⁴; 60:**4, 6, 9; **61:**1; **63:**1², 3, 15³, 16, 17, 19; **64:**7; **65:**9², 14, 16; **66:**6², 20, 23²; **Jer 1:**13, 14; **2:**5, 18², 33; **3:**4, 14², 18, 19, 24, 25; **4:**6, 8, 11, 12, 14, 15²; **5:**6²; **6:**1, 8, 13, 20², 22²; **7:**1, 15, 25, 28; **8:**1, 10, 13, 16, 19; **9:**2, 3, 18, 19, 21²; **10:**9², 11², 13², 20, 22; **11:**1, 7²,

Column 2

19; **12:**2, 12, 14²; **13:**7, 14, 18², 20; **14:**2; **15:**1, 12, 21²; **16:**5, 16, 17²; 19; **17:**5, 12, 13, 16, 18², 26³; **18:**1, 4, 11, 14², 17, 18², 20, 22, 23; **19:**1, 14; **20:**3, 13; **21:**1, 2, 12; **22:**3, 8, 11, 20, 21; **23:**14, 15, 20, 27, 30², 32², 33; **26:**1, 3, 10, 20; **27:**1, 10, 16², 20; **28:**1, 4, 6, 8, 16; **29:**1², 2, 4, 14³, 20, 22, 27; **30:**1, 3, 10, 19, 21; **31:**8², 11, 16³, 23, 34, 36, 38, 39; **32:**1, 9, 30, 31², 37, 40; **33:**5, 7, 8, 15; **34:**1, 3, 8, 21; **35:**1, 15; **36:**1, 2, 3, 6², 7, 8, 9, 10², 11, 13, 14, 21, 29; **37:**5, 11, 17, 21; **38:**10, 11, 14, 18, 23, 25; **40:**1², 4, 12; **41:**5, 6, 15, 16³; **42:**1, 4, 8, 11; **43:**5, 12; **44:**5, 7, 12², 12, 18, 28; **46:**16, 20, 27; **47:**4; **48:**3, 10, 11², 12, 18, 33², 34², 44, 45²; **49:**5, 7, 14, 16, 19², 32, 36; **50:**3, 9²², 16, 26, 28, 39, 41², 44²; **51:**6, 16², 26, 45, 54²; **52:**1, 3, 8, 20², 27, 29, 31; **La 1:**6, 13; **2:**1, 8, 9, 11, 19; **3:**11, 13, 18, 38, 48, 50, 55, 66; **4:**9, 17; **5:**8, 10, 14, 15, 16, 19; **Eze 1:**19, 21, 25, 27²; **3:**17, 18, 19², 20; **4:**8, 14; **5:**4; **6:**9, 14; **7:**22, 26; **8:**2², 6; **9:**2, 3; **10:**2, 4, 6², 16, 18, 19; **11:**15, 17², 19, 23, 24; **12:**3, 16, 27; **13:**20, 21, 22, 23; **14:**6, 7, 8, 9, 11; **15:**3²; **16:**9, 33, 37, 42; **17:**7, 22²; **18:**8, 17, 21, 23, 24, 26, 27, 30; **19:**8, 14; **20:**9, 14, 22, 34², 41², 47; **21:**3², 4, 5, 19, 22:**12²; **23:**3, 17, 18², 22², 28, 40, 42²; **24:**13, 16; **25:**7²; **26:**7; **27:**5, 16², 18, 25; **28:**3, 15, 16², 18, 25; **29:**4, 10, 13, 14, 18; **30:**6, 9, 22; **31:**12²; **32:**13, 21; **33:**7, 8, 9, 11², 12, 14, 18, 19, 21, 30; **34:**10², 12, 13², 27²; **35:**7²; **36:**3, 24, 25², 26, 29, 33; **37:**9, 12, 13, 19, 21, 23², 26; **38:**6, 8³, 12, 15; **39:**2, 3², 10², 17, 18, 22, 23, 24, 25, 27²; **40:**13³, 15, 19, 28, 29, 31²; **41:**7, 11, 20; **42:**3, 5², 9, 20; **43:**2, 6, 9, 14², 15, 23, 25, 27; **44:**10², 15; **45:**7³, 13², 14, 15²; **46:**2, 16, 17, 18; **47:**1², 2, 10, 12, 15, 17, 19; **48:**1, 2, 3, 4, 5, 6, 7, 8², 12, 19², 21², 23, 24, 25, 26, 27, 28, 35; **Da 1:**2, 3, 5, 6; **2:**6, 18, 25; **3:**15, 17²; **4:**3, 12, 13, 14², 16, 23, 25, 31²; **5:**2², 3, 13, 20, 21, 23²; **6:**13, 20, 23, 27; **7:**3, 4, 7, 10, 17, 19, 23, 24²; **8:**4, 5, 7, 11, 16, 22, 27; **9:**2, 5, 13, 16, 25; **11:**7, 26, 29, 41, 45²; **12:**1, 11; **Hos 1:**2, 12; **2:**17, 18; **4:**6; **5:**3, 6; **7:**4, 13, 14²; **8:**6; **9:**6, 12; **10:**5; **11:**2, 4, 7, 10, 11²; **12:**13², 14², 15²; **13:**2, 3, 14², 15², 16²; **2:**7, 13, 20; **3:**6, 11, 16²; **Am 1:**2²; **2:**11²; **3:**5, 12; **4:**7², 8, 11; **5:**19; **6:**2, 14; **7:**11, 15, 17; **8:**12²; **9:**2², 3, 7³, 8, 13², 15; **Ob 1:**1, 4, 18, 19², 20; **Jnh 1:**3², 8², 10; **2:**1, 2, 4, 6, 9; **3:**5, 6, 9, 10; **4:**2, 11; **Mic 1:**2, 3, 7, 11, 12, 16; **2:**3, 4, 8², 9², 3:²; **4:**2², 7; **4:**2²; **7:** 5:²2, 6, 7, 10, 13, 14; **6:**4, 5; **7:**2, 12⁴; **Na 1:**10, 11, 13; **2:**9; **3:**7, 11; **Hab 1:**8; **12:**2:15, 16; **3:**3², 4, 13; **Zep 1:**2, 3, 4, 6, 10³; **3:**10, 11, 18; **Hag 2:**15, 18², 19; **Zec 1:**4, 12²; **2:**6, 13; **3:**2; **4:**1; **6:**1, 5, 10², 12; **8:**7, 23; **9:**7², 10⁴, 11; **10:**4², 10², **11:**6; **13:**1, 2²; **14:**2², 4, 5, 8, 10³, 18; **Mal 1:**9, 10, 11, 13; **2:**3, 6, 7, 8, 12, 13; **3:**7, 11; **4:**2; **Mt 1:**17³, 20, 21; **2:**1, 7, 16; **3:**5, 7, 13, 17; **4:**4, 10, 17, 21, 25; **5:**18, 37, 42²; **6:**1, 13; **7:**5, 16², 23; **8:**1, 13; **9:**9, 15, 16, 20, 27; **10:**27, 29; **11:**1, 12, 25, 29; **12:**15, 38, 42; **13:**12, 27, 49, 53; **14:**2, 13, 24; **15:**1, 5, 8, 18, 22², 27, 28; **16:**1, 21; **17:**5, 9, 18, 20, 25³, 26; **18:**35; **19:**8, 16; **20:**23; **21:**8, 11, 16, 25⁴, 26, 43; **22:**46²; **23:**34, 35; **24:**10, 21, 27, 29, 31², 32; **25:**28, 29, 32², 41; **26:**16, 29, 39, 47; **27:**32, 40, 42, 45, 51, 55², 57, 64; **28:**2, 7, 8; **Mk 1:**9, 11, 45; **2:**20; **3:**7, 8, 9, 22; **4:**25; **5:**2, 6, 29, 30, 34, 35; **6:**6, 14, 16, 33; **7:**1, 4, 6, 11, 18, 21, 23, 33; **8:**1; **9:**7, 9, 10, 21; **11:**14, 20, 30², 31, 32; **12:**2, 34², 13:19, 25, 27², 28; **14:**23, 35, 36, 43; **15:**21², 30, 32, 38, 40, 45; **16:**3, 10, 15², 17; **Lk 1:**2, 3, 15, 48, 50, 52, 71², 74, 78; **2:**4; **3:**7, 22; **4:**1, 9, 22, 38, 42; **5:**3², 8, 10, 17², 26; **6:**17³, 19, 29, 34, 42, 44²; **7:**6, 12, 45; **8:**1, 2, 4, 16, 27, 35, 38, 46, 49; **9:**6, 7, 35, 37, 45, 54; **10:**7, 18, 21, 30, 42; **11:**16, 31, 51; **12:**3, 15, 20, 36, 48², 52; **13:**12, 15, 16, 25, 27², 29; **14:**23, 35, 36, 43; **15:**21²a, 30, 32², 49; **14:**2; **16:**21, 26²; **17:**2, 24, 29, 37; **18:**24, 29; **19:**24, 26; **20:**1, 4; **21:**9, 13², 16, 25⁴; **22:**42²; **40:**35; **Lev 10:**16, 19; **19:**20; **21:**10; **23:**43; **Nu 11:**17, 48²; **3:**4; **5:**4, 18; **7:**11; **8:**4, 13, 24², 26, 28, 34; **12:**1, 10, 14; **13:**22, 31, 32; **14:**2, 6, 36; **16:**2², 19², 27, 32, 47, 49, 50; **17:**8²; **20:**3, 5; **21:**2, 7², 9, 23; **22:**2, 29, 33; **23:**30; **26:**33², 46, 65; **27:**4, 11, 22; **31:**10, 21, 35, 53; **32:**1, 9, 13; **33:**4², 8; **Dt 1:**3, 4²; **2:**15, 14², 15, 20, 30², 35; **3:**6; **4:**25, 42²; **8:**3, 16; **9:**9, 16⁴, 18, 21, 25, 28; **10:**4²², 5, 10; **11:**18, 19, 37, 53, 55; **12:**1, 9, 17², 21, 27, 28, 32, 34, 36, 43²; **13:**3, 4; **14:**7; **15:**5, 15, 26²; **16:**14, 15, 27, 28, 30; **17:**7, 8, 15; **18:**3, 28, 36; **19:**9, 11, 14; **20:**3; **21:**8, 12, 42, 43, 44; **22:**7, 9, 11, 30; **23:**1²; **24:**31², 32, 33;

Column 3

14, 39; **17:**2, 3, 5, 26, 27, 31; **18:**2, 5, 6, 16, 21, 23², 28; **19:**25, 29, 35; **20:**4⁴, 6, 9, 15, 17, 18, 20, 30; **21:**1², 7, 10, 16², 21, 25⁴, 27, 30², 39; **22:**5, 6, 14, 19; **23:**10, 34²; **24:**19; **25:**1, 7, 26:4, 11, 13, 17², 18², 19, 23; **27:**2², 4, 14, 18, 21, 29, 30², 34, 42, 43; **28:**4², 8, 13, 21², 23³; **Ro 1:**4, 5², 7², 13, 17²; **2:**12²; **3:**29; **3:**21², 22, 28; **4:**6, 24; **5:**9, 14; **6:**4, 7, 9, 13, 18, 20, 21, 22; **7:**2, 3, 4, 6, 8, 9, 24; **8:**2, 11², 21, 35, 39; **9:**3, 5, 6, 24²; **10:**3, 7, 9, 17; **11:**1, 15, 17, 26², 36; **13:**3, 14:23²; **15:**19, 22, 31; **16:**2, 17; **1Co 1:**3, 11, 30; **2:**12, 14; **4:**5, 6, 7; **5:**13; **6:**14, 18, 19; **7:**7, 10, 29, 32; **8:**6; **9:**8, 11, 12, 13, 14, 21; **10:**4, 6, 14; **11:**8², 12², 15; **12:**2, 13; **15:**12, 15, 20, 41, 47, 48, 49; **16:**17; **2Co 1:**2, 4, 10, 12, 16; **2:**17²; **3:**1, 3, 5, 13, 18; **4:**7², 14; **5:**1, 6, 8, 9, 16², 18; **6:**12²; **7:**1; **11:**3, 4², 8, 9², 12, 24, 26², 33; **12:**1, 3, 7, 8; **Gal 1:**1², 3, 4, 8, 12², 15; **2:**12²; **3:**2, 13, 15; **4:**1, 17, 24; **5:**4², 7, 8; **6:**8²; **Eph 1:**2, 20; **2:**8, 12²; **3:**15; **4:**16, 18; **5:**14²; **6:**6, 15, 23; **Php 1:**2, 5, 18; **2:**1², 17; **3:**9²; **4:**10, 14, 18; **Col 1:**2, 5, 7, 13, 18, 21, 22, 23; **2:**5, 12, 19; **3:**8, 24; **4:**16; **1Th 1:**8, 9, 10²; **2:**3, 6², 13, 14², 16, 17; **3:**6; **4:**16; **2Th 1:**2, 7, 9²; **2:**2, 13; **3:**2, 3, 6²; **1Ti 1:**2, 5, 6; **4:**3; **5:**13; **6:**2, 10, 11, 20, 21; **2Ti 1:**2, 13, 18; **2:**8², 18, 19, 21, 26; **3:**11, 13, 14, 15; **4:**4, 17, 18; **Tit 1:**4; **2:**10, 14; **Phm 1:**3, 15, 20; **Heb 3:**12; **4:**4, 10², 13; **5:**1, 7, 8, 14; **6:**1; **7:**1², 5², 6², 13, 14, 23, 26; **8:**9, 11; **9:**14, 15; **10:**22; **11:**5, 12, 13, 19, 22, 23, 25²; **13:**5, 10, 20, 24; **Jas 1:**7, 17²; **3:**11, 13, 15, 17; **4:**1, 7; **5:**19, 20²; **1Pe 1:**3, 12, 18², 21, 22; **2:**11; **3:**3, 10², 11, 21; **2Pe 1:**8, 9, 17², 18, 21; **2:**9, 18; **3:**17; **1Jn 1:**1, 5, 7, 9; **2:**13, 14, 16², 19, 20, 24; **3:**11, 14, 22; **4:**1, 2, 3², 5², 6²; **5:**21; **2Jn 1:**3², 5, 6; **3Jn 1:**7, 11; **Jude 1:**14, 23, 24; **Rev 1:**4²; **5³; **2:**5²; 7, 27; **3:**5, 10, 12, 18; **4:**5²; **5:**7, 9; **6:**4, 13, 14, 16²; **7:**1, 2, 4, 5³, 6³, 7³, 8³, 9, 13, 17; **8:**4, 5, 10, 11; **9:**1, 2³, 13; **10:**1, 4, 8, 10; **11:**5, 7, 9, 11, 12, 13; **12:**11, 15; **13:**8, 13; **14:**2, 3, 4, 13³, 18²; **15:**8²; **16:**1, 12, 17, 21; **17:**8; **18:**1, 3, 4, 6, 14, 15, 19²; **19:**3, 5; **20:**3, 7, 9, 11; **21:**2, 3, 4, 6, 10; **22:**1, 19².

HAD (2791)

See also the selected listing for "HAD" in the Main Concordance.

Ge 1:31; **2:**2², 3, 5³, 8², 19, 22; **3:**1, 23; **4:**22, 26; **5:**3², 4, 6, 7, 9, 10, 12, 13, 15, 16, 18, 19, 21, 22, 25, 26, 28², 30; **6:**4, 5, 6, 10, 12²; **7:**9, 14, 16, 22; **8:**2², 3, 6, 7, 8, 11, 13; **9:**24; **10:**1; **11:**1, 11, 12, 13, 14, 15, 16, 17, 18, 19, 20, 21, 22, 23, 24, 25, 26, 30; **12:**1, 4, 5², 7, 20; **13:**1, 2, 3, 4, 5, 14; **14:**4, 13, 14; **15:**17²; **16:**1², 3, 15; **17:**22; **18:**8, 33; **19:**4, 17, 23, 27, 29, 37, 38; **20:**4, 8, 13, 18; **21:**1², 2, 9, 25, 32; **22:**3², 9, 24; **23:**10, 16, 32; **27:**15, 17, 30, 41, 42; **28:**6², 7², 9, 11, 18; **29:**12, 14, 16, 17, 30, 31, 32, 34, 42, 54; **32:**10, 13, 23; **34:**1, 5, 7³, 13, 27; **35:**4, 13, 27; **36:**6, 7³, 11², 15², 16, 18, 29², 30³, 35, 39; **37:**7, 9, 15, 26, 32, 37; **40:**4, 5³, 8, 16², 17², 20²; **41:**1, 5, 7, 11, 14, 15, 19, 21, 43, 54, 56; **42:**24, 29; **43:**2², 6, 10, 25, 26, 31, 33; **44:**4, 24; **45:**4, 16, 21, 27; **46:**5, 6, 12, 18, 25, 27, 29; **47:**22; **49:**33; **50:**4, 12, 13, 14; **Ex 1:**17; **2:**11, 16; **3:**4; **4:**19, 28², 30, 31; **5:**13; **7:**13, 20, 22; **8:**12, 15, 19; **9:**7, 12, 24, 28, 31, 34, 35; **10:**13, 14, 23; **11:**1, 9; **12:**36, 39²; 50; **13:**19²; **14:**5, 6, 19, 25, 28; **16:**3, 17²; **17:**10; **18:**1, 2, 6, 8³, 9, 11; **19:**7, 9, 14; **21:**29, 36; **24:**4; **32:**14, 20, 25, 35; **33:**5; **34:**4, 29, 32, 34; **35:**23, 24, 25, 26², 29; **36:**2, 3, 7², 8, 9², 10, 11², 12, 14; **9:**1, 3, 9, 11, 12, 18, 19, 21, 23, 25; **10:**1, 2, 6, 8, 10, 12, 15; **11:**14, 15, 21; **12:**1, 2, 5, 9, 13, 14; **13:**13, 21; **14:**8, 14; **15:**8², 9, 13, 15, 16, 18; **16:**6, 14; **17:**2, 3, 5, 13; **18:**1, 10, 12, 30; **20:**24, 27, 29, 30, 33; **21:**3², 6, 7, 10, 11³, 19; **22:**1, 4, 6², 7, 8; **23:**8, 9, 14, 18², 21; **24:**3, 7, 9, 14, 16, 24²; **25:**3, 10, 13², 24; **26:**4, 8, 10², 11, 19, 20², 21², 23, 27²; **28:**3, 6, 17, 18, 19², 31; **29:**2, 15², 24, 34²; **30:**3³, 5, 12², 18, 25², 26; **31:**1², 10; **32:**1, 2, 27, 29, 31; **33:**2, 3, 4, 7², 9, 15, 22², 28; **34:**4²², 9, 11, 13, 14², 22, 30, 32, 33; **35:**3, 10, 16, 18², 20, 24; **36:**13, 14, 15; **Ezr 1:**5, 7², 8; **2:**1, 61, 65, 66²; **3:**1, 6, 8², 12; **4:**20; **5:**14² (ft), **6:**13, 20, 21²; **7:**6², 9, 10, 11; **8:**20, 22, 25, 30, 35; **9:**1; **10:**5, 9, 17, 18, 44²; **Ne 2:**1, 9, 10, 12², 12²; **6:**1, 18; **7:**4, 7, 73; **8:**1, 9, 11, 12², 17², 18; **9:**2, 15, 26; **11:**16; **12:**29, 30, 31, 43, 46; **13:**2², 5, 7, 11, 16, 23; **Est 1:**6, 14; **2:**1³, 6, 7⁴, 8²², 10, 15², 20³; **3:**2, 4; **4:**1, 7, 8; **5:**9, 5, 11², 14; **6:**2², 4², 13; **7:**4, 7, 9, 10, 16; **8:**1, 2, 3, 17²; **9:**1, 3, 18, 23²; **24³, 25³, 10, 13², 24; **26:**4, 8, 10², 11, 19, 20², 21², 22; **27:**2, 12, 28:**3, 6, 17, 18, 19², 25²; **26; **31:**1²; 10; **32:**1, 2, 27, 29, 31; **33:**2, 3, 4, 9, 15², 19, 27, 44², 11, 13, 14²; 22, 30, 32, 33; **35:**3, 10, 16, 18², 20, 24; **36:**13, 14, 15; **Ezr 1:**5, 7², 8; **2:**1, 61, 65, 66²; **3:**1, 6, 8², 12; **4:**20; **5:**14²; **6:**13, 20, 21²; **7:**6², 9, 10, 11; **8:**20, 22, 25, 30, 35; **9:**1; **10:**5, 9, 17, 18, 44²; **Ne 2:**1, 9, 10, 12², 12²; **6:**1, 18; **7:**4, 7, 73; **8:**1, 9, 11, 12², 17², 18; **9:**2, 15, 26; **11:**16; **12:**29, 30, 31, 43, 46; **13:**2², 5, 7, 11, 16, 23; **Est 1:**6, 14; **2:**1³, 6, 7⁴, 8²², 10², 15², 20³; **3:**2, 4; **4:**1, 7, 8; **5:**9, 11², 14; **6:**2², 4², 13; **7:**4, 7, 9, 10, 16; **8:**1, 2, 3, 17²; **9:**1, 3, 18, 23², 24², 26:8, 23; **28:**12; **29:**1, 2; **31:**26; **32:**3, 8, 10, 12, 16, 22; **34:**8, 11, 16; **35:**9; **36:**4, 9, 13, 23, 26, 27, 32; **37:**2, 4, 5, 11, 15², 17;

Column 4

Jdg 1:19, 20; **2:**4, 6, 7², 10², 12, 15, 17, 18, 23; **3:**1, 2², 4, 11, 16, 18², 24, 30; **4:**3³, 11, 12; **5:**31; **7:**12, 13, 19; **8:**8, 10, 19, 30², 33, 34, 35; **9:**22, 24, 27, 35, 45, 47, 56; **10:**4; **11:**34, 39; **12:**4, 9, 14; **13:**2, 23; **14:**6, 9, 18, 19, 20; **16:**8, 18, 20, 22, 31; **17:**5, 6, 7; **18:**1², 4, 7, 14, 22, 27, 28, 31; **19:**1, 2, 3, 21², **20:**3, 30, 36², 37, 38, 39, 41; **21:**1, 5, 8, 12, 14, 15, 25; **Ru 1:**4, 6, 7, 12; **2:**1, 14, 17, 18³, 19; **3:**7, 16; **4:**1; **1Sa 1:**2³, 5, 6, 9, 23, 25; **2:**5; **2:**1; **3:**3; **7:**4:6, 13, 18, 19; **5:**1, 4, 9, 12², 9; **10:**11, 16², 26; **11:**5, 9; **13:**3, 13, 19, 22²; **14:**3, 21², 22, 24, 27², 30, 31, 35, 47, 48; **15:**35; **16:**8, 9, 10, 12, 14, 19²; **17:**5, 6, 7; **18:**11², 13, 18, 33; **19:**8, 15, 24, 32, 40; **20:**3, 5, 13; **21:**2²; **8², 11, 12², 13, 19; **23:**21; **24:**8, 10, 11, 19; **1Ki 1:**4, 6; **2:**11, 19, 27, 28, 29, 41²; **3:**2, 10, 15, 17, 18, 21, 28²; **4:**7², 15, 24, 26, 34; **5:**1², 12, 15; **6:**1, 38; **7:**5, 8, 28, 30², 31, 34, 40, 46, 51²; **8:**3, 5, 9, 17, 54², 66; **9:**1³, 2, 11, 12, 14, 16, 19²; **10:**2², 10, 15; **11:**2, 3, 4, 9², 10, 15², 16, 17, 41²; **12:**2, 12², 13, 19, 23; **13:**21; **14:**8, 14; **15:**8, 16, 18, 18, 19; **16:**6, 14; **17:**2, 3, 5, 13; **18:**1, 10, 12, 30; **20:**24, 27, 29, 30, 33; **21:**3², 6, 7, 10, 11³, 19; **22:**1, 4, 6², 7, 8; **2Ki 1:**2, 17²; **2:**7, 9, 13, 14, 22; **3:**2², 3, 4, 9, 21², 26; **4:**17, 20, 44; **5:**1², 2, 4, 8, 14, 19; **6:**15, 18, 23, 29, 30; **7:**6, 8, 15, 16, 17², 18, 19²; **8:**1², 4, 5², 18, 19, 27, 29²; **9:**14, 15², 16, 21, 27, 29; **10:**16, 24, 25, 29, 30, 31; **11:**4, 10, 15, 20; **12:**6, 10, 11, 18; **13:**2, 5, 6, 7², 11, 16, 23, 25; **14:**3, 5, 24, 26, 27, 28; **15:**3, 5, 9, 18, 20, 24, 28, 34; **16:**3², 12, 15, 17², 18³, 19, 3; **17:**3, 42²; **8², 11, 12³, 13, 19; **23:**21; **24:**8, 10, 11, 19; **1Ki 1:**4, 6; **2:**11, 19, 27, 28, 29, 41²; **3:**2², 3, 4, 9, 21², 26; **4:**17, 20, 44; **5:**1², 2, 4, 8, 14, 19; **6:**15, 18, 23, 25, 30; **7:**6, 8, 15, 16, 17², 18, 19²; **8:**1², 4, 5², 18, 19, 27, 29²; **9:**14, 15², 16, 21, 27, 29; **10:**16, 24, 25, 29, 30, 31; **11:**4, 10, 15, 20; **12:**6, 10, 11, 18; **13:**2, 5, 6, 7², 11, 16, 23, 25; **14:**3, 5, 24, 26, 27, 28; **15:**3, 5, 9, 18, 19³; **16:**5¹², 2², 4, 9, 11², 26; **17:**2, 7, 9, 14, 16, 20, 21², 23; **18:**4³, 7², 8², 11, 12³, 13, 15, 21, 26, 32, 37; **19:**8², 15, 24, 7²; **20:**13, 28², 31; **21:**2, 4, 11, 16, 18², 24, 30; **4:**3³, 11, 12; **5:**31; **7:**12, 13, 19; **8:**8, 10, 19, 30², 33, 34, 35; **9:**22, 24, 27, 35, 45, 47, 56; **10:**4; **11:**34, 39; **12:**4, 9, 14; **13:**2, 23; **14:**6, 9, 18, 19, 20; **16:**8, 18, 20, 22, 31; **17:**5, 6, 7; **18:**1², 4, 7, 14, 22, 27, 28, 31; **19:**1, 2, 3, 21²; **20:**3, 30, 36², 37, 38, 39, 41; **21:**1, 5, 8, 12, 14, 15, 25; **1Ch 2:**4, 18, 21, 26, 34²; **4:**5, 9, 18, 27, 40, 43; **5:**9, 18, 25; **6:**49²; **7:**4², 15, 23; **8:**8, 9, 11, 38, 40; **9:**19, 22, 25, 27², 44; **10:**7²; **11:**1, 6, 10, 23; **12:**22, 23, 29, 39; **13:**10, 11, 14; **14:**2²; 9, 12; **15:**1, 3, 15, 26; **16:**1, 2, 40; **18:**9, 10, 11²; **19:**6, 9, 16²; **20:**5; **21:**15, 19, 28, 29; **22:**4, 7; **23:**17, 22; **24:**2, 5, 19, 28; **26:**2, 4, 5, 6, 9, 10², 12²; **32:**27:23; **28:**2, 12; **29:**8, 9, 25; **2Ch 1:**3, 4³, 5, 12, 14; **2:**17; **3:**1; **4:**11, 17; **5:**1², 4, 6, 10, 11; **6:**7, 13²; **7:**6, 7, 9, 10, 11³; **8:**2, 4, 8, 11, 12, 14; **9:**1, 3, 9, 11, 12, 18, 19, 21, 23, 25; **10:**1, 2, 6, 8, 10, 12, 15; **11:**14, 15, 21; **12:**1, 2, 5, 9, 13, 14; **13:**13, 21; **14:**8, 14; **15:**8², 9, 13, 15, 16, 18; **16:**6, 14; **17:**2, 3, 5, 13; **18:**1, 10, 12, 30; **20:**24, 27, 29, 30, 33; **21:**3², 6, 7, 10, 11³, 19; **22:**1, 4, 6², 7, 8; **23:**8, 9, 14, 18², 21; **24:**3, 7, 9, 14, 16, 24²; **25:**3, 10, 13², 24; **26:**4, 8, 10², 11, 19, 20², 21², 23; **29:**15², 24, 34³; **30:**2; **31:**13, 21, 25, 31, 32, 35; **32:**3², 4, 5; **34:**27; **41:**32; **42:**5, 7, 10², 11², 12; **Ps 44:**17, 18², 20; **49:**11, 51:T; **52:**T; **54:**T; **55:**6; **56:**T; **57:**T; **59:**T; **66:**18; **73:**2², 15; **78:**11², 29², 54, 60, 63; **94:**17; **95:**9; **105:**26, 28, 38, 44; **106:**13, 21, 23, 34; **107:**11; **119:**92; **124:**1, 2; **Pr 1:**23; **24:**31; **Ecc 2:**7, 11³, 18; **4:**2, 8; **SS 3:**4²; **5:**6, 6, 11; **8:**11; **Isa 1:**9; **5:**1; **6:**6; **22:**9; **36:**21, 22; **37:**8; **38:**8, 21, 22; **39:**1; **48:**18; **53:**2, 9; **Jer 2:**21; **3:**7, 8; **4:**25; **5:**5; **9:**2; **11:**8, 19²; **13:**7; **15:**17; **16:**15; **18:**10, 19; **19:**14; **20:**2; **23:**8, 22²; **24:**2; **26:**8, 23; **28:**12; **29:**1, 2; **31:**26; **32:**3, 8, 10, 12, 16, 22; **34:**8, 11, 16; **35:**9; **36:**4, 9, 13, 23, 26, 27, 32; **37:**2, 4, 5, 11, 15², 17;

38:6, 7, 14, 27²; **39**:9, 11, 14, 15; **40**:1², 7³, 11², 12; **41**:1, 2, 5, 9², 10, 11, 13, 14, 16³, 18²; **43**:1, 5², 6; **44**:17, 18; **45**:1; **51**:60²; **52**:2, 6, 15, 20, 27; **La 1**:10; **3**:18; **4**:18; **5**:4; **Eze 1**:6, 8², 10³, 11, 23; **3**:6, 23; **8**:4, 11; **9**:2, 3²; **10**:14, 15, 20, 21, 22²; **11**:24, 25; **13**:22; **16**:5, 14; **17**:8, 18; **20**:6, 8, 9, 14, 15, 22, 24², 28, 42; **22**:24; **23**:17, 18, 41; **24**:18; **31**:17; **32**:23, 24, 25, 27, 32; **33**:5, 21; **36**:18², 20, 21²; **38**:8²; **40**:10², 17, 21, 22, 24, 25, 26, 27, 28, 29², 32, 33², 35, 36; **41**:8, 18, 21, 23, 24, 26; **42**:6², 9, 11, 15, 20; **43**:3²; **47**:5; **Da 1**:9, 11; **2**:1, 2, 3, 14, 24; **3**:2, 3, 7, 27; **4**:5, 18, 33; **5**:2, 3, 23; **6**:10², 23, 24; **7**:1, 4, 5, 6², 7², 8, 12, 20; **8**:1², 6; **9**:21; **10**:8; **Hos 1**:8²; **10**:3, 5; **Am 4**:7²; **7**:1, 2, 7; **Ob 1**:16; **Jnh 1**:5, 10; **3**:10²; **Hag 1**:12; **Zec 1**:8; **5**:9; **6**:2; **7**:2, 12; **8**:10, 14; **10**:6; **11**:10; **Mt 1**:6, 19, 20, 22, 24, 25; **2**:4, 7, 9², 13, 15, 16²; **3**:4; **4**:5, 12; **7**:25, 28, 29; **8**:5, 33; **9**:8, 20, 25, 28, 33, 36; **11**:1, 20, 21, 23; **12**:7; **13**:6, 44, 46, 53; **14**:3, 4, 10, 13, 14, 23, 34; **15**:36, 39; **18**:2, 25, 30, 31², 33²; **19**:1, 15, 22; **20**:34; **21**:6, 28; **22**:3, 25, 34; **23**:30; **24**:22, 43; **25**:16, 18, 20, 24; **26**:1, 19, 24, 30, 48, 57², 75; **27**:3, 16, 17, 18, 26, 31, 35, 50, 52, 54, 55, 57, 60; **28**:11, 12, 16; **Mk 1**:19, 32, 34; **2**:1; **3**:10; **4**:6; **5**:4, 8, 14, 15, 16², 18, 19, 20, 21, 25, 26³, 30, 32, 33; **6**:14, 17³, 18, 30, 34, 44, 52, 53; **7**:17; **8**:1, 6, 7, 14²; **23**; **9**:9², 28, 34, 36; **10**:22; **11**:6, 8, 13; **12**:6, 12, 28, 34, 44; **13**:20; **14**:16, 21, 26, 44, 72; **15**:7, 10, 15, 20, 41²; **16**:4, 9, 10, 11, 14², 19; **Lk 1**:7, 22, 58; **2**:15, 17², 20², 21², 22, 26², 36, 39, 49; **3**:19; **4**:9, 13, 16, 32, 40; **5**:4, 6, 9, 17, 25; **6**:18; **7**:1, 10, 21, 29, 30, 37, 39, 42, 43; **8**:2², 6, 27², 29⁴, 30, 34, 35², 36², 38, 39, 43, 47²; **9**:1, 7, 8², 10, 36², 47; **10**:13, 37, 39, 40; **11**:14, 37; **12**:1, 39; **13**:1, 6, 11, 14; **14**:6, 17; **15**:11, 13, 14, 32; **16**:8; **17**:7, 12; **18**:28; **19**:15², 28, 32, 37, 42; **20**:19, 26; **21**:4; **22**:7, 13, 52, 55², 61; **23**:8², 12, 19, 25, 46, 47, 48, 49, 51, 53, 55; **24**:1, 12, 14, 23, 24, 35, 40, 50; **Jn 1**:24, 40²; **2**:2, 9³, 10, 21, 22²; **4**:4, 5, 8, 18, 44, 45³, 46, 47, 53; **5**:5, 6, 10, 13², 15; **6**:2, 6, 12², 13, 17, 19, 22⁴, 23², 26, 64; **7**:10, 30, 39², 50; **8**:20, 31; **9**:8, 13, 14, 15, 18², 22, 24, 35; **10**:40; **11**:11, 13, 17, 19, 21, 28, 30², 31, 32, 33, 43, 45², 46, 57; **12**:1, 9, 12, 16², 18², 29², 36, 37; **13**:1, 2, 3², 10, 12, 21, 29, 30; **15**:22, 24; **17**:5; **18**:1, 2, 9, 10, 14, 16, 18, 26, 32, 40; **19**:1, 19, 30, 32, 39, 41; **20**:1, 7, 8, 9, 12, 18; **21**:7, 15, 20²; **Ac 1**:2, 16; **2**:13, 30, 44, 45; **3**:10, 12, 13, 18; **4**:7, 14, 21, 23, 28, 32, 35; **5**:5, 7, 21, 30, 40, 41; **7**:5, 16, 29, 30, 35, 41, 44³, 60; **8**:4, 9, 11, 14, 16², 25, 27; **9**:23, 27³, 33, 39; **10**:3, 7, 8, 24, 41, 45²; **11**:1, 4, 11, 13, 15, 16, 18, 19; **12**:2, 9, 10, 12², 17, 18, 19, 20, 25; **13**:1, 3, 12, 29, 31, 36, 46; **14**:8, 9, 11, 18, 20, 23, 25, 26², 27²; **15**:3, 4, 12, 23, 38², 39; **16**:9, 10², 13, 16, 23, 27, 34; **17**:1, 3; **18**:2², 16, 18², 25, 27; **19**:9, 12, 16, 19, 21, 41; **20**:1, 13, 16, 36; **21**:1, 9, 10, 19, 29²; **33**, 35; **22**:11, 28, 29, 30; **23**:12, 27, 29; **24**:27; **25**:7, 12, 16, 18, 19, 25; **26**:22, 32; **27**:5, 7, 9², 13, 17, 21, 38; **28**:9, 11, 15, 17, 19, 25; **Ro 1**:13; **2**:25; **3**:25; **4**:2, 11, 12, 18, 21²; **7**:7; **9**:6, 10, 11, 32; **1Co 2**:8; **4**:8; **7**:29; **11**:24; **2Co 2**:3, 12, 13; **5**:21; **7**:5, 7, 14; **8**:6; **9**:5; **10**:14; **11**:32; **Gal 2**:2, 4; **7**:3, 19; **4**:4, 22; **Php 1**:30; **2**:27; **4**:10; **1Th 2**:2, 8; **Tit 3**:5; **Heb 1**:3; **2**:17; **3**:14; **4**:2, 6, 8; **7**:6; **8**:7; **9**:1, 4², 6, 7, 8, 19, 26; **10**:12, 32, 34; **11**:5, 11, 15³, 17, 18, 24, 30, 39, 40; **12**:9; **1Pe 1**:6, 14; **2**:10; **2Pe 1**:21; **1Jn 2**:7, 19; **2Jn 1**:5; **Jude 1**:3; **Rev 4**:1, 3, 4, 7, 8; **5**:6², 8², 6:9², 11; **7**:2; **8**:3, 6, 11; **9**:1, 9, 10², 11, 14, 15; **10**:5, 8, 10; **11**:10; **12**:13², 16; **13**:1, 2, 3², 4, 11, 12, 17; **14**:1, 3, 6, 17, 18²; **15**:2; **16**:2, 9, 11; **17**:1, 3; **18**:1, 19; **19**:20³; **20**:4⁴, 10, 12, 13; **21**:1, 9, 12, 14, 15; **22**:8²

HAS (2407)

See also the selected listing for "HAS" in the Main Concordance.

Ge 1:29, 30; **3**:22; **4**:25; **5**:29; **6**:17; **9**:4, 6; **15**:16; **16**:2, 11; **17**:14²; **18**:19, 21; **19**:13, 19; **21**:6, 17, 26; **22**:20; **24**:27², 35³, 36², 44, 51, 56; **26**:22, 33; **27**:27, 36; **29**:8, 32; **30**:2, 6², 18, 20, 23, 27, 29, 30²; **31**:1², 5, 7³, 9², 12, 15², 16, 32, 42; **33**:5, 11; **34**:8, 21; **35**:3; **37**:33²; **38**:23; **39**:8, 9, 14; **41**:25, 28, 32, 39, 51, 52; **42**:21, 28²; **43**:23; **44**:16, 28; **45**:6, 9; **48**:2, 9, 11, 15, 16; **Ex 3**:9, 13, 14, 15, 16, 18; **4**:5; **5**:3, 23; **7**:16; **9**:18, 19; **11**:6; **15**:1, 2, 4, 21; **16**:7, 8, 9, 15, 16, 29, 32; **19**:8; **20**:20; **21**:3, 8³, 16, 29³; **22**:8, 19, 27; **24**:3, 7, 8; **32**:1, 23, 24, 29, 33; **35**:1, 4, 10, 30, 31, 34, 35; **36**:1²; **Lev 4**:3, 35; **5**:1, 2, 5, 6, 10, 13, 16, 18, 19; **6**:4, 10; **8**:5, 34; **9**:6,

7; **10**:6, 11, 15; **11**:3, 7, 26, 34, 38; **13**:2, 3, 4, 5, 6², 7, 8, 9, 10, 13², 15, 18, 20², 21, 23, 24, 25², 26, 28², 29, 32, 34, 36, 37, 38, 39, 40, 41², 42, 46, 51, 52, 53, 55⁴, 56², 57, 58; **14**:3, 32, 37, 39, 44, 48²; **15**:2, 7, 16, 17, 19, 25³; **16**:20; **17**:2, 4; **19**:8, 20, 22; **20**:3, 9, 11, 15, 17, 18³, 20, 21, 24; **21**:3, 10², 12, 17, 18, 20²; **21**²; **22**:4², 6, 13; **24**:19, 20; **25**:25, 26, 30, 48; **27**:17, 20, 22; **Nu 5**:2, 7², 8, 13, 18, 19, 27, 28; **6**:9, 19, 21; **10**:29; **12**:2; **14**:23, 24, 29, 35; **15**:28, 31; **16**:9, 10, 28, 29, 46²; **19**:2², 13, 16², 18³, 20²; **20**:5; **21**:29; **22**:5, 11, 13; **23**:8², 20, 23; **24**:11, 16, 25:11; **27**:9, 10, 30, 5, 12; **31**:17, 18; **32**:7, 18, 19, 21, 31; **34**:13; **35**:6, 8², 11, 15, 17, 18, 26, 32, 33; **Dt 1**:10, 11, 21; **2**:7³, 30; **3**:18, 20, 21; **4**:19, 23, 32², 33, 34; **5**:12, 15, 16, 24, 26, 32, 33; **6**:17, 20, 25; **7**:2, 6; **8**:10; **9**:3, 4²; **10**:22; **11**:7, 29; **12**:1, 7, 20, 21; **13**:2, 5, 14²; **14**:2, 6, 8, 9; **15**:2², 6, 14, 18, 21²; **16**:10, 17; **17**:1, 3, 4³, 5, 16; **18**:5, 8, 14, 21, 22²; **19**:1; **20**:5, 6, 7, 17; **21**:3⁴, 4, 5, 13, 15, 17, 18, **22**:17, 19, 21, 25, 26, 29; **23**:1, 15; **24**:4, 5²; **26**:11, 18, 19²; **27**:21; **28**:21, 48, 53, 55; **29**:4, 22, 24; **31**:2; **32**:21, 22, 27²; **34**:10, 12; **Jos 1**:13, 15; **2**:9², 24; **5**:9; **6**:16; **7**:8, 11, 15², 20; **8**:8; **10**:4, 14, 19; **14**:10, 14; **17**:14; **18**:3; **20**:6; **22**:4, 22, 25; **23**:3, 9², 13, 14¹, **15**⁴, 16; **24**:20, 27²; **Jdg 1**:7²; **2**:20²; **3**:28; **4**:14²; **6**:13²; **30**; **7**:2, 14, 15; **8**:7; **11**:23, 24, 36; **16**:17, 18, 23, 24; **17**:13; **18**:4, 6, 10, 14; **19**:18, 30; **21**:3, 5; **Ru 1**:13, 20, 21³; **2**:7, 8²; **4**:7², 17², 21, 22²; **6**:3, 4, 9; **7**:12; **9**:12, 16, 24; **10**:1, 2, 11, 22², 24; **11**:13; **12**:13, 24; **13**:4²; 14; **14**:10, 12, 17, 29, 33, 38, 45; **15**:11², 12³, 23, 26, 28², 33; **16**:8, 9, 10; **17**:33, 34, 36, 37; **18**:4³; **20**:3, 13, 15, 22, 29²; **32**; **21**:11; **22**:8, 13; **23**:7², 10, 11, 22; **24**:14; **25**:21, 24, 26, 27, 30², 31, 32, 34, 39³, 40; **26**:19, 27⁶, 12; **28**:9², 15, 16, 17², 18, 21; **29**:3, 5; **30**:23²; **2Sa 2**:7; **3**:29, 38; **4**:8, 9; **5**:20, 24; **6**:12²; 20; **7**:27; **12**:13; **13**:20, 24, 30, 32, 35; **14**:2, 7, 13, 20, 22², 30; **15**:4; **16**:8², 11; **17**:5, 6, 7, 9, 15, 21; **18**:19, 28, 31; **19**:9, 10, 11, 17, 30; **20**:17, 21; **22**:21² 25; **23**:5; **24**:17, 21; **1Ki 1**:11, 13, 18, 19³, 25², 27, 29, 43, 44, 46, 48; **2**:15² 24², 28; **5**:4; **7**:8, 12, 15, 20, 32, 41, 56², 9:8; **10**:9², 12; **12**:19; **13**:3, 26²; **14**:11, 13, 16²; **18**:10, 12, 27; **20**:13, 14, 18, 29²; **22**:23³, 28; **2Ki 1**:14; **2**:2, 4, 6, 16, 22; **3**:7, 10; **4**:2, 14, 27², 31; **7**:6, 14; **8**:1, 4, 7, 9, 10, 13, 22; **9**:18, 20; **10**:10¹; **13**:23; **14**:7; **17**:26; **18**:33, 35; **19**:4² 16, 21, 28; **20**:9; **21**:11³; **22**:4, 10, 13, 16, 18; **1Ch 14**:11, 15; **16**:8, 12; **17**:25; **21**:17; **22**:18²; **23**:25²; **28**:5²; **10**; **29**:1; **2Ch 2**:11, 12; **6**:1, 4, 10, 23, 32; **7**:21; **8**:11; **9**:8²; **10**:19; **13**:5; **14**:7; **16**:7; **18**:22², 27; **21**:10; **23**:6; **24**:20; **25**:8, 9², 27; **29**:8², 11; **30**:8; **31**:10; **32**:14, 15; **34**:16, 18, 21, 24; **35**:21; **36**:23²; **Ezr 1**:2²; **4**:18, 19², 20; **5**:16; **6**:12; **7**:23, 27, 28; **9**:6, 7, 8, 9⁴, 13; **10**:14; **Ne 2**:5; **9**:32, 33; **Est 1**:15, 16; **4**:11; **5**:12; **6**:3², 8²; **13**; **7**:5; **Job 1**:10, 11, 12, 15, 16, 17, 19, 21; **2**:4; **3**:23, 25²; **4**:7; **6**:5², 13; **9**:4; **11**:6²; **12**:9; **14**:6, 13; **15**:12; **16**:8, 11, 12; **17**:6; **18**:17, 19; **19**:6, 8², 9, 13, 21, 26; **20**:4, 19²; **23**; **21**:31; **23**:10, 14, 16; **26**:4; **27**:2²; **8**; **28**:7, 22; **30**:11, 15; **31**:5, 7, 9, 32; **32**:12²; **14**; **33**:4, 11, 23; **36**:23, 25; **37**:7, 21; **38**:37; **40**:16; **41**:11, 15, 26; **42**:7, 8; **Ps 4**:3; **6**:8, 9; **7**:13, 15; **9**:6², 7, 11; **10**:11; **13**:6; **15**:3; **18**:20², 24; **19**:4; **22**:14², 16, 24³, 31; **24**:4; **28**:6; **36**:3; **38**:2, 4, 10; **39**:9; **41**:1, 8, 9; **45**:2, 7; **46**:8; **47**:5; **48**:3; **49**:20; **52**:T; **53**:3; **54**:7; **55**:5; **57**:1; **58**:4; **60**:6; **62**:11, 12; **64**:9; **66**:5, 9, 16, 19, 20; **68**:17, 24; **69**:20²; **71**:11; **73**:25; **74**:3, 18; **77**:8², 9²; **78**:4; **80**:15; **83**:8; **84**:3; **87**:1; **88**:16; **89**:41, 50; **90**:4; **94**:22; **98**:1, 2, 3; **101**:5; **102**:13; **103**:12, 13², 19; **104**:17; **105**:1, 5; **108**:7; **109**:11; **110**:4; **111**:4, 6; **112**:9; **115**:16; **116**:7; **118**:14, 15, 16, 17, 18², 22, 23, 24, 27; **119**:56; **124**:6, 7; **126**:2, 3; **129**:4; **132**:13²; **135**:4; **145**:9², 13, 17; **147**:5, 19, 20; **148**:14; **150**:6; **Pr 2**:17; **3**:30; **6**:7; **7**:19, 26; **9**:1², 2³, 3; **10**:18, 25; **13**:7¹; **14**:26, 29; **15**:15; **17**:16; **18**:21; **19**:17; **20**:12; **21**:20; **23**:24², 29⁶; **24**:5, 7, 12, 20, 29; **28**:2, 11, 23; **30**:4⁴, 15; **31**:11, 21, 31; **Ecc 1**:8, 9², 13, 16; **2**:12, 14, 21; **3**:10, 11³, 15², 19; **4**:3², 10; **5**:4, 10, 14, 18; **6**:5, 8, 10²; **7**:13², 14; **8**:3², 15, 17; **9**:4, 9; **12**:3; **SS 2**:4, 12; **4**:2; **6**:1, 2, 6; **8**:2; **Isa 1**:2, 12, 20, 21, 22; **2**:12, 22; **5**:9; **6**:7, 12; **7**:2; **8**:6, 18; **9**:2, 8, 11²; **10**:7, 9, 12, 22; **12**:1, 2, 4, 5; **14**:4², 5, 11, 24, 27, 32; **16**:13; **19**:12, 14, 20; **21**:2, 4, 9²; **17**; **22**:5, 14, 25; **23**:1, 4, 11²; **24**:3; **25**:8; **26**:20; **27**:7², 11; **28**:2, 22, 25; **29**:10³; **30**:33³; **34**:5, 6, 8, 16; **36**:18, 20; **37**:4², 17, 22, 29; **38**:7, 8, 12², 15²; **40**:2³, 5, 12², 13, 21; **41**:2, 4, 20²; **44**:7, 19, 23; **45**:9, 23; **47**:3, 10, 14²; **48**:8, 14, 16, 20; **49**:1, 5, 7, 10, 14²; **50**:4, 5, 10; **52**:4, 9²; **53**:1, 6², **54**:1, 10; **55**:5; **56**:3; **58**:2, 14; **59**:14; **60**:1, 9; **61**:1², 9, 10; **62**:8, 11; **63**:4, 7²; **64**:4³, 11; **66**:2, 8²;

Jer 2:10, 11, 14, 30, 37; **3**:6³; **4**:7³, 8, 17; **5**:19, 30; **6**:24, 25, 30; **7**:11, 28³, 29; **8**:8, 14, 15, 20; **9**:12², 21³; **11**:17; **12**:8, 9; **13**:15, 22; **14**:17, 19; **16**:10; **17**:8; **18**:13²; **20**:8; **21**:12; **22**:3, 8, 11, 21; **23**:15, 18², 28³, 35, 37; **25**:3, 4, 34; **26**:11, 13, 15, 16; **27**:13; **28**:15; **29**:15, 26, 28, 31², 32; **30**:15; **32**:24, 31, 43; **33**:24; **34**:14², 16, 21; **35**:14; **37**:7; **38**:16, 21; **40**:3², 5, 14; **42**:19²; **44**:23; **45**:3; **46**:10, 17; **47**:4, 7²; **48**:8, 11², 19, 21, 26, 32, 39, 45; **49**:1³, 7², 20², 24³, 25, 30²; **50**:14, 15, 25², 27, 28, 29², 37, 43², 45²; **51**:10², 11, 13, 14, 34⁵, 44; **La 1**:1, 3, 5, 6, 8², 9, 14², 15³, 16, 17²; **2**:1³, 2³, 3⁴, 4³, 5⁴, 6⁴, 7², 9, 17², 22; **3**:1, 2, 3², 4, 5, 7, 9², 15, 16², 28, 37; **4**:1, 8², 11², 16; **5**:1, 2, 15, 16; **Eze 2**:5; **4**:14; **5**:6³; **7**:2, 6⁴, 7², 10⁴, 11, 12², 13, 19; **8**:12; **9**:6, 9; **13**:6; **15**:5; **18**:10, 11, 13, 14, 19², 21, 22², 24², 26, 27, 28; **21**:25²; **29²**; **22**:4, 18, 24, 28, 24**2**; **12², 13; **24**:25; **25**:8; **26**:2; **28**:5; **30**:21; **33**:13², 15, 16; **34**:2; **46**:12; **Da 1**:10; **2**:10, 27, 28, 30, 37, 38², 45; **3**:5, 28; **4**:2, 22, 24, 31; **5**:11, 26; **6**:5, 20, 27; **8**:26; **9**:11, 12², 13; **11**:2, 4, 21; **12**:1, 7; **Hos 2**:5²; **8**; **4**:1; **5**:6; **6**:1²; **8**:3, 6, 7, 9, 14²; **11**:12; **12**:12, 14; **14**:4; **Joel 1**:2, 4, 5, 6², 7, 16, 17, 19, 20; **2**:20, 21, 23, 26, 32; **3**:8; **Am 3**:1, 4², 5, 6, 8², 4:2; **6**:8, 11; **8**:7; **Ob 1**:3, 18; **Jnh 1**:2, 12; **4**:11; **Mic 1**:9²; **12**; **4**:4, 9; **6**:2, 8; **7**:4; **Na 1**:11, 14; **3**:13, 19; **Hab 2**:13, 18; **Zep 1**:7³; **2**:15; **3**:15²; **Hag 1**:12; **Zec 1**:16, 10; **2**:8², 9, 11, 13; **3**:2; **4**:9; **6**:15; **9**:3²; **11**:2²; **13**:5; **Mal 1**:14; **2**:11³, 15; **Mt 2**:2, 5; **4**:16; **5**:23, 28, 31; **6**:34; **8**:20; **9**:6, 18, 22, 33; **10**:25; **11**:11, 12, 15, 18; **12**:11, 28; **13**:9, 11, 12², 15, 21, 43, 52; **14**:2; **15**:13; **16**:27; **17**:9, 12, 15; **19**:6, 11, 29; **20**:7; **21**:42²; **23**:35; **24**:45; **25**:28, 29²; **26**:10, 13, 23, 56, 65; **27**:8, 23, 64; **28**:6, 7, 15, 18; **Mk 1**:15; **2**:10; **3**:26, 30; **4**:9, 11, 13, 23, 25²; **5**:19²; **34**; **6**:2, 14, 16; **7**:29; **37**; **9**:13, 17, 21, 22; **10**:9, 29, 52; **11**:2; **12**:10, 11, 41; **13**:20²; **14**:6, 9, 41; **15**:14; **16**:6; **Lk 1**:13, 25², 45², 48, 49, 51², 52², 53², 54, 61, 68²; **2**:11, 15²; **3**:11²; **4**:6, 18²; **5**:24³; **7**:5, 16², 33, 45, 46, 47, 50; **8**:8, 10, 18², 39, 46, 48; **9**:19, 58; **10**:40, 42; **11**:5, 6, 20, 50; **12**:4²; **3**:6, 10, 14, 44; **5**:5², 17², 19; **6**:16, 17; **7**:11, 13, 14; **8**:1, 12, 22; **9**:2, 7, 9, 14²; **10**:13³, 14, 23; **4**:2², 13², 45; **5**:18², 23; **6**:22², 34²; **7**:5, 16², 33, 45, 46, 47, 50; **8**:8, 10, 18², 39, 46, 48; **9**:19, 58; **10**:40, 42; **11**:5, 6, 20, 50; **12**:4²; **13**:6, 10, 14, 19²; **15**:2; **20**:9; **21**:8; **22**:9, 14, 22²; **7**:6, 8, 19, 38, 47, 48; **8**:10, 28, 29, 35, 40; **9**:32; **10**:4, 39, 41; **11**:10, 11, 39; **12**:19, 23, 38²; **40**, 50; **13**:10; **14**:9, 14²; **15**:9, 13; **16**:21², 32; **17**:1, 10, 14, 18; **19**:11; **35**; **20**:21; **Ac 1**:7, 11; **2**:32, 33², 36; **3**:13, 16, 20; **4**:11; **5**:3, 32; **7**:40, 50; **9**:12, 13, 14, 17; **10**:15, 28, 31, 33, 37; **11**:8, 9, 18; **13**:26, 33, 40, 47; **14**:17²; **15**:14, 21; **17**:7, 31²; **19**:26; **20**:24, 28; **21**:28; **22**:14; **23**:9, 17, 18; **24**:2; **25**:5, 11, 16², 24; **26**:6, 26; **27**:24; **28**:4, 21, 27; **Ro 1**:19, 20; **2**:6, 25; **3**:21; **4**:14; **5**:5²; **6**:7²; **9**; **7**:1; **8**:22, 24, 39; **9**:18, 19; **11**:11, 25²; **32², 34²**, 35; **12**:3, 4; **13**:1, 2, 8, 11; **14**:3, 23; **15**:8, 18, 20; **16**:2, 12, 13, 19; **1Co 1**:9, 20, 24, 30; **2**:7⁴, 9, 10, 12, 16; **3**:5, 10, 14; **4**:9; **5**:1; **6**:1; **7**:7³, 12, 13, 14², 15, 17, 28, 37³; **8**:10; **9**:14; **10**:11, 13, 28; **11**:14, 15; **12**:18, 24²; **26**:16, 36; **15**:12, 13, 14, 16, 17, 20; **24**, 25, 27², 28, 38, 41, 54²; **16**:9, 10, 12; **2Co 1**:10, 19, 20; **2**:5³; **3**:6, 10, 14, 4:4; **5**:5², 17², 19; **6**:16; **7**:11, 13, 14; **8**:1, 12, 22; **9**:2, 7, 9, 14; **10**:13³, 14; **Gal 3**:1, 15, 25; **4**:7, 15, 27; **5**:1, 6, 11; **6**:14; **Eph 1**:3, 6, 18; **2**:14²; **3**:5; **4**:7, 28; **5**:5; **Php 1**:12², 13, 19, 29; **2**:22²; **3**:4, 14; **Col 1**:6²; **12**, 13, 22, 23, 26, 27; **2**:18, 19; **4**:16; **1Th 1**:4, 8; **2**:16, 18; **4**:6, 10³, 14; **Tit 1**:9, 12; **2**:11; **Phm 1**:7, 11, 18; **Heb 1**:2, 4, 9; **2**:5, 6, 13; **3**:3², 12, 15²; **4**:3², 4, 14, 15; **5**:3; **6**:12, 20²; **7**:13, 16, 21, 22, 24, 28; **8**:6; **9**:15, 17, 20, 26; **10**:14, 29³, 36; **11**:16; **12**:26; **13**:5, 23; **Jas 1**:12²; **15**, 25; **2**:5, 13, 14; **5**:2, 15; **1Pe 1**:8; **2**:7; **3**:22; **4**:1, 10; **2Pe 1**:3, 4, 9², 14; **2**:3²; **19**; **3**:4; **1Jn 1**:2, 10; **2**:11, 16, 23², 27, 29; **3**:1, 2, 3, 6, 9, 15, 17²; **4**:2, 7, 12, 13, 14, 16, 18, 20²; **5**:4, 9, 10⁴, 11, 12², 20²; **2Jn 1**:4, 9; **3Jn 1**:11; **Jude 1**:6, 13; **Rev 1**:5, 6; **2**:7, 11, 12, 13, 15, 18²; **12**:10, 12; **13**:9, 18; **14**:7, 10, 15; **16**:18²; **17**:7, 10, 17; **18**:2, 5, 6², 10, 17, 19, 20; **19**:2², 7², 12, 16; **20**:6; **21**:4; **22**:12.

HAVE (4313)

See also the selected listing for "HAVE" in the Main Concordance.

Ge 3:11, 13, 14; **4**:1, 7, 10, 23; **6**:7²; **7**:1, 4, 15; **8**:21; **9**:13, 17; **11**:6; **12**:18; **13**:8; **14**:22², 24²; **15**:3; **16**:8, 11, 13; **17**:5, 20; **18**:3, 5, 10, 12, 13, 14, 19, 30, 31, 31², 19; **19**:5, 8², 12, 19; **20**:3, 5, 6, 9⁴, 17; **21**:7², 23, 29; **22**:12, 16², 18; **24**:14³, 19, 25, 31, 33², 40, 42; **25**:30; **26**:10³, 16, 27; **27**:19, 37³, 38; **28**:15²; **22**; **29**:25², 34; **30**:8², 16, 20, 26, 27², 29, 30, 33, 34; **31**:12, 14, 26, 28, 29, 30, 34, 36, 37², 38³, 42, 43, 51; **32**:4², 5, 10², 12, 28²; **33**:9², 10²; **11**; **34**:30, 31; **35**:2, 3, 17; **37**:17; **38**:24, 29; **40**:15; **41**:15; **42**:2, 9, 10, 12, 36; **43**:7, 10, 21, 22; **44**:4, 5, 9, 10, 15, 16, 17, 19, 20, 28; **45**:1, 10, 13; **46**:30, 31, 32, 34; **47**:1, 4², 5, 9, 23, 25, 29; **49**:6; **50**:4; **Ex 1**:9, 18²; **2**:14, 18, 20, 22; **3**:7³, 8, 9, 12², 16², 17; **4**:10², 21; **5**:15, 21², 22, 23; **6**:5²; **7**:1, 16; **9**:8, 15², 16, 19, 27, 28², 29; **10**:1, 5, 6, 11², 16, 25, 26; **12**:31, 32, 39, 44²; **48**; **14**:5³, 11, 12; **15**:5, 13; **16**:3, 12, 16, 18², 18; **18**:3, 16, 22²; **19**:4, 10; **20**:3, 19, 22²; **22**:15; **23**:7, 13, 20, 30; **24**:12; **25**:8, 10, 20; **27**:19, 11, 17; **28**:1, 3, 5, 7; **29**:35; **31**:2, 6; **32**:4²; **13**²; **14²**, 17², 19, 24; **34**:9, 27; **35**:5; **Lev 6**:17; **7**:33, 34²; **8**:35; **10**:13, 14, 18, 19²; **11**:4², 5, 6, 9, 10, 12, 21, 23; **13**:17; **14**:35, 43; **16**:16; **17**:11, 14; **18**:6, 7, 8, 9, 10, 11, 12, 13, 14, 15², 16, 17², 18, 19, 20, 23²; **19**:10, 30; **20**:12, 13, 16, 17, 19, 25, 26; **22**:25; **23**:24, 38, 39; **24**:22; **25**:4, 5, 9, 32; **26**:2, 10, 35²; **Nu 3**:12; **4**:15, 16; **5**:16, 19, 20², 24, 26, 28, 30; **8**:7², 8, 13, 15, 16, 18, 19; **9**:2, 7, 14; **11**:6, 11, 12, 15, 16, 17, 20², 22²; **12**:11, 14; **14**:11, 14², 15, 17, 19, 20, 27, 31, 34, 35, 40, 43; **15**:15, 25, 39; **16**:3, 5, 7, 11, 13, 15², 30, 38, 41; **18**:6, 8, 9, 20², 24; **20**:14, 17; **21**:5, 22, 30², 34; **22**:5, 20, 28, 29, 30², 32², 33², 34, 38; **23**:4², 11², 20, 22; **24**:7, 8, 10; **25**:5, 12, 17, 20, 19; **31**:15, 19, 49, 50; **32**:4, 5, 11, 17, 24, 33²; **34**:2, 14, 15; **35**:3; **Dt 1**:6, 8, 15, 19, 20, 28, 41; **2**:3, 5, 7, 9, 19, 22, 24, 31; **3**:2, 19², 20², 21, 24; **4**:5, 7, 8, 9, 25², 30, 33; **5**:7, 24², 26, 28; **7**:2, 20; **8**:10, 13, 17; **9**:1, 2, 7¹, 12³, 13, 23, 24²; **10**:9; **11**:8, 10, 28, 31; **12**:6, 7, 9; **11**, 12, 17, 21, 26, 29, 30; **13**:2, 6, 13, 13², 17; **14**:7²; 10, 24, 27, 29; **16**:3; **17**:14; **18**:1, 2, 20; **19**:1; **15**; **20**:9; **21**:8, 9, 12, 14; **22**:7; **23**:13; **24**:5; **25**:1, 2, 13, 14, 15; **26**:1², 3, 10, 12, 13⁴, 14⁵, 15, 17; **27**:2, 3, 4, 8, 9, 12; **28**:20, 33, 40, 41, 54, 64; **29**:2, 22; **30**:1, 3, 4, 12, 13, 19; **31**:15, 17, 20, 27, 29²; **32**:5, 34, 36, 39, 46, 50; **33**:9, 34; **Jos 1**:9, 15, 16; **2**:2, 3, 10, 12; **3**:4; **5**:9, 14²; **6**:2, 3, 4, 5; **7**:3, 11⁵, 12, 19, 20², 25; **8**:1, 6, 8²; **9**:6, 9², 19; **10**:6, 8, 13, 16; **12**:6; **15**:19, 14:14; **17**:14, 16, 18; **18**:6, 7; **22**:2², 3², 17, 23, 24, 25, 27, 31²; **23**:3, 4, 8; **24**:22; **Jdg 1**:2, 7, 15; **2**:2²; **3**:19, 20; **4**:5; **6**:10, 14, 17, 22, 36; **7**:2; **8**:1, 2, 6, 15, 22, 24; **9**:2, 16³, 18, 19, 20, 31, 48; **10**:10, 13, 14, 15; **11**:12², 23, 27, 35², 36; **12**:3; **13**:3, 13, 14, 22, 23², 24; **14**:2, 6, 16, 18³; **15**:3, 10², 11, 16, 18; **16**:7, 10, 11, 13, 15², 17; **17**:2; **18**:9, 10, 11, 24, 25, 27; **31²; 23**:3, 4, 8; **24**:22; **Ru 1**:8, 11, 12; **2**:9²; **10**, 11, 12², 13²; **14**; **3**:2, 10; **4**:9, 10, 11; **1Sa 1**:15, 16, 17, 23; **2**:36; **49**; **4**:16, 20; **5**:8, 10; **6**:7²; **21**; **7**:6; **8**:5, 7², 8, 18; **9**:7², 8, 12, 16, 20, 24; **10**:2, 14, 19²; **12**:1²; **2², 3, 4², 5, 10, 12², 13**, 14, 19; **13**:11, 12, 13², 14, 20; **14**:7, 9, 43; **15**:11, 13, 18, 23, 24, 26, 30; **16**:1², 2, 5, 7, 11, 18; **17**:8², 29, 45, 47; **18**:8, 21, 25; **20**:1², 3, 8, 26, 29, 30, 41; **21**:2, 3, 12, 15; **22**:8², 13, 17, 21, 22, 24², 25, 27, 28, 29, 32³; **32**:5, 34, 36, 39, 46, 50; **23**:3, 7², 9³, 11, 21; **24**:11², 17, 18, 19²; **21**; **25**:8, 28², 29³; **26**:16, 18, 19³, 21³; **27**:5; **28**:9, 12, 15², 21, 22², 23², 29³; **30**:1, 3, 9, 14, 16, 17², 22, 23, 33; **4**:3, 11; **5**:8; **7**:3, 7, 9³, 10, 11, 18, 19, 21, 22, 24², 25, 27, 28, 29; **9**:9; **10**:5; **11**:19; **12**:8, 13, 14, 27; **13**:16, 28; **14**:7, 13, 15; **16**:2, 8², 10, 21; **17**:15, 29; **18**:11, 13, 18, 21, 22, 25; **19**:5², 6, 7, 20², 22; **20**:1; **21**:4²; **5²; 22**:22², 23, 24²; **44**; **24**:10³, 17; **1Ki 1**:11, 14, 24, 34, 35, 44, 45²; **47**; **2**:4, 8, 14, 16, 20; **3**:6³, 7, 8, 11², 12², 13, 26; **5**:6, 8; **8**:13, 16³, 18, 20², 21, 24³, 25², 27, 33², 35², 43, 44², 47⁴, 48³, 50²; **59**; **9**:3⁴, 5, 6, 7², 9²; **10**:7; **11**:11, 13, 22, 32², 33², 34, 36; **12**:10, 16², 18²; **24**¹³; **19**, 25, 33³, 34, 36; **13**:21, 22²; **14**:6, 8, 9³; **17**:4, 9, 10, 12, 13², 18, 20; **18**:5, 9, 12, 18¹, 36; **19**:4, 10², 14², 18²; **20**:4, 18², 31, 36, 40, 42; **21**:2, 10, 19, 20³, 22², 29; **22**:17; **2Ki 1**:13, 14, 16²; **2**:10, 16, 21; **3**:13, 14, 23; **4**:2, 13², 43; **5**:8², 13, 18², 22; **6**:22; **7**:12²; **13**², 9; **8**:19, 22, 31; **10**:2, 8, 13, 27, 30²; **13**:19²; **14**:10; **16**:6; **17**:27, 38; **18**:14, 20, 25, 27, 34; **19**:6², 7, 11², 15, 17, 18, 20², 22³, 23; **20**:3²; **5, 10, 17, 19; **21**:7, 15²; **22**:4², 5², 6, 8, 9²; **13²**, 17²; **19²**; **23**:17; **1Ch 4**:27, 43; **12**:17³; **15**:12; **17**:2, 5, 6³, 8², 10, 16, 17², 19, 20, 22, 23, 25, 26, 27²; **19**:5; **21**:8²; **17**, 22; **22**:8³, 9, 11, 13, 14, 15; **23**:5, 11; **28**:3, 6, 19; **29**:2, 3, 14, 16, 17³, 19; **2Ch 1**:8², 9,

11³, 12; **6:**2, 5³, 6², 8, 10², 11, 15³, 16², 18, 24², 26², 33, 34², 37³, 38², 39; **7:**12², 16, 18, 19, 20², 22²; **9:**6; **10:**10, 16; **12:**5, 7; **13:**8, 10, 11; **14:**7, 11; **16:**9; **18:**16; **19:**3²; **20:**8² 12, 17, 20²; 37²; **21:**12, 13²; **24:**20; **25:**16³, 19; **26:**18²; **28:**9, 11, 23; **29:**9, 18, 19, 31; **30:**6; **31:**10; **32:**13; **33:**7; **34:**15, 17², 21², 25², 27; **Ezr 4:**2, 3, 12; **6:**12; **7:**15, 20, 24; **9:**1, 2³, 7, 10, 11, 13³; **10:**2, 10², 13; **Ne 1:**3, 6, 7², 9; 2:3, 7, 8, 17, 20; **4:**5, 22; **5:**4, 5², 8, 19; **6:**7, 14²; **7:**3; **8:**10; **9:**8, 33², 37; **10:**34; **13:**14; **Est 1:**15, 18; **4:**11, 14; **5:**4, 14²; **6:**8, 10²; **7:**3, 4²; **8:**7²; **9:**12²; 21; **Job 1:**5², 7, 8, 10²; **2:**2, 3; **3:**26²; **4:**3², 4², 8; **5:**3, 16, 23, 27; **6:**3, 8, 10, 11, 12, 13, 14, 21, 22, 24; **7:**1, 3², 16, 20⁴; **9:**21; **10:**2, 4, 20; **12:**3, 4, 5; **13:**1³, 18, 23; **14:**5², 15; **15:**3, 9², 17, 18; **16:**2, 7², 8, 15, 17; **17:**4, 7, 11; **19:**3, 4, 14²,

(index text continues in dense reference format across four columns)

HE (9660)

Ge 1:4, 5, 10, 16, 27², 31; **2:**2², 3², 8², 19², 21², 22²; **3:**1, 6, 8, 10, 11, 15, 16², 17, 22, 23, 24²; **4:**5, 9, 15, 17, 20, 21, 26; **5:**1, 2², 3², 5, 6, 7, 8, 9, 10, 11, 12, 13, 14, 15, 16, 17, 18, 19, 20, 21, 22, 24, 25, 26, 27, 29², 31, 32; **6:**3, 6, 9; **8:**1, 6, 8, 9, 10, 12, 20; **9:**21²; 25², 26, 29; **10:**9, 11²; **11:**10, 11, 12, 13, 14, 15, 16, 17, 18, 19, 20, 21, 22, 23, 24, 25, 26, 32; **12:**4, 5, 7, 8², 12, 16, 18, 19, 20; **13:**1, 3², 4, 18; **14:**12, 14, 15, 16, 18, 19; **15:**5², 6, 7, 10; **16:**4, 8, 12²; **17:**14, 17, 20, 22, 24; **18:**1, 2², 3, 8, 9, 15, 19², 28, 29², 30², 31, 32², 33; **19:**1², 2, 3², 9, 13, 14², 16, 21, 25, 27, 28², 29², 30², 33, 35, 37, 38;

18, 22, 24², 26², 27, 29², 30²; **23:**5, 7, 10, 15, 16, 17, 18², 20, 23, 24, 25, 27, 34², 35²; **24:**5, 22, 23, 24², 26², 27; **25:**5, 6², 12, 14, 15, 16, 20, 22, 24, 25²; **26:**24, 32; **27:**25, 33, 35³, 43; **28:**3, 4, 6, 7, 17, 23², 24, 25, 31; **Ro 1:**2, 28; **2:**6, 7, 28, 29; **3:**25², 26, 29; **4:**2, 6, 10, 11, 14², 12², 16, 17², 19², 20, 21, 25; **5:**5; **6:**9, 10⁴; **7:**1, 2; **8:**3, 9, 11, 24, 27, 29², 30⁶, 32², 34; **9:**15, 18³, 23², 24, 25; **10:**21; **11:**2², 21, 26, 32; **12:**20; **13:**2, 3, 4³, 8; **14:**4², 6², 9, 22, 23; **1Co 1:**8, 28; **2:**14, 15, 16; **3:**7², 10, 14², 15², 18³, 19; **4:**5, 17; **6:**1, 14, 16, 17, 18; **7:**12, 13, 18⁴, 20, 22⁴, 32, 33, 36², 38², 39²; **8:**2², 10; **9:**10²; **10:**13², 22; **11:**7, 23, 24², 25, 26, 28, 34; **12:**11², 18; **14:**2, 4², 5², 11, 13², 16, 24², 25, 37, 38²; **15:**4², 5, 6, 7, 8, 15², 23, 24², 25², 27, 28, 38², 57; **16:**10³, 11, 12²; **2Co 1:**10², 21; **2:**5², 7; **3:**6; **5:**15, 17, 19; **6:**2; **7:**7, 15; **8:**6, 9², 12, 15², 17, 19, 22, 23; **9:**7, 9, 10; **10:**7³, 10; **12:**4, 9, 18; **13:**3, 4²; **Gal 1:**23; **2:**3, 11, 12³; **3:**6, 14; **4:**1² 2; **5:**3, 10; **6:**3³, 4, 7; **Eph 1:**4, 5, 6², 8, 9², 18, 20²; **2:**7, 14, 16, 17²; **3:**11, 16; **4:**8² 9², 10, 11, 28²; **5:**23, 28, 29, 33; **6:**8² 9, 22; **Php 1:**6; **2:**8, 22, 26², 27², 30, 3:4; **Col 1:**13², 15, 17, 18³, 22; **2:**13, 14, 15, 18, 19; **4:**7, 8, 9, 10, 12, 13; **1Th 1:**4, 10; **2:**19; **3:**6, 13; **4:**8; **5:**10, 24; **2Th 1:**6, 8, 10, 11; **2:**4², 6, 7, 14; **3:**3, 10, 14; **1Ti 1:**11, 12; **3:**1, 4, 5, 6², 7²; 16; **5:**1, 8; **6:**4²; **2Ti 1:**12, 16, 17², 18²; **2:**4, 5², 12², 13², 21, 24, 25; **4:**10, 11, 14, 15; **Tit 1:**3, 7, 8, 9²; **3:**5², 6, 11; **Phm 1:**11², 13, 15, 16, 18; **Heb 1:**2³, 3², 4², 5, 6, 7², 8, 10; **2:**5, 9², 12, 13, 14², 16, 17, 18³; **3:**2, 17; **4:**4, 5, 7; **5:**2², 3, 4, 6, 7², 8³, 9; **6:**10, 13, 17, 20; **7:**1, 3, 4, 6, 13, 24, 25², 27³; **8:**4², 5, 6, 13; **9:**7, 11, 12², 15, 19, 20, 21, 24, 25, 26, 28; **10:**5, 8, 9², 11, 12, 13, 14, 15, 17, 23, 36, 38; **11:**4³, 5⁴, 6², 7, 8³, 9², 10, 11², 12, 16, 17, 19, 21², 23², 24, 25, 26², 27³, 28²; **12:**5, 6³, 17⁴, 26; **13:**13, 21, 23; **Jas 1:**5, 6³, 7, 8², 10, 11, 12², 13, 14, 18², 24, 25², 26; **2:**5, 11, 21², 22, 23, 24; **3:**2²; **4:**5, 6, 7, 8, 10, 17; **5:**7, 13, 14, 15², 17, 18; **1Pe 1:**3, 11, 15, 20; **2:**12, 19, 22, 23⁴, 24; **3:**11², 18, 19; **4:**1, 2, 10, 11²; **5:**6, 7; **2Pe 1:**4, 9², 17; **2:**5², 6, 7, 8, 16; **3:**4, 9, 16; **1Jn 1:**7, 9; **2:**2, 4, 11², 16, 22, 25, 28, 29; **3:**2³, 3, 5², 7, 8, 9², 12, 20, 23, 24³; **4:**9, 10, 13², 15, 19, 20², 21; **5:**5, 6, 9, 10, 12², 14, 15, 16², 20; **3Jn 1:**10³; **Jude 1:**6, 9; **Rev 1:**1, 2, 7, 16, 17²; **2:**7, 11², 17, 23, 27², 29; **3:**5, 6, 7², 12, 13, 20, 22; **5:**5, 6, 7, 8; **6:**2², 9, 12; **7:**2, 14, 15, 17; **8:**1, 3; **9:**2; **10:**1, 2; **11:**5², 12⁴, 8, 9, 12², 13², 13:1, 4, 6, 7², 9, 10², 11², 12, 13, 14³, 15, 16, 17; **14:**4, 6, 7, 10², 16, 17; **16:**15²; **17:**8, 10², 11, 14; **18:**1, 2; **19:**2², 9, 10, 11, 12², 13, 15², 16, 20; **20:**2², 9, 13; **21:**3, 4, 5², 6, 7², 10, 16, 17; **22:**7, 9, 10, 12, 20.

HER (1669)

Ge 2:22; **3:**6²; **12:**15², 16, 19²; **16:**2, 3³, 4, 6², 9², 11, 13; **17:**15², 16⁴; **20:**2, 4, 6, 7, 13; **21:**10, 14³, 17, 19; **23:**2; **24:**14, 15², 16², 17, 18, 20, 21, 28, 30, 36, 41, 43, 44, 45³, 46², 47³, 51², 53², 55², 57, 58, 59², 60, 61, 64, 65, 67²; **25:**22, 23, 24²; **26:**9; **27:**6, 15², 17, 42²; **29:**9, 12², 19, 20, 21, 23², 24, 29, 31; **30:**1, 2, 3², 4², 9², 15, 16, 21, 22²; **31:**19, 34, 35; **33:**2, 7; **34:**2³, 3, 8; **35:**17, 18², 20; **38:**2², 6, 8, 11, 14, 15², 16, 18², 19², 20, 22², 23⁴, 24² 25, 26², 27²; **39:**8, 10², 12, 13, 14, 16; **48:**7; **Ex 1:**16; **2:**5², 9, 10; **3:**22²; **4:**25; **11:**5; **15:**20²; **18:**2, 3, 6; **21:**4², 8⁴, 9², 10, 11; **22:**16, 17²; **35:**25; **Lev 12:**2, 4², 5, 6, 7², 8; **15:**19³, 20, 21, 24², 25², 26², 28, 30², 33; **18:**7, 15, 17⁴, 18, 19, 20; **19:**20, 29; **20:**14, 18³; **21:**3, 9; **22:**13³; **27:**4; **Nu 5:**13³, 14², 15², 16², 18², 21², 27, 29; **12:**10, 12, 13, 14³; **22:**23², 25, 27, 33; **30:**3, 4⁴, 5⁸, 6, 7³, 8⁴, 10, 11⁴, 12², 14², 15²; **36:**8; **Dt 20:**7²; **21:**4, 11², 12⁴, 13³, 14²; **22:**13², 14⁴, 16, 17², 19, 21², 22, 23, 25, 27, 28⁴, 29²; **24:**1, 3³, 4³; **25:**5⁴, 8, 11, 12²; **28:**30², 56², 57; **Jos 2:**14, 17; **6:**17², 22³, 23³, 25²; **15:**18³, 19; **Jdg 1:**14³, 15; **4:**5, 8, 18, 20, 22; **5:**26²; **7:**2², 11:34, 35, 38, 39²; **13:**3, 6, 9², 10, 13, 14; **14:**2, 3, 7, 8, 17², **15:**1, 2⁴, 6²; **16:**1, 5, 7, 8, 17, 18, 19; **19:**2, 3², 25⁴, 26, 27², 28²; **20:**6, 21:21; **Ru 1:**3, 5², 6, 7, 8, 10, 14², 15³, 18²; **2:**1, 2, 10, 14², 15, 16³, 18², 19³, 20, 22, 23; **3:**1², 6², 15, 16³; **4:**13²; **1Sa 1:**4, 5², 6⁴, 7², 8², 11, 12, 13³, 14, 18², 19, 22, 23³, 24; **2:**19; **4:**19³, 20, 21²; **7:**14; **18:**17, 21; **25:**3, 19², 20², 23, 35, 39, 41, 42; **28:**7, 10, 12, 13; **2Sa 3:**15², 16³; **6:**16, 23; **11:**3, 4², 26, 27²; **12:**3², 5³, 6, 8, 10, 11, 14², 15⁴, 16, 17, 18², 19³, 20³; **14:**2, 3, 4, 5, 17, 8; **20:**17, 20; **1Ki 1:**3, 4, 31; **2:**19²; **3:**1, 20², 6; **9:**24; **10:**2, 3, 13²; **14:**5², 6; **15:**13; **17:**10, 13, 15², 19, 20; **21:**6; **2Ki 4:**2, 5³, 6, 9, 12, 13, 14², 15², 17, 20,

HERSELF (45)

Ge 18:12; **24:**65; **38:**14²; **Lev 18:**23; **21:**9; **Nu 5:**27, 28, 29; **30:**3, 4, 5, 6, 7, 8, 10, 11, 13; **Jdg 5:**29; **14:**16; **Ru 2:**3; **2Sa 11:**4; **21:**10; **Ps 68:**31; **84:**3; **Pr 14:**33; **Isa 16:**12; **61:**10; **La 1:**8; **Eze 22:**3²; **23:**7², 13; **Hos 2:**13; **8:**9; **Zep 2:**15; **Zec 9:**3; **Mt 9:**21; **Ac 19:**27; **1Ti 5:**10; **Heb 11:**11; **Rev 2:**20; **18:**7; **19:**7.

HIM (5427)

Ge 1:27; **2:**15, 18; **3:**23; **4:**8, 15³, 25², 26; **5:**1, 3, 24, 29; **6:**22; **7:**5, 16, 23; **8:**1, 11, 12; **9:**8, 24; **12:**4², 7, 20; **13:**1, 14; **14:**5, 17², 20; **15:**4, 5², 6, 7, 9, 10, 12, 13; **16:**1, 11, 12, 16; **17:**1, 3, 19³, 20³, 22, 23, 27; **18:**9, 10, 18, 19³, 23, 29; **19:**3, 6, 21, 32, 33, 34², 35, 37, 38; **20:**3, 6, 14; **21:**2, 3, 4², 5, 7, 12, 18²; **22:**1, 2, 3², 9², 11, 12; **23:**9²; 16; **24:**1, 5, 9, 10, 18, 19, 24, 30, 32, 33, 35, 36², 47, 54; **25:**2, 9, 25, 33; **26:**7, 9, 12, 14, 20, 24, 28; **27:**1, 12, 13, 22², 25, 26, 27², 30, 31, 32, 33, 37², 39, 41, 42, 44, 45; **28:**1², 6², 9²; **29:**5, 13³, 14², 15, 20, 28, 32, 33, 34, 35; **30:**4, 5, 6, 8, 11, 13, 16, 18, 20², 24, 27, 29³; **31:**2, 7, 18, 20, 23², 24, 25; **32:**1, 3, 6, 7, 13, 19, 20, 25, 27, 29, 30², 31², 32, 34, 36, 42, 46; **3:**6², 11, 16,

HE – HIM (cont.)

13, 19, 20², 21, 24, 25, 27, 29, 31; **33:**4², 13; **34:**8; **35:**2, 6, 7, 9², 10², 11, 13², 14, 15, 18, 26, 29; **36:**5, 12, 33, 34, 35, 36, 37, 38, 39; **37:**3², 4³, 5, 8², 10, 11, 14², 15², 18², 20³, 21, 22², 23, 24, 25², 27², 28², 33, 35², 38⁴, 4:5², 7, 10, 12, 14, 18; **39:**1², 3², 4, 5, 12, 17, 19, 20, 21³, 23⁴; **40:**7, 9, 12, 23; **41:**8, 12, 33, 42, 43³, 45; **42:**4, 6, 8, 29, 31, 37³, 38; **43:**3, 5, 9³, 17, 19, 26, 28, 32², 33, 34; **44:**7, 14, 18, 20², 21², 22², 26, 28, 29, 32; **45:**2, 3, 9, 14, 15, 26, 27², 28; **46:**5, 7, 28, 29, 31; **47:**4, 7, 8, 18, 29, 31; **48:**1, 10, 13, 18; **49:**9, 23², 28; **50:**1², 2, 3, 4, 7, 9, 12, 14, 17, 18, 26; **Ex 1:**16; **2:**2², 3, 4, 6, 9³, 10³, 12, 20²; **3:**2, 4, 18, 19; **4:**2, 4, 11⁴, 15, 16, 18, 23, 24, 26, 27, 28², 31³; **5:**2; **6:**9, 20, 23, 25, 29; **7:**15, 16; **8:**1, 20; **9:**1, 13; **10:**3, 7; **12:**44; **13:**14, 19; **14:**6, 31; **15:**2², 25; **16:**7, 8; **17:**12; **18:**5, 6, 7, 13, 15, 19; **19:**3, 7, 13, 19, 21; **21:**3, 4², 6, 12, 14², 16², 30, 22:17, 21, 25, 26; **23:**4, 5, 21³; **24:**2; **25:**2; **28:**2; **29:**5, 7, 30; **31:**3, 6, 18; **32:**1, 4, 23, 26; **33:**15; **34:**4, 5, 30, 31², 33, 34²; **35:**21, 31, 34; **38:**23; **40:**13², 16, 19, 21, 23, 25, 27, 29; **Lev 1:**1, 4; **4:**31, 35; **5:**3, 6, 10, 13, 16, 18; **6:**2², 4, 7, 22; **8:**4, 7², 8, 12², 9:9, 12, 13, 18; **13:**3², 5², 6², 8², 10, 11², 13, 14, 15, 17, 20, 21, 22, 23, 25², 26, 27², 28, 33, 34, 37, 43, 44; **14:**3, 7, 11, 18, 20, 21, 29; **15:**3, 10, 24; **16:**4, 17:10, 19:13, 22, 33, 34; **20:**2, 3, 4, 5, 21; **22:**23² 24²; **25:**14, 35, 36, 37², 39, 48, 49, 51, 53; **27:**8; **Nu 3:**4, 6, 7, 9, 42; **5:**8, 9, 6; **11:**7; **7:**89²; **8:**2; **11:**20, 25²; **12:**6², 8; **13:**31; **14:**24, 36; **15:**23, 28, 33², 34², 35, 36²; **16:**5³, 11, 15, 40; **17:**6, 11; **19:**13², 17, 20; **20:**9, 29; **21:**24, 26, 34³, 35; **22:**7, 8, 22², 32, 36, 40; **23:**4, 5, 6, 13, 14, 15, 16, 17³, 18, 22; **25:**12², 13; **26:**10; **27:**6, 13, 14, 22², 23²; **29:**40; **31:**6, 47, 49; **32:**15, 16, 17, 19², 20, 21², 23², 23⁴; **34:**9, 16, 22, 35, 20:12, 13², 14; **Dt 1:**36, 38; **2:**24, 30, 33²; **3:**3, 14, 28; **4:**7, 25, 29², 30, 35; **5:**24; **6:**13; **7:**9, 10, 18; **8:**6, 18, 10, 12, 18, 20; **9:**19, 24, 34²; **10:**6; **11:**13, 22; **13:**3⁴, 8⁵, 9², 10; **15:**8, 9², 10², 13, 14, 18, 20, 5², 6, 8; **21:**15, 17², 18, 19², 21, 23; **22:**1, 2, 4, 18, 19; **23:**15, 16, 17; **25:**2, 7², 18; **26:**16; **28:**7, 8, 20, 44, 48, 54², 10:6; **11:**2, 3, 8, 11, 19, 28, 34; **12:**5, 6², 8, 11, 13; **13:**6², 12, 24²; **14:**5, 6, 16, 17, 18, 19, 20; **15:**1, 10, 12, 13², 14; **16:**2², 5⁴, 8, 9, 12², 14, 15, 16, 19³, 20, 21⁴, 24, 25, 31³; **17:**9, 10, 11⁴; **18:**3, 4, 5, 15, 19, 26; **19:**2³, 3⁴, 4², 7, 11, 22, 25; **Ru 2:**20; **3:**3; **4:**15, 16²; **1Sa 1:**11, 17, 20², 23², 24, 26, 27, 28²; **2:**16, 19²; **3:**17, 27, 36; **3:**7, 8; **4:**16, 18³; **5:**3; **6:**3, 4, 8; **7:**3, 9; **8:**5, 7, 10; **9:**5, 8, 13², 16, 17; **10:**1, 10², 11², 14, 21, 23, 27²; **11:**1, 3, 5, 6; **12:**14, 24; **13:**2, 7, 10, 14, 15², 14²; **13², 14, 15², 16, 17, 18³, 23, 24, 27, 28, 37, 43, 52; **15:**13, 26, 28, 32, 35; **16:**1, 4, 7, 8, 10, 11², 12², 13, 14, 15, 17, 18, 20³, 21³; **17:**3, 10, 12², 16, 21, 22, 24, 26, 27², 30, 31, 33, 34, 35², 38, 40, 41, 44², 45, 52, 53; **2:**6, 8, 9², 13, 15, 19, 22², 29, 31², 32, 34, 36, 42, 46; **3:**6², 11, 16,

19:1³, 11², 15², 17, 21:6, 11, 13, 23, 26, 27; **22:**4, 9, 20²; **23:**13; **24:**19; **25:**5², **26:**10, 14, 28, 6; 9, 12, 13, 18; **29:**21, 22, 23, 25, **28:**30; **2Ch 1:**1², 5, 7, 14; **2:**3, 4², 6⁴, 14; **5:**6; **6:**16; **7:**8, 12; **8:**2, 18; **9:**1², 2, 12, 25, 30; **10:**1, 3, 8³, 10, 18; **11:**13, 19, 20, 22; **12:**1, 3, 8, 11, 12, 16; **13:**3, 7, 10, 11, 19; **14:**1, 5, 6, 7, 10²; **15:**2², 4, 9²; **16:**7, 9, 10, **17:**1, 11; **18:**2³, 7, 12, 13, 14, 15, 20, 21, 25, 26, 31³, 32; **19:**2; **20:**4, 21, 30, 36; **21:**1, 7, 9, 17; **22:**3, 6, 9², 11; **23:**11⁴, 20, 21, 21²; **25:**2, 5, 7, 17, 18, 20²; **27:**2; **28:**5², 9³, 20³, 21, 23, 27; **29:**6², 34:9, 12, 20, 22, **30:**9; **31:**3², 6², 8, 15, 17, 21, 24², 25², 29, 31³, 33²; **33:**6, 11², 13, 17, 18, 20, 23²; **34:**9, **12, 16, 17, 18², 20, 22, 25², 7, 17, 18, 20³; **35:**20, 21, 22², 24², **36:**1, 3, 4, 6³, 8², 10², 13, 20, 23³; **Ezr 1:**2, 3, 4²; **11:**5; **7:**5; **7:**6², 9; **8:**3, 4, 5, 6, 7, 8, 9, 10, 12, 14, 18, 21, 22, 33; **10:**1; **Ne 1:**5, 11; **2:**1, 5, 6, 7; **3:**4², 10, 16, 17², 18, 18, 19; **8:**4, 5; **9:**7², 8; **13:**5, 26², 28; **Est 1:**10, 11, 17, 19; **2:**9, 3:1², 2, 4, 5; **4:**4, 5, 9², 11², 13³, 14; **7:**9; **8:**2, 3, 4, 7; **10:**2; **Job 1:**8, 10; **2:**1, 3², 9, 11², 12², 13², 5:8, 7:10, 17², 18²; **8:**4; **9:**3², 4, 11², 12², 14, 15, 16, 19, 32, 35; **11:**10, 13², 12:16; **13:**7, 8, 15, 16, 18², 19; **14:**5, 6², 20², 15:20, 24², 26, 30, 31; **18:**6, 7, 8, 9, 10, 11, 12², 17; **19:**16, 27, 29; **20:**7, 9, 11, 14, 16, 21, 22², 23⁴; **22:**2, 14, 21, 27; **23:**3, 4, 7, 8, 9², 13, 15², 24:1; **26:**14; **27:**9, 15, 20, 22², 23²; **28:**25, 26, 29, 30, 37², 31:18, 20, 29, 37³; **32:**1, 6², 7, 14²; **33:**13, 17, 23, 24³; **34:**9, 11, 13², 23, 27, 28, 29², 37; **35:**3, 6², 7, 14³; **36:**11, 22, 23², 30; **37:**16, 18, 19, 24; **39:**6, 10, 11², 12, 20, 22², 24¹; **41:**4, 5², 8², 9², 10, 12, 13, 22, 26, 28²; **42:**10², 11⁵; **Ps 2:**12; **3:**2; **4:**3; **7:**4, 5; **8:**4², 5⁵, 6; **10:**4, 5, 15; **13:**4; **18:**T, 6, 11, 23, 30; **20:**6; **21:**2, 3, 4, 5², 6², 22:8⁴, 23³, 24, 26, 27, 29, 30; **24:**6; **25:**12², 14; **27:**4; **28:**7²; **32:**2, 6, 10; **33:**1, 2, 3, 8, 12, 21; **34:**T, 5, 6², 7, 8, 9, 22; **35:**25; **37:**5, 7, 24, 36, 40; **41:**1, 2³, 3², 8; **42:**5, 11; **43:**5; **45:**11; **47:**7; **49:**7; **50:**2³, 18, 23; **51:**T; **52:**T, 6; **55:**12; **56:**T; **59:**T; **61:**7; **62:**1, 3, 4, 5, 8²; **63:**11; **64:**4, 10²; **66:**6, 7, 17; **67:**7; **68:**1, 4², 33, 69:30, 34; **71:**11⁴; **72:**9, 10², 11², 15², 17²; **74:**14; **78:**8, 17, 34², 36², 37, 40², 58, 70, 71; **81:**15; **85:**9, 13; **89:**7, 20, 21², 22², 23, 24, 27, 28², 33, 41, 43, 45; **91:**14², 15⁴; **92:**15; **94:**13; **95:**2³, 4; **96:**6, 9; **97:**2, 3, 7; **98:**1; **100:**2, 4; **101:**5²; **103:**11, 13, 17; **104:**34; **105:**2², 19, 20², 21; **106:**23, 31; **107:**32², 43; **109:**6, 7², 12, 17², 19², 30, 31; **111:**5, 10; **112:**5; **115:**3, 11; **116:**2; **117:**1; **119:**2; **126:**6; **127:**3; **130:**7; **135:**1, 6, 20, 21; **136:**4, 10, 13, 16; **141:**5; **142:**2²; **144:**3²; **145:**18, 19, 20; **147:**1, 11; **148:**1, 2, 3², 4; **149:**3; **150:**1, 2², 3², 4², 5²; **Pr 3:**6; **5:**22²; **6:**15, 16, 31; **7:**10, 13, 21, 23; **10:**13, 24, 26; **11:**26, 27; **12:**14, 15, 25; **13:**24²; **14:**2; **15:**8, 10, 24, 26; **16:**2, 7, 20; **17:**11, 25; **18:**6, 14, 16, 17; **19:**4, 7, 11, 17; **20:**2, 7, 23; **21:**2, 10, 25, 28; **22:**15, 21; **23:**13, 14, 24; **24:**18, 24²; **25:**7², 13, 21; **26:**4, 12, 25, 27; **27:**22²; **28:**11, 17, 22, 24; **29:**20, 23; **30:**5, 31; **31:**1, 12; **Ecc 2:**25, 26; **3:**14, 22²; **4:**10²; **5:**12, 14, 18, 19, 20; **6:**2, 12; **8:**4, 6, 7, 15²; **9:**1; **10:**14², 15; **11:**8²; **12:**6; **SS 1:**2; **3:**1², 2², 4³, 11; **5:**4, 6³, 8², 6:1

Isa 1:4; 5:19; 6:2; 7:4, 14; 8:3, 17; 9:13; 10:6², 15⁴, 20; 11:2, 10; 14:25, 27; 19:1; 20:2; 21:6, 7; 22:21³, 23, 24; 25:9², 10; 26:3; 28:6, 26²; 29:11, 16; 30:18; 31:4, 6; 33:16; 36:3, 6², 21, 22; 37:3, 4, 7², 9, 22, 38²; 38:1; 40:10³, 13, 14⁴, 17², 18; 41:2³, 7; 42:1; 44:7³, 10, 20; 45:1², 9², 10, 24²; 46:7; 48:15²; 49:5, 7; 50:8, 10; 51:2³; 52:14, 15; 53:2³, 3, 4², 5, 6, 10², 12; 55:4, 6, 7²; 56:6²; 57:15, 17, 18³; 58:7; 59:16²; 62:7, 11²; 64:4; Jer 1:2; 3:1; 4:2²; 8:14; 9:8, 24; 10:25; 11:19; 17:7, 11; 18:3, 4, 18; 19:14; 20:3², 9, 10⁴, 15; 21:1; 22:10, 11, 13, 15, 18²; 23:24; 26:8², 19, 21, 23²; 27:6, 7², 11, 12; 28:14²; 29:31; 30:10, 21; 31:20⁴; 32:3, 4², 5, 9; 33:1; 34:2, 3, 14; 36:4, 8, 15, 20, 21, 22, 31; 37:13, 14²; 15, 17³; 38:6, 8, 9, 11, 13², 14, 27³; 39:5³, 7²; 9, 12⁴, 14², 15; 40:1, 2, 3, 5³, 6, 7, 14; 41:2, 7, 11, 12, 13², 16; 42:2, 8, 11; 43:1, 12; 44:20, 23; 45:4; 46:27; 48:10²; 49:8; 50:17, 43; 51:3, 44²; 52:8², 9, 11³, 31, 32²; La 2:19; 3:24, 25², 28², 29, 30³; Eze 1:3, 27, 28; 2:2; 3:18², 20², 27²; 9:1, 4, 5; 12:12, 13², 14; 14:4, 7, 8², 9², 10; 17:6, 7², 12², 15, 16, 17, 20³; 18:20², 22; 19:4², 5, 8², 9³; 21:23, 27, 24:27; 28:12; 29:2, 3, 20; 30:24; 31:11; 32:2, 32; 33:2, 8, 12², 16; 37:16², 19; 38:2, 22³; 40:46; 46:12; 47:23; Da 2:2, 14, 16, 22, 24², 46², 48³; 3:28; 4:8², 15², 16², 23³, 34, 35; 5:11², 13, 17, 19²; 6:3, 4, 12, 14, 15, 16, 18, 23; 7:10³, 14, 16, 25, 27²; 8:4, 6, 7⁴, 11, 13; 9:3, 4, 9, 14, 27; 10:1, 9²; 11:1, 16, 17², 18, 22, 23, 25, 26, 30, 32, 39, 40², 44, 45; 12:7²; Hos 1:2, 3, 4, 9; 4:17; 5:6; 6:3; 7:6, 10²; 8:3; 9:4, 8, 17; 11:1; 12:2, 4³, 13, 14³; 13:11, 13; 14:2; Am 2:3; 5:10, 11, 19; Jnh 1:6, 8, 11, 15, 16; Mic 1:4; 2:7; 3:5; 5:5; 6:6; 7:9; Na 1:5, 6, 7; Hab 2:5, 6², 9, 12, 15, 19, 20; 3:5, 13; Zep 1:6; 2:11; 3:9; Hag 1:12; Zec 1:8; 2:3, 4; 3:1, 4, 5; 4:12; 5:4; 6:12; 8:22; 10:4³; 12:1, 10²; 13:3²; 6; 14:5; Mal 2:5², 12, 17; 3:17; 4:4; Mt 1:20, 21, 23, 24, 25; 2:2, 3, 8², 11², 13; 3:3, 5, 6, 14, 16, 17; 4:3, 5², 7, 8², 10², 11², 20, 22, 24², 25; 5:1, 25, 29, 30, 40, 41; 6:8; 7:8, 9, 10, 11; 8:1, 2, 4, 5, 7², 10, 15, 16, 18, 19, 21, 22, 23, 25, 27, 28, 34²; 9:2, 9², 10, 14, 18, 19, 20, 24, 27, 28, 31; 10:1, 4, 32, 33; 11:3, 15, 27; 12:2, 10, 15, 18, 22², 35², 38, 46, 47, 48; 13:2, 9, 10, 12, 27, 28, 36, 43, 57; 14:2, 3², 4, 5, 13, 15, 22, 26, 31, 33, 35, 36²; 15:10, 11², 12, 20, 22², 25, 30, 32; 16:1², 22², 17:1, 5², 10, 12², 14, 16², 23, 26; 18:2, 6, 15, 17, 24², 26, 27², 28³, 29, 34; 19:2, 3², 10, 13, 27; 20:18, 19, 20, 29, 34; 21:3, 9, 14, 16, 23, 25, 32², 38³, 39³, 41, 46; 22:13², 15, 16, 19, 22, 23, 25², 34², 35, 43, 45, 46; 23:15; 24:1, 3, 44, 46, 47, 50, 51²; 25:6, 10, 28, 29, 31, 32, 37; 26:4, 7, 15², 16, 18, 22, 24², 25, 37, 47, 48, 49, 50, 52, 56, 57, 58, 59, 63, 67², 69, 71; 27:2³, 3, 9, 11, 13, 18, 19², 22, 23, 26, 27², 28², 29², 30², 31⁴, 32, 35, 36, 37, 38, 39, 41, 42², 43², 44², 49², 54, 58; 28:4, 7, 9², 13, 14, 17²; Mk 1:3, 5², 10, 12, 13, 18, 20, 25, 26, 27, 28, 36, 37, 40², 42, 43, 45; 2:3, 4, 13, 14², 15², 16, 19, 24; 3:2², 8, 9², 10, 11², 13², 14, 19, 21, 31, 32², 34; 4:1, 9, 10², 23, 25, 36², 38², 41; 5:2, 3, 4, 6, 8, 9, 18, 19, 20, 21, 23, 24², 27, 30, 33, 37, 40²; 6:2³, 3, 7, 14, 17, 19, 20³, 30, 35, 37, 45, 49, 50, 56²; 7:12, 14, 15², 17, 18, 25, 32², 33, 34; 8:1, 11², 22, 23², 26, 30, 32², 34, 38; 9:2, 7, 11, 13, 15, 17, 18², 20, 22², 25², 26, 27², 28, 31, 32, 36², 38, 39, 42; 10:1, 2, 13, 17², 21², 28, 32, 33², 34⁴, 35, 48²; 49, 51; 11:3, 14, 18², 23, 25, 27, 31; 12:3³, 4, 6, 8³, 12², 14, 17, 18, 26, 28, 32, 33, 34²; 37², 43; 13:1, 3, 36; 14:1, 11², 12², 15, 18, 16:9, 15, 17:14; 19:5², 7, 10, 12, 14, 20; 20:2, 3³, 6, 11; 21:6; 22:3, 11⁴, 17³, 18, 19.

HIMSELF (430)

Ge 8:9; 13:11; 17:17; 22:6, 8; 27:41, 42; 30:36, 40; 32:21; 33:3, 17; 35:7; 39:6, 8; 43:31, 32; 44:18; 45:1²; 50:1; **Ex** 11:3; 21:8; **Lev** 7:8; 9:8; 13:7, 19; 14:9; 15:13; 16:4, 6, 11, 17, 24³, 26, 28; 17:16; 20:6; 21:1, 3, 4², 11; 22:6; 23:29; 25:26, 35, 39, 47, 48, 49, 50; 26:46; **Nu** 5:18; 6:7, 12; 16:9, 10; 19:7, 12², 13, 20; 20:13; 30:2; 31:53; 32:42; **Dt** 3:22; 4:34; 15:12; 17:16, 18, 20; 23:11; 29:19; 31:3, 8; 33:21; **Jos** 11:20; 22:23; 23:5; 24:17; **Jdg** 3:19, 24; 6:31; 13:21; 16:29; **1Sa** 2:14; 3:21; 10:22; 18:1, 3, 11, 17; 19:22; 20:3, 17; 23:7; 24:8; 25:31; 26:10; 27:1, 12; 28:8, 14; **2Sa** 3:31; 6:20; 7:11, 23²; 14:13; 15:1; 16:14; 17:23; 18:18²; **1Ki** 1:5, 52; 12:26; 14:14; 17:21; 18:2; 19:4, 19; 20:38; 21:25, 29²; 22:30; **2Ki** 1:2; 4:34; 5:14, 20; 12:18; 18:25; 24:11; **1Ch** 15:1; 17:21; 29:5; **2Ch** 1:1; 2:1, 12; 12:12, 13; 13:9; 16:14; 17:1, 16; 18:1, 29, 34; 21:4; 26:20; 32:1, 12; 33:12, 19, 23; 35:22; 36:12;

Ezr 7:10; 10:1, 8; **Est** 3:12; 5:10; 6:6; **Job** 1:12; 2:1, 8; 8:6; 14:22; 15:25, 31; 20:20; 21:19; 32:2; **Ps** 4:3; 7:16; 10:6, 11, 13, 14; 36:2, 4; 48:3; 49:15, 18; 50:6; 55:12; 68:16; 87:5; 89:48; 104:2; 130:8; **Pr** 6:32; 8:36; 11:17², 25; 12:23; 15:32; 21:23; 22:9; 26:24; 28:26; 29:11, 15; **Ecc** 4:5; 5:9; 6:8; 12:5; **SS** 3:9; **Isa** 5:16; 7:14; 19:21; 28:21; 36:10; 38:15; 44:5, 15, 16, 20; 45:15; 49:5; 56:3; 58:5; 59:17; 63:10, 12; **Jer** 16:6; 30:21; 34:14; 43:12; 49:10; 51:14; **La** 4:16; **Eze** 14:7; 33:5; 44:3, 25², 27; 45:22; **Da** 1:8²; 2:49; 6:3; 8:25; 11:16, 36, 37; **Hos** 5:6; 10:1; **Am** 6:8; **Jnh** 3:6; 4:5; **Hab** 2:5, 6; **Zec** 2:13; **Mal** 2:16; **Mt** 12:26; 14:23; 16:24; 18:4; 23:12²; 24:48; 26:74; 27:5, 42, 57; **Mk** 3:26; 5:5; 6:17; 8:34; 12:36, 37; 14:54, 67, 71; 15:31; 43; **Lk** 3:23; 7:39; 9:23; 10:29; 11:18; 12:17, 21, 37, 45; 14:11²; 15:15; 16:3; 17:16; 18:4, 11, 14²; 19:12; 20:42; 23:35; 24:12, 15, 27, 36; **Jn** 1:8; 2:24; 4:12, 44; 5:18, 19, 26², 37; 6:15; 7:18; 8:22, 41, 59; 9:9, 21; 12:6, 36; 13:32; 16:27; 18:18, 25; **Ac** 1:3; 5:2; 7:35; 8:13, 34; 12:11; 14:17; 15:14; 16:27; 17:25; 18:5, 19; 20:10, 35; 21:26; 22:29; 25:16; 28:16; **Ro** 8:16, 26; 13:1; 14:7², 12, 22; 15:3; **1Co** 2:15; 3:15; 5:11; 6:15, 16, 17; 11:28; 29; 14:4, 16, 28, 38; 15:27, 28; **2Co** 5:18, 19; 8:19; 10:18; 11:14, 20; **Gal** 1:4; 2:12, 20; 4:14; 5:3; 6:3, 4²; **Eph** 2:14, 15, 20; 5:2, 25, 27, 28, 33; **Php** 2:7, 8, 22; **Col** 1:20; **1Th** 3:11; 4:16; 5:23; **2Th** 2:4³, 16; 3:16; **1Ti** 2:6; **2Ti** 2:13, 21; **Tit** 2:14²; **Heb** 2:18; 5:2, 4, 5; 6:13; 7:27; 9:7, 14, 25, 26; **Jas** 1:24, 26²; **1Pe** 2:23, 24; 5:10; **1Jn** 3:3; **Rev** 19:12; 21:3.

HIS (7165)

Ge 1:27; 2:2, 7, 24², 25; 3:8, 15, 20, 21, 22; 4:1, 2, 4², 5², 8², 17², 21, 23, 25; 5:3²; 6:3, 5, 6, 9; 7:7³, 13³; 8:9, 18³, 21²; 9:1, 5, 6, 8, 22², 24², 25, 27; 10:10, 15, 25²; 11:28², 31⁴; 12:5², 8, 11, 12, 15, 17, 20³; 13:1, 3, 12, 18; 14:12, 14³, 15, 16²; 16:3²; 17:14, 19, 20, 23⁴, 25, 26, 27; 18:1, 2, 19²; 19:1, 3, 14³, 16³, 30²; 20:2, 8, 14, 17²; 21:2, 4, 5, 7, 11, 14, 22, 32; 22:3³, 5, 6, 7, 9, 10, 13, 19, 21, 24; 23:3, 6, 9, 10², 18, 19; 24:2, 7, 9², 10³, 20, 21, 27, 30, 32, 40, 48, 59, 67³; 25:6², 8³, 9, 10, 11, 13, 14, 16², 16², 26², 26²; 27:1², 5, 10, 11, 13, 14², 16², 16², 18², 25², 26², 26²; 27:1², 5, 10, 11, 13, 14², 16², 18, 19, 21, 25, 27, 30², 38, 39, 40, 41; 28:5, 7, 8, 11, 16, 18; 29:1, 6, 10, 11, 13², 18², 20², 23², 30², 31²; 30:14, 35; 31:4, 17², 18², 19, 23, 25², 46, 53, 54, 55²; 32:1, 3, 13, 16², 22², 23, 33:1, 3, 4², 14, 16, 17, 19; 34:3, 4, 5², 8², 13, 19, 20, 24, 26; 35:2, 7, 18, 21, 22, 27, 29¹; 36:2, 6⁵, 24, 32, 35, 39²; 37:1, 2², 3², 4, 5², 8², 9, 10³, 11², 12, 13, 14², 21, 22, 26, 27, 30², 31²; 38:1, 6, 9⁴, 11², 12³, 13, 14, 16, 17, 18, 19²; 40:2, 7, 9, 11, 13², 20², 21, 22; 41:8², 10, 12, 14, 37, 42³, 43, 45, 51; 42:1, 7, 8, 9, 11, 22, 25, 27⁴, 28, 35, 37, 38; 43:7, 8, 9, 16, 18, 21², 29², 30², 31; 44:1², 2, 4, 11, 14, 19, 20⁴, 22², 33; 45:1², 3⁴, 4, 8, 14², 15, 16, 23², 24; 46:1⁵, 6, 7³, 8, 15², 18, 25, 26², 29⁴; 47:2, 7, 10, 11², 12⁴, 18, 19³; 48:1, 2, 9, 10², 12, 13, 14³, 17³, 18, 19¹; 49:1, 10², 11⁴, 12², 13, 17², 16, 24², 26, 31²; 33⁴; 50:1, 2², 7, 8², 10, 14³, 18, 22, 24; **Ex** 1:6, 11, 20; 7:2, 10², 12, 20², 23; 8:6, 13, 4:4, 6², 7³, 11, 14², 15, 18, 20²; 21; 5:21; 6:1, 11, 20; 7:2, 10², 20², 23; 8:6, 13; 9:7, 23, 33, 34; 10:1², 13², 22, 30, 48; 13:9, 16; 14:4, 5, 6, 17³, 18², 21, 22, 27, 30; 11:2², 4⁵; 12:3, 7, 8, 9², 14², 21, 22, 25³, 26², 30, 33; 15:3, 4, 26²; 17:11³, 12², 13, 14; 22:1², 6², 11, 15, 17; 23:5, 8²; 13, 14, 15, 24, 25, 26³, 28; 24:2, 3, 5, 6, 7², 8; 25:1, 3³, 13², 14, 17, 20, 21, 24, 25²; 37², 39³, 40², 42, 43, 44; 26:2, 3, 7², 10, 11, 16, 18, 19, 23, 25, 29²; 27:1, 3², 8, 11, 12; 28:3, 5, 7, 14, 18, 20, 23, 25; 29:2, 4², 5², 11; 30:1, 2²; 31:2²; 4², 5, 6², 7, 8, 9²; 10², 12; **Lev** 1:4, 6², 7, 10, 11², 12, 13, 15; 2:2, 6; 3:2, 8, 13, 17; 4:4², 5, 6², 7, 16, 17², 18, 20, 21, 22²; 5:11, 13, 14, 15, 24, 25, 26, 26³, 27², 34³, 35, 40², 41, 43, 49², 50, 51, 54; 56, 58, 59², 61², 66²; 9:15, 16, 18, 19³, 21, 22, 23²; 10:1, 5³, 6, 11:3, 4³, 6, 8, 9; 17, 19, 21, 23, 26, 27, 28, 34, 35, 36, 43²; 12:6, 8; 13:4², 12, 13, 19, 23, 24²; 14:2², 18, 19, 20²; 21², 22, 31²; 15:2, 3⁴, 4, 5, 8², 10, 11, 12, 13, 14, 15, 6², 7², 9, 13, 26, 28², 34²; 17:19, 23; 18:3, 42², 43, 46²; 19:3², 6, 13², 19, 20, 21²; 20:1, 8, 11, 12, 20², 31, 33², 35, 38², 39, 41,

---

[right column continued:] 11, 12², 14, 15², 17, 21, 22, 23, 24; 22:2, 7, 10, 11², 18; 23:29, 30; 24:9, 11, 19; 25:10², 13, 25³, 27, 28, 30, 41³, 48, 49, 50², 51, 52, 53, 54; 27:14, 15², 16, 17, 18, 19, 22, 31; **Nu** 1:4, 44, 52²; 2:2², 4, 6, 8, 11, 13, 15, 17², 19, 21, 23, 26, 28, 30, 34; 3:9, 10, 38, 48, 51; 4:5, 15, 19², 27; 5:7, 10, 14, 15, 30; 6:5², 6, 7³, 8, 9³, 11, 12, 13, 14, 19²; 21², 23, 25, 26; 7:11, 12, 13, 18, 24, 25, 30, 66, 67, 72, 73, 78, 79; 8:13, 19; 9:13²; 18, 20, 23; 11:1, 10, 29; 12:1, 14:24; 15:4, 30, 31²; 16:5, 17, 18, 19, 40; 17:2, 9; 19:3, 4, 7, 8, 10, 13, 19, 21; 20:11², 24, 25, 26²; 28:1, 22², 24, 26, 29², 33, 34², 35³; 22:5, 18, 21, 22², 23, 27, 31, 36; 23:6, 7, 16, 17, 18, 19, 21, 23², 25; 25:6, 7, 13², 27:3, 4, 8², 9², 10², 11³; 21², 23; 30:2, 16³; 32:13, 18, 21; 35:17, 18, 20², 28, 32; 36:2, 7, 8; **Dt** 1:31, 36²; 41; 2:5, 24, 30², 31², 32, 33²; 34; 3:1, 2², 3, 4, 11; 4:13, 20, 36³, 37², 40, 42²; 47; 5:11, 21², 24³; 6:2, 13, 15, 22; 7:6², 7, 9, 12; 8:2, 5, 6, 11³, 18; 10:6, 8, 10, 12, 15, 20; 11:1⁴, 2³, 3, 22; 12:5², 11, 21; 13:4, 17, 18²; 14:2, 23, 24; 15:2, 17, 18; 16:2, 6, 11; 17:2, 17, 18, 19²; 20³; 18:7², 10, 18; 19:4², 5⁴, 6, 9, 11, 12, 18, 19; 20:8; 21:16³, 17², 18, 19², 21, 22, 23; 22:3, 19, 4, 19, 24, 25⁴; 24:1, 2, 3, 7, 10, 11, 15, 16, 15², 16, 17, 18, 19²; 25:6, 7, 13²; 27:3, 4, 8², 9², 10², 11³; 21², 23; 30:2, 16³; 32:13, 18, 21; 35:17, 18, 20², 28, 32; 36:2, 7, 8; 2, 3, 7, 10, 12, 13, 15, 16; 25:2², 5, 6, 7, 8, 9⁴, 11²; 26:2, 17², 18³; 27:10, 16², 17, 20²; 22³, 23, 24; 28:1, 9², 12, 15, 54², 55; 29:2²; 20:8, 10, 10, 20; 32:4², 5, 9²; 30:8, 10, 16, 20; 32:4², 5, 9²; 43⁴, 50; 33:1, 2, 6, 7³, 9³, 11³, 12, 13, 16, 17, 21, 23, 24², 26; 34:6, 7³, 9, 11²; **Jos** 2:19³; 4:5, 14; 5:13, 14; 6:19, 26; 7:6, 18, 20, 22³, 26; 8:1³, 3, 10, 18, 26, 29; 9:24; 10:2³, 22; 4², 7², 11, 12, 14:24; 15:17, 22, 26², 28²; 18:2, 22², 26, 29², 33, 35, 37³, 45; 11:6², 14², 21; 8:4, 20², 21, 25, 27², 30, 31, 32²; 9:1², 6, 11², 15, 17, 18², 19³, 21, 24, 26, 28, 34, 35, 38², 39, 40, 41; 20:1, 8, 11, 12, 20², 31, 33², 35, 38², 39, 41, 49:1, 10², 11⁴, 13, 16², 24², 26, 31²; 50:1, 2², 7, 8², 10, 14³, 18, 22, 24; **Ru** 1:1, 2², 6; 2:5, 15, 20, 22; 3:4, 7, 8, 14; 4:5, 7, 8, 10³, 13; **1Sa** 1:3, 4, 11², 19, 21², 23, 28; 2:9, 10, 19, 20, 22, 25, 35; 3:2, 9, 12, 13², 18, 19, 21; 4:10, 12², 13², 18², 19; 5:3², 4², 7; 6:3, 5, 9; 7:1, 15, 17; 8:1, 2², 3², 11², 12³, 14, 15, 16, 17, 22; 9:3, 7, 10, 14, 22, 25; 10:11, 14, 16, 25, 26; 11:5, 11; 12:3, 5, 14, 15², 22³; 13:14², 16, 22³; 14:1², 6, 7, 12², 13³, 14, 17, 20, 26, 27³, 34, 45, 49, 50, 52; 15:1, 8, 12, 27, 29², 34; 16:1, 5, 7², 10, 13, 16, 17, 20, 21³, 23; 17:5, 6², 7², 15, 16, 17, 22², 23², 25², 33, 34, 38², 39, 40², 41, 43, 49², 50, 51, 54; 18:2, 4⁴, 7², 10², 22², 25, 27², 28, 29², 30; 19:1, 4², 5², 9³, 10², 15, 16, 17, 20², 21²; 25, 27, 32, 33⁴, 34, 35, 38, 40, 41; 21:11²; 13, 14; 22:1², 6², 11, 15, 17; 23:5, 8², 13, 14, 15, 24, 25, 26³, 28; 24:2, 3, 5, 6, 7², 8; 25:1, 3², 13², 14, 17, 20, 21, 24, 25², 31, 37², 39², 40², 42, 43, 44; 26:2, 3, 7², 10, 11, 16, 18, 19, 20³; 27:1³, 3³, 8², 9, 10, 12; **2Sa** 1:2², 4, 5, 6, 10², 12, 15, 17; 2:2, 3, 16³, 21, 23², 29, 30, 32; 3:2, 3, 6, 8, 12, 20, 27, 29², 30, 38, 39; 4:4², 5, 6, 7², 8, 9, 10, 11³, 12; 5:6, 12²; 6:2, 7, 11, 14, 20, 22³; 7:1², 12, 13, 14, 25; 8:3, 4, 10², 15; 9:9, 11; 10:1, 2², 10, 12; 11:2, 9², 13², 27²; 12:3⁴, 4, 9², 16, 17, 19, 20³, 24, 31, 33², 36, 37; 14:7³, 9, 11, 15, 16, 22², 25², 26³, 30, 33; 15:5, 12, 14, 16, 22², 23², 25², 26², 30, 33; 15:5, 12, 14, 16, 22², 25², 26², 30, 33; 16:5, 9, 11, 13, 18, 22; 17:8, 12, 18, 19, 23², 25; 18:2, 4⁴, 7², 10², 22², 25, 28, 29², 30; 19:1, 4², 5² 9³ 10², 15, 16, 17, 20², 21²; 25, 27, 32, 33⁴, 34, 35, 38, 40, 41; 20:1, 8, 11, 12, 20², 31, 33², 35, 38², 39, 41; **1Ki** 1:2, 6, 9, 10, 15, 21, 23, 27, 37, 46, 47², 51, 52; 2:1, 3³, 4, 5², 6, 9, 10, 12², 19, 24, 33, 34, 40²; 3:1², 3², 6, 15, 27²; 4:2, 10, 13, 21, 25, 27, 31, 32, 34; 5:1³, 7, 9, 11, 15², 18, 28, 31, 32², 38², 39, 46, 54, 56², 58, 59², 61², 66²; 9:15, 16, 18, 19³, 21, 22, 23²; 10:1, 5³, 6, 11:3, 4³, 6, 8, 9; 17, 19, 24, 26, 27, 28, 34, 35, 36, 43²; 12:6, 8; 13:4², 12, 13, 14, 18, 23, 26, 28², 34²; 17:19, 23; 18:3, 42², 43, 46²; 19:3², 6, 13², 19, 20, 21²; 20:1, 8, 11, 12, 20², 31, 33², 35, 38², 39, 41,

42², 43; 21:4, 5, 7, 8, 19, 25, 27, 29³; 22:3, 9, 19³, 20, 22, 31, 34³, 35², 36², 38, 40², 42, 43, 45, 46, 50³, 52, 53; 2Ki 1:2, 8, 9, 10, 11, 12, 13²; 2:8, 12; 3:2², 27; 4:1², 11, 12, 18, 19³, 20, 25, 27, 32, 35, 37, 38, 39, 43; 5:1, 3, 4, 6, 7², 8, 9, 11², 14, 15, 23, 25, 26; 6:7, 8, 10, 11, 12, 17, 24, 30², 31, 32²; 7:12, 13, 17; 8:14, 16, 19², 21³, 24², 26, 29; 9:2, 3, 11, 16, 21, 24³, 25², 26, 27, 28³, 36; 10:3, 10, 11³, 15, 16, 19², 24, 31, 34, 35²; 11:2, 3, 8², 9, 11², 19; 12:1, 18, 20, 21²; 13:3, 8, 9², 12², 13, 16, 21, 23², 24, 25; 14:2, 3², 5², 6, 12, 15², 16², 20, 21, 22, 25, 28, 29²; 15:2, 3, 7², 9, 18, 19², 22², 25, 33, 34, 38³; 16:2², 3, 13³, 15, 20²; 17:13, 15, 18, 20, 23²; 18:2, 3, 12, 17³, 31², 33, 35; 19:1, 4, 7, 19, 37²; 20:2, 13², 20, 21²; 21:1, 3, 6, 7, 9, 10, 11, 18³, 19, 20, 21², 23, 24², 26²; 22:1, 2, 3, 11; 23:3³, 10, 18², 25³, 26, 30³, 31, 32, 34, 36, 37; 24:1², 2, 3, 6², 7², 8, 9, 11, 12², 15², 17², 18, 20; 25:1, 5, 7², 19, 29²; 1Ch 1:13, 19², 46, 50²; 2:13, 18, 25, 35², 42²; 3:3, 9² 10³, 11³, 12³, 13³, 14², 16, 17, 22²; 4:9², 10, 18, 25², 26², 27; 5:1³, 2, 4³, 5³, 6; 6:20³, 21⁴, 22³, 23⁴, 24⁴, 26³, 27⁴, 29³, 30³, 39, 44, 49, 50³, 51³, 52³, 53²; 7:14², 15, 16², 18, 20⁴, 21², 22, 23², 24⁴, 25², 26³, 27², 35; 8:1, 6³, 8, 9, 10, 29, 30, 37³, 39²; 9:5, 19², 35, 36, 43³; 10:2², 4³, 5, 6², 7, 8, 9², 10², 12; 11:10, 11, 20, 23², 25; 12:8, 16, 18, 19³, 21, 28; 13:1, 9, 14², 14²; 15:17, 22; 16:7, 8, 9, 10, 11², 12, 13², 14, 15, 23, 24², 27, 29², 34, 37, 38, 39, 41, 43³; 17:1, 11, 12, 13, 14, 23; 18:3, 4, 10², 14; 19:1, 2³, 3, 7, 11, 13, 15, 17²; 20:3, 8; 21:3, 13, 16, 20, 21, 27²; 22:5, 6, 9³, 10², 17, 18; 23:1, 16, 20, 21, 27², 25; 24:21; 25:3, 4, 9², 10, 11, 12, 13, 14, 15, 16, 17, 18, 19, 20, 21, 22, 23, 24, 25, 26, 27, 28, 29, 30, 31; 26:6, 7, 10, 14, 15, 22, 25², 26, 28, 29, 30; 27:2, 4², 5, 6², 7³, 8, 9, 10, 11, 12, 13, 14, 15; 28:1, 2, 6, 7, 11, 12, 20; 29:23, 28, 30; 2Ch 1:1², 8; 2:11, 15, 17³; 3:1, 2; 5:1, 13; 6:4², 7, 12, 13, 19, 22, 23², 29², 30; 7:3, 6, 10, 11; 8:1, 6³, 8, 9⁴, 14, 18; 9:4², 8², 23, 31³; 10:6², 18; 11:12, 14, 15, 21, 22, 23; 12:13² 14, 16²; 13:2, 5, 6, 12, 17; 14:1³, 2, 4, 5, 12⁴, 13² 14; 15:9, 16, 17, 18; 16:2, 4, 5, 12⁴, 13² 14; 17:1, 2, 3², 4², 5, 6, 7²; 18:8, 18³, 19, 21, 30, 33², 34; 19:1, 10; 20:18, 20, 21², 25, 30, 31, 32; 21:1², 3, 4², 7³, 8, 10, 17, 19⁴; 22:1, 2, 3, 4³, 6, 9², 10², 11, 13; 23:1, 7², 8, 10², 11, 13; 24:1, 16, 22, 25², 27²; 25:1, 3², 4, 11², 14, 17, 22, 28; 26:1, 2, 3, 4, 8, 10, 13, 15, 16³, 19², 20, 21, 23³, 24, 25³, 26, 27⁴; 29:1, 2, 6, 7, 9², 27; 28:1, 3, 5², 6, 7, 9²; 29:1, 2, 3, 10, 19, 25, 30, 36; 30:2, 6, 8, 9, 12, 19², 27; 31:3, 8², 10, 12, 13, 20, 21; 32:3², 9², 14, 15, 16, 17, 31², 26, 27², 31, 32, 33³; 33:3, 6, 7, 10, 11, 12³, 13², 18², 19³, 20³, 22², 23², 24, 25²; 34:2, 3³, 4, 8, 19, 31⁴; 35:3, 4, 8, 9, 23, 24², 26; 36:1, 5, 7, 8, 12, 13, 15³, 16³, 18, 20, 22, 23³; Ezr 1:1³, 2, 7; 2:1; 3:2², 9², 11; 4:7; 5:5, 17; 6:10, 11², 12; 7:6, 9², 14, 15, 23, 28²; 8:17, 19, 22, 25²; 9:8; 10:8, 11, 18; Ne 1:5²; 2:1, 5, 20; 3:1, 10, 12, 17, 23, 28, 29, 30; 4:2, 3, 15, 18², 22, 23; 5:13, 14; 6:5², 10, 11, 18, 19; 7:6; 8:4², 9:8² 10², 32; 11:3, 8, 13, 14, 17, 20; 12:8, 36, 45; 13:6, 30; Est 1:2, 3², 4², 8, 20, 21, 22; 2:3, 7, 9, 15, 16, 17, 18; 3:10², 12; 4:1, 4, 11; 5:1, 2, 9, 10², 11², 14²; 6:1, 3, 5, 12, 13⁴; 7:7³; 8:2, 3, 7, 8; 9:4, 25²; 10:2, 3²; Job 1:4, 10³, 20²; 2:3, 4, 5, 6, 7², 9, 13²; 3:1², 19; 4:9, 17, 18²; 5:3, 4, 5², 18; 6:9, 14; 7:1, 2, 10²; 8:15; 9:4², 5, 13², 33, 34; 11:5; 12:10, 13, 16; 13:11, 15; 14:5, 6, 10, 20, 22; 15:2, 15², 20, 21, 25, 27² 29², 30, 32²; 16:9³ 12, 13, 21; 17:5² 18:5, 6, 7², 8, 10, 11, 13², 14, 14²; 19:6, 11², 12; 20:6², 7, 9, 10³, 11, 12², 13, 14², 15; 18, 20², 21, 22, 23, 25³, 26², 27, 28; 21:17; 22:2², 3², 23², 25³, 26², 27, 28, 29; 22:22²; 23:2, 3, 7, 11³, 12², 14; 24:15, 22, 23; 25:3², 5; 26:8, 9, 11, 12², 14²; 27:1, 8, 9, 14², 17, 19, 21, 23; 28:10; 29:1, 7, 25; 30:18, 24; 31:2, 20, 23, 30, 31, 35; 32:1, 5, 12, 14; 33:10, 18², 19, 20², 21², 22², 23, 25², 26, 30; 34:6, 11, 14², 19, 21, 24, 29, 35, 37³; 35:15, 16; 36:5, 7, 22, 23, 24, 26, 29, 30, 32, 33³; 37:2² 3, 4³; 38:13; 40:4; 41:2², 5², 6, 9; 42:8², 46:6; 47:8; 48:1; 49:12, 16, 17, 19; 50:4, 6; 52:7²; 53:1, 6; 55:20², 21³; 57:2, 3²; 60:6; 61:6; 62:4; 66:2², 5, 7², 8, 17, 20; 67:1; 68:1³, 4², 5, 17,

21, 35; 69:33, 36²; 72:7, 9, 14, 17, 19²; 76:1, 2², 5; 77:7, 8², 9; 78:4, 7², 10, 20, 21², 22, 26, 32, 37, 38², 42, 43², 49², 50, 52, 54², 56, 58, 61², 62², 66, 69, 70, 71²; 79:7; 85:8², 9², 13; 87:1; 89:23², 24, 25², 29³, 30, 36², 39, 40², 41, 42², 43, 44², 45; 91:4³, 11; 94:14²; 95:4, 5², 7³; 96:2², 3, 8², 9, 13; 97:2, 3, 4, 6², 10, 12; 98:1², 2², 3²; 99:5, 6², 7, 9; 100:3³, 4³, 5²; 101:5; 102:T, 16, 19, 21; 103:1, 2, 7², 9, 11, 13, 15, 17, 18², 19²; 21³, 22²; 104:3², 4², 13², 15², 23², 31; 105:1, 2, 3, 4², 5, 6², 7, 8, 18², 21, 22², 24, 25², 26, 27², 28, 42² 43², 45²; 106:1, 2, 8², 12², 13, 23², 24, 40², 45²; 107:1, 8², 15², 20, 21², 22, 24, 31²; 108:7; 109:6, 7, 8², 9², 10, 11, 12, 13, 14², 18³, 31; 110:4, 5, 7; 111:3², 4, 5, 6², 7², 9³, 10; 112:1, 2, 3², 5, 7, 8², 9³, 10; 113:4; 114:2; 116:2, 12, 14, 15, 18; 117:2; 118:1, 2, 3, 4, 27, 29; 119:2, 3, 9; 123:2; 125:2; 128:1; 129:7²; 130:5; 132:7², 13, 18²; 133:2, 3; 135:3, 4², 7, 9², 12, 14²; 136:1, 2, 3, 4, 5², 6, 7, 8, 9, 10, 11, 12, 13, 14, 15², 16², 17³, 18, 19, 20², 21², 22, 23, 24, 25, 26; 138:8; 144:4, 10; 145:3, 13, 17, 21; 146:5; 147:5, 10², 11, 15², 17², 18², 19², 20; 148:2² 8, 13², 14²; 149:1, 3, 4, 9; 150:1²; Pr 2:6, 8; 3:11, 20, 31, 32; 5:21, 22, 23; 6:13³, 14, 27², 28, 30, 31, 33²; 7:20, 23²; 8:22², 29, 30² 31; 9:9; 10:1², 18, 19²; 11:1, 7², 9², 12², 19, 28, 29; 12:4, 8, 10, 11, 13, 14², 16, 23, 27²; 13:1, 2, 3², 9, 18, 16, 22, 24; 14:3, 7, 14, 15, 21, 26, 35; 15:5, 20², 27; 16:4, 7, 9³, 10, 11, 15, 17², 23², 26, 27, 29, 30², 32; 17:12, 13, 18, 25, 28; 18:2, 6, 7³, 9², 10², 12², 13, 16², 18, 22², 25, 26, 27, 30², 32; 19:3² 7², 8, 11, 12, 13, 16², 18, 24², 26²; 20:2, 7, 8², 11², 14, 20², 24, 25, 27, 28; 21:10, 13, 23², 24, 25, 29; 22:5, 8, 9, 11, 16, 25, 29; 23:3, 6, 7, 14; 24:15, 18; 25:5, 13, 18, 22; 26:4, 5², 11, 12, 14, 15², 16, 17, 24², 25², 26²; 27:8, 9, 14, 18, 22; 28:7, 8, 9, 10, 11, 13, 14, 16, 27; 29:3², 5², 6, 11, 12, 14, 15, 21, 24; 30:4⁴, 6, 10, 31; 31:1, 23; Ecc 1:3; 2:14, 21, 23³, 24; 3:9, 13, 22²; 4:4, 5, 8³, 10, 14; 5:10, 11, 15³, 17, 18², 19², 20; 6:2, 3, 6, 7²; 7:14, 15²; 8:5, 8, 9, 15, 16, 17; 9:12, 15, 16; 10:12, 13, 18; 12:5, 13; SS 1:2, 4, 12; 2:3², 4, 6², 16; 3:8², 11³; 4:16; 5:4, 6, 11², 12, 13², 14², 15², 16; 6:2; 7:10; 8:3², 7, 10, 11; Isa 1:2², 31; 2:3², 10, 19, 21, 22; 3:6², 8, 13, 14; 5:1, 7, 12, 16², 19, 25⁴; 6:1, 3, 6; 7:2²; 8:7, 11, 17, 19; 9:6, 7², 12², 17²; 10², 19, 20, 21²; 10:4², 7, 12², 16², 17², 18, 19; 11:1, 3², 4², 5², 8, 10, 11², 15, 16; 12:4²; 13:5, 13, 14², 17², 18, 19, 21, 25², 26; 14:3², 5, 8, 10, 11², 16, 17, 19, 24², 25², 26²; 15:1, 9; 16:6, 12; 17:5, 10², 11; 18:4, 12; 20:9²; 21:7, 9, 14; 22:3, 7; 23:7, 29; 24:8, 11², 12; 25:2, 6², 7, 9, 13; 26:3, 7, 8, 9²; 27:8; 28:3; 30:9², 10, 11, 14, 18, 20, 23, 24, 30, 31; 21:1, 7, 14, 24; Ac 1:3, 7, 14, 18³, 20², 22; 2:6, 8, 14, 29, 30², 31, 41; 3:5, 8, 13, 18, 21, 26, 31, 36, 37, 40; 6:10, 15; 7:4, 5, 8, 10, 13, 14², 17², 20, 23, 24, 25, 60; 8:1, 11, 27, 28², 32, 33², 39²; 9:3, 8, 12², 14; 10:2, 7; 11:3, 13, 16, 17, 32², 34; 12:3, 19³, 34²; 13:5, 11, 26⁴, 27, 39³; 14:8, 14², 23; 15:3, 22²; 16:3; 17:1, 4, 6, 17³, 18:1, 7, 13, 43; 19², 23; 25², 26, 30, 31; 21:1, 7, 14, 24; Ac 1:3, 7, 14, 18³, 20², 22; 2:6, 8, 14, 29, 30², 31, 41; 3:5, 8, 13, 18, 21; 4:26, 32²; 5:1, 2, 6, 7, 10, 17, 21, 26, 31, 36, 37, 40; 6:10, 15; 7:4, 5, 8, 14², 20, 23, 24, 25, 60; 8:1, 11, 27, 28², 32, 33², 39²; 9:3, 8, 12², 14; 10:2, 7; 11:3, 13, 16, 17, 32², 34; 12:3, 19²; 14:10; 15:10, 13², 15, 20, 36; 16:13, 17, 32; 18:1², 2, 10, 17, 19², 25; 19:2, 17, 23, 25², 26², 27, 30, 33, 35, 36, 39, 40, 26, 30, 31; 21:1, 7, 14, 24; Ac 1:3, 7, 14; 2:6, 8, 14, 29, 30², 31, 41; 3:5, 8, 13, 14, 18³, 20², 22; 4:26, 28, 29, 30², 31, 41; 3:5, 8, 13, 8, 14, 29, 30², 31, 41; 3:5, 8, 13, 14, 17, 20, 21, 23, 24, 25, 60; 6:10, 15; 7:4, 5, 8, 9, 10, 13, 14², 17, 20, 23, 24, 25, 26, 31, 36, 40; 6:10, 15; 7:4, 5, 8; 8:1, 2, 6, 8, 14, 29, 30², 31, 41; 3:5, 8, 13, 11, 17², 28, 29, 33²; 34; 12:2, 6, 20; 13:8; 14:4, 9; 12:3, 10:2, 7², 22, 23, 24, 25, 43; 11:13, 15; 12:11, 15, 17, 21²; 13:8, 13, 16, 19, 25, 31, 36²; 14:3, 8; 15:14, 16:3, 6, 27; 32, 33, 34²; 17:2, 7, 28; 18:2, 6, 8, 18; 19:6, 22, 38; 20:10, 18, 22, 38², 29²; 21:11, 19, 32; 22:14², 15, 16, 23:15, 23, 26, 30; 24:2², 25:8, 12, 16, 18, 21, 25, 26, 26; 27:3²; 34; 28:3, 4, 7, 8², 30; Ro 1:2, 3, 4, 5, 9, 20; 2:4, 5, 9, 19²; 3:5², 7, 19, 20; 25²; 4:1³, 9⁴, 13, 23², 25, 26, 27; 6:3, 4, 10:5, 6³; 11:2, 4³, 5², 6, 10², 18, 19, 20, 23, 26²; 12:2; 4:19, 20; 5:26, 27, 28, 31, 37, 38, 41, 45; 12:7²; Hos 3:5; 5:13², 6:2; 7:9², 10; 8:14; 9:8²; 10:1³; 11:10; 12:2², 3, 4, 5, 14³; 13:12, 15⁴; 14:5, 6³, 7²;

Joel 2:11³, 16, 18²; 3:16; Am 1:11³, 13, 15; 2:4, 9², 14, 15²; 3:4, 7²; 4:2, 13²; 5:8, 19²; 6:8; 7:7, 10; 9:6²; Ob 1:6, 11², 12; Jnh 1:5; 2:1; 3:6², 7, 9; 4:6²; Mic 1:2, 3; 2:2²; 3:4, 8², 4:2², 12²; 5:3, 4³; 6:2²; 7:2, 6², 18; Na 1:2³, 3², 5, 6³, 8; 2:3, 5, 12⁴; 3:19²; Hab 1:15², 16¹, 17²; 2:4², 9², 15, 18, 20; 3:3², 4³, 5, 6, 14³; Zep 1:18; 2:13; 3:5, 17; Hag 1:9; 2:12, 22; Zec 1:21; 2:1, 8, 12, 13; 3:1, 4, 5², 10²; 4:1, 9; 5:4; 6:12, 13²; 7:12; 8:4, 10³, 23; 9:10, 14, 16²; 10:3, 12; 11:6², 17⁴; 13:3², 4; 14:4, 9; Mal 1:3² 6², 14; 2:6², 7, 15, 16; 3:1, 2, 14, 16², 17²; Mt 1:2, 11, 18, 21, 24; 2:2, 11, 13, 14, 20, 21, 23²; 3:4², 12⁴; 4:6, 18, 21; 5:11, 17², 18, 21, 22², 24³, 28, 32, 34, 39², 44², 46; 6:25, 27, 29, 33²; 7:9, 24, 26, 28; 8:3², 13, 20, 29; 9:1, 10, 11, 19, 20, 21, 37, 38; 10:1, 2², 10, 11, 21, 24², 25³, 35, 36, 37², 38, 39²; 42; 11:1, 7², 10², 17², 19, 27², 11:1, 2, 20; 12:1, 3, 4, 19, 21, 26, 29², 46, 49; 13:3, 19, 24, 25, 31, 36, 44², 52, 55², 56²; 14:2, 3, 9², 11, 12, 34, 36; 15:4, 5, 6, 11, 23, 30, 32, 33; 16:13, 20, 21, 24², 25², 26², 27², 28; 17:2², 24; 18:6, 15, 23, 25², 26², 28, 29², 34; 19:3, 5², 7, 9, 13, 15, 23, 28; 20:1, 2, 8, 29; 21:18, 29, 31, 34², 35, 37, 38, 41; 22:2, 3, 6, 7, 16², 18, 21, 24², 41², 43, 45, 47, 49; 25:14², 15², 16, 18, 21, 23, 26, 31², 33², 34, 41²; 26:1, 7, 23, 26, 36, 39, 40, 51², 65, 67; 27:19, 24, 25, 29², 31, 35, 37, 38²; 50, 55, 60, 64; 28:3², 7, 8, 9, 13; Mk 1:6, 7, 16, 19, 22, 36, 40, 41; 2:8, 12, 15, 23, 25, 26; 3:5, 7, 9, 17, 20, 21², 26, 27²; 4:2, 3, 34, 35, 40; 5:4, 6, 7, 15, 22, 27, 28, 31, 33; 6:1², 3, 4³, 5, 8, 17, 21², 22, 26², 28, 29, 35, 41, 45, 56; 7:2, 6, 9, 10², 11³, 19², 26, 32, 33, 34; 8:1, 4, 6, 10, 23, 25³, 27, 33, 34², 35², 36, 37, 38; 9:3, 18, 27, 28, 31, 36, 41, 42; 10:1², 7, 30, 34², 38; 11:1², 8, 18, 21², 49; 12:1, 15, 22, 25, 27², 34²; 14:3, 13, 22, 32, 37, 47², 52, 63; 15:20, 21, 24, 27², 37, 39, 41; 16:7, 20; Lk 1:5, 14, 23, 24, 25, 29, 32, 33, 48, 49, 50, 51, 54, 55, 59, 60, 62, 63, 64², 67, 68, 69, 70, 72, 77; 2:3, 14, 28, 34, 41, 43, 47², 48²; 51; 3:1, 17⁴, 19, 23; 4:10, 16, 22, 24, 30, 32², 33, 40; 5:9, 12, 13, 19, 27, 29, 30; 6:1, 3, 4, 10, 13, 14, 17, 20, 40²; 45⁴; 7:2, 3, 11, 12, 13, 15, 16, 38²; 8:5, 9, 22, 25, 26, 28², 29, 35, 41, 42², 44, 47; 9:14, 18, 23, 24², 25, 26, 29², 31, 32², 42, 43, 58, 62; 10:2, 7, 23, 30, 34², 38; 11:1², 8, 18, 21², 49; 12:1, 15, 22, 25, 27, 31, 39, 42, 44, 47²; 13:6, 13, 15, 17, 19, 22; 14:12, 17, 21², 23, 26⁴, 27; 15:5, 6, 12², 13, 15, 16, 17, 20², 22, 28, 29; 16:1², 5, 16, 18, 20, 21, 23, 24; 17:1, 2, 11, 22, 24, 33²; 18:1, 7, 13, 43; 19:13, 14, 17, 19, 22, 24, 29, 48; 20:26, 28, 44, 45; 21:5; 22:14, 39, 44, 50, 71; 23:5, 11, 26, 33², 34, 46, 55; 24:8, 23, 26, 40, 47, 50; Jn 1:6, 11², 12², 14², 16, 35, 41; 2:2, 5, 11³, 12², 17, 21, 22, 23; 3:4, 16, 17, 20, 22, 32, 35; 4:2, 5, 8, 12², 24, 27, 31, 33, 34, 36, 41, 44, 47, 50, 51³, 52, 53; 5:9, 17, 18, 19, 28, 32, 35, 37², 38, 43; 6:3, 8, 15, 18, 23, 24², 25, 26, 29², 31, 32², 42, 43, 58, 62; 10:2, 7, 23; 24², 25, 26, 29², 31, 32², 42, 43, 58, 62; 12:1, 15, 22, 27, 31, 39, 42, 44, 47²; 13:6, 13, 15, 17, 19, 22; 14:12, 17, 21², 23; 23:5, 11, 26, 33², 34, 46, 55; 24:8, 23, 26, 40, 47, 50; Jn 1:6, 11², 12², 14², 16, 35, 41; 2:2, 5, 11³, 12², 17, 21, 22, 23; 3:4, 16, 17, 20, 22, 32, 35; 4:2, 5, 8, 12², 16, 35, 41; 2:2, 5, 11³, 12², 17, 21, 22, 32; 35; 4:2, 5, 8, 12², 13², 16, 17, 23; 6:10; 7:14, 5, 8, 10, 13, 14², 17, 20, 23, 24, 25, 60; 8:1, 11, 27, 28², 32, 33², 39²; 9:3, 8, 12², 14; 10:7, 17, 20, 23, 24, 25, 43; 11:13; 2:6, 14, 20; 13:8; 14:4, 9; Ro 1:2, 3², 4, 5, 9, 20; 2:4, 5, 8; 3:5, 7, 20, 24, 25³, 26²; 4:3, 5, 13, 19², 20; 5:5, 8, 9, 10²; 6:3²; 8:3, 11, 17², 28, 29, 32; 9:7, 19, 22³, 23²; 11:1, 2, 22, 29, 33², 34; 12:2, 6, 20; 13:8; 14:4, 5, 9, 12²; 15:3, 9, 10; 16:13, 15, 21, 23; 1Co 1:4, 9; 2:10; 3:5, 8, 13, 14; 4:5; 5:1, 5; 6:14, 18²; 7:2, 3², 4, 7, 11, 14, 33, 34, 37³; 9:7; 10:24; 11:4², 7; 14:2, 25; 15:10, 23, 25², 27; 16:2, 11; 2Co 1:22²; 2:11; 3:13, 18; 4:6, 11, 14; 5:20; 7:7, 13, 15; 8:9, 17, 18; 9:7, 9², 15; 10:10²; 11:15, 33; Gal 1:15, 16; 2:11, 13; 3:5, 16, 18; 4:2, 4, 6, 23²; 6:4, 5, 6, 8; Eph 1:4, 5², 6, 7, 9², 11, 12, 14, 18, 19², 20, 22, 23; 2:4, 7², 15², 22; 3:7, 10, 11, 15, 16², 20; 4:8, 18²; 5:5³, 6; Php 2:1, 13, 21, 30; 3:10³, 21²; 4:19; Col 1:9, 11, 19, 20, 22, 24, 29; 2:18; 3:25; 4:10; 1Th 1:10; 2:2, 11, 12; 3:13; 4:4, 6, 8; 2Th 1:7, 9, 10, 11²; 2:8², 16; 1Ti 1:12, 16; 3:1, 4², 5, 12²; 5:8²;

18; 6:15; 2Ti 1:8, 9; 2:4, 19, 26; 4:1², 8, 18; Tit 1:3²; 2:14; 3:5, 7; Heb 1:2, 3², 5, 6, 7²; 2:4, 8, 14, 17; 3:6, 7, 15, 18; 4:1, 3, 4, 7, 10²; 5:3, 7; 6:10, 13, 17; 7:2, 6, 10, 16, 21, 22², 26; 8:11²; 9:12, 25; 10:11, 12, 30; 11:4, 7², 8, 9, 17, 21, 22², 26; 12:7, 10, 16, 26; 13:12, 15, 21; Jas 1:9, 10, 11, 14, 23, 26²; 2:16, 21, 22³; 3:2, 6, 13; 4:11; 5:20; 1Pe 1:2, 3; 2:9, 21, 22, 24²; 3:10²; 4:1², 2, 13; 5:10; 2Pe 1:3², 4, 9, 16; 2:8, 16; 3:9, 13, 16²; 1Jn 1:3, 7, 10; 2:3, 5, 9, 10, 11, 16, 27, 28; 3:10, 12³, 15, 16, 17, 19, 22, 23², 24; 4:9², 10, 12, 13, 16, 20; 2Jn 1:6², 11; Jude 1:5, 14, 24; Rev 1:1³, 4, 5, 6, 13², 14², 15², 16³, 17²; 2:1, 13²; 3:5³, 21; 4:8; 6:5; 7:15²; 8:7, 8, 10, 12; 9:1, 13; 10:1³, 2³, 5, 7²; 11:15², 19²; 12:3, 4, 5, 7², 9, 14, 16, 17; 13:1, 2², 5, 6³, 12, 16², 17, 18; 14:1², 7, 9², 10, 11², 14², 16, 19; 15:2², 8; 16:2², 3, 4, 8, 10², 12, 15, 17, 19; 17:8, 11, 14, 17, 18³; 19:2², 5, 7, 10, 12², 13, 15, 16², 19, 20²; 20:1, 4², 7, 11; 21:3, 7; 22:3, 4², 6², 19.

I (8747)

See also selected listing of "I AM" in the Main Concordance.

Ge 1:29, 30; 2:18; 3:10⁴, 11, 12, 13, 15, 16, 17; 4:1, 9², 13, 14², 23; 6:7⁴, 13², 17, 18; 7:1, 4³; 8:21³; 9:3², 5³, 9, 11, 12, 13, 14, 15, 16, 17; 12:1, 2³, 7, 11, 13, 19; 13:15, 16, 17; 14:22, 23², 24; 15:1, 2, 7, 8², 14, 18; 16:2², 5, 10, 13; 17:1, 2, 5, 6², 7, 8², 16², 19, 20⁴, 21; 18:3, 10, 12², 13², 14, 15, 17², 19, 21², 26², 27², 28², 29, 30², 31², 32; 19:8, 19, 21², 22, 34; 20:5, 6³, 9, 11, 13, 16; 21:7, 13, 16, 18, 23, 24, 26², 30; 22:1, 2, 5, 11, 12, 16, 17; 23:4², 11³, 13²; 24:3², 5, 7, 13, 14², 24, 31, 33³, 34, 37, 39, 40, 42³, 43², 45², 46, 47², 48², 49, 56, 58; 25:32; 26:2, 3³, 4, 9², 24³; 27:1, 2, 4³, 6², 7³, 8, 9, 12, 13, 19², 21, 24, 25, 32, 33³, 37³, 41, 43, 45; 28:13³, 15⁴, 16, 20, 21, 22²; 29:19, 21, 25², 33, 34, 35; 30:2, 3, 8², 13, 16, 20, 25, 26², 27², 28, 29, 30³, 31²; 31:3, 5, 10², 11², 12, 13, 27, 29, 31², 35, 36, 38², 39¹, 41², 43, 44, 51, 52; 32:4, 5³, 9, 10⁴, 11², 12², 20³, 26, 30; 33:8, 9, 10, 11², 13, 14²; 34:11, 12, 30; 35:3², 11, 12³; 37:6, 9, 10, 13, 16², 30; 38:18, 22, 23, 25, 26²; 39:9², 14, 18; 40:9, 11, 15², 16; 41:9, 13, 15², 16, 17, 19, 21, 22, 24, 28, 40, 41, 44; 42:2, 14, 18, 22, 33², 34², 37², 43:9² 14², 23; 44:21, 28², 30, 32², 34; 45:3, 4, 11, 12, 18, 28²; 46:2, 3², 4², 30², 31, 34; 47:16, 23, 29, 30²; 48:4³, 5, 7², 9, 11, 19², 21, 22²; 49:1, 7, 18, 29, 31; 50:4, 5³, 17, 19, 21, 24; Ex 2:7, 9, 10, 14, 22; 3:3, 4, 6, 7³, 8, 9, 10, 11², 12², 13², 14³, 15, 16, 17², 18², 19, 20, 21; 4:10², 11, 12, 14, 15, 16, 18, 21², 23²; 5:2³, 10, 23; 6:1, 2, 3⁴, 4, 5³, 6⁴, 7³, 8⁴, 12², 23, 28, 29²; 9:14, 15, 16², 18, 27², 28, 30; 10:1², 2³, 4, 10, 16, 29; 11:1, 4, 8; 12:12³, 13³, 17; 13:8², 15; 14:4³, 17², 18²; 15:1, 2², 9⁴, 26⁴; 16:4², 12², 32²; 17:4, 6, 9, 14; 18:3, 6, 11, 16, 19; 19:4², 9², 20; 20:2, 5, 22⁴, 24²; 21:5, 13; 22:23, 24², 27; 23:7, 13, 15, 20², 22², 23, 25, 26, 27², 28, 29, 30, 31², 24:12²; 25:8, 9, 16, 21, 22; 28:3; 29:35, 42, 43, 44, 45, 46³; 30:6, 36; 31:2, 3, 6², 11, 13; 32:8, 9, 10, 13³, 18, 24², 30³, 33, 34²; 33:1², 2, 3², 5³, 12, 13, 14, 17³, 19², 22, 23; 34:1, 9, 10³, 11², 18, 24, 27²; Lev 6:17²; 7:34; 8:31, 35; 10:3², 13, 18, 19; 11:44², 45²; 14:34², 35; 16:2²; 17:10, 11, 12, 14; 18:2, 3, 4, 5, 6, 21, 24, 25, 30; 19:2, 3, 4, 10, 12, 14, 16, 18, 25, 28, 30, 31, 32, 34, 36, 37; 20:3², 5², 6², 7, 8, 24³, 25, 26², 28³, 30, 31, 35, 37²; 38³; 23:3², 4², 8², 9³, 11, 12, 15, 20², 26²; 24:10, 11², 12, 13², 14, 17²; 25:11², 12; 27:12; 32:8, 11; 33:53, 56²; 35:34²; Dt 1:8, 9, 13, 14, 17⁴, 18, 20, 23, 29, 35, 36, 39, 42, 43; 2:5³, 9², 19², 24, 25, 26, 31; 3:2, 12, 13, 15, 16, 18, 19², 20, 21, 23; 4:1, 2², 5, 8, 21, 22², 26, 40; 5:1, 5, 6, 9, 28, 31²; 6:2, 6; 7:11; 8:1, 11, 19; 9:9³, 12, 13, 14², 15, 16², 17, 18, 21², 23, 24, 25², 26, 28³; 10:2, 3², 5², 10², 11, 13; 11:8, 13, 14, 15, 22, 26, 27, 28, 32; 12:11, 14, 20, 21, 28, 32;

13:18; **15:**5, 11, 15, 16; **18:**18³, 19, 20; **19:**7, 9; **22:**14³, 16, 17; **24:**8, 18, 22; **25:**8; **26:**3², 10, 13³, 14²; **27:**1, 4, 10; **28:**1, 13, 14, 15, 68; **29:**5, 6², 14, 19²; **30:**1, 2, 8, 11, 15, 16, 18, 19²; **31:**2², 5, 14, 16, 17², 18, 20², 21³, 23², 27³, 28, 29²; **32:**1, 3, 20, 21², 23, 24², 26², 27, 34, 35, 39⁵, 40², 41², 42, 46, 49, 52; **33:**9; **34:**4²; **Jos 1:**2, 3², 5³, 6, 9; **2:**4, 5, 9, 12; **3:**7³; **5:**9, 14; **6:**2, 10; **7:**8, 11, 12, 20², 21²; **8:**1, 5, 18; **10:**8; **11:**6; **13:**6²; **14:**7²; 8, 10, 11², 12; **15:**16, 18; **18:**4, 6, 8; **20:**2; **22:**2; **23:**2, 4², 14; **24:**3², 4², 5⁴, 6, 7, 8³, 10²; 11, 12, 13; **Jdg 1:**2, 7, 12, 14; **2:**1⁴, 3², 20, 21, 22; **3:**19, 20; **4:**7, 8², 9, 22; **5:**3³, 7; **6:**8, 9², 10², 14, 15², 16, 17, 18², 22, 37²; **7:**4³, 7, 9, 13, 17², 18; **8:**2, 3, 5, 7, 9², 19, 23, 24; **9:**2, 9, 11, 13, 29²; **10:**12, 13; **11:**9, 27, 31², 35², 37; **12:**2², 3²; **13:**6, 8, 11, 13, 14, 16; **14:**2, 12, 16²; **15:**2², 3², 7², 11, 16², 18; **16:**15, 17², 26²; **17:**2³, 3², 13; **18:**4, 24²; **19:**18³, 24; **20:**4, 6, 28; **Ru 1:**11, 12³, 16², 17², 21; **2:**2, 9, 10, 13², 19; **3:**1, 5, 9, 11, 12², 13; **4:**4⁴, 6³, 9, 10; **1Sa 1:**8, 11, 15³, 16, 20, 22, 26, 27², 28; **2:**1, 23, 24, 27, 28², 29, 30², 31, 33, 35², 36; **3:**4, 5², 6², 8, 11, 12², 13²; 14, **4:**16²; **7:**5; **8:**8; **9:**8², 16², 17, 19², 21, 23², 24², 26, 27; **10:**2, 8, 18², **11:**2²; **12:**1, 2³, 3², 7, 17, 23²; **13:**11, 12²; **14:**7, 24, 29, 37, 40, 43²; **15:**1, 2, 6, 11², 13, 14, 20³, 24³, 25², 26, 30²; **16:**1³, 2², 3², 5, 7, 18, 22; **17:**8, 9, 10, 28, 29², 35², 39², 43, 45, 46, 55, 58; **18:**17², 18², 21; **19:**3², 15, 17; **20:**1³, 5, 8, 9², 12², 13, 14², 20², 21², 22, 23, 29, 30, 36; **21:**2, 4, 5, 8, 15; **22:**3, 9, 15, 22²; **23:**2, 4, 17, 23²; **24:**4, 6, 10³, 11³, 17², 20; **25:**7, 11², 22, 25, 35; **26:**8, 11, 18², 21³, 23, 24; **27:**1³, 5²; **28:**2, 7, 8, 13, 15², 21, 23; **29:**3, 6², 8³, 9; **30:**8², 13², 15; **2Sa 1:**3, 6, 7², 8, 9, 10³, 13, 16, 26; **2:**1², 6, 22²; **3:**8³, 9, 12, 13², 14, 18, 28, 35, 39²; **4:**10²; 11, **5:**19²; **6:**21, 22³; **7:**2, 6³, 7³, 8, 9³, 10, 11², 12³, 13, 14², 15², 18, 27; **9:**1, 3, 7², 9; **10:**2, 11; **11:**5, 11², 12²; **12:**7³, 8³, 11², 12, 13, 22², 23³, 27, 28; **13:**5², 6², 10, 13, 28², 34; **14:**5, 6, 7, 8, 15², 18, 21, 32⁶; **15:**4², 7, 25, 26, 28², 34³; **16:**4², 10, 12, 18², 19⁴; **17:**1, 2³, 11, 15; **18:**2, 4, 10, 11, 12, 13, 18, 22³, 29, 33; **19:**6, 7, 20³, 22³, 26⁴, 28, 29, 33, 34², 35³, 37, 38²; **20:**16, 17; **21:**3², 6; **22:**3, 4², 7², 22², 23, 24, 30², 38², 39, 41, 43², 44, 50²; **24:**2, 10⁴, 12, 13, 14, 17, 21, 24²; **1Ki 1:**5, 14, 21, 30², 35; **2:**2, 7, 8³, 14, 16, 18, 20², 26, 30, 42², 43; **3:**7, 12², 13, 14, 17², 20, 21⁴, 26; **5:**5², 6, 8, 9², **6:**12², 13; **8:**13, 16³, 20³, 21, 27, 43, 44, 48, 59; **9:**3², 4, 5³, 6, 8; **10:**6, 7³; **11:**11², 12², 21, 31, 32, 33, 34³, 35, 36², 37, 38⁴, 39²; **12:**11², 14²; **13:**7, 8², 9, 14, 16², 17, 18, 31; **14:**2, 6, 7, 8, 10³; **15:**19; **16:**2, 3², **17:**1, 4, 9, 10, 12², 20, 24; **18:**1, 9, 12⁴, 13², 15², 18, 22, 23, 24, 36; **19:**2, 4², 10², 14³, 18, **20:**4², 5, 6, 7, 9, 13², 28², 32², 34² 42; **21:**2³, 3, 4, 6³, 20, 21², 22, 29²; **22:**4, 6², 8, 14, 16, 17, 18, 19, 21, 24, 27, 30; **2Ki 1:**2, 10, 12; **2:**2, 3, 4, 5, 6, 9², 10, 18, 21; **3:**7², 14³; **4:**2, 9, 13, 22, 24, 28², 30, 43; **5:**5, 6, 7², 11, 12, 15, 16, 18², 20; **6:**3, 8, 13, 19, 21², 27, 29, 33; **7:**12; **8:**8, 9, 12; **9:**3, 5, 6, 7, 8, 9, 12, 17, 25, 26; **10:**9, 15², 19, 24, 30; **16:**7, 15; **17:**13³, 38; **18:**14², 23, 25, 32; **19:**7, 20, 23³, 24², 25³, 27, 28², 34; **20:**3, 5², 6³, 8, 19; **21:**4, 7², 8³, 12, 13², 14; **22:**8, 16, 19², 20²; **23:**17, 27³; **1Ch 4:**9, 10; **11:**19²; **12:**17; **13:**12; **14:**10²; **15:**12; **16:**18; **17:**1, 5, 6³, 7, 8³, 9, 10³, 11², 12, 13³, 14, 16, 19²; **19:**2, 12; **21:**2, 8³, 10, 12, 13, 17², 22, 23², 24²; **22:**5, 7, 9², 10², 14; **23:**5; **28:**2², 6, 7, 8, 19; **29:**2, 3², 14, 17³, 19; **2Ch 1:**10, 11, 12; **2:**4, 5, 6, 8, 9, 10, 13; **6:**2², 5³, 6², 10³, 11, 18, 33, 34, 38; **7:**12, 13, 14, 16, 17, 18³, 19, 20⁴; **9:**5, 6³; **10:**11², 14²; **12:**5, 7; **16:**3; **18:**3, 5, 7, 13, 14, 15, 16, 17, 18, 20, 21, 26, 29; **25:**9, 16; **28:**23; **29:**10; **32:**13; **33:**7², 8³; **34:**15, 24, 27, 28²; **35:**21², 23; **Ezr 4:**19, 21; **6:**8, 11, 12; **7:**13, 21, 28; **8:**15³, 16, 17², 21, 22, 24, 25, 26, 28; **9:**3², 4, 5, 6; **Ne 1:**1, 2, 4³, 5, 6, 8, 9², 11; **2:**1², 3, 4, 5², 6, 7, 8, 9, 11, 12³, 13, 14, 15², 16³, 17, 18, 20; **4:**13, 14², 19, 22, 23; **5:**6², 7³, 9, 10, 12, 13, 14², 15, 16, 18, 19; **6:**1², 3³, 4, 8, 9, 11, 13, 19; **7:**1, 2, 3, 5²; **12:**31², 38, 40; **13:**6³, 7, 8, 9², 10, 11², 13, 14, 15², 17², 19², 21², 22², 23, 25³, 28, 30, 31; **Est 3:**9; **4:**11, 16⁴; **5:**4, 8², 13; **7:**3, 4²; **8:**6², 7; **Job 1:**15, 16, 17, 19, 21³; **3:**11², 12, 13², 16, 25², 26²; **4:**8, 16²; **5:**3, 8³; **6:**7, 8², 10², 11³, 12, 13, 22², 26, 28; **7:**3, 4⁴, 8, 11³, 12, 13, 15, 16², 20³, 21²; **8:**18; **9:**2, 11², 14², 15³, 16², 20³, 27², 28³, 29² 30, 32, 35²; **10:**1², 2, 7, 13, 14, 15⁴, 16, 18², 19, 20, 21; **11:**4, 5; **12:**3², 4²; **13:**2³, 23; **14:**14, 15; **15:**17²; **16:**2, 4², 6², 15, 22; **17:**10, 13², 14; **19:**4, 7³, 8, 10, 16², 17, 18, 19, 20, 25, 26, 27²; **20:**2, 3; **21:**3², 4, 6², 16, 27; **22:**18; **23:**3², 4, 5, 7², 8², 10², 12, 13², 17; **27:**3, 5³, 6², 11²; **29:**2, 3, 4, 7, 12, 13, 14, 15, 16², 17, 18², 22, 24, 25³; **30:**1², 9, 19, 20², 23, 25, 26², 28², 29; **31:**1, 5, 6, 8, 9, 13,

14², 16, 17, 18², 19, 21², 23², 24, 25, 26, 28, 29, 30, 33, 34², 35², 36², 37², 39²; **32:**6³, 7, 10, 13³, 11², 12, 14, 16, 17³, 18, 19, 20, 21², 22²; **33:**1, 2, 3, 6², 8, 9², 12, 24, 27³, 28, 31, 32, 33; **34:**5, 6³, 16, 31, 32³, 33², 35², 36²; **36:**2³; **37:**20; **38:**3, 4, 9, 10, 11, 23; **39:**6; **40:**4³, 5³, 7, 14; **41:**11, 12; **42:**2, 3², 4², 6, 7, 8; **Ps 2:**6, 7², 8; **3:**4, 5², 6; **4:**1, 3, 8; **5:**2, 3, 7²; **6:**2, 6², 7; **7:**1, 3, 4, 17; **8:**3; **9:**1², 2², 14; **11:**1; **12:**5²; **13:**2, 3, 4², 5, 6; **16:**1, 2², 4, 6, 7, 8²; **17:**3, 4, 6, 15⁴; **18:**1, 2, 3², 6², 21², 22, 23, 29², 37², 38, 40, 42², 43, 49²; **19:**13; **20:**6; **22:**2, 6, 10, 14, 17, 22², 25; **23:**1, 4², 6; **25:**1, 2, 16, 20; **26:**1², 3, 4², 5, 6, 8, 11, 12²; **27:**1², 3, 4², 6², 7, 8, 13², 22², 27²; **30:**1, 2, 6³, 7, 8², 12²; **31:**1, 5, 6², 7, 9, 11², 13², 14², 17, 21, 22³; **32:**3, 5³, 8², **34:**1, 4, 11; **35:**3, 11, 13, 14², 15², 18²; **37:**25³, 35, 36; **38:**6², 8², 13, 14, 15, 16, 17, 18², 20; **39:**1³, 2, 3³, 7², 9, 10, 12, 13², 40:1, 5, 7³, 8, 9², 10³, 12, 17; **41:**4², 9, 10, 11; **42:**2, 4³, 5, 6, 9², 11; **43:**2, 4², 5; **44:**6, 45:1, 17; **46:**10³; **49:**4², 5; **50:**7³, 8, 9, 11, 12², 13, 15, 21³, 22, 23; **51:**3, 4, 5, 7², 13, 16; **52:**8², 9³; **54:**6²; **55:**2, 6³, 7, 8, 9, 12², 14, 16, 17, 23; **56:**3², 4³, 9², 10², 11², 12², 13; **57:**1, 2, 4², 6, 7, 8, 9²; **59:**4, 9, 16², 17; **60:**6, 8²; **61:**2³, 4, 8; **62:**2, 6, 11; **63:**1, 2, 4³, 6², 7; **64:**1; **66:**13, 14, 15², 17, 18; **68:**22²; **69:**2³, 4², 7, 8, 10², 11, 12, 13, 17, 19, 20², 29, 30; **70:**5; **71:**1, 3, 6², 7, 9, 14², 15, 16², 17, 18², 22², 23³; **73:**2, 3², 13², 14², 15, 16, 17², 22², 23, 25², 28²; **75:**2², 3, 4, 9², 10; **77:**1², 2³, 3⁴, 5, 6, 10²; **78:**2², 10, 11², 12; **78:**2²; **81:**6, 7³, 8, 10², 12, 14, 16; **82:**6; **84:**10; **85:**8; **86:**1, 2, 3, 4, 7, 11², 12²; **87:**4; **88:**1, 4², 5, 8, 9², 13, 15²; **89:**1², 2, 3², 4, 19², 20², 23, 25, 27, 28, 29, 32, 33², 34, 35², 50; **91:**2² 14², 15³, 16; **92:**4; **94:**17, 18, 22; **95:**9, 10², 11; **101:**1², 2², 3², 4, 5², 8²; **102:**2², 4, 5, 6, 7², 9, 11, 24; **104:**33³, 34; **105:**11¹; **106:**5²; **108:**1, 2, 3, 7, 9²; **109:**1, 4, 22, 23², 25, 30²; **110:**1; **111:**1; **116:**1, 2, 3, 4, 6, 9, 10³, 11, 12, 13, 14, 16², 17, 18; **118:**5, 6, 7, 10, 11, 12, 13, 17, 19, 21, 28²; **119:**6², 7², 8, 10, 11², 13, 14, 15, 16², 17², 18, 19, 22, 25, 26, 27, 30², 31, 32, 33, 34, 35, 39, 40, 42², 44, 45², 46, 47, 47³, 48³, 51, 52², 54, 55², 56, 57, 58, 59, 60, 61, 62, 63, 66, 67³, 69, 70, 71, 74, 75, 77, 78, 80, 81, 82, 83², 87, 88, 92, 93, 94², 95, 96, 97², 99², 100², 101², 102, 104², 106², 107, 109², 110, 113², 114, 115, 116, 117², 119, 120, 121, 125², 127, 128², 129, 131, 134, 141², 144, 145², 146², 147², 148, 152, 153, 157, 158, 159, 162, 163², 164, 166², 167², 168, 173, 174, 175, 176²; **120:**1, 5², 6, 7²; **121:**1; **122:**1, 8, 9; **123:**1; **130:**1, 5²; **131:**1, 2; **132:**3, 4, 5, 11, 12, 14²; 12:5, 16, 17, 18; **135:**5; **137:**5, 6²; **138:**1², 2, 3, 7; **139:**2², 7², 8², 9², 11, 14³, 15², 18³, 21, 22²; **140:**6, 12; **141:**1², 8, 10; **142:**1², 2, 3, 4, 5², 6, 7, 8³, 9, 12; **144:**2, 9²; **145:**1², 2, 5, 6; **146:**2²; **Pr 1:**23, 24², 26², 28; **4:**2, 3, 10, 11, 20; **5:**7, 12, 13, 14; **7:**6, 7², 14², 15², 16, 17, 24; **8:**4², 6², 12², 13, 14, 17, 19, 20, 24, 25, 27, 30²; **9:**5; **20:**9²; **22:**13, 17, 19, 20; **23:**35³; **24:**30, 32²; **26:**19; **27:**11; **30:**2², 3², 7², 9², 18; **Ecc 1:**12, 13, 14, 16³, 17²; **2:**1², 2, 3², 4, 7, 8², 9, 10², 11², 12, 13, 14, 15³, 17, 18³, 19, 24; **3:**10, 12, 14, 16, 17, 18, 22²; **4:**1¹², 2, 4, 7, 8², 15; **5:**13, 18; **6:**1, 3; **7:**15, 23³, 25, 26, 27, 28²; **8:**2, 9², 10, 12, 14, 15, 16, 17²; **9:**1, 11, 13, 16, 17; **10:**5; **12:**1; **SS 1:**5, 6³, 7², 9; **2:**1, 3, 5, 7, 16, **3:**1², 3⁴, 4, 5; **4:**6; **5:**1⁴, 2, 3⁴, 5, 6², 8³, 6:3, 11, 12, **7:**8³, 10, 12, 13; **8:**1², 2⁴, 4, 5, 10²; **Isa 1:**2, 11², 13, 14, 15², 24, 25², 26; **3:**4, 7²; **5:**1⁴, 4², 5⁴, 6²; **6:**1, 5⁴, 8, 11; **7:**12²; **8:**2, 3, 17², 18; **10:**6², 11²; **12:**1, 2, 13, 17; **14:**13³, 14², 22², 23², 24², 25², 30; **15:**9²; **16:**9², 10; **18:**4; **19:**2, 3, 4, 11; **21:**2, 4, **23:**4²; **24:**16³; **25:**1; **27:**3⁴, 4³; **28:**16, 17, 23, 29:2², 3², 11, 12, 14; **30:**7; **32:**9; **33:**10³, 13, 24; **34:**5; **36:**8, 10, 17; **37:**7², 24³, 25², 26³, 28, 29³, 35; **38:**3, 5², 6², 8, 10², 13, 14, 15⁴, 17², 18², 19², 20, 21; **39:**4; **40:**6²; **41:**4², 8, 9⁴, 10⁴, 13², 14, 15, 17², 18², 19⁴, 20, 21, 22², 23; **42:**1³, 6³, 8², 9², 14⁴, 15, 16², 19²; **43:**1², 2, 3⁴, 4², 5², 6, 7², 10², 11², 12³, 13, 15², 25², 26³, 27, 28; **44:**1, 2, 3, 5, 6², 7, 8², 21², 22, 23², 24, 26², 28; **45:**1², 2, 3⁴, 4², 5², 6², 7², 8⁴, 9¹, 11; **46:**4²; **47:**1, 5, 7², 14; **Da 1:**10; **2:**3², 5², 8², 9, 23, 24, 25, 26, 30; **3:**14, 15, 25, 29; **4:**4, 5², 6, 7, 8, 9², 10², 13³, 18, 30, 34³, 36, 37; **5:**11, 14, 16, 17²; **6:**22², 26; **7:**2, 4, 6, 7, 8, 9, 11², 13, 15, 16, 19, 27³; **9:**2, 3, 4, 5, 6, 7, 13, 15, 16, 17², 18, 19, 27³; **9:**2, 3, 4, 5, 6, 7, 13, 15, 16, 17², 18, 19, 27³; **10:**2, 3², 4, 5, 7, 8³, 9³, 11², 12, 13, 14, 15, 16⁴, 17², 19, 20³, 21; **11:**1, 2; **12:**5, 7, 8³; **Hos 1:**4², 5, 6², 7², 9; **2:**2, 3⁴, 4², 5², 7², 8, 9, 10, 11, 12², 13, 14², 15, 17, 18², 19², 20, 21², 23⁴; **3:**2, 3²; **4:**5, 6², 9, 14, 5:2, 3, 9, 10, 12, 14³, 15, 6:4²; 5:2, 6, 10; **7:**1², 2, 12⁴, 13, 15; **8:**10, 12, 14; **9:**10², 12², 13, 15², 16², 17²; **10:**10²; **11:**1², 2², 3², 4², 8⁴, 9⁴, 11; **12:**8²; **9:**10; **13:**4, 5, 6, 7², 8², 11², 14²; **14:**4, 5, 8³; **Joel 1:**19; **2:**19², 20, 25², 27², 28, 29, 30; **3:**1, 2², 4, 7², 8, 10, 12, 17², 21²; **Am 1:**3, 4, 5², 6, 7, 8², 10, 11, 12, 13, 14; **2:**1, 2, 3, 4, 5, 6, 9², 10², 11, 13; **3:**1, 2², 14², 15; **4:**6, 7², 9², 10⁴, 11², 12²; **5:**1,

4:6, 10, 12, 19⁴, 21, 23, 24, 25, 26, 27, 28²; **5:**1, 4, 5, 7², 9², 14, 15, 18, 22, 29²; **6:**2, 8, 10, 11², 12, 15, 17, 19, 20, 21, 27; **7:**3, 7², 11, 12², 13², 14³, 15², 16, 19, 22², 23², 25, 31, 34; **8:**3, 6², 10, 13², 17, 21³; **9:**1, 2, 7², 10², 11, 12, 15, 16³, 24², 25; **10:**18², 19², 23; **11:**4⁵, 5², 7², 8², 10, 11², 14, 18, 19², 20, 22, 23; **12:**1², 7³, 8, 14³, 15², 17²; **13:**2, 5, 6, 7², 9, 11, 13, 14², 17, 24, 25, 26, 27; **14:**12³, 13², 14, 15, 16, 18², 19³, 20; **15:**3, 4, 6³, 7², 8³, 9³, 10, 11², 13, 14, 15, 16², 17², 19, 20², 21; **16:**5, 9, 13², 15², 16, 18, 21², 17³, 42, 10, 14³, 16²; **17:**3, 4², 10, 14, 16², 22, 27; **18:**2², 6, 7, 8³, 9, 10², 11², 17², 20²; **19:**2, 3, 5, 7³, 8, 9, 11, 12², 15², 20:4², 5, 7², 8², 10, 12², 13, 14², 15³, 16², 17², 19, 20², 21; **16:**5, 9, 13², 17³, 4², 10, 14³, 16²; **22:**5, 6, 7, 14, 21², 24², 25, 26, 23:2, 3², 4, 5, 9, 11, 12², 13, 14, 15, 17, 21, 24, 25³, 30, 31, 32², 33, 34, 38, 39²; 40; **24:**3, 5², 6³, 7³, 8, 9², 10²; **25:**3, 6, 9³, 10, 12, 13², 14, 15, 16, 17, 27, 29²; **26:**2, 3², 4, 6, 15, 16, 22², 23²; **27:**5³, 6², 8², 10, 11, 12², 15², 16, 22²; **28:**2, 3, 4², 7, 11, 14², 16; **29:**4, 7, 9, 10, 11², 12, 14², 18², 19, 20, 21, 23², 25³, 30, 31, 32², 33, 34; 30:2, 3⁴, 4, 5, 9, 10, 11², 13², 14², 18, 19², 21, 22², 23³; 24³, 30, 31, 32², 33, 34, 38, 39²; 40; **43:**10³; **44:**2, 4², 10, 11, 12, 13², 26, 27, 29, 30²; **45:**3, 4², 5², **46:**5, 8², 18, 25, 26, 27, 28⁴; **48:**12, 30, 31³, 32, 33, 35, 38, 44, 47; **49:**2, 5, 6, 8², 10², 11, 13, 14, 15, 16, 19², 25, 27, 32, 35, 36², 37⁴, 38, 39; **50:**9, 18², 19, 20², 21, 24, 31, 32, 34², 44²; **51:**1, 2, 14, 20², 21², 22³, 23³, 24, 25², 36², 39, 40, 44, 47, 52, 53, 57, 64; **La 1:**11, 14, 16, 18, 19, 20⁴, 21², 22³, 23³, 24, 25², 36², 39, 40, 44, 47, 52, 53, 57, 64; **La 1:**11, 14, 16, 18, 19, 20⁴; **2:**11, 13², 22²; **3:**1, 7, 8, 14, 17², 18², 19, 20, 21², 24², 51, 54², 55, 57; **Eze 1:**1², 4², 15², 24, 27, 28³; **2:**1, 2, 3, 4, 8², 3:2², 3², 6, 8, 9, 10, 12, 14, 15², 17², 18², 20², 22², 23, 26, 27²; **4:**5, 6, 8, 13, 14², 15², 16³, 16², 5:2, 5, 8², 9², 10, 11², 12, 13³, 14, 15², 16³, 6:3², 4, 5², **7:**3², 4³, 8², 9², 20, 21, 22, 24², 27²; **8:**1², 4, 5², **10:**1², 2, 9², 13, 15, 19, 20², 22; **11:**1, 5, 7, 8, 9, 10², 11, 12³, 16², 17², 19², 20, 21, 24, 25; **12:**6, 7⁵, 11², 13², 14², 15², 16², 20, 23, 25⁴, 28; **13:**7, 8, 9, 11, 13, 14², 15², 20², 21², 22², **14:**3, 4, 5, 7, 8³, 9², 11, 13, 15, 16, 17², 18, 20, 21, 22², 23; **15:**6², 7³, 8; **16:**6², 7, 8⁴, 9, 10², 11¹, 12, 14, 19², 27², 37², 38², 39, 41, 42, 43, 48, 50, 53, 59⁴, 60¹, 61, 62², 63; **17:**16², 19², 20¹, 21², 22, 23, 24⁴; **18:**3, 23², 30, 32; **20:**3⁴, 5⁴, 7, 9², 10, 12³, 13², 14², 15³, 17, 18, 19, 20, 21², 22³, 23², 25², 26², 31:9, 11², 15³, 16²; **32:**3, 4², 5, 6², 7³, 8², 10², 12², 13, 14, 15², 32²; **33:**2², 6, 7, 8², 11, 14, 15², 16, 19, 20, 21³; **30:**8², 10, 12³, 13², 14, 16, 18, 19², 21, 22², 23², 24², 25², 26³; **31:**9, 11², 15³, 16²; **32:**3, 4², 5, 6², 7³, 8², 10², 12², 13, 14, 15², 32²; **33:**2², 6, 7, 8², 11, 14, 15², 16, 19, 20, 21³; **34:**8, 10³, 11, 12², 13, 14², 15, 16⁴, 17, 20, 22², 23, 24², 25², 26³, 27, 29, 30, 31²; **35:**3, 4², 5, 6, 7³, 8², 9, 11³, 12, 13², 14, 15²; **36:**5, 6, 7, 9, 11, 12², 15, 18, 19², 21², 22², 23⁴, 24², 25², 26², 27, 28, 29², 30², 32², 33³, 36², 37²; **38:**3, 4, 11², 16, 18², 19², 21, 22², 23⁴; **34:**8, 10³, 11, 12², 13, 14², 15, 16⁴, 17, 20, 22², 23, 24², 25², 26³, 27, 29, 30, 31²; **36:**5, 6, 7, 9, 11, 12², 15, 18, 19², 21², 22², 23⁴, 24², 25², 26², 27, 28, 29², 30², 31², 32², 33³, 36², 37², 38; **37:**2, 3, 5, 6³, 7³, 8, 10, 12², 13², 14⁴, 19, 21², 22², 23³, 25², 26³, 27, 28; **38:**3, 4, 11², 16, 18², 19², 21, 22², 23⁴; 3⁴, 6, 7, 9², 44:²², 5, 12, 14, 28²; **46:**12², **47:**1, 5, 7², 14; **Da 1:**10; **2:**3², 5², 8², 9, 23, 24, 25, 26, 29, 30, 34³, 36, 37; **5:**11, 14, 16, 6:22², 26; **7:**2, 4, 6, 7, 8, 9, 11², 13, 15, 16, 19, 27³; **9:**2, 3, 4, 5, 6, 7, 13, 15, 16, 17², 18, 19, 27³;

12, 17, 21³, 22², 23, 27; **6:**8², 14; **7:**2, 5², 8³, 9, 14³; **8:**2², 7, 9, 10³, 11; **9:**1², 2, 3², 4², 7, 8², 9², 11², 14, 15²; **Ob 1:**2, 4, 8; **Jnh 1:**9², 12; **2:**2², 4³, 6, 7, 9³; **3:**2; **4:**2⁴, 9², 11; **Mic 1:**6², 7, 8³, 15; **2:**3, 11, 12²; **3:**1, 8; **4:**6³, 7, 13², 5:10, 11, 12, 13, 14, 15; **6:**4², 6², 7, 10, 11, 13, 14, 16²; **7:**1², 7², 8³, 9³, 15; **Na 1:**12², 13, 14²; **2:**13³; **3:**5³, 6², 7; **Hab 1:**2, 5, 6; **2:**1³; **3:**2², 7, 16², 18²; **Zep 1:**2, 3³, 4², 8, 12, 17; **2:**5, 8, 9, 15; **3:**6², 7, 8², 9, 11, 12, 18, 19³, 20⁴; **Hag 1:**8, 9, 11, 13; **2:**4, 5, 6, 7², 9, 17, 19, 21, 22², 23²; **Zec 1:**3, 6, 8, 9², 14²; **2:**8², 9², 11², 14, 15²; **3:**4², 5, 7, 8, 9³; **4:**2², 4, 5, 11, 12, 13; **5:**1, 2², 4, 6, 9, 10; **6:**1, 4; **7:**3², 12²; **8:**2³, 3, 7², 8, 10, 11², 12, 13, 14, 15, 17, 21; **9:**6, 7, 8², 10, 11², 12³; **10:**3, 6⁴, 8², 9, 11; **11:**5, 6³, 7³, 8², 9², 10, 12, 13, 14; **12:**2, 3, 4³, 6, 9, 10; **13:**2², 5², 6, 7, 9⁴; **14:**2; **Mal 1:**2², 3², 4, 6², 10², 13, 14; **2:**2³, 3², 4, 5, 9, 16²; **3:**1, 5², 6, 7, 10, 11, 17²; **4:**3, 4, 5, 6; **Mt 2:**8, 13, 15², 3:9, 11³, 14, 4:9, 19; **5:**17², 18, 20, 22, 26, 28, 32, 34, 39, 44; **6:**2, 5, 16, 25, 29; **7:**23²; **8:**3, 7, 8, 9², 10², 11, 19, 19²; **9:**13², 22², 28; **10:**15, 16, 23, 27, 32, 33, 34², 35², 42², **11:**9, 10, 11, 16, 22, 24, 25, 28², 29²; **12:**6, 7, 18⁴, 27, 28, 31; **13:**15, 17, 30, 35²; **14:**27²; **15:**24, 32²; **16:**11, 15, 18², 19, 28; **17:**4, 5², 12, 16, 20; **18:**3, 10, 13, 18, 19, 20, 21, 22, 26, 29, 32, 33; **19:**9, 16, 20, 23, 24, 28; **20:**4, 13, 14², 15³, 22; **21:**21, 24³, 27², 29, 30, 31, 43; **22:**4, 8, 32, 44; **23:**34, 36, 37, 39; **24:**2, 5², 25, 34, 47; **25:**12², 20, 21, 22, 23, 24, 26³, 27², 35³, 36⁴, 40, 42², 43⁴, 45; **26:**13, 15, 18, 21, 22, 25, 29³, 31², 32², 33, 34, 35², 36, 39, 42, 48, 53, 55², 61, 63, 64, 70, 72, 74; **27:**4², 19, 22, 24, 43, 63; **28:**5, 7, 20²; **Mk 1:**2, 7², 8, 11², 17, 24, 38², 41; **2:**11, 17; **3:**28; **5:**28², 41; **6:**16, 23, 24, 25, 50; **8:**2, 3, 12, 19, 20, 24, 29², 34; **9:**1, 7, 13, 17, 18, 19, 24, 25, 41; **10:**15, 17, 20², 29, 38², 39², 51; **11:**23, 24, 29³, 33²; **12:**26, 36, 43; **13:**6, 23, 30, 31², 36, 44, 48, 49, 58, 62, 68, **15:**12; **Lk 1:**3, 18², 19³, 34, 38, 43; **2:**10, 48, 49²; **3:**8, 16³, 22²; **4:**6³, 24, 32, 43²; **5:**5, 8, 13, 24, 32; **6:**9, 27, 46, 47; **7:**6, 7, 8², 9³, **8:**10, 28, 46, 50; **9:**9², 18, 20, 27, 35, 38, 40, 41, 44, 45, 47; **10:**3, 12, 18, 19, 20, 21, 22, 24, 29², 35, 36², 40, 42², 43²; **11:**5, 8, 13, 24, 32; **12:**5³, 4, 5, 8², 11, 14, 22, 24², 25, 26³, 27, 28, 30², 32, 34, 36², 37, 38², 44; **13:**3, 5, 18, 20, 24, 32, 33, 34, 35²; **14:**18², 19, 20², 24; **15:**6, 7, 9, 10, 17², 18, 19, 21², 29, 31; **16:**2, 3, 4², 9, 24, 27, 28², 17:4, 8³, 34, 37, 18:4, 11, 13², 14, 17, 18, 21², 29, 41; **19:**5, 8³, 13, 20, 21, 22², 23², 26, 40; **20:**3, 8², 13², 41; **21:**3, 8, 15, 32; **22:**11, 15², 16², 18², 27, 29, 32, 33, 34, 37, 52, 53, 57, 58, 60, 67, 68, 70; **23:**4, 14, 16, 22², 43, 46; **24:**39², 44², 49; **Jn 1:**15, 20, 21, 23, 26, 27, 30², 31², 32, 33, 34, 48, 50²; **2:**19; **3:**3, 5, 11, 12², 28³, 32, 35, 38, 39; **5:**7², 17, 19, 25, 30⁴, 31, 32, 34², 36², 41, 42², 43, 45, 47; **6:**20, 26, 32, 35, 36, 37, 38, 39, 40, 41, 44, 47, 48, 51², 53, 54, 56, 57, 63, 65, 70; **7:**7, 8, 17, 21, 28², 29², 33², 34, 36; **8:**11, 12, 14², 15, 16³, 18², 21², 22², 23³, 24³, 25, 26³, 28³, 29, 34, 37, 38², 40, 42², 43, 45, 46, 49²; 50, 51, 54, 55⁵, 58²; **9:**5², 9, 11², 12, 15², 25⁴, 36, 38, 39, 41; **10:**1, 7², 9, 10, 11, 14², 15², 16², 17, 18³, 25², 27, 28, 30, 32, 34, 36², 37, 38²; **11:**11, 22, 24, 25, 27, 40, 41, 42², 48, 49, 50²; **13:**7, 8, 12, 13, 14, 15², 16, 18³, 19², 20, 21, 26², 33⁴, 34², 36, 37², 38; **14:**2³, 3, 4, 6, 9, 10², 11², 12³, 13, 14, 16, 18², 19, 20, 21², 23, 26², 27, 28³, 29, 30, 31²; **15:**1, 3, 4, 5², 9, 10, 11, 12, 14, 15⁴, 16, 19, 20, 22, 24, 26; **16:**1, 4⁴, 5, 6, 7³, 10, 12, 15, 17², 19², 20, 22, 23, 25, 26², 27, 28², 33²; **17:**4, 5, 6, 8², 9, 11², 12³, 13, 14², 16, 18, 19, 20, 21, 22, 23, 24², 25, 26²; **18:**5, 8, 9, 11, 17, 20³, 21, 23², 25, 26, 34², 36, 37³, 38; **19:**4², 6, 10, 15, 22², 28; **20:**13, 15, 17², 18, 21, 25², 15:1, 13; **Ac 1:**1; **2:**14, 17, 18, 19, 25², 29, 35; **3:**6³, 17; **5:**38; **7:**3, 7, 32, 34³, 43, 56; **8:**19, 23, 31, 36; **9:**15, 16; **10:**14, 20, 26, 28, 29³, 30, 33, 34; **11:**5⁴, 6, 7, 8, 11, 15, 16, 17; **12:**11; **13:**2, 22², 25³, 33, 34, 38, 41, 47; **15:**16³; **16:**18, 30; **17:**3, 22, 23; **18:**6², 10, 15, 21; **19:**13, 15², 21²; **20:**18³, 19², 20, 21, 22, 23, 24², 25², 26², 27, 29, 31, 32, 33, 35²; **21:**13, 37, 39; **22:**3⁴, 4, 5, 6, 7, 8², 10, 13, 17², 19², 20, 21, 27, 28²; **23:**1, 3, 5, 6³, 27², 28², 29, 30³, 35; **24:**4, 10², 11, 14³, 15, 16, 17, 18², 20, 21²; **25:**4, 8, 10³, 11³, 14, 16, 18, 19², 24, 25², 26², 27; **26:**2, 3, 4², 5, 6, 9², 10³, 11³, 12, 13², 14, 15², 16², 17², 19, 20, 22², 25², 26², 27, 29²; **27:**10, 22, 23², 24, 25, 31², 33, 34, 35; **28:**17², 18, 19², 20²; **Ro 1:**8, 9², 10, 11, 12, 13⁴, 14, 15, 16²; **3:**5, 7; **4:**17; **6:**19; **7:**1, 7², 9², 10, 14, 15⁶, 16³, 17, 18³, 19⁴, 20³, 21², 22, 23, 24,

25; **8**:18, 38; **9**:1², 2, 3², 9, 13², 15⁴, 17², 25², 33; **10**:2, 18, 19³, 20², 21; **11**:1², 3, 4, 11, 13³, 14, 19, 25, 27; **12**:1, 3, 19; **14**:11, 14; **15**:8, 9², 14, 15, 17, 18², 19, 20, 22, 23, 24⁴, 25, 28², 29³, 30, 31, 32; **16**:1, 2, 4, 7, 8, 17, 19², 22, 23; **1Co 1**:4, 10, 12⁵, 14², 16³, 19²; **2**:1³, 2², 3; **3**:1, 2, 4², 6, 10; **4**:3³, 6, 8, 14, 15, 16, 17³, 18, 19², 21; **5**:3⁴, 4, 9, 11; **6**:5, 12, 15; **7**:6, 7², 8², 10², 12², 17, 25², 26, 28, 29, 32, 35, 40²; **8**:13³; **9**:1³, 2², 6, 8, 15³, 16⁴, 17³, 18, 19², 20³, 21², 22³, 23², 26², 27³; **10**:1, 15², 19, 20, 29, 30³, 33²; **11**:1, 2³, 3, 17, 18², 22², 23³, 34²; **12**:1, 3, 15², 16², 21², 31; **13**:1², 2³, 3³, 11⁶, 12²; **14**:5², 6³, 11², 14, 15, 18², 19, 21, 37; **15**:1², 2, 3², 9², 10⁴, 11, 31³, 32², 34, 50, 51; **16**:1, 2, 3², 5³, 6², 7², 8, 10, 11, 12, 15, 17, 21; **2Co 1**:13, 15², 16, 17⁴, 22²; **2**:1², 2², 3⁵, 4, 8, 9, 10³, 12, 13³; **4**:13²; **5**:8, 11; **6**:2³, 13, 16², 17, 18; **7**:3², 4³, 8⁴, 9, 12, 14, 16²; **8**:3, 8², 16² 9:2², 3², 5; **10**:1², 2⁴, 8², 9; **11**:1, 2³, 3, 5², 6², 8, 9⁴, 11², 12², 16², 17, 18, 21³, 22³, 23³, 24, 25⁴, 26², 27³, 28, 29² 30², 31, 33; **12**:1², 2², 3², 5², 6², 8, 9, 10³, 11⁴, 13, 14³, 15⁴, 16², 17², 18², 20⁵, 21³; **13**:2⁴, 6, 10⁴; **Gal 1**:6, 9, 10⁴, 11², 12³, 13, 14, 16², 17³, 18, 19, 20², 21; **2**:1², 2⁴, 7, 10, 11, 14², 18⁴, 19², 20⁴, 21; **3**:2, 17², 4:1, 11², 12², 13, 14², 15, 16, 18, 19, 20³; **5**:2, 3, 10, 11², 12, 16, 21²; **6**:11², 14², 17; **Eph 1**:15, 16, 17, 18, 18³; **3**:1, 3, 7, 8, 13, 14, 16, 17²; **4**:1, 17; **5**:32; **6**:19², 20³, 21², 22; **Php 1**:3², 4, 7², 8, 12, 13, 16, 17, 18², 19, 20², 22³, 23², 24, 25³, 27², 30²; **2**:16² 17², 19³, 20, 23², 24², 25, 28²; **3**:4², 7, 8⁴, 10, 12², 13², 14, 18; **4**:1², 2³, 3, 4, 10, 11³, 12², 13, 15, 16², 17², 18³; **Col 1**:23, 24², 25, 29; **2**:1², 4, 5², 4:3, 4², 8, 13, 18; **1Th 2**:18; **3**:5³; **5**:27; **2Th 2**:5²; **3**:17²; **1Ti 1**:3², 12, 13³, 15, 16, 18, 20, 2:1, 7³, 8, 9, 12; **3**:14²; **5**:14, 21; **6**:13³; **2Ti 1**:3³, 4², 5², 6, 11, 12⁶; **2**:7, 9, 10; **3**:11; **4**:1, 6, 7³, 12, 13, 17, 20; **Tit 1**:5²; **3**:8, 12²; **Phm 1**:4², 5, 6, 8, 9², 10², 12, 13², 14, 19², 20², 21², 22; **Heb 1**:5²; **3**:2; **12**:1³; **3**:9, 10², 11; **4**:3; **5**:5; **6**:14; **8**:8, 9³, 10³, 12, **10**:7³, 9², 16³, 17, 30, 38; **11**:32²; **12**:21, 26; **13**:5², 6, 19, 22², 23²; **Jas 2**:16, 18³; **1Pe 1**:16; **2**:6, 11; **5**:1, 12²; **2Pe 1**:12, 13², 14², 15, 17²; **3**:1, 2; **1Jn 2**:1, 4, 7, 8, 12, 13³ 14² 21, 26; **4**:20; **5**:13, 16²; **2Jn 1**:1², 5², 12³; **3Jn 1**:1, 2, 4, 9, 10², 13², 14; **Jude 1**:3³, 5; **Rev 1**:8, 9, 10², 12³, 17³, 18⁴; **2**:2², 4, 5, 6, 7, 9², 10², 13, 14, 16, 17², 19, 20, 21, 22², 23², 24², 25, 26, 27, 28; **3**:1, 2, 3², 5, 8³, 9³, 10, 11, 12³, 15², 16, 17², 18, 19², 20², 21²; **4**:1³, 2; **5**:1, 2, 4, 6, 11, 13; **6**:1², 2, 3, 5², 6, 7, 8, 9, 14; **8**:2, 13²; **9**:1, 13, 16, 17; **10**:1, 4², 5, 8, 9, 10², 11; **11**:1, 3; **12**:10; **13**:1, 2, 11; **14**:1, 2², 6, 13, 14; **15**:1, 2, 5; **16**:1, 5, 7, 13, 15; **17**:1, 3, 6², 7; **18**:1, 4, 7³; **19**:1, 6, 10², 11, 17, 19; **20**:1, 4², 11, 12²; **21**:1, 2, 3, 5, 6², 7, 9, 22; **22**:7, 8³, 9, 12², 13, 16², 18, 20.

I'LL (38)

Ge 13:9²; **19**:19; **24**:14, 19, 44, 46; **27**:45; **29**:18; **30**:1; **33**:12; **34**:12; **38**:17; **Jdg 16**:7, 11, 13, 20; **17**:10; **1Sa 2**:16; **17**:44, 46; **18**:11; **19**:3; **20**:4; **25**:19; **26**:6; **2Sa 24**:21; **1Ki 21**:7; **Ps 10**:6; **Pr 3**:28; **20**:22; **24**:29²; **Mk 6**:22; **Lk 12**:18, 19; **13**:8; **16**:4.

I'M (24)

Ge 16:8; **25**:30; **27**:11, 46; **31**:35; **37**:16; **45**:28; **Jos 14**:11; **Jdg 4**:19; **15**:1; **17**:9²; **1Sa 18**:23; **2Sa 1**:9; **13**:4; **18**:14; **20**:17; **Est 5**:12; **Pr 23**:35; **Lk 14**:19; **16**:3²; **Jn 21**:3; **Ac 10**:21.

IN (11277)

Ge 1:1, 11, 12, 14, 15, 17, 22², 26², 27², 28, 29, 30; **2**:1, 8², 9, 15, 16; **3**:1, 2, 3, 8², 10, 16; **4**:3, 8, 16, 20, 25; **5**:1, 3², 29; **6**:1, 4, 8, 11, 14, 16, 17; **7**:1, 11, 15, 16², 22, 23; **8**:1, 6, 9², 11², 17, 21; **9**:1, 4, 6, 7, 13, 14, 16, 23, 27; **10**:10, 25, 30, 31; **11**:2, 28², 32; **12**:5, 6, 10; **13**:2², 7, 12; **14**:3, 4, 5⁴, 6, 7, 8, 12, 14²; **15**:1, 3, 10², 13, 15, 16; **16**:3, 5, 6, 7, 12; **17**:12, 13², 14, 23², 27²; **18**:1, 3, 9, 11, 24², 26; **19**:1², 2², 8², 12, 13; **20**:1, 3, 6, 9, 11, 18; **21**:2, 7, 10, 14, 15, 20, 21, 22, 33, 34; **22**:4, 13, 17, 19; **23**:2, 6, 10, 11³, 13, 16, 17, 18, 19², 20; **24**:1², 2², 23, 36, 37, 45, 47, 62, 65; **25**:9², 13, 18², 23, 24, 29; **26**:1², 2, 3, 4, 6, 12, 15, 17, 18, 19, 22, 29, 31; **27**:7, 15, 30, 43, 45;

28:9, 12, 16; **29**:2, 17, 18², 26, 27; **30**:2, 15, 16, 27, 33², 35, 38³, 39, 41⁴, 43; **31**:10² 11, 14, 18², 23, 24, 25, 26, 32, 34, 35, 37, 40, 41, 46, 53, 54; **32**:3, 5, 7, 16, 17², 21; **33**:2², 8, 10, 14, 15, 18; **34**:5, 7², 10³, 11, 19, 21² 24, 25, 28², 29, 30²; **35**:3, 4, 6, 11, 17, 22², 26, 27; **36**:5, 6, 8, 9, 16, 17, 20, 21, 24, 30, 31, 35, 43; **37**:1, 3, 7, 11, 15, 18, 22, 24, 31, 35, 36; **38**:7, 10, 11², 18, 20, 27; **39**:2, 3, 4², 5², 6², 8², 9, 12, 13, 14, 20², 21, 22², 23; **40**:3³, 4, 5, 7², 9², 11², 13, 15, 17, 20, 22; **41**:8, 10, 17, 19, 22, 30, 31, 32, 33, 35, 36, 38, 40, 41, 42, 43², 44, 48⁵, 52, 53, 54²; **42**:1, 2, 5, 13, 16, 17, 19, 25, 27, 28, 29, 32, 34, 35, 38; **43**:1, 11, 21, 22, 23, 24, 31, 33; **44**:1, 2, 12, 14², 17, 20, 29, 31, 33; **45**:6, 10, 13, 25, 26; **46**:2, 5, 6, 12, 15², 18, 20, 22, 25², 27² 28, 31, 33, 34; **47**:1², 4², 6³, 7, 11², 13, 14² 16, 17², 19², 20, 24, 25², 26², 27³, 28, 29²; **48**:3, 5, 6, 7, 20; **49**:1, 3², 6, 7², 11², 17, 24, 25², 26², 27³, 28, 29²; **50**:2, 4, 5², 8, 13², 17, 19, 22, 26²; **Ex 1**:5², 8, 14³, 16; **2**:3, 12, 13, 15, 21, 22, 23; **3**:2, 7, 16, 20, 21², 22; **4**:2, 4, 10, 15, 17, 18, 19, 20; **5**:1, 6, 19, 21, 23; **6**:28; **7**:3, 10, 15², 16, 17, 18, 19², 20, 21³; **8**:9, 11, 13², 20, 22, 25, 26, 28; **9**:3, 5, 8, 13, 14, 16, 19³, 21, 24, 25, 27² 28, 31, 33; **10**:5, 6, 7², 12, 14², 15², 17, 19, 23, 26, 28; **11**:2, 5, 7, 8; **12**:3, 4, 7², 8, 11², 12, 16², 19, 20, 22, 24², 26, 31, 37²; **13**:3, 7, 14², 17, 19², 21; **14**:2², 3², 6, 8, 9, 13, 18, 20, 22²; **15**:1², 4², 5, 9, 13, 21, 27; **16**:1, 3², 6, 7, 10, 15², 16², 19, 21, 24, 27, 28, 33²; **17**:5, 6; **18**:8², 9, 10, 11, 14², 15², 16², 19, 20, 22², 23; **19**:1², 2, 5, 9, 13, 21, 27, 23²; **20**:4², 5, 10, 11², 14, 15², 16²; **21**:2, 6, 8, 12, 18², 19, 21, 27, 29, 31, 35²; **22**:2, 4², 5², 6, 9, 13, 21, 27, 23²; **23**:9², 11, 14, 15, 16, 26, 30², 32, 33; **24**:6, 8, 14; **25**:15, 16, 21, 27, 35, 37; **26**:4², 10², 11, 17, 34²; **27**:19, 21²; **28**:3, 10, 11, 17, 18, 19, 20², 30, 38, 43; **29**:3², 8, 9, 11, 24, 29, 30, 31, 32, 39, 41; **30**:6, 18, 34, 36²; **31**:3, 4, 5², 7², 14; **32**:1, 4, 5, 6, 8, 12, 13, 15, 17, 20; **33**:19², 22²; **34**:2, 3, 4², 5, 6³, 9, 10², 12, 15, 18², 26, 27, 29, 35; **35**:3, 19, 31, 32, 33², 35; **36**:11², 17², 22; **37**:14, 21; **38**:23, 25; **39**:1, 6, 10, 11, 12, 13², 23, 41; **40**:3, 4², 10², 11, 17, 34², 38²; **Lev 2**:4, 7, 11, 14; **3**:8; **4**:2, 6, 7, 12, 13, 17, 18, 20, 22, 26, 27, 31, 35; **5**:4², 5², 10, 13², 15², 16, 17, 18; **6**:2, 5, 7, 14, 16², 20², 21, 25, 26², 27, 28², 29², 30; **7**:2, 6², 9², 38; **8**:8, 10, 27; **9**:16, 17; **10**:1, 3, 5, 13, 14, 17, 18, 28, 29, 31, 34², 35; **11**:9, 10², 12², 32³, 33, 36, 37², 49, 51, 52, 53, 57³, 59; **14**:5, 7, 13, 15, 16, 17, 18, 28, 29, 31, 34², 35, 36³, 43, 44, 47, 50, 53², 55²; **15**:15, 25, 30, 31, 33; **16**:2², 15, 16², 17³, 21, 24, 27; **17**:3, 4, 5, 11; **18**:3², 17, 24, 27; **19**:5, 14, 17², 18², 23², 24, 29; **20**:5, 14, 16, 17, 18, 19, 20², 21; **21**:9; **22**:11, 13², 18, 19, 23, 24, 29; **23**:38², 41, 42², 43; **24**:3, 6², 10, 12; **25**:4, 7, 13, 18, 19, 20, 21, 22², 28², 29, 30², 31², 32, 33³, 45, 49, 54²; **26**:1, 4, 5², 6, 16, 20, 22, 25, 27, 28, 31, 33, 34, 35, 36, 39, 44², 45; **27**:21, 24; **Nu 1**:1³, 3², 19, 20, 22, 24, 26, 28, 30, 32, 34, 36, 38, 40, 42, 45, 49, 50, 52; **2**:17³, 32²; **3**:4, 12, 13², 14, 31, 38, 41², 45²; **4**:3⁴, 4, 5, 6, 8, 10, 11, 12², 14, 15, 16², 20, 23, 26, 30, 35², 37², 39, 41, 43, 45; **5**:6, 13, 17, 18, 18², 19, 21², 22²; **7**:2; **8**:2, 3, 14, 16, 17, 18², 24, 26; **9**:1², 3, 5, 14, 18, 21, 22, 23; **10**:9, 12, 14, 18, 22, 25, 31; **11**:1, 5², 6², 7, 8, 14², 16³, 18, 21, 23, 24², 25², 27, 31², 12:5, 6², 7, 8, 14², 16, 19, 20, 21, 22, 24², 4², 5², 9, 13, 21, 27, 27, 31, 32³; **9**:1, 5, 6, 8, 9, 10, 15, 27, 31, 32²; **9**:1, 5, 6, 8, 9, 10, 15, 27, 31, 32²; **9**:1, 5, 6, 8, 9, 10, 15, 27, 31, 32²; **10**:1², 2, 4, 5, 6, 8, 9, 14, 17, 18; **11**:2, 3, 7, 8, 11, 19, 21, 34; **12**:2, 3, 7², 9², 10, 12², 15²; **13**:1, 9, 20, 25; **14**:2, 6, 8, 17, 19; **15**:1, 4, 5, 8², 9, 11, 14, 19², 20; **16**:1, 2, 4², 9², 12, 15, 18, 19, 25, 30, 31, 32, 33², 34; **9**:1²; **18**:1³, 2², 6, 7, 12, 15, 19, 21, 28, 31; **19**:1⁴, 2, 13, 14, 16, 18², 19, 20², 21²; **20**:1, 2, 4, 6, 10², 15², 27, 31, 37, 39², 42, 43; **21**:1, 7², 12, 13, 15, 19, 20², 25², 29, 33, 34, 35; **24**:2, 3, 9, 17, 18, 19, 20; **25**:1, 3, 5, 8, 11, 14, 18⁴, 21, 22, 24, 25; **27**:1, 3², 8, 12, 13², 14, 19², 21²; **29**:2, 3, 6, 8, 10, 11, 12, 15, 18, 21, 22, 23, 25, 27², 29; **2Ch 1**:2, 3, 4, 5², 6, 8, 14²; **2**:2, 3, 7⁴, 8, 14², 16, 17, 18; **3**:1, 2, 10, 15, 17; **4**:2², 5, 7, 8, 11, 17², 20, 22; **5**:1², 3, 5, 7, 9, 10, 12; **6**:1, 2², 5², 6, 7, 10², 12, 13, 14², 16, 19, 22, 24, 28, 31², 37², 38², 40, 41; **7**:7, 10, 11⁴, 15; **8**:2, 4², 6², 8, 11, 12, 14, 15; **9**:4², 5, 8, 11, 14, 16², 20², 22, 23, 25², 27², 29³, 30, 31; **10**:2, 5, 12, 17, 18, 19; **11**:1, 3, 4², 5, 10, 11, 12, 17, 21, 22; **12**:2, 5, 12³, 13², 15, 16; **13**:1, 2, 4, 8, 13, 21, 22; **14**:1², 2, 9, 10, 11; **15**:4, 5², 8², 10, 16; **16**:1, 2, 10, 12², 13, 14², 17²; **17**:2², 7², 12, 13², 19; **18**:2, 3, 9, 15, 16, 21², 22, 27, 30³, 31², 32, 33, 34; **19**:1, 4, 5², 8², 10, 11; **20**:2, 3, 5, 7², 8, 9², 14, 15, 16, 17, 18, 20³, 26, 31, 32², 34², 35; **21**:2, 3, 4, 6, 9, 10², 11, 12²; **22**:1, 3², 4, 6, 9³, 11; **23**:1, 5, 7, 9, 10, 14, 17, 18³, 19; **24**:1, 2, 6, 9², 11, 12, 13, 14, 16², 17, 21, 24², 26, 27, 28; **25**:1, 2, 3, 4, 7, 9, 10³, 5, 17, 19³, 21, 23; **27**:1, 2, 4²; **28**:1, 2², 6, 7, 9, 12, 14, 18², 19, 22, 24, 25², 26, 27²; **29**:1, 2, 3, 4², 6, 9, 15, 22, 24, 25²², 26, 27², 29; **2Ch 1**:2, 3, 4, 5², 6, 8, 14²;

44, 46, 47; **13**:1, 4, 6², 7², 13, 15³, 16³, 19, 22, 23, 25³; **Est 1**:2, 3, 5², 7², 8, 9, 10, 11, 13, 14, 16, 18, 19, 22³; **2**:3², 5, 7, 9, 12, 14³, 15, 16³, 22, 23³; **3**:7³, 8², 12³, 14, 15; **4**:2, 3², 4, 6², 8, 11, 13, 16; **5**:1³, 2², 9², 14; **6**:1, 4, 5², 12; **7**:7, 8; **8**:5, 8³, 9², 10, 11, 12, 13, 14, 17²; **9**:2², 4, 6, 11, 12², 13, 14, 15², 16, 18, 19, 26, 27, 28³, 30, 31, 32; **10**:2, 3²; **Job 1**:1, 4, 5², 7, 12, 19, 20, 22; **2**:2, 6, 10²; **3**:6, 7, 9, 13, 14, 16, 20, 23; **4**:13, 18, 19²; **5**:4, 13, 14², 15, 19, 20², 26²; **6**:4², 6, 10, 17², 19; **7**:11², 21; **8**:14, 16, 22; **9**:5, 29, 32; **10**:1, 12, 13², 15; **11**:4, 10, 14², 18; **12**:6, 10, 25; **13**:14², 15, 17, 27; **14**:6, 8², 13, 17; **15**:8, 15², 31, 32; **16**:4, 9, 10, 15, 19; **17**:6, 12, 13; **18**:3, 4, 6, 10, 15, 17; **19**:8, 12, 24, 25, 26, 28; **20**:11, 12, 13, 14, 22, 26²; **21**:7, 13², 16, 17, 23, 25, 26, 33; **22**:12, 14, 21, 22, 24, 26; **23**:2, 9, 14; **24**:1, 3, 5, 6², 7, 13, 14, 16², 23; **25**:2, 5; **26**:5², 8; **27**:3, 5, 10, 20, 23; **28**:3, 4, 6³, 7, 9, 10, 11, 13, 14, 18, 22, 24, 25; **30**:3, 4, 13, 14, 15; **29**:4, 7, 18, 20², 21, 23; **30**:3, 4, 6³, 7, 9, 10, 11, 13, 14, 18, 22, 24, 25; **31**:5, 6, 15, 21, 24, 26², 32, 33, 35; **32**:1, 6, 8, 22; **33**:8, 11, 12, 15³, 16, 19, 25; **34**:13, 20², 24, 25; **35**:10; **36**:2, 4, 5, 8, 11², 13, 14, 15², 19, 22, 24, 31; **37**:5, 8, 16, 17, 18, 21, 22², 23², 24; **38**:9, 10, 16, 26, 32, 40³; **39**:4, 7, 12, 14, 16, 21, 24; **40**:10, 13², 16², 21, 22²; **41**:1, 22, 30; **42**:6, 11, 15; **Ps 1**:1³, 2, 3, 5²; **2**:1, 4, 5², 12³; **4**:4, 5, 8²; **5**:3³, 4, 5, 7, 8, 11²; **6**:1², 2, 3, 10; **7**:1, 5, 6, 10; **8**:1, 3, 9; **9**:2, 8, 9, 10, 11, 14², 15, 19; **10**:1, 7², 4², 8², 9⁴, 14, 18; **11**:1, 2, 4; **12**:6; **13**:2, 3, 5²; **14**:1, 5; **15**:1; **16**:1, 3², 6, 11; **17**:7, 8, 12, 14, 15; **18**:2, 6, 18, 19, 24, 30, 40, 42; **19**:4, 11, 14; **20**:1, 5, 7³; **21**:1², 7, 9, 13; **22**:4, 5, 8², 9, 15, 22, 25; **23**:1, 2, 5, 6; **24**:1², 3, 7, 8, 9; **25**:2, 3, 5², 8, 9, 12, 13, 14, 20, 21; **26**:1, 3, 6, 10, 12; **27**:4², 5³, 9, 11, 13; **28**:3, 7²; **29**:2, 5, 9; **30**:5, 9²; **31**:1², 6, 7, 8, 9, 14, 15, 16, 17, 19², 20², 21, 22, 23, 24; **32**:2, 4, 8, 10, 11³; **33**:4, 18, 19, 20, 21², 22²; **34**:2, 8, 18, 22; **35**:4, 9², 14, 15, 18, 20, 24, 27²; **36**:2, 7, 9, 10; **37**:3², 4, 5, 7, 9, 19², 23, 27, 29, 31, 32, 33, 35, 39, 40; **38**:1², 3, 7, 8; **39**:1, 6, 7; **40**:3², 7, 9, 10, 14, 16; **41**:1, 2, 5, 12²; **42**:5, 7, 11; **43**:5; **44**:1², 6, 8; **45**:4², 9, 14, 15; **46**:1, 6, 10; **48**:1, 2, 3, 5, 6, 8²; **49**:1, 6, 13, 14², 20; **50**:1, 12, 11, 12, 16, 17, 18; **51**:4, 6², 10, 16²; **52**:1, 7, 8², 9²; **53**:1; **54**:5, 7; **55**:3, 4, 7, 9, 11, 21, 23; **56**:T, 2, 3, 4², 7, 8, 10²; **11**, 13; **57**:1², 4, 6²; **58**:2, 5, 10; **59**:T, 3, 11, 12, 13, 16²; **60**:T, 6, 8; **61**:4², 7; **62**:1, 4², 5, 8, 10²; **63**:T, 1, 2, 4, 7, 11; **64**:5, 8, 10³; **65**:1, 4; **66**:5, 6, 14, 18, 19; **68**:5, 6², 10, 12², 14, 16, 18, 21, 23, 25, 26², 30, 34, 35; **69**:2, 6, 13², 16, 17, 21, 25, 27, 29, 30, 34; **70**:2, 4; **71**:1, 2, 13; **72**:2, 7, 14; **73**:1, 8, 10, 12, 13², 25; **74**:4, 8², 13, 21; **75**:8; **76**:1², 2²; **77**:2, 6, 9, 18; **78**:2, 5, 6, 7, 17, 19, 22², 30, 32², 33², 40², 43², 51, 55; **79**:8; **81**:7; **82**:1, 5; **83**:17; **84**:4, 5, 7, 10³, 12; **85**:6, 9; **86**:2, 5, 7, 11, 15; **87**:4, 5, 6², 7; **88**:5, 6², 11², 12², 13, 15; **89**:2, 5, 6, 7, 11, 15, 16², 19, 37, 39, 43, 49, 50; **90**:4², 5, 6, 8, 14; **91**:1², 2, 6, 11, 12, 15; **92**:2, 13², 14, 15; **93**:1²; **94**:15, 17, 22; **95**:4, 6, 8, 11; **96**:6, 9, 11, 12, 13²; **97**:7, 11, 12; **98**:7²; **99**:2, 4; **101**:2, 5, 6, 7, 8²; **102**:16, 21², 23, 24, 25, 28; **103**:8, 19, 22; **104**:2, 17, 22, 24, 31, 34; **105**:3, 7, 12², 18, 23, 27, 35, 36, 41; **106**:5², 7, 14³, 16, 21, 22, 23, 25, 26, 43, 47; **107**:4, 6, 10³, 13, 19, 23, 24, 26, 28, 32², 40; **108**:7, 9; **109**:4, 17, 26, 29²; 30; **110**:2, 3, 4; **111**:1², 2, 8; **112**:1, 2, 3, 4, 7, 8², 9; **113**:9; **115**:3, 8, 9, 10, 11; **116**:6, 9, 11, 14, 15, 18, 19²; **118**:5, 7, 8², 9², 10, 15, 23, 24, 26, 27²; **119**:3, 5, 11, 14², 16, 18, 25, 32², 40, 42, 43, 45, 47, 50, 52, 55, 66, 70, 74, 75, 81, 83, 89, 92, 109, 114, 118, 120², 147, 149, 162; **120**:1, 5; **122**:2; **123**:1; **124**:8; **125**:1, 4; **126**:4, 5; **127**:1², 2, 4²; **128**:1; **129**:5, 8; **130**:5, 7; **131**:3; **132**:6²; **133**:1; **134**:1, 2; **135**:2², 6², 17, 18, 21; **136**:23; **137**:4; **138**:7; **139**:5, 8, 13, 15², 16, 24²; **140**:2, 7, 11; **141**:4, 8, 10; **142**:T, 3, 5, 6; **143**:1, 3, 8, 9, 11, 12; **144**:2, 12, 13, 14; **145**:8, 17, 18, 21; **146**:3², 5, 6; **147**:5, 10², 11²; **148**:1, 6; **149**:1, 2², 4, 5, 6²; **150**:1²; **Pr 1**:10, 11, 14, 17, 18, 20², 21, 22, 26, 33; **2**:7, 13, 14², 15, 20, 21²; **3**:1, 4, 5, 6, 7, 12², 19, 23, 27; **4**:3, 11, 14; **5**:4, 14, 16², 18, 21; **6**:1, 8, 14, 15, 25; **7**:8, 9, 12²; **8**:20, 25, 27, 30, 31²; **9**:4, 6, 16, 17, 18; **10**:5, 8, 23², 30; **11**:4, 15, 20, 22², 28; **12**:4, 6, 20, 22, 24, 26, 28; **13**:10; **14**:12, 13², 19, 32, 33, 35; **15**:23; **16**:9, 11, 13, 19, 20, 21, 25; **17**:12, 16, 18², 23, 24; **18**:2², 9, 14; **19**:10, 18, 20, 21, 24; **20**:4, 15, 16, 20; **21**:1, 14², 16, 19, 20, 22; **22**:2, 5, 6, 13, 15, 18, 19, 22, 26, 29; **23**:21, 24, 28, 31, 32; **24**:7, 10, 15, 23, 31; **25**:6, 8, 11, 17, 19, 22; **26**:1², 5, 7, 8², 12, 13, 15, 16, 17, 19, 24, 26; **27**:13, 14, 22, 25; **28**:11, 23, 25, 26²; **29**:13, 20, 21, 25; **30**:4², 5, 19, 25, 26, 27, 28, 29; **31**:6, 11, 19, 21, 22; **Ecc 1**:1, 12, 16; **2**:1, 5, 7², 9², 10, 14², 15³, 16, 24; **3**:11², 13, 16², 17; **4**:14;

5:2², 4², 7, 8, 15, 17, 18, 19; **6**:4², 12; **7**:4², 9², 15³, 19, 22, 29; **8**:3, 8, 10, 15; **9**:1, 3², 6, 9, 10, 12², 14, 15; **10**:6, 16, 20²; **11**:3, 5, 6, 9; **12**:1², 5, 9, 12; **SS 1**:4; **2**:3, 12, 14², 15; **3**:3, 8; **4**:7; **5**:7, 12; **6**:2, 10, 11², 12; **7**:11, 12; **8**:5, 10, 11, 13²; **Isa 1**:5, 8², 11, 15, 21, 26, 29; **2**:2, 3, 5, 10, 11, 12, 17, 19², 20, 21, 22²; **3**:7², 13, 14, 18, 25; **4**:1², 2², 3³; **5**:2, 3, 8, 9, 11, 17, 21², 24, 25, 30; **6**:1, 6, 13²; **7**:9, 14, 18, 19³, 20, 21, 22, 23³; **8**:2, 7, 17, 18, 19³, 20, 21, 23; **9**:1³, 2², 4, 5², 14, 17, 18; **10**:5, 6, 7, 12, 17, 20, 24, 26, 27, 31; **11**:3, 10, 11, 15; **12**:1, 4; **13**:3, 5, 8², 9, 10, 14, 16, 20², 21, 22²; **14**:2, 9, 13, 15², 16, 18, 23, 25²; **16**:5³, 10; **17**:4, 5, 7, 9, 14, 18²; **19**:10, 14², 16, 18², 19³, 20, 21, 23, 24; **20**:1, 5², 6; **21**:3, 9, 13, 14; **22**:2, 5, 8², 9², 10, 14, 15, 16, 20, 21, 25; **23**:4, 5, 7, 15, 17; **24**:1, 2, 4², 9, 10, 14, 16², 23²; **25**:1, 4, 9², 10, 12, 15³, 18, 20, 21², 22³, 23; **25**:1, 4, 9⁴, 10, 12, 17, 18², 25; **26**:2, 6, 12², 14, 15, 17; **27**:1, 2, 4, 6, 12, 13⁴; **28**:4, 5, 6, 14, 16, 21, 25³, 29², 29:1², 4, 5, 6, 16, 17², 18; **30**:4, 9, 11, 12, 13², 16², 20², 21, 24; **31**:1², 7, 9²; **32**:1², 2, 10, 16², 18³; **33**:2, 7, 14, 17, 18², 24; **34**:1, 5², 6³, 16; **35**:6², 7, 8³, 9², 12, 19, 23², 25, 27², 30; **36**:1²; **38**:1, 3, 10, 11², 12, 12, 18²; **39**:2²; **40**:3², 7, 9, 10, 14, 16; **41**:2², 7, 9, 15², 18, 20, 21², 22, 23², 24, 25; **43**:3³, 4³, 9, 14², 19, 23, 24, 25; **45**:3, 13, 14, 19³, 23, 24, 25; **46**:7, 8; **47**:1, 5, 8, 9³, 10, 15; **48**:1², 10, 15, 16, 17; **49**:2², 3, 4², 12, 13³, 19, 21, 24, 26², 30²; **50**:10², 11²; **51**:3, 5, 7, 9², 10, 13, 14, 16², 20; **52**:6, 10, 12²; **53**:2, 9², 10; **54**:1, 3, 6, 8, 14; **55**:2, 12²; **56**:7; **57**:1, 2, 5, 6, 11, 15², 17², 19; **58**:4², 10², 11, 14; **59**:6, 8², 9, 12, 14, 17², 20, 21; **60**:9, 10², 11, 17², 18, 22; **61**:3, 6, 7², 8, 10; **62**:3², 4, 9; **63**:1³, 3², 4, 6², 9², 13; **64**:11; **65**:2, 3, 5, 6, 8³, 12, 14, 18², 19², 20, 21, 22, 23; **66**:2, 3, 4, 8³, 11, 17, 20³; **Jer 1**:1, 2, 5, 9, 14, 15, 16³; **2**:2, 5, 17, 23, 24², 27, 28, 30, 34²; **3**:2, 10², 10, 17, 18, 23, 25; **4**:2², 5², 7, 9, 11, 19, 20³, 22, 25, 26, 29; **5**:6, 13, 14, 17, 18, 19², 20, 22, 24, 26, 30, 31; **6**:1, 7, 8, 10, 11³, 12, 16, 23, 24, 26, 29; **7**:3, 4, 6, 7², 8, 10, 12, 14, 17², 23², 30², 31², 32, 34; **8**:7, 16, 18, 19, 22; **9**:2, 3, 6², 8, 9, 19, 21³; **10**:2, 5, 6, 7, 9, 13, 14, 18², 24; **11**:2², 6, 9, 14, 15², 20², 23; **12**:4², 5², 8, 12; **13**:4², 9, 11, 13, 14, 15, 20², 22², 23, 24; **14**:1, 5, 8², 9, 10, 13, 14, 15, 16², 19, 21³; **15**:4, 11, 14, 17, 20; **16**:2, 3, 6, 9², 19; **17**:3, 4, 5, 6³, 7², 11, 16, 18; **18**:4, 5, 8², 14, 17; **19**:2, 3, 4², 5; **20**:1, 2, 6, 9⁴, 16, 17, 18; **21**:2, 4, 7, 9, 11, 12, 13², 14; **22**:3², 6, 7³, 8, 10, 11, 13², 14², 17², 18², 19, 20, 22², 27, 30, 34, 35, 36, 40, 45²; **23**:1, 5², 6, 7, 9, 13, 17², 23, 24, 25², 27, 28, 31, 33, 34², 35, 39, 40, 42, 43², 51², 44², 51, 53, 56; **24**:1², 8², 10, 16, 18²; **25**:4, 10, 11, 22, 26, 27, 28, 31, 34², 35², 36², 37; **26**:1, 2², 7, 9², 11², 15², 16; **27**:1, 11, 15, 21, 22³; **28**:1⁴, 5, 7, 11², 13, 18, 19, 24², 25, 27; **29**:1, 4, 7², 10³, 19²; **30**:2², 3², 11², 16², 18, 20, 24²; **31**:1², 2, 6, 9, 10, 12, 14², 18², 19, 24², 30, 31, 32, 34, 35, 36, 37, 38, 39², 41, 42, 45, 46, 50, 51, 59, 60²; **32**:2, 8, 18, 19; **33**:14; **34**:5, 13, 18, 24, 26, 32, 34, 35, 36, 39, 40, 47, 56; **35**:8, 9, 14, 19, 25, 26; **36**:8, 14, 33, 37, 38, 39², 41, 42, 50; **37**:3, 7, 10, 17; **Hab 1**:4, 5, 14, 15², 16; **2**:8, 17, 18, 19, 20; **3**:2⁴, 7², 11, 12, 14, 17², 18²; **Zep 1**:4, 8, 11, 13, 18²; **2**:4, 7², 10, 11, 14, 15; **3**:2, 7, 11, 12, 13, 17, 19; **Hag 1**:1, 4, 6², 8, 15; **2**:3, 6, 9, 10, 12, 14, 15, 19; **Zec 1**:1, 7, 8, 11; **2**:1, 4, 7, 11, 12; **3**:3, 7, 9², 10; **4**:10; **5**:4, 7, 9, 11; **6**:5, 8, 14; **7**:1, 3, 5, 10; **8**:3, 4², 8, 11, 13, 18², 23; **9**:5, 6, 9, 11, 14, 15, 16²; **10**:1, 2, 3, 5, 7, 8, 9, 12²; **11**:8; **12**:5, 6², 11³, 13³, 4, 8²; **14**:3, 4, 5, 8², 10, 12², 15, 20², 13:3, 4, 8², 10, 11, 13, 18² 2:4, 7², 10, 11, 14, 15; **3**:2, 7, 11, 12, 13, 17, 19; **Mal 1**:1, 14; **2**:5, 6², 9, 11², 15², 16, 17; **3**:3, 4², 8, 10², 11, 16, 17²; **4**:2; **Mt 1**:17, 19, 20²; **2**:1², 2, 5², 6, 9, 12, 13, 16², 18, 19², 22², 23; **3**:1², 3, 6, 8, 12², 16², 19²; **4**:6, 12, 13², 16², 21, 23; **5**:3, 8, 12², 15, 16², 19², 22, 24, 28, 45; **6**:1, 2², 4², 5, 9, 10, 11², 17³, 18, 19, 20, 22, 24, 26², 27, 28, 31, 37, 39²; **9**:1², 2, 8, 11², 17², 19, 22, 23³, 25², 31; **7**:2, 3², 4, 11, 12, 15, 21, 22²; **8**:6, 10, 11, 14, 28, 32; **9**:4, 25, 33, 35; **10**:9, 17, 23, 27³, 28, 32, 33; **11**:1, 2, 8², 11, 16, 20, 21³, 22², 29; **12**:5², 18, 19, 21, 32², 35², 40², 44, 45, 50; **13**:2, 3, 10, 13, 14, 19, 24, 27, 30, 31, 32, 34, 35, 36, 40, 43, 44²; **14**:5³, 7, 33, 34; **15**:9, 33, 36; **16**:3, 13, 28; **17**:12, 19, 22, 24; **18**:1, 4, 5, 6², 10², 14², 18², 19, 20, 32, 34; **19**:21; **20**:1², 3, 4, 7, 21², 21:9², 11, 15, 18, 22, 28, 31², 33², 35, 36, 46; **23**:2, 6, 7, 9, 13, 21, 22², 30², 34, 39; **24**:5, 7, 14, 15, 16, 18, 19, 20, 26², 27, 30, 36, 37, 38², 40, 45², 47; **25**:4, 5, 10, 18, 21, 23, 25, 31², 35, 36, 39, 43², 44; **26**:3, 4², 13, 29, 52, 54, 55, 61, 64, 67, 69; **27**:1, 19, 24, 29², 40, 41, 42, 43, 44, 46, 50, 51, 59, 60²; **28**:18, 19; **Mk 1**:2, 3, 4, 9², 13, 14, 19, 23, 30, 33, 35, 39, 45; **2**:4, 8², 12, 25, 26; **3**:3, 5, 23, 27, 31, 34; **4**:1, 2, 11, 15, 19, 21, 28, 31, 32, 36, 38; **5**:3, 5, 6, 13, 14, 15, 20, 26, 29², 30, 34, 39, 40², 6², 8, 14, 17, 22, 25, 27, 29³, 32, 35, 39, 40, 47, 56; **7**:7, 9, 19, 25, 26; **8**:4, 14, 33, 37, 38²; **9**:3, 17, 33, 36, 37, 38, 39², 41, 42, 50; **10**:10, 16, 21, 30², 37; **11**:1, 11, 13, 14, 20, 22, 24, 25²; **12**:1, 11, 13, 14, 22, 25², 26², 32, 35², 36, 37, 38, 39², 41, 42; **13**:6, 8, 9, 14, 16, 18, 24, 25, 27³, 34, 35; **14**:3, 6, 13², 14, 15, 18, 19, 21², 22², 25, 30, 34, 44; **15**:8, 9, 25, 49, 58, 66; **15**:1², 7, 21, 29, 31, 34, 38, 39, 41, 46²; **16**:5, 17²; **Lk 1**:5, 6, 7, 15, 17, 18, 19, 21, 22, 24, 25, 26², 36², 39, 41, 42, 44, 47, 51, 69, 75, 79²; **80²**; **2**:1, 4, 7³, 8, 11, 12², 14, 16, 19, 23, 24², 27, 28, 29, 31, 34, 43, 44, 46, 49, 51, 52²; **3**:1, 2, 4², 5, 8, 15, 17, 20, 22²; **4**:1, 5, 11, 14, 15, 20, 21, 24², 25, 26², 27², 28, 29, 31, 34, 44, 46, 49, 51, 52²; **5**:7, 12, 19, 22, 25, 35; **6**:1, 8, 9², 10², 12, 14, 16, 18², 20, 21; **Php 1**:1, 4, 9², 10², 12, 14, 16, 18², 20, 21; **7**:10³, 13³, 17, 20, 25, 26, 30, 37; **11**:1, 7, 13, 22, 25, 26, 27, 33², 37, 43², 45, 46, 49, 52, 54; **12**:34, 13, 15, 27, 33, 38, 42, 44, 45, 52, 54; **13**:4², 6, 10, 19², 26, 28, 29, 33, 35; **14**:1, 2, 3, 10, 15, 21, 23, 33; **15**:4, 7², 10², 13, 14², 25, 28; **16**:2, 5, 8, 11, 15², 19², 23²;

24³, 25²; **17**:4, 6, 7, 13, 15, 24, 26², 27, 28, 31, 34; **18**:2, 3, 22, 30²; **19**:15, 17, 20, 21, 22, 27, 37, 38³, 39, 43; **20**:1, 20, 21, 26², 31, 34, 35³, 37, 42, 46³; **21**:2, 3, 4, 8, 11, 13, 21³, 22, 23², 25², 27, 38; 30, 37, 44, 53, 55, 56, 70; **23**:5, 7, 11, 14, 19, 22, 26, 43, 45, 53⁴, 55, 56; **24**:1, 4, 5, 6, 18, 19, 22, 27, 29, 38, 43, 44, 47, 49; **Jn 1**:1, 2, 4, 5, 10, 12, 23², 45, 47; **2**:1, 11², 14, 19, 20, 23², 25; **3**:3, 14, 15, 16, 18², 24, 35, 36; **4**:2, 5, 14, 20, 21, 23, 24², 39, 44, 45²; 46², 47; **5**:2², 6, 7, 26², 33², 35; **6**:6, 10, 24, 29, 31, 35, 40, 49, 53, 55, 56²; 59²; **7**:1, 4, 5, 9, 10, 28, 31², 37, 38, 39, 45, 48²; **8**:2², 3, 4, 5, 6, 12, 17, 20, 21, 24, 25², 26, 30, 35, 38, 44, 48; **9**:3, 5, 7, 34, 35, 36, 37; **10**:1, 5, 9, 23², 24, 25, 34, 38², 40, 42²; **11**:4, 17, 19, 24, 25, 26, 31, 33, 43, 45, 48, 56; **12**:2, 11, 13, 21, 23, 25, 35, 36, 37², 42, 44³, 46²; **13**:1, 21, 26, 17, 18², 19, 24², 25, 27; **14**:2³, 3, 4, 9, 12², 14, 18, 23², 30, 37, 44, 53, 55, 56, 70; **15**:2, 4, 5², 6, 7², 9, 10², 11, 16, 18, 25; **16**:2, 8, 9², 10, 11, 16, 17, 19, 23², 24, 26², 33³; **17**:5, 11², 13, 20, 21³, 23², 26³; **18**:16, 20², 22, 26, 37², 40; **19**:2, 3, 13, 17, 18, 19², 20², 41²; **20**:5², 12, 16, 25, 26, 30², 31; **21**:2, 4, 6, 8; **Ac 1**:1, 5, 8², 10, 11, 14, 15, 17, 19², 20²; **2**:1, 4, 5, 6, 8², 11, 14, 15, 17, 18, 19, 26, 28, 38, 44, 46²; **3**:1, 6, 11, 16, 17, 21; **4**:2, 3, 5, 12, 16, 17, 18², 19, 24², 25, 27, 32; **5**:7, 10, 12, 14, 18, 20, 25², 28, 34, 37², 38, 40², 42; **6**:1², 2, 7, 15; **7**:2², 4, 6², 7, 12, 14, 16, 17, 20, 22, 30², 33, 34, 36², 38², 39, 41², 42², 44, 45, 48; **8**:3, 5, 8, 9, 14, 21, 22, 25, 27, 28, 33, 40; **9**:2, 10², 12, 13, 19, 20, 21, 22, 24, 25², 27², 28², 31², 32, 35, 36, 37, 38, 42, 43; **10**:1, 2, 3, 4, 24, 25², 30, 32, 33, 37, 39², 43, 46, 48; **11**:5², 13, 17, 19, 29; **12**:4, 5, 7, 18; **13**:1, 5, 13, 17, 18, 19, 22, 23³, 24, 27, 33, 34, 36, 41, 43, 51; **14**:8², 11², 15, 16, 17, 21, 23², 25; **15**:15, 21², 23, 35, 36, 38², 16:3, 4, 5², 6, 14, 15, 18, 22, 24², 29, 31, 32, 34, 36; **17**:5³, 13, 16, 17², 22², 24², 28, 30; **18**:4, 6, 8, 9, 10, 13, 17, 18, 23, 25, 26, 28; **19**:4², 6, 7, 9, 10, 13, 17², 20², 24, 27, 29, 32, 33, 34, 39, 40²; **20**:2, 3³, 5, 19, 24, 29, 31, 34, 39, 40; **22**:2, 3³, 5, 19, 24, 29; **23**:1, 6², 11², 13, 21³, 33, 35; **24**:2³, 3, 4, 9, 12², 14, 15, 18²; 20, 21, 24, 27; **25**:1, 17, 23, 24²; **26**:4², 6, 10², 11, 14, 18, 20³, 21, 26, 28; **27**:3, 5, 12², 25, 30, 33, 35, 40, 44²; **28**:8², 10, 12², 17, 23, 30; **Ro 1**:2, 7, 9, 10, 13, 17, 24, 27²; **2**:7, 13, 19, 20; **3**:1², 2, 5, 20, 22, 25², 26; **4**:1, 2, 11, 12, 17², 18, 19, 20, 24; **5**:2², 3, 8, 11, 12, 13, 17, 21; **6**:2, 4, 5², 11², 12, 19⁴, 21, 23; **7**:4, 5, 6², 8, 13², 17², 18², 20, 23²; **8**:1², 3⁴, 5, 9, 10, 11², 17², 18, 19, 20, 22, 24, 26², 27, 28, 31, 37, 39⁴; **9**:1², 2, 8, 11², 17², 19, 22, 23³, 25³, 31; **10**:5, 6, 7, 11, 12, 16, 17, 20; **11**:2, 14, 17², 19, 22, 23³, 25²; **12**:1, 3, 5, 6, 10, 11, 12, 16, 17, 20; **13**:3, 9, 13⁴; **14**:5, 13, 14², 15, 17, 18; **15**:4, 7, 12, 13, 14, 17², 18, 23, 25, 26, 27, 29, 30, 31², 16:1, 2², 3, 5, 7², 8, 9, 10, 11², 12², 13, 17², 22, 23², 25²; **2Co 1**:1, 4², 6, 7², 8, 9, 11, 12³, 14², 17², 19, 20, 21, 22, 23; **2**:3, 9, 10, 11, 14², 17³; **3**:5, 7, 10, 14; **4**:2, 6², 7, 8, 10, 17², 18; **5**:1², 4, 6, 9, 10, 12⁴, 13, 16, 17, 19, 21; **6**:1, 2², 4³, 5², 7⁴, 14, 15; **7**:2, 3, 4³, 9², 11², 13, 16; **8**:2, 4, 5, 7², 10, 14, 19, 21², 22³, 24; **9**:2, 3², 5, 7, 8², 11², 12, 13, 14; **10**:3, 10, 11², 14, 16², 17²; **11**:5, 6, 9, 10, 18², 25, 28², 30; **13**:1, 6, 9, 12²; **14**:2, 4, 5², 6, 7², 10, 12, 13, 14, 18, 19², 20², 21, 22², 24; **15**:2, 15, 17, 18, 19², 23, 28, 31, 32, 41, 43⁴, 52², 54, 58²; **16**:2, 11, 13, 14, 15, 16, 19², 21, 24; **2Co 1**:1, 4², 6, 7², 8, 9, 11, 12³, 14², 17², 19, 20, 21, 22, 23; **2**:3, 9, 10, 11, 14², 17³; **3**:5, 7, 10, 14; **4**:2, 6², 7, 8, 10, 17², 18; **5**:1², 4, 6, 9, 10, 12⁴, 13, 16, 17, 19, 21; **6**:1, 2², 4³, 5², 7⁴, 14, 15; **7**:2, 3, 4³, 9², 11², 13, 16; **8**:2, 4, 5, 7², 10, 14, 19, 21², 22³, 24; **9**:2, 3², 5, 7, 8², 11², 12, 13, 14; **10**:3, 10, 11², 14, 16², 17², 18, 20², 23, 25, 26¹⁰, 32², 33²; **12**:2³, 3, 7, 9, 10⁴, 15, 18, 19², 21; **13**:3, 4², 5², 10, 11; **Gal 1**:2, 13, 14, 16, 22²; **2**:2², 4, 5, 8², 13, 14², 16², 17, 20³; **3**:8, 10, 14, 15, 18, 22, 24, 26, 28; **4**:3, 19², 23, 25, 29, 30; **5**:6, 7, 10, 11, 13, 14, 17, 25; **6**:1, 2, 4, 6, 9, 14; **Eph 1**:1², 3², 4³, 5, 6, 7², 9, 10, 11², 12², 13², 15, 16, 18², 20², 21², 23²; **2**:1, 2², 4, 5, 6², 7⁴, 10² 11, 12², 13, 15², 16, 17², 21², 22²; **3**:4, 5, 6², 9, 10, 11, 12², 15, 16, 17², 17², 18², 19, 21³, 23, 24, 26, 28, 32; **5**:5, 8, 9, 12, 19, 20, 24, 28; **6**:1, 4, 9², 10², 12, 14, 16, 18², 20, 21; **Php 1**:1, 4, 9², 10², 12, 14, 16, 18², 20, 21; **2**:2, 3, 6, 7, 8, 10, 12², 13, 15⁴, 16, 19, 20, 22, 24, 29; **3**:1, 3², 4, 5, 9² 10³, 14, 17, 19, 20; **4**:1, 2, 3², 4, 6, 7, 9, 10, 11², 14², 15, 16², 18, 23; **Col 1**:2, 4, 5², 6, 8, 10⁴, 12², 14, 16, 17, 18, 19, 20, 21, 22, 23², 24³, 25, 27, 28, 29; **2**:2³, 3, 5³, 6, 7², 9², 10, 11², 12², 13², 17, 18, 23; **3**:3, 4, 7², 10²,

11, 14, 15, 16², 17², 18, 20, 22; **4:**1, 3, 5, 7, 12², 15, 16², 17¹, 18; **1Th 1:**1, 2, 3, 6, 7, 8²; **2:**2³, 9, 13, 14², 16², 17², 19²; **3:**1, 2², 4, 5, 7, 8, 9², 10, 13; **4:**1³, 4, 5, 6, 10, 14, 16, 17²; **5:**2, 4, 11, 12, 13³, 18²; **2Th 1:**1, 4, 7, 10, 11, 12²; **2:**3, 4, 9², 10, 12, 13, 14, 17; **3:**4, 6, 9, 12, 14², 16, 17²; **1Ti 1:**2, 3, 13, 14, 16, 18; **2:**2², 6, 8, 11, 15; **3:**8, 11², 13², 15, 16²; **4:**1, 6, 10, 12², 15, 16; **5:**3, 5², 10, 15, 16², 21, 22², 25; **6:**4², 12, 13, 15, 16, 17³, 18, 19, 21; **2Ti 1:**1, 3, 5³, 6, 8, 9, 13, 14, 15, 17, 18²; **2:**1², 2, 4, 10, 16, 20, 25; **3:**1, 9, 11, 12², 14, 15, 16; **4:**1², 2, 5, 8, 11, 20²; **Tit 1:**4, 5², 13, 15; **2:**1, 2³, 3, 7², 9, 10, 12; **3:**3, 8, 14, 15; **Phm 1:**2, 4, 5, 6², 8, 10, 13², 16, 20², 22, 23; **Heb 1:**1², 2, 3, 7, 10; **2:**8, 10, 12, 13, 14, 15, 17³; **3:**1, 2, 5², 8², 11, 14, 15, 17²; **4:**3, 4, 5, 6, 8, 13, 16; **5:**1, 6², 10, 12, 17; **6:**1, 4, 7, 8², 9, 11, 18, 20; **7:**8², 10, 11², 14, 17, 23; **8:**1, 2, 5, 6, 10; **9:**2, 5, 7, 16, 17, 21², 22, 24; **10:**7, 16, 22, 25, 32², 34, 37; **11:**7, 9³, 12, 20, 34, 36, 37², 38³; **12:**4, 10, 14, 22, 23; **13:**3, 18, 21; **Jas 1:**8, 9², 10, 11, 21, 23, 25, 27; **2:**1, 2², 5², 8, 17, 25²; **3:**2³, 9, 13, 14, 18; **4:**5, 11; **5:**3, 5², 10², 13, 14, 15; **1Pe 1:**1, 2, 3, 4, 5, 6, 7, 8, 11, 14, 15, 17, 20²; **2:**2, 6³, 11, 21, 22, 24; **3:**1, 4, 5, 7, 8, 15, 16, 18, 19, 20³, 22²; **4:**1², 3², 6², 10, 11, 13; **5:**1, 5, 6, 9, 10, 12, 13, 14; **2Pe 1:**2, 4², 8², 12, 13, 19² 21; **2:**3, 8, 11, 12, 13², 14, 18, 20, 22; **3:**2, 3, 9, 10, 11, 12, 13, 15, 16², 18; **1Jn 1:**5, 6, 7², 8, 10; **2:**1, 4, 5², 6, 8, 9², 10², 11², 14, 15², 16, 24³, 27², 28³, 3, 4, 5, 6, 9, 14, 15, 17², 18, 19, 23, 24³; **4:**2, 3, 4² 12², 13², 15², 16³, 17², 18²; **5:**8, 10², 11, 13, 14, 20²; **2Jn 1:**1, 2, 3, 4, 6², 7, 9², 11; **3Jn 1:**1, 3, 4, 5, 6; **Jude 1:**2, 4, 6, 7, 8, 11, 16, 18, 20², 21; **Rev 1:**3, 4, 9², 10, 13, 15, 16², 20; **2:**1², 6, 7, 8, 10, 12, 13², 18, 24; **3:**1, 2, 4², 5, 7, 12, 14, 18, 20; **4:**1², 2⁴, 6³; **5:**1, 2, 3, 6, 12, 13², 6:**1, 5, 10, 13², 18², 19², **7:**2², 9², 10, 13, 14, 15; **8:**1, 9, 13², **9:**10, 11², 17, 19²; **10:**1, 2, 6³, 7, 8, 9, 10; **11:**3, 8, 12, 13, 15, 19; **12:**1, 2, 3, 4, 7, 8, 10, 12, 14; **13:**6, 8, 13, 14; **14:**5, 6, 7, 9, 10, 13, 14, 15, 17, 18, 20; **15:**1, 5, 6; **16:**3, 5², 10, 16; **17:**3, 4², 8; **18:**4, 7, 8, 10, 16, 17, 19, 22², 23²; **19:**1, 13², 14, 17³; **20:**1, 6, 8², 12, 13², 15; **21:**8, 10, 16, 22, 27; **22:**3, 7, 18, 19³.

IS (7214)

Ge 2:4, 11², 12, 13, 14², 18, 23; **3:**3, 13, 17; **4:**6, 7³, 9, 13, 24; **5:**1; **6:**3, 9, 13, 17; **8:**17, 21; **9:**12, 17; **10:**1, 9², 12², 11:**9, 10, 27; **12:**12, 19²; **13:**9; **14:**2, 7, 8, 17; **15:**2; **16:**5, 6, 7, 14²; **17:**4, 10, 12, 13; **18:**9, 12, 14, 19, 20, 21, 28; **19:**13, 14, 15, 20², 22, 31³, 37, 38; **20:**2, 3, 5², 6, 7, 11, 12², 13, 15, 16; **21:**12, 13, 17, 22, 29; **22:**7, 14, 20; **23:**2, 9, 11, 15², 19; **24:**5, 8, 23, 50, 51, 65²; **25:**12, 19², 22, 30, 32; **26:**7², 9², 24; **27:**11, 18, 22, 27, 42, 45; **28:**16, 17³, **29:**6², 7², 21, 25, 26, 32; **30:**3, 33², 31:**5, 32, 36, 43, 48², 50², 51² 52²; **32:**2, 4, 6, 18, 20, 26, 27, 30; **33:**10, 17², **34:**10, 14; **35:**6, 10, 19, 27; **36:**1², 8, 9, 19, 24; **37:**2, 10, 14, 27, 32, 33; **38:**13, 14, 21, 24², 26, 29; **39:**9, 19; **40:**8, 12, 18; **41:**25, 26, 28², 32, 38, 39, 51, 52²; **42:**2, 9, 12, 13², 14, 15, 28², 30, 32², 33², 36², 38²; **43:**3, 5, 7, 10, 27², 28, 29, 32; **44:**5, 9, 10, 15, 20, 26², 30², 34; **45:**3, 9, 12, 23, 26², 28; **46:**33; **47:**3, 4, 6, 15, 16, 18², 22, 23; **48:**1, 7, 18, 22; **49:**10, 14, 15², 21, 22, 27, 28; **50:**11², 17, 20, 26, 20; **Ex 1:**16², 22; **2:**6, 20; **3:**5, 12, 13, 14, 15, 22; **4:**2, 5, 11, 14, 22²; **5:**1, 2, 8, 10, 16, 17, 22; **7:**2, 14, 17²; **8:**1, 10, 19, 20, 26; **9:**1, 13, 14, 19, 27, 29; **10:**3, 5, 7, 26; **11:**4; **12:**2, 3, 14, 19², 26², 27, 29; **13:**7, 9, 15; **14:**25; **15:**1, 2², 3², 11², 21, 23², 26; **16:**1, 5, 15², 16², 17; **17:**7, 15; **18:**11, 14, 16, 17, 18; **19:**5, 13; **20:**10, 11, 12, 22²; **21:**23, 30²; **22:**2³, 7, 8, 9, 10³, 11², 14², 15, 16, 25, 27; **23:**15, 21; **24:**2, 8; **25:**39; **26:**6, 12³, 16, 30, 35; **27:**1, 5, 7, 9, 11, 21²; **28:**7, 8, 12, 17, 28²; **29:**1, 9, 14, 18, 22, 23, 28² 30, 32, 34², 38, 42; **30:**2, 10, 12², 21, 23, 31, 32, 35; **31:**14, 15², 32:**17, 18³, 26, 27; **33:**13, 21; **34:**3, 9, 10, 14; **35:**2, 4, 5², 14, 36:**6, 27; **38:**26; **Lev 1:**3², 4, 5, 6, 8, 9³, 10², 11, 12², 13², 14², 16, 17²; **2:**1², 3, 4, 5², 6, 7², 10, 15; **3:**1², 2, 3, 5, 6, 7, 8, 9², 12², 13, 14², 16, 17; **4:**2², 4², 6, 7, 8, 10, 12², 13³, 16, 18, 21, 22², 23, 24², 27², 28, 29, 30, 31, 32, 33³, 35; **5:**2², 3, 4, 5, 7, 8², 9², 11², 12², 15², 17², 18, 19; **6:**2, 6, 9, 11², 12, 15, 16, 17, 18, 20², 22³, 23², 25, 27, 30; **7:**1, 2³, 4, 5, 6, 12, 13, 14, 15, 16², 18², 20, 29, 30², 37; **8:**5, 35; **9:**6, 7, 10:**3, 7, 9, 12, 13, 17; **11:**4, 5, 6, 7, 12, 26, 32, 34², 36, 38, 41², 42; **12:**2, 3, 6, 8; **13:**2, 3², 4², 5³, 6², 8², 10³, 11³, 13², 15, 17, 20², 21³, 22², 23²,

25², 26³, 27³, 28³, 30³, 31², 32², 33, 34, 35, 36², 37³, 39², 40², 41, 42, 43², 44², 47, 49², 50, 51³, 52, 54, 55², 56, 57, 58; **14:**2, 3, 6, 7, 40, 41, 44³, 46, 48, 49, 51, 53, 57; **15:**2², 8, 12, 13², 15, 23, 26, 28, 30, 31, 33; **16:**3², 4², 5, 6, 7, 8, 11, 12, 13, 14, 16², 17, 18, 21, 23², 29, 31², 32², 34²; **17:**2, 5, 6, 7, 11², 14³, 18:**6, 7, 11, 12, 13, 14, 15, 17, 18, 22, 23, 24; **19:**7² 8, 20, 22; **20:**12, 13, 14, 17², 18, 23, 24; **21:**3, 11, 18, 20, 21; **22:**3, 4, 11, 13, 23, 27²; **23:**3², 11², 14, 20, 21, 27, 28²; **25:**4, 5, 10, 12³, 13, 15, 16², 23, 25, 27, 30² 33³, 34, 35, 40², 50, 52, 53, 54; **26:**17, 36, 37; **27:**4, 5, 6, 7, 8, 9², 11², 12, 14, 16, 17, 18, 21, 23, 27², 28, 30; **Nu 1:**4, 51²; **2:**3, 5, 7, 10, 12, 14, 18, 20, 22, 25, 27, 29, 34²; **3:**1; **4:**4, 5, 7³, 9, 15, 16², 19, 24, 27, 28, 31, 32, 33; **5:**2, 6², 8, 12, 13³, 14³, 15², 21, 22, 23, 25², 26², 27, 28, 29, 30²; **6:**4, 5, 7, 8, 11², 13³, 14, 16, 17², 18², 19, 21, 23; **7:**11²; **8:**4, 11, 14, 16, 19², 24, 25; **9:**13, 16; **10:**3, 4, 5, 8, 9, 11², 21, 23, 30³; **11:**13, 15², 24², 28²; **12:**6, 7, 8²; **13:**18, 19, 20²; **14:**3, 7, 8, 9², 13, 14², 18², 19², 23², 24, 31; **19:**2, 3, 4, 5, 6, 9², 13, 14², 18², 19, 20, 21, 20:**5, 14; **21:**5, 8, 13, 14, 27, 30; **22:**4, 16, 32; **23:**19, 21³, 23; **24:**21²; **26:**53, 54, 55, 56; **27:**7, 11, 18, 21; **28:**3, 6, 7, 8, 13, 14², 15, 16, 17, 24, 28; **29:**1; **30:**1, 15; **31:**21, 49; **32:**8, 22, 29; **33:**2; **35:**16, 17, 18, 21, 30²; **36:**5³, 6, 7, 9; **Dt 1:**1, 14, 16, 20, 25³, 30; **2:**29; **3:**9, 11, 14, 16, 20, 24, 26; **4:**1, 6, 7³, 8, 21, 24, 31, 35², 38; **5:**9², 24³, 44, 31, 35², 36², 5, 6, 7, 9, 7; **6:**4, 15², 18, 20, 24; **7:**5, 9², 21²; **8:**7, 13, 18²; **9:**3², 4², 5, 6²; **10:**9, 15, 17², 21, 23², 25, 28; **11:**10, 11, 12, 17, 31; **12:**9, 10, 11, 14, 18², 20, 24²; **15:**2, 9, 12², 16:**18, 21²; **17:**2, 4², 5, 6³, 8, 9; **19:**4, 6²; **20:**5²; **22:**8, 9, 18², 19², 26²; **24:**7, 18²; **25:**15; **27:**4, 9, 15; **28:**3, 5, 6², 18², 19², 23², 24, 31; **29:**18²; **30:**11², 12, 13, 14², 20; **31:**14, 17; **32:**4², 6², 9, 21, 28, 31, 33, 35², 36², 39, 51; **33:**1, 3, 17, 20, 22, 23², 24, 27², 28², 29, 34:**4, 6; **Jos 1:**2, 11, 13, 15; **2:**11, 19²; **3:**10², 15; **4:**5, 24; **5:**4, 15; **6:**17, 26; **7:**2, 12², 13³, 15, 25; **12:**2; **13:**2, 6, 12, 15, 24, 29², 32, 33; **15:**4, 5, 8, 9, 10, 12, 13, 20, 25, 49, 54, 60; **16:**2; **17:**1, 11, 15, 16; **18:**5, 7, 13, 14, 28, 20:**4, 6², 7; **21:**11; **22:**19, 26, 27, 31, 34; **23:**6; **24:**2, 18, 19², **Jdg 1:**2, 26; **4:**14, 20; **5:**9, 28²; **6:**8, 12, 13, 15, 17, 24, 31, 37², 38; **7:**1; **8:**21², 35; **9:**2, 3, 18, 28², 37, 38²; **11:**10, 13:**5, 8, 12, 17, 18; **14:**18²; **15:**19; **16:**2, 15; **18:**9, 12², 19², 19:**9, 10, 23, 24; **20:**9; **21:**6, 11², 19, 23; **Ru 1:**13, 15; **2:**5, 6, 19, 20²; **3:**2, 4, 10, 12², 13, 18; **4:**3, 11, 15, 18; **1Sa 1:**15, 22; **2:**1, 2³, 3, 9, 14, 24, 27, 31, 35; **3:**9, 10, 18²; **4:**4, 14; **5:**5, 7; **6:**18; **8:**7, 11; **9:**6², 7, 11, 12, 17, 18, 19, 20, 21, 24; **10:**2², 5, 7, 11², 12², 18, 24; **11:**5, 7, 9; **12:**5³, 6, 13, 16, 17, 23², 29², 32; **16:**11², 12, 15, 18³, 19; **17:**9, 26, 27, 28, 46, 47², 55, 56; **18:**17, 18, 22, 23; **19:**2, 14, 19, 24, 29²; **20:**1³, 3, 5, 6, 7², 12, 13, 18, 21, 23, 26, 29², 42; **21:**1, 2, 4, 9⁴, 14; **22:**8², 14, 23²; **23:**19, 22, 23, 28; **24:**11, 14, 23²; **25:**6, 7, 10², 17², 25², 29, 41; **26:**1, 15, 16, 17², 18, 22; **27:**11, 11; **28:**7², 14; **29:**3, 10; **30:**20, 24, 2Sa 1:**18; **2:**7, 20², 3:**12, 24; **4:**2, 8, 10; **5:**8²; **6:**2², 8; **7:**3, 5, 8, 13, 18, 19, 22², 23, 26²; **9:**1³, 3⁴, 8; **10:**3; **11:**15, 21, 24; **12:**7, 9, 11², 18, 19², 21, 23; **13:**20, 28, 30, 32, 33; **14:**5², 16, 17, 30; **15:**2, 3, 10, 31; **16:**2, 3², 4, 10, 11², 17²; **17:**2, 7, 8, 9, 11, 12², 13², 14, 16, 17, 18, 21, 22², 23; **18:**13, 18, 20, 25, 28, 29, 32; **19:**1, 2, 8, 9, 11, 27, 35², 37, 42; **20:**11, 19, 21; **21:**1², 22:**2, 3², 4², 31³, 32², 33, 48; **23:**4, 5, 7; **24:**12, 14; **1Ki 1:**16, 21, 23, 27, 35, 51², 52; **2:**22, 30, 38, 42; **3:**8, 9, 22⁴, 23⁴, 27; **5:**4; **6:**3; **7:**28, 37; **8:**19², 21, 23, 24, 28, 31, 35, 38, 46, 60²; **9:**8, 9, 15, 21², 26; **10:**6; **11:**11, 26, 31; **14:**2; **12:**9, 10, 24², 28; **13:**2, 3, 21, 26, 31; **14:**2, 5², 7, 10, 13², 14; **17:**14, 23, 24; **18:**7, 8, 10, 11, 14, 17, 21², 24², 27³, 39², 41, 43, 44; **19:**7, 11; **20:**2, 5, 7, 13, 14, 18, 28², 32², 39, 40, 42²; **21:**2², 7, 14, 15, 18, 22:**7, 8, 11, 27, 32, 33, 48; **2Ki 1:**3², 4, 6², 12, 13; **3:**11², 16, 17, 18; **4:**1², 4, 6, 7, 9, 14, 26², 30, 43, 5:**3, 8, 15, 18, 21, 26², 6:**1, 11, 12, 13², 19² 32²; **7:**1, 4, 9, 20; **8:**5², 12; **9:**3, 6, 11, 16, 17², 18³, 19³, 20, 21, 22, 23, 27; **10:**6, 11²; **11:**14; **12:**9, 10, 24², 28; **13:**2, 3, 21, 26, 31; **14:**4, 11; **16:**14,

25², 30, 32, 34; **17:**1², 2, 4, 7, 12, 16, 20², 21, 24; **19:**3, 13; **21:**10, 11, 13, 24; **22:**1, 5, 10, 13; **23:**24; **25:**1; **27:**1; **28:**6, 7², 18, 20²; **29:**1³, 5, 11³; **2Ch 1:**10, 11; **2:**4, 5, 6, 14²; **5:**13; **6:**9², 11, 14, 15, 19, 22, 26, 29, 36; **7:**3, 13, 21, 22; **8:**8²; **9:**5; **10:**9, 10; **11:**4²; **12:**5, 6; **13:**8, 10, 12²; **14:**7, 11; **15:**2²; **18:**6, 7², 10, 26, 31; **19:**2, 3, 6, 7², 20:**12, 15², 20; **21:**12, 14²; **23:**4, 6; **24:**20; **25:**4², 7; **26:**18; **28:**13, 29:**9, 30:**9, 18, 19; **31:**10, 20; **32:**7, 8², 10, 11; **33:**13; **34:**21⁴, 23, 24, 26; **35:**3, 12, 21³, 26; **36:**23; **Ezr 1:**2, 3; **3:**2, 4, 11²; **4:**11, 13, 14, 15²; **5:**6, 8², 11; **6:**3, 9, 11, 18²; **7:**11, 14, 15; **8:**22²; **9:**7, 11, 13; **10:**2, 4, 13, 14, 23; **Ne 1:**3, 6; **2:**4, 19; **4:**10²; **5:**9; **6:**6², 7, 8; **7:**3; **8:**9, 10², 11, 15; **9:**5, 6², 18; **10:**34², 36, 37, 38; **13:**11, 17; **Est 1:**1, 19², 20; **2:**3, 13; **3:**7, 8²; **4:**11, 16²; **5:**3², 6, 7; **6:**4, 5, 6, 9², 11², 13; **7:**2², 3², 5, 6, 8; **8:**5; **9:**12², 19, 24; **Job 1:**8²; **2:**3²; **3:**3, 19, 20, 23²; **5:**7, 17, 24, 27; **6:**6², 12, 29, 30; **7:**5², 7, 9, 17; **8:**3, 11, 14, 16, 18²; **9:**2, 4², 9, 19³, 22²; **10:**13, 22; **11:**2, 9, 14, 18; **12:**10, 12, 15, 14:**1, 4, 7², 10², 18, 20; **15:**14, 16, 22, 23, 27, 31; **16:**6, 16, 17, 19², 20; **17:**1, 7, 12, 13, 15; **18:**4, 5, 7, 10, 12², 14, 15, 18, 21²; **19:**4, 7, 17, 29; **20:**5, 7, 12, 21, 26, 29; **21:**4, 9, 15, 16, 17, 19, 28, 30², 32², 33, 34; **22:**4, 5, 10, 11, 12, 30; **23:**2², 8, 9, 15; **24:**9², 14, 17, 18, 25; **25:**5, 6², 26:**2, 6; **27:**8, 13, 14, 18, 19, 21; **28:**1², 2², 5, 14², 18, 21, 28²; **30:**15, 31; **31:**2, 3, 12; **32:**6, 8, 9²; **33:**12, 23², 25², 26; **34:**4², 7, 12, 18, 22, 29², 30, 31, 33, 36, 37, 39, 38:**3, 7², 9, 16, 18, 41²; **9², 10², 16, 24, 33, 34; **42:**3, 7, 8; **Ps 1:**1, 2, 3; **5:**9²; **6:**3, 5; **7:**3, 4, 10, 11, 14; **8:**1, 4, 9, 9, 16, 10:**4, 5, 7, 16, 18; **11:**4², 7; **12:**4, 8²; **14:**1² 3, 5, 6; **15:**2²; **16:**3, 8, 9; **17:**2, 14; **18:**2³, 3, 30³, 31², 32, 47; **19:**3², 5, 6, 7, 9, 11²; **21:**1, 5; **22:**11², 15; **23:**1²; **24:**1, 4, 6, 8, 10²; **25:**3, 5, 8, 9, 11, 12, 21; **26:**3; **27:**1², 4; **28:**7, 8; **29:**3², 10³; **31:**4, 14, 19, 20; **32:**1, 2; **33:**1², 4, 5, 12², 16, 17, 18, 20; **34:**8² 16, 18; **35:**10; **36:**1², 4, 6, 7, 9; **37:**13, 30, 31, 37, 39; **38:**3, 7², 9; **39:**4², 5², 6², 7, 11², 12², 13, 20; **40:**4, 7, 8; **41:**1², 13; **42:**3, 6, 8, 10; **44:**1, 4, 5, 7², 8², 15, 19, 20, 24, 28; **45:**1, 5², 6², 9, 11, 14, 18³, 19, 21³, 22; **46:**9², 10, 13; **47:**4², 8, 10, 13, 14, 15², 47:**4², 8, 20, 22, 25; **50:**1², 8², 12², 19³, 28, 34, 35; **51:**5, 7, 13², 19⁴, 30, 31, 33³, 36, 48, 56, 57, 58², 59; **52:**28; **La 1:**1, 2, 4, 12², 16², 17, 18, 20, 21, 22; **2:**4, 5, 9, 11, 12, 13, 15, 16²; **3:**17, 18, 20, 23, 24, 25², 26, 27², 32, 38; **4:**6, 5:**8, 10, 15; **Eze 2:**4; **3:**1, 11, 27; **5:**5², 7, 8; **6:**3, 11, 12²; **7:**2, 3, 5², 7², 9, 10, 12, 14, 15, 23²; **8:**6, 17; **9:**9³; **11:**3, 5³, 7², 8, 16, 17; **12:**10, 19, 22, 23, 27; **13:**3, 8, 10², 11, 12, 13, 15, 18, 20; **14:**4, 6, 9, 21; **15:**2, 3, 4², 5, 6; **16:**3, 19, 34, 36, 59; **17:**3, 9, 10, 19, 22; **18:**4², 5², 9, 19, 20, 21, 24, 25², 27, 29²; **19:**13, 14³; **20:**3, 5, 27, 29, 30, 39, 47; **21:**3, 7, 9, 11², 12², 14, 15², 16, 22, 24, 28; **22:**3, 19, 22, 25, 26, 28; **23:**4², 22, 28, 32, 35, 37, 39, 43², 45, 46; **24:**3, 6, 7, 9, 11, 13, 21; **25:**3, 6, 8, 12, 13, 15, 16; **26:**2, 3, 7, 15, 19; **27:**3; **28:**2, 6, 12, 22, 25; **29:**3², 8, 9, 13, 19; **30:**2, 3², 6, 9, 10, 13, 22; **31:**10, 15, 18; **32:**3, 11, 16, 27², 30; **34:**2, 10, 11, 12, 17², 19, 20, 25, 27; **34:**2, 10, 11, 12, 17, 18², 20, 25, 27; **35:**3, 14, 15; **36:**2, 3, 4, 5, 6, 7, 13, 22², 33, 37; **37:**5, 9, 11, 12, 19², 21, 28; **38:**3, 10, 14, 17, 18; **39:**1, 8², 7, 22²; **40:**4, 45, 46; **41:**4, 22²; **42:**13; **43:**7², 12², 13², 14², 15, 16, 18², 22²; **44:**2², 3, 6, 9², 14, 21, 26, 27; **45:**2, 9², 11, 12, 13, 14, 15, 18, 19, 22, 23, 24, 25; **46:**1³, 2², 4, 5², 6, 7, 8³, 9, 10, 13, 14, 16², 17, 18, 20², 24; **48:**14², 29, 30, 32, 34, 35; **Da 2:**5, 8, 9, 10, 11, 28, 29, 45³, 47; **3:**4, 14, 17; **4:**2, 3, 8², 9³, 17², 18, 24², 25, 27, 30, 31, 32, 34, 37²; **5:**11, 14, 21, 25, 26, 28; **6:**13, 26; **7:**14²; **8:**21²; **9:**9, 13, 14, 27; **10:**17, 21; **11:**12, 36; **12:**1, 11²; **Hos 1:**2; **2:**9; **3:**1²; **4:**1, 2, 13, 17; **5:**1, 3², 4, 9, 11, 13; **6:**4, 8, 10², 11; **7:**8, 9, 11; **8:**1, 3, 6, 8²; **9:**7, 8, 16²; **10:**2, 5, 8, 11, 12, 15; **11:**8², 12; **12:**5, 11; **13:**2, 10, 12, 13, 14; **14:**9²; **Joel 1:**10³, 11, 13², 15; **2:**1, 3², 11, 13², 14, 17², 20³, 22², 27³, 31; **3:**13³, 14; **Am 1:**3, 5, 6, 8, 9, 13; **2:**1, 4, 6, 11; **3:**5, 11, 12; **4:**5, 12, 13; **5:**2, 3, 4, 8, 14, 16, 27; **6:**2, 10²; **7:**1, 2, 4, 5, 7, 10, 11², 13, 17; **8:**1, 2; **9:**6, 9; **Ob 1:**1, 15; **Jnh 1:**7, 8², 12;

4:2², 3; **Mic 1**:3, 5⁵, 9, 11², 15; **2**:1, 4, 7, 10³; **3**:5, 7, 9, 11; **5**:1, 3; **6**:2, 8, 9², 10; **7**:1², 4², 10, 18; **Na 1**:2²; **2**:6, 7, 12; **2**:5, 7, 8², 9, 10, 11; **3**:7, 19; **Hab 1**:3, 4², 11, 15, 17; **2**:4, 5³, 13, 16², 18, 19², 20; **3**:19; **Zep 1**:7, 14; **2**:5, 10, 15²; **3**:5, 15, 17²; **Hag 1**:2, 4, 5, 7, 9; **2**:3, 5, 6, 8², 11, 14², 19; **Zec 1**:3, 4, 14, 16, 17; **2**:2, 8; **3**:2, 7; **4**:1, 6; **5**:3², 5², 6³, 8, 11; **6**:6, 12³, 13; **7**:9, 14; **8**:2, 3, 4, 6, 7, 9, 14, 19, 20, 23²; **9**:1; **10**:1, 5; **11**:3, 4; **12**:1, 5; **13**:7, 9; **14**:1, 12; **Mal 1**:4, 5, 6³, 7, 8², 12², 14²; **2**:1, 7, 14³, 17²; **3**:14; **4**:1²; **Mt 1**:16, 18, 20²; **2**:2, 5, 13, 18; **3**:2, 3, 10, 11, 12, 15, 17; **4**:4, 6, 7, 10, 17; **5**:3, 10, 12, 13, 18, 22², 25, 29, 30, 34, 35², 48; **6**:3, 4, 6², 9, 10, 18², 21, 22, 23², 25, 30³; **7**:4, 6, 13², 14, 19, 21, 24, 26; **8**:27; **9**:3, 5, 12, 14, 15, 24, 34, 37; **10**:2, 7, 10, 13², 24, 25, 26, 27, 37², 38, 41², 42; **11**:5, 6, 10², 11², 14, 19², 30²; **12**:2, 6, 8, 10, 12², 18, 24, 26, 30², 33, 41, 42, 45², 48, 50; **13**:13, 14, 19, 20, 22, 23, 24, 31, 32², 33, 37, 38, 39², 44, 45, 47, 49, 52, 57; **14**:2², 4, 15, 27; **15**:5, 6, 11, 22, 26, 28; **16**:2, 3, 7, 11, 13, 27; **17**:4, 5, 12, 15, 22; **18**:1, 4, 8, 9, 13, 14, 23, 35; **19**:3, 10², 17³, 23, 24, 26; **20**:1, 4, 21, 23; **21**:9, 10, 11, 13, 38, 42; **22**:2, 4, 8, 17², 20, 21², 23, 32, 36, 38, 39, 42, 43; **23**:5, 9, 16, 17, 18, 19, 38, 39; **24**:6, 23², 26², 27, 28, 32, 33, 39, 45, 48², 50; **25**:25; **26**:2, 13, 18, 24, 25, 26, 28², 31, 38, 39, 41², 42, 45², 48, 62, 64, 66; **27**:4, 6², 8, 11, 17, 22, 24, 37; **28**:6, 7; **Mk 1**:2, 15, 27, 37, 38; **2**:9, 17, 18, 19, 24, 26, 28; **3**:4, 21, 22², 24, 25, 26, 29, 35; **4**:11, 15, 22⁴, 26², 29, 30, 31², 41; **5**:9², 23, 35, 39; **6**:4, 14, 15², 18, 35, 50; **7**:2, 6, 11², 15, 20, 27; **8**:16, 36, 38; **9**:5, 7, 12, 13, 17, 23, 31, 40², 43, 45, 47, 48, 50; **10**:2, 18, 23, 24, 25, 27, 40, 46; **11**:9, 10, 17²; **12**:7, 11, 14, 16, 17², 18, 27, 28, 29², 31², 32², 33², 35²; **13**:7, 11², 21², 28, 29; **14**:9, 14, 18, 20, 21, 22, 24², 27, 34, 36, 38², 41, 44, 60, 69; **15**:2, 16, 42; **16**:6, 7, 16; **Lk 1**:15, 18, 28, 36², 37, 42, 45, 49, 60, 61, 63, 66; **2**:11, 23², 24, 34², 36, 43; **4**:4, 8, 10, 17, 18, 21, 24, 36, 43; **5**:21, 23, 31, 34, 39; **6**:2, 4, 5, 9, 20, 23², 26, 32, 33, 34, 35, 40², 44, 47, 48, 49; **7**:7, 22, 23, 27², 28³, 34, 35, 39³, 49; **8**:11², 17, 25², 26, 30, 49, 52; **9**:9, 25, 26, 33, 35, 38, 39, 44, 48², 49, 50², 62; **10**:2, 6, 8, 9, 11, 22², 26, 29, 42²; **11**:7, 8, 15, 18, 23², 26, 27, 29, 31, 32, 34³, 35, 36, 41; **12**:1, 2, 6, 18, 21², 23³, 34, 42, 45, 46, 50, 55, 56, 57; **13**:6, 8, 9, 14, 16, 21; **Jas 1**:6, 8, 10, 11, 12, 13, 14², 15, 17, 21, 23, 26, 27; **2**:6, 10, 14, 15, 16, 17², 19, 20, 24, 26²; **3**:2², 5², 6², 8, 13, 15, 16, 17²; **4**:4, 6, 12², 14, 15, 16²; **5**:1, 7, 8, 9, 11, 13², 14, 16; **1Pe 1**:5, 7, 13, 15, 16, 24, 25; **2**:3, 7, 8, 15, 19², 20²; **3**:4, 5, 6, 12, 13, 14, 17²; **4**:2, 6, 10, 16, 18, 27; **5**:1, 7; **2Pe 1**:9, 13, 17; **2**:6, 9, 10, 13, 17, 19, 22; **3**:1, 4, 8, 9²; **1Jn 1**:3, 5³, 7, 8, 9; **2**:2, 4², 5², 7, 8³, 9, 10, 11², 13, 14, 15, 18⁴, 22⁴, 25, 27, 29²; **3**:1³, 2, 3, 4, 5, 7³, 8², 9, 10⁴, 11, 15, 16², 19, 20, 23, 24; **4**:2², 3⁴, 4³, 6², 8, 9, 10, 12, 15, 16, 17, 18², 20; **5**:1², 2, 3, 4, 5², 6³, 9², 11², 14, 16, 17², 19, 20³; **2Jn** 1:6²; 7; **3Jn** 1:10, 11⁵, 12²; **Jude** 1:14, 24; **Rev 1**:2, 3³, 4², 5, 7, 8², 19, 20; **2**:7, 8, 21; **3**:2, 7, 10, 12; **4**:8³; **5**:2, 5, 12, 13; **8**:11; **9**:11, 12, 13; **10**:6¹, 7, 8; **11**:5, 8, 14, 17; **12**:12²; **13**:4, 10², 17, 18²; **14**:8, 11, 15; **15**:1, 5; **16**:15, 16, 17; **17**:8², 10, 11³, 14, 18; **18**:2, 8, 14; **19**:10, 11, 13²; **20**:2, 5, 12, 14; **21**:3, 6², 8, 16, 23, 27; **22**:7, 10, 11², 12, 17.

26:11, 15, 21; 27:2, 5², 8, 11; 28:10; 29:3, 7², 23², 28; 30:7³; 31:10, 32, 33; 32:3, 7², 8⁴, 10, 23, 24, 28, 29², 31², 34, 35, 36, 43²; 33:2², 6, 9², 10, 16; 34:2, 22²; 35:4; 36:2, 15², 17, 21², 22, 28, 29², 32²; 37:8²; 38:3, 6², 18, 20, 25; 39:1; 40:3, 9, 15; 41:4, 9; 42:6²; 20; 44:6, 22; 46:10², 14², 23; 47:2, 7²; 48:1, 30, 36, 45; 49:2, 12², 14, 18, 27, 33; 50:2, 3, 5, 24, 38, 39, 40; 51:6, 9, 33, 62², 63²; 52:3, 4, 20; La 1:12, 13; 2:3, 16; 3:26, 27, 28, 37², 38; 4:4, 8, 13; 5:18; Eze 1:2, 13², 28; 2:9, 10; 3:3³; 4:1², 2², 3⁴, 9, 10, 11, 12; 5:1, 2; 7:6², 9, 10, 19², 20, 21², 22²; 8:17; 9:3, 4; 10:7³; 11:3, 7, 11, 18, 23; 12:5, 11, 13, 19, 23, 25; 13:5², 10, 11², 12, 14², 15², 14:13², 14, 15², 16, 18, 19, 20, 21, 22², 23; 15:3², 4²; 5³; 17:4², 5², 6³, 7, 8², 9⁴, 10⁵, 22², 23², 24; 18:25, 26, 29; 19:7², 10, 11, 12², 13, 14; 20:9, 14, 22, 29, 47², 48²; 21:5, 7², 11, 12², 14, 15², 23, 26², 27⁴, 29²; 22:14, 20, 30; 23:32², 34³, 39, 41; 24:3², 4², 5², 6³, 7, 8, 11, 12; 25:3², 13; 28:18; 29:3, 9, 11, 15², 20; 30:9, 12, 21, 26; 31:3, 4², 5, 7, 8, 9, 10², 11², 12², 15³, 16, 17; 32:15, 16²; 33:12, 17, 18, 25, 33; 34:10, 18²; 35:2, 6, 7, 13; 36:17, 18, 20, 22, 29, 34, 36; 37:1, 9, 14, 16², 19, 26; 38:14; 39:8², 10, 11², 15²; 40:5, 6, 9, 11, 18, 19, 21, 22, 23, 25, 26, 27, 28, 29, 31, 32, 33, 34, 35², 36², 37, 47, 49; 41:2², 3, 4, 5, 8², 13, 15; 42:7, 16, 17, 18, 19, 20²; 43:14², 18, 20², 21, 22, 23, 26²; 44:1, 2², 11, 14, 24; 45:2, 3, 4², 6, 7, 17²; 46:1, 13, 14, 16, 17³; 47:5, 8², 14², 15, 19, 22; 48:1, 2, 3, 4, 5, 6, 7, 8², 10², 12, 14², 15, 18, 19, 21, 23, 24, 25, 26, 27; Da 1:1; 2:3, 4, 5, 6², 7, 9, 11, 26, 34, 36, 40, 41², 44³; 3:1, 3, 14, 15, 17; 4:2, 7, 9, 11, 12³, 14, 18², 22, 23, 27; 5:5, 7, 8, 15², 16, 17, 26; 6:1, 5, 8², 17², 14², 5², 6², 7⁴, 8, 18, 23³; 8:10³, 11², 12³, 13, 14, 15, 26, 27; 9:13, 25; 10:1, 7; 11:4², 11, 16, 21, 22, 28, 29, 35; 12:6, 7; Hos 1:10; 2:9², 4:3, 9; 7:4, 6, 9; 8:6³, 7³; 9:4, 10², 10:5², 6, 8, 12, 15; 11:3²; 13:2; Joel 1:3², 5, 6, 7³, 15; 2:1, 11², 20; Am 3:6; 4:7; 5:6², 19; 6:2, 8; 7:4; 8:8², 10, 12; 9:5², 8, 11²; Ob 1:7, 15, 17, 18²; Jnh 1:2, 12²; 2:10; 3:2; 4:3, 6, 7, 8, 10³; Mic 1:2, 5², 9², 10; 2:1³, 3, 4, 7, 10²; 4:1²; 5:8; 6:9; 7:10; Na 1:4, 5; 2:7; Hab 2:2², 3⁴, 11, 15, 16, 18², 19³; Zep 2:7²; Hag 1:4, 6, 8, 9; 2:3², 12, 13², 14; Zec 2:2, 4, 5; 3:9; 4:2, 3, 7², 9; 5:3², 4⁴, 6², 11², 6:11, 13; 7:5; 8:6²; 9:2, 5, 13; 10:1, 7; 11:10, 11², 12², 13; 12:3; 13:8; 14:2, 5, 7, 11²; Mal 1:5, 6, 12³, 13, 14; 2:3, 14; 3:10, 14; 4:1; Mt 2:9; 3:15²; 4:4, 6, 7; 5:13², 15³, 21, 25, 27, 29³, 30³, 31, 33, 34, 35², 38, 43; 6:2, 10, 18²; 7:2, 7, 13, 14, 25², 27; 8:9, 13², 26; 9:12, 14, 29, 34; 10:12, 13², 15, 19, 20, 25, 39²; 11:10, 12, 14, 22, 23, 24; 12:10, 11³, 12³, 24, 39, 41, 42, 43⁴, 44³, 45³; 13:2, 4, 5², 8, 17², 19, 20, 22², 23, 30, 32², 33, 40, 44², 46, 48², 49; 14:4, 11, 12, 24, 27; 15:6, 26²; 16:2, 3, 4, 7, 11, 18, 23², 26²; 17:4, 18, 19, 20, 27²; 18:6, 8³, 9³, 13, 17, 19; 19:3, 8, 10, 11, 12, 23, 24; 20:11, 21, 25; 21:13², 19³, 21, 25³, 33², 42, 44; 22:17, 39, 43; 23:16, 18², 20², 22; 24:6, 19, 23, 26, 33, 37² 39, 46; 25:14, 27, 28; 26:12, 24², 25, 26², 27², 29, 31, 39, 42², 51, 54, 61, 64, 70, 72; 27:6², 8, 11, 15, 18, 24, 29, 34², 48², 58, 59, 60; 28:2; Mk 1:2, 35; 2:4, 17, 18; 3:5; 4:1, 4, 5², 8, 15, 16, 19, 20, 21², 24, 29, 30, 31, 32, 37, 39, 50; 7:6, 15, 19, 24, 27², 36; 8:12, 16, 35², 36; 9:5, 12, 13, 18², 20, 22, 28, 32, 42, 43², 45², 47², 50²; 10:2, 5, 15, 23, 25, 42, 47; 11:2³, 3², 4, 7², 11, 13³, 14, 17², 23, 24², 30, 31; 12:1, 11, 14, 15, 21, 35; 13:11, 14, 17, 21, 29; 14:5, 12, 20, 21², 22³, 23², 25, 27, 68, 70; 15:2, 6, 10, 17, 23, 25, 29, 36², 42, 45, 46²; 16:11, 13, 18, 20; Lk 1:3, 38, 57, 66; 2:18, 21, 23, 26, 43; 3:23; 4:4, 6², 7, 8, 10, 11, 12², 20, 39; 5:31, 36; 6:9, 30, 38², 48², 49; 7:8, 14, 27; 8:5², 6, 7, 8, 13, 15, 16³, 21, 29, 36, 45; 9:11, 24², 25, 33, 39², 40, 45³; 10:6, 12, 14, 24², 26, 42²; 11:9, 24³, 26², 29², 32², 33, 40, 44², 46, 48², 49; 14:4, 11, 12, 24, 27; 15:6, 26²; 16:2, 3, 4, 7, 11, 18, 25², 26²; 17:4, 18, 19, 20, 27²; 18:6, 8³, 9³, 13, 17, 19; 19:3, 8, 10, 11, 12, 23, 24; 20:11, 21, 25; 21:13², 19³, 21, 25³, 33², 42, 44; 22:17, 39, 43; 23:16, 18², 20², 22; 24:6, 19, 23, 26, 33, 37² 39, 46; 25:14, 27, 28; 26:12, 24², 25, 26², 27², 29, 31, 39, 42², 51, 54, 61, 64, 70, 72; 27:6², 8, 11, 15, 18, 24, 29, 34², 48², 58, 59, 60; 28:2; Mk 1:2, 35; 2:4, 17, 18; 3:5; 4:1, 4, 5², 8, 15, 16, 19, 20, 21², 24, 29, 30, 31, 32, 37, 39, 50; 7:6, 15, 19, 24, 27², 36; 8:12, 16, 35², 36; 9:5, 12, 13, 18², 20, 22, 28, 32, 42, 43², 45², 47², 50²; 10:2, 5, 15, 23, 25, 42, 47; 11:2³, 3², 4, 7², 11, 13³, 14, 17², 23, 24², 30, 31; 12:1, 11, 14, 15, 21, 35; 13:11, 14, 17, 21, 29; 14:5, 12, 20, 21², 22³, 23², 25, 27, 68, 70; 15:2, 6, 10, 17, 23, 25, 29, 36², 42, 45, 46²; 16:11, 13, 18, 20; Lk 1:3, 38, 57, 66; 2:18, 21, 23, 26, 43; 3:23; 4:4, 6², 7, 8, 10, 11, 12², 20, 39; 5:31, 36; 6:9, 30, 38², 48², 49; 7:8, 14, 27; 8:5², 6, 7, 8, 13, 15, 16³, 21, 29, 36, 45; 9:11, 24², 25, 33, 39², 40, 45³; 10:6, 12, 14, 24², 26, 42²; 11:9, 24³, 26², 29², 32², 33, 40, 44², 46, 48², 49; 12:3, 5, 6, 7, 14², 24³, 25², 27, 28², 29², 36, 47, 49; 13:1, 19², 25, 26, 30; 14:2, 10, 14, 17, 29²; 15:2, 4, 7, 18, 19²; 16:7, 14, 15; 17:16; 18:1, 4, 7, 10, 14, 18, 25, 27, 28, 35², 36, 39; 19:2, 11, 14, 19, 24², 29², 30, 31, 35,

40, 42; 20:1, 14, 15, 25, 27; 21:1, 4, 7³, 9, 11, 12, 13; Ac 1:7, 20², 21; 2:8, 24; 3:16; 4:3, 10, 16, 19, 35², 37; 5:2, 3, 4³, 36, 38, 39; 6:2, 9; 7:41, 44, 45², 47, 53; 8:29, 31; 9:17, 31²; 10:4, 12, 28, 33, 34; 11:4, 5, 6, 10; 12:1, 10², 14, 15²; 13:26, 33, 35, 46; 14:6; 15:11, 15, 16, 19², 28, 31, 38; 16:35; 17:10, 24; 18:14, 15, 21; 19:39, 40²; 20:35; 21:3, 11; 22:25, 26; 23:5, 19; 24:21², 25; 25:16, 27; 26:6, 7, 8, 14, 26; 27:1, 9, 15, 17², 25, 28, 32, 34, 35; 28:2, 3, 11, 20; Ro 1:16, 17, 19, 28; 2:13², 24; 3:4, 10, 19, 26, 27; 4:3, 10³, 13, 16, 17, 18, 22², 29, 30, 31, 32², 33; 10:8², 10², 15; 11:6², 7, 8, 26; 12:6, 7², 8⁵, 18², 19²; 13:5; 14:11, 14, 20, 21; 15:3, 9, 10, 20, 21, 27³; 1Co 1:18, 19, 30, 31; 2:8, 9, 10; 3:2, 6², 10, 13³, 15, 19; 4:2, 4, 7, 9, 12; 5:1, 12; 6:1, 5, 16; 7:1, 8, 9, 14, 21, 26, 30; 8:7²; 9:6, 9³, 11, 12, 18², 25², 27, 26; 10:7, 13, 26, 28, 31; 11:5, 6, 13, 14, 15, 18, 20, 24, 25, 34; 12:12², 15, 16, 20, 24, 26²; 13:4³, 5⁴, 7, 8; 14:9, 12, 21, 35, 36; 15:11, 12, 27², 36, 38, 42², 43⁴, 44², 45; 16:2, 4, 10, 16; 2Co 1:6², 17, 19, 21, 23, 24; 2:5, 3:7, 13, 14²; 4:3, 13; 5:5, 9², 11², 13², 7:8² 12; 8:8, 11², 15, 24, 29²; 5, 9², 10:5, 8, 18; 11:4, 7, 15; 12:2, 8, 11, 16; Gal 1:12³, 13; 2:14, 17; 3:4, 6, 10, 13, 15, 18², 19; 4:9, 13, 18, 22, 27, 29; 5:1; Eph 2:5, 8²; 3:5; 4:7, 8, 11, 17, 29; 5:12, 14², 29; 6:3, 20; Php 1:6, 7, 13, 15, 18, 24, 29; 2:13, 25; 3:1², 3, 13; 4:4, 9, 10, 12², 14; Col 1:6², 7; 2:8, 14², 19, 20; 3:17, 22, 23, 24; 4:4, 16, 17; 1Th 1:8; 2:13² 19; 3:1², 4², 9; 4:3, 11; 5:24; 2Th 2:7; 3:1, 8; 1Ti 1:8; 2:14; 4:4, 5; 5:18, 19; 6:7; 2Ti 1:10, 14; 2:14, 16; 3:14²; 4:16, 17; Tit 1:9²; 2:12; Phm 1:18, 19; Heb 2:4, 5, 10, 16; 3:12, 13, 17; 4:1, 2, 6, 7; 5:11; 6:4, 7², 8, 17, 18, 19; 7:11, 14, 17, 18, 20; 8:3, 5, 6, 9; 9:16², 17², 23; 10:1, 2, 4, 7, 30, 31, 35; 11:6, 18; 12:9, 11³, 15, 19, 20, 25, 26²; 13:2, 14, 16, 17, 29, 34², 33², 43³; 12:19, 20, 22; 24, 25², 26, 29⁴, 31³, 33⁴, 34, 36³, 37, 48; 41:4, 12, 13, 15, 22³; 43:11⁶, 13, 20; 45:6; 46:21; 48:1, 8, 13²; 18, Da 2:32², 33², 34, 48; 4:10, 11, 12³, 14⁴, 15, 19², 20, 21, 23, 26; 7:4, 5³, 6, 7, 9, 11, 19², 20; 8:8; 10:1; 11:21; Hos 10:5³, 6, 7; 12:11; 13:15; Joel 2:20³; Am 9:6, 11²; Ob 1:17; Jnh 1:2; 4:5; Mic 1:1; 2:12; 7:13; Na 2:7, 8, 9; Hab 3:10; Zep 1:12; 2:11; Hag 1:10; 2:3; Zec 1:21; 2:5; 4:3; 5:4², 8, 11; 7:7; 8:12²; 12:4; 14:10; Mal 1:2; Mt 2:16; 5:13, 15; 6:34; 7:25; 12:33³; 13:32; 17:27; 21:43; 24:1, 29, 32²; 26:52; Mk 4:21, 32; 9:50; 13:24, 28²; Lk 6:44, 49; 10:11; 11:33; 13:19; 14:34; 18:34; 19:33; 21:20; 22:37; Jn 3:8; 15:19; 18:12; Ac 2:24; 10:11; 11:5; 15:16, 31; 19:27; 21:3; Ro 6:12; 8:20, 21; 13:10; 1Co 1:17; 7:31; 9:7, 23; 12:12, 25; 15:38; 2Co 3:7; Gal 5:24; Eph 2:3, 15; 3:15; 4:16, 22; Col 1:6, 25²; 2:14, 19, 20; 3:9, 10; 1Ti 2:6; 2Ti 3:5; Heb 2:2; 9:2, 21; 12:2; Jas 1:4, 11²; 5:7, 18; 1Pe 4:10; 2Pe 1:21; 2:5, 22; 3:12; 1Jn 2:8, 17; Rev 1:16; 2:5; 5:5, 9; 6:2, 4, 5, 8, 14; 12:16; 13:12; 14:18, 19; 16:12; 21:11, 15², 17, 22, 23, 24, 25; 22:2.

IT'S (20)

Ge 29:19; 43:23; Jdg 19:9; 1Sa 20:2; 25:21; 2Ki 4:23²; Pr 20:14²; 28:24; Jer 2:25; 18:12; Mt 14:15, 26, 28; Mk 6:35; 13:34; Lk 12:54, 55; Ac 2:15.

ITS (1008)

Ge 1:21, 24; 2:19; 4:11, 12; 7:2², 14³, 22; 8:9, 11; 9:4, 21; 10:5; 15:16; 19:13; 22:13; 28:12; 29:3; 38:18; 40:5, 10; 41:11; 42:6; 49:17; Ex 7:18, 21; 13:13, 22; 14:27; 15:1, 21, 23; 21:28, 34; 23:5, 19; 25:9, 12, 29², 31, 37, 38; 27:3³; 28:7, 8, 32; 29:5, 10, 14², 15, 19, 20, 41; 30:2, 10, 18, 27², 28², 38; 31:8², 9²; 34:20, 26; 35:11², 12, 13², 14, 15, 16⁴, 17, 21; 37:3, 16², 17, 23², 24, 25; 38:3², 4, 8, 30²; 39:4, 5, 33², 35, 36, 37², 39⁴, 40; 40:4, 9, 10, 11; Lev 1:11, 15, 16; 3:8, 9, 13²; 4:4, 11, 33; 5:8²; 7:2, 3, 8; 8:7, 11², 14, 17³, 18, 22, 23; 10:18; 11:32, 42; 13:51, 55; 14:25, 45; 16:15; 17:14²; 18:25²; 19:23, 24, 25; 22:27, 30; 23:10, 19, 29; 26:4², 20², 34²; 27:12, 13, 14, 15, 16, 18, 19, 23², 27², 33; Nu 1:50²; 3:25, 36²; 4:8, 9³, 10, 11, 14, 16, 25, 26, 31; 6:17²; 7:12², 10; 8:4²; 9:3, 12, 14, 21; 12:12³; 13:23, 27; 15:24; 16:30, 32; 19:4, 5; 20:8; 21:25, 32; 26:10, 54, 55; 28:9, 10, 15, 24, 31; 29:11, 16, 19, 22, 25, 28, 31, 34, 38; 32:33, 42; 34:12; Dt 3:12, 17; 8:15; 11:4, 6, 12, 14, 18; 13:15², 16; 14:21; 20:10, 19; 22:4; 28:30; 29:14; 32:11⁴, 22; 33:16; Jos 3:13; 6:2², 26²; 7:8; 8:2²; 9:24; 10:1², 2, 13, 28, 32²; 30², 37², 39⁴; 11:10; 13:17; 15:45, 47²; 17:16, 18; 18:5², 9, 28; 19:49; 21:11; Jdg 1:16; 5:23, 31; 6:19; 7:15; 8:28; 9:26, 45; 11:18; 20:33; 1Sa 5:6, 11; 6:2, 8, 9; 17:7, 20, 35²; 22:19³; 2Sa 2:3; 6:17; 12:27, 30; 14:26; 20:8²; 1Ki 4:13; 6:15, 18²; 7:4, 12, 26, 31²; 8:6, 7, 9; 9:16, 10:19; 13:5, 34²; 16:34²; 21:6; 2Ki 3:25; 4:39; 8:20; 12:9; 15:16; 16:9, 17; 24:29; 18:8; 19:23⁴; 22:16, 19; 25:17; 1Ch 2:23; 4:14; 5:16; 6:55; 7:28⁴; 8:12; 12:15; 18:1;

20:2; 21:27; 23:26; 28:11⁴, 13, 15²; 2Ch 3:8, 11, 12; 4:5; 5:7, 8; 8:16; 21:8; 24:7, 11, 13; 29:18²; 34:24, 27; 36:21²; Ezr 2:68; 3:3; 4:13, 16; 5:15; 6:3, 7; 7:10; 9:9, 11; Ne 1:3; 2:3, 13, 17; 3:1², 3², 6, 13, 14, 15; 4:6; 9:36, 37; 11:25³, 27, 28, 30²; 31; 13:14; Est 1:22²; 6:8; 10:1; Job 1:5; 3:5, 9; 5:16; 8:16, 17, 18, 19; 9:6², 24; 14:7, 8²; 18; 15:33²; 18:8; 24:13²; 27:22, 23; 28:6², 10, 13, 15; 31:26, 38, 39²; 36:32, 33²; 37:1, 9; 38:5, 6², 9, 10, 12, 14, 32, 41; Ps 1:3; 19:6²; 33:17²; 37:35; 46:3²; 48:2; 55:10, 11; 58:4; 60:2; 65:10³; 67:6; 68:13; 69:15, 31; 71:15; 72:16; 75:3²; 8; 80:10², 11², 12²; 85:12; 89:9; 94:20; 103:16; 104:5, 17²; 127:1; 131:2; 137:5, 7; Pr 6:6, 8²; 8:26, 29; 9:1; 14:10²; 15:28; 16:33; 18:21; 24:4; 26:11, 14; 27:8, 18; Ecc 1:6, 8; 3:11; 5:13; 6:4; 7:8, 12; 8:1, 17; 10:10; SS 1:12; 2:13; 3:2, 10⁴; 4:2, 16²; 5:15; 6:6; 7:5, 8; 8:6, 11, 12; Isa 5:5²; 14²; 8:7², 8; 10:14; 13:10, 11, 13, 14; 17, 29, 31; 15:2²; 19:19; 21:9; 22:9, 24²; 23:11, 13; 24:1², 5, 6, 9, 12, 20, 23; 26:1²; 27:10, 11; 28:25³; 30:14, 33; 31:4; 33:8, 20²; 34:5, 10, 15; 37:24⁴; 40:16, 22; 41:9²; 42:5, 11; 44:19, 28; 45:6, 11; 46:7; 48:19; 49:8; 50:3; 51:6, 15, 17; 54:16; 56:5; 58:2; 60:22; 65:18²; Jer 1:18²; 2:7, 11; 4:26; 6:7; 7:28; 10:20; 11:16, 19; 13:23; 14:8; 17:8²; 18:8; 14²; 19:8; 20:5²; 25:9, 18; 27:5, 8, 11²; 28:13; 30:18; 31:23, 24, 35; 33:5, 12; 34:1, 18; 37:7; 46:10; 48:11, 28, 40; 49:1, 2, 13, 17, 19, 22, 31; 50:44, 46; 51:42; 52:22; La 2:2; 4:1, 4; Eze 1:11, 15, 23; 11:6, 18; 13:14; 14:13², 17, 19, 21; 17:4, 6², 7², 9, 22, 23; 19:11³, 12², 14²; 21:3, 5, 25, 29, 30; 22:25; 24:11³, 12; 25:9, 13; 26:2, 3, 19; 29:19; 31:3, 4, 5², 7, 9², 8³, 10², 11, 12³, 13, 15², 16, 17²; 32:7; 34:27, 29; 35:6; 36:5, 13; 38:6²; 40:6, 9, 11, 15, 21³, 22⁴, 24², 25, 26, 29⁴, 31², 33⁴, 34, 36³, 37, 48; 41:4, 12, 13, 15, 22³; 43:11⁶, 13, 20; 45:6; 46:21; 48:1, 8, 13²; 18, Da 2:32², 33², 34, 48; 4:10, 11, 12³, 14⁴, 15, 16, 17; 41:10; 48:13; 50:4, 23; 56:13; 58:5, 8; 60:5; 61:7; 67:1, 2, 3; 4², 5²; 68:1³, 2³, 3², 23, 30; 69:6², 22², 23, 25, 28, 29, 32; 70:2², 3, 4²; 71:13²; 72:15³, 16, 17², 19; 73:26; 74:21; 79:8, 11; 80:3, 7, 19; 83:17²; 84:3; 85:6, 9; 86:11, 17; 88:2; 90:12, 14, 16, 17; 91:7; 101:6; 102:18; 104:31², 34, 35; 106:5², 47; 108:6; 109:7, 8², 9, 10², 11², 12, 13, 14², 15²; 17², 19, 20, 28; 115:14, 15; 116:9; 118:20; 119:18, 38, 41, 74, 76, 77, 78, 79, 80², 115, 125, 134, 144, 148, 169, 170, 171, 172, 173, 175²; 122:6, 7; 128:5²; 6; 129:5, 6, 8; 132:9²; 134:3; 137:5, 6; 138:4, 5; 140:10, 11; 141:2²; 142:7; 143:10; 145:12; 149:6; Pr 5:2²; 18², 19²; 13:8, 23; 14:13²; 18:24; 22:19, 25; 23:25²; 25:10; 26:26; 27:1; 28:11; 30:9² Ecc 2:21; 3:13, 18; 4:12, 14²; 6:3; 7:21, 24; 10:8², 9², 20²; 11:2, 8; SS 4:16; 6:1, 8, 13; 7:8, 9; Isa 2:3; 5:19²; 26:2; 27:3; 30:8; 37:4, 20; 41:20²; 42:9, 43:9, 10, 21; 44:13; 45:3, 6; 46:5; 49:6, 15; 51:23; 55:3, 6; 60:11; 66:5; Jer 5:22²; 6:27; 7:23; 10:18; 13:26; 15:19; 20:14, 16²; 28:6²; 29:6, 18; 38:19, 24; 42:5; 43:3; 50:34; 51:35²; La 1:21²; 2:13; 3:29, 65; 5:21; Eze 3:12; 12:16; 16:54; 20:20; 21:15; 23:48; 24:11; 34:25; 37:9; 38:16; 40:46; 43:10, 11; 44:2, 3, 11², 22, 25, 30; 46:17; Da 2:30²; 4:1, 17, 27; 5:17; 6:16, 25; 11:35; Hos 2:18; 6:2; 13:10; 14:2; Joel 2:14; Am 5:14; 8:5²; 9:12; Jnh 3:9; Mic 1:8; Zec 8:6, 9; 11:1, 17²; 12:7; Mal 1:4²; 2:4, 12²; 3:10; Mt 2:8; 5:16, 25³, 45; 6:4²; 7:6; 9:6; 13:29; 15:32; 17:27; 18:31; 20:1; 21:19; 25:9; 26:5, 39, 42; 27:64; Mk 2:10; 4:12; 7:29; 11:14, 25; 14:2, 14; 15:32; Lk 1:4, 38; 5:24; 8:10², 12; 10:35; 11:33; 12:58; 14:8, 12; 17:8; 20:16; 21:36²; 22:11, 30, 32; Jn 3:15, 21; 4:36, 50; 5:14, 23, 34; 6:30, 50; 7:3, 23; 9:36; 10:10, 38; 11:4, 15, 16, 42; 12:36; 14:3, 13, 14; 15:11²; 16:33; 17:1, 3, 11, 13, 19, 21³, 22, 23, 26²; 19:35; 20:31²; Ac 1:20²; 3:19²; 20; 8:19, 20, 24; 9:17; 10:29; 13:47; 15:17; 17:19; 20:24, 31; 23:24; 24:25; 25:26; 26:18, 29; Ro 1:10, 11, 12, 19; 3:4, 8, 19; 4:16²; 6:1, 4; 8:17; 10:1, 4; 11:9, 10, 14, 25, 31, 32; 13:9; 15:5, 6, 9, 13², 31²; 32; 16:2; 1Co 1:10², 29; 2:12, 16; 3:18; 4:6; 5:5, 7; 7:5, 35; 9:2, 18, 23; 10:33; 11:34; 14:5, 13, 17, 31; 15:28, 35; 16:11; 2Co 4:10, 11, 15; 5:4, 10; 8:11; 9:3; 10:2; 11:3, 6, 16; 12:9, 16, 20; 13:7, 10, 14; Gal 2:16; 4:17, 24; 5:10; 6:1, 13, 14; Eph 1:17²; 18²; 3:12, 16, 17, 18, 19; 4:12, 28, 29; 6:3²; 3:13; 4:3²; 4, 6, 8²; 5:10, 23²; 2Th 1:11²; 12; 2:6, 16; 3:1, 2, 5, 14, 16; 1Ti 1:3, 18; 2:2; 3:6; 4:15; 5:7, 9, 20; 6:1, 19; 2Ti 1:4, 16, 18; 2:10; 4:16; Tit 2:8; 3:8, 11, 14; Phm 1:6, 20; Heb 3:13; 4:1, 11, 16; 6:18; 10:24; 12:10, 13, 27; 13:19, 20, 21; Jas 1:4; 4:3; 5:16; 1Pe 1:6, 7²; 2:2, 9, 12; 3:1, 9, 16; 4:11, 13; 5:6; 2Pe 1:4; 3:17; 1Jn 1:3; 2:28; 5:13, 20; 2Jn 1:8, 12; 3Jn 1:2², 8; Rev 16:15; 19:18; 22:14².

ITSELF (53)

Ge 32:16; Ex 24:10; 29:5; Lev 16:22; 25:2, 5, 11; Jos 10:13; 11:11; 17:8; 2Ki 19:29; 1Ch 26:18; 2Ch 29:17; Job 27:22; Ps 89:2; SS 5:16; Isa 7:2; 10:15; 37:30; 57:9; Eze 7:6; 29:15; Da 2:44; 8:11; Mic 1:9; 7:14; Zec 12:12; Mt 6:34; 12:25², 45; Mk 3:24, 25; 4:28; Lk 11:17², 26; Jn 15:4; 20:7; Ac 12:10; 27:17; 28:3; Ro 8:21; 14:14; 1Co 15:53; 2Co 10:5; Gal 5:6; Eph 4:16; Heb 3:3; 9:24; Jas 2:17; 3:6; 3Jn 1:12.

MAY (1231)

Ge 3:2; 9:26, 27³; 11:4; 16:5; 18:4, 30, 32; 20:7; 24:14², 49, 55, 56, 60²; 27:4, 7, 10, 19, 25, 28, 29³, 31; 28:3, 4²; 30:24, 30; 31:49, 53; 32:5, 8; 38:11; 41:36; 42:2, 16, 20²; 37; 43:8, 14; 47:19², 24, 25; 48:9, 15, 16², 20; Ex 4:5, 8, 23; 5:1, 3, 21; 7:16; 8:1, 9, 10, 20; 9:1, 13, 14, 29; 10:1, 2³, 7, 24; 11:9; 12:5, 16, 44, 45, 48²; 14:26; 18:19; 19:9; 20:12; 21:30; 23:11², 12²; 24:2; 27:20; 28:1, 3, 4, 30, 38, 41; 29:1, 33; 30:30; 31:13; 32:10²; 33:13, 20, 21; 34:3; 40:13, 15; Lev 2:12; 6:3, 18, 29; 7:6, 8, 11, 16, 19, 24, 25; 9:6; 10:6, 14; 11:2, 3, 9, 21, 22, 47²; 13:2; 14:8; 16:26, 28; 17:12², 13; 19:25; 20:22; 21:3, 7, 18, 22²; 22:4, 5, 7, 10², 11, 12, 13²; 18, 19, 23; 23:3; 24:2; 25:7, 20, 29, 36, 44, 45, 48, 49²; 27:26, 27, 28, 29; Nu 4:19; 5:19, 21, 22; 6:5, 20; 7:5; 8:10; 10:35²; 11:16; 14:17; 15:39; 18:4, 7, 11, 13, 31; 19:7; 20:18, 20; 23:10; 24:9; 25:4; 27:11, 16; 30:13; 31:24; 32:22, 23; 35:6, 11, 12, 27, 28; 36:6, 9; Dt 1:11; 3:19, 20; 4:1², 5, 10², 40²; 5:14, 16², 31, 33; 6:2², 3², 18²; 7:17; 8:1², 17; 9:14; 10:11; 11:8, 9, 14, 21; 12:15², 20, 21², 22, 25, 27, 28; 14:4, 6, 7, 9, 10, 11, 12, 20, 21², 22, 25, 27, 28; 14:4, 6, 7, 9, 10, 11, 12, 20, 21², 22, 25, 27, 28; 14:4, 6, 7, 9, 10, 11, 12, 20, 21², 22, 25, 27, 28; 17:19; 18:7, 21; 19:3, 5³, 13, 15; 20:5², 6, 7, 14², 20; 21:11, 13; 22:7²; 8; 23:1, 2, 3, 8, 11, 19, 20, 24; 24:13, 14, 19; 25:15; 26:12; 29:9, 13, 29; 30:6, 12, 13, 14, 19, 20; 31:19; 32:46; 33:13; Jos 1:7, 8, 14, 15, 17, 18; 2:5; 3:7; 8:2; 20:3, 6; 22:23; 23:13; Jdg 5:31²; 7:2, 3; 9:7, 19²; 11:38; 13:5, 17; 16:5, 26; 20:13; Ru 1:8, 9, 17; 2:12²; 13; 4:11²; 12, 14; 1Sa 1:17, 18, 23; 2:20, 25; 3:17; 4:3; 7:8; 9:27; 14:44; 15:25, 30; 18:21²; 19:15; 20:13², 14, 16; 24:12²; 15³, 19; 25:22, 25, 26, 33; 26:19²; 24, 25; 27:5; 28:7; 22; 29:4; 30:22; 2Sa 1:21; 2:6; 3:9, 21², 29², 35, 39; 7:29; 9:10; 11:20²; 12:18, 22; 13:5, 6, 10; 14:7, 14, 17²; 15:20, 21; 16:12; 17:12; 18:20, 22, 23, 32; 19:13, 19², 37; 24:2, 3², 21, 23; 1Ki 1:2, 31, 36, 37, 47; 2:3, 4, 14, 16, 23, 33²; 8:29, 37, 43², 52², 57², 58, 59²; 60; 11:21, 36; 13:6, 18; 17:10, 12; 18:12; 19:2; 20:10, 34; 2Ki 1:10, 12; 3:11; 5:6, 18²; 6:17, 22, 28, 29, 31; 19:4, 19; 1Ch 12:17; 15:2; 16:35²; 17:27; 21:2, 3, 22; 22:11, 12², 14, 19; 28:8; 2Ch 1:10; 6:20², 28, 33², 40, 41²; 7:16; 12:8; 13:9; 19:11; 23:6; 24:22; 30:6, 18; 36:23; Ezr 1:3, 4; 4:15; 6:10, 12; 7:13, 16, 18, 20, 21; Ne 2:3, 7, 8; 5:13²; 9:5; Est 5:5; Job 1:21; 3:3, 4³, 5³, 6², 7³, 8, 9²; 4:10; 13:13; 14:8; 16:18; 24:23; 27:7; 31:8²; 10²; 33:14, 16, 19, 30; 37:7; 38:11; 39:15²; Ps 3:8; 5:11; 9:14; 10:18; 12:3; 15:1²; 17:2²; 19:13, 14; 20:1², 2, 3, 4, 5; 22:26; 24:3², 7, 9; 25:21; 27:4; 30:5, 12; 32:6; 33:22; 34:10, 19; 35:4², 5, 6, 8³, 26²; 27²; 36:11; 39:13; 40:11, 14², 15, 16², 17; 41:10; 48:13; 50:4, 23; 56:13; 58:5, 8; 60:5; 61:7; 67:1, 2, 3; 4², 5²; 68:1³, 2³, 3², 23, 30; 69:6², 22², 23, 25, 28, 29, 32; 70:2², 3, 4²; 71:13²; 72:15³, 16, 17², 19; 73:26; 74:21; 79:8, 11; 80:3, 7, 19; 83:17²; 84:3; 85:6, 9; 86:11, 17; 88:2; 90:12, 14, 16, 17; 91:7; 101:6; 102:18; 104:31², 34, 35; 106:5², 47; 108:6; 109:7, 8², 9, 10², 11², 12, 13, 14², 15²; 17², 19, 20, 28; 115:14, 15; 116:9; 118:20; 119:18, 38, 41, 74, 76, 77, 78, 79, 80², 115, 125, 134, 144, 148, 169, 170, 171, 172, 173, 175²; 122:6, 7; 128:5²; 6; 129:5, 6, 8; 132:9²; 134:3; 137:5, 6; 138:4, 5; 140:10, 11; 141:2²; 142:7; 143:10; 145:12; 149:6; Pr 5:2²; 18², 19²; 13:8, 23; 14:13²; 18:24; 22:19, 25; 23:25²; 25:10; 26:26; 27:1; 28:11; 30:9² Ecc 2:21; 3:13, 18; 4:12, 14²; 6:3; 7:21, 24; 10:8², 9², 20²; 11:2, 8; SS 4:16; 6:1, 8, 13; 7:8, 9; Isa 2:3; 5:19²; 26:2; 27:3; 30:8; 37:4, 20; 41:20²; 42:9, 43:9, 10, 21; 44:13; 45:3, 6; 46:5; 49:6, 15; 51:23; 55:3, 6; 60:11; 66:5; Jer 5:22²; 6:27; 7:23; 10:18; 13:26; 15:19; 20:14, 16²; 28:6²; 29:6, 18; 38:19, 24; 42:5; 43:3; 50:34; 51:35²; La 1:21²; 2:13; 3:29, 65; 5:21; Eze 3:12; 12:16; 16:54; 20:20; 21:15; 23:48; 24:11; 34:25; 37:9; 38:16; 40:46; 43:10, 11; 44:2, 3, 11², 22, 25, 30; 46:17; Da 2:30²; 4:1, 17, 27; 5:17; 6:16, 25; 11:35; Hos 2:18; 6:2; 13:10; 14:2; Joel 2:14; Am 5:14; 8:5²; 9:12; Jnh 3:9; Mic 1:8; Zec 8:6, 9; 11:1, 17²; 12:7; Mal 1:4²; 2:4, 12²; 3:10; Mt 2:8; 5:16, 25³, 45; 6:4²; 7:6; 9:6; 13:29; 15:32; 17:27; 18:31; 20:1; 21:19; 25:9; 26:5, 39, 42; 27:64; Mk 2:10; 4:12; 7:29; 11:14, 25; 14:2, 14; 15:32; Lk 1:4, 38; 5:24; 8:10², 12; 10:35; 11:33; 12:58; 14:8, 12; 17:8; 20:16; 21:36²; 22:11, 30, 32; Jn 3:15, 21; 4:36, 50; 5:14, 23, 34; 6:30, 50; 7:3, 23; 9:36; 10:10, 38; 11:4, 15, 16, 42; 12:36; 14:3, 13, 14; 15:11²; 16:33; 17:1, 3, 11, 13, 19, 21³, 22, 23, 26²; 19:35; 20:31²; Ac 1:20²; 3:19²; 20; 8:19, 20, 24; 9:17; 10:29; 13:47; 15:17; 17:19; 20:24, 31; 23:24; 24:25; 25:26; 26:18, 29; Ro 1:10, 11, 12, 19; 3:4, 8, 19; 4:16²; 6:1, 4; 8:17; 10:1, 4; 11:9, 10, 14, 25, 31, 32; 13:9; 15:5, 6, 9, 13², 31²; 32; 16:2; 1Co 1:10², 29; 2:12, 16; 3:18; 4:6; 5:5, 7; 7:5, 35; 9:2, 18, 23; 10:33; 11:34; 14:5, 13, 17, 31; 15:28, 35; 16:11; 2Co 4:10, 11, 15; 5:4, 10; 8:11; 9:3; 10:2; 11:3, 6, 16; 12:9, 16, 20; 13:7, 10, 14; Gal 2:16; 4:17, 24; 5:10; 6:1, 13, 14; Eph 1:17²; 18²; 3:12, 16, 17, 18, 19; 4:12, 28, 29; 6:3²; 3:13; 4:3²; 4, 6, 8²; 5:10, 23²; 2Th 1:11²; 12; 2:6, 16; 3:1, 2, 5, 14, 16; 1Ti 1:3, 18; 2:2; 3:6; 4:15; 5:7, 9, 20; 6:1, 19; 2Ti 1:4, 16, 18; 2:10; 4:16; Tit 2:8; 3:8, 11, 14; Phm 1:6, 20; Heb 3:13; 4:1, 11, 16; 6:18; 10:24; 12:10, 13, 27; 13:19, 20, 21; Jas 1:4; 4:3; 5:16; 1Pe 1:6, 7²; 2:2, 9, 12; 3:1, 9, 16; 4:11, 13; 5:6; 2Pe 1:4; 3:17; 1Jn 1:3; 2:28; 5:13, 20; 2Jn 1:8, 12; 3Jn 1:2², 8; Rev 16:15; 19:18; 22:14².

ME (4015)

Ge 3:12², 13; 4:10, 14³, 23³, 25; 9:12, 13, 15, 17; 12:12, 18²; 13:8; 14:21, 24; 15:2, 3, 9; 16:2, 5², 13²; 17:1, 2, 4, 7, 11; 18:5, 21, 30, 32; 19:8, 19², 20; 20:5, 6, 9², 11, 13³; 21:6², 23³, 26; 22:12, 18; 23:4, 8², 9², 11, 13², 15²; 24:5, 7³, 12, 17, 23, 27², 37, 39, 43, 44, 45, 48, 49², 54, 56²; 25:22, 30, 31, 32, 33; 26:5, 7, 27³, 27:3, 4², 7², 9, 12, 13², 19², 20, 25, 26, 31, 33, 34², 36², 38; 28:20³, 22; 29:15², 19, 21, 25², 32, 33, 34; 30:1, 3, 6², 13, 14, 16, 18, 20², 24, 25, 26, 27, 31², 32, 33², 31:5², 7², 9, 11, 13, 26, 27², 28, 29, 31, 32, 36, 39, 40, 42², 48, 49, 50, 51, 52; 32:9, 11², 16, 20, 26², 29; 33:10², 11, 14, 15²; 34:4, 11, 12², 30⁴; 35:3²; 37:9, 14, 16; 38:16², 17; 39:7, 8, 9, 12, 14, 15², 17², 18, 19²; 40:8, 9, 14²; 41:10, 24, 51, 52; 42:20, 33, 34, 36²; 43:6, 8, 9, 14, 16, 27, 29; 44:15, 17, 21, 27, 28, 29, 34²; 45:4, 5², 7, 8², 9², 10, 13, 18; 46:31; 47:29², 30², 31; 48:3², 4, 9², 11, 16; 49:6², 29; 50:4, 5², 20; Ex 2:9, 14; 3:9, 13², 14, 15, 16; 4:1², 18, 23, 25; 5:1, 22; 6:12², 30; 7:16²; 8:1, 8, 9, 20, 28; 9:1, 13, 14; 10:3², 17, 28; 11:8²; 12:32; 13:2², 8, 14:15; 17:2, 4; 18:4, 15, 16, 19; 19:5, 6, 9; 20:3, 5, 6, 23, 24, 25; 22:23, 27, 29, 30; 23:14, 15, 18, 33; 24:12; 25:2², 8, 30; 28:1, 3, 4, 41; 29:1, 44; 30:30; 31:13, 17; 32:2, 10, 23, 24, 26, 32, 33, 34; 33:12⁴, 13², 16², 18, 20, 21; 34:2, 19, 20, 25; 40:13, 15; Lev 6:17; 10:3, 19; 20:26; 22:2; 25:55; 26:14, 18, 21², 23, 27², 40², 41; Nu 3:41; 8:16; 11:11, 12, 13, 14, 15³, 16; 14:11², 22², 23, 24, 27, 29, 34, 35; 16:28, 29; 17:10; 18:8³, 9; 20:12²; 22:5, 6, 8, 10, 11, 13, 16, 17, 18, 19, 28, 29, 32, 33², 34, 37; 23:1², 3², 7², 10, 11, 13², 17, 27², 29²; 24:12, 13, 14; 27:14; 28:2²; 32:11; Dt 1:9, 14, 17, 22, 23, 37, 42; 2:1, 2, 9, 17, 31; 3:2, 25, 26³; 4:5, 10³, 14, 21; 5:7, 9, 10, 22, 23, 28², 29, 31; 6:1; 7:4; 8:17; 9:4, 10, 11, 12, 13, 14, 19; 10:1², 4, 5, 10, 11; 18:15, 17; 25:7; 26:10, 14; 31:2, 16, 19, 20, 28; 32:21², 39, 41, 51; Jos 2:4, 12²; 7:19²; 8:5; 10:4, 22; 14:6, 7, 8, 9, 10, 11, 12²; 15:19³; 18:4, 6, 8; 19:46; 22:2; 24:15; Jdg 1:7, 15³; 2:2, 20; 3:28; 4:8²; 19; 5:13; 6:10, 17², 39³; 7:2², 17, 18; 8:15, 24; 9:7, 15, 48, 54; 10:12, 13; 11:7³, 9², 27², 31, 35, 36, 37²; 12:2, 3², 5; 13:6², 7, 10, 16; 14:2², 3², 12², 13², 16³; 15:11, 16:6, 7, 10³, 11, 13³, 15³, 17, 18, 26, 28³, 30; 17:2, 10, 13; 18:4; 19:18, 19, 20, 20:5²; Ru 1:8, 11, 12, 13, 20, 21²; 3:9, 15, 17; 4:4; 1Sa 1:11, 27; 2:29, 30⁴, 36; 3:5, 6, 8, 17²; 8:7, 8; 9:16, 18, 19²; 21; 10:2, 8, 15; 12:1, 2, 3², 12, 23²; 13:9, 12; 14:12, 34, 41, 42, 43, 44; 15:11, 16³, 20, 25, 30²; 16:2, 3, 5, 17, 19; 17:8, 9, 10, 35, 37², 43, 45, 46; 18:8, 17; 19:15, 17³, 20:2², 3, 9, 14, 15; 22:3, 8³, 13³, 17, 23³; 23:7, 10, 11, 12, 21, 22, 23; 24:10, 11, 12², 15³; 17, 18⁴, 19, 21; 25:21, 24, 25, 33, 34², 39; 26:6, 8, 14, 19², 24; 27:1, 5; 28:1, 7, 8², 12, 15⁶, 16, 17, 19, 21, 22; 29:3, 6²; 30:7, 13, 15⁴; 31:4³; 2Sa 1:4, 7², 8, 9², 26²; 2:7, 22; 3:8, 12, 13, 14, 21, 35, 39; 4:9, 10; 5:19, 20; 6:9², 21²; 7:5, 7, 16, 18; 9:8; 10:2, 11; 11:6; 12:10, 22, 23, 28; 13:4, 5, 11, 12, 13², 16², 24; 14:4, 9, 10, 15, 16, 17, 18, 19, 32²; 15:4, 7, 8, 25²; 26, 28, 33², 34, 36; 16:3, 9, 12; 18:13, 19, 22, 27, 29; 19:13, 19, 25, 26, 33², 36, 38² 20:4, 20²; 21:4; 22:3, 5², 6², 17², 18², 19², 20², 21², 23, 25, 33, 34, 36², 37, 40, 44³, 45³, 48², 49³; 23:2, 3, 5², 15, 17²; 24:12, 13, 14, 17, 24; 1Ki 1:12, 13², 17², 26, 29, 30, 51; 2:4², 5, 7, 8², 15, 16, 17, 20, 23, 24², 30, 31, 42; 3:5, 17, 24; 5:4, 6, 8; 8:25²; 9:3, 4, 6, 13; 10:7; 11:21, 22, 33, 36; 12:5, 6, 9, 12, 27; 13:6, 7, 8, 13, 15, 18, 27, 31; 14:2, 8, 9²; 15:19²; 16:2; 17:10, 11, 13², 18², 19; 18:11, 12, 14², 19, 30, 37²; 19:2, 10, 14, 20; 20:10, 32, 35, 36, 37, 39; 21:2, 6, 20, 22; 22:4, 8, 14, 16, 18, 24, 28, 34; 2Ki 2:2, 4, 6, 9², 10, 20; 3:7², 15; 4:2, 6, 22, 24, 27²; 5:7², 8, 11², 17, 22²; 6:11, 19, 26, 28, 31; 8:4, 9, 13, 14; 9:12, 18, 19; 10:6²; 15², 16; 14:8; 16:7²; 18:14², 20, 22, 23², 25, 27, 31, 32; 19:6, 27, 28; 20:8; 21:15; 22:10, 13, 15, 17²; 1Ch 4:10³; 10:4²; 11:17; 12:17⁴; 13:12; 14:10; 17:4, 6, 12, 16, 17; 19:2, 12²; 21:2, 10, 12, 13², 17, 22², 24; 22:8, 18; 28:2, 3, 4², 5, 6, 19²; 2Ch 1:7, 8, 9, 10; 2:3, 7, 8, 9; 6:16²; 7:17; 9:6; 10:5, 6, 9, 12; 12:5, 8; 13:4; 15:2; 16:3²; 18:3, 7, 15, 17, 23, 27, 33; 20:20; 25:17; 28:11, 23; 32:14; 34:18, 21, 23, 25²; 27; 35:21³, 23; 36:23²; Ezr 1:2²; 7:28³; 8:1; 9:1, 4; Ne 1:3, 9; 2:2, 4, 5, 6², 7, 8², 9², 12, 13², 17, 20²; 4:18, 23; 5:15, 18, 19; 6:2², 4, 5, 11², 12, 13³, 14, 19²; 13:14, 22², 28, 31; Est 4:16; 5:8, 12, 13; 6:6; 7:3, 8; 8:5²; Job 2:3; 3:10,

Ge 2:23²; 4:9, 13, 23; 6:3, 18; 9:9, 11, 13,

12, 24, 25²; 4:12, 14; 6:4², 7, 9², 13, 22, 23², 24², 28; 7:3, 8³, 12, 13, 14², 16, 19², 20, 21; 9:11, 16, 17, 18², 20², 28, 31², 32, 34², 35; 10:2³, 3, 7, 8³, 9², 10², 11², 12², 14, 15, 16², 17³, 18², 20; 13:4, 13², 15, 19, 20, 22²; 23, 24, 26²; 14:13⁴; 15:17²; 16:7, 8², 9⁴, 10², 11², 12⁵, 13, 14²; 17:1, 2, 3², 6, 15; 19:2², 3², 5², 6², 9, 10, 11², 12, 13², 14, 15², 18², 19², 21², 22, 27; 20:2, 3²; 21:2, 3, 5, 27, 34; 23:5, 6², 10, 14, 16; 24:15, 25; 27:2², 3, 6; 28:14²; 29:2, 5², 6, 8, 11⁴, 13, 20, 21, 23; 30:1², 9, 10, 11, 12, 13, 15, 16, 18², 19, 20, 21², 22², 23, 27², 31:6, 13, 14, 15, 20, 35², 38; 32:10, 14, 18², 22²; 33:4², 5², 7, 10², 31, 32, 33; 34:2, 5, 10, 32, 33, 34²; 35:3; 36:2; 38:3, 4, 18; 40:7, 8; 41:10, 11², 42:3, 4, 7, 8; Ps 2:7, 8; 3:1, 2, 3², 4, 5, 6, 7; 4:1³; 5:8²; 6:1², 2², 4², 8²; 7:1², 3², 4, 8; 9:13²; 10:6, 13; 11:1; 13:1², 3, 6; 16:1, 5, 6, 7², 8, 10, 11²; 17:3² 6², 8², 9², 11³, 13, 14; 18:4², 5², 16², 17², 18, 19³, 20², 22, 24, 32, 33³, 35, 36, 39, 43³, 44², 47², 48³; 19:13²; 22:1², 7², 9², 11, 12², 13, 14, 15, 16², 17, 19, 21²; 23:2², 3, 4², 5, 6; 25:2², 5², 7, 16², 17, 19, 20³, 21; 26:1, 2², 3, 11²; 27:2², 3², 5³, 6, 7², 9³, 10², 11², 12²; 28:1, 3; 30:1², 2, 3³, 7, 10, 11; 31:1², 2², 3, 4², 5, 8, 9, 11², 13, 15², 16, 17, 21; 32:4², 7; 34:3², 4, 11; 35:1², 3, 7², 11, 12, 13, 15², 16, 19², 20², 22, 23², 24², 26; 36:11²; 38:1², 2², 4, 10, 11, 12, 16, 17, 19, 20, 21², 22; 39:3², 4², 8, 10², 13; 40:1, 2, 7, 11², 12², 13², 15, 17; 41:4², 5, 6, 7², 9², 10², 11², 12²; 42:3, 5, 6, 7, 8, 9, 10², 11; 43:1², 2, 3, 5; 44:6, 15, 16; 49:5, 15; 50:5², 8, 15², 23; 51:1, 2, 3, 5, 6, 7, 8, 10², 11², 12³, 14², 54:1², 4, 5², 7, 55:2², 3², 4², 5², 12², 16, 18³, 23; 56:1², 2², 5, 9, 13², 57:1², 2, 3², 59:1³, 2², 3², 4², 10³; 60:9²; 61:2, 5; 63:8; 64:1, 2; 66:16², 20; 69:1, 2, 4², 6², 9², 11, 12, 13, 14², 15³, 16², 17², 18², 20, 21, 29; 70:1², 3, 5; 71:1², 3, 4, 6, 9², 10², 12², 18, 19, 20², 21, 24; 73:2, 16, 23, 24², 28; 75:9; 77:1; 81:8, 11², 13; 84:8; 86:1, 3, 7, 11², 13², 14, 16², 17³; 87:4²; 88:1, 6, 7²; 14², 16², 17², 18; 89:26, 36; 91:14, 15; 92:4, 10; 94:16², 17, 18, 19; 95:9; 101:2, 3, 4, 6²; 102:2³, 8², 10², 24; 106:4; 108:10²; 109:2², 3², 4, 5, 20, 21², 22, 25, 26²; 116:2², 3, 4, 6, 12, 16; 118:5, 6², 7, 10, 11, 12, 13, 18², 19, 21; 119:8, 10, 12, 19, 22, 23, 26², 27, 28, 29², 31, 33, 34, 41, 42, 49, 51, 53, 58, 61, 64, 66, 68, 69, 71, 72, 73³, 74, 75, 77, 78, 79, 82, 85, 86², 87, 94, 95, 98², 102, 108, 110, 115, 116, 117, 121, 122, 124, 125, 132², 133, 134, 135, 139, 143, 144, 145, 146, 153, 154, 157, 161, 169, 170, 171, 173, 175²; 120:1, 2, 5; 122:1; 129:1, 2², 4; 131:1, 2; 138:2³, 7, 8; 139:1², 5², 6², 10², 11², 13, 16, 17, 19², 23², 24²; 140:1², 4², 5², 9; 141:1, 4, 5³, 8, 9², 10; 142:3², 4, 6³, 7³; 143:3³, 4², 7²; 9, 10², 11; 144:2, 7², 11²; Pr 1:24, 28³, 33; 4:4; 5:7; 7:24; 8:15, 16, 17³, 18, 21, 22, 32, 34, 35, 36²; 9:11; 23:26, 35²; 24:29; 27:11; 30:4, 7, 8³, 18; Ecc 1:16; 2:3, 7, 9², 15, 17, 18; 7:23; 9:13; SS 1:2², 4², 6³, 7, 13, 14; 2:4², 5², 6, 10², 13, 14²; 3:3, 4; 4:8²; 5:2, 7³; 6:5², 12; 7:10; 8:1², 2, 3, 6, 13; Isa 1:2, 11, 12, 13, 14²; 3:7²; 5:3; 6:5, 6, 8; 8:1, 2, 3, 5, 11³, 18; 10:6; 12:1²; 18:4; 21:2, 3, 4², 6, 11, 16; 22:4³; 24:16; 27:4, 5³; 28:22; 29:2, 13⁴, 16; 30:1², 9²; 31:4², 6, 11, 16; 36:5, 7, 10, 16, 17⁴, 18²; 37:6, 21, 28, 29; 38:12³, 13, 15, 16², 17, 20; 39:3; 40:25; 41:1; 42:19; 43:10³, 11, 20, 22³, 23², 24⁴, 26, 27; 44:6, 7, 8, 17, 22; 45:4, 5², 6, 11², 19, 21², 22², 23², 24; 46:3³, 5², 9, 12; 47:8, 10; 48:1², 16², 19², 21², 22, 23³; 49², 15, 16; 49:1², 2²; 50:4², 6, 7, 8³, 9²; 51:1, 4³, 5, 7; 54:9, 17; 55:2², 3², 11; 56:3, 4, 12; 57:8, 11³, 13, 16; 58:2², 59:21; 60:9; 61:1³, 10²; 63:3², 5²; 8; 65:1², 3, 5, 6, 7, 9, 10, 12; 66:1, 4, 22, 23, 24; Jer 1:4, 7, 9, 11, 12, 13, 14, 16; 2:1, 2², 5², 13², 19, 21, 22, 27²; 29², 32, 35; 3:1, 4, 6, 7, 10, 11, 13, 19², 20; 4:1, 12, 17, 19, 22; 5:7, 11, 19, 22; 6:7, 10, 20; 7:10, 16, 18, 23, 26; 8:18, 19, 21; 9:3, 6, 13, 24; 10:19, 20, 24²; 11:4, 6, 7, 9, 11, 14, 17, 18², 19², 20; 12:3², 24², 26, 27; 44:6, 7; 46:6, 7, 8, 17, 22; 45:4, 5², 6, 11², 19, 21², 22², 23², 24; 46:3³, 5², 9, 12; 47:8, 10; 48:1², 16², 19², 21², 22, 23³; 49², 15, 16; 49:1², 2²; 50:4², 6, 7, 8³, 9²; 51:1, 4³, 5, 7; 54:9, 17; 55:2², 3², 11; 56:3, 4, 12; 57:8, 11³, 13, 16; 58:2², 59:21; 60:9; 61:1³, 10²; 63:3², 5²; 8; 65:1², 3, 5, 6, 7, 9, 10, 12; 66:1, 4, 22, 23, 24; Jer 1:4, 7, 9, 11, 12, 13, 14, 16; 2:1, 2², 5², 13², 19, 21, 22, 27²; 29², 32, 35; 3:1, 4, 6, 7, 10, 11, 13, 19², 20; 4:1, 12, 17, 19, 22; 5:7, 11, 19, 22; 6:7, 10, 20; 7:10, 16, 18, 23, 26; 8:18, 19, 21; 9:3, 6, 13, 24; 10:19, 20, 24²; 11:4, 6, 7, 9, 11, 14, 17, 18², 19², 20; 12:3², 24², 26, 27; 13:1, 19; 14:1²; 2, 3, 5, 7², 11, 12, 13²; 26; 13:1, 19; 14:1²; 2, 3, 5, 7², 11, 12, 13;

15:1; 16:1, 20, 26, 43, 50; 17:1, 11, 20; 18:1, 4²; 20:1, 2, 3², 8², 13, 21, 27², 28, 31², 38, 39, 40, 45, 49; 21:1, 8, 18; 22:1, 12, 17, 14, 15, 19, 20; 25:1; 26:1, 2; 27:1; 28:1, 11, 20; 29:1, 17, 20; 30:1, 9, 20; 31:1; 32:1, 17; 33:1, 7, 21, 22², 23; 34:1; 35:1, 13²; 36:16; 37:1³, 2, 3, 4, 9, 10, 11, 15; 38:1, 16; 39:23, 26; 40:1², 2², 13, 15; 43:1, 5², 6², 8, 9, 18, 19; 44:1, 2, 4, 5, 7, 10², 13, 15³, 16; 46:19², 20, 21², 24; 47:1², 2, 3, 4², 6², 8; 48:11; Da 2:3, 5, 6⁴, 9⁴, 23², 24, 26, 30²; 4:2, 5², 6², 7, 9, 18, 19², 27², 28, 31², 33, 34, 35, 36, 37, 38, 41; 24:1, 14, 15, 19, 20; 25:1; 26:1, 2; 27:1; 28:1, 11, 20; 29:1, 17, 20; 30:1, 9, 20; 31:1; 32:1, 17; 33:1, 7, 21, 22², 23; 34:1; 35:1, 13²; 36:16; 37:1³, 2, 3, 4, 9, 10, 11, 15; 38:1, 16; 39:23, 26; 40:1², 2², 13, 15; 43:1, 5², 6², 8, 9, 18, 19; 44:1, 2, 4, 5, 7, 10², 13, 15³, 16; 46:19², 20, 21², 24; 47:1², 2, 3, 4², 6², 8; 48:11; Da 2:3, 5, 6⁴, 9⁴, 23², 24, 26, 30²; 4:2, 5², 6², 7, 9, 18, 19², 27², 28, 31²; 5:7, 15²; 6:22; 7:2, 5, 6, 7, 8, 13, 16, 16², 23; 8:1, 3, 14, 15, 17, 18³, 19², 21; 12:5; Hos 2:5, 13, 16², 19; 3:1, 3; 4:7; 5:3, 15; 6:7; 7:2, 7, 13³, 14², 15; 8:2, 13; 11:2, 7, 8, 12; 12:8; 13:4²; 6, 9, 10; 14:8; Joel 2:12; 3:4³; Am 4:6, 8, 9, 10, 11; 5:4, 22, 25; 7:1, 4, 7, 8, 15²; 8:1, 2; 9:3, 7; Ob 1:3; Jnh 1:2, 12²; 2:2, 3³, 5², 6; 4:3, 8; Mic 2:4; 3:8; 5:2, 15; 6:3; 7:7², 8, 9, 10; Hab 1:3²; 2:1; 3:19; Zep 2:15; 3:7, 8, 10, 11; Hag 2:17; Zec 1:3, 4, 8, 9, 13, 14, 18, 19²; 20; 2:1, 2, 3, 8², 9, 11; 3:1; 4:1², 2, 4, 6, 8, 9; 5:1, 2, 3, 5², 9, 10; 6:1, 4, 5, 8, 9, 15; 7:4, 5; 8:1, 6, 14, 18; 10:9; 11:8, 11, 12², 13², 15; 12:10; 13:7; Mal 1:6²; 2:2, 5, 6; 3:1, 5, 7, 8, 9, 10, 13; Mt 2:8; 3:11, 14; 4:9, 10, 19; 5:11; 7:4, 21, 22, 23; 8:2, 9, 21, 22; 9:9; 10:22, 32, 33, 37², 38², 40³; 11:6, 27, 28, 29; 12:30²; 14:8, 18, 28, 30; 15:5, 8², 9, 22, 25, 32; 16:23²; 24:5; 17:17; 18:5, 6, 21, 26, 28, 29, 32; 19:14, 17, 21, 28; 20:4, 7, 13, 14, 15, 19; 22:19; 23:39; 24:9; 25:20, 22, 35³, 40, 41, 42²; 43³, 45; 26:10, 11, 12, 15, 21, 23², 31, 34, 38, 39, 40, 55², 75; 27:10, 17, 21, 46; 28:10, 18; Mk 1:7, 17, 40; 2:14; 5:7², 31; 6:22, 25, 31; 7:6², 7, 11, 14; 8:2, 33, 34², 35, 38; 9:19, 24, 37⁴, 39, 42; 10:14, 18, 21, 29, 36, 40, 47, 48, 51; 11:29, 30; 12:15³; 13:9, 13; 14:6, 7, 18², 20, 30, 36, 48, 49, 72; 15:9, 34; 14:8³, 23, 27; 6:27, 42, 46, 47; 7:8, 23, 40, 44, 45; 8:28²; 45, 46²; 9:23², 24, 26, 48³, 59²; 61; 10:16⁴, 22, 40²; 11:5, 6, 7², 23³; 12:8, 9, 13, 14; 13:27, 35; 14:18, 19, 26, 27; 15:6, 9, 12, 19, 29, 31; 16:4, 24²; 17:18³, 3², 13, 16, 19, 22, 38, 39, 41; 19:27²; 20:3, 24; 21:17; 22:19, 21, 28, 29, 34², 42, 53, 61, 67; 23:14, 28, 42, 43; 24:39, 44; Jn 1:15³, 30³, 33², 43, 48; 2:4, 17; 4:7, 9, 15, 21, 29, 34, 39; 5:7², 11², 24, 30, 32, 36², 37², 39, 40, 43, 46²; 6:26, 35², 36, 37³, 38, 39², 44², 45, 56, 57³, 65; 7:6, 7, 8, 16, 19, 23, 28², 29, 33, 34², 36³, 37, 38; 8:12, 16, 18, 19, 21, 26, 28, 29³, 37, 40, 42², 45, 46², 49, 54; 9:4, 11, 36; 10:9, 14, 15, 16, 25, 27, 29, 32, 36, 37, 38², 11:25, 26, 41, 42²; 12:8, 26³, 27, 44³, 45², 46, 48, 49², 50; 13:8, 13, 18, 20³, 21, 33, 38²; 14:1, 3, 6, 7², 10², 11², 12, 14, 15, 19², 20, 21², 23, 24²; 28², 30, 31; 15:2, 4², 5, 6, 7, 8, 9, 16, 18², 19², 20, 21², 23, 24², 26², 27; 16:3, 9, 10, 14², 16², 17², 19, 22², 23²; 17:1, 2², 4, 5², 6², 7², 8², 9, 11², 12², 14, 15, 18², 20, 21², 23², 24, 25², 26; 18:5, 8, 11²; 21, 24, 25², 26², 27, 28, 29, 30, 31², 33, 39, 41; 26:8, 17², 18, 19², 20, 21², 23, 24, 25; 27:12; 28:2², 9², 21²; 29:8, 9; 30:13, 15, 23; 2Sa 1:10, 26; 3:7, 13, 14, 18², 26, 48; 5:2, 20; 6:22; 7:5, 6, 7, 8², 10, 11, 13, 14, 15, 18; 9:7, 10, 11; 10:11; 11:11⁴; 13:4, 5²; 6, 10, 11, 12, 13, 20, 25, 26, 32, 34; 14:5, 7, 9², 11, 12, 15, 16, 17², 18, 19²; 18:5, 12³, 13, 18, 22, 28, 31, 32, 33³; 19:4³, 12², 13², 19², 20, 22, 25³, 27²; 28², 30, 35, 37²; 20:9; 22:2³, 3⁴, 4, 7⁴, 18², 19², 21², 22², 25², 29², 30, 33, 34, 35², 37, 38, 39, 40², 41², 44, 47², 49²; 23:2, 5²; 24:3², 17, 21, 22; 24:14; 1Ki 1:13², 17², 18, 20², 21², 24, 27², 30², 31, 33², 36, 37², 48²; 2:15, 17, 20, 22, 24, 26²; 31, 32, 38, 44; 3:6, 7², 14², 17, 18, 20³, 21, 22, 23, 26; 5:3, 4, 5³, 6, 9³; 6:12²; 13; 8:15, 16³, 17, 18², 19, 20, 24, 25, 26, 28, 29³, 9:3³, 4, 7, 13; 10:6, 7; 11:11³, 13, 21, 32, 33³, 34², 36²; 38⁴; 12:10², 11², 14², 24; 13:6, 30, 31; 14:7, 8³; 15:19; 16:2²; 17:1, 14², 20², 21²; 18:7, 10, 11, 12, 13, 14; 19:2², 20; 20:4, 6, 7⁴, 9, 10, 32, 34²; 21:2, 3, 4, 6, 20; 22:4², 28, 49; 2Ki 1:13, 14; 2:12²; 3:7²; 4:1², 13, 16, 19², 28², 29²; 5:3, 6, 11, 13, 18², 20, 22, 26; 6:5, 8, 12, 15, 21, 26, 28, 29, 32; 8:5, 12; 9:7, 21, 32; 10:6, 9, 16, 30; 13:14²; 14:9; 17:13²; 18:23, 24, 27, 29, 34, 35; 19:12, 23, 24, 28³; 34²; 20:5, 6², 15², 19; 21:4, 8, 14, 15; 22:17, 19; 23:27²; 1Ch 4:10; 11:2, 12²; 14:11²; 16:22; 17:4, 6, 7², 9, 10, 13², 14², 16, 25; 21:3³; 17², 23; 22:5, 7³, 8², 10², 11; 28:2³, 3, 4³, 5², 6³, 7, 9, 20; 29:1, 2², 3⁴, 14, 17, 19; 2Ch 1:8, 9, 11; 2:3, 4, 7², 8, 14, 15; 6:4, 5³, 6³, 7, 8², 9, 10², 15, 16², 19, 40; 7:13, 14³, 15³, 16³, 17, 20, 26²; 18:7, 8, 11², 13², 16², 17, 27; 19:6², 7; 21:16; 28:10², 11², 14², 20; 20:4, 6, 7⁴, 9, 10, 32, 34²; 21:2, 3, 4, 6, 20; 22:4², 28, 49; 2Ki 1:13, 14; 2:12²; 3:7²; 4:1², 13, 16, 19², 28², 29²; 5:3, 6, 11, 13, 18², 20, 22, 26; 6:5, 8, 12, 15, 21, 26, 28, 29, 32; 8:5, 12; 9:7, 21, 32; 10:6, 9, 16, 30; 13:14²; 14:9; 17:13²; 18:23, 24, 27, 29, 34, 35; 19:12, 23, 24, 28³; 34²; Ne 1:2, 6, 9²; 2:3², 5, 8²; 4:4, 14, 18; 4:16, 23²; 5:13, 14², 19, 22, 29, 31; Est 4:16; 5:7³, 8²; 7:3⁴, 4; 8:6²; Job 1:5, 8, 21; 2:3; 3:3, 10, 24; 4:12, 14, 15², 16²; 5:8, 9, 10, 12, 15, 22, 29, 30²; 7:5², 6, 7², 11², 13², 16², 21²; 9:15, 17, 18, 20, 21, 25, 27², 28, 30, 31; 10:1³, 8², 12, 14, 15², 16, 18; 11:4; 12:4; 13:14², 16², 17²; 16:4², 5², 6, 7,

---

MY (4597)

Ge 2:23²; 4:9, 13, 23; 6:3, 18; 9:9, 11, 13,

8, 9, 10, 13², 15², 16², 17², 18², 19², 20³; **17:**1², 2, 7², 11³, 13, 14³, 15; **19:**4², 5, 8², 9², 10, 12, 13², 14², 15², 16², 17³, 19, 20, 21, 23, 25, 26², 27²; **20:**2, 3; **21:**2, 4, 6; **23:**2², 4², 7, 11, 12, 16, 17; **24:**25; **27:**3, 4², 5, 6², 7²; **29:**3, 4², 5, 6, 7, 14³, 18², 19², 20², 21, 22, 23, 24; **30:**1, 10, 11², 12², 13, 15², 16, 17², 18, 25, 30², 31²; **31:**1, 4², 5, 7⁴, 8, 9², 10, 13, 17, 18², 20, 21, 22, 24², 25², 27², 29, 30, 31, 32, 33³, 35², 36, 37, 38; **32:**12, 17, 20, 22; **33:**1, 2³, 3², 7, 8, 11², 28; **34:**2; **35:**10; **36:**3², 4; **37:**1; **38:**2; **40:**4², 8²; **42:**3, 5², 7, 8³; **Ps** 2:6², 7; 3:1, 3, 7², 8, 9²; 4:1³, 2, 7; 5:1², 2³, 3², 8; 6:2³, 3, 7², 8, 9², 10; 7:1, 3², 4, 5², 6², 8², 10; 9:1, 3, 4², 13; 13:2³, 3², 4², 5; 14:4; 16:2, 3, 4, 5², 7³, 8, 9³; 17:1³, 2, 3², 5, 6, 9; 18:1, 2⁸, 3, 6⁴, 17², 18², 20², 21, 24², 28³, 29, 32, 33, 34², 36, 37, 38, 39², 40², 46², 48²; 19:12, 14²; 22:1³, 2, 9, 10², 14², 15³, 16², 17, 18², 19, 20², 22, 25²; 23:1, 3, 5³, 6; 25:1, 2², 5², 7², 11, 15², 17², 18³, 19, 20, 21; 26:2², 6, 9², 12; 27:1³, 2, 3, 4, 6, 7, 8, 9²; ...

6:10, 29, 30; **7:**1², 9, 11, 16, 21; **8:**10², 15, 20; **9:**3, 7, 13, 15, 16, 18, 24, 28, 32; **10:**2, 7, 10, 14, 20; **11:**11; **12:**3², 9, 11, 12², 13:2, 11², 20; **14:**2, 7, 12², 16, 21²; **15:**6, 9², 11, 15, 29, 30, 31, 32; **16:**6², 18; **17:**4, 10; **18:**21; **19:**16, 27; **20:**9, 17, 18, 19, 21; **21:**4, 9, 10, 16; **22:**5², 12, 14, 30; **23:**6, 8², 9, 12, 17; **24:**1, 13, 25; **25:**3, 5²; **26:**8; **27:**4, 5, 6, 11, 15; **28:**8, 13, 14², 18; **30:**10, 20, 25², 28; **31:**1, 3, 4, 15², 17, 20, 23, 30, 31, 34; **32:**6, 9², 12, 13², 14²; **33:**12, 14, 27, 33; **34:**18, 19, 32, 33; **35:**3, 12, 13, 14, 15; **36:**4, 5, 6, 7, 12, 13, 18, 19, 20; **37:**23, 24; **39:**4, 7, 16², 17, 22; **40:**23; **41:**12, 28; **42:**3, 7, 8², Ps **1:**1, 3, 4, 5; **3:**2, 6; **4:**4; **5:**4, 9; **6:**1; **7:**12; **9:**12, 18, 19; **10:**4, 12, 15; **14:**3, 4; **15:**5; **16:**4, 8, 10; **17:**1, 3, 5; **18:**21, 22, 36, 37, 38, 41, 43; **19:**3, 13; **21:**2, 7; **22:**2², 5, 6, 11, 19, 24²; **23:**1; **24:**5; **25:**2, 7, 20; **26:**4, 9; **27:**3, 9², 12; **28:**1, 3; **30:**1, 12; **31:**8, 17; **32:**2, 5, 6, 9²; **34:**20; **35:**19², 20, 22², 24, 25; **36:**4, 11, 12; **37:**1, 7, 8, 10, 19, 21, 24, 28, 31, 33, 36; **38:**1, 9, 14, 16, 21²; **39:**2, 6, 8, 9, 12; **40:**4, 6², 9, 10², 11, 17; **41:**2, 11; **44:**3, 6², 17, 18², 21, 23; **46:**2, 5; **49:**9², 12, 16, 17; **50:**3, 8, 12; **51:**11, 16², 17; **52:**7; **53:**3, 4; **54:**T; **55:**1, 23; **56:**4, 8, 11; **57:**T; **58:**T, 5, 8; **59:**T, 11, 15; **60:**10; **62:**6, 10²; **66:**7, 18, 20; **69:**4, 5, 6², 14, 15, 17, 27, 28, 33; **70:**5; **71:**9², 12, 15, 18; **73:**5; **74:**19², 21, 23; **75:**T, 4, 5²; **76:**5; **77:**19; **78:**4, 7, 8³, 10, 22, 32, 37², 38², 39, 42, 44, 50, 56, 64, 67; **79:**6², 8; **80:**18; **81:**5, 9, 11²; **83:**1³; **85:**6, 8; **89:**30, 33, 34, 35, 43, 48; **91:**5, 7, 12; **92:**6²; **94:**7, 9², 10, 14; **95:**8, 10; **101:**3, 5; **102:**2, 17, 18, 24; **103:**2, 9, 10; **105:**15, 28; **106:**7, 11, 13, 23, 24, 25, 34; **107:**38; **108:**11; **109:**1; **110:**4; **115:**1², 17; **118:**6, 17, 18; **119:**6, 8, 10, 11, 16, 19, 31, 36, 43, 46, 51, 60, 61, 80, 83, 87, 92, 102, 109, 110, 116, 121, 122, 136, 141, 153, 155, 157, 158, 176; **121:**3², 6; **124:**1, 2, 6; **125:**3; **127:**5; **129:**2, 8; **131:**1³; **132:**3, 10, 11; **137:**6²; **138:**8; **139:**12, 15, 21; **140:**8², 11; **141:**4², 5, 8; **143:**2, 7; **146:**3; **147:**10, 20; Pr **1:**8, 10, 15², 25, 28², 29, 30; **3:**1, 5, 7, 11², 21, 23, 24, 27, 28, 29, 30, 31; **4:**2, 5, 6, 12², 13, 14, 15, 19, 21, 27; **5:**6, 7, 8, 13; **6:**20, 25, 30, 35; **7:**19, 20, 25; **8:**1², 29, 33; **9:**8; **10:**3, 19, 30; **11:**21; **12:**27; **13:**1; **14:**5, 7, 12, 15; **15:**7, 12; **16:**5, 10, 29; **17:**5, 20, 26; **18:**5; **19:**2, 5², 9, 10, 18, 24; **20:**1, 4, 13, 21, 22, 23; **21:**13²; **22:**6, 20, 22², 24², 26, 28, 29; **23:**3, 4, 6², 7, 9, 10, 13², 17, 18, 20, 22, 23, 31, 35; **24:**1², 12³, 14, 15², 17², 19, 21, 23, 28, 29; **25:**6², 8, 9, 14, 27; **26:**1, 2, 4, 17, 25; **27:**1², 2², 10², 22, 24²; **28:**5, 13, 20, 21, 24; **29:**19, 24; **30:**2, 3, 6, 7, 10, 11, 12, 18; **31:**3, 4³, 12, 18, 27; Ecc **1:**11; **2:**16, 21, 23; **4:**3², 8, 12, 16; **5:**1, 2², 4, 5², 6², 8; **6:**2, 3, 6; **7:**9, 10, 16², 17², 18, 20, 21, 28²; **8:**3², 8, 11, 13³, 16; **9:**2, 11; **10:**4, 15, 17, 20; **11:**2², 4², 5, 6²; **12:**9; SS **1:**6, 8; **2:**7; **3:**1, 2, 4, 5; **4:**2; **5:**6²; **6:**6; **8:**4, 8; Isa **1:**3², 6, 15, 23²; **2:**4, 9; **3:**7, 9; **5:**6, 25, 27⁴; **7:**1, 4, 7², 9², 12², 13; **8:**10, 11, 12², 19, 20; **9:**12, 13, 17, 20, 21; **10:**4, 7², 8², 9², 11, 14, 15, 24; **11:**3, 13; **12:**2; **13:**10², 17, 22; **14:**17, 20, 21, 29, 31; **16:**3; **17:**8, 10; **22:**2, 4, 11, 14; **23:**18; **26:**10², 11, 14, 18²; **27:**4; **28:**8, 12, 18, 25², 27, 28²; **29:**9², 16, 17²; **30:**1², 14; **31:**1, 2, 3², 4, 8²; **32:**10; **33:**1², 16, 20, 23²; **34:**10, 16; **35:**4, 8², 9; **36:**12, 14, 15², 16, 18, 21; **37:**16, 19², 26, 28³, 31², 35; **38:**1, 11; **39:**2, 4; **40:**9, 16, 20², 21⁴, 26, 28³, 31²; **41:**3, 7, 9, 10², 12, 13, 14, 17; **42:**2, 3², 4, 8, 16, 24³, 25²; **43:**1², 2, 5, 6, 12, 18, 19, 22², 23², 24; **44:**2, 8⁴, 20, 21; **45:**1, 4, 5, 13, 18, 19², 21, 23; **46:**7, 13²; **47:**7, 11, 15; **48:**1, 5, 6, 7², 8, 9, 10, 11, 16, 21; **49:**15, 23; **50:**5², 6, 7²; **51:**7, 9, 10, 14, 21; **52:**1, 12, 15², **53:**3, 7²; **54:**2, 4⁴, 9, 10, 11, 14, 15; **55:**2², 5², 8, 10, 11, 13; **56:**3, 5; **57:**4, 10², 11², 12, 16; **58:**1, 2², 6, 7², 13²; **59:**1, 2, 8, 9, 21; **60:**12; **62:**1²; **63:**8, 13, 16, 17, 19²; **64:**3; **65:**1³, 2, 6, 8, 12², 17, 20, 23; **66:**2, 9, 19, 24; Jer **1:**6, 7, 8, 17, 19; **2:**2, 6, 8², 11, 17, 20, 23², 24, 25, 27, 30, 34, 35², 37; **3:**1, 2, 4, 7, 10, 12, 13, 16, 19, 25; **4:**3, 8, 11, 22², 27, 28²; **5:**3, 4, 7, 9², 10², 13, 15², 16, 17, 19, 20², 22², 24, 28², 29²; **6:**14, 15, 16, 17, 19, 20², 25, 29; **7:**4, 6, 9², 10², 13, 15², 16, 17, 19, 20, 22, 24², 26, 27², 28, 31; **8:**2, 4², 6, 7, 11, 12, 19, 20; **9:**3², 4, 9², 10, 13, 20; **10:**2, 4, 5, 7, 11, 16, 21², 23², 24; **11:**3, 8², 11, 12, 14², 21; **12:**4, 6, 9, 17; **13:**1, 11, 15, 17, 21; **14:**9, 10², 11, 12², 13, 14, 15, 18, 21³, 22²; **15:**1, 7, 14, 15, 19², 20; **16:**2, 4, 5², 6, 7, 8, 11, 17, 20; **17:**4, 6, 8, 11, 16², 17, 21, 22, 23², 24, 27²; **18:**6, 8, 10, 15, 17, 18, 23; **19:**5, 15; **20:**3, 9, 11, 14, 17; **21:**10; **22:**3, 5, 6, 10, 12, 13, 16, 18², 21, 28, 30; **24:**2; **25:**3, 4, 6³, 7, 8, 29, 33; **26:**2, 3, 4, 8, 9, 13; **16:**19³, 24; **27:**8, 9², 13, 14², 15, 16, 17, 18, 20; **28:**15; **29:**6, 8², 9, 11, 16, 19², 23, 27, 31; **30:**5, 10², 11², 19², 24; **31:**9, 20, 32; **32:**4, 5, 23², 33²; **33:**3, 24, 25, 26; **34:**3, 4,

14, 17², 18; **35:**6, 13, 14³, 15², 16, 17²; **36:**25², 31; **37:**4, 9², 14³, 19, 20; **38:**4, 14, 15², 17, 18², 20, 23, 24, 25, 26; **39:**16, 17, 18; **40:**3, 4, 7, 9, 14, 16; **41:**8; **42:**5, 10², 11², 13, 14, 17, 19, 21; **43:**2²; **44:**4, 5², 10, 16, 19, 21, 23, 27; **45:**5; **46:**21, 27², 28³; **47:**3; **48:**8, 11², 27, 33; **49:**9², 12², 25, 36²; **50:**5, 7, 9, 13; **51:**3², 5, 6, 9, 39, 46, 50, 57; La **1:**9; **2:**1, 8, 14; **3:**22, 31, 33, 36, 37, 38, 42, 56, 57; **4:**8, 12, 17, 18, 22; **5:**7, 9, 18, 19, 20², 21²; **4:**14; **5:**6, 7², 11; **6:**10; **7:**4, 7, 9, 12, 13³, 19²; **8:**12, 18²; **9:**6, 9, 10; **10:**11, 16; **11:**3, 11, 12; **12:**2², 9, 13; **13:**5, 6, 7², 9, 12, 19²; **14:**16, 18; **15:**5; **16:**4, 16, 20, 22, 28, 29, 43², 47, 49, 51, 56, 61; **17:**9², 10, 12, 18; **18:**6², 7², 8, 12, 13, 14, 15², 16², 17, 19, 20, 21, 23, 25², 28², 29, 30; **20:**3³, 7, 8², 9, 31², 39; **21:**4², 14; **22:**12; **23:**5², 12, 14, 21, 24², 25², 31, 34, 38, 44, 47, 48; **24:**16, 17², 22, 23; **25:**10; **26:**15, 20; **28:**2, 9; **29:**5; **30:**21; **31:**8; **32:**7, 9, 27; **33:**4, 5, 6, 8, 9, 12², 15, 17², 20, 31, 32; **34:**2, 3, 4², 8, 18²; **35:**6, 9; **36:**22, 29, 32; **38:**14, 17; **39:**10, 28; **41:**6; **42:**14; **44:**2, 9, 13, 17, 18, 19, 20, 22, 25, 31; **46:**2, 18; **47:**5, 11, 12; **48:**11, 14²; Da **1:**8²; **2:**1, 5, 9, 10, 11, 18, 24, 30, 34, 43, 45; **3:**6, 11, 14, 15, 16, 18², 27²; **4:**7, 19, 30; **5:**8, 15, 22, 23; **6:**2, 12, 17, 18, 22, 26; **7:**14; **8:**22, 24, 25; **9:**6, 10, 13, 14², 18, 19; **10:**7, 12, 19; **11:**4, 7, 11², 4; **6², 12, 15, 17, 20, 23, 25, 34, 42; **12:**1, 8; Hos **1:**7, 9², 10; **2:**2², 4, 7², 8, 23²; **3:**3; **4:**10², 14, 15⁴; **5:**3, 4², 6²; **6:**6; **7:**2, 4, 8, 9², 10, 14, 16; **8:**6, 13; **9:**1², 2, 3, 4², 17; **10:**3, 9; **11:**3, 5², 9³; **12:**8; **13:**13; **14:**3; Joel **1:**16; **2:**7, 8, 13, 17, 21, 22; **3:**21; Am **1:**3, 6, 9, 11, 13; **2:**1, 4², 6, 11, 12, 14³, 15³; **3:**6²; **4:**6, 8², 9, 10, 11; **5:**5³, 11², 14, 18, 20²; **6:**6, 10, 13; **7:**3, 6, 16; **8:**8, 11, 12; **9:**1, 4, 7², 8, 9, 10; Ob **1:**5², 7, 8, 12, 13, 14; Jnh **1:**6, 13, 14²; **3:**7², 10; **4:**2, 10, 11; Mic **1:**5², 10², 11; **2:**6³, 7, 10; **3:**1, 4, 5, 7², 11, 4:**3, 12; Na **1:**3, 9; **3:**19; Hab **1:**2², 5, 6, 12²; **2:**3², 4, 6, 7²; 13; **3:**17; Zep **1:**13²; **3:**2², 5, 7, 11, 16²; Hag **1:**2, 6; **2:**3, 5, 17, 19; Zec **1:**4²; 6; **3:**2; **4:**5, 6, 13; **7:**6, 7, 10², 12, 13²; **8:**11, 13, 15², 17²; **10:**6, 10; **11:**5, 6, 9, 12, 16; **12:**7²; **13:**4, 5; **14:**2², 12², 19; Mal **1:**2, 8², 10²; **2:**2³, 9, 10², 15², 16; **3:**5, 6², 7, 10², 11, 18; **4:**1; Mt **1:**19; **2:**12²; **3:**9, 10, 11; **4:**4, 6, 7; **5:**17², 18², 20, 21, 26, 27, 33, 34, 36, 39, 42, 46, 47; **6:**1, 2, 3, 5, 7, 8, 13, 15², 16, 18, 19, 20², 25², 26², 28, 29, 30, 31, 34; **7:**1, 6², 19, 21, 22, 25, 26, 29; **8:**8, 10; **9:**12, 13², 14, 19, 20, 23, 24, 26; **10:**5, 9, 14, 19, 20, 23, 24, 26, 28, 29², 34², 37², 38², 42; **11:**6, 8, 11, 17²; 20; **12:**4, 7², 11, 16, 19, 20², 25, 30², 31, 32, 43; **13:**15, 11, 12, 13², 17², 19, 34, 58; **14:**4, 16; **15:**6, 11, 13, 16, 20, 23, 26, 32; **16:**9, 11, 12, 17, 18, 20, 23; **17:**12, 16, 17, 20, 24; **18:**5, 7, 8, 10, 11², 12, 13², 14, 15, 16, 21, 22, 25, 26, 28, 30, 31, 34; **19:**3, 8, 9, 11², 14, 18, 19², 21, 22, 25, 26, 29³; **20:**13², 15, 19, 22², 23, 26², 28; **21:**21², 29, 30, 32², 18, 21, 29, 31, 32; **22:**3², 4, 8, 9, 11, 30, 37, 39, 40, 42, 43, 44, 45²; **23:**3, 9, 13, 24², 26², 27, 28, 30, 31, 34, 37³, 39; **24:**2, 6, 20, 22, 23, 26², 29, 34, 36, 42, 43, 44, 45²; **25:**5, 11, 22, 24, 25, 29, 39, 40, 41, 42, 55, 60, 62²; **27:**14; **28:**5, 6, 10; Mk **1:**7, 22, 34; **2:**2, 4, 17², 18, 27; **3:**12, 20; **4:**5, 7, 25, 27, 34; **5:**3, 10, 19, 37, 39, 43; **6:**5, 9, 11, 18, 19, 26, 31, 52; **7:**3, 4, 24², 27, 36; **8:**17, 21, 30, 32, 37, 38, 39, 40, 41, 48²; **9:**1, 6, 9, 18, 30, 32, 37, 38, 39, 40, 41, 48²; **10:**9, 14, 15, 19⁵, 27, 40, 43, 45; **11:**13, 16, 17, 23; **12:**14, 24², 27, 34²; **13:**2, 7, 11², 14, 18, 20, 21, 24, 30, 32, 33, 35, 36; **14:**2, 7, 19, 21, 25, 29, 36, 37, 38, 40, 44, 49, 55, 56, 58, 59, 60; **15:**23²; **16:**6, 11, 13, 16, 18; Lk **1:**13, 20², 22, 30; **2:**10, 26, 45, 50; **3:**8, 9, 16; **4:**4, 11, 12, 26, 27, 41; **5:**19, 31, 32, 36, 6:**29, 30, 37⁴, 39, 40, 44, 46, 48, 49; **7:**6², 7, 9, 23, 25, 30, 32², 44, 45², 46; **8:**10², 12, 14, 17², 18, 19, 27, 31, 47, 51, 52, 56; **9:**5, 21, 27, 33, 40, 45², 49, 50², 53; **10:**4², 6, 7, 10, 20, 24², 42; **11:**4, 8², 24, 35, 38, 40, 46, 52; **12:**2², 7², 10³, 11, 18, 21, 22, 24, 25², 26, 27², 29², 30, 31, 34², 37², 38², 42; **13:**6, 8, 11, 17², 20; **12:**4, 7², 11, 16, 19, 20², 25, 30², 31, 32, 43; **13:**5, 11, 12, 13², 17², 19, 34, 58; **14:**5, 12, 14, 18, 20, 21, 24, 30, 32, 33, 35, 36; **14:**2, 7, 19, 21, 25, 29, 36, 37, 38, 40, 44, 49, 55, 56, 58, 59, 60; **15:**7², 16², 28, 29, 32², 16:**6, 11, 13, 16, 18; Lk **1:**13, 20², 22, 30; **2:**10, 26, 45, 50; **3:**8, 9, 16; **4:**4, 11, 12, 26, 27, 41; **5:**19, 31, 32, 36, 39; **6:**29, 30, 37⁴, 39, 40, 44, 46, 48, 49; **7:**6², 7, 9, 23, 25, 30, 32², 44, 45², 46; **8:**10², 12, 14, 17², 18, 19, 27, 31, 47, 51, 52, 56; **9:**5, 21, 27, 33, 40, 45², 49, 50², 53; **10:**4², 6, 7, 10, 20, 24², 42; **11:**4, 8², 24, 35, 38, 40, 46, 52; **12:**2², 7², 10³, 11, 18, 21, 22, 24, 25², 26, 27², 29², 30, 31, 34², 37², 38², 42; **13:**6, 8, 11, 17², 20; **14:**5, 12, 14, 18, 20, 21, 24, 30, 32, 33, 35, 36; **16:**6, 11, 13, 16, 18, 21; **17:**8, 10; **18:**4, 7, 19, 10; **20:**4², 5, 15; **21:**22, 23; **22:**5, 9, 10.

30, 35, 37, 39, 42, 44, 47³, 48, 49; **13:**7, 9, 10, 11, 18; **14:**1, 2, 10, 18, 19, 22², 24³, 27³, 30; **15:**6, 15, 16, 19, 24, 26, 30, 32; **17:**9, 14, 15, 16², 20, 25; **18:**9, 11, 17², 25², 28, 30², 36, 40; **19:**11, 21, 24, 31, 33, 36; **20:**5, 9, 14, 17², 23², 24, 25, 29, 30; **21:**4, 8, 11, 18, 23³, 25; Ac **1:**4, 7; **2:**7, 15, 25, 27, 31, 34; **3:**6, 23; **4:**18, 21; **5:**4, 7, 22, 26, 28, 39, 40; **6:**2, 10; **7:**5, 6, 11, 25, 32, 48, 50, 52, 53, 60; **8:**16, 21, 32, 39; **9:**7, 9, 26; **10:**14, 15, 20, 28, 34, 41; **11:**8, 9; **12:**19, 22, 23; **13:**25², 27, 35, 37, 39, 40, 46; **14:**17; **15:**19, 28, 38²; **16:**7; **17:**4, 6, 24, 25, 27, 29; **18:**9²; **19:**2, 27, 30, 31, 32, 34, 36, 40; **20:**20, 22, 27, 29, 33; **21:**4, 12, 13, 14, 21, 34; **22:**9, 18, 22, 23; **23:**5², 12, 14, 21; **24:**4, 12; **25:**7, 10, 11², 16, 17, 18, 24; **26:**19, 25, 26, 29, 31, 32; **27:**7, 15, 21, 22, 24, 34, 39, 41; **28:**4, 18, 19, 21, 24; Ro **1:**13, 16, 28², 32; **2:**4, 11, 13, 14², 21, 26, 27, 28, 29²; **3:**3, 4, 6, 8, 9, 10, 12, 17, 29, 31; **4:**2, 4, 5, 10, 11, 12, 13, 16, 17, 20, 23; **5:**3, 5, 11, 13, 14, 15, 16, 6:**12, 13, 14², 15; **7:**1, 3, 6, 7³, 15², 16, 19², 20; **8:**4, 7, 9³, 12, 15, 18, 20, 23, 25, 26, 32²; **9:**1, 6², 8, 10, 12, 14, 16, 21, 24, 25², 26, 30, 31, 32²; **10:**2, 3², 6, 14², 16, 18, 19², 20²; **11:**2, 4, 7, 8², 11², 18², 20, 21², 23, 25², 26; **12:**2, 3, 4, 14, 16², 17, 19, 21, 23², 13:**4, 5², 9⁴, 13³, 14; **14:**3⁴, 13, 15, 16, 17, 20, 21, 22, 23²; **15:**1, 3, 18, 20², 21²; **16:**4, 18; **1Co **1:**7, 14, 17², 20, 21, 26³, 28; **2:**1, 4, 5, 6, 8, 12, 14, 15³; **3:**1, 2³, 3², 4, 18; **4:**3, 4, 6², 7², 14, 15, 18, 19, 20; **5:**1, 3, 6, 8, 9, 10, 11², 12²; **6:**2³, 3, 7², 9³, 12², 15, 16, 19², 7:**1, 4², 5², 6, 9², 12², 15², 16, 19², 2:**7, 9, 12, 15², 16, 17, 18, 20, 21⁴, 24, 25, 26²; **27:**10, 11, 5, 7, 8, 9, 10, 13, 16², 18, 20² 22³, 28, 29, 32, 33; **11:**6, 7, 8, 11, 14, 20, 22, 31, 32, 34; **12:**1, 14, 15³, 16³; **13:**1, 2, 3, 4³, 5, 6; **14:**2, 8, 11, 16², 17², 21, 22², 23², 24, 33, 34, 39; **15:**9², 10², 13, 14, 15², 16², 17, 29, 29, 32, 33, 36, 37, 39, 46, 51, 58; **16:**7, 22; **2Co **1:**8, 9, 12, 13, 19, 24; **2:**1, 3, 4, 5², 7, 11², 13, 17; **3:**3², 5, 6, 7, 8, 13, 14; **4:**1, 2, 5, 7, 8², 9², 16, 18; **5:**1, 3, 4, 7, 12, 19; **6:**1, 3, 9, 14, 17; **7:**3, 9², 12; **8:**5, 8, 10, 12², 13, 15², 17, 21; **9:**3, 4, 5, 7, 10², 3, 4, 8, 9, 12², 13, 14², 16, 18; **11:**5, 6, 9, 11, 15, 17, 29², 31; **12:**2, 3, 4, 5, 6, 11, 14², 16, 18², 20², 21; **13:**2, 3, 5, 6, 7², 10²; Gal **1:**1, 10, 11, 12, 16, 2:**3, 5, 6, 14², 15, 16², 17, 21; **3:**10, 12, 16, 17, 20, 21; **4:**8², 14, 18, 21, 23, 26, 27, 29; **5:**3, 6, 7², 13, 17, 18; **6:**4, 6, 7, 9, 12; Eph **1:**16, 21; **2:**8, 9; **3:**5, 13; **4:**20, 26², 27, 29, 30; **5:**3, 7, 15, 18; **6:**4, 6, 7, 9, 13; Php **1:**17, 22, 29; **2:**4, 6, 12, 16, 21, 27, 30; **3:**9, 12, 13; **4:**6, 11, 15, 17; Col **1:**9, 23; **2:**1, 11, 16, 18, 21³; **3:**2, 9, 19, 19; **4:**5²; **1Th **1:**5, 8²; **2:**1, 3, 4, 6², 8, 9, 13, 17, 19; **4:**5², 7, 8, 9, 12, 13, 15; **5:**1, 3, 4, 5, 6, 9, 19, 20; **2Th **1:**8²; **2:**2, 3, 12; **3:**2, 6, 7, 8, 9², 10², 11, 14²; **1Ti **1:**3, 7, 9, 20; **2:**7, 9, 12, 14; **3:**4⁴, 5, 6, 7, 8²; **4:**14²; **5:**1, 8, 11, 13², 16, 18, 19, 22², 25; **6:**1, 2, 3, 17; **2Ti **1:**7, 8, 9, 12, 16; **2:**5, 9, 15, 20, 24²; **3:**3, 9; **4:**3, 8, 16; Tit **1:**2, 6, 7², 11, 15; **2:**3, 9, 10, 15; **3:**5, 14; Phm **1:**14²; **19; Heb **1:**14; **2:**1, 5, 8², 11, 16; **3:**8, 10, 15, 16, 17, 18, 19²; **4:**2, 6, 7, 8, 15; **5:**5, 12, 13; **6:**1, 10², 12; **7:**6, 11, 16, 20, 21, 27; **8:**2, 4, 9²; **9:**8, 9, 11, 12, 18, 24, 25, 28; **10:**1, 2, 5, 6, 8, 25, 35, 37, 38, 39; **11:**1, 3, 5², 7, 8, 13, 16, 23, 27, 28, 31, 32, 38; **12:**3, 4, 5², 7, 8², 13, 18, 20, 25²; **13:**2, 6, 9², 14, 16, 17; Jas **1:**4, 6, 7, 17, 20, 22, 23, 25, 26; **2:**4, 5, 6, 7, 11³, 13, 17, 21, 24, 25; **3:**1, 10, 14, 15; **4:**2³, 3, 11³, 14; **5:**6, 12², 17²; **1Pe **1:**8², 12, 14, 18, 23; **2:**7, 10², 16, 18, 23; **3:**1, 3, 6, 9, 14², 21; **4:**2, 4, 12, 15, 16, 17; **5:**2², 3; **2Pe **1:**9, 16; **2:**3, 4, 5, 10, 11, 12, 21; **3:**8, 9², 17; **1Jn **1:**6, 8, 10; **2:**1, 2, 4², 7, 11, 15², 16, 19, 21², 27²; **3:**1², 7, 10³, 12, 13, 14, 18, 21; **4:**1, 3², 6², 8², 10, 18, 20²; **5:**3, 6, 10³, 12, 16, 17, 18; **2Jn **1:**1, 5, 7, 8, 9²; **10²; **12; **3Jn **1:**10, 11², 13; **Jude **1:**5, 6, 9, 10, 19; Rev **1:**17; **2:**2, 3, 5, 9, 10, 11, 13, 24³; **3:**2, 3², 4, 8, 9, 17²; **5:**5; **6:**6; **7:**3, 16; **9:**4², 5, 6, 20³; **10:**4²; **11:**2, 6; **12:**8, 11; **13:**8; **14:**4; **15:**4; **16:**15, 20; **17:**8³, 10, 11, 12; **18:**4², 7; **19:**10; **20:**4², 5, 15; **21:**22, 23; **22:**5, 9, 10.

O (978)

Ge **15:**2, 8; **24:**12, 42; **32:**9²; 49:9, 18; Ex **4:**10, 13; **5:**22; **15:**6², 11, 16, 17²; **32:**4, 8, 11; **34:**9; Nu **10:**35, 36; **12:**13; **14:**14²; **16:**22; **21:**17, 29²; **24:**5²; Dt **3:**24; **4:**1; **5:**1; **6:**3, 4; **9:**1, 26; **10:**12; **18:**21; **26:**10; **27:**9; **32:**1², 6, 43; **33:**7, 11, 29; Jos **7:**8, 13; **10:**12²; Jdg **3:**19; **5:**4, 12², 31; **13:**8; **16:**28²; **21:**3; **1Sa **1:**11; **17:**55; **23:**10, 11, 20; **2Sa**

OF (25210)

Ge **1:**2², 14, 15, 17, 20, 21, 26², 27, 28², 29, 30²; **2:**3, 4, 5², 6, 7², 9⁴, 11², 12, 13², 14², 15², 17³, 19³, 20², 21, 22, 23³; **3:**1, 3, 5, 6, 7², 8³, 14, 17⁴, 18, 19, 20, 21, 22², 23, 24²; **4:**1, 3³, 4², 16², 18³, 20, 21, 22², 23, 25, 26; **5:**1², 6, 7, 9, 10, 12, 18, 19, 21, 22, 25, 26, 29, 32; **6:**2³, 4⁴, 5², 7², 8, 9, 11, 13, 14, 16², 17, 19, 20², 7:**2⁴, 3², 4, 7, 8³, 11⁴, 13, 14, 15², 16, 18, 20, 21², 7:**2⁴, 3², 4, 7, 8³, 14, 16, 17, 19, 20, 21²; **9:**2⁴, 5, 6², 10, 11, 12, 13, 15, 16, 17, 18³, 19, 20,

13², 14², 15², 16², 19; **58**:1, 2, 3, 5, 6³, 8, 9, 10², 12², 14³; **59**:1, 5, 6, 8, 17², 19³, 20, 21²; **60**:1, 3, 5, 6³, 7, 9³, 11, 13³, 14⁴, 15, 16²; 17⁴, 19, 20, 21², 22; **61**:1, 2³, 3¹⁰, 6³, 7², 10²; **62**:2, 3², 7, 9, 11², 12; **63**:1, 2, 4², 7³, 9², 11³, 12, 14, 16, 17, 19; **64**:4, 5, 6, 7², 8; **65**:3², 4², 7, 8², 10, 11, 14⁴, 16², 19², 22³; **66**:5², 6, 8, 9, 12, 14, 15, 17², 18, 19², 20, 21, 24; **Jer 1**:1⁴, 2⁵, 3⁸, 4, 8, 11², 13, 15⁴, 16, 18²; **2**:1, 2³, 3, 4⁴, 6³, 10, 13, 16², 19, 21, 22, 26, 31³, 33, 34²; **3**:3, 6, 8², 10, 16², 17³, 18², 19, 20, 21², 22, 23, 24; **4**:1, 3, 4³, 7², 8, 15, 16, 19², 21, 29, 30, 31⁴; **5**:1, 4², 5², 7, 11², 15, 16, 20, 24², 25, 27², 28²; **6**:1², 2, 4, 9, 10, 11², 14, 15, 17, 19, 22², 23, 24, 27; **7**:2³, 3, 4³, 11, 12², 15, 17², 18², 20², 21, 24, 29, 30, 31²; 32², 33³, 34³; **8**:1⁵, 2, 3, 6, 7², 8², 9², 11, 12, 15, 16², 19, 22; **9**:1³, 2, 4, 6, 7², 10², 11², 14, 15, 17, 19, 20², 22³, 23², 26; **10**:1, 2, 3², 7², 13, 15, 16³, 19, 21, 22²; **11**:2², 3², 4², 6², 8², 9, 10², 12², 13², 14, 16, 17², 19, 21², 23²; **12**:1, 3, 6, 7, 9², 12², 13², 14, 15, 16; **13**:3, 8, 9², 10, 11², 12, 17, 20, 21, 22²; **14**:1, 6, 7, 8², 11, 14, 16², 18, 19, 20, 21, 22²; **15**:3³, 4⁴, 7, 8², 9, 11², 13, 15, 17, 20, 21²; **16**:1, 4³, 9³, 12², 13, 14, 15³, 16, 18, 19²; **17**:1², 3, 6, 8, 12, 13², 15, 16, 17, 18, 19³, 20², 21, 22, 24, 25², 26³, 27²; **18**:5, 6³, 8, 11², 12², 14, 16, 17, 18, 21, 23; **19**:1³, 2², 3⁶, 4³, 5, 6², 7⁴, 8², 9² 13², 14, 15; **20**:1², 2, 4², 5³, 8, 9, 13², 18; **21**:1², 2², 4⁴, 6², 8², 10², 11², 12³; **22**:1², 2², 3, 4, 6³, 9, 11², 16, 18², 19², 22, 23², 24², 25, 26, 29, 30²; **23**:1, 2, 3², 7, 8⁴, 9, 10², 13, 14³, 15, 16, 17, 18², 20², 26², 33, 34, 35, 36², 38², 39; **24**:1³, 4, 5², 8, 9², **25**:1⁶, 2, 3⁴, 5, 9³, 10⁴, 11, 12², 14, 16, 18², 19, 20², 22², 24², 25, 26⁴, 27², 31, 32, 33, 34, 35, 36³, 37², 38³; **26**:1³, 2⁴, 3, 5, 6², 7, 9, 10⁴, 15, 16, 17³, 18⁵, 19², 20², 21, 22², 23², 24; **27**:1³, 2², 3², 6, 8, 9², 11², 12², 13, 14², 17, 18⁴, 20⁴, 21⁴; **28**:1⁶, 3, 4², 5, 6, 7, 10, 11³, 12², 13, 14³, 16, 17; **29**:1, 2, 3³, 4, 7, 8, 18³, 20, 21⁴, 22²

2, 3⁴, 4², 5², 6², 7³, 8², 9³, 10, 13, 14², 15, 18, 22², 26, 27², 30, 31⁴, 32, 35, 36², 37², 38³, 39², 40², 41, 42, 44, 45, 46², 47, 49; **21**:1, 2², 6, 7, 8, 9, 10, 12², 13, 14, 18, 19³, 20, 21², 23, 25², 28, 29², 30; **22**:1, 2², 4³, 5, 6² 16, 17, 18⁴, 23, 24², 25, 26, 29, 30; **23**:1, 2², 6, 7², 13, 14, 15², 17, 19, 20², 21, 23³, 24, 25², 26, 29, 31, 33², 35, 36, 42², 45, 49²; **24**:1², 2², 4², 5, 6, 9, 15, 16², 17², 20, 21³, 22², 23, 25², **25**:1, 2, 3⁴, 4, 6², 8, 9², 10, 12, 14², **26**:1², 2⁴, 7², 9², 10, 11, 13, 15, 16, 17², 18, 20²; **27**:1, 2, 3, 5, 6³, 7², 8, 9², 10, 11², 12², 13, 14, 15, 16, 18², 21², 22³, 23, 25², 26, 27², 31², 33, 34; **28**:1, 2⁵, 5, 7, 8, 9², 10², 11², 12², 13², 14, 16, 17³, 18, 20, 21, 24, 25²; **29**:1, 2², 3, 4, 5³, 6², 10², 11, 12, 13, 14, 15, 16³, 17, 18², 19, 21; **30**:1, 2², 3³, 5, 6, 9³, 10³, 11, 12², 15², 17, 18, 20, 21³, 22, 24² 25⁵; **31**:1, 2⁴, 4, 5², 6², 8², 9, 10², 11, 12³, 13², 15, 16, 17², 18³, 21, 22², 23² 24² 25², 26², 27³, 30, 32; **33**:1, 2³, 5, 6³, 7², 10³, 11², 12⁴, 13, 16, 17, 20³, 21, 22, 23, 24², 26, 27, 28, 29, 30²; **34**:1, 2⁵, 3, 7, 9, 12, 13, 14², 18, 25², 26, 27³, 29², 30, 31; **35**:1, 2, 5, 10, 11, 12, 15³; **36**:1⁴, 2, 3³, 4⁵, 5, 6², 8, 10², 12, 13, 15², 16, 17², 20, 21, 22³, 23, 24, 26², 30² 32², 34³, 35², 37, 38; **37**:1⁴, 2, 3, 4, 9, 11², 12, 15, 16⁴, 19³, 21, 22² 23, 26; **38**:1, 2⁴, 3, 4, 7, 8², 11², 12, 13, 14², 15, 17², 18, 19, 20⁴, 22, 23; **39**:1², 2, 4², 8², 9², 10³, 11², 13³ 14², 15³, 17³, 18⁴, 20², 22, 23, 25, 27², 29; **40**:1⁵, 2², 4², 5², 6, 7, 8, 9, 10, 11, 12, 13³, 14², 15², 16, 18, 19², 20², 26, 27³, 28; **41**:1, 2, 3², 4², 5, 6², 8², 9², 12², 14, 15, 17², 19⁶, 20, 22, 23, 24, 25; **42**:3, 4, 5, 7, 8, 8², 9², 10², 11, 12², 43:2³, 4, 5, 7⁵, 9, 10³, 11², 12³, 13³, 17³, 18, 19², 20³, 21, 27², **44**:1, 2, 3², 4⁴, 5⁴, 6³, 8², 10, 11², 12³, 13², 14², 15³, 17², 19, 20, 22², 27, 30³; **45**:1, 2, 4, 6, 7³, 8, 9, 11², 12, 13⁴, 14⁵, 15², 16³, 18⁴, 19², 20, 22², 23², 24, 25; **46**:1², 2², 3², 5, 6, 7, 8, 9, 11, 14⁵, 16, 17², 18⁴, 19, 22², 23³, 24; **47**:1⁴, 6², 7², 9², 10², 12², 13, 15, 16, 17², 18, 19², 21, 22; **48**:1², 2, 3, 4, 5, 6, 7, 8³, 10², 12³, 13, 14², 15², 18³, 19, 20, 21⁴, 22², 23⁴, 24, 26, 27², 28³, 29, 30, 31⁵, 32³, 33³, 34³, 35; **Da** 1:1⁴, 2⁵, 3², 4², 5, 10, 13, 15², 17³, 18, 20, 21; **2**:1, 5, 10, 12², 14², 18³, 19, 20, 23³, 24², 29, 32², 33³, 34, 37³, 38³, 39, 41⁴, 44², 45³, 47³, 48², 49; **3**:1³, 2, 3, 4, 5³, 7⁴, 10³, 12³, 14, 15², 18, 20, 22, 25, 26³, 27², 28, 29³, 30; **4**:1, 6, 8², 9², 10, 11, 12³, 15², 16³, 17², 18² 21², 22, 23², 25², 26, 29², 30³, 33³, 34, 37³, 38³, 39, 41⁴, 44², 45³, 47³, 48², 49; **3**:1³, 3, 4², 5, 7⁴, 10³, 12³, 14, 15², 18, 20, 22, 25, 26³, 27², 28, 29³, 30; **5**:1, 3, 4², 5², 7, 10, 11⁴, 13, 14, 19², 20, 21³, 23³, 26, 30, 31; **6**:2, 4, 5, 8, 12, 13, 15, 17²

11², 12, 14, 15, 16; **10**:1², 2, 3, 6², 11²; **11**:2, 3³, 6, 7, 8², 11², 12, 13², 15, 16; **12**:1³, 3, 4², 4², 6; **14**:1, 2³, 3, 4⁴, 5², 10³, 13, 14², 16, 17², 18, 19³, 20², 21²; **Mal** 1:1, 4, 5, 10, 11, 12²; **2**:3, 5², 7², 9, 10, 11, 12, 14², 15, 16, 17²; **3**:1, 2, 3, 4, 5², 6, 7, 9, 10, 16; **4**:2, 3, 4, 5, 6², **Mt** 1:1⁴, 2³, 3³, 4³, 5³, 6², 7³, 8², 9³, 10³, 11², 12³, 13³, 14³, 15³, 16³, 18, 20², 24; **2**:1, 2, 4, 6⁴, 9, 11³, 13, 15², 19, 20, 21, 22²; **3**:1, 2, 3⁴, 4, 5, 6, 7, 8, 9, 11³, 13³, 14³, 15², 16³, 17²; **4**:1, 3, 4, 5, 6², 8³, 11, 12², 18, 19, 20², 24; **5**:1, 2, 4, 6⁴, 9, 11³, 13, 15², 19, 20, 21, 22²; **6**:1², 7, 8, 9, 10, 11, 13, 14², 16², 18, 20², 26, 27, 28, 29, 30, 31, 33; **7**:3, 4, 5, 9, 10², 14², 21, 24, 26, 29; **8**:3, 11, 12², 18, 19, 20², 26, 27, 28, 29, 30, 31; **9**:3², 6, 15, 16, 20, 26, 27, 34, 35, 38; **10**:2², 3, 5, 6, 7, 15, 20, 22², 23² 25², 26², 29², 30, 34, 37², 38, 42²; **11**:1, 6, 10, 11², 12³, 19², 20, 22, 24, 25; **12**:1, 4, 8², 11², 15, 23, 24, 28², 32, 34³, 35, 36, 38², 39³, 40², 41², 42, 43, 44, 45, 46, 47², 49, 50, 52⁴, 58²; **13**:3, 5, 6, 8, 9, 10, 17, 20, 21, 22, 25, 29, 31, 33, 35, 36; **15**:1, 2, 3⁶, 4², 6³, 11, 12, 13², 14, 16, 17, 18, 19², 21², 22, 24, 29, 31, 37, 38, 39; **16**:3², 4, 6², 8, 11, 12, 13², 14, 16, 17, 18, 19², 21², 23², 27, 28; **17**:1, 9, 10, 12, 18, 22², 24, 26, 27²; **18**:1, 3, 4, 6², 7, 9, 12, 14, 15, 16, 19, 23, 32, 35; **19**:1², 7, 12², 14, 23, 24², 28³; **20**:1, 10, 12², 13, 18², 20², 21², 25, 28, 30, 31; **21**:1, 2, 5², 9³, 12², 13², 15², 16, 17, 23, 26, 31³, 32, 37, 39, 40, 41, 43, 46; **22**:2, 13, 16², 28², 29², 30, 31², 32², 35, 42², 23:2, 6, 13², 15², 16, 23³, 25² 26, 27, 28, 29², 30², 31, 32², 33, 34, 35³, 39; **24**:3⁴, 6², 8, 9², 14, 15, 17², 21, 22, 27², 29, 30³, 31, 37², 39³, 43², 44, 45, 47, 50², 51; **25**:1, 2, 8, 15, 19, 21, 23, 30, 31, 34, 40², 45², 26², 3², 6, 7, 10, 13, 14, 17², 21, 24², 27, 28², 29², 30, 31², 32, 33, 34, 35³, 39², 45², 46², 26², 3², 6, 7, 10, 13, 14, 17², 21, 24², 27, 28², 29², 30, 31², 32, 33, 34, 35³, 39²; **27**:1, 8, 9, 11, 14, 18, 19, 24², 27², 29³, 30, 31², 32, 33, 37, 38, 41, 42, 45, 46, 47², 48; **28**:1², 2, 9, 10, 15², 17², 18, 19, 27; **Mk** 1:1², 2, 3, 4², 5, 6, 7, 10, 14, 15, 16, 17, 19, 22, 24², 25, 26, 28, 29; **2**:3, 4, 6, 10, 12, 14, 16, 18, 19, 21, 23, 26², 28²; **3**:2, 3, 9, 11, 17², 18, 21², 22², 28, 29; **4**:11², 17, 19², 26, 30, 32², 5:1, 2, 6, 7², 8, 10, 11, 15, 21, 22, 26, 27, 35, 37, 38; **6**:3, 6, 15², 17, 21, 22, 24, 26², 29, 33, 37, 40, 43², 44, 45, 47, 48, 54, 56; **7**:1², 2, 3, 4, 5³, 8³, 9², 13, 15, 19, 20, 21, 24, 26, 31³; **8**:3, 8, 10, 15², 17, 19, 20, 22², 29, 31², 35, 37, 38, 41, 42, 47; **10**:1², 4, 6, 10, 14, 15, 21, 23, 24, 25³, 33², 35, 37, 42, 44², 47; **11**:1², 2, 9, 10, 15², 17², 18, 19, 27; **12**:2², 5, 6, 8, 9, 12, 18, 26², 28, 34, 35², 37, 38³, 38³; **13**:1, 3, 7², 8², 9, 11², 14, 17, 19, 20, 23, 26, 27², 35; **14**:1², 3³, 4², 9, 10, 12², 13², 14, 18², 20, 21², 24, 25³, 26, 28⁴, 34, 35, 36³, 38, 39², 40², 43³, 46², 47, 48, 49, 50²; **15**:1, 2, 3, 4, 9, 10, 12, 16, 18, 21, 22², 26², 31, 32, 35, 38, 39², 40², 43³, 46², 47; **16**:1, 2, 3, 7, 9², 12, 14, 19; **Lk** 1:1, 2, 4, 5⁴, 6², 9², 10, 11³, 14, 15, 16², 17², 18², 19², 27, 29, 32², 33, 35², 39, 43, 44, 48², 65, 68, 69², 70, 71, 74, 76, 77², 78², 79²; **2**:1, 2, 4³, 9², 10, 11, 13, 22², 23, 24², 25, 27, 31, 34, 35, 36³, 38, 39², 40, 41, 43; **3**:1⁶, 2³, 4, 5, 6², 7, 8, 10, 11, 13, 14, 17², 19²; **4**:3², 5, 6, 13⁴, 17, 19, 20, 21, 23²; **5**:2, 4, 9², 10², 14³, 15², 16², 17⁴, 18², 19²; **6**:3, 4, 6, 13⁴, 17, 19, 20, 21, 23²; **7**:2, 4, 6², 8, 23⁴, 24, 25², 26², 27³; **8**:2³, 3, 4, 6, 9² 10³, 11, 13, 14², 15, 17, 19, 20, 21², 22², 23²; **9**:2³, 4, 5, 8, 19, 20², 22, 23²; **10**:4, 8, 12, 13, 14, 15, 17², 18², 19², 20³, 21², 22, 30; **13**:1², 2, 5, 13; **14**:7² 9, 12², 15, 16, 17², 20²; **15**:1, 2, 3, 4, 5, 6², 8², 12, 13², 14², 15², 16³, 18, 19³, 25, 29²; **16**:1, 2, 4, 5, 10, 11, 16, 18, 19, 20², 23, 25², 26; **1Co** 1:2², 4, 8, 10², 12, 13, 14, 16, 17³, 18², 19², 20², 21², 24², 25², 26³, 27², 28³, 29, 30³, 34; **2**:4, 6⁴, 7, 8³, 10², 11³, 12, 14, 16²; **3**:13, 18², 19, 20, 23³; **4**:1², 5, 6, 9, 13², 17², 18, 20³; **5**:1, 2, 4², 5, 6, 7, 8², 10, 12²; **6**:1², 3, 4, 6, 9, 19², 19; **7**:5², 23, 26, 31, 33, 34, 40; **8**:7, 9², 10, 12³; **9**:1, 2, 7², 8, 9, 10, 12², 15², 18², 23; **10**:1, 5, 7, 8², 9, 10, 16³, 17, 18, 20, 21², 24, 25, 27², 28, 30, 31, 32, 33; **11**:1, 3³, 7², 10², 11², 12, 16, 19, 21, 23, 24, 25², 27³, 28², 29, 30; **12**:3, 4, 5, 6², 7, 8³, 9, 10, 11², 12², 13, 16, 17², 18, 22, 24, 27³, 28⁵, 30; **13**:1², 2, 5, 13; **14**:1², 5, 6, 7, 10, 11, 18, 21², 23, 25, 26², 33², 33, 36; **15**:1, 3, 6, 8, 9², 10³, 12², 13², 20, 21, 34, 35, 37², 38, 39, 40², 41, 42, 47², 48², 49², 50, 52, 56, 58; **16**:2³, 3, 10, 13, 15, 19, 23, 24²; **2Co** 1:3³, 3, 5, 6, 8², 9, 11, 14³, 15, 19, 20, 22, 23, 24²; **2**:3, 4², 5, 10, 11, 12, 13, 14², 15, 16², 17²; **3**:1, 3⁴, 6³, 7, 8, 11, 17², 4:2², 4⁶, 6³, 7, 10², 13, 15; **5**:10, 13², 16, 18, 19, 21; **6**:2⁴, 4², 7:1, 5, 6, 12², 13; **8**:2, 4, 6, 7², 8², 9, 16, 20², 21, 22, 23, 24; **9**:2, 4, 10², 12², 13³, 14; **10**:1, 2, 4, 5, 6, 7, 8, 14, 15²; **11**:1, 7², 10³, 13, 14, 15, 20, 23³, 28, 30, 31; **12**:2, 6, 7², 11, 17, 19, 20, 21; **13**:1, 2, 5, 12², 14³; **Gal** 1:4, 6, 7, 10³, 13¹⁴, 19, 22, 24; **2**:5, 7, 8, 9, 14², 20, 21; **3**:7, 9, 10, 13, 14, 19², 21, 22, 25, 26, 27; **4**:3, 4, 5,

6, 13, 14, 19, 21, 23, 25, 27², 28, 29, 30, 31²; **5:**1, 2, 8, 9, 11, 16, 19, 20, 21, 22; **6:**2, 10, 12, 14, 16, 17, 18; **Eph 1:**1², 3, 4, 6, 7², 9, 11², 12, 13², 14², 17², 18², 19, 23; **2:**2⁴, 3², 4, 7, 8, 11, 12, 13, 14, 15, 16, 19, 20; **3:**1², 2, 4, 6, 7³, 8², 9, 10, 13, 16, 18, 19²; **4:**1, 3², 6, 7, 12², 13⁴, 14², 17, 18³, 19, 21, 22, 23, 25², 29, 30², 31²; **5:**1, 2, 3⁴, 4, 5³, 6, 8, 9, 11, 16, 20, 21, 23³, 30, 33; **6:**4, 5, 6², 11, 12², 13², 14², 15, 16², 17³, 18, 19; **Php 1:**1, 4, 5, 6², 7², 8², 9, 10, 11², 14³, 15², 16, 17, 18, 19, 25², 26, 27², 29; **2:**3⁴, 5, 7, 10, 11, 15, 16², 17, 21, 22, 25, 26, 30; **3:**2, 3, 5³, 7, 8, 9, 10², 12², 13, 15², 17, 18²; **4:**3³, 7, 9, 12, 14, 15², 23; **Col 1:**1³, 3, 4², 5, 7, 8, 9, 10², 12², 13², 14, 15, 18, 21, 23, 24, 25, 27²; **2:**2², 3, 8, 9, 11², 12, 13, 15, 17, 18, 20, 23²; **3:**1, 6², 8, 10, 15², 16, 17, 22²; **4:**3, 5, 6, 9, 10, 11, 12³, 16; **1Th 1:**1, 2, 6³, 9; **2:**2², 6, 8, 9, 10, 11, 12, 13³, 14, 16, 17, 19; **3:**2, 6, 7, 9², 13; **4:**2, 4, 6, 12, 13, 15, 16²; **5:**2, 5², 8, 13, 22, 23²; 28; **2Th 1:**1, 3, 5² 8, 9², 11²; 12²; **2:**1, 2, 3, 7², 8³, 9³, 10, 13, 14, 15; **3:**1, 6, 8, 13, 14, 16², 18; **1Ti 1:**1³, 5, 7, 11, 14, 15, 16; **2:**1, 4, 7; **3:**2, 5, 8, 9², 11, 12, 15², 16; **4:**5, 6³, 8, 10², 13, 14; **5:**4, 9, 10², 13, 17², 21², 22², 23, 24²; **6:**1², 3, 5², 7, 10³, 11, 12³, 13³, 15, 17, 19, 20; **2Ti 1:**1³, 5, 6², 7⁴, 8², 9³, 10, 11, 13, 14, 15, 16²; **2:**2, 3, 6, 9, 10², 14, 15, 18, 19, 20² 22², 25, 26; **3:**2², 3, 4², 5, 6, 8, 9, 10, 11², 14, 17; **4:**1³, 2, 3, 5²; 8, 14, 19; **Tit 1:**1⁴, 2², 3, 6², 10, 11, 12, 14; **2:**2, 5, 8, 11, 13; **3:**3, 4, 5², 7; **Phm 1:**1, 6, 7, 9², 21, 25; **Heb 1:**2, 3³, 5, 7², 8, 9, 10², 13; **2:**4, 6², 9, 10, 11, 12, 14, 15, 17; **3:**3², 4, 6, 8, 12, 13, 16, 19²; **4:**1³, 2, 3, 6², 12², 13, 14, 16²; **5:**3, 5, 6, 7², 9, 10, 12; **6:**1², 2², 5², 6, 7, 8, 9, 11, 12², 13, 16³, 17, 22², 23, 27; **8:**1³, 5, 6, 8², 9, 10, 11; **9:**4⁴, 5, 9, 10², 11², 12², 13², 14, 15, 16², 19², 20, 22, 23, 24, 26³, 28; **10:**1, 3, 4, 10², 12, 19, 21, 22, 25, 26, 27³, 28², 29³, 31, 32, 34, 36, 39²; **11:**1², 3, 4, 7, 9, 14, 15, 21², 22, 23, 24, 26³, 28³, 30, 33, 34², 38, 39; **12:**1, 2³, 4, 5², 9, 11, 15, 17, 22², 23³, 24²; 27; **13:**5, 7³, 9², 11, 15², 17, 20³, 22; **Jas 1:**1², 2, 3, 5, 6, 12, 17, 18³, 19, 21; **2:**5, 7, 10², 16; **3:**1, 3, 5, 6³, 7², 8, 10, 15, 17², 18; **4:**4²; 5; **1**, 4², 5; **1**, 2, 7² 14³, 16, 19, 20²; **1Pe 1:**1, 2², 3², 5, 6, 7, 9², 10, 11², 12, 18, 19, 20, 23³, 24, 25; **2:**1² 9² 10, 12, 15, 16, 17, 19², 25; **3:**1² 2, 3, 4³, 5, 7², 8, 12², 16, 20, 21³; **4:**2², 4, 7, 8, 11, 13, 14⁴, 15, 17²; 18; **5:**1, 2, 4, 5, 9, 10, 12², 14²; **2Pe 1:**1², 2³, 3, 8, 11, 12, 13, 16², 19, 20, 21; **2:**2, 5, 6², 7, 9, 10², 11, 12, 13, 14, 15²; **3:**10, 11, 12³, 13, 16, 17, 18; **1Jn 1:**1, 7; **2:**2, 12, 14, 15, 16³, 17, 19, 20, 29; **3:**1, 2, 8² 9² 10³, 17, 23; **4:**2, 3, 5, 6², 7, 13, 14, 15, 17²; **5:**1, 2, 4, 5, 9, 10, 12, 13², 15, 18², 19², 20; **2Jn 1:**2, 4, 9, 13; **3Jn 1:**6, 7, 10, 12²; **Jude 1:**1², 4, 5, 6, 7³, 9, 11, 13, 14, 15², 17, 21; **Rev 1:**1, 2³, 3, 4, 5², 7², 9⁴, 13, 15, 16, 18, 20³; **2:**1², 6, 7², 8², 9², 10⁴, 12², 13, 14, 15, 16, 17, 18³, 20, 21, 22², 23, 24; **3:**1⁴, 2, 5, 7³, 9², 10, 12², 14³, 16, 4:3; 4, 5³, 6, 8; **5:**1, 5⁴, 6², 7, 8², 11; **6:**1², 5, 6², 7, 8², 9³, 10, 11, 12, 15², 16², 17; **7:**1², 2, 3², 4², 5³, 6³, 7³, 8³, 9, 13, 14, 15, 17; **8:**3, 4², 5³, 6³, 7³, 8³, 9, 13, 14²; **9:**1, 2, 4², 5², 7, 9³, 11, 13, 15, 16, 17³, 18³, 19, 20⁴, 21; **10:**3², 7, 8; **11:**1, 4, 6, 8, 10, 11, 13³, 15², 19³; **12:**1, 4, 9², 11², 14³, 16, 17²; **13:**1², 2², 3², 8³, 10, 11, 12, 13, 14⁴, 15, 17², 18; **14:**2², 7², 8, 10⁵, 11, 12²; 14², 15³, 17, 18², 19, 20², 21³; **15:**2², 3, 4³, 5, 6³, 7², 8⁴; **16:**1, 2, 3, 4, 5, 6, 9, 10, 11³, 13⁶, 14³, 17, 18², 19³, 21²; **17:**1², 2³, 4, 5², 6², 7², 8⁴, 14², 18; **18:**3³, 9², 10, 11, 12⁴, 13⁸, 18, 21², 22², 23³, 24³; **19:**1, 2, 6², 7³, 8², 9², 10³, 13, 14, 15⁴, 16², 17, 18³, 19, 20³, 21³; **20:**1, 4⁴, 5, 6², 8, 9², 10, 12, 14², 15²; **21:**2, 3, 4, 6², 8, 9², 10, 12, 14², 15, 18², 19², 21³, 23, 24, 26, 27; **22:**1⁴, 2³, 3², 5², 6², 7, 8, 9², 10², 14, 16, 17², 18², 19², 21.

Ge 1:11, 15, 17, 22, 28, 29, 30; **2:**2, 3, 5²; **3:**14, 24; **4:**4, 5, 12, 14, 15, 26; **6:**1, 4, 5, 6, 12, 17²; **7:**4, 6, 10, 11², 12, 13, 17, 18², 19, 21, 22, 23; **8:**4², 5, 17, 19, 20; **9:**7, 10, 16, 10:8; 12:3, 8⁴, 17, 20; 13:4; 15:11, 18; 17:23, 26; 18:5, 16, 18; 19:2, 9, 24; 20:1; 21:8, 14²; 22:2, 4, 6², 8, 9², 12, 14, 17, 18; 23:8; 24:7, 15, 27, 30, 42, 45, 47, 48, 54, 56, 59; 25:21; 26:4, 7, 9, 22, 25, 31; 27:12, 13, 15; 28:5, 12², 13, 14, 18, 20; 29:1; 30:25, 26, 31, 33, 35, 37; 31:17, 22, 34; 32:1, 20, 21; 33:3, 12, 14, 16; 34:8, 15, 22, 30; 35:14², 16, 19, 21; 36:37; 37:17, 22, 25, 27, 34; 38:9, 13, 14, 19, 28, 30; 39:5; 40:10, 16, 17, 19; 41:3, 5, 17, 22, 42, 45, 50; 42:18, 26, 30, 38; 43:6; 44:3; 45:7, 24; 46:20, 34; 47:31; 48:2, 7, 13², 14², 17, 18, 25²; 50:23, 24; Ex 1:16; 2:25; 3:2, 12, 22; 4:3², 9², 14, 20, 24; 7:4, 15; 8:3, 4, 5, 7, 12, 18, 21², 22; 9:3³, 9, 10, 11², 18, 19, 22², 23, 33; 10:10, 15², 11:1², 5; 12:3, 7, 11, 12², 13, 15, 16³, 17, 22², 23, 29, 34, 37, 42, 51; 13:6, 8, 9³, 11, 16², 17, 20, 21; 14:15, 16, 22³, 29³, 30; 15:9, 17, 19, 26²; 16:1, 5², 14², 22, 25, 26, 27, 29² 30; 17:5, 9, 12³, 14; 18:27; 19:1, 4, 11², 13, 16, 18; 20:4, 10, 11, 24, 25, 26²; 22:8, 11, 30; 23:12, 13, 25; 24:6, 8, 12, 13, 15, 16², 17, 18²; 25:7, 12², 14, 19², 21, 25, 30, 32², 33², 34, 37, 40; 26:5², 13, 26, 27², 30, 32², 34, 35²; 27:7, 8, 10, 11, 13, 14, 15; 28:9, 10², 11, 12², 17, 26, 27, 29, 36², 37, 38², 41; 29:5, 6, 7, 9², 10, 12, 13³, 15, 16, 18, 19, 20², 22², 24, 27², 29²; Lev 1:4², 5, 7², 8², 9, 11, 12², 13, 15², 17²; 2:1², 2, 5, 6, 9, 12, 15; 3:2², 4, 5², 8², 10, 11, 13², 15, 16; 4:3, 4, 7, 9, 10, 12, 15, 18, 19, 24, 25, 26, 29, 30, 31, 33, 34, 35²; 5:11, 12², 6:5, 9² 10², 11, 12³, 13, 15² 20, 21, 27; 7:2, 4, 5, 9, 15, 16², 18, 31, 35, 36, 38²; 8:7², 8, 9², 11, 12², 14, 15, 16, 18, 19, 21, 22, 23³, 24⁴, 26², 28², 30²; 9:1, 9, 10, 12, 13, 14², 17, 18, 20², 24; 10:7; 11:2, 20, 21², 27², 29, 32, 34, 35, 37, 38², 41, 42⁴, 44, 46, 47, 48; 12:3; 13:2, 3, 4, 5, 6, 14, 18, 24, 27², 29², 34, 38, 39, 42², 43, 44, 51; 14:9, 10, 14³, 17⁴, 18, 20, 25, 28⁴, 29, 31, 39³, 41; 15:4², 6², 8, 9, 14, 17, 20², 22, 23, 24, 26²; 29; 16:2, 4³, 13, 14, 15, 18, 19, 21², 22, 23, 24, 25, 29, 30, 32; 17:11; 19:5, 6², 7, 28; 20:9, 11, 12, 13, 16, 27; 21:3, 10; 22:19, 20, 22, 25, 27, 28, 29; 23:5, 6, 7, 8, 11², 12, 21, 24, 28, 29, 30, 34, 36, 40; 24:4, 6, 8, 14; 25:1, 9², 15², 50; 26:9, 30, 46; 27:23, 34; Nu 1:1, 18, 53; 2:3, 10, 18, 25; 3:1, 23, 29, 35, 38; 4:7², 10, 12, 14; 5:15³, 23, 26; 6:5, 7², 9, 10, 27; 7:9, 12, 18, 24, 30, 36, 42, 48, 54, 60, 66, 72, 78, 89; 8:3, 7, 10, 12, 19; 9:3, 5, 6², 10, 11, 13, 15; 10:5, 6, 9, 11; 11:9, 11², 12, 17², 21, 25³, 26, 29; 12:3, 15; 13:17, 20, 23; 14:16, 23; 15:31, 32, 38²; 16:1, 17:2, 3; 18:5, 17, 22; 19:4, 12³, 13², 15, 19², 20; 20:16, 19, 26, 28²; 21:4, 8, 9, 10, 16; 22:6, 11, 12, 17², 22, 23, 24, 26, 36; 23:2, 4, 14², 30; 26:3, 53, 63; 27:18, 23; 28:9, 11, 16, 17, 18, 25, 26; 29:1, 7, 12, 17, 20, 23, 26, 29, 32, 35; 30:9², 14, 15; 31:2, 3, 12, 19, 22, 32², 33:3, 3, 4, 6, 37, 38, 39, 44, 48, 49, 50; 34:3, 4, 6, 9, 11, 12, 15; 35:1, 5⁴, 2, 3, 20², 32, 33, 36:11, 13; Dt 1:3, 33, 36, 41; 2:5, 8, 25, 27, 28, 36, 37; 3:10, 24; 4:13, 17, 32, 36, 39, 48; 5:4, 8, 14, 21, 22²; 6:7, 8², 9² 18, 21; 7:6, 7, 15², 16, 25; 8:1, 3²; 9:4, 5, 9², 10³; 10:1², 2, 3, 4³, 7, 10, 11, 15; 11:4, 12, 14, 18², 20², 29² 12:2², 16, 24, 27; 13:17²; 14:2; 15:23; 16:4, 6, 8; 17:6²; 18:1, 16; 19:8; 21:22, 23²; 22:4, 6³, 8, 23:4², 19; 24:5, 15; 25:6, 7, 18; 26:15; 27:3, 4, 6, 8, 11, 12, 13, 18; 28:1, 8², 9, 10, 12, 20, 25, 48, 53, 54, 55, 57, 59, 61, 68; 29:5, 16, 19², 22², 23, 27; 30:3, 7; 31:17², 18, 20, 21, 23; 32², 27, 11, 13, 36, 41, 43, 48, 50²; 33:1, 10, 16², 19²; 26; 34:4, 9; Jos 1:4, 8; 2:6, 7, 8, 9, 11, 16, 17, 19³; 3:6, 17²; 4:5, 18, 19², 22; 5:4, 7, 10²; 6:4, 5, 14, 15²; 18; 7:5, 6, 7, 10, 25²; 8:4, 5, 8, 19, 22, 29, 30, 31², 32, 33; 9:5, 12, 17, 20; 10:11², 12, 13, 24², 26², 29, 31, 32, 34; 11:2, 4, 8, 13; 12:2; 13:3³, 16, 21, 24², 29²; 14:9², 15:3, 4, 6, 7, 8, 9, 10, 11, 46, 47; 16:1, 4; 17:8, 9; 18:9, 12², 13, 17; 19:5, 8, 9, 12, 14, 18², 20², 27², 28; 20:21, 30, 31², 33, 34, 35, 36, 39, 41, 43, 46, 48; Ru 1:7, 19; 2:1; 3:2, 3, 15; 4:5; 1Sa 1:7, 9, 11, 12, 14; 2:29; 3:2, 3, 15; 4:5; 1Sa 1:7, 9, 11, 12, 14; 2:29;

34: 4:2, 12, 13; 5:3², 4³, 5; 6:6, 8², 9, 11, 12, 15², 18; 7:1, 6, 9, 16; 9:4, 14, 24, 25, 26²; 27; 10:1, 2, 3, 25; 11:2², 7; 12:11; 13:5, 22; 14:1, 2, 4, 22, 23, 24, 25, 32², 47²; 15:12, 18², 19, 20; 16:1, 13; 17:5, 6², 11, 32, 35, 38², 39, 49²; 18:9², 25; 19:2, 13; 20:21, 31, 34; 21:3, 4, 5, 6, 13, 15; 22:6; 23:5, 10, 17, 19, 26²; 24:9; 25:13³, 18, 19, 24, 31, 39, 42; 26:1, 3, 9, 11, 13, 23, 25; 27:6, 11; 28:8, 15, 20, 22, 23; 30:1, 2, 17; 31:1, 4, 5, 8; **2Sa 1:**2², 6², 10², 16, 19, 25; 2:13², 21, 23, 24, 8:20, 23, 25, 27, 32, 34, 39², 41²; 4:7; 5:2, 8; 6:2, 3², 4; 7:23; 8:2, 10; 10:7; 11:2, 13, 21; 12:16, 18, 20, 30; 13:2, 19², 30, 31, 34²; 14:7, 9², 14, 30², 31; 15:12, 22², 23, 32²; 16:2, 6, 22; 17:11, 12², 14; 18:9, 19:2, 25; 19:2, 13; 20:21, 31, 34; 21:3, 4, 5, 6, 19²; 22:1, 16, 18, 22², 25, 34, 43; 23:1, 4, 5, 8; 2Sa 1:2², 6², 10², 16, 19, 25; 2:13² 21, 23, 24, 28, 29, 32; 30:1, 2, 17; 31:1, 4, 5, 8; **1Ki 1:**4, 13, 17, 20², 24, 27, 30, 33, 35, 38, 41, 44, 46, 47, 48; 2:4, 5, 8, 12, 19, 24, 33², 34, 37, 42; 3:3, 4, 6, 19; 4:20, 24, 29; 5:1, 4, 5; 6:8, 29, 32, 35; 7:3, 9, 14, 19, 25², 29², 30², 31, 34, 36², 38, 39², 41², 42, 48, 49²; 8:20, 23, 25, 27, 32, 34, 64, 66; 9:5, 9, 16, 25, 26; 10:2, 5, 9, 20, 26; 11:7, 29; 12:4², 9, 10, 11, 31, 32², 33², 13:2², 3, 24³, 28, 29, 30, 31, 33, 34, 36², 38, 39¹, 41², 42, 48, 49²; 8:20, 23, 25, 27, 32, 34, 64, 66; **2Ki 1:**4, 6, 9, 13, 16; 2:1, 6, 8, 13, 15, 16, 23², 24, 25; 3:11, 21, 22, 25, 27; 4:7, 10, 13, 20, 21, 24, 29, 31², 32, 33, 34, 35, 38; 5:11, 18, 20; 6:10², 11, 26, 30, 31; 7:2, 17; 8:29; 9:3, 6, 10, 13, 15, 17, 25, 26², 27, 32, 36, 37; 10:3, 6, 15, 30; 11:5², 9², 12, 19; 12:9², 11², 20; 13:13, 16, 21; 15:12, 19; 16:4, 12, 13, 14, 15², 17; 17:6, 10; 18:11, 17, 19, 20, 21³, 22, 23, 24, 26, 27; 19:11, 10, 19, 23; 20:5, 8, 11; 21:12²; 22:5, 16, 20; 23:5² 8, 12, 13, 16²; 20², 33; 24:10; 25:1, 6, 8, 17, 27; **1Ch 1:**10, 48; 2:7²; 5:16; 6:49²; 9:2, 18, 24, 32; 10:1, 4, 5, 8; 11:2, 6, 22; 12:40; 13:7, 10; 15:15; 16:8, 40; 17:17, 21; 18:10; 19:8; 20:2, 6²; 21:3, 14, 17, 18, 22, 24, 26², 28, 29; 22:8, 9, 18; 23:29, 31; 26:16, 17³; 27:1, 24²; 28:5, 8, 21; 29:7, 15, 23, 25; 2Ch 1:6; 2:4; 3:1², 2, 7, 13, 15, 16, 4:4⁴, 6², 7², 10², 12, 13, 19; 5:12; 6:10, 13, 14, 16, 18, 23, 27; 7:3, 9, 10, 22; 6:12; 7:9, 1, 4, 8, 18, 19; 10:4², 9, 10, 11; 11:16; 12:7, 10, 14; 13:4, 11², 17, 18²; 14:7, 11; 15:16; 16:7²; 8, 9, 14; 17:10; 18:9, 16, 18³, 24; 19:3, 10; 20:1, 24, 26, 30; 21:11²; 22:6, 8; 23:4², 6, 8³, 11, 15, 20; 24:24, 27; 26:15², 16, 19, 20; 27:3, 5; 28:4, 5, 11, 13, 15; 29:4, 6, 8, 17², 21, 22³, 23, 24, 27; 30:12, 15, 19; 31:3, 19; 32:2, 5, 10, 12, 18, 22, 23, 25², 33; 33:15, 16; 34:5, 10, 11, 24, 25, 28²; 35:1, 3, 16, 20, 22; 36:3, 15²; Ezr 2:68; 3:2, 3², 6, 9; 4:4, 24; 5:8, 15; 6:2, 7², 11, 15, 19, 22; 7:6, 9³, 17, 24, 28; 8:18, 22², 31², 33; 9:5; 10:9, 16; Ne 2:12, 14; 3:26; 4:3, 4, 16; 5:4, 15, 16, 18; 6:2, 3, 15; 7:3; 8:2, 4³, 13, 16, 18; 9:1², 4, 6, 11, 12, 13, 19², 29; 10:31³, 33², 34; 11:1, 3, 22, 30; 12:31², 37², 38, 43; 13:1, 2, 6, 15⁴, 16, 19²; 21³, 25; Est 1:6², 10; 2:17, 23; 3:7, 12, 13, 15; 4:1, 4; 5:1³, 14; 6:4, 8, 9, 11; 7:2, 8, 9, 10; 8:6, 7, 9, 13², 14; 9:1², 10, 13, 15², 16, 17², 18², 25; Job 1:8, 12, 17, 19; 2:1, 3, 9, 12, 13; 3:10; 4:13, 15²; 5:10, 11; 6:2, 22, 30; 7:1, 4; 8:6, 9, 14, 15; 9:8, 26; 10:3; 12:18, 21; 13:7, 11, 27²; 14:3; 15:8, 10, 17², 18², 25; 16:3², 4; 17:2, 10; 18:10, 11; 19:10, 21, 23, 24; 20:4, 9, 28; 21:3, 7; 22:8, 28²; 24:18, 20, 21, 23; 26:10; 28:8; 29:14, 19, 22; 30:12, 21, 24; 31:2, 28, 36²; 33:2, 11, 15, 19, 23, 30; 34:21, 33; 36:25, 28; 37:6; 38:6, 35; 39:11, 14, 27, 28, 30; 40:15; 41:5, 8, 33, 34; Ps 1:2; 2:6; 3:3, 6, 7, 8; 4:4; 7:3, 7, 16²; 9:4; 11:4, 6; 13:3; 14:2, 4; 15:1, 3²; 16:4; 17:6; 18:10, 16, 33, 42, 21:3, 5, 8; 25:15; 26:12; 31:11, 13, 16, 19; 33:2, 14, 18²; 34:1, 15, 35:11, 13, 17; 36:4, 8; 39:1; 40:2; 41:3, 4, 10; 44:16; 46:8; 47:8; 48:9; 49:9, 14; 50:10, 16; 51:1, 19; 53:2, 4; 54:5, 7; 55:10, 22; 56:T, 8; 57:1²; 58:2; 59:4; 62:7, 9, 10; 63:6; 66:6, 11, 17; 67:2; 68:4, 14, 18, 21; 69:9, 11, 24; 71:6; 72:6, 13, 16; 73:18; 74:3; 77:12; 78:9, 27², 32; 79:6³; 80:13, 17, 18; 81:3; 83:10; 84:5, 9; 86:3, 16; 87:1; 89:19; 90:13; 93:4; 94:15, 20; 95:11; 97:3, 11; 99:6²; 101:6; 102:7, 13, 19, 24; 103:13²; 104:3², 5; 105:1, 16, 38; 106:43; 107:23²; 40; 109:12, 17; 110:3, 5; 112:8; 113:5, 6; 116:2, 4, 13, 17; 118:7, 11; 119:15, 19, 23, 27, 30, 48, 78, 97, 99, 112, 132, 148, 158; 120:1; 123:3²; 124:1, 2; 129:6; 132:11, 12, 18; 133:2³, 3; 135:6, 14; 137:2, 7; 138:6; 139:4, 9²; 140:3; 141:5, 8; 143:5, 10; 144:7, 9; 145:5, 9, 18²; 146:4; 147:7, 8; 148:11, 14; 149:5, 7²; Pr 1:15; 3:3, 5, 23, 33; 4:9, 13, 14, 15²; 5:10; 6:14, 28; 7:3²; 19; 8:2, 16, 21, 34; 11:7, 15:3, 14; 16:26, 30; 17:11; 17, 29, 31; 14:7; 15:3, 14; 16:26, 30; 17:11;

19:12, 15; 20:8; 21:9; 22:18; 23:10, 19, 20, 34²; 24:26, 34; 25:19, 20²; 22, 24; 26:14², 27; 27:15; 30:19², 24; 31:3², 26; Ecc 1:6, 13; 3:10; 4:1; 5:2, 11, 20; 6:1; 7:20; 8:14, 16, 17; 9:1; 10:7², 20; SS 2:12, 14, 17; 3:1, 11; 4:4, 16; 5:3, 5, 15; 6:13³; 8:5, 6, 9, 14; Isa 1:4, 24; 3:9, 16, 17, 26; 5:1, 6; 6:1²; 7:3, 17³, 19; 8:1, 8, 18, 19; 9:2, 6, 7², 8, 11, 20², 21²; 10:3, 20²; 11:2, 9, 14²; 12:4; 13:2, 4, 18²; 14:3, 13², 25; 15:3, 5; 16:5; 17:6², 11², 13; 18:3², 4, 6; 19:1, 8, 24; 20:6²; 21:7², 8, 9, 10; 22:1, 12², 16, 22, 24, 25; 23:3, 9, 17; 24:13, 21, 23; 25:6, 7, 10; 26:5, 10; 27:4, 8, 11, 13; 28:1, 4, 10², 13², 20, 24, 28; 29:1; 30:6², 8², 12², 16², 17², 25, 29, 32; 31:1, 4; 32:15; 33:4, 5, 8, 16; 34:5; 35:8²; 9; 36:2, 4, 5, 6³, 7, 8, 9, 11, 12; 37:1, 10, 20, 24, 27; 38:8, 11; 40:7, 9, 12, 15, 24; 41:3, 7, 18, 25²; 42:1, 4, 5, 25; 43:18, 24; 44:3⁴, 5, 20; 45:4, 9; 46:6; 47:1, 6, 7, 9, 12, 15; 48:2, 6; 49:9, 10, 13, 15, 16, 18, 22, 26; 50:10; 51:3, 5, 13; 52:1, 2, 7; 53:6; 54:8, 10; 55:2², 6, 7; 56:7; 57:7, 8, 17, 19; 58:3, 4, 5, 13, 14; 59:4, 13, 17³, 21²; 60:4, 5, 7, 19; 61:1, 3, 6; 62:6², 63:6; 64:4, 7; 65:1, 3, 7², 25; 66:12², 20²; Jer 1:14, 16; 2:17, 20, 34, 35, 37²; 36, 12, 21, 23; 4:8, 30; 5:9, 29; 6:11², 19, 23, 25², 26, 29; 7:20⁴, 29; 8:2, 13²; 9:9, 22, 24; 10:18, 25³; 11:8, 11, 16, 23; 12:2, 5, 13; 13:13, 16, 27; 14:6, 16; 15:5, 6², 7, 8, 15, 17; 16:4, 16, 17; 17:1², 2, 5, 18, 21, 22², 24²; 25², 27; 18:8, 15; 19:3, 9, 11, 15; 20:10²; 21:13; 22:2, 4², 17³, 24, 30; 23:2², 12, 19, 35; 25:26, 29², 30², 31, 33; 26:3, 15³, 19; 27:2, 5; 28:11, 14; 29:16; 30:6, 18², 23; 31:5, 6, 9, 12, 22, 29, 30, 33, 40; 32:10, 29², 42; 33:9, 17, 21, 22, 26, 35:17²; 36:2, 3, 4, 6, 18, 28²; 29, 30, 31, 32; 39:2, 5, 17; 40:4; 41:17²; 42:10, 12, 17, 18²; 44:22², 7; 45:1, 5; 46:2², 4², 5, 9, 10, 25³; 47:5; 48:5, 9, 10², 11, 18, 32, 35, 38, 47; 49:2², 3, 5, 8, 29, 32; 50:6, 15², 19², 38, 42; 51:2, 3, 30, 32, 35, 50, 58, 60; 52:4, 9, 12, 22, 23, 31; La 1:9, 10, 12², 13; 2:4, 7, 10³, 11, 22; 3:28, 55, 65; 4:5, 8; Eze 1:1, 2, 8, 10², 11, 15, 26, 28; 2:1, 10; 4:1, 4², 6, 9; 5:8, 10, 11, 15; 6:10, 13²; 7:4, 8, 9, 18; 8:1, 18; 9:4, 8, 10²; 10:3; 11:9, 10, 11, 21; 12:6, 7, 12; 13:5, 18; 15:2, 3, 4; 16:4, 5², 9, 10, 11², 12², 14, 15, 16, 18, 41, 43, 61; 17:16, 19, 22, 23; 18:2, 13; 19:9, 14; 20:1, 5, 6, 7, 8², 13, 17, 21, 40; 21:14, 29; 22:3, 9, 11, 30, 31²; 23:10, 14, 15, 18, 23, 24, 27, 37, 39, 40, 41², 42², 45; 24:1, 3², 7², 8, 10, 11, 17, 23², 25, 26; 25:11, 12, 14, 17²; 26:1, 6, 8, 16, 17²; 18; 27:3, 4, 9, 10, 11, 27², 29, 30, 31, 33; 28:2, 5, 14, 17, 18, 22, 23, 26; 29:1, 5, 7, 17, 21; 30:9², 14, 15, 19, 20; 31:1, 3, 10, 12, 13, 14, 15; 32:1, 4⁴, 5, 10, 17, 27; 33:4, 5, 21, 26, 34:6, 12, 13, 14, 18, 19; 35:8; 36:9, 11, 18, 25, 33; 37:2, 8, 10, 16², 20, 22; 38:10, 15, 20, 21, 22²; 39:4, 6², 11, 14, 17, 25, 29; 40:1², 10² 19², 21, 23, 26², 27, 32, 34, 37, 39², 40, 41³, 42, 48², 49; 41:1, 2, 3, 6², 11², 12, 14, 15, 17, 19², 20, 25³, 26²; 42:1, 4, 5, 6², 8², 9, 10, 11², 12, 14, 20; 43:12, 14, 20², 22, 24, 27²; 44:18, 19, 27, 30; 45:18, 19³, 20, 21, 22, 25; 46:1³, 3, 4, 6, 12; 47:7, 12, 15, 16², 18, 19, 20; 48:10⁴, 17⁴, 18³, 20, 21, 30, 31, 32, 33, 34, 35; Da 2:10, 28, 34, 35, 48; 3:1, 27; 4:12, 29, 31; 5:5, 27; 6:10, 23, 27; 7:1, 4, 5, 6, 20, 23; 8:7, 10; 9:11, 17, 27²; 10:4², 10; 11:10, 27; 12:5²; Hos 1:10; 2:3, 8; 4:8, 13²; 5:1, 8, 9, 10, 11; 6:2, 3, 9; 7:5, 7; 9:5², 8, 10; 10:8, 11, 12, 13², 14; 12:1, 11; 13:12; Joel 1:13; 2:1, 18, 28, 29, 30, 32²; 3:4, 7, 12; Am 1:14²; 2:7, 8, 16; 3:5, 9, 12², 14; 4:1, 7; 5:9, 11, 15, 19, 24; 6:1, 4³; 5, 12; 9:1, 3, 6, 8; Ob 1:3, 11, 12, 13, 16, 17, 18, 21; Jnh 1:4, 6, 7; 3:4, 5, 8; 4:8; Mic 1:11; 2:1; 5:1, 7; 6:15; 7:16, 17, 19, 20; Na 1:2, 15; 2:3², 5, 13; 3:8, 17, 18; Hab 1:9, 11, 13, 17; 2:1, 2, 6, 9, 15; 3:1, 10, 16, 17, 19²; Zep 1:5, 8, 9², 10, 12, 14, 18; 2:2, 3, 11, 14; 3:8, 9, 11², 16; Hag 1:6, 11⁴, 14, 15; 2:1, 10, 15², 18, 19, 20, 21, 23; Zec 1:7; 3:4, 5²; 9²; 4:2², 3², 11; 5:3²; 6:11, 13²; 7:1; 9:1, 2, 4, 9², 16; 10:6; 11:6, 11; 12:3, 4, 6, 8, 9, 10²; 11; 13:1, 2, 4, 6; 14:4², 6, 8, 9, 12, 13, 18², 20², 21; Mal 1:7, 10; 2:3, 6; 4:1, 3; Mt 2:9, 11; 3:16; 4:4², 5, 16, 17, 21; 5:1, 14, 15, 25, 39, 45²; 6:5, 10, 17, 19; 7:22, 24, 25, 26; 8:15, 24; 9:2, 6, 9, 12, 16, 18, 27², 36; 10:13, 15, 17, 18; 11:1, 6, 22, 24; 12:1, 2, 5, 9, 10, 11, 12, 18, 36; 13:2, 5, 8, 20, 23, 48, 53; 14:6, 8, 11, 13, 14, 19, 22, 23, 25, 26, 28, 29; 15:22, 29, 32; 16:6, 11, 18, 19², 21³; 17:15, 23; 18:10, 12, 18², 19, 26, 27, 33²; 19:13, 15², 28²; 20:8, 19, 30, 31, 34; 21:1, 5², 7², 8², 18, 19, 33, 44²; 22:26, 40, 46; 23:4, 5, 9, 18, 20, 22, 27²; 28²; 35; 24:2, 3, 17, 20, 30, 42, 50; 25:10, 14, 15, 27, 31, 33², 34, 41; 26:7, 12, 16, 17, 29, 31, 33, 53, 64, 74; 27:19², 28, 29, 30², 31, 38², 44, 48, 66; 28:1, 2, 11, 18; Mk 1:10, 31, 40; 2:4, 10, 17, 20, 21, 24; 3:2, 4, 13; 4:1, 5, 8, 11, 16, 20, 21, 26, 38; 5:4, 6,

OUR (1200)

OURS (20)

OURSELVES (45)

OUT (2407)

17:13; **18:**5, 7, 38; **19:**8, 15, 21, 22, 40, 45; **20:**12, 15; **21:**4², 8, 21, 37; **22:**20, 39; **23:**18, 32, 46; **24:**50; **Jn 1:**15; **2:**8, 10, 15, 16; **3:**22; **4:**30, 44; **5:**29; **7:**17, 28, 51, 52; **8:**44; **9:**22, 34, 35; **10:**3, 4, 9, 28, 29; **11:**20, 31, 43, 44, 57; **12:**9, 13, 18, 31, 42, 44; **13:**30; **15:**19, 26; **16:**2; **17:**6, 15; **18:**4, 29, 38; **19:**4², 5, 13, 17; **20:**2, 16, 27; **21:**3², 5, 18; **Ac 1:**18, 21; **2:**17, 18, 33; **3:**19; **4:**30; **5:**6, 9, 10, 19; **7:**7, 19, 36, 40, 45, 58, 60; **8:**1, 7, 27, 39; **9:**1, 40; **10:**17, 18, 23, 45; **12:**4, 9, 15, 17; **13:**17; **14:**6, 10, 14; **15:**24; **16:**11, 18, 30, 37, 40; **17:**5, 27; **18:**6, 23; **19:**13²; 16; **20:**1; **21:**1, 5, 38; **22:**24, 25, 30; **23:**6, 7, 30, 31; **26:**24; **27:**2, 4, 43; **28:**1, 3, 11; **Ro 3:**5; **5:**5; **7:**18; **9:**21, 27, 28; **10:**18, 21; **11:**24, 33; **16:**17; **1Co 4:**19; **5:**2; **9:**9; **10:**13; **14:**23; **2Co 2:**4; **4:**6; **5:**13; **6:**17; **7:**1; **8:**2; **9:**14; **11:**23; **12:**2; **Gal 4:**6, 15; **5:**15; **Eph 1:**11; **2:**15; **3:**16; **4:**29; **5:**4, 10, 21; **Php 1:**15², 17, 19; **2:**3, 12, 16, 17, 21; **3:**2; **4:**15; **Col 1:**23; **1Th 1:**8; **2:**15, 17; **3:**4, 5; **5:**19; **2Th 1:**9; **2:**7; **1Ti 1:**14; **4:**6; **5:**18; **21:**6; **7:** **2Ti 2:**22; **4:**2, 6; **Tit 1:**5; **3:**6; **Heb 1:**11; **3:**16; **8:**9; **11:**3; **12:**1; **Jas 3:**10; **5:**4; **1Pe 1:**11; **2:**9; **2Pe 3:**5; **1Jn 1:**10; **2:**19; **4:**1, 18; **5:**2, 10; **2Jn 1:**7, 8; **3Jn 1:**7, 10; **Jude 1:**5; **Rev 1:**16; **3:**5, 12, 16; **5:**6; **6:**2, 4, 10; **7:**2, 10, 14; **8:**13; **9:**3, 17, 18; **12:**2, 4, 14, 16; **13:**1, 11; **14:**15, 17, 20; **15:**6; **16:**1, 2², 3, 4, 8, 10, 12, 13³, 14, 17²; **17:**8; **18:**4, 16, 19; **19:**15, 21; **20:**1, 8; **21:**2, 10, 16.

SHALL (467)

Ge 2:23; **9:**6; **15:**5; **16:**11; **17:**10; **18:**17; **24:**5; **26:**11; **30:**31; **31:**32; **41:**40; **45:**10; **Ex 2:**7; **3:**13; **4:**15; **12:**14, 22; **13:**7; **19:**12, 13²; **20:**3, 4, 5, 7, 9, 10, 13, 14, 15, 16, 17²; **21:**2, 4², 6, 12; **22:**13, 16; **25:**31, 35, 36; **26:**24; **27:**9, 11, 12, 13, 18; **28:**17, 32; **29:**9, 10, 15, 19; **30:**10, 20, 21, 29, 36; **34:**21²; **35:**2; **Lev 1:**5, 8, 11, 12, 15², 17²; **2:**2, 8, 9, 16; **3:**2, 8, 11, 13, 16; **4:**5, 7², 8, 10, 15, 17, 18, 19, 21, 25, 26, 31², 34, 35²; **5:**6, 8, 10, 12; **6:**10³, 16, 22, 23, 26; **7:**3, 5, 16, 31, 33; **12:**7; **13:**3, 6, 8, 11, 13, 15, 17, 20, 22, 23, 25, 27, 28, 30, 34, 37, 44, 54; **14:**4, 5, 7, 11, 12, 15, 18, 19, 25, 29, 30, 38, 39, 48, 50, 52; **16:**9, 10, 11, 14, 15², 18², 19, 20, 21, 22, 24²; 25; **17:**4; **19:**6; **23:**31; **25:**10, 11, 30; **Nu 1:**51²; **4:**27; **5:**16, 17, 18, 19, 24; **6:**20; **8:**24; **15:**4, 15; **18:**10; **19:**9²; **32:**6; **35:**16, 17, 18, 19², 21²; **36:**7; **Dt 1:**35, 37; **5:**7, 8, 9, 11, 13, 14, 17, 18, 19, 20, 21²; **12:**7²; **13:**17; **14:**26; **15:**2²; **16:**18; **17:**6²; **18:**1, 2; **19:**12; **20:**2, 3, 5, 8, 9, 11²; **21:**2, 3, 5, 6, 7, 13, 19, 20, 21; **22:**15, 17, 18, 19², 21², 24, 25, 29; **24:**16; **25:**2, 5, 6, 7, 8, 9, 10, 12; **26:**4, 5, 11, 12; **27:**8, 12, 13, 14, 15, 16, 17, 18, 19, 20, 21, 22, 23, 24, 25, 26; **31:**2, 11; **Jos 6:**17; **7:**14³, 15; **8:**2; **Jdg 2:**2²; **6:**31; **7:**4²; **20:**18²; 23, 28; **21:**16; **1Sa 5:**8; **6:**2; **10:**2; **11:**12, 13; **14:**37; **23:**2; **28:**11; **30:**8; **2Sa 2:**1²; **5:**19; **15:**20; **19:**23, 38; **21:**3²; **24:**13; **1Ki 1:**13, 17, 24, 30; **2:**24; **3:**26; **8:**25, 29; **9:**5; **18:**31; **22:**6², 15², **2Ki 3:**8; **6:**15, 21²; **14:**6; **17:**12, 36; **20:**9²; **23:**27; **1Ch 14:**10; **2Ch 6:**16; **7:**18; **18:**5², 14²; **23:**5; **25:**4²; **Ezr 9:**14; **Job 2:**10; **38:**3; **40:**7; **42:**4; **Ps 23:**1; **27:**1²; **81:**9²; **95:**11; **101:**4; **SS 8:**8; **Isa 1:**18²; **6:**8; **11:**1; **14:**32; **29:**16; **40:**4²; **6; 44:**19²; **26²; **50:**11; **Jer 15:**2; **Eze 3:**27; **4:**3; **12:**25; **17:**16, 18; **21:**7, 10; **38:**19; **45:**21, 16²; **46:**5, 12, 13, 15; **Da 6:**7; **Hos 13:**4; **Mic 6:**6², 7, 11; **Mt 6:**31³; **16:**22; **17:**17²; **18:**21; **27:**22; **Mk 4:**30²; **6:**24; **9:**19²; **15:**12; **Lk 3:**5²; **9:**41; **12:**17; **13:**18, 20; **16:**3; **20:**13; **Jn 1:**50, 51; **3:**16; **6:**5, 39, 40, 68; **8:**33; **10:**16, 28; **12:**27; **13:**8; **18:**11; **19:**15; **Ac 2:**37; **21:**22; **22:**10; **Ro 3:**5, 9; **4:**1, 18; **5:**9, 10; **6:**1², 14, 15; **7:**7; **8:**31, 35²; **9:**14, 20, 30; **1Co 4:**21; **6:**15; **11:**22²; **13:**12²; **14:**15, 26; **15:**49; **Php 1:**22; **2Th 3:**10; **Heb 2:**3; **3:**11; **4:**3, 5; **11:**32; **1Jn 3:**2²; **Rev 1:**7.

SHE (1011)

Ge 2:23²; **3:**6², 12, 20; **4:**1², 2, 17, 25; **11:**29, 30; **12:**14, 15, 18, 19; **16:**1, 2, 4², 5³, 6, 8, 13²; 15; **17:**16; **18:**12, 15; **19:**26, 33², 35², 37, 38; **20:**2, 3, 5², 12²; **21:**7, 10, 14, 15, 16⁴, 19²; **22:**20; **23:**2; **24:**14, 15, 18, 19², 20, 24, 25, 44, 45, 46², 47, 58, 64, 65, 67; **25:**2, 21, 22²; **26:**7³, 9²; **27:**32³, 33⁴, 34³, 35²; **30:**1³, 3², 4, 5, 6, 8, 9², 11, 13, 15, 16, 17, 18, 20, 21, 23, 24; **35:**17, 18³; **36:**14; **38:**3, 4, 5² 14³, 15², 16², 17, 18², 19², 23, 24, 25⁴, 26, 28, 29; **39:**10, 12, 13, 14², 16, 17; **Ex 2:**2², 3³, 5, 6³, 8, 10²; **4:**25; **26:**6; **21:**3, 4, 7, 9, 10²; **22:**16; **35:**25; **Lev 12:**2, 4, 5², 6, 7, 8³;

15:20², 22, 23, 25², 26², 28³, 29; **18:**7, 9, 11, 12, 13, 14, 15; **19:**20; **20:**18; **21:**3, 9²; **22:**12, 13²; **Nu 5:**13, 14², 27³, 28; **12:**10, 14², 15; **22:**23, 25, 27, 28, 33; **26:**59; **30:**4, 5, 6³, 7, 8, 11, 13; **Dt 21:**13³, 14; **22:**15, 19, 21², 24, 26; **24:**2², 4; **25:**6, 7, 11; **28:**56², 57²; **Jos 2:**4, 6², 8, 15², 16, 21²; **6:**17, 25²; **15:**18³, 19; **Jdg 1:**14³, 15; **4:**5, 6, 18, 19, 21, 22; **5:**25²; 26³, 28, 29; **11:**34, 36, 37, 38², 39²; **13:**9, 14²; **14:**17³; **16:**8, 9, 12, 14, 15, 16, 18, 19, 20; **17:**3, 4; **19:**2³, 3; **20:**5; **Ru 1:**3, 6, 7², 9, 18, 20; **2:**3², 6, 7², 10², 13, 14³, 15², 17², 18⁴, 19², 20, 23; **3:**6, 9, 14, 15, 16; **4:**13²; **1Sa 1:**7, 11, 12, 13, 18², 20, 22, 23, 24, 26; **2:**5²; 19, 20, 21; **4:**19², 20², 21, 22; **18:**19, 21; **25:**3, 18, 19², 20², 23, 24, 35, 36, 41; **28:**12, 14, 21, 24², 25; **2Sa 4:**4; **6:**16²; **11:**4³, 26, 27; **12:**24; **13:**2, 6, 7, 9, 10, 15, 16, 18, 19³; **14:**4², 5, 11, 27; **20:**17²; **18; **21:**8²; 10; **1Ki 1:**2, 4, 17, 22; **2:**14, 16, 18, 19; **3:**17, 19, 20², 27; **10:**1, 2², 5, 6, 10, 13²; **14:**5², 7², 8, 12; **17:**12, 15, 15, 21², 24; **2Ki 4:**2², 5², 6, 7, 9, 12, 13, 14, 15, 16, 17², 21, 22, 23, 24, 25, 26, 27³, 28, 30, 31, 34; **11:**1, 2, 13, 14², 15², 16², 14:2; **14:**2; **15:**2; **21:**19; **22:**1, 14; **23:**31; **36; **24:**8, 18; **1Ch 2:**3, 18; **7:**18; **2Ch 9:**1³, 4, 5, 9, 12³; **11:**19; **12:**13; **15:**16; **22:**10, 11²; **23:**12, 13, 15; **24:**1; **25:**1; **26:**3; **34:**22, 23; **Est 1:**11, 15, 17, 19; **2:**1, 7, 12, 13², 14², 15, 16, 17, 20²; **4:**4²; 10; **5:**12²; **7:**8; **8:**3, 4, 5, 10; **Job 39:**14, 16², 18²; **Ps 45:**14; **46:**5; **84:**3; **Pr 1:**20, 21², **2:**17; **3:**14, 15, 18; **4:**6², 8², 9; **5:**4, 6²; **7:**11, 12, 13², 21², 26; **8:**2, 3; **9:**1, 2², 3², 4, 13, 14, 16; **14:**33; **23:**22, 25, 28; **30:**20; **31:**10, 12, 13, 14, 15², 16², 17, 18, 19, 21, 22², 24, 25², 26, 27, 31; **Ecc 7:**26; **SS 8:**2, 5, 8, 9²; **Isa 1:**21; **3:**26; **8:**3; **13:**20; **16:**12²; **19:**14; **21:**2; **23:**3, 17; **26:**21; **27:**7; **29:**2²; **34:**13, 15; **40:**2; **49:**15²; **51:**18²; **66:**7³, 8; **Jer 3:**1, 6, 7³, 8, 9; **4:**17; **6:**7; **11:**15; **12:**8; **15:**9; **46:**8; **48:**9, 11³, 20, 26, 27, 39, 42; **49:**1, 24; **50:**9, 12², 13, 14, 15² 29²; **51:**6, 7, 8, 9; **52:**1; **La 1:**1², 2³, 4, 8, 9, 10; **Eze 5:**6²; **16:**49; **19:**2, 3, 5²; **23:**5² 7², 8², 9, 10, 11, 12, 13, 14², 16², 17², 18, 19³, 20, 43³; **24:**7³; **26:**2, 5²; **30:**18; **32:**22; **Da 5:**10; **11:**6²; **Hos 1:**3, 8; **2:**2, 3, 5, 6, 7³, 8, 12, 13³, 15²; **3:**1; **8:**8; **Am 1:**3, 6, 9; **Mic 1:**7; **5:**3; **7:**10²; **Na 2:**10; **3:**10; **Zep 2:**15²; **3:**2²; **Zec 9:**3, 4; **Mal 2:**14; **Mt 1:**18, 21, 25; **8:**15; **9:**18, 21, 25; **12:**42; **14:**7, 8; **15:**23, 25, 27; **20:**21; **22:**28; **26:**7, 10, 12², 13, 69; **Mk 1:**31; **5:**23, 26³, 27², 28, 29², 42; **6:**19, 22, 24², 28; **7:**25, 26, 28, 30; **10:**12²; **12:**23, 44²; **14:**3, 6, 8³, 9, 67³, 69; **16:**10, 11; **Lk 1:**25, 36, 40, 42, 45, 57; **2:**7², 36², 37², 38; **4:**39; **7:**12, 37, 38³, 39², 44, 46, 47², 50²; **8:**44, 47⁴, 50, 52, 53, 55; **10:**39, 40; **11:**31; **13:**11, 13; **15:**8²; 9²; **18:**5²; **20:**33; **21:**4²; **22:**56; **Jn 4:**17; **8:**11; **11:**20, 27, 28³, 29³, 31², 32; **12:**3, 7; **16:**21; **20:**2, 11², 13, 14², 15, 16, 18; **Ac 5:**8, 10; **9:**39, 40²; **12:**14³, 15; **16:**15², 16²; 18; **Ro 7:**2, 3⁴; **9:**12; **16:**2²; **1Co 7:**11², 12, 13, 28, 34, 36, 39²; **40³; **11:**6²; **Gal 4:**25, 26; **1Ti 2:**12; **5:**6, 10, 11; **Heb 11:**31; **Jas 2:**25²; **1Pe 5:**13; **Rev 2:**20, 21; **12:**2², 5, 6, 14²; **17:**4, 7; **18:**2, 6², 7², 8, 19, 20.

SO (3003)

For "SO" as a proper name see the Main Concordance.

Ge 1:7², 9, 11, 15, 21, 24, 27, 30; **2:**2, 20, 21; **3:**7, 10, 14, 23; **4:**5, 15², 16; **6:**7, 13, 14; **8:**9, 17, 18; **9:**17, 23; **11:**4, 7, 8; **12:**4, 7, 13, 18, 19; **13:**1, 6, 8, 11, 16, 18; **14:**23; **15:**3, 5, 9; **16:**2, 3, 6, 10, 15; **17:**16; **18:**5, 6, 12, 15, 19², 20², 27, 31; **19:**3, 5, 11, 13, 14, 29, 34, 35, 36, 20:4, 6, 17; **21:**12, 19, 27, 31; **22:**14; **23:**4, 9, 13, 17, 20; **24:**7, 9, 20, 32, 34, 40, 46, 49, 55, 56, 58, 59, 61, 65, 67; **25:**22, 25, 26, 33, 34; **26:**6, 9, 11, 14, 15, 17, 20, 21, 28; **27:**1, 4, 7, 9, 10, 14, 19, 20, 21, 23, 25, 27, 31, 37; **28:**1, 4, 9, 21; **29:**12, 20, 22, 25, 27, 31, 33, 34, 35; **30:**1, 3, 4, 8, 11, 13, 16², 18, 20, 25, 38, 41, 42; **31:**4, 9, 16, 21, 27, 32, 33, 39, 40, 43, 46, 53; **32:**2, 21, 24, 25, 30; **33:**1, 14, 16; **34:**5, 20, 23; **35:**2, 4, 5, 8, 10, 19; **36:**8; **37:**14, 17, 23, 28, 35; **38:**7, 9, 10, 11, 18, 22, 24; **39:**6, 22; **40:**7², 9, 21; **41:**8, 14, 21, 27, 31, 36, 38, 39, 41, 49; **42:**2, 5, 6, 16, 20, 34; **43:**2, 8, 14, 15, 19, 21, 34; **44:**8, 21, 30; **45:**1, 2, 4, 8, 12, 21, 25; **46:**1; **47:**4, 11, 17, 19, 20, 23, 26; **48:**1, 7, 9, 10, 17, 19; **49:**1, 7², 17; **50:**2, 7, 12, 16, 17, 21, 26; **Ex 1:**7, 11, 12, 20; **2:**9, 18, 25; **3:**3, 8, 10, 16, 20; **4:**4, 5; **6:**7, 10, 20, 21, 23², 26, 27; **5:**1, 9, 12; **6:**23, 33, 37; **7:**5, 6, 10, 13, 20, 22²; **8:**6, 7, 13, 16, 19², 24; **9:**1, 2, 4, 10, 11², 14; **12:**8, 10; **13:**13, 17; **14:**7; **15:**15, 16, 19; **16:**10, 16², 17², 21, 22, 24, 32; **17:**6, 7, 10, 11, 12, 13; **18:**7, 23; **19:**7, 8, 9, 20, 21, 25; **20:**12, 20; **22:**2, 6, 31; **23:**12; **25:**37; **26:**6, 13, 25; **27:**2, 5, 7, 20; **28:**1, 3, 4, 7, 28, 30, 32, 35, 38, 41, 43; **29:**1, 29, 44, 46; **30:**8, 20, 21, 29, 30; **31:**13; **32:**1, 3, 4, 6, 10, 24, 25, 26, 31; **33:**6, 11; **34:**1, 4, 16, 27, 28; **35:**5, 21, 22, 26, 29; **36:**1, 4, 6, 14, 15, 17, 18, 19, 37, 38; **37:**17, 19, 22, 24; **38:**1, 7, 8, 18, 24, 30; **39:**1, 5, 7, 8, 22, 26, 30², 32, 42, 43; **40:**16, 19², 21, 23, 25, 27, 29, 32²; **Lev 1:**3; **8:**7, 10, 11², 14, 16, 17, 19, 21, 24, 29, 31²; **9:**5, 9, 10, 11, 15, 16, 18, 21; **10:**1, 5, 11, 14, 15, 19, 24, 33; **13:**4, 6, 11, 14, 15, 21, 26, 28, 31², 32, 34, 53, 54, 56; **14:**11, 42²; **15:**31; **16:**10, 16, 17; **17:**5, 10; **18:**5; **20:**8; **21:**3, 7, 9; **22:**9, 31, 35; **23:**11, 32; **24:**2; **25:**8; **29:**20; **2Ch 1:**5; **4:**11, 18; **5:**6, 9, 12, 16, 21; **6:**10³; **8:**16; **9:**12; **13:**5, 10; **14:**11², 14², 16, 17; **15:**14, 17, 19, 21²; **16:**10, 17, 20, 22, 24, 25; **18:**1, 6, 16; **19:**1, 2², 4, 10; **21:**31; **22:**13, 30, 46; **23:**3, 24; **24:**29, 45; **Jn 1:**7, 39; **2:**7, 8, 15; **3:**8, 14, 16, 21; **4:**5, 15, 16, 36, 40, 53; **5:**10, 12, 16, 21, 26; **6:**9, 13, 30, 57; **7:**3, 18, 23; **8:**28, 36, 52, 53; **9:**7, 11, 16, 36, 39; **10:**12; **11:**3, 4, 14, 15, 41, 53, 57; **12:**10, 19, 34, 36, 40, 46, 50;

13:4, 13, 19, 33, 34; **14**:2, 5, 13, 29; **15**:2, 9, 11; **16**:1, 4, 19, 22, 33; **17**:11, 12, 13, 21; **18**:3, 9, 29, 32; **19**:16, 24, 28, 29, 35, 36; **20**:2, 3, 25; **21**:3, 11; **Ac** 1:6, 19, 23, 26; **3**:5, 19; **4**:6, 15; **5**:3, 15, 22, 32; **6**:2, 7, 12; **7**:4, 10, 19, 24; **8**:8, 19, 24, 27, 31, 32; **9**:2, 8, 17, 28, 38; **10**:20, 22, 29, 33, 48; **11**:2, 17, 18, 26; **12**:5, 8, 14, 15; **13**:3, 35, 51; **14**:1, 3; **15**:2, 25; **16**:3, 5, 8, 18; **17**:5, 17, 27; **18**:11, 16; **19**:3, 9, 10, 12; **20**:31; **21**:23, 24, 35; **23**:10, 11, 18, 24, 28, 31; **24**:6, 10, 16, 26; **25**:20, 26; **26**:1, 3, 18, 19, 22; **27**:3, 9, 13, 15, 25, 32; **28**:14; **Ro** 1:11, 13, 15, 20; **2**:3; **3**:4, 6, 7, 19, 26; **4**:11, 16, 18²; **5**:3, 11, 18, 19, 20, 21²; **6**:1, 6, 12, 19; **7**:3, 4, 5, 6, 12, 13, 21, 25; **8**:3, 7, 23; **10**:4; **11**:5, 7, 8², 10, 11, 16, 19, 25, 26, 31, 32; **12**:5; **13**:2, 12; **14**:6², 8, 9, 12, 22; **15**:4, 6, 9, 13, 16, 19, 20, 24, 28, 32; **16**:19, 26; **1Co** 1:8, 10, 15, 29; **2**:5; **3**:7, 18, 21; **4**:1, 6, 8, 10; **5**:5; **7**:2, 5², 15, 21, 38; **8**:4, 7, 11, 13; **9**:10, 18, 20, 21, 22, 27; **10**:12, 13, 31, 33; **11**:12, 32, 33, 34; **12**:12, 25; **14**:5, 9, 12, 15, 23, 25, 31; **15**:14, 22, 28, 42, 45, 48², 49; **16**:2, 6, 11, 19; **2Co** 1:4, 5, 7, 8, 12, 15, 17, 20; **2**:1, 3, 5, 7, 13, 17; **3**:7; **4**:4, 10, 11, 12, 15, 18; **5**:4, 9, 12, 16², 21; **6**:3; **7**:7, 9, 12, 14; **8**:6, 9, 10, 11, 14, 22; **9**:4, 5, 8, 11; **10**:16; **11**:2, 8, 9, 16, 19, 22³; **12**:6, 9, 15; **Gal** 1:6, 9, 16; **2**:5, 13, 16, 19; **3**:3, 4, 9, 14, 22, 24; **4**:3, 7, 15, 17, 18; **5**:16, 17; **Eph** 1:17; **2**:9; **3**:17; **4**:12, 17, 19, 21; **Php** 1:10, 16, 20, 26; **2**:15, 18, 28; **3**:11, 21; **Col** 1:11, 18, 28, 29; **2**:2, 4, 6; **4**:3, 6; **1Th** 1:7; **2**:8², 10, 16; **3**:1, 3, 13; **4**:10, 12², 14, 17; **5**:4, 6, 10; **2Th** 1:3, 12; **2**:4, 6, 7, 10, 11, 12, 15; **3**:8; **1Ti** 1:3, 7, 16, 18, 19; **3**:7, 14; **4**:15; **5**:4, 7, 14, 16, 20; **6**:1, 17, 19, 21; **2Ti** 1:4; 8; **3**:8, 17; **4**:17, 21; **Tit** 1:9; 13; **2**:5, 8, 10; **3**:7, 8; **Phm** 1:6, 13, 14, 17, 24; **Heb** 1:4; 2:1, 9, 11, 14; **3**:7, 11, 13, 19; **4**:3, 11, 16; **5**:5; **6**:3, 15, 18; **8**:3; **9**:13, 14, 28; **10**:33, 35, 36; **11**:3, 5, 12, 28, 29, 35, 40; **12**:1, 3, 13, 21, 27, 28; **13**:2, 6, 12, 17, 19; **Jas** 1:4, 21, 22; 2:26; **3**:4; **5**:16; **1Pe** 1:7, 15, 21, 22; **2**:2, 24; **3**:1, 7, 9, 16; **4**:6, 7, 11, 13, 19; **5**:13; **2Pe** 1:4, 12; **2**:9; **3**:14, 17; **1Jn** 1:3, 4; 2:1, 28; **3**:5; **4**:11, 16, 17; **5**:13, 20; **2Jn** 1:12; **3Jn** 1:8, 10², 13; **Rev** 1:7; **2**:22; **3**:11, 16, 18³, 19; **8**:12; **10**:9; **11**:6; **12**:4, 11, 14; **13**:15, 17; **14**:16; **16**:5, 15, 18, 21; **18**:4²; **19**:18.

THAT (5758)

Ge 1:4, 10, 11, 12, 18, 21, 24, 25², 26, 28, 29, 30², 31; **2**:3, 9, 12, 19; **3**:3, 5, 6, 11²; **4**:15, 26; **6**:2, 5, 6, 7², 17, 20, 21; **7**:5, 8, 11, 13, 14, 15, 21², 22, 23; **8**:1, 11, 13, 17², 19²; **9**:2, 3, 4, 10², 23; **10**:9, 11, 12; **11**:4², 5, 9; **12**:6, 13, 14, 19; **13**:6, 7, 10, 15, 16; **14**:2, 7, 8, 14, 17, 23², 24; **15**:8, 13, 18; **16**:5, 7, 10, 14; **17**:16, 23, 26; **18**:5, 8, 13, 19², 21², 27, 31; **19**:3, 5, 11, 13, 22, 29, 33, 35; **20**:6, 7, 8, 9²; **21**:7, 9, 10², 12, 22, 23, 25, 30, 31; **22**:12, 14, 16; **23**:2, 11, 15; **24**:2, 3, 6, 7, 14³, 24, 40, 56, 65; **25**:30²; **26**:7, 12, 14, 15, 18, 21, 24, 28, 29, 32; **27**:1, 4, 7, 10, 19, 25, 27, 31, 33; **28**:4; **29**:7, 11, 16², 21, 22²; **29**:2, 12, 19, 31, 33; **30**:1, 3², 9, 15, 16², 27, 33², 35³, 38, 39, 40; **31**:1, 2, 5, 6, 10, 12², 16, 22, 32, 35, 36, 37², 48, 50, 52²; **32**:2, 5, 8, 22, 25²; **33**:10, 11, 13³, 14, 15, 16, 17; **34**:2, 5, 7, 14, 15, 22; **35**:5, 6, 7, 19, 20, 22, 27; **36**:1, 8, 19; **37**:4, 19, 20, 29; **38**:1, 5, 9, 14, 16; **39**:3², 5, 11, 17, 22; **40**:6, 16, 21; **41**:4, 15, 20, 21, 27, 31, 32, 35, 36², 49; **42**:1, 2, 4, 16, 20², 23, 28, 29, 34; **43**:8, 12, 14, 18, 25, 32; **44**:7, 15, 27, 31, 34; **45**:2, 5, 12, 16; **46**:1, 5, 30; **47**:14, 17, 18², 19², 22, 23, 26²; **29**; **48**:7, 20; **49**:17², 21, 25; **50**:3, 11², 15; **Ex** 1:6, 7, 22; **2**:2, 12, 23; **3**:2, 4, 8, 11, 12, 19, 22²; **4**:2, 5², 21², 26, 31; **5**:1, 2, 6, 8, 9, 17; **6**:7; **7**:5, 15, 16, 17², 21; **8**:1, 9², 10, 15, 20, 22³, 28; **9**:1, 4², 7, 11, 13, 14, 15, 16², 18, 19, 20, 29, 30, 34; **10**:1, 2³, 3, 5², 7², 12, 13², 15, 21²; **11**:1, 2, 7, 8, 9, 12; **12**:3, 8, 10, 12, 16, 17, 18, 26, 33, 42, 51; **13**:8, 9, 16, 17, 21; **14**:4, 5, 8, 11, 16, 17, 18, 21, 25, 26, 28, 30; **15**:23; **16**:4, 5, 6, 7, 8, 12, 13, 19², 34; **17**:2, 11, 14; **18**:1, 11, 14, 22, 26; **19**:9, 11, 12, 20, 11; **20**:11, 12, 20, 22; **21**:19, 36; **22**:2, 6, 11, 23²; **23**:12, 15, 24; **24**:8; **25**:22, 37, 40; **26**:6, 12, 14, 22, 24; **27**:2, 5, 20, 21; **28**:3, 28, 32, 35, 38, 43; **29**:37², 39, 42, 46²; **30**:6², 20, 21, 23; **31**:13, 14; **32**:1, 2, 10², 12, 18, 25², 28; **33**:13, 16; **34**:1, 10, 18, 29, 35; **35**:12, 14; **36**:13, 19, 27, 33; **38**:2, 26; **39**:21, 23, 43; **40**:15; **Lev** 1:3, 8, 12, 17; **3**:3, 5, 9, 14; **4**:7, 8, 12, 18; **5**:2, 3, 16; **6**:3, 6, 7, 10, 11; **7**:3, 19, 20, 21, 27, 34², 35, 36; **8**:35; **9**:6, 7, 15; **10**:14², 15², 16; **11**:2, 3², 4, 9, 10, 12, 20, 21³, 23, 27², 29, 31, 32, 34², 35, 37, 39, 41, 42, 44, 46², 47²; **13**:2, 5, 10, 13, 20, 25,

30, 39², 52, 54, 58; **14**:4, 5, 6, 19, 34, 35, 36, 37, 40, 41; **15**:6, 8, 10, 12, 17, 25, 28, 31; **16**:13, 18; **17**:4, 5, 9, 10, 11, 13, 14; **18**:8, 10, 16, 17, 22, 23, 24, 28, 30; **19**:5, 8, 10, 16; **20**:3, 4, 5, 14, 19, 22, 25; **22**:3², 5, 7, 9, 11, 19, 23, 29, 30, 43; **24**:2; **25**:8, 21, 24, 29, 33, 36, 50, 52, 53; **26**:13, 16, 17, 22, 32, 34, 35, 36, 41, 46; **27**:6, 9, 11, 12, 17, 18, 23, 28, 32; **Nu** 1:53; **2**:34²; **4**:6, 7, 8, 9, 11, 12, 15, 18, 19, 26; **5**:6, 8, 18, 19, 22², 24, 26, 27; **6**:4, 11, 18²; **20**³; **7**:5; **8**:3, 11, 19, 22; **9**:6², 13², 16; **11**:3, 11, 16, 17², 25, 29², 32; **12**:10, 14, 16; **13**:24; **14**:1, 8, 14², 31, 45; **15**:30, 31, 39; **16**:5, 9, 11², 13, 28², 30², 40; **17**:8, 10; **18**:5, 9², 13, 14, 15, 24², 26; **19**:2², 7, 13, 14, 19, 20², 21, 22; **20**:4, 8, 14, 29; **21**:1, 7, 11, 14, 15, 18²; **22**:2, 4, 6, 11, 20, 36; **23**:19², 24; **24**:1; **25**:4, 11; **26**:55; **27**:11; **28**:2, 3, 8; **29**:40; **30**:8, 12²; **31**:12, 16, 21, 23², 26, 32, 42, 52; **32**:1, 10, 23; **33**:40; **34**:2, 13; **35**:4, 8², 12, 15, 16, 17², 18², 20, 21², 23², 36:3, 4, 8; **Dt** 1:1, 3, 8, 9, 10, 16, 18, 19², 25, 39; **2**:14, 20, 34, 37; **3**:4², 8, 12², 14, 18, 20², 21², 23, 25, 26, 28; **4**:1², 2, 5, 9, 10, 14², 16, 17, 18, 21, 22, 23, 26², 35², 39, 40², 48; **5**:3, 5, 14, 15², 16², 21, 24, 27², 29², 31, 33²; **6**:1, 2³, 6², 12, 18², 23, 24, 25; **7**:8, 9, 13, 16; **8**:1², 3³, 5, 11², 16, 16, 19²; **9**:1, 3, 4, 5, 6², 8, 9², 11², 14, 17, 21³, 27, 28, 32; **10**:5, 10, 12, 13, 13, 16, 18, 22; **11**:2, 4, 5, 6, 7, 8², 9², 11, 14, 17, 21³, 27, 28, 32; **12**:1, 5, 10, 25, 28, 32; **13**:3, 5, 6, 13, 14, 15, 17, 18; **14**:6², 7² 9, 10, 19, 20, 22, 23, 24, 28, 29²; **15**:7, 9, 15², 18; **16**:3, 12, 17; **17**:1, 4, 5, 8, 9, 16, 18, 19, 20; **18**:1, 19, 22², 19:3, 5, 10², 12, 20, 8, 12, 15, 16, 19, 20; **21**:3, 4, 17, 23; **22**:7, 8, 15, 24, 26; **23**:14, 17, 20², 21, 23, 24; **24**:1; **25**:4, 11; **26**:2, 3, 10, 12, 17², 18², 19²; **27**:1, 10; **28**:7, 10, 13, 33, 35, 51, 56, 57, 60, 67²; **29**:2, 4³, 5, 6², 9, 13, 18, 20, 24, 27, 29; **30**:5, 6, 10, 12, 13, 18, 19² 20; **31**:5, 7, 17², 18, 19, 22, 28, 29; **32**:11², 17, 21, 22, 24, 39, 46, 48, 50; **33**:1, 4, 13; **34**:12² Jos 1:7, 8, 13, 14, 15² 2:7², 9³, 12, 13², 23; **3**:7, 10²; **4**:7, 9, 14, 24³; **5**:2, 5, 6², 11, 12, 6; **15²**; **6**:17, 18, 26; **7**:8, 12, 13, 14³ 15, 24, 26; **8**:2, 9, 11, 13, 14, 18, 21², 22² 24; **9**:9, 10, 13, 16, 20, 24, 27²; **10**:1² 17, 28, 30, 35; **11**:10, 11, 14, 15, 20, 21; **12**:7; **13**:2, 3, 6, 8, 12, 21, 29; **14**:9²; **12³**; **15**:8, 9, 10, 11² 19, 23²; **16**:13; **17**:26, 42, 43, 46, 47², 51, 55; **18**:2, 5, 9, 17, 18, 21²; **27**, 28²; **19**:8, 10, 15, 17, 18, 24²; **20**:1, 3, 7, 9, 14², 30, 33, 34; **21**:5, 6, 7, 9, 10, 15; **22**:6, 8², 13, 15, 18, 22; **23**:7, 9, 10, 15, 28; **24**:6, 11, 16, 20², 21²; **25**:4, 6, 7, 17, 21, 25, 36, 39; **26**:3, 4, 11², 16, 17, 27:4, 7, 11, 21, 22; **28**:1, 16, 20, 21, 25; **29**:4, 30:15, 23², 24, 25; **31**:5, 6, 7²; **2Sa** 1:5, 10², 18, 21, 26; **2**:4, 16, 17, 20, 26, 29; **3**:19, 21³, 23³, 37², 38; **4**:1, 10; **5**:8², 12, 17, 20, 24; **6**:2, 8, 9, 17; **7**:4, 10, 11, 18, 23, 26, 29; **8**:7, 8, 9; **9**:7, 10, 13; **10**:6, 9, 14, 15, 19; **11**:2, 11, 26; **12**:4, 6, 15, 18, 19, 21, 23; **13**:20, 32, 33; **14**:1, 7, 11, 14, 20², 22; **15**:4, 22; **16**:4, 21, 23²; **17**:10², 13, 14, 23; **18**:7, 8, 19, 22, 27, 32; **19**:2³, 3, 6², 7² 20, 22, 30, 34, 37; **20**:12², 18, 19, 21; **21**:3, 5, 14, 17, 18; **22**:32; **23**:4, 5, 29, 41, 41, 44, 51, 2², 4, 16, 17, 27, 31; **24**:1, 3, 21, 23, 24; **1Ki** 1:2, 11, 24², 40, 51; **2**:3, 4, 5, 29, 31, 41, 42; **3**:3, 4², 10, 12, 13, 21, 23, 28; **4**:27, 33; **5**:1, 3, 6², 14; **6**:2, 3, 6, 22, 23; **7**:3, 6, 31, 45, 48; **8**:5³, 8, 9, 12, 21, 26, 28, 29, 40, 43²; 51, 59, 60³, 64, 65; **9**:9, 12, 21; **10**:2, 7, 8, 9; **11**:2, 11, 26; **12**:4, 6, 11, 16, 18, 19, 21, 23; **13**:20, 32, 33; **14**:1, 7, 11, 14, 20², 22; **15**:4; **16**:4, 11, 21, 23², 37³; **17**:9, 10², 14, 24²; **18**:9, 17, 36², 37², 39; **19**:2, 4, 8; **20**:13, 20, 23, 28, 31, 40; **21**:19, 36; **22**:2, 6, 11, 15, 16³, 17, 18, 20, 23, 33, 35, 49; **2Ki** 1:3, 6, 8, 16, 17; **2**:3, 5, 13, 14; **3**:2, 6, 11, 21, 26; **4**:1, 9, 17, 38; **5**:6², 8², 11, 14, 15; **6**:9, 10, 22; **7**:6, 13², 20; **8**:1, 6, 10, 13, 14, 15;

9:20, 21, 25, 26, 34, 36, 37; **10**:10, 19, 23, 36; **11**:1, 5, 7, 10², 17; **12**:4, 8², 9, 10²; **14**:10; **15**:16; **16**:6, 11, 14, 17, 18; **17**:4, 8, 9, 11, 13², 26, 34; **18**:4, 12, 15, 20, 21, 27; **19**:4³, 7, 8, 9, 12, 17, 19², 21, 25, 29, 33, 35; **20**:8², 9, 12, 13², 15, 17, 18; **21**:8, 9, 12, 16²; **22**:4, 9, 13², 19; **23**:11, 13, 15, 16, 17, 19², 24, 26, 33; **24**:10, 13, 20; **25**:3, 13, 15, 23; **1Ch** 1:27; **4**:10², 5:9, 23, 26; **6**:49², 62; **10**:5, 7²; **11**:4, 16, 17, 19; **13**:6, 11, 12; **14**:2², 8, 11, 15; **15**:13, 22; **16**:1, 7, 32, 35²; **17**:3, 9, 10, 16, 24², 25, 27; **18**:8, 9; **19**:6, 10, 15, 16, 19; **20**:4; **21**:2, 19, 22, 24, 28²; **22**:12, 13, 19²; **23**:5, 24; **27**:1²; **28**:8, 12, 18², 29:14, 16, 17, 22, 30; **2Ch** 1:5, 7, 10; **2**:8, 16; **4**:16, 18², 19; **5**:6², 9, 10; **6**:1, 11, 12, 15; **9**:13; **10**:16; **12**:3, 7, 8, 15; **13**:5, 8, 13; **14**:13, 14; **15**:8, 9, 11, 18; **16**:7, 10; **17**:2, 5, 10; **18**:7, 17, 19, 32; **19**:10; **20**:2, 9, 12, 24, 25; **21**:14; **22**:10; **23**:9², 16, **24**:7, 9², 11; **25**:5, 9, 12, 13, 16, 19², 26; **26**:18, 8, 9, 16, 21; **29**:10, 16, 19, 35; **30**:6, 7, 8; **31**:5, 21; **32**:1, 2², 4, 5, 10, 14², 16, 17, 21³, 24, 25; **33**:9, 13; **34**:4, 9, 11, 14², 16, 17, 21³, 24, 25; **35**:3, 16, 17; **36**:8; **Ezr** 2:59; 61; 3:5, 7; **4**:1, 12², 13, 15³, 16, 19, 21; **5**:3, 6, 8, 10, 11², 16; **6**:6, 8, 10, 11, 22; **7**:13, 15, 20, 24; **8**:15, 17, 20, 21, 25, 30, 34; **9**:12; **10**:23; **Ne** 1:2; **2**:5, 7, 10; **3**:8; **4**:1², 10, 15², 16, 22; **5**:15; **6**:1², 6, 12², 13, 16; **7:61**, 63; **8**:8, 12, 14, 15, 17²; **9**:6, 11², 13², 23, 28, 32, 33; **12**:40, 43, 44; **13**:1², 10², 15, 18, 19, 21, 26, 27; **Est** 1:2, 15, 19, 22²; 3:1, 5, 7, 14; **4**:1, 7, 11², 13, 14; **5**:2, 5, 9², 13; **6**:1, 2, 6, 13; **7**:2, 7; **8**:1, 5, 11, 13²; **9**:11, 14, 19, 24, 25², 27²; **Job** 1:10; **2**:11; **3**:4, 6, 7, 8, 12, 21; **4**:21; **5**:9², 12, 24, 25; **6**:8², 9, 10, 11², 13, 15, 17², 18; **8**:18; **9**:2, 10², 22, 31, 32², 34; **10**:6, 7², 9, 13; **11**:5², 14; **12**:9; **13**:5, 9, 13; **15**:3, 9; **16**:5², 14; **19**:4, 6, 23², 24, 25², 29; **20**:3, 5, 9, 11, 21, 15, 30²; **22**:4, 6, 10, 13², 17, 19; **23**:5, 9, 10, 13, 15, 17², 24:18; **26**:2, 5, **28**:7, 28; **30**:11; **31**:6, 11, 12, 21, 27, 29, 34, 35; **32**:5, 6, 8, 16²; **33**:13, 20, 30; **34**:12², 23, 28, 36; **35**:6², 14², 15; **36**:2, 4, 9, 18; **37**:2, 4, 7, 10, 20; **38**:2, 13; **39**:15², 16; **40**:14; **41**:11, 16, 26, 34²; **42**:2, 3; **Ps** 1:4²; **4**:3; **5**:11; **8**:4²; **8**; **9**:14, 17; **10**:15, 18; **12**:4; **14**:7; **17**:3; **18**:36, 38; **20**:6; **24**:7, 9; **25**:2², 27:4; **30**:12; **31**:4; **34**:8; **37**:16; **39**:13; **41**:10, 11; **44**:3; **46**:10; **48**:6, 13; **49**:9, 10, 12, 20; **50**:4, 12, 21²; **51**:4, 5³, 6², 11; **55**:6; **56**:9, 13; **58**:4², 5, 7; **59**:13; **60**:3, 5; **61**:2; **62**:11, 12; **64**:2; **66**:3; **67**:2; **68**:18, 23; **69**:34²; **78**:35²; **39²**, 45², 69; **79**:6², 10; **80**:3, 7, 12, 19; **83**:4, 16, 18²; **85**:6, 9; **86**:11, 17; **87**:5; **89**:2², 11, 36; **90**:4, 11, 12, 14; **91**:5, 6², 12; **92**:7, 10; **94**:11, 20; **95**:8, 10; **96**:11; **100**:3; **101**:6; **102**:18; **103**:5, 14; **104**:15², 16; **105**:45; **106**:5², 26, 47; **107**:25, 37; **108**:6; **109**:15, 27²; **114**:5², 6; **116**:9; **119**:4, 5, 11, 13, 18, 38, 71, 75, 77, 80, 101, 106, 115, 125, 134, 144, 148, 152, 175; **120**:5²; **122**:3, 4; **132**:11; **135**:3, 5²; **139**:14; **140**:12; **141**:6; **142**:7; **144**:3², 5; **145**:12; **146**:4; **148**:6, 8; **150**:6; **Pr** 3:25; **4**:26; **5**:2, 6:16, 17, 18²; **8**:15; **9**:18²; **12**:28; **14**:12; **15**:4; **16**:25, 29; **18**:13; **19**:18, 21; **20**:12²; **21**:30; **22**:19; **23**:3, 24; **24**:14, 27, 29; **26**:7; **27**:8; **28**:3; **29**:26; **30**:15²; **17²**, **18²**, **29²**; **31**:18; **Ecc** 1:13, 14, 17; **2**:1, 11, 13, 14, 17²; **3**:12, 13, 14², 18², 19, 22²; **4**:1, 2, 3, 4, 15; **5**:1, 14, 15, 18; **6**:2, 3, 5, 11; **7**:12, 22; **8**:12, 14, 17; **9**:1, 3, 5, 6, 7, 9, 12, 13, 15²; **10**:5; **11**:6, 9; **SS 2**:15²; **4**:5, 11, 16; **5**:9; **6**:1, 10, 13; **7**:2, 7, 13; **Isa** 1:1, 29; **2**:3, 11, 12, 17, 20; **3**:7, 18; **4**:1; **2**; **5**:29, 30; **6**:1; **7**:18, 20, 21, 23; **8**:12, 14²; **9**:4, 7, 18; **10**:19, 20, 27; **11**:10, 11², 15, 16; **12**:1, 4²; **13**:1, 4; **14**:8, 29³, 32; **17**:4, 7, 9; **18**:7; **19**:14, 19², 18, 19, 21, 23, 24; **20**:1, 2, 6, 22²; **23**:11, 13, 16; **24**:20, 21; **25**:7² 9; **26**:1, 2; **27**:1, 2, 3, 12, 13; **28**:1², 3, 4, 5, 13; **29**:7², 8³, 18; **30**:1, 6, 8, 13, 14, 23², 24, 26, 31:7, 8; **33**:11, 17, 18, 20; **34**:1², 16; **35**:3, 8; **36**:5, 6, 12; **37**:4³, 7, 8, 9, 12, 18, 20², 26, 30, 34; **38**:7, 17, 22²; **39**:1, 2, 4, 6; **40**:2³, 11, 14, 20²; **41**:20³, 22², 27; **42**:5, 7, 8, 10; **43**:9, 10²; **12**, 21; **44**:13, 28; **45**:1², 6, 20, 23; **46**:1, 5, 7, 10, 11²; **47**:11, 15²; **48**:5; **49**:6, 23, 26; **50**:4, 9; **51**:9, 10, 12, 13², 15, 17, 22², 23; **52**:6²; **53**:5, 54:9, 17; **55**:3, 5, 10, 11; **56**:5; **57**:1, 11², 16; **58**:2, 5; **59**:2, 15, 16²; **60**:8, 11, 12, 16, 61:4, 9, 62:2; **63**:5, 14, 17; **64**:1², 3, 11; **65**:1, 5; **66**:5, 6², 19; **Jer** 1:12; **2**:5, 13, 24, 37; **3**:7, 8, 17; **4**:9, 11, 12; **5**:7; **6**:24, 27; **7**:1, 8, 14, 23, 28; **8**:1, 7, 11², 12², 17; **9**:11, 12, 14, 22; **10**:18, 23, 25; **11**:1, 3, 8, 13, 18, 19²; **12**:9; **13**:12, 20, 21, 22, 26; **14**:19; **15**:10, 14, 18; **16**:16, 19, 21; **17**:8, 11, 27; **18**:1, 7, 8, 9, 20; **19**:3, 4; **20**:16; **21**:2, 4, 7, 14; **22**:5; **23**:14, 24, 29, 34, 38, 40; **24**:2, 7; **25**:13²; **29**, 33; **26**:9, 15, 19; **27**:5, 8, 10, 11, 13, 18, 21; **28**:1, 3, 17; **29**:1, 6, 17, 19; **30**:1, 7, 8, 15; **31**:1, 21, 33, 35; **32**:1, 8, 20,

31, 34, 35, 39, 40; **33**:4, 9, 10, 15, 20, 24; **34**:7, 10, 15; **35**:1, 4; **36**:6, 27, 28, 29²; **37**:10, 18; **38**:7, 25; **39**:10, 16, 17; **40**:7, 11, 14; **42**:3, 6, 12, 20; **44**:3, 4, 15, 17, 19, 26, 29³; **46**:1, 7, 10; **47**:1; **48**:2, 20, 27, 28, 38, 41; **49**:10, 13, 22, 24, 26, 31, 34; **50**:4, 5, 8, 17, 20, 30, 32, 34, 38, 43; **51**:29, 31, 39, 48, 60², 61, 62; **52**:3, 6, 17, 19; **La** 1:6, 7, 12², 17; **2**:13, 15; **3**:18, 38, 44; **4**:6, 11, 12, 14, 17, 20; **5**:21; **Eze** 1:5, 26, 27²; **2**:3, 5, 8; **3**:18, 25, 26; **4**:8; **5**:13; **6**:6, 7, 10, 12³, 13, 14²; **7**:4, 9, 11, 27; **8**:2, 3, 6², 13, 15; **9**:4; **10**:1, 7, 14, 20; **11**:1, 5, 10, 12; **12**:6, 9, 12, 15, 16², 20; **13**:5, 9, 11, 14², 20, 21, 23; **14**:8², 9, 15², 17, 19, 23; **15**:2, 7; **16**:8, 19, 28, 54, 62; **17**:8, 9, 14, 19², 21, 24; **18**:9, 25, 29²; **20**:6²; 12, 15, 20², 23, 25, 26², 28, 38, 42, 44, 48; **21**:5, 7, 15, 24; **22**:3, 16, 22, 24, 26²; **23**:3, 13, 20, 38, 39, 41, 43, 48, 49; **24**:8, 24, 27²; **25**:5, 7, 9, 10, 17; **26**:2, 6, 10; **28**:22, 23, 24, 26; **29**:6, 9, 15, 16, 21²; **30**:2, 8, 9, 19, 25, 26; **31**:16; **32**:15, 31; **33**:6, 8, 11, 13, 15, 17, 28, 29, 30, 33; **34**:10, 25, 27, 30²; **35**:4, 9, 12, 15²; **36**:3, 4, 5, 7, 11, 22, 23, 30, 32, 35², 36², 38²; **37**:2, 6, 9, 13, 14, 17, 28; **38**:8, 10, 14, 16², 17², 18, 19², 20, 23; **39**:6², 7, 11, 14, 22², 23, 28; **40**:1, 2, 4, 17; **41**:6, 7, 8, 22; **42**:12, 14; **43**:10, 11, 13; **44**:12, 14, 18, 19, 30; **45**:22; **46**:3, 18²; **47**:3, 4², 5²; **48**:22, 35; **Da** 1:5, 13; **2**:3, 8², 9, 12, 16, 18, 28, 30², 35, 38, 41, 44, 45, 46; **3**:3, 5, 7, 10, 11, 14, 18, 22, 24, 27, 29; **4**:2, 5², 6, 9, 16, 17², 18, 22, 25, 26², 27, 32, 34, 36; **5**:2², 3, 6, 11, 14², 16, 21, 24, 25, 30; **6**:2, 3, 7², 8, 10, 12, 15², 17, 26; **7**:4, 6², 7, 8, 14², 15, 17, 19, 20⁴, 23; **8**:1, 13², 17, 20, 22², 26; **9**:2, 15, 18, 27²; **10**:2, 7, 12; **11**:31, 35; **12**:1¹, 11²; **Hos** 1:1, 5, 6; **2**:6, 8, 16, 18³, 21; **6**:2, 3, 4; **7**:2; **8**:6, 14; **9**:10, 14²; **10**:11, 14, 15; **13**:3, 10; **14**:2; **Joel** 1:1, 15; **2**:5, 25, 27³; **3**:1, 3, 6, 17, 18; **Am** 1:4, 7, 10, 12, 14; **2**:2, 5, 16; **5**:3², 14, 18; **6**:14; **7**:7; **8**:3, 5², 9, 10, 13; **9**:1, 11, 12²; **Ob** 1:8; **Jnh** 1:3, 4, 12², **2**:8; **3**:9; **4**:2², 7, 8, 11; **Mic** 1:1, 2; **2**:4; **3**:4, 9; **4**:2, 6, 7, 9²; **5**:10, 15; **6**:5; **7**:11, 12, 17; **Na** 1:4²; **2**:7; **3**:17; **Hab** 1:1, 4, 5, 6, 14; **2**:2, 13², 15, 18²; **Zep** 1:1, 9, 10, 12, 15; **2**:2, 15; **3**:9, 11, 16; **Hag** 1:8; **2**:12, 21, 23; **Zec** 1:15, 19, 21²; **2**:4, 8, 9², 11², **3**:9, 10; **4**:9; **5**:3, 5; **6**:15; **7**:5, 12, 14; **8**:6, 9, 10, 23; **9**:12, 16; **10**:2²; **11**:1, 11; **12**:2, 3, 4, 6, 7², 8², 9³, 11; **13**:1, 2, 4; **14**:4, 6, 8, 9, 12, 13, 16, 18, 19, 20, 21; **Mal** 1:7, 8², 10²; **2**:4²; **3**:10²; **4**:1², 5; **Mt** 2:8, 16, 22; **3**:9, 10, 16; **4**:4, 6, 12, 17; **5**:16, 17, 20², 21, 22, 23, 27, 28, 32, 33, 38, 43, 45, 46, 47; **6**:4, 18², 23, 29, 30, 32; **7**:13, 14, 19, 22, 25, 27; **8**:4, 9, 11, 13, 24, 28²; **9**:6², 14, 22, 26, 28, 30, 31, 34; **10**:14, 15, 19, 26², 34; **11**:21, 23, 24, 25; **12**:1, 5, 6, 9, 15, 22, 24, 36, 45; **13**:1, 2, 20, 22, 23, 30, 32, 33, 41, 44, 47; **14**:1, 2, 7, 9, 20, 35, 15:5, 11, 12, 13, 17, 18, 21, 22, 27, 28, 37; **16**:11, 12, 18, 20, 21³; **17**:10, 13, 18, 27; **18**:1, 7, 10², 12, 13², 14, 16, 19, 25², 28, 31, 32; **19**:4, 7, 9, 12²; **20**:21, 25, 30; **21**:3, 9², 26, 43, 46; **22**:4, 16, 23, 24, 34, 43, 46; **23**:17, 19, 31, 35; **24**:4, 6, 10, 15, 20, 23, 24, 30, 32, 33, 36, 39, 44, 46, 50; **25**:1, 24, 26, 27, 30; **26**:24, 29, 41, 51, 54, 55³, 56, 59, 62; **27**:3, 4, 8, 16, 18, 19, 24², 51, 54, 58, 60, 63², 64; **28**:4, 5, 11; **Mk** 1:9, 27, 32, 38, 44²; **2**:5; **4**:1², 7, 12, 15, 32, 35, 37; **5**:7, 23, 29, 30; **6**:2², 10, 12, 14², 32, 35, 37; **7**:2², 11², 13², 18², 24²; **8**:8, 15, 31²; **9**:11, 12, 17, 25, 26, 30; **10**:1, 5, 42, 46, 47; **11**:5, 23, 24, 25, 32; **12**:5, 19, 28, 32, 34, 35²; **13**:4, 5, 14, 18, 21, 22, 24, 26, 28, 29, 32, 33; **14**:21, 25, 35, 48, 55, 60, 67²; **15**:10, 16, 32, 42, 44, 45; **16**:1, 4, 11², 20; **Lk** 1:1, 4, 39, 43, 45, 58, 61; **2**:1, 2, 10, 15, 26, 34, 35, 38; **3**:8, 9; **4**:11, 22, 23, 25, 43; **5**:6, 7, 14, 15, 24²; **6**:23², 26, 32, 33², 34, 48, 49; **7**:7, 8, 21, 29², 37, 39; **8**:10, 12, 14, 16, 17², 18, 47, 53; **9**:4, 7, 8², 17, 19, 36², 39, 43, 45; **10**:7, 11, 12², 13, 20², 21, 23, 24, 40²; **11**:14, 18, 26, 33, 35, 38, 48, 50; **12**:1, 2², 4, 12, 28, 30, 33², 36, 43, 46, 47, 56; **13**:1, 2, 21, 31, 14:5, 10, 12, 15, 16, 34, 35, 38; **15**:7, 17²; **16**:4, 9, 15, 20, 25, 28², **17**:1², 8, 31, 34; **18**:1, 3, 5², 8, 11, 14, 31; **19**:4, 11, 22, 23, 26; **20**:6, 11, 17, 18, 20, 21², 28, 35, 37, 41; **21**:7, 8, 15, 20, 22, 27, 30, 34, 36³; **22**:10, 20, 26, 30, 32, 34, 37, 38, 40, 46, 52; **23**:7², 12, 23, 29²; **24**:4, 14, 18, 21, 23, 25, 44; **Jn** 1:3, 4, 7², 9, 11, 31, 33, 34, 39, 41, 50; **2**:9, 17, 22; **3**:15, 16², 20, 21², 26, 28², 31, 32, 33²; **4**:1, 10, 15, 19, 20, 25, 32, 36, 39, 42, 44, 45, 47, 51, 53, 54; **5**:6, 13, 15, 23, 32, 34², 35², 39³, 42², 44, 46; **6**:1, 10, 12, 15, 24, 25, 29, 30, 31², 35, 39, 41; **7**:4, 6, 10, 15, 16, 17, 20, 22, 27, 40, 41, 42³, 49,

7:6, 13², 20; **8**:1, 6, 10, 13, 14, 15; **10**:22, 25; **7**:6, 13², 20; **8**:1, 6, 10, 13, 14, 15;

Column 1 (THAT, continued)

50³, 51², 52, 53, 57²; **12:**7, 9, 12², 16², 17, 18, 29, 34, 36, 46, 48, 50; **13:**1, 3², 5², 11, 13, 14, 15, 17, 19², 35; **14:**3, 8, 10², 11, 13, 20², 28, 29, 31²; **15:**2³, 6, 8, 11², 13, 15, 16, 18, 19; **16:**1, 4², 7, 15², 19, 21, 23, 26², 27, 30³, 33; **17:**1, 2, 3, 7, 8², 11, 12², 13, 15², 19, 21³, 22², 23, 25, 26²; **18:**4, 8, 9, 13, 14, 27, 32, 34; **19:**4, 7, 21, 24, 27, 28², 30, 33, 35², 36; **20:**1, 7, 9, 14, 18, 19, 22, 31³; **21:**3, 4, 15, 16, 17, 20, 22, 23, 24, 25²; **Ac 1:**1, 3, 19²; **2:**3, 8, 29, 30², 31, 41; **3:**14, 16², 17, 18, 19², 20; **4:**10, 13², 23, 32; **5:**3², 8, 10, 15, 26², 31, 34, 42; **6:**14, 15; **7:**5², 7, 12, 16, 19, 20, 25², 37, 41, 46, 53; **8:**1, 8, 9, 14, 15, 18, 19, 23, 24, 26, 29, 35; **9:**2, 17, 20, 22, 26, 27, 35; **10:**8, 15, 22, 28², 34, 37, 42, 43, 45, 48; **11:**1, 9, 17, 28; **12:**1, 9, 11, 15, 19; **13:**8, 10, 17, 25, 26, 27, 29, 34, 38, 40, 41, 47; **14:**1, 9, 10, 21, 27; **15:**7², 8, 10, 11, 17, 19, 24, 39; **16:**3², 10, 12, 18², 19, 26, 33, 38; **17:**3, 7, 13, 16, 22, 26, 27, 29, 33; **18:**5, 28; **19:**2, 4, 10, 12², 16, 23, 26, 27², 35, 40; **20:**2, 15, 20², 21, 23², 25, 26, 29, 31, 34, 35, 38; **21:**11, 22², 24², 25, 29, 31, 34, 36; **22:**10, 13, 19, 24, 29; **23:**3, 5, 6, 8², 10, 22, 24, 27, 29², 34, 35; **24:**4, 9, 10, 11, 15, 21, 26; **25:**6, 15, 16, 24, 26; **26:**5, 6, 7, 8, 9², 10, 18, 20, 21, 23, 26, 28, 29, 31; **27:**1, 10, 12, 17, 18, 25, 28, 29, 32, 40; **28:**1, 7, 11, 15, 19, 20, 22, 28; **Ro 1:**5, 10, 11, 12², 13², 15, 17, 20, 32; **2:**2, 4, 15, 19, 22²; **3:**4, 5, 6, 8², 19², 21; **4:**1, 9, 11², 12, 13², 16, 17, 19²; **5:**3, 15, 17, 18, 20, 21; **6:**1, 3, 4, 6³, 8, 9, 12, 16, 17, 18²; **7:**1, 3, 4², 5, 6, 10², 13³, 14, 16, 18²; **8:**3, 4, 5, 15, 16, 17, 18², 21, 22, 24, 26, 28, 29, 34², 38, 39; **9:**3, 7, 10, 11, 17², 26, 30², 33²; **10:**1, 2, 3, 4, 5, 6², 7, 8, 9², 10², 19; **11:**8², 14, 19, 22, 24, 25, 31, 32, 35; **13:**1²; **14:**9, 14, 20, 21, 23; **15:**4², 6, 8, 13, 14, 16, 20, 23, 29, 31²; **16:**5, 17, 26; **1Co 1:**8, 10, 11, 14, 16, 28², 29, 30²; **2:**5, 7², 12, 14, 16; **3:**16², 17, 18, 20; **4:**2, 3, 4, 5, 6, 7, 8², 9; **5:**1², 5, 6, 7, 10, 11; **6:**2, 3, 5, 7, 9, 13, 14², 15, 16, 19; **7:**5², 7², 12, 14, 16; **8:**1, 4², 7, 9, 13; **9:**9, 13, 14, 15, 18, 22, 23, 24, 25², 27; **10:**1², 4², 12, 13, 16, 19², 33; **11:**3, 14, 15, 18, 30, 32, 34; **12:**2, 3, 9, 15, 16, 22², 24, 25²; **13:**2; **14:**5, 7, 12, 13, 18, 23, 24, 31, 37; **15:**3, 4², 12, 42, 46, 50, 54, 58; **16:**2, 6, 10, 11, 15, 19; **2Co 1:**4, 7, 8, 9, 10, 12², 13, 14, 15, 17, 23², 24; **2:**1, 3², 7, 11, 12; **3:**3, 5, 7, 9², 11; **4:**4, 6, 10, 12, 14, 15², 17; **5:**1, 4, 6, 10, 12, 14, 15, 19, 21; **6:**3; **7:**1², 3², 7, 8², 11, 12², 13; **8:**2, 6, 7², 9², 11, 12, 13; **9:**2, 3², 8, 11, 12, 13; **10:**2², 5, 7², 11, 13, 15, 16; **11:**1, 2, 3, 16, 21², 30; **12:**3, 4, 5, 6², 7⁴, 10; **Gal 1:**6, 11², 16, 20, 22²; **2:**2², 5, 7, 9, 10, 13, 14², 16², 17³, 18, 19; **3:**7, 8, 14², 15, 21, 22², 24, 25; **4:**1, 5, 9², 11, 13, 15, 17, 21; **6:**8, 13; **Eph 1:**8, 12, 17², 18², 19, 21; **2:**7, 9, 11², 12²; **3:**2, 3, 6, 10, 16, 17², 19², 20; **4:**9, 12, 15, 17, 18, 20, 21, 28, 29; **5:**14; **6:**3², 8, 9, 11, 13, 15, 19², 20, 21, 22²; **Php 1:**6, 9, 10, 11, 12, 13, 15, 16, 18, 19, 20², 24, 25, 26, 27, 28³, 30; **2:**5, 9, 10, 11, 15, 16², 19, 22, 24, 28; **3:**8, 9¹, 12², 15, 16², 21; **4:**1, 10, 17, 18; **Col 1:**5³, 6, 10, 11, 18, 23², 26, 28; **2:**2³, 4, 8, 14², 17; **3:**24²; **4:**1, 3², 4, 6, 8², 9, 12, 13, 16², 17; **1Th 1:**4², 5, 8, 11, 16; **3:**3², 4², 5, 6², 10, 13; **4:**3², 4², 6, 12², 14², 15, 17; **5:**2, 4, 10, 15; **2Th 1:**5, 11², 12; **2:**2, 3, 4², 5, 6, 10, 11, 12, 14; **3:**1, 2, 4, 8, 11, 16; **1Ti 1:**3, 8, 9, 11, 12, 14, 15, 16², 18; **2:**1, 2; **3:**4, 7, 14; **4:**1, 6, 9, 10, 15; **5:**7², 16, 20, 25; **6:**1, 4, 5, 8, 9, 19²; **2Ti 1:**1, 4, 12³, 14, 15, 16⁴, 17, 18, 19²; **2:**1, 10², 18², 25; **3:**17; **4:**8, 13, 17; **Tit 1:**1, 5, 9, 11, 13; **2:**5, 8², 10², 11, 14; **3:**7, 8, 10, 11, 13; **Phm 1:**2, 6², 13, 14, 15, 19, 20, 21; **Heb 2:**1, 5, 6², 8, 9, 10, 14², 17²; **3:**10², 12², 13, 18, 19; **4:**1, 3, 6², 11², 16; **6:**1, 7², 8, 9, 18; **7:**5, 9, 13, 14²; **8:**5², 7, 10, 9:4, 7, 8, 9, 11³, 13, 14², 15², 24, 25, 27; **10:**1, 10, 13, 16, 20, 27, 29, 34, 36; **11:**3², 5, 7, 10, 13, 14, 18, 19, 28, 35, 40; **12:**1², 3, 5², 10, 13, 15², 16, 18², 19², 21, 24, 25, 26, 27², 28; **13:**14, 15, 17², 18, 19, 20, 23, 24; **Jas 1:**3, 4, 7, 10, 12, 14, 15, 21, 25, 27; **2:**12, 19², 20, 22, 23, 24; **3:**1, 13, 17²; **4:**1, 3, 4, 5, 6, 13, 14, 15; **5:**1, 16, 17; **1Pe 1:**4, 5, 7, 10, 11, 12², 18², 22², 25; **2:**2, 3², 8², 9, 12, 15, 21, 24; **3:**1, 4, 7, 9, 15, 16, 17², 21; **4:**6, 7, 11², 13², 16², 17; **5:**2, 4, 6, 9, 12; **2Pe 1:**4, 9, 14, 15, 18, 20; **2:**8, 21, 22; **3:**3, 5, 6, 12, 15², 16, 17; **1Jn 1:**1, 3; **2:**1, 3, 18, 19, 22, 24, 26, 27; **3:**1³, 2, 5, 14, 15, 19, 24; **4:**2², 9, 10², 13, 14, 15, 17; **5:**1, 2, 4, 5², 7², 13², 14², 16⁴, 17, 18, 19²; **2Jn 1:**5, 6², 8²; 12; **3Jn 1:**2², 4, 7, 8, 10, 12; **Jude 1:**3, 5, 10; **Rev 1:**2, 9, 12, 20²; **2:**2², 19, 20, 23; **3:**8², 9, 10, 11, 15, 17; **5:**13; **7:**9; **8:**11, 12, 13; **9:**1, 3, 5, 13, 18, 20²; **10:**6², 8²; **11:**4, 6, 7, 13; **12:**4, 9, 12, 13, 14, 16; **13:**2, 6, 15; **14:**2; **15:**5; **16:**3, 13, 15, 16; **17:**3, 6, 18;

Column 2

18:4²; **19:**12, 18, 21; **20:**2, 3, 13²; **21:**11; **22:**6, 14.

THE (55728)

Ge 1:1³, 2⁵, 4³, 5³, 6, 7⁴, 8², 9², 10², 11², 12, 13, 14⁴, 15³, 16⁵, 17³, 18², 19, 20⁴, 21³, 22⁴, 23, 24², 25⁴, 26⁸, 27, 28⁶, 29², 30⁷, 31; **2:**1², 2³, 3², 4⁶, 5⁶, 6³, 7⁶, 8³, 9⁸, 10, 11⁴, 12, 13⁴, 14⁶, 15³, 16⁵, 17², 18² 19⁸, 20⁶, 21⁴, 22⁴, 23; **3:**1⁵, 2³, 3², 4², 6⁴, 7, 8⁹, 9², 10, 11, 12², 13⁴, 14⁵, 15, 16, 17³, 18², 19⁸, 20⁶, 21⁴, 22⁴, 23, 24⁵; **4:**1², 2, 3⁴, 4², 6, 8², 9, 10², 11, 12, 13⁴, 14⁴, 15³, 16², 17³, 18⁴, 19², 20¹, 21², 22³, 23³, 24³, 25²; **5:**1², 6, 7, 9, 10, 12, 13, 15, 16, 18, 19, 21, 22, 25², 26, 29³, 32; **6:**1, 2², 3, 4⁵, 5⁴, 6², 7⁵, 8, 9², 11, 12², 13², 15, 16⁴, 17³, 18, 19, 20², 7:1², 3, 4⁵, 5, 6², 7, 8, 9, 10, 11², 12, 13², 14, 15², 16², 17⁴, 18, 19², 20², 21³, 22³, 23³, 24²; **8:**1⁵, 2⁵, 3⁵, 4⁴, 5⁴, 6², 7², 8³, 9⁴, 10², 11⁴, 12, 13⁴, 14⁴, 15, 16, 17⁵, 18², 19⁴, 20², 21³, 22³; **9:**1², 2², 3², 4², 6, 8², 9, 10², 11, 12, 13, 14, 15, 16, 17², 18², 19, 20², 21³, 22², 23³, 24², 25², 26³, 27³, 28, 29³, 30, 31², 32, 33³, 34, 35²; **10:**1², 2², 3, 5², 6², 7², 8, 9, 10, 12⁴, 14, 15², 16, 19⁴, 20², 21, 22, 23, 24, 25, 26, 27, 28; **11:**1², 2, 3⁴, 4, 5², 6³, 7², 8, 9, 10, 11, 12, 13², 14, 15, 16, 17, 18, 19, 20, 21, 22, 23, 24, 25, 26, 30², 31, 32⁴; **11:**1, 4³, 5⁴, 6², 8³, 9², 10, 11, 12, 13, 14, 15, 16, 17, 18, 19, 20, 21, 22, 23, 24, 25, 26, 27³, 28², 29⁴, 31²; **12:**1⁴, 4, 5³, 6², 7², 8³, 9, 10, 11, 13¹, 14, 15, 16³, 17²; **13:**1⁴, 3², 4², 6, 7³, 9², 10³, 11⁴, 12², 13, 14, 15, 16, 17, 18²; **14:**2⁴, 3⁵, 5⁶, 6³, 7³, 8⁶, 10⁵, 11², 13³, 14⁴, 15³, 16⁴, 17³, 18³, 19³, 20, 22, 23, 25, 26³, 27², 28; **15:**1², 2, 3, 4⁴, 5⁶, 7², 9, 10², 11, 13, 16, 17³, 18⁴; **16:**2, 5², 7⁵, 9, 10, 11³, 13², 14, 15, 16²; **17:**1², 2, 4, 5, 8, 9, 10², 11, 12², 13, 14, 15, 16¹; **18:**1⁵, 2⁶, 7, 8, 9, 10³, 11², 13, 14², 16, 17, 19³, 20², 21², 22²; **19:**1², 2⁴, 3², 4², 5, 6, 8, 9², 10⁴, 11², 12², 13², 14², 15², 16⁵, 17³, 18², 19³, 20, 21², 22², 23, 24², 25³, 26, 27³, 28², 29, 30, 31, 32⁴, 34², 36, 37²; **20:**1, 2³, 4², 5³, 6², 7, 8², 10², 11², 14², 15², 16⁴, 17², 18, 19, 22, 23², 24², 25, 26²; **21:**1³, 5, 6⁴, 8², 9, 10⁴, 12², 13, 15, 16, 17², 21², 22², 23, 24; **22:**1, 2³, 3⁴, 5, 6², 9², 10², 12⁴, 13⁵, 14, 16⁴, 17³, 18⁵, 19², 20³, 21², 22², 23², 24²; **23:**1, 2³, 3², 4², 5³, 6², 7, 8², 9³, 10⁴, 11⁵, 12, 13², 15³, 16², 17, 18², 19³, 20, 21, 22, 23⁴, 24², 25, 26, 27³, 28², 29, 30, 31, 32², 33²; **23:**1, 2³, 3², 4², 5³, 6², 7, 8, 9³, 10⁴, 11⁵, 12, 13²; **Nu 1:**1³, 2, 3⁴, 4, 5², 10, 16⁴, 18⁵, 19², 20⁵, 21², 22⁴, 23⁴, 24³, 25², 26⁴, 27², 28⁴, 29², 30⁴, 31², 32³, 33⁴, 34⁴, 35³, 36⁴, 37², 38⁴, 39, 40⁴, 41², 42⁴, 43², 44³, 45, 46, 47³, 48, 49¹, 50⁴, 51⁴, 52, 53⁸, 54²; **2:**1, 2³, 3⁶, 5³, 7³, 9², 10⁵, 14², 16⁴, 17⁶, 18², 20⁴, 21³, 22², 23, 24⁵, 25, 26⁴, 27², 28⁴, 29²; **3:**1⁴, 2³, 3⁴, 5, 6², 7⁴, 8², 9², 10, 11, 12², 13³, 14², 15, 16², 17³, 18², 19², 20², 21², 22², 23², 24³, 25⁵, 6², 7⁴, 8⁸, 9², 10, 11, 12², 13, 14⁴, 15⁵, 16⁵, 17³, 18⁸, 19⁴, 20⁷, 21⁶; **3:**31², 32², 33³, 34⁴, 35¹, 36², 37², 38⁴, 39, 40⁴, 41⁴, 42⁴, 43², 44⁴, 45, 46, 47³, 48, 49¹, 50⁴, 51⁴, 52, 53⁸, 54²; **2:**1, 2³, 3⁶, 5³, 7³, 8², 9², 10², 11⁴, 12¹, 13⁵, 14², 15², 16³, 17³, 18³, 19, 20⁴, 21⁶, 22, 23, 24, 25, 26², 27³; **7:**1², 2³, 3, 4, 5³, 6³, 7, 8³, 9², 10¹, 11⁵, 12², 13⁵, 14, 16⁴, 17³, 18⁸, 19⁵, 20, 21⁶; **8:**1, 2, 3⁴, 4², 5, 6, 7², 9², 10², 11, 12, 13³, 14⁴, 15², 17³, 18³, 19, 20², 21², 22¹⁰, 23, 24², 26², 27³, 28³, 30³, 31², 32⁴, 34², 36, 37²; **9:**1⁴, 2³, 3⁴, 4⁵, 6, 7, 8, 9², 10³, 11², 12, 13⁴, 14, 15², 16, 17⁵, 18⁴, 19², 20³, 21²², 22⁵, 23⁴; **10:**1², 3², 4, 5³, 6³, 7, 8, 10, 11³, 13², 14, 15³, 16, 17², 18², 19, 20², 21³, 22², 23², 24³, 25², 26³, 27, 28; **11:**1², 4², 5⁶, 6, 7, 8⁴, 9², 10³, 16⁵, 17, 20², 21², 22¹⁰, 24², 25⁶, 26², 27³, 28, 29³; **12:**4³, 5², 6², 7⁶, 8³, 9², 10⁴, 11², 12, 13³, 14, 15³; **13:**1², 3, 4, 5, 6, 7, 8, 9, 10, 11, 12, 13, 14, 16⁴, 17², 18², 19², 21², 22³, 23, 24³; **14:**1, 2³, 5, 7, 8⁴, 9, 10, 11², 13, 14, 15, 16³, 19², 22, 24, 25², 27³, 28³, 30, 31, 32², 33³, 34⁴, 35, 36⁴; **15:**1, 2³, 5, 6, 7, 8, 9, 13, 14, 16³, 17², 18, 19², 20², 21, 22³, 23, 24, 25⁴, 26⁴, 27, 28², 29, 30, 31, 33², 34², 35, 36²; **16:**1², 2³, 5³, 7⁴, 9⁶, 10, 11, 12, 13, 14, 15, 16, 17, 18², 19⁵, 20, 22², 23, 24, 25, 26², 27, 28², 29⁴, 30², 31², 32², 33³, 34⁴, 35³, 36, 37², 38⁴, 39, 40⁴, 41, 42, 43², 44⁴, 45²; **15:**1, 2², 3, 4², 5, 6⁷, 7⁴, 8², 9, 11³, 12⁴, 13², 14, 15², 16²;

Column 3

22; **2:**1, 3⁴, 5⁴, 6², 7², 8², 9², 10², 12², 13², 14², 16, 18, 19², 21, 23², 25; **3:**1⁶, 2³, 3, 4², 5, 6⁴, 7², 8⁴, 9⁴, 10, 11, 12² 13², 14², 15⁷, 16⁴, 17³, 18, 19, 20², 21, 22; **4:**1, 2, 3³, 4³, 5, 7, 8³, 9⁵, 9², 10², 11², 14², 16, 19², 20, 21⁴, 22, 24², 26, 27², 28², 29², 30³, 31³; **5:**1³, 2², 4², 5², 6², 7, 8², 9³, 12, 13², 14, 15, 16, 17⁵, 18², 19, 20², 21³, 22², 24⁴, 25⁴, 25⁵; **6:**1, 2, 3, 4, 5, 6⁴, 7³, 8², 9, 10, 11², 13², 14, 15, 16, 17, 18⁴; **6:**1, 2, 3, 4, 5, 6⁴, 7³, 8², 9, 10, 11², 13², 14, 15, 16, 17, 18, 19, 20, 21, 22², 24², 25², 26², 27², 28, 29, 30; **7:**1, 2, 4, 5³, 6⁴, 7³, 8², 9, 11², 12⁴, 13, 14, 15⁷, 16, 17, 18⁴; **8:**1², 3⁴, 4, 5, 6³, 7³, 8³, 9⁴, 10, 11², 12², 13⁴, 14, 15, 16³, 17³, 18², 19², 20², 21³, 22⁴, 24², 25², 26⁵, 27², 28²; **9:**1⁴, 3⁴, 4², 5⁶, 6², 7³, 8², 9⁴, 10, 11², 12², 13³, 14, 15, 16, 17², 18⁵, 19, 20³, 21², 22³, 23², 24², 25², 26³, 27, 28, 29³, 30², 31³, 32³, 34⁴, 35³, 36³; **22:**1², 2, 4, 5, 6, 8², 9, 10, 11⁵, 12³, 13, 15⁵, 16⁷, 17², 18², 19⁴, 20², 23², 24¹, 25², 28, 29⁴, 30, 31³, 32⁴, 31²; **23:**2⁵, 5, 7, 8², 10, 11⁵, 12³, 13, 15⁵, 16⁷, 17², 18², 19⁴, 20², 23²; **24:**1², 2³, 3³, 4⁵, 5, 6³, 7⁴, 8³, 9, 10, 11, 12, 14, 15², 16²; **25:**1, 2², 3, 6², 7, 9, 12, 14⁴, 15²; **16:**2⁴, 3², 4, 5², 6, 7, 9, 12, 14², 16²; **22:**24², 25, 26³, 27², 28; **26:**1³, 2², 3, 4², 7², 8, 10, 11, 12², 13³, 14, 15⁶, 16³, 17², 18, 19³, 20², 21³; **28:**1, 3, 4, 6², 8, 11, 12², 13, 14, 15², 16, 17, 20, 21³, 22, 23, 24, 25, 26⁴, 27², 28², 29³, 30⁸, 31², 32, 33², 34⁴, 35⁴, 36, 37²; **29:**3², 4⁵, 5⁶, 7, 9, 10, 11³, 12⁴, 13, 14, 15, 16⁴, 17⁵, 18, 19, 20⁵, 21, 22¹⁰, 23², 24³, 26³, 27³, 28², 29, 30³, 31², 32⁴, 34², 36, 37²; **30:**2³, 4², 5, 6², 7, 8³, 10⁴, 11, 12, 13³, 14, 15⁴, 16², 17, 18², 20², 21, 22, 23, 24, 25², 27², 28²; **31:**1, 2, 3, 6², 7⁵, 8², 9², 10⁴, 11², 12, 13², 14, 15³, 16⁵; **32:**1², 2, 3, 6², 7, 8, 9, 11², 12⁴, 13, 16³, 17⁴, 18³, 19⁶, 20⁴, 24², 25, 26³, 27, 28², 29, 30, 31, 32, 33⁴; **33:**1², 3, 4², 5, 6², 7, 8⁴, 9⁴, 10⁵, 11³, 12, 14, 16³, 17², 19², 21, 22; **34:**1⁴, 2², 3⁴, 5², 6³, 7, 8, 9, 11, 12, 13, 14², 15, 16, 17, 27, 28²;

Column 4

30⁶, 31⁴, 32², 33⁵, 34⁵, 35⁵, 36⁴, 37⁷, 38⁵; **8:**1, 15⁵, 16⁵, 17³, 18², 19³, 20⁴, 21², 22³, 23⁴, 24⁵, 25⁷, 26⁴, 27², 28³, 29⁴, 30³, 31³, 32³, 33³, 34, 35³, 36; **9:**1², 2, 3, 4², 5⁶, 6⁴, 7⁵, 8², 9⁸, 10⁷, 11³, 12³, 13³, 14², 15², 16⁴, 17⁵, 18², 19², 20³, 21³, 22², 23³, 24⁵; **10:**1², 3, 4³, 5⁴, 6⁴, 7³, 8, 9², 10⁴, 11², 12⁴, 13², 14³, 15², 16², 17³, 18³, 19³, 21, 26², 27⁴, 29⁴, 30², 31, 33, 38, 39, 40², 41, 42, 44², 45, 46, 47²; **12:**1, 2, 3², 4³, 5, 6⁴, 7², 8²; **13:**1, 2, 3⁴, 4⁴, 5⁴, 6, 7³, 8³, 9, 10⁴, 11, 12⁴, 13², 15³, 16², 17⁴, 19², 20², 21², 22³, 23⁴, 24⁵, 25⁷, 26⁴, 27², 28³, 29⁴, 30³, 31³, 32⁴, 33², 34⁵, 35², 36², 37², 38³, 39, 41, 43², 44³, 45², 46², 47³, 49³, 50¹, 51⁴; **14:**1, 2⁴, 3⁴, 4², 5², 6², 7⁴, 8², 9², 10, 11⁵, 12⁴, 13², 15⁵, 16⁴, 17⁵, 18⁴, 19², 20², 22³, 23², 25; **3:**1⁶, 2³, 3, 4², 5, 6⁴, 7⁸, 8², 9⁸, 10⁷, 11³, 12³, 13³, 14², 15², 16⁴, 17⁵, 18², 19²; **4:**1, 2³, 3⁴, 5, 6⁴, 7³, 8²; **13:**1, 2, 3⁴, 4⁴, 5⁴, 6, 7³, 9⁴, 10², 11, 12⁴, 13², 14², 15³, 16², 17⁴, 19², 20², 21², 22³, 23⁴; **14:**1, 2³, 3⁴, 4², 5², 6², 7⁴, 8², 9², 10, 11⁵, 12⁴, 13², 14², 15⁵, 16⁶, 17⁴, 18⁶, 19², 20⁴, 21⁹, 22², 23³, 24², 25⁴, 25¹; **15:**1, 2², 3², 4², 5, 6⁷, 7⁴, 8², 9, 11³, 12⁴, 13², 14, 15², 16², 17, 18², 19³, 20⁴, 21, 22, 23, 24³, 25⁵, 26⁴, 28³, 29, 30, 31, 33³, 34², 35³, 36, 37³, 38², 39, 40⁴, 41, 42, 43², 44⁴, 45²; **15:**1, 2², 3, 4², 5, 6⁷, 7⁸, 8², 9, 11³, 12⁴, 13², 14, 15², 16².

2³, 3⁶, 4³, 5⁴, 6, 7, 9, 11, 12, 14³, 15³; **2:**1², 2³, 3⁶, 4³, 5², 6², 7, 9, 9⁴, 11⁴, 12⁴, 13⁴; **3:**1, 2², 3, 4², 5³, 8³, 10, 11, 12³, 13, 14⁴, 15², 16⁴, 17², 18, 19; **Hab 1:**1², 4³, 5, 6², 11, 13², 14, 15, 16; **2:**1, 2², 3², 4, 5³, 8, 9, 10, 11⁴, 13⁴, 14⁶, 15, 16², 17, 20²; **3:**1, 3³, 4, 6⁴, 7², 8³, 9², 10², 11³, 12², 13², 14, 15², 16³, 17⁶, 18, 19⁴; **Zep 1:**1⁶, 2³, 3⁸, 4³, 5³, 6², 7⁴, 8⁴, 9², 10⁴, 11, 12, 13, 14⁷, 16², 17², 18³; **2:**2⁵, 3⁴, 5⁴, 6⁷, 8³, 9⁵, 10², 11⁴, 13², 14³, 14³, 15; **3:**1, 2, 3, 4², 5², 7, 8⁶, 9⁴, 10, 11, 13², 14³, 15³, 17, 18², 19, 20³; **Hag 1:**1⁷, 2³, 3³, 5, 7, 8³, 9³, 10², 11³, 12¹⁰, 13⁴, 14⁹, 15³; **2:**1⁵, 2³, 4⁵, 6⁵, 7², 8⁹, 10⁶, 11³, 12², 13, 14, 15, 17², 18⁴, 19⁵, 20⁴, 21², 22³, 23³; **Zec 1:**1⁶, 2, 3⁴, 4³, 5, 6², 7⁸, 8², 9, 10⁵, 11⁵, 12³, 13², 14², 15², 16³, 17², 19⁴, 20, 21⁴; **2:**3, 4, 5, 6², 7, 8³, 9, 10, 11², 12², 13; **3:**1³, 2⁴, 3, 4, 5², 6², 7, 8³, 9² 10⁶, 11⁴, 12, 14³, 15², 16³, 17⁷, 18, 19⁴; **4:**1², 2², 3⁴, 4, 6³, 7², 8², 9², 10², 11², **6:**2², 3⁴, 4, 5⁵, 6⁹, 7⁴, 8³, 9³, 10³, 12⁵, 13³, 14³, 15⁶; **7:**1⁶, 2², 3⁴, 4², 5⁵, 7⁵, 8², 9, 10⁴, 12⁵, 13, 14³; **8:**1², 2, 3⁵, 4, 5, 6², 7⁴, 9⁶, 10³, 13, 14², 16², 17, 18², 19³, 20², 21², 22, 23²; **9:**1⁶, 3², 4², 6², 7³, 9, 10⁷, 11², 14⁵, 15³, 16², 17²; **10:**1⁵, 2², 3⁴, 4³, 5³, 6², 7, 9, 11⁴, 12²; **11:**2³, 3⁴, 4⁵, 5², 6³, 7², 8², 9², 10², 11⁴, 13⁴, 14, 15², 16², 17²; **12:**1², 2³, 3, 4⁴, 5, 6², 7⁴, 8, 9², 10², 11³, 12⁵, 13³, 14², 13:¹², 2⁷, 3, 5, 6², 7⁵, 8², 9², 14:¹, 2³, 3², 4³, 5⁴, 7, 8², 9³, 10⁸, 12², 13², 14², 15³, 16⁵, 17⁴, 18⁵, 19⁴, 20⁷, 21⁴; **Mal 1:**1², 2³, 3, 4⁵, 5², 6³, 7, 8, 9, 10², 11⁸, 12², 13³, 14², **2:**2, 3, 4, 7³, 8³, 9², 10, 11³, 12⁴, 13, 14, 15², 16², 17⁴; **3:**1⁵, 2, 3², 4², 5, 6, 7², 8³, 9⁴, 10⁴, 11², 12², 13, 14, 15², 16³, 17², 18³; **4:**1³, 2², 3⁴, 4², 5², 6⁵; **Mt 1:**1³, 2³, 3³, 4³, 5³, 6², 7³, 8³, 9³ 10³, 11³, 12³, 13⁴, 15², 16³, 17³, 18², 20², 21, 22², 23², 24², 25; **2:**1², 3², 4, 5, 6³, 7, 8, 9⁵, 10, 11², 13³, 14⁵, 16⁴, 17, 19, 20², 21², 22; **3:**1², 2, 3, 4², 5², 6, 7², 10⁴, 11, 12², 13, 16²; **4:**1³, 2, 3⁴, 4, 5⁴, 6, 7², 8³, 10, 11, 13², 14, 15⁴, 16³, 17², 18², 20², 21², 22³, 23³, 24², 25²; **5:**1, 3², 5², 7, 8, 9, 10, 12², 13², 14², 15², 18⁸, 20, 21, 22⁴, 24³, 25⁴, 26², 27², 30², 32; **7:**2², 3², 4², 5², 6, 7², 9, 10³, 13³, 14², 19, 21², 24, 25², 27³, 28, 29; **8:**1, 3⁴, 8², 10, 11⁴, 12³, 13, 15, 16², 17, 18², 19, 20², 22, 23, 24³, 25, 26², 27³, 28, 29², 31², 32⁵, 33³, 34; **9:**2, 3², 6, 7, 8, 9, 11, 12², 13, 14, 15⁴, 16³, 17², 20, 23³, 24, 25³, 28, 31, 33³, 34², 35³, 36, 37² 38²; **10:**2², 3, 4, 5², 6, 8², 10², 12, 13, 14, 15², 17, 18, 20, 22, 23³, 25², 27³, 28³, 29², 30, 34, 36, 40, 42; **11:**1, 3, 5⁶, 6, 7³, 10, 11³, 12³, 13², 14, 16, 17, 19, 20, 21, 22³, 24, 25, 27³; **12:**1², 2², 4³, 5⁵, 6, 7, 8², 10, 11, 12, 13², 14, 17, 18², 19, 20², 21, 22², 23, 24, 25, 27³; **12:**1², 2², 4³, 5⁵, 6, 7, 8², 10, 11, 12, 13², 14, 17, 18², 19, 20², 21², 22, 23³, 24, 25, 27³; **12:**1², 2², 4³, 5⁵, 6, 7, 8², 10, 11, 12, 13², 14, 16, 17, 19, 20, 21², 22³, 24, 25, 27³; **12:**1², 2², 4³, 5⁵, 6, 7, 8², 10, 11, 12, 13², 14, 16, 17, 19, 20, 21², 22³, 24, 25, 27³; **12:**1², 2², 4³, 5⁵, 6, 7, 8², 10, 11, 12, 13², 14, 16, 17, 19, 20, 21², 22³, 24, 25, 27³; **12:**1², 2², 4³, 5⁵, 6, 7, 8², 10, 11, 12, 13², 14, 16, 17, 19, 20, 21², 22³, 24, 25, 27³

29², 31, 32², 33², 34, 35², 38, 41, 42, 44² 45²; **2:**1, 2², 4⁴, 5, 6, 9, 10², 13, 14, 16³, 17³, 18³, 19², 20², 21³, 22³, 23, 24², 26⁴, 27², 28²; **3:**1, 2, 3², 4, 5, 6², 7, 8², 9², 11², 16², 17, 18, 22³, 27, 28², 29; **4:**1⁶, 4³, 5, 6², 7, 10³, 11³, 14², 15, 16, 17, 18, 19⁴, 20, 22, 24, 26², 27², 28³, 29³, 30, 31², 32³, 33, 35, 36², 37², 38² 39³; **5:**1², 2, 3, 4², 5², 7², 10, 11, 12², 13³, 14³, 15², 16³, 17, 18², 19, 20², 21³, 22, 26, 27, 30, 31, 33², 35³, 36, 37, 38², 39, 40³, 41², 42; **9:**1², 3, 7, 9³, 10² 11², 12, 14³, 15, 17, 18³, 19, 20⁴, 21, 24, 25² 26², 27, 31², 32³, 34², 35³, 37, 39, 41, 42, 43, 47, 48; **10:**1², 6, 8, 10², 13, 14², 15², 16, 19, 21, 22, 23², 24², 25², 26, 29², 30, 31, 32² 33⁴, 35, 37, 38², 39², 41, 42, 45, 46³, 48, 49, 51, 52; **11:**1, 2, 3, 4, 6, 7, 10², 11², 12, 13², 14, 15⁴, 16, 18⁴, 19, 20³, 21, 23², 27³, 31², 32³, 33², 34², 35³, 37, 39, 41, 42, 43, 47, 48; **12:**1², 6, 8, 10², 13, 14², 15², 16³, 17³, 18, 20², 23, 24, 25², 26, 29², 30³ 31², 34, 35², 38², 39⁴, 41², 42, 43³, 44; **10:**1², 6, 8, 10², 13, 14², 15², 16, 19, 21, 22, 29², 30, 31, 32² **13:**1, 2, 4, 7, 8, 9, 11, 12², 14³, 16³, 17³, 18³, 19², 20², 21³, 22², 23³, 24², 26², 27², 28², 29; **4:**1⁶, 4³, 5, 6², 7, 10³, 11³, 12², 13, 14², 15², 17, 18², 19², 20², 21³, 22³, 23, 24², 26⁴, 27², 28²

10³, 11, 12², 18, 19, 20, 21², 22, 24², 25, 26, 27², 28, 29, 30, 32², 33, 34, 35³, 44³, 45, 46³, 49, 50, 53; **Jn 1:**1⁴, 2, 4, 5³, 8², 9², 10³, 12, 14⁴, 16, 17, 18², 19, 20, 21, 23⁶, 25², 27², 28², 29⁴, 30, 31, 32, 33⁴, 34, 35, 36, 37, 39, 40, 41³, 43, 44, 45⁴, 48, 49², 50, 51³; **2:**1, 2, 3, 5, 6², 7, 9², 9⁶, 10⁴, 11, 13, 14, 15³, 18, 20, 21, 22³, 23³; **3:**1², 2², 3², 5, 6, 8², 11, 13², 14³, 16, 17³, 18, 19², 20², 21², 22, 25, 26, 28, 29⁵, 31⁶, 33, 34³, 35², 36²; **4:**1, 3, 5, 6³, 8, 9, 10, 11², 12, 14², 15, 18², 19, 20, 21, 22, 23⁴, 25, 28³, 29, 30, 34, 35², 36⁴, 37, 38² 39², 40, 42², 43, 45², 46, 49, 50, 51², 52², 53², 54; **5:**1, 2, 3², 7³, 9², 10⁴, 11, 13², 14, 15², 18², 19², 20², 21², 22³, 24, 25⁴, 26², 27², 28, 29², 31², 32², 33³, 35⁵, 36², 37², 38, 39², 40², 41², 42, 44², 45; **6:**1³, 2², 4, 10², 11³, 12, 13³, 14⁴, 16, 17, 18, 19², 21², 22⁴, 23², 24², 25², 26², 27², 28, 29² 31², 32², 35, 37, 39, 40, 41, 42, 43, 47, 48; **10:**1², 6, 8, 10², 13, 14², 15², 16³, 17³, 18², 19², 20², 21³, 22², 23³, 24², 25⁴, 26², 27², 28, 29²

34, 35⁷, 38, 41; **20:**1², 2, 3, 4, 6², 7⁴, 8, 9², 10, 12², 13, 15³, 16², 17², 18³, 19³, 22, 23, 24⁵, 25, 26, 27, 28³, 29, 30, 32, 34, 35³, 38; **21:**1, 3, 4, 7, 8⁴, 11⁴, 12, 13⁴, 14, 16³, 18³, 19, 20, 21², 24, 25², 26⁶, 27⁴, 28², 29³, 30⁴, 31³, 32³, 33⁴, 35⁴, 36, 37, 38² 39³, 40² 40⁸ 41⁵, 42², 43, 44²; **28:**1, 2, 3², 4², 5², 6, 7², 9³, 10, 11³, 13³, 15⁴, 17⁴, 19, 20, 21, 23⁴, 25³, 28, 31²; **Ro 1:**1, 2², 4³, 5², 7, 8², 9, 10, 11³, 13², 14³, 16, 17³, 18, 19², 20², 23², 24², 25², 27³, 28; **2:**1², 3, 4, 5, 8, 9², 10², 12², 13², 14³, 15², 16, 17, 18², 19², 20², 23², 24, 26, 27³, 29³; **3:**2, 6, 9, 13, 17, 19³, 20², 21², 23, 24, 25, 26², 27, 28, 29², 30¹, 31², 32³, 33³, 34²; **4:**1³, 5³, 6, 8, 9, 10, 11², 14², 15, 18², 19, 20, 21², 22³, 23, 25, 26, 27; **25:**1, 3, 5, 6², 7, 8³, 9, 10, 11², 14, 15, 16, 17, 18, 19², 20³, 22², 24, 25²

Php 1:1², 2, 5², 6, 7, 8, 10, 11², 12, 13, 14³, 16⁴, 17, 18, 19², 22², 23, 24, 25, 27³, 30; **2:**1, 2, 4, 5, 7, 9², 10², 11², 15, 16², 17, 19, 22²,

24, 28, 29, 30²; **3:**1², 2, 3³, 4, 5⁴, 6, 7, 8, 9², 10², 11², 14², 17, 18, 20, 21; **4:**1, 2, 3⁴, 4, 5, 7, 9, 10, 11, 12, 15³, 18, 21², 22, 23²; **Col 1:**1, 2, 3, 4², 5⁴, 6², 8, 9², 10², 12², 13³, 14, 15³, 18³, 20, 23³, 24², 25², 26², 27³; **2:**2², 3, 7, 8, 9², 10, 11⁴, 12², 13, 14², 15², 17², 18², 19²; 20, 23; **3:**1, 6, 7, 10², 13, 15, 16, 17³, 18, 20, 22, 23, 24²; **4:**3, 5², 7², 8, 10, 11², 12, 14, 15², 16³, 17²; **1Th 1:**1⁴, 5, 6⁴, 7, 8, 9, 10², **2:**2, 3, 4², 8, 9, 13³, 14², 15², 16³, 19²; **3:**2, 5, 8, 9², 11, 12, 13; **4:**1², 5, 6, 10, 12, 13, 15³, 16⁵, 17⁴; **5:**2³, 5⁴, 8², 12, 13, 14², 19, 21, 23², 24, 26, 27², 28; **2Th 1:**1³, 2², 3, 4, 5, 7, 8, 9², 10², 12²; **2:**1, 2³, 3³, 6, 7³, 8⁴, 9³, 10, 11, 12, 13³, 14, 15; **3:**1³, 3², 4², 5, 6³, 8, 9, 12², 16², 17, 18; **1Ti 1:**1, 2², 5, 7, 8, 9³, 10⁴, 14², 15², 16, 17², 18², 2:**4, 5, 6, 7³, 14², **3:**2², 6², 7, 9², 11, 12, 15⁴, 16⁴; **4:**1², 3, 5, 6, 8², 10², 12, 13, 14, 15⁴, 16⁴; **5:**5, 6, 7, 8, 9, 10², 13, 14, 16²; 6:**1, 2, 3, 5, 7, 10², 12⁴, 13³, 14, 15², 19², 20, 21²; **2Ti 1:**1², 2, 6², 8², 9, 10², 13, 14³, 15, 16², 17², 18²; **2:**1, 2², 5², 6³, 7, 8, 9, 10³, 15, 18³, 19³, 21², 22², 24, 25², 26²; **3:**1, 3, 6, 7, 8², 9, 11², 15, 17; **4:**1³, 2, 3, 4², 5, 6, 7³, 8³, 13², 14², 17⁴, 18, 19, 21, 22; **Tit 1:**1³, 2², 3², 4, 5, 6², 9, 10, 11, 13², 15; **3:**1, 4, 5², 7, 9, 13, 15; **Phm 1:**2, 3, 5², 7², 9, 13, 15, 16, 20, 25²; **Heb 1:**1², 2, 3⁴, 4², 5, 6, 7, 8², 9, 10², 12, 13; **2:**2, 3, 4, 5, 6, 7, 9², 10, 11², 12², 13, 14³, 17²; **3:**1², 2, 3², 4², 5, 6, 7, 8², 12, 14², 15, 17²; **4:**1², 2, 3², 4², 5, 6, 8, 9², 12, 13, 14³, 16; **5:**3², 5, 6, 7², 9, 10, 12, 13, 14; **6:**1², 2³, 4², 5, 6, 7², 8, 10, 11, 16, 17², 18, 19³, 20; **7:**1², 3, 4², 5³, 6, 7², 8², 9², 10², 11², 12², 13, 16³, 17, 18, 19, 21, 22, 26, 27³, 28⁴; **8:**1⁴, 2³, 4², 5³, 6³, 8², 9², 10², 11³, 13; **9:**1², 2², 3², 4⁵, 5⁴, 6², 7⁴, 8⁴, 9⁴, 10², 11², 12², 13², 14, 15⁴, 16³, 17, 18, 19², 20², 21³, 22² 23³, 24, 25³, 26², 28; **10:**1⁴, 2, 4, 5, 7, 8, 9², 10², 11, 12, 15, 16², 19², 20, 21, 23, 25³, 26², 27, 28², 29⁴, 30, 31², 32⁴, 34, 36; **11:**2, 3, 7², 9², 10, 11, 12⁴, 13, 15, 17, 19, 21, 22², 23, 24, 25², 26², 27, 28⁵, 29³, 30², 31², 32, 33, 34⁴, 37, 38²; **12:**1², 2³, 4, 5, 6, 7², 8, 10, 11, 16, 17², 18, 19, 20, 21, 22², 23⁴, 24³, 26², 27², **13:**4³, 5, 6, 7², 8, 10, 11⁵, 12², 13², 14, 15, 20⁵; **Jas 1:**1³, 3, 6², 7, 9, 10, 11⁴, 12³, 17², 18, 20, 21², 22, 23, 25²; 27; **2:**3³, 5³, 6³, 7², 8, 9, 10, 12, 17, 19, 21, 23, 25³, 26²; **3:**3⁴, 4, 5², 6³, 7², 8, 9, 10, 11, 13, 14², 15, 16, 17², 18³; **4:**2, 4², 5, 6², 7, 10, 11², 12, 15, 17; **5:**1, 3, 4⁶, 5, 7⁴, 8, 9², 10⁴, 11⁴, 15³, 16, 17², 18², 19, 20; **1Pe 1:**1, 2⁴, 3³, 5³, 9², 10³, 11⁴, 12², 13, 14, 18, 19, 20², 21, 22², 23, 24², 25²; **2:**3, 4, 6, 7³, 8, 9, 10³, 11⁴, 12², 13³, 15, 17², 19, 24, 25; **3:**1³, 2, 3, 4, 5³, 7³, 15², 18⁴, 19, 20², 21⁴; **4:**1², 2², 3, 4, 5⁴, 6⁴, 7, 11, 13², 14², 17³, 18³; **5:**1³, 3, 4², 5⁶, 7, 8, 10, 11, 12², 13⁵, 15, 17², 19, 24, 25; **3:**1², 2, 3, 4, 5³, 7², 15², 18⁴, 19, 20²; **1Pe 1:**2, 4³, 10, 11, 12, 13, 14, 18, 19, 20², 21, 22², 24², 25³, 2:**3, 4, 6, 7, 8, 9, 10³, 11², 12³, 13³, 15, 17, 19, 24, 25; **3:**1³, 2, 3, 4, 5³, **2Pe 1:**1, 2, 4³, 10, 11, 12, 13, 16, 19³, 20², 21²; **2:**1², 2, 5², 6, 7, 8, 9, 10², 11², 13, 14, 15, 16⁴, 17, 18, 20⁴, 21², 22²; **3:**2⁴, 3, 4, 5², 6, 7, 8, 9, 10⁵, 12⁵, 13, 15, 16², 17, 18; **1Jn 1:**1², 2³, 3, 5, 6², 7³, 8; **2:**1², 2³, 4², 5², 7², 8, 9, 10, 11³, 13³, 14³, 15⁴, 16³, 17, 18², 19²; 20², 21², 22², 23⁴, 24³, 27; **3:**1⁴, 4, 8⁶, 10³, 11², 12, 13, 17, 19, 23, 24; **4:**1³, 2, 3, 5⁶, 7, 10, 11⁴, 12, 15, 17, 18², 19, 20, 21; **1Pe 1:**1, 2⁴, 3³, 5³, 9², 10³, 11⁴, 12², 13, 14, 18, 19, 20², 21, 22², 23, 24², 25²; **2:**3, 4, 6, 7³, 8, 9, 10³, 11⁴, **2Jn 1:**1², 2, 3², 4, 5, 6, 7⁴, 9⁴, 13; **3Jn 1:**1³, 3², 4, 5, 6, 7³, 8, 9, 10², 12, 14²; **Jude 1:**1, 3³, 4, 5, 6², 7², 8, 9⁴, 10, 11, 12², 13, 14², 15⁴, 17, 18, 19², 20, 21, 23²; 25²; **Rev 1:**1, 2², 3³, 4³, 5⁶, 7³, 8⁴, 9⁴, 10², 11, 12, 13, 15, 16, 17², 20⁶; **2:**1⁵, 2², 5², 6², 7⁴, 8⁵, 9, 10³, 11³, 12⁴, 13, 14², 15², 16, 17⁵, 18³, 19, 20, 23, 24², 26², 28, 29²; **3:**1⁵, 2, 5, 6², 7², 9, 10³, 12², 13², 14°, 15, 16, 20², 21², **4:**1, 2, 5³, 6³, 7⁴, 8², 9², 10³; **5:**1², 2², 3², 4, 5⁶, 6³, 7⁴, 8³, 9, 10², 11, 12², 13², 14⁴, 14⁴, 15², 16⁴, 17⁴, 18³, 19², 21²

THEIR (3701)

Ge 1:11, 12², 21, 24, 25³; **2:**1; **6:**12; **7:**3, 14; **8:**16; **9:**23⁴; **10:**5³, 20², 31², 32², **11:**7; **13:**6; **14:**8, 11, 24; **15:**13³; **17:**8; **18:**16, 20, 26; **19:**33, 35, 36; **22:**17; **23:**13²; **24:**32, 59, 60, 61; **25:**13, 16, 18; **26:**31; **31:**53; **32:**11, 15; **33:**2, 6, 13; **34:**13, 18, 20², 21, 23³, 25, 27, 28, 29²; **35:**4; **36:**7², 19, 30, 40, 43; **37:**2, 4, 12, 16, 21, 25³, 32; **40:**1; **42:**6, 24, 25², 26², 28, 29, 35², 36; **43:**2, 11, 24², 25, 33, 44; **13²; **45:**21, 25, 27; **46:**5³, 6, 17, 32; **47:**11, 12, 17², 20, 22; **48:**6; **49:**5, 6³, 7², 19, 28; **50:**8², 15, 17; **Ex 1:**14², 21; **2:**11, 16, 17², 18, 23³, 24; **3:**7²; **4:**5, 31; **5:**4, 7, 21; **6:**9, 14, 16, 19, 26; **7:**11, 12, 22; **8:**7, 18, 26; **9:**20², 21, 34; **10:**7; **11:**2; **12:**4, 34², 51; **13:**17², 21; **14:**5²; 22², 25, 26, 29²; 31; **18:**19; **19:**8, 9, 10, 14, 21, 24; **22:**9, 23, 30; **23:**6, 24³, 27, 32, 33; **24:**12; **25:**20; **27:**19; **28:**10, 38; **29:**10, 15, 19, 20², 21², 25, 28, 33², 45, 46²; **30:**19, 21; **32:**3, 13, 25, 32, 34; **33:**6, 8; **34:**7, 13³, 15²; 16²; **35:**18, 22; **36:**4, 36, 38²; **37:**9; **38:**17, 19², 28; **40:**15²; 31, 38; **Lev 4:**15; **6:**17; **7:**34, 36, 38; **8:**2, 14, 16, 18, 22, 24; **9:**1, 24², 45²; **10:**1, 5, 19²; **11:**8², 11², 24, 25, 27², 28, 35; **15:**31; **16:**16², 21, 22, 27; **17:**7; **18:**3, 29²; **20:**4, 5, 11², 12², 13², 16², 17, 18, 23, 24, 27²; **21:**5³, 6³, 7², 23:**4, 18, 24:9, 14, 25:3, 32, 33², 34², 45; **26:**4, 20, 36², 39³, 40⁴, 41³, 43, 44², 45³; **Nu 1:**2, 3, 16, 18², 20, 22, 24, 26, 28, 30, 32, 34, 36, 38, 40, 42, 45, 52; **2:**3, 9, 10, 16, 18, 24, 25, 31, 32², 34; **3:**4, 15, 20, 26, 31, 36, 37, 39, 40, 45; **4:**2, 22, 27², 28, 29, 31, 32³, 34, 38, 40, 42, 44, 46; **5:**3; **6:**15²; **7:**3, 7, 8, 9, 10, 80; **8:**7²; 10, 14, 15, 21, 22, 25², 26⁴, 10:4, 18, 20, 22, 26; **11:**1, 12, 24, 33; **13:**4²; **14:**1, 6, 9, 23, 35, 44; **15:**25; **16:**15, 26, 27²; 32², 34, 38; **17:**2, 6², 10; **18:**12², 17², 18, 20, 21, 22, 24; **20:**8²; 11, 21; **21:**2, 3, 24; **23:**21; **24:**7⁴; 8²; **25:**2, 18; **26:**12, 15, 20, 23, 26, 28, 35, 37, 38, 42, 44, 48, 57, 59; **27:**5, 7²; 14, 19; **28:**31; **29:**6, 11, 18, 19, 21, 24, 27, 30, 33, 34, 37, 39; **31:**8, 10, 12, 18², 30², 35²; 36, 48; **32:**16, 17², 24, 33; **33:**29; **Jos 1:**6; **3:**15; **4:**8, 18², 21; **5:**1, 6, 7²; **6:**8, 7:6, 11, 12²; **8:**2, 13, 19, 20, 33; **9:**5²; 14, 17; **10:**5, 19, 20, 24², 40, 42; **11:**4, 6²; 9², 12, 13, 16, 17, 20, 21, 23; **12:**6²; 7²; **13:**12, 14, 23, 28, 33; **14:**2, 3, 4, 12; **15:**2, 4, 12, 32, 36, 41, 44, 46, 51, 54, 57, 59, 60, 62; **16:**4, 5, 9; **17:**2, 4, 11; **18:**1, 2, 7², 8, 10, 11, 12, 14, 19, 20, 21, 28; **19:**1, 6, 7, 9, 10, 15, 16, 18, 22, 23, 25, 30, 31, 33, 38, 39, 41, 47², 48; **20:**4; **21:**3, 8, 16, 18, 19, 20, 25, 26, 29, 31, 32², 35, 37, 39, 41, 43, 44²; **22:**6, 7, 9, 32; **23:**1, 2, 5, 7; **24:**8; **Jdg 1:**2, 3, 4, 7, 17, 27; **2:**2, 3, 10, 12, 14, 17², 18, 19², 20, 22; **3:**4, 6⁴, 7, 18, 25; **4:**5; **5:**18, 20; **6:**3, 5³, 9; **7:**2, 5, 6², 8, 12²; **8:**1, 2, 19², 20²; 27, 29; **9:**24², 26, 27, 35, 57; **10:**12; **12:**1, 2; **13:**20; **14:**19³; 16:18, 23, 24; **18:**1, 2, 7, 8, 10, 12, 21, 27, 30; **19:**21; **20:**2, 13, 14, 15, 22, 33; **21:**6, 12, 16, 22, 23, 24; **1Sa 1:**19; **2:**25; **4:**2; **6:**6, 7, 10, 13, 18; **7:**4; **8:**7; **9:**16; **10:**10, 12; **11:**6; **12:**9; **13:**2, 6², 20; **14:**20, 21, 30, 46, 47; **15:**20; **17:**1, 2, 17, 18, 21, 50, 51, 52, 53; **18:**13, 16, 17; **19:**20; **21:**11, 13²; **22:**5; **23:**5; **25:**10, 13; **28:**1; **29:**1, 2, 5; **30:**2, 3; **31:**7, 9²; 12; **2Sa 1:**11; **2:**25, 26, 27; **3:**18, 30; **4:**12; **5:**2², 21; **6:**5, 19; **7:**7, 10, 23, 24; **10:**3, 4, 8, 17, 18³; **12:**30; **13:**29, 30, 31; **15:**30, 36; **16:**14; **18:**17, 28; **19:**6, 8; **20:**2, 3; **22:**41, 46; **23:**17, 19; **1Ki 1:**7, 41; **2:**4, 5, 15, 33; **4:**28; **6:**27²; **7:**9, 25, 33; **8:**7, 8, 11, 34, 35, 37, 44, 45³, 47, 48³, 49³, 50; **9:**9²; 21; **10:**5; **11:**2, 8; **12:**27²; **13:**11, 12; **14:**15, 22; **15:**16, 32; **16:**2, 13, 26²; **18:**28²; 29, 37; **2Ki 1:**14; **2:**1; **3:**27; **6:**20, 22, 23; **7:**7³, 13, 14, 15; **8:**12²; **9:**13; **10:**7, 32; **11:**12; **13:**5; **14:**6²; **15:**16; **16:**15²; **17:**7, 9², 14², 15, 16, 17, 19, 21, 23, 34, 40, 41³; **18:**12, 27², 30, 34, 40, 41³; **18:**12, 27², 30; **19:**17, 18, 26, 29; **21:**8, 14², 15; **22:**17; **23:**2, 9, 35; **25:**23²; **1Ch 1:**29; **2:**16; **3:**9, 19; **4:**3, 27, 31, 32, 33, 38², 41³; **5:**7², 9, 10, 13, 15, 20², 24², 25; **6:**19, 32, 33, 44, 48, 54², 59, 60, 64, 66, 69, 70, 71, 73, 75, 76, 77, 79, 81; **7:**2², 4, 5, 7, 9², 17², 19, 28, 29, 30, 32, 40; **8:**28, 32, 38; **9:**1, 2, 9², 17², 19, 22, 23, 25³, 32, 34; **10:**7, 9², 10, 12²; **11:**2², 14, 19², 21; **12:**3, 8, 19, 30, 32², 39, 40; **13:**2, 8; **14:**12; **15:**15, 16, 17, 18; **16:**21; **17:**6, 9, 22; **19:**4, 7, 9, 18³; **20:**2; **21:**12;

23:22, 24², 32²; **24:**2, 3, 6, 19³, 30, 31; **25:**3, 6, 7, 8; **26:**6, 8², 12², 13, 20, 31²; **27:**1; **28:**15, 18; **29:**9, 18, 20, 21, 24; **2Ch 2:**11; **3:**13; **4:**4, 14, 20; **5:**8, 9, 11, 12, 14; **6:**25, 26, 28, 34, 35³, 37, 38³, 39³; **7:**3, 6², 10, 14³, 22; **8:**8, 14; **9:**4²; **11:**11, 13, 14, 16²; **13:**12, 14, 15, 16, 18, 19; **14:**4; **15:**4, 12²; **17:**14; **18:**9², 19²; **19:**4; **20:**13, 25, 27, 33²; **21:**3; **22:**5; **24:**10, 18², 23, 24²; **25:**4³, 5, 15; **26:**11, 13, 19; **27:**2; **28:**6, 8, 15, 18; **29:**6, 15, 22²; 23, 24, 26, 30, 34; **30:**7, 9, 16, 17, 22², 27; **31:**1², 2, 5, 6, 10³, 16³, 17³, 19; **32:**13, 17; **33:**17; **34:**5, 25, 30, 32, 33³; **35:**2, 10², 15², 36:15, 17; **Ezr 1:**6; **2:**59, 62, 65, 69, 70², **3:**1, 8², 9, 10², 12²; **4:**5, 9, 17, 23; **5:**3, 5, 6, 8, 10²; **6:**5, 6, 13, 18², 20, 21; **7:**16, 17; **8:**24; **9:**1, 2², 12²; **10:**3, 19²; **Ne 3:**5³, 18, 23; **4:**2, 3, 4², 5², 6², 12, 13, 15, 17; **5:**1², 6, 11, 14, 15; **6:**6, 9, 16; **7:**3², 61, 64, 67, 73²; **8:**6²; 15, 16²; **9:**1, 2³, 3², 4, 6, 9, 11, 15², 17² 19, 20², 21², 23², 24², 26, 27², 28, 29, 35²; 38; **10:**10, 28², 29, 30, 39; **11:**1, 9, 12, 14, 19, 23, 25, 30; **12:**7, 9, 24, 40, 41, 45; **13:**10, 11², 12, 24, 25³; **Est 1:**17, 20; **3:**13; **4:**8; **8:**9, 11²; 13; **9:**2², 5, 10, 15, 16², 22³, 24, 27, 28, 31²; **Job 1:**4²; 5; **2:**11, 12²; **3:**15, 18; **4:**21; **5:**12, 13, 15; **6:**4, 17, 18; **8:**4, 8, 10; **9:**5, 26; **11:**9, 20; **12:**6²; 18, 24; **14:**12; **15:**18, 35; **16:**10; **17:**2, 4, 9; **18:**4; **21:**8³, 9, 10², 11³, 13, 16², 29; **22:**6, 16, 18, 19, 20; **24:**5², 17, 18, 23; **26:**8²; **27:**14, 15; **29:**8, 9², 10², 17, 18, 23; **30:**2², 4, 5, 9, 10², 13², 15; **32:**15, 16; **34:**21, 24, 25, 26; **35:**13; **36:**6, 10, 11², 14, 15², 20, 28; **37:**8; **38:**15², 20², 32, 35, 40; **39:**3², 4; **40:**13, 20, 22; **42:**15²; 16; **Ps 2:**2, 3², 4; **5:**9⁴, 10³; **9:**5, 6, 15, 16; **10:**17; **11:**2², 6; **12:**2; **14:**1, 6; **16:**4²; **17:**7, 10², 14²; **18:**40, 45; **19:**3², 4²; **20:**8²; 11, 12²; **10:**3, 19²; **Ne 3:**5³, **22:**4, 7, 13²; **12:**7, 13, 15²; **18:**25, 26, 32, 33, 39; **38:**12²; **39:**11²; **40:**3; **15:**44:**1, 3², 12, 14; **46:**3; **49:**6², 10, 11³, 13², 14²; **53:**1; **55:**3, 9, 19, 23; **56:**1, 2; **58:**4, 6, 7, 10; **59:**7², 12²; **62:**4²; **64:**3³, 5, 8²; **65:**7; **68:**21, 23; **69:**23²; 25²; **70:**3; **72:**14; **73:**4, 6, 7², 8, 9², 10, 17; **74:**4, 6, 8; **76:**5; **78:**4, 5, 6, 7, 8, 28², 30, 33², 35², 36², 37, 38, 44², 46², 47², 48², 53, 55², 57, 58², 63²; **64²; **79:**10; **81:**6²; 12²; 14², 15; **83:**2, 11², 16; **84:**5; **85:**2; **89:**17, 32²; **90:**10, 16; **91:**12; **93:**3²; **94:**23²; **98:**8; **99:**8; **102:**17, 28; **103:**17; **104:**3, 11, 17, 21²; 22, 27, 29; **105:**14, 16, 24, 29²; 30², 31, 32², 33², 35², 36², 37²; **106:**11, 14, 18, 20, 25, 27, 29, 36, 37, 38², 39, 41, 42², 43, 44², 45; **107:**5, 6², 13², 14, 17², 19², 26², 27, 28², 30, 38², 39, 41²; **109:**2, 10, 13, 15, 25; **113:**8; **115:**2, 4, 7, 9, 10, 11; **119:**2, 70, 118; **123:**2; **124:**3, 6; **125:**3; **127:**5; **129:**3; **130:**8; **132:**12; **135:**6, 12, 17; **136:**21; **140:**2, 3², 5, 8², 9; **141:**4, 6, 10; **144:**12; **145:**15, 19; **146:**4²; **147:**3, 11; **149:**2², 5, 6², 8²; **Pr 1:**5, 15, 16, 18, 31²; **2:**15; **8:**21; **9:**15; **10:**15; **11:**3, 5, 31; **12:**21; **13:**25; **14:**8, 14, 20, 24, 31; **17:**5, 6, 26; **18:**11; **20:**29; **22:**23; **23:**11², **24:**1, 2; **29:**16; **30:**11², 12², 25, 26, 29; **31:**5, 7²; **Ecc 2:**3; **4:**1, 9; **8:**13; **9:**3, 6²; **12:**4, 11, 13; **SS 2:**13; **3:**3; **5:**7; **7:**12, 13; **Isa 1:**4; **2:**4², 7⁴, 8³, 20; **3:**4, 8, 9², 10, 11, 16², 17, 18²; **5:**11, 12, 13², 14², 17, 21², 24², 28⁴, 29²; **6:**2², 4, 10⁵; **8:**19, 21²; **9:**3, 4², 11; **10:**2², 13², 17, 25, 27²; 32; **11:**7; **13:**8, 10², 11, 16, 18², 14:**1, 2², 9, 21², 32; **15:**2, 3, 4, 5, 8, 9², 16:**4, 8, 17:**8², 9, 19:3, 20, 22; **23:**13; **24:**6, 14; **25:**11³; **26:**16, 19, 21; **27:**11²; **28:**9; **29:**13⁴, 15², 22, 23; **30:**4, 6²; **31:**1², 3, 4², 8, 9²; **33:**7, 9, 19; **34:**2, 3³, 7, 17; **35:**10; **36:**12², 37:18, 19, 27, 28², 30; **38:**19; **40:**6, 31; **41:**1, 17, 22, 29²; **42:**4, 14; **43:**9, 11, 18², 26; **45:**1, 12; **46:**1, 6, 7; **48:**19; **49:**22², 23², 26²; **50:**2; **51:**7, 11, 14; **52:**8², 15; **53:**11; **54:**3, 17; **55:**12; **56:**7, 11; **57:**8; **58:**1²; **59:**5, 6³, 7³, 8, 18, 20, 21; **60:**8, 9, 10, 11; **61:**6, 7², 9², **63:**3, 6, 8, 9, 10; **65:**2, 4, 6, 7², 14, 21, 22, 23; **66:**3³, 17, 18², 20, 24²; **Jer 1:**15²; 16²; **2:**11, 13, 26⁴, 27³; **3:**16, 17, 21², 24²; **4:**23³; **5:**3, 4, 5, 6³, 7, 19, 24, 26, 28, 30, 31; **8:**1, 7, 10², 12, 13⁴, 16², 19³; **9:**3, 5, 6, 8, 14², 16; **10:**5, 7, 9, 15, 21; **11:**8, 10², 14, 18, 22², 23; **12:**2², 14; **13:**10; **14:**3¹, 4, 6, 10, 10³, 12, 14, 16³, 15:7, 8², 9²; **16:**3², 4, 15, 17², 18⁴, 20; **17:**1², 22, 23³; **19:**4, 5, 7³, 9²; **20:**4, 5, 11; **21:**7²; **22:**4²; 9, 13; **23:**3, 8, 10, 11, 12, 16, 17, 21², 22², 26, 27, 31, 32; **24:**6, 7, 10; **25:**12, 14³, 16, 27, 34⁴, 36, 38; **26:**10; **27:**4; **29:**23; **30:**3, 8²; 10, 19, 20², 21³; **31:**5, 13, 17, 24, 30², 34², 38, 40; **32:**18, 19, 20², 22, 30², 32³, 33, 34, 35, 38, 39², 44; **33:**8, 12, 20, 26; **34:**10, 11, 20³, 21²; **35:**14, 16; **36:**3², 6, 7, 24, 31; **37:**10; **38:**4, 18, 23; **40:**7, 8, 9; **41:**5²; 12, 17; **43:**1, 12²; **44:**5, 15; **46:**5, 8, 21, 26, 27²; **47:**3³; **48:**34, 35; **49:**7, 11, 18, 20, 21, 29⁴, 32², 35, 37²; **50:**4, 5, 7², 9², 20⁴, 5, 11; **21:**7²²; **22:**4², 9, 13; **23:**3, 8, 10, 11, 12, 16, 17, 21², 22², 26, 27, 31, 32; **24:**6, 7, 10; **25:**12, 14³, 16, 27, 34⁴, 36, 38; **26:**10; **51:**2², 18, 28², 30², 55, 56; **La 1:**11, 22; **2:**9, 10², 12³, 15², 16², 20; **3:**46, 60², 61², 63, 64, 65; **4:**2, 3², 7³, 8², 10³;

14, 20; **5:**7, 8, 12, 14; **Eze 1:**5, 7², 8², 9, 10, 11², 18, 23, 24², 25, 26; **2:**3, 6; **4:**4, 5, 17; **5:**10²; **6:**5, 9⁴, 13⁴; **7:**13, 18², 19³, 20², 24²; **27:**8:16²; 17; **9:**10; **10:**10, 12², 16², 19, 22; **11:**19, 20, 21², 22; **12:**16, 19³; **13:**2, 3, 6³, 17, 18, 22²; **14:**3², 5, 10, 11², 13, 14, 16, 17, 18, 19, 20, 21, 22², 23²; **16:**40, 45²; 47²; **18:**23; **19:**4, 7², 8², **20:**4, 8, 16², 18³, 24², 26, 28³, 30; **21:**15, 23, 28; **22:**6, 27, 31; **23:**3³, 8, 15², 17, 24, 30, 36, 37³, 39², 42, 45, 47³; **24:**25⁵; **25:**4², 13, 15; **26:**16³; **27:**9, 10, 11, 29, 30², 31, 35; **28:**7, 25, 26²; **29:**7³, 8, 14, 16; **30:**7, 11; **31:**4²; 14; **32:**7, 10, 23, 24, 25², 26³, 30²; **33:**2², 11, 17, 31²; **34:**10, 13, 14, 23, 24, 27³, 30; **35:**5³; **36:**5², 12², 17⁴, 18, 19², 23, 37; **37:**10, 20, 21, 23⁴, 25³, 26, 27; **38:**4, 16; **39:**14, 22, 23², 24², 26²; **40:**4³, 9², 10; **44:**10²; 12², 13, 19²; **47:**12⁴; **48:**29; **Da 1:**16; **3:**21, 27³, 28², 29; **6:**24²; **7:**12; **8:**23; **11:**8³, 15, 27, 32; **Hos 1:**7; **2:**5, 17; **3:**5³; **4:**7, 8, 9², 12, 18³, 19; **5:**4³, 5, 6, 7², 15²; **7:**2³, 5², 6², 7³, 14², 16²; **8:**4², 13², 14²; **9:**4, 6², 9², 13, 15²; 16²; **10:**2⁴, 8, 10, 14, 11:4, 6², 11; **12:**11; **13:**2, 16⁴; **14:**4; **Joel 1:**3², 7²; **2:**7, 17, 22²; **3:**6, 13, 21; **Am 2:**4, 8, 14; **3:**10, 12²; **5:**11; **6:**2²; **7:**11, 17; **9:**4, 14², 15; **Ob 1:**12², 13⁴, 14²; **Jnh 1:**13; **3:**8², 10; **4:**11²; **Mic 2:**1², 6, 9², 13²; **3:**2, 3², 7², 9³; **13²; **5:**5; **6:**12, 16; **7:**4, 13, 16⁴, 17; **Na 1:**10, 13; **2:**2, 5, 7, 11; **3:**12, 13; **Hab 1:**6, 7, 8³, 9, 11; **2:**7, 15; **Zep 1:**9, 13², 17²; **18:**2, 7²; **8, 9, 10, 14, 15; **3:**6³, 11, 13; **Hag 1:**10, 12², 14; **2:**22²; **Zec 1:**21; **2:**9; **5:**9; **7:**2, 12, 8; **12:**6; **9:**7²; 16; **10:**6, 7², 9; **11:**3, 5², 6, 16; **12:**5³; 12³, 13³, 14; **14:**12²; **Mal 3:**5, 11; **4:**6²; **Mt 1:**21; **2:**9, 11, 12; **3:**6; **4:**6, 8, 20, 21², 22, 23; **6:**2, 5, 7, 15, 16²; **7:**6, 16, 20, 29; **8:**11, 22, 34; **9:**2, 4, 29, 30, 35; **10:**17, 21; **12:**9, 15, 25; **13:**15³, 43, 54, 58; **14:**14, 15; **15:**2, 8², 9, 26; **16:**8; **17:**12, 25; **18:**10, 31; **20:**8, 25, 34²; **21:**7, 8; **22:**7, 16, 18; **23:**5³; **24:**45; **25:**1, 3, 4, 7, 10; **26:**43, 67; **27:**39; **28:**17; **Mk 1:**5, 18, 19, 20, 23, 39; **2:**5, 8; **3:**5; **5:**17; **6:**6, 52; **7:**3, 5, 6², 7, 29; **8:**17; **9:**48; **10:**32, 42; **11:**7, 8; **12:**15, 41, 44; **13:**12; **14:**40, 56, 59, 65; **15:**19, 29; **16:**2, 14², 18²; **Lk 1:**16, 17, 20, 51, 52, 77; **2:**8, 22, 39, 44²; **3:**15; **4:**6, 11, 15, 20, 30; **6:**1, 18, 23, 26; **8:**3, 12, 14; **9:**5, 47, 60; **10:**38; **11:**17, 48; **12:**36, 42; **13:**1, 29; **16:**4; **8:**18:9; **19:**35, 36; **20:**23; **21:**1, 4²; **23:**23, 24, 25, 48, 51; **24:**5², 11, 17, 31², 43, 45; **Jn 2:**11; **3:**19; **4:**30, 38; **5:**28; **7:**31, 50; **8:**30; **10:**39; **11:**19, 45, 55; **12:**11, 37, 40², 42; **13:**12²; **15:**22, 25; **17:**20; **19:**6; **20:**10; **Ac 1:**9², 19; **2:**41, 45, 46, 47; **4:**23²; 24, 26, 29; **5:**14, 16, 38; **6:**1, 6; **7:**6, 12, 13, 16, 19, 34, 35, 39, 41, 54, 57²; **8:**8:10, 17; **9:**15, 24; **10:**9; **11:**23, 30; **12:**20, 25; **13:**3, 4, 5, 17, 18, 19², 22, 27, 50, 51; **14:**2, 5, 14, 16, 17, 23; **15:**3, 9, 22, 26; **16:**19, 24, 33, 35; **17:**21; **18:**26; **19:**12, 18, 19; **20:**21, 24³; **22:**4, 5, 22, 23, 23; **23:**21, 28, 29, 30, 31; **24:**1, 21; **25:**13, 16, 19; **26:**18, 20²; **27:**19, 43; **28:**6, 27²; **Ro 1:**18, 21², 24², 26, 27, 30²; **2:**15³; **3:**3, 8, 13³, 14, 15, 16, 18; **8:**5²; **10:**2, 3, 18²; **11:**9, 10², 11, 13², 15², 24, 27, 30; **13:**6; **15:**27; **16:**4, 5, 18, 23; **1Co 1:**2; **3:**19; **8:**7, 12; **9:**13, 14; **10:**5; **14:**3, 35; **16:**19; **2Co 3:**14, 15; **6:**16; **8:**2², 3⁴, 14; **9:**14²; **11:**15²; **12:**14²; **13:**13; **Gal 2:**13; **Eph 1:**10; **2:**16; **4:**14, 17, 18²; **29; **5:**24, 28²; **6:**6²; 9; **Php 3:**19²; **Col 2:**23³; **3:**22²; **1Th 2:**16²; **5:**13; **1Ti 1:**9, 19; **3:**11, 13; **4:**14; **5:**4³, 11²; 12, 14; **6:**1, 2, 17²; **2Ti 2:**17, 26; **3:**2, 6, 9; **4:**3², 4; **Tit 1:**12, 15, 16; **2:**4, 5, 9; **3:**13; **Heb 2:**10, 14, 15²; **3:**10, 19; **4:**6, 11; **6:**6; **7:**5², 27; **8:**9, 10³, 12²; **9:**6; **10:**2, 16², 17; **11:**14, 16, 20, 35, 39, 13³, 17², 24; **Jas 1:**27; **5:**3; **1Pe 1:**24; **2:**23; **3:**1, 5², 12, 16; **4:**19; **2Pe 2:**2, 3³, 9, 13²; 21; **3:**3, 16; **1Jn 2:**19; **2Jn 1:**13; **3Jn 1:**6, 10; **Jude 1:**6², 8, 13, 16², 18; **Rev 3:**4; **4:**4, 10, 11; **5:**7, 9, 11, 14, 17²; **7:**9, 11, 14, 17²; **9:**4, 7², 8², 9, 10, 16, 17², 18, 19², 20, 21⁴; **11:**5², 7, 8², 9, 11, 12, 16²; **12:**8, 11²; **14:**1, 2, 5, 11, 13²; **15:**6; **16:**10, 11², 17³, 17²; **18:**11, 15, 17, 19; **19:**18, 19, 21; **20:**4³; **21:**3, 4, 8, 24; **22:**4, 14.

21; **5:**2³; **6:**1, 2, 4, 7, 13², 19, 21; **7:**14, 15; **9:**1, 19; **11:**3, 6, 8, 9; **13:**6; **14:**10, 15³, 24; **15:**5, 10, 11; **17:**23; **18:**2², 8², 16²; **19:**1², 3, 5², 6, 8², 9, 12, 16², 17², 18; **20:**8, 14; **21:**14², 27; **22:**6, 8; **23:**8; **24:**53, 56; **25:**6, 26; **26:**4, 15, 18², 27, 30, 31; **27:**13, 14², 15; **29:**5, 6, 7, 9; **30:**28, 31, 32, 35², 37, 40, 42; **31:**5, 9, 34², 37, 46, 55; **32:**2, 4, 16, 23; **34:**8, 14, 21², 23, 25; **35:**4, 5²; **36:**7²; **37:**2, 4, 6, 13, 17², 18, 22, 25; **38:**18, 26, 28; **39:**14; **40:**3, 4², 6, 8², 11, 17, 22; **41:**3, 6, 8², 12, 13, 19, 21, 23, 30, 38; **42:**7², 9², 12, 14, 17, 18, 23, 24³, 25², 27, 29, 36; **43:**2, 11², 16, 23, 24, 27, 34; **44:**4², 6², 11, 15, 28; **45:**15, 19, 21², 22, 24, 26, 27, 34; **46:**6; **47:**2, 6³, 11, 17², 20, 22; **48:**6, 9², 10², 12, 13², 20; **49:**7², 19, 28², 29; **50:**12, 19, 21²; **Ex** 1:7, 10, 11², 13, 14, 16, 17, 18, 21; **2:**11, 17, 18, 25; **3:**7, 8², 9, 13², 16, 20; **4:**18, 20, 30, 31; **5:**5, 7, 8, 13, 20; **6:**1³, 3, 4², 6, 13; **7:**6, 13; **8:**2, 14; **9:**2², 11, 17, 27, 30, 31; **10:**1, 2, 4, 19, 26, 27; **12:**5, 6², 21, 27, 36, 38, 42; **13:**17, 21³; **14:**4, 5, 7, 9, 10, 17, 19², 23², 25, 27, 28; **15:**5, 7, 9³, 10, 12, 13, 16, 17², 19, 21, 25²; **16:**3, 4, 12, 15, 19, 20², 23; **18:**8, 9, 16, 20², 21², 25; **19:**7, 10², 12, 14, 21, 22, 24, 25; **20:**5², 11; **21:**1; **22:**5, 11, 30²; **23:**13, 23, 24, 27, 29, 30, 31, 32, 33; **24:**14; **25:**3, 8², 10, 12, 13², 19, 20, 26, 28², 37, 40; **26:**1, 6, 11, 19, 37; **27:**6; **28:**5, 9, 12, 20, 25, 26, 27, 33, 40, 41², 43; **29:**1, 3², 4, 8, 9, 13², 17, 22, 24, 25², 29, 30, 33, 35, 46²; **30:**5, 12², 29², 30; **31:**11; **32:**2², 3, 8, 10², 13, 19, 21, 24, 25, 27, 34²; **34:**11, 15, 31², 32, 33, 35²; **35:**1, 23, 29, 35²; **36:**8, 13, 24, 36², 38; **37:**3, 4, 8, 9, 13, 28; **38:**6; **39:**6, 7, 18, 19, 20, 25, 43; **40:**11, 12, 14, 15; **Lev** 1:2, 12; **2:**12; **3:**3, 4, 9, 10, 11, 14, 15, 16; **4:**8, 9, 10, 20; **5:**8; **6:**10, 18; **7:**4, 5, 7, 34, 36; **8:**6, 10, 11, 13³, 27, 28², 30; **9:**2, 7, 11, 13, 14, 22; **10:**1, 2, 4, 5, 11, 14, 17; **11:**4, 11, 26, 31, 32, 33, 35, 43²; **12:**7; **13:**39, 59; **14:**12, 23, 24, 51; **15:**2, 14, 15, 27, 29, 31²; **16:**4, 7, 12, 16, 21, 23, 28; **17:**2, 5², 7, 8², 10; **18:**2, 5², 30; **19:**2, 10, 31, 37; **20:**6, 8, 12, 13, 18, 22, 23, 27; **21:**1, 8², 23; **22:**3, 9², 16³, 18, 25, 31; **23:**2, 10, 22, 43; **24:**6, 12; **25:**2, 3, 21, 43, 44, 46²; **26:**36², 37, 41², 43², 44²; **27:**2; **Nu** 1:19, 49; **2:**5, 12, 20, 27; **3:**6, 16; **4:**12², 19, 27, 37, 41, 45; **5:**3², 4, 12, 23; **6:**2, 7, 16, 20, 23, 27; **7:**5², 6, 10; **8:**6, 7³, 8, 10, 13, 15, 16, 17, 19²; **9:**6, 8; **10:**2, 33², 34; **11:**1³, 3, 4, 12², 16, 17, 21, 22², 24, 25, 26, 28, 29, 31, 32, 33; **12:**4, 5, 9²; **13:**3², 17, 23², 26², 33; **14:**2, 9², 10, 11, 12², 13, 14², 16², 19, 20, 23, 28, 31, 33, 45²; **15:**2, 18, 23, 26, 30², 31, 32, 33, 34, 38, 39; **16:**4, 5, 7; **17:**9²; **18:**1, 5, 7; **19:**4², 5, 10, 16, 17²; **20:**3, 21:1; **22:**2, 4, 14, 18, 23², 3, 5, 19; **25:**7; **26:**32; **29:**8; **2Ch** 1:16, 17; **2:**2, 16², 18²; **3:**10, 16²; **4:**4, 6, 7², 8, 17; **5:**1, 5; **6:**3, 25², 26, 27, 28, 34, 36³; **7:**19, 20, 22²; **8:**2; **9:**8², 11, 16, 18; **10:**7², 9, 10, 13, 16, 17; **11:**11, 12, 14, 23²; **12:**5, 7², 10, 11², 13:7; **14:**7², 15², 17²; **15:**2; **16:**3, 6³; **17:**7³, 9; **18:**5, 9, 31; **19:**4, 6, 9; **10:**20:10², 12², 16², 17, 23, 25, 27², 28³, 21:1; **3:**22:8, 12; **23:**3, 3, 6, 12, 14; **24:**5, 10, 13, 17², 25; **27:**5, 9³, 15², 21, 23², 24; **29:**3, 4, 23, 32, 34; **30:**1, 7, 10, 12, 14, 16, 18, 24, 27; **31:**1, 2, 6, 19; **32:**1², 6, 16, 25, 30², 33; **33:**16; **34:**25, 26²; **36:**7², 13; **Ezr** 1:6, 8²; **2:**62, 63; **3:**3; **4:**4², 5, 20; **5:**1, 2³, 3, 9, 10, 12; **6:**9, 22²; **7:**17; **8:**1, 13, 14, 15, 27, 29², **9:**2, 12; **10:**10; **Ne** 1:2; **2:**9², 17, 18, 20; **3:**2, 7, 23², 27, 29, 30; **4:**4, 11², 12, 15; **5:**7³, 8, 10, 12², 15, 17; **6:**9, 10², 14³, 16, 44; **Est** 2:3²; **3:**4, 8, 9; **4:**4; **5:**8, 11; **6:**8, 9; **8:**10, 11, 17; **9:**1², 2², 3, 5², 16, 24, 26, 27, 28; **Job** 1:4, 5², 6, 15, 17, 19; **2:**1; **5:**14, 15; **8:**4; **9:**5; **11:**20; **12:**15, 23², 24, 25; **15:**19; **17:**4; **20:**15, 19, 29; **21:**8, 9, 17, 26; **22:**6, 19, 29; **24:**17, 20², 23; **26:**5; **27:**5; **29:**24²; **30:**2, 9, 13; **31:**15, 27; **32:**15; **33:**16; **34:**25, 26²; **36:**7², 9, 10², 13, 17; **37:**11, 12, 21; **38:**20; **39:**14, 15²; **40:**13; **42:**9², 15; **Ps** 2:4, 5²; **5:**10², 11², 12; **7:**7; **9:**6, 20; **10:**9, 17; **11:**4²; **12:**5²; **13:**18:14, 37, 38, 41; **19:**11²; **20:**4³; **21:**9³, 12²; **22:**4, 18; **23:**2, 3², 4, 13²; **24:**9; **25:**9, 14; **26:**10; **28:**4³, 5², 9; **30:**3; **31:**12, 20²; **33:**19²; **34:**7, 16, 17²; **35:**6, 8²; **36:**8², 10²; **37:**10, 20, 39²; **38:**16; **39:**2²; **40:**5; **41:**10; **43:**3³; **44:**3²; **45:**16; **47:**6², 13, 14, 15; **48:**6, 7, 13; **49:**13²; **50:**9; **53:**5²; **54:**5; **55:**15²; **56:**7; **58:**7; **59:**8², 11³, 12, 13²; **61:**3, 8², 9; **62:**10; **63:**2², 6, 9⁴, 10, 11², 12, 13, 19; **64:**5, 7, 8³; **65:**8, 9, 21, 22, 23; **66:**4², 19, 20, 21; **68:**2², 25²; **69:**22, 24², 27; **72:**14; **73:**10, 18², 20; **74:**8, 11; **76:**11; **78:**4, 6, 11, 13, 14, 15, 21, 24, 25, 27, 28, 29, 31², 34, 72²; **80:**5²; **81:**12; **82:**4; **83:**4, 8, 9, 13, 15²; **88:**8; **89:**9; **94:**23³; **96:**12; **97:**10; **98:**9; **99:**3, 6, 7²; **102:**14, 26; **104:**8, 24, 27, 28; **105:**14, 17, 24, 27, 38, 40², 44; **106:**4, 8, 9, 10², 11, 15², 21, 23², 26², 27, 29, 32, 34, 36, 41², 42², 43, 46²; **107:**6, 7, 8, 12, 13, 14, 15, 19, 20², 21, 22, 28, 30, 31, 32, 38, 40; **109:**15, 27; **111:**2, 6; **113:**8²; **115:**8²; **118:**10, 11, 12; **119:**33, 47, 52, 93, 129, 140, 152, 165, 167; **126:**2; **127:**5; **132:**12; **135:**18³; **136:**11; **137:**9; **139:**16, 17, 18, 22²; **140:**10; **144:**6; **145:**15, 19; **146:**6; **147:**4, 18; **148:**5, 6, 13; **149:**3, 9; **Pr** 1:10, 12, 16, 26; **21:**7; **22:**2, 5, 17²; **3:**3², 21; **4:**5, 19, 21, 22; **5:**17; **6:**21²; **7:**3²; **8:**8, 9, 10; **10:**6²; **11:**3, 5, 6; **12:**6, 26; **14:**3; **15:**6; **17:**15; **19:**7; **20:**1, 5, 10, 12, 26; **21:**7; **22:**2, 5, 18², 23; **23:**21; **24:**22, 25; **28:**4, 13,

27; **31:**7, 21, 24, 29; **Ecc** 1:14; **2:**5, 14, 18; **3:**5, 18, 19; **4:**16; **5:**8; **6:**2²; **7:**28; **8:**13; **9:**2, 5, 11, 12; **10:**9²; **11:**8; **12:**1, 12; **SS** 3:4; **4:**2, 4; **5:**3; **6:**6; **Isa** 1:2, 14, 23; **2:**9; **3:**4, 9², 10, 11, 12; **5:**25, 27; **8:**7, 14; **10:**6, 19, 20, 26; **11:**6, 14; **13:**2², 8², 17; **14:**1², 2, 9, 20, 22; **16:**14; **17:**2, 11; **18:**16; **19:**2²; **22:**5, 9, 10, 11, 26²; **24:**5, 9, 10, 11, 26, 26²; **25:**5³, 43:6², 7, 13, 14, 15; **48:**3², 5³, 6², 7², 13; **49:**10⁴, 18²; **50:**9; **51:**8², 11; **52:**4, 5; **56:**5², 7, 8; **57:**6, 13², 19; **58:**2; **59:**8², 11, 26; **45:**21; **47:**6², 13, 14, 15; **48:**3², 5³, 6², 7², 12, 21; **49:**10⁴, 18²; **50:**9; **51:**8², 11; **52:**4, 5; **56:**5², 7, 8; **57:**6, 13², 19; **58:**2; **59:**8², 21; **61:**3, 8², 9; **63:**3², 6, 9⁴, 10, 11², 12, 13, 19; **64:**5; **65:**8, 9, 21, 22, 23; **66:**4², 19, 20, 21; **Jer** 1:8, 17³; **2:**3, 25, 28, 34, 37; **4:**12, 29; **5:**3², 5, 6², 9, 10², 13², 16, 19, 29; **6:**9, 10, 15, 18, 21, 24, 30; **7:**16, 22², 23, 27², 28, 33; **8:**3, 4, 13²; **9:**2, 9, 13, 14, 16³, 17, 18, 22; **10:**2, 5, 11, 14, 18; **11:**2, 3, 4, 5, 6, 7, 8², 10, 11², 12, 14, 20, 22, 23; **12:**2, 3, 12, 13, 14²; **13:**10, 12, 13, 14², 19; **14:**10², 12², 13, 14³, 15, 16², 17; **15:**1², 2, 3, 4, 7, 8, 16, 17, 19; **16:**6, 7², 15², 17², 18³, 20; **18:**15², 17², 20, 21, 22, 23²; **19:**7, 9³, 11, 15; **20:**4³, 11; **21:**3, 4, 7²; **22:**7³, 8, 9, 14², 19, 22; **23:**2², 3², 4, 6³, 7, 9, 10², 14, 15², 18, 21, 22, 32², 33; **24:**6², 7, 9², 10²; **25:**6, 9³, 10, 14, 16, 18, 26, 27, 28, 30²; **26:**2, 3, 4, 19², 24; **28:**14; **29:**8, 9, 17³, 18³, 19², 21²; **30:**3, 8, 9, 19², 20, 21; **31:**5, 8³, 9², 10, 11, 13, 23, 28², 32², 34; **32:**14, 18, 20, 22, 23³, 33, 37⁴, 39², 40¹, 41²; **33:**6, 7, 8, 13, 24, 26; **34:**10², 11, 13, 16, 22; **35:**2⁴, 5, 15, 16, 17³; **36:**3², 4, 6, 13, 14, 15, 23², 26; **37:**5; **38:**4, 11, 19, 26, 27; **39:**2², 7², 10², 12, 13, 14²; **40:**7², 8, 9², 10², 12², 14, 15; **41:**3², 7, 10³, 12, 13, 15, 16; **42:**4²; **43:**8², 9³, 10, 11, 12², 13³; **44:**3, 8², 11², 12², 14, 15, 19², 23, 24, 25, 26, 27², 30; **46:**10, 11¹, 16¹, 21², 26; **47:**2, 5, 18², 23; **48:**12; **49:**8, 20², 24², 30², 32; **50:**6, 7², 21, 27³, 33²; **51:**17³, 39², 40²; **52:**3, 26², 27; **La** 1:17, 22; **2:**21²; **3:**20, 40, 63, 64, 65, 66²; **4:**4, 15, 16²; **Eze** 1:6, 8, 19, 20, 21; **2:**4, 5, 6², 7; **3:**4, 6, 9², 11², 13, 15, 17, 26, 27; **4:**9², 13; **5:**2, 3, 4², 13²; **6:**2, 10, 12, 14; **7:**13², 19², 20, 22, 27²; **8:**11², 17, 18⁴; **9:**2, 7, 10², 11¹, 1⁴, 19⁴, 22²; **10:**2, 7, 10, 16, 17², 19²; **11:**1, 5, 7, 19⁴; **12:**6², 7, 10, 11², 12, 14, 15², 16, 19, 20²; **13:**6, 7, 10, 11², 12⁴; **14:**3, 4², 5², 6, 10², 11, 14², 15², 16; **15:**7³; **16:**17, 18², 19, 20, 21, 33, 36, 37², 42³; **17:**6, 17, 18², 19, 20, 21, 33, 36, 37²; **18:**4, 5, 7, 18, 29; **19:**5, 12; **20:**3, 4³, 5³, 7, 8², 9², 10, 11⁴, 12³, 13⁴, 14, 15², 18², 21³, 22², 23³, 25, 26², 27, 28, 30, 38², 40; **21:**6², 28; **22:**13, 14³, 15, 16, 23², 25, 26², 27, 28², 30, 31; **23:**3, 13, 17, 20, 22, 23; **24:**21, 22², 23; **26:**10, 19, 27, 31; **Jl** 2:3, 14, 19;

36, 38, 40, 43, 44, 45, 48, 70, 73, 74; **27:**10, 17, 26, 48, 56; **28:**9, 10, 13, 16, 18, 19, 20; **Mk** 1:20, 22, 31, 44; **2:**2, 3, 8, 12, 13, 17, 19², 20, 27; **3:**12; **4:**2, 11, 13, 15, 21, 33, 34; **5:**10, 12, 13, 19, 39, 40, 43; **6:**4, 5, 7², 11, 13, 31, 33⁴, 34², 37², 39⁴, 41², 46, 48³, 50, 51, 56; **7:**9, 36; **8:**3², 4, 6², 7³, 9, 13, 14, 19, 17, 21, 27, 30, 31; **9:**1, 2³, 3, 4, 7, 8, 9, 14², 16, 31, 33, 36²; **10:**1, 6, 13², 14², 16², 27, 30, 32, 39, 42³; **11:**2, 6², 17; **12:**1, 2, 4, 5, 12, 16, 17, 28²; **13:**5, 9, 12, 20; **14:**7, 10, 13, 16, 23, 24, 27, 34, 37, 40, 41, 60, 69, 70, 71; **15:**8, 12, 15, 40; **16:**12, 13, 14, 15, 18, 19, 20; **Lk** 1:6, 22²; **2:**7, 9², 10, 15, 17, 19, 34, 38, 46², 50, 51²; **3:**13, 16, 18, 20; **4:**2, 11, 23, 26, 27, 35, 39, 40, 41²; **5:**7, 14, 25, 29, 31, 34, 35, 36; **6:**1, 3, 5, 9, 10, 13, 17, 19, 31, 32, 35², 39, 47, 49; **7:**6, 18, 19, 38³, 42²; **8:**3, 31, 32², 37, 55, 56; **9:**1, 2, 3, 5, 10, 11², 13, 14, 16², 18, 23, 34, 45, 46, 47, 49; **12:**6, 16, 24, 30, 37², 38, 42; **13:**4, 23; **14:**5, 7, 19, 23, 25; **15:**2, 3, 4, 12; **16:**15, 28, 29², 30; **17:**14, 15, 23, 27, 29, 31, 34; **19:**11, 13, 27³, 29, 32, 33, 46; **20:**15, 17, 19, 23, 25, 41; **21:**6, 8, 10, 11, 14, 15, 19, 23, 25, 41; **21:**6, 10, 29; **22:**4, 6, 13, 15, 19, 23, 24², 25³, 35, 36, 40, 41, 45, 46, 47, 50, 55, 58, 66; **23:**14, 20, 22, 28, 34; **24:**4, 5, 10, 11, 13, 15, 17, 18, 25, 29, 30², 33, 35, 36², 38, 40, 41, 44, 46, 50², 51²; **Jn** 1:38; **2:**7, 8, 19, 24; **3:**22; **4:**32, 40; **5:**17, 19, 21, 39, 53, 61, 64; **7:**6, 19, 21, 45, 49; **8:**2, 7, 21, 27, 42; **10:**3, 4, 6, 8, 16, 20, 27, 28², 29², 32, 34, 35; **11:**11, 14, 19, 37, 44, 46³, 49, 52²; **12:**35, 36, 40, 47; **13:**1, 5, 12, 17², 20, 22; **14:**21; **15:**2, 3, 4, 7, 8², 12, 15, 17, 18, 19, 20, 21, 22, 23², 26³; **18:**4, 5, 7, 18, 29; **19:**5, 16, 20, 24², 27, 30, 31²; **32:**14, 18, 20, 22, 23³; **17:**2, 5, 6, 7, 8², 9, 10, 11, 12³, 13, 14², 15², 16, 17, 18, 19, 20, 21, 22, 23², 26³; **18:**4, 5, 7, 18, 29; **19:**5, 16, 23², 24, 40; **20:**17, 18, 19, 20, 23, 25, 26²; **21:**3, 6, 11, 16; **Ac** 1:3, 4², 7, 10; **2:**3, 4², 6, 8, 11, 13, 40²; **3:**3, 5², 8, 11, 12; **4:**3, 7², 8, 11, 13, 15², 18², 21², 23, 24, 33, 34²; **5:**13, 15², 16, 18², 21², 23, 24, 33, 34²; **6:**3, 6; **7:**19, 24, 25, 26, 34, 36, 42, 44, 45², 60; **8:**3, 11, 14, 15, 16, 17, 18; **9:**2, 21, 27, 28, 39², 40, 41; **10:**8², 20², 23, 28, 46, 48; **11:**3, 4, 12, 15, 17, 20², 21, 42, 43², 46, 50, 51; **14:**3, 5², 13, 15, 18, 22, 23², 27; **15:**2, 3, 4, 7, 8², 9, 12, 20², 22, 23, 33, 37, 38²; **16:**7, 10, 19, 20, 22, 23, 24, 25, 30, 33, 34², 37, 39³, 40; **17:**2, 5, 6, 7, 9, 13, 16, 18, 26, 32, 34; **18:**2, 3, 6, 11, 16, 20; **19:**2, 6², 9², 12, 13, 19, 25; **20:**1, 18, 30, 36, 38; **21:**1, 4, 7, 19, 20, 21, 22, 23², 27; **22:**2, 3, 4, 5, 13, 15, 24², 25³, 35, 36, 40, 41, 45², 51²; **23:**6, 8, 10², 21², 23, 28, 30; **25:**3, 6, 11, 16; **26:**10, 11⁴, 17, 18, 20², 23, 24, 26³, 28, 29², 30; **27:**9, 21, 33, 35, 40, 42, 43; **28:**14, 17, 23², 27; **Ro** 1:19², 24, 26, 28, 32; **2:**3, 15; **4:**11; **6:**19; **9:**5, 25, 26, 33; **10:**2, 5, 14; **11:**8, 9, 14, 23, 27, 32; **15:**15, 27²; **16:**4, 14, 15, 17; **1Co** 2:14; **6:**13, 15; **7:**8, 31; **10:**4, 5, 7, 8², 9, 10, 11; **11:**2; **12:**6, 11, 18²; **14:**10; **15:**10, 29; **16:**3; **2Co** 2:13; **4:**17; **5:**15, 19; **6:**16²; **8:**22; **9:**2², 13; **11:**8; **Gal** 2:2, 5, 14; **3:**12; **4:**9, 15, 17; **Eph** 2:3, 16; **4:**18; **5:**7, 11; **6:**4, 9; **Php** 1:28; **2:**8; **Col** 1:27; **2:**15²; **3:**14, 19; **1Th** 2:16; **3:**3; **4:**17; **5:**3, 13; **2Th** 2:11; **1Ti** 1:18, 20; **3:**10²; **4:**3, 15, 16; **5:**11, 16²; **24²:** 6:2⁴, 18; **2Ti** 2:14², 17, 25², 26; **3:**5, 11; **4:**3, 16; **Tit** 1:13; **2:**7, 9², 10; **Heb** 1:12; **2:**11; **4:**2, 6, 8; **5:**1; **6:**10; **7:**23, 25; **8:**9³, 10, 11; **9:**13, 15; **10:**8², 16²; **11:**13², 16, 30, 38, 39; **12:**9, 19, 25; **13:**9, 17; **Jas** 2:25; **3:**3; **1Pe** 1:11, 12; **2:**8; **3:**1, 7; **4:**4; **2Pe** 1:4, 9, 12; **2:**1, 3, 4², 6², 8, 17, 19, 21²; **3:**1, 16; **1Jn** 2:19; **3:**24; **4:**4, 5; **3Jn** 1:6, 10; **Jude** 1:10, 11, 23; **Rev** 2:2, 16, 27²; **3:**5, 9; **4:**4; **5:**10, 13; **6:**11; **7:**14, 15, 16, 17; **8:**2, 6, 12; **9:**5², 6, 11; **10:**6; **11:**5², 7, 9, 10, 11, 12; **12:**4, 10, 12; **13:**7, 14; **14:**9, 13, 19; **15:**1, 2; **16:**6, 14; **17:**14; **19:**15, 20, 21; **20:**6, 8, 9, 10, 11, 13; **21:**3², 14; **22:**5, 8², 18.

THEMSELVES (236)

Ge 3:7; **10:**1; **21:**29; **30:**40; **34:**22; **43:**15, 32²; **44:**14; **50:**18; **Ex** 12:39; **18:**22, 26; **19:**22; **32:**8, 31; **34:**15, 16; **Lev** 17:7; **20:**5; **Nu** 8:7, 21, 26; **23:**9, 24; **Dt** 9:12; **31:**14, 16; **Jos** 8:15, 27; **11:**14; **24:**1; **Jdg** 2:17; **5:**2; **6:**2; **8:**27, 33; **9:**8, 51; **18:**30; **19:**22; **20:**22; **1Sa** 2:5; **3:**13; **14:**11; **21:**4; **2Sa** 2:25; **10:**8; **12:**19; **1Ki** 14:23; **18:**23, 28; **2Ki** 3:9; **11:**11; **12:**8; **17:**9, 15; **23:**3; **1Ch** 5:25; **15:**14; **19:**9; **21:**20; **2Ch** 5:11; **7:**14; **12:**6, 7²; **21:**11; **23:**7; **29:**15, 34; **35:**14²; **Ezr** 6:20², 21; **9:**1, 2; **Ne** 4:16; **8:**16; **9:**2, 18; **10:**28, 29; **13:**22; **Est** 8:11, 13; **9:**16, 27, 31; **Job** 1:6; **2:**1; **3:**14; **24:**7, 16; **Ps** 22:29;

35:26; 38:16; 49:11, 13; 57:6; 73:6; 106:28, 39²; Pr 1:18; 23:20; 31:8; Ecc 4:12; Isa 3:9; 34:14; 46:2; 47:14; 56:6; 59:6; 66:17; Jer 2:5, 24; 5:24; 7:19; 9:5; 12:13; 14:22; 25:14; 41:5; 44:10; 50:5; 51:58; La 1:11, 19; Eze 6:9; 14:11, 14, 20; 30:17; 32:4; 34:2, 8, 10; 37:23; Da 10:7; Hos 4:10, 14; 8:4, 10; 9:4, 10; 13:2; Am 9:3; Hab 1:7, 13; 2:13; Zec 12:3, 12; Mt 9:3; 14:15; 16:7; 17:1; 21:25; 23:4; Mk 2:6; 6:32, 36; 9:10; 11:31; 15:31; Lk 5:21; 7:30, 49; 9:10, 36; 20:5; 22:23, 25; 24:12; Jn 6:52; 14:11; Ac 2:42; 15:32; 16:37; 23:12; 27:36; 28:25; Ro 1:27; 2:14; 13:2; 1Co 7:9; 16:15; 2Co 5:15; 8:5; 10:12²; Gal 5:12; Eph 2:11; 4:19; 1Th 1:9; 1Ti 1:4; 3:15; 5:12; 6:10, 19; 2Ti 3:2; Tit 3:8, 14; Heb 5:14; 6:16; 9:23; 10:1; 1Pe 1:12; 3:5; 4:19; 2Pe 2:1, 19; Jude 1:7, 12, 16; Rev 14:4²; 19:21.

THEN (2931)

Ge 1:11, 26, 29; 2:22; 3:7, 8, 13; 4:6, 9, 15, 17, 24; 5:5, 8, 11, 14, 17, 20, 24, 27, 31; 6:3; 7:1, 16; 8:8, 11, 13, 15, 20; 9:1, 8, 23, 29; 10:19; 11:4, 6; 12:9, 12, 19, 20; 13:16; 14:7, 8, 11, 18, 20; 15:4, 5, 11, 13; 16:5, 6, 9; 17:9, 19; 18:4, 5, 7, 8, 10, 13, 17, 20, 23, 27, 30, 32; 19:2, 11, 20, 24, 32; 20:2, 6, 9, 14, 17; 21:4, 16, 19, 25; 22:2, 5, 10, 19; 23:3, 7, 8; 24:5, 8, 10, 12, 23, 26, 33², 39; 41, 47, 53, 54, 55, 57, 61, 66; 25:8, 11, 34²; 26:10, 16, 21, 30, 31; 27:3, 10, 15, 17, 21, 25, 26, 31, 33, 36, 38, 41, 43, 46; 28:5, 8, 20, 21; 29:1, 3, 6, 8, 11, 14, 21, 27, 28, 35; 30:3, 6, 8, 11, 13, 18, 20, 22, 36, 38; 31:3, 8², 14, 17, 24, 26, 55; 32:9, 18, 24, 29; 33:5, 6, 12, 15; 34:6, 11, 16, 30; 35:1, 3, 5, 13, 16, 29; 37:9, 14, 20, 31, 34; 38:8, 11, 14, 23, 30; 39:9, 17; 40:8; 41:4, 7, 9, 17, 21, 25, 30, 39, 42, 44, 55; 42:3, 9, 16, 24, 33, 34, 37; 43:8, 11², 23, 27; 44:2, 10, 12, 13, 18, 21, 25; 45:1, 4, 8, 14, 24; 46:5, 31, 34; 47:7, 10, 16, 31; 48:5, 9, 12, 15, 21; 49:1; 29; 50:2, 5, 18, 21, 24, 25; Ex 1:8, 18, 22; 2:3, 5, 7, 14; 3:6, 13, 18; 4:2, 4, 6, 8, 14, 18, 22, 28; 5:3, 5, 10, 15; 6:1, 7, 10; 7:1, 4, 9, 11, 14, 16; 8:1, 5, 16, 20, 25, 30; 9:1, 8, 13, 22, 27, 33; 10:1, 6, 8, 11, 18, 21, 24; 11:7, 8; 12:7, 21, 27², 48; 13:3, 19; 14:1, 15, 19, 21, 26; 15:1, 20, 22, 25, 27; 16:4, 9, 12, 19, 28, 33; 17:4, 14; 18:7, 12, 27; 19:3, 5, 9, 15, 17, 19; 20:22; 21:6²; 23:11; 24:1, 4, 5, 7, 8, 13, 18; 25:8, 13, 16, 37; 26:6, 11; 28:11, 17; 29:4, 9, 13, 18, 20, 21, 25, 37, 45; 30:11, 12, 17, 22, 26, 34; 31:1, 12; 32:4, 7, 10, 14, 20, 24, 27, 29, 32; 33:1, 11, 15, 18, 21, 23; 34:2, 5, 9, 10, 27, 35; 35:20, 30; 36:2, 6, 11, 13, 17, 19; 37:4, 7, 11; 39:7, 10, 20, 31, 33; 40:1, 4, 10, 13, 19, 21, 28, 33, 34; Lev 1:5, 8, 17; 3:2, 5, 8, 13; 4:5, 7, 10, 16, 21, 25, 30, 34; 5:10; 6:10, 11; 7:12, 21, 37; 8:6, 9, 10, 13, 14, 18, 19, 22, 24, 28, 30, 31, 32; 9:3, 6, 12, 15, 20, 22, 23; 10:3, 6, 8; 11:32; 12:4, 5, 7; 13:17, 21, 26, 31, 54; 14:5, 6, 7, 8, 12, 15, 19, 30, 42, 51, 53; 16:7, 14, 15, 18, 23, 24, 30; 17:15; 23:16, 19; 24:13, 23; 25:9, 19, 27, 28, 41; 26:16, 28, 34², 41; 27:12, 14; Nu 2:17; 4:6, 10, 14; 5:11, 15, 17, 19, 22, 23, 26, 27, 29; 6:10, 18, 20; 7:2; 8:7, 8, 13, 21, 26; 9:9, 20; 10:9, 12, 17, 21; 11:1, 8, 25, 30, 32; 12:5, 8; 13:30; 14:5, 10, 13, 45; 15:4, 24, 35, 40; 16:3, 5, 12, 15, 23, 28, 29, 30, 43, 46, 50; 17:9; 18:8, 32; 19:4, 7, 12, 18; 20:11, 20, 28; 21:2, 6, 9, 11, 17, 18, 33; 22:1, 6, 11, 15, 24, 26, 28, 31, 39; 23:3², 7, 13, 18, 19, 25, 27; 24:10, 15, 20, 21, 23, 25; 25:6, 8; 27:12, 23; 30:4, 7, 11, 12, 14, 15; 31:21, 23, 24, 48; 32:16, 20, 22, 28, 29, 33; 33:56; 34:4, 8, 12; 35:3, 9, 23; 36:3, 5; Dt 1:19, 20, 22, 29, 41; 2:1, 2, 9, 14; 4:12, 13, 25, 30, 41; 5:22, 27; 6:11; 7:2, 12; 8:3, 5, 14; 9:6, 12, 18, 21; 10:2, 5; 11:14, 17, 23; 12:11, 20; 13:9, 11, 14; 14:25, 26; 15:9, 10, 17; 16:7, 10; 17:4, 7, 20; 19:2, 9, 11, 19; 20:8; 21:3, 6, 13, 21; 22:5, 17; 24:4, 13; 25:8; 26:2, 5, 7, 13; 27:9, 15, 16, 17, 18, 19, 20, 21, 22, 23, 24, 25, 26; 28:10, 64; 30:3, 9, 16; 31:1, 7, 10, 15; 34:1, 4, 10; Jos 1:2, 8, 16; 2:1, 14, 18, 22, 23; 3:4; 4:14; 5:9, 14; 6:2, 5, 10, 11, 14, 20; 7:6, 9, 19, 24, 25, 26; 8:1, 9, 18, 30; 9:6, 7, 15, 22; 10:5, 6, 15, 21, 26, 29, 31, 34, 36, 38, 43; 11:23; 12:3; 14:10, 11, 12, 13, 15; 15:3, 4, 7, 8, 9; 16:7; 17:9; 18:4, 8, 10, 13, 27; 19:13, 27; 20:1, 4, 6; 22:1, 6, 11, 21, 27, 32; 23:2, 14; 24:1, 5, 7, 11, 15, 16, 22, 23, 26, 28; Jdg 1:3, 7, 15, 17, 26; 2:11, 16; 3:20, 23; 4:14; 5:11, 13, 22, 31; 6:26, 34, 37, 39; 7:18; 8:7, 13, 15, 18; 9:6, 12, 15, 19, 21, 28, 29, 32, 38, 44, 45; 10:2, 10, 16; 11:12, 17, 19, 21, 29, 32; 12:5; 13:6, 7, 8, 17, 19; 14:7, 16, 19; 15:4, 8, 11, 16, 19; 16:3,

8, 10, 12, 13, 15, 20, 21, 28, 29, 30, 31; 17:2, 10, 12; 18:5, 11, 14, 20, 27; 19:5, 9, 28; 20:1, 3, 10, 24, 26, 29, 34, 36, 39, 41; 21:5, 8, 13, 21, 23; Ru 1:8, 9, 12, 14; 2:4, 17, 19, 21; 3:3, 4, 15, 16, 18; 4:3, 5, 6, 9, 11, 13, 16, 18; 1Sa 1:11, 18, 19; 2:1, 11, 16², 20, 36; 3:4, 8, 10, 15, 18; 5:2; 6:3, 7, 9², 12, 16, 21; 7:3, 5, 9, 12; 8:20, 22; 9:4, 22; 10:1, 3, 21, 24, 25; 11:5², 7, 12, 14; 12:6, 7, 11, 16, 18; 13:3, 15; 14:8, 15, 17, 20, 28, 33, 34, 35, 40, 41, 43, 46; 15:6, 7, 10, 14, 24, 32, 34; 16:5, 8, 9, 12, 19, 22, 23; 17:10, 30, 38, 40, 52; 18:22, 27; 19:5, 13, 18; 20:1, 7, 8, 12, 18, 21², 22, 27, 33, 38, 40, 41, 42; 21:3; 22:11, 17, 18, 22; 23:3, 18, 23, 28; 24:4, 8, 22; 25:1, 9, 11, 19, 35, 37, 39; 26:5, 6, 13, 19, 21, 25; 27:1, 5, 9; 28:2, 7, 11, 14, 25; 30:7, 21; 31:13; 2Sa 1:5, 9, 11, 15; 2:4, 7, 14, 16, 21, 25, 30, 32; 3:12, 14, 16, 19, 21, 22, 26, 31, 35, 38; 4:6; 5:9, 6:8; 7:8, 18; 9:6, 9, 11; 10:5, 11², 13; 11:4², 8, 12, 15, 18, 22, 28, 33, 38, 40, 41, 42; 21:3; 22:11, 17, 18, 22; 23:3, 18, 23, 28; 24:4, 8, 22; 25:1, 9, 11, 19, 35, 37, 39; 26:5, 6, 13, 19, 21, 25; 27:1, 5, 9; 28:2, 7, 11, 14, 25; 30:7, 21; 31:13; 2Sa 1:5, 9, 11, 15; 2:4, 7, 14, 16, 21, 25, 30, 32; 3:12, 14, 16, 19, 21, 22, 26, 31, 35, 38; 4:6; 5:9; 6:8, 19; 7:8, 18, 26; 9:9, 11; 10:5, 11², 13; 11:4², 8, 12, 15, 21, 24; 12:7, 13, 20², 24, 27, 31; 13:5, 9, 10, 15, 26, 28, 29; 14:3, 7, 11, 12, 13, 18, 23; 15:3, 4, 10², 14, 25, 26, 34; 16:3, 4, 9, 11², 16; 17:2, 10, 12, 13, 23; 18:11, 16, 21, 23, 26, 31, 33; 19:5, 15, 18, 22, 28, 30, 31; 20:10, 13, 15, 22; 21, 22, 35; Jn 1:21, 25, 32, 49, 51; 2:8, 9, 10, 18; 3:12; 4:26, 27, 28, 33, 35, 53; 5:8; 6:3, 11, 21, 23, 28, 30, 35, 52, 70; 7:28, 32, 33, 53; 8:11, 19, 28, 32, 39; 9:10, 11, 16, 26, 38; 10:12, 22, 36, 40; 11:7, 14, 16, 36, 40, 41, 47, 48, 49; 12:3, 28, 35, 44; 13:9, 21, 46; 14:22; 15:16, 16:16, 17, 19, 29; 18:8, 28; 19:1, 21:7, 8, 11, 19, 23, 29, 30, 35; 1Ki 1:14, 34, 45; 2:33, 36; 3:12²; 17, 18; 5:4, 9, 12; 6:5, 8, 19; 7:31², 35, 47; 8:8, 9, 14, 16, 21, 23, 29, 35, 46, 60, 64; 9:3²; 10:11; 11:16, 20, 40; 12:1, 25², 30; 13:11², 17, 25; 14:2, 32; 16:16; 17:1, 4, 5, 7, 9, 10, 15; 18:10², 25, 26, 29, 40, 41, 43²; 19:3, 6, 9, 11, 15, 19; 20:40; 21:1, 25; 22:1, 7, 8, 20, 37, 43, 46, 47; 2Ki 1:3, 6, 16; 2:23, 25; 3:11, 20; 4:2, 6, 8², 10, 11, 31, 32, 38, 40, 41; 5:8, 15, 18; 6:2, 6, 9, 14, 20, 25, 30; 7:3, 4, 5, 10; 9:2, 16, 22, 27; 10:1, 15, 17; 11:14, 16; 12:3, 10, 14, 19, 26; 15:4, 35; 16:6; 17:23, 27; 18:5; 19:3, 7, 24, 35, 36; 20:3, 13, 15, 19, 22; 1Ch 3:5, 6, 20; 4:23, 40, 41², 43; 6:31; 7:11, 23; 11:4, 13²; 12:39, 40²; 13:6, 10; 14:4, 11, 12; 16:37; 17:20²; 19:10; 20:3, 6; 21:2, 5, 26, 28; 24:5; 26:17, 18; 27:2, 4, 5, 7, 8, 9, 10, 11, 12, 13, 14, 15; 2Ch 1:3, 5; 2:8; 5:9, 11; 6:5, 9, 16, 14, 20, 26, 36; 7:7, 13, 16²; 9:9; 10:1; 12:12; 13:2, 7; 14:14²; 15:9; 16:3²; 18:6, 7, 19; 19:3, 7; 20:13, 25; 21:9; 22:9; 23:13, 15; 24:11; 25:5, 27; 28:9; 29:35; 30:26²; 31:1; 32:7, 9; 35:7, 18, 21; 36:7, 16, 19; Ezr 1:11; 2:63; 6:6, 12; 7:23; 8:15², 21, 25; 9:4; 10:2, 6, 13; Ne 1:9; 2:11, 12, 14; 4:10, 11, 20; 5:16; 6:7; 7:4, 5, 65, 68; 8:7, 14; 10:36; 12:46; 13:1, 26; Est 1:6, 18; 2:5, 14; 3:8; 4:3; 6:2, 6; 8:17; Job 1:1, 8; 2:3; 3:12, 17²; 19; 6:6, 20, 30; 8:11; 9:33; 11:18; 12:15; 14:7; 19:7, 29; 23:7, 8; 24:13; 28:1, 8; 32:16; 33:23; 34:22; 36:2; 39:28, 29; 40:15; Ps 7:3; 9:14; 10:4; 14:1², 2, 3, 5; 18:41; 19:3, 11; 22:1; 30:9; 31:13; 36:1; 37:37; 38:3, 7; 46:4; 48:6; 51:19; 53:1², 2, 3, 5²; 58:11; 63:1; 68:18, 27³; 69:2, 20, 25, 35, 36; 76:3; 79:3; 86:8; 92:15; 104:17, 25, 26²; 105:31; 107:12, 34, 36; 119:35; 122:5, 7; 130:4; 133:3; 135:17; 137:2, 3; 139:8²; 10, 24; 144:14; Pr 6:9, 16; 8:24², 27; 9:18; 11:10; 12:20, 28; 14:4, 12; 15:17; 16:25; 17:21; 18:24; 19:18; 20:15; 21:30; 22:13; 23:18; 24:14; 26:12, 13; 28:12; 29:9, 18, 20; 30:11, 15, 18, 29; Ecc 1:7, 9, 10, 11; 3:1,

14; 7:4, 9, 27; 8:5, 7, 14, 16; 9:1, 3, 7, 11; 10:4, 7, 15, 18; 11:1, 5, 10, 13, 20, 22, 24; 12:4, 7, 16, 20; 13:9, 21, 23; 14:2, 4, 7, 8, 11; 15:4; 16:6, 29, 39, 42, 52, 61, 63; 17:11, 13, 21; 18:30; 19:8; 20:2, 4, 20, 29, 38, 42, 49; 21:5, 14, 30; 22:13, 19, 30; 23:17, 36, 43, 49; 24:11, 19; 25:5, 11, 17; 26:6, 16, 17, 20; 28:9, 23, 24, 26; 29:6, 9, 16, 21; 30:8, 25, 26; 31:16; 32:14, 15; 33:4, 10, 13, 14, 23, 25, 26, 29, 33; 34:30; 35:4, 9, 12, 15; 36:11, 23, 31, 36, 37, 38; 37:4, 6, 9, 11, 13, 14, 16, 28; 38:23; 39:3, 9, 28; 40:6, 8, 11, 13, 19, 20, 24, 28, 32, 35, 47; 41:1, 3, 5, 13, 15; 42:1, 13, 19; 43:1, 5, 18, 27; 44:1, 4, 25; 46:2, 12, 17, 19, 21; 47:2, 3, 6, 19; 48:28; Da 1:3, 10, 11, 13; 2:4, 8, 9, 15, 17, 19, 24, 35, 46, 48; 3:2, 4, 15, 19, 24, 26, 28, 30; 4:19, 27, 34; 5:8, 17, 29; 6:11, 13, 15, 18, 25; 7:11, 19, 27; 8:13, 14, 18, 27; 10:9, 12, 13, 16; 11:2², 3, 9, 11, 15, 18, 22, 28, 30, 31, 44; 12:5, 6, 7, 8; Hos 1:4, 6, 9; 2:7²; 3:3; 4:16; 5:13, 15; 10:3, 8; 13:6; Joel 2:18, 27; 3:17; Am 2:13; 5:14; 6:2, 10; 7:5, 8, 10, 12, 16; 8:2, 8; 9:5; Jnh 1:4, 7, 14, 15; 3:1, 7; 4:6; Mic 3:1, 4; 5:4; 7:10; Na 3:16; Hab 1:11, 13; 2:2, 7; Zep 3:7, 9; Hag 1:3, 12, 13; 2:13, 14; Zec 1:6, 10, 12, 14, 18, 20; 2:1, 3, 9; 3:1, 4, 5, 7; 4:1, 7, 8, 9, 11; 5:5, 7, 9; 6:8; 7:4; 8:3; 9:14; 11:7, 10, 14, 15; 12:5; 14:3, 5, 16; Mal 1:14; 3:1, 3, 12, 16; 4:3; Mt 2:7, 11, 17; 3:13, 15; 4:1, 5, 11; 5:24; 6:4, 6, 9, 23; 7:5, 6, 11, 23; 8:4, 13, 19, 23, 26, 34; 9:6, 14, 15, 20, 29, 37; 11:9, 20; 12:13, 22, 26, 27, 28, 29, 38, 44, 45; 13:3, 16, 18, 22, 26; 14:5, 9, 10, 12, 23; 15:1, 12, 17, 28, 29, 36; 16:1, 5, 14, 27²; 6:24, 28, 37; 7:4², 5; 8:8, 27; 9:21, 47; 11:29; 14:1, 3, 10; 15:19; 16:3, 27; 18:3, 9, 10, 13, 15, 28², 30; 19:2, 4, 7, 9²; 22:1, 3, 22; 23:13, 21, 29; 24:3; 25:2, 20; 26:2, 3, 7, 13; 27:5; 28:7; 30:16; 2Sa 1:6, 21; 2:2, 4, 18, 23; 3:27; 4:3, 5; 5:6, 14, 20, 21; 6:2, 7; 7:22²; 9:1, 2, 3²; 10:9, 18; 12:1, 31; 13:23, 38; 14:2, 6, 25²; 30, 32; 15:3, 21, 24, 29, 33, 35, 36; 16:1, 5, 14; 17:9; 18:7, 11, 30; 19:31; 20:1, 12; 21:5, 18, 20; 22:42; 23:11, 39; 24:2, 9, 13, 25; Jn 1:21, 25, 32, 49, 51; 2:8, 9, 10, 18; 3:12; 4:26, 27, 28, 33, 35, 53; 5:8; 6:3, 11, 21, 23, 28, 30, 35, 52, 70; 7:28, 32, 33, 53; 8:11, 19, 28, 32, 39; 9:10, 11, 16, 26, 38; 10:12, 22, 36, 40; 11:7, 14, 16, 36, 40, 41, 47, 48, 49; 12:3, 28, 35, 44; 13:6, 9, 11, 21, 25, 27, 31, 36, 37; 14:9, 10; 15:16; 16:16, 17, 19, 29; 18:8, 10, 12, 24, 28, 33, 37; 19:1, 32; 20:6, 10, 27, 29; 21:7, 19; Ac 1:12, 24, 26; 2:8, 14; 3:4, 6, 8, 19; 4:8, 10, 15, 18; 5:3, 6, 10, 17, 25, 35, 40; 6:11; 7:1, 8, 11, 15, 18, 33, 60; 8:17, 24, 30, 35, 38; 9:17, 31, 40, 41; 10:13, 23, 34, 46, 48; 11:7, 10, 11, 16, 18, 25; 12:8, 11, 17, 19; 13:9, 21, 46; 14:19, 21; 15:5, 10, 22; 16:1, 30, 32, 33, 40; 17:9, 15, 19, 22; 18:7, 17, 18, 21, 22; 19:3, 16, 38; 20:11, 38; 21:13, 20, 24, 26, 33; 22:2, 14, 21, 22, 25, 28; 23:11, 39; 24:2, 9, 13, 25; Ro 1:9, 20, 21; 3:1, 9, 27, 31; 4:1, 11; 6:1, 15; 7:3, 7, 12, 13, 25; 8:17, 31; 9:14, 18, 19, 30; 10:14; 11:1, 6, 7, 19; 16, 19, 22; 1Co 12:2; 13:3, 7³; 14:10, 12, 14, 15; 15:7; 2Co 3:21; 4:1, 6, 19; 6:15; 7:5, 38; 8:4; 9:18; 10:19, 28; 11:33; 12:28; 13:12²; 14:11, 21, 22, 26; 15:5, 7², 11, 13, 15, 16, 18, 23, 24, 28, 54; 16:3, 11; 2Co 1:11, 16; 4:12; 5:11; 8:5, 14; 9:5; 11:15, 16; 12:10; Gal 1:18; 2:14; 3:7, 18, 19, 21, 29; 5:1; 6:4; Eph 3:4; 4:1, 14; 5:15; 6:14; Php 1:27; 2:2; Col 2:6; 3:1, 4; 1Th 5:6; 2Th 2:8, 15; 1Ti 2:1; 3:10; 2Ti 2:1; Tit 2:4, 15; 3:10; Phm 1:9; Heb 4:9, 16; 7:2, 27; 9:14, 23, 26; 10:7, 9, 17; 12:8, 11, 25; Jas 1:15; 3:17; 4:7, 14, 17; 5:7; 1Pe 4:19; 2Pe 2:9, 21; 3:14; 1Jn 3:19; Rev 1:17; 2:23; 5:1, 5, 6, 11, 13; 6:1, 4, 6, 11, 15; 7:2, 4, 13; 8:5, 6; 10:1, 5, 8, 11; 11:12, 19; 12:3, 10, 15, 17; 13:11; 14:1, 6, 11, 15; 15:7; 16:1, 5, 13, 16, 18; 17:3, 7, 15; 18:4, 21; 19:5, 6, 9, 19; 20:11, 14; 21:1, 5; 22:1, 10.

THERE (1873)

Ge 1:3², 5², 6, 8², 13², 14, 19², 23², 31²; 2:5, 8, 10, 11, 12; 8:9, 11; 9:11; 11:2, 8, 9², 31; 12:5, 7, 8², 10²; 13:4; 16:14; 18:9, 24, 28, 29, 30², 31, 32; 19:22, 31; 20:1, 2, 11; 21:16, 17, 31, 33; 22:2, 5, 9, 13; 23:13; 24:6, 7, 8, 23, 54; 25:10, 24; 26:1, 8, 17², 19, 22, 23, 25³, 28; 27:45; 28:2, 6, 11, 13; 29:2, 3, 13, 25; 30:42; 31:25, 32, 46, 54²; 32:4, 13, 29; 33:1, 20; 35:1², 7²; 37:24, 29, 30; 38:2, 21², 22², 27; 39:1, 20, 22; 40:8; 41:2, 12, 18, 39, 54²; 42:1, 2², 35, 38; 43:25, 30; 44:20, 31; 45:1, 6², 11; 46:3; 47:13, 18, 27; 48:3, 7; 49:31³; 50:10, 11; Ex 3:2; 8:10, 15, 22; 9:4, 19; 10:14², 26; 11:6²; 12:4, 30², 37; 14:10, 11; 15:25², 27²; 16:3, 10, 13, 26; 17:1, 3, 6; 19:2, 16; 21:22, 23; 23:5; 25:22, 34; 26:25; 28:17, 21, 32; 29:42, 43; 32:5, 17; 33:21; 34:2, 5, 28; 36:30; 39:10, 14; Lev 8:31; 11:4, 21; 13:10², 21, 26, 31, 32; 15:18; 16:23; 19:20; 21:11, 23; 23:3; 25:19; 26:32; Nu 4:7; 5:13; 6:14; 11:16, 17, 34, 35; 12:10; 13:18, 20, 24, 26, 28², 32, 33; 14:5, 43; 17:3; 19:18; 20:1, 2, 5, 15, 26, 28; 21:5², 12, 13, 16, 32; 22:3, 26, 41; 23:13, 14, 15, 23, 27; 26:14; 28:12, 14, 17, 18; 32:39, 40; 33:9², 14, 49; 35:15, 25; Dt 1:28, 31, 46; 2:10, 20; 3:4, 5, 21, 24; 4:22, 28, 29, 35, 39; 5:15, 22; 6:23; 10:5, 6, 7; 11:31; 12:5, 6, 7, 11, 12, 14; 14:26; 15:4, 7, 11; 16:6; 17:12; 18:7, 9; 19:3, 4; 21:4²; 22:21, 27; 23:10; 24:18; 26:5; 27:5, 7; 28:26, 36, 64, 65, 68; 29:18²; 30:4; 31:26; 32:28, 39, 50; 33:19, 20, 26; 34:1, 5; Jos 2:1, 16, 22; 4:9; 5:12; 6:11; 7:3, 6, 22; 8:29, 32, 35; 10:14, 18, 27, 30; 13:1; 14:12; 15:8, 15, 63; 16:1; 17:7, 9, 15; 18:1, 2, 10, 13; 19:14, 15, 22, 30, 38, 50; 21:43; 22:10; 24:5, 25, 26; Jdg 1:5, 7, 11, 21, 29; 2:5; 3:25, 27; 4:17, 22; 5:15, 16, 27²; 6:24, 28, 37; 7:4², 5; 8:8, 27; 9:21, 47; 11:29; 14:1, 3, 10; 15:19; 16:3, 27; 18:3, 9, 10, 13, 15, 28², 30; 19:2, 4, 7, 15, 26, 27, 28; 20:16, 26, 27, 42; 21:9, 10, 14, 19; Ru 1:1, 2, 4, 6, 12, 17; 3:3, 12; 4:1, 17; 1Sa 1:1, 22, 28; 2:2³, 31, 32; 3:1, 10, 21; 4:4, 13; 5:3, 4; 6:14; 7:6, 14, 17²; 9:1, 4, 6², 14; 10:3², 5, 12, 24; 11:14, 15; 14:9, 11, 25, 34, 40, 52; 15:12; 16:11; 17:46; 19:2, 16, 18, 20; 20:3, 6, 11, 23, 29; 21:4, 6², 7, 9²; 22:1, 3, 22; 23:13, 22, 29; 24:3; 25:2, 20; 26:2, 3, 7, 13; 27:5; 28:7; 30:16; 2Sa 1:6, 21; 2:2, 4, 18, 23; 3:27; 4:3, 5; 5:6, 14, 20, 21; 6:2, 7; 7:22²; 9:1, 2, 3²; 10:9, 18; 12:1, 31; 13:23, 38; 14:2, 6, 25²; 30, 32; 15:3, 21, 24, 29, 33, 35, 36; 16:1, 5, 14; 17:9; 18:7, 11, 30; 19:31; 20:1, 12; 21:5, 18, 20; 22:42; 23:11, 39; 24:2, 9, 13, 25; 1Ki 1:14, 34, 45; 2:33, 36; 3:12²; 17, 18; 5:4, 9, 12; 6:5, 8, 19; 7:31², 35, 47; 8:8, 9, 14, 16, 21, 23, 29, 35, 46, 60, 64; 9:3²; 10:11; 11:16, 20, 40; 12:1, 25², 30; 13:11², 17, 25; 14:2, 24, 30; 15:6, 7, 16, 19²; 22, 32; 16:16; 17:1, 4, 5, 7, 9, 10, 15; 18:10², 25, 26, 29, 40, 41, 43²; 19:3, 6, 9, 11, 15, 19; 20:40; 21:1, 25; 22:1, 7, 8, 20, 37, 43, 46, 47; 2Ki 1:3, 6, 16; 2:23, 25; 3:11, 20; 4:2, 6, 8², 10, 11, 31, 32, 38, 40, 41; 5:8, 15, 18; 6:2, 6, 9, 14, 20, 25, 30; 7:3, 4, 5, 10; 9:2, 16, 22, 27; 10:1, 15, 17; 11:14, 16; 12:3, 10, 14, 19, 26; 15:4, 35; 16:6; 17:23, 25, 27; 18:5; 19:3, 7, 24, 35, 36; 20:3, 13, 15, 19, 22; 1Ch 3:5, 6, 20; 4:23, 40, 41², 43; 6:31; 7:11, 23; 11:4, 13²; 12:39, 40²; 13:6, 10; 14:4, 11, 12; 16:37; 17:20²; 19:10; 20:3, 6; 21:2, 5, 26, 28; 24:5; 26:17, 18; 27:2, 4, 5, 7, 8, 9, 10, 11, 12, 13, 14, 15; 2Ch 1:3, 5; 2:8; 5:9, 11; 6:5, 9, 16, 14, 20, 26, 36; 7:7, 13, 16²; 9:9; 10:1; 12:12; 13:2, 7; 14:14²; 15:9; 16:3²; 18:6, 7, 19; 19:3, 7; 20:13, 25; 21:9; 22:9; 23:13, 15; 24:11; 25:5, 27; 28:9; 29:35; 30:26²; 31:1; 32:7, 9; 35:7, 18, 21; 36:7, 16, 19; Ezr 1:11; 2:63; 6:6; 7:23; 8:15², 21, 25; 9:4; 10:2, 6, 13; Ne 1:9; 2:11, 12, 14; 4:10, 11, 20; 5:16; 6:7; 7:4, 5, 65, 68; 8:7, 14; 10:36; 12:46; 13:1, 26; Est 1:6, 18; 2:5, 14; 3:8; 4:3; 6:2, 6; 8:17; Job 1:1, 8; 2:3; 3:12, 17²; 19; 6:6, 20, 30; 8:11; 9:33; 11:18; 12:15; 14:7; 19:7, 29; 23:7, 8; 24:13; 28:1, 8; 32:16; 33:23; 34:22; 36:2; 39:28, 29; 40:15; Ps 7:3; 9:14; 10:4; 14:1², 2, 3, 5; 18:41; 19:3, 11; 22:1; 30:9; 31:13; 36:1; 37:37; 38:3, 7; 46:4; 48:6; 51:19; 53:1², 2, 3, 5²; 58:11; 63:1; 68:18, 27³; 69:2, 20, 25, 35, 36; 76:3; 79:3; 86:8; 92:15; 104:17, 25, 26²; 105:31; 107:12, 34, 36; 119:35; 122:5, 7; 130:4; 133:3; 135:17; 137:2, 3; 139:8²; 10, 24; 144:14; Pr 6:9, 16; 8:24², 27; 9:18; 11:10; 12:20, 28; 14:4, 12; 15:17; 16:25; 17:21; 18:24; 19:18; 20:15; 21:30; 22:13; 23:18; 24:14; 26:12, 13; 28:12; 29:9, 18, 20; 30:11, 15, 18, 29; Ecc 1:7, 9, 10, 11; 3:1,

12, 16², 17, 22; **4**:8², 16; **5**:3², 14; **7**:20; **8**:6, 9, 14; **9**:3, 10, 14, 15; **10**:5, 11; **11**:3; **12**:12; SS **2**:9; **4**:7; **6**:8; **7**:12; **8**:5²; Isa **1**:6; **2**:7²; **3**:24; **4**:5; **5**:6; **7**:23², 24, 25; **9**:1, 7; **11**:16²; **13**:20², 21³; **14**:31; **19**:15, 19, 23; **22**:13, 18²; **23**:12; **27**:4, 10²; **28**:8, 10, 13; **33**:21, 24; **34**:11, 12, 14, 15², 17; **35**:8, 9³; **37**:3, 7, 25, 36, 37; **39**:2, 4, 8; **41**:17, 28; **43**:10, 11, 17; **44**:6, 8²; **45**:5², 6², 14², 18, 21², 22; **46**:7, 9²; **47**:8, 10, 15; **48**:16, 22; **50**:2²; **51**:18²; **52**:11, 14; **57**:7, 21; **59**:8, 15, 16²; **63**:5; **65**:8, 9, 20; Jer **2**:10, 23; **3**:2, 6; **4**:25; **6**:14, 25; **7**:2, 32, 33; **8**:11, 13², 14, 15, 16, 19, 22⁴; **9**:11; **10**:7; **11**:9; **12**:11; **13**:4, 6, 19; **14**:4, 5, 16, 19; **16**:5, 8, 13; **18**:2; **19**:2, 11; **20**:6; **22**:11, 26; **23**:12; **25**:20; **27**:11, 22; **29**:6; **30**:13; **31**:6, 17, 39; **32**:3; **33**:10, 12; **34**:22; **37**:12, 17, 20; **38**:9, 11, 26; **39**:6; **41**:1, 3, 10; **42**:15, 16², 17; **43**:2, 12, 13; **44**:12; **46**:5, 11, 17; **48**:33, 38; **49**:3, 7, 16, 18, 33, 36; **50**:20, 39², 40; **51**:29; **52**:6, 10, 23, 27, 30; La **1**:2, 7, 9, 17, 20, 21; **3**:29; **5**:8; Eze **1**:3, 25, 27; **3**:15, 22², 23; **5**:4; **7**:7, 25; **8**:1, 2, 4, 8, 14, 16; **11**:1, 7; **12**:10, 13, 19, 24; **13**:10, 16; **14**:22; **16**:6; **17**:7, 20; **18**:5; **20**:28, 35, 40³, 43; **22**:25, 26; **23**:2, 20; **26**:17; **28**:26; **29**:11, 14; **30**:13, 18; **32**:15, 22, 24, 26, 29, 30; **34**:5, 14², 26; **35**:10; **37**:7, 8, 22, 25; **38**:19; **39**:11, 16, 17; **40**:1, 3, 17², 23², 41, 42, 49; **41**:6, 11, 22, 25; **42**:7, 12, 13; **47**:7, 8, 9², 10, 23; **48**:35; Da **1**:21; **2**:9, 10, 28, 29, 31, 40; **3**:12, 24, 27; **4**:10, 13; **5**:11; **7**:2, 5, 6, 7, 8, 13, 16; **8**:3, 15; **9**:25; **10**:5, 13²; **11**:4, 5, 11; Hos **2**:15²; **4**:1, 2; **6**:7, 10; **9**:15; **10**:9; **12**:4; Joel **2**:27, 32; **3**:2, 11, 12; Am **3**:5; **5**:16, 17; **6**:2, 10, 12; **7**:12²; **9**:2², 3², 4; Ob **1**:4, 18; Jnh **4**:5; Mic **3**:7; **4**:10²; **7**:1; Na **1**:15; **3**:15; Hab **1**:3; **2**:19; **3**:17²; Zep **1**:14; **2**:7, 14, 15; Hag **2**:14, 16², 19; Zec **1**:8, 16, 18; **2**:1; **3**:9; **4**:3; **5**:1, 7, 9, 11; **6**:1, 13; **8**:5, 9, 10; **10**:10; **14**:6, 7, 9, 21; Mal **3**:10; Mt **1**:17; **2**:13, 22; **4**:21; **5**:23, 24; **6**:21; **7**:4; **8**:12; **9**:9, 27; **10**:11, 26; **11**:1; **12**:10, 45; **13**:42, 50, 53, 58; **14**:23; **15**:29; **17**:2, 3, 20; **18**:20; **19**:2, 15, 17, 27; **21**:2, 12, 28, 33; **22**:11, 13, 23, 25; **24**:7, 21, 23, 26; **25**:9, 30; **26**:5, 36, 71, 73; **27**:34, 36, 47, 55, 57, 61; **28**:2, 7, 10; Mk **1**:38; **2**:2, 6, 15; **3**:1; **4**:36; **5**:15, 22, 25; **6**:1, 5, 10, 33, 55; **7**:32; **9**:2, 4; **11**:2, 5, 15; **12**:18, 20, 31, 32; **13**:8, 21; **14**:15, 54, 69; **15**:39, 41; **16**:7; Lk **1**:5, 61; **2**:5, 6, 7, 8, 25, 36; **4**:25²; **5**:3; **6**:6, 8, 17; **7**:2, 28; **8**:17, 32, 43; **9**:4, 14, 53; **10**:6, 9; **11**:26, 53; **12**:2, 18, 34, 52; **13**:1, 11, 14, 28², 30; **14**:2, 22; **15**:7, 10, 11, 13, 14; **16**:1, 19, 26; **17**:21, 23, 37²; **18**:2, 3; **19**:2, 30; **20**:26, 27, 29; **21**:11, 23, 25; **22**:12, 56; **23**:10, 33, 38, 39, 50; **24**:18, 33; Jn **1**:6, 35, 46, 47; **2**:1, 12; **3**:1, 23; **4**:6, 45, 46; **5**:2, 5, 14, 32; **6**:10, 22, 24, 64; **7**:1, 12, 18, 49; **8**:9, 44, 50; **10**:16; **11**:8, 9, 11, 15, 31, 39²; **12**:9, 20, 29, 41, 42; **20**:5, 6, 14; **21**:9; Ac **1**:18, 20; **2**:5; **4**:6, 12, 14², 34; **5**:22; **7**:12, 52; **8**:1, 5, 8; **9**:2, 7, 10, 33, 36; **10**:1, 18; **12**:18, 19; **13**:1, 4, 6; **14**:1, 3, 5, 8, 27, 28; **15**:33; **16**:12², 13, 26; **17**:1, 7, 10, 13, 17, 21; **18**:2, 23, 27; **19**:1, 2, 7, 8, 21, 23, 27, 32, 38, 39, 40; **20**:8, 13, 15, 22; **21**:1, 4, 5, 10, 12, 23, 24; **22**:5, 10, 12, 20, 25; **23**:3, 8², 9, 29; **24**:15, 18, 19; **25**:4, 5, 9, 14², 20; **27**:4, 6, 12, 37, 44; **28**:7, 12, 13, 14, 15, 21, 30; Ro **2**:8, 9; **3**:1², 10, 11, 12, 18, 22, 30; **4**:15²; **5**:13; **7**:21; **8**:1; **10**:4, 12; **11**:5; **13**:1, 9; **15**:23, 24, 25, 31; **1Co** **1**:10, 11; **3**:3; **5**:1; **6**:5; **7**:2; **8**:4, 5², 6²; **10**:17; **11**:18, 19; **12**:4, 5, 6, 8, 20, 25; **13**:8³; **14**:7, 10, 28; **15**:12, 13, 29, 34, 40², 44²; **16**:9²; **2Co** **2**:10, 13; **3**:17; **6**:15, 16; **8**:12, 13, 14; **9**:1; **12**:1, 7, 20; Gal **3**:28; **5**:23; Eph **4**:4, 14; **5**:3, 4; **6**:9; Php **3**:20; Col **3**:11, 25; **1Ti** **1**:3; **2**:5; **3**:10; **2Ti** **2**:20; **3**:1; **4**:8; Tit **1**:10; **3**:12; Heb **2**:6; **4**:9; **6**:13; **7**:11, 12², 23; **8**:4, 7; **9**:22; **10**:18; **12**:18; Jas **2**:3, 19; **3**:16; **4**:12, 13; **2Pe** **2**:1; **1Jn** **1**:5; **2**:10; **4**:18; **5**:7, 16, 17; **3Jn** **1**:14; Jude **1**:18; Rev **2**:14; **4**:1, 2, 3, 6; **6**:2, 5, 8, 12; **7**:9; **8**:1, 5, 7; **10**:6; **11**:1, 13, 15, 19; **12**:7; **14**:1, 11, 14; **16**:18; **17**:3; **18**:18; **19**:11; **21**:1, 4, 13, 25²; **22**:3, 5.

THESE (1120)

Ge **9**:19; **10**:5, 20, 29, 31, 32²; **14**:3; **15**:10; **18**:8; **19**:8; **21**:29, 30; **22**:23; **24**:28; **25**:4, 13, 16²; **26**:3, 4; **27**:36, 46²; **29**:13; **31**:43; **32**:17, 20; **33**:5, 8; **34**:21; **35**:26; **36**:5, 10, 12, 13, 15, 16, 17, 18, 19², 20, 21, 29, 30, 31, 40, 43; **37**:20; **38**:25²; **41**:35; **43**:16; **44**:1, 6, 46; **48**:15², 18, 22, 25; **48**:8, 16; **49**:26, 28, 29; **50**:16; Ex **1**:1; **4**:9; **6**:14², 15, 16, 19, 24, 25; **10**:1; **11**:8, 10; **12**:16, 24, 43; **17**:4; **18**:14, 18, 23; **19**:6; **20**:1; **21**:1, 11; **24**:8, 11; **25**:3, 39; **26**:24; **28**:4², 41; **29**:24,

33; **30**:25; **32**:4, 8, 9, 21, 22, 31; **33**:4, 12; **34**:27²; **35**:1; **36**:29; **38**:21; Lev **2**:8; **5**:5, 13; **6**:7, 9, 11, 14, 25; **7**:1, 11, 37; **8**:26, 27; **9**:20; **11**:2, 13, 22, 24, 29, 31, 36, 43, 46; **12**:7; **13**:59; **14**:2, 21, 32, 42, 54, 57; **15**:32; **16**:4; **18**:24, 26, 27, 29; **20**:23; **22**:22; **23**:2, 4, 37, 38; **25**:54; **26**:14, 23, 46; **27**:34; Nu **1**:5, 16, 17, 44; **2**:32; **3**:17, 18, 20, 21, 27, 33; **4**:8, 26; **5**:23; **7**:3, 5, 84, 88; **11**:11, 12, 13, 14; **13**:4, 16; **14**:11, 13, 14, 15, 16, 19, 27, 35, 37; **15**:13, 22, 39; **16**:14, 26, 28, 29, 30; **18**:28; **20**:13; **21**:2; **22**:6, 9, 17, 20, 28, 32, 33; **24**:10; **25**:2, 4; **26**:4, 7, 14, 18, 22, 25, 27, 30, 34, 35, 36, 37², 41, 42², 47, 50, 57, 58, 63; **27**:14; **28**:23, 31; **29**:6, 39; **30**:16; **32**:38; **34**:2, 15, 17, 19, 29; **35**:13, 15, 24, 29; **36**:13; Dt **1**:1; **2**:4, 7, 16; **3**:5, 8, 21; **4**:6, 30, 35, 42, 43, 45; **5**:22; **6**:1, 6, 24; **7**:12, 17; **8**:2, 4; **9**:4, 5; **10**:4; **11**:7, 18, 22, 23, 30; **12**:1, 28, 30; **14**:4, 12; **15**:5; **16**:12, 22; **17**:19; **18**:12²; **19**:5, 9, 11; **20**:14; **25**:16; **26**:16; **27**:1, 4, 8, 12, 13; **28**:2, 15, 45; **29**:1; **30**:1, 7; **31**:1, 3, 16, 17, 28; **32**:45; **33**:16; Jos **1**:2, 6; **4**:6, 7, 21; **5**:7; **8**:4; **9**:1, 13; **10**:24², 42; **11**:5, 10, 12, 14, 18; **12**:1, 7; **13**:23, 28; **14**:11; **15**:12; **17**:2; **12**:18; **20**:19; **8**, 16, 23, 31, 39, 48, 51; **20**:4, 9; **21**:8, 10, 16, 26, 42²; **23**:3, 7, 12, 13; **24**:26, 29; Jdg **2**:4, 16; **3**:1; **9**:25, 38; **13**:23; **18**:2, 14, 18; **20**:16; Ru **3**:17; **4**:4; **1Sa** **2**:23; **4**:8; **6**:17; **10**:7, 9; **11**:4, 12; **12**:3; **15**:9; **16**:10, 11; **17**:17, 18, 39; **18**:23, 26; **21**:12; **23**:2; **24**:7; **25**:10, 15, 37; **27**:1, 8; **29**:3; **31**:4; **2Sa** **3**:5, 39; **5**:14; **6**:22; **7**:28; **8**:11; **14**:3; **19**:16²; **18**:21; **22**:23; **23**:1, 8; **24**:17; **1Ki** **4**:2, 8, 21; **7**:9, 45, 47; **8**:8, 54, 59; **9**:10, 13, 20, 21; **10**:7; **12**:6, 7, 9, 10, 27; **14**:27; **18**:36, 37; **21**:27; **22**:11, 17, 23; **2Ki** **1**:13; **4**:38; **6**:18, 20; **7**:13; **10**:7, 9; **16**:15; **17**:41; **18**:27, 35; **19**:17; **21**:11; **22**:5, 12; **23**:16; **24**:3; **1Ch** **1**:23, 29, 31, 33, 43, 54; **2**:1, 3, 18, 23, 33, 50, 53, 55; **3**:1, 4, 5², 9; **4**:2, 3, 4, 6, 12, 18, 22, 31, 33², 42; **5**:14, 17, 24; **6**:17, 19, 31, 50, 54, 60, 64; **7**:8, 11, 17, 29, 33, 40; **8**:6, 10, 28, 38², 40; **9**:9, 18, 34, 44²; **10**:4; **11**:10, 19; **12**:1, 14, 20, 23, 38; **14**:4; **11**:10; **2Ch** **3**:13; **4**:18; **5**:9; **8**:7, 8, 18; **10**:6, 7, 9; **11**:10; **12**:10; **14**:7, 8, 14; **15**:8; **17**:19; **18**:10; **19**:9; **20**:36; **21**:2; **25**:7, 9; **29**:12, 21; **31**:12, 32; **32**:6, 14; **34**:9, 10, 11, 14, 17, 22; **35**:7; **36**:16², 18, 24; **38**:4, 9, 11; **39**:1, 11; **43**:10; **51**:19, 27, 61; La **5**:17; Eze **5**:4; **7**:20; **10**:15, 20; **11**:2; **14**:3, 14, 16, 18; **16**:5, 30, 43, 51; **17**:12, 18; **18**:10, 13; **22**:28; **23**:27; **24**:4, 19; **32**:27; **35**:10; **36**:20, 22; **37**:3, 4, 5, 9; **40**:46; **42**:11, 14; **43**:11, 13, 18, 27; **45**:15; **46**:24; **47**:13; **48**:1, 16, 21, 29, 30; Da **1**:2, 6, 17; **2**:28; **3**:13, 21, 23; **4**:10; **5**:7, 26; **6**:5, 11; **7**:16; **12**:6, 7; Hos **8**:11; **13**:2; **14**:9; Am **9**:12; Mic **2**:6; Hag **1**:2; **2**:13; Zec **1**:9, 12, 19², 21³; **3**:7; **4**:4, 5, 10, 11, 12, 13, 14; **6**:4, 5; **7**:7; **8**:9, 12, 16; **13**:6; Mal **4**:3; Mt **3**:9; **4**:3; **5**:19²; **6**:29, 32, 33; **7**:24, 26, 28; **10**:2, 5, 42; **11**:25; **12**:7; **13**:34, 51, 53, 54, 56; **15**:8, 18, 20, 32; **18**:6, 10, 14; **19**:1, 14, 20; **20**:12, 21, 23; **21**:16, 23, 24, 27; **22**:40; **24**:2, 8, 33, 34; **25**:40, 45; **26**:1, 62; Mk **2**:8; **3**:6; **2**:8; **7**:6, 23; **8**:2; **9**:37, 42; **10**:14, 20, 40; **11**:28, 29, 33; **12**:31; **13**:2, 4, 8, 29, 30; **14**:60; **15**:41; **16**:13, 17; Lk **1**:25, 65; **2**:19, 51; **3**:8; **5**:22; **7**:18; **8**:3; **10**:21, 36; **11**:27, 45; **12**:27, 31; **13**:2; **15**:29; **17**:2; **18**:16, 21; **20**:2, 8; **21**:4, 7, 9, 28, 31, 32; **23**:31, 49; **24**:9, 15, 18, 26, 48; Jn **2**:16; **3**:10; **5**:16, 20, 39; **6**:5; **7**:4; **8**:20; **10**:19, 21, 32, 33; **12**:16³, 37; **13**:17; **18**:8; **19**:36; **20**:18, 31; **21**:15, 24; Ac **1**:3, 22, 24; **2**:7, 15; **3**:24; **4**:13, 16, 17; **7**:12, 50; **10**:44, 47; **11**:12; **13**:34, 42; **14**:15; **15**:17; **16**:17, 20; **17**:6; **19**:36, 37; **20**:5, 34; **21**:24²; **22**:5, 19; **24**:8, 9, 15, 20; **25**:9, 11, 20; **26**:12, 26, 29; **27**:31; **28**:15; Ro **1**:32; **8**:37; **10**:5; **11**:24; **12**:4; **14**:22; **15**:23; **1Co** **4**:6, 19; **9**:15; **10**:6, 11; **12**:11; **13**:13²; **14**:26; **16**:16; **2Co** **7**:1; **8**:24; **12**:7; **13**:10; Gal **3**:12; **4**:24; Eph **5**:3; Php **4**:3;

Col **2**:17, 22; **3**:6, 7, 8, 14; **4**:11; **1Th** **3**:3; **4**:18; **2Th** **2**:5; **1Ti** **1**:4, 6, 19; **3**:14; **4**:6, 11, 15; **5**:4, 7, 21; **6**:2; **2Ti** **2**:14; **3**:8; Tit **2**:15; **3**:8², 9; Heb **1**:2; **4**:4; **7**:13; **9**:5, 23²; **10**:18; **11**:13, 39; **1Pe** **1**:7, 12, 20; **2Pe** **1**:4, 8, 10, 12, 15; **2**:3, 10, 12, 17; **3**:6, 16; **1Jn** **2**:26; **5**:13; Jude **1**:6, 8, 10², 12, 14, 16, 19; Rev **2**:1, 8, 12, 18; **3**:1, 7, 14; **4**:5; **7**:13, 14; **9**:20; **11**:4, 6, 10; **14**:4; **16**:5, 9; **18**:15; **19**:9, 20; **21**:5; **22**:6, 8, 20.

THEY (6563)

Ge **1**:29; **2**:4, 24, 25; **3**:7³, 8; **4**:8; **5**:2; **6**:2², 4; **7**:14, 17, 19; **8**:17; **9**:2, 23²; **10**:30; **11**:2, 3², 4, 6², 7, 8, 31³; **12**:5⁴, 12², 15, 20; **13**:6²; **14**:4², 7², 11, 12; **15**:13, 14²; **16**:10; **17**:13; **18**:5, 8, 9, 16, 21; **19**:2, 3², 4, 5, 8, 9³, 11², 17, 33, 35; **20**:8, 11, 17; **22**:9, 19; **24**:19, 41, 52, 54, 57, 58, 59, 60; **25**:18, 25; **26**:20, 21², 28, 30, 31, 32², 35; **29**:3, 4, 5, 6, 8, 20; **30**:32, 38², 39², 41; **31**:43, 46², 54²; **32**:6, 18²; **33**:4, 5, 7, 13; **34**:5, 7², 13, 14, 19, 21², 22, 23, 26, 28, 29, 30, 31; **35**:4², 5, 16², **36**:7, 16, 17, 43; **37**:4, 5, 8, 16, 17, 18², 19, 23, 24, 25³, 31, 32; **38**:21; **40**:4, 6, 8²; **41**:2, 18, 21³, 27, 35; **42**:6, 7, 8, 10, 20, 21, 23, 26, 27, 28², 32, 33, 34; **44**:1, 4, 7, 13²; **45**:3, 4, 24, 25, 26, 27; **46**:6², 28, 30; **48**:6², 9, 16²; **49**:6², 23; **50**:10², 11, 13, 15, 16, 17, 18, 26; Ex **1**:10, 11², 12², 14, 17, 22; **2**:16, 19; **3**:13; **4**:1, 5, 8², 9, 31³; **5**:1, 3, 8², 9², 20²; **6**:4, 9, 27; **7**:7, 16, 19, 24; **8**:1, 3, 7, 11, 14, 17, 18, 20, 21, 26; **9**:1, 10, 13, 19, 32; **10**:3, 5², 6², 7, 14, 15², 23; **12**:4, 7², 8, 33, 36³, 39³; **13**:17², 19; **14**:2, 3², 4, 7, 12, 18³, 19, 20², 26², 28; **15**:5, 15, 16, 17, 18, 20, 22², 23², 27; **16**:1, 4, 5³, 10, 15², 17, 18, 20, 22, 24, 27, 32, 35²; **17**:1, 2, 3², 4, 7, 12; **18**:7, 8, 13, 16, 19, 24; **19**:1, 3, 7, 11, 14, 17, 18, 20, 21, 26; **20**:18², 21³5; **22**:5, 7, 23; **23**:11, 33; **24**:3, 5, 7, 11²; **25**:15, 37; **26**:24; **27**:7; **28**:1, 3, 4³, 30, 38, 41, 43²; **29**:1, 29, 33², 46; **30**:20⁴, 21³, 29, 30; **31**:10, 11; **32**:1, 4², 6, 8², 9, 15, 20, 23, 24, 31, 33; **33**:4, 10; **34**:12, 15², 16, 30, 35; **35**:19, 22, 28; **36**:3, 6, 7, 10, 11, 12, 13, 14, 16, 17, 18, 19, 20, 22, 23, 25, 27, 31, 33, 34², 35, 36², 37, 38²; **37**:10, 11, 12, 13, 16, 17, 23, 24, 26, 27, 28; **38**:1, 2², 3, 4, 5, 6, 7³, 8, 9, 28, 30; **39**:1², 2, 3, 4, 6, 7, 8², 10, 13, 15, 16, 17, 19, 20, 21, 22, 24, 25, 27, 30, 31, 33, 34, 40; **40**:15, 32², 36, 37; Lev **2**:12; **4**:13, 14², 20; **6**:16; **7**:7, 35, 36; **9**:5, 13, 20, 23²; **10**:1, 2, 5, 7, 14, 19; **11**:8, 13, 28, 31, 35; **14**:7, 42; **15**:7², 8², 10, 11², 12², 18²; **16**:17; **17**:5², 7², 8³, 11, 12²; **18**:3, 24, 27, 30; **19**:7²; **20**:4, 12, 23²; **22**:2, 3, 4, 6²; **24**:6, 8³, 9, 24²; **25**:6, 18²; **26**:7, 26:9, 10, 19, 61, 62², 63, 64, 65; **27**:1, 21; **29**:6; **31**:7, 8, 10, 16, 32:2, 5, 9², 11, 12, 16, 30², 38², 40; **33**:1, 3, 6, 7, 8³, 9², 10, 10, 11, 12, 13, 14, 15, 16, 17, 18, 19, 20, 21, 22, 23, 24, 25, 26, 27, 28, 29, 30, 31, 32, 33, 34, 45, 46, 47, 48, 49, 55; **35**:3, 5, 12; **36**:2², 3, 4, 6³, 12; Dt **1**:24, 25, 28, 39², 44; **2**:4, 11, 12, 13, 14, 14²; **3**:20; **4**:10², 5, 7, 8, 9, 11, 12², 19³, 20, 24, 25, 25², 26³, 26², 27, 34; **5**:1, 28, 29²; **6**:1, 25; **7**:4, 16, 17, 22, 23, 24, 25³; **8**:1; **9**:12, 13, 14; **10**:10, 11; **11**:4, 6, 10, 11, 12, 13, 14, 15², 16, 17, 18², 19, 35², 39, 40², 44; **15**:25²; **16**:3; **17**:9, 10, 20, 33, 33³, 38, 41, 45; **17**:9; **18**:3², 17; **19**:35, 39, 40², 44; **15**:25²; **16**:3; **17**:9, 10, 20, 33, 33³, 38, 41, 45; **18**:6, 7, 20, 21³, 22², 23³, 25²; **19**:4, 11, 17², 15², 12², 13²; **2Sa** **1**:12², 23⁴; **2**:3, 4, 15, 16, 24, 25, 28², 29, 32; **3**:21, 26, 32, 35; **4**:2, 5, 6², 7⁴, 8, 12³; **5**:3, 6, 8, 11; **6**:13, 6, 17; **7**:10²; **9**:2; **10**:5, 6², 13, 14, 13**30, 32; **14**:6, 7²; **15**:11, 17, 24, 30; **16**:22; **17**:8, 17², 18, 20³, 21, 28, 29; **18**:3², 17; **19**:3, 8, 14², 17, 18; **20**:3, 7, 8, 15², 18, 22; **21**:5, 9, 12, 14, 22; **22**:8, 19, 38, 39², 42, 45², 46; **23**:7³, 9; **24**:4, 5, 6, 7³, 23; **1Ki** **1**:1, 3, 7, 23, 25, 32, 39, 41, 44, 45, 53; **2**:4², 7; **3**:22, 24, 28²; **4**:20³, 27, 28; **5**:14, 17; **6**:10; **7**:5, 28, 37; **8**:4, 5, 8, 9, 30, 33³, 35, 40², 44, 46, 47², 48, 50, 51, 52, 65, 66; **9**:9, 13, 22, 23, 28²; **10**:11; **29**:7²; **11**:2², 16, 18², 24, 33, 41; **12**:3, 7, 12, 16, 20, 24, 27²; **13**:11, 13, 20, 25, 27, 30; **14**:15, 18, 22², 23, 28, 29; **15**:7, 22, 23, 31; **16**:5, 14, 16, 20, 26, 27; **18**:6², 10, 26³, 28, 29, 30, 34², 39, 40; **19**:10, 14, 21; **20**:6, 9, 12, 16, 18², 23², 25, 27, 29, 32; **21**:12, 13, 14; **22**:6, 11, 12, 32², 37, 38, 39, 45, 48²; **2Ki** **1**:6, 8, 18; **2**:2, 4, 9, 11, 15, 16, 17², 18, 20, 23; **3**:22, 23, 24, 25², 26, 27; **4**:5, 39, 40³, 43, 44; **5**:23, 24; **6**:4, 14, 20⁴, 22, 23²; **7**:3, 4², 5², 6, 7², 8³, 12³, 13², 21, 27, 33², 36; **10**:4, 7, 8, 13, 14, 20, 21, 24, 25, 26, 27, 34; **11**:12; **12**:8², 9, 11, 15, 13³; **6³, 8, 12, 21²; **14**:15, 18, 19²; **15**:6, 16, 21, 31, 36; **16**:17², 9, 10, 11², 14, 15³, 16³, 17³, 17⁹, 21, 29, 23, 24, 25², 29, 32³, 33⁴, 40, 41; **18**:12²; **17**, 18, 34; **19**:3, 18², 26, 37; **20**:7, 14², 15², 18, 20; **21**:8, 9, 14, 15, 16, 17, 24, 25; **22**:7²; 13, 17, 19, 20; **23**:9, 11, 18, 28; **24**:5; **25**:4, 7², 12, 13, 14, 15², 16², 17, 18, 19, 21, 23, 24, 25³, 29, 32²; 33³, 34², 40, 41; **18**:12², 17, 18, 34; **19**:3, 18², 26, 37; **20**:7, 14², 15², 18, 20; **21**:8, 9, 14, 15, 16, 17, 24, 25; **22**:7²; 13, 17, 19, 20; **23**:9, 11, 18, 28; **24**:5; **25**:4, 7², 12, 13, 14, 15², 16², 17, 18, 19, 21, 23, 24, 25³, 29, 32²; **1Ch** **4**:23²; 28, 33, 39, 40, 41²; 43²; **5**:8, 9, 10², 16, 19, 20³, 21², 22, 23, 24, 25, 26; **6**:32², 54, 55, 60, 65, 67, 71, 72, 74, 76, 77, 78, 80; **7**:4², 21; **8**:28, 32, 40; **9**:13, 22, 23, 27³, 28³, 33, 34, 38; **10**:2, 3, 7, 8, 9, 10, 12; **11**:3, 10, 14², 19; **12**:1, 2², 8², 15², 19, 21², 38; **13**:7, 9; **14**:8, 16; **16**:1², 5, 19, 20, 33; **17**:9²; **18**:2; **19**:5, 6, 7, 11, 14, 15, 16², 17, 18, 19²; **20**:8; **21**:3, 17; **23**:11, 24, 29, 30²; **31**; **24**:2, 4, 5, 19, 31; **25**:5, 7; **26**:6, 8, 22, 27; **29**:7, 9, 20², 22²; **2Ch** **1**:17²; **2**:17; **3**:13; **4**:21; **5**:5, 6, 9, 10, 12, 13; **6**:16, 21, 24², 26, 31², 34, 36, 37², 38², 7³3², 9²; **8**:9, 10, 15, 18; **9**:6, 10, 29, 30; **3**, 7², 16; **11**:4, 17; **12**:2², 7², 8², 11, 15; **13**:11², 14², 18; **14**:7, 10, 13², 14², 15²; **15**:4, 9, 10, 11, 14, 15²; **16**:4, 6, 14³; **17**:9²; 10; **18**:5, 10, 11, 14², 32²; **19**:8; **20**:4, 8, 10², 11, 16, 20², 21, 22², 23³, 25², 26, 29; **21**:17, 19; **22**:4, 6, 9²; **23**:2², 6², 11², 15², 17, 20; **24**:9, 11², 13, 14², 18, 19²; 20, 22², 25²; 25², 29; **26**:18, 20², 28:8², 13, 15⁴, 18, 23²; **29**:6², 7², 15², 16², 17³, 18, 19, 21, 22³, 23, 30; **30**:3, 5, 14, 15, 16, 18, 22, 23; **31**:1², 4, 5, 6, 7, 8, 12, 16, 17, 18²; **32**:3, 4², 18, 19²; **33**:8, 9, 10, 25; **34**:9, 10, 11, 14, 17, 21, 25, 28, 33; **35**:12², 13, 14, 16, 21, 25; **36**:16, 19², 20; Ezr **2**:1, 59, 62, 65, 66, 68, 69; **3**:3, 4, 5, 6, 7², 11, 12; **4**:2, 5, 6, 11, 12, 23; **5**:4, 5, 7, 11; **6**:1, 5, 10, 14, 17, 18, 22; **8**:17, 18, 30; **9**:2, 11, 10; **2**:7, 10, 18; **3**:1², 3, 6, 8, 13²; **4**:2³, 3, 5, 7, 8, 11, 12, 22; **5**:8²; 12², 13; **6**:2, 4, 9, 10, 13, 14, 16, 19; **7**:6, 61, 64, 67; **8**:1, 6, 8, 9, 12, 14, 15, 16, 19; **9**:2², 16, 17²; **10**:38; **11**:30, 32; **12**:26, 27, 30, 37, 39, 43, 44, 45, 47; **13**:2, 3, 15, 21, 29; Est **1**:17; **2**:12, 14; **5**:6; **6**:14; **7**:2, 8, 10; **8**:7, 9; **9**:5², 7, 10, 12, 14; **10**:2; Job **1**:4, 15, 17, 19; **2**:11, 12⁴, 13²; **3**:18, 22; **4**:9², 20², 21;

5:14; 6:18, 20³; 7:6; 8:10², 12; 9:25, 26; 11:8²; 12:7², 15, 25; 14:21; 15:24, 35; 16:10; 17:12; 19:12, 15, 18, 23, 24; 21:8, 11, 12², 13, 14, 18, 26; 22:16, 17; 24:2², 3, 4, 6, 7², 8, 10², 11², 16², 17, 18, 21, 22², 24⁴; 29:22, 23, 24; 30:1, 3, 4, 5², 6, 7, 8, 10², 11, 12², 13², 14²; 31:13; 32:3, 4, 15, 16²; 33:15; 34:19, 20², 23, 25, 27, 28; 35:9; 36:9², 11², 12², 13, 14; 37:8, 12; 38:35, 40; 39:2², 3, 4, 13, 16; 40:12; 41:6, 17², 23, 25; 42:11; Ps 1:4; 2:3; 5:9, 10; 6:7, 10; 7:2; 9:3, 15², 20; 10:10²; 11:2; 14:1, 3, 5; 16:3; 17:10, 11², 12, 14; 18:7, 18, 37, 38², 41, 44², 45²; 19:2², 10², 13; 20:8; 21:11²; 22:4, 5², 7, 16, 18, 26, 31; 23:4; 25:3, 6, 19; 27:2; 28:4, 5; 31:13, 18; 32:6, 9; 33:15; 35:5, 7, 8², 11, 12, 13, 15², 16², 20, 21, 27; 36:8; 37:2², 7, 10, 19², 20, 26, 28, 40; 38:12; 40:5, 12; 41:7; 44:3; 45:15²; 48:4, 5²; 49:11, 14; 52:6; 53:1, 3, 5; 55:3, 10, 21; 56:1, 5², 6³, 8; 57:6³; 58:3, 7, 8, 9, 10², 12; 59:3, 4, 6, 7³, 12, 13, 14, 15; 62:4⁴, 9²; 63:9², 10; 64:3, 4², 5³, 6, 7, 9; 65:13; 66:4², 6; 68:3; 69:21, 23, 26, 28; 71:11; 72:17; 73:4, 5², 6, 8², 11, 12, 19; 74:4, 5, 6, 7², 8²; 76:5²; 78:6, 7, 8, 10, 11, 17, 18², 19, 22, 25, 29³, 30², 32², 34², 35, 36, 37, 39, 40, 41², 42, 44, 53, 56², 57, 58²; 79:1², 3, 7, 12; 82:5³; 83:2², 4, 5², 17²; 84:4, 6², 7; 86:9; 87:7²; 88:17²; 89:16², 31, 51; 90:5, 10; 91:12; 92:7², 12, 13, 14²; 94:2, 4, 5², 6², 7, 11, 21; 95:9, 10², 11; 96:13; 99:6, 7; 101:3, 6; 102:26³; 104:7, 8², 9², 11, 12, 22², 28², 29², 30, 32², 33²; 105:12, 13, 18, 27, 28, 35, 38, 40, 44, 45; 106:3, 7³, 12, 13, 14²; 15, 16, 19, 20, 21, 24², 25, 28, 29³, 32, 33, 34, 35, 36, 37, 38², 39³, 43²; 107:4, 5, 6, 7, 11, 12, 13, 18, 19, 23, 24, 26, 27², 28, 30, 36², 37, 39; 109:2², 4, 5, 16; 111:2, 8; 115:5², 6², 7³; 118:11, 12², 119:1, 2, 3², 24, 74, 87, 98, 111, 138, 150, 155, 158, 165; 120:7; 124:3; 127:5²; 129:1, 2, 6; 135:16², 17; 137:3, 7; 138:4, 5; 139:18, 20; 140:3, 5, 8, 10; 141:7, 9; 142:6; 144:5; 145:4, 5, 6, 7, 11; 146:4; 147:9, 20; 148:5; Pr 1:9, 11, 16, 18, 28², 29, 30, 31; 3:2, 22; 4:16⁴, 17, 19, 22; 6:22³; 7:5; 8:9; 9:18; 15:22; 16:5, 13; 18:8, 11; 19:7; 21:7, 22; 22:22; 23:5², 35²; 24:22; 26:22; 30:15, 24, 25, 26, 27; 31:5; Ecc 1:7; 3:11, 12, 18²; 4:1², 9, 11; 5:1, 11; 8:10; 9:1, 3², 5², 6; 10:13, 11, 8; 12:3; SS 1:4; 3:3; 5:7⁴; 6:5; Isa 1:2, 4², 11, 14, 18³, 23²; 2:4²; 6:8, 12, 20, 21; 3:9³, 10, 11, 12; 5:11, 12², 24, 26, 29³, 30; 6:2³, 3, 10, 13; 7:1, 19, 22, 25; 8:12, 15², 20², 21³, 22²; 9:3, 13, 20²; 10:28³, 29, 32², 11:9, 14³, 16; 13:5, 8², 18²; 14:2, 7, 10², 16²; 27:10², 11; 28:7³, 12, 13; 29:23³; 30:4, 10; 31:8; 33:12; 34:17; 35:2, 9, 10; 36:19; 37:3, 19², 27, 38; 38:19; 39:3², 4², 7; 40:15², 17, 24⁴, 31³; 41:5, 25, 27, 29; 42:9, 16, 22², 24², 25³; 43:2, 9, 14, 17, 21; 44:4, 9², 11, 18⁴, 26; 45:14³, 16, 24; 46:2², 6², 7²; 47:9, 14, 15; 48:3, 5, 7, 13, 21; 49:9, 10, 12, 21, 22, 23², 26; 50:9; 51:11, 14², 20²; 52:6, 8², 15⁴; 56:10⁵, 11⁴; 57:2², 6², 12; 58:2⁴, 3; 59:4², 5, 6, 7², 8², 18, 19; 60:7, 11, 21²; 61:3, 4², 7², 9; 62:4, 6, 12; 63:8, 10, 13, 14, 19; 65:7, 17, 21², 22, 23², 24²; 66:2, 3, 4², 5, 6, 17, 18, 19, 20², 24²; Jer 1:15, 19; 2:5², 6, 11, 13, 15², 24, 26, 27⁴, 28, 30; 3:17², 18, 21; 4:2, 17, 22², 24, 30; 5:2², 3², 4², 5², 7, 8, 12², 13, 17², 22³, 23, 24, 27, 28²; 6:3, 10², 14², 15⁵, 19, 23⁵, 28³, 30; 7:17, 18, 19², 24³, 26², 27², 30, 31, 32; 8:2⁴, 4², 5², 6, 9³, 11², 12⁶, 16, 17, 19; 9:2, 3⁴, 5², 6, 10, 13², 14², 16², 18, 19; 12:2³, 5, 6³, 10, 13², 16³; 13:11, 12; 14:2², 3³, 10², 12², 14, 15, 16, 18; 15:2², 7, 16, 20²; 16:4³, 6, 10, 11, 15², 16², 17, 18, 20, 21; 17:11, 13, 15, 23², 25; 18:12, 15², 18, 20, 22; 19:4⁴, 5, 9, 11, 13, 15; 20:5, 11; 21:6, 11²; 22:4, 5³, 7, 16, 18, 26, 31; 23:3, 4, 10, 17, 24³, 25³, 26, 29²; 37⁴, 38², 39², 40², 42, 49; 21:7, 12; 22:7², 10, 18, 25, 26³, 27, 28, 29, 31; 23:3, 4, 10, 17, 24³, 25³, 26, 29², 37⁴, 38², 39², 40², 42, 44², 45², 47; 24:7; 25:3, 4², 11, 13, 14², 17; 26:4, 6, 10, 12², 16, 17; 27:5², 6², 10, 11², 12, 13, 15, 16, 17, 19, 21, 22, 24, 30², 31², 32²; 28:7, 8, 13, 22, 23, 24, 25², 26³; 29:7², 9, 13, 14, 16, 21; 30:6, 7, 8, 11, 19, 25, 26; 31:14², 16, 17; 32:12², 3², 4², 5, 6, 7, 12, 13², 14², 15, 16³; 8:4², 5, 6, 8, 11, 12², 14, 15³, 16, 17, 25², 26³, 27; 34:18, 23, 26, 34², 36³; 35:12, 15; 36:3, 5², 8, 11, 12, 17, 19², 20², 21, 35, 38; 37:9, 10, 11, 17, 19, 21, 22, 23², 24², 25², 27; 38:8, 17, 23; 39:6, 9, 10³, 14, 15, 16, 18, 23², 26³, 28; 40:18, 24, 48; 41:19; 42:6, 11, 13, 14⁵; 43:7, 8², 10, 11³, 26²; 44:11², 12², 13², 15, 16², 17³, 18⁴, 20²; 22², 23, 24², 29; 46:10²; 47:11, 12, 22; 48:14, 16, 22², 23, 24², 29; Da 1:5², 15, 16, 19; 2:2, 7, 11, 38; 3:3, 7, 9, 12, 14, 24, 27, 28; 4:7; 5:3, 4², 8, 15; 6:4², 12, 13, 16, 22, 24; 7:22; 8:25; 10:7; 11:6, 31, 33, 34², 35; Hos 1:10, 11; 2:4, 8, 21, 22, 23; 3:1, 5; 4:2, 7², 8, 10³, 12², 13, 14², 18; 5:4, 6², 7², 15³; 6:7², 9; 7:1, 2², 3, 4, 6, 7, 12, 13³, 14², 15, 16³; 8:4³, 5, 6, 7, 9, 10², 12, 13³; 9:3, 4, 6, 9³, 10, 11, 16²; 10:2, 3, 4, 8; 11:2³, 3, 5², 7, 10, 11; 12:8, 11; 13:2³, 3, 6⁴, 16²; 14:3, 7; Joel 1:18; 2:4², 5, 7³, 8², 9⁴, 17; 3:2, 3³, 8, 19; Am 2:4², 6, 7, 8², 13², 16²; 4:7³; 5:4², 5, 7, 10³, 11²; 6:2, 7², 8; 7:1², 9, 17, 19³; 8:4, 7², 8², 10; 9:3, 4; Ob 1:5³, 16², 18, 19; Jnh 1:5, 7, 8, 10², 11, 13, 14, 15, 16; 3:5, 10²; Mic 1:7, 16; 2:1, 2², 4, 13; 3:4², 5², 7, 11; 4:3², 11, 12²; 5:1, 4, 6; 7:3², 16, 17³; Na 1:9, 10², 12²; 15; 2:3, 4², 5, 8, 11; 3:12, 13, 16², 17; Hab 1:7², 8, 9, 10³, 11; 2:7, 15; Zep 1:13², 17²; 2:7², 10; 3:4, 7², 13², 16, 18, 19; Hag 1:14²; 2:14²; Zec 1:4, 5, 6, 9, 10, 11, 15; 3:5; 4:10; 5:9², 10; 6:7²; 7:11², 12, 13², 14²; 8:8; 9:2, 15³, 16, 17; 10:2², 5², 6, 8, 9³, 11, 12; 11:6, 13², 12; 6, 10³; 13:2, 9³; 14:12, 13, 17, 18; Mal 1:4²; 2:15; 3:17; 4:3; Mt 1:18, 23; 2:5, 9³, 10², 11³, 12, 13, 18; 3:6; 4:6, 18², 20, 21, 22; 5:4², 5, 6, 7, 8, 9, 12, 15, 16; 6:2, 5², 7², 14, 16³, 26², 28; 7:6, 15²; 8:28, 29, 32, 34²; 9:8², 11, 15, 17², 24, 28; 10:17, 19; 11:16, 18, 19, 20, 21; 12:2, 10, 14, 24, 27, 31, 34, 46, 49; 13:6², 13², 15², 16², 41, 42, 48, 51, 54²; 57; 14:5, 12, 15, 16, 17, 20, 26², 32, 34², 35; 15:2², 9, 12, 14, 31², 32²; 34, 36, 37; 16:5, 7, 12, 14, 28; 17:6, 9, 11, 16, 17², 19³; 18:7, 31; 19:3, 6, 7, 12, 25; 20:5, 7, 10, 11², 12, 18, 22, 23, 24, 30², 31, 33, 34; 21:1², 15, 16, 20², 23, 25, 26, 27, 31, 35, 37, 38, 39, 41, 45, 46²; 22:3, 5, 10, 16, 19², 21, 22², 23, 24, 30, 33, 42; 23:3², 4, 6, 7, 25; 24:3, 30, 31, 39; 25:5, 9, 10, 11², 12, 18, 22, 23, 24, 30²; 31, 33, 34; 21:1², 5, 16, 20², 23, 25, 26, 27, 31, 35, 37, 38, 39, 41, 45, 46²; 26:4², 6², 8²; 15, 21, 22, 26, 30², 59, 60, 66, 67; 27:2, 4, 7, 9, 10, 13, 16, 18, 21, 22, 23, 28, 29², 30, 31³, 32², 33, 34, 35²; 36, 37, 42, 47, 53²; 54, 55, 63, 66; 28:4, 9, 10, 12, 15, 17²; Mk 1:5, 16, 18, 20, 21, 27, 29², 30, 34, 37²; 2:4², 8, 12, 16, 19², 20, 23, 24; 3:2, 4, 6, 8, 11, 13, 14, 21², 30, 31, 32; 4:6², 7, 12², 15, 17³, 33, 36, 41; 5:1, 15³, 35, 38, 40, 42², 49³; 50, 51, 53²; 54, 55², 56²; 7:3, 4², 7, 32, 36, 37; 8:1, 2, 3, 5, 6, 8², 15, 21, 22, 26, 30²; 59, 60, 66, 67; 9:1, 2, 6, 8², 9, 7²; 46, 47², 50, 51, 52, 53²; 54, 55², 56²; 7:3, 4², 7, 32, 36, 37; 8:1, 2, 3, 5, 6, 8², 15, 21, 22, 26, 30², 31, 33, 34, 37², 42², 49³, 50, 51, 53²; 54, 55², 56²; 10:4, 8, 10, 32, 33, 35, 37, 39, 40, 41, 46, 49; 11:1, 4², 6, 7, 8, 12, 18, 19, 20², 21, 23, 24, 28, 29, 30, 31, 32, 33, 34²; 10:4, 8, 10, 32, 33, 35, 37, 39, 40, 41, 46, 49; 11:1, 4², 6, 7, 8, 12, 18, 19, 20, 21, 31, 33, 34²; 10:4, 8, 10, 32, 33, 35, 37, 39, 40, 41, 46, 49; 11:1, 4², 6, 7, 8, 12, 18, 19, 20, 22, 24, 28; 9:1, 2, 6, 8², 9², 11², 12⁶, 16, 17, 19, 20², 31, 33, 34, 34²; 10:4, 8, 10, 32, 33, 35, 37, 39, 40, 41, 46, 49; 11:1, 4², 6, 7, 8, 12, 18, 19, 20, 22, 24, 28; 12:3, 7, 8, 11, 14, 18², 20, 23, 24², 26, 29, 32, 50, 51, 55²; 64, 65; 15:1, 4, 13, 14, 17, 19², 20³, 21, 22, 23, 24², 25, 27, 31, 35; 16:1, 2, 3, 4², 5³, 6, 8², 11², 14, 17², 18⁴; Lk 1:2, 7², 22, 58, 59², 61, 62; 2:6, 9, 16, 17², 20², 39, 42, 43, 44², 45², 46, 48, 50; 3:12; 4:11, 22, 28, 29, 32, 36, 38, 41, 42²; 5:6², 7³, 9, 11, 19², 22, 26, 33, 35; 6:7, 8, 11², 22, 39; 7:4², 9, 19², 20, 29², 30, 31, 32, 39; 8:6, 10², 12², 13⁴, 14³, 19, 22, 23², 25², 26, 31, 33, 34, 35², 37, 40, 45; 9:6, 10², 14, 18, 21, 24, 28, 29², 34; 9:6, 10², 14, 18, 21, 24, 28, 29², 34; 14:4, 6, 14, 18; 15:24; 16:28, 29, 30, 31²; 17:1, 12, 14², 37; 18:1, 8, 15, 32, 34, 37, 43; 19:11, 15, 25, 33, 34, 35, 37, 40, 44²; 48; 20:2, 5, 6, 7, 10, 11, 12, 13, 14², 15, 16, 19², 20³, 21, 22, 23, 24², 25, 27, 31, 35; 16:1, 2, 3, 4², 5³, 6, 8², 17²; 18⁴; Lk 1:2, 7², 22, 58, 59², 61, 62; 21:7², 16, 24, 27, 30; 22:2, 5, 9, 13², 20, 23, 24², 25, 27, 31, 35, 49, 54, 55, 64, 65, 67, 70, 71; 23:2, 5, 11, 12, 18, 21, 23, 25, 33³, 35, 36, 48, 56²; 24:1, 2, 3, 4, 8², 9³, 11, 14, 15, 16, 17, 19, 20, 22, 23², 28, 32³, 36, 41, 42, 45, 52, 53; Jn 1:21, 22, 33², 36, 37², 41, 42, 45, 52, 53; Jn 1:21, 22, 33², 36, 37², 41, 42, 45, 52, 53;

THIS (3712)

Ge 2:4, 23, 24; 3:13, 14; 5:1; 6:9, 15; 7:1; 8:12; 9:12, 17; 10:1; 11:6, 10, 27; 12:7, 12; 13:10; 14:1, 13; 15:1, 4, 7, 18; 16:13; 17:4, 10, 21; 18:4, 10, 12; 19:7, 9, 13, 14, 19, 21; 20:5, 6, 10, 11, 13, 16; 21:6, 26, 30; 22:14; 24:5, 7, 8, 9, 13, 14, 43, 50, 58; 25:12, 19, 22, 26; 26:3, 7, 10, 11, 33; 27:46; 28:15, 16, 17², 20, 22; 29:25, 27, 33; 30:6, 20, 31, 43; 31:1, 13, 40, 41, 48, 51², 52⁴; 32:2, 5, 10, 32; 33:10; 34:4, 30; 35:12, 20; 36:1, 9, 24, 43; 37:2, 6, 9, 17, 19, 22², 32; 38:23, 28, 29; 39:9, 14, 17, 19; 40:12, 14, 17, 19; 41:24, 36, 38, 39; 40:12, 14; 41:24, 28, 33, 38; 42:15², 18, 21, 25, 28, 33; 43:6, 11, 29; 44:5², 7, 13, 15, 16³, 17², 18⁴; Lk 1:2, 7², 22, 58, 59², 61, 62; 2:6, 9, 16, 17², 20², 39, 42, 43, 44², 45², 46, 48, 50; 20:5, 6, 7, 10, 11², 12, 18, 22, 23, 24, 30², 31, 33, 34; 21:1², 15, 16, 20², 23, 25, 26, 27, 31, 35, 37, 38, 39, 41, 45, 46²; 20:3, 4, 8², 15, 21, 22, 26, 30²; 59, 60, 66, 67; 27:2, 4, 7², 12, 15, 17³, 33, 36, 41; 5:1, 11, 35; 6:2, 3, 12, 13, 30, 31, 32, 34, 35, 36, 37, 38², 40², 42, 49³, 50, 51², 53³; 7:3, 4, 8², 15, 21, 26², 30, 32, 36, 48, 49²; 12:1, 24², 27, 36, 53; 13:4, 33; 15:24; 16:28, 29, 30, 31²; 17:1, 12, 14², 37; 18:1, 8, 15, 32, 34, 37, 43; 19:11, 15, 25, 33, 34, 35, 37, 40, 44²; 20:2, 5, 6, 7, 10, 11, 12, 13, 14², 15², 16, 19², 20³, 21, 22, 23, 24², 25, 27, 31, 35; 21:3, 8, 48; Ex 1:18, 22; 2:6, 9, 12, 15; 3:3, 6, 12², 14, 15, 21; 4:5, 17, 22; 5:1, 6, 15, 22², 23; 6:9, 26; 7:17², 23; 8:1, 17, 19, 20, 22, 23, 24, 32; 9:1, 5, 13, 14, 16, 18, 27; 10:3, 6, 7, 17; 11:4; 12:2, 3, 11, 14, 17², 24², 26, 42², 43; 13:3, 5², 8, 9, 10, 14, 15, 19; 14:4; 15:1; 16:3², 4, 16, 22, 23, 32; 17:6, 7, 12; La 1:2, 6, 8, 11², 14², 19², 21²; 2:7, 8, 10, 12², 14², 15, 16, 20; 3:14, 23, 53, 63, 64; 4:8², 9, 14², 15², 19; Eze 1:8, 9², 12², 16, 17², 20, 21², 24², 25; 2:3, 5³, 6², 7²; 3:6, 7, 8, 9, 11, 15, 25, 26,

37, 38, 39; 2:3, 7, 8, 12, 22; 3:26; 4:23, 30, 35, 40, 42, 45²; 5:12, 23; 6:2, 9, 11, 12, 13, 14, 15, 17, 19³, 21², 22, 24, 25², 28, 30, 34, 42, 45, 49, 63; 7:25, 26, 30, 31, 52; 8:3, 6, 7, 10, 11, 12², 14, 15³, 16, 17, 25², 26³, 27; 9:10, 11, 12, 13, 16, 17, 18, 19, 22, 24², 26, 28, 34²; 10:4, 5³, 6, 10, 16, 27, 28, 39, 41; 11:8, 18², 22, 30; 12:10³, 15², 16², 19, 20³, 22, 25; 13:2, 3², 5², 6³, 14²; 27, 28², 29², 31, 45, 48, 50, 51; 14:24; 15:20⁴, 21², 22², 24³, 25; 16:2, 3², 18, 19; 17:3, 6², 7, 8³, 9, 11², 13, 14, 16, 19, 21, 22, 23, 25; 18:3, 5, 6, 7, 12, 18, 21, 28, 30, 40; 19:2, 3, 6, 15, 18, 23, 24², 29, 31, 33², 37², 42; 20:2², 9³, 17, 20, 23³; 21:3², 5, 6, 8², 12, 15; Ac 1:6², 10, 11, 12, 13³, 14, 19, 23, 24, 26; 2:1, 2, 3, 6, 7, 12, 13, 18, 37, 42, 45, 46²; 3:10²; 4:1, 2, 3², 7, 13⁴, 14², 15, 16², 18, 21², 24³, 28, 31, 32², 33²; 5:9, 11, 25, 27, 33, 39, 41, 59; 9:10, 11, 12, 13, 16, 17, 18, 19, 22, 24², 26, 28, 34²; 11:18²; 22, 30; 12:10, 15², 16², 19, 20³, 22, 25; 13:2, 3², 5², 6³, 14²; 27, 28², 29², 31, 45, 48, 50, 51; 14:1, 6, 7, 11, 12², 14, 18, 19, 20², 21, 22, 23, 24, 25², 26³; 15:3², 4³, 7, 14, 17, 19, 36; 16:3, 4², 16; 17:1², 5², 6², 7, 8, 9, 10, 11, 13, 18, 19², 20, 26², 32; 18:3, 13, 17, 19, 20², 23², 28; 19:2, 3, 5, 6, 32, 34; 20:18, 21, 37², 38²; 21:4, 6, 7², 8, 12, 15, 20, 23, 25, 27, 29, 30, 31³, 32, 40; 22:2², 9, 18, 22, 23, 24³; 23:9, 12, 14, 15; 24:2, 15, 27, 32; Ro 1:21², 22², 25, 28, 29³, 30², 31, 32²; 2:14², 15, 26²; 3:2, 12, 17²; 4:7², 17²; 9:7², 26, 32²; 10:1, 2, 3², 14⁴; 11:3², 10, 19, 23², 28², 31²; 14:4, 7, 9², 10, 14, 19, 20²; 25:3², 7, 14, 17, 18, 19, 27, 28²; 29, 30, 36, 38³, 39⁴, 40²; 28:2, 4, 6, 10, 11, 13, 22, 23, 24, 30, 36, 38, 39, 40³; 17:1², 5², 6², 7, 8, 9, 10, 11, 13, 18, 19², 20, 26², 32; 18:3, 13; 1Co 2:8²; 3:13²; 14²; 4:19; 7:9², 14, 29, 30², 36; 8:7²; 9:10, 25; 10:1, 2, 3, 4, 6, 33; 12:12, 19; 13:8²; 14:21, 23, 34, 35², 11:35; 16:4, 15, 17, 18; 2Co 1:20; 4:4; 6:16; 8:3², 4², 5, 14, 23; 10:4; 11:12, 22³, 23; 12:21; Gal 1:23, 24; 2:6, 7, 9³, 10, 12, 14; 4:17²; 5:12, 17; 6:12, 13²; Eph 4:18, 19; Php 1:17, 28; 3:21; 4:18; Col 2:2³, 22, 23; 3:21; 4:9, 11; 1Th 1:9²; 2:15, 16²; 5:3; 2Th 1:9; 2:10², 11; 3:11², 12; 1Ti 1:7⁴; 2:15; 3:9, 10; 4:3; 5:11, 12², 13³; 6:2², 19²; 2Ti 2:10, 18², 23, 26; 3:6, 9; 4:3, 4; Tit 1:11³, 13, 16²; 2:3, 4, 8, 10²; 3:13²; 14; Heb 1:11²; 12; 3:10, 11, 16², 18, 19; 4:2², 3; 6:6²; 8:5, 9, 10, 11; 9:10, 13; 10:2; 11:13⁵, 14, 15³, 16, 23², 29, 35, 37⁴, 38, 40; 12:10, 20, 25²; 13:17²; Jas 2:6, 7; 3:4²; 4:1; 1Pe 1:12²; 2:8³, 12²; 3:1, 2, 5, 14; 4:4²; 5, 6, 11, 14; 1Jn 2:19⁴; 4:1, 5; 3Jn 1:5, 6, 7; Jude 1:4, 7, 10², 11³, 12, 15, 16, 18; Rev 2:9, 22; 3:4², 9; 4:4, 6, 8, 10, 11; 5:8, 9, 10, 11, 12; 6:8, 9, 10, 11²; 16; 7:9, 10, 11, 13², 14², 15, 16²; 9:4, 5², 6, 7, 9, 10², 11, 19, 20, 21; 11:2, 3, 6, 7, 11, 12²; 12:8, 11²; 13:4; 14:3, 4³, 5, 13, 20; 15:2, 6; 16:4², 6², 9³, 11², 13, 14², 16, 21; 17:8, 10, 13, 14, 16², 18:9, 10, 14, 15, 18²; 19:3, 4; 20:4², 6, 8, 9, 10, 12; 21:3; 22:4, 5², 14.

THIS (3712)

Ge 2:4, 23, 24; 3:13, 14; 5:1; 6:9, 15; 7:1; 8:12; 9:12, 17; 10:1; 11:6, 10, 27; 12:7, 12; 13:10; 14:1, 13; 15:1, 4, 7, 18; 16:13; 17:4, 10, 21; 18:4, 10, 12; 19:7, 9, 13, 14, 19, 21; 20:5, 6, 10, 11, 13, 16; 21:6, 26, 30; 22:14; 24:5, 7, 8, 9, 13, 14, 43, 50, 58; 25:12, 19, 22, 26; 26:3, 7, 10, 11, 33; 27:46; 28:15, 16, 17², 20, 22; 29:25, 27, 33; 30:6, 20, 31, 43; 31:1, 13, 40, 41, 48, 51², 52⁴; 32:2, 5, 10, 32; 33:10; 34:4, 30; 35:12, 20; 36:1, 9, 24, 43; 37:2, 6, 9, 17, 19, 22², 32; 38:23, 28, 29; 39:9, 14, 17, 19; 40:12, 14, 18; 41:24, 36, 38, 39; 42:15², 18, 21, 25, 28, 33; 43:6, 11, 29; 44:5², 13, 15, 29; 45:9, 17, 19, 21, 23; 48:4, 15, 18, 20; 49:28; 50:17, 24, 25; Ex 1:18, 22; 2:6, 9, 12, 15; 3:3, 6, 12², 14, 15, 21; 4:5, 17, 22; 5:1, 6, 15, 22², 23; 6:9, 26; 7:17², 23; 8:1, 17, 19, 20, 22, 23, 24, 32; 9:1, 5, 13, 14, 16, 18, 27; 10:3, 6, 7, 17; 11:4; 12:2, 3, 11, 14, 17², 24², 26, 42², 43; 13:3, 5², 8, 9, 10, 14, 15, 19; 14:4; 15:1; 16:3², 4, 16, 22, 23, 32; 17:6; 14:18, 11, 14, 23; 19:3; 20:22; 21:31; 22:9, 21; 23:15; 24:8; 25:9, 15, 30; 26:17, 37; 27:21; 28:32, 43; 29:1, 9, 22², 28, 38, 42; 30:9, 10, 13, 21, 31, 37; 31:13; 32:1, 5, 13, 23, 24, 27, 29; 33:1, 12; 34:9, 18; 35:4; 36:6, 22; 39:23; Lev 2:2; 3:14, 17; 4:20², 21, 26, 31, 35; 5:13, 18; 6:7, 9, 20; 7:12,

35, 36; 8:5; 9:6; 10:3, 9, 15, 19, 20; 12:8; 13:31; 14:8, 31, 36, 53; 15:3, 15, 30; 16:3, 16, 29, 30, 34; 17:2, 5, 7; 18:24; 19:25; 21:24; 22:24; 23:14², 18, 21, 41²; 24:3, 8; 25:13; 26:16, 18, 27, 44; Nu 1:54; 3:1; 4:4, 6, 19, 24, 28, 31, 33, 37, 41, 45; 5:4, 13, 19, 21, 22, 24, 29, 30; 6:13, 21; 7:17, 23, 29, 35, 41, 47, 53, 59, 65, 71, 77, 83; 8:4, 7, 14, 24, 26; 9:3; 10:8, 13, 28; 11:6, 11, 15; 12:2, 7; 13:27; 14:2, 3, 14, 15, 27, 29, 32, 35²; 39, 41; 15:11, 12, 13, 15, 21, 24; 16:4, 6, 21, 28, 30, 40, 45; 17:5, 10; 18:11², 23, 28, 32; 19:2, 10, 14, 21; 20:4, 5, 14, 21:2, 5, 17; 22:4, 10, 16, 30²; 23:5, 16; 24:14, 23; 25:7; 27:11, 12, 16; 28:2, 3, 6, 8, 10, 13, 14, 17, 24; 29:7; 30:1; 31:21, 29; 32:5, 8, 10, 15, 22, 23, 32; 33:2; 34:6, 9, 12, 13; 35:5, 14; 36:5, 6; Dt 1:4, 5, 6, 8, 31, 32, 35, 2:3, 7, 22, 25; 3:14, 18, 26, 27, 28; 4:6², 8, 22, 26, 32, 39, 44, 48; 5:3, 25, 28; 6:25; 7:5; 8:11, 17; 9:4, 6, 7, 13, 27; 10:10; 11:5; 13:14; 15:2, 9, 10, 15; 17:4², 5, 18; 18:3, 16²; 19:4, 7, 10, 20; 20:15; 21:7, 8, 20; 22:5, 14, 16, 19, 25, 26; 24:18; 22; 25:9², 16, 17; 18, 19; 27:3, 8, 26; 28:13, 58³, 61; 29:4, 6, 7, 9, 12, 13, 14, 19², 20, 21, 23, 25, 27², 29; 30:10, 18, 19; 31:7, 9, 11, 12, 13, 19, 21, 22, 23, 24, 25, 26, 30; 32:6, 19, 27, 29, 34, 44, 46², 51; 33:1, 7; 34:4, 6; Jos 1:8, 13; 2:3, 9², 17, 18; 3:4, 10; 4:9, 24; 5:4, 9, 12; 6:3², 9, 14, 25; 7:5, 7, 9, 13, 20, 25, 26; 8:14, 19, 27, 28, 29; 9:12, 20, 24, 27; 10:2, 25, 27; 11:1, 6, 16; 12:2; 13:2, 6, 13, 15, 24, 29, 31, 32; 14:10, 12, 15², 6, 10, 63; 16:5, 8, 10; 17:1, 2, 18:14, 19, 28; 19:8², 21:42, 19, 37, 49; 22:16², 18, 20, 24, 25, 27, 32; 28, 31, 34; 23:9, 13, 15; 24:2, 15, 27, 32; Jdg 1:21, 26, 32; 2:2², 20; 3:2, 12; 4:9, 14; 5:1, 3, 30; 6:8, 13, 20, 24, 26, 29, 39; 7:4², 14; 8:1, 3, 9; 9:3, 7, 24, 25, 29, 42, 46; 10:4; 11:15, 27, 37, 39; 13:20, 23; 14:4; 15:3, 6, 7, 18; 16:15; 17:5, 13; 18:3, 12²; 19:11, 23², 24; 20:3, 9, 10, 11, 12², 25, 29; 21:3, 11, 18; Ru 1:14, 19; 2:10; 3:10; 4:6, 7, 12, 14, 18; 1Sa 1:3, 7, 27; 2:14, 17, 20, 27; 4:6, 7, 14, 16; 5:5; 6:9, 10, 16, 18, 20; 8:6, 8, 11; 9:6, 13, 15, 16, 17, 24; 10:11, 18, 27; 11:2, 5, 8, 9, 12²; 13:12; 14:13², 15², 19², 20; 15:21, 17:14; 17:10, 11, 17, 25, 26³, 27, 28, 32, 33, 37, 46, 56; 18:5, 8; 19:6, 17; 20:2, 3, 16, 21, 31, 39; 21:7, 8, 11, 12²; 14², 24, 28², 33, 39, 42; 21:7, 19², 29; 22:11, 20, 27², 32; 2Ki 1:2, 4, 6, 7, 11², 13, 16²; 2:12, 19, 21², 22; 3:7, 16², 17², 18; 4:9, 13, 16, 43²; 5:6, 7, 8, 18², 20, 26; 6:11, 19², 28, 32, 33; 7:1², 2, 9², 18, 19; 8:5², 8, 9, 22; 9:1, 3, 6, 11, 12, 15, 18, 19, 25, 26, 36, 37; 10:2, 5, 6, 24, 27; 11:5; 12:17; 13:23; 14:7; 15:20; 16:6; 17:7, 12², 17, 34, 41; 18:12, 14, 16, 19², 22, 25², 29, 30, 31; 19:1, 3², 6, 9, 20, 21², 29, 31², 32², 33, 34; 20:1, 5, 6², 9; 21:7, 12, 15, 16², 17, 18, 19, 20; 23:3², 17, 22, 24:20, 25:26; 1Ch 4:14, 41, 43; 5:26; 11:11, 19; 13:4, 11; 16:7; 17:4, 5, 7, 15, 16, 17, 19; 19:8, 17; 20:3; 21:3, 7, 8, 10, 11, 17, 23; 22:8; 24:19; 25:1; 27:1, 6, 24; 28:7, 8, 19; 29:1, 3, 14, 16, 18; 2Ch 1:10², 11; 2:3, 4; 6:8, 18, 20³, 21, 22, 24, 26, 29, 32, 33, 34, 40; 7:12, 15, 16, 20, 21³, 22; 8:8, 14; 10:2, 15, 19; 11:2, 4², 17; 12:5, 7, 14; 13:3, 8, 12; 14:11; 16:5, 7; 18:22; 19:2, 10; 20:1, 7, 9, 12², 15², 16², 17, 26²; 21:10, 12, 18; 23:4; 24:11, 20, 22; 25:15, 16, 17; 29:9, 25, 28; 30:9, 26; 31:1, 7, 10, 11, 20; 32:9, 10, 12, 15, 17, 20; 33:7; 34:21², 23, 24², 25, 26, 27, 28, 31, 32; 35:14, 18, 19, 20, 21, 25; 36:23; Ezr 1:2, 9; 2:69; 3:12; 4:11, 13, 14, 15², 16, 17, 19, 21, 22²; 5:3², 4, 6, 9², 11, 12, 16, 17²; 6:2, 7², 8, 11², 12²; 7:6, 11, 17, 24, 27; 8:23, 35; 9:2, 3, 4, 10, 13, 15; 10:2, 4, 13², 14, 15; Ne 1:11²; 2:2, 10, 18, 19; 3:34; 4:9; 5:11³, 18; 6:2, 3, 7², 8, 13, 16², 17; 7:5; 8:9, 10, 11, 15, 17; 9:10, 18, 32, 38; 13:3, 4, 6, 14, 17, 22, 27; Est 1:18, 21; 2:4, 7, 13, 23; 3:2, 9; 4:11, 13, 14², 15, 16; 5:7, 13, 14; 6:3, 9, 11; 7:2, 8; 8:12; 9:1, 13, 14, 17, 26, 29; 16:23; Job 1:1, 5, 20, 22; 2:10; 3:1; 5:27; 6:10; 7:15; 9:2; 10:13²; 11:2, 6; 12:9; 13:1, 16; 17:8; 21:2, 6; 22:21; 23:15; 24:25; 27:12²;

33:12; 34:16; 35:2; 36:31; 37:1, 14; 38:2, 11, 18; 42:3, 16; Ps 7:3; 17:14²; 18:T; 24:8, 10; 27:4, 13; 34:6; 35:22; 37:5; 39:9; 44:17; 48:14; 49:1², 13; 50:22; 56:9; 62:3²; 69:31; 71:17; 72:20; 73:12, 16; 74:3, 9; 75:9; 77:10; 78:32; 80:14; 81:4; 87:4, 5, 6; 102:18; 106:31; 107:2; 109:20; 118:20, 23, 24; 119:50, 56, 91; 132:14; 144:15; 147:20; 149:5, 9; Pr 3:8; 6:3, 23; 11:21; 16:5; 20:22; 22:2; 24:12; 25:22; 29:13; 30:1, 20; Ecc 1:10, 17; 2:9, 10, 15, 19, 21, 23, 24, 26; 3:13; 4:4, 8, 16; 5:10, 16, 18, 19; 6:2, 9; 7:2, 6, 12, 15, 23², 27, 29; 8:9, 10², 14; 9:1, 3, 9², 13; 11:6; 12:13; SS 3:6; 5:16²; 6:10; 8:5; Isa 1:12²; 2:1; 3:6; 5:25; 6:7, 9, 10; 7:7; 8:6, 11, 20; 9:7, 12, 16, 17, 21; 10:4, 7², 13, 24, 32; 12:5; 13:7; 14:4, 16, 26²; 16:13; 17:14; 18:4; 20:6; 21:3, 6, 16; 22:14², 15², 23:7, 8, 13; 24:3; 25:6, 7, 9², 10; 26:1; 27:9², 11; 28:11, 12², 14, 16, 19, 29; 29:11², 12, 22; 30:11², 12², 13, 15, 21; 31:4; 32:13; 33:6, 16; 36:4², 7, 10², 14, 15, 16; 37:1, 3², 6, 9, 21, 22, 30², 32, 33², 34, 35; 38:1, 5, 6², 7, 11, 15²; 39:6; 40:23; 41:4, 20, 26²; 42:5, 22, 23; 43:1, 9, 14, 16; 44:2, 6, 8, 20, 23, 24; 45:1, 11, 14, 18, 21; 46:8; 48:1, 11, 16, 17, 20; 49:1, 7, 8, 20, 22, 25; 50:1, 11; 51:21, 22; 52:3, 4; 54:9, 17²; 55:13; 56:1, 2, 4; 57:11, 15; 58:5, 6; 59:21²; 60:22; 63:1², 14; 64:12; 65:8, 13; 66:1, 2, 12, 14; Jer 2:5, 10, 12, 17, 31, 34; 3:5; 4:3, 10, 11, 16, 18², 27; 5:1, 9², 14, 19, 20, 21, 29², 31; 6:6², 9, 16, 19, 21, 22; 7:1, 2, 3², 4, 6, 7, 10, 11, 16, 20², 21, 23, 27, 28, 29, 33; 8:3, 4; 9:7, 9², 12, 15², 17, 22, 24; 10:2², 7, 11, 18³, 19; 11:1, 2, 3², 6, 11, 14, 21, 22; 12:14; 13:1, 9, 10, 12, 13², 22, 25; 14:1, 10², 11, 13, 15², 17, 22; 15:1, 2, 19²; 16:2, 3², 5², 6, 9², 10, 13, 21; 17:5, 19, 21, 24, 25²; 18:1, 6, 11, 13²; 19:1, 3², 4², 6, 7, 8, 11⁴, 12³, 13, 15²; 20:4, 5; 21:4²; 22:1², 3², 4, 5, 6, 8², 11², 12, 18, 21, 28, 30²; 23:2, 6, 13, 15, 16, 26, 34, 35, 37, 38⁴; 24:5², 6, 8; 25:3, 8, 9, 11, 13, 15², 27, 28, 32; 26:1, 2, 4, 6², 9², 11² 12², 15, 16, 18, 20²; 27:1, 2, 4², 16, 17, 19², 21, 22; 28:2, 3, 4, 6, 11², 13, 14, 15, 16²; 29:1, 2, 4, 8, 10², 16², 17, 21, 22, 25, 28, 31², 32²; 30:1, 2, 5, 12, 18, 24; 31:2², 7, 15, 16, 23, 26, 33, 35, 37, 38; 32:1, 3², 8, 12, 14, 15²; 20, 22, 23, 28², 29, 31, 36², 37, 41, 42³, 43; 33:2, 4², 5, 9, 10², 12², 16, 17, 20, 25; 34:1, 2³, 4, 5, 6, 10, 13, 14², 17, 18, 19; 36:1, 7, 17, 29², 30; 37:3, 7, 8, 9, 10, 18, 19; 38:2², 3², 4³, 16, 17², 18, 21, 23, 24, 28; 39:16²; 40:2², 3; 42:2, 9, 10, 13, 15, 18², 19, 22; 43:10; 44:1, 2, 4, 7, 10, 11, 23, 25, 29², 30; 45:1, 2, 4²; 46:1, 2, 7, 13, 14; 47:1, 2; 48:1, 40; 49:1, 7, 12, 19, 28, 34, 35; 50:1, 15, 18, 33, 44; 51:1, 33, 36, 46, 58, 59, 62, 63; 52:3, 28; La 1:16; 2:15, 16, 20; 3:21; 5:17; Eze 1:10, 16, 28; 2:3, 4; 3:1, 3, 11, 27; 4:3, 6², 13; 5:5², 7, 8; 6:3, 10, 11; 7:2, 5; 8:5, 15², 17; 9:8; 11:2, 3, 5, 6, 7², 11, 15, 16, 17; 12:10², 19, 22, 23²; 28; 13:3, 8, 13, 18; 14:4, 5, 6, 21; 15:6; 16:3, 29, 36, 44, 49, 59; 17:3, 9, 12, 19, 22; 18:2, 3, 14; 19:14; 20:3, 5, 27², 29², 30, 31, 39, 47; 21:3, 9, 24², 26, 28, 32²; 22:3, 19; 23:11, 22, 28, 30, 32, 35, 38, 46; 24:2³, 3², 6, 9, 21, 24; 25:3, 6, 8, 12, 13, 15, 16; 26:3, 7, 15, 19; 27:3; 28:2, 6, 12, 22, 25; 29:3, 8, 13, 19; 30:2, 6, 10, 13, 22; 31:10, 15, 18; 32:3, 11, 16; 33:10, 25, 27², 33; 34:2, 10, 11, 17, 20; 35:3, 14; 36:2, 3, 4, 5, 6, 7, 13, 22, 32, 33, 35, 37²; 37:5, 9, 12, 18, 19, 21; 38:3, 10, 14, 17, 18; 39:1, 8, 17, 25; 40:18, 27; 41:4, 22; 43:7², 12, 13, 18; 44:2, 6, 9; 45:2, 8, 9, 13, 16, 18; 46:1, 14, 16, 20; 47:6, 8, 9, 13, 14, 18; 48:10, 11, 14, 29; Da 1:8, 14; 2:5, 8, 12, 16, 18, 30, 36, 41, 42, 45, 47; 3:4, 8, 16, 29; 4:18, 24², 28, 30, 31; 5:7, 12, 15, 16, 22, 25, 26; 6:4, 5, 14; 7:6, 8, 16, 21, 23, 24, 28; 8:5, 16; 9:7, 13, 15, 25; 10:8, 11, 15, 19; 12:5, 8; Hos 4:3; 5:1²; 7:10, 16; 8:6; 9:4, 7; Joel 1:2²; 3:9; Am 1:3, 6, 9, 11, 13; 2:1, 4, 6, 11; 3:1, 11, 12, 13; 4:1, 5, 12²; 5:1², 3, 4, 16; 7:1, 3, 6, 7, 11, 13, 17; 8:1, 4, 8; Ob 1:1, 20; Jnh 1:7, 8, 10, 12, 14, 16; 4:2, 10; Mic 1:5, 8; 2:3, 4, 10, 11; 3:5, 9; Na 1:12; Hab 2:1, 6; Zep 1:4; 2:10, 15; 3:11; Hag 1:2, 4, 5, 7, 13; 2:3, 5, 6, 7, 9², 11, 14², 15², 18², 19; Zec 1:3, 4, 14², 16, 17; 2:8; 3:2, 6, 7, 9; 4:6, 9; 5:3, 5, 6, 8; 6:12, 15; 7:9, 14; 8:2, 3, 4, 6², 7, 9, 11, 12, 14, 17, 19, 20, 23; 11:4; 12:1; 13:9; 14:12, 19; Mal 1:4; 2:1, 4, 5, 12; 3:10; Mt 1:18, 20, 22; 2:3, 5; 3:3, 15, 17; 4:9; 5:37; 6:9; 7:12; 8:9², 10, 17, 33; 9:3², 8, 11, 12, 13, 18, 26, 28, 30, 33; 10:7; 11:10, 16, 23, 26; 12:2, 15, 17, 23, 24², 32, 41, 42, 45; 13:13, 15, 19, 22, 28, 49, 54²; 55, 56; 14:2, 13, 15; 15:12, 33; 16:7, 17, 18, 22; 17:5, 6, 20; 18:4, 5, 35; 19:5, 8, 10, 11, 12, 22, 25, 26; 20:24; 21:4, 10, 11, 20, 21, 23, 32, 38, 42; 22:20, 22, 33, 35, 38; 23:36²; 24:3, 14, 32, 34, 43; 26:8², 9, 10²,

12, 13, 26, 28, 29, 31, 34, 39, 42, 54, 56, 61, 62, 71; 27:6, 8, 19, 24, 37, 47, 64; 28:14, 15²; Mk 1:7, 27, 44; 2:7, 8, 12², 17; 3:21, 30; 4:13, 19, 26, 41; 5:3, 8, 14, 39, 42, 43; 6:2², 3², 14, 16, 17, 29, 35²; 7:14, 17, 19, 35; 8:4, 12, 16, 32, 38; 9:7, 21, 29; 10:5, 7, 10, 14, 22, 27, 30, 41; 11:3, 18, 23, 28, 30; 12:4, 7, 10, 11, 16, 29, 31, 43; 13:18, 28, 30; 14:4, 11, 22, 24, 36, 57, 58, 60, 69, 71; 15:32², 35, 39; Lk 1:18, 19, 20, 24, 25, 29, 34, 66²; 2:2, 12, 15, 17, 34, 48; 3:20; 4:3, 13, 21, 22, 23, 28, 36; 5:8, 19, 21, 27, 36; 6:39; 7:1, 4², 8², 9, 17, 27, 31, 39², 44, 45, 49; 8:1, 4, 8, 9, 11, 25, 27, 34, 50; 9:9, 13, 21, 28, 35, 36, 45, 48, 54; 10:1, 5, 11, 21, 28; 11:18, 29, 30, 31, 32, 49, 50, 51; 12:16, 18, 20, 21, 26, 39, 41, 56; 13:2, 6, 7, 16, 17, 31; 14:7, 9, 15, 21, 30; 15:2, 3, 24, 30, 32; 16:2, 8, 14, 24, 26, 28; 17:6, 18, 25, 30; 18:5, 9, 11, 14, 15, 22, 23, 26, 30, 34; 19:7, 9², 11, 13, 14, 28, 42; 20:2, 9, 14, 16², 19, 34²; 21:3, 12, 13, 22, 23, 29, 32; 22:15, 17, 19², 20, 23, 37, 42, 51, 53, 56, 59; 23:2, 4, 6, 12, 14, 18, 22, 38, 41, 46, 47, 48; 24:4, 6, 11, 22, 24, 36, 40, 44, 46; Jn 1:15, 19, 28, 30, 32, 34, 37; 2:11, 12, 18, 19, 20; 3:9, 19, 22, 24, 27; 4:3, 11, 13, 15, 20, 21, 29, 42, 47, 53, 54; 5:6, 9, 12, 17, 18, 19, 28; 6:1, 6, 14, 29, 34, 39, 41, 42, 51², 52, 58², 59, 60, 61², 65, 66; 7:1, 8, 9, 15, 25, 27, 30, 31, 35, 39, 40, 46, 49; 8:4, 6, 9, 22, 23², 52, 59; 9:2, 3², 6, 7, 8, 12, 16, 19², 22, 24, 28, 29, 33, 34, 35, 40; 10:6, 16, 18, 41; 11:2, 4², 9, 11, 26, 28, 29, 37, 39, 42, 43, 47, 48, 51; 12:5, 6, 7, 16, 18, 19, 25, 27³, 30, 31², 33, 34, 38, 39, 41; 13:1, 21, 24, 26, 28; 14:25, 30; 15:8, 11, 12, 13, 17, 21, 25; 16:1, 4², 11, 19, 25, 33; 17:1, 3; 18:9, 15, 22², 29, 32, 36, 37², 38; 19:8, 12, 13, 20, 21, 23, 24², 27, 40; 20:14, 20, 30; 21:1, 14, 19, 20, 23², 24; Ac 1:4, 6, 9, 11, 17, 19, 25; 2:6, 12, 14, 16, 22, 23, 29, 32, 36², 37, 40; 3:12³, 15, 16; 4:7, 10², 17², 24, 27; 5:5, 8, 20, 24², 28², 33; 6:3, 5, 13², 14²; 7:2, 4, 6, 7, 14, 29, 31, 35, 37, 40, 42, 54, 57, 60²; 8:10, 19, 21, 24, 27, 32; 9:13, 15, 21, 30, 42; 10:16, 30; 11:10, 18, 22, 27, 28, 30; 12:1, 3², 12, 17, 22; 13:20², 26, 47, 48; 14:14, 15; 15:2², 3, 10, 13, 16; 16:21; 2Co 1:9, 20, 28; 2:6², 8, 13; 3:12, 18, 19; 4:11, 13, 14, 17; 5:2, 3, 5, 10²; 6:3, 5, 6, 7; 7:6, 10, 12; 8:7, 10; 9:1, 3, 6, 12; 10:2; 11:6, 10, 17, 23; 12:3; 13:1, 10; Gal 2:1, 2, 4; 3:15, 17, 23; 4:24; 5:21; 6:2, 12, 16; Eph 1:15; 2:2, 8, 16; 3:1, 4, 6, 7, 8, 9, 14, 18, 22, 25; 4:28; 5:14, 28, 31, 32; 6:1, 12, 16, 18, 22; Php 1:6, 7, 9, 18, 22, 25, 28; 3:12; 4:11; Col 1:6, 9, 10, 23, 27, 29; 2:4, 8, 20; 3:20; 4:16, 18; 1Th 2:16; 3:5; 4:1, 6, 8; 5:4, 18, 27; 2Th 1:5, 7, 10, 11, 12; 2:11, 14; 3:9, 10, 14, 17²; 1Ti 1:5, 18; 2:3, 7; 4:9, 10; 5:4; 6:11, 14, 17; 2Ti 1:6, 9, 11; 2:7, 8, 19; 3:1; 4:1, 10; Tit 1:13; 2:12; 3:8; Phm 1:19; Heb 2:3, 17; 5:3, 4, 11, 12; 6:9, 11, 18, 19; 7:1, 6, 22; 8:1, 3, 5, 10, 13; 9:2, 4, 6, 8, 9, 11, 15, 18, 20; 10:1, 12, 15, 16; 11:2, 5, 12; 12:17; Jas 1:19, 25, 27; 3:10; 4:13, 15; 5:20; 1Pe 1:6, 10, 25; 2:7, 20, 21; 3:5, 9, 15, 21; 4:6; 5:12; 2Pe 1:5, 13, 17, 18; 2:9, 10; 3:1, 4, 8, 11, 14, 17; 1Jn 1:1, 4, 5; 2:1, 5, 7, 18², 25; 3:3, 10, 11, 16, 19, 23, 24; 4:2, 3, 6, 10, 17², 21; 5:2, 3, 4, 6, 10, 11², 14; 2Jn 1:6, 10; Jude 1:5; Rev 1:3, 20; 2:4, 6, 20; 4:1²; 7:1, 9; 9:15, 17; 13:10, 18; 14:12; 15:5; 17:5, 9; 18:1, 18; 19:1, 10, 16; 20:5; 21:5, 7, 8; 22:7, 9, 10, 16, 18², 19².

THOSE (1368)

Ge 4:20; 6:4; 7:23; 9:10; 12:3; 17:12², 23, 27; 19:25²; 27:23, 29²; 39:22²; 41:3, 48; 42:5; 44:4; 46:26²; 50:8; Ex 8:9; 9:20, 21; 10:6; 13:7; 15:7; 18:11²; 20:5, 6; 23:28, 24; 26:27²; 27:19; 29:27; 30:13, 14; 34:12, 15, 16; 35:24; 36:32; 38:25, 26, 31²; Lev 10:3, 6; 11:21, 27, 31, 47; 15:10; 20:25; 23:38; 24:14; 26:17, 36, 39; Nu 2:32; 3:3, 32, 49;

4:15, 37, 41, 45; 7:2; 10:33; 13:31, 32; 14:6; 15:33; 16:39, 49; 22:6², 12; 23:8²; 24:9²; 25:5, 9; 26:2, 7, 18, 22, 25, 27, 34, 37, 41, 43, 47, 50, 54, 64, 65; 31:36; 32:13; 33:55; Dt 1:44; 5:9, 10; 7:9, 10², 22; 9:25; 10:19, 21; 11:30; 12:3; 13:17; 14:7; 18:12, 14; 28:65; 29:3², 15, 18; 32:21, 41; 33:11, 17; 34:11; Jos 5:4; 8:5, 13, 24, 33; 9:1, 11; 10:22; 13:22; 17:16²; 24:17²; Jdg 1:31, 33²; 2:18, 19, 23; 3:1; 5:14; 7:5²; 8:19; 9:44; 10:18; 12:9; 14:19; 17:6; 18:1²; 19:1, 13; 20:13, 15, 27; 21:7, 10, 25; Ru 4:11; 1Sa 2:4, 5², 10, 30²; 3:1; 5:12; 7:16; 9:13, 22; 10:11; 11:11; 14:6, 15², 21, 48; 15:18; 17:28, 47; 22:2; 28:1; 30:27, 28, 29, 30, 31; 31:7; 2Sa 5:8; 6:13; 16:2, 23; 17:10; 19:6²; 28; 21:13; 1Ki 2:7; 10:10; 11:10; 14:11²; 16:4²; 22, 25; 30; 21:9, 24²; 2Ki 3:23; 6:16²; 10:32; 11:9²; 12:11, 15; 15:37; 19:6; 20:1, 14; 23:5²; 18, 20; 25:11, 19, 28; 1Ch 8:6, 13; 9:3, 22, 33; 12:18; 16:10, 41; 23:27; 24:31; 2Ch 2:14; 9:9; 11:16; 14:6; 15:5; 16:9; 17:19; 19:2, 11; 23:8²; 24:26; 25:5²; 28:12, 13, 15; 30:17, 25; 32:13, 24; 34:4, 22, 28; Ezr 3:5, 9; 8:1; 9:1; 10:3; Ne 1:3, 5; 4:2²; 17; 5:15, 17; 6:17; 7:5; 8:10; 9:2; 10:1; 12:22; 13:15, 23; Est 2:6; 3:8; 9:1, 2, 5, 11, 19; Job 3:8²; 20, 21; 4:4, 8²; 19; 5:11; 7:1; 10:5²; 12:5, 6²; 15:34; 17:9; 19:19; 20:7; 21:29; 24:1, 13, 19; 26:5; 27:15; 29:11; 30:25; 31:3; 36:15; 37:16; 38:14; Ps 5:6, 11; 9:10²; 11:5; 12:5; 14:4; 15:4; 16:4; 17:7, 14; 18:27; 22:25, 29; 24:6; 25:10, 14; 28:1, 3; 31:6, 11, 15, 19²; 33:18²; 34:5, 7, 9, 10, 16, 18; 35:1², 3, 4², 10², 19, 20, 27; 36:10; 37:1, 9, 14, 22²; 38:12², 19²; 20; 40:4, 15, 16; 44:13, 16; 49:6, 13; 53:4, 5; 54:5; 57:3; 59:1, 8, 10; 60:4, 5; 61:5; 65:4, 8; 68:11, 21; 69:4²; 6², 9, 12, 14, 26²; 36; 70:2, 3, 4; 71:10, 13, 24; 73:1, 27; 79:4, 11; 81:15; 83:3²; 84:4, 5, 11; 85:9; 87:4; 88:4, 10; 89:15; 97:7, 10; 99:6; 102:8, 20; 103:11, 13, 17, 18; 105:3; 107:2, 3, 34; 108:6; 109:20, 31; 111:5; 115:8, 13, 17; 118:4; 119:74, 79²; 132, 150; 120:6; 122:1, 6; 125:1, 4², 5; 126:5; 127:2; 129:8; 135:18; 139:21²; 140:9; 142:6; 143:3, 7; 145:14, 19; 146:8; 147:11; Pr 1:12, 19; 2:7; 3:12, 18²; 27; 4:22²; 8:9, 17²; 21, 32; 9:4, 15, 16; 10:26; 29; 11:20, 21; 12:20²; 13:10; 14:22²; 15:9, 26; 16:22; 18:21; 22:23; 23:20, 30; 24:11², 22, 25; 25:13; 26:28; 28:4², 5; 30:5, 11, 12, 13, 14; 31:3; 6², 8; Ecc 1:11²; 4:16; 5:11; 7:11; 8:8, 10; 9:2⁴; 12:3; SS 5:7; 8:12; Isa 1:28; 4:3, 5; 5:11, 18, 19, 20, 21, 22, 26; 9:1, 2, 16²; 10:1², 10; 13:3; 14:9², 16, 19²; 15:9; 17:14²; 19:8, 9; 20:5, 6²; 21:3; 22:21; 23:18; 26:5, 14; 27:7², 13²; 28:1, 6, 9; 29:15, 21, 24²; 30:1; 31:1, 2; 32:3²; 33:19², 24; 35:8; 37:6; 38:1, 11, 18; 39:3; 40:11, 31; 41:11, 12; 42:5, 7, 17; 43:8; 44:9; 45:14, 20; 46:9; 47:13; 49:6, 9, 17, 19, 23, 25; 50:6²; 52:5, 7; 56:8; 57:2, 8, 19; 59:20; 61:3; 62:9²; 63:2; 64:4, 5; 65:1², 9; 66:16, 17², 19, 24; Jer 2:8, 37; 3:16, 18; 5:18, 26; 6:11, 12; 10:18; 11:2, 9; 12:4; 13:13, 20, 21; 14:15, 18; 15:2⁴; 16:7; 17:13, 25; 18:11; 19:7, 10, 12, 13; 21:6; 22:25²; 12:4, 19; 13:2, 11, 15²; 16; 37²; 57, 61²; 19:8; 20:38; 21:23; 22:5²; 9, 10²; 23:20, 22, 25²; 28²; 44; 25:16; 26:20²; 28:9²; 31:14, 16, 17²; 18; 32:18, 20, 21, 24, 25, 28, 29²; 30², 32; 33:24, 27³; 34:27; 35:8; 39:6, 9, 10², 11, 14; 40:21, 22, 46; 44:24; Da 2:44²; 4:17²; 5:19⁴; 7:6, 16; 9:16; 11:6, 14, 26, 30, 32, 33, 39; 12:3²; 10; Hos 2:23; 4:4; 5:10; 10:5; Joel 1:9; 2:11, 16, 20, 29; 3:1; Am 3:12; 9:1, 10; Ob 1:7; Jnh 2:8; Mic 1:11, 12; 2:1², 8; 4:6, 7; Na 1:7; Hab 1:13; Zep 1:5²; 6, 7, 8, 12; 3:11, 19; Zec 3:4; 5:9; 6:8, 15; 8:23; 9:7; 11:5, 9; 12:8; 14:3, 15; Mal 3:5, 15, 16², 18²; Mt 2:20; 3:1; 4:16, 24²; 5:4, 6, 10, 44, 46; 7:11; 8:10; 33; 10:28; 11:5, 8, 11, 27; 14:21, 33; 15:38; 19:11; 13, 20:10, 23; 21:9, 12, 40, 41; 22:3, 4, 7, 8; 23:13, 31, 37; 24:16, 19, 22², 29; 26:57; 73; 27:39, 47, 54; Mk 3:10, 13, 34; 4:11; 5:14, 16; 8:1; 10:32, 40, 42; 11:9², 15²; 12:9; 13:14, 17, 19, 20, 24; 14:4, 47, 69, 70; 15:29, 32; 35; 16:10, 14, 17; Lk 1:2, 50, 51, 79; 2:1; 4:2; 5:35; 6:12, 18, 27, 28²; 32², 33, 34; 7:14, 22, 25, 28; 8:12, 13, 14, 15, 16, 21, 34, 36; 9:7; 10:22; 11:13, 28, 33, 52; 12:4, 37, 38; 13:4, 14, 30, 34; 14:15, 17, 24; 16:26; 18:26, 39; 19:24, 27, 32, 45; 20:16; 21:21³, 23, 25; 22:25, 28; 23:49; 24:33; Jn 1:12, 22; 2:16; 5:25, 29²; 6:11, 13; 7:39; 8:9; 9:8, 39; 12:2, 20; 13:18; 17:2, 6, 9, 20, 24; 18:9; 21; 19:32; 20:29; Ac 1:13, 15, 16; 2:18, 41, 47; 3:2; 4:34; 5:16, 32; 6:1; 7:52;

8:4; 9:21², 35; 10:2; 11:19; 13:31; 15:33; 16:14, 35; 17:17; 18:27; 19:13, 18; 20:32; 22:19, 20, 29; 23:2, 4; 26:18, 20², 30; 27:43; Ro 1:6, 32²; 2:2, 7, 8, 13²; 19, 26; 3:19, 26; 4:14, 16²; 5:14, 17; 6:13, 21; 8:1, 5², 8, 14, 28, 29, 30¹, 33; 9:3; 10:15, 19, 20²; 11:18, 22; 12:14, 15²; 13:2, 3²; 15:3, 21²; 16:10, 11, 22; 1Co 1:2²; 18, 21, 24; 2:9; 4:1, 2; 5:12²; 13; 7:28, 29, 30³; 31; 9:3, 13², 14, 20²; 21²; 10:18; 11:22; 12:22, 28⁴; 14:16; 15:18, 20, 23, 29, 48²; 2Co 1:4; 2:3, 15²; 4:3; 5:12, 15; 11:5, 12; 12:19; 13:2; Gal 1:17; 2:2, 6², 9, 12; 3:7, 9, 22; 4:5, 8, 9, 17; 5:12, 21, 24; 6:10, 12, 13; Eph 1:14; 2:2, 11, 17; 4:28, 29; 5:6; Php 1:28; 2:21; 3:2³, 17; 4:22; Col 2:1; 4:13; 1Th 2:14; 4:13, 14, 15; 5:7², 12, 14; 2Th 1:6, 8, 10; 2:10; 1Ti 1:9, 16; 2:2; 3:13; 4:3, 10; 5:3, 10, 16, 17, 20, 25; 6:2²; 17; 2Ti 2:14, 16, 19, 22, 25; 3:9, 14; Tit 1:9, 10, 14, 15; 2:8; 3:8, 15; Heb 1:14; 2:3, 11, 15, 18; 3:16, 17, 18; 4:2, 6; 5:2; 6:4, 7, 12; 7:23, 25; 9:13, 15, 28; 10:1, 3, 14, 32, 33, 34, 39²; 11:6, 31; 12:6, 11, 19; 13:3², 9, 10, 24; Jas 1:12; 2:5², 12; 5:11; 1Pe 1:12; 2:7, 14², 18²; 3:12, 16; 4:18; 5:3, 5; 2Pe 1:1; 2:10, 18; 1Jn 2:26; 3:24; 5:16; 3Jn 1:10; Jude 1:1, 5, 7, 22; Rev 1:3, 7; 2:2, 9, 15, 22; 3:9, 10, 19; 6:9; 7:4; 9:4, 6; 11:10, 11, 18²; 12:17; 13:2, 6; 14:4, 6, 11; 15:2; 17:6; 19:9, 20; 20:4², 6; 21:8, 27; 22:14, 15.

TO (20933)

Ge 1:6, 9, 11, 12², 14², 15, 16², 17, 18², 21², 24², 25³, 28, 30; 2:5, 9, 15, 16, 18, 19², 20, 21, 22, 24; 3:1, 2, 4, 6², 9, 11, 13, 14, 16², 17², 19², 22, 23, 24²; 4:1, 2, 3, 6, 7, 8², 9, 10, 13, 14, 16²; 17², 19², 22, 23, 24²; 5:1, 3, 6, 7, 8², 9³, 11, 12, 15, 20; 6:1², 3, 7, 8², 13⁴, 15², 16, 17², 18, 20²; 7:1, 2², 4, 5, 13, 15², 16²; 8:1, 4, 6², 7, 8, 9, 13, 18, 20, 21, 22; 9:1, 2, 9³, 10³, 11², 12³, 13, 15, 16, 17, 20, 24, 25; 10:8, 11², 21, 25, 32; 11:3, 4, 5, 6, 31³; 12:1², 7⁴, 8, 9⁴, 14, 15, 18, 19, 20; 13:1³, 6, 8, 9⁴, 14, 15, 17, 18²; 14:2, 4, 7, 10, 13, 15, 17, 21, 22²; 15:1, 4, 5, 6, 7³, 9, 10, 13, 15, 18²; 16:2², 3, 4, 5, 7, 9², 10, 11, 12, 13³, 15; 17:1, 3, 7², 8, 9², 10, 11, 12, 13, 15², 17, 18, 21; 18:1², 2², 5, 6, 7², 8, 9, 10, 13, 14, 16², 17, 19, 25², 27², 29, 31²; 19:1², 2, 4, 5³, 6, 8², 9², 12², 13³, 14³, 16, 17, 18, 19², 20³, 21, 27, 30, 31², 32, 33, 34², 35; 20:3², 5, 6, 9², 11, 13², 14², 16²; 17²; 21:1, 2, 3, 5, 7, 9, 10, 12², 14, 16, 17², 22, 23³, 25, 27, 32; 22:1, 2, 5², 7, 10, 11, 12, 14, 15, 19, 20; 23:1, 2³, 3, 5, 6, 8³, 9³, 10², 11², 13², 15, 16², 18, 20; 24:2, 3, 4, 5³, 7², 8, 9, 10, 11, 12, 13, 14², 16, 17, 18, 20², 21, 23, 24, 25, 27³, 30², 32², 33, 38², 41³, 42², 43², 44, 45², 47, 48, 49², 50, 52, 53³, 54, 56¹, 60², 63², 65; 25:5, 6², 8, 12, 16, 17, 18, 20²; 21, 22, 23, 28; 26:1, 2, 7, 8, 9², 11², 12, 13⁴, 14⁴, 15⁵, 16³, 17,

18^6, 22; **4:**1^2, 2, 4, 5, 8, 9, 10^2, 11, 12, 13, 14, 15^2, 16^2, 18^4, 19^3, 20, 21^3, 22, 23, 24, 25, 26, 27^2, 28^2; 30; **5:**1^2, 3^2, 4, 6, 7, 8^2, 9, 10, 12^2, 15, 17, 18, 19, 20, 21^2, 22, 23^2; **6:**1^2, 2, 3^4, 4, 6^2, 8^6, 9^2, 10, 11, 12^3, 13^2, 16, 19, 26, 27, 28, 29, 30^2; **7:**1^2, 2^2, 4, 7, 8, 9^2, 10, 13, 14^2, 15^3, 16^3, 18, 19^2, 23, 24; **8:**1^3, 2, 5, 8^4, 9^3, 12, 15, 16, 18, 19, 20^3, 25, 26, 27^2, 28^2, 29^3, 30; **9:**1^3, 2^2, 4, 6, 7, 8, 12^2, 13^2, 19^2, 20, 22, 23, 27, 28^2, 29; **10:**1^2, 3^3, 4, 7^2, 8, 9, 12, 17, 19, 21, 25^3, 26^4, 27, 28; **11:**1, 5, 8, 9^3; **12:**1, 2, 3, 4, 7, 8, 11, 14^3, 15, 16^2, 17, 18, 19, 21, 23^2, 26, 27, 29, 33, 37, 39, 41, 42^4, 43^2, 48, 49^2; **13:**1, 2^2, 3, 5^3, 6, 7, 9, 11^2, 12^3, 14^2, 15^2, 17, 19, 21^2; **14:**1, 2^2, 10, 11^4, 12^3, 14, 15^3, 16, 20^2, 26; **15:**1^2, 5, 13, 21^2, 23, 24, 25, 26^2, 27; **16:**1, 3^3, 4^2, 5^2, 6, 8, 9, 10, 11, 15^3, 16, 19, 20^2, 22, 23^3, 25, 26, 27, 28^2, 29^2, 32^2, 33^3, 35; **17:**1^2, 2^2, 3, 4^3, 6, 9^2, 10, 14^2, 16^2; **18:**5, 6^2, 7, 8, 9, 10, 11, 12^3, 13, 15^2, 16, 18, 19^2, 20^2, 22, 23, 24, 26, 27; **19:**1, 3^4, 4^2, 6^2, 7, 8, 9^3, 10^2, 12, 13^3, 14, 15, 17, 20^2, 21^2, 23, 24^2, 25; **20:**5^2, 6, 10, 17, 19^3, 20^2, 22^2, 23, 24^2, 26; **21:**1, 2, 3, 4^2, 8^2, 11, 12^2, 13^2, 14, 15, 16, 17, 18, 21, 23^2, 26, 27, 29, 32, 33, 35; **22:**3, 8, 9^2, 10, 11, 12^2, 13^2, 15, 16, 17^2, 18, 19, 20, 23, 25, 26, 27, 30, 31^2; **23:**3, 4^2, 6, 7^2, 9, 10, 13^2, 14^2, 15, 17, 18, 19, 20, 31^2, 22^2, 24, 28, 30, 31^3, 33^2; **24:**1^3, 2, 5, 7, 12^2, 14^3, 16, 17; **25:**1, 2, 3, 7, 12, 14^3, 16, 17; **25:**1, 2^3, 3, 7, 12, 14, 15^2, 16, 17, 18, 20^2, 22, 23, 24, 25; **26:**2, 6, 8, 11, 12, 13, 16, 17, 19, 24, 28^2, 29, 30, 36; **27:**1, 3, 7, 8, 9, 11, 14, 15, 16, 17, 19, 20, 21^3; **28:**1, 2, 3^2, 4^2, 7^2, 8, 12, 14, 16, 21, 23, 24, 25^2, 26^2, 27^2, 28^3, 34, 36, 37^4, 38, 39, 40, 42, 43^2, 44; **30:**2, 4^2, 8, 10^2, 11, 12, 13^4, 14^2, 15^4, 17, 19, 20^2, 21^2, 22, 24, 26, 31^3, 32, 34, 35, 36^2, 37, 38; **31:**1, 4, 5^3, 6^3, 11, 12, 13^2, 14^2, 15^3, 16^2, 18; **32:**1^2, 3, 5, 6^2, 7, 8^3, 9^2, 12^2, 13, 17, 19, 20, 21^2, 22, 23^2, 25, 26^3, 27^3, 29^2, 30^2, 31, 33, 34^2; **33:**1^4, 3, 4, 5^3, 7^2, 8^2, 10^2, 11^3, 12, 13, 15, 17, 19, 39; **34:**1, 2, 3, 6, 7^2, 8^2, 11, 13, 16, 18, 19, 20, 23, 24, 25, 26, 27, 30, 31^3, 33, 34, 35; **35:**1^2, 3, 4, 5^2, 9, 10, 16, 17, 21, 22, 24, 27, 29^2, 30, 32, 33^3, 34, 35; **36:**1^4, 2^2, 3^2, 5^2, 6, 7, 13, 18, 22, 24, 29, 33, 34, 37; **37:**3, 5, 13, 14^2, 27^2; **38:**4, 5, 8, 15, 18, 24, 25, 26^2, 27, 28^3, 30^2; **39:**3, 4, 16, 17, 18^2, 19^2, 20^2, 21^2, 26, 30, 31^3, 33, 38, 40; **40:**1, 5, 6, 8, 12^2, 15^2, 20, 28, 29, 31, 33; **Lev 1:**1^2, 2^3, 3^2, 4^2, 5^2, 6, 7, 9^3, 10, 13^2, 14^2, 15, 16^2, 17; **2:**1^3, 2^2, 3^2, 4, 5, 7, 8^3, 9, 10^2, 11^3, 12^2, 13, 14, 16; **3:**1, 2^3, 3^3, 5^2, 6^3, 7, 8, 9^4, 11, 12, 13, 14^3, 17; **4:**1, 2, 3, 4^3, 6, 7, 8, 12, 15, 16, 18^2, 24, 29, 30, 31, 32, 33, 35; **5:**1, 4, 6, 7^2, 8^3, 9, 11, 13, 14, 15^4, 16^4, 18^2; **6:**1, 2^2, 4, 5^2, 6^2, 8, 9, 10, 11^2, 12, 14, 15^2, 16^2, 17, 18^2, 19, 20^2, 21^2, 22^2, 24, 25^2, 26, 28, 30; **7:**2^2, 4, 5, 7^2, 9, 10, 11, 12, 13, 14^3, 18, 20, 21, 22, 23, 25, 28, 29^4, 30^3, 31^2, 32^2, 34, 35; 36^2, 38^2; **8:**1, 3, 4, 5^2, 7, 11, 12, 15^2, 21, 28, 31^3, 33, 34, 35; **9:**2, 3, 4^2, 5, 6^2, 7^2, 8, 9, 17, 23; **10:**1, 3, 4, 5^2, 6, 7^2, 8, 9, 17, 19^2; **11:**1, 2, 10, 11, 12^2, 13, 20, 23, 35, 39, 41, 42, 45; **12:**1^2, 2, 3, 4^2, 5^2, 6^2, 7^2; **13:**1, 2^2, 3^2, 4^2, 5^2, 6, 7^2, 8, 10, 11, 12, 13, 16, 17, 19, 20^2, 21, 25^2, 26, 27, 30^2, 31^2, 32^2, 33^2, 34^2, 36^2, 39, 43, 49, 50, 51, 54, 55, 56^2; **14:**1, 2, 3, 4, 6, 7^2, 8^2, 11^2, 12^2, 13^2, 14^2, 17^2, 18, 19^2, 21^2, 23^2, 24, 25, 26, 28^2, 29^2, 31, 33, 36, 37^2, 39, 40, 42, 44, 45, 48, 49, 51, 53^3; **15:**1^2, 2^2, 3, 7, 11, 12^2, 13, 14^3, 15, 29^2, 30; **16:**1, 2^2, 3, 4^3, 5, 6^2, 7^2, 8, 9, 10, 11^2, 12, 13^2, 14^2, 16, 17^2, 18^2, 19^2, 21, 22^2, 23^2, 24, 27^2; **17:**1, 2^3, 4^4, 5^4, 6^3, 7^4, 8, 9^4; **18:**1, 2^2, 3^2, 4, 6^2, 11, 14, 15^2, 18, 19, 20^2; **19:**1, 2^4, 3, 4^2, 5, 6^2, 7^2, 8, 9^4; **20:**1^2, 4, 3, 4^2, 5^2, 6, 7^2,

26:1, 27^2, 28, 29, 30^3; **6:**1, 2^4, 5, 6, 7, 8, 10^2, 11^3, 12, 13^3, 14^2, 16, 17^3, 18^2, 19, 20, 21^3, 22, 23^2, 25; **7:**4, 5, 6, 7, 8, 9^2, 11^2, 13, 17, 19, 23, 25, 29, 31, 35, 37, 41, 43, 47, 49, 53, 55, 59, 61, 65, 67, 71, 73, 77, 79, 83, 85, 86, 87, 88, 89^2; **8:**1, 2^3, 4, 5, 7, 8, 9, 10^2, 11^2, 12^2, 13, 14, 15^2, 16^2, 19^3, 21, 22, 23, 24^2, 26; **9:**1, 4, 6, 7, 9, 11^2, 13, 14, 16; **10:**1, 3^2, 4, 5, 6, 7, 8, 10, 12^2, 21, 29^3, 30, 33^2, 36^2; **11:**2^2, 4^2, 10, 11, 12^3, 13^2, 15^2, 16^3, 17, 18, 21, 26, 30, 31, 35; **12:**1, 4, 6^2, 8^2, 11, 13, 14, 13, 14; **13:**1, 2, 16, 17, 20, 22, 26^3, 27, 33; **14:**2, 3^4, 4^2, 7, 8^2, 9, 10, 14, 15, 16, 18^2, 23, 24, 25, 26, 28, 30, 31, 34, 35, 36, 38, 39, 40, 45; **15:**1, 2^2, 3^2, 4, 7, 8, 10, 11, 13^2, 14^2, 15^2, 16, 17, 18^3, 19, 21^2, 24^2, 25^2, 28, 29, 33, 34, 35, 36, 37, 38^4, 39, 40^2, 41; **16:**3^2, 5^3, 6, 8, 9, 10, 13^2, 15, 16^2, 17^2, 18, 19, 21, 23, 24, 25, 26, 27, 28, 29, 30, 34, 36, 37, 38^2, 39, 40^2, 42, 43, 44, 45, 46, 49, 50^2; **17:**1, 2, 5, 6, 9, 10^4, 12, 13; **18:**1^3, 2, 3^4, 5, 6, 7, 8^3, 9^2, 11, 13, 14, 15, 16, 17, 18, 19^2, 20, 21, 23^2, 24^2, 25, 26^2, 27, 28^2, 29, 30^2; **19:**1, 2, 3, 4, 5, 6, 13, 18, 19^2; **20:**2, 5^2, 6^3, 7, 8, 10, 12^2, 14, 16, 17^2, 19, 21, 22, 23, 24, 26, 29; **21:**1, 2, 3^2, 4^2, 5, 7, 8, 11, 12, 13, 14^2, 15^2, 16, 17, 19, 22, 23, 24^2, 26, 27, 28, 30, 31; **29:**1, 2, 5, 6^2, 8, 11, 12, 13, 16, 18, 19, 21, 24, 26, 28, 30, 31, 33, 34, 36, 37, 38, 39, 40, 41; **23:**3^4, 5, 6, 11, 13^2, 14, 15, 16, 17, 20, 26, 27^3, 28; **24:**1^2, 7, 9, 10^2, 13, 14^3, 20, 24; **25:**1, 2^3, 4, 5^2, 6^2, 10, 11, 15, 16; **26:**1, 2, 52, 53^2, 54^4, 55, 56, 59^2; **27:**1, 2, 6, 7, 8^2, 9, 10, 11^2, 12, 13, 14, 15, 17, 18, 21; **28:**1, 2^4, 3^3, 6, 7^2, 8, 10, 11, 12, 13, 14^2, 16^2, 17, 19, 22, 23, 24^2, 26, 27, 28, 30, 31; **29:**1, 2, 5, 6^2, 8, 11, 12, 13, 16, 18, 19, 22, 23^2, 25, 27, 28^2, 29, 33, 38, 39, 40; **33:**7^2, 9, 14, 49, 50, 51^2, 53, 54^3, 55, 56^3; **34:**1, 2^2, 4, 7, 8^2, 9, 10, 11, 13, 16, 18, 29^2; **35:**1, 2^3, 3, 6, 8^2, 9, 10^2, 11^2, 16, 17, 18, 21^2, 23, 24, 25^2, 26, 28, 29^2, 30^4, 31^2, 32^2; **36:**2^4, 3^2, 4^2, 7, 9, 12, 13; **Dt 1:**1, 2^2, 3, 5, 6, 7, 8^3, 9^2, 14, 15, 17, 18, 20, 22^4, 23, 24, 25, 26, 27^2, 29, 33^3, 35, 38, 39, 40, 41, 42, 44, 45^2; **2:**1, 2, 4, 5, 6^3, 9^2, 10, 12, 14, 17, 18, 19^4, 20, 22, 24, 25, 26, 27^2, 28^2, 30^2, 31^4, 32, 33^2, 34, 35, 36, 37^2; **3:**1, 2^2, 3, 4, 6, 7^2, 8^2, 9, 10, 11^4, 12, 13, 14^3, 15, 19^3, 20, 22, 23, 25, 26, 27^2, 28; **4:**1, 2, 4, 5, 6, 7^2, 8, 9^2, 10^4, 11, 12, 13^2, 14^3, 15, 19^3, 20, 22, 23, 25, 26, 27, 30^2, 31, 32, 36, 38^4, 39, 42, 48; **5:**1, 4^2, 5^2, 9^2, 10, 14, 15, 21, 22^2, 23, 27, 28^3, 29, 30^3, 31^2, 33^2; **6:**1^3, 3, 6, 10^3, 17, 18, 23^2, 24^2, 25; **7:**1, 2, 3, 4, 5^2, 6^2, 8, 9, 10^2, 11, 12^2, 13, 16^2, 17^2, 18^2, 19^2, 20, 21, 26, 28^3; **8:**1^2, 3^3, 2, 3^2, 11, 16, 17, 18^2, 19; **9:**1^3, 4^3, 5^4, 6, 7, 8, 9, 10, 13, 17, 18, 19^2, 20, 21, 26, 28^3; **10:**1, 2^2, 4, 6^2, 8^2, 9^2, 11, 13^2, 14, 16; **11:**1, 2^3, 3^2, 6, 7, 8, 10, 11, 12, 13, 14^2, 15^2, 16, 17, 19, 22, 23^4, 26, 27, 28, 30, 31, 32; **13:**1, 3^2, 4, 5^3, 7, 8^3, 9^2, 10^2, 12, 15, 16^3, 17; **14:**2^2, 8, 9, 10, 11, 12, 17, 21, 23, 24, 25, 26; **15:**2^2, 4, 5, 6, 8^3, 9^2, 10, 11, 12, 14; **16:**2, 7, 8, 9^2, 10^3, 11, 17, 21; **17:**1^2, 3^2, 4, 6, 8, 9, 12, 14, 16, 18^3, 19^3, 20^2; **18:**1^2, 4, 5, 6, 8, 9, 12, 14^2, 15, 17, 19, 20^2, 21, 22^3; **22:**1^2, 2, 4, 7, 15, 16^3, 17, 19^2, 20^3; **21:**1, 2, 3, 4^3, 8, 9, 14, 15^3, 16, 17^2, 18, 19, 20, 21^3; **22:**1^2, 2, 4, 5, 6, 7, 8^2, 10, 11^2, 12, 13, 14, 15, 17, 18, 20, 21^2, 23^2, 25; **24:**1^2, 3, 4, 5^4, 8, 9, 10^2, 11^2, 12, 13, 15, 18, 19, 22; **25:**1^2, 2, 5, 7^4, 8^2, 9^2, 11, 17, 19; **26:**2, 3, 5, 6, 9, 12, 13, 14, 15, 16, 19; **27:**3, 5, 6, 9, 12, 13, 14, 15, 16, 25; **28:**8, 11^2, 12^3, 13, 14^2, 20^2, 21, 25^2, 26, 29, 30^3, 31, 32^2, 35, 36^2, 37, 44^2, 46, 52, 55, 56, 57, 60, 63^3, 64, 68^2; **29:**1^2, 4, 7, 8, 12, 13^2, 18, 20, 21, 24, 26, 29^3; **30:**1, 2^2, 4, 5, 10, 12^3, 13^3, 16^4, 17^2, 18^2, 20^4; **31:**1, 2^2, 4^2, 5^2, 7^2, 9, 11, 12, 13, 17, 18, 19, 20^2, 21, 22, 23, 24, 25, 28, 29^4, 30; **32:**5, 7, 8, 15, 17, 18, 27^2, 35, 38, 39^2, 40, 45, 46, 47, 49, 50^2, 52; **33:**7, 8, 10^2, 19, 23, 26; **34:**1^2, 4^3, 6, 9, 10, 11^4; **Jos 1:**1, 2^4, 4^2, 5, 6^3, 7^3, 8, 11, 12, 14, 18; **2:**2^2, 3^3, 4, 7, 10, 12^3, 13, 16, 17, 22, 23^2; **3:**1, 3^2, 4, 6, 7^2, 9, 14, 16^3; **4:**1, 3^3, 5, 6, 7, 8^2, 9, 11, 12, 13^3, 14^3, 15, 19^2, 20, 22, 23, 24, 28, 30^2, 31, 32^4, 34; **5:**1^2, 2, 4^3, 6, 7, 8^2, 9, 13, 14; **6:**2, 10, 11, 14, 17^2, 18, 19, 21, 22^3, 23, 25^3, 26; **7:**1, 2, 3, 6, 7, 9, 10, 11^2, 12^2, 13, 19^2, 20, 21, 22^3, 23, 24, 26; **8:**1, 2, 3, 4, 7, 8, 9^2, 10, 12, 13^2, 18, 20, 23, 24^2, 27, 29^2, 30, 31, 32, 33^3, 35; **9:**2, 3, 6^2, 7^2, 9, 10, 11^2, 19^2; **10:**1^3, 6, 8^2, 10, 11^2, 12^3, 13, 14, 16, 18, 20, 21, 24, 28^2, 30, 31, 32, 33, 34, 35^2, 36, 37, 39^4, 41^2, 43; **11:**1^2, 2, 3^3, 5, 6^3, 8^3, 9, 10, 11,

12, 14, 17^2, 20, 23^3; **12:**1, 2, 3^2, 5^2, 6^2, 7^3; **13:**1^2, 3, 5^2, 6^3, 8, 10, 13^2, 14^2, 15, 17, 22^2, 24, 26^2, 27, 29^2, 33; **14:**1, 2, 4, 6^2, 7^2, 9, 10, 11^2, 14, 15; **15:**1^2, 3^4, 4, 6^2, 7^3, 8, 10^3, 11^2, 13^2, 16, 17, 18^2, 63; **16:**2, 3^2, 5, 6^3, 7, 8, 10^2; **17:**4^3, 6, 7, 8^2, 9, 10^2, 12^2, 13, 14, 17^2, 18, 19; **19:**11^2, 12^3, 13, 14, 27, 28, 29, 33, 47, 51; **20:**1, 2, 4^2, 6^2, 9^2; **21:**2^2, 8, 10^2, 12, 13, 26, 40, 43, 44^2, 45; **22:**2, 3, 4, 5^3, 6, 7^2, 8, 9^2, 10, 12, 15, 16^3, 17, 19, 20, 21, 22, 23, 24^2, 25, 27^3, 28^2, 29, 30, 31, 32^2, 33^3; **23:**2, 3, 6^3, 7, 8^2, 9^2, 11, 14, 16; **24:**2^2, 4, 6, 7^2, 8, 9^2, 10, 11, 15, 16^2, 17, 18, 19, 20, 22, 23^4, 24, 25, 27^3, 28, 33; **Jdg 1:**1, 2, 3^3, 5, 7^2, 8, 9, 12, 13, 14^2, 16, 19, 20, 22, 24, 25, 26, 27, 29^2, 33; **2:**1^3, 3, 4, 5, 6^2, 10, 12, 14^3, 15^3, 19^2, 20, 22, 23; **3:**1, 2^2, 3, 4, 6, 9, 10, 14, 15^2, 16, 17, 23, 25^2, 26, 28^2, 30; **4:**3, 5, 6^2, 7, 8, 9^2, 12, 13, 14, 17, 18^2, 21, 22; **5:**3^2, 6, 8, 11, 13^2, 23^2, 29; **6:**4, 5^2, 6, 7, 10^2, 11^2, 12, 13, 14, 17, 19, 20, 22, 23^2, 24^2, 25^2, 26, 31^4, 34, 35^2, 36, 39; **7:**2^3, 3, 4^2, 5^2, 6^2, 7^3, 8, 11, 13^2, 15, 17, 20, 22^2, 25; **8:**1, 2, 3^2, 4, 5, 6, 8, 9, 15^2, 20, 24, 25, 26, 27, 29, 33, 35^2; **9:**1^2, 2, 3, 4, 5, 6, 8, 9, 15^2, 16, 17, 20, 24^2, 25^2, 26, 27, 29, 33, 35, 36, 42^2, 44, 45, 47, 50, 51^2; **23:**3, 5, 6, 7, 8, 9, 10, 11, 12, 13, 14, 15, 16^2, 17; **24:**2^2, 3^2, 4, 5, 6^2, 7, 8, 9, 10, 11, 12, 13, 14^2, 16, 17, 18, 19, 20, 21^3, 22, 23^2, 24^2, 25; **1Ki 1:**2^2, 3, 5, 13^3, 14, 15, 17^2, 20, 21, 23, 30, 31, 33^2, 35^2, 37, 38, 47, 48^2, 51^3, 52^2, 53^2, 2:1^2, 2, 4^2, 5, 6^2, 7, 8^4, 9^3, 13, 14^2, 15^3, 16, 17, 18, 19^3, 20, 21, 24, 25^4, 26, 27, 29, 30^2, 36, 39, 40, 41, 42^2, 43, 44^2, 46; **3:**1, 3, 4^2, 5^2, 6, 7^2, 8, 9^3, 11, 15, 16, 21, 25^2, 26, 27, 28; **4:**5, 7, 11, 12^3, 21, 24, 25, 27^2, 28, 31, 33, 34; **5:**1^2, 2, 5, 7^2, 8, 9^2, 11^2, 14, 17; **6:**1, 8^3, 10, 11, 12, 15, 16^2, 18, 19, 22, 24, 33, 38; **7:**1, 3, 7^2, 8, 9^2, 11, 13, 14^2, 16, 18, 20, 21^2, 23^2, 24, 28, 32, 35, 38; **8:**1, 2, 6, 13, 15^2, 16^2, 17, 18^3, 19, 24, 25^4, 28, 31, 33^2, 34^2, 36^2, 37, 39^2, 40; **12:**1^3, 3^2, 5, 9, 13:3^2, 4, 5^3, 6^2, 7^2, 8^4, 9, 10^2, 11^2, 12^5, 16, 19, 20, 21, 22^2, 23, 24, 25, 14:1, 2, 3^4, 4, 5, 6^2, 7, 10^2, 11^2, 12^4, 19^3, 20; **15:**1^2, 2, 3, 4^2, 6^2, 7, 10^3, 11^2, 12^4, 14, 15, 16, 17, 18, 19, 22, 23^3, 25, 26, 28, 31; **17:**2, 3^4, 4, 8^2, 9, 10, 11, 12^3, 18:1^2, 2, 5^4, 6, 7, 9^3, 10, 11^2, 14^2, 15^2, 17^2, 19, 22, 23, 25, 27, 30, 31, 33, 34^3, 37, 38^2, 39, 40, 41, 42^2, 43^2, 44; **5:**1, 3, 4, 5, 6^2, 7^4, 8, 10^2, 11, 13^2, 15, 17, 18, 20, 21, 22^2, 23, 24, 26, 28, 29, 32, 33^2; **7:**2, 3, 4, 5, 6^3, 9^3, 10, 12, 13, 15, 17, 18, 19, 20; **8:**1^2, 3, 4, 5^4, 6, 7^2, 8^2, 9^3, 10^2, 11, 12, 14^2, 19^2, 21, 22, 25, 27, 28, 29^4; **9:**1^2, 2, 4, 7, 11^2, 15, 16^2, 19, 21, 23, 25^2, 27^3, 28, 30, 35, 37; **10:**1^4, 5, 6, 7, 13, 15, 17^3, 18, 19^3, 21, 22, 23, 24, 27, 29, 30^4, 31^2, 32, 33; **11:**1, 2^2, 4, 6, 9^3, 12, 13^2, 14^2, 15^2, 16, 18, 20^2, 21, 22, 12:3^2, 4^3, 5, 7, 9, 11^2, 14^2, 15^2, 16, 18, 20^2, 21, 23^3; **14:**1, 4, 6^2, 8^2, 9^3, 12, 13^2, 14, 19^2, 22, 24, 25, 26, 28; **15:**1, 4, 9, 12^2, 14, 16, 18, 19, 20^2, 28, 29, 32, 35, 37; **16:**1, 5, 6, 7^2, 8, 9^2, 10^2, 15, 18; **17:**3^4, 4, 5, 6, 7^2, 8, 9^2, 11, 13^2, 15, 16, 17, 21, 24, 26, 27, 28^2, 31, 32, 34^2, 35^2, 36^2, 37, 41^2; **18:**1, 4^2, 6, 8, 9, 11, 12, 14, 16, 17^3, 18, 19, 21, 27^3, 30, 34, 32^2, 35, 37, 19:2, 3^2, 4, 5, 6, 7, 9^2, 11, 14, 15, 16, 17^2, 18, 21^3, 22^2, 18^2, 20, 21, 26, 27^2; **20:**1^2, 2, 4, 5, 6, 7, 8, 9, 10, 14, 16, 17, 18; **21:**3, 5, 6, 7^2, 8, 12, 14, 15, 16^2, 21; **22:**3, 4, 5, 6, 7, 8^2, 9, 12, 14^2, 15^2, 16^2, 17, 18, 20^3; **23:**2^2, 3^2, 4^2, 5, 6^2, 8^2, 10^2, 11^2, 12, 15, 16, 17, 19, 20, 21, 22, 24, 26, 29^2, 30, 34^2, 35^2; **24:**2, 3^2, 4, 7, 10, 11, 12, 15^2, 16, 17, 20; **25:**3, 6, 7, 8^2, 9, 11^2, 14, 20, 22, 23, 24, 26, 28; **1Ch 1:**10, 19, 32; **2:**3^2, 9, 35, 49^2; **3:**1, 4, 5; **4:**9, 10, 17, 18, 39^2, 41, 43; **5:**1, 2, 26^2; **6:**19, 31, 32, 48, 54, 56, 70; **7:**4, 5, 11^2, 14, 16, 18, 21, 22, 23, 28^3; **8:**6, 8; **9:**1, 2, 18^2, 19, 21, 22, 25, 27, 29; **10:**4, 8, 9, 11, 12, 13, 14^2; **11:**1, 2, 3, 4, 5, 8, 10, 12, 15^2, 18^2, 19; **12:**1, 2, 17, 18^2, 19^2, 20^2, 23^3, 29, 31, 33, 38^4; **13:**2^3, 4^2, 5, 6^2, 9^2, 11, 12, 13^2; **14:**1^2, 4, 8^2, 9^2, 10, 11, 12, 15^2, 16, 17, 19, 20^2, 21, 23, 24^2, 25; **16:**3, 4^4, 5^2, 6, 7^2, 8, 9^2, 11, 16, 17, 22, 23, 25, 33, 34, 35, 36^2, 37^2, 38, 40^2, 41^2, 43; **17:**1, 2, 3, 4^2, 5^2, 6^2, 7, 10, 11^2, 15, 18, 19, 21^3, 25^2, 26, 27;

18:2, 3, 5, 6, 7, 8^2, 10^2, 11, 13; **19:**2^7, 3^5, 5, 6, 9, 12, 14, 15, 17, 19^2; **20:**1^2, 2, 3^3; **21:**1, 2^3, 3, 4, 5, 6, 8, 9, 10, 11^2, 13, 15^2, 17^2, 18^3, 19, 21, 22^3, 23, 24, 26, 27, 30; **22:**1, 2^3, 3, 4, 5, 6, 7^2, 8^2, 13, 14^3, 17, 18^4, 19^3; **23:**4^2, 5^2, 6, 7, 13^4, 25^2, 26, 27, 28^2, 30^3, 31^2; **24:**7^2, 8^2, 9^2, 10^2, 11^2, 12^2, 13^2, 14^3, 15^2, 16^2, 17^2, 18^2, 19, 30; **25:**5, 9^2, 10, 11, 12, 13, 14, 15, 16, 17, 18, 19, 20, 21, 22, 23, 24, 25, 26, 27, 28, 29, 30, 31; **26:**8, 13, 14^2, 15^2, 16, 18, 21, 31, 32; **27:**23, 24; **28:**1^2, 2^4, 3^4, 4^2, 5, 6^2, 8^2, 10, 13^4, 15, 20; **29:**1, 3, 5^3, 8, 9, 10^2, 12^2, 14, 16, 17, 18, 19^3, 20, 21^2, 22^2, 24, 29; **2Ch 1:**2^4, 3, 4, 6, 7^3, 8, 9, 10, 11^2, 13, 17; **2:**1, 3^3, 4^3, 5, 6^2, 7^2, 9, 11, 12, 14^2, 16^2, 17, 18^3; **3:**1^2, 8, 16, 17^4; **4:**2^3, 3, 6^2, 7, 18, 20, 22; **5:**2^2, 3, 7, 13^2; **6:**2, 4^2, 5^2, 27, 28, 30, 32, 34^2, 36^2, 38, 40, 41, 42; **7:**3^2, 8, 10, 11, 12, 13, 15, 18^2, 19, 21^2; **8:**3, 6, 8, 11, 12, 13, 14^3, 15^2, 17, 18^2; **9:**1^3, 2^2, 5, 8^4, 9, 11^2, 12^2, 14, 18, 23, 26, 29; **10:**1^2, 3^2, 5, 6, 7, 9, 10, 12^2, 15^3, 16^3, 18^3, 19; **11:**1^2, 2, 3^2, 4, 14, 16^2, 22^2, 23; **12:**2, 5^4, 7, 8, 10^3, 11^2, 13, 15; **13:**4, 5, 7, 8^2, 9, 11, 13, 14; **14:**4^2, 7, 10, 11^2, 15; **15:**2^3, 3, 4, 5, 9, 11, 12, 13^2, 14, 17; **16:**1, 2, 7^2, 9^2, 11; **17:**5, 6, 7, 9; **18:**2^4, 4, 5, 9, 12^2, 14, 15^2, 17, 19, 23^2, 24, 25^2, 28, 29, 31; **19:**1, 2^4, 4^2, 8^2, 10^2; **20:**1, 3^4, 7, 9, 10, 11, 12^2, 15, 17^2, 18, 20, 21^4, 22, 23^2, 24, 25^2, 26, 27^2, 28, 34, 36, 37^2; **21:**3, 4, 7^2, 10, 11, 13, 14, 15, 17, 20; **22:**1, 4, 5, 6^4, 7^3, 9^3, 10, 11; **23:**2, 3, 4^2, 5, 6^3, 7, 9, 10, 12, 14^3, 15, 17, 18^2; **24:**4, 5^3, 6^2, 9, 11^2, 13, 14, 17^2, 19, 21, 22, 23; **25:**4^4, 5^3, 7, 8^2, 10, 11, 12^2, 13^2, 14^2, 15, 16^4, 17^2, 18^3, 19, 20, 22^2, 23, 24, 26, 27^2; **26:**2, 6, 8, 11^2, 13, 15, 16^3, 18^3, 19, 20, 22, 23; **28:**5^2, 7, 8, 9^4, 10, 11, 13^2, 15^2, 16, 19, 20, 21, 22, 23^2, 25^3, 26; **29:**5, 7, 10, 11^3, 12, 15, 16^3, 18, 20, 21, 24, 27^2, 30, 31^2, 32, 33, 34; **30:**1^3, 2, 3, 4^2, 5^6, 6^2, 7, 8^2, 9^3, 10, 11, 12^2, 13, 15, 16, 17^2, 18, 19, 21, 22, 23, 27; **31:**1^3, 2^6, 4^2, 6, 10^4, 11, 14^2, 15^2, 16^3, 17^3, 19^3, 21; **32:**1^2, 2, 8^2, 9^2, 11, 12, 13^2, 14, 15, 18^3, 20, 23, 24, 25, 28, 30, 31^3; **33:**3^2, 5, 6, 7^2, 8^2, 10, 11, 13^4, 16, 17^2, 18^2, 22^3, 24^2, 3^4, 7^3, 8^2, 9, 10^2, 11^3, 13, 15^2, 16^3, 17, 20, 22^2, 23^2, 24, 25^2, 26, 28, 30, 31^3; **34:**2^2, 3^4, 7^3, 8^2, 9, 10^2, 11^3, 13, 15, 16^3, 17, 20, 22, 23^2; **35:**1, 2, 3^3, 4, 8, 11, 12^4, 13, 15, 20^2, 21^2, 22^3, 24, 25, 26, 27; **36:**4^2, 6^2, 7, 10, 13, 15, 17, 18, 19, 20^3, 23; **Ezr 1:**1^3, 2, 3, 4, 5, 6, 7, 8, 11; **2:**1^3, 63, 69^2; **3:**2^2, 3, 5, 6^2, 7^3, 8^2, 10, 11^3; **4:**2^3, 3, 4^2, 5^2, 7, 8, 11, 12^2, 14^3, 15, 17, 20, 21^2, 22^3, 24; **5:**1, 2, 3^2, 5, 6, 7, 8^2, 9, 12^2, 13, 14, 16, 17^2; **6:**3^2, 4, 5^4, 8^2, 9, 10, 11^3, 12^3, 14^2, 18, 21; **7:**7, 10^2, 11, 12, 13^2, 14^2, 15^2, 17^2, 19^2, 20, 21, 22, 24^2, 25^3, 27^3, 28^2; **8:**17^4, 20, 22^3, 25, 26, 28^3, 30^2, 31^2, 35^2, 36^4; **9:**1, 5, 6^3, 7^2, 8, 9, 11^2, 12^2, 13, 14; **10:**2^3, 3, 5, 6^2, 7, 8^2, 10^2, 11, 16, 19; **Ne 1:**3, 6, 9^2, 11^3; **2:**1, 3, 4^2, 5, 6, 7^2, 8^2, 9, 10, 11, 12, 14, 16, 17, 18, 20; **3:**1, 2, 4^2, 5, 7, 8, 9, 10, 16, 17, 18, 19^2, 20^2, 21^2, 22, 23, 24^2, 25, 26, 27^2, 29^2, 30^2, 31; **4:**2, 7, 8, 9^2, 11, 14, 15^2, 19, 22; **5:**2, 3, 4^2, 5^3, 7, 8^4, 9, 11, 12, 14, 15^2, 16, 17, 18; **6:**1^2, 2, 3, 5, 6^2, 7^2, 9, 10^3, 11, 13, 14, 17^2, 18^2; **7:**3^2, 5, 6^2, 65, 70^2, 71; **8:**1, 2, 3, 6, 9^3, 10^2, 12^4, 13^2, 14, 15, 18; **9:**4, 5, 6, 8^3, 10, 12^2, 13, 14, 15^2, 17^5, 19^3, 20, 22, 23, 24^2, 25, 26, 27, 28^2, 29^3, 30, 31, 33, 34, 35, 37, 38; **10:**28, 29^2, 30^2, 31, 32, 33, 34, 35, 36^2, 37^3, 38^4, 39^2; **11:**1^3, 2, 24, 30; **12:**23, 24^2, 27^2, 31^3, 37^2, 38, 44^2, 45, 46; **13:**2, 5, 6, 7, 9, 10^3, 13, 16, 19, 22^4, 24, 25^3, 27, 28, 30; **Est 1:**1, 5, 6, 8^2, 11^4, 12, 13, 14^2, 15^3, 17^2, 18, 19^2, 20, 22^3; **2:**3^3, 4, 8^3, 9, 10, 11^2, 12^3, 13^2, 14^3, 15^2, 16, 17^2, 20^2, 21, 22^2, 23; **3:**2, 4, 5, 6^2, 7, 8, 9, 10, 11^2, 12^3, 13^2, 14^3, 15; **4:**2, 3, 4, 5^2, 6, 7, 8^6, 9, 10^2, 11^6, 12, 14, 15, 16; **5:**2, 3, 4, 5, 6, 7^2, 8, 9; **6:**1^2, 2, 4^2, 6^2, 7, 9, 11, 12, 13^2, 14; **7:**1, 2, 5, 7, 8, 9; **8:**1, 2, 3^2, 4, 5^2, 6^2, 7^3, 8, 9^4, 11^3, 12, 13^3; **9:**1^2, 2, 5, 11, 12, 13, 15, 16, 19, 20, 21, 22^3, 23^2, 24, 25, 26, 27, 28, 29, 30, 31^2; **10:**1, 2, 3; **Job 1:**4^2, 6, 7, 8, 11, 12, 14, 15^2, 16, 17^2, 19, 20; **2:**1^2, 2, 3^2, 4, 5, 6, 7, 9^2, 11, 12, 13; **3:**4, 8, 10, 12, 20^2, 21, 23, 24, 25; **4:**5, 12, 20; **5:**1, 7, 8, 11, 16, 26, 27; **6:**7, 9^2, 13, 17, 20, 21, 26, 28^2; **7:**3, 6, 9, 10, 20^2; **8:**4, 5, 6, 15; **9:**3, 7, 12, 14, 33^2, 34; **10:**1, 2, 3^2, 9, 15, 19, 21^2, 22^2; **11:**2^3, 3, 4, 8, 12, 14, 19; **12:**3, 4, 8, 13, 16; **13:**2, 3^2, 6, 13, 15, 17; **14:**14; **15:**4, 8, 11, 17^2, 19, 24, 28, 35; **16:**10, 11, 18, 20; **17:**4, 6, 9, 14^2, 16; **18:**4^2, 14; **19:**17^2; **20:**2, 3, 9, 10, 13, 21; **21:**2, 4, 10, 12^2, 13, 14^2, 15, 21, 22, 29, 30, 31, 32, 33; **22:**2, 7, 15, 17^2, 21^2, 23, 24^2, 26, 27; **23:**3^2, 8^2, 9, 11; **24:**7, 16, 18, 21, 25; **25:**2; **26:**3, 12; **27:**9, 13, 14; **28:**3, 11, 23, 28^2; **29:**7, 8, 10, 12, 15^2, 16, 19, 21, 24; **30:**1, 2, 6, 10, 18, 19, 20, 22^2, 23; **31:**11, 12, 13, 14, 17, 24, 28^2, 29, 30, 32^2, 35; **32:**3, 4, 5, 6, 10, 11, 15, 19, 21; **33:**1^2, 2, 13, 17, 18, 21, 22^2, 23^2, 24, 26, 27, 28^2, 29, 30, 31, 32^2, 33; **34:**2, 9, 10^3, 15, 16, 18^2, 19, 23, 28, 30, 31, 33, 34, 36, 37; **35:**3, 4^3, 6, 7, 11^2, 13^2; **36:**2, 3, 10^2, 15, 16^2, 20, 21^3, 23, 24, 27, 32;

37:2^2, 3, 6^2, 12, 13^2, 14, 19, 20^2; **38:**12, 16, 17, 19, 20^2, 24, 26, 27, 29, 34, 35, 36, 37, 41; **39:**9, 10, 11, 12^2, 18; **40:**1, 4, 6, 8, 14; **41:**3, 4, 10^2, 11, 12, 16, 17, 28, 29; **42:**1, 3, 7^2, 8^2, 16; **Ps 2:**7, 9; **3:**4; **4:**1^2, 3; **5:**1, 2^2; **6:**T, 2; **7:**T, 2^2, 4, 5, 8^2, 9, 14, 17^2; **8:**T, 2; **9:**T, 2, 11, 17; **10:**6, 9, 11, 13^2, 14^2, 15, 17; **11:**1^2, 2; **12:**T, 2; **13:**3, 6^2; **14:**2; **16:**2, 10, 11; **17:**1^2, 5, 6, 11^2; **18:**T, 3, 6^2, 20^2, 24^2, 25^2, 26^2, 33, 35, 41^2, 43, 46, 49^2, 50^2; **19:**4, 5, 6, 8^2; **20:**8; **21:**4; **22:**T, 5, 11, 14, 15, 19, 22, 24, 27, 28, 29, 31; **24:**4; **25:**1, 2, 3^2, 7, 14, 16^2, 20; **26:**5, 11; **27:**2, 4^2, 6, 7, 12; **28:**1^2, 2, 6, 7; **29:**1^2, 2, 11; **30:**2, 4, 8^2, 10, 12; **31:**1, 2^3, 6, 8, 9, 11, 13, 17^2, 21^2, 22^2; **32:**5^2, 6, 9; **33:**1^2, 2, 3, 9, 19; **34:**T, 5, 11, 12, 15, 16, 18; **35:**2, 3, 4, 8, 13, 23, 26; **36:**2, 3^2, 4, 5^2, 10^2, 12; **37:**5, 8, 14^2, 18, 33, 34; **38:**4, 17, 22; **39:**6, 12^2; **40:**1, 2, 3, 4^3, 5^3, 8, 13^2, 14^2, 15; **41:**2, 6, 13^2; **42:**3, 4, 7^2, 8, 10, 12, 14; **43:**3^2, 4^2; **44:**7, 11, 13, 17^2, 20, 22, 25^2; **45:**T, 14^2; **46:**T, 9; **47:**1, 6^2, 7, 9; **48:**3, 10, 13, 14; **49:**4, 7, 10, 15; **50:**1, 5, 14, 16^2, 23; **51:**T, 1^2, 12^2, 13, 19; **52:**T, 5; **53:**T, 2, 5^2; **54:**T, 2, 6; **55:**1, 8, 15, 16; **56:**T, 1, 4, 5, 6, 11, 12^2; **57:**T, 2^2, 10^2; **58:**T; **59:**T, 3^2, 4, 5^2, 13, 17; **60:**T, 4, 9^2; **61:**1, 2^2, 4, 7, 8; **62:**4, 8, 12; **63:**8, 9, 10; **64:**8; **65:**1, 2, 4, 9; **66:**1, 3, 4, 12, 13^2, 15, 17, 20; **67:**1; **68:**4^2, 5, 16, 19^2, 31, 32^2, 33, 35^2; **69:**T, 1, 4^2, 6, 8^2, 13, 16, 25; **70:**1^2, 2, 5; **71:**1, 2, 7^2, 7, 10, 12, 13, 17, 18^3, 19, 22, 23, 24^2; **72:**3, 8^2, 10, 11, 12, 18, 19; **73:**1^2, 5, 9, 10, 16^2, 18, 27, 28; **74:**5, 7, 14, 19; **75:**T, 1, 4^2, 8, 9; **76:**7, 9^2, 11^3; **77:**1^3, 2, 4, 9, 10; **78:**1, 5, 6, 8^2, 10, 17, 18, 23, 24, 31, 34, 36, 44^2, 48^2, 50, 54^2, 55, 56, 62, 64, 66, 71; **79:**1, 2^2, 3, 4^2, 8, 11, 13; **80:**T, 6, 11, 14; **81:**T, 1^2, 8, 9, 11^2, 12^2, 13; **82:**2^3; **83:**8^2, 9^3; **84:**T, 7, 8; **85:**1, 8^3; **86:**2, 3, 4^2, 5^2, 6, 7, 9, 15, 16^2, 17; **88:**T, 2, 4, 8, 9^2, 10, 13, 15; **89:**3, 15, 18^2, 19, 22, 26, 28, 31, 35, 40, 44^2, 49, 52; **90:**2, 3^2, 12, 16^2; **91:**11; **92:**1^2, 2, 3; **94:**2, 19, 21; **95:**1^2, 4; **96:**1^2, 2, 4, 7^2, 8, 13^2; **97:**7; **98:**1, 2, 3, 4, 5, 9; **99:**7, 8; **100:**1, 4; **101:**1, 2, 3, 4, 5, 6, 8; **102:**1, 2, 4, 5, 13^2, 14, 17, 20^2, 22^2; **103:**7^2, 8, 10, 17, 18; **104:**7, 8, 11, 14, 15, 18, 19, 23^2, 26^2, 27^2, 28, 29, 33^2, 34; **105:**1, 2^2, 4, 9, 10^2, 11, 13^2, 14, 19, 22, 25^2, 29, 39, 42, 44; **106:**1, 4^2, 7, 8, 14^2, 16, 23, 26, 28^2, 29, 31^2, 32, 36, 37, 38, 41, 42, 46, 47, 48^2; **107:**1, 4, 6, 7, 8, 12^2, 13, 15, 19, 21, 26^2, 28, 29, 30, 31, 36; **108:**4, 10^2; **109:**6, 12, 16, 17, 20, 25, 28, 31; **110:**1; **111:**4, 10; **112:**5, 9, 10; **113:**3^2, 6; **115:**11, 16, 17; **116:**2, 7, 12, 14, 17, 18; **118:**1, 5, 6, 8^2, 9^2, 13, 18, 19, 27, 29; **119:**1, 4, 6, 9, 12, 17^2, 25, 28, 29, 31^2, 33^2, 37, 38, 41^2, 46, 48, 49, 57, 58^2, 59, 60, 62, 63^2, 65^2, 71, 72, 73, 76^2, 77, 78, 79, 80, 85, 88, 91, 95, 96, 103^2, 105, 107, 112, 116, 121, 124, 126, 130, 132^2, 133, 146, 149, 152, 154, 156, 159, 168, 169, 170, 173; **120:**3, 5; **121:**1; **122:**1^2, 4^2; **123:**1^2, 2; **124:**6; **125:**3^2, 4^2, 5; **126:**1, 6; **127:**2^2, 5; **128:**6; **130:**1, 2; **132:**2^2, 3, 4^2, 7, 8, 11; **135:**3, 4^2, 12, 21^2; **136:**1, 2, 3, 4, 8, 9, 10, 13, 16, 22, 23, 25, 26; **137:**6, 7, 8^2; **139:**6, 8, 12^2, 16, 17, 18; **140:**4, 6, 10; **141:**1, 3^2, 8^2; **142:**1^2, 4, 5, 6, 7; **143:**1^2, 3, 6, 7, 8, 10; **144:**1, 9^2, 10^2, 12; **145:**4, 8, 9, 13, 15, 18^2; **146:**2, 4, 7, 8; **147:**1^3, 6, 7^2, 14, 15, 19^2; **148:**14; **149:**1, 3, 7, 8, 9; **Pr 1:**4^2, 5, 8, 9, 10, 12, 16, 17, 23^3, 28, 29, 33; **2:**2^2, 7, 10, 13, 18^2, 19, 20; **3:**8^2, 10, 18, 22, 27, 28, 34, 35; **4:**1, 13, 20^2, 22, 27; **5:**1^2, 5, 7, 8, 9, 10, 12, 16, 17, 23; **6:**3^2, 4^2, 6, 10, 15, 22, 23, 24^3; **7:**1, 2, 3^3, 4, 5, 6^2, 7^3, 8, 9^4, 12, 15^2, 16, 19, 25, 28, 29; **8:**3^2, 8, 22, 27, 28, 29, 32, 33; **9:**2^2, 7, 10, 13, 18^2, 19, 20; **10:**8, 18, 22, 27, 28, 34, 35; **4:**1, 13, 20^2, 22, 27; **5:**1^2, 2, 5, 6, 7, 8, 9, 10, 11, 12, 14, 16; **6:**3^2, 4^2, 6, 7, 8, 9, 10, 12, 13^2, 15, 16^3, 17, 18; **7:**4, 6, 9, 10, 13^2, 15^2, 16, 19, 25, 28, 29; **8:**1, 3, 8^2, 10, 12, 13, 20, 24, 25^2, 26^2; **18:**5^2, 7, 8, 9, 10, 17, 24; **19:**2^2, 7, 10^2, 11^2, 17^2, 18, 19, 20, 22, 23, 24, 27; **20:**3^3, 6, 8, 13, 17, 25, 28; **21:**2, 3^2, 5^2, 7, 9, 12, 13, 15^2, 16, 19, 25, 28; **22:**1, 7, 16^2, 17, 21, 27, 28, 29, 32, 33; **23:**1^2, 2^2, 4, 5, 6, 7, 9, 12, 22, 26, 30; **24:**7, 11, 12, 13, 14, 23, 24, 28, 29^2, 32, 33; **25:**2^2, 7^3, 8^2, 12, 13, 20, 21^2, 24, 25, 26, 27^2; **26:**2, 4, 5, 8, 11, 15, 21^2, 22; **27:**7, 9, 10, 11, 23, 27^2; **28:**8, 9, 12, 20, 21, 22, 24, 27^2; **29:**3, 9, 10, 11, 12, 13, 15, 17, 25; **30:**1^3, 4, 5, 6, 10, 14, 17^2; **31:**4^2, 6^2, 20^2; **Ecc 1:**5, 6^2, 7, 11, 13^2, 16, 17; **2:**1^2, 3^2, 6, 11, 12, 14, 16, 18, 19, 20, 21, 24, 26^4; **3:**2^4, 3^4, 4^4, 5^4, 6^4, 7^4, 8^2, 11, 12, 14, 15, 17, 20^2, 22^2; **4:**8, 10, 13, 14, 16; **5:**1^3, 2, 4, 5^2, 6, 11^2, 13, 18^2; **6:**2^2, 6^2, 7^2, 8^2, 10, 18, 21, 23, 25^2, 27^2; **8:**3, 4, 5, 7, 8, 9^2, 10, 11, 15^2, 16, 17; **9:**2, 10, 11, 17; **10:**2^2, 4, 15, 16; **11:**2^2, 3^2, 7, 8, 9; **12:**4, 5, 7, 9, 10, 12; **SS 1:**4^2, 9^2, 13, 14; **2:**3^2, 4, 10; **3:**4^2; **4:**6^2; **5:**2, 4, 5; **6:**2^4, 11^3; **7:**9, 10, 11, 12^2; **8:**1, 2^2, 7, 11; **Isa 1:**4, 6, 10, 11, 12, 13, 14, 17, 21, 31; **2:**2, 3^2, 7^2, 8^2, 19^3, 20^2, 21^3; **3:**1, 9, 11, 13; **5:**5^2, 6, 8^3, 11^2, 18, 19, 20, 21, 22, 23,

29: 6:3, 5, 6, 7; **7:**1, 3^3, 4, 8, 10, 12, 13, 14, 15, 16, 20^2, 22; **8:**1, 3^3, 4, 5, 7, 8, 11^2, 13^3, 14, 19, 20^3; **9:**6^2, 13; **10:**1^2, 2, 3, 4, 5, 6^2, 7^3, 14, 15, 21, 25; **11:**10, 11, 14^3; **12:**4, 5^2; **13:**2^3, 3, 5, 9, 11, 14^2, 16; **14:**2^2, 4, 8, 9^2, 10, 11, 12, 13, 15^2, 19, 21^3, 32; **15:**2^3, 4, 5^2; **16:**1^4, 4, 10, 12^3; **17:**2^2, 7^2, 8, 9, 11; **18:**1, 2^2, 4, 6^2, 7^3; **19:**1, 3, 4, 11, 17^2, 18, 19^2, 20^3, 21^2, 22^2, 23^3; **20:**1, 2, 4, 5, 6^2; **21:**2^2, 4, 6, 11, 16^2; **22:**4, 5, 8, 10, 11, 12^3, 15^2, 16, 17, 18, 21^3, 22, 24; **23:**1, 5, 6, 7, 9^2, 12, 15, 17, 18; **24:**1, 9, 10, 11, 12, 15, 16^2, 20; **25:**11, 12^2; **26:**5^2, 10, 11, 14, 16, 17, 18^3, 19, 21; **27:**5, 6, 9^2, 12; **28:**1^3, 2, 6^2, 9^4, 11, 12, 13, 20^2, 21, 28, 29^2, 2, 11^2, 12^2, 13, 15^3, 16^2, 21, 22; **30:**1^2, 2^3, 3, 5^2, 6, 7, 8, 9, 10^2, 18^3, 21^2, 22, 28, 29^2, 30, 32; **31:**1^3, 4^2, 6, 8; **32:**7, 9^2; **33:**1^2, 2, 6, 10, 12, 14^2, 8, 10, 12, 14; **34:**2, 8, 10^2, 18, 21^2, 22, 28, 29^2, 30, 31; **35:**2^4; **36:**2^2, 3, 4, 6, 7^2, 10, 11^3, 12^4, 15, 16, 17, 20, 22; **37:**2^2, 3, 4, 5, 6, 7, 9^2, 10^2, 11, 12, 15, 16, 17, 20, 22, 21^2, 26^2, 27, 28, 37, 38; **38:**1^2, 2^2, 4, 5, 7, 14^2, 15, 16, 18, 21, 22; **39:**3^2, 5, 6, 7, 8; **40:**2^3, 9, 11, 14, 18, 20^2, 21, 22^3, 23; **41:**2^4, 3, 4, 6, 13, 15, 22^2, 27^2, 28^2, 29; **42:**1, 5, 6, 7^3, 8^2, 9, 10^2, 12, 17, 19, 21, 22^2, 23, 24, 25^3, 26^3, 27^3; **43:**6^2, 9^4, 11, 14, 17, 20, 21, 22, 24^2; **46:**2, 3, 4, 5^2, 6, 7^2, 8, 10, 11, 12, 13^2; **47:**8, 10, 11, 14^2; **48:**1, 3, 5, 6, 9, 12, 16, 18, 20; **49:**1, 3, 4, 5^4, 6^3, 7^2, 8^3, 9^3, 18, 20, 22^2, 23; **50:**1, 2^2, 4, 6; **51:**1^3, 2^2, 4^2, 5^2, 6, 9, 16, 17, 18^2, 23^2; **52:**4^2, 7, 8; **53:**1, 2, 4, 5, 8, 11; **54:**3^2, 6, 7, 14, 15, 16; **55:**1, 2, 3^2, 4, 5, 7^2, 10, 11; **56:**3, 4, 5, 6^3, 8, 10, 11; **57:**1, 6, 7, 9^2, 11, 15^2, 18, 19; **58:**1^2, 2^2, 4, 5^2, 6^2, 7^4, 14^2; **59:**1^2, 4, 7, 15, 16, 18^3, 20^2; **60:**3^2, 4, 5^2, 7, 8, 9^2, 13^2; **61:**1^4, 2^2, 3, 11; **62:**11^2; **63:**1, 5, 7, 8^2, 14^2; **64:**2^4, 5^2, 7; **65:**1^2, 3, 13, 15^2, 17, 18, 20, 23; **66:**5, 8, 9^2, 12, 14^2, 17, 18, 19^5, 20^3, 21, 23^2, 24; **Jer 1:**2, 3, 4, 5, 6, 7^3, 9, 10, 11, 12, 13, 14, 15, 16, 17, 18; **2:**1, 3, 9, 7^3, 10^2, 18^4, 24, 27^3, 30, 31^3; **3:**1^2, 2, 3, 4, 6, 7, 9, 10, 11, 13, 15, 18^3, 19, 21, 32; **4:**1, 2^2, 5, 6^2, 7, 11, 13, 16^2, 18, 22, 29, 31; **5:**3, 5^2, 6^2, 7, 10, 11, 12, 13, 15, 17, 18, 19, 23, 25, 26, 28, 29; **7:**1, 2, 6, 9, 10, 11, 12^2, 13, 14, 16, 18^2, 19, 21, 22, 26, 27, 28^2, 31, 33, 34; **8:**2, 3, 4, 5^2, 9, 10^3, 12, 14^3, 16^2, 19^2; **9:**3^2, 5, 6, 8, 12, 17, 20^2; **10:**1, 7, 9^2, 10^4, 11^2, 12^2, 13^2, 14, 17, 18, 19, 20, 23; **11:**1, 2, 12^2, 13^2, 15^3, 18, 19; **12:**3, 4, 8, 9^2, 12, 15, 16; **13:**1, 3, 4, 35, 37^3, 39; **24:**1, 9, 5^2, 6, 7^3, 9, 10; **25:**1, 2^2, 3^2, 4, 5, 6, 7^2, 8, 14, 15^2, 17, 18, 27, 28, 29, 30, 31, 32, 33, 34, 35^2; **26:**2^2, 4^2, 5, 8, 10, 12, 13, 15^3, 16^3, 19^2, 20, 23, 24^3; **27:**1, 2, 3^3, 4, 5, 6, 9^2, 10^2, 11, 12, 14^3, 15, 16, 17, 18, 20, 22^2; **28:**1, 3^2, 6, 7^3, 8, 9, 10^3, 11^2; **29:**1^3, 3^4, 7^2, 8^2, 9, 10, 11^3, 12^4, 14, 18, 19^2, 20, 21, 23^3, 25^4, 26, 28, 29, 30, 31^3; **30:**1, 2, 3, 13, 15, 17, 19, 21^3, 24; **31:**2^2, 3, 4, 6^2, 15, 17, 19, 21, 26, 28^4, 32^3, 34, 35^2, 36, 38, 39, 40^2; **32:**1, 2^2, 5, 8, 10, 11, 12^2, 13, 14, 15^3, 17^4, 18, 19, 21, 23^3, 24, 25^2, 26, 28, 29^2; **33:**1^2, 3, 6, 8, 9, 10, 12^3, 14, 15^2, 16, 17^2, 18^2, 19, 20^2, 21, 22, 25^2, 26; **34:**1, 2^3, 3^2, 5, 7^2, 8, 11^2, 13^3, 16, 18^3, 19, 21, 22; **35:**1^2, 4^4, 5, 6, 9, 11^2, 12, 14^3, 15^4, 18^3, 19; **36:**1^2, 3^2, 4^3, 5^2, 6, 8, 18, 19, 20; **37:**2, 3^2, 4, 6, 7, 10, 12^4, 13, 14^4, 17^2, 18, 19, 20, 21; **38:**2, 3, 4, 5, 8, 9^2, 11, 12, 13^3, 17, 18, 19, 21^2, 22^2, 23, 24, 25^3, 26^2, 27^2; **39:**1, 5, 7, 9^2, 14^3, 15, 16, 17; **40:**1^2, 2, 4^2, 5^2, 6, 7, 8, 9, 10^2, 12^2, 13, 14^3, 15^3, 16; **41:**1, 5, 6^2, 8, 10^2, 12, 14, 15, 17, 18; **42:**1^2, 4, 6, 7, 8, 9, 12^4, 17^3, 18, 19, 20, 21; **43:**1, 2^4, 3^3, 4, 5, 7, 8, 9, 10, 11^3, 12; **44:**1, 3, 5, 8, 10^2, 11^2, 12^4, 14^5, 15^2, 16^2, 17^2, 18^2, 19^5, 20, 24, 25^3, 28^2, 29, 30^3; **45:**2^2, 4^2, 4; **46:**1, 10, 11, 13, 16, 21, 24^2, 25, 26, 27^2; **47:**1, 4^3, 6, 7; **48:**1, 2, 3, 5^2, 9, 11, 21^2, 23, 24^2, 34, 35^3, 39, 46, 47; **49:**9, 12, 14^3, 19, 21, 24, 27, 29, 32, 34, 36, 39; **50:**2^4, 6, 15, 16^2, 17^3, 19, 25, 28^3, 29, 31^3, 34, 39, 42, 44; **51:**2^5, 9^2, 11, 13, 29, 31, 33, 35, 40, 44, 59^2, 61^2, 63, 64; **52:**3, 6, 9, 11, 12, 13, 14, 15, 16^2, 17, 19^2, 21; **La 1:**2, 4^2, 7, 9^2, 10, 11, 12, 14, 15, 16^2, 17, 19^2; **2:**1, 2, 4, 7, 11, 17, 20, 22; **3:**21, 24, 25; **Eze 1:**3, 16, 27; **2:**1^2,

2^2, 3^3, 4^2, 5, 7^2, 8^2, 9; **3:**1^2, 2, 3, 4^3, 5^2, 6^3, 7^4, 10^3, 11^4, 15, 16, 18^3, 21, 22^3, 23, 24^2, 26^2, 27^2; **4:**2^2, 3, 4, 8, 9, 10, 16; **5:**1, 2^4, 4, 7, 9, 10, 12, 15, 16; **6:**1, 3^3, 10, 13, 14; **7:**1, 2, 3, 9, 10, 11, 12, 13, 14, 15, 16; **6:**1, 3^3, 10, 13, 14; **7:**1, 2, 3, 9^2, 10, 14, 15, 16; **8:**2^3, 3^4, 5, 6, 7^2, 8^2, 9, 12, 14, 15^2, 16^2, 17^4, 18; **9:**3^3, 4, 5, 7, 8, 10^2; **10:**2^4, 4, 7, 16, 19; **11:**1^2, 2, 3, 5, 9, 12, 14, 15, 18, 20, 23; **12:**2^4, 4, 7, 9, 11, 12, 15^3, 18, 20, 21^2, 24^3, 26, 28; **13:**1^3, 2, 3, 4, 6^3, 7, 11, 12, 13, 14, 15, 16, 17, 18, 19, 22^3; **14:**1, 3, 9, 10, 11, 12, 14^3, 16^2, 18^2, 20^3, 21; **15:**1^3, 2^3, 3, 4, 5, 6, 7, 10, 11, 15, 19; **16:**1, 5^2, 8^2, 9, 11, 15, 19; **17:**4, 8, 10^3, 11, 13, 15, 17, 18, 19, 20, 21, 23, 24, 26, 27; **18:**1, 2, 3, 4, 5, 7, 9, 10, 11, 13, 16, 18, 19, 20, 21, 22, 23; **19:**2, 3, 4, 5^2, 7, 11, 12^2, 13, 14, 15^2, 20^3, 23, 20^3, 4, 5^2, 6, 9, 10, 12, 13^2; **20:**3, 4, 5, 8^2, 12, 15, 16, 19, 20, 23; **21:**1^2, 4, 7^2, 9, 10, 11, 12, 22; **22:**1, 3, 4, 6, 8, 13, 15, 16, 20, 25^3, 27^3; **23:**1, 2, 3, 5, 8, 12, 14, 16^2, 17^3, 18^2, 20, 21, 22, 23; **24:**1, 3, 5, 6, 7^2, 9, 10; **25:**1, 2^2, 3^4, 4, 5, 6^2, 7^3, 8, 14, 15^2, 17, 18, 27, 28, 29, 30, 31, 32, 33, 34, 35; **26:**2^2, 4^2, 5, 8, 20, 21, 23, 24; **27:**1, 2, 3^3, 4, 5, 6, 9^2, 10^2, 11, 12, 14, 15, 16, 17^2, 18, 19, 20, 21; **28:**1, 3^4, 4, 7, 16; **29:**1^3, 3^4, 7^2, 8^2, 9, 10, 11^3, 12^4, 14, 18, 19^2, 20, 21, 23^3, 25^4, 26, 28, 29; **30:**1, 2, 3, 13, 15, 17, 19, 21^3, 24; **31:**2^2, 3, 4, 6^2; **32:**1, 2^4, 4, 7, 11, 12, 13, 15, 16, 17, 19, 23, 26, 28, 32; **37:**2, 3^2, 4, 6, 7, 10, 12^4, 13, 14^4, 17^2, 18, 19, 20, 21; **38:**2, 3, 4^3, 5, 8, 9, 11^4, 12^3, 13, 14, 16, 19, 21^2, 22^2, 23, 24, 25^3, 26^2, 27^2; **39:**1, 5, 7, 9^2, 14^3, 15, 16, 17, 40; **40:**1, 2, 4^2, 5^2, 6^2, 7^4, 8^2, 9, 10^2, 12^5, 16^3, 17^3, 19, 21, 22, 23, 24^3; **41:**1, 2, 3^3, 4, 5^3, 6, 7^8, 8, 9, 13^3, 14, 15^4, 17, 18, 19^2, 20, 21, 23^3, 24^2, 27^2; **42:**1, 3^2, 4, 6, 10, 13; **43:**2, 3^6, 5, 10^2, 11, 13^2, 14, 15^3, 16^2, 17, 18^2, 19, 20, 24, 28^2; **44:**1, 2, 3, 6, 11, 17, 19^2, 20, 21, 22, 25, 26, 27, 29, 30^4; **45:**1^2, 2, 4, 5^2, 6^2, 7^8, 8^2, 9, 11^2, 12^2, 13^2, 14, 17, 18^3, 19, 20^2, 21, 22, 23, 24, 25; **46:**1^2, 3^2, 4^2, 5, 6^2, 8^2, 9^5, 10, 11, 12, 13^2, 14^3, 16, 17^3, 18, 19; **47:**1, 2, 4, 5, 6, 8, 10, 12, 13, 14^3, 15^2, 17^2, 18, 19, 20, 21^2, 22, 23^2; **48:**1^3, 2, 3, 4, 5, 6, 7, 8^3, 9^2, 12, 14, 21^4, 22^2, 23, 24, 25, 26, 27, 28^2, 29^2; **Da 1:**1, 2, 3, 4^3, 5^2, 7^4, 10^3, 11^4, 15, 16, 17^3, 18^3, 19^2; **2:**2^2, 3, 5, 8, 9, 11, 13^5, 14^3, 15, 16, 17^2, 18, 19^2, 23^2, 24^4, 25, 26, 27, 28^3, 30, 35, 36, 39, 40, 44^2, 45, 46, 47^2; **3:**2^4, 4, 9, 12, 14, 15^2, 16^2, 17, 18, 20, 24, 28^2; **4:**1, 2, 3, 6, 11, 17, 19^2, 20, 21, 22, 25, 26, 27^3, 28, 32, 34, 35, 36^2, 37; **5:**2^2, 7, 11, 12^2, 13, 15, 17^2, 19^6, 23, 26, 28; **6:**1^2, 2, 3, 4^2, 5, 6, 7, 10^2, 12^4, 23, 26, 28; **8:**1^2, 7, 9^2, 11, 12, 13, 14, 15, 16, 17^2, 18, 19, 25; **9:**2^3, 4, 6^3, 7, 11, 12, 13, 14, 15, 16, 17, 18, 19^2, 20, 21, 22, 23^3, 24, 27; **10:**1^4, 9^2, 11^4, 12^3, 13, 14^4, 15, 16, 19, 20^2; **11:**1, 4, 6^2, 7, 8, 9, 16^2, 17^3, 18, 19, 20, 21, 22, 23, 24, 25, 27; **12:**2^3, 3, 4, 6, 10, 13; **Hos 1:**1, 2^3, 4^2, 6, 7^4, 9, 13, 14^2, 19, 21^2, 22^2, 23^2; **3:**1^3, 5; **4:**1, 10, 11^2, 12, 13^2, 14^2, 15^2, 17; **5:**3^2, 4^2, 12, 13^4, 14, 15; **6:**1^2, 3^2, 7, 9, 10; **7:**10, 11^2, 13^3, 14, 16; **8:**1, 2, 4, 7, 9, 10, 13^2; **9:**1, 3, 4^2, 10^2, 12, 13; **10:**6, 8, 10, 11, 14, 15; **11:**2^3, 3, 4, 5^2, 6, 7^2, 12^2; **12:**1, 2^3, 6, 7, 10, 12^3, 13, 14; **13:**13^2, 16; **14:**1, 2, 3, 5, 8; **Joel 1:**1, 3^3, 14^2, 19; **2:**2, 12, 13^2, 19, 24, 25, 31, 32^2; **Am 1:**5, 6, 9, 13, 14; **2:**1, 7, 10, 12; **3:**3, 5, 6, 7, 9^2, 10, 14; **4:**1, 4^5, 5, 6, 8^3, 9, 10, 11, 12, 13^2; **5:**2^2, 4, 5, 6, 11, 16^2, 18, 19^2, 23; **6:**1^3, 2^3, 7, 10^2, 14; **7:**7, 10, 12^2, 15^2; **8:**2, 3, 12^2, 3, 4, 7, 11, 15; **Ob 1:**1^3, 3^2, 5^2, 7, 14, 15, 21; **Jnh 1:**1, 2, 3, 4, 5, 6, 7, 12^2, 13, 14, 16^2, 17; **2:**1, 2, 6, 7, 8^2, 9^3; **3:**1, 2, 3, 5; **4:**2^4, 3, 6^2, 8^3, 9^3; **Mic 1:**1, 7, 9^2, 12^2, 14^2, 15; **2:**1^3, 4, 5, 7; **3:**4, 5, 8^3; **4:**1, 2, 6, 8^2; **5:**3^3, 4, 13; **6:**1^3, 3, 4, 5, 8^3, 9^2, 10, 12^2, 13^3, 16, 14^2, 19; **7:**1, 2, 10, 12^4, 17, 18, 20^3; **Na 1:**3, 9, 14; **2:**5, 11; **3:**11, 7, 10, 13, 18^2; **Hab 1:**2, 5, 6, 7, 8, 12^2, 13, 16^2, 17; **2:**1^4, 5, 6, 9^3, 12, 15, 16, 17, 19^4; **3:**13^3, 14, 16, 19; **Zep 1:**1, 5, 18; **2:**5, 7, 11, 15; **3:**1, 2, 4, 7^2, 8^4, 9, 11^2, 16, 17, 18, 19; **Hag 1:**1^2, 2, 4, 5, 6, 7, 9, 13, 14; **2:**2^3, 3^2, 10, 15, 16^3, 17, 18, 20; **Zec 1:**1, 3^2, 4^2, 6^2, 7, 10, 11, 13, 14, 15, 16, 19, 21^2; **2:**2^2, 3, 4, 6, 8^2; **3:**1, 2, 4^2, 6, 8^2, 10; **4:**2, 6^2, 7, 8, 9, 14; **5:**3^3, 5^2, 10, 11^2; **6:**4, 7, 8, 9, 10, 14, 15^2; **7:**1, 2, 4, 8, 9, 11, 12, 13^2, 14; **8:**2^4, 3, 4, 6, 7, 9, 12, 14, 15^2; **9:**7, 9, 10^3, 12^2; **10:**1^2, 10; **11:**3^2, 6, 13^3, 15, 16, 19; **12:**4^2, 6, 13^2; **13:**7; **14:**2^2, 4, 5, 7, 8^2, 10^4, 16^2, 17^2, 18, 19, 20, 21^2; **Mal 1:**1, 3, 8, 9^2, 11^2, 14^3; **2:**2^3, 5, 7, 8, 9, 12, 13; **3:**1, 4, 5^2, 7^3, 14; **4:**1, 6^2; **Mt**

1:11, 12, 17⁴, 18³, 19³, 20², 21², 22, 23; 2:1, 2, 4, 8², 11, 12³, 13⁴, 16, 18, 19, 20², 21, 22²; 3:5, 7³, 9, 11, 13², 14³, 15²; 4:1, 3², 5, 7, 8, 10, 12, 14, 15, 17, 24; 5:1, 2, 13, 15, 17³, 19, 21², 22³, 24, 25³, 29³, 30³, 32, 33², 39, 40, 41, 42², 45; 6:1², 2³, 3, 5², 6, 16, 18², 24, 27, 33; 7:2, 3, 4, 5, 6², 7², 8, 11³, 12², 13, 14, 15, 21, 22; 8:4³, 5, 7, 8, 9, 10, 11, 13, 15, 16, 17, 18², 19, 20, 21, 25, 29, 32, 33, 34²; 9:1², 2³, 3, 5², 6², 8, 13, 20, 21, 28², 29², 32, 37, 38; 10:1³, 6, 13, 14, 17, 18², 19³, 21², 22², 23, 25, 29, 34³, 35, 42; 11:1³, 2², 4, 5, 7³, 8, 9, 14², 16², 20, 21², 23², 25, 27³, 28; 12:1, 2, 4, 10², 11, 12, 13, 16, 17, 18, 20, 25, 32, 36, 38² 42², 44, 46³, 47², 48, 49; 13:3, 10², 11², 13, 17², 18, 27, 28, 30, 34², 36², 52, 54, 57; 14:2, 4², 5, 7, 11², 13, 15², 16², 18, 19⁴, 22, 23, 25, 27, 28², 30, 35², 36; 15:1, 4, 5², 6, 10, 12, 15, 21, 22, 23, 24, 26², 30, 32³, 33, 35, 36²; 16:1³, 3, 5, 6, 11, 12, 13, 17, 20, 21⁴, 22², 23², 24, 25, 27²; 17:4², 5, 6, 11, 12², 13, 14, 16, 17, 19, 20², 22², 23, 24, 25, 26, 27²; 18:1, 6³, 7³, 8³, 9³, 12, 15, 17⁵, 21², 23, 24, 25², 28, 29, 32, 34²; 19:1³, 3³, 5, 8, 10², 13², 14², 16², 17², 21², 23², 24², 27, 28; 20:1², 2, 7, 8², 10, 11, 12, 13², 14, 15, 17², 18³, 19³, 20, 22², 23⁴, 26, 27, 28³, 31, 32; 21:1², 3, 4, 5², 9, 13, 14, 15, 17, 18, 19², 21², 23, 30, 31, 32², 33²; 22:1, 3, 5², 6, 37, 38, 40, 41², 42², 43, 44, 46; 23:1², 3⁵, 4, 5², 8², 9², 12, 15, 16², 17², 18, 21², 23, 25, 26², 28, 31, 43, 44, 46; 24:1³, 3, 6², 9², 13, 14, 16, 17, 18, 21, 23, 24, 31, 38, 45, 48, 49² 51; 25:1, 6, 8, 9, 10², 14, 15⁴, 16, 25, 28, 34, 35², 36, 37, 39, 41, 42², 46²; 26:1, 2, 4, 7, 9, 10², 12, 14, 16, 17³, 18², 22², 24, 26, 27, 30, 35, 36², 37, 38², 39, 40, 42, 45², 49, 52, 55², 57, 58², 59, 61, 62², 63, 64, 68, 69, 71², 73, 74²; 27:1², 2, 3, 4, 6, 7², 8, 10, 13⁴, 15, 17², 18, 19, 20², 21², 26², 31, 32, 33, 34², 40, 48², 49, 51, 52, 53, 55, 58², 60, 62, 64; 28:1, 2, 5, 8, 9, 10³, 11, 13, 14, 15, 16³, 18², 20²; Mk 1:5, 7, 21², 24, 27, 29, 31², 32, 35, 36, 38, 40, 44³, 45²; 2:2, 3, 4, 5, 6, 8, 9³, 10², 13², 17², 23, 24, 26², 27; 3:2², 3, 4⁵, 5, 6, 7, 8, 9², 10, 12, 13², 14², 16, 17, 20, 21, 23, 31; 4:1, 3, 9, 11², 13, 21², 22², 23, 24, 29, 30, 33, 34, 35², 38, 39, 40; 5:1, 2, 4, 7, 8, 10, 12, 14, 15, 16, 17², 18, 19, 20, 21, 25, 32, 33, 34, 38, 39, 41², 43²; 6:1, 2, 4, 6, 7, 11, 17, 18², 19², 20², 22³, 23, 24, 25², 26, 27, 28², 30, 32², 33², 34², 36², 37², 39, 41³, 45, 46, 48², 50, 55, 56; 7:3, 5, 8, 9², 10, 11², 14², 24², 26, 27², 31, 32², 34², 35, 36; 8:1², 2, 4, 6³, 7, 10, 11², 12, 13, 14, 15³, 18³, 20, 21, 22², 27, 30, 31, 32, 34, 35, 36; 9:1, 5², 6, 7, 9, 10, 12, 13, 14, 15, 16, 17², 18, 19, 20, 21, 25, 27, 30, 31², 32, 33, 35, 36, 38, 41², 43³, 45³, 47³; 10:1, 2, 4, 7, 13², 14³, 17², 21, 23², 24, 25², 26, 28², 30², 32², 33³, 34, 35², 36, 37², 38, 39, 40³, 43, 44, 45⁴, 46, 47, 48, 49, 50², 51²; 11:1, 2², 6, 7, 11², 13, 14, 16, 18, 21, 23, 27, 28; 12:1³, 2², 4, 6, 7², 9, 11², 12, 13, 14, 14⁴, 15, 17³, 18, 23, 26, 33², 34, 36, 37, 38, 43, 44; 13:1, 4, 5, 7, 9², 10, 11², 12², 13, 14, 15, 16, 19, 21², 22², 27, 34, 37²; 14:1, 4, 5, 6, 8, 10³, 11³, 12², 14, 19, 21, 22, 23, 24, 26, 31, 32², 33, 34², 35, 37², 40², 41, 45, 48, 53, 55, 60, 65, 69, 70, 71², 72; 15:1, 4, 6, 8, 9², 10, 15³, 18², 19, 20, 21, 22, 24, 29, 36³, 38, 41, 43, 44, 45; 16:1, 2, 8, 9, 12, 13, 14², 15², 19²; Lk 1:1, 2, 3, 5, 9, 11, 13², 14, 15, 16, 17⁴, 19³, 20², 23, 26, 27³, 28, 30, 31², 35, 36, 38, 43, 45, 50², 54, 55², 57², 59², 60, 61, 62³, 63, 64, 66, 68, 72³, 73, 74³, 76, 77, 78, 79², 80; 2:3², 4³, 5³, 6, 7, 9, 10, 11, 12³, 13, 16, 17², 18, 20; 4:3², 5⁴, 6⁴, 9, 10, 12, 14, 16³, 17, 18⁴, 19, 20, 21, 23², 26², 29²; 31², 34, 36², 38², 39, 40, 41, 42³, 43³; 5:1, 2, 4, 6, 7, 10, 12, 14², 15², 17, 18², 19, 21, 23², 24², 26, 27, 30², 32², 33; 6:1², 4², 5, 7², 8², 9, 10², 11², 12², 13, 18², 19, 24², 25, 27², 29², 30², 31², 32, 33³, 34², 35⁴, 38², 41, 42², 47; 7:2², 3², 4⁴, 6², 7², 8, 9, 10, 11, 13, 14², 15², 16, 19³, 20⁴, 21, 24³, 25, 26, 31, 32, 36², 38, 39, 40, 41, 42, 44, 48, 49, 50; 8:1, 3, 4, 5, 8, 10², 19², 20², 22², 23², 25², 26, 27, 29³, 32², 35², 37, 38, 41², 43, 48, 50, 55², 56; 9:1², 2, 6, 8, 9, 10², 11, 12², 13, 14, 16, 16², 21², 22, 23, 24, 25, 28, 31², 33², 35², 36³, 38, 40, 42², 43, 44³, 45, 46, 48, 49, 51², 52, 54²; 56, 57, 58, 59, 60, 61, 62; 10:1², 2, 5, 6, 7, 11, 13², 16², 17², 19², 22², 23, 25² 27², 29, 30, 31, 32, 34², 35, 36, 38², 39; 11:1², 2³, 5, 37, 39, 41, 42, 43, 44², 46³, 47, 51, 52, 54²; 12:1³, 2², 3, 4⁶, 5, 6, 9³, 10², 11², 12², 15, 17, 18, 19, 21, 24, 26², 27, 30², 31³, 32², 33⁴, 34², 35, 37, 39, 40, 41, 42, 44, 48, 49, 50; 13:6, 7², 12, 14, 15, 16, 17², 18², 19, 20², 21², 24², 31³, 34², 35; 14:1, 3, 6, 8, 9², 10², 12, 15, 17, 18, 19, 21, 25, 26, 28³, 29, 30², 31³, 35; 15:1, 7, 12, 14, 15³, 16, 17³, 18², 19, 20², 21², 22, 24, 28,

---

32; 16:3³, 9, 13, 15, 17², 21, 22, 24², 26³, 27, 28, 29, 30, 31²; 17:1⁴, 2³, 4, 5, 6², 7, 9, 10, 11, 14, 18², 19, 22², 24, 27, 31, 33; 18:1, 3, 4, 6, 7, 9, 10², 13, 15, 16³, 18, 22², 24, 25², 28² 29, 30², 31, 32, 39, 40², 41², 42; 19:3, 4, 5, 7², 8², 9², 10², 11³, 12³, 13, 14², 15², 24², 26², 27, 28, 29, 30, 35, 37, 39, 44², 46, 47, 48; 20:1, 9², 10, 15, 16, 18, 19, 20³, 22³, 23, 25², 26, 27, 33, 38, 40, 41, 42, 45, 46²; 21:4, 5, 7, 10, 12, 13, 14, 15, 16, 21, 24, 28, 36³, 37, 38; 22:2, 4, 5, 6², 7, 8, 9, 10, 11, 15², 19, 21, 22, 23, 24, 26, 27, 29², 34³, 35, 42; 23:1, 2², 4, 7, 8², 11, 14², 15², 18, 20², 22, 24, 25, 28, 30², 32, 33, 48, 51, 52, 54, 56, 64; 24:1, 5², 9, 10², 13, 14, 18, 22², 24, 27, 31, 33, 36³, 39, 40, 41², 42²; Jn 1:7, 8, 9, 11, 12³, 19, 20, 22², 27, 31, 33, 41, 42, 43²; 2:2, 3, 5, 6, 7², 8, 10, 12, 13, 16, 18², 20², 24; 3:2, 4, 6², 11², 12², 13, 16, 18², 19², 20, 21, 23, 26³, 27, 29, 31, 32; 4:3, 4, 5², 7², 8, 9, 10², 13², 14, 15³, 17, 18, 21, 23², 24, 25², 27, 28, 31, 43², 52²; 5:1, 3, 6, 7², 8, 10², 11, 12, 14², 17², 18, 20, 21², 22, 24, 26, 27², 29, 30², 31, 32, 36², 37², 39², 40, 43, 44, 47²; 6:1, 2, 4, 6, 7, 11, 17², 19², 20², 22², 23, 24, 25², 26, 27, 28², 29² 31, 32², 35, 37, 39³, 40, 41, 42, 45², 46, 47, 48; 7:1, 3³, 4, 8², 14², 17, 18, 19, 20, 21², 25², 26, 30, 32, 33², 37, 39⁴, 44, 45, 50, 51, 53; 8:1², 4, 5, 6², 7², 9, 11, 12, 13, 16², 17, 18², 20, 21, 25, 26, 28², 29, 30², 31², 32, 33², 34, 35, 37, 40, 42, 43² 44³, 47², 57, 59²; 9:8, 11², 13, 14², 17, 18, 22, 26, 27², 29³, 31², 34²; 10:3, 8, 10², 16, 17, 18², 20, 27, 28, 29, 31, 32, 33, 35, 39, 40, 41; 11:3, 7², 8, 11², 15, 16, 19², 20, 21, 23, 25, 27, 29, 31², 38, 44, 45, 46, 52, 53, 54², 55, 56; 12:4, 5, 6², 9, 10, 11, 13, 16, 17, 18, 19, 20, 21², 22, 23, 24, 27, 29, 32, 33², 35³, 38², 47², 49², 50²; 13:1², 2, 3, 5, 6³, 10, 11, 12, 18², 21, 22, 23, 24, 26², 27, 28, 29², 14:2, 5, 6², 9, 10, 11, 13, 15², 16², 20, 21, 22, 23, 26, 27, 28²; 15:3, 8², 15, 16, 19², 20, 22, 25, 26, 16:2², 5², 7², 8, 9, 10, 11, 12, 13, 14², 15², 16³, 17, 19, 21, 22, 24², 25², 26³, 27, 28²; 17:3, 4, 5, 7², 8, 9, 11, 15², 16³, 18, 22, 24², 25³, 26, 14:2², 5, 6, 7, 8, 11, 13, 14², 20², 21²; 18:1, 3, 4², 8, 12², 14², 15, 19, 22², 23², 24, 26, 27², 28, 29², 31, 32, 33, 38, 39, 40, 42³, 48; 11:2, 4, 5, 10, 11, 12, 13, 15, 17, 19, 20³, 21, 22, 23², 24, 25², 26, 27, 29²; 20:12², 13, 14, 15², 18, 19², 21, 25, 27, 28, 30², 31²; 21:1⁴, 2³, 4², 5, 6, 7², 10, 11³, 13², 14, 16², 23, 24³; Ac 1:1², 2², 6², 7², 8, 12, 13, 16, 20, 21, 22², 25², 26², 2:3⁴, 4, 11, 14², 20², 22², 23², 24, 29³, 31, 32, 33², 34², 37², 41, 42⁴, 45, 46, 47; 3:1², 2³, 5, 8² 10², 11², 12, 13, 14, 16, 19, 21, 22, 23, 25, 26², 4:1², 4, 7, 8², 9², 12, 15, 16, 17³, 18, 19, 21, 22², 27, 29, 29, 30, 33², 34, 35², 36³, 37², 5:3, 4³, 9², 12, 14², 21², 28², 31², 32², 33², 35³, 36³, 37, 38, 39, 41²; 10:2², 3², 4², 5², 7², 10, 13³, 14, 15, 16, 17, 21, 22³; Heb 1:1, 2, 4², 5, 13, 14; 2:1, 3, 4², 5², 8², 10, 12, 17², 18; 3:2, 5, 6, 12, 14², 20, 22, 23, 24, 26³, 27⁵; 19:4, 9, 12, 13², 17, 19, 21² 22, 30, 31, 33², 36, 39, 40; 20:2, 3², 7³, 9, 13², 14, 16, 19², 20, 25, 26, 27², 28⁴; 10:1, 4, 7, 8, 9², 13, 15, 16, 19, 22³, 23, 29, 30, 31, 33, 36; 11:6², 7, 8², 10, 11, 15, 16, 17, 18, 20, 24, 25², 26, 29, 32, 34, 35², 37², 24:1, 4², 5, 6, 8, 10, 11², 13, 14, 17, 19, 23², 24, 25, 27²; 25:1, 3⁴, 6, 9⁴, 10², 11⁴, 12², 13², 15, 16, 17, 18, 20³, 21², 22², 24, 25, 26³, 27; 26:1², 2, 5, 7, 9, 10, 11⁶, 12², 13, 15, 16², 17, 18, 21, 22², 30, 31, 33, 34², 39, 40, 41, 42³, 44; 28:4², 6², 7³, 8, 10, 11, 14², 15, 16³, 17², 18, 19³, 20²,

---

21; 6:2, 6, 10², 11², 13⁴, 16⁷, 17⁴, 18, 19⁵, 20, 7:1, 2, 4, 6, 9, 10, 11, 13, 14, 15, 16, 18, 19², 20, 21, 25³; 8:3², 4², 5, 7², 9, 11, 12³, 13², 15, 19, 20, 21, 22, 26, 28, 29², 31, 34, 36, 39; 9:15, 17, 18², 19, 20³, 21, 22, 23², 26, 33²; 10:1, 3², 6, 7, 11, 14, 18, 20, 21; 11:3, 4², 5², 6, 9, 11, 13², 22, 24, 25, 30, 31, 32, 35, 36²; 12:1², 2², 3, 5, 6², 8, 9, 10, 16, 17, 19, 20; 13:1, 3, 4², 5², 6, 8, 10, 14; 14:2, 4³, 6², 7², 8, 9, 11, 12, 14, 16, 18, 19³, 20, 21³; 15:1², 2, 4, 7², 8², 9, 10, 13, 16, 18, 19³, 21, 25³, 27; 1Co 1:1, 2³, 3, 7, 8, 10, 17², 18², 21, 23², 24, 27; 2:1² 2, 3, 6, 10, 14, 15; 3:5² 8, 13; 4:1, 5, 6, 9⁵, 11, 13, 14, 16, 17, 18, 19, 21; 5:5, 9, 10, 12²; 6:2², 5², 6, 8; 7:1, 3², 4⁴, 5, 8², 9², 10, 11, 12², 15, 17², 24², 26, 28, 30, 32, 34², 35², 36², 37, 39³; 8:1, 2, 4, 7², 8, 9, 10², 13²; 9:2², 3, 4, 5, 10, 16², 17, 19³, 20⁴, 21², 24, 25², 27; 10:1, 6, 7², 11, 13, 15, 19, 20³, 22², 27², 30, 32, 33; 11:2³, 3, 6, 7, 10, 13², 14, 15, 16, 18, 19², 23, 28, 33; 12:1², 2, 7, 8³, 9², 10⁵, 11, 13², 15², 16², 18, 21², 24, 28, 29, 30, 32, 34, 35², 36², 37, 39³; 8:1, 2, 4, 7², 8, 9, 10³, 13², 14, 15, 16², 17, 18, 19², 20, 21, 22, 23²; 24², 25, 26, 27⁴, 28, 29, 30², 31, 32; 16:1², 3⁵; 4, 5, 10, 13, 17², 19, 21, 25³, 27; 1Co 1:1, 2³, 7, 9, 11, 12³, 15, 19, 20, 21, 22, 25³, 27; 2:1², 2, 3, 6, 10, 14, 15; 3:5² 8, 13; 4:1, 5, 6, 9⁵, 11, 13, 14, 16, 17, 18, 19, 21; 5:5, 9, 10, 12²; 6:2², 5², 6, 8; 7:1, 3², 4⁴, 5, 8², 9², 10, 11, 12², 15, 17², 24², 26, 28, 30, 32, 34², 35², 36², 37, 39³; 8:1, 2, 4, 7², 8, 9, 10², 13²; 9:2², 3, 4, 5, 10, 16², 17, 19³, 20⁴, 21², 24, 25², 27; 10:1², 2, 4, 5², 6, 7², 9³, 10, 11, 12, 13⁴, 14, 15, 16; 11:2³, 3, 4, 5, 6, 7³, 8, 9³, 12² 21³, 23², 31, 32; 12:1², 2, 4², 6, 7², 9³, 11³, 13², 14², 18, 19, 20²; 13:1, 4², 5, 7, 10, 11; 14³, 16, 18, 19, 20², 14:1, 4², 5, 7, 10⁴, 11², 12², 14, 16², 17, 19, 21², 23, 24, 26, 28², 31, 33; 20:1, 2, 9, 11, 12, 14, 17, 17⁵, 18², 25, 27, 28, 29, 31², 32², 42; 4:2, 5, 8, 9³, 14², 15³, 17², 18², 21, 24, 25, 26², 3:2, 5, 7, 9, 11, 12, 13, 15; 4:3³, 4, 8³, 9², 10³, 11, 12, 16, 18², 21; Tit 1:1, 3², 4, 6, 7, 9, 11, 14², 15², 16; 2:2, 4, 5, 6, 8, 9⁶, 10², 11, 12³, 14³; 3:1³, 2³, 8³, 10, 12⁴, 13, 14², 15²; Phm 1:1, 2³, 3², 9, 10, 11³, 12, 13, 14, 16, 18, 19, 21, 22³; Heb 1:1, 2, 4², 5, 13, 14; 2:1, 3, 4², 5², 8², 10, 12, 17², 18; 3:2, 5, 6, 12, 14², 20, 22, 23², 25, 26³, 27; 4:1, 2, 6, 11, 12, 13, 14, 15, 16; 5:1³, 2³, 3, 5, 7, 10, 11³, 12², 14; 6:1², 6⁴, 7, 10, 11³, 12², 13², 15, 16, 18³, 18³; 7:5, 8, 11², 13, 14, 16, 19, 21, 25³, 27; 8:3³, 5², 6², 9, 11, 9:6, 9, 11⁴, 14, 15, 16, 19, 20, 23, 24, 25, 26², 27² 28⁴; 10:1, 4, 7, 8, 9², 13, 15, 16, 19, 22³, 23, 29, 30, 31, 33, 36; 11:6², 7, 8², 10, 11, 15, 16, 17, 18, 20, 24, 25², 26, 29, 32, 34, 35², 37², 12:4, 9, 14², 15², 17, 18², 19, 22², 23³, 24²; Jas 1:1, 5, 9, 12², 15², 18, 19³, 22, 23, 25, 27²; 2:3², 5², 7, 12, 13, 14, 16, 23, 25; 3:1, 2, 3, 4; 4:4, 5, 6, 7, 9², 11², 12; 5:4, 14, 16; 1Pe 1:1, 2, 3, 5, 6, 10, 11², 12³, 13, 14, 18, 25; 2:4², 5², 6, 7, 8, 9, 11², 12, 13, 14², 15, 17, 18³, 20, 21, 23, 24, 25; 3:1², 5², 6, 9, 10, 12², 15³, 17, 18², 19, 22²; 4:3³, 5³, 6⁴, 8, 10, 11, 12, 14; 2Pe 1:1, 5, 9², 10, 12, 13, 15, 18, 19, 21⁴, 22²; 3:1³, 2, 9², 11², 12, 13, 14², 16², 18; 1Jn 1:2³, 3, 4, 5, 6, 8, 10; 2:1², 3, 4, 6, 9, 10, 12, 13, 14², 16², 18; 3:1³, 2, 9³, 11², 12, 13, 14², 20³, 21², 22²; 3:6, 8, 9, 12, 14, 16, 19,

---

23²; 4:1, 5, 6², 11, 14, 18; 5:3, 10, 13, 14, 16⁴, 17, 18; 2Jn 1:1, 4, 6, 10, 12³; 3Jn 1:1; 3³, 4, 5, 6, 8², 9³, 10³, 13², 14³; Jude 1:1, 3³, 5, 7, 9, 11, 15³, 18, 21², 22, 23, 24³, 25; Rev 1:1², 2, 3, 4³, 5, 6³, 8, 11², 12², 13; 2:1, 2, 5, 7³, 8², 10, 13², 13², 14⁴, 15, 16, 17³, 18, 20, 21, 23, 24³, 25, 26², 27, 29; 3:1, 2, 3, 6, 7, 9, 10³, 11, 13, 14, 16, 18³, 21², 22; 4:1, 8, 9, 11; 5:2, 4, 5², 9², 10², 12, 13²; 6:4³, 8, 11², 13, 16; 7:1, 2, 10², 12, 17; 8:2, 3, 6, 13²; 9:1⁴, 4², 5, 6, 10, 12, 14, 15; 10:4, 5, 7², 8, 9³; 11:2, 3, 5², 6², 12³, 12², 42², 5², 6, 9, 11, 12², 13², 14, 15, 17²; 13:3, 4, 5², 6², 7², 8, 10², 13², 14², 15⁴, 16; 14:4, 6³, 12, 15², 18; 15:4, 7; 16:1, 6, 8, 9, 11, 12, 14², 16; 17:1, 6, 7², 8, 11², 13, 15, 16, 17³; 18:5, 6, 14, 17, 19, 21; 19:1, 8, 9², 10³, 15, 17, 19; 20:1, 3, 4², 5, 8², 12, 13; 21:6³, 9, 10, 15, 16, 23; 22:6², 8², 9, 11⁴, 12², 14, 16, 18², 20.

6², 19, 20²; **9:**5, 6, 8, 9, 27; **10:**16, 19, 27; **11:**1, 3², 10, 12², 14; **12:**4, 10, 12; **14:**8, 9, 10, 12, 17, 36², 38; **17:**9, 10; **21:**5; **23:**19; **24:**15; **25:**7, 15², 16, 40; **27:**11; **29:**4², 9; **30:**22, 23⁴; **2Sa** 2:14; 5:2; 10:12; 11:23²; **12:**18; **13:**25, 26; **14:**16; **15:**14³, 19, 20; **16:**20; **17:**6; **18:**3¹⁴; **19:**6, 9², 10, 42, 43; **20:**6²; **21:**5², 6, 17; **24:**14; **1Ki** 1:2; 3:18; **8:**57³; **12:**4², 9, 10; **18:**23, 26; **20:**23, 31; **22:**3; **2Ki** 1:6²; 3:10², 13²; 4:10, 13; 6:1, 2⁴, 11, 12, 16; 7:4², 6, 9, 12; 9:5, 12; **18:**26, 30, 32; **19:**19; **22:**13²; **1Ch** 12:19; **13:**2², 3²; **15:**13; **16:**35³; **19:**13; **2Ch** 10:4², 9, 10; **13:**10, 12; **14:**7², 11; **20:**9³, 11³, 12; **29:**10; **32:**7, 8², 11; **34:**21; **Ezr** 4:2², 3², 12, 14, 18; **5:**11, 17; **8:**17, 18², 21, 22, 31²; **9:**8², 9⁴, 13³, 14³, 15; **10:**2, 3, 14; **Ne** 2:17, 18, 19, 20; **4:**4, 11, 12², 20², 22; **5:**2, 8, 17; 6:2, 7, 9, 10²; **9:**32, 33, 37; **10:**30; **13:**18; **Job** 9:33²; **21:**14; **22:**14, 17²; **31:**15; **34:**4²; 37; **35:**11²; **37:**19; **Ps** 2:3; 4:6²; **12:**7²; **20:**9; **33:**22; **34:**3; **40:**5; **44:**1, 7, 9, 10², 11², 13², 14², 17, 19³, 23, 26²; **46:**7, 11; **47:**3, 4; **54:**T; **59:**7; **60:**1³, 3², 5², 10, 11; **65:**5; **66:**6, 10², 11, 12; **67:**1³, 6, 7; **68:**28; **74:**1, 4, 9; **78:**3, 20; **79:**4, 8², 9²; **80:**1, 2, 3², 6², 7², 14, 18, 19²; **83:**4, 12; **85:**4², 5, 6, 7²; **90:**12, 14, 15², 17²; **95:**1², 2, 6²; **100:**3; **103:**10²; **12; 106:**47²; **108:**6², 11, 12; **115:**1², 12²; **117:**2; **118:**24, 25², 27; **122:**1; **123:**2²; **124:**2, 3², 4², 5, 6; **126:**3; **132:**7²; **136:**23, 24; **137:**3²; **Pr** 1:11, 14; **SS** 1:4; **2:**15; **5:**9²; **7:**11²; **12:** **Isa** 1:9, 18; **2:**3², 5; **4:**1; **6:**8; **7:**6²; **8:**10; **9:**6²; **14:**8, 10; **16:**3; **17:**14²; **22:**13; **25:**9²; **26:**12², 13; **28:**15; **29:**15; **30:**10²; **11; 32:**15; **33:**2, 14², 22; **36:**11, 15, 18; **37:**20; **41:**1, 22³, 23; **43:**9, 26; **49:**20²; **50:**8; **53:**2, 5, 6²; **56:**12; **59:**9², 12²; **63:**7, 15, 16², 17; **64:**6², 7², 9, 12; **Jer** 2:6², 27; **3:**25²; **4:**5, 8, 13; **5:**12, 19, 24²; **6:**4, 5, 24, 26; **8:**14³; **9:**18; **11:**19²; **12:**4; **14:**7, 9², 19, 21²; **16:**10; **18:**12; **21:**2⁴, 13; **26:**16; **29:**15, 28; **31:**3, 6; **35:**6, 8, 10; **36:**15, 17; **37:**3, 9; **38:**16, 25²; **40:**10; **41:**8; **42:**3, 5², 6, 20²; **43:**3⁴; **44:**16; **46:**16; **48:**2; **51:**9, 10², 34⁵; **La** 3:40², 41, 43, 45, 46; **4:**15, 17, 18, 19²; **5:**1, 5, 8², 16, 20², 21, 22²; **Eze** 8:12; **11:**15; **20:**12, 20; **24:**19²; **33:**10, 24; **35:**12; **37:**18; **Da** 1:12; 2:23; 3:17²; **9:**7, 10, 11, 12², 13, 14, 16; **Hos** 6:1⁴, 2², 3¹; **10:**3, 8²; **14:**2, 3; **Am** 4:1²; **9:**10; **Ob** 1:1; **Jnh** 1:6, 7, 8², 11, 14²; **Mic** 2:6; 3:11²; 4:2²; 5:1, 6; 7:19; **Hab** 3:14, 16; **Zec** 1:6; **8:**21, 23; **Mal** 1:2, 9; 2:10; **Mt** 1:23; **3:**15; **6:**11, 12, 13²; **8:**25, 29²; 31²; **9:**27; **13:**28, 36, 56; **15:**15, 23; **17:**4; **19:**27; **20:**7, 12, 30, 31; **22:**17, 24, 25; **24:**3; **25:**8, 9, 11; **26:**17, 46, 63, 68; **27:**4, 25; **Mk** 1:24²; **3:**8; **4:**35; **5:**12²; **6:**3; **9:**5², 22², 38, 40²; **10:**35, 37; **12:**19; **13:**4; **14:**12, 15, 42; **Lk** 1:1, 2, 69, 71, 74²; **2:**15, 48; **4:**34²; **7:**16, 20; **9:**33²; 49, 54; **10:**17; **11:**1, 3, 4³, 45; **12:**41; **13:**25; **16:**26²; **17:**13; **20:**2, 6, 22, 28; **22:**8, 9, 67; **23:**15, 18, 30; **24:**22, 23, 29, 32³; **Jn** 1:14, 22²; **2:**18; **4:**12, 25; **6:**34, 52; **8:**5; **9:**34; **10:**24²; **11:**7, 15, 16; **12:**19; **14:**8², 9, 22, 31; **16:**30; **17:**21; **18:**40; **Ac** 1:21²; **22²**, 24; **2:**8; **3:**4; **12; 5:**28; **6:**2, 14; **7:**27, 38, 40³; **10:**33, 41, 42; **11:**13, 15, 17; **13:**26, 33, 47; **14:**11; **15:**8, 9, 14, 24, 28, 36; **16:**9, 10, 15², 17, 21, 37⁴; **17:**27; **20:**5, 14; **21:**5, 11, 16², 17, 18, 23, 28; **24:**4; **25:**24; **27:**2, 4, 6, 7, 37; **28:**2², 7², 10², 14, 15; **Ro** 3:5, 8; **4:**16, 24²; **5:**5², 8²; **6:**3; 7:6; **8:**4, 18, 26²; 31², 32², 34, 35, 37, 39; **9:**19, 24, 29; **12:**4, 6; **13:**12, 13; **14:**7², 12, 13, 19; **15:**2, 4; **1Co** 1:18, 30; **2:**10, 12, 13; **4:**1, 6, 8, 9; **5:**8; **6:**14; **7:**15; **8:**6, 8; **9:**5, 10²; **10:**6, 11; **15:**30, 32, 57; **2Co** 1:4, 10³, 11², 14², 20²; **2:** **2:**11, 14²; **3:**6; **4:**6, 7, 12, 14²; 17²; **5:**5², 12, 14, 18², 19, 20, 21; **6:**12; **7:**1, 2, 6, 7, 9, 12; **8:**4, 5, 7, 19, 22; **9:**11; **10:**8, 13; **11:**12; **Gal** 1:4; 23; **2:**4; **3:**13², 14, 24; **4:**17; **5:**1, 25, 26; **6:**9, 10; **Eph** 1:3, 4, 5, 6, 8, 9, 19; **2:**3, 4, 5, 6², 7, 10; **3:**20; **4:**7; **5:**2²; **Php** 3:15, 16; **Col** 1:8, 13²; **2:**13, 14²; **4:**3; **1Th** 1:6, 9, 10; **2:**8, 13, 15, 16, 18; **3:**6⁴, 11; **4:**7; **5:**6², 8, 9, 10, 25; **2Th** 1:7; **2:**2, 16²; **3:**1, 6; **1Ti** 6:17; **2Ti** 1:7, 9³, 14; **2:**3, 12; **Tit** 2:8, 12, 14²; **3:**5², 6, 15; **Heb** 1:2; **2:**3; **4:**1, 2, 11, 14, 16²; **6:**1, 18, 20; **9:**24; **10:**15, 20, 22², 23, 24, 25²; **11:**40²; **12:**1³, 2, 9, 10², 25, 28; **13:**13, 15, 18, 21; **Jas** 1:18; **3:**3; **4:**5, 6; **5:**17²; **1Pe** 1:3; **2:**12; **4:**17; **2Pe** 1:3², 4²; **1Jn** 1:2, 3, 7, 8, 9²; **2:**19², 25; **3:**1², 16, 18, 20, 21, 23, 24²; **4:**6², 7, 9, 10, 11, 12², 13², 16, 17, 19, 21; **5:**11, 14, 15, 20; **2Jn** 1:2², 3, 4; **3Jn** 1:9, 10; **Rev** 1:5², 6; **6:**16²; **19:**7.

WAS (4158)

Ge 1:2³, 3, 4, 5², 7, 8², 9, 10, 11, 12, 13², 15, 18, 19², 21, 23², 24, 25, 30, 31³; **2:**5, 10, 19, 20, 21, 23; **3:**1, 6², 8, 10²; **4:**5²; 17, 18⁴, 20, 21², 22²; **5:**4, 24, 30, 32; **6:**5, 6², 9, 11²; **7:**6, 23²; **8:**9, 11, 13, 14; **9:**10, 18; **10:**8, 9,

13, 15, 21², 24, 25³, 26; **11:**9, 10, 28, 29³, 30; **12:**4, 10², 11, 14, 15, 18; **13:**5, 10²; **14:**10, 12, 13, 18; **15:**12; **16:**4, 7, 14, 16; **17:**1, 24², 25, 27; **18:**1, 10², 11, 15; **19:**1, 14, 16, 22, 30, 33, 35; **20:**10; **21:**1, 4, 5², 8², 9, 15, 20, 21, 31; **22:**20, 24; **23:**10, 17; **24:**1, 11, 15², 16, 33, 62, 67; **25:**1, 3, 6, 8, 17, 20, 21, 25², 26², 27, 29, 30; **26:**1, 7, 28, 34; **27:**1, 5, 33, 42, 28:**5, 16, 17; **29:**2, 9², 12, 16², 17, 18, 25, 31², 34; **30:**1; **31:**2, 5, 15, 20, 22, 31, 34, 36, 39, 40, 41², 48, 49; **32:**24, 25, 30, 31, 32, 33; **33:**1, 11; **34:**3; 19²; **35:**7², 8², 17, 18, 19, 22, 29; **36:**22, 24, 32, 35, 39², 43; **37:**2, 24², 29³; **38:**3, 5, 6, 7, 10, 13, 15, 16, 21, 24, 25², 26, 27, 30; **39:**1, 2, 3, 5, 6, 11, 20, 21, 22², 23; **40:**2, 3, 11, 15, 20, 22; **41:**8, 12, 13², 14², 17, 23, 25, 26², 29, 31², 36, 42², 44², 45², 46², 48, 49; **3:**1, 9, 10, 19; **42:**1, 6, 12, 13², 17², 36, 42² 44², 45², 46³, 48; **4:**5, 6, 13, 18, 20, 22², 31², 36, 42², 44², 45² 46, 48; **43:**30; **44:**2, 13, 15²; **45:**1, 46²; **46:**22, 23; **47:**1, 2, 3, 4², 5²; **Da** 1:4; **2:**1, 5, 13, 19, 32, 34, 36; **3:**19, 22, 27²; **4:**4, 5, 10, 11, 12², 13, 19, 29, 33³, 34, 36²; **5:**2, 6, 11, 12, 13, 20, 21², 25, 29³,

16, 19; **18:**2, 3², 4, 7, 13, 26, 28, 29, 30; **19:**3, 6, 11³, 12, 19²; **20:**29, 40; **21:**1², 16, 25; **22:**1, 33, 35, 36, 37, 42², 43, 44, 47, 50; **2Ki** 1:7, 8², 9; **2:**1, 17, 18, 23; **3:**13, 15, 20², 21, 22, 25², 27²; **4:**8, 18, 31, 32, 38², 40, 41; **5:**1³, 14, 20, 26, 27; **6:**5², 8, 10, 25, 26, 32, 33; **7:**2, 5, 7, 10, 11; **8:**4, 5, 7², 16, 17, 19, 31, 35, 36, 11:1, 2, 14² 16, 20; **10:**9, 15, 19, 21, 31, 35, 36; **11:**1, 2, 14², 16, 20, 21; **12:**1², 2, 9, 10, 14, 16, 20, 23; **14:**2³, 3, 5, 7, 12, 16, 20², 21, 22, 25, 26:10, 16, 24, 31²; **27:**2, 3, 4², 5², 6⁴, 7², 8, 9, 10, 11, 12, 13, 14, 15, 24, 25², 26, 27² 28², 29², 30², 31, 32, 33², 34²; **28:**4; **29:**26; **2Ch** 1:1, 3, 5, 12; **2:**14²; **3:**1, 3, 4, 6, 11², 12; **4:**5²; 6, 18, 19; **5:**1, 10, 13; **6:**3, 8; **8:**14, 16³; **9:**2, 4, 6, 13, 18, 20²; **10:**2, 15, 18; **11:**18; **12:**1, 12², 13³, 15, 16; **13:**2², 7, 13²; **14:**1², 2, 5, 6², 14; **15:**3, 4, 5, 6², 8, 9, 15, 17, 19; **16:**2, 3, 10², 12²; **17:**3, 6, 14, 19; **18:**32; **20:**25, 30, 31², 32, 35; **21:**1, 3, 5, 7, 24:1³, 2, 8, 9, 10, 11, 12², 13, 14, 16, 17; **22:**2², 8, 9⁴, 10, 11; **23:**13, 19, 21; **24:**1³, 2, 8, 9, 10, 11, 12², 13, 14, 16, 17; **25:**1³, 3, 16, 22, 28²; **26:**1, 2, 3⁴, 4, 12, 13, 15, 16, 19, 20, 23; **27:**1², 2, 8, 9; **28:**1², 5, 9², 27²; **29:**1², 2, 19, 25, 28, 32, 34, 36; **30:**2, 4; **31:**27, 35, 42, 45, 49², 50², 52; **15:**9², 11, 12, 21, 24, 35, 36:12, 49²; **37:**25, 36; **39:**2, 9; **44:**3²; **50:**21; **51:**5; **53:**5²; **57:**6, 63:7; **66:**14, 17; **68:**11, 14; **69:**20; **73:**16, 21, 22²; **74:**8, 13, 14, 17; **76:**8; **77:**2, 4, 18; **78:**21, 30, 35², 38, 59, 62; **87:**4, 6; **93:**2; **94:**19; **95:**10; **99:**6; **105:**18; **106:**16, 30, 31, 38, 40; **107:**12; **114:**5; **116:**3, 6; **118:**13; **119:**67, 71; **126:**2; **139:**15³; **142:**T; **Pr** 4:3; 7:8, 9; **8:**23, 24, 25, 27, 30²; **24:**31²; **26:**19; **Ecc** 1:10², 12; **2:**3, 10, 11²; 17; **3:**16²; **4:**1², 8², 16; **5:**6; **7:**23, 28; **9:**14; **10:**16; **12:**9, 10; **SS** 1:12; **3:**10; **5:**2, 6; **8:**1, 5, 11; **Isa** 1:21; **6:**4; **7:**1, 2; **11:**16; **22:**3; **23:**3; **36:**12; **37:**9, 38; **38:**1, 17; **39:**2²; **40:**14, 21; **41:**26, 27; **42:**24; **43:**10; **45:**21; **47:**6; **48:**4; **49:**1, 7, 21; **50:**1, 2; **51:**2, 9, 10, 18²; **52:**14; **53:**2³, 5³, 7³, 8², 9², 10, 12; **57:**17; **59:**15², 16³; **63:**3, 4, 5², 9; **65:**1; **Jer** 2:3; **4:**23²; **26:** **8:**15; **13:**7, 20; **15:**17; **18:**4²; **20:**7, 14; **22:**15, 26; **25:**1; **26:**3, 20, 24; **28:**1; **29:**2; **31:**19, 32; **32:**1; **34:**7, 9²; **35:**4², **36:**9, 10, 22², 23; **37:**1, 4, 13, 16, 21; **38:**1, 6, 7, 26, 28²; **39:**2; **41:**1, 9; **44:**6, 30; **45:**1; **46:**2; **48:**13, 27²; **49:**14; **50:**17²; **51:**7; **52:**1³, 7, 9², 12, 15; **3:**54; **4:**6, 18, 20; **Eze** 1:1, 3, 5², 13², 16, 20, 21, 22², 26²; **2:**9; **3:**22, 23; **8:**1, 2, 4, 11², 12; **9:**2, 8, 10:1, 4, 17, 19, 18:13, 16:15², 16:3, 4, 13, 20, 45, 46², 49; 57; **17:**7², 20; **18:**18; **19:**2, 4, 6, 8, 9, 10², 12², **21:**26; **23:**4², 5, 10, 11, 13, 17, 20, 24; **25:**3²; **27:**4, 7, 32; **28:**15; **29:**18; **31:**7, 10, 15; **33:**22³, 24; **34:**5; **35:**10; **36:**17, 20, 35, 36²; **37:**1², 7², 8³, 9², 11, 12²; 13², 14, 15, 16, 17², 18², 19, 21, 22, 23², 25; **38:**16, 36, 47², 48; **49²; 41:**1, 2², 3², 4², 5², 6, 7, 8, 9², **45:**1; **46:**22, 23; **47:**1, 2, 3, 4²; **Da** 1:4; **2:**1, 5, 13, 19, 32, 34, 36; **3:**19, 22, 27²; **4:**4, 5, 10, 11, 12², 13, 19, 29, 33³, 34, 36²; **5:**2, 6, 11, 12, 13, 20, 21², 25, 29³,

30; **6:**2, 4, 14², 17, 22, 23³; **7:**1, 4³, 5³, 6², 7³, 8², 9³, 10²; 11², 13², 14, 15, 19², 21, 28; **8:**2, 3², 5, 7, 8, 11, 12, 15, 17², 18², 22, 27³; **9:**1, 20, 21, 23; **10:**1³, 4, 5, 6, 7, 8², 13, 15²; 19; **11:**29; **12:**6, 7; **Hos** 1:10; **2:**3, 7, 8, 9; **9:**10¹; **10:**1; **11:**1, 3², 13¹; **Joel** 2:2; **Am** 1:1²; 2:9; **4:**7; **7:**1⁴, 4, 7, 14²; **Ob** 1:1; **Jnh** 1:10, 11, 17; **2:**5, 7; **3:**3; **4:**1, 2², 6; **Na** 3:8, 10; **Hab** 3:4²; 8; **Hag** 2:15, 18; **Zec** 1:2, 8², 9, 11, 14, 15, 19; **2:**1, 3; **3:**3; **5:**1, 5, 7, 10; **6:**4²; **7:**5, 12, 14; **8:**9; **11:**11²; **13:**3, 6; **Mal** 1:2; **2:**5; 6², 15; **3:**16; **Mt** 1:2, 3, 5², 6, 12, 16, 18²; 19; **2:**1, 3, 4, 9, 15, 16, 17², 22², 23²; **3:**3, 4, 7, 16²; 4:1, 2, 13, 14, 18, 21, 35, 38; **5:**21, 27, 33, 38, 43; **6:**29; **8:**3, 10, 13, 17², 24, 26, 30; **9:**10, 18, 22, 30, 32², 33³; **10:**1, 5, 14, 16², 17², 20; **11:**2, 3, 14, 18, 19², 24³, 26; **12:**4, 10, 13, 15, 22², 38, 40, 46; **13:**4², 5⁴, 7, 8, 26, 44, 47, 48²; 49, 55; **7:**6, 25, 26, 32, 35; **8:**25; **9:**2, 25, 31, 33, 34, 36, 37; **10:**1, 5, 14, 20, 21², 22, 33, 34²; **22:**10, 11, 12², 14², 17, 20²; **Ac** 1:2, 3, 4, 9, 10, 17, 22, 26; **2:**16, 22, 23, 24, 29, 30, 31², 43; **3:**2²; 16; **4:**3, 6, 9, 14, 22², 31, 32, 33, 35; **5:**4², 34, 36, 37; **6:**1, 9, 15; **7:**2, 9, 12, 13, 20², 21, 22², 23, 25, 27, 31, 35, 38, 41, 47, 52, 53; **8:**1, 8, 9, 13, 18, 28, 32², 33³; **9:**1, 9, 10, 18, 26, 31, 36², 37, 38; **10:**1², 7, 10, 16, 17², 18², 19, 24, 29, 30, 33, 38, 41, 44; **11:**5², 10, 11, 17, 21, 23, 24; **12:**1, 5², 6², 9², 18, 23, 25; **13:**5, 7, 9, 12, 25, 29, 31, 36, 43, 45; **14:**5, 8, 9, 12, 13, 19; **16:**1³, 3, 14², 19, 23, 26, 27, 34, 35; **17:**1, 2, 10, 11, 13, 16³, 18, 34; **18:**3, 5, 12, 14, 24, 27, 28; **19:**1, 4, 17, 29, 32, 34; **20:**3, 4, 9⁴, 13, 16, 18, 19, 38; **21:**3, 5, 16, 30, 31, 33, 35; **22:**3⁴, 9, 12, 13, 19, 23, 26, 27, 34, 35; **23:**5, 7, 9, 10, 27, 29, 30, 34²; **24:**2, 18³, 21, 22, 24, 25, 26, 27; **25:**19, 20, 23; **26:**4, 9²; 12, 13, 19, 26, 27:1, 2, 9, 12², 15, 28², 41; **28:**1, 2, 6, 7, 8, 11, 15, 16, 17, 18, 19, 21, 23; **Ro** 1:3, 4; **4:**2, 3, 9, 10⁴, 11, 12, 13, 19³, 20, 22, 23, 25²; **5:**13³, 14, 18², 20; **6:**4, 6, 9; **7:**4, 7, 9, 10, 13; **8:**3², 20, 34; **9:**9², 12, 26; **10:**20; **11:**4, 15⁴; **14:**5²; 20; **16:**5, 7; **1Co** 1:6, 13, 21²; **2:**2; **7:**18⁴, 20, 22⁴; **9:**10; **10:**4, 5; **11:**9, 23; **15:**11; **15:**4², 10², 11, 47, 48; **16:**12, 17²; **2Co** 1:15, 19², 23; **2:**9, 10; **3:**7², 10, 11, 13; **5:**15, 19; **7:**7, 12, 13, 14; **8:**9, 19; **11:**3, 7, 9², 25³, 33; **12:**2², 4, 7, 13; **13:**2, 4; **Gal** 1:12, 14², 15, 17, 22; **2:**2, 3³, 8², 10², 11, 12, 13; **3:**1, 4, 6, 19³, 22, 24; **4:**13, 14, 23²; **Eph** 2:15; **3:**2, 5, 8, 9, 10; **4:**11; **Php** 2:26, 27; **3:**7; **4:**14, 16²; **Col** 1:19, 24; **2:**14²; **1Th** 2:1; **3:**5; **2Th** 2:5; **3:**11; **1Ti** 1:13²; **14, 16; 2:**7, 13, 14³; **3:**16³; **4:**14; **2Ti** 1:9, 11, 14, 16, 17; **4:**17; **Tit** 1:5²; **Phm** 1:10, 11, 15²; **Heb** 2:2, 3², 9, 10, 18; **3:**2³, 5, 10, 17²; **4:**2, 7, 15; **5:**4, 7, 8, 10; **6:**13, 15, 17; **7:**1, 4, 10, 11², 18, 20; **8:**3, 5²; **9:**2², 3, 8², 18, 23, 24, 28; **11:**3⁴, 4, 5³, 8, 10, 11³, 17, 21, 22, 23³, 26, 31, 33, 34, 38; **12:**17, 20, 21; **Jas** 2:21, 22, 23³, 25; **5:**17; **1Pe** 1:10, 11, 12, 18, 20², 25; **2:**22;

3:18, 20; **4**:6; **2Pe** 2:7, 8, 16, 21; **3**:5, 6; **1Jn** 1:1, 2; **3**:8; **5**:18; **3Jn** 1:7; **Jude** 1:3², 4, 9; **Rev** 1:4, 8, 9, 10, 12, 13, 15, 16, 18; **2**:13; **4**:1, 2², 6, 7³, 8²; **5**:4²; **6**:2; **4²**, 5², 8³, 11², 12, 14; **7**:9; **8**:1, 3, 7³, 8, 12², 13; **9**:1, 5, 8, 9, 16, 18, 19; **10**:1², 2, 4, 11; **11**:1², 8, 13, 17, 19²; **12**:2², 4², 5, 7, 8, 9², 14, 17; **13**:3, 5, 7³, 8, 14², 15; **14**:1, 2, 5, 14², 15, 16²; **15**:5, 8; **16**:8, 10, 12, 18, 21; **17**:3, 4², 5, 6², 8², 11; **18**:1, 18, 24; **19**:4, 8, 11, 20; **20**:10, 11², 12, 13, 15²; **21**:1, 5, 11, 16², 17², 18, 19, 21.

WE (1884)

Ge 3:2; **11**:4; **13**:8; **19**:2, 5, 13, 34; **20**:13; **22**:5²; **24**:25, 50; **26**:22, 28², 29; **29**:5, 8², 27; **31**:14, 49; **32**:6; **34**:14², 15, 16, 21, 30; **37**:7, 26², 32; **38**:23; **40**:8; **41**:12, 38; **42**:2, 11, 21³, 22, 30, 31³, 32; **43**:4, 5, 7², 8², 10², 18, 20, 21³, 22²; **44**:8³, 16², 20², 22, 24²; **46**:³, 47:4, 18, 19⁴, 25²; **48**:7; **50**:15, 18; **Ex** 1:10; **5**:16; **8**:26²; 27; **9**:28; **10**:9², 26²; **12**:33; **14**:5²; 12; **15**:24; **16**:3³, 7, 8; **19**:8; **20**:19²; **24**:3, 7², 14; **32**:1, 23; **Lev** 25:20²; **Nu** 9:7²; **10**:29², 31, 32; **11**:4, 5², 6², 18², 20; **12**:11; **13**:27, 28, 30², 31², 32², 33³; **14**:2, 4, 7, 9, 40²; **16**:12, 14; **17**:12³, 13; **20**:3, 4, 10, 15, 16², 17³, 18, 19⁴; **21**:2, 5, 7², 22³, 30²; **31**:50; **32**:5, 16, 17², 18, 19, 25, 32²; **Dt** 1:19², 22², 28³, 41²; **2**:1², 8², 13, 14², 27², 29, 33, 34², 35²; **3**:1, 3, 4², 6², 7, 8, 10, 12, 29; **4**:7; **5**:24², 25³, 26, 27; **6**:21, 24, 25; **7**:17²; **12**:8, 30; **18**:16, 21; **26**:7; **29**:7, 8, 16², 29; **30**:12, 13; **Jos** 1:16²; 17²; **2**:10, 11, 14², 18, 19, 20²; **4**:23; **5**:1; **6**:17; **7**:7; **8**:5, 6²; **9**:6, 7, 8, 9, 11, 12², 13, 19², 20³, 22, 24², 25²; **17**:14; **22**:17, 23, 24, 26, 27, 28², 31; **24**:15, 17, 18, 21, 22, 24; **Jdg** 1:3, 24; **8**:6, 15; **9**:28²; 38; **10**:10, 15; **11**:6, 8, 10, 24; **13**:15², 17, 22²; **14**:15; **15**:10, 13², 16; **16**:5²; **18**:9; **19**:12²; 18, 19², 22; **20**:13, 23, 28, 32, 39; **21**:7², 16, 18²; **22²**; **Ru** 1:10; **4**:11; **1Sa** 5:8; **6**:2², 4, 9; **7**:6; **8**:19, 20; **9**:7⁴; **10**:14²; **11**:1, 3², 10, 12; **12**:10³, 12, 19²; **14**:8, 9, 10; **15**:15; **16**:11; **17**:9; **20**:42; **23**:3², 20; **25**:7, 8, 15; **30**:14², 22²; **2Sa** 5:1; **7**:22; **11**:23; **12**:18²; **13**:25; **14**:7², 14; **15**:14²; **16**:20; **17**:5, 6, 12²; **18**:3; **19**:10, 42³, 43³; **20**:1, 19; **21**:4², 5; **1Ki** 3:18; **5**:6; **8**:47³; **12**:4, 9, 16; **17**:12; **18**:5²; **20**:23², 25², 31; **22**:3, 7, 8, 15; **2Ki** 2:16; **3**:8, 11, 13; **4**:13; **6**:1, 15, 28, 29²; **7**:3, 4⁶, 9², 10⁴, 5³, 13²; **18**:22, 26; **1Ch** 11:1; **12**:18²; **13**:3; **15**:13; **16**:35²; **17**:20; **29**:13, 14², 15, 16; **2Ch** 2:16; **6**:37²; **10**:4, 9, 16; **13**:10, 11; **14**:7², 11²; **18**:3, 5, 6, 7, 14; **20**:9, 12², 25:16; **28**:13; **29**:18, 19; **31**:10; **Ezr** 4:2, 3, 14², 16; **5**:8, 9, 10², 11², **8**:15, 21, 22, 23, 31, 32², 33; **9**:7, 9, 10², 14, 15²; **10**:2, 4, 12, 13²; **Ne** 1:6, 7²; **2**:17²; 20; **4**:11, 4, 6, 9, 10, 11, 15², 19, 20; **5**:2², 3, 4, 5³, 8, 12³, 16; **9**:33, 36, 37, 38; **10**:30, 31², 32, 34, 35, 36, 37³, 39; **13**:27; **Est** 5:5; **7**:4; **Job** 2:10; **5**:27; **8**:9; **9**:32; **15**:9²; **17**:16; **18**:2, 3; **19**:28; **21**:14, 15²; **26**:14²; **32**:13; **37**:19²; **38**:35; **Ps** 12:4²; **20**:5, 7, 8, 9; **21**:13; **33**:20, 21, 22; **35**:21; **36**:9; **44**:1, 5², 8², 17, 20, 22², 25; **46**:2; **48**:8²; 9; **55**:14; **60**:12; **64**:6; **65**:3, 4; **66**:12; **74**:8, 9; **75**:1²; **78**:3, 4²; **79**:4, 8, 13²; **80**:3, 7, 18; **81**:5²; **90**:7, 9, 10², 12, 14, 15; **95**:7; **100**:3²; **103**:14²; **106**:6², 47; **108**:13; **115**:18; **118**:26; **123**:3, 4; **124**:7²; **126**:1, 3; **129**:8; **132**:6²; **137**:1², 2, 4; **Pr** 1:13, 14; **24**:12; **SS** 1:4²; 11; **6**:1, 13; **8**:8²; 9²; **Isa** 1:9²; 3:2; **4**:1; **5**:19²; **8**:18; **9**:10²; **10**:29; **14**:10; **16**:6; **20**:6²; **22**:13; **24**:16; **25**:9²; **26**:1, 8, 12, 13, 17, 18; **28**:15³; **30**:16²; **33**:2; **36**:7, 11; **38**:20; **41**:22, 23², 26²; **42**:24; **46**:5; **51**:23; **53**:2, 3, 4, 5, 6; **58**:3²; **59**:9², 10³, 11², 12; **63**:17, 19; **64**:3, 5², 6, 8², 9², 11; **66**:5; **Jer** 2:31³; **3**:22, 25³; **4**:13; **5**:12²; **6**:16, 17, 24; **7**:10; **8**:8², 14², 15, 20; **9**:19²; **13**:12; **14**:7, 9, 19², 20²; **15**:2; **16**:10²; **18**:12; **20**:10; **26**:19; **35**:6, 8², 10, 11³; **36**:16²; **38**:25; **41**:8²; 42², 3², 5, 6³, 13, 14; **44**:16, 17⁶, 18², 19², 25; **48**:14, 29; **50**:7; **51**:9, 51²; **La** 2:16³; **3**:22, 42, 47; **4**:17, 18, 20²; **5**:3, 4², 5, 6, 7, 9, 16, 21; **Eze** 11:3; **20**:32; **21**:10; **33**:10², 24; **35**:10; **37**:11; **Da** 2:4, 7, 23, 36; **3**:16, 17², 18; **6**:5; **9**:5³, 6, 7, 8², 9, 10, 11, 13, 14, 15³, 18²; **Hos** 6:2; **8**:2; **10**:3³; **14**:2, 3²; **Am** 6:10, 13; **8**:5²; **Ob** 1:1; **Jnh** 1:6, 11; **3**:9; **Mic** 2:4; **4**:2, 5; **5**:5; **Hab** 1:12; **Zec** 1:11; **8**:23; **Mal** 1:4², 6, 7; **2**:10², 17; **3**:7, 8, 13, 14, 15; **Mt** 2:2; **3**:9; **6**:12, 31²; **7**:22; **9**:14; **11**:3, 17²; **12**:38; **14**:17; **15**:33; **16**:7; **17**:19, 27; **19**:27; **20**:18, 22, 33; **21**:25, 26²; **22**:16, 22²; **23**:30²; **25**:37, 38, 39, 44; **26**:65; **27**:42, 63; **28**:13, 14; **Mk** 2:12; **4**:30²; **5**:9; **6**:37; **8**:16; **9**:28, 38²; **10**:28, 33, 35², 39; **11**:31, 32, 33; **12**:14, 15²; **14**:58, 63; **15**:32; **Lk** 3:8, 10, 12, 14; **4**:23; **5**:26; **7**:19, 20, 32²; **9**:12, 13², 49²; **10**:11; **11**:4; **13**:26; **15**:32; **17**:10²; **18**:28²; 31; **19**:14;

20:5, 6, 7, 21; **22**:49, 71²; **23**:2, 41²; **24**:21; **Jn** 1:14, 16, 41, 45; **3**:2, 11⁴; **4**:20, 22², 42²; **6**:5, 28, 30, 42, 68, 69; **7**:27, 35; **8**:33², 41², 48, 52; **9**:4, 20², 21, 24, 28, 29², 31, 40; **10**:33; **11**:16, 47, 48; **12**:21, 34; **14**:5², 23; **16**:18, 30; **17**:11, 22; **18**:30, 31; **19**:7, 15; **20**:2, 25; **21**:24; **Ac** 2:11, 32, 37; **3**:12, 15; **4**:9, 12, 16², 17, 20²; **5**:23³, 28, 29, 32; **6**:3, 11, 14; **7**:40; **10**:22, 33, 39, 47; **11**:12; **13**:32, 46²; **14**:15²; **15**:10, 11², 19, 20, 24, 25, 27², 36; **16**:10, 11, 12², 13³, 16², 28, 37; **17**:19, 20, 28², 29², 32; **19**:2, 25, 40²; **20**:7, 8, 13², 14, 15², 35; **21**:1³, 2, 3², 4, 5², 6, 7², 8, 10, 12², 14, 15, 16, 17, 22, 23, 25; **23**:9, 14², 15; **24**:2, 3, 5, 6, 8; **26**:14; **27**:1, 2³, 3, 4, 5², 7², 8, 12, 15, 16², 18, 20, 26, 27, 28; **28**:1, 10², 11, 12, 13², 14², 15, 16, 21, 22²; **Ro** 1:5; **2**:2; **3**:5, 8², 9³, 19, 20, 28, 31²; **4**:1, 9; **5**:1², 2³, 3², 6, 8, 9² 10³, 11²; **6**:1², 2², 4², 5², 8², 9³, 10², 11², 12, 13², 14², 15, 16, 21, 22²; **Ro** 1:5; **2**:2; **3**:5, 8², 9³, 19, 20, 28, 31²; **4**:1, 9; **5**:1², 2³, 7², 8, 12, 15, 16², 18, 20, 26, 27, 28²; **6**:1², 2², 3², 4², 5², 6, 9², 10², 11², 15², 16, 17⁴, 22, 23², 24, 25³, 26², 28, 31, 36²; **7**:4, 5, 6, 9²; **8**:12, 15, 16, 17, 22, 23, 24, 26², 28³, 29², 32, 33³, 34, 44²; **11**:2, 10, 19, 24, 26; **12**:1², 2³, 8³, 14, 20, 21², 38², 40; **13**:8; **15**:19, 20, 21, 23, 24², 26²; **16**:5, 7; **17**:17²; **18**:16, 17; **19**:5, 7, 9, 10, 11, 15, 19; **20**:3, 4, 8; **21**:5, 20, 29; **23**:3, 9, 10, 11, 14, 17, 24², 27, 29, 30, 31, 32²; **24**:1, 4², 5, 30, 31; **25**:2², 5², 6²; **26**:6², 7, 8², 9, 11, 13, 14, 17, 18, 19², 20, 21³, 22, 26², 28, 29, 30, 31, 32; **27**:1, 2, 4, 5, 7, 8, 9, 10, 11, 12, 13, 14, 15, 22, 31; **29**:15; **2Ch** 1:16; **2**:17²; **3**:15; **4**:3, 4, 6, 16, 19, 21; **5**:5, 6, 9, 11², 12²; **6**:38; **7**:6²; **8**:7, 9, 10; **9**:18, 20², 28; **10**:8, 17; **11**:10, 12; **13**:14, 17, 18²; **14**:8, 13, 15, 16³; **16**:8; **17**:8, 19; **18**:9, 11; **20**:22³, 33, 34, 36², 37²; **21**:2²; **22**:11; **23**:8², 9, 13³, 14, 18; **24**:13, 14²; **26**:25, 15; **27**:10; **28**:12, 15², 23; **29**:6, 23, 29, 31, 34, 35; **30**:7, 8, 15, 17, 21; **31**:1, 13, 16, 18, 19²; **32**:9², 13, 18, 31; **33**:4², 9, 12; **34**:4², 9, 12², 13, 14, 33; **35**:7, 11, 14, 15, 17, 18; **36**:21; **Ezr** 1:11; **2**:59, 62; **4**:1, 20; **5**:2, 5; **6**:20; **8**:3, 13, 16², 20, 33; **10**:9, 16; **Ne** 2:10, 12; **3**:7, 17, 18, 22; **4**:1², 7, 15, 16, 17; **5**:2, 3, 4, 8, 16, 18²; **6**:2, 9, 16, 17, 18; **7**:1, 4, 61, 64, 68; **8**:2, 4, 7, 9, 14; **9**:3, 4, 12, 20, 26, 27, 28, 30, 35; **10**:1, 8; **11**:1, 13, 14, 20, 21, 22, 23, 30; **12**:1, 7, 8, 12, 22, 23, 24, 25, 27², 28, 44²; **13**:3, 13², 15, 16; **Est** 1:3, 5², 6, 14², 21; **2**:8, 19, 23; **3**:6, 12², 13; **4**:12; **5**:6; **6**:14; **7**:2; **8**:9²; **9**:1, 2, 16, 26; **Job** 1:13, 14², 18; **3**:24², 25; **5**:7; **8**:8, 9, 15, 20², 23; **15**:7²; **16**:4; **19**:23², 24; **22**:3², 8, 16; **29**:5, 10; **30**:5², 6, 8, 22, 34²; **34**:4, 38:4, 6, 21; **39**:16; **42**:15; **Ps** 18:9, 15, 17, 37; **22**:5²; **31**:12; **33**:6, 35:13; **39**:12; **40**:5; **48**:5; **50**:12; **53**:5; **55**:12²; **65**:3; **77**:16, 19; **78**:8², 37², 39, 53, 57, 64; **80**:10; **81**:6; **87**:5; **90**:2; **99**:6, 8; **105**:12; **106**:7, 43; **107**:5, 23, 27, 29, 30, 39; **119**:5; **126**:1, 2; **133**:3; **139**:16, 18; **141**:6; **148**:5; **Pr** 3:20; **8**:24², 25; **Ecc** 2:7; **4**:8, 16²; **7**:10; **SS** 1:6; **6**:11; **8**:1, 7; **Isa** 6:2³, 3; **7**:2, 23; **9**:1; **10**:15; **12**:1; **14**:9²; **22**:2, 3; **26**:17, 18²; **27**:4, 7, 13²; **29**:16; **37**:12²; 19, 36; **40**:15; **41**:22, 25²; **43**:9; **46**:3; **48**:4², 8; **49**:19; **50**:1; **51**:1²; **52**:3, 14², 15; **54**:1, 6; **57**:10; **58**:2; **59**:10; **63**:14; **64**:5; **Jer** 1:5; **2**:3, 36; **4**:24², 25; **6**:14²; **7**:13, 26; **8**:11; **9**:1; **11**:18; **15**:14, 16; **17**:23; **19**:15; **22**:24; **24**:1; **28**:5; **33**:7, 11; **34**:1, 7²; **36**:12, 28, 32; **37**:5, 10², 15; **40**:1, 6, 7²; **41**:1, 2, 3², 7, 10², 11, 13², 16, 18; **42**:1, 6, 7², 10², 11; **43**:1, 8; **44**:1, 2, 3²; **45**:2; **47**:1; **49**:8; **50**:44; **52**:7, 8, 17, 19, 23, 25, 30, 32; **La** 1:7, 14; **2**:4, 14²; **3**:52; **4**:7, 10, 18, 19; **Eze** 1:1, 7², 11², 18², 23; **2**:10; **3**:15; **7**:20; **8**:1, 16²; **9**:6, 8; **10**:3, 12², 15, 20²; **11**:1, 14, 16, 18, 20; **16**:3³, 4³, 5³, 7³, 8, 13², 18²; **17**:22, 24; **19**:2, 10; **20**:16, 21, 25; **21**:30; **23**:2, 3, 4, 20, 42; **26**:17; **27**:7, 8², 9, 11, 15, 21; **28**:12, 13⁴, 14², 15², 16, 18; **29**:7, 11; **31**:3, 4², 7, 9, 10², 11, 13², 16, 18; **32**:27, 31; **34**:5², 6, 12; **36**:17, 19, 35; **37**:2; **38**:8; **39**:18, 23; **40**:2, 7², 9, 10, 12,

28:14:2, 12²; **15**:21, 46, 63; **16**:9; **17**:1, 3, 9, 12²; **18**:2, 20; **19**:15², 16, 22, 23, 30, 31, 35, 38, 39, 48; **21**:4²; 5, 6, 10², 19, 20, 21, 26, 27, 33, 34, 40²; **22**:30, 33; **24**:32; **Jdg** 1:19, 21, 27, 35²; **2**:14, 15; **3**:4, 8, 14; **4**:17; **5**:6, 13, 14, 15; **6**:29; **7**:19, 20, 23, 24; **8**:10²; 19, 26; **9**:3, 7, 27; **10**:17; **11**:12; **12**:2, 6; **14**:4; **15**:6; **16**:2, 12, 17, 25, 27²; **17**:2, 4; **18**:3, 7², 22, 26, 30; **19**:11², 12², 16, 22; **20**:16²; **21**:9, 14², 23; **Ru** 1:2²; 2:23; **1Sa** 1:3, 13; **2**:5², 12, 17, 22, 27; **3**:1, 2; **4**:4, 7, 10, 15, 19; **5**:4, 12; **6**:13; **7**:7, 10, 13, 14; **8**:10; **9**:3, 4, 11, 14, 22, 27; **10**:9, 14; **11**:9, 11²; **13**:2², 4, 7, 11², 15, 16, 17²; **14**:2, 10, 24, 25², 31, 41²; 49, 51; **15**:9, 17; **17**:11, 21, 52; **18**:6; **19**:5; **20**:20; **22**:2², 11, 17; **23**:24, 26²; **24**:3; **25**:7², 16², 20, 43; **26**:7, 12, 16; **29**:2, 4; **30**:2, 6, 10, 16, 21, 26; **2Sa** 1:14, 23⁴; 26; **2**:3, 15, 17, 18, 30, 31; **3**:2, 5, 34², 36; **4**:2², **5**:2, 13; **6**:3, 5, 13; **7**:19; **8**:2, 11, 18; **9**:12; **10**:5, 8, 9, 14, 19²; **11**:7, 16, 16, 22; **12**:1, 18, 19, 31; **13**:23; **14**:27; **15**:4, 18², 24², 24; **16**:5; **17**:17²; **18**:1, 7, 9, 14, 17, 41², 49, 51; **15**:9, 17; **17**:11, 21, 52; **18**:6; **19**:5; **20**:20; **22**:2², 11, 17; **1Ki** 1:9; **3**:2; **4**:2, 10, 13, 20², 21, 22; **5**:12; **6**:5, 7, 10, 25; **7**:4, 5, 6, 9, 10, 11, 19, 20, 22, 24, 25, 28, 29², 32, 33², 33²; **8**:7, 8; **9**:20, 22, 25; **10**:19, 21; **12**:8, 17, 31; **13**:8, 20; **14**:24; **15**:27; **16**:21; **18**:6, 10, 20, 12, 16, 23; **2Ki** 2:1, 11, 15; **4**:6, 39; **6**:20, 32; **7**:3, 10; **9**:25; **10**:1, 4, 6², 11², 7, 10, 12², 21; **12**:3, 21; **13**:21; **14**:4; **15**:4, 35; **17**:9, 14, 23, 41²; **19**:12²; **18**:35; **23**:7, 11, 13, 16; **24**:11, 14; **25**:4, 5, 13, 15, 19, 25, 28; **1Ch** 1:19, 23, 29, 31, 33, 35, 51, 54; **2**:1², 3, 9, 10², 17, 18, 23, 32, 33, 50; **3**:1, 4, 5², 6, 9, 20; **4**:2, 3, 4, 6, 12, 14, 18, 23, 31, 32, 33, 38, 41²; **5**:1, 10, 13, 14, 17, 18, 20, 23, 24², 25; **6**:48, 49, 50, 54³, 55, 56, 57, 60², 61, 62, 63, 66, 67; **7**:3², 8, 11², 12, 16, 17, 19, 21, 29, 33, 40; **8**:3, 6³, 8, 10, 13, 16, 18, 21, 25, 27, 28, 38², 40²; **9**:1, 2, 3, 9, 13², 18, 19, 22, 24, 26², 28³, 33³, 34, 44²; **11**:2, 10, 19, 24, 26; **12**:1, 2³; **13**:8; **15**:19, 20, 21, 23, 24²; **16**:5, 6, 19, 38, 41, 42²; **17**:17²; **18**:16, 17; **19**:5, 7, 9, 10, 11, 15, 19; **20**:3, 4, 8; **21**:2²; **22**:11; **23**:8², 9, 13³, 14, 18; **24**:13, 14²; **26**:25, 15; **27**:10; **28**:12, 15², 23; **29**:6, 23, 29, 31, 34, 35; **30**:7, 8, 15, 17, 21; **31**:1, 13, 16, 18, 19²; **32**:9², 13, 18, 31; **33**:4², 9, 12; **34**:4², 9, 12², 13, 14, 33; **35**:7, 11, 14, 15, 17, 18; **36**:21; **Ezr** 1:11; **2**:59, 62; **4**:1, 20; **5**:2, 5; **6**:20; **8**:3, 13, 16², 20, 33; **10**:9, 16; **Ne** 2:10, 12; **3**:7, 17, 18, 22; **4**:1², 7, 15, 16, 17; **5**:2, 3, 4, 8, 16, 18²; **6**:2, 9, 16, 17, 18; **7**:1, 4, 61, 64, 68; **8**:2, 4, 7, 9, 14; **9**:3, 4, 12, 20, 26, 27, 28, 30, 35; **10**:1, 8; **11**:1, 13, 14, 20, 21, 22, 23, 30; **12**:1, 7, 8, 12, 22, 23, 24, 25, 27², 28, 44²; **13**:3, 13², 15, 16; **Est** 1:3, 5², 6, 14², 21; **2**:8, 19, 23; **3**:6, 12², 13; **4**:12; **5**:6; **6**:14; **7**:2; **8**:9²; **9**:1, 2, 16, 26; **Job** 1:13, 14², 18; **3**:24², 25; **5**:7; **8**:8, 9, 15, 20², 23; **15**:7²; **16**:4; **19**:23², 24; **22**:3², 8, 16; **29**:5, 10; **30**:5², 6, 8, 22, 34²; **38**:4, 6, 21; **39**:16; **42**:15; **Ps** 18:9, 15, 17, 37; **22**:5²; **31**:12; **33**:6; **35**:13; **39**:12; **40**:5; **48**:5; **50**:2; **53**:5; **55**:12²; **65**:3; **77**:16, 19; **78**:8², 37², 39, 53, 57, 64; **80**:10; **81**:6; **87**:5; **90**:2; **99**:6, 8; **105**:12; **106**:7, 43; **107**:5, 23, 27, 29, 30, 39; **119**:5; **126**:1, 2; **133**:3; **139**:16, 18; **141**:6; **148**:5; **Pr** 3:20; **8**:24², 25; **Ecc** 2:7; **4**:8, 16²; **7**:10; **SS** 1:6; **6**:11; **8**:1, 7; **Isa** 6:2³, 3; **7**:2, 23; **9**:1; **10**:15; **12**:1; **14**:9²; **22**:2, 3; **26**:17, 18²; **27**:4, 7, 13²; **29**:16; **37**:12²; 19, 36; **40**:15; **41**:22, 25²; **43**:9; **46**:3; **48**:4², 8; **49**:19; **50**:1; **51**:1²; **52**:3, 14², 15; **54**:1, 6; **57**:10; **58**:2; **59**:10; **63**:14; **64**:5; **Jer** 1:5; **2**:3, 36; **4**:24², 25; **6**:14²; **7**:13, 26; **8**:11; **9**:1; **11**:18; **15**:14, 16; **17**:23; **19**:15; **22**:24; **24**:1; **28**:5; **33**:7, 11; **34**:1, 7²; **36**:12, 28, 32; **37**:5, 10², 15; **40**:1, 6, 7²; **41**:1, 2, 3², 7, 10², 11, 13², 16, 18; **42**:1, 6, 7², 10², 11; **43**:1, 8; **44**:1, 2, 3²; **45**:2; **47**:1; **49**:8; **50**:44; **52**:7, 8, 17, 19, 23, 25, 30, 32; **La** 1:7, 14; **2**:4, 14²; **3**:52; **4**:7, 10, 18, 19; **Eze** 1:1, 7², 11², 18², 23; **2**:10; **3**:15; **7**:20; **8**:1, 16²; **9**:6, 8; **10**:3, 12², 15, 20²; **11**:1, 14, 16, 18, 20; **16**:3³, 4³, 5³, 7³, 8, 13², 18²; **17**:22, 24; **19**:2, 10; **20**:16, 21, 25; **21**:30; **23**:2, 3, 4, 20, 42; **26**:17; **27**:7, 8², 9, 11, 15, 21; **28**:12, 13⁴, 14², 15², 16, 18; **29**:7, 11; **31**:3, 4², 7, 9, 10², 11, 13², 16, 18; **32**:27, 31; **34**:5², 6, 12; **36**:17, 19, 35; **37**:2; **38**:8; **39**:18, 23; **40**:2, 7², 9, 10, 12,

16², 17, 18, 30, 38, 39², 40², 41², 42², 43², 44, 48², 49; **41**:2, 3, 6³, 7, 11, 13, 16, 18, 19, 20, 22, 25, 26; **42**:4, 5, 6, 10, 11, 12; **46**:22; **48**:11; **Da** 1:5², 6, 16; **2**:13, 29, 34, 35, 41, 42, 47; **3**:13, 21, 27, 28; **4**:12, 31, 36; **5**:9, 15; **6**:2, 4, 24; **7**:2, 4, 8, 9², 10, 12; **8**:3, 12; **10**:3, 12; **Hos** 2:12; **6**:7; **8**:7; **10**:14; **13**:6²; **Am** 4:11; **Ob** 1:11; **Jnh** 1:5; **Mic** 1:13²; **Na** 3:9², 10³; **Hab** 1:5; **3**:8, 14; **Zep** 3:7, 19; **Hag** 2:15, 16²; **Zec** 1:8; **18**; **3**:4; **5**:9; **6**:1, 7; **7**:6², 7², 14; **8**:9, 10; **11**:11; **Mt** 1:17; **2**:10, 16, 20; **3**:4, 6; **4**:18²; **5**:12; **7**:28; **8**:16², 27, 28; **9**:8, 32, 36; **11**:7, 21, 23; **12**:1, 3, 23; **13**:6, 54; **14**:20²; 26, 33, 36; **15**:12, 31, 37²; **17**:9, 23; **18**:31; **19**:8, 12², 13, 25; **20**:9, 10, 12, 24, 29, 30; **21**:12, 15, 20, 46; **22**:22, 25, 28, 33, 41; **23**:37; **24**:24, 38; **25**:2², 10²; **26**:8, 21, 22, 26, 43, 59, 69; **27**:32, 38, 44, 52, 54², 55, 56, 61; **28**:3, 4, 11, 13, 15; **Mk** 1:5, 16, 22, 27; **2**:6, 8, 15², 16, 18, 25, 32; **3**:10; **4**:1, 6, 36, 41; **5**:13, 15, 20, 40, 42; **6**:2, 8, 14, 31, 34, 42, 50, 51, 52, 56; **7**:2, 35, 37; **8**:8², 9, 25; **9**:2, 4, 6, 9, 15, 30, 32, 33; **10**:5, 10, 13, 24, 26, 32², 46; **11**:12, 15, 17, 22², 32; **12**:1, 5, 12, 17, 20, 28, 41; **13**:22; **14**:1², 4, 11, 18, 19, 22, 40, 55, 67; **15**:40²; 41; **16**:2, 5, 8, 10, 12, 14; **Lk** 1:2²; 6, 7, 10, 21, 59, 65²; **2**:6, 8, 9, 18, 20, 38, 43², 48, 49; **3**:15²; 21; **4**:20, 22, 25, 27, 28, 32, 36, 42; **5**:2, 9, 17, 22, 26, 29; **6**:3, 7, 8, 11, 18; **7**:16, 21, 39; **8**:1, 3, 4, 19, 23, 35, 37, 40, 52, 56; **9**:7, 14, 17², 18, 32, 33, 34, 43, 45, 57; **10**:33, 38; **11**:52; **12**:1, 49; **13**:1, 2, 4, 17², 34; **14**:24, 25; **15**:1, 16; **16**:14, 16; **17**:10, 14, 17, 27, 28; **18**:9, 15, 19², 32, 33, 45, 47; **20**:19, 26, 29, 33, 45; **21**:5; **22**:2², 5, 63; **23**:10, 32; **24**:4, 13, 14, 16, 28², 31, 32, 36, 37; **Jn** 1:3, 48; **3**:2, 19, 23; **4**:27; **6**:11, 19, 21², 24, 61; **7**:1, 11, 15, 39, 43; **8**:6, 20, 39, 42; **9**:10, 16, 22, 33, 34, 40, 41; **10**:8, 19; **12**:16², 17, 6; **18**:3, 15, 30, 36; **19**:11; **20**:4, 19, 20, 25, 26²; **21**:2, 6, 8, 18, 25; **Ac** 1:10, 13², 2:1, 2, 4, 5, 37, 41², 43, 44, 47; **3**:1, 10, 11; **4**:1, 2², 6, 13², 21, 31², 32, 34; **5**:13, 14, 16, 17², 24, 33, 36, 37; **6**:1; **10**:19; **16**, 26, 54, 59; **8**:1, 7, 12; **9**:17, 21, 26; **10**:2, 9, 38, 45; **11**:24, 26; **12**:11, 12, 16; **13**:1, 2, 42, 45, 48², 52; **14**:4; **15**:1, 2, 4, 22, 30, 31, 32, 33, 36; **16**:5, 15, 16², 23, 25², 26, 33, 38²; **17**:4, 5, 8, 11; **18**:3, 8, 14; **19**:5, 7, 12², 13, 14, 17, 28, 29², 35; **20**:8²; **21**:16, 18, 27, 30, 31, 37, 40; **22**:20, 23, 24, 29; **23**:4, 6, 9, 13, 27, 28; **24**:9; **25**:3, 14, 26; **26**:10, 17², 4, 15, 16, 22, 27², 30, 36, 37, 44; **28**:9, 10, 15, 24; **Ro** 1:21, 27; **2**:26; **3**:6; **4**:17, 23; **5**:6, 8, 10², 19; **6**:3², 4, 17, 20²; **7**:5²; **8**:24; **9**:3, 11, 32; **11**:6, 7, 19, 20, 24², 30; **15**:21, 26, 27; **16**:7; **1Co** 1:13, 15, 26²; **2**:4; **3**:2; **4**:18; **5**:3; **6**:11⁴, 20; **7**:7, 21², 23, 30²; **10**:1, 2, 5, 7, 9, 10, 11; **11**:5, 21; **12**:13², 17², 19; **16**:15; **2Co** 1:8; **3**:14; **5**:20; **7**:5, 9², 13, 15; **8**:3, 10; **9**:2; **11**:21; **12**:2, 13; **Gal** 1:10, 17; **2**:6, 14; **3**:16, 23, 27; **4**:3², 8, 14²; **5**:7, 13; **Eph** 1:11, 12, 13²; **2**:1, 3, 5, 12, 13, 17²; **4**:4²; 21, 22, 30; **5**:8; **6**:7; **Col** 1:16², 21²; **2**:7, 11, 13, 17; **3**:15; **1Th** 2:6, 7, 8, 10, 17; **3**:3, 4, 7; **2Th** 3:7²; 10; **1Ti** 5:1; **6**:12; **Tit** 3:3; **Heb** 2:15; **3**:16²; 19; **8**:4; **9**:2, 5, 9; **10**:6, 8, 33²; **11**:2, 9, 13², 16, 23, 29, 31, 35, 36, 37², 39; **13**:3³; **Jas** 2:22; **5**:6; **1Pe** 1:12, 18; **2**:8, 10, 21, 25; **1Jn** 3:12²; **Rev** 1:14², 15; **3**:15; **4**:4³, 5, 6²; **5**:8, 9, 6, 8, 11², 7:4, 5, 9², 11; **8**:2, 7, 9; **9**:2, 3, 4, 5, 8, 15, 17, 19, 20; **10**:11; **11**:13³, 15, 16, 18; **14**:4, 20; **15**:6, 8; **16**:5, 9; **17**:2; **18**:23²; **19**:14, 20, 21; **20**:3, 4, 5, 12², 13², 14; **21**:12, 13, 14, 19, 21.

WERE (2530)

Ge 2:1, 4, 9², 25; **3**:7², 11, 19; **4**:8; **5**:2; **6**:1, 2, 4²; **7**:11, 16, 19, 23; **8**:1; **9**:18, 19², 23; **10**:10, 21, 25, 29; **11**:5; **12**:6; **13**:6², 7, 13²; **14**:7, 13; **17**:26; **18**:11; **19**:11, 14; **20**:8; **23**:20; **24**:32², 54; **25**:3, 4², 16, 24, 26; **27**:35, 27², 1, 23; **28**:8, 12; **29**:2, 3; **30**:35, 38, 39, 41, 42; **31**:1, 4, 10; **32**:7; **34**:5, 7, 25; **35**:1, 2, 6, 16, 26²; **36**:5², 7², 12, 13, 15, 16², 17², 18, 19², 20², 21, 29, 30, 31, 40, 43; **37**:7, 9, 11, 25²; **38**:12, 27, 29; **40**:5, 6, 7, 10, 13, 16; **41**:4, 5, 50; **42**:5, 13, 30, 32, 35²; 43²; 43:7, 18³, 25, 27, 34; **44**:3; **45**:3², 16, 24; **46**:15², 18, 20, 22², 25, 26, 27, 31; **47**:3, 14, 27, 28; **48**:7, 10; **49**:31²; 32; **50**:8, 23; **Ex** 1:7, 12, 15; **2**:5, 11; **4**:16²; **5**:14², 19²; **6**:14³, 15², 16, 17, 18, 19², 21, 22, 24²; 25, 27; **8**:14, 18; **9**:11, 26, 31, 32; **10**:8, 11; **12**:37; **14**:8, 10², 11, 21, 27; **15**:27; **16**:17; **17**:3, 11², 12; **22**:21; **23**:9; **27**:8; **32**:15, 16, 25, 29; **33**:5; **34**:1, 30; **35**:22, 26, 29; **36**:4, 6, 9, 15, 28, 29, 30; **37**:13, 14, 15², 17, 19, 20, 22, 27, 28; **38**:2, 14, 15, 16, 17³, 19², 20, 21, 25, 27; **39**:4, 13, 14; **Lev** 7:35²; 36; **15**:10; **18**:27, 28, 30; **19**:34; **Nu** 1:16², 18, 20², 22², 24², 26², 28², 30², 32², 34², 36², 38² 40², 42², 44, 45², 47; **2**:33³, 3², 17, 18, 20, 21, 24, 25, 27, 28, 29, 31, 32, 33, 34, 35, 36, 38²; **4**:36, 38, 40, 42, 44, 49; **7**:2², 8, 9², 84, 87, 88; **9**:6; **11**:18, 22², 26², 29; **12**:8; **13**:3; **14**:6, 37; **15**:26, 32; **16**:2, 27, 33, 35, 38; **19**:18; **20**:1³; **21**:32², 23, 29; **24**, 40; **25**:6; **26**:4, 5, 7², 9³, 12, 14², 15, 18², 19, 20, 21, 22², 23, 25², 26², 28, 30, 33, 34, 40; **27**:3², 38, 40, 41², 42², 43, 44, 47², 48, 50², 57², 58, 62; **27**:1, 14; **31**:5, 8, 16², 26, 47, 48; **32**:1, 38, 39, 3², 4², 4:35, 46, 5:5, 15; **6**:21; **7**:7²; **9**:10, 15; **10**:6; **12**:6; **11**:2, 6; **13**:13, 18², 26; **14**:7, 13², 26; **15**:25; **16**:7, 19, 25²; **17**:3, 7²; **18**:12²; 16; **19**:43²; 44; **20**:5², 7; **21**:30; **23**:2, 3, 4, 13⁴, 14², 15², 16, 18; **29**:7; **31**:31, 33; **34**:5², 6, 12; **36**:17, 19, 35; **37**:2; **38**:8; **39**:18, 23; **40**:2, 7², 9, 10, 12,

WHEN (2816)

Ge 2:4², 17; **3**:5, 6; **4**:12; **5**:1, 2, 3, 6, 9, 12, 15, 18, 21, 25, 28; **6**:1, 4; **7**:6; **8**:11; **9**:21, 24; **11**:10, 12, 14, 16, 18, 20, 22, 24, 31; **12**:4, 12, 14, 15; **14**:10, 14, 15; **17**:16, 4, 16; **17**:1, 22, 24; **18**:2, 16, 33; **19**:1, 15, 16, 29, 33², 35²; **20**:8, 13; **21**:4, 5, 15; **22**:3, 9; **24**:14, 22, 41, 42, 52, 54; **25**:20, 24, 26, 29; **26**:7, 8, 34; **27**:1, 5, 27, 34, 40, 42, 45; **28**:6, 11, 16; **29**:3, 10, 13, 23, 25, 31, 33, 34, 35; **30**:1, 9, 16, 30, 38²; **31**:19, 25, 49; **32**:2, 6, 10, 17, 19, 20, 25; **34**:2, 5; **35**:1, 7; **36**:33, 34, 35, 36, 37, 38, 39; **37**:4, 5, 7, 10, 14, 21, 23, 28, 29; **38**:2, 15, 17, 24, 29; **39**:3, 13, 15, 18, 46, 55, 56; **42**:1, 6, 21, 29, 35; **43**:2, 16, 18, 26, 34; **44**:4², 6, 14, 24, 30; **45**:1, 4, 16, 27²; **46**:1, 28, 29³, 10, 23, 25, 31, 33, 34, 35; **30**:1, 9, 16, 30, 38²; **31**:19, 25, 49; **32**:2, 6, 10, 17, 19, 20, 25; **34**:2, 5; **35**:1, 7; **36**:33, 34, 35, 36, 37, 38, 39; **37**:4, 5, 7, 10, 14, 21, 23, 28, 29; **38**:2, 15, 17, 24, 29; **39**:3, 13, 15, 18, 46, 55, 56; **42**:1, 6, 21, 29, 35; **43**:2, 16, 18, 26, 34; **44**:4², 6, 14, 24, 30; **45**:1, 4, 16, 27²; **46**:1, 28, 29; **47**:15, 28, 33; **50**:4, 10, 11, 15, 17; **Ex** 1:16; **2**:2, 3, 10, 15, 18; **3**:4, 12, 21; **4**:6, 7, 14, 21, 31; **5**:13, 19, 20; **6**:28; **7**:5, 7, 9; **8**:15, 17, 18; **9**:23, 29, 34; **11**:1; **12**:6, 13², 23, 25, 26, 27; **13**:5, 8, 14, 15, 17; **14**:5, 18, 31; **15**:19, 23; **16**:8, 14, 15, 18, 21, 32;

17:12; 18:14; 19:13; 20:18; 21:3, 16; 22:27; 23:2, 16; 24:3, 15; 27:7; 28:35³; 30:7, 8, 12², 15, 20; 31:10, 18; 32:1, 5, 17, 19, 34; 33:4, 22; 34:15, 16, 24, 29, 30, 33, 34; 35:19; 39:41; 40:18; Lev 1:2; 2:1; 4:2, 14, 22, 23, 28; 5:1, 3, 4, 5, 15; 6:4; 9:23, 24; 10:3, 16, 20; 11:31, 32; 12:6; 13:2, 3, 9, 15, 18, 21, 24, 31, 38, 40, 53, 56; 14:2, 34, 57; 15:2, 9, 13, 16, 18, 19, 23, 25, 28; 16:1, 20; 19:5, 9, 23, 33, 35; 20:4; 22:7, 21, 27, 29; 23:3, 10, 22, 28, 43; 24:16; 25:2, 16²; 26:10, 17, 25, 26, 41, 44; 27:21; Nu 3:4; 13; 4:5, 15, 19; 5:6, 21, 27, 29, 30; 6:13; 7:1, 10, 84, 89; 8:2, 17, 19; 9:10, 12, 19, 21, 22; 10:3, 5, 9, 34; 11:1, 2, 9, 18², 25; 12:5, 6, 10; 13:17, 23; 14:39; 15:8, 13, 18, 28; 16:4, 19, 22, 42; 18:2, 16, 26, 30; 19:14; 20:3, 16, 29; 21:1, 7, 9, 23; 22:7, 22, 23, 25, 27, 36; 24:1, 2, 22, 23; 25:7, 18²; 26:9, 10, 61, 63, 64; 27:14; 28:26; 30:2, 3, 5, 8, 12, 14; 32:8, 22, 29; 33:1, 8, 39, 51; 34:2; 35:10, 19, 21; 36:2, 4; Dt 1:34; 2:16, 19, 22, 32; 4:10, 19, 30, 45; 5:23, 28; 6:7⁴, 10, 11, 20; 7:1, 2; 8:10, 12², 13; 9:9, 16, 23; 11:6, 19⁴, 29, 31; 12:20, 29; 15:13; 16:6; 17:14, 18; 18:9, 16, 21; 19:11²; 20:1, 2, 9, 10, 13, 19; 21:10, 13, 16, 18; 22:8, 14; 23:4, 9, 13; 24:10, 19, 20, 21; 25:1, 17, 18, 19; 26:1, 12; 27:2, 3, 4, 12; 28:6²; 19²; 29:7, 19, 25; 30:1, 2; 31:11, 20², 21; 32:8², 36, 41, 45; 33:5, 21; 34:4, 7; Jos 2:5, 10, 11, 14, 18, 22; 3:3, 8, 14; 4:1, 6, 7, 21, 23; 5:1, 6, 13; 6:5, 8, 16, 20²; 7:3, 21; 8:5, 6, 8, 14, 21, 24², 33; 9:1, 3, 12; 10:14, 17, 24; 11:1; 13:1, 32; 14:7; 15:18²; 17:13; 19:49; 20:4; 22:7, 10, 11, 15, 20, 30; 24:6, 9; Jdg 1:4, 14², 23, 28, 35; 2:4, 19, 21; 3:9, 25, 27; 4:12; 5:2², 4², 8, 31; 6:7, 12, 13, 22, 28, 29, 31; 7:15, 17, 18, 22; 8:1, 7, 9; 9:7, 16, 30, 33, 36, 43, 47, 55; 10:5, 11, 14, 17; 11:2, 4, 13, 16, 31, 34, 35; 12:3; 13:11, 12, 17, 21; 14:2, 8, 9, 11; 15:6, 17, 19; 16:9, 15, 18, 24, 25, 30; 17:3; 18:3, 8, 10, 18, 22; 19:3, 7, 8, 9, 11, 17, 27, 29; 20:10, 25, 40; 21:9, 21, 22; Ru 1:1, 6, 18, 19; 2:14; 3:4, 7, 15, 16; 4:1; 1Sa 1:9, 21, 25; 2:19, 27, 31; 4:3, 5, 6, 13², 18, 19; 5:3, 4, 7; 6:1, 6, 13; 7:6, 7²; 8:1, 6, 18, 21; 9:5, 17, 26; 10:2, 10, 11, 14, 20, 21; 11:4, 6, 8, 9; 12:12, 17; 13:1, 6, 11; 14:17, 22, 26, 29; 15:2, 6, 13; 16:4²; 6, 16; 17:24, 28, 34, 35, 51, 53; 18:6, 15, 19, 20, 24, 26, 28; 19:5, 14, 16, 18, 20; 20:15, 19, 24, 37; 21:1; 22:1, 8, 22; 23:1, 6, 9, 13, 25²; 24:4, 8, 9, 16, 19; 25:7, 9, 12, 23, 30, 31, 36, 37, 39; 26:3; 27:4, 10; 28:5, 12, 21; 30:3, 13, 26; 31:3, 5, 7, 8, 11; 2Sa 1:2, 7, 16; 2:4, 10, 23; 3:13, 20, 23, 27, 28; 4:1, 4, 10, 11; 5:3, 4, 17; 6:6, 13, 16, 20; 7:12, 14; 8:3, 5, 9; 9:6; 10:2, 5, 6, 14, 17, 19; 11:1, 7, 10, 17, 19, 22, 26; 12:1; 13:5, 6, 11, 21, 23, 28; 14:4, 13, 26; 15:20, 32; 16:1; 17:6, 20, 23, 27; 18:10; 19:3, 8, 18, 25, 40; 20:3, 5, 12; 21:11, 21; 22:1; 23:3², 19, 11; 24:16, 17, 20; 1Ki 1:1²; 32; 2:1, 7, 8, 19, 28, 41; 3:21, 28; 5:1, 5, 7, 7:51; 8:3, 10, 21, 23, 30², 31, 33², 35², 37², 38, 42, 44², 46, 53, 54; 9:1, 5, 12; 10:1, 4; 11:15, 24, 28; 12:2, 16, 20, 21; 13:4, 13, 23, 26, 31; 14:5, 6, 12, 21; 15:21; 16:16, 18; 17:10; 18:12, 17, 39; 19:3, 13, 15; 20:7, 39; 21:16, 27; 22:15, 24, 32², 42; 2Ki 1:5; 2:1, 9, 10, 14, 18; 3:22, 24, 26; 4:6, 11, 25, 27, 32, 36, 39; 5:8, 13, 18², 21, 24, 26; 6:6, 15, 21, 30, 32; 7:5, 17; 8:7, 14, 16, 17, 26; 9:2, 5, 11, 17, 19, 21, 22, 25, 27, 30, 35; 10:7, 8, 17; 11:1, 13, 21; 12:11; 13:16, 21; 14:2; 15:2, 33; 16:2, 12; 17:21, 25, 35; 18:2, 30, 32; 19:1, 3, 5, 7, 8, 10, 27, 35; 20:7, 17, 19; 21:1, 19; 22:1, 11, 19; 23:16, 31, 36; 24:8, 18; 25:23; 1Ch 1:44, 45, 46, 47, 48, 49, 50; 2:19, 21; 5:1; 6:15; 7:21; 9:28²; 10:3, 5, 7, 8, 11; 11:3, 13; 12:15, 17, 19, 20; 13:9; 14:8; 15:29; 16:19; 17:11; 18:3, 5, 9; 19:2, 5, 6, 15, 17, 19; 20:1, 7; 21:21, 28; 22:12; 23:1; 24:19; 2Ch 2:3; 5:1, 4; 6:16, 21², 22, 24², 26², 28², 29², 32, 34², 36; 7:1, 3, 6, 11, 13, 18; 9:1, 3; 10:2, 16; 11:1; 12:7, 9, 13; 13:7; 15:2, 8, 9; 16:5, 8; 18:14, 23, 31, 32; 19:1; 20:10, 24, 29, 31; 21:4, 5, 20; 22:2, 5, 7, 10, 23; 24:11, 14, 25; 25:1, 14; 26:3, 20; 27:1, 8; 28:1, 9; 29:1, 15, 29; 31:1, 8; 32:2, 9, 11, 21, 31, 33; 33:1, 13, 21; 34:1, 19, 27; 35:20; 36:2, 5, 9, 11; Ezr 1:11; 2:68; 3:1, 10, 12; 4:1; 8:15; 9:3, 11; Ne 1:1, 2, 3, 6, 10, 19; 4:1, 7, 15, 23; 5:6, 14; 6:1, 16; 7:73; 9:18², 27, 28; 10:31, 34, 38; 12:30; 13:3, 19; Est 1:5, 10, 12, 20; 2:1, 7, 8, 15, 19, 20, 23; 3:5; 4:1, 4, 12, 16; 5:2, 9; 6:6; 9:22², 25; Job 1:5, 13, 19; 2:11, 12; 3:22²; 4:13; 5:21; 6:5², 16; 7:4, 13; 8:4, 18; 9:11², 23, 24; 11:3, 11, 15:19, 21; 18:2; 19:18; 20:23; 21:6, 21; 22:29; 23:9², 10, 15; 24:14; 27:8²; 9, 19; 28:25, 26; 29:2, 3, 4², 5, 6, 7, 24; 30:24, 26²; 31:13, 14²; 32:5; 33:15; 34:9, 33; 35:12, 14; 36:13; 37:4, 17; 38:4, 8, 9, 10, 11, 30², 38, 40, 41; 39:1², 18, 24; 40:23; 41:25; Ps 3:T; 4:1, 3, 4, 7; 6:5; 8:3; 11:3; 12:8; 13:4; 14:7; 15:4; 17:15;

18:T; 20:1, 5, 9; 21:12; 27:2², 7; 30:6, 7²; 31:21, 22; 32:3, 6; 34:T; 35:13², 15²; 37:7², 33, 34; 38:16, 20; 39:2; 41:5²; 42:2; 48:4²; 49:5², 16², 17, 18; 50:18; 51:T, 4²; 52:T; 53:6; 54:T; 56:T, 3, 9; 57:T; 58:7, 10²; 59:T; 60:T²; 63:T; 65:3; 66:14; 68:7², 14, 18; 69:10, 11; 71:9², 18, 23; 73:3, 16, 20², 21; 75:3; 76:7, 9; 77:2; 78:20, 21, 59; 81:3, 5; 89:9; 94:8, 18, 19; 101:2; 102:T, 2², 22; 104:19, 28² 29², 30; 105:12, 38; 106:4², 7, 44; 107:30; 109:7, 25, 28; 114:1; 116:6; 119:6, 74, 82, 84; 120:7; 124:2, 3; 126:1; 127:5; 133:1; 137:1; 138:3, 4; 139:2², 15²; 18; 141:1; 142:T, 3; 146:4; 147:9; Pr 1:24², 26, 27³; 3:24², 27, 28, 30; 4:3, 12²; 5:11; 6:9, 22³, 30, 34; 8:24², 27², 28, 29²; 10:19, 25; 11:2, 7, 10²; 14:32; 16:7, 15; 18:3; 20:8; 21:11², 15, 27; 22:6, 18; 23:1, 16, 22, 31³, 35; 24:17²; 27:10, 25; 28:2, 12², 28²; 29:2², 16; 31:21; Ecc 2:11; 5:1, 3², 4, 14, 19; 7:14²; 8:9, 11, 16; 9:12; 12:1, 3², 4², 5²; SS 3:4; Isa 1:7; 12, 15; 2:19, 21; 5:4; 6:13; 7:1, 15; 8:19, 21; 9:3; 10:3, 12, 18, 26; 11:16; 16:12²; 17:5²; 6, 11, 13; 18:3³, 5; 19:20; 21:7; 23:5; 24:13²; 26:9, 16; 27:9, 11; 28:7², 15, 18, 24, 25; 29:8², 23; 30:19, 25, 26, 29; 31:3; 32:7; 33:1², 3; 36:2, 15, 18; 37:1, 3, 5, 7, 8, 9, 10, 28, 36; 39:6; 41:28; 43:2³, 13; 47:10; 48:13, 21; 50:2²; 51:2; 52:8; 54:9; 57:13; 58:7; 59:5; 64:2, 3, 5; 65:8; 66:4², 9, 14; Jer 1:2; 2:17, 19, 26, 27, 28; 3:16; 4:10; 5:19; 6:12, 14, 15; 7:22, 27², 32; 8:4² 8, 11, 12; 9:25; 10:10, 13, 15; 11:4, 12, 14, 15; 12:1; 13:21; 15:16; 16:10, 14; 17:6, 8, 11; 18:22; 19:6; 20:1, 3; 21:1; 22:21, 23; 23:5, 7, 33; 25:12, 16; 26:10, 21; 27:20; 29:10, 13; 30:3; 31:6, 23, 27, 31, 32, 38; 33:14; 34:13; 35:11; 36:3, 11, 16; 37:5, 13; 38:1, 9; 39:4; 40:2, 7, 11; 41:6, 7, 11, 13; 42:18, 20; 43:1; 44:19, 22, 25; 47:7²; 48:12, 13; 49:2; 51:16, 18, 46, 47, 52, 59, 61, 63; 52:1; La 1:7; 3:8, 39, 57; 4:10, 15; Eze 1:19²; 21³, 24²; 28; 3:18, 20, 27; 5:2, 13, 15, 16; 6:8, 13; 7:25; 10:3, 5, 6, 16²; 17²; 12:15, 23; 13:6, 7, 10², 12, 14, 16, 22; 14:4, 7, 21, 22, 23; 15:5², 7; 16:8, 22, 30, 31, 61, 63; 17:10, 17; 18:23; 19:5; 20:28, 31, 41, 42, 44; 21:7; 22:10, 16, 28; 23:8, 18, 19, 21, 40, 41; 24:24; 25:3³, 17; 26:10, 15, 19²; 27:28, 33; 28:22, 25, 26; 29:7²; 30:4, 8, 18, 25; 31:16; 32:7, 9, 10, 15²; 33:2, 8, 12², 29, 33; 34:5, 12, 27; 35:11, 15; 36:17, 23; 37:13, 18, 28; 38:14, 16, 18; 39:26, 27; 42:15; 43:3, 8, 18, 23; 44:10, 15, 17, 19, 21; 45:1; 46:8, 9, 10², 12; 47:7, 8; 48:11; Da 2:2, 14; 3:15; 4:7, 26, 31; 5:20; 6:10, 14, 20, 23; 7:22; 8:23, 25; 10:11, 19, 20; 11:2, 12, 21, 24, 34; 12:7; Hos 1:2; 2:9²; 4:14²; 18; 5:6, 13; 7:12²; 9:10³; 12; 10:10, 14, 15; 11:1, 10; 13:1, 6²; 13; Joel 3:1; Am 1:1; 2:13; 3:4², 5, 6², 4:2; 7, 7:2; 8:5, 11; 9:13; Jnh 2:7; 3:6, 10; 4:2, 8; Mic 5:3, 5, 6; 7:15; Na 3:12, 17; Hab 3:8, 14; Zep 1:3; 2:11; 3:20; Hag 2:5, 16², 18; Zec 4:10; 5:11; 6:7; 7:5, 6, 7, 13²; 8:9, 14; 12:3; 13:3; 14:1, 7; Mal 1:8², 13; 3:2, 17; 4:3; Mt 1:2; 3:4, 10, 13, 16, 22; 3:7; 4:12; 5:1, 11; 6:2, 3, 5, 6, 7, 14, 16, 17; 7:4, 28; 8:1, 5, 10, 14, 16, 18, 28, 34; 9:2, 8, 11, 15, 23, 28, 33, 36; 10:14, 19, 23; 11:2; 12:2, 3, 24, 43, 44; 13:6, 19, 21, 26, 32, 44, 46, 48, 53; 14:13, 14, 23, 26, 30; 15:7; 16:2, 5, 13; 17:6, 8, 14, 22, 25, 26; 18:21, 28; 19:1, 15, 22, 25, 28; 20:8, 10, 11, 24, 30; 21:10, 15, 20, 34, 38, 40, 45; 22:11, 22, 33; 23:15; 24:1, 3, 15, 33, 44, 46, 50; 25:27, 31, 37, 38, 39, 44; 26:1, 8, 12, 20, 29, 30, 43; 27:3, 12, 17, 24, 35, 47, 50, 54; 28:12, 17; Mk 1:19, 21, 37; 2:1, 5, 16, 20, 25; 3:8, 21; 4:6, 10, 17, 32, 34, 35; 5:2, 6, 15, 21, 27; 6:2, 11, 16, 20, 22, 34, 38, 47, 49, 53; 7:4, 6; 8:6, 19, 20, 23, 33, 38; 9:8, 9², 25, 30; 10:1, 14, 41, 47, 50; 11:1, 7, 19, 25, 30; 12:25, 34, 43; 13:1, 3, 7, 14, 19, 29; 14:3², 11, 12, 17, 18, 35, 72; 15:7, 20, 30, 34, 36, 41, 44; 16:2, 5, 19, 20, 24; Lk 1:8, 10, 12, 22, 23, 41, 57; 2:15, 17, 21, 27, 39, 42, 45, 48; 3:1, 19, 21, 23; 4:13, 25, 28, 40, 42; 5:4, 6, 8, 12, 19, 20, 35; 6:3, 13, 22², 26, 42, 48; 7:1, 4, 6, 9, 13, 20, 29, 37, 39; 8:6, 8, 13, 27, 28, 33, 34, 35, 40, 45, 51; 9:1, 5, 10, 18, 26, 32, 36, 37, 54; 10:5, 8, 10, 30, 31, 32, 33, 35, 36; 11:1, 11, 14, 22, 34, 36, 54; 12:1; 11, 36, 40, 46, 54, 55; 12:1; 14:1, 7, 8, 10², 12, 13, 15; 15:5, 9, 17, 25, 30; 16:4, 9, 22; 17:7, 10, 14, 15, 20, 22; 18:5, 15, 22, 36, 40; 19:5, 11, 36, 37, 41, 43; 20:14, 16; 21:6, 7, 9, 20, 28, 30, 31; 22:6, 14, 32, 55, 59; 23:7, 8, 29; 24:4³, 9³, 16⁴, 23; 25:2, 5, 9, 14, 15, 18; 26:2, 4, 9, 57, 59; 27:3, 17, 21; 31:6, 14, 16, 17, 18, 19²; 21, 27, 28, 30, 35, 36, 47, 48; 32:1, 11, 13, 39; 33:4, 40; 34:17; 35:6, 11, 15, 25, 30, 31, 32, 33; 36:1, 8; Dt 1:4², 30, 33, 44; 2:4, 8, 20, 21, 22, 23, 29²; 3:2, 24; 4:3, 4, 6, 42, 46; 5:3, 6, 9, 10, 11; 6:12, 15; 7:9, 10², 15, 20, 21; 8:14, 18; 9:2; 10:17, 19, 21, 22; 11:2, 5; 12:12; 13:1, 5, 10, 15; 14:29²; 16:14; 17:5, 9², 12², 15, 18; 18:1, 3, 7, 10², 11², 12, 14, 20²; 19:3, 4², 17; 20:1, 4; 21:1, 18, 23; 22:2, 5, 22, 25, 26, 28; 23:1; 24:1, 4, 8, 14; 25:9; 16², 18; 27:9, 15, 16, 17, 18, 19, 20, 21, 22, 23, 24, 25, 26; 28:7, 43, 62; 29:11, 15²; 22²; 30:7, 12, 13; 31:9, 13, 25; 32:4, 6, 15, 18², 20, 21, 38, 41; 33:3, 11, 16, 20, 26, 29; 34:11; Jos 2:3, 9, 13, 19; 3:3, 8, 13, 15, 17; 4:9, 10; 5:4, 6; 6:9, 17, 22², 23²; 25, 26; 7:5, 15; 8:17, 20, 24, 26, 33², 35; 9:8, 10, 10, 20, 24, 40; 11:2, 19, 20; 12:2, 4; 13:10, 12, 21², 22; 14:8, 15, 15:16, 63; 17:1, 16; 18:2; 20:3, 6, 9; 21:4, 10, 40; 22:20; 23:3, 24², 8, 17, 18, 31²; Jdg 1:1, 12, 20, 21, 30; 2:7², 10, 12, 14, 16, 18; 3:1, 2, 9, 10, 17, 18, 31; 4:2²; 5:10², 13, 14², 31; 6:8, 29; 7:3, 5², 8, 25; 8:31, 34; 9:4, 23, 24, 25², 28², 38²; 10:3, 4, 8; 11:8, 19, 21, 34; 12:14; 13:2, 8, 10, 11; 14:4, 19, 20; 15:6; 16:24, 26; 17:4, 7; 18:3, 14, 17, 22, 29; 19:1, 16, 22², 30; 20:16, 18, 37, 42; 21:5², 7, 11, 12, 14, 16, 18; Ru 1:11; 2:3, 6, 19; 3:2, 9; 4:3, 11², 14, 15²; 1Sa 1:15, 26; 2:3, 4, 5⁴, 10, 14, 15, 22², 25, 30², 35; 3:11; 4:2, 4, 8² 15, 17; 5:5, 12; 6:20; 8:9, 10, 11; 9:5, 13, 22; 10:11, 12², 19; 11:7, 9, 11, 12; 12:6, 8, 9, 14, 13:15, 16, 22; 14:3, 39, 45, 48; 15:29, 16:16, 17, 18, 19; 17:4, 12, 25, 26², 27, 37; 18:18; 20:10, 30; 22:2,

6, 22; 19:5, 8, 13, 23, 26, 30, 33; 20:19, 20, 24; 21:6, 9, 15, 18², 21; Ac 1:6, 8, 10, 13, 22; 2:1, 6, 37; 3:3, 9, 12, 26; 4:13, 24; 5:5, 21, 23, 33; 6:1; 7:12, 21, 23, 29, 31, 45, 54, 60; 8:6, 12, 14, 15, 18, 25, 39; 9:8, 26, 30, 36, 38, 39; 10:7, 29; 11:2, 18, 23, 26; 12:3, 10, 12, 14, 15, 16, 25; 13:5, 12, 29, 36, 43, 45, 48; 14:11, 14, 25; 15:4, 13; 16:7, 15, 16, 19, 27, 35, 38; 17:1, 6, 8, 13, 31, 32; 18:5, 6, 20, 22, 26, 27; 19:2, 6, 17, 19, 28, 34; 20:1, 9, 14, 18, 36; 21:5, 12, 34, 35, 40; 22:1, 9, 14, 20², 21, 30; 23:7, 16, 30, 33, 35; 24:2, 10, 18, 20, 22, 25, 27; 25:7, 15, 17, 18, 21; 26:10, 27; 27:1, 5, 7, 13, 17, 20, 27, 38, 39; 28:4, 9, 10, 16, 17, 19, 25; Ro 2:3, 5, 14, 16; 3:4²; 4:4, 6; 5:6, 10, 13; 6:16, 20; 7:5, 9, 21; 11:27; 13:11; 15:24, 29; 1Co 1:26; 2:1; 3:4; 4:12²; 13; 5:4; 7:18²; 20, 21, 22²; 8:7, 12; 9:10, 16; 10:13; 11:18, 20, 24, 32, 33, 34²; 12:2; 13:10, 11²; 14:26; 15:23, 24, 27, 28, 37, 54; 16:2, 3, 12, 17; 2Co 1:17; 2:3, 12; 3:14, 15; 5:3; 7:5, 15; 10:1², 2, 11², 12; 11:9; 12:10, 20, 21; 13:2, 10²; Gal 1:15; 2:9, 11, 12, 14; 4:3, 4, 8, 18; 6:3; Eph 1:10, 13, 20; 2:2, 5; 4:4, 8; 6:6, 13; Php 2:19, 28; 4:15, 16²; Col 1:3; 2:13; 3:4, 22; 1Th 2:13, 17, 19; 3:1, 4, 5, 13; 2Th 1:7; 2:5; 3:7, 10; 1Ti 1:3; 4:14; 5:11; 6:12; 2Ti 1:17; 4:3, 13; Tit 3:4; Heb 1:6; 2:18; 4:7; 6:13; 7:10, 12, 21, 27; 8:5, 8, 9; 9:6, 11, 17, 19; 10:5, 12, 32, 36; 11:4, 7, 8, 13, 17, 21, 22, 24, 29; 12:5, 17, 25; Jas 1:6, 12, 13, 14, 15; 2:21, 25; 3:3; 4:3, 11; 1Pe 1:7, 11, 12, 13, 14; 2:23²; 3:2, 20; 4:13; 5:4; 2Pe 1:16, 17, 18; 2:4, 5; 1Jn 2:28; 3:2; Jude 1:9; Rev 1:12, 17; 5:8; 6:3, 5, 7, 9, 13; 8:1; 9:2, 5; 10:3, 4, 7, 10; 11:7; 12:13; 17:6, 8, 10; 18:9, 18; 20:7; 22:8.

WHICH (707)

Ge 1:21; 3:17, 23; 4:11; 10:12; 18:10; 23:9, 19; 24:42, 49; 26:18; 27:15; 28:12, 13; 30:14; 31:10; 32:12; 38:14; 46:27; 49:30; 50:13; Ex 3:15; 22; 10:19; 16:1; 17:5; 22:9; 25:16, 21; 29:23, 33; 30:13; 34:1; 38:21; 39:4; Lev 3:4, 10, 15; 4:9; 7:1, 4, 25, 38; 8:26; 14:22, 30, 34; 15:31; 16:16; 20:25; 23:2, 37; 25:32; 26:41; 27:22; Nu 3:47; 5:8; 7:9; 9:19; 13:2, 27; 14:35; 15:18; 17:8; 18:16; 21:13, 30; 22:30; 30:4, 5, 6, 7, 8, 11; 31:37, 38, 39, 40, 42; 35:6, 11, 25, 26, 33; 36:4; Dt 1:20; 2:8; 3:16; 4:13, 27, 28, 31, 40, 42; 7:19; 8:3, 18; 9:28; 10:2; 11:10, 28; 13:2; 19:10; 28:22, 27, 52, 58, 64; 29:22, 23; 32:17; Jos 1:15; 2:15; 18; 3:4; 7:2, 11, 13, 26; 8:29, 31, 32; 10:27; 11:13, 17; 12:2, 7; 14:1, 9; 15:7; 18:17; 20:6; 22:9, 28; 23:13, 16; 24:12, 13, 17, 32, 33; Jdg 1:26; 2:17; 3:4, 16, 22; 8:27; 9:2, 9, 13, 48, 51; 10:4; 14:9; 16:29; 17:2; 21:8; Ru 3:10; 1Sa 6:18; 10:4; 25:2, 27; 26:1; 28:24; 2Sa 6:2; 3; 14:14; 21:20; 23:6; 1Ki 6:5, 21; 7:8, 48; 8:21, 29, 59; 9:3, 10, 26, 28; 10:26; 11:2, 11, 13, 32; 13:12²; 26; 14:21; 15:26, 34; 16:26; 18:30; 22:24; 2Ki 3:3; 6:11; 9:5; 10:29, 31; 13:2, 6, 11, 14; 14:24, 28; 15:9, 18, 24, 28; 17:26, 33; 18:9, 10, 16, 21; 19:6; 20:20; 21:4, 7²; 22:4; 23:2, 7, 8, 10, 26, 27; 25:16; 1Ch 6:60; 16:40; 18:8; 20:6; 21:29; 25:9; 29:19; 2Ch 1:3; 4:3; 15:4; 19:6, 11; 20; 7:6², 20; 8:1, 18; 9:25; 12:13; 13:8; 26:34; 21:12; 25:15; 28:8; 30:6, 8; 33:4, 7²; 34:9, 30; 35:21; 36:14; Ezr 1:7; 5:14; 6:5; 7:6, 14, 25; Ne 2:13²; 3:1; 6:6; 8:1, 2, 14; 9:10, 19; 12:13; Est 1:19; 4:3, 8; 8:2, 3; 10:2; Job 5:1; 12:9; 21:27; 28:5; 36:21, 24, 27; 38:23; 40:15²; Ps 1:3; 7:T; 8:3; 19:5; 31:19²; 32:9; 50:8; 71:3; 74:2³; 78:5, 68; 89:49, 51²; 104:26; 105:30; 106:20, 36; 118:20; 119:48; 125:1; 129:6; Pr 21:22; 30:16²; Ecc 1:3, 10; 2:19, 22; 11:6; SS 3:11; 6:1; Isa 1:29; 2:20; 6:6; 14:6; 16:8; 17:2, 9; 18:2; 36:6; 37:26; 42:23; 43:9, 14; 44:10; 47:12; 48:14; 50:1²; 51:1²; 55:11, 13; 57:20; 62:8; 63:7²; Jer 5:17; 7:10, 11; 8:2²; 9:13; 13:20; 17:19; 18:15; 21:4; 23:6, 18; 24:8; 25:1; 26:4; 27:13, 20; 29:7, 14, 23; 30:11; 32:1, 43; 33:16; 34:21; 35:4; 36:10, 14, 28; 37:7, 15; 38:6; 44:14, 46:2, 28; 49:25, 28; 51:43; 52:20; La 2:17; 4:6; 5:18; Eze 2:10; 5:5; 6:9²; 9:2; 13:20; 20:43; 21:13; 23:41; 24:21; 28:25; 31:18; 36:21, 22, 23; 37:19; 38:8; 40:5, 39, 41; 42:12, 14; 45:14, 21, 25; 46:9, 19; 47:13, 16²; 48:30, 32, 33, 34; Da 1:20; 4:20; 5:23; 6:8, 12; 7:5, 8, 19, 20; 8:9; 9:23; 11:10; Hos 1:10; 2:8, 12; 4:11; Joel 3:7, 21; Am 5:26; Jnh 4:7; Mic 2:3; 5:7, 8; 6:10; 7:14; Hag 1:9; Zec 1:6, 12; 4:10; 9:2; 11:13; 14:12; Mt 1:23; 4:13; 6:30; 7:9; 9:5; 11:20; 12:4; 13:7, 31; 19:18; 21:31; 22:36; 23:17; 26; 26:7, 28; 27:17, 21, 33, 46; Mk 2:9, 26; 3:4, 17; 4:7, 31; 5:41; 7:34; 11:2; 12:28; 14:24; 15:22, 34;

WHO (5081)

Ge 3:6, 11; 4:15, 20, 21, 22; 9:18, 19; 10:1, 8; 12:3, 7; 13:5; 14:7, 13, 20, 24; 15:2, 7; 16:13²; 17:12², 14; 18:7; 19:5, 8, 11, 12, 14, 15; 20:16; 21:6, 7, 26; 23:10, 18; 24:7², 15, 27, 31, 48, 54, 65; 25:11, 28; 26:11, 27:18, 22, 29², 32, 33; 28:5; 30:2; 31:32; 32:7, 9, 17, 19; 33:5; 34:14, 19, 24; 35:1, 2, 3², 26; 36:5, 12, 20, 24, 31, 35; 37:28; 38:3, 12, 21², 22, 25, 30²; 39:1²; 40:5, 7; 42:5, 6, 13, 30, 33; 43:22, 32; 44:16, 17; 45:8, 11, 12; 46:8, 22, 27, 31; 48:8, 15, 16, 22; 49:9, 25²; 50:11, 14; Ex 1:1, 8; 2:14, 21; 3:11, 12, 14; 4:11³, 19; 5:2; 6:7, 20, 27; 9:20, 21; 10:8; 11:5², 8; 12:27, 29², 48; 14:8, 19; 15:7, 11², 16; 16:6, 7, 8, 18²; 18:10², 11, 18, 21²; 19:22; 20:2, 5, 6, 7; 21:8, 12, 15, 16, 17, 19, 22; 22:6, 16, 19, 25; 23:5, 8, 22; 31; 29:30, 46; 30:13, 14; 31:13, 14; 32:1², 4, 8, 23²; 34:12, 15; 35:5, 10, 21, 22, 23, 24, 26, 29; 36:2, 4; 38:8, 25, 26; Lev 2:8; 5:8, 12, 16; 6:22, 26; 7:7, 8, 9, 14, 18², 20, 25, 29, 33; 10:3; 11:28, 36, 40², 45; 12:2, 7; 13:2²; 14:11, 32², 46, 47; 15:5, 7, 9, 19, 33²; 16:1, 26, 28, 32; 17:3, 8, 10², 13, 14, 15; 18:5, 27, 29; 19:20²; 36; 20:2, 5, 6, 8, 24, 27; 21:1, 3, 8, 10², 15, 17, 18², 20³, 21, 23; 22:4, 5, 6, 9, 16, 32, 33; 23:29; 30; 24:9, 14, 16, 18, 25:6, 38; 26:13, 17, 32, 36, 39; 27:8, 12, 15, 19; Nu 1:3, 5, 20, 22, 24, 26, 28, 30, 32, 34, 36, 38, 40, 42, 45, 51; 3:3, 9, 10, 22, 32, 34, 38, 40, 46, 49; 4:3, 23, 30, 35, 37, 39, 41, 43, 47; 5:2²; 6:21; 7:2²; 12; 8:16; 9:13, 14; 10:9, 17; 11:16, 20, 28, 34; 13:18, 28, 31; 14:6², 15, 22², 23, 29², 36, 38, 45; 15:4, 13, 28, 29, 30, 33, 41; 16:2, 5², 7, 11, 35, 38, 39, 49; 17:13, 20, 21², 22; 21:1, 8, 9, 10², 15, 17, 18², 20³, 21, 23; 22:4, 5, 6, 9, 16, 32, 38; 26:13, 17, 32, 36, 39; 27:8, 12, 15, 19; 31:6, 14, 16, 17, 18, 19²; 21, 27, 28, 30, 35, 36, 47, 48; 32:1, 11, 13, 39; 33:4, 40; 34:17; 35:6, 11, 15, 25, 30, 31, 32, 33; 36:1, 8; Dt 1:4², 30, 33, 44; 2:4, 8, 20, 21, 22, 23, 29²; 3:2, 24; 4:3, 4, 6, 42, 46; 5:3, 6, 9, 10, 11; 6:12, 15; 7:9, 10², 15, 20, 21; 8:14, 18; 9:2; 10:17, 19, 21, 22; 11:2, 5; 12:12; 13:1, 5, 10, 15; 14:29²; 16:14; 17:5, 9², 12², 15, 18; 18:1, 3, 7, 10², 11², 12, 14, 20²; 19:3, 4², 17; 20:1, 4; 21:1, 18, 23; 22:2, 5, 22, 25, 26, 28; 23:1; 24:1, 4, 8, 14; 25:9; 16², 18; 27:9, 15, 16, 17, 18, 19, 20, 21, 22, 23, 24, 25, 26; 28:7, 43, 62; 29:11, 15²; 22²; 30:7, 12, 13; 31:9, 13, 25; 32:4, 6, 15, 18², 20, 21, 38, 41; 33:3, 11, 16, 20, 26, 29; 34:11; Jos 2:3, 9, 13, 19; 3:3, 8, 13, 15, 17; 4:9, 10; 5:4, 6; 6:9, 17, 22², 23²; 25, 26; 7:5, 15; 8:17, 20, 24, 26, 33², 35; 9:8, 10, 10, 20, 24, 40; 11:2, 19, 20; 12:2, 4; 13:10, 12, 21², 22; 14:8, 15, 15:16, 63; 17:1, 16; 18:2; 20:3, 6, 9; 21:4, 10, 40; 22:20; 23:3, 24², 8, 17, 18, 31²; Jdg 1:1, 12, 20, 21, 30; 2:7², 10, 12, 14, 16, 18; 3:1, 2, 9, 10, 17, 18, 31; 4:2²; 5:10², 13, 14², 31; 6:8, 29; 7:3, 5², 8, 25; 8:31, 34; 9:4, 23, 24, 25², 28², 38²; 10:3, 4, 8; 11:8, 19, 21, 34; 12:14; 13:2, 8, 10, 11; 14:4, 19, 20; 15:6; 16:24, 26; 17:4, 7; 18:3, 14, 17, 22, 29; 19:1, 16, 22², 30; 20:16, 18, 37, 42; 21:5², 7, 11, 12, 14, 16, 18; Ru 1:11; 2:3, 6, 19; 3:2, 9; 4:3, 11², 14, 15²; 1Sa 1:15, 26; 2:3, 4, 5⁴, 10, 14, 15, 22², 25, 30², 35; 3:11; 4:2, 4, 8² 15, 17; 5:5, 12; 6:20; 8:9, 10, 11; 9:5, 13, 22; 10:11, 12², 19; 11:7, 9, 11, 12; 12:6, 8, 9, 14, 13:15, 16, 22; 14:3, 39, 45, 48; 15:29, 16:16, 17, 18, 19; 17:4, 12, 25, 26², 27, 37; 18:18; 20:10, 30; 22:2,

9, 11, 14, 18, 23; **23**:22; **25**:2, 10², 11, 22, 26, 27, 32, 34, 39, 44; **26**:6, 9, 14², 15; **28**:7; **29**:3, 10; **30**:2, 17, 21², 24³, 26, 27; **2Sa 1**:5, 8, 13, 24²; **2**:3, 4, 31; **3**:20, 29⁴; **4**:2, 4, 8, 9; **5**:2, 6, 8²; **6**:2, 13, 21; **7**:12, 13, 18, 23; **8**:10; **10**:19; **11**:21; **12**:4², 5, 11, 22, 31; **13**:8; **14**:2, 7, 16, 19²; **15**:4, 6, 14, 18, 24; **16**:2, 10, 11, 23; **17**:9, 22, 25; **18**:1, 11, 28, 31, 32; **19**:3, 5, 6², 9, 28; **20**:12, 14; **21**:5, 9, 13, 16, 19; **22**:4, 18, 31, 32², 33, 48², 49; **23**:17, 20; **24**:9, 13, 16, 17²; **1Ki 1**:9, 20, 27, 29, 41, 48; **2**:7, 8, 24, 28; **3**:9; **4**:7, 27, 34; **5**:16; **8**:15, 19², 23², 41, 46², 48, 50, 56; **9**:8, 9, 23, 27; **10**:8, 9, 25; **11**:8, 9, 15, 17, 18, 23, 34; **12**:6, 8, 9, 10², 17, 18, 28; **13**:2, 14, 20, 21, 23, 25, 26², 33; **14**:2, 8, 9, 11², 13, 14; **15**:18; **16**:4², 9; **17**:17; **18**:3, 19, 24; **19**:17²; **20**:11, 14², 17; **21**:8, 11, 18, 24²; **22**:13, 20, 46, 52; **2Ki 1**:6, 7, 9; **2**:15, 17, 18; **3**:13, 21, 27; **4**:8, 9, 18; **5**:3; **6**:12, 16²; **7**:8, 13; **9**:32², 36; **10**:6, 9², 11, 13, 15, 17, 19; **11**:2, 5, 6, 7, 8, 9², 15²; **12**:9, 11, 14, 18, 21; **14**:5, 7, 21, 22, 25; **16**:7; **17**:2, 3, 7, 14, 28, 36, 39; **18**:21, 27, 35; **19**:12, 22; **21**:11, 12, 24; **22**:5, 8, 14, 15, 18; **23**:5, 15, 16, 17, 18, 22, 25; **25**:11², 19², 25³, 28; **1Ch 1**:19, 43, 46; **2**:7, 19, 22, 29, 31, 42², 55², 4; **4**:8, 11, 22, 23, 41, 43; **5**:10, 18³, 26; **6**:10, 33, 39, 49, 54; **7**:5, 15, 24, 31; **8**:6, 7², 12, 13², 32, 34, 40; **9**:3, 13, 16, 26, 33, 40; **11**:2, 4, 19, 22, 23, 42; **12**:1², 4, 15, 18, 20, 23, 32, 38; **13**:2, 6; **15**:26, 27²; **16**:10, 17:12, 16, 21; **18**:10; **19**:7, 9; **20**:3, 5; **21**:5, 12, 15, 17², 20; **22**:9, 10, 20, 28; **24**:28; **25**:1, 2, 3, 36; **26**:6, 28; **28**:6; **29**:5, 8, 14², 17; **2Ch 1**:9, 10, 12; **2**:6², 10, 12²; **5**:5, 11, 12; **6**:4, 9², 14², 32², 36², 39; **7**:14, 21, 22; **8**:18; **9**:7, 8, 24; **10**:6, 8, 9, 10², 17, 18; **11**:16, 18, 20; **12**:5; **13**:10; **15**:9, 13; **16**:2; **17**:16, 19; **18**:12, 19; **19**:2, 6, 10, 11; **20**:6, 15, 22, 35; **21**:13, 16; **22**:1, 8, 9, 11; **23**:4, 7, 8², 14², 18, 19; **24**:12, 22, 26; **25**:3, 10, 15; **26**:1, 2, 5, 7, 18, 19; **28**:5, 12, 15²; **30**:23; **31**:1, 6, 16, 19²; **32**:9, 14, 18, 21, 24, 30; **33**:11, 25; **34**:4, 9, 10, 12, 22, 23, 26, 28, 33; **35**:3², 7, 17, 18, 21; **36**:12, 13, 17, 20; **Ezr 3**:8; **2**:1, 61; **3**:8, 12; **4**:2; **5**:1, 3, 9, 12; **6**:12², 21²; **7**:13, 25², 27, 28; **8**:1, 16², 22², 35, 36; **9**:4, 14; **10**:3, 8, 14, 15, 19², 34, 35; **Ne 1**:3, 5², 11; **2**:16; **4**:3, 12, 14, 17², 18; **5**:8, 13, 17; **6**:10, 14; **7**:5, 6, 63; **8**:2, 3, 9, 10; **9**:4, 5, 7, 18, 24, 26, 27², 32; **10**:1, 28², 37; **11**:2, 3, 6, 12, 13, 14, 16, 17, 19, 22; **12**:1, 8, 24, 25; **13**:3, 16, 23; **Est 1**:1, 5, 10, 13, 14, 18, 19; **2**:3, 4, 6, 7, 8, 14, 15², 21, 22; **3**:6, 8, 9; **4**:11, 14, 16; **6**:2², 4, 6, 10; **7**:5², 9; **8**:10; **9**:1, 5, 16, 27; **Job 1**:8, 15, 16, 17, 19; **2**:3; **3**:8², 14, 15², 16, 21², 22; **4**:2, 4, 7, 8², 19²; **5**:1, 11; **7**:9; **8**:13; **9**:4, 12², 19, 24; **11**:10; **12**:3, 6²; **14**:4; **15**:16², 34; **17**:3, 15; **18**:4, 21; **20**:7; **21**:15, 29, 31²; **22**:18, 30²; **23**:13; **24**:1, 13², 19, 25; **25**:6²; **26**:4, 14; **27**:2², 15; **29**:11, 12², 13, 25; **31**:3, 15, 31; **32**:9²; **34**:7; **37**:17, 18, 19, 29²; **34, 35**:10, 11; **36**:15, 22, 23, 29; **37**:16, 17; **38**:2, 5, 7, 8, 25, 28, 29, 36, 37²; **41**; **39**:5²; **40**:2²; **41**:10, 11, 13², 14; **42**:3, 11; **Ps 1**:1; **2**:12; **4**:6; **5**:4, 5, 6, 11²; **6**:5, 8; **7**:1, 4, 9, 10, 11, 14, 15, 19; **9**:10² 12; **10**:2, 18; **11**:5; **12**:4, 5; **14**:1, 2², 3, 4²; **15**:1², 2², 3, 4, 5²; **16**:3, 4, 7; **17**:7², 9²; **18**:3, 17, 30², 31², 32, 47², 48; **19**:12; **22**:7, 23, 25, 26, 29²; **24**:1, 3², 4², 10; **25**:3, 10, 12, 14; **27**:6; **28**:1, 3²; **31**:6, 11, 15, 19², 24; **32**:6, 10, 11; **33**:14, 15², 18; **34**:T, 5, 7, 8, 9, 10, 16, 18, 22; **35**:1², 3, 4²; **37**:48; **19**:12; **22**:7, 23, 25, 26, 29²; **24**:1, 1², 3², 4², 5²; **17**:9²; **18**:3, 17, 30², 31², 32, 47², 48; **36**:10; **37**:1, 9; **38**:12², 13², 14, 19², 20; **39**:6, 9; **40**:4³, 14², 15, 16²; **41**:1, 9; **44**:4, 16²; **49**:1, 6, 13², 19, 20; **50**:5, 22, 23; **51**:14²; **52**:1, 2, 7; **53**:1, 2², 3, 4²; **54**:4, 5; **55**:19²; **57**:2, 3; **58**:11; **59**:1, 7, 10; **60**:4, 9², 10; **61**:5; **63**:9, 11; **64**:5, 8; **65**:2, 6, 7; **66**:16, 20; **68**:4, 11, 19, 20, 21, 30, 33², 69**:4², 6², 9, 12, 14, 32, 36; **70**:2², 3, 4²; **71**:10, 13, 18, 19², 24; **72**:12, 18; **73**:1, 27²; **74**:13, 14, 15, 17; **75**:2, 3, 7; **76**:7; **77**:14²; **80**:1², 12; **81**:10, 15; **83**:10, 12; **84**:4, 5, 12; **85**:9; **86**:2, 5; **87**:4; **88**:1, 4, 5², 10; **89**:6², 7, 8, 15², 41; **90**:11; **91**:1, 9; **94**:1², 9² 10², 16²; **97**:7², 10, 12; **98**:7; **99**:6; **100**:3; **101**:7²; **102**:8; **103**:3, 4, 5, 11, 13, 17, 18, 20², 21; **104**:32²; **105**:3; **106**:2, 3, 16, 21², 46; **107**:34, 40; **108**:10², 11; **109**:20, 31; **111**:2, 5, 10; **112**:1², 5²; **113**:5², 6; **114**:8²; **115**:8², 11, 13, 17², 18; **118**:4, 26; **119**:1, 2, 21², 42, 53, 63², 74, 79², 118, 132, 150, 157, 162, 165; **120**:6; **121**:3, 4; **122**:6; **124**:6; **125**:1, 4², 5; **126**:1, 5, 6; **128**:1², 4; **129**:5, 7, 8; **130**:3; **134**:1; **135**:2, 18², 20, 21; **136**:4, 5, 6, 7, 10, 13, 16, 17, 12:1³, 3, 8; **13**:7; **14**:21; **Mal 1**:6, 14; **2**:12, 17; **3**:1, 2², 3, 5; **4**:1, 4², 6, 15²; **Mt 1**:16; **2**:2, 6, 16, 20; **3**:3, 7, 11; **4**:24²; **5**:4, 6, 10, 14, 19, 21², 22², 23, 26, 31, 32², 42², 44, 46; **6**:4, 6², 18², 27; **7**:8³, 11, 21³, 24², 26²; **29**:8; **16**:9; **8**:2, 18, 19, 24, 26; **9**:6², 31, 37; **10**:45; **12**:17; **11**:3, 6, 8, 10, 11, 30³, 34, 35; **14**:9, 11²; **16**:17², 25, 26; **17**:18², 19³, 24, 26²; **29**:1, 3, 4, 18, 20; **30**:4³, 5, 9, 11, 12, 22², 23², 30; **31**:3, 6², 8², 10, 30; **Ecc 1**:11²; **2**:7, 18, 19, 21, 25, 26²; **3**:21, 22; **4**:2², 3², 10, 13, 15, 16²; **5**:1, 6; **6**:10, 12²; **7**:11, 13, 18, 20, 24, 26²; **8**:1², 4, 7, 8, 10, 12, 14²; **9**:2⁴, 4; **10**:14; **12**:7; **SS 3**:4, 6; **6**:9, 10; **8**:1, 2, 5², 12, 13; **Isa 1**:12, 28; **2**:22; **3**:14; **4**:3; **5**:8, 11², 18, 19, 20³, 21, 22, 23; **6**:8; **7**:22; **8**:17, 18, 19; **9**:1, 9, 13, 15, 16²; **10**:1², 6, 15⁴, 20, 24²; **13**:3, 15, 17, 14:9², 12, 16², 17², 19, 27²; **15**:9; **16**:5; **17**:14²; **18**:3; **19**:8², 9; **20**:5, 6; **21**:13, 14; **22**:3, 11², 15, 16, 21, 23; **23**:8, 9; **24**:18, 20, 26, 28; **26**:10², 16, 17², 19; **27**:4, 7, 8, 11, 13, 14²; **30**:4², 5, 9, 11, 12, 22², 23², 30; **31**:3, 6², 8², 10, 30; **32**:1, 2², 5, 18, 19; **31**:1³, 2, 3²; **32**:9², 10, 11; **33**:1², 13², 14², 15³, 16, 18, 22, 24; **35**:8; **36**:6, 12, 20; **37**:12, 23; **38**:11, 18; **39**:7; **40**:9²; **12², 13, 14, 15, 18, 19², 20, 21**; **41**:2, 4, 7, 11², 12, 13, 24, 25, 26²; **42**:5⁴, 7, 10², 17², 19², 24; **43**:1², 7, 8², 13, 16, 17, 25; **44**:2³, 7, 9², 10, 24⁴, 25², 26², 27, 28; **45**:3, 9², 10, 12, 15, 18², 20², 21², 24; **46**:3, 4, 12; **47**:13; **48**:1², 2, 17²; **49**:5, 7³, 10, 17, 19, 21², 23, 25; **50**:6², 8³, 9³, 10³, 11; **51**:1², 2, 7², 9², 10², 12², 13³, 15, 16³, 17², 19², 22, 23; **52**:5, 6, 7³, 11, 14; **53**:1, 8; **54**:1³, 6, 10, 16³; **55**:1², 5², **56**:2³, 4, 6³, 8, 11; **57**:2, 13, 15²; **59**:8, 20, 21; **60**:8, 14; **61**:2, 3, 9; **62**:6, 9²; **63**:1², 8, 11², 12², 13; **64**:4², 5², 6; **65**:1², 2, 3, 4², 5, 9, 10, 11², 16, 20⁴; **66**:2, 3⁴, 5², 8², 10², 17², 19, 24; **Jer 1**:14²; **2**:3, 6, 8, 24; **3**:15²; **5**:1, 6, 21², 24²; **26³**; **6**:10, 12; **7**:2; **8**:16; **9**:12, 24², 25, 26; **10**:7², 11, 16, 17, 18, 25; **11**:2, 3, 9, 10, 17; **20**:21; **12**:4, 11, 14; **13**:10², 13², 20, 23; **14**:8, 15, 22; **15**:5³; **16**:3², 7, 14, 15; **17**:5², 7, 9, 11², 13², 20, 25; **18**:13, 16; **19**:3, 7², 11, 12², 13²; **21**:13², 22; **23**:25, 26, 30; **31**:32²; **26**:2, 15, 20, 23; **27³**; **3**:11², 12, 19, 22, 26², 30; **4**:5², 11, 12², 14, 16², 17, 24²; **5**:14², 17²; **6**:3, 7, 13; **7**:1, 4, 17, 20, 24; **8**:1, 4, 5³, 11³, 14, 20, 23, 24, 27, 28³, 31, 32, 33³, 34³, 35, 37²; **9**:5, 6, 8², 12, 19, 20², 25², 30, 31, 33; **10**:4, 5, 6, 7, 11, 12, 13, 15, 16, 19, 20³; **11**:4, 22, 30, 34², 35; **12**:5, 13, 14, 15²; **13**:2², 3², 6, 8; **14³**, 4, 6³, 14, 18, 22, 23; **15**:1, 3, 5, 12, 21²; **16**:5, 6, 7, 10, 11, 12², 13, 17, 22, 23, 25; **1Co 1**:2, 9, 18², 21, 30, 31; **2**:6, 9, 11, 12, 16; **3**:7³, 8²; **4**:2, 4, 7, 17; **5**:2, 3, 10, 11; **6**:16, 17, 18, 19²; **7**:12, 13, 22², 25, 28, 29, 30³, 31, 37²; **38²**; **8**:2, 3, 10; **9**:3, 6, 7³, 13², 14, 25; **10**:17, 18, 28; **11**:4, 5, 22, 29; **12**:3; **14**:2, 3, 4², 5², 8, 13, 16², 23, 24, 38²; **16**:9, 16; **2Co 1**:4, 9, 19, 21; **2**:2, 3, 14, 15², 16; **3**:13, 18², 4**:3, 4, 6, 11, 14²; **5**:12, 15², 18², 21; **7**:6, 12; **8**:15²; **16, 18, 22**; **9**:10; **10**:1, 2, 12, 17, 18²; **11**:9, 12, 20², 29², 31; **12**:2, 21; **13**:2; **Gal 1**:1, 4, 6, 15, 17, 23; **2**:2, 3, 6, 8, 12, 13, 16, 22, 27², 4**:6, 8, 21, 24, 27²; **5**:3, 4, 7, 8, 10, 24; **6**:1, 2, 8², 16²; **Eph 1**:3, 11, 12, 14², 19, 23; **2**:2², 4, 11², 13, 14, 17²; **3**:9, 20; **4**:6, 10², 11, 15, 28, 29²; **5**:6, 28; **6**:9, 24; **Php 1**:6, 28; **2**:6, 13, 20, 25; **3**:4, 15, 17, 21, 22; **Col 1**:7, 8, 12; **2**:1, 10, 12, 18; **3**:4, 25; **4**:9, 11, 12; **1Th 1**:10; **2**:4, 10, 12, 13, 15², 4**:5, 8², 13², 14, 15³, 16; **5**:6, 7², 12³, 14, 24; **2Th 1**:6, 7, 8, 10; **2**:7, 10, 12, 16; **3**:6; **1Ti 1**:9, 12, 16; **2**:4, 6, 10, 14; **3**:13; **4**:3², 10²; **5**:3, 5, 6, 16², 17, 20; **6**:1, 2², 5², 9, 13², 16²; **17²**; **2Ti 1**:9, 10, 14; **2**:2, 14, 15², 16, 18, 19², 22, 25, 26; **3**:6², 8, 12, 14; **4**:1, 8; **Tit 1**:2, 16; **2**:2, 6, 14; **3**:8, 15; **Phm 1**:10, 12; **Heb 1**:14²; **2**:3, 9, 11², 14, 15, 18; **3**:1, 2, 16², 17, 18; **4**:2, 3, 6, 10, 14, 15²; **5**:2, 7, 9, 13, 14; **6**:4³, 5, 12, 18, 20; **7**:5, 6, 8², 9, 16, 25, 26, 28²; **8**:1, 2, 4, 9; **13, 14, 15, 16, 17, 18**; **10**:1, 14, 23, 28, 29³, 30, 33, 37, 39²; **11**:5, 9, 11, 14, 17, 27, 31, 33², 34; **12**:2, 3, 9, 14², 15, 17, 18, 19²; **13**:3, 7, 9, 10, 17, 20; **Jas 1**:5, 6, 10, 12², 17, 23², 25; **2**:5², 6², 7, 11, 12, 13; **3**:1, 9, 13, 18; **4**:4, 11, 12², 13, 17; **5**:4, 6, 10, 11; **1Pe 1**:2, 5, 10, 12, 15, 17; **5**:4, 6, 9, 14³, 18²; **23²; 3**:5; **3**:5, 6, 12, 13, 15, 16, 20, 22; **4**:1, 5, 6, 17, 19; **5**:1, 5, 10, 14, 18²; **1Jn 2**:1, 4, 9, 13, 14, 17², 22², 23, 26, 29; **3**:3, 4, 6², 7, 9, 10⁴, 12, 14, 15, 24; **4**:4², 7, 18, 20; **5**:1², 5², 6², 10², 12², 13, 18, 20²; **2Jn 1**:1, 7, 9, 11; **3Jn 1**:9, 10, 11²; **Jude 1**:1², 4, 5, 6, 7, 12, 18, 19², 22, 24; **Rev 1**:2, 3², 4³, 5², 7, 8³; **2**:1, 2, 7², 8², 9, 11², 12, 13, 14², 15, 17³, 20, 22, 23, 24, 26, 29; **3**:1, 4, 5, 6, 7², 9², 10, 12, 13, 21, 22; **4**:3, 8, 9³, 10³; **5**:1, 2, 4, 7, 12, 13; **6**:9, 11, 16, 17; **7**:2, 4, 9, 10, 14, 15; **8**:2, 3, 6; **9**:14², 15; **10**:6³, 8; **11**:5, 10, 11, 16, 17², 18²; **12**:4, 5, 9, 10, 12, 13, 17; **13**:4², 6, 9, 14, 15; **14**:1, 3, 4, 6, 7, 11², 12, 13, 15, 18³; **15**:2, 4, 7; **16**:2², 5³, 6², 10², 12², 13, 18; **17**:2, 4, 7, 16²; **18**:3, 9, 15, 20; **19**:2, 4, 5, 9, 10, 17, 20²; **20**:2, 4, 6, 10, 11; **21**:5, 6, 7, 8, 9, 15, 27; **22**:7, 8², 9, 11⁴, 14, 15², 17, 18, 20.

WHOM (394)

Ge 6:7; **10**:14; **14**:13; **17**:21; **21**:9; **22**:2; **24**:3, 40, 47; **25**:12; **30**:26; **32**:17; **36**:14; **41**:38; **46**:18, 25; **48**:15; **49**:10; **Ex 6**:5, 26; **22**:9; **28**:3; **32**:7, 11, 13, 33:12, 19²; **36**:1, 2; **Lev 17**:7; **25**:27, 42, 55; **26**:45; **27**:24; **Nu 5**:8; **33**:8²; **27**:18; **33**:4; **Dt 9**:12; **21**:8; **24**:11; **31**:4; **34**:10; **Jos 2**:10; **12**:1; **24**:15; **Jdg 2**:14; **3**:8; **8**:15, 31; **20**:16; **Ru 4**:12; **1Sa 6**:20; **9**:20; **12**:3²; **14**:3; **17**:28, 45; **21**:9; **24**:14²; **28**:11; **30**:13; **2Sa 3**:14; **7**:7, 15, 23; **9**:1, 3; **14**:7; **16**:19, 21; **19**:10; **21**:8²; **22**:3; **23**:8, 18; **1Ki 5**:5; **7**:8; **8**:51; **9**:21; **11**:20, 34; **14**:13; **17**:1; **18**:15, 31; **22**:7, 8; **2Ki 3**:14; **5**:16; **8**:5; **12**:15; **17**:11, 34; **18**:20; **19**:4, 22; **1Ch 1**:12; **4**:18; **5**:6, 25; **11**:11, 20; **12**:29; **17**:6, 21; **29**:1; **2Ch 1**:11; **2**:7; **8**:8; **18**:6, 7; **23**:18; **Ezr 2**:1; **4**:10; **5**:14; **Ne 1**:10; **7**:6; **Est 2**:7; **6**:13; **Job 3**:23; **5**:17; **15**:19; **25**:3; **Ps 16**:3; **18**:2; **27**:1²; **41**:9; **47**:4; **55**:14; **71**:23; **73**:25; **74**:2; **88**:5; **91**:9; **94**:22; **105**:26; **106**:38; **109**:1; **144**:2, 15; **Ecc 4**:8; **9**:9; **SS 1**:7; **Isa 6**:8; **10**:3; **19**:17; **23**:2; **28**:9, 12; **36**:5; **37**:4, 23; **40**:14, 18, 25; **41**:8; **42**:1², 24; **43**:7², 10; **44**:1, 2; **46**:3, 5²; **48**:14; **49**:3; **53**:1, 3; **57**:4², 11; **Jer 6**:10; **11**:12; **15**:10; **20**:6; **24**:5; **25**:15, 17; **26**:5; **29**:3, 20, 22; **30**:9, 17; **31**:20; **40**:5; **41**:2, 10, 16, 18; **42**:6, 9, 11; **43**:6; **La 2**:20; **Eze 2**:4; **11**:15; **16**:20, 37; **21**:27; **23**:9, 37; **Da 1**:11; **2**:24; **3**:12; **5**:12; **6**:22, 16, 20; **Hos 13**:10; **Joel 2**:32; **Am 6**:1; **Mic 1**:16; **Zec 1**:4; **13**:3; **Mal 3**:1; **Mt 1**:16; **3**:17; **11**:10, 27; **12**:18²; **17**:17:5, 25; **18**:7; **19**:11; **20**:23; **21**:44; **23**:35; **24**:45; **Mk 1**:11; **3**:16; **6**:17; **9**:7; **10**:40; **12**:6; **13**:20; **15**:6; **16**:9; **Lk 2**:14; **3**:22; **6**:13, 14, 34; **7**:2, 27; **8**:2, 35, 38; **9**:35; **10**:22; **11**:19, 49; **12**:5, 42, 43; **13**:16; **17**:1; **19**:15; **20**:13, 18; **Jn 1**:15, 33, 45, 47; **3**:34; **5**:21, 45; **6**:68; **7**:39; **8**:54; **10**:35, 36; **12**:1, 9, 38; **13**:23, 26; **14**:26; **15**:26; **17**:3, 6; **19**:26; **21**:7, 20; **Ac 2**:36, 39; **3**:16; **4**:10², 27, 36; **5**:30, 32; **6**:10; **7**:35; **8**:19; **9**:5; **10**:41, 42; **13**:37; **14**:23; **15**:4; **19**:13; **20**:25; **22**:8; **25**:14; **26**:15; **27**:23; **Ro 1**:9; **4**:6, 17, 24; **5**:2, 5, 11; **6**:16; **8**:33; **9**:15², 18², 23, 24; **10**:14; **11**:2; **14**:15; **16**:8; **1Co 1**:24; **3**:5; **4**:17; **6**:19; **8**:6⁴, 11; **10**:11; **15**:6; **2Co 2**:2; **10**:18; **Gal 1**:5; **3**:19; **4**:19; **Eph 3**:15; **4**:30; **Php 2**:25; **4**:1; **Col 1**:14; **2**:3, 19; **1Th 1**:10; **2Th 2**:8; **1Ti 1**:15, 20; **6**:16; **2Ti 1**:3, 12; **3**:14; **Tit 3**:6; **Heb 1**:2; **2**:10²; **3**:1, 17, 18; **4**:13; **6**:7; **7**:13; **13**:21; **Jas 2**:7; **1Pe 3**:19; **5**:12; **2Pe 1**:17; **1Jn 4**:20²; **2Jn 1**:1; **3Jn 1**:1; **Jude 1**:13; **Rev 3**:19.

WHOSE (278)

Ge 10:21; **22**:24; **24**:23, 37, 47; **25**:1; **38**:25; **44**:30; **49**:22; **Ex 1**:15; **25**:2; **34**:14; **35**:21; **Lev 6**:30; **16**:9, 27; **22**:24; **27**:24; **Nu 1**:17; **11**:26; **24**:3, 4, 15, 16; **26**:10, 33; **Dt 19**:1; **21**:6; **28**:49; **29**:18; **Jos 9**:4; **12**:1; **17**:3; **24**:15; **Jdg 5**:14; **6**:10; **16**:4; **19**:12; **Ru 2**:1, 2, 5, 12, 19; **3**:2; **1Sa 1**:3, 2; **4**:15; **9**:1; **10**:26; **12**:3³; **17**:55, 56, 58; **2Sa 3**:12; **16**:8; **17**:10; **21**:16; **1Ki 1**:3; **3**:26; **7**:14²; **13**:11; **19**:18²; **2Ki 7**:2, 17; **8**:1, 5; **18**:22; **1Ch 1**:43; **2**:17, 26; **4**:41; **17**:21; **2Ch 2**:14²; **16**:9; **20**:10; **29**:31; **31**:16; **Ezr 1**:5; **7**:15; **8**:13; **Est 3**:8; **Job 1**:1; **3**:23; **4**:19; **12**:5; **17**:6; **26**:4; **30**:1; **38**:29; **Ps 1**:3; **15**:2; **17**:14; **18**:27; **25**:3; **26**:10²; **32**:1²; **33**:12, 18; **37**:14; **38**:14; **46**:4; **56**:4, 10²; **68**:34²; **78**:8²; **83**:18; **84**:5, 11; **95**:10; **101**:6; **105**:25; **119**:1; **123**:1; **127**:5; **144**:8²; **11²**, 15; **146**:5²; **Pr 2**:7, 12, 15; **11**:20; **14**:2²; **17**:20; **19**:1²; **22**:11; **25**:28; **28**:6²; **18²; 30**:13²; **14²; Ecc 7**:26²; **10**:16², 17²; **Isa 10**:5, 10; **18**:2, 7;

23:7, 8^2; 26:3; 30:7; $31:9^2$; 33:16; 36:7; 45:1; 57:8, 15, 20; 58:11; 65:4; Jer $5:15^2$; 17:5, 7; 32:18; 37:13; 44:28; 46:18; 48:15; 51:57; La 3:25; Eze 3:6; 11:21; $17:16^2$; 20:9, 14, 22; $21:25^2$, 29^2; $23:20^2$; 24:6; 26:10; 32:27; 38:8; 40:2, 3; 42:2; Da 12:1; Hos 7:4; Joel 3:19; Am 5:27; Mic 2:7; 5:2; Hab 1:11; Zec 6:12; Mt 1:3; 5^2, 6; 3:11; $22:20^2$, 28, 42; 24:46; 26:3; Mk 1:7; 7:25; $12:16^2$, 23; Lk 3:16; 6:6; 12:37, 38; 13:1; 16:1; 20:24, 33; Jn 1:27; 4:46; 6:42; 11:2; 18:26; Ac 10:6; 13:25; 14:13; $16:1^2$; 27:23; Ro $4:7^2$, 8; 14:1, 2; 16:23; Php 3:8; 4:3; 1Ti 4:2; 5:17; Tit 1:6; Heb 3:17; 11:10, 34; 12:23; 1Jn 5:16; Jude 1:4; Rev $2:18^2$; 9:11; 13:8, 12; 17:8; 19:11; 21:27.

WILL (10192)

See also the selected listing for "WILL" in the Main Concordance.

Ge 1:29; 2:17, 18, 24^2; 3:3, 4, 5^2, 14^2, 15^3, 16^4, 17, 18^2, 19^2; 4:7, 12^2, 14^3, 15; 5:29; $6:3^2$, 7, 17, 18^2, 20; $7:4^2$; $8:21^2$; 22; 9:2, 3, 5^3, 11^2, 13, 15^2, 16; 11:6, 7; 12:1, 2^4, 3^3, 7, 12^3, 13^2; 13:15, 16; $14:23^2$; 24; 15:2, 3, 4^2, 8, 13^2, 14^2, 15, 16; $16:10^2$, 11, 12^3; $17:2^2$, 4, 5^2, 6^3, 7, 8^2, 11, 14, 15, 16^5, 17^2, 19^3, 20^5, 21^2; $18:10^2$, 12, 13, 14^2, 18^2, 19^2, 21^2, 23, 24, 25, 26, 28^2, 29, 30, 31, 32; 19:2, 15, 17, 19, 20, 21^2; $20:4$, 7^2, 11; 21:6, 10, 12, 13, 18, 23; $22:2$, 5^2, 8, 14^2, 17^2, 18; 23:6, 9, 13^2; 24:3, 4, 7^2, 8, 14, 33, 39, 40, 41^2, 42, 49, 58^2; $25:23^3$; $26:3^4$, 4^3, 22, 24^2, 29; 27:33, 39, 40^3, 41, 46; 28:13, 14^3, 15^2; 30^2, 21, 22^2; 29:8, 27, 32, 34, 35; 30:13, 15, 20, 26, 28, 31^2, 32, 33^2; 31:3, 8^2, 52^2; 32:9, 11, 12^2, 20^2, 26, 28; 33:13; 34:11, 15, 16, 17, 22, 23, 30; 35:3, 10^2, 11^2, 12; 37:8, 10, 26, 28; 38:16, 17, 23; $40:13^2$, 19^2; $41:16$, 30^3, 31^2, 32, 36, 40, 44; $42:15^2$, 16, 18, 33, 34^2, 37, 38^2; $43:3$, 4^2, 5^3, 8, 9^2, 14; $44:9^2$, 10^2, 17, 22, 23, 26, 29, 31^2, 32; 45:6, 11^2, 18, 20, 28; $46:3$, 4^3, 31^2, 34; 47:16, 19, 25, 29, 30; $48:4^3$, 5^2, 6^2, 19^4, 20, 21; 49:1, 4, 7, 8^3, 10^2, 11^2, 12, 13^2, 15, 16, 17, 19^2, 20^3; 50:5, 21, 24, 25; Ex $1:10^2$; 2:9; 3:3, 12^3, 18, 19, 20^3, 21^2, 22^2; 4:9, 12^2, 14, 15^2, 16^2, 21^2, 23; 5:2, 10, 11, 18; $6:1^4$, 6^3, 7^3, 8^2, 12; 7:1, 3, 4^3, 5, 9, 17^3, 18^3, 19^2; 8:2, 3^2, 4, 8, 10, 11^2, 16, 21^2, 22^2, 23^2, 26, 28, 29^2; 9:3, 4^2, 5, 9^2, 14, 17, 18, 19^2, 22, 28, 29^3; 10:3, 4, 5^2, 6, 7, 8, 9, 14, 21, 26, 28, 29; $11:1^3$, 4, 5, 6^2, 7^2; 8^2, 12:4, 12^2, 13^2, 23^2, 25, 33; 13:9, 16, 19; 14:3, 4^4, 13^3, 14, 17^3, 18; $15:1^2$, 2^9, 13^2, 14^2, 15^3, 16^2, 17, 18, 26; $16:4^3$, 6, 7, 8, 12^2, 25, 26, 28; $17:6^2$, 9, 14, 16; 18:15, 18, 19, 22^2, 23^3; 19:5, 6, 8, 9^2, 11, 22, 24; $20:7$, 19^2; 20, 24, 25; 21:6, 13, 19, 28, 34, 36; 22:11, 13, 15, 23, 24^3, 27^2; $23:7$, 21, 22^2, 23^2, 25^2, 26^2, 27^2, 28, 29, 30, 31^3, 33^2; 24:3, 7^2; 12; $25:8$, 9, 16, 21, 22; $26:13^2$, 25, 33; 27:7; $28:28$, 29, 30, 32, 35^2, 38^4, 43; $29:21$, 26, 29, 37^2, 42^2, 43^2, 44^2, 45, 46; 30:6, 8, 12, 16, 20, 21, 25, 29; 36; 31:13, 17; $32:1$, 5, 10, 13^3, 23, 30, 33, 34^2; 33:1, 2, 3, 5, 12, 14^2, 16^2, 17, 19^2, 22^2; 34:1, 10^3, 11, 12, 15^2, 16, 24^2; 40:9, 10, 15^2; Lev 1:3, 4; 3:4, 10, 15; 4:9, 20^2, 26^2, 31^2, 35^2; 5:1, 3, 4, 10, 13^3, 16^2, 17, 18^2; $6:7^2$, 18^2; $7:18^3$; 8:33, 35; 9:4; $10:3^2$, 6^2, 7, 9, 15; $11:24^2$, 25, 26, 27, 28, 31, 32^3, 33, 39, 40^2; 12:2, 5, 7, 8^2; 13:6, 14, 17, 34, 58; 14:8, 9, 20, 31, 36, 46, 53^2; $15:3^2$, 4^2, 5, 6, 7, 8, 9, 10^2, 11, 13, 15, 16, 17, 18, 19^2, 20^2, 21, 23, 24^2, 25^2, 26^2, 27^2, 28, 30, 31; 16:2, 13^2, 16, 22, 30^2; 17:5, 10^2, 15^2, 16; 18:5, 28; 19:5, 7, 8, 17, 22, 24, 25, 27, 29; 23:11, 18, 30, 43; 24:12, 15; 25:6, 18, 19^2, 20, 21^2, 22^2, 28^2, 41, 45, 46; $26:4^2$; 5^3, 6^2, 7^2, 8^3, 9^2, 10^2, 11^2, 12^2, 14^2, 16^4, 17^4, 18^2, 19, 20^3, 21, 22^2, 25^2, 26^4, 28^2, 29^2, 30^2, 31^2, 32^2, 33^3, 34^2, 35, 36^4, 37^2, 38^2, 39^2; 40, 42^2, 43, 44, 45; $27:8^2$, 12^2, 14^2, 15, 18^2; 19, 21^2, 23, 24; Nu $1:53^2$; 2:5, 7, 9, 10, 12, 14, 16, 17^2, 18, 20, 22, 24, 25, 27, 29, 31; 4:15, 20; 5:3, 9, 10, 24, 27^3, 28^2, 31^2; $6:27^2$; 8:14, 19; 9:13; 10:6, 9, 10, 29^2, 30, 32; $11:11^4$, 18^2, 19, 21, 23^2; 14:3, 8^2, 9, 11^2, 12^2, 13, 14, 15, 23^2, 24^2, 27, 28, 29, 30, 31, 32, 33, 34, 35^3, 40, 41, 42, 43^3; 15:10, 16, 25, 26, 28, 39^2; 40^2; $16:5^3$, 7, 12, 14^2, 22, 26, 28, 30; $17:5^2$, 10^2, 12; 18:3, 5, 13, 20^2, 22^2, 23, 24, 30, 32^2; 19:7, 8, 10^2, 12^2, 13^2, 17, 18, 19^2, 21^2, 23, 24, 26^2; $21:2^2$, 7, 16, 22^2; 22:6, 8, 11, 17, 19^2, 34; $23:3^2$, 13, 23, 27; $24:7^2$, 14, 17^2; 18^3, 19, 20, 22, 24; $25:13^2$, 16; 26:55; $27:13$, 17^2; 20, 21^3; $30:4$, 5^2, 7, 8, 10, 11, 12^2; 31:2, 23, 24; $32:11$, 15^2, 17, 18, 19, 20^2, 21, 22, 23^2; 25, 26, 27, 31, 32^2; 33:54, 55^3, 56; $34:2^2$, 3^2, 4, 5, 6^2, 8, 9, 11, 12^2; $35:2$, 3, 4, 5, 6, 12,

13, 15; $36:3^2$, 4^2, 8; Dt 1:13, 17, 22, 30, 36^2, 38^2, 39^3, 41, 42^2; 2:4, 5, 9, 19, 25^3, 27^2; 3:21, 22, 28²; $4:6^2$; 22^2, 26^3, 27^3, 28, 29, 30, 31; 5:11, 25^2, 27, 33; $6:15^2$, 25; $7:4^3$, 10^2, 12, 13^2, 14^2, 15^3, 16, 19, 20, 22^3, 23, 24^4, 25, 26; $8:9^2$, 14^2, 19, 20; $9:3^3$, 5, 14, 28; 10:2, 10; 11:14, 15^2, 16, 17^5, 23^2, 24^2, 25^2; 12:5, 10^3, 11, 14, 18, 25, 26, 28, 29; $13:11^2$, 17^2; 14:23, 24, 25; $15:4$, 6^5, 9^2, 10, 11, 17, 18, 20; 16:2, 6, 7, 11, 15^3, 16; 17:8, 9, 10, 13^2, 17^2; 18:6, 12, 14, 15, 16, 18^3, 19; $19:10^2$, 20^2; 20:1, 8, 18^2; 21:8, 9, 18, 20, 21; 22:9; 23:14, 21^2, 22^2; $24:13^2$; 15; 25:1, 3, 6, 7, 9; 26:2, 17^3, 19^2; 28:1, 2, 3, 4, 5, 6, 7^3, 8^2, 9, 10^2, 11, 12^3, 13, 15^2, 16, 17, 18, 19, 20, 21, 22^2, 23, 24^2, 25^2, 26, 27, 28, 29^3, 30^6, 31^6, 32^2, 33^2, 34, 35, 36^2, 37^2, 38^3, 39^3, 40^3, 41^3, 42, 43^2, 44^4, 45, 46, 48^4, 49^2, 50^2, 51^2, 52^2; 53^2 54, 55^3, 56, 57, 59, 60^2, 61, 62, 63^2 64^2; 65^2, 66, 67^3, 68^3; $29:19^2$, 20^4, 21, 22, 23^2, 24, 25; 30:3, 4, 5^3, 6, 7, 8, 9^2, 12, 13, 16^2, 17^3, 18, 20, 21^2, 23^2, 24^2, 25; $31:3^4$, 4, 5, 6, 8^2, 11, 14, 16^2, 17^5, 18, 20, 21^2, 22^2, 23; 23^2, 24^4; $33:17$, 19^2, 21, 23, 25^2, 27, 28, 29^2; $34:4^2$; Jos 1:3, 4, 5^2, 6, 8, 9, 11, 14^2, 15, 16, 18^2; 2:12, 14, 16, 17, 19^3, 20; 3:4, 5, 7, 10^2, 11, 13; $6:5^2$, 18^2, 26^2; 7:3, 9^2, 12, 25; $8:5^2$, 6^3, 7, 18; $9:20^3$, 23; 10:8, 25; 11:6; 13:6; 14:9, 12; 15:16; 17:17, 18; $18:3$, 4^2, 6, 8; $22:18$, 27^2, 28; $23:5^3$, 15, 16^2, 17:3, 13; $24:15^2$, 18, 19, 20, 21, 24, 27^2; Jdg 1:1, 3, 12, 24; 2:1, 3^3, 21, 22^2; $4:7$, 8, 9^3, 22; $5:3^3$; $6:16^2$, 18, 36, 37^3; $7:4$, 7, 9; 8:7, 9, 23^3; 10:13, 18^2; 11:8, 9, 10, 24^2, 31^2, 37; $13:5^2$; 14:12, 15; 15:3²; 16:5; 17:3, 13; 18:5, 10, 19^2, 20; $20:8^2$, 28; 21:1, 17, 22; Ru 1:9, 10, 16^3, 17^2; $2:22^2$; 3:1, 2, 4, 5, 11, 13, 18; $4:4^4$, 10, 15; 1Sa $1:11^3$, 14, 22^2; 28; $2:9^2$, 10^4, 25^2, 30^2, 31^2, 32^3, 33^2, 34^2, 35^4; 36; 3:11, 12, 14; 4:8, 9; 5:11; $6:3^2$, 5, 9, 20; 7:3, 5; $8:9^2$, 11^4, 12, 13, 14, 15, 16, 17^2 18² 20; 9:5, 6, 8^2, 13^3, 16^2, 17, 19^2, 26; $10:2^2$, 3^3, 5^3, 6, 8; 11:1, 2, 3, 7, 9, 10, 12; 12:10, 15, 17, 22^3, 23^2; 13:12, 14, 19; 14:6, 8, 9, 10^2, 37, 40, 45; 15:2, 26, 33; 16:1, 2, 3, 11, 16^3 17^2; 25^2, 26, 27, 32, 36, 37^2; 2Sa 2:6, 26; 3:12, 13, 18; $5:2^2$, 6, 8^2, 19^2, 24; $6:21$, 22^3; 7:9, 10^3, 11^2, 12^3, 13^2, 14, 15, 16², 21, 26^3, 27, 29; $9:7^3$, 10, 11; $10:2$, 11, 12; 11:11, 12, 15; $12:10$, 11^2, 12, 23², 24; 13:13, 14; $14:7^2$, 8, 9, 11², 15, 17, 20, 21, 22, 24, 28, 33, 34², 36, 38^2; $20:6^2$, 21; $21:3$, 6, 17²; $22:50^2$; 23:5; 24:24; 1Ki 1:5, 13, 14, 17, 20, 21, 24, 30; 2:4, 8, 9, 17, 18, 20, 26, 30, 32, 37², 38, 42^2, 44, 45^2; $3:12^4$, 13^2, 14; $5:5^2$, 6, 8, 9^2; $6:12$, 13^2; $8:19$, 27, 29, 40, 42; 9:3, 5, 7^3, 8^2, 9; $11:2$, 11, 12^2, 13^2, 32, 34, 35, 36, 37^2, 38^3, 39; $12:4$, 7², 11^2, 14^2, 26, 27²; $13:2^3$, 3^2, 7, 22, 32; $14:3^2$, 5, 10^2, 11^2, 12^2, 13^2, 14²; 15:19; $16:3$, 4^2; 17:1, 4, 14^2; 18:1, 5, 12, 14, 15, 21, 23, 24, 37; $19:17^2$, 20; 20:6, 9, 13^2, 14^2, 22, 23, 28^2; 31, 34^2, 36, 39; $21:2^3$, 4, 6^2, 19, 21, 22, 23, 24²; 29²; 22:5, 9^3, 10^4, 13, 19; 2Ki 1:2, 4^2, 6^2; 2:2, 4, 6, 10, 21; $3:7^2$, 17^3, 18, 19^2; 4:16, 30, 43; $5:5$, 8, 10^2, 16, 17^2, 20, 27; 6:8, 13², 17; $7:1$, 2^2, 8, 9, 12^2, 13, 14², 15, 16, 17²; 8:1, 19, 20; $9:7^3$, 8, 9, 10^2, 19; $10:5^2$, 6, 10, 24, 30; 13:17, 19; 15:12; 16:15; 17:39; 18:14, 23, 27, 30^2, 31, 32; $19:4^2$, 7^2, 10, 11, 28^2, 29^2, 30^2, 31, 32, 33^2, 34; $20:1$, 5^2, 6^3, 9, 17^3, 18^3, 19; 21:4, 7, 8³, 13^2, 14²; $22:17^2$, 20^3; $23:27^2$; 25:24; 1Ch 4:10; 10:4; $11:2^2$, 5, 6; 12:18, 19; 13:2; $14:10^2$; 15; $16:18^2$, 33^3; $17:8$, 9^3, 10^2, 11^2, 12^2, 13^2, 14²; 18:2; $21:23^2$, 24; 22:5, 9^3, 10^4, 13, 19; $28:6^2$, 7, 9, 20, 21²; 2Ch $1:12^3$; 2:5, 8, 10, 12, 14, 16^2; 6:9, 18, 31; $7:14^4$, 15, 16, 18, 20^3, 21^2, 22; 10:4, 7^2, 11^2; 14²; $12:7^3$, 8; $13:12^2$; $15:2^2$; 7; 16:3, 9; $18:3^2$, 5, 10, 11, 14, 19, 20, 21², 24, 29; $19:10^2$, 11^3; $20:9^2$, 12, 16^2, 17^3, 20^2, 37; 21:15; 24:20; 25:8; 26:18; 28:13, 23²; 29:10; 30:8, 9^3; 32:11, 15, 17; 33:4, 7, 8^2; $34:25^2$; 28³; 35:21; Ezr 4:3, 13^2, 15, 16, 21; 6:8; 7:18; 10:4, 11; Ne 1:8, 9; $2:6^2$, 7, 8^2, 17, 20^2; $4:2^3$, 12, 20; $5:12^3$; $6:7^2$, 9, 11; 9:29; $10:31^3$, 36, 37^2, 39; 13:21; Est $1:17^2$, 18^2, 20; 3:9; 4:13, 14², 16²; $5:3$, 6^2; 8; $9:12^2$; Job 1:11; 21; 2:4, 5; 4:2; $5:1^3$, 19^2, 20, 21, 22, 23^2, 24^2, 25^2, 26; 6:24; 7:7, 8^3, 10^2, 11³, 13^2, 16, 19^2, 21^3; 8:2, 5, 6, 7, 8, 11, 13^2, 16, 17²; 18^3, 19^2, 20, 21; $9:2^3$, 3^2, 4, 5, 6, 7, 8, 11, 12, 14³, 15, 17, 18^2, 19^2, 20^3; 10:3², 5, 6², 7², 8, 9, 11; $11:3^2$, 15^2, 16, 17^2, 18^2, 19^2, 20^3; $12:2^2$, 3, 7, 8²; $13:7^2$ 8², 15^2, 16, 18, 19, 20, 22, 25^2; 14:3, 7^2, 9, 12, 14^2, 15^2, 16, 17²; $15:17$, 28, 29^3, 30^3, 31, 32^2, 33, 34^2; 16:3, 22; 17:3, 4, 5, 9²; 30^2, 31, 32^2, 33, 34^2;

10, 16^2; 18:2; 19:2, 22, 25, 26, 27, 28, 29^2; $20:7^2$, 9^2, 11, 14^2, 15^2, 16^2, 17, 18, 20, 21, 22^2; $23:10$; $24:15$; $27:4^2$, 5^2, 6^2 10^2, 11^2, 14, 15², 17^2, 19²; 29:18, 19², 20; 30:23; $31:6$, 14²; 32:10, 14, 17², 21^2; 33:28, 31, 33; 34:17, 31, 32; $35:2$, 14; 36:2, 3, 11, 12; 38:3; $39:9^2$, 10, 11²; 40:2, 5, 7, 14; $41:3^2$, 4, 6^2, 8, 12; $42:4^2$, 8^2; Ps 1:5, 6; 2:7, 8, 9^2; 3:2, 6; $4:2^2$, 3, 8; $5:7^2$; $6:10^2$; 7:2, 12^2, 17²; $9:1^2$, 2^3, 12^2, 8^2; 10:6, 16; $11:6^2$; 7; $12:4$, 5^2, 7; $13:1^2$, 2, 3, 4^2, 6; 14:4; 15:5; $16:4^2$, 7, 8, 9, 10^2, 11; $17:3^2$, 6, 15²; $18:49^2$; 19:13; $20:5^2$; $21:7$, 8^2, 9, 10, 12, 13; $22:22^2$, 25, 26, 27², 29², 30², 31; 23:4, 6²; 24:5; $25:3^2$, 12, 13², 15; 26:12; $27:2^2$, 3², 6^3, 8, 10, 13; $28:1$, 5, 7; 30:1, 6, 9², 12; 31:7; 32:5, 6, 7, 8^2; 9; $34:1^2$, 2, 11, 20, 21², 22; 35:9, 10, 17, 18², 28; $37:2^2$, 4, 5, 6, 9^2, 10² 11, 12; $41:2^2$, 3, 5, 6, 11; $42:5$, 6, 11; $43:4^2$; 5; $44:8^2$; $45:6^2$; $46:2$, 5^2, 10²; $48:14$; $49:3^2$, 4², 11, 14³, 15^2, 17^2, 19^2; $50:3$, 7², 15², 21, 22; $51:7^2$, 13², 14, 15, 17, 19²; $52:5^3$, 6², 9³; $53:4$; $54:6^2$, 55:19, 22², 23²; $56:3$, 4, 9², 11, 12; $57:1$, 7, 8, 9²; $58:5$, 9, 10, 11; $59:10^2$, 11, 13; $60:6$, 9², 12²; $61:6$; 62:2², 12^2; $63:3$, 4², 5², 9², 10, 11²; $64:5$, 7², 8²; 65:1, 2; $66:13$, 15²; $67:6^2$, 7²; $68:16$, 21, 22², 29, 31²; $69:30$, 31, 32, 35², 36²; 71:6, 11, 14², 15, 16^2, 20^2, 21, 22², 23, 24; $72:2$, 3, 4², 5, 6, 7², 8, 9², 10², 11², 12, 13, 14, 17²; 73:15, 20, 24, 27, 28; $74:8^2$, 9, 10²; $75:9^2$, 10²; 77:10, 11², 12; $78:2^2$, 4² $79:5^2$, 13²; $80:4$, 18²; 81:8, 10; $82:2$, 7² $83:16$; 85:5², 6, 8², 12²; $86:7^2$; 9², 11, 12; $87:4^2$; 5, 6, 7; $89:1^2$, 2, 4, 21², 22², 23, 24², 25, 26, 27, 28², 29, 32, 33², 34, 35, 36, 37, 46²; 90:13; $91:1$, 2, 3, 4³, 5, 6, 7², 8², 14², 15²; $92:7$, 9², 12², 13, 14²; $94:3^2$, 8, 14², 15² 16², 23²; $96:10$, 12, 13²; 98:9; $101:1^2$, 2³, 4², 5, 6², 7², 8²; $102:13$, 15², 16, 17², 21, 26⁴, 27, 28²; $103:9^2$, 21; 104:9, 33²; 105:11²; $108:1$, 2, 3², 7, 10², 13²; $109:28^3$, 29, 30²; $110:2^2$, 3², 4, 5, 6, 7²; 111:1; $112:2^2$, 5, 6², 7, 8², 9, 10²; $115:8^2$; 12³; $116:2$, 13, 14, 17, 18; $118:6$, 7, 17², 19, 21, 28²; $119:7$, 8, 16, 17², 20, 27, 33, 34, 42, 44, 45, 46², 55, 60, 61, 78, 82, 84, 88, 93, 95, 106, 109, 116, 117², 145, 146; $120:3$, 4; $121:3^2$ 4, 6, 7², 8; $122:8$, 9; 125:3, 5; 126:5, 6; 127:5; $128:2^2$, 3²; $130:8$; $132:3$, 4, 11², 12, 14, 15², 16², 17, 18²; 135:14, 18²; $138:1^2$, 2², 8; $139:10^2$, 11, 12², 140:8, 13²; $141:5$, 6², 7; 142:7; 143:7, 10; $144:9^2$, 12², 13³, 14², 16², 17, 18, 22³, 23²; $145:1^2$, 2, 4², 5², 6², 7, 10², 11, 20, 21; 146:2²; 148:6; Pr 1:9, 13, 14, 22², 26², 28⁴, 31, 32²; $2:5$, 9, 10, 18, 22, 23², 26², $3:2$, 4, 6, 8, 10², 18, 22, 23², 24², $4:4$, 6², 8²; 9, 10², 12², 16², 23; $6:9^2$, 11², 15², 23²; $7:2$, 5, 14, 18, 21, 23², 24; $8:2$, 5, 9, 10², 11², 15², 16², 17², 19, 20, 21, 24, 25, 26, 27, 28², 29^2, 32², 33², 34², 35²; 9:4, 12, 18; $10:3^2$, 6², 7, 9², 13², 14², 15², 16², 17², 18², 19², 23, 24, 25, 26², 27², 28², 29:1, 14, 16, 17², 19, 21, 25; 30:6, 10², 17²; Ecc $1:9^2$, 11; 2:1, 15, 16², 19²; $3:14^2$; 15² 17², 22; 4:11²; $6:12^2$; 7:18, 26²; 8:3, 5², 8, 12, 13², 15; 9:5, 6, 10, 11, 14; $11:3^2$, 4; 12:1, 14; SS 1:4, 11; $3:2^2$; 4:6; 5:8; $7:8^2$; 12; $8:9^2$; Isa $1:15^2$, 19, 20, 24, 25², 26², 27, 28², 29, 30², 31²; $2:2^2$, 3, 4², 9, 11², 12, 17², 18, 19, 20, 21²; $3:4^2$, 5², 6, 7, 10², 11, 17², 18, 24, 25, 26²; $4:1^2$, 2³, 4², 5², 6²; $5:2$, 4, 5², 6³, 7, 11²; 13, 14², 15, 16², 17²; $6:8$, 13²; 7:7², 8, 9, 12², 13, 14², 16, 17²; 18, 19, 20, 21, 22², 23², 24, 25²; $8:2$, 4², 6², 7³, 8, 10², 14³, 15², 17, 18, 21²; $9:1^2$, 5², 6², 7³, 8, 11²; 10:3, 4, 12², 16², 17², 18³, 19, 20², 21², 22², 23², 24²; $11:1^2$, 2, 3, 4⁴, 6, 7, 8³, 9², 10⁴, 11, 12, 13², 15, 16; $12:1^2$, 2³, 3, 4, 5², 6; $13:6$, 7⁴, 8², 10³, 11³, 12, 13², 14²; $14:1^4$, 2³, 3, 4, 13², 15, 16², 17, 18³, 19², 20, 21², 22²; 23²; $15:9$, 16:4², 5², 14²; $17:1^2$, 2², 3², 4², 5, 6, 7, 8², 9², 11, 18³; $19:2$, 3⁴, 4², 5², 6², 7², 9², 10², 11⁴, 12², 14², 16², 17², 18³, 19, 20², 21², 22², 23, 24, 25; 20:4, 5, 6²; $21:2$, 16, 17; 22:14, 18³, 19, 20², 21², 22, 23, 24, 25⁴; $23:5$, 12, 15², 16, 17², 18³; 24:1, 2, 3, 13, 18², 21, 22², 23²; $25:1$, 2³, 4, 5, 7, 8³, 9², 10², 11², 12²; $26:1$, 3, 9², 11², 17, 19⁴, 21²; $27:1^2$, 6², 9³, 12, 13²; $28:7$, 8⁴, 13², 15², 16³, 17², 18², 19³, 6, 7³, 9², 11²; 18³, 19, 3, 6, 7⁴, 8², 9², 10³, 11³, 12, 13², 14²;

19, 20³, 21⁴, 22, 23², 24²; $34:2^2$, 3³, 4², 7³, 9², 10⁴, 11³, 12², 13², 14³, 15³, 16³, 17; $35:1^2$, 2⁴, 3⁴, 5, 6², 7², 8⁵, 9⁴, 10⁵, 15², 16, 18; $37:4^2$, 7, 10, 11, 29², 30², 31, 32², 33², 34²; 35; $38:1$, 5, 6², 7, 8², 12, 15², 20, 22; $39:6^2$, 7³, 8; $40:5^2$, 18², 20², 25, 28, 31⁴; $41:7$, 10², 11², 12², 13, 14, 15², 16⁴, 17², 18², 19², 23; $43:2^4$, 4, 5, 6, 10, 14, 28²; $44:2^3$, 3⁴, 5⁴, 7, 11², 12², 13², 14⁴, 16², 17², 22³, 23², 24²; $45:1^2$, 2¹, 3, 5, 7, 8, 13³, 14⁴, 16³, 17, 18, 19, 21²; $46:1^2$, 4², 5, 11², 12², 13², 14³, 16, 17, 18, 19, 20², 21, 22²; Jer 1:8, 14, 15², 16, 17, 19³; $2:9$, 19², 20, 21, 34, 35, 36, 37²; $3:5^2$, 12, 14, 15², 16⁴, 17³, 18², 22²; $4:1$, 2⁴, 4, 7, 9, 10, 11, 14, 27², 28³; $5:1$, 5, 6³, 12³, 14, 17², 18, 19², 31; $6:2$, 3³, 8, 10, 11, 12, 15², 16², 17, 18, 21², 26; $7:3$, 7, 9, 14, 15, 16, 20, 23³, 32², 33², 34²; $8:1$, 2³, 3, 10, 11, 12, 13, 14, 16³, 17², 18², 19³, 20², 21²; $9:3$, 5, 6, 7³, 9, 10, 11, 13², 15, 16, 20, 22², 23⁴, 24²; $10:4$, 11, 15, 18², 22; $11:3$, 7, 8, 9, 10, 11³, 12, 13, 17², 18, 20²; $12:3$, 4, 7, 8, 10, 11, 12³, 13, 15, 16², 17²; $13:5$, 9⁴, 11³, 12, 13, 14³, 16², 18², 19, 20, 21², 24, 25³, 26², 27²; $14:7$, 8, 9, 10², 12³, 13, 14, 15², 16², 22²; $15:2^4$, 3², 4, 5, 6, 7³, 9, 11², 13, 14², 16³, 18², 19³, 20², 21; $16:4^5$, 6², 7, 9², 13², 14, 15², 16, 18², 19, 21; $17:3^2$, 4², 6, 8, 10², 11, 13², 14², 18², 25³, 26², 27³; $18:2$, 3, 8, 10, 12², 16³, 17², 21², 22²; $19:3$, 6, 7³, 8³, 9², 11², 12², 13; $20:4^4$, 5², 6, 9, 10², 11², 12, 14³; $21:4$, 6, 7⁴, 8, 9, 10², 12², 14²; $22:4$, 5, 6, 7², 8², 9, 10, 11, 12², 14², 18⁴, 19, 21, 22³, 23, 24², 25, 27, 28, 30²; $23:2$, 3³, 4², 5⁴, 6², 7, 8, 12⁴, 15, 17², 19, 20², 26², 27, 33, 34, 39, 40²; $24:6^2$, 7⁴, 8, 9, 10; $25:6$, 9¹, 10², 12², 13, 16, 27, 29², 30¹, 11², 33², 34, 35, 37, 38²; $26:3^2$, 6, 9², 13, 15, 18²; $27:6^2$, 7, 8², 9, 10², 11², 12², 13, 20, 22³; $28:2$, 3, 4², 9, 11, 13, 14³; $29:7$, 10, 12², 13, 14⁴, 17², 18², 21², 22, 28, 32²; $30:3$, 7², 8², 9², 10¹, 11⁴, 14, 16⁴, 17², 18³, 19⁵, 20³, 21⁵, 22², 23, 24²; $31:1^2$, 2, 4³, 5², 6, 8³, 9⁴, 10², 11, 12⁴, 13², 14², 16², 17, 18, 22³, 23, 24, 25, 27, 28, 29, 30², 32, 33, 34⁴, 36, 37, 38, 39, 40²; $32:3^2$, 4³, 5³, 14, 15, 24, 25, 28², 36, 37³, 38², 39², 40⁴, 41², 42, 43, 44³; $33:3^2$, 6², 7, 8², 9², 10, 11, 12, 13, 14, 15², 16³, 17, 18, 21, 22, 26²; $34:2$, 3⁵, 4, 5, 17, 18, 20², 21, 22²; $35:7$, 13, 15, 19; $36:3^2$, 7², 30², 31²; 37:7, 8², 19, 20; $38:2^4$, 3², 9², 10, 19, 20², 22²; 23²; $39:16$, 17², 18³; $40:4$, 9, 10, 15; $42:3$, 4³, 6³, 10², 11, 12, 14², 16³, 17³, 18², 20, 22²; $43:10^3$, 11, 12, 13, 48, 8²; $44:8$, 12, 13, 14², 16, 17³, 25, 26, 27, 28, 29⁴; $45:4$, 5²; $46:8^2$, 10², 12², 15², 16³, 17, 18, 19, 21²; 23, 24, 26², 27³, 28²; $47:2^4$, 3², 5³; $48:1^3$, 2⁴, 4², 7², 8³, 9², 12³, 13, 15², 16, 18, 35, 41², 42, 44³, 47²; $49:2^4$, 3, 4, 5³, 6, 8, 10⁴, 11, 12, 13², 15, 16, 18, 20³, 21³, 22³, 26², 27²; 29³, 32², 33³, 35, 36, 37³, 38, 39; $50:2^3$, 3⁴, 4, 5³, 9⁴, 10², 13³, 16, 18, 20³, 30², 34, 36², 37², 38², 39³, 40², 44², 45², 46²; $51:1^4$, 2², 4, 6, 8, 11, 12, 14², 18, 24, 25, 26, 29, 33, 36², 37, 39, 40, 41²; 42², 43, 44, 47⁴, 48², 52², 53, 55⁴, 56⁴, 57², 58, 62², 64²; La 3:24, 32, 49; $4:21^2$, 22²; Eze 2:1, 5; 3:8; 9, 18³, 19², $4:3^2$, 5, 8, 13², 15, 16², 17³; $5:2$, 4, 8, 9², 10⁴, 11² 12², 13⁴, 14, 15, 16², 17⁴; $6:3$, 4³, 5², 6²; 8², 9, 10, 11, 12⁴, 13, 14², 17³, 18; $7:3^4$, 4³, 8, 9³, 11, 13³, 14, 15, 16, 17², 18, 19⁴, 20, 21, 22², 23²; 24³, 25², 26⁴, 27⁶; $8:6$, 13, 15, 18²; $9:10^2$,

Column 1

23³, 24², 25², 26⁴; **29:**4², 5³, 6, 8, 9², 10, 11², 12³, 13, 14², 15⁴, 16³, 19², 21³; **30:**4³, 5, 6³, 7², 8, 9², 10, 11², 12², 13³, 14, 15, 16⁴, 17², 18⁴, 19², 22, 23, 24³, 25³, 26²; **31:**18²; **32:**3², 4², 5, 6², 7², 8², 9, 10³, 11, 12³, 13, 14, 15, 16³, 20, 21, 28², 31², 32; **33:**4, 5, 6², 8³, 9², 11, 12³, 13⁴, 14, 15², 16², 18, 19, 20, 27², 28⁴, 29, 33²; **34:**10⁴, 11, 12², 13³, 14⁴, 15, 16⁴, 17, 20, 22³, 23³, 24², 25, 26³, 27⁴, 28⁴, 29², 30; **35:**3, 4³, 6³, 7, 8², 9², 10², 11², 12, 14, 15³; **36:**7, 8², 9², 10², 11⁵, 12⁴, 14, 15², 23², 24², 25³, 26², 27, 28³, 29³, 30², 31², 33² 34, 35, 36², 37², 38²; **37:**5², 6², 12, 13, 14⁴, 17, 19, 21², 22³, 23⁵, 24³, 25⁴, 26⁴, 27³, 28; **38:**4, 5, 8², 9², 10², 11³, 12³, 13, 14, 15, 16², 18², 20⁴, 21², 22², 23³; **39:**2², 3, 4², 5, 6², 7³, 8, 9², 10³, 11⁴, 12, 13², 14⁴, 15, 16², 17, 18, 19, 20, 21², 22, 23, 25³, 26, 27, 28², 29²; **42:**13²; **43:**7², 9, 12, 18, 26, 27; **44:**14, 28, 29², 30; **45:**1, 3, 4², 5, 6, 7², 8³, 15, 16, 17²; **46:**2, 12, 16, 17, 18, 20, 24; **47:**9³, 10³, 11² 12⁵, 14, 15, 17², 18², 19², 20²; **48:**1³, 2³, 3², 4², 5², 6², 7², 8⁴, 9, 10³, 11, 12³, 15², 16, 17, 18², 19, 20², 21⁴, 22², 23², 24², 25², 26², 27², 28, 29, 30, 31², 32, 33, 34, 35²; **Da 2:**4, 5, 6, 7, 9², 24, 28, 36, 39², 40², 41², 42³ 44⁵, 45; **3:**6, 11, 15², 17, 18; **4:**25⁴, 26, 27, 32⁴; **5:**7², 12, 16², 17², 6, 18; **6:**5, 26²; **7:**14², 17, 18², 23³, 24³, 25², 26², 27³; **8:**13², 14², 19, 22², 23, 24², 25⁴; **9:**25³, 26², 27³; **10:**14, 20², 21; **11:**2³ 3², 4⁴, 5³, 6⁵, 7³, 8², 9², 10², 11³, 12² 13², 14², 15⁴, 16⁴, 17⁴, 18⁴, 19², 20², 21³, 22² 23², 24⁴, 25³, 26³, 27², 28³, 29⁴, 30³, 31³, 32² 33², 34², 35², 36⁴, 37³, 38², 39⁴, 40³, 41³, 42² 43, 44², 45³; **12:**1³, 2, 3, 4, 6, 7², 8, 10⁴, 11, 13²; **Hos 1:**4², 5, 6, 7², 10², 11⁴; **2:**3², 4, 5, 6², 7², 9², 10², 11², 12³, 13, 14, 15³, 16², 17², 18², 19², 20², 21², 22², 23³; **3:**3, 4, 5²; **4:**5, 6, 9², 10², 14², 19²; **5:**2, 6, 7, 9, 10, 14³, 15³; **6:**1², 2³, 3²; **7:**12³, 16²; **8:**3, 5, 6, 7, 10², 13², 14²; **9:**2², 3², 4⁴, 5, 6⁴, 9, 11, 12, 13, 14, 15², 16, 17², 10:2, 3², 5², 6³, 7, 8³, 10², 11², 14² 15², 11:5², 6², 7, 9³, 10³, 11²; **12:**2, 8, 9, 11, 14²; **13:**3, 7², 8³, 15², 16²; **14:**3² 4, 5² 6², 7⁴, 8, 9²; **Joel 1:**15²; **2:**2, 18, 19², 20³, 24² 25, 26², 27², 28⁴, 29, 30, 31, 32²; **3:**2², 4, 7, 8², 12, 15, 16³, 17³, 18⁵, 19, 20, 21; **Am 1:**3, 4², 5³, 6, 7², 8², 9, 10², 11, 12³, 14², 15; 2:1, 2³, 3, 4, 5², 6, 13, 14³, 15³, 16; **3:**2, 8, 11², 12, 14², 15³, 4:2², 3², 12²; **5:**3² 6³, 11², 14, 15, 16², 17², 18, 19, 20, 22², 23, 27; **6:**7² 8, 9, 10, 11, 14²; **7:**3, 6, 8, 9³, 11², 17²; **8:**2, 3, 5, 7, 8³, 9, 10³, 11², 12², 13, 14; **9:**1³ 2², 3², 4², 8², 9², 10², 11², 12², 13, 14², 15²; **Ob 1:**2², 4, 6, 7⁴, 8, 9², 10², 15², 16², 17³ 18⁴, 19⁴, 20², 21²; **Jnh 1:**6², 12; **2:**4, 9²; **3:**4, 9; **Mic 1:**6², 7⁴, 8³, 11, 14², 15², 16; **2:**3², 4², 9, 10, 12⁴, 13³; **3:**4³, 6², 7, 11, 12², 4:1³ 2³, 3⁵, 4², 5, 6², 7², 8², 10³, 13⁴; **5:**1, 2³, 4, 4³ 5², 6², 7³, 8², 9⁵, 10⁴, 11, 12, 13, 15; **6:**7³ 14¹, 15³, 16²; **7:**7, 8², 9³, 10⁴, 11, 12, 13, 15, 16³, 17⁴, 19², 20; **Na 1:**3, 8², 9³, 10², 12, 13, 14³, 15²; **2:**2, 13³; **3:**5², 6², 7², 11², 15²; **Hab 1:**12²; **2:**1³, 3³, 4, 6, 7³, 8, 11², 14, 16², 17²; **3:**16, 18²; **Zep 1:**2², 3³, 4², 8, 9, 10, 11², 12² 13³, 14, 15, 17³, 18³; **2:**3, 4², 5, 6, 7³, 9³, 10, 11², 12, 13, 14⁵; **3:**6, 7, 8², 9, 10, 11², 12³, 15, 16, 17³, 18, 19³, 20²; **Hag 2:**6³, 7³, 9², 19, 21, 22³, 23²; **Zec 1:**3, 9, 12, 16³, 17²; **2:**4, 5², 9³, 10², 11, 12⁴, 13³; **3:**4, 7³, 9³, 10²; **4:**7²; **5:**3², 4³, 11; **6:**12, 13⁵, 14, 15³; **8:**3³, 4, 5, 6, 7, 8³, 11, 12⁵, 13², 19, 20, 21, 22, 23³, 4¹, 5⁴, 6², 7², 8², 10⁴, 11, 12, 13, 14⁴, 15⁴, 16², 17²; **10:**3², 4², 5², 6⁴, 7⁴, 8³, 9³, 10³, 11⁵, 12²; **11:**6⁴, 9, 16²; **12:**2, 4³, 5, 6³, 7³, 8, 9³, 10³, 11³, 13:1², 3², 4², 5, 6, 7², 8², 9⁶; **14:**1, 2⁴, 3, 4², 5⁴, 6, 7², 8², 9², 10², 11³, 12⁴, 13³, 14, 15, 16, 17, 18², 19², 20²; **Mal 1:**4³, 5, 9, 10, 11³; **2:**2², 3³, 4; **3:**1⁴, 2, 3⁴, 4, 5², 7, 8, 10², 11², 12², 17², 18; **4:**1⁴, 2³, 3, 5, 6²; **Mt 1:**21², 23³; **2:**6², 23²; **3:**10, 11², 12²; **4:**6³, 9²; **5:**4², 5, 6, 7, 8, 9, 18, 19², 20, 21², 22², 26, 46; **6:**1, 4, 6, 7, 10, 14, 15, 18², 21, 22, 23, 24², 25², 30, 33, 34; **7:**1, 2², 5, 7³, 8, 9, 10, 11, 16, 20, 21², 22³; **8:**7, 8, 11², 12, 13², 15², 16, 17³, 18, 21, 29; **10:**14, 15, 17, 18, 19, 20, 21², 22², 23, 26², 29², 32, 33, 36, 39², 41², 42; **11:**10² 22, 23², 24, 28, 29; **12:**11, 18², 19², 20², 21², 22³, 27, 31², 32², 33², 36, 37², 39, 40, 41, 42², 44, 45, 50; **15:**13, 14; **16:**2, 3, 4, 18², 19³, 25², 26, 27, 28; **17:**4, 11, 20², 23², 27; **18:**3, 12, 16, 18², 19, 26, 29, 35, 19:5², 21, 27, 28, 29², 30²; **20:**4, 16², 18², 19², 23², 21:2, 3, 13, 21, 22⁴, 25, 27, 29, 30, 37, 40, 41³, 43²; 44²; **22:**13, 28, 30²; **23:**11, 12², 13, 26, 33³, 34²; 35, 36, 39; **24:**2³, 5², 6, 7², 9², 10² 11, 12, 13, 14², 19, 22, 24, 27, 28, 30, 34², 37, 39, 40², 41², 42, 44, 46, 47, 50, 51²; **25:**1, 14, 21, 23, 29³, 30, 31, 32², 33, 34, 37, 40, 41, 44, 45, 46; **26:**2, 11², 13, 21, 23, 24, 29, 31², 32, 33, 34, 35, 61², 62, 64; **28:**7, 10, 14; **Mk 1:**2², 7, 11², 20², 21², 22²; **3:**28, 29, 35; **4:**13, 24, 25²; **5:**23, 28; **6:**11, 23; **8:**3, 12, 35², 38; **9:**1, 31², 41, 49;

Column 2

10:7, 8, 15², 21, 30, 31, 33³, 34², 39; **11:**2, 3, 17, 23², 24, 29², 31, 33; **12:**6, 7, 9², 23, 25², 40; **13:**2², 4², 6², 8², 9², 12², 13², 17, 18, 19, 22, 24², 25², 26, 27, 30, 31², 33, 35; **14:**7², 9, 13, 15, 18, 21, 25, 27³, 28, 29, 30, 31, 36², 38, 58², 62, 72; **16:**3, 7, 16², 17³, 18⁴; **Lk 1:**13, 14², 15², 16, 17, 20², 31, 32³, 33², 34, 35³, 42, 45, 48, 76², 78; **2:**10, 12², 34, 35²; **3:**6, 9, 16², 17²; **4:**6, 7, 10, 11², 23³; **5:**5, 10, 35³, 36², 37²; **6:**21², 25², 35³, 37³, 38³, 39, 40, 41, 46², 47, 48³, 52, 53, 59; **13:**3, 5, 24², 25², 26, 27, 28, 29² 30², 32²; 35; **14:**5, 9², 10², 11, 12³, 13, 14², 15; **15:**7, 18; **16:**4, 9, 10, 11, 12, 13², 28, 30, 31², 32², 35³, 36², 37³, 38³, 39, 40, 41, 46², 47², 48³, 52, 53, 59; **13:**3, 5, 24², 25², 26, 27, 28, 29², 30², 35; **14:**5, 9², 10², 11, 12³, 13, 14², 15; **15:**7, 18; **16:**4, 9, 10, 11, 12, 13², 28, 30, 31², 9:24², **11:**4, 9, 12, 22, 23, 24, 25, 26, 48²; **12:**8², 25², 26², 28, 31, 32, 34, 48; **13:**7, 17, 19, 26, 32², 33², 35, 36, 37, 38²; **14:**3, 8, 12², 13, 14, 15, 16², 17, 18², 19³, 20, 21², 23², 24², 25³, 26², 27, 32, 33², 34², 35, 37; **22:**10, 12, 16, 18, 22, 34, 40, 42, 46, 61, 67, 69; **23:**16, 34, 37, 42, 44, 45, 46; **28:**12, 15, 20; **29:**2, 6, 9², 14, 18, 19, 21, 23, 28, 30; **30:**2, 3, 4, 8, 15, 16³, 20², 40; **31:**3, 5, 6, 10, 12, 18, 21, 23², 24, 32, 38, 42, 50; **32:**4, 6, 7, 11, 13, 15, 20, 24, 25², 28²; **33:**1, 5, 15; **34:**5, 6, 7², 9, 16, 19, 22, 24; **35:**2², 3, 6, 13, 14, 15, 22; **37:**2, 14², 25; **38:**1, 2, 8, 9, 12, 14, 16², 18, 26; **39:**2, 3, 6², 7, 8², 10², 12, 14, 19, 21, 23; **40:**2, 7, 14; **41:**10, 12, 40; **42:**4, 6, 13, 21, 25, 32, 33, 38; **43:**3, 4, 5, 8, 12, 14, 16², 21, 22², 32², 34; **44:**1, 2, 3, 4², 6, 12², 18, 23, 26², 30², 33, 34; **45:**1, 5, 15, 23²; **46:**1, 4, 6, 7, 26, 27; **47:**1, 6, 17, 19, 30; **48:**1, 12, 21, 22; **49:**23²; 25, 29, 30; **50:**9, 13, 14², 22; **Ex 1:**1², 7, 10, 11, 14²; **2:**3, 21, 24²; **3:**8, 12, 12, 30; **7:**4, 17; **8:**2, 3, 5, 17, 22; **9:**15; **10:**2, 38, 39; **13:**3, 5, 7, 9, 13, 14, 16, 19²; **14:**6, 7², 11, 22, 29; **15:**10, 15, 20; **16:**2, 20, 31; **16:**7, 8, 9, 14, 17, 18, 24; **20:**18, 20, 25; **21:**3, 6, 8, 11, 18², 19, 20, 30; **23:**2, 5, 7, 11, 16, 18, 32²; **24:**2, 3, 8², 12, 14; **25:**11, 12, 13, 19, 20, 22, 24, 28²; **26:**1², 3, 4, 5, 17, 29², 31, 32², 37; **27:**2, 6, 10², 11², 12, 14, 15, 16, 18²; **28:**1, 8⁴, 21, 28, 32, 33³; **29:**2², 3, 4, 5, 12, 13, 17, 20, 28, 32, 36, 37; **31:**3², 7, 9; **32:**4, 11, 12, 15, 35²; **33:**3², 5, 17, 12², 13², 14, 15, 16², 17, 22; **34:**3, 5, 9, 10, 12, 20, 22, 25, 27³, 28, 29², 34, 35; **35:**11, 12, 13, 14, 15, 16², 17, 25, 31², 35; **36:**8², 10, 11, 12², 34², 35, 36, 38²; **37:**2, 3, 4, 8, 9, 11, 15, 17, 19, 20, 22, 25, 26, 28, 38²; **39:**5⁴, 6, 14, 21, 23, 25, 26, 28, 30³; **40:**3, 12, 10², 11, 12², 13², 15, 16, 18², 19, 20, 24; **21:**19; **22:**2, 6, 9, 11, 20, 22, 27; **23:**13², 17, 18², 20, 24, 26, 34; **24:**11; **26:**9² 13, 42², 44, 45; **Nu 1:**47; **2:**2, 33, 34; **3:**1, 4, 20; **4:**5, 6, 8, 9, 11, 12, 26, 32; **5:**8², 13, 19, 20; **6:**15³, 17, 20, 21; **7:**1², 89, 14², 19², 20, 25, 26, 31², 32, 37², 38, 43², 44, 49², 50, 55², 56, 61², 62, 67², 68, 73², 74, 79², 80, 86, 87, 89²; **8:**8², 20, 22; **9:**3, 7, 11, 14, 20, 22; **10:**7, 29, 32²; **11:**4, 8², 9, 11, 12, 14, 19, 23, 30, 42, 43; **15:**4, 6², 9², 24, 38; **16:**2, 3, 13, 18, 22, 27, 31, 35², 39, 40; **23:**3, 4, 6, 13, 15, 16, 19, 24, 25, 28; **26:**3, 10, 61, 62; **28:**5², 7, 8, 9², 12⁴, 13², 14³, 20², 21, 28, 31; **29:**3³, 4, 6, 9, 10, 11, 14³, 15, 16, 19, 21, 22, 24, 25, 27, 28, 30, 31, 33, 34, 37, 38; **30:**10; **31:**6², 8, 14, 17, 18, 23, 35², 37, 42, 44, 47, 50, 52; **32:**14, 15, 29, 30, 33; **34:**12; **35:**5, 7, 16, 20, 21, 25, 26², 27; **Dt 1:**25, 28, 37, 42; **2:**7, 33, 37; **3:**1, 2, 5², 6, 12, 21, 23, 26, 27; **4:**3, 11², 21, 23, 29², 31, 40², 42, 46, 13, 21; **5:**3³; **6:**3², 5³, 10, 11, 18, 21; **7:**2, 3, 8, 12, 16, 19, 20³, 35², 36, 37²; **38²; **11:**18; **12:**3, 14, 25, 26; **13:**4, 5², 6, 17, 21, 23; **Jas 1:**5, 7, 10, 11, 12, 25; **2:**13, 31; **3:**1; **4:**7, 8, 10, 13, 14, 15²; **5:**3, 9, 12², 15²; 20; **1Pe 2:**6, 15; **3:**7, 17; **4:**2, 5, 17, 18, 19; **5:**1, 4², 10; **2Pe 1:**8, 10, 11, 12, 14, 15²; **2:**1², 2², 3, 12, 13², 3:3, 4, 10⁴, 11, 12²; **1Jn 1:**9; **2:**1, 17, 24; **3:**2, 9, 4:17; **5:**14, 16; **2Jn 1:**2, 3; **3Jn 1:**6, 9, 10, 14; **Jude 1:**18²; **Rev 1:**7², 19; **2:**5, 7, 10³, 11, 16², 17², 22³, 23³, 24, 26², 27², 28³, 3:3³, 4, 5³, 9², 11², 14², 20, 21; **4:**1, 11; **5:**10²; **7:**15, 16³, 17²; **9:**6⁴; **10:**6, 7, 9²; **11:**2², 3, 6, 7, 8, 9, 10², 15; **12:**5; **13:**8, 10², 14¹; **14:**10², 13²; **15:**4²; **17:**1, 7, 9, 10, 11, 14, 18², 21; **18:**4², 7, 8, 10, 14, 19, 23², 23²; **19:**15; **20:**6², 7, 8, 10; **21:**3², 4², 6, 7³, 8, 9², **25², 26, 27²; **22:**3³, 4², 5⁴, 12, 18, 19.

WITH (5912)

Column 3

Ge 1:11, 12, 20, 21, 29; **2:**21; **3:**6, 12, 16; **4:**1², 4, 5, 17, 25; **5:**22, 24; **6:**3, 6, 9, 13, 14, 18², 19²; **7:**2, 13, 14², 23; **8:**1, 17, 18; **9:**8, 9², 10³, 11, 12; **10:**5; **11:**4; **12:**4, 8, 20; **13:**1², 5; **14:**5, 13, 16, 17, 24; **15:**9, 14, 17, 18; **16:**2, 4, 6, 11; **17:**4, 10, 12, 13, 19, 21, 22, 23, 27; **18:**16, 23, 25, 33; **19:**1, 3, 5, 8², 11, 15, 31, 32, 33, 34²; **20:**5, 6, 16; **21:**6, 10, 14, 19, 20, 22, 23; **22:**3, 5; **23:**8; **24:**5, 8, 10, 15, 26; **26:**3, 10, 15, 20, 24, 26, 28²; **27:**11, 16, 34, 37, 42, 44, 45, 46; **28:**12, 15, 20; **29:**2, 6, 9², 14, 18, 19, 21, 23, 28, 30; **30:**2, 3, 4, 8, 15, 16³, 40; **31:**3, 5, 6, 10, 12, 18, 21, 23², 24, 32, 38, 42, 50; **33:**1, 5, 15; **34:**5, 6, 7², 9, 16, 19, 22, 24; **35:**2², 3, 6, 13, 14, 15, 22; **37:**2, 14², 25; **38:**1, 2, 8, 9, 12, 14, 16², 18, 26; **39:**2, 3, 6², 7, 8², 10², 12, 14, 19, 21, 23; **40:**2, 7, 14; **41:**10, 12, 40; **42:**4, 6, 13, 21, 25, 32, 33, 38; **43:**3, 4, 5, 8, 12, 14, 16², 21, 22², 32², 34; **44:**1, 2, 3, 4², 6, 12², 18, 23, 26², 30², 33, 34; **45:**1, 5, 15, 23²; **46:**1, 4, 6, 7, 26, 27; **47:**1, 6, 17, 19, 30; **48:**1, 12, 21, 22; **49:**23²; 25, 29, 30; **50:**9, 13, 14², 22; **Ex 1:**1², 7, 10, 11, 14²; **2:**3, 21, 24²; **3:**8, 12, 12, 30; **7:**4, 17; **8:**2, 3, 5, 17, 22; **9:**15; **10:**2, 38, 39; **13:**3, 5, 7, 9, 13, 14, 16, 19²; **14:**6, 7², 11, 22, 29; **15:**10, 15, 20; **16:**2, 20, 31; **17:**2², 4, 5², 9, 12; **18:**5, 6, 12, 22; **19:**9, 13, 16, 17, 18, 24; **20:**18, 20, 25; **21:**3, 6, 8, 11, 18², 19, 20, 30; **23:**2, 5, 7, 11, 16, 18, 32²; **24:**2, 3, 8², 12, 14; **25:**11, 12, 13, 19, 20, 22, 24, 28²; **26:**1², 3, 4, 5, 17, 29², 31, 32², 37; **27:**2, 6, 10², 11², 12, 14, 15, 16, 18²; **28:**1, 8⁴, 21, 28, 32, 33³; **29:**2², 3, 4, 5, 12, 13, 17, 20, 28, 32, 36, 37; **31:**3², 7, 9; **32:**4, 11, 12, 15, 35²; **33:**3², 5, 17, 12², 13², 14, 15, 16², 17, 22; **34:**3, 5, 9, 10, 12, 20, 22, 25, 27³, 28, 29², 34, 35; **35:**11, 12, 13, 14, 15, 16², 17, 25, 31², 35; **36:**8², 10, 11, 12², 34², 35, 36, 38²; **37:**2, 3, 4, 8, 9, 11, 15, 17, 19, 20, 22, 25, 26, 28, 38²; **39:**5⁴, 6, 14, 21, 23, 25, 26, 28, 30³; **40:**3, 12, 10², 11, 12², 13², 15, 16, 18², 19, 20, 24; **21:**19; **22:**2, 6, 9, 11, 20, 22, 27; **23:**13², 17, 18², 20, 24, 26, 34; **24:**11; **26:**9² 13, 42², 44, 45; **Nu 1:**47; **2:**2, 33, 34; **3:**1, 4, 20; **4:**5, 6, 8, 9, 11, 12, 26, 32; **5:**8², 13, 19, 20; **6:**15³, 17, 20, 21; **7:**1², 89, 14², 19², 20, 25, 26, 31², 32, 37², 38, 43², 44, 49², 50, 55², 56, 61², 62, 67², 68, 73², 74, 79², 80, 86, 87, 89²; **8:**8², 20, 22; **9:**3, 7, 11, 14, 20, 22; **10:**7, 29, 32²; **11:**4, 8², 9, 11, 12, 14, 19, 23, 30, 42, 43; **15:**4, 6², 9², 24, 38; **16:**2, 3, 13, 18, 22, 27, 31, 35², 39, 40; **23:**3, 4, 6, 13, 15, 16, 19, 24, 25, 28; **26:**3, 10, 61, 62; **28:**5², 7, 8, 9², 12⁴, 13², 14³, 20², 21, 28, 31; **29:**3³, 4, 6, 9, 10, 11, 14³, 15, 16, 19, 21, 22, 24, 25, 27, 28, 30, 31, 33, 34, 37, 38; **30:**10; **31:**6², 8, 14, 17, 18, 23, 35², 37, 42, 44, 47, 50, 52; **32:**14, 15, 29, 30, 33; **34:**12; **35:**5, 7, 16, 20, 21, 25, 26², 27; **Dt 1:**25, 28, 37, 42; **2:**7, 33, 37; **3:**1, 2, 5², 6, 12, 21, 23, 26, 27; **4:**3, 11², 21, 23, 29², 31, 40², 42, 46, 13, 21; **5:**3³; **6:**3², 5³, 10, 11, 18, 21; **7:**2, 3, 8, 12, 16, 19, 20³, 35², 36, 37²; **8:**1, 4, 5, 9, 11², 13, 14, 18; **9:**1, 4, 8, 12, 21², 24, 25; **10:**1, 4, 5, 7, 15, 24, 29, 31, 34, 36, 37, 38, 40, 43; **11:**4, 16, 19, 13:21, 17; **14:**4, 6, 7; **15:**13, 45, 46, 63; **17:**4, 11; **19:**46; **20:**4; **21:**2, 11, 16, 19, 21, 24², 34, 25, 27, 29, 31, 32, 33, 35, 37, 39, 41; **22:**5, 7, 8⁴, 9, 14, 16, 18, 19, 24, 27, 31, 32; **23:**7, 12³, 14; **24:**6, 7, 12, 14; **Jdg 1:**3³, 7, 16, 17, 18, 19, 21, 22;

Column 4

2:1, 2, 18, 20; **3:**15, 21, 27², 31; **4:**6, 7, 8², 9², 10, 13, 22²; **5:**9², 13, 14, 15²; **6:**5, 12, 13, 16, 21, 28, 32, 39, 40; **7:**3, 4², 5, 6, 7, 10, 13, 16, 18, 19, 22; **8:**7, 10, 16, 18, 19; **9:**26, 44, 48; **10:**7, 15, 17; **11:**8, 11, 12², 20, 25², 37; **12:**1, 2; **13:**9, 19, 20; **14:**5, 6, 7, 9, 18, 19; **15:**3, 5, 13, 16²; **16:**1, 3, 4, 7, 8, 9, 11, 12², 13², 14², 16, 18, 27, 28, 30²; **17:**2, 10, 11; **18:**7, 19, 20, 23, 24, 25, 27, 28; **19:**3, 4, 5, 9, 10, 19, 22, 27; **20:**2, 25, 28², 35, 38; **21:**10, 12, 16; **Ru 1:**1, 3, 7, 10, 11, 15, 17, 18; **2:**4, 6, 8, 10, 11, 14, 19, 21, 22, 23; **3:**2; **4:**5, 10; **1Sa 1:**19, 21, 24²; **2:**4, 8, 13², 17, 19, 22, 26², 28, 33; **3:**17, 19; **4:**3, 4, 8; **5:**6, 7, 8, 9, 11, 12; **6:**2, 7, 11, 15, 18; **7:**3, 5, 10; **8:**11, 20; **9:**3, 5, 19, 24, 25; **10:**5, 6, 7, 11; **11:**1, 2, 5, 6; **12:**2, 7, 20, 24; **13:**2², 5, 7², 15, 16, 22; **14:**2, 7, 13, 17, 18, 20, 21² 27, 32, 34, 39, 43, 44, 45, 52; **15:**6, 8, 25, 26, 30, 31; **16:**1, 2, 5, 12, 18, 19, 20², 22; **17:**3, 19, 20, 22, 23, 28³, 37, 40, 41, 43, 45, 50, 51, 52, 57; **18:**1³, 2, 4, 6³, 8², 12, 14, 20, 22, 28, 30; **19:**3, 7, 8, 9, 10, 19, 22², 23; **20:**5, 8, 13³, 16, 30, 35², 41, 42; **21:**1, 2; **22:**2, 3, 4², 6, 8, 9, 17, 19, 23²; **23:**6, 7, 23²; **24:**4, 7, 8, 10; **25:**7, 13², 22, 23, 25, 26, 33, 39, 41, 42; **26:**2, 5, 6², 7, 8, 25²; **27:**2, 3², 5; **28:**14, 19, 20; **29:**2³, 4, 6², 8, 9, 10²; **30:**9, 21, 22², 23, 24; **31:**5; **2Sa 1:**2², 6, 11, 12, 14, 21, 24; **2:**2, 3², 12, 31; **3:**7, 9, 12, 13, 16, 17, 20, 21, 22², 23, 27, 31, 35; **4:**7; **5:**3, 10, 11, 6:4, 5³, 10, 12, 14, 15², 7:3, 6, 7, 9, 12², 14² 19, 22, 29; **8:**2, 10², 11; **10:**6, 7, 13, 16, 19; **11:**1, 4, 9, 11, 13, 14; **12:**3, 5, 9², 11, 16, 17, 24, 30, 31²; **13:**1, 4, 11, 15, 20, 26², 27, 31; **14:**4, 6, 17, 19, 22, 33; **15:**1², 2, 13, 14, 16, 17, 18, 19², 20², 22, 23, 27, 30, 31, 33, 35, 36²; **16:**1, 6, 12, 13, 14, 15, 17, 18, 21², 22; **17:**2², 8, 10², 11, 16, 22, 24, 14, 18:1, 2, 5, 27, 28; **19:**7, 9, 13, 16, 17², 25, 26, 31, 33², 34, 36, 37, 38, 40, 41, 43; **20:**3, 8, 9, 13, 15, 22; **21:**8², 10, 13; **22:**21, 30², 33, 40; **23:**5², 6, 9, 21²; **24:**2, 20; **1Ki 1:**4, 6², 7², 21, 22, 23, 25, 31, 33, 35, 37², 40, 41, 44, 45, 51; **2:**4, 5, 6, 8, 10, 23²; **28², 32, 35; **3:**1, 17, 26; **4:**13; **5:**1, 6, 10; **6:**9, 15², 16, 18, 20, 21², 22², 27, 28, 30, 32, 35; **7:**2, 3, 7, 9, 10, 12, 24, 30², 31, 36, 43; **8:**9³, 15, 21, 23, 24², 39, 46, 47, 48, 54, 57², 62, 65; **9:**11, 12², 15, 17, 24; **10:**1, 2², 7, 13, 17, 18², 19, 22, 26; **11:**2, 4, 9, 15, 17, 18², 19, 20, 21, 38, 43; **12:**8, 10, 11², 14², 18², 13:6² 7, 8, 15, 16², 18, 19, 24, 25, 28; **14:**3, 6, 8, 20, 31²; **15:**8, 19, 20, 22, 24²; **16:**6, 12, 17, 28, 34; **17:**9, 16, 20, 18:4, 13, 20, 26; **19:**1, 2, 10, 14, 19, 20; **20:**20, 24, 25, 31, 34, 35, 38, 39; **21:**8, 22:4, 10, 11, 13, 19, 31, 39, 40, 44, 49, 50²; **2Ki 1:**8², 9, 11, 13, 15²; **2:**8, 14; **3:**4², 7², 9², 12, 13, 17, 19, 20, 25, 26; **4:**18, 38, 42; **5:**5, 6, 6:9, 15², 16, 18, 20, 21², 22², 27, 28, 30, 31, 32, 35; **7:**2, 3, 7, 9, 10, 12, 24, 30², 31, 36; **8:**1, 8, 9, 11, 12, 14, 21², 24, 28, 29; **9:**1, 15, 19, 16, 28; **10:**2, 6, 15², 16, 23, 24, 25, 31, 35; **11:**3, 4, 8, 11, 12, 19, 20; **12:**11, 15, 21; **13:**9, 13², 19; **14:**6, 8, 16², 20, 22, 25, 29, 29; **15:**5, 7, 22, 25² 38²; **16:**10, 11, 20²; **17:**13, 15, 18, 33, 35, 36, 38²; **18:**7, 16, 17, 23, 31, 37; **19:**6, 7, 9, 23, 24, 32, 37; **20:**3; **21:**11, 18; **22:**13; **23:**2, 3, 5, 9, 14, 16, 25⁴; **24:**2, 4, 6; **25:**1, 7, 11, 17², 24, 25², 26, 28; **1Ch 2:**21, 23, 41; **4:**21, 27, 40; **5:**1; **6:**32, 33, 49², 55, 59, 60, 69, 70, 71, 73, 75, 76, 77, 79, 81; **7:**23, 29; **8:**12; **9:**20, 26, 31; **11:**3, 9, 10, 13, 23², 42; **12:**23², 38, 19, 27, 28, 32, 33³, 34, 37, 39; **13:**1, 2, 6, 7, 8³, 13, 14; **14:**15³, 18, 25, 28²; **16:**16, 38, 40, 41; **17:**2, 6, 8, 11, 20, 18:10, 11; **19:**7, 8, 14, 16, 19; **20:**2³, 4², 5², 6; **21:**12², 16, 20, 21, 26; **22:**11, 16, 18, 23:5, 11; **24:**3; **25:**1, 6, 7; **26:**8; **28:**1, 9², 15, 20; **29:**2, 17³, 21, 22, 30; **2Ch 1:**1, 14; **2:**7, 8, 9, 12, 14³, 18; **3:**4, 5³, 6, 7⁴, 8, 10, 14, 15; **4:**3, 9, 14, 20; **5:**10, 13²; **6:**4², 11, 14, 15², 18, 30, 36, 37, 38, 41; **7:**3, 6, 8, 18; **8:**5², 14, 18; **9:**1⁴, 6, 12, 16, 17², 18, 23, 25, 31; **10:**8, 10, 11² 14²; **11:**11, 13; **12:**1, 7², 11, 15, 16; **13:**3², 8, 9, 12², 19; **14:**1, 6, 7, 8⁴, 9, 15², 23, 14³; **16:**3, 4, 6, 8, 10, 12, 13, 14; **17:**3, 8, 9, 10, 14, 15, 16, 17², 18²; **18:**1, 3, 9, 10, 11²; **20:**1, 13, 17, 19, 28, 35, 36, 37; **21:**1², 4, 7, 9, 14, 15, 17, 18; **22:**1, 5, 6, 7, 9, 12; **23:**1, 3, 7, 9, 13, 11, 16, 18, 20, 21; **24:**14, 16, 24; **25:**4, 7³, 10, 24, 26, 27, 17, 23; **27:**9; **28:**9, 15, 18, 27; **29:**8, 10, 18², 22², 24, 25, 26², 29, 30², 35; **30:**6, 21, 24, 25, 32:3, 6, 7³, 8², 9, 21, 33³; **33:**11, 20; **34:**8, 21, 22, 30, 32², 33; **35:**5, 9, 10, 12, 18² 21³; **36:**6, 10, 17, 23; **Ezr 1:**3, 4³, 6³; **2:**2, 63, 70; **3:**2, 4², 10²; **4:**3, 9, 16; **5:**2, 8²; **6:**4, 7, 12, 13, 16, 21, 22²; **7:**13, 14, 15, 16, 17², 18², 21, 23, 25, 28; **8:**1³, 3, 4, 5, 6, 7, 8, 9, 10, 11, 12, 13, 14, 16, 18, 22; **9:**4, 8, 12; **10:**3, 8, 12, 14, 17; **Ne 1:**2, 3, 5; **2:**6, 9, 12², 17; **3:**12; **4:**6, 13, 16, 17, 20, 22, 23, 30; **5:**1; **6:**16; **7:**2, 7, 65, 73; **8:**6, 12, 13, 18; **9:**4, 8, 12, 15, 24², 25, 30; **10:**28, 29; **11:**20, 25; **12:**1¹, 8, 27², 33,

35, 36, 38, 40, 41, 44; **13:**2, 4, 5, 9, 15, 31; **Est 1:**6, 7, 12, 13, 21; **2:**6, 9, 12², 13, 14, 18; **3:**11, 12, 13; **4:**3, 8; **5:**2, 4, 8, 9, 12, 14; **6:**8, 12, 14; **7:**1, 3, 8; **8:**3, 5², 8², 10, 17; **9:**5, 29²; **10:**2; **Job 1:**4, 6, 22; **2:**1, 7, 8, 11, 13; **3:**14, 15², 22; **4:**2, 18; **5:**23²; **6:**16; **7:**5, 14²; **8:**5, 21²; **9:**3, 14², 15, 17, 18, 30², 35; **10:**11², **11:**19; **12:**2, 25; **13:**3, 4, 21; **15:**2², 3², 24, 26, 27²; **16:**12, 16, 21; **17:**7, 9; **18:**20; **19:**2, 16, 20, 24, 27; **20:**11, 17; **21:**3, 24, 34; **22:**18, 21; **23:**4, 6; **24:**12, 16, 17; **28:**14, 15, 16², 17, 19²; **29:**5, 6, 9; **30:**1, 21, 30; **31:**1, 10, 17, 20, 38; **32:**2, 3, 4, 16; **33:**10, 16, 19, 26; **34:**8²; **35:**4, 16; **36:**2, 4, 7, 16, 17, 32; **37:**4, 11; **38:**2, 26, 27, 32, 34, 36; **39:**10, 13, 17, 19, 20, 23; **40:**2, 10, 15, 19; **41:**1², 2, 3, 4, 7², 13, 14; **42:**7, 8, 11, 15; **Ps 2:**9, 11²; **4:**T, 7; **5:**4, 9², 12²; **6:**T, 6², 7; **7:**2, 4, 14; **8:**5; **9:**1, 8, 20; **12:**2, 4; **13:**2; **14:**5; **16:**11²; **17:**10, 11, 15; **18:**12, 20, 29², 32, 39; **20:**6; **21:**3, 6, 12; **23:**4, 5; **26:**4², 5, 9²; **27:**6; **28:**3³; **29:**7, 11; **30:**11; **31:**9²; **18; **32:**7; **33:**2; **34:**3; **35:**1², 5, 13, 21, 26; **36:**9; **37:**24; **38:**7, 17, 20; **39:**3, 12; **41:**11; **42:**2, 4², 8; **43:**4; **44:**1, 2, 9, 15, 19; **45:**2, 3, 7, 8², 12, 13, 15; **46:**3, 7, 9, 11; **47:**1; **48:**10; **49:**4, 17²; **50:**5, 18², 22; **51:**T, 7; **53:**5, 54:T; **55:**T, 14²; **60:**5, 10, 12; **61:**T; **62:**4; **63:**5²; **64:**7; **65:**4, 5, 6, 9², 10, 11², 12, 13²; **66:**1, 13, 17; **67:**T; **68:**6, 13², 25, 33; **69:**13, 27, 30, 31; **71:**8, 13, 22²; **72:**1², 2, 19; **73:**6, 8, 23, 24; **74:**4, 6; **75:**5, 8; **76:**T, 4²; **77:**15, 17; **78:**9, 14², 36², 47², 58², 62, 72²; **80:**5, 10², 16; **81:**16²; **83:**3, 5, 7, 15², 16; **84:**6, 9; **85:**5; **86:**8, 12; **87:**4; **88:**5, 7, 9; **89:**1, 3, 6, 10, 13, 20, 24, 28, 32², 38, 39, 45, 51²; **90:**9, 14; **91:**4, 8, 15, 16; **93:**1; **94:**20; **95:**2², 10; **96:**10; **98:**4, 5², 6, 9; **100:**2², 4²; **101:**2, 4, 6; **102:**9; **103:**4, 5, 17², 18; **104:**1, 2, 6², 25, 28; **105:**9, 18, 30, 32, 37, 40, 43²; **106:**26, 35, 40; **107:**9, 22; **108:**1, 6, 11, 13; **109:**2, 3, 21, 26, 29, 30; **111:**1; **112:**5; **113:**8²; **115:**7; **118:**6, 7, 27; **119:**2, 7, 10, 13, 20, 28, 34, 58, 61, 64, 69², 81, 98, 124, 145, 149, 158, 171; **120:**4²; **122:**1; **125:**5; **126:**2², 3, 5, 6²; **127:**5; **129:**7; **130:**4, 7²; **131:**1, 2; **132:**9, 15², 16, 18; **135:**7; **136:**12; **138:**1, 7; **139:**3, 18, 20; **140:**9; **141:**4; **144:**13; **147:**7, 8², 14; **149:**3², 4, 8²; **150:**3², 4², 5²; **Pr 1:**11, 13, 14, 15, 31; **2:**16; **3:**5, 9², 10, 15, 28; **4:**4, 9; **5:**17; **6:**3, 12, 13², 14, 25, 29; **7:**5, 10, 13, 16, 17, 18, 20, 21²; **8:**11, 12, 18, 24, 30; **11:**2, 9; **12:**8, 14; **13:**20; **14:**1, 18; **15:**16², 17, 19, 22; **16:**7, 8², 19, 30; **17:**1², 27; **18:**3, 20; **19:**6, 7; **20:**8, 17; **21:**9, 19, 24, 27, 31; **22:**9, 24²; **23:**1, 7, 13, 14; **24:**4, 21, 25, 31; **25:**7, 9, 24; **26:**23, 24; **27:**11, 16, 22, 26²; **29:**9, 14, 26; **30:**14, 16, 19, 28, 29, 31; **31:**13, 19, 24, 25, 26; **Ecc 1:**18; **2:**1, 3², 9, 21, 22; **4:**6², 8, 16; **5:**2, 10, 17, 20; **6:**10; **8:**11, 12, 13; **9:**2¹, 7², 8, 9, 10, 14; **SS 1:**2, 4, 6, 10², 11; **2:**5¹, 10, 13; **3:**6, 8, 10, 11; **4:**4, 8², 9², 13², 14²; **5:**1, 2², 5², 8, 13, 14²; **6:**1, 4; **7:**6; **8:**9, 13; **Isa 1:**4, 6, 7, 22, 27², 30, 31; **2:**6; **3:**10, 16²; **5:**2, 11, 13, 14, 18², 29; **6:**2⁴, 4, 6², 7, 10²; **7:**2, 14, 24²; **8:**1, 7, 10, 11; **9:**7, 9, 10², 12; **10:**11², 24, 26, 33, 34; **11:**3² 4⁴, 6², 7, 15; **12:**1, 3; **13:**9, 18; **14:**1, 6², 11, 19², 21, 23; **15:**3; **16:**4, 9; **17:**2, 5; **18:**5; **19:**9, 16, 21, 24, **20:**4; **21:**3, 7, 9; **22:**6, 21; **23:**17²; **24:**9, 16; **26:**17, 18; **27:**1, 5², 6, 8², 11; **28:**7, 8, 11, 15², 18², 27³; **29:**3, 6², 7², 8³, 12, 14, 21²; **30:**11, 20, 22², 24, 27, 29, 30², 31, 32², 33; **32:**1, 6, 7, 13; **33:**5, 14², 19, 21; **34:**2, 3, 6, 7³, 14, 15; **35:**4³, 10; **36:**2, 8, 16, 22; **37:**6, 7, 9, 24, 25, 33, 38; **38:**3, 11, 20; **40:**9, 10², 12, 19; **41:**2², 4², 7, 10², 15, 21, 23; **42:**13, 22²; **43:**2, 5, 23², 24²; **44:**12³, 13⁴; **45:**8, 9, 14², 17²; **46:**11, 12², 15², 48:**16, 20; **49:**4, 23, 25², 26; **50:**1, 3, 11; **51:**3, 9, 11, 16, 20, 21; **52:**1, 8; **53:**9², 12²; **54:**7, 8, 9, 11²; **55:**3, 5; **56:**11; **57:**5, 8, 9, 15; **58:**4, 7², 9²; **12; **59:**2², 4, 6, 12, 21; **60:**5, 9², 15; **61:**8, 10²; **62:**11; **63:**1, 3, 11; **64:**11; **65:**23; **66:**10², 15³, 16²; **Jer 1:**8, 19; **2:**8, 12, 22, 35, 37²; **3:**1, 2, 3, 9, 10, 15; **4:**4, 30; **5:**5, 17; **6:**3, 6, 11, 12, 23, 26, 29; **7:**5, 16, 23; **8:**19²; **9:**5, 8², 16, 18, 22; **10:**3, 4², 10; **11:**5, 10, 15, 16²; **12:**1, 5²; **13:**12², 13, 17; **14:**3, 12, 17, 21; **15:**7, 10, 11, 17², 20; **16:**18²; **17:**1², 3; **18:**6, 12, 18, 20, 23; **19:**4, 10; **20:**4, 11, 17; **21:**5, 9, 10, 12; **22:**7, 14², 15; **23:**16, 21, 24, 32, 39; **24:**7; **25:**6, 7, 15, 26; **26:**11, 14, 18, 22, 23; **27:**5, 8, 13, 18, 20; **29:**13, 16, 18, 20, 23; **30:**6, 20²; **31:**19²; **32:**4², 7, 8, 9, 11, 13; **34:**5, 8, 10², **32:**9, 2², 21², 25; **34:**3², 8, 13; **36:**14, 22, 23; **37:**3², 15; **38:**22, 10, 11², 13, 20, 25, 26, 27; **39:**1, 7, 9, 18; **40:**4, 5, 6, 9; **41:**1, 2², 3, 5, 7, 8, 9², 10, 11, 12, 13²; **42:**5, 6, 8, 11; **43:**6, 9; **44:**8, 13, 15; **45:**3, 5; **46:**4, 10, 22, 28²; **48:**7, 9, 33, 37; **49:**3, 18, 29, 37; **50:**2², 16, 36, 38, 40, 42; **51:**14², 16, 22², 23², 27, 33², 34, 39, 59; **52:**4, 11, 15, 22², 32; **La 1:**16, 22²; **2:**1, 3², 7, 9, 13; **3:**5, 7, 9, 13, 15², 16, 30, 43, 44; **4:**9, 10, 14; **5:**18, 22; **Eze 1:**4, 15, 20, 21, 25; **3:**3, 14, 25; **4:**7, 8;

5:2³, 5, 11², 12, 15, 16; **7:**4, 9², 18², 19, 27²; **8:**16, 17, 18²; **9:**1, 2², 6, 7, 10, 11; **10:**2, 17, 19; **11:**6, 22; **12:**7, 14; **13:**10, 11, 12, 13, 14, 15, 20, 22; **14:**4, 11; **16:**2, 4², 5, 8, 9, 10², 11, 13, 17, 25, 26², 28, 29, 36, 37, 40, 43, 46², 50, 53, 55², 59, 60², 61, 62; **17:**3, 7, 12, 13, 17; **18:**6; **19:**4, 9; **20:**4, 5², 6, 7, 15², 17, 18, 23, 26, 31, 33², 34², 39, 40, 42, 44; **21:**6, 11, 12, 21; **22:**2, 7, 11, 14, 20, 21, 31; **23:**7, 8, 10, 15, 23, 24⁴, 25, 27, 29, 30, 33, 36, 37, 41, 42, 44³, 47; **24:**4, 16, 19, 27; **25:**6, 10, 14, 15²; **26:**7², 8, 9, 10, 11, 16, 20²; **27:**6, 12, 13, 15², 16, 17, 18, 20, 21, 22, 23, 24², 25³ 31³, 33, 34, 35²; **28:**11, 16, 23²; **29:**4; **30:**5, 11; **31:**2², 3, 7, 8, 9, 11, 14, 15², 16, 17, 18³, 32:2², 5, 6², 9, 15, 22², 27², 28; **33:**6, 14, 30; **34:**4, 13, 14, 16; **36:**2², 5, 8, 12, 13, 23; **37:**1, 20, 21², 22, 23², 25, 26; **38:**2, 39, 40, 41, 43; **Hos 2:**3, 6, 13, 18; **3:**3³; **4:**5, 14²; **5:**5, 6, 14; **6:**4²; **5², 8²; **7:**3², 5², 6, 8, 9; **8:**4, 13²; **9:**8; **10:**14; **11:**4²; **12:**1², 3, 4²; **14:**2, 8; **Joel 2:**5, 12², 20, 24²; **3:**18²; **Am 1:**3, 11; **2:**3, 13; **3:**15²; **4:**2², 9, 10³; **5:**2, 14, 23; **6:**4, 10, 12; **7:**7, 9; **8:**4, 5, 6²; **9:**1; **Ob 1:**10; **Jnh 2:**9; **3:**6, 8, 9; **Mic 1:**7; **2:**4, 12; **3:**8³, 10², 12; **5:**1, 6²; **6:**6³, 7², 8, 11²; **7:**2, 5, 10; **Na 1:**2, 8; **2:**11, 12², 3:6², 8, 12, 18; **Hab 1:**15; **2:**2, 6, 12, 14, 16, 19; **3:**8², 9, 14, 15; **Zep 1:**9, 11, 12; **3:**6, 14, 15, 17³, 19; **Hag 1:**6, 9, 13; **2:**4, 5, 7, 13, 14, 17; **Zec 1:**2, 9, 12, 13, 15, 16, 17; **2:**1, 11; **4:**1, 2², 4; **5:**9; **6:**6³, 13; **7:**2, 14; **8:**2, 4, 5, 6, 8, 10, 13², 14, 15, 16², 17²; **3:**16; **4:**2, 6; **Mt 1:**18, 23², 25; **2:**3, 11², 16; **3:**8, 11³, 12, 17; **4:**21, 24; **5:**22, 25², 28², 41; **6:**2, 7², 27; **8:**2, 9, 10, 14, 16, 29, 34; **9:**8, 10, 11, 15, 19; **10:**5; **12:**10, 30², 41, 42, 45²; **13:**15⁴, 20, 29, 56; **14:**7; **15:**6, 8, 20, 32; **16:**27; **17:**1, 3, 5, 17², 20; **18:**9, 20, 23, 26, 29; **19:**26²; **20:**8, 15, 20, 24, 26; **21:**2², 22:10, 16², 23, 35, 37²; **23:**30; **24:**30, 31, 41, 49, 51; **25:**3, 4, 10, 17, 19, 20, 21, 22², 23, 27²; 31; **26:**7, 11, 18, 20, 29, 35, 36, 37, 39², 40, 47², 48, 51, 55, 58, 67, 69, 71, 72; **27:**3, 19, 22, 30, 34, 38, 44, 48, 54; **28:**8, 12, 20; **Mk 1:**6, 8², 11, 3, 10, 24, 26, 27, 29, 30, 40, 43, 45; **2:**15, 16²; **3:**1, 3, 6, 7, 10, 14²; **4:**16, 24, 32, 33, 34, 36; **5:**2, 3, 5, 7, 17, 18, 23, 24, 33, 38, 40; **6:**3, 13, 23, 25, 31, 51; **7:**2, 5, 6, 34, 37; **8:**2, 10, 14, 16, 34, 38; **9:**1, 2, 4, 8, 14, 15, 16, 19², 42, 43, 47, 49, 50; **10:**27² 30, 32², 39², 41, 43, 46; **11:**11; **12:**14, 18, 21, 30⁴, 33³, 37; **13:**26, 34; **14:**3, 7, 14, 17², 18, 31, 33, 34, 43², 44, 48, 49, 54, 65; **67; **15:**1, 7, 12, 19, 23, 27, 32, 36, 37, 41; **16:**10, 18, 20; **Lk 1:**12, 15, 28, 30, 31, 37, 41, 51, 53, 56, 66, 67; **2:**5, 13, 24, 36, 40, 51, 52; **3:**8, 11², 14, 16³, 17, 18, 22; **4:**27, 34, 36; **5:**1, 12², 26, 29, 30, 34, 36; **6:**8, 11, 38; **7:**4, 6, 8, 11, 12, 16, 36, 38²; **44²; **8:**1, 7, 13, 15, 28, 37, 38, 41, 45; **9:**10, 18, 28, 31, 32, 41²; **10:**17, 27⁴; **11:**7, 23²; **12:**37, 46, 53³, 58; **13:**1, 17, 26; **14:**15, 25, 31²; **15:**2, 6, 9, 16, 20, 28, 29, 30, 34, 44, 54; **16:**8, 10⁴, 11, 12, 20, 23; **17:**2, 20, 31, 18:3, 31, 34, 34³, 44, 48, 49, 54, 65; **67; **15:**1, 7, 12, 19, 23, 27, 32, 36, 37, 41;

39; 28:10, 11, 14, 16, 20², 27⁴; **Ro 1:**4, 9, 24, 27³, 29; **3:**2; **5:**1; **6:**4, 5², 6², 8², 7:21; **8:**5, 16, 17, 18, 26, 27, 32; **9:**22, 28; **10:**9, 10²; **11:**27; **12:**3², 4, 13, 15², 16², 18, 21; **13:**14; **15:**1, 6, 10, 13², 16, 27, 32², 33; **16:**7, 14, 15, 16, 20; **1Co 1:**2, 9, 10, 17; **2:**1, 2, 3, 4²; **3:**13; **4:**1, 8, 12, 17, 21²; **5:**2, 3, 4, 4², 8², 9, 11², 6:**1, 15, 16², 17², 20; **7:**9, 12, 13; **8:**10; **9:**5, 12; **10:**5, 20, 30; **11:**4, 5, 13, 32; **12:**12, 23², 26², 28; **13:**6; **14:**2, 9², 12, 15⁴, 16, 36; **15:**10, 35, 42, 53²; **54²; **16:**2, 3, 6, 7, 10, 11, 12, 20, 23; **2Co 1:**1, 4, 12, 20, 24; **2:**4, 17; **3:**3², 7, 10, 11, 18²; **4:**13, 14²; **5:**2, 4, 8; **6:**7, 14², 15, 16; **7:**3, 15; **8:**4, 5, 8, 17, 18, 22, 24; **9:**4, 13²; **10:**1, 4, 9, 12², 14; **11:**1, 2, 4, 9, 12, 19, 20, 25; **12:**8, 12, 18; **13:**2, 3, 4, 11, 12, 14; **Gal 1:**2, 18²; **2:**1, 3, 5, 7, 12, 14, 20; **3:**3, 9, 17, 27; **4:**12, 14, 18, 20, 25, 30; **5:**17, 24, 25; **6:**6, 11, 18; **Eph 1:**3, 5, 7, 8, 11, 13; **2:**5, 6², 15, 19, 20; **3:**6, 12, 16, 18; **4:**2, 19, 21, 22, 28², 30, 31; **5:**6, 7, 11, 18, 19, 26; **6:**2, 3, 5², 9, 14², 15², 16, 18², 23, 24; **Php 1:**1, 4, 7, 8, 11, 23, 25, 26; **2:**1², 6, 12, 17, 18, 22², 23, 29; **3:**17, 18; **4:**2², 3, 6, 9, 15²; 21, 23; **Col 1:**9, 11, 28, 29; **2:**5, 7, 11², 12², 13, 14, 16, 18, 19, 20, 22, 23; **3:**1, 3, 4, 9, 12, 13, 16², 19, 22, 23; **4:**1, 6, 9, 18; **1Th 1:**5⁴, 6; **2:**2, 4, 8, 11²; **3:**4, 13; **4:**11, 14, 16; 17², 18; **5:**10, 13, 14, 20, 26, 28; **2Th 1:**7, 9, 11; **25; 8, 9; **3:**1, 7, 10, 14, 16, 18; **1Ti 1:**14, 18; **2:**9²; **10, 15; **3:**4, 7, 9; **4:**2, 3, 4, 7; **6:**6, 8, 10, 17, 21; **2Ti 1:**3, 4, 8, 13, 14; **2:**3, 10, 11², 12, 19, 22, 23; **3:**5, 6; **4:**2, 3, 11², 13, 22²; **Tit 1:**7; **2:**1, 15; **3:**10, 15²; **Phm 1:**13, 19, 25; **Heb 1:**9; **2:**7, 9; **3:**10, 17², 4:12, 13, 16; **5:**2, 7, 13; **6:**17²; **7:**21; **8:**7, 8³, 9, 10; **9:**19, 21, 22, 23², 25, 26; **10:**6, 8, 16, 22², 33, 34, 38; **11:**9, 10, 25, 31, 40; **12:**1, 14, 17, 18, 21, 28; **13:**5, 6, 16², 21, 22; **Jas 1:**11; **2:**4; **3:**9²; **4:**3, 4; **5:**14; **1Pe 1:**2, 4; **3:**9², 10, 11, 16, 19²; **20², 26³, 27², 30², 31, 32²; **19:**2; **20:**4, 5, 8², 10², 12², 14, 18², 20, 24; **21:**2, 5, 7, 29²; **34²; **22:**6², 8, 9, 12, 13, 16, 17², 20²; 28², 29², 30², 32², 33, 34², 35, 37², 38; **23:**3, 11³, 13², 26, 27²; **24:**9²; **10², 11², 12, 14, 22²; **25:**5, 18²; **27:**7, 13², 14; **28:**2, 3, 8, 22, 26, 30; **29:**1, 5, 7, 39; **31:**2, 15, 19², 24², 26; **32:**6, 7, 14, 15, 22², 40²; **26², 29², 30², **33:**51, 52, 53, 55⁴, 56; **34:**2², 17; **35:**4, 6, 7, 8, 10, 13, 29², 33, 34; **36:**2; **Dt 1:**6, 8, 9², 10, 11², 13, 14, 15, 17, 18², 19, 20², 21²; 22, 23, 26², 27, 29, 30², 31⁴, 32, 33⁴, 34, 37², 39, 40, 41², 42³, 43⁴, 44³, 45², 46²; 2:3, 4², 5, 6³, 7³, 9, 18, 19², 25³, 31, 37; **3:**2¹, 18², 19, 20³, 21², 22, 24², 26, 27, 28²; **4:**1³, 2², 3², 4, 5³, 8, 9, 10, 11², 12³, 14³, 15⁴, 16, 19, 20⁴, 21³, 22, 23, 25², 26⁴, 27, 28, 29², 30³, 31, 33, 34, 35², 36⁴, 37, 38⁴, 40², 5:4, 5³, 6, 7, 8, 9, 11, 12², 13³, 14⁵, 15⁵, 16⁴, 17⁴, 18², 19, 20⁴, 21³, 22, 24², 25², 26³, 27, 28⁴, 29³, 30, 31, 32²; **6:**1², 2⁴, 3⁵, 6, 7³, 10⁴, 11², 12, 13, 14³, 15³, 16⁴, 17, 18²; 19, 20², 21, 22, 24², 25²; 26², 27, 28; **4:**1³, 2², 3², 4, 5⁵, 15, 16, 19, 20⁴, 21³, 22, 23, 24, 25²; **5:**3, 6, 7, 9, 13, 14³, 15⁴, 16⁴, 19, 20, 21², 22, 23⁴; **24:**4, 7², 8², 9, 10, 11², 13, 14²; 15², 18³, 19⁴, 21², 22; **25:**12, 15³, 17², 18², 19⁴; **26:**1², 2², 5, 10, 11³, 12², 13, 14, 15², 16, 17⁸, 18², 19²; **27:**1, 2², 3³, 4², 8², 9, 10, 12², 13, 14², 15³, 16², 18⁴; **28:**1³, 2, 3, 6², 7⁴, 8⁴, 9², 10⁴, 11², 12⁴, 13⁴, 14², 15⁴, 16⁴, 17², 18⁴, 19³, 20²; **31:**2², 3³, 5, 6⁵, 7⁴, 8², 9, 10³, 11², 12², 13, 14², 16⁴, 17², 18⁴, 19³, 20³; **32:**6³, 7², 14, 18⁴, 38², 46², 47²; **50²; **51², 52²; **33:**3², 8³, 10, 18, 26, 27, 29⁴; **34:**4²; **Jos 1:**2, 3³, 5⁴, 6, 7³, 8⁵, 9³, 10⁴, 11, 12², 13³, 14²; 15³, 16², 17², 18; **2:**3, 5, 9³, 10⁴, 11, 12², 13²,

YOU (13727)

Ge 1:29; **2:**16, 17³; **3:**1, 3⁴, 4, 5², 9, 10, 11⁴, 12, 13, 14⁴, 15², 16⁴, 17⁵, 18², 19⁵; **4:**6, 7⁵, 10, 11, 12³, 14, 6²; **6:**15, 18⁴, 19², 20, 21²; **7:**1², 2; **8:**16, 17; **9:**2, 3³, 4, 7, 9², 10², 11, 12², 15; **12:**1², 3³, 7, 11, 12², 13², 18², 19; **13:**8, 9³, 14, 15², 17; **14:**23²; **15:**2, 3, 5, 7², 15; **16:**5², 6, 8², 11³, 13; **17:**2², 6, 6², 7³, 7³, 8², 9⁴, 10⁴, 11², 12, 15, 16, 19², 20, 21; **18:**4, 5⁴, 10, 14, 15, 23, 24, 25², 28; **19:**2, 5, 9², 12², 15, 17, 19, 21, 22, 34; **20:**3², 4, 6², 7³, 9⁴, 13, 15², 16³; **21:**12, 22², 23², 26, 29; **22:**2, 5, 12⁴, 16, 17, 18, 23:4⁴, 6², 8, 9, 11³, 13, 15; **24:**3², 5, 6, 7², 8⁴, 14², 15², 37, 38², 40², 41⁴, 42, 47, 49, 50, 55, 58, 60; **25:**18, 23; **26:**2², 3, 9², 16, 24², 27², 28³, 29⁴, 27:4, 7, 8, 10, 19², 20, 24, 25, 28, 29⁵ 31, 32, 33, 36, 37², 38, 40⁴, 42, 45⁴; **28:**3⁴, 4³, 13², 14², 15⁵, 22²; **29:**4, 5, 14, 15, 25³, 26⁴; **30:**2², 15³, 16², 26³, 27, 29², 30²; **31:**3², 34, 38³; **31:**3, 6, 12, 13², 16, 26, 27³, 28², 29, 30², 31, 32, 36, 37², 38, 39², 41², 42², 43, 44, 48, 49, 50³, 51, 52², **32:**4, 6, 9, 10², 17⁴, 18, 19², 20², 28, 29; **33:**5, 8, 9, 10, 11, 12, 15; **34:**10², 11², 12², 15³, 16³, 17, 30; **35:**1³, 2², 10, 11, 12², 17; **37:**8², 10², 13², 15, 16; **38:**16³, 17, 18²; **39:**9²; 17, 40:13⁴, 14, 19; **41:**15³, 39², 40², 41, 55; **42:**1, 7, 9², 12, 14², 15², 16⁴, 18, 19², 21³, 23², 25⁴, 28², 33, 34², 36², 37², 38³; **43:**3², 6², 7², 8, 10², 15², 17, 18, 19, 21, 23², 27, 29²; **44:**4², 5, 8, 10², 15², 17, 18, 19, 21², 23, 27, 29², 32²; **45:**4, 5, 7², 8, 10³, 11³, 12², 13, 18², 19; **46:**3, 4², 30, 34²; **47:**5, 6², 8, 16, 18, 23³, 24, 25, 29, 30, 34²; **48:**2, 4³, 5, 6, 20, 21², 22; **49:**1³, 4², 8², 9², 25²; **50:**6, 17³, 20, 21, 24, 25; **Ex 1:**16, 18; **2:**7, 9, 13, 14³, 18, 20; **3:**5, 10, 12², 13, 14², 15, 16², 17², 18², 19, 20, 21, 22²; **4:**1, 5, 8, 9², 10, 12², 14², 15³, 16², 17, 18, 19², 21², 23², 25; **5:**4, 5, 7, 10, 11, 13, 14, 17²; **6:**1, 6³, 7³, 8², 7:1, 2, 4, 9, 16, 16², 17, 19, 28², 29, 30; **10:**2², 3, 4, 5, 7, 10³, 11, 16, 24, 28, 29³; **11:**1², 7, 8²; **12:**2, 4, 5², 10 11³, 13, 14, 15, 16, 18, 20², 22, 23, 24, 25², 26, 27², 31², 32, 44, 48, 49; **13:**3⁴, 5², 8², 9, 11³, 13², 14³, 16⁴, 17², 19; **14:**11², 12, 13⁴, 14²; **15:**7³, 10, 11², 12, 13³, 16, 17², 26⁴; **16:**3, 4, 6, 7, 8⁵, 12, 15², 16, 19³, 23, 28, 29⁴, 32², 33²; **17:**2²; **18:**2³, 6, 14, 18², 20³, 21⁵, 22²; **19:**4³, 5, 6; **20:**1², 2, 3, 4, 7³, 9², 10², 11⁴, 13, 14², 17³, 20³; **21:**1, 8, 9², 10², 11³, 13, 14², 21², 23³; **22:**1², 3, 4, 6, 7, 9², 13, 14³, 15, 16, 18, 20⁴, 21³; **22:**2², 24³, 25³; **24:**4, 7², 8², 9, 12², **25:**12, 15², 17² 18², 19⁴; **26:**1², 2², 5, 10, 11³, 12², 13, 14, 15², 16, 17², 18², 19⁴; **27:**1, 2², 3³, 4², 8², 9, 10, 12², 13, 14², 15³, 16², 18⁴; **28:**1³, 2, 3, 6², 7⁴, 8⁴, 9², 10⁴, 11², 12⁴, 13⁴, 14², 15⁴, 16⁴, 17², 18⁴, 19³, 20²; **29:**1, 5, 7, 9²; 10², 11, 16, 24, 25²; **30:**1⁴, 2³, 3⁴, 5³, 6², 7, 8⁴, 9², 10⁴; **31:**2³, 6, 11, 13², 14, 16², 27, 29⁴; **32:**6³, 7², 14, 18⁴, 38², 46², 47²; **50²; **51², 52²; **33:**3², 8³, 10, 18, 26, 27, 29⁴; **34:**4²; **Jos 1:**2, 3³, 5⁴, 6, 7³, 8⁵, 9³, 10⁴, 11, 12², 13³, 14²; 15³, 16², 17², 18; **2:**3, 5, 9³, 10⁴, 11, 12², 13²,

2:10, 11, 12², 29², 31, 48², 49²; **3:**7², 8, 13, 16², 22²; **4:**3, 6, 7, 9, 10², 11², 23², 24, 25, 34³, 41; **5:**5, 10, 12², 22, 24², 30, 34; **6:**2, 3, 9, 20, 21⁴, 22⁴, 24², 25⁴, 26², 27², 28², 29, 30², 31², 32³, 33³, 34³, 35, 37³, 38³, 41, 42⁴, 46, 47; **7:**4, 6, 7, 9, 14, 19, 20², 22, 24, 25, 26², 27², 28, 32³, 33, 34, 40, 43, 44², 45, 46, 47, 50; **8:**10, 18, 20, 28², 39, 45, 48; **9:**4², 5², 13, 20², 27, 33, 38, 41², 44, 48, 50², 54, 57², 60, 61; **10:**3, 5, 6, 7, 8², 9, 10, 11, 12, 13¹, 14, 15¹, 16¹, 19², 20, 21², 23, 24², 26, 28², 35², 36, 40, 41; **11:**2, 5, 7, 8, 9⁴, 11, 13², 18, 20, 27², 35, 36, 39², 40, 41, 42⁴, 43², 44², 45², 46⁴, 47², 48³, 51, 52⁴; **12:**2³, 4, 5⁴, 7, 8, 11³, 12², 14, 19, 20², 23, 24, 25, 26², 27, 28², 29, 30, 31, 32, 37, 40², 41, 44, 51², 54² 55, 56², 57, 58², 59³; **13:**2, 3⁴, 5², 12, 15², 25³, 26³, 27³, 28², 31, 34³, 35⁴; **14:**5², 8², 9³, 10³, 12⁴, 13, 14², 22, 24, 28, 33; **15:**4, 7, 10, 18, 21, 29², 30, 31; **16:**2², 5, 7, 9², 11², 12², 13, 15, 25², 26², 27; **17:**4², 6³, 7, 8, 10³, 19, 21, 22², 23, 34; **18:**8, 11, 14, 17, 19, 20, 22³, 28, 29, 41², 42; **19:**17, 19, 21³, 22⁴, 23, 26, 30³, 31², 33, 40, 42³, 43⁴, 44⁴, 46; **20:**2², 3, 5, 8, 21²; **21:**3, 6, 8, 9, 12⁴, 14, 15, 16², 17, 19, 20², 30, 31², 32, 34, 36²; **22:**9, 10², 12, 15, 16, 17, 18, 19, 20, 26², 27, 28, 29, 30, 31², 33, 34³, 35², 36², 37, 40, 42, 46², 48, 52, 53², 58, 61, 64, 67³, 68², 70²; **23:**3², 14, 15, 29, 34, 39, 41, 44², 48, 49²; **24:**5, 6², 17² 18, 25, 36, 38, 39, 41, 44², 48, 49²; **Jn 1:**21³, 22², 25², 26², 33, 38², 39, 42², 48⁴, 49², 50⁴, 51²; **2:**4, 5, 10, 16, 18, 20; **3:**2², 3, 5, 7, 8², 10², 11², 12³, 26², 28; **4:**7, 9², 10⁴, 11², 12, 17³, 18³, 19, 20, 21, 22², 26, 27², 32, 35², 38³, 42, 48², 50; **5:**6, 10, 12, 14², 19², 20, 26², 27, 28, 33, 34, 35, 37, 38², 39², 40², 42², 43², 44², 45, 46², 47²; **6:**25, 26⁴, 27, 30³, 32³, 36³, 47, 53⁴, 61, 62, 63, 64, 65, 67², 68, 69, 70²; **7:**3², 4, 6, 7, 8, 19³, 20², 21, 22², 23, 28³, 33, 34³, 36³, 45, 47², 52²; **8:**5, 7, 10, 11, 13, 14, 19³, 21³, 22, 23², 24², 25, 26, 28², 31², 32², 33, 34, 36², 37³, 38³, 39², 40², 41, 42, 43², 44³, 45, 46², 47², 48, 49, 51, 52², 53³, 54, 55², 57², 58; **9:**17, 19, 26, 27⁴, 28, 30, 34², 35, 37², 41⁴; **10:**1², 7, 24², 25², 26², 32², 33², 34, 36, 38², 11:3, 8², 15, 21, 22², 26, 27, 28, 32, 34, 40³, 41², 42², 49, 50², 56; **12:**8³, 24, 34, 35³, 36²; **13:**6, 7², 8³, 10², 12², 13, 14, 15³, 16, 17³, 18, 19², 20, 21², 27, 33⁴, 34³, 35², 36³, 37², 38², 14:2², 3³, 4, 5, 7, 9², 10², 11², 12, 13, 14, 15², 16², 17³, 18², 19², 20³, 22, 24, 25, 26², 27³, 28⁴, 29², 30, 15:3⁴, 4², 5², 6², 7³, 8, 9², 10, 11², 12, 13, 14², 15³, 16, 17³, 18, 19², 20, 21², 27, 33⁴, 34³; 35², 36, 37³, 38²; 14:2², 3³, 4, 5, 7, 9², 10², 12, 13, 14, 15², 16², 17³, 18², 19², 20³, 22; 16:1², 2⁴, 4², 5², 6², 7³, 10, 12², 13⁴, 14, 15, 16⁵, 18, 19⁶, 20², 21, 26, 27²; 16:1², 2⁴, 4², 5², 6², 7³, 10, 12², 13², 14, 15, 16⁵, 17², 19³, 20, 21², 27, 33⁴, 34³; 17:1, 2³, 3², 4², 5, 6³, 7² 8³, 9, 10, 11², 12, 13, 15², 18, 21³, 22², 23³, 24³, 25³, 26³; 18:4, 7, 8², 17², 22, 23, 25², 26, 29, 30, 33, 34, 35², 37², 39²; 19:4, 6, 9, 10⁴, 11³, 12², 35; 20:13, 15⁴, 19, 21², 23², 26, 29², 31²; 21:3, 5, 6, 10, 12, 15³, 16³, 17⁵, 18⁸, 20, 22², 23; **Ac 1:**4, 5, 6, 7, 8, 11³, 24², 14², 15, 22³, 23², 27², 28², 29, 33, 36, 38², 39; **3:**6, 12², 13², 14², 15, 16², 17, 20, 22³, 25, 26³; **4:**7, 10, 15, 19, 24, 25, 27; 5:3², 4³, 8, 9², 25, 28², 30, 35, 38, 39²; 6:3; 7:3, 4, 26², 27, 28², 33, 34, 35, 37, 42, 43³, 49, 51², 52, 53; 8:20³, 21, 22, 23, 24, 30²; 9:4, 5², 6², 17², 34; 10:19, 21, 22², 28, 29, 33³, 36, 37; 11:3, 14², 16; 12:8; 13:10³ 11³, 15, 16, 25, 26, 32, 33, 34, 35, 38², 39, 40, 41³, 46², 47²; 14:15⁴, 17²; 15:1², 7², 10, 24, 25, 28, 29²; 16:15, 17, 18, 31², 36²; 17:3, 19, 20, 22², 23²; 18:10², 14², 19:2³, 3, 13, 15, 25, 26, 36, 37, 39; 20:18², 20³, 25, 26, 27, 28, 29, 31, 32², 33³, 34, 35; 21:13, 20, 21, 22, 23, 24², 37², 38; 22:3, 7, 8², 10², 14, 15², 16, 19, 21, 25, 26, 27; 23:3⁴, 4, 11², 15², 18², 19, 20, 22, 30²; 24:2, 4², 8, 10, 11, 13, 19, 21, 25²; 25:9, 10, 12², 22, 24, 26², 26:1, 2, 3², 8, 14², 15², 16⁴, 17², 24², 27²; 27:21², 22², 24³, 31, 33², 34²; 28:20², 21², 26², 28; **Ro 1:**6, 7, 8, 9, 10, 11³, 12, 13³, 15; 2:1⁵, 3³, 4², 5, 17³, 18², 19², 20, 21⁴, 22⁴, 23², 24, 25⁴, 27², 3:4¹, 17; 5:6; 6:3, 12, 14, 16⁵, 17³, 18, 19², 20, 21², 22²; 7:1, 4²; 8:9², 10, 11², 13⁴, 15², 9:17²; 10, 19, 20; 10:8, 9², 10², 19²; 11:2, 13, 17, 18³, 19, 20, 21², 22³, 24, 25², 30, 31; 12:1, 2, 3³, 14, 18, 20; 13:3², 4², 6, 7², 11; 14:4, 10⁵, 15², 16², 15:3, 5², 6, 7, 8, 9, 11², 13², 14², 15², 22, 23, 24², 28, 29, 30, 32², 33; 16:1, 2², 6, 17², 19², 20, 21, 22, 23², 25; **1Co 1:**3, 4², 5, 6, 7², 8², 9, 10⁴, 11, 12, 13², 14, 15, 26, 30²; 2:1², 2, 3², 3³, 4², 5, 9, 16³, 17, 18, 23; 4:3, 6², 7⁴, 8⁶, 10³, 14², 15², 16, 17², 18², 19, 21²; 5:1, 2², 3, 4², 6, 7³, 8², 9, 11⁴, 15, 16, 19⁴; 7:1, 5², 16⁴, 21⁴, 23², 26⁴, 27, 28³, 32² 35², 36³, 37, 38², 39³, 40; 8:10, 12², 12² 2², 11², 12, 13, 21², 27², 31; 9:1⁴, 12²; 10:1, 13, 23, 25, 26, 31, 36⁴, 37⁵, 50, 51, 58²; 16:2, 3, 5, 6², 7², 10, 12, 15², 17, 19², 20,

23, 24; **2Co 1:**2, 6, 7³, 8, 11, 12, 13², 14⁴, 15², 16³, 18, 19, 21, 23, 24²; **2:**1, 2³, 3², 4⁴, 5, 7, 8, 9², 10; **3:**1², 2, 3²; **4:**12, 14, 15:12³, 13, 20; **6:**1, 2³, 11², 12², 17, 18²; **7:**3³, 4², 7, 8², 9³, 11³, 12², 13, 14⁴, 15², 16; **8:**1, 7², 8, 9², 10³, 13, 14, 16, 17, 22, 23, 24; **9:**1, 2, 3³, 4², 5², 8³, 11², 12, 13, 14³; **10:**1², 2, 7, 8², 9, 13, 14², 15, 16; **11:**1² 2³, 4⁵, 6, 7, 8, 9², 11, 12², 13⁴, 15⁵, 16², 17², 18³, 19², 20⁴, 21; **13:**1, 2², 3³, 4, 5⁴, 6, 7³, 9, 10², 11, 14; **Gal 1:**3, 6², 7, 8, 9² 11, 13, 20²; **2:**5, 14³; **3:**1², 3², 4, 5⁴, 8, 26, 27, 28, 29²; **4:**6, 7³, 8², 9³, 10, 11², 12³, 13², 14³, 15², 16, 17³, 18, 19, 20², 21², 28; **5:**2³, 4², 7³, 8, 10², 13⁵, 15, 16, 17², 18², 21; **6:**1², 2, 11, 12, 13; **Eph 1:**2, 13³, 16², 17², 18²; **2:**1², 2³, 5, 8, 11, 12, 13, 17, 19, 22; **3:**1, 2², 4, 13², 16, 17, 19; **4:**1², 4², 17², 20, 21, 22, 25, 26, 30, 32²; **5:**3, 5, 6², 8⁴, 14, 15, 33; **6:**3², 5, 6, 7, 8, 9, 11, 13², 16, 21², 22²; **Php 1:**2, 3, 4, 6, 7³, 8, 10, 12, 24, 25, 26, 27³, 28², 29, 30²; **2:**1, 4, 12², 13², 16, 17, 18, 19², 22, 25², 26², 28², 30; **3:**1², 15², 17, 18; **4:**1², 3, 9², 10³, 14, 15², 16, 18, 22²; **Col 1:**2, 3, 4, 5², 6³, 7, 9³, 10, 11, 12, 21, 22², 23², 24, 25, 27; **2:**1², 4², 5³, 6, 7, 8, 10, 11, 13², 16², 18, 20³, 3:1, 3, 4, 7², 8, 9, 13², 15, 16³, 17, 22, 23, 24³; **4:**1², 5, 6, 7, 8², 9², 10³, 12³, 13, 16², 17², 18; **1Th 1:**1², 2, 4², 5, 6², 7, 8, 9², 10², 11², 12², 13⁴, 14², 17², 18, 19, 20; **3:**2, 3, 4³, 5, 6⁴, 7, 8, 9, 10³, 11, 12, 13, 15², 16, 17², 18; **1Ti 1:**3², 18³; **3:**14²; **5:**4³; **6:**3¹ 12²; **2Ti 1:**3, 4, 5, 6², 13, 14, 15, 18; **2:**1, 2, 7, 23; **3:**10, 14²; **4:**1, 5⁴, 6², 7, 8², 9, 10, 11², 12², 14, 16²; **Tit 1:**5³; **2:**1, 8, 15²; **3:**8, 11, 12, 13, 15²; **Phm 1:**3, 4, 6², 7, 8², 9, 10, 11², 12, 14, 15², 16, 17², 18²; **Heb 1:**5, 9³, 10, 11, 12²; **2:**6², 7³; **3:**7, 8, 12, 13, 15²; **4:**1, 7; **5:**5, 6, 11, 12²; **6:**10², 11, 12, 14²; **7:**17, 21; **8:**5²; **9:**20, **10:**5², 6, 8², 25, 29, 32², 33³, 34³, 36²; **12:**3, 4, 5³, 7, 8², 17, 18, 22², 23, 25; **13:**3² 5³, 7, 17², 19², 21, 22², 23², 24, 25; **Jas 1:**2, 3, 4, 5, 21²; **2:**3³, 4, 6³, 7, 8², 9², 11², 16², 18², 19, 20², 22, 24; **3:**1², 13, 14, 16²; **4:**1¹ 2⁵, 3², 5, 7³, 8³, 9, 10², 11², 12², 13³; **5:**1, 4, 5, 7, 8², 9, 11, 12², 13, 14², 16, 19²; **1Pe 1:**4, 6², 8⁴, 9, 10, 12³, 13, 14², 17², 18, 19, 21, 22³, 23, 25; **2:**2, 3, 4, 5, 7, 9³, 10⁴, 11, 12, 15, 20³, 21⁴, 24, 25²; **3:**6², 7², 9², 12⁴, 13, 14³, 15², 16, 21³; **4:**3, 4², 7, 12², 13³, 14³, 15, 16²; **5:**1, 2³, 3, 4, 5, 6, 7, 9, 10⁴, 12², 14; **2Pe 1:**4, 8², 10², 11, 12², 15, 16, 19, 20; **2:**1, 3, 3:1², 2, 3, 9, 11², 12, 14, 15, 17², **1Jn 1:**2, 3², 5; **2:**1², 7³, 8², 13³, 14⁶, 18, 20², 21³, 24³, 26², 27³, 29²; **3:**5, 7, 11, 13, 15; **4:**2, 3, 4², 5:13³; **2Jn 1:**5, 6², 8³, 10, 12³; **3Jn 1:**2², 3, 5, 6, 12, 13, 14²; **Jude 1:**3², 6², 12, 18, 19, 20, 21², 24²; **Rev 1:**4, 11, 19, 20; **2:**2³, 3, 4², 5⁴, 6², 9, 10⁶, 13³, 14², 15, 16, 19², 20², 23, 24³, 25; **3:**1², 3⁴, 4, 8³, 9, 10², 11, 15², 16², 17³, 18⁴; **4:**1, 11²; **5:**9³, 10; **6:**10; **7:**14; **10:**11; **11:**17²; **12:**12³; **15:**4³; **16:**5³, 6; **17:**1, 7², 8, 12, 15, 16, 18; **18:**4², 14², 20, 22³, 23²; **19:**5², 10, 18; **21:**9; **22:**9, 16.

YOUR (6631)

Ge 3:5, 14², 15², 16³, 17², 19²; **4:**6, 7, 9, 10, 11², 14; **6:**18³; **7:**1; **8:**16²; **9:**2, 5, 9; **12:**1³, 2, 7, 13, 18, 19; **13:**8, 14, 15, 16²; **14:**20²; **15:**1², 4³, 5, 13, 15, 16, 18; **16:**5, 6², 9, 10, 11², 12⁵, 7, 8³, 9, 10², 12², 13³, 15, 18, 19; **18:**3² 4, 5², 9, 10; **19:**2³, 15², 17, 19²; **20:**10, 13, 16; **21:**12², 13; **22:**2², 12², 16², 17², 18, 20; **23:**6², 11, 15; **24:**2, 5, 7, 14³, 17, 19, 23, 40, 43, 44, 46, 51, 60; **25:**23, 31; **26:**3², 4², 9, 10, 24²; **27:**3², 6², 9, 14³, 17, 19, 23, 31², 32², 35², 39², 40², 42, 44, 45; **28:**2², 3, 4, 13², 14²; **29:**15, 18; **30:**14, 15, 27, 28, 29, 31, 32², 31:3², 5, 6, 7, 8², 9, 13, 29, 30, 31, 32, 35, 37², 38², 41³, 52; **32:**4, 5, 6, 9², 10, 12, 18, 20, 27, 28, 29; **33:**5, 8, 10², 34:8², 9, 11, 15, 16, 35:1, 2, 10², 11, 12; **37:**7, 10², 13, 14, 32; **38:**8³, 11, 13, 18², 24; **39:**19; **40:**7, 8, 13², 19²; **41:**40, 44; **42:**10, 11, 13, 15, 16², 19², 20², 33³; **43:**3, 5, 7², 11, 12, 13, 14, 23⁴, 27, 28, 29; **44:**7, 8, 9, 16, 17, 18², 21, 23², 24, 27, 28, 29; **45:**4, 7, 9, 10², 11, 17², 18², 19, 20, 21, 23²; **46:**3, 4, 33, 34; **47:**3³, 4², 5⁶, 11², 18, 20, 21, 22, 24, 29²; **48:**1, 2, 4², 5, 11², 18, 20, 21, 22; **49:**2, 4, 8⁴, 18, 25, 26; **50:**4, 6, 16, 17², 18, 21, 24, 25; **Ex 2:**13; **3:**5, 6, 13, 15, 16, 18², 19², 22²; **4:**2, 3, 6, 7, 8, 10, 11, 13⁴, 14², 15, 17, 23², 4:2, 4², 5, 8, 9³, 14², 15, 19, 22, 30; **10:**2, 4, 5, 6⁴, 8, 10, 12,

16, 17, 21, 24²; **12:**2, 11⁶, 15, 17, 19, 21, 23, 24, 26, 32; **13:**5, 7, 8, 9³, 11, 12, 13, 14, 16², 19; **14:**16², 26; **15:**6², 7², 8, 10, 12, 13³, 16², 17³, 26; **16:**7, 8, 9, 12, 16, 17⁵; **17:**5; **18:**6²; **20:**2, 5, 7, 9, 12, 16, 17³, 24³, 26; **22:**24², 26, 28, 29, 30²; **23:**4, 6, 10, 11³, 12, 13², 15, 16, 17³, 18, 19², 20², 21², 25², 26; **24:**1, 2, 9, 11³, 13, 16², 19², 21, 22, 25, 26, 27, 28, 31, 33; **28:**1, 2, 4, 41; **29:**12, 26; **30:**15, 16; **32:**2³, 4, 7, 8, 11², 12², 13⁴, 29, 30; **33:**1, 5, 13², 15, 16², 18, 19, 34:9², 10, 16², 19, 20, 23, 24³; **35:**2, 3; **Lev 1:**2; **2:**5, 7, 13⁴; **7:**32; **8:**33²; **9:**2², 7²; **10:**4, 6², 9, 13², 14⁴, 15; **11:**44, 45; **14:**34; **16:**2, 30; **18:**2, 4, 7³, 8², 9³, 10², 11³, 12², 13², 14², 15², 16², 18², 20, 21²; **19:**2, 3, 4, 5, 9³, 10², 12, 13, 14, 15, 16², 17³, 18³, 19, 25², 27², 28, 29³, 30², 31², 36; **20:**7, 19², 24; **21:**8, 17; **22:**3, 19, 20, 24, 25², 29, 33; **23:**11, 14, 22⁴, 28, 32, 38, 40, 43², 24:22²; **25:**3², 4², 5, 6, 7², 9, 14, 15, 17², 19, 25, 35, 36, 38², 39, 43, 44, 45², 46², 47, 55; **26:**1², 5, 6, 7, 8, 9, 12², 13², 16², 17, 18, 19, 20, 26², 31³, 32², 33, 36, 39, 42², 45; **27:**13², 18, 20, 23²; **31:**2, 3, 14, 35:11, 14, 15, 18, 24:5² 14, 21²; **25:**5; **27:**13², 18, 20, 29:39³; **31:**2, 3, 19, 24, 49; **32:**4, 5², 6, 8, 14, 22², 23, 24², 25, 27, 31, 33:54² 55²; **34:**3², 6², 7, 9, 10, 12²; **35:**11, 14; **Dt 1:**8, 10², 11, 12², 13, 15, 16², 21², 26, 27, 30², 31, 32, 33, 38, 39, 42², 43, 45; **2:**3, 4, 5, 7⁴, 24, 25, 30², 3:18³, 19², 20², 21², 22, 24³, 27; **4:**1, 2, 3⁴, 6, 9³, 10, 19, 21², 23², 24, 25, 26⁴, 28², 29, 31²; **5:**1, 6, 9, 11, 12, 14², 16, 18², 19, 20; **7:**1, 2, 3⁴, 4², 6², 7, 10², 13², 15, 16, 17, 18, 19, 20; **8:**1, 2, 3, 5⁴, 6², 7, 12, 16, 17, 23, 26³, 27, 29⁴; **10:**9, 11, 1², 2², 5, 7, 9, 10, 12³, 13, 14, 15, 16⁴, 17², 18³, 19², 20³, 26, 27, 31³; **20:**8, 14, 16, 17², 19; **21:**22²; **22:**13, 30, 32²; **23:**13, 15, 24:5², 6; **25:**5; **27:**13², 18, 20, 29:39³; **31:**2, 3, 19, 24, 49; **32:**4, 5², 6, 8, 14, 22², 23, 24², 25, 27, 31, 33:54², 55²; **34:**3², 6², 7, 9, 10, 12²; **35:**11, 14; **Jos 1:**3, 4, 6, 8, 9, 11³, 13, 14⁶, 15², 17⁴, 18², 2:3, 11, 14, 16, 18⁴, 19; **3:**3², 9; **4:**5, 6, 21, 23²; **24:**5, 15; 6:2, 10, 18, 22; 7:9, 10, 13; 8:1, 7², 18; 9:8², 9, 11², 24², 25; 10:6, 8, 19³, 24; 14:9³; 18:3; 22:3², 4³, 5³, 8⁴, 24, 25, 27; 23:3³, 4³, 8, 10, 11, 13⁴, 14², 15, 16; 24:2, 3, 6, 7, 8, 11, 12, 14, 15, 19², 23, 27; **Jdg 2:**1, 3, 3:28²; 4:7, 14; 5:10, 12, 31; 6:9, 10, 17, 25², 26, 30; 7:7, 9, 10, 15; 8:3, 6², 7, 15², 22², 24; 9:2, 18, 19, 29, 32, 33, 38, 54; 11:9, 17, 19, 24, 36²; 12:1²; 13:12, 13, 16, 17²; 14:3, 13, 15²; 15:2, 18; 16:6, 15, 17²; 17:10² 18:6, 10, 23, 25²; 19:9, 19²; 20:7, 28; 21:22; Ru 1:8², 10, 11, 15, 16²; 2:10, 11⁴, 13³; 3:3, 9²; 17; 4:4, 11, 12, 15³; 1Sa 1:11², 14, 16, 18²; 2:1, 3, 27, 28², 29, 30², 31³, 32, 33³, 34, 36; 3:9, 10; 4:17; 6:4², 5, 6, 21; 7:3; 8:5², 11, 13, 14, 15², 16², 17; 9:19, 20, 26; 10:2, 7, 19²; 12:2², 6, 7, 8, 11, 12², 14, 15, 16, 19², 20, 24, 25; 13:13²; 14:19²; 28, 34; 15:15, 17, 21, 24, 28, 30, 33²; 16:1, 58; 17:9, 10, 28, 32, 34, 36, 44, 46, 58; 19:2, 11; 20:1, 3², 6, 7, 8², 10, 15, 18, 29, 30, 31, 41, 42; 21:2²; 22:14³, 15², 16, 22, 23; 23:4, 10, 11², 21; 24:4², 10, 11², 15, 16, 18, 20; 25:6, 7, 8³, 13, 24², 26², 27, 28, 29, 31, 33, 35², 41; 26:8², 15², 16², 17, 22, 24; 27:5²; 28:1, 2, 16, 17², 19, 21, 22²; 29:8, 10; 31:4; 2Sa 1:14, 16¹, 19², 24, 25, 26², 2:5, 7, 22, 26; 3:8, 17, 21, 25, 31, 34²; 4:8² 11; 5:6, 21; 7:9², 11, 12⁴, 16³, 19³, 20, 21³, 23²; 24²; 25, 26², 27² 28³, 29²; 9:2, 6, 7, 7², 8, 9, 10⁴; 10:3, 5; 11:8², 21, 24²; 12:8³, 9, 10²; 13:5, 7, 10, 20², 24, 35; 14:6, 7, 8, 11, 12, 15, 17², 19², 20, 22²; 31; 15:2, 3, 8, 15, 19, 20, 21, 27², 34³; 16:3, 4, 8, 17², 19, 21, 22²; 17, 19, 20, 26, 32; **13:**5, 7, 8, 9³, 11, 12, 13, 14, 16², 19;

16, 17, 21, 24²; **12:**2, 11⁶, 15, 17, 19, 21, 23, 24, 26, 32; **13:**5, 7, 8, 9³, 11, 12, 13, 14, 16², 19; 20, 21²; **17:**6, 8², 9, 10; **18:**13, 28, 29; **19:**5⁴, 7², 14, 19, 20, 26, 27, 28², 35², 36, 37²; **20:**6, 17, 18; **22:**28, 30, 36, 50; **24:**3, 10, 13³, 16, 17, 21, 23; **1Ki 1:**12², 13², 17³, 19, 24, 26²; 30, 33, 47, 53; **2:**3, 4, 6, 7², 21, 26, 37², 38, 39, 43, 44²; **3:**6, 7, 8, 9², 11, 13, 14, 20, 23²; **5:**5², 6; **6:**12; **8:**18², 19², 23³, 24⁴, 25², 26², 28³, 29², 30³, 31, 32, 33², 34, 35², 36³, 38, 39, 41², 42³, 43⁴, 44², 48, 49, 50, 51², 52³, 53², 61; **9:**4, 5², 6; **10:**6², 8³, 9; **11:**2, 11², 12³, 22, 37; **12:**4, 7, 9², 10, 14, 16², 24, 28; **13:**6, 8, 18, 21, 22²; **14:**9, 12; **15:**19²; **16:**3; **17:**12, 13, 19, 23, 24; **18:**8, 9, 10, 12, 18, 24, 25, 31, 36, 44; **19:**2, 10, 14³; **20:**3², 5², 6, 9, 13, 22, 28, 31, 32, 33, 34², 35, 39², 40², 42²; **21:**2, 13, 30, 49; **2Ki 1:**10, 12, 13; **2:**3, 5, 9, 16²; **3:**7², 13², 17²; **4:**1, 2², 3, 4, 7², 13, 16², 26², 29³, 36; **5:**8, 10, 15, 17², 18², 25, 27; **6:**3, 12, 22, 28, 29, 7²; **7:**2, 19; **8:**1, 9, 13; **9:**1², 7, 22, 31; **10:**2, 3², 5, 6, 15, 24², 26², 27; **13:**16; **14:**9², 10², 12:7, 14, 15², 16:7; **17:**13², 39²; **18:**26, 27, 32; **19:**4², 6, 16, 20, 22², 23, 28³; **20:**1, 3², 5, 6, 15, 17²; **21:**2, 9, 19², 20²; **23:**21; **1Ch 4:**10; **10:**4; **11:**1, 2; **12:**18; **15:**12; **16:**35²; **17:**8², 10, 11⁴, 13, 17², 18², 19², 21², 22², 23, 24², 25, 26², 27²; **19:**3, 5; **21:**8, 11, 12, 15, 17², 22; **22:**11, 12, 18, 19²; **28:**6, 8², 9, 21; **29:**12, 13, 14, 15, 16², 17, 18, 19, 20; **2Ch 1:**9, 11²; **2:**8, 10, 14²; **6:**8² 14³, 15⁴, 16² 17², 19², 20³, 21³, 22, 23, 24², 25, 26² 27², 29, 30, 31, 32⁴, 33⁴, 38, 39², 40² 41⁵, 42²; **7:**12, 17, 18²; **9:**5², 6, 7³, 8³; **10:**4, 7, 9², 10, 14, 16²; **11:**4; **13:**8, 9, 12, 14¹¹; **15:**7; **16:**3²; **7²**, 8; **18:**3, 12, 14, 29; **19:**3, 10²; **20:**6, 7, 8, 9², 17, 20; **21:**12², 13², 14³, 15; **24:**5; **25:**15, 18, 19; **28:**9², 10², 19; **29:**5, 30:7, 8, 9³; **32:**10, 14, 15; **33:**8; **34:**16, 27², 28²; **35:**3², 4, 5, 6; **Ezr 4:**2, 11, 15; **5:**10; **7:**14², 17⁴, 18²; **Ne 1:**6⁴, 7, 8, 9, 10⁴, 11⁵; **2:**2, 5, 6; **4:**5, 14⁵; **5:**7, 8; **6:**8; **8:**9, 10; **9:**5², 8, 14², 16, 18, 19, 20², 25, 26², 27, 28² 29², 30², 31, 32², 35; **13:**18, 22, 25²; **Est 4:**8, 14⁴; **5:**3, 6², **6:**13; **7:**2², 3; **9:**12²; **Job 1:**11², 12, 17, 18; **2:**5², 6, 9; **4:**4, 6⁴; **5:**24², 25²; **6:**22, 25, 27, 28; **7:**20²; **8:**2, 4, 6², 7², 21², 22; **10:**3, 5², 7, 8, 12, 13², 16, 17²; **11:**3, 4, 6, 13, 14², 15, 16, 18, 19; **13:**12², 17, 21², 24²; **14:**3, 13, 15, 15², 15:5², 6², 10, 12², 13²; **16:**3, 18:3, 4²; **21:**5², 14, 34²; **22:**3, 4, 5², 6, 22, 23, 24², 25, 26, 27, 28, 30; **26:**4²; 30:21; 32:11, 14, 34:33; 35:4, 6, 7, 8², 14; 36:16, 19²; 37:17; 38:11, 34, 39:9, 11, 12², 26, 27; 40:9, 11, 14; 41:4, 5; 42:7, 8; **Ps 2:**7, 8², 12; 3:8²; 4:4³, 6; 5:5, 7³, 8², 11², 12; 6:1³, 4; 7:6; 8:1², 2, 3², 6, 9; 9:1, 2, 4, 10, 14², 19; 10:5, 12; 11:1, 5²; 15:1²; 16:10, 11²; 17:2, 4, 5, 7², 8², 13, 14, 15²; 18:15², 29, 35², 49; 19:11, 13, 14; 20:3², 4², 5; 21:1, 6, 8⁴, 9, 13²; 22:22, 26, 23:4²; 24:6, 7, 9, 25:4², 5, 6, 7, 11; 26:3², 6, 7, 27; 27:8, 9¹, 11; 28:2, 9²; 30:7, 9; 31:1, 2, 3, 5, 7, 15, 16³, 19, 20, 22²; 32:4; 33:22; 34:13³; 35:3, 24, 28²; 36:5², 6², 7², 8², 9, 10²; 37:4, 5, 6²; 38:1², 2, 3; 39:10²; 40:8², 10⁴, 11³, 16; 41:12; 42:3, 5, 7², 10, 11; 43:3², 5; 44:2, 3², 5, 8, 12, 17, 18, 22, 24, 26, 45:2, 3², 4², 6², 7², 8, 9, 10², 11², 12, 16, 17; 47:1; 48:9², 10³, 11; 50:7, 8², 9², 14, 16, 18, 19²; 20², 21; 51:1², 4, 9, 11², 12, 13, 14, 15, 18, 19; 52:2, 5, 9³; 54:1², 5, 6, 55:22; 56:7, 8²; 57:1, 5, 10², 11; 58:2², 9; 59:11, 16²; 60:3, 5; 61:4², 5, 7, 8; 62:8², 63:2², 3, 4, 7, 8; 65:4³, 6, 8, 11²; 66:3³, 4, 13; 67:2²; 68:7, 9, 10², 18, 23³, 24, 28², 29, 35; 69:7, 9, 13³, 16², 17², 24², 27, 29, 32; 70:4²; 71:2², 8², 15² 16², 17, 18², 19, 22, 24; 72:1², 2², 73:15, 24, 28; 74:1², 2, 3, 4, 7², 10, 11³, 13, 18, 19²; 20, 21, 22, 23²; 75:1², 4, 5; 76:6, 10², 11; 77:11, 12², 13, 14, 15², 17, 18², 19³, 20; 79:1², 2⁵, 6, 8², 9, 10, 11, 13³; 80:2, 3, 4, 7, 15, 16³, 17², 18, 19; 81:7, 10²; 82:8; 83:2², 3, 15², 16; 84:1, 3, 4, 9, 10; 85:1, 2, 3², 4, 5, 6, 9, 11³, 12, 13, 16³, 17; 88:2, 5, 7², 10, 11², 12², 14, 15, 16²; 89:1, 2², 4, 5², 6², 8², 14³, 15, 16², 17, 19, 38, 39, 46, 49², 50, 51²; 90:4, 7², 8, 9, 11³, 13, 14, 16³; 91:4, 7², 8, 9, 10, 11, 12; 92:1, 2², 4², 5², 9²; 93:2, 5²; 94:5², 12, 18, 19; 95:8, 9; 97:8; 99:3; 101:1; 102:2², 10, 12, 14, 15, 24, 25, 27, 28²; 103:3², 4, 5²; 104:7², 24², 29, 30; 106:4, 5³, 7², 47²; 108:4², 5, 6; 109:21², 26, 27, 28; 110:1², 2² 3², 5; 115:11², 14; 116:16³, 19; 119:5, 6, 7, 8, 9, 10, 11, 12, 13, 15², 16², 17³, 18, 19, 20, 21, 22, 24, 25, 26, 27², 28, 29, 30, 31, 32, 33, 34, 35, 36, 37, 38², 39, 40², 41³ 42, 43, 44, 45, 46, 47, 48², 49², 50, 51, 52, 53, 54, 55², 56, 57, 58², 59, 60, 61, 62, 63, 64², 65², 66, 67, 68, 69, 70, 71, 72, 73², 74, 75, 76², 77², 78, 79, 80, 81², 83, 84, 85, 86, 87, 88², 89, 90, 91, 92, 93, 94, 95, 96, 97, 98, 99, 100, 101, 102, 103, 104, 105, 106, 107, 108, 109, 110, 111, 112, 113, 114, 116, 117, 118, 119, 120, 122, 123², 124³, 125², 126, 127, 128, 129, 130, 131, 132, 133,

134, 135³, 136, 137, 139, 140², 141, 142²,
143, 144, 145, 146, 147, 148, 149², 150, 151,
152, 153, 154, 155, 156², 157, 158, 159²,
160², 161, 162, 163, 164, 165, 166², 167,
168², 169, 170, 171, 172², 173², 174², 175,
176²; **121**:3, 5², 7, 8; **122**:2, 7², 9; **128**:2, 3⁴,
5, 6; **130**:2, 7; **131**:3; **132**:8², 9², 10², 11²,
12²; **134**:2; **135**:9, 13²; **137**:9; **138**:1, 2⁶, 4,
7², 8²; **139**:5, 7², 10², 14, 16², 17, 20²;
140:13; **142**:7²; **143**:1, 2, 5², 7, 8, 10², 11²,
12²; **144**:5, 6, 7; **145**:1, 2, 4², 5², 6², 7², 10,
11², 12², 13², 16; **146**:3, 10; **147**:12, 13², 14;
Pr 1:8², 9², 14, 22, 26; **2**:2², 10²; **3**:1, 2, 3²,
5², 6², 7, 8², 9², 10², 11, 20², 21, 22, 23², 24, 26², 27,
28, 29; **4**:4, 9, 10, 12, 13, 15, 21², 23, 24²,
25², 26, 27; **5**:2, 9², 10², 11², 15², 16², 18²;
6:1, 2, 3³, 4², 9, 20², 21², 25, 26; **7**:2, 3², 4,
25; **9**:6, 11², 12; **16**:3; **19**:18; **22**:17, 18², 19,
27, 28; **23**:2, 8, 9, 12², 15, 16, 17, 18, 19,
22², 25, 26², 33²; **24**:10, 12, 13, 14², 17², 27²,
28²; **25**:7, 8, 9, 10, 17, 21; **27**:2², 10², 23²,
27², 29:17²; **30**:32²; **31**:3²; **Ecc** 5:1, 2³, 4, 6²;
7:9, 17, 21, 22; **9**:7², 8, 9⁴, 10²; **10**:4, 20³;
11:1, 6², 9⁴, 10²; **12**:1², **SS** 1:2, 3², 4, 7, 8,
10², 15; **2**:14⁴; **4**:1³, 2, 3⁴, 4, 5, 9², 10³, 11³,
13; **5**:1, 9², 6:1², 5², 6, 7²; **7**:1², 2², 3, 4³, 5²,
6, 7², 8², 9; **8**:5, 6², 13; **Isa** 1:5², 6², 7³, 11,
13², 14², 15², 16, 18, 22², 23, 25², 26²; **2**:6;
3:12, 14, 25²; **4**:1; **6**:7³; **7**:3, 5, 9, 11, 17²,
20³; **8**:8, 10²; **10**:3, 22, 27²; **12**:1; **14**:9, 11²,
13, 16, 19, 20², 30²; **16**:3, 9²; **17**:10²; **19**:12;
20:2²; **22**:2, 3, 7, 12, 14, 16², 18²; **19**² 20² 21³;
23:7, 10, 12, 14; **25**:1, 12; **26**:8², 9, 11⁴, 13,
17, 19², 20; **28**:17², 18², 22²; **29**:1, 4³, 5, 10²;
30:3, 15², 16, 20², 21, 22², 23, 29; **31**:7²;
32:11², 12, 20²; **33**:3, 4, 6, 11, 17, 18, 20,
23; **35**:4; **36**:11, 12, 17; **37**:4², 6, 17, 23⁴, 24,
29³; **38**:1, 3, 5⁴, 17², 18², 19; **39**:4, 6², 7²;
40:1, 9², 26; **41**:10, 12, 13², 14, 21², 22, 24;
42:6, 20; **43**:3⁴, 4, 5, 14², 15², 23, 24³, 25²,
26, 27², 28; **44**:3² 22², 23, 24, 27; **45**:9;
46:3, 4; **47**:2³, 3², 6, 8, 9, 10², 12², 13;
48:4², 8, 17², 18², 19², **49**:16, 17, 18², 19²,
20², 21, 22², 23³, 25, 26²; **50**:1⁴, 11; **51**:2, 6,
7, 13, 15, 16, 20², 22³, 23²; **52**:1, 2², 7, 8,
12; **54**:2⁴, 3, 4², 5³, 6, 8, 11, 12³, 13²; **55**:2²,
3, 5, 8², 9²; **57**:4, 5, 6², 7², 8⁴, 9², 10², 11,
12², 13; **58**:1, 3², 4², 7², 8, 10² 11² 12², 13²,
14²; **59**:2³, 3⁴, 12, 21³; **60**:1, 3², 4³, 5, 6, 9²,
10, 11, 14², 16², 17², 18⁴, 19⁴, 20⁴, 21; **61**:5²;
62:2², 3, 4³, 5², 6, 8², 11; **63**:2, 14, 15⁴, 16,
17³, 18³, 19; **64**:2², 5, 7², 8, 9, 10; **65**:7², 15;
66:5², 9, 14, 20, 22; **Jer** 1:9; **2**:2, 5, 9, 16,
17, 19³, 20², 22, 25², 30², 33, 34, 36, 37²;
3:2, 5, 13³, 14, 16, 18; **4**:1, 3, 4, 7², 14, 18²,
30³; **5**:3, 7, 14, 17⁴, 19², 25²; **6**:8, 9, 16, 20²;
7:3², 5², 6, 7, 14, 15, 21², 22, 23, 25, 29;
9:4², 20²; **10**:6, 7, 17, 24, 25²; **11**:4², 5, 7,
15², 20, 21; **12**:1, 6², 13; **13**:1, 4, 16², 17,
18³, 20, 21, 22³, 25, 26³, 27²; **14**:7, 9, 21³;
15:11, 13⁴, 14, 15, 16², 17; **16**:9², 11, 12, 13;
17:3⁴, 4², 16, 22²; **18**:11³, 20, 23²; **20**:4², 6²,
12; **21**:4, 14²; **22**:2², 7, 15, 17², 20², 21², 22³,
25; **23**:39; **25**:5³, 6, 7, 28, 34; **26**:11, 13³, 14,
15; **27**:2, 4, 6, 9⁵, 10, 12, 13; **28**:7; **29**:6²,
13, 16, 21, 25; **30**:10, 12², 13², 14³, 15³, 16,
17, 22; **31**:4, 7², 16³, 17², 21; **32**:7², 8, 17,
19³, 21, 23, 34:3³, 5, 13, 14, 16, 17²; **35**:6,
15³, 18; **37**:18, 19; **38**:5, 12, 16, 17², 20, 22²,
23; **39**:16, 18; **40**:2, 4, 10, 14, 15; **42**:2, 3,
4, 5, 9, 12, 13, 20, 21; **44**:3, 8, 9², 10, 21³,
22², 25³; **45**:5; **46**:3, 4³, 12², 14, 15, 19, 27;
47:6; **48**:6, 7, 18², 27², 28, 32², 46²; **49**:4³,
11², 16²; **50**:12, 14, 31; **51**:6, 13, 24, 36, 45;

La 1:10; **2**:13, 14³, 15, 16, 17, 18², 19³, 21;
3:23, 55, 56, 65; **4**:22⁴; **5**:19; **Eze** 2:1, 8;
3:3, 9, 11, 24, 26², 27; **4**:3, 4², 6, 7, 8, 9,
15; **5**:1², 2, 3, 9, 10², 11, 12², 16; **6**:2, 3, 4⁴,
5², 6³, 7, 11²; **7**:3², 4, 8², 9; **9**:8; **10**:2; **11**:5,
15³; **12**:3, 4, 5, 6², 18², 25; **13**:4, 8, 17², 18,
20², 21³, 22, 23; **14**:6²; **16**:3³, 4, 6², 7², 8,
11², 12³, 13² 14³, 15⁴, 16², 18, 20², 22⁴, 23,
25³, 26², 27³, 29, 31², 32, 33², 34², 36², 37²,
39³, 41³, 43³, 45⁴, 46², 47, 48², 49, 51, 52³,
53, 54, 55², 56², 57, 58², 60, 61², 63²; **17**:5;
18:25, 29, 30²; **19**:2, 10²; **20**:5, 7², 18, 19,
20, 27, 30, 31³, 36, 39², 40³, 42, 43, 44², 46,
47; **21**:2, 12, 14, 16, 24³, 30, 32²; **22**:4² 12,
13, 14², 15; **23**:21³, 22, 25³, 26², 29², 31², 32,
33, 34, 35², 40², 49²; **24**:13², 14², 16, 17⁴,
21², 22, 23², 27; **25**:2, 4², 6³; **26**:8², 9², 10²,
11³, 12³, 13², 15, 17², 18², 20; **27**:4³, 5, 6², 7³,
8³, 9², 10², 11⁴, 12², 13, 14, 15, 16², 17, 18,
19², 21, 22, 24, 25, 26, 27², 28, 33³, 34²;
28:2, 4², 5⁴, 7², 13, 15, 16, 17⁴, 18², 21; **29**:2,
3, 4³, 5, 8, 10, 21; **32**:2², 5², 6², 8, 9, 10, 12;
33:2, 11, 12, 17, 25, 26, 30, 31, 32; **34**:18³,
19, 21, 31; **35**:2, 4, 8⁴, 9, 11, 36; **36**:13, 14, 15,
22, 24, 25², 26, 28², 29, 31², 32², 33²; **37**:12,
13, 14, 17, 18, 25; **38**:2, 4², 9, 10, 13, 15;
39:3⁴, 4, 20; **40**:4²; **43**:27; **44**:6, 7, 8, 30³;
45:9; **47**:14²; **Da** 1:10², 12, 13; **2**:4, 5, 28³,
29, 30, 38, 47²; **3**:12, 17, 18; **4**:19² 22² 26,
27³, 31; **5**:11⁴, 16, 17², 18, 23³, 26, 28; **6**:16,
20; **7**:5; **9**:5, 6², 11, 13, 15, 16⁴, 17³, 18³, 19⁴,
24²; **10**:12³, 14, 17, 21; **11**:14; **12**:1², 9, 13²;
Hos 1:9; **2**:1², 2; **3**:1²; **4**:4, 5, 6², 13², 14²;
5:13; **6**:4; **8**:1, 5; **9**:1, 5, 7², 10; **10**:12, 13²,
14², 15; **12**:6²; **9**:2; **13**:4, 9, 10³, 14²; **14**:1³, 8;
Joel 1:2², 3², 5, 13, 14; **2**:12, 13³, 14, 17²,
23, 26, 27, 28³; **3**:4, 5, 7, 8, 10², 11, 17; **Am**
2:11²; **3**:2, 11²; **4**:1, 4², 5, 9², 10⁴, 12; **5**:12²,
17, 21², 23², 26³; **6**:2, 4, 5, 7; **7**:12², 17²;
8:10³, 14; **9**:15; **Ob** 1:3², 4, 7³, 9, 10, 12,
15²; **Jnh** 1:6, 8; **2**:3, 4², 7; **Mic** 1:16²; **2**:10;
4:9, 10; **5**:1, 9³, 10², 11², 14³; **6**:1, 5,
8, 9, 10, 13, 14, 16; **7**:4, 5², 10, 11², 14³; **Na**
1:13², 14³, 15²; **2**:1, 13³; **3**:5⁴, 12, 13³, 14, 16,
17², 18³, 19⁴; **Hab** 1:5, 13; **2**:7, 10²; **3**:2²,
3:2², 8³, 9, 11², 13², 15; **Zep** 1:11; **3**:14, 15³,
16, 17, 20²; **Hag** 1:4, 5, 6, 7, 11; **2**:17²; **Zec**
1:2, 4³, 5, 6, 3:4, 8; **6**:15; **7**:10; **8**:9, 13, 14,
16, 17; **9**:9, 11, 12, 13²; **11**:1², 9; **13**:6; **14**:1;
Mal 1:5, 6, 8, 9, 10, 13; **2**:2³, 3³, 8, 13², 14³,
15², 16, 17; **3**:7, 11², 4:3; **Mt** 1:20²; **4**:6, 7,
10; **5**:12, 16³, 20, 23², 24³, 25, 29³, 30³, 33,
36, 37², 40², 43², 44, 45, 47, 48; **6**:1² 3², 4²,
6³, 8, 9, 10⁴, 14, 15², 17², 18², 21², 22² 23²,
25², 26, 32²; **7**:3² 4², 5, 6, 11², 22²; **9**:2, 4, 5,
6, 11, 14, 18, 22, 29; **10**:9, 12, 13², 14² 17,
20, 27, 29, 30; **11**:10, 26, 29; **12**:2, 13, 27²,
37², 47; **13**:16², 27²; **15**:2, 3, 4, 6, 28;
16:6, 11²; **17**:16, 24, 27; **18**:8³, 9, 14, 15², 33,
35²; **19**:8⁴, 19², 21; **20**:14, 21³, 26, 27; **21**:5²;
22:17, 37⁴, 39, 44²; **23**:11, 23, 32, 34, 37,
38; **24**:3, 20, 42; **25**:8, 21, 23, 25, 34; **26**:18,
42, 52, 73; **27**:4, 24; **Mk** 1:2, 44; **2**:5, 9²,
11; **3**:5, 32; **5**:9, 19, 23, 34², 35; **6**:8, 11, 18;
7:5, 9, 10², 13, 29; **8**:17; **9**:18, 38, 43, 45,
47; **10**:5, 19, 37³, 43, 49, 52; **11**:25²; **12**:30⁵,
31, 33⁴, 36²; **13**:9, 23; **Lk** 1:13², 36, 44, 61;
2:29, 30, 32, 35, 48; **3**:14; **4**:8, 11, 12, 21,
23; **5**:14, 20, 22, 23, 24; **6**:10, 22, 23, 24,
27, 29², 35², 36, 38, 41², 42⁵; **7**:27, 44, 48,
50; **8**:20, 25, 30, 48, 49; **9**:5, 40, 41, 49;
10:6, 11, 17, 20, 21, 27⁶; **11**:2², 11, 13², 19²,
34⁵, 36, 42, 47, 48; **12**:1, 7, 15, 20, 22², 29,
30, 32, 33, 34², 35, 58; **13**:12, 34, 35; **14**:9,

10², 12³; **15**:19² 21, 27², 29, 30; **16**:2, 6, 7,
12, 15, 25²; **17**:3, 19, 20; **18**:20, 42²; **19**:5,
16, 18, 20, 22, 39, 42, 43, 44; **20**:43²; **21**:13,
14, 15, 18, 28², 34; **22**:32², 36, 53; **23**:14²,
28, 42, 46; **24**:38; **Jn** 2:17, 18; **4**:16, 18, 35,
50, 53; **5**:8, 10, 11, 20, 42, 45²; **6**:26, 49, 58;
7:3; **8**:11, 13², 17, 19, 21, 24², 38, 41, 42,
44², 52, 54, 56; **9**:10, 17, 19, 26, 41; **10**:34;
11:15, 23; **12**:15, 28, 30, 36; **13**:14², 38;
14:1, 27; **15**:11; **16**:7, 20, 22², 24, 26; **17**:1²
5, 6, 11, 14, 17; **18**:11, 31, 34, 35², 39;
19:14, 15, 26, 27; **20**:17², 27²; **21**:6, 18; **Ac**
2:17³, 27, 28, 35², 38, 39; **3**:17, 19, 22², 25²,
26; **4**:25, 27, 28, 29², 30²; **5**:3, 4, 9, 28; **7**:3²,
6, 32, 33, 37, 43, 51, 52; **8**:20, 21, 22; **9**:13,
14, 34; **10**:4, 31²; **11**:14; **12**:8², 15; **13**:33,
35, 41; **14**:10, 17; **15**:23, 24; **16**:31; **17**:23,
28; **18**:6², 15; **20**:30, 31; **22**:13, 16, 18, 20;
23:5, 21, 35²; **24**:2, 22; **25**:5; **26**:16, 17, 24²;
27:22, 25; **28**:22, 25; **Ro** 1:8; **2**:5², 17; **4**:18;
6:12, 13², 14, 19²; **8**:10², 11, 36; **9**:7; **10**:6,
8², 9², 10²; **11**:3², 28; **12**:1², 2, 11, 20; **13**:9,
11; **14**:10², 13², 15³, 21; **15**:9, 24; **16**:17, 19,
20; **1Co** 1:5²; **2**:5; **4**:6, 15; **5**:2, 6, 6:8², 15,
19², 20; **7**:5, 14, 16², 21, 35; **8**:9, 11, 12;
11:17, 14:9, 16², 20, 23; **15**:1, 14, 17², 34²
55², 58; **16**:3, 13; **2Co** 1:6², 11, 24²; **2**:8, 10;
4:5, 15; **5**:11; **6**:13; **7**:2, 7³, 9; **8**:6, 7, 8, 9,
23², 24; **9**:2; **10**:7, 11, 12²; **11**:3², 10:6, 15;
11:3² 12:14, 19; **13**:9; **Gal** 3:1, 3, 16; **4**:15²,
16; **5**:13, 14; **6**:13, 18; **Eph** 1:13, 15², 18;
2:1; **3**:13, 16, 17; **4**:22², 23, 26, 29; **5**:19,
22, 25; **6**:1, 2, 4, 5, 6, 9, 11, 13, 14, 15;
Php 1:9, 19, 25, 26; **2**:4, 5, 12, 17, 20,
25; **4**:5, 6, 7², 10, 15, 17, 19, 23; **Col** 1:4, 8,
21², 23; **2**:5, 12, 13²; **3**:1, 2, 3, 4, 5, 8, 9,
15, 16, 18, 19, 20, 21, 22, 23; **4**:1, 6, 8; **1Th**
1:3³, 5, 8; **2**:14; **3**:2, 5, 6, 7, 10, 12, 13;
4:11³, 12; **5**:23; **2Th** 1:3, 4, 11; **2**:17; **3**:5;
1Ti 4:14, 15, 16²; **5**:1, 23²; **6**:12, 20; **2Ti**
1:4, 5³; **2**:15; **4**:5² 9, 15, 21, 22; **Tit** 2:7;
3:12; **Phm** 1:2, 5², 6, 7, 13, 14, 19, 21, 22,
25; **Heb** 1:5, 8²; **4**:10, 12, 13²; **2**:12²; **3**:1,
8, 9, 15; **4**:7; **5**:5; **6**:9, 10, 11; **10**:7, 9, 32,
34, 35; **11**:18; **12**:4²; 12, 13; **13**:5, 7, 17, 24;
Jas 1:3; **2**:2, 8, 18; **3**:14; **4**:1, 3, 8², 9², 12,
14; **5**:2², 3², 4, 12², 16; **1Pe** 1:7², 9², 13², 17,
18, 20, 21, 22; **2**:2², 16; **3**:8, 13², 16, 21; **5**:6,
5:1, 2, 3, 4, 7², 15, 16; **5**:2, 7, 8, 9; **2Pe** 1:5,
8, 10, 13, 19; **3**:2, 17²; **1Jn** 2:12; **2Jn** 1:4,
10, 13; **3Jn** 1:2, 3, 6; **Jude** 1:12, 20; **Rev**
1:9; **2**:2³, 4, 5, 6, 9², 13², 19³, 23; **3**:1, 2, 8,
9, 11, 15, 18²; **4**:11; **5**:9; **10**:9²; **11**:17, 18⁴;
14:15, 18; **15**:3²², 4²; **16**:6, 7; **18**:10, 14, 23²;
19:10²; **22**:9.

YOURS (86)

Ge 1:29; **20**:7; **31**:32; **45**:20; **48**:6; **Ex** 11:8;
Nu 18:11, 13, 14, 15, 18²; **Dt** 9:21; **11**:24;
20:1; **Jos** 17:18; **Jdg** 1:3; **4**:9; **7**:18; **1Sa**
2:23; **25**:6; **2Sa** 16:4; **1Ki** 1:47²; **3**:9, 22²;
5:6; **20**:4; **21**:19; **22**:23; **2Ki** 2:10; **18**:19;
1Ch 12:18; **21**:24; **29**:11³; **2Ch** 1:10; **2**:8;
18:22; **20**:15; **21**:14; **Job** 42:2; **Ps** 71:16;
74:16²; **86**:8; **89**:11²; **119**:94; **128**:2; **Pr** 5:17;
Isa 36:4; **45**:14; **63**:19; **Jer** 32:20; **38**:22; **Da**
2:39; **Am** 6:2; **Mal** 3:12; **Mt** 17:27; **18**:32;
Mk 2:18; **11**:24; **Lk** 4:7; **5**:33; **6**:20; **15**:30,
31, 32; **22**:42; **Jn** 15:20; **17**:6, 9, 10; **1Co**

3:21, 22; **10**:29; **16**:18; **2Co** 6:12; **Eph** 6:9;
2Th 1:11; **1Pe** 1:2; **2Pe** 1:2; **Jude** 1:2.

YOURSELF (191)

Ge 6:14; **14**:21; **28**:2; **31**:32; **33**:9; **Ex** 9:17;
10:3; **19**:23; **20**:4, 19; **34**:2; **Lev** 9:7; **18**:20,
23; **19**:18, 34; **25**:6; **Nu** 5:20; **Dt** 5:8; **8**:17;
9:4; **23**:12, 13; **Jos** 14:12; **Jdg** 8:21; **19**:5, 6,
8, 9; **Ru** 3:3; **4**:6, 8; **1Sa** 20:8; **25**:26; **28**:2;
2Sa 16:21; **17**:11; **20**:4; **22**:26², 27²; **1Ki**
1:17²; **2**:2, 5, 36; **3**:11; **11**:31; **14**:2, 9; **17**:13;
18:1; **20**:40; **21**:20; **2Ki** 5:10; **22**:19; **1Ch**
17:21; **2Ch** 21:15; **25**:19; **34**:27²; **Ne** 9:10;
Job 5:27; **15**:8; **18**:4; **33**:5; **35**:8; **38**:3, 34;
40:7, 8, 10²; **Ps** 10:1; **18**:25², 26²; **37**:4;
44:23; **45**:3; **59**:5; **65**:6; **80**:15, 17; **89**:46;
119:102; **Pr** 6:3², 5; **22**:25; **23**:4; **25**:6; **26**:4;
30:32; **Ecc** 7:16, 22; **Isa** 22:16; **26**:15; **47**:8,
10; **51**:9; **52**:1, 2; **63**:14; **64**:12; **Jer** 1:17;
2:22; **4**:30²; **13**:22; **20**:4; **32**:8; **38**:18, 23;
45:5; **La** 2:18; **3**:43, 44; **5**:21; **Eze** 3:19, 21,
24; **4**:4, 9; **16**:17, 24; **23**:30, 40; **28**:4; **33**:9;
Da 5:17, 22, 23; **9**:15; **10**:12; **Hos** 1:2; **Am**
7:17; **Ob** 1:3; **Mal** 2:15, 16; **Mt** 4:6; **8**:4;
19:19; **21**:21; **22**:39; **27**:40; **Mk** 1:44; **11**:23;
12:31, 33; **14**:30; **15**:30; **Lk** 4:9, 23; **5**:14;
6:42; **7**:6; **10**:27; **12**:20; **17**:8; **23**:37, 39; **Jn**
1:22; **7**:4; **14**:22; **21**:18; **Ac** 5:3; **16**:28;
21:24; **23**:3; **24**:8; **25**:10; **26**:1; **Ro** 2:1, 5,
17, 21; **12**:3²; **13**:9; **14**:22; **Gal** 5:14; **6**:1;
1Ti 4:7, 13, 15, 16; **5**:22; **2Ti** 2:15; **Jas** 2:8.

YOURSELVES (213)

Ge 34:9; **35**:2; **45**:5, 12; **47**:24; **Ex** 18:18;
19:4, 15; **20**:22, 23; **23**:9; **30**:37; **Lev** 11:24,
43², 44², **16**:29, 31; **17**:11; **18**:24, 30; **19**:4,
28; **20**:7, 25; **23**:27, 32; **26**:1; **Nu** 11:18;
15:39; **16**:3, 21; **29**:7; **31**:18, 19; **32**:20; **Dt**
4:9, 15, 16, 23; **7**:17, 25; **9**:16; **10**:19; **14**:1;
18:21; **19**:2, 7; **20**:14; **21**:9; **28**:68; **29**:16;
31:14, 19; **Jos** 2:16; **3**:5; **7**:13, 14; **8**:2;
17:15; **22**:16, 19; **23**:3, 12; **24**:15, 22; **Jdg**
15:12; **1Sa** 2:29; **7**:3²; **8**:17; **10**:19; **16**:5; **2Ki**
11:8; **1Ch** 15:12; **2Ch** 29:5, 31; **35**:4, 6; **Ezr**
10:11; **Ne** 13:25; **Job** 19:5, 29; **27**:12; **42**:8;
Isa 1:16; **26**:20; **29**:9; **43**:22; **48**:2; **50**:11;
58:10; **62**:6; **Jer** 2:17, 28; **4**:4; **7**:21; **25**:7;
26:15; **37**:9; **44**:7², 8²; **47**:5; **49**:14; **Eze**
18:31; **20**:7, 18, 30, 31, 43³; **24**:23; **34**:3;
36:31; **47**:21, 22; **Hos** 10:12; **Am** 3:9; **5**:26;
Mic 1:16; **2**:3; **6**:15; **Na** 2:1; **Hag** 1:4; **Zec**
7:6; **Mt** 3:9; **6**:19, 20; **16**:8; **23**:13, 31; **25**:9;
Mk 6:31; **9**:50; **Lk** 3:8; **11**:46, 52; **12**:11,
33, 57; **13**:28; **16**:9, 15; **17**:3, 14; **21**:14, 30;
23:28; **Jn** 3:28; **6**:43; **15**:8; **18**:31; **Ac** 2:22,
40; **4**:19; **5**:39; **13**:46; **18**:15; **20**:28, 34;
27:21; **Ro** 6:11, 13, 16; **12**:10; **13**:14; **15**:5,
14; **1Co** 3:16, 18; **6**:8; **7**:5; **10**:15; **11**:13;
15:58; **2Co** 3:2; **7**:11², 12; **9**:13; **13**:5²; **Gal**
3:27; **5**:1, 2; **Eph** 2:8; **Php** 1:27; **2**:3; **Col**
3:8, 12; **4**:2; **1Th** 4:9; **2Th** 3:7; **Heb** 10:34;
13:3; **Jas** 1:22; **2**:4; **4**:7, 10; **5**:5; **1Pe** 1:22;
2:1, 13, 18; **4**:1; **5**:5, 6; **1Jn** 5:21; **Jude**
1:20, 21.

BIBLICAL–LANGUAGE
INDEX–LEXICONS

FEATURES OF THE HEBREW TO ENGLISH AND ARAMAIC TO ENGLISH INDEX–LEXICONS

G/K NUMBER	**LEXICAL FORM and TRANSLITERATION**	**FREQUENCY COUNT**
Matches the number at the end of context lines; one- to four-digit numbers are Hebrew, five-digit numbers are Aramaic (see the introduction, pages xii, xv).	See the transliteration and pronunciation table below.	Indicates the total number of occurrences of this Hebrew or Aramaic word in the biblical text (see the introduction, page xv).

10008 אֱדַיִן 'ᵉdayin (57)

NIV WORD and (FREQUENCY COUNT)
NIV words are listed according to their exact textual spelling and are organized according to frequency (see the introduction, page xv).

then (11)

MULTIPLE WORDS / MULTIPLE NUMBERS
More than one NIV word and/or more than one G/K number indicate multiple-word translations (see the introduction, pages xii, xiii, xv).

as soon as (1) +10168+10427

SUPERSCRIPT "S"
Indicates "substitution" translation (see the introduction, pages xiii-xv).

that dayˢ (1)

UNTRANSLATED
Always the final entry, indicates the number of times the NIV did not translate the Hebrew or Aramaic word for stylistic reasons (see the introduction, pages xv, xvi).

untranslated (11)

VARIANT; NOT USED
Notes words of variant spelling and variant readings in the G/K number list that were not used in translating the NIV (see the introduction, pages xv, xvi).

Variant; not used

HEBREW AND ARAMAIC TRANSLITERATION AND PRONUNCIATION TABLE

Hebrew	English	Sound	Hebrew	English	Sound	Vowel	Sound
	Hebrew	*English* . . *Sound*	כ ך	k̲	Bach	ā	father
			ל	l	let	ē	they
א	'	[no sound]	מ ם	m	mother	ō	phone
ב	b	boy	נ ן	n	not	ô	phone
ב	b̲	vote	ס	s	sip	û	tune
ג	g	girl	ע	'	[no sound]	a	father
ג	g̲	girl	פ	p	pot	e	get
ד	d	dog	פ ף	p̲	phone	i	pin, machine
ד	d̲	dog	צ ץ	ṣ	sits	o	phone
ה	h	hot	ק	q	torque	u	sure
ו	w	vote	ר	r	rot	ᵉ	select
ז	z	zip	שׂ	ś	sip		[if vocal]
ח	ḥ	Bach	שׁ	š	ship	ᵃ	baton
ט	ṭ	tip	ת	t	tip	ᵉ	select
י	y	yes	ת	t̲	tip	ᵒ	motel
כ	k	kit					

HEBREW TO ENGLISH INDEX–LEXICON OF THE OLD TESTAMENT

1 א '
Variant; not used

2 אַ - ā' (1)
untranslated (1)

3 אָב 'āḇ (1209)
father (527)
fathers (264)
father's (121)
forefathers (80)
families (57) +1074
families (36)
family (25) +1074
family (14)
forefather (11)
ancestral (9)
them[s] (9) +2257
fathers' (5)
father's (4) +4200
parents (3) +562+2256
ancestor (2)
ancestors (2)
clans (2)
forefathers (2) +3
grandfather's (2)
he[s] (2) +3870
him[s] (2) +2257
parents (2)
clan (1) +1074+5476
clans (1) +1074
family possessions (1)
fatherless (1) +401
forefather's (1)
forefathers (1) +8037
grandfather (1)
group (1) +1074+2755
he[s] (1) +2023
he[s] (1) +3276
him[s] (1) +2023
him[s] (1) +3276
his[s] (1) +2023
his[s] (1) +2257
them[s] (1) +3870
them[s] (1) +4013
they[s] (1) +4013
untranslated (10)

4 אֵב 'ēḇ (2)
growing (1)
new growth (1)

5 אֲבַגְתָא 'aḇagtā' (1)
Abagtha (1)

6 אָבַד 'āḇad (185)
perish (43)
destroy (28)
destroyed (18)
lost (11)
perished (9)
destruction (5)
gone (5)
perishes (4)
perishing (4)
ruined (4)
annihilate (3)
come to nothing (3)
comes to nothing (2)
destroys (2)
lose (2)
wipe out (2)
annihilation (1)
banish (1)
be destroyed (1)
broken (1)
brought ruin (1)
certainly be destroyed (1) +6
come to ruin (1)
corrupts (1)
dead (1)
demolish (1)
destroy completely (1) +6
destroying (1)
die (1)
died (1)
dying (1)
elude (1)
expelled (1)
exterminate (1)
give up (1)
have no (1) +4946
have nowhere (1) +4946
kill (1)
loses (1) +8
not escape (1) +4960
perish (1) +6
ruin (1)
silence (1)
squanders (1)
surely be destroyed (1) +6
swept (1)
vanished (1)
wandering (1)
wiped out (1)
without (1)
untranslated (2)

7 אֹבֵד 'ōḇēd (2)
ruin (2)

8 אֲבֵדָה 'aḇēdāh (4)
lost property (2)
loses (1) +6
lost (1)

9 אֲבַדֹּה 'aḇaddōh (1)
destruction (1)

10 אֲבַדּוֹ 'aḇaddô (1)
untranslated (1)

11 אֲבַדּוֹן 'aḇaddôn (5)
destruction (5)

12 אַבְדָן 'aḇdān (1)
destroying (1)

13 אָבְדָן 'āḇdān (1)
destruction (1)

14 אָבָה 'āḇāh (53)
would (13)
refused (11) +4202
willing (11)
unwilling (7) +4202
accept (2)
refuse (2) +4202
will (2)
agree to demands (1)
consent (1)
submit (1)
would have (1)
yield (1)

15 אֵבֶה 'ēḇeh (1)
papyrus (1)

16 אֲבוֹי 'aḇôy (1)
sorrow (1)

17 אֵבוּס 'ēḇûs (3)
manger (3)

18 אִבְחָה 'iḇḥāh (1)
slaughter (1)

19 אֲבַטִּיחַ 'aḇaṭṭiyaḥ (1)
melons (1)

20 אֲבִי1 'āḇiy1 (1)
oh that (1)

21 אֲבִי2 'āḇiy2
Variant; not used

22 אֲבִי3 'āḇiy3
Variant; not used

23 אֲבִי 'aḇiy (1)
Abijah (1)

24 אֲבִיאֵל 'aḇiy'ēl (3)
Abiel (3)

25 אֲבִיאָסָף 'aḇiy'āsāp (1)
Abiasaph (1)

26 אָבִיב 'āḇiyḇ (8)
Abib (5)

headed (1)
heads (1)
that^s (1)

27 אֲבִיבַעַל *'ᵃbiyba'al*
Variant; not used

28 אֲבִיגַיִל *'ᵃbiygayil* (19)
Abigail (17)
untranslated (2)

29 אֲבִידָן *'ᵃbiydān* (5)
Abidan (5)

30 אֲבִידָע *'ᵃbiydā'* (2)
Abida (2)

31 אֲבִיָּה *'ᵃbiyyāh* (28)
Abijah (25)
Abijah's (3)

32 אֲבִיָּהוּ *'ᵃbiyyāhû* (2)
Abijah (2)

33 אֲבִיהוּא *'ᵃbiyhû'* (12)
Abihu (12)

34 אֲבִיהוּד *'ᵃbiyhûd* (1)
Abihud (1)

35 אֲבִיהַיִל *'ᵃbiyhayil* (2)
Abihail (2)

36 אֶבְיוֹן *'ebyôn* (61)
needy (46)
poor (14)
needy (1) +132

37 אֲבִיּוֹנָה *'ᵃbiyyônāh* (1)
desire (1)

38 אֲבִיחַיִל *'ᵃbiyhayil* (4)
Abihail (4)

39 אֲבִיטוּב *'ᵃbiytûb* (1)
Abitub (1)

40 אֲבִיטָל *'ᵃbiytāl* (2)
Abital (2)

41 אֲבִים *'ᵃbiyyām*
Variant; not used

42 אֲבִימָאֵל *'ᵃbiymā'ēl* (2)
Abimael (2)

43 אֲבִימֶלֶךְ *'ᵃbiymelek* (66)
Abimelech (60)
Abimelech's (2)
he^s (1)
him^s (1)
his^s (1)

44 אֲבִינָדָב *'ᵃbiynādāb* (12)
Abinadab (9)
Abinadab's (2)
untranslated (1)

45 אֲבִינֹעַם *'ᵃbiynō'am* (4)
Abinoam (4)

46 אֲבִינֵר *'ᵃbiynēr* (1)
Abner (1)

47 אֶבְיָסָף *'ebyāsāp* (3)
Ebiasaph (3)

48 אֲבִיעֶזֶר *'ᵃbiy'ezer* (7)
Abiezer (6)
Abiezrites (1)

49 אֲבִי עֶזְרִי *'ᵃbiy 'ezriy* (3)
Abiezrites (2)
Abiezrite (1)

50 אֲבִי־עַלְבּוֹן *'ᵃbiy-'albôn* (1)
Abi-Albon (1)

51 אָבִיר *'ābiyr* (6)
mighty one (6)

52 אַבִּיר *'abbiyr* (17)
mighty (4)
bulls (2)

stallions (2)
warriors (2)
angels (1)
great (1)
head (1)
steeds (1)
strong (1)
stubborn-hearted (1) +4213
valiant men (1) +4213

53 אֲבִירָם *'ᵃbiyrām* (11)
Abiram (11)

54 אֲבִישַׁג *'ᵃbiyšag* (5)
Abishag (5)

55 אֲבִישׁוּעַ *'ᵃbiyšûa'* (5)
Abishua (5)

56 אֲבִישׁוּר *'ᵃbiyšûr* (2)
Abishur (1)
Abishur's (1)

57 אֲבִישַׁי *'ᵃbiyšay* (19)
Abishai (19)

58 אֲבִישָׁלוֹם *'ᵃbiyšālôm* (2)
Abishalom (2)

59 אֶבְיָתָר *'ebyātār* (30)
Abiathar (28)
he^s (1)
them^s (1) +2256+7401

60 אָבָךְ *'ābak* (1)
rolls upward (1)

61 אָבַל1 *'ābal1* (32)
mourn (11)
mourned (9)
mourns (4)
mourning (2)
grieve (1)
grieving (1)
in mourning (1)
lament (1)
made lament (1)
pretend in mourning (1)

62 אָבַל2 *'ābal2* (7)
parched (3)
dries up (2)
dried up (1)
dry up (1)

63 אָבֵל1 *'ābēl1* (8)
mourn (2)
mourners (2)
grief (1)
grieve (1)
mourning (1)
weeping (1)

64 אָבֵל2 *'ābēl2* (1)
Abel (1)

65 אֵבֶל *'ēbel* (24)
mourning (15)
mourn (2)
ceremony of mourning (1)
moan (1)
mourn (1) +6913
period of mourning (1)
sorrow (1)
time of mourning (1)
weep (1)

66 אֲבָל *'ᵃbāl* (11)
but (3)
however (2)
indeed (1)
not at all (1)
now (1)
surely (1)
well (1)
yes but (1)

67 אֻבָל *'ubāl* (3)
canal (3)

68 אָבֵל בֵּית מַעֲכָה *'ābēl bēyt ma'ᵃkāh* (4)
Abel Beth Maacah (4)

69 אָבֵל הַשִּׁטִּים *'ābēl haššittiym* (1)
Abel Shittim (1)

70 אָבֵל כְּרָמִים *'ābēl kᵉrāmiym* (1)
Abel Keramim (1)

71 אָבֵל מְחוֹלָה *'ābēl mᵉhôlāh* (3)
Abel Meholah (3)

72 אָבֵל מַיִם *'ābēl mayim* (1)
Abel Maim (1)

73 אָבֵל מִצְרַיִם *'ābēl misrayim* (1)
Abel Mizraim (1)

74 אֶבֶן *'eben* (273)
stone (93)
stones (89)
rock (8)
rocks (7)
stone (5) +928+2021+8083
weights (5)
gems (4)
stoned (4) +8083
hailstones (3) +453
slingstones (3) +7845
blocks (2)
differing weights (2) +74+2256
onyx (2) +8732
ore (2)
sapphire (2) +6209
some^s (2)
stone (2) +928+2021+6232
stoned (2) +928+2021+6232
another^s (1)
capstone (1) +8036
charm (1) +2834
chrysolite (1) +9577
cornerstone (1) +7157
cover (1)
fieldstones (1) +8969
gem (1)
hail (1) +1352
hailstones (1)
hailstones (1) +1352
jewels (1)
marble (1) +8880
masons (1) +3093
plumb line (1)
plumb line (1) +974
sling stones (1) +928+2021
sparkling jewels (1) +734
standard (1)
stone (1) +8083
stonecutters (1) +2935
stoned (1) +928+2021+8083
stoned to death (1) +8083
stonemasons (1) +3093+7815
stoning (1) +928+2021+8083
them (1) +928+2021+4392
them^s (1)
them^s (1) +2021+9109
these^s (1) +2021
two differing weights (1) +74+2256
untranslated (4)

75 אֶבֶן הָעֵזֶר *'eben hā'ēzer* (3)
Ebenezer (3)

76 אֲבָנָה *'ᵃbānāh* (1)
Abana (1)

77 אַבְנֵט *'abnēt* (9)
sash (6)
sashes (3)

78 אָבְנַיִם *'obnayim* (2)
delivery stool (1)
wheel (1)

79 אַבְנֵר *'abnēr* (62)
Abner (55)
Abner's (3)
him^s (2)

heˢ (1)
untranslated (1)

80 אָבַס *'ābas* (2)
choice (1)
fattened (1)

81 אֲבַעְבֻּעֹת *'ᵃba'bu'ōṯ* (2)
festering (2)

82 אֶבֶץ *'ebeṣ* (1)
Ebez (1)

83 אִבְצָן *'ibṣān* (2)
Ibzan (2)

84 אָבַק *'ābaq* (2)
wrestled (2)

85 אָבָק *'ābāq* (6)
dust (4)
fine dust (1)
powder (1)

86 אֲבָקָה *'ᵃbāqāh* (1)
spices (1)

87 אָבַר *'ābar* (1)
take flight (1)

88 אֵבֶר *'ēber* (3)
wings (2)
feathers (1)

89 אֶבְרָה *'ebrāh* (4)
feathers (2)
pinions (2)

90 אַבְרָהָם *'abrāhām* (175)
Abraham (153)
Abraham's (11)
heˢ (6)
himˢ (2)
hisˢ (1)
hisˢ (1) +4200
untranslated (1)

91 אַבְרֵךְ *'abrēk* (1)
make way (1)

92 אַבְרָם *'abrām* (61)
Abram (50)
Abram's (5)
himˢ (3)
heˢ (1)
hisˢ (1)
untranslated (1)

93 אַבְשַׁי *'abšay* (6)
Abishai (6)

94 אַבְשָׁלוֹם *'abšālôm* (109)
Absalom (88)
Absalom's (10)
heˢ (6)
himˢ (2)
Absalom's (1) +4200
untranslated (2)

95 אֹבֹת *'ōbōṯ* (4)
Oboth (4)

96 אָגֵא *'āgē'* (1)
Agee (1)

97 אֲגַג *'ᵃgag* (8)
Agag (7)
untranslated (1)

98 אֲגָגִי *'ᵃgāgiy* (5)
Agagite (5)

99 אֲגֻדָּה *'ᵃguddāh* (4)
bunch (1)
cords (1)
foundation (1)
group (1)

100 אֱגוֹז *'ᵉgôz* (1)
nut trees (1)

101 אָגוּר *'āgûr* (1)
Agur (1)

102 אֲגוֹרָה *'ᵃgôrāh* (1)
piece (1)

103 אֶגֶל *'ēgel* (1)
drops (1)

104 אֶגְלַיִם *'eglayim* (1)
Eglaim (1)

105 אֲגַם *'ᵃgam*
Variant; not used

106 אֲגַם1 *'ᵃgam1* (9)
pools (3)
ponds (2)
marshes (1)
pool (1)
pool (1) +4784
swampland (1) +4784

107 אֲגַם2 *'ᵃgam2*
Variant; not used

108 אָגֵם *'āgēm* (1)
sick (1)

109 אַגְמוֹן *'agmôn* (5)
reed (3)
cord (1)
reeds (1)

110 אַגָּן *'aggān* (3)
bowls (2)
goblet (1)

111 אֲגַף *'ᵃgap* (7)
troops (7)

112 אָגַר *'āgar* (3)
gather grapes (1)
gathers (1)
gathers crops (1)

113 אֲגַרְטָל *'ᵃgarṭāl* (2)
dishes (2)

114 אֶגְרֹף *'egrōp* (2)
fist (1)
fists (1)

115 אִגֶּרֶת *'iggereṯ* (10)
letters (6)
letter (4)

116 אֵד *'ēd* (2)
streams (2)

117 אָדַב *'ādab* (1)
grieve (1)

118 אַדְבְּאֵל *'adbᵉ'ēl* (2)
Adbeel (2)

119 אֲדַר *'ᵃdad* (1)
Hadad (1)

120 אִדּוֹ *'iddô* (2)
Iddo (2)

121 אֱדוֹם *'ᵉdôm* (104)
Edom (79)
Edom (11) +824
Edomites (10)
Edom's (2)
Edomites (1) +1201
untranslated (1)

122 אֱדוֹמִי *'ᵉdômiy* (12)
Edomite (8)
Edomites (4)

123 אָדוֹן *'ādôn* (332)
lord (142)
master (105)
master's (28)
Lord (17)
lords (5)
lord's (4) +4200
masters (4)
sir (3)

youˢ (3) +3276
lord's (2)
sovereign (2)
fellow officers (1) +6269
gods (1)
heˢ (1) +3276
herˢ (1) +851+2257
himˢ (1) +3276
husbands (1)
owner (1)
supervisors (1)
the Lord (1)
yourˢ (1) +3276
untranslated (7)

124 אַדּוֹן *'addôn* (1)
Addon (1)

125 אֲדוֹנִיָּה *'ᵃdôniyyāh*
Variant; not used

126 אֲדוֹרַיִם *'ᵃdôrayim* (1)
Adoraim (1)

127 אֲדוֹרָם *'ᵃdôrām*
Variant; not used

128 אֹדוֹת *'ōdôṯ* (11)
because of (4) +6584
about (3) +6584
concerned (1)
for sake (1) +6584
untranslated (2)

129 אַדִּיר *'addiyr* (27)
nobles (7)
mighty (6)
leaders (3)
majestic (3)
mighty one (2)
glorious (1)
leader (1)
mightier (1)
picked troops (1)
splendid (1)
stately (1)

130 אֲדַלְיָא *'ᵃdalyā'* (1)
Adalia (1)

131 אָדֵם *'ādēm* (10)
dyed red (6)
red (3)
ruddy (1)

132 אָדָם1 *'ādām1* (549)
man (278)
men (82)
men (23) +1201
people (20)
human (13)
man's (13)
one (13)
man (10) +1201
mankind (10)
anyone (9)
mankind (6) +1201
person (5)
men's (3)
persons (3)
someone (3)
body (2)
everyone (2)
man's (2) +1201
man's (2) +4200
mortal men (2) +1201
all mankind (1) +1201
all men (1) +1201+2021
anotherˢ (1) +2021
any (1)
anyone (1) +3972
charioteers (1) +8207
deserted (1) +401+4946
elseˢ (1)
every (1)
everyone (1) +2021+3972

everyone (1) +3972
giver^s (1)
he^s (1)
him^s (1) +2021
his^s (1)
his^s (1) +2021
human (1) +1201
human being (1)
low (1) +1201
low among men (1) +1201
lowborn men (1) +1201
man-made (1) +3338+5126
men (1) +1201+2021
mortals (1)
natural (1) +2021+3869+3972
needy (1) +36
nobody (1) +4202
other^s (1)
others^s (1)
people (1) +1201
people (1) +5883
rabble (1) +8044
reflects the man (1) +2021+4200
scoundrel (1) +1175
slaves (1) +5883
son (1)
successor (1) +339+995+8611
they^s (1) +2021
those^s (1)
whoever (1) +2021+3972
untranslated (8)

133 אָדָם2 'ādām2
Variant; not used

134 אָדָם3 'ādām3 (12)
Adam (11)
Adam's (1)

135 אָדָם4 'ādām4
Variant; not used

136 אָדָם5 'ādām5 (2)
Adam (1)
untranslated (1)

137 אָדֹם 'ādōm (9)
red (7)
ruddy (1)
untranslated (1)

138 אֹדֶם 'ōdem (3)
ruby (3)

139 אֲדֹם 'ᵃdōm
Variant; not used

140 אֲדַמְדָם 'ᵃdamdām (6)
reddish-white (4) +4237
reddish (2)

141 אֲדָמָה1 'ᵃdāmāh1 (226)
land (120)
ground (42)
earth (30)
soil (11)
dust (4)
lands (3)
clay (2)
country (2)
crops (2)
fields (2)
native land (2)
below (1) +2021+6584
crops (1) +2021+7262
farmer (1) +408+6268
her^s (1) +3776
home (1)
homeland (1)

142 אֲדָמָה2 'ᵃdāmāh2 (1)
Adamah (1)

143 אֲדָמָה3 'ᵃdāmāh3
Variant; not used

144 אַדְמָה 'admāh (5)

Admah (5)

145 אַדְמוֹנִי 'admôniy (3)
ruddy (2)
red (1)

146 אַדְמִי הַנֶּקֶב 'ᵃdāmiy hanneqeb (1)
Adami Nekeb (1)

147 אֲדֻמִּים 'ᵃdummiym (2)
Adummim (2)

148 אַדְמָתָא 'admātā' (1)
Admatha (1)

149 אֶדֶן 'eden (58)
bases (41)
base (2)
footings (1)
those^s (1)
untranslated (13)

150 אַדָּן 'addān (1)
Addon (1)

151 אֲדֹנָי 'ᵃdōnāy (442)
sovereign (291)
the Lord (91)
Lord (57)
the Lord's (3)

152 אֲדֹנִי בֶזֶק 'ᵃdōniy bezeq (3)
Adoni-Bezek (3)

153 אֲדֹנִיָּה 'ᵃdōniyyāh (7)
Adonijah (7)

154 אֲדֹנִיָּהוּ 'ᵃdōniyyāhû (19)
Adonijah (17)
Adonijah's (1) +4200
untranslated (1)

155 אֲדֹנִי־צֶדֶק 'ᵃdōniy-ṣedeq (2)
Adoni-Zedek (2)

156 אֲדֹנִיקָם 'ᵃdōniyqām (3)
Adonikam (3)

157 אֲדֹנִירָם 'ᵃdōniyrām (4)
Adoniram (4)

158 אָדַר 'ādar (3)
majestic (2)
glorious (1)

159 אֶדֶר 'eder (2)
handsome (1)
rich (1)

160 אֲדָר 'ᵃdār (8)
Adar (8)

161 אַדָּר1 'addār1 (1)
Addar (1)

162 אַדָּר2 'addār2 (1)
Addar (1)

163 אֲדַרְכֹנִים 'ᵃdarkōniym (2)
darics (2)

164 אַדְרָם 'ᵃdōrām
Variant; not used

165 אַדְרַמֶּלֶךְ1 'adrammelek1 (1)
Adrammelech (1)

166 אַדְרַמֶּלֶךְ2 'adrammelek2 (2)
Adrammelech (2)

167 אֶדְרֶעִי 'edre'iy (8)
Edrei (8)

168 אַדֶּרֶת 'adderet (12)
cloak (5)
robe (2)
garment (1)
prophet's garment (1)
rich pastures (1)
royal robes (1)
splendid (1)

169 אָדַשׁ 'ādaš
Variant; not used

170 אָהַב 'āhab (217)
love (93)
loves (38)
loved (33)
lovers (12)
friends (8)
allies (4)
friend (4)
in love with (3)
fell in love with (2)
like (2)
liked (2)
adore (1)
attracted to (1)
both^s (1) +2021+2021+2256+8533
chosen ally (1)
dearly (1)
desires (1)
likes (1)
on friendly terms (1)
resents (1) +4202
show love (1)
showed love (1)
value (1)
was loved (1)
were loved (1)
untranslated (2)

171 אֹהַב 'ōhab (2)
love (1)
thing loved (1)

172 אָהֵב 'ahab (2)
lovers (1)
loving (1)

173 אַהֲבָה1 'ahᵃbāh1 (33)
love (26)
friendship (2)
loved (2)
lovingly (1)
that^s (1)
untranslated (1)

174 אַהֲבָה2 'ahᵃbāh2
Variant; not used

175 אֲהַבְהַבִי 'ᵃhabhābay
Variant; not used

176 אֹהַד 'ōhad (2)
Ohad (2)

177 אֲהָהּ 'ᵃhāh (15)
Ah (9)
oh (3)
Alas (1)
not so (1)
what (1)

178 אַהֲוָא 'ahᵃwā' (3)
Ahava (3)

179 אֵהוּד 'ēhûd (9)
Ehud (8)
untranslated (1)

180 אֱהִי 'ᵉhiy (3)
where (2)
where (1) +686

181 אֶהְיֶה 'ehyeh
Variant; not used

182 אָהַל1 'āhal1 (3)
moved tents (1)
pitch tent (1)
pitched tents (1)

183 אָהַל2 'āhal2 (1)
bright (1)

184 אֹהֶל 'āhāl
Variant; not used

185 אֹהֶל1 'ōhel1 (351)
tent (260)
tents (45)
home (10)

homes (9)
dwellings (3)
it[s] (3) +2021
house (2)
tabernacle (2)
another[s] (1)
broke camp (1) +4946+5825
camps (1)
house (1) +1074
household (1)
nomads (1) +928+8905
sanctuary (1)
tent site (1)
tent-dwelling (1) +928+2021
untranslated (8)

186 2אֹהֶל *'ōhel2* (1)
Ohel (1)

187 אֶהֶל *'ēhel*
Variant; not used

188 אָהֳלָה *'oh°lāh* (5)
Oholah (5)

189 אֲהָלוֹת *'°hālôt* (2)
aloes (2)

190 אָהֳלִיאָב *'oh°liy'āb* (5)
Oholiab (5)

191 אָהֳלִיבָה *'oh°liybāh* (6)
Oholibah (6)

192 אָהֳלִיבָמָה *'oh°liybāmāh* (8)
Oholibamah (8)

193 1אֲהָלִים *'°hāliym1* (2)
aloes (2)

194 2אֲהָלִים *'°hāliym2*
Variant; not used

195 אַהֲרוֹן *'ah°rôn* (347)
Aaron (300)
Aaron's (31)
he[s] (5)
his[s] (3)
Aaron's (1) +4200
Aaronic (1) +1201
family of Aaron (1)
him[s] (1)
untranslated (4)

196 או *'ô* (320)
or (247)
whether or (13)
either or (4)
if (3)
when (3)
whether (3)
and (2)
also (1)
at all (1) +1524+7785
either (1)
if (1) +4537
nor (1)
or else (1)
or so (1)
over a year (1) +2296+2296+3427+9102
rather than (1)
which way (1) +3545+6584+6584+8520
untranslated (35)

197 או *'aw* (1)
crave (1)

198 אוּאֵל *'û'ēl* (1)
Uel (1)

199 1אוֹב *'ôb1* (1)
wineskins (1)

200 2אוֹב *'ôb2* (16)
mediums (9)
medium (2)
ghostlike (1) +3869
medium (1) +1266
medium (1) +8626

one[s] (1) +1266
spirit (1)

201 אוֹבִיל *'ôbiyl* (1)
Obil (1)

202 אוּד *'ûd* (3)
burning stick (2)
firewood (1)

203 1אָנָה *'āwāh1* (29)
crave (4)
desired (3)
desires (3)
craves (2)
longed for (2)
crave other food (1) +9294
craved other food (1)
craves for more (1) +9294
desire (1)
enthralled (1)
gave in to craving (1) +9294
like (1)
long for (1)
pleases (1)
set desire on (1)
want (1)
yearns for (1)
untranslated (3)

204 2אָנָה *'āwāh2* (1)
run a line (1)

205 אַוָּה *'awwāh* (7)
want (3)
craving (1) +5883
earnestness (1) +5883
please (1)
pleases (1)

206 אוּזַי *'ûzay* (1)
Uzai (1)

207 אוּזָל *'ûzāl* (3)
Uzal (3)

208 אוֹי *'ôy* (24)
woe (19)
Alas (2)
Ah (1)
alas (1)
in trouble (1)

209 אֱוִי *'°wiy* (2)
Evi (2)

210 אוֹיָה *'ôyāh* (1)
woe (1)

211 1אֱוִיל *'°wiyl1* (25)
fool (16)
fools (7)
fool's (1)
wicked fools (1)

212 2אֱוִיל *'°wiyl2*
Variant; not used

213 אֱוִיל מְרֹדַךְ *'°wiyl mrōdak* (2)
Evil-Merodach (2)

214 1אוּל *'ûl1* (1)
bodies (1)

215 2אוּל *'ûl2* (1)
untranslated (1)

216 אֱוִלִי *'°wiliy* (1)
foolish (1)

217 1אוּלַי *'ûlay1* (2)
Ulai (2)

218 2אוּלַי *'ûlay2* (45)
perhaps (25)
what if (9)
it may be (3)
maybe (3)
but (1)
but perhaps (1)

if not (1)
may yet (1)
were it to (1)

219 1אוּלָם *'ûlām1* (19)
but (5) +2256
but (4)
nevertheless (2) +2256
though (2)
but if (1)
however (1) +2256
if (1)
otherwise (1)
yet (1)
untranslated (1)

220 2אוּלָם *'ûlām2* (4)
Ulam (4)

221 3אוּלָם *'ûlām3*
Variant; not used

222 אִוֶּלֶת *'iwwelet* (25)
folly (22)
foolish (2)
sinful folly (1)

223 אוֹמָר *'ômār* (3)
Omar (3)

224 אָוֶן *'āwen* (77)
evil (23)
evildoers (16) +7188
wicked (6)
sin (3)
wrong (3)
calamity (1)
deceit (1)
disaster (1)
distress (1)
evildoer (1) +7188
false (1)
hardship (1)
harm (1)
idol (1)
iniquity (1)
injustice (1)
malice (1)
malicious (1)
misfortune (1)
nothing (1)
on no account (1) +6584
punishment (1)
sins (1)
slander (1)
sorrow (1)
suffering (1)
trouble (1)
unjust (1)
villain (1) +408
wicked men (1) +7188
wickedness (1)

225 2אָוֶן *'āwen2* (2)
Aven (1)
Heliopolis (1)

226 1אוֹן *'ôn1* (12)
power (3)
manhood (2)
man (1)
sign of strength (1)
strength (1)
vigor (1)
weak (1) +401
wealth (1)
wealthy (1)

227 2אוֹן *'ôn2* (1)
on (1)

228 3אוֹן *'ôn3* (3)
on (3)

229 אוֹנוֹ *'ônô* (5)
Ono (5)

230 אוֹנִי 'ôniy (1)
mourners (1)

231 אוֹנָם 'ônām (4)
Onam (4)

232 אוֹנָן 'ônān (8)
Onan (7)
untranslated (1)

233 אוּפָז 'ûpāz (2)
finest gold (1) +4188
Uphaz (1)

234 1אוֹפִיר 'ôpiyr1 (13)
Ophir (11)
gold of Ophir (1)
there^s (1)

235 2אוֹפִיר 'ôpiyr2
Variant; not used

236 אוֹפָן 'ôpan (35)
wheels (23)
wheel (8)
cartwheel (1) +6322
untranslated (3)

237 אוּץ 'ûs (10)
delayed (1) +4202
eager (1)
haste (1)
hasty (1) +928+8079
in haste (1)
pressing (1)
run (1)
small (1)
try (1)
urged (1)

238 אוֹצָר 'ôsār (79)
treasures (22)
treasuries (20)
storehouses (9)
treasury (7)
riches (2)
storehouse (2)
supplies (2)
treasure (2)
arsenal (1)
fortune (1)
put in charge of the storerooms (1)
　　　　　　　　　　　　+732+6584
storehouse (1) +1074
storerooms (1)
storerooms (1) +4200+5969
stores (1)
treasury (1) +1074
vats (1)
vaults (1)
wealth (1)
untranslated (2)

239 1אוֹר 'ôr1 (45)
shine (8)
give light (6)
make shine (6)
light (4)
brightened (2)
gives light (2)
brightens (1)
dawned (1)
daybreak (1)
give light (1) +240
gives sight (1)
giving light (1)
keep burning (1)
leaves glistening (1)
light fires (1)
lights up (1)
lit up (1)
look with favor (1) +7156
made light shine (1)
make fires (1)
radiant (1)
resplendent with light (1)

shining ever brighter (1) +2143+2256

240 2אוֹר 'ôr2 (119)
light (83)
lightning (7)
daybreak (3) +1332+2021
daylight (3)
dawn (2) +1332+2021
shining (2)
sun (2)
brightens (1)
broad daylight (1) +3427
dawn (1)
daybreak (1)
daylight (1) +1332+2021
give light (1) +239
gleam (1)
glint (1)
lamp (1)
light of day (1)
lights (1)
new day (1)
shine (1) +2118
sunlight (1) +2780
sunrise (1)
sunshine (1)
untranslated (1)

241 1אוּר 'ûr1 (6)
fire (4)
east (1)
light (1)

242 2אוּר 'ûr2 (7)
Urim (7)

243 3אוּר 'ûr3 (4)
Ur (4)

244 4אוּר 'ûr4 (1)
Ur (1)

245 1אוֹרָה 'ôrāh1 (3)
light (1)
morning (1)
time of happiness (1)

246 2אוֹרָה 'ôrāh2 (1)
herbs (1)

247 אוּרִי 'ûriy (7)
Uri (7)

248 אוּרִיאֵל 'ûriy'ēl (4)
Uriel (4)

249 אוּרִיָּה 'ûriyyāh (36)
Uriah (29)
him^s (3)
Uriah's (2)
untranslated (2)

250 אוּרִיָּהוּ 'ûriyyāhû (3)
Uriah (3)

251 אוּרִים 'ûriym
Variant; not used

252 אוּת 'ût (4)
give consent (2)
agreed (1)
consent (1)

253 1אוֹת 'ôt1 (79)
sign (36)
miraculous signs (17)
signs (14)
miraculous sign (3)
symbols (2)
accounts (1)
banners (1)
example (1)
mark (1)
standards (1)
wonders (1)
untranslated (1)

254 2אוֹת 'ôt2
Variant; not used

255 אָז 'āz (141)
then (65)
at that time (11)
and (5)
long ago (5) +4946
ever since (2) +4946
now (2)
since (2) +4946
so (2)
time (2)
about this time (1)
after (1)
already (1)
already (1) +4946
and (1) +2256
distant past (1)
from (1) +4946
meanwhile (1)
now (1) +4946
of old (1)
old (1)
once (1)
past (1)
that will mean (1)
thus (1)
when (1) +4946
untranslated (29)

256 אֶזְבַּי 'ezbāy (1)
Ezbai (1)

257 אֵזוֹב 'ēzôb (10)
hyssop (10)

258 אֵזוֹר 'ēzôr (14)
belt (9)
belt (1) +5516
belts (1) +2513
it^s (1) +2021
loincloth (1)
sash (1)

259 אֲזַי 'azay (3)
untranslated (3)

260 אַזְכָּרָה 'azkārāh (7)
memorial portion (6)
memorial offering (1)

261 אָזַל 'āzal (5)
gone (2)
disappears (1)
go about (1)
off goes (1)

262 אֶזֶל 'ezel (1)
Ezel (1)

263 1אָזַן 'āzan1 (41)
listen (19)
hear (11)
pay attention (3)
give ear (2)
ear perceived (1)
give a hearing (1) +7754
listened (1)
paid attention (1)
pays attention (1)
turned a deaf ear (1) +4202

264 2אָזַן 'āzan2 (1)
pondered (1)

265 אֹזֶן 'ōzen (188)
ears (58)
ear (25)
hearing (24)
to (19) +928
pay attention (7) +5742
give ear (6) +5742
heard (3) +928
before (2) +928
let know (2) +906+1655
listen (2) +5742
revealed (2) +1655
tells (2) +906+1655

they[s] (2)
bring to attention (1) +1655
confiding in (1) +906+1655
ear lobe (1)
hear (1) +5742
heard (1)
heard (1) +606+928
in person (1) +928
listen (1) +7992
listen carefully (1) +928+9048
listen closely (1) +928+9048
listen closely (1) +5742
listen well (1) +5742
listened (1) +928
listened attentively to (1) +448
listens (1) +9048
make sure hears (1) +928+8492
makes listen (1) +1655
news (1) +2245
paid any attention (1) +4200+5742+9048
paid attention (1) +5742
revealed (1) +906+1655
speaks (1) +1655
tell (1) +906+1655
tell (1) +928+1819
told (1) +928+1819
wearing (1) +928
whoever[s] (1)
untranslated (7)

266 אֹזֶן 'ōzēn (1)
equipment (1)

267 אֹזֶן שֶׁאֱרָה 'uzzēn še''rāh (1)
Uzzen Sheerah (1)

268 אַזְנוֹת תָּבוֹר 'aznôt tābôr (1)
Aznoth Tabor (1)

269 אָזְנִי 'āzniy1 (1)
Ozni (1)

270 אָזְנִי 'āzniy2 (1)
Oznite (1)

271 אֲזַנְיָה 'ªzanyāh (1)
Azaniah (1)

272 אֲזִקִּים 'ªziqqiym (2)
chains (2)

273 אָזַר 'āzar (17)
armed (4)
arms (2)
brace (2) +2743
prepare for battle (2)
armed yourself (1)
binds (1)
clothed (1)
get ready (1) +5516
provide (1)
strengthen (1)
untranslated (1)

274 אֶזְרוֹעַ 'ezrôa' (2)
arm (1)
it[s] (1) +3276

275 אֶזְרָח 'ezrāh (17)
native-born (12)
born (1)
citizens (1)
native soil (1)
native-born (1) +824
native-born (1) +824+2021

276 אֶזְרָחִי 'ezrāhiy (3)
Ezrahite (3)

277 אָח 'āh1 (2)
Alas (1)
oh (1)

278 אָח 'āh2 (632)
brother (211)
brothers (201)
relatives (67)
fellow (19)

associates (17)
brother's (17)
other[s] (15)
countrymen (10)
another[s] (7)
fellow countrymen (5)
kinsmen (5)
relative (5)
family (3)
people (3)
brother Israelite (2)
countryman (2)
cousins (2)
friends (2)
he[s] (2) +3870
nephew (2) +1201
others[s] (2)
among yourselves (1) +408+448
anyone else[s] (1)
associate (1)
brother Israelites (1)
brotherhood (1)
brothers (1) +562
companions (1)
each (1) +408+2257
equally (1) +408+2257+3869
equally among them (1) +408+2257+3869
families (1)
fellow Jews (1)
fellow Levites (1)
him[s] (1) +3870
people from Benjamin (1) +2157
people from Judah (1) +2157
priests[s] (1) +2157
them[s] (1)
them[s] (1) +2257
two men (1) +408+2256+3481
uncle (1)
uncle's (1) +562
very own brother (1) +562+1201+3870
untranslated (10)

279 אָח 'ah (3)
firepot (2)
untranslated (1)

280 אֹחַ 'ōah (1)
jackals (1)

281 אַחְאָב 'ah'āb (92)
Ahab (79)
Ahab's (7)
he[s] (3)
he[s] (1) +1201+6687
untranslated (2)

282 אֶחָב 'ehāb (1)
Ahab (1)

283 אַחְבָּן 'ahbān (1)
Ahban (1)

284 אָחַד 'āhad
Variant; not used

285 אֶחָד 'ehād (976)
one (466)
a (78)
each (58)
first (39)
same (32)
other[s] (27)
any (16)
single (13)
another[s] (12)
eleven (6) +6926
once (6)
the (6)
certain (5)
an (4)
eleventh (4) +6926
forty-one (4) +752+2256
man[s] (4)
only (4)
twenty-first (4) +2256+6929

twenty-one (4) +2256+6929
unit (4)
any (3) +3972
common (3)
eleven (3) +6925
next (3)
once (3) +7193
one and the same (3)
some (3)
thirty-one (3) +2256+8993
together (3) +285+448
41,500 (2)
      +547+752+2256+2256+2822+4395
621 (2) +2256+4395+6929+9252
agree (2) +2118+3869
alike (2)
all (2)
identical (2)
numbered (2) +3869
second (2)
the other[s] (2)
unique (2)
yearly (2) +928+9102
151,450 (1)   +547+547+752+2256+2256
      +2256+2256+2822+2822+4395+4395
61 (1) +2256+9252
61,000 (1) +547+2256+9252
721 (1) +2256+2256+4395+6929+8679
all (1) +928
all the same (1)
all together (1) +408+3869
alone (1) +928
annual (1) +928+2021+9102
another (1)
appointed (1)
back and forth (1) +285+2178+2178+2256
daily (1) +3427+4200
did the same[s] (1) +285+448+2489
each one (1)
equally (1) +3869
fellow[s] (1)
few (1)
for a while (1) +3427
forty-first (1) +752+2256
in unison (1) +3869
joined together (1) +3869+6641
none (1) +4202
once for all (1)
one time (1)
one way (1) +928
one-tenth (1) +6928
only a few (1)
over here (1) +4200+6298
over there (1) +4200+6298
same one (1)
shoulder to shoulder (1) +8900
singleness (1)
some other[s] (1)
someone (1)
someone (1) +2021+6639
suddenly (1) +928
third[s] (1)
thirty-first (1) +2256+8993
time and again (1) +2256+4202+4202+9109
together (1) +3869
undivided (1)
unheard-of (1)
unity (1)
whatever[s] (1)
wherever (1) +889+928+2021+5226
whose[s] (1) +2021+2021+9108
untranslated (81)

286 אָחוּ 'āhû (3)
reeds (3)

287 אֵחוּד 'ēhûd (1)
Ehud (1)

288 אַחֲוָה 'ah°wāh1 (1)
brotherhood (1)

289 אַחֲוָה 'ah°wāh2 (1)
what say (1)

290 אָחֻז 'āḥuz
Variant; not used

291 אֲחוֹחַ 'aḥôaḥ (1)
Ahoah (1)

292 אֲחוֹחִי 'aḥôḥiy (5)
Ahohite (4)
Ahohite (1) +1201

293 אֲחוּמַי 'aḥûmay (1)
Ahumai (1)

294 אָחוֹר 'āḥôr (41)
back (14)
backs (2)
backward (2)
behind (2)
hindquarters (2)
rear (2)
west (2)
away (1)
backsliding (1)
backward (1) +4200
behind (1) +4946
deserted (1) +6047
drawn back (1) +6047
future (1)
is driven back (1) +6047
made retreat (1) +8740
on both sides (1) +2256+7156
overthrows (1) +8740
retreating (1) +6047
time to come (1)
under control (1) +928
withdrawn (1) +8740

295 אָחוֹת 'āḥôt (119)
sister (88)
sisters (11)
other⁵ (4)
sister's (4)
together (2) +448+851
another⁵ (1)
untranslated (9)

296 1אָחַז 'āḥaz1 (65)
seized (9)
grip (4)
seizes (3)
caught (2)
grips (2)
hold (2)
seize (2)
supports (2)
take (2)
took (2)
took hold (2)
accept possession (1)
acquire property (1)
acquired (1)
acquired property (1)
are caught (1)
are taken (1)
bar (1)
being taken (1)
catch (1)
clinging (1)
closely followed (1)
did so⁵ (1)
embracing (1)
fastened (1)
grasp (1)
grasping (1)
grasps (1)
handle (1)
held (1)
hold fast (1)
hold out (1)
in (1)
inserted (1)
kept from closing (1) +9073
see (1)
share (1)

steady (1)
take hold (1)
take on (1)
wearing (1)
untranslated (3)

297 2אָחַז 'āḥaz2 (3)
attached to (1)
covers (1)
was attached (1)

298 אָחָז 'āḥāz (42)
Ahaz (41)
untranslated (1)

299 אֲחֻזָּה 'aḥuzzāh (66)
property (28)
possession (14)
land (4) +824
possess (4)
family land (3) +8441
place (2)
site (2)
family property (1)
hold (1)
hold as a possession (1)
lands (1)
occupied (1)
property (1) +824
territory (1)
that⁵ (1)
untranslated (1)

300 אַחְזַי 'aḥzay (1)
Ahzai (1)

301 אֲחַזְיָה 'aḥazyāh (7)
Ahaziah (7)

302 אֲחַזְיָהוּ 'aḥazyāhû (31)
Ahaziah (27)
Ahaziah's (4)

303 אֲחֻזָּם 'aḥuzzām (1)
Ahuzzam (1)

304 אֲחֻזַּת 'aḥuzzat (1)
Ahuzzath (1)

305 אֵחִי 'eḥiy (1)
Ehi (1)

306 אֲחִי 'aḥiy (2)
Ahi (2)

307 אֲחִיאָם 'aḥiy'ām (2)
Ahiam (2)

308 אֲחִיָּה 'aḥiyyāh (18)
Ahijah (16)
Ahiah (1)
Ahijah's (1)

309 אֲחִיָּהוּ 'aḥiyyāhû (5)
Ahijah (5)

310 אֲחִיהוּד 'aḥiyhûd (1)
Ahihud (1)

311 אַחְיוֹ 'aḥyô (6)
Ahio (6)

312 אֲחִיחֻד 'aḥiyḥud (1)
Ahihud (1)

313 אֲחִיטוּב 'aḥiyṭûb (15)
Ahitub (15)

314 אֲחִילוּד 'aḥiylûd (5)
Ahilud (5)

315 אֲחִימוֹת 'aḥiymôt (1)
Ahimoth (1)

316 אֲחִימֶלֶךְ 'aḥiymelek (18)
Ahimelech (18)

317 אֲחִימָן 'aḥiyman (4)
Ahiman (4)

318 אֲחִימַעַץ 'aḥiyma'as (15)
Ahimaaz (15)

319 אֶחְיָן 'aḥyān (1)
Ahian (1)

320 אֲחִינָדָב 'aḥiynādāb (1)
Ahinadab (1)

321 אֲחִינֹעַם 'aḥiynō'am (7)
Ahinoam (7)

322 אֲחִיסָמָךְ 'aḥiysāmāk (3)
Ahisamach (3)

323 אֲחִיעֶזֶר 'aḥiy'ezer (6)
Ahiezer (6)

324 אֲחִיקָם 'aḥiyqām (20)
Ahikam (20)

325 אֲחִירָם 'aḥiyrām (1)
Ahiram (1)

326 אֲחִירָמִי 'aḥiyrāmiy (1)
Ahiramite (1)

327 אֲחִירַע 'aḥiyra' (5)
Ahira (5)

328 אֲחִישָׁחַר 'aḥiyšāḥar (1)
Ahishahar (1)

329 אֲחִישָׁר 'aḥiyšār (1)
Ahishar (1)

330 אֲחִיתֹפֶל 'aḥiytōpel (20)
Ahithophel (17)
Ahithophel's (3)

331 אַחְלָב 'aḥlāb (1)
Ahlab (1)

332 אַחְלַי 'aḥ'lay (2)
if only (1)
oh that (1)

333 אַחְלַי 'aḥlāy (2)
Ahlai (2)

334 אַחְלָמָה 'aḥlāmāh (2)
amethyst (2)

335 אֲחַסְבַּי 'aḥasbay (1)
Ahasbai (1)

336 אָחַר 'āḥar (17)
delay (5)
delayed (2)
slow (2)
detain (1)
hold back (1)
late (1)
linger (1)
lost time (1)
remained (1)
stay up late (1)
took longer (1)

337 1אַחֵר 'aḥēr1 (166)
other (83)
another (39)
others (12)
else (4)
next (4)
another (3) +6388
different (2)
more (2)
more (2) +6388
additional (1)
changed (1) +2200
new (1)
other gods (1)
second (1)
set farther back (1) +2021+2958
someone else (1)
someone else's (1)
strange (1)
sword⁵ (1)
various (1)
what⁵ (1)
untranslated (3)

338 2אַחֵר 'aḥēr2 (1)
Aher (1)

339 אַחַר 'ahar (716)
after (205)
behind (42)
followed (27) +2143
follow (20) +2143
next to (17)
with (16)
afterward (14) +4027
to (13)
follow (12)
from (12) +4946
followed (11)
following (11)
after that (10)
then (10)
behind (9) +4946
in the course of time (8) +4027
afterward (7)
back (6)
followed (6) +995
following (6) +2143
some time later (6) +465+1821+2021+2021
pursue (5)
pursuing (5)
since (5)
after (4) +4027
of (4)
west (4)
later (3)
later (3) +4027
now (3)
some time later (3) +4027
succeed (3)
after this (2)
against (2)
around (2)
away from (2) +4946
back (2) +4946
beyond (2)
chasing (2)
finished (2)
flee (2)
follow (2) +2118
followers (2)
follows (2) +995
in addition to (2)
join (2)
outlived (2) +799+3427
pursue (2) +8938
pursuing (2) +4946
rear (2)
tending (2)
then (2) +4027
after (1) +4946
after a while (1) +465+1821+2021+2021
after the time of (1)
afterward (1) +4026
again (1)
at (1)
back (1) +7155
backs (1)
butt (1)
calling to arms (1) +2410
chasing (1) +1944
departing from (1) +4946
descendants (1)
deserted (1) +4946+6590
devoted to (1) +2143
ends up (1)
ever (1)
far side (1)
follow (1) +995
follow (1) +1815
follow (1) +3655
follow (1) +4946+7756
follow (1) +6296
follow (1) +7756
followed (1) +2118
followed (1) +3655
followed (1) +7756
followed in (1) +995

followers (1) +889+2021+6639
followers (1) +2143
follows (1)
follows (1) +4027
for (1)
from then on (1) +4027+4946
future (1)
gave support (1) +6468
go over the branches a second time (1)
                           +6994
go over the vines again (1) +6618
greedy (1) +2143
how long (1) +5503+6388
imitated (1)
in (1)
in hot pursuit (1)
in the course of time (1) +4027+4946
last of all (1)
later (1) +465+1821+2021+2021
later (1) +2296
later (1) +4027+4946
lead on (1) +3870
lead to do the same^s (1) +466+2177+2388
leaves behind (1)
led (1) +2143
left (1) +4946
loyal to (1)
lust after (1) +2388
lusted after (1) +2388
next (1)
next after (1)
next in line (1)
over (1)
pursue (1) +2143
pursue (1) +3655
pursued (1) +2143
pursuing (1) +2143
pursuit (1)
right behind (1)
runs after for favors (1) +2388
shortly after (1)
since (1) +889
some time after (1)
some time later (1)
succeeded (1)
successive years (1) +9102+9102
successor (1)
successor (1) +132+995+8611
supported (1)
supported (1) +2118
then (1) +2256
those^s (1) +889+2021+6639
toward (1)
under the command of (1)
when (1)
worshiping (1)
untranslated (83)

340 אַחֲרוֹן 'ah^rôn (51)
last (11)
end (10)
next (4)
western (4)
future (2)
later (2)
rear (2)
second (2)
then (2) +928+2021
to come (2)
end (1) +928+2021+2118
follow (1)
he^s (1) +408+2021+2021
later (1) +928+2021
present (1)
then (1)
this^s (1)
time (1)
west (1)
yet to come (1)

341 אַחְרַח 'ahrah (1)
Aharah (1)

342 אַחְרְחֵל '^aharhēl (1)
Aharhel (1)

343 אַחֲרֵי 'ah^ray (1)
in the end (1)

344 אַחֲרִית 'ah^riyt (61)
end (20)
to come (8)
future (7)
last (4)
future hope (3)
left (3)
descendants (2)
at last (1)
end of life (1)
far side (1)
final destiny (1)
final outcome (1)
future (1) +3427
later (1)
later in time (1) +928
latter part (1)
latter part of life (1)
least (1)
outcome (1)
what happens (1)
what might happen (1)

345 אַחֲרַנִּית '^ōranniyt (7)
back (2)
backward (2)
go back (1) +8740
gone down (1) +3718
turned the other way (1)

346 אֲחַשְׁדַּרְפָּן '^ahašdarpān (4)
satraps (4)

347 אֲחַשְׁוֵרוֹשׁ '^ahašwērôš (31)
Xerxes (31)

348 אֲחַשְׁרֹשׁ '^ahašērōš (1)
untranslated (1)

349 אֲחַשְׁתָּרִי '^ahaštāriy
Variant; not used

350 אֲחַשְׁתְּרָן '^ahašťrān (2)
for king (1)
royal (1)

351 אַט 1 'at1 (5)
gently (2) +4200
gentle (1)
meekly (1)
slowly (1) +4200

352 אַט 2 'at2
Variant; not used

353 אָטָד 1 'ātād1 (4)
thornbush (3)
thorns (1)

354 אָטָד 2 'ātād2 (2)
Atad (2)

355 אֵטוּן 'ētûn (1)
linens (1)

356 אִטִּים 'ittiym (1)
spirits of the dead (1)

357 אָטַם 'ātam (8)
narrow (4)
holds (1)
shuts (1)
stopped (1)
stops (1)

358 אָטַר 'ātar (1)
close (1)

359 אָטֵר 'ātēr (5)
Ater (5)

360 אִטֵּר 'ittēr (2)
left-handed (2) +3338+3545

361 אִי 'êy (40)
where (16)
where (9) +2296
what (3) +2296
which (2) +2296
by what (1) +2296
no more (1)
what (1)
where (1) +5226
which way (1) +2006+2021+2296
which way (1) +2296
why (1) +2296+4200
untranslated (3)

362 1אִי 'iyl (36)
islands (15)
coastlands (8)
coasts (5)
island (2)
coast (1)
distant shores (1)
distant shores (1) +3542
maritime (1)
shore (1)
shores (1)

363 2אִי 'iy2 (3)
hyenas (3)

364 3אִי 'iy3 (1)
not (1)

365 4אִי 'iy4 (2)
pity (1)
woe (1)

366 אָיַב 'āyab (1)
enemy (1)

367 אֹיֵב 'ōyēb (284)
enemies (191)
enemy (70)
foes (12)
foe (3)
enemy's (1)
his own^s (1) +2021
their^s (1) +3870
whom^s (1)
untranslated (4)

368 אֵיבָה 'êybāh (5)
hostility (4)
enmity (1)

369 אֵיד 'êyd (24)
disaster (16)
calamity (3)
destruction (2)
fall (1)
ruin (1)
siege ramps (1) +784

370 1אַיָּה 'ayyāh1 (4)
black kite (2)
falcon's (1)
vultures (1)

371 2אַיָּה 'ayyāh2 (6)
Aiah (4)
Aiah's (2)

372 אַיֵּה 'ayyēh (44)
where (43)
untranslated (1)

373 אִיּוֹב 'iyyôb (58)
Job (49)
Job's (5)
he^s (3)
untranslated (1)

374 אִיזֶבֶל 'iyzebel (22)
Jezebel (18)
Jezebel's (3)
she^s (1)

375 אֵיךְ 'êyk (61)
how (47)

why (6)
what (4)
how gladly (1)
too (1)
what else (1)
untranslated (1)

376 אִיכָבוֹד 'iykābôd (2)
Ichabod (1)
Ichabod's (1)

377 אֵיכָה 'êykāh (17)
how (12)
where (2)
but how (1)
see how (1)
what (1)

378 אֵיכֹה 'êykōh (1)
where (1)

379 אֵיכָכָה 'êykākāh (4)
how (2)
untranslated (2)

380 1אַיִל 'ayill (161)
ram (88)
rams (61)
its^s (4) +2021
it^s (2) +2021
leading men (2)
leaders (2)
ruler (1)
rulers (1)
untranslated (1)

381 2אַיִל 'ayil2 (5)
oaks (4)
sacred oaks (1)

382 3אַיִל 'ayil3 (30)
jambs (9)
projecting walls (9)
jambs (1) +4647
untranslated (11)

383 4אַיִל 'ayil4
Variant; not used

384 אֱיָל 'eyāl (1)
strength (1)

385 אַיָּל 'ayyāl (12)
deer (9)
young stag (3) +6762

386 אֵיל פָּארָן 'êyl pā'rān (1)
El Paran (1)

387 אַיָּלָה 'ayyālāh (10)
doe (5)
deer (3)
does (2)

388 אִילוֹ 'iylô
Variant; not used

389 אַיָּלוֹן 'ayyālôn (10)
Aijalon (10)

390 1אֵילוֹן 'êylôn1 (4)
Elon (4)

391 2אֵילוֹן 'êylôn2 (1)
Elon (1)

392 אֵילוֹן בֵּית חָנָן 'êylôn bêyt hānān (1)
Elon Bethhanan (1)

393 אֵילוֹת 'êylôt (4)
Elath (3)
untranslated (1)

394 אֱיָלוּת 'eyālût (1)
strength (1)

395 אֵילָם 'êylām (64)
portico (44)
hall (3)
colonnade (1) +6647
porticoes (1)

temple porch (1)
untranslated (14)

396 אֵילִם 'êylim (6)
Elim (5)
where^s (1) +928

397 אֵילַת 'êylat (4)
Elath (4)

398 אָיֹם 'āyōm (3)
majestic (2)
feared (1)

399 אֵימָה 'êymāh (17)
terror (7)
terrors (4)
fear (2)
dreadful (1)
fearsome (1)
great fear (1)
wrath (1)

400 אֵימִים 'êymiym (3)
Emites (3)

401 1אַיִן 'ayin1 (790)
no (209)
there is no (98)
not (93)
nothing (32)
there was no (29)
without (29)
is not (20)
none (10)
cannot (9)
without (9) +4946
gone (8)
there will be no (8)
be no more (7)
never (7)
lack (6)
there is none (6)
are no more (5)
beyond (5)
don't (5)
is no more (5)
neither (5)
be no (4)
is no (4)
is there no (4)
no (4) +4946
nor (4) +2256
there is not (4)
there was none (4)
there were no (4)
were not (4)
it is not (3)
nothing (3) +3972
there is no (3) +1172
was not (3)
is that not (2)
is there not (2)
isn't (2)
it's not (2)
lacks (2)
none (2) +408
nothing (2) +1821
nothing (2) +4399
senseless (2) +4213
there are no (2)
there is nothing (2)
there is nothing (2) +4399
there was not (2)
there was nothing (2)
there will be none (2)
was no more (2)
was there no (2)
waterless (2) +4784
without (2) +928
won't (2)
all alone (1) +9108
allowed (1) +646
am no more (1)

any^s (1)

any[s] (1)
are not (1)
aren't (1)
bare (1) +928+4399
be nothing (1) +1194
before (1) +3954
boundless (1) +7897
cannot (1) +3946
countless (1) +5031
deserted (1) +132+4946
deserted (1) +3782
deserted (1) +3782+4946
disappeared (1)
endless (1) +7891
endless (1) +7897
fatherless (1) +3
free from (1)
gone from (1) +907
here are no (1)
in vain (1)
incomprehensible (1) +1069
incurable (1) +5340
innumerable (1) +5031
is never (1)
is nothing (1)
isn't there (1)
it was impossible (1)
it was not (1)
kept secret (1) +5583
lack (1) +928
lack (1) +4200
loses (1)
more (1) +4200
more than (1) +4200
naught (1)
nearly (1) +3869
neither (1) +4946
never (1) +4200+6409
none (1) +4946
none will be (1) +4946
nor (1) +677
nor (1) +1685+2256
nor (1) +2256+4946
nothing at all (1) +700+2256
nothing whatever (1) +1821+3972
or (1)
or (1) +561+2256
otherwise (1) +561
powerless (1) +445+3338+4200
powerless (1) +445+4200
powerless (1) +3946
regardless (1) +4200+9068
so[s] (1)
surely (1) +561
than (1)
there is neither (1)
there is no (1) +3972
there is no (1) +4946
there is nothing (1) +3972
there were no (1) +1172
there were not (1)
there will not be (1)
too (1)
unclean (1) +3196
uncovered (1) +4064
unless (1)
unsearchable (1) +2984
was no (1)
weak (1) +226
will not (1)
without (1) +4200
without (1) +6330
without any payment (1) +2855
without equal (1) +3202+4946
worthless (1) +2914
wouldn't (1)
untranslated (18)

402 אַיִן2 *'ayin2* (17)
where (12)
where (5) +4946

403 אִין *'iyn* (1)
don't (1)

404 אִיעֶזֶר *'iy'ezer* (1)
Iezer (1)

405 אִיעֶזְרִי *'iy'ezriy* (1)
Iezerite (1)

406 אֵיפָה *'ēypāh* (40)
ephah (29)
basket (4)
differing measures (1) +406+2256
measure (1)
measures (1)
measuring basket (1)
two differing measures (1) +406+2256

407 אֵיפֹה *'ēypōh* (10)
where (8)
what (1)
where from (1)

408 אִישׁ1 *'iyšl* (2189)
man (612)
men (523)
each (160)
one (106)
husband (64)
man's (32)
anyone (29)
every (18)
everyone (18)
people (16)
Israelites (14) +3776
soldiers (12) +4878
someone (12)
any (11)
some[s] (10)
they[s] (9) +2021
person (8)
they[s] (7)
everyone (6) +3972
he[s] (6) +2021
Israelite (6) +1074+3776+4946
those[s] (6)
he[s] (5)
Israelite (5) +3776
none (5) +4202
swordsmen (5) +2995+8990
them[s] (5)
warrior (5) +4878
all (4)
army (4) +4878
husbands (4)
male (4)
those[s] (4) +2021
another[s] (3)
anyone (3) +2021+4769
foot soldiers (3) +8081
him[s] (3)
him[s] (3) +2021
they (3)
who (3)
anyone (2) +408
anyone (2) +3972
at war with (2) +4878
champion (2) +1227+2021
each (2) +408
father (2)
fellow (2)
Israelite (2) +1201+3776+4946
mankind (2)
merchants (2) +9365
mourners[s] (2)
neighbor[s] (2)
none (2) +401
servants (2)
their[s] (2)
them[s] (2) +2021
valiant fighter (2) +1201+2657
valiant fighters (2) +2657
warriors (2) +2657

whoever (2)
whoever (2) +889
whoever (2) +2021+4769
you[s] (2)
a[s] (1)
accuser (1) +8190
adulteress (1) +851
all together (1) +285+3869
allies (1) +1382
among yourselves (1) +278+448
another creature[s] (1)
any (1) +408
any (1) +3972
any man (1) +408
any man (1) +2021+4769
anyone (1) +2021
anyone (1) +2021+3972
anyone's (1)
archers (1) +928+2021+4619+8008
army (1)
Benjamin (1) +1201+3549
Benjamite (1) +1228
Benjamite (1) +3549
Benjamites (1) +1228+4946
blood relatives (1) +1460
Boaz[s] (1) +2021
brother (1)
captive (1)
census (1) +6296
champions (1) +2657
child (1)
close friend (1) +8934
counselor (1) +6783
counselors (1) +6783
cubs (1)
descendant (1) +2446+4946
deserve to (1)
deserved (1)
each (1) +278+2257
eloquent (1) +1821
enemies (1) +5194
Ephraimites (1) +713
equally (1) +278+2257+3869
equally among them (1) +278+2257+3869
everyone (1) +2021+3972
everyone's (1) +928
experienced fighter (1) +4878
experienced fighting men (1)
              +1475+2657+4878
famous (1) +9005
farmer (1) +141+6268
fellow townsmen (1) +6551
fellowman (1)
followers (1) +889+2143+6640
forces (1)
friend[s] (1)
friends (1) +8934
Gibeonites (1) +1500
Gileadites (1) +1680
give in marriage (1) +4200+5989
great soldiers (1) +4878
group (1)
guards (1) +5464
he[s] (1) +340+2021+2021
he[s] (1) +2021+2021+6640+8886
he[s] (1) +2021+5283
high (1) +1201
highborn (1) +1201
himself[s] (1) +2021
his[s] (1) +2021
hunter (1) +7473
husband's (1)
in the prime of life (1)
Israel (1) +3776
Israelite (1) +2021+3778
kings[s] (1)
leaders (1) +8031
liar (1) +3942
madman (1) +8713
man (1) +408+2256
man's body (1)

mankind (1) +1414
marries (1) +2118+2118+4200
marries (1) +2118+4200
marry (1) +2118+4200
members (1)
men (1) +1201
men's (1)
Moabites (1) +4566
mockers (1) +4371
more[s] (1)
neighbor's (1)
Ninevites (1) +5770
none[s] (1)
officials (1)
one and all (1)
one party[s] (1)
one[s] (1) +2424
opponent (1)
oppressor (1) +9412
ready for battle (1) +2021+4200+4878+7372
remain unmarried (1)
        +1194+2118+4200+4200+6328
sailors (1) +641
scoffers (1) +4371
scoundrel (1) +1175
scoundrel (1) +1175+2021
slanderers (1) +4383
slept with (1) +3359+4200+5435
soldier (1) +7372
soldiers (1) +1505+4878
soldiers (1) +7372
soldiers (1) +8081
some of them[s] (1)
son (1)
son (1) +2446
spies (1) +8078
steward[s] (1)
steward[s] (1) +889+1074+2021+6584
strongest defenders (1) +2657
talker (1) +8557
tall (1) +4500
tend livestock (1) +2118+5238
tended livestock (1) +2118+5238
the parties (1) +2084+2256+8276
their[s] (1) +2021
their[s] (1) +3373
them (1)
they[s] (1) +3315
they[s] (1) +7159
this[s] (1)
together (1) +907+2084+8276
townspeople (1) +6551
tribe of Benjamin (1) +3549
troublemaker (1) +1175
trusted friends (1) +8934
two men (1) +278+2256+3481
unmarried (1) +2118+4200+4202
untraveled (1) +1172+4946+6296
villain (1) +224
virgin (1) +3359+4202
voluntarily (1) +4213+6584+6590
well-known (1) +9005
who (1) +2021+6504
whoever (1) +889+3972
untranslated (243)

409 אִישׁ2 'iyš2
Variant; not used

410 אִישׁ־בֹּשֶׁת 'iyš-bōšet (11)
Ish-Bosheth (11)

411 אִישׁ־טוֹב 'iyš-tôb
Variant; not used

412 אִישְׁהוֹד 'iyšhôd (1)
Ishhod (1)

413 אִישׁוֹן 'iyšôn (5)
apple (2)
apple (1) +1426
dark (1) +696
untranslated (1)

414 אִישַׁי 'iyšay (1)
Jesse (1)

415 אִיתוֹן 'iytôn (2)
entrance (1)
untranslated (1)

416 אִיתַי 'iytay (1)
Ithai (1)

417 אִיתִיאֵל 'iytiy'ēl (3)
Ithiel (3)

418 אִיתָמָר 'iytāmār (21)
Ithamar (19)
Ithamar's (2)

419 אֵיתָן1 'ēytān1 (13)
rich (2)
constant (1)
enduring (1)
ever flowing (1)
everlasting (1)
flowing stream (1)
hard (1)
long established (1)
never-failing (1)
place (1)
secure (1)
steady (1)

420 אֵיתָן2 'ēytān2 (8)
Ethan (8)

421 אַךְ 'ak (161)
but (31)
surely (21)
only (16)
however (8)
but only (5)
nevertheless (5)
yet (5)
alone (4)
just (4)
nothing but (4)
also (2)
and (2)
indeed (2)
so (2)
after (1)
although (1)
as long as (1)
as surely as (1)
be sure (1)
both (1)
but (1) +3954
but also (1)
but too (1)
complete (1)
completely (1)
except (1)
fully (1)
furthermore (1)
just after (1)
mere (1)
once more (1) +2021+7193
only (1) +8370
provided (1) +561
really (1)
scarcely (1)
surely (1) +6964
though (1)
very (1)
untranslated (26)

422 אַכַּד 'akkad (1)
Akkad (1)

423 אַכְזָב 'akzāb (2)
deceptive (2)

424 אַכְזִיב 'akziyb (4)
Aczib (4)

425 אַכְזָר 'akzār (4)
deadly (1)
fierce (1)

heartless (1)
ruthlessly (1) +4200

426 אַכְזָרִי 'akzāriy (8)
cruel (7)
merciless (1)

427 אַכְזְרִיּוּת 'akzᵉriyyût (1)
cruel (1)

428 אֲכִילָה 'ᵃkiylāh (1)
food (1)

429 אָכִישׁ 'ākiyš (21)
Achish (19)
untranslated (2)

430 אָכַל 'ākal (820)
eat (359)
ate (70)
devour (44)
consume (31)
be eaten (25)
eats (25)
eaten (23)
devoured (22)
eating (22)
consumed (19)
devours (10)
consuming (9)
food (8)
consumes (6)
feed on (6)
be consumed (5)
enjoy (5)
ate up (4)
burns (4)
gave to eat (4)
eaten (3) +430
eater (3)
feast (3)
fed (3)
be devoured (2)
been destroyed (2)
destroy (2)
destroyed (2)
devouring (2)
eat up (2)
enjoys (2)
feasting (2)
feed (2)
give[s] (2)
had to eat (2)
make eat (2)
make eat food (2)
needed (2)
shared (2)
burn up (1)
burned (1)
burned up (1)
claimed (1)
crushed completely (1) +2256+4730
dine on (1)
dined (1)
dried up (1)
earn (1)
eat away (1)
eaten away (1)
eaten provisions (1) +430
eats away (1)
enjoyed (1)
feast on (1)
feasting (1) +2256+9272
feeding (1)
feeds on (1)
free to eat (1) +430
get food (1)
give to eat (1)
had food enough (1)
have food (1)
have plenty to eat (1) +430
have[s] (1)
is eaten (1)
is eaten (1) +430

kept (1)
lick up (1)
like (1)
live on (1)
meal (1) +4312
must eat (1) +430
needs (1)
pests (1)
prepare food to eat (1)
prepares (1)
provided for (1) +2118+2256+4200+4312
put an end (1)
ruins (1)
sap (1)
sat (1)
scarce (1) +928+5017
share in (1)
sharing (1) +4946
stay for a meal (1) +4312
stripped (1)
stripped clean (1)
supposed to dine (1) +3782+3782
taste (1)
took space (1)
use (1)
used up (1) +430
would[s] (1)
untranslated (16)

431 אֹכֶל *'ōkel* (39)
food (36)
it[s] (1)
mealtime (1) +2021+6961
prey (1)

432 אֻכָל *'ukāl* (1)
Ucal (1)

433 אָכְלָה *'oklāh* (17)
food (11)
fuel (3)
eat (2)
devour (1)

434 1אָכֵן *'ākēn1* (18)
surely (7)
but (4)
yet (2)
actually (1)
because surely (1)
how (1)
truly (1)
untranslated (1)

435 2אָכֵן *'ākēn2*
Variant; not used

436 אָכַף *'ākap* (1)
drives on (1)

437 אֶכֶף *'ekep* (1)
hand (1)

438 אִכָּר *'ikkār* (7)
farmers (4)
farmer (1)
people (1)
work fields (1)

439 אַכְשָׁף *'akšāp* (3)
Acshaph (3)

440 1אַל *'al1* (730)
not (511)
don't (64)
no (52)
nor (14) +2256
never (11)
or (5)
nor (3)
without (3)
cannot (2)
from (2)
neither (2)
never (2) +4200+6409
nothing (2)

stop (2)
abstain from sexual relations (1)
+448+851+5602
always (1) +2893
better than (1)
beware (1) +9068
forget (1) +2349
immortality (1) +4638
instead of (1)
neither (1) +2256
never (1) +6524
or (1) +2256
overlook (1) +7155
untranslated (44)

441 2אֵל *'al2*
Variant; not used

442 1אֵל *'ēl1*
Variant; not used

443 2אֵל *'ēl2*
Variant; not used

444 3אֵל *'ēl3*
Variant; not used

445 4אֵל *'ēl4* (5)
power (3) +3338
powerless (1) +401+3338+4200
powerless (1) +401+4200

446 5אֵל *'ēl5* (237)
God (199)
god (19)
God's (5)
mighty (4)
gods (3)
mighty one (3)
great (1)
heavenly beings (1) +1201
his[s] (1)
mighty (1) +1201

447 6אֵל *'ēl6* (9)
these (7)
those (2)

448 אֶל *'el* (5516)
to (3052)
into (160)
against (128)
on (114)
in (102)
at (91)
for (74)
toward (57)
with (51)
enter (36) +995
before (30)
over (23)
upon (20)
concerning (17)
entered (17) +995
of (16)
about (16)
reached (13) +995
among (12)
by (12)
into (11) +9348
around (10)
lay with (7) +995
near (7)
because of (6)
sleep with (6) +995
enters (5) +995
slept with (5) +995
along (4)
arrived (4) +995
attack (4)
attack (4) +6590
in front of (4) +7156
lie with (4) +995
after (3)
as for (3)

at (3) +4578
attack (3) +995
decorated (3)
facedown (3) +7156
facing (3) +7156
from (3)
in front of (3) +4578
straight ahead (3) +6298+7156
together (3) +285+285
up to (3)
wherever (3) +889+3972
above (2)
above (2) +1068
all the way to (2)
along with (2)
approaches (2) +995
be buried (2) +665+7700
beside (2)
down to (2)
faced (2) +7156
facing each other (2) +4691+4691
fall in (2) +6015
hands together (2) +4090+4090
in addition to (2)
in front of (2)
include (2)
inside (2) +9348
into presence (2)
next to (2) +3338
next to (2) +6298
on (2) +4578
onto (2)
received (2) +995
together (2) +295+851
under (2)
abstain from sexual relations (1)
+440+851+5602
abutted (1)
according to (1)
across (1)
adjoining (1) +7156
among (1) +9348
among yourselves (1) +278+408
and (1)
approached (1) +995
arrive (1) +995
as (1)
as far as (1)
as far as (1) +4578
at the sight of (1)
ate (1) +995+7931
attack (1) +7756
attacked (1) +7756
attacking (1) +6590
attentive to (1)
away (1) +2021+2025+2575
because (1)
befall (1) +628
before (1) +7156
belonged to (1)
belonged to (1) +2118
belongs to (1)
beside (1) +3338
bordering (1)
both and (1)
buried (1) +995+7700
call to mind (1) +4213+8740
care (1) +4213+8492
care about (1) +4213+8492
checked on (1) +8938
committed adultery with (1) +995
concerned about (1) +4213+8492
concerned for (1)
consult (1)
consult (1) +2143
counting on (1) +906+5883+5951
covered (1)
decorated with (1)
definitely (1) +3922
did the same[s] (1) +285+285+2489
done so[s] (1) +995+7931

during (1)
entered (1) +6073
entering (1) +995
entrusted to (1) +3338
every kind (1) +2385+2385+4946
faced (1)
faced forward (1) +4578+7156
filled with gladness (1) +1637+8524
find (1) +995
fit for (1)
fixed on (1)
follow (1) +3338
for the sake of (1)
from (1) +7156
go sleep with (1) +995
guest (1) +995+1074
have (1)
have on hand (1) +3338+9393
here (1)
impressed (1)
in accordance with (1)
in charge of (1)
in front of (1) +4578+7156
in the front line (1) +4578+7156
in vain (1) +2855
inherit (1) +2118
inquire of (1) +2011
inquire of (1) +7928
inquired of (1) +606
inside (1)
inside (1) +1074+2021
into (1) +7163
invade (1) +995
invaded (1) +995
invaded (1) +6590
invader (1) +995
join (1)
joining (1)
keep away (1) +3870+7928
lie with (1) +7928
listened attentively to (1) +265
look in the face (1) +5951+7156
lusted after (1) +6311
lying on (1)
lying with (1) +995
make turn (1) +5989
married (1) +995
meet (1)
meet (1) +7156
occupied (1) +6641
occupy (1) +995
on account of (1)
on the faces of (1)
on the side of (1)
onto (1) +9348
opposite (1)
opposite (1) +7156
out of (1)
overboard (1) +2021+3542
overruled (1) +2616
overtook (1) +995
participate in (1) +2118
reach (1) +995
reached (1) +6590
reaches (1) +995
reflected on (1) +4213+5989
rejoined (1) +2143
replace (1) +995+9393
right in (1)
see (1) +6524
showed concern for (1) +7155
sleeps with (1) +995
southern (1) +5582+6991
southward (1) +2021+3545
square (1) +752+8062+8063
square (1) +752+8063
stops to think (1) +4213+8740
surmounted by (1)
that (1)
their (1) +2157
thought (1) +606+3276

to (1) +4578
to (1) +9348
to within (1)
took (1) +995
touched (1) +995
toward (1) +2006
toward (1) +5790
toward (1) +7156
use (1) +2143
went in to spend the night with (1) +995
untranslated (1171)

449 אֵל אֱלֹהֵי יִשְׂרָאֵל ʾēl ʾᵉlōhēy yiśrāʾēl (1)
El Elohe Israel (1)

450 אֵל בֵּית־אֵל ʾēl bēyṯ-ʾēl (1)
El Bethel (1)

451 אֵל בְּרִית ʾēl bʾriyṯ (1)
El-Berith (1)

452 אֵלָא ʾēlāʾ (1)
Ela (1)

453 אֶלְגָּבִישׁ ʾelgāḇiyš (3)
hailstones (3) +74

454 אַלְגּוּמִּים ʾalgûmmiym (3)
algumwood (2) +6770
algum (1)

455 אֶלְדָּד ʾeldāḏ (2)
Eldad (2)

456 אֶלְדָּעָה ʾeldāʿāh (2)
Eldaah (2)

457 אָלָה1 ʾālāh1 (8)
swears the oath (2)
take an oath (2)
bound under an oath (1)
cursing (1)
take oaths (1)
utter a curse (1)

458 אָלָה2 ʾālāh2 (1)
mourn (1)

459 אָלָה3 ʾālāh3
Variant; not used

460 אָלָה4 ʾālāh4 (34)
oath (10)
curses (8)
curse (7)
object of cursing (3)
required (2) +928+5957
accursed (1)
public charge (1)
put under oath (1) +9048
sworn agreement (1)

461 אֵלָה1 ʾēlāh1 (13)
oak (6)
oak tree (3)
terebinth (2)
great tree (1)
tree (1)

462 אֵלָה2 ʾēlāh2 (13)
Elah (12)
Elah's (1)

463 אֵלָה3 ʾēlāh3 (3)
Elah (3)

464 אַלָּה ʾallāh (1)
oak (1)

465 אֵלֶּה ʾēlleh (747)
these (481)
this (55)
those (15)
them (12)
they (12)
this (12) +1821+2021+2021
such (10)
others (7)
some time later (6) +339+1821+2021+2021

some (5)
following (4)
the (4)
here (3)
who (3)
altogether (2) +2256
men (2)
now (2) +928+2021+2021+3427
one group (2)
that (2)
us (2)
what (2) +1821+2021+2021
after a while (1) +339+1821+2021+2021
all this (1)
all (1)
animals (1)
as follows (1)
case (1)
each other (1)
everything (1) +1821+2021+2021+3972
gave the message (1)
          +1819+1821+2021+2021+3972
his (1)
impartially (1) +465+6640
later (1) +339+1821+2021+2021
next (1)
share their duties (1) +6640
she (1)
that happened (1) +1821+2021+2021
that (1) +1821+2021+2021
the craftsmen (1)
the first (1)
the men of the ambush (1)
the men (1)
the others (1)
the total (1)
their (1) +2021
things (1)
this is how (1) +928+3972
this is how (1) +1821+2021+2021+3869
this is why (1) +6584
two (1)
very (1)
what (1)
who (1)
whose (1) +1426+2257
your (1)
untranslated (69)

466 אֱלֹהִים ʾᵉlōhiym (2602)
God (2242)
gods (205)
god (59)
God's (25)
he (7)
he (7) +3378+3870
judges (4)
him (3) +3378+3870
angels (2) +1201+2021
goddess (2)
he (2) +2021
his (2) +3378+3870
angels (1) +1201
divine (1)
God's (1) +4200
God's (1) +4946
God-fearing (1) +2021+3710
godly (1)
great (1)
he (1) +824+2021
he (1) +3378
he (1) +3378+5646
heavenly beings (1)
high (1)
him (1)
him (1) +2021
him (1) +3378+4013
his (1) +3276
I (1)
idols (1)
it (1) +778+2021

lead to do the same[s] (1) +339+2177+2388
majestic (1)
mighty (1)
sacred (1)
shrine (1) +1074
spirit (1)
them[s] (1) +1074+2021+3998
them[s] (1) +2157
there[s] (1) +928+1074
very (1) +4200
untranslated (13)

467 אֵלוּ 'illû (2)
if (2)

468 אֱלוֹהַּ 'lôah (58)
God (46)
god (7)
God's (4)
untranslated (1)

469 אֱלוּל1 'lûl1 (1)
Elul (1)

470 אֱלוּל2 'lûl2 (1)
untranslated (1)

471 אֵלוֹן1 'ēlôn1 (10)
great tree (4)
great trees (4)
large tree (1)
tree (1)

472 אֵלוֹן2 'ēlôn2 (2)
Elon (2)

473 אַלּוֹן1 'allôn1 (8)
oak (4)
oaks (4)

474 אַלּוֹן2 'allôn2 (1)
Allon (1)

475 אַלּוֹן בָּכוּת 'allôn bākût (1)
Allon Bacuth (1)

476 אַלּוּף1 'allûp1 (9)
close friends (2)
friend (2)
allies (1)
companion (1)
gentle (1)
oxen (1)
partner (1)

477 אַלּוּף2 'allûp2 (60)
chiefs (16)
leaders (3)
divisions (1)
untranslated (40)

478 אָלוּשׁ 'ālûš (2)
Alush (2)

479 אֶלְזָבָד 'elzābād (2)
Elzabad (2)

480 אָלַח 'ālah (3)
corrupt (3)

481 אֶלְחָנָן 'elhānān (4)
Elhanan (4)

482 אֱלִיאָב 'liy'āb (21)
Eliab (20)
he[s] (1)

483 אֱלִיאֵל 'liy'ēl (10)
Eliel (10)

484 אֱלִיאָתָה 'liy'ātāh (1)
Eliathah (1)

485 אֱלִידָד 'liydād (1)
Elidad (1)

486 אֶלְיָדָע 'elyādā' (4)
Eliada (4)

487 אַלְיָה 'alyāh (5)
fat tail (5)

488 אֵלִיָּה 'ēliyyāh (8)
Elijah (8)

489 אֵלִיָּהוּ 'ēliyyāhû (63)
Elijah (60)
Elijah's (1)
him[s] (1)
untranslated (1)

490 אֱלִיהוּ 'liyhû (4)
Elihu (4)

491 אֱלִיהוּא 'liyhû' (7)
Elihu (6)
he[s] (1)

492 אֶלְיְהוֹעֵינַי 'ely'hô'ēynay (2)
Eliehoenai (2)

493 אֶלְיוֹעֵינַי 'elyô'ēynay (7)
Elioenai (7)

494 אֱלִיחְבָּא 'elyahbā' (2)
Eliahba (2)

495 אֱלִיחֹרֶף 'liyhōrep (1)
Elihoreph (1)

496 אֱלִיל 'liyl (20)
idols (15)
worthless (2)
idolatries (1)
images (1)
untranslated (1)

497 אֱלִימֶלֶךְ 'liymelek (6)
Elimelech (6)

498 אֶלְיָסָף 'elyāsāp (6)
Eliasaph (6)

499 אֱלִיעֶזֶר 'liy'ezer (14)
Eliezer (14)

500 אֱלִיעָם 'liy'ām (2)
Eliam (2)

501 אֱלִיעֵנַי 'liy'ēnay (1)
Elienai (1)

502 אֱלִיפַז 'liypaz (15)
Eliphaz (14)
him[s] (1)

503 אֱלִיפָל 'liypal (1)
Eliphal (1)

504 אֱלִיפְלֵהוּ 'liyp'lēhû (2)
Eliphelehu (2)

505 אֱלִיפֶלֶט 'liypelet (8)
Eliphelet (8)

506 אֱלִיצוּר 'liysûr (5)
Elizur (5)

507 אֱלִיצָפָן 'liysāpān (4)
Elizaphan (4)

508 אֱלִיקָא 'liyqā' (1)
Elika (1)

509 אֶלְיָקִים 'elyāqiym (12)
Eliakim (12)

510 אֱלִישֶׁבַע 'liyšeba' (1)
Elisheba (1)

511 אֱלִישָׁה 'liyšāh (3)
Elishah (3)

512 אֱלִישׁוּעַ 'liyšûa' (3)
Elishua (3)

513 אֶלְיָשִׁיב 'elyāšiyb (17)
Eliashib (15)
Eliashib's (1)
it[s] (1) +1074

514 אֱלִישָׁמָע 'liyšāmā' (16)
Elishama (16)

515 אֱלִישָׁע 'liyšā' (58)
Elisha (54)
Elisha's (3)

he[s] (1)

516 אֱלִישָׁפָט 'liyšāpāt (1)
Elishaphat (1)

517 אֱלִיָּתָה 'liyyātāh (1)
Eliathah (1)

518 אַלְלַי 'allay (2)
what misery (1)
woe (1)

519 אָלַם1 'ālam1 (8)
silent (6)
be silenced (1)
speechless (1)

520 אָלַם2 'ālam2 (1)
binding (1)

521 אֵלֶם 'ēlem
Variant; not used

522 אִלֵּם 'illēm (6)
mute (4)
that cannot speak (1)
those who cannot speak (1)

523 אַלְמֻגִּים 'almuggiym (3)
almugwood (3) +6770

524 אֲלֻמָּה 'lummāh (5)
sheaves (2)
it[s] (1)
sheaf (1)
sheaves of grain (1)

525 אַלְמוֹדָד 'almôdād (2)
Almodad (2)

526 אַלַּמֶּלֶךְ 'allammelek (1)
Allammelech (1)

527 אַלְמָן1 'almān1 (1)
forsaken (1)

528 אַלְמָן2 'almān2 (1)
strongholds (1)

529 אַלְמֹן 'almōn (1)
widowhood (1)

530 אַלְמָנָה 'almānāh (54)
widow (31)
widows (18)
widow's (4)
untranslated (1)

531 אַלְמָנוּת 'almānût (4)
widow's (2)
widowhood (1)
widows (1)

532 אַלְמֹנִי 'almōniy (3)
certain (1) +7141
friend (1) +7141
such and such (1) +7141

533 אֶלֹנִי 'ēlōniy (1)
Elonite (1)

534 אֶלְנַעַם 'elnā'am (1)
Elnaam (1)

535 אֶלְנָתָן 'elnātān (7)
Elnathan (7)

536 אֶלָּסָר 'ellāsār (2)
Ellasar (2)

537 אֶלְעָד 'el'ād (1)
Elead (1)

538 אֶלְעָדָה 'el'ādāh (1)
Eleadah (1)

539 אֶלְעוּזַי 'el'ûzay (1)
Eluzai (1)

540 אֶלְעָזָר 'el'āzār (72)
Eleazar (70)
Eleazar's (2)

541 אֶלְעָלֵא 'el'ālē' (1)
Elealeh (1)

542 אֶלְעָלֵה 'el'ālēh (4)
Elealeh (4)

543 אֶלְעָשָׂה 'el'āśāh (6)
Eleasah (4)
Elasah (2)

544 1אָלַף 'ālap1 (4)
learn (1)
prompts (1)
teach (1)
teaches (1)

545 2אָלַף 'ālap2 (1)
increase by thousands (1)

546 1אֶלֶף 'elep1 (7)
herds (5)
oxen (2)

547 2אֶלֶף 'elep2 (495)
thousand (223)
thousands (31)
24,000 (14) +752+2256+6929
25,000 (14) +2256+2822+6929
10,000 (9) +6930
4,500 (8) +752+2256+2822+4395
1,000 (5)
1,254 (4) +752+2256+2822+4395
36,000 (3) +2256+8993+9252
40,500 (3) +752+2256+2822+4395
5,000 (3) +2822
53,400 (3)
    +752+2256+2256+2822+4395+8993
603,550 (3)   +547+2256+2256+2256
    +2822+2822+4395+4395+8993+9252
eleven hundred (3) +2256+4395
1,052 (2) +2256+2822+9109
1,247 (2) +752+2256+4395+8679
1,775 (2)
    +2256+2256+2256+2822+4395+8679+8679
16,000 (2) +6925+9252
18,000 (2) +6925+9046
200,000 (2) +4395
30,500 (2) +2256+2822+4395+8993
32,200 (2) +2256+2256+4395+8993+9109
35,400 (2)
    +752+2256+2256+2822+4395+8993
4,600 (2) +752+2256+4395+9252
41,500 (2)
    +285+752+2256+2256+2822+4395
45,650 (2)   +752+2256+2256+2256
    +2822+2822+4395+9252
46,500 (2)
    +752+2256+2256+2822+4395+9252
54,400 (2)
    +752+752+2256+2256+2822+4395
57,400 (2)
    +752+2256+2256+2822+4395+8679
59,300 (2)
    +2256+2256+2822+4395+8993+9596
6,720 (2) +2256+4395+6929+8679+9252
62,700 (2)
    +2256+2256+4395+8679+9109+9252
7,337 (2)
    +2256+4395+8679+8679+8993+8993
74,600 (2)
    +752+2256+2256+4395+8679+9252
fourteen hundred (2) +752+2256+4395
million (2) +547
seventeen hundred (2) +2256+4395+8679
units of a thousand (2)
1,017 (1) +2256+6925+8679
1,017 (1) +6925+8679
1,222 (1) +2256+4395+6929+9109
1,290 (1) +2256+4395+9596
1,335 (1) +2256+2822+4395+8993+8993
1,365 (1)
    +2256+2256+2256+2822+4395+8993+9252
1,760 (1) +2256+2256+4395+8679+9252
108,100 (1)
    +547+2256+2256+4395+4395+9046
120,000 (1) +2256+4395+6929

14,700 (1) +752+2256+4395+6925+8679
151,450 (1)   +285+547+752+2256
    +2256+2256+2256+2822+2822+4395+4395
153,600 (1)   +547+2256+2256+2256
    +2822+4395+4395+8993+9252
157,600 (1)   +547+2256+2256+2256
    +2822+4395+4395+8679+9252
16,750 (1)
    +2256+2822+4395+6925+8679+9252
17,200 (1) +2256+4395+6925+8679
180,000 (1) +2256+4395+9046
186,400 (1)   +547+547+752+2256+2256
    +2256+4395+4395+9046+9252
2,000 (1)
2,056 (1) +2256+2822+9252
2,067 (1) +2256+8679+9252
2,172 (1) +2256+2256+4395+8679+9109
2,172 (1) +2256+4395+8679+9109
2,200 (1) +2256+4395
2,300 (1) +2256+4395+8993
2,322 (1) +2256+4395+6929+8993+9109
2,400 (1) +752+2256+4395
2,600 (1) +2256+4395+9252
2,630 (1) +2256+2256+4395+8993+9252
2,750 (1) +2256+2822+4395+8679
2,812 (1) +2256+4395+6925+9046+9109
2,818 (1) +2256+4395+6925+9046+9046
20,000 (1) +6929
20,200 (1) +2256+4395+6929
20,800 (1) +2256+4395+6929+9046
22,000 (1) +2256+6929+9109
22,034 (1)
    +752+2256+2256+2256+6929+8993+9109
22,200 (1) +2256+2256+4395+6929+9109
22,273 (1)   +2256+2256+2256
    +4395+6929+8679+8993+9109
22,600 (1)
    +2256+2256+4395+6929+9109+9252
23,000 (1) +2256+6929+8993
25,100 (1) +2256+2256+2822+4395+6929
26,000 (1) +2256+6929+9252
28,600 (1)
    +2256+2256+4395+6929+9046+9252
280,000 (1) +2256+4395+9046
3,000 (1) +8993
3,023 (1) +2256+2256+6929+8993+8993
3,200 (1) +2256+4395+8993
3,600 (1) +2256+4395+8993+9252
3,630 (1)
    +2256+2256+4395+8993+8993+9252
3,700 (1) +2256+4395+8679+8993
3,930 (1) +2256+4395+8993+8993+9596
300,000 (1) +4395+8993
307,500 (1)   +547+2256+2256+2822
    +4395+4395+8679+8993
32,000 (1) +2256+8993+9109
32,500 (1)
    +2256+2256+2822+4395+8993+9109
337,500 (1)   +547+547+2256+2256+2256
    +2822+4395+4395+8679+8993+8993
337,500 (1)   +547+547+2256+2256
    +2822+4395+4395+8679+8993+8993
37,000 (1) +2256+8679+8993
40,000 (1) +752
42,360 (1)
    +752+2256+4395+8052+8993+9252
42,360 (1) +752+4395+8052+8993+9252
43,730 (1)   +752+2256+2256+2256
    +4395+8679+8993+8993
44,760 (1)   +752+752+2256+2256
    +2256+4395+8679+9252
45,400 (1)
    +752+752+2256+2256+2822+4395
45,600 (1)
    +752+2256+2256+2822+4395+9252
5,400 (1) +752+2256+2822+4395
50,000 (1) +2822
52,700 (1)
    +2256+2256+2822+4395+8679+9109
6,200 (1) +2256+4395+9252
6,800 (1) +2256+4395+9046+9252

60,500 (1) +2256+2822+4395+9252
601,730 (1)   +547+2256+2256+4395
    +4395+8679+8993+9252
61,000 (1) +285+2256+9252
61,000 (1) +2256+8052+9252
64,300 (1)
    +752+2256+2256+4395+8993+9252
64,400 (1)
    +752+752+2256+2256+4395+9252
675,000 (1)   +547+547+2256+2256
    +2822+4395+8679+9252
7,000 (1) +8679
7,100 (1) +2256+4395+8679
7,500 (1) +2256+2822+4395+8679
70,000 (1) +8679
72,000 (1) +2256+8679+9109
76,500 (1)
    +2256+2256+2822+4395+8679+9252
8,580 (1)
    +2256+2256+2822+4395+9046+9046
8,600 (1) +2256+4395+9046+9252
80,000 (1) +9046
87,000 (1) +2256+8679+9046
eighteen thousand (1) +2256+8052+9046
fifteen hundred feet (1) +564
five hundred yards (1) +564
thirty-six hundred (1)
    +2256+4395+8993+9252
thirty-three hundred (1)
    +2256+4395+8993+8993
three thousand feet (1) +564
twelve hundred (1) +2256+4395
twenty-seven hundred (1) +2256+4395+8679
twenty-six hundred (1) +2256+4395+9252
units of 1,000 (1)
vast (1) +547
untranslated (6)

548 3אֶלֶף 'elep3 (12)
clans (9)
clan (1)
unit (1)
units (1)

549 4אֶלֶף 'elep4
Variant; not used

550 אֶלְפֶּלֶט 'elpelet (1)
Elpelet (1)

551 אֶלְפַּעַל 'elpa'al (3)
Elpaal (3)

552 אָלַץ 'ālas (1)
prodded (1)

553 אֶלְצָפָן 'elsāpān (2)
Elzaphan (2)

554 אַלְקוּם 'alqûm (1)
army (1)

555 אֶלְקָנָה 'elqānāh (21)
Elkanah (20)
untranslated (1)

556 אֶלְקֹשִׁי 'elqōšiy (1)
Elkoshite (1)

557 אֶלְתּוֹלַד 'eltôlad (2)
Eltolad (2)

558 אֶלְתְּקֵא 'elt'qē' (1)
Eltekeh (1)

559 אֶלְתְּקֵה 'elt'qēh (1)
Eltekeh (1)

560 אֶלְתְּקֹן 'elt'qôn (1)
Eltekon (1)

561 אִם 'im (1070)
if (522)
but (39) +3954
or (39)
not (34)
when (27)
except (24) +3954

though (22)
whether (16)
surely (14) +4202
only (11) +3954
if (10) +3954
even if (9)
that (8)
no (7)
only (7)
but if (6)
since (6)
unless (6) +3954
although (5)
or (5) +2256
never (4)
unless (4) +4202
whenever (4)
yet if (4)
and (3)
however (3) +3954
neither (3)
only if (3)
until (3) +6330
but (2) +4202
but only (2) +3954
don't (2)
if (2) +3907
instead (2) +3954
nor (2)
other than (2) +3954
surely (2) +3954
than (2) +3954
that (2) +4202
though (2) +3954
till (2) +4202
until (2) +889+6330
whether (2) +4202
without (2) +3954
after (1) +3983
although (1) +3954
as (1)
as if (1)
as long as (1) +6388
because (1)
because (1) +3610+4202
but (1)
cannot (1)
certainly (1) +4202
even (1) +3954
even though (1)
except (1) +1194
however (1)
if even (1)
if indeed (1)
if only (1)
indeed (1) +3954
never (1) +2721
never (1) +4200+5905
never (1) +6330+6409
nor (1) +2256
not (1) +3954
not even (1)
not one (1)
nothing (1) +3972+4946
or (1) +401+2256
other than (1)
otherwise (1) +401
please (1)
provided (1) +421
rather (1)
rather (1) +3954
so (1) +3610+4202
suppose (1)
surely (1) +401
till (1) +6330
unless (1) +1194
unless (1) +3954+4200+7156
unless (1) +3954+4202
until (1) +3954
whether (1) +2022+4202
while (1)

why (1) +4027+4200+4537
won't until (1) +3954
yet (1) +3954
you (1) +3870
untranslated (145)

562 אֵם 'ēm (220)
mother (134)
mother's (60)
mothers (8)
parents (3) +3+2256
birth (2) +1061
grandmother (2)
she^s (2) +2257
birth (1) +5055
brothers (1) +278
fork (1)
grandmother's (1)
mothers' (1)
uncle's (1) +278
very own brother (1) +278+1201+3870
untranslated (2)

563 אָמָה 'āmāh (56)
maidservant (16)
servant (14)
maidservants (9)
slave girls (4)
female (3)
servant's (2)
slave girl (2)
her^s (1) +3870
me^s (1) +3870
slave born in household (1) +1201
slave woman (1)
slave woman's (1)
slaves (1) +2256+6269

564 1אַמָּה 'ammāh1 (255)
cubits (163)
cubit (37)
about six hundred feet (2) +752+4395
long cubits (2)
seventy-five feet (2) +2822
18 inches (1)
45 feet (1) +8993
450 feet (1) +4395+8993
75 feet (1) +2822
doorposts (1)
fifteen feet (1) +928+2021+6924
fifteen hundred feet (1) +547
five hundred yards (1) +547
four and a half feet (1) +8993
more than thirteen feet (1) +9596
over nine feet (1) +2256+2455+9252
seven and a half feet (1) +928+2021+2822
six feet (1) +752
thirty feet (1) +928+2021+6929
three feet (1)
three thousand feet (1) +547
time (1)
twenty feet (1) +2822+6926
twenty-seven feet (1) +6926+9046
yards (1)
untranslated (29)

565 2אַמָּה 'ammāh2 (1)
Ammah (1)

566 3אַמָּה 'ammāh3
Variant; not used

567 4אַמָּה 'ammāh4
Variant; not used

568 אֵמָה 'ēmāh
Variant; not used

569 אֻמָּה 'ummāh (3)
tribal (2)
peoples (1)

570 1אָמוֹן 'āmôn1 (2)
craftsman (1)
craftsmen (1)

571 2אָמוֹן 'āmôn2 (17)
Amon (15)
Amon's (2)

572 3אָמוֹן 'āmôn3 (1)
Amon (1)

573 1אֵמוּן 'ēmûn1 (2)
faithful (2)

574 2אֵמוּן 'ēmûn2 (6)
faithful (2)
faith (1)
trustworthy (1)
truthful (1)
unfaithful (1) +4202

575 אֱמוּנָה 'ẹmûnāh (49)
faithfulness (20)
truth (6)
faithful (5)
faithfully (5) +928
entrusted with (2) +928
trustworthy (2)
truthful (2)
complete honesty (1)
faith (1)
integrity (1)
safe (1)
steady (1)
sure foundation (1)
trust (1)

576 אָמוֹץ 'āmôs (13)
Amoz (13)

577 אָמִי 'āmiy (1)
Ami (1)

578 אֲמִינוֹן 'ạmiynôn (1)
Amnon (1)

579 אַמִּיץ 'ammiys (6)
mighty (2)
bravest (1) +4213
strength (1)
strong (1)
vast (1)

580 אָמִיר 'āmiyr (2)
branches (1)
undergrowth (1)

581 1אָמַל 'āmal1 (16)
languish (2)
wither (2)
fade (1)
fails (1)
faint (1)
languishes (1)
pine away (1)
pines away (1)
waste away (1)
wasted away (1)
wastes away (1)
weak-willed (1) +4226
withered (1)
withers (1)

582 2אָמַל 'āmal2
Variant; not used

583 אֻמְלַל 'umlal (1)
faint (1)

584 אֲמֵלָל 'ạmēlāl (1)
feeble (1)

585 אֲמָם 'ạmām (1)
Amam (1)

586 1אָמַן 'āman1 (97)
believe (20)
faithful (15)
trust (8)
believed (7)
trustworthy (4)
be established (2)

come true (2)
firm (2)
have faith (2)
places trust (2)
put trust (2)
be confirmed (1)
be trusted (1)
be upheld (1)
be verified (1)
believes (1)
certain (1)
confident (1)
despairs (1) +4202
endure (1)
enduring (1)
fails (1) +4202
firmly (1)
have assurance (1)
lasting (1)
lingering (1)
loyal (1)
never fail (1)
not fail (1)
prolonged (1)
reliable (1)
stand (1)
stand firm (1) +4394
stand firm in faith (1)
stand still (1)
sure (1)
trusted (1)
trusted advisers (1)
trusting (1)
trusts (1)
trustworthy (1) +8120
was attested (1)

587   אָמַן2   'āman2 (9)
nurse (1)
are carried (1)
brought up (1)
cared (1)
foster fathers (1)
guardians (1)
guardians of children (1)
nurtured (1)

588   אָמָן   'āmmān (1)
craftsman's (1)

589   אָמֵן   'āmēn (30)
amen (26)
truth (2)
amen so be it (1) +589

590   אֹמֶן   'ōmen (1)
perfect (1)

591   אֲמָנָה1   'ᵃmānāh1 (2)
binding agreement (1)
regulated (1)

592   אֲמָנָה2   'ᵃmānāh2 (2)
Amana (1)
untranslated (1)

593   אָמְנָה1   'omnāh1 (2)
really (1)
true (1)

594   אָמְנָה2   'omnāh2 (1)
bringing up (1)

595   אֹמְנָה   'ōmnāh (1)
doorposts (1)

596   אַמְנוֹן   'amnôn (27)
Amnon (25)
Amnon's (1)
himˢ (1)

597   אָמְנָם   'omnām (9)
true (4)
indeed (2)
be assured (1)
doubtless (1)

unthinkable (1) +4202

598   אֻמְנָם   'umnām (5)
really (3)
indeed (1)
really (1) +677

599   אָמֵץ   'āmēṣ (41)
courageous (11)
strong (4)
strengthen (3)
managed (2)
raised up (2)
determined (1)
encourage (1)
established (1)
hardened (1)
hardhearted (1) +906+4222
increases (1)
let grow (1)
marshal (1)
muster (1)
obstinate (1)
opposed (1) +6584
reinforced (1)
steady (1)
strengthened (1)
stronger (1)
supported (1)
take heart (1) +4213
take heart (1) +4222
victorious (1)

600   אָמֹץ   'āmōṣ (2)
powerful (2)

601   אֹמֶץ   'ōmeṣ (1)
grow stronger (1) +3578

602   אָמְצָה   'amṣāh (1)
strong (1)

603   אַמְצִי   'amṣiy (2)
Amzi (2)

604   אֲמַצְיָה   'ᵃmaṣyāh (9)
Amaziah (9)

605   אֲמַצְיָהוּ   'ᵃmaṣyāhû (31)
Amaziah (29)
Amaziah's (2)

606   אָמַר1   'āmar1 (5317)
said (1958)
says (610)
say (506)
asked (215)
replied (185)
answered (161)
saying (138)
tell (93)
told (84)
thought (47)
ask (45)
ordered (28)
message (18)
added (15)
spoke (14)
commanded (13)
answer (12)
speak (12)
promised (10)
declared (9)
shouted (9)
continued (8)
word (8)
thinking (7)
uttered (7) +2256+5951
called (6)
cried (6)
prayed (6)
think (6)
call (5)
exclaimed (5)
gave orders (5)

asking (4)
declare (4)
reply (4)
reported (4)
spoken (4)
tells (4)
asks (3)
be called (3)
be said (3)
called out (3)
cried out (3)
intend (3)
suggested (3)
announced (2)
be (2)
challenge (2)
claim (2)
claims (2)
command (2)
commands (2)
cry out (2)
demanded (2)
is said (2)
name (2)
order (2)
read (2)
replied (2) +8938
responded (2)
say (2) +606
set (2)
shout (2)
shouting (2)
talked (2)
telling (2)
thinks (2)
want (2)
add (1)
advised (1)
afraidˢ (1)
agreed (1)
assured (1)
be named (1)
be told (1)
been given (1)
boast (1)
boasted (1)
boasts (1)
brought up (1)
call out (1)
called back (1)
calling out (1)
came (1)
claimed (1)
commemorate (1)
complain (1)
confessed (1)
cries (1)
cry (1)
cry out (1) +4200+5951
declares (1) +606
demand (1)
demanding (1)
directed (1)
exclaim (1)
explain (1)
gave (1)
gave an order (1)
gave the order (1)
give (1)
goes (1)
greeted (1)
heard (1) +265+928
indicate (1)
indicated (1)
inquired of (1) +448
insisted (1)
instructed (1)
intended (1)
issued orders (1)
keep saying (1) +606
makes speech (1) +609

news (1)
objected (1)
offered (1)
plan (1)
plead (1)
proclaiming (1)
promised (1) +606
proposed (1)
protest (1)
provided (1)
question (1)
realize (1) +4200+4222
recite (1)
recite (1) +2256+6699
repeated (1)
replies (1)
report (1)
reporting (1)
respond (1)
say (1) +2256+6699
saying (1) +4200
search (1) +928
sent word (1)
shows (1)
snorts (1)
so sure (1) +606
speaks (1)
spoke up (1)
suggest (1)
swear (1)
talking (1)
tell (1) +1821
think (1) +928+4213
think (1) +928+4222
thinks (1) +928+4222
thought (1) +448+3276
told (1) +4200+8938
urged (1)
use (1)
used (1)
uttered (1)
wanted (1)
warned (1)
warning (1)
was said (1)
was told (1)
words (1)
untranslated (878)

607 2אָמַר *'āmar2* (2)
boast (1)
full of boasting (1)

608 אֹמֶר *'ōmer* (5)
speech (2)
promise (1)
what[s] (1)
word (1)

609 1אֵמֶר *'ēmer1* (48)
words (33)
arguments (2)
what say (2) +7023
words (2) +7023
answers (1)
appointed (1)
keeps saying (1) +8740
lies (1) +9214
makes speech (1) +606
pleading (1)
those[s] (1)
what said (1) +7023
what say (1)

610 2אֵמֶר *'ēmer2*
Variant; not used

611 1אִמֵּר *'immēr1* (1)
fawns (1)

612 2אִמֵּר *'immēr2* (8)
Immer (8)

613 3אִמֵּר *'immēr3* (2)
Immer (2)

614 אִמְרָה *'imrāh* (37)
word (13)
promise (11)
words (4)
promises (2)
speech (2)
command (1)
prayer (1)
what have to say (1)
what say (1)
untranslated (1)

615 אֶמְרָה *'emrāh*
Variant; not used

616 אֱמֹרִי *'ᵉmōriy* (87)
Amorites (76)
Amorite (10)
it[s] (1) +1473+2021

617 אִמְרִי *'imriy* (2)
Imri (2)

618 אֲמַרְיָה *'ᵃmaryāh* (13)
Amariah (12)
Amariah's (1)

619 אֲמַרְיָהוּ *'ᵃmaryāhû* (3)
Amariah (3)

620 אַמְרָפֶל *'amrāpel* (2)
Amraphel (2)

621 אֶמֶשׁ *'emeš* (5)
last night (3)
night (1)
yesterday (1)

622 אֱמֶת *'ᵉmet* (127)
faithfulness (34)
truth (29)
true (20)
faithful (5)
sure (5)
faithfully (4)
faithfully (4) +928
security (3)
truthful (3)
honorably (2) +928
reliable (2)
right (2)
truly (2) +928
trustworthy (2)
assurance (1)
assuredly (1) +928
fairly (1)
fairness (1)
faithful (1) +928+2143
faithfully (1) +6913
integrity (1)
lasting (1)
really (1) +928
sound (1)

623 אַמְתַּחַת *'amtaḥaṯ* (15)
sack (7)
sacks (7)
it[s] (1) +2257

624 אֲמִתַּי *'ᵃmitay* (2)
Amittai (2)

625 אָן *'ān* (42)
where (17) +2025
how long (12) +2025+6330
anywhere else (2) +625+2025+2025+2256
where (2)
which way (2) +2025
anywhere (1) +625+2025+2025+2256
how long (1) +6330
when (1) +2025+6330
wherever (1) +2025
untranslated (1)

626 אָנָּא *'ānnā'* (7)
O (5)
I ask (1)

oh (1)

627 1אָנַח *'ānāh1* (3)
groan (1)
lament (1)
mourning (1)

628 2אָנַח *'ānāh2* (4)
befall (1) +448
befalls (1) +4200
lets happen (1) +3338+4200
trying to pick a quarrel (1)

629 אָנָּה *'ānnāh* (6)
O (6)

630 אָנוּ *'ānû* (1)
untranslated (1)

631 אָנוּשׁ *'ānûš* (8)
incurable (3)
beyond cure (1)
despair (1)
grievous (1)
incurable wound (1)
no cure (1)

632 1אֱנוֹשׁ *'ᵉnôš1* (42)
man (20)
men (9)
mortal (4)
man's (2)
friends (1) +8934
he[s] (1)
his[s] (1)
mankind (1)
one (1)
ordinary (1)
very few (1) +4663

633 2אֱנוֹשׁ *'ᵉnôš2* (7)
Enosh (7)

634 אָנַח *'ānah* (13)
groan (7)
groaning (2)
grieve (1)
groaned (1)
groans (1)
moan (1)

635 אֲנָחָה *'ᵃnāḥāh* (11)
groaning (6)
sighing (4)
groans (1)

636 אֲנַחְנוּ *'ᵃnaḥnû* (121)
we (103)
us (6)
we're (2)
our (1)
untranslated (9)

637 אֲנָחֲרַת *'ᵃnāḥᵃraṯ* (1)
Anaharath (1)

638 אֲנִי *'ᵃniy* (874)
I (790)
me (26)
myself (21)
we (6)
I'll (3)
my (2)
each of us (1) +2085+2256
I'm (1)
me alone (1) +3276
mine (1)
my life (1)
yes[s] (1)
untranslated (20)

639 אֳנִי *'ᵒniy* (7)
ships (3)
fleet (1)
fleet of trading ships (1) +9576
galley (1)
it[s] (1) +9576

640 אֲנִיָּה 'ᵃniyyāh (2)
lament (1)
lamentation (1)

641 אֳנִיָּה 'ᵒniyyāh (32)
ships (16)
ship (3)
boats (1)
cargo (1) +889+928+2021+3998
fleet of ships (1)
fleet of trading ships (1) +2143+4200+9576
fleet of trading ships (1) +2143+9576
fleet of trading ships (1) +9576
itˢ (1) +9576
sail (1) +928+2021+2143
sailors (1) +408
theseˢ (1)
theyˢ (1)
trading ship (1) +9576
untranslated (1)

642 אֲנִיעָם 'ᵃniy'ām (1)
Aniam (1)

643 אֲנָךְ 'ᵃnāḵ (4)
plumb line (3)
true to plumb (1)

644 אָנֹכִי 'ānōḵiy (359)
I (326)
I'm (8)
me (5)
myself (5)
I'll (3)
itˢ (1)
we (1)
untranslated (10)

645 אָנַן 'ānan (2)
complain (1)
complained (1)

646 אָנַס 'ānas (1)
allowed (1) +401

647 אָנַף 'ānap (14)
angry (14)

648 אָנָף 'ānāp
Variant; not used

649 אֲנָפָה 'ᵃnāpāh (2)
heron (2)

650 אָנַק 'ānaq (4)
groan (3)
lament (1)

651 1אֲנָקָה 'ᵃnāqāh1 (4)
groans (2)
groaning (1)
wail (1)

652 2אֲנָקָה 'ᵃnāqāh2 (1)
gecko (1)

653 אָנַשׁ 'ānaš (1)
ill (1)

654 אָסָא 'āsā' (58)
Asa (50)
Asa's (7)
untranslated (1)

655 אָסוּךְ 'āsûḵ (1)
littleˢ (1)

656 אָסוֹן 'āsôn (5)
harm (3)
serious injury (2)

657 אֵסוּר 'ēsûr (3)
bindings (1)
chains (1)
imprisoned (1) +1074+2021+5989

658 אָסִיף 'āsiyp (3)
ingathering (2)
harvest (1)

659 אָסִיר 'āsiyr (14)

prisoners (8)
captives (2)
captive (1)
held (1)
untranslated (2)

660 1אָסִיר 'assiyr1 (4)
captives (2)
captive (1)
prisoners (1)

661 2אַסִּיר 'assiyr2 (4)
Assir (4)

662 אָסָם 'āsām (2)
barns (2)

663 אַסְנָה 'asnāh (1)
Asnah (1)

664 אָסְנַת 'āsnaṯ (3)
Asenath (3)

665 אָסַף 'āsap (199)
gathered (18)
gather (17)
assembled (14)
be gathered (9)
assemble (6)
harvest (5)
rear guard (5)
was gathered (5)
brought together (4)
called together (4) +2256+8938
gathered together (4)
take away (4)
are taken away (3)
collected (3)
cure (3)
gather together (3)
gathered up (3)
mustered (3)
accumulated (2)
be buried (2) +448+7700
gather in (2)
gather up (2)
gathers (2)
gathers up (2)
no longer shine (2) +5586
put (2)
withdraw (2)
admit (1)
are gathered (1)
assembling (1)
banded together (1) +2021+2653+4200
be brought back (1)
be collected (1)
be gathered (1) +665
be gathered up (1)
be herded together (1) +669
be recovered (1)
been brought (1)
been gathered (1)
bring (1)
bring back (1)
brought (1)
brought back (1)
called together (1)
came together (1)
cured (1)
do so more (1)
drew up (1)
dying (1)
gather around (1)
gathering (1)
get (1)
gone (1)
got together (1)
had brought (1)
harvested (1)
is gathered in (1)
is harvested (1)
join (1)
join forces (1)

joined forces (1)
joined forces (1) +3481
lose (1)
massing together (1)
muster (1)
rallied (1)
receive (1)
regrouped (1) +3480
remove (1)
return (1)
returned (1)
set aside (1)
steal away (1)
store away (1)
summon (1)
surely gather (1) +665
sweep away (1) +6066
take (1)
taken (1)
taken away (1)
together (1)
took (1)
took into service (1)
victims (1)
wane (1)
wasˢ (1)
were brought together (1)
were caught (1)
were gathered (1)
were mustered (1)
withdrawn (1)
withdraws (1)
withdrew (1)

666 אָסָף 'āsāp (46)
Asaph (45)
Asaph's (1)

667 אָסֹף 'āsōp (3)
storehouse (1)
storehouse (1) +1074
storerooms (1)

668 אֹסֶף 'ōsep (3)
gathers (1)
harvest of fruit (1)
untranslated (1)

669 אֲסֵפָה 'ᵃsēpāh (1)
be herded together (1) +665

670 אֲסֻפָּה 'ᵃsuppāh (1)
collected sayings (1) +1251

671 אֲסַפְסֻף 'ᵃsapsup (1)
rabble (1)

672 אַסְפָּתָא 'aspāṯā' (1)
Aspatha (1)

673 אָסַר 'āsar (73)
bound (9)
obligated (4)
obligates (4)
be tied (2)
hitch up (2)
prison (2) +1074
prisoners (2)
tie up (2)
tied (2)
ties (2)
are bound (1)
be kept in prison (1)
be tied up (1)
been captured (1)
bind (1)
binding (1)
captives (1)
fetters (1)
had made ready (1)
harness (1)
hitch (1)
hitched (1)
hitched up (1)
instruct (1)

is held captive (1)
join in (1)
made ready (1)
obligate (1)
obligation taken (1)
prison (1) +1074+2021
put (1)
put in bonds (1)
put in chains (1)
start (1)
stay (1)
take prisoner (1)
tether (1)
tethered (1)
tie up (1) +673
ties securely (1) +673
was confined (1)
went into (1)
were bound (1)
were confined (1)
were held (1)
were taken prisoner (1)
wore (1)
untranslated (3)

674 אָסָר *'issār* (11)
pledge (6)
pledges (5)

675 אֵסַר־חַדֹּן *'ēsar-haddōn* (3)
Esarhaddon (3)

676 אֶסְתֵּר *'estēr* (55)
Esther (42)
Esther's (5)
she^s (4)
her^s (1)
who^s (1)
untranslated (2)

677 1אַף *'ap1* (134)
and (8)
too (7)
and (6) +2256
even (6)
how much less (6) +3954
also (4)
how much more (4)
how much more (4) +3954
how much worse (3) +3954
no sooner (3) +1153
surely (3)
all (2)
and also (2)
how much more so (2) +3954
now (2)
then (2)
too (2) +2256
yes (2)
also (1) +2256
but also (1)
but even (1)
but now (1)
even (1) +2256
even (1) +2256+3954
how (1)
how much better (1) +3954
how much less (1) +3954+4202
how much more (1) +2256+3954
if (1)
in all this (1)
indeed (1)
indeed (1) +2256+3954
moreover (1)
no (1)
nor (1) +401
or (1)
really (1)
really (1) +598
really (1) +3954
rejoice greatly (1) +1635+1638
though (1)
till (1) +2256

together with (1) +2256
true (1)
very (1)
whether (1)
yet (1) +2256
untranslated (37)

678 2אַף *'ap2* (277)
anger (173)
wrath (15)
face (14)
nostrils (12)
angry (11) +3013
nose (10)
angry (4)
faces (4)
very angry (4) +3013
patient (3) +800
fury (2)
noses (2)
anger (1) +3013
angry (1) +3019
before (1) +928
before (1) +4200
breath (1)
brow (1)
double (1)
fell facedown (1) +2556+4200
furious (1) +3013+4394
gives patience (1) +799
great rage (1) +3034
hot-tempered (1)
life breath (1) +8120
long-suffering (1) +800
not angry (1) +8740
passion (1)
patience (1) +802
pride (1) +1470
quick-tempered (1) +7920
resentment (1)
snout (1)
which^s (1) +2257
untranslated (1)

679 אָפַד *'āpad* (2)
fasten (1)
fastened (1)

680 1אֵפֹד *'ēpōd1* (49)
ephod (46)
it^s (1) +2021
untranslated (2)

681 2אֵפֹד *'ēpōd2* (1)
Ephod (1)

682 אֲפֻדָּה *'ăpuddāh* (3)
skillfully woven (2)
covered (1)

683 אַפֶּדֶן *'appeden* (1)
royal (1)

684 אָפָה *'āpāh* (13)
bake (5)
baked (5)
bakes (1)
baking (1)
be baked (1)

685 אֹפֶה *'ōpeh* (11)
baker (8)
bakers (2)
baked goods (1) +4407+5126

686 אֵפוֹא *'ēpô* (15)
then (7)
now (3)
so (2)
how (1) +928+4537
oh (1) +4769+5989
where (1) +180

687 אֲפוּנָה *'āpûnāh*
Variant; not used

688 אָפִיח *'ăpiyah* (1)

Aphiah (1)

689 אָפִיל *'āpiyl* (1)
ripen later (1)

690 1אַפַּיִם *'appayim1*
Variant; not used

691 2אַפַּיִם *'appayim2* (2)
Appaim (2)

692 1אָפִיק *'āpiyq1* (18)
ravines (8)
streams (4)
valleys (2)
channels (1)
rows (1)
streams (1) +5707
tubes (1)

693 2אָפִיק *'āpiyq2* (1)
mighty (1)

694 אֹפֶל *'ōpel* (9)
darkness (4)
thick darkness (2)
deepest night (1) +4017+6547
gloom (1)
shadows (1)

695 אָפֵל *'āpēl* (1)
pitch-dark (1)

696 אֲפֵלָה *'ăpēlāh* (10)
gloom (2)
dark (1)
dark (1) +413
darkness (1)
deep darkness (1)
deep shadows (1)
night (1)
total darkness (1) +3125
utter darkness (1)

697 אֶפְלָל *'eplāl* (2)
Ephlal (2)

698 אֹפֶן *'ōpen* (1)
aptly (1) +6584

699 אָפֵס *'āpēs* (5)
come to an end (1)
gone (1)
used up (1)
vanish (1)
vanished (1)

700 אֶפֶס *'epes* (43)
ends (14)
no (5)
none (5)
without (3) +928
but (2) +3954
not (2)
only (2)
amount to nothing (1)
but (1)
however (1) +3954
lately (1) +928
nothing (1)
nothing at all (1) +401+2256
or (1) +2256
vanish away (1)
whether (1) +2256
yet (1) +3954

701 אֹפֶס *'ōpes* (1)
ankle-deep (1)

702 אֶפֶס דַּמִּים *'epes dammiym* (1)
Ephes Dammim (1)

703 אָפַע *'epa'* (1)
worthless (1)

704 אֶפְעֶה *'ep'eh* (3)
adder (2)
adders (1)

705 אָפַף *'āpap* (5)
entangled (2)

engulfing (1)
surround (1)
swirled about (1)

706 אָפַק 'āpaq (7)
are withheld (1)
control himself (1)
controlling himself (1)
felt compelled (1)
held myself back (1)
hold yourself back (1)
restrained himself (1)

707 אֲפֵק 'ăpēq (9)
Aphek (9)

708 אֲפֵקָה 'ăpēqāh (1)
Aphekah (1)

709 אֵפֶר 'ēper (22)
ashes (20)
dust (2)

710 אֲפֵר 'ăpēr (2)
headband (2)

711 אֶפְרֹחַ 'eprōah (5)
young (2)
young ones (1)
untranslated (2)

712 אַפִּרְיוֹן 'appiryôn (1)
carriage (1)

713 אֶפְרַיִם 'eprayim (180)
Ephraim (148)
Ephraim's (12)
Ephraim (6) +1201
Ephraimites (4) +1201
Ephraim (2) +824
Ephraimite (2) +1201
Ephraimites (2)
Ephraimite (1)
Ephraimites (1) +408
Ephraimites (1) +4946
untranslated (1)

714 אֶפְרָת 1 'eprāt1 (4)
Ephrath (4)

715 אֶפְרָת 2 'eprāt2 (1)
Ephrath (1)

716 אֶפְרָתָה 1 'eprātāh1 (3)
Ephrathah (3)

717 אֶפְרָתָה 2 'eprātāh2 (2)
Ephrathah (2)

718 אֶפְרָתִי 'eprātiy (5)
Ephraimite (3)
Ephrathite (1)
Ephrathites (1)

719 אֶצְבֹּן 'esbōn (2)
Ezbon (2)

720 אֶצְבַּע 'esba' (31)
finger (17)
fingers (11)
forefinger (2)
toes (1)

721 אָצִיל 1 'āsiyl1 (1)
farthest corners (1)

722 אָצִיל 2 'āsiyl2 (1)
leaders (1)

723 אַצִּיל 'assiyl (3)
arms (1) +3338
long (1)
wrists (1) +3338

724 אָצַל 'āsal (5)
denied (1)
reserved (1)
smaller (1)
take (1)
took (1)

725 אֵצֶל 'ēsel (61)
beside (30)
near (6)
side (4)
at (2)
at side (2)
away (2) +4946
by (2)
next to (2)
with (2)
close to (1)
close to (1) +7940
go to bed with (1) +8886
neared (1) +2143
next to (1) +4946
to (1)
untranslated (3)

726 אֵצֶל 2 'ēsel2
Variant; not used

727 אָצֵל 1 'āsēl1 (6)
Azel (6)

728 אָצֵל 2 'āsēl2 (1)
Azel (1)

729 אֲצַלְיָהוּ 'ăsalyāhû (2)
Azaliah (2)

730 אֹצֶם 'ōsem (2)
Ozem (2)

731 אֶצְעָדָה 'es'ādāh (2)
armlets (1)
band (1)

732 אָצַר 'āsar (5)
stored up (2)
be stored up (1)
hoard (1)
put in charge of the storerooms (1)
+238+6584

733 אֵצֶר 'ēser (5)
Ezer (5)

734 אֶקְדָּח 'eqdāh (1)
sparkling jewels (1) +74

735 אַקּוֹ 'aqqô (1)
wild goat (1)

736 אֲרָא 'ărā' (1)
Ara (1)

737 אֶרְאֵל 'er'ēl (1)
brave men (1)

738 אֲרִאֵל 'ări'ēl (2)
best men (2)

739 אַרְאֵלִי 1 'ar'ēliy1 (2)
Areli (2)

740 אַרְאֵלִי 2 'ar'ēliy2 (1)
Arelite (1)

741 אָרַב 'ārab (41)
ambush (9)
lie in wait (8)
lies in wait (5)
in ambush (3)
set an ambush (3)
hidden (2)
lay in wait (2)
ambush set (1)
ambushes (1)
bandits (1)
hide (1)
lurked (1)
lurks (1)
lying in wait (1)
took up concealed positions (1)
untranslated (1)

742 אֲרָב 'ărāb (1)
Arab (1)

743 אֶרֶב 'ereb (2)

cover (1)
wait (1)

744 אֹרֶב 'ōreb (2)
intrigue (1)
trap (1)

745 אַרְבְּאֵל 'arbē'l
Variant; not used

746 אַרְבֶּה 'arbeh (24)
locusts (15)
locust (5)
great locusts (2)
great locust (1)
they^s (1) +2021

747 אָרְבָה 'ārbāh (1)
cleverness (1)

748 אֲרֻבָּה 'ărubbāh (9)
floodgates (6)
nests (1)
window (1)
windows (1)

749 אֲרֻבּוֹת 'ărubbôt (1)
Arubboth (1)

750 אַרְבִּי 'arbiy (1)
Arbite (1)

751 ארנבן 'rnbn
Variant; not used

752 אַרְבַּע 1 'arba'1 (456)
four (172)
forty (78)
fourteenth (19) +6925
24,000 (14) +547+2256+6929
fourteen (12) +6925
twenty-fourth (9) +2256+6929
4,500 (8) +547+2256+2822+4395
fourteen (7) +6926
forty-two (5) +2256+9109
fourth (5)
twenty-four (5) +2256+6929
1,254 (4) +547+2256+2822+4395
all fours (4)
forty-one (4) +285+2256
fourteenth (4) +6926
40,500 (3) +547+2256+2822+4395
430 (3) +2256+4395+8993
53,400 (3)
+547+2256+2256+2822+4395+8993
fortieth (3)
forty-five (3) +2256+2822
1,247 (2) +547+2256+4395+8679
345 (2) +2256+2822+4395+8993
35,400 (2)
+547+2256+2256+2822+4395+8993
4,600 (2) +547+2256+4395+9252
403 (2) +2256+4395+8993
41,500 (2)
+285+547+2256+2256+2822+4395
42 (2) +2256+9109
435 (2) +2256+2822+4395+8993
45,650 (2)   +547+2256+2256+2256
+2822+2822+4395+9252
46,500 (2)
+547+2256+2256+2822+4395+9252
54,400 (2)
+547+752+2256+2256+2822+4395
57,400 (2)
+547+2256+2256+2822+4395+8679
74 (2) +2256+8679
74,600 (2) +547+2256+4395+8679+9252
about six hundred feet (2) +564+4395
forty-eight (2) +2256+9046
fourteen hundred (2) +547+2256+4395
14,700 (1) +547+2256+4395+6925+8679
148 (1) +2256+4395+9046
151,450 (1)   +285+547+547+2256+2256
+2256+2256+2822+2822+4395+4395
186,400 (1)   +547+547+547+2256
+2256+2256+4395+4395+9046+9252

2,400 (1) +547+2256+4395
22,034 (1)
   +547+2256+2256+2256+6929+8993+9109
242 (1) +2256+4395+9109
245 (1) +2256+2256+2822+4395
245 (1) +2256+2822+4395
284 (1) +2256+4395+9046
324 (1) +2256+4395+6929+8993
34 (1) +2256+8993
40 (1)
40,000 (1) +547
410 (1) +2256+4395+6927
42,360 (1)
   +547+2256+4395+8052+8993+9252
42,360 (1) +547+4395+8052+8993+9252
420 (1) +2256+4395+6929
43,730 (1)   +547+2256+2256+2256
   +4395+8679+8993+8993
44,760 (1)   +547+752+2256+2256
   +2256+4395+8679+9252
45,400 (1)
   +547+752+2256+2256+2822+4395
45,600 (1)
   +547+2256+2256+2822+4395+9252
454 (1) +752+2256+2822+4395
468 (1) +2256+4395+9046+9252
5,400 (1) +547+2256+2822+4395
64,300 (1)
   +547+2256+2256+4395+8993+9252
64,400 (1)
   +547+752+2256+2256+4395+9252
642 (1) +2256+2256+4395+9109+9252
642 (1) +2256+4395+9109+9252
648 (1) +2256+4395+9046+9252
743 (1) +2256+2256+4395+8679+8993
743 (1) +2256+4395+8679+8993
745 (1) +2256+2822+4395+8679
840 (1) +2256+4395+9046
845 (1) +2256+2822+4395+9046
945 (1) +2256+2256+2822+4395+9596
each[s] (1)
forty-first (1) +285+2256
forty-nine (1) +2256+9596
forty-seven (1) +2256+8679
four-fifths (1) +3338
six feet (1) +564
square (1) +448+8062+8063
square (1) +448+8063
untranslated (8)

753 אַרְבַּע 2 'arba'2
Variant; not used

754 אַרְבָּעִים 'arbā'iym
Variant; not used

755 אָרַג 'ārag (14)
weaver's (4)
weaver (3)
weavers (2)
did weaving (1) +1428
spin (1)
weave (1)
wove (1)
woven (1) +5126

756 אֶרֶג 'ereg (2)
loom (1)
weaver's shuttle (1)

757 אַרְגָּב 'argāḇ
Variant; not used

758 אַרְגֹּב 1 'argōḇ1 (4)
Argob (4)

759 אַרְגֹּב 2 'argōḇ2 (1)
Argob (1)

760 אַרְגְּוָן 'arg'wān (1)
purple (1)

761 אַרְגַּז 'argaz (3)
chest (3)

762 אָרְגְּנִים 'ōrgiym

Variant; not used

763 אַרְגָּמָן 'argāmān (38)
purple (36)
purple material (1)
tapestry (1)

764 אַרְדְּ 'ard (3)
Ard (3)

765 אַרְדּוֹן 'ardôn (1)
Ardon (1)

766 אַרְדִּי 'ardiy (1)
Ardite (1)

767 אֲרִדַי "riday (1)
Aridai (1)

768 אָרָה 'ārāh (2)
gathered (1)
pick (1)

769 אֲרוֹד "rôḏ
Variant; not used

770 אַרְוָד 'arwāḏ (2)
Arvad (2)

771 אֲרוֹדִי 1 "rôḏiy1 (2)
Arodi (2)

772 אֲרוֹדִי 2 "rôḏiy2 (1)
Arodite (1)

773 אַרְוָדִי 'arwāḏiy (2)
Arvadites (2)

774 אֻרְוָה 'urwāh (4)
stalls (3)
pens (1)

775 אָרוּז 'ārûz (1)
tightly knotted (1)

776 אֲרוּכָה "rûḵāh (6)
health (2)
repairs (2)
healing (1)
healing for wound (1)

777 אֲרוּמָה "rûmāh (1)
Arumah (1)

778 אֲרוֹן "rôn (202)
ark (181)
chest (10)
it[s] (4) +2021
it[s] (2)
coffin (1)
it[s] (1) +466+2021
it[s] (1) +1382+2021
untranslated (2)

779 אֲרַוְנָה "rawnāh (11)
Araunah (8)
he[s] (1)
untranslated (2)

780 אֶרֶז 'erez (73)
cedar (53)
cedars (19)
them[s] (1) +6770

781 אַרְזָה 'arzāh (1)
beams of cedar (1)

782 אָרַח 1 'āraḥ1 (7)
traveler (4)
going out (1)
keeps company (1) +2495+4200
travelers (1)

783 אָרַח 2 'āraḥ2 (4)
Arah (4)

784 אֹרַח 'ōraḥ (56)
path (17)
paths (11)
way (9)
ways (5)
course (4)

roads (2)
age of childbearing (1) +851+2021+3869
conduct (1)
destiny (1)
end (1)
journey (1)
path (1) +2006
siege ramps (1) +369
untranslated (1)

785 אֹרְחָה 'ōrḥāh (4)
caravans (3)
caravan (1)

786 אֲרֻחָה "ruḥāh (6)
allowance (2)
meal (1)
provisions (1)
untranslated (2)

787 אֲרִי "riy (34)
lion (17)
lions (12)
lions' (2)
fierce lion (1)
lion's (1)
young lion (1) +4097

788 אוּרִי 'uriy (1)
Uri (1)

789 אֲרִיאֵל 1 "riy'ēl1 (5)
altar hearth (2)
hearth (1)
untranslated (2)

790 אֲרִיאֵל 2 "riy'ēl2 (4)
Ariel (4)

791 אֲרִיאֵל 3 "riy'ēl3 (1)
Ariel (1)

792 אֲרִידָתָא "riyḏātā' (1)
Aridatha (1)

793 אַרְיֵה 1 'aryēh1 (46)
lion (34)
lion's (4)
lions (4)
cubs (1) +1594
it[s] (1) +1581+2021
untranslated (2)

794 אַרְיֵה 2 'aryēh2 (1)
Arieh (1)

795 אוּרְיָה 'uryāh
Variant; not used

796 אַרְיוֹךְ 'aryôḵ (2)
Arioch (2)

797 אוּרִים 'uriym
Variant; not used

798 אֲרִיסַי "riysay (1)
Arisai (1)

799 אָרַךְ 'āraḵ (35)
live long (8) +3427
long (4)
lengthen (2)
outlived (2) +339+3427
prolong (2)
been long (1)
delay (1)
endure (1)
enjoy a long life (1) +3427
enjoy long life (1) +3427
give long (1)
gives patience (1) +678
go by (1)
have long (1)
lives a long time (1)
living long (1)
made long (1)
maintains (1)
patient (1)
remained (1)

stayed (1) +8905
stick out (1)

800 אָרֵךְ *'ārēk* (15)
slow (9)
patient (3) +678
long (1)
long-suffering (1) +678
patience (1) +8120

801 אָרֹךְ *'ārōk* (3)
long time (2)
longer (1)

802 אֹרֶךְ *'ōrek* (94)
long (65)
length (12)
wide (2)
endless (1)
extended (1)
forever (1) +3427+4200
lengthwise (1)
longer (1)
many years (1) +3427
patience (1) +678
prolong (1)
so long (1) +3427
spreading (1)
square (1) +2256+8145
total wingspan (1) +4053
untranslated (3)

803 אֶרֶךְ1 *'erek1*
Variant; not used

804 אֶרֶךְ2 *'erek2* (1)
Erech (1)

805 אַרְכִּי *'arkiy* (6)
Arkite (5)
Arkites (1)

806 אֲרָם *'arām* (129)
Aram (69)
Arameans (42)
Aramean (7)
Aramean kingdom (2)
their[s] (2)
them[s] (2)
they[s] (2)
it[s] (1)
untranslated (2)

807 אֲרַם מַעֲכָה *'aram maʿakāh* (1)
Aram Maacah (1)

808 אֲרַם נַהֲרַיִם *'aram nahᵃrayim* (5)
Aram Naharaim (5)

809 אֲרַם צוֹבָה *'aram sôbāh* (1)
Aram Zobah (1)

810 אַרְמוֹן *'armôn* (33)
fortresses (19)
citadels (4)
citadel (3)
palaces (3)
fortress (1)
palace (1)
stronghold (1)
strongholds (1)

811 אֲרָמִי *'arāmiy* (5)
in Aramaic (5)

812 אֲרַמִּי *'arammiy* (13)
Aramean (8)
Arameans (4)
untranslated (1)

813 אַרְמֹנִי *'armōniy* (1)
Armoni (1)

814 אֲרָן *'arān* (2)
Aran (2)

815 אֹרֶן1 *'ōren1* (1)
pine (1)

816 אֹרֶן2 *'ōren2* (1)

Oren (1)

817 אַרְנֶבֶת *'arnebet* (2)
rabbit (2)

818 אַרְנוֹן *'arnôn* (25)
Arnon (24)
Arnon's (1)

819 אֲרַנְיָה *'aranyāh*
Variant; not used

820 אַרְנָן *'arnān* (1)
Arnan (1)

821 אָרְנָן *'ārnān* (12)
Araunah (9)
he[s] (1)
him[s] (1)
untranslated (1)

822 אַרְפַּד *'arpād* (6)
Arpad (6)

823 אַרְפַּכְשַׁד *'arpakšad* (9)
Arphaxad (9)

824 אֶרֶץ *'eres* (2505)
land (1150)
earth (524)
Egypt (184) +5213
ground (160)
country (92)
countries (39)
lands (34)
Canaan (29) +4046
world (20)
region (18)
territory (17)
Edom (11) +121
Gilead (8) +1680
Israel (7) +3776
around[s] (6)
it[s] (6) +2021
Judah (6) +3373
wild (6)
area (5)
earth's (5)
fields (5)
Moab (5) +4566
countryside (4)
district (4)
Goshen (4) +1777
land (4) +299
neighboring (4)
soil (4)
territories (4)
dust (3)
floor (3)
its[s] (3) +2021
Assyria (2) +855
cities (2) +9133
community (2)
empire (2)
Ephraim (2) +713
Judah[s] (2) +2021
lower Egypt (2) +5213
Midian (2) +4518
Negev (2) +5582
Shinar (2) +9114
the other[s] (2) +2021+7895
there[s] (2) +2021
they[s] (2) +2021+6639
upper Egypt (2) +7356
areas of land (1)
army (1)
Babylon (1) +951
Babylon (1) +4169
Babylonia (1) +9114
Bashan (1) +1421
battlefield (1)
Benjamin (1) +1228
clay (1)
community (1) +2021+6639
desert (1) +4497

districts (1)
down (1) +2025
fail (1) +2025+5877
field (1)
floor space (1)
foreign (1)
Galilee (1) +1665
he[s] (1) +466+2021
here[s] (1) +928+2021
here[s] (1) +2021
homeland (1) +4580
homeland (1) +5226
in midair (1)
      +1068+1068+2021+2021+2256+9028
it[s] (1) +2021+2021+2296
land's (1) +928
little distance (1) +3896
Naphtali (1) +5889
nations (1)
nations (1) +1580
native land (1)
native-born (1) +275
native-born (1) +275+2021
native-born (1) +928+2021+3528
neighbors (1)
on foot (1) +2021+6584
other nationalities (1) +2021+6639
peoples (1)
Philistines (1) +7149
place (1)
plain (1) +6677
plateau (1) +4793
property (1) +299
shore (1)
soil (1) +6760
some distance (1) +2021+3896
some distance (1) +3896
suitable (1)
Tema (1) +9401
their[s] (1) +2021+6639
them[s] (1) +2021+6551
there (1) +928
there[s] (1) +928+2021
there[s] (1) +928+2257
there[s] (1) +2025+4046
tracts of land (1)
Uz (1) +6420
vicinity (1)
where[s] (1)
whole earth (1) +9315
whole world (1) +9315
untranslated (42)

825 אַרְצָא *'arsā'* (1)
Arza (1)

826 אָרַר *'ārar* (63)
cursed (32)
curse (11)
be cursed (7)
brings a curse (5)
put a curse on (2)
under a curse (2)
curse (1) +4423
curse bitterly (1) +826
this[s] (1)

827 אֲרָרַט *'ᵃrārat* (4)
Ararat (4)

828 אֲרָרִי *'ᵃrāriy*
Variant; not used

829 אָרַשׂ *'āraś* (11)
pledged to be married (5)
betroth (3)
betrothed (2)
pledged (1)

830 אֲרֶשֶׁת *'ᵃrešet* (1)
request (1)

831 אַרְתַּחְשַׁסְתָּא *'artahšast'* (10)
Artaxerxes (9)
untranslated (1)

832 אֲשַׂרְאֵל *'ᵃśar'ēl* (1)
Asarel (1)

833 אֲשַׂרְאֵלָה *'ᵃśar'ēlāh* (1)
Asarelah (1)

834 אַשְׂרְאֵלִי *'aśri'ēliy* (1)
Asrielite (1)

835 אַשְׂרִיאֵל *'aśriy'ēl* (3)
Asriel (3)

836 אֵשׁ1 *'ēš1* (379)
fire (259)
burn down (9) +928+2021+8596
fiery (9)
set on fire (9) +928+2021+3675
burned (8) +928+2021+8596
lightning (7)
burning (6)
be burned up (4) +928+2021+8596
burn (4) +928+2021+8596
burned up (4) +928+2021+8596
set fire (4) +3675
set on fire (4) +928+2021+8596
burn up (4) +928+2021+8596
burned down (3) +928+2021+8596
burning (3) +2021+6584
flame (3)
coals (2)
fire (2) +4258
fires (2)
flaming (2)
it^s (2) +2021
use for fuel (2) +1277
are burned up (1) +928+2021+8596+8596
be burned (1) +928+2021+8596
be burned down (1) +928+2021+8596
blazing (1)
burn (1) +4805
burn to death (1) +928+2021+8596
burned (1) +928+2021+8938
burned down (1) +2021+8596
burned to death (1) +928+2021+8596
charred (1) +928+1277+2021
firepot (1) +3963
flashes (1) +928
fuel for fire (1) +928+1896
fuel for flames (1) +928+1896
kindled (1) +7706
lightning (1) +4259
lit (1) +1277
on fire (1) +928+1277+2021
set ablaze (1) +928+2021+3675
set fire to (1) +928+2021+8596
set fire to (1) +928+2021+8938
set on fire (1) +3675
used for fuel (1) +1198+8596
untranslated (5)

837 אֵשׁ2 *'ēš2*
Variant; not used

838 אֵשׁ *'iš* (1)
one (1)

839 אַשְׁבֵּל *'ašbēl* (3)
Ashbel (3)

840 אַשְׁבֵּלִי *'ašbēliy* (1)
Ashbelite (1)

841 אֶשְׁבָּן *'ešbān* (2)
Eshban (2)

842 אַשְׁבֵּעַ *'ašbēa'*
Variant; not used

843 אֶשְׁבַּעַל *'ešba'al* (2)
Esh-Baal (2)

844 אָשֵׁד *'āšēd* (7)
slopes (5)
mountain slopes (2)

845 אֶשֶׁד *'ešed*
Variant; not used

846 אַשְׁדּוֹד *'ašdôd* (17)
Ashdod (15)
untranslated (2)

847 אַשְׁדּוֹדִי *'ašdôdiy* (6)
people of Ashdod (2)
Ashdod (1)
from Ashdod (1)
men of Ashdod (1)
untranslated (1)

848 אַשְׁדּוֹדִית *'ašdôdiyt* (1)
language of Ashdod (1)

849 אַשְׁדּוֹת הַפִּסְגָּה *'ašdôt happisgāh*
Variant; not used

850 אֲשֵׁדַת *'ēšdāt* (1)
mountain slopes (1)

851 אִשָּׁה *'iššāh* (781)
wife (253)
woman (167)
women (103)
wives (91)
married (10) +4374
wife's (9)
each (7)
give in marriage (7) +4200+5989
her^s (6) +2021
mother (6)
one (6)
she^s (6) +2021
widow (6)
gave in marriage (5) +4200+5989
harem (5) +1074
marry (5) +2118+4200
married (4) +4200+4374
marry (4) +4200+4374
marry (4) +4374
woman's (4)
married (3) +2118+4200
adulteress (2) +2424
harem (2)
her^s (2)
mate (2)
together (2) +295+448
abstain from sexual relations (1)
           +440+448+5602
adulteress (1) +408
age of childbearing (1) +784+2021+3869
be given in marriage (1) +4200+5989
become wife (1) +4200+4374
gave in marriage (1) +5989
girl (1) +3251
give in marriage (1) +2021+5989
her^s (1) +123+2257
her^s (1) +2257
married (1) +2118
married (1) +2257+4200+4200+4374
married (1) +5951
married to (1) +2118+4200
Naomi^s (1) +2021
others^s (1) +2021
period (1) +2006
queens^s (1)
she^s (1) +2257
stillborn child (1) +5878
them^s (1)
they^s (1) +1201+2021
they^s (1) +2021
took in marriage (1) +4200+4374
was given in marriage (1) +4200+5989
widow (1) +4637
wife (1) +1249
women's (1)
untranslated (32)

852 אִשֶּׁה *'iššeh* (65)
offering made by fire (38)
offerings made by fire (19)
made by fire (2)
offering by fire (2)
sacrifice made by fire (2)

offering made by fire (1) +7933
offerings made with fire (1)

853 אֲשׁוּיָה *'ᵃšûyāh*
Variant; not used

854 אֶשּׁוּן *'ēšûn* (1)
pitch darkness (1) +3125

855 אַשּׁוּר *'aššûr* (151)
Assyria (120)
Assyrian (9)
Asshur (7)
Assyrians (5)
Assyrians (5) +1201
Assyria (2) +824
Assyria's (1)
Shalmaneser^s (1) +4889
untranslated (1)

856 אַשּׁוּרִי *'ᵃšûriy* (1)
Ashuri (1)

857 אַשּׁוּרִם *'aššûrim* (1)
Asshurites (1)

858 אַשְׁחוּר *'ašhûr* (2)
Ashhur (2)

859 אַשְׁיָה *'āšyāh* (2)
towers (1)
untranslated (1)

860 אֲשִׁימָא *'ᵃšiymā'* (1)
Ashima (1)

861 אָשִׁישׁ *'āšiyš* (1)
men (1)

862 אֲשִׁישָׁה *'ᵃšiyšāh* (4)
cake of raisins (2)
raisins (1)
sacred cakes (1)

863 אֶשֶׁךְ *'ešek* (1)
testicles (1)

864 אֶשְׁכּוֹל1 *'eškôl1* (9)
cluster of grapes (3)
clusters (3)
cluster (2)
clusters of fruit (1)

865 אֶשְׁכּוֹל2 *'eškôl2* (4)
Eshcol (4)

866 אֶשְׁכֹּל3 *'eškōl3* (2)
Eshcol (2)

867 אַשְׁכְּנַז *'ašk°naz* (3)
Ashkenaz (3)

868 אֶשְׁכָּר *'eškār* (2)
gifts (1)
paid (1) +8740

869 אֵשֶׁל *'ēšel* (3)
tamarisk tree (3)

870 אָשַׁם *'āšam* (35)
guilty (15)
bear guilt (3)
condemned (2)
sin (2)
admit guilt (1)
declare guilty (1)
devastated (1)
guilty of wrongdoing (1) +870
held guilty (1)
innocent (1)
pay for it (1)
suffering (1)
unpunished (1) +4202
very guilty (1) +870
wronged (1)

871 אָשָׁם *'āšam* (47)
guilt offering (29)
guilt offerings (5)
penalty (4)
guilt (2)

wrong (2)
its^s (1) +2021
making amends for sin (1)
restitution (1) +8740
sins (1)
untranslated (1)

872 אָשֵׁם '*āšēm* (2)
convict (1)
punished (1)

873 אַשְׁמָה '*ašmāh* (19)
guilt (13)
guilty (2)
guilt offering (1)
guilty of sins (1)
requiring payment (1)
shame (1)

874 אַשְׁמוּרָה '*ašmûrāh* (7)
watches of the night (3)
watch (2)
last watch of the night (1) +1332
last watch of the night (1) +1332+2021

875 אַשְׁמָן '*ašmān* (1)
strong (1)

876 אֶשְׁנָב '*ešnāb* (2)
lattice (2)

877 אַשְׁנָה '*ašnāh* (2)
Ashnah (2)

878 אֶשְׁעָן '*eš'ān* (1)
Eshan (1)

879 אַשָּׁף '*aššāp* (2)
enchanters (2)

880 אַשְׁפָּה '*ašpāh* (6)
quiver (5)
quivers (1)

881 אַשְׁפְּנַז '*ašp^enaz* (1)
Ashpenaz (1)

882 אֶשְׁפָּר '*ešpār* (2)
cake of dates (2)

883 אַשְׁפֹּת '*ašpōt* (7)
dung (4)
ash heap (2)
ash heaps (1)

884 אַשְׁקְלוֹן '*ašq^elôn* (12)
Ashkelon (12)

885 אֶשְׁקְלוֹנִי '*ešq^elôniy* (1)
Ashkelon (1)

886 אָשַׁר1 '*āšar1* (6)
walk (2)
are guided (1)
guide (1)
guides (1)
keep right (1)

887 אָשַׁר2 '*āšar2* (11)
call blessed (4)
be blessed (1)
bless (1)
call happy (1)
called blessed (1)
encourage (1)
spoke well of (1)
untranslated (1)

888 אָשֵׁר '*āšēr* (43)
Asher (37)
Asher (5) +1201
Asher's (1) +4946

889 אֲשֶׁר '*^ašer* (5501)
that (538)
who (527)
as (270) +3869
which (222)
what (178)
whom (120)

where (79)
just as (58) +3869
whose (42)
those (41)
when (41)
when (38) +3869
until (30) +6330
whatever (30) +3972
because (28)
for (28)
how (28)
just as (24) +3869+3972
because (21) +3610
as (18)
what (18) +3869
whatever (18)
just as (17) +3869+4027
after (14) +3869
because (14) +6584
if (13)
as (12) +3869+4027
like (12) +3869
so that (11)
the one^s (10)
wherever (10) +928+3972
though (8)
administrator^s (7) +6584
whatever (7) +3869
anyone (6)
because (6) +9393
he^s (6)
so (6)
them^s (6)
as (5) +3869+3972
because (5) +3869
since (5)
whatever (5) +3869+3972
him^s (4)
of (4)
something (4)
the covenant^s (4)
things (4)
whoever (4)
at (3)
because (3) +6813
before (3) +4202+6330
for (3) +3610
if (3) +3869
just as (3)
since (3) +3610
territory^s (3)
the land^s (3)
these (3)
this (3)
wherever (3) +448+3972
wherever (3) +928+2006+2021
wherever (3) +928+5226
although (2)
as much as (2) +3869
as soon as (2) +3869
because (2) +928
even as (2) +3869
even though (2)
exactly as (2) +3869+4027
for (2) +9393
here (2)
how much (2)
it^s (2)
just the way (2) +3869
just what (2) +3869+4027
one^s (2)
others^s (2)
peoples^s (2)
sometimes (2) +3780
such (2)
the creatures^s (2)
the day^s (2)
the man^s (2)
the men^s (2)
the name^s (2)
the ones^s (2)

the property^s (2)
the steward^s (2) +6584
the way^s (2)
the ways^s (2)
there (2)
they^s (2)
until (2) +561+6330
what (2) +3869+4027
whatever (2) +3869+4027
where (2) +928
wherever (2)
wherever (2) +928+2021+3972+5226
whoever (2) +408
whoever (2) +4769
with (2)
abundantly (1) +3907+6330+6330
according to (1)
according to (1) +3869
although (1) +928+3972
any (1)
anything (1) +3972
as (1) +928
as (1) +928+3972
as easily as (1) +3869
as long as (1) +3869
as soon as (1)
as though (1) +3869
because (1) +3869+7023
because (1) +4946
because of (1) +3869
but (1)
by (1)
cargo (1) +641+928+2021+3998
closest friend (1) +3869+3870+5883+8276
covenant^s (1)
creature^s (1)
creatures^s (1)
crowd (1) +3972+6641
disaster^s (1)
do not know where am going (1)
               +2143+2143+6584

edict^s (1)
else^s (1)
everything else (1)
exactly as (1) +3869+3972
exactly like (1) +3869+3972+4027
except (1) +4202
finally (1) +6330
followers (1) +339+2021+6639
followers (1) +408+2143+6640
for (1) +928
for (1) +6584
from (1) +928
gods^s (1)
governor^s (1) +6584
have (1) +4200
houses^s (1)
if only (1) +3869
in (1)
in accordance with (1) +3869
in accordance with (1) +3972
in proportion to (1) +3869+5002
in the end (1) +6330
including (1)
instead of (1) +9393
it (1)
just as (1) +3869+3972+4027
just as (1) +3972+4200
just what (1) +3869
keeper^s (1) +6584
kind (1) +3869
lest (1) +4202
life (1) +2118+3427
like (1)
like (1) +3869+3972
like (1) +3869+4027
living thing^s (1)
make countless (1) +4202+6218+8049
man^s (1)
matter^s (1)
men^s (1)

mission (1) +1821+8938
more (1) +3869
moving from place to place (1)
    +928+2143+2143
my people^s (1)
no sooner than (1) +3869
nothing (1) +3972+4202
now that (1) +3869
one (1)
or (1)
or (1) +4202
other^s (1) +907
otherwise (1) +4202+5100
people^s (1) +928+3972
place^s (1)
possessions^s (1)
predecessor (1) +2118+4200+7156
proper place (1) +2118+5226+9004
property^s (1)
property^s (1) +2118+4200
replies^s (1)
responsible for (1) +928+4200
robe^s (1)
same (1) +3869
same as (1)
share (1) +3869+4200
shared hardships (1) +928+6700+6700
she^s (1)
since (1) +339
since (1) +928
since (1) +4946
since (1) +9393
so (1) +3869
so that (1) +3610
so with (1) +3869
some other place^s (1)
some^s (1)
someone (1)
son^s (1)
steward^s (1) +408+1074+2021+6584
steward^s (1) +1074+6584
such as (1)
surviving (1) +3855+3856
than (1) +4946
that (1) +6330
the areas^s (1)
the celebration^s (1)
the cup^s (1)
the girl^s (1)
the gods^s (1)
the person^s (1)
the place^s (1)
the places^s (1)
the plans^s (1)
the storehouses^s (1) +928+2157+3972
the temple^s (1)
the terms^s (1)
the territory^s (1)
the total^s (1)
the vineyard^s (1)
then (1)
then (1) +3869
this is how (1) +3869
those^s (1) +339+2021+6639
till (1) +6330
town^s (1)
under (1)
very things (1) +3869+4027
vows^s (1)
what (1) +4017
whatever (1) +928+3972
whatever (1) +3869+3972+4027
when (1) +6584
whenever (1) +928+3972
whenever (1) +3869
wherever (1) +285+928+2021+5226
wherever (1) +928
wherever (1) +928+2021+5226
wherever (1) +2021+3972+5226+6584
wherever (1) +2025+9004
wherever (1) +3972+6584

wherever (1) +3972+9004
wherever (1) +4946
wherever^s (1) +5226
while (1)
while (1) +3869
whoever (1) +408+3972
whose (1) +4200
yet (1)
yet (1) +1172+4946
you^s (1)
untranslated (2620)

890 אֶשֶׁר 'ešer (2)
blessed (1)
happy (1)

891 אֹשֶׁר 'ōšer (1)
happy (1)

892 אָשֻׁר 'āšur (9)
steps (4)
feet (2)
foothold (1)
place to stand (1)
tracked down (1)

893 1אַשֻּׁר 'aššur1
Variant; not used

894 2אַשֻּׁר 'aššur2
Variant; not used

895 אֲשֵׁרָה 'ašērāh (40)
Asherah poles (22)
Asherah pole (14)
Asherah (3)
Asherahs (1)

896 אָשֵׁרִי 'āšēriy (1)
people of Asher (1)

897 אַשְׁרֵי 'ašrēy (44)
blessed (37)
how happy (4)
blessings (1)
happy (1)
untranslated (1)

898 אֲשֻׁרִים 'ašuriym
Variant; not used

899 אָשַׁשׁ 'āšaš (1)
fix in mind (1)

900 אֶשְׁתָּאֹל 'eštā'ôl (7)
Eshtaol (7)

901 אֶשְׁתָּאֻלִי 'eštā'uliy (1)
Eshtaolites (1)

902 אֶשְׁתּוֹן 'eštôn (2)
Eshton (2)

903 אֶשְׁתְּמֹה 'eštᵉmōh (1)
Eshtemoh (1)

904 אֶשְׁתְּמֹעַ 'eštᵉmōa' (5)
Eshtemoa (5)

905 אַתְּ 'at (65)
you (50)
how did it go (1) +4769
untranslated (14)

906 1אֵת 'ēt1 (10942)
aloud (5) +5951+7754
entreat (3) +2704+7156
ordained (3) +3338+4848
sought the favor of (3) +2704+7156
take a census (3) +5951+8031
installed (2) +3338+4848
let know (2) +265+1655
openhanded (2) +3338+7337+7337
ordination (2) +3338+4848
tells (2) +265+1655
accepted (1) +5951+7156
began (1) +5951+7754
come into presence (1) +7156+8011
confiding in (1) +265+1655

consecrated (1) +3338+4848
count (1) +5951+8031
counted (1) +5951+8031
counting on (1) +448+5883+5951
did so^s (1) +2021+6913+7175
did^s (1) +3877+4213+4392
disheartened (1) +4222+5022
given word (1) +7023+7198
hardhearted (1) +599+4222
has sexual relations with (1) +1655+6872
have sexual relations (1) +6872+8011
helped (1) +2616+3338
helped find strength (1) +2616+3338
include in the census (1) +5951+8031
inquire of (1) +7023+8626
intercede with (1) +2704+7156
interceded with (1) +2704+7156
keep themselves alive (1) +4392+5883+8740
let go (1) +3338+5663
looked (1) +6524
offering body (1) +7316+8079
ordain (1) +3338+4848
out (1) +5951
relieve himself (1) +2257+6114+8079
relieving himself (1) +2257+6114+8079
revealed (1) +265+1655
saw (1) +5951+6524
seek favor (1) +2704+7156
sent on way (1) +8938
sought favor (1) +2704+7156
stared with a fixed gaze (1)
    +2256+6641+7156+8492
sulking (1) +6015+7156
sworn (1) +3338+5951
tell (1) +265+1655
tightfisted (1) +3338+7890
undergo circumcision (1) +1414+4576+6889
uttered a word (1) +3076+4383
wanted (1) +5883+8626
wanted to kill (1) +1335+5883
wept so loudly (1) +928+1140+5989+7754
worry (1) +4213+8492
untranslated (10870)

907 2אֵת 'ēt2 (935)
with (405)
from (93) +4946
against (34)
to (28)
among (14)
along with (13)
his (13) +2257
before (9) +7156
and (8)
have (8)
near (7)
of (7) +4946
for (5)
in (5)
slept with (5) +8886
by (4)
left (4) +2143+4946
through (4) +4946
upon (4)
doing (3) +4946
had (3) +5162
lies with (3) +8886
pronounced on (3) +1819
sleeps with (3) +8886
the LORD's (3) +3378+4946
allied with (2)
away from (2) +4946
before (2)
close to (2)
has (2)
have (2) +3780
help (2)
in front of (2) +7156
lay with (2) +8886
leave (2) +2143+4946
of (2)

within (2)
about (1)
accompanied (1) +2143
accompanied (1) +6590
accompanied by (1)
accompany (1) +3655
according to (1)
account for (1) +3108
adding to (1) +2256
all around (1)
alongside (1)
among (1) +4946
among (1) +8905
and (1) +2256
and together (1)
any of (1) +4946
as (1)
as well as (1)
ask (1) +8626
assist (1) +6641
away (1) +4946
because of (1)
both and (1)
bring (1) +995
by (1) +4946
by myself (1) +3276+4946
company (1) +2118
concern (1)
confide in (1) +4213
decreed (1)
determined (1) +4946
fighting with (1) +2118
following (1) +6639
for (1) +4946
forsaking (1) +4946
gain support (1) +2118+3338
given to (1)
gone from (1) +401
had (1)
help (1) +2118
helped (1)
helping (1)
in addition to (1)
in hand (1)
in possession (1)
in sight (1) +7156
in view (1) +7156
inquire of (1) +2011+4946
into (1)
know (1)
leaves (1) +2143+4946
left (1) +4946
lie with (1) +8886
lies with (1) +8886+8886
lost (1) +4946+5877
lying with (1) +8886
my (1) +3276
near (1) +2143
next to (1)
on (1)
on (1) +4946
on behalf of (1) +4946
on side (1)
oppose (1)
other^s (1) +889
out of (1) +4946
over (1)
own (1)
past (1) +4946
representative (1) +4946
send (1) +995+4946
sent by (1) +4946
served (1) +6641+7156
shared with (1)
show (1)
sleeping with (1) +2446+8886+8887
sleeps with (1) +2446+8886+8887
some (1) +4946
supported (1) +2118+3338
through (1)
to (1) +7156

together (1)
together (1) +408+2084+8276
together with (1)
told (1) +4946+9048
toward (1)
under (1)
under (1) +7156
under care (1)
with (1) +7156
with the help of (1)
with the help of (1) +4946
within sight of (1) +7156
your (1) +3870
untranslated (130)

908 אֵת3 'ēṯ3 (5)
plowshares (3)
mattocks (2)

909 אֶתְבַּעַל 'eṯbaʻal (1)
Ethbaal (1)

910 אָתָה 'āṯāh (21)
come (7)
bring (2)
comes (2)
advance (1)
assembled (1)
be restored (1)
came (1)
come forward (1)
coming (1)
holds (1)
pass (1)
sweeps over (1)
things to come (1)

911 אַתָּה 'aṯāh (745)
you (621)
yourself (17)
your (4)
you're (2)
your own (2)
it (1)
you alone (1) +911
you yourself (1)
you'll (1)
yours (1)
untranslated (93)

912 אָתוֹן 'āṯôn (34)
donkey (13)
donkeys (12)
female donkeys (2)
her^s (2) +2021
colt (1) +1201
donkey's (1)
female (1)
she^s (1) +2021
them^s (1) +2021

913 אָתוּק 'atûq (1)
untranslated (1)

914 אִתִּי 'atiy (7)
untranslated (7)

915 אִתַּי 'itay (8)
Ittai (7)
Ithai (1)

916 אַתִּיק 'atiyq (5)
galleries (3)
gallery (2)

917 אַתֶּם 'atem (283)
you (244)
yourselves (10)
your (3)
yours (2)
people^s (1)
you and your men (1)
untranslated (22)

918 אֵתָם 'ēṯām (4)
Etham (4)

919 אֶתְמוֹל 'etmôl (8)
before (2) +8997
day (1) +3427
formerly (1) +4946+8997
in the past (1) +1685+1685+8997
lately (1)
long (1) +4946
previously (1) +3869+8997

920 אַתֵּן 'atēn (4)
you (4)

921 אֶתְנָה 'etnāh (1)
pay (1)

922 אֶתְנִי 'etniy (1)
Ethni (1)

923 אֵתָנִים 'ēṯāniym (1)
Ethanim (1)

924 אֶתְנַן 'etnan (11)
earnings (2)
payment (2)
wages (2)
hire as a prostitute (1)
pay (1) +5989
temple gifts (1)
wages of a prostitute (1)
untranslated (1)

925 אֶתְנָן 'etnān (1)
Ethnan (1)

926 אֲתָרִים 'aṯāriym (1)
Atharim (1)

927 ב b
Variant; not used

928 בְּ- bᵊ- (15567)
in (4676)
with (1047)
on (956)
at (580)
by (501)
when (497)
of (303)
to (281)
into (274)
against (260)
among (241)
through (183)
for (160)
among (111) +9348
from (98)
over (89)
as (80)
through (62) +3338
because of (59)
during (59)
among (52) +7931
according to (50)
while (48)
throughout (47) +3972
in (45) +9348
when (45) +3427
before (36) +3270
obey (36) +7754+9048
hand over (35) +3338+5989
upon (34)
under (33)
there^s (28) +2023
after (27)
throughout (26)
along (25)
enter (25) +995
in (24) +7931
handed over (23) +3338+5989
follow (22) +2143
about (20)
whenever (20)
with (20) +3338
within (20)
within (20) +7931

to (19) +265
by (18) +3338
near (18)
obeyed (18) +7754+9048
with (17) +9348
because (16)
how (16) +4537
if (16)
has (15)
inquired of (15) +8626
inside (15) +9348
to (15) +3338
to (15) +7754
within (15) +9348
used (14)
have (12)
here (12) +2296
had (11)
when (11) +6961
with (11) +7931
around (10)
followed (10) +2143
seems (10) +6524
where (10)
wherever (10) +889+3972
wherever (10) +3972
burn down (9) +836+2021+8596
east (9) +6298
inside (9)
into (9) +9348
safely (9) +8934
set on fire (9) +836+2021+3675
without (9) +4202
and (8)
be handed over (8) +3338+5989
burned (8) +836+2021+8596
entered (8) +995
in spite of (8)
seemed (8) +6524
think (8) +6524
through (8) +9348
before (7)
outside (7) +2021+2575
pleased (7) +3512+6524
that (7)
toward (7)
along with (6) +9348
amid (6)
any (6)
before (6) +2021+8037
despite (6)
invade (6) +995
like (6)
secretly (6) +2021+6260
there^s (6) +3731
this is how (6) +2296
unintentionally (6) +8705
use (6)
within (6) +6388
against (5) +7156
always (5) +3972+6961
at the cost of (5)
beyond (5) +6298
displeased (5) +6524+8317
faithfully (5) +575
has (5) +2118
on account of (5)
pleased with (5) +2834+5162+6524
pleases (5) +3202+6524
ruthlessly (5) +7266
stone (5) +74+2021+8083
using (5)
accidentally (4) +8705
accompanied by (4)
across (4) +6298
allotted (4) +1598+2021
be burned up (4) +836+2021+8596
beside (4)
burn (4) +836+2021+8596
burned up (4) +836+2021+8596
consult (4) +2011

every morning (4)
               +928+1332+1332+2021+2021
faithfully (4) +622
have (4) +3338
in exchange for (4)
inner room (4) +2540+2540
inquire of (4) +2011
invaded (4) +995
near (4) +7931
out of (4)
seem (4) +6524
set on fire (4) +836+2021+8596
there^s (4) +1195+2021
there^s (4) +2023+9348
there^s (4) +2257
to (4) +6524
touch (4) +2118
unintentionally (4) +1172+1981
wearing (4)
whether (4)
with (4) +6524
as (3) +2006
at the risk of (3)
at the time of (3)
before (3) +4202
between (3) +9348
burn up (3) +836+2021+8596
burned down (3) +836+2021+8596
called out (3) +1524+7754+7924
cost (3)
daily (3) +3427+3427
each year (3) +9102+9102
early (3) +8040
every last male (3) +7815+8874
favorably disposed toward (3) +2834+6524
first (3) +2021+9378
follows (3) +2143
has (3) +3780
heard (3) +265
including (3)
king's (3) +4889
later (3)
like (3) +3202+6524
made (3)
male (3) +7815+8874
on high (3) +2021+5294
on the basis of (3)
saw (3) +6524
secret (3) +4537
share (3) +5951
some (3)
though (3)
through (3) +7931
throughout (3) +1473+3972
under (3) +3338
upon (3) +7931
whenever (3) +3972
wherever (3) +889+2006+2021
wherever (3) +889+5226
wild (3) +2021+8441
without (3) +700
all (2)
all day long (2) +2021+2021+2085+3427
allotted (2) +1598+2021+5989
alone (2) +1727+2257
along with (2)
anywhere (2) +3972+5226
as (2) +6961
as before (2) +3869+7193+7193
as long as (2)
as long as live (2) +6388
as soon as (2)
assassinate (2) +3338+8938
associate with (2) +995
at (2) +6961
because (2) +889
because of (2) +1673
before (2) +265
before (2) +3270+4202
bloodshed (2) +995+1947
boldly (2) +3338+8123

by (2) +6524
by means of (2)
by what means (2) +4537
certainly be handed over (2)
               +3338+5989+5989
chosen (2) +7924+9005
deceitfully (2) +5327
disobeyed (2) +4202+7754+9048
distressed (2) +6524+8317
do (2)
down (2)
each (2)
each day (2) +3427+3427
earlier (2) +2021+9378
entrusted with (2) +575
everywhere (2) +3972
exceedingly (2) +4394+4394
fill (2)
first (2) +2021+8037
fleet-footed (2) +7824+8079
following (2)
following (2) +8079
for each day (2) +1821+3427+3427
for nothing (2) +1896+8198
from (2) +9348
fully obey (2) +7754+9048+9048
greatly (2) +4394+4394
guilty (2) +3338
had (2) +3338
hand over (2) +3338+6037
handed over (2) +3338+6037
have respect for (2) +3700+6524
honorably (2) +622
in charge of (2)
in obedience to (2)
in return for (2)
inside (2) +1074+2021
intersecting (2) +9348
invades (2) +995
its (2) +2023
joyfully (2) +8525
just as (2)
led by (2) +8031
make a survey of (2) +2143
my (2) +3276+8079
near (2) +6298
now (2) +465+2021+2021+3427
on (2) +7931
on high (2) +7757
over (2) +8031
overwhelmed (2) +2118+4202+6388+8120
play (2) +3338+5594
playing the harp (2) +3338+5594
please (2) +3202+6524
please (2) +3837+6524
pleased (2) +3202+6524
pleased (2) +3837+6524
privately (2) +2021+6260
purchased (2) +4374+4697
quietly (2) +2021+4319
reached (2) +995
required (2) +460+5957
sees (2) +6524
sell (2) +4084+5989
sold for (2) +2118
stone (2) +74+2021+6232
stoned (2) +74+2021+6232
struck (2) +2118
supervising (2)
taking with (2) +3338
then (2) +340+2021
there^s (2) +1074+2021
there^s (2) +9076
thought (2) +6524
throughout (2) +6017
throughout (2) +9348
truly (2) +622
up to (2)
very (2) +4394+4394
what (2)
what (2) +4537

when (2) +2021+3427
where (2) +889
where[s] (2) +2023
wherever (2)
wherever (2) +889+2021+3972+5226
wherever goes (2) +928+995+2256+3655
while (2) +3427
wholeheartedly (2) +3972+4213
wholeheartedly (2) +3972+4222
wholeheartedly (2) +4222+8969
with help (2)
without (2) +401
withstand (2) +995
withstand (2) +6641+7156
wounds (2) +995
yearly (2) +285+9102
ability (1) +2683+4213
aboard (1)
above (1) +2021+5294
accuse (1) +1821+8492
across (1)
affected (1)
after (1) +1821
after (1) +1896+4946
after (1) +3427
after (1) +8079
after (1) +9005
again (1) +1685+2021+2021+2085+7193
against (1) +6330
alive (1) +5883
all (1) +285
all night long (1) +2021+4326
allotted (1) +1598+2021+2118
alone (1) +285
along (1) +6298
along (1) +9348
along with (1) +3338
along with (1) +7931
alongside (1)
aloud (1) +1524+7754
aloud (1) +7754
already (1) +2021+9378
although (1) +889+3972
angry (1) +3013+6524
annual (1) +285+2021+9102
annual (1) +2021+7193+9102
annually (1) +2256+3972+9102+9102
anywhere in (1) +1473+3972
appealed to (1) +3512+6524
appear (1) +2118+3869+6524
approve of (1) +3202+6524
archers (1) +408+2021+4619+8008
archers (1) +2021+4619+8008
are burned up (1) +836+2021+8596+8596
arrayed in (1)
as (1) +889
as (1) +889+3972
as directs (1)
as done before (1) +3869+7193+7193
as long as (1) +3427
as long as (1) +3972+6961
as long as (1) +6388
as one (1) +9348
as usually did (1) +3427+3427+3869
assaults (1) +8938
assemble (1) +2021+6590+7736
assisted (1) +2616+3338
assuredly (1) +622
at (1) +2006+2021
at (1) +6298
at (1) +7931
at (1) +9348
at once (1) +2021+2021+2085+3427
at once (1) +2021+2021+2085+6961
at once (1) +2021+3427
at other times (1) +7193+7193
at stake (1)
at the blast (1) +1896
at the time (1)
attached to (1)
attack (1) +3338+8938

attack (1) +3718
attack (1) +5877
attacked (1) +3338+8938
attacked (1) +5877
attacked (1) +6590
attacks (1) +3338+8938
bare (1) +401+4399
based on (1)
be a virgin (1) +1436
be burned (1) +836+2021+8596
be burned down (1) +836+2021+8596
be defeated (1) +3338+5989
be taken captive (1) +2021+4090+9530
bears (1)
because (1) +2256+3610+3610
because (1) +3610
because (1) +3610+3610
because of (1) +3338
been handed over (1) +3338+5989
before (1) +678
before (1) +2021+9378
beginning with (1)
behind (1)
belong to (1) +2118
belonged to (1) +8079
bent on (1) +6783
beset (1) +995
beside (1) +2668
beside (1) +3338
besiege (1) +995+2021+5189
besieged (1) +2837
between (1)
bind themselves with (1) +995
blind (1) +2021+5782+6427
boasted (1) +1540+7023
borrowed (1) +5957
bought (1) +2021+4084+7864
bring about (1) +2118
brings (1)
brought (1) +3338
brought with (1) +2118+3338
brutally (1) +7266
burn to death (1) +836+2021+8596
burned (1) +836+2021+8938
burned to death (1) +836+2021+8596
buy (1) +4084
by (1) +9348
by day (1) +3429
by means (1)
cargo (1) +641+889+2021+3998
carried (1) +3338+4374
carry off (1) +995+2021+8660
carrying (1)
cause (1) +3338
centrally located in (1) +9348
charred (1) +836+1277+2021
close to (1)
clung to (1)
come into (1) +5877
commit (1) +2143
committed (1) +2143
compels (1)
concealed in (1)
concerning (1)
consider (1) +4222
consider (1) +6524
considered (1) +6524
constantly (1) +3972+6961
consult (1) +1821+2011
containing (1)
contrary to (1) +3869+4202
counted off (1) +5031+6296
covered (1) +2118
covers (1) +995
cruelly (1) +2622
customary (1) +3869+7193+7193
daily (1) +1821+3427+3427
daily (1) +2257+3427+3427
day by day (1) +1821+2257+3427+3427
day by day (1) +1821+3427+3427
dealing with (1)

debtor (1) +5957
deceived (1) +5792+5793
deceptively (1) +6817
defiantly (1) +7418
delegation (1) +3338+6269
deliberately (1) +6893
delivered (1) +3338
despise (1) +1022+6524
despise (1) +6524+7837
despises (1) +1022+6524
despises (1) +6524+7837
despite (1) +4200+8611
diligently obey (1) +7754+9048+9048
disapprove (1) +6524+8317
disobedience (1) +4202+7754+9048
disobey (1) +1194+7754+9048
displease (1) +2834+4202+5162+6524
displease (1) +6524+8273
displeasing (1) +2834+4202+5162+6524
displeasing (1) +6524+8273
distributed among (1)
do that[s] (1) +2118+2257+3338
done by (1) +3338
doubly (1) +2021+9109
drew (1) +3338+4848
driving (1)
due annually (1) +1896+4946+9102+9102
during (1) +3427
each day's (1) +2257+3427+3427
each day's (1) +3427+3427
each morning (1)
　　　　+928+1332+1332+2021+2021
eagerly (1) +3972+8356
east (1) +2025+4667+6298
east (1) +2025+4667+6298+9087
east (1) +4667+6298+9087
encounter (1) +995
end (1) +340+2021+2118
entered (1) +995+9348
entering (1) +995
entering (1) +995+7931
entering (1) +995+9348
enters (1) +995
entrusted to (1) +3338
even after (1)
even if (1)
evening (1) +928+2021+2021+6847+6847
every (1)
every day (1) +3427+3427
every evening (1)
　　　　+928+2021+2021+6847+6847
every Sabbath (1) +8701+8701
everyone's (1) +408
everywhere (1) +3972+5226
fairly (1) +7406
faithful (1) +622+2143
far back in (1) +3752
far off (1) +8158
fault (1) +4200+8611
favorable toward (1) +2834+5162+6524
feeds (1) +5966+9094
few (1) +5031+5071
fiercely (1) +2021+6677
fifteen feet (1) +564+2021+6924
filled (1) +2118+3972
filled with (1) +7931
flashed back and forth (1) +4374+9348
flashes (1) +836
follow (1) +2143+8079
follow (1) +8079
followed (1)
followed (1) +6590+8079
for (1) +889
for (1) +1685+8611
for (1) +3338
for (1) +6524
for (1) +9348
forcefully (1) +3338
formerly (1) +2021+8037
fought in (1) +3655
free from (1) +4202

from (1) +889
from (1) +3338
from (1) +6524
from now (1) +6388
from the time (1)
fuel for fire (1) +836+1896
fuel for flames (1) +836+1896
fully determined (1) +4222+8969
galled (1) +6524+8317
gave in (1) +7754+9048
gave victory (1) +3338+5989
get (1)
give (1) +3338+5989
given by (1)
giving credit to (1) +9005
glad (1) +3512+6524
gladly (1) +3206+4222
go (1) +2006+2143
gone (1) +2118+4202
gone (1) +4202+6641
had (1) +2118
had (1) +7023
had (1) +7931
had chance (1) +2118+3338
hand over (1) +3338+4835
hand over (1) +3338+5162
hand over to (1) +3338+5989
handed (1) +3338+5989
handed over (1) +3338+5162
handed over (1) +3338+5796
handing over (1) +3338+5989
handing over (1) +3338+6037
harbor (1) +4328+7931
harbor in (1)
harnessed to (1)
harshly (1) +2622
has (1) +3338
hasty (1) +237+8079
have (1) +2118
have (1) +3338+5162
have (1) +3780
have (1) +5055
have (1) +7023
have a claim on (1)
heard (1) +265+606
here^s (1) +824+2021
here^s (1) +2021+2021+2296+5226
here^s (1) +2021+4497
here^s (1) +2023
here^s (1) +5226
his (1) +2257
his^s (1) +2021+4889
hold (1) +2118+3338
holding (1) +3338
holds (1) +2118+3338
how (1)
how (1) +686+4537
hurl insults (1) +7080+8557
if (1) +3427
imagine (1) +5381
imprisoned (1) +5464+5989
in (1) +1068
in (1) +4213
in (1) +4595
in accordance with (1)
in charge of (1) +3338
in each corner (1) +928+5243+5243
in equal amounts (1) +963+963
in keeping with (1)
in payment for (1)
in person (1) +265
in possession (1)
in regard to (1)
in response to (1)
in the name of (1)
in view of (1)
include (1) +9348
inquire of (1) +8626
inquires of (1) +1821+8626
inquiring of (1) +8626
inserted into (1)

inside (1) +5055
inside (1) +7931
insist on paying for (1) +4697+7864+7864
inspire (1) +4222+5989
intentionally (1) +7402
interwoven (1) +2021+8054
into (1) +7931
invade (1) +6296
invade (1) +6590
invaded (1) +6590
invoke (1) +7023+7924
involved in (1)
Israel's (1) +3776
Israelite (1) +1201+3776
Israelite (1) +3776
its^s (1) +2021+6551
join (1) +2118
joined in (1) +9348
just before (1) +3270
keep (1) +2143
keeping watch (1) +6524+8011
kept (1) +2143
killing (1) +3338+8938
lack (1) +401
lack (1) +4202
laden with (1)
laid siege (1) +995+2021+5189
lamb (1) +2021+3897+8445
lamb (1) +2021+4166+8445
land's (1) +824
lately (1) +700
later (1) +340+2021
later in time (1) +344
lead life (1) +2143
leads (1) +2021+8037
leave (1)
led life (1) +2143
let get away (1) +2006+8938
let touch (1) +995
leveled completely (1) +2021+9164+9168
lie in state (1) +3883+8886
like (1) +9348
liked (1) +3837+6524
likes (1) +2021+3202+4200
listen carefully (1) +265+9048
listen carefully (1) +7754+9048
listen closely (1) +265+9048
listened (1) +265
live (1) +2021+2644
live (1) +2143
lived (1) +1074+2021
living in (1)
long ago (1) +2021+8037
look (1) +6524
look carefully (1) +6524+8011
looked (1) +2118+6524
lose heart (1) +1327+7931+8120
lost self-confidence (1) +4394+5877+6524
loudly (1) +1524+7754
made (1) +4374
made a fatal mistake (1) +5883+9494
made pay for (1) +8031+8740
made with (1)
make enter (1) +995
make fine speeches (1) +2488+4863
make full restitution (1) +8031+8740
make sure hears (1) +265+8492
makes (1)
mark (1)
measured out (1) +4500+9419
mention (1) +7023+9019
monthly (1) +2544+2544
mortal (1) +5883
mounted (1) +2021+6061
moving from place to place (1)
+889+2143+2143
must sell (1) +2021+4084+4835+4835
my (1) +3276
nails down (1) +2616+5021
named (1) +7924+9005
native-born (1) +824+2021+3528

nomads (1) +185+8905
not please (1) +6524+8317
not want (1) +6524+8273
now (1)
obey (1) +2143
obey fully (1) +7754+9048+9048
obeying (1) +7754+9048
obeys (1) +7754+9048
of (1) +9348
off (1)
offer (1)
on (1) +9348
on board (1)
on board (1) +9348
on each side (1)
on fire (1) +836+1277+2021
on side (1)
on the condition that (1) +2296
on the tip of tongue (1) +2674+4383
once (1)
one (1)
one by one (1) +5031
one of^s (1)
one way (1) +285
only (1) +1727+2257
only if (1)
oppose (1) +995
oppressed (1) +2021+6913+6945
out here (1) +2021+2575
outdoor (1) +2021+2575
over (1) +9348
overrun (1)
paid (1)
painted (1) +2021+7037+8531
parallel (1) +7156
part of (1)
pay with (1)
peaceably (1) +8934
peacefully (1) +8934
penned up (1) +1074+2021+3973
people^s (1) +889+3972
pierce (1)
pierce (1) +995
pierced (1) +995
pierced (1) +5737
placed seal (1) +2597+3159
please (1) +2256+3202+3838+6524
please (1) +3838+6524
pleased (1) +3201+6524
pleased (1) +3838+6524
pleased with (1) +2834+5951+6524
pleased with (1) +3202+6524
pleased with (1) +3512+6524
pleased with (1) +3837+6524
pleases (1) +3512+6524
plot against (1) +3108+4222
prefer (1) +3202+6524
present in (1)
preserved (1) +2021+2645+8492
presumptuously (1) +2295
prevailed upon (1) +2616
privately (1) +2021+4319
privately (1) +2021+8952
proclaim (1) +7924
proclaimed (1) +7924
promised (1) +1819+7023
prone to (1)
protect (1) +3829+8883
pursues (1) +8740
put in jeopardy (1) +1414+5951+9094
put on (1) +5516+8492
puts up a bold front (1) +6451+7156
quickly (1) +4559
raiding (1) +995
rationed (1) +5374
rationed (1) +5486
reached (1) +2118
reached (1) +9048
reaches to (1)
ready for battle (1) +2021+4878+7372
really (1) +622

regarding (1)
regards (1) +5162+6524
regular flow (1) +1414+2307
regularly (1) +3427+3427+4200
repay (1) +8031+8740
responsible for (1) +889+4200
responsible for (1) +4200+8611
responsible for (1) +6015
result of (1)
ride (1) +2143
risked (1)
roars (1) +5989+7754
Sabbath after Sabbath (1)
  +928+2021+2021+3427+3427+8701+8701
sacrificed (1) +5989+6296
sail (1) +641+2021+2143
sandaled (1) +2021+5837
satisfied (1) +3512+6524
satisfied (1) +8934
scarce (1) +430+5017
scorned the idea (1) +1022+6524
screamed (1) +1524+7754+7924
search (1) +606
seem (1) +2118+6524
seem (1) +4017+6524
seemed (1) +2118+6524
seize (1) +3338+8492
sell for (1) +2118
set ablaze (1) +836+2021+3675
set fire to (1) +836+2021+8596
set fire to (1) +836+2021+8938
set on (1)
set with (1)
seven and a half feet (1) +564+2021+2822
shamefully (1) +2365
shared hardships (1) +889+6700+6700
sharply (1) +2622
shoot (1) +2021+8008
shout (1) +7754+7924
shout aloud (1) +1744+7924
shouted (1) +7754+7924
shouted (1) +7754+8123+9558
since (1) +889
sing (1) +7023+8492
sing songs (1) +4200+7754+8123+9048
sins defiantly (1) +3338+6913+8123
sins unintentionally (1) +6913+8705
sleeping with (1) +5989+8888
sling stones (1) +74+2021
smoothly (1) +4797
so quickly (1) +7328
some of (1)
someone else's (1) +3338
soon (1) +7940
speak (1) +7023
spreads feathers to run (1)
      +2021+5257+5294
stargazers (1) +2600+3919
stationed at (1)
stoned (1) +74+2021+8083
stoning (1) +74+2021+8083
strike (1) +2118
striking (1) +2118
suddenly (1) +285
suddenly (1) +7328+7353
suddenly (1) +7353
suffer (1)
suffered (1) +2118
surely hand over (1) +3338+5989+5989
surrender (1) +3338+6037
surrounded by (1) +9348
sweep away (1) +4053+7674
take great delight (1) +8464+8525
take hold of (1) +2118
take in (1)
taken (1) +3338
taken great pains (1) +6715
taken into account (1)
takes the stand (1) +7756
tell (1) +265+1819
tent-dwelling (1) +185+2021

that (1) +3907
the storehouses[s] (1) +889+2157+3972
their[s] (1) +2157+4090
them[s] (1) +74+2021+4392
then[s] (1) +2296
then[s] (1) +2021+2021+2085+3427
there[s] (1)
there[s] (1) +824
there[s] (1) +1195+2021
there[s] (1) +2021+2215
there[s] (1) +466+1074
there[s] (1) +824+2021
there[s] (1) +824+2257
there[s] (1) +951
there[s] (1) +1014+2021
there[s] (1) +1028
there[s] (1) +1074+2021+3752
there[s] (1) +1078
there[s] (1) +1618
there[s] (1) +2006+2021
there[s] (1) +2021+2215
there[s] (1) +2021+4722
there[s] (1) +2021+5207
there[s] (1) +2021+6551
there[s] (1) +2023+8148
there[s] (1) +2025+9463
there[s] (1) +2157
there[s] (1) +2257+7931
there[s] (1) +2257+9348
there[s] (1) +2972
there[s] (1) +4392+9348
there[s] (1) +5213
there[s] (1) +5707+7724
there[s] (1) +8931
think (1) +606+4213
think (1) +606+4222
thinks (1) +606+4222
thirty feet (1) +564+2021+6929
this (1) +3907
this is how (1) +465+3972
this is the way (1) +4392
thoughtlessly (1) +1051+4200+8557
thoughts (1) +5883+6783
through fault (1)
throughout (1) +7931
thunders (1) +5989+7754
till (1)
timely (1) +6961
to (1) +4200+6288
to (1) +4213
to avenge (1)
to each man (1) +9005
to get (1)
together with (1)
told (1) +265+1819
told (1) +7023+8492
took (1)
took with (1) +3338
tried (1) +4213+9365
troubled (1) +6524+8273
under control (1) +294
under cover (1) +9564
underfoot (1) +8079
unharmed (1) +8934
unintentionally (1) +4202+7402
unnoticed (1) +2021+4319
unscathed (1) +8934
upset (1) +6524+8317
urgently (1) +2622
use name as a curse (1) +8678
used (1) +3338
used for (1)
uses (1) +3338
value (1) +1540+6524
valued (1) +1540+6524
very old (1) +995+2021+2416+3427
vigorously (1) +6437
walk (1) +2006+2143
walking along (1) +2006+2021
wanted to do (1) +3202+6524
watch (1) +6524

waylaid (1) +2006+2021+8492
wearing (1) +265
went aboard (1) +3718
wept so loudly (1) +906+1140+5989+7754
were put in chains (1) +2414+8415
west (1) +6298
whatever (1) +889+3972
when (1) +8040
when began (1) +3427
whenever (1) +889+3972
whenever (1) +3427
whenever (1) +3972+6961
whenever (1) +6961
where[s] (1) +396
where[s] (1) +2021+5226
where[s] (1) +2177
where[s] (1) +2257
where[s] (1) +5226
where[s] (1) +6152+8234
wherever (1) +285+889+2021+5226
wherever (1) +889
wherever (1) +889+2021+5226
wherever (1) +2021+3972+5226
wholeheartedly (1) +4213+8969
why (1) +4537
willfully (1) +4222
wish (1) +3202+6524
wish (1) +3512+6524
wished (1) +3202+6524
with (1) +2118
with (1) +8079
with in hand (1)
within (1) +2668
within (1) +3752
within (1) +5055+9348
without (1) +1172
without meaning (1) +2021+2039
withstood (1) +6641+7156
won (1) +5951+6524
workmen (1) +2021+4856+6913
worn (1) +5432
worth (1)
your (1) +2257
your (1) +3870
untranslated (2479)

929 בִּאָה *bi'āh* (1)
entrance (1)

930 בָּאַר *bā'ar* (3)
clearly (1)
expound (1)
make plain (1)

931 בְּאֵר1 *b'ēr1* (39)
well (30)
pit (2)
wells (2)
full of pits (1) +931
well (1) +4784
well's (1)
wells (1) +4784

932 בְּאֵר2 *b'ēr2* (2)
Beer (2)

933 בְּאֵר3 *b'ēr3*
Variant; not used

934 בֹּאר *bō'r*
Variant; not used

935 בְּאֵר אֵילִים *b'ēr 'ēyliym* (1)
Beer Elim (1)

936 בְּאֵר לַחַי רֹאִי *b'ēr lahay rō'iy* (3)
Beer Lahai Roi (3)

937 בְּאֵר שֶׁבַע *b'ēr šeba'* (34)
Beersheba (34)

938 בְּאֵרָא *b'ērā'* (1)
Beera (1)

939 בְּאֵרָה *b'ērāh* (1)
Beerah (1)

940 בְּאֵרוֹת *bᵉʾērôṭ* (5)
Beeroth (5)

941 בְּאֵרִי *bᵉʾēriy* (2)
Beeri (2)

942 בְּאֵרֹת בְּנֵי־יַעֲקָן *bᵉʾērōṭ bᵉnēy-yaʿᵃqān*
Variant; not used

943 בְּאֵרֹתִי *bᵉʾērōṭiy* (5)
Beerothite (4)
people of Beeroth (1)

944 בָּאַשׁ *bāʾaš* (17)
stench (3)
stink (2)
bring shame (1)
give a bad smell (1) +5580
loathsome (1)
made stench (1) +8194
made yourself a stench (1)
making a stench (1)
reeked (1)
rot (1)
smell (1)
smelled bad (1)
so odious (1) +944

945 בְּאֹשׁ *bᵉʾōš* (3)
stench (3)

946 בְּאֻשׁ *bᵉʾuš* (2)
bad (1)
bad fruit (1)

947 בָּאֲשָׁה *bāʾᵃšāh* (1)
weeds (1)

948 בַּאֲשֶׁר *baʾᵃšer*
Variant; not used

949 בָּבָה *bābāh* (1)
apple (1)

950 בֵּבַי *bēbay* (6)
Bebai (6)

951 בָּבֶל *bābel* (262)
Babylon (242)
Babylon's (3)
Babylonians (2) +1201
Babel (1)
Babylon (1) +824
Babylonia (1)
Babylonian (1) +1201
heˢ (1) +4889
himˢ (1) +4889
hisˢ (1) +4889
thereˢ (1) +928
untranslated (7)

952 בַּג *bag* (1)
untranslated (1)

953 בָּגַד *bāgad* (49)
unfaithful (16)
betrayed (5)
broken faith (4)
treacherous (4)
betray (2)
betrays (2)
break faith (2)
faithless (2)
traitor (2)
acted treacherously (1)
betraying (1)
breaking faith (1)
faithless (1) +954
how treacherous (1) +953
traitors (1)
undependable (1)
utterly unfaithful (1) +953

954 1בֶּגֶד *beged1* (2)
faithless (1) +953
treachery (1)

955 2בֶּגֶד *beged2* (217)
clothes (79)

garments (48)
clothing (23)
robes (17)
garment (14)
cloak (8)
cloth (8)
tunic (2)
wardrobe (2)
articles of clothing (1)
blankets (1) +2927
cloaks (1)
clothed (1)
clothed (1) +4252
clothes (1) +6886
covers (1)
fold of cloak (1)
rags (1)
thoseˢ (1)
untranslated (6)

956 בֹּגְדוֹת *bōgᵉḏôṭ* (1)
treacherous (1)

957 בָּגוֹד *bāgôḏ* (2)
unfaithful (2)

958 בִּגְוַי *bigway* (6)
Bigvai (6)

959 בִּגְלַל *biglal*
Variant; not used

960 בִּגְתָא *bigṭāʾ* (1)
Bigtha (1)

961 בִּגְתָן *bigṭān* (1)
Bigthana (1)

962 בִּגְתָנָא *bigṭānāʾ* (1)
Bigthana (1)

963 1בַּד *bad1* (162)
alone (40) +4200
in addition to (18) +4200+4946
only (16) +4200
besides (9) +4200+4946
only one (8) +4200
by themselves (4) +4200+4392
apart (3) +4200
as well as (2) +4200+4946
in addition to (2) +4200
limbs (2)
not counting (2) +4200+4946
not including (2) +4200+4946
set (2)
all (1) +4200
all alone (1) +4200
all by myself (1) +3276+4200
along with (1) +4200+4946
also (1) +4200
anyone (1) +4200
besides (1) +4200
by himself (1) +2257+4200
by itself (1) +2257+4200
by itself (1) +4200
by myself (1) +3276+4200
even though (1) +4200
in addition (1) +4200
in addition (1) +4200+4946
in equal amounts (1) +928+963
into another set (1) +4200
into one set (1) +4200
more than (1) +4200+4946
myself (1) +3276
only (1) +2314+4200
only exception (1) +4200
only one (1) +2257+4200
other than (1) +1194+4200
other than (1) +4200+4946
parts (1)
separate (1) +3657+4200
separate (1) +4200
this one (1) +4200
untranslated (23)

964 2בַּד *bad2* (41)
poles (31)

carrying poles (2)
theirˢ (2) +2021
bars of gates (1)
branches (1)
gates (1)
main branches (1) +4751
theyˢ (1) +2021
untranslated (1)

965 3בַּד *bad3* (23)
linen (22)
undergarments (1) +4829

966 4בַּד *bad4* (3)
boasts (2)
idle talk (1)

967 5בַּד *bad5* (2)
false prophets (2)

968 בָּדָא *bāḏāʾ* (2)
choosing (1)
making up (1)

969 בָּדַד *bāḏad* (3)
alone (1)
straggler (1)
wandering alone (1)

970 בָּדָד *bāḏāḏ* (11)
alone (6)
alone (1) +4200
apart (1) +4200
by itself (1) +4200
deserted (1)
desolate (1)

971 בְּדַד *bᵉdad* (2)
Bedad (2)

972 בְּדֵי *bᵉḏēy*
Variant; not used

973 בְּדְיָה *bēḏᵉyāh* (1)
Bedeiah (1)

974 בְּדִיל *bᵉḏiyl* (5)
tin (4)
plumb line (1) +74

975 בָּדִיל *bāḏiyl* (1)
impurities (1)

976 בָּדַל *bāḏal* (42)
set apart (7)
separate (5)
separated (4)
distinguish (3)
separated themselves (3)
set aside (3)
separate yourselves (2)
severing completely (2)
be expelled (1)
defected (1)
dismissed (1)
employed (1)
excluded (1)
kept themselves separate (1)
make a distinction (1)
selected (1)
single out (1)
singled out (1)
surely exclude (1) +976
was set apart (1)

977 בָּדָל *bāḏāl* (1)
piece (1)

978 בְּדֹלַח *bᵉḏōlaḥ* (2)
aromatic resin (1)
resin (1)

979 בְּדָן *bᵉḏān* (1)
Bedan (1)

980 בָּדַק *bāḏaq* (1)
repaired (1)

981 בֶּדֶק *bedeq* (10)
damage (2)

repair (1) +2616
repairing (1)
seams (1)
shipwrights (1) +2616
untranslated (4)

982 בִּדְקַר *bidqar* (1)
Bidkar (1)

983 בֹּהוּ *bōhû* (3)
empty (2)
desolation (1)

984 בְּהוֹן *bᵉhôn* (2)
thumbs (2) +3338

985 בַּהַט *bahat* (1)
porphyry (1)

986 בָּהִיר *bāhiyr* (1)
bright (1)

987 בָּהַל *bāhal* (39)
terrified (10)
dismayed (3)
hurried (2)
make afraid (2)
terrifies (2)
alarm (1)
alarmed (1)
am bewildered (1)
dismayed (1) +4394
eager (1)
hurry (1)
immediately (1)
in a hurry (1)
in agony (1)
in anguish (1) +4394
quick (1)
quickly (1)
quickly gained (1)
raced (1)
sudden (1)
terrify (1)
terror (1)
terror seize (1)
tremble (1)
was shaken (1)

988 בֶּהָלָה *behālāh* (4)
terror (2)
misfortune (1)
sudden terror (1)

989 בְּהֵמָה *bᵉhēmāh* (190)
animals (63)
animal (44)
livestock (33)
cattle (17)
beasts (13)
beast (5)
herds (3)
anotherˢ (1)
beasts of burden (1) +2256+2651
brute beast (1)
kinds of cattle (1) +989+2256
livestock (1) +5238
mount (1)
mounts (1)
oneˢ (1)
wild beasts (1)
untranslated (2)

990 בְּהֵמוֹת *bᵉhēmôt* (1)
behemoth (1)

991 בֹּהֶן *bōhen* (14)
big toe (5)
thumb (5)
big toes (2)
thumbs (2)

992 בֹּהַן *bōhan* (2)
Bohan (2)

993 בֹּהַק *bōhaq* (1)
harmless rash (1)

994 בֶּהֶרֶת *baheret* (12)
spot (7)
bright spot (2)
spots (2)
untranslated (1)

995 בּוֹא *bô'* (2581)
come (374)
came (285)
bring (177)
went (174)
brought (165)
go (105)
coming (71)
comes (67)
arrived (48)
enter (36) +448
enter (31)
returned (29)
enter (25) +928
took (22)
bringing (19)
entered (19)
go in (19)
went in (18)
entered (17) +448
take (14)
bring in (13)
gone (13)
reached (13) +448
come in (12)
entering (12)
brought in (11)
came in (11)
reached (11) +6330
bring back (10)
went into (10)
brings (8)
entered (8) +928
enters (8)
brought back (7)
fulfilled (7)
lay with (7) +448
put (7)
set (7)
well advanced (7)
followed (6) +339
get (6)
go into (6)
invade (6) +928
reached (6)
sleep with (6) +448
sunset (6) +2021+9087
went back (6)
attack (5) +6584
enters (5) +448
goes (5)
happened (5)
slept with (5) +448
approached (4) +6330
arrived (4) +448
back (4)
came back (4)
carried off (4)
entrance (4)
flee (4)
flows (4)
going (4)
going on duty (4)
included (4)
invaded (4) +928
lie with (4) +448
overtake (4)
reached (4) +2025
return (4)
arriving (3)
attack (3) +448
attack (3) +4200
bring about (3)
bring into (3)
brought into (3)

comes true (3)
entered (3) +4200
get in (3)
give (3)
going in (3)
is brought (3)
marched (3)
overtakes (3)
returning (3)
sailed (3)
setting (3)
taken (3)
toward (3) +2025+3870
was brought (3)
advance (2)
approach (2)
approaches (2) +448
approaching (2)
arrival (2)
arrives (2)
associate with (2) +928
at hand (2)
attack (2)
attacked (2) +6584
be brought (2)
been brought into (2)
bloodshed (2) +928+1947
bow (2)
bring down (2)
bringing in (2)
brought to pass (2)
came home (2)
came to pass (2)
carried (2)
carry (2)
certainly come (2) +995
come into (2)
come true (2)
delivered (2)
enter (2) +6584
entering (2) +4200
follows (2) +339
get there (2)
go back (2)
go now (2) +2143
goes down (2)
goes in (2)
happens (2)
inserted (2)
invade (2)
invades (2) +928
kept (2)
led (2)
led in campaigns (2)
             +2256+3655+4200+7156
led on military campaigns (2) +2256+3655
left (2) +4946
march (2)
placed (2)
present (2)
presented (2)
put in (2)
reach (2) +6330
reached (2) +928
received (2) +448
set out (2)
sets (2)
sunset (2) +2021+6961+9087
were brought (2)
wherever goes (2) +928+928+2256+3655
withstand (2) +928
wounds (2) +928
accompanied (1) +8079
actually come (1) +995
admitted (1)
advanced (1)
advancing (1)
all the way to (1)
all the way to (1) +3870+6330
all the way to (1) +6330
appear (1)

appeared (1)	encounter (1) +928	made attack (1)
apply (1)	encroach (1)	make (1)
approached (1)	enter (1) +4200	make enter (1) +928
approached (1) +448	entered (1) +928+9348	make go down (1)
are^s (1)	entered (1) +2025	married (1) +448
are brought (1)	entered (1) +6584	migration (1)
arrive (1)	entered and went (1)	moved (1)
arrive (1) +448	entering (1) +448	moved into (1)
arrive (1) +6330	entering (1) +928	moved out (1)
arrived (1) +6330	entering (1) +928+7931	moves (1)
arrives (1) +7024	entering (1) +928+9348	moving (1)
assembled (1) +7736	entering (1) +2025	occupy (1) +448
associate (1)	entering (1) +6330	offer (1)
at hand (1) +4200+7940	enters (1) +928	on (1)
at hand (1) +7940	enters (1) +2025	on duty (1) +2256+3655
ate (1) +448+7931	enters (1) +4200	oppose (1) +928
attacking (1) +6584	escort (1)	out (1)
attacks (1) +6584	every spring (1) +9102	over (1)
awaits (1)	extending (1)	overtook (1) +448
away (1)	fallen (1)	overwhelm (1) +6584
be^s (1)	find (1) +448	pass (1)
be brought in (1)	fled (1)	passed (1)
be heard^s (1)	float (1)	pierce (1) +928
be inserted (1)	flowing (1)	pierced (1) +928
be right there (1)	follow (1) +339	place (1)
be taken (1)	followed in (1) +339	placing (1)
became (1)	fulfill (1)	poured (1)
been brought (1)	future (1)	produce (1)
been taken into (1)	gain (1)	provide (1)
begin (1)	gave (1)	pulled back (1)
beset (1) +928	give in (1)	put (1) +4200+7156
besiege (1) +928+2021+5189	given (1)	put (1) +4200+9202
bind themselves with (1) +928	go (1) +2143	putting (1)
blessed (1) +1388	go about business (1) +2256+3655	raiding (1) +928
border (1)	go at once (1) +2143+2256	reach (1)
bound (1)	go down (1)	reach (1) +448
break into (1)	go home (1)	reached (1) +4200
bring (1) +907	go in (1) +2143+2256	reaches (1) +448
bring home (1)	go sleep with (1) +448	received (1)
bring out (1)	going down (1)	received (1) +4200
bringing into (1)	gone into (1)	reentered (1) +2256+8740
broke (1)	granted (1)	replace (1) +448+9393
brought about (1)	guest (1) +448+1074	report back (1)
brought in as wives (1)	had (1)	reported (1)
built up (1)	had brought (1)	resound (1)
buried (1)	had brought in (1)	rest (1)
buried (1) +448+7700	had^s (1)	return (1) +995
by all means go (1) +2143	hand over (1)	return (1) +2143
calling together (1) +2256+8938	happen (1)	return (1) +6388
came along (1)	harbor (1)	rose (1)
came back (1) +2143+2256	harvested (1)	sank in (1)
came bringing (1)	has (1)	send (1)
came up (1)	have (1)	send (1) +907+4946
came with (1)	here (1)	sent (1)
carried away (1)	hid in (1)	serve (1) +2256+3655
carried back (1)	imported (1)	set foot (1)
carry back (1)	in (1)	share (1)
carry off (1)	insert (1)	shave head in mourning (1) +7947
carry off (1) +928+2021+8660	intermarry (1)	shed (1)
carry out duties (1) +2256+3655	into (1)	sleeps with (1) +448
caused to come (1)	invade (1) +448	stay (1) +4202
check (1) +4200+7156	invade (1) +2025+9004	stayed away (1) +4202
collapses (1) +8691	invaded (1) +448	stepped (1)
come back (1)	invaded (1) +6584	stole into (1) +1704+4200
come home (1)	invader (1) +448	successor (1) +132+339+8611
come on (1)	invading (1) +4200	sunset (1) +2021+3064
come to rest (1)	invited (1)	swarm (1)
comes (1) +995	is (1)	sweep on (1) +995
comes by (1)	join (1) +6330	swept in (1)
comes in (1)	journeyed (1)	take (1) +1198
comes true (1) +995	laid siege (1) +928+2021+5189	take (1) +6584
committed adultery with (1) +448	last (1)	take along (1)
confront (1)	lead (1)	take back (1)
consort (1)	lead (1) +2256+3655	take home (1)
covers (1) +928	lead (1) +2256+3655+4200+7156	take into (1)
crept (1)	led into (1)	take out (1)
crowded into (1)	ledges (1)	take part (1)
deported (1) +1583	let touch (1) +928	taken place (1)
does^s (1)	lie with (1) +6584	takes place (1)
done so^s (1) +448+7931	listed (1)	taking (1)
edge (1)	lying with (1) +448	time is ripe (1) +7891

to the vicinity of (1) +3870+6330
took (1) +448
took back (1)
took back (1) +2256+8938
took into (1)
touch (1)
touched (1) +448
toward (1) +3870
travel about (1) +2256+3655
traveled (1)
treads (1)
turn (1)
very old (1) +928+2021+2416+3427
visit (1)
was brought into (1)
was taken (1)
went in to spend the night with (1) +448
went inside (1)
went on (1)
went out (1)
went over (1)
were (1)
were taken (1)
what[s] (1) +2021
wielding (1) +2025+4200+5087
will[s] (1)
work (1)
untranslated (88)

996 בּוּז1 *bûz1* (13)
despises (4)
despise (3)
scorns (2)
derides (1)
scorn (1)
utterly scorned (1) +996

997 בּוּז2 *bûz2* (11)
contempt (9)
despised (1)
laughingstock (1)

998 בּוּז3 *bûz3* (3)
Buz (3)

999 בּוּזָה *bûzāh* (1)
despised (1)

1000 בּוּזִי1 *bûziy1* (2)
Buzite (2)

1001 בּוּזִי2 *bûziy2* (1)
Buzi (1)

1002 בַּנִּי *bawway*
Variant; not used

1003 בּוּךְ *bûk* (3)
bewildered (1)
mill about (1)
wandering around in confusion (1)

1004 בּוּל1 *bûl1* (1)
Bul (1)

1005 בּוּל2 *bûl2* (1)
block (1)

1006 בּוּל3 *bûl3* (1)
produce (1)

1007 בּוּנָה *bûnāh* (1)
Bunah (1)

1008 בּוּס *bûs* (12)
trample down (4)
kicking about (2)
loathes (1)
trample (1)
trampled (1)
trampled down (1)
trampled underfoot (1)
trampling (1)

1009 בּוּץ *bûs* (8)
fine linen (6)
linen (1)
white linen (1)

1010 בּוֹצֵץ *bôṣēṣ* (1)
Bozez (1)

1011 בּוּקָה *bûqāh* (1)
pillaged (1)

1012 בּוֹקֵר *bôqēr* (1)
shepherd (1)

1013 בּוּר *bûr* (1)
concluded (1)

1014 בּוֹר *bôr* (71)
pit (26)
cistern (19)
well (7)
cisterns (5)
dungeon (3)
dungeon (2) +1074
wells (2)
death (1)
hole (1)
one[s] (1)
quarry (1) +5217
slimy pit (1) +8622
there[s] (1) +928+2021
untranslated (1)

1015 בּוֹר הַסִּרָה *bôr hassirāh*
Variant; not used

1016 בּוֹר־עָשָׁן *bôr-'āšān* (1)
Bor Ashan (1)

1017 בּוֹשׁ1 *bôš1* (120)
put to shame (41)
ashamed (24)
disgraced (8)
shame (6)
shamed (4)
disappointed (3)
disgrace (3)
disgraceful (3)
dismayed (3)
be disgraced (2)
despair (2)
have shame at all (2) +1017
bear shame (1)
bring shame (1)
brings shame (1)
disgraces (1)
distressed (1)
embarrassment (1)
felt ashamed (1)
felt shame (1)
frustrate (1)
humiliated (1)
infamy (1)
let be dashed (1)
let be put to shame (1)
shameful (1)
shamelessly (1) +4202
suffer shame (1)
utter shame (1) +1425
untranslated (1)

1018 בּוֹשׁ2 *bôš2* (2)
so long (2)

1019 בּוּשָׁה *bûšāh* (4)
shame (4)

1020 בַּז *baz* (25)
plunder (15)
plundered (4)
loot (2) +1024
despoil (1) +4200+5989
looted (1)
plunder (1) +1024
taken captive (1)

1021 בְּזָא *bāzā'* (2)
divided (2)

1022 בָּזָה *bāzāh* (44)
despised (19)
despise (7)

contemptible (3)
was despised (3)
be despised (2)
despises (2)
contemptuous (1)
despise (1) +928+6524
despises (1) +928+6524
is despised (1)
ridiculed (1)
scorned the idea (1) +928+6524
show contempt (1)
shown contempt (1)

1023 בִּזָּה *bizzāh* (10)
plunder (7)
booty (1)
pillage (1)
plundered (1)

1024 בָּזַז *bāzaz* (43)
plunder (11)
carried off (4)
carry off (4)
plundered (3)
loot (2)
loot (2) +1020
looted (2)
took (2)
be plundered (1)
collect (1)
make spoil (1)
plunder (1) +1020
plunderers (1)
robbing (1)
snatch (1)
take (1)
taken plunder (1)
taking as plunder (1)
took as plunder (1)
totally plundered (1) +1024

1025 בִּזָּיוֹן *bizzāyôn* (1)
disrespect (1)

1026 בִּזְיוֹתְיָה *bizyôtyāh* (1)
Biziothiah (1)

1027 בָּזָק *bāzāq* (1)
flashes of lightning (1)

1028 בֶּזֶק *bezeq* (3)
Bezek (2)
there[s] (1) +928

1029 בָּזַר *bāzar* (2)
distribute (1)
scatter (1)

1030 בִּזְּתָא *bizz'tā'* (1)
Biztha (1)

1031 בָּחוֹן *bāhôn* (1)
tester of metals (1)

1032 בַּחוּן *bahûn* (1)
siege towers (1)

1033 בָּחוּר1 *bāhûr1* (50)
young men (34)
young man (6)
able (3)
men (3)
bridegrooms (1)
sons (1)
strong young men (1)
younger men (1)

1034 בָּחוּר2 *bāhûr2*
Variant; not used

1035 בְּחוּרוֹת *b'hûrôt* (2)
youth (2)

1036 בְּחוּרִים *b'hûriym* (1)
youth (1)

1037 בָּחוּרִים1 *bahûriym1*
Variant; not used

1038 בַּחוּרִים2 *bahûriym2* (5)
Bahurim (5)

1039 בָּחִין *bahiyn* (1)
untranslated (1)

1040 בָּחִיר *bāhiyr* (13)
chosen (13)

1041 1בָּחַל *bāhal1* (1)
detested (1)

1042 2בָּחַל *bāhal2* (1)
untranslated (1)

1043 בָּחַן *bāhan* (29)
test (11)
be tested (3)
examine (3)
tested (3)
tests (2)
challenge (1)
examines (1)
probe (1)
searches (1)
testing (1)
tried (1)
untranslated (1)

1044 בָּחַן *bahan* (1)
watchtower (1)

1045 1בֹּחַן *bōhan1*
Variant; not used

1046 2בֹּחַן *bōhan2* (1)
tested (1)

1047 1בָּחַר *bāhar1* (166)
chosen (63)
choose (42)
chose (27)
chooses (7)
choice (4)
best (3)
prefer (3)
selected (2)
acceptable (1)
adopt (1)
choose (1) +7864
decide (1)
desirable (1)
desire (1)
discern (1)
find (1)
finest (1)
selects (1)
sided with (1) +4200
tested (1)
would rather be (1)
untranslated (2)

1048 2בָּחַר *bāhar2*
Variant; not used

1049 בַּחֲרוּמִי *bahªrûmiy* (1)
Baharumite (1)

1050 בַּחֲרֻמִי *bahurimiy*
Variant; not used

1051 בָּטָא *bātā'* (4)
carelessly (1)
rash words came (1)
reckless words (1)
thoughtlessly (1) +928+4200+8557

1052 בָּטוּחַ *bātûah*
Variant; not used

1053 1בָּטַח *bātah1* (119)
trust (45)
trusts (15)
trusted (10)
depending (8)
depend (4)
feel secure (4)
put trust (4)
rely (3)

secure (3)
confident (2)
let persuade to trust (2)
on basing (2)
put confidence (2)
relied (2)
trusting (2)
unsuspecting (2)
basing confidence (1)
bold (1)
depended (1)
has full confidence (1) +4213
led to believe (1)
made trust (1)
persuaded to trust (1)
reckless (1)
safe (1)

1054 2בָּטַח *bātah2* (1)
stumble (1)

1055 1בֶּטַח *betah1* (42)
safety (24)
secure (4)
confidence (2)
safely (2) +4200
securely (2)
unsuspecting (2)
complacency (1)
feeling of security (1)
security (1)
trustfully (1) +4200
unsuspecting (1) +4200
without a care (1)

1056 2בֶּטַח *betah2*
Variant; not used

1057 בִּטְחָה *bithāh* (1)
trust (1)

1058 בַּטֻּחָה *battuhāh* (1)
secure (1)

1059 בִּטָּחוֹן *bittāhôn* (3)
confidence (2)
hope (1)

1060 בָּטֵל *bātal* (1)
cease (1)

1061 1בֶּטֶן *beten1* (72)
womb (28)
belly (4)
birth (4)
abdomen (3)
stomach (3)
birth (2) +562
body (2)
heart (2)
inmost being (2) +2540
inmost parts (2) +2540
bodies (1)
born (1)
borne (1)
bowl-shaped part (1)
brothers (1) +1201
children (1) +2021+7262
children (1) +7262
conceived (1)
craving (1)
depths (1)
descendants (1) +7262
infants (1) +7262
inside (1)
offspring (1)
pregnancy (1)
still hunger (1) +4848
waist (1)
within (1)
untranslated (2)

1062 2בֶּטֶן *beten2* (1)
Beten (1)

1063 בָּטְנָה *botnāh* (1)

pistachio nuts (1)

1064 בְּטֹנִים *b'tōniym* (1)
Betonim (1)

1065 בִּי *biy* (12)
O (4)
please (3)
but (2)
please (1) +5528
untranslated (2)

1066 בְּיִי *bāyay*
Variant; not used

1067 בִּין *biyn* (171)
understand (29)
discerning (16)
understanding (11)
consider (8)
understood (5)
give understanding (4)
have understanding (4)
instructed (4)
understands (4)
discern (3)
discernment (3)
gain (3)
perceive (3)
clever (2)
gain understanding (2)
gives thought (2)
gives understanding (2)
look (2)
ponder (2)
realized (2)
show regard (2)
skilled (2)
able (1)
acted wisely (1)
brilliant (1)
cared for (1)
checked (1)
comprehended (1)
consider carefully (1)
considers (1)
distinguish (1)
dwell on (1)
enlighten (1)
explain (1)
explaining (1)
feel (1)
find (1)
gave full attention (1)
give discernment (1)
give thought (1)
have concern (1) +1981
insight (1)
insights have (1)
instruct (1)
instructing (1)
intelligent (1)
know (1)
knows (1)
learned (1)
learning (1)
let understand (1)
look lustfully (1)
looked closely (1)
master (1)
note well (1) +1067
noticed (1)
observe (1)
pays heed (1)
prudent (1)
quick to understand (1) +4529
realize (1)
regard (1)
see (1)
sensible (1)
show (1)
show favor (1)
skillful (1)

take heed (1)
take note (1)
teacher (1)
tell the meaning (1)
think (1)
thinking (1)
understand clearly (1) +1069
well (1)
untranslated (2)

1068 בַּיִן *bayin* (410)
between (164)
among (31)
at twilight (11) +2021+6847
from (6)
at (3)
between (3) +4946
above (2) +448
as (2)
on forehead (2) +6524
on foreheads (2) +6524
or (2)
whether (2)
with (2)
above (1)
above (1) +6584
against (1)
alternated with (1)
among (1) +4946
attached to (1)
difference between (1)
distinction between (1)
every (1)
from (1) +4200
front of heads (1) +6524
have (1) +2118
in (1) +928
in midair (1)
    +824+1068+2021+2021+2256+9028
in the midst of (1)
midst (1)
of (1) +4946
on (1)
out (1) +4946
out of (1) +4946
relationships between (1)
separate (1) +5911
separated (1) +7233
slung on back (1) +4190
the difference between (1)
to (1)
together (1)
using (1)
witness (1) +9048
womb (1) +8079
untranslated (147)

1069 בִּינָה *biynāh* (38)
understanding (24)
insight (2)
wisdom (2)
discernment (1)
good sense (1)
great skill (1) +2682+3359
incomprehensible (1) +401
intelligence (1)
understand (1)
understand (1) +3359
understand clearly (1) +1067
understood (1) +3359
untranslated (1)

1070 בֵּיצָה *bēyṣāh* (6)
eggs (5)
untranslated (1)

1071 בַּיִר *bayir*
Variant; not used

1072 בִּירָה *biyrāh* (18)
citadel (14)
forts (2)
palatial structure (2)

1073 בִּירָנִיָּה *biyrāniyyāh*
Variant; not used

1074 1בַּיִת *bayit1* (2045)
house (770)
temple (436)
palace (120)
household (81)
houses (81)
home (71)
family (67)
families (57) +3
family (25) +3
people (21)
land (15)
palace (15) +4889
homes (10)
hold (8)
buildings (6)
households (6)
Israelite (6) +408+3776+4946
place (6)
prison (6) +2021+6045
estate (5)
harem (5) +851
inside (5) +4946
Israel (5) +3776
shrines (5)
behind (4) +4946
building (4)
families (4)
family line (4)
hall (4)
it^s (4) +2021
Judah (4) +3373
prison (4) +2021+3975
room (4)
that^s (4)
dynasty (3)
armory (2) +3998
center (2)
court (2)
division (2)
dungeon (2) +1014
inside (2) +928+2021
inside (2) +2025
its^s (2) +2021
its^s (2) +3378
palace grounds (2) +4889
prison (2) +673
prison (2) +2021+3989
prison (2) +3975
quarters (2)
residence (2)
sanctuary (2)
shelter (2)
storehouses (2) +5800
temple area (2)
temples (2)
there^s (2) +928+2021
those^s (2)
tribe (2)
tribes (2)
web (2)
apartment (1)
banquet hall (1) +3516
born in the same home (1) +4580
bottles (1)
camps (1) +5661
clan (1)
clan (1) +3+5476
clans (1) +3
descendants (1)
descendants (1) +5270
dungeon (1) +3975
dwellings (1)
full (1) +6017
group (1) +3+2755
guest (1) +448+995
guests (1) +1591
house (1) +185
house (1) +4632

imprisoned (1) +657+2021+5989
in (1) +2021+2025
inner (1)
inside (1)
inside (1) +448+2021
inside (1) +4200+4946
interior (1)
interior (1) +2025+4946
inward (1) +2025
Israelite (1) +3776
Israelites (1) +3776
it^s (1) +513
it^s (1) +1251
it^s (1) +3378
kitchens (1) +1418
lived (1) +928+2021
living with (1)
lodge (1) +4472
main hall (1)
mansions (1)
mansions (1) +8041
palace (1) +4895
palaces (1)
pen up (1) +2025
penned up (1) +928+2021+3973
possessions (1)
prison (1)
prison (1) +673+2021
prison (1) +2021+4551
prison (1) +2021+7213
prison (1) +5464
prisons (1) +3975
realm (1)
sanctuary (1) +5219
shrine (1)
shrine (1) +466
slave by birth (1) +3535
stall (1)
steward^s (1) +408+889+2021+6584
steward^s (1) +889+6584
storehouse (1) +238
storehouse (1) +667
strong fortress (1) +5181
that^s (1) +2021+2021+2296
them^s (1) +466+2021+3998
them^s (1) +2023
there^s (1) +466+928
there^s (1) +928+2021+3752
there^s (1) +7281
there^s (1) +8235
they^s (1) +3441
tomb (1)
town (1)
treasury (1) +238
under (1) +4200
underneath (1) +4946
wall (1)
where^s (1)
wine stewards (1) +8042
workers (1) +6275
untranslated (42)

1075 2בַּיִת *bayit2* (3)
among (1)
between (1)
meet (1)

1076 3בַּיִת *bayit3*
Variant; not used

1077 בֵּית אָוֶן *bēyt 'āwen* (7)
Beth Aven (7)

1078 בֵּית־אֵל *bēyt-'ēl* (71)
Bethel (70)
there^s (1) +928

1079 בֵּית אַרְבֵּאל *bēyt 'arbē'l* (1)
Beth Arbel (1)

1080 בֵּית אַשְׁבֵּעַ *bēyt 'ašbēa'* (1)
Beth Ashbea (1)

1081 בֵּית בַּעַל מְעוֹן *bēyt ba'al mᵉ'ôn* (1)
Beth Baal Meon (1)

1082 בֵּית בִּרְאִי *bēyṭ bir'iy* (1)
Beth Biri (1)

1083 בֵּית בָּרָה *bēyṭ bārāh* (2)
Beth Barah (2)

1084 בֵּית־גָּדֵר *bēyṭ-gāḏēr* (1)
Beth Gader (1)

1085 בֵּית גָּמוּל *bēyṭ gāmûl* (1)
Beth Gamul (1)

1086 בֵּית דִּבְלָתַיִם *bēyṭ diḇlāṭayim* (1)
Beth Diblathaim (1)

1087 בֵּית־דָּגוֹן *bēyṭ-dāḡôn* (2)
Beth Dagon (2)

1088 בֵּית הָאֱלִי *bēyṭ hā'ĕliy* (1)
of Bethel (1)

1089 בֵּית הָאָצֵל *bēyṭ hā'ēsel* (1)
Beth Ezel (1)

1090 בֵּית הַגִּלְגָּל *bēyṭ haggilgāl* (1)
Beth Gilgal (1)

1091 בֵּית הַגָּן *bēyṭ haggān* (1)
Beth Haggan (1)

1092 בֵּית הַמֶּרְחָק *bēyṭ hammerhāq*
Variant; not used

1093 בֵּית הַיְשִׁימוֹת *bēyṭ hay'šiymôṭ* (4)
Beth Jeshimoth (4)

1094 בֵּית־הַכֶּרֶם *bēyṭ-hakkerem* (2)
Beth Hakkerem (2)

1095 בֵּית־הַלַּחְמִי *bēyṭ-hallahmiy* (4)
of Bethlehem (3)
the Bethlehemite (1)

1096 בֵּית־הַמַּרְכָּבוֹת *bēyṭ-hammarkāḇôṭ* (1)
Beth Marcaboth (1)

1097 בֵּית הָעֵמֶק *bēyṭ hā'ēmeq* (1)
Beth Emek (1)

1098 בֵּית הָעֲרָבָה *bēyṭ hā''rāḇāh* (4)
Beth Arabah (4)

1099 בֵּית הָרָם *bēyṭ hārām* (1)
Beth Haram (1)

1100 בֵּית הָרָן *bēyṭ hārān* (1)
Beth Haran (1)

1101 בֵּית הַשִּׁטָּה *bēyṭ haššittāh* (1)
Beth Shittah (1)

1102 בֵּית־חָגְלָה *bēyṭ-hoglāh* (3)
Beth Hoglah (3)

1103 בֵּית־חוֹרוֹן *bēyṭ-hôrôn* (14)
Beth Horon (14)

1104 בֵּית חָנָן *bēyṭ hānān*
Variant; not used

1105 בֵּית כָּר *bēyṭ kār* (1)
Beth Car (1)

1106 בֵּית לְבָאוֹת *bēyṭ l'ḇā'ôṭ* (1)
Beth Lebaoth (1)

1107 בֵּית לֶחֶם *bēyṭ lehem* (41)
Bethlehem (40)
untranslated (1)

1108 בֵּית לְעַפְרָה *bēyṭ l''aprāh* (1)
Beth Ophrah (1)

1109 בֵּית מִלּוֹא *bēyṭ millô'* (4)
Beth Millo (4)

1110 בֵּית מְעוֹן *bēyṭ m''ôn* (1)
Beth Meon (1)

1111 בֵּית מַעֲכָה *bēyṭ ma''ḵāh*
Variant; not used

1112 בֵּית מַרְכָּבוֹת *bēyṭ markāḇôṭ* (1)
Beth Marcaboth (1)

1113 בֵּית נִמְרָה *bēyṭ nimrāh* (2)
Beth Nimrah (2)

1114 בֵּית עֶדֶן *bēyṭ 'eden* (1)
Beth Eden (1)

1115 בֵּית־עַזְמָוֶת *bēyṭ-'azmāweṭ* (1)
Beth Azmaveth (1)

1116 בֵּית־עֲנוֹת *bēyṭ-''nôṭ* (1)
Beth Anoth (1)

1117 בֵּית־עֲנָת *bēyṭ-''nāṭ* (3)
Beth Anath (3)

1118 בֵּית־עֵקֶד *bēyṭ-'ēqeḏ* (2)
Beth Eked (2)

1119 בֵּית עַשְׁתָּרוֹת *bēyṭ 'aštārôṭ*
Variant; not used

1120 בֵּית פֶּלֶט *bēyṭ peleṭ* (2)
Beth Pelet (2)

1121 בֵּית פְּעוֹר *bēyṭ p''ôr* (4)
Beth Peor (4)

1122 בֵּית פַּצֵּץ *bēyṭ passēs* (1)
Beth Pazzez (1)

1123 בֵּית־צוּר *bēyṭ-sûr* (4)
Beth Zur (4)

1124 בֵּית־רְחוֹב *bēyṭ-r'hôḇ* (2)
Beth Rehob (2)

1125 בֵּית רָפָא *bēyṭ rāpā'* (1)
Beth Rapha (1)

1126 בֵּית־שְׁאָן *bēyṭ-š''ān* (9)
Beth Shan (9)

1127 בֵּית שֶׁמֶשׁ *bēyṭ šemeš* (20)
Beth Shemesh (20)

1128 בֵּית־שִׁמְשִׁי *bēyṭ-šimšiy* (2)
of Beth Shemesh (2)

1129 בֵּית תּוֹגַרְמָה *bēyṭ tôḡarmāh* (2)
Beth Togarmah (2)

1130 בֵּית־תַּפּוּחַ *bēyṭ-tappûaḥ* (1)
Beth Tappuah (1)

1131 בִּיתָן *biyṭān* (3)
palace (3)

1132 בָּכָא 1 *bāḵā' 1* (4)
balsam trees (4)

1133 בָּכָא 2 *bāḵā' 2* (1)
Baca (1)

1134 בָּכָה *bāḵāh* (114)
wept (36)
weep (26)
weeping (16)
wailing (5)
mourned (3)
wept (3) +1140
mourn (2)
wailed (2)
bitterly weeps (1) +1134
cried (1)
crying (1)
grieved (1)
mourning (1)
sob (1)
sobbing (1)
tears (1)
weep (1) +1134
weep at all (1) +1134
weep bitterly (1) +1134
weeping (1) +1140
wept aloud (1)
wept bitterly (1) +1135+2221
wept much (1) +1134
wet with tears (1)

1135 בֶּכֶה *bekeh* (1)
wept bitterly (1) +1134+2221

1136 בִּכּוּרָה *bikkûrāh* (4)
early figs (1)
early fruit (1)

fig ripe (1)
ripen early (1)

1137 בִּכּוּרִים *bikkûriym* (17)
firstfruits (12)
first ripe (1)
first ripe fruit (1)
first ripe grain (1)
untranslated (2)

1138 בְּכוֹרַת *b'ḵôraṭ* (1)
Becorath (1)

1139 בָּכוּת *bāḵûṭ*
Variant; not used

1140 בְּכִי *b'ḵiy* (29)
weeping (14)
weep (4)
wept (3) +1134
weeps (2)
tears (1)
weep (1) +5951
weeping (1) +1134
weeping bitterly (1) +1140
wept so loudly (1) +906+928+5989+7754

1141 בֹּכִים *bōḵiym* (2)
Bokim (2)

1142 בְּכִירָה *b'ḵiyrāh* (6)
older (6)

1143 בְּכִית *b'ḵiyṭ* (1)
mourning (1)

1144 בָּכַר *bāḵar* (4)
bear (1)
bearing first child (1)
firstborn belongs to (1) +4200
give the rights of the firstborn (1)

1145 בֶּכֶר *bēḵer* (1)
young camels (1)

1146 בֶּכֶר *beker* (5)
Beker (5)

1147 בְּכוֹר *b'ḵôr* (122)
firstborn (108)
oldest (1)
firstborn male (2)
first (1)
first male offspring (1)
first male offspring (1) +7081+8167
poorest of the poor (1) +1924
untranslated (5)

1148 בְּכוֹרָה *b'ḵôrāh* (10)
birthright (6)
ages (1) +7584
firstborn (1)
rights as firstborn (1)
rights of the firstborn (1)

1149 בִּכְרָה *bikrāh* (1)
she-camel (1)

1150 בֹּכְרוּ *bōḵrû* (2)
Bokeru (2)

1151 בַּכְרִי *bakriy* (1)
Bekerite (1)

1152 בִּכְרִי *bikriy* (8)
Bicri (8)

1153 בַּל *bal 1* (69)
not (34)
cannot (6)
no (5)
never (3)
no sooner (3) +677
never (2) +4200+5905
never (2) +4200+6409
nor (2) +2256
nothing (2)
blind (1) +8011
don't (1)
ignorant (1) +3359

immovable (1) +4572
in order that no (1)
never (1) +2256+6329+6409
untouched (1) +7212
without (1)
worthless (1) +3603
untranslated (1)

1154 בַּל‎ *bal2*
Variant; not used

1155 בֵּל‎ *bēl* (3)
Bel (3)

1156 בַּלְאֲדָן‎ *bal'ᵃdān* (2)
Baladan (2)

1157 בֵּלְאשַׁצַּר‎ *bēl'šassar* (1)
Belshazzar's (1)

1158 בָּלַג‎ *bālag* (4)
flashes (1)
have joy (1)
rejoice (1)
smile (1)

1159 בִּלְגָּה‎ *bilgāh* (3)
Bilgah (2)
Bilgah's (1)

1160 בִּלְגַּי‎ *bilgay* (1)
Bilgai (1)

1161 בִּלְדַּד‎ *bildad* (5)
Bildad (5)

1162 בָּלָה‎ 1 *bālāh1* (16)
wear out (6)
worn out (2)
decay (1)
did^s (1)
long enjoy (1)
made grow old (1)
oppress (1)
wasted away (1)
wastes away (1)
untranslated (1)

1163 בָּלָה‎ 2 *bālāh2* (1)
Balah (1)

1164 בָּלָה‎ 3 *bālah3* (1)
untranslated (1)

1165 בָּלֶה‎ *bāleh* (5)
old (2)
worn (1)
worn out (1)
worn-out (1)

1166 בַּלָּהָה‎ *ballāhāh* (10)
terrors (6)
horrible end (3)
sudden terror (1)

1167 בִּלְהָה‎ 1 *bilhāh1* (10)
Bilhah (9)
she^s (1)

1168 בִּלְהָה‎ 2 *bilhāh2* (1)
Bilhah (1)

1169 בִּלְהָן‎ *bilhān* (4)
Bilhan (4)

1170 בְּלוֹי‎ *b'lôy* (3)
old (2)
worn-out (1)

1171 בֵּלְטְשַׁאצַּר‎ *bēlt'ša'ssar* (2)
Belteshazzar (2)

1172 בְּלִי‎ *b'liy* (58)
no (9)
not (7)
lack (6)
without (6)
unintentionally (4) +928+1981
there is no (3) +401
no (2) +4946
without (2) +4200

deserted (1) +3782+4946
destruction (1)
guiltless (1) +7322
lacking (1)
lacking (1) +4946
nameless (1) +9005
no longer (1)
no more (1)
nothing (1) +4537
relentless (1) +3104
there were no (1) +401
unnoticed (1) +4946+8492
untraveled (1) +408+4946+6296
without (1) +928
without (1) +3869
without (1) +4946
yet (1) +889+4946
untranslated (2)

1173 בְּלִיל‎ *b'liyl* (3)
fodder (3)

1174 בְּלִימָה‎ *b'liymāh*
Variant; not used

1175 בְּלִיַּעַל‎ *b'liyya'al* (27)
wicked (6)
scoundrels (3) +1201
wicked (3) +1201
destruction (2)
vile (2)
corrupt (1)
evil men (1)
scoundrel (1) +132
scoundrel (1) +408
scoundrel (1) +408+2021
troublemaker (1) +408
troublemakers (1)
troublemakers (1) +1201
wickedness (1)
worthless (1)
untranslated (1)

1176 בָּלַל‎ 1 *bālal1* (44)
mixed (38)
confuse (1)
confused (1)
fed (1)
mixes (1)
poured (1)
untranslated (1)

1177 בָּלַל‎ 2 *bālal2*
Variant; not used

1178 בָּלַם‎ *bālam* (1)
controlled (1)

1179 בָּלַס‎ *bālas* (1)
took care of (1)

1180 בָּלַע‎ 1 *bāla'1* (44)
swallowed up (9)
swallow up (7)
swallowed (7)
swallow (3)
be swallowed up (2)
destroy (2)
swallows (2)
consumed (1)
destroying (1)
devoured (1)
devours (1)
for an instant (1) +6330+8371
gulps down (1)
is swallowed up (1)
moment (1)
ruin (1)
torn (1)
uneaten (1) +4202
untranslated (1)

1181 בָּלַע‎ 2 *bāla'2*
Variant; not used

1182 בָּלַע‎ 3 *bāla'3* (6)

are led astray (1)
at wits' end (1) +2683+3972
befuddled (1)
bring to nothing (1)
confuse (1)
turn (1)

1183 בֶּלַע‎ 1 *bela'1* (1)
what swallowed (1)

1184 בֶּלַע‎ 2 *bela'2* (1)
harmful (1)

1185 בֶּלַע‎ 3 *bela'3* (12)
Bela (12)

1186 בֶּלַע‎ 4 *bela'4* (2)
Bela (2)

1187 בַּלְעֲדֵי‎ *bal'ᵃdēy* (17)
apart from (3) +4946
besides (3) +4946
cannot (2)
other than (2) +4946
without (2) +4946
besides (1)
except (1) +4946
not (1) +4946
nothing (1)
without (1)

1188 בַּלְעִי‎ *bal'iy* (1)
Belaite (1)

1189 בִּלְעָם‎ 1 *bil'ām1* (60)
Balaam (53)
Balaam's (4)
he^s (1)
him^s (1)
the two of them^s (1) +1192+2256

1190 בִּלְעָם‎ 2 *bil'ām2* (1)
Bileam (1)

1191 בָּלַק‎ *bālaq* (2)
devastate (1)
stripped (1)

1192 בָּלָק‎ *bālāq* (43)
Balak (34)
Balak's (2)
the two of them^s (1) +1189+2256
them^s (1) +6269
untranslated (5)

1193 בִּלְשָׁן‎ *bilšān* (2)
Bilshan (2)

1194 בִּלְתִּי‎ *biltiy* (112)
not (37)
no (14)
keep from (5)
nothing (5)
neither (4)
without (3)
except (2)
fail (2)
never (2)
prevent (2) +5989
unless (2)
avoid (1)
be kept from (1) +1757+4200
be nothing (1) +401
besides (1)
but (1)
ceremonially unclean (1) +3196
didn't (1)
disobey (1) +928+7754+9048
except (1) +561
except for (1)
failing (1)
forbidden (1) +7422
free from (1)
from (1)
insatiable (1) +8425
instead of (1) +4200
no more (1)

not (1) +4946
only (1) +4202
other than (1) +963+4200
refusing (1)
remain unmarried (1)
+408+2118+4200+4200+6328
stop (1)
unable (1)
unceasing (1) +6239
unless (1) +561
worthless (1) +3603
untranslated (7)

1195 בָּמָה1 *bāmāh1* (105)
high places (62)
high place (20)
heights (9)
there[s] (4) +928+2021
mound (2)
shrines (1)
there (1) +928+2021
tops (1)
waves (1)
untranslated (4)

1196 בָּמָה2 *bāmāh2* (1)
Bamah (1)

1197 בִּמְהָל *bimhāl* (1)
Bimhal (1)

1198 בְּמוֹ *bᵉmô* (12)
from (2)
in (2)
with (2)
take (1) +995
through (1)
used for fuel (1) +836+8596
untranslated (3)

1199 בָּמוֹת *bāmôṯ* (2)
Bamoth (2)

1200 בָּמוֹת בַּעַל *bāmôṯ baʿal* (2)
Bamoth Baal (2)

1201 בֵּן1 *bēn1* (4932)
son (1847)
sons (814)
Israelites (483) +3776
descendants (229)
children (175)
old (153)
people (85)
Ammonites (79) +6648
young (54)
Israelite (50) +3776
men (35)
men (23) +132
Israel (21) +3776
Benjamites (17) +1228
Reubenites (17) +8017
Gadites (16) +1514
Levites (15) +4290
Benjamin (13) +1228
descendant (12)
son's (12)
them[s] (12) +3776
Judah (11) +3373
age (10)
foreigners (10) +5797
man (10) +132
Ammon (9) +6648
children's (9)
company (9)
Danites (9) +1968
Hittites (9) +3147
Merarites (9) +5356
they[s] (9) +3776
Ammonite (8) +6648
people (8) +6639
Gad (7) +1514
Kohathite (7) +7740
Merarite (7) +5356

countrymen (6) +6639
Ephraim (6) +713
exiles (6) +1583
Gershonites (6) +1767
grandson (6)
mankind (6) +132
Reuben (6) +8017
Asher (5) +888
Assyrians (5) +855
boy (5)
foreigner (5) +5797
line (5)
Manasseh (5) +4985
Naphtali (5) +5889
peoples (5)
Simeon (5) +9058
sons' (5)
their[s] (5) +2257
year-old (5) +9102
Zebulun (5) +2282
able men (4) +2657
age (4) +9102
Anakites (4) +6737
brave (4) +2657
Dan (4) +1968
descended (4)
Ephraimites (4) +713
grandchildren (4) +1201
grandsons (4)
Issachar (4) +3779
Kohathites (4) +7740
man (4)
Simeonites (4) +9058
child (3)
cousin (3) +1856
grandson (3) +1201
grandsons (3) +1201
Israelites' (3) +3776
Kohathites (3) +7741
Levites (3) +4291
one[s] (3)
princes (3)
princes (3) +4889
scoundrels (3) +1175
their[s] (3) +3870
whose[s] (3)
wicked (3) +1175
ages (2) +9102
angels (2) +466+2021
Babylonians (2) +951
born (2)
calf (2) +1330
calves (2)
common people (2) +6639
condemned to (2)
cubs (2)
Ephraimite (2) +713
father[s] (2)
fruitful vine (2) +7238
Gershonite (2) +1767
grandchildren (2)
him[s] (2) +3870
hostages (2) +9510
Israelite (2) +408+3776+4946
Israelites (2) +3776+4946
Joseph (2) +3441
lambs (2) +7366
lay people (2) +6639
man's (2) +132
Manassites (2) +4985
mortal men (2) +132
nephew (2) +278
overnight (2) +4326
they[s] (2) +5797
valiant fighter (2) +408+2657
young men (2)
Aaronic (1) +195
able (1) +2657
able-bodied (1) +2657
Ahohite (1) +292
all mankind (1) +132

all men (1) +132+2021
angels (1) +466
anointed (1) +2021+3658
army (1)
arrows (1) +8008
arrows[s] (1)
babies (1)
Babylonian (1) +951
Benjamin (1) +408+3549
birth (1)
bravely (1) +2657+4200
bravest soldier (1) +2657
brood (1)
brothers (1) +1061
bull (1) +1330
calves (1) +1330
children (1) +1887
children's (1) +4200
choice (1)
clans (1)
colt (1) +912
courageous (1) +2657
cousins on their father's side (1) +1856
Cushites (1) +3934
deserve to (1)
deserves (1)
deserves to (1)
destitute (1) +2710
disciple (1)
Edomites (1) +121
Egyptians (1) +5213
especially bred (1) +2021+8247
evildoers (1) +6594
families (1)
fertile (1) +9043
fighting (1) +2657
foal (1)
foreigner (1) +2021+5797
foreigners (1) +2021+5797
Gad (1) +1532
Gershonite (1) +1769
Gershonites (1) +1768
Gershonites (1) +1769
Gilead (1) +1680
goats (1) +6436
granddaughters (1) +1426
Greeks (1) +3436
Hacmonite (1) +2685
he[s] (1) +281+6687
heavenly beings (1) +446
high (1) +408
highborn (1) +408
him[s] (1) +2021+3778
him[s] (1) +2023
his people[s] (1) +3147
human (1) +132
Israelite (1) +928+3776
Israelite (1) +3776+4200
Israelite (1) +3776+4946
Israelites (1) +3776+6639
Jaakanites (1) +3622
Judah's (1) +3373
Kedar (1) +7723
Kohathite (1) +7741
Korahites (1) +7948
low (1) +132
low among men (1) +132
lowborn men (1) +132
Maacathite (1) +5084
members (1)
men (1) +132+2021
men (1) +408
mighty (1) +446
Moabites (1) +4566
murderer (1) +8357
must die (1) +4638
my[s] (1) +2257
native (1) +6639
nephews (1) +2157
noisy boasters (1) +8623
of Gilead (1) +1682

of Judah (1) +3373
one (1)
one who will inherit (1) +5479
opening of the womb (1) +5402
oppressed (1) +6715
people (1) +132
prince (1) +4889
proud (1) +8832
proud beasts (1) +8832
rebellious (1) +5308
Reuben (1) +8018
Reubenite (1) +8017
servant (1)
singers (1) +8876
slave born in household (1) +563
soldiers (1) +2657
some[s] (1)
sparks (1) +8404
successors (1)
their[s] (1)
their[s] (1) +1769+2021
their[s] (1) +6648
them[s] (1) +3620
them[s] (1) +4013
them[s] (1) +6648
these men[s] (1) +2021+5566
they[s] (1) +851+2021
they[s] (1) +1201+1514+2256+8017
they[s] (1) +1228
they[s] (1) +1968
they[s] (1) +2257
they[s] (1) +6648
tribe (1)
tribes (1)
troops (1) +1522
troublemakers (1) +1175
vassal (1)
very own brother (1) +278+562+3870
vultures (1) +5979
warriors (1) +2657
who[s] (1) +3776
Zadokites (1) +7401
Zerahites (1) +2438
untranslated (237)

1202 בֵּן *bēn2*
Variant; not used

1203 בֶּן־אֲבִינָדָב *ben-'ᵃbiynādāb* (1)
Ben-Abinadab (1)

1204 בֶּן־אוֹנִי *ben-'ôniy* (1)
Ben-Oni (1)

1205 בֶּן־גֶּבֶר *ben-geber* (1)
Ben-Geber (1)

1206 בֶּן־דֶּקֶר *ben-deqer* (1)
Ben-Deker (1)

1207 בֶּן־הֲדַד *ben-hᵃdad* (25)
Ben-Hadad (24)
Ben-Hadad's (1)

1208 בֶּן־הִנֹּם *ben-hinnōm* (10)
Ben Hinnom (10)

1209 בֶּן־זוֹחֵת *ben-zôhēt* (1)
Ben-Zoheth (1)

1210 בֶּן־חוּר *ben-hûr* (1)
Ben-Hur (1)

1211 בֶּן־חַיִל *ben-hayil* (1)
Ben-Hail (1)

1212 בֶּן־חָנָן *ben-hānān* (1)
Ben-Hanan (1)

1213 בֶּן־חֶסֶד *ben-hesed* (1)
Ben-Hesed (1)

1214 בֶּן־עַמִּי *ben-'ammiy* (1)
Ben-Ammi (1)

1215 בָּנָה *bānāh* (377)
built (114)
build (96)

building (24)
rebuilt (23)
rebuild (14)
be rebuilt (12)
built up (12)
builders (9)
build up (7)
builds (6)
be built (4)
fortified (4)
rebuilding (3)
been built (2)
been rebuilt (2)
build a family (2)
erect (2)
is built (2)
made (2)
rebuilt (2) +2256+8740
set up (2)
using[s] (2)
be established (1)
be restored (1)
besieged (1) +6584
builds up (1)
constructed (1)
construction (1)
craftsmen (1)
did work (1)
done this[s] (1) +3378+4200+4640
erected (1)
establish (1)
form (1)
indeed built (1) +1215
lined (1)
make firm (1)
newly built (1)
partitioned off (1)
prosper (1)
rebuild (1) +2256+8740
repairing (1)
restored (1)
stands firm (1)
was built (1)
were used (1)
worked (1)
untranslated (5)

1216 בְּנֹב *bᵉnōb*
Variant; not used

1217 בְּנוֹ *bᵉnô* (2)
Beno (2)

1218 בִּנּוּי *binnûy* (8)
Binnui (8)

1219 בְּנוֹת *bᵉnôt*
Variant; not used

1220 בָּנִי *bāniy* (13)
Bani (13)

1221 בֻּנִּי *bunniy* (3)
Bunni (3)

1222 בְּנֵי־בְרַק *bᵉnēy-bᵉraq* (1)
Bene Berak (1)

1223 בְּנֵי יַעֲקָן *bᵉnēy ya'ᵃqān* (2)
Bene Jaakan (2)

1224 בִּנְיָה *binyāh* (1)
building (1)

1225 בְּנָיָה *bᵉnāyāh* (11)
Benaiah (11)

1226 בְּנָיָהוּ *bᵉnāyāhû* (31)
Benaiah (31)

1227 בֵּנַיִם *bēnayim* (2)
champion (2) +408+2021

1228 בִּנְיָמִין *binyāmiyn* (168)
Benjamin (111)
Benjamites (17) +1201
Benjamin (13) +1201
Benjamites (11)

Benjamite (4)
Benjamin's (2)
tribe of Benjamin (2)
Benjamin (1) +824
Benjamite (1) +408
Benjamite (1) +4946
Benjamites (1) +408+4946
Benjamites (1) +4946
they[s] (1) +1201
untranslated (2)

1229 בֶּן־יְמִינִי *ben-yᵉmiyniy* (10)
Benjamite (7)
Benjamites (1)
men of Benjamin (1)
untranslated (1)

1230 בִּנְיָן *binyān* (7)
building (4)
outer wall (2)
wall (1)

1231 בְּנִינוּ *bᵉniynû* (1)
Beninu (1)

1232 בִּנְעָא *bin'ā'* (2)
Binea (2)

1233 בְּסוֹדְיָה *bᵉsôdᵉyāh* (1)
Besodeiah (1)

1234 בֵּסַי *bēsay* (2)
Besai (2)

1235 בֹּסֶר *bōser* (5)
sour grapes (3)
grape (1)
unripe grapes (1)

1236 בַּעֲבוּר *ba'ᵃbûr*
Variant; not used

1237 בַּעַד 1 *ba'ad1* (104)
for (48)
through (8)
behind (5)
from (4)
behind (3) +4946
in (3)
around (2)
on behalf of (2)
around (1) +4946+6017
barred in (1) +1378
by (1)
for (1) +3954
of (1)
on (1)
on behalf (1)
over (1)
seals off (1) +3159
untranslated (20)

1238 בַּעַד 2 *ba'ad2*
Variant; not used

1239 בָּעָה 1 *bā'āh1* (3)
ask (2)
pillaged (1)

1240 בָּעָה 2 *bā'āh2* (2)
bulging (1)
causes to boil (1)

1241 בְּעוּלָה *bᵉ'ûlāh* (1)
Beulah (1)

1242 בְּעוֹר *bᵉ'ôr* (10)
Beor (10)

1243 בְּעוּת *bi'ût* (2)
terrors (1)

1244 בֹּעַז 1 *bō'az1* (22)
Boaz (22)

1245 בֹּעַז 2 *bō'az2* (2)
Boaz (2)

1246 בָּעַט *bā'at* (2)
kicked (1)

scorn (1)

1247 בְּעִי *bᵉˤiy*
Variant; not used

1248 בְּעִיר *bᵉˤiyr* (7)
livestock (4)
animals (1)
cattle (1)
untranslated (1)

1249 1בַּעַל *bāˤal1* (15)
husband (4)
be married (1)
has a husband (1)
married (1)
married (1) +1251
marries (1)
marries (1) +2256+4374
marry (1)
marrying (1)
ruled (1)
ruled over (1)
wife (1) +851

1250 2בַּעַל *bāˤal2*
Variant; not used

1251 1בַּעַל *baˤal1* (164)
Baal (55)
Baals (18)
citizens (18)
owner (14)
husband (6)
Baal worship (3)
Baal's (3)
husbands (2)
two-horned (2) +2021+7967
with (2)
accuser (1) +5477
allied (1) +1382
archers (1) +2932
bird on the wing (1) +4053
birds (1) +4053
captain (1)
charmer (1) +4383
collected sayings (1) +670
creditor (1) +2257+3338+5408
dreamer (1) +2021+2706
filled with (1)
given to gluttony (1) +5883
has (1)
himˢ (1) +2023
hot-tempered (1) +2779
husband's (1)
involved in (1)
itˢ (1) +1074
man (1)
man's (1)
married (1) +1249
master (1)
men (1)
one who destroys (1) +5422
one who gives (1)
owned (1)
owner's (1)
people (1)
possessor (1)
practice (1)
related by marriage (1)
riders (1) +7304
rulers (1)
schemer (1) +4659
tenants (1)
theyˢ (1) +3972+4463+8901
those who deserve (1)
those who get (1)
those who have (1)
under oath (1) +8652
whoˢ (1) +8901

1252 2בַּעַל *baˤal2* (3)
Baal (3)

1253 בַּעַל בְּרִית *baˤal bᵉriyt* (2)

Baal-Berith (2)

1254 בַּעַל גָּד *baˤal gād* (3)
Baal Gad (3)

1255 בַּעַל הָמוֹן *baˤal hāmôn* (1)
Baal Hamon (1)

1256 בַּעַל זְבוּב *baˤal zᵉbûb* (4)
Baal-Zebub (4)

1257 בַּעַל חָנָן *baˤal hānān* (5)
Baal-Hanan (5)

1258 בַּעַל חָצוֹר *baˤal hāsôr* (1)
Baal Hazor (1)

1259 בַּעַל חֶרְמוֹן *baˤal hermôn* (2)
Baal Hermon (2)

1260 בַּעַל מְעוֹן *baˤal mᵉˤôn* (3)
Baal Meon (3)

1261 בַּעַל פְּעוֹר *baˤal pᵉˤôr* (2)
Baal Peor (2)

1262 בַּעַל־פְּרָצִים *baˤal-pᵉrāsiym* (4)
Baal Perazim (4)

1263 בַּעַל צָפֹן *baˤal sᵉpōn* (3)
Baal Zephon (3)

1264 בַּעַל שָׁלִשָׁה *baˤal šālišāh* (1)
Baal Shalishah (1)

1265 בַּעַל תָּמָר *baˤal tāmār* (1)
Baal Tamar (1)

1266 1בַּעֲלָה *baˤᵃlāh1* (4)
medium (1) +200
mistress (1)
oneˢ (1) +200
owned (1)

1267 2בַּעֲלָה *baˤᵃlāh2* (6)
Baalah (6)

1268 בְּעָלוֹת *bᵉˤālôt* (1)
Bealoth (1)

1269 בְּעֶלְיָדָע *bᵉˤelyādāˤ* (1)
Beeliada (1)

1270 בְּעַלְיָה *bᵉˤalyāh* (1)
Bealiah (1)

1271 בַּעֲלִיס *baˤᵃliys* (1)
Baalis (1)

1272 בַּעֲלָת *baˤᵃlāt* (4)
Baalath (4)

1273 בַּעֲלַת בְּאֵר *baˤᵃlat bᵉˀēr* (1)
Baalath Beer (1)

1274 בְּעֹן *bᵉˤōn* (1)
Beon (1)

1275 בַּעֲנָא *baˤᵃnāˀ* (3)
Baana (3)

1276 בַּעֲנָה *baˤᵃnāh* (9)
Baanah (9)

1277 1בָּעַר *bāˤar1* (63)
burn (11)
burned (5)
burning (5)
blazed (4)
burn up (3)
fire (3)
light (3)
ablaze (2)
blazing (2)
burned up (2)
burns (2)
consume (2)
set ablaze (2)
use for fuel (2) +836
blazed forth (1)
blazes (1)
charred (1) +836+928+2021
consumed (1)

consumes (1)
fires (1)
flare up (1)
kindled (1)
lit (1) +836
on fire (1) +836+928+2021
raged (1)
sacrificed (1)
sets ablaze (1)
started (1)
use for fuel (1)

1278 2בָּעַר *bāˤar2* (24)
purge (12)
rid (3)
destroyed (2)
removed (2)
got rid of (1)
graze (1)
grazes (1)
laid waste (1)
ruined (1)

1279 3בָּעַר *bāˤar3* (7)
senseless (5)
brutal (1)
give senseless (1)

1280 בַּעַר *baˤar* (5)
senseless (3)
ignorant (1)
stupid (1)

1281 בַּעֲרָא *baˤᵃrāˀ* (1)
Baara (1)

1282 בְּעֵרָה *bᵉˤērāh* (1)
fire (1)

1283 בַּעֲשֵׂיָה *baˤᵃśēyāh* (1)
Baaseiah (1)

1284 בַּעְשָׁא *baˤšāˀ* (28)
Baasha (25)
Baasha's (2)
heˢ (1)

1285 בְּעֶשְׁתְּרָה *bᵉˤeštᵉrāh* (1)
Be Eshtarah (1)

1286 בָּעַת *bāˤat* (16)
overwhelmed (2)
terrified (2)
terrify (2)
afraid (1)
alarm (1)
fill with terror (1)
frighten (1)
frightening (1)
makes tremble (1)
overwhelm (1)
startle (1)
tormented (1)
tormenting (1)

1287 בְּעָתָה *bᵉˤātāh* (2)
terror (2)

1288 בֹּץ *bōs* (1)
mud (1)

1289 בִּצָּה *bissāh* (4)
marsh (2)
swamps (1)
untranslated (1)

1290 בָּצוּר *bāsûr* (26)
fortified (22)
walls (2)
unsearchable (1)
untranslated (1)

1291 בֵּצַי *bēsay* (3)
Bezai (3)

1292 1בָּצִיר *bāsiyr1* (7)
grape harvest (4)
full grape harvest (1)
grapes (1)

sal'ēl (9)

(9)

baṣlûṭ (2)
ṣazluth (2)

1297 בַּצְלִית *baṣliyṭ*
Variant; not used

1298 בָּצַע *bāṣa'* (16)
cut off (3)
greedy (3)
breaking ranks (1)
bring down (1)
builds (1)
complete (1)
finished (1)
fulfilled (1)
go after ill-gotten gain (1) +1299
greedy (1) +1299
make unjust gain (1)
make unjust gain (1) +1299

1299 בֶּצַע *besa'* (23)
gain (9)
dishonest gain (3)
unjust gain (2)
cut off (1)
go after ill-gotten gain (1) +1298
greed (1)
greedy (1) +1298
ill-gotten gain (1)
ill-gotten gains (1)
make unjust gain (1) +1298
plunder (1)
selfish gain (1)

1300 בְּצַעֲנִנִים *b'ṣa''nanniym*
Variant; not used

1301 בָּצֵק *bāṣēq1* (2)
swell (1)
swollen (1)

1302 בָּצֵק *bāṣēq2* (5)
dough (5)

1303 בִּצְקָלוֹן *biṣqālôn*
Variant; not used

1304 בָּצְקַת *bāṣqaṭ* (2)
Bozkath (2)

1305 בָּצַר *bāṣar1* (7)
grape pickers (2)
harvest (2)
gathered (1)
gathering grapes (1)
harvest grapes (1)

1306 בָּצַר *bāṣar2* (1)
breaks (1)

1307 בָּצַר *bāṣar3* (4)
be thwarted (1)
fortifies (1)
impossible (1)
strengthen (1)

1308 בָּצַר *bāṣar4*
Variant; not used

1309 בֶּצֶר *beṣer1* (2)
gold (1)
nuggets (1)

1310 בֶּצֶר *beṣer2* (1)
Bezer (1)

1311 בֶּצֶר *beṣer3* (4)
Bezer (4)

1312 בָּצְרָה *boṣrāh1* (1)

pen (1)

1313 בָּצְרָה *boṣrāh2* (8)
Bozrah (8)

1314 בַּצָּרָה *bassārāh* (3)
trouble (1)
drought (2)

1315 בִּצָּרוֹן *biṣṣārôn* (1)
fortress (1)

1316 בַּצֹּרֶת *bassōreṯ* (1)
drought (1)

1317 בַּקְבּוּק *baqbûq* (2)
Bakbuk (2)

1318 בַּקְבֻּק *baqbuq* (3)
jar (3)

1319 בַּקְבֻּקְיָה *baqbuqyāh* (3)
Bakbukiah (3)

1320 בַּקְבַּקַּר *baqbaqqar* (1)
Bakbakkar (1)

1321 בֻּקִּי *buqqiy* (5)
Bukki (5)

1322 בֻּקִּיָּהוּ *buqqiyyāhû* (2)
Bukkiah (2)

1323 בָּקִיעַ *bāqiya'* (2)
bits (1)
breaches in defenses (1)

1324 בָּקַע *bāqa'* (51)
divided (3)
ripped open (3)
split (3)
was broken through (3)
broke (2)
burst forth (2)
cracked (2)
divide (2)
hatch (2)
opened up (2)
split apart (2)
were divided (2)
be split (1)
been broken through (1)
break forth (1)
break through (1)
breaks up (1)
burst (1)
chopped up (1)
conquer (1)
cut (1)
gush forth (1)
invaded (1)
is hatched (1)
mauled (1)
ready to burst (1)
rip open (1)
shook (1)
splits (1)
taken by storm (1)
tear apart (1)
tore open (1)
tunnels (1) +3284
unleash (1)
were dashed to pieces (1)

1325 בֶּקַע *beqa'* (2)
beka (2)

1326 בִּקְעָה *biq'āh* (20)
plain (9)
valley (7)
valleys (4)

1327 בָּקַק *bāqaq1* (8)
be completely laid waste (1) +1327
destroyers (1)
devastate (1)
laid waste (1)
lay waste (1)
lose heart (1) +928+7931+8120

ruin (1)

1328 בָּקַק *bāqaq2* (1)
spreading (1)

1329 בָּקַר *bāqar* (7)
look after (2)
consider (1)
look (1)
pick out (1)
seek (1)
seeking guidance (1)

1330 בָּקָר *bāqār* (184)
cattle (40)
herds (32)
oxen (31)
bull (27) +7228
bulls (14)
herd (10)
bulls (5) +7228
bull (4)
ox (4)
animals (2)
calf (2) +1201
heifer (2) +6320
bull (1) +1201
calves (1) +1201
cattle (1) +5238
cow (1)
cows (1)
cows' (1)
herds (1) +5238
herds (1) +6373
oxgoad (1) +4913
plowing (1)
young cow (1) +6320

1331 בֹּקֶר *bōqer1*
Variant; not used

1332 בֹּקֶר *bōqer2* (212)
morning (179)
every morning (4)
 +928+928+1332+2021+2021
dawn (3)
daybreak (3) +240+2021
dawn (2) +240+2021
morning's (2)
mornings (2)
break of day (1) +7155
daybreak (1) +2021+7155
daybreak (1) +7155
daylight (1) +240+2021
each morning (1)
 +928+928+1332+2021+2021
each morning (1)
 +1332+2021+2021+4200+4200
hold back overnight (1) +4328+6330
last watch of the night (1) +874
last watch of the night (1) +874+2021
morning light (1)
untranslated (4)

1333 בַּקָּרָה *baqqārāh* (1)
looks after (1)

1334 בִּקֹּרֶת *biqqōreṯ* (1)
due punishment (1)

1335 בָּקַשׁ *bāqaš* (225)
seek (58)
seeking (12)
look for (10)
looked for (10)
search for (10)
searched for (7)
looking for (6)
sought (5)
tried (5)
searched (4)
seeks (4)
find (3)
hold accountable (3) +3338+4946
search (3)

search out (3)
trying (3)
bent on (2)
call to account (2)
conspired (2)
demand (2)
in search of (2)
intend (2)
searching for (2)
seek out (2)
sought out (2)
take (2)
trying to take (2)
want (2)
about to (1)
ask for (1)
asked (1)
asked for (1)
asked for permission (1)
asking for (1)
be sought (1)
beg (1)
begging (1)
call to account (1) +3338+4946
carefully investigated (1) +2011+2256
demanded (1)
demanded payment (1)
finds (1)
gone in search of (1)
hold responsible (1) +3338+4946
inquiring of (1)
intended (1)
invites (1)
looking for a chance (1)
looks for (1)
looks to (1)
petitioned (1)
plans (1)
plead with (1)
pleaded (1)
pleaded with (1)
promote (1)
promotes (1)
pursue (1)
pursues (1)
pursuing (1)
questioned (1)
search be made for (1)
search made for (1)
searching (1)
seek an audience with (1) +7156
seek help (1)
seek to (1)
set out (1)
snare (1)
sought to (1)
straining (1)
tried to take (1)
try to find (1)
try to get (1)
trying to (1)
trying to get (1)
want to (1)
want to do (1)
wanted to (1)
wanted to kill (1) +906+5883
wanted to make (1) +4200
was investigated (1)
went in search of (1)

1336 בַּקָּשָׁה *baqqāšāh* (8)
request (7)
asked (1)

1337 1בַּר *bar1* (4)
son (4)

1338 2בַּר *bar2* (7)
pure (3)
bright (1)
empty (1)
favorite (1)
radiant (1)

1339 3בַּר *bar3* (13)
grain (11)
wheat (2)

1340 4בַּר *bar4* (1)
wilds (1)

1341 1בֹּר *bōr1* (5)
cleanness (5)

1342 2בֹּר *bōr2* (2)
thoroughly purge away (1)　　　+2021+3869+7671
washing soda (1)

1343 1בָּרָא *bārā'1* (48)
created (21)
create (10)
were created (6)
creator (3)
are created (2)
creating (2)
brings about (1)
creates (1)
done (1)
not yet created (1)

1344 2בָּרָא *bārā'2* (1)
fattening (1)

1345 3בָּרָא *bārā'3* (5)
clear (1)
clear land (1)
cut down (1)
make (1)
untranslated (1)

1346 4בָּרָא *bārā'4*
Variant; not used

1347 בְּרֹאדַךְ־בַּלְאֲדָן *bʳrō'dak-balʰdān*
Variant; not used

1348 בְּרָאִי *bir'iy*
Variant; not used

1349 בְּרָאיָה *bʳrā'yāh* (1)
Beraiah (1)

1350 בַּרְבֻּר *barbur* (1)
fowl (1)

1351 בָּרַד *bārad* (1)
hail (1)

1352 בָּרָד *bārād* (29)
hail (21)
hail (1) +74
hailstones (1)
hailstones (1) +74
hailstorm (1)
hailstorm (1) +2443
it^s (1) +2021
storm (1)
untranslated (1)

1353 בָּרֹד *bārōd* (4)
dappled (2)
spotted (2)

1354 1בֶּרֶד *bered1* (1)
Bered (1)

1355 2בֶּרֶד *bered2* (1)
Bered (1)

1356 1בָּרָה *bārāh1* (6)
eat (3)
food (1)
give to eat (1)
urged to eat (1)

1357 2בָּרָה *bārāh2*
Variant; not used

1358 בָּרוּךְ *bārûk* (26)
Baruch (26)

1359 בָּרוּר *bārûr* (2)
purify (1) +2200
sincerely (1)

1360 בְּרוֹשׁ *bʳrôš* (19)
pine (7)
pine trees (4)
pine tree (3)
pines (3)
pine (1) +6770
spears of pine (1)

1361 בְּרוֹת *bʳrôṯ* (1)
firs (1)

1362 בָּרוּת *bārûṯ* (1)
food (1)

1363 בֵּרוֹתָה *bērôṯāh* (1)
Berothah (1)

1364 בִּרְזוֹת *birzāwiṯ* (1)
untranslated (1)

1365 בִּרְזָיִת *birzāyiṯ* (1)
Birzaith (1)

1366 בַּרְזֶל *barzel* (76)
iron (62)
iron-smelting (3)
ax (2)
iron tool (2)
blacksmith (1) +3093
head (1)
iron axhead (1)
iron chains (1)
irons (1)
tool of iron (1)
untranslated (1)

1367 בַּרְזִלַּי *barzillay* (12)
Barzillai (12)

1368 1בָּרַח *bārah1* (65)
fled (32)
flee (5)
fleeing (3)
running away (3)
come away (1)
drives out (1)
drove away (1)
drove out (1)
escaping (1)
extend (1)
extended (1)
flees (1)
flees headlong (1) +1368
fleeting (1)
fly away (1)
go back (1)
gone back (1)
leave at once (1)
make flee (1)
put to flight (1)
ran away (1)
ran off (1)
run away (1)
run off (1)
takes to flight (1)

1369 2בָּרַח *bārah2*
Variant; not used

1370 3בָּרַח *bārah3*
Variant; not used

1371 בָּרִחַ *bāriah* (4)
fugitives (2)
gliding (2)

1372 בַּרְחֻמִי *barhumiy* (1)
Barhumite (1)

1373 בֵּרִי *bēriy* (1)
Beri (1)

1374 בָּרִיא *bāriy'* (14)
fat (4)
healthy (3)
fat (2) +1414
choice (1)
choice sheep (1)

choicest (1)
nourished (1) +1414
stall-fed (1)

1375 בְּרִיאָה *bʳriy'āh* (1)
something totally new (1)

1376 בִּרְיָה *biryāh* (3)
food (3)

1377 בָּרִיחַ *bāriyah* (1)
Bariah (1)

1378 בְּרִיחַ *bʳriyah* (41)
bars (17)
crossbars (11)
crossbar (2)
bar (1)
barred gates (1)
barred in (1) +1237
bars of gates (1)
gate (1)
gate bars (1)
untranslated (5)

1379 בֵּרִים *bēriym* (1)
Berites (1)

1380 בְּרִיעָה *bʳriy'āh* (11)
Beriah (11)

1381 בְּרִיעִי *bʳriy'iy* (1)
Beriite (1)

1382 בְּרִית *bʳriyt* (284)
covenant (246)
treaty (26)
agreement (3)
compact (3)
agreements (1)
alliance (1)
allied (1) +1251
allies (1) +408
itˢ (1) +778+2021
marriage covenant (1)

1383 בֹּרִית *bōriyt* (2)
soap (2)

1384 1בָּרַךְ *bārak1* (3)
had kneel down (1)
kneel (1)
knelt down (1) +1386+6584

1385 2בָּרַךְ *bārak2* (327)
blessed (86)
bless (79)
praise (63)
be blessed (23)
praised (8)
blesses (7)
give blessing (6)
congratulate (3)
curse (3)
cursed (3)
extol (3)
pronounce blessings (3)
blessing (2)
gave blessing (2)
be praised (1)
bless (1) +1385
bless abundant (1) +1385
bless at all (1) +1385
blessed (1) +1385
blessed again and again (1) +1385
blessings given (1)
commended (1)
counted blessed (1)
do soˢ (1)
done nothing but bless (1) +1385
give greetings (1)
given (1)
giving blessing (1) +1388
greet (1)
greet (1) +7925
greeted (1)
greets (1)

invokes a blessing (1)
invokes a blessing on himself (1)
is blessed (1)
pronounce blessing (1)
pronounced (1)
richly bless (1) +1385
surely bless (1) +1385
thank (1)
worships (1)
untranslated (1)

1386 בֶּרֶךְ *berek* (26)
knees (15)
knee (3)
lap (2)
for (1) +6584
knee-deep (1)
kneel (1)
kneeling (1) +4156+6584
knelt down (1) +1384+6584
untranslated (1)

1387 בַּרַכְאֵל *barak'ēl* (2)
Barakel (2)

1388 1בְּרָכָה *bʳrākāh1* (68)
blessing (37)
blessings (14)
blessed (2)
blessed (2) +5989
gift (2)
peace (2)
present (2)
special favor (2)
bless (1) +5989
blessed (1) +995
generous (1)
giving blessing (1) +1385
good (1)

1389 2בְּרָכָה *bʳrākāh2* (1)
Beracah (1)

1390 3בְּרָכָה *bʳrākāh3* (2)
Beracah (2)

1391 בְּרֵכָה *bʳrēkāh* (18)
pool (13)
pools (2)
pool (1) +4784
reservoirs (1) +4784
untranslated (1)

1392 בֶּרֶכְיָה *berekyāh* (7)
Berekiah (7)

1393 בֶּרֶכְיָהוּ *berekyāhû* (4)
Berekiah (4)

1394 בְּרֹמִים *bʳrōmiym* (1)
multicolored (1)

1395 בַּרְנֵעַ *barnēa'*
Variant; not used

1396 בֶּרַע *bera'* (1)
Bera (1)

1397 בָּרַק *bāraq* (1)
send forth lightning (1) +1398

1398 1בָּרָק *bārāq1* (21)
lightning (11)
flash like lightning (3)
bolts of lightning (2)
flashing (1)
gleaming point (1)
glittering (1)
lightning bolts (1)
send forth lightning (1) +1397

1399 2בָּרָק *bārāq2* (14)
Barak (12)
Barak's (1)
heˢ (1)

1400 בְּרָק *bʳraq*
Variant; not used

1401 בַּרְקוֹס *barqôs* (2)
Barkos (2)

1402 בַּרְקָן *barqōn* (2)
briers (2)

1403 בָּרֶקֶת *bāreqet* (2)
beryl (2)

1404 בָּרְקַת *borqat* (1)
beryl (1)

1405 1בָּרַר *bārar1* (15)
pure (3)
choice (2)
chosen (2)
show yourself pure (2)
be purified (1)
choose (1)
cleanse (1)
purge (1)
purified (1)
tests (1)

1406 2בָּרַר *bārar2* (2)
polished (1)
sharpen (1)

1407 בִּרְשַׁע *birša'* (1)
Birsha (1)

1408 בֵּרֹתַי *bērōtay* (1)
Berothai (1)

1409 בֵּרֹתִי *bērōtiy* (1)
Berothite (1)

1410 בְּשׂוֹר *bʳśôr* (3)
Besor (2)
untranslated (1)

1411 בֹּשֶׂם *bōśem* (30)
spices (21)
spice (3)
fragrance (2)
fragrant (2)
perfumes (1)
spice-laden (1)

1412 בָּשְׂמַת *bāśʳmat* (7)
Basemath (7)

1413 בָּשַׂר *bāśar* (24)
proclaim (4)
bring good tidings (2)
bringing good news (2)
brought the news (2)
proclaim the news (2)
take the news (2)
bring good news (1)
bring tidings (1)
bringing news (1)
brings good news (1)
do soˢ (1)
hear good news (1)
messenger of good tidings (1)
preach good news (1)
proclaimed (1)
proclaiming (1)

1414 בָּשָׂר *bāśār* (270)
flesh (75)
meat (64)
body (21)
himself (10) +2257
mankind (10)
skin (8) +6425
creature (7)
bodies (5)
people (5)
life (4)
flesh and blood (3)
men (3)
creatures (2)
everyone (2) +3972
fat (2) +1374
gaunt (2) +1987
itˢ (2)

kind (2)
living thing (2)
mortal man (2)
skin (2)
be circumcised (1) +4576+6889
blood relative (1) +8638
bodily (1) +4946
body (1) +6872
circumcised (1) +4576+6889
close relative (1) +8638
completely (1) +2256+4946+5883+6330
genitals (1)
lean (1) +8369
lustful (1) +1541
mankind (1) +408
meal (1)
mortal (1)
myself (1) +3276
nothing but skin (1) +2256+6425
nourished (1) +1374
one^s (1) +3972
put in jeopardy (1) +928+5951+9094
regular flow (1) +928+2307
that^s (1)
them (1) +4392
those^s (1)
undergo circumcision (1) +906+4576+6889
was circumcised (1) +4576+6889
you (1) +3870
untranslated (12)

1415 בְּשֹׂרָה b'śōrāh (6)
news (3)
good news (2)
reward for news (1)

1416 בְּשֶׁבֶת baššebet
Variant; not used

1417 בְּשַׁגַּם b'šaggam
Variant; not used

1418 בָּשַׁל bāšal (28)
cook (10)
cooked (5)
boiled (3)
boil (2)
baked (1)
burned to cook (1)
cooked (1) +1419
kitchens (1) +1074
ripe (1)
ripened (1)
roast (1)
roasted (1)

1419 בָּשֵׁל bāšēl (2)
boiled (1)
cooked (1) +1418

1420 בִּשְׁלָם bišlām (1)
Bishlam (1)

1421 1בָּשָׁן bāšān1 (60)
Bashan (59)
Bashan (1) +824

1422 2בָּשָׁן bāšān2
Variant; not used

1423 בָּשְׁנָה bošnāh (1)
disgraced (1) +4374

1424 בָּשַׂס bāśas (1)
trample (1)

1425 בֹּשֶׁת bōšet (30)
shame (20)
disgraced (2)
disgrace (1) +7156
humiliation (1) +7156
shame (1) +6872
shameful god (1)
shameful gods (1)
shameful idol (1)
shaming (1)
utter shame (1) +1017

1426 1בַּת bat1 (588)
daughter (245)
daughters (205)
women (15)
people (14) +6639
surrounding settlements (10)
settlements (9)
villages (7)
surrounding villages (6)
granddaughter (5)
woman (5)
owls (4) +3613
daughter's (3)
girl (3)
girls (2)
horned owl (2) +3613
maidens (2)
owl (2) +3613
year-old (2) +9102
young women (2)
adopted (1) +4200+4374
age (1) +9102
apple (1) +413
branches (1)
city (1)
cousin (1) +1856
descendant (1)
Egypt (1) +5213
eyes (1) +6524
granddaughters (1) +1201
inhabitants (1)
old (1)
outlying villages (1)
people (1)
princess (1) +4889
she^s (1) +7281
sister (1)
songs (1) +8877
whose^s (1) +465+2257
whose^s (1) +7524
young (1)
untranslated (24)

1427 2בַּת bat2 (14)
baths (8)
bath (6)

1428 3בַּת bat3 (1)
did weaving (1) +755

1429 בָּתָה bātāh (1)
wasteland (1)

1430 בֹּתָה bōtāh
Variant; not used

1431 בַּתָּה batāh (1)
steep (1)

1432 1בְּתוּאֵל b'tû'ēl1 (9)
Bethuel (9)

1433 2בְּתוּאֵל b'tû'ēl2 (1)
Bethuel (1)

1434 בְּתוּל b'tûl (1)
Bethul (1)

1435 בְּתוּלָה b'tûlāh (51)
virgin (25)
maidens (7)
virgins (6)
young women (4)
maiden (3)
daughters (1)
girl (1)
girls (1) +5855
unmarried (1)
women (1)
young woman (1)

1436 בְּתוּלִים b'tûliym (9)
proof of virginity (3)
never marry (2)
be a virgin (1) +928
proof that a virgin (1)

to be a virgin (1)
virgin (1)

1437 בִּתְיָה bityāh (1)
Bithiah (1)

1438 בָּתַק bātaq (1)
hack to pieces (1)

1439 בָּתַר bātar (2)
cut (1)
cut in half (1)

1440 1בֶּתֶר beter1 (3)
pieces (2)
halves (1)

1441 2בֶּתֶר beter2 (1)
rugged (1)

1442 בַּת־רַבִּים bat-rabbiym (1)
Bath Rabbim (1)

1443 בִּתְרוֹן bitrôn (1)
Bithron (1)

1444 בַּת־שֶׁבַע bat-šeba' (12)
Bathsheba (12)

1445 בַּת־שׁוּעַ bat-šûa'
Variant; not used

1446 ג g
Variant; not used

1447 גֵּא gē' (1)
pride (1)

1448 גָּאָה gā'āh (6)
highly exalted (2) +1448
grow tall (1)
hold head high (1)
risen (1)

1449 גֵּאָה gē'āh (1)
pride (1)

1450 גֵּאֶה gē'eh (8)
proud (7)
pride (1)

1451 גְּאוּאֵל g'û'ēl (1)
Geuel (1)

1452 גַּאֲוָה ga'awāh (18)
pride (7)
arrogance (2)
majesty (2)
back (1)
conceit (1)
glorious (1)
proud (1)
proud (1) +6913
surging (1)
triumph (1)

1453 גְּאוּלִים g'ûliym (1)
redemption (1)

1454 גָּאוֹן gā'ôn (49)
pride (23)
majesty (6)
arrogance (5)
proud (5)
thickets (3)
splendor (2)
arrogant (1)
glory (1)
lush thicket (1)
majestic (1)
pomp (1)

1455 גֵּאוּת gē'ût (8)
majesty (2)
pride (2)
arrogance (1)
column (1)
glorious things (1)
surging (1)

1456 גַּאֲיוֹן ga'ayôn (1)
arrogant (1)

1457 1 גָּאַל *gāʾal1* (103)
redeemed (18)
redeem (17)
redeemer (17)
avenger (13)
kinsman-redeemer (7)
be redeemed (3)
do itˢ (2)
redeem (2) +1457
redeems (2)
relative (2)
rescue (2)
claim (1)
close relative (1)
defender (1)
delivered (1)
do soˢ (1)
has the right to do itˢ (1)
is redeemed (1)
kinsman-redeemers (1)
near of kin (1)
redeem himself (1)
redeemable (1)
redeems (1) +1457
untranslated (4)

1458 2 גָּאַל *gāʾal2* (11)
defiled (4)
defile himself (2)
unclean (2)
are defiled (1)
are stained (1)
stained (1)

1459 גֹּאֶל *gōʾal* (1)
defiled (1)

1460 גְּאֻלָּה *gᵉʾullāh* (14)
redemption (4)
redeem (3)
right of redemption (2)
as nearest relative duty (1)
blood relatives (1) +408
itˢ (1) +3276
redeemed (1)
right to redeem (1)

1461 1 גַּב *gab1* (10)
rims (3)
mounds (2)
back (1)
backs (1)
eyebrows (1) +6524
mound (1)
strong (1)

1462 2 גַּב *gab2* (2)
defenses (2)

1463 1 גֵּב *gēb1* (3)
cisterns (1)
full of ditches (1) +1463

1464 2 גֵּב *gēb2* (1)
beams (1)

1465 גֶּבֶא *gebeʾ* (2)
cistern (1)
marshes (1)

1466 גֵּבָה *gēbāh* (1)
locusts (1)

1467 גָּבַהּ *gābah* (33)
proud (5)
exalted (3)
haughty (3)
towered (3)
high (2)
higher (2)
soar (2)
arrogant (1)
build high (1)
builds high (1)
devoted (1)
exalts (1)

highest (1)
made higher (1)
make grow tall (1)
pride (1)
pride (1) +4213
taller (1)
tower proudly (1)
upward (1)

1468 גָּבֵהַּ *gābēah* (4)
haughty (1)
pride (1) +8120
proud (1)
towered (1)

1469 גָּבֹהַּ *gābōah* (38)
high (19)
tall (2)
arrogant (1)
exalted (1)
haughty (1)
height (1) +7757
heights (1)
lofty (1)
long (1)
longer (1)
official (1)
oneˢ (1)
othersˢ (1)
proud (1)
so proudly (1) +1469
taller (1)
towers (1)
untranslated (1)

1470 גֹּבַהּ *gōbah* (18)
height (4)
high (3)
tall (2)
conceit (1)
haughty (1)
heights (1)
higher (1)
pride (1)
pride (1) +678
raised (1)
splendor (1)
untranslated (1)

1471 גַּבְהוּת *gabhût* (2)
arrogance (1)
arrogant (1)

1472 גָּבוֹל *gābôl*
Variant; not used

1473 גְּבוּל *gᵉbûl* (249)
territory (58)
boundary (44)
border (36)
borders (10)
boundaries (10)
itˢ (9) +2021
country (7)
land (7)
area (4)
boundary stone (4)
region (3)
rim (3)
throughout (3) +928+3972
coastline (2)
vicinity (2)
allotted portions (1)
allotted territory (1)
anywhere (1) +3972
anywhere in (1) +928+3972
areas (1)
bank (1)
borderland (1)
boundary stones (1)
coast (1)
districts (1)
domain (1)
Egypt (1) +5213

end (1) +7895
homeland (1)
itˢ (1)
itˢ (1) +616+2021
limits (1)
neighboring territory (1)
part (1)
parts (1)
places (1)
the borders (1)
wall (1)
walls (1)
untranslated (23)

1474 גְּבוּלָה *gᵉbûlāh* (2)
boundary stones (1)
field (1)

1475 גִּבּוֹר *gibbôr* (160)
warriors (27)
mighty (23)
mighty men (17)
fighting men (12) +2657
warrior (11)
brave warriors (6) +2657
mighty man (4)
strong (4)
heroes (3)
man (3)
special guard (3)
able men (2) +2657
best fighting men (2) +2657
fighting men (2)
hero (2)
mighty warrior (2)
mighty warriors (2)
powerful (2)
standing (2) +2657
valiant soldier (2) +2657
warrior's (2)
anotherˢ (1)
blameless (1) +9459
brave fighting men (1) +2657
brave man (1) +2657
brave warrior (1) +2657
capable men (1) +2657
champion (1)
experienced fighting men (1)
　　　　　　　+408+2657+4878
fighter (1)
fighters (1)
good fighters (1)
leaders (1)
men (1)
mighty (1) +3946
mighty men (1) +2657
mighty warrior (1) +2657
military staff (1)
noblest (1) +4946
officers (1)
principal (1)
soldiers (1)
strong man (1)
troops (1) +2657
very capable men (1) +2657
warriors (1) +2657
untranslated (2)

1476 גְּבוּרָה *gᵉbûrāh* (62)
power (16)
strength (14)
might (11)
achievements (8)
mighty acts (4)
thingsˢ (2)
acts of power (1)
mighty power (1)
mighty works (1)
source of strength (1)
victory (1)
warriors (1)
untranslated (1)

1477 גֻּבַּח *gibbēah* (1)
bald forehead (1)

1478 גַּבַּחַת *gabbahat* (4)
forehead (3)
other[s] (1)

1479 גֹּבַי *gōbay* (2)
locusts (1)
swarms of locusts (1)

1480 גַּבַּי *gabbay* (1)
Gabbai (1)

1481 גֵּבִים *gēbiym* (1)
Gebim (1)

1482 גְּבִינָה *g'biynāh* (1)
cheese (1)

1483 גָּבִיעַ *gābiya'* (14)
cups (6)
cup (4)
bowls (1)
one[s] (1)
untranslated (2)

1484 גְּבִיר *g'biyr* (2)
lord (2)

1485 גְּבִירָה *g'biyrāh* (13)
mistress (7)
queen mother (3)
position as queen mother (2)
queen (1)

1486 גָּבִישׁ *gābiyš* (1)
jasper (1)

1487 גָּבַל *gābal* (5)
borders (1)
formed the boundary (1)
put limits (1)
put limits around (1)
set up (1)

1488 גְּבַל *g'bal* (1)
Gebal (1)

1489 גְּבָל *g'bāl* (1)
Gebal (1)

1490 גִּבְלִי *gibliy* (2)
Gebalites (1)
men of Gebal (1)

1491 גַּבְלֻת *gablut* (2)
braided (2)

1492 גִּבֵּן *gibbēn* (1)
hunchbacked (1)

1493 גַּבְנֹן *gabnôn* (2)
rugged (2)

1494 גֶּבַע *geba'* (15)
Geba (15)

1495 גִּבְעָא *gib'ā'* (1)
Gibea (1)

1496 1גִּבְעָה *gib'āh1* (67)
hills (36)
hill (26)
heights (2)
hilltops (2)
untranslated (1)

1497 2גִּבְעָה *gib'āh2* (49)
Gibeah (48)
untranslated (1)

1498 גִּבְעֹנִי *gib'ôniy* (8)
Gibeonites (6)
Gibeonite (1)
of Gibeon (1)

1499 גִּבְעֹל *gib'ōl* (1)
in bloom (1)

1500 גִּבְעֹן *gib'ōn* (39)
Gibeon (38)
Gibeonites (1) +408

1501 גִּבְעַת *gib'at*
Variant; not used

1502 גִּבְעַת הָעֲרָלוֹת *gib'at hā'arālôt* (1)
Gibeath Haaraloth (1)

1503 גִּבְעָתִי *gib'ātiy* (1)
Gibeathite (1)

1504 גָּבַר *gābar* (25)
rose (3)
triumph (3)
great (2)
strengthen (2)
winning (2)
arrogantly (1)
confirm (1)
flooded (1)
greater (1)
increasing (1)
needed (1)
overpowered (1)
overwhelmed (1)
prevailed (1)
prevails (1)
stronger (1)
strongest (1)
vaunts himself (1)

1505 1גֶּבֶר *geber1* (66)
man (39)
men (7)
one (3)
man's (2)
any[s] (1)
blameless (1) +9459
boy (1)
each[s] (1)
families (1)
he[s] (1)
him[s] (1)
husband's (1)
men's (1)
mighty man (1)
ruler (1) +8031
soldiers (1) +408+4878
strong man (1)
whoever[s] (1)
untranslated (1)

1506 2גֶּבֶר *geber2* (1)
Geber (1)

1507 גִּבָּר *gibbār* (1)
Gibbar (1)

1508 גַּבְרִיאֵל *gabriy'ēl* (2)
Gabriel (2)

1509 גְּבֶרֶת *g'beret* (2)
queen (2)

1510 גִּבְּתוֹן *gibb'tôn* (6)
Gibbethon (5)
it[s] (1)

1511 גָּג *gāg* (31)
roof (18)
roofs (7)
top (3)
roof of house (1)
top of the wall (1)
untranslated (1)

1512 1גַּד *gad1* (2)
coriander (2)

1513 2גַּד *gad2* (3)
fortune (1)
good fortune (1)
untranslated (1)

1514 גָּד *gād* (70)
Gad (43)
Gadites (16) +1201
Gad (7) +1201
Gad's (1)
they[s] (1) +1201+1201+2256+8017

untranslated (2)

1515 גִּדְגָּד *gidgād*
Variant; not used

1516 גֻּדְגֹּדָה *gudgōdāh* (2)
Gudgodah (1)
untranslated (1)

1517 1גָּדַד *gādad1* (5)
cut yourselves (2)
cut himself (1)
cut themselves (1)
slashed themselves (1)

1518 2גָּדַד *gādad2* (3)
band together (1)
marshal troops (1)
thronged (1)

1519 גָּדָה *gādāh*
Variant; not used

1520 גַּדָּה *gaddāh*
Variant; not used

1521 1גְּדוּד *g'dûd1* (1)
ridges (1)

1522 2גְּדוּד *g'dûd2* (33)
troops (5)
raiders (3)
raiding bands (3)
band of raiders (2)
bands (2)
forces (2)
raiding party (2)
troop (2)
band of rebels (1)
bandits (1)
divisions (1)
invaders (1)
marauders (1)
men ready for battle (1) +4878+7372
raid (1)
them[s] (1) +2021
troops (1) +1201
untranslated (3)

1523 גְּדוּדָה *g'dûdāh* (1)
slashed (1)

1524 גָּדוֹל *gādôl* (529)
great (244)
large (41)
high (23)
greatest (17)
loud (16)
greater (9)
mighty (9)
older (9)
heavy (8)
old (7)
vast (7)
very (6)
greatly (5)
terrible (5)
bitterly (4)
important (4)
much (4)
oldest (4)
powerful (4)
strong (4)
called out (3) +928+7754+7924
even more (3)
larger (3)
many (3)
aloud (2) +7754
awful (2)
became more and more powerful (2)
              +2143+2143+2256
deep (2)
fierce (2)
great (2) +4394
huge (2)
louder (2)

loudly (2)
more (2)
such (2)
wealthy (2)
wonders (2)
all (1)
aloud (1) +928+7754
at all (1) +196+7785
awful (1) +2098
became more and more powerful (1)
        +2143+2256
better (1)
big (1)
boastful (1) +1819
chief (1)
deeds (1)
destroyed (1) +4394+4804+5782
devastated (1) +4394+4804+5782
difficult (1)
far (1)
feat (1) +1821
fine (1) +2256+3202
great amount (1)
grievous (1)
hard (1)
harsh (1)
highly regarded (1) +4394
hot-tempered (1) +2779
huge (1) +4200+4394+6330
immense (1)
imposing (1) +4200+5260
intense (1) +4394
large (1) +4394
leaders (1)
leading (1)
loud (1) +4394+6330
loudly (1) +928+7754
main (1)
most important (1)
nobles (1)
noisy din (1) +7754
nothing (1) +1821+2256+4202+7785
older (1) +4946
power (1)
preeminent (1)
prominent (1)
rich (1)
screamed (1) +928+7754+7924
serious (1)
shout (1) +7754+7924
so much (1)
solemn (1)
strange (1)
stronger (1)
such (1) +2296
terrified (1) +3707+3711
thick (1)
top (1)
total (1) +4394
trembled violently (1)
        +3006+3010+4394+6330
utterly (1)
vast (1) +4394
vast (1) +4394+4394
violent (1)
well-to-do (1)
untranslated (2)

1525 גְּדוּלָה gᵉdûllāh (13)
great (3)
greatness (3)
great thing (2)
great deeds (1)
honor (1)
majesty (1)
recognition (1)
untranslated (1)

1526 גִּדּוּף giddûp (2)
scorn (1)
taunts (1)

1527 גְּדוּפָה gᵉdûpāh (1)

taunt (1)

1528 גִּדּוּפָה giddûpāh (1)
insults (1)

1529 גְּדוֹר1 gᵉdôr1 (4)
Gedor (4)

1530 גְּדוֹר2 gᵉdôr2 (3)
Gedor (3)

1531 גְּדִי gᵉdiy (17)
young goat (7) +6436
young goat (5)
goat (1)
goatskins (1) +6425+6436
lambs (1)
young goats (1)
young goats (1) +6436

1532 גָּדִי1 gādiy1 (15)
Gadites (12)
Gad (1)
Gad (1) +1201
of Gad (1)

1533 גָּדִי2 gādiy2 (2)
Gadi (2)

1534 גַּדִּי gaddiy (1)
Gaddi (1)

1535 גַּדִּיאֵל gaddiy'ēl (1)
Gaddiel (1)

1536 גִּדְיָה gidyāh (5)
banks (2)
at flood stage (1) +3972+4848+6584
at flood stage (1) +3972+6584
untranslated (1)

1537 גְּדִיָּה gᵉdiyyāh (1)
young goats (1)

1538 גָּדִישׁ1 gādiyš1 (3)
sheaves (1)
shocks (1)
shocks of grain (1)

1539 גָּדִישׁ2 gādiyš2 (1)
tomb (1)

1540 גָּדַל gādal (117)
great (17)
greater (8)
grown up (7)
exalted (6)
grew up (6)
exalt (5)
grew (5)
reared (4)
defied (2) +6584
gives great (2)
glorify (2)
honored (2)
make great (2)
wealthy (2)
boast (1)
boast so much (1) +3870+7023
boasted (1) +928+7023
boosting (1)
brought up (1)
developed (1)
displayed (1)
exalt himself (1)
great (1) +4394
great things done (1)
greatness (1)
grew older (1)
grow long (1)
grown (1)
grows up (1)
increased (1)
lifted up (1)
made great (1)
made grow (1)
made threats (1)
magnificent (1)

magnify (1)
make greater (1)
make grow (1)
make so much of (1)
mocking (1)
most (1)
nourished (1)
pile high (1)
powerful (1)
raised (1)
raising (1)
reached (1) +6330
rear (1)
rearing (1)
rich (1)
set up to be great (1)
show greatness (1)
superior (1)
trained (1)
triumphed (1)
undertook great (1)
value (1) +928+6524
valued (1) +928+6524
well-nurtured (1)
yielding (1)
untranslated (1)

1541 גָּדֵל gādēl (4)
lustful (1) +1414
more and more powerful (1)
        +2025+2143+2256+4200+5087+6330
stature (1)
wealth (1)

1542 גֹּדֶל gōdel (13)
majesty (4)
greatness (3)
arrogance (1)
beauty (1)
great (1)
great power (1)
strength (1)
willful pride (1) +7262

1543 גִּדֵּל giddēl (4)
Giddel (4)

1544 גָּדִיל gādil (2)
festooned (1)
tassels (1)

1545 גְּדַלְיָה gᵉdalyāh (6)
Gedaliah (6)

1546 גְּדַלְיָהוּ gᵉdalyāhû (26)
Gedaliah (25)
Gedaliah's (1)

1547 גִּדַּלְתִּי giddaltiy (2)
Giddalti (2)

1548 גָּדַע gāda' (23)
cut down (4)
cut off (3)
broke (2)
cut to pieces (2)
be cut off (1)
be felled (1)
be sheared off (1)
been cast down (1)
been felled (1)
broke down (1)
broken (1)
broken down (1)
cut short (1)
cut through (1)
cuts through (1)
is cut off (1)

1549 גִּדְעוֹן gid'ôn (39)
Gideon (35)
heˢ (3)
Gideon's (1)

1550 גִּדְעֹם gid'ōm (1)
Gidom (1)

1551 גִּדְעֹנִי *gid'ōniy* (5)
Gideoni (5)

1552 גָּדַף *gādap* (7)
blasphemed (5)
blasphemes (1)
revile (1)

1553 גָּדַר *gādar* (10)
masons (2)
repair (2)
barred (1)
blocked (1)
build up (1)
repairer of walls (1)
wall in (1) +1555
walled (1)

1554 גְּדֵר *geder* (1)
Geder (1)

1555 גָּדֵר *gādēr* (14)
wall (7)
walls (3)
fence (1)
wall in (1) +1553
wall of protection (1)
untranslated (1)

1556 גְּדֵרָה1 *g'dērāh1* (9)
pens (4)
walls (3)
pens (1) +7366
wall (1)

1557 גְּדֵרָה2 *g'dērāh2* (2)
Gederah (2)

1558 גְּדֵרוֹת *g'dērôt* (2)
Gederoth (2)

1559 גְּדֵרִי *g'dēriy* (1)
Gederite (1)

1560 גִּדֶרֶת *gideret*
Variant; not used

1561 גְּדֵרָתִי *g'dērātiy* (1)
Gederathite (1)

1562 גְּדֵרֹתַיִם *g'dērōtayim* (1)
Gederothaim (1)

1563 גֶּה *gēh*
Variant; not used

1564 גָּהָה *gāhāh* (1)
heal (1)

1565 גֵּהָה *gēhāh* (1)
medicine (1)

1566 גָּהַר *gāhar* (3)
stretched out (2)
bent down (1)

1567 גַּו *gaw* (3)
back (2)
backs (1)

1568 גֵּו1 *gēw1* (7)
back (5)
backs (2)

1569 גֵּו2 *gēw2* (1)
fellow men (1)

1570 גּוֹב1 *gôb1* (2)
Gob (2)

1571 גּוֹב2 *gôb2* (1)
swarms (1)

1572 גּוּב *gûb*
Variant; not used

1573 גּוֹג *gôg* (10)
Gog (10)

1574 גּוּד *gûd* (3)
attack (1)
attacked (1)
invading (1)

1575 גֵּוָה1 *gēwāh1* (3)
pride (2)
lift up (1)

1576 גֵּוָה2 *gēwāh2* (1)
back (1)

1577 גּוּז *gûz* (2)
drove in (1)
pass (1)

1578 גּוֹזָל *gôzāl* (2)
young (1)
young pigeon (1)

1579 גּוֹזָן *gôzān* (5)
Gozan (5)

1580 גּוֹי *gôy* (561)
nations (410)
nation (114)
people (8)
gentiles (5)
gentile (2)
peoples (2)
another[s] (1)
countries (1)
each national group (1) +1580
foreign (1)
it[s] (1) +2021
kind (1)
nations (1) +824
pagan nations (1)
they[s] (1)
untranslated (10)

1581 גְּוִיָּה *g'wiyyāh* (13)
bodies (4)
body (4)
carcass (1)
corpses (1)
dead (1)
it[s] (1) +793+2021
untranslated (1)

1582 גּוֹיִם *gôyim* (3)
Goiim (2)
Goyim (1)

1583 גּוֹלָה *gôlāh* (41)
exile (16)
exiles (15)
exiles (6) +1201
captive (1)
deported (1) +995
those[s] (1) +2021
took (1) +2143

1584 גּוֹלָן *gôlān* (6)
Golan (4)
untranslated (2)

1585 גּוּמָץ *gûmmāṣ* (1)
pit (1)

1586 גּוּנִי1 *gûniy1* (4)
Guni (4)

1587 גּוּנִי2 *gûniy2* (1)
Gunite (1)

1588 גָּוַע *gāwa'* (24)
die (8)
died (4)
breathed his last (4)
perish (3)
perished (2)
breathes his last (1)
close to death (1)
fell dead (1)

1589 גּוּף *gûp* (1)
shut (1)

1590 גּוּפָה *gûpāh* (2)
bodies (1)
untranslated (1)

1591 גּוּר1 *gûr1* (81)

living (24)
dwell (10)
live (7)
settle (6)
stay (4)
stayed (3)
aliens (2)
live for a while (2)
lived (2)
settled (2)
stay for a while (2)
staying (2)
strangers (2)
alien (1)
can[s] (1)
for a while stayed (1)
gather together (1)
guests (1) +1074
linger (1)
live awhile (1)
lived as an alien (1)
lives (1)
living as an alien (1)
nomads (1)
settles (1)
untranslated (1)

1592 גּוּר2 *gûr2* (6)
conspire (2)
attack (1) +1592
attacks (1)
stir up (1)

1593 גּוּר3 *gûr3* (10)
afraid (3)
fear (2)
revere (2)
terrified (2)
dreaded (1)

1594 גּוּר4 *gûr4* (7)
cubs (3)
cub (2)
cubs (1) +793
young (1)

1595 גּוּר5 *gûr5* (1)
Gur (1)

1596 גּוֹר *gôr* (2)
cubs (2)

1597 גּוּר־בַּעַל *gûr-bā'al* (1)
Gur Baal (1)

1598 גּוֹרָל *gôrāl* (77)
lot (37)
lots (17)
allotment (5)
allotted (4) +928+2021
allotted (3)
allotted (2) +928+2021+5989
allotted (2) +2118
allotted (1) +928+2021+2118
allotted inheritance (1)
drawing lots (1)
portions (1)
territory allotted (1)
untranslated (2)

1599 גּוּשׁ *gûš* (1)
scabs (1) +6760

1600 גֵּז *gēz* (4)
fleece (1)
harvested (1)
mown field (1)
wool from shearing (1)

1601 גִּזְבָּר *gizbār* (1)
treasurer (1)

1602 גָּזָה *gāzāh* (1)
brought forth (1)

1603 גִּזָּה *gizzāh* (7)
fleece (6)

untranslated (1)

1604 גִּזוֹנִי *gizôniy* (1)
Gizonite (1)

1605 גָּזַז *gāzaz* (15)
shear (3)
shearers (3)
shearing (3)
be cut off (1)
cut off (1)
shave heads (1) +7942
shaved (1)
sheep-shearing time (1)
sheepshearers (1)

1606 גָּזֵז *gāzēz* (2)
Gazez (2)

1607 גָּזִית *gāziyt* (11)
dressed (3)
dressed stone (3)
cut (2)
blocks of stone (1)
dressed stones (1)
stone (1)

1608 גָּזַל *gāzal* (30)
rob (3)
snatched (3)
been robbed (2)
commit robbery (2) +1611
seized (2)
are robbed (1)
be forcibly taken (1)
caught (1)
commit robbery (1) +1610
commits robbery (1) +1611
exploit (1)
injured (1)
robbed (1)
robbed (1) +1609
robs (1)
seize (1)
snatch away (1)
steal (1)
stolen (1)
stolen (1) +1611
take by force (1)
tear (1)
withhold (1)

1609 גֵּזֶל *gēzel* (2)
denied (1)
robbed (1) +1608

1610 גָּזֵל *gāzēl* (4)
commit robbery (1) +1608
robbery (1)
stolen (1)
stolen goods (1)

1611 גְּזֵלָה *gᵉzēlāh* (6)
commit robbery (2) +1608
commits robbery (1) +1608
plunder (1)
stolen (1) +1608
what stolen (1)

1612 גָּזָם *gāzām* (3)
locust swarm (2)
locusts (1)

1613 גַּזָּם *gazzām* (2)
Gazzam (2)

1614 גֶּזַע *geza'* (3)
stump (2)
take root (1) +9245

1615 גָּזַר1 *gāzar1* (12)
are cut off (2)
be cut off (1)
cut (1)
cut down (1)
cut in two (1)
decide (1)

decreed (1)
divided (1)
excluded (1)
there are no (1)
was cut off (1)

1616 גָּזַר2 *gāzar2* (1)
devour (1)

1617 גֶּזֶר1 *gezer1* (2)
asunder (1)
pieces (1)

1618 גֶּזֶר2 *gezer2* (15)
Gezer (14)
thereˢ (1) +928

1619 גִּזְרָה *gizrāh* (8)
courtyard (7)
appearance (1)

1620 גְּזֵרָה *gᵉzērāh*
Variant; not used

1621 גִּזְרִי *gizriy* (1)
untranslated (1)

1622 גָּחָה *gāhāh*
Variant; not used

1623 גָּחוֹן *gāhôn* (2)
belly (2)

1624 גַּחַל *gahal* (16)
coals (6)
burning coals (5)
bolts (2)
embers (1)
hot coals (1)
untranslated (1)

1625 גַּחֶלֶת *gahelet* (2)
burning coal (1)
coals (1)

1626 גַּחַם *gaham* (1)
Gaham (1)

1627 גַּחַר *gahar* (2)
Gahar (2)

1628 גַּיְא *gay'* (60)
valley (50)
valleys (7)
itˢ (1) +2215
untranslated (2)

1629 גֵּיְא חֲרָשִׁים *gēy' hᵉrāšiym* (1)
Ge Harashim (1)

1630 גִּיד *giyd* (7)
sinews (3)
tendon (2) +5962
tendons (2)

1631 גִּיחַ1 *giyah1* (6)
brought (1)
burst (1)
charged out (1)
in agony (1)
surge (1)
thrashing about (1)

1632 גִּיחַ2 *giyah2* (1)
Giah (1)

1633 גִּיחוֹן *giyhôn* (6)
Gihon (6)

1634 גֵּיחֲזִי *gēyhᵃziy* (12)
Gehazi (12)

1635 גִּיל1 *giyl1* (47)
rejoice (25)
glad (11)
rejoices (3)
great joy (1) +1635
joy (1)
joyful (1)
rejoice greatly (1) +677+1638
rejoiced (1)

untranslated (2)

1636 גִּיל2 *giyl2* (1)
age (1)

1637 גִּיל3 *giyl3* (8)
gladness (5)
delight (1)
filled with gladness (1) +448+8524
jubilant (1)

1638 גִּילָה *giylāh* (2)
delight (1)
rejoice greatly (1) +677+1635

1639 גִּילֹנִי *giylōniy* (2)
Gilonite (2)

1640 גִּינַת *giynat* (2)
Ginath (2)

1641 גִּישׁ *giyš* (1)
untranslated (1)

1642 גֵּישָׁן *gēyšān* (1)
Geshan (1)

1643 גַּל1 *gal1* (18)
heap (8)
heap of ruins (2)
pile (2)
piles of stone (2) +5898
heap of rubble (1)
pile of rocks (1)
piles of stones (1)
rubble (1)

1644 גַּל2 *gal2* (16)
waves (13)
breakers (1)
fountain (1)
surging (1)

1645 גֵּל *gēl* (3)
dung (1)
excrement (1)
excrement (1) +7362

1646 גֹּל *gōl*
Variant; not used

1647 גַּלָּב *gallāb* (1)
barber's (1)

1648 גִּלְבֹּעַ *gilbōa'* (8)
Gilboa (8)

1649 גַּלְגַּל1 *galgal1* (9)
wheels (3)
wagons (2)
chariot wheels (1)
wheel (1)
whirling wheels (1)
whirlwind (1)

1650 גַּלְגַּל2 *galgal2* (2)
tumbleweed (2)

1651 גִּלְגָּל1 *gilgāl1* (1)
wheels (1)

1652 גִּלְגָּל2 *gilgāl2* (40)
Gilgal (39)
untranslated (1)

1653 גֻּלְגֹּלֶת *gulgōlet* (12)
one by one (4) +4200+4392
skull (2)
each (1) +5031
each one (1)
head (1)
individually (1) +4200
person (1)
total (1)

1654 גֶּלֶד *gēled* (1)
skin (1)

1655 גָּלָה *gālāh* (188)
carried into exile (11)
have sexual relations with (11) +6872

deported (7)
be exposed (4)
dishonored (4) +6872
expose (4)
uncovered (4)
exposed (3)
go into exile (3)
have sexual relations (3) +6872
open (3)
opened (3)
revealed (3)
taken captive (3)
taken into exile (3)
be revealed (2)
been carried into exile (2)
been revealed (2)
betray (2)
betrays (2)
committed (2)
departed (2)
exile (2)
exiled (2)
have relations with (2) +6872
laid bare (2)
let know (2) +265+906
made known (2)
revealed (2) +265
revealed himself (2)
sent into exile (2)
surely go into exile (2) +1655
tells (2) +265+906
took captive (2)
took into exile (2)
uncover (2)
unsealed (2)
went into captivity (2)
went into exile (2)
airing (1)
banished (1)
bare (1)
be carried into exile (1)
be exiled (1)
be laid bare (1)
been shown (1)
been torn off (1)
being carried into exile (1)
bring to attention (1) +265
brought (1)
captive (1)
captivity (1)
carried away (1)
carried into exile (1) +1655
carried on openly (1)
carry away (1)
carry into exile (1)
carry off (1)
certainly go into exile (1) +1655
clearly reveal myself (1) +1655
confiding in (1) +265+906
disclose (1)
dishonor bed (1) +4053
dishonor bed (1) +6872
dishonor by having sexual relations with (1)
          +6872
dishonor by to have sexual relations (1)
          +6872
dishonors bed (1) +4053
disrobing (1)
driven out (1)
free (1)
go (1)
go into exile (1) +1655
gone into exile (1)
has sexual relations with (1) +906+6872
lay bare (1)
led captive (1)
let enjoy (1)
let see (1)
lift (1)
makes listen (1) +265
remove (1)

removed (1)
revealed (1) +265+906
revealing (1)
reveals (1)
send into exile (1)
set out (1)
showed themselves (1)
speak (1)
speaks (1) +265
strip (1) +6872
strip off (1)
stripped (1)
stripped away (1)
take off (1)
taken (1)
tell (1) +265+906
was given (1)
was uncovered (1)
were taken captive (1)
word come (1)
would[s] (1) +1655
untranslated (2)

1656 גִּלֹה gilōh (2)
Giloh (2)

1657 גֻּלָּה gullāh (15)
bowl-shaped (6)
springs (4)
bowl (3)
untranslated (2)

1658 גִּלּוּלִים gillûliym (48)
idols (46)
idolatry (2)

1659 גְּלוֹם g'lôm (1)
fabric (1)

1660 גָּלוֹן gālôn
Variant; not used

1661 גָּלוּת gālûṯ (15)
exiles (7)
exile (5)
captives (1)
communities (1)
communities of captives (1)

1662 גָּלַח gālaḥ (23)
shave (5)
shave off (5)
shaved off (3)
cut hair (2)
shaved (2)
be shaved (1)
been shaved (1)
were shaved (1)
untranslated (3)

1663 גִּלָּיוֹן gillāyôn (2)
mirrors (1)
scroll (1)

1664 גָּלִיל 1 gāliyl1 (4)
rings (1)
rods (1)
turned in sockets (1)
untranslated (1)

1665 גָּלִיל 2 gāliyl2 (6)
Galilee (5)
Galilee (1) +824

1666 גְּלִילָה g'liylāh (3)
regions (2)
region (1)

1667 גְּלִילוֹת g'liylôṯ (3)
Geliloth (3)

1668 גַּלִּים galliym (2)
Gallim (2)

1669 גָּלְיָת golyāṯ (6)
Goliath (6)

1670 גָּלַל 1 gālal1 (17)

roll (4)
rolled (3)
commit (2)
attack (1)
come rolling in (1)
lay wallowing (1)
roll on (1)
rolled away (1)
rolled up (1)
rolls (1)
trusts (1)

1671 גָּלָל 2 gālal2
Variant; not used

1672 גָּלָל 1 gālāl1 (2)
dung (1)
filth (1)

1673 גָּלָל 2 gālāl2 (10)
because of (7)
because of (2) +928
because (1)

1674 גָּלָל 3 gālāl3 (3)
Galal (3)

1675 גִּלֲלַי gilᵃlay (1)
Gilalai (1)

1676 גָּלַם gālam (1)
rolled up (1)

1677 גֹּלֶם gōlem (1)
unformed body (1)

1678 גַּלְמוּד galmûḏ (4)
barren (3)
Haggard (1)

1679 גָּלַע gāla' (3)
breaks out (1)
defies (1)
quick to quarrel (1)

1680 גִּלְעָד gil'āḏ (102)
Gilead (85)
Gilead (8) +824
Gileadites (3)
Gilead (1) +1201
Gilead's (1)
Gileadites (1) +408
them[s] (1) +2418
there[s] (1) +5206
untranslated (1)

1681 גַּלְעֵד gal'ēḏ (2)
Galeed (2)

1682 גִּלְעָדִי gil'āḏiy (11)
Gileadite (8)
of Gilead (2)
of Gilead (1) +1201

1683 גָּלַשׁ gālaš (2)
descending (2)

1684 גֻּלֹּת gullōṯ
Variant; not used

1685 גַּם gam (769)
also (106)
even (64)
too (62)
and (53) +2256
and (49)
also (26) +2256
even (15) +2256
both (13)
then (9)
moreover (8) +2256
but (6)
or (6)
yes (6)
either (5)
moreover (5)
now (5)
though (5)

as well (4)
neither (4) +4202
or (4) +2256
too (4) +2256
again (3)
as well as (3) +2256
indeed (3)
just as (3)
nor (3)
nor (3) +4202
now (3) +2256
then (3) +2256
and also (2)
another (2)
as for (2)
besides (2) +2256
but (2) +2256
but also (2)
even (2) +3954
in turn (2)
indeed (2) +2256
more (2)
neither (2)
no (2)
so (2) +2256
surely (2)
therefore (2) +2256
together with (2) +2256
yes (2) +2256
yet (2)
yet (2) +2256
after (1) +2256
again (1) +928+2021+2021+2085+7193
along with (1) +2256
although (1) +3954
and even (1)
and indeed (1)
and now (1)
as well as (1)
besides (1)
both and (1)
but even (1)
but even (1) +2256
certainly (1)
even if (1)
ever (1)
finally (1) +2256
for (1) +928+8611
for some time (1) +1685+8997+9453
furthermore (1)
furthermore (1) +2256
in spite of (1)
in the past (1) +919+1685+8997
including (1) +2256
instead (1) +2256
joined (1) +2256
kept provoking (1) +4087+4088
mere (1)
moreover (1) +3954
next (1)
no sooner than (1)
nor (1) +401+2256
nor (1) +2256
nor (1) +2256+4202
or (1) +3954
rather (1) +2256
since (1)
so (1)
still (1) +2256
than (1) +2256
that (1) +2256
therefore (1)
very well (1)
when (1)
whether (1)
with (1)
with (1) +2256
untranslated (200)

1686 גָּמָא *gāmā'* (2)
eats up (1)
give (1)

1687 גֹּמֶא *gōme'* (4)
papyrus (4)

1688 גֹּמֶד *gōmed* (1)
about a foot and a half (1)

1689 גַּמָּדִים *gammādiym* (1)
men of Gammad (1)

1690 גָּמוּל *gāmûl* (1)
Gamul (1)

1691 גְּמוּל *gᵉmûl* (19)
what done (4)
what deserve (3)
retribution (2)
benefits (1)
deeds (1)
deserve (1)
deserves (1) +3338
due (1)
kindness (1)
something done (1)
what deserves (1)
whatˢ (1)
work (1)

1692 גְּמוּלָה *gᵉmûlāh* (3)
retribution (1)
wayˢ (1)
what done (1)

1693 גִּמְזוֹ *gimzô* (1)
Gimzo (1)

1694 גָּמַל *gāmal* (37)
weaned (7)
done (5)
dealt with (2)
repay (2)
treated (2)
was weaned (2)
been good (1)
benefits (1)
brings (1)
brought (1)
brought up (1)
committed (1)
did (1)
do good (1)
good (1)
goodness (1)
is weaned (1)
paying back (1)
produced (1)
repaying (1)
reward (1)
ripening (1)
young child (1)

1695 גָּמָל *gāmāl* (54)
camels (46)
camel (3)
camels' (2)
camel's (1)
camel-loads (1) +5362
untranslated (1)

1696 גְּמַלִּי *gᵉmalliy* (1)
Gemalli (1)

1697 גַּמְלִיאֵל *gamliy'ēl* (5)
Gamaliel (5)

1698 גָּמַר *gāmar* (5)
bring to an end (1)
failed (1)
fulfill (1)
fulfills (1)
no more (1)

1699 1גֹּמֶר *gōmer1* (5)
Gomer (5)

1700 2גֹּמֶר *gōmer2* (1)
Gomer (1)

1701 גְּמַרְיָה *gᵉmaryāh* (1)

Gemariah (1)

1702 גְּמַרְיָהוּ *gᵉmaryāhû* (4)
Gemariah (4)

1703 גַּן *gan* (41)
garden (39)
gardens (2)

1704 גָּנַב *gānab* (40)
steal (9)
stolen (3)
steals (2)
stole (2)
stole away (2)
are stolen (1)
be considered stolen (1)
deceive (1)
deceived (1) +4213
deceived (1) +4222
kidnapping (1) +5883
kidnaps (1)
snatches away (1)
steal away (1)
steal in (1)
stealing (1)
stole into (1) +995+4200
swept away (1)
taken secretly (1)
thief (1)
was forcibly carried off (1) +1704
was secretly brought (1)
was stolen (1)
was stolen (1) +1704
untranslated (1)

1705 גַּנָּב *gannāb* (17)
thief (9)
thieves (7)
kidnapper (1)

1706 גְּנֵבָה *gᵉnēbāh* (2)
stolen (1)
theft (1)

1707 גְּנֻבַת *gᵉnubat* (2)
Genubath (2)

1708 גַּנָּה *gannāh* (16)
gardens (9)
garden (6)
grove (1)

1709 גֶּנֶז *genez1* (2)
treasury (2)

1710 2גֶּנֶז *genez2* (1)
rugs (1)

1711 גַּנְזַךְ *ganzak* (1)
storerooms (1)

1712 גַּנִּים *ganniym* (1)
Variant; not used

1713 גָּנַן *gānan* (8)
defend (4)
shield (4)

1714 גִּנְּתוֹי *ginnᵉtôy*
Variant; not used

1715 גִּנְּתוֹן *ginnᵉtôn* (3)
Ginnethon (2)
Ginnethon's (1)

1716 גָּעָה *gā'āh* (2)
bellow (1)
lowing (1)

1717 גֹּעָה *gō'āh* (1)
Goah (1)

1718 גָּעַל *gā'al* (10)
abhor (4)
despised (2)
abhorred (1)
despise (1)
fail (1)
was defiled (1)

1719 גֹּעַל *gō'al* (1)
despised (1)

1720 גָּעַל *ga'al* (9)
Gaal (9)

1721 גָּעַר *gā'ar* (14)
rebuke (7)
rebuked (3)
rebukes (2)
prevent (1)
reprimanded (1)

1722 גְּעָרָה *g'ārāh* (15)
rebuke (12)
threat (3)

1723 גָּעַשׁ *gā'aš* (10)
trembled (4)
surging (2)
are shaken (1)
roll (1)
stagger (1)
untranslated (1)

1724 גַּעַשׁ *ga'aš* (4)
Gaash (4)

1725 גַּעְתָּם *ga'tām* (3)
Gatam (3)

1726 1גַּף *gap1* (1)
highest point (1) +5294

1727 2גַּף *gap2* (3)
alone (2) +928+2257
only (1) +928+2257

1728 גֶּפֶן *gepen* (55)
vine (36)
vines (16)
grapevine (2) +3516
grapevines (1)

1729 גֹּפֶר *gōper* (1)
cypress (1)

1730 גָּפְרִית *gopriyt* (7)
burning sulfur (4)
sulfur (3)

1731 גֵּר *gēr* (92)
alien (61)
aliens (26)
stranger (3)
alien's (1)
strangers (1)

1732 גִּר *gir* (1)
chalk (1)

1733 גֵּרָא *gērā'* (9)
Gera (9)

1734 גָּרָב *gārāb* (3)
festering (2)
festering sores (1)

1735 1גָּרֵב *gārēb1* (2)
Gareb (2)

1736 2גָּרֵב *gārēb2* (1)
Gareb (1)

1737 גַּרְגַּר *gargar* (1)
olives (1)

1738 גַּרְגְּרֹת *garg'rôt* (4)
neck (4)

1739 גִּרְגָּשִׁי *girgāšiy* (7)
Girgashites (7)

1740 גָּרַד *gārad* (1)
scraped himself (1)

1741 גָּרָה *gārāh* (15)
stirs up (3)
ask (2)
provoke to war (2)
carry the battle (1) +2256+8740
engage (1)

opposed (1)
prepare for war (1)
provoke (1)
resist (1)
wage war (1) +2021+4200+4878
untranslated (1)

1742 1גֵּרָה *gērāh1* (11)
cud (11)

1743 2גֵּרָה *gērāh2* (5)
gerahs (5)

1744 גָּרוֹן *gārôn* (9)
throat (3)
mouths (1)
neck (1)
necks (1)
shout aloud (1) +928+7924
throats (1)
untranslated (1)

1745 גֵּרוּת כְּמְהָם *gērût kimhām* (1)
Geruth Kimham (1)

1746 גָּרַז *gāraz* (1)
am cut off (1)

1747 גִּרְזִי *girziy* (1)
Girzites (1)

1748 גְּרִזִּים *g'riziym* (4)
Gerizim (4)

1749 גַּרְזֶן *garzen* (4)
ax (3)
chisel (1)

1750 1גָּרַם *gāram1* (1)
leave (1)

1751 2גָּרַם *gāram2* (2)
break in pieces (1)
dash (1)

1752 גֶּרֶם *gerem* (5)
bare (1)
bone (1)
bones (1)
limbs (1)
rawboned (1)

1753 גַּרְמִי *garmiy* (1)
Garmite (1)

1754 גָּרֹל *gārōl* (1)
untranslated (1)

1755 גֹּרֶן *gōren* (36)
threshing floor (32)
threshing floors (3)
threshing floor (1) +1841

1756 גָּרַס *gāras* (2)
broken (1)
consumed (1)

1757 1גָּרַע *gāra'1* (21)
be reduced (2)
be taken (2)
cut off (2)
be kept from (1) +1194+4200
be taken away (1)
deprive (1)
disappear (1)
hinder (1)
limit (1)
omit (1)
reduce (1)
reduce the number (1)
reduced (1)
subtract (1)
take (1)
take away (1)
taken (1)
withdraw favor (1)

1758 2גָּרַע *gāra'2* (1)
draws up (1)

1759 גָּרַף *gārap* (1)
swept away (1)

1760 גָּרַר *gārar* (5)
catches (1)
chew (1)
drag away (1)
driving (1)
trimmed (1)

1761 גְּרָר *g'rār* (10)
Gerar (10)

1762 גֶּרֶשׂ *gereś* (2)
crushed (1)
crushed grain (1)

1763 1גָּרַשׁ *gāraš1* (46)
drive out (8)
drive (7)
divorced (5)
drove out (5)
drove away (3)
driven (2)
driving out (2)
drove (2)
be driven (1)
been banished (1)
been driven out (1)
cast aside (1)
drive away (1)
drive out (1) +1763
driving (1)
emptied (1)
get rid of (1)
removed (1)
were banished (1)

1764 2גָּרַשׁ *gāraš2* (3)
be stirred up (1)
cast up (1)
tossing (1)

1765 גֶּרֶשׁ *gereš* (1)
yield (1)

1766 גְּרֻשָׁה *g'rušāh* (1)
dispossessing (1)

1767 גֵּרְשׁוֹן *gēršôn* (17)
Gershon (9)
Gershonites (6) +1201
Gershonite (2) +1201

1768 גֵּרְשֹׁם *gēršōm* (14)
Gershom (7)
Gershon (6)
Gershonites (1) +1201

1769 גֵּרְשֻׁנִּי *gēršunniy* (13)
Gershonite (7)
Gershonites (3)
Gershonite (1) +1201
Gershonites (1) +1201
their[s] (1) +1201+2021

1770 גְּשׁוּר *g'šûr* (9)
Geshur (8)
they[s] (1) +2256+5083

1771 גְּשׁוּרִי *g'šûriy* (6)
Geshurites (3)
people of Geshur (3)

1772 גָּשַׁם *gāšam* (1)
bring rain (1)

1773 1גֶּשֶׁם *gešem1* (35)
rain (24)
showers (3)
rains (2)
rainy (2)
abundant showers (1)
downpour (1) +4764
shower (1)
winter rains (1)

1774 2גֶּשֶׁם *gešem2* (3)
Geshem (3)

1775 גֹּשֶׁם *gōšem* (1)
showers (1)

1776 גַּשְׁמוּ *gašmû* (1)
Geshem (1)

1777 גֹּשֶׁן *gōšen* (15)
Goshen (11)
Goshen (4) +824

1778 גִּשְׁפָּא *gišpā'* (1)
Gishpa (1)

1779 גָּשַׁשׁ *gāšaš* (2)
feeling way (1)
grope along (1)

1780 1גַּת *gat1* (5)
winepress (4)
winepresses (1)

1781 2גַּת *gat2* (34)
Gath (34)

1782 3גַּת *gat3*
Variant; not used

1783 גַּת הַחֵפֶר *gat haḥēper* (2)
Gath Hepher (2)

1784 גַּת־רִמּוֹן *gat-rimmôn* (4)
Gath Rimmon (4)

1785 גִּתִּי *gitiy* (10)
Gittite (8)
Gath (1)
Gittites (1)

1786 גִּתַּיִם *gitayim* (2)
Gittaim (2)

1787 גִּתִּית *gitiyt* (3)
gittith (3)

1788 גֶּתֶר *geter* (2)
Gether (2)

1789 ד *d*
Variant; not used

1790 דָּאַב *dā'ab* (3)
dim (1)
faint (1) +5883
sorrow (1)

1791 דְּאָבָה *d'ābāh* (1)
dismay (1)

1792 דְּאָבוֹן *d'ābôn* (1)
despairing (1)

1793 דָּאַג *dā'ag* (7)
afraid (1)
dread (1)
dreaded (1)
has worries (1)
troubled (1)
worried (1)
worrying (1)

1794 דָּאג *dā'g* (1)
fish (1)

1795 דֹּאֵג *dō'ēg* (8)
Doeg (6)
untranslated (2)

1796 דְּאָנָה *d'āgāh* (6)
anxiety (2)
fear (2)
anxious (1)
restless (1)

1797 1דָּאָה *dā'āh1* (5)
soared (2)
swooping down (2)
swoop down (1)

1798 2דָּאָה *dā'āh2* (1)
red kite (1)

1799 דֹּאר *dō'r* (1)
Dor (1)

1800 דֹּב *dōb* (12)
bear (10)
bears (2)

1801 דֹּבֶא *dōbe'* (1)
strength (1)

1802 דְּבָאָה *d'bā'āh*
Variant; not used

1803 דְּבַב *dābab* (1)
flowing gently (1)

1804 דִּבָּה *dibbāh* (9)
slander (3)
bad report (2)
report (2)
bad reputation (1)
whispering (1)

1805 1דְּבוֹרָה *d'bôrāh1* (4)
bees (3)
swarm of bees (1)

1806 2דְּבוֹרָה *d'bôrāh2* (10)
Deborah (10)

1807 דִּבְיוֹנִים *dibyōniym* (1)
seed pods (1)

1808 1דְּבִיר *d'biyr1* (15)
inner sanctuary (14)
most holy place (1) +7731

1809 2דְּבִיר *d'biyr2* (1)
Debir (1)

1810 3דְּבִיר *d'biyr3* (13)
Debir (11)
untranslated (2)

1811 דְּבֵלָה *d'bēlāh* (5)
poultice (2)
cake of pressed figs (1)
cakes of pressed figs (1)
fig cakes (1)

1812 דִּבְלָה *diblāh* (1)
Diblah (1)

1813 דִּבְלַיִם *diblayim* (1)
Diblaim (1)

1814 דִּבְלָתַיְם *diblātayim*
Variant; not used

1815 דָּבַק *dābaq* (54)
hold fast (7)
cling (5)
bound (2)
clung (2)
held fast (2)
keep (2)
make stick (2)
stay (2)
sticks (2)
ally (1)
almost upon (1)
are joined fast (1)
caught up (1)
clings (1)
defiled (1) +4583
drawn (1)
follow (1) +339
found (1)
froze (1)
joined (1)
laid low (1)
not escape (1)
overtake (1)
overtook (1)
plague (1)
pressed hard (1)
pressed hard after (1)
pressing (1)
reduced to (1)
stayed (1)
stayed close (1)
stick together (1)

sticking (1)
stuck (1)
tightly joined (1)
united (1)
untranslated (1)

1816 דָּבֵק *dābēq* (3)
held fast (1)
sticks closer (1)
touched (1)

1817 דֶּבֶק *debeq* (3)
sections (2)
welding (1)

1818 1דָּבַר *dābar1* (5)
departure (1)
destroy (1)
destroyed (1)
subdued (1)
subdues (1)

1819 2דָּבַר *dābar2* (1140)
said (197)
speak (170)
spoken (99)
spoke (85)
say (67)
promised (51)
tell (49)
speaking (38)
told (37)
speaks (18)
talked (17)
says (14)
talking (14)
talk (11)
saying (10)
gave (6)
pronounced (6)
reported (6)
declared (5)
decreed (5)
directed (5)
made (5)
proclaimed (5)
repeated (5)
replied (5)
say (5) +1821
warned (5)
asked (4)
given (4)
praying (4)
promise (4)
speak out (4)
words (4)
ask (3)
give (3)
instructed (3)
preached (3)
pronounce (3)
pronounced on (3) +907
spoke up (3)
telling (3)
threatened (3)
announce (2)
answered (2)
declare (2)
foretold (2)
full of (2)
give answer (2) +1821
give message (2)
liars (2) +9214
proclaim (2)
promises made (2)
propose (2)
sang (2)
speak up (2)
spreads (2)
tells (2)
threaten (2)
address (1)
announced (1)

are said (1)
argued (1)
asking (1)
asks (1)
boastful (1) +1524
break out (1)
commanded (1)
complain (1)
contend (1)
decree (1)
described (1)
dictate (1)
discussed (1)
encourage (1) +4213+6584
encouraged (1) +4222+6584
ever say (1) +1821
explained (1)
fluent (1) +4200+4554
fomenting (1)
gave the message (1)
            +465+1821+2021+2021+3972
give an answer (1)
give opinion (1)
gives (1)
giving (1)
imagine (1)
instructed (1) +7023
invite (1)
is spoken (1)
lie (1) +3942
lie (1) +9214
lied (1) +3942
lies (1) +8736
lying (1) +3942
lying (1) +9214
made request (1)
make (1)
make many promises (1) +1821
make promise (1) +1821
make request (1)
mention (1)
mentioned (1)
message (1)
message came (1)
named (1)
ordered (1)
persuade (1) +4213+6584
plea (1)
pleaded (1)
pleads (1)
predicted (1)
proclaiming (1)
proclaims (1)
promise (1) +1821
promised (1) +928+7023
promises (1)
promises (1) +1821
prophesied (1) +5553
rebukes (1)
recited (1)
reciting (1)
recommended (1)
request (1) +1821
requested (1)
ridicule (1)
said (1) +1821
said (1) +1821+2021
said a word (1)
shouted (1)
silent (1) +4202
slander (1)
speak well (1) +1819
speak with words (1)
speech (1) +4537
spoken (1) +1821
spoken (1) +7023
spoken kindly (1) +4213+6584
state (1)
suggested (1)
talking together (1)
taught (1)

tell (1) +265+928
thought (1)
told (1) +265+928
urging (1)
used to say (1) +1819
utter (1)
will^s (1) +1821
untranslated (26)

1820   3רָבָ *dābar3*
Variant; not used

1821   רָבָד *dābār* (1455)
word (339)
words (226)
events (51)
this^s (44) +2021+2021+2296
annals (37) +3427
things (33)
message (31)
what^s (31) +2021
thing (27)
matter (24)
what said (21)
nothing (19) +4202
promise (15)
anything (14)
say (13)
this^s (12) +465+2021+2021
command (11)
everything (11) +2021+3972
what^s (11)
said (10)
answer (9)
answer (8) +8740
report (8)
what say (8)
anything (7) +3972
records (7)
terms (7)
because of (6) +6584
case (6)
commandments (6)
it^s (6) +2021
reported (6) +8740
some time later (6) +339+465+2021+2021
asked (5)
cases (5)
everything (5) +3972
instructions (5)
promises (5)
say (5) +1819
this^s (5) +2021
account (4)
advice (4)
commanded (4)
it^s (4) +2021+2021+2296
plan (4)
promised (4)
sayings (4)
something (4)
told (4)
affairs (3)
annals (3)
answered (3) +8740
because (3) +6584
commands (3)
concerning (3) +6584
conversation (3)
instruction (3)
lies (3) +9214
questions (3)
request (3)
speak (3)
way (3)
what^s (3) +2021+2021+2296
about (2) +6584
achievements (2)
affair (2)
bidding (2)
charge (2)
conduct (2)

counsel (2)
decree (2)
deeds (2)
dispute (2)
doing (2)
empty words (2) +8557
for (2) +6584
for each day (2) +928+3427+3427
give answer (2) +1819
nothing (2) +401
nothing (2) +3972+4202
occasion (2)
order (2)
predicting (2)
regulations (2)
relationship (2)
required (2)
requirement (2)
requirements (2)
saying (2)
some (2)
speaks (2)
spoke (2)
story (2)
thoughts (2)
verdict (2) +5477
voice (2)
what asks (2)
what written (2)
what^s (2) +465+2021+2021
written (2)
accusations (1)
accuse (1) +928+8492
activity (1)
after (1) +928
after a while (1) +339+465+2021+2021
amount (1)
animal^s (1)
answer (1) +6699
answers (1) +8740
anything (1) +1821+2021+3972+4946
anything (1) +2021+3972
anything (1) +3972+4946
as a result of (1) +6584
ask (1) +2011
at all (1)
behavior (1)
business (1)
cases (1) +8191
cause (1)
charges (1)
claims (1)
compliments (1) +5833
concerned (1)
conferred (1)
conferred (1) +2118
consult (1) +928+2011
curses (1)
customary (1) +4027
daily (1) +928+3427+3427
danger (1)
day by day (1) +928+2257+3427+3427
day by day (1) +928+3427+3427
decided (1) +6641
decisions (1)
deed (1)
defiance (1)
demand (1)
details (1)
directed (1)
disease (1)
disputes (1)
done (1)
duties (1)
duty (1)
edict (1)
eloquent (1) +408
else (1)
enough (1)
ever say (1) +1819
everything (1) +465+2021+2021+3972

feat (1) +1524
flaw (1) +8273
fulfilled (1)
gave the message (1)
      +465+1819+2021+2021+3972
harm (1) +8273
how (1)
idea (1)
in behalf of (1) +6584
inquires of (1) +928+8626
instructed (1)
it^s (1)
language (1)
later (1) +339+465+2021+2021
lesson (1)
lies (1) +3942
make many promises (1) +1819
make promise (1) +1819
matters (1)
mere talk (1) +8557
mission (1) +889+8938
need (1)
news (1)
nothing (1) +1524+2256+4202+7785
nothing whatever (1) +401+3972
offering (1)
one^s (1)
ones^s (1)
ordered (1)
plans (1)
plot (1)
prediction (1)
promise (1) +1819
promises (1) +1819
prophecy (1)
proposal (1)
proposed (1)
question (1)
record (1)
refrain (1)
reports (1)
request (1) +1819
requested (1)
responded (1)
revelation (1)
rule (1)
said (1) +1819
said (1) +1819+2021
says (1)
secret (1)
sins (1) +6411
situation (1)
slandered (1) +6613+8492
slanders (1) +6613+8492
something to say (1)
songs (1) +8877
speak up (1)
speaking (1)
speaking (1) +7754
speech (1)
speeches (1)
spoken (1)
spoken (1) +1819
such^s (1)
suggested (1) +2021+2021+2296
suggestion (1)
tell (1) +606
text (1)
that happened (1) +465+2021+2021
that said (1)
that^s (1) +465+2021+2021
the word (1)
them^s (1) +2021+2021+2296
them^s (1) +3870
theme (1)
they^s (1) +3870
this (1) +2021+2021+2296
this is how (1) +465+2021+2021+3869
this^s (1)
thought (1)
threatened (1)

threats (1)
through (1) +3869
times (1)
transfer of property (1) +3972+9455
trouble (1)
what foretold (1)
what happened (1)
what have to say (1)
what said (1) +7754
what says (1)
what spoke (1)
what^s (1) +7754
whatever (1) +4537
whisper (1)
why (1)
will^s (1) +1819
words (1) +7023
work (1)
year (1) +9102
untranslated (48)

1822 1הֶבֶר *deber1* (49)
plague (43)
plagues (3)
pestilence (2)
diseases (1)

1823 2הֶבֶר *deber2*
Variant; not used

1824 דֹּבֶר *dōber* (2)
pasture (2)

1825 הִבֵּר *dibbēr* (1)
word (1)

1826 הִבְרָה *dibrāh* (5)
as for (1) +6584
because (1) +6584
cause (1)
order (1)
therefore (1) +6584+8611

1827 דֹּבְרוֹת *dōbrôt* (1)
rafts (1)

1828 דִּבְרִי *dibriy* (1)
Dibri (1)

1829 דָּבְרַת *dāberrat* (3)
Daberath (3)

1830 דַּבֶּרֶת *dabberet* (1)
instruction (1)

1831 דְּבַשׁ *debaš* (54)
honey (52)
honeycomb (1) +3626
honeycomb (1) +7430

1832 1דַּבֶּשֶׁת *dabbešet1* (1)
humps (1)

1833 2דַּבֶּשֶׁת *dabbešet2* (1)
Dabbesheth (1)

1834 דָּג *dāg* (18)
fish (17)
fishing (1)

1835 1דָּגָה *dāgāh1* (1)
increase (1)

1836 2דָּגָה *dāgāh2* (15)
fish (15)

1837 דָּגוֹן *dāgôn* (13)
Dagon (8)
Dagon's (2)
his^s (1)
his body^s (1)
untranslated (1)

1838 1דָּגַל *dāgal1* (1)
outstanding (1)

1839 2דָּגַל *dāgal2* (3)
in procession (1)
lift up banners (1)
troops with banners (1)

1840 דֶּגֶל *degel* (14)
standard (11)
standards (2)
banner (1)

1841 דָּגָן *dāgān* (40)
grain (38)
bread (1)
threshing floor (1) +1755

1842 דָּגַר *dāgar* (2)
care for young (1)
hatches eggs (1)

1843 דַּד *dad* (4)
bosom (2)
bosoms (1)
breasts (1)

1844 דָּדָה *dādāh* (2)
leading (1)
walk humbly (1)

1845 דֹּדָוָהוּ *dōdāwāhû* (1)
Dodavahu (1)

1846 דֹּדִי *dōdiy*
Variant; not used

1847 דְּדָן *dedān* (10)
Dedan (10)

1848 דְּדָנִי *dedāniy* (1)
Dedanites (1)

1849 דֹּדָנִים *dōdāniym*
Variant; not used

1850 דָּהַם *dāham* (1)
taken by surprise (1)

1851 דָּהַר *dāhar* (1)
galloping (1)

1852 דַּהֲרָה *dahᵃrāh* (2)
galloping (2)

1853 דּוּב *dûb* (1)
drain away (1)

1854 דַּוָּג *dawwāg* (2)
fishermen (1)
untranslated (1)

1855 דּוּגָה *dûgāh* (1)
fishhooks (1) +6106

1856 דּוֹד *dôd* (61)
lover (28)
uncle (11)
love (8)
cousin (3) +1201
beloved (2)
others^s (2)
cousin (1)
cousin (1) +1426
cousins on their father's side (1) +1201
lover's (1) +4200
lovers (1)
relative (1)
untranslated (1)

1857 דּוּד *dûd* (8)
basket (3)
baskets (2)
caldrons (1)
kettle (1)
pot (1)

1858 דָּוִד *dāwid* (1075)
David (906)
David's (69)
he^s (47)
him^s (18)
David's (8) +4200
his^s (4)
David's line (1)
you^s (1)
untranslated (21)

1859 דּוּדָאִים *dûdā'iym* (6)
mandrakes (5)
mandrake plants (1)

1860 דּוֹדָה *dôdāh* (3)
aunt (2)
father's sister (1)

1861 דּוֹדוֹ *dôdô* (4)
Dodo (3)
untranslated (1)

1862 דּוֹדַי *dôday* (3)
Dodai (3)

1863 דּוּדַי *dûday*
Variant; not used

1864 דָּוָה *dāwāh* (1)
monthly period (1) +5614

1865 דָּוֶה *dāweh* (5)
faint (2)
menstrual cloth (1)
monthly period (1)
monthly period (1) +5614

1866 דּוּחַ *dûah* (3)
cleanse (1)
rinsed (1)
washed (1)

1867 דְּוַי *dᵉway* (2)
ill (1)
sickbed (1) +6911

1868 דַּוָּי *dawwāy* (3)
faint (2)
afflicted (1)

1869 דּוֹיֵג *dôyēg* (1)
untranslated (1)

1870 דּוּך *dûk* (1)
crushed (1)

1871 דּוּכִיפַת *dûkiypat* (2)
hoopoe (2)

1872 דּוּמָה1 *dûmāh1* (2)
silence (1)
silence of death (1)

1873 דּוּמָה2 *dûmāh2* (1)
Dumah (1)

1874 דּוּמָה3 *dûmāh3* (3)
Dumah (3)

1875 דּוּמִיָּה *dûmiyyāh* (4)
awaits (1)
rest (1)
silent (1)
still (1)

1876 דּוּמָם *dûmām* (3)
lifeless (1)
quietly (1)
silence (1)

1877 דּוּמֶשֶׂק *dûmmeśeq* (1)
Damascus (1)

1878 דּוֹן *dôn*
Variant; not used

1879 דּוּן *dûn*
Variant; not used

1880 דּוֹנַג *dônag* (4)
wax (4)

1881 דּוּץ *dûs* (1)
goes (1)

1882 דּוּק *dûq*
Variant; not used

1883 דּוּר1 *dûr1* (1)
pile wood (1)

1884 דּוּר2 *dûr2* (1)
dwell (1)

1885 דּוּר3 *dûr3* (2)
all around (1) +2021+3869
ball (1)

1886 דּוֹר1 *dôr1* (1)
house (1)

1887 דּוֹר2 *dôr2* (151)
generation (44)
generations to come (37)
all generations (14) +1887+2256
generations (12)
descendants (6)
thoseˢ (4)
generations (3) +1887+2256
all generations (2) +1887
age-old (1) +1887+2256
all time (1) +1887+2256
always (1) +1887+2256+4200
anotherˢ (1)
children (1) +1201
company (1)
endless generations (1) +1887+2256
generations long past (1) +1887+2256+9102
generations to come (1) +1887+2256
many generations (1) +1887+2256
people (1)
people of time (1)
through all generations (1) +1887
to come (1) +1887+2256
untranslated (3)

1888 דּוֹר3 *dôr3* (3)
Dor (3)

1889 דּוּשׁ *dûš* (16)
thresh (3)
threshed (2)
be trampled (2)
go on threshing (1) +1889
is threshed (1)
is trampled down (1)
tear (1)
threshing (1)
threshing grain (1)
threshing time (1)
trample (1)
treading out grain (1)

1890 דָּחָה *dāhāh* (7)
are brought down (1)
driving away (1)
pushed back (1) +1890
thrown down (1)
tottering (1)
trip (1)

1891 דָּחַח *dāhah*
Variant; not used

1892 דְּחִי *dᵉhiy* (2)
stumbling (2)

1893 דֹּחַן *dōhan* (1)
millet (1)

1894 דָּחַף *dāhap* (4)
spurred on (2)
eager (1)
rushed (1)

1895 דָּחַק *dāhaq* (2)
afflicted (1)
jostle (1)

1896 דַּי *day* (39)
whenever (5) +4946
enough (4)
from (3) +4946
as much as wanted (2)
as often as (2) +4946
for nothing (2) +928+8198
afford (1) +3338+5162
afford (1) +3338+5595
after (1) +928+4946
as far as possible (1) +3869
at the blast (1) +928

deserves (1) +3869
due annually (1) +928+4946+9102+9102
enough (1) +4200+4537
fuel for fire (1) +836+928
fuel for flames (1) +836+928
just enough (1)
means (1)
no end (1) +3869
often (1) +4946
plenty (1)
room enough (1)
sufficient (1)
sufficient means (1) +3869
swarms (1)
whatever (1)
whenever (1) +3954+4946

1897 דִּיבוֹן *diybôn* (9)
Dibon (9)

1898 דִּיבוֹן גָּד *diybôn gād* (2)
Dibon Gad (2)

1899 דִּיג *diyg* (1)
catch (1)

1900 דַּיָּג *dayyāg* (2)
fishermen (2)

1901 דַּיָּה *dayyāh* (2)
falcon (1)
falcons (1)

1902 דְּיוֹ *dᵉyô* (1)
ink (1)

1903 דִּי זָהָב *diy zāhāb* (1)
Dizahab (1)

1904 דִּימוֹן *diymôn* (2)
Dimon (1)
Dimon's (1)

1905 דִּימוֹנָה *diymônāh* (1)
Dimonah (1)

1906 דִּין1 *diyn1* (24)
judge (8)
contend (2)
govern (2)
plead (2)
vindicate (2)
administer (1)
arguing with each other (1)
defend rights (1)
defended (1)
governs (1)
provide justice (1)
punish (1)
vindicated (1)

1907 דִּין2 *diyn2* (19)
cause (3)
judgment (3)
justice (3)
rights (3)
case (2)
judge (2)
lawsuits (1) +1907+4200
quarrels (1)
untranslated (1)

1908 דַּיָּן *dayyān* (2)
defender (1)
judge (1)

1909 דִּינָה *diynāh* (8)
Dinah (7)
Dinah's (1)

1910 דִּיפַת *diypat*
Variant; not used

1911 דָּיֵק *dāyēq* (6)
siege works (6)

1912 דַּיִשׁ *dayiš* (1)
threshing (1)

1913 דִּישׁוֹן1 *diyšôn1* (1)
ibex (1)

1914 דִּישׁוֹן2 *diyšôn2* (8)
Dishon (7)
Dishan (1)

1915 דִּישָׁן *diyšān* (4)
Dishan (4)

1916 דַּךְ *dak* (4)
oppressed (3)
hurts (1)

1917 דָּכָא *dākā'* (18)
crush (7)
crushed (4)
broke (1)
contrite (1)
crushes (1)
crushing (1)
dejected (1)
humbled themselves (1)
was crushed (1)

1918 דַּכָּא1 *dakkā'1* (3)
contrite (1)
crushed (1)
crushing (1)

1919 דַּכָּא2 *dakkā'2* (1)
dust (1)

1920 דָּכָה *dākāh* (6)
crushed (4)
contrite (1)
untranslated (1)

1921 דַּכָּה *dakkāh*
Variant; not used

1922 דֳּכִי *dŏkiy* (1)
pounding waves (1)

1923 דַּל1 *dall* (1)
door (1)

1924 דַּל2 *dal2* (48)
poor (36)
weak (4)
grew weaker and weaker (1) +2143+2256
haggard (1)
helpless (1)
humble (1)
needy (1)
poorest of the poor (1) +1147
scrawny (1)
weakest (1)

1925 דָּלַג *dālag* (5)
scale (2)
avoid stepping (1)
leap (1)
leaping (1)

1926 דָּלָה1 *dālāh1* (5)
draw water (1)
draws out (1)
drew water (1) +1926
lifted out of the depths (1)

1927 דָּלָה2 *dālāh2* (1)
hang limp (1)

1928 דָּלָה3 *dālāh3*
Variant; not used

1929 דַּלָּה1 *dallāh1* (2)
hair (1) +8031
loom (1)

1930 דַּלָּה2 *dallāh2* (5)
poorest (5)

1931 דָּלַח *dālah* (3)
churning (1)
muddied (1)
stirred (1)

1932 דְּלִי *dŏliy* (2)
bucket (1)

buckets (1)

1933 דְּלָיָה *dŏlāyāh* (4)
Delaiah (4)

1934 דְּלָיָהוּ *dŏlāyāhû* (3)
Delaiah (3)

1935 דְּלִילָה *dŏliylāh* (6)
Delilah (6)

1936 דָּלִית *dāliyt* (8)
branches (6)
boughs (2)

1937 דָּלַל1 *dālal1* (7)
in need (2)
dwindle (1)
fade (1)
impoverished (1)
in great need (1)
weak (1)

1938 דָּלַל2 *dālal2* (1)
dangles (1)

1939 דִּלְעָן *dil'ān* (1)
Dilean (1)

1940 דָּלַף1 *dālap1* (2)
leaks (1)
pour out tears (1)

1941 דָּלַף2 *dālap2* (1)
weary (1)

1942 דֶּלֶף *delep* (2)
constant dripping (2) +3265

1943 דַּלְפוֹן *dalpôn* (1)
Dalphon (1)

1944 דָּלַק *dālaq* (9)
chased (1)
chasing (1) +339
fervent (1)
flaming (1)
hunt down (1)
hunts down (1)
inflamed (1)
kindle (1)
set on fire (1)

1945 דַּלֶּקֶת *dalleqet* (1)
inflammation (1)

1946 דֶּלֶת *delet* (88)
doors (46)
door (21)
gates (10)
leaves (2)
columns (1)
gate (1)
it[s] (1) +2021
lid (1)
outside (1) +4946
untranslated (4)

1947 דָּם *dām* (359)
blood (282)
bloodshed (17)
bloodthirsty (6)
guilty of bloodshed (4)
it[s] (4) +2021
guilt of blood (3)
lifeblood (3) +5883
bleeding (2)
bloodguilt (2)
bloodshed (2) +928+995
bloodshed (2) +1947+4200
guilt of bloodshed (2)
guilt of shedding blood (2)
blood shed (1)
blood vengeance (1)
blood-stained (1)
bloodshed (1) +5477
bloodshed (1) +9161
bloodstains (1)
death (1)

destruction (1)
do anything that endangers life (1)
            +6584+6641
flow (1)
guilt of murder (1) +5883
guilty of blood (1)
guilty of murder (1)
innocent man (1) +5929
it[s] (1)
it[s] (1) +2023+4946
it[s] (1) +2257
killing (1)
massacre (1)
murder (1)
murdering (1)
other[s] (1)
person[s] (1)
shedding of blood (1)
untranslated (3)

1948 דָּמָה1 *dāmāh1* (29)
compare (4)
compared (3)
is like (3)
be like (2)
am like (1)
are like (1)
been like (1)
equal (1)
intending (1)
intends (1)
like (1)
liken (1)
make myself like (1)
match (1)
meditate (1)
plan (1)
planned (1)
plotted (1)
think (1)
thought (1)
told parables (1)

1949 דָּמָה2 *dāmāh2* (4)
be silenced (1)
ceasing (1)
silence (1)
unceasingly (1) +4202

1950 דָּמָה3 *dāmāh3* (13)
ruined (3)
destroy (2)
perish (2)
are destroyed (1)
be completely destroyed (1) +1950
be wiped out (1)
disaster awaits (1)
float away (1)

1951 דֻּמָה *dumāh* (1)
silenced (1)

1952 דְּמוּת *dŏmût* (25)
likeness (5)
like (4)
looked like (4)
looked (3)
figure (2)
appearance (1)
figures (1)
form (1)
image (1)
like (1) +3869
sketch (1)
untranslated (1)

1953 דְּמִי *dŏmiy* (1)
prime (1)

1954 דֳּמִי *dŏmiy* (3)
rest (2)
silent (1)

1955 דִּמְיוֹן *dimyôn* (1)
like (1)

1956 דַּמִּים *dammiym*
Variant; not used

1957 1דָּמַם *damam1* (24)
silent (6)
be silenced (2)
be still (2)
ceasing (1)
find rest (1)
keeps quiet (1)
quieted (1)
quietly (1)
rest (1)
silence (1)
silenced (1)
stand still (1)
still (1)
stood still (1)
stops (1)
wait (1)
waiting in silence (1)

1958 2דָּמַם *damam2*
Variant; not used

1959 3דָּמַם *damam3* (5)
be destroyed (1)
be silenced (1)
doomed to perish (1)
perish (1)
will be laid waste (1)

1960 דְּמָמָה *dᵉmāmāh* (3)
hushed (1)
whisper (1)
whisper (1) +7754

1961 דֹּמֶן *dōmen* (6)
refuse (6)

1962 דִּמְנָה *dimnāh* (1)
Dimnah (1)

1963 דָּמַע *dāma'* (2)
weep bitterly (1) +1963

1964 דֶּמַע *dema'* (1)
vats (1)

1965 דִּמְעָה *dim'āh* (23)
tears (21)
weeping (2)

1966 דַּמֶּשֶׂק *dammeśeq* (39)
Damascus (37)
untranslated (2)

1967 דְּמֶשֶׂק *dᵉmeśeq*
Variant; not used

1968 1דָּן *dān1* (50)
Dan (33)
Danites (9) +1201
Dan (4) +1201
Danite (1) +4200+4751
Danites (1)
they⁵ (1) +1201
untranslated (1)

1969 2דָן *dān2* (20)
Dan (20)

1970 דָּן יַעַן *dān ya'an* (1)
Dan Jaan (1)

1971 דָּנְאֵל *dāni'ēl* (3)
untranslated (3)

1972 דַּנָּה *dannāh* (1)
Dannah (1)

1973 דִּנְהָבָה *dinhābāh* (2)
Dinhabah (2)

1974 דָּנִי *dāniy* (5)
Danites (3)
Dan (1)
men of Dan (1)

1975 דָּנִיֵּאל *dāniyyē'l* (29)
Daniel (29)

1976 דֵּעַ *dēa'* (5)
what know (3)
knowledge (2)

1977 דָּעָה *dā'āh*
Variant; not used

1978 דֵּעָה *dē'āh* (6)
knowledge (4)
knows (1)
teach (1) +3723

1979 דְּעוּאֵל *dᵉ'û'ēl* (5)
Deuel (5)

1980 דָּעַךְ *dā'ak* (9)
snuffed out (5)
died out (1)
extinguished (1)
goes out (1)
vanish (1)

1981 1דַּעַת *da'at1* (91)
knowledge (68)
know (5)
unintentionally (4) +928+1172
acknowledgment (2)
experienced (1) +2256+9312
has knowledge (1) +3359
have concern (1) +1067
have knowledge (1) +3359
it⁵ (1)
learning (1)
man of knowledge (1) +3359
notions (1)
understanding (1)
well informed (1) +3359
what know (1)
what teach (1)

1982 2דַּעַת *da'at2*
Variant; not used

1983 3דַּעַת *da'at3*
Variant; not used

1984 דְּפִי *dᵉpiy* (1)
slander (1) +5989

1985 דָּפַק *dāpaq* (3)
driven hard (1)
knocking (1)
pounding (1)

1986 דָּפְקָה *dopqāh* (2)
Dophkah (2)

1987 דַּק *daq* (14)
thin (6)
fine (2)
gaunt (2) +1414
dwarfed (1)
finely ground (1)
gentle (1)
untranslated (1)

1988 דֹּק *dōq* (1)
canopy (1)

1989 דִּקְלָה *diqlāh* (2)
Diklah (2)

1990 דָּקַק *dāqaq* (13)
powder (3)
ground (2)
be ground (1)
break to pieces (1)
broke to pieces (1)
broke up (1)
crush (1)
fine (1)
grind (1)
pounded (1)

1991 דָּקַר *dāqar* (11)
run through (3)
be thrust through (1)
drove through (1)
fatally wounded (1)
pierced (1)
racked with hunger (1)
ran through (1)
stab (1)
wounded (1)

1992 דֶּקֶר *deqer*
Variant; not used

1993 דַּר *dar* (1)
mother-of-pearl (1)

1994 דֵּרָאוֹן *dērā'ôn* (2)
contempt (1)
loathsome (1)

1995 דָּרְבָן *dārbān* (1)
goads (1)

1996 דָּרְבֹנָה *dārbōnāh* (1)
goads (1)

1997 דַּרְדַּע *darda'* (2)
Darda (2)

1998 דַּרְדַּר *dardar* (2)
thistles (2)

1999 דָּרוֹם *dārôm* (19)
south (17)
south wind (1)
southward (1)

2000 1דְּרוֹר *dᵉrôr1* (2)
swallow (2)

2001 2דְּרוֹר *dᵉrôr2* (1)
liquid (1)

2002 3דְּרוֹר *dᵉrôr3* (7)
freedom (5)
freedom for slaves (1)
liberty (1)

2003 דָּרְיָוֵשׁ *dāryāweš* (10)
Darius (10)

2004 דַּרְיוֹשׁ *daryôš*
Variant; not used

2005 דֶּרֶךְ *dārak* (63)
bend (4)
trampled (4)
treads (4)
draw (3)
tread (3)
treading (2)
guide (2)
marches (2)
set (2)
strung (2)
trodden (2)
aim (1)
archer (1)
bent (1)
come (1)
cross over (1)
direct (1)
directs (1)
draw the bow (1)
drew (1)
enables to go (1)
go (1)
guides (1)
handle (1)
lead (1)
led (1)
make ready to shoot (1)
march on (1)
overran (1)
press (1)
set feet (1)
set foot on (1)
step (1)
string (1)
trample down (1)
treads out (1)
trod (1)

use (1)
walked (1)
walks (1)
with bows (1) +8008
untranslated (2)

2006 דֶּרֶךְ *derek* (713)
ways (180)
way (177)
road (61)
journey (30)
path (21)
conduct (18)
toward (15)
direction (9)
roads (9)
through (8)
route (7)
life (5)
what done (5)
pass by (4) +6296
paths (4)
side (4)
to (4)
as (3) +928
by (3)
highway (3)
mission (3)
on (3)
roadside (3)
wherever (3) +889+928+2021
works (3)
all do (2)
course (2)
distance (2)
does (2)
facing (2)
go to (2)
passageway (2)
street (2)
trackless (2) +4202
what[s] (2) +2021
action (1)
along (1)
at (1) +928+2021
behavior (1)
by way of (1)
course of life (1)
crossroads (1)
custom (1)
did (1)
dispersed (1) +2143+4200
distant (1) +2021+8049
do so[s] (1) +4946+8740
done (1)
everything do (1)
extending (1)
fate (1)
favors (1)
follow (1)
following (1)
go (1) +928+2143
god (1)
how behaved (1)
how live (1)
in the way should go (1) +6584+7023
justice (1)
leads (1)
leads to (1)
let get away (1) +928+8938
line (1)
long (1)
main road (1) +2006
man of integrity (1) +9448
march (1)
missions (1)
northward (1) +2021+7600
on way (1) +6913
path (1) +784
period (1) +851
place (1)
room (1)

routes (1)
running here and there (1) +8592
siege ramp (1)
skilled (1) +3512
streets (1)
strength (1)
teaching (1)
that[s] (1)
there[s] (1) +928+2021
things did (1)
toward (1) +448
toward (1) +6584
toward (1) +6584+7156
travel (1) +6296
traveled (1)
traveled (1) +2143
traveling (1)
upright (1) +3838
vigor (1)
walk (1)
walk (1) +928+2143
walked (1)
walking along (1) +928+2021
waylaid (1) +928+2021+8492
what did (1)
where[s] (1) +2021
which way (1) +361+2021+2296
untranslated (40)

2007 דַּרְכְּמוֹנִים *darkmôniym* (4)
drachmas (4)

2008 דַּרְמֶשֶׂק *darmeśeq* (6)
Damascus (6)

2009 דָּרַע *dāraʿ*
Variant; not used

2010 דַּרְקוֹן *darqôn* (2)
Darkon (2)

2011 דָּרַשׁ *dāraš* (164)
seek (34)
inquire of (19)
sought (11)
consult (5)
seeking (5)
consult (4) +928
inquire of (4) +928
call to account (3)
demand an accounting (3)
cares for (2)
consults (2)
hold accountable (2) +3338+4946
investigate (2)
let inquire of (2) +4200
look (2)
require (2)
search for (2)
searches (2)
seek help (2)
seek out (2)
seeks (2)
sought out (2)
study (2)
appeal (1)
are pondered (1)
ask (1)
ask (1) +1821
asked (1)
avenges (1)
call to account (1) +4946+6640
care about (1)
care for (1)
carefully investigated (1) +1335+2256
cares (1)
certainly demand (1) +2011
comes looking for (1)
consult (1) +928+1821
consulted (1)
find out (1)
follow (1)
give an accounting (1)
guidance (1)

inquire (1)
inquire of (1) +448
inquire of (1) +907+4946
inquire of (1) +4200
inquired about (1) +2011
inquired of (1)
inquiring (1)
let inquire of (1)
let inquire of at all (1) +2011+4200
look for (1)
look to (1)
make investigation (1)
probe (1)
rally (1)
required (1) +6584
revealed myself (1)
search was made (1)
searched (1)
searches for (1)
seek will (1)
selects (1)
sought after (1)
worked for (1)
would (1)
yield to the plea (1)
untranslated (1)

2012 דָּשָׁא *dāšā'* (2)
green (1)
produce (1)

2013 דֶּשֶׁא *deše'* (14)
grass (4)
green (4)
vegetation (3)
grass (1) +4604
new grass (1)
new growth (1)

2014 דָּשֵׁן1 *dāšēn1* (11)
prosper (2)
remove ashes (2)
accept (1)
anoint (1)
are fully satisfied (1)
be soaked (1)
gives health (1)
is covered (1)
thrive (1)

2015 דָּשֵׁן2 *dāšēn2* (2)
fresh (1)
rich (1)

2016 דֶּשֶׁן *dešen* (16)
ashes (7)
abundance (3)
ash (1)
choice food (1)
oil (1)
rich (1)
richest of fare (1)
richest of foods (1) +2256+2693

2017 דָּת *dāṭ* (22)
edict (8)
law (6)
laws (2)
command (1)
customs (1)
order (1)
orders (1)
prescribed (1)
untranslated (1)

2018 דָּתָן *dāṭān* (10)
Dathan (10)

2019 דֹּתָן *dōṭān* (3)
Dothan (3)

2020 ה *h*
Variant; not used

2021 הַ־ *ha-* (30369)
the (16201)

a (759)
who (468)
that (205)
his[s] (157)
this (150)
those (145)
today (137) +3427
their[s] (95)
an (78)
what (67)
your[s] (59)
these (54)
he[s] (44)
this[s] (44) +1821+2021+2296
each (40)
today (39) +2021+2296+3427
O (35)
my[s] (31)
what[s] (31) +1821
him[s] (29) +4889
they[s] (28) +6639
he[s] (26) +4889
one (26)
its[s] (25)
her[s] (22)
any (21)
always (18) +3427+3972
anyone (18)
they[s] (18)
which (18)
whoever (18)
now (17) +2021+2296+3427
other[s] (17)
he[s] (16) +3913
them[s] (16) +6639
now (14) +3427
our[s] (14)
you[s] (13)
this[s] (12) +465+1821+2021
at twilight (11) +1068+6847
everything (11) +1821+3972
whatever (11)
him[s] (10)
it[s] (10) +6551
tonight (10) +4326
burn down (9) +836+928+8596
it[s] (9) +1473
set on fire (9) +836+928+3675
some[s] (9)
they[s] (9) +408
burned (8) +836+928+8596
every (8)
everyone (7) +3972+5883
it[s] (7)
outside (7) +928+2575
before (6) +928+8037
he[s] (6) +408
her[s] (6) +851
his[s] (6) +4889
it[s] (6) +824
it[s] (6) +1821
prison (6) +1074+6045
secretly (6) +928+6260
she[s] (6) +851
some time later (6) +339+465+1821+2021
sunset (6) +995+9087
as long as (5) +3427+3972
it[s] (5) +4640
stone (5) +74+928+8083
this[s] (5) +1821
those[s] (5) +6639
allotted (4) +928+1598
be burned up (4) +836+928+8596
burn (4) +836+928+8596
burned up (4) +836+928+8596
day after day (4) +3427+3972
every morning (4)
                +928+928+1332+1332+2021
falsely (4) +4200+9214
first (4) +3427+3869
his own[s] (4)

in vain (4) +4200+8736
it[s] (4) +1074
it[s] (4) +1821+2021+2296
it[s] (4) +1947
it[s] (4) +3542
its[s] (4) +380
prison (4) +1074+3975
set on fire (4) +836+928+8596
them[s] (4) +7931
there[s] (4) +928+1195
those[s] (4) +408
Trans-Euphrates (4) +5643+6298
who[s] (4) +3913
anyone (3) +408+4769
burn up (3) +836+928+8596
burned down (3) +836+928+8596
burning (3) +836+6584
daybreak (3) +240+1332
east (3) +4667+9087
ever since (3) +2021+2296+3427+6330
first (3) +928+9378
forever (3) +3427+3972
he[s] (3) +7149
him[s] (3) +408
his own[s] (3) +4889
it[s] (3) +185
it[s] (3) +778
it[s] (3) +2215
it[s] (3) +5438
it[s] (3) +5596
it[s] (3) +5999
it[s] (3) +6219
its[s] (3) +824
its[s] (3) +4640
men[s] (3)
misuse (3) +4200+5951+8736
on high (3) +928+5294
she[s] (3) +5855
them (3) +6639
them[s] (3) +3913
them[s] (3) +7971
what[s] (3)
what[s] (3) +1821+2021+2296
what[s] (3) +5126
wherever (3) +889+928+2006
whose (3)
wild (3) +928+8441
all day long (2) +928+2021+2085+3427
allotted (2) +928+1598+5989
Amaziah[s] (2) +4889
angels (2) +466+1201
anyone (2) +3972+5883
anything (2)
anything (2) +3972+3998
certain (2)
champion (2) +408+1227
chief officer (2) +7372+8569
completely (2) +3972+4200
continual (2) +3427+3972
continually (2) +3427+3972
dawn (2) +240+1332
daybreak (2) +6590+8840
earlier (2) +928+9378
east (2) +2025+4667+9087
everyone (2) +3972+6639
first (2) +928+8037
forever (2) +6330+6409
he[s] (2) +466
he[s] (2) +2021+2085+5883
he[s] (2) +8357
her[s] (2) +912
her[s] (2) +5855
here[s] (2) +2021+2296+5226
him[s] (2) +5853
his own[s] (2) +3913
inside (2) +928+1074
it[s] (2) +380
it[s] (2) +836
it[s] (2) +4966
it[s] (2) +5577
it[s] (2) +7228

it[s] (2) +7339
it[s] (2) +8120
its[s] (2) +1074
its[s] (2) +2958
its[s] (2) +3284
its[s] (2) +7228
its[s] (2) +9133
Judah[s] (2) +824
misuses (2) +4200+5951+8736
never (2) +3427+3972+4202
now (2) +465+928+2021+3427
now (2) +3869+6961
one's (2)
one[s] (2) +6639
prison (2) +1074+3989
privately (2) +928+6260
quietly (2) +928+4319
someone (2)
someone[s] (2)
something[s] (2)
still (2) +2021+2296+3427+6330
stone (2) +74+928+6232
stoned (2) +74+928+6232
sunrise (2) +2436+9087
sunset (2) +995+6961+9087
the other[s] (2) +824+7895
their own[s] (2)
their[s] (2) +964
their[s] (2) +6639
them[s] (2)
them[s] (2) +408
them[s] (2) +3051
them[s] (2) +3338
them[s] (2) +3972+6639
them[s] (2) +4131
them[s] (2) +5853
them[s] (2) +8993
then (2) +340+928
there[s] (2) +824
there[s] (2) +928+1074
they[s] (2) +824+6639
they[s] (2) +3913
they[s] (2) +7366
this very (2)
those[s] (2) +5877
two-horned (2) +1251+7967
used to (2) +4200+8037
what[s] (2) +465+1821+2021
what[s] (2) +2006
when (2) +928+3427
where[s] (2) +5226
wherever (2) +889+928+3972+5226
whoever (2) +408+4769
whose[s] (2)
above (1) +928+5294
abroad (1) +2575+4200
accuses (1) +4200+5477+7756
after a while (1) +339+465+1821+2021
afternoon (1) +3427+5742
again (1) +928+1685+2021+2085+7193
age of childbearing (1) +784+851+3869
ago (1) +3427
Ai[s] (1) +6551
all around (1) +1885+3869
all men (1) +132+1201
all night long (1) +928+4326
all-night (1) +3972+4326
allotted (1) +928+1598+2118
already (1) +928+9378
annual (1) +285+928+9102
annual (1) +928+7193+9102
anointed (1) +1201+3658
another[s] (1)
another[s] (1) +132
another[s] (1) +2215+2296+4946
another[s] (1) +9019
any man (1) +408+4769
anyone (1) +408
anyone (1) +408+3972
anyone[s] (1) +4637
anything (1) +1821+1821+3972+4946

anything (1) +1821+3972
anything[s] (1)
archers (1) +408+928+4619+8008
archers (1) +928+4619+8008
are burned up (1) +836+928+8596+8596
around (1) +2575+4946
assemble (1) +928+6590+7736
at (1) +928+2006
at last (1) +7193
at once (1) +928+2021+2085+3427
at once (1) +928+2021+2085+6961
at once (1) +928+3427
at once (1) +3427
at this time (1) +3427
away (1) +448+2025+2575
awhile (1) +3427+3869
banded together (1) +665+2653+4200
be burned (1) +836+928+8596
be burned down (1) +836+928+8596
be taken captive (1) +928+4090+9530
before (1) +928+9378
below (1) +141+6584
below deck (1) +3752+6208
besiege (1) +928+995+5189
blind (1) +928+5782+6427
Boaz[s] (1) +408
both[s] (1) +170+2021+2256+8533
bought (1) +928+4084+7864
breeding (1) +3501+7366
brings to ruin (1) +4200+6156+8273
burn to death (1) +836+928+8596
burned (1) +836+928+8938
burned down (1) +836+8596
burned to death (1) +836+928+8596
callous (1) +2693+3869
captain (1) +2480+8042
cargo (1) +641+889+928+3998
carry off (1) +928+995+8660
charred (1) +836+928+1277
children (1) +1061+7262
commander in chief (1) +6584+7372
community (1) +824+6639
crops (1) +141+7262
daily (1) +3427+4200
David's[s] (1)
daybreak (1) +1332+7155
daylight (1) +240+1332
did so[s] (1) +906+6913+7175
distant (1) +2006+8049
doing this[s] (1) +3569+6894
doubly (1) +928+9109
dreamer (1) +1251+2706
each day (1) +2021+3427+3427+4200+4200
each day (1) +3427+4200
each morning (1)
　　　　　+928+928+1332+1332+2021
each morning (1)
　　　　　+1332+1332+2021+4200+4200
each[s] (1) +4090
end (1) +340+928+2118
enthrones (1) +3782+4058+4200
especially bred (1) +1201+8247
evening (1) +928+928+2021+6847+6847
evening (1) +6847+6961
ever (1) +3427+3972
every day (1) +3427+4200
every evening (1)
　　　　　+928+928+2021+6847+6847
everyone (1) +132+3972
everyone (1) +408+3972
everyone[s] (1)
everything (1) +465+1821+2021+3972
everything (1) +3972
everything (1) +3972+4856
everywhere (1) +3972+5226
fiercely (1) +928+6677
fifteen feet (1) +564+928+6924
fight (1) +3655+4200+4878
followers (1) +339+889+6639
for life (1) +3427+3972
foreigner (1) +1201+5797

foreigners (1) +1201+5797
forevermore (1) +6330+6409
formerly (1) +928+8037
from now on (1) +3427+3972
furthermore (1) +2256+9108
gave the message (1)
　　　　　+465+1819+1821+2021+3972
get out of here (1) +2025+2575+8938
give in marriage (1) +851+5989
God-fearing (1) +466+3710
hard (1) +3668+4200+4607
he himself[s] (1) +3913
he[s] (1) +340+408+2021
he[s] (1) +408+2021+6640+8886
he[s] (1) +408+5283
he[s] (1) +466+824
he[s] (1) +3381+3913
he[s] (1) +3758+5566
he[s] (1) +4855
he[s] (1) +5853
he[s] (1) +7595
her[s] (1) +6320
here[s] (1) +824
here[s] (1) +824+928
here[s] (1) +928+2021+2296+5226
here[s] (1) +928+4497
here[s] (1) +5226
him[s] (1) +132
him[s] (1) +466
him[s] (1) +1201+3778
him[s] (1) +3450
him[s] (1) +3759+5566
him[s] (1) +4889+6460
him[s] (1) +5782
him[s] (1) +5999
him[s] (1) +7127
him[s] (1) +7140
him[s] (1) +7149
him[s] (1) +8357
himself[s] (1) +408
his own[s] (1) +367
his own[s] (1) +2021+2418+5566
his[s] (1) +132
his[s] (1) +408
his[s] (1) +928+4889
his[s] (1) +4637
his[s] (1) +5566
immediately (1) +3427+3869
imprisoned (1) +657+1074+5989
in (1) +1074+2025
in broad daylight (1)
　　　　　+2021+2296+4200+6524+9087
in broad daylight (1) +5584+9087
in midair (1)
　　　　　+824+1068+1068+2021+2256+9028
infamous (1) +3238+9005
inside (1) +448+1074
interwoven (1) +928+8054
Israel's[s] (1)
Israelite (1) +408+3778
it[s] (1) +778
it[s] (1) +3136
it[s] (1) +4058
it[s] (1) +4114
it[s] (1) +4640
it's[s] (1) +3427
it[s] (1) +258
it[s] (1) +466+778
it[s] (1) +616+1473
it[s] (1) +680
it[s] (1) +778+1382
it[s] (1) +793+1581
it[s] (1) +824+2021+2296
it[s] (1) +1352
it[s] (1) +1580
it[s] (1) +1946
it[s] (1) +2021+2085+5226
it[s] (1) +2021+2296+6551
it[s] (1) +2021+2296+8878
it[s] (1) +2021+2645+7606
it[s] (1) +2162

it[s] (1) +2570
it[s] (1) +2633
it[s] (1) +2706
it[s] (1) +2851
it[s] (1) +3051
it[s] (1) +3855
it[s] (1) +4084
it[s] (1) +4223
it[s] (1) +4258
it[s] (1) +4722
it[s] (1) +4784
it[s] (1) +4889+9133
it[s] (1) +4963
it[s] (1) +5120
it[s] (1) +5261
it[s] (1) +6130
it[s] (1) +6174
it[s] (1) +6322
it[s] (1) +6592
it[s] (1) +6639
it[s] (1) +6727
it[s] (1) +6770
it[s] (1) +7498
it[s] (1) +7663
it[s] (1) +7815
it[s] (1) +8288
it[s] (1) +8367
it[s] (1) +8385
it[s] (1) +8407
it[s] (1) +8441
it[s] (1) +8538
it[s] (1) +8701
it[s] (1) +8947
it[s] (1) +9024
it[s] (1) +9043
it[s] (1) +9310
its[s] (1) +871
its[s] (1) +928+6551
its[s] (1) +2633
its[s] (1) +3720
its[s] (1) +4058+4200
its[s] (1) +6425
its[s] (1) +6592
its[s] (1) +7175
Jacob's[s] (1)
Jether[s] (1) +5853
just (1) +3427
just now (1) +3427
laid siege (1) +928+995+5189
lamb (1) +928+3897+8445
lamb (1) +928+4166+8445
last night (1) +4326
last watch of the night (1) +874+1332
lasting (1) +2021+2296+3427+6330
later (1) +339+465+1821+2021
later (1) +340+928
leads (1) +928+8037
leveled completely (1) +928+9164+9168
likes (1) +928+3202+4200
live (1) +928+2644
lived (1) +928+1074
long ago (1) +928+8037
long life (1) +2644+4200
man's[s] (1)
mealtime (1) +431+6961
men (1) +132+1201
midnight (1) +2942+4326
mounted (1) +928+6061
must sell (1) +928+4084+4835+4835
Naomi[s] (1) +851
native-born (1) +275+824
native-born (1) +824+928+3528
natural (1) +132+3869+3972
nightfall (1) +4326
noon (1) +3427+4734
northward (1) +2006+7600
nothing (1) +3972+4202
now (1) +7193
on each side (1)　　　+2021+2296+2296+4946
　　　　　+4946+4946+4946+6298+6298
on fire (1) +836+928+1277

on foot (1) +824+6584
on high (1) +4200+5294
on high (1) +5294
on the west (1) +4427+9087
once again (1) +3869+8037
once more (1) +421+7193
one another (1) +6639
one[s] (1) +4131
one[s] (1) +5566
oppressed (1) +928+6913+6945
other nationalities (1) +824+6639
others[s] (1)
others[s] (1) +851
out here (1) +928+2575
outdoor (1) +928+2575
outer (1) +2575+4200
outside the family (1) +2025+2424+2575
overboard (1) +448+3542
painted (1) +928+7037+8531
penned up (1) +928+1074+3973
people[s] (1)
perjurers (1) +4200+8678+9214
perjury (1) +4200+8678+9214
permanently (1) +4200+7552
places[s] (1)
plotting (1) +3086+8288
preserved (1) +928+2645+8492
prison (1) +673+1074
prison (1) +1074+4551
prison (1) +1074+7213
privately (1) +928+4319
privately (1) +928+8952
put out (1) +2575+3655
ready for battle (1) +408+4200+4878+7372
ready for battle (1) +928+4878+7372
recently (1) +3427
reflects a face (1) +2021+4200+7156+7156
reflects the man (1) +132+4200
regular (1) +3427+3972
Sabbath after Sabbath (1)
    +928+928+2021+3427+3427+8701+8701
safely (1) +4200+8934
said (1) +1819+1821
sail (1) +641+928+2143
sandaled (1) +928+5837
Saul's[s] (1)
scoundrel (1) +408+1175
see (1) +4200+6524+8011
set ablaze (1) +836+928+3675
set farther back (1) +337+2958
set fire to (1) +836+928+8596
set fire to (1) +836+928+8938
seven and a half feet (1) +564+928+2822
seven-day periods (1) +3427+8679
she[s] (1)
she[s] (1) +912
she[s] (1) +4893
shoot (1) +928+8008
similar (1) +3869+5260
sling stones (1) +74+928
sober (1) +3516+3655+4946
some distance (1) +824+3896
someone (1) +285+6639
someone[s] (1) +5877
someone[s] (1) +8011
southward (1) +448+3545
spreads feathers to run (1) +928+5257+5294
spring (1) +4784+6524
spring (1) +9102+9588
steward[s] (1) +408+889+1074+6584
still (1) +2021+2296+3427+3869
stoned (1) +74+928+8083
stoning (1) +74+928+8083
such (1)
such[s] (1) +6913
suggested (1) +1821+2021+2296
sunset (1) +995+3064
tent-dwelling (1) +185+928
that happened (1) +465+1821+2021
that[s] (1) +465+1821+2021
that[s] (1) +1074+2021+2296

the place[s] (1)
their[s] (1) +408
their[s] (1) +465
their[s] (1) +824+6639
their[s] (1) +1201+1769
their[s] (1) +2498+4200
their[s] (1) +3913
their[s] (1) +4131
them[s] (1) +74+928+4392
them[s] (1) +3192
them[s] (1) +74+9109
them[s] (1) +466+1074+3998
them[s] (1) +824+6551
them[s] (1) +912
them[s] (1) +1522
them[s] (1) +1821+2021+2296
them[s] (1) +2021+2296+6639
them[s] (1) +2143
them[s] (1) +3192
them[s] (1) +3192+9109
them[s] (1) +4283
them[s] (1) +4291
them[s] (1) +5566
them[s] (1) +5987
them[s] (1) +6109
them[s] (1) +6296
them[s] (1) +6929+7983
them[s] (1) +7194
them[s] (1) +7700
them[s] (1) +7736
them[s] (1) +7983
them[s] (1) +9149
then[s] (1) +928+2021+2085+3427
then[s] (1) +2021+2085+6961
there[s] (1) +928+1195
there[s] (1) +928+2215
there[s] (1) +824+928
there[s] (1) +928+1014
there[s] (1) +928+1074+3752
there[s] (1) +928+2006
there[s] (1) +928+2215
there[s] (1) +928+4722
there[s] (1) +928+5207
there[s] (1) +928+6551
there[s] (1) +3720
there[s] (1) +8441
there[s] (1) +9399
these men[s] (1) +1201+5566
these men[s] (1) +4856+6913
these[s] (1) +74
these[s] (1) +2693
they[s] (1) +132
they[s] (1) +746
they[s] (1) +851
they[s] (1) +851+1201
they[s] (1) +964
they[s] (1) +2256+2657+3405+8569
they[s] (1) +3374
they[s] (1) +3452
they[s] (1) +3972+6639
they[s] (1) +4291
they[s] (1) +4619
they[s] (1) +4784
they[s] (1) +4855
they[s] (1) +5954
they[s] (1) +6296
they[s] (1) +7736
they[s] (1) +8103
they[s] (1) +8569
they[s] (1) +9133
thirty feet (1) +564+928+6929
this (1) +1821+2021+2296
this is how (1) +465+1821+2021+3869
this kind of sore (1) +5596+5999
this[s] (1) +2021+2296+5126
this[s] (1) +9108
thoroughly purge away (1)
    +1342+3869+7671
those[s] (1) +339+889+6639
those[s] (1) +1583
those[s] (1) +2651

those[s] (1) +7156
those[s] (1) +7239
those[s] (1) +8599
those[s] (1) +8636
tomorrow[s] (1)
two[s] (1)
unnoticed (1) +928+4319
useless (1) +4200+9214
very old (1) +928+995+2416+3427
wage war (1) +1741+4200+4878
walking along (1) +928+2006
waylaid (1) +928+2006+8492
what[s] (1) +995
what[s] (1) +2021+2296+5184
what[s] (1) +4856
whatever[s] (1) +3655
where[s] (1) +928+5226
where[s] (1) +2006
where[s] (1) +2021+2667+2958
wherever (1) +285+889+928+5226
wherever (1) +889+3972+5226+6584
wherever (1) +889+928+5226
wherever (1) +928+3972+5226
wherever (1) +3972+4946+5226
which way (1) +361+2006+2296
which[s] (1) +7366
which[s] (1) +8965
who (1) +408+6504
whoever (1) +132+3972
whoever[s] (1)
whom (1)
whose[s] (1) +285+2021+9108
without meaning (1) +928+2039
woman's monthly uncleanness (1)
    +3240+5614
workmen (1) +928+4856+6913
year (1) +3427+4200
years (1) +6961+9102
yet (1) +2021+2085+3427+6330
yet (1) +2021+2156+3427+6330
yet (1) +3427
Ziklag[s] (1) +6551
untranslated (10017)

2022   הֲ *ha-* (743)
whether (12)
if (11)
not (8)
when (4)
don't (3)
as you know (2) +4202
or (2)
rather (2)
aren't (1)
isn't (1)
not only (1)
only (1) +4202
so (1)
surely (1)
unless (1) +4202
what about (1) +4202
whether (1) +561+4202
untranslated (690)

2023   ָה *-āh* (3129)
her (1141)
it (539)
its (257)
the[s] (95)
she (67)
their (67)
them (28)
there[s] (28) +928
his (13)
the city[s] (12)
the land[s] (12)
whose (12)
herself (8)
herself (7) +5883
this (7)
which[s] (7)
there[s] (6) +6584

your (6)
a^s (5)
her (5) +4200
her own (5)
there^s (4) +928+9348
him (3)
one (3)
that city^s (3)
there^s (3)
this^s (3)
Hagar^s (2)
hers (2)
its (2) +928
its (2) +4200
its land^s (2)
its^s (2)
Jerusalem^s (2)
land^s (2)
she (2) +5883
that^s (2)
the town^s (2)
where^s (2) +928
which (2)
wisdom^s (2)
you (2)
all this^s (1)
an^s (1)
another^s (1)
city^s (1)
Dinah's^s (1)
Edom's^s (1)
Edom^s (1)
Egypt^s (1)
Hannah^s (1)
he^s (1) +3
here^s (1) +928
hers (1) +4200
herself (1) +4222
herself (1) +7931
him^s (1) +3
him^s (1) +1201
him^s (1) +1251
his former righteousness^s (1)
his nurse^s (1)
his^s (1) +3
in (1)
Israel's^s (1)
it^s (1) +1947+4946
its (1) +6584
its inhabitants^s (1)
its own (1)
its people^s (1)
Judah^s (1)
Moab^s (1)
my law^s (1)
Nineveh^s (1) +5226
piece^s (1)
that (1)
that day^s (1)
that place^s (1)
that time^s (1)
that's (1)
the (1)
the courtyard^s (1)
the daughter's^s (1)
the dove^s (1)
the earth^s (1)
the fire^s (1)
the first woman^s (1)
the girl^s (1)
the goat^s (1)
the kingdom^s (1)
the lampstand^s (1)
the pit^s (1)
the place^s (1)
the plot^s (1)
the spring^s (1)
the sword^s (1)
the temple^s (1)
their land^s (1)
their lands^s (1)

them^s (1) +1074
themselves (1)
there^s (1) +928+8148
there^s (1) +5226
these^s (1)
this city^s (1)
this land^s (1)
those (1)
tongue^s (1)
Tyre^s (1)
what happened^s (1)
whom (1)
word^s (1)
your own (1)
your wife^s (1)
yourself (1) +4222
Zion^s (1)
untranslated (687)

2024 הֹ - *ōh* (53)
his (9)
they (4)
them (3)
its (1)
it (1)
their (1)
those (1)
untranslated (32)

2025 2הָ - *āh2* (1116)
to (292)
on (95)
at (58)
there (58) +9004
into (51)
in (37)
more (36) +5087
west (28) +3542
north (26) +7600
toward (25)
where (17) +625
where (16) +9004
east (13) +7708
how long (12) +625+6330
for (9)
northern (9) +7600
south (9) +5582
outside (8) +2575
east (7) +4667
east (7) +7711
upward (6) +4200+5087
out (5) +2575
south (5) +9402
above (4) +4200+4946+5087
reached (4) +995
the Jordan^s (4) +9004
above (3) +4200+5087
eastern (3) +7711
from (3)
in it^s (3) +9004
on (3) +5087
over (3) +4200+4946+5087
south (3) +5582+9402
southern (3) +5582
toward (3) +995+3870
westward (3) +3542
after (2)
anywhere else (2) +625+625+2025+2256
each year (2) +3427+3427+4946
east (2) +2021+4667+9087
eastern (2) +4667
head (2) +2256+4946+5087+8900
higher (2) +5087
highly (2) +4200+5087
in the presence of (2) +5584
inside (2)
inside (2) +1074
it^s (2) +9004
outside (2) +2575+4946
south (2) +2025+5582+9402
top (2) +4200+4946+5087
up (2) +4200+5087

very (2) +4200+5087
western (2) +3542
wherever (2) +9004
which way (2) +625
across (1)
advance (1) +7156
against (1)
along (1)
among (1)
annual (1) +3427+3427+4946
anywhere (1) +625+625+2025+2256
as far as (1)
at each successive level (1)
        +2025+4200+4200+5087+5087
away (1) +448+2021+2575
back^s (1) +9004
beyond (1) +5087
deep (1) +5087
depth (1) +4200+5087
down (1) +824
downstream (1) +4200+4946+5087
east (1) +928+4667+6298
east (1) +928+4667+6298+9087
east (1) +4667+6298
eastern (1) +7708
eastward (1) +2025+4667+7711
eastward (1) +4667
eastward (1) +7708
eastward (1) +7711
entered (1) +995
entering (1) +995
enters (1) +995
exceedingly (1) +4200+5087
extend eastward (1) +7708
extend out (1) +2575
extend westward (1) +3542
facing (1)
fail (1) +824+5877
get out of here (1) +2021+2575+8938
heights (1) +4200+5087
here (1) +2178
here^s (1) +5213
high above (1) +4200+4946+5087
higher than (1) +4200+5087+8049
in (1) +1074+2021
in ascending stages (1)
        +2025+4200+4200+5087+5087
inside^s (1) +9004
interior (1) +1074+4946
invade (1) +995+9004
inward (1) +1074
join (1)
magnificence (1) +5087
more (1) +4200+5087
more and more powerful (1)
        +1541+2143+2256+4200+5087+6330
northern (1) +4946+7600
older (1) +5087
on to (1)
onto (1)
outer (1) +4200+4946+5087
outside (1) +2667
outside (1) +7339
outside the family (1) +2021+2424+2575
over (1)
over and above (1) +4200+5087
overturned (1) +2200+4200+5087
pen up (1) +1074
project upward (1) +4200+5087
severe (1) +4200+5087
southeast (1) +2025+5582+7711
southeast (1) +5582+7711
the land^s (1) +9004
there^s (1) +824+4046
there^s (1) +928+9463
to (1) +9004
top (1) +4200+5087
top (1) +5087
top of (1) +4200+4946+5087
upstream (1) +4200+5087
upward (1) +4200+4946+5087

very (1) +4200+5087+6330
west (1) +5115
western[s] (1) +4667
when (1) +625+6330
where[s] (1) +7730
wherever (1) +625
wherever (1) +889+9004
wielding (1) +995+4200+5087
young and old (1) +2256+5087
untranslated (115)

2026 הֵא *hē'* (2)
here (1)
surely (1)

2027 הֶאָח *he'āḥ* (12)
Aha (11)
Ah (1)

2028 הָאֲחַשְׁתָּרִי *hā'aḥaštāriy* (1)
Haahashtari (1)

2029 הָאֱלִי *hā'ĕliy*
Variant; not used

2030 הָאֶלֶף *hā'elep̄* (1)
Haeleph (1)

2031 הָאַמָּה *hā'ammāh*
Variant; not used

2032 הָאָצֵל *hā'ēsel*
Variant; not used

2033 הָאַרְבַּע *hā'arba'*
Variant; not used

2034 הָאָרְרִי *hā'rāriy*
Variant; not used

2035 הַב1 *hab1* (33)
give (12)
ascribe (9)
come (5)
bring (2)
appoint (1)
choose (1)
do (1)
praise (1)
put (1)

2036 הַב2 *hab2*
Variant; not used

2037 הַבְהַב *habhab* (1)
given (1)

2038 הָבַל *hāb̄al* (5)
worthless (2)
fill with false hopes (1)
meaningless talk (1) +2039
take pride (1)

2039 הֶבֶל1 *hebel1* (73)
meaningless (34)
worthless idols (9)
breath (5)
in vain (5)
worthless (4)
dishonest (1)
empty talk (1)
fleeting (1)
futile (1)
futility (1)
less meaning (1) +8049
meaningless talk (1) +2038
mere breath (1)
no meaning (1)
nonsense (1)
utterly meaningless (1) +2039
utterly useless (1) +2256+8198
vapor (1)
without meaning (1) +928+2021
worthless idols (1) +8736

2040 הֶבֶל2 *hebel2* (8)
Abel (8)

2041 הָבְנִים *hob̄niym* (2)

ebony (1)
untranslated (1)

2042 הָבַר *hāb̄ar* (2)
astrologers (1) +9028
untranslated (1)

2043 הֵגֵא *hēgē'* (1)
Hegai (1)

2044 הַגִּדְגָּד *haggidḡād̄*
Variant; not used

2045 הַגְּדוֹלִים *hagged̄ôliym* (1)
Haggedolim (1)

2046 הַגּוֹיִם *haggôyim*
Variant; not used

2047 הָגָה1 *hāḡāh1* (25)
meditate (3)
plot (3)
growls (1)
lament (1)
meditates (1)
moan (1)
moan mournfully (1) +2047
moaned (1)
mutter (1)
mutters (1)
ponder (1)
speak (1)
speaks (1)
tell (1)
think (1)
utter (1)
utter a sound (1)
uttering (1)
utters (1)
weighs (1)

2048 הָגָה2 *hāḡāh2* (3)
remove (2)
drives out (1)

2049 הֶגֶה *hegeh* (3)
moan (1)
mourning (1)
rumbling (1)

2050 הָגוּת *hāḡût̄* (1)
utterance (1)

2051 הֵגַי *hēḡay* (3)
Hegai (3)

2052 הָגִיג *hāḡiyḡ* (2)
meditated (1)
sighing (1)

2053 הִגָּיוֹן *higḡāyôn* (4)
Higgaion (1)
meditation (1)
melody (1)
mutter (1)

2054 הָגִין *hāḡiyn* (1)
corresponding (1)

2055 הַגִּלְגָּל *haggilḡāl*
Variant; not used

2056 הַגָּן *haggān*
Variant; not used

2057 הָגָר *hāḡār* (12)
Hagar (11)
she[s] (1)

2058 הַגְרִי *haḡriy* (7)
Hagrites (4)
Hagri (2)
Hagrite (1)

2059 הֵד *hēd̄* (1)
joy (1)

2060 הֲדַד *hᵃd̄ad̄* (13)
Hadad (12)
untranslated (1)

2061 הֲדַדְעֶזֶר *hᵃd̄ad̄'ezer* (21)
Hadadezer (17)
Hadadezer's (2)
who[s] (2)

2062 הֲדַדְרִמּוֹן *hᵃd̄ad̄-rimmôn* (1)
Hadad Rimmon (1)

2063 הָדָה *hād̄āh* (1)
put (1)

2064 הֹדּוּ *hôddû* (2)
India (2)

2065 הֲדוּרִים *hᵃd̄ûriym* (1)
mountains (1)

2066 הֲדוֹרָם1 *hᵃd̄ôrām1* (2)
Hadoram (2)

2067 הֲדוֹרָם2 *hᵃd̄ôrām2* (2)
Adoniram (1)
Hadoram (1)

2068 הִדַּי *hidday* (1)
Hiddai (1)

2069 הֹדַיְוָהוּ *hôd̄aywāhû* (1)
untranslated (1)

2070 הָדַךְ *hād̄ak̄* (1)
crush (1)

2071 הֲדֹם *hᵃd̄ōm* (6)
footstool (5) +8079
footstool (1)

2072 הֲדַס *hᵃd̄as* (6)
myrtle trees (3)
myrtle (2)
myrtles (1)

2073 הֲדַסָּה *hᵃd̄assāh* (1)
Hadassah (1)

2074 הָדַף *hād̄ap̄* (11)
shoves (2)
depose (1)
drive out (1)
driven (1)
driven out (1)
push away (1)
push down (1)
shove (1)
thrusting out (1)
thwarts (1)

2075 הָדַר *hād̄ar* (6)
are shown respect (1) +7156
exalt yourself (1)
favoritism (1) +7156
show favoritism (1)
show respect (1)
splendor (1)

2076 הֲדַר *hᵃd̄ar*
Variant; not used

2077 הָדָר *hād̄ār* (30)
splendor (12)
majesty (10)
majestic (2)
blessing (1)
choice (1)
dignity (1)
glory (1)
honor (1)
nobles (1)

2078 הֶדֶר *hed̄er* (1)
splendor (1)

2079 הֲדָרָה *hᵃd̄ārāh* (5)
splendor (4)
glory (1)

2080 הֲדַרְעֶזֶר *hᵃd̄ar'ezer*
Variant; not used

2081 הָהּ *hāh* (1)
Alas (1)

2082 הוֹ *hô* (2)
anguish (1) +2082

2083 וּ *hû* (1)
it (1)

2084 ־הוּ *-hû* (1083)
him (484)
it (147)
his (137)
them (36)
he (20)
their (18)
its (13)
the[s] (10)
his own (6)
a[s] (4)
David[s] (4)
they (4)
which (4)
someone (3)
each (2)
Moses[s] (2)
Pekahiah[s] (2)
whose (2)
your (2)
Abram[s] (1)
Asahel's[s] (1)
Ben-Hadad[s] (1)
both of you (1) +2256+3870
Cyrus[s] (1)
God[s] (1)
idol[s] (1)
Joab[s] (1)
meal[s] (1)
my (1)
Nadab[s] (1)
one's (1)
that day[s] (1)
the altar[s] (1)
the child[s] (1)
the clouds[s] (1)
the idol[s] (1)
the inside[s] (1)
the lamb[s] (1)
the lion[s] (1)
thc manna[s] (1)
the mountain[s] (1)
the parties (1) +408+2256+8276
the stand[s] (1)
the water[s] (1)
their own (1)
theirs (1)
this (1)
together (1) +408+907+8276
who (1)
whom (1)
you (1)
untranslated (146)

2085 הוּא *hû'* (1888)
he (438)
that (379)
it (191)
she (82)
this (54)
they (40)
that is (34)
who (32)
himself (22)
that same (19)
one (11)
same (10)
which (9)
him (7)
his (6)
those (6)
these (4)
Jotham[s] (3)
the man[s] (3)
this city[s] (3)
Abram[s] (2)
all day long (2) +928+2021+2021+3427

far and wide (2) +2134+2256+4946
he[s] (2) +2021+2021+5883
its (2)
only[s] (2)
that man[s] (2)
that very (2)
the animal[s] (2)
the LORD[s] (2)
them (2)
what (2)
you (2)
again (1) +928+1685+2021+2021+7193
any[s] (1)
anyone (1)
at once (1) +928+2021+2021+3427
at once (1) +928+2021+2021+6961
Baal[s] (1)
Balaam[s] (1)
Beerah[s] (1)
daughter[s] (1)
David[s] (1)
death[s] (1)
each of us (1) +638+2256
Elah[s] (1)
Elijah[s] (1)
Elisha[s] (1)
else (1)
fire[s] (1)
Gaal[s] (1)
Gehazi[s] (1)
Hannah[s] (1)
he alone (1)
he himself (1)
herself (1)
it[s] (1) +2021+2021+5226
joy[s] (1)
let it be (1) +4027
man[s] (1)
mine (1)
my vow[s] (1)
Naaman[s] (1)
Naomi[s] (1)
other[s] (1)
priests[s] (1)
regular[s] (1)
Ruth[s] (1)
she's (1)
Shem[s] (1)
something[s] (1)
such (1)
that part[s] (1)
that person[s] (1)
that slave[s] (1)
that son[s] (1)
that's (1)
the city[s] (1)
the father[s] (1)
the key[s] (1)
the Makirites[s] (1)
the person[s] (1)
the prophet[s] (1)
the slave[s] (1)
the woman[s] (1)
then[s] (1) +928+2021+2021+3427
then[s] (1) +2021+2021+6961
things[s] (1)
this man[s] (1)
this same (1)
very (1)
which[s] (1)
who[s] (1)
whoever (1)
whose (1)
yet (1) +2021+2021+3427+6330
untranslated (444)

2086 1הוֹד *hôd1* (24)
splendor (10)
majesty (3)
glory (2)
honor (2)
proud (2)

authority (1)
best strength (1)
face (1)
glorious (1)
majestic (1)

2087 2הוֹד *hôd2* (1)
Hod (1)

2088 הוֹדְנָה *hôdwāh* (2)
Hodaviah (2)

2089 הוֹדַרְוְיָה *hôdawyāh* (3)
Hodaviah (3)

2090 הוֹדַרְוְיָהוּ *hôdawyāhû* (1)
Hodaviah (1)

2091 הוֹדִרְיָה *hôdiyyāh* (6)
Hodiah (5)
Hodiah's (1)

2092 1הָוָה *hāwāh1* (1)
fall (1)

2093 2הָוָה *hāwāh2* (5)
be (2)
become (1)
get (1)
lie (1)

2094 1הַוָּה *hawwāh1* (3)
craving (1)
desire (1)
evil desires (1)

2095 2הַוָּה *hawwāh2* (13)
destroying (2)
destruction (2)
ruin (2)
corrupt (1)
deadly (1)
destructive forces (1)
disaster (1)
malice (1)
malicious (1)
misery (1)

2096 הוֹוָה *hôāh* (3)
calamity (3)

2097 הוֹהָם *hôhām* (1)
Hoham (1)

2098 הוֹי *hôy* (51)
woe (36)
Alas (5)
come (4)
Ah (3)
oh (2)
awful (1) +1524

2099 הוֹלֵלוֹת *hôlēlôt* (4)
madness (4)

2100 הוֹלֵלוּת *hôlēlût* (1)
madness (1)

2101 הוּם *hûm* (4)
distraught (1)
shook (1)
stirred (1)
throng (1)

2102 הוֹמָם *hômām* (1)
Homam (1)

2103 הוּן *hûn* (1)
thinking it easy (1)

2104 הוֹן *hôn* (26)
wealth (15)
enough (2)
wealth of goods (2)
money (1)
pittance (1) +4202
possessions (1)
rich (1)
riches (1)
treasures (1)

valuable things (1) +3701

2105 הוֹר *hôr*
Variant; not used

2106 הוֹשָׁמָע *hôšāmā'* (1)
Hoshama (1)

2107 הוֹשֵׁעַ *hôšēa'* (16)
Hoshea (12)
Hosea (2)
him[s] (1)
Joshua (1)

2108 הוֹשַׁעְיָה *hôša'yāh* (3)
Hoshaiah (3)

2109 הוּת *hût* (1)
assault (1)

2110 הוֹתִיר *hôṯiyr* (2)
Hothir (2)

2111 הָזָה *hāzāh* (1)
dream (1)

2112 הַחִירוֹת *hahiyrôṯ*
Variant; not used

2113 הִי *hiy* (1)
woe (1)

2114 ־הִי *-hiy* (1)
his (1)

2115 הִיא *hiy'*
Variant; not used

2116 הֵידָד *hêydāḏ* (7)
shouts of joy (3)
shout (1)
shout in triumph (1) +6702
shouting (1)
shouts (1)

2117 הָיְדוֹת *huyy'ḏôṯ* (1)
songs of thanksgiving (1)

2118 הָיָה *hāyāh* (3577)
be (715)
was (305)
came (165)
become (164)
were (159)
is (97)
been (77)
are (76)
became (59)
had (50) +4200
have (48) +4200
come (26)
happened (26)
will (19)
am (17)
had (16)
happen (16)
have (16)
remain (14)
lived (12) +3427
belong to (11) +4200
has (11)
hold (10)
becomes (9)
fall (9)
comes (8)
lived (8)
remained (8)
set (8)
go (7)
bring (6)
continue (6)
done (6)
fell (6)
has (6) +4200
lie (6)
made (6)
serve (6)
went (6)

belonged to (5) +4200
bring (5) +4200
consider (5) +4200
ended (5) +9362
fallen (5)
has (5) +928
left (5)
marry (5) +851+4200
stay (5)
stayed (5)
belongs to (4) +4200
endure (4)
included (4)
keep (4)
last (4)
leave (4)
numbered (4)
one day (4) +2256
rest (4)
spread (4)
took place (4)
touch (4) +928
appears (3)
coming (3)
end (3) +9362
ending (3) +9362
extend (3)
given (3)
keep (3) +4200
kept (3)
lay (3)
make (3)
married (3) +851+4200
may (3)
put (3)
stand (3)
taken (3)
use (3)
used (3)
wear (3) +6584
agree (2) +285+3869
allotted (2) +1598
applies (2)
arose (2)
bind (2) +3213+4200
brought (2)
come what may (2) +4537
connecting (2)
did (2)
do (2)
extended (2)
follow (2) +339
fulfilled (2)
get (2)
help (2) +6640
lies (2)
living (2)
lying (2)
occur (2)
overwhelmed (2) +928+4202+6388+8120
owned (2) +5238
preceded (2) +4200+7156
reached (2)
receive (2) +4200
regard as (2) +4200
rule (2) +6584
serve as (2)
served (2)
settled (2)
sold for (2) +928
spent (2)
struck (2) +928
take place (2)
turn to (2)
turned into (2) +4200
use (2) +4200
wear (2)
abound (1) +7172
acquired (1) +4200
act (1)
allotted (1) +928+1598+2021

amount to (1)
amounted to (1)
appear (1)
appear (1) +928+3869+6524
appeared (1)
apply (1)
aroused (1) +6584
arranged (1) +4595
attach (1)
be (1) +2118
be treated as (1)
become (1) +4200
becoming (1)
began (1)
beginning (1)
being (1)
belong (1)
belong to (1) +928
belonged to (1) +448
belonging to (1) +4200
belongs (1)
bring about (1) +928
brings (1)
broke out (1)
brought about (1) +4946
brought with (1) +928+3338
came (1) +2118
came into being (1)
came on (1)
came to (1)
came to be (1)
carried by (1) +6584
caught (1)
cause (1) +4946
certainly come true (1) +2118
come into being (1) +2118
comes of (1)
committed (1)
company (1) +907
compare with (1) +3869
complete (1) +4946+7891
condemn (1) +2631+4200
conferred (1) +1821
consist of (1)
continued (1) +2143
controlled (1) +4200
could not (1) +6584
count (1) +4200
covered (1) +928
decide (1) +6584+7023
decided (1) +4213+6640
designate (1)
do that[s] (1) +928+2257+3338
downcast (1) +4200
drove back (1) +6584
earlier (1)
end (1) +340+928+2021
ends (1)
endure (1) +4200
engaged in (1)
escapes (1) +7129
exhausted (1)
exists (1)
extending (1)
fared (1)
feared (1) +3007
fighting with (1) +907
filled (1) +928+3972
find (1)
follow (1)
followed (1) +339
formed (1)
fulfilled (1) +4027
future (1) +4537+8611
gain support (1) +907+3338
gained (1)
give (1)
give (1) +4200
give shelter (1) +6261
goes (1) +8079
gone (1)

gone (1) +928+4202
got (1) +4200
grew worse and worse (1)
    +2617+2716+4394
had (1) +928
had (1) +6584
had chance (1) +928+3338
had part in (1) +4946
had to (1) +6584
happening (1)
happens (1)
harbor (1) +4222+6640
harbored (1) +4200
has (1) +6640
have (1) +928
have (1) +1068
have (1) +6584
having (1) +4200
help (1) +907
help (1) +4200
hold (1) +928+3338
holds (1) +928+3338
in office (1)
inclined (1) +2296
include (1)
increase (1)
incurs (1)
inherit (1) +448
into marry (1) +4200
join (1) +928
joined (1)
lasted (1)
led the way (1) +3338+8037
left (1) +4200
lend (1)
let (1)
life (1) +889+3427
looked (1) +928+6524
made angry (1) +7911
made fall (1) +4200+4842
make sport of (1) +4200+5442
making (1)
married (1) +851
married to (1) +851+4200
marries (1) +408+2118+4200
marries (1) +408+4200
marries (1) +4200
marry (1) +408+4200
marry into (1) +4200
mattered (1)
mount (1) +4853
moved (1)
observe (1)
occurred (1)
once (1)
owes (1)
own (1) +4200
participate in (1) +448
passed (1)
predecessor (1) +889+4200+7156
prepare (1) +3922
produced (1)
proper place (1) +889+5226+9004
propertys (1) +889+4200
prove to be (1)
proved to be (1)
provided for (1) +430+2256+4200+4312
raise (1)
raised (1)
reached (1) +928
reaching (1)
ready (1)
rebel (1) +5308
received (1)
received (1) +4200
regard (1) +4200+7156
remain unmarried (1)
    +408+1194+4200+4200+6328
remains (1)
required (1)
rested (1)

restored (1)
retains (1)
retains (1) +4200
ruled (1) +4889
run (1)
seem (1)
seem (1) +928+6524
seemed (1)
seemed (1) +928+6524
sell for (1) +928
serve (1) +4200
serve (1) +4200+7156
served (1) +4200+7156
served as (1)
serving (1)
share (1) +4200
shed (1)
shine (1) +240
show (1) +4200
shows to be (1) +4200
sprang up (1)
standing (1)
start (1)
started (1)
staying (1)
steals forth (1)
stretched (1)
strike (1)
strike (1) +928
striking (1) +928
suffer (1)
suffered (1) +928
suffered (1) +4200
supply (1) +4200
supported (1) +339
supported (1) +907+3338
surely become (1) +2118
surely take place (1)
surround (1) +4946+6017
take (1)
take (1) +4200
take care of (1) +4200+5466
take care of (1) +6125
take command (1) +4200+5464
take hold of (1) +928
take the place of (1) +9393
tasted (1)
taught (1) +3723
tend livestock (1) +408+5238
tended livestock (1) +408+5238
testify (1) +6332
took care of (1) +6125
touches (1) +6584
treated (1)
treated (1) +6640
treating (1)
turn against (1) +4200+8477
turned (1)
turned out (1)
unite (1) +3480+4200+4222
unmarried (1) +408+4200+4202
used to (1)
using (1)
wants (1)
was altogether (1) +2118
was committed (1)
wasn't (1) +4202
weighed (1)
went over (1) +6017
when (1) +4946
with (1) +928
work (1)
you (1)
untranslated (887)

2119 הַיָּה *hayyāh* (1)
untranslated (1)

2120 הֵיךְ *hēyk* (2)
how (2)

2121 הֵיכָל *hēykāl* (80)

temple (54)
outer sanctuary (7)
palace (7)
main hall (6)
palaces (4)
sanctuary (1)
temples (1)

2122 הֵילֵל *hēylēl* (1)
morning star (1)

2123 הֵימָם *hēymām* (1)
Homam (1)

2124 הֵימָן *hēymān* (17)
Heman (16)
hiss (1)

2125 הִין *hiyn* (22)
hin (22)

2126 הַיַּרְקוֹן *hayyarqôn*
Variant; not used

2127 הַיְשִׁימוֹת *hayšiymôt*
Variant; not used

2128 הָכַר *hākar*
Variant; not used

2129 הַכָּרָה *hakkārāh* (1)
look (1)

2130 הַכֶּרֶם *hakkerem*
Variant; not used

2131 הַל *hal*
Variant; not used

2132 הֲלֹא *hᵉlō'*
Variant; not used

2133 הָלָא *hālā'* (1)
driven away (1)

2134 הָלְאָה *hāl'āh* (16)
on (4)
beyond (2) +2256+4946
far and wide (2) +2085+2256+4946
beyond (1) +4200+4946
beyond (1) +4946
continuing (1)
forward (1)
on the other side of (1) +2256+4946+6298
outside (1) +4946
some distance away (1)
way (1)

2135 הַלּוֹחֵשׁ *hallôhēš* (2)
Hallohesh (2)

2136 הִלּוּלִים *hillûliym* (2)
festival (1)
offering of praise (1)

2137 הַלָּז *hallāz* (7)
this (3)
that (2)
the (1)
there's (1)

2138 הַלָּזֶה *hallāzeh* (3)
that (2)
this (1)

2139 הַלֵּזוּ *hallēzû*
Variant; not used

2140 הַלַּחְמִי *hallahmiy*
Variant; not used

2141 הָלִיךְ *hāliyk* (1)
path (1)

2142 הֲלִיכָה *hᵉliykāh* (7)
procession (2)
affairs (1)
traveling merchants (1)
way (1)
ways (1)
untranslated (1)

2143 הָלַךְ *hālak* (1556)

go (327)
went (171)
come (94)
walk (87)
walked (38)
left (32)
gone (29)
followed (27) +339
follow (22) +928
follow (20) +339
going (15)
moved (15)
set out (15)
led (14)
came (11)
went away (11)
followed (10) +928
take (10)
walking (10)
went out (9)
walks (8)
go about (7)
go back (7)
goes (7)
leave (7)
continue (6)
continued (6)
following (6) +339
live (6)
go out (5)
left (5) +4946
marched (5)
returned (5)
run (5)
traveled (5)
went off (5)
went on (5)
brought (4)
coming (4)
fled (4)
go (4) +2256+8740
go away (4)
go off (4)
lead (4)
leave (4) +4946
left (4) +907+4946
be (3)
did^s (3)
follow (3)
followed (3)
follows (3) +928
go ahead (3)
going about (3)
grow (3)
on way (3)
ran (3)
taking (3)
wandered (3)
withdrew (3)
advanced (2)
away (2)
bandit (2)
be on way (2)
became more and more powerful (2)
        +1524+2143+2256
been (2)
began (2)
carry (2)
departs (2)
disappears (2)
done^s (2)
flow (2)
flowed (2)
get (2)
get out (2)
go (2) +2143
go now (2) +995
go way (2)
goes about (2)
going back (2)

going back and forth (2)
gossip (2) +8215
leader (2) +4200+7156
leads away (2)
leave (2) +907+4946
make a survey of (2) +928
march (2)
marched out (2)
marching (2)
minister (2)
move (2)
moved about (2)
remain (2)
return (2)
rode (2)
sent (2)
set sail (2)
spread (2)
stay (2)
took (2)
travel (2)
walk about (2)
way (2)
weak as (2)
went on way (2)
went over (2)
went up (2)
were on way (2)
about (1)
accompanied (1) +907
accompanied by (1) +6640
accompany (1) +4200+5584
advances (1)
all the way (1)
all this time (1)
associates (1)
attended by (1) +4200+8079
banish (1)
be on way (1) +2256+5825
became more and more powerful (1)
        +1524+2256
blows (1)
by all means go (1) +995
came back (1) +995+2256
cause to walk (1)
climbed up (1)
closer and closer (1) +2256+7929
comes (1)
commit (1) +928
committed (1) +928
concern (1)
conduct (1)
consult (1) +448
continued (1) +2118
continued to grow (1)
course (1)
crawl (1)
depart (1)
departed (1)
deported (1)
devoted to (1)
devoted to (1) +339
disappeared (1) +4946+6524
dispersed (1) +2006+4200
do not know where am going (1)
        +889+2143+6584
drive (1)
driven (1)
drove back (1)
enabled to walk (1)
entered (1) +6330
escape (1)
escorted (1)
exiled (1)
fade away (1)
faithful (1) +622+928
flashed back and forth (1)
flashed down (1)
fleeing (1)
fleet of trading ships (1) +641+4200+9576
fleet of trading ships (1) +641+9576

floated (1)
flowing (1)
flows (1)
flows away (1)
flying (1)
follow (1) +928+8079
follow along (1)
followers (1) +339
followers (1) +408+889+6640
freely strut (1)
get away (1)
get back (1)
get rid of (1)
go (1) +928+2006
go (1) +995
go aside (1)
go at once (1) +995+2256
go at once (1) +2143
go forward (1)
go in (1) +995+2256
go on (1)
go on way (1)
go over (1)
go to and fro (1)
go up (1)
goes down (1)
goes out (1) +2143
goes to and fro (1)
going around (1)
going off (1)
gone (1) +2143
gone away (1)
gone off (1) +2143
gone up (1)
greedy (1) +339
grew even wilder (1) +2256+6192
grew louder and louder (1)
        +2256+2618+4394
grew stronger and stronger (1) +2256+2618
grew stronger and stronger (1) +2256+7997
grew weaker and weaker (1) +1924+2256
have go (1)
hurry (1) +4559
increased more and more (1)
        +2143+2256+8041
invaded (1) +4200
join (1) +6584
join (1) +6640
journey (1)
journeyed (1)
keep (1) +928
keep on (1)
keeping all the way (1) +2143
kept (1)
kept (1) +928
kept coming (1) +2143
kept on (1)
kept on (1) +8743
lead (1) +4200+7156
lead life (1) +928
lead on (1) +2256+5627
leading (1)
leads (1)
leads a life (1)
leave (1) +4946+6640
leave (1) +4946+6643
leaves (1) +907+4946
leaving (1)
led (1) +339
led life (1) +928
left (1) +4946+6640
live (1) +928
lived (1)
made walk (1)
made way (1)
make flow (1)
man^s (1)
marches (1)
melting away (1) +2256+4570
more and more powerful (1)
        +1541+2025+2256+4200+5087+6330

moved back and forth (1)
moves (1)
moves about (1)
moves along (1)
moving (1)
moving about (1)
moving from place to place (1)
moving from place to place (1)
                    +889+928+2143
near (1) +907
neared (1) +725
obey (1) +928
off (1)
passed away (1)
passing (1)
persisted (1)
proceed (1)
proceeded (1)
prowled (1)
prowling (1)
pursue (1) +339
pursued (1) +339
pursuing (1) +339
ran down (1)
receded steadily (1) +2256+8740+8740
rejoined (1) +448
resort to (1) +4200+7925
return (1) +995
return (1) +2256+7155
return (1) +8740
ride (1) +928
rides (1)
roam (1) +2256+3718
roamed (1)
rode off (1)
rougher and rougher (1) +2256+6192
roving (1)
runs along (1)
sail (1) +641+928+2021
sending (1)
sending on (1)
set off (1)
shining ever brighter (1) +239+2256
slanderer (1) +8215
stalks (1)
stream (1)
surely leave (1) +2143+4946+6584
sweep (1)
take back (1)
take part (1) +6640
take possession (1)
take turns (1) +3427
taken (1)
them^s (1) +2021
took (1) +1583
took to (1)
travel along (1)
traveled (1) +2006
travelers (1) +5986
traveling (1)
tripping along with mincing steps (1)
                    +2256+3262
trudge (1)
turned (1)
turning (1)
use (1) +448
very well go (1) +2143
walk (1) +928+2006
walk continually (1)
walked along (1)
walked along (1) +2143
walked around (1)
walked back and forth (1)
walked on (1)
walking along (1)
walking along (1) +2143
walking around (1)
walks around (1)
wanders (1)
ways (1)
went (1) +2143

went about (1)
went along (1) +2143
went around (1)
went back (1)
went down (1)
went forth (1)
went forward (1)
went home (1)
went in (1)
went out (1) +2143
will^s (1)
with (1)
withdraw (1)
withdrew (1) +4946
untranslated (78)

2144 הֵלֶךְ *hēlek* (2)
oozing out (1)
traveler (1)

2145 הָלַל1 *hālal1* (4)
radiance (1)
shone (1)
show (1)
throws out flashes (1)

2146 הָלַל2 *hālal2* (146)
praise (89)
boast (11)
praised (7)
worthy of praise (6)
boasts (4)
glory (4)
give praise (3)
praises (3)
be praised (2)
praising (2)
bring praise (1)
cheering (1)
extol (1)
exult (1)
gave thanks (1)
giving praise (1)
had wedding songs (1)
is praised (1)
make boast (1)
renown (1)
sang (1)
sang praises (1)
sing praise (1)
sing praises (1)
that purpose^s (1)

2147 הָלַל3 *hālal3* (16)
arrogant (3)
go mad (2)
makes fools of (2)
acted like a madman (1)
boast (1)
drive furiously (1)
foolish (1)
gone mad (1)
mock (1)
rail (1)
storm (1)
turns into a fool (1)

2148 הִלֵּל *hillēl* (2)
Hillel (2)

2149 הַלְלוּיָהּ *har'lûyāh*
Variant; not used

2150 הָלַם *hālam* (8)
beat (1)
laid low (1)
smashed (1)
strike (1)
strikes (1)
struck (1)
thundered (1)
trampled down (1)

2151 הֲלֹם *hᵃlōm* (12)
here (4)

this far (2) +6330
in all directions (1)
now (1)
over here (1)
to (1)
untranslated (2)

2152 הֵלֶם *hēlem* (1)
Helem (1)

2153 הַלְמוּת *halmût* (1)
hammer (1)

2154 הָם1 *hām1* (1)
Ham (1)

2155 הָם2 *hām2* (1)
wealth (1)

2156 הֵם *hēm* (562)
they (321)
those (39)
them (14)
these (13)
that (10)
who (6)
it (5)
themselves (4)
things^s (3)
men^s (2)
such^s (2)
the gatekeepers^s (2)
this (2)
all^s (1)
his net^s (1)
Israelites^s (1)
our own^s (1)
people^s (1)
the (1)
the Benjamites^s (1)
the Israelites^s (1)
the others^s (1)
the people^s (1)
the places^s (1)
the priests^s (1)
the spies^s (1)
their idols^s (1)
those same (1)
yet (1) +2021+2021+3427+6330
you (1)
untranslated (122)

2157 הֶם *-hem* (3048)
them (1103)
their (915)
they (116)
the^s (54)
their (35) +4200
themselves (27)
their own (20)
those (18)
the people^s (11)
it (9)
these (7)
whose (7)
men^s (6)
who (6)
her (5)
his (5)
its (5)
their own (5) +4200
theirs (4)
which (4)
whom (4)
him (3)
Israel^s (3)
Moses and Aaron^s (3)
my people^s (3)
the idols^s (3)
the Israelites^s (3)
theirs (3) +4200
a^s (2)
each (2)
its own (2)

peoples (2)
the (2)
the Gibeonitess (2)
the Hagritess (2)
the postss (2)
thems (2) +4053
theses (2)
you (2)
your (2)
boths (1)
doing sos (1)
each others (1) +9109
Elijah and Elishas (1) +9109
enemiess (1)
his descendantss (1)
his followerss (1)
his preceptss (1)
Israelitess (1)
its (1)
itself (1)
loverss (1)
man'ss (1)
my accuserss (1)
nephews (1) +1201
officialss (1)
one kind after another (1) +4200+5476
ones (1) +4200
others (1) +4946
people from Benjamin (1) +278
people from Judah (1) +278
priestss (1) +278
relateds (1)
such thingss (1)
that (1)
the Ammonitess (1)
the bodiess (1)
the brotherss (1)
the cherubims (1)
the Egyptianss (1)
the envoyss (1)
the gatekeeperss (1)
the heavenss (1)
the Hebronitess (1)
the Kohathites (1)
the Levitess (1)
the man and the womans (1)
the mens (1)
the messengerss (1)
the Philistiness (1)
the potss (1)
the processions (1)
the seas (1)
the shepherdss (1)
the spiess (1)
the standss (1)
the storehousess (1) +889+928+3972
the storeroomss (1)
the waters (1)
their (1) +448
their (1) +928+4090
their (1) +4946
their (1) +6584
their own (1) +7156
theirs (1) +4946
thems (1) +466
thems (1) +8533
themselves (1) +7156
theres (1) +928
theres (1) +6584
these dayss (1)
these mens (1)
these thingss (1)
this threats (1)
thornss (1)
those Israelitess (1)
us (1) +2256+3276
wheres (1) +6584
womens (1)
your troopss (1)
untranslated (567)

2158 הַמְּדָתָא *hamm‛dātā’* (5)

Hammedatha (5)

2159 הָמָה *hāmāh* (34)
roar (5)
disturbed (3)
laments (3)
loud (2)
rage (2)
roaring (2)
snarling (2)
astir (1)
brawler (1)
bustles about (1)
cry out (1)
groaned (1)
growl (1)
in uproar (1)
moaning (1)
noise (1) +7754
noisy (1)
pound (1)
pounds (1)
raging (1)
tumult (1)
yearns (1)

2160 הֵמָּה *hēmmāh*
Variant; not used

2161 ־הֵמָה *-hēmāh* (1)
thes (1)

2162 הָמוֹן *hāmôn* (84)
hordes (18)
army (11)
crowd (7)
wealth (5)
many (4)
all (2) +3972
commotion (2)
masses (2)
multitudes (2)
noise (2)
noisy (2)
roar (2)
vast army (2)
abundance (1)
army (1) +2657
clamor (1)
confusion (1)
great amount (1)
heavy (1)
its (1) +2021
large (1)
multitude (1)
people (1)
populace (1)
raging (1)
roaring (1)
rumble (1)
tenderness (1) +5055
throng (1)
thunder (1)
troops (1)
tumult (1)
turmoil (1)
uproar (1) +7754
untranslated (2)

2163 הֲמוֹן גּוֹג *h‛môn gôg* (2)
Hamon Gog (2)

2164 הֲמוֹנָה *h‛mônāh* (1)
Hamonah (1)

2165 הַמַּחְלְקוֹת *hammahl‛qôt*
Variant; not used

2166 הֶמְיָה *hemyāh* (1)
noise (1)

2167 הֲמֻלָּה *h‛mullāh* (2)
storm (1)
tumult (1) +7754

2168 הַמֹּלֶכֶת *hammōleket* (1)
Hammoleketh (1)

Hammedatha (5)

2169 1הָמַם *hāmam1* (17)
routed (3)
threw into confusion (2)
drives over (1)
eliminated (1)
resounds (1)
rout (1)
ruin (1)
threw into a panic (1)
throw into confusion (1)
throwing into confusion (1) +4539
thrown into confusion (1)
troubling (1)
untranslated (2)

2170 2הָמַם *hāmam2*
Variant; not used

2171 הָמַן *hāman* (1)
unruly (1)

2172 הָמָן *hāmān* (54)
Haman (43)
Haman's (5)
hes (5)
untranslated (1)

2173 הֲמָסִים *h‛māsiym* (1)
twigs (1)

2174 הַמִּצְפֶּה *hammispeh*
Variant; not used

2175 הַמַּרְכָּבוֹת *hammarkābôt*
Variant; not used

2176 1הֵן *hēn1* (100)
if (15)
but (7)
surely (7)
see (6)
look (4)
now (4)
when (4)
since (2)
though (2)
yet (2)
agreed (1)
but if (1)
even (1)
for (1)
full well (1)
heres (1)
oh (1)
only (1)
what if (1)
untranslated (38)

2177 ־הֵן *-hen* (183)&
their (77)
them (46)
they (8)
thes (3)
it (2)
its (2)
their (2) +4200
their own (2)
boths (1)
lead to do the sames (1) +339+466+2388
the girlss (1)
the roomss (1)
the woman and her sisters (1)
theirs (1)
theses (1)
things (1)
wheres (1) +928
which (1)
whichs (1)
untranslated (30)

2178 1הֵנָּה *hēnnāh1* (51)
here (25)
lefts (2)
now (2)
rights (2)
back and forth (1) +285+285+2178+2256

here (1) +2025
here (1) +6330
in any direction (1) +2178+2256
nearby (1)
on this side (1)
opposite (1)
since (1) +6330
the present time (1)
then (1)
there (1)
this (1)
this day^s (1)
thus far (1) +6330
toward it (1)
yet (1) +6330
untranslated (2)

2179 הֵנָּה2 *hēnnāh2* (47)
they (8)
these (5)
them (4)
things^s (2)
those (2)
both (1)
cows^s (1)
given even more (1)
              +2179+2256+3578+3869+3869
people^s (1)
plans^s (1)
such (1)
their (1) +4200
themselves (1)
what is the meaning (1) +4537
untranslated (16)

2180 הִנֵּה *hinnēh* (1061)
see (81)
look (61)
here (57)
there (57)
saw (43)
now (33)
if (28)
surely (24)
found (12)
yes (9)
how (6)
indeed (6)
listen (6)
suddenly (6)
but (5)
this (4)
beware (3)
even (3)
that (3)
already (2)
appeared (2)
as soon as (2)
discovered (2)
just (2)
just then (2) +2256
remember (2)
so (2)
suppose (2)
very well (2)
very well then (2)
what (2)
when (2)
after all (1)
all at once (1) +2296
be sure (1)
behold (1)
certainly (1)
come (1)
come then (1)
consider (1)
for (1)
heard (1)
here now (1)
it is still there (1)
just as (1)
meanwhile (1)

nevertheless (1)
not (1)
now then (1)
ready (1)
ready to do (1)
realized (1)
right now (1)
showed (1)
since (1)
soon (1)
suddenly appeared (1)
sure (1)
surely (1) +3954
then (1)
therefore (1)
think (1)
this is how (1)
this is why (1)
though (1)
too (1)
unless (1)
very well (1) +5528
well (1)
what can do (1)
untranslated (550)

2181 הֵנָה *-hᵉnāh* (3)&
its (1)
them (1)
they (1)

2182 הֲנָחָה *hᵃnāḥāh* (1)
holiday (1)

2183 הִנֹּם *hinnōm* (3)
Hinnom (3)

2184 הֵנַע *hēnaʿ* (3)
Hena (3)

2185 הֲנָפָה *hᵃnāpāh*
Variant; not used

2186 הַנֶּקֶב *hanneqeb*
Variant; not used

2187 הַס *has* (7)
be silent (2)
be still (2)
hush (1)
quiet (1)
silence (1)

2188 הָסָה *hāsāh* (1)
silenced (1)

2189 הַסְּנָאָה *hassᵉnāʾāh* (1)
Hassenaah (1)

2190 הַסְּנֻאָה *hassᵉnuʾāh* (2)
Hassenuah (2)

2191 הַסֹּפֶרֶת *hassōperet* (1)
Hassophereth (1)

2192 הָעֲבָרִים *hāʿᵃbāriym*
Variant; not used

2193 הָעֵזֶר *hāʿēzer*
Variant; not used

2194 הָעַמֹּנִי *hāʿammōniy*
Variant; not used

2195 הָעֵמֶק *hāʿēmeq*
Variant; not used

2196 הָעֲרָבָה *hāʿᵃrābāh*
Variant; not used

2197 הָעֲרָלוֹת *hāʿᵃrālōt*
Variant; not used

2198 הֲפֻגָה *hᵃpugāh* (1)
relief (1)

2199 הַפּוּךְ *happûk*
Variant; not used

2200 הָפַךְ *hāpak* (94)
turned (21)

turn (8)
overthrew (5)
changed (4)
overthrow (4)
be changed (2)
be turned (2)
turned back (2)
was changed (2)
wheel around (2) +3338
are (1)
be brought (1)
be overturned (1)
been turned over (1)
came tumbling (1)
change (1)
changed (1) +337
deceitful (1)
devastate (1)
distort (1)
disturbed (1)
flashing back and forth (1)
got down (1)
is transformed (1)
lays bare (1)
left (1)
overcome (1)
overthrown (1)
overthrows (1)
overturn (1)
overturned (1) +2025+4200+5087
overturns (1)
overwhelm (1)
purify (1) +1359
restore (1)
routed (1) +6902
swirl (1)
takes shape (1)
the tables were turned (1)
turn into (1)
turned about (1) +3338
turned and became (1)
turned around (1)
turned into (1)
turned over (1)
turning (1)
turns (1)
unreliable (1)
was overcome (1)
was overthrown (1)
was sapped (1)
was turned (1)

2201 הֵפֶךְ *hēpek* (3)
opposite (1)
turn upside down (1)
very opposite (1)

2202 הֲפֵכָה *hᵃpēkāh* (1)
catastrophe (1)

2203 הֲפַכְפַּךְ *hᵃpakpak* (1)
devious (1)

2204 הַפִּצֵץ *happisṣēs* (1)
Happizzez (1)

2205 הֻצַּב *hussab*
Variant; not used

2206 הַצֹּבֵבָה *hassōbēbāh* (1)
Hazzobebah (1)

2207 הַצְּבָרִים *hassᵉbāyim*
Variant; not used

2208 הַצָּלָה *hassālāh* (1)
deliverance (1)

2209 הַצְּלֶלְפּוֹנִי *hassᵉlelpôniy* (1)
Hazzelelponi (1)

2210 הֹצֶן *hōsen* (1)
weapons (1)

2211 הַצֻּרִים *hassuriym*
Variant; not used

2212 הַקּוֹץ *haqqôs* (5)
Hakkoz (5)

2213 הַקּוֹרֵא *haqqôrē'*
Variant; not used

2214 הַקָּטָן *haqqātān* (1)
Hakkatan (1)

2215 הַר *har* (560)
mountains (143)
mount (119)
mountain (114)
hill country (82)
hills (40)
hill (32)
mountain shrines (4)
mountaintops (4) +8031
it^s (3) +2021
another^s (1) +2021+2296+4946
hillside (1)
hillside (1) +7521
hilltop (1)
hilltop (1) +8031
hilltops (1) +8031
it^s (1) +1628
mountain clefts (1)
mountain haunts (1)
mountain regions (1)
mountaintop (1) +8031
range (1)
there (1) +928+2021
there^s (1) +928+2021
untranslated (5)

2216 הֹר *hōr* (12)
Hor (12)

2217 הָרָא *hārā'* (1)
Hara (1)

2218 הָרֹאֶה *hārō'eh* (1)
Haroeh (1)

2219 הַרְאֵל *har'ēl* (1)
altar hearth (1)

2220 הַרְבָּה *harbāh*
Variant; not used

2221 הַרְבֵּה *harbēh* (50)
much (10)
many (8)
great (4)
great quantity (4) +4394
more (3)
quantities (2)
abundance (1)
abundance (1) +4394
abundant supply (1)
all (1)
extensive (1)
full (1)
great (1) +4394
great numbers (1) +4394
greatly (1)
greatly (1) +4394
large (1)
large amount (1) +4394
large number (1)
overrighteous (1) +7404
overwicked (1) +8399
seldom (1) +4202
so much (1)
very (1) +4394
wept bitterly (1) +1134+1135

2222 הָרַג *hārag* (167)
killed (53)
kill (46)
slain (9)
put to death (7)
killing (6)
murdered (4)
slay (4)
kills (3)

put (3)
destroyed (2)
slaughter (2)
slayer (2)
be killed (1)
be ravaged (1)
been killed (1)
destroy (1)
destroying (1)
executed (1)
face death (1)
murder (1)
murderer (1)
murderers (1)
murdering (1)
murders (1)
must certainly put to death (1) +2222
put to death (1) +2222
put to death (1) +4638
ravage (1)
slaughter (1) +4200+5422
slaughter takes place (1) +2223
slaughtered (1)
slaughtering (1)
slew (1)
untranslated (3)

2223 הֶרֶג *hereg* (5)
slaughter (2)
killed (1)
killing (1)
slaughter takes place (1) +2222

2224 הֲרֵגָה *hᵃrēgāh* (5)
slaughter (5)

2225 הָרָה *hārāh* (45)
conceived (16)
pregnant (16)
conceive (7)
with child (2)
conceives (1)
gave birth (1)
is born (1)
untranslated (1)

2226 הָרֶה *hāreh* (12)
pregnant (7)
with child (2)
enlarged (1)
expectant mothers (1)
pregnant women (1)

2227 הָרֻם *hārûm* (1)
Harum (1)

2228 הֵרוֹן *hērôn* (1)
childbearing (1)

2229 הֲרוֹרִי *hᵃrôriy* (1)
Harorite (1)

2230 הָרִיָּה *hāriyyāh* (1)
pregnant women (1)

2231 הֵרָיוֹן *hērāyôn* (2)
conceive (1)
conception (1)

2232 הֲרִיסָה *hᵃriysāh* (1)
ruins (1)

2233 הֲרִיסוּת *hᵃriysût* (1)
waste (1)

2234 הָרֶם *hārām*
Variant; not used

2235 הֹרָם *hōrām* (1)
Horam (1)

2236 הַרְמוֹן *harmôn* (1)
Harmon (1)

2237 הָרָן *hārān* (7)
Haran (7)

2238 הָרַס *hāras* (43)
tear down (7)

overthrow (3)
tears down (3)
broken down (2)
destroyed (2)
force way through (2)
in ruins (2)
torn down (2)
are torn down (1)
be overturned (1)
been broken down (1)
being destroyed (1)
break (1)
break down (1)
demolish (1)
demolished (1)
destroy (1)
is destroyed (1)
laid waste (1) +2256+2990
left in ruins (1)
must demolish (1) +2238
ousted (1)
overthrew (1)
overthrown (1)
pull down (1)
threw down (1)
was destroyed (1)

2239 הֶרֶס *heres* (1)
destruction (1)

2240 הֲרָרִי *hᵃrāriy* (5)
Hararite (5)

2241 הַשַּׁחַר *haššahar*
Variant; not used

2242 הַשִּׁטָּה *haššittāh*
Variant; not used

2243 הַשִּׁטִּים *haššittiym*
Variant; not used

2244 הָשֵׁם *hāšēm* (1)
Hashem (1)

2245 הַשְׁמָעוּת *hašmā'ût* (1)
news (1) +265

2246 הַתַּאֲוָה *hata'ᵃwāh*
Variant; not used

2247 הִתּוּךְ *hitûk* (1)
melted (1)

2248 הִתְחַבְּרוּת *hithabbᵉrût*
Variant; not used

2249 הִתְיַחֵשׂ *hityahēś*
Variant; not used

2250 הַתִּיכוֹן *hatiykôn*
Variant; not used

2251 הֲתָךְ *hᵃtāk* (4)
Hathach (3)
him^s (1)

2252 הָתַל *hātal* (1)
taunt (1)

2253 הֲתֻלִּים *hᵃtuliym* (1)
mockers (1)

2254 הָתַת *hātat*
Variant; not used

2255 ו *w*
Variant; not used

2256 וְ *wᵉ-* (50531)
and (19275)
but (1877)
then (1821)
so (1179)
or (931)
when (596)
with (333)
also (251)
now (246)
so that (236)

led in campaigns (2) +995+3655+4200+7156
led on military campaigns (2) +995+3655
neither (2)
nevertheless (2) +219
ninety-nine (2) +9596+9596
ninety-six (2) +9252+9596
nor (2) +1153
now when (2)
or (2) +3954
rather than (2) +4202
rebuilt (2) +1215+8740
send for (2) +4374+8938
seventeen hundred (2) +547+4395+8679
sixty-six (2) +9252+9252
sixty-two (2) +9109+9252
slaves (2) +6269+9148
so (2) +1685
still (2)
summoned (2) +7924+8938
them[s] (2) +2286+7518
therefore (2) +1685
thirty-eight (2) +8993+9046
thirty-eighth (2) +8993+9046
thirty-second (2) +8993+9109
thirty-seven (2) +8679+8993
together with (2) +1685
too (2) +677
treaty of friendship (2) +3208+8934
twenty-second (2) +6929+9109
twenty-seven (2) +6929+8679
us (2) +3276+3870
various kinds of service (2) +6275+6275
where (2)
wherever goes (2) +928+928+995+3655
with the help of (2)
yes (2) +1685
yet (2) +1685
1,017 (1) +547+6925+8679
1,222 (1) +547+4395+6929+9109
1,290 (1) +547+4395+9596
1,335 (1) +547+2822+4395+8993+8993
1,365 (1) +547+2256+2256+2822+4395+8993+9252
1,760 (1) +547+2256+4395+8679+9252
105 (1) +2822+4395
108,100 (1) +547+547+2256+4395+4395+9046
110 (1) +4395+6927
119 (1) +4395+6926+9596
120,000 (1) +547+4395+6929
122 (1) +2256+4395+6929+9109
122 (1) +4395+6929+9109
133 (1) +2256+4395+8993+8993
138 (1) +4395+8993+9046
139 (1) +4395+8993+9596
14,700 (1) +547+752+4395+6925+8679
148 (1) +752+4395+9046
151,450 (1) +285+547+547+752+2256+2256+2256+2822+2822+4395+4395
153,600 (1) +547+547+2256+2256+2822+4395+4395+8993+9252
156 (1) +2822+4395+9252
157,600 (1) +547+547+2256+2256+2822+4395+4395+8679+9252
16,750 (1) +547+2822+4395+6925+8679+9252
160 (1) +4395+9252
162 (1) +2256+4395+9109+9252
17,200 (1) +547+4395+6925+8679
172 (1) +4395+8679+9109
180 (1) +4395+9046
180,000 (1) +547+4395+9046
182 (1) +2256+4395+9046+9109
186,400 (1) +547+547+547+752+2256+2256+4395+4395+9046+9252
187 (1) +2256+4395+8679+9046
188 (1) +4395+9046+9046
2,056 (1) +547+2822+9252
2,067 (1) +547+8679+9252
2,172 (1) +547+2256+4395+8679+9109
2,172 (1) +547+4395+8679+9109

2,200 (1) +547+4395
2,300 (1) +547+4395+8993
2,322 (1) +547+4395+6929+8993+9109
2,400 (1) +547+752+4395
2,600 (1) +547+4395+9252
2,630 (1) +547+2256+4395+8993+9252
2,750 (1) +547+2822+4395+8679
2,812 (1) +547+4395+6925+9046+9109
2,818 (1) +547+4395+6925+9046+9046
20,200 (1) +547+4395+6929
20,800 (1) +547+4395+6929+9046
205 (1) +2822+4395
207 (1) +4395+8679
209 (1) +4395+9596
212 (1) +4395+6925+9109
218 (1) +4395+6925+9046
22 (1) +6929+9109
22,000 (1) +547+6929+9109
22,034 (1) +547+752+2256+2256+6929+8993+9109
22,200 (1) +547+2256+4395+6929+9109
22,273 (1) +547+2256+2256+4395+6929+8679+8993+9109
22,600 (1) +547+2256+4395+6929+9109+9252
23,000 (1) +547+6929+8993
232 (1) +4395+8993+9109
242 (1) +752+4395+9109
245 (1) +752+2256+2822+4395
245 (1) +752+2822+4395
25,100 (1) +547+2256+2822+4395+6929
26,000 (1) +547+6929+9252
273 (1) +2256+4395+8679+8993
28 (1) +6929+9046
28,600 (1) +547+2256+4395+6929+9046+9252
280,000 (1) +547+4395+9046
284 (1) +752+4395+9046
288 (1) +4395+9046+9046
3,023 (1) +547+2256+6929+8993+8993
3,200 (1) +547+4395+8993
3,600 (1) +547+4395+8993+9252
3,630 (1) +547+2256+4395+8993+8993+9252
3,700 (1) +547+4395+8679+8993
3,930 (1) +547+4395+8993+8993+9596
307,500 (1) +547+547+2256+2822+4395+4395+8679+8993
318 (1) +4395+6925+8993+9046
32,000 (1) +547+8993+9109
32,500 (1) +547+2256+2822+4395+8993+9109
323 (1) +4395+6929+8993+8993
324 (1) +752+4395+6929+8993
328 (1) +4395+6929+8993+9046
337,500 (1) +547+547+547+2256+2256+2822+4395+4395+8679+8993+8993
337,500 (1) +547+547+547+2256+2822+4395+4395+8679+8993+8993
34 (1) +752+8993
35 (1) +2822+8993
350 (1) +2822+4395+8993
365 (1) +2256+2822+4395+8993+9252
37,000 (1) +547+8679+8993
410 (1) +752+4395+6927
42,360 (1) +547+752+4395+8052+8993+9252
420 (1) +752+4395+6929
43,730 (1) +547+752+2256+2256+4395+8679+8993+8993
44,760 (1) +547+752+752+2256+2256+4395+8679+9252
45,400 (1) +547+752+752+2256+2822+4395
45,600 (1) +547+752+2256+2822+4395+9252
454 (1) +752+752+2822+4395
468 (1) +752+4395+9046+9252
5,400 (1) +547+752+2822+4395
52,700 (1) +547+2256+2822+4395+8679+9109
530 (1) +2822+4395+8993

550 (1) +2822+2822+4395
56 (1) +2822+9252
595 (1) +2256+2822+2822+4395+9596
6,200 (1) +547+4395+9252
6,800 (1) +547+4395+9046+9252
60,500 (1) +547+2822+4395+9252
601,730 (1) +547+547+2256+4395+4395+8679+8993+9252
61 (1) +285+9252
61,000 (1) +285+547+9252
61,000 (1) +547+8052+9252
62 (1) +9109+9252
623 (1) +4395+6929+8993+9252
628 (1) +4395+6929+9046+9252
64,300 (1) +547+752+2256+4395+8993+9252
64,400 (1) +547+752+752+2256+4395+9252
642 (1) +752+2256+4395+9109+9252
642 (1) +752+4395+9109+9252
648 (1) +752+4395+9046+9252
650 (1) +2822+4395+9252
655 (1) +2822+2822+4395+9252
666 (1) +2256+4395+9252+9252+9252
667 (1) +4395+8679+9252+9252
67 (1) +8679+9252
675 (1) +2822+4395+8679+9252
675,000 (1) +547+547+547+2256+2822+4395+8679+9252
690 (1) +4395+9252+9596
7,100 (1) +547+4395+8679
7,500 (1) +547+2822+4395+8679
72 (1) +8679+9109
72,000 (1) +547+8679+9109
721 (1) +285+2256+4395+6929+8679
725 (1) +2822+4395+6929+8679
730 (1) +4395+8679+8993
736 (1) +4395+8679+8993+9252
743 (1) +752+2256+4395+8679+8993
743 (1) +752+4395+8679+8993
745 (1) +752+2822+4395+8679
76,500 (1) +547+2256+2822+4395+8679+9252
775 (1) +2822+4395+8679+8679
777 (1) +2256+4395+8679+8679+8679
782 (1) +2256+4395+8679+9046+9109
8,580 (1) +547+2256+2822+4395+9046+9046
8,600 (1) +547+4395+9046+9252
807 (1) +4395+8679+9046
815 (1) +2822+4395+6926+9046
822 (1) +4395+6929+9046+9109
830 (1) +4395+8993+9046
832 (1) +4395+8993+9046+9109
840 (1) +752+4395+9046
845 (1) +752+2822+4395+9046
87,000 (1) +547+8679+9046
895 (1) +2256+2822+4395+9046+9596
905 (1) +2822+4395+9596
910 (1) +4395+6924+9596
912 (1) +4395+6926+9109+9596
928 (1) +4395+6929+9046+9596
930 (1) +4395+8993+9596
945 (1) +752+2256+2822+4395+9596
950 (1) +2822+4395+9596
956 (1) +2256+2822+4395+9252+9596
962 (1) +2256+4395+9109+9252+9596
969 (1) +2256+4395+9252+9596+9596
accompanied by (1)
adding to (1) +907
after (1) +1685
after this (1)
again and again (1) +8899+8938
age-old (1) +1887+1887
all time (1) +1887+1887
along with (1) +1685
also (1) +677
also included (1)
alternate[s] (1) +2298+7194+8232
alternated[s] (1) +7194+8232
always (1) +1887+1887+4200
and (1) +255

and (1) +907
and (1) +6330
and again (1)
and alike (1)
and after (1)
and as (1)
and as for (1)
and either (1)
and even after (1)
and even though (1)
and likewise (1)
and still (1)
and that is why (1)
and what about (1)
and whenever (1)
and with (1)
annually (1) +928+3972+9102+9102
anywhere (1) +625+625+2025+2025
army (1) +6639+7736
as far as (1)
as surely as live (1) +2644+2644+5883
as well (1)
as well as (1) +3869
assassinated (1) +4637+5782
at that (1)
back and forth (1) +285+285+2178+2178
be on way (1) +2143+5825
bearing (1)
beasts of burden (1) +989+2651
became more and more powerful (1)
　　　　　　　　　　　　　　+1524+2143
because (1) +928+3610+3610
because (1) +4202
been brought to attention (1) +5583+9048
bordering each side[s] (1)
　　　　　　　　+2296+2296+4946+4946
both of you (1) +2084+3870
both[s] (1) +170+2021+2021+8533
bring (1) +3655+4374
but (1) +3463
but (1) +8370
but even (1) +1685
but too (1)
but while (1)
by the time (1)
by then (1)
calling together (1) +995+8938
came back (1) +995+2143
carefully investigated (1) +1335+2011
carry out duties (1) +995+3655
carry the battle (1) +1741+8740
cities (1) +6551+6551
closer and closer (1) +2143+7929
commander-in-chief (1) +8031+8569
completely (1) +1414+4946+5883+6330
cover up (1) +4059+8740
crushed completely (1) +430+4730
deception (1) +4213+4213
did so[s] (1) +2932+4374+8008
differing measures (1) +406+406
each of us (1) +638+2085
each table (1) +8947+8947
each town (1) +6551+6551
eighteen thousand (1) +547+8052+9046
eighty-six (1) +9046+9252
eighty-three (1) +8993+9046
endless generations (1) +1887+1887
enslaved (1) +3899+4200+4200+6269+9148
especially (1)
even (1) +677
even (1) +677+3954
even then (1)
even while (1)
every city (1) +6551+6551
every day (1) +3427+3427+3972
every family (1) +5476+5476
every province (1) +4519+4519
except for (1) +4202
executed (1) +4637+5782
exorbitant interest (1) +5968+9552
experienced (1) +1981+9312

feasting (1) +430+9272
fifteen (1) +2822+6927
fifty-second (1) +2822+9109
finally (1) +1685
fine (1) +1524+3202
for instance (1)
forty-first (1) +285+752
forty-nine (1) +752+9596
forty-seven (1) +752+8679
fully obeyed (1) +6913+9048
furthermore (1) +1685
furthermore (1) +2021+9108
furthermore (1) +6388
furthermore (1) +6964
generations long past (1) +1887+1887+9102
generations to come (1) +1887+1887
given even more (1)
　　　　　　　+2179+2179+3578+3869+3869
go about business (1) +995+3655
go at once (1) +995+2143
go in (1) +995+2143
grapes or raisins (1) +3313+4300+6694
great wrath (1) +2405+7912
grew even wilder (1) +2143+6192
grew louder and louder (1)
　　　　　　　　　　　+2143+2618+4394
grew stronger and stronger (1) +2143+2618
grew stronger and stronger (1) +2143+7997
grew weaker and weaker (1) +1924+2143
had brought (1) +4374+8938
had executed (1) +4637+5782
had removed (1) +4374+8938
harem (1) +8721+8721
have to do with (1) +4200+4200
here is what (1) +2296+2296+3869+3869
how much more (1) +677+3954
however (1) +219
if then (1)
in addition (1)
in addition to (1)
in any direction (1) +2178+2178
in any direction (1) +3907+3907
in midair (1)
　　　　　　+824+1068+1068+2021+2021+9028
in order for (1)
including (1) +1685
including and (1)
increased more and more (1)
　　　　　　　　　　+2143+2143+8041
indeed (1) +677+3954
instead (1) +1685
interest of any kind (1) +5968+9552
invite (1) +7924+8938
joined (1) +1685
just who (1) +4769+4769
kills (1) +4637+5782+5883
kinds of cattle (1) +989+989
laid waste (1) +2238+2990
later (1)
lead (1) +995+3655
lead (1) +995+3655+4200+7156
lead on (1) +2143+5627
likewise (1)
made good escape (1) +4880+5674
man (1) +408+408
many generations (1) +1887+1887
many years (1) +3427+9102
marauding (1) +6296+8740
marries (1) +1249+4374
meanwhile (1) +3907+3907+6330+6330
melting away (1) +2143+4570
more and more powerful (1)
　　　　　+1541+2025+2143+4200+5087+6330
movements (1) +4569+4604
much too numerous (1) +6786+8041
neither (1) +440
never (1) +1153+6329+6409
nine-and-a-half (1) +2942+9596
ninety-eight (1) +9046+9596
no more than (1)
nor (1) +401+1685

nor (1) +401+4946
nor (1) +561
nor (1) +1685
nor (1) +1685+4202
nothing (1) +1524+1821+4202+7785
nothing at all (1) +401+700
nothing but skin (1) +1414+6425
now (1) +6964
numbers increased greatly (1) +7238+8049
obey (1) +6913+9068
on both (1) +2296+2296+4946+4946
on both sides (1) +294+7156
on both sides[s] (1) +2296+2296+4946
on duty (1) +995+3655
on each side[s] (1) +2296+2296+4946+4946
on the other side of (1) +2134+4946+6298
once more (1)
one of the other peoples (1) +6639+6639
or (1) +401+561
or (1) +440
or (1) +700
or even (1)
otherwise (1) +4202
over nine feet (1) +564+2455+9252
pay close attention (1) +7992+9048
please (1) +928+3202+3838+6524
provided for (1) +430+2118+4200+4312
raised (1) +5951+5989
raped (1) +6700+8886
rapes (1) +2616+6640+8886
rapes (1) +6640+8886+9530
rather (1)
rather (1) +1685
realize (1) +3359+8011
realized (1) +3359+8011
reappears (1) +7255+8740
rebuild (1) +1215+8740
recaptured (1) +4374+8740
receded steadily (1) +2143+8740+8740
recite (1) +606+6699
reentered (1) +995+8740
reopened (1) +2916+8740
return (1) +2143+7155
richest of foods (1) +2016+2693
roam (1) +2143+3718
rougher and rougher (1) +2143+6192
ruined (1) +2472+2476
say (1) +606+6699
scream for help (1) +7754+7924+8123
screamed for help (1) +7754+7924+8123
sent for (1) +4374+8938
sent word (1) +5583+8938
sent word (1) +7924+8938
serve (1) +995+3655
seventeen (1) +6927+8679
shining ever brighter (1) +239+2143
shouted (1) +5951+7754+7924
similarly (1)
sixty-eight (1) +9046+9252
sixty-five (1) +2822+9252
slaves (1) +563+6269
square (1) +802+8145
square (1) +4946+4946+7024+7024
staggering burden (1) +4842+7050
stared with a fixed gaze (1)
　　　　　　　　+906+6641+7156+8492
stayed night (1) +3782+4328
still (1) +1685
strip off clothes (1) +6910+7320
summon (1) +4374+8938
suppose (1)
surely (1)
than (1) +1685
than (1) +4202
that (1) +1685
the parties (1) +408+2084+8276
the two of them[s] (1) +1189+1192
them[s] (1) +59+7401
then (1) +339
then (1) +6964
they[s] (1) +1201+1201+1514+8017

they^s (1) +1770+5083
they^s (1) +2021+2657+3405+8569
thirty-fifth (1) +2822+8993
thirty-first (1) +285+8993
thirty-six (1) +8993+9252
thirty-six hundred (1)
                +547+4395+8993+9252
thirty-sixth (1) +8993+9252
thirty-three hundred (1)
                +547+4395+8993+8993
through (1)
tightly shut up (1) +6037+6037
till (1) +677
time and again (1) +285+4202+4202+9109
to come (1) +1887+1887
together with (1) +677
together with (1) +6330
took back (1) +995+8938
travel about (1) +995+3655
tripping along with mincing steps (1)
                +2143+3262
twelve hundred (1) +547+4395
twenty-seven hundred (1) +547+4395+8679
twenty-six (1) +6929+9252
twenty-six hundred (1) +547+4395+9252
twenty-sixth (1) +6929+9252
two differing measures (1) +406+406
two differing weights (1) +74+74
two men (1) +278+408+3481
two-and-a-half (1) +2942+9109
undivided loyalty (1) +4202+4213+4213
upon (1)
us (1) +2157+3276
us (1) +3276+4013
utterly useless (1) +2039+8198
various gates (1) +9133+9133
various peoples (1) +6639+6639
various provinces (1) +4519+4519
violated (1) +6700+8886
what (1) +2296+2296+3869+3869
what (1) +2296+2297+3869+3869
what about (1)
when also (1)
whether (1)
whether (1) +700
who (1)
whoever he may be (1) +6424+6699
whole assembly (1) +6337+7736
with (1) +1685
with both (1)
yet (1) +677
yet (1) +6964
yet also (1)
young and old (1) +2025+5087
untranslated (20271)

2257 י ֑ -ô (12080)
his (4456)
him (2172)
he (548)
it (499)
its (373)
the^s (338)
their (286)
them (182)
his own (140)
his (81) +4200
whose (56)
himself (55)
a^s (40)
her (36)
they (31)
whom (26)
your (26)
himself (18) +5883
his (13) +907
one (13)
who (13)
David^s (11)
that^s (11)
the altar^s (11)

himself (10) +1414
himself (10) +4213
its own (10)
the king^s (10)
the king's^s (10)
their own (10)
each (9)
them^s (9) +3
you (9)
God^s (8)
his own (8) +4200
those^s (8)
he (7) +5883
God's^s (6)
man's^s (6)
the man^s (6)
the LORD^s (6)
the value^s (5)
their^s (5) +1201
this^s (5)
Aaron^s (4)
an^s (4)
David's^s (4)
Elijah^s (4)
Elisha^s (4)
Gideon^s (4)
its (4) +4200
Jacob^s (4)
Jehoram^s (4)
Jehu^s (4)
Moses^s (4)
she (4)
the gateway^s (4)
their (4) +4200
there^s (4) +928
which (4)
Abram^s (3)
any^s (3)
anyone (3)
Eliakim's^s (3)
Jehoiachin^s (3)
Joseph^s (3)
Moses'^s (3)
my (3)
same^s (3)
Saul's^s (3)
Solomon^s (3)
there^s (3)
these^s (3)
whose (3) +4200
Aaron's^s (2)
Abraham^s (2)
Ahab^s (2)
Ahaziah^s (2)
alone (2) +928+1727
Amnon^s (2)
Gehazi^s (2)
he (2) +3338
here^s (2)
him^s (2) +3
his (2) +6640
Hosea^s (2)
Isaac^s (2)
Israel's^s (2)
Jehoiachin's^s (2)
Jehoram's^s (2)
Jeremiah^s (2)
Joab^s (2)
Joash^s (2)
Job's^s (2)
Joseph's^s (2)
Josiah^s (2)
Josiah's^s (2)
man^s (2)
Nebuchadnezzar^s (2)
Noah^s (2)
own (2)
owner (2) +4200
Saul^s (2)
she^s (2) +562
Solomon's^s (2)

the area^s (2)
the ark^s (2)
the king of the south^s (2)
the lamps^s (2)
the LORD's^s (2)
the man himself^s (2)
the man's^s (2)
the neighbor^s (2)
the person^s (2)
the table^s (2)
their own (2) +4200
them^s (2) +6269
they^s (2) +6269
tribe^s (2)
your own (2)
Zedekiah's^s (2)
Abijah's^s (1)
Abishai^s (1)
Abraham's^s (1)
Absalom's^s (1)
Achan^s (1)
Adonijah^s (1)
Ahab's^s (1)
Ahaz^s (1)
Amasa^s (1)
Amon's^s (1)
animal^s (1)
another^s (1)
any such thing^s (1)
Baal's^s (1)
Baruch^s (1)
Benaiah^s (1)
both^s (1)
by himself (1) +963+4200
by itself (1) +963+4200
consecrate himself (1) +3338+4848
creditor (1) +1251+3338+5408
daily (1) +928+3427+3427
day by day (1) +928+1821+3427+3427
did this^s (1) +3338+5742
did^s (1) +3338+5989
do that^s (1) +928+2118+3338
each (1) +278+408
each day's (1) +928+3427+3427
Egypt^s (1)
Ehud^s (1)
Eleazar^s (1)
Elisha's^s (1)
enemy^s (1)
equally (1) +278+408+3869
equally among them (1) +278+408+3869
every (1)
every^s (1)
God's name^s (1)
Gog^s (1)
Hadad^s (1)
Haman^s (1)
Hanun^s (1)
he himself (1)
Heman's^s (1)
her husband^s (1)
her son^s (1)
her^s (1) +123+851
her^s (1) +851
herself (1)
him (1) +3338
him (1) +5883
him^s (1) +3162
him^s (1) +6660
himself (1) +4222
himself (1) +8031
himself (1) +8638
himself (1) +9005
his (1) +928
his (1) +6584
his body^s (1)
his descendants^s (1)
his father's^s (1)
his father^s (1)
his neighbor^s (1)
his own (1) +4213+4946

his own (1) +5883
his^s (1) +3
inner sanctuary^s (1)
Israel^s (1)
it^s (1)
it^s (1) +623
it^s (1) +1947
it^s (1) +2308
it^s (1) +2942
it^s (1) +3338
it^s (1) +8031
it^s (1) +9005
its own (1) +5883
itself (1)
Jacob's^s (1)
Jehoahaz^s (1)
Jehoiakim's^s (1)
Jehu's^s (1)
Jeriah^s (1)
Jesse^s (1)
Jethro^s (1)
Joab's^s (1)
Job^s (1)
Joshua^s (1)
Judah's^s (1)
Laban^s (1)
Lot's^s (1)
Manasseh^s (1)
married (1) +851+4200+4200+4374
my companion^s (1)
my^s (1) +1201
Naaman's^s (1)
Naboth's^s (1)
Neco^s (1)
not circumcised (1) +4200+6889
Obed-Edom^s (1)
of his own (1) +3655+3751
one's (1)
one^s (1)
only (1) +928+1727
only one (1) +963+4200
opposite^s (1)
others^s (1)
Othniel^s (1)
person^s (1)
Pharaoh's^s (1)
pillar^s (1)
Potiphar^s (1)
Rehoboam^s (1)
relieve himself (1) +906+6114+8079
relieving himself (1) +906+6114+8079
riches^s (1)
royal^s (1)
Sennacherib's^s (1)
servant^s (1)
Shalmaneser's^s (1) +4200
Shaul's^s (1)
she^s (1) +851
she^s (1) +3304
she^s (1) +7108
Sheba^s (1)
Sherebiah's^s (1)
Shimei^s (1)
soldier^s (1)
someone (1)
someone's (1)
something^s (1)
stolen goods (1) +4200+4202
such^s (1)
that man's line^s (1)
that month^s (1)
that nation^s (1)
that person^s (1)
the angel^s (1)
the animal^s (1)
the article^s (1)
the basket^s (1)
the bells^s (1)
the Benjamites^s (1)
the boy's^s (1)
the boy^s (1)

the bread^s (1)
the calf^s (1)
the captain^s (1)
the cloud^s (1)
the coming storm^s (1)
the contaminated part^s (1)
the country^s (1)
the defender^s (1)
the enemy's^s (1)
the ephod^s (1)
the gold^s (1)
the grapes^s (1)
the injured man^s (1)
the lambs^s (1)
the offender^s (1)
the one (1)
the other half of Manasseh^s (1)
the other man^s (1)
the people^s (1)
the person (1)
the Philistine's^s (1)
the pillar^s (1)
the platform^s (1)
the pot^s (1)
the priest^s (1)
the rim^s (1)
the robe^s (1)
the scroll^s (1)
the servant^s (1)
the shore^s (1)
the slave^s (1)
the snake^s (1)
the successor^s (1)
the tribe^s (1)
the value^s (1)
the wicked^s (1)
the wood^s (1)
their^s (1)
theirs (1) +4200
them^s (1) +278
them^s (1) +6639
them^s (1) +7366
themselves (1) +5883
there^s (1) +824+928
there^s (1) +928+7931
there^s (1) +928+9348
they (1) +5883
they^s (1)
they^s (1) +1201
this (1)
this altar^s (1)
this god's^s (1)
this matter^s (1)
this^s (1) +3769+4202
Uzziah^s (1)
walled (1) +2570+4200
where^s (1) +928
which^s (1) +678
which^s (1) +7366
who^s (1)
whose^s (1) +465+1426
your (1) +928
your brother's^s (1)
your father^s (1)
your side^s (1)
your tithe^s (1)
yourself (1)
yourself (1) +4213
yourself (1) +5883
Zechariah's^s (1)
Zechariah^s (1)
untranslated (2076)

2258 וְדָן wᵉdān
Variant; not used

2259 וָהֵב wāhēb (1)
Waheb (1)

2260 וָו wāw (13)
hooks (13)

2261 וָזָר wāzār (1)
guilty (1)

2262 וַיְזָתָא wayzātā' (1)
Vaizatha (1)

2263 וָלָד wālād (1)
children (1)

2264 וַנְיָה wanyāh (1)
Vaniah (1)

2265 וָפְסִי wopsiy (1)
Vophsi (1)

2266 וַשְׁנִי wašniy
Variant; not used

2267 וַשְׁתִּי waštiy (10)
Vashti (10)

2268 ז z
Variant; not used

2269 זְאֵב1 zᵉ'ēb1 (7)
wolf (4)
wolves (3)

2270 זְאֵב2 zᵉ'ēb2 (6)
Zeeb (6)

2271 זֹאת zō't
Variant; not used

2272 זָבַד zābad (1)
presented (1)

2273 זֶבֶד zēbed (1)
gift (1)

2274 זָבָד zābād (8)
Zabad (8)

2275 זַבְדִי zabdiy (3)
Zabdi (3)

2276 זַבְדִּיאֵל zabdiy'ēl (2)
Zabdiel (2)

2277 זְבַדְיָה zᵉbadyāh (6)
Zebadiah (6)

2278 זְבַדְיָהוּ zᵉbadyāhû (3)
Zebadiah (3)

2279 זְבוּב zᵉbûb (2)
flies (2)

2280 זָבוּד zābûd (2)
Zabud (2)
untranslated (1)

2281 זְבוּדָה zᵉbûddāh (1)
untranslated (1)

2282 זְבוּלוּן zᵉbûlûn (45)
Zebulun (40)
Zebulun (5) +1201

2283 זְבוּלֹנִי zᵉbûlōniy (3)
Zebulun (1)
Zebulunite (1)
untranslated (1)

2284 זָבַח zābah (134)
sacrifice (39)
sacrificed (18)
offer sacrifices (17)
offered (10)
offer (9)
offered sacrifices (8)
sacrificing (6)
sacrifices (4)
slaughter (3)
slaughtered (3)
made sacrifices (2) +2285
preparing (2)
sacrifice (2) +2285
butchered (1)
do^s (1)
making (1)
offer sacrifice (1)

offered a sacrifice (1)
offering (1)
offering sacrifices (1)
offers (1)
sacrifices offer (1)
untranslated (2)

2285 1זֶבַח *zebah1* (162)
sacrifices (57)
sacrifice (47)
offering (24)
offerings (15)
sacrificed (13)
made sacrifices (2) +2284
sacrifice (2) +2284
feasting (1)
it[s] (1) +8968

2286 2זֶבַח *zebah2* (12)
Zebah (10)
them[s] (2) +2256+7518

2287 זַבַּי *zabbay* (2)
Zabbai (2)

2288 זְבִידָה *z'biydāh* (1)
Zebidah (1)

2289 זְבִינָא *z'biynā'* (1)
Zebina (1)

2290 זָבַל *zābal* (1)
treat with honor (1)

2291 1זְבֻל *z'bul1* (6)
Zebul (6)

2292 2זְבֻל *z'bul2* (5)
magnificent (2)
heavens (1)
lofty throne (1)
princely mansions (1)

2293 זַג *zāg* (1)
skins (1)

2294 זֵד *zēd* (13)
arrogant (10)
haughty (1)
proud (1)
willful sins (1)

2295 זָדוֹן *zādôn* (11)
pride (4)
arrogant (2)
arrogance (1)
conceited (1)
contempt (1)
overweening pride (1) +6301
presumptuously (1) +928

2296 זֶה *zeh* (1778)
this (1082)
these (109)
that (49)
this[s] (44) +1821+2021+2021
today (39) +2021+2021+3427
here (17)
now (17) +2021+2021+3427
one (17)
such (16)
it (13)
here (12) +928
he (9)
where (9) +361
another[s] (7)
on both sides[s] (6) +2256+2296+4946+4946
this is how (6) +928
this very (6)
other[s] (5)
what (5)
it[s] (4) +1821+2021+2021
side[s] (4)
the (4)
the other[s] (4)
ever since (3) +2021+2021+3427+6330
now (3)

really (3)
same (3)
so (3) +6584
such (3) +3869
that same (3)
thing[s] (3)
those (3)
very (3)
what (3) +361
what[s] (3) +1821+2021+2021
another messenger[s] (2)
at either end[s] (2) +2256+2296+4946+4946
here[s] (2) +2021+2021+5226
how (2)
man[s] (2)
she (2)
so (2) +3869
still (2) +2021+2021+3427+6330
them (2)
there (2)
therefore (2) +6584
this is how (2)
which (2)
which (2) +361
who (2)
all at once (1) +2180
an (1)
another messenger (1)
another[s] (1) +2021+2215+4946
back[s] (1)
bordering each side[s] (1)
         +2256+2296+4946+4946
by what (1) +361
except for (1)
from (1) +4946
front[s] (1)
he's (1)
her (1)
here is what (1) +2256+2296+3869+3869
here[s] (1) +928+2021+2021+5226
how (1) +4537
in broad daylight (1)
         +2021+2021+4200+6524+9087
inclined (1) +2118
it[s] (1) +824+2021+2021
it[s] (1) +2021+2021+6551
it[s] (1) +2021+2021+8878
its[s] (1)
just (1) +6964
lasting (1) +2021+2021+3427+6330
later (1) +339
Leah[s] (1)
long for[s] (1)
neither (1) +4202
now (1) +3954
now[s] (1) +6964
of what use (1) +4200+4537
on both (1) +2256+2296+4946+4946
on both sides[s] (1) +2256+2296+4946
on each side (1)   +2021+2021+2296
    +4946+4946+4946+4946+6298+6298
on each side[s] (1) +2256+2296+4946+4946
on the condition that (1) +928
once (1)
one condition[s] (1)
over a year (1) +196+2296+3427+9102
right where (1)
same amount[s] (1)
so (1)
still (1) +2021+2021+3427+3869
such (1) +1524
such offerings[s] (1)
such questions[s] (1)
suggested (1) +1821+2021+2021
that's (1)
that[s] (1) +1074+2021+2021
the condition[s] (1)
the first one[s] (1)
the younger one[s] (1)
the[s] (1)
them[s] (1) +1821+2021+2021

them[s] (1) +2021+2021+6639
then (1)
then (1) +928
this (1) +1821+2021+2021
this fellow's[s] (1) +4200
this is what (1)
this[s] (1) +2021+2021+5126
today (1) +3427
what (1) +2256+2296+3869+3869
what (1) +2256+2297+3869+3869
what (1) +4769
what do I care about (1)
         +3276+4200+4200+4537
what[s] (1) +2021+2021+5184
which way (1) +361
which way (1) +361+2006+2021
whom (1)
why (1) +361+4200
why (1) +6584
woman (1)
you[s] (1)
untranslated (145)

2297 זֹה *zōh* (11)
this (6)
one (1)
such (1) +3869
what (1) +2256+2296+3869+3869
untranslated (2)

2298 זָהָב *zāhāb* (388)
gold (365)
golden (9)
Gold (2)
pure gold (2) +2298
alternate[s] (1) +2256+7194+8232
nuggets of gold (1)
untranslated (7)

2299 זָהַם *zāham* (1)
finds repulsive (1)

2300 זַהַם *zaham* (1)
Zaham (1)

2301 1זָהַר *zāhar1* (1)
shine (1)

2302 2זָהַר *zāhar2* (22)
warn (8)
take warning (3)
dissuade (2)
give warning (2)
be warned (1)
is warned (1)
taken warning (1)
teach (1)
took warning (1)
warned (1)
untranslated (1)

2303 זֹהַר *zōhar* (2)
bright (1)
brightness (1)

2304 זִו *ziw* (2)
Ziv (2)

2305 זֹו *zô* (2)
for this (1)
untranslated (1)

2306 זוּ *zû* (15)
the (4)
as (1)
it (1)
such (1)
that (1)
things (1)
where (1)
who (1)
whose (1)
untranslated (3)

2307 זוּב *zûb* (42)
flowing (19)

discharge (9)
gushed out (3)
man^s (3)
bodily discharge (1)
discharge (1) +2308
flow (1)
fruitful (1)
has a discharge (1) +2308
regular flow (1) +928+1414
running sore (1)
waste away (1)

2308 זוֹב *zôḇ* (13)
discharge (7)
discharge (1) +2307
discharge (1) +3240
has a discharge (1) +2307
it^s (1) +2257
untranslated (2)

2309 זוּזִים *zûziym* (1)
Zuzites (1)

2310 זוּחַ *zûaḥ*
Variant; not used

2311 זוֹחֵת *zôḥēṯ* (1)
Zoheth (1)

2312 זָוִית *zāwiyṯ* (2)
corners (1)
pillars (1)

2313 זוּל *zûl* (1)
pour out (1)

2314 זוּלָה *zûlāh* (16)
but (6)
except (4)
besides (2)
apart from (1)
only (1)
only (1) +963+4200
only (1) +4202

2315 זוּן *zûn*
Variant; not used

2316 זוּעַ *zûa'* (3)
make tremble (1)
showed fear (1)
tremble (1)

2317 זְוָעָה *z'wā'āh* (6)
abhorrent (4)
object of dread (1)
terror (1)

2318 1זוּר *zûr1* (4)
broken (1)
cleansed (1)
crush (1)
squeezed (1)

2319 2זוּר *zûr2* (6)
turned (2)
deserted (1)
estranged (1)
go astray (1)
stranger (1)

2320 3זוּר *zûr3* (1)
offensive (1)

2321 זָזָא *zāzā'* (1)
Zaza (1)

2322 זָחַח *zāḥaḥ* (2)
swing out (2)

2323 1זָחַל *zāhal1* (2)
crawl (1)
glide (1)

2324 2זָחַל *zāhal2* (1)
fearful (1)

2325 זֹחֶלֶת *zōḥeleṯ* (1)
Zoheleth (1)

2326 זִיד *ziyḏ* (10)

arrogant (2)
arrogance (1)
arrogantly treated (1)
contemptuous (1)
cooking (1)
defied (1)
presumes (1)
schemes (1)
treated arrogantly (1)

2327 זֵידוֹן *zēyḏôn* (1)
raging (1)

2328 1זִיז *ziyz1* (2)
creatures (2)

2329 2זִיז *ziyz2* (1)
overflowing (1)

2330 זִיזָא *ziyzā'* (3)
Ziza (3)

2331 זִיזָה *ziyzāh* (1)
Ziza (1)

2332 זִינָא *ziynā'*
Variant; not used

2333 זִיעַ *ziya'* (1)
Zia (1)

2334 1זִיף *ziyp1* (8)
Ziph (7)
there^s (1) +4497

2335 2זִיף *ziyp2* (2)
Ziph (2)

2336 זִיפָה *ziypāh* (1)
Ziphah (1)

2337 זִיפִי *ziypiy* (3)
Ziphites (3)

2338 זִיקוֹת *ziyqôṯ* (2)
flaming torches (1)
torches (1)

2339 זַיִת *zayiṯ* (38)
olive (9)
olive tree (8)
olive groves (7)
olives (7)
olive trees (4)
olive grove (1)
olive trees (1) +3658
olives from trees (1)

2340 זֵיתָן *zēyṯān* (1)
Zethan (1)

2341 זַךְ *zak* (11)
pure (6)
clear (2)
flawless (1)
innocent (1)
upright (1)

2342 זָכָה *zākāh* (8)
kept pure (2)
pure (2)
acquit (1)
justified (1)
keep pure (1)
make yourselves clean (1)

2343 זְכוֹכִית *z'kôkiyṯ* (1)
crystal (1)

2344 זְכוּר *z'kûr* (4)
men (4)

2345 זָכוּר *zākûr*
Variant; not used

2346 זַכּוּר *zakkûr* (10)
Zaccur (10)

2347 זַכַּי *zakkay* (3)
Zaccai (2)
untranslated (1)

2348 זָכַךְ *zākak* (4)
pure (2)
brighter (1)
untranslated (1)

2349 1זָכַר *zākar1* (225)
remember (116)
remembered (23)
be remembered (15)
remembers (8)
invoke (4)
mention (4)
consider (2)
mentioned (2)
petition (2)
proclaim (2)
recalled (2)
remind (2)
tell (2)
are remembered (1)
be invoked (1)
brought to mind (1)
burns memorial (1)
call on (1)
carry on the memory (1)
cause to be honored (1)
commemorate (1)
disregarding (1) +4202
done this^s (1)
draw attention to (1)
forget (1) +440
hold (1)
honor (1)
made mention of (1)
make petition (1)
mindful (1)
perpetuate memory (1) +9005
praise (1)
recalling (1)
record (1)
reflect on (1)
reflects on (1)
remember (1) +2349
remember well (1) +2349
reminded (1)
reminder (1)
review the past (1)
summons (1)
think about (1)
thought (1)
trust (1)
well remember (1) +2349
worthy of mention (1)
untranslated (4)

2350 2זָכַר *zākar2* (1)
males (1)

2351 זָכָר *zākār* (82)
male (37)
men (17)
males (11)
man (9)
son (3)
boy (1)
boys (1) +3251
not a virgin (1) +3359+5435
slept with (1) +3359+4200+5435
slept with (1) +3359+5435

2352 זֵכֶר *zēker* (23)
memory (11)
renown (3)
name (2)
remembered (2)
celebrate (1) +5580
fame (1)
name by which remembered (1)
name of renown (1)
remembers (1)

2353 1זֵכֶר *zeker1* (1)
Zeker (1)

2354 זֵכֶר‎ *zeker2*
Variant; not used

2355 זִכָּרוֹן‎ *zikkārôn* (24)
memorial (9)
reminder (3)
remembered (2)
remembrance (2)
chronicles (1)
commemorate (1)
commemorated (1)
historic right (1)
maxims (1)
pagan symbols (1)
remind (1)
something remembered (1)

2356 זִכְרִי‎ *zikriy* (12)
Zicri (12)

2357 זְכַרְיָה‎ *z⁸karyāh* (25)
Zechariah (24)
Zechariah's (1)

2358 זְכַרְיָהוּ‎ *z⁸karyāhû* (16)
Zechariah (16)

2359 זְלוּת‎ *zullût* (1)
vile (1)

2360 זַלְזַל‎ *zalzal* (1)
shoots (1)

2361 1זָלַל‎ *zālal1* (7)
gluttons (2)
despise (1)
despised (1)
gorge (1)
profligate (1)
worthless (1)

2362 2זָלַל‎ *zālal2* (2)
tremble (1)
trembled (1)

2363 זַלְעָפָה‎ *zal'āpāh* (3)
feverish (1)
indignation (1)
scorching (1)

2364 זִלְפָּה‎ *zilpāh* (7)
Zilpah (7)

2365 1זִמָּה‎ *zimmāh1* (29)
lewdness (6)
wickedness (3)
consequences of lewdness (2)
lewd (2)
wicked schemes (2)
evil (1)
evil intent (1)
evil schemes (1)
lewd act (1)
lewd acts (1)
penalty for lewdness (1)
plans (1)
schemes (1)
shameful (1)
shameful crimes (1)
shamefully (1) +928
shameless (1)
wicked (1)
untranslated (1)

2366 2זִמָּה‎ *zimmāh2* (3)
Zimmah (3)

2367 זְמוֹרָה‎ *z⁸môrāh* (5)
branch (3)
vines (2)

2368 זַמְזֻמִּים‎ *zamzummiym* (1)
Zamzummites (1)

2369 1זָמִיר‎ *zāmiyr1* (7)
singing (2)
songs (2)
music and song (1)
song (1)

theme of song (1)

2370 2זָמִיר‎ *zāmiyr2*
Variant; not used

2371 זְמִירָה‎ *z⁸miyrāh* (1)
Zemirah (1)

2372 זָמַם‎ *zāmam* (13)
determined (3)
plot (2)
carry out purpose (1)
considers (1)
decided (1)
intended (1)
plan (1)
planned (1)
planned evil (1)
resolved (1)

2373 זָמָם‎ *zāmām* (1)
plans (1)

2374 זָמַן‎ *zāman* (3)
set (2)
designated (1)

2375 זְמָן‎ *z⁸mān* (4)
time (2)
designated times (1)
time appointed (1)

2376 1זָמַר‎ *zāmar1* (45)
sing praise (18)
make music (10)
sing praises (8)
sing (7)
music (1)
praise (1)

2377 2זָמַר‎ *zāmar2* (3)
prune (2)
pruned (1)

2378 זֶמֶר‎ *zemer* (1)
mountain sheep (1)

2379 1זִמְרָה‎ *zimrāh1* (7)
song (3)
music (2)
singing (2)

2380 2זִמְרָה‎ *zimrāh2* (1)
best products (1)

2381 1זִמְרִי‎ *zimriy1* (17)
Zimri (16)
Zimri's (1)

2382 2זִמְרִי‎ *zimriy2* (1)
Zimri (1)

2383 זִמְרָן‎ *zimrān* (2)
Zimran (2)

2384 זִמְרָת‎ *zimrāt*
Variant; not used

2385 זַן‎ *zan* (3)
every kind (1) +448+2385+4946
various (1)

2386 זָנַב‎ *zānab* (2)
attack from the rear (1)
cut off (1)

2387 זָנָב‎ *zānāb* (11)
tail (9)
stubs (1)
tails (1)

2388 1זָנָה‎ *zānāh1* (62)
prostitute (12)
prostituted (5)
unfaithful (5)
engaged in prostitution (4)
turn to prostitution (3)
committed adultery (2)
lusted after (2) +339
prostitutes (2)
adulterous (1)

carried on prostitution (1)
caused to prostitute themselves (1)
commit adultery (1)
continue prostitution (1) +2388
did⁸ (1)
engage in prostitution (1)
engaging in prostitution (1)
guilty of prostitution (1)
guilty of the vilest adultery (1) +2388
indulge in sexual immorality (1)
lead to do the same⁸ (1) +339+466+2177
led to prostitute themselves (1)
lust after (1) +339
making a prostitute (1)
ply her trade (1)
promiscuous (1)
prostituting (1)
prostitution (1)
runs after for favors (1) +339
that⁸ (1) +4392
turned to prostitution (1)
use as a prostitute (1) +9373
untranslated (2)

2389 2זָנָה‎ *zānāh2*
Variant; not used

2390 זוֹנָה‎ *zônāh* (33)
prostitute (20)
prostitutes (7)
harlot (2)
prostitution (2)
harlots (1)
prostitute's (1)

2391 1זָנוֹחַ‎ *zānôah1* (4)
Zanoah (4)

2392 2זָנוֹחַ‎ *zānôah2* (1)
Zanoah (1)

2393 זְנוּנִים‎ *z⁸nûniym* (12)
prostitution (4)
adulterous (1)
adulterous look (1)
adultery (1)
idolatry (1)
unfaithfulness (1)
wanton lust (1)
untranslated (2)

2394 זְנוּת‎ *z⁸nût* (9)
prostitution (7)
immorality (1)
unfaithfulness (1)

2395 1זָנַח‎ *zānah1* (1)
stink (1)

2396 2זָנַח‎ *zānah2* (19)
rejected (11)
reject (4)
cast off (1)
deprived (1)
removed (1)
throw out (1)

2397 זָנַק‎ *zānaq* (1)
springing out (1)

2398 זָעָה‎ *zā'āh*
Variant; not used

2399 זֵעָה‎ *zē'āh* (1)
sweat (1)

2400 זַעֲוָה‎ *za'⁸wāh* (7)
terror (1)
thing of horror (1)
untranslated (5)

2401 זַעֲוָן‎ *za'⁸wān* (2)
Zaavan (2)

2402 זְעֵיר‎ *z⁸'êyr*
Variant; not used

2403 זָעַךְ‎ *zā'ak* (1)
are cut short (1)

2404 זָעַם *zā'am* (12)
denounce (3)
angry (2)
accursed (1)
denounced (1)
expresses wrath (1)
fury shown (1)
under the wrath (1)
under wrath (1)
vent fury (1)

2405 זַעַם *za'am* (22)
wrath (15)
indignation (3)
anger (1)
fierce (1)
great wrath (1) +2256+7912
insolent (1)

2406 1זָעַף *zā'ap1* (3)
angry (1)
rages (1)
raging (1)

2407 2זָעַף *zā'ap2* (2)
dejected (1)
looking worse (1)

2408 זַעַף *za'ap* (6)
rage (2)
raging (2)
enraged (1)
wrath (1)

2409 זָעֵף *zā'ēp* (2)
angry (2)

2410 זָעַק *zā'aq* (74)
cry out (18)
cried out (16)
cried (5)
cries out (4)
called (3)
cry (3)
crying out (2)
summon (2)
assembled (1)
call out (1)
called out to fight (1)
calling to arms (1) +339
cried for help (1)
cried out for help (1)
cry for help (1) +7754
cry out for help (1)
gathered together (1)
howl (1)
issued a proclamation (1)
make appeals (1)
sent up a cry (1)
summoned (1)
summoning (1)
wail (1)
wailing (1) +2411
weeping aloud (1)
were called (1)
were called together (1)
untranslated (1)

2411 זְעָקָה *z''āqāh* (18)
cry (7)
outcry (3)
cry out (1) +7754
cry out (1) +9048
crying (1)
lament (1) +6424
lamentation (1)
shouts (1)
wailing (1)
wailing (1) +2410

2412 זִפְרוֹן *ziprôn* (1)
Ziphron (1)

2413 זֶפֶת *zepet* (3)
pitch (3)

2414 זֵק *zēq1* (4)
chains (2)
fetters (1)
were put in chains (1) +928+8415

2415 2זֵק *zēq2* (1)
firebrands (1)

2416 1זָקֵן *zāqēn1* (26)
old (22)
aged (1) +4394
grew old (1)
grow old (1)
very old (1) +928+995+2021+3427

2417 זָקָן *zāqān* (19)
beard (11)
beards (5)
chin (2)
hair (1)

2418 2זָקֵן *zāqēn2* (180)
elders (122)
old (32)
aged (5)
dignitaries (2)
leaders (2)
leading (2)
chief (1)
elder (1)
elderly (1)
his own[s] (1) +2021+2021+5566
of ripe old age (1)
older (1)
older (1) +3427+4200
them[s] (1) +1680
veteran (1)
women[s] (1)
untranslated (5)

2419 זֹקֶן *zōqen* (1)
old age (1)

2420 זִקְנָה *ziqnāh* (6)
old age (3)
old (2)
grew old (1)

2421 זְקֻנִים *z'quniym* (4)
old age (4)

2422 זָקַף *zāqap* (2)
lifts up (2)

2423 זָקַק *zāqaq* (7)
refined (3)
distill (1)
finest (1)
purified (1)
refine (1)

2424 זָר *zār* (70)
foreigners (14)
foreign (8)
strangers (7)
another (4)
anyone else (4)
adulteress (3)
else (3)
stranger (3)
unauthorized (3)
adulteress (2) +851
alien (2)
aliens (2)
anyone other than a priest (2)
strange (2)
distant sources (1)
enemies (1)
foreigners' (1)
illegitimate (1)
imported (1)
one[s] (1)
one[s] (1) +408
other (1)
outside a priest's family (1)
outside the family (1) +2021+2025+2575

unauthorized person (1)

2425 זֵר *zēr* (10)
molding (10)

2426 זָרָא *zārā'* (1)
loathe (1)

2427 זָרַב *zārab* (1)
dry (1)

2428 זְרֻבָּבֶל *z'rubbābel* (21)
Zerubbabel (21)

2429 זֶרֶד *zered* (4)
Zered (3)
untranslated (1)

2430 1זָרָה *zārāh1* (38)
scatter (18)
scattered (5)
winnow (4)
spread (3)
winnows out (2)
are scattered (1)
is scattered (1)
spread out (1)
throw away (1)
were scattered (1)
winnowing (1)

2431 2זָרָה *zārāh2* (1)
discern (1)

2432 זְרוֹעַ *z'rôa'* (90)
arm (53)
arms (15)
strength (6)
power (4)
shoulder (2)
allies (1)
arm of power (1)
armed forces (1)
army (1)
forces (1)
power (1) +3946
powerful (1)
shoulders (1)
strengthened (1) +2616
strong arms (1) +3338

2433 זֵרוּעַ *zērûa'* (2)
seeds (1)
seeds (1) +2446

2434 זַרְזִיף *zarziyp*
Variant; not used

2435 זַרְזִיר *zarziyr* (1)
strutting rooster (1) +5516

2436 זָרַח *zārah* (18)
rises (5)
rise (2)
rose (2)
sunrise (2) +2021+9087
appears (1)
broke out (1)
dawned (1)
dawns (1)
shine (1)
shining (1)
sunrise (1) +9087

2437 1זֶרַח *zerah1* (1)
dawn (1)

2438 2זֶרַח *zerah2* (21)
Zerah (20)
Zerahites (1) +1201

2439 זַרְחִי *zarhiy* (6)
Zerahite (4)
Zerahites (2)

2440 זְרַחְיָה *z'rahyāh* (5)
Zerahiah (5)

2441 1זָרַם *zāram1* (1)
sweep away (1)

2442 זָרַם 2 *zăram2* (1)
poured down (1)

2443 זֶרֶם *zerem* (9)
storm (4)
driving rain (1) +4784
hailstorm (1) +1352
rains (1)
thunderstorm (1)
torrents (1)

2444 זִרְמָה *zirmāh* (2)
emission (1)
that[s] (1)

2445 זָרַע *zāra'* (56)
sow (16)
plant (9)
planted (4)
sown (4)
planted crops (2)
seed-bearing (2) +2446
sower (2)
sows (2)
be able to have children (1) +2446
be planted (1)
bearing (1)
have descendants (1)
is shed (1)
plant (1) +2446
plant seed (1)
plant with seed (1)
planting (1)
pregnant (1)
scatter (1)
scattered (1)
seed (1) +2446
sowed (1)
sowing seed (1)

2446 זֶרַע *zera'* (230)
descendants (82)
offspring (35)
seed (25)
children (20)
family (5)
grain (5)
semen (5)
line (4)
people (4)
descent (3)
blood (2)
descendant (2)
descended (2)
family line (2)
posterity (2)
seed-bearing (2) +2445
be able to have children (1) +2445
brood (1)
child (1)
crops (1)
descendant (1) +408+4946
fertile (1)
have sexual relations (1) +4200+5989+8888
Jews[s] (1)
origin (1)
plant (1)
plant (1) +2445
planter (1) +5432
planting (1)
produce (1) +3655+9311
race (1)
righteous (1) +7404
seed (1) +2445
seed to sow (1) +5433
seeds (1) +2433
seedtime (1)
sleeping with (1) +907+8886+8887
sleeps with (1) +907+8886+8887
son (1) +408
sons (1)
stock (1)
their[s] (1) +3870

them[s] (1) +3870
various kinds (1)
untranslated (2)

2447 זֵרֹעִים *zĕrō'iym* (1)
vegetables (1)

2448 זֵרְעֹנִים *zĕr'ōniym* (1)
vegetables (1)

2449 זָרַף *zārap* (1)
watering (1)

2450 זָרַק 1 *zāraq1* (35)
sprinkled (15)
sprinkle (11)
been sprinkled (2)
scatter (2)
scattered (1)
sprinkles (1)
sprinkling (1)
toss (1)
tossed (1)

2451 זָרַק 2 *zāraq2*
Variant; not used

2452 זָרַר 1 *zārar1*
Variant; not used

2453 זָרַר 2 *zārar2* (1)
sneezed (1)

2454 זֶרֶשׁ *zereš* (4)
Zeresh (4)

2455 זֶרֶת *zeret* (7)
span (5)
breadth of hand (1)
over nine feet (1) +564+2256+9252

2456 זַתּוּא *zatû'* (4)
Zattu (4)

2457 זֵתָם *zētām* (2)
Zetham (2)

2458 זֵתָר *zētar* (1)
Zethar (1)

2459 ח *h*
Variant; not used

2460 חֹב *hōb* (1)
heart (1)

2461 חָבָא *hābā'* (36)
hid (7)
hidden (7)
hiding (5)
hide (3)
hid themselves (2)
be protected (1)
become hard (1)
force into hiding (1)
hidden away (1)
hidden himself (1)
hide themselves (1)
hide yourselves (1)
hushed (1)
secretly (1)
stay there (1)
stepped aside (1)
uses[s] (1)

2462 חָבַב *hābab* (1)
love (1)

2463 חֹבָב *hōbāb* (2)
Hobab (2)

2464 חָבָה *hābāh* (2)
conceal himself (1)
hide (1)

2465 חֻבָּה *hubbāh* (1)
Hubbah (1)

2466 חָבוֹר *hābôr* (3)
Habor (3)

2467 חַבּוּרָה *habbûrāh* (7)

bruise (2)
wounds (2)
Blows (1)
injuring (1)
welts (1)

2468 חָבַט *hābat* (5)
beat (1)
is beaten out (1)
thresh (1)
threshed (1)
threshing (1)

2469 חֲבַיָּה *h°bayyāh* (2)
Hobaiah (2)

2470 חֶבְיוֹן *hebyôn* (1)
hidden (1)

2471 חָבַל 1 *hābal1* (12)
hold in pledge (2)
demanded security (1)
require a pledge for a loan (1) +2478
seized for a debt (1)
take as a pledge (1)
take as a pledge (1) +2471
take as security for a debt (1)
take in pledge (1)
taken in pledge (1)
taking as security (1)

2472 חָבַל 2 *hābal2* (12)
destroy (3)
acted very wickedly (1) +2472
be broken (1)
is broken (1)
offend (1)
pay for it (1)
ruin (1)
ruined (1) +2256+2476
work havoc (1)

2473 חָבַל 3 *hābal3* (3)
conceived (1)
in labor (1)
pregnant (1)

2474 חֶבֶל 1 *hebel1* (2)
procession (2)

2475 חֶבֶל 2 *hebel2* (49)
cords (11)
ropes (9)
region (4)
portion (3)
land (2)
rope (2)
share (2)
allotted (1)
boundary lines (1)
by (1)
cord (1)
district (1)
fate (1)
it[s] (1)
lands (1)
length (1)
length of cord (1)
lengths (1)
line (1)
measured (1)
noose (1)
portions (1)
rigging (1)

2476 חֶבֶל 3 *hebel3* (1)
ruined (1) +2256+2472

2477 חֵבֶל *hēbel* (8)
pain (3)
pains (2)
anguish (1)
labor pains (1)
pangs (1)

2478 חֲבֹל *h°bōl* (3)
require a pledge for a loan (1) +2471

what took in pledge (1)
what took in pledge for a loan (1)

2479 חִבֵּל *hibbēl* (1)
rigging (1)

2480 חֹבֵל *hōbēl* (5)
seamen (3)
captain (1) +2021+8042
seamen (1) +3542

2481 חֲבֹלָה *hᵃbōlāh* (1)
what took in pledge (1)

2482 חֹבְלִים *hōbliym* (2)
union (2)

2483 חֲבַצֶּלֶת *hᵃbasselet* (2)
crocus (1)
rose (1)

2484 חֲבַצִּנְיָה *hᵃbassinyāh* (1)
Habazziniah (1)

2485 חָבַק *hābaq* (13)
embrace (3)
embraced (3)
embraces (2)
folds (1)
hold in arms (1)
hug (1)
lie (1)
untranslated (1)

2486 חִבֻּק *hibbuq* (2)
folding (2)

2487 חֲבַקּוּק *hᵃbaqqûq* (2)
Habakkuk (2)

2488 1חָבַר *hābar1* (1)
make fine speeches (1) +928+4863

2489 2חָבַר *hābar2* (28)
attached (2)
be fastened (2)
fasten (2)
fasten together (2)
joined (2)
made an alliance (2)
agreed (1)
allied with (1)
allies (1)
among (1)
casts spells (1) +2490
coming to an agreement (1)
did the sameˢ (1) +285+285+448
do the sameˢ (1)
enchanter (1) +2490
is closely compacted (1)
join (1)
join together (1)
joined forces (1)
joined to (1)
touched (1)
touching (1)

2490 1חֶבֶר *heber1* (7)
bands (1)
casts spells (1) +2489
enchanter (1) +2489
magic spells (1)
share (1)
share with (1)
spells (1)

2491 2חֶבֶר *heber2* (11)
Heber (10)
Heber's (1)

2492 חָבֵר *hābēr* (15)
associated with (3)
companions (2)
friend (2)
friends (2)
kind (1)
partner (1)
united (1)

untranslated (3)

2493 חַבָּר *habbār* (1)
traders (1)

2494 חֲבַרְבֻּרוֹת *hᵃbarburôt* (1)
spots (1)

2495 חֶבְרָה *hebrāh* (1)
keeps company (1) +782+4200

2496 1חֶבְרוֹן *hebrôn1* (63)
Hebron (62)
untranslated (1)

2497 2חֶבְרוֹן *hebrôn2* (10)
Hebron (10)

2498 חֶבְרוֹנִי *hebrôniy* (6)
Hebronites (4)
Hebronite (1)
theirˢ (1) +2021+4200

2499 חֶבְרִי *hebriy* (1)
Heberite (1)

2500 חֲבֶרֶת *hᵃberet* (1)
partner (1)

2501 חֹבֶרֶת *hōberet* (4)
set (4)

2502 חָבַשׁ *hābaš* (32)
saddled (9)
bind up (3)
binds up (3)
put (2)
saddle (2)
bandaged (1)
been bound up (1)
bound up (1)
did soˢ (1)
dressed (1)
fastened (1)
govern (1)
have saddled (1)
remedy (1)
shroud (1)
twisted (1)
wrapped around (1)
untranslated (1)

2503 חֲבִתִּים *hᵃbitiym* (1)
offering bread (1)

2504 חַג *hag* (62)
feast (33)
festival (19)
festivals (4)
religious feasts (2)
festal procession (1)
festival offerings (1)
festival sacrifices (1)
yearly festivals (1)

2505 חָגָּא *hāggā'* (1)
terror (1)

2506 1חָגָב *hāgāb1* (5)
grasshopper (2)
grasshoppers (2)
locusts (1)

2507 2חָגָב *hāgāb2* (1)
Hagab (1)

2508 חֲגָבָא *hᵃgābā'*
Variant; not used

2509 חֲגָבָה *hᵃgābāh* (2)
Hagaba (1)
Hagabah (1)

2510 חָגַג *hāgag* (16)
celebrate (9)
celebrate a festival (1)
celebrate the feast (1)
festive (1)
hold a festival (1)
reeled (1)

reveling (1)
untranslated (1)

2511 חָגוּ *hāgû* (3)
clefts (3)

2512 חֲגוֹר *hᵃgôr* (3)
belt (2)
sashes (1)

2513 חָגוֹר *hāgôr* (3)
belts (1) +258

2514 חֲגוֹרָה *hᵃgôrāh* (5)
bear arms (1) +2520
belt (1)
coverings (1)
sash (1)
warrior's belt (1)

2515 חַגִּי *haggiy* (3)
Haggi (2)
Haggite (1)

2516 חַגַּי *haggay* (9)
Haggai (9)

2517 חַגִּיָּה *haggiyyāh* (1)
Haggiah (1)

2518 חַגִּית *haggiyt* (5)
Haggith (5)

2519 חָגְלָה *hoglāh* (4)
Hoglah (4)

2520 חָגַר *hāgar* (43)
put on (13)
wearing (4)
armed (3) +3998
tied around (3)
tuck cloak into belt (2) +5516
wear (2)
bear arms (1) +2514
belt (1)
cloak tucked into belt (1) +5516
clothed (1)
fastened on (1)
gird (1)
in (1)
put sackcloth around (1)
puts on armor (1)
restrained (1)
sets about work (1) +5516
strapped (1)
tie (1)
tie around (1)
tied (1)
was armed (1)

2521 1חַד *had1* (4)
sharp (3)
sharpened (1)

2522 2חַד *had2* (1)
each (1)

2523 חָדַד *hādad* (5)
sharpened (2)
fiercer (1)
is sharpened (1)
slash (1)

2524 חֲדַד *hᵃdad* (2)
Hadad (2)

2525 1חָדָה *hādāh1* (2)
delighted (1)
made glad (1)

2526 2חָדָה *hādāh2* (1)
be included (1)

2527 3חָדָה *hādāh3* (2)
sharpens (2)

2528 חַדָּה *haddāh*
Variant; not used

2529 חַדּוּד *haddûd* (1)
jagged (1)

2530 חֶדְוָה *hedwāh* (2)
joy (2)

2531 חָדִיד *hādiyd* (3)
Hadid (3)

2532 1חָדַל *hādal1* (59)
stopped (10)
stop (8)
refrain (5)
fail (4)
ceased (3)
give up (3)
let alone (3)
not (2)
abandoned (1)
absent (1)
always be (1) +4202
cease (1)
do not (1)
don't (1)
failing (1)
fails (1)
gone away (1)
keep (1)
leave alone (1) +4946
no enough (1)
no more (1)
over (1)
past (1)
refrain from (1)
refuse (1)
show restraint (1)
silent (1)
stop trusting in (1) +4946
untranslated (1)

2533 2חָדַל *hādal2*
Variant; not used

2534 חָדֵל *hādēl* (3)
fleeting (1)
refuse (1)
rejected (1)

2535 חֶדֶל *hedel* (1)
this world (1)

2536 חַדְלָי *hadlāy* (1)
Hadlai (1)

2537 חֶדֶק *hēdeq* (2)
brier (1)
thorns (1)

2538 חִדֶּקֶל *hiddeqel* (2)
Tigris (2)

2539 חָדַר *hādar* (1)
closing in from every side (1)

2540 חֶדֶר *heder* (35)
room (6)
bedroom (4) +5435
inner room (4) +928+2540
rooms (3)
bedroom (2)
bedroom (2) +4753
chambers (2)
inmost being (2) +1061
inmost parts (2) +1061
bedrooms (1)
chamber (1)
constellations (1)
homes (1)
inner room (1)
private room (1)
shrine (1)

2541 חַדְרָךְ *hadrāk* (1)
Hadrach (1)

2542 חָדַשׁ *hādaš* (10)
renew (4)
restore (2)
bring new (1)
is renewed (1)
reaffirm (1)
repaired (1)

2543 חָדָשׁ *hādāš* (53)
new (50)
fresh (1)
recently (1)
recently (1) +4946+7940

2544 1חֹדֶשׁ *hōdeš1* (283)
month (193)
months (30)
new Moon (7)
new Moons (7)
new Moon festivals (4)
new Moon festival (3)
another⁵ (1)
mating time (1)
monthly (1)
monthly (1) +928+2544
new moon (1)
new Moon festivals (1) +8031
whole month (1) +3427
untranslated (31)

2545 2חֹדֶשׁ *hōdeš2* (1)
Hodesh (1)

2546 חֲדָשָׁה *hᵉdāšāh* (1)
Hadashah (1)

2547 חָדְשִׁי *hodšiy*
Variant; not used

2548 חֲדַתָּה *hᵉdatāh*
Variant; not used

2549 חוּב *hûb* (1)
because of (1)

2550 חוֹב *hôb* (1)
loan (1)

2551 חוֹבָה *hôbāh* (1)
Hobah (1)

2552 1חוּג *hûg1* (1)
marks out (1)

2553 2חוּג *hûg2* (3)
circle (1)
horizon (1)
vaulted (1)

2554 חוּד *hûd* (4)
tell (2)
given (1)
set forth (1)

2555 1חָוָה *hāwāh1* (6)
tell (3)
display (1)
explain (1)
show (1)

2556 2חָוָה *hāwāh2* (173)
worship (39)
bow down (33)
bowed down (30)
worshiped (23)
pay honor (7)
worshiping (7)
bowed (6)
bowing down (5)
bowed in worship (2)
prostrated himself (2)
worships (2)
bow (1)
bow down to worship (1)
bowed low (1)
bows down (1)
fell facedown (1) +678+4200
fell prostrate (1)
honor (1)
humbly bow (1)
kneeling (1)
knelt (1)
paid homage (1)

paid honor (1)
reverence (1)
worshiped leaned (1)
untranslated (3)

2557 1חַוָּה *hawwāh1* (3)
settlements (3)

2558 2חַוָּה *hawwāh2* (2)
eve (2)

2559 חוֹזָי *hôzāy*
Variant; not used

2560 1חוֹחַ *hôah1* (12)
thistle (4)
hook (2)
thorns (2)
brambles (1)
briers (1)
thickets (1)
thornbush (1)

2561 2חוֹחַ *hôah2*
Variant; not used

2562 חוּט *hût* (7)
circumference (1) +6015
cord (1)
cord (1) +9535
line (1)
ribbon (1)
thread (1)
threads (1)

2563 חִוִּי *hiwwiy* (25)
Hivites (23)
Hivite (2)

2564 חֲוִילָה *hᵃwiylāh* (7)
Havilah (7)

2565 1חוּל *hûl1* (10)
swirling down (2)
dancing (1)
fall (1)
flash (1)
join (1)
turned (1)
wait (1)
wait patiently (1)
untranslated (1)

2566 2חוּל *hûl2* (2)
Hul (2)

2567 1חוֹל *hôl1* (23)
sand (21)
grains of sand (2)

2568 2חוֹל *hôl2*
Variant; not used

2569 חוּם *hûm* (4)
dark-colored (4)

2570 חוֹמָה *hômāh* (133)
wall (81)
walls (43)
city wall (2)
walled (2)
it⁵ (1) +2021
walled (1) +2257+4200
untranslated (3)

2571 חוּס *hûs* (24)
look with pity (6) +6524
show pity (4) +6524
concerned (2)
looked with pity (2) +6524
show mercy (2)
have pity (1)
look with compassion (1) +6524
mercy (1)
mind (1)
showing pity (1) +6524
spare (1)
spared (1)
take pity (1)

2572 חוֹף *hôp* (7)
coast (4) +3542
coast (1)
haven (1)
seashore (1) +3542

2573 חוּפָם *hûpām* (1)
Hupham (1)

2574 חוּפָמִי *hûpāmiy* (1)
Huphamite (1)

2575 חוּץ *hûs* (164)
outside (49) +4946
streets (38)
street (13)
outside (8)
outside (8) +2025
outside (7) +928+2021
out (5) +2025
out (4) +4946
outer (3)
fields (2)
outside (2) +2025+4946
abroad (1) +2021+4200
area (1) +4946
around (1) +2021+4946
away (1) +448+2021+2025
countryside (1)
elsewhere (1)
extend out (1) +2025
get out of here (1) +2021+2025+8938
land (1)
market areas (1)
out (1)
out here (1) +928+2021
outdoor (1) +928+2021
outer (1) +2021+4200
outside the family (1) +2021+2025+2424
put out (1) +2021+3655
relieve yourself (1) +3782
without (1) +4946
untranslated (7)

2576 חוֹק *hôq*
Variant; not used

2577 חוּקֹק *hûqōq* (1)
Hukok (1)

2578 חָוַר *hāwar1* (1)
grow pale (1)

2579 חָוַר *hāwar2*
Variant; not used

2580 חוּר *hûr1* (2)
white (2)

2581 חוּר *hûr2* (15)
Hur (15)

2582 חוֹרוֹן *hôrôn*
Variant; not used

2583 חוֹרִי *hôrāy* (1)
fine linen (1)

2584 חוּרַי *hûray* (1)
Hurai (1)

2585 חוּרִי *hûriy* (1)
Huri (1)

2586 חוּרָם *hûrām* (11)
Hiram (6)
Huram (2)
he[s] (1)
Hiram's (1)
untranslated (1)

2587 חוּרָם אֲבִי *hûrām 'ăbiy* (2)
Huram-Abi (2)

2588 חַוְרָן *hawrān* (2)
Hauran (2)

2589 חוֹרֹנַיִם *hôrōnayim* (5)
Horonaim (5)

2590 חוּשׁ *hûš1* (18)
come quickly (7)
hasten (2)
do swiftly (1)
go quickly (1)
hurried (1)
hurry (1)
ready (1)
rushes (1)
sudden (1)
swooping (1)
untranslated (1)

2591 חוּשׁ *hûš2* (3)
dismayed (1)
find enjoyment (1)
greatly disturbed (1)

2592 חוּשָׁה *hûšāh* (1)
Hushah (1)

2593 חוּשִׁי *hûšay* (14)
Hushai (12)
untranslated (2)

2594 חוּשִׁים *hûšiym* (2)
Hushim (2)

2595 חוּשָׁם *hûšām* (4)
Husham (4)

2596 חַוֹּת יָאִיר *hawwōt yā'iyr* (4)
Havvoth Jair (4)

2597 חוֹתָם *hôtām1* (14)
seal (10)
signet ring (2)
placed seal (1) +928+3159
sealed together (1) +6037

2598 חוֹתָם *hôtām2* (2)
Hotham (2)

2599 חֲזָאֵל *hăzā'ēl* (23)
Hazael (21)
he[s] (1)
his[s] (1)

2600 חָזָה *hāzāh* (54)
see (13)
saw (5)
seen (5)
visions (5)
gaze (3)
look (3)
see visions (3)
sees (3)
are[s] (1)
gave (1)
give visions (1)
gloat (1)
looked (1)
looks (1)
observed (1)
observes (1)
prophesy (1)
received (1)
saw visions (1) +2606
select (1)
stargazers (1) +928+3919
vision saw (1)

2601 חָזֶה *hāzeh* (13)
breast (11)
breasts (2)

2602 חֹזֶה *hōzeh1* (17)
seer (11)
seers (5)
prophets (1)

2603 חֹזֶה *hōzeh2* (1)
agreement (1)

2604 חֲזָהאֵל *hăzāh'ēl*
Variant; not used

2605 חֲזוֹ *hăzô* (1)
Hazo (1)

2606 חָזוֹן *hāzôn* (35)
vision (22)
visions (8)
revelation (4)
saw visions (1) +2600

2607 חָזוּת *hāzût* (5)
prominent (2)
vision (2)
agreement (1)

2608 חֲזוֹת *hăzôt* (1)
visions (1)

2609 חֲזִיאֵל *hăziy'ēl* (1)
Haziel (1)

2610 חֲזָיָה *hăzāyāh* (1)
Hazaiah (1)

2611 חֶזְיוֹן *hezyôn* (1)
Hezion (1)

2612 חִזָּיוֹן *hizzāyôn* (9)
vision (5)
visions (2)
dreams (1)
revelation (1)

2613 חֲזִיז *hăziyz* (3)
thunderstorm (2) +7754
storm clouds (1)

2614 חֲזִיר *hăziyr* (7)
pig (2)
pig's (2)
pigs (2)
boars (1)

2615 חֵזִיר *hēziyr* (2)
Hezir (2)

2616 חָזַק *hāzaq* (290)
strong (41)
repaired (18)
made repairs (14)
strengthen (12)
repair (10)
took hold (7)
hardened (6)
severe (5)
strengthened (5)
stronger (5)
encourage (4)
firmly (4)
hard (4)
repairs made (4)
take hold (4)
took (4)
gripped (3)
harden (3)
hold fast (3)
powerful (3)
seizes (3)
armed (2)
embraced (2)
encouraged (2)
encouraged (2) +3338
established himself firmly (2)
fasten (2)
fight bravely (2)
grabbed (2)
held (2)
help (2)
holds fast (2)
seize (2)
take (2)
took courage (2)
urged (2)
assisted (1) +928+3338
assisted (1) +3338
be sure (1)
began (1) +3338
brace yourselves (1) +5516
captured (1)
carried out repairs (1)

caught (1)
caught hold (1)
caulk (1)
cling (1)
clings (1)
come (1)
conquered (1) +6584
courage (1)
courageously (1)
devote (1)
devoted (1)
do best (1)
embrace (1)
encourages (1)
equipped (1)
fortified (1)
found strength (1)
gave power (1)
gave strength (1)
gave strong support (1) +6640
give strength (1)
given strength (1)
gone^S (1)
grasped (1)
grasping (1)
grew in strength (1)
grips (1)
harsh (1)
have strength (1)
heavier (1)
held secure (1)
help (1) +3338
helped (1)
helped (1) +906+3338
helped find strength (1) +906+3338
hold back (1)
hold on (1)
holding (1)
holding on (1)
join (1) +6584
kept (1)
lay hold (1)
leans (1)
made harder (1)
made strong (1)
maintain (1)
maintains (1)
marshaled strength (1)
nails down (1) +928+5021
overpowered (1)
overruled (1) +448
overruled (1) +6584
preserve (1)
press (1)
prevailed upon (1) +928
proved stronger (1)
rallied strength (1)
rapes (1) +2256+6640+8886
recovery (1)
reinforce (1)
reinforced (1)
repair (1) +981
repairing (1)
resist (1)
restored (1)
restoring (1)
seized (1)
shipwrights (1) +981
showed strength (1)
stay (1)
strengthen position (1)
strengthened (1) +2432
strengthened himself (1)
strengthening his own position (1)
strengthens (1)
strong (1) +3338
support (1)
supported (1)
supports (1) +6640
take courage (1)
take firm hold (1)

take up (1)
takes hold (1)
triumphed (1)
unswerving (1)
victorious (1)
was strengthened (1)
worked hard (1)
untranslated (3)

2617 חָזָק *hāzāq* (57)
mighty (23)
strong (12)
powerful (6)
hardened (2) +5195
power (2)
stronger (2)
bitter (1)
fiercest (1)
good (1)
grew worse and worse (1)
            +2118+2716+4394
hard (1)
harder (1)
loud (1)
severe (1)
stubborn (1) +4213
unyielding (1) +7156

2618 חָזֵק *hāzēq* (2)
grew louder and louder (1)
            +2143+2256+4394
grew stronger and stronger (1) +2143+2256

2619 חֵזֶק *hēzeq* (1)
strength (1)

2620 חֹזֶק *hōzeq* (5)
mighty (3)
power (1)
strength (1)

2621 חִזְקָה *hezqāh* (4)
became powerful (1)
become strong (1)
gained power (1)
strong (1)

2622 חָזְקָה *hāzqāh* (5)
cruelly (1) +928
force (1)
harshly (1) +928
sharply (1) +928
urgently (1) +928

2623 חִזְקִי *hizqiy* (1)
Hizki (1)

2624 חִזְקִיָּה *hizqiyyāh* (13)
Hezekiah (9)
he^S (1)
Hezekiah's (1)
Hezekiah's (1) +4200
Hizkiah (1)

2625 חִזְקִיָּהוּ *hizqiyyāhû* (74)
Hezekiah (66)
Hezekiah's (5)
he^S (2)
Hezekiah's (1) +4200

2626 חָח *hāh* (8)
hooks (4)
hook (2)
brooches (1)
untranslated (1)

2627 חָטָא *hātā'* (239)
sinned (68)
committed (23)
sin (23)
caused to commit (20)
sins (19)
purify (9)
sinning (6)
sinner (5)
caused to sin (4)

wronged (4)
purify himself (3)
bear the blame (2)
do wrong (2)
done wrong (2)
led into sin (2)
purified (2)
sinful (2)
wrongs (2)
a sin committed (1) +2631
be purified (1)
bore the loss (1)
bring sin (1)
cause to sin (1)
cleanse (1)
commit (1)
commit a sin (1)
commits sin (1)
committed (1) +2628
committed a sin (1) +2631
crime committed (1)
failed to do (1)
fails to find (1)
fails to reach (1)
fault (1)
find missing (1)
forfeiting (1)
forfeits (1)
lead into sin (1)
make out to be guilty (1)
make sin (1)
miss (1)
miss the way (1)
offended (1)
offered for a sin offering (1)
offers (1)
presented for a sin offering (1)
purified themselves (1)
purify yourselves (1)
purifying (1)
retreat (1)
sin offerings (1)
sinned greatly (1) +2628
sinner's (1)
wicked (1)
untranslated (5)

2628 חֵטְא *hēt'* (34)
sins (8)
sin (5)
guilty of sin (3)
consequences of sin (2)
guilty (2)
held responsible (2) +5951
sinful (2)
become guilty (1) +5951+6584
committed (1) +2627
consequences of sins (1)
errors (1)
guilt (1)
guilty (1) +5951
punished for sins (1)
shortcomings (1)
sinned greatly (1) +2627
untranslated (1)

2629 חַטָּא *hattā'* (19)
sinners (13)
criminals (1)
sinful (1)
sinned (1)
sinner (1)
sinning (1)
wicked people (1)

2630 חֶטְאָה *het'āh* (1)
sinning (1)

2631 חֲטָאָה *hªtā'āh* (8)
sin (2)
a sin committed (1) +2627
committed a sin (1) +2627
condemn (1) +2118+4200

guilt (1)
sin offerings (1)
sins (1)

2632 חַטָּאָה *hattā'āh*
Variant; not used

2633 חַטָּאת *hattā't* (298)
sin offering (105)
sin (85)
sins (74)
sin offerings (8)
punishment (3)
cleansing (1)
iniquities (1)
it^s (1) +2021
its^s (1) +2021
offense (1)
purification from sin (1)
purification offering (1)
sinful thing (1)
sinner (1)
sinning (1)
that^s (1)
wickedness (1)
wronged (1)
wrongs (1)
wrongs (1) +6913
untranslated (8)

2634 חָטַב *hātab* (9)
woodcutters (3) +6770
cut (2)
carved (1)
chop (1)
cut down (1)
woodsmen (1)

2635 חֲטֻבוֹת *h^tubôt* (1)
colored (1)

2636 חִטָּה *hittāh* (30)
wheat (30)

2637 חַטּוּשׁ *hattûš* (5)
Hattush (5)

2638 חֲטִיטָא *h^tiytā'* (2)
Hatita (2)

2639 חַטִּיל *hattiyl* (2)
Hattil (2)

2640 חֲטִיפָא *h^tiypā'* (2)
Hatipha (2)

2641 חָטַם *hātam* (1)
hold back (1)

2642 חָטַף *hātap* (3)
catch (1)
catches (1)
seize (1)

2643 חֹטֶר *hōter* (2)
rod (1)
shoot (1)

2644 1חַי *hay1* (238)
life (108)
as surely as lives (46)
as surely as live (23)
live (12)
lived (9)
as live (6)
lives (6)
as lives (3)
living (3)
as surely as live (2) +5883
lifetime (2)
as surely as live (1) +2256+2644+5883
creature (1)
life will not be worth living (1) +4200+4537
life-giving (1)
lifetime (1) +3427
live (1) +928+2021
long life (1) +2021+4200
nourish (1)

old (1) +3427+9102
untranslated (8)

2645 2חַי *hay2* (146)
living (62)
alive (34)
live (15)
fresh (8)
raw (5)
lives (3)
life (2)
lifetime (2)
next year (2)
next year (2) +6961
as surely as live (1)
flowing (1)
green (1)
it^s (1) +2021+2021+7606
lived (1)
living creatures (1)
living thing (1)
others^s (1)
preserved (1) +928+2021+8492
raw (1) +4695
vigorous (1)

2646 3חַי *hay3* (1)
family (1)

2647 חִיאֵל *hiy'ēl* (1)
Hiel (1)

2648 חִידָה *hiydāh* (17)
riddle (8)
hard questions (2)
riddles (2)
allegory (1)
answer (1)
hidden things (1)
intrigue (1)
scorn (1)

2649 חָיָה *hāyāh* (275)
live (90)
lived (43)
preserve life (12)
spared (10)
long live (9)
surely live (9) +2649
keep alive (7)
let live (7)
recover (6)
revive (5)
save life (5)
kept alive (3)
leave alive (3)
preserve (3)
restored to life (3)
allowed to live (2)
bring back to life (2)
came to life (2)
certainly recover (2) +2649
come to life (2)
preserves life (2)
revived (2)
save (2)
save lives (2)
spare (2)
survive (2)
survived (2)
allow to live (1)
bring to life (1)
brought back to life (1)
choose life (1)
die (1) +4202
flourish (1)
give life (1)
gives life (1)
healed (1)
live again (1)
live on (1)
lives (1)
makes alive (1)
preserved life (1)

protect lives (1)
raised (1)
recovered (1)
recovery (1) +2716+4946
renew (1)
restore life (1)
restored (1)
saved lives (1)
saving (1)
spare life (1)
spare lives (1)
spared lives (1)
sparing (1)
stay alive (1)
will^s (1)
untranslated (5)

2650 חָיֶה *hāyeh* (1)
vigorous (1)

2651 1חַיָּה *hayyāh1* (103)
animals (25)
beasts (25)
living creatures (13)
living (8)
animal (7)
wild animals (6)
beast (4)
creatures (3)
living creature (2)
wild beasts (2)
animal (1) +7473
beasts of burden (1) +989+2256
creature (1)
livestock (1)
living things (1)
ones^s (1)
those^s (1) +2021
wild animal (1)

2652 2חַיָּה *hayyāh2* (13)
life (3)
hunger (1)
live (1)
lives (1)
me (1) +3276
renewal (1)
them (1) +4392
very being (1)
untranslated (3)

2653 3חַיָּה *hayyāh3* (3)
band (1)
banded together (1) +665+2021+4200
people (1)

2654 חַיּוּת *hayyût* (1)
living (1)

2655 1חִיל *hiyl1* (47)
in anguish (4)
in labor (4)
tremble (4)
gave birth (2)
shakes (2)
was given birth (2)
wounded (2)
writhe (2)
writhe in pain (2)
writhed (2)
writhes (2)
at birth (1)
be born (1)
bears (1)
brings (1)
brought forth (1)
brought to birth (1)
felt pain (1)
goes into labor (1)
in deep anguish (1)
in distress (1)
suffers torment (1)
trembles (1)
twists (1)

were brought forth (1)
writhe in agony (1) +2655
writhe in agony (1) +4394
writhed in pain (1)
untranslated (1)

2656 חִיל 2 *hiyl2* (2)
endure (1)
prosperous (1)

2657 חַיִל *hayil* (246)
army (77)
wealth (25)
fighting men (12) +1475
strength (11)
brave warriors (6) +1475
riches (5)
able men (4) +1201
brave (4) +1201
force (4)
troops (4)
valiant (4)
capable (3)
forces (3)
noble character (3)
soldiers (3)
strong (3)
able men (2) +1475
able-bodied (2)
best fighting men (2) +1475
caravan (2)
might (2)
mighty things (2)
power (2)
standing (2)
standing (2) +1475
valiant fighter (2) +408+1201
valiant fighters (2) +408
valiant soldier (2) +1475
victory (2)
warriors (2) +408
worthy (2)
able (1)
able (1) +1201
able-bodied (1) +1201
armed force (1)
armed forces (1) +7372
armies (1)
army (1) +2162
army (1) +7372
battle (1)
brave (1)
brave fighting men (1) +1475
brave man (1) +1475
brave warrior (1) +1475
bravely (1) +1201+4200
bravest soldier (1) +1201
capable men (1) +1475
champions (1) +408
company (1)
courageous (1) +1201
experienced fighting men (1)
                +408+1475+4878
fighting (1)
fighting (1) +1201
goods (1)
mighty (1)
mighty men (1) +1475
mighty warrior (1) +1475
military (1)
military leaders (1)
noble (1)
one^s (1)
profit (1)
skills (1)
soldiers (1) +1201
special ability (1)
strongest defenders (1) +408
they^s (1) +2021+2256+3405+8569
troops (1) +1475
valiantly (1)
very capable men (1) +1475

warriors (1) +1201
warriors (1) +1475
wealthy (1)
untranslated (3)

2658 חֵיל *hēyl* (7)
ramparts (3)
defense (1)
outer fortifications (1)
wall (1)
walls (1)

2659 חִיל 3 *hiyl3* (6)
pain (5)
anguish (1)

2660 חִילָה *hiylāh* (1)
pain (1)

2661 חִילֵז *hiylēz*
Variant; not used

2662 חֵילֵךְ *hēylēk* (1)
Helech (1)

2663 חֵילָם *hēylām* (2)
Helam (2)

2664 חִילֵן *hiylēn* (1)
Hilen (1)

2665 חִין *hiyn* (1)
graceful (1)

2666 חַיִץ *hayis* (1)
flimsy wall (1)

2667 חִיצוֹן *hiysôn* (25)
outer (20)
away from (1)
both outer (1)
outside (1)
outside (1) +2025
where^s (1) +2021+2021+2958

2668 חֵיק *hēyq* (39)
arms (6)
cloak (5)
lap (4)
laps (4)
gutter (3)
breast (2)
heart (2)
loves (2)
beside (1) +928
bosom (1)
embrace (1)
floor (1)
garment (1)
love (1)
returned unanswered (1) +8740
secret (1)
within (1) +928
untranslated (2)

2669 חִירָה *hiyrāh* (2)
Hirah (2)

2670 חִירוֹם *hiyrôm* (3)
Hiram (2)
he^s (1)

2671 חִירָם *hiyrām* (22)
Hiram (15)
Huram (3)
he^s (1)
Hiram's (1)
untranslated (2)

2672 חִירֹת *hiyrōt*
Variant; not used

2673 חִישׁ *hiyš* (1)
quickly (1)

2674 חֵךְ *hēk* (18)
mouth (6)
roof of mouth (3)
taste (3)
tongue (2)

lips (1)
on the tip of tongue (1) +928+4383
roof of mouths (1)
speech (1)

2675 חָכָה *hākāh* (14)
wait (7)
delay (1)
lie in ambush (1)
long for (1)
longs (1)
wait in hope (1)
waited (1)
waits for (1)

2676 חַכָּה *hakkāh* (3)
hooks (2)
fishhook (1)

2677 חֲכִילָה *hᵃkiylāh* (3)
Hakilah (3)

2678 חֲכַלְיָה *hᵃkalyāh* (2)
Hacaliah (2)

2679 חַכְלִילִי *hakliyliy* (1)
darker (1)

2680 חַכְלִלוּת *haklilût* (1)
bloodshot (1)

2681 חָכַם *hākam* (28)
wise (13)
skillful (2)
wisdom (2)
wiser (2)
deal shrewdly (1)
extremely wise (1) +2682
make wiser (1)
makes wiser (1)
making wise (1)
overwise (1) +3463
skill (1)
teach wisdom (1)
untranslated (1)

2682 חָכָם *hākām* (138)
wise (105)
skilled (7)
skilled (6) +4213
wisdom (4)
craftsmen (2)
skilled craftsmen (2)
wiser (2)
advisers (1)
craftsmen (1) +4213
extremely wise (1) +2681
great skill (1) +1069+3359
shrewd (1)
skillful (1)
those^s (1)
unwise (1) +4202
wise (1) +4213
wisest (1)

2683 חָכְמָה *hokmāh* (149)
wisdom (131)
skill (7)
learning (2)
skilled (2)
ability (1) +928+4213
at wits' end (1) +1182+3972
skill (1) +4213
that^s (1)
wisdom (1) +8120
wise (1)
wise advice (1)

2684 חָכְמוֹת *hokmôt* (4)
wisdom (4)

2685 חַכְמוֹנִי *hakmôniy* (2)
Hacmoni (1)
Hacmonite (1) +1201

2686 חָכַר *hākar* (1)
attack (1)

2687 חֹל *ḥōl* (7)
common (4)
common use (1)
not holy (1)
ordinary (1)

2688 חָלָא *ḥālā'* (1)
afflicted with a disease (1)

2689 חֶלְאָה1 *ḥel'āh1* (5)
deposit (3)
encrusted (1)
untranslated (1)

2690 חֶלְאָה2 *ḥel'āh2* (2)
Helah (2)

2691 חֵלְאָם *ḥēlā'm*
Variant; not used

2692 חָלָב *ḥālāb* (44)
milk (41)
cheeses (1) +3043
suckling (1)
well nourished (1) +4848

2693 חֵלֶב1 *ḥēleb1* (92)
fat (64)
fat portions (7)
finest (5)
best (3)
callous hearts (2)
callous (1) +2021+3869
curds (1)
fattened (1)
flesh (1)
richest of foods (1) +2016+2256
these^s (1) +2021
untranslated (5)

2694 חֵלֶב2 *ḥēleb2*
Variant; not used

2695 חֶלְבָּה *ḥelbāh* (1)
Helbah (1)

2696 חֶלְבּוֹן *ḥelbôn* (1)
Helbon (1)

2697 חֶלְבְּנָה *ḥelb'nāh* (1)
galbanum (1)

2698 חֶלֶד *ḥeled* (5)
world (2)
fleeting life (1)
life (1)
span of years (1)

2699 חֵלֶד *ḥēled* (2)
Heled (2)

2700 חֹלֶד *ḥōled* (1)
weasel (1)

2701 חֻלְדָּה *ḥuldāh* (2)
Huldah (2)

2702 חֶלְדַּי *ḥelday* (3)
Heldai (3)

2703 חָלָה1 *ḥālāh1* (56)
ill (13)
weak (8)
illness (4)
diseased (3)
faint (3)
wounded (3)
been wounded (2)
grievous (2)
afflicted (1)
beyond healing (1)
cause to suffer (1)
concerned (1)
crushing (1) +4394
fatal (1)
grieve (1)
hurt (1)
incurable (1)
inflamed (1) +2779

injured (1)
lay ill (1)
makes sick (1)
pretend to be ill (1)
pretended to be ill (1)
sick (1)
suffering (1)
wear themselves out (1)

2704 חָלָה2 *ḥālāh2* (17)
entreat (3) +906+7156
sought the favor of (3) +906+7156
appeal (1)
court favor (1) +7156
curry favor with (1) +7156
implore (1) +7156
intercede with (1) +906+7156
interceded with (1) +906+7156
seek favor (1) +906+7156
seek favor (1) +7156
sought (1)
sought favor (1) +906+7156
sought favor (1) +7156

2705 חַלָּה *ḥallāh* (14)
cakes (6)
cake (3)
loaf (2)
cake (1) +4312
loaves of bread (1)
untranslated (1)

2706 חֲלוֹם *ḥ'lôm* (65)
dream (28)
dreams (14)
had a dream (6) +2731
dream had (2) +2731
dreamer (2) +2731
had dream (2) +2731
had dreams (2) +2731
dreamed (1)
dreamer (1) +1251+2021
dreaming (1)
dreams (1) +2731
dreams encourage to have (1) +2731
foretells by dreams (1) +2731
interpreters of dreams (1)
it^s (1) +2021
untranslated (1)

2707 חַלּוֹן *ḥallôn* (32)
window (13)
windows (10)
openings (7)
parapet openings (1)
untranslated (1)

2708 חֹלוֹן *ḥōlôn* (3)
Holon (3)

2709 חַלּוֹנַי *ḥallônāy*
Variant; not used

2710 חֲלוֹף *ḥ'lôp* (1)
destitute (1) +1201

2711 חֲלוּשָׁה *ḥ'lûšāh* (1)
defeat (1)

2712 חֲלַח *ḥ'laḥ* (3)
Halah (3)

2713 חַלְחוּל *ḥalḥûl* (1)
Halhul (1)

2714 חַלְחָלָה *ḥalḥālāh* (4)
anguish (2)
pain (1)
tremble (1)

2715 חָלַט *ḥālaṭ* (1)
pick up (1)

2716 חֲלִי *ḥ'liy* (24)
disease (5)
illness (5)
sickness (4)
affliction (1)

evil (1)
grew worse and worse (1)
              +2118+2617+4394
ill (1)
illnesses (1)
infirmities (1)
injured (1)
injury (1)
recovery (1) +2649+4946
suffering (1)

2717 חֲלִי1 *ḥ'liy1* (2)
jewels (1)
ornament (1)

2718 חֲלִי2 *ḥ'liy2* (1)
Hali (1)

2719 חֶלְיָה *ḥelyāh* (1)
jewelry (1)

2720 חָלִיל1 *ḥāliyl1* (6)
flutes (4)
flute (2)

2721 חָלִיל2 *ḥāliyl2* (21)
far be it (12)
forbid (4)
never (3)
never (1) +561
of course not (1)

2722 חֲלִיפָה *ḥ'liypāh* (12)
sets (6)
change (1)
clothes (1)
new (1)
renewal (1)
shifts (1)
wave upon wave (1)

2723 חֲלִיצָה *ḥ'liysāh* (2)
belongings (1)
weapons (1)

2724 חֶלְכָּה *ḥēl'kāh* (3)
victims (2)
victim (1)

2725 חָלַל1 *ḥālal1* (135)
began (25)
desecrated (11)
profane (11)
begin (8)
desecrate (7)
profaned (7)
begun (6)
defile (5)
defiled (5)
desecrating (5)
enjoy (4)
started (4)
beginning (3)
being profaned (3)
first time (2)
grew (2)
violate (2)
am profaned (1)
be defamed (1)
be desecrated (1)
becoming (1)
been defiled (1)
been profaned (1)
break (1)
bring low (1)
defiles herself (1)
degrade (1)
desecrates (1)
disgrace (1)
disgraces (1)
dishonor (1)
drove in disgrace (1)
launch (1)
let be profaned (1)
proceeded (1)
treating with contempt (1)

undertook (1)
violates (1)
was desecrated (1)
untranslated (3)

2726 חָלַל2 *ḥālal2* (8)
killed (1)
pierce (1)
pierced (1)
pierced through (1)
slay (1)
was pierced (1)
wounded (1)
wounds (1)

2727 חָלַל3 *ḥālal3* (2)
make music (1)
playing (1)

2728 חָלָל1 *ḥālāl1* (92)
slain (38)
killed (21)
dead (6)
wounded (5)
casualties (4)
body (3)
victims (3)
slaughter (2)
bodies (1)
dead bodies (1)
die (1)
fall in battle (1) +5877
flattering (1)
hurt (1)
mortally wounded man (1)
people (1)
slain in battle (1)
violent (1)

2729 חָלָל2 *ḥālāl2* (3)
defiled (2)
profane (1)

2730 חָלַם1 *ḥālam1* (2)
grow strong (1)
restored to health (1)

2731 חָלַם2 *ḥālam2* (27)
had a dream (6) +2706
had a dream (5)
dream had (2) +2706
dreamer (2) +2706
dreams (2)
had dream (2) +2706
had dreams (2) +2706
dream (1)
dreamed (1)
dreams (1) +2706
dreams encourage to have (1) +2706
foretells by dreams (1) +2706
untranslated (1)

2732 חֵלֶם *ḥēlem*
Variant; not used

2733 חַלָּמוּת *ḥallāmût* (1)
egg (1)

2734 חַלָּמִישׁ *ḥallāmiyš* (5)
flint (1)
flinty (1)
flinty rock (1)
hard (1)
hard rock (1)

2735 חֵלוֹן *ḥēlōn* (5)
Helon (5)

2736 חָלַף1 *ḥālap1* (26)
changed (3)
new (3)
change (2)
changing (1)
comes along (1)
disappear (1)
discarded (1)
exchange (1)

glided past (1)
go (1)
goes by (1)
let renew (1)
over (1)
renew (1)
replace (1)
skim past (1)
sprout (1)
sweep on (1)
sweep past (1)
sweeping (1)
violated (1)

2737 חָלַף2 *ḥālap2* (2)
pierced (1)
pierces (1)

2738 חֵלֶף1 *ḥēlep1* (1)
Heleph (1)

2739 חֵלֶף2 *ḥēlep2* (2)
for (1)
in return for (1)

2740 חָלַץ1 *ḥālaṣ1* (23)
deliver (4)
rescued (3)
be delivered (2)
delivers (2)
torn out (2)
delivered (1)
escape (1)
is rescued (1)
offer (1)
rescue (1)
robbed (1)
take off (1)
unsandaled (1) +5837
withdrawn (1)
untranslated (1)

2741 חָלַץ2 *ḥālaṣ2* (21)
armed (12)
armed guard (2)
arm (1)
arm ourselves (1)
arm yourselves (1)
armed for battle (1)
army (1)
soldiers (1)
strengthen (1)

2742 חֶלֶץ *ḥeleṣ* (5)
Helez (5)

2743 חֲלָצַיִם *ḥᵃlāṣayim* (11)
brace (2) +273
flesh and blood (2) +3655+4946
waist (2)
body (1)
heart (1)
stomach (1)
waists (1)
untranslated (1)

2744 חָלַק1 *ḥālaq1* (9)
flatters (2)
seductive (2)
deceitful (1)
flattering (1)
smooth (1)
smooths (1)
speak deceit (1)

2745 חָלַק2 *ḥālaq2* (56)
divide (9)
divided (6)
dividing (3)
share (3)
be divided (2)
distribute (2)
gave (2)
parcel out (2)
accomplice (1) +6640
allots (1)

allotting (1)
apportioned (1)
assigns (1)
be allotted (1)
be distributed (1)
be divided up (1)
distributed (1)
distributes (1)
distributing supplies (1)
divide up (1)
divided up (1)
divides (1)
get share of property (1)
give a portion (1)
give a share (1)
given (1)
is dispersed (1)
is distributed (1)
made assignments (1)
received (1)
scatter (1)
scattered (1)
separated into divisions (1)
took some of the things (1)
were split (1)

2746 חָלַק3 *ḥālaq3*
Variant; not used

2747 חָלָק1 *ḥālāq1* (9)
flattering (3)
smooth (2)
flattery (1)
pleasant (1)
slippery (1)
smoother (1)

2748 חָלָק2 *ḥālāq2* (2)
Halak (2)

2749 חֵלֶק1 *ḥēleq1* (1)
smooth (1)

2750 חֵלֶק2 *ḥēleq2* (66)
share (16)
portion (14)
lot (6)
allotment (4)
portions (4)
parts (3)
reward (3)
fate (2)
plot of ground (2)
benefits (1)
fields (1)
have say (1) +6699
inheritance (1)
land (1)
lives (1)
owns (1)
part (1)
plot (1)
possession (1)
that⁵ (1)
untranslated (1)

2751 חֵלֶק3 *ḥēleq3* (2)
Helek (2)

2752 חָלֻק *ḥalluq* (1)
smooth (1)

2753 חֶלְקָה1 *ḥelqāh1* (2)
smooth (2)

2754 חֶלְקָה2 *ḥelqāh2* (23)
field (10)
field (4) +8441
plot (2)
plot of ground (2)
portion (2)
another⁵ (1)
piece (1)
tract (1)

2755 חֲלֻקָּה *ḥᵃluqqāh* (1)
group (1) +3+1074

2756 חֲלֻקָּה *ḥᵃluqqāh*
Variant; not used

2757 חֶלְקִי *ḥelqiy* (1)
Helekite (1)

2758 חֶלְקַי *ḥelqāy* (1)
Helkai (1)

2759 חִלְקִיָּה *ḥilqiyyāh* (15)
Hilkiah (13)
heˢ (1)
Hilkiah's (1)

2760 חִלְקִיָּהוּ *ḥilqiyyāhû* (19)
Hilkiah (18)
heˢ (1)

2761 חֲלַקְלַק *ḥᵃlaqlaq* (4)
slippery (2)
intrigue (1)
not sincere (1)

2762 חֶלְקַת *ḥelqat* (2)
Helkath (2)

2763 חֶלְקַת הַצֻּרִים *ḥelqat haṣṣuriym* (1)
Helkath Hazzurim (1)

2764 חָלַשׁ1 *ḥālaš1* (1)
laid low (1)

2765 חָלַשׁ2 *ḥālaš2* (2)
laid low (1)
overcame (1)

2766 חַלָּשׁ *hallāš* (1)
weakling (1)

2767 חָם1 *ḥām1* (4)
father-in-law (4)

2768 חָם2 *ḥām2* (2)
swelter (1)
warm (1)

2769 חָם3 *ḥām3* (16)
Ham (15)
Hamites (1)

2770 חֹם *ḥōm* (9)
heat (8)
hot (1)

2771 חֵמָא *ḥēmā'*
Variant; not used

2772 חֶמְאָה *hem'āh* (10)
curds (6)
cream (2)
butter (1)
curdled milk (1)

2773 חָמַד *ḥāmad* (21)
covet (6)
desire (2)
treasure (2)
choice (1)
chooses (1)
coveted (1)
delight (1)
delight in (1)
delighted (1)
desirable (1)
lust after (1)
pleasing (1)
precious (1)
wealth (1)

2774 חֶמֶד *ḥemed* (6)
handsome (3)
fruitful (1)
lush (1)
pleasant (1)

2775 חֶמְדָּה *ḥemdāh* (16)
pleasant (3)
desired (2)
fine (2)
treasures (2) +3998
desirable (1)

desire (1)
regret (1)
stately (1)
valuable (1)
valuables (1)
value (1)

2776 חֲמֻדוֹת *ḥᵃmudôt* (9)
highly esteemed (3)
best (1)
choice (1)
costly gifts (1)
precious (1)
riches (1)
value (1)

2777 חֶמְדָּן *hemdān* (2)
Hemdan (2)

2778 חָמָה *hāmāh* (1)
careful (1)

2779 חֵמָה *hēmāh* (123)
wrath (75)
anger (12)
fury (8)
rage (5)
venom (4)
angry (2)
burning (2)
fierce (2)
furious (2)
poison (2)
easily angered (1)
enraged (1) +4848
hot (1)
hot-tempered (1)
hot-tempered (1) +1251
hot-tempered (1) +1524
indignation (1)
inflamed (1) +2703
stinging (1)

2780 חַמָּה *hammāh* (6)
sun (4)
heat (1)
sunlight (1) +240

2781 חַמּוּאֵל *hammû'ēl* (1)
Hammuel (1)

2782 חֲמוּטַל *ḥᵃmûṭal* (3)
Hamutal (3)

2783 חָמוּל *ḥāmûl* (3)
Hamul (3)

2784 חָמוּלִי *ḥāmûliy* (1)
Hamulite (1)

2785 חַמּוֹן *hammôn* (2)
Hammon (2)

2786 חָמוּץ *hāmûṣ*
Variant; not used

2787 חָמוֹץ *hāmôṣ* (1)
oppressed (1)

2788 חַמּוּק *hammûq* (1)
graceful (1)

2789 חֲמוֹר1 *ḥᵃmôr1* (98)
donkey (47)
donkeys (45)
donkey's (3)
donkeys (1) +2789
male donkeys (1)

2790 חֲמוֹר2 *ḥᵃmôr2*
Variant; not used

2791 חֲמוֹר3 *ḥᵃmôr3* (13)
Hamor (12)
hisˢ (1)

2792 חָמוֹת *ḥāmôt* (11)
mother-in-law (11)

2793 חֹמֶט *ḥōmet* (1)

skink (1)

2794 חֻמְטָה *humtāh* (1)
Humtah (1)

2795 חֲמִיטַל *ḥᵃmiyṭal* (2)
untranslated (2)

2796 חָמִיץ *hāmiys* (1)
mash (1)

2797 חֲמִישִׁי *ḥᵃmiyšiy* (45)
fifth (43)
five-sided (1)
one fifth (1)

2798 חָמַל *hāmal* (41)
spare (12)
pity (6)
spared (4)
had pity (2)
have pity (2)
mercy (2)
allow pity (1)
bear (1)
compassion (1)
concern (1)
felt sorry (1)
had compassion (1)
had concern (1)
in compassion spares (1)
mercilessly (1) +4202
refrained (1)
show mercy (1)
take pity (1)
unrelenting (1) +4202

2799 חֶמְלָה *hemlāh* (2)
merciful (1)
mercy (1)

2800 חֻמְלָה *humlāh*
Variant; not used

2801 חָמַם *hāmam* (23)
warm (8)
hot (6)
warms (2)
aroused (1)
burn with lust (1)
heat (1)
in a rage (1) +4222
lets warm (1)
warming (1)
untranslated (1)

2802 חַמָּן *hammān* (8)
incense altars (8)

2803 חָמַס1 *hāmas1* (8)
do violence (2)
harms (1)
laid waste (1)
mistreated (1)
stripped (1)
violence (1)
wrong (1)

2804 חָמַס2 *hāmas2*
Variant; not used

2805 חָמָס *hāmās* (60)
violence (43)
violent (5)
destroyed (2)
malicious (2)
crime (1)
fiercely (1)
plunder (1)
ruthless (1)
terror (1)
violent (1) +4848
wrong (1)
wronged (1)

2806 חָמֵץ1 *hāmēs1* (4)
rises (1)
was grieved (1)

yeast (1)
yeast added (1)

2807 חָמֵץ 2 *hāmēs2* (1)
cruel (1)

2808 חָמֵץ 3 *hāmēs3* (1)
stained crimson (1)

2809 חָמֵץ 4 *hāmēs4* (11)
yeast (3)
anything containing yeast (2)
anything with yeast in it (1)
bread made with yeast (1)
containing yeast (1)
leavened bread (1)
made with yeast (1)
with yeast in it (1)

2810 חֹמֶץ *hōmes* (6)
vinegar (4)
wine vinegar (1)
untranslated (1)

2811 חָמַק *hāmaq* (2)
left (1)
wander (1)

2812 חָמַר 1 *hāmar1* (2)
foam (1)
foaming (1)

2813 חָמַר 2 *hāmar2* (4)
in torment (2)
red (1)
untranslated (1)

2814 חָמַר 3 *hāmar3* (1)
coated (1)

2815 חֶמֶר *hemer* (1)
foaming (1)

2816 חֹמֶר 1 *hōmer1* (1)
churning (1)

2817 חֹמֶר 2 *hōmer2* (17)
clay (11)
mortar (4)
mud (2)

2818 חֹמֶר 3 *hōmer3* (13)
homer (10)
heaps (1) +2818
homers (1)

2819 חֵמָר *hēmār* (3)
tar (3)

2820 חַמְרָן *hamrān*
Variant; not used

2821 חָמַשׁ *hāmaš* (5)
armed (1)
armed for battle (1)
fully armed (1)
outposts (1) +7895
take a fifth (1)

2822 חָמֵשׁ *hāmēš* (504)
five (164)
fifty (77)
twenty-five (23) +2256+6929
fifteenth (15) +6925
25,000 (14) +547+2256+6929
250 (10) +2256+4395
4,500 (8) +547+752+2256+4395
fifteen (8) +6926
fifteen (6) +6925
500 (5) +4395
captain (5) +8569
fifth (5)
1,254 (4) +547+752+2256+4395
eighty-five (4) +2256+9046
fifties (4)
40,500 (3) +547+752+2256+4395
5,000 (3) +547
50 (3)

53,400 (3)
  +547+752+2256+2256+4395+8993
603,550 (3)   +547+547+2256+2256+2256
  +2822+4395+4395+8993+9252
fiftieth (3)
fifty-two (3) +2256+9109
forty-five (3) +752+2256
seventy-five (3) +2256+8679
thirty-five (3) +2256+8993
twenty-fifth (3) +2256+6929
1,052 (2) +547+2256+9109
1,775 (2)
  +547+2256+2256+2256+4395+8679+8679
150 (2) +2256+4395
30,500 (2) +547+2256+4395+8993
345 (2) +752+2256+4395+8993
35,400 (2) +547+752+2256+2256+4395+8993
41,500 (2) +285+547+752+2256+2256+4395
435 (2) +752+2256+4395+8993
45,650 (2)   +547+752+2256+2256
  +2256+2822+4395+9252
46,500 (2) +547+752+2256+2256+4395+9252
52 (2) +2256+9109
54,400 (2) +547+752+752+2256+2256+4395
57,400 (2) +547+752+2256+2256+4395+8679
59,300 (2)+547+2256+2256+4395+8993+9596
65 (2) +2256+9252
652 (2) +2256+4395+9109+9252
95 (2) +2256+9596
fifteenth (2) +6926
fifty-five (2) +2256+2822
menˢ (2)
seventy-five feet (2) +564
1,335 (1) +547+2256+4395+8993+8993
1,365 (1)
  +547+2256+2256+2256+4395+8993+9252
105 (1) +2256+4395
151,450 (1)   +285+547+547+752+2256
  +2256+2256+2822+4395+4395
153,600 (1)   +547+547+2256+2256
  +2256+4395+4395+8993+9252
156 (1) +2256+4395+9252
157,600 (1)   +547+547+2256+2256+2256
  +4395+4395+8679+9252
16,750 (1)+547+2256+2256+4395+6925+8679+9252
2,056 (1) +547+2256+9252
2,750 (1) +547+2256+4395+8679
205 (1) +2256+4395
245 (1) +752+2256+2256+4395
245 (1) +752+2256+4395
25,100 (1) +547+2256+2256+4395+6929
307,500 (1)   +547+547+2256+2256
  +4395+4395+8679+8993
32,500 (1)+547+2256+2256+4395+8993+9109
337,500 (1)   +547+547+547+2256+2256
  +2256+4395+4395+8679+8993+8993
337,500 (1)   +547+547+547+2256+2256
  +4395+4395+8679+8993+8993
35 (1) +2256+8993
350 (1) +2256+4395+8993
365 (1) +2256+2256+4395+8993+9252
45,400 (1) +547+752+752+2256+2256+4395
45,600 (1) +547+752+2256+2256+4395+9252
454 (1) +752+752+2256+4395
5,400 (1) +547+752+2256+4395
50,000 (1) +547
52,700 (1)
  +547+2256+2256+4395+8679+9109
530 (1) +2256+4395+8993
550 (1) +2256+2822+4395
56 (1) +2256+9252
595 (1) +2256+2256+2822+4395+9596
60,500 (1) +547+2256+4395+9252
650 (1) +2256+4395+9252
655 (1) +2256+2822+4395+9252
675 (1) +2256+4395+8679+9252
675,000 (1)   +547+547+547+2256
  +2256+4395+8679+9252
7,500 (1) +547+2256+4395+8679
725 (1) +2256+4395+6929+8679
745 (1) +752+2256+4395+8679

75 feet (1) +564
76,500 (1)
  +547+2256+2256+4395+8679+9252
775 (1) +2256+4395+8679+8679
8,580 (1) +547+2256+2256+4395+9046+9046
815 (1) +2256+4395+6926+9046
845 (1) +752+2256+4395+9046
895 (1) +2256+2256+4395+9046+9596
905 (1) +2256+4395+9596
945 (1) +752+2256+2256+4395+9596
950 (1) +2256+4395+9596
956 (1) +2256+2256+4395+9252+9596
captains (1) +8569
fifteen (1) +2256+6927
fifty-second (1) +2256+9109
seven and a half feet (1) +564+928+2021
sixty-five (1) +2256+9252
thirty-fifth (1) +2256+8993
twenty feet (1) +564+6926
untranslated (13)

2823 חֹמֶשׁ 1 *hōmeš1* (1)
fifth (1)

2824 חֹמֶשׁ 2 *hōmeš2* (4)
stomach (3)
belly (1)

2825 חֲמִשִּׁים *hᵃmiššiym*
Variant; not used

2826 חֲמֻשִׁים *hᵃmušiym*
Variant; not used

2827 חֵמֶת *hēmet* (4)
skin (3)
wineskin (1)

2828 חֲמָת *hᵃmāt* (24)
Hamath (24)

2829 חַמַּת 1 *hammat1* (1)
Hammath (1)

2830 חַמַּת 2 *hammat2* (1)
Hammath (1)

2831 חַמֹּת דֹּאר *hammōt dō'r* (1)
Hammoth Dor (1)

2832 חֲמָת צוֹבָה *hᵃmāt sôbāh* (1)
Hamath Zobah (1)

2833 חֲמָתִי *hᵃmātiy* (2)
Hamathites (2)

2834 חֵן 1 *hēn1* (69)
favor (41)
grace (5)
pleased with (5) +928+5162+6524
favorably disposed toward (3) +928+6524
bless (2)
gracious (2)
alluring (1) +3202
charm (1)
charm (1) +74
displease (1) +928+4202+5162+6524
displeasing (1) +928+4202+5162+6524
esteemed (1)
favorable toward (1) +928+5162+6524
graceful (1)
kindhearted (1)
ornament to grace (1)
pleased with (1) +928+5951+6524

2835 חֵן 2 *hēn2* (1)
Hen (1)

2836 חֵנָדָד *hēnādād* (4)
Henadad (4)

2837 חָנָה 1 *hānāh1* (143)
camped (77)
encamped (12)
camp (11)
encamp (9)
set up camp (4)
took up positions (3)

besiege (2) +6584
made camp (2)
pitched camp (2)
set up tents (2)
attacked (1)
besieged (1) +928
besieged (1) +6584
camping (1)
defend (1)
encamps (1)
laid siege to (1) +6584
living (1)
nearly over (1)
remain in camp (1)
remained in camp (1)
set up (1)
settle (1)
settled (1)
stay (1)
untranslated (4)

2838   2חָנָה   hānāh2
Variant; not used

2839   חַנָּה   hannāh (13)
Hannah (12)
her^s (1)

2840   1חֲנוֹךְ   ḥᵃnôk1 (16)
Enoch (10)
Hanoch (6)

2841   2חֲנוֹךְ   ḥᵃnôk2
Variant; not used

2842   חָנוּן   hānûn (11)
Hanun (11)

2843   חַנּוּן   hannûn (13)
gracious (12)
compassionate (1)

2844   חָנוּת   hānût (1)
vaulted cell (1)

2845   1חָנַט   hānat1 (1)
forms (1)

2846   2חָנַט   hānat2 (3)
embalmed (2)
embalm (1)

2847   חֲנֻטִים   ḥᵃnutiym (1)
embalming (1)

2848   חַנִּיאֵל   hanniy'ēl (2)
Hanniel (2)

2849   חָנִיךְ   hāniyk (1)
trained men (1)

2850   חֲנִינָה   ḥᵃniynāh (1)
favor (1)

2851   חֲנִית   ḥᵃniyt (49)
spear (38)
spears (8)
it^s (1) +2021
its^s (1)
untranslated (1)

2852   חָנַךְ   hānak (5)
dedicated (3)
dedicate (1)
train (1)

2853   חֲנֻכָּה   ḥᵃnukkāh (8)
dedication (6)
offerings for dedication (2)

2854   חֲנֹכִי   ḥᵃnōkiy (1)
Hanochite (1)

2855   חִנָּם   hinnām (32)
without cause (7)
for nothing (5)
for no reason (4)
needless (2)
useless (2)
without reason (2)

at no cost (1)
cost nothing (1)
costs nothing (1)
harmless soul (1) +5929
in vain (1) +448
innocent (1)
undeserved (1)
without any payment (1) +401
without any reason (1)
without paying anything (1)

2856   חֲנַמְאֵל   ḥᵃnam'ēl (4)
Hanamel (4)

2857   חֲנָמַל   ḥᵃnāmal (1)
sleet (1)

2858   1חָנַן   hānan1 (78)
have mercy (14)
gracious (13)
merciful (8)
kind (4)
plead (3)
begged (2)
generous (2)
have pity (2)
making supplication (2)
pleaded (2)
show mercy (2)
beg (1)
beg for mercy (1)
begged for favor (1)
charming (1)
cried for mercy (1)
do a kindness (1)
favor (1)
generously (1)
gets mercy (1)
grace is shown (1)
gracious (1) +2858
graciously given (1)
lift up for mercy (1)
made^s (1)
moves to pity (1)
pity (1)
plead for mercy (1)
prayed (1)
show favor (1)
shows favor (1)
shows mercy (1)
take pity (1)
untranslated (1)

2859   2חָנַן   hānan2 (1)
loathsome (1)

2860   חָנָן   hānān (12)
Hanan (12)

2861   חֲנַנְאֵל   ḥᵃnan'ēl (4)
Hananel (4)

2862   חֲנָנִי   ḥᵃnāniy (11)
Hanani (11)

2863   חֲנַנְיָה   ḥᵃnanyāh (25)
Hananiah (24)
he^s (1)

2864   חֲנַנְיָהוּ   ḥᵃnanyāhû (3)
Hananiah (3)

2865   חָנֵס   hānēs (1)
Hanes (1)

2866   1חָנֵף   hānēp1 (11)
defiled (4)
completely defiled (1) +2866
corrupt (1)
desecrated (1)
godless (1)
pollute (1)
pollutes (1)

2867   2חָנֵף   hānēp2
Variant; not used

2868   3חָנֵף   hānēp3 (13)

godless (10)
ungodly (3)

2869   חֹנֶף   hōnep (1)
ungodliness (1)

2870   חֲנֻפָּה   ḥᵃnuppāh (1)
ungodliness (1)

2871   חָנַק   hānaq (2)
hanged himself (1)
strangled (1)

2872   חֲנָתוֹן   hannātôn (1)
Hannathon (1)

2873   1חָסַד   hāsad1 (1)
shame (1)

2874   2חָסַד   hāsad2 (2)
show yourself faithful (2)

2875   1חֶסֶד   hesed1 (3)
disgrace (3)

2876   2חֶסֶד   hesed2 (248)
love (129)
kindness (41)
unfailing love (32)
great love (6)
mercy (6)
loving (5)
kindnesses (3)
unfailing kindness (3)
acts of devotion (2)
devotion (2)
favor (2)
approval (1)
devout (1)
faithful (1)
faithfully (1)
glory (1)
good favor (1)
grace (1)
kind (1)
kindly (1)
loving-kindness (1)
loyal (1)
merciful (1)
well (1)
untranslated (4)

2877   3חֶסֶד   hesed3
Variant; not used

2878   חֲסַדְיָה   ḥᵃsadyāh (1)
Hasadiah (1)

2879   חָסָה   hāsāh (37)
take refuge (23)
find refuge (3)
takes refuge (3)
taken refuge (2)
trust (2)
have a refuge (1)
makes refuge (1)
refuge (1)
took refuge (1)

2880   1חֹסָה   hōsāh1 (4)
Hosah (4)

2881   2חֹסָה   hōsāh2 (1)
Hosah (1)

2882   חָסוּת   hāsût (1)
untranslated (1)

2883   חָסִיד   hāsiyd (35)
saints (15)
faithful (6)
godly (4)
loving (2)
consecrated (1)
devoted (1)
favored (1)
holy (1)
merciful (1)
ungodly (1) +4202

untranslated (2)

2884 חֲסִידָה *ḥᵉsiydāh* (6)
stork (6)

2885 חָסִיל *ḥāsiyl* (6)
grasshoppers (2)
locusts (2)
grasshopper (1)
young locusts (1)

2886 חֲסִין *ḥᵉsiyn* (1)
mighty (1)

2887 חָסַל *ḥāsal* (1)
devour (1)

2888 חָסַם *ḥāsam* (2)
block the way (1)
muzzle (1)

2889 חָסַן *ḥāsan* (1)
hoarded (1)

2890 חֹסֶן *ḥōsen* (5)
rich store (1)
riches (1)
treasure (1)
treasures (1)
wealth (1)

2891 חָסֹן *ḥāsōn* (2)
mighty (1)
strong (1)

2892 חַסְפַּס *ḥaspas* (1)
flakes (1)

2893 1חָסֵר *ḥāsēr1* (23)
lack (3)
lacks (3)
lacked (2)
run dry (2)
always (1) +440
depriving (1)
goes hungry (1)
gone down (1)
had nothing (1) +3972
have too little (1)
in want (1)
made lower (1)
needs (1) +4728
number is less than (1)
recede (1)
scarce (1)
withholds (1)

2894 2חָסֵר *ḥāsēr2* (17)
lacks (9)
lack (3)
lacked (2)
have no (1)
lacking (1)
short (1)

2895 חֶסֶר *ḥeser* (2)
poverty (1)
want (1)

2896 חֹסֶר *ḥōser* (3)
lack (1)
poverty (1)
untranslated (1)

2897 חַסְרָה *ḥasrāh* (1)
Hasrah (1)

2898 חֶסְרוֹן *ḥesrôn* (1)
lacking (1)

2899 1חַף *ḥap1* (1)
clean (1)

2900 2חַף *ḥap2*
Variant; not used

2901 חָפָא *ḥāpā'* (1)
secretly did (1)

2902 חָפָה *ḥāpāh* (12)
covered (4)

overlaid (3)
cover (2)
are sheathed (1)
paneled (1)
was covered (1)

2903 1חֻפָּה *ḥuppāh1* (3)
canopy (1)
chamber (1)
pavilion (1)

2904 2חֻפָּה *ḥuppāh2* (1)
Huppah (1)

2905 חָפַז *ḥāpaz* (10)
alarm (1)
alarmed (1)
dismay (1)
fled (1)
headlong flight (1)
hurried (1)
hurrying (1)
terrified (1)
took to flight (1)
untranslated (1)

2906 חִפָּזוֹן *ḥippāzôn* (3)
haste (3)

2907 חֻפִּים *ḥuppiym* (3)
Huppites (2)
Huppim (1)

2908 חֹפֶן *ḥōpen* (6)
handfuls (2) +4850
hands (2)
hollow of hands (1)
two handfuls (1) +4850

2909 חָפְנִי *ḥopniy* (5)
Hophni (5)

2910 חָפַף *ḥāpap* (1)
shields (1)

2911 1חָפֵץ *ḥāpēṣ1* (74)
pleased (9)
desire (7)
delights (6)
delighted (5)
pleases (5)
want (5)
delight (4)
desires (3)
delight in (2)
displeases (2) +4202
eager (2)
take pleasure (2)
will (2)
delights in (1)
desired (1) +3139
favors (1)
find delight (1)
find pleasure (1)
finds delight (1)
finds pleasure (1)
fond (1)
found pleasure (1)
have delight (1)
have desire (1)
have pleasure (1)
meant (1)
pleasure (1)
rather (1)
take any pleasure in (1) +2911
take delight (1)
willing (1)
wished (1)

2912 2חָפַץ *ḥāpas2* (1)
sways (1)

2913 3חָפֵץ *ḥāpēṣ3* (12)
desire (3)
delight (2)
delight in (1)
delights in (1)

loves (1)
prefer (1)
takes pleasure in (1)
wanted (1)
willing (1)

2914 חֵפֶץ *ḥēpeṣ* (38)
please (5)
delight (3)
desire (3)
desired (3)
pleasure (3)
wants (3)
activity (2)
wanted (2)
care (1)
delightful (1)
desires (1)
eager (1)
just right (1)
matter (1)
pleased (1)
precious (1)
purpose (1)
such things^s (1)
want (1)
will (1)
wish (1)
worthless (1) +401

2915 חֶפְצִי־בָהּ *ḥepsiy-bāh* (2)
Hephzibah (2)

2916 1חָפַר *ḥāpar1* (22)
dug (10)
spy out (3)
dig a hole (1)
digs (1)
dug up (1)
look about (1)
paws (1)
reopened (1) +2256+8740
scoops out (1)
search for (1)
seeks out (1)

2917 2חָפַר *ḥāpar2* (17)
confusion (4)
disgrace (3)
disgraced (3)
humiliated (2)
abashed (1)
ashamed (1)
covered with shame (1)
disappointed (1)
dismay (1)

2918 1חֵפֶר *ḥēper1* (7)
Hepher (7)

2919 2חֵפֶר *ḥēper2* (2)
Hepher (2)

2920 חֶפְרִי *ḥepriy* (1)
Hepherite (1)

2921 חֲפָרַיִם *ḥᵃpārayim* (1)
Hapharaim (1)

2922 חָפְרַע *ḥopra'* (1)
Hophra (1)

2923 חֲפַרְפָּרָה *ḥᵃparpārāh* (1)
rodents (1)

2924 חָפַשׂ *ḥāpaś* (24)
disguised himself (5)
search (3)
in disguise (2)
searches (1)
be ransacked (1)
becomes like (1)
devised (1)
examine (1)
go into hiding (1)
hunt down (1)
inquired (1)

look around (1)
plot (1)
search for (1)
searched (1)
track down (1)

2925 חֵפֶשׂ *hēpeś* (1)
plan (1)

2926 חָפַשׂ *hāpaš* (1)
been freed (1)

2927 חֹפֶשׂ *hōpeš* (1)
blankets (1) +955

2928 חֻפְשָׁה *hupšāh* (1)
freedom (1)

2929 חָפְשׁוּת *hopšût* (1)
untranslated (1)

2930 חָפְשִׁי *hopšiy* (17)
free (9)
free (2) +8938
exempt from taxes (1) +6913
freed (1)
freed (1) +8938
set apart (1)
set free (1) +8938
untranslated (1)

2931 חָפְשִׁית *hopšiyt* (2)
separate (2)

2932 חֵץ *hēs* (55)
arrows (38)
arrow (12)
archers (1) +1251
did so^s (1) +2256+4374+8008
untranslated (3)

2933 חָצֵב1 *hāsēb1* (16)
dug (3)
cut out (2)
dig (2)
cut in pieces (1)
cut to pieces (1)
engraved (1)
hewing (1)
hewn out (1)
prepare (1)
swings (1)
were cut (1)
untranslated (1)

2934 חָצַב2 *hāsab2* (1)
strikes (1)

2935 חֹצֵב *hōsēb* (8)
stonecutters (5)
masons (2)
stonecutters (1) +74

2936 חָצָה *hāsāh* (15)
divided (5)
be divided (1)
divide (1)
divide equally (1)
divide up (1)
dividing (1)
live out half (1)
parceled out (1)
rising up (1)
set apart (1)
untranslated (1)

2937 חָצוֹר1 *hāsôr1* (18)
Hazor (18)

2938 חָצוֹר2 *hāsôr2*
Variant; not used

2939 חָצוֹר חֲדַתָּה *hāsôr hᵃdatāh* (1)
Hazor Hadattah (1)

2940 חֲצֹת *hᵃsôt* (3)
midnight (2) +4326
middle (1)

2941 חֲצוֹת *husôt*

Variant; not used

2942 חֲצִי *hᵃsiy* (125)
half (79)
half-tribe (18) +8657
middle (6)
half-tribe (5) +4751
half-district (4) +7135
halfway (2)
two (2)
half-tribe (1)
it^s (1) +2257
midnight (1) +2021+4326
midst (1)
nine-and-a-half (1) +2256+9596
two-and-a-half (1) +2256+9109
untranslated (3)

2943 חֵצִי1 *hēsiy1* (5)
arrow (5)

2944 חֵצִי2 *hēsiy2*
Variant; not used

2945 חָצִיר1 *hāsiyr1* (20)
grass (19)
hay (1)

2946 חָצִיר2 *hāsiyr2* (1)
leeks (1)

2947 חָצִיר3 *hāsiyr3*
Variant; not used

2948 חָצִיר4 *hāsiyr4* (1)
home (1)

2949 חֵצֶן *hēsen*
Variant; not used

2950 חֹצֶן *hōsen* (3)
arms (2)
folds of robe (1)

2951 חָצַץ1 *hāsas1* (2)
come to an end (1)
in ranks (1)

2952 חָצַץ2 *hāsas2* (1)
singers (1)

2953 חָצָץ *hāsās* (2)
gravel (2)

2954 חַצְצוֹן תָּמָר *hassôn tāmār* (2)
Hazazon Tamar (2)

2955 חַצְצֵר *hassar* (12)
blew (1)
blew trumpets (1)
blow (1)
played (1)
sounding (1)
trumpeters (1)
untranslated (6)

2956 חֲצֹצְרָה *hᵃsōsᵉrāh* (29)
trumpets (25)
trumpeters (3)
horn (1)

2957 חָצֵר *hāsar*
Variant; not used

2958 חָצֵר *hāsēr* (191)
courtyard (59)
court (48)
villages (45)
courts (21)
courtyards (4)
its^s (2) +2021
settlements (2)
enclosed (1)
set farther back (1) +337+2021
surrounding villages (1)
where^s (1) +2021+2021+2667
untranslated (6)

2959 חָצֵר2 *hāsēr2*
Variant; not used

2960 חֲצַר־אַדָּר *hᵃsar-'addār* (1)
Hazar Addar (1)

2961 חֲצַר גַּדָּה *hᵃsar gaddāh* (1)
Hazar Gaddah (1)

2962 חָצֵר הַתִּיכוֹן *hāsēr hatiykôn* (1)
Hazer Hatticon (1)

2963 חֲצַר סוּסָה *hᵃsar sûsāh* (1)
Hazar Susah (1)

2964 חֲצַר סוּסִים *hᵃsar sûsiym* (1)
Hazar Susim (1)

2965 חֲצַר עֵינוֹן *hᵃsar 'êynôn* (1)
Hazar Enan (1)

2966 חֲצַר עֵינָן *hᵃsar 'êynān* (3)
Hazar Enan (3)

2967 חֲצַר שׁוּעָל *hᵃsar šû'āl* (4)
Hazar Shual (4)

2968 חֶצְרוֹ *hesrô* (2)
Hezro (2)

2969 חֶצְרוֹן1 *hesrôn1* (16)
Hezron (16)

2970 חֶצְרוֹן2 *hesrôn2* (1)
Hezron (1)

2971 חֶצְרוֹנִי *hesrôniy* (2)
Hezronite (2)

2972 חֲצֵרוֹת *hᵃsērôt* (6)
Hazeroth (5)
there^s (1) +928

2973 חֲצֵרִים *hᵃsēriym*
Variant; not used

2974 חֶצְרַי *hesray* (1)
untranslated (1)

2975 חֲצַרְמָוֶת *hᵃsarmāwet* (2)
Hazarmaveth (2)

2976 חֹק *hōq* (129)
decrees (75)
share (11)
decree (8)
statutes (4)
limits (2)
ordinance (2)
allotment (1)
appointed time (1)
barrier (1)
boundaries (1)
boundary (1)
conditions (1)
custom (1)
daily bread (1)
daily bread (1) +4312
horizon (1)
law (1)
laws (1)
limit (1)
make laws (1) +2980
portions (1)
precepts (1)
prescribed portion (1)
quota (1)
regular allotment (1)
regular share (1)
regulations (1)
statute (1)
territory (1)
time (1)
tradition (1)
untranslated (2)

2977 חָקָה *hāqāh* (4)
portrayed (2)
carvings (1)
putting marks (1)

2978 חֻקָּה *huqqāh* (104)
decrees (52)

ordinance (23)
regulations (7)
statutes (5)
customs (3)
practices (3)
requirement (3)
rules (3)
fixed laws (1)
laws (1)
regular (1)
requirements (1)
share (1)

2979 חֲקוּפָא *ḥᵃqûpā'* (2)
Hakupha (2)

2980 חָקַק *ḥāqaq* (19)
marked out (2)
scepter (2)
captains (1)
chiseling (1)
decrees (1)
draw (1)
engraved (1)
inscribe (1)
lawgiver (1)
leader's (1)
make laws (1)
make laws (1) +2976
portrayed (1)
princes (1)
ruler's staff (1)
scepters (1)
were written (1)

2981 חֵקֶק *ḥēqeq*
Variant; not used

2982 חֻקֹּק *ḥuqqōq* (1)
Hukkok (1)

2983 חָקַר *ḥāqar* (27)
explore (4)
search (3)
examined (2)
was determined (2)
be searched out (1)
dense (1) +4202
discovered (1)
probe (1)
questions (1)
sample (1)
search out (1)
searched (1)
searched out (1)
searches for (1)
searching for (1)
sees through (1)
sound out (1)
test (1)
tested (1)
took up (1)

2984 חֵקֶר *ḥēqer* (13)
fathom (2)
fathomed (2)
searching (2)
finding out (1)
inquiry (1)
mysteries (1)
recesses (1)
seek (1)
unsearchable (1) +401
what learned (1)

2985 חֹר1 *ḥōr1* (13)
nobles (12)
noble (1)

2986 חֹר2 *ḥōr2* (7)
hole (2)
holes (2)
lairs (1)
latch-opening (1)
sockets (1)

2987 חֻר *ḥur* (2)
hole (1)
pits (1)

2988 חֹר הַגִּדְגָּד *ḥōr haggidgād* (2)
Hor Haggidgad (2)

2989 חֲרָאִים *ḥᵃrā'iym* (3)
filth (2)
untranslated (1)

2990 חָרֵב1 *ḥārēb1* (37)
laid waste (6)
dried up (5)
dry up (5)
desolate (3)
ruined (3)
been dried (2)
dry (2)
parched (2)
devastated (1)
horror (1)
laid waste (1) +2238+2256
lay waste (1)
left deserted (1)
lies in ruins (1)
makes run dry (1)
utterly ruined (1) +2990

2991 חָרֵב2 *ḥārēb2* (4)
kill (2)
must have fought (1) +2991

2992 חָרֵב3 *ḥārēb3* (10)
in ruins (3)
dry (2)
ruin (2)
desolate (1)
desolate waste (1)
ruined (1)

2993 חָרֵב4 *ḥārēb4*
Variant; not used

2994 חָרֵב5 *ḥārēb5*
Variant; not used

2995 חֶרֶב *ḥereb* (412)
sword (362)
swords (31)
swordsmen (5) +408+8990
dagger (3)
knives (3)
war (2)
killed (1) +4200+5782+7023
tool (1)
weapons (1)
untranslated (4)

2996 חֹרֶב1 *ḥōreb1* (13)
heat (6)
drought (3)
dry (3)
fever (1)

2997 חֹרֶב2 *ḥōreb2* (4)
object of horror (1)
rubble (1)
ruined (1)
waste (1)

2998 חֹרֵב *ḥōrēb* (17)
Horeb (17)

2999 חָרְבָּה *ḥorbāh* (43)
ruins (21)
ruin (7)
desolate (5)
in ruins (3)
deserts (1)
desolation (1)
places lying in ruins (1)
ruined (1)
ruined homes (1)
waste (1)
wasteland (1)

3000 חָרָבָה *ḥārābāh* (8)

dry ground (4)
dry land (3)
dry up (1) +5989

3001 חֶרָבוֹן *ḥᵃrābôn* (1)
heat (1)

3002 חַרְבוֹנָא *harbônā'* (1)
Harbona (1)

3003 חַרְבוֹנָה *harbônāh* (1)
Harbona (1)

3004 חָרַג *ḥārag* (2)
come trembling (2)

3005 חַרְגֹּל *hargōl* (1)
cricket (1)

3006 חָרַד *ḥārad* (39)
make afraid (9)
tremble (5)
trembled (4)
come trembling (2)
frighten away (2)
trembling (2)
alarm (1)
fear (1)
frighten (1)
gone to trouble (1) +3010
pounds (1)
quaking with fear (1)
routing (1)
shudder (1)
startled (1)
strike with terror (1)
terrify (1)
terror filled (1) +4394
trembled violently (1)
　　　　　+1524+3010+4394+6330
trembles (1)
untranslated (1)

3007 חָרֵד *ḥārēd* (6)
trembles (2)
fear (1)
feared (1) +2118
tremble (1)
trembled (1)

3008 חֲרֹד1 *ḥᵃrōd1* (1)
Harod (1)

3009 חֲרֹד2 *ḥᵃrōd2*
Variant; not used

3010 חֲרָדָה1 *ḥᵃrādāh1* (9)
fear (2)
panic (2)
terror (2)
gone to trouble (1) +3006
horror (1)
trembled violently (1)
　　　　　+1524+3006+4394+6330

3011 חֲרָדָה2 *ḥᵃrādāh2* (2)
Haradah (2)

3012 חֲרֹדִי *ḥᵃrōdiy* (2)
Harodite (2)

3013 חָרָה1 *ḥārāh1* (92)
angry (22)
burned (18)
angry (11) +678
burn (6)
aroused (4)
burns (4)
fret (4)
very angry (4) +678
burned (2) +4394
anger (1) +678
angry (1) +928+6524
burning (1)
compete (1)
flared (1)
flared up (1)
furious (1) +678+4394

furious (1) +4394
fury (1) +4394
have more and more (1)
loses temper (1) +3013
rage (1)
raged (1)
troubled (1)
zealously (1)
untranslated (1)

3014 חָרָה2 *hārāh2*
Variant; not used

3015 חַרְהֲיָה *harhªyāh* (1)
Harhaiah (1)

3016 חֲרוּזִים *hªrûziym* (1)
strings of jewels (1)

3017 חָרוּל *hārûl* (3)
weeds (2)
undergrowth (1)

3018 חֲרוּמַף *hªrûmap* (1)
Harumaph (1)

3019 חָרוֹן *hārôn* (40)
fierce (28)
wrath (5)
burning (2)
angry (1) +678
burning anger (1)
dry (1)
heat (1)
hot (1)

3020 חֲרוּפִי *hªrûpiy* (1)
Haruphite (1)

3021 חָרוּץ1 *hārûs1* (6)
gold (5)
untranslated (1)

3022 חָרוּץ2 *hārûs2* (1)
trench (1)

3023 חָרוּץ3 *hārûs3* (4)
sharp (1)
sledge (1)
sledges (1)
threshing sledge (1)

3024 חָרוּץ4 *hārûs4* (1)
maimed (1)

3025 חָרוּץ5 *hārûs5* (2)
decision (2)

3026 חָרוּץ6 *hārûs6* (5)
diligent (5)

3027 חָרוּץ7 *hārûs7* (1)
Haruz (1)

3028 חַרְחוּר *harhûr* (2)
Harhur (2)

3029 חַרְחֲיָה *harhªyāh*
Variant; not used

3030 חַרְחַס *harhas* (1)
Harhas (1)

3031 חַרְחֻר *harhur* (1)
scorching heat (1)

3032 חֶרֶט *heret* (2)
pen (1)
tool (1)

3033 חַרְטֹם *hartōm* (11)
magicians (10)
themˢ (1)

3034 חֲרִי *hªriy* (6)
fierce (3)
burning (1)
great rage (1) +678
hot (1)

3035 חֹרִי1 *hōriy1* (1)
bread (1)

3036 חֹרִי2 *hōriy2* (3)
Hori (3)

3037 חֹרִי3 *hōriy3* (7)
Horite (4)
Horites (3)

3038 חָרִיט *hāriyt* (2)
bags (1)
purses (1)

3039 חִרְיֹונִים *hiryyôniym*
Variant; not used

3040 חָרִיף *hāriyp* (2)
Hariph (2)

3041 חֲרִיפוֹת *hªriypôt*
Variant; not used

3042 חֲרִיפִי *hªriypiy* (1)
untranslated (1)

3043 חָרִיץ1 *hāriys1* (1)
cheeses (1) +2692

3044 חָרִיץ2 *hāriys2* (2)
picks (2)

3045 חָרִישׁ *hāriyš* (3)
ground (1)
plowing (1)
plowing season (1)

3046 חֲרִישִׁי *hªriyšiy* (1)
scorching (1)

3047 חָרַךְ *hārak* (1)
roast (1)

3048 חֲרַכִּים *hªrakkiym* (1)
lattice (1)

3049 חָרַם1 *hāram1* (50)
totally destroyed (13)
completely destroyed (6)
completely destroy (4)
totally destroy (3)
destroy completely (2)
destroyed (2)
destroying completely (2)
annihilate (1)
be destroyed (1)
bring about destruction (1)
Completely destroy (1)
Completely destroy (1) +3049
destroy (1)
destroy totally (1)
destroying (1)
devote (1)
devoted and destroyed (1)
devoted to destruction (1) +3051
devotes (1)
exterminate (1)
forfeit (1)
kill (1)
must destroy totally (1) +3049

3050 חָרַם2 *hāram2* (1)
disfigured (1)

3051 חֵרֶם1 *hērem1* (29)
devoted things (6)
devoted (4)
destruction (3)
set apart for destruction (2)
themˢ (2) +2021
condemned things (1)
curse (1)
destroyed (1)
determined should die (1)
devoted to destruction (1)
devoted to destruction (1) +3049
devoted to God (1)
devoted to the LORD (1)
itˢ (1) +2021
that which is devoted (1)
totally destroyed (1)
untranslated (1)

3052 חֵרֶם2 *hērem2* (9)
net (5)
fishnets (2)
nets (1)
trap (1)

3053 חָרִם *hārim* (11)
Harim (10)
Harim's (1)

3054 חָרֵם *hªrēm* (1)
Horem (1)

3055 חָרְמָה *hormāh* (9)
Hormah (9)

3056 חֶרְמוֹן *hermôn* (14)
Hermon (13)
heights of Hermon (1)

3057 חֶרְמֹנִים *hermōniym*
Variant; not used

3058 חֶרְמֵשׁ *hermēš* (3)
sickle (2)
sickles (1)

3059 חָרָן1 *hārān1* (10)
Haran (10)

3060 חָרָן2 *hārān2* (2)
Haran (2)

3061 חֹרֹנִי *hōrōniy* (3)
Horonite (3)

3062 חַרְנֶפֶר *harneper* (1)
Harnepher (1)

3063 חֶרֶס1 *heres1* (1)
itch (1)

3064 חֶרֶס2 *heres2* (2)
sun (!)
sunset (1) +995+2021

3065 חֶרֶס3 *heres3* (2)
Heres (2)

3066 חַרְסָה *harsāh*
Variant; not used

3067 חַרְסוּת *harsût* (1)
untranslated (1)

3068 חַרְסִית *harsiyt* (1)
Potsherd (1)

3069 חָרַף1 *hārap1* (1)
all winter (1)

3070 חָרַף2 *hārap2* (39)
taunted (4)
defied (3)
defy (3)
insult (3)
insulted (3)
insulting (3)
mocked (3)
heaped insults on (2)
reproach (2)
ridicule (2)
shows contempt (2)
taunt (2)
discredit (1)
hurled (1)
mock (1)
rebuking (1)
risked (1) +4200+4637
taunts (1)
treats with contempt (1)

3071 חָרַף3 *hārap3*
Variant; not used

3072 חָרַף4 *hārap4* (1)
promised (1)

3073 חָרֵף *hārēp* (1)
Hareph (1)

3074 חֹרֶף *hōrep* (7)
winter (5)

prime (1)
season (1)

3075 חֶרְפָּה *herpāh* (73)
disgrace (17)
reproach (16)
scorn (10)
insults (5)
object of scorn (5)
shame (4)
contempt (3)
scorned (3)
insolence (2)
humiliation (1)
insult (1)
insulted (1)
mock (1)
mocked (1)
objects of reproach (1)
offensive (1)
slur (1)

3076 1חָרַץ *hāras1* (10)
been decreed (2)
decreed (2)
bark (1) +4383
been determined (1)
determined (1)
is decreed (1)
pronounced (1)
uttered a word (1) +906+4383

3077 2חָרַץ *hāras2* (1)
move quickly (1)

3078 חַרְצֹב *harsōb* (2)
chains (1)
struggles (1)

3079 חַרְצָן *harsān* (1)
seeds (1)

3080 חָרַק *hāraq* (5)
gnash (3)
gnashed (1)
gnashes (1)

3081 1חָרַר *hārar1* (9)
be charred (1)
burn (1)
burned up (1)
burns (1)
chars (1)
glows (1)
is charred (1)
kindling (1)
parched (1)

3082 2חָרַר *hārar2*
Variant; not used

3083 חֲרֵרִים *herēriym* (1)
parched places (1)

3084 חֶרֶשׂ *hereś* (17)
clay (9)
potsherd (2)
potsherds (2)
earthenware (1)
fragment (1)
piece of broken pottery (1)
pieces (1)

3085 חֲרֶשֶׂת *hereśet*
Variant; not used

3086 1חָרַשׂ *hāraś1* (27)
plow (6)
plot (3)
be plowed (2)
plowed (2)
plowing (2)
craftsman (1)
devises (1)
farmer (1)
inscribed (1)
plan (1)

planted (1)
plots (1)
plotting (1) +2021+8288
plowman (1)
plowmen (1)
plows (1)
tools (1)

3087 2חָרֵשׁ *hārēš2* (47)
silent (15)
quiet (8)
says nothing (3)
deaf (2)
altogether silent (1) +3087
fail to speak (1)
holds tongue (1)
keeps silent (1)
kept quiet (1)
made no move (1)
reduce to silence (1)
remain silent (1) +3087
said no more (1)
say nothing (1)
saying nothing (1)
says nothing (1) +3087
still (1)
stop (1)
turn a deaf ear (1)
without saying a word (1)

3088 1חֶרֶשׁ *hereš1*
Variant; not used

3089 2חֶרֶשׁ *hereš2* (1)
secretly (1)

3090 3חֶרֶשׁ *hereš3* (1)
Heresh (1)

3091 1חֹרֶשׁ *hōreš1* (3)
forest (1)
thickets (1)
wooded areas (1)

3092 2חֹרֶשׁ *hōreš2* (4)
Horesh (4)

3093 חָרָשׁ *hārāš* (38)
craftsmen (11)
craftsman (8)
carpenters (4)
carpenters (3) +6770
blacksmith (2)
blacksmith (1) +1366
carpenter (1) +6770
craftsman's (1)
cutter (1)
makers (1)
masons (1) +74
skilled (1)
stonemasons (1) +74+7815
stonemasons (1) +7815
workers (1)

3094 חֵרֵשׁ *hērēš* (9)
deaf (8)
untranslated (1)

3095 חַרְשָׁא *haršā'* (2)
Harsha (2)

3096 חֲרָשִׁים *herāšiym*
Variant; not used

3097 חֲרֶשֶׁת *herešet*
Variant; not used

3098 1חֲרֹשֶׁת *herōšet1* (4)
cut (2)
work (2)

3099 חֲרֹשֶׁת הַגּוֹיִם *herōšet haggôyim* (3)
Harosheth Haggoyim (3)

3100 חָרַת *hārat* (1)
engraved (1)

3101 חֶרֶת *heret* (1)
Hereth (1)

3102 חֲשׁוּפָא *hešûpā'* (2)
Hasupha (2)

3103 חֲשׁוּפַי *hešûpay*
Variant; not used

3104 חָשַׂךְ *hāśak* (27)
hold back (3)
withheld (3)
kept (2)
bring relief (1)
halted (1)
hesitate (1)
holds (1)
is relieved (1)
is spared (1)
keep (1)
keep silent (1) +7023
preserve (1)
punished less (1) +4200+4752
relentless (1) +1172
reserve (1)
restrain (1)
spare (1)
spares (1)
sparing (1)
too easy on (1)
uses with restraint (1)
withholds (1)

3105 חָשִׂף *hāśip* (1)
small flocks (1)

3106 1חָשַׂף *hāśap1* (11)
bared (1)
draw (1)
lay bare (1)
lift up (1)
pull up (1)
scooping (1)
strip bare (1)
stripped off bark (1) +3106
strips bare (1)

3107 2חָשַׂף *hāśap2*
Variant; not used

3108 חָשַׁב *hāšab* (112)
think (6)
devised (5)
plot (5)
plan (4)
plots (4)
are regarded (3)
count (3)
devise (3)
plotting (3)
thought (3)
was considered (3)
are considered (2)
be considered (2)
be reckoned (2)
considered (2)
determine (2)
devises (2)
intended (2)
make (2)
planning (2)
purposed (2) +4742
seem (2)
seems (2)
were considered (2)
account (1)
account for (1) +907
am counted (1)
be credited (1)
be taken (1)
care for (1)
compute (1)
consider (1)
consider themselves (1)
considers (1)
counted (1)
counts (1)

credited (1)
determine the value (1)
determined (1)
devise plans (1)
devising (1)
esteemed (1)
execute (1)
has in mind (1) +4222
hold (1)
honored (1)
imagine (1)
improvise (1)
is considered (1)
is thought (1)
make plans (1) +4742
mean (1)
planned (1)
plans (1)
plans have (1) +4742
plot against (1) +928+4222
plotted (1)
plotted (1) +4742
regard (1)
regarded (1)
require an accounting (1)
respected (1)
scheming (1)
threatened (1)
treats (1)
tried (1)
was credited (1)
were thought (1)

3109 חֵשֶׁב *hēšeb* (8)
waistband (7)
skillfully woven waistband (1)

3110 חֹשֵׁב *hōšēb* (12)
skilled craftsman (8)
designer (1)
designers (1)
designers (1) +4742
skillful men (1)

3111 חַשְׁבַּדָּנָה *hašbaddānāh* (1)
Hashbaddanah (1)

3112 חֲשֻׁבָה *hᵃšubāh* (1)
Hashubah (1)

3113 1חֶשְׁבּוֹן *hešbôn1* (3)
scheme of things (2)
planning (1)

3114 2חֶשְׁבּוֹן *hešbôn2* (38)
Heshbon (38)

3115 חִשָּׁבוֹן *hiššābôn* (2)
machines (1)
schemes (1)

3116 חֲשַׁבְיָה *hᵃšabyāh* (12)
Hashabiah (12)

3117 חֲשַׁבְיָהוּ *hᵃšabyāhû* (3)
Hashabiah (3)

3118 חֲשַׁבְנָה *hᵃšabnāh* (1)
Hashabnah (1)

3119 חֲשַׁבְנְיָה *hᵃšabnᵉyāh* (2)
Hashabneiah (2)

3120 חָשָׁה *hāšāh* (16)
silent (8)
not speak (2)
aren't do something (1)
calmed (1)
doing nothing (1)
hushed (1)
keeping it to ourselves (1)
not saying (1)

3121 חָשׁוּב *haššûb* (5)
Hasshub (5)

3122 חָשׁוּק *hāšûq* (8)
bands (8)

3123 חֻשִׁים *hušiym* (1)
Hushim (1)

3124 חָשַׁךְ *hāšak* (17)
dark (5)
darkened (3)
darkens (2)
dim (2)
black (1)
blacker (1)
brings darkness (1)
darken (1)
made dark (1)

3125 חֹשֶׁךְ *hōšek* (80)
darkness (70)
dark (4)
black (1)
dark place (1)
dusk (1)
gloom (1)
pitch darkness (1) +854
total darkness (1) +696

3126 חָשֹׁךְ *hāšōk* (1)
obscure (1)

3127 חָשְׁכָה *hāšᵉkāh* (1)
darkness (1)

3128 חֲשֵׁכָה *hᵃšēkāh* (7)
darkness (4)
dark (3)

3129 חָשַׁל *hāšal* (1)
lagging (1)

3130 חָשֻׁם *hāšum* (5)
Hashum (5)

3131 חֻשִׁם *hušim* (1)
Hushites (1)

3132 חֶשְׁמוֹן *hešmôn* (1)
Heshmon (1)

3133 חַשְׁמַל *hašmal* (3)
glowing metal (3)

3134 חַשְׁמַן *hašman* (1)
envoys (1)

3135 חַשְׁמֹנָה *hašmōnāh* (2)
Hashmonah (2)

3136 חֹשֶׁן *hōšen* (25)
breastpiece (23)
it (1) +2021
untranslated (1)

3137 1חָשַׁק *hāšaq1* (8)
desired (2) +3139
set affection (2)
attracted (1)
in love kept (1)
loves (1)
set (1)

3138 2חָשַׁק *hāšaq2* (3)
bands (2)
make bands (1)

3139 חֵשֶׁק *hēšeq* (4)
desired (2) +3137
desired (1) +2911
longed for (1)

3140 חִשֻּׁק *hiššuq* (1)
spokes (1)

3141 חִשֻּׁר *hiššur* (1)
hubs (1)

3142 חֲשְׂרָה *hašrāh*
Variant; not used

3143 חֲשַׁשׁ *hᵃšaš* (2)
chaff (1)
dry grass (1)

3144 חֻשָׁתִי *hušātiy* (5)
Hushathite (5)

3145 1חַת *hat1* (2)
dread (1)
fear (1)

3146 2חַת *hat2* (2)
broken (1)
terrified (1)

3147 חֵת *hēt* (14)
Hittites (9) +1201
Hittite (2)
Hittites (2)
his peopleˢ (1) +1201

3148 חָטָא *hātā'*
Variant; not used

3149 חָתָה *hātāh* (4)
heap (1)
scoop (1)
snatch up (1)
taking (1)

3150 חִתָּה *hitāh* (1)
terror (1)

3151 חִתּוּל *hitûl* (1)
splint (1)

3152 חַתְחַת *hathat* (1)
dangers (1)

3153 חִתִּי *hitiy* (48)
Hittites (25)
Hittite (23)

3154 חִתִּית *hitiyt* (9)
terror (8)
untranslated (1)

3155 חָתַךְ *hātak* (1)
are decreed (1)

3156 חָתַל *hātal* (2)
wrapped in cloths (1) +3156

3157 חֲתֻלָּה *hᵃtullāh* (1)
wrapped (1)

3158 חֶתְלוֹן *hetlôn* (2)
Hethlon (2)

3159 חָתַם *hātam* (26)
sealed (12)
seal (2)
seal up (2)
affixing seals (1)
be sealed up (1)
blocked (1)
enclosed (1)
model (1)
placed seal (1) +928+2597
seals off (1) +1237
shut in (1)
stops (1)
untranslated (1)

3160 חֹתֶמֶת *hōtemet* (1)
seal (1)

3161 חָתַן *hātan* (11)
son-in-law (5)
intermarry (4)
allied himself by marriage (1)
made an alliance (1)

3162 חֹתֵן *hōtēn* (21)
father-in-law (19)
brother-in-law (1)
himˢ (1) +2257

3163 חָתָן *hātān* (20)
bridegroom (10)
son-in-law (6)
sons-in-law (3)
related by marriage (1)

3164 חֲתֻנָּה *hᵃtunnāh* (1)
wedding (1)

3165 חֹתֶנֶת *hōtenet* (1)
mother-in-law (1)

3166 חָתַף *ḥāṯap̄* (1)
snatches away (1)

3167 חֶתֶף *ḥeṯep̄* (1)
bandit (1)

3168 חָתַר *ḥāṯar* (8)
dug (3)
dig (2)
break into (1)
dig down (1)
row (1)

3169 חָתַת *ḥāṯaṯ* (54)
discouraged (10)
terrified (9)
dismayed (7)
shattered (7)
filled with terror (3)
terrify (3)
afraid (2)
be shattered (2)
shatter (2)
broken (1)
cracked (1)
dreaded (1)
fail (1)
frighten (1)
frightened (1)
panic (1)
stood in awe (1)
terror (1)

3170 1חֲתַת *ḥᵃṯaṯ1* (1)
something dreadful (1)

3171 2חֲתַת *ḥᵃṯaṯ2* (1)
Hathath (1)

3172 ט *ṭ*
Variant; not used

3173 טֵאטֵא *ṭē'ṭē'* (1)
sweep (1)

3174 טָבְאַל *ṭāḇ''al* (1)
Tabeel (1)

3175 טָבְאֵל *ṭāḇ''ēl* (1)
Tabeel (1)

3176 טָבַב *ṭāḇaḇ*
Variant; not used

3177 טִבָּה *ṭibbāh*
Variant; not used

3178 טְבוּלִים *ṭᵊḇûliym* (1)
turbans (1)

3179 טַבּוּר *ṭabbûr* (2)
center (2)

3180 טָבַח *ṭāḇaḥ* (11)
slaughter (3)
slaughtered (3)
be slaughtered (1)
prepared (1)
slaughter (1) +3181
slaughters (1)
slay (1)

3181 1טֶבַח *ṭeḇaḥ1* (12)
slaughter (9)
animal (1)
meat (1)
slaughter (1) +3180

3182 2טֶבַח *ṭeḇaḥ2* (1)
Tebah (1)

3183 3טֶבַח *ṭeḇaḥ3* (1)
Tebah (1)

3184 טַבָּח *ṭabbāḥ* (32)
guard (13)
imperial guard (12)
cook (2)
untranslated (5)

3185 טַבָּחָה *ṭabbāḥāh* (1)
cooks (1)

3186 טִבְחָה *ṭibḥāh* (3)
butchered (1)
meat (1)
slaughtered (1)

3187 טִבְחַת *ṭibḥaṯ* (1)
Tebah (1)

3188 טָבַל *ṭāḇal* (16)
dip (8)
dipped (4)
bathe (1)
plunge (1)
soaked (1)
touched (1)

3189 טְבַלְיָהוּ *ṭᵊḇalyāhû* (1)
Tabaliah (1)

3190 טָבַע *ṭāḇa'* (10)
sink (2)
sunk (2)
are drowned (1)
fallen (1)
sank (1)
sank down (1)
were set (1)
were settled in place (1)

3191 טַבָּעוֹת *ṭabbā'ōṯ* (2)
Tabbaoth (2)

3192 טַבַּעַת *ṭabba'aṯ* (50)
rings (34)
ring (5)
signet ring (5)
signet rings (2)
them (1) +2021
themˢ (1) +2021
themˢ (1) +2021+9109
untranslated (1)

3193 טַבְרִמֹּן *ṭaḇrimmōn* (1)
Tabrimmon (1)

3194 טֵבֵת *ṭēḇēṯ* (1)
Tebeth (1)

3195 טַבָּת *ṭabbāṯ* (1)
Tabbath (1)

3196 טָהוֹר *ṭāhôr* (95)
pure (42)
clean (32)
ceremonially clean (13)
unclean (3) +4202
ceremonially unclean (1) +1194
flawless (1)
free from impurity (1)
unclean (1) +401
untranslated (1)

3197 טָהֵר *ṭāhēr* (93)
clean (23)
be cleansed (12)
cleanse (12)
pronounce clean (9)
cleansed (8)
purify (7)
purified (4)
ceremonially clean (3)
purify themselves (3)
purified themselves (2)
make ceremonially clean (1)
pronounces clean (1)
pronouncing clean (1)
pure (1)
purge (1)
purged (1)
purified themselves ceremonially (1)
purifier (1)
purify yourselves (1)
unclean (1) +4202

3198 טֹהַר *ṭōhar* (4)
purification (2)

clean (1)
clear (1)

3199 טְהָר *ṭᵊhār* (1)
splendor (1)

3200 טׇהֳרָה *ṭohᵒrāh* (13)
cleansing (3)
ceremonial cleansing (2)
pronounced clean (2)
purification (2)
purified (2)
clean (1)
cleansed (1)

3201 1טוֹב *ṭôḇ1* (29)
pleases (7)
in high spirits (5) +4213
did well (2)
feel better (2)
beautiful (1)
better (1) +3201
doing good (1)
done well (1)
favorably disposed (1)
go well (1)
make prosper (1)
pleased (1) +928+6524
pleasing (1)
prosper (1)
well off (1)
untranslated (1)

3202 2טוֹב *ṭôḇ2* (489)
good (241)
better (64)
best (17)
well (10)
fine (9)
prosperity (9)
right (7)
better off (6)
gracious (6)
pleases (6)
beautiful (5) +5260
pleases (5) +928+6524
favorable (4)
goodness (4)
precious (4)
choice (3)
kind (3)
like (3) +928+6524
beautiful (2)
favorably (2)
glad (2)
happy (2)
please (2)
please (2) +928+6524
pleased (2) +928+6524
pleasing (2)
prospers (2) +5162
rich (2)
satisfaction (2)
success (2)
very well (2)
alluring (1) +2834
approve of (1) +928+6524
attractive (1)
benefited (1)
better (1) +4946
bounty (1)
celebrating (1) +3427
celebration (1)
cheerful (1)
delightful (1)
favor (1)
festive (1)
fine (1) +1524+2256
finest (1)
flourishing (1)
generous man (1) +6524
graciously (1)
handsome (1)

handsome (1) +5260
handsome (1) +9307
happiness (1)
healthier (1)
help (1)
impressive (1)
intelligent (1) +8507
joyful (1)
likes (1) +928+2021+4200
lovely (1)
mean more (1)
noble (1)
pleasant (1)
please (1) +928+2256+3838+6524
pleased with (1) +928+6524
prefer (1) +928+6524
profitable (1)
profitable (1) +6087
prosper (1)
prosper (1) +5162
prospered (1)
prosperous (1)
relief (1)
sinful (1) +4202
sound (1)
the other^s (1)
valid (1)
wanted to do (1) +928+6524
wealth (1)
well off (1)
well-being (1)
wicked (1) +4202
wish (1) +928+6524
wished (1) +928+6524
without equal (1) +401+4946
worthwhile (1)
wrong (1) +4202
untranslated (2)

3203 שׁוֹב3 *tôb3* (1)
sweet (1)

3204 שׁוֹב4 *tôb4* (4)
Tob (4)

3205 שׁוֹב5 *tôb5*
Variant; not used

3206 שׁוּב *tûb* (32)
good things (7)
goodness (6)
best (3)
prosperity (3)
bounty (2)
good (2)
attractive (1)
best things (1)
blessings (1)
fair (1)
finest wares (1)
gladly (1) +928+4222
joy (1)
prosper (1)
rich produce (1)

3207 שׁוֹב אֲדוֹנִיָּה *tôb 'ᵃdôniyyāh* (1)
Tob-Adonijah (1)

3208 שׁוֹבָה *tôbāh* (67)
good (22)
prosperity (9)
good things (7)
favor (3)
well (3)
bounty (2)
good thing (2)
kindly (2)
treaty of friendship (2) +2256+8934
enjoyment (1)
fair (1)
good deeds (1)
good do (1) +3512
good work (1)
goodness (1)

goods (1)
gracious (1)
in behalf (1) +6584
joy (1)
prosperous (1)
satisfaction (1)
unharmed (1)
welfare (1)
well-being (1)

3209 טוֹבִיָּה *tôbiyyāh* (17)
Tobiah (14)
Tobijah (2)
Tobiah's (1)

3210 טוֹבִיָּהוּ *tôbiyyāhû* (1)
Tobijah (1)

3211 טָוָה *tāwāh* (2)
spun (2)

3212 טוּחַ *tûah* (11)
covered (3)
cover (2)
been plastered (1)
overlaying (1)
plaster (1)
plastered (1)
whitewash (1) +9521
whitewashed (1)

3213 טוֹטָפֹת *tôtāpōt* (3)
bind (2) +2118+4200
symbol (1)

3214 טוּל *tûl* (14)
hurl (2)
hurled (2)
threw (2)
throw (2)
be hurled out (1)
fall (1)
hurl away (1) +3232
is cast (1)
overpowering (1)
sent (1)

3215 טוּר *tûr* (26)
row (9)
rows (9)
course (2)
courses (2)
ledge of stone (1)
sets (1)
untranslated (2)

3216 טוּשׂ *tûś* (1)
swooping down (1)

3217 טָחָה *tāhāh* (1)
bowshot (1) +8008

3218 טְחוֹן *tᵉhôn* (1)
millstones (1)

3219 טְחוֹת *tuhôt* (2)
heart (1)
inner parts (1)

3220 טָחַח *tāhah* (1)
plastered over (1)

3221 טָחַן *tāhan* (7)
grinding (2)
ground (2)
grind (1)
grind grain (1)
ground to powder (1) +3512

3222 טַחֲנָה *tahᵃnāh* (1)
grinding (1)

3223 טֹחֲנָה *tōhᵃnāh* (1)
grinders (1)

3224 טְחֹרִים *tᵉhōriym* (8)
tumors (1)
untranslated (6)

3225 טִיחַ *tiyah* (1)

whitewash (1)

3226 טִיט *tiyt* (13)
mud (7)
clay (2)
mire (2)
dirt (1)
muddy (1)

3227 טִירָה *tiyrāh* (7)
camps (3)
ledge (1)
locations (1)
place (1)
towers (1)

3228 טַל *tal* (31)
dew (31)

3229 טָלָא *tālā'* (8)
spotted (6)
gaudy (1)
patched (1)

3230 טְלָאִים *tᵉlā'iym* (1)
Telaim (1)

3231 טָלֶה *tāleh* (3)
lamb (1)
lambs (1)

3232 טַלְטֵלָה *taltēlāh* (1)
hurl away (1) +3214

3233 טָלַל *tālal* (1)
roofing over (1)

3234 1טֶלֶם *telem1* (1)
Telem (1)

3235 2טֶלֶם *telem2* (1)
Telem (1)

3236 טַלְמוֹן *talmôn* (5)
Talmon (5)

3237 1טָמֵא *tāmē'1* (163)
unclean (62)
defiled (28)
defile (12)
pronounce unclean (8)
defile yourselves (6)
defiles (5)
defiled herself (4)
ceremonially unclean (3)
defiling (3)
desecrated (3)
make himself unclean (3)
defile themselves (2)
defiled yourself (2)
impure (2)
make himself ceremonially unclean (2)
make yourselves unclean (2)
be made unclean (1)
became defiled (1)
been defiled (1)
corrupt (1)
defile himself (1)
defiled yourselves (1)
defiles herself (1)
desecrate (1)
impurity (1)
let become defiled (1)
make unclean (1)
pronounce ceremonially unclean (1)
pronounce unclean (1) +3237
pronounced unclean (1)
remains unclean (1) +3238

3238 2טָמֵא *tāmē'2* (87)
unclean (64)
ceremonially unclean (12)
defiled (7)
impure (1)
infamous (1) +2021+9005
pagan (1)
remains unclean (1) +3237

3239 טָמְאָה *tom'āh*
Variant; not used

3240 טֻמְאָה *tum'āh* (36)
uncleanness (16)
unclean (6)
impurity (4)
impurities (2)
ceremonially unclean (1)
discharge (1) +2308
filthiness (1)
impure (1)
things that make unclean (1)
unclean practices (1)
woman's monthly uncleanness (1)
              +2021+5614
untranslated (1)

3241 טָמָה *tāmāh* (1)
considered stupid (1)

3242 טָמַם *tāmam*
Variant; not used

3243 טָמַן *tāman* (31)
hidden (10)
hid (6)
hide (3)
buried (2)
buries (2)
bury (2)
hiding (2)
grave (1)
lies in wait (1)
set (1)
treasures hidden (1) +8561

3244 טֶנֶא *tene'* (4)
basket (4)

3245 טָנַף *tānap* (1)
soil (1)

3246 טָעָה *tā'āh* (1)
lead astray (1)

3247 טָעַם *tā'am* (11)
taste (4)
tasted (2)
tastes (2)
merely tasted (1) +3247
sees (1)

3248 טַעַם *ta'am* (13)
pretended to be insane (2) +9101
tasted (2)
decree (1)
discernment (1)
discreetly (1)
discretion (1)
flavor (1)
good judgment (1)
judgment (1)
tastes (1)
untranslated (1)

3249 1טַעַן *tā'an1* (1)
pierced (1)

3250 2טָעַן *tā'an2* (1)
load (1)

3251 1טַף *tap1* (42)
children (27)
women and children (6)
little ones (4)
little children (2)
boys (1) +2351
families (1)
girl (1) +851

3252 2טַף *tap2*
Variant; not used

3253 1טָפַח *tāpah1* (1)
spread out (1)

3254 2טָפַח *tāpah2* (1)
cared for (1)

3255 טֶפַח *tepah* (2)
handbreadth (2)

3256 טֹפַח *tōpah* (5)
handbreadth (5)

3257 1טִפְחָה *taphāh1* (1)
handbreadth (1)

3258 2טִפְחָה *taphāh2* (1)
eaves (1)

3259 טִפֻּחִים *tippuhiym* (1)
cared for (1)

3260 טָפַל *tāpal* (3)
cover (1)
smear (1)
smeared (1)

3261 טִפְסָר *tipsār* (2)
commander (1)
officials (1)

3262 טָפַף *tāpap* (1)
tripping along with mincing steps (1)
              +2143+2256

3263 טָפַשׁ *tāpaš* (1)
unfeeling (1)

3264 טֶפַת *tāpat* (1)
Taphath (1)

3265 טָרַד *tārad* (2)
constant dripping (2) +1942

3266 טְרוֹם *t'rôm* (1)
untranslated (1)

3267 טָרַח *tārah* (1)
loads (1)

3268 טֹרַח *tōrah* (2)
burden (1)
problems (1)

3269 טָרִי *tāriy* (2)
fresh (1)
open (1)

3270 טֶרֶם *terem* (56)
before (36) +928
before (9)
not yet (4)
before (2) +928+4202
before (1) +4946
just before (1) +928
no yet (1)
no yet (1) +3972
still not (1)

3271 טָרַף *tārap* (25)
tear to pieces (4)
tear (3)
tearing (3)
been torn to pieces (1) +3271
give (1)
killed (1)
mangles (1)
prey (1)
raged (1)
ravenous (1)
surely been torn to pieces (1) +3271
tearing prey (1)
tears (1)
torn to pieces (1)
was torn to pieces by a wild animal (1)
              +3271

3272 טֶרֶף *terep* (22)
prey (13)
food (4)
victims (2)
game (1)
kill (1)
torn (1)

3273 טָרָף *tārāp* (2)
freshly plucked (1)

new (1)

3274 טְרֵפָה *t'rēpāh* (9)
torn by wild animals (5)
animal torn by beasts (1)
animals torn by wild beasts (1)
prey (1)
remains (1)

3275 י *y*
Variant; not used

3276 יִ- *-iy* (6489)
my (3486)
me (1800)
I (381)
my (77) +4200
the^s (52)
my own (43)
me (35) +5883
mine (33) +4200
I (29) +5883
myself (27)
our (25)
us (18)
mine (16)
a^s (9)
myself (9) +5883
I'm (4)
my (4) +5883
my own (4) +4200
her (3)
his (3)
me (3) +7156
myself (3) +4213
we (3)
you^s (3) +123
here^s (2)
him (2)
I've (2)
me (2) +3883
my (2) +928+8079
this^s (2)
us (2) +2256+3870
you (2)
all by myself (1) +963+4200
an^s (1)
by myself (1) +907+4946
by myself (1) +963+4200
he^s (1) +3
he^s (1) +123
her (1) +4200
her own (1)
here^s (1) +6584
here^s (1) +6640
him^s (1) +3
him^s (1) +123
his^s (1) +466
I (1) +4213
I (1) +5055
I (1) +7023
I (1) +8120
it^s (1) +274
it^s (1) +1460
it^s (1) +4213
it^s (1) +7754
its (1)
me (1) +2652
me (1) +8120
me alone (1) +638
mine (1) +4200+8611
mine (1) +6643
mine (1) +9393
my (1) +907
my (1) +928
my (1) +4200+7156
my (1) +6640
my (1) +7156
my life (1)
my life's (1)
my own (1) +4200+8611
myself (1) +963
myself (1) +1414

myself (1) +3338
our own (1)
ours (1) +4200
theirˢ (1) +3776+6639
themˢ (1) +6639
theyˢ (1) +7366
thought (1) +448+606
us (1) +2157+2256
us (1) +2256+4013
what do I care about (1)
            +2296+4200+4200+4537
your (1)
yourˢ (1) +123
untranslated (353)

3277 יָאַב *yā'ab* (1)
longing for (1)

3278 יָאָה *yā'āh* (1)
due (1)

3279 יַאֲזַנְיָה *ya'ᵃzanyāh* (2)
Jaazaniah (2)

3280 יַאֲזַנְיָהוּ *ya'ᵃzanyāhû* (2)
Jaazaniah (2)

3281 יָאִיר *yā'iyr* (8)
Jair (8)

3282 1יָאַל *yā'al1* (4)
become fools (2)
foolish (1)
foolishly (1)

3283 2יָאַל *yā'al2* (19)
determined (3)
pleased (3)
agreed (2)
bold (2)
be so kind as (1)
began (1)
by all means (1)
content (1)
intent on (1)
please (1) +5528
tried (1)
willing (1)
untranslated (1)

3284 יְאֹר *yᵉ'ōr* (65)
Nile (31)
river (13)
streams (10)
canals (2)
itsˢ (2) +2021
riverbank (1) +8557
rivers (1)
streams of the Nile (1)
tunnels (1) +1324
untranslated (3)

3285 יָאִרִי *yā'iriy* (1)
Jairite (1)

3286 יָאַשׁ *yā'aš* (6)
despair (1)
despairing (1)
give up (1)
hopeless (1)
no use (1)
use (1)

3287 יֹאשִׁיָה *yō'šiyyāh* (1)
Josiah (1)

3288 יֹאשִׁיָהוּ *yō'šiyyāhû* (52)
Josiah (47)
Josiah's (3)
himˢ (1)
untranslated (1)

3289 יִאתוֹן *yi'tôn*
Variant; not used

3290 יְאָתְרַי *yᵉ'ātᵉray* (1)
Jeatherai (1)

3291 יְבַב *yābab* (1)

cried out (1)

3292 יְבוּל *yᵉbûl* (12)
crops (7)
harvest (2)
grapes (1)
harvests (1)
produce (1)

3293 יְבוּס *yᵉbûs* (4)
Jebus (3)
untranslated (1)

3294 יְבוּסִי *yᵉbûsiy* (41)
Jebusites (32)
Jebusite (9)

3295 יִבְחָר *yibḥār* (3)
Ibhar (3)

3296 יָבִין *yābiyn* (8)
Jabin (6)
himˢ (1) +4046+4889
Jabin's (1)

3297 יָבַל *yābal* (18)
bring (5)
are led in (1)
be brought (1)
be carried (1)
be led forth (1)
been carried (1)
bring back (1)
is carried (1)
is delivered (1)
is led (1)
led (1)
sends (1)
taken (1)
was led (1)

3298 1יָבָל *yābāl1* (2)
flow (1)
flowing streams (1) +4784

3299 2יָבָל *yābāl2* (1)
Jabal (1)

3300 יִבְלְעָם *yiblᵉ'ām* (3)
Ibleam (3)

3301 יַבֶּלֶת *yabbelet* (1)
anything with warts (1)

3302 יָבַם *yābam* (3)
fulfill the duty of a brother-in-law (2)
fulfill duty as a brother-in-law (1)

3303 יָבָם *yābām* (2)
husband's brother (2)

3304 יְבָמָה *yᵉbāmāh* (5)
brother's widow (1)
brother's wife (1)
herˢ (1) +3871
sheˢ (1) +2257
sister-in-law (1)

3305 יַבְנְאֵל *yabnᵉ'ēl* (2)
Jabneel (2)

3306 יַבְנֶה *yabnēh* (1)
Jabneh (1)

3307 יִבְנְיָה *yibnᵉyāh* (1)
Ibneiah (1)

3308 יִבְנִיָּה *yibniyyāh* (1)
Ibnijah (1)

3309 יַבֹּק *yabbōq* (7)
Jabbok (7)

3310 יְבֶרֶכְיָהוּ *yᵉberekyāhû* (1)
Jeberekiah (1)

3311 יִבְשָׂם *yibśām* (1)
Ibsam (1)

3312 1יָבֵשׁ *yābēš1* (63)
dried up (15)
withered (8)

dry up (7)
wither (6)
dry (5)
withers (5)
dries up (2)
wither away (2)
completely dry (1)
completely withered (1) +3312
drought (1)
fail (1)
made shrivel (1)
make dry (1)
overthrow (1)
parched (1)
shriveled up (1)
wither completely (1) +3312
withered away (1)

3313 2יָבֵשׁ *yābēš2* (10)
dry (8)
grapes or raisins (1) +2256+4300+6694
lost (1)

3314 3יָבֵשׁ *yābēš3* (3)
Jabesh (3)

3315 4יָבֵשׁ *yābēš4* (9)
Jabesh (8)
theyˢ (1) +408

3316 יָבֵשׁ גִּלְעָד *yābēš gil'ād* (12)
Jabesh Gilead (12)

3317 יַבָּשָׁה *yabbāšāh* (14)
dry ground (10)
dry land (2)
land (2)

3318 יַבֶּשֶׁת *yabbešet* (2)
dry land (1)
ground (1)

3319 יִגְאָל *yig'āl* (3)
Igal (3)

3320 יָגַב *yāgab* (2)
fields (2)

3321 יָגֵב *yāgēb* (1)
fields (1)

3322 יָגְבְּהָה *yogbᵉhāh* (2)
Jogbehah (2)

3323 יִגְדַּלְיָהוּ *yigdalyāhû* (1)
Igdaliah (1)

3324 1יָגָה *yāgāh1* (7)
brings grief (1)
brought (1)
brought grief (1)
grief (1)
grieve (1)
torment (1)
tormentors (1)

3325 2יָגָה *yāgāh2* (1)
been removed (1)

3326 יָגוֹן *yāgôn* (14)
sorrow (13)
anguish (1)

3327 יָגוּר *yāgûr* (1)
Jagur (1)

3328 יָגוֹר *yāgôr* (2)
fear (2)

3329 יָגִיעַ *yāgiya'* (1)
weary (1) +3946

3330 יְגִיעַ *yᵉgiya'* (16)
labor (4)
fruits of labor (2)
products (2)
fruit of labor (1) +4090
heavy work (1)
possessions (1)
produce (1)

toil (1)
wealth (1)
work (1)
worked (1)

3331 יְגִיעָה *y*ᵉ*giy'āh* (1)
wearies (1)

3332 יָגְלִי *yogliy* (1)
Jogli (1)

3333 יָגַע *yāga'* (26)
wearied (6)
weary (5)
labored (3)
worn out (3)
toil (2)
exhaust (1)
labor (1)
struggle (1)
tired (1)
toiled (1)
wear out (1)
wearies (1)

3334 יָגָע *yāgā'* (1)
what toiled for (1)

3335 יָגֵעַ *yāgēa'* (3)
wearisome (1)
weary (1)
worn out (1)

3336 יָגֹר *yāgōr* (5)
dread (2)
dreaded (2)
feared (1)

3337 יְגַר שָׂהֲדוּתָא *y*ᵉ*gar śāhᵃdûtā'* (1)
Jegar Sahadutha (1)

3338 יָד *yād* (1627)
hand (538)
hands (349)
through (62) +928
hand over (35) +928+5989
power (34)
from (33) +4946
handed over (23) +928+5989
with (20) +928
by (18) +928
to (15) +928
care (14)
to (12) +6584
be handed over (8) +928+5989
afford (7) +5952
arm (7)
next to (7) +6584
arms (6)
command (6)
control (5)
direction (5)
next section (5) +6584
side (5)
supervision (5)
against (4) +4946+9393
finger (4)
have (4) +928
possession (4)
spacious (4) +8146
clutches (3)
fist (3)
hands (3) +4090
hold accountable (3) +1335+4946
next (3) +6584
ordained (3) +906+4848
power (3) +445
special gifts (3) +9556
strength (3)
under (3) +928
along (2) +6584
armrests (2)
as much as pleases (2) +5522
assassinate (2) +928+8938
authority (2)

axles (2)
bank (2)
be sure of this (2) +3338+4200
boldly (2) +928+8123
by (2) +6584
certainly be handed over (2)
            +928+5989+5989
encouraged (2) +2616
grasp (2)
guilty (2) +928
had (2) +928
hand over (2) +928+6037
handed (2)
handed over (2) +928+6037
he (2) +2257
hold accountable (2) +2011+4946
installed (2) +906+4848
left-handed (2) +360+3545
liberality (2)
monument (2)
next to (2) +448
openhanded (2) +906+7337+7337
ordain (2) +4848
ordination (2) +906+4848
paw (2)
place (2)
play (2) +928+5594
playing the harp (2) +928+5594
projection (2)
projections (2)
prospers (2) +5952
rebelled (2) +8123
seized (2) +8492
supports (2)
taking with (2) +928
themˢ (2) +2021
thumbs (2) +984
times (2)
wheel around (2) +2200
wrist (2)
you (2) +3870
abandon (1) +4946+8332
accompanied by (1) +6584
actions (1)
adjoining (1) +6584
adjoining section (1) +6584
afford (1) +1896+5162
afford (1) +1896+5595
against (1) +4946
agent (1) +4200
along (1)
along (1) +4200
along with (1) +928
arms (1) +723
as a direct result (1) +9393
as prescribed by (1) +6584
assistant (1) +6584
assisted (1) +928+2616
assisted (1) +2616
assisted (1) +6584
attack (1) +928+8938
attack (1) +6584+6590
attacked (1) +928+8938
attacks (1) +928+8938
be defeated (1) +928+5989
because of (1) +928
beckon (1) +5677
beckon (1) +5951
been handed over (1) +928+5989
began (1) +2616
beside (1) +448
beside (1) +928
beside (1) +4200
beside (1) +6584
body (1)
border (1)
borders (1)
bounty (1)
bracelets (1) +6584+7543
broad (1) +8146
brought (1) +928

brought with (1) +928+2118
call to account (1) +1335+4946
carried (1) +928+4374
cause (1) +928
commanded (1)
companies (1)
consecrate himself (1) +2257+4848
consecrate himself (1) +4848
consecrated (1) +906+4848
creditor (1) +1251+2257+5408
custody (1)
customers (1) +6086
customers (1) +6088
debts (1) +5391
dedicate (1) +4848
dedicated (1) +4848
delegation (1) +928+6269
delivered (1) +928
deserves (1) +1691
did thisˢ (1) +2257+5742
didˢ (1) +2257+5989
discourage (1) +8332
discouraging (1) +8332
do (1) +5126
do thatˢ (1) +928+2118+2257
don't say a word (1) +6584+7023+8492
done by (1) +928
drew (1) +928+4848
entrusted to (1) +448
entrusted to (1) +928
fists (1)
follow (1) +448
for (1) +928
for (1) +6584
force (1)
forcefully (1) +928
four-fifths (1) +752
from (1) +928
gain support (1) +907+2118
gave victory (1) +928+5989
give (1) +928+5989
give up (1) +8332
given over (1) +5599+6584
had chance (1) +928+2118
hand over (1) +928+4835
hand over (1) +928+5162
hand over to (1) +928+5989
handed (1) +928+5989
handed (1) +4946
handed over (1) +928+5162
handed over (1) +928+5796
handing over (1) +928+5989
handing over (1) +928+6037
handiwork (1) +5126
has (1) +928
have (1) +928+5162
have (1) +3780+9393
have on hand (1) +448+9393
have on hand (1) +3780+9393
help (1) +2616
help (1) +4200
help (1) +6640
help (1) +6640+8883
helped (1) +906+2616
helped find strength (1) +906+2616
him (1) +2257
hold (1)
hold (1) +928+2118
hold responsible (1) +1335+4946
holding (1) +928
holds (1) +928+2118
in charge of (1) +928
itˢ (1) +2257
itˢ (1) +3870
killing (1) +928+8938
labor (1)
large (1) +8146
leadership (1)
led the way (1) +2118+8037
let go (1) +906+5663
lets happen (1) +628+4200

little by little (1) +6584
lost courage (1) +8332
made subject to (1) +4044+9393
man-made (1) +132+5126
marched past (1) +6296+6584
memorial (1)
myself (1) +3276
nakedness (1)
near (1) +6584
nearby (1) +6584
of (1) +4946
ordain (1) +906+4848
ordained (1) +4848
ordered (1)
overpowered (1) +6451+6584
pledged (1) +5989
plenty of room (1) +8146
portion (1)
powerless (1) +401+445+4200
put in charge (1) +6584+6641
put up security (1) +4200+9546
reached out (1) +8938
reaches out (1) +8938
reaching (1) +8938
remaining (1)
reward earned (1) +7262
rich (1) +5952
ruled (1) +4939
seize (1) +928+8492
set apart (1) +4848
set free (1) +4946+8938
shapes (1) +5126
shares (1)
shed by (1) +4946
shores (1)
sided with (1) +6640
signpost (1)
sins defiantly (1) +928+6913+8123
snare (1)
someone else^S (1) +928
stroke (1)
strong (1) +2616
strong arms (1) +2432
submit (1) +5989
submit (1) +8132
submitted (1) +5989
supported (1) +907+2118
surely hand over (1) +928+5989+5989
surrender (1) +928+6037
surrenders (1) +5989
swore (1) +5951
sworn (1) +906+5951
take charge of (1) +9393
taken (1) +928
things did (1) +5126
those^S (1)
tightfisted (1) +906+7890
to (1) +9393
took with (1) +928
turned about (1) +2200
unable to support (1) +4572
under (1) +4946
under care (1)
used (1) +928
uses (1) +928
vicinity (1)
wants to give (1) +5952
war clubs (1) +5234
waves (1)
weak (1) +8333
with (1) +4200
with (1) +6584
wrists (1)
wrists (1) +723
untranslated (72)

3339 יִדְאֲלָה *yid'ᵃlāh* (1)
Idalah (1)

3340 יִדְבָּשׁ *yidbāš* (1)
Idbash (1)

3341 יָדַד *yāḏaḏ* (3)
cast (3)

3342 יְדִדוּת *yᵉḏiḏûṯ* (1)
love (1)

3343 יָדָה1 *yāḏāh1* (3)
shoot (1)
threw (1)
throw down (1)

3344 יָדָה2 *yāḏāh2* (111)
praise (44)
give thanks (35)
confess (10)
thanksgiving (3)
confessed (2)
confessing (2)
extol (2)
admit (1)
brings praise (1)
confesses (1)
confession (1)
gave thanks (1)
led in thanksgiving (1) +9378
praised (1)
praises (1)
praising (1)
psalm of thanks (1)
thank (1)
thanking (1)
thanks (1)

3345 יַדּוּ *yaddaw* (1)
untranslated (1)

3346 יִדּוֹ *yiddô* (1)
Iddo (1)

3347 יָדוֹן *yāḏôn* (1)
Jadon (1)

3348 יַדּוּעַ *yaddûaʿ* (3)
Jaddua (3)

3349 יְדוּתוּן *yᵉḏûtûn* (16)
Jeduthun (15)
his^S (1)

3350 יַדַּי *yadday* (1)
Jaddai (1)

3351 יָדִיד *yāḏiyḏ* (8)
love (3)
beloved (2)
loved one (1)
lovely (1)
loves (1)

3352 יְדִידָה *yᵉḏiyḏāh* (1)
Jedidah (1)

3353 יְדִידוֹת *yᵉḏiyḏôṯ* (1)
wedding (1)

3354 יְדִידְיָה *yᵉḏiyḏyāh* (1)
Jedidiah (1)

3355 יְדָיָה *yᵉḏāyāh* (2)
Jedaiah (2)

3356 יְדִיעֲאֵל *yᵉḏiyʿᵃʾēl* (6)
Jediael (6)

3357 יְדִיתוּן *yᵉḏiytûn* (4)
Jeduthun (1)
untranslated (3)

3358 יִדְלָף *yidlāp̄* (1)
Jidlaph (1)

3359 יָדַע *yāḏaʿ* (949)
know (422)
knows (43)
knew (39)
known (23)
acknowledge (21)
understand (15)
teach (13)
realize (12)

make known (11)
tell (11)
made known (10)
learned (9)
aware (8)
find out (8)
know how (8)
show (7)
know about (6)
knowing (6)
learn (6)
be sure (5) +3359
knew about (5)
knowledge (5)
realized (5)
be known (4)
experienced (4)
knows how (4)
lay with (4)
see (4)
understanding (4)
acknowledged (3)
answer (3)
be sure (3)
confront (3)
consider (3)
find out (3) +2256+8011
is known (3)
know (3) +3359
make myself known (3)
observe (3)
see (3) +2256+8011
skilled (3)
unknown (3) +4202
cares for (2)
chosen (2)
concern (2)
concerned about (2)
found out (2)
friends (2)
gain (2)
have (2)
have sex with (2)
ignorant (2) +4202
is made aware (2)
learns (2)
let know (2)
recognized (2)
respected (2)
revealed myself (2)
take notice (2)
unaware (2) +4202
understood (2)
able (1)
acknowledges (1)
acquaintances (1)
agreed (1)
apply (1)
approval (1)
are known (1)
assured (1)
assured (1) +3359
attaining (1)
be found out (1)
be made known (1)
be recognized (1)
be remembered (1)
be sure know (1) +3359
become aware (1)
become known (1)
been discovered (1)
been known (1)
behaved (1)
by surprise (1) +4202
can (1)
can read (1) +6219
cannot read (1) +4202+6219
care about (1)
care for (1)
cared for (1)
close friend (1)

close friends (1)
closest friend (1)
closest friends (1)
come to (1)
comprehend (1)
decide (1)
display (1)
displayed (1)
endowed with (1)
enjoy (1)
experts (1)
familiar with (1)
feel (1)
find (1)
foresee (1)
great skill (1) +1069+2682
had experience (1)
had intimate relations with (1)
had regard for (1)
had the least inkling (1) +3359
has knowledge (1) +1981
have concern for (1)
have knowledge (1) +1981
have to do with (1)
ignorant (1) +1153
inform (1)
instructed (1)
is respected (1)
know all about (1)
know for certain (1) +3359
know how to read (1) +6219
know what it is like (1)
know what means (1)
knowing about (1)
knowing how (1)
knows very well (1) +3359
lain with (1)
leading (1)
learn the difference between (1)
learned about (1)
learning (1)
lets be known (1)
letting know (1)
made himself known (1)
make himself known (1)
make predictions (1)
makes known (1)
man of knowledge (1) +1981
mourners (1) +5631
must understand (1) +3359
not a virgin (1) +2351+5435
note (1)
notice (1)
noticed (1)
perceive (1)
perceiving (1)
proclaim (1)
raped (1)
realize (1) +2256+8011
realized (1) +2256+8011
realizing (1)
recognizes (1)
remember (1)
reveal myself (1)
revealed (1)
show how to distinguish (1)
showed (1)
shown (1)
shown himself (1)
shows (1)
skillful (1)
sleep with (1)
slept with (1)
slept with (1) +408+4200+5435
slept with (1) +2351+4200+5435
slept with (1) +2351+5435
slept with (1) +5435
stranger (1) +4202
strangers (1) +4202
suffer (1)
taught a lesson (1)

teaching (1)
tell the difference (1)
think (1)
think it over (1)
think over (1)
told (1)
trained (1)
understand (1) +1069
understands (1)
understood (1) +1069
unfamiliar (1) +4202
virgin (1) +408+4202
want to do with (1)
was discovered (1)
was known (1)
watched over (1)
watches over (1)
well informed (1) +1981
were seen (1)
untranslated (14)

3360 יָדַע yāḏā‘ (2)
Jada (2)

3361 יִרְעְיָה yᵉḏa‘yāh (11)
Jedaiah (9)
Jedaiah's (2)

3362 יִדְּעֹנִי yiddᵉ‘ōniy (11)
spiritists (9)
spiritist (2)

3363 יָהּ yāh (49)
the LORD (44)
LORD (4)
heˢ (1)

3364 יָהַב yāhaḇ
Variant; not used

3365 יְהַב yᵉhaḇ (1)
cares (1)

3366 יָהַד yāhaḏ (1)
became Jews (1)

3367 יָהְדָּי yāhdāy (1)
Jahdai (1)

3368 יְהַדְיָה yᵉhuḏiyyāh
Variant; not used

3369 יֵהוּא yēhû’ (58)
Jehu (52)
heˢ (4)
Jehu's (2)

3370 יְהוֹאָחָז yᵉhô’āḥāz (20)
Jehoahaz (18)
Ahaziah (2)

3371 יְהוֹאָשׁ yᵉhô’āš (17)
Jehoash (9)
Joash (8)

3372 יְהוּד yᵉhûḏ (1)
Jehud (1)

3373 יְהוּדָה yᵉhûḏāh (819)
Judah (772)
Judah (11) +1201
Judah's (11)
Judah (6) +824
Judah (4) +1074
Jews (3)
Judean (2)
Judah's (1) +1201
of Judah (1) +1201
theirˢ (1) +408
theyˢ (1)
Yaudi (1)
untranslated (5)

3374 יְהוּדִי yᵉhûḏiy1 (82)
Jews (57)
Jew (10)
Jewish (4)
men of Judah (3)

Judean (1)
theyˢ (1) +2021
untranslated (6)

3375 יְהוּדִי2 yᵉhûḏiy2 (4)
Jehudi (4)

3376 יְהוּדִית1 yᵉhûḏiyt1 (6)
in Hebrew (5)
language of Judah (1)

3377 יְהוּדִית2 yᵉhûḏiyt2 (1)
Judith (1)

3378 יהוה yhwh (6829)&
the LORD (6030)
LORD (399)
the LORD's (243)
heˢ (35)
the LORD's (27) +4200
himˢ (16)
hisˢ (13)
heˢ (7) +466+3870
himˢ (3) +466+3870
itsˢ (3) +1074
the LORD's (3) +907+4946
hisˢ (2) +466+3870
meˢ (2)
done thisˢ (1) +1215+4200+4640
heˢ (1) +466
heˢ (1) +466+5646
heˢ (1) +4855
himˢ (1) +466+4013
the angel (1) +4855
the LORD's (1) +4946+6640
the LORD himself (1) +7156
untranslated (38)

3379 יְהוֹזָבָד yᵉhôzāḇāḏ (4)
Jehozabad (4)

3380 יְהוֹחָנָן yᵉhôḥānān (9)
Jehohanan (9)

3381 יְהוֹיָדָע yᵉhôyāḏā‘ (51)
Jehoiada (50)
heˢ (1) +2021+3913

3382 יְהוֹיָכִין yᵉhôyāḵiyn (10)
Jehoiachin (10)

3383 יְהוֹיָקִים yᵉhôyāqiym (36)
Jehoiakim (34)
Jehoiakim's (2)

3384 יְהוֹיָרִיב yᵉhôyāriyḇ (2)
Jehoiarib (2)

3385 יְהוּכַל yᵉhûḵal (1)
Jehucal (1)

3386 יְהוֹנָדָב yᵉhônāḏāḇ (8)
Jonadab (5)
Jehonadab (3)

3387 יְהוֹנָתָן yᵉhônāṯān (82)
Jonathan (68)
heˢ (3)
Jonathan's (3)
Jehonathan (2)
meˢ (1)
untranslated (5)

3388 יְהוֹסֵף yᵉhôsēp̄ (1)
Joseph (1)

3389 יְהוֹעַדָּה yᵉhô‘addāh (2)
Jehoaddah (2)

3390 יְהוֹעַדִּין yᵉhô‘addiyn (1)
Jehoaddin (1)

3391 יְהוֹעַדָּן yᵉhô‘addān (2)
Jehoaddin (1)
untranslated (1)

3392 יְהוֹצָדָק yᵉhôṣāḏāq (8)
Jehozadak (8)

3393 יְהוֹרָם yᵉhôrām (29)
Jehoram (16)

Joram (13)

3394 יְהוֹשֶׁבַע yᵉhôšebaʿ (1)
Jehosheba (1)

3395 יְהוֹשַׁבְעַת yᵉhôšabʿat (2)
Jehosheba (2)

3396 יְהוֹשָׁמָע yᵉhôšāmāʿ
Variant; not used

3397 יְהוֹשֻׁעַ yᵉhôšuaʿ (218)
Joshua (203)
heˢ (8)
himˢ (2)
untranslated (5)

3398 1יְהוֹשָׁפָט yᵉhôšāpāṭ1 (82)
Jehoshaphat (79)
Jehoshaphat's (2)
untranslated (1)

3399 2יְהוֹשָׁפָט yᵉhôšāpāṭ2 (2)
Jehoshaphat (2)

3400 יָהִיר yāhiyr (2)
arrogant (2)

3401 יְהַלֶּלְאֵל yᵉhallelʾēl (2)
Jehallelel (2)

3402 יָהֲלֹם yāhᵃlōm (3)
emerald (3)

3403 יַהַץ yahaṣ (7)
Jahaz (7)

3404 יַהְצָה yahṣāh (2)
Jahzah (2)

3405 יוֹאָב yôʾāb (145)
Joab (132)
Joab's (8)
heˢ (2)
theyˢ (1) +2021+2256+2657+8569
whoˢ (1)
untranslated (1)

3406 יוֹאָח yôʾāh (11)
Joah (11)

3407 יוֹאָחָז yôʾāḥāz (4)
Jehoahaz (3)
Joahaz (1)

3408 יוֹאֵל yôʾēl (20)
Joel (20)

3409 יוֹאָשׁ yôʾāš (47)
Joash (30)
Jehoash (16)
himˢ (1)

3410 יוֹב yôb
Variant; not used

3411 1יוֹבָב yôbāb1 (2)
Jobab (2)

3412 2יוֹבָב yôbāb2 (7)
Jobab (7)

3413 יוֹבֵל yôbēl (27)
jubilee (20)
trumpets (3) +8795
ram's horn (1)
rams' horns (1)
trumpets (1) +7967
year of jubilee (1)

3414 1יוּבַל yûbal1 (1)
stream (1)

3415 2יוּבַל yûbal2 (1)
Jubal (1)

3416 יוֹזָבָד yôzābād (11)
Jozabad (11)

3417 יוֹזָכָר yôzākār
Variant; not used

3418 יוֹחָא yôḥāʾ (2)
Joha (2)

3419 יוֹחָנָן yôḥānān (24)
Johanan (24)

3420 יוּטָּה yûṭṭāh (3)
Juttah (3)

3421 יוֹיָדָע yôyādāʿ (5)
Joiada (5)

3422 יוֹיָכִין yôyākiyn (1)
Jehoiachin (1)

3423 יוֹיָקִים yôyāqiym (4)
Joiakim (4)

3424 יוֹיָרִיב yôyāriyb (5)
Joiarib (4)
Joiarib's (1)

3425 יוֹכֶבֶד yôkebed (2)
Jochebed (2)

3426 יוּכַל yûkal (1)
Jehucal (1)

3427 1יוֹם yôm1 (2298)
day (950)
days (474)
today (137) +2021
time (122)
when (45) +928
today (39) +2021+2021+2296
annals (37) +1821
years (21)
always (18) +2021+3972
life (17)
now (17) +2021+2021+2296
reign (17)
now (14) +2021
lived (12) +2118
times (10)
as long as (9) +3972
lifetime (9)
period (9)
live long (8) +799
years (8) +9102
year (7)
reigns (6)
as long as (5) +2021+3972
day after day (4) +2021+3972
first (4) +2021+3869
three-day (4) +8993
annual (3)
as long as lived (3) +3972
daily (3) +928+3427
day's (3)
ever since (3) +2021+2021+2296+6330
forever (3) +2021+3972
some time (3)
thoseˢ (3)
all day long (2) +928+2021+2021+2085
always (2) +3972
as long as lives (2) +3972
continual (2) +2021+3972
continually (2) +2021+3972
daily (2) +3427
date (2)
daytime (2)
during (2)
each day (2) +928+3427
each year (2) +2025+3427+4946
for each day (2) +928+1821+3427
live (2)
never (2) +2021+3972+4202
now (2) +465+928+2021+2021
outlived (2) +339+799
rest (2) +3972
some time later (2) +4946
still (2) +2021+2021+2296+6330
weeks (2) +8651
when (2) +928+2021
while (2) +928
whole (2)
after (1) +928
afternoon (1) +2021+5742

age (1)
age (1) +8044
ago (1) +2021
allotted time (1)
annual (1) +2025+3427+4946
as long as (1) +928
as long as endure (1) +3869
as long as live (1) +3972
as long as live (1) +3972+4200+6409
as long as live (1) +4946
as usually did (1) +928+3427+3869
at once (1) +928+2021
at once (1) +928+2021+2021+2085
at once (1) +2021
at this time (1) +2021
awhile (1) +2021+3869
based on the rate paid (1) +3869
birthday (1) +3528
broad daylight (1) +240
celebrating (1) +3202
daily (1) +285+4200
daily (1) +928+1821+3427
daily (1) +928+2257+3427
daily (1) +2021+4200
day (1) +919
day after day (1)
day by day (1) +928+1821+2257+3427
day by day (1) +928+1821+3427
daylight (1)
days as (1)
days of life (1)
distant future (1) +8041
during (1) +928
during that time (1)
each day (1) +2021+2021+3427+4200+4200
each day (1) +2021+4200
each day's (1) +928+2257+3427
each day's (1) +928+3427
each day's (1) +3427
eachˢ (1)
endures (1)
enjoy a long life (1) +799
enjoy long life (1) +799
enjoyed long life (1) +8428
ever (1) +2021+3972
ever (1) +3972
ever (1) +4946
ever since (1) +4946
every day (1)
every day (1) +928+3427
every day (1) +2021+4200
every day (1) +2256+3427+3972
fate (1)
first (1) +3869
for a while (1) +285
for life (1) +2021+3972
forever (1) +802+4200
from now on (1) +2021+3972
full (1)
full moon (1) +4057
full years (1) +9102
future (1) +344
future (1) +4737
how long must wait (1) +3869+4537
if (1) +928
immediately (1) +2021+3869
in lifetime (1) +3972
in little more than (1) +6584
in the course of time (1) +3427+4200+4946
in trouble (1) +7997
it's (1) +2021
itˢ (1)
just (1) +2021
just now (1) +2021
lasting (1) +2021+2021+2296+6330
later on (1) +4946
length of days (1) +9102
life (1) +889+2118
life span (1) +5031
lifetime (1) +2644
light (1)

lingering (1) +3427+6584
lived (1)
lives (1) +9102
long ago (1) +4946+7710
many years (1) +802
many years (1) +2256+9102
never (1) +4202+4946
night (1)
noon (1) +2021+4734
old (1) +2644+9102
old (1) +4946+7710
older (1) +2418+4200
older (1) +3888
one month (1) +3732
other days (1) +3427
over a year (1) +196+2296+2296+9102
past (1) +8037
recently (1) +2021
regular (1) +2021+3972
regularly (1) +928+3427+4200
Sabbath after Sabbath (1)
     +928+928+2021+2021+3427+8701+8701
season (1)
select a day (1) +3427+4200+4946
set time (1) +4595
seven-day (1) +8679
seven-day periods (1) +2021+8679
since (1) +4200+4946
so long (1) +802
span of life (1)
still (1) +2021+2021+2296+3869
sun (1)
take turns (1) +2143
that day (1) +3427
then[s] (1) +928+2021+2021+2085
this[s] (1)
today (1)
today (1) +2296
tomorrow (1) +4737
two[s] (1)
used to be (1) +6409
very old (1) +928+995+2021+2416
when (1)
when (1) +4946
when began (1) +928
whenever (1) +928
while (1) +3972
while continues (1) +3972
whole month (1) +2544
year (1) +2021+4200
yet (1) +2021
yet (1) +2021+2021+2085+6330
yet (1) +2021+2021+2156+6330
younger (1) +4200+7582
untranslated (65)

3428 יוֹם2 *yôm2*
Variant; not used

3429 יוֹמָם *yômām* (51)
day (23)
by day (19)
in the daytime (2)
by day (1) +928
constant (1)
day after day (1) +9458
during the day (1)
during the daytime (1)
every day (1)
in daytime (1)

3430 יָוָן *yāwān* (11)
Greece (6)
Javan (4)
Greeks (1)

3431 יָוֵן *yāwēn* (2)
mire (1)
miry (1)

3432 יוֹנָדָב *yônādāb* (7)
Jonadab (7)

3433 יוֹנָה1 *yônāh1* (32)
dove (14)

doves (8)
pigeons (8)
pigeon (2)

3434 יוֹנָה2 *yônāh2* (19)
Jonah (18)
Jonah's (1)

3435 יוֹנָה3 *yônāh3*
Variant; not used

3436 יְוָנִי *y'wāniy* (1)
Greeks (1) +1201

3437 יוֹנֵק *yônēq* (12)
infants (6)
infant (2)
infant's (1)
nursed (1)
nursing (1)
tender shoot (1)

3438 יוֹנֶקֶת *yôneqet* (6)
shoots (4)
new shoots (1)
young shoots (1)

3439 יוֹנַת אֵלֶם רְחֹקִים *yônat 'ēlem r'hōqiym*
Variant; not used

3440 יוֹנָתָן *yônātān* (42)
Jonathan (42)

3441 יוֹסֵף *yôsēp* (213)
Joseph (180)
Joseph's (19)
he[s] (5)
him[s] (4)
Joseph (2) +1201
his[s] (1)
they[s] (1) +1074
untranslated (1)

3442 יוֹסִפְיָה *yôsipyāh* (1)
Josiphiah (1)

3443 יוֹעֵאלָה *yô'ē'lāh* (1)
Joelah (1)

3444 יוֹעֵד *yô'ēd* (1)
Joed (1)

3445 יוֹעֶזֶר *yô'ezer* (1)
Joezer (1)

3446 יוֹעֵץ *yô'ēs* (21)
counselor (7)
advisers (6)
counselors (5)
adviser (1)
encouraged (1)
one to give counsel (1)

3447 יוֹעָשׁ *yô'āš* (2)
Joash (2)

3448 יוֹצֵאת *yôsē't* (1)
going into captivity (1)

3449 יוֹצָדָק *yôsādāq* (4)
Jozadak (4)

3450 יוֹצֵר *yôsēr* (20)
potter (11)
potter's (4)
him[s] (1) +2021
potters (1)
pottery (1)
pottery (1) +3998
pottery (1) +5574

3451 יוֹקִים *yôqiym* (1)
Jokim (1)

3452 יוֹרֶה1 *yôreh1* (2)
archers (1)
they[s] (1) +2021

3453 יוֹרֶה2 *yôreh2* (3)
autumn (2)

untranslated (1)

3454 יוֹרָה *yôrāh* (1)
Jorah (1)

3455 יוֹרַי *yôray* (1)
Jorai (1)

3456 יוֹרָם *yôrām* (20)
Joram (14)
Jehoram (4)
him[s] (1)
Jehoram's (1)

3457 יוּשַׁב חֶסֶד *yûšab hesed* (1)
Jushab-Hesed (1)

3458 יוֹשִׁבְיָה *yôšibyāh* (1)
Joshibiah (1)

3459 יוֹשָׁה *yôšāh* (1)
Joshah (1)

3460 יוֹשַׁוְיָה *yôšawyāh* (1)
Joshaviah (1)

3461 יוֹשָׁפָט *yôšāpāt* (2)
Joshaphat (2)

3462 יוֹתָם *yôtām* (24)
Jotham (22)
Jotham's (2)

3463 יוֹתֵר *yôtēr* (10)
advantage (1)
anything in addition (1)
benefits (1)
but (1) +2256
gain (1)
not only (1)
overwise (1) +2681
profit (1)
rest (1)
than (1) +4946

3464 יְזוּאֵל *y'zû'ēl* (1)
untranslated (1)

3465 יְזִיאֵל *y'ziy'ēl* (1)
Jeziel (1)

3466 יִזִּיָּה *yizziyyāh* (1)
Izziah (1)

3467 יָזִיז *yāziyz* (1)
Jaziz (1)

3468 יִזְלִיאָה *yizliy'āh* (1)
Izliah (1)

3469 יָזַן *yāzan* (1)
lusty (1)

3470 יְזַנְיָה *y'zanyāh* (1)
Jezaniah (1)

3471 יְזַנְיָהוּ *y'zanyāhû* (1)
Jaazaniah (1)

3472 יֶזַע *yeza'* (1)
perspire (1)

3473 יִזְרָח *yizrāh* (1)
Izrahite (1)

3474 יִזְרַחְיָה *yizrahyāh* (3)
Izrahiah (2)
Jezrahiah (1)

3475 יִזְרְעֵאל1 *yizr''ē'l1* (2)
Jezreel (2)

3476 יִזְרְעֵאל2 *yizr''ē'l2* (34)
Jezreel (34)

3477 יִזְרְעֵאלִי *yizr''ē'liy* (13)
Jezreelite (7)
of Jezreel (5)
untranslated (1)

3478 יְחֻבָּה *y'hubbāh* (1)
untranslated (1)

3479 יַחַד *yāhad* (3)
join (2)

give undivided (1)

3480 יַחַד *yahad* (46)
together (14)
all (8)
alike (3)
completely (2)
each other (2)
alone (1)
along with (1)
also (1)
both (1)
by no means (1) +4202
in force (1)
now (1)
regrouped (1) +665
side by side (1)
together in unity (1)
unite (1) +2118+4200+4222
with (1)
untranslated (5)

3481 יַחְדָּו *yahdāw* (96)
together (57)
all (7)
both (4)
alike (3)
as well (2)
fitted (2) +9447
together with (2)
alone (1)
altogether (1)
assemble (1) +5602
assemble (1) +7695
be reunited (1) +7695
came together (1) +7695
each other (1)
even (1)
joined forces (1) +665
people[s] (1)
two men (1) +278+408+2256
with (1)
with one accord (1)
untranslated (6)

3482 יַחְדּוֹ *yahdô* (1)
Jahdo (1)

3483 יַחְדִּי *yahdōy*
Variant; not used

3484 יַחְדִּיאֵל *yahdiy'ēl* (1)
Jahdiel (1)

3485 יֶחְדְּיָהוּ *yehd'yāhû* (2)
Jehdeiah (2)

3486 יְחוּאֵל *y'hû'ēl* (1)
untranslated (1)

3487 יַחֲזִיאֵל *yah"ziy'ēl* (6)
Jahaziel (6)

3488 יַחְזְיָה *yahz'yāh* (1)
Jahzeiah (1)

3489 יְחֶזְקֵאל *y'hezqē'l* (3)
Ezekiel (2)
Jehezkel (1)

3490 יְחִזְקִיָּה *y'hizqiyyāh* (3)
Hezekiah (3)

3491 יְחִזְקִיָּהוּ *y'hizqiyyāhû* (41)
Hezekiah (37)
Hezekiah's (2)
he[s] (1)
Jehizkiah (1)

3492 יַחְזֵרָה *yahzērāh* (1)
Jahzerah (1)

3493 יְחִיאֵל *y'hiy'ēl* (14)
Jehiel (14)

3494 יְחִיאֵלִי *y'hiy'ēliy* (2)
Jehieli (2)

3495 יָחִיד *yāhiyd* (12)
only son (5)

only child (3)
lonely (2)
precious life (2)

3496 יְחִיָּה *y'hiyyāh* (1)
Jehiah (1)

3497 יְחִיל *yāhiyl* (1)
wait (1)

3498 יָחַל *yāhal* (45)
put hope (14)
hope (7)
wait (7)
waited (6)
expect (1)
expectantly (1)
given hope (1)
hope unfulfilled (1)
linger (1)
looked (1)
looking (1)
wait for (1)
wait in hope (1)
untranslated (2)

3499 יַחְלְאֵל *yahl'ēl* (2)
Jahleel (2)

3500 יַחְלְאֵלִי *yahl'ēliy* (1)
Jahleelite (1)

3501 יָחַם *yāham* (6)
in heat (2)
breeding (1) +2021+7366
conceived (1)
mate (1)
mated (1)

3502 יַחְמוּר *yahmûr* (2)
roe deer (1)
roebucks (1)

3503 יַחְמַי *yahmay* (1)
Jahmai (1)

3504 יָחֵף *yāhēp* (5)
barefoot (4)
bare (1)

3505 יַחְצְאֵל *yahs'ēl* (2)
Jahzeel (1)
Jahziel (1)

3506 יַחְצְאֵלִי *yahs'ēliy* (1)
Jahzeelite (1)

3507 יַחֲצִיאֵל *yah"siy'ēl* (1)
Jahziel (1)

3508 יָחַר *yāhar* (1)
untranslated (1)

3509 יָחַשׂ *yāhaś* (20)
family (2)
listed (2)
listed in genealogy (2)
be listed in the genealogical record (1)
deal with genealogies (1)
enrolled in the genealogical records (1)
genealogical record listed (1)
kept a genealogical record (1)
listed in genealogical records (1)
names in the genealogical records (1)
registered (1)
registration by families (1)
was listed in the genealogies (1)
were entered in the genealogical records (1)
were recorded in the genealogies (1)
were registered (1)
were registered by genealogy (1)

3510 יַחַשׂ *yahaś* (1)
genealogical (1)

3511 יַחַת *yahat* (8)
Jahath (7)
Jehath (1)

3512 יָטַב *yātab* (115)

go well (14)
do good (10)
good (10)
pleased (7) +928+6524
reform (4)
make prosper (3)
well (3)
do what is right (2)
enjoy (2)
thoroughly (2)
treated well (2)
adorned (1)
appealed to (1) +928+6524
arranged (1)
best (1)
better (1)
brought success (1)
cheer up (1) +4213
commends (1)
correctly (1)
delighted (1)
do right (1)
do[s] (1)
doing good (1)
enjoying (1)
found favor (1)
give joy (1)
gives (1)
glad (1) +928+6524
glad (1) +4213
goes well (1)
good do (1) +3208
good done (1)
greater (1)
ground to powder (1) +3221
have a right (1)
have any right (1)
in good spirits (1) +4213
inclined (1)
kind (1)
make famous (1)
make more prosperous (1)
makes cheerful (1)
please (1)
pleased (1)
pleased with (1) +928+6524
pleases (1) +928+6524
prosper (1)
really change (1) +3512
satisfied (1) +928+6524
share (1)
show kindness (1)
skilled (1)
skilled (1) +2006
skillfully (1)
stately (1)
stately bearing (1)
surely make prosper (1) +3512
tends (1)
thorough (1)
to pieces (1)
treat well (1)
very (1)
well provided for (1)
wish (1) +928+6524

3513 יָטְבָה *yot'bāh* (1)
Jotbah (1)

3514 יָטְבָתָה *yot'bātāh* (3)
Jotbathah (3)

3515 יְטוּר *y'tûr* (3)
Jetur (3)

3516 יַיִן *yayin* (141)
wine (132)
grapevine (2) +1728
wineskins (2) +5532
banquet (1) +5492
banquet hall (1) +1074
old wine (1)
sober (1) +2021+3655+4946

wine offerings (1)

3517 יַךְ *yak*
Variant; not used

3518 יְכָנְיָה *yᵉkônyāh*
Variant; not used

3519 יָכַח *yākaḥ* (59)
rebuke (14)
punish (3)
rebuked (3)
rebukes (3)
chosen (2)
judge (2)
settle disputes (2)
accuse (1)
accuses (1)
arbitrate (1)
are vindicated (1)
argue (1)
argue case (1)
arguments (1)
be chastened (1)
complained (1)
convict (1)
correct (1)
correction (1)
corrects (1)
decide (1)
defend (1)
defender (1)
disciplines (1)
give decisions (1)
lodging a charge (1)
pleads (1)
present case (1)
prove (1)
proved wrong (1)
reason together (1)
rebuke frankly (1) +3519
reproves (1)
surely rebuke (1) +3519
useˢ (1)

3520 יָכִין1 *yākiyn1* (6)
Jakin (6)

3521 יָכִין2 *yākiyn2* (2)
Jakin (2)

3522 יָכִינִי *yākiyniy* (1)
Jakinite (1)

3523 יָכֹל *yākōl* (194)
cannot (45) +4202
could (38)
able (23)
can (22)
can't (7) +4202
overcome (5)
must (4)
overpower (3)
prevail (3)
succeed (3)
allowed (2)
bear (2)
can do (2)
overcame (2)
allowed to (1)
attain (1)
avail (1)
can (1) +3523
can certainly do (1) +3523
cannot bear (1) +4202
cannot stand (1) +4202
could do (1)
could risk (1)
dare (1)
dares (1)
endure (1)
ever able (1) +3523
failed (1) +4202
gained the victory (1)
have time (1) +4538

incapable (1) +4202
powerless (1) +4202
prevailed (1)
surely triumph (1) +3523
too heavy a burden to carry (1) +4202+5951
troubled (1) +4202+9200
unable (1) +4202
will (1)
won (1)
untranslated (4)

3524 יְכָלְיָה *yᵉkolyāh* (2)
Jecoliah (1)
untranslated (1)

3525 יְכָלְיָהוּ *yᵉkolyāhû* (1)
Jecoliah (1)

3526 יְכָנְיָה *yᵉkonyāh* (7)
Jehoiachin (6)
untranslated (1)

3527 יְכָנְיָהוּ *yᵉkonyāhû* (1)
Jehoiachin (1)

3528 יָלַד *yālad* (495)
father (147)
bore (49)
gave birth (46)
had (31)
born (24)
were born (20)
give birth (16)
borne (13)
in labor (12)
gives birth (8)
have (7)
midwives (7)
was born (7)
is born (5)
be born (4)
bear children (4)
has (4)
mother (4)
bear (3)
bears (3)
given birth (3)
having children (3)
baby (2)
been born (2)
birth (2)
borne children (2)
childless (2) +4202
descendants (2)
had a baby (2)
had a son (2)
had children (2)
have children (2)
in childbirth (2)
midwife (2)
was descended (2)
arrives (1)
be brought forth (1)
bear a child (1)
bearing children (1)
begotten (1)
birthday (1) +3427
bore a child (1)
bore young (1)
bring forth (1)
bring to delivery (1)
child was born (1)
childbirth (1)
children (1)
children born (1)
daughter (1)
descendant (1)
fathered (1)
fathers (1)
forefather (1)
gave life (1)
give delivery (1)
giving birth (1)
had sons (1)

has son (1)
have a child (1)
have a son (1)
help in childbirth (1)
indicated ancestry (1)
lay (1)
making bud (1)
menˢ (1)
native-born (1) +824+928+2021
near the time of delivery (1)
newborn (1)
placed at birth (1)
remained childless (1) +4202
son be born (1)
womenˢ (1)
yet unborn (1)
untranslated (10)

3529 יֶלֶד *yeled* (90)
child (21)
children (20)
young men (11)
boy (8)
boys (5)
baby (4)
boy's (3)
young (3)
sons (2)
youth (2)
babies (1)
baby's (1)
brood (1)
gives birth prematurely (1) +3655
little ones (1)
pagans (1) +5799
son (1)
young man (1)
youths (1)
untranslated (2)

3530 יַלְדָּה *yaldāh* (3)
girls (2)
girl (1)

3531 יַלְדוּת *yaldût* (3)
youth (2)
young (1)

3532 יָלָה *yālah* (1)
wasted away (1)

3533 יִלּוֹד *yillôd* (5)
born (4)
children born (1)

3534 יָלוֹן *yālôn* (1)
Jalon (1)

3535 יָלִיד *yāliyd* (13)
descendants (6)
born (3)
those born (3)
slave by birth (1) +1074

3536 יָלַל *yālal* (30)
wail (26)
turn to wailing (1)
wails (1)
weep (1)
untranslated (1)

3537 יְלֵל *yᵉlēl* (1)
howling (1)

3538 יְלָלָה *yᵉlālāh* (5)
wailing (3)
lamentation (1)
wail (1)

3539 יַלֶּפֶת *yallepet* (2)
running sores (2)

3540 יֶלֶק *yeleq* (9)
grasshoppers (3)
locusts (2)
young locusts (2)
swarm of locusts (1)

young locust (1)

3541 יַלְקוּט *yalqût* (1)
pouch (1)

3542 יָם *yām* (395)
sea (262)
west (37)
west (28) +2025
seas (21)
seashore (5)
seashore (5) +8557
western (5)
coast (4) +2572
it's (4) +2021
high seas (3) +4213
westward (3) +2025
coast (2)
river (2)
western (2) +2025
coast (1) +8557
distant shores (1) +362
extend westward (1) +2025
lake (1)
overboard (1) +448+2021
seafarers (1) +6296
seamen (1) +2480
seashore (1) +2572
shore (1) +8557
south (1)
waters (1)
untranslated (1)

3543 יְמוּאֵל *y'mû'ēl* (2)
Jemuel (2)

3544 יְמִימָה *y'miymāh* (1)
Jemimah (1)

3545 יָמִין1 *yāmiyn1* (140)
right (118)
south (12)
left-handed (2) +360+3338
south (2) +4946
hand (1)
southward (1) +448+2021
which way (1) +196+6584+6584+8520
untranslated (3)

3546 יָמִין2 *yāmiyn2* (6)
Jamin (6)

3547 יָמִינִי *yāmiyniy* (1)
Jaminite (1)

3548 יְמָינִי *y'māyniy* (2)
untranslated (2)

3549 יְמִינִי *y'miyniy* (4)
Benjamin (1)
Benjamin (1) +408+1201
Benjamite (1) +408
tribe of Benjamin (1) +408

3550 יִמְלָא *yimlā'* (2)
Imlah (2)

3551 יִמְלָה *yimlāh* (2)
Imlah (2)

3552 יַמְלֵךְ *yamlēk* (1)
Jamlech (1)

3553 יָמִם *yēmim* (1)
hot springs (1)

3554 יָמַן *yāman* (5)
turn to the right (2)
go to the right (1)
right-handed (1)
to the right (1)

3555 יִמְנָה *yimnāh* (5)
Imnah (4)
Imnite (1)

3556 יְמָנִי *y'māniy* (33)
right (24)
south (9)

3557 יִמְנָע *yimnā'* (1)
Imna (1)

3558 יָמַר *yāmar* (1)
changed (1)

3559 יִמְרָה *yimrāh* (1)
Imrah (1)

3560 יָמַשׁ *yāmaš* (1)
untranslated (1)

3561 יָנָה *yānāh* (19)
oppress (5)
oppressor (3)
mistreat (2)
oppressors (2)
take advantage of (2)
crush (1)
do wrong (1)
driving (1)
mistreated (1)
oppresses (1)

3562 יָנוֹחַ *yānôah* (3)
Janoah (3)

3563 יָנוֹחָה *yānôhāh*
Variant; not used

3564 יָנוּם *yānûm* (1)
untranslated (1)

3565 יָנִים *yāniym* (1)
Janim (1)

3566 יְנִיקָה *y'niyqāh* (1)
shoot (1)

3567 יָנַק *yānaq* (16)
nurse (7)
nursed (4)
drink (1)
feast on (1)
female (1)
nourished (1)
suck (1)

3568 יַנְשׁוּף *yanšûp* (3)
great owl (3)

3569 יָסַד1 *yāsad1* (41)
laid the foundations (5)
the foundation was laid (4)
established (3)
laid the foundation (3)
founded (2)
ordained (2)
set (2)
the foundation laid (2)
assigned (1)
assigned to positions (1)
begun (1)
doing this's (1) +2021+6894
foundations (1)
foundations be laid (1)
instructed (1)
laid foundations (1)
lay (1)
lay foundations (1)
lays the foundation (1)
made a place (1)
provide a foundation (1)
sets (1)
sure (1)
the foundation been laid (1)
the foundations were laid (1)
was founded (1)

3570 יָסַד2 *yāsad2* (2)
conspire (1)
gather (1)

3571 יְסֻד *y'sud*
Variant; not used

3572 יְסוֹד *y'sôd* (20)
base (9)
foundations (6)

foundation (2)
foot (1)
restoration (1)
stand firm (1)

3573 יְסוּדָה *y'sûdāh* (1)
foundation (1)

3574 יִסּוֹר *yissôr* (1)
correct (1)

3575 יָסַךְ *yāsak*
Variant; not used

3576 יִסְכָּה *yiskāh* (1)
Iscah (1)

3577 יִסְמַכְיָהוּ *yismakyāhû* (1)
Ismakiah (1)

3578 יָסַף *yāsap* (217)
again (26)
again (22) +6388
add (21)
severely (12)
more (9)
longer (8)
more (7) +6388
added (6)
longer (5) +6388
once more (5)
anymore (4) +6388
continued (4)
make even heavier (4)
anymore (3)
do again (3)
multiply (3)
adding (3)
adds (2)
all the more (2) +6388
enlarged (2)
far exceeded (2)
increased (2)
never (2) +4202
once again (2)
once again (2) +6388
once more (2) +6388
promote (2)
adds length (1)
another (1)
another (1) +6388
any longer (1)
any longer (1) +6388
back (1) +6388
be added (1)
bring (1)
bring more and more (1)
brings (1)
by far (1)
carried still further (1)
continued (1) +6388
destroy (1)
do again (1) +6388
else (1)
ever (1)
farther (1)
gains (1)
gave (1)
given even more (1)
        +2179+2179+2256+3869+3869
grow stronger (1) +601
had reaffirm (1)
heap (1)
heaping (1)
increase (1)
increase (1) +6584
join (1)
later (1)
make again (1) +6388
make increase (1)
making more (1)
more (1) +8041
more and more (1)
more and more (1) +3972+6584

more besides (1)
multiplies (1)
over (1)
persist (1)
prolong (1)
reach out[s] (1)
still another (1) +6388
still more (1)
stirring up more (1)
stop (1) +4202
stopped (1) +4202+6388
were added (1) +6388
untranslated (6)

3579 1יָסַר *yāsar1* (42)
discipline (10)
punish (5)
scourged (4)
disciplines (2)
instructs (2)
scourge (2)
take warning (2)
accept correction (1)
be corrected (1)
be warned (1)
been disciplined (1)
catch (1)
chastened severely (1) +3579
correct (1)
corrects (1)
disciplined (1)
instructed (1)
taught (1)
trained (1)
warning (1)

3580 2יָסַר *yāsar2*
Variant; not used

3581 יֹסֵר *yāsōr*
Variant; not used

3582 יָע *yā'* (9)
shovels (9)

3583 1יַעְבֵּץ *ya'bēs1* (1)
Jabez (1)

3584 2יַעְבֵּץ *ya'bēs2* (3)
Jabez (3)

3585 יָעַד *yā'ad* (28)
meet (8)
banded together (3)
assemble (2)
challenge (2)
gathered (2)
joined forces (2)
appointed (1)
met by agreement (1)
ordered (1)
placed (1)
selected (1)
selects (1)
set (1)
summon (1)
turned (1)

3586 יַעְדָּה *ya'dāh* (2)
Jadah (2)

3587 יֶעְדּוֹ *ye'dô* (1)
Iddo (1)

3588 יֶעְדִּי *ye'diy* (1)
untranslated (1)

3589 יָעָה *yā'āh* (1)
sweep away (1)

3590 יְעוּאֵל *y'û'ēl* (6)
Jeuel (2)
untranslated (4)

3591 יְעוּץ *y'ûs* (1)
Jeuz (1)

3592 יָעוּר *yā'ûr* (1)

untranslated (1)

3593 יְעוּשׁ *y'ûš* (9)
Jeush (9)

3594 יָעַז *yā'az* (1)
arrogant (1)

3595 יַעֲזִיאֵל *ya'³ziy'ēl* (1)
Jaaziel (1)

3596 יַעֲזִיָּהוּ *ya'³ziyyāhû* (2)
Jaaziah (2)

3597 יַעְזֵיר *ya'zēyr* (13)
Jazer (13)

3598 יָעַט *yā'at* (1)
arrayed (1)

3599 יְעִיאֵל *y'iy'ēl* (13)
Jeiel (13)

3600 יָעִיר *yā'iyr* (1)
Jair (1)

3601 יְעִישׁ *y'iyš* (3)
untranslated (3)

3602 יַעְכָּן *ya'kān* (1)
Jacan (1)

3603 יָעַל *yā'al* (23)
gain (3)
of value (2)
succeed (2)
worthless idols (2) +4202
advantage (1)
benefit (1)
benefit in the least (1) +3603
best (1)
did good (1)
do good (1)
have value (1)
profit (1)
unprofitable (1) +4202
useless (1) +4202
worthless (1) +1153
worthless (1) +1194
worthless (1) +4202

3604 1יָעֵל *yā'ēl1* (3)
wild goats (2)
goats (1)

3605 2יָעֵל *yā'ēl2* (6)
Jael (6)

3606 יַעֲלָא *ya'³lā'* (1)
Jaala (1)

3607 1יַעֲלָה *ya'³lāh1* (1)
deer (1)

3608 2יַעֲלָה *ya'³lāh2* (1)
Jaala (1)

3609 יַעְלָם *ya'lām* (4)
Jalam (4)

3610 1יַעַן *ya'an1* (99)
because (34)
because (21) +889
because (3) +3954
because of (3)
for (3) +889
since (3) +889
for (2)
because (1) +561+4202
because (1) +928
because (1) +928+2256+3610
because (1) +928+3610
but since (1)
in (1)
since (1)
since (1) +3954
so (1) +561+4202
so that (1) +889
therefore (1) +4027+4200
while (1)

why (1) +4537
untranslated (15)

3611 2יַעַן *ya'an2*
Variant; not used

3612 יָעֵן *yā'ēn* (1)
ostriches (1)

3613 יַעֲנָה *ya'³nāh* (8)
owls (4) +1426
horned owl (2) +1426
owl (2) +1426

3614 יַעֲנַי *ya'nay* (1)
Janai (1)

3615 1יָעֵף *yā'ēp1* (8)
faint (2)
tired (2)
exhaust (1)
fall (1)
labor (1)
tire (1)

3616 2יָעֵף *yā'ēp2* (1)
swift flight (1) +3618

3617 3יָעֵף *yā'ēp3* (3)
weary (2)
exhausted (1)

3618 יְעָף *y'āp* (1)
swift flight (1) +3616

3619 יָעַץ *yā'as* (59)
consulted (5)
advice gave (3) +6783
advise (3)
advised (3)
planned (3)
advice (2)
advice given (2) +6783
counsels (2)
determined (2)
planned (2) +6783
plot (2)
plotted (2)
purposed (2)
advice offered (1)
advise (1) +6783
agreed (1)
confer (1)
conferred (1)
conferring (1)
conspire (1)
consult (1)
consulted advisers (1)
consulting (1)
counsel (1)
counseled (1)
decided (1)
give advice (1)
give counsel (1)
giving advice (1) +6783
intend (1)
makes plans (1)
makes up (1)
planning (1) +6783
plotted (1) +6783
promote (1)
seeking advice (1)
take advice (1)
take counsel (1)
warn (1)

3620 יַעֲקֹב *ya'³qōb* (349)
Jacob (316)
Jacob's (17)
he[s] (7)
him[s] (5)
his[s] (2)
Jacob's (1) +4200
them[s] (1) +1201

3621 יַעֲקֹבָה *ya'³qōbāh* (1)
Jaakobah (1)

3622 יַעְקָן *ya'ᵃqān* (1)
Jaakanites (1) +1201

3623 יַעַר1 *ya'ar1* (57)
forest (38)
forests (7)
thickets (3)
woods (3)
finest of forests (2) +4149
thicket (2)
forested (1)
groves (1)

3624 יַעַר2 *ya'ar2* (1)
honeycomb (1)

3625 יַעַר3 *ya'ar3* (1)
Jaar (1)

3626 יַעְרָה1 *ya'ᵃrāh1* (1)
honeycomb (1) +1831

3627 יַעְרָה2 *ya'ᵃrāh2*
Variant; not used

3628 יַעְרָה *ya'rāh*
Variant; not used

3629 יַעְרֵי אֹרְגִים *ya'ᵃrēy 'ōrᵉgiym* (1)
Jaare-Oregim (1)

3630 יְעָרִים *yᵉ'āriym* (1)
Jearim (1)

3631 יַעֲרֶשְׁיָה *ya'ᵃrešyāh* (1)
Jaareshiah (1)

3632 יַעֲשׂוּ *ya'ᵃśû* (1)
Jaasu (1)

3633 יַעֲשַׂי *ya'ᵃśay* (1)
untranslated (1)

3634 יַעֲשִׂיאֵל *ya'ᵃśiy'ēl* (2)
Jaasiel (2)

3635 יִפְדְיָה *yipdᵉyāh* (1)
Iphdeiah (1)

3636 יָפָה *yāpāh* (8)
beautiful (3)
adorn (1)
adorn yourself (1)
delightful (1)
majestic (1)
most excellent (1)

3637 יָפֶה *yāpeh* (42)
beautiful (23)
beautiful (3) +5260
lovely (3)
beautiful (2) +9307
handsome (2) +5260
sleek (2) +5260
fair (1)
fine (1)
handsome (1)
handsome appearance (1)
proper (1)
sleek (1) +9307
well-built (1) +9307

3638 יְפֵה־פִיָה *yᵉpēh-piyyāh*
Variant; not used

3639 יָפוֹ *yāpô* (4)
Joppa (4)

3640 יָפַח *yāpah* (1)
gasping for breath (1)

3641 יָפֵחַ *yāpēah* (1)
breathing out (1)

3642 יְפִי *yᵉpiy* (19)
beauty (18)
beautiful (1)

3643 יָפִיעַ1 *yāpiya'1* (1)
Japhia (1)

3644 יָפִיעַ2 *yāpiya'2* (4)
Japhia (4)

3645 יְפִיפִיָה *yᵉpēypiyyāh* (1)
beautiful (1)

3646 יַפְלֵט *yaplēt* (3)
Japhlet (2)
Japhlet's (1)

3647 יַפְלֵטִי *yaplētiy* (1)
Japhletites (1)

3648 יְפֻנֶה *yᵉpunneh* (16)
Jephunneh (16)

3649 יָפַע *yāpa'* (8)
shine forth (2)
light (1)
makes flash (1)
shine (1)
shines forth (1)
shone forth (1)
smile (1)

3650 יִפְעָה *yip'āh* (2)
shining splendor (1)
splendor (1)

3651 יֶפֶת *yepet* (11)
Japheth (11)

3652 יִפְתָּח1 *yiptāh1* (1)
Iphtah (1)

3653 יִפְתָּח2 *yiptāh2* (29)
Jephthah (22)
himˢ (2)
heˢ (1)
hisˢ (1)
Jephthah's (1)
untranslated (2)

3654 יִפְתַּח־אֵל *yiptah-'ēl* (2)
Iphtah El (2)

3655 יָצָא *yāsā'* (1076)
brought out (100)
came out (84)
went out (82)
go out (57)
go (40)
come out (39)
left (38)
bring out (35)
leave (24)
come (21)
went (20)
serve (14)
marched out (12)
gone out (11)
out (11)
set out (10)
bring (8)
brought (8)
coming out (8)
came (7)
comes (7)
get out (7)
going out (7)
spread (7)
goes out (6)
take (6)
comes out (5)
extending (5)
took (5)
bring forth (4)
bringing out (4)
brings out (4)
coming (4)
escape (4)
go free (4)
gone (4)
leaving (4)
march out (4)
produces (4)
released (4)
removed (4)
returned (4)
spreading (4)
surrender (4)
took out (4)
came forward (3)
fell (3)
free (3)
going (3)
had brought (3)
lead out (3)
led out (3)
marching out (3)
projecting (3)
send out (3)
sent (3)
went on (3)
withdrew (3)
be brought out (2)
began (2)
break out (2)
bringing (2)
brings (2)
burst out (2)
come forth (2)
come up (2)
continued (2)
depart (2)
departed (2)
departure (2)
didˢ (2)
drive out (2)
experienced soldiers (2) +7372
exported (2)
flesh and blood (2) +2743+4946
flow out (2)
flows (2)
forth (2)
given (2)
goes (2)
going off duty (2)
gone from (2)
has (2)
imported (2) +2256+6590
is (2)
led (2)
led in campaigns (2) +995+2256+4200+7156
led on military campaigns (2) +995+2256
marches out (2)
move out (2)
produce (2)
promised (2) +4946+7023
ready for military service (2) +7372
ready to go out (2) +7372
remove (2)
said (2) +4946+7023
sank (2)
stepped forward (2)
take out (2)
taken (2)
taken out (2)
took from (2)
utter (2)
wherever goes (2) +928+928+995+2256
your own flesh and blood (2) +3870+4946
accompany (1) +907
advance (1)
advanced (1)
advancing (1)
announced (1)
appearing (1)
arise (1)
arisen (1)
arises (1)
avoid (1)
away (1)
become known (1)
been brought out (1)
born (1) +4946+8167
breaks out (1)
breathed her last (1) +5883

bring (1) +2256+4374
bringing forth (1)
budded (1) +7258
burst forth (1)
call out (1)
came out (1) +3655
carried away (1)
carried out (1)
carry (1)
carry out (1)
carry out duties (1) +995+2256
charges (1)
cleared (1)
collapse (1)
coming forth (1)
continue (1)
crawling out (1)
crossed (1)
dart (1)
departs (1)
descendants (1) +3751+5883
descended (1)
direct descendants (1) +3751
do[s] (1)
draw (1)
drawn (1)
drew out (1)
empties (1)
empty (1)
encamped (1) +4722
end (1)
escaped (1)
escapes (1)
ever goes outside (1) +3655
exacted (1)
extend (1)
extended (1)
falls (1)
fight (1) +2021+4200+4878
flash (1)
flashed (1)
flashed out (1)
flowed (1)
flowing (1)
flying (1)
follow (1)
follow (1) +339
followed (1)
followed (1) +339
followed (1) +6640
forges (1)
fought in (1) +928
fought in (1) +4200
found (1)
freed (1)
gives (1)
gives birth prematurely (1) +3529
gives vent to (1)
go about (1)
go about business (1) +995+2256
go into (1)
go off (1)
go off duty (1)
go off to war (1)
go up (1)
goes over (1)
grows out (1)
gushed out (1) +8041
had difficulty taking possession of (1) +4946
have leave (1)
headed (1)
imported (1)
issue (1)
joined (1)
lay (1)
lead (1) +995+2256
lead (1) +995+2256+4200+7156
leads forth (1)
leaves (1)
led out (1) +4200+7156
left (1) +3655

made come out (1)
make shine (1)
make spew out (1) +4946+7023
makes come up (1)
march on (1)
marched into (1)
met expenses (1)
of (1) +4946
of his own (1) +2257+3751
on duty (1) +995+2256
on the way (1)
on way (1)
out came (1)
out comes (1)
out goes (1)
paid (1)
passing (1)
pierced (1)
pour out (1)
pours (1)
prevails (1)
produce (1) +2446+9311
produced (1)
promote (1)
pursue (1) +339
put away (1)
put out (1) +2021+2575
reached (1)
release (1)
risen (1)
rises (1)
rising (1)
rode out (1)
rush (1)
rushed out (1)
say (1) +4946+7023
send away (1)
sent out (1)
serve (1) +995+2256
serve in (1)
set free (1)
sets free (1)
shines out (1)
slip out (1)
sober (1) +2021+3516+4946
sow (1)
speak (1)
spoke (1)
spreads (1)
spring (1)
spring up (1)
springs up (1)
starting (1)
stepped out (1)
stretch (1)
surely come out (1) +3655
surely march out (1) +3655
surrender (1) +3655
surrendered (1)
take back (1)
telling (1)
took part in (1) +4200
travel about (1) +995+2256
turned out (1)
undertook (1)
unsheathed (1) +4946+9509
uttered (1) +4946
venture out (1)
vindicated (1) +7407
was brought out (1)
went away (1)
went outside (1)
were (1)
whatever[s] (1) +2021
untranslated (18)

3656 יָצַב‎ *yāṣaḇ* (49)
stood (6)
stand (5)
confront (3)
stand up (3)

took stand (3)
present themselves (2)
present yourselves (2)
presented themselves (2)
serve (2)
stay (2)
take positions (2)
commits himself (1)
kept distance (1) +4946+5584
place (1)
present himself (1)
sided (1)
stand firm (1)
stand out (1)
stand still (1)
standing (1)
station myself (1)
take a stand (1)
take place (1)
take stand (1)
take up positions (1)
took places (1)
wait (1)
withstand (1) +6640

3657 יָצַג‎ *yāṣag* (17)
set (4)
made (2)
placed (2)
leave (1)
leave behind (1)
maintain (1)
make bare (1)
place (1)
presented (1)
separate (1) +963+4200
touch (1)
untranslated (1)

3658 יִצְהָר1‎ *yishār1* (23)
oil (20)
anointed (1) +1201+2021
olive oil (1)
olive trees (1) +2339

3659 יִצְהָר2‎ *yishār2* (9)
Izhar (9)

3660 יִצְהָרִי‎ *yishāriy* (4)
Izharites (4)

3661 יָצוּעַ1‎ *yāṣûaʻ1* (5)
bed (2)
bed (1) +6911
couch (1)
marriage bed (1)

3662 יָצוּעַ2‎ *yāṣûaʻ2* (3)
untranslated (3)

3663 יִצְחָק‎ *yiṣḥāq* (110)
Isaac (102)
Isaac's (3)
he[s] (2)
his[s] (1)
who[s] (1)
untranslated (1)

3664 יִצְחָר‎ *yiṣḥār* (1)
untranslated (1)

3665 יָצִיא‎ *yāṣiy'* (2)
sons (1) +5055
untranslated (1)

3666 יָצִיעַ‎ *yāṣiyaʻ* (3)
floor (1)
side rooms (1)
structure (1)

3667 יָצַע‎ *yāṣaʻ* (4)
are spread out (1)
lay (1)
lying (1)
make bed (1)

3668 יָצַק‎ *yāṣaq* (52)
pour (11)

cast (10)
poured (6)
poured out (4)
firm (2)
hard (2)
pouring (2)
were cast (2)
been anointed (1)
beset (1)
frozen (1)
hard (1) +2021+4200+4607
is smelted (1)
pour out (1)
ran (1)
serve (1)
served (1)
set down (1)
spread out (1)
washed away (1)
untranslated (1)

3669 יְצֻקָה *yᵉsuqāh* (1)
one piece with (1)

3670 יָצַר *yāsar* (43)
formed (15)
maker (4)
planned (4)
forms (3)
made (2)
preparing (2)
shapes (2)
brings on (1)
creator (1)
fashioned (1)
forged (1)
form (1)
make (1)
makes (1)
man (1)
ordained (1)
was formed (1)
untranslated (1)

3671 1 יֵצֶר *yēser1* (9)
inclination (2)
creation (1)
desire (1) +4742
disposed (1)
formed (1)
mind (1)
motive (1)
pot (1)

3672 2 יֵצֶר *yēser2* (3)
Jezer (3)

3673 יִצְרִי *yisriy* (2)
Izri (1)
Jezerite (1)

3674 יְצֻרִים *yᵉsuriym* (1)
frame (1)

3675 יָצַת *yāsat* (28)
set on fire (9) +836+928+2021
set fire (4) +836
kindle (3)
been burned (2)
are burned (1)
burn (1)
burns (1)
kindled (1)
set ablaze (1) +836+928+2021
set on fire (1)
set on fire (1) +836
sets ablaze (1)
untranslated (2)

3676 יֶקֶב *yeqeb* (16)
winepress (7)
vats (3)
winepresses (3)
presses (2)
wine vat (1)

3677 יְקַבְצְאֵל *yᵉqabsᵉ'ēl* (1)
Jekabzeel (1)

3678 יָקַד *yāqad* (8)
be kept burning (3)
burn (2)
burning (1)
burns (1)
kindled (1)

3679 יְקֹד *yᵉqōd* (2)
blazing (1)
fire (1)

3680 יָקְדְעָם *yoqdᵉ'ām* (1)
Jokdeam (1)

3681 יָקֶה *yāqeh* (1)
Jakeh (1)

3682 יִקְהָה *yᵉqāhāh* (2)
obedience (2)

3683 יָקוּד *yāqûd* (1)
hearth (1)

3684 יָקוֹט *yāqôt* (1)
fragile (1)

3685 יְקוּם *yᵉqûm* (3)
living thing (2)
living creature (1)

3686 יָקוֹשׁ *yāqôš*
Variant; not used

3687 יָקוּשׁ *yāqûš* (4)
fowler (1)
fowler's (1)
men who snare birds (1)
snares (1) +7062

3688 יְקוּתִיאֵל *yᵉqûtiy'ēl* (1)
Jekuthiel (1)

3689 יָקַח *yāqah* (1)
insolent (1)

3690 יָקְטָן *yoqtān* (6)
Joktan (6)

3691 יָקִים *yāqiym* (2)
Jakim (2)

3692 יַקִּיר *yaqqiyr* (1)
dear (1)

3693 יְקַמְיָה *yᵉqamyāh* (3)
Jekamiah (3)

3694 יְקַמְעָם *yᵉqam'ām* (2)
Jekameam (2)

3695 יָקְמְעָם *yāqm'ām* (2)
Jokmeam (2)

3696 יָקְנְעָם *yoqnᵉ'ām* (4)
Jokneam (4)

3697 יָקַע *yāqa'* (8)
killed and exposed (2)
turned away in disgust (2)
been killed and exposed (1)
kill and expose (1)
turn away (1)
wrenched (1)

3698 יְקַפָּאוֹן *yᵉqippā'ôn*
Variant; not used

3699 יָקַץ *yāqas* (11)
awoke (6)
woke up (3)
awakened (1)
wake up (1)

3700 יָקַר *yāqar* (11)
precious (4)
have respect for (2) +928+6524
costly (1)
make scarcer (1)
priced (1)
seldom (1)

well known (1) +4394

3701 יָקָר *yāqār* (35)
precious (18)
high-grade (2)
rare (2)
beauty (1)
fine (1)
good quality (1)
honored (1)
outweighs (1) +4946
priceless (1)
prizes (1)
quality (1)
splendor (1)
valuable things (1) +2104
very (1)
worthy (1)
untranslated (1)

3702 יְקָר *yᵉqār* (17)
honor (7)
riches (2)
honor (1) +6913
precious things (1)
price (1)
rare (1)
respect (1) +5989
splendor (1)
treasures (1)
valuables (1)

3703 יְקָרָה *yiqrāh*
Variant; not used

3704 יָקֹשׁ *yāqaš* (9)
are ensnared (1)
are trapped (1)
be ensnared (1)
be snared (1)
been trapped (1)
fowler's (1)
laid (1)
set a trap (1)
snared (1)

3705 יָקְשָׁן *yoqšān* (4)
Jokshan (4)

3706 יָקְתְאֵל *yoqtᵉ'ēl* (2)
Joktheel (2)

3707 1 יָרֵא *yārē'1* (332)
afraid (118)
fear (91)
awesome (24)
feared (12)
revere (11)
worship (10)
be feared (4)
dreadful (4)
revered (4)
terrified (4) +4394
awesome wonders (3)
fears (3)
intimidate (3)
stand in awe (3)
alarmed (2)
frightened (2)
have fear (2)
have reverence (2)
revering (2)
worshiped (2)
are feared (1)
awesome deeds (1)
awesome works (1)
believer (1)
despair (1)
dreaded (1)
dreadful (1) +4394
feared (1) +3711
fearfully (1)
fearing (1)
filled with fear (1) +4394
frighten (1)

held in awe (1)
is feared (1)
made afraid (1)
not daring (1)
overawed (1)
respect (1)
respects (1)
reverent (1)
shown reverence (1)
stood in awe (1) +4394
terrified (1) +1524+3711
terrified (1) +4394+4394
terrify (1)
terror (1)

3708 יָרֵא yārē'2
Variant; not used

3709 יָרֵא yārē'3
Variant; not used

3710 יָרֵא yārē'4 (52)
fear (32)
fears (7)
afraid (4)
feared (3)
worshiped (2)
God-fearing (1) +466+2021
revere (1)
worship (1)
worshiping (1)

3711 יִרְאָה yir'āh (45)
fear (34)
piety (3)
reverence (2)
awesome (1)
feared (1)
feared (1) +3707
fears (1)
revere (1)
terrified (1) +1524+3707

3712 יִרְאוֹן yir'ôn (1)
iron (1)

3713 יִרְאִייָה yir'iyyāyh (2)
Irijah (2)

3714 יָרֵב yārēb (2)
great (2)

3715 יְרֻבַּעַל yᵉrubba'al (14)
Jerub-Baal (11)
Jerub-Baal's (3)

3716 יָרָבְעָם yārāb''ām (104)
Jeroboam (94)
Jeroboam's (6)
heˢ (4)

3717 יְרֻבֶּשֶׁת yᵉrubbešet (1)
Jerub-Besheth (1)

3718 יָרַד yārad (384)
went down (63)
go down (61)
come down (28)
came down (24)
bring down (19)
down (13)
brought down (8)
gone down (8)
go (7)
take down (7)
coming down (6)
fall (6)
going down (5)
took down (4)
come (3)
comes down (3)
descend (3)
descended (3)
gone (3)
leave (3) +4946
let down (3)

lowered (3)
overflow (3)
be brought down (2)
continued down (2)
descending (2)
falling (2)
fell (2)
flowing (2)
goes down (2)
lead down (2)
pull down (2)
went (2)
abandon (1) +4946
abandoned (1)
are brought down (1)
attack (1)
attack (1) +928
been brought down (1)
been taken down (1)
bowed (1)
brings down (1)
brought (1)
came (1)
came down (1) +3718
came out (1)
carried down (1)
climbed down (1)
consign (1)
continued (1)
cut down (1)
descends (1)
do soˢ (1)
fail (1)
fall down (1)
fallen (1)
falls (1)
flattens (1)
flow (1)
flow from (1)
flowed down (1)
flowing down (1)
goes down (1) +4200+4752
gone down (1) +345
got off (1) +4946+6584
haul down (1)
leading down (1)
leave (1) +4946+9348
led down (1)
let flow (1)
let go down (1)
letting run down (1)
made flow down (1)
march down (1)
moved down (1)
overflowing (1)
poured (1)
prostrate (1)
pulls down (1)
puts (1)
ran down (1)
removed (1)
road down (1)
roam (1) +2143+2256
running down (1)
sank (1)
sank down (1)
send down (1)
sends (1)
sent down (1)
settled (1)
sink (1)
soˢ (1)
step down (1)
stepped down (1)
subdue (1)
subdued (1)
take (1)
take off (1) +4946+6584
taken (1)
toward evening (1) +4394
was taken down (1)

went aboard (1) +928
went out (1)
willˢ (1)
untranslated (5)

3719 יֶרֶד yered (7)
Jared (6)
Jered (1)

3720 יַרְדֵּן yardēn (183)
Jordan (172)
Jordan's (3)
river (2)
itsˢ (1) +2021
thereˢ (1) +2021
untranslated (4)

3721 יָרָה yārāh1 (27)
shoot (10)
shot (3)
cast (1)
fallen (1)
hurled (1)
laid (1)
motions (1)
overthrown (1)
set up (1)
shoot arrows (1)
shooting (1)
shot arrows (1)
shot with arrows (1) +3721
throws (1)
untranslated (1)

3722 יָרָה yārāh2 (3)
be refreshed (1)
showers (1)
water (1)

3723 יָרָה yārāh3 (45)
teach (25)
instruct (3)
teaches (3)
taught (2)
determine (1)
direct (1)
display (1)
get directions (1)
give guidance (1)
guide (1)
instructed (1)
instruction (1)
instructs (1)
showed (1)
taught (1) +2118
teach (1) +1978

3724 יָרָה yārah (1)
afraid (1)

3725 יְרוּאֵל yᵉrû'ēl (1)
Jeruel (1)

3726 יָרוֹחַ yārôah (1)
Jaroah (1)

3727 יָרוּם yārûm
Variant; not used

3728 יָרוֹק yārôq (1)
green thing (1)

3729 יְרוּשָׁא yᵉrûšā' (1)
Jerusha (1)

3730 יְרוּשָׁה yᵉrûšāh (1)
Jerusha (1)

3731 יְרוּשָׁלַם yᵉrûšālami (643)
Jerusalem (631)
thereˢ (6) +928
Jerusalem's (3)
the cityˢ (1)
untranslated (2)

3732 יֶרַח yerah1 (12)
month (5)
months (5)

moon (1)
one month (1) +3427

3733 יֶרַח 2 *yerah2* (2)
Jerah (2)

3734 יָרֵחַ *yārēah* (27)
moon (27)

3735 יְרִחוֹ *yᵉrihô* (57)
Jericho (56)
thereˢ (1)

3736 יְרֹחָם *yᵉrōhām* (10)
Jeroham (10)

3737 יְרַחְמְאֵל *yᵉrahmᵉ'ēl* (8)
Jerahmeel (8)

3738 יְרַחְמְאֵלִי *yᵉrahmᵉ'ēliy* (2)
Jerahmeel (1)
Jerahmeelites (1)

3739 יַרְחָע *yarhā'* (2)
Jarha (2)

3740 יָרַט *yārat* (2)
reckless (1)
thrown (1)

3741 יְרִיאֵל *yᵉriy'ēl* (1)
Jeriel (1)

3742 יָרִיב1 *yāriybl* (3)
contend (2)
accusers (1)

3743 יָרִיב2 *yāriyb2* (3)
Jarib (3)

3744 יְרִיבַי *yᵉriybay* (1)
Jeribai (1)

3745 יְרִיָּה *yᵉriyyāh* (1)
Jeriah (1)

3746 יְרִיָּהוּ *yᵉriyyāhû* (2)
Jeriah (2)

3747 יְרִיחה *yᵉriyhōh*
Variant; not used

3748 יְרִימוֹת *yᵉriymôt* (7)
Jerimoth (7)

3749 יְרִיעָה *yᵉriy'āh* (54)
curtains (18)
curtain (14)
otherˢ (4)
tent (3)
shelter (2)
dwellings (1)
shelters (1)
tent curtains (1)
untranslated (10)

3750 יְרִיעוֹת *yᵉriy'ôt* (1)
Jerioth (1)

3751 יָרֵךְ *yārēk* (34)
side (9)
thigh (9)
hip (5)
base (3)
breast (2)
attacked viciously (1) +5782+6584+8797
descendants (1) +3655+5883
direct descendants (1) +3655
leg (1)
legs (1)
of his own (1) +2257+3655

3752 יְרֵכָה *yᵉrēkāh* (30)
far end (6)
ends (4)
utmost heights (4)
far (3)
depths (2)
remote area (2)
below deck (1) +2021+6208
border (1)

end (1)
far back in (1) +928
rear (1)
thereˢ (1) +928+1074+2021
within (1) +928
untranslated (2)

3753 יָרָם *yāram*
Variant; not used

3754 יַרְמוּת *yarmût* (7)
Jarmuth (7)

3755 יְרָמוֹת *yᵉrāmôt*
Variant; not used

3756 יְרֵמוֹת *yᵉrēmôt* (7)
Jeremoth (5)
Jerimoth (2)

3757 יְרֵמַי *yᵉrēmay* (1)
Jeremai (1)

3758 יִרְמְיָה *yirmᵉyāh* (18)
Jeremiah (16)
heˢ (1) +2021+5566
Jeremiah's (1)

3759 יִרְמְיָהוּ *yirmᵉyāhû* (129)
Jeremiah (123)
heˢ (2)
himˢ (2)
himˢ (1) +2021+5566
Jeremiah's (1)

3760 יָרַע *yāra'* (1)
faint (1)

3761 יַרְפְּאֵל *yirpᵉ'ēl* (1)
Irpeel (1)

3762 יָרַק *yāraq* (3)
spit (1)
spit (1) +3762

3763 יָרָק *yārāq* (3)
vegetable (2)
vegetables (1)

3764 יֶרֶק *yereq* (8)
green (4)
tender shoots (2)
grass (1)
plants (1)

3765 יַרְקוֹן *yarqôn*
Variant; not used

3766 יֵרָקוֹן *yērāqôn* (6)
mildew (5)
deathly pale (1)

3767 יָרְקְעָם *yorqᵉ'ām* (1)
Jorkeam (1)

3768 יְרַקְרַק *yᵉraqraq* (3)
greenish (2)
shining (1)

3769 יָרַשׁ1 *yāraš1* (232)
possess (48)
take possession (31)
drive out (24)
driven out (11)
inherit (11)
drove out (9)
took possession (9)
take over (6)
took over (6)
dispossess (5)
taken over (5)
heir (4)
occupy (4)
taken possession (4)
dislodge (3)
destroy (2)
possessed (2)
take (2)
become poor (1)
belonged (1)

capturing (1)
certainly drive out (1) +3769
conquer (1)
conqueror (1)
destitute (1)
displaces (1)
dispossessing (1)
drive from (1)
drive out completely (1) +3769
drove (1)
drove out completely (1) +3769
fell heir (1)
gain possession (1)
gave as an inheritance (1)
give (1)
given (1)
gives (1)
grow poor (1)
heirs (1)
inheritance (1)
inherited (1)
inherits (1)
leave as an inheritance (1)
make inherit (1)
make vomit up (1)
new owners (1)
occupied (1)
own (1)
poor (1)
prosperous (1) +6807
push out (1)
rob (1)
seize (1)
seized property (1)
sends poverty (1)
share in the inheritance (1)
take away possessions (1)
thisˢ (1) +2257+4202
won (1)
untranslated (2)

3770 יָרַשׁ2 *yāraš2*
Variant; not used

3771 יְרֵשָׁה *yᵉrēšāh* (2)
conquered (2)

3772 יְרֻשָּׁה *yᵉruššāh* (14)
possession (7)
own (2)
heirs (1)
heritage (1)
inheritance (1)
part (1)
possess (1)

3773 יִשְׂחָק *yiśhāq* (2)
Isaac (2)

3774 יְשִׂימְאֵל *yᵉśiymi'ēl* (1)
Jesimiel (1)

3775 יָשָׂם *yāśam*
Variant; not used

3776 יִשְׂרָאֵל *yiśrā'ēl* (2506)
Israel (1712)
Israelites (483) +1201
Israelites (72)
Israelite (50) +1201
Israel's (35)
Israel (21) +1201
Israelite (16)
Israelites (14) +408
themˢ (12) +1201
theyˢ (9) +1201
Israel (7) +824
themˢ (7)
Israelite (6) +408+1074+4946
Israel (5) +1074
Israelite (5) +408
Israel's (3) +4200
Israelites' (3) +1201
Israelite (2) +408+1201+4946
Israelites (2) +1201+4946

their^s (2)

them^s (2) +3972+7736

her^s (1)

her^s (1) +141

Israel (1) +408

Israel (1) +6639

Israel's (1) +928

Israelite (1) +928

Israelite (1) +928+1201

Israelite (1) +1074

Israelite (1) +1201+4200

Israelite (1) +1201+4946

Israelite (1) +4946

Israelites (1) +1074

Israelites (1) +1201+6639

Israelites (1) +4946

the whole land^s (1)

their^s (1) +3276+6639

their^s (1) +6584

them^s (1) +3972

they^s (1) +3972

who^s (1) +1201

untranslated (18)

3777 יִשַׂרְאֵלָה *y'śar'ēlāh* (1)
Jesarelah (1)

3778 יִשְׂרְאֵלִי *yiśr'ēliy* (5)
Israelite (3)
him^s (1) +1201+2021
Israelite (1) +408+2021

3779 יִשָּׂשׂכָר *yiśśāśkār* (43)
Issachar (38)
Issachar (4) +1201
untranslated (1)

3780 יֵשׁ *yēš* (138)
there is (27)
have (12) +4200
is (11)
is there (8)
be (5)
are (4)
have (4)
will (4)
am (3)
has (3) +928
there are (3)
there was (3)
has (2)
have (2) +907
owned (2) +4200
sometimes (2) +889
are there (1)
continue (1)
do (1)
had (1)
had (1) +4200
have (1) +928
have (1) +3338+9393
have on hand (1) +3338+9393
it is (1)
lies (1)
owns (1) +4200
so^s (1)
there were (1)
there will be (1)
this is (1)
wealth (1)
were (1)
yes (1)
untranslated (25)

3781 יִשְׂאָל *yiś'āl*
Variant; not used

3782 יָשַׁב *yāšab* (1093)
live (141)
lived (91)
people (73)
live in (68)
sit (59)
settled (43)

stay (40)
living (39)
sitting (39)
living in (33)
stayed (32)
sat (31)
inhabitants (30)
sat down (22)
remained (18)
dwell (13)
inhabited (13)
lived in (12)
settle (12)
enthroned (11)
sits (11)
dwelling (10)
lives (10)
remain (9)
seated (9)
dwell in (8)
occupied (8)
reigned (8)
staying (8)
wait (6)
married (5)
settle down (5)
sit enthroned (5)
men (4)
sits enthroned (4)
be (3)
inhabitant (3)
left (3)
lived at (3)
sit down (3)
at rest (2)
be inhabited (2)
dwells (2)
dwelt (2)
everyone (2) +3972
king (2)
lies (2)
make dwell (2)
marrying (2)
occupy (2)
reign (2)
resettle (2)
resettled (2)
residents (2)
ruling (2)
seat (2)
seats (2)
situated (2)
stand (2)
stays (2)
took seat (2)
took up residence (2)
were (2)
avoid (1) +4946
brought to live (1)
citizens (1)
continually (1)
crouching (1)
deserted (1) +401
deserted (1) +401+4946
deserted (1) +1172+4946
deserted (1) +4202
did so^s (1)
dwellers (1)
dwellings (1)
endures (1)
enthrones (1) +2021+4058+4200
give (1)
go (1)
had live (1)
have a home (1)
held court (1)
hide in (1)
hold out (1)
intact (1)
kings (1)
lay in wait (1)

let live (1)
lie (1)
live securely (1)
living at (1)
lounging (1)
made dwell (1)
make live (1)
makes dwell (1)
meet (1)
meeting (1)
mounted like jewels (1) +4859+6584
occupants (1)
peopled (1)
reigns (1)
relieve yourself (1) +2575
remains (1)
rest (1)
rested (1)
restore (1)
rule (1)
sat up (1)
sat waiting (1)
securely (1)
set up (1)
sets (1)
settle in (1)
settle on (1)
settles (1)
sit as judge (1)
spent (1)
stay (1) +3782
stay in (1)
stay up (1)
stayed at home (1)
stayed night (1) +2256+4328
stopping (1)
succeeded (1)
successor (1)
supposed to dine (1) +430+3782
taken seat (1)
takes (1) +6584
takes seat (1)
throne (1)
thrones (1)
took place (1)
took places (1)
took seats (1)
was (1)
withdrew (1)
untranslated (27)

3783 יֹשֵׁב בַּשֶּׁבֶת *yōšēb baššebet* (1)
Josheb-Basshebeth (1)

3784 יֶשֶׁבְאָב *yešeb'āb* (1)
Jeshebeab (1)

3785 יִשְׁבּוֹ בְּנֹב *yišbô b'nōb* (1)
untranslated (1)

3786 יִשְׁבָּח *yišbāh* (1)
Ishbah (1)

3787 יִשְׁבִּי בְּנֹב *yišbiy b'nōb* (1)
Ishbi-Benob (1)

3788 יָשֻׁבִי לֶחֶם *yāšubiy lehem* (1)
Jashubi Lehem (1)

3789 יִשְׁבַּעַל *yišba'al*
Variant; not used

3790 יָשָׁבְעָם *yāšāb'ām* (3)
Jashobeam (3)

3791 יִשְׁבָּק *yišbāq* (2)
Ishbak (2)

3792 יָשְׁבְּקָשָׁה *yošb'qāšāh* (2)
Joshbekashah (2)

3793 יָשׁוּב1 *yāšûb1* (4)
Jashub (4)

3794 יָשׁוּב2 *yāšûb2*
Variant; not used

3795 יָשׁוּבִי *yāšûḇiy* (1)
Jashubite (1)

3796 יִשְׁוָה *yišwāh* (2)
Ishvah (2)

3797 יְשׁוֹחָיָה *yᵉšôḥāyāh* (1)
Jeshohaiah (1)

3798 1יִשְׁוִי *yišwiy1* (4)
Ishvi (4)

3799 2יִשְׁוִי *yišwiy2* (1)
Ishvite (1)

3800 1יֵשׁוּעַ *yēšûaʿ1* (28)
Jeshua (27)
Joshua (1)

3801 2יֵשׁוּעַ *yēšûaʿ2* (1)
Jeshua (1)

3802 יְשׁוּעָה *yᵉšûʿāh* (78)
salvation (47)
deliverance (9)
savior (6)
victories (5)
save (2)
victorious (2)
deliver (1)
deliverer (1)
rescue (1)
safety (1)
saves (1)
saving (1)
victory (1)

3803 יֶשַׁח *yešaḥ* (1)
empty (1)

3804 יָשַׁט *yāšaṭ* (3)
extend (1)
extended (1)
held out (1)

3805 יִשַׁי *yišay* (41)
Jesse (34)
Jesse's (5)
him^s (1)
untranslated (1)

3806 יָשִׁיב *yāšiyḇ* (1)
untranslated (1)

3807 יִשִּׁיָּה *yiššiyyāh* (6)
Isshiah (5)
Ishijah (1)

3808 יִשִּׁיָּהוּ *yiššiyyāhû* (1)
Isshiah (1)

3809 יְשִׁימָה *yᵉšiymāh* (1)
Variant; not used

3810 יְשִׁימוֹן *yᵉšiymôn* (13)
wasteland (7)
Jeshimon (4)
waste (1)
wastelands (1)

3811 יְשִׁימוֹת *yᵉšiymôṯ*
Variant; not used

3812 יַשִּׁימָוֶת *yaššiymāweṯ* (1)
untranslated (1)

3813 יָשִׁישׁ *yāšiyš* (4)
aged (2)
old (1)
old men (1)

3814 יְשִׁישַׁי *yᵉšiyšay* (1)
Jeshishai (1)

3815 יָשַׁם *yāšam*
Variant; not used

3816 יִשְׁמָא *yišmāʾ* (1)
Ishma (1)

3817 יִשְׁמָעֵאל *yišmāʿēʾl* (48)
Ishmael (47)
he^s (1)

3818 יִשְׁמְעֵאלִי *yišmᵉʿēʾliy* (8)
Ishmaelites (6)
Ishmaelite (2)

3819 יִשְׁמַעְיָה *yišmaʿyāh* (1)
Ishmaiah (1)

3820 יִשְׁמַעְיָהוּ *yišmaʿyāhû* (1)
Ishmaiah (1)

3821 יִשְׁמְרַי *yišmᵉray* (1)
Ishmerai (1)

3822 1יָשֵׁן *yāšēn1* (18)
sleep (8)
fell asleep (2)
sleep (2) +9104
sleeping (2)
asleep (1)
put to sleep (1)
sleeps (1)
smolders (1)

3823 2יָשֵׁן *yāšēn2* (3)
chronic (1)
last year's harvest (1) +3824
lived a long time (1)

3824 יָשָׁן *yāšān* (6)
old (3)
it^s (2)
last year's harvest (1) +3823

3825 3יָשֵׁן *yāšēn3* (7)
asleep (2)
sleep (2)
sleeping (2)
slept (1)

3826 4יָשֵׁן *yāšēn4* (1)
Jashen (1)

3827 יְשָׁנָה *yᵉšānāh* (3)
Jeshanah (3)

3828 יָשַׁע *yāšaʿ* (184)
save (86)
saved (22)
be saved (11)
saves (10)
rescue (8)
help (7)
deliver (5)
gave victory (4)
rescued (3)
worked salvation (3)
am saved (2)
avenging (2)
bring victory (2)
give victory (2)
are saved (1)
avenged (1)
be delivered (1)
brought about victory (1) +9591
came to rescue (1)
deliverance (1)
get help for (1)
having salvation (1)
help at all (1) +3828
is saved (1)
kept safe (1)
preserve (1)
salvation (1)
saving (1)
spare (1)
untranslated (1)

3829 יֶשַׁע *yešaʿ* (36)
salvation (15)
savior (6)
safety (2)
victory (2)
deliver (1)
protect (1) +928+8883
save (1)

saving (1)

3830 יֹשָׁע *yōšaʿ*
Variant; not used

3831 יִשְׁעִי *yišʿiy* (5)
Ishi (4)
who^s (1)

3832 יְשַׁעְיָה *yᵉšaʿyāh* (4)
Jeshaiah (4)

3833 יְשַׁעְיָהוּ *yᵉšaʿyāhû* (35)
Isaiah (30)
Jeshaiah (3)
untranslated (2)

3834 יִשְׁפָּה *yišpāh* (1)
Ishpah (1)

3835 יָשְׁפֵה *yāšpēh* (3)
jasper (3)

3836 יִשְׁפָּן *yišpān* (1)
Ishpan (1)

3837 יָשַׁר *yāšar* (27)
make straight (4)
right (3)
please (2) +928+6524
pleased (2) +928+6524
best (1)
channeled (1)
consider right (1)
fix directly (1)
go straight (1)
good (1)
hammered evenly (1)
keeps straight (1)
level (1)
liked (1) +928+6524
makes straight (1)
pleased with (1) +928+6524
upright (1)
went straight (1)
untranslated (2)

3838 1יָשָׁר *yāšār1* (117)
upright (48)
right (44)
fit (3)
just (2)
straight (2)
alliance (1)
conscientious (1) +4222
faultless (1)
in accord with (1) +4222
innocent (1)
level (1)
please (1) +928+2256+3202+6524
please (1) +928+6524
pleased (1) +928+6524
reliable (1)
right and true (1)
righteous (1)
safe (1)
stretched out (1)
truth (1)
upright (1) +2006
uprightness (1)
worthy (1)

3839 2יָשָׁר *yāšār2* (2)
Jashar (2)

3840 יֵשֶׁר *yēšer* (1)
Jesher (1)

3841 יֹשֶׁר *yōšer* (14)
upright (4)
honest (2)
straight (2)
uprightness (2)
integrity (1)
integrity (1) +4222
right (1)
unduly (1) +4946

3842 יִשְׁרָה *yišrāh* (1)
upright (1)

3843 יְשֻׁרוּן *y'šurûn* (4)
Jeshurun (4)

3844 יָשֵׁשׁ *yāšēš* (1)
aged (1)

3845 יָתֵד *yātēd* (25)
tent pegs (7)
peg (4)
pin (3)
tent peg (3)
stakes (2)
those^s (2)
firm place (1)
pegs (1)
something to dig with (1)
untranslated (1)

3846 יָתוֹם *yātôm* (42)
fatherless (36)
orphans (2)
fatherless child (1)
fatherless children (1)
orphan (1)
orphan's (1)

3847 יְתוּר *y'tûr*
Variant; not used

3848 יַתִּיר *yatiyr* (4)
Jattir (4)

3849 יִתְלָה *yitlāh* (1)
Ithlah (1)

3850 יִתְמָה *yitmāh* (1)
Ithmah (1)

3851 1יָתַן *yātan1*
Variant; not used

3852 2יָתַן *yātan2*
Variant; not used

3853 יַתְנִיאֵל *yatniy'ēl* (1)
Jathniel (1)

3854 יִתְנָן *yitnān* (1)
Ithnan (1)

3855 יָתַר *yātar* (105)
left (24)
rest (20)
remaining (7)
left over (6)
remain (5)
be left (3)
leave (3)
spare (3)
had left over (2)
remains (2)
some (2)
allow to remain (1)
are left (1)
be left alive (1)
been left alive (1)
escaped (1)
excel (1)
grant abundant (1)
had some left over (1)
have left over (1)
holding out (1)
it^s (1) +2021
keep (1)
kept (1)
leaving (1)
more (1)
most (1)
preserve (1)
remained (1)
sparing (1)
still (1)
stopped (1) +4202
survived (1)

surviving (1) +889+3856
survivors (1)
was detained (1)
was left (1)
untranslated (2)

3856 1יֶתֶר *yeter1* (95)
other (45)
rest (21)
left (5)
survivors (3)
excelling (2)
last (2)
remaining (2)
wealth (2)
arrogant (1)
even far (1) +4394
full (1)
leave (1)
little left (1) +7129+8636
others (1)
power (1)
remnant (1)
surviving (1)
surviving (1) +889+3855
untranslated (3)

3857 2יֶתֶר *yeter2* (7)
thongs (3)
bow (1)
cords of tent (1)
strings (1)
untranslated (1)

3858 3יֶתֶר *yeter3* (9)
Jether (8)
Jethro (1)

3859 יִתְרָא *yitrā'* (1)
Jether (1)

3860 יִתְרָה *yitrāh* (2)
wealth (2)

3861 יִתְרוֹ *yitrô* (9)
Jethro (8)
he^s (1)

3862 יִתְרוֹן *yitrôn* (10)
gain (3)
better (2)
advantage (1)
gained (1)
increase (1)
profit (1)
success (1)

3863 יִתְרִי *yitriy* (5)
Ithrite (4)
Ithrites (1)

3864 יִתְרָן *yitrān* (3)
Ithran (3)

3865 יִתְרְעָם *yitr''ām* (2)
Ithream (2)

3866 יֹתֶרֶת *yōteret* (11)
covering (11)

3867 יְתֵת *y'tēt* (2)
Jetheth (2)

3868 כ *k*
Variant; not used

3869 כְּ *k'-* (2914)
like (899)
as (425)
as (270) +889
when (112)
according to (86)
just as (58) +889
about (41)
when (38) +889
in (30)
in accordance with (30)
as soon as (24)

just as (24) +889+3972
what (21)
for (20)
what (18) +889
just as (17) +889+4027
just as (16)
same (16)
such (15)
after (14) +889
at (13)
after (12)
as (12) +889+4027
like (12) +889
to (12)
as if (11)
same as (11)
while (9)
as though (8)
by (8)
such as (8)
with (8)
whatever (7) +889
because (6)
like (6) +5126
similar (6)
as (5) +889+3972
because (5) +889
following (5)
whatever (5) +889+3972
alike (4)
first (4) +2021+3427
in keeping with (4)
unlike (4) +4202
whenever (4)
as common as (3)
how (3) +4537
if (3) +889
into (3)
like (3) +5260
so (3)
soon (3) +5071
such (3) +2296
whatever (3)
according to (2) +6584
agree (2) +285+2118
almost (2) +5071
as before (2) +928+7193+7193
as much as (2) +889
as soon as (2) +889
at once (2) +8092
because of (2)
but (2)
compared to (2)
conformed to (2) +6913
equal (2)
even as (2) +889
exactly as (2) +889+4027
follow (2) +6913
followed (2)
had (2)
how many (2) +4537+6330
how often (2) +4537
imitate (2) +6913
in the order of (2)
in way (2)
indeed (2)
just the way (2) +889
just what (2) +889+4027
now (2) +2021+6961
numbered (2) +285
out of (2)
so (2) +2296
way (2)
what (2) +889+4027
what deserve (2) +5126
whatever (2) +889+4027
whatever (2) +3972
according to (1) +889
according to (1) +7023
according to the rules (1)
accordingly (1) +7023

adhere to (1) +6913
after (1) +9005
against (1) +4202
age of childbearing (1) +784+851+2021
all (1)
all around (1) +1885+2021
all together (1) +285+408
among (1)
and (1)
appear (1) +928+2118+6524
appropriate (1)
as (1) +4027
as (1) +6961
as (1) +8611
as deserve (1)
as done before (1) +928+7193+7193
as easily as (1) +889
as far as (1)
as far as possible (1) +1896
as for (1)
as good as (1)
as in the case of (1)
as in times past (1) +3972
as is the case (1)
as long as (1) +889
as long as endure (1) +3427
as many (1)
as many as (1)
as measureless as (1)
as much as (1)
as much as (1) +7023
as soon as (1) +4027
as surely as (1)
as though (1) +889
as usual (1) +8997+9453
as usually (1)
as usually did (1) +928+3427+3427
as well as (1)
as well as (1) +2256
as with (1)
at (1) +6590
awhile (1) +2021+3427
based on the rate paid (1) +3427
because (1) +889+7023
because of (1) +889
both alike (1)
both and (1)
by the time (1)
callous (1) +2021+2693
closest friend (1) +889+3870+5883+8276
compare with (1)
compare with (1) +2118
contrary to (1) +928+4202
contrary to (1) +4202
customary (1) +928+7193+7193
deserves (1) +1896
desire (1)
equal to (1)
equally (1)
equally (1) +278+408+2257
equally (1) +285
equally among them (1) +278+408+2257
even (1)
even for (1)
exactly as (1) +889+3972
exactly like (1) +889+3972+4027
exactly like (1) +4027
fared like (1)
few (1) +5071
first (1) +3427
follow (1)
followed the example (1) +6913+6913
from (1)
fulfill (1) +4027+6913+7023
ghostlike (1) +200
given even more (1)
    +2179+2179+2256+3578+3869
heart and soul (1) +4222
here is what (1) +2256+2296+2296+3869
how (1)
how long (1) +4537

how long must wait (1) +3427+4537
how many (1) +4537
how many more (1) +4537
how quickly (1) +5071
if (1)
if only (1) +889
immediately (1) +2021+3427
in a moment (1) +5071
in accordance with (1) +889
in accordance with (1) +4027
in proportion to (1)
in proportion to (1) +889+5002
in proportion to (1) +7023
in the way (1)
in unison (1) +285
joined together (1) +285+6641
just as (1) +889+3972+4027
just as (1) +3972
just as (1) +4027
just like (1)
just like (1) +4027
just like (1) +7023
just what (1) +889
kind (1)
kind (1) +889
large enough (1)
like (1) +889+3972
like (1) +889+4027
like (1) +1952
like (1) +5477
like (1) +6524
like (1) +6886
might well have (1) +5071
mistake for (1) +8011
more (1)
more (1) +889
natural (1) +132+2021+3972
nearly (1) +401
no end (1) +1896
no sooner than (1)
no sooner than (1) +889
not(s) (1)
nothing but (1)
nothing more than (1)
now that (1) +889
obeyed (1) +7756
of (1)
of little value (1) +5071
once again (1) +2021+8037
one for each (1) +5031
only (1)
or (1)
outcome different (1) +4202
persisted in (1) +6913
prescribed (1) +5477
previously (1) +919+8997
quotas (1) +5477
remains (1)
same (1) +889
scarcely (1) +5071
share (1) +889+4200
similar (1) +2021+5260
so (1) +889
so (1) +6584
so many (1) +4537
so that (1) +7023
so with (1)
so with (1) +889
some (1)
some (1) +5071
soon (1) +5071+7775
sort (1)
spokesman (1) +7023
standing (1)
still (1) +2021+2021+2296+3427
such (1) +2297
suddenly (1) +8092
sufficient means (1) +1896
suitable (1) +5584
suitable for (1) +5584
than (1)

the same as (1)
then (1) +889
this is how (1) +465+1821+2021+2021
this is how (1) +889
thoroughly purge away (1)
    +1342+2021+7671
though (1)
through (1) +1821
together (1) +285
too (1)
treated as (1)
usual (1)
very things (1) +889+4027
what (1) +2256+2296+2296+3869
what (1) +2256+2296+2297+3869
what deserve (1)
what deserve for (1)
what deserves (1)
whatever (1) +889+3972+4027
whenever (1) +889
whether (1)
while (1) +889
without (1) +1172
yet (1)
untranslated (264)

3870 ךָ -kā (7096)
your (3454)
you (2610)
the(s) (85)
your own (65)
yourself (43)
your (28) +4200
yours (24) +4200
you (21) +5883
yours (19)
him (10)
a(s) (8)
your (8) +4200
he(s) (7) +466+3378
yourselves (7)
his (6)
your (5)
its (4)
my (4)
your own (4) +4200
yourself (4) +4222
yourself (4) +5883
him(s) (3) +466+3378
their(s) (3) +1201
toward (3) +995+2025
what are you doing (3) +4200+4537
an(s) (2)
he(s) (2) +3
he(s) (2) +278
him(s) (2) +1201
his(s) (2) +466+3378
their (2)
this(s) (2)
us (2) +2256+3276
you (2) +3338
your own flesh and blood (2) +3655+4946
your very own (2) +4200
yourself (2) +4213
yourselves (2) +4222
yourselves (2) +5883
all the way to (1) +995+6330
any(s) (1)
boast so much (1) +1540+7023
both of you (1) +2084+2256
closest friend (1) +889+3869+5883+8276
each other(s) (1)
he(s) (1) +6269
her (1)
her(s) (1) +563
here(s) (1) +6584
him(s) (1) +278
him(s) (1) +6269
his(s) (1) +8276
I(s) (1) +6269
Israelite(s) (1)

it[s] (1) +3338
its[s] (1)
keep away (1) +448+7928
lead on (1) +339
me (1)
me[s] (1) +563
me[s] (1) +6269
one[s] (1)
their[s] (1) +367
their[s] (1) +2446
them[s] (1) +3
them[s] (1) +1821
them[s] (1) +2446
them[s] (1) +4621
they[s] (1) +1821
to the vicinity of (1) +995+6330
toward (1) +995
very own brother (1) +278+562+1201
what right have you (1) +4200+4537
whose (1)
you (1) +561
you (1) +1414
you (1) +4213
you (1) +8120
you yourself (1) +7156
you[s] (1)
your (1) +907
your (1) +928
your own self (1)
untranslated (592)

3871 ךָ -*k* (1287)
your (615)
you (484)
the[s] (13)
your (10) +4200
you (4) +5883
you (3)
her (2)
their (2)
whose (2)
you (2) +7156
your own (2)
yours (2)
yourself (2)
yourselves (2)
her[s] (1) +3304
these[s] (1)
this city[s] (1)
what is the matter (1) +4200+4537
whom (1)
your (1) +4946
your (1) +6584
yours (1) +4200
yourself (1) +4213
yourself (1) +4222
untranslated (132)

3872 כְּאַב *kā'ab* (8)
in pain (2)
ache (1)
brought grief (1)
feels pain (1)
ruin (1)
sharp (1)
wounds (1)

3873 כְּאֵב *k'ēb* (6)
pain (3)
anguish (2)
suffering (1)

3874 כָּאָה *kā'āh* (3)
brokenhearted (1) +4222
disheartened (1) +4213
lose heart (1)

3875 כָּאֶה *kā'eh* (1)
untranslated (1)

3876 כַּאֲשֶׁר *ka'ášer*
Variant; not used

3877 1כָּבֵד *kābēd1* (115)
honor (19)

heavy (8)
honored (6)
hardened (4)
honors (4)
be honored (3)
gain glory (3)
honorable (3)
glorify (2)
glorious (2)
highly respected (2)
honoring (2)
made heavy (2)
multiply (2)
nobles (2)
put heavy (2)
renowned (2)
was held in honor (2)
abounding (1)
am glorified (1)
am honored (1)
be held in honor (1)
bring glory (1)
bring honor (1)
burden (1)
did[s] (1) +906+4213+4392
distinguished (1)
distinguished himself (1)
dull (1)
failing (1)
fierce (1)
gain glory for myself (1)
gained glory for yourself (1)
give glory (1)
glorified (1)
glory (1)
grew fierce (1)
grievous (1)
harden (1)
harder (1)
heavy (1) +3878
heavy (1) +4394
held in honor (1)
increased (1)
is honored (1)
laid heavy (1)
make dull (1)
makes wealthy (1)
outweigh (1) +4946
placed a heavy burden (1)
pretend to be somebody (1)
proud (1)
reward (1)
reward handsomely (1) +3877
reward handsomely (1) +3877+4394
stopped up (1) +4946+9048
unyielding (1)
was honored (1)
wealthy (1)
weighed down (1)
untranslated (1)

3878 2כָּבֵד *kābēd2* (40)
heavy (8)
great (4)
large (4)
severe (4)
difficult (2)
worst (2) +4394
bitterly (1) +4394
dense (1)
great numbers (1) +4394
heavier (1)
heavy (1) +3877
large (1) +4394
loaded (1)
severe (1) +4394
slow (1)
solemn (1)
strong (1)
terrible (1) +4394
thick (1)
tired (1)

unyielding (1)
untranslated (1)

3879 3כָּבֵד *kābēd3* (14)
liver (13)
heart (1)

3880 כֹּבֶד *kōbed* (4)
dense (1)
heat (1)
heavy (1)
piles (1)

3881 כְּבֵדֻת *k'bēdut* (1)
difficulty (1)

3882 כָּבָה *kābāh* (24)
quenched (7)
quench (4)
go out (3)
put out (2)
snuff out (2)
extinguished (1)
goes out (1)
gone out (1)
quench fire (1)
snuffed out (1)
unquenchable (1) +4202

3883 1כָּבוֹד *kābôd1* (200)
glory (120)
honor (33)
glorious (10)
splendor (6)
pomp (3)
wealth (3)
dignity (2)
honored (2)
me (2) +3276
riches (2)
soul (2)
vast (2)
abundance (1)
gloriously (1)
heart (1)
honor (1) +5989
honorable (1)
honored (1) +6913
honoring (1)
lie in state (1) +928+8886
men of rank (1)
respect (1)
rewarded (1)
splendid (1)
tongue (1)

3884 2כָּבוֹד *kābôd2* (2)
elegant (1)
glorious (1)

3885 כְּבוּדָּה *k'bûddāh* (1)
possessions (1)

3886 כָּבוּל *kābûl* (2)
Cabul (2)

3887 כַּבּוֹן *kabbôn* (1)
Cabbon (1)

3888 כַּבִּיר *kabbiyr* (10)
mighty (4)
blustering (1)
feeble (1) +4202
flooding downpour (1) +8851
fortune (1)
great (1)
older (1) +3427

3889 כָּבִיר *kābiyr* (2)
goats' hair (2) +6436

3890 כֶּבֶל *kebel* (2)
shackles (2)

3891 כָּבַס *kābas* (51)
wash (36)
washed (5)
washerman's (3)

be washed (2)
been washed (2)
launderer's (1)
wash away (1)
untranslated (1)

3892 כָּבַר *kābar* (2)
abundance (1)
multiplies (1)

3893 כְּבָר1 *k'bār1* (9)
already (5)
before (1)
long since (1)
now (1)
untranslated (1)

3894 כְּבָר2 *k'bār2* (8)
Kebar (8)

3895 כְּבָרָה1 *k'bārāh1* (1)
sieve (1)

3896 כְּבָרָה2 *k'bārāh2* (3)
little distance (1) +824
some distance (1) +824
some distance (1) +824+2021

3897 כֶּבֶשׂ *kebeś* (107)
male lambs (35)
lambs (25)
lamb (19)
male lamb (15)
sheep (3)
lamb (1) +928+2021+8445
sheep (1) +7366
untranslated (8)

3898 כִּבְשָׂה *kibśāh* (8)
ewe lamb (4)
ewe lambs (2)
lamb (1)
lambs (1)

3899 כָּבַשׁ *kābaš* (15)
is subdued (2)
been enslaved (1)
enslaved (1) +2256+4200+4200+6269+9148
forced (1)
is subject (1)
make men slaves (1) +6269
molest (1)
overcome (1)
subdue (1)
subdued (1)
subject (1)
tread underfoot (1)
was brought under control (1)
untranslated (1)

3900 כֶּבֶשׁ *kebeš* (1)
footstool (1)

3901 כִּבְשָׁן *kibšān* (4)
furnace (4)

3902 כַּד *kad* (18)
jar (12)
jars (3)
large jars (1)
pitcher (1)
untranslated (1)

3903 כַּדּוּר *kaddûr*
Variant; not used

3904 כְּרֵי *k'dēy*
Variant; not used

3905 כַּדְכֹּד *kadkōd* (2)
rubies (2)

3906 כְּדָרְלָעֹמֶר *k'dārlā'ōmer* (5)
Kedorlaomer (5)

3907 כֹּה *kōh* (577)
this is what (471)
this (16)
ever so (12)

here (4)
so (3)
if (2) +561
this is how (2)
abundantly (1) +889+6330+6330
in any direction (1) +2256+3907
like this (1)
meanwhile (1) +2256+3907+6330+6330
now (1)
over there (1)
same (1)
such (1)
that (1)
that (1) +928
that is what (1)
there (1)
this (1) +928
this way (1)
what (1)
what happened (1)
untranslated (49)

3908 כָּהָה1 *kāhāh1* (12)
faded (5)
weak (2)
faint (1)
falter (1)
grown dim (1)
totally blinded (1) +3908

3909 כָּהָה2 *kāhāh2* (1)
restrain (1)

3910 כֵּהֶה *kēheh* (4)
despair (1)
dull (1)
smoldering (1)
weak (1)

3911 כֵּהָה *kēhāh* (1)
heal (1)

3912 כָּהַן *kāhan* (23)
serve as priests (12)
priest (2)
priests (2)
serve as priest (2)
served as priests (2)
high priest (1)
served as priest (1)
serving as priests (1)

3913 כֹּהֵן *kōhēn* (750)
priest (390)
priests (300)
he[s] (16) +2021
priest's (5)
who[s] (4) +2021
them[s] (3) +2021
his own[s] (2) +2021
priestly (2)
they[s] (2) +2021
he himself[s] (1) +2021
he[s] (1) +2021+3381
idolatrous priests (1)
priesthood (1)
Priests (1)
royal advisers (1)
their[s] (1) +2021
untranslated (19)

3914 כְּהֻנָּה *k'hunnāh* (14)
priesthood (9)
priestly office (2)
priests (2)
priestly service (1)

3915 כּוּב *kûb*
Variant; not used

3916 כּוֹבַע *kôba'* (6)
helmets (4)
helmet (2)

3917 כָּוָה *kāwāh* (2)
be burned (1)

being scorched (1)

3918 כְּוִיָּה *k'wiyyāh* (2)
burn (2)

3919 כּוֹכָב *kôkāb* (37)
stars (33)
star (2)
stargazers (1) +928+2600
starry (1)

3920 כּוּל *kûl* (37)
contain (3)
endure (3)
held (3)
hold (3)
provide (3)
provided (3)
feed (2)
supplied (2)
supplied provisions (2)
sustain (2)
bear (1)
conducts (1)
given provisions (1)
hold in (1)
holding (1)
holding in (1)
holds (1)
provide supplies (1)
supply with food (1)
sustained (1)
sustains (1)

3921 כּוּמָז *kûmāz* (2)
necklaces (1)
ornaments (1)

3922 כּוּן1 *kûn1* (219)
established (23)
prepared (14)
establish (10)
prepare (10)
be established (9)
provided (9)
steadfast (6)
ready (5)
founded (4)
get ready (4)
made preparations (4)
formed (3)
is firmly established (3)
provide (3)
right (3)
set (3)
set in place (3)
been proved (2)
direct (2)
establishes (2)
firm (2)
is established (2)
loyal (2)
turn (2)
was carried out (2)
was established (2)
about to (1)
aim (1)
appear (1) +4604
appointed (1)
are prepared (1)
be restored (1)
be secure (1)
be set (1)
be trusted (1)
been firmly decided (1)
been made ready (1)
bent on (1)
brought about (1)
build (1)
built (1)
commit (1)
confirmed (1)
could (1)
definite information (1)

definitely (1) +448
determines (1)
devote (1)
devoted (1)
done^s (1)
encourage (1) +4213
endure (1)
erected (1)
establishing (1)
fashions (1)
find out (1)
finish (1)
form (1)
full (1)
gave a firm (1)
have ready (1)
is (1)
is made ready (1)
keep loyal (1)
lays up (1)
made plans (1)
made ready (1)
make (1)
make preparation (1)
make preparations (1)
make secure (1)
makes firm (1)
makes secure (1)
on the alert (1)
ordained (1)
piles (1)
prepare (1) +2118
preparing (1)
provides (1)
put in place (1)
refreshed (1)
secure (1)
set in order (1)
set on (1)
set up (1)
sets (1)
spread (1)
stand (1)
steadfastly (1)
stood (1)
stood (1) +5163+8079
store up (1)
stores (1)
string (1)
succeed (1)
supplied provisions (1)
supplies (1)
supply (1)
support (1)
sustain (1)
took (1)
was arranged (1)
was firmly established (1)
was reestablished (1)
were attached (1)
were formed (1)
were prepared (1)
untranslated (4)

3923 כּוּן2 *kûn2* (1)
Cun (1)

3924 כַּוָּן *kawwān* (2)
cakes (1)
cakes of bread (1)

3925 כּוֹנַנְיָהוּ *kônanyāhû* (3)
untranslated (3)

3926 1כּוֹס *kôs1* (31)
cup (26)
goblet (2) +7694
cups (1)
give a drink (1) +9197
lot (1) +4987

3927 2כּוֹס *kôs2* (3)
little owl (2)
owl (1)

3928 1כּוּר *kûr1*
Variant; not used

3929 2כּוּר *kûr2* (9)
furnace (9)

3930 כּוּר עָשָׁן *kôr 'āšān*
Variant; not used

3931 כּוֹרֶשׁ *kôreš* (15)
Cyrus (15)

3932 1כּוּשׁ *kûš1* (29)
Cush (26)
Cushite (3)

3933 2כּוּשׁ *kûš2* (1)
Cush (1)

3934 1כּוּשִׁי *kûšiy1* (25)
Cushite (14)
Cushites (7)
Cushites (1) +1201
Ethiopian (1)
Nubians (1)
untranslated (1)

3935 2כּוּשִׁי *kûšiy2* (2)
Cushi (2)

3936 כּוּשָׁן *kûšān* (1)
Cushan (1)

3937 כּוּשַׁן רִשְׁעָתַיִם *kûšan riš'ātayim* (4)
Cushan-Rishathaim (2)
him^s (1)
whom^s (1)

3938 כּוּשָׁרָה *kôšārāh* (1)
singing (1)

3939 כּוּת *kût* (1)
Cuthah (1)

3940 כּוּתָה *kûtāh* (1)
Cuthah (1)

3941 כָּזַב *kāzab* (16)
lie (3)
false (2)
lying (2)
prove false (2)
considered a liar (1)
deceive (1)
fail (1)
liar (1) +8120
liars (1)
mislead (1)
prove a liar (1)

3942 כָּזָב *kāzāb* (31)
lies (11)
lying (5)
lie (4)
false gods (3)
false (2)
deceptive (1)
liar (1) +408
lie (1) +1819
lied (1) +1819
lies (1) +1821
lying (1) +1819

3943 כֹּזֵבָא *kōzēbā'* (1)
Cozeba (1)

3944 כָּזְבִּי *kāzbiy* (2)
Cozbi (2)

3945 כְּזִיב *kᵉziyb* (1)
Kezib (1)

3946 1כֹּחַ *kōah1* (126)
strength (56)
power (31)
might (4)
powerful (4)
ability (2)
able (2) +6806
helpless (2) +4202+6806

powerless (2) +4202
wealth (2)
cannot (1) +401
crops (1)
firm (1)
great (1)
helpless (1) +4946
mighty (1)
mighty (1) +1475
power (1) +2432
powerless (1) +401
qualified (1)
resources (1)
shout (1)
strengthened (1)
very strong (1) +6793
vigorous (1)
weakness (1) +4202
weary (1) +3329
yield (1)
untranslated (3)

3947 2כֹּחַ *kōah2* (1)
monitor lizard (1)

3948 כָּחַד *kāhad* (32)
hide (8)
hidden (3)
conceal (2)
hiding (2)
annihilated (1)
are destroyed (1)
denied (1)
destroy (1)
got rid of (1)
hides (1)
keep (1)
keep back (1)
led to downfall (1)
lost (1)
perish (1)
perishing (1)
ruined (1)
was hidden (1)
were destroyed (1)
wipe out (1)
wiped (1)

3949 כָּחַל *kāhal* (1)
painted (1)

3950 כָּחַשׁ *kāhaš* (22)
cringe (3)
lied (3)
lying (2)
come cringing (1)
cower (1)
deceive (1)
deceiving (1)
disown (1)
disowns (1)
fail (1)
fails (1)
lie (1)
lies (1)
thin (1)
treachery (1)
unfaithful (1)
untrue (1)

3951 כַּחַשׁ *kahaš* (6)
lies (4)
deception (1)
gauntness (1)

3952 כֶּחָשׁ *kehāš* (1)
deceitful (1)

3953 1כִּי *kiy1* (1)
branding (1)

3954 2כִּי *kiy2* (4486)
for (1059)
that (564)
because (531)

when (221)
if (149)
but (108)
though (54)
since (46)
surely (43)
but (39) +561
how (39)
except (24) +561
and (20)
yet (19)
even (14)
so (14)
although (12)
only (12)
only (11) +561
if (10) +561
as (8)
now (8)
why (8)
because of (6)
by (6)
even though (6)
how much less (6) +677
unless (6) +561
because (5) +6584
indeed (5)
whenever (5)
yes (5)
after (4)
how much more (4) +677
however (4)
if not (4) +4295
then (4)
because (3) +3610
even if (3)
how much worse (3) +677
however (3) +561
if not (3)
instead (3)
just (3)
now that (3)
or (3)
therefore (3)
until (3) +6330
while (3)
after all (2)
as for (2)
because (2) +4027+6584
because (2) +6813
but (2) +700
but only (2)
but only (2) +561
certainly (2)
even (2) +1685
for (2) +4027+6584
how much more so (2) +677
in fact (2)
instead (2) +561
nevertheless (2)
no (2)
or (2) +2256
other than (2) +561
out of (2)
perhaps (2)
so that (2)
still (2)
suppose (2)
surely (2) +561
than (2) +561
though (2) +561
too (2)
what (2)
whether (2)
without (2) +561
all (1)
although (1) +561
although (1) +1685
as well (1)
at (1)
at all (1)

at least (1)
because (1) +4200+4537
because (1) +9393
because of (1) +4946+7156
because that will mean (1)
before (1) +401
but (1) +421
clearly (1) +8011
despite (1)
even (1) +561
even (1) +677+2256
even when (1)
ever (1)
for (1) +1237
for otherwise (1)
for surely (1)
greater (1)
how much better (1) +677
how much less (1) +677+4202
how much more (1) +677+2256
how well (1)
however (1) +700
if anything but (1)
if so (1) +6964
in doing this (1)
in order to (1)
indeed (1) +561
indeed (1) +677+2256
is that why (1)
it was the custom of (1)
just because (1)
moreover (1)
moreover (1) +1685
not (1) +561
not only (1)
now (1) +2296
on the contrary (1)
once (1)
or (1) +1685
other than (1)
rather (1)
rather (1) +561
rather (1) +4202
really (1)
really (1) +677
rightly (1)
since (1) +3610
since (1) +4027+6584
since (1) +9393
so (1) +4394
surely (1) +2180
surely (1) +6964
that if (1)
that really (1)
this (1)
till (1) +6330
truly (1)
unless (1) +561+4200+7156
unless (1) +561+4202
until (1) +561
very well then (1)
well (1)
what more (1) +4537
when (1) +4200+7023
whenever (1) +1896+4946
where (1)
with (1)
won't until (1) +561
yes (1) +4202
yet (1) +561
yet (1) +700
untranslated (1232)

3955 כִּי־אָם *kiy-'im*
Variant; not used

3956 כִּי עַל כֵּן *kiy 'al kēn*
Variant; not used

3957 כִּיד *kiyd* (1)
destruction (1)

3958 כִּידוֹר *kiydôd* (1)

sparks (1)

3959 כִּידוֹן *kiydôn* (9)
javelin (5)
lance (2)
spear (1)
spears (1)

3960 כִּידוֹר *kiydôr* (1)
attack (1)

3961 כִּידֹן *kiydōn* (1)
Kidon (1)

3962 כִּיּוּן *kiyyûn* (1)
pedestal (1)

3963 כִּיּוֹר *kiyyôr* (23)
basin (12)
basins (6)
firepot (1) +836
pan (1)
platform (1)
untranslated (2)

3964 כִּילַי *kiylay* (2)
scoundrel (1)
scoundrel's (1)

3965 כֵּילַפּוֹת *kēylappôt* (1)
hatchets (1)

3966 כִּימָה *kiymāh* (3)
Pleiades (3)

3967 כִּיס *kiys* (6)
bag (3)
bags (1)
purse (1)
untranslated (1)

3968 כִּיר *kiyr* (1)
cooking pot (1)

3969 כִּישׁוֹר *kiyšôr* (1)
distaff (1)

3970 כָּכָה *kākāh* (37)
so (5)
this (4)
this is how (4)
this is what (4)
in this way (3)
in the same way (2)
such a thing (2)
as (1)
because of (1) +6584
in this manner (1)
like this (1)
such (1)
such and such (1)
that (1)
thus (1)
true (1)
untranslated (4)

3971 כִּכָּר *kikkār* (68)
talents (38)
plain (10)
talent (9)
bread (2) +4312
loaf (2)
cover (1)
crust (1)
loaf (1) +4312
loaves (1)
region (1)
surrounding region (1)
whole region (1)

3972 כֹּל *kōl* (5417)
all (3246)
every (311)
whole (265)
everything (189)
any (155)
entire (82)
everyone (49)

throughout (47) +928
anyone (38)
anything (37)
no (31) +4202
whatever (30) +889
each (26)
just as (24) +889+3869
whoever (22)
always (18) +2021+3427
whatever (17)
a (16)
altogether (14)
none (14) +4202
throughout (14)
one (13)
rest (13)
everything (11) +1821+2021
nothing (11) +4202
total (11)
wherever (10) +889+928
wherever (10) +928
as long as (9) +3427
other^s (9)
those^s (9)
anything (7) +1821
anywhere (7)
everyone (7) +2021+5883
full (7)
everyone (6) +408
always (5) +928+6961
as (5) +889+3869
as long as (5) +2021+3427
completely (5)
everything (5) +1821
whatever (5) +889+3869
both (4)
day after day (4) +2021+3427
everything (4) +5126
in all (4)
much (4)
some (4) +4946
any (3) +285
as long as lived (3) +3427
at all (3)
everything (3) +4213
everywhere (3)
forever (3) +2021+3427
fully (3)
nothing (3) +401
throughout (3) +928+1473
throughout (3) +4200
whenever (3) +928
wherever (3) +448+889
all (2) +2162
always (2) +3427
an (3)
anyone (2) +408
anyone (2) +2021+5883
anyone (2) +5883
anything (2) +2021+3998
anything (2) +4399
anywhere (2) +928+5226
as long as (2) +6388
as long as lives (2) +3427
completely (2) +2021+4200
continual (2) +2021+3427
continually (2) +2021+3427
during (2)
even (2)
ever (2)
everyone (2) +1414
everyone (2) +2021+6639
everyone (2) +3782
everyone (2) +5883
everything (2) +3998
everywhere (2) +928
everywhere (2) +5226
great (2)
great (2) +8044
in full force (2)
it^s (2)

never (2) +2021+3427+4202
no (2) +4202+4946
nothing (2) +1821+4202
rest (2) +3427
something (2)
them^s (2) +2021+6639
them^s (2) +3776+7736
this^s (2)
together (2)
totaled (2)
various (2)
what^s (2)
whatever (2) +3869
wherever (2) +889+928+2021+5226
wholeheartedly (2) +928+4213
wholeheartedly (2) +928+4222
your^s (2)
abundant (1)
all kinds (1) +4946
all over (1)
all-night (1) +2021+4326
although (1) +889+928
always (1)
among (1) +4200
annually (1) +928+2256+9102+9102
any (1) +408
anyone (1) +132
anyone (1) +408+2021
anything (1) +889
anything (1) +1821+1821+2021+4946
anything (1) +1821+2021
anything (1) +1821+4946
anything (1) +3998
anywhere (1) +1473
anywhere in (1) +928+1473
around (1)
as (1)
as (1) +889+928
as (1) +6645+8611
as in times past (1) +3869
as long as (1)
as long as (1) +928+6961
as long as live (1) +3427
as long as live (1) +3427+4200+6409
at flood stage (1) +1536+4848+6584
at flood stage (1) +1536+6584
at random (1)
at wits' end (1) +1182+2683
body (1)
constantly (1) +928+6961
covered with (1)
crowd (1) +889+6641
depth (1)
detailed (1)
details (1)
dire (1)
eagerly (1) +928+8356
ever (1) +2021+3427
ever (1) +3427
everlasting (1) +6409
every day (1) +2256+3427+3427
every way (1)
everyone (1) +132
everyone (1) +132+2021
everyone (1) +408+2021
everyone else (1) +7736
everyone's (1)
everything (1) +465+1821+2021+2021
everything (1) +2021
everything (1) +2021+4856
everything (1) +5626
everything (1) +8214
everywhere (1) +928+5226
everywhere (1) +2021+5226
exactly as (1) +889+3869
exactly like (1) +889+3869+4027
farthest recesses (1) +9417
filled (1) +928+2118
four^s (1)
from now on (1) +2021+3427

full force (1)
gave the message (1)
         +465+1819+1821+2021+2021
had nothing (1) +2893
in accordance with (1) +889
in lifetime (1) +3427
just as (1) +889+3869+4027
just as (1) +889+4200
just as (1) +3869
like (1) +889+3869
long (1)
men^s (1)
more (1)
more and more (1) +3578+6584
natural (1) +132+2021+3869
no yet (1) +3270
none (1) +4202+4946
none (1) +4202+5883
nothing (1) +561+4946
nothing (1) +889+4202
nothing (1) +2021+4202
nothing but (1)
nothing whatever (1) +401+1821
numbered (1)
one^s (1) +1414
only (1)
open (1)
people^s (1) +889+928
prosperity (1) +8044
regular (1) +2021+3427
rest^s (1)
shrub (1) +8489
so far as (1) +4200
solid (1)
something (1) +3998
sound (1)
still (1) +6388
such (1)
such (1) +4946
that^s (1)
the storehouses^s (1) +889+928+2157
them^s (1) +3776
them^s (1) +6551
there is no (1) +401
there is nothing (1) +401
these things^s (1)
these^s (1)
they^s (1) +1251+4463+8901
they^s (1) +2021+6639
they^s (1) +3776
things (1) +3998
this is how (1) +465+928
throng (1)
through (1)
throughout (1) +4946
throughout (1) +6584+7156
total (1) +4200+5031
total (1) +7212
transfer of property (1) +1821+9455
utter (1)
vast (1)
we (1) +5646
whatever (1) +889+3869+4027
whatever (1) +889+928
whenever (1)
whenever (1) +889+928
whenever (1) +928+6961
whenever (1) +4200
wherever (1) +889+2021+5226+6584
wherever (1) +889+6584
wherever (1) +889+9004
wherever (1) +928+2021+5226
wherever (1) +2021+4946+5226
while (1) +3427
while continues (1) +3427
who^s (1)
whoever (1) +132+2021
whoever (1) +408+889
untranslated (310)

3973 כָּלָא 1 *kālā' 1* (17)
    were restrained (2)

am confined (1)
confined (1)
contain (1)
hold back (1)
imprisoned (1)
keeping (1)
kept (1)
penned up (1) +928+1074+2021
refuse (1)
seal (1)
stop (1)
stopped falling (1)
withheld (1)
withhold (1)
untranslated (1)

3974 כָּלָא 2 *kālā' 2* (1)
finish (1)

3975 כֶּלֶא *kele'* (10)
prison (4) +1074+2021
prison (2)
prison (2) +1074
dungeon (1) +1074
prisons (1) +1074

3976 כִּלְאָב *kil'āb* (1)
Kileab (1)

3977 כִּלְאַיִם *kil'ayim* (4)
two kinds (3)
different kinds (1)

3978 כֶּלֶב *keleb* (32)
dogs (19)
dog (10)
dog's (2)
male prostitute (1)

3979 כָּלֵב *kālēb* (35)
Caleb (29)
Caleb's (6)

3980 כָּלֵב אֶפְרָתָה *kālēb 'eprātāh* (1)
Caleb Ephrathah (1)

3981 כָּלִבּוּ *kālibbiw*
'Variant; not used

3982 כָּלִבִּי *kālibbiy* (2)
Calebite (1)
untranslated (1)

3983 כָּלָה 1 *kālāh1* (206)
finished (55)
destroyed (14)
destroy (11)
fail (9)
spend (8)
completed (6)
finish (6)
perish (6)
end (4)
put an end (4)
consume (3)
ended (3)
gone (3)
spent (3)
vanish (3)
cease (2)
come to an end (2)
complete (2)
completely (2)
consumed (2)
determined (2)
fails (2)
finishing (2)
fulfill (2)
used up (2)
very (2)
after (1)
after (1) +561
all (1)
bent on (1)
blind (1)
came to an end (1)

completely (1) +6330
completely destroyed (1) +6330
completion (1)
concludes (1)
crushed (1)
decided (1)
destroy completely (1)
destroys (1)
disappear (1)
done (1)
eliminate (1)
ending (1)
failed (1)
faints (1)
faints with longing (1)
finally (1)
full (1)
given full vent (1)
grow weary (1)
hanging (1)
intended (1)
longed (1)
made an end (1)
make an end (1)
meet (1)
overcome (1)
ravage (1)
settled (1)
stopped (1)
strip bare (1)
vanishes (1)
wastes away (1)
wear out (1)
were completed (1)
wipe (1)
wiped (1)
wiped out (1)
yearns (1)
untranslated (2)

3984 כָּלָה 2 *kālāh2*
Variant; not used

3985 כָּלֶה *kāleh*
Variant; not used

3986 כָּלָה 3 *kālāh3* (21)
end (6)
completely destroy (5) +6913
destroy completely (3) +6913
destruction (2)
bad (1)
completely (1)
destructive (1)
power to destroy (1)
totally (1)

3987 כַּלָּה *kallāh* (34)
bride (15)
daughter-in-law (14)
daughters-in-law (5)

3988 כְּלֻהִי *k'luhiy* (1)
Keluhi (1)

3989 כְּלוּא *k'lû'* (2)
prison (2) +1074+2021

3990 כְּלוּב 1 *k'lûb1* (3)
basket (2)
cages (1)

3991 כְּלוּב 2 *k'lûb2* (2)
Kelub (2)

3992 כְּלוּבָי *k'lûbāy* (1)
Caleb (1)

3993 כְּלוּהוּ *k'lûhû* (1)
untranslated (1)

3994 כְּלוּלֹת *k'lûlōt* (1)
bride (1)

3995 כֶּלַח 1 *kelah1* (2)
full vigor (1)
vigor (1)

3996 כֶּלַח 2 *kelah2* (2)
Calah (2)

3997 כָּל-חֹזֶה *kol-hōzeh* (2)
Col-Hozeh (2)

3998 כְּלִי *k'liy* (325)
articles (67)
furnishings (21)
armor-bearer (18) +5951
weapons (14)
utensils (13)
instruments (11)
jar (9)
pot (9)
article (8)
equipment (8)
accessories (7)
jars (7)
weapon (7)
things (6)
armor (5)
jewelry (5)
belongings (4)
goods (4)
objects (4)
supplies (4)
armed (3) +2520
object (3)
vessels (3)
anything (2)
anything (2) +2021+3972
armor-bearers (2) +5951
armory (2) +1074
bag (2)
bags (2)
everything (2) +3972
goblets (2) +5482
household articles (2)
jewels (2)
one[s] (2)
packed (2)
pottery (2)
treasures (2) +2775
another[s] (1)
anything (1) +3972
baggage (1)
basket (1)
boats (1)
cargo (1) +641+889+928+2021
clothing (1)
container (1)
dishes (1)
goblets (1)
instruments (1) +8877
it[s] (1)
jewel (1)
kinds (1)
material (1)
methods (1)
other[s] (1)
possessions (1)
pots (1)
pottery (1) +3450
sacks (1)
something (1) +3972
specific things (1) +5466
storage jar (1)
storage jars (1)
them[s] (1) +466+1074+2021
thing (1)
things (1) +3972
tool (1)
weapon (1) +4878
weapon (1) +4878+7372
weapon (1) +5424
weapons (1) +4878
yokes (1)
untranslated (23)

3999 כְּלִיא *k'liy'* (2)
untranslated (2)

4000 כִּלְיָה *kilyāh* (31)
kidneys (18)
heart (4)
mind (3)
inmost being (2)
hearts (1)
kernels (1)
minds (1)
spirit (1)

4001 כִּלָּיוֹן *killāyôn* (2)
destruction (1)
weary with longing (1)

4002 כִּלְיוֹן *kilyôn* (3)
Kilion (3)

4003 כָּלִיל *kāliyl* (15)
perfect (3)
whole (3)
completely (2)
entirely (2)
perfection (1)
solid (1)
totally (1)
whole burnt offering (1)
whole burnt offerings (1)

4004 כַּלְכֹּל *kalkōl* (2)
Calcol (2)

4005 כָּלַל *kālal* (2)
brought to perfection (2)

4006 כְּלָל *kʿlāl* (1)
Kelal (1)

4007 כָּלַם *kālam* (38)
ashamed (6)
disgraced (6)
humiliated (3)
blush (2)
disgrace (2)
mistreat (2)
be disgraced (1)
be put to shame (1)
been in disgrace (1)
blush with shame (1)
despairing (1)
disgraces (1)
embarrass (1)
fear disgrace (1)
humbled (1)
in disgrace (1)
lacked (1)
put to shame (1)
puts to shame (1)
rebuke (1)
reproached (1)
shameful treatment (1)
were shocked (1)

4008 כִּלְמַד *kilmad* (1)
Kilmad (1)

4009 כְּלִמָּה *kʿlimmāh* (30)
disgrace (12)
shame (9)
scorn (3)
dishonor (1)
dishonors (1)
humiliation (1)
mocking (1)
shamed (1)
taunts (1)

4010 כְּלִמּוּת *kʿlimmût* (1)
shame (1)

4011 כַּלְנֵה *kalnēh* (2)
Calneh (2)

4012 כַּלְנוֹ *kalnô* (1)
Calno (1)

4013 כֶּם *-kem* (2658)
you (1268)
your (940)

the^s (52)
your (48) +4200
yourselves (36)
your own (18)
yourselves (12) +5883
their (4)
yours (4) +4200
your own (3) +4200
yours (3)
them^s (2) +7700
you (2) +5883
yourselves (2) +7156
a^s (1)
an^s (1)
every^s (1)
him^s (1) +466+3378
see for yourselves (1) +6524+8011
the (1)
the people^s (1)
their (1) +4200
them (1)
them^s (1) +3
them^s (1) +1201
they (1)
they^s (1) +3
think (1) +4200+8492
us (1) +2256+3276
what do you mean (1) +4200+4537
you (1) +6795
you (1) +7156
you're (1)
your (1) +4946
your (1) +6584
yourselves (1) +4222
yourselves (1) +7418
untranslated (241)

4014 כָּמַהּ *kāmah* (1)
longs for (1)

4015 כַּמָּה *kammāh*
Variant; not used

4016 כִּמְהָם *kimhām* (3)
Kimham (3)

4017 כְּמוֹ *kʿmô* (141)
like (80)
as (25)
according to (2)
with (2)
all (1)
as though (1)
as well as (1)
but (1)
deepest night (1) +694+6547
equal (1)
equal to (1)
even so (1)
for (1)
in a moment (1) +8092
kind (1)
or (1)
same (1)
seem (1) +928+6524
such (1) +4027
such as (1)
thus (1)
what (1) +889
whether (1)
worse (1) +4202
worth (1)
untranslated (11)

4018 כְּמוֹהֶם *kimwhām* (1)
untranslated (1)

4019 כְּמוֹשׁ *kʿmôš* (9)
Chemosh (8)
untranslated (1)

4020 כְּמִישׁ *kʿmiyš*
Variant; not used

4021 כַּמֹּן *kammōn* (3)
cummin (3)

4022 כָּמַס *kāmas* (1)
kept in reserve (1)

4023 כָּמַר *kāmar* (4)
aroused (1)
deeply moved (1) +8171
filled with (1)
hot (1)

4024 כֹּמֶר *kōmer* (3)
idolatrous priests (1)
pagan (1)
pagan priests (1)

4025 כַּמְרִיר *kamriyr* (1)
blackness (1)

4026 כֵּן *kēn1* (20)
right (7)
honest (5)
afterward (1) +339
agreed (1)
aright (1)
correctly (1)
order (1)
truly (1)
unjustly (1) +4202
yes (1)

4027 כֵּן *kēn2* (752)
therefore (146) +4200
so (88)
therefore (52) +6584
that is why (34) +6584
this (32)
so (25) +6584
same (23)
that (20)
just as (17) +889+3869
afterward (14) +339
as (12) +889+3869
so (10) +4200
in the course of time (8) +339
such (7)
as (6)
because (5) +6584
but (5) +4200
this is why (5) +6584
after (4) +339
true (4)
what (4)
in this way (3)
it^s (3)
later (3) +339
some time later (3) +339
that is what (3)
then (3) +4200
this is what (3)
and (2)
because (2) +3954+6584
exactly (2)
exactly as (2) +889+3869
for (2) +3954+6584
for (2) +4200
in way (2)
just what (2) +889+3869
like (2)
like that (2)
like this (2)
more (2)
no (2) +4202
no wonder (2) +6584
so that (2) +6584
surely (2) +4200
that is how (2)
that is the way (2)
then (2) +339
this is how (2)
very well (2) +4200
what (2) +889+3869
whatever (2) +889+3869
accordingly (1)
alike (1)
also (1)

also sweet[s] (1)
and (1) +4200
and (1) +6584
and so (1) +6584
as (1) +3869
as soon as (1) +3869
as well (1)
because (1) +4200
because of (1) +6584
because of this (1) +4200
because of this (1) +6584
custom (1) +6913
customary (1) +1821
empty (1) +4202
enough (1)
exactly like (1) +889+3869+3972
exactly like (1) +3869
follow (1) +6913
follow lead (1) +6913
followed (1) +6913
follows (1) +339
for (1)
from then on (1) +339+4946
fulfill (1) +3869+6913+7023
fulfilled (1) +2118
further (1)
futile (1) +4202
greatly (1)
happening[s] (1)
how (1) +6584
however (1) +4200
in accordance with (1) +3869
in the course of time (1) +339+4946
in the same order (1)
in the same way (1)
it must be (1)
just as (1)
just as (1) +889+3869+3972
just as (1) +3869
just for that (1) +4200
just like (1) +3869
later (1) +339+4946
let it be (1) +2085
like (1) +889+3869
nevertheless (1) +4200
not (1)
nothing (1) +4202
particularly (1) +4200
similar (1)
since (1) +3954+6584
since (1) +6584
so much (1)
so then (1) +4200
still (1) +4200
such (1) +4017
that (1) +6584
that was how (1)
that's why (1) +6584
then (1)
then (1) +6584
therefore (1) +3610+4200
this reason (1)
this was the kind (1)
this was what (1)
this way (1)
thus (1)
too (1)
tried (1) +6913
unlike (1) +4202+6913
very things (1) +889+3869
very well (1)
whatever (1) +889+3869+3972
why (1) +561+4200+4537
yes (1)
yet (1)
yet (1) +4200
untranslated (85)

4028 3כֵן kēn3
Variant; not used

4029 4כֵן kēn4 (10)
stand (8)

basework (1) +5126
mast (1) +9568

4030 5כֵן kēn5 (6)
position (2)
instead of (1) +6584
place (1)
succeeded (1) +6584+6641
successor (1) +6584+6641

4031 6כֵן kēn6 (5)
gnats (4)
flies (1)

4032 ־כֵן -ken (19)
your (13)
you (5)
your own (1)

4033 כָּנָה kānāh (4)
bestow a title of honor (1)
flatter (1)
flattery (1)
take (1)

4034 כַּנֵּה kannēh (1)
Canneh (1)

4035 כַּנָּה kannāh (1)
root (1)

4036 כִּנּוֹר kinnôr (42)
harp (21)
harps (19)
lutes (1)
lyre (1)

4037 כָּנְיָהוּ konyāhû (3)
Jehoiachin (3)

4038 כִּנָּם kinnām (2)
gnats (2)

4039 כְּנָנִי kᵉnāniy (1)
Kenani (1)

4040 כְּנַנְיָה kᵉnanyāh (1)
Kenaniah (1)

4041 כְּנַנְיָהוּ kᵉnanyāhû (2)
Kenaniah (2)

4042 כָּנַנְיָהוּ kānanyāhû (3)
Conaniah (3)

4043 כָּנַס kānas (11)
gather (3)
gathers (2)
amassed (1)
assemble (1)
bring (1)
gather together (1)
storing up wealth (1)
wrap around (1)

4044 כָּנַע kāna' (36)
humbled himself (5)
subdued (5)
humbled themselves (4)
humbled yourself (3)
subdue (3)
humble himself (2)
subjected (2)
were subdued (2)
are humbled (1)
humble (1)
humble themselves (1)
humbled (1)
made subject to (1) +3338+9393
repented (1)
silence (1)
was subdued (1)
were subjugated (1)
untranslated (1)

4045 כִּנְעָה kin'āh (1)
belongings (1)

4046 1כְּנַעַן kᵉna'an1 (89)
Canaan (51)

Canaan (29) +824
Canaanite (5)
him[s] (1) +3296+4889
Phoenicia (1)
there[s] (1) +824+2025
untranslated (1)

4047 2כְּנַעַן kᵉna'an2 (4)
merchants (2)
merchant (1)
merchants (1) +6639

4048 כִּנְעָן kin'ān (1)
traders (1)

4049 כְּנַעֲנָה kᵉna'ᵃnāh (5)
Kenaanah (5)

4050 1כְּנַעֲנִי kᵉna'ᵃniy1 (71)
Canaanites (56)
Canaanite (13)
Canaan (1)
in Canaan (1)

4051 2כְּנַעֲנִי kᵉna'ᵃniy2 (2)
merchants (2)

4052 כָּנַף kānap (1)
hidden (1)

4053 כָּנָף kānāp (111)
wings (56)
wing (14)
corner (3)
corners (3)
corner of garment (2)
ends (2)
flying (2)
fold (2)
them[s] (2) +2157
bird (1) +7606
bird on the wing (1) +1251
birds (1) +1251
birds (1) +7606
clothes (1)
dishonor bed (1) +1655
dishonors bed (1) +1655
each[s] (1)
edges (1)
folds of garment (1)
hem (1)
hem of robe (1)
kind[s] (1)
kinds[s] (1)
other[s] (1)
piece (1)
quarters (1)
sweep away (1) +928+7674
those[s] (1)
total wingspan (1) +802
winged (1)
untranslated (4)

4054 כִּנְרוֹת kinrôt (3)
Kinnereth (3)

4055 כִּנֶּרֶת kinneret (4)
Kinnereth (4)

4056 כְּנָת kᵉnāt (2)
associates (1)
untranslated (1)

4057 כֶּסֶא kese' (3)
full moon (1)
full moon (1) +3427
moon full (1)

4058 כִּסֵּא kissē' (135)
throne (110)
thrones (8)
chair (4)
seat (3)
seat of honor (3)
those[s] (2)
authority (1)
enthrones (1) +2021+3782+4200

its (1) +2021
its^s (1) +2021+4200
untranslated (1)

4059 כָּסָה *kāsāh* (153)
covered (37)
cover (26)
covers (15)
covering (7)
decorating (4)
be covered (3)
cover (3) +4832
cover up (3)
hide (3)
put on (3)
wearing (3)
were covered (3)
around (2)
clothed (2)
conceal (2)
concealed (2)
conceals (2)
keeps (2)
overwhelms (2)
provides (2)
put over (2)
are covered (1)
bathing (1)
blindfolds (1) +7156
buried (1)
closed (1)
clothe (1)
cover themselves (1)
cover up (1) +2256+8740
covered herself (1)
covered up (1)
covers over (1)
decorate (1)
engulfed (1)
fills (1)
flood (1)
is shrouded (1)
keep (1)
overlooks (1)
overwhelm (1)
overwhelmed (1)
shield (1)
was covered (1)
wear (1)
untranslated (2)

4060 כֶּסֶה *kēseh*
Variant; not used

4061 כִּסֶּה *kisseh*
Variant; not used

4062 כָּסוּי *kāsûy* (2)
cover (1) +5989
covering (1)

4063 כְּסוּלוֹת *k'sûlōt* (1)
Kesulloth (1)

4064 כְּסוּת *k'sût* (9)
covering (2)
cloak (2)
clothing (1)
cover (1)
cover the offense (1) +6524
garment (1)
uncovered (1) +401
untranslated (1)

4065 כָּסַח *kāsah* (2)
cut (1)
is cut down (1)

4066 כְּסִיה *kēsyāh*
Variant; not used

4067 1כְּסִיל *k'siyl1* (70)
fool (36)
fools (21)
foolish (9)
fool's (4)

4068 2כְּסִיל *k'siyl2* (4)
Orion (3)
constellations (1)

4069 3כְּסִיל *k'siyl3* (1)
Kesil (1)

4070 כְּסִילוּת *k'siylût* (1)
folly (1)

4071 כָּסַל *kāsal* (1)
foolish (1)

4072 1כֶּסֶל *kesel1* (7)
loins (5)
back (1)
waist (1)

4073 2כֶּסֶל *kesel2* (6)
trust (3)
confidence (1)
stupidity (1)
trusts in (1)

4074 כִּסְלָה *kislāh* (2)
confidence (1)
folly (1)

4075 כִּסְלֵו *kislēw* (3)
Kislev (2)
untranslated (1)

4076 כְּסָלוֹן *k'sālôn* (1)
Kesalon (1)

4077 כִּסְלוֹן *kislôn* (1)
Kislon (1)

4078 כַּסְלֻחִים *kasluhiym* (2)
Casluhites (2)

4079 כִּסְלֹת תָּבוֹר *kislōt tābôr* (1)
Kisloth Tabor (1)

4080 כָּסַם *kāsam* (2)
keep hair trimmed (1) +4080

4081 כֻּסֶּמֶת *kussemet* (3)
spelt (3)

4082 כָּסַס *kāsas* (1)
determine amount needed (1)

4083 כָּסַף *kāsap* (6)
hungry (1)
long for (1)
longed (1) +4083
shameful (1) +4202
yearns (1)

4084 כֶּסֶף *kesep* (401)
silver (303)
money (61)
price (7)
bought (2) +5239
sell (2) +928+5989
shekels (2)
silver (2) +4084
value (2) +6886
bought (1) +928+2021+7864
buy (1) +928
it^s (1) +2021
must sell (1) +928+2021+4835+4835
pay (1) +5989
pay (1) +8740
pay (1) +9202
payment (1)
property (1)
value (1)
what paid (1)
untranslated (8)

4085 כָּסְפְּיָא *kāsipyā'* (2)
Casiphia (2)

4086 כֶּסֶת *keset* (2)
magic charms (2)

4087 כָּעַס *kā'as* (54)
provoked to anger (19)
provoke to anger (7)
provoking to anger (6)
provoked (4)
angered (3)
angry (2)
provoke (2)
provoked to anger (2) +4088
incensed (1)
kept provoking (1) +1685+4088
make angry (1)
provoke to anger (1) +4088
provoking (1)
thrown insults (1)
trouble (1)
vexed (1)
untranslated (1)

4088 כַּעַס *ka'as* (22)
grief (4)
sorrow (4)
provoked to anger (2) +4087
anger (1)
angered (1)
annoyance (1)
anxiety (1)
displeasure (1)
frustration (1)
ill-tempered (1)
kept provoking (1) +1685+4087
provocation (1)
provoke to anger (1) +4087
provoked to anger (1)
taunt (1)

4089 כַּעַשׂ *ka'aś* (4)
anger (1)
anguish (1)
grief (1)
resentment (1)

4090 כַּף *kap* (193)
hands (76)
hand (32)
dish (12)
dishes (12)
palm (6)
soles (6)
feet (5) +8079
foot (4) +8079
sole (4)
hands (3) +3338
socket (3)
grasp (2)
handful (2) +4850
hands together (2) +448+4090
palm of hand (2)
arms (1)
be taken captive (1) +928+2021+9530
clutches (1)
each^s (1) +2021
earnings (1) +7262
fingers (1)
from (1) +4946
fruit of labor (1) +3330
handles (1)
palms of hands (1)
paws (1)
pocket (1)
their^s (1) +928+2157
those^s (1) +8079
took a handful (1) +4848
untranslated (6)

4091 כֵּף *kēp* (2)
rocks (2)

4092 כָּפָה *kāpāh* (1)
soothes (1)

4093 כִּפָּה *kippāh* (4)
palm branch (2)
branches (1)
fronds (1)

4094 כְּפוֹר1 *k'pôr1* (8)
bowls (3)

each dish (2) +2256+4094
untranslated (2)

4095 כְּפוֹר2 *kᵉpôr2* (3)
frost (3)

4096 כָּפִיס *kāpiys* (1)
beams (1)

4097 כְּפִיר *kᵉpiyr* (30)
lion (7)
lions (7)
great lion (4)
young lions (4)
strong lion (3)
great lions (1)
heˢ (1)
young (1)
young lion (1)
young lion (1) +787

4098 כְּפִירָה *kᵉpiyrāh* (4)
Kephirah (4)

4099 כְּפִירִים *kᵉpiyriym* (2)
villages (2)

4100 כָּפַל *kāpal* (5)
folded double (2)
fold double (1)
strike twice (1)
untranslated (1)

4101 כֶּפֶל *kepel* (3)
bridle (1) +8270
double (1)
two sides (1)

4102 כָּפַן *kāpan* (1)
sent out (1)

4103 כָּפָן *kāpān* (2)
famine (1)
hunger (1)

4104 כָּפַף *kāpap* (5)
are bowed down (2)
bow down (1)
bowed down in distress (1)
bowing (1)

4105 כָּפַר1 *kāpar1* (101)
make atonement (58)
making atonement (6)
atonement made (5)
made atonement (4)
atone (3)
be atoned for (3)
forgave (2)
forgive (2)
makes atonement (2)
accept atonement (1)
appease (1)
atoned for (1)
atonement (1)
atonement be made (1)
atonement made (1) +4113
atonement was made (1)
be annulled (1)
be atoned (1)
is atoned for (1)
make amends (1)
pacify (1) +7156
pardon (1)
ward off with a ransom (1)
untranslated (2)

4106 כָּפַר2 *kāpar2* (1)
coat (1)

4107 כָּפָר *kāpār* (2)
villages (2)

4108 כֹּפֶר1 *kōper1* (1)
villages (1)

4109 כֹּפֶר2 *kōper2* (1)
pitch (1)

4110 כֹּפֶר3 *kōper3* (2)
henna (1)
henna blossoms (1)

4111 כֹּפֶר4 *kōper4* (13)
ransom (8)
bribe (2)
bribes (1)
compensation (1)
payment (1)

4112 כְּפַר הָעַמֹּנִי *kᵉpar hā'ammōniy* (1)
Kephar Ammoni (1)

4113 כִּפֻּרִים *kippuriym* (8)
atonement (6)
atonement made (1) +4105
atoning (1)

4114 כַּפֹּרֶת *kappōret* (27)
atonement cover (15)
cover (10)
atonement (1)
it (1) +2021

4115 כָּפַשׁ *kāpaš* (1)
trampled (1)

4116 כַּפְתּוֹר1 *kaptôr1* (3)
Caphtor (3)

4117 כַּפְתּוֹר2 *kaptôr2* (18)
buds (8)
bud (6)
columns (1)
tops of the pillars (1)
untranslated (2)

4118 כַּפְתֹּרִי *kaptōriy* (3)
Caphtorites (3)

4119 כַּר1 *kar1* (12)
lambs (8)
battering rams (3)
choice lambs (1) +4946+7366

4120 כַּר2 *kar2* (3)
meadows (2)
fields (1)

4121 כַּר3 *kar3* (1)
saddle (1)

4122 כַּר *kār*
Variant; not used

4123 כֹּר *kōr* (7)
cors (6)
cor (1)

4124 כִּרְבֵּל *kirbēl* (1)
was clothed (1)

4125 כָּרָה1 *kārāh1* (15)
dug (5)
digs (3)
pierced (2)
cut out (1)
dig (1)
is dug (1)
plots (1)
sank (1)

4126 כָּרָה2 *kārāh2* (4)
barter (1)
barter away (1)
bought (1)
untranslated (1)

4127 כָּרָה3 *kārāh3* (1)
prepared a feast (1) +4130

4128 כָּרָה4 *kārāh4*
Variant; not used

4129 כָּרָה5 *kārāh5*
Variant; not used

4130 כֵּרָה *kērāh* (1)
prepared a feast (1) +4127

4131 כְּרוּב1 *kᵉrûb1* (91)

cherubim (66)
cherub (15)
themˢ (2) +2021
oneˢ (1) +2021
theirˢ (1) +2021
untranslated (6)

4132 כְּרוּב2 *kᵉrûb2* (2)
Kerub (2)

4133 כָּרִי *kāriy* (3)
Carites (2)
untranslated (1)

4134 כְּרִית *kᵉriyt* (2)
Kerith (2)

4135 כְּרִיתוּת *kᵉriytût* (4)
divorce (4)

4136 כַּרְכֹּב *karkōb* (2)
ledge (2)

4137 כַּרְכֹּם *karkōm* (1)
saffron (1)

4138 כַּרְכְּמִישׁ *karkᵉmiyš* (3)
Carchemish (3)

4139 כַּרְכַּס *karkas* (1)
Carcas (1)

4140 כִּרְכָּרָה *kirkārāh* (1)
camels (1)

4141 כֶּרֶם *kāram*
Variant; not used

4142 כֶּרֶם1 *kerem1* (93)
vineyards (49)
vineyard (41)
grapes (1)
vintage (1)
untranslated (1)

4143 כֶּרֶם2 *kerem2*
Variant; not used

4144 כֹּרֵם *kōrēm* (5)
work vineyards (2)
vine growers (1)
vineyards (1)
working fields and vineyards (1)

4145 כַּרְמִי1 *karmiy1* (8)
Carmi (8)

4146 כַּרְמִי2 *karmiy2* (1)
Carmite (1)

4147 כַּרְמִיל *karmiyl* (3)
crimson (3)

4148 כְּרָמִים *kᵉrāmiym*
Variant; not used

4149 כַּרְמֶל1 *karmel1* (15)
fertile field (5)
finest of forests (2) +3623
orchards (2)
fertile (1)
fertile fields (1)
fertile lands (1)
fertile pasturelands (1)
fruitful land (1)
untranslated (1)

4150 כַּרְמֶל2 *karmel2* (7)
Carmel (7)

4151 כַּרְמֶל3 *karmel3* (15)
Carmel (15)

4152 כַּרְמֶל4 *karmel4* (3)
new grain (2)
heads of new grain (1)

4153 כַּרְמְלִי *karmᵉliy* (7)
of Carmel (5)
Carmelite (2)

4154 כְּרָן *kᵉrān* (2)
Keran (2)

4155 כִּרְסֵם kirsēm (1)
ravage (1)

4156 כָּרַע kāraʻ (36)
sank (3)
bow (2)
bow down (2)
fell (2)
kneel down (2)
knelt down (2)
made bow (2)
bend down (1)
bowed down (1)
bows down (1)
bring down (1)
brought to knees (1)
cringe (1)
crouch (1)
crouch down (1)
crouches (1)
cutting down (1)
down (1)
faltering (1)
got down (1)
kneel (1)
kneeling (1) +1386+6584
knelt (1)
made miserable (1) +4156
sleep with (1) +6584
slumped down (1)
went into labor (1)

4157 כֶּרַע keraʻ (9)
legs (8)
leg bones (1)

4158 כַּרְפַּס karpas (1)
hangings of linen (1)

4159 כָּרַר kārar (2)
danced (1)
dancing (1)

4160 כָּרֵשׂ kārēś (1)
stomach (1)

4161 כַּרְשְׁנָא karš°nā' (1)
Carshena (1)

4162 כָּרַת kārat (289)
cut off (56)
made (45)
be cut off (37)
make (27)
cut down (20)
destroy (14)
cut (8)
fail to have (8) +4200
kill (6)
be destroyed (4)
destroyed (4)
making (4)
be cut down (3)
made a covenant (3)
be ruined (2)
covenanted (2)
put an end (2)
renewed (2)
was cut off (2)
are cut off (1)
banish (1)
be broken (1)
be consumed (1)
be cut out (1)
be rid of (1)
be struck down (1)
be taken (1)
be without (1) +4946
been broken off (1)
been cut off (1)
been snatched (1)
cease (1)
chop down (1)
conquered (1)
cut up (1)

cutting (1)
cutting (1) +9163
cutting off (1)
destruction (1)
disappear (1)
entered (1)
fell (1)
felling (1)
form (1)
is cut down (1)
killing (1)
killing off (1)
leave no (1)
made a pact (1)
make a treaty (1)
makes (1)
makes a covenant (1)
must surely be cut off (1) +4162
take away (1)
vanished (1)
were cut off (1)
wipe out (1)
untranslated (1)

4163 כְּרֹת k°rōt
Variant; not used

4164 כְּרֻתוֹת k°rutôt (3)
trimmed beams (3)

4165 כְּרֵתִי k°rētiy (11)
Kerethites (10)
Kerethite (1)

4166 כֶּשֶׂב keśeb (13)
lamb (5)
sheep (4)
lamb (1) +928+2021+8445
lambs (1)
sheep (1) +8445
young of the flock (1)

4167 כִּשְׂבָּה kiśbāh (1)
lamb (1)

4168 כֶּשֶׂד keśed (1)
Kesed (1)

4169 כַּשְׂדִּים kaśdiym (82)
Babylonians (49)
Babylonian (12)
Chaldeans (8)
Babylonia (5)
astrologers (2)
Chaldea (2)
Babylon (1) +824
Babylonians' (1)
untranslated (2)

4170 כָּשָׂה kāśāh (1)
sleek (1)

4171 כָּשַׂח kāśah
Variant; not used

4172 כַּשִּׂיל kaśśiyl (1)
axes (1)

4173 כָּשַׁל kāšal (65)
stumble (23)
fall (5)
stumbled (4)
stumbles (3)
be brought down (2)
downfall (2)
give way (2)
overthrow (2)
are brought down (1)
bring to ruin (1)
cause to fall (1)
caused to stumble (1)
fails (1)
faltered (1)
feeblest (1)
giving out (1)
made stumble (1)
make fall (1)

overthrown (1)
sapped (1)
stagger (1)
staggers (1)
stumble and fall (1) +4173
stumbling (1)
weak (1)
without success (1)
untranslated (3)

4174 כִּשָּׁלוֹן kiššālôn (1)
fall (1)

4175 כָּשַׁף kāšap (6)
sorcerers (3)
engages in witchcraft (1)
sorceress (1)
witchcraft (1)

4176 כֶּשֶׁף kešep (6)
sorceries (3)
witchcraft (3)

4177 כַּשָּׁף kaššāp (1)
sorcerers (1)

4178 כָּשֵׁר kāšēr (3)
bring (1)
succeed (1)
thinks right (1)

4179 כִּשְׁרוֹן kišrôn (3)
achievement (1) +5126
benefit (1)
skill (1)

4180 כָּתַב kātab (225)
written (107)
write (25)
wrote (23)
recorded (9)
write down (6)
wrote down (5)
be written (3)
inscribed (3)
signed (3)
were recorded (3)
be listed (2)
engraved (2)
was recorded (2)
were written (2)
write a description (2)
writes (2)
wrote out (2)
been recorded (1)
copied (1) +5467
decree be issued (1)
issue decrees (1) +4180
listed (1)
lodged (1)
map out (1)
order be written (1)
put in writing (1)
putting in writing (1)
record (1)
record (1) +9005
register (1)
was written (1)
was written down (1)
were listed (1)
words (1)
writing (1)
written descriptions (1)
wrote description (1)
untranslated (3)

4181 כְּתָב k°tāb (17)
script (5)
records (3)
text (3)
book (1)
directions written (1)
document (1)
letter (1)
prescribed (1)
writing (1)

4182 כְּתֹבֶת *k'tōbet* (1)
marks (1)

4183 כִּתִּיִּים *kitiyyiym* (10)
Kittim (4)
Cyprus (3)
western coastlands (1)
untranslated (2)

4184 כָּתִית *kātiyt* (5)
pressed (2)
pressed olives (2)
pressed olive (1)

4185 כֹּתֶל *kōtel* (1)
wall (1)

4186 כִּתְלִישׁ *kitliyš* (1)
Kitlish (1)

4187 כָּתַם *kātam* (1)
stain (1)

4188 כֶּתֶם *ketem* (9)
gold (5)
fine gold (1)
finest gold (1) +233
pure gold (1)
purest gold (1) +7058

4189 כֻּתֹנֶת *kutōnet* (29)
robe (13)
tunics (6)
tunic (5)
garments (4)
garment (1)

4190 כָּתֵף *kātēp* (68)
side (18)
shoulders (10)
shoulder pieces (8)
slope (8)
shoulder (5)
backs (3)
projecting walls (2)
slopes (2)
arm (1)
flank (1)
handles (1)
ones (1)
sides (1)
sidewalls (1)
slung on back (1) +1068
supports (1) +7193
wall (1)
untranslated (3)

4191 כְּתֵף *k'tōp*
Variant; not used

4192 1כָּתַר *kātar1* (1)
bear (1)

4193 2כָּתַר *kātar2* (4)
encircle (1)
gather about (1)
hem in (1)
surrounded (1)

4194 3כָּתַר *kātar3* (1)
crowned (1)

4195 כֶּתֶר *keter* (3)
crown (2)
crest (1)

4196 כֹּתֶרֶת *kōteret* (24)
capitals (11)
capital (5)
circular frame (1)
untranslated (7)

4197 כָּתַשׁ *kātaš* (1)
grind (1)

4198 כָּתַת *kātat* (16)
beat (3)
crushed (3)
are broken to pieces (1)

---

are defeated (1)
battered to pieces (1) +8625
be broken to pieces (1)
beat down (1)
broke into pieces (1)
crush (1)
oppress (1)
shattered (1)
was crushed (1)

4199 לְ *l*
Variant; not used

4200 1לְ- *r-* (20495)
to (4730)
for (1684)
of (756)
before (542) +7156
in (365)
with (219)
as (210)
by (209)
why (165) +4537
from (157)
therefore (146) +4027
forever (137) +6409
on (137)
into (110)
at (102)
have (94)
against (91)
had (90)
his (81) +2257
through (79)
my (77) +3276
that (74)
before (71)
in front of (66) +7156
according to (61)
so that (60)
had (50) +2118
has (50)
to (50) +7156
have (48) +2118
your (48) +4013
ahead (45) +7156
about (42)
alone (40) +963
over (40)
your (36) +3870
their (35) +2157
mine (33) +3276
belongs to (28)
so (26)
the LORD's (26) +3378
belong to (25)
to (25) +7023
upon (25)
when (25)
before (24) +4946+7156
yours (24) +3870
belonging to (23)
our (22) +5646
by (21) +7156
in order to (21)
among (20)
like (19)
presence (19) +7156
and (18)
every (18)
forever (18) +5905
in addition to (18) +963+4946
toward (17)
belonged to (16)
concerning (16)
only (16) +963
against (13) +7156
before (13) +5584
as for (12)
forever (12) +6329
have (12) +3780
after (11)

---

belong to (11) +2118
from (11) +4946+7156
for (10) +7156
so (10) +4027
under (10)
your (10) +3871
besides (9) +963+4946
to (9) +7754
David's (8) +1858
fail to have (8) +4162
from (8) +7156
his own (8) +2257
never (8) +4202+6409
only one (8) +963
formerly (7) +7156
give in marriage (7) +851+5989
meet (7) +7156
on behalf (7)
Solomon's (7) +8976
with (7) +7156
because of (6)
has (6) +2118
near (6)
near (6) +7156
serve (6) +6641+7156
their (6) +4564
upward (6) +2025+5087
before (5) +6524
belonged to (5) +2118
bring (5) +2118
but (5) +4027
close to (5) +6645
consider (5) +2118
destined for (5)
ever (5) +6409
for sake (5)
gave in marriage (5) +851+5989
have to do with (5)
her (5) +2023
marry (5) +851+2118
on side (5)
sent for (5) +2256+7924+8938
their own (5) +2157
used to (5) +7156
what (5) +4537
while (5)
with (5) +7023
above (4) +2025+4946+5087
always (4) +5905
belongs to (4) +2118
by themselves (4) +963+4392
concerns (4)
escape with (4) +8965
falsely (4) +2021+9214
father's (4) +3
given to (4)
great (4) +8044
greet (4) +8626+8934
greeted (4) +8626+8934
in honor (4)
in vain (4) +2021+8736
in vain (4) +8198
its (4) +2257
king's (4) +4889
lord's (4) +123
married (4) +851+4374
marry (4) +851+4374
my own (4) +3276
one by one (4) +1653+4392
owned (4)
owns (4)
plentiful (4) +8044
received (4)
Saul's (4) +8620
their (4) +2257
throughout (4)
till (4)
to belong (4)
within (4)
your own (4) +3870
yours (4) +4013

above (3) +2025+5087
along (3)
apart (3) +963
as if (3)
as soon as (3)
attack (3) +995
awaits (3)
become (3)
below (3) +4752
between (3)
by (3) +7023
down (3) +4752
entered (3) +995
eternal (3) +6409
face (3) +7156
faced (3)
get (3)
great amount (3) +8044
greatly (3) +8044
in abundance (3) +8044
in behalf of (3)
Israel's (3) +3776
keep (3) +2118
large numbers (3) +8044
leading (3) +7156
leads to (3)
married (3) +851+2118
mean by (3)
misuse (3) +2021+5951+8736
never (3) +4202+5905
opposite (3) +7156
over (3) +2025+4946+5087
related to (3)
sight (3) +7156
theirs (3) +2157
then (3) +4027
throughout (3) +3972
to belonged (3)
until (3)
watch (3) +6524
watched (3) +6524
what are you doing (3) +3870+4537
whose (3) +2257
whose (3) +4769
without (3) +4202
your own (3) +4013
a matter of (2)
accompanies (2) +7156
according to (2) +7023
across (2)
after (2) +7891
along with (2) +6645
always (2) +6409
any (2)
applies to (2)
as (2) +6645
as long as (2) +7156
as much as (2) +7023
as well as (2) +963+4946
assigned to (2)
at (2) +7156
at random (2) +9448
at table^s (2) +7156
at the point of (2)
be sure of this (2) +3338+3338
Belonging to (2)
bent on (2)
beside (2) +6645
beside (2) +7156
bind (2) +2118+3213
bloodshed (2) +1947+1947
bottom (2) +4752+4946
brings (2)
cause (2)
clan by clan (2) +5476
completely (2) +2021+3972
covered with (2) +7156
do for (2)
during (2)
each (2)
entered service (2) +6641+7156

entering (2) +995
eternal (2) +6329
ever (2) +6329
extensive (2) +8044
for (2) +4027
forever (2) +6330+6409
gently (2) +351
give (2)
given (2)
have in common (2)
highly (2) +2025+5087
his (2) +4564
his^s (2) +8976
holding (2)
in (2) +5584
in (2) +6961
in accordance with (2)
in addition to (2) +963
in behalf (2)
in connection with (2)
in front of (2) +5584
in order that (2)
in presence (2) +5584+6524
in such a way that (2)
in way (2) +7156
inside (2) +7156
its (2) +2023
just as (2) +6645
large quantities (2) +8044
leader (2) +2143+7156
led in campaigns (2) +995+2256+3655+7156
let inquire of (2) +2011
liable to (2)
long ago (2) +4946+8158
man's (2) +132
many (2) +8044
mean to (2)
misuses (2) +2021+5951+8736
much (2) +8044
never (2) +440+6409
never (2) +1153+5905
never (2) +1153+6409
never again (2) +4202+6409
not counting (2) +963+4946
not including (2) +963+4946
of (2) +4946+7156
of (2) +7156
on account of (2)
on behalf of (2)
opposite (2) +5584
ours (2) +5646
own (2)
owned (2) +3780
owner (2) +2257
parallel to (2) +6645
Pharaoh's (2) +7281
plenty (2) +8044
preceded (2) +2118+7156
preceded (2) +7156
receive (2) +2118
regard (2) +5584+8492
regard as (2) +2118
representing (2)
resist (2) +6641+7156
safely (2) +1055
see (2) +7156
seems to (2) +7156
served (2) +6641+7156
serving (2) +6641+7156
some (2)
surely (2) +4027
their (2) +2177
their own (2) +2257
to (2) +6524
to belongs (2)
top (2) +2025+4946+5087
turned into (2) +2118
under (2) +7156
up (2) +2025+5087
use (2) +2118

used to (2) +2021+8037
very (2) +2025+5087
very well (2) +4027
watching (2) +6524
when (2) +6961
when (2) +7023
without (2) +1172
withstand (2) +6641+7156
won (2) +5951+7156
your very own (2) +3870
Aaron's (1) +195
above (1)
above (1) +4946+4946+5087+6645
abroad (1) +2021+2575
Absalom's (1) +94
abundant (1) +8044
accompanied (1)
accompany (1) +2143+5584
accused of (1)
accuses (1) +2021+5477+7756
acquired (1) +2118
adjoining (1) +6645
Adonijah's (1) +154
adopted (1) +1426+4374
adorned (1) +7596+9514
affects (1)
again (1) +6409
agent (1) +3338
agreed with (1) +7754+9048
ahead (1)
ahead (1) +4946+7156
alike (1) +6645
all (1) +963
all alone (1) +963
all by myself (1) +963+3276
allotted (1)
allowed (1)
alone (1) +970
along (1) +3338
along with (1)
along with (1) +963+4946
alongside (1) +6645
alongside of (1) +6645
also (1) +963
always (1) +1887+1887+2256
always (1) +6329
among (1) +3972
and (1) +4027
anyone (1) +963
apart (1) +970
around (1)
as (1) +6961
as a result (1)
as in (1)
as long as live (1) +3427+3972+6409
as well as (1) +6645
asked how they were (1) +8626+8934
assaults (1) +5596+5596
assigned (1)
assistant (1) +6641+7156
at (1) +6645
at (1) +7023
at advance (1) +7156
at each successive level (1)
                +2025+2025+4200+5087+5087
at hand (1) +995+7940
at sanctuary^s (1) +7156
at the head of (1) +7156
attack (1)
attack (1) +6913
attains (1)
attend (1) +6641+7156
attend (1) +7156
attended by (1) +2143+8079
attending (1) +7156
attention (1) +7156
avoid (1) +4202+6843
awaits (1) +7156
backward (1) +294
bake thoroughly (1) +8596+8599
banded together (1) +665+2021+2653

be given in marriage (1) +851+5989
be kept from (1) +1194+1757
became (1)
because (1)
because (1) +3954+4537
because (1) +4027
because of this (1) +4027
become (1) +2118
become wife (1) +851+4374
befalls (1) +628
before (1) +678
before (1) +5584+6524
before eyes (1) +7156
before time (1) +4946+7156
beforehand (1) +4946+7156
belonging to (1) +2118
beside (1) +3338
besides (1)
besides (1) +963
beyond (1) +2134+4946
bodyguard (1) +8031+9068
bordering (1) +6645
borne by (1)
bravely (1) +1201+2657
bring (1)
bringing (1)
brings to ruin (1) +2021+6156+8273
brought (1)
but (1)
but why (1) +4537
by (1) +4946
by (1) +6524
by himself (1) +963+2257
by itself (1) +963
by itself (1) +963+2257
by itself (1) +970
by myself (1) +963+3276
call in honor of (1) +7727
check (1) +995+7156
children's (1) +1201
choose (1)
come across (1) +7156+7925
committed (1)
condemn (1) +2118+2631
consult (1) +7156
contains (1)
continually (1) +6329
continually (1) +8092
controlled (1)
controlled (1) +2118
corresponding to (1)
count (1) +2118
covered (1) +8492
crown (1)
crowns (1) +8031
cry out (1) +606+5951
daily (1) +285+3427
daily (1) +2021+3427
Danite (1) +1968+4751
depth (1) +2025+5087
despite (1) +928+8611
despoil (1) +1020+5989
directed to (1)
directly in front of (1) +5790
directly opposite (1) +5790+7156
dispersed (1) +2006+2143
done this^s (1) +1215+3378+4640
doomed to (1)
downcast (1) +2118
downstream (1) +2025+4946+5087
droves (1) +8044
each day (1) +2021+2021+3427+3427+4200
each day (1) +2021+3427
each morning (1)
          +1332+1332+2021+2021+4200
each^s (1) +5031
endless (1) +5905
endure (1) +2118
enough (1) +1896+4537
enslaved (1) +2256+3899+4200+6269+9148
enter (1) +995

enter service (1) +6641+7156
entered the service (1) +6641+7156
enters (1) +995
enthrones (1) +2021+3782+4058
even though (1) +963
ever (1) +7156
ever again (1) +5905+5905
ever since (1) +4946
everlasting (1) +5905
everlasting (1) +6409
every day (1) +2021+3427
exceedingly (1) +2025+5087
extends to (1) +4946
faced (1) +7156
far and wide (1) +4946+6330+8158
far away (1) +4946+6330+8158
fault (1) +928+8611
fell facedown (1) +678+2556
fight (1) +2021+3655+4878
find (1)
finds (1)
firstborn belongs to (1) +1144
fit for (1)
fleet of trading ships (1) +641+2143+9576
fluent (1) +1819+4554
for life (1) +6409
for relief from (1) +4946+7156
for the sake of (1)
for the use of (1)
forced to (1)
forever (1) +802+3427
forward (1) +7156
fought in (1) +3655
found (1) +7156+8011
from (1) +1068
from (1) +4946
from among (1)
from place to place (1) +5023
gain (1)
gave permission (1)
girl's (1) +5855
give (1) +2118
give (1) +7156
give in marriage (1) +408+5989
given over to (1)
God's (1) +466
goes down (1) +3718+4752
going (1)
got (1) +2118
great number (1) +8044
great numbers (1) +8044
great quantities (1) +4394+8044
had (1) +3780
had (1) +5162
had been (1) +7156
harbored (1) +2118
hard (1) +2021+3668+4607
has (1) +5162
has to do with (1)
have (1) +889
have (1) +5989
have part (1)
have regard for (1) +5564
have right (1)
have sexual relations (1) +2446+5989+8888
have the right (1)
have to do with (1) +2256+4200
having (1)
having (1) +2118
hear (1) +5877+7156
heights (1) +2025+5087
help (1)
help (1) +2118
help (1) +3338
help (1) +6913
her (1) +3276
here (1) +7156
hers (1) +2023
Hezekiah's (1) +2624
Hezekiah's (1) +2625
high above (1) +2025+4946+5087

higher than (1) +2025+5087+8049
his^s (1) +90
his^s (1) +4889+5213
his^s (1) +5557
his^s (1) +8620
hold (1)
how was (1) +8934
how was going (1) +8934
how were (1) +8934
however (1) +4027
huge (1) +1524+4394+6330
hunt down (1) +4511+7421
imposing (1) +1524+5260
in (1) +7156
in accordance with (1) +7023
in addition (1) +963
in addition (1) +963+4946
in ascending stages (1)
          +2025+2025+4200+5087+5087
in broad daylight (1)
          +2021+2021+2296+6524+9087
in charge of (1)
in debt (1) +5957
in earlier times (1) +7156
in eyes (1) +7156
in front of (1) +6524
in fulfillment of (1)
in large numbers (1) +8044
in opposition to (1)
in path (1) +7156
in possession (1)
in preparation for (1)
in service (1) +7156
in the course of time (1) +3427+3427+4946
in the eyes of (1) +7156
in the face of (1) +5584
in the sight of (1)
in this way (1)
inclines to (1)
individually (1) +1653
inner (1) +7156
inner (1) +7163
inquire of (1) +2011
inside (1) +1074+4946
inside (1) +7163
instead of (1)
instead of (1) +1194
instead of (1) +7156
intimate with (1)
into (1) +7163
into another set (1) +963
into marry (1) +2118
into one set (1) +963
invaded (1) +2143
invading (1) +995
involved in (1)
Israelite (1) +1201+3776
it means (1)
its^s (1) +2021+4058
Jacob's (1) +3620
jointed (1) +4946+5087+8079
just as (1) +889+3972
just for that (1) +4027
keep (1)
keeps company (1) +782+2495
kept (1)
killed (1) +2995+5782+7023
Korah's (1) +7946
lack (1) +401
large amount (1) +8044
larger (1) +8044
lasting (1) +6409
later (1)
later (1) +7891
lawsuits (1) +1907+1907
lead (1) +995+2256+3655+7156
lead (1) +2143+7156
lead (1) +7156
lead across (1) +6296+7156
lead to (1)
leading into (1)

leading into (1) +7023
leading to (1)
learned (1) +5583
leaves (1)
led (1) +7156
led out (1) +3655+7156
led to (1)
left (1) +2118
length (1) +6645
let inquire of at all (1) +2011+2011
lets happen (1) +628+3338
life will not be worth living (1) +2644+4537
like (1) +6645
likes (1) +928+2021+3202
long (1) +6409
long ago (1) +6409
long life (1) +2021+2644
lover's (1) +1856
made fall (1) +2118+4842
make serve (1) +8492
make sport of (1) +2118+5442
married (1) +851+2257+4200+4374
married to (1) +851+2118
marries (1) +408+2118
marries (1) +408+2118+2118
marries (1) +2118
marry (1) +408+2118
marry into (1) +2118
match for (1)
mighty (1) +8044
mine (1) +3276+8611
more (1) +401
more (1) +2025+5087
more (1) +8044
more and more powerful (1)
　　　+1541+2025+2143+2256+5087+6330
more for (1)
more quickly than (1) +7156
more readily than (1) +7156
more than (1) +401
more than (1) +963+4946
Moses' (1) +5407
my (1) +3276+7156
my own (1) +3276+8611
Nebuchadnezzar's (1) +5557
never (1) +401+6409
never (1) +561+5905
never (1) +4202+7156
nevertheless (1) +4027
next to (1)
next to (1) +5584
next to (1) +6298
not circumcised (1) +2257+6889
numerous (1) +8044
obey (1)
obey (1) +7754+9048
of (1) +4946+8611
of what use (1) +2296+4537
of what use (1) +4537
offered a kiss of homage (1) +5975+7023
older (1) +2418+3427
on behalf of (1) +5466
on behalf of (1) +5790
on high (1) +2021+5294
once for all (1) +5905
one kind after another (1) +2157+5476
one[s] (1) +2157
only (1) +963+2314
only exception (1) +963
only one (1) +963+2257
open (1) +7156
opposite (1) +6645
other than (1) +963+1194
other than (1) +963+4946
ours (1) +3276
ours (1) +5646+7156
out (1)
out of way (1) +4946+7156
outer (1) +2021+2575
outer (1) +2025+4946+5087
over (1) +4946+6584

over (1) +7156
over and above (1) +2025+5087
over here (1) +285+6298
over there (1) +285+6298
overlooking (1) +7156
overtake (1)
overtakes (1)
overturned (1) +2025+2200+5087
own (1) +2118
owning (1)
owns (1) +3780
paid any attention (1) +265+5742+9048
particularly (1) +4027
pay (1)
people's (1) +6639
per (1)
perjurers (1) +2021+8678+9214
perjury (1) +2021+8678+9214
permanently (1) +2021+7552
permanently (1) +7552
piece by piece (1) +5984
plentifully (1) +7859
powerless (1) +401+445
powerless (1) +401+445+3338
preceding (1) +7156
predecessor (1) +889+2118+7156
present (1) +5877+7156
present (1) +7156
previous (1) +7156
project upward (1) +2025+5087
property[s] (1) +889+2118
provide with (1)
provided for (1) +430+2118+2256+4312
provides for (1)
punished less (1) +3104+4752
put (1) +995+7156
put (1) +995+9202
put up security (1) +3338+9546
quantities (1) +8044
quarrel between (1)
quite innocently (1) +9448
reached (1) +995
ready for (1)
ready for battle (1) +408+2021+4878+7372
realize (1) +606+4222
receive (1)
received (1) +995
received (1) +2118
receives (1) +5989
reduced to servitude (1) +6268+6269
referring to (1)
reflects a face (1) +2021+2021+7156+7156
reflects the man (1) +132+2021
regard (1) +2118+7156
regarded (1)
regarded in the sight of (1) +7156
regardless (1) +401+9068
regards (1) +5162+7156
regularly (1) +928+3427+3427
relating to (1)
relation to (1)
remain unmarried (1)
　　　+408+1194+2118+4200+6328
renowned (1) +9005
represent (1)
represented (1)
resisted (1) +5584+6641
resort to (1) +2143+7925
responding to (1) +6645
responsible for (1)
responsible for (1) +889+928
responsible for (1) +928+8611
responsible for (1) +5584
rests with (1)
retains (1) +2118
reward (1)
right before (1)
right before (1) +5584
right for (1)
risked (1) +3070+4637
ruined (1) +7914

ruthlessly (1) +425
safely (1) +2021+8934
safely (1) +8934
same as (1)
saying (1) +606
see (1) +2021+6524+8011
see (1) +6524
see to it (1) +6524
seeks (1)
select a day (1) +3427+3427+4946
self-control (1) +5110+8120
sent for (1) +7924+8938
separate (1) +963
separate (1) +963+3657
servants' (1) +6269
serve (1) +2118
serve (1) +2118+7156
serve (1) +7156
served (1) +2118+7156
service of (1)
setting the time (1) +5503
severe (1) +2025+5087
Shalmaneser's[s] (1) +2257
share (1) +889+3869
share (1) +2118
Shimei's (1) +9059
show (1) +2118
show (1) +7156
shows to be (1) +2118
sided with (1) +1047
since (1) +3427+4946
sing songs (1) +928+7754+8123+9048
slaughter (1) +2222+5422
slept with (1) +408+3359+5435
slept with (1) +2351+3359+5435
slow down (1) +6806+8206
slowly (1) +351
so as (1)
so as to (1)
so far as (1) +3972
so many (1) +8044
so then (1) +4027
Solomon's (1) +8611+8976
some years later (1) +7891+9102
started (1) +6991
stationed at (1)
still (1) +4027
stole into (1) +995+1704
stolen goods (1) +2257+4202
storerooms (1) +238+5969
straight ahead (1) +5790
straight to (1)
struck (1)
subject to (1)
succeed against (1) +5584
such as (1)
suffered (1) +2118
summoned (1) +7924+8938
supply (1) +2118
take (1) +2118
take care of (1) +2118+5466
take command (1) +2118+5464
take for (1) +5989+7156
taken (1)
taken from (1) +4946+7156
testify (1) +6332+6699
than (1)
that[s] (1) +8079
the LORD's (1) +3378
their (1) +2179
their (1) +4013
their[s] (1) +2021+2498
theirs (1) +2257
therefore (1) +3610+4027
think (1) +4013+8492
this fellow's[s] (1) +2296
this one (1) +963
thoughtlessly (1) +928+1051+8557
thus (1)
to (1) +928+6288
to (1) +4946

to (1) +6584+7156
to fulfill (1)
to honor (1)
to the point of (1)
to the very end (1) +6409+6813
to turned (1)
together with (1)
told (1) +606+8938
took in marriage (1) +851+4374
took part in (1) +3655
top (1) +2025+5087
top of (1) +2025+4946+5087
tore apart (1) +7973+7974+9109
total (1)
total (1) +3972+5031
treated the same as (1) +6645
troubles (1)
trustfully (1) +1055
tuned to (1)
turn against (1) +2118+8477
turn into (1)
under (1) +1074
under blessing (1) +7156
under direction (1) +7156
under supervision (1) +7156
unintentionally (1) +8705
unite (1) +2118+3480+4222
unless (1) +561+3954+7156
unmarried (1) +408+2118+4202
unsuspecting (1) +1055
unto (1)
upstream (1) +2025+5087
upward (1) +2025+4946+5087
used as (1)
used by (1)
used for (1)
used in (1)
useless (1) +2021+9214
uses (1)
valued at (1)
very (1) +466
very (1) +2025+5087+6330
wage war (1) +1741+2021+4878
walled (1) +2257+2570
want (1)
wanted to make (1) +1335
was given in marriage (1) +851+5989
watched (1) +7156
wear (1)
were fettered (1) +5602+5733
what do I care about (1)
    +2296+3276+4200+4537
what do you mean (1) +4013+4537
what is doing (1) +4537
what is the matter (1) +3871+4537
what right have you (1) +3870+4537
when (1) +3954+7023
whenever (1) +3972
whenever (1) +7023
where[s] (1) +4564
where[s] (1) +7156
wherever (1)
wherever (1) +8079
whether (1)
while (1) +6961
whose (1) +889
why (1) +361+2296
why (1) +561+4027+4537
why (1) +4537+8611
wielding (1) +995+2025+5087
wish well (1) +8934
with (1) +3338
with (1) +6645
without (1) +401
worship (1) +7156
year (1) +2021+3427
yet (1) +4027
younger (1) +3427+7582
yours (1) +3871
Zedekiah's (1) +7409
untranslated (7405)

4201   לְ־2   *l̂-2*
  Variant; not used

4202   לֹא   *lō'* (5189)
not (2963)
no (613)
never (155)
nor (109) +2256
cannot (101)
nothing (68)
without (67)
cannot (45) +3523
neither (42)
don't (33)
no (31) +3972
didn't (30)
none (29)
nothing (19) +1821
isn't (14)
none (14) +3972
or (14)
or (14) +2256
surely (14) +561
won't (13)
before (12)
haven't (11)
nor (11)
nothing (11) +3972
refused (11) +14
without (9) +928
failed (8)
never (8) +4200+6409
can't (7) +3523
nothing (7) +4399
refused (7)
unwilling (7) +14
aren't (5)
forbidden (5) +6913
hasn't (5)
never (5) +6388
none (5) +408
refuse (5)
little (4)
neither (4) +1685
unjust (4) +9419
unless (4) +561
unlike (4) +3869
wouldn't (4)
before (3) +889+6330
before (3) +928
beyond (3)
fail (3)
fails (3)
injustice (3) +5477
instead of (3)
more than (3)
neither (3) +2256
never (3) +4200+5905
nor (3) +1685
unclean (3) +3196
unknown (3) +3359
without (3) +4200
as you know (2) +2022
before (2) +928+3270
but (2) +561
can't (2)
childless (2) +3528
disobeyed (2) +928+7754+9048
disobeyed (2) +9048
displeases (2) +2911
doesn't (2)
forbidden (2) +7422
free from (2)
from (2)
hardly (2)
helpless (2) +3946+6806
ignorant (2) +3359
lack (2)
never (2) +2021+3427+3972
never (2) +3578
never (2) +6330+6409

never again (2) +4200+6409
no (2) +3972+4946
no (2) +4027
nothing (2) +1821+3972
overwhelmed (2) +928+2118+6388+8120
powerless (2) +3946
rather than (2)
rather than (2) +2256
refuse (2) +14
shouldn't (2)
that (2) +561
till (2) +561
trackless (2) +2006
unable (2)
unaware (2) +3359
useless (2) +7503
whether (2) +561
worthless idols (2) +3603
against (1) +3869
agreed (1)
always be (1) +2532
anything[s] (1)
as[s] (1)
avoid (1) +4200+6843
barely (1)
because (1) +561+3610
because (1) +2256
before (1) +6330
before (1) +6388
before elapsed (1) +4848
better than (1)
bottled-up (1) +7337
but (1)
by no means (1) +3480
by surprise (1) +3359
can hardly breathe (1) +5972+8636
cannot bear (1) +3523
cannot read (1) +3359+6219
cannot stand (1) +3523
certainly (1) +561
cloudless (1) +6265
contrary (1)
contrary to (1)
contrary to (1) +928+3869
contrary to (1) +3869
couldn't (1)
delayed (1) +237
dense (1) +2983
denying (1)
deserted (1) +3782
despairs (1) +586
die (1) +2649
disobedience (1) +928+7754+9048
disobey (1) +9048
disorder (1) +6043
displease (1) +928+2834+5162+6524
displeasing (1) +928+2834+5162+6524
disregarding (1) +2349
either (1)
else (1)
empty (1) +4027
ever (1)
except (1) +889
except for (1) +2256
fail (1) +8505
failed (1) +3523
failed (1) +6388+7756
fails (1) +586
feeble (1) +3888
feeble (1) +6437
free from (1) +928
free of (1)
futile (1) +4027
gives way (1) +6641
go unanswered (1) +6699
gone (1) +928+2118
gone (1) +928+6641
hidden (1) +8011
how much less (1) +677+3954
if (1)
ignored (1) +4213+8492

in vain (1)
incapable (1) +3523
keeps (1) +4614
lack (1) +928
lest (1) +889
little value (1) +4399
make countless (1) +889+6218+8049
many (1) +5071
measureless (1) +4499
mercilessly (1) +2798
neglected (1) +5757
neither (1) +2296
never (1) +3427+4946
never (1) +4200+7156
never (1) +5905+6330
never (1) +6409
never (1) +8041
never (1) +9458
nobody (1) +132
none (1) +285
none (1) +3972+4946
none (1) +3972+5883
none (1) +4399
nor (1) +1685+2256
nothing (1) +889+3972
nothing (1) +1524+1821+2256+7785
nothing (1) +2021+3972
nothing (1) +4027
nothing (1) +4312
nothing (1) +5126
Nowhere (1)
nowhere (1)
of no account (1)
only (1) +1194
only (1) +2022
only (1) +2314
only (1) +8370
only^s (1)
or (1) +889
other than (1)
otherwise (1) +889+5100
otherwise (1) +2256
outcome different (1) +3869
past (1)
pittance (1) +2104
powerless (1)
powerless (1) +3523
precious (1) +5877
rather (1) +3954
refused (1) +9048
remained childless (1) +3528
resents (1) +170
scarcely (1)
seldom (1) +2221
shameful (1) +4083
shamelessly (1) +1017
silent (1) +1819
since (1)
sinful (1) +3202
so (1) +561+3610
stay (1) +995
stayed away (1) +995
still to come (1) +6913
stolen goods (1) +2257+4200
stop (1)
stop (1) +3578
stopped (1) +3578+6388
stopped (1) +3855
stops (1)
stranger (1) +3359
strangers (1) +3359
surely (1)
than (1) +2256
this^s (1) +2257+3769
till (1)
time and again (1) +285+2256+4202+9109
too (1)
too heavy a burden to carry (1) +3523+5951
troubled (1) +3523+9200
turned a deaf ear (1) +263
unable (1) +3523

unafraid (1) +7064
unceasingly (1) +1949
unchanged (1) +4614
unclean (1) +3197
uncut (1) +7786
undivided loyalty (1) +2256+4213+4213
uneaten (1) +1180
unfaithful (1) +574
unfamiliar (1) +3359
unfanned (1) +5870
ungodly (1) +2883
unintentionally (1) +928+7402
unjust (1) +5477
unjustly (1) +4026
unless (1)
unless (1) +561+3954
unless (1) +2022
unlike (1)
unlike (1) +4027+6913
unmarried (1) +408+2118+4200
unprofitable (1) +3603
unpunished (1) +870
unquenchable (1) +3882
unrelenting (1) +2798
unrighteousness (1) +7406
unruly (1) +4340
unsharpened (1) +7837
unsuccessful (1) +7503
unsuited (1) +5534
unthinkable (1) +597
untiring (1) +7028
unwise (1) +2682
useless (1)
useless (1) +3603
useless (1) +6122
virgin (1) +408+3359
wasn't (1) +2118
weakness (1) +3946
what about (1) +2022
whether (1) +561+2022
who^s (1)
wicked (1) +3202
withheld^s (1) +4763
withhold (1)
worse (1) +4017
worthless (1) +3603
wrong (1) +3202
yes (1) +3954
untranslated (329)

4203 לֹא דְבָר *lō' dā_bār* (2)
Lo Debar (2)

4204 לֹא עַמִּי *lō' 'ammiy* (1)
Lo-Ammi (1)

4205 לֹא רֻחָמָה *lō' ruḥāmāh* (2)
Lo-Ruhamah (2)

4206 לָאָה *lā'āh* (19)
weary (3)
worn out (3)
try patience (2)
burdened (1)
can no longer (1)
cannot (1)
could not (1)
discouraged (1)
frustrated (1)
impatient (1)
lazy (1)
not be able (1)
wears herself out (1)
weary themselves (1)

4207 לֵאָה *lē'āh* (34)
Leah (28)
Leah's (5)
untranslated (1)

4208 לָאז *lā'z*
Variant; not used

4209 לָאט *lā'aṭ*

Variant; not used

4210 לָאֵל *lā'ēl* (1)
Lael (1)

4211 לְאֹם *l'ōm* (35)
peoples (18)
nations (8)
people (4)
nation (1)
nations' (1)
other^s (1)
others^s (1)
subjects (1)

4212 לְאָמִּים *l'ummiym* (1)
Leummites (1)

4213 לֵב *lē_b* (600)
heart (310)
hearts (74)
mind (21)
judgment (11)
himself (10) +2257
attention (7)
minds (7)
skilled (6) +2682
in high spirits (5) +3201
understanding (5)
brokenhearted (3) +8689
everything (3) +3972
high seas (3) +3542
myself (3) +3276
tenderly (3) +6584
arrogant (2) +5951
conscience-stricken (2) +5782
considered (2) +8492
courage (2)
imagination (2)
senseless (2) +401
thoughts (2)
wholehearted devotion (2) +8969
wholeheartedly (2) +928+3972
will (2)
willing (2) +5618
willing (2) +5951
wise (2)
yourself (2) +3870
ability (1)
ability (1) +928+2683
accord (1)
again give allegiance (1) +8740
am forgotten (1) +4946+8894
anxious striving (1) +8301
attitude (1)
bravest (1) +579
call to mind (1) +448+8740
care (1) +448+8492
care about (1) +448+8492
careful attention (1)
cares (1) +6584+8492
cheer up (1) +3512
chest (1)
concerned about (1) +448+8492
confide in (1) +907
conscience (1)
consider (1) +6584+8492
consider (1) +8492
consider well (1) +8883
craftsmen (1) +2682
dared (1) +4848
deceived (1) +1704
deception (1) +2256+4213
decided (1) +2118+6640
desire (1)
did^s (1) +906+3877+4392
discourage (1) +5648
discouraged (1) +5648
disheartened (1) +3874
encourage (1) +1819+6584
encourage (1) +3922
encouragingly (1) +6584
enraged (1) +6192

faithless (1) +6047
glad (1) +3512
has full confidence (1) +1053
head (1)
heartache (1) +6780
his own (1) +2257+4946
I (1) +3276
idea (1) +4946
ignored (1) +4202+8492
in (1) +928
in good spirits (1) +3512
inclined (1) +5742
intent (1)
intention (1) +8492
it^s (1) +3276
kindly (1)
led astray (1) +5742
merrymakers (1) +8524
obstinate (1) +7997
opinions (1)
persist in own way (1) +9244
persuade (1) +1819+6584
pride (1) +1467
proud (1) +8123
purpose (1)
reason (1)
reflected on (1) +448+5989
refreshed (1) +6184
resolved (1) +6584+8492
rip open (1) +6033+7973
sense (1)
skill (1) +2683
spirit (1)
spoken kindly (1) +1819+6584
stops to think (1) +448+8740
stubborn (1) +2617
stubborn-hearted (1) +52
stunned (1) +7028
take heart (1) +599
take note (1) +8883
them (1) +4392
themselves (1) +4392
think (1) +606+928
think (1) +5989
think about (1) +6584+6590
to (1) +928
tried (1) +928+9365
undivided loyalty (1) +2256+4202+4213
valiant men (1) +52
very (1)
voluntarily (1) +408+6584+6590
wholeheartedly (1) +928+8969
willful (1)
willing (1) +5605
willingly (1) +4946
wisdom (1)
wise (1) +2682
worry (1) +906+8492
you (1) +3870
yourself (1) +2257
yourself (1) +3871
untranslated (3)

4214 לֵב קָמָי *lēb qāmāy* (1)
Leb Kamai (1)

4215 לָבֹא *lābō'* (1)
Variant; not used

4216 לֶבֶא *lebe'* (1)
lions (1)

4217 לְבֹא חֲמָת *l'bō' ḥ^emāt* (12)
Lebo Hamath (12)

4218 לִבְאָה *lib'āh* (1)
mate (1)

4219 לְבָאֹת *l'bā'ôt* (1)
Lebaoth (1)

4220 1לָבַב *lābab1* (3)
stolen heart (2)
become wise (1)

4221 2לָבַב *lābab2* (2)
made bread (1)
make special bread (1) +4223

4222 לֵבָב *lēbāb* (252)
heart (120)
hearts (46)
mind (10)
give careful thought (5) +8492
yourself (4) +3870
conscience (3)
heart's (2)
minds (2)
understanding (2)
wholehearted devotion (2) +8969
wholeheartedly (2) +928+3972
wholeheartedly (2) +928+8969
yourselves (2) +3870
breasts (1)
brokenhearted (1) +3874
conscientious (1) +3838
consider (1) +928
consider better (1) +8123
convictions (1) +6640
courage (1)
deceived (1) +1704
disheartened (1) +906+5022
downhearted (1) +8317
encouraged (1) +1819+6584
enticed (1) +7331
fainthearted (1) +8205
fainthearted (1) +8216
filled with pride (1) +8123
fully determined (1) +928+8969
gladly (1) +928+3206
harbor (1) +2118+6640
hardhearted (1) +599+906
has in mind (1) +3108
heart and soul (1) +3869
herself (1) +2023
himself (1) +2257
in a rage (1) +2801
in accord with (1) +3838
indecisive (1) +8205
inspire (1) +928+5989
integrity (1) +3841
intend (1) +6640
intent (1)
plot against (1) +928+3108
profound (1)
proud (1) +8123
purpose (1)
realize (1) +606+4200
take heart (1) +599
themselves (1) +4392
think (1) +606+928
think (1) +5989
think (1) +6584+6590
thinks (1) +606+928
unite (1) +2118+3480+4200
willfully (1) +928
yourself (1) +2023
yourself (1) +3871
yourselves (1) +4013
untranslated (4)

4223 לִבְכָה *l'bibāh* (3)
bread (1)
it^s (1) +2021
make special bread (1) +4221

4224 לְבַד *l'bad*
Variant; not used

4225 לַבָּה *labbāh* (1)
flames (1)

4226 לִבָּה *libbāh* (1)
weak-willed (1) +581

4227 1לְבוֹנָהו *l'bônāh1*
Variant; not used

4228 2לְבוֹנָה *l'bônāh2* (1)
Lebonah (1)

4229 לָבוּשׁ *lābûš* (15)
clothed (7)
in (3)
armed (1)
covered (1)
dress (1)
dressed (1)
wore (1)

4230 לְבוּשׁ *l'bûš* (31)
clothing (5)
garments (5)
garment (4)
robe (4)
clothed (3)
clothes (2)
coat (1)
dressed (1)
gown (1)
military tunic (1) +4496
put on (1)
put on (1) +5989
robed (1)
robes (1)

4231 לָבַט *lābat* (3)
comes to ruin (2)
come to ruin (1)

4232 לְבִי *l'biy*
Variant; not used

4233 לָבִיא *lābiy'* (11)
lioness (7)
lion (3)
lions (1)

4234 לְבִיָּא *l'biyyā'* (1)
lioness (1)

4235 1לָבֵן *lāban1* (5)
made spotless (2)
leaving white (1)
white (1)
whiter (1)

4236 2לָבֵן *lāban2* (3)
bricks (1)
make bricks (1) +4246
making bricks (1) +4246

4237 1לָבָן *lābān1* (29)
white (24)
reddish-white (4) +140
whiter (1)

4238 2לָבָן *lābān2* (54)
Laban (45)
Laban's (5)
he^s (2)
him^s (1)
untranslated (1)

4239 3לָבָן *lābān3* (1)
Laban (1)

4240 לָבֵן *labēn*
Variant; not used

4241 לְבָנָא *l'bānāh'*
Variant; not used

4242 לִבְנֶה *libneh* (2)
poplar (2)

4243 לִבְנָה *libnāh* (18)
Libnah (17)
it^s (1)

4244 1לְבָנָה *l'bānāh1* (3)
moon (3)

4245 2לְבָנָה *l'bānāh2* (2)
Lebana (1)
Lebanah (1)

4246 לְבֵנָה *l'bēnāh* (12)
bricks (5)
brick (2)
altars of brick (1)

clay tablet (1)
make bricks (1) +4236
making bricks (1) +4236
pavement (1)

4247 לְבֹנָה l⁰bōnāh (21)
incense (20)
frankincense (1)

4248 לְבָנוֹן l⁰bānôn (71)
Lebanon (68)
cedar of Lebanon (2)
thereˢ (1)

4249 לִבְנִי1 libniy1 (5)
Libni (5)

4250 לִבְנִי2 libniy2 (2)
Libnite (1)
Libnites (1)

4251 לִבְנָת libnāt
Variant; not used

4252 לָבַשׁ lābaš (98)
put on (23)
clothed (15)
clothe (10)
wear (9)
dress (5)
came upon (3)
dressed (3)
dressed in (3)
robed (3)
covered (2)
wore (2)
clad (1)
clothed (1) +955
clothes (1)
dress in (1)
provide (1)
provided with clothes (1)
put clothes on (1)
put on (1) +9432
put on as clothing (1)
put on clothes (1)
put on robes (1)
puts on (1)
putting on (1)
robe (1)
vestments (1)
wear clothes (1)
worn (1)
untranslated (3)

4253 לֹג lōg (5)
log (5)

4254 לֹד lōd (4)
Lod (4)

4255 לִדְבִר lidbir
Variant; not used

4256 לֵדָה lēdāh (4)
deliver (2)
birth (1)
in labor (1)

4257 לֹה lōh (1)
untranslated (1)

4258 לַהַב lahab (12)
flames (3)
fire (2) +836
flame (2)
flashing (2)
aflame (1)
blade (1)
itˢ (1) +2021

4259 לֶהָבָה lehābāh (19)
flame (6)
flames (3)
flaming (3)
blaze (2)
blazing (1)
burned (1)

flashes (1)
lightning (1) +836
point (1)

4260 לְהָבִים l⁰hābiym (2)
Lehabites (2)

4261 לַהַג lahag (1)
study (1)

4262 לָהַד lāhad (1)
Lahad (1)

4263 לָהַהּ lāhah (1)
madman (1)

4264 לָהָהּ lāhāh
Variant; not used

4265 לָהַט1 lāhat1 (10)
sets ablaze (2)
blazes (1)
burned up (1)
consumed (1)
consumes (1)
flames (1)
in flames (1)
set afire (1)
set on fire (1)

4266 לָהַט2 lāhat2 (1)
ravenous beasts (1)

4267 לַהַט lahat (1)
flaming (1)

4268 לְהָטִים l⁰hātiym (1)
secret arts (1)

4269 לָהֵם lāham (2)
choice morsels (2)

4270 לָהֵן lāhēn
Variant; not used

4271 לְהֵלֶּה lihlēah
Variant; not used

4272 לַהֲקָה lah⁰qāh (1)
group (1)

4273 לוּ lû (25)
if (12)
if only (8)
let (1)
oh (1)
what if (1)
will (1)
untranslated (1)

4274 לוֹ דְבָר lô d⁰bār (2)
Lo Debar (2)

4275 לוּב lûb (6)
Libyans (4)
Libya (2)

4276 לוּד lûd (9)
Lud (2)
Ludites (2)
Lydia (2)
Lydians (1)
men of Lydia (1)
untranslated (1)

4277 לָוָה1 lāwāh1 (12)
join (5)
bind themselves (2)
accompany (1)
attached (1)
be joined (1)
bound himself (1)
joined (1)

4278 לָוָה2 lāwāh2 (14)
lend (4)
borrow (3)
borrower (2)
lender (2)
lend freely (1)
lends (1)

lends freely (1)

4279 לוּז1 lûz1 (6)
devious (2)
let out (1)
deceit (1)
perverse (1)

4280 לוּז2 lûz2 (1)
almond (1)

4281 לוּז3 lûz3 (8)
Luz (7)
untranslated (1)

4282 לוּזָה lûzāh
Variant; not used

4283 לוּחַ lûah (43)
tablets (33)
tablet (3)
boards (2)
panels (1)
surfaces (1)
themˢ (1) +2021
theyˢ (1)
timbers (1)

4284 לוּחִית lûhiyt (2)
Luhith (2)

4285 לוֹחֵשׁ lôhēš
Variant; not used

4286 לוּט lût (4)
covered (1)
enfolds (1)
pulled over (1)
wrapped (1)

4287 לוֹט1 lôt1 (1)
shroud (1)

4288 לוֹט2 lôt2 (33)
Lot (30)
heˢ (1)
Lot's (1)
untranslated (1)

4289 לוֹטָן lôtān (7)
Lotan (5)
Lotan's (2)

4290 לֵוִי1 lēwiy1 (62)
Levi (42)
Levites (15) +1201
Levite (2)
Levites (2)
Levites (1) +4751

4291 לֵוִי2 lēwiy2 (288)
Levites (245)
Levite (26)
Levi (5)
Levites (3) +1201
Levitical (2)
themˢ (2) +2021
Levites (1) +5476
theyˢ (1) +2021
untranslated (3)

4292 לוְיָה liwyāh (2)
garland (2)

4293 לוְיָתָן liwyātān (6)
Leviathan (4)
leviathan (2)

4294 לוּל lûl (1)
stairway (1)

4295 לוּלֵא lûlē' (14)
if not (5)
if not (4) +3954
unless (2)
but (1)
not (1)
still (1)

4296 לוּן lûn (19)
grumbled (7)

grumble (3)
constant grumbling (1) +9442
grumbling (1)
grumbling (1) +9442
howl (1)
made grumble (1)
untranslated (4)

4297 לוּשׁ *lûš* (6)
knead (2)
kneaded (2)
kneading (1)
untranslated (1)

4298 לוֹשׁ *lāwiš* (1)
untranslated (1)

4299 לָזוּת *lāzûṯ* (1)
corrupt talk (1)

4300 לַח *lah* (6)
fresh (2)
green (2)
fresh-cut (1)
grapes or raisins (1) +2256+3313+6694

4301 לֵחַ *lēah* (1)
strength (1)

4302 1לְחוּם *lᵉhûm1* (1)
entrails (1)

4303 2לְחוּם *lᵉhûm2* (1)
blows (1)

4304 לֻחֹת *luhôṯ* (1)
untranslated (1)

4305 1לְחִי *lᵉhiy1* (20)
cheeks (4)
jawbone (4)
cheek (3)
jaws (3)
face (2)
jaw (2)
jowls (1)
neck (1)

4306 2לְחִי *lᵉhiy2* (4)
Lchi (4)

4307 לֶחִי רֹאִי *lahay rō'iy*
Variant; not used

4308 לָחַךְ *lāhak* (6)
lick (3)
lick up (1)
licked up (1)
licks up (1)

4309 1לְחַם *lāham1* (171)
fight (70)
fought (30)
attacked (15)
fighting (11)
attack (7)
attacking (5)
battle (5)
make war (5)
fights (4)
war (3)
made war (2)
at war (1)
engage in battle (1)
fight (1) +4309
fight battle (1)
military (1)
military exploits (1)
overpower (1)
overpower (1) +6584
pressed attack (1)
stormed (1)
waging war (1)
wars (1)
untranslated (1)

4310 2לְחַם *lāham2* (6)
eat (4)

consuming (1)
dine (1)

4311 לָחֶם *lāhem* (1)
war (1)

4312 לֶחֶם *lehem* (299)
food (124)
bread (116)
loaves of bread (6)
somethingˢ (3)
bread (2) +3971
meal (2)
provisions (2)
something to eat (2) +7326
baked (1)
cake (1) +2705
crops (1)
daily bread (1) +2976
eat (1)
feast (1)
feed (1)
food (1) +7326
fruit (1)
loaf (1) +3971
loaves (1)
meal (1) +430
nothing (1) +4202
overfed (1) +8430
provided for (1) +430+2118+2256+4200
stay for a meal (1) +430
swallow up (1)
untranslated (25)

4313 לַחְמִי *lahmiy* (1)
Lahmi (1)

4314 לַחְמָס *lahmās* (1)
Lahmas (1)

4315 לָחַץ *lāhas* (19)
oppressed (6)
oppress (4)
oppressors (2)
confined (1)
crushing (1)
hold shut (1)
oppressing (1)
press (1)
pressed close (1)
severely oppressing (1) +4316

4316 לַחַץ *lahas* (12)
affliction (2)
nothing but (2)
oppressed (2)
oppression (2)
severely oppressing (1) +4315
wayˢ (1)
untranslated (2)

4317 לָחַשׁ *lāhaš* (3)
charmer (1)
whisper (1)
whispering among themselves (1)

4318 לַחַשׁ *lahaš* (5)
charmed (2)
barely whisper a prayer (1) +7440
charms (1)
enchanter (1)

4319 לָט *lāt* (7)
secret arts (3)
quietly (2) +928+2021
privately (1) +928+2021
unnoticed (1) +928+2021

4320 לֹט *lōt* (2)
myrrh (2)

4321 לְטָאָה *lᵉtā'āh* (1)
wall lizard (1)

4322 לְטוּשִׁים *lᵉtûšiym* (1)
Letushites (1)

4323 לָטַשׁ *lātaš* (5)

sharpened (2)
fastens piercing (1)
forged (1)
sharpen (1)

4324 לֹיָה *lōyāh* (3)
wreaths (3)

4325 לַיִל *layil* (8)
night (6)
untranslated (2)

4326 לַיְלָה *laylāh* (227)
night (189)
nights (14)
tonight (10) +2021
midnight (2) +2940
overnight (2) +1201
all night long (1) +928+2021
all-night (1) +2021+3972
dark (1)
last night (1) +2021
midnight (1) +2021+2942
nightfall (1)
nightfall (1) +2021
nighttime (1)
nocturnal (1)
untranslated (1)

4327 לִילִית *liyliyṯ* (1)
night creatures (1)

4328 לִין *liyn* (69)
spend the night (17)
spent the night (6)
stay (6)
remain (4)
spent (3)
dwell (2)
spend (2)
stay at night (2)
at home (1)
camp (1)
camped (1)
endure (1)
for the night (1)
harbor (1) +928+7931
hold back overnight (1) +1332+6330
kept (1)
leave overnight (1)
left (1)
lie all night (1)
remains (1)
resides (1)
rest (1)
resting (1)
rests (1)
roost (1)
sleeping (1)
spend days (1)
spend nights (1)
spent the nights (1)
stay night (1)
stay tonight (1)
stayed night (1) +2256+3782
stays at night (1)
stays only a night (1) +5742
stopped for the night (1)

4329 לִיץ *liys* (6)
mock (2)
mocks (2)
mocker (1)
mocking (1)

4330 1לַיִשׁ *layiš1* (3)
lion (2)
lionesses (1)

4331 2לַיִשׁ *layiš2* (2)
Laish (2)

4332 3לַיִשׁ *layiš3* (4)
Laish (4)

4333 לַיְשָׁה *layšāh* (1)
Laishah (1)

4334 לָכַד *lāka_d* (121)
captured (33)
took (17)
capture (9)
be captured (6)
was taken (6)
be caught (4)
take (4)
takes (4)
caught (3)
taken (3)
was chosen (3)
captures (2)
ensnare (2)
was captured (2)
are caught (1)
are trapped (1)
assumed (1)
be taken captive (1)
catch (1)
catch (1) +4334
catches (1)
cling together (1)
conquered (1)
ensnared (1)
entangle (1)
frozen (1)
held fast (1)
is captured (1)
is caught (1)
seize (1)
taking possession (1)
took prisoner (1)
trapped (1)
was caught (1)
were caught (1)
were taken (1)

4335 לֶכֶד *leke_d* (1)
snared (1)

4336 לֵכָה *lēkāh* (1)
Lecah (1)

4337 לָכִישׁ *lākiyš* (24)
Lachish (24)

4338 לָכֵן *lāk_ēn*
Variant; not used

4339 לֻלָאוֹת *lulā'ô_t* (13)
loops (11)
untranslated (2)

4340 לָמַד *lāma_d* (87)
teach (30)
learn (15)
taught (14)
learned (3)
teaches (3)
trains (3)
teaching (2)
train (2)
trained (2)
accept (1)
adopted (1)
cultivated (1)
experienced (1)
imparted (1)
instructors (1)
learn well (1) +4340
teachers (1)
unruly (1) +4202
were trained (1)
untranslated (2)

4341 לִמֻּד *limmu_d* (6)
accustomed to (2)
disciples (1)
instructed (1)
one taught (1)
taught (1)

4342 לָמָּה *lāmmāh*
Variant; not used

4343 לָמוֹ *lāmô*
Variant; not used

4344 לָמוֹ *l'mô* (4)
for (1)
in (1)
over (1)
untranslated (1)

4345 לְמוּאֵל *l'mû'ēl* (2)
Lemuel (2)

4346 לְמוֹאֵל *l'mô'l*
Variant; not used

4347 לֶמֶךְ *lemek* (11)
Lamech (11)

4348 לְמַעַן *l'ma'an*
Variant; not used

4349 לֵן *lēn*
Variant; not used

4350 לֹעַ *lōa'* (1)
throat (1)

4351 לָעַב *lā'ab* (1)
mocked (1)

4352 לָעַג *lā'ag* (21)
mock (6)
mocks (6)
ridiculed (3)
maliciously mocked (1) +4352
mocked (1)
scoff (1)
scoffs (1)
strange (1)

4353 לַעַג *la'ag* (7)
scorn (3)
derision (1)
foreign (1)
ridicule (1)
ridiculed (1)

4354 לָעֵג *lā'ēg*
Variant; not used

4355 לַעְדָּה *la'dāh* (1)
Laadah (1)

4356 לַעְדָּן *la'dān* (7)
Ladan (7)

4357 לָעֵז *lā'ez* (1)
foreign tongue (1)

4358 לָעַט *lā'at* (1)
let have (1)

4359 לָעִיר *lā'iyr*
Variant; not used

4360 לַעֲנָה *la'⁽nāh* (8)
bitter (3)
gall (3)
bitterness (2)

4361 לַעֲנוֹת *l'annô_t* (1)
leannoth (1)

4362 לָעַע1 *lā'a'l* (2)
impetuous (1)
rashly (1)

4363 לָעַע2 *lā'a'2* (1)
drink (1)

4364 לְעָפְרָה *l'aprāh*
Variant; not used

4365 לַפִּיד *lappiy_d* (13)
torches (5)
torch (4)
firebrands (1)
flaming torches (1)
lightning (1)
untranslated (1)

4366 לַפִּידוֹת *lappiydô_t* (1)
Lappidoth (1)

4367 לִפְנֵי *lipnēy*
Variant; not used

4368 לִפְנַי *lipnay*
Variant; not used

4369 לָפַת *lāpa_t* (3)
reached toward (1)
turn aside (1)
turned (1)

4370 לֵץ *lēs* (16)
mocker (11)
mockers (4)
proud mockers (1)

4371 לָצוֹן *lāsôn* (3)
mockers (1) +408
mockery (1)
scoffers (1) +408

4372 לָצַץ *lāsas* (1)
mockers (1)

4373 לַקּוּם *laqqûm* (1)
Lakkum (1)

4374 לָקַח *lāqah* (966)
take (238)
took (238)
get (46)
taken (32)
accept (23)
bring (20)
brought (20)
married (16)
taking (14)
take away (12)
receive (11)
received (11)
married (10) +851
took away (10)
marry (8)
accepted (7)
choose (7)
accepts (6)
carried off (6)
got (6)
selected (6)
takes (6)
capture (5)
captured (5)
marries (5)
bring back (4)
married (4) +851+4200
marry (4) +851
marry (4) +851+4200
put (4)
seize (4)
seized (4)
taken away (4)
was taken (4)
be taken (3)
been captured (3)
carried (3)
carried away (3)
collected (3)
respond to (3)
select (3)
took hold (3)
use (3)
am taken (2)
carry away (2)
collect (2)
found (2)
is taken (2)
keep (2)
kill (2) +5883
led away (2)
picked up (2)
purchased (2) +928+4697
send for (2) +2256+8938
takes away (2)
took as prisoners (2)
was taken away (2)

were taken (2)
accepting (1)
acquiring (1)
adopted (1) +1426+4200
appoint (1)
are gathered (1)
are taken (1)
arrest (1)
be brought (1)
be taken away (1)
become wife (1) +851+4200
been taken (1)
been taken away (1)
being led away (1)
blow away (1)
bring (1) +2256+3655
buy (1)
buys (1)
captivate (1)
carried (1) +928+3338
catch (1)
caught (1)
choose as wives (1)
chose (1)
come back (1)
did[s] (1)
did so[s] (1)
did so[s] (1) +2256+2932+8008
disgraced (1) +1423
drew (1)
find (1)
flashed back and forth (1) +928+9348
flashing (1)
force to give (1)
get back (1)
gets (1)
given (1)
grabbed (1)
had brought (1)
had brought (1) +2256+8938
had removed (1) +2256+8938
have (1)
have come (1)
invites (1)
kept (1)
learn (1)
learned (1)
loaded (1)
made (1) +928
make (1)
married (1) +851+2257+4200+4200
marries (1) +1249+2256
need (1)
open to (1)
pledged to marry (1)
prefer (1)
prepare (1)
recaptured (1) +2256+8740
receives (1)
removed (1)
responded to (1)
retake (1)
sampled (1)
sent for (1)
sent for (1) +2256+8938
share (1)
snatched (1)
strip of (1)
stripped (1)
suffer (1)
summon (1) +2256+8938
take up (1)
takes life (1)
taking hold (1)
took down (1)
took in marriage (1) +851+4200
took out (1)
took over (1)
took prisoner (1)
use as (1)
wag (1)

want (1)
was captured (1)
wins (1)
untranslated (22)

4375 לֶקַח *leqaḥ* (9)
instruction (3)
learning (3)
beliefs (1)
persuasive words (1)
teaching (1)

4376 לִקְחִי *liqḥiy* (1)
Likhi (1)

4377 לָקַט *lāqaṭ* (37)
gather (11)
gathered (8)
glean (6)
pick up (3)
be gathered up (1)
collected (1)
gather up (1)
gathering (1)
gathers (1)
gleaned (1)
gleans (1)
picked up (1)
picked up scraps (1)

4378 לֶקֶט *leqeṭ* (2)
gleanings (2)

4379 לָקַק *lāqaq* (7)
lapped (2)
licked up (2)
lap (1)
lick up (1)
untranslated (1)

4380 לָקַשׁ *lāqaš* (1)
glean (1)

4381 לֶקֶשׁ *leqeš* (2)
second crop (1)
untranslated (1)

4382 לָשָׁד *lāšād* (2)
something made (1)
strength (1)

4383 לָשׁוֹן *lāšôn* (117)
tongue (62)
tongues (23)
language (11)
bay (3)
languages (3)
wedge (2)
words (2)
bark (1) +3076
charmer (1) +1251
deceit (1) +9567
fangs (1)
gulf (1)
lips (1)
object of malicious talk (1)
          +6584+6590+8557
on the tip of tongue (1) +928+2674
slanderers (1) +408
speech (1)
uttered a word (1) +906+3076

4384 לִשְׁכָּה *liškāh* (47)
rooms (21)
room (13)
storerooms (5)
side rooms (2)
chambers (1)
hall (1)
priests' rooms (1) +7731
that[s] (1)
untranslated (2)

4385 לֶשֶׁם1 *lešem1* (2)
jacinth (2)

4386 לֶשֶׁם2 *lešem2* (2)
Leshem (2)

4387 לָשָׁן *lāšan* (3)
slander (1)
slanders (1)
untranslated (1)

4388 לֶשַׁע *lešaʻ* (1)
Lasha (1)

4389 לַשָּׁרוֹן *laššārôn* (1)
Lasharon (1)

4390 לֶתֶךְ *lētek* (1)
lethek (1)

4391 מ *m*
Variant; not used

4392 ם ָ- *ām* (3952)
them (1550)
their (1012)
they (251)
the[s] (124)
their own (43)
it (31)
whose (15)
a[s] (14)
these (12)
those (12)
you (11)
its (10)
which[s] (10)
the people[s] (9)
themselves (9) +5883
his (7)
Israel[s] (6)
men[s] (6)
themselves (6)
who (6)
the Israelites[s] (5)
them (5) +5883
by themselves (4) +963+4200
he (4)
one by one (4) +1653+4200
the creatures[s] (4)
they (4) +5883
this (4)
us (4)
all[s] (3)
each (3)
her (3)
him (3)
our (3)
she (3)
that[s] (3)
the cherubim[s] (3)
the Levites[s] (3)
the men[s] (3)
the rest[s] (3)
your (3)
courts[s] (2)
gods[s] (2)
Judah[s] (2)
my people[s] (2)
our fathers[s] (2)
that (2)
the enemies[s] (2)
the shields[s] (2)
the wicked[s] (2)
these articles[s] (2)
whom (2)
almost to a man (1) +6330+9462
an[s] (1)
anyone (1)
Babylon[s] (1)
battle[s] (1)
did[s] (1) +906+3877+4213
each[s] (1)
Egypt[s] (1)
else's (1)
extremes[s] (1)
him (1)
his enemies[s] (1)
his offerings[s] (1)

his own (1)
his sons[s] (1)
its people[s] (1)
keep themselves alive (1) +906+5883+8740
man's[s] (1)
man[s] (1)
men (1)
Moses and Aaron[s] (1)
one's own (1)
priests[s] (1)
prophets[s] (1)
that person[s] (1)
that[s] (1) +2388
the Arameans[s] (1)
the army[s] (1)
the Canaanites[s] (1)
the case[s] (1)
the censers[s] (1)
the days[s] (1)
the enemies[s] (1)
the flock[s] (1) +5883
the forces[s] (1)
the Gibeonites[s] (1)
the goats[s] (1)
the gods[s] (1)
the hair[s] (1)
the Horites[s] (1)
the kings[s] (1)
the Midianite[s] (1)
the Midianites[s] (1)
the nations[s] (1)
the nobles and officials[s] (1)
the others[s] (1)
the people (1)
the priests[s] (1)
the procession[s] (1)
the ropes[s] (1)
the servants[s] (1)
the stones[s] (1)
the things[s] (1)
the water[s] (1)
their enemies[s] (1)
their gods[s] (1)
their leaders[s] (1)
their sons[s] (1)
their temples[s] (1)
theirs (1)
them (1) +74+928+2021
them (1) +1414
them (1) +2652
them (1) +4213
themselves (1) +4213
themselves (1) +4222
there[s] (1) +928+9348
these offerings[s] (1)
they (1) +9307
this is the way (1) +928
those nations[s] (1)
your brothers[s] (1)
your lovers[s] (1)
your sons[s] (1)
untranslated (637)

4393 מַאֲבוּס *ma'ăbûs* (1)
granaries (1)

4394 מְאֹד *m''ōd* (296)
very (71)
greatly (22)
great (18)
so (7)
large (6)
most (6)
very (6) +6330
great quantity (4) +2221
terrified (4) +3707
very much (4)
beyond measure (3) +6330
how (3)
all (2)
burned (2) +3013
closely (2)

deep (2)
desperate (2)
exceedingly (2) +928+4394
exceedingly (2) +4394
fully (2)
great (2) +1524
greatly (2) +928+4394
large (2) +8041
much (2)
overweening (2)
strength (2)
thoroughly (2)
utterly (2)
utterly (2) +6330
very (2) +928+4394
worst (2) +3878
abundance (1) +2221
abundantly (1)
accumulate large amounts (1) +8049
aged (1) +2416
almost (1)
at a distance (1) +8158
badly (1)
behaved in the vilest manner (1) +9493
beyond number (1) +8041
bitterly (1)
bitterly (1) +3878
boundless (1) +8146
come quickly (1) +4554
coming quickly (1) +4554
completely (1)
critically (1)
crushing (1) +2703
destroyed (1) +1524+4804+5782
devastated (1) +1524+4804+5782
devout (1)
dismayed (1) +987
dreadful (1) +3707
enough (1)
even far (1) +3856
even more (1)
ever-present (1) +5162
exceedingly (1)
exhausted (1) +6545
far (1)
filled with fear (1) +3707
firmly (1)
full well (1)
furious (1) +678+3013
furious (1) +3013
furious (1) +7911
fury (1) +3013
great (1) +1540
great (1) +2221
great numbers (1) +2221
great numbers (1) +3878
great quantities (1) +4200+8044
greatly (1) +2221
greatly (1) +4394
grew louder and louder (1)
        +2143+2256+2618
grew worse and worse (1)
        +2118+2617+2716
heavy (1) +3877
highly (1)
highly regarded (1) +1524
huge (1)
huge (1) +1524+4200+6330
in anguish (1) +987
intense (1) +1524
kept bringing pressure (1) +7210
large (1) +1524
large (1) +3878
large amount (1) +2221
least (1)
long way (1) +8158
lost self-confidence (1) +928+5877+6524
loud (1) +1524+6330
make as great as you like (1) +8049
many (1) +8041
more (1)

more than (1)
much (1) +6330
quickly (1)
reward handsomely (1) +3877+3877
severe (1) +3878
severe (1) +8041
so (1) +3954
so (1) +4394
so highly (1)
so much (1)
stand firm (1) +586
stood in awe (1) +3707
strongly (1)
tempest rages (1) +8548
terrible (1) +3878
terrified (1) +3707+4394
terror filled (1) +3006
too (1)
total (1) +1524
toward evening (1) +3718
trembled violently (1)
        +1524+3006+3010+6330
utter (1)
vast (1) +1524
vast (1) +1524+4394
very (1) +2221
very (1) +6786
violently (1)
well known (1) +3700
without restraint (1) +6330
writhe in agony (1) +2655
untranslated (3)

4395 מֵאָה 1 *mē'āh1* (581)
hundred (233)
hundreds (18)
250 (10) +2256+2822
100 (8)
4,500 (8) +547+752+2256+2822
units of a hundred (6)
120 (5) +2256+6929
200 (5)
500 (5) +2822
1,254 (4) +547+752+2256+2822
128 (4) +2256+6929+9046
127 (3) +2256+2256+6929+8679
40,500 (3) +547+752+2256+2822
430 (3) +752+2256+8993
53,400 (3)
        +547+752+2256+2256+2822+8993
603,550 (3)   +547+547+2256+2256+2256
        +2822+2822+4395+8993+9252
eleven hundred (3) +547+2256
1,247 (2) +547+752+2256+8679
1,775 (2)
        +547+2256+2256+2256+2822+8679+8679
112 (2) +2256+6925+9109
123 (2) +2256+6929+8993
130 (2) +2256+8993
137 (2) +2256+2256+8679+8993
150 (2) +2256+2822
200,000 (2) +547
220 (2) +2256+6929
223 (2) +2256+6929+8993
30,500 (2) +547+2256+2822+8993
300 (2) +8993
32,200 (2) +547+2256+2256+8993+9109
320 (2) +2256+6929+8993
345 (2) +752+2256+2822+8993
35,400 (2)
        +547+752+2256+2256+2822+8993
372 (2) +2256+8679+8993+9109
390 (2) +2256+8993+9596
392 (2) +2256+8993+9109+9596
4,600 (2) +547+752+2256+9252
403 (2) +752+2256+8993
41,500 (2) +285+547+752+2256+2256+2822
435 (2) +752+2256+2822+8993
45,650 (2)   +547+752+2256+2256
        +2256+2822+2822+9252
46,500 (2)
        +547+752+2256+2256+2822+9252

54,400 (2) +547+752+752+2256+2256+2822
57,400 (2)
        +547+752+2256+2256+2822+8679
59,300 (2)
        +547+2256+2256+2822+8993+9596
6,720 (2) +547+2256+6929+8679+9252
62,700 (2)
        +547+2256+2256+8679+9109+9252
621 (2) +285+2256+6929+9252
652 (2) +2256+2822+9109+9252
666 (2) +2256+9252+9252+9252
7,337 (2)
        +547+2256+8679+8679+8993+8993
74,600 (2)
        +547+752+2256+2256+8679+9252
760 (2) +2256+8679+9252
800 (2) +9046
973 (2) +2256+8679+8993+9596
about six hundred feet (2) +564+752
fourteen hundred (2) +547+752+2256
hundredth (2)
seventeen hundred (2) +547+2256+8679
units of hundreds (2)
1,222 (1) +547+2256+6929+9109
1,290 (1) +547+2256+9596
1,335 (1) +547+2256+2822+8993+8993
1,365 (1)
   +547+2256+2256+2256+2822+8993+9252
1,760 (1) +547+2256+2256+8679+9252
105 (1) +2256+2822
108,100 (1)
      +547+547+2256+2256+4395+9046
110 (1) +2256+6927
112 (1) +6925+9109
119 (1) +2256+6926+9596
120,000 (1) +547+2256+6929
122 (1) +2256+2256+6929+9109
122 (1) +2256+6929+9109
133 (1) +2256+2256+8993+8993
138 (1) +2256+8993+9046
139 (1) +2256+8993+9596
14,700 (1) +547+752+2256+6925+8679
148 (1) +752+2256+9046
151,450 (1) +285+547+547+752+2256+2256
        +2256+2256+2822+2822+4395
153,600 (1)   +547+547+2256+2256
        +2256+2822+4395+8993+9252
156 (1) +2256+2822+9252
157,600 (1)   +547+547+2256+2256
        +2256+2822+4395+8679+9252
16,750 (1)
      +547+2256+2822+6925+8679+9252
160 (1) +2256+9252
162 (1) +2256+2256+9109+9252
17,200 (1) +547+2256+6925+8679
172 (1) +2256+8679+9109
180 (1) +2256+9046
180,000 (1) +547+2256+9046
182 (1) +2256+2256+9046+9109
186,400 (1)   +547+547+547+752+2256
        +2256+2256+4395+9046+9252
187 (1) +2256+2256+8679+9046
188 (1) +2256+9046+9046
2,172 (1) +547+2256+2256+8679+9109
2,172 (1) +547+2256+8679+9109
2,200 (1) +547+2256
2,300 (1) +547+2256+8993
2,322 (1) +547+2256+6929+8993+9109
2,400 (1) +547+752+2256
2,600 (1) +547+2256+9252
2,630 (1) +547+2256+2256+8993+9252
2,750 (1) +547+2256+2822+8679
2,812 (1) +547+2256+6925+9046+9109
2,818 (1) +547+2256+6925+9046+9046
20,200 (1) +547+2256+6929
20,800 (1) +547+2256+6929+9046
205 (1) +2256+2822
207 (1) +2256+8679
209 (1) +2256+9596
212 (1) +2256+6925+9109
218 (1) +2256+6925+9046

22,200 (1) +547+2256+2256+6929+9109
22,273 (1)   +547+2256+2256+2256
        +6929+8679+8993+9109
22,600 (1)
      +547+2256+2256+6929+9109+9252
232 (1) +2256+8993+9109
242 (1) +752+2256+9109
245 (1) +752+2256+2256+2822
245 (1) +752+2256+2822
25,100 (1) +547+2256+2256+2822+6929
273 (1) +2256+2256+8679+8993
28,600 (1)
      +547+2256+2256+6929+9046+9252
280,000 (1) +547+2256+9046
284 (1) +752+2256+9046
288 (1) +2256+9046+9046
3,200 (1) +547+2256+8993
3,600 (1) +547+2256+8993+9252
3,630 (1)
      +547+2256+2256+8993+8993+9252
3,700 (1) +547+2256+8679+8993
3,930 (1) +547+2256+8993+8993+9596
300,000 (1) +547+8993
307,500 (1)   +547+547+2256+2256
        +2822+4395+8679+8993
318 (1) +2256+6925+8993+9046
32,500 (1)
      +547+2256+2256+2822+8993+9109
323 (1) +2256+6929+8993+8993
324 (1) +752+2256+6929+8993
328 (1) +2256+6929+8993+9046
337,500 (1)   +547+547+547+2256+2256
        +2256+2822+4395+8679+8993+8993
337,500 (1)   +547+547+547+2256+2256
        +2822+4395+8679+8993+8993
350 (1) +2256+2822+8993
365 (1) +2256+2256+2822+8993+9252
410 (1) +752+2256+6927
42,360 (1)
      +547+752+2256+8052+8993+9252
42,360 (1) +547+752+8052+8993+9252
420 (1) +752+2256+6929
43,730 (1)   +547+752+2256+2256
        +2256+8679+8993+8993
44,760 (1)   +547+752+752+2256
        +2256+8679+9252
45,400 (1) +547+752+752+2256+2256+2822
45,600 (1)
      +547+752+2256+2256+2822+9252
450 feet (1) +564+8993
454 (1) +752+752+2256+2822
468 (1) +752+2256+9046+9252
5,400 (1) +547+752+2256+2822
52,700 (1)
      +547+2256+2256+2822+8679+9109
530 (1) +2256+2822+8993
550 (1) +2256+2822+2822
595 (1) +2256+2256+2822+2822+9596
6,200 (1) +547+2256+9252
6,800 (1) +547+2256+9046+9252
60,500 (1) +547+2256+2822+9252
601,730 (1)   +547+547+2256+2256
        +4395+8679+8993+9252
623 (1) +2256+6929+8993+9252
628 (1) +2256+6929+9046+9252
64,300 (1)
      +547+752+2256+2256+8993+9252
64,400 (1) +547+752+752+2256+2256+9252
642 (1) +752+2256+2256+9109+9252
642 (1) +752+2256+9109+9252
648 (1) +752+2256+9046+9252
650 (1) +2256+2822+9252
655 (1) +2256+2822+2822+9252
666 (1) +2256+2256+9252+9252+9252
667 (1) +2256+8679+9252+9252
675 (1) +2256+2822+8679+9252
675,000 (1)
 +547+547+547+2256+2256+2822+8679+9252
690 (1) +2256+9252+9596
7,100 (1) +547+2256+8679
7,500 (1) +547+2256+2822+8679

721 (1) +285+2256+2256+6929+8679
725 (1) +2256+2822+6929+8679
730 (1) +2256+8679+8993
736 (1) +2256+8679+8993+9252
743 (1) +752+2256+2256+8679+8993
743 (1) +752+2256+8679+8993
745 (1) +752+2256+2822+8679
76,500 (1)
      +547+2256+2256+2822+8679+9252
775 (1) +2256+2822+8679+8679
777 (1) +2256+2256+8679+8679+8679
782 (1) +2256+2256+8679+9046+9109
8,580 (1)
      +547+2256+2256+2822+9046+9046
8,600 (1) +547+2256+9046+9252
807 (1) +2256+8679+9046
815 (1) +2256+2822+6926+9046
822 (1) +2256+6929+9046+9109
830 (1) +2256+8993+9046
832 (1) +2256+8993+9046+9109
840 (1) +752+2256+9046
845 (1) +752+2256+2822+9046
895 (1) +2256+2256+2822+9046+9596
905 (1) +2256+2822+9596
910 (1) +2256+6924+9596
912 (1) +2256+6926+9109+9596
928 (1) +2256+6929+9046+9596
930 (1) +2256+8993+9596
945 (1) +752+2256+2256+2822+9596
950 (1) +2256+2822+9596
956 (1) +2256+2256+2822+9252+9596
962 (1) +2256+2256+9109+9252+9596
969 (1) +2256+2256+9252+9596+9596
hundredfold (1) +9134
thirty-six hundred (1)
        +547+2256+8993+9252
thirty-three hundred (1)
        +547+2256+8993+8993
twelve hundred (1) +547+2256
twenty-seven hundred (1) +547+2256+8679
twenty-six hundred (1) +547+2256+9252
two hundred (1)
untranslated (7)

4396   מֵאָה 2*mē'āh2* (2)
hundred (2)

4397   מַאֲוַיִּים *ma'ᵃwiyyiym* (1)
desires (1)

4398   מְאוּם *mᵉ'ûm* (1)
untranslated (1)

4399   מְאוּמָה *mᵉ'ûmāh* (32)
anything (10)
nothing (7) +4202
anything (2) +3972
nothing (2) +401
there is nothing (2) +401
all (1)
any kind (1)
bare (1) +401+928
fault (1)
little value (1)
little value (1) +4202
none (1) +4202
something (1)
untranslated (1)

4400   מָאוֹס *mā'ôs* (1)
refuse (1)

4401   מָאוֹר *mā'ôr* (19)
light (13)
lights (4)
cheerful (1)
moon (1)

4402   מְאוּרָה *mᵉ'ûrāh* (1)
nest (1)

4403   מֵאָז *mē'āz*
Variant; not used

4404   מֹאזְנַיִם *mō'znayim* (15)
scales (12)

balance (2)
set of scales (1) +5486

4405 מֵאיוֹת *mᵉʾāyôṯ*
Variant; not used

4406 מֵאַיִן *mēʾayin*
Variant; not used

4407 מַאֲכָל *maʾᵃḵāl* (30)
food (21)
fruit (4)
baked goods (1) +685+5126
devoured (1)
meal (1)
something to eat (1)
supplies (1)

4408 מַאֲכֶלֶת *maʾᵃḵeleṯ* (4)
knife (3)
knives (1)

4409 מַאֲכֹלֶת *maʾᵃḵōleṯ* (2)
fuel (2)

4410 מַאֲמָץ *maʾᵃmāṣ* (1)
efforts (1)

4411 מַאֲמָר *maʾᵃmār* (3)
command (1)
decree (1)
instructions (1)

4412 מָאֵן *māʾan* (46)
refused (22)
refuse (15)
refuses (2)
refusing (2)
absolutely refuses (1) +4412
incurable (1) +8324
rejected (1)
resist (1)

4413 מָאֵן *māʾēn*
Variant; not used

4414 מֵאֵן *mēʾēn*
Variant; not used

4415 מָאַס1 *māʾas1* (74)
rejected (34)
reject (12)
despise (8)
despised (3)
despises (3)
be rejected (1)
denied (1)
disdained (1)
refuse (1)
rejected completely (1) +4415
rejects (1)
ridiculed (1)
scorn (1)
spurn (1)
spurned (1)
utterly rejected (1) +4415
vile (1)

4416 מָאַס2 *māʾas2* (2)
festering (1)
vanish (1)

4417 מֵאֱסֵף *mᵉʾassēp*
Variant; not used

4418 מַאֲפֶה *maʾᵃpeh* (1)
baked (1)

4419 מַאֲפֵל *maʾᵃpēl* (1)
darkness (1)

4420 מַאְפֵלְיָה *maʾpēlyāh* (1)
great darkness (1)

4421 מָאַר *māʾar* (4)
destructive (3)
painful (1)

4422 מַאֲרָב *maʾᵃrāḇ* (5)
ambush (1)

hiding place (1)
place of ambush (1)
troops (1)
wait (1)

4423 מְאֵרָה *mᵉʾērāh* (5)
curse (2)
curses (2)
curse (1) +826

4424 מֵאֲשֵׁר *mēʾᵃšer*
Variant; not used

4425 מֵאֵת *mēʾēṯ*
Variant; not used

4426 מִבְדָּלוֹת *miḇdālôṯ* (1)
set aside (1)

4427 מָבוֹא *māḇôʾ* (24)
entrance (7)
enter (2)
place where sets (2)
setting (2)
west (2) +9087
do⁵ (1)
entrances (1) +7339
entryway (1)
gateway (1)
go down (1)
how to get into (1)
on the west (1) +2021+9087
outskirts (1)
untranslated (1)

4428 מְבוּכָה *mᵉḇûḵāh* (2)
confusion (1)
terror (1)

4429 מַבּוּל *mabbûl* (14)
flood (11)
floodwaters (3) +4784

4430 מְבוֹנִים *mᵉḇôniym*
Variant; not used

4431 מְבוּסָה *mᵉḇûsāh* (3)
aggressive (2)
trampling (1)

4432 מַבּוּעַ *mabbûaʿ* (3)
bubbling springs (1) +4784
spring (1)
springs (1)

4433 מְבוּקָה *mᵉḇûqāh* (1)
plundered (1)

4434 מְבוּשִׁים *mᵉḇûšiym* (1)
private parts (1)

4435 מִבְחוֹר *miḇḥôr* (2)
choicest (1)
major (1)

4436 מִבְחָר1 *miḇḥār1* (12)
choicest (4)
best (3)
choice possessions (1)
elite (1)
fine (1)
finest (1)
pick (1)

4437 מִבְחָר2 *miḇḥār2* (1)
Mibhar (1)

4438 מַבָּט *mabbāṭ* (3)
hope (1)
relied on (1)
trusted in (1)

4439 מִבְטָא *miḇṭāʾ* (2)
rash promise (2)

4440 מִבְטָח *miḇṭāḥ* (15)
trust (4)
confidence (2)
secure (2)
security (2)

hope (1)
reliance (1)
source of confidence (1)
trusted (1)
what relies on (1)

4441 מַבָּךְ *mabbāḵ* (1)
sources (1)

4442 מַבֵּל *mabbēl* (1)
fire (1)

4443 מַבְלִיגִית *maḇliygiyṯ* (1)
comforter (1)

4444 מְבֻלָּקָה *mᵉḇulāqāh*
Variant; not used

4445 מִבְנֶה *miḇneh* (1)
buildings (1)

4446 מְבֻנַּי *mᵉḇunnay* (1)
Mebunnai (1)

4447 מַבְנִית *maḇniyṯ*
Variant; not used

4448 מִבְצָר1 *miḇṣār1* (36)
fortified (21)
strongholds (5)
fortresses (3)
fortified cities (2)
defenses (1)
fortified city (1)
fortified places (1)
fortress (1)
mightiest fortresses (1) +5057

4449 מִבְצָר2 *miḇṣār2* (2)
Mibzar (2)

4450 מִבְצָר3 *miḇṣār3* (1)
ore (1)

4451 מִבְרָח *miḇrāḥ* (2)
fleeing (1)
untranslated (1)

4452 מִבְשָׂם *miḇśām* (3)
Mibsam (3)

4453 מְבַשְּׁלוֹת *mᵉḇaššᵉlôṯ* (1)
places for fire (1)

4454 מַג *māg* (2)
official (2)

4455 מַגְבִּישׁ *maḡbiyš* (1)
Magbish (1)

4456 מִגְבָּלוֹת *miḡbālôṯ* (1)
braided (1)

4457 מִגְבָּעָה *miḡbāʿāh* (4)
headbands (3)
headbands (1) +6996

4458 מֶגֶד *meḡeḏ* (12)
best (2)
choice (2)
valuable gifts (2)
articles of value (1)
costly gifts (1)
delicacy (1)
finest (1)
fruitfulness (1)
precious (1)

4459 מְגִדּוֹ *mᵉḡiddô* (11)
Megiddo (11)

4460 מִגְדּוֹל *miḡdôl* (1)
untranslated (1)

4461 מְגִדּוֹן *mᵉḡiddôn* (1)
Megiddo (1)

4462 מַגְדִּיאֵל *maḡdiyʾēl* (2)
Magdiel (2)

4463 מִגְדָּל1 *miḡdāl1* (48)
tower (28)
towers (13)

watchtower (2)
watchtower (2) +5915
high platform (1)
they[s] (1) +1251+3972+8901
watchtowers (1)

4464 מִגְדָּל2 *migdāl2*
Variant; not used

4465 מִגְדֹּל *migdōl* (6)
Migdol (6)

4466 מִגְדַּל־אֵל *migdal-'ēl* (1)
Migdal El (1)

4467 מִגְדַּל־גָּד *migdal-gad* (1)
Migdal Gad (1)

4468 מִגְדַּל־עֵדֶר *migdal-'ēder* (1)
Migdal Eder (1)

4469 מִגְדָּנוֹת *migdānôt*
Variant; not used

4470 מָגוֹג *māgôg* (4)
Magog (4)

4471 מָגוֹר1 *māgôr1* (8)
terror (7)
terrors (1)

4472 מָגוֹר2 *māgôr2* (11)
pilgrimage (2)
alien (1)
live as an alien (1)
lived (1)
living (1)
lodge (1) +1074
lodging (1)
stayed (1)
staying (1)
where lived (1)

4473 מָגוֹר3 *māgôr3*
Variant; not used

4474 מָגוֹר מִסָּבִיב *māgôr missābiyb* (1)
Magor-Missabib (1)

4475 מְגוֹרָה *megôrāh* (3)
dread (1)
dreads (1)
fears (1)

4476 מְגוּרָה *megûrāh* (1)
barn (1)

4477 מַגְזֵרָה *magzērāh* (1)
axes (1)

4478 מַגָּל *maggāl* (2)
sickle (2)

4479 מְגִלָּה *megillāh* (21)
scroll (17)
scroll (4) +6219

4480 מְגַמָּה *megammāh* (1)
hordes (1)

4481 מָגַן *māgan* (3)
delivered (1)
hand over (1)
present (1)

4482 מָגֵן1 *māgēn1* (63)
shield (34)
shields (17)
small shields (6)
armed (2)
kings (1)
large[s] [shields] (1)
rulers (1)
shields small (1)

4483 מָגֵן2 *māgēn2*
Variant; not used

4484 מָגֵן *megen*
Variant; not used

4485 מְגִנָּה *meginnāh* (1)
veil (1)

4486 מִגְעֶרֶת *mig'eret* (1)
rebuke (1)

4487 מַגֵּפָה *maggēpāh* (26)
plague (19)
blow (2)
casualties (1)
losses (1)
plagues (1)
slaughter (1)
untranslated (1)

4488 מַגְפִּיעָשׁ *magpiy'āš* (1)
Magpiash (1)

4489 מָגַר *māgar* (2)
cast (1)
thrown (1)

4490 מְגֵרָה *megērāh* (4)
saws (2)
axes (1)
saw (1)

4491 מִגְרוֹן *migrôn* (2)
Migron (2)

4492 מִגְרָעוֹת *migrā'ôt* (1)
offset ledges (1)

4493 מְגְרָפָה *megrāpāh* (1)
clods (1)

4494 מִגְרָשׁ *migrāš* (119)
pasturelands (41)
pastureland (5)
farm (1)
open land (1)
pastureland (1) +8441
shorelands (1)
untranslated (69)

4495 מִגְרָשׁוֹת *migrešôt*
Variant; not used

4496 מַד *mad* (11)
tunic (3)
clothes (2)
clothing (1)
decreed (1)
garment (1)
military tunic (1) +4230
robes (1)
saddle blankets (1)

4497 מִדְבָּר1 *midbār1* (270)
desert (256)
open (3)
wasteland (2)
wilderness (2)
barren wilderness (1)
desert (1) +824
deserts (1)
here[s] (1) +928+2021
open country (1)
there[s] (1)
there[s] (1) +2334

4498 מִדְבָּר2 *midbār2* (1)
mouth (1)

4499 מָדַד *mādad* (51)
measured (30)
measured off (5)
measure off (3)
be measured (2)
measure (2)
consider (1)
drags on (1)
measure distance (1)
measure the full payment (1)
measureless (1) +4202
poured into measures (1)
stretched himself out (1)
untranslated (2)

4500 מִדָּה1 *middāh1* (55)
measurements (12)

size (10)
measuring (9)
section (7)
huge (2)
at regular intervals (1)
district (1)
great (1)
great size (1)
length (1)
long (1)
measure (1)
measured out (1) +928+9419
measures (1)
number (1)
standard (1)
tall (1)
tall (1) +408
untranslated (2)

4501 מִדָּה2 *middāh2* (1)
tax (1)

4502 מַדְהֵבָה *madhēbāh* (1)
fury (1)

4503 מַדּוּ *mādû* (2)
garments (2)

4504 מַדְוֶה2 *madweh2* (2)
diseases (2)

4505 מַדּוּחִים *maddûhiym* (1)
misleading (1)

4506 מָדוֹן1 *mādôn1* (29)
dissension (7)
quarrelsome (6)
disputes (2)
quarrel (2)
strife (2)
conflict (1)
contends (1)
source of contention (1)
untranslated (7)

4507 מָדוֹן2 *mādôn2* (2)
Madon (2)

4508 מַדּוּעַ *maddûa'* (72)
why (70)
what (1)
what's the meaning of (1)

4509 מְדוּרָה *medûrāh* (2)
fire pit (1)
wood (1)

4510 מִדְחֶה *midheh* (1)
ruin (1)

4511 מַדְחֵפָה *madhēpāh* (1)
hunt down (1) +4200+7421

4512 מָדַי *māday* (16)
Media (7)
Medes (5)
Madai (2)
Mede (1)
Median (1)

4513 מָדַי *mādiy* (1)
Mede (1)

4514 מַדַּי *madday*
Variant; not used

4515 מָדִין *mādiyn* (1)
untranslated (1)

4516 מִדִּין *middiyn* (1)
Middin (1)

4517 מִדְיָן1 *midyān1*
Variant; not used

4518 מִדְיָן2 *midyān2* (59)
Midian (32)
Midianites (12)
Midianite (8)
Midian (2) +824

Midian's (2)
them[s] (1)
untranslated (2)

4519 מְדִינָה m'diynāh (51)
provinces (20)
province (10)
provincial (5)
each province (3) +2256+4519
district (1)
every province (1) +2256+4519
parts (1)
regions (1)
various provinces (1) +2256+4519
untranslated (5)

4520 מִדְיָנִי midyāniy (8)
Midianite (5)
Midianites (3)

4521 מְדֹכָה m'dōkāh (1)
mortar (1)

4522 מַדְמֵן madmēn (1)
Madmen (1)

4523 1מַדְמֵנָה madmēnāh1 (1)
manure (1)

4524 2מַדְמֵנָה madmēnāh2 (1)
Madmenah (1)

4525 1מַדְמַנָּה madmannāh1 (1)
Madmannah (1)

4526 2מַדְמַנָּה madmannāh2 (1)
Madmannah (1)

4527 1מְדָן m'dān1 (2)
Medan (2)

4528 2מְדָן m'dān2
Variant; not used

4529 מַדָּע maddā' (6)
knowledge (4)
quick to understand (1) +1067
thoughts (1)

4530 מֹדָע mōdā' (2)
kinsman (1)
relative (1)

4531 מֹדַעַת mōda'at (1)
kinsman (1)

4532 מַדְקָרָה madqērāh (1)
pierce (1)

4533 מַדְרֵגָה madrēgāh (2)
cliffs (1)
mountainside (1)

4534 מִדְרָךְ midrāk (1)
put on (1)

4535 מִדְרָשׁ midrāš (2)
annotations (2)

4536 מְדֻשָׁה m'dušāh (1)
crushed (1)

4537 מָה māh (755)
what (343)
why (165) +4200
how (69)
why (33)
how (16) +928
why (13) +6584
whatever (7)
what (5) +4200
how long (4) +6330
what mean (4)
who (4)
how (3) +3869
O (3)
secret (3) +928
what are you doing (3) +3870+4200
what's the matter (3)
by what means (2) +928
come what may (2) +2118

how many (2) +3869+6330
how often (2) +3869
not (2)
what (2) +928
anything (1)
because (1) +3954+4200
but why (1) +4200
enough (1) +1896+4200
ever so (1)
future (1) +2118+8611
how (1) +686+928
how (1) +2296
how find things (1)
how long (1) +3869
how long must wait (1) +3427+3869
how many (1) +3869
how many more (1) +3869
how much (1)
if (1) +196
life will not be worth living (1) +2644+4200
not[s] (1)
nothing (1) +1172
of what use (1) +2296+4200
of what use (1) +4200
so many (1) +3869
speech (1) +1819
that (1)
this is how (1)
what (1) +6584
what about (1)
what do I care about (1)
                     +2296+3276+4200+4200
what do you mean (1) +4013+4200
what is doing (1) +4200
what is the matter (1) +3871+4200
what is the meaning (1)
what is the meaning (1) +2179
what is the meaning of (1)
what is troubling (1)
what is wrong (1)
what kind (1)
what like (1)
what more (1) +3954
what right have you (1) +3870+4200
what's (1)
whatever (1) +1821
when (1) +6330
where (1)
whether (1)
which (1)
why (1) +561+4027+4200
why (1) +928
why (1) +3610
why (1) +4200+8611
why (1) +9393
untranslated (15)

4538 מָהַהּ māhah (8)
wait (2)
delay (1)
delayed (1)
have time (1) +3523
hesitated (1)
linger (1)
waited (1)

4539 מְהוּמָה m'hûmāh (12)
panic (4)
turmoil (3)
confusion (2)
throwing into confusion (1) +2169
tumult (1)
unrest (1)

4540 מְהוּמָן m'hûmān (1)
Mehuman (1)

4541 מְהֵיטַבְאֵל m'hēytab'ēl (3)
Mehetabel (3)

4542 מָהִיר māhiyr (4)
skilled (1)
skillful (1)
speeds (1)

well versed (1)

4543 מָהַל māhal (1)
diluted (1)

4544 מַהֲלָךְ mah'lāk (5)
journey (1)
passageway (1)
place (1)
visit (1)
untranslated (1)

4545 מַהֲלָל mah'lāl (1)
praise (1)

4546 מַהֲלַלְאֵל mah'lal'ēl (7)
Mahalalel (7)

4547 מַהֲלֻמוֹת mah'lumôt (2)
beating (1)
beatings (1)

4548 מָהֵם māhēm
Variant; not used

4549 מַהֲמֹרוֹת mah'mōrôt (1)
miry pits (1)

4550 מַהְפֵּכָה mahpēkāh (6)
overthrown (3)
overthrew (2)
destruction (1)

4551 מַהְפֶּכֶת mahpeket (4)
stocks (3)
prison (1) +1074+2021

4552 מְחוֹלָה m'hôlāh
Variant; not used

4553 מְחִקְצָעוֹת m'huqsā'ôt
Variant; not used

4554 1מָהַר māhar1 (82)
quickly (26)
hurried (9)
quick (6)
at once (4)
hurry (4)
bring at once (3)
soon (3)
swift (3)
immediately (2)
act at once (1)
all at once (1)
are swept away (1)
come quickly (1)
come quickly (1) +4394
coming quickly (1) +4394
darting (1)
dash (1)
do now (1)
early (1)
fearful (1)
fluent (1) +1819+4200
go at once (1)
hasten (1)
hastily (1)
hasty (1)
impetuous (1)
lost no time (1)
move quickly (1)
rash (1)
run after (1)
sudden (1)

4555 2מָהַר māhar2 (2)
must pay bride-price (1) +4555

4556 1מָהֵר mahēr1
Variant; not used

4557 2מָהֵר mahēr2
Variant; not used

4558 מֹהַר mōhar (3)
bride-price (1)
price for bride (1)
price for the bride (1)

4559 מְהֵרָה *m'hērāh* (20)
quickly (7)
at once (2)
soon (2)
hurriedly (1)
hurry (1)
hurry (1) +2143
immediately (1)
quickly (1) +928
speedily (1)
swiftly (1)
swiftly (1) +6330
very soon (1)

4560 מַהֲרַי *mah'ray* (3)
Maharai (3)

4561 מַהֵר שָׁלָל חָשׁ בַּז
mahĕr šālāl hāš baz (2)
Maher-Shalal-Hash-Baz (2)

4562 מַהֲתַלָּה *mah'tallāh* (1)
illusions (1)

4563 מוֹ *mô*
Variant; not used

4564 ־מוֹ *-mô* (119)
them (47)
their (23)
their (6) +4200
themselves (5)
him (3)
they (3)
us (3)
his (2) +4200
it (2)
the[s] (2)
each other[s] (1)
he (1)
his (1)
his people[s] (1)
its (1)
my enemies[s] (1)
Shem[s] (1)
those (1)
water[s] (1)
where[s] (1) +4200
who (1)
untranslated (12)

4565 מוֹאָב1 *mô'āb1* (2)
Moab (2)

4566 מוֹאָב2 *mô'āb2* (179)
Moab (136)
Moabites (12)
Moab (7) +8441
Moab's (7)
Moabite (7)
Moab (5) +824
its[s] (1)
Moabites (1) +408
Moabites (1) +1201
there[s] (1) +8441
they[s] (1)

4567 מוֹאָבִי *mô'ābiy* (16)
Moabitess (6)
Moabite (5)
Moabites (4)
Moab (1)

4568 מוֹאָל *mô'l*
Variant; not used

4569 מוֹבָא *môbā'* (3)
entrances (1)
movements (1) +2256+4604
untranslated (1)

4570 מוּג *mûg* (17)
melt away (3)
melting in fear (2)
melts (2)
collapses (1)
disheartened (1)
flow (1)
made waste away (1)
melt (1)
melted away (1)
melting away (1) +2143+2256
quake (1)
soften (1)
toss about (1)

4571 מוּד *môd* (1)
shook (1)

4572 מוֹט1 *môt1* (41)
be shaken (8)
fall (5)
be moved (4)
removed (2)
slip (2)
slipping (2)
topple (2)
are shaken (1)
be uprooted (1)
be uprooted (1) +9247
bring down (1)
gives way (1)
immovable (1) +1153
is thoroughly shaken (1) +4572
let fall (1)
quaking (1)
shake (1)
slipped (1)
slips (1)
staggering (1)
unable to support (1) +3338
untranslated (1)

4573 מוֹט2 *môt2* (4)
carrying frame (2)
pole (1)
yoke (1)

4574 מוֹטָה *môtāh* (12)
yoke (8)
bars (2)
crossbars (1)
poles (1)

4575 מוּךְ *mûk* (5)
poor (4)
poor to pay (1)

4576 מוּל1 *mûl1* (31)
circumcised (7)
be circumcised (4)
been circumcised (2)
was circumcised (2)
are[s] (1)
be circumcised (1) +1414+6889
been circumcised (1) +6889
circumcise (1)
circumcise (1) +6889
circumcise yourselves (1)
circumcised (1) +1414+6889
circumcising (1)
did so[s] (1)
had[s] (1)
must be circumcised (1) +4576
undergo circumcision (1) +906+1414+6889
was circumcised (1) +1414+6889
were circumcised (1)
untranslated (1)

4577 מוּל2 *mûl2* (3)
cut off (3)

4578 מוּל3 *mûl3* (35)
at (3) +448
in front of (3) +448
corner (2)
in front of (2) +4946
near (2)
on (2) +448
on (2) +4946
opposite (2)
toward (2)
as far as (1) +448
before (1)
border (1)
faced forward (1) +448+7156
facing (1)
from (1) +4946
in front of (1) +448+7156
in the front line (1) +448+7156
in the front part (1)
in the vicinity of (1)
next to (1) +4946
off (1) +4946
opposite direction (1)
to (1)
to (1) +448

4579 מוֹלָדָה *môlādāh* (4)
Moladah (4)

4580 מוֹלֶדֶת *môledet* (22)
native (4)
relatives (3)
birth (2)
family (2)
family background (2)
people (2)
born (1)
born in the same home (1) +1074
children (1)
homeland (1) +824
natives (1)
untranslated (2)

4581 מוּלָה *mûlāh* (1)
circumcision (1)

4582 מוֹלִיד *môliyd* (1)
Molid (1)

4583 מוּם *mûm* (21)
defect (8)
blemish (3)
flaw (2)
shame (2)
abuse (1)
defects (1)
defiled (1) +1815
injured (1) +5989
injures (1) +5989
physical defect (1)

4584 מוּמְכָן *m'wmukān* (1)
untranslated (1)

4585 מוּסָב *mûsāb*
Variant; not used

4586 מוּסָד *mûsād* (2)
foundation (1)
foundation laid (1)

4587 מוֹסָד *môsād* (8)
foundations (8)

4588 מוּסָדָה *mûsādāh* (2)
foundation (1)
untranslated (1)

4589 מוֹסָדָה *môsādāh* (5)
foundations (3)
foundation (1)
founded (1)

4590 מוּסָךְ *mûsāk* (1)
canopy (1)

4591 מוֹסֵר *môsēr* (5)
chains (2)
noose (1) +6577
shackles (1)

4592 מוּסָר *mûsār* (50)
discipline (21)
instruction (10)
correction (6)
disciplined (2)
lesson (2)
punishment (2)

punished (1)
punishing (1)
rebuke (1)
taught (1)
teaches (1)
warning (1)
warnings (1)

4593 מֹוסֵרָה1 *môsērāh1* (8)
bonds (3)
chains (2)
ropes (1)
shackles (1)
yoke of straps (1)

4594 מֹוסֵרָה2 *môsērāh2* (1)
Moserah (1)

4595 מֹועֵד *mô'ēd* (223)
meeting (147)
appointed feasts (24)
appointed time (15)
time (7)
appointed (2)
festivals (2)
seasons (2)
anniversary (1)
appointed feast (1)
appointed seasons (1)
appointed times (1)
army (1)
arranged (1) +2118
assembly (1)
assigned portion (1)
certain place (1)
council (1)
designated (1)
feast (1)
feasts (1)
festival offerings (1)
in (1) +928
occasion (1)
opportunity (1)
place of meeting (1)
place where met (1)
place where worshiped (1)
ready (1)
set time (1) +3427
time set (1)
times (1)

4596 מֹועָד *mô'ād* (1)
ranks (1)

4597 מֹועָרָה *mû'ādāh* (1)
designated (1)

4598 מֹועַדְיָה *mô'adyāh* (1)
Moadiah's (1)

4599 מֹועָף *mû'āp* (1)
gloom (1)

4600 מֹועֵצָה *mô'ēsāh* (7)
counsel (1)
devices (1)
inclinations (1)
intrigues (1)
plans (1)
schemes (1)
traditions (1)

4601 מֹועָקָה *mû'āqāh* (1)
burdens (1)

4602 מֹופַעַת *môpa'at* (1)
untranslated (1)

4603 מֹופֵת *môpēt* (36)
wonders (17)
sign (7)
wonder (3)
miracles (2)
miraculous sign (2)
portent (2)
miracle (1)
symbolic of things to come (1)

symbols (1)

4604 מֹוצָא1 *môsā'1* (27)
exits (3)
flowing springs (2) +4784
imported (2)
spring (2) +4784
stages (2)
appear (1) +3922
came from (1)
east (1)
go (1)
grass (1) +2013
issuing (1)
mine (1)
movements (1) +2256+4569
outlet (1)
rises (1)
springs (1) +4784
utter (1)
what passes (1)
what uttered (1)
where dawns (1)
word that comes from (1)

4605 מֹוצָא2 *môsā'2* (5)
Moza (5)

4606 מֹוצָאָה *môsā'āh* (2)
origins (1)
untranslated (1)

4607 מֹוצָק1 *mûsāq1* (7)
cast metal (3)
cast (1)
cast bronze (1)
cast in molds (1)
hard (1) +2021+3668+4200

4608 מֹוצָק2 *mûsāq2* (2)
distress (1)
restriction (1)

4609 מֹוצָקָה *mûsāqāh* (2)
channels (1)
one piece with (1)

4610 מוּק *mûq* (1)
scoff (1)

4611 מֹוקֵד *môqēd* (2)
burning (1)
glowing embers (1)

4612 מֹוקְדָה *môq'dāh* (1)
hearth (1)

4613 מֹוקֵשׁ *môqēš* (27)
snare (12)
snares (6)
trap (3)
traps (3)
ensnared (1)
snared (1)
trapped (1)

4614 מוּר1 *mûr1* (14)
exchanged (3)
divided up (1)
exchange (1)
give way (1)
keeps (1) +4202
make a substitution (1) +4614
make substitution (1)
substitute (1)
substitute (1) +4614
unchanged (1) +4202

4615 מוּר2 *mûr2*
Variant; not used

4616 מֹורָא *môrā'* (12)
fear (4)
terror (3)
awesome (1)
awesome deeds (1)
feared (1)
respect (1)

reverence (1)

4617 מֹורַג *môrag* (3)
threshing sledges (2)
threshing sledge (1)

4618 מֹורָד *môrād* (5)
road down (2)
hammered (1)
slope (1)
slopes (1)

4619 מֹורֶה1 *môreh1* (5)
archers (1)
archers (1) +408+928+2021+8008
archers (1) +928+2021+8008
they[s] (1) +2021
untranslated (1)

4620 מֹורֶה2 *môreh2* (3)
autumn rains (2)
autumn (1)

4621 מֹורֶה3 *môreh3* (4)
teachers (2)
teacher (1)
them[s] (1) +3870

4622 מֹורֶה4 *môreh4* (3)
Moreh (3)

4623 מֹורָה1 *môrāh1* (3)
razor (3)

4624 מֹורָה2 *môrāh2*
Variant; not used

4625 מֹורָשׁ1 *môrāš1* (2)
inheritance (1)
place (1)

4626 מֹורָשׁ2 *môrāš2* (1)
desires (1)

4627 מֹורָשָׁה *môrāšāh* (9)
possession (9)

4628 מֹורֶשֶׁת גַּת *môrešet gat* (1)
Moresheth Gath (1)

4629 מֹורַשְׁתִּי *môraštiy* (2)
of Moresheth (2)

4630 מוּשׁ1 *mûš1* (3)
feel (2)
touch (1)

4631 מוּשׁ2 *mûš2* (21)
leave (3)
depart (2)
shaken (2)
departed (1)
fails (1)
give way (1)
go away (1)
left place (1)
move (1)
moved (1)
moving (1)
remove (1)
save (1)
takes (1)
vanish (1)
without (1)
untranslated (1)

4632 מֹושָׁב *môšāb* (43)
live (12)
settlements (5)
seat (3)
dwelling (2)
seating (2)
where settle (3)
council (1)
dwelling place (1)
dwellings (1)
home (1)
house (1) +1074
houses (1)

length of time (1)
members (1)
place (1)
places where lived (1)
region where lived (1)
settled (1)
situated (1)
stood (1)
throne (1)
untranslated (1)

4633 מוּשִׁי1 *mûšiy1* (8)
Mushi (8)

4634 מוּשִׁי2 *mûšiy2* (2)
Mushite (1)
Mushites (1)

4635 מוֹשִׁיעַ *môšiya'* (21)
savior (11)
deliverer (3)
rescue (3)
deliverers (2)
rescues (1)
save (1)

4636 מוֹשָׁעָה *môšā'āh* (1)
saves (1)

4637 מוּת *mût* (809)
die (200)
died (162)
dead (103)
put to death (43)
kill (36)
killed (31)
death (30)
be put to death (26)
dies (25)
must be put to death (19) +4637
surely die (7) +4637
assassinated (5)
die (5) +4637
dying (5)
kill (4) +4637
must die (4) +4637
shall be put to death (4) +4637
slay (4)
surely be put to death (4) +4637
certainly die (3) +4637
putting to death (3)
be murdered (2)
brings death (2)
causing to die (2)
destroy (2)
died a natural death (2)
killing (2)
kills (2)
perish (2)
put^s (2)
slain (2)
anyone^s (1) +2021
as good as dead (1)
assassinated (1) +2256+5782
assassination (1)
be killed (1)
body (1)
bring about death (1)
certainly be put to death (1) +4637
die out (1)
doomed to die (1) +4637
end (1)
executed (1) +2256+5782
failed (1)
fell dead (1)
go down (1)
had executed (1) +2256+5782
his^s (1) +2021
in fact die (1) +4637
is put to death (1)
killed (1) +5782
killing off (1)
kills (1) +2256+5782+5883
lifeless (1)

lives (1)
lose life (1)
make die (1)
man^s (1)
messengers of death (1)
mortal (1)
murder (1)
must be put to death (1)
put death (1)
put to death (1) +4637
ready to die (1)
risked (1) +3070+4200
slays (1)
someone^s (1)
stillborn infant (1)
struck down and died (1)
was killed (1)
was put to death (1)
were put to death (1)
widow (1) +851
untranslated (10)

4638 מָוֶת *māwet* (151)
death (109)
die (11)
died (11)
dies (5)
deadly (3)
dead (2)
capital offense (1) +5477
deadly plague (1)
death's (1)
dying (1)
immortality (1) +440
kill (1)
must die (1) +1201
plague (1)
put to death (1) +2222
untranslated (1)

4639 מוֹתָר *môtār* (3)
profit (2)
advantage (1)

4640 מִזְבֵּחַ *mizbēah* (403)
altar (337)
altars (50)
it^s (5) +2021
its^s (4) +2021
done this^s (1) +1215+3378+4200
untranslated (6)

4641 מֶזֶג *mezeg* (1)
blended wine (1)

4642 מָזֶה *māzeh* (1)
wasting (1)

4643 מַזֶּה *mazzeh*
Variant; not used

4644 מִזֶּה *mizzeh*
Variant; not used

4645 מִזָּה *mizzāh* (3)
Mizzah (3)

4646 מָזוּ *māzû* (1)
barns (1)

4647 מְזוּזָה *mĕzûzāh* (19)
doorposts (4)
doorframe (3)
doorframes (3)
doorpost (2)
doorway (1) +7339
doorways (1) +7339
gatepost (1) +9133
gateposts (1) +9133
jambs (1)
jambs (1) +382
posts (1)

4648 מָזוֹן *māzôn* (2)
provisions (2)

4649 מָזוֹר1 *māzôr1* (3)
sores (2)

sore (1)

4650 מָזוֹר2 *māzôr2* (1)
trap (1)

4651 מֵזַח1 *mēzah1* (1)
harbor (1)

4652 מֵזַח2 *mēzah2* (1)
belt (1)

4653 מָזִיחַ *māziyah* (1)
disarms (1) +8332

4654 מַזְכִּיר *mazkiyr* (9)
recorder (9)

4655 מַזָּל *mazzāl* (1)
constellations (1)

4656 מִזְלָג *mizlāg*
Variant; not used

4657 מַזְלֵג *mazlēg* (7)
meat forks (4)
fork (2)
forks (1)

4658 מִזְלָגָה *mizlāgāh*
Variant; not used

4659 מְזִמָּה *mĕzimmāh* (19)
discretion (4)
crafty (2)
purposes (2)
schemes (2)
wicked schemes (2)
discernment (1)
evil intent (1)
evil schemes (1)
plan (1)
purpose (1)
schemer (1) +1251
thoughts (1)

4660 מִזְמוֹר *mizmôr* (57)
psalm (57)

4661 מַזְמֵרָה *mazmērāh* (4)
pruning hooks (3)
pruning knives (1)

4662 מְזַמֶּרֶת *mĕzammeret* (5)
wick trimmers (5)

4663 מִזְעָר *miz'ār* (4)
in a very short time (1) +5071+6388
very few (1) +632
very few (1) +5071
very soon (1) +5071+6388

4664 מָזַר *māzar*
Variant; not used

4665 מִזְרֶה *mizreh* (2)
shovel (1)
winnowing fork (1)

4666 מַזָּרוֹת *mazzārôt* (1)
constellations (1)

4667 מִזְרָח *mizrāh* (74)
east (34)
east (7) +2025
rising (6)
sunrise (5)
east (3) +2021+9087
sunrise (3) +9087
east (2) +2021+2025+9087
east (2) +9087
eastern (2) +2025
east (1) +928+2025+6298
east (1) +928+2025+6298+9087
east (1) +928+6298+9087
east (1) +2025+6298
eastern (1)
eastern (1) +9087
eastward (1) +2025
eastward (1) +2025+2025+7711
western^s (1) +2025

untranslated (1)

4668 מְזָרִים *m'zāriym* (1)
driving winds (1)

4669 מִזְרָע *mizrā'* (1)
sown field (1)

4670 מִזְרָק *mizrāq* (32)
sprinkling bowls (15)
sprinkling bowl (13)
bowl used for sprinkling (1)
bowlful (1)
bowls (1)
sacred bowls (1)

4671 מֵחַ *mēah* (2)
fat animals (1)
rich (1)

4672 מֹחַ *mōah* (1)
marrow (1)

4673 1מָחָא *māhā'1* (3)
clap (2)
clapped (1)

4674 2מָחָא *māhā'2*
Variant; not used

4675 מַחֲבֵא *mah"bē'* (1)
shelter (1)

4676 מַחֲבֹא *mah"bō'* (1)
hiding places (1)

4677 מְחַבְּרוֹת *m'habb'rôt* (2)
fittings (1)
joists (1)

4678 מַחְבֶּרֶת *mahberet* (8)
set (6)
seam (2)

4679 מַחֲבַת *mah"bat* (5)
griddle (3)
baking (1)
pan (1)

4680 מַחֲגֹרֶת *mah"gōret* (1)
sackcloth (1) +8566

4681 1מָחָה *māhāh1* (34)
blot out (11)
be blotted out (3)
blotted out (2)
wipe (2)
wiped out (2)
wipes (2)
be wiped away (1)
be wiped out (1)
blots out (1)
completely blot out (1) +4681
ruin (1)
swept away (1)
wash off (1)
wipe away (1)
wipe out (1)
wiped (1)
wiping (1)

4682 2מָחָה *māhāh2* (1)
continue (1)

4683 3מָחָה *māhāh3* (1)
meats (1)

4684 מְחוּגָה *m'hûgāh* (1)
compasses (1)

4685 מָחוֹז *māhôz* (1)
haven (1)

4686 מְחוּיָאֵל *m'hûyā'ēl* (2)
Mehujael (2)

4687 מָחֳיִם *mah"wiym* (1)
Mahavite (1)

4688 1מָחוֹל *māhôl1* (6)
dancing (4)
dance (2)

4689 2מָחוֹל *māhôl2* (1)
Mahol (1)

4690 מַחֲזֶה *mah"zeh* (4)
vision (3)
visions (1)

4691 מֶחֱזָה *meh'zāh* (3)
facing each other (2) +448+4691

4692 מַחֲזִיאוֹת *mah"ziy'ôt* (2)
Mahazioth (2)

4693 מְחִי *m'hiy* (1)
blows (1)

4694 מְחִירָא *m'hiydā'* (2)
Mehida (2)

4695 מִחְיָה *mihyāh* (8)
food (1)
living thing (1)
new life (1)
raw (1) +2645
raw flesh (1)
recover (1)
relief (1)
save lives (1)

4696 מְחִיָּיאֵל *m'hiyyāy'ēl*
Variant; not used

4697 1מְחִיר *m'hiyr1* (15)
price (6)
purchased (2) +928+4374
charge (1)
cost (1)
insist on paying for (1) +928+7864+7864
money (1)
sale (1)
worth (1)
untranslated (1)

4698 2מְחִיר *m'hiyr2* (1)
Mehir (1)

4699 מַחֲלֵב *mah"lēb*
Variant; not used

4700 מַחֲלֶה *mah"leh* (2)
disease (1)
sickness (1)

4701 מַחֲלָה *mah"lāh* (4)
disease (2)
diseases (1)
sickness (1)

4702 מַחְלָה *mahlāh* (5)
Mahlah (5)

4703 מְחֹלָה *m'hōlāh* (8)
dancing (5)
dances (2)
dance (1)

4704 מְחִלָּה *m'hillāh* (1)
holes (1)

4705 מַחְלוֹן *mahlôn* (4)
Mahlon (3)
Mahlon's (1)

4706 1מַחְלִי *mahliy1* (12)
Mahli (12)

4707 2מַחְלִי *mahliy2* (2)
Mahlite (1)
Mahlites (1)

4708 מַחֲלֻיִים *mah"luyiym* (2)
wounded (1)
untranslated (1)

4709 מַחֲלָף *mah"lāp* (1)
pans (1)

4710 מַחֲלָפָה *mah"lāpāh* (3)
braids (3)

4711 מַחֲלָצוֹת *mah"lāsôt* (2)
fine robes (1)

rich garments (1)

4712 מַחְלְקוֹת *mahl'qôt* (1)
Variant; not used

4713 מַחֲלֹקֶת *mah"lōqet* (42)
divisions (19)
division (17)
tribal divisions (2)
army divisions (1)
groups (1)
portions (1)
untranslated (1)

4714 1מַחֲלַת *māh"lat1* (2)
mahalath (2)

4715 2מַחֲלַת *māh"lat2* (2)
Mahalath (2)

4716 מְחֹלָתִי *m'hōlātiy* (2)
Meholathite (1)
of Meholah (1)

4717 מַחְמָאֹת *mahmā'ōt* (1)
butter (1)

4718 מַחְמָד *mahmād* (13)
treasures (4)
delight (3)
cherished (1)
lovely (1)
pleasing (1)
treasured (1)
value (1)
value (1) +6524

4719 מַחְמֹד *mahmōd* (2)
treasures (1)
untranslated (1)

4720 מַחְמָל *mahmāl* (1)
object (1)

4721 מַחְמֶצֶת *mahmeset* (2)
anything with yeast in it (1)
made with yeast (1)

4722 מַחֲנֶה *mah"neh* (214)
camp (144)
army (23)
camps (8)
forces (5)
troops (3)
armies (2)
dwelling (2)
fighting (2)
group (2)
groups (2)
lines (2)
attendants (1)
band (1)
company (1)
droves (1)
encamped (1) +3655
force (1)
its (1) +2021
its (1) +5213
Midianites (1)
there (1) +928+2021
tribes (1)
units (1)
unwalled (1)
untranslated (6)

4723 מַחֲנֵה־דָן *mah"nēh-dān* (2)
Mahaneh Dan (2)

4724 מַחֲנַיִם *mah"nayim* (14)
Mahanaim (14)

4725 מַחֲנָק *mah"nāq* (1)
strangling (1)

4726 מַחְסֶה *mahseh* (20)
refuge (18)
shelter (2)

4727 מַחְסוֹם *mahsôm* (1)
muzzle (1)

4728 מַחְסוֹר *mahsôr* (13)
poverty (4)
lack (2)
need (2)
scarcity (2)
lacks (1)
needs (1) +2893
poor (1)

4729 מַחְסֵיָה *mahsēyāh* (2)
Mahseiah (2)

4730 מָחַץ *māhas* (13)
crush (3)
crushed (2)
crushed completely (1) +430+2256
crushing (1)
cut to pieces (1)
injures (1)
pierce (1)
shattered (1)
smite (1)
wounded (1)

4731 מַחַץ *mahas* (1)
wounds (1)

4732 מַחְצֵב *mahsēb* (3)
dressed (3)

4733 מֶחֱצָה *meh'sāh* (2)
half (2)

4734 מַחֲצִית *mah'siyt* (16)
half (13)
half as much (1)
half share (1)
noon (1) +2021+3427

4735 מָחַק *māhaq* (1)
crushed (1)

4736 מֶחְקָר *mehqār* (1)
depths (1)

4737 מָחָר *māhār* (52)
tomorrow (43)
in the future (4)
days to come (1)
ever (1)
future (1) +3427
some day (1)
tomorrow (1) +3427

4738 מַחֲרָאָה *mah'rā'āh* (1)
latrine (1)

4739 מַחֲרֵשָׁה *mah'rēšāh* (2)
plowshares (2)

4740 מָחֳרָת *moh'rāt* (32)
next day (22)
day after (6)
next (3)
following (1)

4741 מַחְשֹׂף *mahsōp* (1)
exposing (1)

4742 מַחֲשָׁבָה *mah'šābāh* (56)
thoughts (14)
plans (9)
plan (3)
plots (3)
purposes (3)
artistic designs (2)
imaginations (2)
purposed (2) +3108
scheme (2)
schemes (2)
artistic craftsmanship (1)
design (1)
designed (1)
designers (1) +3110
desire (1) +3671
devised (1)
make plans (1) +3108
overthrow (1)

plans have (1) +3108
plotted (1) +3108
plotting (1)
things planned (1)
ways (1)
what thinking (1)

4743 מַחְשָׁךְ *mahšāk* (7)
darkness (5)
dark places (1)
darkest (1)

4744 מַחַת *mahat* (3)
Mahath (3)

4745 מְחִתָּה *m'hitāh* (11)
ruin (4)
terror (1)
object of horror (1)
ruined (1)
ruins (1)
undoing (1)

4746 מַחְתָּה *mahtāh* (22)
censers (11)
censer (4)
firepans (3)
trays (3)
it^s (1)

4747 מַחְתֶּרֶת *mahteret* (2)
breaking in (2)

4748 מַטְאֲטֵא *mat''tē'* (1)
broom (1)

4749 מַטְבֵּחַ *matbēah* (1)
place to slaughter (1)

4750 מָטֶה *māteh*
Variant; not used

4751 מַטֶּה *matteh* (253)
tribe (124)
staff (37)
tribes (21)
tribal (8)
rod (6)
half-tribe (5) +2942
staffs (5)
supply (4)
club (3)
branches (2)
scepter (2)
arrows (1)
bar (1)
branch (1)
Danite (1) +1968+4200
family (1)
Levites (1) +4290
main branches (1) +964
one^s (1)
spear (1)
supplies (1)
them^s (1)
untranslated (25)

4752 מַטָּה *mattāh* (19)
below (3) +4200
bottom (3)
down (3) +4200
bottom (2) +4200+4946
lower (2)
goes down (1) +3718+4200
going down to (1)
less (1)
punished less (1) +3104+4200
untranslated (2)

4753 מִטָּה *mittāh* (28)
bed (17)
couch (4)
bedroom (2) +2540
beds (2)
bier (1)
carriage (1)
couches (1)

4754 מֻטֶּה *mutteh* (1)
injustice (1)

4755 מֻטָּה *muttāh* (1)
Variant; not used

4756 מִטְהָר *mithār*
Variant; not used

4757 מַטְוֶה *matweh* (1)
what spun (1)

4758 מָטִיל *mātiyl* (1)
rods (1)

4759 מַטְמוֹן *matmôn* (5)
hidden treasure (2)
hidden (1)
riches (1)
treasure (1)

4760 מַטָּע *mattā'* (7)
planted (2)
planting (2)
base (1)
land for crops (1)
untranslated (1)

4761 מַטְעָם *mat'ām* (8)
tasty food (6)
delicacies (2)

4762 מִטְפַּחַת *mitpahat* (2)
cloaks (1)
shawl (1)

4763 מָטַר *mātar* (18)
rained down (3)
had rain (2)
rain down (2)
sent rain (2)
had^s (1)
pour down (1)
rain (1)
rain (1) +4764
rained (1)
send (1)
send rain (1)
water (1)
withheld^s (1) +4202

4764 מָטָר *mātār* (38)
rain (34)
showers (2)
downpour (1) +1773
rain (1) +4763

4765 מַטְרֵד *matrēd* (2)
Matred (2)

4766 מַטָּרָה *mattārāh* (16)
guard (13)
target (3)

4767 מַטְרִי *matriy* (1)
Matri's (1)

4768 מַי *may*
Variant; not used

4769 מִי *miy* (424)
who (285)
whom (34)
what (17)
which (11)
whose (11)
if only (10) +5989
oh (8) +5989
anyone (7)
whoever (6)
anyone (3) +408+2021
if only (3)
whose (3) +4200
how (2)
one (2)
someone (2)
whoever (2) +408+2021
whoever (2) +889
any man (1) +408+2021

how did it go (1) +905
how I long for (1) +5761+5989
I wish (1) +5989
just who (1) +2256+4769
oh (1) +686+5989
oh how I wish (1) +5989
others^s (1)
what (1) +2296
untranslated (6)

4770 מֵי הַיַּרְקוֹן *mēy hayyarqôn* (1)
Me Jarkon (1)

4771 מֵי זָהָב *mēy zāhāb* (2)
Me-Zahab (2)

4772 מֵידְבָא *mēydbā'* (5)
Medeba (5)

4773 מֵידָד *mēydād* (2)
Medad (2)

4774 מֵיטָב *mēytāb* (6)
best (5)
untranslated (1)

4775 מִיכָא *miykā'* (4)
Mica (4)

4776 מִיכָאֵל *miykā'ēl* (13)
Michael (13)

4777 מִיכָה *miykāh* (33)
Micah (24)
Micah's (6)
his^s (1)
Mica (1)
Micaiah (1)

4778 מִיכָהוּ *miykāhû* (1)
untranslated (1)

4779 מִיכָיָה *miykāyāh* (4)
Micaiah (3)
untranslated (1)

4780 מִיכָיְהוּ *miykāyāhû* (1)
Micaiah (1)

4781 מִיכָיְהוּ *miykāy'hû* (21)
Micaiah (19)
Micah (1)
Micah's (1)

4782 מִיכָל *miykāl* (1)
brook (1) +4784

4783 מִיכַל *miykal* (17)
Michal (17)

4784 מַיִם *mayim* (581)
water (359)
waters (140)
flood (3)
floodwaters (3) +4429
rain (3)
springs (3) +5078
tears (3)
flowing springs (2) +4604
river (2)
sea (2)
spring (2)
spring (2) +4604
spring (2) +6524
springs (2) +6524
that^s (2)
waterless (2) +401
well-watered (2) +9272
brook (1) +4782
bubbling springs (1) +4432
dam (1)
driving rain (1) +2443
floodwaters (1) +8041
floodwaters (1) +8673
flow (1)
flowing streams (1) +3298
it^s (1) +2021
melted (1)
pool (1)

pool (1) +106
pool (1) +1391
reservoirs (1) +1391
reservoirs (1) +5224
seas (1)
spring (1) +2021+6524
spring of water (1)
springs (1) +4604
stream (1)
swampland (1) +106
they^s (1) +2021
water supply (1)
water's (1)
watercourse (1) +7104
watering (1)
waves (1)
well (1) +931
wells (1) +931
untranslated (18)

4785 מִיָּמִין *miyyāmiyn* (4)
Mijamin (4)

4786 מִין *miyn* (31)
kind (18)
kinds (9)
various kinds (1)
untranslated (3)

4787 מֵינֶקֶת *mēyneqet* (6)
nurse (4)
nursing mothers (1)
untranslated (1)

4788 מֵיסָךְ *mēysāk* (1)
untranslated (1)

4789 מֵיפַעַת *mēypa'at* (4)
Mephaath (4)

4790 מִיץ *miys* (3)
churning (1)
stirring up (1)
twisting (1)

4791 מֵישָׁא *mēyšā'* (1)
Mesha (1)

4792 מִישָׁאֵל *miyšā'ēl* (7)
Mishael (7)

4793 מִישׁוֹר *miyšôr* (23)
plateau (9)
justice (2)
level (2)
level ground (2)
plains (2)
justly (1)
plain (1)
plateau (1) +824
smooth (1)
straight (1)
uprightness (1)

4794 מֵישַׁךְ *mēyšak* (1)
Meshach (1)

4795 מֵישַׁע *mēyša'* (1)
Mesha (1)

4796 מֵישָׁע *mēyšā'* (1)
Mesha (1)

4797 מֵישָׁרִים *mēyšāriym* (19)
right (6)
equity (3)
fair (2)
uprightly (2)
alliance (1)
integrity (1)
justice (1)
level (1)
smoothly (1) +928
straight (1)

4798 מֵיתָר *mēytār* (9)
ropes (7)
cords (1)

drawn bow (1)

4799 מַכְאֹב *mak'ōb* (16)
pain (7)
suffering (4)
sorrows (2)
grief (1)
pains (1)
woes (1)

4800 מַכְבֵּנָה *makbēnāh* (1)
Macbenah (1)

4801 מַכְבַּנַּי *makbannay* (1)
Macbannai (1)

4802 מַכְבֵּר *makbēr* (1)
thick cloth (1)

4803 מִכְבָּר *mikbār* (6)
grating (6)

4804 מַכָּה *makkāh* (48)
wounds (9)
wound (4)
losses (3)
struck down (3)
blow (2)
injury (2)
plagues (2)
slaughter (2)
afflictions (1)
attack (1)
beatings (1)
blows (1)
calamities (1)
casualties (1)
destroyed (1) +1524+4394+5782
devastated (1) +1524+4394+5782
disaster (1)
disasters (1)
flogged (1) +5782
force (1)
ground (1)
inflicted (1)
plague (1)
slaughtered (1)
sores (1)
struck down (1) +5782
victory (1)
untranslated (2)

4805 מִכְוָה *mikwāh* (5)
burn (4)
burn (1) +836

4806 מָכוֹן *mākôn* (17)
place (11)
foundation (1)
dwelling place (1)
foundations (1)
site (1)
untranslated (1)

4807 מְכוֹנָה *m'kônāh* (25)
movable stands (7)
stand (6)
stands (6)
foundation (1)
place (1)
untranslated (4)

4808 מְכוּרָה *m'kûrāh* (3)
ancestry (3)

4809 מָכִי *mākiy* (1)
Maki (1)

4810 מָכִיר *mākiyr* (22)
Makir (20)
Makir's (1)
Makirites (1)

4811 מָכִירִי *mākiyriy* (1)
Makirite (1)

4812 מָכַךְ *mākak* (3)
are brought low (1)

sag (1)
wasted away (1)

4813 מִכְלָא *miklā'* (3)
pens (2)
pen (1)

4814 מִכְלוֹל *miklôl* (2)
full (1)
fully (1)

4815 מַכְלוּל *maklûl* (1)
beautiful garments (1)

4816 מִכְלוֹת *miklôt* (1)
solid (1)

4817 מִכְלָל *miklāl* (1)
perfect (1)

4818 מַכֹּלֶת *makkōlet* (1)
food (1)

4819 מִכְמָן *mikmān* (1)
treasures (1)

4820 מִכְמָס *mikmās* (2)
Micmash (2)

4821 מִכְמָר *mikmār* (2)
net (1)
nets (1)

4822 מַכְמֹר *makmōr*
Variant; not used

4823 מִכְמֶרֶת *mikmeret* (3)
dragnet (2)
nets (1)

4824 מִכְמֹרֶת *mikmōret*
Variant; not used

4825 מִכְמָשׂ *mikmāś* (9)
Micmash (9)

4826 מִכְמְתָת *mikm'tāt* (2)
Micmethath (2)

4827 מַכְנַדְבַי *maknadbay* (1)
Macnadebai (1)

4828 מְכֹנָה *m'kōnāh* (1)
Meconah (1)

4829 מִכְנָס *miknās* (5)
undergarments (4)
undergarments (1) +965

4830 מֶכֶס *mekes* (6)
tribute (6)

4831 מִכְסָה *miksāh* (2)
number (1)
value (1) +6886

4832 מִכְסֶה *mikseh* (16)
covering (12)
cover (3) +4059
coverings (1)

4833 מְכַסֶּה *m'kasseh* (4)
awnings (1)
clothes (1)
cover (1)
layer of fat (1)

4834 מַכְפֵּלָה *makpēlāh* (6)
Machpelah (6)

4835 מָכַר *mākar* (80)
sold (19)
sell (17)
selling (7)
sells (7)
be sold (5)
sold himself (4)
seller (3)
sells himself (3)
been sold (2)
were sold (2)
be sold back (1)
enslaved (1)

hand over (1) +928+3338
must be sold (1) +4929
must sell (1) +928+2021+4084+4835
offer yourselves for sale (1)
sell land (1) +4928
sellers (1)
sold themselves (1)
sold yourself (1)

4836 מֶכֶר *meker* (3)
merchandise (1)
pay (1) +5989
worth (1)

4837 מַכָּר *makkār* (2)
treasurers (2)

4838 מִכְרֶה *mikreh* (1)
pits (1)

4839 מְכֵרָה *m'kērāh* (1)
swords (1)

4840 מִכְרִי *mikriy* (1)
Micri (1)

4841 מְכֵרָתִי *m'kērātiy* (1)
Mekerathite (1)

4842 מִכְשׁוֹל *mikšôl* (14)
stumbling block (4)
obstacles (2)
downfall (1)
fallen (1)
made fall (1) +2118+4200
make stumble (1)
makes fall (1)
staggering burden (1) +2256+7050
stumble (1)
stumbling blocks (1)

4843 מַכְשֵׁלָה *makšēlāh* (2)
heap of ruins (1)
heaps of rubble (1)

4844 מִכְתָּב *miktāb* (9)
writing (5)
inscription (1) +7334
letter (1)
written (1)
untranslated (1)

4845 מְכִתָּה *m'kitāh* (1)
pieces (1)

4846 מִכְתָּם *miktām* (6)
miktam (6)

4847 מַכְתֵּשׁ *maktēš* (3)
hollow place (1)
market district (1)
mortar (1)

4848 1מָלֵא *mālē' 1* (253)
filled (46)
fill (38)
full (35)
be filled (10)
over (8)
wholeheartedly (7)
completed (5)
covered (5)
fulfilled (5)
was filled (4)
filling (3)
fills (3)
ordained (3) +906+3338
satisfy (3)
set (3)
installed (2) +906+3338
laden with (2)
ordain (2) +3338
ordination (2) +906+3338
passed (2)
aloud (1)
are filled (1)
at flood stage (1) +1536+3972+6584
bathed in (1)

be paid in full (1)
bear (1)
before elapsed (1) +4202
came (1)
come (1)
come to an end (1)
confirm (1)
consecrate himself (1) +2257+3338
consecrate himself (1) +3338
consecrated (1) +906+3338
cover (1)
cover (1) +7156
crowded (1)
dared (1) +4213
dedicate (1) +3338
dedicated (1) +3338
did completely (1)
drenched (1)
drew (1) +928+3338
enraged (1) +2779
enriched (1)
finish (1)
finished (1)
fulfilling (1)
fulfillment (1)
give full (1)
given (1)
gorge (1)
grant (1)
have fill (1)
heaping up (1)
highly (1)
is satisfied (1)
last (1)
live out (1)
make succeed (1)
making full (1)
midst (1)
mount (1) +4853
mounted (1)
numbered (1)
ordain (1) +906+3338
ordained (1) +3338
overflowing (1)
presented the full number (1)
prosper (1)
provide (1)
racked with (1)
set apart (1) +3338
shown (1)
still hunger (1) +1061
take up (1)
taking full (1)
took a handful (1) +4090
unite (1)
uses (1)
violent (1) +2805
well nourished (1) +2692
were filled (1)
untranslated (2)

4849 2מָלֵא *mālē' 2* (60)
filled (31)
full (21)
abundance (1)
loaded (1)
loud (1)
mother's⁵ (1)
strewn with (1)
strong (1)
weighed down (1)
untranslated (1)

4850 מְלֹא *m'lō'* (38)
everything in (8)
all that is in (5)
filled (3)
full (3)
handful (2) +4090
handfuls (2) +2908
take a handful (2) +7858+7859
all that in (1)

all who are in (1)
all who were in (1)
bowlful (1) +6210
cover (1)
fullness (1)
group (1)
length (1)
take (1)
third^s (1)
two handfuls (1) +2908
whole band (1)
untranslated (1)

4851 מִלֹּא *millō'*
Variant; not used

4852 מְלֵאָה *m'lē'āh* (3)
crops (1)
granaries (1)
juice (1)

4853 מִלֻּאָה *millu'āh* (4)
mount (1) +2118
mount (1) +4848
mounted (1)
settings (1)

4854 מִלֻּאִים *millu'iym* (14)
ordination (7)
mounted (2)
ordination offering (2)
ordination offerings (1)
ordination ram (1)
settings (1)

4855 מַלְאָךְ *mal'āk* (213)
angel (98)
messengers (60)
messenger (23)
angels (9)
men (8)
envoys (6)
delegation (1)
he^s (1) +2021
he^s (1) +3378
men^s (1)
official (1)
spies (1)
the angel (1) +3378
they^s (1) +2021
untranslated (1)

4856 מְלָאכָה *m'lā'kāh* (167)
work (87)
regular work (12) +6275
workers (7) +6913
anything (3)
duties (3)
task (3)
workmen (3) +6913
business (2)
crafts (2)
project (2)
property (2)
service (2)
use (2) +6913
administrators (1) +6913
anything useful (1)
assist (1)
been used (1) +6913
building (1)
craftsmanship (1)
deeds (1)
details (1)
do (1)
done (1)
droves (1)
everything (1) +2021+3972
kinds (1)
made (1)
master craftsmen (1) +6913
matter (1)
merchants (1) +6913
part (1)

performed (1)
projects (1)
purpose (1)
responsible (1)
responsible (1) +6275
settings (1) +9513
something useful (1)
supplies (1)
these men^s (1) +2021+6913
what^s (1) +2021
work (1) +6913
worked (1)
working (1) +6913
workmen (1)
workmen (1) +928+2021+6913
untranslated (4)

4857 מַלְאֲכוּת *mal'ăkût* (1)
message (1)

4858 מַלְאָכִי *mal'ăkiy* (1)
Malachi (1)

4859 מִלֵּאת *millē't* (1)
mounted like jewels (1) +3782+6584

4860 מַלְבּוּשׁ *malbûš* (8)
robes (4)
clothes (3)
clothing (1)

4861 מַלְבֵּן *malbēn* (3)
brick pavement (1)
brickmaking (1)
brickwork (1)

4862 מָלָה *mālāh*
Variant; not used

4863 מִלָּה *millāh* (38)
words (24)
speaking (2)
speeches (2)
word (2)
anything to say (1)
byword (1)
make fine speeches (1) +928+2488
reply (1) +8740
said (1)
say (1)
what say (1)
what^s (1)

4864 מִלּוֹא *millô'* (6)
supporting terraces (6)

4865 מַלּוּחַ *mallûah* (1)
salt herbs (1)

4866 מַלּוּךְ *mallûk* (6)
Malluch (6)

4867 מְלוּכָה *m'lûkāh* (25)
kingdom (11)
royal (7)
kingship (3)
dominion (1)
king (1)
queen (1)
rule (1)

4868 מַלּוּכִי *mallûkiy* (1)
Malluch's (1)

4869 מָלוֹן *mālôn* (8)
lodging place (2)
camp (1)
camp overnight (1)
parts (1)
place (1)
place where they stopped for the night (1)
place where we stopped for the night (1)

4870 מְלוּנָה *m'lûnāh* (2)
hut (2)

4871 מַלּוֹתִי *mallôtiy* (2)
Mallothi (2)

4872 מָלַח1 *mālah1* (1)
vanish (1)

4873 מָלַח2 *mālah2* (4)
be salted (1)
season (1)
were rubbed with salt (1) +4873

4874 מֶלַח1 *melah1* (2)
clothes (2)

4875 מֶלַח2 *melah2* (30)
salt (29)
untranslated (1)

4876 מַלָּח *mallāh* (4)
mariners (2)
sailors (2)

4877 מְלֵחָה *m'lēhāh* (3)
salt (1)
salt flats (1)
salt waste (1)

4878 מִלְחָמָה *milhāmāh* (319)
battle (135)
war (74)
fighting (16)
fight (14)
soldiers (12) +408
wars (6)
warrior (5) +408
army (4) +408
army (4) +6639
battles (4)
military (3)
warfare (3)
at war with (2) +408
battle formation (2)
battle lines (2)
fighting (2) +6913
military age (2)
armed (1)
at war (1)
at war (1) +6913
attack (1)
attacked (1)
battle (1) +7372
experienced fighter (1) +408
experienced fighting men (1)
           +408+1475+2657
fight (1) +2021+3655+4200
force (1) +6639
great soldiers (1) +408
men ready for battle (1) +1522+7372
ready for battle (1) +408+2021+4200+7372
ready for battle (1) +928+2021+4200+7372
soldiers (1) +408+1505
soldiers (1) +9530
struggle (1)
that^s (1)
time of war (1)
wage war (1) +1741+2021+4200
war cry (1)
weapon (1) +3998
weapon (1) +3998+7372
weapons (1) +3998
well-trained (1) +6913
went to war (1) +6913
untranslated (3)

4879 מֶלֶט *melet* (1)
clay (1)

4880 מָלַט1 *mālat1* (95)
escaped (20)
escape (17)
save (7)
flee (5)
rescued (4)
run (4)
be delivered (3)
rescue (3)
saved (3)
deliver (2)

delivers (2)
go free (2)
got away (2)
let get away (2)
be saved (1)
escape (1) +4880
escape (1) +7127
escaping (1)
get away (1)
is kept safe (1)
lay eggs (1)
made escape (1)
made good escape (1) +2256+5674
release (1)
retrieved (1)
save (1) +4880
shoot out (1)
slip out (1)
slipped away (1)
spared (1)
were saved (1)

4881 מָלַט2 *mālat2*
Variant; not used

4882 מְלַטְיָה *mᵉlaṭyāh* (1)
Melatiah (1)

4883 מְלִיכוּ *mᵉliykû* (1)
untranslated (1)

4884 מְלִילָה *mᵉliylāh* (1)
kernels (1)

4885 מֵלִיץ *mēliyṣ* (5)
envoys (1)
intercessor (1)
interpreter (1)
mediator (1)
spokesmen (1)

4886 מְלִיצָה *mᵉliyṣāh* (2)
parables (1)
ridicule (1)

4887 מָלַךְ1 *mālak1* (350)
king (151)
reigned (70)
reign (37)
made king (24)
reigns (9)
ruled (9)
make king (7)
rule (5)
proclaimed king (3)
set up king (2) +4889
acknowledged as king (1)
appoint as king (1)
came to power (1)
confirmed as king (1)
crown (1)
extend (1)
give king (1) +4889
intend to reign (1) +4887
king (1) +4889
kingship (1)
made king (1) +4889
made queen (1)
make king (1) +4889
put on throne (1)
queen (1)
reigned (1) +4889
ruled over (1)
ruling (1)
set a king (1) +4889
set up kings (1)
surely be king (1) +4887
took control (1)
was made ruler (1)
untranslated (8)

4888 מָלַךְ2 *mālak2* (1)
pondered (1)

4889 מֶלֶךְ1 *melek1* (2527)
king (1840)

kings (271)
king's (172)
royal (65)
himˢ (29) +2021
heˢ (26) +2021
palace (15) +1074
hisˢ (6) +2021
king's (4) +4200
his ownˢ (3) +2021
king's (3) +928
princes (3) +1201
reign (3)
Amaziahˢ (2) +2021
palace grounds (2) +1074
ruled (2)
set up king (2) +4887
give king (1) +4887
heˢ (1) +951
himˢ (1) +951
himˢ (1) +2021+6460
himˢ (1) +3296+4046
hisˢ (1) +928+2021
hisˢ (1) +951
hisˢ (1) +4200+5213
itˢ (1) +2021+9133
king (1) +4887
kingdom (1)
kingdoms (1)
kings' (1)
made king (1) +4887
majesty (1)
make king (1) +4887
prince (1) +1201
princess (1) +1426
reigned (1) +4887
rule over (1)
ruled (1) +2118
rulers (1)
set a king (1) +4887
Shalmaneserˢ (1) +855
untranslated (55)

4890 מֶלֶךְ2 *melek2* (2)
Melech (2)

4891 מֹלֶךְ *mōlek* (9)
Molech (9)

4892 מַלְכֹּדֶת *malkōdet* (1)
trap (1)

4893 מַלְכָּה *malkāh* (35)
queen (30)
queen's (2)
queens (2)
sheˢ (1) +2021

4894 מִלְכָּה *milkāh* (11)
Milcah (11)

4895 מַלְכוּת *malkût* (90)
kingdom (35)
reign (19)
royal (16)
realm (5)
empire (2)
kingdoms (2)
royal position (2)
became king (1)
king (1)
kingship (1)
palace (1) +1074
position as king (1)
royalty (1)
rule (1)
untranslated (2)

4896 מַלְכִּיאֵל *malkiy'ēl* (3)
Malkiel (3)

4897 מַלְכִּיאֵלִי *malkiy'ēliy* (1)
Malkielite (1)

4898 מַלְכִּיָּה *malkiyyāh* (15)
Malkijah (15)

4899 מַלְכִּיָּהוּ *malkiyyāhû* (1)
Malkijah (1)

4900 מַלְכִּי־צֶדֶק *malkiy-ṣedeq* (2)
Melchizedek (2)

4901 מַלְכִּירָם *malkiyrām* (1)
Malkiram (1)

4902 מַלְכִּי־שׁוּעַ *malkiy-šûa'* (5)
Malki-Shua (5)

4903 מַלְכָּם *malkām* (4)
Molech (3)
Malcam (1)

4904 מִלְכֹּם *milkōm* (3)
Molech (3)

4905 מַלְכֵּן *malkēn* (1)
untranslated (1)

4906 מְלֶכֶת *mᵉleket* (5)
queen (5)

4907 מֹלֶכֶת *mōleket*
Variant; not used

4908 מָלַל1 *mālal1* (5)
wither (2)
be blunted (1)
dry (1)
withers away (1)

4909 מָלַל2 *mālal2* (2)
are cut off (1)
circumcise (1)

4910 מָלַל3 *mālal3* (4)
proclaim (1)
said (1)
say (1)
speak (1)

4911 מָלַל4 *mālal4* (1)
signals (1)

4912 מִלֲלַי *milᵃlay* (1)
Milalai (1)

4913 מַלְמָד *malmād* (1)
oxgoad (1) +1330

4914 מָלַץ *mālaṣ* (1)
sweet (1)

4915 מֶלְצָר *melṣar* (2)
guard (2)

4916 מָלַק *mālaq* (2)
wring (1)
wring off (1)

4917 מַלְקוֹחַ *malqôaḥ* (7)
spoils (4)
plunder (2)
allˢ (1)

4918 מַלְקוֹחַיִם *malqôḥayim* (1)
roof of mouth (1)

4919 מַלְקוֹשׁ *malqôš* (8)
spring rains (4)
rain in spring (1)
spring (1)
spring rain (1)
springtime (1) +6961

4920 מֶלְקָחַיִם *melqāḥayim* (6)
tongs (3)
wick trimmers (3)

4921 מֶלְתָּחָה *meltāḥāh* (1)
wardrobe (1)

4922 מַלְתָּעוֹת *maltā'ôt* (1)
fangs (1)

4923 מַמְּגוּרָה *mamᵉgûrāh* (1)
granaries (1)

4924 מֵמַד *mēmad* (1)
dimensions (1)

4925 מְמוּכָן *m'mûkān* (3)
  Memucan (3)

4926 מָמוֹת *māmôt* (2)
  deadly (1)
  death (1)

4927 מַמְזֵר *mamzēr* (2)
  foreigners (1)
  one born of a forbidden marriage (1)

4928 מִמְכָּר *mimkār* (10)
  sold (2)
  what sold (2)
  goods (1)
  land sold (1)
  money from sale (1)
  release (1)
  sale (1)
  sell land (1) +4835

4929 מִמְכֶּרֶת *mimkeret* (1)
  must be sold (1) +4835

4930 מַמְלָכָה *mamlākāh* (117)
  kingdom (58)
  kingdoms (45)
  royal (7)
  kings (2)
  kingship (2)
  reign (2)
  royal power (1)

4931 מַמְלָכוּת *mamlākût* (9)
  kingdom (4)
  realm (3)
  reign (1)
  royal (1)

4932 מִמְסָךְ *mimsāk* (2)
  bowls of mixed wine (2)

4933 מֶמֶר *memer* (1)
  bitterness (1)

4934 1מַמְרֵא *mamrē' 1* (8)
  Mamre (8)

4935 2מַמְרֵא *mamrē' 2* (2)
  Mamre (2)

4936 מַמְרֹרִים *mamm'rōriym* (1)
  misery (1)

4937 מִמְשַׁח *mimšah* (1)
  anointed (1)

4938 מִמְשָׁל *mimšāl* (3)
  power (2)
  leaders (1)

4939 מֶמְשָׁלָה *memšālāh* (17)
  dominion (4)
  govern (4)
  kingdom (3)
  ruled (2)
  authority (1)
  forces (1)
  rule (1)
  ruled (1) +3338

4940 מִמְשָׁק *mimšāq* (1)
  place (1)

4941 מַמְתַקִּים *mamtaqiym* (2)
  sweet (1)
  sweetness (1)

4942 1מָן *mān1* (13)
  manna (13)

4943 2מָן *mān2* (1)
  what (1)

4944 1מֵן *mēn1* (2)
  music of strings (1)
  strings (1)

4945 2מֵן *mēn2* (1)
  share (1)

4946 מִן *min* (7531)
  from (2540)
  of (592)
  than (182)
  out of (179)
  from (155) +6584
  some (123)
  in (116)
  on (98)
  at (94)
  from (93) +907
  more than (93)
  before (82) +7156
  because of (54) +7156
  too (54)
  by (50)
  outside (49) +2575
  from (45) +7156
  with (44)
  because of (43)
  any (40)
  for (39)
  to (37)
  from (33) +3338
  one (32)
  from (25) +6640
  before (24) +4200+7156
  among (23)
  since (21)
  above (19) +5087
  in addition to (18) +963+4200
  below (17) +9393
  of (17) +7156
  because (16)
  from (16) +7931
  from (16) +9348
  on every side (16) +6017
  not (15)
  as (14)
  above (13) +6584
  out of (13) +9348
  through (13)
  without (13)
  from (12) +339
  no (12)
  above (11)
  after (11)
  from (11) +4200+7156
  from among (11)
  part (11)
  away from (10)
  away from (10) +6584
  on each side (10) +2256+4946+7024+7024
  rather than (10)
  against (9)
  behind (9) +339
  besides (9) +963+4200
  of one piece with (9)
  on (9) +6584
  so (9)
  when (9)
  without (9) +401
  because (8) +7156
  off (8) +6584
  around (7) +6017
  better than (7)
  by (7) +7156
  north (7) +7600
  of (7) +907
  under (7) +9393
  whether (7)
  Israelite (6) +408+1074+3776
  on both sides[s] (6) +2256+2296+2296+4946
  over (6)
  before (5)
  far away (5) +8158
  from (5) +5584
  greater than (5)
  inside (5) +1074
  left (5) +2143
  long ago (5) +255

  off (5)
  toward (5)
  whenever (5) +1896
  where (5) +402
  above (4) +2025+4200+5087
  against (4) +3338+9393
  among (4) +7931
  at (4) +7156
  behind (4) +1074
  beneath (4) +9393
  beyond (4)
  both (4)
  far from (4)
  later (4) +7891
  leave (4) +2143
  left (4) +907+2143
  malice aforethought (4) +8533+8997+9453
  most (4)
  no (4) +401
  of (4) +6640
  of (4) +9348
  on either side (4) +2256+4946+7024+7024
  out (4) +2575
  out of (4) +6584
  some (4) +3972
  south (4) +5582
  that (4)
  through (4) +907
  until (4)
  within (4)
  across (3) +6298
  after (3) +7891
  against (3) +6584
  against (3) +7156
  ancient (3) +6409
  apart from (3) +1187
  away (3)
  away from (3) +6640
  back (3) +9004
  behind (3) +1237
  belong to (3)
  besides (3) +1187
  between (3) +1068
  between (3) +2256+6330
  doing (3) +907
  east (3) +7710
  either (3)
  escape (3) +7156
  ever since (3)
  from (3) +1896
  higher than (3) +6584
  hold accountable (3) +1335+3338
  into (3)
  leave (3) +3718
  left (3) +7756
  northern (3) +7600
  out (3) +9004
  over (3) +2025+4200+5087
  so that (3)
  the LORD's (3) +907+3378
  unaware of (3) +6623
  under (3)
  about (2)
  along (2)
  as often as (2) +1896
  as well as (2) +963+4200
  at either end[s] (2) +2256+2296+2296+4946
  at set times (2) +6330+6961+6961
  away (2) +725
  away (2) +9004
  away from (2) +339
  away from (2) +907
  back (2) +339
  before (2) +6584
  beside (2) +7396
  between (2)
  beyond (2) +2134+2256
  beyond (2) +6298
  bottom (2) +4200+4752
  by (2) +6640
  cannot (2)

caused by (2)
dictated (2) +7023
distant (2) +5305
distant (2) +8158
each year (2) +2025+3427+3427
east (2) +6298
even more than (2)
ever (2) +6409
ever since (2) +255
excluded from (2)
extend from (2)
extended from (2)
extending from (2)
far and wide (2) +2085+2134+2256
far from (2) +5584
flesh and blood (2) +2743+3655
from (2) +6584+7156
from (2) +9393
from every side (2) +6017
from out of (2) +9348
future (2) +8158
got off (2) +6584+7563
had the habit (2) +8997+9453
head (2) +2025+2256+5087+8900
hold accountable (2) +2011+3338
in front of (2) +4578
in regard to (2)
instead of (2)
Israelite (2) +408+1201+3776
Israelites (2) +1201+3776
just above (2) +5087
leave (2) +907+2143
leave alone (2) +6073
left (2) +995
left of (2)
less than (2)
like (2)
long ago (2) +4200+8158
long ago (2) +6409
long ago (2) +7710
long ago (2) +8158
made of (2)
mine (2) +5761
nearby (2) +5584
never (2)
no (2) +1172
no (2) +3972+4202
north (2) +8520
not counting (2) +963+4200
not including (2) +963+4200
nothing but (2)
of (2) +4200+7156
of one piece (2)
on (2) +4578
only (2)
other than (2) +1187
out (2)
out from (2)
outside (2) +2025+2575
over (2) +5087
over (2) +6584
promised (2) +3655+7023
pursuing (2) +339
said (2) +3655+7023
separated from (2) +6584
since (2) +255
so many (2) +8044
so not (2)
so that not (2)
some (2) +7921
some of (2)
some time later (2) +3427
south (2) +3545
speak (2) +7023
to (2) +6640
top (2) +2025+4200+5087
turning from (2)
upon (2)
where (2) +9004
without (2) +1187
your own flesh and blood (2) +3655+3870

abandon (1) +3338+8332
abandon (1) +3718
about to (1) +6964+7940
above (1) +4200+4946+5087+6645
above (1) +5087+6584
according to (1)
across from (1) +6298
across the way (1) +5584
after (1) +339
after (1) +928+1896
after (1) +7895
after (1) +7921
against (1) +3338
ahead (1) +4200+7156
all around (1) +6017
all kinds (1) +3972
all life (1) +6388
all sorts (1) +7896
all the way from (1)
allots (1)
along (1) +6298
along with (1) +963+4200
alongside (1) +6298
aloof (1) +5584
already (1) +255
always (1) +6388
am forgotten (1) +4213+8894
among (1) +907
among (1) +1068
annual (1) +2025+3427+3427
another[s] (1) +2021+2215+2296
any (1) +6388
any of (1) +907
anything (1) +1821+1821+2021+3972
anything (1) +1821+3972
area (1) +2575
around (1) +1237+6017
around (1) +2021+2575
as long as (1)
as long as live (1) +3427
as much as (1) +8049
Asher's (1) +888
avert (1) +6296+6584
avoid (1)
avoid (1) +3782
away (1) +907
away (1) +6584
away (1) +6640
away from (1) +5584
away from (1) +7156
be without (1) +4162
because (1) +889
because of (1) +3954+7156
because of (1) +5584
because of (1) +6584
because of (1) +9004
before (1) +3270
before (1) +6640
before (1) +8997+9453
before time (1) +4200+7156
beforehand (1) +4200+7156
behind (1) +294
belonging to (1)
belongs to (1)
Benjamite (1) +1228
Benjamites (1) +408+1228
Benjamites (1) +1228
beside (1) +6584
better (1) +3202
beyond (1) +2134
beyond (1) +2134+4200
bodily (1) +1414
bordering each side[s] (1)
                    +2256+2296+2296+4946
born (1) +3655+8167
branch of (1) +9348
brief (1) +7940
broke camp (1) +185+5825
broke off (1) +8740
brought about (1) +2118
by (1) +907

by (1) +4200
by (1) +6298
by (1) +6584
by (1) +7023
by (1) +9348
by myself (1) +907+3276
by not (1)
call to account (1) +1335+3338
call to account (1) +2011+6640
cause (1) +2118
causes (1)
certain (1)
choice lambs (1) +4119+7366
citizens of[s] (1)
complete (1) +2118+7891
completely (1) +1414+2256+5883+6330
concerning (1)
confront (1)
confronting (1) +7156
consent (1)
constant (1) +5584
deaf (1) +9048
defense against (1) +7156
departing from (1) +339
deprived of (1)
descendant (1) +408+2446
deserted (1) +132+401
deserted (1) +339+6590
deserted (1) +401+3782
deserted (1) +1172+3782
determined (1) +907
dictate (1) +7023
dictated (1) +7023+7924
dictating (1) +7023
dictation (1) +7023
directed by (1)
directly from (1)
disappeared (1) +2143+6524
do away with (1) +6073+9348
do so[s] (1) +2006+8740
down (1)
down (1) +8031
downstream (1) +2025+4200+5087
driven from (1)
driven from (1) +928+1896+9102+9102
during (1)
eastward (1) +7710
eluded (1) +6015+7156
entire (1) +7895
enveloped (1) +6017
Ephraimites (1) +713
escaped from (1)
even beyond (1) +6584
ever (1) +3427
ever since (1) +3427
ever since (1) +4200
every (1) +7891
every kind (1) +448+2385+2385
excelled (1)
except (1) +1187
except for (1)
extends to (1) +4200
face (1) +7156
faced (1)
facing (1)
facing (1) +5584
fail (1) +6073
failed (1) +6980
failed to keep (1) +6073
far and wide (1) +4200+6330+8158
far away (1) +4200+6330+8158
far away (1) +5305
few (1)
follow (1) +339+7756
for (1) +907
for (1) +6584
for (1) +7156
for fear of (1)
for fear of (1) +7156
for lack of (1)
for relief from (1) +4200+7156

for sake (1) +7156
former (1) +7710
formerly (1) +919+8997
forsaking (1) +907
free from (1)
from (1) +255
from (1) +2296
from (1) +4090
from (1) +4200
from (1) +4578
from (1) +5584+6524
from (1) +6017
from (1) +6298
from (1) +6524
from (1) +6640+7156
from (1) +7891
from inside (1)
from then on (1) +339+4027
frontal (1) +5584
gaunt (1) +9043
give up (1) +8740
God's (1) +466
gone from (1) +9348
got off (1) +3718+6584
had difficulty taking possession of (1) +3655
had part in (1) +2118
handed (1) +3338
have no (1) +6
have no (1) +6259+6524
have nowhere (1) +6
helpless (1) +3946
high above (1) +2025+4200+5087
higher (1) +5087
higher (1) +6584
his (1) +5647
his own (1) +2257+4213
hold responsible (1) +1335+3338
idea (1) +4213
in (1) +6584
in (1) +7931
in (1) +9348
in addition (1) +963+4200
in deference to (1) +7156
in front of (1) +7156
in presence (1)
in the course of time (1) +339+4027
in the course of time (1) +3427+3427+4200
including (1)
inquire of (1) +907+2011
inside (1) +1074+4200
inside (1) +7163
interior (1) +1074+2025
Israelite (1) +1201+3776
Israelite (1) +3776
Israelites (1) +3776
it^s (1) +1947+2023
its^s (1) +5288
jointed (1) +4200+5087+8079
just (1) +6964
keep from (1)
kept distance (1) +3656+5584
kept from (1)
Lacking (1) +1172
larger share of (1)
later (1)
later (1) +339+4027
later on (1) +3427
leave (1)
leave (1) +2143+6640
leave (1) +2143+6643
leave (1) +3718+9348
leave (1) +6015
leave (1) +6590
leave (1) +7756
leave (1) +9004
leave alone (1) +2532
leave alone (1) +6641
leaves (1) +907+2143
leaving (1) +5825
leaving (1) +6296
left (1)

left (1) +339
left (1) +907
left (1) +2143+6640
left (1) +5825
left (1) +6590
left (1) +7756+9348
lived (1)
long (1) +919
long (1) +6409
long (1) +8158
long ago (1) +3427+7710
lost (1)
lost (1) +907+5877
lost (1) +5877
lower (1) +9393
made from (1)
made up of (1)
make room for (1) +7156
make spew out (1) +3655+7023
meet (1) +7156
member (1)
more (1)
more than (1) +963+4200
most of (1)
much more than (1)
near (1)
near (1) +7396
nearby (1) +7940
neither (1) +401
never (1) +3427+4202
next to (1) +725
next to (1) +4578
next to (1) +7396
no longer be (1) +6073
no more (1)
noblest (1) +1475
none (1) +401
none (1) +3972+4202
none will be (1) +401
nor (1) +401+2256
northern (1) +2025+7600
not (1) +1187
not (1) +1194
not harm (1) +5927
nothing (1) +561+3972
now (1) +255
obscure (1) +6680+9048
of (1) +1068
of (1) +3338
of (1) +3655
of (1) +4200+8611
of (1) +6584
of (1) +7895
of all (1) +9348
off (1) +4578
often (1) +1896
old (1) +3427+7710
older (1) +1524
on (1) +907
on behalf of (1) +907
on both (1) +2256+2296+2296+4946
on both sides^s (1) +2256+2296+2296
on each side (1)   +2021+2021+2296+2296
                     +4946+4946+4946+6298+6298
on each side^s (1) +2256+2296+2296+4946
on high (1) +5087
on high (1) +5294
on terms (1) +6640
on the basis of (1)
on the other side of (1) +2134+2256+6298
on this side of (1) +6298
once (1)
opposing (1)
opposite (1) +5584
or (1)
other than (1) +963+4200
others^s (1) +2157
out (1) +1068
out (1) +7156
out of (1) +907
out of (1) +1068

out of (1) +5584
out of (1) +7156
out of (1) +7931
out of way (1) +4200+7156
outer (1) +2025+4200+5087
outnumber (1) +8045
outnumber (1) +8049
outside (1) +1946
outside (1) +2134
outweigh (1) +3877
outweighs (1) +3701
over (1) +4200+6584
pad (1) +9393
past (1) +907
past (1) +6584
peels (1) +6584
permission (1)
poured out (1) +9161
presence (1) +6584
prevent from (1)
projecting from (1)
protection from (1) +7156
received from (1)
recently (1) +2543+7940
recovery (1) +2649+2716
reject (1) +6584+7156+8938
reject (1) +6584+7156+8959
representative (1) +907
represented (1)
rest of (1)
resting on (1) +9393
rid (1) +6584+8959
risked (1) +5584+8959
say (1) +3655+7023
select a day (1) +3427+3427+4200
send (1) +907+995
sent by (1) +907
set free (1) +3338+8938
sharing (1) +430
shed by (1) +3338
side (1) +6298
sides (1) +6017+6298
since (1) +889
since (1) +3427+4200
so cannot (1)
so that no (1)
sober (1) +2021+3516+3655
some (1) +907
some distance away (1) +8158
some distance away (1) +8178
some distance from (1) +7156
southern (1) +5582
southernmost (1) +7895
southward (1) +9402
spared from (1) +7156
spoke the word (1) +7023
square (1) +2256+4946+7024+7024
started (1)
starting out from (1)
stop trusting in (1) +2532
stopped (1)
stopped (1) +6590
stopped up (1) +3877+9048
such (1) +3972
surely leave (1) +2143+2143+6584
surpasses (1)
surround (1) +2118+6017
take off (1) +3718+6584
taken (1)
taken from (1) +4200+7156
than (1) +889
than (1) +3463
than deserved (1)
the LORD's (1) +3378+6640
their (1) +2157
theirs (1) +2157
there (1) +9004
there is no (1) +401
those^s (1)
throughout (1) +3972
till no more (1)

tilting away from (1) +7156
to (1) +4200
to (1) +6584
to (1) +7156
to (1) +9393
to nothing (1) +8024
told (1) +907+9048
top of (1) +2025+4200+5087
unaware (1) +6524+6623
under (1) +3338
under (1) +7156
underneath (1) +1074
underneath (1) +9393
unduly (1) +3841
unnoticed (1) +1172+8492
unsheathed (1) +3655+9509
untraveled (1) +408+1172+6296
upward (1) +2025+4200+5087
used (1)
uttered (1) +3655
utterly (1)
was spent for making (1) +6913
west (1) +6298
when (1) +255
when (1) +2118
when (1) +3427
whenever (1) +1896+3954
wherever (1) +889
wherever (1) +2021+3972+5226
while (1)
will (1)
willingly (1) +4213
with (1) +7396
with the help of (1) +907
withdrew (1) +2143
without (1) +1172
without (1) +2575
without being aware (1) +6524
without equal (1) +401+3202
worked (1)
worse than (1)
yet (1) +889+1172
your (1) +3871
your (1) +4013
untranslated (1167)

4947 מַנְגִּינָה *mangiynāh* (1)
mock in songs (1)

4948 1מָנָה *mānāh1* (28)
counted (4)
provided (4)
assigned (3)
count (3)
be counted (2)
number (2)
take a census (2)
appoint (1)
appointed (1)
counts (1)
destine (1)
determines (1)
raise (1)
was numbered (1)
were assigned (1)

4949 מָנֶה *māneh* (5)
minas (4)
mina (1)

4950 2מָנָה *mānāh2* (12)
share (3)
piece of meat (1)
portion (1)
portions (1)
portions of food (1)
portions of meat (1)
presents (1)
presents of food (1)
some[s] (1)
special food (1)

4951 מֹנֶה *mōneh* (2)
times (2)

4952 מִנְהָג *minhāg* (2)
driving (1)
that[s] (1)

4953 מִנְהָרָה *minhārāh* (1)
shelters (1)

4954 מָנוֹד *mānôd* (1)
shake (1)

4955 1מָנוֹחַ *mānôah1* (7)
resting place (2)
came to rest (1)
home (1)
place to set (1)
places of rest (1)
rest (1)

4956 2מָנוֹחַ *mānôah2* (18)
Manoah (15)
he[s] (1)
untranslated (2)

4957 מְנוּחָה *mᵉnûhāh* (21)
rest (6)
resting place (6)
place of rest (2)
easily (1)
peace and rest (1)
place to rest (1)
places of rest (1)
quiet (1)
resting (1)
staff (1)

4958 מָנוּל *mānôl*
Variant; not used

4959 מָנוֹן *mānôn* (1)
grief (1)

4960 מָנוֹס *mānôs* (8)
refuge (4)
escape (1)
flee (1)
flee in haste (1) +5674
not escape (1) +6

4961 מְנוּסָה *mᵉnûsāh* (2)
fleeing (1)
flight (1)

4962 מָנוֹר *mānôr* (4)
rod (4)

4963 מְנוֹרָה *mᵉnôrāh* (41)
lampstand (26)
lampstands (5)
each lampstand (2) +2256+4963
each lampstand (1) +4963
it[s] (1) +2021
lamp (1)
untranslated (3)

4964 מִנְּזָר *minnᵉzār* (1)
guards (1)

4965 מְנָח *munnāh* (3)
open area (3)

4966 מִנְחָה *minhāh* (211)
grain offering (92)
grain offerings (42)
offering (18)
tribute (13)
gift (11)
offerings (9)
gifts (8)
sacrifice (5)
grain (2)
it[s] (2) +2021
offering of grain (2)
sacrifices (2)
evening sacrifice (1) +6590
sacrifice (1) +6590
untranslated (3)

4967 מְנָחוֹת *mᵉnuhôt*
Variant; not used

4968 מְנַחֵם *mᵉnahēm* (8)
Menahem (7)
Menahem's (1)

4969 1מָנַחַת *mānahat1* (2)
Manahath (2)

4970 2מָנַחַת *mānahat2* (1)
Manahath (1)

4971 מָנַחְתִּי *mānahtiy* (2)
Manahathites (2)

4972 מְנִי *mᵉniy* (1)
destiny (1)

4973 1מִנִּי *minniy1* (1)
Minni (1)

4974 2מִנִּי *minniy2* (34)
from (12)
than (3)
with (3)
by (2)
from (2) +4200
out of (2)
since (2)
before (1)
ever since (1)
of (1)
untranslated (5)

4975 מִנְיָמִין *minyāmiyn* (3)
Miniamin (2)
Miniamin's (1)

4976 1מִנִּית *minniyt1* (2)
Minnith (2)

4977 2מִנִּית *minniyt2*
Variant; not used

4978 מִנְלֶה *minleh* (1)
possessions (1)

4979 מָנַע *māna'* (29)
kept (4)
withheld (4)
withhold (4)
keep (2)
keeps (2)
refuse (2)
are denied (1)
been withheld (1)
denied (1)
deprived (1)
do not run (1)
held back (1)
hoards (1)
keep back (1)
not set (1)
refused (1)
restrain (1)

4980 מַנְעוּל *man'ûl* (6)
bolts (5)
lock (1)

4981 מִנְעָל *min'āl* (1)
bolts of gates (1)

4982 מַנְעַמִּים *man'ammiym* (1)
delicacies (1)

4983 מְנַעַנְעִים *mᵉna'an'iym* (1)
sistrums (1)

4984 מְנַקִּית *mᵉnaqiyt* (4)
bowls (3)
bowls used for drink offerings (1)

4985 מְנַשֶּׁה *mᵉnaššeh* (145)
Manasseh (130)
Manasseh's (6)
Manasseh (5) +1201
Manassites (2) +1201
tribe of Manasseh (1)
untranslated (1)

4986 מְנַשִּׁי *mᵉnaššiy* (4)
Manasseh (3)

Manassites (1)

4987 מְנָת *m'nāt* (9)
portions (3)
portion (2)
assigned (1)
contributed (1)
food (1)
lot (1) +3926

4988 מָס *mās* (1)
despairing man (1)

4989 מַס *mas* (23)
forced labor (14)
slave (2)
forced laborers (1)
labor force (1)
laborers (1)
slave labor (1)
slave labor force (1)
tribute (1)
untranslated (1)

4990 מֵסַב *mēsab* (4)
around (2)
surround (1)
table (1)

4991 מְסִבָּה *m'sibbāh* (1)
around (1)

4992 מִסָּבִיב *missābiyb*
Variant; not used

4993 1מַסְגֵּר *masgēr1* (3)
prison (3)

4994 2מַסְגֵּר *masgēr2* (4)
artisans (4)

4995 מִסְגֶּרֶת *misgeret* (18)
rim (6)
panels (5)
side panels (2)
strongholds (2)
dens (1)
untranslated (2)

4996 מַסַּד *massad* (1)
foundation (1)

4997 מִסְדְּרוֹן *misd'rôn* (1)
porch (1)

4998 מָסָה *māsāh* (4)
consume (1)
drench (1)
made melt with fear (1)
melts (1)

4999 1מַסָּה *massāh1* (3)
trials (2)
testings (1)

5000 2מַסָּה *massāh2* (1)
despair (1)

5001 3מַסָּה *massāh3* (5)
Massah (5)

5002 מִסָּה *missāh* (1)
in proportion to (1) +889+3869

5003 מַסְוֶה *masweh* (3)
veil (3)

5004 מְסוּכָה *m'sûkāh* (1)
thorn hedge (1)

5005 מַסָּח *massāh* (1)
take turns (1)

5006 מִסְחָר *mishar* (1)
revenues (1)

5007 מָסָךְ *māsak* (5)
mixed (2)
mingle (1)
mixing (1)
poured (1)

5008 מֶסֶךְ *mesek* (1)
mixed with spices (1)

5009 מָסָךְ *māsāk* (25)
curtain (17)
shielding (3)
covering (2)
curtains (1)
defenses (1)
shields (1)

5010 מְסֻכָה *m'sukāh* (1)
adorned (1)

5011 1מַסֵּכָה *massēkāh1* (26)
cast idol (5)
idol cast (3)
images (3)
cast (2)
cast idols (2)
idol (2)
image (2)
cast images (1)
cast metal (1)
forming an alliance (1) +5818
idol cast from metal (1)
idols (1)
idols cast (1)
idols made of metal (1)

5012 2מַסֵּכָה *massēkāh2* (2)
blanket (1)
sheet (1)

5013 3מַסֵּכָה *massēkāh3*
Variant; not used

5014 מִסְכֵּן *miskēn* (4)
poor (4)

5015 מְסֻכָּן *m'sukkān*
Variant; not used

5016 מִסְכְּנוֹת *misk'nôt* (7)
store (6)
buildings to store (1)

5017 מִסְכֵּנֻת *miskēnut* (1)
scarce (1) +430+928

5018 מַסֶּכֶת *masseket* (3)
fabric (3)

5019 מְסִלָּה *m'sillāh* (27)
road (10)
highway (6)
roads (3)
highways (2)
courses (1)
main road (1)
pilgrimage (1)
steps (1)
straight ahead (1)
ways (1)

5020 מַסְלוּל *maslûl* (1)
highway (1)

5021 מַסְמֵר *masmēr* (4)
nails (3)
nails down (1) +928+2616

5022 מָסַס *māsas* (21)
melt (6)
melted (3)
melted away (2)
be soaked (1)
disheartened (1) +906+4222
dropped (1)
made lose (1)
melt with fear (1) +5022
melts (1)
waste away (1)
wastes away (1)
weak (1)

5023 מַסַּע *massa'* (12)
journey (2)
travels (2)

from place to place (1) +4200
having set out (1)
order of march (1)
setting out (1)
stages in journey (1)
traveled from place to place (1)
traveling from place to place (1)
way (1)

5024 1מַסָּע *massā'1* (1)
quarry (1)

5025 2מַסָּע *massā'2* (1)
dart (1)

5026 מִסְעָד *mis'ād* (1)
supports (1)

5027 מִסְפֵּד *mispēd* (16)
wailing (5)
mourning (4)
wail (2)
weeping (2)
howl (1) +6913
lamented (1) +6199
mourns (1)

5028 מִסְפּוֹא *mispô'* (5)
fodder (4)
feed (1)

5029 מִסְפָּחָה *mispāhāh* (2)
veils (2)

5030 מִסְפַּחַת *mispahat* (3)
rash (3)

5031 1מִסְפָּר *mispār1* (133)
number (47)
listed (15)
counted (8)
few (7)
list (6)
as many as (3)
how many (2)
number (2) +5152
numbered (2)
numbers (2)
account (1)
all (1)
allotted (1)
any (1)
bowmen (1) +8008
census (1)
count (1)
counted off (1) +928+6296
countless (1) +401
during (1)
each (1) +1653
each[s] (1) +4200
few (1) +928+5071
in all (1)
innumerable (1) +401
inventory (1)
length (1)
life span (1) +3427
limit (1)
listing (1)
many (1)
measure (1)
one by one (1) +928
one for each (1) +3869
only a few (1)
only a few (1) +5493
so many (1) +8041
total (1) +3972+4200
very few (1) +5493
untranslated (10)

5032 2מִסְפָּר *mispār2* (1)
Mispar (1)

5033 מִסְפֶּרֶת *misperet* (1)
Mispereth (1)

5034 מָסַר *māsar* (2)
supplied (1)

the means of (1)

5035 מֹסְרוֹת *mōsĕrôṯ* (2)
Moseroth (2)

5036 מֹסְרָם *mōsārām*
Variant; not used

5037 מָסֹרֶת *māsōreṯ* (1)
bond (1)

5038 מִסָּת *missaṯ*
Variant; not used

5039 מִסְתּוֹר *mistôr* (1)
hiding place (1)

5040 מַסְתֵּר *mastēr* (1)
hide (1)

5041 מִסְתָּר *mistār* (10)
ambush (2)
hiding (2)
secret places (2)
cover (1)
hiding places (1)
secret (1)
untranslated (1)

5042 מַעֲבָד *ma'ăḇāḏ* (1)
deeds (1)

5043 מַעֲבֶה *ma'ăḇeh* (1)
molds (1)

5044 מַעֲבָר *ma'ăḇār* (3)
ford (1)
pass (1)
stroke (1)

5045 מַעְבָּרָה *ma'bārāh* (8)
fords (5)
pass (2)
river crossings (1)

5046 1מַעְגָּל *ma'gāl1* (3)
camp (3)

5047 2מַעְגָּל *ma'gāl2* (13)
paths (8)
path (2)
carts (1)
way (1)
ways (1)

5048 מָעַד *mā'aḏ* (8)
turn (2)
bent (1)
lame (1)
slip (1)
slipping (1)
wavering (1)
wrenched (1)

5049 מַעֲדַי *ma'ăday* (1)
Maadai (1)

5050 מַעַדְיָה *ma'adyāh* (1)
Moadiah (1)

5051 מַעֲדַנּוֹת *ma'ădannôṯ* (2)
beautiful (1)
confidently (1)

5052 מַעֲדַנִּים *ma'ădanniym* (3)
delicacies (2)
delight (1)

5053 מַעְדֵּר *ma'dēr* (1)
hoe (1)

5054 מְעָה *mā'āh* (1)
numberless grains (1)

5055 מֵעֶה *mē'eh* (33)
body (4)
bowels (4)
heart (4)
anguish (2)
inside (2)
stomach (2)
within (2)

birth (1) +562
children (1) +7368
flesh (1)
have (1) +928
I (1) +3276
inside (1) +928
intestines (1)
line (1)
sons (1) +3665
stomachs (1)
tenderness (1) +2162
within (1) +928+9348
womb (1)

5056 מָעוֹג *mā'ôg* (1)
bread (1)

5057 מָעוֹז *mā'ôz* (35)
fortress (8)
refuge (8)
stronghold (7)
fortresses (2)
helmet (2) +8031
protection (2)
height (1)
mightiest fortresses (1) +4448
protect (1)
strength (1)
strong (1)
untranslated (1)

5058 מָעוֹזֵן *mā'ôzen* (1)
fortresses (1)

5059 מָעוֹךְ *mā'ôk* (1)
Maoch (1)

5060 1מָעוֹן *mā'ôn1*
Variant; not used

5061 2מָעוֹן *mā'ôn2* (18)
dwelling (7)
dwelling place (4)
haunt (4)
den (1)
refuge (1)
where live (1)

5062 3מָעוֹן *mā'ôn3* (3)
Maon (2)
Maonites (1)

5063 4מָעוֹן *mā'ôn4* (6)
Maon (6)

5064 מְעוֹנִים *mĕ'ûniym* (5)
Meunites (3)
Meunim (2)

5065 מְעוֹנֹתַי *mĕ'ônōṯay* (2)
Meonothai (2)

5066 מָעוּף *mā'ûp* (1)
gloom (1)

5067 מָעוֹר *mā'ôr* (1)
naked bodies (1)

5068 מַעֲזְיָה *ma'azyāh* (1)
Maaziah (1)

5069 מַעַזְיָהוּ *ma'azyāhû* (1)
Maaziah (1)

5070 מָעַט *mā'aṭ* (22)
few (4)
decrease (2)
smaller (2)
decreased (1)
dwindles away (1)
gathered little (1)
give less (1)
just a few (1)
let diminish (1)
little (1)
make few in number (1)
make weak (1)
no less than (1)
numbers decreased (1)

reduce to nothing (1)
small (1)
trifling (1)

5071 מְעַט *mĕ'aṭ* (101)
little (33)
few (12)
not enough (5)
only a few (5)
little while (3)
smaller (3)
soon (3) +3869
almost (2) +3869
isn't enough (2)
short distance (2)
soon (2) +6388
almost (1) +6388
brief (1)
brink (1)
few (1) +928+5031
few (1) +3869
few in number (1) +5493
fewest (1)
how quickly (1) +3869
in a moment (1) +3869
in a very short time (1) +4663+6388
little more (1)
little while (1) +6388
little while (1) +8092
many (1) +4202
might well have (1) +3869
moment's (1)
of little value (1) +3869
only a little (1)
scarcely (1) +3869
short (1)
some (1)
some (1) +3869
soon (1) +3869+7775
too few (1)
too little (1)
very few (1) +4663
very soon (1) +4663+6388
wasn't enough (1)
waste away (1)

5072 מְעֻטָּה *mĕ'uṭṭāh*
Variant; not used

5073 מַעֲטֶה *ma'ăṭeh* (1)
garment (1)

5074 מַעֲטָפֹת *ma'ăṭepeṯ* (1)
capes (1)

5075 מְעִי *mĕ'iy* (1)
heap (1)

5076 מָעַי *mā'ay* (1)
Maai (1)

5077 מְעִיל *mĕ'iyl* (28)
robe (20)
cloak (4)
robes (2)
garment (1)
untranslated (1)

5078 מַעְיָן *ma'yān* (23)
springs (10)
spring (5)
springs (3) +4784
fountain (2)
fountains (1)
well (1)
wells (1)

5079 מַעְיָנִים *mĕ'iyniym* (2)
untranslated (2)

5080 מָעַךְ *mā'ak* (4)
bruised (1)
fondled (1)
stuck (1)
were fondled (1)

5081 1מַעֲכָה *ma'ăkāh1* (3)
Maacah (3)

5082 מַעֲכָה2 *ma"ᵃkāh2* (19)
Maacah (19)

5083 מַעֲכָת *ma"ᵃkāt* (1)
theyˢ (1) +1770+2256

5084 מַעֲכָתִי *ma"ᵃkātiy* (8)
Maacah (3)
Maacathite (3)
Maacathite (1) +1201
Maacathites (1)

5085 מָעַל *mā'al* (36)
unfaithful (13)
unfaithful (7) +5086
acted unfaithfully (2) +5086
acted unfaithfully (1)
betray (1)
break faith (1) +5086
broke faith (1)
commits a violation (1) +5086
forsaking (1) +5086
more and more unfaithful (1) +5086+8049
most unfaithful (1) +5086
treachery (1) +5086
unfaithfulness (1) +5086
unfaithfulness guilty of (1) +5086
unfaithfulness showed (1) +5086
violating the ban (1)
untranslated (1)

5086 1מַעַל *ma'all* (29)
unfaithful (7) +5085
unfaithfulness (6)
acted unfaithfully (2) +5085
break faith (1) +5085
commits a violation (1) +5085
disobedience (1)
falsehood (1)
forsaking (1) +5085
matter (1)
more and more unfaithful (1) +5085+8049
most unfaithful (1) +5085
treachery (1) +5085
turning away (1)
unfaithfulness (1) +5085
unfaithfulness guilty of (1) +5085
unfaithfulness showed (1) +5085
untranslated (1)

5087 2מַעַל *ma'al2* (140)
more (36) +2025
above (19) +4946
upward (6) +2025+4200
above (4) +2025+4200+4946
above (3) +2025+4200
on (3) +2025
over (3) +2025+4200+4946
head (2) +2025+2256+4946+8900
higher (2) +2025
highly (2) +2025+4200
just above (2) +4946
over (2) +4946
top (2) +2025+4200+4946
up (2) +2025+4200
very (2) +2025+4200
above (1) +4200+4946+4946+6645
above (1) +4946+6584
at each successive level (1)
     +2025+2025+4200+4200+5087
beyond (1) +2025
deep (1) +2025
depth (1) +2025+4200
downstream (1) +2025+4200+4946
exceedingly (1) +2025+4200
heights (1) +2025+4200
high above (1) +2025+4200+4946
higher (1) +4946
higher than (1) +2025+4200+8049
in ascending stages (1)
     +2025+2025+4200+4200+5087
jointed (1) +4200+4946+8079
magnificence (1) +2025
more (1) +2025+4200

more and more powerful (1)
     +1541+2025+2143+2256+4200+6330
older (1) +2025
on high (1) +4946
outer (1) +2025+4200+4946
over and above (1) +2025+4200
overturned (1) +2025+2200+4200
project upward (1) +2025+4200
severe (1) +2025+4200
top (1)
top (1) +2025
top (1) +2025+4200
top of (1) +2025+4200+4946
upstream (1) +2025+4200
upward (1) +2025+4200+4946
very (1) +2025+4200+6330
wielding (1) +995+2025+4200
young and old (1) +2025+2256
untranslated (15)

5088 מֵעַל *mē'al*
Variant; not used

5089 מֹעַל *mō'al* (1)
lifted (1)

5090 מַעֲלֶה *ma"ᵃleh* (16)
pass (7)
hill (2)
way (2)
ascent (1)
going up (1)
mount (1)
stairs (1)
way up (1)

5091 1מַעֲלֶה *ma"ᵃlāhl* (1)
what is going through (1)

5092 2מַעֲלֶה *ma"ᵃlāh2* (48)
steps (22)
ascents (15)
stairway (2)
flight of stairs (1)
journey (1)
lofty palace (1)
most exalted (1) +9366
untranslated (5)

5093 מַעֲלָה *ma'lāh*
Variant; not used

5094 מַעֲלִיל *ma"ᵃliyl* (1)
untranslated (1)

5095 מַעֲלָל *ma"ᵃlāl* (42)
deeds (16)
actions (8)
done (6)
practices (3)
dealings (1)
do (1)
evil practices (1)
sins (1)
ways (1)
what doing (1)
wicked deeds (1)
work (1)
untranslated (1)

5096 מַעֲמָד *ma"ᵃmād* (5)
attending (2)
duty (1)
places (1)
position (1)

5097 מָעֳמָד *mo"ᵒmād* (1)
foothold (1)

5098 מַעֲמָסָה *ma"ᵃmāsāh* (1)
immovable (1)

5099 מַעֲמַקִּים *ma"ᵃmaqqiym* (5)
depths (3)
deep (2)

5100 מַעַן *ma'an* (271)
so that (78)

to (36)
that (24)
for sake (22)
for the sake of (22)
because of (17)
so (17)
then (10)
and (7)
in order to (6)
for (5)
therefore (4)
bent on (1)
for then (1)
in behalf of (1)
in this way (1)
otherwise (1) +889+4202
that is why (1)
this (1)
thus (1)
till (1)
untranslated (14)

5101 1מַעֲנֶה *ma"ᵃnehl* (7)
answer (2)
giving an apt reply (1) +7023
reply (1)
respond (1)
say (1)
way to refute (1)

5102 2מַעֲנֶה *ma"ᵃneh2* (1)
ends (1)

5103 מַעֲנָה *ma"ᵃnāh* (2)
acre (1) +7538
furrows (1)

5104 מְעֹנָה *m'ᵒōnāh* (9)
dens (5)
refuge (2)
den (1)
dwelling place (1)

5105 מַעֲנִית *ma"ᵃniyt* (1)
untranslated (1)

5106 מַעַץ *ma'as* (1)
Maaz (1)

5107 מַעֲצֵבָה *ma"ᵃsēbāh* (1)
torment (1)

5108 מַעֲצָד *ma"ᵃsād* (2)
chisel (1)
tool (1)

5109 מַעְצוֹר *ma'sôr* (1)
hinder (1)

5110 מַעְצָר *ma'sār* (1)
self-control (1) +4200+8120

5111 מַעֲקֶה *ma"ᵃqeh* (1)
parapet (1)

5112 מַעֲקַשִּׁים *ma"ᵃqaššiym* (1)
rough places (1)

5113 מַעַר *ma'ar* (2)
available space (1)
nakedness (1)

5114 1מַעֲרָב *ma"ᵃrābl* (9)
wares (8)
merchants (1) +6842

5115 2מַעֲרָב *ma"ᵃrāb2* (15)
west (12)
place of setting (1)
west (1) +2025
untranslated (1)

5116 מַעֲרֶה *ma"ᵃreh*
Variant; not used

5117 מְעָרָה *m'ᵃ'ārāhl* (40)
cave (30)
caves (6)
den (1)
untranslated (3)

5118 מְעָרָה2 *mᵉ'ārāh2* (1)
wasteland (1)

5119 מַעֲרָךְ *ma'ᵃrāḵ* (1)
plans (1)

5120 מַעֲרָכָה *ma'ᵃrāḵāh* (19)
armies (3)
battle line (3)
ranks (3)
lines (2)
battle lines (1)
battle positions (1)
battlefield (1) +8441
facing each other (1) +7925
forces (1)
itˢ (1) +2021
proper kind (1)
row (1)

5121 מַעֲרֶכֶת *ma'ᵃreḵeṯ* (10)
set out on the table (3)
consecrated bread (2)
row (2)
rows (1)
set out (1)
setting out the consecrated bread (1)

5122 מַעֲרֹם *ma'ᵃrōm* (1)
naked (1)

5123 מַעֲרָץ *ma'ᵃrāṣ*
Variant; not used

5124 מַעֲרָצָה *ma'ᵃrāṣāh* (1)
great power (1)

5125 מַעֲרָת *ma'ᵃrāṯ* (1)
Maarath (1)

5126 מַעֲשֶׂה *ma'ᵃśeh* (236)
work (60)
works (17)
made (14)
what done (11)
what made (10)
deeds (8)
things (7)
like (6) +3869
everything (4) +3972
worked (4)
do (3)
like (3)
practices (3)
whatˢ (3) +2021
crops (2)
deed (2)
done (2)
done (2) +6913
fashioned (2)
labor (2)
network (2) +8407
objects (2)
occupation (2)
products (2)
shape (2)
what deserve (2) +3869
what did (2)
working (2)
accomplished (1)
achievement (1) +4179
acting (1)
actions (1)
acts (1)
baked goods (1) +685+4407
baking (1)
basework (1) +4029
construction (1)
crafted (1)
creature made (1)
crime (1) +8288
crop (1)
customs (1)
design (1)
do (1) +3338

does (1)
duties (1)
formed (1)
fruit (1)
handiwork (1) +3338
how made (1)
idols made (1)
interwoven chains (1) +9249
is done (1) +6913
making (1)
man-made (1) +132+3338
network (1) +8422+8422
nothing (1) +4202
performance (1)
perfumes (1) +5351
projects (1)
property (1)
sculptured (1) +7589
shapes (1) +3338
structure (1)
that does (1)
that done (1)
that made (1)
things did (1)
things did (1) +3338
thisˢ (1) +2021+2021+2296
trouble (1)
undertook (1)
verses (1)
way (1)
well-dressed hair (1) +5250
what do (1)
what make (1)
whatever do (1)
work (1) +6913
woven (1) +755
wrongdoing (1)
untranslated (2)

5127 מַעֲשַׂי *ma'ᵃśay* (1)
Maasai (1)

5128 מַעֲשֵׂיָה *ma'ᵃśēyāh* (16)
Maaseiah (16)

5129 מַעֲשֵׂיָהוּ *ma'ᵃśēyāhû* (7)
Maaseiah (7)

5130 מַעֲשֵׂר *ma'ᵃśēr* (32)
tithe (13)
tithes (13)
tenth (5)
setting aside a tenth (1) +6923

5131 מַעֲשַׁקּוֹת *ma'ᵃšaqqôṯ* (2)
extortion (1)
tyrannical (1) +8041

5132 מֹף *mōp̄* (1)
Memphis (1)

5133 מִפְגָּע *mip̄gā'* (1)
target (1)

5134 מַפָּח *mappāḥ* (1)
gasp (1)

5135 מַפֻּחַ *mappuaḥ* (1)
bellows (1)

5136 מְפִיבֹשֶׁת *mᵉp̄iyḇōšeṯ* (15)
Mephibosheth (15)

5137 מֻפִּים *muppiym* (1)
Muppim (1)

5138 מֵפִיץ *mēp̄iyṣ* (1)
club (1)

5139 מַפָּל *mappāl* (2)
folds (1)
sweepings (1)

5140 מִפְלָאוֹת *mip̄lā'ôṯ* (1)
wonders (1)

5141 מִפְלַגָּה *mip̄laggāh* (1)
subdivisions (1)

5142 מַפָּלָה *mappālāh* (1)
ruins (1)

5143 מַפֵּלָה *mappēlāh* (2)
ruin (2)

5144 מִפְלָט *mip̄lāṭ* (1)
place of shelter (1)

5145 מִפְלֶצֶת *mip̄leṣeṯ* (4)
poleˢ (2)
repulsive (2)

5146 מִפְלָשׂ *mip̄lāś* (1)
hang poised (1)

5147 מַפֶּלֶת *mappeleṯ* (8)
fall (3)
downfall (2)
carcass (1)
fallen (1)
shipwreck (1)

5148 מִפְעָל *mip̄'āl* (1)
deeds (1)

5149 מִפְעָלָה *mip̄'ālāh* (2)
what done (1)
works (1)

5150 מַפָּץ *mappāṣ* (1)
deadly (1)

5151 מַפֵּץ *mappēṣ* (1)
war club (1)

5152 מִפְקָד *mip̄qāḏ* (5)
number (2) +5031
appointment (1)
designated part (1)
inspection (1)

5153 מִפְרָץ *mip̄rāṣ* (1)
coves (1)

5154 מַפְרֶקֶת *map̄reqeṯ* (1)
neck (1)

5155 מִפְרָשׂ *mip̄rāś* (2)
sail (1)
spreads out (1)

5156 מִפְשָׂעָה *mip̄śā'āh* (1)
buttocks (1)

5157 מִפְתָּח *mip̄tāḥ* (1)
open (1)

5158 מַפְתֵּחַ *map̄tēaḥ* (3)
key (2)
key for opening (1)

5159 מִפְתָּן *mip̄tān* (8)
threshold (8)

5160 מֵץ *mēṣ* (1)
oppressor (1)

5161 מֹץ *mōṣ* (8)
chaff (8)

5162 מָצָא *māṣā'* (456)
found (108)
find (85)
be found (25)
finds (16)
was found (12)
is found (11)
were (9)
been found (8)
were found (8)
come upon (7)
meet (7)
discovered (6)
finding (6)
is caught (6)
met (6)
pleased with (5) +928+2834+6524
present (5)
are (3)
came upon (3)

discover (3)
had (3) +907
handed (3)
came (2)
comprehend (2)
fathom (2)
happened (2)
have enough (2)
is (2)
lived (2)
overtook (2)
prospers (2) +3202
reach (2)
still (2)
survives (2)
was (2)
acquire (1)
acquired (1)
acquires (1)
afford (1) +1896+3338
are found (1)
be room enough (1)
be seen (1)
become (1)
been brought (1)
before (1)
bring a reward (1)
brings (1)
brings upon (1)
came across (1)
captured (1)
catch (1)
caught up (1)
comes (1)
detect (1)
discover meaning (1)
displease (1) +928+2834+4202+6524
displeasing (1) +928+2834+4202+6524
do (1)
doing (1)
enough (1)
ever-present (1) +4394
fall on (1)
favorable toward (1) +928+2834+6524
find out (1)
following (1)
found courage (1)
found out (1)
found to be true (1)
gain (1)
gained (1)
get (1)
had (1)
had (1) +4200
hand over (1) +928+3338
handed over (1) +928+3338
happened to (1)
has (1) +4200
have (1)
have (1) +928+3338
here (1)
hit (1)
is attained (1)
is captured (1)
is found (1) +5162
lay hold (1)
lay on (1)
lies (1)
lift (1)
looking for (1)
lot (1)
overcome (1)
overtake (1)
possess (1)
probe (1)
prosper (1) +3202
reaches (1)
reaped (1)
regards (1) +928+6524
regards (1) +4200+7156
search (1)

seize (1)
seized (1)
solved (1)
spreads (1)
still out (1)
took (1)
uncovered (1)
was caught (1)
were caught (1)
win (1)
untranslated (9)

5163 מַצָּב *maṣṣāb* (10)
outpost (4)
detachment (1)
garrison (1)
office (1)
outposts (1)
stood (1) +3922+8079
stood (1) +8079

5164 מֻצָּב *muṣṣāb* (2)
pillar (1)
towers (1)

5165 מַצָּבָה *maṣṣābāh* (1)
outpost (1)

5166 מִצָּבָה *miṣṣābāh*
Variant; not used

5167 מַצֵּבָה *maṣṣēbāh* (34)
sacred stones (14)
pillar (10)
sacred stone (5)
monument (1)
pillars (1)
sacred pillars (1)
stone pillars (1)
untranslated (1)

5168 מְצֹבָיָה *mᵉṣōbāyāh* (1)
Mezobaite (1)

5169 1מַצֶּבֶת *maṣṣebet1* (2)
stump (1)
stumps (1)

5170 2מַצֶּבֶת *maṣṣebet2* (2)
pillar (2)

5171 מְצָד *mᵉṣād* (11)
strongholds (7)
fortress (2)
stronghold (2)

5172 מָצָה *māṣāh* (7)
be drained out (2)
drain dry (1)
drained to dregs (1) +9272
drink down (1)
drink up (1)
wrung out (1)

5173 מֹצָה *mōṣāh* (1)
Mozah (1)

5174 1מַצָּה *maṣṣāh1* (53)
bread made without yeast (14)
unleavened bread (20)
without yeast (5)
bread without yeast (3)
bread (2)
made without yeast (2)
feast of unleavened bread (1)
prepared without yeast (1)
unleavened (1)
untranslated (4)

5175 2מַצָּה *maṣṣāh2* (3)
quarrel (1)
quarrels (1)
strife (1)

5176 מִצְהָב *muṣhāb*
Variant; not used

5177 מִצְהָלוֹת *mishālôt* (2)
lustful neighings (1)

neighing (1) +7754

5178 1מָצוֹד *māṣôd1* (2)
net (1)
snare (1)

5179 2מָצוֹד *māṣôd2* (1)
plunder (1)

5180 1מְצוּדָה *mᵉṣûdāh1* (3)
snare (2)
prey (1)

5181 2מְצוּדָה *mᵉṣûdāh2* (18)
fortress (9)
stronghold (7)
prison (1)
strong fortress (1) +1074

5182 1מְצוֹדָה *mᵉṣôdāh1* (1)
net (1)

5183 2מְצוֹדָה *mᵉṣôdāh2* (2)
fortress (1)
prison (1)

5184 מִצְוָה *miṣwāh* (184)
commands (138)
command (11)
commanded (4)
ordered (4)
commandments (3)
prescribed (3)
admonition (2)
commanded (2) +7422
instructions (2)
law (2)
commandment (1)
gave (1)
laws (1)
order (1)
orders (1)
rules (1)
terms (1)
way prescribed (1)
what ordered (1)
what[s] (1) +2021+2021+2296
untranslated (3)

5185 מְצוּלָה *mᵉṣôlāh* (12)
depths (9)
deep (2)
ravine (1)

5186 מָצוֹק *māṣôq* (6)
distress (3)
suffering (2)
stress (1)

5187 מָצוּק *māṣûq* (2)
foundations (1)
stood (1)

5188 מְצוּקָה *mᵉṣûqāh* (7)
distress (4)
anguish (3)

5189 1מָצוֹר *māṣôr1* (22)
siege (15)
besieged (2)
besiege (1) +928+995+2021
laid siege (1) +928+995+2021
ramparts (1)
siege works (1)
siegeworks (1)

5190 2מָצוֹר *māṣôr2* (4)
fortified (2)
defense (1)
stronghold (1)

5191 3מָצוֹר *māṣôr3* (5)
Egypt (5)

5192 4מָצוֹר *māṣôr4*
Variant; not used

5193 מְצוּרָה *mᵉṣûrāh* (8)
fortified (5)

defenses (1)
fortress (1)
siege works (1)

5194 מְצוּרוֹת *maṣṣûṯ* (1)
enemies (1) +408

5195 מֵצַח *mēsaḥ* (13)
forehead (8)
hardened (2) +2617
brazen look (1)
foreheads (1)
untranslated (1)

5196 מִצְחָה *mishāh* (1)
greaves (1)

5197 מְצִלָּה *mᵉsillāh* (1)
bells (1)

5198 מְצֻלָּה *mᵉsulāh*
Variant; not used

5199 מְצִלְתַּיִם *mᵉsiltayim* (13)
cymbals (13)

5200 מִצְנֶפֶת *misnepet* (12)
turban (11)
untranslated (1)

5201 מַצָּע *massāʿ* (1)
bed (1)

5202 מִצְעָד *misʿād* (3)
steps (2)
submission (1)

5203 1מִצְעָר *misʿār1* (5)
small (2)
humble (1)
little while (1)
only a few (1)

5204 2מִצְעָר *misʿār2* (1)
Mizar (1)

5205 1מִצְפֶּה *mispeh1* (2)
place that overlooks (1)
watchtower (1)

5206 2מִצְפֶּה *mispeh2* (5)
Mizpah (4)
thereˢ (1) +1680

5207 מִצְפָּה *mispāh* (41)
Mizpah (39)
thereˢ (1) +928+2021
untranslated (1)

5208 מַצְפּוֹן *maspôn* (1)
hidden treasures (1)

5209 מָצַץ *māsas* (1)
drink deeply (1)

5210 מֵצַר *mēsar* (3)
anguish (2)
distress (1)

5211 מְצָרָה *massārāh*
Variant; not used

5212 מִצְרִי *misriy* (24)
Egyptian (21)
Egyptian's (2)
Egyptians (1)

5213 מִצְרַיִם *misrayim* (687)
Egypt (374)
Egypt (184) +824
Egyptians (82)
Egyptian (10)
Egypt's (5)
Mizraim (4)
lower Egypt (2) +824
themˢ (2)
country (1)
Egypt (1) +1426
Egypt (1) +1473
Egyptians (1) +1201
hereˢ (1) +2025

hisˢ (1) +4200+4889
itˢ (1) +4722
lower Egypt (1)
the Egyptians (1)
thereˢ (1)
thereˢ (1) +928
theyˢ (1)
whoˢ (1)
untranslated (11)

5214 מַצְרֵף *masrēp̄* (2)
crucible (2)

5215 מַק *maq* (2)
decay (1)
stench (1)

5216 1מַקֶּבֶת *maqqebeṯ1* (4)
hammer (3)
hammers (1)

5217 2מַקֶּבֶת *maqqebeṯ2* (1)
quarry (1) +1014

5218 מַקֵּדָה *maqqēḏāh* (9)
Makkedah (9)

5219 מִקְדָּשׁ *miqdāš* (75)
sanctuary (61)
sanctuaries (4)
holy place (2)
holiest (1)
holy places (1)
holy things (1)
itˢ (1)
most holy place (1) +7731
sanctuary (1) +1074
shrine (1)
temple (1)

5220 מַקְהֵל *maqhēl* (2)
great assembly (1)
great congregation (1)

5221 מַקְהֵלוֹת *maqhēlôṯ* (2)
Makheloth (2)

5222 מִקְוֵא *miqwē'*
Variant; not used

5223 1מִקְוֶה *miqweh1* (5)
hope (5)

5224 2מִקְוֶה *miqweh2* (3)
collecting (1)
gathered (1)
reservoirs (1) +4784

5225 מִקְוֶה *miqwāh* (1)
reservoir (1)

5226 מָקוֹם *māqôm* (401)
place (268)
home (14)
places (12)
land (5)
room (5)
site (4)
spot (4)
whereˢ (4)
dwelling place (3)
wherever (3) +889+928
anywhere (2) +928+3972
dwell (2)
everywhere (2) +3972
hereˢ (2) +2021+2021+2296
seat (2) +8699
sites (2)
space (2)
thereˢ (2)
whereˢ (2) +2021
wherever (2) +889+928+2021+3972
area (1)
base (1)
channels (1)
commands (1)
countries (1)
direction (1)

dwelling (1)
everywhere (1) +928+3972
everywhere (1) +2021+3972
haunt (1)
hereˢ (1) +928
hereˢ (1) +928+2021+2021+2296
hereˢ (1) +2021
homeland (1)
homeland (1) +824
homes (1)
itˢ (1)
itˢ (1) +2021+2021+2085
Ninevehˢ (1) +2023
points (1)
position (1)
positions (1)
post (1)
proper place (1) +889+2118+9004
regions (1)
reside (1)
rest (1)
sanctuary (1) +7731
seated (1) +5989
somewhere (1)
suitable (1)
thereˢ (1) +2023
town (1)
town records (1) +9133
way (1)
where (1) +361
where dwells (1)
where lived (1)
whereˢ (1) +928
whereˢ (1) +928+2021
wherever (1) +285+889+928+2021
wherever (1) +889+2021+3972+6584
wherever (1) +889+928+2021
wherever (1) +928+2021+3972
wherever (1) +2021+3972+4946
whereverˢ (1) +889
untranslated (13)

5227 מָקוֹר *māqôr* (18)
fountain (9)
spring (3)
assembly (1)
flow (1)
itˢ (1)
source of (1)
springs (1)
well (1)

5228 מִקָּח *miqqāḥ* (1)
bribery (1) +8816

5229 מַקָּחוֹת *maqqāḥôṯ* (1)
merchandise (1)

5230 מִקְטָר *miqtār* (1)
burning (1)

5231 מֻקְטָר *muqtār* (1)
incense (1)

5232 מְקַטֶּרֶת *mᵉqatteret* (1)
incense altars (1)

5233 מִקְטֶרֶת *miqteret* (2)
censer (2)

5234 מַקֵּל *maqqēl* (18)
staff (7)
branches (6)
branch (1)
staffs (1)
stick of wood (1)
sticks (1)
war clubs (1) +3338

5235 מִקְלוֹת *miqlôṯ* (4)
Mikloth (4)

5236 מִקְלָט *miqlāt* (20)
refuge (17)
place of refuge (1)
protection (1)

untranslated (1)

5237 מִקְלַעַת *miqla'aṯ* (4)
carved (2) +7844
carved (1)
engraving (1)

5238 מִקְנֶה *miqneh* (76)
livestock (45)
cattle (4)
flocks (4)
herdsmen (2) +8286
owned (2) +2118
acquired (1)
animal (1)
animals (1)
bought (1)
cattle (1) +1330
droves of livestock (1)
flocks (1) +7366
flocks and herds (1)
herds (1)
herds (1) +1330
herds and flocks (1)
herds of livestock (1)
herdsmen (1)
livestock (1) +989
sheep and goats (1) +7366
tend livestock (1) +408+2118
tended livestock (1) +408+2118
that[s] (1)
untranslated (1)

5239 מִקְנָה *miqnāh* (15)
bought (4)
purchase (3)
bought (2) +4084
price (2)
paid (1)
property (1)
untranslated (1)

5240 מִקְנֵיָהוּ *miqnēyāhû* (2)
Mikneiah (2)

5241 מִקְסָם *miqsām* (2)
divinations (2)

5242 מָקֵץ *māqas* (1)
Makaz (1)

5243 מִקְצוֹעַ *miqsôa'* (12)
corners (5)
angle (4)
angle of the wall (1)
in each corner (1) +928+928+5243

5244 מַקְצֻעָה *maqsu'āh* (1)
chisels (1)

5245 מָקַק *māqaq* (10)
waste away (4)
rot (3)
be dissolved (1)
fester (1)
wasting away (1)

5246 מִקְרָא *miqrā'* (23)
assembly (15)
assemblies (3)
another[s] (1) +7731
assemble (1)
calling together (1)
convocations (1) +7924
read (1)

5247 מִקְרֶה *miqreh* (10)
fate (4)
destiny (2)
as it turned out (1) +7936
by chance (1)
something happened (1)
that[s] (1)

5248 מְקָרֶה *mᵉqāreh* (1)
rafters (1)

5249 מְקֵרָה *mᵉqērāh* (2)

house (1)
summer palace (1)

5250 מִקְשֶׁה *miqšeh* (1)
well-dressed hair (1) +5126

5251 1מִקְשָׁה *miqšāh1* (9)
hammered (5)
hammered out (2)
hammer out (1) +6913
untranslated (1)

5252 2מִקְשָׁה *miqšāh2* (2)
field of melons (1)
melon patch (1)

5253 1מַר *mar1* (41)
bitter (18)
bitterness (7)
bitterly (4)
anguish (3)
bitter suffering (2)
bitter anguish (1)
deadly (1)
discontented (1) +5883
fierce (1) +5883
hot-tempered (1) +5883
in anguish (1) +5883
ruthless (1)

5254 2מַר *mar2* (1)
drop (1)

5255 מֹר *mōr* (12)
myrrh (12)

5256 1מָרָא *mārā'1*
Variant; not used

5257 2מָרָא *mārā'2* (1)
spreads feathers to run (1) +928+2021+5294

5258 3מָרָא *mārā'3*
Variant; not used

5259 4מָרָא *mārā'4* (1)
Mara (1)

5260 מַרְאֶה *mar'eh* (103)
appearance (14)
looked (10)
vision (10)
appears (5)
beautiful (5) +3202
appear (3)
appeared (3)
beautiful (3) +3637
like (3) +3869
that[s] (3)
face (2)
handsome (2) +3637
sight (2)
sleek (2) +3637
ugly (2) +8273
what sees (2)
clearly (1)
eye (1)
features (1)
handsome (1) +3202
huge (1)
imposing (1) +1524+4200
look (1)
look at (1)
looked (1) +8011
pattern (1)
saw (1) +6524
see (1)
see (1) +6524
seem (1)
sights (1)
sights (1) +6524
similar (1) +2021+3869
what[s] (1)
untranslated (14)

5261 1מַרְאָה *mar'āh1* (11)
vision (5)

visions (5)
it[s] (1) +2021

5262 2מַרְאָה *mar'āh2* (1)
mirrors (1)

5263 מֻרְאָה *mur'āh* (1)
crop (1)

5264 מְרֹאוֹן *mᵉr'ôn*
Variant; not used

5265 מְרַאֲשׁוֹת *mᵉra'ᵃšōṯ* (13)
near head (4)
head (2)
under head (2)
by head (1)
heads (1)
untranslated (3)

5266 מֵרַב *mērab* (4)
Merab (4)

5267 מַרְבַד *marbad* (2)
covered (1) +8048
coverings bed (1)

5268 מִרְבָּה *mirbāh* (1)
so much (1)

5269 מַרְבֶּה *marbeh* (3)
abundance (1)
increase (1)
untranslated (1)

5270 מַרְבִּית *marbiyṯ* (5)
most (2)
descendants (1) +1074
greatness (1)
profit (1)

5271 מַרְבֵּץ *marbēs* (2)
lair (1)
resting place (1)

5272 מַרְבֵּק *marbēq* (4)
fattened (3)
stall (1)

5273 מַרְגּוֹעַ *margôa'* (1)
rest (1)

5274 מַרְגְּלוֹת *margᵉlōṯ* (6)
feet (4)
legs (1)
untranslated (1)

5275 מַרְגֵּמָה *margēmāh* (1)
sling (1)

5276 מַרְגֵּעָה *margē'āh* (1)
place of repose (1)

5277 מָרַד *mārad* (25)
rebelled (12)
rebel (7)
revolt (2)
rebelling (1)
rebellion (1)
rebellious (1)
untranslated (1)

5278 1מֶרֶד *mered1* (1)
rebellion (1)

5279 2מֶרֶד *mered2* (2)
Mered (2)

5280 מַרְדּוּת *mardûṯ* (1)
rebellious (1)

5281 מְרֹדָךְ *mᵉrōdāk* (1)
Marduk (1)

5282 מְרֹדַךְ־בַּלְאֲדָן *mᵉrōdak-bal'ᵃdān* (2)
Merodach-Baladan (2)

5283 מָרְדְּכַי *mordᵉkay* (60)
Mordecai (49)
Mordecai's (5)
he[s] (3)
him[s] (2)

heˢ (1) +408+2021

5284 מֻרְדָּף *murdāp* (1)
aggression (1)

5285 מָרָה *mārāh*
Variant; not used

5286 1מָרָה *mārāh1* (44)
rebelled (20)
rebellious (9)
rebel (3)
defied (2)
rebels (2)
defying (1)
disobedient (1)
disobeyed (1)
hostility (1)
most rebellious (1) +5286
rebelling (1)
rebellion (1)

5287 2מָרָה *mārāh2*
Variant; not used

5288 3מָרָה *mārāh3* (5)
Marah (4)
itsˢ (1) +4946

5289 מֹרָה *mōrāh* (2)
bitterness (1)
source of grief (1) +8120

5290 מַרְהֵבָה *marhēbāh*
Variant; not used

5291 מָרוּד *mārûd* (3)
wandering (2)
wanderer (1)

5292 מֵרוֹז *mērôz* (1)
Meroz (1)

5293 מָרוֹחַ *mārôah* (1)
damaged (1)

5294 מָרוֹם *mārôm* (54)
on high (10)
heights (9)
heavens (4)
exalted (3)
high (3)
on high (3) +928+2021
pride (3)
above (1) +928+2021
arrogance (1)
exalted (1) +6639
haughty (1)
heaven (1)
height (1)
heights (1) +8031
heights above (1)
heights of heaven (1)
high positions (1)
highest point (1)
highest point (1) +1726
lofty (1)
on heights (1)
on high (1) +2021
on high (1) +2021+4200
on high (1) +4946
skies (1)
spreads feathers to run (1) +928+2021+5257

5295 מֵרוֹם *mērôm* (2)
Merom (2)

5296 מֵרוֹץ *mērôs* (1)
race (1)

5297 1מְרוּצָה *mᵉrûsāh1* (5)
course (2)
runs (1)
untranslated (2)

5298 2מְרוּצָה *mᵉrûsāh2* (1)
extortion (1)

5299 מְרוּקִים *mᵉrûqiym* (1)
beauty treatments (1)

5300 מָרוֹת *mārôt* (1)
Maroth (1)

5301 מַרְזֵחַ *marzēah* (2)
feasting (1)
funeral meal (1)

5302 מָרַח *mārah* (1)
apply (1)

5303 מֶרְחָב *merhāb* (6)
spacious place (3)
meadow (1)
setting free (1)
whole (1)

5304 מַרְחָבְיָה *merhābyāh*
Variant; not used

5305 מֶרְחָק *merhāq* (18)
afar (4)
distant (4)
distant (2) +4946
far away (2)
distant lands (1)
far away (1) +4946
far-off (1)
faraway (1)
some distance away (1)
stretches afar (1)

5306 מַרְחֶשֶׁת *marheset* (2)
pan (2)

5307 מָרַט *mārat* (14)
polished (5)
lost hair (2) +8031
smooth-skinned (2)
burnished (1)
made raw (1)
pulled (1)
pulled out beard (1)
pulled out hair (1)

5308 מְרִי *mᵉriy* (23)
rebellious (17)
rebellion (3)
bitter (1)
rebel (1) +2118
rebellious (1) +1201

5309 מְרִיא *mᵉriy'* (8)
fattened calves (3)
fattened animals (2)
choice (1)
fattened calf (1)
yearling (1)

5310 מְרִיב *mᵉriyb*
Variant; not used

5311 מְרִיב בַּעַל *mᵉriyb ba'al* (3)
Merib-Baal (2)
whoˢ (1)

5312 1מְרִיבָה *mᵉriybāh1* (2)
quarreling (1)
rebelled (1)

5313 2מְרִיבָה *mᵉriybāh2* (7)
Meribah (7)

5314 מְרִי־בַעַל *mᵉriy-ba'al* (1)
whoˢ (1)

5315 מְרִיבַת קָדֵשׁ *mᵉriybat qādēš* (4)
Meribah Kadesh (4)

5316 מְרָיָה *mᵉrāyāh* (1)
Meraiah (1)

5317 מֹרִיָּה *mōriyyāh* (2)
Moriah (2)

5318 מְרָיוֹת *mᵉrāyôt* (6)
Meraioth (6)

5319 מִרְיָם *miryām* (15)
Miriam (13)
herˢ (1)
sheˢ (1)

5320 מְרִירוּת *mᵉriyrût* (1)
bitter grief (1)

5321 מְרִירִי *mᵉriyriy* (1)
deadly (1)

5322 מֹרֶךְ *mōrek* (1)
fearful (1)

5323 מֶרְכָּב *merkāb* (3)
chariot (1)
seat (1)
sits (1)

5324 מֶרְכָּבָה *merkābāh* (44)
chariots (21)
chariot (20)
untranslated (3)

5325 מַרְכְּבוֹת *markābôt*
Variant; not used

5326 מַרְכֹּלֶת *markōlet* (1)
marketplace (1)

5327 1מִרְמָה *mirmāh1* (39)
deceit (12)
deceitful (9)
dishonest (4)
lies (4)
deception (3)
false (3)
deceitfully (2) +928
deceitfully (1)
treachery (1)

5328 2מִרְמָה *mirmāh2* (1)
Mirmah (1)

5329 מְרֵמוֹת *mᵉrēmôt* (7)
Meremoth (6)
Meremoth's (1)

5330 מִרְמָס *mirmās* (7)
trampled underfoot (2)
beaten down (1)
trample down (1) +8492
trampled (1)
what trampled (1) +8079
where run (1)

5331 מְרֹנֹתִי *mᵉrōnōtiy* (2)
Meronothite (1)
of Meronoth (1)

5332 מֶרֶס *meres* (1)
Meres (1)

5333 מַרְסְנָא *marsᵉnā'* (1)
Marsena (1)

5334 מֶרַע *mēra'* (1)
evil (1)

5335 1מֵרֵעַ *mērēa'1* (8)
friend (3)
friends (3)
companions (1)
personal adviser (1)

5336 2מֵרֵעַ *mērēa'2*
Variant; not used

5337 מִרְעֶה *mir'eh* (13)
pasture (12)
place where fed (1)

5338 מַרְעִית *mar'iyt* (10)
pasture (8)
fed (1)
flock (1)

5339 מַרְעֲלָה *mar'ᵃlāh* (1)
Maralah (1)

5340 1מַרְפֵּא *marpē'1* (14)
healing (8)
remedy (3)
healed (1)
health (1)
incurable (1) +401

5341 מַרְפֵּא2 *marpē'2* (2)
at peace (1)
calmness (1)

5342 מַרְפֵּה *marpēh*
Variant; not used

5343 מִרְפָּשׂ *mirpāś* (1)
what muddied (1)

5344 מָרַץ *māras* (4)
ails (1)
beyond all remedy (1)
bitter (1)
painful (1)

5345 מַרְצֵעַ *marsēa'* (2)
awl (2)

5346 מַרְצֶפֶת *marsepet* (1)
base (1)

5347 מָרַק *māraq* (4)
be scoured (1)
cleanse away (1)
polish (1)
polished (1)

5348 מָרָק *mārāq* (3)
broth (3)

5349 מֶרְקָח *merqāh* (1)
perfume (1)

5350 מֶרְקָחָה *merqāhāh* (2)
pot of ointment (1)
spices (1)

5351 מִרְקַחַת *mirqahat* (3)
fragrant (1)
perfumes (1) +5126
took care of mixing (1) +8379

5352 מָרַר *mārar* (14)
bitter (2)
made bitter (2)
bitterly (1)
bitterness attacked (1)
furiously (1)
grieve bitterly (1)
grieves (1)
in bitter distress (1)
made taste bitterness (1)
rage (1)
rebel (1)
suffered (1)

5353 מָרֹר *mārōr* (5)
bitter herbs (3)
bitter things (1)
bitterness (1)

5354 מְרֵרָה *m'rērāh* (1)
gall (1)

5355 מְרֹרָה *m'rōrāh* (2)
liver (1)
venom (1)

5356 מְרָרִי1 *m'rāriy1* (39)
Merari (21)
Merarites (9) +1201
Merarite (7) +1201
Merarite (2)

5357 מְרָרִי2 *m'rāriy2* (1)
Merarite (1)

5358 מָרֵשָׁה1 *mārēšāh1* (6)
Mareshah (6)

5359 מָרֵשָׁה2 *mārēšāh2* (2)
Mareshah (2)

5360 מִרְשַׁעַת *mirša'at* (1)
wicked (1)

5361 מְרָתַיִם *m'rātayim* (1)
Merathaim (1)

5362 מַשָּׂא1 *maśśā'1* (36)

burden (8)
load (7)
carry (5)
burdens (2)
carrying (2)
singing (2)
what to carry (2)
camel-loads (1) +1695
carried about (1)
desire (1)
loads (1)
oppression (1)
take away (1) +5911
that5 (1)
tribute (1)

5363 מַשָּׂא2 *maśśā'2* (30)
oracle (27)
oracles (1)
prophecies (1)
prophecy (1)

5364 מַשָּׂא3 *maśśā'3* (2)
Massa (2)

5365 מַשָּׂא *maśśō'* (1)
partiality (1) +7156

5366 מַשָּׂאָה *maśśā'āh* (1)
clouds of smoke (1)

5367 מַשְׂאוֹת *maś'ôt*
Variant; not used

5368 מַשְׂאֵת *maś'ēt* (15)
gifts (2)
tax (2)
burden (1)
cloud (1)
gift (1)
lifting up (1)
portion (1)
portions (1)
present (1)
signal (1)
smoke (1)
untranslated (2)

5369 מִשְׂגָּב1 *miśgāb1* (17)
fortress (9)
stronghold (5)
refuge (2)
high (1)

5370 מִשְׂגָּב2 *miśgāb2*
Variant; not used

5371 מַשֶּׂגֶת *maśśeget*
Variant; not used

5372 מְשׂוּכָה *m'śûkkāh* (1)
hedge (1)

5373 מַשּׂוֹר *maśśôr* (1)
saw (1)

5374 מְשׂוּרָה *m'śûrāh* (4)
measure out (1)
measurements of quantity (1)
quantity (1)
rationed (1) +928

5375 מָשׂוֹשׂ1 *māśôś1* (16)
joy (6)
delight (2)
gaiety (2)
rejoices (2)
celebrations (1)
joyful (1)
merriment (1)
rejoice greatly (1) +8464

5376 מָשׂוֹשׂ2 *māśôś2* (1)
withers away (1)

5377 מִשְׂחָק *mishāq* (1)
scoff (1)

5378 מַשְׂטֵמָה *maśtēmāh* (2)

hostility (2)

5379 מְשֻׁכָה *m'śukāh* (1)
blocked (1)

5380 מַשְׂכִּיל *maśkiyl* (14)
maskil (13)
psalm of praise (1)

5381 מַשְׂכִּית *maśkiyt* (6)
carved (1)
carved images (1)
evil conceits (1)
idol (1)
imagine (1) +928
settings (1)

5382 מַשְׂכֹּרֶת *maśkōret* (4)
wages (3)
rewarded (1)

5383 מַשְׂמֵרָה *maśmērāh* (1)
nails (1)

5384 מִשְׂפָּח *miśpāh* (1)
bloodshed (1)

5385 מִשְׂרָה *miśrāh* (2)
government (2)

5386 מִשְׂרְפוֹת *miśrāpôt* (2)
burned (1)
funeral fire (1)

5387 מִשְׂרְפוֹת מַיִם *miśr'pôt mayim* (2)
Misrephoth Maim (2)

5388 מַשְׂרֵקָה *maśrēqāh* (2)
Masrekah (2)

5389 מַשְׂרֵת *maśrēt* (1)
pan (1)

5390 מָשׁ *maš*
Variant; not used

5391 מַשָּׁא *maššā'* (4)
debts (1)
debts (1) +3338
exacting of usury (1)
usury (1)

5392 מֵשָׁא *mēšā'* (1)
Mesha (1)

5393 מַשְׁאָב *maš'āb* (1)
watering places (1)

5394 מַשָּׁאָה *maššā'āh* (1)
make a loan (1) +5957

5395 מַשָּׁאָה *maššu'āh*
Variant; not used

5396 מַשָּׁאוֹן *maššā'ôn* (1)
deception (1)

5397 מַשֻּׁאוֹת *maššu'ôt* (2)
ruin (1)
ruins (1)

5398 מַשְׁאָל *miš'āl* (2)
Mishal (2)

5399 מִשְׁאָלָה *miš'ālāh* (2)
desires (1)
requests (1)

5400 מִשְׁאֶרֶת *miš'eret* (4)
kneading trough (2)
kneading troughs (2)

5401 מִשְׁבְּצוֹת *mišb'sôt* (9)
filigree (3)
settings (3)
filigree settings (2)
interwoven (1)

5402 מַשְׁבֵּר *mašbēr* (3)
point of birth (1)
opening of the womb (1) +1201

5403 מִשְׁבָּר *mišbār* (5)
waves (3)

breakers (2)

5404 מִשְׁבָּת *mišbāṭ* (1)
destruction (1)

5405 מִשְׁגֶּה *mišgeh* (1)
mistake (1)

5406 מָשָׁה *māšāh* (3)
drew out (2)
drew (1)

5407 מֹשֶׁה *mōšeh* (767)
Moses (709)
he[s] (19)
him[s] (17)
Moses' (13)
his[s] (3)
Moses' (1) +4200
untranslated (5)

5408 מַשֶּׁה *maššeh* (1)
creditor (1) +1251+2257+3338

5409 מְשׁוֹאָה *mᵉšô'āh* (3)
ruin (1)
wasteland (1)
wastelands (1)

5410 מַשּׁוּאָה *maššû'āh* (1)
Variant; not used

5411 מְשׁוֹבָב *mᵉšôḇāḇ* (1)
Meshobab (1)

5412 מְשׁוּבָה *mᵉšûḇāh* (14)
backsliding (4)
faithless (4)
waywardness (2)
backslidings (1)
turn away (1)
turn from (1)
untranslated (1)

5413 מְשׁוּגָה *mᵉšûgāh* (1)
error (1)

5414 מָשׁוֹט *māšôṭ* (1)
oars (1)

5415 מִשּׁוֹט *miššôṭ* (1)
oars (1)

5416 מְשׁוּסָה *mᵉšiwssāh* (1)
untranslated (1)

5417 מָשַׁח *māšaḥ* (71)
anointed (33)
anoint (24)
spread (4)
anointing (3)
was anointed (2)
been anointed (1)
decorates (1)
oil (1)
rubbed (1)
use (1)

5418 1מִשְׁחָה *mišḥāh1* (21)
anointing (21)

5419 2מִשְׁחָה *mišḥāh2* (2)
portion (1)
untranslated (1)

5420 1מָשְׁחָה *mošḥāh1* (1)
anointing (1)

5421 2מָשְׁחָה *mošḥāh2* (1)
portion (1)

5422 מַשְׁחִית *mašḥiyṭ* (16)
destroyer (4)
destructive (2)
corruption (1)
deathly pale (1)
destroy (1)
destroyers (1)
destroys (1)
destruction (1)
one who destroys (1) +1251

slaughter (1) +2222+4200
traps (1)
undoing (1)

5423 מִשְׁחָר *mišḥār* (1)
dawn (1)

5424 מַשְׁחֵת *mašḥēṭ* (1)
weapon (1) +3998

5425 מִשְׁחַת *mišḥaṭ* (1)
disfigured (1)

5426 מָשְׁחָת *mošḥāṭ* (1)
deformed (1)

5427 מִשְׁטוֹחַ *mišṭôaḥ* (3)
place to spread (2)
places for spreading (1)

5428 מִשְׁטָר *mišṭār* (1)
dominion (1)

5429 מֶשִׁי *mešiy* (2)
costly fabric (1)
costly garments (1)

5430 מְשֵׁיזַבְאֵל *mᵉšēyzaḇ'ēl* (3)
Meshezabel (3)

5431 מָשִׁיחַ *māšiyaḥ* (38)
anointed (38)

5432 מָשַׁךְ *māšak* (36)
drew (2)
tall (2)
archers (1) +8008
be delayed (1)
be prolonged (1)
bear (1)
cheering (1)
continue (1)
deferred (1)
delay (1)
drag away (1)
dragged off (1)
drags away (1)
drags off (1)
draw along (1)
drawn (1)
extend (1)
follow (1)
go at once (1)
joins (1)
lead the way (1)
led (1)
lure (1)
patient (1)
planter (1) +2446
prolong (1)
pull in (1)
pulled (1)
pulled up (1)
sound long (1)
sounds a long blast (1)
spread out (1)
take away (1)
worn (1) +928

5433 1מֶשֶׁךְ *mešek1* (2)
price (1)
seed to sow (1) +2446

5434 2מֶשֶׁךְ *mešek2* (10)
Meshech (10)

5435 מִשְׁכָּב *miškāḇ* (46)
bed (23)
beds (6)
bedroom (4) +2540
lies with (2)
bedding (1)
bier (1)
couch (1)
lie in death (1)
mat (1)
not a virgin (1) +2351+3359
slept with (1) +408+3359+4200

slept with (1) +2351+3359
slept with (1) +2351+3359+4200
slept with (1) +3359
taking rest (1) +8886

5436 מֹשְׁכוֹת *mōšᵉkôṭ* (1)
cords (1)

5437 מְשֻׁכֶּלֶת *mᵉšukkeleṭ*
Variant; not used

5438 מִשְׁכָּן *miškān* (139)
tabernacle (102)
dwelling place (8)
tents (5)
dwellings (4)
dwelling (3)
it[s] (3) +2021
dwelling places (2)
where dwells (2)
habitat (1)
homes (1)
houses (1)
lived (1)
place where dwell (1)
resting place (1)
tent (1)
untranslated (3)

5439 1מָשַׁל *māšal1* (17)
be like (2)
is like (2)
quote (2)
tell (2)
become like (1)
byword (1)
liken (1)
poets (1)
quote proverb (1)
quotes proverbs (1)
quoting (1)
reduced to (1)
telling (1)

5440 2מָשַׁל *māšal2* (81)
rule (28)
ruler (16)
rules (7)
ruled (6)
rulers (4)
ruler's (3)
govern (2)
ruling (2)
actually rule (1) +5440
controls (1)
dominion (1)
exercised (1)
gain control (1)
has right (1)
in charge (1)
made ruler (1)
make rulers (1)
master (1)
untranslated (2)

5441 3מָשַׁל *māšal3*
Variant; not used

5442 1מָשָׁל *māšāl1* (40)
oracle (7)
proverb (7)
proverbs (7)
byword (6)
discourse (2)
parable (2)
parables (2)
saying (2)
make sport of (1) +2118+4200
object of scorn (1)
ridicule (1) +5951
taunt (1)
taunt (1) +5951

5443 2מָשָׁל *māšāl2* (1)
Mashal (1)

5444 מֹשֵׁל‎ 1 *mōšel1* (1)
equal (1)

5445 מֹשֵׁל‎ 2 *mōšel2* (2)
power (1)
rule (1)

5446 מְשֹׁל‎ *m'šōl*
Variant; not used

5447 מִשְׁלוֹחַ‎ *mišlôah* (3)
giving (2)
lay (1)

5448 מִשְׁלָח‎ *mišlāh* (7)
put to (6)
places where turned loose (1)

5449 מִשְׁלַחַת‎ *mišlahat* (2)
band (1)
discharged (1)

5450 מְשֻׁלָּם‎ *m'šullām* (25)
Meshullam (25)

5451 מְשִׁלֵּמוֹת‎ *m'šillēmôt* (2)
Meshillemoth (2)

5452 מְשֶׁלֶמְיָה‎ *m'šelemyāh* (1)
Meshelemiah (1)

5453 מְשֶׁלֶמְיָהוּ‎ *m'šelemyāhû* (3)
Meshelemiah (3)

5454 מְשִׁלֵּמִית‎ *m'šillēmiyt* (1)
Meshillemith (1)

5455 מְשֻׁלֶּמֶת‎ *m'šullemet* (1)
Meshullemeth (1)

5456 מִשְׁלֹשׁ‎ *mišlōš*
Variant; not used

5457 מְשַׁמָּה‎ *m'šammāh* (7)
waste (4)
dried up (2)
object of horror (1)

5458 מִשְׁמָן‎ *mišmān* (5)
fat (2)
richest (1)
sturdiest (1)
sturdy (1)

5459 מִשְׁמַנָּה‎ *mišmannāh* (1)
Mishmannah (1)

5460 מַשְׁמַנִּים‎ *mašmanniym* (1)
choice food (1)

5461 מִשְׁמָע‎ 1 *mišmā'1* (1)
what hears (1)

5462 מִשְׁמָע‎ 2 *mišmā'2* (4)
Mishma (4)

5463 מִשְׁמַעַת‎ *mišma'at* (4)
bodyguard (3)
subject to (1)

5464 מִשְׁמָר‎ 1 *mišmār1* (22)
custody (6)
guard (4)
else[s] (1)
guarded (1) +9068
guards (1)
guards (1) +408
imprisoned (1) +928+5989
other[s] (1)
posts (1)
prison (1) +1074
section (1)
services (1)
take command (1) +2118+4200
under guard (1) +6584

5465 מִשְׁמָר‎ 2 *mišmār2*
Variant; not used

5466 מִשְׁמֶרֶת‎ *mišmeret* (78)
duties (10)
requirements (7)
care (5)
responsibilities (4)
kept (3)
responsible (3)
service (3)
duty (2)
guarding (2) +9068
have charge of (2) +9068
keep (2)
order (2)
responsible for care (2)
what requires (2)
assigned (1)
guard (1)
guard (1) +9068
guarding (1)
guards (1)
in charge (1)
lead (1)
loyal (1) +9068
mission (1)
obligations (1)
on behalf of (1) +4200
positions (1)
post (1)
responsibility (1)
responsible (1) +9068
safe (1)
services (1)
serving (1)
specific things (1) +3998
take care of (1)
take care of (1) +2118+4200
under guard (1)
use (1)
watch (1)
untranslated (5)

5467 מִשְׁנֶה‎ *mišneh* (34)
second (8)
next in rank (5)
double (4)
twice as much (4)
second District (3)
double portion (2)
copied (1) +4180
copy (1)
matching (1)
new quarter (1)
other (1)
second in rank (1)
second-in-command (1)
twice (1)

5468 מְשִׁסָּה‎ *m'šissāh* (6)
plundered (3)
loot (2)
victim (1)

5469 מִשְׁעוֹל‎ *miš'ôl* (1)
narrow path (1)

5470 מִשְׁעִי‎ *miš'iy* (1)
make clean (1)

5471 מִשְׁעָם‎ *miš'ām* (1)
Misham (1)

5472 מִשְׁעָן‎ *miš'ān* (4)
supplies (2)
support (2)

5473 מַשְׁעֵן‎ *maš'ēn* (1)
supply (1)

5474 מַשְׁעֵנָה‎ *maš'ēnāh* (1)
support (1)

5475 מִשְׁעֶנֶת‎ *miš'enet* (11)
staff (9)
cane (1)
staffs (1)

5476 מִשְׁפָּחָה‎ *mišpāhāh* (304)
clan (131)
clans (124)
peoples (8)
families (7)
family (7)
clan by clan (2) +4200
people (2)
clan (1) +3+1074
each clan (1) +5476
every family (1) +2256+5476
kinds (1)
kingdoms (1)
Levites (1) +4291
nation (1)
one kind after another (1) +2157+4200
untranslated (13)

5477 מִשְׁפָּט‎ *mišpāt* (424)
justice (94)
laws (83)
just (28)
judgment (24)
right (13)
cause (11)
judgments (11)
regulations (11)
specified (8)
ordinances (7)
punishment (6)
law (5)
sentence (5)
case (4)
prescribed (4)
rights (4)
standards (4)
decision (3)
injustice (3) +4202
ordinance (3)
prescribed way (3)
requirements (3)
what requires (3)
commands (2)
court (2)
custom (2)
decisions (2)
judge (2)
judging (2)
justly (2)
legal (2)
practice (2)
practices (2)
proper procedure (2)
sentenced (2)
specifications (2)
trial (2)
verdict (2) +1821
what do[s] (2)
accuser (1) +1251
accuses (1) +2021+4200+7756
always do (1)
bloodshed (1) +1947
capital offense (1) +4638
charges (1)
customs (1)
decided (1)
defense (1)
deserve (1)
deserving (1)
dimensions (1)
disputes decided (1)
do (1)
due (1)
honest (1)
honestly (1)
inquiring (1)
judge (1) +9149
judges (1) +6913
justice of cause (1)
kind (1)
lawsuits (1)
like (1) +3869
making decisions (1)
manner (1)
means of making decisions (1)

place of judgment (1)
plan (1)
precepts (1)
prescribed (1) +3869
proper place (1)
punish (1) +6913
quotas (1) +3869
regulation (1)
regulations prescribed (1)
render judgment (1) +9149
right way (1)
rightfully (1)
rule (1)
share (1)
standards measuring (1)
statutes (1)
unjust (1) +4202
verdict (1)
vindication (1)
way prescribed (1)
untranslated (5)

5478 מִשְׁפְּתַיִם *mišp'tayim* (2)
campfires (1)
two saddlebags (1)

5479 מֶשֶׁק *mešeq* (1)
one who will inherit (1) +1201

5480 מַשָּׁק *maššāq* (1)
swarm (1)

5481 מְשֻׁקָּד *m'šuqqād* (6)
shaped like almond flowers (4)
untranslated (2)

5482 1מַשְׁקֶה *mašqeh1* (19)
cupbearer (10)
cupbearers (2)
goblets (2) +3998
liquid (1)
position (1)
water (1)
well watered (1)
well-watered (1)

5483 2מַשְׁקֶה *mašqeh2*
Variant; not used

5484 מִשְׁקוֹל *mišqôl* (1)
weigh out (1)

5485 מַשְׁקוֹף *mašqôp* (3)
top (2)
tops (1)

5486 מִשְׁקָל *mišqāl* (49)
weight (20)
weighing (16)
weighed (6)
exact weight (1)
force (1)
paid (1) +5989
rationed (1) +928
set of scales (1) +4404
weighed out (1)
untranslated (1)

5487 מִשְׁקֶלֶת *mišqelet* (2)
plumb line (2)

5488 מִשְׁקָע *mišqā'* (1)
clear (1)

5489 מִשְׁרָה *mišrāh* (1)
juice (1)

5490 מִשְׁרָעִי *mišrā'iy* (1)
Mishraites (1)

5491 מָשַׁשׁ *māšaš* (9)
grope (2)
searched through (2)
felt (1)
grope about (1)
touched (1)
touches (1)
untranslated (1)

5492 מִשְׁתֶּה *mišteh* (46)
banquet (12)
feast (12)
feasting (8)
drink (3)
drinking (2)
banquet (1) +3516
banquets (1)
dinner (1)
feasts (1)
meal (1)
table (1)
that[s] (1)
untranslated (2)

5493 1מֹת *môt1* (20)
men (11)
few (3)
few in number (1) +5071
friends (1)
little (1)
only a few (1) +5031
people (1)
very few (1) +5031

5494 2מֹת *môt2*
Variant; not used

5495 מַתְבֵּן *matbēn* (1)
straw (1)

5496 מֶתֶג *meteg* (4)
bit (3)
halter (1)

5497 מֶתֶג הָאַמָּה *meteg hā'ammāh* (1)
Metheg Ammah (1)

5498 מָתוֹק *mātôq* (12)
sweet (10)
sweeter (2)

5499 מְתוּשָׁאֵל *m'tûšā'ēl* (2)
Methushael (2)

5500 מְתוּשֶׁלַח *m'tûšelah* (6)
Methuselah (6)

5501 מָתַח *mātah* (1)
spreads out (1)

5502 מִתְחָה *mithāh*
Variant; not used

5503 מָתַי *mātay* (43)
how long (27) +6330
when (11)
how long (2)
for how long (1) +6330
how long (1) +339+6388
setting the time (1) +4200

5504 מַתְכֹּנֶת *matkōnet* (5)
formula (2)
number (1)
original design (1)
standard measure (1)

5505 מַתְלָאָה *matlā'āh*
Variant; not used

5506 מְתַלְּעוֹת *m'tall''ôt* (3)
fangs (2)
jaws (1)

5507 מְתֹם *m'tōm* (4)
health (2)
all (1)
soundness (1)

5508 1מַתָּן *matān1* (5)
gift (3)
gifts (2)

5509 2מַתָּן *matān2* (3)
Mattan (3)

5510 1מַתָּנָה *matānāh1* (17)
gifts (9)
gift (5)

bribe (1)
bribes (1)
given (1)

5511 2מַתָּנָה *matānāh2* (2)
Mattanah (2)

5512 מִתְנִי *mitniy* (1)
Mithnite (1)

5513 מַתְנַי *matnay* (3)
Mattenai (3)

5514 מַתַּנְיָה *matanyāh* (13)
Mattaniah (13)

5515 מַתַּנְיָהוּ *matanyāhû* (3)
Mattaniah (3)

5516 מָתְנַיִם *mātnayim* (47)
waist (16)
side (4)
waists (4)
backs (3)
body (2)
loins (2)
there[s] (2)
tuck cloak into belt (2) +2520
armor (1)
belt (1) +258
bodies (1)
brace yourselves (1) +2616
cloak tucked into belt (1) +2520
get ready (1) +273
heart (1)
make wear (1) +6584+6590
put on (1) +928+8492
sets about work (1) +2520
strutting rooster (1) +2435
tucking cloak into belt (1) +9113

5517 מָתַק *mātaq* (6)
sweet (4)
enjoyed sweet (1)
feasts on (1)

5518 מָתֵק *mātēq* (2)
pleasant (1)
pleasantness (1)

5519 מֹתֶק *môteq* (1)
sweet (1)

5520 מִתְקָה *mitqāh* (2)
Mithcah (2)

5521 מִתְרְדָת *mitr'dāt* (2)
Mithredath (2)

5522 מַתָּת *matat* (6)
gift (3)
as much as pleases (2) +3338
gifts he does not give (1) +9214

5523 מַתַּתָּה *matatāh* (1)
Mattattah (1)

5524 מַתִּתְיָה *matityāh* (4)
Mattithiah (4)

5525 מַתִּתְיָהוּ *matityāhû* (4)
Mattithiah (4)

5526 נ *n*
Variant; not used

5527 ן ָ *-ān* (36)
their (9)
they (5)
them (4)
each (2)
the creatures[s] (1)
the rooms[s] (1)
the[s] (1)
you (1)
untranslated (12)

5528 1נָא *nā'1* (405)
please (59)
now (22)

I beg you (5)
then (4)
come now (3) +6964
I would like (2)
all right (1)
but (1)
I pray (1)
if you will (1)
O (1)
please (1) +1065
please (1) +3283
quick (1)
right now (1)
so (1)
therefore (1)
very well (1) +2180
we pray (1)
untranslated (297)

5529 נָא2 *nā'2* (1)
raw (1)

5530 נֹא *nō'* (4)
Thebes (4)

5531 נֹא אָמוֹן *nō' 'āmôn* (1)
Thebes (1)

5532 נֹאד *nō'd* (7)
skin (2)
wineskins (2) +3516
jars (1)
scroll (1)
wineskin (1)

5533 נָאָה *nā'āh* (3)
beautiful (2)
adorns (1)

5534 נָאוֶה *nā'weh* (10)
fitting (4)
lovely (4)
beautiful (1)
unsuited (1) +4202

5535 נָאַם *nā'am* (1)
declare (1)

5536 נְאֻם *n'um* (376)
declares (363)
oracle (9)
says (3)
declared (1)

5537 נָאַף *nā'ap* (31)
commit adultery (7)
adulterers (6)
committed adultery (5)
adulteress (3)
adulterer (2)
adulterous (2)
adultery (2)
commits adultery (2)
adulteries (1)
untranslated (1)

5538 נַאֲפוּפִים *na'ăpûpiym* (1)
unfaithfulness (1)

5539 נִאֻפִים *ni'upiym* (2)
adulteries (1)
adultery (1)

5540 נָאַץ *nā'as* (24)
spurned (5)
despise (4)
revile (2)
treated with contempt (2)
despised (1)
is blasphemed (1)
made show utter contempt (1) +5540
rejected (1)
rejecting (1)
reviled (1)
reviles (1)
spurns (1)
treat with contempt (1)
treating with contempt (1)

5541 נְאָצָה *n'āsāh* (2)
disgrace (2)

5542 נֶאָצָה *ne'āsāh* (3)
blasphemies (2)
contemptible things (1)

5543 נָאַק *nā'aq* (2)
groan (1) +5544
groans (1)

5544 נְאָקָה *n'āqāh* (4)
groaning (2)
groan (1) +5543
groaned (1)

5545 נָאַר *nā'ar* (2)
abandoned (1)
renounced (1)

5546 נֹב *nōb* (6)
Nob (6)

5547 נָבָא *nābā'* (115)
prophesy (47)
prophesying (28)
prophesied (26)
prophesies (8)
acts like a prophet (1)
frantic prophesying (1)
poses as a prophet (1)
prophetic (1)
untranslated (2)

5548 נָבַב *nābab*
Variant; not used

5549 נְבוֹ1 *n'bô1* (11)
Nebo (11)

5550 נְבוֹ2 *n'bô2* (1)
Nebo (1)

5551 נְבוֹ3 *n'bô3* (1)
Nebo (1)

5552 נְבוּ שַׁר־סְכִים *n'bû śar-s'kiym* (1)
Nebo-Sarsekim (1)

5553 נְבוּאָה *n'bû'āh* (3)
prophecy (2)
prophesied (1) +1819

5554 נָבוּב *nābûb* (4)
hollow (3)
witless (1)

5555 נְבוּזַרְאֲדָן *n'bûzar'ădān* (15)
Nebuzaradan (15)

5556 נְבוּכַדְנֶאצַּר *n'bûkadne'ssar* (28)
Nebuchadnezzar (26)
his[s] (1)
untranslated (1)

5557 נְבוּכַדְרֶאצַּר *n'bûkadre'ssar* (34)
Nebuchadnezzar (31)
his[s] (1) +4200
Nebuchadnezzar's (1) +4200
untranslated (1)

5558 נְבוּשַׁזְבָּן *n'bûšazbān* (1)
Nebushazban (1)

5559 נָבוֹת *nābôt* (22)
Naboth (17)
Naboth's (4)
he[s] (1)

5560 נָבַח *nābah* (1)
bark (1)

5561 נֹבַח1 *nōbah1* (1)
Nobah (1)

5562 נֹבַח2 *nōbah2* (2)
Nobah (2)

5563 נִבְחַז *nibhaz* (1)
Nibhaz (1)

5564 נָבַט *nābat* (70)
look (20)

looked (7)
consider (6)
see (3)
tolerate (3)
gaze (2)
have regard for (2)
look down (2)
look up (2)
looks (2)
seen (2)
detect (1)
esteem (1)
have regard for (1) +4200
let look (1)
look around (1)
look on (1)
look with favor (1) +7156
looked around (1)
looked over (1)
looks down (1)
observe (1)
sees (1)
stare (1)
viewed (1)
views (1)
watch (1)
watches over (1)
watching (1)
untranslated (1)

5565 נְבָט *n'bāt* (25)
Nebat (25)

5566 נָבִיא *nābiy'* (316)
prophet (152)
prophets (150)
he[s] (1) +2021+3758
him[s] (1) +2021+3759
his own[s] (1) +2021+2021+2418
his[s] (1) +2021
one[s] (1) +2021
prophecy (1)
prophesy (1)
prophet's (1)
them[s] (1) +2021
these men[s] (1) +1201+2021
those who prophesy (1)
untranslated (3)

5567 נְבִיאָה *n'biy'āh* (6)
prophetess (6)

5568 נְבָיוֹת *n'bāyôt* (5)
Nebaioth (5)

5569 נֵבֶךְ *nēbek* (1)
springs (1)

5570 נָבֵל1 *nābēl1* (20)
fading (3)
fall (3)
wither (3)
lose heart (2)
withers (2)
crumbles (1)
die away (1)
only wear out (1) +5570
shrivel up (1)
shriveled (1)
withered (1)

5571 נָבֵל2 *nābal2* (5)
dishonor (1)
dishonors (1)
played the fool (1)
rejected (1)
treat with contempt (1)

5572 נָבָל1 *nābāl1* (19)
fool (9)
foolish (4)
fools (2)
base (1)
lawless (1)
no understanding (1)

wicked fools (1)

5573 2 נָבָל *nābāl2* (21)
Nabal (18)
Nabal's (2)
he[s] (1)

5574 1 נֵבֶל *nēbel1* (11)
skin (3)
wineskin (2)
jars (1)
jugs (1)
pots (1)
pottery (1) +3450
skins (1)
water jars (1)

5575 2 נֵבֶל *nēbel2* (27)
lyres (15)
lyre (7)
harps (4)
harp (1)

5576 נְבָלָה *n'bālāh* (13)
disgraceful thing (4)
folly (3)
disgraceful (2)
vileness (2)
outrageous things (1)
wicked thing (1)

5577 נְבֵלָה *n'bēlāh* (48)
body (13)
carcasses (13)
carcass (5)
dead bodies (5)
anything found dead (3)
it[s] (2) +2021
already dead (1)
animal found dead (1)
bodies (1)
found dead (1)
lifeless forms (1)
untranslated (2)

5578 נַבְלוּת *nablût* (1)
lewdness (1)

5579 נְבַלָּט *n'ballāt* (1)
Neballat (1)

5580 נָבַע *nāba'* (11)
gushes (2)
bubbling (1)
celebrate (1) +2352
give a bad smell (1) +944
overflow (1)
pour forth (1)
pour out (1)
poured out (1)
spew (1)
utter (1)

5581 נִבְשָׁן *nibšān* (1)
Nibshan (1)

5582 נֶגֶב *negeb* (111)
south (38)
Negev (36)
south (9) +2025
southern (6)
south (4) +4946
south (3) +2025+9402
southern (3) +2025
Negev (2) +824
south (2) +2025+2025+9402
south (2) +9402
southeast (1) +2025+2025+7711
southeast (1) +2025+7711
southern (1) +448+6991
southern (1) +4946
southland (1)
southland (1) +8441

5583 נָגַד *nāgad* (372)
tell (93)
told (87)

was told (23)
reported (15)
declare (14)
proclaim (11)
announce (8)
explain (6)
report (5)
answered (4)
give (4)
inform (4)
revealed (4)
said (4)
declared (3)
explained (3)
foretold (3)
show (3)
brought report (2)
denounces (2)
foretell (2)
heard (2)
informed (2)
messenger (2)
speak (2)
telling (2)
tells (2)
warned (2)
admit (1)
announces (1)
announcing (1)
assured (1) +5583
be sure to tell (1) +5583
been brought to attention (1) +2256+9048
been shown (1)
been told (1)
been told about (1) +5583
confess (1)
confront (1)
declares (1)
declaring (1)
describe (1)
disclose (1)
do so[s] (1)
explaining (1)
expose (1)
exposed (1)
give an answer (1)
give answer (1) +5583
kept secret (1) +401
learn (1)
learned (1) +4200
let know (1)
made clear (1)
make known (1)
message (1)
messenger[s] (1)
must report (1) +5583
parade (1)
proclaiming (1)
report came back (1)
reveals (1)
sent word (1) +2256+8938
showed (1)
shown (1)
speak up (1)
spoke (1)
tell answer (1)
tell the news (1)
testify (1)
testimony (1)
told answer (1)
utter (1)
was reported (1)
were clearly told (1) +5583
word came (1)
untranslated (4)

5584 נֶגֶד *neged* (151)
before (29)
opposite (15)
before (13) +4200
in the presence of (7)
in front of (6)

from (5) +4946
facing (3)
in (3)
near (3)
presence (3)
before (2) +7156
by (2)
distance (2)
far from (2) +4946
in (2) +4200
in front of (2) +4200
in presence (2) +4200+6524
in the presence of (2) +2025
in the sight of (2)
nearby (2) +4946
opposite (2) +4200
regard (2) +4200+8492
straight in (2)
accompany (1) +2143+4200
across the way (1) +4946
against (1)
aloof (1) +4946
away from (1) +4946
because of (1) +4946
before (1) +4200+6524
bent on (1) +7156
beyond (1)
constant (1) +4946
defend (1) +6641
directly (1)
facing (1) +4946
from (1) +4946+6524
frontal (1) +4946
in broad daylight (1) +2021+9087
in sight (1)
in the face of (1) +4200
kept distance (1) +3656+4946
known to (1)
next to (1) +4200
opposite (1) +4946
out of (1) +4946
resisted (1) +4200+6641
responsible for (1) +4200
right before (1) +4200
risked (1) +4946+8959
some distance (1)
straight (1)
straight through (1)
succeed against (1) +4200
suitable (1) +3869
suitable for (1) +3869
to (1)
with (1)
untranslated (3)

5585 נָגַהּ *nāgah* (6)
turns into light (2)
burning (1)
dawned (1)
give (1)
shine (1)

5586 1 נֹגַהּ *nōgah1* (19)
brightness (5)
brilliant light (2)
dawn (2)
no longer shine (2) +665
radiance (2)
bright (1)
flashing (1)
glow (1)
light (1)
ray of brightness (1)
splendor (1)

5587 2 נֹגַהּ *nōgah2* (2)
Nogah (2)

5588 נֹגְהָה *nōghāh* (1)
brightness (1)

5589 נְגוֹ *n'gô*
Variant; not used

5590 נָגַח *nāgaḥ* (11)
gore (3)
gores (3)
butting (1)
charged (1)
engage in battle (1)
push back (1)
untranslated (1)

5591 נַגָּח *naggāḥ* (2)
goring (2)

5592 נָגִיד *nāgiyd* (44)
leader (13)
ruler (12)
prince (3)
in charge (2)
officers (2)
official in charge (2)
administrators (1)
chief (1)
commanders (1)
leaders (1)
nobles (1)
officer (1)
officer in charge (1)
rulers (1)
supervisor (1)
worthy things (1)

5593 נְגִינָה *nᵉgiynāh* (14)
stringed instruments (9)
mock in song (2)
music (1)
song (1)
songs (1)

5594 נָגַן *nāgan* (15)
harpist (2)
play (2)
play (2) +928+3338
play the harp (2)
playing the harp (2) +928+3338
musicians (1)
playing (1)
plays (1)
plays an instrument (1)
sing (1)

5595 נָגַע *nāga'* (150)
touches (43)
touched (24)
touch (17)
came (6)
come (4)
reached (4)
arrived (3)
reaches (3)
struck (3)
afflicted (2)
get (2)
reach (2)
reaching (2)
strike (2)
strikes (2)
add (1)
afford (1) +1896+3338
approach (1)
are plagued (1)
attack (1)
befall (1)
bother (1)
bring down (1)
brought down (1)
casts down (1)
draws near (1)
drew near (1)
extend (1)
follows (1)
happened (1)
inflicted (1)
isˢ (1)
laid (1)
let themselves be driven back (1)

level (1)
molest (1)
molests (1)
near (1)
pierces (1)
plagued (1)
put (1)
seize (1)
stricken (1)
touching (1)
went (1)
untranslated (1)

5596 נֶגַע *nega'* (78)
mildew (15)
infectious (11)
sore (11)
contamination (3)
disaster (3)
infected person (3)
itˢ (3) +2021
affected article (2)
afflictions (2)
contaminated (2)
diseases (2)
articleˢ (1)
assault (1)
assaults (1) +4200+5596
Blows (1)
contaminated article (1)
flogging (1)
floggings (1)
infected person (1) +5999
infection (1)
personˢ (1)
plague (1)
scourge (1)
sores (1)
spreading mildew (1) +7669
stricken (1)
this kind of sore (1) +2021+5999
wounds (1)
untranslated (3)

5597 נָגַף *nāgap* (49)
be defeated (5)
strike (5)
been defeated (4)
strike down (3)
struck down (3)
were defeated (3)
afflicted (2)
been routed (2)
struck (2)
stumble (2)
was defeated (2)
was routed (2)
bring defeat upon (1)
defeated (1)
defeating (1)
defeating (1) +5597
hit (1)
inflicts (1)
injures (1)
plague (1)
routed (1)
strike with a plague (1)
struck with a plague (1)
were beaten (1)
were routed (1)

5598 נֶגֶף *negep* (7)
plague (6)
causes to stumble (1)

5599 נָגַר *nāgar* (10)
rushing (2)
delivered over (1)
flow (1)
given over (1) +3338+6584
hand over (1)
pour (1)
pours out (1)

spilled (1)
stretched out (1)

5600 נִגְרֶת *niggeret*
Variant; not used

5601 נָגַשׂ *nāgaś* (23)
slave drivers (5)
oppressor (3)
require payment (2)
ruler (2)
driver's (1)
exacted (1)
exploit (1)
hard pressed (1)
in distress (1)
oppress (1)
oppress each other (1)
oppressors (1)
slave driver's (1)
tax collector (1)
was oppressed (1)

5602 נָגַשׁ *nāgaš* (125)
approached (12)
bring (11)
come near (11)
brought (7)
came (7)
approach (6)
went up (5)
come (4)
take (4)
went (3)
advanced (2)
brought close (2)
came up (2)
close (2)
come close (2)
come forward (2)
come here (2)
get so close (2)
go (2)
go up (2)
presented (2)
abstain from sexual relations (1)
+440+448+851
assemble (1) +3481
be brought (1)
be overtaken (1)
bring in (1)
bring near (1)
brings (1)
came forward (1)
came near (1)
came over (1)
confront (1)
done soˢ (1)
draw near (1)
drew near (1)
get out (1)
give more space (1)
go near (1)
march out (1)
moved forward (1)
offered (1)
overtake (1)
place (1)
present (1)
sacrifice (1)
set (1)
set forth (1)
step forward (1)
stepped forward (1)
took (1)
touch (1)
went close (1)
went over (1)
were fettered (1) +4200+5733

5603 נֵד *nēḏ* (4)
heap (2)
wall (2)

5604 נָדָא *nādā'* (1)
untranslated (1)

5605 נָדַב *nādab* (17)
brought as freewill offerings (1) +5607
freewill offerings (1)
gave freewill offerings (1)
gave willingly (1)
give generously (1)
given freely (1)
given willingly (1)
prompts to give (1)
volunteered (1)
volunteered himself for service (1)
willing (1)
willing (1) +4213
willing (1) +8120
willing response (1)
willing volunteers (1)
willingly given (1)
willingly offer themselves (1)

5606 נָדָב *nādāb* (20)
Nadab (19)
Nadab's (1)

5607 נְדָבָה *nᵉdābāh* (26)
freewill offerings (10)
freewill offering (7)
freely (2)
willing (2)
abundant (1)
brought as freewill offerings (1) +5605
freewill (1)
voluntarily (1)
untranslated (1)

5608 נְדַבְיָה *nᵉdabyāh* (1)
Nedabiah (1)

5609 נִדְגָּלוֹת *nidgālôt*
Variant; not used

5610 נָדַד *nādad* (28)
flee (5)
fled (3)
banished (2)
fugitives (2)
strays (2)
be cast aside (1)
could not (1)
flapped (1)
flee in haste (1) +5610
flown away (1)
fluttering (1)
fly away (1)
in flight (1)
nothing (1)
refugees (1)
strayed (1)
wanderers (1)
wanders about (1)

5611 נְדֻדִים *nᵉdudiym* (1)
toss (1) +8425

5612 נָדָה *nādāh* (2)
exclude (1)
put off (1)

5613 נֵדֶה *nēdeh* (1)
fee (1)

5614 נִדָּה *niddāh* (29)
period (7)
cleansing (6)
monthly period (3)
unclean thing (3)
act of impurity (1)
corruption (1)
defilement (1)
impurity (1)
impurity of monthly period (1)
monthly flow (1)
monthly period (1) +1864
monthly period (1) +1865

polluted (1)
woman's monthly uncleanness (1)
+2021+3240

5615 1נָדַח *nādah1* (55)
banish (6)
banished (6)
exiles (5)
been scattered (3)
drive (2)
fugitives (2)
led astray (2)
strays (2)
are drawn away (1)
be driven away (1)
be enticed (1)
be thrust (1)
been banished (1)
been driven (1)
chased away (1)
disperses (1)
drive out (1)
driven (1)
driven away (1)
enticed (1)
estranged (1)
exiled (1)
hunted (1)
outcast (1)
pushing (1)
scatter (1)
scattered (1)
seduced (1)
spewed out (1)
straying (1)
topple (1)
turn (1)
turn away (1)
were exiled (1)
untranslated (1)

5616 2נָדַח *nādah2* (3)
bring (1)
putting (1)
swings (1)

5617 נֹדִי *nōdiy*
Variant; not used

5618 נָדִיב *nādiyb* (27)
nobles (8)
princes (5)
willing (3)
noble (2)
ruler (2)
willing (2) +4213
great man's (1)
nobleman (1)
officials (1)
prince's (1)
royal (1)

5619 נְדִיבָה *nᵉdiybāh* (3)
noble (2)
dignity (1)

5620 1נָדָן *nādān1* (1)
sheath (1)

5621 2נָדָן *nādān2* (1)
gifts (1)

5622 נָדַף *nādap* (9)
windblown (3)
blow away (2)
blows away (1)
fleeting (1)
is blown away (1)
refute (1)

5623 נָדַר *nādar* (31)
made a vow (4) +5624
vowed (3) +5624
made vow (2) +5624
make a vow (2) +5624
makes a vow (2) +5624

vow (2)
vow made (2) +5624
made a vow (1)
made vow (1)
made vows (1) +5624
make a special vow (1) +7098
make a vow (1)
make vows (1)
make vows (1) +5624
makes a vow (1)
making a vow (1)
making vow (1)
vowed (1)
vows (1)
vows made (1) +5624
vows to give (1)

5624 נֶדֶר *nēder* (60)
vows (21)
vow (13)
made a vow (4) +5623
vowed (3)
vowed (3) +5623
made vow (3) +5623
make a vow (2) +5623
makes a vow (2) +5623
vow made (2) +5623
fulfill a special vow (1) +7098
made vows (1) +5623
make vows (1) +5623
makes a special vow (1) +7098
special vow (1) +7098
special vows (1) +7098
vows made (1) +5623
what promised (1)

5625 נֹהַ *nōah* (1)
value (1)

5626 נָה *-nāh* (214)
it (84)
her (22)
them (9)
its (6)
whichˢ (5)
they (4)
she (3)
that (3)
the lampstandˢ (3)
him (2)
theˢ (2)
this (2)
everything (1) +3972
himself (1)
incenseˢ (1)
one (1)
soˢ (1)
the animalˢ (1)
the cityˢ (1)
the flockˢ (1)
the foodˢ (1)
the landˢ (1)
their (1)
themselves (1)
which (1)
widowˢ (1)
untranslated (55)

5627 1נָהַג *nāhag1* (30)
carried off (3)
guiding (3)
lead (3)
led (3)
drive (2)
guide (2)
drive away (1)
driven away (1)
drives (1)
driving (1)
drove (1)
drove ahead (1)
guided (1)
lead away (1)

lead on (1) +2143+2256
led forth (1)
led in triumphal procession (1)
led out (1)
made blow (1)
take (1)

5628 נָהַג nāhag2 (1)
moan (1)

5629 נָהָה 1 nāhāh1 (3)
mourned (1)
taunt (1)
wail (1)

5630 נָהָה 2 nāhāh2
Variant; not used

5631 נְהִי nᵉhiy (7)
wail (2)
mourners (1) +3359
mournful song (1)
mourning (1)
wail (1) +5951
wailing (1)

5632 נִהְיָה nihyāh
Variant; not used

5633 נָהַל nāhal (10)
guide (3)
brought (1)
gently leads (1)
lead (1)
leads (1)
move along (1)
put (1)
took care of (1)

5634 נַהֲלָל naĥᵉlāl (2)
Nahalal (2)

5635 נַהֲלֹל 1 naĥᵉlōl1 (1)
water holes (1)

5636 נַהֲלֹל 2 naĥᵉlōl2 (1)
Nahalol (1)

5637 נָהַם nāham (5)
groan (2)
growl (1)
roar (1)
roaring (1)

5638 נַהַם naham (2)
roar (2)

5639 נְהָמָה nᵉhāmāh (2)
anguish (1)
roaring (1)

5640 נָהַק nāhaq (2)
bray (1)
brayed (1)

5641 נָהַר 1 nāhar1 (3)
stream (3)

5642 נָהַר 2 nāhar2 (3)
radiant (2)
rejoice (1)

5643 נָהָר nāhār (119)
river (58)
rivers (23)
streams (12)
Trans-Euphrates (4) +2021+6298
canal (3)
seas (3)
Euphratesˢ (2)
flood (2)
riverbed (2)
waters (2)
canals (1)
currents (1)
riversˢ (1) +5707
untranslated (5)

5644 נְהָרָה nᵉhārāh (1)
light (1)

5645 נַהֲרַיִם naĥᵉrayim
Variant; not used

5646 נוּל 1 -nûl (1656)
us (701)
our (670)
we (94)
our (22) +4200
our own (12)
ourselves (10)
ours (7)
theˢ (6)
it (5)
we (5) +5883
ourselves (3) +5883
us (3) +5883
me (2)
ours (2) +4200
aˢ (1)
each other (1) +9109
heˢ (1) +466+3378
hereˢ (1)
one (1)
ours (1) +4200+7156
that (1)
us (1) +6524
us deserve (1)
we (1) +3972
we're (1)
whatˢ (1)
you (1)
untranslated (101)

5647 נוּן 2 -nû2 (511)
him (174)
it (85)
them (48)
he (24)
his (10)
my wrathˢ (8)
they (8)
animalˢ (2)
its (2)
the altarˢ (2)
the ephodˢ (2)
the servantˢ (2)
themselves (2)
whom (2)
Abimelechˢ (1)
Absalomˢ (1)
all he hasˢ (1)
allˢ (1)
anotherˢ (1)
anyˢ (1)
drinkˢ (1)
Edomˢ (1)
hers (1)
his (1) +4946
his own (1)
Jeremiahˢ (1)
Judahˢ (1)
manˢ (1)
mannaˢ (1)
one (1)
the bloodˢ (1)
the manˢ (1)
the meatˢ (1)
the oilˢ (1)
the roofˢ (1)
the sacred portionˢ (1)
the wickedˢ (1)
their (1)
their own (1)
thereˢ (1)
these tithesˢ (1)
this breadˢ (1)
thoseˢ (1)
what (1)
who (1)
untranslated (109)

5648 נוּא nû' (9)
forbids (2)

discourage (1) +4213
discouraged (1) +4213
forbid (1)
forbidden (1)
refuse (1)
thwarts (1)
untranslated (1)

5649 נוּב nûb (4)
bear fruit (1)
brings forth (1)
increase (1)
make thrive (1)

5650 נוֹב nôb (1)
untranslated (1)

5651 נוֹבַי nôbāy (1)
untranslated (1)

5652 נוּג nûg (1)
sorrows (1)

5653 נוּד nûd (26)
flee (3)
mourn (3)
wanderer (2)
away (1)
comfort (1)
comforted (1)
drive away (1)
fluttering (1)
go astray (1)
make wander (1)
moaning (1)
mourn loss (1)
shake (1)
shake head in scorn (1)
shake heads in scorn (1)
show sympathy (1)
swaying (1)
sways (1)
sympathize (1)
sympathy (1)
untranslated (1)

5654 נוֹד 1 nôd1 (1)
lament (1)

5655 נוֹד 2 nôd2 (1)
Nod (1)

5656 נוֹדָב nôdāb (1)
Nodab (1)

5657 נָוָה 1 nāwāh1 (1)
at rest (1)

5658 נָוָה 2 nāwāh2 (1)
praise (1)

5659 נָוֶה 1 nāweh1 (32)
pasture (9)
dwelling (3)
house (3)
grazing land (2)
homeland (2)
pastureland (2)
abode (1)
dwelling place (1)
dwelling places (1)
haunt (1)
haunts (1)
home (1)
land (1)
pastures (1)
pleasant place (1)
property (1)
settlement (1)

5660 נָוֶה 2 nāweh2
Variant; not used

5661 נָוָה 3 nāwāh3 (15)
pastures (7)
camps (1) +1074
dwell (1)
dwellings (1)

grasslands (1)
haunts (1)
meadows (1)
pasturelands (1)
place (1)

5662 נָוֹת *nāwôt* (1)
untranslated (1)

5663 1נוּחַ *nûah1* (143)
leave (11)
given rest (8)
put (8)
rest (7)
left (6)
kept (5)
rested (5)
set (5)
at rest (4)
give rest (4)
leave alone (4)
place (4)
placed (4)
find rest (3)
gave rest (3)
gives rest (3)
settle (3)
subside (3)
allowed (2)
came to rest (2)
granted rest (2)
laid (2)
put down (2)
set up (2)
allied (1)
allowed to remain (1)
be set (1)
brought (1)
cast (1)
comes to rest (1)
deposited (1)
forsake (1)
get relief (1)
give peace (1)
gives relief (1)
giving rest (1)
got relief (1)
have rest (1)
lay (1)
lay to rest (1)
lays (1)
left unweighed (1)
let be idle (1)
let go (1) +906+3338
let remain (1)
lowered (1)
permits (1)
remain (1)
reposes (1)
resides (1)
resting (1)
safely (1)
save (1)
saved (1)
set down (1)
settled (1)
settled down (1)
store (1)
store up (1)
subsided (1)
throw (1)
tolerate (1)
touch (1)
wait patiently (1)
waited (1)

5664 2נוּחַ *nûah2*
Variant; not used

5665 נוֹחַ *nôah* (1)
resting place (1)

5666 נוֹחָה *nôhāh* (1)
Nohah (1)

5667 נוּט *nût* (1)
shake (1)

5668 נָוִית *nāwiyt* (5)
untranslated (5)

5669 נָזֵל *nāzel*
Variant; not used

5670 נוּם *nûm* (6)
slumber (3)
sleep (2)
slumbers (1)

5671 נוּמָה *nûmāh* (1)
drowsiness (1)

5672 1נוּן *nûn1* (2)
continue (1)
untranslated (1)

5673 2נוּן *nûn2* (30)
Nun (30)

5674 נוּס *nûs* (160)
fled (63)
flee (38)
flees (7)
ran (7)
fleeing (6)
run (5)
escape (3)
flee away (3)
escaped (2)
fugitives (2)
draining away (1)
drives along (1)
fled back (1)
fled up (1)
flee in haste (1) +4960
flight (1)
forced to flee (1) +5674
fugitive (1)
get away (1)
get away (1) +5674
gone (1)
hurried to bring (1)
keep (1)
leave (1)
made good escape (1) +2256+4880
on the run (1)
put to flight (1)
retreat (1)
routed (1)
running away (1)
turned and ran (1)
untranslated (1)

5675 נוּעַ *nûa'* (42)
shake (5)
hold sway (3)
shaken (3)
make wander about (2)
restless (2)
stagger (2)
staggered (2)
tosses (2)
wander about (2)
crooked (1)
disturb (1)
grope (1)
is shaken (1)
made wander (1)
moving (1)
reels (1) +5675
set trembling (1)
shaking (1)
shook (1)
sways (1)
tremble (1)
trembled (1)
wander (1)
wandering (1)
untranslated (3)

5676 נוֹעַדְיָה *nô'adyāh* (2)

Noadiah (2)

5677 1נוּף *nûp1* (35)
wave (12)
waved (4)
presented (3)
present (2)
use (2)
beckon (1) +3338
put (1)
raise (1)
raised (1)
raises (1)
shake (1)
shakes (1)
sweep (1)
used (1)
uses (1)
was waved (1) +9485
wield (1)

5678 2נוּף *nûp2* (2)
gave (1)
perfumed (1)

5679 נוֹף *nôp* (1)
loftiness (1)

5680 נוּץ *nûs* (1)
flee (1)

5681 נוֹצָה *nôsāh* (3)
plumage (2)
feathers (1)

5682 נוּק *nûq*
Variant; not used

5683 נוּשׁ *nûš* (1)
helpless (1)

5684 1נָזָה *nāzāh1* (24)
sprinkle (17)
spattered (2)
sprinkled (2)
is spattered (1)
sprinkles (1)
untranslated (1)

5685 2נָזָה *nāzāh2*
Variant; not used

5686 נָזִיד *nāziyd* (6)
stew (6)

5687 נָזִיר *nāziyr* (16)
Nazirite (8)
Nazirites (2)
prince (2)
untended vines (2)
princes (1)
separation (1)

5688 נָזַל *nāzal* (11)
flow (3)
descend (1)
made flow (1)
pour down moisture (1)
quaked (1)
shower down (1)
spread abroad (1)
streaming down (1)
streams (1)

5689 נֹזֵל *nōzēl* (5)
streams (3)
running water (1)
surging (1)

5690 נֶזֶם *nezem* (17)
ring (5)
earrings (4)
rings (4)
earring (2)
nose ring (2)

5691 נֶזֶק *nēzeq* (1)
disturbing (1)

5692 נָזַר1 *nāzar1* (5)
consecrated themselves (1)
fast (1)
keep separate (1)
separates himself (1)
treat with respect (1)

5693 נָזַר2 *nāzar2* (5)
separation (2)
abstain (1)
dedicate (1)
Nazirite (1)

5694 נֵזֶר *nēzer* (25)
crown (7)
separation (6)
dedicated (3)
diadem (3)
Nazirite (2)
dedication (1)
hair (1)
symbol of separation (1)
untranslated (1)

5695 נֹחַ *nōah* (47)
Noah (40)
Noah's (3)
he^s (2)
his^s (2)

5696 נַחְבִּי *nahbiy* (1)
Nahbi (1)

5697 נָחָה1 *nāhāh1* (35)
lead (11)
guide (9)
led (6)
guided (4)
guides (2)
disperses (1)
lead out (1)
ushers (1)

5698 נָחָה2 *nāhāh2*
Variant; not used

5699 נַחוּם *nahûm* (1)
Nahum (1)

5700 נְחוּם *n'hûm* (1)
Nehum (1)

5701 נָחוֹר *nāhôr* (18)
Nahor (16)
Nahor's (2)

5702 נָחוּשׁ *nāhûš* (1)
bronze (1)

5703 נְחוּשָׁה *n'hûšāh* (10)
bronze (8)
bronze-tipped (1)
copper (1)

5704 נְחִילוֹת *n'hiylôt* (1)
flutes (1)

5705 נָחִיר *nāhiyr* (1)
nostrils (1)

5706 נָחַל *nāhal* (59)
inherit (6)
assign as an inheritance (2)
distribute (2)
gave inheritance (2)
giving as an inheritance (2)
inheritance (2)
lead to inherit (2)
receive inheritance (2)
received (2)
received inheritance (2)
allotted (1)
assign inheritance (1)
assigned (1)
been allotted (1)
bestowing (1)
cause to inherit (1)
divide (1)

divide as inheritance (1)
divide for an inheritance (1)
dividing (1)
gave (1)
get inheritance (1)
give as an inheritance (1)
give inheritance (1)
has inherit (1)
have inheritance (1)
have inheritance (1) +5709
help assign (1)
heritage (1)
inherit land (1)
inheritance given (1)
inherits (1)
leaves an inheritance (1)
pass on as an inheritance (1)
possess (1)
possessed (1)
reassign (1)
receive (1)
receive inheritance (1) +5709
received as an inheritance (1)
take as inheritance (1)
take possession (1)
will (1)
wills (1)
untranslated (1)

5707 נַחַל1 *nahal1* (139)
valley (34)
gorge (19)
river (17)
streams (12)
ravine (11)
ravines (9)
stream (8)
wadi (7)
brook (5)
torrent (3)
torrents (2)
valleys (2)
course (1)
intermittent streams (1)
poplars (1) +6857
rivers (1)
rivers (1) +5643
shaft (1)
stream beds (1)
streams (1) +692
there^s (1) +928+7724
untranslated (1)

5708 נַחַל2 *nahal2*
Variant; not used

5709 נַחֲלָה1 *nah°lāh1* (222)
inheritance (185)
heritage (5)
inherit (3)
part (3)
property (3)
inheritances (2)
one^s (2)
territory (2)
that^s (2)
ancestral property (1)
estate (1)
have inheritance (1) +5706
inherited (1)
it^s (1)
land (1)
land inherited (1)
land inherits (1)
lands (1)
place (1)
receive inheritance (1) +5706
territories (1)
territory inherit (1)
untranslated (2)

5710 נַחֲלָה2 *nah°lāh2* (1)
disease (1)

5711 נַחֲלָה3 *nah°lāh3* (2)
wadi (2)

5712 נַחֲלִיאֵל *nah°liy'ēl* (2)
Nahaliel (2)

5713 נֶחְלָמִי *neh°lāmiy* (3)
Nehelamite (3)

5714 נָחַם *nāham* (108)
comfort (23)
comforted (5)
express sympathy (5)
relent (5)
be comforted (4)
change mind (4)
comforts (4)
was grieved (4)
console (3)
grieved (3)
have compassion (3)
relented (3)
am grieved (2)
be consoled (2)
comforter (2)
comforters (2)
compassion (2)
consoled (2)
give comfort (2)
relents (2)
be avenged (1)
change minds (1)
consoling himself (1)
find comfort (1)
get relief (1)
given comfort (1)
giving comfort (1)
had compassion (1)
have pity (1)
look with compassion (1)
pity (1)
reassured (1)
reconsider (1)
recovered from grief (1)
relent and do not bring (1)
relent and not bring (1)
relent so that not bring (1)
relented and did not (1)
repent (1)
repented (1)
repents (1)
show compassion (1)
showed pity (1)
was comforted (1)
was consoled (1)
were consoled (1)

5715 נַחַם *naham* (1)
Naham (1)

5716 נֹחַם *nōham* (1)
compassion (1)

5717 נֶחָמָה *nehāmāh* (2)
comfort (1)
consolation (1)

5718 נְחֶמְיָה *n'hemyāh* (8)
Nehemiah (8)

5719 נִחֻמִים *nihumiym* (3)
comfort (1)
comforting (1)
compassion (1)

5720 נַחֲמָנִי *nah°māniy* (1)
Nahamani (1)

5721 נַחְנוּ *nahnû* (6)
we (5)
untranslated (1)

5722 נָחַץ *nāhas* (1)
urgent (1)

5723 נָחַר *nāhar* (2)
angry (1)

blow fiercely (1)

5724 נָחַר *nahar* (1)
snorting (1)

5725 נַחֲרָה *nahᵃrāh* (1)
snorting (1)

5726 נַחְרִי *nahray* (2)
Naharai (2)

5727 נָחַשׁ *nāhaš* (11)
divination (2)
find things out by divination (1) +5727
interprets omens (1)
learned by divination (1)
practice divination (1)
sorcery (1)
took as a good sign (1)
uses for divination (1) +5727

5728 נַחַשׁ *nahaš* (2)
sorcery (2)

5729 1נָחָשׁ *nāhāš1* (31)
snake (14)
serpent (11)
snakes (3)
serpent's (2)
venomous snakes (1)

5730 2נָחָשׁ *nāhāš2*
Variant; not used

5731 3נָחָשׁ *nāhāš3* (9)
Nahash (8)
himˢ (1)

5732 נַחְשׁוֹן *nahšôn* (10)
Nahshon (10)

5733 1נְחֹשֶׁת *nᵉhōšet1* (140)
bronze (128)
bronze shackles (5)
copper (4)
chains (1)
wealth (1)
were fettered (1) +4200+5602

5734 2נְחֹשֶׁת *nᵉhōšet2*
Variant; not used

5735 נְחֻשְׁתָּא *nᵉhuštā'* (1)
Nehushta (1)

5736 נְחֻשְׁתָּן *nᵉhuštān* (1)
Nehushtan (1)

5737 נָחַת *nāhat* (10)
bend (2)
bring down (1)
come (1)
come down (1)
descend (1)
go down (1)
impresses (1)
level (1)
pierced (1) +928

5738 1נַחַת *nahat1* (1)
coming down (1)

5739 2נַחַת *nahat2* (6)
rest (2)
comfort (1)
peace (1)
quiet (1)
tranquillity (1)

5740 3נַחַת *nahat3* (5)
Nahath (5)

5741 נָחֵת *nāhēt* (1)
going down (1)

5742 נָטָה *nātāh* (217)
stretch out (22)
stretched out (20)
outstretched (18)
turn (12)
pitched (10)

pay attention (7) +265
turned (7)
give ear (6) +265
stretches out (5)
upraised (5)
deprive (4)
deny (3)
pervert (3)
spread out (3)
took aside (3)
turn aside (3)
turned away (3)
deprive of justice (2)
evening (2)
extended (2)
held out (2)
listen (2) +265
parted (2)
pitch (2)
spread (2)
swerve (2)
afternoon (1) +2021+3427
applying (1)
be stretched out (1)
bend (1)
bent down (1)
brandishes (1)
conspired (1)
did thisˢ (1) +2257+3338
directs (1)
extend (1)
get back on (1)
get off (1)
giving (1)
go ahead (1)
go forward (1)
grow long (1)
hear (1) +265
hold out (1)
inclined (1) +4213
kept away (1)
lay (1)
lead (1)
leaning (1)
led astray (1)
led astray (1) +4213
let be drawn (1)
let down (1)
lie down (1)
listen closely (1) +265
listen well (1) +265
measures (1)
misleads (1)
outspread (1)
paid any attention (1) +265+4200+9048
paid attention (1) +265
part (1)
perverted (1)
plot (1)
pushed (1)
raised (1)
set (1)
shakes (1)
showed (1)
shown (1)
siding (1)
slipped (1)
spreads out (1)
stay (1)
stays only a night (1) +4328
strayed (1)
stretch wide (1)
stretched (1)
throw (1)
thrust (1)
turn away (1)
turned aside (1)
turning (1)
turning aside (1)
went over (1)
withholds (1)

won over (1)
yield (1)
untranslated (3)

5743 נְטוֹפָתִי *nᵉtôpātiy* (11)
Netophathite (8)
Netophathites (3)

5744 נָטִיל *nātiyl* (1)
who trade with (1)

5745 נָטִיעַ *nātiya'* (1)
plants (1)

5746 נְטִישׁוֹת *nᵉtiyšôt* (3)
branches (2)
spreading branches (1)

5747 נָטַל *nātal* (4)
giving (1)
laid (1)
lifted up (1)
weighs (1)

5748 נֵטֶל *nētel* (1)
burden (1)

5749 נָטַע *nāta'* (59)
plant (28)
planted (19)
are planted (1)
farmers (1)
firmly embedded (1)
implanted (1)
pitch (1)
plants (1)
replanted (1)
set in place (1)
set out (1)
set up (1)
untranslated (2)

5750 נֶטַע *neta'* (4)
garden (1)
plant (1)
plants (1)
set out (1)

5751 נְטָעִים *nᵉtā'iym* (1)
Netaim (1)

5752 נָטַף *nātap* (18)
drip (3)
prophesy (3)
preach (2)
dripped (1)
dripping (1)
drop (1)
fell gently (1)
poured (1)
poured down (1)
poured down rain (1)
preaching (1)
prophet (1)
prophets say (1)

5753 נָטָף *nātāp* (1)
gum resin (1)

5754 נֵטֶף *netep* (1)
drops (1)

5755 נְטִפָה *nᵉtipāh* (2)
earrings (1)
pendants (1)

5756 נְטֹפָה *nᵉtōpāh* (2)
Netophah (2)

5757 1נָטַר *nātar1* (9)
angry (2)
bear a grudge against (1)
harbor anger (1)
maintains wrath (1)
neglected (1) +4202
take care of (1)
tenants (1)
tend (1)

5758 נָטַר2 *nātar2*
Variant; not used

5759 נָטַשׁ *nātaš* (40)
abandoned (5)
forsake (5)
left (4)
leave (3)
reject (3)
spread out (3)
abandon (1)
be abandoned (1)
brought down (1)
cast out (1)
deserted (1)
drawn (1)
drop (1)
forgo (1)
hangs loose (1)
let (1)
rejected (1)
scattered (1)
spread (1)
spreading out (1)
stopped thinking (1)
throw (1)
unused (1)

5760 נִי *niy* (1)
wail (1)

5761 נִי- *-niy* (1315)
me (1011)
I (204)
my (28)
us (12)
myself (3)
him (2)
mine (2) +4946
we (2)
how I long for (1) +4769+5989
I'll (1)
untranslated (49)

5762 נִיב *niyḇ* (2)
itˢ (1)
praise (1)

5763 נֵיבָי *nēybāy* (1)
Nebai (1)

5764 נִיד *niyd* (1)
comfort (1)

5765 נִידָה *niydāh* (1)
unclean (1)

5766 נָיוֹת *nāyôṯ* (6)
Naioth (6)

5767 נִיחֹחַ *niyhôah* (43)
pleasing (39)
fragrant incense (4) +8194

5768 נִין1 *niyn1*
Variant; not used

5769 נִין2 *niyn2* (3)
offspring (2)
children (1)

5770 נִינְוֵה *niynᵉwēh* (17)
Nineveh (16)
Ninevites (1) +408

5771 נִיס *niys* (1)
untranslated (1)

5772 נִיסָן *niysān* (2)
Nisan (2)

5773 נִיצוֹץ *niysôs* (1)
spark (1)

5774 נִיר1 *niyr1* (2)
break up (2)

5775 נִיר2 *niyr2* (5)
lamp (5)

5776 נִיר3 *niyr3* (3)
unplowed ground (2)
field (1)

5777 נָכָא1 *nākā'1* (1)
were driven out (1)

5778 נָכָא2 *nākā'2* (1)
grieve (1)

5779 נָכֵא *nākē'* (3)
crushed (2)
crushes (1)

5780 נִכֹאת *nᵉkō'ṯ* (2)
spices (2)

5781 נֶכֶד *neked* (3)
descendants (3)

5782 נָכָה *nākāh* (501)
struck down (57)
killed (39)
struck (34)
defeated (32)
strike (28)
put (24)
attacked (21)
kill (15)
attack (13)
beat (10)
kills (10)
strike down (9)
inflicted (7)
conquered (5)
cut down (5)
destroy (5)
afflict (4)
afflicted (4)
attacks (4)
fought (4)
hits (4)
murdered (4)
slain (4)
subdued (4)
take (4)
assassinated (3)
defeat (3)
hit (3)
killing (3)
pin (3)
punished (3)
put to death (3)
slaughtered (3)
stabbed (3)
strikes (3)
beat down (2)
beaten (2)
broke through (2)
conscience-stricken (2) +4213
defeating (2)
destroyed (2)
flog (2)
had beaten (2)
inflict (2)
kill (2) +5883
overpowered (2)
punish (2)
slapped (2)
slaughtering (2)
strike together (2)
striking (2)
striking down (2)
takes life (2) +5883
victory (2)
were destroyed (2)
wounded (2)
annihilate (1)
assailant (1)
assassinated (1) +2256+4637
assassins (1)
attacked viciously (1) +3751+6584+8797
be beaten (1)
be struck down (1)

beating (1)
beats (1)
being beaten (1)
blazed (1)
blighted (1)
blind (1) +928+2021+6427
break up (1)
chewed (1)
clapped (1)
conquers (1)
dealt (1)
destroyed (1) +1524+4394+4804
devastated (1) +1524+4394+4804
drove (1)
executed (1)
executed (1) +2256+4637
fall (1)
fallen (1)
fell upon (1)
flogged (1) +4804
give lashes (1)
had executed (1) +2256+4637
had struck down (1)
harm (1)
have flogged (1)
himˢ (1) +2021
hitting (1)
indeed defeated (1) +5782
inflicted casualties (1)
injured (1)
is blighted (1)
is struck (1)
killed (1) +2995+4200+7023
killed (1) +4637
killed (1) +8357
killed off (1)
kills (1) +2256+4637+5883
lashes (1)
must certainly put (1) +5782
overthrow (1)
personˢ (1)
plunge (1)
plunged (1)
putting to death (1)
putting to rout (1)
routed (1)
sacked (1)
send down (1)
shot (1)
slay (1)
smash (1)
smitten (1)
strikes down (1)
strikes the blow (1)
struck (1) +5782
struck down (1) +4804
struck the blow (1)
tear down (1)
thrust (1)
was killed (1)
was put to death (1)
were afflicted (1)
were beaten (1)
wound (1)
wounds was given (1)
untranslated (4)

5783 נָכֵה *nākeh* (3)
contrite (1)
crippled (1)
lame (1)

5784 נְכֵה *nēkeh* (1)
attackers (1)

5785 נְכֹה *nᵉkōh* (4)
Neco (3)
untranslated (1)

5786 נְכוֹ *nᵉkô* (4)
Neco (4)

5787 נָכוֹן1 *nākôn1* (1)
fate (1)

5788 נָכוֹן2 *nākôn2*
Variant; not used

5789 נָכוֹן3 *nākôn3* (1)
Nacon (1)

5790 נֹכַח *nōkah* (25)
opposite (5)
before (4)
facing (3)
faces (2)
approval (1)
directly in front of (1) +4200
directly opposite (1) +4200+7156
in front of (1)
in full view (1) +6524
in the presence of (1) +7156
on behalf of (1) +4200
open before (1) +7156
straight ahead (1) +4200
toward (1) +448
toward (1) +6330
vicinity (1)

5791 נָכֹחַ *nākōah* (8)
right (3)
honest (1)
honesty (1)
proper (1)
uprightly (1)
uprightness (1)

5792 נָכַל *nākal* (4)
cheat (1)
conspire (1)
deceived (1) +928+5793
plotted (1)

5793 נֵכֶל *nēkel* (1)
deceived (1) +928+5792

5794 נְכָסִים *nᵉkāsiym* (5)
possessions (2)
riches (2)
wealth (1)

5795 נָכַר1 *nākar1* (45)
recognized (9)
recognize (5)
acknowledge (4)
show partiality (4) +7156
know (2)
are recognized (1)
concerned (1)
disguises himself (1)
distinguish (1)
examine to see (1)
favor (1)
is known (1)
know how (1)
make friends with (1)
misunderstand (1)
notice (1)
paid regard (1)
realized (1)
regard (1)
remembers (1)
see (1)
takes note of (1)
tell (1)
took note (1)
took notice (1)
untranslated (1)

5796 נָכַר2 *nākar2* (5)
handed over (1) +928+3338
made foreign (1)
pretend to be someone else (1)
pretended to be a stranger (1)
pretense (1)

5797 נֵכָר *nēkār* (36)
foreign (16)
foreigners (10) +1201
foreigner (5) +1201
they^s (2) +1201

alien (1)
foreigner (1) +1201+2021
foreigners (1) +1201+2021

5798 נֵכֶר *nēker* (2)
disaster (1)
misfortune (1)

5799 נָכְרִי *nokriy* (46)
foreign (14)
foreigner (10)
wayward (6)
alien (4)
foreigners (4)
another (1)
another man's (1)
foreigners (1) +6639
pagans (1) +3529
someone else (1)
stranger (1)
wild (1)
untranslated (1)

5800 נְכֹת *nᵉkōt* (3)
storehouses (2) +1074
untranslated (1)

5801 נָלָה *nālāh* (1)
stop (1)

5802 נְמִבְזָה *nᵉmibzāh*
Variant; not used

5803 נְמוּאֵל *nᵉmû'ēl* (3)
Nemuel (3)

5804 נְמוּאֵלִי *nᵉmû'ēliy* (1)
Nemuelite (1)

5805 נְמָלָה *nᵉmālāh* (2)
ant (1)
ants (1)

5806 נָמֵס *nāmēs*
Variant; not used

5807 נָמֵר *nāmēr* (6)
leopard (4)
leopards (2)

5808 נִמְרֹד *nimrōd* (4)
Nimrod (4)

5809 נִמְרָה *nimrāh* (1)
Nimrah (1)

5810 נִמְרִים *nimriym* (2)
Nimrim (2)

5811 נִמְשִׁי *nimšiy* (5)
Nimshi (5)

5812 נֵס *nēs* (21)
banner (14)
battle standard (2)
pole (2)
sail (1)
signal (1)
warning sign (1)

5813 נְסִבָּה *nᵉsibbāh* (1)
turn of events (1)

5814 נָסָה *nāsāh* (36)
test (14)
tested (8)
put to the test (6)
used to (2)
did^s (1)
testing (1)
tried (1)
try (1)
venture (1)
ventures (1)

5815 נָסַח *nāsah* (4)
be uprooted (1)
tear (1)
tears down (1)
torn (1)

5816 נָסִיךְ1 *nāsiyk1* (2)
drink offerings (1)
metal images (1)

5817 נָסִיךְ2 *nāsiyk2* (4)
princes (3)
leaders (1)

5818 נָסַךְ1 *nāsak1* (23)
poured out (7)
pour out (6)
pouring out (3)
casts (2)
brought (1)
forming an alliance (1) +5011
pour (1)
pouring out of drink offerings (1)
pouring out of offerings (1)

5819 נָסַךְ2 *nāsak2* (1)
covers (1)

5820 נָסַךְ3 *nāsak3* (2)
installed (1)
was appointed (1)

5821 נֶסֶךְ1 *nesek1* (60)
drink offerings (32)
drink offering (27)
libations (1)

5822 נֶסֶךְ2 *nesek2* (4)
images (3)
metal god (1)

5823 נָסַס1 *nāsas1* (1)
sick (1)

5824 נָסַס2 *nāsas2* (2)
be unfurled (1)
sparkle (1)

5825 נָסַע *nāsa'* (146)
set out (49)
left (43)
moved on (6)
traveled (5)
went (5)
move (3)
broke camp (2)
brought out (2)
move on (2)
moved (2)
pulled up (2)
withdrew (2)
advance (1)
are pulled up (1)
be on way (1) +2143+2256
been pulled down (1)
broke camp (1) +185+4946
journeyed (1)
leaving (1) +4946
led (1)
left (1) +4946
let loose (1)
marching (1)
move about (1)
move out (1)
out (1)
put to one side (1)
quarries (1)
removed from quarry (1)
setting out (1)
tore loose (1)
uproots (1)
wander (1)
went out (1)
untranslated (1)

5826 נָסַק *nāsaq*
Variant; not used

5827 נִסְרֹךְ *nisrōk* (2)
Nisroch (2)

5828 נֵעָה *nē'āh* (1)
Neah (1)

5829 נֹעָה *nō'āh* (4)
Noah (4)

5830 נְעוּרִים *n°'ûriym* (46)
youth (37)
young (5)
childhood (3)
boyhood (1)

5831 נְעוּרוֹת *n°'ûrôṯ* (1)
youth (1)

5832 נְעִיאֵל *n°'iy'ēl* (1)
Neiel (1)

5833 נָעִים1 *nā'iym1* (11)
pleasant (4)
beautiful (1)
charming (1)
compliments (1) +1821
contentment (1)
gracious (1)
pleasing (1)
pleasures (1)

5834 נָעִים2 *nā'iym2* (2)
melodious (1)
singer (1)

5835 נָעַל1 *nā'al1* (6)
locked (2)
bolt (1)
bolted (1)
locked up (1)
sealed (1)

5836 נָעַל2 *nā'al2* (2)
put sandals on (1)
sandals (1)

5837 נַעַל *na'al* (22)
sandals (14)
sandal (6)
sandaled (1) +928+2021
unsandaled (1) +2740

5838 נָעֵם *nā'ēm* (8)
pleasant (2)
dear (1)
delicious (1)
go well (1)
more favored (1)
pleasing (1)
well (1)

5839 נַעַם *na'am* (1)
Naam (1)

5840 נֹעַם *nō'am* (7)
favor (3)
pleasant (2)
beauty (1)
pleasing (1)

5841 נַעֲמָה1 *na'ªmāh1* (4)
Naamah (4)

5842 נַעֲמָה2 *na'ªmāh2* (1)
Naamah (1)

5843 נָעֳמִי *nā'ºmiy* (21)
Naomi (19)
Naomi's (1)
she[s] (1)

5844 נַעֲמִי *na'ªmiy* (1)
Naamite (1)

5845 נַעֲמָן *na'ªmān* (16)
Naaman (14)
Naaman's (2)

5846 נַעֲמָנִים *na'ªmāniym* (1)
finest (1)

5847 נַעֲמָתִי *na'ªmātiy* (4)
Naamathite (4)

5848 נַעֲצוּץ *na'ªṣûṣ* (2)
thornbush (1)
thornbushes (1)

5849 נָעַר1 *nā'ar1* (1)
growl (1)

5850 נָעַר2 *nā'ar2* (11)
swept (2)
am shaken off (1)
drop leaves (1)
keeps (1)
shake (1)
shake myself free (1)
shake off (1)
shake out (1)
shaken out (1)
shook out (1)

5851 נָעַר3 *nā'ar3*
Variant; not used

5852 נַעַר1 *na'ar1*
Variant; not used

5853 נַעַר2 *na'ar2* (253)
boy (48)
servant (29)
young (25)
young man (23)
men (21)
servants (14)
child (13)
young men (11)
boy's (4)
boys (4)
young officers (4)
children (3)
youth (3)
foreman (2) +5893
him[s] (2) +2021
steward (2)
them[s] (2) +2021
underlings (2)
aide (1)
assistants (1)
attendants (1)
attendants (1) +9250
boy (1) +7783
child's (1)
he[s] (1)
he[s] (1) +2021
helper (1)
Jether[s] (1) +2021
man (1)
men's (1)
personal attendants (1) +9250
personal servant (1) +9250
servant's (1)
sons (1)
workers (1)
youths (1)
youths (1) +7783
untranslated (22)

5854 נֹעַר *nō'ar* (4)
youth (3)
child's (1)

5855 נַעֲרָה1 *na'ªrāh1* (63)
girl (19)
girl's (10)
maids (7)
servant girls (5)
girls (4)
she[s] (3) +2021
young (3)
her[s] (2) +2021
young woman (2)
attendants (1)
girl's (1) +4200
girls (1) +1435
she[s] (1)
untranslated (4)

5856 נַעֲרָה2 *na'ªrāh2* (3)
Naarah (3)

5857 נַעֲרָה3 *na'ªrāh3* (1)
Naarah (1)

5858 נַעֲרַי *na'ªray* (1)
Naarai (1)

5859 נְעַרְיָה *n°'aryāh* (3)
Neariah (3)

5860 נַעֲרָן *na'ªrān* (1)
Naaran (1)

5861 נְעֹרֶת *n°'ōreṯ* (2)
piece of string (1) +7348
tinder (1)

5862 נֹף *nōp̄* (7)
Memphis (7)

5863 נֶפֶג *nepeg* (4)
Nepheg (4)

5864 נָפָה1 *nāp̄āh1* (1)
sieve (1)

5865 נָפָה2 *nāp̄āh2*
Variant; not used

5866 נְפוּסִים *n°p̄ûsiym* (1)
Nephussim (1)

5867 נְפוּשְׁסִים *n°p̄ûš°siym* (1)
Nephussim (1)

5868 נָפוֹת *nāp̄ôṯ* (1)
Naphoth (1)

5869 נָפוֹת דֹּאר *nāp̄ôṯ dō'r* (3)
Naphoth Dor (3)

5870 נָפַח *nāp̄ah* (11)
boiling (2)
blast (1)
blew away (1)
blow (1)
breathe last (1) +5883
breathed (1)
broken (1)
fans (1)
sniff contemptuously (1)
unfanned (1) +4202

5871 נֹפַח *nōp̄ah* (1)
Nophah (1)

5872 נְפִילִים *n°p̄iyliym* (3)
Nephilim (3)

5873 נְפִיסִים *n°p̄iysiym* (1)
untranslated (1)

5874 נָפִישׁ *nāp̄iyš* (3)
Naphish (3)

5875 נְפִישְׁסִים *n°p̄iyš°siym* (1)
untranslated (1)

5876 נֹפֶךְ *nōp̄ek* (4)
turquoise (4)

5877 נָפַל *nāp̄al* (435)
fall (102)
fell (67)
fallen (40)
falls (23)
cast (13)
allotted (4)
collapsed (4)
down (4)
downfall (4)
failed (4)
gone over (4)
make fall (4)
allot (3)
bring down (3)
came (3)
cut down (3)
fall down (3)
falling (3)
fell down (3)
put (3)
bring (2)
brought down (2)
defected (2)

deserting (2)
downcast (2)
falls prostrate (2)
fell prostrate (2)
going to death (2)
got down (2)
have cut down (2)
inferior (2)
lay (2)
lie fallen (2)
lying (2)
seized (2) +6584
surrender (2)
those^s (2) +2021
threw (2)
threw arms around (2) +6584+7418
threw down (2)
waste away (2)
afraid (1) +6584+7065
allocate (1)
allots (1)
assail (1) +6584
attack (1) +928
attacked (1)
attacked (1) +928
become (1)
bowed down (1) +6584+7156
bowed down to the ground (1) +6584+7156
brings on (1)
cast down (1)
casting (1)
cause to fall (1)
caused to fall (1)
collapse (1)
collapses (1)
come into (1) +928
come over (1)
confined (1)
consisted of (1)
cracked (1) +7288
crumble (1)
cutting down (1)
defeated (1)
deserts (1)
died (1)
do not count (1)
down came (1)
dropped out (1)
drops (1)
erodes (1)
fail (1) +824+2025
fall in battle (1) +2728
fall limp (1)
fallen down (1)
falls down (1)
fell dead (1)
frown (1) +7156
give birth (1)
give up (1)
given birth (1)
gone down (1)
happens (1)
have fall (1)
hear (1) +4200+7156
hurtling down (1)
killed (1)
knocks out (1)
lay prostrate (1)
left (1)
let fall (1)
lie (1)
lived in hostility toward (1) +6584+7156
lose (1)
lost (1) +907+4946
lost (1) +4946
lost self-confidence (1) +928+4394+6524
made come down (1)
make (1)
make drop (1)
make lie down (1)
making (1)

neglect (1)
overpower (1)
overwhelmed (1) +6584
perish (1)
pleading (1) +9382
plunge (1)
precious (1) +4202
present (1) +4200+7156
reach (1)
settled (1)
settles (1)
sink (1)
slaughter (1)
slay (1)
someone^s (1) +2021
stilled (1)
strewn (1)
stumble (1)
such force^s (1)
surely come to ruin (1) +5877
surrenders (1)
those^s (1)
threw arms around (1) +6584
throw (1)
throw in (1)
throwing himself down (1)
thrown (1)
tumbles (1)
wastes away (1)
were^s (1)
untranslated (2)

5878 נֵפֶל *nēpel* (3)
stillborn child (2)
stillborn child (1) +851

5879 1נָפַץ *nāpas1* (17)
shatter (9)
smash (2)
broke (1)
broken (1)
crushed to pieces (1)
dash to pieces (1)
dashes (1)
separate (1)

5880 2נָפַץ *nāpas2* (3)
scatter (1)
scattered (1)
scattering (1)

5881 נֶפֶץ *nepes* (1)
cloudburst (1)

5882 נָפַשׁ *nāpaš* (3)
be refreshed (1)
refreshed himself (1)
rested (1)

5883 נֶפֶשׁ *nepeš* (757)
life (129)
soul (105)
lives (36)
me (35) +3276
I (29) +3276
person (22)
you (21) +3870
himself (18) +2257
heart (16)
yourselves (12) +4013
people (11)
myself (9) +3276
themselves (9) +4392
anyone (7)
everyone (7) +2021+3972
he (7) +2257
herself (7) +2023
appetite (6)
creatures (6)
spirit (5)
them (5) +4392
we (5) +5646
body (4)
creature (4)

dead body (4)
death (4)
man (4)
my (4) +3276
one (4)
souls (4)
they (4) +4392
you (4) +3871
yourself (4) +3870
breath (3)
dead (3)
desire (3)
hearts (3)
lifeblood (3) +1947
needs (3)
ourselves (3) +5646
persons (3)
someone (3)
those^s (3)
us (3) +5646
anyone (2) +2021+3972
anyone (2) +3972
as surely as live (2) +2644
desires (2)
everyone (2) +3972
he^s (2) +2021+2021+2085
hunger (2)
hungry (2) +8281
kill (2) +4374
kill (2) +5782
long (2) +5951
members (2)
mind (2)
neck (2)
she (2) +2023
takes life (2) +5782
thing (2)
you (2) +4013
yourselves (2) +3870
affection (1)
alive (1) +928
all (1)
another^s (1)
appetites (1)
as surely as live (1) +2256+2644+2644
be a willing party (1) +5951
being (1)
breathe last (1) +5870
breathed her last (1) +3655
closest friend (1) +889+3869+3870+8276
completely (1) +1414+2256+4946+6330
corpse (1)
cost (1)
counting on (1) +448+906+5951
courage (1)
craved (1)
craving (1)
craving (1) +205
descendants (1) +3655+3751
die (1)
discontented (1) +5253
dying (1)
earnest (1)
earnestness (1) +205
enemies (1) +8533
faint (1) +1790
feel (1)
fierce (1) +5253
given to gluttony (1) +1251
greed (1)
greedy man (1) +8146
guilt of murder (1) +1947
he^s (1)
heart's (1)
hearts' (1)
herself (1)
him (1) +2257
him^s (1)
his own (1) +2257
hot-tempered (1) +5253
how it feels (1)

hunger (1) +8199
impatient (1) +7918
in all^s (1)
in anguish (1) +5253
its own (1) +2257
just what wanted (1)
keep themselves alive (1) +906+4392+8740
keep themselves alive (1) +8740
kidnapping (1) +1704
kill (1)
kills (1) +2256+4637+5782
livelihood (1)
living soul (1)
made a fatal mistake (1) +928+9494
member (1)
minds (1)
mortal (1) +928
murders (1) +8357
none (1) +3972+4202
people (1) +132
perfume (1)
personal vows (1) +6886
pleased (1)
plunder (1) +7693
relish (1) +5951
slave (1)
slaves (1) +132
stouthearted (1) +6437
that^s (1)
the flock^s (1) +4392
themselves (1) +2257
these^s (1)
they (1) +2257
thirst (1)
thirsty (1) +8799
thoughts (1) +928+6783
threatened (1) +6330
throats (1)
wait to kill (1) +9068
wanted (1) +906+8626
wanted to kill (1) +906+1335
weary (1) +6546
willing (1)
wished (1)
wishes (1)
yourself (1) +2257
zeal (1)
untranslated (46)

5884 נֶפֶת *nepet*
Variant; not used

5885 נֹפֶת *nōpet* (5)
honey (3)
honey from the comb (1)
sweetness as the honeycomb (1)

5886 נִפְתּוֹחַ *neptôah* (2)
Nephtoah (2)

5887 נַפְתּוּלִים *naptûliym* (1)
had a struggle (1) +7349

5888 נַפְתֻּחִים *naptuhiym* (2)
Naphtuhites (2)

5889 נַפְתָּלִי *naptāliy* (51)
Naphtali (44)
Naphtali (5) +1201
Naphtali (1) +824
untranslated (1)

5890 1נֵץ *nēs1* (2)
blossomed (1) +6590
flowers (1)

5891 2נֵץ *nēs2* (3)
hawk (3)

5892 נָצָא *nāsā'*
Variant; not used

5893 1נָצַב *nāsab1* (74)
standing (14)
set up (9)
set (5)

stood (5)
stand (3)
district officers (2)
foreman (2) +5853
officials (2)
attendants (1)
attending (1)
decreed (1)
deputy (1)
district governors (1)
erected as a monument (1)
establish (1)
foremen (1) +8569
healthy (1)
is (1)
keeps intact (1)
leader (1)
life (1)
made (1)
made stand firm (1)
piled up (1)
present yourself (1)
presides (1)
ready (1)
repointing (1)
resting (1)
stands firm (1)
stay (1)
stood by (1)
stood firm (1)
stood upright (1)
takes place (1)
takes stand (1)
wait (1)
waiting (1)
untranslated (2)

5894 2נָצַב *nāsab2*
Variant; not used

5895 1נִצָּב *nissāb1*
Variant; not used

5896 2נִצָּב *nissāb2* (1)
handle (1)

5897 1נָצָה *nāsāh1* (8)
fighting (3)
rebelled (2)
fight broke out (1)
fought (1)
got into a fight (1)

5898 2נָצָה *nāsāh2* (8)
lie in ruins (2)
piles of stone (2) +1643
desolate (1)
laid waste (1)
laid waste (1) +5898

5899 3נָצָה *nāsāh3*
Variant; not used

5900 נִצָּה *nissāh* (2)
blossoms (1)
flower (1)

5901 1נֹצָה *nōsāh1* (1)
contents (1)

5902 2נֹצָה *nōsāh2*
Variant; not used

5903 נְצוּרִים *n^sûriym*
Variant; not used

5904 נָצַח *nāsah* (65)
director of music (56)
foremen (2)
supervise (2)
direct (1)
directing (1)
does always (1)
supervised (1)
supervising (1)

5905 1נֵצַח *nēsah1* (43)

forever (18) +4200
always (4) +4200
never (3) +4200+4202
never (2) +1153+4200
endless (1) +4200
eternal (1)
ever again (1) +4200+5905
everlasting (1)
everlasting (1) +4200
flamed unchecked (1) +9068
forever (1)
glory (1)
majesty (1)
never (1) +561+4200
never (1) +4202+6330
once for all (1) +4200
splendor (1)
unending (1)
utmost (1)

5906 2נֵצַח *nēsah2* (2)
blood (2)

5907 1נְצִיב *n^siyb1* (12)
garrisons (4)
outpost (3)
garrison (1)
governor (1)
pillar (1)
untranslated (2)

5908 2נְצִיב *n^siyb2* (1)
Nezib (1)

5909 נְצִיחַ *n^siyah* (2)
Neziah (2)

5910 נָצִיר *nāsiyr* (1)
untranslated (1)

5911 נָצַל *nāsal* (212)
rescue (42)
deliver (40)
save (32)
delivered (17)
rescued (12)
delivers (6)
saved (6)
be saved (3)
snatched (3)
be delivered (2)
defended (2)
escape (2)
free yourself (2)
protect (2)
recovered (2)
rescues (2)
saves (2)
surely deliver (2) +5911
be rescued (1)
come to rescue (1)
defender (1)
deliverance (1)
delivering (1)
ease (1)
escapes (1)
ever delivered (1) +5911
free (1)
plunder (1)
plundered (1)
protected (1)
rescued at all (1) +5911
rescuing (1)
retake (1)
safe (1)
separate (1) +1068
snatch (1)
spared (1)
stripped off (1)
succeed in the rescue (1) +5911
take (1)
take away (1) +5362
take back (1)
taken away (1)

taken refuge (1)
took away (1)
was spared (1)
untranslated (1)

5912 נִצָּנִים *nissāniym*
Variant; not used

5913 1נָצַץ *nāsas1* (1)
gleamed (1)

5914 2נָצַץ *nāsas2* (3)
in bloom (2)
blossoms (1)

5915 נָצַר *nāsar* (61)
keep (15)
protect (8)
guards (5)
guard (4)
obey (4)
guarded (2)
preserve (2)
watch over (2)
watchtower (2) +4463
crafty (1)
guard well (1)
hidden (1)
is spared (1)
keep safe (1)
keep watch over (1)
keeping secret vigil (1)
keeps (1)
kept (1)
maintaining (1)
observe (1)
preserves (1)
tends (1)
watcher (1)
watchman (1)
watchmen (1)
untranslated (1)

5916 נֵצֶר *nēser* (4)
branch (2)
family line (1) +9247
shoot (1)

5917 נִצְרָה *niss'rāh* (1)
watch (1)

5918 1נָקַב *nāqab1* (16)
designated (3)
pierce (2)
pierces (2)
been given (1)
bestow (1)
bored (1)
holes (1)
name (1)
notable (1)
pierced (1)
were designated (1)
were registered (1)

5919 2נָקַב *nāqab2* (3)
blasphemes (2)
blasphemed (1)

5920 1נֶקֶב *neqeb1* (1)
mountings (1)

5921 2נֶקֶב *neqeb2*
Variant; not used

5922 נְקֵבָה *n'qēbāh* (22)
female (16)
woman (3)
daughter (1)
girl (1)
women (1)

5923 נָקֹד *nāqōd* (9)
speckled (9)

5924 נֹקֵד *nōqēd* (2)
raised sheep (1)
shepherds (1)

5925 נְקֻדָּה *n'quddāh* (1)
studded (1)

5926 נִקֻּדִים *niqqudiym* (3)
moldy (2)
cakes (1)

5927 נָקָה *nāqāh* (41)
go unpunished (9)
innocent (3)
leave the guilty unpunished (3) +5927
be banished (2)
be released (2)
hold guiltless (2)
let go entirely unpunished (2) +5927
be cleared of guilt (1)
consider innocent (1)
destitute (1)
forgive (1)
go unpunished (1) +5927
guiltless (1)
have a right to get even (1)
hold innocent (1)
indeed go unpunished (1) +5927
let go unpunished (1)
not be held responsible (1)
not harm (1) +4946
pardon (1)
pardoned (1)

5928 נְקוֹדָא *n'qôdā'* (4)
Nekoda (4)

5929 נָקִי *nāqiy* (43)
innocent (30)
released (2)
clean (1)
exempt (1)
free (1)
free from blame (1)
free from obligation (1)
harmless soul (1) +2855
innocent man (1) +1947
not binding (1)
not held responsible (1)
not responsible (1)
without guilt (1)

5930 נָקִיא *nāqiy'*
Variant; not used

5931 נִקָּיוֹן *niqqāyôn* (5)
innocence (2)
clean (1)
empty stomachs (1) +9094
purity (1)

5932 נָקִיק *nāqiyq* (3)
crevices (2)
crevice (1)

5933 נָקַם *nāqam* (35)
avenge (6)
takes vengeance (2)
took revenge (2) +5934
avenge (1) +5934
avenge (1) +5935
avenge myself (1)
avenge themselves (1)
avenge wrongs (1)
avenged (1)
avenged myself (1)
avenger (1)
avenging (1)
be punished (1)
bent on revenge (1)
doing so (1)
get revenge (1)
get revenge (1) +5934
is avenged (1)
must be punished (1) +5933
punished (1)
seek revenge (1)
suffer vengeance (1)
take revenge (1)
take revenge (1) +5934

take vengeance (1)
take vengeance (1) +5935
vengeance (1)

5934 נָקָם *nāqām* (17)
vengeance (7)
take vengeance (2) +8740
took revenge (2) +5933
avenge (1)
avenge (1) +5933
avenged (1)
get revenge (1) +5933
revenge (1)
take revenge (1) +5933

5935 נְקָמָה *n'qāmāh* (27)
vengeance (17)
avenges (2)
avenges (2) +5989
avenge (1)
avenge (1) +5933
avenged (1) +5989
avenged (1) +6913
revenge (1)
take vengeance (1) +5933

5936 נָקַע *nāqa'* (3)
turned away in disgust (2)
turned away (1)

5937 1נָקַף *nāqap1* (2)
cut down (1)
destroyed (1)

5938 2נָקַף *nāqap2* (17)
surrounded (2)
circling (1)
cut hair (1)
cycle go on (1)
drawn (1)
echoes along (1)
encircled (1)
engulfed (1)
go around (1)
march around (1) +6015
run course (1)
station themselves (1)
station yourselves (1)
surround (1)
untranslated (2)

5939 נֹקֵף *nōqep* (2)
beaten (2)

5940 נִקְפָּה *niqpāh* (1)
rope (1)

5941 נָקַר *nāqar* (6)
gouge out (2)
gouged out (1)
pecked out (1)
pierces (1)
were hewn (1)

5942 נְקָרָה *n'qārāh* (2)
caverns (1)
cleft (1)

5943 נָקַשׁ *nāqaš* (4)
be ensnared (1)
seize (1)
set a trap (1)
set traps (1)

5944 1נֵר *nēr1* (44)
lamps (23)
lamp (16)
lights (2)
them[s] (1)
untranslated (2)

5945 2נֵר *nēr2* (17)
Ner (17)

5946 נֵרְגַל *nērgal* (1)
Nergal (1)

5947 נֵרְגַל שַׂר־אֶצֶר *nērgal śar-'eser* (3)
Nergal-Sharezer (3)

5948 גֵרְדְּ *nērd* (3)
nard (2)
perfume (1)

5949 נֵרִיָּה *nēriyyāh* (7)
Neriah (7)

5950 נֵרִיָּהוּ *nēriyyāhû* (3)
Neriah (3)

5951 נָשָׂא *nāśā'* (656)
carry (36)
bear (35)
lift up (32)
carried (26)
carrying (26)
up (26)
armor-bearer (18) +3998
lifted up (16)
take up (14)
took (12)
forgive (10)
raise (10)
brought (8)
held responsible (7) +6411
lifted (7)
take (7)
uttered (7) +606+2256
bring (6)
carried off (6)
took up (6)
aloud (5) +906+7754
bearing (5)
carries (5)
lift (5)
look (5) +6524
swore with uplifted (5)
take away (5)
accept (4) +7156
aloud (4) +7754
carry off (4)
endure (4)
exalted (4)
get (4)
loaded (4)
lofty (4)
pick up (4)
picks up (4)
rose (4)
show partiality (4) +7156
spread (4)
suffer (4)
be carried off (3)
bore (3)
forgiving (3)
looked (3) +6524
married (3)
misuse (3) +2021+4200+8736
offer (3)
picked up (3)
put (3)
share (3) +928
sworn with uplifted (3)
take a census (3) +906+8031
armor-bearers (2) +3998
arrogant (2) +4213
be lifted up (2)
be raised (2)
bearer (2)
brought back (2)
carried away (2)
forgave (2)
held responsible (2) +2628
long (2) +5883
misuses (2) +2021+4200+8736
pay (2)
pray (2) +9525
receive (2)
released (2) +8031
rise (2)
rise up (2)
shows partiality (2) +7156

spare (2)
suffered (2)
support (2)
take a census (2) +8031
taken (2)
wear (2)
willing (2) +4213
with uplifted swore (2)
won (2) +4200+7156
abounds (1)
accept (1)
accepted (1) +906+7156
are forgiven (1)
armed (1)
at all forgive (1) +5951
be a willing party (1) +5883
be carried (1)
be exalted (1)
be forgiven (1)
be raised up (1)
be taken away (1)
bear up (1)
bear with (1)
beckon (1) +3338
become guilty (1) +2628+6584
been exalted (1)
began (1) +906+7754
begin (1)
borne fruit (1)
bring upon (1)
carried (1) +6673
carriers (1) +6025
carries off (1)
carry about (1)
carry away (1)
carry back (1)
casts (1)
caught up (1)
chose (1)
clothed with (1)
containing (1)
continued on journey (1) +8079
count (1) +906+8031
counted (1) +906+8031
counting on (1) +448+906+5883
cry out (1) +606+4200
disdainful (1)
ease (1)
elevated (1)
elevating (1)
equipped (1)
exalt itself (1)
exalted yourself (1)
gather (1)
gave assistance (1)
grant (1) +7156
granted request (1) +7156
guilty (1)
guilty (1) +2628
had (1)
handle (1)
have respect for (1)
helped (1)
high (1)
highly regarded (1) +7156
honored (1) +7156
include in the census (1) +906+8031
incur (1)
is carried off (1)
is exalted (1)
let shine (1)
lifts up (1)
loaded up (1)
look in the face (1) +448+7156
look with longing (1) +6524
looked about (1) +6524
looks (1) +6524
loudly (1) +7754
made (1)
make (1)
man of rank (1) +7156

married (1) +851
mount up (1)
mourn (1) +7806
moved (1)
must be carried (1) +5951
out (1)
out (1) +906
pardon (1)
pardoned (1)
pardons (1)
partial (1) +7156
placed (1)
pleased with (1) +928+2834+6524
prepare (1)
produce (1)
prominent (1) +7156
provide (1)
pull up (1)
put himself forward (1)
put in jeopardy (1) +928+1414+9094
raised (1)
raised (1) +2256+5989
raising (1)
rear (1)
rebel (1)
receive (1) +7156
relish (1) +5883
respect (1) +7156
responsible for (1)
ridicule (1) +5442
rise again (1)
rises high (1)
rouse themselves (1)
saw (1) +906+6524
served (1)
set yourselves (1)
share (1)
share in (1) +6584
shouted (1) +2256+7754+7924
showed partiality (1) +7156
shown honor (1) +7156
shown partiality (1) +7156
sing (1)
snatch up (1)
suffer for (1)
suffering for (1)
supplied (1)
swear with uplifted (1)
sweep away (1)
sweeps away (1)
swore (1) +3338
sworn (1) +906+3338
take in marriage (1)
taken anything (1) +5951
taken as wives (1)
taken up (1)
takes (1)
takes up (1)
taunt (1) +5442
toil (1)
too heavy a burden to carry (1) +3523+4202
took away (1)
took notice (1) +6524
transport (1)
trembles (1)
turn (1)
uplifted (1)
wail (1) +5631
was highly regarded (1)
was raised (1)
wearing (1)
weep (1) +1140
won (1) +928+6524
wore (1)
untranslated (11)

5952 נָשַׂג *nāśag* (50)
overtake (14)
afford (7) +3338
overtook (6)
catch up (2)

continue until (2)
overtaken (2)
prospers (2) +3338
accompany (1)
attain (1)
catch (1)
caught up (1)
certainly overtake (1) +5952
equal (1)
move (1)
overtaking (1)
put (1)
reach (1)
reaches (1)
rich (1) +3338
wants to give (1) +3338
untranslated (1)

5953 נְשׂוּאָה *n°śû'āh* (1)
images that are carried about (1)

5954 1נָשִׂיא *nāśiy'1* (131)
leader (43)
leaders (29)
prince (29)
princes (10)
chiefs (3)
ruler (3)
rulers (2)
chief (1)
chief leader (1) +5954
himself[s] (1)
leaders' (1)
they[s] (1) +2021
untranslated (6)

5955 2נָשִׂיא *nāśiy'2* (4)
clouds (4)

5956 נָשַׂק *nāśaq* (3)
broke out (1)
burn up (1)
kindles a fire (1)

5957 1נָשָׁא *nāšā'1* (18)
creditor (3)
required (2) +460+928
borrowed (1) +928
creditors (1)
debtor (1) +928
exacting (1)
in debt (1) +4200
lending (1)
lent (1)
loan made (1)
make a loan (1) +5394
making loan (1)
moneylender (1)
subject to tribute (1)
usury charging (1)

5958 2נָשָׁא *nāšā'2* (15)
deceive (4)
let deceive (4)
deceived (3)
are deceived (1)
completely deceived (1) +5958
take by surprise (1)

5959 נָשַׁב *nāšab* (3)
blows (1)
drove away (1)
stirs up (1)

5960 1נָשָׁה *nāšāh1* (9)
forget (3)
forgotten (2)
made forget (1)
not endow (1)
surely forget (1) +5960

5961 2נָשָׁה *nāšāh2*
Variant; not used

5962 נָשֶׁה *nāšeh* (2)
tendon (2) +1630

5963 נְשִׁי *n°šiy* (2)
debts (1)
untranslated (1)

5964 נְשִׁיָּה *n°šiyyāh* (1)
oblivion (1)

5965 נְשִׁיקָה *n°šiyqāh* (2)
kisses (2)

5966 1נָשַׁךְ *nāšak1* (11)
bite (3)
bites (3)
bitten (2)
bit (1)
feeds (1) +928+9094
is bitten (1)

5967 2נָשַׁךְ *nāšak2* (5)
charge interest (1)
charge interest (1) +5968
debtors (1)
earn interest (1)
untranslated (1)

5968 נֶשֶׁךְ *nešek* (12)
usury (5)
interest (2)
charge interest (1) +5967
exorbitant interest (1) +2256+9552
interest of any kind (1) +2256+9552
untranslated (2)

5969 נִשְׁכָּה *niškāh* (3)
living quarters (1)
room (1)
storerooms (1) +238+4200

5970 נָשַׁל *nāšal* (7)
take off (2)
drive out (1)
drives out (1)
driving out (1)
drop off (1)
fly off (1)

5971 נָשַׁם *nāšam* (1)
gasp (1)

5972 נְשָׁמָה *n°šāmāh* (24)
breath (11)
breathed (4)
blast (2)
spirit (2)
breath (1) +8120
breathes (1)
breathing (1)
can hardly breathe (1) +4202+8636
life (1)

5973 נָשַׁף *nāšap* (2)
blew (1)
blows (1)

5974 נֶשֶׁף *nešep* (12)
dusk (4)
twilight (3)
dawn (2)
darkening (1)
morning (1)
night (1)

5975 1נָשַׁק *nāšaq1* (30)
kissed (17)
kiss (9)
kiss good-by (2)
kissed good-by (1)
offered a kiss of homage (1) +4200+7023

5976 2נָשַׁק *nāšaq2* (5)
armed (2)
armed (1) +8227
brushing (1)
submit (1)

5977 1נֶשֶׁק *nešeq1* (10)
weapons (6)
armory (1)

battle (1)
fray (1)
weapon (1)

5978 2נֶשֶׁק *nešeq2*
Variant; not used

5979 נֶשֶׁר *nešer* (26)
eagle (15)
eagles (5)
eagle's (2)
vulture (2)
eagles' (1)
vultures (1) +1201

5980 נָשַׁת *nāšat* (4)
cease (1)
dry up (1)
exhausted (1)
parched (1)

5981 נִשְׁתְּוָן *ništ°wān*
Variant; not used

5982 נְתוּנִים *n°tûniym*
Variant; not used

5983 נָתַח *nātah* (9)
cut (4)
cut into pieces (4)
cut up (1)

5984 נֵתַח *nētah* (13)
pieces (8)
piece (2)
parts (2)
piece by piece (1) +4200
pieces of meat (1)

5985 נָתִיב *nātiyb* (5)
path (3)
hidden path (1)
wake (1)

5986 נְתִיבָה *n°tiybāh* (21)
paths (11)
path (3)
way (2)
bypaths (1)
road (1)
roads (1)
streets (1)
travelers (1) +2143

5987 נָתִין *nātiyn* (17)
temple servants (15)
them[s] (1) +2021
untranslated (1)

5988 נָתַךְ *nātak* (21)
poured out (7)
be melted (3)
melt (2)
paid out (2)
pour out (2)
poured down (2)
be poured out (1)
been poured out (1)
is poured out (1)

5989 נָתַן *nātan* (2016)
give (344)
gave (231)
put (169)
given (147)
giving (58)
make (55)
gives (45)
made (37)
set (36)
hand over (35) +928+3338
handed over (23) +928+3338
placed (23)
let (19)
be given (18)
grant (14)
pay (14)
place (14)

yield (13)
bring (12)
delivered (12)
granted (11)
appointed (10)
if only (10) +4769
send (9)
spread (9)
assigned (8)
be handed over (8) +928+3338
entrusted (8)
hand over (8)
oh (8) +4769
deliver (7)
exchanged (7)
give in marriage (7) +851+4200
give over (7)
sent (7)
lay (6)
offered (6)
repay (6)
sell (6)
allow (5)
attach (5)
gave in marriage (5) +851+4200
get (5)
give in marriage (5)
give up (5)
paid (5)
set up (5)
show (5)
take (5)
allowed (4)
been given (4)
bring down (4)
fasten (4)
fastened (4)
gave over (4)
laid (4)
makes (4)
offer (4)
provide (4)
provided (4)
provides (4)
setting (4)
thunders (4) +7754
was given (4)
applied (3)
attached (3)
bringing down (3)
brought (3)
cause (3)
caused (3)
deal (3)
do (3)
establish (3)
give back (3)
given over (3)
paying (3)
produce (3)
resounded (3)
stationed (3)
surrender (3)
treat (3)
turn (3)
turned (3)
was issued (3)
allotted (2) +928+1598+2021
appoint (2)
are (2)
are given (2)
attaching (2)
avenges (2) +5935
be given wholly (2) +5989
be issued (2)
been put (2)
bestows (2)
blessed (2) +1388
causes (2)
certainly be handed over (2)
           +928+3338+5989

contributed (2)
dedicated (2)
deliver over (2)
delivered over (2)
delivers (2)
direct (2)
distributing (2)
do so[s] (2)
entrust (2)
established (2)
gifts (2)
handed over (2)
hang (2)
is given (2)
kept (2)
left (2)
lend (2)
lends (2)
lifting (2)
made turn (2)
maintain (2)
making (2)
permit (2)
presented (2)
prevent (2) +1194
proclaim (2)
providing (2)
puts (2)
putting (2)
raised (2)
received (2)
reported (2)
reward (2)
sell (2) +928+4084
thrown (2)
thunder (2) +7754
turn into (2)
turn over (2)
wrap (2)
yields (2)
abandoned (1)
allotted (1)
allow to possess (1)
allowing (1)
allows (1)
announced (1)
announces (1)
appoints (1)
are laid (1)
are put (1)
arranged (1)
ascribe (1)
avenged (1) +5935
barter (1)
be (1)
be bought (1)
be defeated (1) +928+3338
be given in marriage (1) +851+4200
be handed over (1)
be injured (1)
be left (1)
be supplied (1)
bears (1)
became (1)
been allotted (1)
been committed (1)
been handed over (1) +928+3338
been published (1)
been subjected (1)
bestow (1)
bestowed (1)
bless (1) +1388
bow (1)
bowed (1)
breeds (1)
bringing (1)
brings (1)
bury (1)
buy (1)
called together (1)
came (1)

carry out (1)
cast (1)
charge (1)
charging (1)
choose (1)
committed (1)
confirm (1)
consign (1)
costs (1)
cover (1) +4062
credited (1)
cry aloud (1) +7754
cut (1) +8582
deliver (1) +5989
demand (1)
designate (1)
designated (1)
despoil (1) +1020+4200
destined (1)
devote (1)
devoted (1)
did[s] (1) +2257+3338
dispenses (1)
display (1)
distribute (1)
distributed (1)
does (1)
drop (1)
dry up (1) +3000
enabled (1)
endow (1)
exchange (1)
falls (1)
filled (1)
flourishes (1)
from (1)
gave in marriage (1)
gave in marriage (1) +851
gave in pledge (1)
gave up (1)
gave victory (1) +928+3338
give (1) +928+3338
give (1) +5989
give away (1)
give generously (1) +5989
give in marriage (1) +408+4200
give in marriage (1) +851+2021
give permission (1)
given in pledge (1)
given up (1)
gives gifts (1)
gives over (1)
glad to give (1) +5989
granted requests (1)
granting (1)
grants (1)
growl (1) +7754
growled (1) +7754
hand over to (1) +928+3338
handed (1) +928+3338
handing over (1) +928+3338
hands over (1)
has sexual relations (1) +8888
have (1)
have (1) +4200
have sexual relations (1) +2446+4200+8888
have sexual relations (1) +8888
healing (1) +8337
hold (1)
hold accountable (1) +6584
honor (1) +3883
how I long for (1) +4769+5761
I wish (1) +4769
imparts (1)
imposed (1)
imprisoned (1) +657+1074+2021
imprisoned (1) +928+5464
inflict (1)
injured (1) +4583
injures (1) +4583
inserted (1)

inspire (1) +928+4222
instruct (1)
is drawn (1)
is thrown (1)
issued (1)
join (1)
keep (1)
leave (1)
let be heard (1)
let have (1)
let out (1)
lifts (1)
made face (1) +7156
made ready (1)
make restitution (1)
make turn (1) +448
marry (1)
must certainly give (1) +5989
oh (1) +686+4769
oh how I wish (1) +4769
open (1) +7341
ordained (1)
paid (1) +5486
pay (1) +924
pay (1) +4084
pay (1) +4836
pay (1) +8510
perform (1)
permitted to do (1)
pile (1)
piled (1)
pitch (1)
plant (1)
pledged (1) +3338
pour (1)
pour out (1)
produces (1)
producing (1)
prove to be (1)
pulled (1)
push (1)
put in place (1)
put on (1) +4230
put out (1)
put up (1)
raise (1)
raised (1) +2256+5951
raises (1)
raising (1)
receive (1)
receives (1) +4200
recite (1)
reduced (1)
reflected on (1) +448+4213
replaced (1) +9393
resolved (1) +7156
resound (1)
respect (1) +3702
reward (1) +7190
rewarded (1) +8510
rises (1)
roared (1) +7754
roars (1) +928+7754
sacrificed (1) +928+6296
seated (1) +5226
send down (1)
send out (1)
share (1)
shares (1)
sing (1) +7754
slander (1) +1984
sleeping with (1) +928+8888
sparkles (1) +6524
spend (1)
spreads (1)
stained (1)
store (1)
stored (1)
strike (1)
subjected (1)
submit (1) +3338

submitted (1) +3338
suffer (1) +6584
supplied (1)
supplies (1)
supply (1)
surely hand over (1) +928+3338+5989
surrenders (1) +3338
take for (1) +4200+7156
think (1) +4213
think (1) +4222
thunders (1) +928+7754
tie (1) +6584
tie up (1)
traded (1)
treated (1)
turned (1) +7156
turned into (1)
turned over (1)
turns (1)
use (1)
was entrusted (1)
was given in marriage (1) +851+4200
was left hanging (1)
wept so loudly (1) +906+928+1140+7754
were assigned (1)
were given (1)
were given over (1)
wins (1)
untranslated (34)

5990 נָתַן *nāṯān* (42)
Nathan (42)

5991 נְתַנְאֵל *n⁸tan'ēl* (14)
Nethanel (14)

5992 נְתַנְיָה *n⁸tanyāh* (15)
Nethaniah (15)

5993 נְתַנְיָהוּ *n⁸tanyāhû* (5)
Nethaniah (5)

5994 נְתַן־מֶלֶךְ *n⁸tan-melek* (1)
Nathan-Melech (1)

5995 נָתַס *nāṯas* (1)
break up (1)

5996 נָתַע *nāṯa'* (1)
are broken (1)

5997 נָתַץ *nāṯas* (42)
broke down (6)
tore down (6)
break down (4)
demolished (4)
tear down (3)
torn down (3)
demolish (2)
destroyed (2)
pulled down (2)
be broken up (1)
been torn down (1)
breaks down (1)
bring down to ruin (1)
broken down (1)
destroy (1)
lay in ruins (1)
shattered (1)
tear out (1)
tears down (1)

5998 נָתַק *nāṯaq* (27)
break (2)
broken (2)
snapped (2)
are purged out (1)
are shattered (1)
are snapped (1)
broke away (1)
drag off (1)
draw away (1)
is broken (1)
is torn (1)
lured away (1)

pull off (1)
set (1)
snaps (1)
tear (1)
tear away (1)
tear off (1)
tore off (1)
torn (1)
torn off (1)
uprooted (1) +9247
were drawn away (1)
were lured away (1)

5999 נֶתֶק *neteq* (14)
itch (7)
itˢ (3) +2021
diseased area (1)
himˢ (1) +2021
infected person (1) +5596
this kind of sore (1) +2021+5596

6000 1נָתַר *nāṯar1* (1)
let loose (1)

6001 2נָתַר *nāṯar2* (3)
hopping (1)
leaps (1)
made tremble (1)

6002 3נָתַר *nāṯar3* (3)
released (1)
sets free (1)
untie (1)

6003 נֶתֶר *neter* (2)
soda (2)

6004 נָתַשׁ *nāṯaš* (20)
uproot (11)
be uprooted (3)
uprooted (3)
completely uproot (1) +6004
was uprooted (1)

6005 ס *s*
Variant; not used

6006 סְאָה *s⁸'āh* (9)
seahs (6)
seah (3)

6007 סְאוֹן *s⁸'ôn* (1)
boot (1)

6008 סָאַן *sā'an* (1)
warrior's (1)

6009 סַאסְּאָה *sa'ss⁸'āh* (1)
warfare (1)

6010 1סָבָא *sābā'1* (6)
drink fill (1)
drink too much (1)
drunk (1)
drunkard (1)
drunkards (1)
untranslated (1)

6011 סֹבֵא *sōḇe'* (3)
choice wine (1)
drinks (1)
wine (1)

6012 2סָבָא *sābā'2*
Variant; not used

6013 סְבָא *s⁸ḇā'* (4)
Seba (4)

6014 סְבָאִי *s⁸ḇā'iy* (2)
Sabeans (2)

6015 סָבַב *sāḇaḇ* (163)
surrounded (15)
turned (12)
surround (10)
turn (8)
changed (4)
go about (3)

moved (3)
prowl about (3)
turning (3)
circle around (2)
coiled around (2)
curved (2)
fall in (2) +448
led around (2)
made rounds (2)
made way around (2)
march around (2)
marched around (2)
measure around (2) +6017
pass (2)
round (2)
settings (2)
turn about (2)
turned around (2)
turned away (2)
turns (2)
went around (2)
winds through (2)
all around (1)
around (1)
be turned over (1)
become (1)
began (1)
bring back (1)
bring over (1)
brought around (1)
carried around (1)
change (1)
changing (1)
circled (1)
circuit (1)
circumference (1) +2562
coming around (1)
cross (1)
curved around (1)
dragged (1)
eluded (1) +4946+7156
encircled (1) +6017
encircled (1) +6017+6017
encircling (1)
engulf (1)
gather around (1)
gathered around (1)
go (1)
go around (1)
hinged (1)
is rolled (1)
leave (1) +4946
march around (1) +5938
on every side (1)
once again (1)
put around (1)
responsible for (1) +928
returned home (1)
roundabout (1)
sent around (1)
shielded (1)
sit down (1)
skirted (1)
stand aside (1)
stepped aside (1)
sulking (1) +906+7156
surrounding (1)
surrounds (1)
swarmed around (1)
swirled about (1)
swung open (1)
took away (1)
turn against (1)
turn away (1) +7156
turn over (1)
turned (1) +7156
turned over (1)
waged against from all sides (1)
walk about (1)
walk through (1)
went (1)

went throughout (1)
were changed (1)
were mounted (1)
untranslated (2)

6016 סִבָּה *sibbāh* (1)
turn of events (1)

6017 סָבִיב *sābiyb* (319)
around (108)
surrounding (27)
all around (23)
all around (17) +6017
on every side (16) +4946
on all sides (13)
on every side (9)
around (7) +4946
all (5)
neighbors (5)
surround (5)
every side (4)
surrounded (4)
around (3) +6017
about (2)
circular in shape (2) +6318
from every side (2) +4946
measure around (2) +6015
neighboring (2)
surrounds (2)
throughout (2) +928
all around (1) +4946
all over (1) +6017+6584
along (1)
area around (1)
around (1) +1237+4946
back and forth (1) +6017
circular band (1) +6318
completely (1)
completely surrounding (1) +6017
course (1)
covered with (1) +6017+8470
encircled (1) +6015
encircled (1) +6015+6017
encircling (1)
enveloped (1) +4946
escorted by (1)
everything around (1)
everywhere (1)
from (1) +4946
full (1) +1074
in (1)
on (1)
outside walls (1)
overrun (1)
ringed about (1)
round about (1)
sides (1) +4946+6298
stationed around (1)
surround (1) +2118+4946
surrounding (1) +6017
turn (1)
went over (1) +2118
untranslated (19)

6018 סָבַךְ *sābak* (2)
entangled (1)
entwines (1)

6019 סְבַךְ *sˀbak* (3)
thickets (2)
thicket (1)

6020 סְבֹךְ *sˀbōk* (2)
lair (1)
thicket (1)

6021 סִבְּכַי *sibbˀkay* (4)
Sibbecai (4)

6022 סָבַל *sābal* (9)
bear (2)
sustain (2)
burden (1)
carried (1)

carry (1)
drags himself along (1)
draw heavy loads (1)

6023 סֵבֶל *sēbel* (3)
burden (1)
labor force (1)
materials (1)

6024 סֹבֶל *sōbel* (3)
burden (2)
burdens (1)

6025 סַבָּל *sabbāl* (5)
carriers (2)
laborers (2)
carriers (1) +5951

6026 סִבְלוֹת *siblôt* (6)
yoke (2)
forced labor (1)
hard labor (1)
work (1)
working (1)

6027 סִבֹּלֶת *sibbōlet* (1)
Sibboleth (1)

6028 סִבְרַיִם *sibrayim* (1)
Sibraim (1)

6029 סַבְתָּא *sabtā'* (1)
Sabta (1)

6030 סַבְתָּה *sabtāh* (1)
Sabtah (1)

6031 סַבְתְּכָא *sabtˀkā'* (2)
Sabteca (2)

6032 סְגַד *sˀgad* (5)
bow down (2)
bows down (2)
untranslated (1)

6033 סְגוֹר *sˀgôr* (1)
rip open (1) +4213+7973

6034 סָגוּר *sāgûr* (9)
pure (8)
finest gold (1)

6035 סְגֻלָּה *sˀgullāh* (8)
treasured possession (6)
personal treasures (1)
treasure (1)

6036 סֶגֶן *segen* (17)
officials (12)
commanders (3)
officers (1)
rulers (1)

6037 סָגַר *sāgar* (82)
shut (21)
put in isolation (5)
be shut (4)
gave over (3)
be shut up (2)
close (2)
close up (2)
closed (2)
closed up (2)
delivered (2)
hand over (2)
hand over (2) +928+3338
handed over (2) +928+3338
isolate (2)
keep in isolation (2)
sold (2)
surrender (2)
are closed (1)
closed in (1)
confine (1)
confined (1)
confines in prison (1)
deliver up (1)
delivered up (1)

filled in (1)
given up (1)
handing over (1) +928+3338
hemmed in (1)
imprisoned himself (1)
imprisons (1)
is barred (1)
locked (1)
sealed together (1) +2597
shut yourself (1)
shuts (1)
surrender (1) +928+3338
tightly shut up (1) +2256+6037
turned over (1)
will[s] (1)

6038 סָגָר *sāgār* (1)
javelin (1)

6039 סַגְרִיר *sagriyr* (1)
rainy (1)

6040 סַד *sad* (2)
shackles (2)

6041 סָדִין *sādiyn* (4)
linen garments (4)

6042 סְדֹם *s⁽e⁾dōm* (39)
Sodom (38)
the city[s] (1)

6043 סֵדֶר *sēder* (1)
disorder (1) +4202

6044 סָהַר *sahar* (1)
rounded (1)

6045 סֹהַר *sōhar* (8)
prison (6) +1074+2021
untranslated (2)

6046 סוֹא *sô'* (1)
So (1)

6047 1סוּג *sûg1* (24)
be turned (5)
move (4)
deserted (1) +294
disloyal (1)
drawn back (1) +294
faithless (1) +4213
is driven back (1) +294
moves (1)
overtake (1)
retreating (1) +294
store up (1)
turn (1)
turn away (1)
turn back (1)
turned (1)
turned away (1)
turning (1)

6048 2סוּג *sûg2* (1)
encircled (1)

6049 3סוּג *sûg3* (1)
untranslated (1)

6050 סוּגַר *sûgar* (1)
cage (1)

6051 סוֹד *sôd* (21)
council (7)
confidence (4)
company (1)
confides (1)
conspiracy (1)
conspire (1)
counsel (1)
fellowship (1)
gathered (1)
intimate (1)
intimate friendship (1)
plan (1)

6052 סוֹדִי *sôdiy* (1)
Sodi (1)

6053 סוּחַ *sûah* (1)
Suah (1)

6054 סוּחָה *sûhāh* (1)
refuse (1)

6055 סוֹטַי *sôtay* (2)
Sotai (2)

6056 1סוּךְ *sûk1* (2)
spurred on (1)
stir up (1)

6057 2סוּךְ *sûk2* (10)
use (3)
healing balm (1)
perfume (1)
pour (1)
put on (1)
put on lotions (1)
used lotions at all (1) +6057

6058 3סוּךְ *sûk3*
Variant; not used

6059 סְוֵנֵה *s⁽e⁾wēnēh* (3)
Aswan (3)

6060 סְוֵנִים *s⁽e⁾wēniym*
Variant; not used

6061 1סוּס *sûs1* (138)
horses (87)
horse (30)
horseman (3) +8206
horseback (2)
horses' (2)
mounted (2) +8206
war-horses (2)
horse's (1)
horsemen (1) +8206
mounted (1) +928+2021
stallions (1)
them[s] (1)
work horses (1)
untranslated (4)

6062 2סוּס *sûs2* (1)
untranslated (1)

6063 סוּסָה *sûsāh* (1)
mare (1)

6064 סוּסִי *sûsiy* (1)
Susi (1)

6065 סוּסִים *sûsiym*
Variant; not used

6066 1סוּף *sûp1* (6)
sweep away (2)
demolished (1)
die out (1)
meet end (1)
sweep away (1) +665

6067 סוֹף *sôp* (5)
end (2)
conclusion (1)
destiny (1)
rear (1)

6068 2סוּף *sûp2* (28)
red (24)
reeds (2)
rushes (1)
seaweed (1)

6069 3סוּף *sûp3* (1)
Suph (1)

6070 1סוּפָה *sûpāh1* (15)
whirlwind (6)
gale (2)
storm (2)
tempest (2)
stormy (1)
whirlwinds (1)
windstorm (1)

6071 2סוּפָה *sûpāh2* (1)
Suphah (1)

6072 סוֹפֶרֶת *sôperet* (1)
Sophereth (1)

6073 1סוּר *sûr1* (301)
removed (31)
remove (28)
turn away (22)
turn (10)
turned away (10)
away (7)
take away (7)
cut off (6)
leave (6)
turn aside (6)
take (5)
turned (5)
depart (4)
got rid of (4)
left (4)
shuns (4)
stop (4)
took off (4)
turned aside (4)
get rid of (3)
keep (3)
lifted (3)
taken away (3)
turning (3)
turning aside (3)
avoids (2)
cease (2)
come (2)
come in (2)
deny (2)
departed (2)
deposed (2)
go (2)
gone (2)
is removed (2)
leave alone (2) +4946
put away (2)
rejected (2)
rid (2)
shun (2)
stopped (2)
stray (2)
take off (2)
throw away (2)
took (2)
took away (2)
turned in (2)
abolish (1)
banish (1)
been removed (1)
broke away (1)
carry away (1)
circumcise (1) +6889
clear (1)
cleared away (1)
come over (1)
denied (1)
denies (1)
deprives (1)
dethroned (1)
deviate (1)
did away with (1)
do away with (1) +4946+9348
dragged (1)
end (1)
entered (1) +448
escape (1)
expelled (1)
fail (1) +4946
failed to keep (1) +4946
far (1)
give up (1)
give up pursuit (1)
go away (1)
go over (1)

gone over (1)
hardened rebels (1) +6253
instead of (1)
is abolished (1)
keep free (1)
lay aside (1)
led astray (1)
left undone (1)
made come off (1)
make leave (1)
move (1)
move back (1)
moved away (1)
no longer be (1) +4946
pass away (1)
past (1)
put aside (1)
put out (1)
removal (1)
removes (1)
return (1)
sent away (1)
set aside (1)
shows no (1)
shunned (1)
silences (1)
slip (1)
snatch away (1)
stay (1)
strip off (1)
take back (1)
taken (1)
turns (1)
turns away (1)
vanish (1)
ward off (1)
went over (1)
went up (1)
untranslated (2)

6074 סוּר2 *sûr2* (1)
corrupt (1)

6075 סוּר3 *sûr3* (1)
Sur (1)

6076 סוֹרִי *sôriy*
Variant; not used

6077 סוּת1 *sût1* (18)
incited (4)
urged (3)
entices (2)
misleading (2)
drew away (1)
inciting (1)
let mislead (1)
mislead (1)
misled (1)
urged on (1)
wooing (1)

6078 סוּת2 *sût2* (2)
robes (1)
untranslated (1)

6079 סָחַב *sāhab* (5)
dragged away (3)
drag away (1)
drag down (1)

6080 סְחָבָה *sᵉhābāh* (3)
rags (2)
untranslated (1)

6081 סָחָה *sāhāh* (1)
scrape away (1)

6082 סְחִי *sᵉhiy* (1)
scum (1)

6083 סְחִיפָה *sᵉhiypāh*
Variant; not used

6084 סָחִישׁ *sāhiyš* (1)
what springs from (1)

6085 סָחַף *sāhap* (2)
be laid low (1)
driving (1)

6086 סָחַר *sāhar* (21)
merchants (8)
did business with (4)
trade (3)
customers (1) +3338
gone (1)
merchant (1)
pounds (1)
traders (1)
trafficked (1)

6087 סַחַר *sahar* (7)
marketplace (1)
merchandise (1)
profit (1)
profitable (1) +3202
profits (1)
trading (1)
untranslated (1)

6088 סְחֹרָה *sᵉhōrāh* (1)
customers (1) +3338

6089 סֹחֵרָה *sōhērāh* (1)
rampart (1)

6090 סֹחֶרֶת *sōheret* (1)
costly stones (1)

6091 סֵט *sēt* (1)
faithless (1)

6092 סִיג *siyg* (7)
dross (7)

6093 סִיד *siyd*
Variant; not used

6094 סִיוָן *siywān* (1)
Sivan (1)

6095 סִיחוֹן *siyhôn* (37)
Sihon (34)
heˢ (2)
Sihon's (1)

6096 סִין1 *siyn1* (2)
Pelusium (2)

6097 סִין2 *siyn2* (4)
sin (4)

6098 סִינִי *siyniy* (2)
Sinites (2)

6099 סִינַי *siynay* (35)
Sinai (35)

6100 סִינִים *siyniym*
Variant; not used

6101 סִיס *siys* (2)
swift (2)

6102 סִיסְרָא *siysᵉrā'* (21)
Sisera (20)
Sisera's (1)

6103 סִיעָא *siy'ā'* (1)
Sia (1)

6104 סִיעֲהָא *siyˊᵃhā'* (1)
Siaha (1)

6105 סִיר *siyr* (29)
pot (11)
pots (11)
cooking pot (2)
washbasin (2) +8176
caldron (1)
cooking pots (1)
pan (1)

6106 סִירָה *siyrāh* (5)
thorns (3)
fishhooks (1) +1855
thornbushes (1)

6107 סָךְ *sāk* (1)
multitude (1)

6108 סֹךְ *sōk* (4)
cover (1)
dwelling (1)
lair (1)
tent (1)

6109 סֻכָּה *sukkāh* (32)
tabernacles (9)
booths (7)
shelter (3)
tents (3)
canopy (2)
dwelling (1)
hut (1)
pavilion (1)
shelters (1)
shrine (1)
tent (1)
themˢ (1) +2021
thicket (1)

6110 סִכּוּת *sikkût*
Variant; not used

6111 סֻכּוֹת *sukkôt* (18)
Succoth (18)

6112 סֻכּוֹת בְּנוֹת *sukkôt bᵉnôt* (1)
Succoth Benoth (1)

6113 סֻכִּיִּים *sukkiyyiym* (1)
Sukkites (1)

6114 סָכַךְ1 *sākak1* (18)
covered (2)
guardian (2)
overshadowing (2)
conceal (1)
cover (1)
hedged in (1)
overshadowed (1)
relieve himself (1) +906+2257+8079
relieving himself (1) +906+2257+8079
shelter (1)
shield (1)
shielded (1)
shields (1)
shut up (1)
spread protection (1)

6115 סָכַךְ2 *sākak2* (2)
knit together (2)

6116 סֹכֵךְ *sōkēk* (1)
protective shield (1)

6117 סְכָכָה *sᵉkākāh* (1)
Secacah (1)

6118 סָכַל *sākal* (8)
done a foolish thing (3)
acted foolishly (1)
acted like a fool (1)
foolish (1)
turn into foolishness (1)
turns into nonsense (1)

6119 סָכָל *sākāl* (8)
fool (4)
foolish (1)
senseless (1)
stupid (1)
untranslated (1)

6120 סֶכֶל *sekel* (1)
fools (1)

6121 סִכְלוּת *siklût* (6)
folly (6)

6122 סָכַן1 *sākan1* (9)
be of benefit (1)
been in the habit of (1) +6122
benefit (1)
familiar with (1)
profit (1)

profits (1)
submit (1)
useless (1) +4202

6123 סָכַן2 *sākan2* (1)
too poor (1)

6124 סָכַן3 *sākan3* (1)
be endangered (1)

6125 סֹכֵן *sōkēn* (3)
steward (1)
take care of (1) +2118
took care of (1) +2118

6126 סָכַר1 *sākar1* (2)
be silenced (1)
been closed (1)

6127 סָכַר2 *sākar2* (1)
hand over (1)

6128 סָכַר3 *sākar3* (1)
hired (1)

6129 סָכַת *sākat* (1)
silent (1)

6130 סַל *sal* (15)
basket (12)
baskets (2)
it's (1) +2021

6131 סָלָא *sālā'* (1)
worth their weight (1)

6132 סַלּוּא *sallu'* (2)
Sallu (2)

6133 סִלָּא *sillā'* (1)
Silla (1)

6134 סָלַד *sālad* (1)
joy (1)

6135 סֶלֶד *seled* (2)
Seled (2)

6136 סָלָה1 *sālāh1* (2)
reject (1)
rejected (1)

6137 סָלָה2 *sālāh2* (2)
be bought (2)

6138 סֶלָה *selāh* (74)
Selah (74)

6139 סַלּוּ *sallû* (2)
Sallu (1)
Sallu's (1)

6140 סָלוּא *sālû'* (1)
Salu (1)

6141 סִלּוֹן *sillôn* (2)
briers (1)
thorns (1)

6142 סָלַח *sālah* (47)
forgive (26)
be forgiven (13)
release (3)
forgiven (1)
forgives (1)
pardon (1)
untranslated (1)

6143 סַלָּח *sallāh* (1)
forgiving (1)

6144 סַלַּי *sallay* (1)
Sallai (1)

6145 סְלִיחָה *sᵉliyhāh* (3)
forgiving (2)
forgiveness (1)

6146 סַלְכָה *salkāh* (4)
Salecah (4)

6147 סָלַל1 *sālal1* (2)
esteem (1)
set yourself (1)

6148 סָלַל2 *sālal2* (10)
build up (4)
build (2)
built up (1)
extol (1)
is a highway (1)
pile up (1)

6149 סֹלְלָה *sōlᵉlāh* (11)
siege ramps (4)
ramp (3)
siege ramp (3)
ramps (1)

6150 סֻלָּם *sullām* (1)
stairway (1)

6151 סַלְסִלָּה *salsillāh* (1)
branches (1)

6152 סֶלַע1 *sela'1* (58)
rock (30)
rocks (9)
crags (4)
cliff (2)
cliffs (2)
mountain (2)
cliff (1) +9094
rocky (1)
rocky crag (1)
rocky crags (1)
stone (1)
stronghold (1)
where's (1) +928+8234
untranslated (2)

6153 סֶלַע2 *sela'2* (4)
Sela (4)

6154 סֶלַע הַמַּחְלְקוֹת *sela' hammahlᵉqôt* (1)
Sela Hammahlekoth (1)

6155 סָלְעָם *sāl'ām* (1)
katydid (1)

6156 סָלַף *sālap* (7)
overthrows (2)
twists (2)
brings to ruin (1) +2021+4200+8273
frustrates (1)
ruins (1)

6157 סֶלֶף *selep* (2)
deceitful (1)
duplicity (1)

6158 סָלַק *sālaq* (1)
go up (1)

6159 סֹלֶת *sōlet* (53)
fine flour (46)
flour (6)
fine (1)

6160 סַם *sam* (16)
fragrant (14)
fragrant spices (1)
untranslated (1)

6161 סַמְגַּר *samgar* (1)
Samgar (1)

6162 סַמְגַּר־נְבוֹ *samgar-nᵉbô*
Variant; not used

6163 סְמָדַר *sᵉmādar* (3)
blossoming (1)
blossoms (1)
in bloom (1)

6164 סָמַךְ *sāmak* (48)
lay (17)
laid (6)
sustained (3)
upholds (3)
leans (2)
steadfast (2)
sustain (2)
sustains (2)

allies (1)
bracing (1)
gained confidence (1)
gave support (1)
laid siege (1)
lies heavily (1)
relied (1)
rely (1)
rested (1)
secure (1)
strengthen (1)

6165 סְמַכְיָהוּ *sᵉmakyāhû* (1)
Semakiah (1)

6166 סֶמֶל *semel* (5)
idol (2)
image (2)
shape (1)

6167 סָמַם *sāmam*
Variant; not used

6168 סָמַן *sāman* (1)
plot (1)

6169 סָמַר *sāmar* (2)
stood on end (1)
trembles (1)

6170 סָמָר *sāmār* (1)
swarm (1)

6171 סְנָאָה *sᵉnā'āh* (2)
Senaah (2)

6172 סַנְבַּלַּט *sanballat* (10)
Sanballat (10)

6173 סַנָּה *sannāh*
Variant; not used

6174 סְנֶה *sᵉneh* (6)
bush (5)
it's (1) +2021

6175 סְנֶּה *senneh* (1)
Seneh (1)

6176 סְנוּאָה *sᵉnû'āh*
Variant; not used

6177 סַנְוֵרִים *sanwēriym* (3)
blindness (3)

6178 סַנְחֵרִיב *sanhēriyb* (13)
Sennacherib (13)

6179 סַנְסַנָּה *sansannāh* (1)
Sansannah (1)

6180 סַנְסִנָּה *sansinnāh* (1)
fruit (1)

6181 סְנַפִּיר *sᵉnappiyr* (5)
fins (5)

6182 סָס *sās* (1)
worm (1)

6183 סִסְמַי *sismay* (2)
Sismai (2)

6184 סָעַד *sā'ad* (12)
refresh (2)
sustains (2)
grant support (1)
have something to eat (1)
made secure (1)
refreshed (1) +4213
supported (1)
sustain (1)
uphold (1)
upholding (1)

6185 סָעָה *sā'āh* (1)
tempest (1) +8120

6186 סָעִיף1 *sā'iyp1* (4)
cave (2)
overhanging (2)

6187 סָעִיף2 *sā'iyp2* (2)
boughs (1)

branches (1)

6188 סָעַף *sā'ap* (1)
lop off (1)

6189 סֵעֵף *sē'ēp* (1)
double-minded (1)

6190 סְעַפָּה *s^e'appāh* (2)
boughs (2)

6191 סְעִפִּים *s^e'ippiym* (1)
opinions (1)

6192 סָעַר *sā'ar* (7)
enraged (1) +4213
grew even wilder (1) +2143+2256
lashed by storms (1)
rougher and rougher (1) +2143+2256
scattered with a whirlwind (1)
stormed out (1)
swirling (1)

6193 סַעַר *sa'ar* (8)
storm (4)
tempest (1)
violent winds (1)
whirlwind (1)
wind (1)

6194 סְעָרָה *s^e'ārāh* (18)
storm (5)
whirlwind (3)
gale (1)
storms (1)
stormy (1)
tempest (1)
tempest (1) +8120
violent wind (1) +8120
violent winds (1) +8120
windstorm (1) +8120
untranslated (2)

6195 1סַף *sap1* (7)
basins (3)
basin (1)
bowls (1)
cup (1)
untranslated (1)

6196 2סַף *sap2*
Variant; not used

6197 3סַף *sap3* (25)
threshold (7)
doorkeepers (5) +9068
thresholds (5)
doorway (2)
doorframes (1)
doorkeeper (1) +9068
doors (1)
doorways (1)
entrance (1)
untranslated (1)

6198 4סַף *sap4* (1)
Saph (1)

6199 סָפַד *sāpad* (30)
mourn (12)
mourned (8)
lament (3)
be mourned (2)
beat (1)
lamented (1) +5027
mourners (1)
walk in mourning (1)
weep (1)

6200 סָפָה *sāpāh* (16)
be swept away (4)
sweep away (2)
are caught (1)
be destroyed (1)
being swept away (1)
bring disaster (1)
perish (1)
perished (1)

sweeps away (1)
swept away (1)
take (1)
take off (1)

6201 סָפוּן *sāpôn*
Variant; not used

6202 1סָפַח *sāpah1* (4)
appoint (1)
huddled (1)
share (1)
unite (1)

6203 2סָפַח *sāpah2* (1)
pouring (1)

6204 סַפַּחַת *sappahat* (2)
rash (2)

6205 סִפַּי *sippay* (1)
Sippai (1)

6206 1סָפִיחַ *sāpiyah1* (4)
what grows by itself (2)
what grows of itself (2)

6207 2סָפִיחַ *sāpiyah2* (1)
torrents (1)

6208 סְפִינָה *s^epiynāh* (1)
below deck (1) +2021+3752

6209 סַפִּיר *sappiyr* (11)
sapphires (5)
sapphire (4)
sapphire (2) +74

6210 סֵפֶל *sēpel* (2)
bowl (1)
bowlful (1) +4850

6211 סָפַן *sāpan* (6)
covered (1)
paneled (1)
panels (1)
roofing (1)
was kept (1)
was roofed (1)

6212 סִפֻּן *sippun* (2)
ceiling (2)

6213 סַפְסִינ *sapsiyg* (1)
glaze (1)

6214 סָפַף *sāpap* (1)
doorkeeper (1)

6215 1סָפַק *sāpaq1* (6)
beat (2)
clap (1)
punishes (1)
scornfully claps hands (1)
struck together (1)

6216 2סָפַק *sāpaq2* (1)
wallow (1)

6217 סֶפֶק *sepeq* (1)
riches (1)

6218 סָפַר *sāpar* (105)
tell (18)
told (17)
count (12)
count off (6)
declare (6)
proclaim (4)
counted (3)
telling (3)
be recorded (2)
be told (2)
recount (2)
talk (2)
were told (2)
acknowledge (1)
appraised (1)
be counted (1)
boasted (1)

census taken (1) +6222
conscripted (1)
counted out (1)
declared (1)
gave account (1)
inform (1)
is declared (1)
keeping records (1)
make countless (1) +889+4202+8049
proclaimed (1)
recite (1)
record (1)
recounted (1)
repeated (1)
speak (1)
state (1)
took a census (1)
utter (1)
wait (1)
were counted (1)
write (1)
untranslated (1)

6219 1סֵפֶר *sēper1* (188)
book (104)
scroll (23)
letter (12)
letters (10)
deed (6)
certificate (4)
dispatches (4)
scroll (4) +4479
it^s (3) +2021
literature (2)
written (2)
books (1)
can read (1) +3359
cannot read (1) +3359+4202
deeds (1)
documents (1)
indictment (1)
know how to read (1) +3359
record (1)
records (1)
scriptures (1)
them^s (1)
untranslated (3)

6220 2סֵפֶר *sēper2*
Variant; not used

6221 סֹפֵר *sōpēr* (56)
secretary (28)
scribe (11)
secretaries (4)
scribes (2)
teacher (2)
writing (2)
chief officer (1)
commander's (1)
man learned (1)
officer in charge (1)
scribe's (1)
secretary's (1)
writer (1)

6222 1סְפָר *s^epār1* (1)
census taken (1) +6218

6223 2סְפָר *s^epār2* (1)
Sephar (1)

6224 סְפָרַד *s^epārad* (1)
Sepharad (1)

6225 סִפְרָה *siprāh* (1)
record (1)

6226 סְפָרְוַיִם *s^eparwayim* (7)
Sepharvaim (6)
untranslated (1)

6227 סְפָרְוִים *s^eparwiym* (1)
Sepharvites (1)

6228 סְפֹרוֹת *s^epōrôt* (1)
measure (1)

6229 סֹפְרִים *sōpᵉrîm*
Variant; not used

6230 סֹפֶרֶת *sōperet*
Variant; not used

6231 סְפֵת *sepet*
Variant; not used

6232 סָקַל *sāqal* (22)
stone (5)
be stoned (2)
been stoned (2)
stone (2) +74+928+2021
stoned (2) +74+928+2021
cleared of stones (1)
must be stoned to death (1) +6232
pelted (1)
remove (1)
stoning (1)
surely be stoned (1) +6232
throwing (1)

6233 סָר *sār* (1)
captain (1)

6234 סַר *sar* (3)
sullen (3)

6235 סָרָב *sārāb* (1)
briers (1)

6236 סַרְגוֹן *sargôn* (1)
Sargon (1)

6237 סֶרֶד *sered* (2)
Sered (2)

6238 סַרְדִּי *sardiy* (1)
Seredite (1)

6239 1סָרָה *sārāh1* (1)
unceasing (1) +1194

6240 2סָרָה *sārāh2* (7)
rebellion (4)
crime (1)
revolt (1)
revolted against (1)

6241 סִרָה *sirāh* (1)
Sirah (1)

6242 סָרוּחַ *sārûaḥ* (3)
flowing (1)
lounge (1)
lounging (1)

6243 1סָרַח *sāraḥ1* (3)
hang (1)
hang down (1)
spreading (1)

6244 2סָרַח *sāraḥ2* (1)
decayed (1)

6245 סֶרַח *seraḥ* (1)
length (1)

6246 סִרְיוֹן *siryôn* (2)
armor (2)

6247 סָרִיס *sāriys* (45)
eunuchs (10)
official (9)
officials (9)
officer (5)
court officials (4)
eunuch (4)
officers (2)
attendants (1)
palace officials (1)

6248 1סֶרֶן *seren1* (1)
axles (1)

6249 2סֶרֶן *seren2* (21)
rulers (21)

6250 סַרְעַפָּה *sar'appāh* (1)
boughs (1)

6251 סָרַף *sārap* (1)
burn (1)

6252 סִרְפָּד *sirpād* (1)
briers (1)

6253 1סָרַר *sārar1* (17)
stubborn (6)
rebellious (4)
obstinate (2)
stubbornly (2)
defiant (1)
hardened rebels (1) +6073
rebels (1)

6254 2סָרַר *sārar2* (1)
in charge (1)

6255 סְתָו *sᵉtāw* (1)
winter (1)

6256 סְתוּר *sᵉtûr* (1)
Sethur (1)

6257 סְתָיו *sᵉtāyw* (1)
untranslated (1)

6258 סָתַם *sātam* (12)
stopped up (3)
blocked (2)
being closed (1)
blocking off (1)
close up (1)
closed up (1)
inmost place (1)
seal up (1)
stop up (1)

6259 סָתַר *sātar* (83)
hide (35)
hidden (10)
hid (9)
hiding (4)
conceal (2)
concealed (2)
is hidden (2)
secret (2)
are hidden (1)
away (1)
be sheltered (1)
certainly hide (1) +6259
covers (1)
go into hiding (1)
have no (1) +4946+6524
hide yourself (1)
hides (1)
hides himself (1)
hiding place (1)
take refuge (1)
takes refuge (1)
undetected (1)
vanish (1)
untranslated (1)

6260 סֵתֶר *sēter* (35)
secret (8)
secretly (6) +928+2021
shelter (5)
hiding place (2)
privately (2) +928+2021
refuge (2)
concealed (1)
covering (1)
hidden (1)
hiding (1)
hiding places (1)
ravine (1)
secret place (1)
sly (1)
thundercloud (1) +8308
veil (1)

6261 סִתְרָה *sitrāh* (1)
give shelter (1) +2118

6262 סִתְרִי *sitriy* (1)
Sithri (1)

6263 ע '
Variant; not used

6264 1עָב *'āb1* (3)
overhang (1)
overhanging roof (1)
overhangs (1)

6265 2עָב *'āb2* (30)
clouds (19)
cloud (7)
clouds of the sky (2) +8836
cloudless (1) +4202
thick clouds (1)

6266 3עָב *'āb3* (1)
thickets (1)

6267 עָב *'ab*
Variant; not used

6268 עָבַד *'ābad* (290)
serve (88)
worship (37)
served (28)
worshiped (13)
do (11)
work (10)
serving (8)
subject to (8)
ministers (6)
enslave (3)
enslaved (3)
labor (3)
subject (3)
work for (3)
worked (3)
worked for (3)
worshiping (3)
burdened (2)
farm (2)
hold in bondage (2)
serves (2)
till (2)
used (2)
work (2) +6275
workers (2)
works (2)
be cultivated (1)
be plowed (1)
been plowed (1)
been worked (1)
beenˢ (1)
bondage (1) +6275
cultivate (1)
do work (1)
doˢ (1)
doing (1)
done (1)
drove (1)
efforts (1)
enslaving (1)
farmer (1) +141+408
fulfilling by doing (1)
keep working (1)
laborer (1)
led (1)
make slaves (1)
make work (1)
making work (1)
observe (1)
perform (1)
profits (1)
put to work (1)
reduced to servitude (1) +4200+6269
servant (1)
serve as slaves (1)
services (1)
slave (1)
subjects (1)
subjugate (1)
submit (1)
to subject (1)
worship (1) +6275

untranslated (3)

6269 עֶבֶד 1 *'ebed1* (806)
servant (325)
servants (156)
officials (77)
men (48)
slaves (30)
officers (16)
menservants (15)
slave (15)
attendants (14)
slavery (14)
manservant (8)
male slaves (7)
servant's (7)
subject (7)
official (4)
subjects (3)
attendant (2)
in bondage (2)
male slave (2)
officer (2)
retinue (2)
serve (2)
slaves (2) +2256+9148
them[s] (2) +2257
they[s] (2) +2257
vassal (2)
vassals (2)
as a slave (1) +6275
court (1)
delegation (1) +928+3338
enslaved (1) +2256+3899+4200+4200+9148
envoys (1)
fellow officers (1) +123
government officials (1)
he[s] (1) +3870
him[s] (1) +3870
I[s] (1) +3870
in service (1)
lowest of slaves (1) +6269
make men slaves (1) +3899
me[s] (1) +3870
messengers (1)
reduced to servitude (1) +4200+6268
servants men (1)
servants the (1)
servants' (1)
servants' (1) +4200
served (1)
service (1)
slaves (1) +563+2256
slaves male (1)
subordinates (1)
them[s] (1) +1192
they[s] (1) +8620
worship (1)
untranslated (9)

6270 עֶבֶד 2 *'ebed2* (6)
Ebed (6)

6271 עֲבַד *'ăbad* (1)
what do (1)

6272 עַבְדָּא *'abdā'* (2)
Abda (2)

6273 עֹבֵד־אֱדוֹם *'ōbēd-'ĕdôm* (20)
Obed-Edom (18)
him[s] (1)
his[s] (1)

6274 עַבְדְּאֵל *'abd'ēl* (1)
Abdeel (1)

6275 עֲבֹדָה *'ăbōdāh* (144)
work (39)
service (24)
regular work (12) +4856
labor (7)
duties (5)
serving (5)
use (5)

ceremony (3)
ministering (3)
campaign (2)
constructing (2)
job (2)
ministry (2)
slavery (2)
task (2)
various kinds of service (2) +2256+6275
work (2) +6268
as a slave (1) +6269
assist (1)
bondage (1)
bondage (1) +6268
by (1)
craft (1)
cultivate (1)
demands (1)
doing (1)
doing work (1)
effect (1)
farmed (1)
posts (1)
regular service (1) +7372
required (1)
responsible (1)
responsible (1) +4856
served (1)
slaves (1)
tasks (1)
workers (1) +1074
worship (1) +6268
untranslated (2)

6276 עֲבֻדָּה *'ăbuddāh* (2)
servants (2)

6277 עַבְדּוֹן 1 *'abdôn1* (6)
Abdon (6)

6278 עַבְדּוֹן 2 *'abdôn2* (3)
Abdon (3)

6279 עַבְדִּי *'abdiy* (3)
Abdi (3)

6280 עַבְדִּיאֵל *'abdiy'ēl* (1)
Abdiel (1)

6281 עֹבַדְיָה *'ōbadyāh* (11)
Obadiah (11)

6282 עֹבַדְיָהוּ *'ōbadyāhû* (9)
Obadiah (9)

6283 עֶבֶד־מֶלֶךְ *'ebed-melek* (6)
Ebed-Melech (6)

6284 עֲבֵד נְגוֹ *'ăbēd n'gô* (1)
Abednego (1)

6285 עַבְדֻת *'abdut* (3)
bondage (2)
slavery (1)

6286 עָבָה *'ābāh* (3)
thicker (2)
heavy (1)

6287 עֲבוֹט *'ăbôt* (4)
pledge (2)
offering as a pledge (1)
untranslated (1)

6288 עֲבוּר 1 *'ăbûr1* (49)
for the sake of (11)
because of (6)
so that (5)
for sake (4)
to (4)
because (3)
for (2)
in order to (2)
on account of (2)
so (2)
that (2)
for this purpose (1)
then (1)

to (1) +928+4200
while (1)
untranslated (2)

6289 עֲבוּר 2 *'ăbûr2* (2)
food (1)
produce (1)

6290 עָבוֹת 1 *'ābôt1* (4)
leafy (3)
shade (1)

6291 עָבוֹת 2 *'ābôt2* (5)
thick foliage (4)
boughs (1)

6292 עָבַט 1 *'ābat1* (5)
borrow (1)
freely lend (1) +6292
get (1)
lend (1)

6293 עָבַט 2 *'ābat2* (1)
swerving (1)

6294 עַבְטִיט *'abtiyt* (1)
extortion (1)

6295 עֲבִי *'ăbiy* (6)
thick (2)
thickness (2)
dense (1)
molds (1)

6296 עָבַר 1 *'ābar1* (551)
crossed (31)
pass (30)
cross (28)
cross over (23)
passed (21)
crossed over (17)
go (17)
crossing (12)
went (10)
passed by (9)
pass by (8)
pass through (8)
went on (8)
go over (7)
sacrificed (6)
violated (6)
come (5)
go on (5)
moved on (5)
swept (5)
pass by (4) +2006
sacrifice (4)
take away (4)
advanced (3)
came along (3)
come over (3)
continued (3)
going (3)
led (3)
over (3)
pass away (3)
passed through (3)
spread (3)
traveled (3)
bring across (2)
broken (2)
came by (2)
comes (2)
disobey (2)
get through (2)
go beyond (2)
go on way (2)
go past (2)
going down (2)
gone (2)
gone by (2)
had pass (2)
journey (2)
led through (2)
make (2)

marched (2)
pass on (2)
passed along (2)
passer-by (2)
passes (2)
passing by (2)
passing through (2)
past (2)
put (2)
send (2)
spare (2)
sweep through (2)
sweeps by (2)
swept by (2)
taken away (2)
travel (2)
travelers (2)
travels (2)
turn over (2)
walked (2)
according to the weight current (1)
advance (1)
avert (1) +4946+6584
be over (1)
been (1)
beyond (1)
blown (1)
blows (1)
breed (1)
bring across (1) +6296
brought (1)
brought over (1)
came to the other side (1)
carried over (1)
carry over (1)
cast off (1)
cause to pass (1)
cease (1)
census (1) +408
coming (1)
coming over (1)
continue on (1)
continued along (1)
continued on (1)
counted off (1) +928+5031
cover (1)
cover (1) +6584
cross over without fail (1) +6296
crosses over (1)
crossing over (1)
did so[s] (1)
disobeyed (1)
disobeying (1)
disregarded (1)
driven (1)
enter (1)
exceed (1)
expelled (1)
explored (1) +9365
extended (1)
fail (1)
fall (1)
felt (1)
fleeting (1)
flowing (1)
follow (1) +339
forded (1)
forgive (1)
forgives (1)
forth (1)
give over (1)
go away (1)
goes (1)
goes across (1)
goes through (1)
going over (1)
gone on (1)
had pass by (1)
have no limit (1)
have shave (1) +9509
have sounded (1)

invade (1)
invade (1) +928
irresistible (1)
issued (1)
jealous (1) +6584+7863+8120
kept on going (1)
know no limits (1)
laid (1)
lead across (1) +4200+7156
leaving (1) +4946
led around (1)
let pass (1)
made work (1)
make cross (1)
marauding (1) +2256+8740
march on (1)
marched on (1)
marched past (1) +3338+6584
marching (1)
missed (1)
moved on ahead (1)
moved on beyond (1)
moves on (1)
on the way (1)
on way (1)
outran (1)
over going (1)
overcome (1)
overflow (1)
overlook (1)
overrun (1)
overstep (1)
overwhelmed (1) +8031
overwhelming (1)
pass into other hands (1)
passed away (1)
passes by (1)
passing (1)
perish (1)
perishing (1)
provide safe-conduct (1)
put a yoke (1)
put an end (1)
ran (1)
ran past (1)
reclaimed (1)
remove (1)
removed (1)
repealed (1)
roam (1)
sacrificed (1) +928+5989
sacrifices (1)
sail (1)
seafarers (1) +3542
send out (1)
sent (1)
sent across (1)
sent over (1)
sent throughout (1)
set free (1)
shave (1)
sin (1)
sound (1)
spreading among (1)
surrounded (1)
sweep (1)
sweeps on (1)
swept away (1)
swim (1)
take note as pass (1)
take over (1)
taken from (1)
taken over (1)
them[s] (1) +2021
they[s] (1) +2021
through (1)
took (1)
took off (1)
transfer (1)
transgressed (1)
travel (1) +2006

traveled along (1)
traveling through (1)
turn away (1)
turned aside (1)
untraveled (1) +408+1172+4946
used (1)
vanishes (1)
violate (1)
violation (1)
wade through (1)
walk on (1)
walk over (1)
walked over (1)
went as far as (1)
went away (1)
went forward (1)
went over (1)
went up (1)
untranslated (11)

6297　2עָבַר　‘ābar2 (8)
very angry (4)
angers (1)
angry (1)
hotheaded (1)
meddles (1)

6298　1עֵבֶר　‘ēber1 (92)
east (9) +928
side (9)
other side (6)
beyond (5) +928
across (4) +928
beyond (4)
Trans-Euphrates (4) +2021+5643
across (3) +4946
straight ahead (3) +448+7156
beyond (2) +4946
east (2) +4946
near (2) +928
next to (2) +448
across from (1) +4946
along (1)
along (1) +928
along (1) +4946
alongside (1) +4946
at (1) +928
by (1) +4946
east (1)
east (1) +928+2025+4667
east (1) +928+2025+4667+9087
east (1) +928+4667+9087
east (1) +2025+4667
east side (1)
from (1) +4946
goes on (1)
land beyond (1)
next to (1) +4200
on each side (1)　+2021+2021+2296+2296
　　　　　+4946+4946+4946+4946+6298
on the other side of (1) +2134+2256+4946
on this side of (1) +4946
over here (1) +285+4200
over there (1) +285+4200
side (1) +4946
sides (1)
sides (1) +4946+6017
space (1)
this side (1)
west (1)
west (1) +928
west (1) +4946
untranslated (6)

6299　2עֵבֶר　‘ēber2 (15)
Eber (15)

6300　עָבָר　‘ābār
Variant; not used

6301　עֶבְרָה　‘ebrāh (34)
wrath (21)
anger (4)

fury (4)
insolence (2)
rage (2)
overweening pride (1) +2295

6302 עֶבְרָה ʿᵃbārāh (3)
fords (2)
ford (1)

6303 1עִבְרִי ʿibriy1 (34)
Hebrew (16)
Hebrews (16)
womanˢ (1)
untranslated (1)

6304 2עִבְרִי ʿibriy2 (1)
Ibri (1)

6305 עֲבָרִים ʿᵃbāriym (5)
Abarim (5)

6306 עֶבְרֹן ʿebrōn
Variant; not used

6307 עַבְרֹנָה ʿabrōnāh (2)
Abronah (2)

6308 עָבַשׁ ʿābaš (1)
shriveled (1)

6309 עָבַת ʿābat (1)
conspire (1)

6310 עֲבֹת ʿᵃbōt (19)
ropes (7)
chains (4)
rope (3)
chains (1) +9249
cords (1)
fetters (1)
harness (1)
ties (1)

6311 עָגַב ʿāgab (8)
lusted after (3) +6584
lovers (1)
lusted (1)
lusted after (1)
lusted after (1) +448
untranslated (1)

6312 עֲגָבָה ʿᵃgābāh (2)
love (1)
lust (1)

6313 עֲגָבִים ʿᵃgābiym (1)
devotion (1)

6314 עֻגָה ʿugāh (7)
cake of bread (2)
cakes (2)
bread (1)
cake (1)
flat cake (1)

6315 עָגוּר ʿāgûr (2)
thrush (2)

6316 עָגִיל ʿāgiyl (2)
earrings (2)

6317 עֲגִילָה ʿᵃgiylāh (1)
shields (1)

6318 עָגֹל ʿāgōl (6)
circular in shape (2) +6017
round (2)
circular band (1) +6017
rounded (1)

6319 עֵגֶל ʿēgel (36)
calf (19)
calves (10)
shape of a calf (3)
calf-idol (2)
calf-idols (1)
shape of calves (1)

6320 1עֶגְלָה ʿeglāh1 (11)
heifer (6)

heifer (2) +1330
heifer's (1)
herˢ (1) +2021
young cow (1) +1330

6321 2עֶגְלָה ʿeglāh2 (2)
Eglah (2)

6322 עֲגָלָה ʿᵃgālāh (24)
cart (13)
carts (8)
cartwheel (1) +236
itˢ (1) +2021
threshing cart (1)

6323 1עֶגְלוֹן ʿeglôn1 (5)
Eglon (4)
whoˢ (1)

6324 2עֶגְלוֹן ʿeglôn2 (8)
Eglon (8)

6325 עֶגְלַיִם ʿeglayim
Variant; not used

6326 עֶגְלַת שְׁלִשִׁיָּה ʿeglat šᵉlišiyyāh (2)
Eglath Shelishiyah (2)

6327 עָגַם ʿāgam (1)
grieved (1)

6328 עָגַן ʿāgan (1)
remain unmarried (1)
      +408+1194+2118+4200+4200

6329 1עַד ʿad1 (48)
ever (16)
forever (12) +4200
forever (3) +6330
ancient (2)
eternal (2) +4200
ever (2) +4200
ever and ever (2)
everlasting (2)
always (1) +4200
continually (1) +4200
eternal (1)
ever (1) +6330
forever (1)
never (1) +1153+2256+6409
of old (1)

6330 2עַד ʿad2 (1261)
to (322)
until (224)
till (94)
as far as (70)
forever (44) +6409
until (30) +889
how long (27) +5503
up to (21)
and (13)
all the way to (12)
how long (12) +625+2025
reached (11) +995
before (9)
at (8)
or (8)
as (7)
by (7)
for (6)
until (6) +8611
very (6) +4394
ever (5) +6409
forevermore (5) +6409
while (5)
after (4)
approached (4) +995
even (4)
from (4)
how long (4) +4537
still (4)
always (3) +6409
among (3)
and alike (3)
before (3) +889+4202

between (3) +2256+4946
beyond measure (3) +4394
but (3)
ever since (3) +2021+2021+2296+3427
forever (3) +6329
out to (3)
reaches to (3)
through (3)
until (3) +561
until (3) +3954
when (3)
as far away as (2)
at set times (2) +4946+6961+6961
come to (2)
down to (2)
enough (2)
everlasting (2) +6409
forever (2) +2021+6409
forever (2) +4200+6409
from beginning to (2)
how many (2) +3869+4537
in (2)
in the end (2)
lasts (2)
more (2) +6409
never (2) +4202+6409
of (2)
reach (2) +995
still (2) +2021+2021+2296+3427
this far (2) +2151
till (2) +8611
until (2) +561+889
up (2)
utterly (2) +4394
with (2)
abundantly (1) +889+3907+6330
against (1) +928
all the way to (1) +995
all the way to (1) +995+3870
all the way up (1)
almost to a man (1) +4392+9462
and (1) +2256
arrive (1) +995
arrived (1) +995
as long as (1)
at the point of (1)
before (1) +4202
by then (1)
completely (1) +1414+2256+4946+5883
completely (1) +3983
completely destroyed (1) +3983
down to (1) +9462
end (1)
endless (1) +6409
ends (1)
entered (1) +2143
entering (1) +995
even as far as (1)
even enough (1)
ever (1) +6329
extends to (1)
far and wide (1) +4200+4946+8158
far and wide (1) +8158
far away (1) +4200+4946+8158
finally (1) +889
for an instant (1) +1180+8371
for how long (1) +5503
forevermore (1) +2021+6409
founded on (1)
here (1) +2178
hold back overnight (1) +1332+4328
how long (1) +625
huge (1) +1524+4200+4394
in the end (1) +889
including (1)
into (1)
join (1) +995
lasted so long (1)
lasting (1) +2021+2021+2296+3427
lasting (1) +6409
led to (1)

loud (1) +1524+4394
meanwhile (1) +2256+3907+3907+6330
more and more powerful (1)
　　　　+1541+2025+2143+2256+4200+5087
much (1) +4394
near (1)
never (1) +561+6409
never (1) +4202+5905
on (1) +6964
only (1)
over (1)
prior (1)
reach to (1)
reached (1) +1540
reached height (1) +8003
reaching to (1)
reduces to (1)
since (1)
since (1) +2178
so much (1)
so much that (1)
still in force (1)
swiftly (1) +4559
that (1) +889
this far (1) +7024
though (1)
threatened (1) +5883
thus far (1) +2178
till (1) +561
till (1) +889
till (1) +3954
till (1) +6961
to the point of (1)
to the vicinity of (1) +995+3870
together with (1) +2256
toward (1)
toward (1) +5790
trembled violently (1)
　　　　+1524+3006+3010+4394
until the end of (1)
until the time for (1)
very (1) +2025+4200+5087
waited (1)
when (1) +625+2025
when (1) +4537
when (1) +8611
while (1) +8611
while still (1)
without (1) +401
without restraint (1) +4394
yet (1)
yet (1) +2021+2021+2085+3427
yet (1) +2021+2021+2156+3427
yet (1) +2178
yet (1) +6964
untranslated (91)

6331 3עַד ‘ad3 (1)
prey (1)

6332 עֵד ‘ēd (73)
witness (38)
witnesses (18)
testify (3)
testimony (3)
call in as witnesses (1) +6386
evidence (1)
had witnessed (1) +6386
have the transaction witnessed (1) +6386
testify (1) +2118
testify (1) +4200+6699
those who speak up for (1)
witnessed (1) +6386
untranslated (3)

6333 עִדֹּא ‘iddō’ (1)
Iddo (1)

6334 1עָדָה ‘ādāh1 (2)
prowls (1)
takes away (1)

6335 2עָדָה ‘ādāh2 (8)
adorned (2)

adorn (1)
adorns (1)
decked (1)
put on (1)
put on jewelry (1) +6344
take up (1)

6336 3עָדָה ‘ādāh3 (8)
Adah (8)

6337 1עֵדָה ‘ēdāh1 (148)
community (69)
assembly (50)
followers (10)
people (4)
band (2)
company (2)
assembled (1)
community's (1)
flocking together (1)
herd (1)
household (1)
swarm (1)
whole assembly (1) +2256+7736
untranslated (4)

6338 2עֵדָה ‘ēdāh2 (5)
witness (4)
witnesses (1)

6339 3עֵדָה ‘ēdāh3
Variant; not used

6340 עִדָּה ‘iddāh (1)
filthy (1)

6341 עִדֹּו ‘iddô (4)
Iddo (4)

6342 עִדֹּוא ‘iddô’ (3)
Iddo (2)
Iddo's (1)

6343 עֵדוּת ‘ēdût (83)
testimony (37)
statutes (29)
stipulations (4)
copy of covenant (2)
covenant (2)
regulations (2)
requirements (2)
statute (2)
demands (1)
warnings gave (1) +6386
warnings given (1) +6386

6344 עֲדִי ‘ⁿdiy (14)
ornaments (5)
jewelry (2)
beautiful jewelry (1) +7382
bridle (1) +8270
desires (1)
jewels (1)
most beautiful of jewels (1) +6344
put on jewelry (1) +6335

6345 עַדְיָא ‘ⁿdāyā’ (1)
untranslated (1)

6346 עֲדִיאֵל ‘ⁿdiy’ēl (3)
Adiel (3)

6347 עֲדָיָה ‘ⁿdāyāh (8)
Adaiah (8)

6348 עֲדָיָהוּ ‘ⁿdāyāhû (1)
Adaiah (1)

6349 1עָדִין ‘ādiyn1 (1)
wanton (1)

6350 2עָדִין ‘ādiyn2 (4)
Adin (4)

6351 עֲדִינָא ‘ⁿdiynā’ (1)
Adina (1)

6352 עֲדִינֹו ‘ⁿdiynô
Variant; not used

6353 עֲדִיתָיִם ‘ⁿdiytayim (1)
Adithaim (1)

6354 עַדְלַי ‘adlay (1)
Adlai (1)

6355 עֲדֻלָּם ‘ⁿdullām (8)
Adullam (8)

6356 עֲדֻלָּמִי ‘ⁿdullāmiy (3)
Adullamite (2)
of Adullam (1)

6357 עָדָן ‘ādan (1)
reveled (1)

6358 1עֵדֶן ‘ēden1 (3)
delicacies (1)
delights (1)
finery (1)

6359 2עֵדֶן ‘ēden2 (14)
Eden (14)

6360 3עֵדֶן ‘ēden3 (2)
Eden (2)

6361 עֶדֶן ‘eden (3)
Eden (3)

6362 עַדֶּן ‘ⁿden (1)
yet (1)

6363 עַדְנָא ‘adnā’ (2)
Adna (2)

6364 עַדְנָה ‘ⁿdenāh (1)
still (1)

6365 עַדְנָה ‘adnāh (1)
Adnah (1)

6366 עֶדְנָה ‘ednāh (1)
pleasure (1)

6367 עַדְנַח ‘adnah (1)
Adnah (1)

6368 עַדְעָדָה ‘ad‘ādāh (1)
Adadah (1)

6369 עָדַף ‘ādap (9)
additional (2)
left (2)
balance (1)
exceed number (1)
exceeded number (1)
have too much (1)
left over (1)

6370 1עָדַר ‘ādar1 (2)
help (1)
volunteered to serve (1)

6371 2עָדַר ‘ādar2 (2)
cultivated (2)

6372 3עָדַר ‘ādar3 (7)
missing (3)
fail (1)
left (1)
nowhere to be found (1)
saw to it that was lacking (1)

6373 1עֵדֶר ‘ēder1 (39)
flock (15)
flocks (15)
herds (3)
each herd (1) +6373
flocks and herds (1)
herds (1) +1330
sheep (1)
untranslated (1)

6374 2עֵדֶר ‘ēder2 (2)
Eder (2)

6375 3עֵדֶר ‘ēder3 (1)
Eder (1)

6376 עֶדֶר ‘eder (1)
Eder (1)

6377 עַדְרִיאֵל *'aḏriy'ēl* (2)
Adriel (2)

6378 עֲדָשִׁים *'ᵃdāšiym* (4)
lentils (3)
lentil (1)

6379 עַוָּא *'awwā'* (1)
Avva (1)

6380 עוּב *'ûḇ* (1)
covered with the cloud (1)

6381 עוֹבֵד *'ôḇēḏ* (10)
Obed (10)

6382 עוֹבָל *'ôḇāl* (2)
Obal (2)

6383 עוּג *'ûg* (1)
bake (1)

6384 עוֹג *'ôg* (22)
Og (20)
Og's (2)

6385 עוּגָב *'ûgāḇ* (4)
flute (4)

6386 1עוּד *'ûḏ1* (44)
warned (5)
warn (4)
testify (3)
admonished (2)
call as witnesses (2)
sustains (2)
acting as witness (1)
been warned (1)
bind (1)
brought charges against (1)
call in as witnesses (1) +6332
call to testify (1)
commended (1)
gave charge (1)
give warning (1)
had witnessed (1) +6332
have testify (1)
have the transaction witnessed (1) +6332
say (1)
solemnly declared (1)
stand firm (1)
testified (1)
warn solemnly (1) +6386
warned (1) +6386
warned solemnly (1) +6386
warnings gave (1) +6343
warnings given (1) +6343
witnessed (1) +6332
untranslated (1)

6387 2עוּד *'ûḏ2*
Variant; not used

6388 עוֹד *'ôḏ* (491)
longer (74)
again (72)
still (54)
more (35)
again (22) +3578
while still (16)
other (11)
another (9)
anymore (8)
continued (8)
more (7) +3578
yet (7)
further (6)
within (6) +928
longer (5) +3578
never (5) +4202
also (4)
anymore (4) +3578
besides (4)
once again (4)
another (3) +337
any longer (3)
any more (3)

else (3)
all the more (2) +3578
as long as (2) +3972
as long as live (2) +928
even (2)
ever (2)
left (2)
more (2) +337
once again (2) +3578
once more (2) +3578
overwhelmed (2) +928+2118+4202+8120
remain (2)
remained (2)
remains (2)
soon (2) +5071
still another (2)
while (2)
added (1)
all life (1) +4946
almost (1) +5071
always (1) +4946
another (1) +3578
any (1) +4946
any longer (1) +3578
as long as (1)
as long as (1) +561
as long as (1) +928
awaits (1)
back (1)
back (1) +3578
before (1) +4202
but also (1)
continue (1)
continued (1) +3578
do again (1) +3578
even as (1)
even more (1)
ever again (1)
failed (1) +4202+7756
for (1)
from now (1) +928
from now on (1)
furthermore (1) +2256
how long (1) +339+5503
in (1)
in a very short time (1) +4663+5071
kept on (1)
left now (1)
little while (1) +5071
long time (1)
make again (1) +3578
moreover (1)
next (1)
not enough (1) +7781
now (1)
on (1)
once more (1)
only (1)
others (1)
reappears (1) +8011
reconsider (1) +8740
regain (1) +6806
return (1) +995
since then (1)
something else (1)
stands (1)
still (1) +3972
still (1) +8636
still another (1) +3578
stopped (1) +3578+4202
time (1)
very soon (1) +4663+5071
were added (1) +3578
yet to come (1)
untranslated (29)

6389 עוֹדֵד *'ôḏēḏ* (3)
Oded (3)

6390 1עָוָה *'āwāh1* (17)
done wrong (6)
perverted (2)

am staggered (1)
bowed down (1)
did wrong (1)
does wrong (1)
made crooked (1)
perverse (1)
ruin (1)
sinning (1)
warped (1)

6391 2עָוָה *'āwāh2*
Variant; not used

6392 1עַוָּה *'awwāh1* (3)
ruin (3)

6393 2עַוָּה *'awwāh2*
Variant; not used

6394 עִוָּה *'iwwāh* (3)
Ivvah (3)

6395 עוּז *'ûz* (6)
flee for safety (2)
bring to a place of shelter (1)
look for help (1)
strong (1)
take cover (1)

6396 1עֲוִיל *'ᵃwiyl1* (2)
children (1)
little boys (1)

6397 2עֲוִיל *'ᵃwiyl2* (1)
evil men (1)

6398 1עַוִּים *'awwiym1* (3)
Avvites (3)

6399 2עַוִּים *'awwiym2* (1)
Avvim (1)

6400 עֲוִית *'ᵃwiyṯ* (2)
Avith (2)

6401 1עָוֶל *'āwal1* (2)
doing evil (1)
evil (1)

6402 2עוּל *'ûl2* (5)
calved (1)
have young (1)
nursing young (1)
sheep (1)
such⁵ (1)

6403 3עוּל *'ûl3* (3)
infant (2)
baby at breast (1)

6404 עָוֶל *'āwel* (22)
evil (5)
sin (4)
dishonest (3)
wrong (3)
dishonestly (1)
doing wrong (1)
fault (1)
guilt (1)
pervert (1) +6913
unjust (1)
ways (1)

6405 עַוָּל *'awwāl* (5)
wicked (2)
evil man (1)
unjust (1)
unrighteous (1)

6406 עַוְלָה *'awlāh* (32)
wicked (7)
wickedness (7)
evil (5)
wrong (5)
injustice (3)
crime (1)
false (1)
iniquity (1)
unjust (1)

wickedly (1)

6407 עֹלֵל *'ôlēl* (11)
children (7)
infant (1)
infants (1)
little children (1)
little ones (1)

6408 עֹלָל *'ôlāl* (9)
children (7)
infants (2)

6409 עוֹלָם *'ôlām* (440)
forever (137) +4200
everlasting (56)
forever (44) +6330
lasting (26)
forever (21)
ancient (13)
ever (9)
regular (9)
never (8) +4200+4202
of old (7)
eternal (5)
ever (5) +4200
ever (5) +6330
for ever (5)
forevermore (5) +6330
long ago (4)
always (3)
always (3) +6330
ancient (3) +4946
eternal (3) +4200
old (3)
age-old (2)
always (2) +4200
ancient times (2)
eternity (2)
ever (2) +4946
everlasting (2) +6330
for life (2)
forever (2) +2021+6330
forever (2) +4200+6330
long (2)
long ago (2) +4946
more (2) +6330
never (2) +440+4200
never (2) +1153+4200
never (2) +4202+6330
never again (2) +4200+4202
permanent (2)
again (1) +4200
ages (1)
all eternity (1)
all time (1)
any time (1)
as long as live (1) +3427+3972+4200
continue (1)
continued (1)
early times (1)
endless (1) +6330
everlasting (1) +3972
everlasting (1) +4200
for life (1) +4200
forevermore (1) +2021+6330
gone by (1)
lasting (1) +4200
lasting (1) +6330
lasting (1) +9458
life (1)
long (1) +4200
long (1) +4946
long ago (1) +4200
long time (1)
never (1) +401+4200
never (1) +561+6330
never (1) +1153+2256+6329
never (1) +4202
to come (1)
to the very end (1) +4200+6813
used to be (1) +3427
untranslated (2)

6410 עוּן *'ûn*
Variant; not used

6411 עָוֺן *'āwōn* (234)
sin (59)
sins (49)
guilt (35)
wickedness (13)
iniquity (12)
iniquities (10)
punishment (9)
held responsible (7) +5951
crime (4)
guilty (4)
wicked (4)
consequences of sin (3)
responsibility for offenses (3)
blame (2)
offense (2)
sinful (2)
wrong (2)
affliction (1)
crimes (1)
evil deeds (1)
faults (1)
offenses (1)
punished (1)
punished (1) +7936
punishment for sins (1)
sins (1) +1821
wrongdoing (1)
wrongdoings (1)
wrongs (1)
untranslated (2)

6412 עֹנָה *'ônāh*
Variant; not used

6413 עַוְעִים *'iw'iym* (1)
dizziness (1)

6414 עוּף 1 *'ûp1* (26)
fly away (4)
darting (3)
flew (3)
fly (3)
flying (3)
flies (2)
cast (1)
flies away (1)
fly along (1)
fly off (1)
hovering overhead (1)
swoop down (1)
untranslated (2)

6415 עוּף 2 *'ûp2*
Variant; not used

6416 עוֹף *'ôp* (71)
birds (54)
bird (12)
flying (2)
winged (2)
winged creature (1)

6417 עוֹפִי *'ôpay* (1)
untranslated (1)

6418 עוּץ 1 *'ûṣ1* (2)
consider (1)
devise (1)

6419 עוּץ 2 *'ûṣ2* (5)
Uz (5)

6420 עוּץ 3 *'ûṣ3* (3)
Uz (2)
Uz (1) +824

6421 עוּק *'ûq* (2)
crush (1)
crushes (1)

6422 עָוַר 1 *'āwar1* (5)
put out (3)
blinds (2)

6423 עוּר 2 *'ûr2* (1)
uncovered (1) +6880

6424 עוּר 3 *'ûr3* (82)
awake (16)
stir up (8)
awaken (6)
rouse (6)
stirred up (6)
wake up (5)
raised (4)
arouse (3)
moved (3)
arise (2)
aroused (2)
be roused (2)
stirs up (2)
wakens (2)
being stirred up (1)
gloated (1)
is wakened (1)
lament (1) +2411
lash (1)
raise up (1)
rising (1)
roused (1)
roused himself (1)
rouses (1)
stir (1)
strives (1)
thrive (1)
wakened (1)
whoever he may be (1) +2256+6699

6425 עוֹר *'ôr* (99)
skin (39)
leather (14)
hides (13)
hide (8)
skin (8) +1414
skins (6)
face (3) +7156
body (1)
flesh (1)
goatskins (1) +1531+6436
its[s] (1) +2021
nothing but skin (1) +1414+2256
untranslated (3)

6426 עִוֵּר *'iwwēr* (26)
blind (26)

6427 עִוָּרוֹן *'iwwārôn* (2)
blind (1) +928+2021+5782
blindness (1)

6428 עַוֶּרֶת *'awweret* (1)
blind (1)

6429 עוּשׁ *'ûš* (1)
quickly (1)

6430 עָוַת *'āwat* (11)
pervert (3)
cheating (1)
deprive (1)
frustrates (1)
is twisted (1)
made crooked (1)
stoop (1)
wronged (1)
wronging (1)

6431 עוּת *'ût* (1)
sustains (1)

6432 עַוָּתָה *'awwātāh* (1)
wrong done (1)

6433 עוּתַי *'ûtay* (2)
Uthai (2)

6434 עַז *'az* (23)
strong (5)
mighty (4)
fierce (3)
powerful (3)

fierce-looking (1) +7156
fortified (1)
great (1)
harshly (1)
stern-faced (1) +7156
strength (1)
stronger (1)
stronghold (1)

6435 עַז *'āz* (1)
power (1)

6436 עֵז *'ēz* (74)
male goat (24) +8538
goats (11)
goat (8)
goat hair (7)
young goat (7) +1531
goat (2) +7618
goat (2) +8538
goat (2) +8544
goats' hair (2) +3889
male goats (2) +8538
goat (1) +8445
goats (1) +1201
goats' (1)
goatskins (1) +1531+6425
male goats (1) +7618
young goat (1)
young goats (1) +1531

6437 עֹז *'ōz* (94)
strength (38)
strong (12)
power (11)
mighty (8)
might (6)
fortified (3)
stronghold (3)
praise (2)
feeble (1) +4202
firm (1)
fortress (1)
great (1)
great power (1)
hard (1)
stouthearted (1) +5883
strongholds (1)
stubborn (1)
vigorously (1) +928
untranslated (1)

6438 עֻזָּא *'uzzā'* (11)
Uzzah (6)
Uzza (5)

6439 עֲזָאזֵל *'"zā'zēl* (4)
scapegoat (4)

6440 1עָזַב *'āzabl* (212)
forsake (37)
forsaken (34)
leave (28)
left (19)
abandoned (18)
deserted (11)
forsook (8)
abandon (6)
forsaking (5)
free (5)
rejected (4)
neglect (3)
desert (2)
deserts (2)
fails (2)
leaves (2)
rejecting (2)
be abandoned (1)
be laid waste (1)
be left (1)
been abandoned (1)
change (1)
commits (1)
disregarded (1)

forfeit (1)
forsakes (1)
gave up (1)
give free rein (1)
give up (1)
go (1)
ignores (1)
is forsaken (1)
is neglected (1)
lays (1)
left behind (1)
left destitute (1)
renounces (1)
stop (1)
stopped showing (1)
turn from (1)
vanish (1)

6441 2עָזַב *'āzab2* (4)
be sure help (1) +6441
restore wall (1)
restored (1)

6442 עִזְּבוֹנִים *'izbôniym* (7)
merchandise (7)

6443 עַזְבּוּק *'azbûq* (1)
Azbuk (1)

6444 עַזְגָּד *'azgād* (4)
Azgad (4)

6445 עַזָּה *'azzāh* (20)
Gaza (20)

6446 עֻזָּה *'uzzāh* (3)
Uzzah (3)

6447 1עַזּוּבָה *'"zûbāhl*
Variant; not used

6448 2עֲזוּבָה *'"zûbāh2* (4)
Azubah (4)

6449 עָזוּז *'zûz* (3)
power (2)
violence (1)

6450 עִזּוּז *'izzûz* (2)
reinforcements (1)
strong (1)

6451 עָזַז *'āzaz* (10)
brazen (1)
fixed securely (1)
makes powerful (1)
oppressive (1)
overpowered (1) +3338+6584
puts up a bold front (1) +928+7156
show strength (1)
strong (1)
triumph (1)
triumphant (1)

6452 עָזָז *'āzāz* (1)
Azaz (1)

6453 עֲזַזְיָהוּ *'"zazyāhû* (3)
Azaziah (3)

6454 עֻזִּי *'uzziy* (11)
Uzzi (11)

6455 עֻזִּיָּא *'uzziyyā'* (1)
Uzzia (1)

6456 עֲזִיאֵל *'"ziy'ēl* (1)
Aziel (1)

6457 עֻזִּיאֵל *'uzziy'ēl* (16)
Uzziel (16)

6458 עֻזִּיאֵלִי *'"zziy'ēliy* (2)
Uzzielites (2)

6459 עֻזִּיָּה *'uzziyyāh* (8)
Uzziah (8)

6460 עֻזִּיָּהוּ *'uzziyyāhû* (19)
Uzziah (17)
him[s] (1) +2021+4889

Uzziah's (1)

6461 עֲזִיזָא *'"ziyzā'* (1)
Aziza (1)

6462 1עַזְמָוֶת *'azmāwetl* (6)
Azmaveth (6)

6463 2עַזְמָוֶת *'azmāwet2* (2)
Azmaveth (2)

6464 עַזָּן *'azzān* (1)
Azzan (1)

6465 עָזְנִיָּה *'ozniyyāh* (2)
black vulture (2)

6466 עָזַק *'āzaq* (1)
dug up (1)

6467 עֲזֵקָה *'"zēqāh* (7)
Azekah (7)

6468 עָזַר *'āzar* (82)
help (42)
helped (12)
helps (6)
helper (2)
added (1)
allied with (1)
allies (1)
am helped (1)
assist (1)
came to rescue (1)
cohorts (1)
gave support (1) +339
give support (1)
helpers (1)
helping (1)
is helped (1)
protect (1)
receive help (1) +6469
support (1)
supported (1)
sustain (1)
was helped (1)
were helped (1)
untranslated (1)

6469 1עֵזֶר *'ēzer1* (22)
help (13)
helper (5)
receive help (1) +6468
staff (1)
strength (1)
untranslated (1)

6470 2עֵזֶר *'ēzer2* (4)
Ezer (4)

6471 1עֶזֶר *'ezer1*
Variant; not used

6472 2עֶזֶר *'ezer2* (1)
Ezer (1)

6473 עַזּוּר *'azzur* (3)
Azzur (3)

6474 עֶזְרָא *'ezrā'* (22)
Ezra (21)
Ezra's (1)

6475 עֲזַרְאֵל *'"zar'ēl* (6)
Azarel (6)

6476 1עֶזְרָה *'ezrāhl* (26)
help (19)
aid (3)
allies (1)
helper (1)
influence (1)
support (1)

6477 2עֶזְרָה *'ezrāh2* (1)
Ezrah (1)

6478 עֲזָרָה *'"zārāh* (9)
ledge (6)
court (2)

outer court (1)

6479 עֶזְרִי *'ezriy* (1)
Ezri (1)

6480 עֲזְרִיאֵל *'azriy'ēl* (3)
Azriel (3)

6481 עֲזַרְיָה *'azaryāh* (32)
Azariah (31)
Azariah's (1)

6482 עֲזַרְיָהוּ *'azaryāhû* (16)
Azariah (14)
Azariah's (1)
Azariahu (1)

6483 עַזְרִיקָם *'azriyqām* (6)
Azrikam (6)

6484 עַזָּתִי *'azzātiy* (2)
Gaza (1)
people of Gaza (1)

6485 עֵט *'ēt* (4)
pen (2)
tool (2)

6486 1עָטָה *'ātāh1* (15)
cover (5)
wrapped (2)
covered (1)
covered with a mantle (1)
veiled (1)
wearing (1)
wrap around himself (1)
wrapped himself (1)
wraps around him (1)
wraps himself (1)

6487 2עָטָה *'ātāh2* (3)
is grasped (1)
take firm hold (1) +6487

6488 עָטוּף *'ātûp* (2)
faint (1)
weak (1)

6489 עֲטִין *'atiyn* (1)
body (1)

6490 עֲטִישָׁה *'atiyšāh* (1)
snorting (1)

6491 עֲטַלֵּף *'atallēp* (3)
bat (2)
bats (1)

6492 עָטָם *'ātām*
Variant; not used

6493 1עָטַף *'ātap1* (3)
clothe (1) +8884
mantled (1)
turns (1)

6494 2עָטַף *'ātap2* (11)
faint (8)
ebbed away (1)
ebbing away (1)
weak (1)

6495 3עָטַף *'ātap3*
Variant; not used

6496 1עָטַר *'ātar1* (2)
closing in (1)
surround (1)

6497 2עָטַר *'ātar2* (5)
crowned (2)
bestower of crowns (1)
crown (1)
crowns (1)

6498 1עֲטָרָה *'atārāh1* (23)
crown (18)
wreath (3)
crowns (2)

6499 2עֲטָרָה *'atārāh2* (1)
Atarah (1)

6500 עֲטָרוֹת *'atārôt* (4)
Ataroth (4)

6501 עֲטָרוֹת אַדָּר *'atārôt 'addār* (2)
Ataroth Addar (2)

6502 עֲטָרוֹת בֵּית יוֹאָב *'atārôt bêt yô'āb* (1)
Atroth Beth Joab (1)

6503 עֲטָרוֹת שׁוֹפָן *'atārôt šôpān* (1)
Atroth Shophan (1)

6504 עַי *'ay* (38)
Ai (36)
city^s (1)
who (1) +408+2021

6505 עִי *'iy* (5)
heap of rubble (3)
broken man (1)
rubble (1)

6506 1עֵיבָל *'êybāl1* (4)
Ebal (4)

6507 2עֵיבָל *'êybāl2* (3)
Ebal (3)

6508 3עֵיבָל *'êybāl3*
Variant; not used

6509 עַיָּה *'ayyāh* (2)
Aija (1)
Ayyah (1)

6510 עִיּוֹן *'iyyôn* (3)
Ijon (3)

6511 עֲיּוֹת *'ayôt* (1)
untranslated (1)

6512 1עִיט *'iyt1* (1)
hurled insults (1)

6513 2עִיט *'iyt2* (2)
pounce (1)
pounced (1)

6514 עַיִט *'ayit* (8)
bird of prey (3)
birds of prey (3)
birds (1)
carrion birds (1) +7606

6515 עֵיטָם *'êytām* (5)
Etam (5)

6516 עִיֵּי הָעֲבָרִים *'iyyēy hā'abāriym* (2)
Iye Abarim (2)

6517 עִיִּים *'iyyiym* (2)
Iim (1)
Iyim (1)

6518 עֵילוֹם *'êylôm*
Variant; not used

6519 עֵילַי *'iylay* (1)
Ilai (1)

6520 1עֵילָם *'êylām1* (16)
Elam (15)
Elam's (1)

6521 2עֵילָם *'êylām2* (13)
Elam (12)
untranslated (1)

6522 עֲיָם *'ayām* (1)
scorching (1)

6523 עַיַן *'āyan* (2)
kept jealous eye on (1)
untranslated (1)

6524 1עַיִן *'ayin1* (896)
eyes (437)
sight (63)
eye (36)
looked (25)
presence (14)
seems (10) +928
spring (10)

seemed (8) +928
think (8) +928
pleased (7) +928+3512
face (6)
look (6)
look with pity (6) +2571
before (5) +4200
displeased (5) +928+8317
look (5) +5951
pleased with (5) +928+2834+5162
pleases (5) +928+3202
seem (4) +928
show pity (4) +2571
to (4) +928
with (4) +928
favorably disposed toward (3) +928+2834
fountain (3)
like (3) +928+3202
looked (3) +5951
saw (3) +928
watch (3) +4200
watched (3) +4200
watching (3)
appearance (2)
by (2) +928
distressed (2) +928+8317
full view (2)
have respect for (2) +928+3700
in presence (2) +4200+5584
look after (2) +6584+8492
looked with pity (2) +2571
on forehead (2) +1068
on foreheads (2) +1068
please (2) +928+3202
please (2) +928+3837
pleased (2) +928+3202
pleased (2) +928+3837
sees (2) +928
sparkled (2)
spring (2) +4784
springs (2) +4784
thought (2) +928
to (2) +4200
watching (2) +4200
angry (1) +928+3013
appealed to (1) +928+3512
appear (1) +928+2118+3869
approve of (1) +928+3202
before (1) +4200+5584
begrudge (1) +8317
by (1) +4200
consider (1) +928
considered (1) +928
cover the offense (1) +4064
despise (1) +928+1022
despise (1) +928+7837
despises (1) +928+1022
despises (1) +928+7837
disappeared (1) +2143+4946
disapprove (1) +928+8317
displease (1) +928+2834+4202+5162
displease (1) +928+8273
displeasing (1) +928+2834+4202+5162
displeasing (1) +928+8273
downcast (1) +8814
eyebrows (1) +1461
eyes (1) +1426
eyesight (1)
favorable toward (1) +928+2834+5162
for (1) +928
fountains (1)
from (1) +928
from (1) +4946
from (1) +4946+5584
front of heads (1) +1068
galled (1) +928+8317
generous man (1) +3202
glad (1) +928+3512
glance (1)
gleam (1)
have no (1) +4946+6259

have no compassion (1) +8317
in broad daylight (1)
             +2021+2021+2296+4200+9087
in front of (1) +4200
in full view (1) +5790
judgment (1)
keeping watch (1) +928+8011
like (1) +3869
liked (1) +928+3837
look (1) +928
look carefully (1) +928+8011
look with compassion (1) +2571
look with longing (1) +5951
looked (1) +906
looked (1) +928+2118
looked about (1) +5951
looks (1) +5951
lost self-confidence (1) +928+4394+5877
never (1) +440
not please (1) +928+8317
not want (1) +928+8273
outward appearance (1)
please (1) +928+2256+3202+3838
please (1) +928+3838
pleased (1) +928+3201
pleased (1) +928+3838
pleased with (1) +928+2834+5951
pleased with (1) +928+3202
pleased with (1) +928+3512
pleased with (1) +928+3837
pleases (1) +928+3512
pools (1)
prefer (1) +928+3202
regards (1) +928+5162
satisfied (1) +928+3512
saw (1) +906+5951
saw (1) +5260
scorned the idea (1) +928+1022
see (1) +448
see (1) +2021+4200+8011
see (1) +4200
see (1) +5260
see (1) +8011
see (1) +8492
see for yourselves (1) +4013+8011
see to it (1) +4200
seem (1) +928+2118
seem (1) +928+4017
seemed (1) +928+2118
show (1)
show ill will (1) +8317
showing pity (1) +2571
sights (1) +5260
sparkles (1) +5989
sparkling (1)
spring (1) +2021+4784
springs (1)
stay awake (1) +7219
stingy (1) +8273
stingy man (1) +8273
those[s] (1)
took notice (1) +5951
troubled (1) +928+8273
unaware (1) +4946+6623
upset (1) +928+8317
us (1) +5646
value (1) +928+1540
value (1) +4718
valued (1) +928+1540
wanted to do (1) +928+3202
watch (1)
watch (1) +928
watches (1)
well (1)
what see (1)
winks maliciously (1) +7975
wish (1) +928+3202
wish (1) +928+3512
wished (1) +928+3202
without being aware (1) +4946
won (1) +928+5951

untranslated (36)

6525 עַיִן 2 'ayin2
Variant; not used

6526 עַיִן 3 'ayin3 (5)
Ain (5)

6527 עֵין גֶּדִי 'ēyn gediy (6)
En Gedi (6)

6528 עֵין גַּנִּים 'ēyn ganniym (3)
En Gannim (3)

6529 עֵין־דֹּאר 'ēyn-dō'r (3)
Endor (3)

6530 עֵין הַקּוֹרֵא 'ēyn haqqôrē' (1)
En Hakkore (1)

6531 עֵין הַתַּנִּין 'ēyn hatanniyn
Variant; not used

6532 עֵין חַדָּה 'ēyn haddāh (1)
En Haddah (1)

6533 עֵין חָצוֹר 'ēyn hāsôr (1)
En Hazor (1)

6534 עֵין חֲרֹד 'ēyn hᵉrōd
Variant; not used

6535 עֵין מִשְׁפָּט 'ēyn mišpāt (1)
En Mishpat (1)

6536 עֵין עֶגְלַיִם 'ēyn 'eglayim (1)
En Eglaim (1)

6537 עֵין רֹגֵל 'ēyn rōgēl (4)
En Rogel (4)

6538 עֵין רִמּוֹן 'ēyn rimmôn (1)
En Rimmon (1)

6539 עֵין שֶׁמֶשׁ 'ēyn šemeš (2)
En Shemesh (2)

6540 עֵין תַּפּוּחַ 'ēyn tappûah (1)
En Tappuah (1)

6541 עֵינוֹן 'ēynôn
Variant; not used

6542 עֵינַיִם 'ēynayim (2)
Enaim (2)

6543 עֵינָם 'ēynām (1)
Enam (1)

6544 עֵינָן 'ēynān (5)
Enan (5)

6545 עָיֵף 'iyp (5)
exhausted (2)
exhausted (1) +4394
faint (1)
fainting (1)

6546 עָיֵף 'āyēp (18)
weary (6)
exhausted (3)
famished (2)
tired (2)
faint (1)
parched (1)
thirsty (1)
weary (1) +5883
worn out (1)

6547 עֵיפָה 1 'ēypāh1 (2)
darkness (1)
deepest night (1) +694+4017

6548 עֵיפָה 2 'ēypāh2 (1)
ephah (1)

6549 עֵיפָה 3 'ēypāh3 (4)
ephah (4)

6550 עֵיפַי 'ēypay (1)
Ephai (1)

6551 עִיר 1 'iyr1 (1092)
city (512)

towns (262)
cities (126)
town (100)
it[s] (10) +2021
villages (8)
hometown (3)
Ai[s] (1) +2021
another[s] (1)
citadel (1)
cities (1) +2256+6551
each town (1) +2256+6551
each towns (1) +6551
every city (1) +2256+6551
fellow townsmen (1) +408
inner shrine (1)
it[s] (1) +2021+2021+2296
its[s] (1)
its[s] (1) +928+2021
places (1)
them[s] (1)
them[s] (1) +824+2021
them[s] (1) +3972
there[s] (1) +928+2021
townspeople (1) +408
villages (1) +7252
which[s] (1)
Ziklag[s] (1) +2021
untranslated (46)

6552 עִיר 2 'iyr2 (2)
anguish (1)
wrath (1)

6553 עִיר 3 'iyr3 (1)
Ir (1)

6554 עִיר 4 'iyr4 (2)
donkey (1)
untranslated (1)

6555 עַיִר 'ayir (7)
donkeys (3)
colt (2)
donkeys' (1)
male donkeys (1)

6556 עִיר הַחֶרֶס 'iyr haheres
Variant; not used

6557 עִיר הַחֶרֶס 'iyr haheres
Variant; not used

6558 עִיר הַמֶּלַח 'iyr hammelah
Variant; not used

6559 עִיר הַתְּמָרִים 'iyr hattᵉmāriym
Variant; not used

6560 עִיר נָחָשׁ 'iyr nāhāš (1)
Ir Nahash (1)

6561 עִיר שֶׁמֶשׁ 'iyr šemeš (1)
Ir Shemesh (1)

6562 עִירָא 'iyrā' (6)
Ira (6)

6563 עִירָד 'iyrād (2)
Irad (2)

6564 עִירוּ 'iyrû (1)
Iru (1)

6565 עִירִי 'iyriy (1)
Iri (1)

6566 עִירָם 'iyrām (2)
Iram (2)

6567 עֵירֹם 'ēyrōm (10)
naked (9)
nakedness (1)

6568 עַיִשׁ 'ayiš (1)
bear (1)

6569 עַיִת 'ayyat (1)
Aiath (1)

6570 עַכְבּוֹר 'akbôr (7)
Acbor (7)

6571 עַכָּבִישׁ 'akkāḇîš (2)
spider's (2)

6572 עַכְבָּר 'akbār (6)
rats (5)
rat (1)

6573 עַכּוֹ 'akkô (1)
Acco (1)

6574 עָכוֹר 'āḵôr (5)
Achor (5)

6575 עָכָן 'āḵān (6)
Achan (6)

6576 עָכַס 'āḵas (1)
ornaments jingling (1)

6577 עֶכֶס 'eḵes (2)
bangles (1)
noose (1) +4591

6578 עַכְסָה 'aḵsāh (5)
Acsah (5)

6579 עָכַר 'āḵar (14)
brings trouble (4)
brought trouble (3)
bring trouble (2)
made trouble (2)
increased (1)
troubler (1)
wretched (1)

6580 עָכָר 'āḵār (1)
Achar (1)

6581 עֶכְרָן 'okrān (5)
Ocran (5)

6582 עַכְשׁוּב 'aḵšûḇ (1)
vipers (1)

6583 עַל 1 'al1 (4)
Most High (4)

6584 עַל 2 'al2 (5780)
on (1149)
against (400)
over (376)
to (319)
for (250)
in (248)
upon (166)
from (155) +4946
at (128)
by (92)
with (79)
of (61)
because of (57)
about (53)
therefore (52) +4027
above (45)
in charge of (43)
that is why (34) +4027
concerning (31)
along (29)
because (29)
around (27)
near (26)
beside (25)
so (25) +4027
into (24)
according to (18)
from (18)
facedown (15) +7156
under (15)
because (14) +889
above (13) +4946
on (13) +7156
why (13) +4537
to (12) +3338
attack (10)
away from (10) +4946
bears (10) +7924
border (10)
over (10) +7156

within (10)
on (9) +4946
toward (9)
after (8)
along with (8)
as (8)
before (8)
near (8) +7156
off (8) +4946
on top of (8)
together with (8)
administrator[s] (7) +889
next to (7) +3338
wearing (7)
attacked (6) +6590
because of (6) +1821
in (6) +7156
in front of (6) +7156
next to (6)
there[s] (6) +2023
among (5)
attack (5) +995
attack (5) +6590
because (5) +3954
because (5) +4027
before (5) +7156
east (5) +7156
for sake (5)
had charge of (5)
next section (5) +3338
this is why (5) +4027
across (4)
bear (4) +7924
because of (4) +128
connected to (4)
enter (4) +6590
have (4)
in accordance with (4)
in addition to (4)
in command (4) +7372
out of (4) +4946
than (4)
upon (4) +7156
about (3) +128
according to (3) +7023
against (3) +4946
attacking (3) +7756
because (3) +1821
burning (3) +836+2021
concerning (3) +1821
covered with (3)
faces (3) +7156
facing (3) +7156
had to (3)
higher than (3) +4946
in opposition to (3)
in spite of (3)
invaded (3) +6590
lusted after (3) +6311
next (3) +3338
on account of (3)
oppose (3)
past (3)
responsible for (3)
rested on (3)
so (3) +2296
tenderly (3) +4213
throughout (3)
top (3)
toward (3) +7156
up to (3)
wear (3) +2118
when (3)
about (2) +1821
according to (2) +3869
across (2) +7156
across from (2) +7156
along (2) +3338
and (2)
as for (2)
as though (2)

as well as (2)
attached to (2)
attacked (2) +995
await (2)
because (2) +3954+4027
before (2) +4946
besides (2)
besiege (2) +2837
by (2) +3338
cover (2)
crown (2)
decorated with (2)
defied (2) +1540
enter (2) +995
fighting (2)
for (2) +1821
for (2) +3954+4027
from (2) +4946+7156
from (2) +7156
got off (2) +4946+7563
in behalf (2)
in front of (2)
inner (2)
look after (2) +6524+8492
lying on (2) +7156
mating with (2) +6590
more than (2)
no wonder (2) +4027
on behalf (2)
onto (2)
outside (2)
over (2) +4946
prostrate (2) +7156
protect (2) +6641
responsibility for (2)
rests on (2)
rule (2) +2118
rule over (2)
seized (2) +5877
separated from (2) +4946
set on (2)
so that (2) +4027
the steward[s] (2) +889
therefore (2) +2296
though (2)
threw arms around (2) +5877+7418
to (2) +7931
too (2)
wore (2)
above (1) +1068
above (1) +4946+5087
above (1) +7156
accompanied by (1) +3338
accuse (1) +7212
add (1)
adjoining (1) +3338
adjoining section (1) +3338
adorned (1) +6590
afraid (1) +5877+7065
against (1) +7156
against side (1)
ahead (1) +7156
all over (1) +6017+6017
all the way to (1)
although (1)
and (1) +4027
and alike (1)
and so (1) +4027
anoint (1)
apart from (1)
aptly (1) +698
aroused (1) +2118
as a result of (1) +1821
as far as (1)
as for (1) +1826
as part of (1)
as prescribed by (1) +3338
assail (1) +5877
assaults (1) +7756
assistant (1) +3338
assisted (1) +3338

assume the responsibility for carrying out (1) +6641
at (1) +6813
at (1) +7156
at flood stage (1) +1536+3972
at flood stage (1) +1536+3972+4848
at heels (1) +7418
at side (1)
attack (1) +3338+6590
attacked (1) +7756
attacked viciously (1) +3751+5782+8797
attacking (1)
attacking (1) +995
attacks (1) +995
attacks (1) +7756
attendants (1) +6641
avert (1) +4946+6296
away (1) +4946
because (1) +1826
because of (1) +3970
because of (1) +4027
because of (1) +4946
because of (1) +6813
because of this (1) +4027
become guilty (1) +2628+5951
been under (1) +6590
below (1) +141+2021
beside (1) +3338
beside (1) +4946
beside (1) +7156
besieged (1) +1215
besieged (1) +2837
better than (1)
between (1)
beyond (1)
binding on (1)
blessed (1)
bordering (1)
borne on (1) +7156
bowed down (1) +5877+7156
bowed down to the ground (1) +5877+7156
bracelets (1) +3338+7543
by (1) +4946
by (1) +7023
care for (1)
cares (1) +4213+8492
carried by (1) +2118
carry on (1) +7756
charged against (1)
commander in chief (1) +2021+7372
confronted (1) +6641
confronted (1) +7756
conquered (1) +2616
consider (1) +4213+8492
contribute (1)
corresponding to (1) +7156
could not (1) +2118
cover (1) +6296
credited to (1)
crossing (1) +7156
crowns (1)
deal with (1)
decide (1) +2118+7023
demanded (1) +7023
depend on (1)
directed to (1)
do anything that endangers life (1) +1947+6641
do not know where am going (1) +889+2143+2143
don't say a word (1) +3338+7023+8492
drove back (1) +2118
during (1)
east (1) +7156+7710
embraced (1) +7418
encircle (1) +7443
encourage (1) +1819+4213
encouraged (1) +1819+4222
encouragingly (1) +4213
entered (1) +995
even beyond (1) +4946

expressed (1) +7023
extend toward (1)
extended (1) +7156
falsely (1) +9214
feed on (1)
fight (1)
follows (1) +7925
for (1) +889
for (1) +1386
for (1) +3338
for (1) +4946
for sake (1) +128
gave a high rank in (1) +8492
given over (1) +3338+5599
got off (1) +3718+4946
governor[s] (1) +889
had (1)
had (1) +2118
had to (1) +2118
hanging on (1)
has (1)
have (1) +2118
help (1)
here[s] (1) +3276
here[s] (1) +3870
higher (1) +4946
highest (1) +8031
his (1) +2257
hold accountable (1) +5989
how (1)
how (1) +4027
in (1) +4946
in accordance with (1) +7023
in behalf (1) +3208
in behalf of (1)
in behalf of (1) +1821
in charge (1) +6641
in control (1)
in hands (1)
in hostility toward (1) +7156
in little more than (1) +3427
in preference to (1) +7156
in presence (1)
in presence of (1)
in store for (1)
in the light of (1)
in the presence of (1)
in the way should go (1) +2006+7023
including (1)
increase (1) +3578
instead of (1) +4030
invade (1) +6590
invaded (1) +995
its (1) +2023
jealous (1) +6296+7863+8120
join (1) +2143
join (1) +2616
keeper[s] (1) +889
kneeling (1) +1386+4156
knelt down (1) +1384+1386
laid siege to (1) +2837
leader (1)
leads to (1)
lie with (1) +995
lingering (1) +3427+3427
little by little (1) +3338
lived in hostility toward (1) +5877+7156
load (1)
loaded with (1)
longed for (1)
make wear (1) +5516+6590
manned (1)
marched past (1) +3338+6296
more and more (1) +3578+3972
mounted like jewels (1) +3782+4859
near (1) +3338
nearby (1)
nearby (1) +3338
nearest (1) +7156
object of malicious talk (1) +4383+6590+8557

obligates (1)
of (1) +4946
on (1) +7023
on behalf of (1)
on foot (1) +824+2021
on no account (1) +224
on side (1)
opposed (1) +599
opposed (1) +6641
over (1) +4200+4946
over higher (1)
overflow (1) +6590
overpower (1) +4309
overpowered (1) +3338+6451
overruled (1) +2616
overwhelm (1) +995
overwhelmed (1) +5877
part (1)
part of (1)
past (1) +4946
peels (1) +4946
persuade (1) +1819+4213
placed on (1)
presence (1) +4946
protects (1) +6641
put in charge (1) +3338+6641
put in charge of the storerooms (1) +238+732
reaches to (1)
reason (1)
received gladly (1) +8523
reclining (1)
regarding (1)
reign over (1)
reject (1) +4946+7156+8938
reject (1) +4946+7156+8959
repay (1) +8031+8740
required (1) +2011
required of (1)
resolved (1) +4213+8492
responsible (1)
rest on (1)
rid (1) +4946+8959
ring (1)
ruled over (1)
serve (1) +6641
set against (1)
share in (1) +5951
shave (1) +7947
simply (1) +7023
since (1)
since (1) +3954+4027
since (1) +4027
sleep with (1) +4156
so (1) +3869
spoken kindly (1) +1819+4213
stand up (1) +6641+6642
steward[s] (1) +408+889+1074+2021
steward[s] (1) +889+1074
strike (1)
succeeded (1) +4030+6641
successor (1) +4030+6641
suffer (1) +5989
supervised (1)
supporting (1)
surely leave (1) +2143+2143+4946
take (1) +995
take care of (1)
take off (1) +3718+4946
takes (1) +3782
that (1) +4027
that's why (1) +4027
the duty of (1)
their (1) +2157
their[s] (1) +3776
then (1) +4027
there[s] (1) +2157
therefore (1) +1826+8611
think (1) +4222+6590
think about (1) +4213+6590
this is why (1) +465

threw arms around (1) +5877
throughout (1) +3972+7156
tie (1) +5989
to (1) +4200+7156
to (1) +4946
to reach (1)
took up (1) +6641
touches (1) +2118
toward (1) +2006
toward (1) +2006+7156
under guard (1) +5464
upside down (1) +7156
used (1)
used for (1)
using (1)
voluntarily (1) +408+4213+6590
watch over (1) +8492
wear (1) +6590
wearing around (1)
weigh down (1)
what (1) +4537
when (1) +889
where[s] (1) +2157
where[s] (1) +6642
wherever (1) +889+2021+3972+5226
wherever (1) +889+3972
which way (1) +196+3545+6584+8520
while still alive (1) +7156
why (1) +2296
will (1) +7023
with (1) +3338
with (1) +7156
worn (1)
yet (1)
your (1) +3871
your (1) +4013
untranslated (913)

6585 עֹל *'ōl* (40)
yoke (36)
it[s] (3)
yoked (1) +6590

6586 עַל־כֵּן *'al-kēn*
Variant; not used

6587 עֻלָּא *'ullā'* (1)
Ulla (1)

6588 עַלְבוֹן *'albôn*
Variant; not used

6589 עִלֵּג *'illēg* (1)
stammering (1)

6590 עָלָה *'ālāh* (901)
went up (111)
go up (76)
brought up (46)
came up (31)
go (24)
bring up (23)
come up (23)
offered (14)
come (13)
sacrificed (13)
offer (12)
up (12)
attack (11)
sacrifice (11)
gone up (10)
bring (9)
coming up (9)
lifted (9)
rise (8)
rises (8)
went (8)
climbed (7)
attacked (6) +6584
led up (6)
marched up (6)
set up (6)
ascended (5)
attack (5) +6584

attacked (5)
came (5)
chews (5)
marched (5)
presented (5)
rising (5)
sacrificing (5)
take up (5)
ascend (4)
attack (4) +448
brought (4)
chew (4)
climb up (4)
conscripted (4)
enter (4) +6584
goes up (4)
going up (4)
grow (4)
return (4)
rose (4)
send up (4)
took (4)
climbed up (3)
grew up (3)
growing (3)
invaded (3) +6584
lying on (3)
makes rise (3)
march (3)
offered sacrifices (3)
offerings (3)
present (3)
returned (3)
used (3)
withdraw (3)
withdrew (3)
advance (2)
advances (2)
aroused (2)
assemble (2)
attacking (2)
carried (2)
carried up (2)
carry up (2)
climb (2)
climbs (2)
daybreak (2) +2021+8840
get (2)
go back (2)
go on up (2)
go straight up (2)
gone (2)
got on (2)
imported (2) +2256+3655
invaded (2)
is (2)
lift (2)
made (2)
mating with (2) +6584
offered up (2)
offering (2)
raged (2)
reached (2)
reaches (2)
sets up (2)
soar (2)
spring up (2)
sprinkled (2)
take (2)
taken (2)
withdrawn (2)
accompanied (1) +907
adorned (1) +6584
advanced (1)
appeared (1)
approach (1)
are exalted (1)
are recorded (1)
ascending (1)
ascent (1)
assemble (1) +928+2021+7736

at (1) +3869
attack (1) +3338+6584
attacked (1) +928
attacking (1) +448
attacks (1)
back (1)
been under (1) +6584
billowed up (1)
blazed up (1)
blossomed (1) +5890
blow away (1)
blowing in (1)
bring back (1)
bringing up (1)
brought along (1)
brought back (1)
building (1)
burning (1)
carried away (1)
casting up (1)
charge (1)
charged (1)
charging (1)
chosen (1)
climbed in (1)
climbing up (1)
come back (1)
comes (1)
comes out (1)
coming (1)
coming out (1)
consider (1)
continued (1)
continued up (1)
decorated (1)
deserted (1) +339+4946
drag away (1)
entered (1)
evening sacrifice (1) +4966
exalted (1)
falls (1)
filled (1)
first light of dawn (1) +8840
flare up (1)
flared (1)
flourishing (1)
flowed over (1)
followed (1) +928+8079
gathered (1)
get up (1)
goes (1)
going (1)
gone ahead (1)
grow up (1)
had come up (1)
had go up (1)
haul up (1)
have (1)
headed (1)
helped up (1)
invade (1) +928
invade (1) +6584
invaded (1) +448
invaded (1) +928
is on way (1)
kept burning (1)
lead (1)
leading to (1)
leave (1) +4946
left (1) +4946
lights (1)
made come up (1)
made grow up (1)
make come (1)
make come up (1)
make offerings (1)
make wear (1) +5516+6584
makes offering (1)
making (1)
mount (1)
mounted up (1)

move away (1)
moved away (1)
moved up (1)
object of malicious talk (1)
                  +4383+6584+8557
offer up (1)
offers (1)
on (1)
on way (1)
on way up (1)
overflow (1) +6584
overgrown (1)
overrun (1)
paid (1)
passed (1)
presented offerings (1)
progressed (1)
pull out (1)
pulls up (1)
put on (1)
raises up (1)
ran (1)
ran up (1)
reached (1) +448
restore (1)
retreated (1)
sacrifice (1) +4966
sacrifice (1) +6592
scale (1)
send (1)
serve (1)
should go up (1) +6590
sprinkle (1)
stepped out (1)
steps (1)
stir up (1)
stirs up (1)
stopped (1) +4946
surely bring back (1) +6590
surpass (1)
swarm (1)
take away (1)
taken up (1)
think (1) +4222+6584
think about (1) +4213+6584
took up (1)
upper (1)
voluntarily (1) +408+4213+6584
walking (1)
wear (1)
wear (1) +6584
weighed (1)
went back (1)
went off (1)
went over (1)
worked (1)
yoked (1) +6585
untranslated (22)

6591 עָלֶה *'āleh* (18)
leaves (7)
leaf (5)
branches (1)
green leaf (1)
untranslated (4)

6592 1עֹלָה *'ōlāh1* (288)
burnt offering (159)
burnt offerings (109)
offering (7)
sacrifice (2)
burnt (1)
it^s (1) +2021
its^s (1) +2021
offerings (1)
sacrifice (1) +6590
sacrifices (1)
them^s (1)
untranslated (4)

6593 2עֹלָה *'ōlāh2*
Variant; not used

6594 1עַלְוָה *'alwāh1* (1)
evildoers (1) +1201

6595 2עַלְוָה *'alwāh2* (2)
Alvah (2)

6596 עֲלוּמִים *'ălûmiym* (5)
youth (3)
youthful vigor (1)
untranslated (1)

6597 עַלְוָן *'alwān* (2)
Alvan (2)

6598 עֲלוּקָה *'ălûqāh* (1)
leech (1)

6599 עָלוֹת *'ālôt* (1)
Aloth (1)

6600 עָלַז *'ālaz* (17)
rejoice (7)
jubilant (2)
triumph (2)
glad (1)
leaps for joy (1)
made merry (1)
reveling (1)
shout with laughter (1)
untranslated (1)

6601 עָלֵז *'ālēz* (1)
revelers (1)

6602 עֲלָטָה *'ălāṭāh* (4)
dusk (3)
darkness (1)

6603 1עֵלִי *'ēliy1* (33)
Eli (27)
Eli's (4)
who^s (1)
untranslated (1)

6604 2עֵלִי *'ēliy2* (1)
Most High (1)

6605 עֱלִי *'ĕliy* (1)
pestle (1)

6606 עִלִּי *'illiy* (2)
upper (2)

6607 עֲלָיָה *'ălāyāh* (1)
untranslated (1)

6608 עֲלִיָּה *'ăliyyāh* (19)
upper room (6)
room (4)
room above (2)
upper chambers (2)
upper parts (2)
upper rooms (2)
room over (1)

6609 1עֶלְיוֹן *'elyôn1* (22)
upper (15)
high (2)
imposing (2)
top (2)
most exalted (1)

6610 2עֶלְיוֹן *'elyôn2* (31)
Most High (31)

6611 עַלִּיז *'alliyz* (7)
revelry (3)
rejoice (2)
carefree (1)
revelers (1)

6612 עֲלִיל *'ăliyl* (1)
furnace (1)

6613 עֲלִילָה *'ăliylāh* (24)
actions (6)
what done (5)
deeds (4)
did (1)
do (1)
done (1)

mighty deeds (1)
misdeeds (1)
practices (1)
slandered (1) +1821+8492
slanders (1) +1821+8492
works (1)

6614 עֲלִילִיָּה *'ăliyliyyāh* (1)
deeds (1)

6615 עַלְיָן *'alyān*
Variant; not used

6616 עָלִיץ *'āliyṣ*
Variant; not used

6617 עֲלִיצֻת *'ăliyṣut* (1)
gloating (1)

6618 1עָלַל *'ālal1* (18)
abuse (2)
abused (1)
brings grief (1)
cut down (1)
deal (1)
dealt (1)
dealt harshly (1)
glean thoroughly (1) +6618
go over a second time (1)
go over the vines again (1) +339
made a fool (1)
mistreat (1)
take part in (1)
treated (1)
treated harshly (1)
was inflicted (1)

6619 2עָלַל *'ālal2* (1)
buried (1)

6620 3עָלַל *'ālal3* (1)
youths (1)

6621 4עָלַל *'ālal4*
Variant; not used

6622 עֹלֵלוֹת *'ōlēlôt* (6)
few grapes (2)
gleanings (2)
gleaning (1)
gleanings of grapes (1)

6623 עָלַם *'ālam* (29)
hidden (4)
ignore (4)
unaware of (3) +4946
hard (2)
hide (2)
bring (1)
close (1)
close (1) +6623
closes (1)
hiding (1)
hypocrites (1)
make shut (1)
obscures (1)
secret (1)
shut (1)
swollen (1)
turn away (1)
unaware (1) +4946+6524

6624 עֶלֶם *'elem* (2)
boy (1)
young man (1)

6625 עַלְמָה *'almāh* (7)
maiden (2)
maidens (2)
girl (1)
virgin (1)
virgins (1)

6626 עַלְמוֹן *'almôn* (1)
Almon (1)

6627 עַלְמוֹן דִּבְלָתָיִם *'almôn diblātayim* (2)
Almon Diblathaim (2)

6628 עֲלָמוֹת *'ǎlāmôṯ* (2)
alamoth (2)

6629 עַל־מוּת *'al-mûṯ*
Variant; not used

6630 1עָלֶמֶת *'ālemeṯ1* (1)
Alemeth (1)

6631 2עָלֶמֶת *'ālemeṯ2* (3)
Alemeth (3)

6632 עָלַס *'ālas* (3)
enjoy (1)
enjoy ourselves (1)
flap joyfully (1)

6633 עָלַע *'āla'* (1)
feast on (1)

6634 עָלַף *'ālap* (6)
faint (2)
decorated (1)
disguise herself (1)
fainted (1)
withered away (1)

6635 עָלְפֶּה *'ulpeh*
Variant; not used

6636 עָלַץ *'ālas* (8)
rejoice (3)
rejoices (2)
triumph (2)
jubilant (1)

6637 עָלָתָה *'ōlāṯāh* (2)
injustice (1)
untranslated (1)

6638 1עַם *'am1* (32)
people (32)

6639 2עַם *'am2* (1836)
people (1261)
peoples (100)
nations (90)
men (72)
army (48)
troops (31)
they^s (28) +2021
them^s (16) +2021
people (14) +1426
soldiers (10)
nation (9)
people (8) +1201
people's (7)
countrymen (6) +1201
fighting men (6)
those^s (5) +2021
army (4) +4878
Israelites^s (4)
nationality (4)
others^s (4)
each people (3) +2256+6639
them (3) +2021
common people (2) +1201
creatures (2)
everyone (2) +2021+3972
humble (2) +6714
lay people (2) +1201
lives (2)
one^s (2) +2021
their^s (2) +2021
them^s (2) +2021+3972
they^s (2) +824+2021
those^s (2)
anyone else^s (1)
army (1) +2256+7736
common people (1)
community (1) +824+2021
everyone (1)
exalted (1) +5294
fellow townsmen (1) +9133
followers (1) +339+889+2021
following (1) +907
force (1) +4878

force of men (1)
forces (1)
foreigners (1) +5799
guests (1)
Israel (1) +3776
Israelites (1) +1201+3776
it^s (1) +2021
leaders (1) +8031
man (1)
merchants (1) +4047
multitude (1)
nationalities (1)
native (1) +1201
one another (1) +2021
one of the other peoples (1) +2256+6639
other nationalities (1) +824+2021
people's (1) +4200
person (1)
population (1)
soldier (1)
soldiers (1) +7372
someone (1) +285+2021
their^s (1) +824+2021
their^s (1) +3276+3776
them^s (1) +2021+2021+2296
them^s (1) +2257
them^s (1) +3276
they^s (1)
they^s (1) +2021+3972
those^s (1) +339+889+2021
various peoples (1) +2256+6639
untranslated (37)

6640 עִם *'im* (1049)
with (527)
to (63)
against (42)
and (25)
from (25) +4946
among (24)
in (15)
for (13)
near (12)
along with (11)
toward (10)
together with (8)
at (7)
before (7)
like (7)
on (5)
sleeps with (5) +8886
join (4)
lie with (4) +8886
of (4) +4946
away from (3) +4946
beside (3)
by (3)
have (3)
help (3)
slept with (3) +8886
accompanied by (2)
accompany (2)
also (2)
around (2)
as well as (2)
by (2) +4946
come to bed with (2) +8886
has sexual relations with (2) +8886
help (2) +2118
his (2) +2257
in company with (2)
into (2)
lay with (2) +8886
sleep with (2) +8886
to (2) +4946
to belong (2)
accompanied by (1) +2143
accomplice (1) +2745
allies^s (1) +8611
allots to (1)
and alike (1)
and all (1)

as long as (1)
aside (1)
attitude (1)
away (1) +4946
because of (1)
bed with (1) +8886
before (1) +4946
belong to (1)
besides (1)
both and (1)
call to account (1) +2011+4946
concerning (1)
convictions (1) +4222
decided (1) +2118+4213
demand (1)
desire (1)
despite (1)
done this^s (1) +8886
dwell with (1)
endued with (1)
even as (1)
followed (1)
followed (1) +3655
followers (1) +408+889+2143
from (1)
from (1) +4946+7156
gave strong support (1) +2616
give (1)
harbor (1) +2118+4222
has (1)
has (1) +2118
he^s (1) +408+2021+2021+8886
help (1) +3338
help (1) +3338+8883
here (1)
here^s (1) +3276
impartially (1) +465+465
in mind (1)
in spite of (1)
in store (1)
in the care of (1)
in the presence of (1)
intend (1) +4222
join (1) +2143
leave (1) +2143+4946
left (1) +2143+4946
lies with (1) +8886
manned by (1)
my (1) +3276
of (1)
on terms (1) +4946
present (1)
rapes (1) +2256+2616+8886
rapes (1) +2256+8886+9530
share their duties (1) +465
sided with (1) +3338
sleeping with (1) +8886
support (1)
supports (1) +2616
take part (1) +2143
the LORD's (1) +3378+4946
took care of (1)
treated (1) +2118
treated (1) +6913
when (1)
where (1)
with help (1)
with the help of (1)
withstand (1) +3656
untranslated (106)

6641 עָמַד *'āmaḏ* (525)
stood (82)
stand (64)
standing (53)
stopped (19)
appointed (10)
stationed (8)
stands (7)
stay (7)
stop (7)
assigned (6)

present (6)
serve (6) +4200+7156
stood still (6)
endure (5)
stand up (5)
stood up (5)
arise (4)
endures (4)
have stand (4)
ministering (4)
put in place (4)
set (4)
stayed (4)
had stand (3)
presented (3)
raised (3)
remain (3)
remains (3)
serve (3)
set in place (3)
stand firm (3)
appear (2)
appoint (2)
came to a halt (2)
confirmed (2)
delay (2)
enables to stand (2)
entered service (2) +4200+7156
last (2)
minister (2)
perform (2)
propped up (2)
protect (2) +6584
remained (2)
resist (2) +4200+7156
rise (2)
rose up (2)
served (2)
served (2) +4200+7156
serving (2) +4200+7156
set up (2)
stand ground (2)
stayed behind (2)
take stand (2)
took places (2)
took stand (2)
unchanged (2)
unchanged (2) +9393
upright (2)
wait (2)
withstand (2) +928+7156
withstand (2) +4200+7156
act (1)
appeared (1)
appointing (1)
as did[s] (1)
assist (1) +907
assistant (1) +4200+7156
assume the responsibility for carrying out (1)
    +6584
attend (1) +4200+7156
attendants (1) +6584
avoid (1)
be (1)
be presented (1)
broke out (1)
built (1)
calm (1)
can[s] (1)
claim (1)
come (1)
come forward (1)
confronted (1) +6584
crowd (1) +889+3972
decided (1) +1821
defend (1) +5584
do anything that endangers life (1)
    +1947+6584
emerge (1)
enduring (1)
enter service (1) +4200+7156

entered the service (1) +4200+7156
establish (1)
face (1)
fulfillment (1)
gets up (1)
gives stability (1)
gives way (1) +4202
gone (1) +928+4202
had pledge (1)
had serve (1)
halt (1)
halted (1)
held (1)
in charge (1) +6584
installed (1)
joined together (1) +285+3869
keep on (1)
leave alone (1) +4946
linger (1)
live (1)
made stand (1)
making strong (1)
muster (1)
occupied (1) +448
on duty (1)
opposed (1) +6584
performed (1)
persists (1)
pillar (1)
pledged (1)
position (1)
post (1)
posted (1)
posting (1)
protects (1) +6584
put in charge (1) +3338+6584
putting in place (1)
raise (1)
raised up (1)
reach (1)
rebuilding (1)
rebuilt (1)
rely (1)
repair (1)
replaced (1) +9393
represent (1)
resist (1)
resisted (1) +4200+5584
rise up (1)
rises (1)
serve (1) +6584
served (1) +907+7156
sets up (1)
stand the strain (1)
stand up (1) +6584+6642
standing trial (1)
stands firm (1)
stared with a fixed gaze (1)
    +906+2256+7156+8492
staying (1)
stays (1)
stirred up (1)
stood by (1)
stood firm (1)
stood in places (1)
stood waiting (1)
succeed (1)
succeeded (1) +4030+6584
successor (1) +4030+6584
successor (1) +9393
surviving (1)
to feet (1)
tolerated (1)
took (1)
took up (1) +6584
uphold (1)
was (1)
were (1)
withstood (1) +928+7156
worked (1)
untranslated (9)

6642 עֹמֵד *'ōmeḏ* (8)
feet (1)
place where standing (1)
places (1)
positions (1)
posts (1)
stand up (1) +6584+6641
standing (1)
where[s] (1) +6584

6643 עִמָּד *'immāḏ* (45)
with (16)
to (6)
against (2)
in (2)
besides (1)
for (1)
leave (1) +2143+4946
mine (1) +3276
oppose (1)
oppose (1) +8189
surround (1)
toward (1)
untranslated (11)

6644 עֶמְדָה *'emdāh* (1)
protection (1)

6645 1עֻמָּה *'ummāh1* (32)
close to (5) +4200
along with (2) +4200
as (2) +4200
beside (2) +4200
just as (2) +4200
parallel to (2) +4200
above (1) +4200+4946+4946+5087
adjoining (1) +4200
alike (1) +4200
alongside (1) +4200
alongside of (1) +4200
as (1) +3972+8611
as well as (1) +4200
at (1) +4200
bordering (1) +4200
length (1) +4200
like (1) +4200
opposite (1) +4200
responding to (1) +4200
treated the same as (1) +4200
with (1) +4200
untranslated (2)

6646 2עֻמָּה *'ummāh2* (1)
Ummah (1)

6647 עַמּוּד *'ammûḏ* (112)
pillars (38)
posts (36)
pillar (25)
columns (2)
colonnade (1) +395
column (1)
one[s] (1)
untranslated (8)

6648 עַמּוֹן *'ammôn* (106)
Ammonites (79) +1201
Ammon (9) +1201
Ammonite (8) +1201
Ammon (5)
Ammonites (1)
their[s] (1) +1201
them[s] (1) +1201
they[s] (1) +1201
untranslated (1)

6649 עַמּוֹנִי *'ammôniy* (21)
Ammonite (13)
Ammonites (6)
Ammon (1)
untranslated (1)

6650 עָמוֹס *'āmôs* (7)
Amos (7)

6651 עָמוֹק 'āmôq (2)
Amok (1)
Amok's (1)

6652 עַמִּי 'ammiy
Variant; not used

6653 עַמִּיאֵל 'ammiy'ēl (6)
Ammiel (6)

6654 עַמִּיהוּד 'ammiyhûd (10)
Ammihud (10)

6655 עַמִּיזָבָד 'ammiyzābād (1)
Ammizabad (1)

6656 עַמִּיחוּר 'ammiyhûr (1)
untranslated (1)

6657 עַמִּינָדָב 'ammiynādāb (13)
Amminadab (13)

6658 עָמִיר 'āmiyr (4)
sheaves (1)
cut grain (1)
grain (1)

6659 עַמִּישַׁדָּי 'ammiyšaddāy (5)
Ammishaddai (5)

6660 עָמִית 'āmiyt (12)
neighbor (4)
anotherˢ (1)
close (1)
countryman (1)
countrymen (1)
himˢ (1)
himˢ (1) +2257
neighbor's (1)
otherˢ (1)

6661 עָמָל 'āmal (11)
labor (3)
toils (2)
efforts (1)
poured effort (1)
tend (1)
toiled (1)
worked (1)
works (1)

6662 1עָמָל 'āmāl1 (55)
trouble (15)
work (8)
labor (5)
misery (5)
toil (5)
oppressive (2)
toilsome (2)
wrong (2)
abuse (1)
bitter labor (1)
burdens (1)
distress (1)
efforts (1)
making trouble (1)
miserable (1)
suffering (1)
thingsˢ (1)
what toiled for (1)
whatˢ (1)

6663 2עָמָל 'āmāl2 (1)
Amal (1)

6664 1עָמֵל 'āmēl1 (4)
misery (2)
laborer's (1)
workman's (1)

6665 2עָמֵל 'āmēl2 (5)
labors (1)
toil (1)
toiled for (1)
toiling (1)
toilsome (1)

6666 עַמְלֵק 'amlēs
Variant; not used

6667 עֲמָלֵק 'ᵃmālēq (39)
Amalekites (25)
Amalek (12)
Amalekite (1)
theirˢ (1)

6668 עֲמָלֵקִי 'ᵃmālēqiy (12)
Amalekites (9)
Amalekite (3)

6669 1עָמַם 'āmam1 (1)
rival (1)

6670 2עָמַם 'āmam2 (2)
hidden (1)
lost luster (1)

6671 עַמֹּנָה 'ammōnāh (1)
untranslated (1)

6672 עִמָּנוּ אֵל 'immānû 'ēl (2)
Immanuel (2)

6673 עָמַס 'āmas (9)
laid (2)
bears burdens (1)
burdensome (1)
carried (1) +5951
loaded (1)
loading (1)
move (1)
upheld (1)

6674 עֲמַסְיָה 'ᵃmasyāh (1)
Amasiah (1)

6675 עַמְעָד 'am'ād (1)
Amad (1)

6676 עָמַק 'āmaq (9)
deep (3)
deepest (1)
go to great depths (1)
greatly (1)
made deep (1)
profound (1)
sunk deep (1)

6677 עֵמֶק 'ēmeq (68)
valley (52)
valleys (11)
plain (2)
fiercely (1) +928+2021
plain (1) +824
plains (1)

6678 עָמֹק 'āmōq (17)
deep (13)
cunning (1)
deeper (1)
most profound (1) +6678

6679 עֹמֶק 'ōmeq (2)
deep (1)
depths (1)

6680 עָמֵק 'āmēq (3)
obscure (2)
obscure (1) +4946+9048

6681 עֵמֶק קָצִיץ 'ēmeq q'siys (1)
Emek Keziz (1)

6682 1עָמַר 'āmar1 (1)
gathers (1)

6683 2עָמַר 'āmar2 (2)
treat as a slave (1)
treats as a slave (1)

6684 1עֹמֶר 'ōmer1 (8)
sheaf (4)
sheaves (3)
sheaf of grain (1)

6685 2עֹמֶר 'ōmer2 (6)
omer (5)
omers (1)

6686 עֲמֹרָה 'ᵃmōrāh (19)
Gomorrah (19)

6687 עָמְרִי 'omriy (18)
Omri (15)
Omri's (2)
heˢ (1) +281+1201

6688 עַמְרָם 'amrām (14)
Amram (13)
Amram's (1)

6689 עַמְרָמִי 'amrāmiy (2)
Amramites (2)

6690 עֲמָשָׂא 'ᵃmāśā' (16)
Amasa (15)
whoseˢ (1)

6691 עֲמָשַׂי 'ᵃmāśay (5)
Amasai (5)

6692 עֲמַשְׂסַי 'ᵃmaśsay (1)
Amashsai (1)

6693 עֲנָב 'ᵃnāb (2)
Anab (2)

6694 עֵנָב 'ēnāb (19)
grapes (12)
good grapes (2)
grape (1)
grapes or raisins (1) +2256+3313+4300
raisin (1)
untranslated (1)

6695 עָנַג 'ānag (10)
delight (2)
find delight (2)
delicate (1)
delight yourself (1)
enjoy (1)
find joy (1)
mocking (1)
sensitive (1)

6696 עֹנֶג 'ōneg (2)
delight (1)
luxurious (1)

6697 עָנֹג 'ānōg (3)
sensitive (2)
delicate (1)

6698 עָנַד 'ānad (2)
fasten (1)
put on (1)

6699 1עָנָה 'ānāh1 (314)
answered (74)
answer (73)
replied (41)
said (29)
answers (9)
asked (7)
respond (7)
responded (6)
testify (5)
reply (4)
testifies (4)
spoke (3)
answering (2)
declare (2)
give (2)
help (2)
said in reply (2)
spoke up (2)
accept (1)
accuse (1)
answer (1) +1821
answer given (1)
arguing (1)
be answered (1)
come to relief (1)
dispute (1)
echo (1)
explained (1)
gave ruling (1)
get response (1)
give answer (1)

give testimony (1)
gives (1)
gives back answer (1)
giving testimony (1)
go unanswered (1) +4202
had[s] (1)
have answer (1)
have say (1) +2750
recite (1) +606+2256
reported (1)
said a word (1)
save (1)
say (1)
say (1) +606+2256
says (1)
shout (1)
shouted (1)
tell (1)
testified (1)
testify (1) +4200+6332
testimony (1)
told (1)
whoever he may be (1) +2256+6424
untranslated (4)

6700 2עָנָה ʿānāh2 (81)
afflicted (12)
deny (6)
oppress (5)
humble (4)
oppressed (4)
humbled (3)
subdue (3)
afflict (2)
humble yourself (2)
mistreated (2)
raped (2)
violated (2)
be afflicted (1)
bring affliction (1)
broke (1)
bruised (1)
deny himself (1)
disgraced (1)
dishonored (1)
disturbed (1)
do[s] (1) +6700
force (1)
hardships endured (1)
humble ourselves (1)
made suffer (1)
mistreat (1)
oppressors (1)
overwhelmed (1)
punish (1)
raped (1) +2256+8886
ravished (1)
shared hardships (1) +889+928+6700
stilled (1)
stoop down (1)
subdued (1)
submit (1)
suffered (1)
suffered affliction (1)
take advantage of (1)
use (1)
violate women (1)
violated (1) +2256+8886
violates (1)
untranslated (1)

6701 3עָנָה ʿānāh3 (3)
burden (2) +6721
keeps occupied (1)

6702 4עָנָה ʿānāh4 (15)
sing (6)
sang (4)
sound (2) +7754
howl (1)
shout in triumph (1) +2116
singing (1)

6703 עֹנָה ʿōnāh (1)
marital rights (1)

6704 עֲנָה ʿᵃnāh (12)
Anah (12)

6705 עָנָו ʿānāw (25)
humble (7)
afflicted (4)
poor (4)
oppressed (2)
afflicted (1) +6714
helpless (1)
meek (1)
needy (1)
them[s] (1)
untranslated (3)

6706 עֻנּוֹ ʿunnô (1)
untranslated (1)

6707 עָנוּב ʿānûḇ (1)
Anub (1)

6708 עֲנָוָה ʿᵃnāwāh (6)
humility (5)
stoop down (1)

6709 עַנְוָה ʿanwāh
Variant; not used

6710 עֲנוֹק ʿᵃnôq (1)
Anak (1)

6711 עֲנוּשִׁים ʿᵃnûšiym (1)
fines (1)

6712 עֲנוֹת ʿᵃnôṯ
Variant; not used

6713 עֲנוּת ʿᵃnûṯ (1)
suffering (1)

6714 עָנִי ʿāniy (79)
poor (40)
afflicted (14)
oppressed (4)
needy (3)
helpless (2)
humble (2) +6639
weak (2)
afflicted (1) +6705
distress (1)
gentle (1)
humble (1)
meek (1)
suffer (1)
wretched (1)
untranslated (5)

6715 עֱנִי ʿᵉniy (37)
affliction (14)
suffering (9)
misery (8)
distress (1)
grief (1)
hardship (1)
oppressed (1) +1201
persecute (1)
taken great pains (1) +928

6716 עֻנִּי ʿunniy (3)
Unni (3)

6717 עֲנָיָה ʿᵃnāyāh (2)
Anaiah (2)

6718 עָנָיו ʿānāyw
Variant; not used

6719 עָנִים ʿāniym (1)
Anim (1)

6720 עֵנִים ʿêniym (1)
untranslated (1)

6721 עִנְיָן ʿinyān (8)
burden (2) +6701
business (1)
cares (1)

labor (1)
misfortune (1) +8273
task (1)
work (1)

6722 עֲנֵם ʿᵃnêm (1)
Anem (1)

6723 עֲנָמִים ʿᵃnāmiym (2)
Anamites (2)

6724 עֲנַמֶּלֶךְ ʿᵃnammelek̲ (1)
Anammelech (1)

6725 1עָנַן ʿānan1 (1)
bring clouds (1) +6727

6726 2עָנַן ʿānan2 (10)
practiced sorcery (2)
sorcery (2)
cast spells (1)
mediums (1)
practice divination (1)
practice sorcery (1)
soothsayers' (1)
sorceress (1)

6727 1עָנָן ʿānān1 (87)
cloud (63)
clouds (17)
mist (2)
bring clouds (1) +6725
it[s] (1) +2021
morning mist (1)
smoke (1)
them[s] (1)

6728 2עָנָן ʿānān2 (1)
Anan (1)

6729 עֲנָנָה ʿᵃnānāh (1)
cloud (1)

6730 עֲנָנִי ʿᵃnāniy (1)
Anani (1)

6731 1עֲנַנְיָה ʿᵃnanʿyāh1 (1)
Ananiah (1)

6732 2עֲנַנְיָה ʿᵃnanʿyāh2 (1)
Ananiah (1)

6733 עָנָף ʿānāp̲ (7)
branches (6)
branch (1)

6734 עָנֵף ʿānêp̲ (1)
full of branches (1)

6735 עָנַק ʿānaq (3)
necklace (1)
supply liberally (1) +6735

6736 1עֲנָק ʿᵃnāq1 (3)
chain (1)
chains (1)
jewel (1)

6737 2עֲנָק ʿᵃnāq2 (17)
Anakites (7)
Anak (6)
Anakites (4) +1201

6738 1עָנֵר ʿānêr1 (2)
Aner (2)

6739 2עָנֵר ʿānêr2 (1)
Aner (1)

6740 עָנַשׁ ʿānaš (8)
suffer (2)
fine (1)
imposed a levy (1)
must be fined (1) +6740
punish (1)
punished (1)

6741 עֹנֶשׁ ʿōneš (2)
levy (1)
penalty (1)

6742 עֲנָת ʿᵃnāṯ (2)
Anath (2)

6743 1עֲנָתוֹת *'ᵃnātôt1* (13)
Anathoth (13)

6744 2עֲנָתוֹת *'ᵃnātôt2* (2)
Anathoth (2)

6745 עֲנְתֹתִי *'ann'tōtiy* (5)
from Anathoth (3)
Anathothite (2)

6746 עֲנְתֹתִיָּה *'antōtiyyāh* (1)
Anthothijah (1)

6747 עָסִיס *'āsiys* (5)
new wine (3)
nectar (1)
wine (1)

6748 עָסַס *'āsas* (1)
trample down (1)

6749 עָעַר *'ā'ar*
Variant; not used

6750 עֲפָאִים *'ᵃpā'yim*
Variant; not used

6751 עֳפִי *'ᵒpiy* (1)
branches (1)

6752 1עָפַל *'āpal1* (1)
puffed up (1)

6753 2עָפַל *'āpal2* (1)
presumption (1)

6754 1עֹפֶל *'ōpel1* (6)
tumors (6)

6755 2עֹפֶל *'ōpel2* (8)
hill of Ophel (4)
citadel (1)
hill (1)
Ophel (1)
stronghold (1)

6756 עָפְנִי *'opniy* (1)
Ophni (1)

6757 עַפְעַפַּיִם *'ap'appayim* (10)
eyelids (3)
eyes (3)
first rays (1)
gaze (1)
glances (1)
rays (1)

6758 עָפַף *'āpap* (1)
brandish (1)

6759 עָפַר *'āpar* (1)
showering (1)

6760 עָפָר *'āpār* (110)
dust (81)
earth (5)
rubble (5)
soil (4)
ground (3)
ashes (2)
powder (2)
clay (1)
dirt (1)
earthen ramps (1)
material (1)
plaster (1)
sand (1)
scabs (1) +1599
soil (1) +824

6761 עֵפֶר *'ēper* (4)
Epher (4)

6762 עֹפֶר *'ōper* (5)
young stag (3) +385
fawns (2)

6763 1עָפְרָה *'oprāh1* (1)
Ophrah (1)

6764 2עָפְרָה *'oprāh2* (7)
Ophrah (7)

6765 עַפְרָה *'aprāh*
Variant; not used

6766 1עֶפְרוֹן *'eprôn1* (12)
Ephron (8)
Ephron's (2)
he^s (1)
him^s (1)

6767 2עֶפְרוֹן *'eprôn2* (2)
Ephron (2)

6768 עֶפְרָיִן *'eprayin* (1)
untranslated (1)

6769 עֹפֶרֶת *'ōperet* (9)
lead (9)

6770 עֵץ *'ēs* (329)
wood (100)
trees (69)
tree (61)
timber (12)
wooden (10)
gallows (9)
logs (9)
stick (7)
shaft (4)
almugwood (3) +523
carpenters (3) +3093
stick of wood (3)
sticks (3)
woodcutters (3) +2634
algumwood (2) +454
timbers (2)
beams (1)
branches (1) +8457
carpenter (1) +3093
carpenters (1)
firewood (1)
it^s (1) +2021
loads of wood (1)
lumber (1)
olive (1) +9043
paneling (1) +7596
piece of wood (1)
pine (1) +1360
plant life (1)
stalks (1)
that^s (1)
them^s (1) +780
wooden idol (1)
woodpile (1)
woodwork (1)
untranslated (10)

6771 1עָצָב *'āsab1* (2)
like image (1)
shaped (1)

6772 2עָצָב *'āsab2* (14)
distressed (2)
grieve (2)
grieved (2)
be grieved (1)
be injured (1)
filled with grief (1)
grieving (1)
interfered with (1)
twist (1)
was filled with pain (1)
was grieved (1)

6773 עָצָב *'āsāb* (17)
idols (13)
images (4)

6774 עָצָב *'assāb* (1)
workers (1)

6775 1עֶצֶב *'eseb1* (1)
pot (1)

6776 2עֶצֶב *'eseb2* (6)
hard work (1)
harsh (1)
pain (1)
toil (1)
toiling (1)
trouble (1)

6777 1עֹצֶב *'ōseb1* (1)
idols (1)

6778 2עֹצֶב *'ōseb2* (4)
pain (2)
offensive (1)
suffering (1)

6779 עִצָּבוֹן *'issābôn* (3)
painful toil (2)
pains (1)

6780 עַצֶּבֶת *'assebet* (5)
grief (1)
heartache (1) +4213
sorrows (1)
sufferings (1)
wounds (1)

6781 עָצָה *'āsāh* (1)
winks (1)

6782 עָצֶה *'āseh* (1)
backbone (1)

6783 1עֵצָה *'ēsāh1* (88)
counsel (23)
advice (15)
plans (9)
plan (4)
advice gave (3) +3619
purpose (3)
schemes (3)
strategy (3)
advice given (2) +3619
planned (2) +3619
purposes (2)
advise (1) +3619
bent on (1) +928
consultation (1)
counselor (1) +408
counselors (1) +408
decision (1)
giving advice (1) +3619
harmony (1) +8934
planned (1)
planning (1) +3619
plot (1)
plots (1)
plotted (1) +3619
predictions (1)
sense (1)
that^s (1)
thoughts (1) +928+5883
verdict (1)
untranslated (1)

6784 2עֵצָה *'ēsāh2*
Variant; not used

6785 3עֵצָה *'ēsāh3* (2)
trees (1)
wooden idols (1)

6786 עָצוּם *'āsûm* (31)
mighty (8)
powerful (7)
stronger (6)
strong (4)
great (1)
much too numerous (1) +2256+8041
power (1)
strength (1)
throngs (1)
very (1) +4394

6787 עֶצְיוֹן גֶּבֶר *'esyôn geber* (7)
Ezion Geber (7)

6788 עָצַל *'āsal* (1)
hesitate (1)

6789 עָצֵל *'āsēl* (14)
sluggard (13)

sluggard's (1)

6790 עַצְלָה 'aslāh (1)
laziness (1)

6791 עַצְלוּת 'aslût (1)
idleness (1)

6792 עֲצַלְתַּיִם ⁿsaltayim (1)
lazy (1)

6793 1עָצַם 'āsam1 (18)
many (6)
numerous (3)
crush bones (1)
height of power (1)
made numerous (1)
more (1)
power (1)
powerful (1)
strength (1)
vast (1)
very strong (1) +3946

6794 2עָצַם 'āsam2 (2)
sealed (1)
shuts (1)

6795 1עֶצֶם 'esem1 (126)
bones (80)
very (11)
blood (6)
bone (6)
body (3)
same (3)
bodies (2)
being (1)
frame (1)
itself (1)
limb (1)
thoseˢ (1)
vigor (1)
you (1) +4013
untranslated (8)

6796 2עֶצֶם 'esem2 (3)
Ezem (3)

6797 1עֹצֶם 'ōsem1 (3)
strength (2)
might (1)

6798 2עֹצֶם 'ōsem2 (1)
frame (1)

6799 עָצְמָה 'asmāh
Variant; not used

6800 עָצְמָה 'osmāh (2)
potent (1)
power (1)

6801 עַצְמוֹן 'asmôn (3)
Azmon (2)
whereˢ (1)

6802 עֲצֻמוֹת ⁿsumôt (1)
arguments (1)

6803 עֶצֶן 'ēsen
Variant; not used

6804 עֶצְנִי 'esniy (1)
untranslated (1)

6805 עָצַץ 'āsas
Variant; not used

6806 עָצַר 'āsar (46)
slave (5)
shut up (4)
able (2) +3946
be stopped (2)
helpless (2) +3946+4202
retain (2)
stopped (2)
was stopped (2)
able (1)
been kept (1)
close up (1)

closed up (1) +6806
confined (1)
detain (1)
detained (1)
govern (1)
holds back (1)
keep (1)
kept (1)
prevail (1)
refrained (1)
regain (1) +6388
restricted (1)
seized (1)
shut (1)
slow down (1) +4200+8206
stay (1)
stops (1)
was banished (1)
was checked (1)
was confined (1)
was shut in (1)

6807 עֵצֶר 'eser (1)
prosperous (1) +3769

6808 עֹצֶר 'ōser (3)
oppression (2)
barren (1)

6809 עֲצָרָה ⁿsārāh (11)
assembly (5)
assemblies (2)
sacred assembly (2)
closing assembly (1)
crowd (1)

6810 עָקַב 'āqab (5)
deceived (1)
deceiver (1) +6810
grasped heel (1)
holds back (1)

6811 1עָקֵב 'āqēb1 (13)
heel (4)
heels (2)
ambush (1)
body (1)
footprints (1)
hoofs (1)
step (1)
steps (1)
tracks (1)

6812 2עָקֵב 'āqēb2 (1)
deceivers (1)

6813 עֵקֶב 'ēqeb (15)
because (3) +889
because (2) +3954
for (2)
at (1) +6584
because (1)
because of (1) +6584
bring (1)
if (1)
reward (1)
to the end (1)
to the very end (1) +4200+6409

6814 1עָקֹב 'āqōb1 (1)
footprints (1)

6815 2עָקֹב 'āqōb2 (2)
deceitful (1)
rough ground (1)

6816 עֹקֶב 'ōqeb
Variant; not used

6817 עָקְבָּה 'āqbāh (1)
deceptively (1) +928

6818 עָקַד 'āqad (1)
bound (1)

6819 עָקֹד 'āqōd (7)
streaked (7)

6820 עֶקֶד 'ēqed
Variant; not used

6821 עָקָה 'āqāh (1)
stares (1)

6822 עַקּוּב 'aqqûb (8)
Akkub (8)

6823 עָקַל 'āqal (1)
perverted (1)

6824 עֲקַלְקַל ⁿqalqāl (2)
crooked ways (1)
winding (1)

6825 עֲקַלָּתוֹן ⁿqallātôn (1)
coiling (1)

6826 עֲקָן ⁿqān (2)
Akan (2)

6827 1עָקַר 'āqar1 (2)
uproot (1)
uprooted (1)

6828 2עָקַר 'āqar2 (5)
hamstrung (4)
hamstring (1)

6829 עָקָר 'āqār (12)
barren (8)
sterile (2)
childless (1)
without young (1)

6830 1עֵקֶר 'ēqer1 (1)
member (1)

6831 2עֵקֶר 'ēqer2 (1)
Eker (1)

6832 עַקְרָב 'aqrāb (9)
scorpions (6)
scorpion (3)

6833 עֶקְרוֹן 'eqrôn (22)
Ekron (22)

6834 עֶקְרוֹנִי 'eqrôniy (2)
Ekron (1)
people of Ekron (1)

6835 עָקַשׁ 'āqaš (5)
distort (1)
perverse (1)
pronounce guilty (1)
takes crooked (1)
turned crooked (1)

6836 1עִקֵּשׁ 'iqqēš1 (11)
perverse (6)
crooked (3)
warped (1)
wicked (1)

6837 2עִקֵּשׁ 'iqqēš2 (3)
Ikkesh (3)

6838 עִקְּשׁוּת 'iqq'šût (2)
corrupt (1)
perversity (1)

6839 1עָר 'ār1 (2)
adversaries (1)
enemy (1)

6840 2עָר 'ār2 (6)
Ar (6)

6841 עֵר 'ēr (10)
Er (9)
untranslated (1)

6842 1עָרַב 'ārab1 (17)
puts up security (4)
make a bargain (2)
come to aid (1)
devote (1)
ensure (1)
guarantee safety (1)
guaranteed safety (1)

merchants (1) +5114
mortgaging (1)
pledge (1)
put up security (1)
puts up security (1) +6859
trade (1)

6843 עֲרַב 2 *'ārab2* (5)
mingled (2)
avoid (1) +4200+4202
join (1)
share (1)

6844 עֲרַב 3 *'ārab3* (8)
please (2)
sweet (2)
acceptable (1)
found pleasure (1)
pleasant (1)
pleasing (1)

6845 עֲרַב 4 *'ārab4* (3)
evening (2)
turns to gloom (1)

6846 עֶרֶב 1 *'ereb1*
Variant; not used

6847 עֶרֶב 2 *'ereb2* (134)
evening (110)
at twilight (11) +1068+2021
dusk (2)
evenings (2)
night (2)
evening (1) +928+928+2021+2021+6847
evening (1) +2021+6961
every evening (1)
　　　　　　+928+928+2021+2021+6847
fading (1)
untranslated (1)

6848 עֶרֶב 3 *'ereb3*
Variant; not used

6849 עֵרֶב 1 *'ēreb1* (9)
knitted material (9)

6850 עֵרֶב 2 *'ēreb2* (5)
foreign people (2)
foreigners (1)
of foreign descent (1)
other people (1)

6851 עֲרָב 1 *'ªrab1* (7)
Arabia (6)
Arabian (1)

6852 עֲרָב 2 *'ªrab2*
Variant; not used

6853 עָרֵב *'ārēb* (2)
sweet (1)
tastes sweet (1)

6854 עֹרֵב 1 *'ōrēb1* (10)
raven (6)
ravens (4)

6855 עֹרֵב 2 *'ōrēb2* (7)
Oreb (7)

6856 עָרֹב *'ārōb* (9)
swarms of flies (5)
flies (4)

6857 עֲרָבָה 1 *'ªrābāh1* (5)
poplars (3)
poplar trees (1)
poplars (1) +5707

6858 עֲרָבָה 2 *'ªrābāh2* (58)
Arabah (28)
plains (17)
desert (4)
wasteland (3)
wastelands (2)
wilderness (2)
deserts (1)
untranslated (1)

6859 עֲרֻבָּה *'ªrubbāh* (2)
assurance (1)
puts up security (1) +6842

6860 עֵרָבוֹן *'ērābôn* (3)
pledge (3)

6861 עַרְבִי *'arbiy* (8)
Arabs (5)
Arab (2)
untranslated (1)

6862 עֲרָבִי *'ªrābiy* (2)
Arab (1)
nomad (1)

6863 עַרְבָתִי *'arbātiy* (2)
Arbathite (2)

6864 עָרַג *'ārag* (3)
pants (2)
pant (1)

6865 עֲרָד 1 *'ªrād1* (1)
Arad (1)

6866 עֲרָד 2 *'ªrād2* (4)
Arad (4)

6867 עָרָה 1 *'ārāh1* (14)
exposed (2)
tear down (2)
dishonor (1)
emptied (1)
empty (1)
give over to death (1)
is poured (1)
make bald (1)
poured out (1)
stripped (1)
stripped naked (1)
uncovers (1)

6868 עָרָה 2 *'ārāh2* (1)
plants (1)

6869 עָרָה 3 *'ārāh3* (1)
Arah (1)

6870 עֲרוּגָה *'ªrûgāh* (4)
beds (2)
plot (2)

6871 עָרוֹד *'ārôd* (1)
his[s] (1)

6872 עֶרְוָה *'erwāh* (54)
have sexual relations with (11) +1655
nakedness (11)
dishonored (4) +1655
dishonor (3)
have sexual relations (3) +1655
have relations with (2) +1655
indecent (2)
shame (2)
unprotected (2)
body (1) +1414
dishonor bed (1) +1655
dishonor by having sexual relations with (1)
　　　　　　+1655
dishonor by to have sexual relations (1)
　　　　　　+1655
has sexual relations with (1) +906+1655
have sexual relations (1) +906+8011
naked (1)
shame (1) +1425
strip (1) +1655
untranslated (5)

6873 עָרוֹם *'ārôm* (16)
naked (12)
stripped (3)
that way[s] (1)

6874 עָרוּם *'ārûm* (11)
prudent (8)
crafty (3)

6875 עֲרוֹעֵר 1 *'ªrô'ēr1*
Variant; not used

6876 עֲרוֹעֵר 2 *'ªrô'ēr2* (16)
Aroer (16)

6877 עָרוּץ *'ārûs* (1)
dry (1)

6878 עֵרִי 1 *'ēriy1* (2)
Eri (2)

6879 עֵרִי 2 *'ēriy2* (1)
Erite (1)

6880 עֶרְיָה *'eryāh* (6)
bare (4)
nakedness (1)
uncovered (1) +6423

6881 עֲרִיסָה *'ªriysāh* (4)
ground meal (4)

6882 עֲרִיפִים *'ªriypiym* (1)
clouds (1)

6883 עָרִיץ *'āriys* (21)
ruthless (17)
fierce (2)
cruel (1)
warrior (1)

6884 עֲרִירִי *'ªriyriy* (4)
childless (4)

6885 עָרַךְ *'ārak* (75)
took up positions (5)
arrange (4)
deployed (4)
prepared (4)
arranged (3)
compare (3)
prepare (3)
spread (3)
drew up (2)
drew up line (2)
formed battle lines (2)
judge quality (2)
marshaled (2)
set (2)
set out (2)
take up positions (2)
accuse (1)
been prepared (1)
compare with (1)
deployed forces (1)
draw up case (1)
drawing up (1)
drawn up (1)
drew up lines (1)
formation (1)
formed lines (1)
handle (1)
in formation (1)
keep (1)
laid out (1)
lay (1)
lay out (1)
line up (1)
ready (1)
recount (1)
set out (1) +6886
set up (1)
set value (1)
state (1)
stationed (1)
sustain (1)
taxed (1)
tend (1)
tended (1)
value sets (1)
untranslated (1)

6886 עֵרֶךְ *'ērek* (33)
value (11)
proper value (3)
set value (3)
value (2) +4084
assessments (1)

clothes (1) +955
equivalent values (1)
form (1)
like (1) +3869
personal vows (1) +5883
price set (1)
set out (1) +6885
specified amount (1)
that⁵ (1)
value (1) +4831
what belongs (1)
worth (1)
untranslated (1)

6887 עֲרַל 'āral (2)
be exposed (1)
regard as forbidden (1) +6889

6888 עָרֵל 'ārēl (35)
uncircumcised (29)
faltering (2)
closed (1)
forbidden (1)
untranslated (2)

6889 עׇרְלָה 'orlāh (15)
foreskins (3)
be circumcised (1) +1414+4576
been circumcised (1) +4576
circumcise (1) +4576
circumcise (1) +6073
circumcised (1) +1414+4576
flesh (1)
foreskin (1)
not circumcised (1) +2257+4200
regard as forbidden (1) +6887
undergo circumcision (1) +906+1414+4576
was circumcised (1) +1414+4576
untranslated (1)

6890 1עָרַם 'āram1 (1)
piled up (1)

6891 2עָרַם 'āram2 (6)
craftiness (1)
cunning (1)
learn prudence (1)
shows prudence (1)
very crafty (1) +6891

6892 עֹרֶם 'ōrem
Variant; not used

6893 עׇרְמָה 'ormāh (5)
prudence (3)
deliberately (1) +928
ruse (1)

6894 עֲרֵמָה ⁿᵃrēmāh (11)
heaps (3)
doing this⁵ (1) +2021+3569
grain (1)
grain pile (1)
heap (1)
heaps of grain (1)
in heaps (1) +6894
mound (1)

6895 עַרְמוֹן 'ermôn (2)
plane trees (2)

6896 עֶרֶן 'ērān (1)
Eran (1)

6897 עֵרָנִי 'ērāniy (1)
Eranite (1)

6898 עַרְעוֹר 'ar'ôr
Variant; not used

6899 עַרְעָר 'ar'ār (3)
bush (2)
destitute (1)

6900 עֲרָעָרה 'ar'ārāh
Variant; not used

6901 עֲרֹעֵרִי ⁿᵃrō'ēriy (1)
Aroerite (1)

6902 עֹרֶף 'ōrep (33)
stiff-necked (11) +7996
backs (7)
stiff-necked (7) +7997
neck (4)
back (2)
routed (1) +2200
untranslated (1)

6903 1עָרַף 'ārap1 (2)
drop (1)
fall (1)

6904 2עָרַף 'ārap2 (6)
break neck (3)
breaks neck (1)
demolish (1)
neck was broken (1)

6905 עׇרְפָּה 'ārpāh (2)
Orpah (2)

6906 עֲרָפֶל ⁿᵃrāpel (15)
thick darkness (4)
blackness (2)
dark cloud (2)
dark clouds (2)
darkness (2)
deep darkness (2)
deep gloom (1)

6907 עָרַץ 'āras (15)
terrified (4)
dread (2)
shake (2)
cause terror (1)
feared (1)
give way to panic (1)
is feared (1)
stand in awe (1)
terrify (1)
torment (1)

6908 עָרַק 'āraq (2)
gnawing pains (1)
roamed (1)

6909 עָרְקִי 'arqiy (2)
Arkites (2)

6910 עָרַר 'ārar (4)
be leveled (1) +6910
strip off clothes (1) +2256+7320
stripped bare (1)

6911 עֶרֶשׂ 'ereś (10)
bed (4)
couches (2)
bed (1) +3661
couch (1)
sickbed (1) +1867
untranslated (1)

6912 עֵשֶׂב 'ēśeb (33)
grass (11)
plants (8)
growing (4)
plant (4)
vegetation (2)
green thing (1)
pasture (1)
tender plants (1)
untranslated (1)

6913 1עָשָׂה 'āśāh1 (2637)
do (405)
did (286)
made (270)
done (263)
make (161)
doing (61)
does (55)
follow (39)
prepare (30)
celebrate (25)
deal (24)

built (22)
obey (22)
maker (21)
show (21)
carry out (20)
be done (18)
act (17)
sacrifice (16)
committed (14)
inflict (14)
provide (14)
celebrated (13)
prepared (13)
keep (11)
acted (10)
bring (10)
been done (9)
gave (9)
observe (9)
performed (9)
shown (9)
accomplish (8)
makes (8)
offer (8)
treated (8)
work (8)
brought (7)
making (7)
present (7)
treat (7)
workers (7) +4856
bear (6)
build (6)
perform (6)
worked (6)
commits (5)
completely destroy (5) +3986
deal with (5)
forbidden (5) +4202
is done (5)
obeys (5)
produce (5)
showed (5)
uphold (5)
acquired (4)
appointed (4)
be made (4)
carried out (4)
exploits (4)
give (4)
grant (4)
observed (4)
provided (4)
put (4)
use (4)
used (4)
working (4)
yield (4)
achieve (3)
acting (3)
be granted (3)
brought about (3)
caused (3)
conduct (3)
destroy completely (3) +3986
do work (3)
engage (3)
gain (3)
gained (3)
held (3)
instituted (3)
offered (3)
performs (3)
practice (3)
produced (3)
sends (3)
showing (3)
shows (3)
supervise (3)
used to make (3)
waged (3)

were carved (3)
workmen (3) +4856
works (3)
achieved (2)
acts (2)
are done (2)
bake (2)
be fulfilled (2)
be prepared (2)
been made (2)
been observed (2)
behaved (2)
busy (2)
carrying out (2)
carved (2)
conformed to (2) +3869
consulted (2)
deal (2) +6913
deals (2)
dealt (2)
done (2) +5126
dug (2)
establishes (2)
fight (2)
fighting (2) +4878
follow (2) +3869
formed (2)
fought (2)
fulfill (2)
fully accomplishes (2) +2256+7756
get (2)
happen (2)
happens (2)
harm (2) +8273
harm (2) +8288
imitate (2) +3869
inflicted (2)
introduced (2)
kept (2)
maintain (2)
obeyed (2)
open (2)
ordained (2)
practices (2)
put into practice (2)
responsible (2)
serve (2)
set up (2)
shaping (2)
undertaken (2)
use (2) +4856
was celebrated (2)
worship (2)
yielded (2)
accomplished (1)
accomplishing (1)
add (1)
adhere to (1) +3869
administer (1)
administrators (1) +4856
am (1)
amassed (1)
answer (1)
applies (1)
apply (1)
are (1)
artificial (1)
assign (1)
assigned (1)
at war (1) +4878
at work (1)
attack (1) +4200
attend to (1)
avenged (1) +5935
be (1)
be carried out (1)
be completed (1)
be paid back (1)
be presented (1)
be used (1)
bearing (1)

became famous (1) +9005
been (1)
been committed (1)
been constructed (1)
been followed (1)
been used (1) +4856
began (1)
behave (1)
behaves (1)
bring up (1)
bulges with flesh (1) +7089
cancel debts (1) +9024
careful to carry out (1) +6913
carried on (1)
carried through (1)
carrying on (1)
carves (1)
cast (1)
celebrating (1)
celebration (1)
certainly carry out (1) +6913
certainly do (1) +6913
certainly make (1) +6913
comes (1)
commit (1)
committing (1)
construct (1)
constructed (1)
continue (1)
continued (1)
cooked (1)
copied (1)
created (1)
creature (1)
crop (1)
custom (1)
custom (1) +4027
customary (1)
deeds (1)
defends (1)
defiled$ (1)
deserve (1)
did so$ (1) +906+2021+7175
diligent (1)
displayed (1)
do (1) +6913
do great things (1) +6913
do something (1)
dressed (1)
earners (1)
earns (1)
engaged in (1)
erected (1)
establish (1)
established (1)
evildoer (1) +8288
evildoer (1) +8402
evildoers (1) +8402
executed (1)
exempt from taxes (1) +2930
exercises (1)
express (1)
faithfully (1) +622
fashion (1)
fashioned (1)
finished (1)
fit for (1)
follow (1) +4027
follow lead (1) +4027
followed (1) +4027
followed the example (1) +3869+6913
fulfill (1) +3869+4027+7023
fulfilled (1)
fulfills (1)
fully obeyed (1) +2256+9048
gains (1)
get ready (1)
give over (1)
given (1)
goes on (1)

going (1)
got ready (1)
granted (1)
grow (1)
hammer (1) +8393
hammer out (1) +5251
handle (1)
handled (1)
have (1)
have$ (1)
help (1)
help (1) +4200
holding (1)
honor (1) +3702
honored (1) +3883
howl (1) +5027
in charge (1)
is built (1)
is carried out (1)
is done (1) +5126
is made (1)
judge$ (1)
judges (1) +5477
keeping (1)
keeps (1)
make provision (1)
make up (1)
manage (1)
marks off (1)
master craftsmen (1) +4856
may do (1)
measured (1)
meet (1)
merchants (1) +4856
molded (1)
mount (1)
mounted (1)
mourn (1) +65
move (1)
obey (1) +2256+9068
observance (1)
occurs (1)
officiate (1)
on way (1) +2006
oppressed (1) +928+2021+6945
Pack (1)
pack (1)
passes through (1)
persist (1)
persisted in (1) +3869
pervert (1) +6404
piled (1)
presents (1)
proclaimed (1)
proud (1) +1452
provides (1)
providing (1)
punish (1) +5477
put forth (1)
put in jeopardy (1) +9214
ready (1)
received (1)
reduces (1)
render (1)
rescued (1) +9591
resist (1)
resorted (1)
rich (1)
roughs out (1)
sacrificed (1)
secures (1)
serve (1) +7372
set (1)
shapes (1)
sins defiantly (1) +928+3338+8123
sins unintentionally (1) +928+8705
still to come (1) +4202
stir up (1)
such$ (1) +2021
surely show (1) +6913
surely sprout (1) +6913

take (1)
take action (1)
take part (1) +7928
take place (1)
taken care of (1)
taking place (1)
these men[s] (1) +2021+4856
trained (1)
treated (1) +6640
tried (1) +4027
trim (1)
trimmed (1)
turns to (1)
unlike (1) +4027+4202
upheld (1)
upholds (1)
use to make (1)
useful (1)
wage (1)
waging (1)
was happening (1)
was made (1)
was spent for making (1) +4946
well-trained (1) +4878
went about (1)
went on (1)
went to war (1) +4878
were made (1)
were practiced (1)
were prepared (1)
were[s] (1)
won (1)
work (1) +4856
work (1) +5126
worker (1)
workers (1)
working (1) +4856
workmen (1) +928+2021+4856
works out (1)
wrongdoing (1) +8400
wrongs (1) +2633
untranslated (97)

6914 עָשָׂה 2 'āśāh2 (3)
caressed (3)

6915 עֲשָׂהאֵל 'ᵃśāh'ēl (18)
Asahel (17)
he[s] (1)

6916 עֵשָׂו 'ēśāw (97)
Esau (79)
Esau's (14)
he[s] (3)
untranslated (1)

6917 עָשׂוֹר 'āśôr (16)
tenth (12)
ten-stringed (3)
ten (1)

6918 עֲשִׂיאֵל 'ᵃśiy'ēl (1)
Asiel (1)

6919 עֲשָׂיָה 'ᵃśāyāh (8)
Asaiah (8)

6920 עֲשִׂירִי 'ᵃśiyriy (29)
tenth (29)

6921 עָשַׂק 'āśaq (1)
disputed (1)

6922 עֵשֶׂק 'ēśeq (1)
Esek (1)

6923 עָשַׂר 'āśar (9)
take a tenth (2)
be sure to set aside a tenth (1) +6923
collect tithes (1)
give a tenth (1) +6923
receive tithes (1)
setting aside a tenth (1) +5130

6924 עֶשֶׂר 'eśer (59)
ten (57)
910 (1) +2256+4395+9596

fifteen feet (1) +564+928+2021

6925 עָשָׂר 'āśār (205)
twelve (51) +9109
12 (24) +9109
fourteenth (19) +752
fifteenth (15) +2822
twelfth (15) +9109
fourteen (12) +752
eleventh (8) +6954
thirteenth (8) +8993
fifteen (6) +2822
eighteen (4) +9046
seventeenth (4) +8679
sixteen (4) +9252
eleven (3) +285
sixteenth (3) +9252
112 (2) +2256+4395+9109
16,000 (2) +547+9252
18 (2) +9046
18,000 (2) +547+9046
eighteenth (2) +9046
nineteenth (2) +9596
thirteen (2) +8993
1,017 (1) +547+2256+8679
1,017 (1) +547+8679
112 (1) +4395+9109
13 (1) +8993
14,700 (1) +547+752+2256+4395+8679
16,750 (1)
     +547+2256+2822+4395+8679+9252
17,200 (1) +547+2256+4395+8679
2,812 (1) +547+2256+4395+9046+9109
2,818 (1) +547+2256+4395+9046+9046
212 (1) +2256+4395+9109
218 (1) +2256+4395+9046
318 (1) +2256+4395+8993+9046
eleven (1) +6954
nineteen (1) +9596
untranslated (1)

6926 עֶשְׂרֵה 'eśrēh (136)
twelve (30) +9109
sixteen (14) +9252
thirteen (10) +8993
eighteenth (9) +9046
fifteen (8) +2822
eighteen (7) +9046
fourteen (7) +752
twelfth (7) +9109
eleven (6) +285
eleventh (5) +6954
seventeen (5) +8679
eleven (4) +6954
eleventh (4) +285
fourteenth (4) +752
thirteenth (3) +8993
fifteenth (2) +2822
nineteenth (2) +9596
seventeenth (2) +8679
119 (1) +2256+4395+9596
815 (1) +2256+2822+4395+9046
912 (1) +2256+4395+9109+9596
hundred and twenty thousand (1)
     +8052+9109
nineteen (1) +9596
twenty feet (1) +564+2822
twenty-seven feet (1) +564+9046

6927 עֲשָׂרָה 'ᵃśārāh (65)
ten (59)
110 (1) +2256+4395
410 (1) +752+2256+4395
fifteen (1) +2256+2822
seventeen (1) +2256+8679
untranslated (2)

6928 עִשָּׂרוֹן 'iśśārôn (33)
two-tenths (11) +9109
three-tenths (8) +8993
one-tenth (4)
tenth (4)
one-tenth (1) +285

untranslated (5)

6929 עֶשְׂרִים 'eśriym (316)
twenty (119)
twenty-five (23) +2256+2822
twenty-two (15) +2256+9109
24,000 (14) +547+752+2256
25,000 (14) +547+2256+2822
twentieth (9)
twenty-fourth (9) +752+2256
twenty-third (7) +2256+8993
twenty-seventh (6) +2256+8679
twenty-three (6) +2256+8993
120 (5) +2256+4395
twenty-four (5) +752+2256
twenty-nine (5) +2256+9596
128 (4) +2256+4395+9046
twenty-eight (4) +2256+9046
twenty-first (4) +285+2256
twenty-one (4) +285+2256
127 (3) +2256+2256+4395+8679
29 (3) +2256+9596
twenty-fifth (3) +2256+2822
123 (2) +2256+4395+8993
20 (2)
220 (2) +2256+4395
223 (2) +2256+4395+8993
320 (2) +2256+4395+8993
6,720 (2) +547+2256+4395+8679+9252
621 (2) +285+2256+4395+9252
twenty-second (2) +2256+9109
twenty-seven (2) +2256+8679
1,222 (1) +547+2256+4395+9109
120,000 (1) +547+2256+4395
122 (1) +2256+2256+4395+9109
122 (1) +2256+4395+9109
2,322 (1) +547+2256+4395+8993+9109
20,000 (1) +547
20,200 (1) +547+2256+4395
20,800 (1) +547+2256+4395+9046
22 (1) +2256+9109
22,000 (1) +547+2256+9109
22,034 (1)
     +547+752+2256+2256+2256+8993+9109
22,200 (1) +547+2256+2256+4395+9109
22,273 (1)   +547+2256+2256+2256
     +4395+8679+8993+9109
22,600 (1)
     +547+2256+2256+4395+9109+9252
23,000 (1) +547+2256+8993
25,100 (1) +547+2256+2256+2822+4395
26,000 (1) +547+2256+9252
28 (1) +2256+9046
28,600 (1)
     +547+2256+2256+4395+9046+9252
3,023 (1) +547+2256+2256+8993+8993
323 (1) +2256+4395+8993+8993
324 (1) +752+2256+4395+8993
328 (1) +2256+4395+8993+9046
420 (1) +752+2256+4395
623 (1) +2256+4395+8993+9252
628 (1) +2256+4395+9046+9252
721 (1) +285+2256+2256+4395+8679
725 (1) +2256+2822+4395+8679
822 (1) +2256+4395+9046+9109
928 (1) +2256+4395+9046+9596
them[s] (1) +2021+7983
thirty feet (1) +564+928+2021
twenty-six (1) +2256+9252
twenty-sixth (1) +2256+9252
untranslated (2)

6930 עֲשֶׂרֶת 'ᵃśeret (52)
ten (39)
10,000 (9) +547
tens (3)
ten-acre (1) +7538

6931 עָשׁ 1 'āš1 (7)
moth (4)
moths (2)
moth's cocoon (1)

6932 2עֵשׁ ʿāš2
Variant; not used

6933 3עֵשׁ ʿāš3 (1)
bear (1)

6934 עָשׁוֹק ʿāšôq (1)
oppressor (1)

6935 עֲשׁוּקִים ʿašûqiym (3)
oppression (3)

6936 עָשׂוֹת ʿāśôt (1)
wrought (1)

6937 עֲשָׂוָת ʿaśwāt (1)
Ashvath (1)

6938 עָשִׁיר ʿāšiyr (23)
rich (21)
wealth (1)
wealthy (1)

6939 עָשַׁן ʿāšan (6)
smoke (2)
anger smolder (1)
burn (1)
covered with smoke (1)
smolder (1)

6940 1עָשָׁן ʿāšān1 (25)
smoke (23)
cloud of smoke (1)
smoking (1)

6941 2עָשָׁן ʿāšān2 (4)
Ashan (4)

6942 עָשֵׁן ʿāšēn (2)
in smoke (1)
smoldering (1)

6943 עָשַׁק ʿāšaq (37)
oppress (7)
oppressed (7)
defraud (4)
oppresses (3)
cheated (2)
oppressor (2)
oppressors (2)
cheats (1)
crushed (1)
mistreat (1)
oppression (1)
practice extortion (1) +6945
practiced extortion (1) +6945
rages (1)
take advantage (1)
taken by extortion (1) +6945
tormented (1)

6944 עֵשֶׁק ʿēšeq (1)
Eshek (1)

6945 עֹשֶׁק ʿōšeq (15)
oppression (6)
extortion (3)
oppressed (1)
oppressed (1) +928+2021+6913
practice extortion (1) +6943
practiced extortion (1) +6943
taken by extortion (1) +6943
tyranny (1)

6946 עָשְׁקָה ʿošqāh (1)
troubled (1)

6947 עָשַׁר ʿāšar (17)
rich (7)
bring wealth (1)
brings wealth (1)
enrich (1)
enriched (1)
get rich (1)
give wealth (1) +6948
made rich (1)
pretends to be rich (1)
richer (1) +6948
wealth (1)

6948 עֹשֶׁר ʿōšer (37)
wealth (21)
riches (14)
give wealth (1) +6947
richer (1) +6947

6949 עָשַׁשׁ ʿāšaš (3)
weak (3)

6950 1עָשַׁת ʿāšat1 (1)
sleek (1)

6951 2עָשַׁת ʿāšat2 (1)
take notice (1)

6952 עֶשֶׁת ʿešet (1)
polished (1)

6953 עַשְׁתּוּת ʿaštût (1)
have (1)

6954 עַשְׁתֵּי ʿaštēy (18)
eleventh (8) +6925
eleventh (5) +6926
eleven (4) +6926
eleven (1) +6925

6955 עֶשְׁתֹּנֶת ʿeštōnet (1)
plans (1)

6956 עַשְׁתֹּרֶת ʿaštōret (9)
Ashtoreths (6)
Ashtoreth (3)

6957 עַשְׁתְּרֶת ʿašteret (4)
lambs (4)

6958 עַשְׁתָּרֹת ʿaštārōt (6)
Ashtaroth (6)

6959 עַשְׁתְּרֹת קַרְנַיִם ʿašt'rōt qarnayim (1)
Ashteroth Karnaim (1)

6960 עֶשְׁתְּרָתִי ʿšt'rātiy (1)
Ashterathite (1)

6961 עֵת ʿēt (297)
time (179)
times (26)
season (12)
when (11) +928
always (5) +928+3972
when (3)
as (2) +928
at (2) +928
at set times (2) +4946+6330+6961
days (2)
in (2) +4200
next year (2) +2645
now (2)
now (2) +2021+3869
proper time (2)
sunset (2) +995+2021+9087
when (2) +4200
appointed time (1)
as (1) +3869
as (1) +4200
as long as (1) +928+3972
at once (1) +928+2021+2021+2085
circumstances (1)
constantly (1) +928+3972
doom (1)
due time (1)
end (1)
evening (1) +2021+6847
future (1)
hour (1)
mealtime (1) +431+2021
occasion (1)
old (1)
past (1) +8037
punishment (1)
ripens (1)
seasons (1)
spring (1) +9102+9588
springtime (1) +4919
then[s] (1) +2021+2021+2085
till (1) +6330

time after time (1) +8041
timely (1) +928
whenever (1) +928
whenever (1) +928+3972
while (1) +4200
years (1) +2021+9102
untranslated (8)

6962 עֵת קָצִין ʿēt qāsiyn (1)
Eth Kazin (1)

6963 עָתָד ʿātad (2)
crumbling (1)
get ready (1)

6964 עַתָּה ʿatāh (434)
now (317)
then (10)
come now (3) +5528
therefore (3)
already (2)
but (2)
longer (2)
soon (2)
when (2)
about to (1) +4946+7940
although (1)
always (1)
further (1)
furthermore (1)
furthermore (1) +2256
going to (1)
if so (1) +3954
just (1) +2296
just (1) +4946
now (1) +2256
now (1) +2296
now then (1)
on (1) +6330
right now (1)
so (1)
surely (1) +421
surely (1) +3954
that day (1)
that time on (1)
then (1) +2256
this (1)
this day (1)
this time on (1)
yet (1) +2256
yet (1) +6330
untranslated (65)

6965 עָתוּד ʿātûd (2)
treasures (1)
untranslated (1)

6966 עַתּוּד ʿatûd (29)
male goats (15)
goats (12)
leaders (2)

6967 עִתִּי ʿitiy (1)
appointed for the task (1)

6968 עַתַּי ʿatay (4)
Attai (4)

6969 עָתִיד ʿātiyd (6)
ready (3)
doom (1)
poised (1)
untranslated (1)

6970 עֲתָיָה ʿatāyāh (1)
Athaiah (1)

6971 עַתִּיק ʿatiyq (1)
fine (1)

6972 עַתִּיק ʿatiyq (2)
from ancient times (1)
taken (1)

6973 עֲתָךְ ʿatāk (1)
Athach (1)

6974 עַתְלַי ʿatlāy (1)
Athlai (1)

6975 עֲתַלְיָה *ʿᵃtalyāh* (7)
Athaliah (7)

6976 עֲתַלְיָהוּ *ʿᵃtalyāhû* (10)
Athaliah (10)

6977 עָתַם *ʿātam* (1)
be scorched (1)

6978 עָתְנִי *ʿotniy* (1)
Othni (1)

6979 עָתְנִיאֵל *ʿotniyʾēl* (7)
Othniel (7)

6980 עָתַק *ʿātaq* (9)
moved (2)
copied (1)
fail (1)
failed (1) +4946
growing old (1)
moved on (1)
moves (1)
went on (1)

6981 עָתָק *ʿātāq* (4)
arrogance (1)
arrogant (1)
arrogantly (1)
outstretched (1)

6982 עָתֵק *ʿātēq* (1)
enduring (1)

6983 1עָתַר *ʿātar1* (20)
pray (7)
answered prayer (4)
prayed (4)
was moved by entreaty (2)
answered prayers (1)
prays (1)
respond to pleas (1)

6984 2עָתַר *ʿātar2* (2)
multiplies (1)
without restraint (1)

6985 1עָתָר *ʿātār1* (1)
worshipers (1)

6986 2עָתָר *ʿātār2* (1)
fragrant (1)

6987 עֶתֶר *ʿeter* (2)
Ether (2)

6988 עֲתֶרֶת *ʿᵃteret* (1)
abundant (1)

6989 פ *p*
Variant; not used

6990 פָּאָה *pāʾāh* (1)
scatter (1)

6991 1פֵּאָה *pēʾāh1* (85)
side (33)
boundary (4)
edges (4)
end (4)
corners (2)
distant places (2) +7899
foreheads (2)
border (1)
edge (1)
front (1)
places (1)
sides (1)
southern (1) +448+5582
started (1) +4200
untranslated (27)

6992 2פֵּאָה *pēʾāh2* (1)
remotest frontiers (1)

6993 3פֵּאָה *pēʾāh3*
Variant; not used

6994 1פָּאַר *pāʾar1* (1)
go over the branches a second time (1)
             +339

6995 2פָּאַר *pāʾar2* (13)
display splendor (3)
adorn (2)
endowed with splendor (2)
boast (1)
bring honor (1)
crowns (1)
displays glory (1)
leave the honor (1)
raise itself (1)

6996 פְּאֵר *pᵉʾēr* (7)
turbans (2)
adorns head (1)
crown of beauty (1)
headbands (1) +4457
headdresses (1)
turban (1)

6997 פֹּארָה *pōʾrāh* (7)
branches (5)
leafy boughs (1)
untranslated (1)

6998 פֻּארָה *puʾrāh* (1)
boughs (1)

6999 פָּארוּר *pāʾrûr* (2)
grows pale (1) +7695
turns pale (1) +7695

7000 פָּארָן *pāʾrān* (10)
Paran (10)

7001 פַּג *pag* (1)
early fruit (1)

7002 פִּגּוּל *piggûl* (4)
impure (2)
unclean (1)
unclean meat (1)

7003 פָּגַע *pāgaʿ* (46)
touched (6)
strike down (4)
struck down (4)
meet (2)
meets (2)
plead (2)
strike (2)
attack (1)
attacked (1)
bordered (1)
come across (1)
come to the help of (1)
doˢ (1)
extended (1)
find (1)
found (1)
harmed (1)
intercede (1)
intervene (1)
kill (1)
laid (1)
made intercession (1)
make plead (1)
met (1)
praying (1)
reached (1)
spare (1)
strike mark (1)
urge (1)
urged (1)
untranslated (1)

7004 פֶּגַע *pegaʿ* (2)
chance (1)
disaster (1) +8273

7005 פַּגְעִיאֵל *pagʿiyʾēl* (5)
Pagiel (5)

7006 פָּגַר *pāgar* (2)
exhausted (2)

7007 פֶּגֶר *peger* (21)
bodies (7)
dead bodies (7)
carcasses (2)
lifeless idols (2)
corpse (1)
dead (1)
lifeless forms (1)

7008 פָּגַשׁ *pāgaš* (14)
met (6)
have in common (2)
meet (2)
attack (1)
comes (1)
meet together (1)
meets (1)

7009 פָּדָה *pādāh* (60)
redeem (22)
redeemed (15)
ransom (4)
delivered (2)
ransomed (2)
be ransomed (1)
be redeemed (1)
been ransomed (1) +7009
buy back (1)
let be redeemed (1)
must redeem (1) +7009
ransoms (1)
redeem (1) +7009
redeems (1)
redemption (1)
rescued (1)
untranslated (1)

7010 פְּדַהְאֵל *pᵉdahʾēl* (1)
Pedahel (1)

7011 פְּדָהצוּר *pᵉdāhsûr* (5)
Pedahzur (5)

7012 פְּדוּיִם *pᵉdûyim* (3)
redemption (2)
redeem (1)

7013 פָּדוֹן *pādôn* (2)
Padon (2)

7014 פְּדוּת *pᵉdût* (3)
redemption (2)
ransom (1)

7015 פְּדָיָה *pᵉdāyāh* (7)
Pedaiah (7)

7016 פְּדָיָהוּ *pᵉdāyāhû* (1)
Pedaiah (1)

7017 פִּדְיוֹם *pidyôm* (1)
redemption (1)

7018 פִּדְיוֹן *pidyôn* (2)
ransom (1)
redeem (1)

7019 פַּדָּן *paddān* (1)
Paddan (1)

7020 פַּדָּן אֲרָם *paddan ʿᵃrām* (10)
Paddan Aram (10)

7021 פָּדַע *pādaʿ* (1)
spare (1)

7022 פֶּדֶר *peder* (3)
fat (3)

7023 פֶּה *peh* (498)
mouth (199)
mouths (40)
command (39)
to (25) +4200
lips (13)
opening (8)
face (7)
with (5) +4200
word (5)
commanded (4)
end (4)

speech (4)
spoken (4)
testimony (4)
according to (3) +6584
by (3) +4200
number (3)
according to (2) +4200
as much as (2) +4200
commands (2)
dictated (2) +4946
man (2)
other^s (2)
promised (2) +3655+4946
pronounced (2)
required (2)
said (2)
said (2) +3655+4946
speak (2)
speak (2) +4946
speak up (2) +7337
what say (2) +609
when (2) +4200
words (2) +609
according to (1) +3869
accordingly (1) +3869
amount (1)
as much as (1) +3869
at (1) +4200
beak (1)
because (1) +889+3869
big talk (1)
boast so much (1) +1540+3870
boasted (1) +928+1540
by (1) +4946
by (1) +6584
collar (1)
collar (1) +9389
consulting (1) +8626
decide (1) +2118+6584
demanded (1) +6584
dictate (1) +4946
dictated (1)
dictated (1) +4946+7924
dictating (1) +4946
dictation (1) +4946
direction (1)
don't say a word (1) +3338+6584+8492
double-edged (1)
double-edged (1) +9109
drank in (1) +7196
expressed (1) +6584
fruit (1)
fulfill (1) +3869+4027+6913
gape (1) +8143
give command (1) +7337
given word (1) +906+7198
giving an apt reply (1) +5101
had (1) +928
have (1) +928
hunger (1)
I (1) +3276
in accordance with (1) +4200
in accordance with (1) +6584
in proportion to (1) +3869
in the way should go (1) +2006+6584
inquire of (1) +906+8626
instructed (1) +1819
invoke (1) +928+7924
jaws (1)
just like (1) +3869
keep silent (1) +3104
killed (1) +2995+4200+5782
leading into (1) +4200
made a vow (1) +7198
make spew out (1) +3655+4946
mention (1) +928+9019
neck (1)
offered a kiss of homage (1) +4200+5975
on (1) +6584
orders (1)
portion (1)

promised (1) +928+1819
requires (1)
say (1)
say (1) +3655+4946
say (1) +7337
sayings (1)
share (1)
simply (1) +6584
sing (1) +928+8492
sneer (1) +8143
so that (1) +3869
speak (1) +928
speaks (1) +7337
spoke the word (1) +4946
spoken (1) +1819
spokesman (1) +3869
talk (1)
taste (1)
told (1) +928+8492
two-thirds (1) +9109
what said (1) +609
when (1) +3954+4200
whenever (1) +4200
will (1) +6584
words (1) +1821
words (1) +7339
untranslated (10)

7024 פֹּה *pōh* (70)
here (43)
on each side (10) +2256+4946+4946+7024
on either side (4) +2256+4946+4946+7024
other^s (2)
side (2)
arrives (1) +995
square (1) +2256+4946+4946+7024
this far (1) +6330
untranslated (3)

7025 פוּאָה *pû'āh* (3)
Puah (3)

7026 פּוּאָה *puww'āh* (1)
Puah (1)

7027 פוּאִי *pû'iy* (1)
Puite (1)

7028 פוּג *pûg* (4)
feeble (1)
paralyzed (1)
stunned (1) +4213
untiring (1) +4202

7029 פוּנָה *pûgāh* (1)
relief (1)

7030 פֻּוָּה *puwwāh*
Variant; not used

7031 פוּחַ 1 *pûah1* (3)
breaks (2)
blow (1)

7032 פוּחַ 2 *pûah2* (12)
pours out (4)
breathe (1)
breathe out (1)
gives (1)
malign (1)
sneers (1)
speaks (1)
stir up (1)
witness (1)

7033 פוּט *pût* (7)
Put (7)

7034 פוּטִיאֵל *pûṭiy'ēl* (1)
Putiel (1)

7035 פוֹטִיפַר *pôṭiypar* (2)
Potiphar (2)

7036 פוֹטִי פֶרַע *pôṭiy pera'* (3)
Potiphera (3)

7037 פוּךְ *pûk* (4)

turquoise (2)
paint (1)
painted (1) +928+2021+8531

7038 פוֹל *pôl* (2)
beans (2)

7039 פוּל 1 *pûl1*
Variant; not used

7040 פוּל 2 *pûl2* (3)
Pul (2)
him^s (1)

7041 פוּן *pûn* (1)
in despair (1)

7042 פוּנֶה *pôneh*
Variant; not used

7043 פוּנִי *pûniy*
Variant; not used

7044 פוּנֹן *pûnōn* (2)
Punon (2)

7045 פוּעָה *pû'āh* (1)
Puah (1)

7046 פוּץ *pûṣ* (67)
scattered (21)
scatter (11)
disperse (7)
were scattered (5)
been scattered (4)
dispersed (2)
overflow (2)
attacker (1)
be scattered (1)
blow away (1)
broken (1)
dog (1)
driven (1)
go out (1)
is scattered (1)
scattering (1)
scatters (1)
separated (1)
sow (1)
spread out (1)
unleash (1)
untranslated (1)

7047 פוּץ 2 *pûṣ2*
Variant; not used

7048 פוּק 1 *pûq1* (2)
stumble (1)
totter (1)

7049 פוּק 2 *pûq2* (7)
receives (2)
gains (1)
let succeed (1)
obtains (1)
provision (1)
spend (1)

7050 פוּקָה *pûqāh* (1)
staggering burden (1) +2256+4842

7051 פוּר 1 *pûr1*
Variant; not used

7052 פוּר 2 *pûr2* (8)
Purim (5)
pur (3)

7053 פוּרָה *pûrāh* (2)
measures (1)
winepress (1)

7054 פוּרָתָא *pôrāṯā'* (1)
Poratha (1)

7055 פוּשׁ 1 *pûšl* (4)
frolic (1)
gallops headlong (1)
leap (1)
untranslated (1)

7056 פּוּשׁ2 *pûš2* (1)
scattered (1)

7057 פּוּתִי *pûtiy* (1)
Puthites (1)

7058 פָּז *paz* (9)
pure gold (5)
gold (2)
fine gold (1)
purest gold (1) –4188

7059 פָּזַז1 *pāzaz1* (1)
fine (1)

7060 פָּזַז2 *pāzaz2* (2)
leaping (1)
limber (1)

7061 פָּזַר *pāzar* (10)
scattered (5)
been scattered (1)
dispersed (1)
gives freely (1)
scattered abroad (1)
scatters (1)

7062 פַּח1 *pahl* (24)
snare (14)
snares (5)
trap (4)
snares (1) +3687

7063 פַּח2 *pah2* (2)
sheets (1)
thin sheets (1)

7064 פָּחַד *pāhad* (25)
afraid (3)
fear (2)
overwhelmed with dread (2) +7065
terrified (2)
brought down to terror (1)
come trembling (1)
feared (1)
fears (1)
fill (1)
filled with dread (1)
in awe (1)
live in terror (1)
looked in fear (1)
made shake (1)
showed fear (1)
throb (1)
tremble (1)
trembles (1)
turn in fear (1)
unafraid (1) +4202

7065 פַּחַד1 *pahadl* (49)
fear (14)
terror (13)
dread (8)
calamity (2)
overwhelmed with dread (2) +7064
afraid (1) +5877+6584
awe (1)
cares (1)
disaster (1)
dreaded (1)
peril (1)
terrifying (1)
terrors (1)
threat (1)
what[s] (1)

7066 פַּחַד2 *pahad2* (2)
thighs (1)
untranslated (1)

7067 פַּחְדָּה *pahdāh* (1)
awe (1)

7068 פֶּחָה *pehāh* (28)
governors (15)
governor (10)
officer (2)

officers (1)

7069 פָּחַז *pāhaz* (2)
adventurers (1)
arrogant (1)

7070 פַּחַז *pahaz* (1)
turbulent (1)

7071 פַּחֲזוּת *pahᵃzût* (1)
reckless (1)

7072 פָּחַח *pāhah* (1)
trapped (1)

7073 פֶּחָם *pehām* (4)
coals (3)
charcoal (1)

7074 פַּחַת *pahat* (10)
pit (7)
cave (2)
pitfalls (1)

7075 פַּחַת מוֹאָב *pahat mô'āb* (6)
Pahath-Moab (6)

7076 פְּחֶתֶת *pᵉhetet* (1)
mildew (1)

7077 פִּטְדָה *pitdāh* (4)
topaz (4)

7078 פְּטִירִים *pᵉtiyriym* (1)
untranslated (1)

7079 פַּטִּישׁ *pattiyš* (3)
hammer (3)

7080 פָּטַר *pātar* (9)
open (4)
breaching (1)
eluded (1)
hurl insults (1) +928+8557
released (1)
were exempt from duties (1)

7081 פֶּטֶר *peter* (11)
first offspring (5)
firstborn (3)
first male offspring (1) +1147+8167
firstborn (1) +8167
firstborn (1) +8715

7082 פִּטְרָה *pitrāh* (1)
firstborn (1)

7083 פִּי־בֶסֶת *piy-beset* (1)
Bubastis (1)

7084 פִּי הַחִירוֹת *piy hahiyrôt* (4)
Pi Hahiroth (4)

7085 פִּיד *piyd* (4)
misfortune (2)
calamities (1)
distress (1)

7086 פִּיחַ *piyah* (2)
soot (2)

7087 פִּיכֹל *piykōl* (3)
Phicol (3)

7088 פִּים *piym* (1)
two thirds of a shekel (1)

7089 פִּימָה *piymāh* (1)
bulges with flesh (1) +6913

7090 פִּינְחָס *piynhās* (25)
Phinehas (25)

7091 פִּינֹן *piynōn* (2)
Pinon (2)

7092 פִּיפִיּוֹת *piypiyyôt* (2)
double-edged (1)
many teeth (1)

7093 פִּישׁוֹן *piyšôn* (1)
Pishon (1)

7094 פִּיתוֹן *piytôn* (2)
Pithon (2)

7095 פַּךְ *pak* (3)
flask (3)

7096 פָּכָה *pākāh* (1)
flowing (1)

7097 פֹּכֶרֶת הַצְּבָיִים *pōkeret hassᵉbāyiym* (2)
Pokereth-Hazzebaim (2)

7098 פָּלָא *pālā'* (73)
wonders (17)
wonderful (15)
marvelous (10)
miracles (5)
amazing (3)
hard (3)
difficult (2)
am wonderfully made (1)
are wonderful (1)
astound (1)
astounding (1)
display awesome power (1)
fulfill a special vow (1) +5624
greatly (1)
impossible (1)
magnificent (1)
make a special vow (1) +5623
makes a special vow (1) +5624
send fearful (1)
show wonder (1)
showed wonderful (1)
special vow (1) +5624
special vows (1) +5624
unheard-of (1)
wonder (1)

7099 פֶּלֶא *pele'* (13)
wonders (4)
miracles (3)
wonderful (2)
astonishing things (1)
astounding (1)
marvelous things (1)
wonder (1)

7100 פִּלְאִי *pil'iy* (3)
beyond understanding (1)
wonderful (1)
untranslated (1)

7101 פַּלֻּאִי *pallu'iy* (1)
Palluite (1)

7102 פְּלָאיָה *pᵉlā'yāh* (2)
Pelaiah (2)

7103 פָּלַג *pālag* (4)
was divided (2)
confound (1)
cuts (1)

7104 פֶּלֶג1 *peleg1* (10)
streams (9)
watercourse (1) +4784

7105 פֶּלֶג2 *peleg2* (7)
Peleg (7)

7106 פְּלַגָּה *pᵉlaggāh* (3)
districts (2)
streams (1)

7107 פְּלֻגָּה *pᵉluggāh* (1)
subdivision (1)

7108 פִּלֶגֶשׁ *pilegeš* (37)
concubine (21)
concubines (14)
lovers (1)
she[s] (1) +2257

7109 פִּלְדָּשׁ *pildāš* (1)
Pildash (1)

7110 פְּלָדֹת *pᵉlādōt* (1)
metal (1)

7111 פָּלָה *pālāh* (5)
deal differently (1)

distinguish (1)
make a distinction (1)
makes a distinction (1)
set apart (1)

7112 פַּלּוּא *pallû'* (5)
Pallu (5)

7113 פְּלֹנִי *p⁽ᵉ⁾lôniy* (3)
Pelonite (3)

7114 פָּלַח *pālah* (5)
pierces (2)
bring forth (1)
cut up (1)
plows (1)

7115 פְּלַח *pelah* (6)
millstone (3)
halves (2)
part (1)

7116 פִּלְחָא *pilhā'* (1)
Pilha (1)

7117 פָּלַט *pālat* (26)
deliverer (5)
rescue (5)
delivered (4)
deliver (3)
delivers (2)
save (2)
calve (1)
carry off (1)
let escape (1)
saves (1)
survive (1)

7118 פֶּלֶט *pelet* (2)
Pelet (2)

7119 פַּלֵּט *pallēt* (1)
deliverance (1)

7120 פַּלְטִי *paltiy1* (2)
Palti (1)
Paltiel (1)

7121 פַּלְטִי *paltiy2* (1)
Paltite (1)

7122 פִּלְטָי *piltāy* (1)
Piltai (1)

7123 פַּלְטִיאֵל *paltiy'ēl* (2)
Paltiel (2)

7124 פְּלַטְיָה *p⁽ᵉ⁾latyāh* (3)
Pelatiah (3)

7125 פְּלַטְיָהוּ *p⁽ᵉ⁾latyāhû* (2)
Pelatiah (2)

7126 פְּלָיָה *p⁽ᵉ⁾lāyāh* (1)
Pelaiah (1)

7127 פָּלִיט *pāliyt* (18)
escape (6)
escaped (2)
fugitives (2)
anyoneˢ (1)
escape (1) +4880
fugitive (1)
himˢ (1) +2021
man who escaped (1)
manˢ (1)
renegades (1)
survivor (1)

7128 פָּלֵיט *pālēyt* (4)
escaped (1)
fugitives (1)
refugees (1)
survive (1)

7129 פְּלֵיטָה *p⁽ᵉ⁾lēytāh* (30)
remnant (6)
deliverance (4)
escape (4)
survivors (4)

escaped (3)
fugitives (3)
band of survivors (2)
escapes (1) +2118
little left (1) +3856+8636
place to escape (1)
survivor (1)

7130 פָּלִיל *pāliyl* (2)
concede (1)
court (1)

7131 פְּלִילָה *p⁽ᵉ⁾liylāh* (1)
decision (1)

7132 פְּלִילִי *p⁽ᵉ⁾liyliy* (2)
to be judged (2)

7133 פְּלִילִיָּה *p⁽ᵉ⁾liyliyyāh* (1)
rendering decisions (1)

7134 פֶּלֶךְ1 *pelek1* (2)
crutch (1)
spindle (1)

7135 פֶּלֶךְ2 *pelek2* (8)
district (4)
half-district (4) +2942

7136 פָּלַל1 *pālal1* (4)
expected (1)
furnished justification (1)
intervened (1)
mediate (1)

7137 פָּלַל2 *pālal2* (80)
pray (30)
prayed (28)
praying (10)
prays (5)
intercede (2)
prayer (2)
offer prayer (1) +9525
plead (1)
untranslated (1)

7138 פָּלָל *pālāl* (1)
Palal (1)

7139 פְּלַלְיָה *p⁽ᵉ⁾lalyāh* (1)
Pelaliah (1)

7140 פַּלְמֹנִי *palmōniy* (1)
himˢ (1) +2021

7141 פְּלֹנִי *p⁽ᵉ⁾lôniy* (3)
certain (1) +532
friend (1) +532
such and such (1) +532

7142 פָּלַס1 *pālas1* (4)
make level (1)
make smooth (1)
mete out (1)
prepared (1)

7143 פָּלַס2 *pālas2* (2)
examines (1)
gives thought (1)

7144 פֶּלֶס *peles* (2)
balances (1)
scales (1)

7145 פָּלַץ *pālas* (1)
makes tremble (1)

7146 פַּלָּצוּת *pallāsût* (4)
fear (1)
horror (1)
terror (1)
trembling (1)

7147 פָּלַשׁ *pālaš* (5)
roll (4)
untranslated (1)

7148 פְּלֶשֶׁת *p⁽ᵉ⁾lešet* (9)
Philistia (7)
Philistines (2)

7149 פְּלִשְׁתִּי *p⁽ᵉ⁾lištiy* (289)
Philistines (200)
Philistine (62)
theyˢ (8)
Philistine's (4)
heˢ (3) +2021
themˢ (3)
himˢ (1) +2021
hisˢ (1)
Philistia (1)
Philistines (1) +824
theirˢ (1)
untranslated (4)

7150 פֶּלֶת *pelet* (2)
Peleth (2)

7151 פְּלֻת *p⁽ᵉ⁾lut* (1)
distinction (1)

7152 פְּלֵתִי *p⁽ᵉ⁾lētiy* (7)
Pelethites (7)

7153 פֵּן *pen* (133)
or (49)
not (16)
otherwise (9)
lest (8)
so that not (6)
if (4)
might (4)
no (3)
and (2)
because (2)
for (2)
so not (2)
that no (2)
that not (2)
can't (1)
for if (1)
in order that not (1)
may (1)
not be allowed (1)
or else (1)
perhaps (1)
so cannot (1)
so that no (1)
that (1)
too (1)
won't (1)
would (1)
untranslated (9)

7154 פַּנַּג *pannag* (1)
confections (1)

7155 פָּנָה *pānāh* (134)
turned (27)
turn (18)
facing (14)
looked (4)
prepare (4)
look (3)
return (3)
turning (3)
turns (3)
faces (2)
give attention (2)
left (2)
look with favor (2)
turned back (2)
turns away (2)
accept (1)
approaches (1)
back (1)
back (1) +339
break camp (1)
break of day (1) +1332
cleared ground (1)
daybreak (1) +1332
daybreak (1) +1332+2021
emptied (1)
expected (1)
face (1)

faced (1)
fading (1)
fled (1)
glancing (1)
go (1)
goes (1)
looked around (1)
looking (1)
looking back (1)
notice (1)
overlook (1) +440
pass away (1)
pays attention (1)
prepared (1)
respond (1)
return (1) +2143+2256
showed concern for (1) +448
surveyed (1)
tied (1)
turn around (1)
turn back (1)
turn to help (1)
turned (1) +8900
turned around (1)
turned away (1)
turns back (1)
untranslated (5)

7156 פָּנֶה pāneh (2127)
before (542) +4200
face (211)
presence (108)
before (82) +4946
in front of (66) +4200
because of (54) +4946
to (50) +4200
ahead (45) +4200
from (45) +4946
faces (35)
front (25)
before (24) +4200+4946
by (21) +4200
before (19)
presence (19) +4200
of (17) +4946
sight (17)
facedown (15) +6584
against (13) +4200
on (13) +6584
from (11) +4200+4946
for (10) +4200
over (10) +6584
surface (10)
before (9) +907
facing (9)
because (8) +4946
from (8) +4200
near (8) +6584
open (8)
by (7) +4946
formerly (7) +4200
meet (7) +4200
with (7) +4200
in (6) +6584
in front of (6) +6584
near (6) +4200
serve (6) +4200+6641
against (5) +928
before (5) +6584
east (5) +6584
used to (5) +4200
accept (4) +5951
at (4) +4946
determined (4) +8492
in front of (4) +448
show partiality (4) +5795
show partiality (4) +5951
upon (4) +6584
against (3) +4946
east (3)
entreat (3) +906+2704

escape (3) +4946
face (3) +4200
face (3) +6425
facedown (3) +448
faces (3) +6584
facing (3) +448
facing (3) +6584
leading (3) +4200
me (3) +3276
opposite (3) +4200
sight (3) +4200
sought the favor of (3) +906+2704
straight ahead (3) +448+6298
toward (3) +6584
accompanies (2) +4200
across (2) +6584
across from (2) +6584
advisers (2) +8011
as long as (2) +4200
at (2) +4200
at tableˢ (2) +4200
attitude (2)
audience (2)
before (2) +5584
beside (2) +4200
covered with (2) +4200
entered service (2) +4200+6641
face to face (2)
faced (2)
faced (2) +448
faced each other (2) +8011
floor (2)
from (2) +4946+6584
from (2) +6584
in front of (2)
in front of (2) +907
in way (2) +4200
inside (2) +4200
leader (2) +2143+4200
led in campaigns (2) +995+2256+3655+4200
looking (2)
lying on (2) +6584
of (2) +4200
of (2) +4200+4946
preceded (2) +2118+4200
preceded (2) +4200
prostrate (2) +6584
reject (2) +8740
repulse (2) +8740
resist (2) +4200+6641
see (2) +4200
seems to (2) +4200
served (2) +4200+6641
serving (2) +4200+6641
shows partiality (2) +5951
top (2)
under (2) +4200
withstand (2) +928+6641
withstand (2) +4200+6641
won (2) +4200+5951
you (2) +3871
yourselves (2) +4013
above (1) +6584
accepted (1) +906+5951
adjoining (1) +448
advance (1) +2025
against (1) +6584
ahead (1) +4200+4946
ahead (1) +6584
all (1)
appear before (1) +8011
appearance (1)
appearing (1)
approach (1)
are shown respect (1) +2075
assistant (1) +4200+6641
at (1) +6584
at advance (1) +4200
at sanctuaryˢ (1) +4200
at the head of (1) +4200
attend (1) +4200

attend (1) +4200+6641
attending (1) +4200
attention (1)
attention (1) +4200
awaits (1) +4200
away from (1) +4946
because of (1) +3954+4946
before (1) +448
before eyes (1) +4200
before time (1) +4200+4946
beforehand (1) +4200+4946
beginning (1)
bent on (1) +5584
beside (1) +6584
blade (1)
blindfolds (1) +4059
border (1)
borne on (1) +6584
bowed down (1) +5877+6584
bowed down to the ground (1) +5877+6584
check (1) +995+4200
come across (1) +4200+7925
come into presence (1) +906+8011
condition (1)
confronting (1) +4946
consult (1) +4200
corresponding to (1) +6584
countenance (1)
court favor (1) +2704
cover (1) +4848
crossing (1) +6584
curry favor with (1) +2704
defense against (1) +4946
determine (1) +8492
determined (1) +8492+8492
directly opposite (1) +4200+5790
disgrace (1) +1425
earlier times (1)
east (1) +6584+7710
edge (1)
eluded (1) +4946+6015
end (1)
enter service (1) +4200+6641
entered the service (1) +4200+6641
ever (1) +4200
expression (1)
extended (1) +6584
face (1) +4946
faced (1) +4200
faced forward (1) +448+4578
favoritism (1) +2075
field (1)
fierce-looking (1) +6434
for (1)
for (1) +4946
for fear of (1) +4946
for relief from (1) +4200+4946
for sake (1) +4946
forward (1) +4200
found (1) +4200+8011
from (1) +448
from (1) +4946+6640
front columns (1)
frown (1) +5877
give (1) +4200
grant (1) +5951
granted request (1) +5951
ground (1)
had been (1) +4200
had special access to (1) +8011
head (1)
headed for (1) +8492
hear (1) +4200+5877
here (1) +4200
highly regarded (1) +5951
honored (1) +5951
humiliation (1) +1425
implore (1) +2704
in (1)
in (1) +4200
in deference to (1) +4946

in earlier times (1) +4200
in eyes (1) +4200
in front (1)
in front of (1) +448+4578
in front of (1) +4946
in hostility toward (1) +6584
in path (1) +4200
in preference to (1) +6584
in service (1) +4200
in sight (1) +907
in the eyes of (1) +4200
in the front line (1) +448+4578
in the presence of (1) +5790
in view (1) +907
inner (1) +4200
instead of (1) +4200
intended (1)
intercede with (1) +906+2704
interceded with (1) +906+2704
lead (1)
lead (1) +995+2256+3655+4200
lead (1) +2143+4200
lead (1) +4200
lead across (1) +4200+6296
led (1) +4200
led out (1) +3655+4200
lifetime (1)
lived in hostility toward (1) +5877+6584
look in the face (1) +448+5951
look with favor (1) +239
look with favor (1) +5564
looked (1)
looked (1) +8492
looks (1)
made face (1) +5989
make room for (1) +4946
man of rank (1) +5951
meet (1) +448
meet (1) +4946
meet with (1) +8011
more quickly than (1) +4200
more readily than (1) +4200
mouth (1)
my (1) +3276
my (1) +3276+4200
nearest (1) +6584
never (1) +4200+4202
obstinate (1) +7997
on both sides (1) +294+2256
open (1) +4200
open before (1) +5790
opening (1)
opposite (1) +448
ours (1) +4200+5646
out (1) +4946
out of (1) +4946
out of way (1) +4200+4946
outer (1)
over (1) +4200
overlooking (1) +4200
pacify (1) +4105
parallel (1) +928
partial (1) +5951
partiality (1) +5365
preceding (1) +4200
predecessor (1) +889+2118+4200
present (1)
present (1) +4200
present (1) +4200+5877
previous (1) +4200
prominent (1) +5951
protection from (1) +4946
put (1) +995+4200
puts up a bold front (1) +928+6451
receive (1) +5951
reflects a face (1) +2021+2021+4200+7156
regard (1) +2118+4200
regarded in the sight of (1) +4200
regards (1) +4200+5162
region (1)
reject (1) +4946+6584+8938

reject (1) +4946+6584+8959
renounce (1) +8740
resist (1)
resolved (1) +5989
respect (1) +5951
scalp (1)
see (1) +8011
seek an audience with (1) +1335
seek favor (1) +906+2704
seek favor (1) +2704
seen for myself (1) +8011
serve (1) +2118+4200
serve (1) +4200
served (1) +907+6641
served (1) +2118+4200
show (1) +4200
showed partiality (1) +5951
shown honor (1) +5951
shown partiality (1) +5951
some distance from (1) +4946
sought favor (1) +906+2704
sought favor (1) +2704
spared from (1) +4946
stared with a fixed gaze (1)
        +906+2256+6641+8492
stern-faced (1) +6434
sulking (1) +906+6015
table^s (1)
take for (1) +4200+5989
taken from (1) +4200+4946
that^s (1)
the LORD himself (1) +3378
their own (1) +2157
themselves (1) +2157
those^s (1) +2021
throughout (1) +3972+6584
tilting away from (1) +4946
to (1) +907
to (1) +4200+6584
to (1) +4946
toward (1)
toward (1) +448
toward (1) +2006+6584
turn away (1) +6015
turned (1) +5989
turned (1) +6015
turned (1) +8492
under (1) +907
under (1) +4946
under blessing (1) +4200
under direction (1) +4200
under supervision (1) +4200
unless (1) +561+3954+4200
unyielding (1) +2617
upside down (1) +6584
watched (1) +4200
way (1)
where^s (1) +4200
while still alive (1) +6584
with (1) +907
with (1) +6584
within sight of (1) +907
withstood (1) +928+6641
worship (1) +4200
you (1) +4013
you yourself (1) +3870
untranslated (121)

7157 פִּנָּה *pinnāh* (31)
corner (15)
corners (5)
cornerstone (3)
leaders (2)
capstone (1) +8031
corner defenses (1)
cornerstone (1) +74
cornerstones (1)
street corner (1)
strongholds (1)

7158 1פְּנוּאֵל *p'nû'ēl1* (2)
Penuel (2)

7159 2פְּנוּאֵל *p'nû'ēl2* (6)
Peniel (5)
they^s (1) +408

7160 1פְּנִיאֵל *p'niy'ēl1* (1)
untranslated (1)

7161 2פְּנִיאֵל *p'niy'ēl2* (1)
Peniel (1)

7162 פְּנִיִים *p'niyyyim*
Variant; not used

7163 פְּנִימָה *p'niymāh* (13)
inside (2)
within (2)
in (1)
inner (1) +4200
inner sanctuary (1)
inside (1) +4200
inside (1) +4946
into (1) +448
into (1) +4200
inward (1)
untranslated (1)

7164 פְּנִימִי *p'niymiy* (31)
inner (25)
inner sanctuary (2)
innermost (2)
far end (1)
inside (1)

7165 פְּנִינִים *p'niyniym* (7)
rubies (6)
untranslated (1)

7166 פְּנִנָּה *p'ninnāh* (3)
Peninnah (3)

7167 פָּנַק *pānaq* (1)
pampers (1)

7168 פַּס *pas* (5)
richly ornamented (3)
ornamented (2)

7169 פַּס דַּמִּים *pas dammiym* (1)
Pas Dammim (1)

7170 פָּסַג *pāsag* (1)
view (1)

7171 פִּסְגָּה *pisgāh* (8)
Pisgah (8)

7172 פִּסָּה *pissāh* (1)
abound (1) +2118

7173 1פָּסַח *pāsah1* (4)
pass over (3)
passed over (1)

7174 2פָּסַח *pāsah2* (3)
became crippled (1)
danced (1)
waver (1)

7175 פֶּסַח *pesah* (49)
Passover (36)
Passover lamb (4)
Passover lambs (3)
Passover offerings (3)
did so^s (1) +906+2021+6913
its^s (1) +2021
Passover animals (1)

7176 פָּסֵחַ *pāsēah* (4)
Paseah (4)

7177 פִּסֵּחַ *pissēah* (14)
lame (11)
crippled (3)

7178 פָּסִיל *pāsiyl* (23)
idols (16)
images (5)
carved idols (1)
carved images (1)

7179 פָּסַך *pāsak* (1)
Pasach (1)

7180 פָּסַל *pāsal* (6)
chisel out (2)
chiseled out (2)
carved (1)
cut (1)

7181 פֶּסֶל *pesel* (31)
idol (11)
idols (7)
carved image (5)
image (4)
carved (2)
carved images (1)
images (1)

7182 פָּסַס *pāsas* (1)
vanished (1)

7183 פִּסְפָּה *pispāh* (1)
Pispah (1)

7184 פָּעָה *pā'āh* (1)
cry out (1)

7185 פָּעוּ *pā'û* (2)
Pau (2)

7186 פְּעוֹר *p⁽ᵉ⁾'ôr* (9)
Peor (9)

7187 פָּעִי *pā'iy*
Variant; not used

7188 פָּעַל *pā'al* (57)
evildoers (16) +224
do (12)
done (9)
does (2)
made (2)
act (1)
affect (1)
bestow (1)
bring (1)
devise (1)
did (1)
evildoer (1) +224
fashions (1)
forges (1)
maker (1)
makes ready (1)
plot (1)
practice (1)
wicked men (1) +224
works (1)
works out (1)

7189 פֹּעַל *pō'al* (37)
deeds (8)
work (7)
works (5)
what done (4)
conduct (2)
labor (2)
performed exploits (2)
acts (1)
did (1)
made (1)
something (1)
wages (1)
what did (1)
whatˢ (1)

7190 פְּעֻלָּה *p⁽ᵉ⁾'ullāh* (14)
wages (3)
deeds (2)
recompense (2)
reward (2)
work (2)
payment (1)
reward (1) +5989
works (1)

7191 פְּעֻלְּתַי *p⁽ᵉ⁾'ull⁽ᵉ⁾tay* (1)
Peullethai (1)

7192 פָּעַם *pā'am* (5)
troubled (3)

stir (1)
troubles (1)

7193 פַּעַם *pa'am* (117)
times (44)
time (14)
feet (10)
twice (5)
now (3)
once (3) +285
once more (3)
as before (2) +928+3869+7193
encounter (2)
footsteps (2)
one more (2)
steps (2)
again (1) +928+1685+2021+2021+2085
annual (1) +928+2021+9102
anvil (1)
as done before (1) +928+3869+7193
at last (1) +2021
at other times (1) +928+7193
campaign (1)
clatter (1)
customary (1) +928+3869+7193
forms (1)
level (1)
moment (1)
now (1) +2021
once (1)
once more (1) +421+2021
otherˢ (1)
sets (1)
supports (1) +4190
thrust (1)
twice over (1)
untranslated (1)

7194 פַּעֲמוֹן *pa'ᵃmôn* (7)
bells (4)
alternateˢ (1) +2256+2298+8232
alternatedˢ (1) +2256+8232
themˢ (1) +2021

7195 פַּעֲנֵחַ *pa'nēah*
Variant; not used

7196 פָּעַר *pā'ar* (4)
open (2)
drank in (1) +7023
opens (1)

7197 פַּעֲרַי *pa'ᵃray* (1)
Paarai (1)

7198 פָּצָה *pāsāh* (15)
opened (3)
deliver (2)
open wide (2)
opens (2)
delivers (1)
given word (1) +906+7023
made a vow (1) +7023
open (1)
opened wide (1)
promised (1)

7199 1פָּצַח *pāsah1*
Variant; not used

7200 2פָּצַח *pāsah2* (9)
burst (6)
break (1)
break in pieces (1)
untranslated (1)

7201 פְּצִירָה *p⁽ᵉ⁾siyrāh* (1)
sharpening (1)

7202 פָּצַל *pāsal* (2)
peeled (1)
peeling (1)

7203 פְּצָלוֹת *p⁽ᵉ⁾sālôt* (1)
stripes (1)

7204 פָּצַם *pāsam* (1)
torn open (1)

7205 פָּצַע *pāsa'* (3)
been emasculated (1)
bruised (1)
wounded (1)

7206 פֶּצַע *pesa'* (8)
wounds (4)
wound (2)
bruises (1)
wounding (1)

7207 פָּצַץ *pāsas* (3)
breaks in pieces (1)
crumbled (1)
crushed (1)

7208 פָּצֵץ *passēs*
Variant; not used

7209 פִּצֵּץ *pissēs*
Variant; not used

7210 פָּצַר *pāsar* (7)
insisted (2)
arrogance (1)
kept bringing pressure (1) +4394
persisted (1)
persuaded (1)
urged (1)

7211 פַּק *piq* (1)
give way (1)

7212 פָּקַד *pāqad* (301)
punish (45)
counted (23)
number (19)
numbered (13)
numbers (12)
appoint (11)
were counted (11)
appointed (9)
assigned (9)
count (8)
mustered (8)
care for (6)
missing (6)
put in charge (6)
appointed as governor (5)
punished (5)
come (3)
empty (3)
punishes (3)
surely come to aid (3) +7212
assign (2)
be punished (2)
deal (2)
enroll (2)
examine (2)
gracious (2)
mobilized (2)
officers (2)
punishing (2)
supervisors (2)
total (2)
were appointed (2)
accuse (1) +6584
assembled (1)
be called to arms (1)
be missed (1)
be missing (1)
be robbed (1)
bestow punishment (1)
bestowed care on (1)
bring (1)
bring punishment (1)
called to account (1)
came (1)
come to aid (1)
come to the aid of (1)
commit (1)
concerned about (1)
counted (1) +7212
destroy (1)
didˢ (1)

experience (1)
fails to come (1)
harm (1)
in charge (1)
in charge of (1)
lack (1)
listed (1)
longed for (1)
missed (1)
misses at all (1) +7212
missing (1) +7212
muster forces (1)
mustering (1)
numbering (1)
placed (1)
post (1)
posted (1)
prescribed (1)
punishments come (1)
put (1)
put away (1)
see (1)
send (1)
sets (1)
store (1)
summoned (1)
take care of (1)
take stock of (1)
total (1) +3972
untouched (1) +1153
visit (1)
was counted (1)
was entrusted (1) +7214
watch over (1)
watched over and seen (1) +7212
were counted in the census (1)
were found missing (1)
were recorded (1)
were registered (1)
untranslated (6)

7213 פְּקֻדָּה *p⁽e⁾quddāh* (32)
punished (4)
punishment (3)
appointed (2)
appointed order (2)
guards (2)
judgment (2)
assignment (1)
charge (1)
enrollment (1)
governor (1)
having charge (1)
in charge (1)
mustered (1)
officials (1)
oversight (1)
place of leadership (1)
prison (1) +1074+2021
providence (1)
reckoning (1)
responsible (1)
stored up (1)
visits (1)
what usually happens (1)

7214 פִּקָּדוֹן *piqqādôn* (3)
held in reserve (1)
something entrusted (1)
was entrusted (1) +7212

7215 פְּקִדֻת *p⁽e⁾qidut* (1)
guard (1)

7216 פְּקוֹד *p⁽e⁾qôd* (2)
Pekod (2)

7217 פְּקוּדִים *p⁽e⁾qûdiym* (1)
amounts (1)

7218 פִּקּוּדִים *piqqûdiym* (24)
precepts (24)

7219 פָּקַח *pāqah* (20)
open (7)

opened (4)
be opened (2)
fix (1)
gives sight (1)
keep watchful (1)
opens (1)
stay awake (1) +6524
were opened (1)
untranslated (1)

7220 פֶּקַח *peqah* (11)
Pekah (10)
Pekah's (1)

7221 פִּקֵּחַ *piqqēah* (2)
see (1)
sight (1)

7222 פְּקַחְיָה *p⁽e⁾qahyāh* (3)
Pekahiah (2)
Pekahiah's (1)

7223 פְּקַח־קוֹחַ *p⁽e⁾qah-qôah* (1)
release from darkness (1)

7224 פָּקִיד *pāqiyd* (13)
chief officer (3)
in charge (3)
commissioners (2)
officer (2)
deputy (1)
direction (1)
supervisors (1)

7225 פְּקָעִים *p⁽e⁾qā'iym* (3)
gourds (3)

7226 פַּקֻּעֹת *paqqu'ōt* (1)
gourds (1)

7227 פֶּקֶר *peqer*
Variant; not used

7228 פַּר *par* (132)
bull (47)
bulls (30)
bull (27) +1330
bull's (9)
bulls (5) +1330
young bulls (3)
itˢ (2) +2021
itsˢ (2) +2021
bull calves (1)
itsˢ (1)
oneˢ (1)
oxen (1)
untranslated (3)

7229 פָּרָא *pārā'* (1)
thrives (1)

7230 פֶּרֶא *pere'* (9)
wild donkey (4)
wild donkeys (3)
donkeys (1)
wild donkey's (1)

7231 פִּרְאָם *pir'ām* (1)
Piram (1)

7232 פַּרְבָּר *parbār* (2)
court (2)

7233 פָּרַד *pārad* (26)
separates (3)
spread out (3)
are scattered (1)
be parted (1)
be scattered (1)
be separated (1)
consort (1)
deserts (1)
divided (1)
keeps apart (1)
left (1)
out of joint (1)
part company (1)
parted (1)

parted company (1)
scattered (1)
separated (1)
separated (1) +1068
set apart by themselves (1)
unfriendly (1)
was separated (1)
were parted (1)

7234 פֶּרֶד *pered* (14)
mules (10)
mule (4)

7235 פִּרְדָּה *pirdāh* (3)
mule (3)

7236 פַּרְדֵּס *pardēs* (3)
forest (1)
orchard (1)
parks (1)

7237 פְּרֻדֹת *p⁽e⁾rudōt* (1)
seeds (1)

7238 1פָּרָה *pārāh1* (29)
fruitful (14)
make fruitful (5)
fruitful vine (2) +1201
made fruitful (2)
bear fruit (1)
flourish (1)
increased (1)
numbers increased greatly (1) +2256+8049
produces (1)
spring up (1)

7239 2פָּרָה *pārāh2* (26)
cows (18)
heifer (6)
cow (1)
thoseˢ (1) +2021

7240 3פָּרָה *pārāh3* (1)
Parah (1)

7241 פֶּרֶה *pereh* (1)
wild donkey (1)

7242 פֻּרָה *purāh* (2)
Purah (2)

7243 פְּרוּדָא *p⁽e⁾rûdā'* (1)
Peruda (1)

7244 פְּרוֹזִים *p⁽e⁾rôziym* (1)
untranslated (1)

7245 פָּרוּחַ *pārûah* (1)
Paruah (1)

7246 פַּרְוַיִם *parwayim* (1)
Parvaim (1)

7247 פַּרְוָר *parwār* (1)
court (1)

7248 פָּרוּר *pārûr* (3)
pot (3)

7249 פֵּרוֹת *pērôt*
Variant; not used

7250 פָּרַז *pāraz* (2)
warriors (1)
untranslated (1)

7251 פְּרָזוֹן *p⁽e⁾rāzôn* (2)
village life (1)
warriors (1)

7252 פְּרָזוֹת *p⁽e⁾rāzôt* (2)
city without walls (1)
villages (1) +6551

7253 פְּרָזִי *p⁽e⁾rāziy* (4)
country (1)
rural (1)
unwalled (1)
unwalled villages (1)

7254 פְּרִזִּי *p⁽e⁾rizziy* (23)
Perizzites (23)

7255 1פָּרַח *pārah1* (34)
flourish (5)
blossom (4)
broken out (3)
budded (3)
bud (2)
spring up (2)
blossomed (1)
break out (1)
breaking out (1)
breaks out all over (1) +7255
bring to bud (1)
broke out (1)
burst into bloom (1) +7255
make flourish (1)
reappears (1) +2256+8740
spreading (1)
sprout (1)
sprouted (1)
thrive (1)

7256 2פָּרַח *pārah2* (2)
birds (2)

7257 3פָּרַח *pārah3*
Variant; not used

7258 פֶּרַח *perah* (17)
blossoms (8)
blossom (3)
floral work (2)
budded (1) +3655
flowers (1)
untranslated (2)

7259 פִּרְחַח *pirhah* (1)
tribe (1)

7260 פָּרַט *pārat* (1)
strum away (1)

7261 פֶּרֶט *peret* (1)
grapes that have fallen (1)

7262 פְּרִי *pᵉriy* (120)
fruit (80)
crops (7)
produce (4)
young (4)
fruits (3)
deserve (2)
firstfruits (2) +8040
fruitful (2)
children (1) +1061
children (1) +1061+2021
crops (1) +141+2021
descendants (1)
descendants (1) +1061
earnings (1) +4090
fruitage (1)
fruitfulness (1)
infants (1) +1061
offspring (1)
result (1)
reward earned (1) +3338
rewarded (1)
what deserve (1)
willful pride (1) +1542
untranslated (1)

7263 פְּרִידָא *pᵉriydā'* (1)
Perida (1)

7264 1פָּרִיץ *pāriys1* (1)
ferocious (1)

7265 2פָּרִיץ *pāriys2* (5)
violent (3)
robbers (2)

7266 פֶּרֶךְ *perek* (6)
ruthlessly (5) +928
brutally (1) +928

7267 פָּרֹכֶת *pārōket* (25)
curtain (25)

7268 פָּרַם *pāram* (3)

tear (2)
torn (1)

7269 פַּרְמַשְׁתָּא *parmaštā'* (1)
Parmashta (1)

7270 פַּרְנָךְ *parnāk* (1)
Parnach (1)

7271 1פָּרַס *pāras1* (14)
split (11)
hoofs (1)
offer food (1)
share (1)

7272 פֶּרֶס *peres* (2)
vulture (2)

7273 2פָּרַס *pāras2* (28)
Persia (26)
Persian (2)

7274 פַּרְסָה *parsāh* (21)
hoof (12)
hoofs (6)
untranslated (3)

7275 פַּרְסִי *pārsiy* (1)
Persian (1)

7276 1פָּרַע *pāra'1* (1)
take the lead (1)

7277 2פָּרַע *pāra'2* (15)
unkempt (3)
ignores (2)
avoid (1)
cast off restraint (1)
get out of control (1)
hold back (1)
ignore (1)
ignored (1)
loosen (1)
promoted wickedness (1)
running wild (1)
taking away (1)

7278 1פֶּרַע *pera'1* (2)
leaders (1)
princes (1)

7279 2פֶּרַע *pera'2* (2)
hair (1) +8552
hair long (1)

7280 3פֶּרַע *pera'3*
Variant; not used

7281 פַּרְעֹה *par'ōh* (274)
Pharaoh (206)
Pharaoh's (51)
hisˢ (5)
heˢ (4)
himˢ (2)
Pharaoh's (2) +4200
royal (1)
sheˢ (1) +1426
thereˢ (1) +1074
untranslated (1)

7282 1פַּרְעֹשׁ *par'ōš1* (2)
flea (2)

7283 2פַּרְעֹשׁ *par'ōš2* (6)
Parosh (6)

7284 פִּרְעָתוֹן *pir'ātôn* (1)
Pirathon (1)

7285 פִּרְעָתוֹנִי *pir'ātôniy* (5)
Pirathonite (3)
from Pirathon (1)
untranslated (1)

7286 פַּרְפַּר *parpar* (1)
Pharpar (1)

7287 פָּרַץ *pāras* (50)
broken out (4)
broke down (3)
broken down (3)

urged (3)
break down (2)
break out (2)
increased (2)
spread (2)
spread out (2)
again and again bursts (1) +7288+7288
are broken down (1)
break (1)
break all bounds (1)
breaking away (1)
breaks open (1)
breaks through (1)
brim over (1)
broke out (1)
broke out in anger (1)
broken (1)
broken into (1)
broken out (1) +7288
broken through (1)
burst forth (1)
cuts (1)
destroy (1)
dispersing (1)
far and wide (1)
gaps (1)
increase (1)
many (1)
prosperous (1)
tear down (1)
urging (1)
went out (1)
untranslated (1)

7288 1פֶּרֶץ *peres1* (19)
gap (3)
breach (2)
break out (2)
wrath (2)
again and again bursts (1) +7287+7288
breaching of walls (1)
breaks (1)
breaks in the wall (1)
broken (1)
broken out (1) +7287
broken places (1)
cracked (1) +5877
gap in the wall (1)

7289 2פֶּרֶץ *peres2* (15)
Perez (15)

7290 פֶּרֶץ עֻזָּא *peres 'uzzā'* (2)
Perez Uzzah (2)

7291 פַּרְצִי *parsiy* (1)
Perezite (1)

7292 פְּרָצִים *pᵉrāsiym* (1)
Perazim (1)

7293 פָּרַק *pāraq* (10)
take off (2)
free (1)
freed (1)
rip to pieces (1)
tearing off (1)
throw off (1)
took off (1)
tore apart (1)
was stripped (1)

7294 פֶּרֶק *pereq* (2)
crossroads (1)
plunder (1)

7295 פָּרָק *pārāq* (1)
untranslated (1)

7296 1פָּרַר *pārar1* (48)
break (8)
broken (6)
breaking (5)
broke (4)
foils (2)
frustrate (2)

nullifies (2) +7296
be broken (1)
be thwarted (1)
discredit (1)
fail (1)
frustrated (1)
frustrating (1)
no longer stirred (1)
nullified (1)
nullifies (1)
nullify (1)
put away (1)
revoking (1)
take (1)
thwart (1)
thwarts (1)
undermine (1)
violate (1)
was revoked (1)

7297 פָּרַר pārar2 (4)
is split asunder (1) +7297
shattered (1)
split open (1)

7298 פָּרַשׂ pāraś (68)
spread (21)
spread out (19)
spreading (4)
scattered (3)
spreading out (2)
throw (2)
be scattered (1)
cast (1)
chop up (1)
display (1)
exposes (1)
extended (1)
gives (1)
held out (1)
laid (1)
opens (1)
scatters (1)
spreads (1)
spreads out (1)
stretch out (1)
stretches out (1)
stretching out (1)
unrolled (1)

7299 פָּרְשֵׁז parśēz (1)
spreading (1)

7300 פָּרַשׁ pāraš1 (3)
clear (1)
made clear (1)
making clear (1)

7301 פָּרַשׁ pāraš2 (1)
poisons (1)

7302 פֶּרֶשׁ pereš1 (7)
offal (6)
untranslated (1)

7303 פֶּרֶשׁ pereš2 (1)
Peresh (1)

7304 פָּרָשׁ pārāš1 (18)
horses (14)
war horses (2)
riders (1) +1251
steeds (1)

7305 פָּרָשׁ pārāš2 (38)
horsemen (27)
charioteers (6)
cavalry (5)

7306 פַּרְשֶׁגֶן parśegen (1)
copy (1)

7307 פַּרְשְׁדֹן parš⁰dōn (1)
back (1)

7308 פָּרָשָׁה pārāšāh (2)
exact amount (1)

---

full account (1)

7309 פַּרְשַׁנְדָתָא paršandātā' (1)
Parshandatha (1)

7310 פְּרָת p⁰rāt (19)
Euphrates (15)
Perath (4)

7311 פֹּרָת pōrāt
Variant; not used

7312 פַּרְתְּמִים partmiym (3)
most noble (1)
nobility (1)
princes (1)

7313 פָּשָׂה pāśāh (20)
spread (14)
spread (2) +7313
spreading (2) +7313

7314 פָּשַׂע pāśa' (1)
march (1)

7315 פֶּשַׂע peśa' (1)
step (1)

7316 פָּשַׂק pāśaq (2)
offering body (1) +906+8079
speaks rashly (1) +8557

7317 פַּשׁ paš (1)
wickedness (1)

7318 פָּשַׁח pāšāh (1)
mangled (1)

7319 פַּשְׁחוּר pashûr (14)
Pashhur (13)
heˢ (1)

7320 פָּשַׁט pāšat (43)
raided (7)
strip (7)
stripped (4)
take off (4)
skin (2)
stripped off (2)
took off (2)
advance (1)
go raiding (1)
made a dash (1)
raiding (1)
remove (1)
removed (1)
rob (1)
rushed (1)
rushed forward (1)
skinned (1)
strip off (1)
strip off clothes (1) +2256+6910
strip the dead (1)
swept down (1)
taken off (1)

7321 פָּשַׁע pāša' (41)
rebelled (13)
in rebellion (4)
rebels (3)
transgressors (3)
committed (2)
rebel (2)
rebellion (2)
revolted (2)
sin (2)
sinned (2)
do wrong (1)
in revolt (1)
offended (1)
rebellious (1)
sinners (1)
wrongs (1)

7322 פֶּשַׁע peša' (93)
sins (20)
offenses (14)
rebellion (13)

---

transgressions (11)
transgression (8)
sin (7)
offense (5)
rebellious (3)
crime (1)
disobeys (1)
guilt of rebellion (1)
guiltless (1) +1172
illegal possession (1)
penalty of sin (1)
rebels (1)
sinful (1)
sinfulness (1)
sinned (1)
wrong (1)
wrongs (1)

7323 פֵּשֶׁר pēšer (1)
explanation (1)

7324 פֵּשֶׁת pēšet (16)
linen (12)
flax (4)

7325 פִּשְׁתָּה pištāh (4)
flax (2)
wick (2)

7326 פַּת pat (14)
piece (2)
something to eat (2) +4312
bread (1)
crumble (1) +7359
crust (1)
food (1)
food (1) +4312
itˢ (1)
little (1)
pebbles (1)
pieces (1)
some (1)

7327 פֹּת pōt (2)
scalps (1)
sockets (1)

7328 פִּתְאֹם pit'ōm (25)
suddenly (13)
sudden (4)
in an instant (2)
all at once (1)
at once (1)
by surprise (1)
so quickly (1) +928
suddenly (1) +928+7353
unexpectedly (1)

7329 פַּת־בַּג pat-bag (6)
food (4)
choice food (1)
provisions (1)

7330 פִּתְגָם pitgām (2)
edict (1)
sentence (1)

7331 פָּתָה pātāh1 (27)
entice (5)
deceive (2)
enticed (2)
enticing (2)
allure (1)
be deceived (1)
be persuaded (1)
been enticed (1)
coax (1)
deceived (1)
easily deceived (1)
enticed (1) +4222
entices (1)
flatter (1)
is enticed (1)
lure (1)
seduces (1)
simple (1)

talks too much (1) +8557
was deceived (1)

7332 פָּתָה2 *pātāh2* (1)
extend the territory (1)

7333 פְּתוּאֵל *pᵉtû'ēl* (1)
Pethuel (1)

7334 פִּתּוּחַ *pitûaḥ* (11)
engraved (2)
art of engraving (1) +7338
carved paneling (1)
engrave (1) +7338
engraved (1) +7338
engraves (1)
experienced in engraving (1) +7338
inscription (1)
inscription (1) +4844
untranslated (1)

7335 פְּתוֹר *pᵉtôr* (2)
Pethor (2)

7336 פְּתוֹת *pᵉtôt* (1)
scraps (1)

7337 פָּתַח1 *pātaḥ1* (136)
open (44)
opened (33)
be opened (4)
loose (2)
openhanded (2) +906+3338+7337
speak up (2) +7023
takes off (2)
were opened (2)
are opened (1)
be poured out (1)
be released (1)
be set free (1)
bottled-up (1) +4202
break open (1)
breaking up (1)
draw (1)
drawn (1)
expose (1)
expound (1)
free yourself (1)
freed (1)
freeing (1)
give command (1) +7023
go (1)
loosened (1)
make flow (1)
market (1)
open wide (1)
opened up (1)
opens (1)
reach (1)
release (1)
removed (1)
say (1) +7023
set free (1)
speaks (1) +7023
strip (1)
take off (1)
throw open (1)
thrown open (1)
uncovers (1)
unloaded (1)
unlocked (1)
unsealed (1)
unstopped (1)
unstrung (1)
untied (1)
was opened (1)
wide open (1) +7337
untranslated (2)

7338 פִּתַּח2 *pātaḥ2* (9)
engrave (3)
art of engraving (1) +7334
carved (1)
engrave (1) +7334
engraved (1)

engraved (1) +7334
experienced in engraving (1) +7334

7339 פֶּתַח *petaḥ* (163)
entrance (110)
door (15)
doorway (9)
doors (5)
entrances (3)
doorways (2)
gate (2)
gates (2)
itˢ (2) +2021
doorway (1) +4647
doorways (1) +4647
entrance (1) +9133
entrances (1) +4427
gateways (1) +9133
mouth (1)
oneˢ (1)
outside (1)
outside (1) +2025
parapet opening (1)
words (1) +7023
untranslated (2)

7340 פֵּתַח *pētaḥ* (1)
unfolding (1)

7341 פִּתָחוֹן *pitāḥôn* (2)
open (1)
open (1) +5989

7342 פְּתַחְיָה *pᵉtaḥyāh* (4)
Pethahiah (4)

7343 פֶּתִי1 *petiy1* (16)
simple (15)
simplehearted (1)

7344 פֶּתִי2 *petiy2* (3)
simple ways (2)
ignorance (1)

7345 פְּתִיגִיל *pᵉtiygiyl* (1)
fine clothing (1)

7346 פְּתַיּוּת *pᵉtayyût* (1)
undisciplined (1)

7347 פְּתִיחָה *pᵉtiyḥāh* (2)
drawn sword (1)
drawn swords (1)

7348 פָּתִיל *pātiyl* (11)
cord (8)
fastened (1)
piece of string (1) +5861
strands (1)

7349 פָּתַל *pātal* (5)
show yourself shrewd (2)
crooked (1)
had a struggle (1) +5887
wily (1)

7350 פְּתַלְתֹּל *pᵉtaltōl* (1)
crooked (1)

7351 פִּתֹם *pitōm* (1)
Pithom (1)

7352 פֶּתֶן *peten* (6)
cobra (3)
serpents (2)
cobras (1)

7353 פֶּתַע *peta'* (7)
suddenly (3)
instant (1)
suddenly (1) +928
suddenly (1) +928+7328

7354 פָּתַר *pātar* (9)
interpret (4)
interpreted (2)
given interpretation (1)
giving interpretation (1)
said in interpretation (1)

7355 פִּתָרוֹן *pitārôn* (5)
meaning (2)
means (2)
interpretations (1)

7356 פַּתְרוֹס *patrôs* (5)
Upper Egypt (2)
Upper Egypt (2) +824
Upper [Egypt] (1)

7357 פַּתְרֻסִים *patrusiym* (2)
Pathrusites (2)

7358 פַּתְשֶׁגֶן *patšegen* (3)
copy (3)

7359 פָּתַת *pātat* (1)
crumble (1) +7326

7360 צ *s*
Variant; not used

7361 צֵא *ṣē'*
Variant; not used

7362 צֵאָה *ṣē'āh* (2)
excrement (1)
excrement (1) +1645

7363 צוֹאָה *ṣô'āh* (5)
filth (3)
untranslated (2)

7364 צוֹאִי *ṣô'iy* (2)
filthy (2)

7365 צֶאֱלִים *ṣe'ᵉliym* (2)
lotus plants (1)
lotuses (1)

7366 צֹאן *ṣō'n* (275)
sheep (97)
flocks (69)
flock (66)
sheep and goats (11)
animals (6)
shepherds (3) +8286
lambs (2) +1201
theyˢ (2) +2021
animal from flock (1)
breeding (1) +2021+3501
choice lambs (1) +4119+4946
ewes (1)
flocks (1) +5238
goats (1)
pens (1) +1556
restˢ (1)
sheep (1) +3897
sheep and goats (1) +5238
sheep goats or (1)
sheep or goats (1)
themˢ (1) +2257
theyˢ (1) +3276
whichˢ (1) +2021
whichˢ (1) +2257
untranslated (3)

7367 צַאֲנָן *ṣa'ᵃnān* (1)
Zaanan (1)

7368 צֶאֱצָאִים *ṣe'ᵉṣā'iym* (11)
offspring (4)
descendants (3)
all that comes out (1)
children (1) +5055
crops (1)
that comes out (1)

7369 צָב1 *ṣāb1* (2)
covered (1)
wagons (1)

7370 צָב2 *ṣāb2* (1)
great lizard (1)

7371 צָבָא1 *ṣābā'1* (14)
conscripting (2)
fight (2)
fought (2)

attack (1)
do battle (1)
fighting (1)
serve (1) +7372
served (1)
served (1) +7371
take part (1) +7372

7372 2אָבָצ *sābā'2* (487)
Almighty (285)
army (59)
divisions (21)
division (20)
battle (12)
host (8)
hosts (8)
armies (6)
war (6)
forces (5)
in command (4) +6584
serve (4)
starry host (4)
stars (4)
hard service (3)
chief officer (2) +2021+8569
experienced soldiers (2) +3655
heavenly hosts (2)
ready for military service (2) +3655
ready to go out (2) +3655
troops (2)
armed forces (1) +2657
army (1) +2657
array (1)
battle (1) +4878
commander in chief (1) +2021+6584
commanders (1) +8569
company (1)
men ready for battle (1) +1522+4878
multitudes (1)
powers (1)
ready for battle (1) +408+2021+4200+4878
ready for battle (1) +928+2021+4878
regular service (1) +6275
serve (1) +6913
serve (1) +7371
soldier (1) +408
soldiers (1)
soldiers (1) +408
soldiers (1) +6639
starry hosts (1)
take part (1) +7371
vast array (1)
weapon (1) +3998+4878
untranslated (3)

7373 3אָבָצ *sābā'3* (1)
gazelles (1)

7374 הָאָבְצ *sᵉbā'āh* (2)
gazelles (2)

7375 םיאבצ *sᵉbō'iym* (5)
Zeboiim (5)

7376 הָבֵבֹצ *sōbēbāh*
Variant; not used

7377 הָבָצ *sābāh* (2)
swell (1)
swells (1)

7378 הֶבֹצ *sōbeh*
Variant; not used

7379 הֶבָצ *sābeh* (1)
swell (1)

7380 עַבֻצ *sābûa'* (1)
speckled (1)

7381 טֶבְצ *sābat* (1)
offered (1)

7382 1יִבְצ *sᵉbiy1* (18)
beautiful (6)
glory (4)
beauty (2)

most beautiful (2)
beautiful jewelry (1) +6344
jewel (1)
most beautiful (1) +7382

7383 2יִבְצ *sᵉbiy2* (11)
gazelle (10)
gazelles (1)

7384 אָיְבִצ *sibyā'* (1)
Zibia (1)

7385 הָיְבִצ *sibyāh* (2)
Zibiah (2)

7386 הָיִבְצ *sᵉbiyyāh* (2)
gazelle (2)

7387 םיִיֹבְצ *sᵉbōyiym* (3)
untranslated (3)

7388 עַבָצ *sāba'*
Variant; not used

7389 עַבֶצ *seba'* (3)
colorful garments (2)
garments (1)

7390 ןֹעְבִצ *sib'ôn* (8)
Zibeon (8)

7391 םיִעֹבְצ *sᵉbō'iym* (2)
Zeboim (2)

7392 רַבָצ *sābar* (7)
build (1)
heaped up (1)
heaps up (1)
heaps up wealth (1)
piled (1)
store up (1)
stored up (1)

7393 רֶבֹצ *sibbur* (1)
piles (1)

7394 ןֹרְבִצ *sibbārôn*
Variant; not used

7395 תֶבֶצ *sebet* (1)
bundles (1)

7396 1דַצ *sad1* (34)
side (14)
sides (5)
arm (2)
beside (2) +4946
opposite sides (2) +7521
backs (1)
flank (1)
near (1) +4946
next to (1) +4946
otherˢ (1)
vicinity (1)
with (1) +4946
untranslated (2)

7397 2דַצ *sad2*
Variant; not used

7398 דָדָצ *sādād* (2)
Zedad (2)

7399 1הָדָצ *sādāh1* (2)
do intentionally (1)
hunting down (1)

7400 2הָדָצ *sādāh2* (1)
are destroyed (1)

7401 קֹדָצ *sādôq* (53)
Zadok (51)
themˢ (1) +59+2256
Zadokites (1) +1201

7402 הָיְדִצ *sᵉdiyyāh* (2)
intentionally (1) +928
unintentionally (1) +928+4202

7403 םיִדִצ *siddiym* (1)
Ziddim (1)

7404 קיִדַצ *saddiyq* (206)
righteous (178)
innocent (13)
just (3)
right (2)
righteous one (2)
upright (2)
honest (1)
in the right (1)
overrighteous (1) +2221
righteous (1) +2446
righteousness (1)
untranslated (1)

7405 קַדָצ *sādaq* (40)
righteous (11)
innocent (3)
acquit (2)
acquitting (2)
declare not guilty (2)
justify (2)
vindicated (2)
admit in the right (1)
appear righteous (1)
be reconsecrated (1)
cleared (1)
innocence (1)
justifying (1)
lead to righteousness (1)
made appear righteous (1)
made seem righteous (1)
maintain rights (1)
prove innocence (1)
prove right (1)
proved right (1)
right (1)
see that gets justice (1)
vindicates (1)

7406 קֶדֶצ *sedeq* (118)
righteousness (58)
righteous (16)
honest (8)
right (7)
justice (5)
accurate (3)
fairly (3)
just (3)
righteously (2)
truth (2)
cleared (1)
fairly (1) +928
integrity (1)
justly (1)
rightful (1)
rights (1)
true (1)
unrighteousness (1) +4202
vindication (1)
untranslated (2)

7407 הָקָדְצ *sᵉdāqāh* (159)
righteousness (98)
right (20)
righteous (9)
righteous acts (7)
righteous things (4)
innocence (2)
justice (2)
prosperity (2)
vindication (2)
claim (1)
honesty (1)
integrity (1)
just (1)
righteous act (1)
righteous deeds (1)
righteous state (1)
righteous will (1)
righteously (1)
salvation (1)
vindicated (1) +3655
untranslated (2)

7408 צִדְקִיָּה *sidqiyyāh* (7)
Zedekiah (7)

7409 צִדְקִיָּהוּ *sidqiyyāhû* (57)
Zedekiah (53)
Zedekiah's (2)
his[s] (1)
Zedekiah's (1) +4200

7410 צָהַב *sāhab* (1)
polished (1)

7411 צָהֹב *sāhōb* (3)
yellow (3)

7412 1צָהַל *sāhal1* (9)
acclaim (1)
cry out (1) +7754
held a celebration (1)
neigh (1)
neighing (1)
shout (1)
shout aloud (1)
shout for joy (1)
untranslated (1)

7413 2צָהַל *sāhal2* (1)
make shine (1)

7414 צָהַר *sāhar* (1)
crush olives (1)

7415 צֹהַר *sōhar* (1)
roof (1)

7416 צָהֳרַיִם *soherayim* (23)
noon (11)
midday (7)
noonday (3)
high noon (1)
noonday sun (1)

7417 צוּ *saw* (1)
idols (1)

7418 צַוָּאר *sawwā'r* (42)
neck (25)
necks (7)
threw arms around (2) +5877+6584
at heels (1) +6584
defiantly (1) +928
embraced (1) +6584
head (1)
shoulders (1)
yourselves (1) +4013
untranslated (2)

7419 צוֹבָא *sôbā'* (2)
Zobah (2)

7420 צוֹבָה *sôbāh* (10)
Zobah (10)

7421 צוּד *sûd* (17)
ensnare (4)
hunt (3)
hunts (2)
hunt down (1)
hunt down (1) +4200+4511
hunted (1)
hunted (1) +7421
preys upon (1)
stalk (1)
stalked (1)

7422 צָוָה *sāwāh* (504)
commanded (210)
command (45)
gave (25)
ordered (22)
commands (13)
giving (13)
gave orders (10)
give (10)
instructed (9)
appointed (8)
do (8)
told (8)
gave order (7)
directed (6)
gave command (5)
order (5)
tell (5)
been commanded (4)
give command (4)
given (4)
orders (4)
charged (3)
commission (3)
decreed (3)
gave instructions (3)
give orders (3)
instructions (3)
laid down (3)
put in order (3)
was commanded (3)
commanded (2) +5184
forbidden (2) +4202
given order (2)
given orders (2)
giving orders (2)
ordained (2)
send (2)
appoint (1)
are directed (1)
bestows (1)
commander (1)
commanding (1)
commissioned (1)
decree (1)
decrees (1)
determined (1)
direct (1)
directs (1)
dispatch (1)
forbidden (1)
forbidden (1) +1194
gave a charge (1)
gave an order (1)
gave commands (1)
gave the order (1)
give a message (1)
give commands (1)
give the order (1)
given a command (1)
given an order (1)
given the command (1)
giving instructions (1)
issue an order (1)
left instructions (1)
marshaled (1)
prescribed (1)
put in charge (1)
puts in command (1)
say (1)
sent (1)
sent word (1)
summon (1)
urge (1)
untranslated (2)

7423 צָוַח *sāwah* (1)
shout (1)

7424 צְוָחָה *sewāhāh* (4)
cries (1)
cry (1)
cry of distress (1)
cry out (1)

7425 צוּלָה *sûlāh* (1)
watery deep (1)

7426 צוּם *sûm* (21)
fasted (12)
fast (5)
fasted (1) +7426
fasted (1) +7427
fasting (1)

7427 צוֹם *sôm* (26)
fasting (10)
fast (9)
day of fasting (1)
fasted (1) +7426
fasts (1)
time of fasting (1)
untranslated (3)

7428 צוּעָר *sû'ār* (5)
Zuar (5)

7429 1צוּף *sûp1* (3)
closed (1)
made float (1)
overwhelmed (1)

7430 2צוּף *sûp2* (2)
comb (1)
honeycomb (1) +1831

7431 3צוּף *sûp3* (3)
Zuph (3)

7432 צוֹפַח *sôpah* (2)
Zophah (2)

7433 צוֹפִי *sôpay* (1)
Zophai (1)

7434 צוּפִי *sûpiy* (1)
Zuphite (1)

7435 צוֹפִים *sôpiym*
Variant; not used

7436 צוֹפַר *sôpar* (4)
Zophar (4)

7437 1צוּץ *sûs1* (8)
flourish (2)
blossomed (1) +7488
bud (1)
budded (1)
flourishes (1)
resplendent (1)
springs up (1)

7438 2צוּץ *sûs2* (1)
peering (1)

7439 צוּק *sûq* (11)
inflict (3)
besiege (2)
oppressor (2)
compels (1)
imposed (1)
nagging (1)
press (1)

7440 2צוּק *sûq2* (1)
barely whisper a prayer (1) +4318

7441 צוֹק *sôq* (1)
trouble (1)

7442 צוּקָה *sûqāh* (3)
distress (1)
fearful (1)
trouble (1)

7443 1צוּר *sûr1* (35)
besieging (7)
besieged (6)
laid siege (5)
besiege (3)
lay siege (3)
besieges (1)
encircle (1) +6584
enclose (1)
hem in (1)
put into bags (1)
siege (1)
stirring up (1)
take (1)
tied up (1)
tuck away (1)
under siege (1)

7444 2צוּר *sûr2* (4)
harass (2)
attack (1)

oppose (1)

7445 צוּר3 *sûr3* (2)
cast (1)
fashioning (1)

7446 צוּר4 *sûr4* (74)
rock (60)
rocks (8)
rocky (3)
crag (1)
crags (1)
strength (1)

7447 צוּר5 *sûr5*
Variant; not used

7448 צוּר6 *sûr6* (5)
Zur (5)

7449 צוּר7 *sûr7*
Variant; not used

7450 צוּר *sôr* (42)
Tyre (42)

7451 צוּרָה *sûrāh* (6)
design (3)
forms (1)
untranslated (2)

7452 צוּרִיאֵל *sûriy'ēl* (1)
Zuriel (1)

7453 צוּרִישַׁדָּי *sûriyšadday* (5)
Zurishaddai (5)

7454 צוּרֹנִים *saww⁽ᵉ⁾rōniym* (1)
necklace (1)

7455 צוּת *sût* (1)
set on fire (1)

7456 צַח *sah* (4)
clear (1)
radiant (1)
scorching (1)
shimmering (1)

7457 צָחָה *siheh* (1)
parched (1)

7458 צָחַח *sāhah* (1)
whiter (1)

7459 צְחִחִי *s⁽ᵉ⁾hihiy* (1)
untranslated (1)

7460 צְחִיחַ *sāhiyah* (5)
bare (4)
exposed places (1)

7461 צְחִיחָה *s⁽ᵉ⁾hiyhāh* (1)
sun-scorched land (1)

7462 צְחָנָה *sah⁽ᵃ⁾nāh* (1)
smell (1)

7463 צַחְצָחוֹת *sahsāhôt* (1)
sun-scorched land (1)

7464 צָחַק *sāhaq* (13)
laugh (4)
laughed (2)
make sport (2)
caressing (1)
indulge in revelry (1)
joking (1)
mocking (1)
performed (1)

7465 צְחֹק *s⁽ᵉ⁾hōq* (2)
laughter (1)
scorn (1)

7466 צָחַר *sāhar* (1)
Zahar (1)

7467 צָחֹר *sāhōr* (1)
white (1)

7468 צֹחַר *sōhar* (5)
Zohar (5)

7469 צִי *siy1* (4)
ships (3)
ship (1)

7470 צִי *siy2* (6)
desert creatures (4)
creatures of the desert (1)
desert tribes (1)

7471 צִיבָא *siybā'* (16)
Ziba (15)
Ziba's (1)

7472 צִיר *siyd* (1)
packed (1)

7473 צַיִד *sayid1* (14)
game (7)
hunter (2)
wild game (2)
animal (1) +2651
hunter (1) +408
hunting (1)

7474 צַיִד *sayid2* (5)
food (2)
provisions (2)
food supply (1)

7475 צַיָּד *sayyād* (1)
hunters (1)

7476 צֵידָה *sēydāh* (10)
provisions (6)
food (2)
supplies (1)
untranslated (1)

7477 צִידוֹן *siydôn* (20)
Sidon (20)

7478 צִידוֹן רַבָּה *siydôn rabbāh* (2)
Greater Sidon (2)

7479 צִידֹנִי *siydōniy* (16)
Sidonians (15)
people of Sidon (1)

7480 צִיָּה *siyyāh* (16)
dry (5)
parched (4)
desert (2)
drought (2)
parched land (2)
dry land (1)

7481 צִיּוֹן *sāyôn* (2)
desert (2)

7482 צִיּוֹן *siyyôn* (154)
Zion (152)
Zion's (2)

7483 צִיּוּן *siyyûn* (3)
marker (1)
road signs (1)
tombstone (1)

7484 צִיחָא *siyhā'* (3)
Ziha (3)

7485 צִינֹק *siynōq* (1)
neck-irons (1)

7486 צִיעֹר *siy'ōr* (1)
Zior (1)

7487 צִיף *siyp* (1)
untranslated (1)

7488 צִיץ *siys1* (14)
flowers (7)
flower (3)
plate (3)
blossomed (1) +7437

7489 צִיץ *siys2* (1)
Ziz (1)

7490 צִיץ *siys3* (1)
salt (1)

7491 צִיצָה *siysāh* (1)
flower (1)

7492 צִיצִת *siysit* (4)
tassels (2)
hair (1)
tassel (1)

7493 צִיר *siyr1* (1)
delegation (1)

7494 צִיר *siyr2* (1)
hinges (1)

7495 צִיר *siyr3* (6)
envoy (3)
ambassadors (1)
envoys (1)
messenger (1)

7496 צִיר *siyr4* (5)
anguish (1)
labor pains (1)
pain (1)
pangs (1)
those⁽ˢ⁾ (1)

7497 צִיר *siyr5* (2)
idols (1)
untranslated (1)

7498 צֵל *sēl* (53)
shadow (27)
shade (16)
shadows (4)
protection (2)
shelter (2)
evening shadows (1)
it⁽ˢ⁾ (1) +2021

7499 צָלָה *sālāh* (3)
roast (1)
roasted (1)
roasts (1)

7500 צִלָּה *sillāh* (3)
Zillah (3)

7501 צָלוּל *s⁽ᵉ⁾lûl* (1)
round loaf (1)

7502 צָלַח *sālah1* (10)
came in power (6)
came forcefully (1)
come in power (1)
rushed (1)
sweep through (1)

7503 צָלַח *sālah2* (55)
prosper (7)
succeed (7)
prospered (5)
victorious (4)
gave success (3)
successful (3)
give success (2)
grant success (2)
have success (2)
thrive (2)
useless (2) +4202
achieve purpose (1)
avail (1)
granted success (1)
helped (1)
made successful (1)
make success (1)
prevail (1)
prosperous (1)
prospers (1)
rose (1)
succeeded (1)
succeeded in carrying out (1)
unsuccessful (1) +4202
useful (1)
victoriously (1)
win (1)

7504 צְלֹחִית *s⁽ᵉ⁾lōhiyt* (1)
bowl (1)

7505 צַלַּחַת *sallahaṯ* (4)
dish (3)
pans (1)

7506 צְלַחַת *sēlahaṯ*
Variant; not used

7507 צְלִי *sāliy* (3)
meat (1)
roast (1)
roasted (1)

7508 צְלִיל *seliyl* (1)
untranslated (1)

7509 1צָלַל *sālal1* (4)
tingle (2)
make tingle (1)
quivered (1)

7510 2צָלַל *sālal2* (1)
sank (1)

7511 3צָלַל *sālal3* (2)
evening shadows fell (1)
overshadowing (1)

7512 1צֶלֶם *selem1* (15)
idols (6)
image (5)
models (2)
figures (1)
untranslated (1)

7513 2צֶלֶם *selem2* (2)
fantasies (1)
phantom (1)

7514 1צַלְמוֹן *salmôn1* (1)
Zalmon (1)

7515 2צַלְמוֹן *salmôn2* (2)
Zalmon (2)

7516 צַלְמָוֶת *salmāweṯ* (18)
deep shadow (4)
shadow of death (3)
darkness (2)
deep darkness (2)
deep shadows (2)
deepest gloom (2)
blackest (1)
blackness (1)
thick darkness (1)

7517 צַלְמֹנָה *salmōnāh* (2)
Zalmonah (2)

7518 צַלְמֻנָּע *salmunnā'* (12)
Zalmunna (10)
them[S] (2) +2256+2286

7519 צָלַע *sāla'* (4)
lame (3)
limping (1)

7520 צֶלַע *sela'* (4)
fall (1)
falls (1)
slip (1)
stumbled (1)

7521 1צֵלָע *sēlā'1* (41)
side (10)
side rooms (9)
sides (4)
boards (2)
opposite sides (2) +7396
another[S] (1)
beams (1)
floor (1)
hillside (1) +2215
leaves (1)
one[S] (1)
planks (1)
rib (1)
ribs (1)
side room (1)
untranslated (4)

7522 2צֵלָע *sēlā'2* (12)
Zela (1)
Zelah (1)

7523 צָלָף *sālāp* (1)
Zalaph (1)

7524 צְלָפְחָד *selāp̄ḥāḏ* (11)
Zelophehad (5)
Zelophehad's (4)
who[S] (1)
whose[S] (1) +1426

7525 צֶלְצַח *selsah* (1)
Zelzah (1)

7526 צִלְצַל *selāsal* (1)
swarms of locusts (1)

7527 1צִלְצָל *silsāl1* (1)
whirring (1)

7528 2צִלְצָל *silsāl2* (1)
spears (1)

7529 צְלְצְלִים *selseliym* (3)
cymbals (3)

7530 צֶלֶק *seleq* (2)
Zelek (2)

7531 צִלְּתַי *silltay* (2)
Zillethai (2)

7532 1צָמֵא *sāmē'1* (11)
thirsty (6)
thirst (2)
thirsts (2)
suffer thirst (1)

7533 צָמָא *sāmā'* (17)
thirst (15)
parched ground (1)
thirsty (1)

7534 2צָמֵא *sāmē'2* (9)
thirsty (8)
dry (1)

7535 צִמְאָה *sim'āh* (1)
dry (1)

7536 צִמָּאוֹן *simmā'ôn* (3)
thirsty ground (2)
thirsty (1)

7537 צָמַד *sāmaḏ* (5)
joined in worshiping (2)
harness (1)
strapped (1)
yoked themselves (1)

7538 צֶמֶד *semeḏ* (15)
yoke (3)
pair (2)
two (2)
acre (1) +5103
oxen (1)
string (1)
team (1)
teams (1)
ten-acre (1) +6930
together (1)
yoke of oxen (1)

7539 צַמָּה *sammāh* (4)
veil (4)

7540 צִמּוּקִים *simmûqiym* (4)
cakes of raisins (3)
raisin cakes (1)

7541 צָמַח *sāmah* (33)
grow (3)
grown (3)
sprouted (3)
make grow (2)
make sprout (2)
makes grow (2)
appear (1)
branch out (1)

bring to fruition (1)
causes to grow (1)
flourish (1)
flourishing (1)
grew (1)
growing (1)
made grow (1)
make spring up (1)
produce (1)
spring into being (1)
spring up (1)
springs forth (1)
springs up (1)
sprout (1)
sprouting (1)
sprung up (1)

7542 צֶמַח *semah* (12)
branch (5)
crops (1)
grew (1)
growth (1)
head (1)
plant (1)
sprout (1)
vegetation (1)

7543 1צָמִיד *sāmiyḏ1* (6)
bracelets (5)
bracelets (1) +3338+6584

7544 2צָמִיד *sāmiyḏ2* (1)
lid (1)

7545 צַמִּים *sammiym* (1)
snare (1)

7546 צָמַק *sāmaq* (1)
dry (1)

7547 צֶמֶר *semer* (16)
wool (13)
woolen (2)
woolen garment (1)

7548 צְמָרִי *semāriy* (2)
Zemarites (2)

7549 צְמָרַיִם *semārayim* (2)
Zemaraim (2)

7550 צַמֶּרֶת *sammereṯ* (5)
top (3)
shoot (1)
tops (1)

7551 צָמַת *sāmaṯ* (15)
destroy (4)
destroyed (3)
put to silence (2)
cease to flow (1)
end (1)
seek to destroy (1)
silence (1)
silenced (1)
wears out (1)

7552 צְמִתֻת *semituṯ* (2)
permanently (1) +2021+4200
permanently (1) +4200

7553 צֵן *sēn* (3)
thorns (2)
hooks (1)

7554 צִן *sin* (10)
Zin (10)

7555 צֹנֵא *sōnā'*
Variant; not used

7556 צֹנֶה *sōneh* (1)
flocks (1)

7557 1צִנָּה *sinnāh1* (1)
coolness (1)

7558 2צִנָּה *sinnāh2* (20)
shield (9)
large[S] [shields] (4)

large shields (3)
shields (3)
buckler (1)

7559 צִנָּה3 *sinnāh3*
Variant; not used

7560 צָנוּעַ *sānûa'* (1)
humility (1)

7561 צָנוּף *sānûp*
Variant; not used

7562 צִנּוֹר *sinnôr* (2)
water shaft (1)
waterfalls (1)

7563 צָנַח *sānah* (3)
got off (2) +4946+6584
untranslated (1)

7564 צְנִינִים *s'niyniym* (2)
thorns (2)

7565 צָנִיף *sāniyp* (5)
turban (3)
diadem (1)
untranslated (1)

7566 צְנִיפָה *s'niypāh* (1)
tiaras (1)

7567 צָנַם *sānam*
Variant; not used

7568 צָנֻם *sānum* (1)
withered (1)

7569 צְנָן *s'nān* (1)
Zenan (1)

7570 צָנַע *sāna'* (1)
humbly (1)

7571 צָנַף *sānap* (3)
put on (1)
roll up tightly (1) +7571+7572

7572 צְנֵפָה *s'nēpāh* (1)
roll up tightly (1) +7571+7571

7573 צִנְצֶנֶת *sinsenet* (1)
jar (1)

7574 צַנְתָּרוֹת *santārôt* (1)
pipes (1)

7575 צָעַד *sā'ad* (8)
marched (2)
climb (1)
marched off (1)
strode through (1)
taken steps (1) +7576
walk (1)
walking along (1)

7576 צַעַד *sa'ad* (14)
step (5)
steps (5)
path (2)
stride (1)
taken steps (1) +7575

7577 צְעָדָה1 *s'‘ādāh1* (2)
marching (2)

7578 צְעָדָה2 *s'‘ādāh2* (1)
ankle chains (1)

7579 צָעָה *sā'āh* (5)
cowering prisoners (1)
lay down (1)
pour (1)
pour out (1)
striding forward (1)

7580 צָעוֹר *sā'ôr* (2)
untranslated (2)

7581 צָעִיף *sā'iyp* (3)
veil (3)

7582 צָעִיר1 *sā'iyr1* (23)
younger (7)

young (3)
youngest (3)
least (2)
little (2)
small (2)
lowly (2)
servants (1)
smallest (1)
younger (1) +3427+4200

7583 צָעִיר2 *sā'iyr2* (1)
Zair (1)

7584 צְעִירָה *s'‘iyrāh* (1)
ages (1) +1148

7585 צָעַן *sā'an* (1)
moved (1)

7586 צֹעַן *sō'an* (7)
Zoan (7)

7587 צְעֻנִים *s'‘anniym* (1)
untranslated (1)

7588 צַעֲנַנִּים *sa'ananniym* (2)
Zaanannim (2)

7589 צַעֲצֻעִים *sa'asu'iym* (1)
sculptured (1) +5126

7590 צָעַק *sā'aq* (55)
cried out (16)
cry out (9)
cried for help (3)
cries out (3)
beg (2)
called out (2)
cried (2)
crying out (2)
were called out (2)
appealed (1)
burst out (1)
cried out for help (1) +7754
cry (1)
cry aloud (1)
cry out (1) +7590
scream for help (1)
screamed (1)
shout (1)
summoned (1)
was called up (1)
were called to arms (1)
were summoned (1)

7591 צְעָקָה *s'‘āqāh* (21)
cry (9)
outcry (3)
cries (2)
cry (2) +7754
wailing (2)
cries of distress (1)
crying out (1)
outcry (1) +7754

7592 צָעַר *sā'ar* (3)
brought low (1)
disdained (1)
little ones (1)

7593 צֹעַר *sō'ar* (10)
Zoar (10)

7594 צָפַד *sāpad* (1)
shriveled (1)

7595 צָפָה1 *sāpāh1* (38)
watchman (11)
lookout (4)
watchmen (4)
watch (3)
he[s] (1) +2021
keep watch (1)
keeping watch (1)
lie in wait (1)
look (1)
looking (1)
lookouts (1)

marked (1)
standing watch (1)
wait in expectation (1)
watch in hope (1)
watched (1)
watches over (1)
watching (1)
untranslated (2)

7596 צָפָה2 *sāpāh2* (47)
overlaid (27)
overlay (11)
covered (4)
adorned (1) +4200+9514
coating (1)
paneling (1) +6770
spread (1)
untranslated (1)

7597 צָפָה3 *sāpāh3* (1)
flowing (1)

7598 צְפוֹ *s'pô* (3)
Zepho (3)

7599 צִפּוּי *sippûy* (5)
overlaid (3)
overlay (2)

7600 צָפוֹן1 *sāpôn1* (151)
north (97)
north (26) +2025
northern (9) +2025
north (7) +4946
northern (4)
northern (3) +4946
north wind (1)
northern (1) +2025+4946
northward (1) +2006+2021
sacred mountain (1)
untranslated (1)

7601 צָפוֹן2 *sāpôn2* (3)
Zaphon (3)

7602 צְפוֹן *s'pôn* (2)
Zephon (2)

7603 צְפוֹנִי1 *s'pôniy1* (1)
northern (1)

7604 צְפוֹנִי2 *s'pôniy2* (1)
Zephonite (1)

7605 צָפוּעַ *sāpûa'* (1)
untranslated (1)

7606 צִפּוֹר1 *sippôr1* (40)
bird (18)
birds (12)
bird's (2)
sparrow (2)
bird (1) +4053
birds (1) +4053
carrion birds (1) +6514
it[s] (1) +2021+2021+2645
poultry (1)
untranslated (1)

7607 צִפּוֹר2 *sippôr2* (7)
Zippor (7)

7608 צַפַּחַת *sappahat* (7)
jug (6)
jar (1)

7609 צְפִי *s'piy*
Variant; not used

7610 צְפִיָּה *sippiyyāh* (1)
towers (1)

7611 צִפְיוֹן *sipyôn*
Variant; not used

7612 צִפְיוֹנִי *sipyôniy*
Variant; not used

7613 צַפִּיחִת *sappiyhit* (1)
wafers (1)

7614 צֹפִים *sōp̄iym* (1)
Zophim (1)

7615 צָפִין *sāp̄iyn* (1)
untranslated (1)

7616 צָפִיַע *sāp̄iya'* (1)
manure (1)

7617 צְפִיעָה *sᵉp̄iy'āh* (1)
offshoots (1)

7618 צָפִיר *sāp̄iyr* (6)
goat (2) +6436
goat (1)
male goats (1)
male goats (1) +6436
untranslated (1)

7619 צְפִירָה *sᵉp̄iyrāh* (3)
doom (2)
crown (1)

7620 צָפִית *sāp̄iyt* (1)
rugs (1)

7621 צָפַן *sāp̄an* (34)
store up (3)
stored up (3)
cherish (2)
hidden (2)
hide (2)
keep safe (2)
restraining (2)
waylay (2)
closed (1)
concealed (1)
hid (1)
holds in store (1)
is concealed (1)
is stored up (1)
kept on record (1)
lurk (1)
secret (1)
set (1)
stores up (1)
treasured (1)
treasured place (1)
treasures (1)
untranslated (2)

7622 צְפַנְיָה *sᵉp̄anyāh* (8)
Zephaniah (8)

7623 צְפַנְיָהוּ *sᵉp̄anyāhû* (2)
Zephaniah (2)

7624 צָפְנַת פַּעְנֵחַ *sāp̄ᵉnat pa'nēah* (1)
Zaphenath-Paneah (1)

7625 צֶפַע *sepa'* (1)
viper (1)

7626 צִפְעֹנִי *sip̄'ōniy* (4)
vipers (2)
viper (1)
viper's (1)

7627 צָפַף *sāp̄ap* (4)
whisper (2)
chirp (1)
cried (1)

7628 צַפְצָפָה *sap̄sāp̄āh* (1)
willow (1)

7629 צָפַר *sāp̄ar* (1)
leave (1)

7630 צְפַרְדֵּעַ *sᵉp̄ardēa'* (13)
frogs (13)

7631 צִפֹּרָה *sippōrāh* (3)
Zipporah (3)

7632 צִפֹּרֶן *sippōren* (2)
nails (1)
point (1)

7633 צֶפֶת *sepet* (1)
capital (1)

7634 צְפַת *sᵉp̄at* (1)
Zephath (1)

7635 צְפָתָה *sᵉp̄ātāh* (1)
Zephathah (1)

7636 צָקוּן *sāqûn*
Variant; not used

7637 צִקְלַג *siqlag* (15)
Ziklag (14)
itˢ (1)

7638 צִקָּלוֹן *siqqālôn* (1)
untranslated (1)

7639 1צַר *sar1* (47)
distress (20)
trouble (11)
narrow (3)
small (3)
distressed (2)
adversity (1)
anguish (1)
anguished (1)
critical (1)
grieve (1)
misery (1)
pent-up (1)
tightly (1)

7640 2צַר *sar2* (68)
enemies (28)
foes (19)
enemy (11)
foe (3)
adversaries (2)
adversary (2)
hostile (1)
opponent (1)
oppressor (1)

7641 3צַר *sar3* (1)
flint (1)

7642 4צַר *sar4*
Variant; not used

7643 צֵר *sēr* (1)
Zer (1)

7644 1צֹר *sōr1* (5)
flint (3)
edge (1)
flint knife (1)

7645 2צֹר *sōr2*
Variant; not used

7646 צָרַב *sārab* (1)
be scorched (1)

7647 צָרָב *sārāb* (1)
scorching (1)

7648 צָרֶבֶת *sārebet* (2)
scar (2)

7649 צְרֵדָה *sᵉrēdāh* (1)
Zeredah (1)

7650 1צָרָה *sārāh1* (70)
trouble (24)
distress (22)
troubles (8)
anguish (4)
calamity (2)
difficulties (2)
adversity (1)
calamities (1)
distressed (1)
distresses (1)
groan (1)
hardship (1)
hostility (1)
oppressed (1)

7651 2צָרָה *sārāh2* (1)
rival (1)

7652 צָרָה *sirāh*
Variant; not used

7653 צְרוּיָה *sᵉrûyāh* (26)
Zeruiah (25)
Zeruiah's (1)

7654 צְרוּעָה *sᵉrû'āh* (1)
Zeruah (1)

7655 1צְרוֹר *sᵉrôr1* (7)
purse (2)
bag (1)
bundle (1)
pouch (1)
pouches (1)
sachet (1)

7656 2צְרוֹר *sᵉrôr2* (2)
pebble (1)
piece (1)

7657 3צְרוֹר *sᵉrôr3* (1)
Zeror (1)

7658 צָרַח *sārah* (2)
raise the battle cry (1)
shouting (1)

7659 צֶרַח *serah*
Variant; not used

7660 צֹרִי *sōriy* (5)
from Tyre (1)
men from Tyre (1)
of Tyre (1)
Tyre (1)
Tyrians (1)

7661 צֳרִי *sᵉriy* (6)
balm (6)

7662 צְרִי *sᵉriy* (1)
Zeri (1)

7663 צְרִיחַ *sᵉriyah* (4)
stronghold (2)
itˢ (1) +2021
pits (1)

7664 צְרֶךְ *sōrek* (1)
need (1)

7665 צָרַע *sāra'* (20)
had leprosy (6)
leprosy (4)
leprous (4)
diseased (2)
disease (1)
has an infectious skin disease (1)
infectious skin disease (1)
personˢ (1)

7666 צָרְעָה *sor'āh* (10)
Zorah (10)

7667 צִרְעָה *sir'āh* (3)
hornet (3)

7668 צָרְעִי *sor'iy* (1)
Zorites (1)

7669 צָרַעַת *sāra'at* (35)
skin disease (10)
infectious disease (7)
mildew (6)
leprosy (5)
disease (2)
infectious skin diseases and mildew (1)
itˢ (1)
leprous (1)
spreading mildew (1)
spreading mildew (1) +5596

7670 צָרְעָתִי *sor'ātiy* (2)
Zorathites (2)

7671 צָרַף *sārap* (34)
goldsmith (6)
refined (5)
flawless (3)

goldsmiths (2)
refine (2)
silversmith (2)
been tested (1)
examine (1)
fashions (1)
proved true (1)
refiner (1)
refiner's (1)
refining goes on (1) +7671
sift (1)
test (1)
thoroughly purge away (1)
+1342+2021+3869
untranslated (3)

7672 צֹרְפִי *sōrpiy* (1)
goldsmiths (1)

7673 צָרְפַת *sār'pat* (3)
Zarephath (3)

7674 1צָרַר *sārar1* (30)
distress (3)
bring distress (2)
in distress (2)
in labor (2)
besiege (1)
bind up (1)
bound securely (1)
distressed (1)
frustrated (1)
gave trouble (1)
hampered (1)
kept in confinement (1)
lay siege (1)
mended (1)
oppress (1)
oppressed (1)
small (1)
stored up (1)
sweep away (1) +928+4053
trouble (1)
tying (1)
weakened (1)
wrapped (1)
wrapped up (1)
wraps up (1)

7675 2צָרַר *sārar2* (26)
enemies (7)
enemy (4)
foes (4)
oppressed (2)
adversaries (1)
foe (1)
give trouble (1)
hostile (1)
oppose (1)
oppressing (1)
rival wife (1)
treat as enemies (1)
treated as enemies (1)

7676 3צָרַר *sārar3*
Variant; not used

7677 4צָרַר *sārar4*
Variant; not used

7678 צְרֵרָה *s'rērāh* (1)
Zererah (1)

7679 צֶרֶת *seret* (1)
Zereth (1)

7680 צֶרֶת הַשַּׁחַר *seret haššahar* (1)
Zereth Shahar (1)

7681 צָרְתָן *sār'tān* (4)
Zarethan (4)

7682 ק *q*
Variant; not used

7683 קָא *qē'* (1)
vomit (1)

7684 קָאַת *qā'at* (5)
desert owl (4)
owl (1)

7685 קַב *qab* (1)
cab (1)

7686 קָבַב *qābab* (14)
curse (8)
cursed (2)
put a curse on (2)
curse at all (1) +7686

7687 קֵבָה *qēbāh* (2)
body (1)
inner parts (1)

7688 קֻבָּה *qubbāh* (1)
tent (1)

7689 קִבּוּץ *qibbûs* (1)
collection (1)

7690 קְבוּרָה *q'bûrāh* (14)
tomb (5)
grave (4)
burial (2)
buried (1)
have burial (1) +7699
proper burial (1)

7691 קָבַל *qābal* (14)
accept (3)
took (3)
opposite (2)
received (2)
agreed (1)
take choice (1)
untranslated (2)

7692 קְבֹל *q'bōl* (2)
battering rams (1)
in front of (1)

7693 קָבַע *qāba'* (6)
rob (3)
plunder (1)
plunder (1) +5883
robbing (1)

7694 קֻבַּעַת *qubba'at* (2)
goblet (2) +3926

7695 קָבַץ *qābas* (127)
gather (38)
gathered (15)
assembled (12)
assemble (10)
gathers (5)
called together (4)
brought together (3)
gather together (3)
bring (2)
came together (2)
collect (2)
come together (2)
were assembled (2)
amasses (1)
assemble (1) +3481
assemble yourselves (1)
be gathered (1)
be reunited (1) +3481
bring back (1)
bring together (1)
came together (1) +3481
collected (1)
come and join (1)
gather in (1)
gathered together (1)
grows pale (1) +6999
join (1)
joined forces (1)
mobilized (1)
mustered (1)
picked up (1)
rallied (1)
shepherd (1)

stored up (1)
surely bring together (1) +7695
takes captive (1)
turns pale (1) +6999
were brought (1)
were gathered (1)

7696 קַבְצְאֵל *qabs''ēl* (3)
Kabzeel (3)

7697 קְבֻצָה *q'busāh* (1)
gather (1)

7698 קִבְצַיִם *qibsayim* (1)
Kibzaim (1)

7699 קָבַר *qābar* (133)
buried (54)
was buried (31)
bury (30)
burying (7)
be buried (4)
be sure to bury (1) +7699
gravediggers (1)
have burial (1) +7690
is buried (1)
untranslated (2)

7700 קֶבֶר *qeber* (68)
grave (18)
tomb (16)
graves (10)
tombs (9)
burial (5)
be buried (2) +448+665
buried (2)
them[s] (2) +4013
burial place (1)
burial site (1)
buried (1) +448+995
them[s] (1) +2021

7701 קִבְרוֹת הַתַּאֲוָה *qibrôt hata''wāh* (5)
Kibroth Hattaavah (5)

7702 קָדַד *qādad* (15)
bowed down (7)
bowed low (5)
bowed (2)
bowed heads (1)

7703 קִדָּה *qiddāh* (2)
cassia (2)

7704 קְדוּמִים *q'dûmiym* (1)
age-old (1)

7705 קָדוֹשׁ *qādôš* (116)
holy (62)
holy one (43)
consecrated (4)
sacred (4)
saints (2)
untranslated (1)

7706 קָדַח *qādah* (5)
kindle (1)
kindled (1)
kindled (1) +836
light (1)
sets ablaze (1)

7707 קַדַּחַת *qaddahat* (2)
fever (2)

7708 קָדִים *qādiym* (67)
east (38)
east (13) +2025
east wind (7)
eastward (2)
desert wind (1)
east winds (1)
eastern (1) +2025
eastward (1) +2025
extend eastward (1) +2025
hot east wind (1)
untranslated (1)

7709 קָדַם *qādam* (26)
come before (4)
confronted (4)
come to meet (2)
confront (2)
bring (1)
come (1)
comes before (1)
go (1)
go before (1)
has a claim against (1)
in front (1)
meet (1)
met (1)
quick (1)
receive (1)
rise (1)
stay open (1)
welcomed (1)

7710 קֶדֶם *qedem* (61)
east (17)
of old (8)
eastern (7)
long ago (5)
ancient (3)
east (3) +4946
before (2)
gone by (2)
long ago (2) +4946
ancient times (1)
before began (1)
days of old (1)
east (1) +6584+7156
eastward (1) +4946
eternal (1)
everlasting (1)
forever (1)
former (1) +4946
long ago (1) +3427+4946
old (1) +3427+4946
past (1)

7711 קֶדֶם *qēdem* (26)
east (10)
east (7) +2025
eastern (3) +2025
eastward (1) +2025
eastward (1) +2025+2025+4667
southeast (1) +2025+2025+5582
southeast (1) +2025+5582
untranslated (2)

7712 קִדְמָה *qadmāh* (6)
before (3)
old (1)
past (1)
untranslated (1)

7713 קִדְמָה *qidmāh* (4)
east (4)

7714 קֵדְמָה1 *qēdmāh1*
Variant; not used

7715 קֵדְמָה2 *qēdmāh2* (2)
Kedemah (2)

7716 קַדְמוֹן *qadmôn* (1)
eastern (1)

7717 קְדֵמוֹת *qᵉdēmôt* (4)
Kedemoth (4)

7718 קַדְמִיאֵל *qadmiy'ēl* (8)
Kadmiel (8)

7719 קַדְמֹנִי1 *qadmôniy1* (10)
eastern (3)
east (2)
former (2)
old (1)
past (1)
untranslated (1)

7720 קַדְמֹנִי2 *qadmôniy2* (1)
Kadmonites (1)

7721 קָדְקֹד *qodqōd* (12)
top of head (3)
brow (2)
head (2)
skulls (2)
crown of head (1)
crowns (1)
heads (1)

7722 קָדַר *qādar* (17)
darkened (3)
mourning (3)
darken (2)
mourn (2)
black (1)
blackened (1)
clothed with gloom (1)
dark (1)
go dark (1)
grief (1)
wail (1)

7723 קֵדָר *qēdār* (12)
Kedar (10)
Kedar (1) +1201
Kedar's (1)

7724 קִדְרוֹן *qidrôn* (11)
Kidron (10)
there[s] (1) +928+5707

7725 קַדְרוּת *qadrût* (1)
darkness (1)

7726 קַדְרַנִּית *qᵉdōranniyt* (1)
mourners (1)

7727 קָדַשׁ *qādaš* (171)
consecrate (30)
consecrated (22)
dedicated (10)
consecrate yourselves (9)
consecrated themselves (7)
dedicates (7)
holy (7)
keep holy (7)
makes holy (7)
show myself holy (7)
set apart (6)
prepare (5)
consecration (3)
made holy (3)
been consecrated (2)
declare holy (2)
dedicate (2)
honor as holy (2)
keeping holy (2)
make holy (2)
regard as holy (2)
sacred (2)
set aside (2)
acknowledge holiness (1)
be acknowledged as holy (1)
be consecrated (1)
call in honor of (1) +4200
celebrate holy (1)
consecrate themselves (1)
consecrating (1)
consecrating themselves (1)
consecrating themselves (1) +7731
defiled (1)
done[s] (1)
have purified (1)
holiness (1)
purified herself (1)
send (1)
set apart as holy (1)
show himself holy (1)
show holiness (1)
showed himself holy (1)
solemnly consecrate (1) +7727
uphold holiness (1)
untranslated (1)

7728 קָדֵשׁ1 *qādēš1* (11)

shrine prostitutes (5)
shrine prostitute (4)
prostitutes of the shrines (1)
untranslated (1)

7729 קָדֵשׁ2 *qādēš2* (14)
Kadesh (14)

7730 קֶדֶשׁ *qedeš* (12)
Kedesh (11)
where[s] (1) +2025

7731 קֹדֶשׁ *qōdeš* (433)
holy (136)
sanctuary (72)
sacred (65)
most holy (23) +7731
holy place (14)
most holy place (11) +7731
holy things (10)
holiness (9)
most holy place (8)
sacred offerings (8)
consecrated (7)
holy offerings (5)
most holy offerings (5) +7731
most holy things (3) +7731
sacred offering (3)
dedicated (2)
dedicated things (2)
holy furnishings (2)
sacred gifts (2)
sacred objects (2)
something holy (2)
things dedicated (2)
another[s] (1) +5246
consecrated gifts (1) +7731
consecrated things (1)
consecrating themselves (1) +7727
dedicate (1)
dedicated gifts (1)
gifts dedicated (1)
holy one (1)
holy ones (1)
holy precincts (1)
it[s] (1)
most holy place (1) +1808
most holy place (1) +5219
most sacred (1) +7731
most sacred food (1) +7731
offering (1)
offerings (1)
priests' rooms (1) +4384
sacred portion (1)
sacred things (1)
sanctuary (1) +5226
sanctuary area (1)
set apart (1)
temple (1)
things[s] (1)
what holy (1)
untranslated (7)

7732 קָדֵשׁ בַּרְנֵעַ *qādēš barnēa'* (10)
Kadesh Barnea (10)

7733 קָהָה *qāhāh* (4)
set on edge (3)
dull (1)

7734 קֵהָיוֹן *qēhāyôn*
Variant; not used

7735 קָהַל *qāhal* (39)
gathered (9)
assembled (8)
assemble (5)
came together (3)
gather (2)
gathered together (2)
mustered (2)
summoned (2)
called together (1)
came as a group (1)
convenes a court (1)

crowded (1)
gather together (1)
summoned to assemble (1)

7736 קָהָל *qāhāl* (123)
assembly (72)
community (13)
company (5)
horde (4)
crowd (3)
mob (3)
throng (3)
army (2)
gathered (2)
hordes (2)
alliance (1)
army (1) +2256+6639
assemble (1) +928+2021+6590
assembled (1) +995
congregation (1)
everyone else (1) +3972
people (1)
them[s] (1) +3776+3972
them[s] (1) +2021
them[s] (1) +3776+3972
they[s] (1) +2021
whole assembly (1) +2256+6337
untranslated (2)

7737 קְהִלָּה *qᵉhillāh* (2)
assembly (1)
meeting (1)

7738 קֹהֶלֶת *qōhelet* (7)
teacher (7)

7739 קְהֵלָתָה *qᵉhēlātāh* (2)
Kehelathah (2)

7740 קְהָת *qᵉhāt* (32)
Kohath (18)
Kohathite (7) +1201
Kohathites (4) +1201
Kohath's (2)
untranslated (1)

7741 קְהָתִי *qᵉhātiy* (15)
Kohathite (7)
Kohathites (3)
Kohathites (3) +1201
Kohath (1)
Kohathite (1) +1201

7742 קָו *qāw1* (20)
rule (8)
measuring line (7)
line (4)
measure (1)

7743 קָו *qāw2* (3)
strange speech (2) +7743

7744 קָו *qāw3*
Variant; not used

7745 קָוֵא *qᵉwē'* (2)
Kue (2)

7746 קוֹבַע *qôbaʿ* (2)
helmet (1)
helmets (1)

7747 קָוָה *qāwāh1* (47)
hope in (7)
wait (7)
look (5)
looked for (4)
hope (3)
hoped (2)
trusted (2)
wait for (2)
eager (1)
expect (1)
hope for (1)
hoped for (1)
in hope (1)
long for (1)

look for (1)
look in hope (1)
put trust (1)
waited for (1)
waited patiently for (1) +7747
waiting (1)
waiting eagerly (1)
waits (1)

7748 קָוָה *qāwāh2* (2)
be gathered (1)
gather (1)

7749 קָוֶה *qāweh* (3)
untranslated (3)

7750 קְוֵה *qᵉwēh* (2)
Kue (2)

7751 קוֹחַ *qôaḥ*
Variant; not used

7752 קוּט *qût* (7)
loathe (4)
abhor (1)
angry (1)
loathing (1)

7753 קוּט *qôt*
Variant; not used

7754 קוֹל *qôl* (506)
voice (101)
sound (62)
obey (36) +928+9048
obeyed (18) +928+9048
voices (17)
to (15) +928
listen (12)
thunder (12)
noise (11)
to (9) +4200
cry (8)
cry for mercy (6) +9384
sounds (6)
aloud (5) +906+5951
proclamation (5)
roar (5)
aloud (4) +5951
thunders (4) +5989
blast (3)
called out (3) +928+1524+7924
cries (3)
plea (3)
word (3)
aloud (2)
aloud (2) +1524
crackling (2)
cry (2) +7591
crying (2)
disobeyed (2) +928+4202+9048
fully obey (2) +928+9048+9048
hear (2)
heard (2)
heard (2) +9048
lowing (2)
response (2)
shout (2)
shouts of joy (2) +8262
sound (2) +6702
sounding (2)
speech (2)
thunder (2) +5989
thunderstorm (2) +2613
what say (2)
what says (2)
words (2)
acclamation (1)
agreed with (1) +4200+9048
aloud (1) +928
aloud (1) +928+1524
argue (1) +9048
began (1) +906+5951
blast (1) +8795
bleating (1)

calling (1) +7924
calls (1)
clamor (1)
clatter (1) +8323
command (1)
cooing (1)
crack (1)
cried out (1)
cried out for help (1) +7590
cry aloud (1) +5989
cry for help (1) +2410
cry for help (1) +8776
cry out (1) +2411
cry out (1) +7412
diligently obey (1) +928+9048+9048
disobedience (1) +928+4202+9048
disobey (1) +928+1194+9048
gave in (1) +928+9048
give a hearing (1) +263
growl (1)
growl (1) +5989
growled (1) +5989
hears (1) +9048
hears (1) +9048+9048
hiss (1)
it[s] (1) +3276
listen (1) +9048
listen carefully (1) +928+9048
loud (1)
loudly (1) +928+1524
loudly (1) +5951
music (1)
neighing (1) +5177
news (1)
noise (1) +2159
noisy din (1) +1524
obey (1) +4200+9048
obey fully (1) +928+9048+9048
obeying (1) +928+9048
obeys (1) +928+9048
outcry (1) +7591
rebuke (1)
resound (1)
roared (1) +5989
roaring (1) +8614
roars (1) +928+5989
say (1)
scream for help (1) +2256+7924+8123
screamed (1) +928+1524+7924
screamed for help (1) +2256+7924+8123
shout (1) +928+7924
shout (1) +1524+7924
shout (1) +8123
shouted (1) +928+7924
shouted (1) +928+8123+9558
shouted (1) +2256+5951+7924
shouting (1) +9558
shouts (1)
sing (1) +5989
sing songs (1) +928+4200+8123+9048
song (1)
sound (1) +8123
speaking (1) +1821
taunts (1)
thunders (1) +928+5989
tumult (1) +2167
tune (1)
uproar (1) +2162
uproar (1) +9558
very (1)
war cry (1)
weeping (1)
wept so loudly (1) +906+928+1140+5989
what have to say (1)
what said (1)
what said (1) +1821
what saying (1)
what[s] (1)
what[s] (1) +1821
whisper (1) +1960
untranslated (23)

7755 קוֹלָיָה *qôlāyāh* (2)
  Kolaiah (2)

7756 קוּם *qûm* (630)
  got up (50)
  rise (28)
  rise up (28)
  get up (24)
  arise (22)
  set up (17)
  rose (16)
  stand (16)
  establish (13)
  raise up (11)
  set out (11)
  fulfill (10)
  come (9)
  go (9)
  raised up (9)
  at once (8)
  established (8)
  stood up (8)
  restore (7)
  rose up (7)
  stand up (7)
  foes (5)
  stood (5)
  arose (4)
  confirm (4)
  erected (4)
  keep (4)
  prepared (4)
  adversaries (3)
  attacking (3) +6584
  carried out (3)
  confirms (3)
  endure (3)
  enemies (3)
  fulfilled (3)
  help up (3)
  kept (3)
  left (3) +4946
  now (3)
  proceeded (3)
  rises (3)
  rises up (3)
  set (3)
  standing (3)
  up (3)
  begin (2)
  build (2)
  came (2)
  confirmed (2)
  decreed (2)
  deeded (2)
  fully accomplishes (2) +2256+6913
  get ready (2)
  gets up (2)
  got ready (2)
  grows up (2)
  hurry (2)
  maintain (2)
  place (2)
  raise (2)
  raises (2)
  raising up (2)
  rise to power (2)
  risen up (2)
  rouse (2)
  stands (2)
  start (2)
  stepped forward (2)
  succeeded (2) +9393
  supported (2)
  survive (2)
  went (2)
  accomplish (1)
  accuses (1) +2021+4200+5477
  all right do itˢ (1)
  appear (1)
  appears (1)
  appointed (1)
  arise and come (1)
  assaults (1) +6584
  attack (1)
  attack (1) +448
  attacked (1) +448
  attacked (1) +6584
  attacks (1)
  attacks (1) +6584
  be (1)
  become (1)
  been kept (1)
  began (1)
  belong (1)
  binding (1)
  break out (1)
  brighter (1)
  bring (1)
  came out (1)
  came to power (1)
  carries out (1)
  carry on (1)
  carry on (1) +6584
  carry out (1)
  changed (1) +7756
  come forward (1)
  come on (1)
  come out (1)
  confirming (1)
  confronted (1) +6584
  confronts (1)
  convict (1)
  crept up (1)
  doˢ (1)
  done (1)
  erect (1)
  establish the custom (1)
  exalted (1)
  failed (1) +4202+6388
  final (1)
  follow (1) +339
  follow (1) +339+4946
  followed (1) +339
  gave (1)
  get away (1)
  get it to its feet (1) +7756
  go up (1)
  gone (1)
  grew up (1)
  grown (1)
  has effect (1)
  have (1)
  heaped up (1)
  hold (1)
  hurried (1)
  in turn (1)
  incited (1)
  keep (1) +7756
  leave (1) +4946
  left (1)
  left (1) +4946+9348
  lift up (1)
  made (1)
  make good (1)
  makes rise (1)
  moved (1)
  moved out (1)
  obeyed (1) +3869
  opposed (1)
  opposite (1)
  piled up (1)
  prevails (1)
  produce (1)
  provide (1)
  raised (1)
  rebelled (1)
  remain (1)
  remains (1)
  revolted (1)
  risen (1)
  send (1)
  set to work (1)
  setting up (1)
  sit up (1)
  soon (1)
  started (1)
  station (1)
  stilled (1)
  stir up (1)
  stood ground (1)
  strengthen (1)
  succeed (1)
  surely stand (1) +7756
  surged forward (1)
  take place (1)
  takes the stand (1) +928
  turned (1)
  undertakes (1)
  uphold (1)
  was set up (1)
  went out (1)
  went to work (1)
  withdrew (1)
  withstand (1)
  untranslated (64)

7757 קוֹמָה *qômāh* (46)
  high (28)
  height (2)
  on high (2) +928
  tallest (2)
  deep (1)
  diameter (1)
  height (1) +1469
  higher (1)
  length (1)
  lengths (1)
  lofty trees (1) +8123
  low (1) +9166
  on high (1)
  stature (1)
  untranslated (2)

7758 קוֹמְמִיּוּת *qômᵉmiyyût* (1)
  with heads held high (1)

7759 קוֹנֵן *qônēn*
  Variant; not used

7760 קוֹעַ *qôaʿ* (1)
  Koa (1)

7761 קוֹף *qôp̄* (2)
  apes (2)

7762 קוּץ1 *qûṣ1* (8)
  dread (2)
  abhorred (1)
  detest (1)
  disgusted (1)
  filled with dread (1)
  hostile (1)
  resent (1)

7763 קוּץ2 *qûṣ2* (1)
  tear apart (1)

7764 קוֹץ1 *qôṣ1* (12)
  thorns (10)
  thornbushes (2)

7765 קוֹץ2 *qôṣ2*
  Variant; not used

7766 קוֹץ3 *qôṣ3* (1)
  Koz (1)

7767 קוּצּוֹת *qᵉwussôṯ* (2)
  hair (2)

7768 קוּקוּ *qawqāw*
  Variant; not used

7769 קוּר1 *qûr1* (2)
  dug wells (2)

7770 קוּר2 *qûr2* (2)
  cobwebs (1)
  web (1)

7771 קוֹרָה *qôrāh* (5)
beams (1)
ceiling beams (1)
pole (1)
roof (1)
tree (1)

7772 קוּשׁ *qûš* (1)
ensnare (1)

7773 קוּשָׁיָהוּ *qûšāyāhû* (1)
Kushaiah (1)

7774 קַח *qāh*
Variant; not used

7775 קָט *qāt* (1)
soon (1) +3869+5071

7776 קֶטֶב *qeteb* (4)
plague (2)
destruction (1)
destructive (1)

7777 קְטוֹרָה *q'tôrāh* (1)
incense (1)

7778 קְטוּרָה *q'tûrāh* (4)
Keturah (4)

7779 קָטַל *qātal* (3)
slay (2)
kills (1)

7780 קֶטֶל *qetel* (1)
slaughter (1)

7781 קָטֹן1 *qātōn1* (4)
not enough (1)
not enough (1) +6388
skimping (1)
unworthy (1)

7782 קֹטֶן *qōten* (2)
little finger (2)

7783 קָטָן1 *qātān1* (47)
small (12)
least (9)
younger (8)
young (5)
youngest (4)
little (2)
boy (1) +5853
lesser (1)
light (1)
low (1)
smaller (1)
smallest (1)
youths (1) +5853

7784 קָטָן2 *qātān2*
Variant; not used

7785 קָטֹן2 *qātōn2* (54)
small (14)
youngest (14)
least (7)
young (7)
little (3)
younger (3)
simple (2)
at all (1) +196+1524
brief (1)
lesser (1)
nothing (1) +1524+1821+2256+4202

7786 קָטַף *qātap* (5)
break off (1)
broke off (1)
gathered (1)
pick (1)
uncut (1) +4202

7787 קָטַר1 *qātar1* (115)
burn (35)
burn incense (18)
burned incense (14)
burned (12)

burning incense (11)
burned sacrifices (4)
burn sacrifices (3)
make offerings (2)
be burned (1)
burn offerings (1)
burned up (1) +7787
burning (1)
burns incense (1)
make offering (1)
offer (1)
offer sacrifices (1)
offered up (1)
perfumed (1)
present (1)
presented offerings (1)
presenting (1)
untranslated (2)

7788 קָטַר2 *qātar2* (1)
enclosed (1)

7789 קִטֵּר *qittēr* (1)
incense (1)

7790 קִטְרוֹן *qitrôn* (1)
Kitron (1)

7791 קְטֻרוֹת *q'turôt*
Variant; not used

7792 קְטֹרֶת *q'tōret* (60)
incense (59)
offering (1)

7793 קַטָּת *qattāt* (1)
Kattath (1)

7794 קִיא1 *qiy'1* (9)
vomit (2)
vomit out (2)
vomited out (2)
spit out (1)
vomit up (1)
vomited (1)

7795 קִיא2 *qiy'2* (3)
vomit (3)

7796 קָיָה *qāyāh*
Variant; not used

7797 קַיִת *qayit*
Variant; not used

7798 קִיטוֹר *qiytôr* (4)
smoke (2)
clouds (1)
dense smoke (1)

7799 קִים *qiym* (1)
foes (1)

7800 קִימָה *qiymāh* (1)
standing (1)

7801 קִין *qiyn* (8)
chant (3)
composed laments (1)
sang lament (1)
take up a lament (1)
took up lament (1) +7806
wailing (1)

7802 קַיִן1 *qayin1* (1)
spearhead (1)

7803 קַיִן2 *qayin2* (16)
Cain (16)

7804 קַיִן3 *qayin3* (2)
Kenites (2)

7805 קַיִן4 *qayin4* (1)
Kain (1)

7806 קִינָה1 *qiynāh1* (18)
lament (13)
laments (2)
mourn (1) +5951
took up lament (1) +7801

weeping (1)

7807 קִינָה2 *qiynāh2* (1)
Kinah (1)

7808 קֵינִי *qēyniy* (12)
Kenites (7)
Kenite (5)

7809 קֵינָן *qēynān* (6)
Kenan (6)

7810 קִיץ *qiys* (23)
awake (7)
wake up (4)
awakens (2)
rouse (2)
all summer (1)
awakened (1)
awakes (1)
awoke (1)
come to life (1)
rise (1)
roused (1)
wake (1)

7811 קַיִץ *qayis* (20)
summer (10)
summer fruit (3)
ripe fruit (2)
ripened fruit (2)
cakes of figs (1)
fruit (1)
harvest (1)

7812 קִיצוֹן *qiysôn* (4)
end (4)

7813 קִיקָיוֹן *qiyqāyôn* (5)
vine (5)

7814 קִיקָלוֹן *qiyqālôn* (1)
disgrace (1)

7815 קִיר1 *qiyr1* (74)
wall (38)
walls (16)
every last male (3) +928+8874
male (3) +928+8874
sides (3)
side (2)
agony (1)
ceiling (1)
city (1)
it⁸ (1) +2021
roof (1)
stonemasons (1) +74+3093
stonemasons (1) +3093
untranslated (2)

7816 קִיר2 *qiyr2* (1)
Kir (1)

7817 קִיר3 *qiyr3* (4)
Kir (4)

7818 קִיר־חֶרֶשׂ *qiyr-hereś* (3)
Kir Hareseth (3)

7819 קִיר חֲרֶשֶׂת *qiyr h' reśet* (2)
Kir Hareseth (2)

7820 קֵירֹס *qēyrōs* (2)
Keros (2)

7821 קִישׁ *qiyš* (21)
Kish (21)

7822 קִישׁוֹן *qiyšôn* (6)
Kishon (6)

7823 קִישִׁי *qiyšiy* (1)
Kishi (1)

7824 קַל *qal* (13)
swift (7)
fleet-footed (2) +928+8079
foam (1)
speedily (1)
swifter (1)
swiftly (1)

7825 קֹל1 qōl1 (1)
little (1)

7826 קֹל2 qōl2
Variant; not used

7827 קָלָה qālah (1)
untranslated (1)

7828 קָלָה1 qālāh1 (4)
burned (1)
roasted (1)
roasted grain (1)
searing pain (1)

7829 קָלָה2 qālāh2 (7)
base (1)
be a nobody (1)
be degraded (1)
be despised (1)
dishonors (1)
little known (1)
small (1)

7830 קָלוֹן qālôn (17)
shame (9)
disgrace (3)
insult (2)
disgraceful (1)
insults (1)
shameful ways (1)

7831 קַלַּחַת qallahat (2)
caldron (1)
pot (1)

7832 קָלַט qālat (1)
stunted (1)

7833 קָלִי qāliy (6)
roasted grain (4)
roasted (1)
untranslated (1)

7834 קַלָּי qallāy (1)
Kallai (1)

7835 קֵלָיָה qēlāyāh (1)
Kelaiah (1)

7836 קְלִיטָא qᵉliytā' (3)
Kelita (3)

7837 קָלַל qālal (81)
curse (12)
cursed (8)
curses (7)
lighten (5)
swifter (5)
cursing (3)
make lighter (3)
blasphemer (2)
not serious (2)
receded (2)
be considered accursed (1)
become undignified (1)
blaspheme (1)
call a curse down (1)
called curses down (1)
called down a curse (1)
called down curses (1) +7839
cast lots (1)
comes easily (1)
considered trivial (1)
despise (1) +928+6524
despises (1) +928+6524
disdained (1)
easy (1)
humble (1)
humbled (1)
is cursed (1)
lift (1)
made contemptible (1)
pronounce a curse on (1)
put a curse on (1)
revile (1)
simple (1)

small (1)
swaying (1)
swift (1)
treat with contempt (1)
treated with contempt (1)
trivial (1)
unsharpened (1) +4202
unworthy (1)
vile (1)

7838 קָלָל qālāl (2)
burnished (2)

7839 קְלָלָה qᵉlālāh (33)
curse (12)
curses (7)
cursing (5)
object of cursing (4)
condemnation (2)
accursed (1)
called down curses (1) +7837
pronounce curses (1)

7840 קָלַס qālas (4)
deride (1)
jeered (1)
mock (1)
scorned (1)

7841 קֶלֶס qeles (3)
derision (2)
reproach (1)

7842 קַלָּסָה qallāsāh (1)
laughingstock (1)

7843 קָלַע1 qāla'1 (4)
hurl away (1)
hurl out (1)
sling (1)
slung (1)

7844 קָלַע2 qāla'2 (3)
carved (2) +5237
carved (1)

7845 קֶלַע1 qela'1 (6)
sling (3)
slingstones (3) +74

7846 קֶלַע2 qela'2 (15)
curtains (15)

7847 קַלָּע qallā' (1)
men armed with slings (1)

7848 קִלְקֵל qᵉlōqēl (1)
miserable (1)

7849 קִלְּשׁוֹן qill'šôn (1)
forks (1)

7850 קָמָה qāmāh (8)
standing grain (6)
grainfield (1)
stalk (1)

7851 קְמוּאֵל qᵉmû'ēl (3)
Kemuel (3)

7852 קָמוֹן qāmôn (1)
Kamon (1)

7853 קִמּוֹשׂ qimmôś (3)
briers (1)
nettles (1)
thorns (1)

7854 קֶמַח qemah (14)
flour (13)
meal (1)

7855 קָמַט qāmat (2)
bound (1)
were carried off (1)

7856 קָמַי qāmay
Variant; not used

7857 קָמַל qāmal (2)
wither (1)

withers (1)

7858 קָמַץ qāmas (3)
take a handful (2) +4850+7859
take a handful (1)

7859 קֹמֶץ qōmes (4)
take a handful (2) +4850+7858
handful (1)
plentifully (1) +4200

7860 קֵן qēn (13)
nest (11)
house (1)
rooms (1)

7861 קָנָא qānā' (33)
jealous (5)
envy (4)
envious (3)
suspects (3)
envied (2)
jealous (2) +7863
made jealous (2)
very zealous (2) +7861
zealous (2)
aroused jealousy (1)
jealousy (1)
make envious (1)
provokes to jealousy (1)
stirred up jealous anger (1)
zeal (1)
zealous (1) +7863

7862 קַנָּא qannā' (6)
jealous (6)

7863 קִנְאָה qin'āh (43)
jealousy (15)
zeal (15)
jealous anger (4)
envy (3)
jealous (2) +7861
jealous (1)
jealous (1) +6296+6584+8120
zealous (1) +7861
untranslated (1)

7864 קָנָה1 qānāh1 (78)
buy (20)
bought (19)
get (7)
buyer (6)
acquire (2)
be bought (2)
purchase (2)
purchased (2)
acquired (1)
acquires (1)
bought (1) +928+2021+4084
bought back (1)
buyers (1)
buying (1)
buys (1) +7871
choose (1) +1047
gains (1)
gets (1)
insist on paying (1) +7864
insist on paying for (1) +928+4697+7864
master (1)
reclaim (1)
taken (1)
untranslated (1)

7865 קָנָה2 qānāh2 (6)
creator (3)
brought forth (2)
created (1)

7866 קָנֶה qāneh (58)
rod (12)
branches (10)
reed (5)
branch (4)
reeds (4)
calamus (3)

shaft (2)
stalk (2)
cane (1)
fragrant calamus (1)
joint (1)
measuring rod (1)
scales (1)
untranslated (11)

7867 קָנֶה3 *qānāh3* (3)
Kanah (3)

7868 קַנּוֹא *qannô'* (2)
jealous (2)

7869 קְנַז *qᵉnaz* (11)
Kenaz (11)

7870 קְנִזִּי *qᵉnizziy* (4)
Kenizzite (3)
Kenizzites (1)

7871 קִנְיָן *qinyān* (11)
goods (3)
buys (1) +7864
creatures (1)
have (1)
herds (1)
livelihood (1)
possessed (1)
property (1)
untranslated (1)

7872 קִנָּמוֹן *qinnāmôn* (3)
cinnamon (3)

7873 קָנַן *qānan* (6)
make nests (1)
makes nest (1)
nest (1)
nested (1)
nestled (1)
untranslated (1)

7874 קֵנֵץ *qenes* (1)
end (1) +8492

7875 קְנָת *qᵉnāt* (2)
Kenath (2)

7876 קָסַם *qāsam* (22)
diviners (6)
divination (2)
divinations (2)
consult (1)
omen (1)
practice divination (1) +7877
practiced divination (1)
practiced divination (1) +7877
practices divination (1) +7877
seek an omen (1) +7877
soothsayer (1)
tell fortunes (1)
utter divinations (1)
untranslated (2)

7877 קֶסֶם *qesem* (11)
divination (2)
divinations (2)
fee for divination (1)
lot (1)
oracle (1)
practice divination (1) +7876
practiced divination (1) +7876
practices divination (1) +7876
seek an omen (1) +7876

7878 קָסַס *qāsas* (1)
stripped (1)

7879 קֶסֶת *qeset* (3)
kit (2)
writing kit (1)

7880 קָעָה *qā'āh*
Variant; not used

7881 קְעִילָה *qᵉ'iylāh* (18)
Keilah (18)

7882 קַעֲקַע *qa'ᵃqa'* (1)
tattoo (1)

7883 קְעָרָה *qᵉ'ārāh* (17)
plate (13)
plates (4)

7884 קָפָא *qāpā'* (4)
complacent (1)
congealed (1)
curdle (1)
untranslated (1)

7885 קִפָּאוֹן *qippā'ôn* (1)
frost (1)

7886 קָפַד *qāpad* (1)
rolled up (1)

7887 קִפֹּד *qippōd* (3)
screech owl (2)
owls (1)

7888 קְפָדָה *qᵉpādāh* (1)
terror (1)

7889 קִפּוֹז *qippôz* (1)
owl (1)

7890 קָפַץ *qāpas* (7)
shut (2)
bounding (1)
gathered up (1)
shuts (1)
tightfisted (1) +906+3338
withheld (1)

7891 קֵץ *qēs* (67)
end (40)
later (4) +4946
after (3) +4946
climax (3)
after (2) +4200
remotest (2)
afar (1)
complete (1) +2118+4946
course (1)
endless (1) +401
every (1) +4946
from (1) +4946
fulfilled (1)
later (1) +4200
limit (1)
passed (1)
prospects (1)
some years later (1) +4200+9102
time is ripe (1) +995

7892 קָצַב *qāsab* (2)
cut (1)
sheep just shorn (1)

7893 קֶצֶב *qeseb* (3)
shape (2)
roots (1)

7894 קָצָה1 *qāsāh1* (4)
cutting off (1)
reduce size (1)
scraped (1)
scraped off (1)

7895 קָצֶה *qāseh* (93)
end (28)
ends (16)
edge (11)
border (3)
mouth (3)
otherˢ (4)
outskirts (3)
foot (2)
frontier (2)
part (2)
the otherˢ (2) +824+2021
after (1) +4946
distant (1)
end (1) +1473
entire (1) +4946

every part (1)
extreme (1)
far end (1)
farthest (1)
most distant land (1)
of (1) +4946
otherˢ (1) +9028
outposts (1) +2821
southernmost (1) +4946
tip (1)
untranslated (3)

7896 קָצָה2 *qāsāh2* (35)
ends (11)
corners (9)
end (4)
all sorts (2)
tip (2)
all (1)
all sorts (1) +4946
otherˢ (1)
outer fringe (1)
quarters (1)
ruin (1)
untranslated (1)

7897 קֵצֶה *qēseh* (5)
end (2)
boundless (1) +401
endless (1) +401
number (1)

7898 קָצוּ *qāsû* (3)
ends (2)
borders (1)

7899 קָצוּץ *qāsûs* (3)
distant places (2) +6991
distant (1)

7900 קָצוּר *qāsûr* (1)
narrower (1)

7901 קְצוֹת *qᵉsôt*
Variant; not used

7902 קֶצַח *qesah* (3)
caraway (3)

7903 קָצִין *qāsiyn* (12)
commander (4)
rulers (3)
leader (2)
commanders (1)
leaders (1)
ruler (1)

7904 קְצִיעָה1 *qᵉsiy'āh1* (1)
cassia (1)

7905 קְצִיעָה2 *qᵉsiy'āh2* (1)
Keziah (1)

7906 קְצִיץ *qᵉsiys*
Variant; not used

7907 קָצִיר1 *qāsiyr1* (49)
harvest (37)
harvests (3)
harvest time (2)
harvesting (2) +7917
harvesting grain (1)
reap (1) +7917
reaper (1)
reaping (1)
untranslated (1)

7908 קָצִיר2 *qāsiyr2* (5)
branches (2)
boughs (1)
shoots (1)
twigs (1)

7909 קָצַע1 *qāsa'1* (1)
have scraped (1)

7910 קָצַע2 *qāsa'2* (3)
corners (3)

7911 קָצַף *qāṣap̄* (34)
angry (23)
angered (2)
enraged (2)
anger (1)
angry (1) +7912
aroused wrath (1)
furious (1) +4394
made angry (1) +2118
provoked to anger (1)
very angry (1) +7912

7912 1קֶצֶף *qeṣep̄1* (28)
wrath (13)
anger (7)
angry (3)
angry (1) +7911
discord (1)
fury (1)
great wrath (1) +2256+2405
very angry (1) +7911

7913 2קֶצֶף *qeṣep̄2* (1)
twig (1)

7914 קְצָפָה *q⁺ṣāp̄āh* (1)
ruined (1) +4200

7915 1קָצַץ *qāṣaṣ1* (11)
cut off (4)
took away (3)
cut (1)
cut free (1)
shatters (1)
stripped off (1)

7916 2קָצַץ *qāṣaṣ2*
Variant; not used

7917 1קָצַר *qāṣar1* (36)
reap (15)
harvesters (5)
reaper (3)
harvesting (2) +7907
gather (1)
harvest (1)
harvesting (1)
harvests (1)
reap (1) +7907
reaped (1)
reapers (1)
reaps (1)
untranslated (3)

7918 2קָצַר *qāṣar2* (14)
cut short (3)
short (2)
angry (1)
bear no longer (1)
grew weary (1)
impatient (1)
impatient (1) +5883
short (1) +7918
tired (1)
too short (1)

7919 קֹצֶר *qōṣer* (1)
discouragement (1) +8120

7920 קָצֵר *qāṣēr* (5)
drained (2)
few (1)
quick-tempered (1) +678
quick-tempered (1) +8120

7921 קְצָת *q⁺ṣāt* (9)
end (2)
some (2) +4946
after (1) +4946
corners (1)
far away (1)
untranslated (2)

7922 קַר *qar* (3)
cold (1)
cool (1)
even-tempered (1) +8120

7923 קֹר *qōr* (1)
cold (1)

7924 1קָרָא *qārā'1* (737)
called (139)
call (81)
named (55) +9005
summoned (45)
read (33)
called (27) +9005
proclaim (23)
summon (18)
calls (15)
be called (14)
invited (12)
proclaimed (12)
called out (11)
calling (11)
bears (10) +6584
cried out (9)
call out (7)
cry out (7)
gave (7)
invite (7)
call (6) +9005
cry (6)
shouted (6)
is called (5)
sent for (5) +2256+4200+8938
bear (4) +6584
call upon (4)
called together (4)
name (4) +9005
proclaiming (4)
summons (4)
are called (3)
call on (3)
called out (3) +928+1524+7754
cried (3)
guests (3)
named (3)
sent for (3) +2256+8938
was called (3)
announced (2)
asks (2)
be called (2) +9005
be reckoned (2)
call in (2)
chosen (2) +928+9005
declared (2)
famous (2) +9005
gave name (2)
given (2)
read aloud (2)
say (2)
summoned (2) +2256+8938
were summoned (2)
announce (1)
appeal (1)
be known as (1)
be known as (1) +9005
be mentioned (1)
be named (1) +9005
been called (1)
been invited as guests (1)
been named (1) +9005
being called (1)
being summoned (1)
bleat (1)
blurts out (1)
brag (1)
bring out (1)
call back (1)
call for help (1)
call yourselves (1)
called down (1)
called in (1)
calling (1) +7754
calling (1) +9005
calling down (1)
calling for help (1)
calling forth (1)

calling out (1)
calls in (1)
claims (1)
convocations (1) +5246
cries out (1)
decreed (1)
dictated (1) +4946+7023
did⁵ (1)
exclaim (1)
foretold (1)
get (1)
give (1)
got (1)
grasping (1)
herald (1)
invitation (1)
invite (1) +2256+8938
invites (1)
invoke (1) +928+7023
is called (1) +9005
is called together (1)
known as (1)
make an offer (1)
make proclamation (1)
men of high rank (1)
name (1)
named (1) +928+9005
offer (1)
pray (1)
prayed (1)
preach (1)
proclaim (1) +928
proclaimed (1) +928
pronounced (1)
raised a cry (1)
reading (1)
scream for help (1) +2256+7754+8123
screamed (1) +928+1524+7754
screamed for help (1) +2256+7754+8123
sent for (1) +4200+8938
sent word (1) +2256+8938
shout (1)
shout (1) +928+7754
shout (1) +1524+7754
shout aloud (1) +928+1744
shouted (1) +928+7754
shouted (1) +2256+5951+7754
shouted the news (1)
summoned (1) +4200+8938
voices (1)
was called (1) +9005
was read aloud (1)
were appointed (1)
were called (1)
were counted (1)
were invited (1)
word (1)
untranslated (8)

7925 2קָרָא *qārā'2* (138)
meet (78)
against (13)
met (5)
happened (4)
toward (3)
attack (2)
came toward (2)
come upon (2)
follows (2)
meet in battle (2)
oppose (2)
breaks out (1)
brought upon (1)
come (1)
come across (1) +4200+7156
comes (1)
facing each other (1) +5120
fall upon (1)
fight (1)
follows (1) +6584
greet (1) +1385
happen (1)

happened to be (1) +7936
help (1)
into (1)
opposite (1)
out came to meet (1)
resort to (1) +2143+4200
seized (1)
wage (1)
welcomed (1)
went to meet (1)
untranslated (2)

7926 קֹרֵא1 *qōrē'1* (2)
partridge (2)

7927 קֹרֵא2 *qōrē'2* (3)
Kore (3)

7928 קָרַב *qārab* (280)
bring (36)
present (36)
offer (22)
brought (15)
come near (11)
approached (9)
come (9)
presented (9)
brings (7)
go near (7)
offers (7)
approach (6)
came (6)
near (6)
offered (5)
went (5)
brought forward (4)
brought near (3)
came near (3)
come forward (3)
drew near (3)
had come forward (3)
about (2)
acceptable (2)
advance (2)
bring near (2)
came forward (2)
come here (2)
join (2)
made an offering (2)
offering (2)
sacrificed (2)
add (1)
appear (1)
approaches (1)
approaching (1)
bring forward (1)
bring here (1)
bringing (1)
bringing near (1)
brought offering (1)
brought to a close (1)
came together (1)
cause to come near (1)
closer (1)
come closer (1)
comes (1)
comes near (1)
draw near (1)
draws near (1)
encroach (1)
go (1)
gone near (1)
have brought (1)
have come near (1)
inquire of (1) +448
joined (1)
keep away (1) +448+3870
lie with (1) +448
made (1)
made offerings (1)
make (1)
march up (1)
meet (1)

offer sacrifices (1)
offer up (1)
present yourselves (1)
presenting (1)
presents (1)
reach (1)
reached (1)
soon (1)
stood (1)
take part (1) +6913
went near (1)
untranslated (2)

7929 קָרֵב *qārēb* (12)
draw near (2)
approached (1)
approaches (1)
came (1)
closer (1)
closer and closer (1) +2143+2256
comes near (1)
even comes near (1) +7929
goes near (1)
going (1)

7930 קְרָב *q'rāb* (9)
war (5)
battle (4)

7931 קֶרֶב *qereb* (225)
among (52) +928
in (24) +928
within (20) +928
among (18)
from (16) +4946
inner parts (16)
with (11) +928
midst (6)
heart (5)
among (4) +4946
near (4) +928
them⁵ (4) +2021
through (3) +928
upon (3) +928
inmost being (2)
on (2) +928
to (2) +6584
along with (1) +928
at (1) +928
ate (1) +448+995
body (1)
done so⁵ (1) +448+995
entering (1) +928+995
filled with (1) +928
folds (1)
had (1) +928
harbor (1) +928+4328
hearts (1)
herself (1) +2023
in (1) +4946
inside (1) +928
into (1) +928
lose heart (1) +928+1327+8120
middle (1)
mind (1)
minds (1)
out of (1) +4946
presence (1)
ranks (1)
stomach (1)
there⁵ (1) +928+2257
thick (1)
throughout (1) +928
untranslated (7)

7932 קִרְבָה *qirbāh* (2)
come near (1)
near (1)

7933 קָרְבָּן *qorbān* (80)
offering (58)
offerings (7)
gifts (2)
offers (2)

gift (1)
offered (1)
offering made by fire (1) +852
sacrifice (1)
untranslated (7)

7934 קֻרְבָּן *qurbān* (2)
contribution (1)
contributions (1)

7935 קַרְדֹּם *qardōm* (5)
axes (4)
ax (1)

7936 קָרָה1 *qārāh1* (27)
met (4)
happen (3)
happened (3)
laid beams (1)
as it turned out (1) +5247
beams (1)
come (1)
come true (1)
comes (1)
gave success (1)
give success (1)
happened to be (1) +7925
lays beams (1)
make beams (1)
meet (1)
overtake (1)
overtakes (1)
punished (1) +6411
select (1)

7937 קָרֶה *qāreh* (1)
emission (1)

7938 קָרָה2 *qārāh2* (6)
cold (5)
icy blast (1)

7939 קָרָה3 *qārāh3*
Variant; not used

7940 קָרוֹב *qārôb* (77)
near (38)
nearest (5)
neighbors (3)
approach (2)
close (2)
warriors (2)
about to (1) +4946+6964
always (1)
at hand (1) +995
at hand (1) +995+4200
brief (1) +4946
close at hand (1)
close relative (1)
close relative (1) +8638
close to (1) +725
close to heart (1)
closely associated (1)
closely related (1)
closest (1)
come near (1)
dependent (1)
fellowman (1)
invites (1)
kinsmen (1)
nearby (1)
nearby (1) +4946
nearer (1)
neighbor (1)
recently (1) +2543+4946
shorter (1)
soon (1) +928

7941 קָרוּת *qārût*
Variant; not used

7942 קָרַח *qārah* (6)
must shave (1) +7947
shave head (1)
shave heads (1) +1605
shave heads (1) +7947

was rubbed bare (1)
untranslated (1)

7943 קֶרַח *qerah* (7)
ice (4)
cold (1)
frost (1)
hail (1)

7944 קֵרֵחַ *qērēah* (3)
baldhead (2)
bald (1)

7945 קָרֵחַ *qārēah* (14)
Kareah (14)

7946 קֹרַח *qōrah* (37)
Korah (34)
Korah's (2)
Korah's (1) +4200

7947 קָרְחָה *qorhāh* (11)
shaved (3)
baldness (1)
make bald (1) +8143
must shave (1) +7942
shave (1) +6584
shave (1) +8492
shave head in mourning (1) +995
shave heads (1) +7942
tear out hair (1)

7948 קָרְחִי *qorhiy* (8)
Korahite (3)
Korahites (3)
Korah (1)
Korahites (1) +1201

7949 קָרַחַת *qārahat* (4)
head (2)
bald head (1)
side^s (1)

7950 קְרִי *q'riy* (7)
hostile (6)
hostility (1)

7951 קָרִיא *qāriy'* (3)
appointed (1)
officials (1)
untranslated (1)

7952 קְרִיאָה *q'riy'āh* (1)
message (1)

7953 קִרְיָה *qiryāh* (29)
city (20)
town (5)
cities (3)
one^s (1)

7954 קְרִיּוֹת *q'riyyôt* (3)
Kerioth (3)

7955 קְרִיּוֹת חֶצְרוֹן *q'riyyôt hesrôn* (1)
Kerioth Hezron (1)

7956 קִרְיַת *qiryat* (1)
Kiriath (1)

7957 קִרְיַת אַרְבַּע *qiryat 'arba'* (7)
Kiriath Arba (7)

7958 קִרְיַת־בַּעַל *qiryat-ba'al* (2)
Kiriath Baal (2)

7959 קִרְיַת הָאַרְבַּע *qiryat hā'arba'* (2)
Kiriath Arba (2)

7960 קִרְיַת חֻצוֹת *qiryat husôt* (1)
Kiriath Huzoth (1)

7961 קִרְיַת יְעָרִים *qiryat y'āriym* (19)
Kiriath Jearim (19)

7962 קִרְיַת־סַנָּה *qiryat-sannāh* (1)
Kiriath Sannah (1)

7963 קִרְיַת־סֵפֶר *qiryat-sēper* (4)
Kiriath Sepher (4)

7964 קִרְיָתַיִם *qiryātayim* (7)
Kiriathaim (6)

untranslated (1)

7965 קָרַם *qāram* (2)
cover (1)
covered (1)

7966 קָרַן *qāran* (4)
radiant (3)
horns (1)

7967 קֶרֶן *qeren* (75)
horns (44)
horn (23)
two-horned (2) +1251+2021
brow (1)
hillside (1)
him^s (1)
rays (1)
trumpets (1) +3413
tusks (1)

7968 קֶרֶן הַפּוּךְ *qeren happûk* (1)
Keren-Happuch (1)

7969 קַרְנַיִם *qarnayim* (1)
Karnaim (1)

7970 קָרַס *qāras* (2)
stoop (1)
stoops low (1)

7971 קֶרֶס *qeres* (10)
clasps (7)
them^s (3) +2021

7972 קַרְסֹל *qarsōl* (2)
ankles (2)

7973 קָרַע *qāra'* (63)
tore (26)
torn (12)
tear (10)
rend (2)
tore away (2)
be split apart (1)
cut off (1)
makes large (1)
most certainly tear away (1) +7973
rip open (1) +4213+6033
shade (1)
slandered (1)
tear off (1)
tore apart (1) +4200+7974+9109
was split apart (1)

7974 קְרָעִים *q'rā'iym* (4)
pieces (2)
rags (1)
tore apart (1) +4200+7973+9109

7975 קָרַץ *qāras* (5)
been taken (1)
maliciously wink (1)
purses (1)
winks (1)
winks maliciously (1) +6524

7976 קֶרֶץ *qeres* (1)
gadfly (1)

7977 קַרְקַע 1 *qarqa'1* (7)
floor (5)
bottom (1)
floors (1)

7978 קַרְקַע 2 *qarqa'2* (1)
Karka (1)

7979 קַרְקַר *qarqar*
Variant; not used

7980 קַרְקֹר *qarqōr* (1)
Karkor (1)

7981 קָרַר 1 *qārar1* (2)
pours out (2)

7982 קָרַר 2 *qārar2* (1)
battering down (1)

7983 קֶרֶשׁ *qereš* (51)
frames (27)

frame (8)
those^s (2)
deck (1)
them^s (1) +2021
them^s (1) +2021+6929
untranslated (11)

7984 קֶרֶת *qeret* (5)
city (5)

7985 קַרְתָּה *qartāh* (2)
Kartah (2)

7986 קַרְתָּן *qartān* (1)
Kartan (1)

7987 קַשְׂוָה *qaśwāh* (4)
pitchers (3)
jars (1)

7988 קְשִׂיטָה *q'śiytāh* (3)
pieces of silver (2)
piece of silver (1)

7989 קַשְׂקֶשֶׂת *qaśqeśet* (8)
scales (7)
coat of scale armor (1) +9234

7990 קַשׁ *qaš* (16)
stubble (7)
chaff (6)
straw (2)
piece of straw (1)

7991 קִשֻּׁאָה *qiššu'āh* (1)
cucumbers (1)

7992 קָשַׁב *qāšab* (46)
listen (14)
pay attention (12)
hear (4)
listened (3)
listens (2)
paid attention (2)
alert (1) +7993
attendance (1)
attentively (1)
gave heed (1)
heard (1)
heed (1)
listen (1) +265
pay close attention (1) +2256+9048
turning (1)

7993 קֶשֶׁב *qešeb* (4)
alert (1)
alert (1) +7992
paid attention (1)
response (1)

7994 קַשָּׁב *qaššāb* (2)
attentive (2)

7995 קַשֻּׁב *qaššub* (3)
attentive (3)

7996 קָשָׁה *qāšāh* (29)
stiff-necked (11) +6902
harden (2)
put heavy (2)
cruel (1)
difficult (1)
distressed (1)
great difficulty (1)
hard (1)
hardens (1)
hardship (1)
harshly (1)
having great difficulty (1)
heavy (1)
made stubborn (1)
resisted (1)
stubbornly refused (1)
treats harshly (1)

7997 קָשֶׁה *qāšeh* (36)
stiff-necked (7) +6902
harshly (5)

cruel (3)
fierce (3)
hard (2)
harsh (2)
stubborn (2)
bad news (1)
deeply troubled (1) +8120
desperate times (1)
difficult (1)
dire (1)
grew stronger and stronger (1) +2143+2256
in trouble (1) +3427
obstinate (1) +4213
obstinate (1) +7156
strong (1)
surly (1)
unyielding (1)

7998 קָשַׁח *qāšah* (1)
harden (1)

7999 קֹשְׁט *qōšt* (1)
true (1)

8000 קֹשֶׁט *qōšet* (1)
bow (1)

8001 קְשִׁי *qᵉšiy* (1)
stubbornness (1)

8002 קִשְׁיוֹן *qišyôn* (2)
Kishion (2)

8003 קָשַׁר *qāšar* (44)
conspired (10)
plotted (7)
bind (4)
conspired (4) +8004
tie (3)
tied (3)
became one with (1)
carried out (1)
closely bound up (1)
conspiracy led (1) +8004
conspirators (1)
hold (1)
is bound up (1)
put on (1)
put on a leash (1)
raising a conspiracy (1)
reached height (1) +6330
strong (1)
stronger (1)

8004 קֶשֶׁר *qešer* (16)
conspiracy (5)
conspired (4) +8003
treason (4)
conspiracy led (1) +8003
rebellion (1)
traitor (1)

8005 קְשָׁרִים *qiššuriym* (2)
sashes (1)
wedding ornaments (1)

8006 1קָשַׁשׁ *qāšaš1* (8)
gathering (4)
gather (2)
gather together (2)

8007 2קָשַׁשׁ *qāšaš2*
Variant; not used

8008 קֶשֶׁת *qešet* (76)
bow (45)
bows (14)
rainbow (4)
archer (1) +9530
archers (1) +408+928+2021+4619
archers (1) +928+2021+4619
archers (1) +5432
archers (1) +8227
arrow (1)
arrows (1)
arrows (1) +1201

bowmen (1) +5031
bowshot (1) +3217
did so[s] (1) +2256+2932+4374
shoot (1) +928+2021
with bows (1) +2005

8009 קַשָּׁת *qaššāt* (1)
archer (1) +8050

8010 ר *r*
Variant; not used

8011 1רָאָה *rā'āh1* (1303)
see (342)
saw (305)
seen (102)
look (52)
looked (37)
appeared (33)
sees (27)
examine (25)
show (23)
appear (20)
showed (17)
shown (12)
consider (10)
be seen (9)
realized (9)
find out (8)
seeing (8)
appears (7)
watching (7)
examines (6)
enjoy (5)
looks (5)
watch (5)
find (4)
have regard for (4)
learned (4)
noticed (4)
watched (4)
been seen (3)
find out (3) +2256+3359
observe (3)
remember (3)
see (3) +2256+3359
advisers (2) +7156
be shown (2)
decide (2)
face (2)
faced each other (2) +7156
had[s] (2)
here (2)
inspect (2)
knows (2)
let see (2)
look after (2)
look around (2)
look down on (2)
look for (2)
look over (2)
looking (2)
meet (2)
notice (2)
observed (2)
present himself (2)
provide (2)
revealed (2)
view (2)
were exposed (2)
Ah (1)
allowed to see (1)
appear before (1) +7156
appearing (1)
are given (1)
attract (1)
be found (1)
be provided (1)
bear in mind (1)
beheld (1)
being seen (1)
blind (1) +1153

catch glimpse (1)
caught sight of (1)
cherished (1)
choose (1)
chose (1)
chosen (1)
clearly (1) +3954
come into presence (1) +906+7156
come into view (1)
compare (1)
consider carefully (1)
considers (1)
conspicuous (1)
contemplating (1)
display (1)
displayed (1)
ever seeing (1) +8011
experienced (1)
faced (1)
found (1)
found (1) +4200+7156
gaze (1)
gazing (1)
glimpse (1)
gloat (1)
had a vision (1)
had special access to (1) +7156
have sexual relations (1) +906+6872
hidden (1) +4202
indeed seen (1) +8011
inspected (1)
keeping watch (1) +928+6524
knew (1)
knowing (1)
let gloat (1)
listen (1)
listen carefully (1)
look carefully (1) +928+6524
looked (1) +5260
looked things over (1)
looking at each other (1)
lookout (1)
looks down on (1)
made see (1)
make look (1)
make see (1)
meet with (1) +7156
met (1)
mistake for (1) +3869
only look (1) +8011
paid attention (1)
please (1)
present (1)
present myself (1)
present yourself (1)
probe (1)
realize (1)
realize (1) +2256+3359
realized (1) +2256+3359
realizing (1)
reappears (1) +6388
reason (1)
recognize (1)
regard (1)
regarded (1)
respect (1)
revealing (1)
reveals (1)
saw clearly (1) +8011
see (1) +2021+4200+6524
see (1) +6524
see (1) +7156
see for yourselves (1) +4013+6524
see visions (1)
seems (1)
seen for myself (1) +7156
selected (1)
show himself (1)
showing (1)
sight (1)
someone[s] (1) +2021

stare (1)
suffered (1)
took note (1)
turn (1)
uncovered (1)
understand (1)
very well (1)
viewed (1)
visible (1)
visit (1)
was seen (1)
were shown (1)
untranslated (37)

8012 רָאָה2 *rā'āh2* (1)
red kite (1)

8013 רָאֶה *rā'eh*
Variant; not used

8014 רֹאֶה1 *rō'eh1* (12)
seer (10)
seer's (1)
seers (1)

8015 רֹאֶה2 *rō'eh2* (1)
seeing visions (1)

8016 רֹאֶה3 *rō'eh3*
Variant; not used

8017 רְאוּבֵן *r''ûbēn* (72)
Reuben (45)
Reubenites (17) +1201
Reuben (6) +1201
Reubenite (1) +1201
theyˢ (1) +1201+1201+1514+2256
untranslated (2)

8018 רְאוּבֵנִי *r''ûbēniy* (18)
Reubenites (13)
Reuben (2)
men of Reuben (1)
Reuben (1) +1201
Reubenite (1)

8019 רַאֲוָה *ra'ʰwāh* (1)
spectacle (1)

8020 רְאוּמָה *r''ûmāh* (1)
Reumah (1)

8021 רְאוּת *r''ût* (1)
feast on (1)

8022 רֹאִי *rō'iy*
Variant; not used

8023 רְאִי *r''iy* (1)
mirror (1)

8024 רֳאִי *r'ʰiy* (4)
features (1)
sees (1)
spectacle (1)
to nothing (1) +4946

8025 רְאָיָה *r''āyāh* (4)
Reaiah (4)

8026 רְאִית *r''iyt* (1)
untranslated (1)

8027 רָאַם *rā'am* (1)
raised up (1)

8028 רְאֵם *r''ēm* (9)
wild ox (6)
wild oxen (2)
himˢ (1)

8029 רָאמוֹת1 *rā'môt1* (2)
coral (2)

8030 רָאמוֹת2 *rā'môt2* (5)
Ramoth (5)

8031 רֹאשׁ1 *rō'š1* (603)
head (217)
heads (124)
top (45)

chief (33)
leaders (19)
first (16)
tops (10)
beginning (8)
hair (8)
chiefs (6)
companies (6)
leader (6)
mountaintops (4) +2215
summit (3)
take a census (3) +906+5951
topmost (3)
ends (2)
finest (2)
helmet (2) +5057
high (2)
leading (2)
led by (2) +928
lost hair (2) +5307
over (2) +928
prominent place (2)
released (2) +5951
take a census (2) +5951
all (1)
any (1)
authority (1)
begin (1)
bodyguard (1) +4200+9068
branches off (1)
capstone (1) +7157
choicest gifts (1)
command (1)
commander-in-chief (1) +2256+8569
commanders (1)
company (1)
count (1) +906+5951
counted (1) +906+5951
crest (1)
crowns (1) +4200
detachments (1)
director (1)
directors (1)
divisions (1)
down (1) +4946
each (1)
fine (1)
foremost (1)
full (1)
hair (1) +1929
headwaters (1)
heights (1) +5294
highest (1)
highest (1) +6584
hilltop (1) +2215
hilltops (1) +2215
himself (1) +2257
include in the census (1) +906+5951
itˢ (1) +2257
itˢ (1) +8552
junction (1)
leaders (1) +408
leaders (1) +6639
leading men (1)
made pay for (1) +928+8740
make full restitution (1) +928+8740
masters (1)
men (1)
mountaintop (1) +2215
new Moon festivals (1) +2544
oldest (1)
outstanding (1)
overwhelmed (1) +6296
peaks (1)
raiding parties (1)
reaches (1)
repay (1) +928+8740
repay (1) +6584+8740
ruler (1) +1505
rulers (1)
special (1)

sum (1)
tip (1)
untranslated (11)

8032 רֹאשׁ2 *rō'š2* (12)
poison (5)
poisoned (3)
bitterness (2)
gall (1)
poisonous weeds (1)

8033 רֹאשׁ3 *rō'š3* (1)
Rosh (1)

8034 רֹאשׁ4 *rō'š4*
Variant; not used

8035 רִאשָׁה *ri'šāh* (1)
before (1)

8036 רֹאשָׁה *rō'šāh* (1)
capstone (1) +74

8037 רִאשׁוֹן *ri'šôn* (182)
first (100)
former (19)
beginning (13)
before (6) +928+2021
earlier (6)
before (4)
first (2) +928+2021
old (2)
used to (2) +2021+4200
ancestors (1)
chief (1)
chief officials (1)
days of old (1)
early (1)
fathers (1)
forefathers (1) +3
formerly (1) +928+2021
front (1)
highest (1)
lead (1)
leads (1) +928+2021
led the way (1) +2118+3338
long (1)
long ago (1) +928+2021
of old (1)
older (1)
once again (1) +2021+3869
one in the lead (1)
past (1)
past (1) +3427
past (1) +6961
predecessors (1)
previous (1)
used to (1)
untranslated (3)

8038 רִאשׁוֹנִי *ri'šôniy* (1)
first (1)

8039 רַאֲשׁוֹת *ra'ʰšôt*
Variant; not used

8040 רֵאשִׁית *rē'šiyt* (51)
first (13)
firstfruits (8)
beginning (7)
best (6)
early (3) +928
firstfruits (2) +7262
beginnings (1)
choice (1)
choice parts (1)
early (1)
finest (1)
firstfruits of harvest (1)
foremost (1)
leaders (1)
mainstay (1)
starting (1)
supreme (1)
when (1) +928

8041 רֵב rab1 (425)
many (162)
great (73)
long (18)
numerous (14)
abundant (12)
mighty (10)
much (10)
abounding (8)
large (8)
enough (6)
larger (6)
vast (6)
full (4)
more (4)
greatly (3)
number (3)
plenty (3)
crowd (2)
deep (2)
fully (2)
gone too far (2)
great deal (2)
heavy (2)
large (2) +4394
large amount (2)
long enough (2)
rushing (2)
so great (2)
so many (2)
weighs heavily (2)
abundantly (1)
all abound (1)
beyond number (1) +4394
chief (1)
convinced (1)
distant (1)
distant future (1) +3427
floodwaters (1) +4784
gone far enough (1)
great quantities (1)
greater (1)
greater power (1)
gushed out (1) +3655
high (1)
huge (1)
increased more and more (1)
           +2143+2143+2256
increasing (1)
larger number (1)
mansions (1) +1074
many (1) +4394
more (1) +3578
most (1)
much too numerous (1) +2256+6786
multitude (1)
multitudes (1)
never (1) +4202
numbers (1)
old (1)
older (1)
powerful (1)
quantities (1)
quantity (1)
rich (1)
richly (1)
severe (1) +4394
severely (1)
so (1)
so many (1) +5031
so much (1)
stronger (1)
surging (1)
time after time (1) +6961
too long (1)
tyrannical (1) +5131
utterly (1)
very (1)
what (1)
whole (1)
wide (1)

8042 2רֵב rab2 (33)
commander (23)
chief (3)
high (2)
officers (2)
captain (1) +2021+2480
wine stewards (1) +1074
untranslated (1)

8043 3רֵב rab3 (3)
archers (2)
archer (1)

8044 רֹב rōb (152)
many (31)
great (24)
numerous (6)
all (5)
great (4) +4200
much (4)
plentiful (4) +4200
abundant (3)
great amount (3) +4200
greatly (3) +4200
in abundance (3) +4200
large numbers (3) +4200
abundance (2)
extensive (2) +4200
great (2) +3972
great numbers (2)
greatness (2)
large (2)
large quantities (2) +4200
many (2) +4200
much (2) +4200
plenty (2) +4200
so many (2) +4946
abound (1)
abundant (1) +4200
advanced (1)
age (1) +3427
droves (1) +4200
great number (1)
great number (1) +4200
great numbers (1) +4200
great quantities (1) +4200+4394
harsh (1)
in abundance (1)
in large numbers (1) +4200
increased (1)
large amount (1) +4200
larger (1) +4200
load (1)
long (1)
mighty (1) +4200
more (1) +4200
multitude (1)
numerous (1) +4200
prosperity (1) +3972
quantities (1) +4200
rabble (1) +132
size (1)
so many (1)
so many (1) +4200
surpassing (1)
thick (1)
widespread (1)
untranslated (7)

8045 1רֵבַב rābab1 (20)
many (7)
great (3)
numerous (3)
increased (2)
abound (1)
do[s] (1)
increase in number (1)
outnumber (1) +4946
tens of thousands (1)

8046 2רֵבַב rābab2 (1)
shot (1)

8047 רְבָבָה r°bābāh (18)
ten thousand (6)
tens of thousands (5)
countless (1)
grow (1)
myriads (1)
ten thousands (1)
thousands (1)
untranslated (2)

8048 רְבַד rābad (1)
covered (1) +5267

8049 1רָבָה rābāh1 (179)
increase (14)
many (10)
increase in number (9)
increased (9)
increase numbers (8)
numerous (8)
multiplied (5)
make numerous (4)
multiply (4)
thrive (4)
great (3)
greater (3)
greatly (3)
increases (3)
much (3)
multiplies (3)
gave many (2)
give larger (2)
had many (2)
increase the number (2)
increasing (2)
keep (2)
long (2)
make great (2)
more (2)
reared (2)
take many (2)
abundant (1)
accumulate large amounts (1) +4394
acquire great numbers (1)
add to numbers (1)
adding (1)
as much as (1) +4946
before[s] (1)
built many (1)
built more (1)
distant (1) +2006+2021
done more (1)
enlarge (1)
enlarged (1)
freely (1)
gaining (1)
gathered much (1)
generously gave (1)
get more (1)
give more (1)
greatly increase (1) +8049
grew up (1)
grow large (1)
have many (1)
heap (1)
higher than (1) +2025+4200+5087
increased in number (1)
increased number (1)
increased numbers (1)
kept on (1)
lavished (1)
less meaning (1) +2039
made many (1)
made numerous (1)
make as great as you like (1) +4394
make countless (1) +889+4202+6218
make many (1)
make numerous (1) +8049
make plentiful (1)
makes grow (1)
many times (1)
more and more (1)

more and more unfaithful (1) +5085+5086
multiply the number (1)
numbers increased (1)
numbers increased greatly (1) +2256+7238
offer many (1)
outnumber (1) +4946
piles up (1)
repeatedly (1)
so does⁵ (1)
so increase (1) +8049
time after time (1)
too much (1)
use an abundance (1)
whole (1)
yet more (1)
untranslated (5)

8050 רָבָה rābāh2 (1)
archer (1) +8009

8051 רַבָּה rabbāh (15)
Rabbah (15)

8052 רִבּוֹא ribbô' (11)
20,000 (2) +9109
42,360 (1)
     +547+752+2256+4395+8993+9252
42,360 (1) +547+752+4395+8993+9252
61,000 (1) +547+2256+9252
eighteen thousand (1) +547+2256+9046
hundred and twenty thousand (1)
     +6926+9109
many thousands (1)
ten thousand (1)
tens of thousands (1)
untranslated (1)

8053 רְבִיבִים r'biybiym (6)
showers (5)
abundant rain (1)

8054 רָבִיד rābiyd (3)
chain (1)
interwoven (1) +928+2021
necklace (1)

8055 רְבִיעִי r'biy'iy (57)
fourth (44)
quarter (9)
fourth generation (2)
four-sided (1)
square (1)

8056 רַבִּית rabbiyt (1)
Rabbith (1)

8057 רָבַךְ rābak (3)
mixing (1)
well-kneaded (1)
well-mixed (1)

8058 רִבְלָה riblāh (11)
Riblah (11)

8059 רַב מָג rab māg
Variant; not used

8060 רַב־סָרִיס rab-sāriys
Variant; not used

8061 רָבַע rāba'1 (4)
have sexual relations with (2)
lying down (1)
mate (1)

8062 רָבַע rāba'2 (12)
square (9)
rectangular (2)
square (1) +448+752+8063

8063 רֶבַע reba'1 (7)
directions (2)
quarter (2)
sides (1)
square (1) +448+752
square (1) +448+752+8062

8064 רֶבַע reba'2 (2)
Reba (2)

8065 רֹבַע rōba'1 (2)
fourth part (1)
quarter (1)

8066 רֹבַע rōba'2
Variant; not used

8067 רִבֵּעַ ribbēa' (4)
fourth generation (4)

8068 רְבֻעַת r'bu'at
Variant; not used

8069 רָבַץ rābaṣ (30)
lie down (11)
lay down (2)
lie (2)
lying (2)
rest (2)
build (1)
crouching (1)
fall (1)
fallen down (1)
have lie down (1)
lies (1)
lies down (1)
lying down (1)
makes lie down (1)
rest flocks (1)
sitting (1)

8070 רֵבֶץ rēbes (4)
resting place (2)
dwelling place (1)
where lay (1)

8071 רִבְקָה ribqāh (30)
Rebekah (29)
Rebekah's (1)

8072 רַב־שָׁקֵה rab-šāqēh (16)
field commander (12)
commander (4)

8073 רֶגֶב regeb (2)
clods of earth (1)
soil (1)

8074 רָגַז rāgaz (41)
tremble (7)
rage (4)
shook (4)
disturbed (3)
shakes (2)
trembled (2)
all astir (1)
anger (1)
come trembling (1)
convulsed (1)
enraged (1)
in anguish (1)
made tremble (1)
make tremble (1)
pounded (1)
provoke (1)
quake (1)
quarrel (1)
rages (1)
rouse (1)
shake (1)
shaken (1)
shudder (1)
trembles (1)
unrest (1)

8075 רֹגֶז rōgez (7)
turmoil (3)
excitement (1)
roar (1)
trouble (1)
wrath (1)

8076 רַגָּז raggāz (1)
anxious (1)

8077 רְגָזָה rogzāh (1)
shudder (1)

8078 רָגַל rāgal (26)
spies (8)
spied out (4)
spy out (4)
spying (2)
explore (1)
explored (1)
scouts (1)
secret messengers (1)
slander (1)
slandered (1)
spies (1) +408
taught to walk (1)

8079 רֶגֶל regel (252)
feet (131)
foot (43)
legs (6)
feet (5) +4090
footstool (5) +2071
foot (4) +4090
times (4)
steps (3)
big toes (2)
fleet-footed (2) +928+7824
following (2) +928
footsteps (2)
my (2) +928+3276
accompanied (1) +995
after (1) +928
ankles (1)
attended by (1) +2143+4200
belonged to (1) +928
continued on journey (1) +5951
follow (1) +928
follow (1) +928+2143
followed (1) +928+6590
goes (1) +2118
hasty (1) +237+928
jointed (1) +4200+4946+5087
letting range free (1) +8938
offering body (1) +906+7316
pace (1)
relieve himself (1) +906+2257+6114
relieving himself (1) +906+2257+6114
service (1)
step (1)
stood (1) +3922+5163
stood (1) +5163
that⁵ (1) +4200
those⁵ (1) +4090
underfoot (1) +928
underfoot (1) +9393
what trampled (1) +5330
wherever (1) +4200
with (1) +928
womb (1) +1068
untranslated (12)

8080 רֹגֶל rōgēl
Variant; not used

8081 רַגְלִי ragliy (12)
foot soldiers (6)
foot soldiers (3) +408
on foot (2)
soldiers (1) +408

8082 רֹגְלִים rōg'liym (2)
Rogelim (2)

8083 רָגַם rāgam (16)
stone (5) +74+928+2021
stoned (4) +74
must stone (1) +8083
stone (1)
stone (1) +74
stoned (1) +74+928+2021
stoned to death (1) +74
stoning (1) +74+928+2021

8084 רֶגֶם regem (1)
Regem (1)

8085 רֶגֶם מֶלֶךְ regem melek (1)
Regem-Melech (1)

8086 רִגְמָה *rigmāh* (1)
great throng (1)

8087 רָגַן *rāgan* (7)
gossip (4)
grumbled (2)
complain (1)

8088 1רָגַע *rāga'1* (7)
become (1)
churned up (1)
churns up (1)
in an instant (1)
instant (1)
moment (1)
stirs up (1)

8089 2רָגַע *rāga'2* (5)
bring rest (1)
cease (1)
find repose (1)
give rest (1)
repose (1)

8090 3רָגַע *rāga'3* (1)
broken (1)

8091 רָגֵעַ *rāgēa'* (1)
live quietly (1)

8092 רֶגַע *rega'* (22)
moment (9)
at once (2) +3869
in a moment (2)
at another time (1)
at any time (1)
continually (1) +4200
in a moment (1) +4017
in an instant (1)
little while (1) +5071
peace (1)
sudden (1)
suddenly (1) +3869

8093 רָגַשׁ *rāgaš* (1)
conspire (1)

8094 רֶגֶשׁ *regeš* (1)
throng (1)

8095 רִגְשָׁה *rigšāh* (1)
noisy crowd (1)

8096 רָדַד *rādad* (2)
beaten (1)
subdues (1)

8097 1רָדָה *rādāh1* (23)
rule (11)
ruled (3)
officials (2)
directed (1)
leading (1)
rule over (1)
ruler (1)
subdued (1)
subdues (1)
trample the grapes (1)

8098 2רָדָה *rādāh2* (2)
scooped out (1)
taken (1)

8099 רַדַּי *radday* (1)
Raddai (1)

8100 רְדִיד *r'diyd* (2)
cloak (1)
shawls (1)

8101 רָדַם *rādam* (7)
fell into a deep sleep (2)
in a deep sleep (1)
lay fast asleep (1)
lie still (1)
sleep (1)
sleeps (1)

8102 רֹדָן *rōdān* (3)
Rodanim (2)
Rhodes (1)

8103 רָדַף *rādap* (144)
pursue (33)
pursued (27)
pursuing (11)
pursues (9)
chased (8)
pursuers (7)
chase (6)
persecute (5)
persecutors (4)
follow (3)
pursuit (3)
went in pursuit (3)
chases (2)
go (2)
in pursuit (2)
came by in pursuit (1)
devise (1)
driven (1)
driven away (1)
hound (1)
hounded (1)
hunts (1)
hurried (1)
past (1)
plague (1)
press on (1)
pursuer (1)
put to flight (1)
routs (1)
run after (1)
set out in pursuit (1)
theyˢ (1) +2021
untranslated (2)

8104 רָהַב *rāhab* (4)
made bold (1)
overwhelm (1)
press plea (1)
rise up (1)

8105 רַהַב *rahab* (6)
Rahab (6)

8106 רֹהַב *rōhab*
Variant; not used

8107 רָהָב *rāhāb* (1)
proud (1)

8108 רָהְגָה *rāhgāh* (1)
Rohgah (1)

8109 רָהָה *rāhāh*
Variant; not used

8110 1רַהַט *rahat1* (3)
troughs (2)
troughs (1) +9216

8111 2רַהַט *rahat2* (1)
tresses (1)

8112 רָהִיט *rāhiyt* (1)
rafters (1)

8113 רוּד *rûd* (4)
restless (1)
roam (1)
trouble (1)
unruly (1)

8114 רוֹדָנִים *rôdāniym*
Variant; not used

8115 רָוָה *rāwāh* (14)
drench (2)
satisfy (2)
drenched (1)
drink deep (1)
drunk its fill (1)
feast (1)
lavished on (1)
quenched its thirst (1)
refresh (1)
refreshes (1)

sated (1)
watering (1)

8116 רָוֶה *rāweh* (4)
well-watered (2)
drowned (1)
watered land (1)

8117 רוֹחֲנָה *rôḥªgāh* (1)
untranslated (1)

8118 רָוַח *rāwaḥ* (3)
find relief (1)
relief come (1)
spacious (1)

8119 רֶוַח *rewaḥ* (2)
relief (1)
space (1)

8120 רוּחַ *rûaḥ* (379)
spirit (176)
wind (79)
breath (31)
winds (13)
mind (5)
heart (4)
side (4)
spirits (4)
blast (3)
sides (3)
anger (2)
courage (2)
feelings (2)
itˢ (2) +2021
overwhelmed (2) +928+2118+4202+6388
air (1)
breath (1) +5972
breeze (1)
breezes (1)
cool (1)
deep sleep (1) +9554
deeply troubled (1) +7997
discouragement (1) +7919
empty (1)
even-tempered (1) +7922
hostility (1)
I (1) +3276
inspired (1)
inspires (1)
jealous (1) +6296+6584+7863
liar (1) +3941
life (1)
life breath (1) +678
long-winded (1)
lose heart (1) +928+1327+7931
me (1) +3276
motives (1)
pant (1) +8634
patience (1) +800
pride (1) +1468
quick-tempered (1) +7920
rage (1)
resentment (1)
revived (1) +8740
self-control (1) +4200+5110
source of grief (1) +5289
strength (1)
temper (1)
tempest (1) +6185
tempest (1) +6194
trustworthy (1) +586
violent wind (1) +6194
violent winds (1) +6194
whirlwind (1)
willing (1) +5605
windstorm (1) +6194
wisdom (1) +2683
you (1) +3870
untranslated (4)

8121 רְוָחָה *r'wāḥāh* (2)
relief (2)

8122 רְוָיָה *r'wāyāh* (2)
overflows (1)

place of abundance (1)

8123 רוּם1 *rûm1* (194)
exalted (20)
exalt (16)
present (10)
high (9)
lift up (7)
raised (6)
haughty (5)
lifted high (5)
raise (5)
remove (5)
provided (4)
tall (4)
exalts (3)
lift (3)
raised up (3)
be exalted (2)
boldly (2) +928+3338
brought up (2)
lifted (2)
lifted up (2)
lifts (2)
lofty (2)
offer (2)
presenting (2)
proud (2)
rebelled (2) +3338
rose (2)
take (2)
as a special gift set aside (1)
be lifted up (1)
brandish (1)
build on high (1)
consider better (1) +4222
contributed (1)
displays (1)
donated (1)
exalt himself (1)
exult (1)
filled with pride (1) +4222
greater (1)
heights (1)
held up (1)
higher (1)
highest (1)
holds up (1)
honored (1)
is removed (1)
let triumph (1)
lift out (1)
lifts up (1)
lofty trees (1) +7757
loud (1)
made grow tall (1)
picked up (1)
present (1) +9556
present a portion (1)
presented (1)
proud (1) +4213
proud (1) +4222
raised and taken an oath (1)
rebuild (1)
rise (1)
rise up (1)
rises (1)
scream for help (1) +2256+7754+7924
screamed for help (1) +2256+7754+7924
set apart (1)
set high (1)
set up (1)
shout (1) +7754
shouted (1) +928+7754+9558
sing songs (1) +928+4200+7754+9048
sins defiantly (1) +928+3338+6913
sound (1) +7754
stop (1)
take out (1)
take up (1)
taller (1)
took away (1)

took up (1)
towering (1)
triumph (1)
triumphed (1)
turn (1)
upraised (1)
very top (1)
was presented (1) +9556
untranslated (4)

8124 רוּם2 *rûm2* (6)
haughty (2)
pride (2)
haughtiness (1)
high (1)

8125 רוֹם *rôm* (1)
high (1)

8126 רוּמָה *rûmāh* (1)
Rumah (1)

8127 רוֹמָה *rômāh* (1)
proudly (1)

8128 רוֹמֵם *rômām* (2)
praise (2)

8129 רוֹמֵמֻת *rômēmut* (1)
rise up (1)

8130 רוּן *rûn* (1)
wakes from stupor (1)

8131 רוּעַ *rûa'* (45)
shout (8)
shout aloud (4)
shout for joy (4)
shouted (3)
gave a shout (2) +9558
shout in triumph (2)
shouting (2)
cry aloud (1) +8275
cry out (1)
crying out (1)
extol (1)
give a shout (1) +9558
give a war cry (1)
made noise (1) +9558
raise the battle cry (1)
raise the war cry (1)
raised a shout (1) +9558
raised the battle cry (1)
shout with joy (1)
shouted for joy (1)
shouts (1)
signal (1)
sound (1)
sound a blast (1)
sound alarm (1)
sound of battle cry (1)
triumph (1)

8132 רוּץ *rûs* (103)
run (20)
ran (19)
guards (10)
couriers (6)
running (5)
hurried (4)
guard (3)
hurry (3)
rush (3)
advance (2)
chase (2)
guardroom (2) +9288
anotherˢ (1)
attack (1)
busy (1)
charge (1)
charged (1)
charging (1)
courier (1)
dart about (1)
gallop along (1)
go (1)

go quickly (1)
hasten (1)
quickly brought (1)
raced (1)
ran off (1)
runner (1)
runs (1)
rushed forward (1)
rushes (1)
served quickly (1)
submit (1) +3338
untranslated (3)

8133 רוּשׁ *rûš* (23)
poor (19)
oppressed (1)
poverty (1)
pretends to be poor (1)
weak (1)

8134 רוּת *rût* (12)
Ruth (12)

8135 רָזָה *rāzāh* (2)
destroys (1)
waste away (1)

8136 רָזֶה *rāzeh* (2)
lean (1)
poor (1)

8137 רָזוֹן1 *rāzôn1* (3)
wasting disease (2)
short (1)

8138 רָזוֹן2 *rāzôn2* (1)
prince (1)

8139 רְזוֹן *r'zôn* (1)
Rezon (1)

8140 רָזִי *rāziy* (2)
waste away (2)

8141 רָזַם *rāzam* (1)
flash (1)

8142 רָזַן *rāzan* (6)
rulers (5)
princes (1)

8143 רָחַב *rāhab* (25)
enlarges (3)
broaden (2)
enlarge (2)
boasts (1)
broad (1)
enlarged (1)
extend (1)
gape (1) +7023
give relief (1)
given room (1)
greedy (1)
make bald (1) +7947
multiplied (1)
open wide (1)
opened wide (1)
opens the way (1)
set free (1)
sneer (1) +7023
swell with joy (1)
wide (1)
wider (1)

8144 רַחַב *rahab* (2)
spacious place (1)
vast expanses (1)

8145 רֹחַב *rōhab* (103)
wide (69)
width (11)
breadth (3)
thick (3)
deep (2)
distance (2)
broad (1)
from front to back (1)
length (1)

projected (1)
span (1)
square (1) +802+2256
widened (1)
untranslated (6)

8146 1רָחָב *rāhāb̲1* (21)
spacious (4) +3338
broad (2)
proud (2)
spacious (2)
boundless (1) +4394
broad (1) +3338
freedom (1)
gaping (1)
greedy man (1) +5883
large (1)
large (1) +3338
plenty of room (1) +3338
spread out (1)
thick (1)
wider (1)

8147 2רָחָב *rāhāb̲2* (5)
Rahab (5)

8148 1רְחֹב *rᵉhōb̲1* (43)
streets (15)
square (10)
public square (6)
public squares (5)
squares (4)
oneˢ (1)
open square (1)
thereˢ (1) +928+2023

8149 2רְחֹב *rᵉhōb̲2* (7)
Rehob (7)

8150 3רְחֹב *rᵉhōb̲3* (3)
Rehob (3)

8151 רְחֹבוֹת *rᵉhōb̲ōt̲* (3)
Rehoboth (3)

8152 רְחַבְיָה *rᵉhab̲yāh* (2)
Rehabiah (2)

8153 רְחַבְיָהוּ *rᵉhab̲yāhû* (3)
Rehabiah (2)
hisˢ (1)

8154 רְחַבְעָם *rᵉhab̲'ām* (50)
Rehoboam (43)
heˢ (3)
Rehoboam's (3)
untranslated (1)

8155 רְחֹבֹת עִיר *rᵉhōb̲ōt̲ 'iyr* (1)
Rehoboth Ir (1)

8156 רְחוּם *rᵉhûm* (4)
Rehum (4)

8157 רַחוּם *rahûm* (13)
compassionate (10)
merciful (3)

8158 רָחוֹק *rāhôq* (85)
far (12)
distant (11)
afar (10)
distance (10)
far away (9)
far away (5) +4946
distant (2) +4946
distant place (2)
future (2) +4946
long ago (2) +4200+4946
long ago (2) +4946
long way (2)
at a distance (1) +4394
away (1)
beyond (1)
beyond reach (1)
far and wide (1) +4200+4946+6330
far and wide (1) +6330
far away (1) +4200+4946+6330

far off (1)
far off (1) +928
far-off (1)
farthest (1)
long (1) +4946
long way (1) +4394
past (1)
some distance away (1) +4946
widely (1)

8159 רָחִיט *rāhiyt̲* (1)
untranslated (1)

8160 רֵחַיִם *rēhayim* (5)
millstones (2)
hand mill (1)
handmill (1)
pair of millstones (1)

8161 1רָחֵל *rāhēl1* (4)
sheep (3)
ewes (1)

8162 2רָחֵל *rāhēl2* (47)
Rachel (40)
Rachel's (5)
herˢ (1)
sheˢ (1)

8163 רָחַם *rāham* (47)
have compassion (15)
compassion (4)
has compassion (4)
show love (4)
mercy (3)
show compassion (3)
have mercy (2)
loved (2)
show mercy (2)
find compassion (1)
finds mercy (1)
full of compassion (1)
had compassion (1)
have great compassion (1) +8163
love (1)
pity (1)

8164 רָחָם *rāhām* (1)
osprey (1)

8165 1רַחַם *raham1* (1)
Raham (1)

8166 2רַחַם *raham2*
Variant; not used

8167 רֶחֶם *rehem* (31)
womb (20)
birth (4)
born (1) +3655+4946
first male offspring (1) +1147+7081
firstborn (1) +7081
girl (1)
mothers (1)
woman (1)
wombs (1)

8168 רָחָמָה *rāhāmāh* (1)
osprey (1)

8169 רַחֲמָה *rahᵃmāh* (1)
twoˢ (1)

8170 רֻחָמָה *ruhāmāh*
Variant; not used

8171 רַחֲמִים *rahᵃmiym* (40)
compassion (18)
mercy (11)
compassions (1)
deeply moved (1) +4023
favor (1)
great mercy (1)
kindest acts (1)
merciful (1)
pitied (1)
pity (1)
sympathy (1)

untranslated (2)

8172 רַחֲמָנִי *rahᵃmāniy* (1)
compassionate (1)

8173 1רָחַף *rāhap1* (3)
hovering (1)
hovers (1)
tremble (1)

8174 2רָחַף *rāhap2*
Variant; not used

8175 רָחַץ *rāhas* (73)
bathe (25)
wash (23)
washed (10)
bathed (4)
washing (4)
are cleansed (1)
bathing (1)
drenched (1)
plunge (1)
wash away (1)
washed myself (1)
were washed (1)

8176 רַחַץ *rahas* (2)
washbasin (2) +6105

8177 רַחְצָה *rahsāh* (2)
washing (2)

8178 רָחַק *rāhaq* (58)
far (12)
far away (7)
drive far (3)
keep far (3)
put away (2)
remove far (2)
sent far away (2)
stand aloof (2)
taken (2)
alienated (1)
avoid (1)
away (1)
distance away (1)
extended (1)
extending (1)
far off (1)
far removed (1)
go far (1)
gone some distance (1)
have nothing to do (1)
is severed (1)
keep distance (1)
must very far (1) +8178
no near (1)
refrain (1)
send far (1)
some distance away (1) +4946
stays far (1)
strayed far (1)
went far (1)
withdraw far (1)

8179 רָחֵק *rāhēq* (1)
far (1)

8180 רָחַשׁ *rāhaš* (1)
stirred (1)

8181 רַחַת *rahat̲* (1)
fork (1)

8182 רָטַב *rātab̲* (1)
drenched (1)

8183 רָטֹב *rātōb̲* (1)
well-watered plant (1)

8184 רָטָה *rātāh*
Variant; not used

8185 רֶטֶט *retet̲* (1)
panic (1)

8186 רֻטֲפַשׁ *rut̲ᵃpaš* (1)
is renewed (1)

8187 רָטַשׁ *rātaš* (6)
be dashed to pieces (1)
be dashed to the ground (1)
dash to the ground (1)
strike down (1)
were dashed to pieces (1)
were dashed to the ground (1)

8188 רִי *riy* (1)
moisture (1)

8189 רִיב1 *riyb1* (71)
quarreled (7)
bring charges (6)
contend (4)
defend (4)
accuse (3)
rebuked (3)
complain (2)
quarrel (2)
rebuke (2)
take up (2)
accused (1)
argue (1)
argue the case (1)
bring a case (1)
bring a charge (1)
charges (1)
contended (1)
contends (1)
criticized (1)
defender (1)
defends (1)
defends cause (1)
dispute (1)
fights (1)
in court (1)
judgment (1)
oppose (1)
oppose (1) +6643
plead (1)
plead case (1)
plead cause (1)
plead the case (1)
pleads (1)
quarrel (1) +8189
quarrels (1)
took to task (1)
took up (1)
upheld (1)
uphold (1)
uphold cause (1)
vigorously defend (1) +8189
untranslated (3)

8190 רִיב2 *riyb2* (60)
case (11)
cause (9)
strife (7)
dispute (4)
attacks (2)
charge (2)
complaint (2)
disputes (2)
lawsuit (2)
quarrel (2)
quarreling (2)
accusation (1)
accuser (1) +408
accusing (1)
cases of dispute (1)
charges (1)
contend (1)
court (1)
distress (1)
grievance (1)
justice (1)
lawsuits (1)
oppose (1)
strives (1)
struggle (1)
taunts (1)

8191 רִיבָה *riybāh* (2)
cases (1) +1821
plea (1)

8192 רִיבַי *riybay* (2)
Ribai (2)

8193 רִיחַ *riyah* (11)
smell (2)
accept (1)
catches the scent (1)
caught the smell (1) +8194
comes close (1)
delight (1)
enjoy fragrance (1)
smelled (1)
stand (1)
take delight (1)

8194 רֵיחַ *rēyah* (58)
aroma (40)
fragrance (8)
fragrant incense (4) +5767
smell (2)
caught the smell (1) +8193
made stench (1) +944
scent (1)
that⁵ (1)

8195 רִיפוֹת *riypôt* (2)
grain (2)

8196 רִיפַת *riypat* (2)
Riphath (2)

8197 רִיק1 *riyq1* (19)
draw (3)
drawn (3)
emptying (2)
pour out (2)
poured out (2)
brandish (1)
called out (1)
draw out (1)
empty (1)
leaves empty (1)
pour (1)
poured (1)

8198 רִיק2 *riyq2* (12)
in vain (4) +4200
for nothing (2) +928+1896
in vain (2)
delusions (1)
empty (1)
no purpose (1)
utterly useless (1) +2039+2256

8199 רֵיק *rēyq* (14)
empty (4)
fantasies (2)
worthless (2)
adventurers (1)
emptied (1)
hunger (1) +5883
idle (1)
reckless (1)
vulgar (1)

8200 רֵיקָם *rēyqām* (16)
empty-handed (9)
empty (3)
unfilled (1)
unsatisfied (1)
without cause (1)
without excuse (1)

8201 רִיר1 *riyr1* (1)
flowing (1)

8202 רִיר2 *riyr2* (2)
saliva (1)
white (1)

8203 רֵישׁ *rēyš* (7)
poverty (7)

8204 רֹךְ *rōk* (1)

gentle (1)

8205 רַךְ *rak* (18)
gentle (5)
tender (5)
inexperienced (2)
responsive (2)
weak (2)
fainthearted (1) +4222
indecisive (1) +4222

8206 רָכַב *rākab* (78)
riding (10)
mounted (6)
rider (6)
put (4)
rode (4)
horseman (3) +6061
ride (3)
riders (3)
rides (3)
drive (2)
mounted (2) +6061
ridden (2)
ride on (2)
rode off (2)
set (2)
came riding (1)
cause to ride (1)
driver (1)
drivers (1)
got into chariot (1)
got on (1)
had ride (1)
had ride along (1)
horsemen (1) +6061
in a chariot (1)
lead (1)
led on horseback (1)
let ride (1)
made ride (1)
mount (1)
moved (1)
ride forth (1)
ride off (1)
rides on (1)
riding in chariots (1)
slow down (1) +4200+6806
take (1)
taken (1)
took by chariot (1)

8207 רֶכֶב *rekeb* (121)
chariots (78)
chariot (26)
charioteers (3)
riders (3)
chariot horses (2)
upper (2)
charioteers (1) +132
chariots and charioteers (1)
upper one (1)
untranslated (4)

8208 רַכָּב *rakkāb* (3)
chariot driver (2)
horseman (1)

8209 רֵכָב *rēkāb* (13)
Recab (13)

8210 רִכְבָּה *rikbāh* (1)
saddle (1)

8211 רֵכָבִי *rēkābiy* (4)
Recabite (2)
Recabites (2)

8212 רֵכָה *rēkāh* (1)
Recah (1)

8213 רְכוּב *r'kûb* (1)
chariot (1)

8214 רְכוּשׁ *r'kûš* (28)
possessions (11)

goods (7)
property (3)
wealth (2)
equipment (1)
equipped (1)
everything (1) +3972
flocks (1)
riches (1)

8215 רָכִיל rāḵiyl (6)
gossip (2) +2143
slander (1)
slanderer (1) +2143
slanderous (1)
spreading slander (1)

8216 רָכַך rāḵaḵ (6)
lose (2)
fainthearted (1) +4222
made faint (1)
soothed (1)
soothing (1)

8217 רָכַל rāḵal (17)
merchants (6)
traded (6)
merchant (2)
traders (2)
traded with (1)

8218 רָכָל rāḵāl (1)
Racal (1)

8219 רְכֻלָּה rᵉḵullāh (4)
trade (2)
merchandise (1)
trading (1)

8220 רָכַס rāḵas (2)
tied (2)

8221 רֶכֶס reḵes (1)
rugged places (1)

8222 רֹכֶס rōḵes (1)
intrigues (1)

8223 רָכַשׁ rāḵaš (5)
accumulated (2)
acquired (2)
untranslated (1)

8224 רְכֵשׁ reḵeš (4)
chariot horses (1)
fast horses (1)
horses (1)
team (1)

8225 1רָם rām1
Variant; not used

8226 2רָם rām2 (7)
ram (7)

8227 1רָמָה rāmāh1 (4)
hurled (2)
archers (1) +8008
armed (1) +5976

8228 2רָמָה rāmāh2 (8)
betrayed (2)
deceive (2)
deceived (2)
betray (1)
deceives (1)

8229 3רָמָה rāmāh3 (5)
lofty shrines (3)
hill (1)
lofty shrine (1)

8230 4רָמָה rāmāh4 (36)
Ramah (33)
Ramoth (2)
untranslated (1)

8231 רִמָּה rimmāh (7)
maggots (2)
worm (2)
worms (2)

maggots (1)

8232 1רִמּוֹן rimmôn1 (32)
pomegranates (24)
pomegranate (4)
alternateˢ (1) +2256+2298+7194
alternatedˢ (1) +2256+7194
pomegranate tree (1)
untranslated (1)

8233 2רִמּוֹן rimmôn2 (3)
Rimmon (3)

8234 3רִמּוֹן rimmôn3 (9)
Rimmon (8)
whereˢ (1) +928+6152

8235 4רִמּוֹן rimmôn4 (3)
Rimmon (2)
thereˢ (1) +1074

8236 רִמּוֹן פֶּרֶץ rimmôn peres (2)
Rimmon Perez (2)

8237 רִמּוֹנוֹ rimmônô (1)
Rimmono (1)

8238 רָמֹת rāmōṯ (1)
untranslated (1)

8239 רָמוּת rāmûṯ (1)
remains (1)

8240 רָמֹת גִּלְעָד rāmōṯ gilʿāḏ (20)
Ramoth Gilead (20)

8241 רָמוֹת־נֶגֶב rāmôṯ-negeḇ (1)
Ramoth Negev (1)

8242 רֹמַח rōmah (15)
spears (10)
spear (5)

8243 רַמְיָה ramyāh (1)
Ramiah (1)

8244 1רְמִיָּה rᵉmiyyāh1 (7)
faulty (2)
lazy (2)
lax (1)
laziness (1)
shiftless (1)

8245 2רְמִיָּה rᵉmiyyāh2 (8)
deceit (4)
deceitful (2)
deceitfully (2)

8246 רַמִּים rammiym
Variant; not used

8247 רַמָּכָה rammāḵāh (1)
especially bred (1) +1201+2021

8248 רְמַלְיָהוּ rᵉmalyāhû (13)
Remaliah (11)
Remaliah's (2)

8249 1רְמַם rāmam1 (1)
full (1)

8250 2רְמַם rāmam2 (5)
rose (2)
exalted (1)
get away (1)
rose upward (1)

8251 רֹמַמְתִּי עֶזֶר rōmamtiy ʿezer (2)
Romamti-Ezer (2)

8252 רָמַס rāmas (19)
trample (4)
trampled (4)
trampled underfoot (3)
aggressor (1)
be trampled (1)
mauls (1)
trample down (1)
trampling (1)
tread (1)
treading (1)
trod down (1)

8253 רָמַשׂ rāmaś (17)
moves (5)
move (4)
moves along (2)
creature that moves (1)
creatures that move (1)
moved (1)
moves about (1)
moving (1)
prowl (1)

8254 רֶמֶשׂ remeś (17)
creatures that move (5)
creature (2)
creatures (2)
crawling things (1)
creature that moves (1)
creatures that move along the ground (1)
moves (1)
reptiles (1)
sea creatures (1)
small creatures (1)
teeming creatures (1)

8255 רֶמֶת remet (1)
Remeth (1)

8256 רָמַת הַמִּצְפֶּה rāmat hammispeh (1)
Ramath Mizpah (1)

8257 רָמַת לֶחִי rāmat lᵉhiy (1)
Ramath Lehi (1)

8258 רָמָתִי rāmātiy (1)
Ramathite (1)

8259 רָמָתַיִם rāmātayim (1)
Ramathaim (1)

8260 רֹן rōn (1)
songs (1)

8261 רָנָה rānāh (1)
rattles (1)

8262 1רִנָּה rinnāh1 (33)
cry (10)
singing (4)
song (4)
songs of joy (4)
shouts of joy (3)
plea (2)
shouts of joy (2) +7754
joy (1)
pride (1)
rejoicing (1)
sing (1)

8263 2רִנָּה rinnāh2 (1)
Rinnah (1)

8264 רָנַן rānan (53)
sing for joy (15)
shout for joy (11)
sing (9)
cry out (2)
rejoice (2)
call forth songs of joy (1)
calls aloud (1)
cries aloud (1)
ever sing for joy (1) +8264
joyfully sing (1)
jubilant song (1)
made sing (1)
sang (1)
shout (1)
shouted for joy (1)
sing joyfully (1)
sings (1)
songs of joy (1)

8265 רְנָנָה rᵉnānāh (4)
joyful songs (1)
mirth (1)
shout of joy (1)
singing (1)

8266 רְנָנִים rᵉnāniym (1)
ostrich (1)

8267 רִסָּה *rissāh* (2)
Rissah (2)

8268 רָסִיס1 *rāsiys1* (1)
dampness (1)

8269 רָסִיס2 *rāsiys2* (1)
pieces (1)

8270 רֶסֶן1 *resen1* (4)
bit (1)
bridle (1) +4101
bridle (1) +6344
restraint (1)

8271 רֶסֶן2 *resen2* (1)
Resen (1)

8272 רָסַס *rāsas* (1)
moisten (1)

8273 רַע *ra'* (351)
evil (190)
wicked (24)
bad (23)
wrong (10)
harm (8)
trouble (8)
disaster (5)
wild (4)
poor (3)
ugly (3)
deadly (2)
ferocious (2)
grievous (2)
harm (2) +6913
heavy (2)
malice (2)
no good (2)
painful (2)
ruin (2)
sad (2)
sin (2)
terrible (2)
ugly (2) +5260
bitter (1)
brings to ruin (1) +2021+4200+6156
crimes (1)
cruel (1)
destroying (1)
destruction (1)
difficult (1)
disaster (1) +7004
displease (1) +928+6524
displeasing (1) +928+6524
distressing (1)
dreadful (1)
flaw (1) +1821
great (1)
hardships (1)
harm (1) +1821
harmful (1)
horrible (1)
hurt (1)
immoral (1)
impure (1)
look sad (1)
mean (1)
miserable (1)
misery (1)
misfortune (1) +6721
not want (1) +928+6524
not[s] (1)
one way[s] (1)
savage (1)
serious (1)
severe (1)
stern (1)
stingy (1) +6524
stingy man (1) +6524
surely suffer (1) +8317
troubled (1) +928+6524
ugly (1) +9307
undesirable (1)

unfavorable (1)
unjust (1)
vile (1)
violence (1)
worse (1)
worst (1)
wretched (1)
untranslated (1)

8274 רַע2 *ra'2*
Variant; not used

8275 רֵעַ1 *rēa'1* (3)
cry aloud (1) +8131
shouting (1)
thunder (1)

8276 רֵעַ2 *rēa'2* (188)
neighbor (52)
other[s] (29)
friend (26)
neighbor's (18)
friends (15)
another[s] (12)
neighbors (7)
companions (3)
countrymen (3)
another man's (2)
companion (2)
fellow Israelite (2)
another's[s] (1)
associates (1)
closest friend (1) +889+3869+3870+5883
each other[s] (1)
fellow (1)
friendship (1)
his[s] (1) +3870
husband (1)
lovers (1)
neighbors' (1)
one who is close (1)
opponent (1)
opponent's (1)
the parties (1) +408+2084+2256
together (1) +408+907+2084
untranslated (2)

8277 רֵעַ3 *rēa'3* (2)
thoughts (2)

8278 רֹעַ *rōa'* (19)
evil (9)
bad (4)
wicked (2)
sad (2)
sadness (1)
sinful (1)
ugly (1)

8279 רָעֵב1 *rā'ēb1* (13)
hungry (6)
causing to hunger (1)
famished (1)
feel the famine (1)
goes hungry (1)
hunger (1)
let go hungry (1)
starving (1)

8280 רָעָב *rā'āb* (101)
famine (91)
hunger (6)
starvation (2)
starve (2)

8281 רָעֵב2 *rā'ēb2* (20)
hungry (17)
hungry (2) +5883
starving (1)

8282 רְעָבוֹן *r'ābôn* (3)
starving (2)
famine (1)

8283 רָעַד *rā'ad* (3)
greatly distressed (1)

trembles (1)
trembling (1)

8284 רַעַד *ra'ad* (2)
trembling (2)

8285 רְעָדָה *r'ādāh* (4)
trembling (4)

8286 רָעָה1 *rā'āh1* (172)
shepherd (42)
shepherds (37)
tend (8)
feed (7)
graze (7)
tending (6)
pasture (5)
feed on (4)
feeds on (3)
grazing (3)
herdsmen (3)
shepherds (3) +7366
take care of (3)
browse (2)
browses (2)
eat (2)
find pasture (2)
grazed (2)
herdsmen (2) +5238
pastured (2)
rule (2)
shepherd's (2)
cared for (1)
devour (1)
drive away (1)
enjoy pasture (1)
graze flock (1)
grazing flocks (1)
grazing the flocks (1)
herding (1)
keeping (1)
kept (1)
lead (1)
leaders (1)
nourish (1)
prey on (1)
shaved (1)
shepherd flock (1)
shepherded (1)
shepherdess (1)
tends (1)
untranslated (4)

8287 רָעָה2 *rā'āh2* (5)
companion (3)
attended at wedding (1)
make friends (1)

8288 רָעָה3 *rā'āh3* (318)
disaster (79)
evil (48)
wickedness (32)
harm (26)
calamity (18)
trouble (17)
ruin (8)
wrong (8)
wicked (6)
calamities (4)
disasters (4)
troubles (4)
wrongdoing (4)
bad (3)
distress (3)
misfortune (3)
badly (2)
crimes (2)
danger (2)
destruction (2)
evil deeds (2)
evil thing (2)
harm (2) +6913
misery (2)
another[s] (1)

awful crime (1)
awful thing (1)
crime (1) +5126
cruelty (1)
deeds of evildoers (1)
defeat (1)
discomfort (1)
displeased (1) +8317
downfall (1)
evil intent (1)
evildoer (1) +6913
fate (1)
fault (1)
harming (1)
it⁵ (1) +2021
malice (1)
offense (1)
peril (1)
plotting (1) +2021+3086
punishment (1)
sin (1)
sins (1)
something desperate (1)
very disturbed (1) +8317
wicked thing (1)
wickedness is great (1) +8288
worst (1)
wrongs (1)
untranslated (5)

8289 רָעָה4 *rā'āh4*
Variant; not used

8290 רָעָה5 *rā'āh5*
Variant; not used

8291 רֵעֶה *rē'eh* (4)
friend (2)
personal adviser (1)
untranslated (1)

8292 רֵעָה *rē'āh* (4)
companions (1)
friends (1)
girls (1)
untranslated (1)

8293 רְעוּ *r' û* (5)
Reu (5)

8294 רְעוּאֵל *r'û'ēl* (10)
Reuel (10)

8295 רְעוּת1 *r'ût1* (6)
mate (2)
another's⁵ (1)
another⁵ (1)
someone else (1)
untranslated (1)

8296 רְעוּת2 *r'ût2* (7)
chasing after (7)

8297 רְעִי *r'iy* (1)
pasture-fed (1)

8298 רֵעִי *rē'iy* (1)
Rei (1)

8299 רַעְיָה *ra'yāh* (9)
darling (9)

8300 רֵעְיָה *rē'yāh*
Variant; not used

8301 רַעְיוֹן *ra'yôn* (3)
chasing after (2)
anxious striving (1) +4213

8302 רָעַל *rā'al* (1)
brandished (1)

8303 רַעַל *ra'al* (1)
reeling (1)

8304 רְעָלָה *r'ālāh* (1)
veils (1)

8305 רְעֵלָיָה *r'ēlāyāh* (1)
Reelaiah (1)

8306 רָעַם1 *rā'am1* (11)
resound (1)
thundered (3)
thunders (3)
thunder (2)

8307 רָעַם2 *rā'am2* (2)
distorted with fear (1)
irritate (1)

8308 רַעַם *ra'am* (6)
thunder (4)
shout (1)
thundercloud (1) +6260

8309 רַעְמָא *ra'mā'* (2)
Raamah (2)

8310 רַעְמָה1 *ra'māh1* (1)
flowing mane (1)

8311 רַעְמָה2 *ra'māh2* (3)
Raamah (3)

8312 רַעְמָה3 *ra'māh3*
Variant; not used

8313 רַעַמְיָה *ra'amyāh* (1)
Raamiah (1)

8314 רַעְמְסֵס *ra'm'sēs* (5)
Rameses (5)

8315 רָעַן *rā'an* (1)
flourish (1)

8316 רַעֲנָן *ra'ănān* (19)
spreading (11)
green (3)
fine (1)
flourishing (1)
green tree (1)
thriving (1)
verdant (1)

8317 רָעַע1 *rā'a'1* (95)
evil (10)
wicked (10)
harm (6)
displeased (5) +928+6524
evildoers (5)
bring disaster (4)
bad (3)
brought trouble (3)
do harm (3)
distressed (2) +928+6524
doing evil (2)
mistreated (2)
acted wickedly (1)
begrudge (1) +6524
bring trouble (1)
brought misfortune (1)
brought to grief (1)
brought tragedy (1)
crushed (1)
destruction brought (1)
did evil (1)
disapprove (1) +928+6524
displeased (1)
displeased (1) +8288
do evil (1)
do wicked thing (1)
doing wrong (1)
done evil (1)
done wrong (1) +8317
downhearted (1) +4222
galled (1) +928+6524
grudging (1)
harming (1)
have no compassion (1) +6524
hurts (1)
leads to evil (1)
look sad (1)
not please (1) +928+6524
persist in doing evil (1) +8317
show ill will (1) +6524
sinned (1)

suffers harm (1)
surely suffer (1) +8273
treat worse (1)
trouble came (1)
upset (1) +928+6524
very disturbed (1) +8288
vile (1)
wickedly (1)
wronged (1)

8318 רָעַע2 *rā'a'2* (6)
break (1)
broken (1)
come to ruin (1)
is broken up (1) +8318
shatters (1)

8319 רָעַף *rā'ap* (5)
overflow (2)
let drop (1)
rain down (1)
showers fall (1)

8320 רָעַץ *rā'as* (2)
shattered (2)

8321 רָעַשׁ1 *rā'aš1* (30)
shake (6)
tremble (6)
trembles (4)
quake (3)
quaked (3)
made tremble (2)
shook (2)
make leap (1)
quaking (1)
shaken (1)
sway (1)

8322 רָעַשׁ2 *rā'aš2*
Variant; not used

8323 רַעַשׁ *ra'aš* (17)
earthquake (7)
rumbling (2)
battle (1)
clatter (1) +7754
commotion (1)
frenzied (1)
noise (1)
rattling (1)
rattling sound (1)
tremble (1)

8324 רָפָא1 *rāpā'1* (69)
heal (21)
healed (10)
heals (5)
be healed (4)
physicians (4)
recover (3)
be cured (2)
cure (2)
dress (2)
fresh (2)
are healed (1)
be repaired (1)
been healed (1)
gone (1)
incurable (1) +4412
makes fresh (1)
mend (1)
physician (1)
repaired (1)
see that is completely healed (1) +8324
wholesome (1)
untranslated (2)

8325 רָפָא2 *rāpā'2* (3)
Rapha (3)

8326 רִפְאוּת *rip'ût* (1)
health (1)

8327 רְפָאִים1 *r'pā'iym1* (8)
dead (5)

departed spirits (1)
spirits of the dead (1)
spirits of the departed (1)

8328 רְפָאִים2 rᵉpā'iym2 (11)
Rephaites (10)
whoˢ (1)

8329 רְפָאִים3 rᵉpā'iym3 (8)
Rephaim (8)

8330 רְפָאֵל rᵉpā'ēl (1)
Rephael (1)

8331 רָפַד rāpad (3)
leaving a trail (1)
refresh (1)
spread out (1)

8332 רָפָה1 rāpāh1 (46)
leave (4)
go limp (3)
hang limp (3)
lazy (3)
let alone (3)
let go (3)
abandon (2)
give (2)
lowered (2)
withdraw (2)
abandon (1) +3338+4946
almost (1)
disarms (1) +4653
discourage (1) +3338
discouraging (1) +3338
fail (1)
falter (1)
feeble (1)
give up (1) +3338
leave alone (1)
lost courage (1) +3338
refrain (1)
sinks down (1)
slack (1)
still (1)
stop (1)
subsided (1)
wait (1)
weak (1)

8333 רָפֶה rāpeh (4)
feeble (2)
weak (1)
weak (1) +3338

8334 רָפָה2 rāpāh2 (1)
Raphah (1)

8335 רָפָה3 rāpāh3 (4)
Rapha (4)

8336 רָפוּא rāpû' (1)
Raphu (1)

8337 רְפוּאָה rᵉpû'āh (3)
healing (1) +5989
remedies (1)
remedy (1)

8338 רֶפַח repah (1)
Rephah (1)

8339 רְפִידָה rᵉpiydāh (1)
base (1)

8340 רְפִידִים rᵉpiydiym (5)
Rephidim (5)

8341 רְפָיָה rᵉpāyāh (5)
Rephaiah (5)

8342 רִפָּיוֹן rippāyôn (1)
hang limp (1)

8343 רַפְסֹדוֹת rapsōdôt (1)
rafts (1)

8344 רָפַף rāpap (1)
quake (1)

8345 רָפַק rāpaq (1)
leaning (1)

8346 רָפַשׂ rāpaś (5)
humble yourself (1)
humbled (1)
muddied (1)
muddy (1)
muddying (1)

8347 רֶפֶשׁ repeš (1)
mire (1)

8348 רֶפֶת repet (1)
stalls (1)

8349 רָץ ras (1)
bars (1)

8350 רָץ rās
Variant; not used

8351 רָצָא1 rāsā'1 (1)
sped forth (1)

8352 רָצָא2 rāsā'2
Variant; not used

8353 רָצַד rāsad (1)
gaze in envy (1)

8354 רָצָה1 rāsāh1 (52)
accept (10)
be accepted (5)
pleased with (4)
enjoy (3)
pleased (3)
delights in (2)
please (2)
approve (1)
be acceptable (1)
dear to (1)
delight (1)
devotion (1)
enjoyed (1)
favored (1)
favors (1)
finds favor with (1)
held in high esteem (1)
in delight (1)
join (1)
loved (1)
pleasing (1)
put in (1)
received favorably (1)
regain favor (1)
show favor (1)
showed favor (1)
take delight in (1)
take pleasure (1)
take pleasure in (1)
takes delight (1)

8355 רָצָה2 rāsāh2 (4)
pay for (2)
been paid for (1)
make amends (1)

8356 רָצוֹן rāsôn (56)
favor (15)
accepted (7)
acceptable (5)
pleased (4)
pleases (4)
will (4)
delights (3)
desires (2)
goodwill (2)
pleasure (2)
delight (1)
eagerly (1) +928+3972
favored (1)
fitting (1)
good pleasure (1)
please (1)
pleasing (1)
wished (1)

8357 רָצַח rāsah (47)
murderer (12)
accused of murder (7)
murder (6)
accused (3)
heˢ (2) +2021
killed (2)
murdered (2)
anyoneˢ (1)
be murdered (1)
himˢ (1) +2021
kill (1)
killed (1) +5782
killed a person (1)
kills a man (1)
kills another (1)
murderer (1) +1201
murderers (1)
murders (1) +5883
put to death (1)
throw down (1)

8358 רֶצַח resah (2)
mortal agony (1)
slaughter (1)

8359 רִצְיָא risyā' (1)
Rizia (1)

8360 רְצִין rᵉsiyn (11)
Rezin (10)
Rezin's (1)

8361 רָצַע rāsa' (1)
pierce (1)

8362 רָצַף rāsap (1)
inlaid (1)

8363 רֶצֶף1 resep1 (1)
baked over hot coals (1)

8364 רֶצֶף2 resep2 (2)
Rezeph (2)

8365 רִצְפָּה1 rispāh1 (1)
live coal (1)

8366 רִצְפָּה2 rispāh2 (4)
Rizpah (4)

8367 רִצְפָּה rispāh (7)
pavement (5)
itˢ (1) +2021
mosaic pavement (1)

8368 רָצַץ rāsas (20)
oppressed (4)
splintered (3)
broken (2)
crushed (2)
bruised (1)
brutally oppressed (1)
cracked (1)
cruel (1)
crush (1)
discouraged (1)
jostled each other (1)
smashed to pieces (1)
trampled (1)

8369 רַק1 raq1 (3)
lean (2)
lean (1) +1414

8370 רַק2 raq2 (109)
only (30)
but (22)
however (13)
except (5)
nevertheless (4)
surely (3)
yet (3)
always (2)
except that (2)
although (1)
and (1)
as for (1)

be sure (1)
but (1) +2256
but also (1)
but only (1)
moreover (1)
nothing but (1)
only (1) +421
only (1) +4202
really (1)
sheer (1)
untranslated (12)

8371 רֹק *rōq* (3)
for an instant (1) +1180+6330
spit (1)
spitting (1)

8372 רָקַב *rāqab* (2)
rot (2)

8373 רָקָב *rāqāb* (5)
decay (2)
rot (1)
rots (1)
something rotten (1)

8374 רָקָב *rōqeb*
Variant; not used

8375 רִקָּבוֹן *riqqābôn* (1)
rotten (1)

8376 רָקַד *rāqad* (9)
skipped (2)
dance (1)
dance about (1)
dancing (1)
jolting (1)
leap (1)
leap about (1)
makes skip (1)

8377 רַקָּה *raqqāh* (5)
temple (3)
temples (2)

8378 רַקּוֹן *raqqôn* (1)
Rakkon (1)

8379 רָקַח *rāqaḥ* (8)
perfumer (3)
blended (1)
makes perfume (1)
mixing in (1)
perfume (1) +9043
took care of mixing (1) +5351

8380 רֶקַח *reqaḥ* (1)
spiced (1)

8381 רֹקַח *rōqaḥ* (2)
blend (1)
fragrant blend (1)

8382 רַקָּח *raqqāḥ* (1)
perfume-makers (1)

8383 רִקֻּח *riqquaḥ* (1)
perfumes (1)

8384 רַקָּחָה *raqqāḥāh* (1)
perfumers (1)

8385 רָקִיעַ *rāqiya'* (17)
expanse (13)
heavens (2)
itˢ (1) +2021
skies (1)

8386 רָקִיק *rāqiyq* (8)
wafers (5)
wafer (3)

8387 רָקַם *rāqam* (9)
embroiderer (7)
embroiderers (1)
was woven together (1)

8388 רֶקֶם *rāqem* (1)
Rakem (1)

8389 1רֶקֶם *reqem1* (1)
Rekem (1)

8390 2רֶקֶם *reqem2* (4)
Rekem (4)

8391 רִקְמָה *riqmāh* (12)
embroidered (4)
embroidered work (2)
embroidered cloth (1)
embroidered dress (1)
embroidered garments (1)
highly embroidered (1)
varied colors (1)
various colors (1)

8392 רָקַע *rāqa'* (11)
spread out (3)
hammered out (2)
hammered (1)
overlays (1)
spreading out (1)
stamp (1)
stamped (1)
trampled (1)

8393 רִקַּע *riqqua'* (1)
hammer (1) +6913

8394 רָקַק *rāqaq* (1)
spits (1)

8395 רַקַּת *raqqaṭ* (1)
Rakkath (1)

8396 רֹשׁ *rōš*
Variant; not used

8397 רִשְׁיוֹן *rišyôn* (1)
authorized (1)

8398 רָשַׁם *rāšam* (1)
written (1)

8399 רָשַׁע *rāša'* (35)
condemn (7)
acted wickedly (3)
condemning (3)
guilty (3)
condemns (2)
done evil (2)
wicked (2)
condemned (1)
declare guilty (1)
did wrong (1)
do wrong (1)
doing wrong (1)
done wrong (1)
guilty of wickedness (1)
inflicted punishment (1)
let be condemned (1)
overwicked (1) +2221
refute (1)
violated (1)
untranslated (1)

8400 רֶשַׁע *reša'* (30)
wickedness (16)
wicked (5)
evil (2)
ill-gotten (2)
dishonest (1)
evil deeds (1)
injustice (1)
itˢ (1)
wrongdoing (1) +6913

8401 רָשָׁע *rāšā'* (264)
wicked (237)
guilty (9)
evil (3)
wickedness (3)
heˢ (2)
himˢ (2)
deserves (1)
evildoers (1)
in the wrong (1)

one in the wrong (1)
outlaw (1)
theyˢ (1)
ungodly (1)
untranslated (1)

8402 רִשְׁעָה *riš'āh* (15)
wickedness (11)
crime (1)
evildoer (1) +6913
evildoers (1) +6913
wicked (1)

8403 רִשְׁעָתַיִם *riš'ātayim*
Variant; not used

8404 1רֶשֶׁף *rešep1* (7)
pestilence (2)
blazing (1)
bolts of lightning (1)
burns (1)
flashing (1)
sparks (1) +1201

8405 2רֶשֶׁף *rešep2* (1)
Resheph (1)

8406 רָשַׁשׁ *rāšaš* (2)
been crushed (1)
destroy (1)

8407 רֶשֶׁת *rešeṭ* (22)
net (16)
network (2) +5126
itˢ (1) +2021
network (1)
snare (1)
trap (1)

8408 רָתוֹק *ratôq* (2)
chains (1)
untranslated (1)

8409 רָתַח *rātaḥ* (3)
bring to a boil (1) +8410
churning (1)
makes churn (1)

8410 רֶתַח *retaḥ* (1)
bring to a boil (1) +8409

8411 רְתִיקָה *ratiyqāh* (1)
chains (1)

8412 רָתַם *rātam* (1)
harness (1)

8413 רֹתֶם *rōtem* (4)
broom tree (3)
tree (1)

8414 רִתְמָה *ritmāh* (2)
Rithmah (2)

8415 רָתַק *rātaq* (2)
were put in chains (1) +928+2414
untranslated (1)

8416 רְתֻקוֹת *r'tuqôt* (1)
chains (1)

8417 רְתֵת *r'tēt* (1)
trembled (1)

8418 שׂ *ś*
Variant; not used

8419 שְׂאֹר *ś'ōr* (5)
yeast (5)

8420 1שְׂאֵת *ś'ēt1* (7)
honor (2)
splendor (2)
accepted (1)
lofty place (1)
rises up (1)

8421 2שְׂאֵת *ś'ēt2* (7)
swelling (6)
swollen (1)

8422 שְׂבָכָה *ś'bākāh* (17)
network (12)

lattice (1)
mesh (1)
network (1) +5126+8422
untranslated (1)

8423 שְׂבָם *ś^ebām* (1)
Sebam (1)

8424 שִׂבְמָה *śibmāh* (5)
Sibmah (5)

8425 שָׂבַע *śāba'* (100)
satisfied (30)
filled (9)
satisfy (9)
full (6)
get enough (3)
have enough (3)
satisfies (3)
endured (2)
fill (2)
had enough (2)
has enough (2)
have abundant (2)
too much (2)
all want (1)
all wanted (1)
content (1)
eat fill (1)
eaten enough (1)
eats fill (1)
enjoy (1)
enjoy plenty (1)
feast on (1)
fully repaid (1)
gorge (1)
had fill (1)
had plenty (1)
have fill (1)
have more than enough (1)
have plenty (1)
have to spare (1)
have too much (1)
insatiable (1) +1194
overwhelm (1)
satisfy fully (1)
supplied all needs (1)
toss (1) +5611
well watered (1)
untranslated (1)

8426 שָׂבַע *śāba'* (8)
abundance (7)
overflowing (1)

8427 שֹׂבַע *śōba'* (7)
all want (2)
fill (2)
all could eat (1)
all wanted (1)
content (1)

8428 שָׂבֵעַ *śābēa'* (10)
full (7)
abounding (1)
content (1)
enjoyed long life (1) +3427

8429 שָׂבְעָה *śob'āh* (4)
abundant (1)
enough (1)
glutted (1)
satisfy (1)

8430 שִׂבְעָה *śib'āh* (1)
overfed (1) +4312

8431 שָׂבַר1 *śābar1* (2)
examining (2)

8432 שָׂבַר2 *śābar2* (6)
look (2)
wait (2)
hope (1)
hoped (1)

8433 שֶׂבֶר *śēber* (2)

hope (1)
hopes (1)

8434 שָׂגָא *śāgā'* (2)
extol (1)
makes great (1)

8435 שָׂגַב *śāgab* (20)
protect (4)
be exalted (2)
exalted (2)
is exalted (2)
lifted (2)
lofty (2)
high (1)
is kept safe (1)
safe (1)
strengthened (1)
strong (1)
unscalable (1)

8436 שָׂגָה *śāgāh* (4)
grow (1)
increase (1)
prosperous (1)
thrive (1)

8437 שְׂגוּב *ś^egûb* (3)
Segub (3)

8438 שַׂגִּיא *śaggiy'* (2)
exalted (1)
great (1)

8439 שְׂגִיב *ś^egiyb* (1)
untranslated (1)

8440 שָׂדַד *śādad* (3)
break up the ground (1)
harrowing (1)
till (1)

8441 שָׂדֶה *śādeh* (322)
field (128)
fields (76)
wild (24)
country (17)
land (11)
open country (8)
Moab (7) +4566
field (4) +2754
ground (4)
open (4)
territory (4)
family land (3) +299
region (3)
wild (3) +928+2021
area (2)
countryside (2)
mainland (2)
open field (2)
soil (2)
battlefield (1) +5120
it^s (1) +2021
lands (1)
outlying districts (1)
pastureland (1) +4494
place (1)
southland (1) +5582
there^s (1) +2021
there^s (1) +4566
untranslated (7)

8442 שָׂדַי *śāday* (13)
field (9)
fields (1)
slopes (1)
wild (1)

8443 שִׂדִּים *śiddiym* (3)
Siddim (3)

8444 שְׂדֵרָה *ś^edērāh* (4)
ranks (3)
planks (1)

8445 שֶׂה *śeh* (47)
sheep (26)

lamb (11)
another^s (2)
flock (2)
animals (1)
goat (1) +6436
lamb (1) +928+2021+3897
lamb (1) +928+2021+4166
one^s (1)
sheep (1) +4166

8446 שָׂהֵד *śāhēd* (1)
advocate (1)

8447 שָׂהֲדוּתָא *śāh^adûtā'*
Variant; not used

8448 שַׂהֲרֹנִים *śah^arōniym* (3)
ornaments (2)
crescent necklaces (1)

8449 שֹׂבֶךְ *śōbek* (1)
thick branches (1)

8450 שׂוּג1 *śûg1*
Variant; not used

8451 שׂוּג2 *śûg2* (1)
make grow (1)

8452 שׂוּחַ *śûah* (1)
meditate (1)

8453 שַׂוְחָט *śawhāt*
Variant; not used

8454 שׂוּט *śût* (1)
turn aside (1)

8455 שׂוּךְ *śûk* (2)
block (1)
put a hedge (1)

8456 שׂוֹךְ *śôk* (1)
branches (1)

8457 שׂוֹכָה *śôkāh* (1)
branches (1) +6770

8458 שׂוֹכֹה *śôkōh* (5)
Socoh (5)

8459 שׂוֹכוֹ *śôkô* (3)
Soco (3)

8460 שׂוּכָתִי *śûkātiy* (1)
Sucathites (1)

8461 שׂוּמָה *śûmāh* (1)
intention (1)

8462 שׂוּר *śûr*
Variant; not used

8463 שׂוֹרָה *śôrāh* (1)
place (1)

8464 שׂוּשׂ *śûś* (27)
rejoice (11)
delight (2)
glad (2)
rejoicing (2)
delight greatly (1) +8464
delighted (1)
gladly (1)
happy (1)
please (1)
pleased (1)
rejoice greatly (1) +5375
take delight (1)
take great delight (1) +928+8525

8465 שֵׂחַ *śēah* (1)
thoughts (1)

8466 שָׂחָה *śāhāh* (3)
flood (1)
swim (1)
swimmer (1)

8467 שָׂחוּ *śāhû* (1)
deep enough to swim in (1)

8468 שְׂחוֹק *ś^ehôq* (15)
laughter (7)

laughingstock (3)
object of ridicule (3)
pleasure (1)
ridiculed (1)

8469 שָׁחַט *śāhat* (1)
squeezed (1)

8470 שָׁחִיף *śāhiyp* (1)
covered with (1) +6017+6017

8471 שָׁחַק *śāhaq* (36)
laugh (7)
laughs (6)
celebrating (3)
rejoicing (3)
celebrate (1)
danced (1)
entertain (1)
fight hand to hand (1)
frolic (1)
joking (1)
joyful (1)
laughed (1)
make a pet (1)
mock (1)
perform (1)
play (1)
playing (1)
revelers (1)
scoffs (1)
scorned (1)
smiled (1)

8472 שָׁחֹת *śuhōt*
Variant; not used

8473 שֵׁט *śēt* (1)
rebels (1)

8474 שָׂטָה *śātāh* (6)
goes astray (2)
gone astray (2)
turn (2)

8475 שָׂטַם *śātam* (6)
assails (1)
attack (1)
held a grudge against (1)
holds a grudge against (1)
hostility (1)
revile (1)

8476 שָׂטַן *śātan* (6)
accusers (3)
accuse (2)
slander (1)

8477 שָׂטָן *śātān* (27)
Satan (18)
adversary (4)
oppose (2)
accuser (1)
adversaries (1)
turn against (1) +2118+4200

8478 1שִׂטְנָה *śitnāh1* (1)
accusation (1)

8479 2שִׂטְנָה *śitnāh2* (1)
Sitnah (1)

8480 שִׂיא *śiy'* (1)
pride (1)

8481 שִׂיאוֹן *śiy'ôn* (1)
Siyon (1)

8482 שִׂיב *śiyb* (2)
gray (1)
gray-haired (1)

8483 שֵׂיב *śēyb* (1)
age (1)

8484 שֵׂיבָה *śēybāh* (19)
old age (6)
gray head (5)
gray hair (2)

aged (1)
gray (1)
gray hairs (1)
gray-haired (1)
hair gray (1)
white hair (1)

8485 שִׂיג *śiyg* (1)
busy (1)

8486 1שִׂיד *śiyd1* (2)
coat (2)

8487 2שִׂיד *śiyd2* (4)
lime (2)
plaster (2)

8488 1שִׂיחַ *śiyah1* (21)
meditate (7)
consider (3)
speak (3)
mused (2)
tell (2)
complain (1)
deep in thought (1)
in distress (1)
mock (1)

8489 2שִׂיחַ *śiyah2* (4)
bushes (2)
brush (1)
shrub (1) +3972

8490 3שִׂיחַ *śiyah3* (13)
complaint (7)
anguish (1)
complaints (1)
lament (1)
meditation (1)
sort of things he says (1)
thoughts (1)

8491 שִׂיחָה *śiyhāh* (3)
meditate (2)
devotion (1)

8492 שִׂים *śiym* (587)
put (106)
set (50)
make (48)
made (35)
placed (16)
set up (13)
give (11)
laid (11)
appointed (8)
lay (8)
makes (7)
place (7)
turn (7)
established (5)
gave (5)
give careful thought (5) +4222
puts (5)
bring (4)
determined (4) +7156
put in place (4)
put up (4)
putting (4)
took (4)
turned (4)
appoint (3)
brought (3)
fasten (3)
named (3) +9005
performed (3)
provide (3)
take (3)
assign (2)
attached (2)
charges (2)
considered (2) +4213
consigning to labor (2)
fastened (2)
fix (2)

given (2)
giving (2)
leaving (2)
look after (2) +6524+6584
mark out (2)
pay (2)
planted (2)
posted (2)
prepare (2)
prepares (2)
reduce (2)
reduced (2)
regard (2) +4200+5584
seized (2) +3338
served (2)
sets (2)
turn into (2)
accuse (1) +928+1821
added (1)
applied (1)
attach (1)
avenged (1)
be sure to appoint (1) +8492
become (1)
care (1) +448+4213
care about (1) +448+4213
cares (1) +4213+6584
caused to turn (1)
charge (1)
clap (1)
concerned about (1) +448+4213
consider (1)
consider (1) +4213
consider (1) +4213+6584
controls (1)
covered (1) +4200
depends on (1)
designate (1)
destroy (1) +9039
determine (1) +7156
determined (1) +7156+8492
did[s] (1)
displayed (1)
does (1)
don't say a word (1) +3338+6584+7023
drew up (1)
end (1) +7874
erected (1)
establish (1)
establishes (1)
exacted (1)
examine (1)
fastens (1)
float (1)
formed (1)
gave a high rank in (1) +6584
grants (1)
had (1)
had brought (1)
had take up positions (1)
harbor (1)
headed for (1) +7156
hung (1)
ignored (1) +4202+4213
imposed (1)
increased (1)
inflict (1)
intention (1) +4213
keep (1)
keeps (1)
lay up (1)
left (1)
lifted (1)
light (1)
list (1)
loaded (1)
looked (1) +7156
make serve (1) +4200
make sure hears (1) +265+928
making (1)
marked off (1)

offers (1)
piled (1)
pitched (1)
plant (1)
pondered (1)
ponders (1)
poured (1)
prepared (1)
presented (1)
preserve (1)
preserved (1) +928+2021+2645
press charges (1)
pressed (1)
provided (1)
put in charge (1)
put on (1) +928+5516
repay (1)
replace (1) +9393
replaced (1)
require (1)
resolved (1) +4213+6584
see (1) +6524
seize (1) +928+3338
separated (1)
serve (1)
set in place (1)
sets up (1)
setting (1)
shave (1) +7947
shedding (1)
showed (1)
shrouded (1)
sing (1) +928+7023
slandered (1) +1821+6613
slanders (1) +1821+6613
spread (1)
stared with a fixed gaze (1)
　　　　　　+906+2256+6641+7156
stationed (1)
stirs up (1)
strap (1)
take up positions (1)
think (1) +4013+4200
throw (1)
thrown (1)
told (1) +928+7023
trample down (1) +5330
treat (1)
turned (1) +7156
turned into (1)
unnoticed (1) +1172+4946
use (1)
used (1)
was placed (1)
was set (1)
watch over (1) +6584
waylaid (1) +928+2006+2021
worry (1) +906+4213
untranslated (20)

8493 שֵׂךְ *śēk* (1)
barbs (1)

8494 שׂךְ *śōk* (1)
dwelling (1)

8495 שָׂכָה *śākāh*
Variant; not used

8496 שֻׂכָּה *śukkāh* (1)
harpoons (1)

8497 שְׂכוּ *śekû* (1)
Secu (1)

8498 שֶׂכְוִי *śekwiy* (1)
mind (1)

8499 שְׂכִיָה *śāk*yāh* (1)
Sakia (1)

8500 שְׂכִיָה *śkiyyāh* (1)
vessel (1)

8501 שַׂכִּין *śakkiyn* (1)
knife (1)

8502 שָׂכִיר *śāk̲iyr* (18)
hired man (5)
hired worker (4)
hired (3)
servant bound by contract (2)
hired hand (1)
laborers (1)
man hired (1)
mercenaries (1)

8503 שָׂכַךְ 1 *śāk̲ak1* (2)
cover (1)
hide (1)

8504 שָׂכַךְ 2 *śāk̲ak2*
Variant; not used

8505 שָׂכַל 1 *śāk̲al1* (61)
wise (13)
understand (6)
successful (4)
prosper (3)
prudent (3)
understanding (3)
instruct (2)
act wisely (1)
careful (1)
fail (1) +4202
gaining wisdom (1)
gave thought (1)
gave understanding (1)
give attention (1)
give insight (1)
gives heed (1)
giving attention (1)
guides (1)
had great success (1)
had regard for (1)
has regard for (1)
have insight (1)
insight (1)
instructed (1)
met with success (1)
ponder (1)
showed understanding (1) +8507
showing aptitude (1)
skilled (1)
succeeds (1)
successfully (1)
takes note (1)
understands (1)
wisely (1)

8506 שָׂכַל 2 *śāk̲al2* (1)
crossing (1)

8507 שֶׂכֶל *śek̲el* (16)
understanding (4)
wisdom (3)
capable (1)
discretion (1)
intelligence (1)
intelligent (1) +3202
meaning (1)
name (1)
showed understanding (1) +8505
wise (1)
untranslated (1)

8508 שִׂכְלוּת *śik̲lût̲* (1)
folly (1)

8509 שָׂכַר *śāk̲ar* (20)
hired (9)
hire (3)
been hired (1)
earn wages (1) +8509
hire themselves out (1)
hired (1) +8509
hires (1)
untranslated (1)

8510 שָׂכָר 1 *śāk̲ār1* (28)
wages (10)
reward (6)

pay (2)
rewarded (2)
fare (1)
money paid for hire (1)
paid (1) +9202
pay (1) +5989
return (1)
rewarded (1) +5989
worth (1)
untranslated (1)

8511 שָׂכָר 2 *śāk̲ār2* (2)
Sacar (2)

8512 שֶׂכֶר *śek̲er* (2)
reward (1)
wage (1)

8513 שְׂלָו *śᵉlāw* (4)
quail (4)

8514 שַׂלְמָא *śalmā'* (2)
Salma (2)

8515 שַׂלְמָה 1 *śalmāh1* (16)
clothes (5)
cloak (4)
garment (2)
robes (2)
clothing (1)
garments (1)
robe (1)

8516 שַׂלְמָה 2 *śalmāh2*
Variant; not used

8517 שַׂלְמוֹן *śalmôn* (4)
Salmon (4)

8518 שַׂלְמַי *śalmay*
Variant; not used

8519 שָׂלַק *śālaq*
Variant; not used

8520 שְׂמֹאל *śᵉmō'l* (54)
left (45)
north (6)
north (2) +4946
which way (1) +196+3545+6584+6584

8521 שְׂמֹאל *śim'ēl* (5)
to the left (3)
go to the left (1)
left-handed (1)

8522 שְׂמָאלִי *śᵉmā'liy* (9)
north (4)
left (3)
untranslated (2)

8523 שָׂמַח *śāmah* (157)
rejoice (42)
glad (30)
rejoiced (11)
gloat (5)
rejoices (5)
brings joy (4)
bring joy (3)
delight (3)
happy (3)
joy (3)
make glad (3)
rejoicing (3)
enjoy (2)
gladly (2)
joyful (2)
let gloat (2)
pleased (2)
beˢ (1)
bring happiness (1)
cheers (1)
cheers up (1)
delights (1)
elated (1)
exult (1)
filled with joy (1)
give joy (1)

given cause to rejoice (1)
given joy (1) +8525
giving joy (1)
gladdens (1)
gladness (1)
glee (1)
gloats (1)
happy (1) +8525
held a celebration (1)
joyous (1)
made rejoice (1)
made very glad (1) +8523
make merry (1)
makes glad (1)
makes merry (1)
received gladly (1) +6584
rejoiced (1) +8525
share joy (1) +8525
shines brightly (1)
take pleasure (1)
untranslated (2)

8524 שָׂמֵחַ *śāmēaḥ* (20)
happy (5)
joyful (2)
rejoicing (2)
cheerful (1)
cheering (1)
delight (1)
delight in (1)
filled with gladness (1) +448+1637
filled with joy (1)
gloat (1)
joy (1)
merrymakers (1) +4213
rejoice (1)
rejoicing (1) +8525

8525 שִׂמְחָה *śimḥāh* (94)
joy (46)
gladness (10)
rejoicing (6)
pleasure (5)
rejoice (3)
joyful (2)
joyfully (2)
joyfully (2) +928
rejoiced (2)
celebrate (1)
delight (1)
delights (1)
enjoyment (1)
given joy (1) +8523
glad occasions (1)
glee (1)
happiness (1)
happy (1) +8523
joyful songs (1)
pleased (1)
rejoiced (1) +8523
rejoicing (1) +8524
revelry (1)
share joy (1) +8523
take great delight (1) +928+8464

8526 שְׂמִיכָה *śᵉmiykāh* (1)
covering (1)

8527 שָׂמַךְ *śāmak*
Variant; not used

8528 שַׂמְלָה *śamlāh* (4)
Samlah (4)

8529 שִׂמְלָה *śimlāh* (31)
clothes (12)
clothing (7)
cloak (4)
garment (3)
cloth (2)
best clothes (1)
untranslated (2)

8530 שַׂמְלַי *śamlay*
Variant; not used

8531 שָׁמֵם *śāmam* (1)
painted (1) +928+2021+7037

8532 שְׁמָמִית *śᵉmāmiyṯ* (1)
lizard (1)

8533 שָׂנֵא *śānē'* (148)
hate (59)
hated (16)
hates (14)
foes (11)
enemies (9)
malice aforethought (4) +4946+8997+9453
adversaries (3)
dislikes (3)
enemy (3)
foe (2)
unloved (2)
abhor (1)
am not loved (1)
are shunned (1)
bothˢ (1) +170+2021+2021+2256
detest (1)
enemies (1) +5883
enemy's (1)
hate (1) +8534
have hatred (1) +8534
hostile (1)
is hated (1)
malicious (1)
not love (1)
not loved (1)
notˢ (1)
refuses (1)
shunned (1)
themˢ (1) +2157
thoroughly hated (1) +8533
untranslated (2)

8534 שִׂנְאָה *śin'āh* (17)
hatred (8)
hate (2)
hate (1) +8533
hated (1)
hates (1)
have hatred (1) +8533
malice (1)
malice aforethought (1)
untranslated (1)

8535 שָׂנִיא *śāniy'* (1)
not love (1)

8536 שְׂנִיר *śᵉniyr* (4)
Senir (4)

8537 1שָׂעִיר *śā'iyr1* (3)
hairy (2)
shaggy (1)

8538 2שָׂעִיר *śā'iyr2* (54)
male goat (24) +6436
goat (10)
male goat (7)
goat's (3)
goats (3)
goat (2) +6436
male goats (2) +6436
wild goats (2)
itˢ (1) +2021

8539 3שָׂעִיר *śā'iyr3* (2)
goat idols (2)

8540 4שָׂעִיר *śā'iyr4* (1)
showers (1)

8541 1שֵׂעִיר *śē'iyr1* (35)
Seir (35)

8542 2שֵׂעִיר *śē'iyr2* (1)
Seir (1)

8543 3שֵׂעִיר *śē'iyr3* (3)
Seir (3)

8544 1שְׂעִירָה *śᵉ'iyrāh1* (2)
goat (2) +6436

8545 2שְׂעִירָה *śᵉ'iyrāh2* (1)
Seirah (1)

8546 שְׂעִפִּים *śᵉ'ippiym* (2)
disquieting (1)
troubled thoughts (1)

8547 1שַׂעַר *śā'ar1* (3)
shudder (3)

8548 2שַׂעַר *śā'ar2* (4)
storm out (1)
sweeps out (1)
swept away (1)
tempest rages (1) +4394

8549 3שַׂעַר *śā'ar3* (1)
fear (1)

8550 1שַׂעַר *śa'ar1* (3)
horror (3)

8551 2שַׂעַר *śa'ar2* (1)
wind (1)

8552 שֵׂעָר *śē'ār* (28)
hair (23)
hairy (2)
garment of hair (1)
hair (1) +7279
itˢ (1) +8031

8553 שַׂעֲרָה *śa'ᵃrāh* (7)
hair (3)
hair of head (2)
hairs (2)

8554 שְׂעָרָה *śᵉ'ārāh* (2)
storm (2)

8555 שְׂעֹרָה *śᵉ'ōrāh* (34)
barley (33)
untranslated (1)

8556 שְׂעֹרִים *śᵉ'ōriym* (1)
Seorim (1)

8557 שָׂפָה *śāpāh* (178)
lips (97)
rim (14)
edge (10)
bank (7)
language (6)
seashore (5) +3542
speech (5)
chattering (2)
empty words (2) +1821
mouth (2)
talk (2)
tongue (2)
band (1)
banks (1)
border (1)
coast (1) +3542
hurl insults (1) +928+7080
mere talk (1) +1821
object of malicious talk (1)
           +4383+6584+6590
riverbank (1) +3284
shore (1)
shore (1) +3542
speaks rashly (1) +7316
talker (1) +408
talks too much (1) +7331
thoughtlessly (1) +928+1051+4200
what said (1)
whisper (1)
words (1)
untranslated (7)

8558 שָׂפַח *śāpaḥ* (1)
bring sores on (1)

8559 שָׂפָם *śāpām* (5)
lower part of face (3)
faces (1)
mustache (1)

8560 שִׂפְמוֹת *śipmôṯ* (1)
Siphmoth (1)

8561 שָׁפַן *šāp̄an* (1)
treasures hidden (1) +3243

8562 1שָׁפַק *šāp̄aq1* (2)
claps in derision (1)
clasp hands (1)

8563 2שָׁפַק *šāp̄aq2* (1)
enough (1)

8564 שֶׁפֶק *šep̄eq*
Variant; not used

8565 שֵׁפֶק *šēp̄eq* (1)
plenty (1)

8566 שַׂק *śaq* (48)
sackcloth (42)
sack (3)
sacks (2)
sackcloth (1) +4680

8567 שָׁקַד *šāqad* (1)
been bound (1)

8568 שָׁקַר *šāqar* (1)
flirting (1)

8569 שַׂר *śar* (421)
officials (78)
commanders (74)
princes (41)
commander (36)
officers (31)
leaders (29)
nobles (18)
chief (17)
ruler (14)
prince (10)
leader (8)
captain (7)
rulers (7)
captain (5) +2822
leading (3)
officials in charge (3)
warden (3)
chief officer (2) +2021+7372
command (2)
governor (2)
in charge (2)
captains (1) +2822
chief men (1)
chief officials (1)
commander-in-chief (1) +2256+8031
commanders (1) +7372
dignitaries (1)
foremen (1) +5893
head (1)
heads (1)
masters (1)
mighty (1)
officer (1)
they[s] (1) +2021
they[s] (1) +2021+2256+2657+3405
untranslated (15)

8570 שַׂרְאֶצֶר *śar'eser* (3)
Sharezer (3)

8571 שָׂרַג *śārag* (2)
close-knit (1)
woven together (1)

8572 שָׂרַד *śārad* (1)
left (1)

8573 שְׂרַד *śᵉrad* (4)
woven (4)

8574 שְׂרֵד *śered* (1)
marker (1)

8575 1שָׂרָה *śārāh1* (3)
struggled (3)

8576 2שָׂרָה *śārāh2* (5)
ladies (1)
of royal birth (1)
queen (1)
queens (1)
women of nobility (1)

8577 3שָׂרָה *śārāh3* (38)
Sarah (35)
Sarah's (1)
she[s] (1)
untranslated (1)

8578 שְׂרוּג *śᵉrûg* (5)
Serug (5)

8579 שְׂרוֹךְ *śᵉrôk* (2)
thong (2)

8580 שֶׂרַח *śerah* (3)
Serah (3)

8581 שָׂרַט *śārat* (3)
cut (1) +8583
injure themselves (1) +8581

8582 שֶׂרֶט *śeret* (1)
cut (1) +5989

8583 שָׂרֶטֶת *śāretet* (1)
cut (1) +8581

8584 שָׂרַי *śāray* (17)
Sarai (15)
she[s] (1)
untranslated (1)

8585 שָׂרִיג *śāriyg* (3)
branches (3)

8586 1שָׂרִיד *śāriyd1* (29)
survivors (17)
survive (4)
left (2)
survivor (2)
few (1)
men who were left (1)
survived (1)
untranslated (1)

8587 2שָׂרִיד *śāriyd2* (2)
Sarid (2)

8588 שְׂרָיָה *śᵉrāyāh* (19)
Seraiah (17)
Seraiah's (1)
untranslated (1)

8589 שְׂרָיָהוּ *śᵉrāyāhû* (1)
Seraiah (1)

8590 שִׂרְיוֹן *śiryôn* (2)
Sirion (2)

8591 שָׂרִיק *śāriyq* (1)
combed (1)

8592 שָׂרַךְ *śārak* (1)
running here and there (1) +2006

8593 שַׂר־סְכִים *śar-sᵉkiym*
Variant; not used

8594 שָׂרַע *śāra'* (3)
deformed (2)
stretch out (1)

8595 שַׂרְעַפִּים *śar'appiym* (2)
anxiety (1)
anxious thoughts (1)

8596 שָׂרַף *śārap̄* (117)
burned (27)
burn (13)
burn down (9) +836+928+2021
burned (8) +836+928+2021
be burned up (4) +836+928+2021
burn (4) +836+928+2021
burned up (4) +836+928+2021
burns (4)
set on fire (4) +836+928+2021
burn up (3) +836+928+2021
burned down (3) +836+928+2021
set fire to (3)
be burned (2)
been burned up (2)
burn up (2)
are burned up (1) +836+928+2021+8596
bake thoroughly (1) +4200+8599
be burned (1) +836+928+2021
be burned down (1) +836+928+2021
be destroyed (1)
being burned (1)
burn as sacrifices (1)
burn down (1)
burn to death (1) +836+928+2021
burned as sacrifices (1)
burned down (1) +836+2021
burned to death (1)
burned to death (1) +836+928+2021
burned up (1)
destroy (1)
destroyed (1)
destroyed by fire (1)
is burned (1)
made (1)
make a fire (1)
set fire to (1) +836+928+2021
used for fuel (1) +836+1198
untranslated (2)

8597 1שָׂרָף *śārāp̄1* (7)
seraphs (2)
venomous (2)
snake (1)
snakes (1)
venomous serpent (1)

8598 2שָׂרָף *śārāp̄2* (1)
Saraph (1)

8599 שְׂרֵפָה *śᵉrēp̄āh* (13)
fire (3)
burned (2)
burning (2)
bake thoroughly (1) +4200+8596
burned-out (1)
burning waste (1)
smoldering remains (1)
those[s] (1) +2021
untranslated (1)

8600 שָׂרַק *śāraq*
Variant; not used

8601 1שָׂרֹק *śārōq1* (1)
brown (1)

8602 2שָׂרֹק *śārōq2* (1)
choicest vines (1)

8603 1שֹׂרֵק *śōrēq1* (2)
choice vine (1)
choicest vines (1)

8604 2שֹׂרֵק *śōrēq2* (1)
Sorek (1)

8605 שְׂרֵקָה *śᵉrēqāh* (1)
choicest branch (1)

8606 שָׂרַר *śārar* (7)
choose princes (1)
govern (1)
governed (1)
lord it (1) +8606
rule (1)
ruler (1)

8607 שָׂשׂוֹן *śāśôn* (22)
joy (14)
gladness (6)
joyful (1)
rejoicing (1)

8608 שָׂתַם *śātam* (1)
shuts out (1)

8609 שָׂתַר *śātar* (1)
outbreak (1)

8610 שׁ *š*
Variant; not used

8611 שֶׁ־ *ša-* (142)
that (15)
who (15)
which (7)
until (6) +6330
the one[s] (4)
whose (4)
because (3)
whom (3)
he[s] (2)
till (2) +6330
allies[s] (1) +6640
as (1) +3869
as (1) +3972+6645
body[s] (1)
despite (1) +928+4200
fault (1) +928+4200
for (1) +928+1685
future (1) +2118+4537
how (1)
it[s] (1)
mine (1) +3276+4200
my own (1) +3276+4200
of (1) +4200+4946
responsible for (1) +928+4200
since (1)
so that (1)
Solomon's (1) +4200+8976
successor (1) +132+339+995
than (1)
the produce[s] (1)
therefore (1) +1826+6584
when (1) +6330
where (1)
while (1) +6330
why (1) +4200+4537
wisdom[s] (1)
untranslated (55)

8612 שָׁאַב *šā'ab* (19)
draw water (5)
draw (4)
drew (4)
carriers (3)
carry (1)
drew water (1)
filled (1)

8613 שָׁאַג *šā'ag* (21)
roar (7)
roaring (4)
roared (3)
roars (2)
comes roar (1)
groan (1)
roar mightily (1) +8613
untranslated (1)

8614 שְׁאָגָה *š'āgāh* (7)
roar (3)
groaning (2)
groans (1)
roaring (1) +7754

8615 1שָׁאָה *šā'āh1* (4)
turned into (2)
lie ruined (1)
ruined (1)

8616 2שָׁאָה *šā'āh2* (2)
roar (2)

8617 3שָׁאָה *šā'āh3* (1)
watched closely (1)

8618 שַׁאֲוָה *ša'ăwāh* (1)
untranslated (1)

8619 שְׁאוֹל *š'ôl* (66)
grave (55)
death (6)
depths (2)
depths of the grave (2)
realm of death (1)

8620 שָׁאוּל *šā'ûl* (406)

Saul (327)
Saul's (34)
he[s] (12)
Shaul (9)
him[s] (6)
Saul's (4) +4200
his[s] (3)
his[s] (1) +4200
they[s] (1) +6269
untranslated (9)

8621 שָׁאוּלִי *šā'ûliy* (1)
Shaulite (1)

8622 1שָׁאוֹן *šā'ôn1* (1)
slimy pit (1) +1014

8623 2שָׁאוֹן *šā'ôn2* (17)
uproar (5)
roaring (3)
roar (2)
brawlers (1)
great tumult (1)
loud noise (1)
noise (1)
noisy boasters (1) +1201
roar of battle (1)
tumult (1)

8624 שְׁאָט *š'āt* (3)
malice (3)

8625 שְׁאִיָּה *š'iyyāh* (1)
battered to pieces (1) +4198

8626 שָׁאַל *šā'al* (174)
ask (39)
asked (36)
inquired of (15) +928
question (6)
asks (5)
greet (4) +4200+8934
greeted (4) +4200+8934
request (4)
consult (3)
questioned (3)
asking (2)
have request to make (2) +8629
ask (1) +907
asked how they were (1) +4200+8934
be given over (1)
beg (1)
beggars (1)
borrows (1)
consulted (1)
consulting (1) +7023
demand (1)
demanding (1)
demands (1)
desired (1)
earnestly asked for permission (1) +8626
earnestly asked permission (1) +8626
find out (1)
gave (1)
gave what asked for (1)
get answer (1) +8626
give (1)
have request (1) +8629
inquire (1)
inquire of (1) +906+7023
inquire of (1) +928
inquires of (1) +928+1821
inquiring of (1) +928
investigate (1)
invoking (1)
looks (1)
make[s] (1)
medium (1) +200
obtain decisions (1)
pray (1)
prayed (1)
questioned closely (1) +8626
require (1)
said (1)

tell (1)
took (1)
wanted (1) +906+5883
was borrowed (1)
wish (1)
untranslated (7)

8627 שְׁאָל *š'āl* (1)
Sheal (1)

8628 שְׁאָלָה *š'ālāh*
Variant; not used

8629 שְׁאֵלָה *š'ēlāh* (13)
petition (6)
have request to make (2) +8626
have request (1) +8626
prayed for (1)
request (1)
what asked for (1)
what[s] (1)

8630 שְׁאַלְתִּיאֵל *š'altiy'ēl* (6)
Shealtiel (6)

8631 שָׁאַן *šā'an* (5)
security (2)
at ease (1)
at rest (1)
enjoy ease (1)

8632 שְׁאָן *š'ān*
Variant; not used

8633 שַׁאֲנָן *ša'ănān* (10)
complacent (3)
insolence (2)
at ease (1)
feel secure (1)
peaceful (1)
proud (1)
undisturbed (1)

8634 1שָׁאַף *šā'ap1* (11)
pant (3)
hotly pursue (2)
hurries back (1)
long for (1)
longing for (1)
pant (1) +8120
pursue (1)
sniffing (1)

8635 2שָׁאַף *šā'ap2* (3)
trample (2)
hounded (1)

8636 שָׁאַר *šā'ar* (133)
left (52)
remained (10)
remain (9)
leave (7)
left behind (6)
leaving (5)
rest (5)
survived (5)
survive (3)
survivors (3)
have left (2)
leave alive (2)
spare (2)
been kept (1)
can hardly breathe (1) +4202+5972
left alone (1)
left survivor (1)
little left (1) +3856+7129
remains (1)
remnant (1)
remnant spare (1)
reserve (1)
sparing (1)
still (1)
still (1) +6388
survives (1)
those[s] (1) +2021
untranslated (8)

8637 שְׁאָר *š°'ār* (25)
rest (10)
remnant (9)
survivors (3)
other (1)
remainder (1)
remaining (1)

8638 שְׁאֵר *š°'ēr* (18)
flesh (5)
close relative (3)
meat (2)
blood relative (1) +1414
body (1)
close relative (1) +1414
close relative (1) +7940
close relatives (1)
food (1)
himself (1) +2257
relative (1)

8639 שְׁאָר יָשׁוּב *š°'ār yāšûb* (1)
Shear-Jashub (1)

8640 שַׁאֲרָה *ša'arāh*
Variant; not used

8641 שֶׁאֱרָה *še'erāh* (1)
Sheerah (1)

8642 שְׁאֵרִית *š°'ēriyt* (66)
remnant (44)
rest (7)
survivors (7)
remain (2)
remaining (2)
descendant (1)
last (1)
left (1)
other (1)

8643 שְׁאֵת *š°'t* (1)
ruin (1)

8644 שְׁבָא *š°bā'* (23)
Sheba (22)
Sabeans (1)

8645 שְׁבָאִים *š°bā'iym* (1)
Sabeans (1)

8646 שְׁבָבִים *š°bābiym* (1)
broken in pieces (1)

8647 שָׁבָה *šābāh* (46)
captors (4)
carried off (4)
taken captive (4)
captured (3)
took captive (3)
are held captive (2)
captives (2)
conquerors (2)
take captive (2)
takes captive (2) +8647
be taken captive (1)
been captured (1)
been carried captive (1)
been taken captive (1)
captured (1) +8660
carried away (1)
held captive (1)
is taken away (1)
led in train (1)
made captives of (1)
make captives (1)
seized (1)
take captives (1) +8660
taken (1)
taken as prisoners (1) +8664
takes captive (1)
took as prisoners (1) +8664

8648 שְׁבוֹ *š°bô* (2)
agate (2)

8649 שְׁבוּאֵל *š°bû'ēl* (3)
Shubael (3)

8650 שְׁבוּל *š°bûl*
Variant; not used

8651 שָׁבוּעַ *šābûa'* (20)
weeks (7)
sevens (4)
seven (3)
weeks (2) +3427
bridal week (1)
feast of weeks (1)
week (1)
untranslated (1)

8652 שְׁבוּעָה *š°bû'āh* (29)
oath (17)
swear (2)
curse (1)
denounce (1)
oath swore (1)
put oath (1) +8678
sworn (1)
sworn allegiance (1) +8678
sworn judgments (1)
takes an oath (1) +8678
them^s (1)
under oath (1) +1251

8653 שָׁבוּר *šābûr* (1)
injured (1)

8654 שְׁבוּת *š°bût* (29)
fortunes (14)
captivity (7)
exiled (1)
made prosperous again (1) +8740
untranslated (6)

8655 1שָׁבַח *šābah1* (9)
commend (2)
extol (2)
glory (2)
declared (1)
glorify (1)
receive praise (1)

8656 2שָׁבַח *šābah2* (3)
keeps (1)
still (1)
stilled (1)

8657 שֵׁבֶט *šēbet* (190)
tribes (74)
tribe (44)
rod (23)
half-tribe (18) +2942
scepter (15)
tribal (3)
club (2)
staff (2)
chief men (1)
javelins (1)
peoples (1)
punish (1)
rulers (1)
shepherd's rod (1)
stick (1)
untranslated (2)

8658 שְׁבָט *š°bāt* (1)
Shebat (1)

8659 שָׁבִי *šābiy*
Variant; not used

8660 שְׁבִי *š°biy* (48)
captivity (17)
exile (13)
captives (8)
captured (4)
prisoners (2)
captured (1) +8647
carry off (1) +928+995+2021
prisoner (1)
take captives (1) +8647

8661 שֹׁבִי *šôbiy* (1)
Shobi (1)

8662 שֹׁבַי *šôbay* (2)
Shobai (2)

8663 שָׁבִיב *šābiyb* (1)
flame (1)

8664 שִׁבְיָה *šibyāh* (9)
prisoners (3)
captives (2)
captivity (2)
taken as prisoners (1) +8647
took as prisoners (1) +8647

8665 שְׁבִיָּה *š°biyyāh* (1)
captive (1)

8666 שְׁבִיל *š°biyl* (3)
paths (1)
way (1)
untranslated (1)

8667 שָׁבִיס *šābiys* (1)
headbands (1)

8668 שְׁבִיעִי *š°biy'iy* (97)
seventh (97)

8669 שְׁבִית *š°biyt* (14)
fortunes (4)
captives (1)
untranslated (9)

8670 שֹׁבֶל *šôbel* (1)
skirts (1)

8671 שַׁבְּלוּל *šabb°lûl* (1)
slug (1)

8672 1שִׁבֹּלֶת *šibbōlet1* (16)
heads of grain (8)
heads (3)
grain (2)
branches (1)
leftover grain (1)
Shibboleth (1)

8673 2שִׁבֹּלֶת *šibbōlet2* (3)
floods (1)
floodwaters (1) +4784
flowing (1)

8674 שֶׁבְנָא *šebnā'* (7)
Shebna (7)

8675 שֶׁבְנָה *šebnāh* (2)
Shebna (2)

8676 שְׁבַנְיָה *š°banyāh* (5)
Shebaniah (5)

8677 שְׁבַנְיָהוּ *š°banyāhû* (1)
Shebaniah (1)

8678 שָׁבַע *šāba'* (186)
swore (35)
swear (29)
promised on oath (21)
sworn (21)
took an oath (7)
swore an oath (6)
charge (5)
made swear (4)
take oaths (4)
made swear an oath (3)
made take an oath (3)
make swear (3)
oath (3)
put under oath (3)
taken an oath (3)
solemnly swore (2)
swears (2)
swore oath (2)
takes an oath (2)
bound under a strict oath (1) +8678
bound with the oath (1)
confirmed by oath (1)
declared on oath (1)
gave oath (1)
gave solemn oath (1)

given oath (1)
made swear an oath (1) +8678
perjurers (1) +2021+4200+9214
perjury (1) +2021+4200+9214
pledged on oath (1)
pronounced solemn oath (1)
put oath (1) +8652
ratified by oath (1)
solemnly promised (1)
swear allegiance (1)
swearing (1)
swears falsely (1)
sworn allegiance (1) +8652
sworn an oath (1)
taken oath (1)
takes an oath (1) +8652
took oath (1)
took the oath (1)
use name as a curse (1) +928
want to swear (1)

8679 1שֶׁבַע *šeba'1* (487)
seven (286)
seventy (57)
seventh (9)
twenty-seventh (6) +2256+6929
70 (5)
seventeen (5) +6926
seventeenth (4) +6925
127 (3) +2256+2256+4395+6929
seventy-five (3) +2256+2822
seventy-seven (3) +2256+8679
thirty-seventh (3) +2256+8993
1,247 (2) +547+752+2256+4395
1,775 (2)   +547+2256+2256
                  +2256+2822+4395+8679
137 (2) +2256+2256+4395+8993
372 (2) +2256+4395+8993+9109
57,400 (2)
          +547+752+2256+2256+2822+4395
6,720 (2) +547+2256+4395+6929+9252
62,700 (2)
          +547+2256+2256+4395+9109+9252
7,337 (2)
          +547+2256+4395+8679+8993+8993
74 (2) +752+2256
74,600 (2)
          +547+752+2256+2256+4395+9252
760 (2) +2256+4395+9252
973 (2) +2256+4395+8993+9596
seven (2) +8679
seventeen hundred (2) +547+2256+4395
seventeenth (2) +6926
thirty-seven (2) +2256+8993
twenty-seven (2) +2256+6929
1,017 (1) +547+2256+6925
1,017 (1) +547+6925
1,760 (1) +547+2256+2256+4395+9252
14,700 (1) +547+752+2256+4395+6925
157,600 (1)   +547+547+2256+2256
                  +2256+2822+4395+4395+9252
16,750 (1)
          +547+2256+2822+4395+6925+9252
17,200 (1) +547+2256+4395+6925
172 (1) +2256+4395+9109
187 (1) +2256+2256+4395+9046
2,067 (1) +547+2256+9252
2,172 (1) +547+2256+2256+4395+9109
2,172 (1) +547+2256+4395+9109
2,750 (1) +547+2256+2822+4395
207 (1) +2256+4395
22,273 (1)   +547+2256+2256+2256
                  +4395+6929+8993+9109
273 (1) +2256+2256+4395+8993
3,700 (1) +547+2256+4395+8993
307,500 (1)   +547+547+2256+2256
                  +2822+4395+4395+8993
337,500 (1)   +547+547+547+2256+2256
                  +2256+2822+4395+4395+8993+8993
337,500 (1)   +547+547+547+2256+2256
                  +2822+4395+4395+8993+8993
37,000 (1) +547+2256+8993

43,730 (1)   +547+752+2256+2256
                  +2256+4395+8993+8993
44,760 (1)   +547+752+752+2256
                  +2256+2256+4395+9252
52,700 (1)
          +547+2256+2256+2822+4395+9109
601,730 (1)   +547+547+2256+2256
                  +4395+4395+8993+9252
667 (1) +2256+4395+9252+9252
67 (1) +2256+9252
675 (1) +2256+2822+4395+9252
675,000 (1)   +547+547+547+2256
                  +2256+2822+4395+9252
7,000 (1) +547
7,100 (1) +547+2256+4395
7,500 (1) +547+2256+2822+4395
70,000 (1) +547
72 (1) +2256+9109
72,000 (1) +547+2256+9109
721 (1) +285+2256+2256+4395+6929
725 (1) +2256+2822+4395+6929
730 (1) +2256+4395+8993
736 (1) +2256+4395+8993+9252
743 (1) +752+2256+2256+4395+8993
743 (1) +752+2256+4395+8993
745 (1) +752+2256+2822+4395
76,500 (1)
          +547+2256+2256+2822+4395+9252
775 (1) +2256+2822+4395+8679
777 (1) +2256+2256+4395+8679+8679
782 (1) +2256+2256+4395+9046+9109
807 (1) +2256+4395+9046
87,000 (1) +547+2256+9046
forty-seven (1) +752+2256
many (1)
seven-day (1) +3427
seven-day periods (1) +2021+3427
sevenfold (1)
seventeen (1) +2256+6927
twenty-seven hundred (1) +547+2256+4395
untranslated (7)

8680 2שֶׁבַע *šeba'2* (9)
Sheba (9)

8681 3שֶׁבַע *šeba'3* (1)
Sheba (1)

8682 4שֶׁבַע *šeba'4*
Variant; not used

8683 שִׁבְעָה *šib'āh* (1)
Shibah (1)

8684 שִׁבְעִים *šib'iym*
Variant; not used

8685 שִׁבְעָנָה *šib'ānāh* (1)
seven (1)

8686 שִׁבְעָתַיִם *šib'ātayim*
Variant; not used

8687 שָׁבֵץ *šābas* (2)
filigree settings (1)
weave (1)

8688 שָׁבָץ *šābās* (1)
throes of death (1)

8689 1שָׁבַר *šābar1* (147)
break (19)
broken (16)
smashed (10)
be broken (9)
broke (9)
be destroyed (5)
break down (4)
cut off (4)
shattered (4)
smash (4)
brokenhearted (3) +4213
injured (3)
is broken (3)
are broken (2)
are crushed (2)
breaking to pieces (2)

breaks (2)
broke up (2)
crush (2)
destroy (2)
destroyed (2)
is injured (2)
mauled (2)
was broken off (2)
were wrecked (2)
abolish (1)
are broken off (1)
are shattered (1)
be broken off (1)
be broken up (1)
be injured (1)
be smashed (1)
been broken (1)
been grieved (1)
break to pieces (1)
break to pieces (1) +8689
break up (1)
breaks down (1)
breaks in pieces (1)
bring to the moment of birth (1)
broke off (1)
broken off (1)
crushed (1)
demolish (1)
desolate (1)
fixed (1)
is shattered (1)
quench (1)
shattering (1)
stripped (1)
suffered (1)
was broken (1)
were crushed (1)
untranslated (1)

8690 2שָׁבַר *šābar2* (21)
buy (11)
sell (3)
buy grain (2)
sold grain (2)
buying (1)
pay for (1)
selling (1)

8691 1שֶׁבֶר *šeber1* (44)
destruction (14)
wound (7)
destroyed (3)
disaster (2)
fracture (2)
break in pieces (1)
broken (1)
brokenness (1)
bruises (1)
collapses (1) +995
crash (1)
crippled (1)
crushed (1)
crushes (1)
downfall (1)
fractures (1)
injury (1)
ruin (1)
thrashing (1)
untranslated (2)

8692 2שֶׁבֶר *šeber2* (9)
grain (9)

8693 3שֶׁבֶר *šeber3* (1)
Sheber (1)

8694 שֵׁבֶר *šēber* (1)
interpretation (1)

8695 שִׁבָּרוֹן *šibbārôn* (2)
broken (1)
destruction (1)

8696 שְׁבָרִים *š'bāriym* (1)
stone quarries (1)

8697 שָׁבַת *šābat* (72)
put an end (14)
rested (4)
stopped (4)
come to an end (3)
remove (3)
rest (3)
stop (3)
bring an end (2)
cease (2)
ended (2)
gone (2)
put a stop (2)
abandoned (1)
abstained from work (1)
blot out (1)
bring to an end (1)
cause to stop (1)
cut off (1)
did away with (1)
disappear (1)
discard (1)
do away with (1)
do not work (1)
have rest (1)
have[s] (1)
leave (1)
left without (1)
makes cease (1)
must observe a sabbath (1) +8701
need not (1)
no (1)
observe sabbath (1) +8701
removed (1)
revert (1)
rid (1)
ruined (1)
settles (1)
silence (1)
stilled (1)
stopping (1)

8698 2שָׁבַת *šābat2*
Variant; not used

8699 1שֶׁבֶת *šebet1* (6)
seat (2) +5226
home (1)
lie (1)
reign (1)
site (1)

8700 2שֶׁבֶת *šebet2* (2)
Do-Nothing (1)
loss of time (1)

8701 שַׁבָּת *šabbāt* (111)
sabbath (66)
sabbaths (30)
another[s] (1)
every sabbath (1) +928+8701
every sabbath (1) +8701
it[s] (1) +2021
must observe a sabbath (1) +8697
observe sabbath (1) +8697
sabbath after sabbath (1)
    +928+928+2021+2021+3427+3427+8701
sabbath days (1)
sabbath rests (1)
weeks (1)
untranslated (2)

8702 שַׁבָּתוֹן *šabbātôn* (11)
rest (7)
day of rest (4)

8703 שַׁבְּתַי *šabb'tay* (3)
Shabbethai (3)

8704 שָׁגַג *šāgag* (4)
deceived (1)
erred (1)
went astray (1)
wrong committed unintentionally (1) +8705

8705 שְׁגָגָה *š'gāgāh* (19)
unintentionally (6) +928
accidentally (4) +928
mistake (2)
error (1)
not intentional (1)
sins unintentionally (1) +928+6913
unintentional wrong (1)
unintentionally (1) +4200
wrong (1)
wrong committed unintentionally (1) +8704

8706 שָׁגָה *šāgāh* (21)
stagger (3)
stray (3)
captivated (2)
led astray (2)
sins unintentionally (2)
deceiver (1)
erred (1)
gone astray (1)
leads (1)
leads astray (1)
let stray (1)
unintentionally (1)
wandered (1)
wrong (1)

8707 שָׁגֵה *šāgēh* (1)
Shagee (1)

8708 שָׁגַח *šāgah* (3)
gazing (1)
stare (1)
watches (1)

8709 שְׁגִיאָה *š'giy'āh* (1)
errors (1)

8710 שִׁגָּיוֹן *šiggāyôn* (2)
shiggaion (1)
shigionoth (1)

8711 שָׁגַל *šāgal* (4)
been ravished (1)
raped (1)
ravish (1)
ravished (1)

8712 שֵׁגָל *šēgal* (2)
queen (1)
royal bride (1)

8713 שָׁגַע *šāga'* (7)
carry on (1)
drive mad (1)
insane (1)
madman (1)
madman (1) +408
madmen (1)
maniac (1)

8714 שִׁגָּעוֹן *šiggā'ôn* (3)
madness (2)
madman (1)

8715 שֶׁגֶר *šeger* (5)
calves (4)
firstborn (1) +7081

8716 שַׁד *šad* (21)
breasts (17)
breast (4)

8717 שֵׁד *šēd* (2)
demons (2)

8718 1שֹׁד *šōd1* (3)
breasts (2)
breast (1)

8719 2שֹׁד *šōd2* (25)
destruction (13)
ruin (4)
violence (3)
oppression (2)
havoc (1)
loot (1)

untranslated (1)

8720 שָׁדַד *šādad* (59)
destroyer (7)
destroyed (6)
destroy (5)
ruined (4)
destroyers (3)
is destroyed (3)
are destroyed (2)
be destroyed (2)
destroying (2)
destroys (2)
devastated (2)
marauders (2)
are ruined (1)
assail (1)
be devastated (1)
be ruined (1)
been destroyed (1)
dead (1)
doomed to destruction (1)
in ruins (1)
lies in ruins (1)
looter (1)
perish (1)
raid (1)
ravage (1)
robbers (1)
robs (1)
shatter (1)
takes loot (1)
utterly ruined (1) +8720

8721 שִׁדָּה *šiddāh* (2)
harem (1) +2256+8721

8722 שָׁדוּד *šādûd*
Variant; not used

8723 שִׁדּוֹן *šaddûn* (1)
judgment (1)

8724 שַׁדַּי *šadday* (48)
Almighty (48)

8725 שְׁדֵיאוּר *š'dēy'ûr* (5)
Shedeur (5)

8726 שַׁדִּין *šaddiyn* (1)
untranslated (1)

8727 שְׁדֵמָה *š'dēmāh* (5)
fields (4)
terraces (1)

8728 שָׁדַף *šādap* (3)
scorched (3)

8729 שְׁדֵפָה *š'dēpāh* (2)
scorched (2)

8730 שִׁדָּפוֹן *šiddāpôn* (5)
blight (5)

8731 שַׁדְרַךְ *šadrak* (1)
Shadrach (1)

8732 1שֹׁהַם *šōham1* (11)
onyx (9)
onyx (2) +74

8733 2שֹׁהַם *šōham2* (1)
Shoham (1)

8734 שָׁו *šāw*
Variant; not used

8735 שׁוּא *šû'*
Variant; not used

8736 שָׁוְא *šāw'* (54)
false (15)
in vain (4) +2021+4200
worthless (4)
in vain (3)
lies (3)
misuse (3) +2021+4200+5951
deceitful (2)
falsehood (2)

futility (2)
misuses (2) +2021+4200+5951
deceit (1)
destruction (1)
empty plea (1)
falsely (1)
futile (1)
idol (1)
idols (1)
lies (1) +1819
meaningless (1)
nothing (1)
worthless idols (1)
worthless idols (1) +2039
worthless things (1)
untranslated (1)

8737 שָׁוְא *š*ʷwāʾ (2)
Sheva (2)

8738 שׁוֹא *šôʾ* (1)
ravages (1)

8739 שׁוֹאָה *šôʾāh* (12)
ruin (3)
desolate (2)
storm (2)
catastrophe (1)
destroyed (1)
disaster (1)
ruins (1)
trouble (1)

8740 שׁוּב *šûbl* (1069)
return (157)
returned (99)
turn (50)
bring back (39)
go back (37)
again (34)
restore (34)
turn back (34)
come back (23)
brought back (21)
went back (21)
back (20)
turned (16)
turn away (15)
restored (14)
turned away (13)
put back (10)
repent (10)
turned back (10)
give back (9)
send back (9)
answer (8) +1821
repay (8)
came back (7)
take back (7)
turns (7)
turns away (7)
recovered (6)
reported (6) +1821
returns (6)
answer (5)
bring (5)
change (5)
go (5)
took back (5)
go (4) +2143+2256
pay back (4)
refuse (4)
relent (4)
rewarded (4)
take (4)
withdrew (4)
answered (3) +1821
bringing back (3)
make return (3)
regain (3)
restores (3)
returning (3)
started back (3)

stop (3)
stopped (3)
turned around (3)
again and again (2)
be sure to take back (2) +8740
bring down (2)
brought (2)
come (2)
coming back (2)
ever return (2) +8740
give (2)
keep (2)
left (2)
once more (2)
oppose (2)
pay (2)
rebuilt (2) +1215+2256
reject (2) +7156
repaid (2)
repented (2)
reply (2)
repulse (2) +7156
restrain (2)
retreat (2)
revert (2)
revoked (2)
rewards (2)
sent (2)
sent back (2)
take vengeance (2) +5934
turn around (2)
turn away (2) +8740
turning (2)
withdraw (2)
withholds (2)
again (1) +9108
again be used (1)
again give allegiance (1) +4213
another (1)
answer give (1)
answered (1)
answers (1) +1821
arrived (1)
back again (1)
be brought back (1)
been returned (1)
break (1)
bring in (1)
broke off (1) +4946
brought down (1)
by all means send (1) +8740
call to mind (1) +448+4213
came again (1)
carry the battle (1) +1741+2256
caused to roam (1)
changed (1)
changed mind (1)
changed minds (1)
continually (1)
cover up (1) +2256+4059
depart (1)
departs (1)
didˢ (1)
do soˢ (1) +2006+4946
dole out (1)
draw back (1)
drew back (1)
drives (1)
dwell (1)
escaping (1)
flow back (1)
flowed back (1)
forced to restore (1)
gave (1)
get back (1)
give up (1) +4946
gives back (1)
go back (1) +345
go on (1)
going back (1)
hold back (1)

keep themselves alive (1) +906+4392+5883
keep themselves alive (1) +5883
keeps saying (1) +609
left behind (1)
lose (1)
made go back (1)
made pay for (1) +928+8031
made prosperous again (1) +8654
made retreat (1) +294
make full restitution (1) +928+8031
make go (1)
make right (1)
marauding (1) +2256+6296
mislead (1)
no longer (1)
not angry (1) +678
overruling (1)
overthrows (1) +294
paid (1)
paid (1) +868
paid back (1)
pass again (1)
passed (1)
pay (1) +4084
pays back (1)
pays back (1) +8740
penitent (1)
prompt to answer (1)
pull back (1)
pursues (1) +928
raised (1)
ran (1)
reappears (1) +2256+7255
rebuild (1) +1215+2256
recaptured (1) +2256+4374
receded steadily (1) +2143+2256+8740
recoil (1)
recoils (1)
reconsider (1) +6388
recover (1)
reentered (1) +995+2256
refreshes (1)
refund (1)
renew (1)
renounce (1) +7156
reopened (1) +2256+2916
repay (1) +928+8031
repay (1) +6584+8031
repaying (1)
repents (1)
reply (1) +4863
rescue (1)
respond (1)
responded (1)
rest (1)
restitution (1) +871
restitution made (1)
restore again (1)
restorer (1)
restrained (1)
retire (1)
retreats (1)
return (1) +2143
return (1) +8740
returned unanswered (1) +2668
reverse (1)
reversed (1)
revived (1) +8120
reviving (1)
revoke (1)
roll back (1)
say (1)
send (1)
sending back (1)
shy away (1)
something else (1)
stops to think (1) +448+4213
strayed (1)
subsides (1)
supply (1)
surely return (1) +8740

take away (1)
take back (1) +8740
taken back (1)
takes back (1) +8740
try again (1)
turn again (1)
turned again (1)
turned to go (1)
turning away (1)
vent (1)
ward off (1)
were brought back (1)
withdrawn (1) +294
withheld (1)
withhold (1)
untranslated (33)

8741 שׁוּב2 *šûb2*
Variant; not used

8742 שׁוּבָאֵל *šûbā'ēl* (3)
Shubael (3)

8743 שׁוֹבָב1 *šôbāb1* (3)
faithless (2)
kept on (1) +2143

8744 שׁוֹבָב2 *šôbāb2* (4)
Shobab (4)

8745 שׁוֹבֵב *šôbēb* (3)
unfaithful (2)
traitors (1)

8746 שׁוּבָה *šûbāh* (1)
repentance (1)

8747 שׁוֹבָךְ *šôbak* (2)
Shobach (2)

8748 שׁוֹבָל *šôbāl* (9)
Shobal (9)

8749 שׁוֹבֵק *šôbēq* (1)
Shobek (1)

8750 שָׁוָה1 *šāwāh1* (14)
compare (2)
be like (1)
count equal (1)
equal (1)
get what deserved (1)
gives satisfaction (1)
in best interest (1)
is like (1)
justify (1)
leveled (1)
liken (1)
stilled (1)
waited patiently (1)

8751 שָׁוָה2 *šāwāh2* (7)
bestowed (2)
makes (2)
brought forth (1)
set (1)
set heart (1)

8752 שׁוּה *šāweh*
Variant; not used

8753 שָׁוֵה *šāwēh* (1)
Shaveh (1)

8754 שָׁוֵה קִרְיָתַיִם *šāwēh qiryātayim* (1)
Shaveh Kiriathaim (1)

8755 שׁוּחַ1 *šûaḥ1* (1)
leads down (1)

8756 שׁוּחַ2 *šûaḥ2* (2)
Shuah (2)

8757 שׁוּחָה1 *šûḥāh1* (5)
pit (4)
rifts (1)

8758 שׁוּחָה2 *šûḥāh2* (1)
Shuhah's (1)

8759 שַׁוְחָט *šawḥāt*
Variant; not used

8760 שׁוּחִי *šûḥiy* (5)
Shuhite (5)

8761 שׁוּחָם *šûḥām* (1)
Shuham (1)

8762 שׁוּחָמִי *šûḥāmiy* (2)
Shuhamite (2)

8763 שׁוּט1 *šûṭ1* (13)
oarsmen (2)
range (2)
roaming (2)
go (1)
go here and there (1)
go up and down (1)
gone (1)
rush here and there (1)
wander (1)
went around (1)

8764 שׁוּט2 *šûṭ2* (3)
despise (1)
malicious (1)
maligned (1)

8765 שׁוֹט1 *šôṭ1* (12)
whips (5)
scourge (3)
whip (2)
lash (1)
untranslated (1)

8766 שׁוֹט2 *šôṭ2*
Variant; not used

8767 שׁוּל *šûl* (11)
hem (5)
skirts (4)
train of robe (1)
untranslated (1)

8768 שׁוֹלָל *šôlāl* (4)
stripped (2)
barefoot (1)
untranslated (1)

8769 שׁוּלַמִּית *šûlammiyt* (2)
Shulammite (2)

8770 שׁוּמִים *šûmiym* (1)
garlic (1)

8771 שׁוּנִי1 *šûniy1* (2)
Shuni (2)

8772 שׁוּנִי2 *šûniy2* (1)
Shunite (1)

8773 שׁוּנֵם *šûnēm* (3)
Shunem (3)

8774 שׁוּנַמִּי *šûnammiy* (8)
Shunammite (8)

8775 שָׁוַע *šāwa'* (22)
cry for help (7)
cried for help (4)
call for help (3)
called for help (3)
cry out (3)
cry out for help (1)
plead for relief (1)

8776 שֶׁוַע *šewa'* (1)
cry for help (1) +7754

8777 שׁוֹעַ1 *šôa'1* (2)
highly respected (1)
rich (1)

8778 שׁוֹעַ2 *šôa'2* (1)
Shoa (1)

8779 שׁוֹעַ3 *šôa'3* (1)
crying out (1)

8780 שׁוּעַ1 *šûa'1* (1)
cries for help (1)

8781 שׁוּעַ2 *šûa'2* (3)
Shua (3)

8782 שׁוּעַ3 *šûa'3* (1)
wealth (1)

8783 שׁוּעָא *šû'ā'* (1)
Shua (1)

8784 שַׁוְעָה *šaw'āh* (11)
cry (7)
cry for help (3)
outcry (1)

8785 שׁוּעָל1 *šû'āl1* (7)
foxes (3)
jackals (3)
fox (1)

8786 שׁוּעָל2 *šû'āl2* (1)
Shual (1)

8787 שׁוּעָל3 *šû'āl3* (1)
Shual (1)

8788 שׁוֹעֵר *šô'ēr* (37)
gatekeepers (29)
doorkeepers (4)
gatekeeper (2)
keep watch (1)
keeper of gate (1)

8789 שׁוּף1 *šûp1* (2)
crush (2)

8790 שׁוּף2 *šûp2* (1)
strike (1)

8791 שׁוֹפָךְ *šôpak* (2)
Shophach (2)

8792 שׁוּפָם *šûpām* (1)
Shupham (1)

8793 שׁוּפָמִי *šûpāmiy* (1)
Shuphamite (1)

8794 שׁוֹפָן *šôpān*
Variant; not used

8795 שׁוֹפָר *šôpār* (72)
trumpet (44)
trumpets (18)
trumpets (3) +3413
ram's horn (2)
blast (1) +7754
horns (1)
rams' horns (1)
trumpet (1) +9558
untranslated (1)

8796 שׁוּק1 *šûq1* (3)
overflow (2)
water (1)

8797 שׁוֹק *šôq* (19)
thigh (12)
legs (5)
attacked viciously (1) +3751+5782+6584
leg (1)

8798 שׁוּק2 *šûq2* (4)
street (2)
streets (2)

8799 שׁוֹקֵק *šôqēq* (2)
thirsty (1) +5883
unquenched (1)

8800 שׁוּר1 *šûr1* (14)
see (5)
behold (1)
care for (1)
gaze (1)
lie in wait (1)
look (1)
lurk (1)
pays attention (1)
perceive (1)
view (1)

8801 שׁוּר2 *šûr2* (4)
carriers (1)
comes (1)

descend (1)
went (1)

8802 שׁוֹר *šôr* (79)
ox (38)
bull (16)
cattle (13)
animal (2)
bulls (2)
calf (2)
herd (2)
oxen (2)
cow (1)
one[s] (1)

8803 3שׁוּר *šûr3* (3)
wall (3)

8804 4שׁוּר *šûr4* (6)
Shur (6)

8805 שׁוּרָה *šûrāh* (1)
terraces (1)

8806 שׁוֹרֵר *šôrēr* (6)
slander (2)
adversaries (1)
enemies (1)
oppressors (1)
slanderers (1)

8807 שַׁוְשָׁא *šawšā'* (1)
Shavsha (1)

8808 1שׁוּשַׁן *šûšan1* (17)
lilies (11)
lily (6)

8809 2שׁוּשַׁן *šûšan2* (21)
Susa (21)

8810 שׁוּשַׁק *šûšaq* (1)
untranslated (1)

8811 שׁוּתֶלַח *šûtelah* (4)
Shuthelah (4)

8812 שָׁזַף *šāzap* (3)
darkened (1)
saw (1)
seen (1)

8813 שָׁזַר *šāzar* (21)
finely twisted (21)

8814 שַׁח *šah* (1)
downcast (1) +6524

8815 שָׁחַד *šāhad* (2)
bribing (1)
pay a ransom (1)

8816 שֹׁחַד *šōhad* (23)
bribe (12)
bribes (6)
gift (2)
bribery (1) +5228
reward (1)
those who love bribes (1)

8817 שָׁחָה *šāhāh* (2)
fall prostrate (1)
weighs down (1)

8818 שְׁחוֹר *šᵉhôr* (1)
soot (1)

8819 שְׁחוּת *šᵉhût* (1)
trap (1)

8820 שָׁחַח *šāhah* (19)
brought low (3)
be brought low (2)
bow down (1)
bowed head (1)
bowing (1)
bring down (1)
collapse (1)
collapsed (1)
cowered (1)
crouch (1)

downcast (1)
faint (1)
humbled (1)
humbles (1)
mumble (1)
untranslated (1)

8821 1שָׁחַט *šāhat1* (81)
slaughtered (35)
slaughter (23)
killed (5)
sacrifices (2)
be slaughtered (1)
butchered (1)
dead (1)
deadly (1)
kill (1)
killing (1)
offer (1)
sacrifice (1)
sacrificed (1)
sacrifices slaughtered (1)
slaughtering (1)
slay (1)
was killed (1)
were slaughtered (1)
untranslated (2)

8822 2שָׁחַט *šāhat2* (5)
hammered (5)

8823 שַׁחֲטָה *šahᵉtāh* (1)
slaughter (1)

8824 שְׁחִיטָה *šᵉhiytāh* (1)
kill (1)

8825 שְׁחִין *šᵉhiyn* (13)
boil (6)
boils (5)
sores (1)
untranslated (1)

8826 שָׁחִיס *šāhiys* (1)
what springs from (1)

8827 שְׁחִית *šᵉhiyt* (2)
grave (1)
traps (1)

8828 שַׁחַל *šahal* (7)
lion (6)
untranslated (1)

8829 שְׁחֵלֶת *šᵉhēlet* (1)
onycha (1)

8830 שַׁחַף *šahap* (2)
gull (2)

8831 שַׁחֶפֶת *šahepet* (2)
wasting disease (1)
wasting diseases (1)

8832 שָׁחִץ *šahas* (2)
proud (1) +1201
proud beasts (1) +1201

8833 שַׁחֲצוּמָה *šahᵉsûmāh* (1)
Shahazumah (1)

8834 שַׁחֲצִימָה *šahᵉsiymāh* (1)
untranslated (1)

8835 שָׁחַק *šāhaq* (4)
beat fine (2)
grind (1)
wears away (1)

8836 שַׁחַק *šahaq* (21)
clouds (8)
skies (8)
clouds of the sky (2) +6265
dust (1)
skies above (1)
sky (1)

8837 1שָׁחַר *šāhar1* (1)
grows black (1)

8838 2שָׁחַר *šāhar2* (13)
earnestly seek (2)
careful (1)
conjure away (1)
eagerly (1)
foraging (1)
longs for (1)
look (1)
look for (1)
looked for (1)
search for (1)
seek (1)
seeks (1)

8839 שָׁחֹר *šāhōr* (6)
black (5)
dark (1)

8840 שַׁחַר *šahar* (24)
dawn (14)
daybreak (2)
daybreak (2) +2021+6590
day dawns (1)
first light of dawn (1) +6590
light of dawn (1)
morning (1)
sun rises (1)
untranslated (1)

8841 שַׁחֲרוּת *šahᵉrût* (1)
vigor (1)

8842 שְׁחַרְחֹר *šᵉharhōr* (1)
dark (1)

8843 שְׁחַרְיָה *šᵉharyāh* (1)
Shehariah (1)

8844 שַׁחֲרַיִם *šahᵉrayim* (1)
Shaharaim (1)

8845 שָׁחַת *šāhat* (146)
destroy (60)
destroyed (11)
corrupt (10)
destroying (5)
cut down (3)
destroys (3)
ruin (3)
ruined (3)
act corruptly (2)
corrupted (2)
depraved (2)
destruction (2)
devastate (2)
raiding parties (2)
ravage (2)
acted corruptly (1)
afflicting (1)
allowed to fall into ruin (1)
battering (1)
blemished (1)
cause devastation (1)
cause of destruction (1)
clip off (1)
corrupt practices (1)
corruption (1)
devastated (1)
devouring (1)
doing so[s] (1)
downfall (1)
endanger (1)
given to corruption (1)
killed (1)
laid waste (1)
overthrow (1)
polluted (1)
ravaging (1)
ravening (1)
spilled (1)
steal (1)
stifling (1)
struck down (1)
sure to become utterly corrupt (1) +8845
tear down (1)

violated (1)
was marred (1)
was ruined (1)
wasted (1)
untranslated (1)

8846 שַׁחַת *šahat* (23)
pit (17)
corruption (2)
decay (2)
dungeon (1)
slime pit (1)

8847 שִׁטָּה *šittāh* (29)
acacia (25)
acacia wood (3)
acacias (1)

8848 שָׂטַח *šātah* (6)
enlarges (1)
exposed (1)
scattered (1)
spread out (1)
spread out (1) +8848

8849 שׁוֹטֵט *šōtēt* (1)
whips (1)

8850 שִׁטִּים *šittiym* (4)
Shittim (4)

8851 שָׁטַף *šātap* (31)
overwhelming (3)
torrents (3)
engulf (2)
flood (2)
overflow (2)
wash away (2)
washed (2)
be rinsed (1)
be swept away (1)
charging (1)
engulfed (1)
flooding (1)
flooding downpour (1) +3888
flowed (1)
flowed abundantly (1)
overflowing (1)
rinsed (1)
rinsing (1)
rushing (1)
sweep over (1)
swept away (1)
swirling over (1)

8852 שֶׁטֶף *šetep* (6)
flood (2)
overwhelming (2)
rise (1)
torrents of rain (1)

8853 שֹׁטֵר *šātar* (25)
officials (10)
officers (6)
foremen (5)
officer (1)
overseer (1)
scribes (1)
serve as officials (1)

8854 שֹׁטֵר *šōtēr*
Variant; not used

8855 שִׁטְרַי *šitray* (1)
Shitrai (1)

8856 שַׁי *šay* (3)
gifts (3)

8857 שֵׁיָא *šᵉyā'* (1)
untranslated (1)

8858 שִׁיאָן *šiy'ōn* (1)
Shion (1)

8859 1שִׁיבָה *šiybāh1* (1)
stay (1)

8860 2שִׁיבָה *šiybāh2* (1)
captives (1)

8861 שָׁיָה *šāyāh* (1)
deserted (1)

8862 שִׁיזָא *šiyzā'* (1)
Shiza (1)

8863 שִׁיחַ *šiyah* (5)
downcast (4)
down (1)

8864 שִׁיחָה *šiyhāh* (3)
pit (1)
pitfalls (1)
untranslated (1)

8865 שִׁיחוֹר *šiyhôr* (4)
Shihor (4)

8866 שִׁיחוֹר לִבְנָת *šiyhôr libnāt* (1)
Shihor Libnath (1)

8867 שִׁיט *šiyt*
Variant; not used

8868 שַׁיִט *šayit* (1)
oars (1)

8869 שִׁילֹה *šiylōh*
Variant; not used

8870 שִׁילוֹ *šiylô* (3)
Shiloh (3)

8871 שֵׁילָל *šēylāl*
Variant; not used

8872 שִׁילֹנִי *šiylōniy* (6)
Shilonite (4)
of Shiloh (1)
Shilonites (1)

8873 שִׁימוֹן *šiymôn* (1)
Shimon (1)

8874 שִׁין *šiyn* (6)
every last male (3) +928+7815
male (3) +928+7815

8875 שַׁיִן *šayin* (2)
urine (2)

8876 1שִׁיר *šiyr1* (87)
sing (33)
singers (27)
musicians (6)
sang (5)
womenˢ (5)
choirs (2)
be sung (1)
echo (1)
musician (1)
praised in song (1)
sang song (1)
singers (1) +1201
singing (1)
sings (1)
untranslated (1)

8877 2שִׁיר *šiyr2* (79)
song (47)
songs (11)
musical (6)
music (5)
singing (4)
instruments (1) +3998
sing (1)
singers (1)
songs (1) +1426
songs (1) +1821
untranslated (1)

8878 שִׁירָה *šiyrāh* (13)
song (11)
itˢ (1) +2021+2021+2296
songs (1)

8879 שִׁירָה *šᵉyārāh*
Variant; not used

8880 שַׁיִשׁ *šayiš* (1)
marble (1) +74

8881 שִׁישָׁא *šiyšā'* (1)
Shisha (1)

8882 שִׁישַׁק *šiyšaq* (7)
Shishak (7)

8883 1שִׁית *šiyt1* (86)
make (9)
put (9)
set (7)
made (6)
laid (3)
bring (2)
give (2)
granted (2)
is demanded (2)
lay (2)
place (2)
take (2)
turn (2)
alert (1)
applied (1)
apply (1)
appointed (1)
assign (1)
change (1)
close (1)
consider well (1) +4213
demands (1)
drawn up (1)
endowed (1)
establish (1)
gave a place (1)
halt (1)
harbors (1)
have (1)
help (1) +3338+6640
hold (1)
make turn (1)
makes (1)
pay (1)
perform (1)
placed (1)
placing (1)
posted (1) +8883
protect (1) +928+3829
set out (1)
strike (1)
take note (1) +4213
treat (1)
turned (1)
wrestle (1)
untranslated (3)

8884 2שִׁית *šiyt2* (2)
clothe (1) +6493
dressed (1)

8885 שַׁיִת *šayit* (7)
thorns (7)

8886 שָׁכַב *šākab* (211)
rested (36)
lie down (20)
lie (18)
lay down (13)
lying (10)
lay (8)
rest (8)
lies (7)
sleep (5)
sleeps with (5) +6640
slept with (5) +907
lie with (4) +6640
lying down (4)
lies down (3)
lies with (3) +907
sleeps with (3) +907
slept with (3) +6640
be laid (2)
come to bed with (2) +6640
has sexual relations with (2) +6640
laid (2)
lay with (2) +907

lay with (2) +6640
put (2)
sleep with (2) +6640
slept (2)
bed with (1) +6640
done this[s] (1) +6640
go (1)
go to bed with (1) +725
go to sleep (1)
gone to bed (1)
he[s] (1) +408+2021+2021+6640
laid low (1)
laid to rest (1)
lain down (1)
lay down to sleep (1)
lie around (1)
lie in state (1) +928+3883
lie with (1) +907
lies with (1) +907+8886
lies with (1) +6640
lying with (1) +907
made lie down (1)
raped (1) +2256+6700
rapes (1) +2256+2616+6640
rapes (1) +2256+6640+9530
resting (1)
sleeping (1)
sleeping with (1) +907+2446+8887
sleeping with (1) +6640
sleeps (1)
sleeps with (1) +907+2446+8887
stayed (1)
take rest (1)
taking rest (1) +5435
tip over (1)
violated (1) +2256+6700
untranslated (5)

8887 שִׁכְבָה *šikbāh* (9)
emission (4)
layer (1)
sleeping with (1) +907+2446+8886
sleeps with (1) +907+2446+8886
untranslated (2)

8888 שְׁכֹבֶת *š*kōbet* (4)
has sexual relations (1) +5989
have sexual relations (1) +2446+4200+5989
have sexual relations (1) +5989
sleeping with (1) +928+5989

8889 שָׁכָה *šākāh* (1)
well-fed (1)

8890 שְׁכוֹל *š*kôl* (3)
loss of children (2)
forlorn (1)

8891 שַׁכּוּל *šakkûl* (6)
alone (2)
robbed of cubs (2)
childless (1)
robbed (1)

8892 שְׁכוּלָה *š*kûlāh* (1)
bereaved (1)

8893 שִׁכּוֹר *šikkôr* (13)
drunkards (4)
drunk (3)
drunkard (2)
getting drunk (2) +9272
drunkard's (1)
drunken (1)
drunken men (1)

8894 שָׁכַח *šākah* (101)
forget (42)
forgotten (22)
forgot (11)
be forgotten (9)
ignore (4)
forgets (2)
ignored (2)
am forgotten (1) +4213+4946
ever forget (1) +8894

is forgotten (1)
made forget (1)
make forget (1)
neglect (1)
overlook (1)
unmindful (1)

8895 שָׁכֵחַ *šākēah* (2)
forget (2)

8896 שָׁכַךְ *šākak* (5)
subsided (2)
receded (1)
rid (1)
untranslated (1)

8897 שָׁכַל *šākal* (23)
miscarry (3)
bereaved (2)
deprive of children (2)
leave childless (2)
make childless (2)
bereave (1)
bereaves (1)
bring bereavement (1)
cast fruit (1)
childless (1)
deprived of children (1)
lose (1)
made childless (1)
make unproductive (1)
miscarried (1)
rob of children (1)
unproductive (1)

8898 שִׁכֻּלִים *šikkuliym* (1)
bereavement (1)

8899 שָׁכַם *šākam* (66)
early (18)
again and again (11)
got up early (5)
get up early (4)
got up (4)
early got up (3)
early in the morning (3)
rose (3)
rose early (3)
early the next morning (2)
again and again (1) +2256+8938
eager (1)
early arose (1)
early morning get up (1)
go early (1)
laid (1)
morning (1)
rise early (1)
untranslated (2)

8900 שְׁכֶם1 *š*kem1* (22)
shoulders (9)
shoulder (7)
head (2) +2025+2256+4946+5087
backs (1)
ridge of land (1)
shoulder to shoulder (1) +285
turned (1) +7155

8901 שְׁכֶם2 *š*kem2* (48)
Shechem (43)
there[s] (2)
its[s] (1)
they[s] (1) +1251+3972+4463
who[s] (1) +1251

8902 שְׁכֶם3 *š*kem3* (15)
Shechem (12)
Shechem's (3)

8903 שֶׁכֶם *šekem* (3)
Shechem (3)

8904 שִׁכְמִי *šikmiy* (1)
Shechemite (1)

8905 שָׁכַן *šākan* (131)
live (26)

dwell (21)
dwelling (8)
live in (6)
settled (5)
dwell in (4)
dwells (4)
nest (3)
stayed (3)
dwelt (2)
dwelt in (2)
have a home (2) +9393
let live (2)
lived in (2)
lives (2)
living (2)
remain (2)
rest (2)
set up (2)
settle (2)
abode (1)
allow to dwell (1)
among (1) +907
at rest (1)
came to rest (1)
camp (1)
come to dwell (1)
dwells in (1)
encamped (1)
find shelter (1)
inhabit (1)
inhabited (1)
let settle (1)
lie (1)
lie down to rest (1)
lived (1)
lives in (1)
made a dwelling (1)
make home (1)
make sleep (1)
nomads (1) +185+928
placed (1)
resides (1)
rests (1)
settled in (1)
stands (1)
stay (1)
stayed (1) +799
untranslated (1)

8906 שֵׁכֶן *šēken*
Variant; not used

8907 שָׁכֵן *šākēn* (21)
neighbors (11)
neighbor (3)
neighboring (2)
living (1)
neighboring peoples (1)
one living in (1)
people who live in (1)
untranslated (1)

8908 שְׁכַנְיָה *š*kanyāh* (9)
Shecaniah (8)
Shecaniah's (1)

8909 שְׁכַנְיָהוּ *š*kanyāhû* (2)
Shecaniah (2)

8910 שָׁכַר *šākar* (18)
drunk (6)
make drunk (4)
made drunk (3)
drank freely (1)
drink fill (1)
get drunk (1)
have fill (1)
keep on getting drunk (1)

8911 שֵׁכָר *šēkār* (23)
beer (11)
fermented drink (9)
drinks (2)
drunkards (1) +9272

8912 שָׁכֻר *šākur* (1)
made drunk (1)

8913 1שִׁכָּרוֹן *šikkārôn1* (3)
drunkenness (2)
drunk (1)

8914 2שִׁכָּרוֹן *šikkārôn2* (1)
Shikkeron (1)

8915 שָׁל *šal* (1)
irreverent act (1)

8916 שַׁלְאֲנַן *šal'ªnan* (1)
secure (1)

8917 שָׁלַב *šālab* (2)
set parallel (2)

8918 שָׁלָב *šālāb* (3)
uprights (3)

8919 שָׁלַג *šālag* (1)
snow fallen (1)

8920 1שֶׁלֶג *šeleg1* (19)
snow (16)
snowy (2)
snows (1)

8921 2שֶׁלֶג *šeleg2* (1)
soap (1)

8922 1שָׁלָה *šālāh1* (7)
at ease (1)
have peace (1)
live at ease (1)
negligent (1)
raise hopes (1)
secure (1)
undisturbed (1)

8923 2שָׁלָה *šālāh2* (1)
takes away (1)

8924 1שֵׁלָה *šēlāh1* (1)
what[s] (1)

8925 2שֵׁלָה *šēlāh2* (8)
Shelah (8)

8926 שִׁלֹה *šilōh* (22)
Shiloh (22)

8927 שַׁלְהֶבֶת *šalhebet* (2)
flame (2)

8928 שַׁלְהֶבְתְיָה *šalhebetyāh* (1)
mighty flame (1)

8929 שָׁלֵו *šālēw* (8)
at ease (2)
carefree (2)
prosperous (1)
quiet (1)
respite (1)
well (1)

8930 שָׁלוּ *šālû* (1)
felt secure (1)

8931 שִׁלוֹ *šilô* (7)
Shiloh (6)
there[s] (1) +928

8932 שַׁלְוָה *šalwāh* (8)
feel secure (3)
complacency (1)
felt secure (1)
peace and quiet (1)
security (1)
unconcerned (1) +9200

8933 שִׁלּוּחִים *šillûhiym* (3)
parting gifts (1)
sent away (1)
wedding gift (1)

8934 שָׁלוֹם *šālôm* (236)
peace (113)
all right (9)
safe (9)

safely (9) +928
come in peace (5)
prosperity (5)
greet (4) +4200+8626
greeted (4) +4200+8626
well (4)
how are (3)
success (3)
cordially (2)
good health (2)
in peace (2)
peaceful (2)
peacefully (2)
prosper (2)
treaty of friendship (2) +2256+3208
triumph (2)
all is well (1)
asked how they were (1) +4200+8626
benefit (1)
blessing (1)
close friend (1) +408
completely (1)
contentment (1)
desires (1)
friendly relations (1)
friends (1)
friends (1) +408
friends (1) +632
good (1)
goodwill (1)
greet (1)
grow well (1)
harmony (1) +6783
how is (1)
how was (1)
how was (1) +4200
how was going (1) +4200
how were (1) +4200
kind (1)
order (1)
peace and prosperity (1)
peaceably (1)
peaceably (1) +928
peaceful relations (1)
peacefully (1) +928
peacetime (1)
perfect peace (1) +8934
prospers (1)
safely (1) +2021+4200
safely (1) +4200
satisfied (1) +928
secure (1)
sound (1)
soundness (1)
trusted friends (1) +408
unharmed (1)
unharmed (1) +928
unscathed (1)
unscathed (1) +928
welcome (1)
welfare (1)
well-being (1)
wish well (1) +4200
yes[s] (1)
untranslated (3)

8935 שַׁלּוּם *šallûm* (26)
Shallum (25)
Shallum's (1)

8936 שִׁלּוּם *šillûm* (4)
retribution (2)
bribes (1)
reckoning (1)

8937 שַׁלּוּן *šallûn* (1)
Shallun (1)

8938 שָׁלַח *šālah* (847)
sent (310)
send (113)
let go (55)
sent away (22)

sending (20)
sent out (17)
lay (11)
sent word (11)
reached out (10)
sends (10)
send away (9)
stretched out (7)
send on way (5)
sent for (5) +2256+4200+7924
sent on way (5)
set free (5)
called together (4) +665+2256
lift (4)
release (4)
send word (4)
sent off (4)
set (4)
stretch out (4)
divorce (3)
reach out (3)
sent back (3)
sent for (3)
sent for (3) +2256+7924
shoot (3)
stirs up (3)
assassinate (2) +928+3338
been sent (2)
dismissed (2)
divorced (2)
drive out (2)
extend (2)
free (2)
free (2) +2930
gave orders (2)
gave over (2)
pursue (2) +339
raise (2)
reached (2)
reached down (2)
replied (2) +606
send back (2)
send for (2) +2256+4374
send forth (2)
send out (2)
sent message (2)
shot (2)
summoned (2) +2256+7924
thrust (2)
unleashed (2)
was sent (2)
abandoned (1)
again and again (1) +2256+8899
appealed (1)
assaults (1) +928
assigned (1)
attack (1) +928+3338
attacked (1) +928+3338
attacks (1) +928+3338
banished (1)
be sent (1)
be sure to let go (1) +8938
being sent (1)
brought (1)
burned (1) +836+928+2021
calling together (1) +995+2256
cast (1)
checked on (1) +448
come back (1)
delivered (1)
demanded (1)
directed (1)
dispatched (1)
divorces (1)
do let go (1) +8938
does[s] (1)
ended (1)
exile (1)
extends (1)
force (1)
freed (1) +2930

gave (1)
gave away in marriage (1)
get out of here (1) +2021+2025+2575
give an order (1)
had brought (1) +2256+4374
had removed (1) +2256+4374
holds (1)
invite (1) +2256+7924
killing (1) +928+3338
laid (1)
lay snares (1)
lays (1)
leave (1)
left to himself (1)
let down (1)
let get away (1)
let get away (1) +928+2006
let grow (1)
let loose (1)
lets loose (1)
lets stray (1)
letting go (1)
letting range free (1) +8079
lowered (1)
made flourish (1)
makes pour (1)
mission (1) +889+1821
ordered (1)
pointing (1)
provided (1)
pushed (1)
put (1)
put out (1)
putting (1)
reach down (1)
reached out (1) +3338
reaches out (1) +3338
reaching (1) +3338
reject (1) +4946+6584+7156
released (1)
releases (1)
remove (1)
return (1)
rushing (1)
see on way (1)
seize (1)
send a message (1)
send for (1)
send urgent (1) +8938
sending away (1)
sends out (1)
sent a message (1)
sent for (1) +2256+4374
sent for (1) +4200+7924
sent for help (1)
sent forth (1)
sent messengers (1)
sent on way (1) +906
sent word (1) +2256+5583
sent word (1) +2256+7924
set fire to (1) +836+928+2021
set free (1) +2930
set free (1) +3338+4946
shooting (1)
spared (1)
specify (1)
spreading (1)
summon (1)
summon (1) +2256+4374
summoned (1)
summoned (1) +4200+7924
swing (1)
throw off (1)
told (1) +606+4200
took back (1) +995+2256
turned (1)
unleash (1)
use (1)
use to do (1)
vent (1)
was sent away (1)

were sent (1)
were sent on way (1)
untranslated (17)

8939 1חלַשֶׁ *šelah1* (7)
weapon (3)
sword (2)
defenses (1)
weapons (1)

8940 2חלַשֶׁ *šelah2* (1)
Siloam (1)

8941 3חלַשֶׁ *šelah3* (9)
Shelah (9)

8942 חַלֹשִׁ *šilōah* (1)
Shiloah (1)

8943 תוֹחלְֻשׁ *šᵉluhōt* (1)
shoots (1)

8944 יחְלַשׁ *šilhiy* (2)
Shilhi (2)

8945 םיחִלָֻשׁ *šᵉlāhiym* (1)
plants (1)

8946 םיחִלְשׁ *šilhiym* (1)
Shilhim (1)

8947 ןחָלֻשׁ *šulhān* (71)
table (52)
tables (12)
each table (1) +2256+8947
itˢ (1) +2021
untranslated (4)

8948 טלַשׁ *šālat* (8)
enable (1)
enables (1)
got the upper hand (1)
have control (1)
let rule (1)
lorded it over (1)
lords it over (1)
overpower (1)

8949 טלֶשֶׁ *šelet* (7)
shields (6)
small shields (1)

8950 ןֹטלְשׁ *šiltôn* (2)
power (1)
supreme (1)

8951 תטֶלֶֹשׁ *šalletet* (1)
brazen (1)

8952 ילְשׁ *šᵉliy* (1)
privately (1) +928+2021

8953 היָלְשׁ *šilyāh* (1)
afterbirth (1)

8954 טילִשַׁ *šalliyt* (4)
governor (1)
power (1)
ruler (1)
rulers (1)

8955 1שׁילִשׁ *šāliyš1* (2)
basket (1)
bowlful (1)

8956 2שׁילִשׁ *šāliyš2* (1)
lutes (1)

8957 3שׁילִשׁ *šāliyš3* (16)
officers (5)
officer (3)
captains (2)
chariot officers (2)
chariot officer (1)
chief officers (1)
untranslated (2)

8958 ישִׁילִשׁ *šᵉliyšiy* (105)
third (93)
three (7)
day after (1)

day after tomorrow (1)
one-third (1)
thatˢ (1)
upper (1)

8959 ךלַשׁ *šālak* (125)
threw (26)
throw (14)
cast (8)
thrust (7)
thrown (6)
put (5)
throw away (3)
throw down (3)
thrown down (3)
get rid of (2)
hurled (2)
hurled down (2)
threw down (2)
thrown away (2)
thrown out (2)
throws (2)
toss (2)
are cast (1)
banish (1)
be thrown (1)
be thrown out (1)
cast away (1)
cast out (1)
didˢ (1)
divide (1)
dropped (1)
dropping (1)
flung (1)
hurl (1)
hurls (1)
hurls down (1)
in ruins (1)
knocked (1)
pelt (1)
pushed back (1)
pushed down (1)
reject (1) +4946+6584+7156
rid (1) +4946+6584
risked (1) +4946+5584
scatter (1)
scattered (1)
set down (1)
shedding (1)
snatched (1)
sprinkle (1)
threw away (1)
threw out (1)
throw off (1)
thrown aside (1)
was brought low (1)
were thrown out (1)

8960 ךלָשׁ *šālāk* (2)
cormorant (2)

8961 1תכֶלֶּשַׁ *šalleket1* (1)
cut down (1)

8962 2תכֶלֶּשַׁ *šalleket2* (1)
Shalleketh (1)

8963 1ללַשׁ *šālal1* (2)
pull out (1) +8963

8964 2ללַשׁ *šālal2* (14)
plunder (4)
plundered (4)
plunder (2) +8965
seize (2)
becomes prey (1)
loot (1) +8965

8965 ללָשׁ *šālāl* (74)
plunder (49)
escape with (4) +4200
spoils (4)
loot (3)
plunder (2) +8964

booty (1)
goods (1)
loot (1) +8964
plundered (1)
prey (1)
property (1)
share of plunder (1)
spoil (1)
value (1)
which[s] (1) +2021
untranslated (2)

8966 שָׁלֵם1 *šālēm1* (117)
repay (18)
fulfill (12)
pay (9)
make restitution (6)
pay back (6)
reward (6)
at peace (4)
finished (3)
made peace (3)
repays (3)
made a treaty of peace (2)
made an end (2)
must make restitution (2) +8966
repaying (2)
restore (2)
accomplish (1)
be fulfilled (1)
be repaid (1)
bring punishment (1)
carries out (1)
committed (1)
completed (1)
end (1)
fulfilled (1)
fulfilled obligations (1)
fulfilling (1)
fulfills (1)
is rewarded (1)
keep (1)
make good (1)
make pay (1)
make peace (1)
makes live at peace (1)
must certainly make restitution (1) +8966
must pay (1) +8966
offer (1)
paid back (1)
pay back in full (1)
pay for the loss (1)
pays back (1)
peaceful (1)
present (1)
receive due (1)
repaid (1)
repay in full (1) +8966
restitution (1)
returns (1)
unscathed (1)

8967 שְׁלָם *šᵉlām*
Variant; not used

8968 שֶׁלֶם *šelem* (87)
fellowship (34)
fellowship offerings (32)
fellowship offering (20)
it[s] (1) +2285

8969 שָׁלֵם2 *šālēm2* (27)
fully committed (4)
accurate (2)
fully devoted (2)
whole (2)
wholehearted devotion (2) +4213
wholehearted devotion (2) +4222
wholeheartedly (2) +928+4222
allies (1)
dressed (1)
fieldstones (1) +74
friendly (1)

full measure (1)
fully determined (1) +928+4222
richly (1)
safely (1)
uncut (1)
wholeheartedly (1) +928+4213
untranslated (1)

8970 שָׁלֵם3 *šālēm3* (2)
Salem (2)

8971 שָׁלֵם4 *šālēm4*
Variant; not used

8972 שִׁלֵּם1 *šillēm1*
Variant; not used

8973 שִׁלֵּם2 *šillēm2* (3)
Shillem (3)

8974 שִׁלֻּמָה *šillumāh* (1)
punishment (1)

8975 שַׁלָּמָה *šallāmāh*
Variant; not used

8976 שְׁלֹמֹה *šᵉlōmōh* (293)
Solomon (235)
Solomon's (26)
he[s] (12)
Solomon's (7) +4200
him[s] (6)
his[s] (2)
his[s] (2) +4200
Solomon's (1) +4200+8611
untranslated (2)

8977 שְׁלֹמוֹת *šᵉlōmôt* (4)
Shelomoth (3)
untranslated (1)

8978 שַׁלְמַי *šalmay* (2)
Shalmai (2)

8979 שְׁלֹמִי *šᵉlōmiy* (1)
Shelomi (1)

8980 שִׁלֵּמִי *šillēmiy* (1)
Shillemite (1)

8981 שְׁלֻמִיאֵל *šᵉlumiy'ēl* (5)
Shelumiel (5)

8982 שֶׁלֶמְיָה *šelemyāh* (5)
Shelemiah (5)

8983 שֶׁלֶמְיָהוּ *šelemyāhû* (5)
Shelemiah (5)

8984 שְׁלֹמִית1 *šᵉlōmiyt1* (7)
Shelomith (6)
untranslated (1)

8985 שְׁלֹמִית2 *šᵉlōmiyt2* (2)
Shelomith (2)

8986 שַׁלְמַן *šalman* (1)
Shalman (1)

8987 שַׁלְמַנְאֶסֶר *šalman'eser* (2)
Shalmaneser (2)

8988 שַׁלְמֹנִים *šalmōniym* (1)
gifts (1)

8989 שֵׁלָנִי *šēlāniy* (2)
of Shelah (1)
Shelanite (1)

8990 שָׁלַף *šālap* (25)
swordsmen (5) +408+2995
draw (4)
drawn (4)
armed (3)
handle (2)
drew (1)
grow (1)
pull out (1)
pulls (1)
removed (1)
took off (1)
untranslated (1)

8991 שֶׁלֶף *šelep* (2)
Sheleph (2)

8992 שָׁלַשׁ *šālaš* (10)
did the third time (1)
divide into three (1)
do a third time (1)
day after tomorrow (1)
third (1)
three (1)
three years old (1)
three-year-old (1)
untranslated (2)

8993 שָׁלֹשׁ *šālōš* (601)
three (282)
thirty (83)
third (12)
thirteen (10) +6926
thirteenth (8) +6925
three-tenths (8) +6928
twenty-third (7) +2256+6929
thirty-three (6) +2256+8993
thirty-two (6) +2256+9109
twenty-three (6) +2256+6929
30 (5)
three-day (4) +3427
32 (3) +2256+9109
36,000 (3) +547+2256+9252
430 (3) +752+2256+4395
53,400 (3)
          +547+752+2256+2256+2822+4395
603,550 (3)   +547+547+2256+2256+2256
                +2822+2822+4395+4395+9252
thirteenth (3) +6926
thirty-five (3) +2256+2822
thirty-ninth (3) +2256+9596
thirty-one (3) +285+2256
thirty-seventh (3) +2256+8679
123 (2) +2256+4395+6929
130 (2) +2256+4395
137 (2) +2256+2256+4395+8679
223 (2) +2256+4395+6929
30,500 (2) +547+2256+2822+4395
300 (2) +4395
32,200 (2) +547+2256+2256+4395+9109
320 (2) +2256+4395+6929
345 (2) +752+2256+2822+4395
35,400 (2)
          +547+752+2256+2256+2822+4395
372 (2) +2256+4395+8679+9109
390 (2) +2256+4395+9596
392 (2) +2256+4395+9109+9596
403 (2) +752+2256+4395
435 (2) +752+2256+2822+4395
59,300 (2)
          +547+2256+2256+2822+4395+9596
7,337 (2)
          +547+2256+4395+8679+8679+8993
973 (2) +2256+4395+8679+9596
them[s] (2) +2021
thirteen (2) +6925
thirty-eight (2) +2256+9046
thirty-eighth (2) +2256+9046
thirty-second (2) +2256+9109
thirty-seven (2) +2256+8679
1,335 (1) +547+2256+2822+4395+8993
1,365 (1)   +547+2256+2256
                    +2256+2822+4395+9252
13 (1) +6925
133 (1) +2256+2256+4395+8993
138 (1) +2256+4395+9046
139 (1) +2256+4395+9596
153,600 (1)   +547+547+2256+2256
                    +2822+2256+4395+4395+9252
2,300 (1) +547+2256+4395
2,322 (1) +547+2256+4395+6929+9109
2,630 (1) +547+2256+2256+4395+9252
22,034 (1)   +547+752+2256+2256
                    +2256+6929+9109
22,273 (1)   +547+2256+2256+2256
                    +4395+6929+8679+9109

23,000 (1) +547+2256+6929
232 (1) +2256+4395+9109
273 (1) +2256+2256+4395+8679
3,000 (1) +547
3,023 (1) +547+2256+2256+6929+8993
3,200 (1) +547+2256+4395
3,600 (1) +547+2256+4395+9252
3,630 (1)
          +547+2256+2256+4395+8993+9252
3,700 (1) +547+2256+4395+8679
3,930 (1) +547+2256+4395+8993+9596
300,000 (1) +547+4395
307,500 (1)   +547+547+2256+2256
                    +2822+4395+4395+8679
318 (1) +2256+4395+6925+9046
32,000 (1) +547+2256+9109
32,500 (1)
          +547+2256+2256+2822+4395+9109
323 (1) +2256+4395+6929+8993
324 (1) +752+2256+4395+6929
328 (1) +2256+4395+6929+9046
337,500 (1)   +547+547+547+2256+2256
               +2256+2822+4395+4395+8679+8993
337,500 (1)   +547+547+547+2256
               +2256+2822+4395+4395+8679+8993
34 (1) +752+2256
35 (1) +2256+2822
350 (1) +2256+2822+4395
365 (1) +2256+2256+2822+4395+9252
37,000 (1) +547+2256+8679
42,360 (1)
          +547+752+2256+4395+8052+9252
42,360 (1) +547+752+4395+8052+9252
43,730 (1)   +547+752+2256
               +2256+2256+4395+8679+8993
45 feet (1) +564
450 feet (1) +564+4395
530 (1) +2256+2822+4395
601,730 (1)   +547+547+2256+2256
               +4395+4395+8679+9252
623 (1) +2256+4395+6929+9252
64,300 (1)
          +547+752+2256+2256+4395+9252
730 (1) +2256+4395+8679
736 (1) +2256+4395+8679+9252
743 (1) +752+2256+2256+4395+8679
743 (1) +752+2256+4395+8679
830 (1) +2256+4395+9046
832 (1) +2256+4395+9046+9109
930 (1) +2256+4395+9596
eighty-three (1) +2256+9046
four and a half feet (1) +564
peoples (1) +9109
thirtieth (1)
thirty-fifth (1) +2256+2822
thirty-first (1) +285+2256
thirty-six (1) +2256+9252
thirty-six hundred (1)
               +547+2256+4395+9252
thirty-sixth (1) +2256+9252
thirty-three hundred (1)
               +547+2256+4395+8993
this times (1) +9102
three-pronged (1) +9094
untranslated (9)

8994 שֶׁלֶשׁ šēleš (1)
Shelesh (1)

8995 שְׁלִשָׁה šālišāh (1)
Shalisha (1)

8996 שִׁלְשָׁה šilšāh (1)
Shilshah (1)

8997 שִׁלְשׁוֹם šilšôm (25)
before (6) +9453
malice aforethought (4) +4946+8533+9453
before (2) +919
had the habit (2) +4946+9453
as usual (1) +3869+9453
before (1) +4946+9453
for some time (1) +1685+1685+9453

formerly (1) +919+4946
had been (1) +9453
in the past (1) +919+1685+1685
in the past (1) +9453
past (1) +9453
previously (1) +919+3869
untranslated (2)

8998 שְׁלִשִׁי šālišiy (2)
three (2)

8999 שְׁלִשִׁיָּה šᵉlišiyyāh
Variant; not used

9000 שִׁלֵּשִׁים šillēšiym (5)
third (4)
third generation (1)

9001 שְׁלֹשִׁים šᵉlōšiym
Variant; not used

9002 שִׁלְתָּה šiltāh
Variant; not used

9003 שְׁלַתִּיאֵל šaltiy'ēl (3)
Shealtiel (3)

9004 שָׁם šām (836)
there (400)
where (101)
there (58) +2025
whichs (18)
its (17)
where (16) +2025
here (9)
in whichs (5)
in its (4)
the Jordans (4) +2025
back (3) +4946
in its (3) +2025
out (3) +4946
away (2) +4946
behind (2)
in (2)
in Zions (2)
its (2) +2025
that places (2)
thems (2)
where (2) +4946
wherever (2) +2025
whoms (2)
among whichs (1)
at Pas Dammims (1)
back (1)
backs (1) +2025
because of (1) +4946
beside (1)
Gaths (1)
Hebrons (1)
in such placess (1)
in that places (1)
in thems (1)
insides (1) +2025
into its (1)
invade (1) +995+2025
leave (1) +4946
nearby (1)
place (1)
proper place (1) +889+2118+5226
right there (1)
Samarias (1)
see (1)
that lands (1)
the chests (1)
the citys (1)
the lands (1) +2025
the norths (1)
thems (1)
there (1) +4946
to (1) +2025
whats (1)
when (1)
wherever (1)
wherever (1) +889+2025
wherever (1) +889+3972

untranslated (141)

9005 1שֵׁם šēm1 (864)
name (563)
names (62)
named (55) +7924
named (44)
called (27) +7924
called (10)
fame (10)
name's (7)
call (6) +7924
renown (6)
famous (5)
name (4) +7924
honor (3)
named (3) +8492
be called (2) +7924
chosen (2) +928+7924
famous (2) +7924
after (1) +928
after (1) +3869
be known as (1) +7924
be named (1) +7924
became famous (1) +6913
been named (1) +7924
byword (1)
calling (1) +7924
famous (1) +408
giving credit to (1) +928
himself (1) +2257
infamous (1) +2021+3238
is called (1) +7924
its (1) +2257
memorable (1)
named (1) +928+7924
nameless (1) +1172
perpetuate memory (1) +2349
record (1) +4180
renowned (1) +4200
thats (1)
to each man (1) +928
was called (1) +7924
well-known (1) +408
word (1)
untranslated (28)

9006 2שֵׁם šēm2 (17)
Shem (17)

9007 שַׁמָּא šammā' (2)
Shamma (1)
Shammah (1)

9008 שְׁמְאֵבֶר šem'ēber (1)
Shemeber (1)

9009 שִׁמְאָה šim'āh (1)
Shimeah (1)

9010 שִׁמְאָם šim'ām (1)
Shimeam (1)

9011 שַׁמְגַּר šamgar (2)
Shamgar (2)

9012 שָׁמַד šāmad (90)
destroy (31)
destroyed (24)
be destroyed (6)
are destroyed (5)
destruction (3)
demolish (2)
wipe out (2)
annihilate (1)
annihilation (1)
be overthrown (1)
been decimated (1)
been destroyed (1)
brought to ruin (1)
certainly be destroyed (1) +9012
completely destroyed (1)
crushed (1)
cut off (1)
exterminating (1)

get rid of (1)
perished (1)
shatter (1)
totally destroy (1) +9012

9013 שֶׁמֶד *šemed* (1)
Shemed (1)

9014 1שַׁמָּה *šammāh1* (40)
desolate (7)
waste (7)
horror (6)
object of horror (5)
ruin (4)
laid waste (3)
desolation (1)
desolations (1)
destroyed (1)
devastate (1)
horrible (1)
in ruins (1)
thing of horror (1)
wasteland (1)

9015 2שַׁמָּה *šammāh2* (7)
Shammah (7)

9016 שַׂמְהוּת *šamhût* (1)
Shamhuth (1)

9017 שְׁמוּאֵל *šᵉmû'ēl* (141)
Samuel (127)
heˢ (5)
Samuel's (4)
himˢ (2)
Shemuel (1)
untranslated (2)

9018 שַׁמּוּעַ *šammûa'* (5)
Shammua (5)

9019 שְׁמוּעָה *šᵉmû'āh* (27)
news (8)
report (7)
message (5)
rumor (3)
anotherˢ (1) +2021
mention (1) +928+7023
reports (1)
rumors (1)

9020 שָׁמוּר *šāmûr* (1)
untranslated (1)

9021 שַׁמּוֹת *šammôt* (1)
Shammoth (1)

9022 שָׂמַח *šāmah*
Variant; not used

9023 שָׁמַט *šāmat* (10)
stumbled (2)
be thrown down (1)
cancel (1)
cancel debt (1)
lie unplowed (1)
lose (1)
threw down (1)
throw down (1)
untranslated (1)

9024 שְׁמִטָּה *šᵉmittāh* (5)
canceling debts (2)
cancel debts (1) +6913
itˢ (1) +2021
time for canceling debts (1)

9025 שַׁמַּי *šammay* (6)
Shammai (5)
Shammai's (1)

9026 שְׁמִידָע *šᵉmiydā'* (3)
Shemida (3)

9027 שְׁמִידָעִי *šᵉmiydā'iy* (1)
Shemidaite (1)

9028 שָׁמַיִם *šāmayim* (416)
heaven (154)

heavens (141)
sky (46)
air (40)
starry (9)
highest heavens (6) +9028
skies (6)
heavenly (2)
astrologers (1) +2042
heaven's (1)
highest heaven (1) +9028
horizon (1)
in midair (1)
                    +824+1068+1068+2021+2021+2256
otherˢ (1) +7895
skies above (1) +9028
untranslated (2)

9029 שְׁמִינִי *šᵉmiyniy* (28)
eighth (27)
followingˢ (1)

9030 שְׁמִינִית *šᵉmiyniyt* (3)
sheminith (3)

9031 1שָׁמִיר *šāmiyr1* (8)
briers (8)

9032 2שָׁמִיר *šāmiyr2* (3)
as hard as flint (1)
flint (1)
hardest stone (1)

9033 3שָׁמִיר *šāmiyr3* (1)
Shamir (1)

9034 4שָׁמִיר *šāmiyr4* (3)
Shamir (3)

9035 שְׁמִירָמוֹת *šᵉmiyrāmôt* (5)
Shemiramoth (4)
untranslated (1)

9036 שַׁמְלַי *šamlay* (1)
untranslated (1)

9037 1שָׁמֵם *šāmēm1* (94)
appalled (19)
desolate (15)
causes desolation (4)
deserted (4)
devastated (4)
lay waste (4)
lies desolate (4)
completely destroy (2)
demolished (2)
destitute (2)
destroyed (2)
horrified (2)
ruin (2)
was laid waste (2)
are appalled (1)
are demolished (1)
astonished (1)
be demolished (1)
be destroyed (1)
be laid waste (1)
brought devastation (1)
cause to be appalled (1)
desolation (1)
desolations (1)
destroy yourself (1)
dismayed (1)
fill with horror (1)
himˢ (1)
in ruins (1)
laid waste (1)
made desolate (1)
overwhelmed (1)
ravaged (1)
ruined (1)
strip (1)
stripped (1)
was left so desolate (1)
were terrified (1)
without help (1)
untranslated (1)

9038 2שָׁמֵם *šāmēm2* (2)
desolate (2)

9039 שְׁמָמָה *šᵉmāmāh* (56)
desolate (30)
waste (5)
desolation (3)
ruins (3)
wasteland (3)
desolate place (2)
laid waste (2)
barren (1)
demolished (1)
desolate waste (1)
despair (1)
destroy (1) +8492
ravaged (1)
ruined (1)
utterly desolate (1)

9040 שִׁמְמָה *šimmāh* (1)
desolate (1)

9041 שִׁמָּמוֹן *šimmāmôn* (2)
despair (2)

9042 1שָׁמֵן *šāmēn1* (5)
fat (1)
filled with food (1)
grew fat (1)
make calloused (1)
well-nourished (1)

9043 שֶׁמֶן *šemen* (193)
oil (155)
olive oil (13)
olive (4)
perfume (3)
fertile (2)
best (1)
cosmetic lotions (1)
fat (1)
fertile (1) +1201
fine perfume (1)
gaunt (1) +4946
itˢ (1) +2021
lotions (1)
oils (1)
ointments (1)
olive (1) +6770
perfume (1) +8379
perfumes (1)
rich food (1)
wild olive (1)
untranslated (1)

9044 שָׁמָן *šāmān* (2)
richness (2)

9045 2שָׁמֵן *šāmēn2* (10)
fertile (3)
rich (3)
luxury (1)
plentiful (1)
sleek (1)
vigorous (1)

9046 שְׁמֹנֶה *šᵉmōneh* (147)
eight (29)
eighty (16)
eighteenth (9) +6926
eighteen (7) +6926
128 (4) +2256+4395+6929
eighteen (4) +6925
eighty-five (4) +2256+2822
twenty-eight (4) +2256+6929
eighth (3)
18 (2) +6925
18,000 (2) +547+6925
80 (2)
800 (2) +4395
98 (2) +2256+9596
eighteenth (2) +6925
forty-eight (2) +752+2256
thirty-eight (2) +2256+8993

thirty-eighth (2) +2256+8993
108,100 (1)
　　　+547+547+2256+2256+4395+4395
138 (1) +2256+4395+8993
148 (1) +752+2256+4395
180 (1) +2256+4395
180,000 (1) +547+2256+4395
182 (1) +2256+2256+4395+9109
186,400 (1)　　　+547+547+547+752+2256
　　　　　+2256+2256+4395+4395+9252
187 (1) +2256+2256+4395+8679
188 (1) +2256+4395+9046
2,812 (1) +547+2256+4395+6925+9109
2,818 (1) +547+2256+4395+6925+9046
20,800 (1) +547+2256+4395+6929
218 (1) +2256+4395+6925
28 (1) +2256+6929
28,600 (1)
　　　+547+2256+2256+4395+6929+9252
280,000 (1) +547+2256+4395
284 (1) +752+2256+4395
288 (1) +2256+4395+9046
318 (1) +2256+4395+6925+8993
328 (1) +2256+4395+6929+8993
468 (1) +752+2256+4395+9252
6,800 (1) +547+2256+4395+9252
628 (1) +2256+4395+6929+9252
648 (1) +752+2256+4395+9252
782 (1) +2256+2256+4395+8679+9109
8,580 (1)
　　　+547+2256+2256+2822+4395+9046
8,600 (1) +547+2256+4395+9252
80,000 (1) +547
807 (1) +2256+4395+8679
815 (1) +2256+2822+4395+6926
822 (1) +2256+4395+6929+9109
830 (1) +2256+4395+8993
832 (1) +2256+4395+8993+9109
840 (1) +752+2256+4395
845 (1) +752+2256+2822+4395
87,000 (1) +547+2256+8679
895 (1) +2256+2256+2822+4395+9596
928 (1) +2256+4395+6929+9596
eighteen thousand (1) +547+2256+8052
eightieth (1)
eighty-six (1) +2256+9252
eighty-three (1) +2256+8993
ninety-eight (1) +2256+9596
sixty-eight (1) +2256+9252
twenty-seven feet (1) +564+6926

9047 שְׁמֹנִים *š°mōnîym*
Variant; not used

9048 שָׁמַע *šāma'* (1161)
heard (293)
hear (238)
listen (225)
listened (40)
obey (36) +928+7754
hears (27)
obey (19)
obeyed (18) +928+7754
proclaim (15)
obeyed (13)
agreed (9)
be heard (9)
hearing (8)
listening (8)
understand (8)
is heard (6)
listen carefully (4) +9048
listens (4)
paid attention (4)
was heard (4)
do (3)
heed (3)
let hear (3)
pay attention (3)
proclaimed (3)
resound (3)
sound (3)

agree (2)
are heard (2)
declare (2)
discerning (2)
disobeyed (2) +928+4202+7754
disobeyed (2) +4202
foretold (2)
fully obey (2) +928+7754+9048
give (2)
heard (2) +7754
mark my words (2)
obedient (2)
obeying (2)
proclaiming (2)
raise (2)
received a report (2)
sang (2)
summon (2)
administering (1)
agreed with (1) +4200+7754
announce (1)
announced (1)
are heeded (1)
argue (1) +7754
be heeded (1)
been brought to attention (1) +2256+5583
been heard (1)
been heard of (1)
been proclaimed (1)
been^s (1)
boast (1)
bring word (1)
called up (1)
careful to obey (1) +9048
cause to hear (1)
caused to hear (1)
certainly hear (1) +9048
complied (1)
comply (1)
cry out (1)
cry out (1) +2411
deaf (1) +4946
did (1)
diligently obey (1) +928+7754+9048
disobedience (1) +928+4202+7754
disobey (1) +928+1194+7754
disobey (1) +4202
ever hearing (1) +9048
expect to be heard (1)
faithfully obey (1) +9048
find out (1)
fully obeyed (1) +2256+6913
gave in (1) +928+7754
get back to (1)
have^s (1)
heard (1) +9051
heard definitely (1) +9048
hears (1) +7754
hears (1) +7754+9048
hears (1) +9048
heeds (1)
is proclaimed (1)
is reported (1)
issued an order (1)
learn (1)
let be heard (1)
listen (1) +7754
listen carefully (1) +265+928
listen carefully (1) +928+7754
listen closely (1) +265+928
listen in (1)
listened to (1)
listens (1) +265
made hear (1)
made known (1)
made proclamation (1)
make hear (1)
make heard (1)
obedience (1)
obey (1) +4200+7754
obey fully (1) +928+7754+9048

obeying (1) +928+7754
obeys (1)
obeys (1) +928+7754
obscure (1) +4946+6680
overheard (1)
paid any attention (1) +265+4200+5742
pay close attention (1) +2256+7992
playing (1)
plots (1)
proclaims (1)
pronounced (1)
put under oath (1) +460
reached (1)
reached (1) +928
received (1)
received message (1)
refused (1) +4202
resounds (1)
sing songs (1) +928+4200+7754+8123
sound be heard (1)
sounding (1)
stopped up (1) +3877+4946
summoned (1)
surely heard (1) +9048
tell (1)
told (1)
told (1) +907+4946
was overheard (1)
were heard (1)
witness (1) +1068
word came (1)
untranslated (10)

9049 שֶׁמַע 1 *šema'1* (1)
clash (1)

9050 שֶׁמַע 2 *šema'2* (5)
Shema (5)

9051 שֵׁמַע *šēma'* (17)
fame (4)
report (3)
reports (3)
hear (2)
news (2)
heard (1) +9048
rumor (1)
word (1)

9052 שָׁמָע *šāmā'* (1)
Shama (1)

9053 שֹׁמַע *šōma'* (4)
reports (2)
fame (1)
reputation (1)

9054 שְׁמַע *š°ma'* (1)
Shema (1)

9055 שִׁמְעָא *šim'ā'* (5)
Shimea (4)
Shammua (1)

9056 שִׁמְעָה *šim'āh* (3)
Shimeah (3)

9057 שְׁמָעָה *š°mā'āh* (1)
Shemaah (1)

9058 שִׁמְעוֹן *šim'ôn* (44)
Simeon (30)
Simeon (5) +1201
Simeonites (4) +1201
Simeonites (3)
Shimeon (1)
untranslated (1)

9059 שִׁמְעִי 1 *šim'iy1* (45)
Shimei (42)
he^s (1)
Shimei's (1) +4200
untranslated (1)

9060 שִׁמְעִי 2 *šim'iy2* (2)
Shimei (1)
Shimeites (1)

9061 שְׁמַעְיָה *š^ema'yāh* (34)
Shemaiah (32)
his^s (1)
Shemaiah's (1)

9062 שְׁמַעְיָהוּ *š^ema'yāhû* (7)
Shemaiah (7)

9063 שִׁמְעֹנִי *šim'ōniy* (4)
Simeon (1)
Simeonite (1)
Simeonites (1)

9064 שִׁמְעָת *šim'āt* (2)
Shimeath (2)

9065 שִׁמְעָתִי *šim'ātiy* (1)
Shimeathites (1)

9066 שֶׁמֶץ *šēmes* (2)
faint (1)
whisper (1)

9067 שִׁמְצָה *šimsāh* (1)
laughingstock (1)

9068 שָׁמַר *šāmar* (469)
keep (83)
careful (46)
obey (21)
observe (20)
kept (19)
carefully (16)
guard (16)
keeps (9)
watch (9)
watchmen (8)
keeping (7)
guards (6)
watches over (6)
doorkeepers (5) +6197
in charge (5)
keeper (5)
maintain (5)
obeyed (5)
protect (5)
take care of (5)
watch over (5)
celebrate (4)
responsible (4)
be sure (3)
care (3)
do (3)
guarded (3)
guarding (3)
heeds (3)
observed (3)
on guard (3)
protects (3)
watched over (3)
watchman (3)
be careful (2)
beware (2)
carried out (2)
carrying out (2)
cling (2)
faithful (2)
follow (2)
followed (2)
guard yourself (2)
guarding (2) +5466
have charge of (2) +5466
keep safe (2)
kept myself (2)
make sure (2)
obeys (2)
perform (2)
protected (2)
safekeeping (2)
see (2)
serve (2)
waiting (2)
watches (2)
watching (2)
watching over (2)

assures (1)
be protected (1)
be sure to keep (1) +9068
beware (1) +440
bodyguard (1) +4200+8031
cared for (1)
careful (1) +9068
careful to do (1)
carefully observe (1) +9068
cherishes (1)
consider (1)
continue (1)
continued (1)
defending (1)
did^s (1)
done (1)
doorkeeper (1) +6197
eyed (1)
faithfully carried out (1)
flamed unchecked (1) +5905
give (1)
guard (1) +5466
guarded (1) +5464
had charge of (1)
have charge of (1)
heed (1)
hoarded (1)
keep away (1)
keep close watch on (1)
keep penned up (1)
keep track of (1)
keepers (1)
keeps close watch (1)
kept a record (1)
kept in mind (1)
kept penned up (1)
kept themselves (1)
kept watch (1)
living (1)
looks after (1)
loyal (1) +5466
must (1)
obey (1) +2256+6913
obeying (1)
observing (1)
on duty (1)
on duty at (1)
paid attention (1)
pay attention (1)
performed (1)
performing (1)
preserve (1)
preserved (1)
put (1)
regardless (1) +401+4200
remains (1)
responsible (1) +5466
responsible for (1)
secured (1)
see to it (1)
shepherd (1)
spare (1)
spies (1)
take care (1)
tended sheep (1)
under siege (1)
wait to kill (1) +5883
was set aside (1)
watch carefully (1)
untranslated (1)

9069 שֶׁמֶר1 *šemer1* (5)
dregs (3)
aged wine (1)
wines (1)

9070 שֶׁמֶר2 *šemer2* (3)
Shemer (3)

9071 שֹׁמֵר *šōmēr* (3)
Shomer (3)

9072 שְׁמָרָה *šāmrāh* (1)
guard (1)

9073 שְׁמֻרָה *š^emurāh* (1)
kept from closing (1) +296

9074 שִׁמְרוֹן1 *šimrôn1* (2)
Shimron (2)

9075 שִׁמְרוֹן2 *šimrôn2* (3)
Shimron (3)

9076 שֹׁמְרוֹן *šōmrôn* (109)
Samaria (105)
the city^s (2)
there^s (2) +928

9077 שִׁמְרוֹן מְראוֹן *šimrôn m^er'ôn* (1)
Shimron Meron (1)

9078 שִׁמְרִי *šimriy* (4)
Shimri (4)

9079 שְׁמַרְיָה *š^emaryāh* (3)
Shemariah (3)

9080 שְׁמַרְיָהוּ *š^emaryāhû* (1)
Shemariah (1)

9081 שִׁמֻּרִים *šimmuriym* (2)
vigil (2)

9082 שְׁמְרִימוֹת *š^emiriymôt*
Variant; not used

9083 שְׁמְרִית *šimriyt* (1)
Shimrith (1)

9084 שִׁמְרֹנִי *šimrōniy* (1)
Shimronite (1)

9085 שֹׁמְרֹנִי *šōmrōniy* (1)
people of Samaria (1)

9086 שִׁמְרָת *šimrāt* (1)
Shimrath (1)

9087 שֶׁמֶשׁ *šemeš* (135)
sun (102)
sunset (6) +995+2021
east (3) +2021+4667
sunrise (3) +4667
east (2) +2021+2025+4667
east (2) +4667
sunrise (2) +2021+2436
sunset (2) +995+2021+6961
west (2) +4427
battlements (1)
broad daylight (1)
east (1) +928+2025+4667+6298
east (1) +928+4667+6298
eastern (1) +4667
in broad daylight (1)
       +2021+2021+2296+4200+6524
in broad daylight (1) +2021+5584
on the west (1) +2021+4427
sunlight (1)
sunrise (1) +2436
sunshine (1)

9088 שִׁמְשׁוֹן *šimšôn* (38)
Samson (33)
Samson's (3)
he^s (2)

9089 שִׁמְשַׁי *šimšay*
Variant; not used

9090 שִׁמְשִׁי *šimšiy*
Variant; not used

9091 שַׁמְשְׁרַי *šamš^eray* (1)
Shamsherai (1)

9092 שֻׁמָתִי *šumātiy* (1)
Shumathites (1)

9093 שָׁן *šan*
Variant; not used

9094 שֵׁן1 *šēn1* (56)
teeth (26)
ivory (10)
tooth (9)
cliff (1)

cliff (1) +6152
crag (1)
empty stomachs (1) +5931
fangs (1)
feeds (1) +928+5966
put in jeopardy (1) +928+1414+5951
three-pronged (1) +8993
untranslated (3)

9095 שֵׁן2 *šēn2* (1)
Shen (1)

9096 שְׁנָא *šānā'* (1)
dull (1)

9097 שְׁנָא *šēnā'* (1)
sleep (1)

9098 שִׁנְאָב *šin'āḇ* (1)
Shinab (1)

9099 שִׁנְאָן *šin'ān* (1)
thousands (1)

9100 שֶׁנְאַצַּר *šen'aṣṣar* (1)
Shenazzar (1)

9101 שָׁנָה1 *šānāh1* (24)
change (2)
different (2)
do again (2)
pretended to be insane (2) +3248
put aside (2)
repeats (2)
again (1)
alter (1)
changes (1)
changing (1)
deprive (1)
did again (1)
disguise yourself (1)
more (1)
moved (1)
rebellious (1)
strike twice (1)
was given (1)

9102 שָׁנָה2 *šānāh2* (878)
years (409)
year (303)
years (8) +3427
year-old (5) +1201
age (4) +1201
each year (3) +928+9102
spring (3) +9588
ages (2) +1201
them[s] (2)
year-old (2) +1426
yearly (2) +285+928
age (1) +1426
ages (1)
annual (1) +285+928+2021
annual (1) +928+2021+7193
annually (1) +928+2256+3972+9102
day (1)
due annually (1) +928+1896+4946+9102
each year (1) +9102
every spring (1) +995
full years (1) +3427
generations long past (1) +1887+1887+2256
it[s] (1)
its[s] (1)
length of days (1) +3427
lives (1) +3427
many years (1) +2256+3427
old (1) +2644+3427
over a year (1) +196+2296+2296+3427
some years later (1) +4200+7891
spring (1) +2021+9588
spring (1) +6961+9588
successive years (1) +339+9102
this time[s] (1) +8993
time (1)
year (1) +1821
year's (1)

years (1) +2021+6961
untranslated (103)

9103 שָׁנָה3 *šānāh3*
Variant; not used

9104 שֵׁנָה *šēnāh* (23)
sleep (19)
sleep (2) +3822
sleep of death (1)
slumber (1)

9105 שֶׁנְהַבִּים *šenhabbiym* (2)
ivory (2)

9106 שָׁנִי1 *šāniy1* (42)
scarlet yarn (31) +9357
scarlet (7)
scarlet thread (2)
scarlet (1) +9357
scarlet wool (1) +9357

9107 שָׁנִי2 *šāniy2*
Variant; not used

9108 שֵׁנִי *šēniy* (157)
second (75)
other (33)
another (12)
second time (10)
again (5)
after (3)
again (1) +8740
all alone (1) +401
another part (1)
each (1)
following (1)
furthermore (1) +2021+2256
middle (1)
next (1)
one (1)
second in command (1)
this time (1)
this[s] (1) +2021
whose[s] (1) +285+2021+2021
untranslated (8)

9109 שְׁנַיִם *šnayim* (772)
two (374)
both (52)
twelve (51) +6925
twelve (30) +6926
12 (24) +6925
each (16)
twelfth (15) +6925
twenty-two (15) +2256+6929
second (12)
two-tenths (11) +6928
pair (9)
double (8)
twelfth (7) +6926
thirty-two (6) +2256+8993
forty-two (5) +752+2256
32 (3) +2256+8993
fifty-two (3) +2256+2822
together (3)
1,052 (2) +547+2256+2822
112 (2) +2256+4395+6925
20,000 (2) +8052
32,200 (2) +547+2256+2256+4395+8993
372 (2) +2256+4395+8679+8993
392 (2) +2256+4395+8993+9596
42 (2) +752+2256
52 (2) +2256+2822
62,700 (2)
       +547+2256+2256+4395+8679+9252
652 (2) +2256+2822+4395+9252
other (2)
pairs (2) +9109
sides (2)
sixty-two (2) +2256+9252
thirty-second (2) +2256+8993
twenty-second (2) +2256+6929
twice (2)
1,222 (1) +547+2256+4395+6929

112 (1) +4395+6925
122 (1) +2256+2256+4395+6929
122 (1) +2256+4395+6929
162 (1) +2256+2256+4395+9252
172 (1) +2256+4395+8679
182 (1) +2256+2256+4395+9046
2,172 (1) +547+2256+2256+4395+8679
2,172 (1) +547+2256+4395+8679
2,322 (1) +547+2256+4395+6929+8993
2,812 (1) +547+2256+4395+6925+9046
212 (1) +2256+4395+6925
22 (1) +2256+6929
22,000 (1) +547+2256+6929
22,034 (1)
      +547+752+2256+2256+2256+6929+8993
22,200 (1) +547+2256+2256+4395+6929
22,273 (1)   +547+2256+2256+2256
             +4395+6929+8679+8993
22,600 (1)
      +547+2256+2256+4395+6929+9252
232 (1) +2256+4395+8993
242 (1) +752+2256+4395
32,000 (1) +547+2256+8993
32,500 (1)
      +547+2256+2256+2822+4395+8993
52,700 (1)
      +547+2256+2256+2822+4395+8679
62 (1) +2256+9252
642 (1) +752+2256+2256+4395+9252
642 (1) +752+2256+4395+9252
72 (1) +2256+8679
72,000 (1) +547+2256+8679
782 (1) +2256+2256+4395+8679+9046
822 (1) +2256+4395+6929+9046
832 (1) +2256+4395+8993+9046
912 (1) +2256+4395+6926+9596
962 (1) +2256+2256+4395+9252+9596
another (1)
both sides (1)
double-edged (1) +7023
doubly (1) +928+2021
each other (1) +5646
each other[s] (1) +2157
each[s] (1)
Elijah and Elisha[s] (1) +2157
few (1)
fifty-second (1) +2256+2822
hundred and twenty thousand (1)
                 +6926+8052
inner and outer[s] (1)
people[s] (1) +8993
some[s] (1)
them[s] (1) +74+2021
them[s] (1) +2021+3192
time and again (1) +285+2256+4202+4202
tore apart (1) +4200+7973+7974
two at a time (1) +9109
two-and-a-half (1) +2256+2942
two-thirds (1) +7023
untranslated (38)

9110 שְׁנִינָה *šniynāh* (4)
object of ridicule (3)
ridicule (1)

9111 שָׁנַן1 *šānan1* (8)
sharp (4)
sharpen (2)
embittered (1)
make sharp (1)

9112 שָׁנַן2 *šānan2* (1)
impress (1)

9113 שָׁנַס *šānas* (1)
tucking cloak into belt (1) +5516

9114 שִׁנְעָר *šin'ār* (8)
Babylonia (3)
Shinar (2)
Shinar (1) +824
Babylonia (1) +824

9115 שָׁסָה *šāsāh* (11)
plundered (4)

raiders (2)
loot (1)
looted (1)
looting (1)
pillage (1)
plunderers (1)

9116 שָׁסַס *šāsas* (6)
plundered (3)
be looted (1)
plunder (1)
ransacked (1)

9117 שָׁסַע *šāsa'* (9)
completely divided (3) +9118
completely divided (1)
divided (1) +9118
rebuked (1)
tear open (1)
tore apart (1)
torn (1)

9118 שֶׁסַע *šesa'* (4)
completely divided (3) +9117
divided (1) +9117

9119 שָׁסַף *šāsap* (1)
put to death (1)

9120 שָׁעָה *šā'āh* (11)
look (6)
have regard (1)
look with favor (1)
looked with favor (1)
pay attention (1)
turn away (1)

9121 שְׁעָטָה *š°'āṭāh* (1)
galloping (1)

9122 שַׁעַטְנֵז *ša'aṭnēz* (2)
woven (1)
woven material (1)

9123 שֹׁעַל *šō'al* (3)
handful (1)
handfuls (1)
hollow of hand (1)

9124 שַׁעַלְבִים *ša'albiym* (2)
Shaalbim (2)

9125 שַׁעֲלַבִּין *ša'alabbiyn* (1)
Shaalabbin (1)

9126 שַׁעַלְבֹנִי *ša'albōniy* (2)
Shaalbonite (2)

9127 שַׁעֲלִים *ša'aliym* (1)
Shaalim (1)

9128 שָׁעַן *šā'an* (22)
rely (5)
lean (3)
leaning (3)
relied (3)
leaned (2)
rest (2)
depended (1)
leans (1)
lie (1)
untranslated (1)

9129 1שָׁעַע *šā'a'1* (4)
blind yourselves (1)
close (1)
closed (1)
sightless (1)

9130 2שָׁעַע *šā'a'2* (6)
delight (3)
brought joy (1)
dandled (1)
play (1)

9131 שָׁעַף *ša'ap* (2)
Shaaph (2)

9132 שָׁעַר *šā'ar* (1)
thinking (1)

9133 1שַׁעַר *ša'ar1* (374)
gate (177)
gates (75)
gateway (29)
towns (18)
city gate (11)
entrance (10)
cities (6)
court (5)
city gates (4)
courts (4)
gateways (4)
town (3)
cities (2) +824
each gate (2) +2256+9133
its^s (2) +2021
town gate (2)
assembly at the gate (1)
end^s (1)
entrance (1) +7339
fellow townsmen (1) +6639
gatepost (1) +4647
gateposts (1) +4647
gateways (1) +7339
it^s (1) +2021+4889
opposite^s (1)
other^s (1)
they^s (1) +2021
town records (1) +5226
various gates (1) +2256+9133
untranslated (5)

9134 2שַׁעַר *ša'ar2* (1)
hundredfold (1) +4395

9135 שֹׁעָר *šō'ār* (1)
poor (1)

9136 שַׁעֲרוּר *ša'ᵃrûr* (2)
shocking thing (1)
something horrible (1)

9137 שַׁעֲרוּרִי *ša'ᵃrûriy* (3)
horrible thing (2)
untranslated (1)

9138 שְׁעַרְיָה *š°'aryāh* (2)
Sheariah (2)

9139 שַׁעֲרַיִם *ša'ᵃrayim* (3)
Shaaraim (3)

9140 שַׁעֲשְׁגַז *ša'ašgaz* (1)
Shaashgaz (1)

9141 שַׁעֲשׁוּעִים *ša'ᵃšû'iym* (9)
delight (7)
delighting (1)
filled with delight (1)

9142 שָׁפָה *šāpāh* (2)
bare (1)
stick out (1)

9143 שְׁפוֹ *š°pô* (2)
Shepho (2)

9144 שְׁפוֹט *š°pôṭ* (2)
judgment (1)
punishment (1)

9145 שְׁפוּפָם *š°pûpām*
Variant; not used

9146 שְׁפוּפָן *š°pûpān* (1)
Shephuphan (1)

9147 שְׁפוֹת *š°pôṭ* (1)
cheese (1)

9148 שִׁפְחָה *šiphāh* (63)
servant (19)
maidservant (12)
maidservants (11)
female (7)
servant girl (3)
maid (2)
slave girl (2)
slaves (2) +2256+6269

women (2)
enslaved (1) +2256+3899+4200+4200+6269
servant girls (1)
serve (1)

9149 שָׁפַט *šāpat* (204)
judge (69)
judges (26)
led (12)
rulers (8)
execute judgment (6)
govern (5)
decide (4)
judged (4)
judging (4)
vindicate (4)
defend (3)
lead (3)
leaders (3)
defend the cause (2)
delivered (2)
governed (2)
rule (2)
ruler (2)
sentence (2)
administer (1)
argue (1)
be judged (1)
bring judgment (1)
bring justice (1)
bring to judgment (1)
brought to trial (1)
condemn (1)
confront with evidence (1)
decide dispute (1)
decided (1)
defend cause (1)
defending (1)
enter into judgment (1)
executing judgment (1)
given^s (1)
gives judgment (1)
goes to court (1)
is tried (1)
judge (1) +5477
judge in office (1)
judges decide (1)
judges in office (1)
leader (1)
leading (1)
pass judgment (1)
play the judge (1) +9149
pleads case (1)
punish (1)
render judgment (1) +5477
ruled (1)
serve as judge (1)
serve as judges (1)
served (1)
served as judges (1)
them^s (1) +2021
uphold (1)
untranslated (3)

9150 שֶׁפֶט *šepet* (16)
punishment (9)
judgment (3)
acts of judgment (2)
judgments (1)
Penalties (1)

9151 שָׁפָט *šāpāt* (8)
Shaphat (8)

9152 שְׁפַטְיָה *š°paṭyāh* (10)
Shephatiah (10)

9153 שְׁפַטְיָהוּ *š°paṭyāhû* (3)
Shephatiah (3)

9154 שִׁפְטָן *šipṭān* (1)
Shiphtan (1)

9155 1שְׁפִי *š°piy1* (10)
barren heights (7)

barren height (1)
barren hill (1)
untranslated (1)

9156 שָׁפִי2 *š∘piy2*
Variant; not used

9157 שֻׁפִּים1 *šuppiyml* (1)
Shuppim (1)

9158 שֻׁפִּים2 *šuppiym2* (2)
Shuppites (2)

9159 שְׁפִיפֹן *š∘piypōn* (1)
viper (1)

9160 שָׁפִיר *šāpiyr* (1)
Shaphir (1)

9161 שָׁפַךְ *šāpak* (117)
pour out (33)
shed (25)
poured out (11)
build (6)
shedding (4)
outpoured (3)
pours out (3)
be poured out (2)
be shed (2)
built (2)
pour (2)
pours (2)
sheds (2)
am poured out (1)
be poured (1)
been shed (1)
bloodshed (1) +1947
build up (1)
drain out (1)
dumped (1)
ebb away (1)
ebbs away (1)
flowed (1)
lavished (1)
lost (1)
outpouring (1)
poured out (1) +4946
pouring out (1)
scattered (1)
spilled out (1)
spills (1)
untranslated (2)

9162 שֶׁפֶךְ *šepek* (2)
heap (1)
where thrown (1)

9163 שְׁפָכָה *šopkāh* (1)
cutting (1) +4162

9164 שָׁפֵל1 *šāpēll* (30)
humbled (6)
brought low (4)
bring low (3)
bring down (2)
brings down (1)
brings low (1)
casts (1)
come down (1)
descended (1)
fades (1)
humble (1)
humbles (1)
humiliate (1)
lay low (1)
lays low (1)
leveled completely (1) +928+2021+9168
levels (1)
low (1)
stoops down (1)

9165 שֶׁפֶל *šēpel* (2)
low (1)
low estate (1)

9166 שָׁפָל *šāpāl* (18)
lowly (8)

deep (3)
humiliated (2)
low (2)
deeper (1)
low (1) +7757
lowliest (1)

9167 שָׁפֵל2 *šāpēl2*
Variant; not used

9168 שִׁפְלָה *šiplāh* (1)
leveled completely (1) +928+2021+9164

9169 שְׁפֵלָה *š∘pēlāh* (20)
western foothills (13)
foothills (7)

9170 שִׁפְלוּת *šiplûṭ* (1)
idle (1)

9171 שָׁפָם *šāpām* (1)
Shapham (1)

9172 שְׁפָם *š∘pām* (2)
Shepham (2)

9173 שֻׁפִּם *šuppim*
Variant; not used

9174 שִׁפְמוֹת *šip∘môṭ*
Variant; not used

9175 שִׁפְמִי *šipmiy* (1)
Shiphmite (1)

9176 שָׁפָן1 *šāpānl* (4)
coney (1)
coneys (2)

9177 שָׁפָן2 *šāpān2* (30)
Shaphan (30)

9178 שָׁפַע *šāpa‘*
Variant; not used

9179 שֶׁפַע *šepa‘* (1)
abundance (1)

9180 שִׁפְעָה *šip‘āh* (6)
flood (2)
troops (2)
herds (1)
many (1)

9181 שִׁפְעִי *šip‘iy* (1)
Shiphi (1)

9182 שָׁפַר *šāpar* (1)
delightful (1)

9183 שֶׁפֶר1 *šeperl* (1)
beautiful (1)

9184 שֶׁפֶר2 *šeper2* (2)
Shepher (2)

9185 שִׁפְרָה1 *šiprāhl* (1)
fair (1)

9186 שִׁפְרָה2 *šiprāh2* (1)
Shiphrah (1)

9187 שַׁפְרוּר *šaprûr* (1)
untranslated (1)

9188 שַׁפְרִיר *šapriyr* (1)
royal canopy (1)

9189 שָׁפַת *šāpaṭ* (5)
put on (3)
establish (1)
lay (1)

9190 שְׁפַתַּיִם1 *š∘patayiml* (1)
campfires (1)

9191 שְׁפַתַּיִם2 *š∘patayim2* (1)
double-pronged hooks (1)

9192 שֶׁצֶף *šesep* (1)
surge (1)

9193 שָׁקַד1 *šāqadl* (12)
watching (3)
did not hesitate (1)

guard (1)
have an eye for (1)
lie awake (1)
lie in wait (1)
stand guard (1)
watch (1)
watch kept (1)
watched (1)

9194 שָׁקַד2 *šāqad2*
Variant; not used

9195 שָׁקַד3 *šāqad3*
Variant; not used

9196 שָׁקֵד *šāqēd* (4)
almond tree (2)
almonds (2)

9197 שָׁקָה *šāqāh* (62)
water (10)
watered (6)
drink (5)
made drink (4)
gave a drink (3)
give to drink (3)
gave (2)
get a drink (2)
get to drink (2)
give drink (2)
got to drink (2)
have drink (2)
drench (1)
gave water (1)
give (1)
give a drink (1)
give a drink (1) +3926
give water (1)
given (1)
given a drink (1)
given to drink (1)
gives drink (1)
irrigated (1)
let drink (1)
made to drink (1)
make drink (1)
rich (1)
watering (1)
waters (1)
wine served (1)
untranslated (1)

9198 שִׁקּוּי *šiqqûy* (3)
drink (2)
nourishment (1)

9199 שִׁקּוּץ *šiqqûṣ* (28)
vile images (9)
abomination (3)
detestable god (3)
detestable idols (3)
abominable idols (1)
abominations (1)
detestable acts (1)
detestable images (1)
detestable things (1)
filth (1)
forbidden food (1)
vile (1)
vile god (1)
vile goddess (1)

9200 שָׁקַט *šāqaṭ* (42)
at peace (5)
quiet (5)
rest (4)
had peace (3)
peaceful (3)
quietness (3)
calm (2)
had rest (2)
have peace (2)
in peace (2)
calms (1)
enjoyed peace (1)

grant relief (1)
left (1)
lies hushed (1)
silent (1)
still (1)
troubled (1) +3523+4202
unconcerned (1) +8932
unsuspecting (1)
untranslated (1)

9201 שֶׁקֶט *šeqet* (1)
quiet (1)

9202 שָׁקַל *šāqal* (23)
weighed out (7)
pay (2)
weigh (2)
weigh out (2)
be weighed (1)
be weighed (1) +9202
paid (1) +8510
pay (1) +4084
put (1) +995+4200
spend (1)
took revenue (1)
weighed (1)
untranslated (1)

9203 שֶׁקֶל *šeqel* (88)
shekels (45)
shekel (39)
price (1)
weighs (1)
which$ (1)
untranslated (1)

9204 שִׁקְמָה *šiqmāh* (7)
sycamore-fig trees (5)
fig trees (1)
sycamore-figs (1)

9205 שָׁקַע *šāqa'* (6)
sink (2)
died down (1)
let settle (1)
sinks (1)
tie down (1)

9206 שְׁקַעֲרוּרָה *š⁽e⁾qa⁽a⁾rûrāh* (1)
depressions (1)

9207 שָׁקַף *šāqap* (22)
looked down (6)
looks down (4)
looked out (2)
overlooking (2)
watched (2)
appears (1)
look down (1)
looked (1)
looms (1)
overlooks (1)
peered (1)

9208 שֶׁקֶף *šāqep* (1)
frames (1)

9209 שְׁקֻפִים *š⁽e⁾qupiym* (2)
clerestory (1)
windows placed high (1)

9210 שָׁקַץ *šāqas* (7)
defile (2)
detest (2)
disdained (1)
utterly abhor (1) +9210

9211 שֶׁקֶץ *šeqes* (11)
detestable (7)
detest (3)
abominable things (1)

9212 שָׁקַק *šāqaq* (4)
charging (1)
pounce (1)
rush (1)
rushing back and forth (1)

9213 שָׁקַר *šāqar* (6)
false (2)
betray (1)
deal falsely (1)
deceive (1)
lie (1)

9214 שֶׁקֶר *šeqer* (113)
lies (21)
lying (16)
false (14)
deceptive (4)
falsely (4) +2021+4200
lie (4)
without cause (4)
deceit (3)
deceitful (3)
falsehood (3)
falsely (3)
fraud (3)
lies (3) +1821
not true (3)
false gods (2)
liar (2)
liars (2) +1819
wrong (2)
deceiver (1)
deception (1)
disillusionment (1)
falsely (1) +6584
gifts he does not give (1) +5522
in vain (1)
liars (1)
lie (1) +1819
lies (1) +609
lying (1) +1819
perjurers (1) +2021+4200+8678
perjury (1) +2021+4200+8678
pretense (1)
put in jeopardy (1) +6913
useless (1) +2021+4200
vain hope (1)
without reason (1)

9215 שַׁקָּר *šaqqār*
Variant; not used

9216 שֹׁקֶת *šōqet* (2)
trough (1)
troughs (1) +8110

9217 שֵׁר1 *šēr1* (1)
bracelets (1)

9218 שֵׁר2 *šēr2*
Variant; not used

9219 שֹׁר *šōr* (3)
body (1)
cord (1)
navel (1)

9220 שָׁרָב *šārāb* (2)
burning sand (1)
desert heat (1)

9221 שֵׁרֵבְיָה *šērēbyāh* (8)
Sherebiah (8)

9222 שַׁרְבִיט *šarbiyt* (4)
scepter (4)

9223 שָׁרָה1 *šārāh1* (2)
deliver (1)
unleashes (1)

9224 שָׁרָה2 *šārāh2* (1)
vineyards (1)

9225 שָׁרָה *šērāh*
Variant; not used

9226 שָׁרוּחֶן *šārûhen* (1)
Sharuhen (1)

9227 שָׁרוֹן *šārôn* (6)
Sharon (6)

9228 שָׁרוֹנִי *šārôniy* (1)
Sharonite (1)

9229 שְׁרוּקָה *š⁽e⁾rûqāh* (1)
untranslated (1)

9230 שֵׁרוּת *šērût*
Variant; not used

9231 שִׁרְטַי *širtay* (1)
untranslated (1)

9232 שָׁרַי *šāray* (1)
Sharai (1)

9233 שִׁרְיָה *širyāh* (1)
javelin (1)

9234 שִׁרְיוֹן *širyôn* (8)
armor (3)
breastplate (1)
coat of armor (1)
coat of scale armor (1) +7989
coats of armor (1)
untranslated (1)

9235 שָׁרִיר *šāriyr* (1)
muscles (1)

9236 שְׁרֵמוֹת *š⁽e⁾rēmôt* (1)
untranslated (1)

9237 שָׁרַץ *šāras* (14)
moves about (3)
multiply (2)
move about (1)
multiplied (1)
swarm (1)
swarms (1)
teem (1)
teem (1) +9238
teemed (1)
teems (1)
untranslated (1)

9238 שֶׁרֶץ *šeres* (15)
creatures (4)
creature (3)
animals (1)
crawling thing (1)
creatures that move along the ground (1)
insects (1)
insects that swarm (1)
move along (1)
swarming things (1)
teem (1) +9237

9239 שָׁרַק *šāraq* (12)
scoff (7)
hiss (1)
hisses (1)
signal (1)
whistle (1)
whistles (1)

9240 שְׁרֵקָה *š⁽e⁾rēqāh* (7)
scorn (5)
derision (1)
object of scorn (1)

9241 שְׁרִקָה *š⁽e⁾riqāh* (2)
object of scorn (1)
whistling (1)

9242 שָׁרַר *šārar*
Variant; not used

9243 שָׁרָר *šārār* (1)
Sharar (1)

9244 שְׁרִרוּת *š⁽e⁾rirût* (10)
stubbornness (7)
stubborn (2)
persist in own way (1) +4213

9245 שָׁרַשׁ *šāraš* (8)
be uprooted (1)
take root (1)
take root (1) +1614
taken root (1)
taking root (1)

took root (1) +9247
uproot (1)
uprooted (1)

9246 שֶׁרֶשׁ *šereš* (1)
Sheresh (1)

9247 שֹׁרֶשׁ *šōreš* (33)
roots (15)
root (12)
be uprooted (1) +4572
depths (1)
family line (1) +5916
soles (1)
took root (1) +9245
uprooted (1) +5998

9248 שָׁרְשָׁה *šaršāh*
Variant; not used

9249 שַׁרְשְׁרָה *šarš°rāh* (8)
chains (5)
chain (1)
chains (1) +6310
interwoven chains (1) +5126

9250 שָׁרַת *šārat* (100)
minister (29)
ministering (14)
serve (8)
service (6)
aide (4)
assist (4)
servants (4)
served (4)
ministered (3)
servant (3)
attendant (2)
attending (2)
ministers (2)
attendants (1)
attendants (1) +5853
attended (1)
ministering (1) +9251
officials (1)
on duty (1)
personal attendants (1) +5853
personal servant (1) +5853
serving (1)
supply (1)
take care of (1)
waited on (1)
untranslated (3)

9251 שָׁרֵת *šārēt* (1)
ministering (1) +9250

9252 1שֵׁשׁ *šēš1* (271)
six (116)
sixty (23)
sixteen (14) +6926
sixteen (4) +6925
36,000 (3) +547+2256+8993
603,550 (3)　　　　　+547+547+2256+2256
　　　　　+2256+2822+2822+4395+4395+8993
sixteenth (3) +6925
16,000 (2) +547+6925
4,600 (2) +547+752+2256+4395
45,650 (2)　　　　　+547+752+2256+2256
　　　　　+2256+2822+2822+4395
46,500 (2)
　　　　　+547+752+2256+2256+2822+4395
6,720 (2) +547+2256+4395+6929+8679
62,700 (2)
　　　　　+547+2256+2256+4395+8679+9109
621 (2) +285+2256+4395+6929
65 (2) +2256+2822
652 (2) +2256+2822+4395+9109
666 (2) +2256+4395+9252+9252
74,600 (2)
　　　　　+547+752+2256+2256+4395+8679
760 (2) +2256+4395+8679
ninety-six (2) +2256+9596
sixty-six (2) +2256+9252

sixty-two (2) +2256+9109
1,365 (1)　　　　　+547+2256+2256
　　　　　+2256+2822+4395+8993
1,760 (1) +547+2256+2256+4395+8679
153,600 (1)　　　　　+547+547+2256+2256
　　　　　+2256+2822+4395+4395+8993
156 (1) +2256+2822+4395
157,600 (1)　　　　　+547+547+2256+2256
　　　　　+2256+2822+4395+4395+8679
16,750 (1)
　　　　　+547+2256+2822+4395+6925+8679
160 (1) +2256+4395
162 (1) +2256+2256+4395+9109
186,400 (1)　　　　　+547+547+547+752+2256
　　　　　+2256+2256+4395+4395+9046
2,056 (1) +547+2256+2822
2,067 (1) +547+2256+8679
2,600 (1) +547+2256+4395
2,630 (1) +547+2256+2256+4395+8993
22,600 (1)
　　　　　+547+2256+2256+4395+6929+9109
26,000 (1) +547+2256+6929
28,600 (1)
　　　　　+547+2256+2256+4395+6929+9046
3,600 (1) +547+2256+4395+8993
3,630 (1)
　　　　　+547+2256+2256+4395+8993+8993
365 (1) +2256+2256+2822+4395+8993
42,360 (1)
　　　　　+547+752+2256+4395+8052+8993
42,360 (1) +547+752+4395+8052+8993
44,760 (1)　　　　　+547+752+752+2256
　　　　　+2256+2256+4395+8679
45,600 (1)
　　　　　+547+752+2256+2256+2822+4395
468 (1) +752+2256+4395+9046
56 (1) +2256+2822
6,200 (1) +547+2256+4395
6,800 (1) +547+2256+4395+9046
60 (1)
60,500 (1) +547+2256+2822+4395
601,730 (1)　　　　　+547+547+2256+2256
　　　　　+4395+4395+8679+8993
61 (1) +285+2256
61,000 (1) +285+547+2256
61,000 (1) +547+2256+8052
62 (1) +2256+9109
623 (1) +2256+4395+6929+8993
628 (1) +2256+4395+6929+9046
64,300 (1)
　　　　　+547+752+2256+2256+4395+8993
64,400 (1) +547+752+752+2256+2256+4395
642 (1) +752+2256+2256+4395+9109
642 (1) +752+2256+4395+9109
648 (1) +752+2256+4395+9046
650 (1) +2256+2822+4395
655 (1) +2256+2822+2822+4395
666 (1) +2256+2256+4395+9252+9252
667 (1) +2256+4395+8679+9252
67 (1) +2256+8679
675 (1) +2256+2822+4395+8679
675,000 (1)　　　　　+547+547+547+2256
　　　　　+2256+2822+4395+8679
690 (1) +2256+4395+9596
736 (1) +2256+4395+8679+8993
76,500 (1)
　　　　　+547+2256+2256+2822+4395+8679
8,600 (1) +547+2256+4395+9046
956 (1) +2256+2256+2822+4395+9596
962 (1) +2256+2256+4395+9109+9596
969 (1) +2256+2256+4395+9596+9596
eighty-six (1) +2256+9046
over nine feet (1) +564+2256+2455
sixth (1)
sixty-eight (1) +2256+9046
sixty-five (1) +2256+2822
thirty-six (1) +2256+8993
thirty-six hundred (1)
　　　　　+547+2256+4395+8993
thirty-sixth (1) +2256+8993
twenty-six (1) +2256+6929

twenty-six hundred (1) +547+2256+4395
twenty-sixth (1) +2256+6929
untranslated (3)

9253 2שֵׁשׁ *šēš2* (3)
marble (3)

9254 3שֵׁשׁ *šēš3* (39)
linen (21)
fine linen (17)
untranslated (1)

9255 שָׁשָׁא *šāšā'* (1)
drag along (1)

9256 שֵׁשְׁבַּצַּר *šēšbassar* (2)
Sheshbazzar (2)

9257 שָׁשָׁה *šāšāh* (1)
sixth (1)

9258 שָׁשַׁי *šāšay* (1)
Shashai (1)

9259 שֵׁשַׁי *šēšay* (3)
Sheshai (3)

9260 שֵׁשִׁי *šēšiy*
Variant; not used

9261 שִׁשִּׁי *šiššiy* (28)
sixth (28)

9262 שִׁשִּׁים *šiššiym*
Variant; not used

9263 שֵׁשַׁךְ *šēšak* (2)
Sheshach (2)

9264 שֵׁשָׁן *šēšān* (5)
Sheshan (4)
he^s (1)

9265 שָׁשַׁק *šāšaq* (2)
Shashak (2)

9266 שָׁשַׁר *šāšar* (2)
red (2)

9267 שָׁת *šāt*
Variant; not used

9268 1שֵׁת *šēt1* (3)
buttocks (2)
foundations (1)

9269 2שֵׁת *šēt2* (9)
Seth (8)
Sheth (1)

9270 3שֵׁת *šēt3*
Variant; not used

9271 1שָׁתָה *šātāh1* (1)
workers in cloth (1)

9272 2שָׁתָה *šātāh2* (215)
drink (127)
drank (28)
drinking (23)
drinks (8)
drunk (6)
must drink (3) +9272
drinkers (2)
getting drunk (2) +8893
well-watered (2) +4784
be drunk (1)
dine (1)
drained to dregs (1) +5172
drinks in (1)
drinks up (1)
drunkards (1) +8911
feasted (1)
feasting (1) +430+2256
get a drink (1)
have a drink (1)
refresh (1)
untranslated (2)

9273 שָׁתוֹת *šātôt*
Variant; not used

9274 שְׁתִי1 *š°tiy1* (9)
woven (9)

9275 שְׁתִי2 *š°tiy2* (1)
drunkenness (1)

9276 שְׁתִיָּה *š°tiyyāh* (1)
drink in own way (1)

9277 שָׁתִיל *šātiyl* (1)
shoots (1)

9278 שָׁתַל *šātal* (10)
planted (5)
plant (1)
been planted (1)
is planted (1)
is transplanted (1)

9279 שֻׁתַלְחִי *šutalhiy* (1)
Shuthelahite (1)

9280 שָׁתַם *šātam* (2)
sees clearly (2)

9281 שְׁתֻם *š°tum*
Variant; not used

9282 שָׁתָן *šātan*
Variant; not used

9283 שָׁתַע *šāta'* (2)
dismayed (2)

9284 שָׁתַק *šātaq* (4)
calm (2)
calm down (1)
dies down (1)

9285 שֵׁתָר *šētār* (1)
Shethar (1)

9286 שָׁתַת *šātat* (2)
destined (1)
lay claim (1)

9287 ת *t*
Variant; not used

9288 תָּא *tā'* (17)
alcoves (8)
alcove (2)
guardroom (2) +8132
alcoves for the guards (1)
untranslated (4)

9289 תָּאַב1 *tā'ab1* (2)
long for (2)

9290 תָּאַב2 *tā'ab2* (1)
abhor (1)

9291 תַּאֲבָה *ta'ăbāh* (1)
longing (1)

9292 תָּאָה *tā'āh* (2)
run a line (1)
untranslated (1)

9293 תְּאוֹ *t°'ô* (2)
antelope (2)

9294 תַּאֲוָה1 *ta'ăwāh1* (21)
desire (5)
longing (2)
longings (2)
bounty (1)
choicest (1)
crave other food (1) +203
craved (1)
craves for more (1) +203
craving (1)
cravings (1)
desires (1)
gave in to craving (1) +203
pleasing (1)
selfish ends (1)
what craved (1)

9295 תַּאֲוָה2 *ta'ăwāh2*
Variant; not used

9296 תְּאוֹמִים *t°'ômiym*
Variant; not used

9297 תַּאֲלָה *ta'ălāh* (1)
curse (1)

9298 תָּאַם *tā'am* (2)
has twin (2)

9299 תַּאֲנָה *ta'ănāh* (1)
in heat (1)

9300 תְּאֵנָה *t°'ēnāh* (39)
fig tree (15)
figs (13)
fig trees (6)
fig (2)
ones[s] (1)
those[s] (1)
tree (1)

9301 תֹּאֲנָה *tō'ănāh* (1)
occasion (1)

9302 תַּאֲנִיָּה *ta'ăniyyāh* (2)
mourn (1)
mourning (1)

9303 תְּאֻנִים *t°'uniym* (1)
efforts (1)

9304 תַּאֲנַת שִׁלֹה *ta'ănat šilōh* (1)
Taanath Shiloh (1)

9305 תָּאַר1 *tā'ar1* (6)
turned (3)
curved (1)
headed (1)
went down (1)

9306 תָּאַר2 *tā'ar2* (2)
makes an outline (1)
marks (1)

9307 תֹּאַר *tō'ar* (15)
form (4)
beautiful (2) +3637
bearing (1)
beauty (1)
fine-looking (1)
handsome (1) +3202
look like (1)
sleek (1) +3637
they (1) +4392
ugly (1) +8273
well-built (1) +3637

9308 תָּאֲרֵעַ *tā'rēa'* (1)
Tarea (1)

9309 תְּאַשּׁוּר *t°'aššûr* (3)
cypress (2)
cypress wood (1)

9310 תֵּבָה *tēbāh* (28)
ark (25)
basket (2)
it[s] (1) +2021

9311 תְּבוּאָה *t°bû'āh* (43)
harvest (11)
crops (6)
income (4)
produce (4)
brings forth (1)
comes (1)
crop (1)
crop comes in (1)
enough (1)
fruit (1)
gain (1)
harvesting crops (1)
produce (1) +2446+3655
produced (1)
produces (1)
product (1)
revenue (1)
what is taken (1)
yield (1)

yields returns (1)
untranslated (2)

9312 תְּבוּנָה *t°bûnāh* (42)
understanding (28)
ability (3)
insight (2)
cleverly fashioned (1)
detect (1)
discernment (1)
experienced (1) +1981+2256
judgment (1)
reasoning (1)
skillful (1)
wisdom (1)
words of insight (1)

9313 תְּבוּסָה *t°bûsāh* (1)
downfall (1)

9314 תָּבוֹר *tābôr* (10)
Tabor (10)

9315 תֵּבֵל *tēbēl* (36)
world (30)
earth (3)
whole earth (1) +824
whole world (1) +824
world's (1)

9316 תֶּבֶל *tebel* (2)
perversion (2)

9317 תֻּבַל *tubal* (8)
Tubal (8)

9318 תַּבְלִית *tabliyt* (1)
destruction (1)

9319 תְּבַלֻּל *t°ballul* (1)
defect (1)

9320 תֶּבֶן *teben* (17)
straw (17)

9321 תִּבְנִי *tibniy* (3)
Tibni (3)

9322 תַּבְנִית *tabniyt* (20)
plans (3)
looked like (2)
pattern (2)
plan (2)
adorn (1)
form (1)
formed (1)
image (1)
kinds (1)
replica (1)
untranslated (5)

9323 תַּבְעֵרָה *tab'ērāh* (2)
Taberah (2)

9324 תֵּבֵץ *tēbēṣ* (3)
Thebez (2)
it[s] (1)

9325 תִּגְלַת פְּלָאֶסֶר *tiglat pil'eser* (3)
Tiglath-Pileser (3)

9326 תַּגְמוּל *tagmûl* (1)
goodness (1)

9327 תִּגְרָה *tigrāh* (1)
blow (1)

9328 תֹּגַרְמָה *tōgarmāh* (2)
Togarmah (2)

9329 תִּדְהָר *tidhār* (2)
fir (2)

9330 תַּדְמֹר *tadmōr* (2)
Tadmor (2)

9331 תִּדְעָל *tid'āl* (2)
Tidal (2)

9332 תֹּהוּ *tōhû* (20)
nothing (3)
empty (2)

formless (2)
waste (2)
barren (1)
chaos (1)
confusion (1)
empty space (1)
false (1)
in vain (1)
ruined (1)
useless (1)
useless idols (1)
wasteland (1)
worthless (1)

9333 תְּהוֹם *t'hôm* (36)
deep (19)
depths (6)
deep waters (3)
deep springs (2)
ocean depths (2)
deeps (1)
oceans (1)
seas (1)
springs (1)

9334 תָּהֳלָה *toh'lāh* (1)
error (1)

9335 תְּהִלָּה *t'hillāh* (58)
praise (46)
praised (2)
praises (2)
boast (1)
glory (1)
hymn of praise (1)
praiseworthy deeds (1)
psalm of praise (1)
renown (1)
theme of praise (1)
untranslated (1)

9336 תַּהֲלוּכָה *tah'lûkāh*
Variant; not used

9337 תַּהְפֻּכוֹת *tahpukôt* (10)
perverse (6)
confusing things (1)
deceit (1)
perverseness (1)
perversity (1)

9338 תָּו *tāw* (3)
mark (1)
put a mark (1) +9344
sign (1)

9339 תּוֹאֲמִים *tô'ᵃmiym* (6)
twin (3)
double (2)
twins (1)

9340 תּוּבַל קַיִן *tûbal qayin* (2)
Tubal-Cain (1)
Tubal-Cain's (1)

9341 תּוּבְנָה *tûb'nāh* (1)
untranslated (1)

9342 תּוּגָה *tûgāh* (4)
grief (3)
sorrow (1)

9343 תּוֹדָה *tôdāh* (32)
thanksgiving (9)
thank offerings (8)
thank (4)
praise (2)
songs of thanksgiving (2)
choir (1)
choirs that gave thanks (1)
choirs to give thanks (1)
confession (1)
expression of thankfulness (1)
giving thanks (1)
thank offering (1)

9344 1תָּוָה *tāwāh1* (3)
making marks (1)

put a mark (1) +9338
untranslated (1)

9345 2תָּוָה *tāwāh2* (1)
vexed (1)

9346 תּוֹחַ *tôah* (1)
Toah (1)

9347 תּוֹחֶלֶת *tôhelet* (5)
hope (2)
expected (1)
hoped (1)
prospect (1)

9348 תָּוֶךְ *tāwek* (420)
among (111) +928
in (45) +928
middle (27)
with (17) +928
from (16) +4946
inside (15) +928
within (15) +928
midst (13)
out of (13) +4946
among (12)
center (11)
into (11) +448
into (9) +928
through (8) +928
along with (6) +928
within (5)
of (4) +4946
there^s (4) +928+2023
between (3) +928
from (2) +928
from out of (2) +4946
heart (2)
inside (2) +448
intersecting (2) +928
presence (2)
throughout (2) +928
along (1) +928
among (1) +448
as one (1) +928
at (1) +928
branch of (1) +4946
by (1) +928
by (1) +4946
central (1)
centrally located in (1) +928
do away with (1) +4946+6073
entered (1) +928+995
entering (1) +928+995
flashed back and forth (1) +928+4374
for (1) +928
gone from (1) +4946
in (1) +4946
include (1) +928
inner part (1)
interior (1)
joined in (1) +928
leave (1) +3718+4946
left (1) +4946+7756
like (1) +928
of (1) +928
of all (1) +4946
on (1) +928
on board (1) +928
onto (1) +448
over (1) +928
ranks (1)
surrounded by (1) +928
there^s (1) +928+2257
there^s (1) +928+4392
to (1) +448
two (1)
within (1) +928+5055
untranslated (25)

9349 תּוֹכֵחָה *tôkēhāh* (4)
rebuke (2)
punishment (1)
reckoning (1)

9350 תּוֹכַחַת *tôkahat* (24)
correction (8)
rebuke (8)
argument (1)
arguments (1)
complaint (1)
corrections (1)
punish (1)
punished (1)
rebukes (1)
reply (1)

9351 תּוֹלָד *tôlād* (1)
Tolad (1)

9352 תּוֹלֵדוֹת *tôlēdôt* (39)
records (14)
account (10)
listed genealogy (3)
genealogical records (2)
genealogy (2)
account of line (1)
account of the family (1)
birth (1)
descendants (1)
family line (1)
genealogical record (1)
lines of descent (1)
order of birth (1)

9353 תּוֹלוֹן *tôlôn* (1)
untranslated (1)

9354 תּוֹלָל *tôlāl* (1)
tormentors (1)

9355 1תּוֹלָע *tôlā'1* (2)
crimson (1)
purple (1)

9356 2תּוֹלָע *tôlā'2* (6)
Tola (6)

9357 תּוֹלֵעָה *tôlē'āh* (41)
scarlet yarn (31) +9106
worm (5)
worms (2)
maggots (1)
scarlet (1) +9106
scarlet wool (1) +9106

9358 תּוֹלָעִי *tôlā'iy* (1)
Tolaite (1)

9359 תּוֹעֵבָה *tô'ēbāh* (118)
detestable practices (30)
detestable (19)
detestable things (18)
detests (13)
detestable thing (7)
detest (6)
detestable idols (6)
detestable ways (3)
things detestable (3)
loathsome (2)
things^s (2)
abhors (1)
abominations (1)
detestable god (1)
detestable offense (1)
detestable sins (1)
repulsive (1)
thing detestable (1)
what detestable (1)
untranslated (1)

9360 תּוֹעָה *tô'āh* (2)
error (1)
trouble (1)

9361 תּוֹעָפוֹת *tô'āpôt* (4)
strength (2)
choicest (1)
peaks (1)

9362 תּוֹצָאוֹת *tôsā'ôt* (25)
ended (5) +2118

out (5)
end (3) +2118
ending (3) +2118
escape (1)
exits (1)
extended (1)
farthest limits (1)
wellspring (1)
untranslated (4)

9363 תּוֹקַהַת *tāwqᵉhaṭ* (1)
untranslated (1)

9364 תּוֹקְעִים *tôqᵉ'iym* (1)
strike hands in pledge (1)

9365 תּוּר *tûr* (24)
explore (6)
explored (5)
merchants (2) +408
cautious (1)
explored (1) +6296
exploring (1)
find (1)
going (1)
investigate (1)
ranges (1)
search out (1)
searched out (1)
sent to spy out (1)
tried (1) +928+4213

9366 תּוֹר1 *tôr1* (5)
earrings (2)
turn (2)
most exalted (1) +5092

9367 תּוֹר2 *tôr2* (14)
doves (9)
dove (5)

9368 תּוֹרָה *tôrāh* (223)
law (168)
laws (16)
regulations (15)
teaching (8)
instruction (5)
instructions (2)
matters of law (1)
teaching of law (1)
teaching of the law (1)
teachings (1)
usual way of dealing (1)
untranslated (4)

9369 תּוֹשָׁב *tôšāb* (13)
temporary resident (5)
stranger (2)
guest (1)
living (1)
people living (1)
strangers (1)
temporary residents (1)
tenants (1)

9370 תּוּשִׁיָּה *tûšiyyāh* (11)
sound judgment (3)
success (2)
victory (2)
wisdom (2)
insight (1)
true wisdom (1)

9371 תּוֹתָח *tôṭāh* (1)
club (1)

9372 תַּזַז *tāzaz* (1)
cut down (1)

9373 תַּזְנוּת *taznûṭ* (22)
prostitution (8)
promiscuity (5)
lust (2)
favors (1)
illicit favors (1)
promiscuous (1)
prostitute (1)

use as a prostitute (1) +2388
untranslated (2)

9374 תַּחְבֻּלוֹת *taḥbulôṭ* (7)
guidance (4)
advice (1)
direction (1)
untranslated (1)

9375 תֹּהוּ *tōhû* (1)
Tohu (1)

9376 תַּחְכְּמֹנִי *taḥkᵉmōniy* (1)
Tahkemonite (1)

9377 תַּחֲלֻאִים *taḥᵃlu'iym* (5)
diseases (3)
pain (1)
ravages (1)

9378 תְּחִלָּה *tᵉhillāh* (23)
beginning (7)
first (3) +928+2021
began (2)
earlier (2) +928+2021
first (2)
first time (2)
already (1) +928+2021
before (1) +928+2021
led in thanksgiving (1) +3344
untranslated (2)

9379 תַּחְמָס *taḥmās* (2)
screech owl (2)

9380 תַּחַן *taḥan* (2)
Tahan (2)

9381 תַּחֲנָה *taḥᵃnāh* (1)
set up camp (1)

9382 תְּחִנָּה1 *tᵉhinnāh1* (25)
plea (10)
petition (4)
plea for mercy (2)
supplication (2)
cry for mercy (1)
gracious (1)
mercy (1)
pleading (1) +5877
pleas (1)
request (1)
supplications (1)

9383 תְּחִנָּה2 *tᵉhinnāh2* (1)
Tehinnah (1)

9384 תַּחֲנוּן *taḥᵃnûn* (18)
cry for mercy (6) +7754
cry for mercy (2)
pray (2)
begging for mercy (1)
mercy (1)
petition (1)
petitions (1)
pleading (1)
requests (1)
supplication (1)
supplications (1)

9385 תַּחֲנִי *taḥᵃniy* (1)
Tahanite (1)

9386 תַּחֲנֹתִי *taḥᵃnōṭiy*
Variant; not used

9387 תַּחְפַּנְחֵס *taḥpanḥēs* (8)
Tahpanhes (7)
untranslated (1)

9388 תַּחְפְּנֵיס *taḥpᵉnēys* (3)
Tahpenes (3)

9389 תַּחְרָא *taḥrā'* (2)
collar (1)
collar (1) +7023

9390 תַּחְרַע *taḥrēa'* (1)
Tahrea (1)

9391 תַּחַשׁ1 *taḥaš1* (14)
sea cows (12)
hides of sea cows (1)
leather (1)

9392 תַּחַשׁ2 *taḥaš2* (1)
Tahash (1)

9393 תַּחַת1 *taḥaṭ1* (511)
under (150)
succeeded (65)
for (34)
in place of (24)
in place (23)
instead of (18)
below (17) +4946
beneath (15)
below (10)
under (7) +4946
because (6) +889
succeed (5)
against (4) +3338+4946
beneath (4) +4946
instead (4)
where (4)
with (4)
at feet (3)
in (3)
in return for (3)
place (3)
replace (3)
while married to (3)
among (2)
at the foot of (2)
for (2) +889
from (2) +4946
have a home (2) +8905
in exchange for (2)
on (2)
succeeded (2) +7756
to (2)
to compensate for (2)
unchanged (2) +6641
underneath (2)
although (1)
amid (1)
as a direct result (1) +3338
at foot of (1)
at the spot (1)
because (1) +3954
by (1)
from (1)
have (1) +3338+3780
have on hand (1) +448+3338
have on hand (1) +3338+3780
homes (1)
in exchange (1)
in position (1)
in stead (1)
in the place of (1)
instead of (1) +889
landˢ (1)
legs (1)
lower (1) +4946
made subject to (1) +3338+4044
mine (1) +3276
on behalf (1)
on the spot (1)
pad (1) +4946
position (1)
replace (1) +448+995
replace (1) +8492
replaced (1) +5989
replaced (1) +6641
resting on (1) +4946
riding (1)
since (1) +889
since (1) +3954
submission (1)
succeeds (1)
successor (1) +6641
supported (1)

take charge of (1) +3338
take the place of (1)
take the place of (1) +2118
to (1) +3338
to (1) +4946
underfoot (1) +8079
underneath (1) +4946
undersides (1)
when (1)
where stand (1)
why (1) +4537
untranslated (26)

9394 תַּחַת2 *tahat2* (4)
Tahath (4)

9395 תַּחַת3 *tahat3* (2)
Tahath (2)

9396 תַּחְתּוֹן *tahtôn* (14)
lower (11)
lowest (3)

9397 תַּחְתִּי *tahtiy* (19)
below (7)
depths (4)
lower (4)
lowest (2)
beneath (1)
foot (1)

9398 תַּחְתִּים חָדְשִׁי *tahtiym hodšiy* (1)
Tahtim Hodshi (1)

9399 תִּיכוֹן *tiykôn* (10)
middle (7)
center (2)
there^s (1) +2021

9400 תִּילוֹן *tiylôn* (1)
Tilon (1)

9401 תֵּימָא *têymā'* (5)
Tema (4)
Tema (1) +824

9402 תֵּימָן1 *têymān1* (23)
south (8)
south (5) +2025
south (3) +2025+5582
south (2) +2025+2025+5582
south (2) +5582
south wind (2)
southward (1) +4946

9403 תֵּימָן2 *têymān2* (11)
Teman (11)

9404 תֵּימָנִי *têymāniy* (8)
Temanite (6)
Temanites (2)

9405 תֵּימְנִי *têym'niy* (1)
Temeni (1)

9406 תִּימָרָה *tiymārāh* (2)
billows (1)
column (1)

9407 תִּיצִי *tiysiy* (1)
Tizite (1)

9408 תִּירוֹשׁ *tiyrôš* (38)
new wine (34)
grapes (1)
juice (1)
new (1)
wine (1)

9409 תִּירְיָא *tiyryā'* (1)
Tiria (1)

9410 תִּירָס *tiyrās* (2)
Tiras (2)

9411 תַּיִשׁ *tayiš* (4)
male goats (2)
goats (1)
he-goat (1)

9412 תֹּךְ *tōk* (4)

threats (2)
oppression (1)
oppressor (1) +408

9413 תָּכָה *tākāh* (1)
bow down (1)

9414 תְּכוּנָה *t'kûnāh* (3)
arrangement (1)
dwelling (1)
supply (1)

9415 תֻּכִּיִּים *tukkiyyiym* (2)
baboons (2)

9416 תִּכְלָה *tiklāh* (1)
perfection (1)

9417 תַּכְלִית *takliyt* (5)
boundary (1)
end (1)
farthest recesses (1) +3972
limits (1)
nothing but (1)

9418 תְּכֵלֶת *t'kēlet* (49)
blue (42)
blue yarn (3)
blue cloth (2)
blue material (2)

9419 תָּכַן *tākan* (18)
just (5)
unjust (4) +4202
weighs (2)
amount been determined (1)
are weighed (1)
hold firm (1)
marked off (1)
measured out (1) +928+4500
understood (1)
weighed (1)

9420 תֹּכֶן1 *tōken1* (2)
full quota (1)
size (1)

9421 תֹּכֶן2 *tōken2* (1)
token (1)

9422 תָּכְנִית *tokniyt* (2)
perfection (1)
plan (1)

9423 תַּכְרִיךְ *takriyk* (1)
robe (1)

9424 תֵּל *tēl* (5)
heap of ruins (1)
mound (1)
mounds (1)
ruin (1)
ruins (1)

9425 תֵּל אָבִיב *tēl 'ābiyb* (1)
Tel Abib (1)

9426 תֵּל חַרְשָׁא *tēl haršā'* (2)
Tel Harsha (2)

9427 תֵּל מֶלַח *tēl melah* (2)
Tel Melah (2)

9428 תָּלָא *tālā'* (3)
determined (1)
hung (1)
suspense (1)

9429 תַּלְאֻבוֹת *tal'ubôt* (1)
burning heat (1)

9430 תְּלָאָה *t'lā'āh* (5)
hardship (2)
hardships (2)
burden (1)

9431 תְּלַאשַּׂר *t'la'śśār* (2)
Tel Assar (2)

9432 תִּלְבֹּשֶׁת *tilbōšet* (1)
put on (1) +4252

9433 תִּלְגַת פִּלְנְאֶסֶר *till'gat piln''eser* (3)
Tiglath-Pileser (3)

9434 תָּלָה *tālāh* (28)
hanged (8)
hung (7)
hang (5)
hanging (3)
been hung up (1)
is hung (1)
suspends (1)
were hanged (1)
untranslated (1)

9435 תָּלוּל *tālûl* (1)
lofty (1)

9436 תֶּלַח *telah* (1)
Telah (1)

9437 תְּלִי *t'liy* (1)
quiver (1)

9438 תָּלַל *tālal* (9)
deceive (2)
made a fool of (2)
act deceitfully (1)
cheated (1)
deceives (1)
deluded (1)
making a fool of (1)

9439 תֶּלֶם *telem* (5)
furrows (2)
plowed (2)
furrow (1)

9440 תַּלְמַי *talmay* (6)
Talmai (6)

9441 תַּלְמִיד *talmiyd* (1)
student (1)

9442 תְּלֻנּוֹת *t'lunnôt* (8)
grumbling (5)
complaints (1)
constant grumbling (1) +4296
grumbling (1) +4296

9443 תָּלַע *tāla'* (1)
clad in scarlet (1)

9444 תַּלְפִּיּוֹת *talpiyyôt* (1)
elegance (1)

9445 תְּלַשַּׂר *t'laśśār*
Variant; not used

9446 תַּלְתַּל *taltāl* (1)
wavy (1)

9447 תָּם *tām* (16)
blameless (8)
fitted (2) +3481
flawless (1)
innocent (1)
integrity (1)
perfect (1)
quiet (1)
strong (1)

9448 תֹּם *tōm* (25)
blameless (8)
integrity (6)
at random (2) +4200
clear (2)
full (2)
full measure (1)
last (1)
man of integrity (1) +2006
quite innocently (1) +4200
righteous (1)

9449 תָּמַהּ *tāmah* (10)
aghast (1)
amazed (1)
appalled (1)
astounded (1)
look aghast (1)

looked in astonishment (1)
stunned (1)
surprised (1)
utterly amazed (1) +9449

9450 תֻּמָּה *tummāh* (5)
integrity (4)
blameless (1)

9451 תִּמָּהוֹן *timmāhôn* (2)
confusion (1)
panic (1)

9452 תַּמּוּז *tammûz* (1)
Tammuz (1)

9453 תְּמוֹל *t'môl* (23)
before (6) +8997
malice aforethought (4) +4946+8533+8997
yesterday (4)
had the habit (2) +4946+8997
as usual (1) +3869+8997
before (1) +4946+8997
for some time (1) +1685+1685+8997
had been (1) +8997
in the past (1) +8997
past (1) +8997
untranslated (1)

9454 תְּמוּנָה *t'mûnāh* (10)
form (7)
image (1)
kind (1)
likeness (1)

9455 תְּמוּרָה *t'mûrāh* (6)
substitute (2)
had for (1)
return (1)
trading (1)
transfer of property (1) +1821+3972

9456 תְּמוּתָה *t'mûtāh* (2)
death (1)
die (1)

9457 תֶּמַח *temah* (2)
Temah (2)

9458 תָּמִיד *tāmiyd* (104)
always (23)
regular (23)
continually (12)
regularly (12)
ever (8)
daily sacrifice (5)
forever (3)
constantly (2)
at all times (1)
constant (1)
continual (1)
continued (1)
continuing (1)
continuously (1)
daily (1)
day after day (1) +3429
endless (1)
keep on (1)
kept (1)
lasting (1) +6409
long (1)
never (1) +4202
often (1)
untranslated (1)

9459 תָּמִים *tāmiym* (91)
without defect (47)
blameless (19)
perfect (8)
full (3)
good faith (2)
whole (2)
all (1)
blameless (1) +1475
blameless (1) +1505
entire (1)

right answer (1)
truth (1)
untranslated (4)

9460 תֻּמִּים *tummiym* (5)
Thummim (5)

9461 תָּמַךְ *tāmak* (21)
uphold (3)
gains (2)
holds (2)
lay hold (2)
accepting (1)
gain (1)
grasps (1)
held (1)
held up (1)
hold fast (1)
lead straight (1)
made secure (1)
support (1)
taken hold (1)
took hold (1)
upholds (1)

9462 תָּמַם *tāmam* (63)
gone (5)
completely (4)
end (3)
perish (3)
all (2)
blameless (2)
completed (2)
finished (2)
over (2)
put an end (2)
show yourself blameless (2)
vanish (2)
all gone (1)
almost to a man (1) +4392+6330
burn away (1)
burned (1)
burned away (1)
consumed (1)
cook well (1)
destroy (1)
destroyed (1)
die (1)
died (1)
done (1)
doomed (1)
down to (1) +6330
ended (1)
fail (1)
have get ready (1)
last (1)
meet end (1)
overtaken (1)
perfect (1)
perished (1)
perishing (1)
settled (1)
spent (1)
stop (1)
untranslated (5)

9463 תִּמְנָה *timnāh* (12)
Timnah (11)
there[s] (1) +928+2025

9464 תִּמְנִי *timniy* (1)
Timnite's (1)

9465 תִּמְנָע *timna'* (6)
Timna (6)

9466 תִּמְנַת־חֶרֶס *timnat-heres* (1)
Timnath Heres (1)

9467 תִּמְנַת־סֶרַח *timnat-serah* (2)
Timnath Serah (2)

9468 תָּמֵס *temes* (1)
melting away (1)

9469 תָּמָר1 *tāmār1* (12)
palms (5)

palm (3)
palm tree (2)
palm trees (2)

9470 תָּמָר2 *tāmār2* (22)
Tamar (22)

9471 תָּמָר3 *tāmār3* (4)
Tamar (3)
untranslated (1)

9472 תֹּמֶר1 *tōmer1* (1)
palm (1)

9473 תֹּמֶר2 *tōmer2* (1)
scarecrow (1)

9474 תִּמֹרָה *timōrāh* (20)
palm trees (14)
palm tree (2)
palm tree decorations (2)
palm tree designs (1)
untranslated (1)

9475 תַּמְרוּק *tamrûq* (3)
beauty treatments (2)
cosmetics (1)

9476 תַּמְרוּרִים1 *tamrûriym1* (3)
bitter (1)
bitterly (1)
great (1)

9477 תַּמְרוּרִים2 *tamrûriym2* (1)
guideposts (1)

9478 תַּן *tan* (15)
jackals (13)
jackal (1)
untranslated (1)

9479 תָּנָה1 *tānāh1* (2)
sold (2)

9480 תָּנָה2 *tānāh2* (1)
commemorate (1)

9481 תְּנוּאָה *t'nû'āh* (2)
against (1)
fault (1)

9482 תְּנוּבָה *t'nûbāh* (5)
fruit (3)
crops (1)
food (1)

9483 תְּנוּךְ *t'nûk* (8)
lobe (5)
lobes (2)
untranslated (1)

9484 תְּנוּמָה *t'nûmāh* (5)
slumber (5)

9485 תְּנוּפָה *t'nûpāh* (30)
wave offering (21)
waved (5)
blows (1)
uplifted (1)
was waved (1) +5677
wave offerings (1)

9486 תַּנּוּר *tannûr* (15)
oven (8)
furnace (3)
ovens (3)
firepot (1)

9487 תַּנְחוּמוֹת *tanhûmôt* (2)
consolation (1)
consolations (1)

9488 תַּנְחוּמִים *tanhûmiym* (3)
comforting (1)
consolation (1)
console (1)

9489 תַּנְחֻמֶת *tanhumet* (2)
Tanhumeth (2)

9490 תַּנִּין *tanniyn* (15)
monster (5)

snake (3)
serpent (2)
creatures of the sea (1)
great sea creatures (1)
jackal (1)
monster of the deep (1)
serpents (1)

9491 1תִּנְשֶׁמֶת *tinšemet1* (1)
chameleon (1)

9492 2תִּנְשֶׁמֶת *tinšemet2* (2)
white owl (2)

9493 תָּעַב *tāʿab* (22)
vile (4)
abhor (3)
detest (3)
abhorred (2)
despise (2)
abhors (1)
behaved in the vilest manner (1) +4394
degraded (1)
detest (1) +9493
loathed (1)
rejected (1)
repulsive (1)

9494 תָּעָה *tāʿāh* (51)
led astray (6)
leads astray (4)
go astray (3)
lead astray (3)
wandered (3)
went astray (3)
reel (2)
stray (2)
strayed (2)
wayward (2)
deceive himself (1)
did^s (1)
error (1)
falters (1)
go about (1)
gone astray (1)
had wander (1)
made a fatal mistake (1) +928+5883
made wander (1)
make stagger (1)
make wander (1)
makes stagger (1)
mislead (1)
sends wandering (1)
spread (1)
staggers around (1)
strays (1)
wander about (1)
wandering around (1)
wandering off (1)
untranslated (1)

9495 תֹּעוּ *tōʿû* (2)
Tou (2)

9496 תְּעוּדָה *tᵉʿûdāh* (3)
testimony (2)
method of legalizing transactions (1)

9497 תֹּעִי *tōʿiy* (3)
Tou (2)
he^s (1)

9498 1תְּעָלָה *tᵉʿālāh1* (9)
aqueduct (3)
trench (3)
channel (1)
channels (1)
tunnel (1)

9499 2תְּעָלָה *tᵉʿālāh2* (2)
healing (2)

9500 תַּעֲלוּלִים *taʿᵃlûliym* (2)
harsh treatment (1)
mere children (1)

9501 תַּעֲלֻם *taʿᵃlum*

Variant; not used

9502 תַּעֲלֻמָה *taʿᵃlumāh* (3)
secrets (2)
hidden things (1)

9503 תַּעֲנוּג *taʿᵃnûg* (5)
delight (1)
delights (1)
delights of the heart (1)
live in luxury (1)
pleasant (1)

9504 תַּעֲנִית *taʿᵃniyt* (1)
self-abasement (1)

9505 תַּעֲנָךְ *taʿᵃnak* (7)
Taanach (7)

9506 תָּעַע *tāʿaʿ* (2)
scoffed (1)
tricking (1)

9507 תְּעֻפָה *tᵉʿupāh* (1)
darkness (1)

9508 תַּעֲצֻמוֹת *taʿᵃsumôt* (1)
strength (1)

9509 תַּעַר *taʿar* (13)
scabbard (5)
razor (4)
have shave (1) +6296
knife (1)
sheath (1)
unsheathed (1) +3655+4946

9510 תַּעֲרוּבוֹת *taʿᵃrûbôt* (2)
hostages (2) +1201

9511 תַּעְתֻּעִים *taʿtuʿiym* (2)
mockery (2)

9512 1תֹּף *tōp1* (16)
tambourines (9)
tambourine (4)
music of tambourines (2)
music of tambourine (1)

9513 2תֹּף *tōp2* (1)
settings (1) +4856

9514 תִּפְאָרֶת *tipʾeret* (51)
glorious (11)
glory (11)
splendor (9)
honor (7)
fine (3)
beautiful (2)
boasted (2)
adorned (1) +4200+7596
elation (1)
finery (1)
look (1)
pride (1)
untranslated (1)

9515 1תַּפּוּחַ *tappûah1* (6)
apple tree (3)
apples (3)

9516 2תַּפּוּחַ *tappûah2* (1)
Tappuah (1)

9517 3תַּפּוּחַ *tappûah3* (5)
Tappuah (5)

9518 תְּפוּצָה *tᵉpûsāh* (1)
shattered (1)

9519 תֻּפִינִים *tupiyniym* (1)
broken (1)

9520 תָּפֵל *tāpal*
Variant; not used

9521 1תָּפֵל *tāpēl1* (5)
whitewash (4)
whitewash (1) +3212

9522 2תָּפֵל *tāpēl2* (2)
tasteless (1)

worthless (1)

9523 תֹּפֶל *tōpel* (1)
Tophel (1)

9524 תִּפְלָה *tiplāh* (3)
wrongdoing (2)
repulsive thing (1)

9525 תְּפִלָּה *tᵉpillāh* (77)
prayer (60)
prayers (10)
petition (2)
pray (2) +5951
offer prayer (1) +7137
plea (1)
pray (1)

9526 תִּפְלֶצֶת *tipleset* (1)
terror (1)

9527 תִּפְסַח *tipsah* (2)
Tiphsah (2)

9528 תָּפַף *tāpap* (2)
beat (1)
playing tambourines (1)

9529 תָּפַר *tāpar* (4)
mend (1)
sew (1)
sewed (1)
sewed together (1)

9530 תָּפַשׂ *tāpaś* (65)
captured (8)
seize (4)
seized (4)
take (4)
took (4)
capture (3)
arrested (2)
be caught (2)
caught (2)
grasped (2)
taken (2)
was trapped (2)
archer (1) +8008
are caught (1)
be captured (1)
be taken captive (1) +928+2021+4090
been caught in the act (1)
brandishing (1)
capturing (1)
carry (1)
covered (1)
deal with (1)
dishonor (1)
handle (1)
hold (1)
occupy (1)
play (1)
rapes (1) +2256+6640+8886
reaper (1)
recapture (1)
soldiers (1) +4878
surely be captured (1) +9530
take captive (1)
take hold (1)
taken over (1)
took hold (1)
untranslated (1)

9531 1תֹּפֶת *tōpet1* (1)
spit (1)

9532 2תֹּפֶת *tōpet2* (9)
Topheth (9)

9533 תָּפְתֶּה *topteh* (1)
Topheth (1)

9534 תָּקְהַת *toqhat* (1)
Tokhath (1)

9535 1תִּקְוָה *tiqwāh1* (2)
cord (1)
cord (1) +2562

9536 תִּקְוָה2 *tiqwāh2* (32)
hope (30)
expectation (1)
hopes (1)

9537 תִּקְוָה3 *tiqwāh3* (2)
Tikvah (2)

9538 תְּקוּמָה *tᵉqûmāh* (1)
able to stand (1)

9539 תְּקוֹמֵם *tᵉqômēm*
Variant; not used

9540 תָּקוֹעַ *tāqôaʿ* (1)
trumpet (1)

9541 תְּקוֹעַ *tᵉqôaʿ* (7)
Tekoa (7)

9542 תְּקוֹעִי *tᵉqôʿiy* (7)
from Tekoa (4)
men of Tekoa (2)
Tekoite (1)

9543 תְּקוּפָה *tᵉqûp̄āh* (4)
turn (2)
circuit (1)
course (1)

9544 תַּקִּיף *taqqiyp̄* (2)
stronger (1)
untranslated (1)

9545 תָּקַן *tāqan* (3)
set in order (1)
straighten (1)
straightened (1)

9546 תָּקַע *tāqaʿ* (70)
blow (10)
sounded (10)
blew (7)
sound (7)
blowing (5)
sounding (3)
plunged (2)
sounds (2)
strikes in pledge (2)
blow trumpets (1)
blows (1)
camped (1)
carried (1)
clap (1)
claps (1)
drive (1)
driven (1)
drove (1)
fastened (1)
had blown (1)
hung up (1)
pitch (1)
pitched (1)
put up security (1) +3338+4200
signal (1)
sounded blast (1)
struck in pledge (1)
tighten (1)
tightened (1)
untranslated (2)

9547 תֵּקַע *tēqaʿ* (1)
sounding (1)

9548 תָּקַף *tāqap̄* (3)
overpower (1)
overpowered (1)
overwhelm (1)

9549 תֹּקֶף *tōqep̄* (3)
authority (1)
might (1)
power (1)

9550 תַּרְאֵלָה *tarʾᵃlāh* (1)
Taralah (1)

9551 תַּרְבוּת *tarbût* (1)
brood (1)

9552 תַּרְבִּית *tarbiyt* (7)
excessive interest (4)
exorbitant interest (1) +2256+5968
interest of any kind (1) +2256+5968
untranslated (1)

9553 תִּרְגַּם *tirgēm* (1)
language (1)

9554 תַּרְדֵּמָה *tardēmāh* (7)
deep sleep (6)
deep sleep (1) +8120

9555 תִּרְהָקָה *tirhāqāh* (2)
Tirhakah (2)

9556 תְּרוּמָה *tᵉrûmāh* (76)
offering (19)
portion (12)
contributions (8)
offerings (7)
presented (4)
contribution (3)
special gifts (3) +3338
part (2)
set aside (2)
special gift (2)
bribes (1)
district (1)
gift (1)
portion as a special gift (1)
present (1) +8123
present an offering (1)
special gifts (1)
special portion (1)
was presented (1) +8123
untranslated (5)

9557 תְּרוּמִיָּה *tᵉrûmiyyāh* (1)
special gift (1)

9558 תְּרוּעָה *tᵉrûʿāh* (36)
battle cry (5)
shouts (3)
shouts of joy (3)
blast (2)
cry (2)
gave a shout (2) +8131
war cries (2)
acclaim (1)
give a shout (1) +8131
made noise (1) +8131
raised a shout (1) +8131
resounding (1)
shout (1)
shout for joy (1)
shouted (1) +928+7754+8123
shouting (1)
shouting (1) +7754
shouts for joy (1)
signaling (1)
sound the trumpets (1)
trumpet (1) +8795
trumpet blast (1)
trumpet blasts (1)
uproar (1) +7754

9559 תְּרוּפָה *tᵉrûp̄āh* (1)
healing (1)

9560 תִּרְזָה *tirzāh* (1)
cypress (1)

9561 תֶּרַח *terah* (11)
Terah (10)
heˢ (1)

9562 תָּרַח *tārah* (2)
Terah (2)

9563 תִּרְחֲנָה *tirhᵃnāh* (1)
Tirhanah (1)

9564 תָּרְמָה *tormāh* (1)
under cover (1) +928

9565 תַּרְמוּק *tarmûq* (1)
Variant; not used

9566 תַּרְמוּת *tarmût* (1)
untranslated (1)

9567 תַּרְמִית *tarmiyt* (5)
delusions (2)
deceit (1)
deceit (1) +4383
deceitfulness (1)

9568 תֹּרֶן *tōren* (3)
flagstaff (1)
mast (1)
mast (1) +4029

9569 תַּרְעִית *tarʿiyt*
Variant; not used

9570 תַּרְעֵלָה *tarʿēlāh* (3)
makes stagger (2)
made stagger (1)

9571 תִּרְעָתִים *tirʿātiym* (1)
Tirathites (1)

9572 תְּרָפִים *tᵉrāp̄iym* (15)
household gods (8)
idol (3)
idols (3)
idolatry (1)

9573 תִּרְצָה1 *tirsāh1* (5)
Tirzah (5)

9574 תִּרְצָה2 *tirsāh2* (13)
Tirzah (13)

9575 תֶּרֶשׁ *tereš* (2)
Teresh (2)

9576 תַּרְשִׁישׁ1 *taršiyš1* (25)
Tarshish (16)
fleet of trading ships (1) +639
fleet of trading ships (1) +641
fleet of trading ships (1) +641+2143
fleet of trading ships (1) +641+2143+4200
itˢ (1) +639
itˢ (1) +641
that portˢ (1)
trade (1)
trading ship (1) +641

9577 תַּרְשִׁישׁ2 *taršiyš2* (7)
chrysolite (6)
chrysolite (1) +74

9578 תַּרְשִׁישׁ3 *taršiyš3* (3)
Tarshish (3)

9579 תִּרְשָׁתָא *tiršātā* (5)
governor (5)

9580 תַּרְתָּן *tartān* (2)
supreme commander (2)

9581 תַּרְתָּק *tartāq* (1)
Tartak (1)

9582 תְּשׂוּמָה *tᵉśûmāh* (1)
left (1)

9583 תְּשֻׁאָה *tᵉšuʾāh* (5)
commotion (1)
shout (1)
shouts (1)
storm (1)
thunders (1)

9584 תִּשְׁבֶּה *tišbeh*
Variant; not used

9585 תִּשְׁבִּי *tišbiy* (6)
Tishbite (6)

9586 תִּשְׁבֵּי *tišbēy* (1)
Tishbe (1)

9587 תַּשְׁבֵּץ *tašbēs* (1)
woven (1)

9588 תְּשׁוּבָה *tᵉšûbāh* (8)
spring (3) +9102
answering (1)

answers (1)
spring (1) +2021+9102
spring (1) +6961+9102
went back (1)

9589 תְּשֻׁוֶה *t'šuwwāh* (1)
untranslated (1)

9590 תַּשְׁוִית *tašwiyṭ*
Variant; not used

9591 תְּשׁוּעָה *t'šû'āh* (34)
salvation (12)
victory (12)
help (2)
brought about victory (1) +3828
deliverance (1)
delivered (1)
rescue (1)
rescued (1) +6913
save (1)
saves (1)
savior (1)

9592 תְּשׁוּקָה *t'šûqāh* (3)
desire (2)
desires (1)

9593 תְּשׁוּרָה *t'šûrāh* (1)
gift (1)

9594 תֻּשִׁיָּה *tušiyyāh*
Variant; not used

9595 תְּשִׁיעִי *t'šiy'iy* (18)
ninth (18)

9596 תֵּשַׁע *tēša'* (77)
nine (12)
ninth (5)
twenty-nine (5) +2256+6929
29 (3) +2256+6929
thirty-ninth (3) +2256+8993
390 (2) +2256+4395+8993
392 (2) +2256+4395+8993+9109
59,300 (1)
            +547+2256+2256+2822+4395+8993
95 (2) +2256+2822
973 (2) +2256+4395+8679+8993
98 (2) +2256+9046
nineteenth (2) +6925
nineteenth (2) +6926
ninety (2)
ninety-nine (2) +2256+9596
ninety-six (2) +2256+9252
1,290 (1) +547+2256+4395
119 (1) +2256+4395+6926

139 (1) +2256+4395+8993
209 (1) +2256+4395
3,930 (1) +547+2256+4395+8993+8993
595 (1) +2256+2256+2822+2822+4395
690 (1) +2256+4395+9252
895 (1) +2256+2256+2822+4395+9046
90 (1)
905 (1) +2256+2822+4395
910 (1) +2256+4395+6924
912 (1) +2256+4395+6926+9109
928 (1) +2256+4395+6929+9046
930 (1) +2256+4395+8993
945 (1) +752+2256+2256+2822+4395
950 (1) +2256+2822+4395
956 (1) +2256+2256+2822+4395+9252
962 (1) +2256+2256+4395+9109+9252
969 (1) +2256+2256+4395+9252+9596
forty-nine (1) +752+2256
more than thirteen feet (1) +564
nine-and-a-half (1) +2256+2942
nineteen (1) +6925
nineteen (1) +6926
ninety-eight (1) +2256+9046

9597 תִּשְׁעִים *tiš'iym*
Variant; not used

ARAMAIC TO ENGLISH
INDEX-LEXICON
OF THE OLD TESTAMENT

10001 א '
Variant; not used

10002 אָ - ā' (831)
the (412)
O (26)
a (15)
this (7)
his^s (4)
these (4)
he^s (3) +10421
him^s (3) +10421
that (3)
an (2)
continually (2) +10089+10753
ever (2) +10550
he^s (2) +10421+10453
his^s (2) +10421
immediately (2) +10734
my^s (2)
as soon as (1) +10089+10168+10530
as soon as (1) +10168+10232+10341
certainly (1) +10327
cordial greetings (1) +10002+10353+10720
ever (1) +10527+10550
forever (1) +10378+10550
forever (1) +10509+10527
forever (1) +10527+10550
forever (1) +10550
it^s (1)
it^s (1) +10418
it^s (1) +10424
it^s (1) +10614
its^s (1)
never end (1) +10509+10527
order (1) +10302+10682
she^s (1) +10423
sundown (1) +10436+10728
them^s (1) +10038
they^s (1) +10353+10553
this^s (1) +10418
Trans-Euphrates (1) +10468+10526
what^s (1) +10418
when (1) +10089+10530
who^s (1) +10131
untranslated (314)

10003 אַב 'ab (9)
father (6)
fathers (2)
predecessors (1)

10004 אֵב 'ēb (3)
fruit (3)

10005 אֲבַד '^abad (7)
execute (2)
completely destroyed (1) +10221+10722

destroyed (1)
executed (1)
execution (1)
perish (1)

10006 אֶבֶן 'eben (8)
rock (3)
stone (3)
large stones (2) +10146

10007 אִגְּרָה 'igg^erāh (3)
letter (3)

10008 אֱדַיִן '^dayin (57)
then (13) +10089
then (11)
so (8) +10089
so (3)
when (2) +10089
also (1) +10358
and (1) +10221
as soon as (1) +10168+10427
at this (1)
finally (1)
now (1)
that day^s (1)
therefore (1) +10089
thus (1) +10089
untranslated (11)

10009 אֲדָר '^dār (1)
Adar (1)

10010 אִדַּר 'iddar (1)
threshing floor (1)

10011 אֲדַרְגָּזַר '^dargāzar (2)
advisers (2)

10012 אֲדְרַזְדָּא 'adrazdā' (1)
with diligence (1)

10013 אֶדְרָע 'edrā' (1)
force (1)

10014 אַזְדָּא 'azdā' (2)
firmly (2)

10015 אֲזָה '^zāh (3)
heated (1)
hot (1)
hotter (1)

10016 אֲזַל '^zal (7)
returned (2)
went (2)
go (1)
untranslated (2)

10017 אָח 'ah (2)
brother Jews (1)
untranslated (1)

10018 אַחֲוָיָה 'ah^wāyāh
Variant; not used

10019 אֲחִידָה '^hiydāh (1)
riddles (1)

10020 אַחְמְתָא 'ahm^tā' (1)
Ecbatana (1)

10021 אַחַר 'ahar (3)
after (1)
in the future (1) +10180
to come (1) +10180+10201

10022 אַחֲרִי 'ah^riy (1)
to come (1)

10023 אָחֳרִי 'oh^riy (6)
another (3)
a^s (1)
one (1)
other (1)

10024 אָחֳרֵין 'oh^rēyn (1)
finally (1) +10221+10527

10025 אָחֳרָן 'oh^rān (5)
another (2)
one (1)
other (1)
someone else (1)

10026 אֲחַשְׁדַּרְפַּן '^hašdarpan (9)
satraps (9)

10027 אִילָן 'iylān (6)
tree (6)

10028 אֵימְתָן 'ēym^tān (1)
frightening (1)

10029 אִיתַי 'iytay (19)
there is (3)
are (2)
do (1)
have (1) +10089
in fact (1)
there are (1)
unharmed (1) +10244+10379
will be left with (1) +10378
untranslated (8)

10030 אֲכַל '^kal (7)
devoured (2)
ate (1)
denounced (1) +10642
devour (1)
eat (1)
falsely accused (1) +10642

10031 אַל 'al (4)
don't (2)

not (2)

10032 אֵל ’ēl (1)
these (1)

10033 אֱלָה ’ĕlāh (96)
God (73)
gods (15)
god (6)
untranslated (2)

10034 אֵלֶּה ’ēlleh (2)
untranslated (2)

10035 אִלּוּ ’ĕlû (5)
there (4)
untranslated (1)

10036 אִלֵּין ’illēyn (5)
the others[s] (1)
those (1)
untranslated (3)

10037 אִלֵּךְ ’illēk (14)
these (8)
untranslated (6)

10038 אֲלַף ’ălap (5)
thousands (2)
them[s] (1) +10002
thousand (1)
untranslated (1)

10039 אַמָּה ’ammāh (4)
ninety feet (3) +10749
nine feet (1) +10747

10040 אֻמָּה ’ummāh (8)
nations (6)
nation (1)
people (1)

10041 אֲמַן ’ăman (3)
trustworthy (2)
trusted (1)

10042 אֲמַר ’ămar (71)
said (6)
tell (6)
told (5)
asked (3)
command (3)
commanded (2)
gave orders (2)
interpret (2) +10600
ordered (2)
say (2)
decreed (1)
gave explanation (1)
gave the order (1)
saying (1)
spoke (1)
summoned (1) +10085+10378
untranslated (32)

10043 אִמַּר ’immar (3)
male lambs (3)

10044 אֲנָה ’ănāh (16)
I (15)
me (1)

10045 אִנּוּן ’innûn (4)
those (1)
untranslated (3)

10046 אֱנוֹשׁ ’ĕnôš (2)
untranslated (2)

10047 אֲנַחְנָא ’ănaḥnā’ (4)
we (4)

10048 אֲנַס ’ănas (1)
difficult (1)

10049 אֲנַף ’ănap (2)
attitude (1) +10614
prostrate (1) +10542

10050 אֱנָשׁ ’ĕnāš (25)
man (8)

men (6)
people (3)
anyone (2) +10353
everyone (1) +10353
human (1)
mankind (1) +10120
people (1) +10120
people (1) +10240
whoever (1) +10168+10353

10051 אַנְתְּ ’ant (14)
untranslated (14)

10052 אַנְתָּה ’antāh (15)
you (13)
untranslated (2)

10053 אַנְתּוּן ’antûn (1)
you (1)

10054 אֱסוּר ’ĕsûr (3)
bound (2)
imprisonment (1)

10055 אָסְנַפַּר ’āsĕnapar (1)
Ashurbanipal (1)

10056 אָסְפַּרְנָא ’āsĕparnā’ (7)
with diligence (3)
be sure (1)
diligence (1)
fully (1)
surely (1)

10057 אֱסַר ’ĕsar (7)
decree (7)

10058 אָע ’ā‘ (5)
timbers (2)
wood (2)
beam (1)

10059 אַף ’ap (4)
also (2) +10221
even (1) +10221
nor (1) +10221+10379

10060 אֲפָרְסָי ’ăpārĕsāy (1)
Persia (1)

10061 אֲפַרְסְכָי ’ăparsĕkāy (2)
officials (2)

10062 אֲפַרְסַתְכָי ’ăparsatĕkāy (1)
officials (1)

10063 אַפְּתֹם ’appĕtōm (1)
revenues (1)

10064 אֶצְבַּע ’eṣba‘ (3)
fingers (1)
toes (1)
toes (1) +10655

10065 אַרְבַּע ’arba‘ (8)
four (8)

10066 אַרְגְּוָן ’argĕwān (3)
purple (3)

10067 אֲרוּ ’ărû (5)
there (5)

10068 אֹרַח ’ōraḥ (2)
ways (2)

10069 אַרְיֵה ’aryēh (10)
lions’ (5)
lions (4)
lion (1)

10070 אַרְיוֹךְ ’aryôk (5)
Arioch (4)
untranslated (1)

10071 אֲרִיךְ ’ărik (1)
proper (1)

10072 אַרְכֻּבָּה ’arkubbāh (1)
knees (1)

10073 אַרְכָה ’arkāh (2)
continue (1)

live (1) +10089+10261

10074 אַרְכְּוָי ’arkĕwāy (2)
Erech (1)
untranslated (1)

10075 אֲרַע ’ăra‘ (21)
earth (14)
ground (3)
land (2)
inferior (1)
world (1)

10076 אַרְעִי ’ar‘iy (1)
floor (1)

10077 אֲרַק ’ăraq (1)
earth (1)

10078 אַרְתַּחְשַׁשְׂתְּא ’artaḥšaśt’ (7)
Artaxerxes (6)
untranslated (1)

10079 אֹשׁ ’ōš (3)
foundations (3)

10080 אֶשָּׁא ’eššā’ (1)
fire (1)

10081 אָשַׁף ’āšap (6)
enchanters (4)
enchanter (2)

10082 אֻשַּׁרְנָא ’uššarnā’ (2)
structure (2)

10083 אֶשְׁתַּדּוּר ’eštadûr (2)
rebellion (1)
sedition (1)

10084 אָת ’āt (3)
signs (2)
miraculous signs (1)

10085 אֲתָה ’ătāh (16)
brought (3)
brought in (2)
came (2)
come (2)
bring in (1)
coming (1)
gone (1)
summoned (1) +10042+10378
was brought (1)
went (1)
were brought (1)

10086 אַתּוּן ’atûn (10)
furnace (10)

10087 אֲתַר ’ătar (5)
site (2)
place (1)
places (1)
trace (1)

10088 ב b
Variant; not used

10089 בְּ- bĕ- (227)
in (79)
then (13) +10008
with (11)
on (9)
at (8)
so (8) +10008
over (7)
by (6)
of (6)
from (4)
have (3)
continually (2) +10002+10753
throughout (2) +10353
to (2)
under (2)
underfoot (2) +10655
when (2) +10008
about (1)
among (1)

as soon as (1) +10002+10168+10530
be handed over (1) +10311+10314
because (1)
daily (1) +10317+10317
Daniel's (1) +10181
during (1)
had (1)
handed over (1) +10311+10314
have (1) +10029
his (1) +10192
immediately (1) +10096
in (1) +10135
in (1) +10135+10464
live (1) +10073+10261
loudly (1) +10264
on (1) +10135
place^s (1) +10135+10193
place^s (1) +10193
possess (1) +10311
something to do with (1)
therefore (1) +10008
thus (1) +10008
wearing (1)
when (1) +10002+10530
wherever (1) +10168+10353
while (1)
with regard to (1)
untranslated (32)

10090 בְּאִישׁ *bi'yš* (1)
wicked (1)

10091 בְּאֵשׁ *bᵉ'ēš* (1)
distressed (1)

10092 בָּאתַר *bā'tar* (3)
after (3)

10093 בָּבֶל *bābel* (25)
Babylon (24)
its^s (1)

10094 בָּבְלִי *bāb'liy* (1)
Babylon (1)

10095 בְּדַר *bᵉdar* (1)
scatter (1)

10096 בְּהִילוּ *bᵉhiylû* (1)
immediately (1) +10089

10097 בְּהַל *bᵉhal* (11)
terrified (3)
alarm (1)
alarmed (1)
amazement (1) +10755
at once (1)
disturbed (1)
frightened (1)
hurried (1)
troubled (1)

10098 בְּטַל *bᵉtal* (6)
stop (2)
came to a standstill (1)
stop work (1)
stopped (1)
untranslated (1)

10099 בֵּין *bēyn* (3)
among (1)
between (1)
untranslated (1)

10100 בִּינָה *biynāh* (1)
discerning (1) +10313

10101 בִּירָה *biyrāh* (1)
citadel (1)

10102 בִּית *biyt* (1)
spent the night (1)

10103 בַּיִת *bayit* (44)
house (17)
temple (16)
home (2)
houses (2)

archives (1) +10148
archives (1) +10515
hall (1)
residence (1)
treasury (1)
treasury (1) +10148
untranslated (1)

10104 בָּל *bāl* (1)
determined (1) +10682

10105 בֵּלְאשַׁצַּר *bēl'šassar* (2)
Belshazzar (2)

10106 בְּלָה *bᵉlāh* (1)
oppress (1)

10107 בְּלוֹ *bᵉlô* (3)
tribute (3)

10108 בֵּלְטְשַׁאצַּר *bēlt'ša'ssar* (8)
Belteshazzar (8)

10109 בֵּלְשַׁאצַּר *bēlša'ssar* (5)
Belshazzar (4)
Belshazzar's (1)

10110 בֵּן *bēn*
Variant; not used

10111 בְּנָה *bᵉnāh* (22)
rebuild (7)
built (3)
be rebuilt (2)
building (2)
is built (2)
rebuilding (2)
build (1)
constructing (1)
construction (1)
under construction (1)

10112 בִּנְיָן *binyān* (1)
building (1)

10113 בְּנַס *bᵉnas* (1)
angry (1)

10114 בְּעָה *bᵉ'āh* (12)
asked (2)
prays (2) +10115
asked for (1)
look for (1)
plead (1)
praying (1)
prays (1)
request (1)
sought out (1)
tried (1)

10115 בָּעוּ *bā'û* (2)
prays (2) +10114

10116 בְּעֵל *bᵉ'ēl* (3)
commanding officer (3) +10302

10117 בִּקְעָה *biq'āh* (1)
plain (1)

10118 בְּקַר *bᵉqar* (5)
a search made (2)
a search be made (1)
inquire (1)
searched (1)

10119 בַּר1 *bar1* (8)
field (5)
wild (3)

10120 בַּר2 *bar2* (19)
son (5)
exiles (4) +10145
descendant (2)
sons (2)
age (1) +10732
children (1)
mankind (1) +10050
people (1)
people (1) +10050
young (1)

10121 בְּרַךְ1 *bᵉrak1* (1)
got down (1)

10122 בְּרַךְ2 *bᵉrak2* (4)
praise (2)
praised (2)

10123 בְּרֵךְ *bᵉrēk* (1)
knees (1)

10124 בְּרַם *bᵉram* (5)
but (3)
however (1)
nevertheless (1)

10125 בְּשַׂר *bᵉśar* (3)
creature (1)
flesh (1)
men (1)

10126 בַּת *bat* (2)
baths (2)

10127 ג *g*
Variant; not used

10128 גַּב *gab* (2)
back (1)
untranslated (1)

10129 גֹּב *gōb* (10)
den (10)

10130 גְּבוּרָה *gᵉbûrāh* (2)
power (2)

10131 גְּבַר *gᵉbar* (21)
men (12)
some^s (3)
man (2)
soldiers (1)
who^s (1) +10002
untranslated (2)

10132 גִּבָּר *gibbar* (1)
strongest soldiers (1) +10264

10133 גְּדָבַר *gᵉdābar* (2)
treasurers (2)

10134 גְּדַד *gᵉdad* (2)
cut down (2)

10135 גַּו *gaw* (13)
into (6) +10378
in (1) +10089
in (1) +10089+10464
middle (1)
of (1) +10427
on (1) +10089
place^s (1) +10089+10193
untranslated (1)

10136 גֵּוָה *gēwāh* (1)
pride (1)

10137 גּוּחַ *gûah* (1)
churning up (1)

10138 גּוֹן *gôn*
Variant; not used

10139 גִּזְבַּר *gizbar* (1)
treasurers (1)

10140 גְּזַר *gᵉzar* (6)
diviners (3)
cut out (1)
diviner (1)
was cut out (1)

10141 גְּזֵרָה *gᵉzērāh* (3)
announced (1)
decree (1)
solitary (1)

10142 גִּיר *giyr* (1)
plaster (1)

10143 גַּלְגַּל *galgal* (1)
wheels (1)

10144 גְּלָה *gᵉlāh* (9)
deported (2)

revealer (2)
reveals (2)
been revealed (1)
reveal (1)
was revealed (1)

10145 גָּלוּ *gālû* (4)
exiles (4) +10120

10146 גְּלָל *g⁰lāl* (2)
large stones (2) +10006

10147 גְּמַר *g⁰mar* (1)
greetings (1)

10148 גְּנַז *g⁰naz* (3)
archives (1) +10103
treasury (1)
treasury (1) +10103

10149 גַּף *gap̱* (3)
wings (3)

10150 גְּרַם *g⁰ram* (1)
bones (1)

10151 גְּשֵׁם *g⁰šēm* (6)
body (3)
bodies (1)
lives (1)
untranslated (1)

10152 ד *d*
Variant; not used

10153 דְּ־ *d⁰-*
Variant; not used

10154 דָּא *dā'* (6)
this (2)
each (1)
others^s (1)
together (1) +10154+10378

10155 דֹּב *dōḇ* (1)
bear (1)

10156 דְּבַח *d⁰baḥl* (1)
present (1)

10157 דְּבַח *d⁰baḥ2* (1)
sacrifices (1)

10158 דְּבַק *d⁰baq* (1)
united (1) +10180+10180+10554

10159 דִּבְרָה *dibᵉrāh* (2)
so that (1) +10168+10527
so that (1) +10168+10542

10160 דְּהַב *d⁰haḇ* (23)
gold (23)

10161 דְּהוּא *d⁰hû'*
Variant; not used

10162 דְּהָיֵא *dehāyē'*
Variant; not used

10163 דּוּר *dûr* (13)
live (2)
peoples (2)
lived (1)
shelter (1)
untranslated (7)

10164 דּוּרָא *dûrā'* (1)
Dura (1)

10165 דּוּשׁ *dûš* (1)
trampling down (1)

10166 דַּחֲוָה *daḥᵉwāh* (1)
entertainment (1)

10167 דְּחַל *d⁰ḥal* (6)
terrifying (2)
awesome (1)
feared (1)
made afraid (1)
reverence (1)

10168 דִּי *diy* (348)
of (46)

that (46)
who (18)
which (9)
until (8) +10527
whom (8)
so that (6)
those (5)
anyone (4) +10426
from (4)
because (3)
because (3) +10353+10619
for (3) +10353+10619
in (3)
when (3) +10341
with (3)
but (2)
for (2)
just as (2)
what (2)
whatever (2) +10353
whoever (2) +10426
any more than (1) +10195+10341
as (1)
as (1) +10527
as soon as (1) +10002+10089+10530
as soon as (1) +10002+10232+10341
as soon as (1) +10008+10427
because (1) +10427
because of (1) +10378+10619
by (1) +10353+10619
during (1)
even as (1) +10353+10619
hoping (1) +10527
if (1)
just as (1) +10353+10619
one (1)
over (1)
since (1) +10353+10619
so that (1) +10159+10527
so that (1) +10159+10542
surely (1) +10427+10643
this is the meaning (1) +10353+10619
though (1) +10353+10619
whatever (1) +10408
when (1) +10427
wherever (1) +10089+10353
while (1) +10527
whoever (1) +10050+10353
whoever (1) +10353
whose (1)
untranslated (135)

10169 דִּין *diyn1* (2)
administer justice (1)
untranslated (1)

10170 דִּין *diyn2* (5)
court (2)
judgment (1)
just (1)
punished (1) +10191+10522

10171 דַּיָּן *dayyān* (2)
judges (2)

10172 דִּינָיֵא *diynāyē'*
Variant; not used

10173 דֵּךְ *dēk* (13)
this (12)
untranslated (1)

10174 דִּכֵּן *dikkēn* (3)
that (1)
this (1)
untranslated (1)

10175 דְּכַר *d⁰kar* (3)
rams (3)

10176 דִּכְרוֹן *dikrôn* (1)
memorandum (1)

10177 דָּכְרָן *dokrān* (2)
archives (1) +10515
records (1) +10515

10178 דְּלַק *d⁰laq* (1)
all ablaze (1) +10471

10179 דְּמָה *d⁰māh* (2)
like (1)
looked like (1)

10180 דְּנָה *d⁰nāh* (58)
this (30)
that (2)
ago (1) +10427+10622
as follows (1) +10341
before (1) +10427+10622
in the future (1) +10021
so (1) +10353+10619
such (1) +10341
that is why (1) +10542
the (1)
then (1) +10353+10619
therefore (1) +10353+10619
these (1)
this (1) +10341
this made (1) +10353+10619
to come (1) +10021+10201
united (1) +10158+10180+10554
untranslated (10)

10181 דָּנִיֵּאל *dāniyyē'l* (52)
Daniel (46)
Daniel's (1)
Daniel's (1) +10089
he^s (1)
him^s (1)
untranslated (2)

10182 דְּקַק *d⁰qaq* (10)
crushed (3)
crush (2)
breaks (1)
broke to pieces (1)
broken to pieces (1)
crushing (1)
smashed (1)

10183 דָּר *dār* (4)
generation (4)

10184 דָּרְיָוֶשׁ *dārᵉyāweš* (15)
Darius (15)

10185 דְּרַע *d⁰rā'* (1)
arms (1)

10186 דָּת *dāṯ* (14)
law (7)
laws (4)
decree (2)
penalty (1)

10187 דֶּתֶא *dete'* (2)
grass (2)

10188 דְּתָבַר *d⁰ṯāḇar* (2)
judges (2)

10189 ה *h*
Variant; not used

10190 הֲ־ *hᵃ-* (7)
is it true (1) +10609
untranslated (6)

10191 ה ָ ־ *-āh* (63)
the (15)
Trans-Euphrates (12) +10468+10526
its^s (1)
immediately (1) +10734
it^s (1) +10424
punished (1) +10170+10522
suddenly (1) +10734
that (1)
that province^s (1) +10468+10526
this (1)
your^s (1)
untranslated (26)

10192 ה ֵ ־ *-ēh* (159)
his (47)

him (24)
it (16)
its (10)
he (7)
the^s (5)
their (3)
a^s (1)
his (1) +10089
his (1) +10378
his own (1)
man^s (1)
same^s (1)
untranslated (41)

10193 הָ‍ָ *-ah* (52)
it (15)
its (7)
them (5)
place^s (1) +10089
place^s (1) +10089+10135
the^s (1)
which (1)
untranslated (21)

10194 הָא *hā'* (1)
look (1)

10195 הֵא *hē'* (1)
any more than (1) +10168+10341

10196 הַדָּבַר *haddābar* (4)
advisers (4)

10197 הַדָּם *haddām* (2)
pieces (2)

10198 הֲדַר1 *h^adar1* (3)
glorified (1)
glorify (1)
honor (1)

10199 הֲדַר2 *h^adar2* (3)
honor (1)
majesty (1)
splendor (1)

10200 הוּא *hû'* (16)
he (5)
it (1)
that (1)
that tree^s (1)
untranslated (8)

10201 הֲוָה *h^wāh* (71)
be (11)
was (7)
became (2)
happen (2)
were (2)
appear (1)
continued (1)
had (1) +10542
have (1)
keep (1)
kept (1)
must (1)
remain (1)
stay (1)
take place (1)
to come (1) +10021+10180
untranslated (36)

10202 הוּךְ *hûk*
Variant; not used

10203 הוֹן *-hôn* (61)
their (17)
them (17)
the^s (3)
their own (1)
they (1)
untranslated (22)

10204 הִי *-hiy* (76)
his (26)
its (14)
him (11)

he (5)
it (4)
one (1)
the^s (1)
untranslated (14)

10205 הִיא *hiy'* (8)
it (1)
itself (1)
there (1)
this (1)
untranslated (4)

10206 הֵיכַל *hēykal* (13)
temple (8)
palace (5)

10207 הֲלַךְ *h^lak* (7)
go (3)
walk (1)
walking (1)
walking around (1)
untranslated (1)

10208 הֲלָךְ *h^lāk* (3)
duty (3)

10209 הֹם *-hōm* (12)
their (5)
them (4)
untranslated (3)

10210 הִמּוֹ *himmô* (12)
them (6)
they (1)
untranslated (5)

10211 הִמּוֹנְךְ *hmwnk* (3)
untranslated (3)

10212 הַמְיָנַךְ *hamyānak* (3)
chain (3)

10213 הֵן *hēn* (16)
if (11)
even if (1)
then (1)
untranslated (3)

10214 הֵן *-hēn* (8)
the others^s (1)
them (1)
untranslated (6)

10215 הַנְזָקָה *hanzāqāh*
Variant; not used

10216 הַצְדָּא *hasdā'*
Variant; not used

10217 הַרְהֹר *harhōr* (1)
images (1)

10218 הִתְבְּהָלָה *hitb^hālāh*
Variant; not used

10219 הִתְנַדָּבוּ *hit naddābû*
Variant; not used

10220 ו *w*
Variant; not used

10221 וְ־ *w^-* (751)
and (400)
or (20)
but (19)
then (9)
now (5)
so (5)
so that (5)
moreover (3)
nor (3) +10379
that (3)
together with (3)
with (3)
also (2)
also (2) +10059
120 (1) +10395+10574
and (1) +10008
and now (1)

and that (1)
and when (1)
as (1)
as for (1)
at this (1)
completely destroyed (1) +10005+10722
even (1) +10059
finally (1)
finally (1) +10024+10527
furthermore (1)
including (1)
instead (1)
next (1)
nor (1)
nor (1) +10059+10379
period of time (1) +10232+10530
set to work (1) +10624+10742
sixty-two (1) +10749+10775
therefore (1)
till (1)
until (1)
when (1)
while (1)
yes (1)
yet (1)
untranslated (241)

10222 ז *z*
Variant; not used

10223 זְבַן *z^ban* (1)
gain (1)

10224 זְהִיר *z^hiyr* (1)
careful (1)

10225 זוּד *zûd* (1)
pride (1)

10226 זוּן *zûn* (1)
was fed (1)

10227 זוּעַ *zû'a* (4)
dreaded (1)
fear (1)
untranslated (2)

10228 זִיו *ziyw* (6)
face pale (3)
dazzling (1)
look so pale (1) +10731
splendor (1)

10229 זָכוּ *zākû* (1)
innocent (1)

10230 זְכַרְיָה *z^karyāh* (2)
Zechariah (2)

10231 זְמָן1 *z^man1* (2)
conspired (1)
untranslated (1)

10232 זְמָן2 *z^man2* (11)
time (5)
times (2)
as soon as (1) +10002+10168+10341
period of time (1) +10221+10530
seasons (1)
set times (1)

10233 זְמָר *z^mār* (4)
music (4)

10234 זַמָּר *zammār* (1)
singers (1)

10235 זַן *zan* (4)
kinds (4)

10236 זְעֵיר *z^'ēyr* (6)
little (5)
little longer (1)

10237 זְעִק *z^'iq* (1)
called (1)

10238 זְקַף *z^qap* (1)
be lifted up (1)

10239 זְרֻבָּבֶל *z^erubbābel* (1)
Zerubbabel (1)

10240 זְרַע *z^era'* (1)
people (1) +10050

10241 ח *h*
Variant; not used

10242 חֲבוּלָה *h^abûlāh* (1)
wrong (1)

10243 חֲבַל *h^abal* (6)
be destroyed (3)
destroy (2)
hurt (1)

10244 חֲבָל *h^abāl* (3)
threat (1)
unharmed (1) +10029+10379
wound (1)

10245 חֲבַר *h^abar* (3)
friends (3)

10246 חַבְרָה *habrāh* (1)
others (1)

10247 חַגַּי *haggay* (2)
Haggai (2)

10248 חַד *had* (15)
a (5)
one (5)
first (3)
same (1)
times (1)

10249 חֲדֶה *h^adēh* (1)
chest (1)

10250 חֶדְוָה *hedwāh* (1)
joy (1)

10251 חֲדַת *h^adat*
Variant; not used

10252 חֲוָה *h^awāh* (15)
interpret (5) +10600
tell (4)
explain (2)
do^s (1)
explain (1) +10600
reveal (1)
tells (1)

10253 חוּט *hût* (1)
repairing (1)

10254 חִוָּר *hiwwār* (1)
white (1)

10255 חֲזָה *h^azāh* (31)
looked (8)
saw (7)
had^s (3)
see (3)
watched (3)
looking (1)
realize (1)
usual (1)
vision (1)
watch (1)
watching (1)
untranslated (1)

10256 חֵזוּ *h^ezû* (12)
visions (6)
vision (4)
dream (1) +10267
looked (1)

10257 חֱזוֹת *h^azôt* (2)
visible (2)

10258 חֲטָאָה *hattā'āh* (3)
sin (1)
wickedness (1)
untranslated (1)

10259 חֲטָי *h^atāy* (2)
sins (1)

10260 חַטָּיָא *hattāyā'* (1)
sin offering (1)

10261 חַי *hay* (7)
living (4)
live (1) +10073+10089
lives (1)
well-being (1)

10262 חֲיָה *h^ayāh* (6)
live (5)
spared (1)

10263 חֵיוָה *hêywāh* (20)
beasts (7)
beast (6)
animals (5)
animal (2)

10264 חַיִל *hayil* (7)
army (1)
compelled (1)
loud (1)
loudly (1) +10089
powers (1)
strongest soldiers (1) +10132
untranslated (1)

10265 חַכִּים *hakkiym* (14)
wise (14)

10266 חָכְמָה *hokmāh* (8)
wisdom (7)
that^s (1)

10267 חֵלֶם *hēlem* (22)
dream (20)
dream (1) +10256
dreams (1)

10268 חֲלַף *h^alap* (4)
pass by (4)

10269 חֲלָק *h^alāq* (3)
live (2)
nothing (1) +10379

10270 חֲמָה *h^amāh* (2)
furious (1)
furious (1) +10416

10271 חֲמַר *h^amar* (6)
wine (6)

10272 חִנְטָה *hintāh* (2)
wheat (2)

10273 חֲנֻכָּה *h^anukkāh* (4)
dedication (4)

10274 חֲנַן *h^anan* (2)
asking for help (1)
kind (1)

10275 חֲנַנְיָה *h^ananyāh* (1)
Hananiah (1)

10276 חַסִּיר *hassiyr* (1)
wanting (1)

10277 חֲסַן *h^asan* (2)
possess (1)
possessed (1)

10278 חֲסֵן *h^asēn* (2)
mighty (1)
power (1)

10279 חֲסַף *h^asap* (9)
clay (5)
baked clay (2)
baked clay (1) +10298
clay (1) +10298

10280 חֲצַף *h^asap* (2)
harsh (1)
urgent (1)

10281 חֲרַב *h^arab* (1)
was destroyed (1)

10282 חַרְטֹם *hartōm* (5)
magicians (3)
magician (2)

10283 חֲרַךְ *h^arak* (1)
was singed (1)

10284 חֲרַץ *h^aras* (1)
legs (1) +10626

10285 חֲשַׁב *h^ašab* (1)
are regarded (1)

10286 חֲשׁוֹךְ *h^ašôk* (1)
darkness (1)

10287 חֲשַׁח *h^ašah* (1)
need (1)

10288 חַשְׁחָה *hašhāh* (1)
needed (1)

10289 חַשְׁחוּ *hašhû* (1)
needed (1)

10290 חֲשַׁל *h^ašal* (1)
smashes (1)

10291 חֲתַם *h^atam* (1)
sealed (1)

10292 ט *t*
Variant; not used

10293 טְאָב *t^e'ēb* (1)
overjoyed (1) +10678

10294 טָב *tāb* (2)
pleases (1)
pure (1)

10295 טַבָּח *tabbāh* (1)
guard (1)

10296 טוּר *tûr* (2)
mountain (2)

10297 טְוָת *t^ewāt* (1)
without eating (1)

10298 טִין *tiyn* (2)
baked clay (1) +10279
clay (1) +10279

10299 טַל *tal* (5)
dew (5)

10300 טְלַל *t^elal* (1)
found shelter (1)

10301 טְעֵם1 *t^e'ēm1* (3)
eat (2)
ate (1)

10302 טְעֵם2 *t^e'ēm2* (30)
decree (5)
decree (4) +10682
commanding officer (3) +10116
order (3)
attention (2)
authorized (2) +10682
accountable (1)
command (1)
commanded (1) +10682
decreed (1) +10682
decrees (1)
drinking (1)
order (1) +10002+10682
order (1) +10682
prescribed (1) +10427
report (1)
tact (1)

10303 טְפַר *t^epar* (2)
claws (1)
nails (1)

10304 טְרַד *t^erad* (4)
driven away (2)
was driven away (2)

10305 טַרְפְּלָי *tarp^elāy* (1)
men from Tripolis (1)

10306 י *y*
Variant; not used

10307 יִ ־ *-iy* (72)
my (33)
I (14)
me (12)
my (1) +10621
myself (1) +10380
untranslated (11)

10308 יְבַל *yᵉbal* (3)
brought (2)
take (1)

10309 יַבֶּשָׁה *yabbᵉšāh* (1)
earth (1)

10310 יְגַר *yᵉgar*
Variant; not used

10311 יַד *yad* (17)
hand (7)
hands (3)
hand (2) +10589
be handed over (1) +10089+10314
direction (1)
handed over (1) +10089+10314
possess (1) +10089
power (1)

10312 יְדָה *yᵉdāh* (2)
giving thanks (1)
thank (1)

10313 יְדַע *yᵉda'* (47)
know (11)
tell (8)
acknowledge (3)
interpret (3) +10600
explained (2)
inform (2)
made known (2)
shown (2)
understand (2)
acknowledged (1)
certain (1) +10327+10427
discerning (1) +10100
gave (1)
information (1)
knew (1)
knows (1)
learned (1)
remember (1)
showed (1)
teach (1)
untranslated (1)

10314 יְהַב *yᵉhab* (28)
given (4)
gave (3)
was given (3)
be given (1)
be handed over (1)
be handed over (1) +10089+10311
be paid (1)
entrusted (1)
give (1)
give up (1)
gives (1)
handed over (1) +10089+10311
laid (1)
lavished (1)
made (1)
paid (1)
placed (1)
pronounced (1)
thrown (1)
were allowed (1)
were paid (1)

10315 יְהוּד *yᵉhûd* (7)
Judah (6)
untranslated (1)

10316 יְהוּדָי *yᵉhûdāy* (10)
Jews (9)

Jewish (1)

10317 יוֹם *yôm* (16)
days (6)
day (3)
time (3)
daily (1) +10089+10317
long history (1) +10427+10550
times (1)

10318 יוֹצָדָק *yôsādāq* (1)
Jozadak (1)

10319 יְחַת *yᵉhat*
Variant; not used

10320 יְטַב *yᵉṭab* (1)
seems best (1)

10321 יְכֵל *yᵉkil* (14)
able (5)
can (5)
defeating (1)
unable (1) +10379
untranslated (2)

10322 יָם *yam* (2)
sea (2)

10323 יְסַף *yᵉsap* (1)
became even greater (1) +10339+10650

10324 יְעַט *yᵉ'at* (1)
agreed (1)

10325 יָעֵט *yā'ēt* (2)
advisers (2)

10326 יְצַב *yᵉṣab* (1)
know the true meaning (1)

10327 יַצִּיב *yaṣṣiyb* (5)
certain (1) +10313+10427
certainly (1) +10002
stands (1)
true (1)
true meaning (1)

10328 יְקַד *yᵉqad* (8)
blazing (8) +10471

10329 יְקֵדָה *yᵉqēdāh* (1)
blazing (1)

10330 יַקִּיר *yaqqiyr* (2)
honorable (1)
too difficult (1)

10331 יְקָר *yᵉqār* (7)
glory (6)
honor (1)

10332 יְרוּשְׁלֶם *yᵉrûšᵉlem* (26)
Jerusalem (26)

10333 יְרַח *yᵉrah* (2)
month (1)
months (1)

10334 יַרְכָה *yarkāh* (1)
thighs (1)

10335 יִשְׂרָאֵל *yiśrā'ēl* (8)
Israel (7)
Israelites (1) +10553

10336 יֵשׁוּעַ *yēšû'a* (1)
Jeshua (1)

10337 יָת *yāt* (1)
untranslated (1)

10338 יְתִב *yᵉtib* (5)
living (1)
seated (1)
settled (1)
sit (1)
took seat (1)

10339 יַתִּיר *yatiyr* (8)
became even greater (1) +10323+10650
exceptional (1)
keen (1)

most (1)
outstanding (1)
so (1)
very (1)
untranslated (1)

10340 כ *k*
Variant; not used

10341 כְּ־ *kᵉ-* (41)
like (14)
as (6)
in accordance with (4)
when (3) +10168
at (2)
how (2) +10408
according to (1)
after (1)
any more than (1) +10168+10195
as follows (1) +10180
as soon as (1) +10002+10168+10232
for (1)
in way (1)
such (1) +10180
this (1) +10180
when (1)

10342 ־ךְ *-k* (118)
your (46)
you (40)
there[s] (1) +10444
yours (1)
yourself (1)
yourself (1) +10381
untranslated (28)

10343 כְּדַב *kᵉdab* (1)
misleading (1)

10344 כִּדְבָה *kidbāh*
Variant; not used

10345 כָּה *kāh* (1)
this (1) +10527

10346 כְּהַל *kᵉhal* (4)
could (2)
able (1)
can (1)

10347 כָּהֵן *kāhēn* (8)
priests (6)
priest (2)

10348 כַּוָּה *kawwāh* (1)
windows (1)

10349 ־כוֹן *-kôn* (10)
you (8)
your (2)

10350 כּוֹרֶשׁ *kôreš* (8)
Cyrus (7)
untranslated (1)

10351 כִּיל *kiyl*
Variant; not used

10352 כַּכַּר *kakkar* (1)
talents (1)

10353 כֹּל *kōl* (105)
all (36)
any (9)
whole (7)
no (4) +10379
because (3) +10168+10619
for (3) +10168+10619
anyone (2) +10050
every (2)
everything (2)
throughout (2) +10089
whatever (2) +10168
a[s] (1)
anyone (1)
by (1) +10168+10619
cordial greetings (1) +10002+10002+10720
do so[s] (1) +10544+10708

entire (1)
even as (1) +10168+10619
everyone (1) +10050
just as (1) +10168+10619
none (1) +10379
other^s (1)
since (1) +10168+10619
so (1) +10180+10619
then (1) +10180+10619
therefore (1) +10168+10619
they^s (1) +10002+10553
this is the meaning (1) +10168+10619
this made (1) +10180+10619
though (1) +10168+10619
wherever (1) +10089+10168
whoever (1) +10050+10168
whoever (1) +10168
untranslated (11)

10354 כְּלַל k°lal (8)
are restored (2)
finished (2)
restore (2)
restoring (1)
untranslated (1)

10355 ־כֹם -kōm (5)
you (3)
your (2)

10356 כְּמָה k°māh
Variant; not used

10357 כֵּן kēn (8)
this (2)
untranslated (6)

10358 כְּנֵמָא k°nēmā' (5)
also (1) +10008
as follows (1)
this (1)
untranslated (2)

10359 כְּנַשׁ k°naš (3)
assembled (1)
crowded around (1)
summoned (1) +10378+10714

10360 כְּנָת k°nāt (7)
associates (6)
fellow (1)

10361 כַּסְדִּי kasday
Variant; not used

10362 כְּסַף k°sap (13)
silver (12)
money (1)

10363 כְּעַן k°'an (13)
now (6)
furthermore (1)
now then (1)
the present (1)
untranslated (4)

10364 כְּעֶנֶת k°'enet (3)
now (1)
untranslated (2)

10365 כְּעֶת k°'et (1)
untranslated (1)

10366 כְּפַת k°pat (4)
firmly tied (1)
tie up (1)
tied up (1)
were bound (1)

10367 כֹּר kōr (1)
cors (1)

10368 כַּרְבְּלָה karb°lāh (1)
turbans (1)

10369 כְּרָה k°rāh (1)
troubled (1)

10370 כָּרוֹז kārôz (1)
herald (1)

10371 כְּרַז k°raz (1)
proclaimed (1)

10372 כָּרְסֵא korsē' (3)
throne (2)
thrones (1)

10373 כַּשְׂדִּי kaśday (15)
astrologers (6)
astrologer (1)
Babylonians (1)
Chaldean (1)
untranslated (6)

10374 כְּתַב k°tab (8)
wrote (4)
read (1)
was written (1)
write down (1)
wrote down (1)

10375 כְּתָב k°tāb (12)
writing (5)
inscription (1)
put in writing (2) +10673
decree (1)
limit (1)
what written (1)

10376 כְּתַל k°tal (2)
wall (1)
walls (1)

10377 ל l
Variant; not used

10378 ־לְ l°- (364)
to (102)
for (22)
of (11)
into (7)
forever (6) +10550
had (6)
into (6) +10135
in (3)
against (2)
as (2)
before (2) +10619
on (2)
why (2) +10408
against (1) +10608
applied to (1)
at (1)
because of (1) +10168+10619
by (1)
extends to (1)
forever (1) +10002+10550
his (1) +10192
in favor of (1)
later (1) +10636
near (1) +10619
never (1) +10379+10550
so that (1)
summoned (1) +10042+10085
summoned (1) +10359+10714
together (1) +10154+10154
toward (1)
what (1) +10408
will be left with (1) +10029
with (1)
with (1) +10619
untranslated (170)

10379 לָא lā' (82)
not (38)
no (10)
cannot (4)
no (4) +10353
without (4)
nor (3) +10221
never (2)
before (1)
neither (1)
never (1) +10378+10550
none (1) +10353

nor (1) +10059+10221
nothing (1)
nothing (1) +10269
rather than (1)
unable (1) +10321
unharmed (1) +10029+10244
weren't (1)
untranslated (6)

10380 לֵב lēb (1)
myself (1) +10307

10381 לְבַב l°bab (7)
mind (3)
heart (2)
mind (1) +10669
yourself (1) +10342

10382 לְבוּשׁ l°bûš (2)
clothes (1)
clothing (1)

10383 לְבַשׁ l°baš (3)
clothed (3)

10384 לָה lāh
Variant; not used

10385 לָהֵן1 lāhēn1 (3)
so (1)
so then (1)
therefore (1)

10386 לָהֵן2 lāhēn2 (7)
except (4)
but (2)
unless (1)

10387 לֵוָי lēwāy (4)
Levites (4)

10388 לְוָת l°wāt (1)
from (1) +10427

10389 לְחֶם l°hem (1)
banquet (1)

10390 לְחֵנָה l°hēnāh (3)
concubines (3)

10391 לֵילִי lēylēy (5)
night (5)

10392 לִשָּׁן liššān (7)
men of every language (6)
language (1)

10393 מ m
Variant; not used

10394 מָא mā'
Variant; not used

10395 מְאָה m°'āh (8)
hundred (7)
120 (1) +10221+10574

10396 מֹאזְנֵא mō'z°nē' (1)
scales (1)

10397 מֵאמַר mē'mar (2)
declare (1)
requested (1)

10398 מָאן mā'n (7)
articles (4)
goblets (3)

10399 מְגִלָּה m°gillāh (1)
scroll (1)

10400 מְגַר m°gar (1)
overthrow (1)

10401 מַדְבַּח madbah (1)
altar (1)

10402 מִדָּה middāh (4)
taxes (3)
revenues (1)

10403 מְדוֹר m°dôr (3)
live (2)

lived (1)

10404 מָדַי *māday* (7)
Medes (4)
Mede (1)
Media (1)
untranslated (1)

10405 מָדָיָא *mādāyā'*
Variant; not used

10406 מְדִינָה *m'dīynāh* (11)
province (7)
provincial (2)
district (1)
provinces (1)

10407 מְדָר *m'dār* (1)
live (1)

10408 מָה *māh* (14)
what (5)
how (2) +10341
why (2) +10378
things (1)
what (1) +10378
whatever (1)
whatever (1) +10168
why (1) +10542

10409 מוֹת *mōt* (1)
death (1)

10410 מָזוֹן *māzôn* (2)
food (2)

10411 מְחָא *m'hā'* (4)
struck (2)
hold back (1)
impaled (1)

10412 מַחְלְקָה *mahl'qāh* (1)
groups (1)

10413 מְטָא *m'tā'* (8)
approached (1)
came (1)
happened (1)
issued (1)
reached (1)
reaches (1)
touched (1)
touching (1)

10414 מִישָׁאֵל *mîyšā'ēl* (1)
Mishael (1)

10415 מֵישַׁךְ *mēyšak* (14)
Meshach (13)
untranslated (1)

10416 מְלָא *m'lā'* (2)
filled (1)
furious (1) +10270

10417 מַלְאַךְ *mal'ak* (2)
angel (2)

10418 מִלָּה *millāh* (24)
matter (4)
words (3)
command (2)
decided (2)
things (2)
decree (1)
dream[s] (1)
it[s] (1) +10002
speak (1) +10425
substance (1) +10646
thing (1)
this[s] (1) +10002
voices (1)
what asks (1)
what said (1)
what[s] (1) +10002

10419 1מְלַח *m'lah1* (1)
under obligation (1) +10420

10420 2מְלַח *m'lah2* (3)
salt (2)
under obligation (1) +10419

10421 מֶלֶךְ *melek* (180)
king (137)
kings (11)
royal (9)
king's (6)
he[s] (3) +10002
him[s] (3) +10002
he[s] (2) +10002+10453
his[s] (2) +10002
kingdoms (1)
royal interests (1)
them[s] (1)
untranslated (4)

10422 מְלַךְ *m'lak* (1)
advice (1)

10423 מַלְכָּה *malkāh* (2)
queen (1)
she[s] (1) +10002

10424 מַלְכוּ *malkû* (57)
kingdom (30)
kingdoms (7)
reign (5)
royal (4)
sovereignty (2)
dominion (1)
government affairs (1)
it[s] (1) +10002
it[s] (1) +10191
realm (1)
royal authority (1)
sovereign power (1)
throne (1)
untranslated (1)

10425 מְלַל *m'lal* (5)
spoke (2)
answered (1)
speak (1) +10418
speaking (1)

10426 מַן *man* (10)
anyone (4) +10168
what (2)
who (2)
whoever (2) +10168

10427 מִן *min* (125)
from (41)
of (8)
partly (7)
to (5)
with (3)
because of (2)
before (2) +10621
from (2) +10621
one (2)
out of (2)
according to (1)
ago (1) +10180+10622
among (1)
as soon as (1) +10008+10168
because (1) +10168
before (1) +10180+10622
by (1)
by (1) +10621
certain (1) +10313+10327
for (1)
from (1) +10388
greater than (1)
in (1) +10608
issue (1) +10621
long history (1) +10317+10550
more than (1)
of (1) +10135
on (1)
over (1) +10543
partly (1) +10636
prescribed (1) +10302
some (1)

surely (1) +10168+10643
when (1) +10168
untranslated (27)

10428 מְנֵא *m'nē'* (3)
mene (3)

10429 מִנְדָּה *mindāh*
Variant; not used

10430 מַנְדַּע *manda'* (4)
knowledge (2)
sanity (2)

10431 מְנָה *m'nāh* (5)
appointed (2)
appoint (1)
numbered (1)
set (1)

10432 מִנְחָה *minhāh* (2)
grain offerings (1)
offering (1)

10433 מִנְיָן *minyān* (1)
each (1)

10434 מַעֲבָד *ma''bād* (1)
does (1)

10435 מְעֵה *m''ēh* (1)
belly (1)

10436 מֵעָל *me'āl* (1)
sundown (1) +10002+10728

10437 מָרֵא *mārē'* (6)
Lord (2)
lord (2)
untranslated (2)

10438 מְרַד *m'rad* (1)
rebellion (1)

10439 מְרַד *mārād* (2)
rebellious (2)

10440 מְרַט *m'rat* (1)
were torn off (1)

10441 מֹשֶׁה *mōšeh* (1)
Moses (1)

10442 מְשַׁח *m'šah1* (2)
oil (1)
olive oil (1)

10443 מְשַׁח *m'šah2*
Variant; not used

10444 מִשְׁכַּב *miškab* (6)
bed (5)
there[s] (1) +10342

10445 מִשְׁכַּן *miškan* (1)
dwelling (1)

10446 מַשְׁרוֹקִי *mašrôqiy* (4)
flute (4)

10447 מִשְׁתֵּא *mištē'* (1)
banquet (1)

10448 מַתְּנָה *mat'nāh* (3)
gifts (3)

10449 נ *n*
Variant; not used

10450 נָא *-nā'* (11)
us (7)
our (1)
the[s] (1)
we (1)
untranslated (1)

10451 נְבָא *n'bā'* (1)
prophesied (1)

10452 נְבוּאָה *n'bû'āh* (1)
preaching (1)

10453 נְבוּכַדְנֶצַּר *n'bûkadnessar* (31)
Nebuchadnezzar (28)

he[s] (2) +10002+10421
untranslated (1)

10454 נְבִזְבָּה n°bizbāh (2)
rewards (2)

10455 נְבִיא n°biy' (8)
prophet (3)
prophets (1)
untranslated (4)

10456 נֶבְרְשָׁה nebr°šāh (1)
lampstand (1)

10457 נְגַד n°gad (1)
flowing (1)

10458 נֶגֶד neged (1)
toward (1)

10459 נְגַהּ n°gah (1)
first light (1)

10460 נְגוּ n°gô
Variant; not used

10461 נְדַב n°dab (4)
freely given (1)
freewill offerings (1)
wish (1)
untranslated (1)

10462 נִדְבָּךְ nidbāk (2)
courses (1)
untranslated (1)

10463 נְדַד n°dad (1)
could not (1)

10464 נִדְנֶה nidneh (1)
in (1) +10089+10135

10465 נְהוֹר n°hôr (1)
untranslated (1)

10466 נְהִיר n°hiyr (1)
light (1)

10467 נָהִירוּ nahiyrû (2)
insight (2)

10468 נְהַר n°har (15)
Trans-Euphrates (12) +10191+10526
river (1)
that province[s] (1) +10191+10526
Trans-Euphrates (1) +10002+10526

10469 נוּד nûd (1)
flee (1)

10470 נְוָלוּ n°wālû (3)
piles of rubble (2)
pile of rubble (1)

10471 נוּר nûr (17)
blazing (8) +10328
fire (8)
all ablaze (1) +10178

10472 נְזַק n°zaq (4)
detriment (1)
suffer (1)
suffer loss (1)
troublesome (1)

10473 נְחָשׁ n°hāš (9)
bronze (9)

10474 נְחַת n°hat (6)
coming down (2)
deposit (1)
deposited (1)
stored (1)
was deposed (1)

10475 נְטַל n°tal (2)
raised (1)
was lifted (1)

10476 נְטַר n°tar (1)
kept (1)

10477 ־נִי -niy (18)
me (17)

untranslated (1)

10478 נִיחוֹחַ niyhôha (2)
incense (1)
pleasing (1)

10479 נְכַס n°kas (2)
property (1)
treasury (1)

10480 נְמַר n°mar (1)
leopard (1)

10481 נְסַח n°sah (1)
be pulled (1)

10482 נְסַךְ1 n°sak1 (1)
presented (1)

10483 נְסַךְ2 n°sak2 (1)
drink offerings (1)

10484 נְפַל n°pal (12)
fall down (5)
fell (3)
came (1)
fell down (1)
have occasion (1)
untranslated (1)

10485 נְפַק n°paq (12)
taken (3)
appeared (1)
came out (1)
come out (1)
coming out (1)
gone out (1)
issued (1)
removed (1)
took (1)
untranslated (1)

10486 נִפְקָה nipqāh (2)
costs (1)
expenses (1)

10487 נִצְבָּה nisbāh (1)
strength (1)

10488 נְצַח n°sah (1)
distinguished himself (1)

10489 נְצַל n°sal (3)
save (2)
saves (1)

10490 נְקֵא n°qē' (1)
white (1)

10491 נְקַשׁ n°qaš (1)
knocked (1)

10492 נְשָׂא n°śā' (3)
revolt (1)
swept away (1)
take (1)

10493 נְשִׁין n°šiyn (1)
wives (1)

10494 נִשְׁמָה nišmāh (1)
life (1)

10495 נְשַׁר n°šar (2)
eagle (2)

10496 נִשְׁתְּוָן ništ°wān (5)
letter (4)
written reply (1)

10497 נְתִין n°tiyn (1)
temple servants (1)

10498 נְתַן n°tan (7)
gives (3)
paid (1)
provide (1)
supply (1)
untranslated (1)

10499 נְתַר n°tar (1)
strip off (1)

10500 ס s
Variant; not used

10501 סַבְּכָא sabb°kā'
Variant; not used

10502 סְבַל s°bal (1)
be laid (1)

10503 סְבַר s°bar (1)
try (1)

10504 סְגִד s°gid (12)
worship (10)
paid honor (1)
worshiped (1)

10505 סְגַן s°gan (5)
prefects (4)
in charge (1) +10647

10506 סְגַר s°gar (1)
shut (1)

10507 סוּמְפֹּנְיָה sûmpōnyāh (4)
pipes (3)
untranslated (1)

10508 סוּף sûp (2)
bring to an end (1)
fulfilled (1)

10509 סוֹף sôp (5)
distant parts (1)
end (1)
ends (1)
forever (1) +10002+10527
never end (1) +10002+10527

10510 סוּפֹּנְיָא sûpōnyā'
Variant; not used

10511 סְתַר s°tar
Variant; not used

10512 סִיפֹּנְיָא siypōnyā'
Variant; not used

10513 סְלַק s°laq (8)
came up (4)
lift out (1)
took up (1)
turned (1)
was lifted (1)

10514 סְעַד s°'ad (1)
helping (1)

10515 סְפַר s°par (5)
archives (1) +10103
archives (1) +10177
book (1)
books (1)
records (1) +10177

10516 סָפַר sāpar (6)
secretary (4)
teacher (2)

10517 סַרְבָּל sarbāl (2)
robes (2)

10518 סָרַךְ sārak (5)
administrators (5)

10519 סְתַר1 s°tar1 (1)
hidden (1)

10520 סְתַר2 s°tar2 (1)
destroyed (1)

10521 ע '
Variant; not used

10522 עֲבַד '°bad (28)
done (3)
do (2)
made (2)
be carried out (1)
be cut into (1)
be done (1)
be made (1)

being carried on (1)
carried out (1)
celebrated (1)
cut into (1)
does (1)
gave (1)
make (1)
neglect (1) +10712
obey (1)
performed (1)
performs (1)
provide (1)
punished (1) +10170+10191
waging (1)
untranslated (3)

10523 עֲבַד *ᵃbēd* (9)
servants (6)
servant (1)
untranslated (2)

10524 עֲבֵד נְגוֹ *ᵃbēd nᵉgô* (14)
Abednego (13)
untranslated (1)

10525 עֲבִידָה *ᵃbiydāh* (6)
work (3)
administrators (1)
affairs (1)
service (1)

10526 עֲבַר *ᵃbar* (14)
Trans-Euphrates (12) +10191+10468
that provinceˢ (1) +10191+10468
Trans-Euphrates (1) +10002+10468

10527 עַר *ᶜad* (35)
until (8) +10168
until (4)
for (3)
during (2)
as (1) +10168
ever (1) +10002+10550
finally (1) +10024+10221
forever (1) +10002+10509
forever (1) +10002+10550
hoping (1) +10168
never end (1) +10002+10509
on (1)
so that (1) +10159+10168
this (1) +10345
to (1)
up to (1)
while (1) +10168
untranslated (5)

10528 עֲדָה *ᵃdāh* (9)
repealed (2)
stripped (2)
deposes (1)
pass away (1)
taken (1)
taken away (1)
was (1)

10529 עִדּוֹא *iddô'* (2)
Iddo (2)

10530 עִדָּן *iddān* (13)
times (6)
time (3)
as soon as (1) +10002+10089+10168
period of time (1) +10221+10232
situation (1)
when (1) +10002+10089

10531 עוֹד *ôd* (1)
still (1)

10532 עֲוָיָה *ᵃwāyāh* (1)
wickedness (1)

10533 עוֹף *ôp* (2)
bird (1)
birds (1)

10534 עוּר *ûr* (1)
chaff (1)

10535 עֵז *ēz* (1)
male goats (1) +10615

10536 עִזְקָה *izqāh* (2)
rings (1)
signet ring (1)

10537 עֶזְרָא *ezrā'* (3)
Ezra (3)

10538 עֲזַרְיָה *ᵃzaryāh* (1)
Azariah (1)

10539 עֵטָה *ēṭāh* (1)
wisdom (1)

10540 עַיִן *ayin* (5)
eyes (4)
eye (1)

10541 עִיר *iyr* (3)
messenger (2)
messengers (1)

10542 עַל *al* (114)
to (16)
on (13)
over (8)
for (7)
against (6)
about (4)
in (4)
around (3)
lying in (3)
of (3)
among (1)
concerning (1)
had (1) +10201
lying (1)
lying on (1)
prostrate (1) +10049
rule (1)
so that (1) +10159+10168
than (1)
that is why (1) +10180
toward (1)
why (1) +10408
untranslated (35)

10543 עֶלָּא *ēllā'* (1)
over (1) +10427

10544 עִלָּה *illāh* (3)
basis for charges (1)
do soˢ (1) +10353+10708
grounds for charges (1)

10545 עֲלָוָה *ᵃlāwāh* (1)
burnt offerings (1)

10546 עִלָּי *illāy* (20)
most High (10)
untranslated (10)

10547 עִלִּי *illiy* (1)
upstairs room (1)

10548 עֶלְיוֹן *elyôn* (4)
most High (3)
hisˢ (1)

10549 עֲלַל *ᵃlal* (17)
brought (3)
came (2)
went (2)
came in (1)
came into (1)
take (1)
took (1)
was brought (1)
went in (1)
were brought (1)
untranslated (3)

10550 עָלַם *ālam* (20)
forever (6) +10378
eternal (2)
ever (2) +10002
everlasting (2)

ancient (1)
ever (1)
ever (1) +10002+10527
forever (1) +10002
forever (1) +10002+10378
forever (1) +10002+10527
long history (1) +10317+10427
never (1) +10378+10379

10551 עֵלְמָי *ēlmāy* (1)
Elamites (1)

10552 עֲלַע *ᵃla'* (1)
ribs (1)

10553 עַם *am* (15)
people (7)
peoples (6)
Israelites (1) +10335
theyˢ (1) +10002+10353

10554 עִם *im* (22)
with (10)
for (2)
to (2)
against (1)
among (1)
as well as (1)
at (1)
like (1)
of (1)
united (1) +10158+10180+10180
untranslated (1)

10555 עַמִּיק *ammiyq* (1)
deep (1)

10556 עֲמַר *ᵃmar* (1)
wool (1)

10557 עֵן *an*
Variant; not used

10558 עֲנָה *ᵃnāh* (30)
said (13)
answered (5)
replied (5)
asked (3)
ordered (1)
shouted (1)
untranslated (2)

10559 עֲנֵה *ᵃnēh* (1)
oppressed (1)

10560 עֲנָן *ᵃnān* (1)
clouds (1)

10561 עֲנַף *ᵃnap* (4)
branches (4)

10562 עֲנַשׁ *ᵃnāš* (1)
confiscation (1)

10563 עֲנֵת *enet*
Variant; not used

10564 עֲפִי *ᵃpiy* (3)
leaves (3)

10565 עֲצִיב *ᵃsiyb* (1)
anguished (1)

10566 עֲקַר *ᵃqar* (2)
were uprooted (1)
untranslated (1)

10567 עִקַּר *iqqar* (3)
stump (3)

10568 עֲר *ār* (2)
adversaries (1)
untranslated (1)

10569 עֲרַב *ᵃrab* (4)
mixed (2)
mixes (1)
mixture (1)

10570 עֲרָד *ᵃrād* (1)
wild donkeys (1)

10571 עַרְוָה 'arwāh (1)
dishonored (1)

10572 עֲשַׂב "śab (5)
grass (4)
plants (1)

10573 עֲשַׂר "śar (6)
ten (4)
twelve (2) +10775

10574 עֶשְׂרִין 'eśriyn (1)
120 (1) +10221+10395

10575 עֲשֵׁת "šat (1)
planned (1)

10576 עֵת 'et
Variant; not used

10577 עֲתִיד "tiyd (1)
ready (1)

10578 עַתִּיק 'atiyq (3)
ancient (3)

10579 פ p
Variant; not used

10580 פֶּחָה pehāh (10)
governor (6)
governors (4)

10581 פֶּחָר pehār (1)
untranslated (1)

10582 פַּטִּישׁ pattiyš (2)
trousers (1)
untranslated (1)

10583 1פְּלַג p'lag1 (1)
divided (1)

10584 2פְּלַג p'lag2 (1)
half (1)

10585 פְּלֻגָּה p'luggāh (1)
divisions (1)

10586 פְּלַח p'lah (10)
serve (7)
workers (1)
worship (1)
worshiped (1)

10587 פָּלְחָן polhān (1)
worship (1)

10588 פֻּם pum (6)
mouth (4)
lips (1)
mouths (1)

10589 פַּס pas (2)
hand (2) +10311

10590 פְּסַנְתֵּרִין p'santēriyn (4)
harp (4)

10591 פַּרְזֶל parzel (20)
iron (20)

10592 פְּרַס p'ras (1)
is divided (1)

10593 פְּרֵס p'rēs (2)
parsin (1)
Peres (1)

10594 פָּרַס pāras (6)
Persians (4)
Persia (2)

10595 פַּרְסָי parsāy (2)
Persian (1)
untranslated (1)

10596 פְּרַק p'raq (1)
renounce (1)

10597 פְּרַשׁ p'raš (1)
translated (1)

10598 פַּרְשֶׁגֶן paršegen (3)
copy (3)

10599 1פְּשַׁר p'šar1 (2)
give interpretations (1) +10600
interpret (1)

10600 2פְּשַׁר p'šar2 (32)
means (7)
interpret (5) +10252
interpretation (4)
interpret (3)
interpret (3) +10313
interpret (2) +10042
meaning (2)
explain (1)
explain (1) +10252
give interpretations (1) +10599
mean (1)
meant (1)
untranslated (1)

10601 פִּתְגָם pitgām (6)
answer (1)
decision (1)
defend (1) +10754
edict (1)
reply (1)
report (1)

10602 פְּתַח p'tah (2)
opened (1)
were opened (1)

10603 פְּתָי p'tāy (2)
wide (2)

10604 צ s
Variant; not used

10605 צְבָה s'bāh (10)
wanted to (4)
wishes (4)
pleases (1)
wanted (1)

10606 צְבוּ s'bû (1)
situation (1)

10607 צְבַע s'ba' (5)
be drenched (2)
was drenched (2)
drenched (1)

10608 צַד sad (2)
against (1) +10378
in (1) +10427

10609 צְדָא s'dā' (1)
is it true (1) +10190

10610 צִדְקָה sidqāh (1)
right (1)

10611 צַוַּאר sawwa'r (3)
neck (3)

10612 צְלָה s'lāh (2)
pray (1)
prayed (1)

10613 צְלַח s'lah (4)
making rapid progress (1)
promoted (1)
prosper (1)
prospered (1)

10614 צְלֵם s'lēm (17)
image (10)
statue (5)
attitude (1) +10049
it^s (1) +10002

10615 צְפִיר s'piyr (1)
male goats (1) +10535

10616 צִפַּר sippar (4)
birds (3)
bird (1)

10617 ק q
Variant; not used

10618 קְבַל q'bal (3)
receive (2)

took over (1)

10619 קֳבֵל q°bēl (29)
because (3) +10168+10353
for (3) +10168+10353
before (2) +10378
because of (1) +10168+10378
by (1) +10168+10353
even as (1) +10168+10353
just as (1) +10168+10353
near (1) +10378
since (1) +10168+10353
so (1) +10180+10353
then (1) +10180+10353
therefore (1) +10180+10353
this is the meaning (1) +10168+10353
this made (1) +10180+10353
though (1) +10168+10353
with (1) +10378
untranslated (8)

10620 קַדִּישׁ qaddiyš (13)
holy (7)
saints (5)
they^s (1)

10621 קֳדָם q°dām (46)
to (11)
before (7)
before (2) +10427
from (2) +10427
by (1) +10427
former (1)
in presence (1)
in sight (1)
into presence (1)
issue (1) +10427
my (1) +10307
presence (1)
untranslated (16)

10622 קַדְמָה qadmāh (2)
ago (1) +10180+10427
before (1) +10180+10427

10623 קַדְמָי qadmāy (3)
first (2)
earlier (1)

10624 קוּם qûm (36)
set up (9)
stood (4)
issue (2)
rise (2)
sets (2)
appoint (1)
appointed (1)
arise (1)
come (1)
endure (1)
get up (1)
got up (1)
installed (1)
issues (1)
leaped to feet (1)
set (1)
set to work (1) +10221+10742
sets up (1)
standing (1)
was raised up (1)
untranslated (2)

10625 קְטַל q'tal (7)
put to death (4)
was slain (2)
killed (1)

10626 קְטַר q'tar (3)
difficult problems (2)
legs (1) +10284

10627 קַיִט qayit (1)
summer (1)

10628 קְיָם q'yām (2)
edict (2)

10629 קָיָם *qayyām* (2)
endures (1)
restored (1)

10630 קִיתָרֹס *qiytrōs* (4)
zither (4)

10631 קָל *qāl* (7)
sound (4)
voice (2)
untranslated (1)

10632 קְנָה *qᵉnāh* (1)
buy (1)

10633 קְצַף1 *qᵉsap1* (1)
furious (1)

10634 קְצַף2 *qᵉsap2* (1)
wrath (1)

10635 קְצַץ *qᵉsas* (1)
trim off (1)

10636 קְצָת *qᵉsāt* (3)
end (1)
later (1) +10378
partly (1) +10427

10637 קְרָא *qᵉrā'* (11)
read (4)
been read (1)
call (1)
called (1)
called out (1)
proclaimed (1)
reads (1)
was read (1)

10638 קְרֵב *qᵉrēb* (9)
approached (2)
came forward (1)
came near (1)
led (1)
offer sacrifices (1)
offered (1)
sacrifice (1)
went (1)

10639 קְרָב *qᵉrāb* (1)
war (1)

10640 קִרְיָה *qiryāh* (9)
city (9)

10641 קֶרֶן *qeren* (14)
horn (9)
horns (5)

10642 קְרַץ *qᵉras* (2)
denounced (1) +10030
falsely accused (1) +10030

10643 קְשֹׁט *qᵉšōt* (2)
right (1)
surely (1) +10168+10427

10644 קַתְרֹוס *qatrôs* (4)
untranslated (4)

10645 ר *r*
Variant; not used

10646 רֵאשׁ *rē'š* (14)
head (4)
mind (4)
heads (2)
saw (2)
leaders (1)
substance (1) +10418

10647 רַב *rab* (23)
great (11)
boastfully (2)
chief (2)
boastful (1)
commander (1)
enormous (1)
huge (1)
imposing (1)

in charge (1) +10505
large (1)
many (1) +10678

10648 רְבָה *rᵉbāh* (6)
grew large (2)
great (1)
grew (1)
grown (1)
placed in a high position (1)

10649 רִבּוֹ *ribbô* (3)
ten thousand (2)
untranslated (1)

10650 רְבוּ *rᵉbû* (5)
greatness (3)
became even greater (1) +10323+10339
high position (1)

10651 רְבִיעִי *rᵉbiy'āy* (10)
fourth (6)
untranslated (4)

10652 רַבְרְבָנִין *rabᵉrᵉbāniyn* (9)
nobles (8)
untranslated (1)

10653 רְגַז1 *rᵉgaz1* (1)
angered (1)

10654 רְגַז2 *rᵉgaz2* (1)
rage (1)

10655 רְגַל *rᵉgal* (8)
feet (4)
underfoot (2) +10089
toes (1) +10064
untranslated (1)

10656 רְגַשׁ *rᵉgaš* (3)
went as a group (3)

10657 רֵו *rēw* (2)
appearance (1)
looks (1)

10658 רוּחַ *rûha* (11)
spirit (6)
mind (1)
qualities (1)
wind (1)
winds (1)
untranslated (1)

10659 רוּם1 *rûm1* (4)
arrogant (1)
exalt (1)
promoted (1)
set up (1)

10660 רוּם2 *rûm2* (5)
high (2)
top (2)
height (1)

10661 רָז *rāz* (9)
mystery (6)
mysteries (3)

10662 רְחוּם *rᵉhûm* (4)
Rehum (4)

10663 רַחִיק *rahiyq* (1)
away (1)

10664 רַחֲמִין *rahᵃmiyn* (1)
mercy (1)

10665 רְחַץ *rᵉhas* (1)
trusted (1)

10666 רֵיחַ *rēyha* (1)
smell (1)

10667 רְמָה *rᵉmāh* (12)
be thrown (5)
threw (2)
thrown (2)
impose (1)
throw (1)

were set in place (1)

10668 רֵעוּ *rᵉ''û* (2)
decision (1)
will (1)

10669 רַעְיוֹן *ra'yôn* (6)
thoughts (2)
mind (1)
mind (1) +10381
untranslated (2)

10670 רַעֲנָן *ra'ᵃnan* (1)
prosperous (1)

10671 רְעַע *rᵉ'a'* (2)
break (1)
breaks to pieces (1)

10672 רְפַס *rᵉpas* (2)
trampled (2)

10673 רְשַׁם *rᵉšam* (7)
put in writing (2) +10375
been published (1)
publish (1)
put in writing (1)
was written (1)
wrote (1)

10674 שׂ *ś*
Variant; not used

10675 שָׂב *śāb* (5)
elders (5)

10676 שַׂבְּכָא *śabbᵉkā'* (4)
lyre (4)

10677 שְׂנָא *śᵉgā'* (3)
greatly (2)
grow (1)

10678 שַׂגִּיא *śaggiy'* (13)
abundant (2)
deeply (1)
enormous (1)
even more (1)
fill (1)
great (1)
greatly (1)
large (1)
many (1)
many (1) +10647
overjoyed (1) +10293
so (1)

10679 שָׂהֲרוּ *śāhᵃdû*
Variant; not used

10680 שְׂטַר *śᵉtar* (1)
sides (1)

10681 שִׂיב *śiyb*
Variant; not used

10682 שִׂים *śiym* (26)
issued (5)
decree (4) +10302
issue (3)
authorized (2) +10302
appointed (1)
called (1) +10721
commanded (1) +10302
decreed (1) +10302
determined (1) +10104
order (1) +10002+10302
order (1) +10302
pay (1)
pays (1)
placed (1)
placing (1)
turned into (1)

10683 שְׂכַל *śᵉkal* (1)
thinking (1)

10684 שָׂכְלְתָנוּ *śāklᵉtānû* (3)
intelligence (2)
understanding (1)

10685 שִׁלָּה *śillāh* (1)
untranslated (1)

10686 שְׂנָא *śᵉnā'* (2)
enemies (1)
untranslated (1)

10687 שְׂעַר *śᵉ'ar* (3)
hair (3)

10688 שׁ *š*
Variant; not used

10689 שְׁאֵל *šᵉ'ēl* (6)
asked (3)
ask (1)
asks (1)
questioned (1)

10690 שְׁאֵלָה *šᵉ'ēlāh* (1)
verdict (1)

10691 שְׁאַלְתִּיאֵל *šᵉ'altiy'ēl* (1)
Shealtiel (1)

10692 שְׁאָר *šᵉ'ār* (12)
rest (5)
elsewhere (2)
left (2)
other (2)
anything else (1)

10693 שְׁבַח *šᵉbah* (5)
praise (2)
praised (2)
honored (1)

10694 שְׁבַט *šᵉbat* (1)
tribes (1)

10695 שְׁבִיב *šᵉbiyb* (2)
flames (1)
flaming (1)

10696 שְׁבַע *šᵉba'* (6)
seven (6)

10697 שְׁבַק *šᵉbaq* (5)
leave (2)
be left (1)
not interfere (1)
remain (1)

10698 שְׁבַשׁ *šᵉbaš* (1)
baffled (1)

10699 שֵׁגַל *šēgal* (3)
wives (3)

10700 שְׁדַר *šᵉdar* (1)
made every effort (1)

10701 שַׁדְרַךְ *šadrak* (14)
Shadrach (13)
untranslated (1)

10702 שְׁוָה *šᵉwāh* (3)
be turned into (1)
given (1)
untranslated (1)

10703 שׁוּר *šûr* (4)
walls (3)
untranslated (1)

10704 שׁוּשַׁנְכִי *šûšankāy* (1)
of Susa (1)

10705 שְׁחַת *šᵉhat* (3)
corrupt (1)
corruption (1)
wicked (1)

10706 שֵׁיזִב *šēyzib* (9)
rescue (5)
rescued (2)
rescues (1)
save (1)

10707 שֵׁיצִיא *šēysiy'* (1)
completed (1)

10708 שְׁכַח *šᵉkah* (18)
was found (5)

find (4)
found (4)
do so⁵ (1) +10353+10544
leaving (1)
obtain (1)
untranslated (2)

10709 שְׁכַן *šᵉkan* (2)
caused to dwell (1)
nesting places (1)

10710 שְׁלֵה *šᵉlēh* (1)
contented (1)

10711 שָׁלַה *šāluh*
Variant; not used

10712 שְׁלוּ *šᵉlû* (4)
anything (1)
fail (1)
neglect (1) +10522
negligent (1)

10713 שַׁלְוָה *šᵉlēwāh* (1)
prosperity (1)

10714 שְׁלַח *šᵉlah* (14)
sent (9)
are sent (1)
lifts (1)
send (1)
sending message (1)
summoned (1) +10359+10378

10715 שְׁלֵט *šᵉlēt* (7)
made ruler (2)
ruler (2)
harmed (1)
overpowered (1)
rule (1)

10716 שִׁלְטֹן *šiltōn* (2)
officials (2)

10717 שָׁלְטָן *šolᵉtān* (14)
dominion (7)
authority (2)
power (2)
authority to rule (1)
part (1)
rulers (1)

10718 שַׁלִּיט *šalliyt* (10)
sovereign (4)
authority (1)
mighty (1)
officer (1)
ruler (1)
rules (1)
ruling (1)

10719 שְׁלִם *šᵉlim* (3)
brought to an end (1)
deliver (1)
finished (1)

10720 שְׁלָם *šᵉlām* (4)
prosper (2)
cordial greetings (1) +10002+10002+10353
greetings (1)

10721 שֻׁם *šum* (12)
name (4)
called (3)
names (3)
called (1) +10682
named (1)

10722 שְׁמַד *šᵉmad* (1)
completely destroyed (1) +10005+10221

10723 שְׁמַיִן *šᵉmayin* (38)
heaven (29)
air (3)
heavens (3)
sky (3)

10724 שְׁמַם *šᵉmam* (1)
greatly perplexed (1)

10725 שְׁמַע *šᵉma'* (9)
heard (4)
hear (3)
hears (1)
obey (1)

10726 שָׁמְרָיִן *šomrayin* (2)
Samaria (2)

10727 שְׁמַשׁ *šᵉmaš1* (1)
attended (1)

10728 שְׁמַשׁ *šᵉmaš2* (1)
sundown (1) +10002+10436

10729 שִׁמְשַׁי *šimšay* (4)
Shimshai (4)

10730 שֵׁן *šēn* (5)
teeth (3)
untranslated (2)

10731 שְׁנָה1 *šᵉnāh1* (22)
different (5)
changed (4)
change (3)
changes (2)
turned (2)
altered (1)
defied (1)
grew (1)
look so pale (1) +10228
scorched (1)
untranslated (1)

10732 שְׁנָה2 *šᵉnāh2* (7)
year (5)
age (1) +10120
years (1)

10733 שְׁנָה3 *šᵉnāh* (1)
sleep (1)

10734 שָׁעָה *šā'āh* (5)
immediately (2) +10002
immediately (1) +10191
suddenly (1) +10191
time (1)

10735 שְׁפַט *šᵉpat* (1)
magistrates (1)

10736 שַׁפִּיר *šappiyr* (2)
beautiful (2)

10737 שְׁפַל1 *šᵉpal1* (4)
humbled (2)
humble (1)
subdue (1)

10738 שְׁפַל2 *šᵉpal2* (1)
lowliest (1)

10739 שְׁפַר *šᵉpar* (3)
pleased (2)
pleasure (1)

10740 שְׁפַרְפָּר *šᵉparpār* (1)
dawn (1)

10741 שָׁק *šāq* (1)
legs (1)

10742 שְׁרָה *šᵉrāh* (6)
solve (2)
dwells (1)
gave way (1)
set to work (1) +10221+10624
unbound (1)

10743 שְׁרֹשׁ *šᵉrōš* (3)
roots (3)

10744 שְׁרֹשׁוּ *šᵉrōšû* (1)
banishment (1)

10745 שְׁרֹשִׁי *šᵉrōšiy* (1)
untranslated (1)

10746 שֵׁשְׁבַּצַּר *šēšbassar* (2)
Sheshbazzar (2)

10747 שֵׁת *šēt* (2)
nine feet (1) +10039
sixth (1)

10748 שְׁתָה *š⁵tāh* (5)
drank (4)
drink (1)

10749 שִׁתִּין *šitiyn* (4)
ninety feet (3) +10039
sixty-two (1) +10221+10775

10750 שְׁתַר בּוֹזְנַי *š⁵tar bôz⁵nay* (4)
Shethar-Bozenai (4)

10751 ת *t*
Variant; not used

10752 תְּבַר *t⁵bar* (1)
brittle (1)

10753 תְּדִיר *t⁵diyr* (2)
continually (2) +10002+10089

10754 תּוּב *tûb* (8)
restored (2)
returned (2)
defend (1) +10601
gave (1)
received (1)
spoke (1)

10755 תְּוַה *t⁵wah* (1)
amazement (1) +10097

10756 תּוֹר *tôr* (7)
cattle (4)
bulls (3)

10757 תְּחוֹת *t⁵hôt* (5)
under (4)
untranslated (1)

10758 תְּלַג *t⁵lag* (1)
snow (1)

10759 תְּלִיתָי *t⁵liytāy* (2)
third (1)
untranslated (1)

10760 תְּלָת *t⁵lāt* (11)
three (10)
third (1)

10761 תַּלְתָּא *taltā'* (3)
third highest (3)

10762 תְּלָתִין *t⁵lātiyn* (2)
thirty (2)

10763 תְּמַהּ *t⁵mah* (3)
wonders (3)

10764 תַּמָּה *tammāh* (4)
there (2)
untranslated (2)

10765 תִּנְיָן *tinyān* (1)
second (1)

10766 תִּנְיָנוּת *tinyānût* (1)
once more (1)

10767 תִּפְתָּי *tiptāy* (2)
magistrates (2)

10768 תַּקִּיף *taqqiyp* (5)
powerful (2)
strong (2)
mighty (1)

10769 תְּקַל *t⁵qal* (1)
been weighed (1)

10770 תְּקֵל *t⁵qēl* (2)
tekel (2)

10771 תְּקַן *t⁵qan* (1)
was restored (1)

10772 תְּקֵף *t⁵qip* (5)
strong (3)
enforce (1)
hardened (1)

10773 תְּקֹף *t⁵qōp* (1)
might (1)

10774 תְּקָף *t⁵qāp* (1)
power (1)

10775 תְּרֵין *t⁵rēyn* (4)
twelve (2) +10573
second (1)
sixty-two (1) +10221+10749

10776 תְּרַע *t⁵ra'* (2)
court (1)
opening (1)

10777 תָּרָע *tārā'* (1)
gatekeepers (1)

10778 תַּרְתֵּין *tartēyn*
Variant; not used

10779 תַּתְּנַי *tat⁵nay* (4)
Tattenai (4)

FEATURES OF THE GREEK TO ENGLISH
INDEX–LEXICON

G/K NUMBER	LEXICAL FORM and TRANSLITERATION	FREQUENCY COUNT
Matches the number at the end of context lines (see the introduction, pages xii, xv).	See the transliteration and pronunciation table below.	Indicates the total number of occurrences of this Greek word in the biblical text (see the introduction, page xv).

257 ἄλλος *allos* (155)

another (42)

NIV WORD and (FREQUENCY COUNT)
NIV words are listed according to their exact textual spelling and are organized according to frequency (see the introduction, page xv).

one another (1) +257+4639

MULTIPLE WORDS / MULTIPLE NUMBERS
More than one NIV word and/or more than one G/K number indicate multiple-word translations (see the introduction, pages xii, xiii, xv).

gospel^s (1)

SUPERSCRIPT "S"
Indicates "substitution" translation (see the introduction, pages xiii-xv).

untranslated (5)

UNTRANSLATED
Always the final entry, indicates the number of times the NIV did not translate the Greek word for stylistic reasons (see the introduction, pages xv, xvi).

Variant; not used

VARIANT; NOT USED
Notes words of variant spelling and variant readings in the G/K number list that were not used in translating the NIV (see the introduction, pages xv, xvi).

GREEK TRANSLITERATION
AND PRONUNCIATION TABLE

Greek	English	Sound
Greek	*English*	*Sound*
Α, α	A, a	father
Β, β	B, b	boy
Γ, γ	G, g	girl
Δ, δ	D, d	dog
Ε, ε	E, e	get
Ζ, ζ	Z, z	adze
Η, η	Ē, ē	they
Θ, θ	Th, th	they
Ι, ι	I, i	pin, machine
Κ, κ	K, k	kit
Λ, λ	L, l	let
Μ, μ	M, m	mother
Ν, ν	N, n	not
Ξ, ξ	X, x	fox
Ο, ο	O, o	hot
Π, π	P, p	pot
Ρ, ρ	R, r	rot
Σ, σ, ς	S, s, s	sip
Τ, τ	T, t	tip
Υ, υ	Y, y	put

Greek	English	Sound
Φ, φ	Ph, ph	phone
Χ, χ	Ch, ch	Bach
Ψ, ψ	Ps, ps	lips
Ω, ω	Ō, ō	phone
γγ	ng	thing
γκ	nk	think
γξ	nx	thinks
γχ	nch	think
ευ	eu	you
ηυ	ēu	say you
ου	ou	through
υι	hui	hwee
ʽ	h	hot
ῥ	rh	myrrh
α	ā	father
η	ē	they
ω	ō	phone

GREEK TO ENGLISH
INDEX–LEXICON
OF THE NEW TESTAMENT

1 α *a*
Variant; not used

2 Ἀαρών *Aarōn* (5)
Aaron (4)
Aaron's (1)

3 Ἀβαδδών *Abaddōn* (1)
Abaddon (1)

4 ἀβαρής *abarēs* (1)
burden (1)

5 ἀββά *abba* (3)
Abba (3)

6 Ἅβελ *Habel* (4)
Abel (4)

7 Ἀβιά *Abia* (3)
Abijah (3)

8 Ἀβιαθάρ *Abiathar* (1)
Abiathar (1)

9 Ἀβιληνή *Abilēnē* (1)
Abilene (1)

10 Ἀβιούδ *Abioud* (2)
Abiud (2)

11 Ἀβραάμ *Abraam* (73)
Abraham (64)
Abraham's (9)

12 ἄβυσσος *abyssos* (9)
Abyss (8)
deep (1)

13 Ἅγαβος *Hagabos* (2)
Agabus (2)

14 ἀγαθοεργέω *agathoergeō* (2)
do good (1)
shown kindness (1)

15 ἀγαθοεργός *agathoergos*
Variant; not used

16 ἀγαθοποιέω *agathopoieō* (9)
do good (3)
doing good (3)
are good (1)
do what is right (1)
does what is good (1)

17 ἀγαθοποιία *agathopoiia* (1)
do good (1)

18 ἀγαθοποιός *agathopoios* (1)
who do right (1)

19 ἀγαθός *agathos* (102)
good (89)
kind (2)

right (2)
better (1)
clear (1)
favor (1)
generous (1)
goods (1)
helpful (1)
pleasant (1)
useful (1)
untranslated (1)

20 ἀγαθωσύνη *agathōsynē* (4)
goodness (3)
good (1)

21 ἀγαλλίασις *agalliasis* (5)
joy (2)
delight (1)
glad (1)
great joy (1)

22 ἀγαλλιάω *agalliaō* (11)
rejoices (2)
be glad (1)
enjoy (1)
filled with joy (1)
filled with joy (1) +5915
full of joy (1)
glad (1)
greatly rejoice (1)
overjoyed (1) +5897
rejoiced (1)

23 ἄγαμος *agamos* (4)
unmarried (4)

24 ἀγανακτέω *aganakteō* (7)
indignant (6)
saying indignantly (1)

25 ἀγανάκτησις *aganaktēsis* (1)
indignation (1)

26 ἀγαπάω *agapaō* (143)
love (74)
loved (40)
loves (22)
love (2) +27
truly love (2)
longed for (1)
loving (1)
showed love (1)

27 ἀγάπη *agapē* (116)
love (109)
love (2) +26
love (2) +2400
it^s (1) +3836
love feasts (1)
loves (1)

28 ἀγαπητός *agapetos* (61)
dear friends (22)
dear (13)
love (11)
dear friend (9)
loved (3)
dearly loved (1)
friends (1)
so dear (1)

29 Ἀγάρ *Hagar* (2)
Hagar (2)

30 ἀγγαρεύω *angareuō* (3)
forced (2)
forces (1)

31 ἀγγεῖον *angeion* (1)
jars (1)

32 ἀγγελία *angelia* (2)
message (2)

33 ἀγγέλλω *angellō* (1)
with the news (1)

34 ἄγγελος *angelos* (176)
angel (86)
angels (81)
messenger (4)
angel's (2)
messengers (2)
spies (1)

35 ἄγγος *angos* (1)
baskets (1)

36 ἀγέλη *agelē* (7)
herd (7)

37 ἀγενεαλόγητος *agenealogētos* (1)
without genealogy (1)

38 ἀγενής *agenēs* (1)
lowly (1)

39 ἁγιάζω *hagiazō* (28)
sanctified (7)
sanctify (4)
made holy (3)
hallowed (2)
make holy (2)
makes sacred (2)
sanctified (2) +1639
set apart (2)
consecrated (1)
holy (1)
made holy (1) +1639
makes holy (1)

40 ἁγιασμός *hagiasmos* (10)
holiness (4)

holy (2)
sanctifying (2)
be sanctified (1)
holy life (1)

41 ἅγιος *hagios* (234)
holy (161)
saints (45)
God's people (9)
sacred (4)
holy people (3)
sanctuary (3)
believers (1)
consecrated (1) +2813
devoted (1)
God's holy people (1)
holy one (1)
holy ones (1)
holy place (1)
most holy place (1) +41

42 ἁγιότης *hagiotēs* (1)
holiness (1)

43 ἁγιωσύνη *hagiōsynē* (3)
holiness (2)
holy (1) +1877

44 ἀγκάλη *ankalē* (1)
arms (1)

45 ἄγκιστρον *ankistron* (1)
line (1)

46 ἄγκυρα *ankyra* (4)
anchors (3)
anchor (1)

47 ἄγναφος *agnaphos* (2)
unshrunk (2)

48 ἁγνεία *hagneia* (2)
purity (2)

49 ἁγνίζω *hagnizō* (7)
purified (2)
ceremonial cleansing (1)
ceremonially clean (1)
purification rites (1)
purifies (1)
purify (1)

50 ἁγνισμός *hagnismos* (1)
purification (1)

51 ἀγνοέω *agnoeō* (22)
ignorant (5)
not understand (3)
unknown (3)
not know (2)
unaware (2)
don't know (1)
ignorance (1)
ignored (1)
ignores (1)
not realizing (1)
not recognize (1)
uninformed (1)

52 ἀγνόημα *agnoēma* (1)
sins committed in ignorance (1)

53 ἄγνοια *agnoia* (4)
ignorance (4)

54 ἁγνός *hagnos* (8)
pure (6)
innocent (1)
purity (1)

55 ἁγνότης *hagnotēs* (2)
pure (1)
purity (1)

56 ἁγνῶς *hagnōs* (1)
sincerely (1)

57 ἀγνωσία *agnōsia* (2)
are ignorant (1) +2400
ignorant (1)

58 ἄγνωστος *agnōstos* (1)
unknown (1)

59 ἀγορά *agora* (11)
marketplaces (6)
marketplace (5)

60 ἀγοράζω *agorazō* (30)
buy (13)
bought (9)
purchased (2)
selling (2)
buying (1)
buys (1)
redeemed (1)
spend (1)

61 ἀγοραῖος *agoraios* (2)
courts are open (1) +72
marketplace (1)

62 ἄγρα *agra* (2)
catch (2)

63 ἀγράμματος *agrammatos* (1)
unschooled (1)

64 ἀγραυλέω *agrauleō* (1)
living out (1)

65 ἀγρεύω *agreuō* (1)
catch (1)

66 ἀγριέλαιος *agrielaios* (2)
olive tree that is wild (1)
wild olive shoot (1)

67 ἄγριος *agrios* (3)
wild (3)

68 Ἀγρίππας *Agrippas* (11)
Agrippa (11)

69 ἀγρός *agros* (36)
field (22)
countryside (5)
fields (5)
country (3)
itˢ (1) +3836

70 ἀγρυπνέω *agrypneō* (4)
alert (1)
keep watch (1)
on guard (1)
on the watch (1)

71 ἀγρυπνία *agrypnia* (2)
have gone without sleep (1) +1877
sleepless nights (1)

72 ἄγω *agō* (69)
brought (25)
bring (10)
led (8)
go (6)
took (3)
bringing (2)
listen (2)
take (2)
brought to trial (1)
courts are open (1) +61
for (1)
influenced (1)
leads (1)
leave (1) +1949
led away (1)
swayed (1)
taken (1)
took (1) +4161
untranslated (1)

73 ἀγωγή *agōgē* (1)
way of life (1)

74 ἀγών *agōn* (6)
fight (2)
opposition (1)
race (1)
struggle (1)

struggling (1)

75 ἀγωνία *agōnia* (1)
anguish (1)

76 ἀγωνίζομαι *agōnizomai* (8)
fight (2)
competes in the games (1)
fought (1)
make every effort (1)
strive (1)
struggling (1)
wrestling (1)

77 Ἀδάμ *Adam* (9)
Adam (9)

78 ἀδάπανος *adapanos* (1)
free of charge (1)

79 Ἀδδί *Addi* (1)
Addi (1)

80 ἀδελφή *adelphē* (25)
sister (15)
sisters (8)
believing wife (1) +1222
woman (1)

81 ἀδελφός *adelphos* (342)
brothers (204)
brother (104)
brothers (12) +467
brother's (8)
believers (3)
himˢ (2) +899+3836
man (2)
own people (2)
anotherˢ (1)
believing man (1)
fellow (1)
himˢ (1) +1609+3836
people (1)

82 ἀδελφότης *adelphotēs* (2)
brotherhood of believers (1)
brothers (1)

83 ἄδηλος *adēlos* (2)
not clear (1)
unmarked (1)

84 ἀδηλότης *adēlotēs* (1)
uncertain (1)

85 ἀδήλως *adēlōs* (1)
aimlessly (1)

86 ἀδημονέω *adēmoneō* (3)
troubled (2)
distressed (1)

87 ᾅδης *hadēs* (10)
Hades (5)
depths (2)
grave (2)
hell (1)

88 ἀδιάκριτος *adiakritos* (1)
impartial (1)

89 ἀδιάλειπτος *adialeiptos* (2)
constantly (1)
unceasing (1)

90 ἀδιαλείπτως *adialeiptōs* (4)
continually (3)
constantly (1)

91 ἀδιαφθορία *adiaphthoria*
Variant; not used

92 ἀδικέω *adikeō* (28)
harm (5)
done wrong (3)
do wrong (2)
does wrong (2)
hurt (2)
wronged (2)
damage (1)

did wrong (1)
do harm (1)
guilty (1)
harm done (1)
inflict injury (1)
injured (1)
mistreated (1)
mistreating (1)
torment (1)
unfair (1)
wrong (1)

93 ἀδίκημα *adikēma* (3)
crime (1)
crimes (1)
misdemeanor (1)

94 ἀδικία *adikia* (25)
wickedness (9)
evil (4)
unjust (2)
unrighteousness (2)
dishonest (1)
evildoers (1) +2239
harm (1)
nothing false (1) +4024
sin (1)
worldly (1)
wrong (1)
wrongdoing (1)

95 ἀδικοκρίτης *adikokritēs*
Variant; not used

96 ἄδικος *adikos* (13)
unjust (3)
unrighteous (3)
dishonest (2)
wicked (2)
evildoers (1)
ungodly (1)
worldly (1)

97 ἀδίκως *adikōs*
Variant; not used

98 Ἀδμίν *Admin*
Variant; not used

99 ἀδόκιμος *adokimos* (8)
depraved (1)
disqualified (1)
fail the test (1) +1639
failed the test (1) +1639
rejected (1)
to have failed (1) +1639
unfit (1)
worthless (1)

100 ἄδολος *adolos* (1)
pure (1)

101 Ἀδραμυττηνός *Adramyttēnos* (1)
from Adramyttium (1)

102 Ἀδρίας *Adrias* (1)
Adriatic sea (1)

103 ἁδρότης *hadrotēs* (1)
liberal (1)

104 ἀδυνατέω *adynateō* (2)
impossible (2)

105 ἀδύνατος *adynatos* (10)
impossible (7)
crippled (1)
powerless (1)
weak (1)

106 ᾄδω *adō* (5)
sang (3)
sing (2)

107 ἀεί *aei* (7)
always (7)

108 ἀετός *aetos* (5)
eagle (3)

vultures (2)

109 ἄζυμος *azymos* (9)
feast of unleavened Bread (4)
unleavened Bread (2)
bread without yeast (1)
feast of unleavened Bread (1) +2465
without yeast (1)

110 Ἀζώρ *Azōr* (2)
Azor (2)

111 Ἄζωτος *Azōtos* (1)
Azotus (1)

112 ἀηδία *aēdia*
Variant; not used

113 ἀήρ *aēr* (7)
air (6)
sky (1)

114 ἀθανασία *athanasia* (3)
immortality (2)
immortal (1)

115 ἀθάνατος *athanatos*
Variant; not used

116 ἀθέμιτος *athemitos* (2)
against law (1)
detestable (1)

117 ἄθεος *atheos* (1)
without God (1)

118 ἄθεσμος *athesmos* (2)
lawless (2)

119 ἀθετέω *atheteō* (16)
rejects (6)
reject (2)
rejected (2)
set aside (2)
broken (1)
frustrate (1)
refuse (1)
setting aside (1)

120 ἀθέτησις *athetēsis* (2)
do away (1)
set aside (1)

121 Ἀθῆναι *Athēnai* (4)
Athens (4)

122 Ἀθηναῖος *Athēnaios* (2)
Athenians (1)
Athens (1)

123 ἀθλέω *athleō* (2)
competes (1)
competes as an athlete (1)

124 ἄθλησις *athlēsis* (1)
contest (1)

125 ἀθροίζω *athroizō* (1)
assembled together (1)

126 ἀθυμέω *athymeō* (1)
become discouraged (1)

127 ἄθῷος *athōos* (2)
innocent (2)

128 αἴγειος *aigeios* (1)
goatskins (1) +1293

129 αἰγιαλός *aigialos* (6)
shore (3)
beach (2)
sandy beach (1)

130 Αἰγύπτιος *Aigyptios* (5)
Egyptian (3)
Egyptians (2)

131 Αἴγυπτος *Aigyptos* (25)
Egypt (20)
Egypt (5) +1178

132 ἀΐδιος *aidios* (2)

eternal (1)
everlasting (1)

133 αἰδώς *aidōs* (1)
decency (1)

134 Αἰθίοψ *Aithiops* (2)
Ethiopian (1) +467
Ethiopians (1)

135 αἷμα *haima* (97)
blood (87)
man (2) +2779+4922
subject to bleeding (2) +1877+4868
bleeding (1) +3836+4868
bleeding (1) +3836+4380
blood money (1) +5507
blood red (1) +6055
natural descent (1)
shedding blood (1)

136 αἱματεκχυσία *haimatekchysia* (1)
shedding of blood (1)

137 αἱμορροέω *haimorroeō* (1)
subject to bleeding (1)

138 Αἰνέας *Aineas* (2)
Aeneas (2)

139 αἴνεσις *ainesis* (1)
praise (1)

140 αἰνέω *aineō* (8)
praising (5)
praise (3)

141 αἴνιγμα *ainigma* (1)
poor (1) +1877

142 αἶνος *ainos* (2)
praise (1)
praised (1) +1443

143 Αἰνών *Ainōn* (1)
Aenon (1)

144 αἴξ *aix*
Variant; not used

145 αἱρέομαι *haireomai* (3)
chose (2)
choose (1)

146 αἵρεσις *hairesis* (9)
sect (4)
party (2)
differences (1)
factions (1)
heresies (1)

147 αἱρετίζω *hairetizō* (1)
chosen (1)

148 αἱρετικός *hairetikos* (1)
divisive (1)

149 αἴρω *airō* (101)
take (15)
picked up (9)
take away (7)
pick up (6)
taken (6)
get (5)
took (5)
taken away (4)
takes away (4)
took away (4)
carry (3)
take up (3)
takes (3)
away with (2)
go (2)
lift up (2)
pull away (2)
raised (2)
called out in a loud voice (1) +5889
carried (1)
cuts off (1)
deprived (1)

get out (1)
get rid of (1)
hoisted aboard (1)
keep in suspense (1) +3836+6034
looked (1) +3836+4057
put (1)
removed (1)
rid (1)
take out (1)
taken down (1)
taking out (1)
weighed anchor (1)
untranslated (1)

150 αἰσθάνομαι *aisthanomai* (1)
grasp (1)

151 αἴσθησις *aisthēsis* (1)
insight (1)

152 αἰσθητήριον *aisthētērion* (1)
themselves (1)

153 αἰσχροκερδής *aischrokerdēs* (2)
pursuing dishonest gain (2)

154 αἰσχροκερδῶς *aischrokerdōs* (1)
greedy for money (1)

155 αἰσχρολογία *aischrologia* (1)
filthy language (1)

156 αἰσχρός *aischros* (4)
disgrace (1)
disgraceful (1)
dishonest (1)
shameful (1)

157 αἰσχρότης *aischrotēs* (1)
obscenity (1)

158 αἰσχύνη *aischynē* (6)
shame (3)
shameful (2)
humiliated (1) +3552

159 αἰσχύνομαι *aischynomai* (5)
ashamed (4)
unashamed (1) +3590

160 αἰτέω *aiteō* (70)
ask (23)
asked for (9)
ask for (8)
asked (8)
asks (6)
asks for (4)
asking (3)
asked (1) +161
asked favor (1)
beg (1) +1797+3836
called for (1)
demand (1)
demanded (1)
pray (1)
request (1)
urgently requested (1) +4151

161 αἴτημα *aitēma* (3)
asked (1) +160
demand (1)
requests (1)

162 αἰτία *aitia* (20)
basis for a charge (3)
reason (3)
why (3) +1328+4005
charge (1)
charge (1) +5770
charge against (1)
charges (1)
guilty of crime (1)
proper ground (1)
situation (1)
so (1) +1328+4005
that is why (1) +1328+4005
therefore (1) +1328+4005
untranslated (1)

163 αἰτίαμα *aitiama*
Variant; not used

164 αἰτιάομαι *aitiaomai*
Variant; not used

165 αἴτιος *aitios* (5)
basis (1)
basis for a charge (1)
grounds for the death penalty (1) +2505
reason (1)
source (1)

166 αἰτίωμα *aitiōma* (1)
charges (1)

167 αἰφνίδιος *aiphnidios* (2)
suddenly (1)
unexpectedly (1)

168 αἰχμαλωσία *aichmalōsia* (3)
captivity (2)
led captives in his train (1) +169

169 αἰχμαλωτεύω *aichmalōteuō* (1)
led captives in his train (1) +168

170 αἰχμαλωτίζω *aichmalōtizō* (4)
gain control over (1)
making a prisoner (1)
take captive (1)
taken as prisoners (1)

171 αἰχμάλωτος *aichmalōtos* (1)
prisoners (1)

172 αἰών *aiōn* (122)
ever (44)
forever (23) +1650+3836
age (20)
ages (7)
never (4) +1650+3590+3836+4024
world (4)
eternal (2)
never (2) +1650+3836+4024
universe (2)
again (1) +1650+3836
ages past (1)
ever (1) +1650+3836
ever (1) +1666+3836
forever (1) +1650
forever (1) +1650+2465
forevermore (1) +1650+3836+4246
life (1)
long ago (1)
long ago (1) +608
never again (1) +1650+3590+3836+4024
time (1)
ways (1)
untranslated (1)

173 αἰώνιος *aiōnios* (71)
eternal (63)
beginning of time (2) +5989
everlasting (2)
ages (1)
forever (1)
never (1) +1650+3590+3836+4024
untranslated (1)

174 ἀκαθαρσία *akatharsia* (10)
impurity (6)
impure (1)
sexual impurity (1)
to be impure (1) +2093
unclean (1)

175 ἀκαθάρτης *akathartēs*
Variant; not used

176 ἀκάθαρτος *akathartos* (31)
evil (23)
unclean (6)
filth (1)
impure (1)

177 ἀκαιρέομαι *akaireomai* (1)
had no opportunity (1)

178 ἀκαίρως *akairōs* (1)
out of season (1)

179 ἄκακος *akakos* (2)
blameless (1)
naive (1)

180 ἄκανθα *akantha* (14)
thorns (9)
thornbushes (2)
which[s] (2) +3836
untranslated (1)

181 ἀκάνθινος *akanthinos* (2)
of thorns (2)

182 ἄκαρπος *akarpos* (7)
unfruitful (3)
unproductive (2)
fruitless (1)
without fruit (1)

183 ἀκατάγνωστος *akatagnōstos* (1)
cannot be condemned (1)

184 ἀκατακάλυπτος *akatakalyptos* (2)
uncovered (2)

185 ἀκατάκριτος *akatakritos* (2)
hasn't been found guilty (1)
without a trial (1)

186 ἀκατάλυτος *akatalytos* (1)
indestructible (1)

187 ἀκατάπαστος *akatapastos*
Variant; not used

188 ἀκατάπαυστος *akatapaustos* (1)
never stop (1)

189 ἀκαταστασία *akatastasia* (5)
disorder (3)
revolutions (1)
riots (1)

190 ἀκατάστατος *akatastatos* (2)
restless (1)
unstable (1)

191 ἀκατάσχετος *akataschetos*
Variant; not used

192 Ἁκελδαμάχ *Hakeldamach* (1)
Akeldama (1)

193 ἀκέραιος *akeraios* (3)
innocent (2)
pure (1)

194 ἀκηδεμονέω *akēdemoneō*
Variant; not used

195 ἀκλινής *aklinēs* (1)
unswervingly (1)

196 ἀκμάζω *akmazō* (1)
ripe (1)

197 ἀκμήν *akmēn* (1)
still (1)

198 ἀκοή *akoē* (24)
message (4)
ears (3)
heard (3)
ever hearing (2) +201
news (2)
rumors (2)
what heard (2)
ear (1)
hearing (1)
learn (1)
reports (1)
sense of hearing (1)
what ears want to hear (1)

199 ἀκολουθέω *akoloutheō* (90)
followed (41)
follow (32)
following (6)
accompanied (2)

behind (1)
come (1)
follow (1) +3958
followed out (1) +2002
following behind (1)
follows (1)
is one of us (1) +1609+3552
went with (1)
untranslated (1)

200 ἀκουστός *akoustos*
Variant; not used

201 ἀκούω *akouō* (428)
heard (199)
hear (99)
listen (40)
hears (18)
hearing (14)
heard about (10)
listens (9)
listening (8)
listened (5)
heard of (3)
ever hearing (2) +198
understand (2)
accept (1)
aware of (1)
ever hearing (1) +201
hear (1) +1639+4047
hear (1) +4015
heard (1) +1639
hearers (1)
it[s] (1) +608+794+4005
learned (1)
obey (1)
reached (1) +1650
reported (1)
say (1) +1609+1666
told (1)
understands (1)
whispered[s] (1)
untranslated (2)

202 ἀκρασία *akrasia* (2)
lack of self-control (1)
self-indulgence (1)

203 ἀκρατής *akratēs* (1)
without self-control (1)

204 ἄκρατος *akratos* (1)
full strength (1)

205 ἀκρίβεια *akribeia* (1)
thoroughly (1) +2848

206 ἀκριβέστατος *akribestatos*
Variant; not used

207 ἀκριβής *akribēs* (1)
strictest (1)

208 ἀκριβόω *akriboō* (2)
found out exact (1)
learned (1)

209 ἀκριβῶς *akribōs* (9)
accurate (2)
accurately (1)
careful (1)
carefully (1)
more adequately (1)
very careful (1)
very well (1)
well (1)

210 ἀκρίς *akris* (4)
locusts (4)

211 ἀκροατήριον *akroatērion* (1)
audience room (1)

212 ἀκροατής *akroatēs* (4)
hear (1)
heard (1) +1181
listen (1)
listens (1) +1639

213 ἀκροβυστία *akrobystia* (20)
uncircumcised (5)
not circumcised (4)
uncircumcision (4)
before circumcised (1) +1877
gentiles (1)
they (1) +899+3836
uncircumcised (1) +1877
uncircumcised (1) +2400
untranslated (2)

214 ἀκρογωνιαῖος *akrogōniaios* (2)
chief cornerstone (1) +1639
cornerstone (1)

215 ἀκροθίνιον *akrothinion* (1)
plunder (1)

216 ἄκρον *akron* (6)
ends (2)
end (1)
other[s] (1)
tip (1)
top (1)

217 Ἀκύλας *Akylas* (6)
Aquila (6)

218 ἀκυρόω *akyroō* (3)
nullify (2)
set aside (1)

219 ἀκωλύτως *akōlytōs* (1)
without hindrance (1)

220 ἄκων *akōn* (1)
not voluntarily (1)

221 ἅλα *hala*
Variant; not used

222 ἀλάβαστρον *alabastron*
Variant; not used

223 ἀλάβαστρος *alabastros* (4)
alabaster jar (3)
jar (1)

224 ἀλαζονεία *alazoneia* (2)
boasting (1)
brag (1) +1877+3836

225 ἀλαζών *alazōn* (2)
boastful (2)

226 ἀλαλάζω *alalazō* (2)
clanging (1)
wailing (1)

227 ἀλάλητος *alalētos* (1)
words cannot express (1)

228 ἄλαλος *alalos* (3)
mute (2)
robbed him of speech (1)

229 ἅλας *halas* (8)
salt (6)
it[s] (2) +3836

230 ἀλείφω *aleiphō* (9)
poured on (4)
anoint (2)
anointed (1)
put oil on (1)
put on (1)

231 ἀλεκτοροφωνία *alektorophōnia* (1)
when the rooster crows (1)

232 ἀλέκτωρ *alektōr* (11)
rooster (11)

233 Ἀλεξανδρεύς *Alexandreus* (2)
Alexandria (1)
of Alexandria (1)

234 Ἀλεξανδρῖνος *Alexandrinos* (2)
Alexandrian (2)

235 Ἀλέξανδρος *Alexandros* (6)
Alexander (5)

he[s] (1) +3836

236 ἄλευρον *aleuron* (2)
flour (1)
large amount of flour (1) +4929+5552

237 ἀλήθεια *alētheia* (109)
truth (93)
true (5)
assure (1) +2093+3306
certainly (1) +2093
deny truth (1) +2848+6017
how true (1) +2093
right (1) +2093
true (1) +1877
truly (1) +1877
truthful (1)
truthfully (1)
truthfulness (1)
untranslated (1)

238 ἀληθεύω *alētheuō* (2)
speaking truth (1)
telling truth (1)

239 ἀληθής *alēthēs* (26)
true (9)
valid (5)
real (3)
truth (3)
integrity (2)
genuine (1)
really (1)
reliable (1)
truthful (1)

240 ἀληθινός *alēthinos* (28)
true (26)
right (1)
sincere (1)

241 ἀλήθω *alēthō* (2)
grinding (1)
grinding grain (1)

242 ἀληθῶς *alēthōs* (18)
surely (6)
really (3)
the truth (3)
truly (2)
actually (1)
true (1)
with certainty (1)
without a doubt (1)

243 ἁλιεύς *halieus* (5)
fishermen (3)
fishers (2)

244 ἁλιεύω *halieuō* (1)
fish (1)

245 ἁλίζω *halizō* (2)
made salty (1)
salted (1)

246 ἀλίσγημα *alisgēma* (1)
polluted (1)

247 ἀλλά *alla* (638)
but (414)
instead (20)
yet (16)
no (14)
rather (11)
on the contrary (10)
only (7)
and (6)
in fact (5)
indeed (5)
but rather (4)
nevertheless (4)
but only (3)
however (3)
now (3)
if not (2)
so (2)

again (1)
although (1)
and what is more (1)
      +1145+2779+4047+4246+5250
but (1) +2445
but instead (1)
certainly (1)
even (1)
even though (1)
except (1)
except that (1)
for (1)
if (1)
in addition (1) +2779
indeed (1) +2779
instead (1) +3437
instead of (1)
just (1)
on contrary (1) +1883
on the contrary (1) +3437+4498
surely (1) +1145
then (1)
though (1)
to some extent (1) +608+3538
what (1)
what is more (1) +1254+2779+3667+4024
what is more (1) +3529
yes (1)
untranslated (82)

248 ἀλλάσσω *allassō* (6)
changed (3)
change (2)
exchanged (1)

249 ἀλλαχόθεν *allachothen* (1)
other way (1)

250 ἀλλαχοῦ *allachou* (1)
somewhere else (1)

251 ἀλληγορέω *allēgoreō* (1)
taken figuratively (1)

252 ἀλληλουϊά *hallēlouia* (4)
Hallelujah (4)

253 ἀλλήλων *allēlōn* (100)
one another (46)
each other (32)
themselves (3)
each other's (2)
together (2) +4639
yourselves (2)
all the others (1)
mutual (1)
one another's (1)
one body (1)
others (1)
parted company (1) +608+714
talked the matter over (1) +1368+4639
them (1)
untranslated (5)

254 ἀλλογενής *allogenēs* (1)
foreigner (1)

255 ἀλλοιόω *alloioō*
Variant; not used

256 ἅλλομαι *hallomai* (3)
jumped up (1)
jumping (1)
welling up (1)

257 ἄλλος *allos* (155)
another (42)
other (34)
others (33)
someone else (6)
else (5)
some (5)
more (4)
still another (2)
still others (2)
that one (2)

another (1) +5516
another's (1)
anyone else (1)
anything (1)
gospelˢ (1)
one (1)
one (1) +1651+4024
one another (1) +257+4639
other (1) +1254
other than (1)
others (1) +1254
some (1) +1254
some more (1)
someone (1)
untranslated (5)

258 ἀλλοτριεπίσκοπος *allotriepiskopos* (1)
meddler (1)

259 ἀλλότριος *allotrios* (14)
others (4)
someone else's (3)
stranger (2)
another (1)
foreign (1)
not his own (1)
not their own (1)
stranger's (1)

260 ἀλλόφυλος *allophylos* (1)
gentile (1)

261 ἄλλως *allōs* (1)
not (1)

262 ἀλοάω *aloaō* (3)
treading out the grain (2)
thresher (1)

263 ἄλογος *alogos* (3)
brute (1)
unreasonable (1)
unreasoning (1)

264 ἀλόη *aloē* (1)
aloes (1)

265 ἅλς *hals*
Variant; not used

266 ἁλυκός *halykos* (1)
salt spring (1)

267 ἄλυπος *alypos* (1)
less anxiety (1)

268 ἅλυσις *halysis* (11)
chains (6)
chain (3)
chained hand (1) +1297
chained hand (1) +1313

269 ἀλυσιτελής *alysitelēs* (1)
no advantage (1)

270 ἄλφα *alpha* (3)
Alpha (3)

271 Ἀλφαῖος *Halphaios* (5)
Alphaeus (5)

272 ἅλων *halōn* (2)
threshing floor (2)

273 ἀλώπηξ *alōpēx* (3)
foxes (2)
fox (1)

274 ἅλωσις *halōsis* (1)
caught (1)

275 ἅμα *hama* (10)
together (3)
at the same time (2)
and (1)
besides (1)
early in the morning (1) +4745
one thing more (1)
with (1)

276 ἀμαθής *amathēs* (1)

ignorant (1)

277 ἀμαράντινος *amarantinos* (1)
never fade away (1)

278 ἀμάραντος *amarantos* (1)
fade (1)

279 ἁμαρτάνω *hamartanō* (43)
sin (14)
sinned (12)
sinning (7)
sins (5)
commit a sin (1) +281
doing wrong (1)
done wrong (1)
leave your life of sin (1) +3600
sinful (1)

280 ἁμάρτημα *hamartēma* (4)
sins (3)
sin (1)

281 ἁμαρτία *hamartia* (173)
sins (74)
sin (73)
be guilty of sin (3) +2400
sin (2) +4472
sin offering (2)
sin offerings (2) +4309
sinful (2)
sinning (1)
commit a sin (1) +279
guilt (1)
guilty of sin (1) +2400
promotes sin (1) +1356
sin (1) +2237
sin's (1)
sinned (1) +1639+4472
sins (1) +1639
sins (1) +3836+4472
sins (1) +4472
what is sinful (1)
what sin was (1)
without sin (1) +4024

282 ἀμάρτυρος *amartyros* (1)
without testimony (1)

283 ἁμαρτωλός *hamartōlos* (47)
sinners (29)
sinner (9)
sinful (6)
sinful life (1)
sinner (1) +467
sinner (1) +476

284 Ἀμασίας *Amasias*
Variant; not used

285 ἄμαχος *amachos* (2)
not quarrelsome (1)
peaceable (1)

286 ἀμάω *amaō* (1)
mowed (1)

287 ἀμέθυστος *amethystos* (1)
amethyst (1)

288 ἀμελέω *ameleō* (4)
ignore (1)
neglect (1)
paid no attention (1)
turned away (1)

289 ἄμεμπτος *amemptos* (5)
blameless (2)
blamelessly (1)
faultless (1) +1181
nothing wrong with (1)

290 ἀμέμπτως *amemptōs* (2)
blameless (2)

291 ἀμέριμνος *amerimnos* (2)
free from concern (1)
out of trouble (1)

292 ἀμετάθετος *ametathetos* (2)
unchangeable (1)
unchanging (1)

293 ἀμετακίνητος *ametakinētos* (1)
nothing move (1)

294 ἀμεταμέλητος *ametamelētos* (2)
irrevocable (1)
no regret (1)

295 ἀμετανόητος *ametanoētos* (1)
unrepentant (1)

296 ἄμετρος *ametros* (2)
beyond limits (2) *+1650+3836*

297 ἀμήν *amēn* (123)
the truth (74)
amen (30)
untranslated (18)

298 ἀμήτωρ *amētōr* (1)
mother (1)

299 ἀμίαντος *amiantos* (4)
pure (2)
faultless (1)
spoil (1)

300 Ἀμιναδάβ *Aminadab* (3)
Amminadab (3)

301 ἄμμον *ammon*
Variant; not used

302 ἄμμος *ammos* (5)
sand (4)
shore (1)

303 ἀμνός *amnos* (4)
lamb (4)

304 ἀμοιβή *amoibē* (1)
repaying (1) *+625*

305 ἄμορφος *amorphos*
Variant; not used

306 ἄμπελος *ampelos* (9)
vine (7)
grapes (1)
grapevine (1)

307 ἀμπελουργός *ampelourgos* (1)
took care of the vineyard (1)

308 ἀμπελών *ampelōn* (23)
vineyard (23)

309 Ἀμπλιᾶτος *Ampliatos* (1)
Ampliatus (1)

310 ἀμύνομαι *amynomai* (1)
went to defense (1)

311 ἀμφιβάλλω *amphiballō* (1)
casting a net (1)

312 ἀμφίβληστρον *amphiblēstron* (1)
net (1)

313 ἀμφιέζω *amphiezō* (1)
clothes (1)

314 ἀμφιέννυμι *amphiennymi* (3)
dressed (2)
clothes (1)

315 Ἀμφίπολις *Amphipolis* (1)
Amphipolis (1)

316 ἄμφοδον *amphodon* (1)
street (1)

317 ἀμφότεροι *amphoteroi* (14)
both (11)
all (1)
them all (1) *+3836*
two (1)

318 ἀμώμητος *amōmētos* (1)
blameless (1)

319 ἄμωμον *amōmon* (1)
spice (1)

320 ἄμωμος *amōmos* (8)
blameless (3)
without blemish (2)
without fault (2)
unblemished (1)

321 Ἀμών *Amōn* (2)
Amon (2)

322 Ἀμώς *Amōs* (1)
Amos (1)

323 ἄν *an* (166)
would (39)
whoever (19) *+4005*
if (17)
until (13) *+2401*
anyone (7)
before (4) *+2401*
whom (4) *+4005*
anyone who (3) *+4005*
whatever (2) *+4005*
whatever (2) *+4005+5516*
when (2) *+6055*
wherever (2) *+3963*
whoever (2) *+4015*
all who (1) *+4012*
all whom (1) *+4012*
any (1)
any (1) *+4005+5516*
as (1) *+2776*
as soon as (1) *+6055*
before (1) *+2445+4570*
could (1)
everyone (1) *+4246*
everything (1) *+4012+4246*
except (1) *+1623+3614*
had (1) *+2400*
if any (1) *+4005*
might (1)
once (1) *+608+4005*
pray (1) *+2377*
so that (1) *+3968*
somehow or other (1) *+6055*
survive (1) *+5392*
the one (1) *+4005*
till (1) *+2401*
until (1) *+948+4005*
what (1) *+5516*
what going on (1) *+4047+5515*
whatever (1) *+1650+4005*
whatever (1) *+4012*
whatever (1) *+5516*
when (1)
when (1) *+2471*
when (1) *+4005*
when (1) *+1650+4005*
which (1) *+5515*
whoever (1) *+3836*
untranslated (17)

324 ἀνά *ana* (13)
each (2)
among (1) *+3545*
at (1)
between (1) *+3545*
each (1) *+1651+1667*
each one (1) *+3836*
extra (1) *+1545*
from (1)
into (1) *+3545*
one at a time (1) *+3538*
two by two (1) *+1545+1545*
untranslated (1)

325 ἀναβαθμός *anabathmos* (2)
steps (2)

326 ἀναβαίνω *anabainō* (82)
went up (23)
going up (7)
come up (5)
go up (4)

went (4)
ascend (3)
ascended (3)
came up (3)
climbed (3)
coming (2)
coming up (2)
grew up (2)
ascending (1)
climbed aboard (1)
climbs in (1)
comes up (1)
conceived (1)
decided (1) *+2093+2840+3836*
go (1)
goes up (1)
gone (1)
grows (1)
left (1)
marched (1)
reached (1)
returned (1)
returning (1)
rise (1)
rises (1)
rose (1)
went upstairs (1)
were up (1) *+1639*
untranslated (1)

327 ἀναβάλλω *anaballō* (1)
adjourned the proceedings (1)

328 ἀναβιβάζω *anabibazō* (1)
pulled up (1)

329 ἀναβλέπω *anablepō* (24)
looked up (5)
received sight (5)
receive sight (4)
looking up (3)
see (3)
see again (2)
able to see (1)
restore sight (1)

330 ἀνάβλεψις *anablepsis* (1)
recovery of sight (1)

331 ἀναβοάω *anaboaō* (1)
cried out (1)

332 ἀναβολή *anabolē* (1)
delay (1) *+4472*

333 ἀνάγαιον *anagaion* (2)
upper room (2)

334 ἀναγγέλλω *anangellō* (14)
told (4)
reported (2)
declare (1)
explain (1)
make known (1)
making known (1)
openly confessed (1) *+2018*
preach (1)
proclaim (1)
tell (1)

335 ἀναγεννάω *anagennaō* (2)
born again (1)
given new birth (1)

336 ἀναγινώσκω *anaginōskō* (32)
read (24)
reading (5)
reader (2)
reads (1)

337 ἀναγκάζω *anankazō* (9)
compelled (2)
force (2)
made (2)
compel (1)
drove to it (1)
make (1)

338 ἀναγκαῖος *anankaios* (8)
necessary (2)
close (1)
daily necessities (1) +5970
had (1) +1639
indispensable (1)
more necessary (1)
necessary for (1)

339 ἀναγκαστῶς *anankastōs* (1)
must (1)

340 ἀνάγκη *anankē* (17)
necessary (3)
compulsion (2)
distress (2)
hardships (2)
must (2)
compelled (1) +2130
crisis (1)
forced (1) +2848
had (1)
must (1) +2400
need (1) +2400

341 ἀναγνωρίζω *anagnōrizō* (1)
told (1)

342 ἀνάγνωσις *anagnōsis* (3)
public reading (1)
read (1)
reading (1)

343 ἀνάγω *anagō* (23)
put out to sea (5)
sail (4)
brought (2)
sailed (2)
set sail (2)
bring out (1)
bring up (1)
brought back (1)
led (1)
led up (1)
set out (1)
taken upstairs (1)
took (1)

344 ἀναδείκνυμι *anadeiknymi* (2)
appointed (1)
show (1)

345 ἀνάδειξις *anadeixis* (1)
appeared publicly (1)

346 ἀναδέχομαι *anadechomai* (2)
received (1)
welcomed (1)

347 ἀναδίδωμι *anadidōmi* (1)
delivered (1)

348 ἀναζάω *anazaō* (3)
alive again (2)
sprang to life (1)

349 ἀναζητέω *anazēteō* (3)
look for (2)
looking for (1)

350 ἀναζώννυμι *anazōnnymi* (1)
prepare for action (1) +3836+4019

351 ἀναζωπυρέω *anazōpyreō* (1)
fan into flame (1)

352 ἀναθάλλω *anathallō* (1)
renewed (1)

353 ἀνάθεμα *anathema* (6)
cursed (2)
eternally condemned (2)
curse (1)
taken a solemn oath (1) +354

354 ἀναθεματίζω *anathematizō* (4)
bound with an oath (1)
call down curses (1)
taken a solemn oath (1) +353

taken an oath (1)

355 ἀναθεωρέω *anatheōreō* (2)
consider (1)
looked carefully at (1)

356 ἀνάθημα *anathēma* (1)
gifts dedicated to God (1)

357 ἀναίδεια *anaideia* (1)
boldness (1)

358 ἀναίρεσις *anairesis* (1)
death (1)

359 ἀναιρέω *anaireō* (24)
kill (9)
killed (4)
put to death (4)
executed (2)
get rid of (1)
killing (1)
overthrow (1)
sets aside (1)
took (1)

360 ἀναίτιος *anaitios* (2)
innocent (2)

361 ἀνακαθίζω *anakathizō* (2)
sat up (2)

362 ἀνακαινίζω *anakainizō* (1)
brought back (1)

363 ἀνακαινόω *anakainoō* (2)
renewed (2)

364 ἀνακαίνωσις *anakainōsis* (2)
renewal (1)
renewing (1)

365 ἀνακαλύπτω *anakalyptō* (2)
removed (1)
unveiled (1)

366 ἀνακάμπτω *anakamptō* (4)
return (2)
come back (1)
go back (1)

367 ἀνάκειμαι *anakeimai* (14)
reclining at the table (4)
at the table (2)
guests (2)
at the meal (1) +3836
dinner guests (1)
eating (1)
having dinner (1)
reclining (1)
seated (1)

368 ἀνακεφαλαιόω *anakephalaioō* (2)
bring together under one head (1)
summed up (1)

369 ἀνακλίνω *anaklinō* (6)
take places at the feast (2)
have recline at the table (1)
have sit down (1)
placed (1)
sit down (1)

370 ἀνακόπτω *anakoptō*
Variant; not used

371 ἀνακράζω *anakrazō* (5)
cried out (5)

372 ἀνακραυγάζω *anakraugazō*
Variant; not used

373 ἀνακρίνω *anakrinō* (16)
examined (3)
judged (2)
raising questions (2)
called to account (1)
cross-examined (1)
discerned (1)
examining (1)
judge (1)

judges (1)
judgment (1)
makes judgments about (1)
sit in judgment on (1)

374 ἀνάκρισις *anakrisis* (1)
investigation (1)

375 ἀνακυλίω *anakyliō*
Variant; not used

376 ἀνακύπτω *anakyptō* (4)
straightened up (2)
stand up (1)
straighten up (1)

377 ἀναλαμβάνω *analambanō* (13)
taken up (4)
get (1)
lifted up (1)
put on (1)
take aboard (1)
take up (1)
taken (1)
taken back (1)
took (1)
took aboard (1)

378 ἀνάλημψις *analēmpsis* (1)
taken up (1)

379 ἀναλίσκω *analiskō*
Variant; not used

380 ἀνάλλομαι *anallomai*
Variant; not used

381 ἀναλογία *analogia* (1)
proportion (1)

382 ἀναλογίζομαι *analogizomai* (1)
consider (1)

383 ἄναλος *analos* (1)
saltiness (1)

384 ἀναλόω *analoō* (2)
destroy (1)
destroyed (1)

385 ἀνάλυσις *analysis* (1)
departure (1)

386 ἀναλύω *analyō* (2)
depart (1)
to return (1) +4536

387 ἀναμάρτητος *anamartētos* (1)
without sin (1)

388 ἀναμένω *anamenō* (1)
wait for (1)

389 ἀναμιμνῄσκω *anamimnēskō* (6)
remembered (2)
remember (1)
remembers (1)
remind (1)
remind of (1)

390 ἀνάμνησις *anamnēsis* (4)
remembrance (3)
reminder (1)

391 ἀνανεόομαι *ananeoomai* (1)
made new (1)

392 ἀνανήφω *ananēphō* (1)
come to senses (1)

393 Ἀνανίας *Hananias* (11)
Ananias (11)

394 ἀναντίρρητος *anantirrētos* (1)
undeniable (1)

395 ἀναντιρρήτως *anantirrētōs* (1)
without raising any objection (1)

396 ἀνάξιος *anaxios* (1)
not competent (1)

397 ἀναξίως *anaxiōs* (1)
unworthy manner (1)

398 ἀνάπαυσις *anapausis* (5)
rest (4)
stop (1) +2400

399 ἀναπαύω *anapauō* (12)
refreshed (3)
resting (2)
get rest (1)
give rest (1)
refresh (1)
rest (1)
rests (1)
take life easy (1)
wait (1)

400 ἀναπείθω *anapeithō* (1)
persuading (1)

401 ἀνάπειρος *anapeiros* (2)
crippled (2)

402 ἀναπέμπω *anapempō* (5)
sent back (2)
send (1)
sending back (1)
sent (1)

403 ἀναπηδάω *anapēdaō* (1)
jumped to his feet (1)

404 ἀναπίπτω *anapiptō* (12)
sit down (3)
reclined at the table (2)
sat down (2)
leaned back (1)
leaning back (1)
returned to place (1) +4099
sit down to eat (1)
take (1) +1650

405 ἀναπληρόω *anaplēroō* (6)
finds himself (1)
fulfill (1)
fulfilled (1)
heap up to the limit (1)
make up for (1)
supplied (1)

406 ἀναπολόγητος *anapologētos* (2)
no excuse (1)
without excuse (1)

407 ἀναπράσσω *anaprassō*
Variant; not used

408 ἀναπτύσσω *anaptyssō* (1)
unrolling (1)

409 ἀνάπτω *anaptō* (2)
kindled (1)
set on fire (1)

410 ἀναρίθμητος *anarithmētos* (1)
countless (1)

411 ἀνασείω *anaseiō* (2)
stirred up (1)
stirs up (1)

412 ἀνασκευάζω *anaskeuazō* (1)
troubling (1)

413 ἀνασπάω *anaspaō* (2)
pull out (1)
pulled up (1)

414 ἀνάστασις *anastasis* (42)
resurrection (37)
rise (3)
raised to life again (1)
rising (1)

415 ἀναστατόω *anastatoō* (3)
agitators (1)
caused trouble (1)
revolt (1)

416 ἀνασταυρόω *anastauroō* (1)
crucifying all over again (1)

417 ἀναστενάζω *anastenazō* (1)

sighed deeply (1) +3836+4460

418 ἀναστρέφω *anastrephō* (10)
live (3)
conduct (1)
conducted ourselves (1)
lived (1)
overturned (1)
return (1)
treated (1)
went back (1)

419 ἀναστροφή *anastrophē* (13)
way of life (4)
lives (3)
behavior (2)
life (2)
do (1)
live (1)

420 ἀνασῴζω *anasōzō*
Variant; not used

421 ἀνατάσσομαι *anatassomai* (1)
draw up (1)

422 ἀνατέλλω *anatellō* (9)
came up (2)
rises (2)
causes to rise (1)
dawned (1)
descended (1)
just after sunrise (1) +2463+3836
rising (1)

423 ἀνατίθημι *anatithēmi* (2)
discussed (1)
set before (1)

424 ἀνατολή *anatolē* (10)
east (7)
east (2) +2463
rising sun (1)

425 ἀνατολικός *anatolikos*
Variant; not used

426 ἀνατρέπω *anatrepō* (2)
destroy (1)
ruining (1)

427 ἀνατρέφω *anatrephō* (3)
brought up (2)
cared for (1)

428 ἀναφαίνω *anaphainō* (2)
appear (1)
sighting (1)

429 ἀναφέρω *anapherō* (10)
offer (2)
offered (2)
bore (1)
led (1)
led up (1)
offering (1)
take away (1)
taken up (1)

430 ἀναφωνέω *anaphōneō* (1)
exclaimed (1)

431 ἀνάχυσις *anachysis* (1)
flood (1)

432 ἀναχωρέω *anachōreō* (14)
withdrew (5)
left (3)
returned (2)
drew (1)
go away (1)
gone (1)
withdrew (1) +1696

433 ἀνάψυξις *anapsyxis* (1)
refreshing (1)

434 ἀναψύχω *anapsychō* (1)
refreshed (1)

435 ἀνδραποδιστής *andrapodistēs* (1)
slave traders (1)

436 Ἀνδρέας *Andreas* (13)
Andrew (13)

437 ἀνδρίζομαι *andrizomai* (1)
men of courage (1)

438 Ἀνδρόνικος *Andronikos* (1)
Andronicus (1)

439 ἀνδροφόνος *androphonos* (1)
murderers (1)

440 ἀνεγκλησία *anenklēsia*
Variant; not used

441 ἀνέγκλητος *anenklētos* (5)
blameless (3)
free from accusation (1)
nothing against them (1)

442 ἀνεκδιήγητος *anekdiēgētos* (1)
indescribable (1)

443 ἀνεκλάλητος *aneklalētos* (1)
inexpressible (1)

444 ἀνέκλειπτος *anekleiptos* (1)
not be exhausted (1)

445 ἀνεκτός *anektos* (5)
more bearable (5)

446 ἀνελεήμων *aneleēmōn* (1)
ruthless (1)

447 ἀνέλεος *aneleos* (1)
without mercy (1)

448 ἀνεμίζω *anemizō* (1)
blown by the wind (1)

449 ἄνεμος *anemos* (31)
wind (19)
winds (10)
squall (2) +3278

450 ἀνένδεκτος *anendektos* (1)
bound to come (1) +2262+3590

451 ἀνεξεραύνητος *anexeraunētos* (1)
unsearchable (1)

452 ἀνεξίκακος *anexikakos* (1)
not resentful (1)

453 ἀνεξιχνίαστος *anexichniastos* (2)
beyond tracing out (1)
unsearchable (1)

454 ἀνεπαίσχυντος *anepaischyntos* (1)
does not need to be ashamed (1)

455 ἀνεπίλημπτος *anepilēmptos* (3)
above reproach (1)
blame (1)
no open to blame (1)

456 ἀνέρχομαι *anerchomai* (3)
went up (2)
go up (1)

457 ἄνεσις *anesis* (5)
freedom (1)
peace (1)
relief (1)
relieved (1)
rest (1)

458 ἀνετάζω *anetazō* (2)
question (1)
questioned (1)

459 ἄνευ *aneu* (3)
without (2)
apart from (1)

460 ἀνεύθετος *aneuthetos* (1)
unsuitable (1)

461 ἀνευρίσκω *aneuriskō* (2)
finding (1)

found (1)

462 ἀνέχομαι *anechomai* (15)
put up with (8)
bear with (2)
bearing with (1)
doing that[s] (1)
endure (1)
enduring (1)
listen (1)

463 ἀνεψιός *anepsios* (1)
cousin (1)

464 ἄνηθον *anēthon* (1)
dill (1)

465 ἀνήκω *anēkō* (3)
fitting (1)
out of place (1) +4024
what you ought to do (1) +3836

466 ἀνήμερος *anēmeros* (1)
brutal (1)

467 ἀνήρ *anēr* (217)
men (64)
man (63)
husband (37)
brothers (12) +81
husbands (12)
husband's (2)
Jew (2) +2681
man's (2)
characters (1)
divorced (1) +608+668
Ethiopian (1) +134
faithful to her husband (1) +1222+1651
he[s] (1) +3836
him[s] (1) +3836
Jews (1) +2681
marriage (1)
mature (1) +5455
murderer (1) +5838
owner of (1) +4005
prophet (1) +4737
sinner (1) +283
terrorists (1) +3836+4974
you (1)
untranslated (8)

468 ἀνθίστημι *anthistēmi* (14)
opposed (4)
resist (4)
do so[s] (1)
oppose (1)
rebelling against (1)
resists (1)
stand up against (1)
stand your ground (1)

469 ἀνθομολογέομαι *anthomologeomai* (1)
gave thanks (1)

470 ἄνθος *anthos* (4)
flowers (2)
blossom (1)
flower (1)

471 ἀνθρακιά *anthrakia* (2)
fire (1)
fire of burning coals (1)

472 ἄνθραξ *anthrax* (1)
coals (1)

473 ἀνθρωπάρεσκος *anthrōpareskos* (2)
win favor (2)

474 ἀνθρώπινος *anthrōpinos* (7)
human (3)
among men (1)
common to man (1)
I put this in human terms (1) +3306
man (1)

475 ἀνθρωποκτόνος *anthrōpoktonos* (3)
murderer (3)

476 ἄνθρωπος *anthrōpos* (550)
man (277)
men (136)
people (18)
man's (12)
human (9)
everyone (6) +4246
men's (5)
him[s] (4) +3836
self (4)
child (3)
fellow (3)
mankind (3)
being (2)
everybody (2) +4246
everyone (2)
king (2) +995
landowner (2) +3867
men (2) +3836+3836+5626
others (2)
pay attention who they are (2) +1063+4725
person (2)
they[s] (2) +3836
you[s] (2)
all (1) +4246
all the world (1) +1639+4005+5515
anyone[s] (1) +3836
cripple (1) +822
enemy (1) +2398
friend (1)
from everyday life (1) +2848
from human point of view (1) +2848
he[s] (1) +1697+3836
he[s] (1) +3836
him[s] (1) +1877+3836+4047
human (1) +2848
human being (1)
human reasons (1)
husband (1)
Jew (1) +2681
judge by external appearance (1)
                        +3284+4725
merchant (1) +1867
no one (1) +4029
one[s] (1)
outwardly (1) +2032+3836
owner of a house (1) +3867
Roman citizen (1) +4871
Roman citizens (1) +4871
self (1) +2840+3836
sinner (1) +283
someone[s] (1)
something man made up (1) +2848
suppose one (1) +5515
them[s] (1)
them[s] (1) +3836
those[s] (1)
who[s] (1) +3836
untranslated (15)

477 ἀνθυπατεύω *anthypateuō*
Variant; not used

478 ἀνθύπατος *anthypatos* (5)
proconsul (4)
proconsuls (1)

479 ἀνίημι *aniēmi* (4)
came loose (1)
leave (1)
not (1)
untied (1)

480 ἀνίλεως *anileōs*
Variant; not used

481 ἄνιπτος *aniptos* (2)
unwashed (2)

482 ἀνίστημι *anistēmi* (107)
got up (15)
get up (13)
stood up (13)
rise (9)

raise up (5)
rose (5)
rise again (4)
stand up (3)
appeared (2)
arise (2)
come back to life (2)
appears (1)
became ruler (1)
came forward (1)
come (1)
got ready (1)
have children (1) +5065
helped to her feet (1)
left (1)
left (1) +608
opposes (1) +2093
opposition arose (1)
raised (1)
raised again (1)
raised from the dead (1)
raised to life (1)
raised up (1)
raising (1)
raising up (1)
risen (1)
rises (1)
rising (1)
rose again (1)
send (1)
set out (1)
stand up (1) +3981
standing up (1)
started out (1) +2002
stood (1)
untranslated (6)

483 Ἅννα *Hanna* (2)
Anna (1)
Annas (1)

484 Ἅννας *Hannas* (3)
Annas (3)

485 ἀνόητος *anoētos* (6)
foolish (5)
how foolish you are (1) +6043

486 ἄνοια *anoia* (2)
folly (1)
furious (1) +4398

487 ἀνοίγω *anoigō* (77)
opened (38)
open (21)
opening (3)
opens (3)
standing open (2)
began to speak (1) +3306+3836+5125
broke open (1)
flew open (1)
lay open (1)
restored (1)
speak (1) +3836+5125
spoken freely (1) +3836+5125
untranslated (3)

488 ἀνοικοδομέω *anoikodomeō* (2)
rebuild (2)

489 ἄνοιξις *anoixis* (1)
open (1)

490 ἀνομία *anomia* (15)
wickedness (5)
lawlessness (3)
breaks law (1) +4472
ever-increasing wickedness (1)
                        +490+1650+3836
evil (1)
evildoers (1) +2237+3836
lawless acts (1)
transgressions (1)

491 ἄνομος *anomos* (9)
not having the law (3)

lawless (2)
free from law (1)
lawbreakers (1)
transgressors (1)
wicked (1)

492 ἀνόμως *anomōs* (2)
apart from the law (2)

493 ἀνόνητος *anonētos*
Variant; not used

494 ἀνορθόω *anorthoō* (3)
restore (1)
straightened up (1)
strengthen (1)

495 ἀνόσιος *anosios* (2)
unholy (2)

496 ἀνοχή *anochē* (2)
forbearance (1)
tolerance (1)

497 ἀνταγωνίζομαι *antagōnizomai* (1)
struggle (1)

498 ἀντάλλαγμα *antallagma* (2)
in exchange for (2)

499 ἀνταναπληρόω *antanaplēroō* (1)
fill up (1)

500 ἀνταποδίδωμι *antapodidōmi* (7)
repay (4)
in return (1)
pay back (1)
repaid (1)

501 ἀνταπόδομα *antapodoma* (2)
repaid (1)
retribution (1)

502 ἀνταπόδοσις *antapodosis* (1)
reward (1)

503 ἀνταποκρίνομαι *antapokrinomai* (2)
say (1)
talk back (1)

504 ἀντέχω *antechō* (4)
devoted to (2)
help (1)
hold firmly to (1)

505 ἀντί *anti* (22)
for (9)
because (4) *+4005*
instead (2)
with (2)
after (1)
as (1)
for this reason (1) *+4047*
in place (1)
untranslated (1)

506 ἀντιβάλλω *antiballō* (1)
discussing (1)

507 ἀντιδιατίθημι *antidiatithēmi* (1)
oppose (1)

508 ἀντίδικος *antidikos* (5)
adversary (2)
adversary who is taking to court (1)
enemy (1)
he[s] (1) *+3836*

509 ἀντίθεσις *antithesis* (1)
opposing ideas (1)

510 ἀντικαθίστημι *antikathistēmi* (1)
resisted (1)

511 ἀντικαλέω *antikaleō* (1)
invite back (1)

512 ἀντίκειμαι *antikeimai* (8)
oppose (3)
adversaries (1)
contrary (1)
enemy (1)

in conflict (1)
opponents (1)

513 ἄντικρυς *antikrys* (1)
off (1)

514 ἀντιλαμβάνω *antilambanō* (3)
benefit (1)
help (1)
helped (1)

515 ἀντιλέγω *antilegō* (11)
say (2)
contradict (1)
objected (1)
obstinate (1)
oppose (1)
opposes (1)
spoken against (1)
talk back (1)
talked against (1)
talking against (1)

516 ἀντίλημψις *antilēmpsis* (1)
those able to help (1)

517 ἀντιλογία *antilogia* (4)
argument (1)
doubt (1)
opposition (1)
rebellion (1)

518 ἀντιλοιδορέω *antiloidoreō* (1)
retaliate (1)

519 ἀντίλυτρον *antilytron* (1)
ransom (1)

520 ἀντιμετρέω *antimetreō* (1)
measured (1)

521 ἀντιμισθία *antimisthia* (2)
exchange (1)
penalty (1)

522 Ἀντιόχεια *Antiocheia* (18)
Antioch (18)

523 Ἀντιοχεύς *Antiocheus* (1)
from Antioch (1)

524 ἀντιπαρέρχομαι *antiparerchomai* (2)
passed by on the other side (2)

525 Ἀντιπᾶς *Antipas* (1)
Antipas (1)

526 Ἀντιπατρίς *Antipatris* (1)
Antipatris (1)

527 ἀντιπέρα *antipera* (1)
across (1)

528 ἀντιπίπτω *antipiptō* (1)
resist (1)

529 ἀντιστρατεύομαι *antistrateuomai* (1)
waging war against (1)

530 ἀντιτάσσω *antitassō* (5)
opposes (2)
opposed (1)
opposing (1)
rebels against (1)

531 ἀντίτυπος *antitypos* (2)
copy (1)
symbolizes (1)

532 ἀντίχριστος *antichristos* (5)
antichrist (4)
antichrists (1)

533 ἀντλέω *antleō* (4)
draw (1)
draw out (1)
draw water (1)
drawn (1)

534 ἄντλημα *antlēma* (1)
to draw with (1)

535 ἀντοφθαλμέω *antophthalmeō* (1)

head into (1)

536 ἄνυδρος *anydros* (4)
arid (2)
without rain (1)
without water (1)

537 ἀνυπόκριτος *anypokritos* (6)
sincere (6)

538 ἀνυπότακτος *anypotaktos* (4)
disobedient (1)
not subject (1)
rebellious (1)
rebels (1)

539 ἄνω *anō* (9)
above (5)
up (2)
heavenward (1)
the brim (1)

540 ἄνωθεν *anōthen* (13)
from above (3)
top (3)
again (2)
from (2)
all over again (1) *+4099*
for a long time (1)
from the beginning (1)

541 ἀνωτερικός *anōterikos* (1)
interior (1) *+3538*

542 ἀνώτερος *anōteros* (2)
first (1)
up (1)

543 ἀνωφελής *anōphelēs* (2)
unprofitable (1)
useless (1)

544 ἀξίνη *axinē* (2)
ax (2)

545 ἄξιος *axios* (41)
worthy (17)
deserves (5)
deserving (4)
deserve (3) *+1639*
deserve (2)
in keeping with (2)
worth (2)
advisable (1) *+1639*
deserved (1)
deserves (1) *+1639*
rightly so (1) *+1639*
untranslated (2)

546 ἀξιόω *axioō* (7)
consider worthy (1)
count worthy (1)
deserves (1)
found worthy of (1)
think it wise (1)
want (1)
worthy (1)

547 ἀξίως *axiōs* (6)
worthy (3)
in a manner worthy (2)
in a way worthy (1)

548 ἀόρατος *aoratos* (5)
invisible (5)

549 Ἀουλία *Aoulia*
Variant; not used

550 ἀπαγγέλλω *apangellō* (45)
told (13)
reported (12)
tell (6)
report (4)
proclaim (3)
confirm (1)
declare (1)
exclaimed (1)
exclaiming (1)

preached (1)
said (1)
tell about (1)

551 ἀπάγχω *apanchō* (1)
hanged (1)

552 ἀπάγω *apagō* (15)
led away (4)
leads (2)
took (2)
brought (1)
executed (1)
lead away (1)
lead out (1)
led (1)
led astray (1)
take (1)

553 ἀπαίδευτος *apaideutos* (1)
stupid (1)

554 ἀπαίρω *apairō* (3)
taken from (3)

555 ἀπαιτέω *apaiteō* (2)
demand back (1)
demanded from (1)

556 ἀπαλγέω *apalgeō* (1)
lost all sensitivity (1)

557 ἀπαλλάσσω *apallassō* (3)
cured (1)
free (1)
reconciled to (1)

558 ἀπαλλοτριόω *apallotrioō* (3)
alienated from (1)
excluded (1)
separated (1)

559 ἀπαλός *hapalos* (2)
tender (2)

560 ἀπαντάω *apantaō* (2)
meet (1)
met (1)

561 ἀπάντησις *apantēsis* (3)
meet (3)

562 ἅπαξ *hapax* (14)
once (7)
once for all (4)
again (2)
already (1)

563 ἀπαράβατος *aparabatos* (1)
permanent (1)

564 ἀπαρασκεύαστος *aparaskeuastos* (1)
unprepared (1)

565 ἀπαρνέομαι *aparneomai* (10)
disown (7)
deny (3)

566 ἀπαρτί *aparti*
Variant; not used

567 ἀπάρτι *aparti*
Variant; not used

568 ἀπαρτισμός *apartismos* (1)
complete (1)

569 ἀπαρχή *aparchē* (8)
firstfruits (6)
first (1)
first convert (1)

570 ἅπας *hapas* (34)
all (18)
everything (7)
whole (3)
everyone (2)
everybody (1)
none (1) +4024
unlimited (1)
untranslated (1)

571 ἀπασπάζομαι *apaspazomai* (1)
saying good-by to (1)

572 ἀπατάω *apataō* (3)
deceive (1)
deceived (1)
deceives (1)

573 ἀπάτη *apatē* (7)
deceitfulness (3)
deceitful (1)
deceives (1)
deceptive (1)
pleasures (1)

574 ἀπάτωρ *apatōr* (1)
without father (1)

575 ἀπαύγασμα *apaugasma* (1)
radiance (1)

576 ἀπαφρίζω *apaphrizō* (1)
Variant; not used

577 ἀπείθεια *apeitheia* (6)
disobedience (4)
disobedient (2)

578 ἀπειθέω *apeitheō* (14)
disobedient (4)
disobeyed (2)
refused to believe (2)
disobey (1)
do not believe (1)
not obey (1)
reject (1)
rejects (1)
unbelievers (1)

579 ἀπειθής *apeithēs* (6)
disobedient (5)
disobey (1)

580 ἀπειλέω *apeileō* (2)
made threats (1)
warn (1)

581 ἀπειλή *apeilē* (3)
threats (2)
threaten (1)

582 ἄπειμι1 *apeimi1* (7)
absent (3)
absent from (1)
away (1)
in absence (1)
not present (1)

583 ἄπειμι2 *apeimi2* (1)
went (1)

584 ἀπεῖπον *apeipon* (1)
renounced (1)

585 ἀπείραστος *apeirastos* (1)
cannot tempted (1)

586 ἄπειρος *apeiros* (1)
not acquainted with (1)

587 ἀπεκδέχομαι *apekdechomai* (8)
eagerly await (1)
eagerly await for (1)
eagerly wait for (1)
wait for (1)
wait eagerly for (1)
waited (1)
waiting for (1)
waits (1)

588 ἀπεκδύομαι *apekdyomai* (2)
disarmed (1)
taken off (1)

589 ἀπέκδυσις *apekdysis* (1)
putting off (1)

590 ἀπελαύνω *apelaunō* (1)
had ejected from (1)

591 ἀπελεγμός *apelegmos* (1)

lose good name (1) +1650+2262

592 ἀπελεύθερος *apeleutheros* (1)
freedman (1)

593 Ἀπελλῆς *Apellēs* (1)
Apelles (1)

594 ἀπελπίζω *apelpizō* (1)
expecting to get back (1)

595 ἀπέναντι *apenanti* (5)
before (1)
defying (1) +4556
in front of (1)
opposite (1)
you can see (1) +5148

596 ἀπέραντος *aperantos* (1)
endless (1)

597 ἀπερισπάστως *aperispastōs* (1)
undivided (1)

598 ἀπερίτμητος *aperitmētos* (1)
uncircumcised (1)

599 ἀπέρχομαι *aperchomai* (118)
went (25)
go (21)
went away (18)
left (6)
went off (5)
went back (4)
go away (3)
gone (3)
leave (3)
crossed (2)
passed away (2)
returned (2)
went out (2)
came (1)
cross (1)
drew (1)
followed (1) +3958
go on (1)
go over (1)
go running off after (1) +1503+3593
goes away (1)
going away (1)
gone away (1)
gone from (1)
hurried away from (1) +5444
left from (1)
on their way (1)
passed (1)
past (1)
perversion (1) +2283+3958+4922
spread (1)
turned back (1) +1650+3836+3958
went up (1)
withdraw (1)
withdrew (1)

600 ἀπέχω *apechō* (19)
abstain from (4)
received in full (3)
are from (2)
avoid (2)
was from (2)
about from (1)
enough (1)
have back (1)
received (1)
received payment (1)
was (1)

601 ἀπιστέω *apisteō* (8)
not believe (6)
faithless (1)
not have faith (1)

602 ἀπιστία *apistia* (11)
unbelief (6)
lack of faith (4)
unbelieving (1)

603 ἄπιστος *apistos* (23)
unbelievers (7)
unbelieving (6)
unbeliever (5)
not a believer (2)
doubting (1) +1181
incredible (1)
not believe (1)

604 ἁπλόος *haploos* (2)
good (2)

605 ἁπλότης *haplotēs* (8)
generosity (2)
sincerity (2)
generous (1)
generously (1) +1877
holiness (1)
sincere devotion (1)

606 ἁπλοῦς *haplous*
Variant; not used

607 ἁπλῶς *haplōs* (1)
generously (1)

608 ἀπό *apo* (647)
from (335)
of (36)
by (23)
on (12)
in (11)
since (11)
for (10)
against (9)
at (7)
with (7)
away (4)
because of (4)
far off (3) +3427
because (2)
ever since (2) +4005
in part (2) +3538
out of (2)
since (2) +4005
some (2)
after (1)
again (1) +785
again (1) +3814+3836
ago (1) +4005
alike (1) +1651
as (1)
at the hands of (1)
before (1)
before (1) +4725
belonged to (1)
beyond (1)
both (1)
cut off from (1)
deserting (1) +3572
divorced (1) +467+668
down from (1)
elude (1) +5771
far away (1) +3427
for a distance of (1)
from among (1)
from the time (1) +4005
given (1) +2400
in the future (1) +785
it⁵ (1) +201+794+4005
leaving (1) +4513
left (1)
left (1) +482
long ago (1) +172
now (1) +785
now (1) +3814+3836
now (1) +4005
on some points (1) +3538
once (1) +323+4005
out (1)
part (1)
parted company (1) +253+714
some of (1)
some time ago (1) +792+2465

sound asleep (1) +2965+3836+5678
that had touched (1) +3836+5999
to (1)
to some extent (1) +247+3538
unmarried (1) +1222+3395
who belonged to (1)
with ever-increasing glory (1)
+1518+1518+1650
untranslated (118)

609 ἀποβαίνω *apobainō* (4)
happened (1)
landed (1) +1178+1650+3836
left (1)
result (1)

610 ἀποβάλλω *apoballō* (2)
throw away (1)
throwing aside (1)

611 ἀποβλέπω *apoblepō* (1)
looking ahead (1)

612 ἀπόβλητος *apoblētos* (1)
rejected (1)

613 ἀποβολή *apobolē* (2)
lost (1)
rejection (1)

614 ἀπογίνομαι *apoginomai* (1)
die (1)

615 ἀπογραφή *apographē* (2)
census (2)

616 ἀπογράφω *apographō* (4)
register (2)
census be taken of (1)
written (1)

617 ἀποδείκνυμι *apodeiknymi* (4)
accredited (1)
proclaiming (1)
prove (1)
put on display (1)

618 ἀπόδειξις *apodeixis* (1)
demonstration (1)

619 ἀποδεκατεύω *apodekateuō*
Variant; not used

620 ἀποδεκατόω *apodekatoō* (4)
give a tenth of (2)
collect a tenth from (1) +2400
give God a tenth of (1)

621 ἀπόδεκτος *apodektos* (2)
pleases (1)
pleasing (1)

622 ἀποδέχομαι *apodechomai* (7)
welcomed (3)
accepted (1)
acknowledge (1)
received (1)
welcome (1)

623 ἀποδημέω *apodēmeō* (6)
went away on a journey (2)
going on a journey (1)
set off (1)
went away (1)
went on journey (1)

624 ἀπόδημος *apodēmos* (1)
going away (1)

625 ἀποδίδωμι *apodidōmi* (48)
give (9)
pay back (6)
reward (4)
pay (3)
repay (3)
gave back (2)
given (2)
paid (2)
sold (2)
account (1) +3364

award (1)
fulfill (1)
give account for (1)
give back (1)
give share of (1)
got (1)
keep (1)
pays back (1)
produces (1)
reimburse (1)
repay the debt (1)
repaying (1) +304
to testify to (1) +3457
yielding (1)

626 ἀποδιορίζω *apodiorizō* (1)
divide (1)

627 ἀποδοκιμάζω *apodokimazō* (9)
rejected (9)

628 ἀποδοχή *apodochē* (2)
acceptance (2)

629 ἀπόθεσις *apothesis* (2)
put aside (1) +1639
removal from (1)

630 ἀποθήκη *apothēkē* (6)
barn (4)
barns (2)

631 ἀποθησαυρίζω *apothēsaurizō* (1)
lay up treasure (1)

632 ἀποθλίβω *apothlibō* (1)
pressing (1)

633 ἀποθνήσκω *apothnēskō* (112)
died (49)
die (33)
dies (11)
dead (9)
dying (5)
death (2)
put to death (1) +1877+5840
who die (1)
untranslated (1)

634 ἀποκαθιστάνω *apokathistanō*
Variant; not used

635 ἀποκαθίστημι *apokathistēmi* (8)
completely restored (3)
restored (2)
restore (2)
restores (1)

636 ἀποκαλύπτω *apokalyptō* (26)
revealed (19)
reveal (3)
disclosed (2)
a revelation comes (1)
make clear (1)

637 ἀποκάλυψις *apokalypsis* (18)
revelation (9)
revealed (7)
revelations (2)

638 ἀποκαραδοκία *apokaradokia* (2)
eager expectation for (1)
eagerly expect (1)

639 ἀποκαταλλάσσω *apokatallassō* (3)
reconcile (2)
reconciled (1)

640 ἀποκατάστασις *apokatastasis* (1)
restore (1)

641 ἀπόκειμαι *apokeimai* (4)
destined (1)
in store (1)
laid away (1)
stored up (1)

642 ἀποκεφαλίζω *apokephalizō* (4)
beheaded (4)

643 ἀποκλείω *apokleiō* (1)
closes (1)

644 ἀποκόπτω *apokoptō* (6)
cut off (3)
cut (1)
cutting off (1)
emasculate (1)

645 ἀπόκριμα *apokrima* (1)
sentence (1)

646 ἀποκρίνομαι *apokrinomai* (231)
answered (80)
replied (59)
asked (17)
said (11)
answer (9)
gave answer (4)
declared (3)
spoke up (3)
going to answer (2)
made reply (2)
reply (2)
say (2)
answers (1)
demanded (1)
given answer (1)
in reply (1)
insisted (1)
replied (1) +3306+4022
replied (1) +5774
responded (1)
retorted (1)
say in reply (1)
spoke (1)
tell (1)
told (1)
untranslated (24)

647 ἀπόκρισις *apokrisis* (4)
answer (3)
answers (1)

648 ἀποκρύπτω *apokryptō* (4)
hidden (2)
hidden from (1)
kept hidden for (1)

649 ἀπόκρυφος *apokryphos* (3)
concealed (2)
hidden (1)

650 ἀποκτείνω *apokteinō* (74)
kill (34)
killed (26)
put to death (4)
kills (2)
take life (2)
die (1)
died (1)
execute (1)
killing (1)
strike dead (1)
untranslated (1)

651 ἀποκτέννω *apoktennō*
Variant; not used

652 ἀποκυέω *apokyeō* (2)
give birth (1)
gives birth to (1)

653 ἀποκυλίω *apokyliō* (4)
rolled away (2)
roll away (1)
rolled back (1)

654 ἀπολαλέω *apolaleō*
Variant; not used

655 ἀπολαμβάνω *apolambanō* (10)
receive (2)
received (2)
getting (1)
has back (1)
receive from (1)

repaid (1)
rewarded (1) +3635
took away from (1)

656 ἀπόλαυσις *apolausis* (2)
enjoyment (1)
pleasures (1)

657 ἀπολείπω *apoleipō* (7)
left (4)
remains (2)
abandoned (1)

658 ἀπολείχω *apoleichō*
Variant; not used

659 ἀπολιμπάνω *apolimpanō*
Variant; not used

660 ἀπόλλυμι *apollymi* (90)
lose (14)
lost (12)
destroyed (9)
perish (9)
destroy (8)
kill (7)
loses (7)
killed (4)
perishing (4)
drown (3)
ruined (3)
die (2)
bring to end (1)
executed (1)
kill (1) +3836
perishes (1)
spoils (1)
starving to death (1) +3350
vanished (1)
wasted (1)

661 Ἀπολλύων *Apollyōn* (1)
Apollyon (1)

662 Ἀπολλωνία *Apollōnia* (1)
Apollonia (1)

663 Ἀπολλῶς *Apollōs* (10)
Apollos (10)

664 ἀπολογέομαι *apologeomai* (10)
defend yourselves (2)
defense (2)
make defense (2)
defending (1)
defending ourselves (1)
made defense (1)
make a defense (1) +2527

665 ἀπολογία *apologia* (8)
defense (4)
answer (1)
defend (1)
defending (1)
eagerness clear (1)

666 ἀπολούω *apolouō* (2)
wash away (1)
washed (1)

667 ἀπολύτρωσις *apolytrōsis* (10)
redemption (8)
ransom (1)
released (1)

668 ἀπολύω *apolyō* (66)
release (15)
send away (7)
divorces (6)
let go (6)
dismissed (5)
released (5)
divorce (4)
sent away (4)
sent off (3)
set free (3)
dismiss (1)
divorced (1)

divorced (1) +467+608
forgive (1)
forgiven (1)
free (1)
leave (1)
send (1)

669 ἀπομάσσω *apomassō* (1)
wipe off against (1)

670 ἀπομένω *apomenō*
Variant; not used

671 ἀπονέμω *aponemō* (1)
treat (1)

672 ἀπονίπτω *aponiptō* (1)
washed (1)

673 ἀποπέμπω *apopempō*
Variant; not used

674 ἀποπίπτω *apopiptō* (1)
fell (1)

675 ἀποπλανάω *apoplanaō* (2)
deceive (1)
wandered from (1)

676 ἀποπλέω *apopleō* (4)
sailed (2)
sail (1)
set sail (1)

677 ἀποπλύνω *apoplynō*
Variant; not used

678 ἀποπνίγω *apopnigō* (2)
choked (1)
drowned (1)

679 ἀπορέω *aporeō* (6)
at a loss (2)
perplexed (2)
puzzled (1)
wondering (1)

680 ἀπορία *aporia* (1)
perplexity (1)

681 ἀπορίπτω *aporiptō* (1)
jump overboard (1)

682 ἀπορφανίζω *aporphanizō* (1)
torn away from (1)

683 ἀποσκευάζω *aposkeuazō*
Variant; not used

684 ἀποσκίασμα *aposkiasma* (1)
shifting (1)

685 ἀποσπάω *apospaō* (4)
draw away (1)
drew out (1)
torn away (1)
withdrew (1)

686 ἀποστασία *apostasia* (2)
rebellion (1)
to turn away from (1)

687 ἀποστάσιον *apostasion* (3)
divorce (2)
certificate of divorce (1)

688 ἀποστάτης *apostatēs*
Variant; not used

689 ἀποστεγάζω *apostegazō* (1)
made an opening in (1)

690 ἀποστέλλω *apostellō* (132)
sent (93)
send (15)
sending (5)
sent out (4)
send back (2)
send out (2)
sending out (2)
gave orders (1)
given orders (1)

ordered (1)
puts (1)
release (1) *+912+1877*
sent away (1)
sent for (1) *+3559*
sent message (1)
sent word (1)

691 ἀποστερέω *apostereō* (6)
cheat (1)
cheated (1)
defraud (1)
deprive (1)
failed to pay (1)
robbed (1)

692 ἀποστολή *apostolē* (4)
apostleship (2)
apostolic (1)
ministry of an apostle (1)

693 ἀπόστολος *apostolos* (80)
apostles (51)
apostle (19)
apostles' (5)
messenger (2)
super-apostles (2) *+5663*
representatives (1)

694 ἀποστοματίζω *apostomatizō* (1)
besiege with questions (1) *+4309+4498*

695 ἀποστρέφω *apostrephō* (9)
turn away from (4)
deserted (1)
put back (1)
turning from (1)
who inciting to rebellion (1)
who reject (1)

696 ἀποστυγέω *apostygeō* (1)
hate (1)

697 ἀποσυνάγωγος *aposynagōgos* (3)
put out of the synagogue (2)
put out of the synagogue (1) *+4472*

698 ἀποτάσσω *apotassō* (6)
left (2)
give up (1)
leaving (1)
said good-by (1)
say good-by (1)

699 ἀποτελέω *apoteleō* (2)
full-grown (1)
heal people (1) *+2617*

700 ἀποτίθημι *apotithēmi* (9)
put off (2)
rid of (2)
get rid of (1)
laid (1)
put (1)
put aside (1)
throw off (1)

701 ἀποτινάσσω *apotinassō* (2)
shake off (1)
shook off (1)

702 ἀποτίνω *apotinō* (1)
pay back (1)

703 ἀποτολμάω *apotolmaō* (1)
boldly (1)

704 ἀποτομία *apotomia* (2)
sternness (2)

705 ἀποτόμως *apotomōs* (2)
harsh (1)
sharply (1)

706 ἀποτρέπω *apotrepō* (1)
have nothing to do with (1)

707 ἀπουσία *apousia* (1)
absence (1)

708 ἀποφέρω *apopherō* (6)
carried away (2)
carried (1)
led away (1)
taken (1)
untranslated (1)

709 ἀποφεύγω *apopheugō* (3)
escape (1)
escaped (1)
escaping from (1)

710 ἀποφθέγγομαι *apophthengomai* (3)
addressed (1)
saying (1)
untranslated (1)

711 ἀποφορτίζομαι *apophortizomai* (1)
unload (1)

712 ἀπόχρησις *apochrēsis* (1)
use (1)

713 ἀποχωρέω *apochōreō* (3)
away from (1)
leaves (1)
left (1)

714 ἀποχωρίζω *apochōrizō* (2)
parted company (1) *+253+608*
receded (1)

715 ἀποψύχω *apopsychō* (1)
faint (1)

716 Ἄππιος *Appios* (1)
Appius (1)

717 ἀπρόσιτος *aprositos* (1)
unapproachable (1)

718 ἀπρόσκοπος *aproskopos* (3)
blameless (1)
clear (1)
not cause to stumble (1)

719 ἀπροσωπολήμπτως *aprosōpolēmptōs* (1)
impartially (1)

720 ἄπταιστος *aptaistos* (1)
falling (1)

721 ἅπτω *haptō* (39)
touched (20)
touch (10)
lights (2)
built (1)
handle (1)
harm (1)
hold on to (1)
light (1)
marry (1) *+1222*
touching (1)

722 Ἀπφία *Apphia* (1)
Apphia (1)

723 ἀπωθέω *apōtheō* (6)
reject (3)
rejected (2)
pushed aside (1)

724 ἀπώλεια *apōleia* (18)
destruction (10)
doomed to destruction (2)
destroyed (1)
destroyed (1) *+1650*
destructive (1)
perish (1) *+1639+1650*
waste (1)
waste (1) *+1181*

725 ἀρά *ara* (1)
cursing (1)

726 ἄρα *ara* (49)
then (12)
so (8)
therefore (5) *+4036*
consequently (2) *+4036*

therefore (2)
as to (1)
consequently (1)
if in fact (1) *+1642*
in that case (1)
in that case (1) *+2075*
otherwise (1) *+2075*
perhaps (1) *+1145+1623*
perhaps (1) *+1623*
so then (1)
then (1) *+1145*
thus (1) *+1145*
untranslated (9)

727 ἆρα *ara* (3)
does that mean that (1)
untranslated (2)

728 Ἀραβία *Arabia* (2)
Arabia (2)

729 Ἄραβοι *Araboi*
Variant; not used

730 Ἀράμ *Aram* (3)
ram (3)

731 ἄραφος *araphos* (1)
seamless (1)

732 Ἄραψ *Araps* (1)
Arabs (1)

733 ἀργέω *argeō* (1)
untranslated (1)

734 ἀργός *argos* (8)
doing nothing (2)
careless (1)
idle (1)
idlers (1)
ineffective (1)
lazy (1)
useless (1)

735 ἀργύρεος *argyreos* (3)
silver (3)

736 ἀργύριον *argyrion* (20)
money (12)
silver (3)
silver coins (3)
coins (1)
drachmas (1)

737 ἀργυροκόπος *argyrokopos* (1)
silversmith (1)

738 ἄργυρος *argyros* (5)
silver (5)

739 ἀργυροῦς *argyrous*
Variant; not used

740 Ἄρειος πάγος *Areios pagos* (2)
meeting of the Areopagus (2)

741 Ἀρεοπαγίτης *Areopagitēs* (1)
member of the Areopagus (1)

742 ἀρεσκεία *areskeia* (1)
please (1)

743 ἀρέσκω *areskō* (17)
please (10)
pleased (3)
trying to please (2)
displease (1) *+3590*
try to please (1)

744 ἀρεστός *arestos* (4)
pleases (2)
pleased (1) *+1639*
right (1)

745 Ἀρέτας *Haretas* (1)
Aretas (1)

746 ἀρετή *aretē* (5)
goodness (3)
excellent (1)

praises (1)

747 Ἀρηΐ *Arēi*
Variant; not used

748 ἀρήν *arēn* (1)
lambs (1)

749 ἀριθμέω *arithmeō* (3)
numbered (2)
count (1)

750 ἀριθμός *arithmos* (18)
number (12)
in number (1) +3836+4005
numbering (1) +1639
numbers (1)
untranslated (3)

751 Ἀριμαθαία *Harimathaia* (4)
Arimathea (4)

752 Ἀρίσταρχος *Aristarchos* (5)
Aristarchus (5)

753 ἀριστάω *aristaō* (3)
breakfast (1)
eat (1)
eating (1)

754 ἀριστερός *aristeros* (4)
left (3)
left hand (1)

755 Ἀριστόβουλος *Aristoboulos* (1)
Aristobulus (1)

756 ἄριστον *ariston* (4)
dinner (1)
feast (1)
luncheon (1)
meal (1)

757 ἀρκετός *arketos* (3)
enough (3)

758 ἀρκέω *arkeō* (8)
content (3)
enough (3)
satisfied (1)
sufficient (1)

759 ἄρκος *arkos* (1)
bear (1)

760 ἄρκτος *arktos*
Variant; not used

761 ἅρμα *harma* (4)
chariot (3)
chariots (1)

762 Ἁρμαγεδών *Harmagedōn* (1)
Armageddon (1)

763 Ἀρμίν *Armin*
Variant; not used

764 ἁρμόζω *harmozō* (1)
promised (1)

765 ἁρμός *harmos* (1)
joints (1)

766 ἀρνέομαι *arneomai* (34)
denied (10)
disown (5)
deny (4)
denies (3)
disowned (3)
denying (2)
disowns (2)
fail (1)
refused (1)
rejected (1)
renounce (1)
say no to (1)

767 Ἀρνί *Arni*
Variant; not used

768 ἀρνίον *arnion* (30)

lamb (28)
lamb's (1)
lambs (1)

769 ἀροτριάω *arotriaō* (3)
plowing (1)
plowman (1)
plows (1)

770 ἄροτρον *arotron* (1)
plow (1)

771 ἁρπαγή *harpagē* (3)
greed (2)
confiscation (1)

772 ἁρπαγμός *harpagmos* (1)
something to be grasped (1)

773 ἁρπάζω *harpazō* (14)
caught up (3)
snatch (1)
attacks (1)
carry off (1)
force (1)
lay hold of (1)
snatched up (1)
snatches away (1)
suddenly took away (1)
take by force (1)

774 ἅρπαξ *harpax* (5)
swindlers (2)
ferocious (1)
robbers (1)
swindler (1)

775 ἀρραβών *arrabōn* (3)
deposit guaranteeing (2)
deposit (1)

776 ἄρρην *arrēn*
Variant; not used

777 ἄρρητος *arrētos* (1)
inexpressible (1)

778 ἀρρωστέω *arrōsteō*
Variant; not used

779 ἄρρωστος *arrōstos* (5)
sick (5)

780 ἀρσενοκοίτης *arsenokoitēs* (2)
homosexual offenders (1)
perverts (1)

781 ἄρσην *arsēn* (9)
male (6)
men (3)

782 Ἀρτεμᾶς *Artemas* (1)
Artemas (1)

783 Ἄρτεμις *Artemis* (5)
Artemis (5)

784 ἀρτέμων *artemōn* (1)
foresail (1)

785 ἄρτι *arti* (36)
now (20)
now on (3)
still (3) +2401
again (1) +608
at last (1)
at once (1)
in the future (1) +608
just (1)
just now (1)
now (1) +608
this moment (1)
this very (1)
this very day (1)

786 ἀρτιγέννητος *artigennētos* (1)
newborn (1)

787 ἄρτιος *artios* (1)
thoroughly (1)

788 ἄρτος *artos* (95)
bread (63)
loaves (18)
food (4)
loaf (3)
loaves of bread (3)
consecrated bread (1) +4606
untranslated (3)

789 ἀρτύω *artyō* (3)
made salty (1)
make salty (1)
seasoned (1)

790 Ἀρφαξάδ *Arphaxad* (1)
Arphaxad (1)

791 ἀρχάγγελος *archangelos* (2)
archangel (2)

792 ἀρχαῖος *archaios* (11)
ancient (3)
long ago (2)
people long ago (2)
earliest (1)
early (1)
old (1)
some time ago (1) +608+2465

793 Ἀρχέλαος *Archelaos* (1)
Archelaus (1)

794 ἀρχή *archē* (56)
beginning (31)
first (5)
rulers (5)
corners (2)
power (2)
all along (1) +3836
demons (1)
dominion (1)
early (1)
elementary (1)
elementary truths (1) +3836+5122
it[s] (1) +201+608+4005
positions of authority (1)
powers (1)
rule (1)
ruler (1)

795 ἀρχηγός *archēgos* (4)
author (3)
prince (1)

796 ἀρχιερατικός *archieratikos* (1)
high priest's (1)

797 ἀρχιερεύς *archiereus* (122)
chief priests (64)
high priest (51)
high priest's (3)
high priests (1)
chief priest (1)
high priesthood (1)

798 ἀρχιλῃστής *archilēstēs*
Variant; not used

799 ἀρχιποίμην *archipoimēn* (1)
chief shepherd (1)

800 Ἄρχιππος *Archippos* (2)
Archippus (2)

801 ἀρχισυνάγωγος *archisynagōgos* (9)
synagogue ruler (7)
synagogue rulers (2)

802 ἀρχιτέκτων *architektōn* (1)
builder (1)

803 ἀρχιτελώνης *architelōnēs* (1)
chief tax collector (1)

804 ἀρχιτρίκλινος *architriklinos* (3)
master of the banquet (2)
he[s] (1) +3836

805 ἀρχοστασία *archostasia*
Variant; not used

806 ἄρχω *archō* (86)
began (52)
beginning (7)
begin (3)
begins (2)
became (1)
first (1)
late in afternoon (1) +2465+3111
rule over (1)
rulers (1)
started (1)
went on (1)
untranslated (15)

807 ἄρχων *archōn* (37)
rulers (12)
ruler (9)
prince (7)
leaders (3)
authorities (2)
magistrate (1)
prominent (1)
ruler's (1)
ruling (1)

808 ἄρωμα *arōma* (4)
spices (4)

809 Ἀσά *Asa* (2)
Asa (2)

810 ἀσάλευτος *asaleutos* (2)
cannot be shaken (1)
would not move (1) +3531

811 Ἀσάφ *Asaph*
Variant; not used

812 ἄσβεστος *asbestos* (3)
unquenchable (2)
never goes out (1)

813 ἀσέβεια *asebeia* (6)
ungodly (3)
godlessness (2)
ungodliness (1)

814 ἀσεβέω *asebeō* (1)
done in ungodly way (1)

815 ἀσεβής *asebēs* (10)
ungodly (8)
godless (1)
wicked (1)

816 ἀσέλγεια *aselgeia* (10)
debauchery (4)
filthy (1)
lewdness (1)
license for immorality (1)
lustful desires (1) +2123
sensuality (1)
shameful (1)

817 ἄσημος *asēmos* (1)
ordinary (1)

818 Ἀσήρ *Asēr* (2)
Asher (2)

819 ἀσθένεια *astheneia* (24)
weakness (8)
weaknesses (4)
weak (2)
crippled (1) +2400
diseases (1)
illness (1) +3836+4922
illnesses (1)
infirmities (1)
infirmity (1)
invalid (1)
sick (1) +2400
sickness (1)
sicknesses (1)

820 ἀσθενέω *astheneō* (34)
sick (12)
weak (11)

ill (2)
lay sick (2)
disabled (1)
feel weak (1)
invalid (1)
powerless (1)
sickness (1) +3798
weakened (1)
weakening (1)

821 ἀσθένημα *asthenēma* (1)
failings (1)

822 ἀσθενής *asthenēs* (25)
weak (14)
sick (6)
weaker (2)
cripple (1) +476
unimpressive (1)
weakness (1)

823 Ἀσία *Asia* (18)
province of Asia (15)
Asia (3)

824 Ἀσιανός *Asianos* (1)
from the province of Asia (1)

825 Ἀσιάρχης *Asiarchēs* (1)
officials of the province (1)

826 ἀσιτία *asitia* (1)
without food (1)

827 ἄσιτος *asitos* (1)
without food (1)

828 ἀσκέω *askeō* (1)
strive (1)

829 ἀσκός *askos* (12)
wineskins (9)
skins (3)

830 ἀσμένως *asmenōs* (1)
warmly (1)

831 ἄσοφος *asophos* (1)
unwise (1)

832 ἀσπάζομαι *aspazomai* (59)
greet (30)
send greetings (11)
sends greetings (6)
greeted (4)
call out to (1)
give greeting (1)
give greetings to (1)
greets (1)
pay respects to (1)
said good-by (1)
sends greetings to (1)
welcomed (1)

833 ἀσπασμός *aspasmos* (10)
greeting (6)
greeted (3)
greetings (1)

834 ἄσπιλος *aspilos* (4)
defect (1)
from being polluted (1)
spotless (1)
without spot (1)

835 ἀσπίς *aspis* (1)
vipers (1)

836 ἄσπονδος *aspondos* (1)
unforgiving (1)

837 ἀσσάριον *assarion* (2)
pennies (1)
penny (1)

838 Ἀσσάρων *Assarōn*
Variant; not used

839 ἆσσον *asson* (1)
along the shore (1)

840 Ἄσσος *Assos* (2)
Assos (2)

841 ἀστατέω *astateō* (1)
homeless (1)

842 ἀστεῖος *asteios* (2)
no ordinary (2)

843 ἀστήρ *astēr* (27)
stars (16)
star (11)

844 ἀστήρικτος *astēriktos* (2)
unstable (1)
unstable (1) +6034

845 ἄστοργος *astorgos* (2)
heartless (1)
without love (1)

846 ἀστοχέω *astocheō* (3)
turned (1)
wandered (1)
wandered away (1)

847 ἀστραπή *astrapē* (9)
flashes of lightning (4)
lightning (4)
light (1)

848 ἀστράπτω *astraptō* (2)
that gleamed like lightning (1)
which flashes (1)

849 ἄστρον *astron* (1)
star (1)

850 Ἀσύγκριτος *Asynkritos* (1)
Asyncritus (1)

851 ἀσύμφωνος *asymphōnos* (1)
disagreed (1) +1639

852 ἀσύνετος *asynetos* (5)
dull (2)
foolish (1)
no understanding (1)
senseless (1)

853 ἀσύνθετος *asynthetos* (1)
faithless (1)

854 ἀσφάλεια *asphaleia* (3)
certainty (1)
safety (1)
securely (1) +1877+4246

855 ἀσφαλής *asphalēs* (5)
definite (1)
exactly (1)
firm (1)
get at truth (1) +1182
safeguard (1)

856 ἀσφαλίζω *asphalizō* (4)
made secure (2)
fastened (1)
make secure (1)

857 ἀσφαλῶς *asphalōs* (3)
assured (1) +1182
carefully (1)
under guard (1)

858 ἀσχημονέω *aschēmoneō* (2)
acting improperly (1)
rude (1)

859 ἀσχημοσύνη *aschēmosynē* (2)
indecent acts (1)
shamefully (1)

860 ἀσχήμων *aschēmōn* (1)
unpresentable (1)

861 ἀσωτία *asōtia* (3)
debauchery (1)
dissipation (1)
wild (1)

862 ἀσώτως *asōtōs* (1)
wild (1)

863 ἀτακτέω atakteō (1)
　idle (1)

864 ἄτακτος ataktos (1)
　idle (1)

865 ἀτάκτως ataktōs (2)
　idle (1)
　idle (1) +4344

866 ἄτεκνος ateknos (2)
　childless (1)
　no children (1)

867 ἀτενίζω atenizō (14)
　looked straight (2)
　fastened (1)
　gazing (1)
　look steadily (1)
　looked (1)
　looked (1) +2917
　looked closely at (1)
　looked directly at (1)
　looked intently (1)
　looked straight at (1)
　looking intently (1)
　stare at (1)
　stared at (1)

868 ἄτερ ater (2)
　when no was present (1)
　without (1)

869 ἀτιμάζω atimazō (6)
　dishonor (2)
　degrading of (1)
　insulted (1)
　suffering disgrace (1)
　treated shamefully (1)

870 ἀτιμάω atimaō (1)
　treated shamefully (1)

871 ἀτιμία atimia (7)
　dishonor (2)
　common (1)
　disgrace (1)
　ignoble (1)
　shameful (1)
　to my shame (1) +2848

872 ἄτιμος atimos (4)
　without honor (2)
　dishonored (1)
　less honorable (1)

873 ἀτιμόω atimoō
　Variant; not used

874 ἀτμίς atmis (2)
　billows (1)
　mist (1)

875 ἄτομος atomos (1)
　flash (1)

876 ἄτοπος atopos (4)
　wrong (2)
　unusual (1)
　wicked (1)

877 Ἀττάλεια Attaleia (1)
　Attalia (1)

878 αὐγάζω augazō (1)
　see (1)

879 αὐγή augē (1)
　daylight (1)

880 Αὔγουστος Augoustos (1)
　Augustus (1)

881 αὐθάδης authadēs (2)
　arrogant (1)
　overbearing (1)

882 αὐθαίρετος authairetos (2)
　entirely on their own (1)
　on own initiative (1)

883 αὐθεντέω authenteō (1)
　have authority over (1)

884 αὐλέω auleō (3)
　played the flute (2)
　played (1)

885 αὐλή aulē (12)
　courtyard (6)
　palace (2)
　court (1)
　house (1)
　pen (1)
　sheep pen (1)

886 αὐλητής aulētēs (2)
　flute players (2)

887 αὐλίζομαι aulizomai (2)
　spend the night (1)
　spent the night (1)

888 αὐλός aulos (1)
　flute (1)

889 αὐξάνω auxanō (23)
　grew (4)
　grow (4)
　grow up (2)
　growing (2)
　grows (2)
　become greater (1)
　enlarge (1)
　greatly increased (1) +2779+4437
　increase (1)
　made grow (1)
　makes grow (1)
　rises (1)
　spread (1)
　spread widely (1)

890 αὔξησις auxēsis (2)
　grow (1)
　grows (1) +4472

891 αὔξω auxō
　Variant; not used

892 αὔριον aurion (14)
　tomorrow (8)
　next day (3)
　tomorrow (3) +3836

893 αὐστηρός austēros (2)
　hard (2)

894 αὐτάρκεια autarkeia (2)
　contentment (1)
　need (1)

895 αὐτάρκης autarkēs (1)
　content (1)

896 αὐτοκατάκριτος autokatakritos (1)
　self-condemned (1)

897 αὐτόματος automatos (2)
　all by itself (1)
　by itself (1)

898 αὐτόπτης autoptēs (1)
　eyewitnesses (1)

899 αὐτός autos (5593)
　him (1382)
　his (899)
　them (807)
　their (275)
　he (219)
　her (198)
　it (185)
　Jesus[s] (141)
　they (124)
　its (49)
　himself (37)
　same (37)
　Paul[s] (19)
　the people[s] (17)
　Jesus'[s] (15)

the man[s] (15)
she (14)
his own (12)
God's[s] (11)
the man's[s] (10)
Christ[s] (9)
these (9)
yourselves (9)
myself (8)
that (8)
those (8)
you (8)
his disciples[s] (7)
themselves (7)
John[s] (6)
the city[s] (5)
the disciples[s] (5)
the Jews[s] (5)
whose (5)
God[s] (4)
itself (4)
ourselves (4)
the apostles[s] (4)
the beast[s] (4)
the boy[s] (4)
their own (4)
very (4)
which (4)
whom (4)
Abraham[s] (3)
he himself (3)
I (3)
Jesus and his disciples[s] (3)
John's[s] (3)
Moses[s] (3)
others (3)
own (3)
Peter and John[s] (3)
Peter[s] (3)
Saul[s] (3)
Stephen[s] (3)
that (3) +3836
the crowd[s] (3)
the plants[s] (3)
theirs (3)
them (3) +4639
them[s] (3) +3412+3836
there (3) +1877
this (3)
together (3) +2093+3836
we (3)
who (3)
here (2)
herself (2)
him[s] (2) +81+3836
his master[s] (2)
home (2) +1650+3875
home (2) +3836+3875
Joseph[s] (2)
Lazarus[s] (2)
love[s] (2)
named (2) +3950
Paul and Barnabas[s] (2)
Paul and Silas[s] (2)
Peter's[s] (2)
that is how (2) +2848+3836
that very (2)
the body[s] (2)
the child[s] (2)
the children[s] (2)
the Lord[s] (2)
the men[s] (2)
the servant[s] (2)
the vineyard[s] (2)
the women[s] (2)
the young man[s] (2)
there (2)
they themselves (2)
to himself (2) +1877+2840+3836
your (2)
yourself (2)

a fig tree[s] (1)
a man's[s] (1)
agree (1) +3306+3836
alive (1) +1877
along (1) +5250
Ananias[s] (1)
Apollos[s] (1)
as I did (1) +4047
as usual (1) +2848+3836
at once (1) +3836+6052
at their hands (1) +5679
Barnabas and Saul[s] (1)
before their very eyes (1) +1063
being like-minded (1) +3836+5858
believers[s] (1) +1666
both of you (1) +2779+5148
boy's[s] (1)
by himself (1) +3668
child's[s] (1)
Christ's[s] (1)
come together (1) +1639+2093+3836
comes together (1) +2093+3836+5302
death[s] (1)
Elizabeth[s] (1)
Elymas[s] (1)
equal (1) +3836
faith[s] (1)
Festus[s] (1)
for the express purpose (1) +1650+4047
for this very reason (1) +4047
governing[s] (1) +4047
had[s] (1)
he (1) +1328+3836+5931
he (1) +5679
he and his disciples (1)
he's (1)
he's (1) +1639+6034
he[s] (1) +899+1877+3836+4460
here (1) +1877
him (1) +4639
him (1) +5679
himself (1) +2840
himself[s] (1) +3836+3950
his fellow (1) +3836+5250
his own (1)
his parents[s] (1)
home (1) +1650+3836+3875
I (1) +1609
I myself (1)
immediately (1) +1877+3836+6052
in his sight (1) +1967
in one place (1) +2093+3836
in same way (1)
Isaac[s] (1)
Israel[s] (1)
its (1) +1877
its own (1)
its[s] (1) +3836+4725
Jairus[s] (1)
James[s] (1)
Jesus (1) +2652
Jesus' body[s] (1)
Jews'[s] (1)
John's (1) +2722
just as though (1) +1651+2779+3836
just like this (1) +2848+3836
Levi's[s] (1)
Levi[s] (1)
lies[s] (1)
live in harmony (1) +3836+5858
Lydda[s] (1)
Mary[s] (1)
men's[s] (1)
men[s] (1)
money[s] (1)
nearby (1) +3836
of the scrolls[s] (1)
of them (1) +5201
one (1) +3836
one another (1)
Paul's[s] (1)

perfectly united (1) +2936+3836
Pilate[s] (1)
pointing (1) +1753+3836+5931
put on board (1) +1650+1837
rider (1) +2093+2764
riders (1) +2093+2764
same things (1)
same way (1)
Saul's[s] (1)
serpent's (1) +4058
she (1) +5679
Simeon[s] (1)
spirit of unity (1) +3836+5858
such (1)
such beings (1)
surrounding (1) +4309
than they (1)
that country[s] (1)
that God[s] (1)
that one sheep[s] (1)
that rest[s] (1)
that same (1)
the ark[s] (1)
the beggar[s] (1)
the blessing[s] (1)
the commander's[s] (1)
the commander[s] (1)
the commandment[s] (1)
the council[s] (1)
the cross[s] (1)
the firstborn[s] (1)
the flock[s] (1)
the gentiles[s] (1)
the gospel[s] (1)
the island[s] (1)
the Israelites[s] (1)
the kings[s] (1)
the land[s] (1)
the messengers[s] (1)
the money[s] (1)
the net[s] (1)
the officers[s] (1)
the one[s] (1)
the other[s] (1)
the others (1)
the perfume[s] (1)
the pigs[s] (1)
the prophets[s] (1)
the same (1)
the servants[s] (1)
the slave girl[s] (1)
the son[s] (1)
the spirit[s] (1)
the star[s] (1)
the sun[s] (1)
the tongue[s] (1)
the tree[s] (1)
the two of you (1) +2779+5148
the two[s] (1)
the very one (1)
the very thing (1) +4047
the widow[s] (1)
the wine[s] (1)
their (1) +3836
their homes[s] (1)
their own number (1)
them out (1)
them[s] (1) +3836+4546
them[s] (1) +3836+5284
themselves (1) +2840+3836
themselves (1) +3836+6034
these men[s] (1)
they (1) +213+3836
they (1) +1328
they (1) +3836+4057
they (1) +4123
they (1) +4639
they (1) +5679
they[s] (1) +899+2779+3412+3836
they[s] (1) +1204+3836
they[s] (1) +3412+3836

they[s] (1) +3836+6001
this is why (1) +1328
this man[s] (1)
this perfume[s] (1)
this[s] (1) +3836+4246
Timothy[s] (1)
to their number (1) +2093+3836
told him (1) +1181+4639
Trembling (1) +2400+5571
two Israelites[s] (1)
what we are writing[s] (1) +3836
who are there (1) +1877
who belonged to their sect (1)
whole (1)
whose (1) +4005
widow (1) +1222
with a great crash (1)
　　　　　+1639+3489+3836+4774
with them (1) +1328+5931
you yourself (1)
you yourselves (1)
your slaves[s] (1)
Zechariah's[s] (1)
untranslated (675)

900　αὐτόφωρος *autophōros* (1)
caught in the act (1) +2093+2898

901　αὐτόχειρ *autocheir* (1)
with own hands (1)

902　αὐχέω *aucheō* (1)
makes boasts (1)

903　αὐχμηρός *auchmēros* (1)
dark (1)

904　ἀφαιρέω *aphaireō* (10)
cutting off (3)
take away (2)
take away from (1)
taken away (1)
taken away from (1)
takes away from (1)
taking away (1)

905　ἀφανής *aphanēs* (1)
hidden from (1)

906　ἀφανίζω *aphanizō* (5)
destroy (2)
disfigure (1)
perish (1)
vanishes (1)

907　ἀφανισμός *aphanismos* (1)
disappear (1)

908　ἄφαντος *aphantos* (1)
disappeared (1) +1181

909　ἀφεδρών *aphedrōn* (2)
untranslated (2)

910　ἀφειδία *apheidia* (1)
harsh treatment (1)

911　ἀφελότης *aphelotēs* (1)
sincere (1)

912　ἄφεσις *aphesis* (17)
forgiveness (13)
forgiven (1)
forgiven (1) +2400
freedom (1)
release (1) +690+1877

913　ἁφή *haphē* (2)
ligament (1)
ligaments (1)

914　ἀφθαρσία *aphtharsia* (7)
imperishable (3)
immortality (2)
imperishable (1) +1877
undying (1)

915　ἄφθαρτος *aphthartos* (7)
immortal (2)

imperishable (2)
can never perish (1)
last forever (1)
unfading (1)

916 ἀφθονία *aphthonia*
Variant; not used

917 ἀφθορία *aphthoria* (1)
integrity (1)

918 ἀφίημι *aphiēmi* (145)
left (37)
forgive (22)
forgiven (22)
let (19)
leave (8)
leave alone (5)
leaving (4)
deserted (3)
divorce (3)
canceled (2)
let go (2)
abandoned (1)
abandons (1)
allow (1)
consented (1)
forgives (1)
forsaken (1)
gave up (1)
have neglected (1)
leaves (1)
leaving behind (1)
let be (1)
let go of (1)
let go on (1)
neglecting (1)
refuse (1) +4024
tolerate (1)
untranslated (2)

919 ἀφικνέομαι *aphikneomai* (1)
heard about (1)

920 ἀφιλάγαθος *aphilagathos* (1)
not lovers of good (1)

921 ἀφιλάργυρος *aphilargyros* (2)
free from the love of money (1)
not a lover of money (1)

922 ἄφιξις *aphixis* (1)
leave (1)

923 ἀφίστημι *aphistēmi* (12)
left (3)
abandon (1)
away from (1)
fall away (1)
leave alone (1)
led in revolt (1)
take away from (1)
turn away from (1)
turns away from (1)
withdrew (1)

924 ἄφνω *aphnō* (3)
suddenly (3)

925 ἀφόβως *aphobōs* (4)
fearlessly (1)
nothing to fear (1)
without fear (1)
without the slightest qualm (1)

926 ἀφομοιόω *aphomoioō* (1)
like (1)

927 ἀφοράω *aphoraō* (2)
fix eyes (1)
see (1)

928 ἀφορίζω *aphorizō* (10)
separate (4)
set apart (3)
exclude (1)
separates (1)
took (1)

929 ἀφορμή *aphormē* (7)
opportunity (5)
ground (1)
indulge (1)

930 ἀφρίζω *aphrizō* (2)
foaming at the mouth (1)
foams at the mouth (1)

931 ἀφρός *aphros* (1)
foams at the mouth (1)

932 ἀφροσύνη *aphrosynē* (4)
as a fool (1) +1877
folly (1)
fool (1)
foolishness (1)

933 ἄφρων *aphrōn* (11)
fool (5)
foolish (5)
fools (1)

934 ἀφυπνόω *aphypnoō* (1)
fell asleep (1)

935 ἀφυστερέω *aphystereō*
Variant; not used

936 ἄφωνος *aphōnos* (4)
mute (1)
silent (1)
without meaning (1)
without speech (1)

937 Ἀχάζ *Achaz* (2)
Ahaz (2)

938 Ἀχαΐα *Achaia* (10)
Achaia (10)

939 Ἀχαϊκός *Achaikos* (1)
Achaicus (1)

940 ἀχάριστος *acharistos* (2)
ungrateful (2)

941 Ἀχάς *Achas*
Variant; not used

942 ἀχειροποίητος *acheiropoiētos* (3)
not built by human hands (1)
not done by the hands of men (1)
not made by man (1)

943 Ἀχίμ *Achim* (2)
Akim (2)

944 ἀχλύς *achlys* (1)
mist (1)

945 ἀχρεῖος *achreios* (2)
unworthy (1)
worthless (1)

946 ἀχρειόω *achreioō* (1)
become worthless (1)

947 ἄχρηστος *achrēstos* (1)
useless (1)

948 ἄχρι *achri* (48)
until (16)
to (10)
until (5) +4005
as far as (2)
up to (2)
as high as (1)
as long as (1) +4005
before (1)
even to (1)
even to the point of (1)
for (1)
just before (1) +4005
later (1)
right up to (1)
so much as (1)
then (1) +4005
to where (1)
until (1) +323+4005

949 ἄχυρον *achyron* (2)
chaff (2)

950 ἀψευδής *apseudēs* (1)
not lie (1)

951 ἀψίνθιον *apsinthion* (1)
Variant; not used

952 ἄψινθος *apsinthos* (2)
bitter (1)
wormwood (1)

953 ἄψυχος *apsychos* (1)
lifeless (1)

954 β *b*
Variant; not used

955 Βάαλ *Baal* (1)
Baal (1)

956 Βαβυλών *Babylōn* (12)
Babylon (11)
untranslated (1)

957 βαθμός *bathmos* (1)
standing (1)

958 βάθος *bathos* (8)
deep (3)
depth (2)
extreme (1) +2848
shallow (1) +2400+3590
shallow (1) +3590

959 βαθύνω *bathynō* (1)
down deep (1)

960 βαθύς *bathys* (4)
deep (3)
very early in the morning (1) +3986

961 βάϊον *baion* (1)
branches (1)

962 Βαλαάμ *Balaam* (3)
Balaam (2)
Balaam's (1)

963 Βαλάκ *Balak* (1)
Balak (1)

964 βαλλάντιον *ballantion* (4)
purse (3)
purses (1)

965 βάλλω *ballō* (122)
thrown (26)
put (18)
throw (16)
threw (6)
hurled (4)
bring (3)
cast (3)
casting (3)
lying (3)
hurled down (2)
pour (2)
poured (2)
pours (2)
putting (2)
spewed (2)
swung (2)
toss (2)
did[s] (1)
drives (1)
drop (1)
entice (1) +1967+4998
fertilize (1) +3162
flinging (1)
flung (1)
gave (1)
gave (1) +1650
help (1)
impose (1)
jumped (1) +1571
laid (1)
lay (1)

let down (1)
lies (1)
planted (1)
prompted (1) +1650+2840+3836
scatters (1)
stone (1) +2093
swept (1)
thrown down (1)
untranslated (2)

966 βαπτίζω *baptizō* (77)
baptized (47)
baptize (12)
baptizing (8)
Baptist (2)
wash (2)
baptism (1)
baptism receive (1)
baptism undergo (1) +967
baptized (1) +967
baptized (1) +3836
baptized (1) +5639

967 βάπτισμα *baptisma* (20)
baptism (17)
baptism undergo (1) +966
baptized (1) +966
baptizing (1)

968 βαπτισμός *baptismos* (3)
baptisms (1)
ceremonial washings (1)
washing (1)

969 βαπτιστής *baptistēs* (12)
Baptist (12)

970 βάπτω *baptō* (4)
dipped (2)
dip (1)
dipping (1)

971 βαρ *bar*
Variant; not used

972 Βαραββᾶς *Barabbas* (11)
Barabbas (11)

973 Βαράκ *Barak* (1)
Barak (1)

974 Βαραχίας *Barachias* (1)
Berekiah (1)

975 βάρβαρος *barbaros* (6)
foreigner (2)
islanders (2)
barbarian (1)
non-Greeks (1)

976 βαρέω *bareō* (6)
burdened (2)
heavy (1)
under pressure (1)
very sleepy (1) +5678
weighed down (1)

977 βαρέως *bareōs* (2)
hardly (2)

978 Βαρθολομαῖος *Bartholomaios* (4)
Bartholomew (4)

979 Βαριησοῦς *Bariēsous* (1)
Bar-Jesus (1)

980 Βαριωνᾶ *Bariōna* (1)
son of Jonah (1)

981 Βαριωνᾶς *Bariōnas*
Variant; not used

982 Βαρναβᾶς *Barnabas* (28)
Barnabas (28)

983 βάρος *baros* (6)
burden (3)
burdens (1)
that far outweighs them all (1)
+1650+2848+5651+5651

to burden (1) +2202

984 Βαρσαββᾶς *Barsabbas* (2)
Barsabbas (2)

985 Βαρτιμαῖος *Bartimaios* (1)
Bartimaeus (1)

986 βαρύνω *barynō*
Variant; not used

987 βαρύς *barys* (6)
burdensome (1)
heavy (1)
important matters (1)
savage (1)
serious (1)
weighty (1)

988 βαρύτιμος *barytimos* (1)
very expensive (1)

989 βασανίζω *basanizō* (12)
tormented (4)
torture (4)
buffeted (1)
pain (1)
straining (1)
suffering (1)

990 βασανισμός *basanismos* (6)
torment (3)
agony (1)
sting (1)
torture (1)

991 βασανιστής *basanistēs* (1)
jailers to be tortured (1)

992 βάσανος *basanos* (3)
torment (2)
severe pain (1)

993 βασιλεία *basileia* (162)
kingdom (154)
kingdoms (3)
itˢ (1) +1847+3836+3836
king (1)
made king (1) +3284+3836
rule (1)
rules (1) +2400

994 βασίλειος *basileios* (2)
palaces (1)
royal (1)

995 βασιλεύς *basileus* (115)
king (82)
kings (27)
king (2) +476
king's (2)
heˢ (1) +3836
kings' (1)

996 βασιλεύω *basileuō* (21)
reign (10)
reigned (4)
kings (3)
king (2)
reigning (1)
reigns (1)

997 βασιλικός *basilikos* (5)
royal (2)
royal official (2)
king's (1)

998 βασιλίσκος *basiliskos*
Variant; not used

999 βασίλισσα *basilissa* (4)
queen (4)

1000 βάσις *basis* (1)
feet (1)

1001 βασκαίνω *baskainō* (1)
bewitched (1)

1002 βαστάζω *bastazō* (27)
carry (5)

carrying (4)
bear (3)
carried (3)
bear with (1)
borne (1)
carried away (1)
endured hardships (1)
gave birth (1)
help himself to (1)
pay (1)
picked up (1)
rides (1)
support (1)
take (1)
tolerate (1)

1003 βάτος1 *batos1* (5)
bush (4)
briers (1)

1004 βάτος2 *batos2* (1)
eight hundred gallons (1) +1669

1005 βάτραχος *batrachos* (1)
frogs (1)

1006 βατταλογέω *battalogeō* (1)
babbling (1)

1007 βδέλυγμα *bdelygma* (6)
abomination (2)
abominable (1)
abominations (1)
detestable (1)
what is shameful (1)

1008 βδελυκτός *bdelyktos* (1)
detestable (1)

1009 βδελύσσομαι *bdelyssomai* (2)
abhor (1)
vile (1)

1010 βέβαιος *bebaios* (8)
binding (1)
certain (1)
firm (1)
firmly (1)
guaranteed (1)
in force (1)
secure (1)
sure (1)

1011 βεβαιόω *bebaioō* (8)
confirmed (3)
strengthened (2)
confirm (1)
keep strong (1)
makes stand firm (1)

1012 βεβαίωσις *bebaiōsis* (2)
confirming (1)
confirms (1) +1650

1013 βέβηλος *bebēlos* (5)
godless (4)
irreligious (1)

1014 βεβηλόω *bebēloō* (2)
desecrate (2)

1015 Βεελζεβούλ *Beelzeboul* (7)
Beelzebub (7)

1016 Βελιάρ *Beliar* (1)
Belial (1)

1017 βελόνη *belonē* (1)
needle (1)

1018 βέλος *belos* (1)
arrows (1)

1019 βελτίων *beltiōn* (1)
very well (1)

1020 Βενιαμείν *Beniamein*
Variant; not used

1021 Βενιαμίν *Beniamin* (4)
Benjamin (4)

1022 Βερνίκη *Bernikē* (3)
Bernice (3)

1023 Βέροια *Beroia* (2)
Berea (2)

1024 Βεροιαῖος *Beroiaios* (1)
from Berea (1)

1025 Βέρος *Beros*
Variant; not used

1026 Βεωορσόρ *Beōorsor*
Variant; not used

1027 Βεώρ *Beōr* (1)
Beor (1)

1028 Βηθαβαρά *Bēthabara*
Variant; not used

1029 Βηθανία *Bēthania* (12)
Bethany (12)

1030 Βηθαραβά *Bētharaba*
Variant; not used

1031 Βηθεσδά *Bēthesda* (1)
Bethesda (1)

1032 Βηθζαθά *Bēthzatha*
Variant; not used

1033 Βηθλέεμ *Bēthleem* (8)
Bethlehem (8)

1034 Βηθσαϊδά *Bēthsaida* (7)
Bethsaida (7)

1035 Βηθσαϊδάν *Bēthsaidan*
Variant; not used

1036 Βηθφαγή *Bēthphagē* (3)
Bethphage (3)

1037 βῆμα *bēma* (12)
court (4)
judge's seat (2)
judgment seat (2)
convened the court (1) +2093+2767+3836
court (1) +2093
foot of ground (1) +4546
throne (1)

1038 Βηρεύς *Bēreus*
Variant; not used

1039 βήρυλλος *bēryllos* (1)
beryl (1)

1040 βία *bia* (3)
pounding (1)
use force (1) +3552
violence (1)

1041 βιάζω *biazō* (2)
forcefully advancing (1)
forcing way (1)

1042 βίαιος *biaios* (1)
violent (1)

1043 βιαστής *biastēs* (1)
forceful (1)

1044 βιβλαρίδιον *biblaridion* (3)
little scroll (3)

1045 βιβλιδάριον *biblidarion*
Variant; not used

1046 βιβλίον *biblion* (34)
book (13)
scroll (13)
books (3)
certificate (2)
it^s (2) +3836
scrolls (1)

1047 βίβλος *biblos* (10)
book (8)
record (1)
scrolls (1)

1048 βιβρώσκω *bibrōskō* (1)
eaten (1)

1049 Βιθυνία *Bithynia* (2)
Bithynia (2)

1050 βίος *bios* (10)
property (2)
to live on (2)
civilian affairs (1) +4548
life (1)
life's (1)
lives (1)
possessions (1)
what he has and does (1)

1051 βιόω *bioō* (1)
live (1)

1052 βίωσις *biōsis* (1)
way lived (1)

1053 βιωτικός *biōtikos* (3)
life (1)
of this life (1)
such matters^s (1)

1054 βλαβερός *blaberos* (1)
harmful (1)

1055 βλάπτω *blaptō* (2)
hurt (1)
injuring (1)

1056 βλαστάνω *blastanō* (4)
budded (1)
produced (1)
sprouted (1)
sprouts (1)

1057 βλαστάω *blastaō*
Variant; not used

1058 Βλάστος *Blastos* (1)
Blastus (1)

1059 βλασφημέω *blasphēmeō* (34)
slander (4)
blaspheme (3)
cursed (3)
hurled insults at (3)
blasphemed (2)
blasphemes (2)
blaspheming (2)
abusive (1)
abusively (1)
blasphemies (1) +1060
blasphemy (1)
bring into disrepute (1)
denounced (1)
heap abuse on (1)
insulting (1)
malign (1)
slandered (1)
slandering (1)
slanderously reported (1)
speak abusively against (1)
spoken blasphemy (1)
spoken of as evil (1)

1060 βλασφημία *blasphēmia* (18)
blasphemy (5)
slander (5)
blasphemous (2)
blaspheme (1)
blasphemies (1)
blasphemies (1) +1059
blasphemy against (1)
malicious talk (1)
slanderous (1)

1061 βλάσφημος *blasphēmos* (4)
abusive (1)
blasphemer (1)
blasphemy (1)
slanderous (1)

1062 βλέμμα *blemma* (1)

saw (1)

1063 βλέπω *blepō* (129)
see (49)
saw (8)
seen (6)
watch out (6)
see to it (5)
seeing (5)
sees (5)
ever seeing (3) +1063
look (3)
blind (2) +3590
careful (2)
consider carefully (2)
look at (2)
pay attention who they are (2) +476+4725
unseen (2) +3590
alert (1)
be (1)
be unable to see (1) +3590
before their very eyes (1) +899
careful that (1)
consider (1)
do^s (1)
exposed (1)
facing (1)
gaze on (1)
has^s (1)
have^s (1)
looked at (1)
looking on (1)
looks (1)
looks at (1)
on guard (1)
on your guard (1)
saw that (1)
sight (1)
stared (1)
take care (1)
think (1)
watch out (1) +4932
watch out for (1)
untranslated (2)

1064 βλητέος *blēteos* (1)
must be poured (1)

1065 Βοανηργές *Boanērges* (1)
Boanerges (1)

1066 βοάω *boaō* (12)
calling (4)
called out (2)
shouting (2)
cried out (1)
cry aloud (1)
cry out (1)
shrieks (1) +3489+5889

1067 Βόες *Boes* (2)
Boaz (2)

1068 βοή *boē* (1)
cries (1)

1069 βοήθεια *boētheia* (2)
help (1)
ropes (1)

1070 βοηθέω *boētheō* (8)
help (6)
helped (2)

1071 βοηθός *boēthos* (1)
helper (1)

1072 βόθρος *bothros*
Variant; not used

1073 βόθυνος *bothynos* (3)
pit (3)

1074 βολή *bolē* (1)
throw (1)

1075 βολίζω *bolizō* (2)
took soundings (2)

1076 βολίς *bolis*
Variant; not used

1077 Βοόζ *Booz*
Variant; not used

1078 Βόος *Boos* (1)
Boaz (1)

1079 βόρβορος *borboros* (1)
mud (1)

1080 βορρᾶς *borras* (2)
north (2)

1081 βόσκω *boskō* (9)
feed (3)
feeding (3)
tending (3)

1082 Βοσόρ *Bosor*
Variant; not used

1083 βοτάνη *botanē* (1)
crop (1)

1084 βότρυς *botrys* (1)
clusters of grapes (1)

1085 βουλευτής *bouleutēs* (2)
member of the council (2)

1086 βουλεύω *bouleuō* (6)
consider (1)
decided (1)
made plans (1)
make plans (1)
plotted (1)
untranslated (1)

1087 βουλή *boulē* (12)
purpose (6)
will (2)
decided that (1) +5502
decision (1)
motives (1)
planned (1) +1181

1088 βούλημα *boulēma* (3)
choose (1)
plan (1)
will (1)

1089 βούλομαι *boulomai* (37)
want (9)
wanted (9)
chooses (3)
planned (2)
wanting (2)
willing (2)
chose (1)
counsel (1)
determined (1)
determines (1)
had in mind (1)
intended (1)
like (1)
liked (1)
wants (1)
will (1)

1090 βουνός *bounos* (2)
hill (1)
hills (1)

1091 βοῦς *bous* (8)
ox (4)
cattle (2)
oxen (2)

1092 βραβεῖον *brabeion* (2)
prize (2)

1093 βραβεύω *brabeuō* (1)
rule (1)

1094 βραδύνω *bradynō* (2)
delayed (1)
slow (1)

1095 βραδυπλοέω *bradyploeō* (1)

made slow headway (1)

1096 βραδύς *bradys* (3)
slow (2)
how slow (1)

1097 βραδύτης *bradytēs* (1)
slowness (1)

1098 βραχίων *brachiōn* (3)
arm (2)
power (1)

1099 βραχύς *brachys* (7)
little (3)
for a little while (1)
short (1)
short (1) +1328
untranslated (1)

1100 βρέφος *brephos* (8)
baby (4)
babies (2)
infancy (1)
newborn babies (1)

1101 βρέχω *brechō* (7)
rain (3)
wet (2)
rained (1)
sends rain (1)

1102 βριμάομαι *brimaomai*
Variant; not used

1103 βροντή *brontē* (12)
peals of thunder (4)
thunder (3)
thunders (3)
peal of thunder (1)
thundered (1)

1104 βροχή *brochē* (2)
rain (2)

1105 βρόχος *brochos* (1)
restrict (1) +2095

1106 βρυγμός *brygmos* (7)
gnashing (7)

1107 βρύχω *brychō* (1)
gnashed (1)

1108 βρύω *bryō* (1)
flow (1)

1109 βρῶμα *brōma* (17)
food (10)
foods (2)
what eat (2)
eating (1)
solid food (1)

1110 βρώσιμος *brōsimos* (1)
to eat (1)

1111 βρῶσις *brōsis* (11)
food (6)
rust (2)
eat (1)
eating (1)
meal (1)

1112 βυθίζω *bythizō* (2)
plunge (1)
sink (1)

1113 βυθός *bythos* (1)
open sea (1)

1114 βυρσεύς *byrseus* (3)
tanner (3)

1115 βύσσινος *byssinos* (5)
fine linen (5)

1116 βύσσος *byssos* (1)
fine linen (1)

1117 βωμός *bōmos* (1)
altar (1)

1118 γ *g*
Variant; not used

1119 Γαββαθᾶ *Gabbatha* (1)
Gabbatha (1)

1120 Γαβριήλ *Gabriēl* (2)
Gabriel (2)

1121 γάγγραινα *gangraina* (1)
gangrene (1)

1122 Γάδ *Gad* (1)
Gad (1)

1123 Γαδαρηνός *Gadarēnos* (1)
Gadarenes (1)

1124 Γάζα1 *Gaza1* (1)
Gaza (1)

1125 γάζα2 *gaza2* (1)
treasury (1)

1126 γαζοφυλάκιον *gazophylakion* (5)
place where the offerings were put (2)
temple treasury (2)
treasury (1)

1127 Γάιος *Gaios* (5)
Gaius (5)

1128 γάλα *gala* (5)
milk (5)

1129 Γαλάτης *Galatēs* (1)
Galatians (1)

1130 Γαλατία *Galatia* (4)
Galatia (3)
Galatian (1)

1131 Γαλατικός *Galatikos* (2)
Galatia (1)
of Galatia (1)

1132 γαλήνη *galēnē* (3)
calm (3)

1133 Γαλιλαία *Galilaia* (62)
Galilee (62)

1134 Γαλιλαῖος *Galilaios* (10)
Galileans (5)
Galilean (4)
Galilee (1)

1135 Γαλλία *Gallia*
Variant; not used

1136 Γαλλίων *Galliōn* (3)
Gallio (3)

1137 Γαμαλιήλ *Gamaliēl* (2)
Gamaliel (2)

1138 γαμέω *gameō* (28)
marry (12)
marries (7)
married (5)
marrying (2)
get married (1)
got married (1) +1222

1139 γαμίζω *gamizō* (7)
given in marriage (4)
giving in marriage (1)
marries (1)
marry (1)

1140 γαμίσκω *gamiskō* (1)
given in marriage (1)

1141 γάμος *gamos* (16)
wedding (6)
wedding banquet (5)
banquet (2)
marriage (1)
wedding feast (1)
wedding hall (1)

1142 γάρ *gar* (1040)
for (502)

because (85)
but (10)
and (9)
now (7)
indeed (6)
in fact (4)
since (4)
after all (3)
why (3)
as (2)
in fact (2) +2779
so (2)
yes (2)
as for (1)
as it is (1) +2779
because of (1)
even though (1) +1569
even though (1) +3525
for (1) +3590
for example (1)
for to be sure (1)
how (1) +3590
if (1)
in (1)
likewise (1) +2779
moreover (1)
no (1)
rather (1)
suppose (1) +1569
surely (1)
the fact is (1)
the reason (1) +1650+4047
though (1)
what does it matter (1) +5515
yet (1)
you see (1)
untranslated (376)

1143 γαστήρ *gastēr* (9)
pregnant women (3) +1877+2400
with child (2) +1877+2400
gluttons (1)
pregnant (1) +1877+2400
pregnant woman (1) +1877+2400
with child (1) +1877+5197

1144 Γαύδη *Gaudē*
Variant; not used

1145 γέ *ge* (24)
do[s] (3) +3590
does[s] (2) +3590
really (2)
surely (2) +1623
yet (2)
and what is more (1)
                +247+2779+4047+4246+5250
perhaps (1) +726+1623
surely (1) +247
then (1)
then (1) +726
though (1) +2779
thus (1) +726
untranslated (6)

1146 Γεδεών *Gedeōn* (1)
Gideon (1)

1147 γέεννα *geenna* (12)
hell (12)

1148 Γεθσημανή *Gethsēmanē*
Variant; not used

1149 Γεθσημανί *Gethsēmani* (2)
Gethsemane (2)

1150 γείτων *geitōn* (4)
neighbors (4)

1151 γελάω *gelaō* (2)
laugh (2)

1152 γέλως *gelōs* (1)
laughter (1)

1153 γεμίζω *gemizō* (9)

filled (5)
fill (2)
full (1)
swamped (1)

1154 γέμω *gemō* (11)
full (5)
covered with (3)
filled (2)
full of (1)

1155 γενεά *genea* (43)
generation (29)
generations (5)
descendants (1)
it[s] (1) +3836+4047
kind (1)
past (1) +4233
times (1)
untranslated (4)

1156 γενεαλογέω *genealogeō* (1)
trace descent (1)

1157 γενεαλογία *genealogia* (2)
genealogies (2)

1158 γενέθλια *genethlia*
Variant; not used

1159 γενέθλιος *genethlios*
Variant; not used

1160 γενέσια *genesia* (2)
birthday (2)

1161 γένεσις *genesis* (5)
birth (2)
genealogy (1)
life (1)
untranslated (1)

1162 γενετή *genetē* (1)
birth (1)

1163 γένημα *genēma* (4)
fruit (3)
harvest (1)

1164 γεννάω *gennaō* (97)
father (40)
born (37)
become father (3)
gives birth to (2)
bear (1)
bears children (1)
became (1)
became father (1)
became the father of (1)
birth (1)
bore (1)
came descendants (1)
child (1)
conceived (1)
gave birth to (1)
had (1)
illegitimate children (1) +1666+4518
native (1) +1877+4005
produce (1)

1165 γέννημα *gennēma* (4)
brood (4)

1166 Γεννησαρέτ *Gennēsaret* (3)
Gennesaret (3)

1167 γέννησις *gennēsis*
Variant; not used

1168 γεννητός *gennētos* (2)
born (2)

1169 γένος *genos* (20)
kinds (3)
offspring (3)
people (3)
family (2)
native (2)
born (1)

children (1) +5626
countrymen (1)
Jews (1) +1609+1877+3836
kind (1)
sorts (1)
untranslated (1)

1170 Γερασηνός *Gerasēnos* (3)
Gerasenes (3)

1171 Γεργεσηνός *Gergesēnos*
Variant; not used

1172 γερουσία *gerousia* (1)
assembly of elders (1)

1173 γέρων *gerōn* (1)
old (1)

1174 γεύομαι *geuomai* (15)
taste (6)
tasted (4)
eat (2)
ate (1)
get a taste (1)
tasting (1)

1175 γεωργέω *geōrgeō* (1)
farmed (1)

1176 γεώργιον *geōrgion* (1)
field (1)

1177 γεωργός *geōrgos* (19)
tenants (12)
farmers (3)
farmer (2)
gardener (1)
them[s] (1) +3836

1178 γῆ *gē* (250)
earth (151)
land (31)
ground (20)
soil (13)
Egypt (5) +131
shore (5)
earthly (3)
country (2)
landed (2) +2093+2262+3836
region (2)
Sodom (2) +5047
world (2)
ashore (1) +1650+3836
ashore (1) +2093
Canaan (1) +5913
countryside (1)
earth's (1)
its[s] (1) +3836
landed (1) +609+1650+3836
Midian (1) +3409
them[s] (1) +2093+2997+3836+3836
world's (1)
untranslated (2)

1179 γῆρας *gēras* (1)
old age (1)

1180 γηράσκω *gēraskō* (2)
aging (1)
old (1)

1181 γίνομαι *ginomai* (668)
was (54)
be (49)
become (46)
came (41)
happened (28)
became (26)
were (20)
done (13)
happen (13)
is (13)
been (11)
made (11)
performed (8)
take place (8)

come (6)
are (5)
do (5)
took place (5)
be done (4)
become (4) +1650
by no means (4) +3590
get (4)
making (4)
not at all (4) +3590
appeared (3)
approached (3)
became (3) +1650
becomes (3)
being (3)
broke out (3)
comes (3)
happening (3)
happens (3)
absolutely not (2) +3590
arrived (2)
becoming (2)
born (2)
brought (2)
came up (2)
certainly not (2) +3590
had (2)
lived (2)
marries (2)
occurred (2)
once (2) +1254
perform (2)
promised (2) +2039
reached (2) +2093
seized (2) +2093
share (2) +5171
stood (2)
surpassed (2) +1869
taken place (2)
turned (2)
turned into (2)
went (2)
accomplished (1)
agreed (1) +3924
am (1)
and (1) +2779
approaching (1) +1584
arose (1)
arose (1) +1254
arriving (1)
at daybreak (1) +2002+2465
at hour (1) +6052
bear (1)
became (1) +1639
become of (1)
been (1) +1639
been (1) +1650
been turned into (1)
belong (1)
betrayed (1) +4595
brought about (1)
came about (1)
changed (1) +2283
come of (1)
come true (1)
complained (1) +1198
dawn (1) +2465+3516
daybreak (1) +2465
decided (1) +1191
developed (1)
did (1)
died (1) +2505
died (1) +3738
disappeared (1) +908
do (1) +4475
does (1)
does^s (1) +4048
doing (1)
doubting (1) +603
early in the morning (1) +4746
entered (1) +1656

experienced (1)
faultless (1) +289
fell (1)
fell headlong (1) +4568
fell into trance (1) +1749+2093
finds (1) +2351
finished (1)
follow example (1) +3629
fright (1) +1873
gain freedom (1) +1801
given (1)
go (1)
grant (1)
granted (1)
grew (1)
grown up (1) +3489
happened (1) +1639
has (1)
have (1)
heard (1) +212
heard about (1) +1196
heard sound (1) +5889
held accountable (1) +5688
imitate (1) +3629
in fear (1) +1873
in the morning (1) +2465
introduced (1)
join with others following example (1)
+5213
learned about (1) +5745
look somber (1) +5034
looked so much like (1) +6059
loses (1)
make (1)
man-made (1) +1328+5931
may never (1) +3590
moths have eaten (1) +4963
neared (1) +1581
need (1) +2400+5970
never (1) +3590
now (1) +2779
obey (1) +5675
on (1)
once (1) +2779
one day (1) +1254
one day (1) +2779
owns (1)
participate in (1) +3128
planned (1) +1087
plunged into (1)
praying (1) +4666
proved (1)
proved to be (1)
rang out (1)
reach (1) +1650
reached (1)
reaching (1) +2093
receive (1)
result (1)
result in (1) +1666
revealed (1) +1871
rewards (1) +3633
served (1)
set (1)
shared in (1) +3581
shouted (1) +3189
show (1) +5745
so (1) +1254
spending time (1) +5990
spent (1)
split (1)
spoken (1)
stand firm (1) +1612
starting (1)
suffered (1)
suffering (1)
supply (1)
take charge of (1) +2062
taken (1)
that are (1)
that evening (1) +4070

the next morning (1) +2465
the time came when (1) +1254
thinking (1) +3836+5856
to marry^s (1) +4048
told him (1) +899+4639
trembled with fear (1) +1958
trembling (1) +1958
turn (1)
turned (1) +1650
turned out (1)
undergoes (1) +3581
unequaled (1) +3888+4024
unequaled (1) +3888+4024+5525
used (1)
visit (1)
wake up (1) +1213
was born (1)
was filled with (1)
was going on (1)
waste (1) +724
went on (1)
wept (1) +2653+3088
woke up (1) +2031
work together (1) +5301
untranslated (66)

1182 γινώσκω *ginōskō* (222)
know (91)
understand (17)
known (15)
knows (12)
knew (11)
learned (6)
find out (5)
aware (4)
knowing (4)
recognize (4)
recognized (4)
found out (3)
aware of (2)
know that (2)
knowledge (2)
made known (2)
understood (2)
acknowledge (1)
assured (1) +857
concluded (1)
discover (1)
do so^s (1)
evidence (1)
evident (1)
felt (1)
find out about (1)
get at truth (1) +855
had (1)
keep in mind (1)
knew about (1)
know about (1)
know how (1)
knows about (1)
knows thoughts (1)
learn (1)
learned about (1)
mark (1)
not clear (1) +4024
realize (1)
realized (1)
receive news (1)
regarded (1)
remember (1)
saw (1)
see if (1)
speak (1)
sure (1)
sure (1) +3857
sure of (1)
unaware (1) +4024
union with (1)
untranslated (2)

1183 γλεῦκος *gleukos* (1)
wine (1)

1184 γλυκύς *glykys* (4)
fresh (1)
fresh water (1)
sweet (1)
tasted sweet (1) *+1639*

1185 γλῶσσα *glōssa* (50)
tongue (21)
tongues (19)
language (5)
languages (2)
speaking in tongues (2)
untranslated (1)

1186 γλωσσόκομον *glōssokomon* (2)
keeper of money bag (1) *+2400*
money (1)

1187 γναφεύς *gnapheus* (1)
untranslated (1)

1188 γνήσιος *gnēsios* (4)
true (2)
loyal (1)
sincerity (1)

1189 γνησίως *gnēsiōs* (1)
genuine (1)

1190 γνόφος *gnophos* (1)
darkness (1)

1191 γνώμη *gnōmē* (9)
judgment (2)
purpose (2)
advice (1)
agreeing (1) *+1651+4472*
consent (1)
decided (1) *+1181*
thought (1)

1192 γνωρίζω *gnōrizō* (25)
made known (5)
make known (5)
tell (4)
known (3)
know (2)
told about (2)
know about (1)
present (1)
remind of (1)
spread (1)

1193 γνώριμος *gnōrimos*
Variant; not used

1194 γνῶσις *gnōsis* (29)
knowledge (25)
considerate (1) *+2848*
knowing (1)
knows (1)
understanding (1)

1195 γνώστης *gnōstēs* (1)
well acquainted with (1)

1196 γνωστός *gnōstos* (15)
known (6)
know (3) *+1639*
explain (1) *+1639*
friends (1)
heard about (1) *+1181*
knew (1)
know (1)
outstanding (1)

1197 γογγύζω *gongyzō* (8)
grumble (3)
grumbling (2)
complained (1)
did[s] (1)
whispering (1)

1198 γογγυσμός *gongysmos* (4)
complained (1) *+1181*
complaining (1)
grumbling (1)
whispering (1)

1199 γογγυστής *gongystēs* (1)
grumblers (1)

1200 γόης *goēs* (1)
impostors (1)

1201 Γολγοθᾶ *Golgotha* (3)
Golgotha (3)

1202 Γόμορρα *Gomorra* (4)
Gomorrah (4)

1203 γόμος *gomos* (3)
cargoes (2)
cargo (1)

1204 γονεύς *goneus* (20)
parents (19)
they[s] (1) *+899+3836*

1205 γόνυ *gony* (12)
knees (5)
knee (3)
kneel (1) *+2828+3836*
knelt (1) *+3836+5502*
knelt down (1) *+3836+5502*
knelt down (1) *+5502*

1206 γονυπετέω *gonypeteō* (4)
fell on knees before (1)
knelt (1)
knelt before (1)
on knees (1)

1207 γράμμα *gramma* (14)
letters (3)
bill (2)
letter (2)
written (2)
get learning (1) *+3857*
learning (1)
scriptures (1)
written code (1)
wrote (1)

1208 γραμματεύς *grammateus* (63)
teachers of the law (57)
teacher of the law (2)
clerk (1)
scholar (1)
teachers (1)
untranslated (1)

1209 γραπτός *graptos* (1)
written (1)

1210 γραφή *graphē* (50)
scripture (30)
scriptures (18)
writings (2)

1211 γράφω *graphō* (191)
written (105)
write (40)
wrote (15)
writing (11)
described (2)
make it (2)
recorded (2)
write down (2)
written down (2)
wrote down (2)
describes (1)
do so[s] (1)
had a notice prepared (1) *+5518*
read (1) *+1639*
sent the letter (1)
with writing (1)
write an account (1)
wrote about (1)

1212 γραώδης *graōdēs* (1)
old wives' tales (1)

1213 γρηγορέω *grēgoreō* (22)
keep watch (8)
watch (3)
alert (2)

on guard (2)
awake (1)
kept watch (1)
stays awake (1)
wake up (1)
wake up (1) *+1181*
watchful (1)
watching (1)

1214 γυμνάζω *gymnazō* (4)
trained (2)
experts (1) *+2840*
train (1)

1215 γυμνασία *gymnasia* (1)
training (1)

1216 γυμνητεύω *gymnēteuō*
Variant; not used

1217 γυμνιτεύω *gymniteuō* (1)
in rags (1)

1218 γυμνός *gymnos* (16)
naked (7)
needed clothes (2)
needing clothes (2)
taken it off (1)
uncovered (1)
wearing nothing (1) *+2093+4314*
without clothes (1)
untranslated (1)

1219 γυμνότης *gymnotēs* (2)
nakedness (2)

1220 γυναικάριον *gynaikarion* (1)
weak-willed women (1)

1221 γυναικεῖος *gynaikeios* (1)
wives (1)

1222 γυνή *gynē* (215)
woman (90)
wife (58)
women (30)
wives (12)
dear woman (2)
widow (2)
wife's (2)
believing wife (1) *+80*
bride (1)
faithful to her husband (1) *+467+1651*
got married (1) *+1138*
leaves wife (1) *+2400*
married (1) *+1313*
married (1) *+3284*
married a woman (1) *+3284*
married to (1)
marry (1) *+721*
mother (1)
she[s] (1)
she[s] (1) *+3836*
unmarried (1) *+608+3395*
widow (1) *+899*
widow (1) *+5939*
woman's (1)
women's (1)
untranslated (1)

1223 Γώγ *Gōg* (1)
Gog (1)

1224 γωνία *gōnia* (9)
capstone (5) *+3051*
corners (3)
corner (1)

1225 δ *d*
Variant; not used

1226 Δαβίδ *Dabid*
Variant; not used

1227 δαιμονίζομαι *daimonizomai* (13)
demon-possessed (10)
possessed by a demon (1)
possessed by demons (1)

suffering from demon-possession (1)

1228 δαιμόνιον *daimonion* (63)
demons (42)
demon (15)
demon-possessed (5) +2400
gods (1)

1229 δαιμονιώδης *daimoniōdēs* (1)
of the devil (1)

1230 δαίμων *daimōn* (1)
demons (1)

1231 δάκνω *daknō* (1)
biting (1)

1232 δάκρυον *dakryon* (10)
tears (8)
tear (2)

1233 δακρύω *dakryō* (1)
wept (1)

1234 δακτύλιος *daktylios* (1)
ring (1)

1235 δάκτυλος *daktylos* (8)
finger (6)
fingers (1)
lift a finger (1)

1236 Δαλμανουθά *Dalmanoutha* (1)
Dalmanutha (1)

1237 Δαλματία *Dalmatia* (1)
Dalmatia (1)

1238 δαμάζω *damazō* (4)
tamed (2)
subdue (1)
tame (1)

1239 δάμαλις *damalis* (1)
heifer (1)

1240 Δάμαρις *Damaris* (1)
Damaris (1)

1241 Δαμασκηνός *Damaskēnos* (1)
the Damascenes (1)

1242 Δαμασκός *Damaskos* (15)
Damascus (15)

1243 Δάν *Dan*
Variant; not used

1244 δανείζω *daneizō*
Variant; not used

1245 δάνειον *daneion* (1)
debt (1)

1246 δανειστής *daneistēs*
Variant; not used

1247 δανίζω *danizō* (4)
lend (3)
borrow (1)

1248 Δανιήλ *Daniēl* (1)
Daniel (1)

1249 δάνιον *danion*
Variant; not used

1250 δανιστής *danistēs* (1)
moneylender (1)

1251 δαπανάω *dapanaō* (5)
spend (2)
spent (2)
pay expenses (1)

1252 δαπάνη *dapanē* (1)
cost (1)

1253 Δαυίδ *Dauid* (59)
David (57)
David's (2)

1254 δέ *de* (2787)
but (669)
and (257)

then (89)
now (82)
he (70) +3836
they (49) +3836
so (37)
Jesus[s] (25) +3836
however (23)
yet (17)
when (9)
she (8) +3836
while (7)
instead (6)
meanwhile (5)
another (4) +4005
even (4)
the man[s] (4) +3836
also (3)
and yet (3)
at this (3)
others (3) +3836
another (2)
as (2)
as it is (2) +3814
for (2)
if he does (2) +1623+3590
moreover (2)
nevertheless (2)
once (2) +1181
or (2)
others (2) +4005
rather (2)
some (2)
still (2)
that (2)
the disciples[s] (2) +3836
the men[s] (2) +3836
those (2) +3836
though (2)
where (2)
after this (1)
again (1)
and now (1)
and some (2) +4005
another (1) +3836
another man (1) +4005
arose (1) +1181
as for (1)
as it is (1) +4022
at other times (1) +4047
at this point (1) +4047
because (1)
but (1) +1883+3836
but (1) +4022
but as far as (1)
but in the other case (1) +1695
by (1)
by now (1)
Cornelius[s] (1) +3836
finally (1)
former (1)
if (1)
in addition (1)
in addition (1) +2093
in fact (1) +2779
indeed (1) +2779
instead (1) +3814
Jesus' followers[s] (1) +3836
just (1)
just as (1)
Mary[s] (1) +3836
nor anyone (1) +4029
not until (1) +2453
now that (1)
on (1)
once (1)
one day (1) +1181
or (1) +4005
or at least (1) +1623+3590
other (1) +257
others (1) +257
otherwise (1) +1623+3590

Pilate[s] (1) +3836
rather (1) +3437
remember this (1) +4047
similarly (1)
simply (1)
so (1) +1181
so he (1) +3836
so they (1) +3836
some (1) +257
still another (1)
still others (1) +3836
the expert in the law[s] (1) +3836
the father[s] (1) +3836
the man's[s] (1) +3836
the manager[s] (1) +3836
the other (1) +4005
the people[s] (1) +3836
the rioters[s] (1) +3836
the time came when (1) +1181
those who (1) +3836
to the other (1) +4005
what is more (1) +247+2779+3667+4024
when (1) +1623
when (1) +6055
which (1)
yes (1)
untranslated (1303)

1255 δέησις *deēsis* (18)
prayers (6)
prayer (4)
pray (2) +4472
praying (2)
requests (2)
petition (1)
pray for help (1)

1256 δεῖ *dei* (101)
must (57)
ought (13)
should (9)
had (8)
have (3)
belong (1)
due (1)
for work (1) +1877+2237+4005
had (1) +1639
necessary (1)
ought to (1)
should be (1)
shouldn't (1) +4024
have (1)
untranslated (2)

1257 δεῖγμα *deigma* (1)
example (1)

1258 δειγματίζω *deigmatizō* (2)
expose to public disgrace (1)
made spectacle (1)

1259 δείκνυμι *deiknymi* (33)
show (20)
showed (6)
shown (3)
bring about (1)
explain (1)
showing (1)
shows (1)

1260 δεικνύω *deiknyō*
Variant; not used

1261 δειλία *deilia* (1)
timidity (1)

1262 δειλιάω *deiliaō* (1)
afraid (1)

1263 δειλινός *deilinos*
Variant; not used

1264 δειλός *deilos* (3)
afraid (1)
cowardly (1)
so afraid (1)

1265 δεῖνα *deina* (1)
certain (1)

1266 δεινός *deinos*
Variant; not used

1267 δεινῶς *deinōs* (2)
fiercely (1)
terrible (1)

1268 δειπνέω *deipneō* (4)
supper (2)
eat (1)
my supper (1) +5515

1269 δειπνοκλήτωρ *deipnoklētor*
Variant; not used

1270 δεῖπνον *deipnon* (16)
banquet (4)
supper (4)
banquets (3)
dinner (2)
evening meal (1)
meal (1)
untranslated (1)

1271 δεῖπνος *deipnos*
Variant; not used

1272 δεισιδαιμονία *deisidaimonia* (1)
religion (1)

1273 δεισιδαίμων *deisidaimōn* (1)
very religious (1)

1274 δέκα *deka* (25)
ten (24)
eighteen (1) +2779+3893

1275 δεκαδύο *dekadyo*
Variant; not used

1276 δεκαέξ *dekaex*
Variant; not used

1277 δεκαοκτώ *dekaoktō* (2)
eighteen (2)

1278 δεκαπέντε *dekapente* (3)
fifteen (1)
ninety feet deep (1) +3976
two miles (1) +5084

1279 Δεκάπολις *Dekapolis* (3)
Decapolis (3)

1280 δεκατέσσαρες *dekatessares* (5)
fourteen (5)

1281 δέκατος *dekatos* (7)
tenth (7)

1282 δεκατόω *dekatoō* (2)
collected a tenth (1)
paid the tenth (1)

1283 δεκτός *dektos* (5)
favor (2)
acceptable (1)
accepted (1)
accepts (1) +1639

1284 δελεάζω *deleazō* (3)
entice (1)
enticed (1)
seduce (1)

1285 δένδρον *dendron* (25)
tree (17)
trees (8)

1286 δεξιοβόλος *dexiobolos*
Variant; not used

1287 δεξιολάβος *dexiolabos* (1)
spearmen (1)

1288 δεξιός *dexios* (54)
right hand (31)
right (21)
right side (2)

1289 δέομαι *deomai* (22)
pray (5)
beg (4)
begged (3)
ask (2)
please (2) +5148
prayed (2)
implore (1)
plead (1)
pleaded with (1)
prayed to (1)

1290 δέος *deos* (1)
awe (1)

1291 Δερβαῖος *Derbaios* (1)
from Derbe (1)

1292 Δέρβη *Derbē* (3)
Derbe (3)

1293 δέρμα *derma* (1)
goatskins (1) +128

1294 δερμάτινος *dermatinos* (2)
leather (2)

1295 δέρρις *derris*
Variant; not used

1296 δέρω *derō* (15)
beat (7)
beaten with blows (2)
beating (2)
flogged (2)
slaps (1)
strike (1)

1297 δεσμεύω *desmeuō* (3)
arresting (1)
chained hand (1) +268
tie up (1)

1298 δεσμέω *desmeō*
Variant; not used

1299 δέσμη *desmē* (1)
bundles (1)

1300 δέσμιος *desmios* (16)
prisoner (11)
in prison (2)
prisoners (2)
arrested (1)

1301 δεσμός *desmos* (18)
chains (11)
chained (2)
imprisonment (2)
bound (1)
prison (1)
untranslated (1)

1302 δεσμοφύλαξ *desmophylax* (3)
jailer (3)

1303 δεσμωτήριον *desmōtērion* (4)
jail (2)
prison (2)

1304 δεσμώτης *desmōtēs* (2)
prisoners (2)

1305 δεσπότης *despotēs* (10)
masters (4)
sovereign Lord (4)
master (1)
sovereign (1)

1306 δεῦρο *deuro* (9)
come (7)
go (1)
now (1)

1307 δεῦτε *deute* (12)
come (12)

1308 δευτεραῖος *deuteraios* (1)
on the following day (1)

1309 δεύτερον *deuteron* (6)

second time (2)
again (1)
again (1) +4099
later (1)
second (1)

1310 δευτερόπρωτος *deuteroprōtos*
Variant; not used

1311 δεύτερος *deuteros* (37)
second (27)
second time (4) +1666
second time (2) +1666+4099
another (1)
inner (1)
second (1) +4099
twice (1)

1312 δέχομαι *dechomai* (56)
welcomes (9)
welcome (7)
welcomed (7)
receive (6)
receives (6)
received (5)
accept (3)
accepted (3)
take (3)
obtained (1)
receiving (1)
refused (1) +4024
taking (1)
took (1)
welcomed (1) +1645+3552
untranslated (1)

1313 δέω *deō* (43)
bound (16)
tied (5)
bind (4)
prisoners (3)
in prison (2)
tie (2)
ties up (2)
wrapped (2)
arrest (1)
chained (1)
chained hand (1) +268
compelled (1)
in chains (1)
married (1) +1222
put in chains (1)

1314 δή *dē* (5)
therefore (1)
untranslated (4)

1315 δηλαυγῶς *dēlaugōs*
Variant; not used

1316 δῆλος *dēlos* (3)
clear (1)
clearly (1)
gives away (1) +4472

1317 δηλόω *dēloō* (7)
bring to light (1)
indicate (1)
informed (1)
made clear (1)
pointing (1)
showing (1)
told of (1)

1318 Δημᾶς *Dēmas* (3)
Demas (3)

1319 δημηγορέω *dēmēgoreō* (1)
delivered a public address (1)

1320 Δημήτριος *Dēmētrios* (3)
Demetrius (3)

1321 δημιουργός *dēmiourgos* (1)
builder (1)

1322 δῆμος *dēmos* (4)
crowd (2)

people (1)
they[s] (1) +3836

1323 δημόσιος *dēmosios* (4)
public (2)
publicly (2)

1324 δηνάριον *dēnarion* (16)
denarius (7)
a day's wages (2)
denarii (2)
eight months of a man's wages (1) +1357
eight months' wages (1) +1357
silver coins (1)
the money worth a year's wages (1) +5559
untranslated (1)

1325 δήποτε *dēpote*
Variant; not used

1326 δηποτοῦν *dēpotoun*
Variant; not used

1327 δήπου *dēpou* (1)
surely (1)

1328 διά *dia* (666)
through (180)
by (80)
because of (65)
for (30)
because (23)
therefore (23) +4047
why (23) +5515
with (15)
in (13)
because (10) +3836
for this reason (9) +4047
for sake (8)
for the sake of (8)
from (7)
that is why (5) +4047
the reason (5) +4047
at (4)
out of (4)
so (4) +4047
this is why (4) +4047
always (3) +4246
because (3) +4047
during (3)
for benefit (3)
how is it that (3) +5515
on (3)
on account of (3)
the result of (3)
afforded by (2)
continually (2) +4246
regularly (2) +4246
since (2)
so then (2) +4047
that was why (2) +4047
why (2) +162+4005
who (2) +4005
after (1)
as the result of (1)
briefly (1) +3900
bring about (1)
by all this (1) +4047
by means of (1)
by the authority of (1)
causes (1)
compared to (1)
days (1) +2465
due to (1)
enabling (1) +1443+3836+5931
for (1) +3836
for sakes (1)
for that very reason (1) +4047
for the benefit of (1)
for this very reason (1) +4047
forever (1) +4246
go through (1)
he (1) +899+3836+5931
in answer to (1)

in keeping with (1)
in the presence of (1)
in view of (1)
man-made (1) +1181+5931
night (1) +3816+4246
of (1)
on account (1)
on the basis of (1)
on the evidence of (1)
over a period (1)
patiently (1) +5705
reaching more and more (1)
            +3836+4429+4498
short (1) +1099
since (1) +3836
so (1) +162+4005
so (1) +4005
terrified (1) +5832
that is why (1) +162+4005
therefore (1) +162+4005
they (1) +899
this is why (1) +899
to bottom (1) +3910
traveled about the country (1) +1451+4246
under (1)
use (1)
using (1) +5931
visit on the way (1)
when (1)
why (1) +4005
with (1) +899+5931
with the help of (1)
untranslated (54)

1329 διαβαίνω *diabainō* (3)
come over (1)
go (1)
passed through (1)

1330 διαβάλλω *diaballō* (1)
accused (1)

1331 διαβεβαιόομαι *diabebaioomai* (2)
confidently affirm (1)
stress (1)

1332 διαβλέπω *diablepō* (3)
see clearly (2)
eyes opened (1)

1333 διάβολος *diabolos* (38)
devil (31)
devil's (3)
he[s] (1) +3836
malicious talkers (1)
slanderers (1)
slanderous (1)

1334 διαγγέλλω *diangellō* (3)
give notice of (1)
proclaim (1)
proclaimed (1)

1335 διαγίνομαι *diaginomai* (3)
later (1)
lost (1)
was over (1)

1336 διαγινώσκω *diaginōskō* (2)
decide (1)
information (1)

1337 διαγνωρίζω *diagnōrizō*
Variant; not used

1338 διάγνωσις *diagnōsis* (1)
decision (1)

1339 διαγογγύζω *diagongyzō* (2)
mutter (1)
muttered (1)

1340 διαγρηγορέω *diagrēgoreō* (1)
fully awake (1)

1341 διάγω *diagō* (2)
live (1)
lived (1)

1342 διαδέχομαι *diadechomai* (1)
received (1)

1343 διάδημα *diadēma* (3)
crowns (3)

1344 διαδίδωμι *diadidōmi* (3)
distributed (1)
divides up (1)
give (1)

1345 διάδοχος *diadochos* (1)
succeeded (1) +3284

1346 διαζώννυμι *diazōnnymi* (3)
wrapped around (2)
wrapped around waist (1)

1347 διαθήκη *diathēkē* (33)
covenant (25)
covenants (3)
covenant make (2) +1416
will (2)
covenant made (1) +1416

1348 διαίρεσις *diairesis* (3)
different (3)

1349 διαιρέω *diaireō* (2)
divided between (1)
gives (1)

1350 διακαθαίρω *diakathairō* (1)
clear (1)

1351 διακαθαρίζω *diakatharizō* (1)
clear (1)

1352 διακατελέγχομαι *diakatelenchomai* (1)
refuted (1)

1353 διακελεύω *diakeleuō*
Variant; not used

1354 διακονέω *diakoneō* (37)
serves (6)
wait on (6)
served (4)
serve (3)
administer (2)
attended (2)
help (2)
helped (2)
care for (1)
cared for needs (1)
do the work (1)
helpers (1)
helping (1)
helping to support (1)
in the service of (1)
ministry (1)
serve as deacons (1)
serving (1)

1355 διακονία *diakonia* (34)
ministry (14)
service (9)
serve (3)
distribution (1)
help (1)
mission (1)
preparations to be made (1)
service that perform (1) +3311+3836+4047
serving (1)
task (1)
work (1)

1356 διάκονος *diakonos* (29)
servant (13)
servants (7)
minister (3)
deacons (2)
attendants (1)
deacon (1)
ministers (1)
promotes sin (1) +281

1357 διακόσιοι *diakosioi* (8)
1,260 (2) +2008+5943

two hundred (2)
276 (1) +1573+1971
eight months of a man's wages (1) +1324
eight months' wages (1) +1324
hundred yards (1) +4388

1358 διακούω *diakouō* (1)
hear case (1)

1359 διακρίνω *diakrinō* (19)
doubt (4)
doubts (2)
criticized (1)
discriminated (1)
disputing (1) +1363
hesitate (1)
hesitation (1)
interpret (1)
judge a dispute (1)
judged (1)
made distinction (1)
makes different (1)
recognizing (1)
waver (1)
weigh carefully (1)

1360 διάκρισις *diakrisis* (3)
distinguish from (')
distinguishing between (1)
passing judgment (1)

1361 διακωλύω *diakōlyō* (1)
deter (1)

1362 διαλαλέω *dialaleō* (2)
discuss (1)
talking about (1)

1363 διαλέγομαι *dialegomai* (13)
reasoned (4)
arguing (2)
addresses (1)
argued about (1)
discoursed (1)
discussions (1)
disputing (1) +1359
spoke to (1)
talked (1)

1364 διαλείπω *dialeipō* (1)
stopped (1)

1365 διάλεκτος *dialektos* (6)
in Aramaic (3) +1579
language (3)

1366 διαλιμπάνω *dialimpanō*
Variant; not used

1367 διαλλάσσομαι *diallassomai* (1)
reconciled (1)

1368 διαλογίζομαι *dialogizomai* (16)
thinking (5)
discussed (4)
arguing about (1)
talked the matter over (1) +253+4639
talking (1)
talking about (1)
thought (1)
wondered (1)
wondering (1)

1369 διαλογισμός *dialogismos* (14)
thoughts (6)
thinking (3)
arguing (1)
argument (1)
disputable (1)
disputing (1)
doubts (1)

1370 διαλύω *dialyō* (1)
dispersed (1)

1371 διαμαρτύρομαι *diamartyromai* (15)
testified (3)
declared (2)

warn (2)
warned (2)
charge (1)
give charge (1)
testify (1)
testifying (1)
testifying to (1)
warns (1)

1372 διαμάχομαι *diamachomai* (1)
argued vigorously (1)

1373 διαμένω *diamenō* (5)
remain (2)
goes on (1)
remained (1)
stood (1)

1374 διαμερίζω *diamerizō* (11)
divided (4)
divided up (2)
divide (1)
divided among (1)
dividing up (1)
gave (1)
separated (1)

1375 διαμερισμός *diamerismos* (1)
division (1)

1376 διανέμω *dianemō* (1)
spreading (1)

1377 διανεύω *dianeuō* (1)
making signs (1) +1639

1378 διανόημα *dianoēma* (1)
thoughts (1)

1379 διάνοια *dianoia* (12)
minds (4)
mind (3)
thoughts (2)
understanding (2)
thinking (1)

1380 διανοίγω *dianoigō* (8)
opened (5)
explaining (1)
firstborn (1) +3616
open (1)

1381 διανυκτερεύω *dianyktereuō* (1)
spent the night (1) +1639

1382 διανύω *dianyō* (1)
continued (1)

1383 διαπαντός *diapantos*
Variant; not used

1384 διαπαρατριβή *diaparatribē* (1)
constant friction between (1)

1385 διαπεράω *diaperaō* (6)
crossed over (4)
cross over (1)
crossing over (1)

1386 διαπλέω *diapleō* (1)
sailed across (1)

1387 διαπονέομαι *diaponeomai* (2)
greatly disturbed (1)
troubled (1)

1388 διαπορεύομαι *diaporeuomai* (5)
going by (1)
going through (1)
passing through (1)
traveled (1)
went through (1)

1389 διαπορέω *diaporeō* (4)
perplexed (2)
puzzled (1)
wondering about (1)

1390 διαπραγματεύομαι *diapragmateuomai* (1)
gained (1)

1391 διαπρίω *diapriō* (2)
furious (2)

1392 διαρήγνυμι *diarēgnymi*
Variant; not used

1393 διαρήσσω *diarēssō*
Variant; not used

1394 διαρθρόω *diarthroō*
Variant; not used

1395 διαρπάζω *diarpazō* (3)
rob (2)
carry off (1)

1396 διαρρήγνυμι *diarrēgnymi* (5)
tore (3)
break (1)
broken (1)

1397 διασαφέω *diasapheō* (2)
explain (1)
told (1)

1398 διασείω *diaseiō* (1)
extort money (1)

1399 διασκορπίζω *diaskorpizō* (9)
scattered (5)
scattered seed (2)
squandered (1)
wasting (1)

1400 διασπάω *diaspaō* (2)
tore apart (1)
torn to pieces (1)

1401 διασπείρω *diaspeirō* (3)
scattered (3)

1402 διασπορά *diaspora* (3)
people live scattered among (1) +3836
scattered (1)
scattered throughout (1)

1403 διαστέλλω *diastellō* (7)
commanded (2)
gave orders (2)
authorization (1)
did so[s] (1)
warned (1)

1404 διάστημα *diastēma* (1)
later (1)

1405 διαστολή *diastolē* (3)
difference (2)
distinction (1)

1406 διαστρέφω *diastrephō* (7)
perverse (2)
depraved (1)
distort the truth (1) +3281
perverting (1)
subverting (1)
turn (1)

1407 διασώζω *diasōzō* (8)
safely (2)
escaped (1)
heal (1)
healed (1)
in safety (1)
saved through (1)
spare (1)

1408 διαταγή *diatagē* (1)
put into effect (1)

1409 διάταγμα *diatagma* (1)
edict (1)

1410 διαταράσσω *diatarassō* (1)
greatly troubled (1)

1411 διατάσσω *diatassō* (17)
directed (2)
ordered (2)
told (2)
told to do (2)

commanded (1)
give directions (1)
instituted (1)
instructing (1)
made arrangement (1)
orders (1)
put into effect (1)
required (1)
the rule lay down (1)

1412 διατελέω *diateleō* (1)
last (1)

1413 διατηρέω *diatēreō* (2)
avoid (1)
treasured (1)

1414 διατί *diati*
Variant; not used

1415 διατίθεμαι *diatithemai*
Variant; not used

1416 διατίθημι *diatithēmi* (7)
covenant make (2) +1347
made (2)
confer (1)
conferred (1)
covenant made (1) +1347

1417 διατρίβω *diatribō* (9)
stayed (3)
spending (2)
remained (1)
spent (1)
spent some time (1)
stayed a while (1)

1418 διατροφή *diatrophē* (1)
food (1)

1419 διαυγάζω *diaugazō* (1)
dawns (1)

1420 διαυγής *diaugēs* (1)
transparent (1)

1421 διαφανής *diaphanēs*
Variant; not used

1422 διαφέρω *diapherō* (13)
valuable (2)
worth more than (2)
carry (1)
different from (1)
differs (1)
driven (1)
makes difference (1)
more valuable than (1)
spread (1)
superior (1)
what is best (1) +3836

1423 διαφεύγω *diapheugō* (1)
escaping (1)

1424 διαφημίζω *diaphēmizō* (3)
spread the news about (1)
spreading (1)
widely circulated (1)

1425 διαφθείρω *diaphtheirō* (6)
corrupt (1)
destroy (1)
destroyed (1)
destroying (1)
destroys (1)
wasting away (1)

1426 διαφθορά *diaphthora* (6)
decay (4)
body decayed (1) +3972
decay (1) +1650+5715

1427 διάφορος *diaphoros* (4)
superior (2)
different (1)
various (1)

1428 διαφυλάσσω *diaphylassō* (1)

guard carefully (1) +3836

1429 διαχειρίζω *diacheirizō* (2)
kill (1)
killed (1)

1430 διαχλευάζω *diachleuazō* (1)
made fun of (1)

1431 διαχωρίζω *diachōrizō* (1)
leaving (1)

1432 διγαμία *digamia*
Variant; not used

1433 δίγαμος *digamos*
Variant; not used

1434 διδακτικός *didaktikos* (2)
able to teach (1)

1435 διδακτός *didaktos* (3)
taught (3)

1436 διδασκαλία *didaskalia* (21)
teaching (10)
doctrine (5)
teach (2)
teachings (2) +1438
teachings (1)
things taught (1)

1437 διδάσκαλος *didaskalos* (59)
teacher (50)
teachers (8)
master (1)

1438 διδάσκω *didaskō* (97)
teach (35)
teaching (31)
taught (20)
teaches (4)
taught (2) +1639
teachings (2) +1436
instructed (1)
lecture (1)
teachings (1)

1439 διδαχή *didachē* (30)
teaching (23)
instruction (3)
taught (2)
careful instruction (1)
teachings (1)

1440 δίδραχμον *didrachmon* (2)
two-drachma (1)
untranslated (1)

1441 Δίδυμος *Didymos* (3)
Didymus (3)

1442 διδῶ *didō*
Variant; not used

1443 δίδωμι *didōmi* (416)
give (116)
given (107)
gave (74)
gives (13)
put (9)
pay (5)
grant (4)
granted (4)
offered (4)
giving (3)
let (3)
make (3)
offer (3)
arranged (2)
commanded (2) +1953
enable (2)
gave up (2)
give to the poor (2) +1797
perform (2)
placed (2)
produced (2)
show (2)
struck in the face (2) +4825

appointed (1)
assigned (1)
bear (1)
benefit (1) +5921
bring (1)
buy (1)
cast (1)
caused (1)
distributed (1)
does (1)
enabled (1)
enabled (1) +1639
enabling (1) +1328+3836+5931
entrusted (1)
gifts (1)
give (1) +3836
glorified (1) +1518
glorify (1) +1518
hinder (1) +1600
is (1)
is^s (1)
lavished (1)
leave (1)
pass on (1)
payment (1)
plot (1) +5206
poured (1)
praised (1) +142
presented (1)
punish (1) +1689
puts (1)
receive (1)
repay (1)
rescue (1) +5401
rewarding (1) +3635+3836
set (1)
sound (1)
speak (1)
strengthen (1) +3194
take back (1)
took (1)
try hard (1) +2238
venture (1)
untranslated (5)

1444 διεγείρω *diegeirō* (6)
got up (2)
grew rough (1)
refresh (1)
stimulate to (1)
woke (1)

1445 διενθυμέομαι *dienthymeomai* (1)
thinking (1)

1446 διεξέρχομαι *diexerchomai*
Variant; not used

1447 διέξοδος *diexodos* (1)
corners (1)

1448 διερμηνεία *diermēneia*
Variant; not used

1449 διερμηνευτής *diermēneutēs* (1)
interpreter (1)

1450 διερμηνεύω *diermēneuō* (6)
interpret (3)
explained what said (1)
interprets (1)
translated (1)

1451 διέρχομαι *dierchomai* (42)
go through (4)
traveled through (3)
go (2)
go over (2)
goes through (2)
going through (2)
passing through (2)
traveled throughout (2)
went (2)
came (1)
come (1)

coming (1)
gone about (1)
gone through (1)
passed (1)
passed through (1)
pierce (1)
spread (1)
took the road through (1)
traveled (1)
traveled about (1)
traveled about the country (1) +1328+4246
traveled along (1)
visit on way (1)
walked around (1)
walked right through (1)
was coming (1) +3516
went around (1)
went on (1) +4134
went through (1)

1452 διερωτάω *dierōtaō* (1)
found out (1)

1453 διετής *dietēs* (1)
two years old (1)

1454 διετία *dietia* (2)
two years (2)

1455 διηγέομαι *diēgeomai* (8)
tell (3)
told (2)
described (1)
reported (1)
speak of (1)

1456 διήγησις *diēgēsis* (1)
account (1)

1457 διηνεκής *diēnekēs* (4)
forever (2) +1650+3836
endlessly (1) +1650+3836
for all time (1) +1650+3836

1458 διθάλασσος *dithalassos* (1)
sandbar (1) +5536

1459 διϊκνέομαι *diikneomai* (1)
penetrates (1)

1460 διΐστημι *diistēmi* (3)
later (1)
left (1)
untranslated (1)

1461 διϊστορέω *diistoreō*
Variant; not used

1462 διϊσχυρίζομαι *diischyrizomai* (2)
asserted (1)
insisting that (1)

1463 δικάζω *dikazō*
Variant; not used

1464 δικαιοκρισία *dikaiokrisia* (1)
righteous judgment (1)

1465 δίκαιος *dikaios* (79)
righteous (53)
right (11)
just (8)
upright (3)
innocent (2)
honest (1)
righteousness (1)

1466 δικαιοσύνη *dikaiosynē* (91)
righteousness (74)
justice (5)
what is right (5)
right (2)
acts of righteousness (1)
are justified (1) +1650
itˢ (1)
righteous (1) +1877
righteous life (1)

1467 δικαιόω *dikaioō* (39)

justified (19)
justify (4)
justifies (3)
proved right (3)
considered righteous (2)
declared righteous (2)
acknowledged that right (1)
acquitted (1)
freed (1)
justified before God (1)
make innocent (1)
vindicated (1)

1468 δικαίωμα *dikaiōma* (10)
regulations (3)
righteous (2)
act of righteousness (1)
justification (1)
requirements (1)
righteous decree (1)
righteous requirements (1)

1469 δικαίως *dikaiōs* (5)
justly (2)
as ought (1)
righteous (1)
upright (1)

1470 δικαίωσις *dikaiōsis* (2)
justification (2)

1471 δικαστής *dikastēs* (2)
judge (2)

1472 δίκη *dikē* (3)
justice (1)
punished (1) +5514
punishment (1)

1473 δίκτυον *diktyon* (12)
nets (8)
net (4)

1474 δίλογος *dilogos* (1)
sincere (1) +3590

1475 διό *dio* (53)
therefore (27)
so (12)
that is why (5)
this is why (4)
for this reason (1)
now (1)
so then (1)
untranslated (2)

1476 διοδεύω *diodeuō* (2)
passed through (1)
traveled about (1)

1477 Διονύσιος *Dionysios* (1)
Dionysius (1)

1478 διόπερ *dioper* (2)
therefore (2)

1479 διοπετής *diopetēs* (1)
image which fell from heaven (1)

1480 διόρθωμα *diorthōma* (1)
reforms (1)

1481 διόρθωσις *diorthōsis* (1)
the new order (1)

1482 διορύσσω *dioryssō* (4)
break in (2)
broken into (2)

1483 Διόσκουροι *Dioskouroi* (1)
twin gods Castor and Pollux (1)

1484 διότι *dioti* (23)
because (10)
for (6)
therefore (2)
since (1)
so (1)
untranslated (3)

1485 Διοτρέφης *Diotrephēs* (1)
Diotrephes (1)

1486 διπλόος *diploos* (4)
double (2)
pay back double (1) +1488
twice as much (1)

1487 διπλοῦς *diplous*
Variant; not used

1488 διπλόω *diploō* (1)
pay back double (1) +1486

1489 δίς *dis* (6)
twice (4)
again (2)

1490 δισμυριάς *dismyrias* (1)
two hundred million (1) +3689

1491 διστάζω *distazō* (2)
doubt (1)
doubted (1)

1492 δίστομος *distomos* (3)
double-edged (3)

1493 δισχίλιοι *dischilioi* (1)
two thousand (1)

1494 διϋλίζω *diylizō* (1)
strain out (1)

1495 διχάζω *dichazō* (1)
turn (1)

1496 διχοστασία *dichostasia* (2)
dissensions (1)
divisions (1)

1497 διχοτομέω *dichotomeō* (2)
cut to pieces (2)

1498 διψάω *dipsaō* (16)
thirsty (13)
thirst (2)
thirst for (1)

1499 δίψος *dipsos* (1)
thirst (1)

1500 δίψυχος *dipsychos* (2)
double-minded (2)

1501 διωγμός *diōgmos* (10)
persecution (5)
persecutions (5)

1502 διώκτης *diōktēs* (1)
persecutor (1)

1503 διώκω *diōkō* (45)
persecuted (15)
persecute (11)
pursue (5)
persecuting (4)
make every effort (2)
press on (2)
pursued (2)
follow (1)
go running off after (1) +599+3593
practice (1)
try (1)

1504 δόγμα *dogma* (5)
regulations (2)
decree (1)
decrees (1)
untranslated (1)

1505 δογματίζω *dogmatizō* (1)
submit to rules (1)

1506 δοκέω *dokeō* (62)
think (20)
thought (7)
thinks (6)
seems (3)
thinking (3)
expect (2)
seem (2)

seemed good (2)
think that (2)
considered (1)
considers himself (1) +1639
convinced (1)
decided (1)
found (1)
men[s] (1)
opinion (1)
regarded (1)
reputed (1)
seemed (1)
seemed to be leaders (1)
supposing (1)
take for (1) +1639
wants (1)
untranslated (1)

1507 δοκιμάζω dokimazō (22)
test (6)
approve (2)
approved (1)
approves (1)
be tested (1)
discern (1)
examine (1)
find out (1)
how interpret (1)
interpret (1)
proved (1)
refined (1)
test and approve (1)
tests (1)
think it worthwhile (1)
try out (1)

1508 δοκιμασία dokimasia (1)
tried (1)

1509 δοκιμή dokimē (7)
character (2)
proved (2)
proof (1)
severe trial (1) +2568
would stand the test (1)

1510 δοκίμιον dokimion (2)
proved genuine (1)
testing (1)

1511 δόκιμος dokimos (7)
approved (3)
approval (1)
stood the test (1)
test (1)
tested and approved (1)

1512 δοκός dokos (6)
plank (6)

1513 δόλιος dolios (1)
deceitful (1)

1514 δολιόω dolioō (1)
practice deceit (1)

1515 δόλος dolos (11)
deceit (5)
deceitful (1)
false (1)
sly (1) +1877
sly way (1)
trick (1)
trickery (1)

1516 δολόω doloō (1)
distort (1)

1517 δόμα doma (4)
gifts (3)
gift (1)

1518 δόξα doxa (165)
glory (112)
glorious (15)
praise (9)
splendor (9)

honor (5)
celestial beings (2)
brilliance (1)
glories (1)
glorified (1) +1443
glorify (1) +1443
glorious (1) +1877
glorious presence (1)
glorious splendor (1)
honored (1)
majesty (1)
shone with glory (1) +2400
with ever-increasing glory (1)
              +608+1518+1650
untranslated (2)

1519 δοξάζω doxazō (61)
glorify (12)
glorified (11)
praised (11)
honored (4)
praising (4)
bring glory to (3)
praise (3)
glorious (2)
glory (2)
brought glory (1)
gave praise to (1)
glorifies (1)
glorifying (1)
glory come to (1)
glory gave (1)
honor (1)
make much of (1)
take glory (1)

1520 Δορκάς Dorkas (2)
Dorcas (2)

1521 δόσις dosis (2)
giving (1)
untranslated (1)

1522 δότης dotēs (1)
giver (1)

1523 Δουβέριος Douberios
Variant; not used

1524 δουλαγωγέω doulagōgeō (1)
make slave (1)

1525 δουλεία douleia (5)
slavery (2)
bondage (1)
makes a slave (1)
slaves (1)

1526 δουλεύω douleuō (25)
serve (10)
serving (3)
slaves (3)
enslaved (2)
served (2)
in slavery (1)
serve as slaves (1)
serves (1)
slave (1)
slaving (1)

1527 δούλη doulē (3)
servant (2)
untranslated (1)

1528 δοῦλος1 doulos1 (124)
servant (54)
servants (38)
slave (18)
slaves (11)
servant's (2)
slavery (1)

1529 δοῦλος2 doulos2 (2)
in slavery (2)

1530 δουλόω douloō (8)
become slaves (2)

addicted (1)
be enslaved (1)
bound (1)
in slavery (1)
make a slave (1)
slave (1)

1531 δοχή dochē (2)
banquet (2)

1532 δράκων drakōn (13)
dragon (13)

1533 δράσσομαι drassomai (1)
catches (1)

1534 δραχμή drachmē (3)
coin (1)
silver coins (1)
untranslated (1)

1535 δρέπανον drepanon (8)
sickle (8)

1536 δρόμος dromos (3)
race (2)
work (1)

1537 Δρούσιλλα Drousilla (1)
Drusilla (1)

1538 δύναμαι dynamai (210)
can (85)
cannot (40) +4024
could (35)
able (24)
can't (5) +4024
cannot (3) +3590
couldn't (2) +4024
ready (2)
and cannot (1) +4028
can do (1)
cannot (1) +4046
cannot do (1) +4024
cannot do (1) +4028
competent (1)
enables (1)
may (1)
possible (1)
right (1)
unable (1) +3590
unable (1) +4024
untranslated (2)

1539 δύναμις dynamis (119)
power (73)
miracles (16)
ability (3)
miraculous powers (3)
powerful (3)
powers (3)
mighty (2)
as much as were able (1) +2848
bodies (1)
brilliance (1)
enabled (1)
excessive (1)
fury (1)
grasp the meaning (1) +3836+3857
heavenly bodies (1) +3836+4041
mighty one (1)
miracle (1)
miraculous powers (1) +1920
so powerfully (1) +1877
strength (1)
work miracles (1)
workers of miracles (1)
untranslated (1)

1540 δυναμόω dynamoō (2)
strengthened (1)
turned to strength (1)

1541 δυνάστης dynastēs (3)
important official (1)
ruler (1)
rulers (1)

1542 δυνατέω *dynateō* (3)
able (2)
powerful (1)

1543 δυνατός *dynatos* (32)
possible (10)
able (4)
strong (3)
could (2)
power (2)
powerful (2)
can (1) +1639
could have done so (1)
had power (1) +1639
impossible (1) +4024
influential (1)
leaders (1)
mighty (1)
possible (1) +1639
thorough (1)

1544 δύνω *dynō* (2)
setting (1)
sunset (1) +2463

1545 δύο *dyo* (134)
two (122)
extra (2)
seventy-two (2) +1573
42 (1) +5477
both^s (1) +3836
extra (1) +324
forty-two (1) +5477
twenty to thirty gallons (1)
+2445+3583+5552
two by two (1) +1545
two by two (1) +324+1545

1546 δυσβάστακτος *dysbastaktos* (1)
hardly carry (1)

1547 δυσεντερία *dysenteria*
Variant; not used

1548 δυσεντέριον *dysenterion* (1)
dysentery (1)

1549 δυσερμήνευτος *dysermēneutos* (1)
hard to explain (1)

1550 δύσις *dysis*
Variant; not used

1551 δύσκολος *dyskolos* (1)
hard (1)

1552 δυσκόλως *dyskolōs* (3)
hard (3)

1553 δυσμή *dysmē* (5)
west (5)

1554 δυσνόητος *dysnoētos* (1)
hard to understand (1)

1555 δυσφημέω *dysphēmeō* (1)
slandered (1)

1556 δυσφημία *dysphēmia* (1)
bad report (1)

1557 δώδεκα *dōdeka* (75)
twelve (61)
12,000 (13) +5942
untranslated (1)

1558 δωδέκατος *dōdekatos* (1)
twelfth (1)

1559 δωδεκάφυλον *dōdekaphylon* (1)
twelve tribes (1)

1560 δῶμα *dōma* (7)
roof (4)
roofs (2)
roof of house (1)

1561 δωρεά *dōrea* (11)
gift (10)
it^s (1) +3836

1562 δωρεάν *dōrean* (9)
freely (3)
for nothing (1)
free gift (1)
free of charge (1)
without cost (1)
without paying for it (1)
without reason (1)

1563 δωρέομαι *dōreomai* (3)
given (2)
gave (1)

1564 δώρημα *dōrēma* (2)
gift (2)

1565 δῶρον *dōron* (19)
gift (8)
gifts (8)
gift devoted to God (1)
help (1)
offerings (1)

1566 δωροφορία *dōrophoria*
Variant; not used

1567 ε *e*
Variant; not used

1568 ἔα *ea* (1)
Ha (1)

1569 ἐάν *ean* (351)
if (205)
unless (31) +3590
whatever (11) +4005
whoever (6) +4005
when (5)
wherever (5) +3963
anyone (3)
suppose (3)
though (3)
what (3) +4005
whatever (3) +5516
anything (2) +4005
whatever (2) +4012
whenever (2) +3963
whenever (2) +4006
whoever (2) +5516
all who (1) +4012
anyone (1) +4005
anyone (1) +4012
anyone (1) +4246+6034
anyone (1) +5516
anyone who (1) +4005
anyone who (1) +5516
anything (1) +4005+4246+4547
anything (1) +5516
as for (1)
at least (1) +2779
but (1) +3590
even (1) +2779
even if (1)
even though (1) +1142
everyone (1)
everything (1) +4012+4246
fail (1) +3590
in keeping with income (1)
+2338+4005+5516
just (1) +2779
like (1) +6055
man (1)
on (1)
only (1) +3590
provided that (1)
since (1)
suppose (1) +1142
suppose a (1) +5515
those whom (1) +4005
until (1) +3590+4754
what (1) +4012
whatever (1)
whatever (1) +4005+5516
whenever (1)
whenever (1) +2471

wherever (1) +4023
whether (1)
who (1) +5516
whoever (1) +4015
whom (1) +4005
without (1) +3590
would (1)
untranslated (21)

1570 ἐάνπερ *eanper* (3)
if (2)
untranslated (1)

1571 ἑαυτοῦ *heautou* (267)
himself (77)
themselves (29)
his own (16)
ourselves (15)
his (14)
itself (12)
their (11)
their own (9)
them (6)
each other (4)
one another (4)
he (3)
herself (3)
yourselves (3)
her (2)
they (2)
appeared (1) +5746
bringing (1) +2400+3552
claimed to be (1) +4472
claims to be (1) +4472
her own (1)
him (1)
his heart (1)
his self (1)
his senses (1)
inwardly (1) +1877
it (1)
jumped (1) +965
myself (1)
oneself (1)
others (1)
our (1)
our hearts (1)
own (1)
proper (1)
renounced marriage (1) +2335+2336
self-seeking (1) +2426+3836
their hearts (1)
to himself (1) +1877
we (1)
your hearts (1)
yours (1)
yourself (1)
untranslated (30)

1572 ἐάω *eaō* (11)
let (6)
allow (2)
allowed (1)
left (1)
no more (1)

1573 ἑβδομήκοντα *hebdomēkonta* (5)
seventy-two (2) +1545
276 (1) +1357+1971
seventy (1)
seventy-five (1) +4297

1574 ἑβδομηκοντάκις *hebdomēkontakis* (1)
seventy-seven times (1) +2231

1575 ἕβδομος *hebdomos* (9)
seventh (9)

1576 Ἔβερ *Eber* (1)
Eber (1)

1577 Ἑβραϊκός *Hebraikos*
Variant; not used

1578 Ἑβραῖος *Hebraios* (4)
Hebrews (2)

Hebraic Jews (1)
Hebrew (1)

1579 Ἑβραΐς *Hebrais* (3)
in Aramaic (3) +*1365*

1580 Ἑβραϊστί *Hebraisti* (7)
in Aramaic (5)
in Hebrew (2)

1581 ἐγγίζω *engizō* (42)
near (13)
approached (9)
approaching (3)
came near (2)
came up (2)
come near (2)
comes (2)
almost (1)
almost here (1)
comes near (1)
draw near (1)
drawing near (1)
drew near (1)
gathering around (1)
gets here (1)
neared (1) +*1181*

1582 ἐγγράφω *engraphō* (3)
written (1)
written in (1)
written on (1)

1583 ἔγγυος *engyos* (1)
guarantee (1)

1584 ἐγγύς *engys* (31)
near (22)
almost time (2)
approaching (1) +*1181*
from (1)
in danger of (1)
nearby (1)
nearer (1)
Sabbath day's walk from (1)
        +*2400+3847+4879*
soon (1)

1585 ἐγγύτερον *engyteron*
Variant; not used

1586 ἐγείρω *egeirō* (143)
raised (45)
get up (15)
got up (11)
risen (10)
rise (8)
raised to life (7)
raised from the dead (6)
raise (5)
appear (3)
raise up (3)
raises (3)
woke up (3)
gets up (2)
helped up (2)
wake up (2)
woke (2)
appeared (1)
come (1)
come now (1)
go (1)
lift out (1)
lifted (1)
made (1)
made get up (1)
on your feet (1)
raise again (1)
raised again (1)
raised up (1)
rise again (1)
rising (1)
stand up (1)
stir up (1)

1587 ἔγερσις *egersis* (1)

resurrection (1)

1588 ἐγκάθετος *enkathetos* (1)
spies (1)

1589 ἐγκαίνια *enkainia* (1)
feast of Dedication (1)

1590 ἐγκαινίζω *enkainizō* (2)
opened (1)
put into effect (1)

1591 ἐγκακέω *enkakeō* (6)
lose heart (2)
become weary (1)
discouraged (1)
give up (1)
tire of (1)

1592 ἐγκαλέω *enkaleō* (7)
accusing (2)
accusation (1)
accusations (1)
being charged with (1)
bring any charge (1)
press charges (1)

1593 ἐγκαταλείπω *enkataleipō* (10)
abandoned (2)
deserted (2)
forsaken (2)
abandon (1)
forsake (1)
give up (1)
left (1)

1594 ἐγκατοικέω *enkatoikeō* (1)
living among (1)

1595 ἐγκαυχάομαι *enkauchaomai* (1)
boast (1)

1596 ἐγκεντρίζω *enkentrizō* (6)
grafted in (2)
graft in (1)
grafted (1)
grafted in among (1)
grafted into (1)

1597 ἐγκλείω *enkleiō*
Variant; not used

1598 ἔγκλημα *enklēma* (2)
charge (1)
charges (1)

1599 ἐγκομβόομαι *enkomboomai* (1)
clothe with (1)

1600 ἐγκοπή *enkopē* (1)
hinder (1) +*1443*

1601 ἐγκόπτω *enkoptō* (5)
cut in on (1)
hinder (1)
hindered from (1)
stopped (1)
weary (1)

1602 ἐγκράτεια *enkrateia* (4)
self-control (4)

1603 ἐγκρατεύομαι *enkrateuomai* (2)
control themselves (1)
goes into training (1)

1604 ἐγκρατής *enkratēs* (1)
disciplined (1)

1605 ἐγκρίνω *enkrinō* (1)
classify (1)

1606 ἐγκρύπτω *enkryptō* (2)
mixed (2)

1607 ἔγκυος *enkyos* (1)
expecting a child (1)

1608 ἐγχρίω *enchriō* (1)
put on (1)

1609 ἐγώ *egō* (2670)

me (748)
I (500)
my (481)
us (362)
our (289)
we (176)
mine (11)
I myself (7)
ours (6)
my own (5)
I (2) +*1877*
our own (2)
your (2)
as for me (1)
as surely as I live (1) +*2409*
equal with us (1) +*2777+2779*
for myself (1)
here (1) +*1877*
him^s (1) +*81+3836*
I (1) +*899*
I (1) +*3836+6034*
I (1) +*6034*
I'm (1) +*1639*
intelligible (1) +*3808+3836*
is one of us (1) +*199+3552*
it^s (1) +*3836+5013*
Jews (1) +*1169+1877+3836*
me (1) +*3836+3950*
me (1) +*3836+6034*
me (1) +*6034*
me say (1) +*4123*
myself (1) +*6034*
of mine (1) +*1650*
our companions (1) +*3836+5250*
ourselves (1)
say (1) +*201+1666*
them^s (1) +*3836+4252*
this^s (1) +*3364+3836+4047*
we'll (1)
what business is it of mine (1) +*5515*
with us (1)
yes (1) +*2627*
untranslated (50)

1610 ἐδαφίζω *edaphizō* (1)
dash to the ground (1)

1611 ἔδαφος *edaphos* (1)
ground (1)

1612 ἑδραῖος *hedraios* (3)
firm (1)
settled the matter (1) +*2705*
stand firm (1) +*1181*

1613 ἑδραίωμα *hedraiōma* (1)
foundation (1)

1614 Ἑζεκίας *Hezekias* (2)
Hezekiah (2)

1615 ἐθελοθρησκία *ethelothrēskia* (1)
self-imposed worship (1)

1616 ἐθίζω *ethizō* (1)
custom (1)

1617 ἐθνάρχης *ethnarchēs* (1)
governor (1)

1618 ἐθνικός *ethnikos* (4)
pagans (3)
pagan (1)

1619 ἐθνικῶς *ethnikōs* (1)
like a gentile (1)

1620 ἔθνος *ethnos* (162)
gentiles (81)
nations (37)
nation (23)
pagans (6)
people (6)
Nation (3)
gentile (2)
country (1)
gentile (1) +*1666*

heathen (1)
pagan (1)

1621 ἔθος *ethos* (12)
customs (6)
custom (4)
as usual (1) +2848+3836
in the habit of (1)

1622 ἔθω *ethō*
Variant; not used

1623 εἰ *ei* (502)
if (313)
except (36) +3590
but (10) +3590
only (10) +3590
since (10)
that (6)
though (6)
whether (6)
only (5) +3590+4024
though (4) +2779
never (3)
but only (2) +3590
if he does (2) +1254+3590
surely (2) +1145
unless (2) +1760+3590
unless (2) +3590
unless (2) +3614
whatever (2) +5516
but (1) +2779
even though (1)
evidently (1) +3590
except (1) +323+3614
except for (1) +3590
hoping (1) +4803
if (1) +3525
in the hope that (1)
nevertheless (1) +3590
no (1)
now that (1)
only (1)
only (1) +3590+3668
only to (1) +3590+4029
or at least (1) +1254+3590
otherwise (1) +1254+3590
otherwise (1) +1760+3590
perhaps (1) +726
perhaps (1) +726+1145
perhaps (1) +5593
somehow (1) +4803
surely (1) +3605
that (1) +4803
to see if (1)
undoubtedly (1) +5593
unless (1) +4024
until (1) +3590+4020
what (1) +5516
what if (1)
when (1)
when (1) +1254
whether or not (1)
untranslated (47)

1624 εἰδέα *eidea* (1)
appearance (1)

1625 εἶδον *eidon*
Variant; not used

1626 εἶδος *eidos* (5)
form (2)
appearance (1)
kind (1)
sight (1)

1627 εἰδωλεῖον *eidōleion* (1)
idol's temple (1)

1628 εἰδωλόθυτος *eidōlothytos* (9)
food sacrificed to idols (5)
sacrificed to idols (2)
sacrifice offered to an idol (1)
such food (1)

1629 εἰδωλολάτρης *eidōlolatrēs* (7)
idolaters (5)
idolater (2)

1630 εἰδωλολατρία *eidōlolatria* (4)
idolatry (4)

1631 εἴδωλον *eidōlon* (11)
idols (8)
idol (2)
it's (1) +3836

1632 εἰκῇ *eikē* (6)
for nothing (2)
idle notions (1)
nothing (1)
vain (1)
wasted (1)

1633 εἴκοσι *eikosi* (11)
twenty-four (6) +5475
twenty (2)
a hundred and twenty feet deep (1) +3976
three or three and a half miles (1)
                  +2445+4297+5084+5558
twenty-three (1) +5552

1634 εἴκω *eikō* (1)
give in (1) +3836+5717

1635 εἰκών *eikōn* (23)
image (13)
likeness (4)
portrait (2)
images (1)
it's (1) +2563+3836+3836
portrait (1) +2400
realities (1)

1636 εἰλικρίνεια *eilikrineia* (3)
sincerity (3)

1637 εἰλικρινής *eilikrinēs* (2)
pure (1)
wholesome (1)

1638 εἰ μήν *ei mēn*
Variant; not used

1639 εἰμί *eimi* (2462)
is (705)
are (369)
was (302)
be (263)
am (130)
were (128)
been (36)
come (14)
have (14)
had (12)
means (9)
comes (8)
happen (7)
be (6) +1650
lived (6)
do (5)
isn't (5) +4024
mean (5)
means (5) +3493
stands for (5)
become (4) +1650
belong to (4) +1666
belonged to (4) +1666
has (4)
live (4)
stay (4)
stayed (4)
as (3)
become (3)
being (3)
belong (3)
belongs to (3) +1666
calls for (3)
deserve (3) +545
hate (3) +3631
it's (3)

know (3) +1196
remain (3)
will (3)
with (3)
aren't (2) +4024
aren't (2) +4049
began (2)
belongs to (2)
cannot (2) +4024
cease to be (2) +4024
companions (2) +3552+3836
companions (2) +3836+5250
controlled (2)
deserve (2) +2653
did (2)
follow (2)
form (2)
go (2)
had (2) +2400
leads to (2)
mean (2) +2527
meant (2)
pleases (2) +2298
sanctified (2) +39
saved (2) +5392
taught (2) +1438
to (2)
would (2)
accepts (1) +1283
advisable (1) +545
after he was circumcised (1) +1877+4364
all the world (1) +476+4005+5515
am present (1)
are (1) +1650
at work (1)
be diligent (1)
be that as it may (1)
bears (1) +4472
became (1) +1181
because are (1)
been (1) +1181
before this been (1) +4732
believer (1) +4412
belong to Lord (1) +3261
belong to (1)
belonged to (1)
belonging to Simon (1) +4981
belongs (1)
belongs to Christ (1) +5986
betray (1) +3836+4140
binds together (1) +5278
boast (1) +3017
break (1) +4127
bring (1) +1650
came about (1)
can (1) +1543
care very little (1) +1650+1788
catch (1) +2436
chief cornerstone (1) +214
come together (1) +899+2093+3836
come together (1) +5251
come upon (1) +2158
considers himself (1) +1506
consist (1)
continued (1)
cured (1) +2543
cut (1) +3300
deserves (1) +545
devoted to (1) +4674
disagreed (1) +851
does belong to (1)
done (1)
done (1) +2237
done (1) +4472
done (1) +4556
enabled (1) +1443
end (1) +4639
enjoy long life (1) +3432
enter (1) +1656
envious (1) +3836+4057+4505
equality (1) +2698+3836

exist (1)
existed (1)
exists (1)
explain (1) +1196
fail the test (1) +99
failed the test (1) +99
fall (1) +4406
find (1)
find (1) +2351
forgive (1) +2664
gathered (1)
gathered (1) +2190
get (1)
given fullness (1) +4444
gives life (1) +2443
had (1) +338
had (1) +1256
had (1) +1877
had authority (1) +1877+2026
had power (1) +1543
had taken part in a rebellion (1) +3334
had too much (1) +3551
happened (1)
happened (1) +1181
have (1) +2400
have all you want (1) +3170
have an obligation (1) +4050
have being (1)
have hope (1) +1827
have such a place (1)
he's (1)
he's (1) +899+6034
hear (1) +201+4047
heard (1) +201
hold terror (1) +5832
how far will they go (1) +4047+5515
I'm (1) +1609
in charge of (1) +2093
in other words (1) +4047
including (1) +4005
involves (1)
is (1) +3493
is now (1)
isn't (1) +4049
keep (1)
kept on (1)
know (1) +5745
last (1)
lasts (1)
leaders (1) +4755
let be (1)
listens (1) +212
lived (1) +1695
longs for (1) +2160
looks like (1)
looks like (1) +3927
made (1)
made holy (1) +39
make complete (1) +4444
making a complaint about[s] (1)
making signs (1) +1377
marveled (1) +2513
may (1)
meaning (1)
means (1) +3306
means (1) +4005
meet (1)
numbering (1) +750
of you (1) +1877+3836+5148
on (1)
on the evening (1) +4070
one (1)
one of (1) +1666
only (1) +3666
owe (1) +4050
owed money to (1) +5971
owns (1) +2625
owns (1) +3261
participate (1) +3128
perish (1) +724+1650
place (1)

please (1) +2298
pleased (1) +744
possible (1) +1543
previously seen (1) +4632
put aside (1) +629
put trust (1) +4275
read (1) +1211
read (1) +2108
receive (1)
rely (1) +4275
rely on (1) +1666
represent (1)
resembled (1) +3927
rest (1)
rightly so (1) +545
riot (1) +2573
Romans (1) +4871
sat (1) +5153
say (1)
settle matters (1) +2333
share (1) +3128
share with (1) +5171
show favoritism (1) +4720
show favoritism (1) +4721
sided with (1) +5250
sinned (1) +281+4472
sins (1) +281
spent the night (1) +1381
spread (1)
standing (1)
standing (1) +2705
stood (1) +2392
stood (1) +2705
stood (1) +3023
stood opposed (1) +5641
sums up (1)
take (1) +2400
take for (1) +1506
taken part (1) +3128
takes captive (1) +5194
tasted sweet (1) +1184
testify (1) +3457
testify (1) +3459
though (1)
to have failed (1) +99
treat (1)
valued highly (1) +1952
want (1)
was present (1)
went (1)
were (1) +4537
were present (1)
were up (1) +326
what shall we do (1) +4036+5515
while (1) +1877+3836
with a great crash (1)
          +899+3489+3836+4774
withdrew (1) +5723
wore clothing (1) +1907
work with (1) +5301
untranslated (120)

1640 εἰμι *eimi*
Variant; not used

1641 εἵνεκεν *heineken* (2)
because (1) +4005
untranslated (1)

1642 εἴπερ *eiper* (6)
if (2)
if in fact (1) +726
if indeed (1)
since (1)
untranslated (1)

1643 εἴπως *eipōs*
Variant; not used

1644 εἰρηνεύω *eirēneuō* (4)
live in peace (2)
be at peace (1)
live at peace (1)

1645 εἰρήνη *eirēnē* (92)
peace (82)
peace be with (4)
go I wish you well (1) +1877+5632
peacemakers (1) +4472
reconcile (1) +1650+5261
safe (1) +1877
the blessing of peace (1)
welcomed (1) +1312+3552

1646 εἰρηνικός *eirēnikos* (2)
peace (1)
peace-loving (1)

1647 εἰρηνοποιέω *eirēnopoieō* (1)
making peace (1)

1648 εἰρηνοποιός *eirēnopoios* (1)
peacemakers (1)

1649 εἴρω *eirō*
Variant; not used

1650 εἰς *eis* (1762)
to (467)
into (249)
in (165)
for (143)
on (48)
at (37)
as (26)
forever (23) +172+3836
against (17)
to (15) +3836
so that (14) +3836
among (12)
so that (11)
that (7) +3836
be (6) +1639
of (6)
with (6)
about (5)
before (5)
until (5)
back (4) +3836+3958
become (5) +1181
become (4) +1639
entered (4) +2262
for purpose (4)
leads to (4)
never (4) +172+3590+3836+4024
toward (4)
why (4) +5515
and so (3) +3836
brought (3)
in order that (3) +3836
leading to (3)
reached (3) +2262
where (3) +4005
among (2) +3545+3836
became (2) +1181
beyond limits (2) +296+3836
down upon (2)
forever (2) +1457+3836
home (2) +899+3875
never (2) +172+3836+4024
on to (2)
over (2)
that (2)
through (2)
throughout (2) +3910
to bring (2)
to do (2)
whatever (2) +323+4005
aboard (1)
across (1) +3836+4305
again (1) +172+3836
all over (1) +3910
and thus (1) +3836
are (1) +1639
are justified (1) +1466
are saved (1) +5401
arrived (1) +2262

as a result (1) +3836
as far as (1)
ashore (1) +1178+3836
at all (1) +3836+4117
attaining to (1)
away^s (1) +2557+3836
be saved (1) +5401
become (1)
been (1) +1181
before (1) +3545+3836
before them (1) +3545
belonging (1) +4348
bring (1) +1639
brings into (1) +1652
burial (1) +3645+5502
by (1)
by itself (1) +1651+3023+5536+6006
care very little (1) +1639+1788
completely (1) +3836+4117
condemned (1) +2262+3213
confirms (1) +1012
decay (1) +1426+5715
destroyed (1) +724
discredited (1) +3357+4029
doing (1)
endlessly (1) +1457+3836
enter (1) +4513
Ephesus (1)
eventually (1) +5465
ever (1) +172+3836
ever-increasing wickedness (1)
　　　　　　　　+490+490+3836
faith from first to last (1) +4411+4411
far off (1) +3426
for (1) +3836
for all time (1) +1457+3836
for the express purpose (1) +899+4047
for this reason (1) +4047
forever (1) +172
forever (1) +172+2465
forevermore (1) +172+3836+4246
from (1)
full of (1)
gave (1) +965
greatly (1) +4353
grew (1) +2262+3836
hand over to (1) +4140+5931
has enough (1) +2400
home (1) +899+3836+3875
home (1) +3836+3875
home (1) +3836+3875+5148
in agreement (1) +1651+3836
in dealing with (1)
in order that (1)
in order to (1)
in regard to (1)
indoors (1) +3836+3864
indoors (1) +3875
intended to bring (1)
it^s (1) +3795
landed (1) +609+1178+3836
led to (1)
listen carefully (1)
　　　　+3836+4044+5148+5148+5502
lose good name (1) +591+2262
make one (1) +1651
never (1) +173+3590+3836+4024
never again (1) +172+3590+3836+4024
next (1) +3516+3836
of mine (1) +1609
onto (1)
perish (1) +724+1639
prompted (1) +965+2840+3836
put on board (1) +899+1837
reach (1) +1181
reached (1) +201
reaching (1) +2262
reconcile (1) +1645+5261
regarding (1)
result (1) +3836
result in (1)

return (1) +2262+3836+4099
return (1) +5715
right into (1) +2276+2401
saved (1) +4348+6034
so (1) +3836
so as (1) +3836
so as to (1)
so then (1) +3836
spur on (1) +4237
take (1) +404
take (1) +2884
testifying (1) +3457
that far outweighs them all (1)
　　　　　　　+983+2848+5651+5651
that is why (1) +4047
the full extent of (1) +5465
the reason (1) +1142+4047
the reason (1) +4047
then will be able (1) +3836
there^s (1) +2038+3836
this is the reason (1) +4047
this very reason (1) +4047
throughout (1)
throughout (1) +4246
till (1)
to (1) +4047
to be (1)
to cause (1)
to serve (1)
to this end (1) +4005
treat (1) +4472
turned (1) +1181
turned around (1) +3836+3958+5138
turned back (1) +599+3836+3958
under (1)
under power (1) +5931
unto (1)
up (1)
visit in advance (1) +4601
visited (1) +2262
what (1) +5515
where (1)
where (1) +5536
where^s (1) +3836+5596
will turn out (1)
with (1) +3836
with ever-increasing glory (1)
　　　　　　　+608+1518+1518
without (1) +3590
untranslated (279)

1651 εἰς *heis* (343)
one (241)
a (16)
first (8)
a single (7)
the other^s (6)
each (5) +1667
man (4)
alone (3)
an (3)
one (3) +5516
a unit (1)
agreeing (1) +1191+4472
alike (1) +608
among (1) +1666
another (1)
any (1)
by itself (1) +1650+3023+5536+6006
detail (1) +1667
each (1)
each (1) +324+1667
each (1) +1651+2848
each other (1) +1651+3836
everyone (1) +1667
faithful to her husband (1) +467+1222
first day (1)
in agreement (1) +1650+3836
in turn (1) +2848
in unison (1)
just as though (1) +899+2779+3836

make one (1) +1650
nothing (1) +4028
once (1)
one (1) +257+4024
one (1) +1666
one (1) +3836
one after the other (1) +1667
one at a time (1) +1651+2848
only (1) +4028
some (1) +3538+3836
someone (1)
the next day (1) +2465+3552
the one (1)
the only (1)
the same (1)
unity (1)
untranslated (12)

1652 εἰσάγω *eisagō* (11)
brought in (2)
brought into (2)
bring in (1)
brings into (1) +1650
brought (1)
led into (1)
take into (1)
taken into (1)
took into (1)

1653 εἰσακούω *eisakouō* (5)
heard (4)
listen (1)

1654 εἰσδέχομαι *eisdechomai* (1)
receive (1)

1655 εἴσειμι *eiseimi* (4)
enter (1)
entered into (1)
went (1)
went to (1)

1656 εἰσέρχομαι *eiserchomai* (195)
enter (54)
entered (34)
went into (16)
go into (7)
went in (7)
come in (6)
enters (6)
go in (6)
come (5)
came in (4)
went inside (4)
went to (4)
comes in (3)
fall into (3)
went (3)
arrived in (2)
came into (2)
entering (2)
gone (2)
arrived (1)
came (1)
came to (1)
come at (1)
come in among (1)
come to (1)
comes into (1)
enter (1) +1639
enter into (1)
entered (1) +1181
entered into (1)
get in (1)
go (1)
goes into (1)
going into (1)
gone into (1)
got to (1)
hurried (1) +3552+5082
reached (1)
reaped the benefits of (1)
started (1)

went into (1) +4513
untranslated (3)

1657 εἰσκαλέομαι *eiskaleomai* (1)
invited (1)

1658 εἴσοδος *eisodos* (5)
coming (1)
enter (1)
reception (1)
visit (1)
welcome into (1)

1659 εἰσπηδάω *eispēdaō* (1)
rushed in (1)

1660 εἰσπορεύομαι *eisporeuomai* (17)
enter (3)
enters (3)
come in (2)
going into (2)
came (1)
go into (1)
going (1)
moved about freely (1) +1744+2779
went in (1)
went into (1)
went to (1)

1661 εἰστρέχω *eistrechō* (1)
ran (1)

1662 εἰσφέρω *eispherō* (8)
lead into (2)
bringing to (1)
brought (1)
brought into (1)
carries (1)
do thisˢ (1)
take into (1)

1663 εἶτα *eita* (15)
then (10)
after that (1)
and (1)
moreover (1)
once more (1) +4099
when (1)

1664 εἴτε *eite* (65)
or (28)
whether (18)
if (11)
where (3)
as for (1)
as for (1) +5642
such as (1)
untranslated (2)

1665 εἴωθα *eiōtha* (4)
custom (4)

1666 ἐκ *ek* (917)
from (314)
of (207)
by (53)
out of (45)
at (20)
with (19)
in (17)
on (13)
out (7)
for (6)
some of (6)
from among (5)
belong to (5)
belong to (4) +1639
belonged to (4) +1639
second time (4) +1311
through (4)
among (3)
because of (3)
belongs to (3) +1639
circumcised (3) +4364
since (3)
whose mother was (3)

because (2)
belonged to (2)
depends on (2)
have faith (2) +4411
over (2)
part of (2)
second time (2) +1311+4099
under (2)
according to means (1) +2400+3836
after (1)
among (1) +1651
as (1)
away from (1)
based on (1)
believe (1) +4411
believersˢ (1) +899
between (1)
completely (1) +3336+4356
descendant (1) +2588+3836
descendant (1) +3875
descended from (1)
descended from (1) +5065
ever (1) +172+3836
followed (1)
free and belong to no man (1) +1801+4246
from then on (1) +4047
gentile (1) +1620
heavenly (1) +4041
his native language (1) +2625+3836
illegitimate children (1) +1164+4518
imperfect (1) +3538
in answer to (1)
in front of (1) +1885
it depends on you (1) +3836+5148
Jews (1) +4364
lose (1) +3496
might say (1) +3836+5125
on account of (1)
one (1) +1651
one of (1)
one of (1) +1639
oppose (1) +1885
physically (1) +5882
reluctantly (1) +3383
rely on (1) +1639
result in (1) +1181
say (1) +201+1609
they the kind (1) +4047
third time (1) +5569
this is how (1) +4047
to (1)
wholeheartedly (1) +2840
whose mother (1)
without (1) +4024
untranslated (104)

1667 ἕκαστος *hekastos* (82)
each (54)
each (5) +1651
every (3)
everyone (3)
a manˢ (2)
anyone (1)
daily (1) +2465+2848
detail (1) +1651
each (1) +324+1651
each of (1)
each one (1)
every one (1)
everyone (1) +1651
everyone (1) +4246
him (1)
his (1)
one (1)
one after the other (1) +1651
yourself (1)
untranslated (1)

1668 ἑκάστοτε *hekastote* (1)
always (1)

1669 ἑκατόν *hekaton* (17)
hundred (8)

144,000 (3) +5475+5477+5942
144 (1) +5475+5477
153 (1) +4299+5552
eight hundred gallons (1) +1004
hundreds (1)
seventy-five pounds (1) +3354
thousand bushels (1) +3174

1670 ἑκατονταετής *hekatontaetēs* (1)
hundred years old (1)

1671 ἑκατονταπλασίων *hekatontaplasiōn* (3)
hundred times (3)

1672 ἑκατοντάρχης *hekatontarchēs* (20)
centurion (16)
centurions (2)
centurion's (1)
officers (1)

1673 ἑκατόνταρχος *hekatontarchos*
Variant; not used

1674 ἐκβαίνω *ekbainō* (1)
left (1)

1675 ἐκβάλλω *ekballō* (81)
drive out (20)
driving out (8)
drove out (5)
drives out (3)
take out (3)
threw (3)
thrown (3)
brings (2)
driven (2)
get rid of (2)
remove from (2)
send out (2)
threw out (2)
brings out (1)
brought out (1)
dragged (1)
drive (1)
driven out (1)
drove from (1)
exclude (1)
expelled (1)
leads (1)
out (1)
pluck out (1)
put out (1)
put outside (1)
puts out (1)
reject (1)
sent (1)
sent away (1)
sent off (1)
sent out (1)
take out of (1)
throw (1)
throw outside (1)
throwing (1)
took out (1)

1676 ἔκβασις *ekbasis* (2)
outcome (1)
way out (1)

1677 ἐκβλαστάνω *ekblastanō*
Variant; not used

1678 ἐκβολή *ekbolē* (1)
throw the cargo overboard (1)

1679 ἐκγαμίζω *ekgamizō*
Variant; not used

1680 ἐκγαμίσκω *ekgamiskō*
Variant; not used

1681 ἔκγονος *ekgonos* (1)
grandchildren (1)

1682 ἐκδαπανάω *ekdapanaō* (1)
everything I have expend (1)

1683 ἐκδέχομαι *ekdechomai* (6)

expecting (1)
looking forward to (1)
wait for (1)
waiting for (1)
waits (1)
waits for (1)

1684 ἔκδηλος *ekdēlos* (1)
clear (1)

1685 ἐκδημέω *ekdēmeō* (3)
away from (2)
away (1)

1686 ἐκδίδωμι *ekdidōmi* (4)
rented (3)
rent (1)

1687 ἐκδιηγέομαι *ekdiēgeomai* (2)
told (1)
told how (1)

1688 ἐκδικέω *ekdikeō* (6)
avenge (1)
avenged (1)
justice (1)
punish (1)
see that gets justice (1)
take revenge (1) +4932

1689 ἐκδίκησις *ekdikēsis* (9)
avenge (2)
justice (2)
avenged (1) +4472
punish (1)
punish (1) +1443
punishment (1)
readiness to see justice done (1)

1690 ἔκδικος *ekdikos* (2)
agent to bring punishment (1)
punish (1)

1691 ἐκδιώκω *ekdiōkō* (1)
drove out (1)

1692 ἔκδοτος *ekdotos* (1)
handed over (1)

1693 ἐκδοχή *ekdochē* (1)
expectation (1)

1694 ἐκδύω *ekdyō* (5)
took off (2)
stripped (1)
stripped of clothes (1)
unclothed (1)

1695 ἐκεῖ *ekei* (106)
there (72)
where (13)
here (2)
nearby (2)
at Berea[s] (1)
at his house (1)
but in the other case (1) +1254
in (1)
in that place (1)
lived (1) +1639
stayed (1) +3531
to the grove[s] (1)
untranslated (9)

1696 ἐκεῖθεν *ekeithen* (37)
from there (12)
that place (3)
there (3)
from that place (2)
from (1)
left (1) +2002
left that place (1)
left there (1) +3553
on (1)
on each side (1) +1949+2779
that (1)
that town[s] (1)
the synagogue[s] (1)
then (1)

where (1)
withdrew (1) +432
untranslated (5)

1697 ἐκεῖνος *ekeinos* (264)
that (99)
he (29)
those (28)
they (15)
this (9)
them (7)
him (6)
his (3)
she (3)
the (3)
these (3)
he himself (2)
that same (2)
that very (2)
the former[s] (2)
the man[s] (2)
the one (2)
their (2)
who (2)
he[s] (1) +476+3836
himself (1)
his disciples[s] (1)
it (1)
Jesus Christ[s] (1)
Jesus[s] (1)
John[s] (1)
Judas[s] (1)
Mary[s] (1)
next (1)
others (1)
Priscilla and Aquila[s] (1)
same (1)
that was the time (1) +1877+2465+3836
the disciples[s] (1)
the father[s] (1)
the other (1)
your brother[s] (1)
untranslated (25)

1698 ἐκεῖσε *ekeise* (2)
there (1)
where (1)

1699 ἐκζητέω *ekzēteō* (7)
earnestly seek (1)
held responsible (1)
held responsible for (1)
searched intently and with the greatest care
　　　　　　(1) +2001+2779
seek (1)
seeks (1)
sought (1)

1700 ἐκζήτησις *ekzētēsis* (1)
controversies (1)

1701 ἐκθαμβέω *ekthambeō* (4)
alarmed (2)
deeply distressed (1)
overwhelmed with wonder (1)

1702 ἔκθαμβος *ekthambos* (1)
astonished (1)

1703 ἐκθαυμάζω *ekthaumazō* (1)
amazed (1)

1704 ἔκθετος *ekthetos* (1)
throw out (1)

1705 ἐκκαθαίρω *ekkathairō* (2)
cleanses (1)
get rid of (1)

1706 ἐκκαίω *ekkaiō* (1)
inflamed (1)

1707 ἐκκακέω *ekkakeō*
Variant; not used

1708 ἐκκεντέω *ekkenteō* (2)
pierced (2)

1709 ἐκκλάω *ekklaō* (3)
broken off (3)

1710 ἐκκλείω *ekkleiō* (2)
alienate (1)
excluded (1)

1711 ἐκκλησία *ekklēsia* (114)
church (74)
churches (34)
assembly (4)
congregation (1)
congregations (1)

1712 ἐκκλίνω *ekklinō* (3)
away (1)
turn (1)
turned away (1)

1713 ἐκκολυμβάω *ekkolymbaō* (1)
swimming away (1)

1714 ἐκκομίζω *ekkomizō* (1)
carried out (1)

1715 ἐκκοπή *ekkopē*
Variant; not used

1716 ἐκκόπτω *ekkoptō* (10)
cut down (5)
cut off (3)
cut from under (1)
cut out (1)

1717 ἐκκρεμάννυμι *ekkremannymi* (1)
hung on (1)

1718 ἐκλαλέω *eklaleō* (1)
tell (1)

1719 ἐκλάμπω *eklampō* (1)
shine (1)

1720 ἐκλανθάνομαι *eklanthanomai* (1)
forgotten (1)

1721 ἐκλέγομαι *eklegomai* (22)
chosen (9)
chose (8)
choose (3)
made a choice (1)
picked (1)

1722 ἐκλείπω *ekleipō* (4)
end (1)
fail (1)
gone (1)
stopped shining (1)

1723 ἐκλεκτός *eklektos* (22)
chosen (12)
elect (10)

1724 ἐκλογή *eklogē* (7)
chosen (3)
election (3)
elect (1)

1725 ἐκλύω *eklyō* (5)
collapse (2)
give up (1)
lose (1)
lose heart (1)

1726 ἐκμάσσω *ekmassō* (5)
wiped (4)
drying (1)

1727 ἐκμυκτηρίζω *ekmyktērizō* (2)
sneered at (1)
sneering at (1)

1728 ἐκνεύω *ekneuō* (1)
slipped away (1)

1729 ἐκνήφω *eknēphō* (1)
come back to senses (1)

1730 ἑκούσιος *hekousios* (1)
spontaneous (1) +2848

1731 ἑκουσίως *hekousiōs* (2)

deliberately (1)
willing (1)

1732 ἔκπαλαι *ekpalai* (2)
long (1)
long ago (1)

1733 ἐκπειράζω *ekpeirazō* (4)
put to the test (2)
test (2)

1734 ἐκπέμπω *ekpempō* (2)
sent away (1)
sent on way (1)

1735 ἐκπερισσῶς *ekperissōs* (1)
emphatically (1)

1736 ἐκπετάννυμι *ekpetannymi* (1)
held out (1)

1737 ἐκπηδάω *ekpēdaō* (1)
rushed out (1)

1738 ἐκπίπτω *ekpiptō* (10)
run aground (2)
dashed (1)
failed (1)
fall (1)
fall away (1)
fall from (1)
fallen away from (1)
falls (1)
fell off (1)

1739 ἐκπλέω *ekpleō* (3)
sailed (3)

1740 ἐκπληρόω *ekplēroō* (1)
fulfilled (1)

1741 ἐκπλήρωσις *ekplērōsis* (1)
end (1)

1742 ἐκπλήσσω *ekplēssō* (13)
amazed (9)
astonished (3)
overwhelmed with amazement (1) +5669

1743 ἐκπνέω *ekpneō* (3)
breathed his last (2)
died (1)

1744 ἐκπορεύομαι *ekporeuomai* (33)
come out (3)
comes out (3)
leaving (3)
out came (2)
went out (2)
came from (1)
came out (1)
come (1)
comes (1)
comes from (1)
coming out (1)
flowing from (1)
from came (1)
go out (1)
goes out (1)
going (1)
leave (1)
left (1)
moved about freely (1) +1660+2779
out come (1)
out comes (1)
out of (1)
spread (1)
started (1)
went (1)

1745 ἐκπορνεύω *ekporneuō* (1)
gave up to sexual immorality (1)

1746 ἐκπτύω *ekptyō* (1)
scorn (1)

1747 ἐκπυρόω *ekpyroō*
Variant; not used

1748 ἐκριζόω *ekrizoō* (4)

uprooted (2)
pulled up by the roots (1)
root up (1)

1749 ἔκστασις *ekstasis* (7)
trance (2)
amazed (1) +3284
amazement (1)
astonished (1) +2014
bewildered (1)
fell into trance (1) +1181+2093

1750 ἐκστρέφω *ekstrephō* (1)
warped (1)

1751 ἐκσῴζω *eksōzō*
Variant; not used

1752 ἐκταράσσω *ektarassō* (1)
throwing into an uproar (1)

1753 ἐκτείνω *ekteinō* (16)
stretch out (5)
reached out (4)
stretched out (2)
lay (1)
lower (1)
motioned with (1)
pointing (1) +899+3836+5931
reached for (1) +3836+5931

1754 ἐκτελέω *ekteleō* (2)
finish (2)

1755 ἐκτένεια *ekteneia* (1)
earnestly (1) +1877

1756 ἐκτενής *ektenēs* (1)
deeply (1)

1757 ἐκτενῶς *ektenōs* (3)
earnestly (2)
deeply (1)

1758 ἐκτίθημι *ektithēmi* (4)
explained (3)
placed outside (1)

1759 ἐκτινάσσω *ektinassō* (4)
shake off (2)
shook from (1)
shook out (1)

1760 ἐκτός *ektos* (8)
outside (2)
unless (2) +1623+3590
beyond (1)
not include (1)
otherwise (1) +1623+3590
out of (1)

1761 ἕκτος *hektos* (14)
sixth (13)
noon (1) +6052

1762 ἐκτρέπω *ektrepō* (5)
disabled (1)
turn aside (1)
turn away from (1)
turned away (1)
wandered away from (1)

1763 ἐκτρέφω *ektrephō* (2)
bring up (1)
feeds (1)

1764 ἔκτρομος *ektromos*
Variant; not used

1765 ἔκτρωμα *ektrōma* (1)
abnormally born (1)

1766 ἐκφέρω *ekpherō* (8)
carried out (2)
bring (1)
brought (1)
carry out (1)
led (1)
produces (1)
take out of (1)

1767 ἐκφεύγω *ekpheugō* (8)
escape (5)
escaped (1)
ran out (1)
slipped through (1)

1768 ἐκφοβέω *ekphobeō* (1)
frighten (1)

1769 ἔκφοβος *ekphobos* (2)
so frightened (1)
with fear (1)

1770 ἐκφύω *ekphyō* (2)
come out (2)

1771 ἐκφωνέω *ekphōneō*
Variant; not used

1772 ἐκχέω *ekcheō* (27)
poured out (14)
shed (5)
pour out (3)
run out (2)
rushed (1)
scattered (1)
spilled out (1)

1773 ἐκχύννομαι *ekchynnomai*
Variant; not used

1774 ἐκχωρέω *ekchōreō* (1)
get out (1)

1775 ἐκψύχω *ekpsychō* (3)
died (3)

1776 ἑκών *hekōn* (2)
by its own choice (1)
voluntarily (1)

1777 ἐλαία *elaia* (15)
olives (10)
mount of olives (2)
olive (1)
olive tree (1)
olive trees (1)

1778 ἔλαιον *elaion* (11)
oil (9)
olive oil (2)

1779 ἐλαιών *elaiōn* (1)
mount of olives (1)

1780 Ἐλαμίτης *Elamitēs* (1)
Elamites (1)

1781 ἐλάσσων *elassōn* (4)
cheaper (1)
lesser (1)
younger (1)
untranslated (1)

1782 ἐλαττονέω *elattoneō* (1)
have too little (1)

1783 ἐλαττόω *elattoō* (3)
made lower (2)
less (1)

1784 ἐλάττων *elattōn*
Variant; not used

1785 ἐλαύνω *elaunō* (5)
driven (3)
oars (1)
rowed (1)

1786 ἐλαφρία *elaphria* (1)
lightly (1)

1787 ἐλαφρός *elaphros* (2)
light (2)

1788 ἐλάχιστος *elachistos* (14)
least (7)
very little (3)
very small (2)
care very little (1) +1639+1650
trivial (1)

1789 Ἐλεάζαρ *Eleazar* (2)
Eleazar (2)

1790 ἐλεάω *eleaō*
Variant; not used

1791 ἐλεγμός *elegmos* (1)
rebuking (1)

1792 ἔλεγξις *elenxis* (1)
rebuked (1) +2400

1793 ἔλεγχος *elenchos* (1)
certain (1)

1794 ἐλέγχω *elenchō* (17)
rebuke (3)
exposed (2)
rebuked (2)
convict (1)
convict of guilt (1)
convicted (1)
convinced that is a sinner (1)
correct (1)
expose (1)
prove guilty (1)
rebukes (1)
refute (1)
show fault (1)

1795 ἐλεεινός *eleeinos* (2)
pitied more than (1)
pitiful (1)

1796 ἐλεέω *eleeō* (32)
have mercy on (11)
mercy (4)
had mercy on (3)
received mercy (3)
shown mercy (3)
have pity (2)
be merciful to (1)
had[s] (1)
has mercy on (1)
receive mercy (1)
showing mercy (1)
to show mercy (1)

1797 ἐλεημοσύνη *eleēmosynē* (13)
gifts to the poor (2)
give to the needy (2) +4472
give to the poor (2) +1443
beg (1) +160+3836
begging (1) +3836+4639
gave to in need (1) +4472
gifts for the poor (1)
giving (1)
helping the poor (1) +4472
money (1) +3284

1798 ἐλεήμων *eleēmōn* (2)
merciful (2)

1799 ἔλεος *eleos* (27)
mercy (24)
merciful (2)
tender mercy (1) +5073

1800 ἐλευθερία *eleutheria* (11)
freedom (10)
be free (1)

1801 ἐλεύθερος *eleutheros* (23)
free (18)
exempt (1)
free and belong to no man (1) +1666+4246
gain freedom (1) +1181
released (1)
set free (1)

1802 ἐλευθερόω *eleutheroō* (7)
set free (5)
liberated (1)
sets free (1)

ἔλευσις *eleusis* (1)
...ning (1)

...άντινος *elephantinos* (1)

ivory (1)

1805 Ἐλιακείμ *Eliakeim*
Variant; not used

1806 Ἐλιακίμ *Eliakim* (3)
Eliakim (3)

1807 ἕλιγμα *heligma*
Variant; not used

1808 Ἐλιέζερ *Eliezer* (1)
Eliezer (1)

1809 Ἐλιούδ *Elioud* (2)
Eliud (2)

1810 Ἐλισάβετ *Elisabet* (9)
Elizabeth (9)

1811 Ἐλισαῖος *Elisaios* (1)
Elisha (1)

1812 Ἐλισσαῖος *Elissaios*
Variant; not used

1813 ἑλίσσω *helissō* (2)
roll up (1)
rolling up (1)

1814 ἕλκος *helkos* (3)
sores (3)

1815 ἑλκόω *helkoō* (1)
covered with sores (1)

1816 ἑλκύω *helkyō* (8)
dragged (3)
dragging (1)
draw (1)
draws (1)
drew (1)
haul in (1)

1817 Ἑλλάς *Hellas* (1)
Greece (1)

1818 Ἕλλην *Hellēn* (25)
Greeks (14)
Greek (5)
gentile (4)
gentiles (2)

1819 Ἑλληνικός *Hellēnikos* (1)
Greek (1)

1820 Ἑλληνίς *Hellēnis* (2)
Greek (2)

1821 Ἑλληνιστής *Hellēnistēs* (3)
Grecian Jews (2)
Greeks (1)

1822 Ἑλληνιστί *Hellēnisti* (2)
Greek (2)

1823 ἐλλογάω *ellogaō* (1)
charge (1)

1824 ἐλλογέω *ellogeō* (1)
taken into account (1)

1825 Ἐλμαδάμ *Elmadam* (1)
Elmadam (1)

1826 Ἐλμωδάμ *Elmōdam*
Variant; not used

1827 ἐλπίζω *elpizō* (31)
hope (11)
put hope (4)
hope for (2)
hoped (2)
hoping (2)
set hope (2)
expect (1)
expected (1)
have hope (1) +1639
hopes (1)
hopes are set (1)
hopes for (1)
puts hope (1)
trust (1)

1828 ἐλπίς *elpis* (53)
hope (51)
all hope (1)
untranslated (1)

1829 Ἐλύμας *Elymas* (1)
Elymas (1)

1830 ἐλωΐ *elōi* (4)
Eloi (4)

1831 ἐμαυτοῦ *emautou* (37)
myself (17)
my own (7)
me (4)
my (3)
I (2)
my own accord (2)
my (1) +3836+4309
untranslated (1)

1832 ἐμβαίνω *embainō* (16)
got (10)
get (2)
got into (2)
getting (1)
stepped (1)

1833 ἐμβάλλω *emballō* (1)
throw (1)

1834 ἐμβαπτίζω *embaptizō*
Variant; not used

1835 ἐμβάπτω *embaptō* (2)
dipped (1)
dips (1)

1836 ἐμβατεύω *embateuō* (1)
goes into great detail about (1)

1837 ἐμβιβάζω *embibazō* (1)
put on board (1) +899+1650

1838 ἐμβλέπω *emblepō* (12)
looked at (4)
saw (2)
blinded (1) +4024
look at (1)
looked closely at (1)
looked directly at (1)
looked straight at (1)
looking (1)

1839 ἐμβριμάομαι *embrimaomai* (5)
deeply moved (2)
rebuked harshly (1)
strong warning (1)
warned sternly (1)

1840 ἐμέω *emeō* (1)
spit (1)

1841 ἐμμαίνομαι *emmainomai* (1)
obsession (1) +4360

1842 Ἐμμανουήλ *Emmanouēl* (1)
Immanuel (1)

1843 Ἐμμαοῦς *Emmaous* (1)
Emmaus (1)

1844 ἐμμένω *emmenō* (4)
continue (1)
remain faithful to (1)
remain true to (1)
stayed in (1)

1845 ἐμμέσω *emmesō*
Variant; not used

1846 Ἐμμώρ *Hemmōr* (1)
Hamor (1)

1847 ἐμός *emos* (73)
my (43)
my own (9)
mine (5)
I (4)
me (4)
for me (3)

I have (2) +3836
itˢ (1) +993+3836+3836
itˢ (1) +3836
myself (1)

1848 ἐμπαιγμονή *empaigmonē* (1)
scoffing (1)

1849 ἐμπαιγμός *empaigmos* (1)
jeers (1)

1850 ἐμπαίζω *empaizō* (13)
mocked (8)
mock (2)
mocking (1)
outwitted (1)
ridicule (1)

1851 ἐμπαίκτης *empaiktēs* (2)
scoffers (2)

1852 ἐμπέμπω *empempō*
Variant; not used

1853 ἐμπεριπατέω *emperipateō* (1)
walk among (1)

1854 ἐμπιμπλάω *empimplaō*
Variant; not used

1855 ἐμπίμπλημι *empimplēmi* (5)
enjoyed company (1)
filled (1)
had enough (1)
provides with plenty (1)
well fed (1)

1856 ἐμπίμπρημι *empimprēmi* (1)
burned (1)

1857 ἐμπιπλάω *empiplaō*
Variant; not used

1858 ἐμπίπλημι *empiplēmi*
Variant; not used

1859 ἐμπίπρημι *empiprēmi*
Variant; not used

1860 ἐμπίπτω *empiptō* (7)
fall (5)
falls (1)
fell (1)

1861 ἐμπλέκω *emplekō* (2)
entangled in (1)
involved in (1)

1862 ἐμπλοκή *emplokē* (1)
braided (1)

1863 ἐμπνέω *empneō* (1)
breathing out (1)

1864 ἐμπορεύομαι *emporeuomai* (2)
carry on business (1)
exploit (1)

1865 ἐμπορία *emporia* (1)
business (1)

1866 ἐμπόριον *emporion* (1)
market (1) +3875

1867 ἔμπορος *emporos* (5)
merchants (4)
merchant (1) +476

1868 ἐμπρήθω *emprēthō*
Variant; not used

1869 ἔμπροσθεν *emprosthen* (47)
before (19)
in front of (7)
ahead (4)
at (2)
in presence (2)
in the presence (3)
surpassed (2) +1181
in faces (1)
in front (1)
in full view of (1)

on ahead (1)
to (1)
your (1) +5148
untranslated (2)

1870 ἐμπτύω *emptyō* (6)
spit on (3)
spit (2)
spit at (1)

1871 ἐμφανής *emphanēs* (2)
revealed (1) +1181
seen (1)

1872 ἐμφανίζω *emphanizō* (10)
show (3)
brought charges (2)
appear (1)
appeared (1)
appeared and presented the charges (1)
petition (1)
reported (1)

1873 ἔμφοβος *emphobos* (5)
afraid (1)
fright (1) +1181
frightened (1)
in fear (1) +1181
terrified (1)

1874 ἐμφυσάω *emphysaō* (1)
breathed on (1)

1875 ἔμφυτος *emphytos* (1)
planted in (1)

1876 ἐμφωνέω *emphōneō*
Variant; not used

1877 ἐν *en* (2749)
in (1415)
with (152)
by (140)
at (134)
on (92)
among (87)
to (37)
through (34)
when (24)
of (23)
as (17)
for (17)
among (14) +3545
during (10)
into (10)
about (8)
when (8) +3836
within (8)
because of (6)
this is how (6) +4047
throughout (6) +3910
when (6) +4005
on account of (5)
soon (5) +5443
under (5)
against (4)
from (4)
how (4) +5515
out of (4)
where (4) +4005
while (4)
according to (3)
everywhere (3) +4246+5536
pregnant women (3) +1143+2400
there (3) +899
while (3) +3836
while (3) +4005
along (2)
as (2) +3836
here (2) +4047
how (2)
I (2) +1609
in (2) +3545
over (2)
subject to bleeding (2) +135+4868

throughout (2)
to himself (2) +899+2840+3836
while in (2)
with child (2) +1143+2400
a public figure (1) +4244
across (1)
after he was circumcised (1) +1639+4364
after this (1) +2759+3836
alive (1) +899
always (1) +2789+4246
as a fool (1) +932
as a man (1) +4922
as has just been said (1) +3306+3836
as of first importance (1) +4755
at the time of (1)
because (1) +4005
before (1)
before (1) +3545
before (1) +3545+3836
before circumcised (1) +213
before the group (1) +3545
believe (1) +4409
belong to (1)
besides (1)
both of them (1) +4005
brag (1) +224+3836
briefly (1) +3900
by (1) +5931
by the power of (1)
caused by (1)
cheerfully (1) +2660
clearly (1) +4244
complete (1) +4246
conceived (1) +3120+3836+5197
confident (1) +5712
contained (1) +2400
contained (1) +5639
diligently (1) +5082
doesˢ (1) +3531+5148
done by (1)
down (1)
earnestly (1) +1755
elsewhere (1) +2283
enemies (1) +2397
figuratively (1) +4231
figuratively speaking (1) +4130
for (1) +3545+3836
for work (1) +1256+2237+4005
from among (1)
generously (1) +605
gently (1) +4460+4559
gently (1) +4559
glorious (1) +1518
go I wish you well (1) +1645+5632
had (1) +1639
had authority (1) +1639+2026
have gone without sleep (1) +71
heˢ (1) +899+899+3836+4460
heavenly things (1) +3836+4041
here (1) +899
here (1) +1609
himˢ (1) +476+3836+4047
holy (1) +43
humbly (1) +4559
immediately (1) +899+3836+6052
immediately (1) +5443
imperishable (1) +914
in accordance with (1)
in presence (1)
in spite of (1)
in the cause of (1)
inside (1)
inwardly (1) +1571
inwardly (1) +3220+3836
its (1) +899
Jews (1) +1169+1609+3836
legalistic (1) +3795
made think (1) +2840+3836+5502
make up mind (1) +2840+3836+5502
meanwhile (1) +3568+3836
met personally (1) +3836+3972+4725+4922

native (1) +1164+4005
near (1)
next (1)
observing (1) +4513
of you (1) +1639+3836+5148
old (1) +2465+4581
on board (1) +3836+4450
on journey (1) +4513
one Sabbath (1) +3836+4879
one Sabbath (1) +4879
outward (1) +3836+5745
outwardly (1) +3836+5745
outwardly (1) +4922
painful (1) +3383
perfectly (1) +4246
perishable (1) +5785
poor (1) +141
preaching (1) +3364
pregnant (1) +1143+2400
pregnant woman (1) +1143+2400
put to death (1) +633+5840
quick (1) +5443
quickly (1) +5443
relationship to (1)
release (1) +690+912
returned (1) +2059+3836
righteous (1) +1466
safe (1) +1645
secret (1) +3696
securely (1) +854+4246
short time (1) +3900
show favoritism (1) +4721
sleeping (1) +2761
sly (1) +1515
so powerfully (1) +1539
soon afterward (1) +2009+3836
staying away from (1) +4024+4344
that was the time (1) +1697+2465+3836
there (1) +3545
there (1) +3836+5536
there^s (1) +2639+3836
there^s (1) +3836+4047+4484
Thessalonians (1) +2553
this kind of^s (1) +4231
this makes (1) +4047
thus (1) +4047
to himself (1) +1571
today (1) +2465+3836+4958
true (1) +237
truly (1) +237
uncircumcised (1) +213
united with (1)
unseen (1) +3220+3836
unseen (1) +3224+3836
until (1) +4005
use deception (1) +4111+4344
wear (1)
what (1) +5515
when (1) +2465
where (1) +4005+5536
while (1) +1639+3836
who are there (1) +899
with (1) +3545
with child (1) +1143+5197
with regard to (1) +3538
with the help of (1)
within (1) +3517+3836
wondered about (1) +2840+3836+5502
you have (1) +5148
your (1) +5148
untranslated (267)

1878 ἐναγκαλίζομαι *enankalizomai* (2)
taking in his arms (1)
took in arms (1)

1879 ἐνάλιος *enalios* (1)
creatures of sea (1)

1880 ἐνάλλομαι *enallomai*
Variant; not used

        ἀνθρωπέω *enanthrōpeō*

Variant; not used

1882 ἔναντι *enanti* (2)
before (2)

1883 ἐναντίον *enantion* (9)
before (2)
against (1)
but (1) +1254+3836
in public (1) +3295+3836
in the sight (1)
instead (1) +3437+3836
on contrary (1) +247
untranslated (1)

1884 ἐναντιόομαι *enantioomai*
Variant; not used

1885 ἐναντίος *enantios* (7)
against (3)
hostile (1)
in front of (1) +1666
oppose (1)
oppose (1) +1666

1886 ἐναργής *enargēs*
Variant; not used

1887 ἐνάρχομαι *enarchomai* (2)
began (1)
beginning (1)

1888 ἔνατος *enatos* (10)
ninth (7)
three in the afternoon (2)
three in the afternoon (1)
+2465+3836+6052

1889 ἐναφίημι *enaphiēmi*
Variant; not used

1890 ἐνδεής *endeēs* (1)
needy (1)

1891 ἔνδειγμα *endeigma* (1)
evidence (1)

1892 ἐνδείκνυμι *endeiknymi* (11)
show (5)
display (2)
show that (2)
did (1)
shown (1)

1893 ἔνδειξις *endeixis* (4)
demonstrate (2)
proof (1)
sign (1)

1894 ἔνδεκα *hendeka* (6)
eleven (6)

1895 ἐνδέκατος *hendekatos* (3)
eleventh (3)

1896 ἐνδέχομαι *endechomai* (1)
can (1)

1897 ἐνδημέω *endēmeō* (3)
at home (3)

1898 ἐνδιδύσκω *endidyskō* (2)
dressed in (1)
put on (1)

1899 ἔνδικος *endikos* (2)
deserved (1)
just (1)

1900 ἐνδόμησις *endomēsis*
Variant; not used

1901 ἐνδοξάζομαι *endoxazomai* (2)
glorified (2)

1902 ἔνδοξος *endoxos* (4)
expensive (1)
honored (1)
radiant (1)
wonderful (1)

1903 ἔνδυμα *endyma* (8)
clothes (7)

clothing (1)

1904 ἐνδυναμόω *endynamoō* (7)
strong (2)
gave strength (1)
given strength (1)
gives strength (1)
powerful (1)
strengthened (1)

1905 ἐνδύνω *endynō* (1)
worm way (1)

1906 ἔνδυσις *endysis* (1)
untranslated (1)

1907 ἐνδύω *endyō* (28)
put on (7)
clothe with (3)
clothed with (3)
dressed in (3)
wear (2)
wearing (2)
clothed (1)
in place (1)
putting on (1)
wore clothing (1) +1639
worn (1)
untranslated (3)

1908 ἐνδώμησις *endōmēsis* (1)
untranslated (1)

1909 ἐνέδρα *enedra* (2)
ambush (1)
plot (1)

1910 ἐνεδρεύω *enedreuō* (2)
waiting (1)
waiting in ambush for (1)

1911 ἔνεδρον *enedron*
Variant; not used

1912 ἐνειλέω *eneileō* (1)
wrapped in (1)

1913 ἔνειμι *eneimi* (7)
is (3)
change (1) +4164
inside (1)
untranslated (2)

1914 ἔνεκα *heneka*
Variant; not used

1915 ἔνεκεν *heneken* (24)
for (4)
because (4)
for reason (2)
for the sake of (2)
on account (4)
sake (2)
for sake (1)
of (1)
that (1)
why (1)
why (1) +5515
untranslated (1)

1916 ἐνενήκοντα *enenēkonta* (4)
ninety-nine (4) +1933

1917 ἐνεός *eneos* (1)
speechless (1)

1918 ἐνέργεια *energeia* (8)
power (2)
work (2)
working (2)
energy (1)
powerful (1)

1919 ἐνεργέω *energeō* (21)
at work in (8)
works in (2)
act (1)
at work (1)
at work within (1)

effective (1)
exerted in (1)
expressing (1)
produces in (1)
work (1)
work among (1)
works (1)
works out (1)

1920 ἐνέργημα *energēma* (2)
miraculous powers (1) *+1539*
working (1)

1921 ἐνεργής *energēs* (3)
active (2)
effective work (1)

1922 ἐνευλογέω *eneulogeō* (2)
blessed (1)
blessed through (1)

1923 ἐνέχω *enechō* (3)
burdened (1)
nursed a grudge against (1)
oppose (1)

1924 ἐνθάδε *enthade* (8)
here (6)
back (1)
there (1)

1925 ἔνθεν *enthen* (2)
from here (2)

1926 ἐνθυμέομαι *enthymeomai* (2)
considered (1)
entertain thoughts (1)

1927 ἐνθύμησις *enthymēsis* (4)
thoughts (3)
design (1)

1928 ἔνι *eni*
Variant; not used

1929 ἐνιαυτός *eniautos* (14)
year (10)
years (2)
annual (1) *+2848*
year after year (1) *+2848*

1930 ἐνίοτε *eniote*
Variant; not used

1931 ἐνίστημι *enistēmi* (7)
present (3)
the present (2)
be (1)
come (1)

1932 ἐνισχύω *enischyō* (2)
regained strength (1)
strengthened (1)

1933 ἐννέα *ennea* (5)
ninety-nine (4) *+1916*
nine (1)

1934 ἐννεός *enneos*
Variant; not used

1935 ἐννεύω *enneuō* (1)
made signs (1)

1936 ἔννοια *ennoia* (2)
attitude (1)
attitudes (1)

1937 ἔννομος *ennomos* (2)
legal (1)
under law (1)

1938 ἐννόμως *ennomōs*
Variant; not used

1939 ἔννυχος *ennychos* (1)
while it was still dark (1)

1940 ἐνοικέω *enoikeō* (5)
lives in (2)
dwell in (1)
live with (1)

lived in (1)

1941 ἐνορκίζω *enorkizō* (1)
charge before (1)

1942 ἑνότης *henotēs* (2)
unity (2)

1943 ἐνοχλέω *enochleō* (2)
cause trouble (1)
troubled (1)

1944 ἔνοχος *enochos* (10)
guilty (2)
subject (2)
worthy (2)
answerable (1)
guilty of sinning against (1)
held (1)
in danger (1)

1945 ἔνταλμα *entalma* (3)
rules (2)
commands (1)

1946 ἐνταφιάζω *entaphiazō* (2)
burial (1)
prepare for burial (1)

1947 ἐνταφιασμός *entaphiasmos* (2)
burial (2)

1948 ἐντέλλω *entellō* (15)
command (6)
commanded (4)
commanded to keep (1)
gave instructions (1)
giving instructions (1)
instructed (1)
tells (1)

1949 ἐντεῦθεν *enteuthen* (9)
from (1)
from another place (1)
from here (1)
here (1)
leave (1) *+72*
of here (1)
on each side (1) *+1696+2779*
one on each side (1) *+1949+2779*
this place (1)

1950 ἔντευξις *enteuxis* (2)
intercession (1)
prayer (1)

1951 ἐντίθημι *entithēmi*
Variant; not used

1952 ἔντιμος *entimos* (5)
precious (2)
honor (1) *+2400*
person more distinguished than (1)
valued highly (1) *+1639*

1953 ἐντολή *entolē* (67)
command (17)
commands (15)
commandment (13)
commandments (10)
commanded (2) *+1443*
orders (2)
commanded (1) *+3284*
instructions (1)
law (1)
one^s (1)
regulation (1)
requires (1)
with instructions (1) *+3284*
untranslated (1)

1954 ἐντόπιος *entopios* (1)
people there (1)

1955 ἐντός *entos* (2)
inside (1)
within (1)

1956 ἐντρέπω *entrepō* (9)

respect (3)
ashamed (1)
care about (1)
cared about (1)
feel ashamed (1)
respected (1)
shame (1)

1957 ἐντρέφω *entrephō* (1)
brought up (1)

1958 ἔντρομος *entromos* (3)
trembled with fear (1) *+1181*
trembling (1)
trembling (1) *+1181*

1959 ἐντροπή *entropē* (2)
shame (2)

1960 ἐντρυφάω *entryphaō* (1)
reveling (1)

1961 ἐντυγχάνω *entynchanō* (5)
appealed (1)
intercede (1)
intercedes (1)
interceding (1)
petitioned (1)

1962 ἐντυλίσσω *entylissō* (3)
wrapped (2)
folded up (1)

1963 ἐντυπόω *entypoō* (1)
engraved (1)

1964 ἐνυβρίζω *enybrizō* (1)
insulted (1)

1965 ἐνυπνιάζομαι *enypniazomai* (2)
dream (1)
dreamers (1)

1966 ἐνύπνιον *enypnion* (1)
dreams (1)

1967 ἐνώπιον *enōpion* (94)
before (37)
in the presence (9)
in the sight (5)
in front of (4)
in the eyes (4)
to (4)
against (2)
in presence (2)
in sight (2)
on behalf (2)
publicly (2) *+4246*
sight (2)
at (1)
by (1)
entice (1) *+965+4998*
in full view of (1)
in his sight (1) *+899*
on behalf of (1)
publicly (1) *+3836+4436*
with (1)
untranslated (11)

1968 Ἐνώς *Enōs* (1)
Enosh (1)

1969 ἐνωτίζομαι *enōtizomai* (1)
listen carefully (1)

1970 Ἑνώχ *Henōch* (3)
Enoch (3)

1971 ἕξ *hex* (13)
six (7)
half (2) *+3604*
276 (1) *+1357+1573*
666 (1) *+1980+2008*
a half (1) *+3604*
forty-six (1) *+2779+5477*

1972 ἐξαγγέλλω *exangellō* (1)
declare (1)

1973 ἐξαγοράζω *exagorazō* (4)
make the most of opportunity (1)
+2789+3836

making the most of (1)
redeem (1)
redeemed from (1)

1974 ἐξάγω *exagō* (12)
led out (6)
brought out (2)
escort out (1)
escorted (1)
lead out (1)
leads out (1)

1975 ἐξαιρέω *exaireō* (8)
rescued (3)
gouge out (2)
rescue (2)
set free (1)

1976 ἐξαίρω *exairō* (1)
expel (1)

1977 ἐξαιτέω *exaiteō* (1)
asked (1)

1978 ἐξαίφνης *exaiphnēs* (5)
suddenly (5)

1979 ἐξακολουθέω *exakoloutheō* (3)
follow (3)

1980 ἐξακόσιοι *hexakosioi* (2)
1,600 (1) +5943
666 (1) +1971+2008

1981 ἐξαλείφω *exaleiphō* (5)
blot out from (1)
canceled (1)
wipe away from (1)
wipe from (1)
wiped out (1)

1982 ἐξάλλομαι *exallomai* (1)
jumped (1)

1983 ἐξανάστασις *exanastasis* (1)
resurrection (1)

1984 ἐξανατέλλω *exanatellō* (2)
sprang up (2)

1985 ἐξανίστημι *exanistēmi* (3)
have children (2) +5065
stood up (1)

1986 ἐξανοίγω *exanoigō*
Variant; not used

1987 ἐξαπατάω *exapataō* (6)
deceive (3)
deceived (3)

1988 ἐξάπινα *exapina* (1)
suddenly (1)

1989 ἐξαπορέω *exaporeō* (2)
despaired (1)
in despair (1)

1990 ἐξαποστέλλω *exapostellō* (12)
sent (7)
sent away (3)
send (1)
sent off (1)

1991 ἐξαρτάω *exartaō*
Variant; not used

1992 ἐξαρτίζω *exartizō* (2)
equipped (1)
up (1)

1993 ἐξαστράπτω *exastraptō* (1)
flash of lightning (1)

1994 ἐξαυτῆς *exautēs* (6)
at once (2)
immediately (1)
right now (1)
right then (1)

untranslated (1)

1995 ἐξεγείρω *exegeirō* (2)
raise (1)
raised up (1)

1996 ἔξειμι1 *exeimi1* (4)
get (1)
leave (1)
leaving (1)
left (1)

1997 ἔξειμι2 *exeimi2*
Variant; not used

1998 ἐξελέγχω *exelenchō*
Variant; not used

1999 ἐξέλκω *exelkō* (1)
dragged away (1)

2000 ἐξέραμα *exerama* (1)
vomit (1)

2001 ἐξεραυνάω *exeraunaō* (1)
searched intently and with the greatest care
(1) +1699+2779

2002 ἐξέρχομαι *exerchomai* (217)
went out (37)
left (21)
came out (19)
come out (14)
go out (11)
leave (11)
came (8)
gone out (7)
went (6)
spread (5)
come (4)
go (4)
set out (4)
gone (3)
leaving (3)
out came (3)
came out of (2)
comes out (2)
coming (2)
get out (2)
go away (2)
going out (2)
got out (2)
landed (2)
leave (2) +2032
out of come (2)
went on (2)
went out from (2)
went out of (2)
at daybreak (1) +1181+2465
bringing (1)
came from (1)
come from (1)
come out of (1) +4047
comes (1)
coming from (1)
descended from (1) +4019
driven out (1)
escaped (1)
flowed out (1)
followed out (1) +199
issued (1)
known (1)
led out (1)
left (1) +1696
left (1) +3854
originate (1)
out (1)
out come (1)
rode out (1)
slipping away from (1)
started (1)
started out (1) +482
stepped (1)
take (1)
walked out (1)

went out (1) +2032
went out (1) +4513
went through (1)
untranslated (1)

2003 ἔξεστι *exesti* (31)
lawful (10)
permissible (4)
unlawful (4) +4024
right (3)
can (1)
have right (1)
have the right (1)
lawful for (1)
lawful for (1) +4024
legal (1)
may (1)
permitted (1)
the law (1)
the law forbids (1) +4024

2004 ἐξετάζω *exetazō* (3)
ask (1)
make a search (1)
search for (1)

2005 ἐξέφνης *exephnēs*
Variant; not used

2006 ἐξέχω *exechō*
Variant; not used

2007 ἐξηγέομαι *exēgeomai* (6)
told (2)
described (1)
made known (1)
reported (1)
telling about (1)

2008 ἐξήκοντα *hexēkonta* (9)
sixty (5)
1,260 (2) +1357+5943
666 (1) +1971+1980
seven miles (1) +5084

2009 ἑξῆς *hexēs* (5)
next (4)
soon afterward (1) +1877+3836

2010 ἐξηχέω *exēcheō* (1)
rang out (1)

2011 ἕξις *hexis* (1)
use (1)

2012 ἐξιστάνω *existanō*
Variant; not used

2013 ἐξιστάω *existaō*
Variant; not used

2014 ἐξίστημι *existēmi* (17)
amazed (7)
astonished (6)
out of mind (2)
astonished (1) +1749
utterly amazed (1) +2513

2015 ἐξισχύω *exischyō* (1)
power (1)

2016 ἔξοδος *exodos* (3)
departure (2)
exodus from Egypt (1)

2017 ἐξολεθρεύω *exolethreuō* (1)
completely cut off from (1)

2018 ἐξομολογέω *exomologeō* (10)
confess (3)
praise (3)
confessing (2)
consented (1)
openly confessed (1) +334

2019 ἐξορκίζω *exorkizō* (1)
charge under oath (1)

2020 ἐξορκιστής *exorkistēs* (1)
driving out evil spirits (1)

2021 ἐξορύσσω *exoryssō* (2)
digging through (1)
torn out (1)

2022 ἐξουδενέω *exoudeneō* (1)
rejected (1)

2023 ἐξουδενόω *exoudenoō*
Variant; not used

2024 ἐξουθενέω *exoutheneō* (11)
look down on (2)
treat with contempt (2)
amounts to nothing (1)
despised (1)
looked down on (1)
of little account (1)
refuse to accept (1)
rejected (1)
ridiculed (1)

2025 ἐξουθενόω *exouthenoō*
Variant; not used

2026 ἐξουσία *exousia* (102)
authority (53)
power (11)
right (9)
authorities (8)
authority over (2)
charge (2)
control (2)
ability (1)
disposal (1)
dominion (1)
exercise of freedom (1)
had authority (1) +1639+1877
in charge (1)
jurisdiction (1)
kingdom (1)
must (1) +2400
on authority (1) +3284
reigns (1)
rights (1)
with authority (1) +2400
untranslated (2)

2027 ἐξουσιάζω *exousiazō* (4)
belong to (2)
exercise authority over (1)
mastered (1)

2028 ἐξουσιαστικός *exousiastikos*
Variant; not used

2029 ἐξοχή *exochē* (1)
leading (1)

2030 ἐξυπνίζω *exypnizō* (1)
wake up (1)

2031 ἔξυπνος *exypnos* (1)
woke up (1) +1181

2032 ἔξω *exō* (62)
outside (25)
out (17)
away (3)
from (2)
leave (2) +2002
out of (2)
outsiders (2) +3836
foreign (1)
outwardly (1) +476+3836
went out (1) +2002
untranslated (6)

2033 ἔξωθεν *exōthen* (13)
outside (6)
on the outside (2)
from outward (1)
from the outside (1)
outer (1)
outsiders (1)
untranslated (1)

2034 ἐξωθέω *exōtheō* (2)
drove out (1)

run aground (1)

2035 ἐξώτερος *exōteros* (3)
outside (2)
untranslated (1)

2036 ἔοικα *eoika* (2)
like (2)

2037 ἑορτάζω *heortazō* (1)
keep the Festival (1)

2038 ἑορτή *heortē* (25)
feast (22)
Passover feast (1)
religious festival (1)
there[s] (1) +1650+3836

2039 ἐπαγγελία *epangelia* (52)
promise (23)
promised (9)
promises (9)
promised (2) +1181
what was promised (2) +3836
consent (1)
has promised (1)
promised (1) +2040
was promised (1)
what had been promised (1) +3836
what has been promised (1) +3836
what was promised (1)

2040 ἐπαγγέλλομαι *epangellomai* (15)
promised (8)
made promise (2)
promise (2)
profess (1)
professed (1)
promised (1) +2039

2041 ἐπάγγελμα *epangelma* (2)
promise (1)
promises (1)

2042 ἐπάγω *epagō* (3)
bringing on (1)
brought on (1)
make guilty of (1) +2093

2043 ἐπαγωνίζομαι *epagōnizomai* (1)
contend (1)

2044 ἐπαθροίζω *epathroizō* (1)
increased (1)

2045 Ἐπαίνετος *Epainetos* (1)
Epenetus (1)

2046 ἐπαινέω *epaineō* (6)
praise (2)
commended (1)
have praise (1)
sing praises to (1)
untranslated (1)

2047 ἔπαινος *epainos* (11)
praise (7)
commend (1)
commend (1) +2400
praised (1)
praiseworthy (1)

2048 ἐπαίρω *epairō* (19)
looked up (3) +3836+4057
lift up (2)
lifted up (2)
raised (2)
called out (1) +5889
hoisted (1)
look up (1) +3836+4057
looked (1) +3836+4057
looking (1) +3836+4057
open eyes (1) +4057
pushes forward (1)
sets up (1)
shouted (1) +3836+5889
taken up (1)

2049 ἐπαισχύνομαι *epaischynomai* (11)

ashamed of (7)
ashamed (4)

2050 ἐπαιτέω *epaiteō* (2)
beg (1)
begging (1)

2051 ἐπακολουθέω *epakoloutheō* (4)
accompanied (1)
devoting (1)
follow (1)
trail behind (1)

2052 ἐπακούω *epakouō* (1)
heard (1)

2053 ἐπακροάομαι *epakroaomai* (1)
listening (1)

2054 ἐπάν *epan* (3)
when (2)
as soon as (1)

2055 ἐπάναγκες *epanankes* (1)
requirements (1)

2056 ἐπανάγω *epanagō* (3)
put out (2)
on way back (1)

2057 ἐπαναμιμνήσκω *epanamimnēskō* (1)
remind again (1)

2058 ἐπαναπαύομαι *epanapauomai* (2)
rely on (1)
rest on (1)

2059 ἐπανέρχομαι *epanerchomai* (2)
return (1)
returned (1) +1877+3836

2060 ἐπανίστημι *epanistēmi* (2)
rebel against (2)

2061 ἐπανόρθωσις *epanorthōsis* (1)
correcting (1)

2062 ἐπάνω *epanō* (19)
on (7)
over (4)
above (3)
more than (2)
of (1)
take charge of (1) +1181
untranslated (1)

2063 ἐπάρατος *eparatos* (1)
curse on (1)

2064 ἐπαρκέω *eparkeō* (3)
help (2)
helping (1)

2065 ἐπαρχεία *eparcheia* (2)
province (2)

2066 ἐπάρχειος *eparcheios*
Variant; not used

2067 ἐπαρχικός *eparchikos*
Variant; not used

2068 ἔπαυλις *epaulis* (1)
place (1)

2069 ἐπαύριον *epaurion* (17)
next day (15)
following day (2)

2070 ἐπαυτοφώρῳ *epautophōrō*
Variant; not used

2071 Ἐπαφρᾶς *Epaphras* (3)
Epaphras (3)

2072 ἐπαφρίζω *epaphrizō* (1)
foaming up (1)

2073 Ἐπαφρόδιτος *Epaphroditos* (2)
Epaphroditus (2)

2074 ἐπεγείρω *epegeirō* (2)
stirred up (1)
stirred up against (1)

2075 ἐπεί *epei* (26)
since (9)
because (4)
if it could (1)
if it were (1)
if that were so (1)
in that case (1) +726
now if (1)
otherwise (1)
otherwise (1) +726
so (1)
then (1)
untranslated (4)

2076 ἐπειδή *epeidē* (10)
since (4)
because (2)
for (1)
when (1)
untranslated (2)

2077 ἐπειδήπερ *epeidēper* (1)
untranslated (1)

2078 ἐπεῖδον *epeidon* (2)
consider (1)
shown favor (1)

2079 ἔπειμι *epeimi* (5)
next day (3)
following (1)
next (1)

2080 ἐπείπερ *epeiper*
Variant; not used

2081 ἐπεισαγωγή *epeisagōgē* (1)
introduced (1)

2082 ἐπεισέρχομαι *epeiserchomai* (1)
come upon (1)

2083 ἔπειτα *epeita* (16)
then (10)
after that (2)
later (2)
also (1)
and after (1)

2084 ἐπέκεινα *epekeina* (1)
beyond (1)

2085 ἐπεκτείνομαι *epekteinomai* (1)
straining toward (1)

2086 ἐπενδύομαι *ependyomai* (2)
clothed (2)

2087 ἐπενδύτης *ependytēs* (1)
outer garment (1)

2088 ἐπέρχομαι *eperchomai* (9)
happen to (2)
attacks (1)
came (1)
come upon (1)
comes on (1)
coming (1)
coming on (1)
coming upon (1)

2089 ἐπερωτάω *eperōtaō* (56)
asked (35)
ask (5)
question (4)
ask questions (2)
asking (2)
questioned (2)
ask about (1)
ask for (1)
asked about (1)
asking questions (1)
demanded (1)
plied (1)

2090 ἐπερώτημα *eperōtēma* (1)
pledge (1)

2091 ἐπέχω *epechō* (5)
attention (1)
hold out (1)
noticed (1)
stayed a little longer (1) +5989
watch closely (1)

2092 ἐπηρεάζω *epēreazō* (2)
mistreat (1)
speak maliciously against (1)

2093 ἐπί *epi* (888)
on (260)
in (73)
to (71)
at (39)
over (38)
against (34)
for (33)
of (21)
before (15)
upon (14)
by (12)
with (9)
about (8)
because of (5)
around (3)
from (3)
together (3) +899+3836
above (2)
after (2)
among (2)
as long as (2) +4012+5989
because (2)
because (2) +4005
during (2)
generously (2) +2330
in accordance with (2)
in the account (2)
into (2)
landed (2) +1178+2262+3836
reached (2) +1181
reached (2) +2262
right at (2)
seized (2) +1181
seized (2) +2095+3836+5931
toward (2)
whatever (2) +4012
when (2)
a long time (1) +4498
across (1)
along (1)
any further (1) +4498
arrest (1) +2095+3836+5931
arrested (1) +2095+3836+5931
as long as (1) +4012
ashore (1) +1178
assure (1) +237+3306
at the time (1)
bedridden (1) +2879+3187
beside (1)
between (1)
caught in the act (1) +900+2898
certainly (1) +237
come together (1) +899+1639+3836
comes together (1) +899+3836+5302
convened the court (1) +1037+2767+3836
court (1) +1037
covers (1) +3023
decided (1) +326+2840+3836
died (1) +3738
drive out (1)
embraced (1) +2158+3836+5549
facedown (1) +4725
fell into trance (1) +1181+1749
from bad to worse (1) +3836+5937
get very far (1) +4498+4621
holding in (1)
how true (1) +237
in addition (1) +1254
in charge of (1) +1639
in connection with (1)
in front of (1)

in one place (1) +899+3836
in the days of (1)
in the time of (1)
inasmuch as (1) +3525+4012+4036
just then (1) +4047
make guilty of (1) +2042
more and more (1) +4498
near (1)
on and on (1) +4498
on the basis of (1)
only as long as (1) +4012+5989
opposes (1) +482
reached (1)
reaching (1) +1181
resting on (1)
rider (1) +899+2764
riders (1) +899+2764
riders (1) +2764+3836
right (1) +237
spend time (1) +3531+5989
stone (1) +965
struck (1) +2262
that is why (1) +4047
them[s] (1) +1178+2997+3836+3836
threw himself (1) +4406+4725
threw his arms around (1)
                      +2158+3836+5549
throughout (1) +4246
to be impure (1) +174
to face (1)
to overcome (1)
to their number (1) +899+3836
to where (1)
trusted personal servant (1) +3131+3836
under (1)
up to (1)
wearing nothing (1) +1218+4314
what (1) +4005
where (1) +4005
while (1) +4012
you (1) +5148
untranslated (133)

2094 ἐπιβαίνω *epibainō* (6)
arriving in (1)
boarded (1)
came (1)
go on (1)
riding (1)
went on board (1)

2095 ἐπιβάλλω *epiballō* (18)
laid on (2)
seized (2) +2093+3836+5931
seized (2) +3836+5931
sews on (2)
arrest (1) +2093+3836+5931
arrested (1) +2093+3836+5931
arrested (1) +3836+5931
broke (1)
broke down (1)
lay on (1)
puts to (1)
restrict (1) +1105
share (1) +3538
threw over (1)

2096 ἐπιβαρέω *epibareō* (3)
be a burden to (2)
put it too severely (1)

2097 ἐπιβιβάζω *epibibazō* (3)
put on (2)
taken (1)

2098 ἐπιβλέπω *epiblepō* (3)
look at (1)
mindful of (1)
show special attention to (1)

2099 ἐπίβλημα *epiblēma* (4)
patch (4)

2100 ἐπιβοάω *epiboaō*
Variant; not used

2101 ἐπιβουλή *epiboulē* (4)
plot (2)
plan (1)
plots (1)

2102 ἐπιγαμβρεύω *epigambreuō* (1)
marry (1)

2103 ἐπίγειος *epigeios* (7)
earthly (4)
earthly things (2)
on earth (1)

2104 ἐπιγίνομαι *epiginomai* (1)
came up (1)

2105 ἐπιγινώσκω *epiginōskō* (44)
recognized (6)
know (5)
recognize (4)
known (3)
learned (3)
realized (3)
knew (2)
knows (2)
understood (2)
acknowledge (1)
come to understand (1)
find out (1)
found out (1)
fully known (1)
know fully (1)
learn the truth (1)
realize (1)
realized that (1)
recognition (1)
recognizing (1)
took note (1)
understand (1)
verify (1)

2106 ἐπίγνωσις *epignōsis* (20)
knowledge (14)
acknowledge (1) +2262
conscious (1)
full understanding (1)
know (1)
know better (1)
knowing (1)

2107 ἐπιγραφή *epigraphē* (5)
inscription (3)
written notice (2)

2108 ἐπιγράφω *epigraphō* (5)
write on (2)
read (1) +1639
this inscription (1) +4005
written (1)

2109 ἐπιδείκνυμι *epideiknymi* (7)
show (3)
call attention to (1)
make clear (1)
proving (1)
showing (1)

2110 ἐπιδέχομαι *epidechomai* (2)
have (1)
welcome (1)

2111 ἐπιδημέω *epidēmeō* (2)
lived there (1)
visitors from (1)

2112 ἐπιδιατάσσομαι *epidiatassomai* (1)
add to (1)

2113 ἐπιδίδωμι *epididōmi* (9)
give (5)
delivered (1)
gave (1)
gave way (1)
handed (1)

2114 ἐπιδιορθόω *epidiorthoō* (1)
straighten out (1)

2115 ἐπιδύω *epidyō* (1)
go down (1)

2116 ἐπιείκεια *epieikeia* (1)
kind (1)

2117 ἐπιεικής *epieikēs* (6)
considerate (3)
gentleness (2)
gentle (1)

2118 ἐπιζητέω *epizēteō* (13)
looking for (5)
a thorough search made for (1)
asks for (1)
looks for (1)
run after (1)
runs after (1)
sought so earnestly (1)
want to bring up (1)
wanted (1)

2119 ἐπιθανάτιος *epithanatios* (1)
condemned to die (1)

2120 ἐπίθεσις *epithesis* (4)
laying on (3)
laid on (1)

2121 ἐπιθυμέω *epithymeō* (16)
long (3)
covet (2)
desires (2)
longed (2)
want (2)
coveted (1)
did[s] (1)
eagerly desired (1) +2123
longing (1)
lustfully (1) +3836+4639

2122 ἐπιθυμητής *epithymētēs* (1)
setting hearts on (1)

2123 ἐπιθυμία *epithymia* (38)
desires (11)
evil desires (8)
desire (3)
cravings (2)
lust (2)
passions (2)
covetous desire (1)
desire (1) +2400
eagerly desired (1) +2121
evil desire (1)
longed for (1)
longing (1)
lustful desires (1) +816
passionate (1)
sinful desires (1)
what coveting was (1)

2124 ἐπιθύω *epithyō*
Variant; not used

2125 ἐπικαθίζω *epikathizō* (1)
sat (1)

2126 ἐπικαλέω *epikaleō* (29)
called (8)
call on (7)
appeal to (2)
calls on (2)
appealed (1)
appealed to (1)
bear (1)
belong (1)
call (1)
calling on (1)
known as (1)
made appeal (1)
made appeal to (1)
prayed (1)

2127 ἐπικάλυμμα *epikalymma* (1)
cover-up (1) +2400

2128 ἐπικαλύπτω *epikalyptō* (1)

covered (1)

2129 ἐπικατάρατος *epikataratos* (2)
cursed (2)

2130 ἐπίκειμαι *epikeimai* (7)
applying (1)
compelled (1) +340
continued raging (1) +3900+4024
crowding around (1)
insistently (1)
laid across (1)
on (1)

2131 ἐπικέλλω *epikellō* (1)
ran aground (1)

2132 ἐπικερδαίνω *epikerdainō*
Variant; not used

2133 ἐπικεφάλαιον *epikephalaion*
Variant; not used

2134 Ἐπικούρειος *Epikoureios* (1)
Epicurean (1)

2135 ἐπικουρία *epikouria* (1)
help (1)

2136 ἐπικράζω *epikrazō*
Variant; not used

2137 ἐπικρίνω *epikrinō* (1)
decided (1)

2138 ἐπιλαμβάνομαι *epilambanomai* (19)
took (6)
seized (2)
take hold (2)
arrested (1)
catch (1)
caught (1)
helps (1)
seizing (1)
taking hold of (1)
trap in (1)
turned on (1)
untranslated (1)

2139 ἐπιλάμπω *epilampō*
Variant; not used

2140 ἐπιλανθάνομαι *epilanthanomai* (8)
forget (3)
forgotten (2)
forgets (1)
forgetting (1)
forgot (1)

2141 ἐπιλέγω *epilegō* (2)
called (1)
chose (1)

2142 ἐπιλείπω *epileipō* (1)
not have (1)

2143 ἐπιλείχω *epileichō* (1)
licked (1)

2144 ἐπιλησμονή *epilēsmonē* (1)
forgetting (1)

2145 ἐπίλοιπος *epiloipos* (1)
rest (1)

2146 ἐπίλυσις *epilysis* (1)
interpretation (1)

2147 ἐπιλύω *epilyō* (2)
explained (1)
must be settled (1)

2148 ἐπιμαρτυρέω *epimartyreō* (1)
testifying that (1)

2149 ἐπιμέλεια *epimeleia* (1)
for needs (1)

2150 ἐπιμελέομαι *epimeleomai* (3)
look after (1)
take care of (1)
took care of (1)

2151 ἐπιμελῶς *epimelōs* (1)
carefully (1)

2152 ἐπιμένω *epimenō* (16)
stayed (3)
continue in (2)
kept on (2)
been there (1)
go on (1)
persevere in (1)
persist in (1)
remain (1)
spend (1)
spend time (1) +5989
stay (1)
stay on (1)

2153 ἐπινεύω *epineuō* (1)
declined (1) +4024

2154 ἐπίνοια *epinoia* (1)
thought (1)

2155 ἐπιορκέω *epiorkeō* (1)
break oath (1)

2156 ἐπίορκος *epiorkos* (1)
perjurers (1)

2157 ἐπιούσιος *epiousios* (2)
daily (2)

2158 ἐπιπίπτω *epipiptō* (11)
came on (2)
come upon (1) +1639
embraced (1) +2093+3836+5549
fallen on (1)
gripped with fear (1) +5832
pushing forward (1)
seized with fear (1) +5832
struck (1)
threw himself on (1)
threw his arms around (1)
            +2093+3836+5549

2159 ἐπιπλήσσω *epiplēssō* (1)
rebuke harshly (1)

2160 ἐπιποθέω *epipotheō* (9)
long (3)
crave (1)
hearts go out to (1)
intensely (1)
long for (1)
longing (1)
longs for (1) +1639

2161 ἐπιπόθησις *epipothēsis* (2)
longing (2)

2162 ἐπιπόθητος *epipothētos* (1)
long for (1)

2163 ἐπιποθία *epipothia* (1)
longing (1)

2164 ἐπιπορεύομαι *epiporeuomai* (1)
coming (1)

2165 ἐπιράπτω *epiraptō* (1)
sews (1)

2166 ἐπιρίπτω *epiriptō* (2)
cast on (1)
threw on (1)

2167 ἐπισείω *episeiō*
Variant; not used

2168 ἐπίσημος *episēmos* (2)
notorious (1)
outstanding (1)

2169 ἐπισιτισμός *episitismos* (1)
food (1)

2170 ἐπισκέπτομαι *episkeptomai* (11)
look after (2)
visit (2)
care for (1)
choose (1)

come (1)
come to (1)
come to help (1)
looked after (1)
showed concern (1)

2171 ἐπισκευάζομαι *episkeuazomai* (1)
got ready (1)

2172 ἐπισκηνόω *episkēnoō* (1)
rest on (1)

2173 ἐπισκιάζω *episkiazō* (5)
enveloped (3)
fall on (1)
overshadow (1)

2174 ἐπισκοπέω *episkopeō* (2)
see to it (1)
serving as overseers (1)

2175 ἐπισκοπή *episkopē* (4)
coming (1)
overseer (1)
place of leadership (1)
visits (1)

2176 ἐπίσκοπος *episkopos* (5)
overseer (3)
overseers (2)

2177 ἐπισπάομαι *epispaomai* (1)
become uncircumcised (1)

2178 ἐπισπείρω *epispeirō* (1)
sowed (1)

2179 ἐπίσταμαι *epistamai* (14)
know (6)
understand (2)
familiar (1)
knew (1)
know about (1)
know that (1)
understands (1)
well aware (1)

2180 ἐπίστασις *epistasis* (2)
pressure (1)
stirring up (1) +4472

2181 ἐπιστάτης *epistatēs* (7)
master (7)

2182 ἐπιστέλλω *epistellō* (3)
written (2)
write (1)

2183 ἐπιστήμη *epistēmē*
Variant; not used

2184 ἐπιστήμων *epistēmōn* (1)
understanding (1)

2185 ἐπιστηρίζω *epistērizō* (4)
strengthening (3)
strengthen (1)

2186 ἐπιστολή *epistolē* (24)
letter (15)
letters (9)

2187 ἐπιστομίζω *epistomizō* (1)
silenced (1)

2188 ἐπιστρέφω *epistrephō* (36)
turn (4)
turn to (4)
turned (4)
go (3)
turned around (3)
return (2)
returned (2)
turned to (2)
turning to (2)
turns (2)
bring back (1)
bring back to (1)
comes back (1)
go back (1)

returned to (1)
returns to (1)
turned back (1)
turning (1)

2189 ἐπιστροφή *epistrophē* (1)
had been converted (1) +3836

2190 ἐπισυνάγω *episynagō* (8)
gather (3)
gather together (2)
gathered (1)
gathered (1) +1639
gathers (1)

2191 ἐπισυναγωγή *episynagōgē* (2)
gathered to (1)
meeting together (1)

2192 ἐπισυντρέχω *episyntrechō* (1)
running (1)

2193 ἐπισυρράπτω *episyrraptō*
Variant; not used

2194 ἐπισύστασις *episystasis*
Variant; not used

2195 ἐπισφαλής *episphalēs* (1)
dangerous (1)

2196 ἐπισχύω *epischyō* (1)
insisted (1)

2197 ἐπισωρεύω *episōreuō* (1)
gather around (1)

2198 ἐπιταγή *epitagē* (7)
command (5)
authority (1)
commanding (1) +2848+3306

2199 ἐπιτάσσω *epitassō* (10)
gives orders (2)
order (2)
ordered (2)
command (1)
commands (1)
directed (1)
orders (1)

2200 ἐπιτελέω *epiteleō* (10)
attain goal (1)
bring to completion (1)
build (1)
carry it on to completion (1)
carry on (1)
completed (1)
completion (1)
finish (1)
perfecting (1)
undergoing (1)

2201 ἐπιτήδειος *epitēdeios* (1)
needs (1)

2202 ἐπιτίθημι *epitithēmi* (39)
put on (10)
placed on (6)
gave (2)
laying on (2)
place (2)
place on (2)
add to (1)
adds to (1)
attack (1)
beat (1) +4435
flogged (1) +4435
furnished with (1)
laid on (1)
lay on (1)
on lay (1)
placed (1)
placing on (1)
puts on (1)
putting on (1)
set on (1)
to burden (1) +983

2203 ἐπιτιμάω *epitimaō* (30)
rebuked (17)
rebuke (6)
warned (2)
gave orders (1)
said sternly (1)
sternly (1)
strictly warned (1) *+4133*
warning (1)

2204 ἐπιτιμία *epitimia* (1)
punishment (1)

2205 ἐπιτρέπω *epitrepō* (18)
let (5)
allowed (3)
gave permission (2)
permission (2)
permitted (2)
permit (1)
permits (1)
permitting (1)
received permission (1)

2206 ἐπιτροπεύω *epitropeuō*
Variant; not used

2207 ἐπιτροπή *epitropē* (1)
commission (1)

2208 ἐπίτροπος *epitropos* (3)
foreman (1)
guardians (1)
manager (1)

2209 ἐπιτυγχάνω *epitynchanō* (5)
gained (1)
have (1)
obtain (1)
received (1)
untranslated (1)

2210 ἐπιφαίνω *epiphainō* (4)
appeared (3)
shine on (1)

2211 ἐπιφάνεια *epiphaneia* (6)
appearing (5)
splendor (1)

2212 ἐπιφανής *epiphanēs* (1)
glorious (1)

2213 ἐπιφαύσκω *epiphauskō* (1)
shine on (1)

2214 ἐπιφέρω *epipherō* (2)
bring against (1)
bringing (1)

2215 ἐπιφωνέω *epiphōneō* (4)
shouted (2)
shouting (1)
shouting at (1)

2216 ἐπιφώσκω *epiphōskō* (2)
about to begin (1)
dawn (1)

2217 ἐπιχειρέω *epicheireō* (3)
tried (2)
undertaken (1)

2218 ἐπιχείρησις *epicheirēsis*
Variant; not used

2219 ἐπιχέω *epicheō* (1)
pouring on (1)

2220 ἐπιχορηγέω *epichorēgeō* (5)
add (1)
give (1)
receive (1)
supplies (1)
supported (1)

2221 ἐπιχορηγία *epichorēgia* (2)
help given (1)
supporting (1)

2222 ἐπιχρίω *epichriō* (2)

put on (2)

2223 ἐπιψαύω *epipsauō*
Variant; not used

2224 ἐποικοδομέω *epoikodomeō* (7)
build up (1)
building on (1)
builds (1)
builds on (1)
built (1)
built on (1)
built up (1)

2225 ἐποκέλλω *epokellō*
Variant; not used

2226 ἐπονομάζω *eponomazō* (1)
call (1)

2227 ἐποπτεύω *epopteuō* (2)
see (2)

2228 ἐπόπτης *epoptēs* (1)
eyewitnesses (1)

2229 ἔπος *epos* (1)
one might even say (1) *+3306+6055*

2230 ἐπουράνιος *epouranios* (19)
heavenly (8)
heavenly realms (5)
heaven (4)
heavenly things (1)
in heaven (1)

2231 ἑπτά *hepta* (88)
seven (85)
seventh (1)
seventy-seven times (1) *+1574*
week (1) *+2465*

2232 ἑπτάκις *heptakis* (4)
seven times (4)

2233 ἑπτακισχίλιοι *heptakischilioi* (1)
seven thousand (1)

2234 ἑπταπλασίων *heptaplasiōn*
Variant; not used

2235 Ἔραστος *Erastos* (3)
Erastus (3)

2236 ἐρανάω *eraunaō* (6)
searches (3)
diligently study (1)
look into (1)
trying to find out (1)

2237 ἐργάζομαι *ergazomai* (41)
work (7)
do (5)
worked (3)
does (2)
doing (2)
done (2)
administered (1)
at work (1)
bring about (1)
brings (1)
busy (1)
carrying on (1)
done (1) *+1639*
earn (1)
earn living (1)
evildoers (1) *+490+3836*
for work (1) *+1256+1877+4005*
let do (1)
put to work (1)
sin (1) *+281*
work for a living (1)
work for (1)
work hard (1) *+3159*
worked for (1)
working (1)
works (1)

2238 ἐργασία *ergasia* (6)

business (2)
indulge (1)
making money (1)
money (1)
try hard (1) *+1443*

2239 ἐργάτης *ergatēs* (16)
workers (5)
worker (3)
workmen (3)
do (1)
evildoers (1) *+94*
men to work (1)
them[s] (1) *+3836*
workman (1)

2240 ἔργον *ergon* (169)
work (35)
deeds (29)
done (9)
works (9)
doing (8)
observing (8)
actions (7)
do (6)
miracles (6)
things (5)
acts (4)
deed (3)
action (2)
task (2)
thing (2)
what he did (2)
act (1)
actions deserve (1) *+2848*
activity (1)
behavior (1)
did (1)
did (1) *+3836*
does (1)
had done (1)
it[s] (1)
it[s] (1) *+3836+5516*
labor (1)
made (1)
miracle (1)
observe (1)
practices (1)
requirements (1)
something (1)
these[s] (1) *+2819*
ways (1)
what he does (1)
what she did (1)
what[s] (1) *+3836*
what[s] (1) *+3836+5516*
will (1)
untranslated (8)

2241 ἐρεθίζω *erethizō* (2)
embitter (1)
stirred to action (1)

2242 ἐρείδω *ereidō* (1)
stuck fast (1)

2243 ἐρεύγομαι *ereugomai* (1)
utter (1)

2244 ἐρημία *erēmia* (4)
remote place (2)
country (1)
deserts (1)

2245 ἔρημος *erēmos* (49)
desert (32)
solitary (4)
desolate (3)
remote (3)
desert region (1)
deserted (1)
lonely (1)
lonely places (1)
open country (1)
quiet (1)

solitary places (1)

2246 ἐρημόω *erēmoō* (5)
brought to ruin (2)
ruined (2)
ruin (1)

2247 ἐρήμωσις *erēmōsis* (3)
desolation (3)

2248 ἐρίζω *erizō* (1)
quarrel (1)

2249 ἐριθεία *eritheia* (7)
selfish ambition (5)
factions (1)
self-seeking (1)

2250 ἔριον *erion* (2)
wool (2)

2251 ἔρις *eris* (9)
quarreling (2)
strife (2)
arguments (1)
discord (1)
dissension (1)
quarrels (1)
rivalry (1)

2252 ἐρίφιον *eriphion* (1)
goats (1)

2253 ἔριφος *eriphos* (2)
goats (1)
young goat (1)

2254 Ἑρμᾶς *Hermas* (1)
Hermas (1)

2255 ἑρμηνεία *hermēneia* (2)
interpretation (2)

2256 ἑρμηνευτής *hermēneutēs*
Variant; not used

2257 ἑρμηνεύω *hermēneuō* (3)
means (2)
translated (1)

2258 Ἑρμῆς *Hermēs* (2)
Hermes (2)

2259 Ἑρμογένης *Hermogenēs* (1)
Hermogenes (1)

2260 ἑρπετόν *herpeton* (4)
reptiles (4)

2261 ἐρυθρός *erythros* (2)
red (2)

2262 ἔρχομαι *erchomai* (632)
come (195)
came (130)
comes (58)
coming (57)
went (47)
arrived (13)
go (10)
returned (6)
return (5)
entered (4) +1650
arrives (3)
came back (3)
come back (3)
going (3)
gone (3)
reached (3)
reached (3) +1650
traveled (3)
visit (3)
went back (3)
went out (3)
joined (2) +4639
landed (2) +1178+2093+3836
on way (2)
reached (2) +2093
returns (2)
rose (2)

accompanied by (1) +2779
acknowledge (1) +2106
approaching (1) +4639
arrival (1)
arrived (1) +1650
been (1)
bound to come (1) +450+3590
bring (1)
brought (1)
brought out (1)
comes home (1)
coming (1) +3836
coming back (1)
coming of (1)
condemned (1) +1650+3213
entered (1)
fall (1)
falling (1)
follow (1) +3958
followed (1)
gathered (1)
get here (1)
get in (1)
goes (1)
going to happen (1)
going to rain (1) +3915
grew (1) +1650+3836
has served (1)
here (1)
hurried off (1) +5067
join (1) +4639
landed (1)
lighting (1)
lose good name (1) +591+1650
made their way (1)
make visit (1)
next (1)
occurs (1)
on his way (1)
on their way (1)
passed by (1)
reaching (1) +1650
rest (1)
result (1)
return (1) +1650+3836+4099
returning (1)
see (1) +4639
set off (1)
struck (1) +2093
to come (1) +3516
visited (1) +1650
visited (1) +4639
went on (1)
untranslated (9)

2263 ἐρωτάω *erōtaō* (63)
asked (19)
ask (18)
urged (3)
asks (2)
begged (2)
invited (2)
please (2) +5148
pray (2)
prayer is (2)
questioned (2)
ask questions (1)
asked for (1)
asking (1)
beg (1)
praying (1)
question (1)
questioning (1)
request (1)
requesting (1)

2264 ἐσθής *esthēs* (8)
clothes (5)
dressed (1)
robe (1)
robes (1)

2265 ἔσθησις *esthēsis*

Variant; not used

2266 ἐσθίω *esthiō* (158)
eat (92)
ate (19)
eating (19)
eats (10)
eaten (4)
do[s] (2)
food (2)
abstains (1) +3590
consume (1)
does so[s] (1) +4024
drink (1)
eating of (1)
get food (1)
have a feast (1)
have dinner (1)
untranslated (2)

2267 ἔσθω *esthō*
Variant; not used

2268 Ἑσλί *Hesli* (1)
Esli (1)

2269 ἔσοπτρον *esoptron* (2)
mirror (1)
reflection mirror (1)

2270 ἑσπέρα *hespera* (3)
evening (3)

2271 ἑσπερινός *hesperinos*
Variant; not used

2272 Ἑσρώμ *Hesrōm* (3)
Hezron (3)

2273 ἑσσόομαι *hessoomai* (1)
inferior (1)

2274 ἔσχατος *eschatos* (52)
last (42)
end (2)
ends (2)
final (2)
last of all (1)
least important (1)
lowest (1)
now (1)

2275 ἐσχάτως *eschatōs* (1)
dying (1)

2276 ἔσω *esō* (9)
inner (2)
inside (2)
in (1)
into (1)
inwardly (1) +3836
right into (1) +1650+2401
untranslated (1)

2277 ἔσωθεν *esōthen* (12)
inside (4)
on the inside (2)
from inside (1)
from within (1)
inwardly (1)
on both sides (1) +2779+3957
under (1)
within (1)

2278 ἐσώτερος *esōteros* (2)
inner (2)

2279 ἑταῖρος *hetairos* (3)
friend (3)

2280 ἑτερόγλωσσος *heteroglōssos* (1)
strange tongues (1)

2281 ἑτεροδιδασκαλέω *heterodidaskaleō* (2)
teach false doctrines (1)
teaches false doctrines (1)

2282 ἑτεροζυγέω *heterozygeō* (1)
yoked together (1)

2283 ἕτερος *heteros* (98)
another (29)
other (29)
others (13)
different (4)
else (4)
some (3)
different from (2)
another (1) +3836
changed (1) +1181
day after (1)
elsewhere (1) +1877
foreigners (1)
his fellowmanˢ (1) +3836
next (1)
perversion (1) +599+3958+4922
somebody else (1)
someone else (1)
still others (1)
untranslated (3)

2284 ἑτέρως *heterōs* (1)
differently (1)

2285 ἔτι *eti* (93)
still (31)
more (9)
again (7)
longer (7)
continue (5)
any more (4)
even (3)
any longer (2)
anymore (1)
as (1)
as long as still (1)
before long (1) +3625
besides (1)
just as (1) +2317
left (1)
longer (1) +5989
never again (1) +4024
never again (1) +4028
now (1)
on (1)
only (1)
other (1)
still (1) +3814
very while (1) +4012+4012
while still (1)
yes (1) +5445
untranslated (7)

2286 ἑτοιμάζω *hetoimazō* (40)
prepared (19)
prepare (10)
make preparations (5)
get ready (3)
kept ready (1)
made ready (1)
make ready (1)

2287 Ἕτοιμας *Hetoimas*
Variant; not used

2288 ἑτοιμασία *hetoimasia* (1)
readiness (1)

2289 ἕτοιμος *hetoimos* (17)
ready (14)
prepared (1)
right (1)
work already done (1)

2290 ἑτοίμως *hetoimōs* (3)
ready (2)
ready (1) +2400

2291 ἔτος *etos* (49)
years (40)
year (3)
years old (3)
eighty-four (1) +3837+5475
untranslated (2)

2292 εὖ *eu* (5)

well (2)
well done (2)
help (1) +4472

2293 Εὕα *Heua* (2)
eve (2)

2294 εὐαγγελίζω *euangelizō* (54)
preach the gospel (7)
preached (7)
preaching the gospel (5)
preached the good news (3)
preach (2)
preach the good news (2)
preached the gospel (2)
proclaiming the good news (2)
the good news preached (2)
the gospel preached (2)
announced (1)
bring good news (1)
bring news (1)
bringing good news (1)
brought good news about (1)
gospel preached (1) +2295
gospel to proclaim (1) +2295
had the gospel preached (1)
preach a gospel (1)
preach good news (1)
preaching (1)
preaching a gospel (1)
preaching the good news (1)
preaching gospel (1) +2295
tell good news (1)
tell the good news (1)
telling the good news (1)
telling the good news about (1)
the good news is preached (1)
told the good news about (1)

2295 εὐαγγέλιον *euangelion* (76)
gospel (60)
good news (6)
preaching gospel (2)
gospel preached (1) +2294
gospel to proclaim (1) +2294
itˢ (1) +3836
preach gospel (1)
preaching (1)
preaching gospel (1) +2294
proclaiming gospel (1)
spreading gospel (1)

2296 εὐαγγελιστής *euangelistēs* (3)
evangelist (2)
evangelists (1)

2297 εὐαρεστέω *euaresteō* (3)
pleased (2)
please (1)

2298 εὐάρεστος *euarestos* (9)
pleasing (5)
pleases (2) +1639
please (1)
please (1) +1639

2299 εὐαρέστως *euarestōs* (1)
acceptably (1)

2300 Εὔβουλος *Euboulos* (1)
Eubulus (1)

2301 εὖγε *euge* (1)
well done (1)

2302 εὐγενής *eugenēs* (3)
noble birth (1)
of more noble character than (1)
of noble birth (1)

2303 εὐγλωττία *euglōttia*
Variant; not used

2304 εὐδία *eudia* (1)
fair weather (1)

2305 εὐδοκέω *eudokeō* (21)
pleased (8)

well pleased (5)
delight (2)
delighted (2)
pleased with (1)
prefer (1) +3437
thought it best (1)
with pleased (1)

2306 εὐδοκία *eudokia* (9)
good pleasure (3)
desire (1)
good purpose (1)
goodwill (1)
on whom favor rests (1)
pleasure (1)
purpose (1)

2307 εὐεργεσία *euergesia* (2)
act of kindness shown to (1)
service (1)

2308 εὐεργετέω *euergeteō* (1)
doing good (1)

2309 εὐεργέτης *euergetēs* (1)
benefactors (1)

2310 εὔθετος *euthetos* (3)
fit (1)
fit for service (1)
useful (1)

2311 εὐθέως *eutheōs* (36)
immediately (19)
at once (8)
as soon as (1)
at that moment (1)
at this (1)
now (1)
quickly (1)
right away (1)
soon (1)
suddenly (1)
untranslated (1)

2312 εὐθυδρομέω *euthydromeō* (2)
sailed straight (2)

2313 εὐθυμέω *euthymeō* (3)
keep up courage (2)
happy (1)

2314 εὔθυμος *euthymos* (1)
encouraged (1)

2315 εὐθύμως *euthymōs* (1)
gladly (1)

2316 εὐθύνω *euthynō* (2)
go (1)
make straight (1)

2317 εὐθύς1 *euthys1* (51)
immediately (13)
at once (8)
as soon as (6)
quickly (4)
as soon as (2) +4020
at once (2) +4020
at this (1)
just as (1)
just as (1) +2285
just then (1)
right away (1)
shortly (1)
sudden (1)
the moment (1)
then (1)
very early in the morning (1) +4745
when (1)
without delay (1)
untranslated (5)

2318 εὐθύς2 *euthys2* (8)
straight (6)
right (2)

2319 εὐθύτης *euthytēs* (1)
righteousness (1)

2320 εὐκαιρέω *eukaireō* (3)
has the opportunity (1)
have a chance (1)
spent time (1)

2321 εὐκαιρία *eukairia* (2)
opportunity (2)

2322 εὔκαιρος *eukairos* (2)
opportune (1)
time of need (1)

2323 εὐκαίρως *eukairōs* (2)
in season (1)
opportunity (1)

2324 εὔκοπος *eukopos* (7)
easier (7)

2325 εὐλάβεια *eulabeia* (2)
reverence (1)
reverent (1)

2326 εὐλαβέομαι *eulabeomai* (1)
holy fear (1)

2327 εὐλαβής *eulabēs* (4)
devout (2)
God-fearing (1)
godly (1)

2328 εὐλογέω *eulogeō* (40)
blessed (19)
gave thanks (6)
bless (5)
praising (3)
blessing (2)
bless (1) +2328
gave thanks for (1)
give thanks (1)
praise (1)
praised (1)

2329 εὐλογητός *eulogētos* (8)
praise (4)
praised (3)
blessed (1)

2330 εὐλογία *eulogia* (16)
blessing (6)
praise (4)
generous gift (2)
generously (2) +2093
flattery (1)
thanksgiving (1)

2331 εὐμετάδοτος *eumetadotos* (1)
generous (1)

2332 Εὐνίκη *Eunikē* (1)
Eunice (1)

2333 εὐνοέω *eunoeō* (1)
settle matters (1) +1639

2334 εὔνοια *eunoia* (1)
wholeheartedly (1) +3552

2335 εὐνουχίζω *eunouchizō* (2)
made that way^s (1) +2336
renounced marriage (1) +1571+2336

2336 εὐνοῦχος *eunouchos* (8)
eunuch (5)
eunuchs (1)
made that way^s (1) +2335
renounced marriage (1) +1571+2335

2337 Εὐοδία *Euodia* (1)
Euodia (1)

2338 εὐοδόω *euodoō* (4)
go well (1)
in keeping with income (1)
+1569+4005+5516
is getting along well (1)
way opened for (1)

2339 εὐπάρεδρος *euparedros* (1)
devotion (1)

2340 εὐπειθής *eupeithēs* (1)
submissive (1)

2341 εὐπερίσπαστος *euperispastos*
Variant; not used

2342 εὐπερίστατος *euperistatos* (1)
easily entangles (1)

2343 εὐποιΐα *eupoiia* (1)
do good (1)

2344 εὐπορέω *euporeō* (1)
ability (1)

2345 εὐπορία *euporia* (1)
good income (1)

2346 εὐπρέπεια *euprepeia* (1)
beauty (1)

2347 εὐπρόσδεκτος *euprosdektos* (5)
acceptable (4)
favor (1)

2348 εὐπρόσεδρος *euprosedros*
Variant; not used

2349 εὐπροσωπέω *euprosōpeō* (1)
make a good impression (1)

2350 εὐρακύλων *eurakylōn* (1)
the northeaster (1)

2351 εὑρίσκω *heuriskō* (176)
found (83)
find (53)
finds (13)
met (3)
finding (2)
appeared (1)
bring about (1)
considered (1)
decide (1)
discovered (1)
enjoyed (1)
evident (1)
find (1) +1639
find out (1)
finds (1) +1181
found that (1)
laid bare (1)
obtained (1)
prove (1)
provide (1)
recovered (1)
result (1)
were looking for (1) +2671
when found (1)
untranslated (3)

2352 εὐροκλύδων *euroklydōn*
Variant; not used

2353 εὐρύχωρος *eurychōros* (1)
broad (1)

2354 εὐσέβεια *eusebeia* (15)
godliness (12)
godly (3)

2355 εὐσεβέω *eusebeō* (2)
put religion into practice by caring for (1)
worship (1)

2356 εὐσεβής *eusebēs* (3)
devout (2)
godly (1)

2357 εὐσεβῶς *eusebōs* (2)
godly (1)
godly life (1)

2358 εὔσημος *eusēmos* (1)
intelligible (1)

2359 εὔσπλαγχνος *eusplanchnos* (2)
compassionate (2)

2360 εὐσχημονέω *euschēmoneō*
Variant; not used

2361 εὐσχημόνως *euschēmonōs* (3)
decently (1)
fitting (1)
win the respect (1)

2362 εὐσχημοσύνη *euschēmosynē* (1)
modesty (1)

2363 εὐσχήμων *euschēmōn* (5)
prominent (2)
high standing (1)
presentable (1)
right (1)

2364 εὐτόνως *eutonōs* (2)
vehemently (1)
vigorously (1)

2365 εὐτραπελία *eutrapelia* (1)
coarse joking (1)

2366 Εὔτυχος *Eutychos* (1)
Eutychus (1)

2367 εὐφημία *euphēmia* (1)
good report (1)

2368 εὔφημος *euphēmos* (1)
admirable (1)

2369 εὐφορέω *euphoreō* (1)
produced a good crop (1)

2370 εὐφραίνω *euphrainō* (14)
celebrate (5)
rejoice (3)
glad (2)
held a celebration (1)
lived (1)
make glad (1)
merry (1)

2371 Εὐφράτης *Euphratēs* (2)
Euphrates (2)

2372 εὐφροσύνη *euphrosynē* (2)
fills with joy (1)
joy (1)

2373 εὐχαριστέω *eucharisteō* (38)
thank (13)
gave thanks (7)
giving thanks (5)
given thanks (4)
give thanks (2)
gives thanks (2)
thanked (2)
give thanks for (1)
grateful (1)
thankful (1)

2374 εὐχαριστία *eucharistia* (15)
thanksgiving (8)
thanks (2)
expressions of thanks (1)
gratitude (1)
thank (1)
thankful (1)
thankfulness (1)

2375 εὐχάριστος *eucharistos* (1)
thankful (1)

2376 εὐχή *euchē* (3)
vow (2)
prayer (1)

2377 εὔχομαι *euchomai* (7)
pray (3)
pray (1) +323
prayed for (1)
prayer for (1)
wish (1)

2378 εὔχρηστος *euchrēstos* (3)
useful (2)
helpful (1)

2379 εὐψυχέω *eupsycheō* (1)
cheered (1)

2380 εὐωδία *euōdia* (3)
fragrant (2) +4011
aroma (1)

2381 εὐώνυμος *euōnymos* (9)
left (8)
south of (1)

2382 εὐωχία *euōchia*
Variant; not used

2383 ἐφάλλομαι *ephallomai* (1)
jumped on (1)

2384 ἐφάπαξ *ephapax* (5)
once for all (4)
at the same time (1)

2385 Ἐφεσῖνος *Ephesinos*
Variant; not used

2386 Ἐφέσιος *Ephesios* (5)
Ephesians (2)
of Ephesus (2)
Ephesian (1)

2387 Ἔφεσος *Ephesos* (16)
Ephesus (15)
he (1)

2388 ἐφευρετής *epheuretēs* (1)
invent (1)

2389 ἐφημερία *ephēmeria* (2)
division (1)
priestly division (1)

2390 ἐφήμερος *ephēmeros* (1)
daily (1)

2391 ἐφικνέομαι *ephikneomai* (2)
come (1)
reaches (1)

2392 ἐφίστημι *ephistēmi* (21)
appeared (2)
came (2)
came up (2)
stood beside (2)
bent (1)
close (1)
come (1)
come on (1)
coming up (1)
it was (1)
prepared (1)
rushed to (1)
stood (1) +1639
stood near (1)
stopped (1)
stopped at (1)
untranslated (1)

2393 ἐφοράω *ephoraō*
Variant; not used

2394 Ἐφραίμ *Ephraim* (1)
Ephraim (1)

2395 ἐφφαθά *ephphatha* (1)
Ephphatha (1)

2396 ἐχθές *echthes* (3)
yesterday (3)

2397 ἔχθρα *echthra* (6)
hatred (2)
hostility (2)
enemies (1) +1877
hostile (1)

2398 ἐχθρός *echthros* (32)
enemies (21)
enemy (10)
enemy (1) +476

2399 ἔχιδνα *echidna* (5)
vipers (4)
viper (1)

2400 ἔχω *echō* (708)

have (209)
has (91)
had (72)
need (25) +5970
with (21)
having (11)
is (7)
sick (7) +2809
are (6)
held (6)
was (6)
demon-possessed (5) +1228
get (5)
needs (5) +5970
possessed by (5)
without (5) +3590
hold (4)
take (4)
am (3)
be (3)
be guilty of sin (3) +281
hold to (3)
holding (3)
holds (3)
keep (3)
pregnant women (3) +1143+1877
thank (3) +5921
able (2)
belongs to (2)
excuse (2) +4148
felt (2)
had (2) +1639
have (2) +3836
love (2) +27
married to (2)
needed (2) +5970
possess (2)
reap (2)
rich (2) +3836+5975
were (2)
who had (2)
with child (2) +1143+1877
accompanied by (1)
according to means (1) +1666+3836
accusers (1) +2991
approach (1) +4643
are ignorant (1) +57
as follows (1) +3836+4047+5596
be bold (1) +4244+4498
be dependent on (1) +5970
be encouraged (1) +4155
been (1)
believe (1) +4411
believers (1) +3836+4411
belongs to you (1) +5050
benefit (1) +5921
bring (1)
bringing (1) +1571+3552
can (1)
can⁵ (1)
cannot (1) +4024
collect a tenth from (1) +620
come (1)
commend (1) +2047
confident (1) +4244
consider (1)
considered (1) +6055
contained (1) +1877
could (1)
cover-up (1) +2127
covered (1) +2848
crippled (1) +819
demon-possessed (1)
+3836+3836+4460+4505
desire (1) +2123
distressed (1) +3383
doing (1)
dwell (1) +3531
end (1) +5465
enjoy (1)
enjoyed (1)

enjoying favor (1) +5921
eyes (1) +4057
face (1)
filled with (1)
finish (1) +5455
following (1)
for now (1) +3814+3836
forgiven (1) +912
gave (1)
gave (1) +4639
give (1)
given (1) +608
glory in (1) +3018
glory over (1) +3018
got (1)
guilty of sin (1) +281
had (1) +323
had charge of (1)
harbor (1)
hard (1) +4498
hardened (1) +4800
has enough (1) +1650
has given (1)
has hold (1)
have (1) +1639
have kept (1)
have made (1)
haven't (1) +3590
holding on to (1)
honor (1) +1952
in leaf (1) +5877
in need (1) +5970
is ours (1)
is time of grief (1) +3383
is under (1)
it was so (1) +4048
keep hold of (1)
keeper of money bag (1) +1186
keeping (1)
leaves wife (1) +1222
live (1)
lived (1) +2998+3836
living (1) +3836+6034
made (1)
made up of (1)
maintained (1)
must (1) +340
must (1) +2026
nearby (1)
need (1) +340
need (1) +1181+5970
next (1)
next day (1)
obey (1) +5717
one who had (1)
persevered (1) +5702
portrait (1) +1635
preached (1) +3062
pregnant (1) +1143+1877
pregnant woman (1) +1143+1877
reaching (1)
ready (1) +2290
rebuked (1) +1792
remember (1) +3644
retain (1)
rules (1) +993
Sabbath day's walk from (1)
+1584+3847+4879
sealed with (1) +5382
shallow (1) +958+3590
shone with glory (1) +1518
short (1) +3900
sick (1) +819
since going through (1)
spare (1) +3590
spread (1) +3786
stop (1) +398
suffer persecution (1) +2568
surrounded by (1)
take (1) +1639
taken (1)

thankful (1) +5921
that accompany (1)
their breastplates were (1) +2606
their hair (1) +2582
there is a judge (1) +3212+3836
treated with (1)
trembling (1) +899+5571
uncircumcised (1) +213
want (1)
was sick (1) +2809
was with (1)
were ill (1) +2809
which had (1)
who are (1)
who have (1)
who need (1) +5970
whose (1) +4005
whose^s (1)
with (1) +4005
with authority (1) +2026
wounded (1) +3836+4435
untranslated (18)

2401 ἕως *heōs* (146)
to (31)
until (31)
until (13) +323
until (13) +4005
before (4) +323
how long (4) +4536
till (4)
how (3)
still (3) +785
until (3) +4015
up to (3)
while (3)
even (2)
for (2)
to the point (2)
while (2) +4005
and (1)
as far as (1)
as long as (1)
before (1)
before (1) +4005
fully (1) +5465
going on to (1)
of this (1) +4047
right into (1) +1650+2276
right on down to (1)
right up to (1)
till (1) +323
to where (1)
when (1) +4005
while (1) +4015
untranslated (8)

2402 ς *[stigma]*
Variant; not used

2403 ζ *z*
Variant; not used

2404 Ζαβουλών *Zaboulōn* (3)
Zebulun (3)

2405 Ζακχαῖος *Zakchaios* (3)
Zacchaeus (3)

2406 Ζάρα *Zara* (1)
Zerah (1)

2407 ζαφθάνι *zaphthani*
Variant; not used

2408 Ζαχαρίας *Zacharias* (11)
Zechariah (10)
Zechariah's (1)

2409 ζάω *zaō* (139)
live (50)
living (42)
alive (18)
lives (15)
lived (4)
came to life (2)

as surely as I live (1) +1609
belonged (1)
brought to life (1)
come to life (1)
life (1)
live on (1)
receive living (1)
returned to life (1)

2410 ζβέννυμι *zbennymi*
Variant; not used

2411 Ζεβεδαῖος *Zebedaios* (12)
Zebedee (10)
Zebedee's (2)

2412 ζεστός *zestos* (3)
hot (2)
the other^s (1)

2413 ζεύγνυμι *zeugnymi*
Variant; not used

2414 ζεῦγος *zeugos* (2)
pair (1)
yoke (1)

2415 ζευκτηρία *zeuktēria* (1)
ropes (1)

2416 Ζεύς *Zeus* (2)
Zeus (2)

2417 ζέω *zeō* (2)
fervor (1)
with great fervor (1) +3836+4460

2418 ζηλεύω *zēleuō* (1)
earnest (1)

2419 ζῆλος *zēlos* (16)
jealousy (7)
envy (2)
zeal (2)
ardent concern (1)
concern (1)
enthusiasm (1)
raging (1)
zealous (1)

2420 ζηλόω *zēloō* (11)
eagerly desire (2)
zealous (2)
covet (1)
eager (1)
envy (1)
jealous (1)
jealous for (1)
jealous of (1)
zealous for (1)

2421 ζηλωτής *zēlōtēs* (8)
eager (3)
Zealot (2)
zealous (2)
zealous for (1)

2422 ζημία *zēmia* (4)
loss (4)

2423 ζημιόω *zēmioō* (6)
forfeit (2)
forfeits (1)
harmed (1)
lost (1)
suffer loss (1)

2424 Ζηνᾶς *Zēnas* (1)
Zenas (1)

2425 Ζήνων *Zēnōn*
Variant; not used

2426 ζητέω *zēteō* (117)
looking for (18)
seek (14)
look for (10)
tried (9)
trying (6)
seeking (5)

want (5)
seeks (4)
looked for a way (3)
watched for (3)
ask for (2)
in search of (2)
searching for (2)
try (2)
wanting (2)
asked for (1)
asking (1)
asking for (1)
asks for (1)
attempt (1)
demanded (1)
demanding (1)
determined (1)
gain (1)
got ready (1)
looks out for (1)
make effort to obtain (1)
ready (1)
required (1)
search (1)
search for (1)
searched for (1)
self-seeking (1) +1571+3836
set heart on (1)
set hearts on (1)
sought (1)
sought for (1)
tries (1)
trying to kill (1) +3836+6034
trying to take (1)
waiting (1)
wanted (1)
wants (1)
watching for (1)
works for (1)

2427 ζήτημα *zētēma* (5)
questions (2)
controversies (1)
points of dispute (1)
question (1)

2428 ζήτησις *zētēsis* (7)
controversies (2)
argument (1)
arguments (1)
debate (1)
discussion (1)
investigate (1)

2429 ζιζάνιον *zizanion* (8)
weeds (8)

2430 Ζμύρνα *Zmyrna*
Variant; not used

2431 Ζοροβαβέλ *Zorobabel* (3)
Zerubbabel (3)

2432 ζόφος *zophos* (5)
blackest (2)
darkness (1)
gloom (1)
gloomy (1)

2433 ζυγός *zygos* (6)
yoke (5)
pair of scales (1)

2434 ζύμη *zymē* (13)
yeast (12)
that^s (1) +3836

2435 ζυμόω *zymoō* (4)
worked through the dough (2)
works through (2)

2436 ζωγρέω *zōgreō* (2)
catch (1) +1639
taken captive (1)

2437 ζωή *zōē* (135)
life (128)

living (2)
alive (1)
brings life (1)
lifetime (1)
live (1)
untranslated (1)

2438 ζώνη *zōnē* (8)
belt (4)
belts (2)
sash (1)
sashes (1)

2439 ζώννυμι *zōnnymi* (3)
dress (1)
dressed (1)
put on clothes (1)

2440 ζωννύω *zōnnyō*
Variant; not used

2441 ζωογονέω *zōogoneō* (3)
die (1) +3590
gives life to (1)
preserve (1)

2442 ζῷον *zōon* (23)
living creatures (13)
living creature (4)
animals (2)
beasts (1)
untranslated (3)

2443 ζωοποιέω *zōopoieō* (11)
gives life (4)
made alive (2)
come to life (1)
give life (1)
gives life (1) +1639
impart life (1)
life-giving (1)

2444 η *ē*
Variant; not used

2445 ἤ *ē* (341)
or (244)
than (31)
and (9)
before (3) +4570
either (2)
instead of (2) +3437
before (1) +323+4570
but (1)
but (1) +247
more than (1)
nor (1)
only (1) +4024+4498
some (1)
than (1) +3437
three or three and a half miles (1)
+1633+4297+5084+5558
twenty to thirty gallons (1)
+1545+3583+5552
unless (1)
whether (1)
untranslated (38)

2446 ἢ *ē*
Variant; not used

2447 ἦ μήν *ē mēn*
Variant; not used

2448 ἡγεμονεύω *hēgemoneuō* (2)
governor (2)

2449 ἡγεμονία *hēgemonia* (1)
reign (1)

2450 ἡγεμών *hēgemōn* (20)
governor (13)
governors (4)
governor's (2)
rulers (1)

2451 ἡγέομαι *hēgeomai* (28)
consider (8)

leaders (4)
considered (2)
ruler (2)
think (2)
bear in mind (1)
chief (1)
hold (1)
idea (1)
regard (1)
regarded (1)
rules (1)
thought (1)
understand (1)
who treated (1)

2452 ἡδέως *hēdeōs* (5)
gladly (2)
liked (1)
very gladly (1)
with delight (1)

2453 ἤδη *ēdē* (61)
already (33)
now (5)
by now (2)
by this time (2)
as good as dead (1) +3739
as soon as (1) +4020
at last (1) +4537
even now (1)
nearly (1)
not until (1) +1254
now at last (1) +4537
still (1)
untranslated (11)

2454 ἡδονή *hēdonē* (5)
pleasures (3)
desires (1)
pleasure (1)

2455 ἡδύοσμον *hēdyosmon* (2)
mint (1)
spices mint (1)

2456 ἦθος *ēthos* (1)
character (1)

2457 ἥκω *hēkō* (25)
come (18)
has come (2)
have come (2)
arrived (1)
here (1)
overtake (1)

2458 ἠλί1 *ēli1*
Variant; not used

2459 Ἡλί2 *Ēli2* (1)
Heli (1)

2460 Ἡλίας *Ēlias* (29)
Elijah (28)
Elijah's (1)

2461 ἡλικία *hēlikia* (8)
life (2)
of age (2)
age (1)
short (1) +3625+3836
stature (1)
untranslated (1)

2462 ἡλίκος *hēlikos* (3)
how much (1)
small (1)
what a great (1)

2463 ἥλιος *hēlios* (32)
sun (28)
east (2) +424
just after sunrise (1) +422+3836
sunset (1) +1544

2464 ἧλος *hēlos* (2)
nail (1)
nails (1)

2465 ἡμέρα *hēmera* (389)
day (180)
days (114)
time (32)
daily (5) +2848
daylight (4)
day after day (2) +2848
every day (2) +2848
some time ago (2) +3836+4047+4574
this^s (2) +3836+4047
very day (2) +4958
years (2)
a week later (1) +3552+3893
always (1) +3836+4246
another^s (1)
at daybreak (1) +1181+2002
broad daylight (1)
court (1)
daily (1) +1667+2848
dawn (1) +1181+3516
day after day (1) +4246
day by day (1) +2848+4246
daybreak (1) +1181
days (1) +1328
daytime (1)
during (1)
each day (1) +3836
feast of unleavened Bread (1) +109
forever (1) +172+1650
in the morning (1) +1181
late in afternoon (1) +806+3111
long (1) +4498
morning (1)
nine in the morning (1) +3836+5569+6052
noon (1) +3545
old (1) +1877+4581
Sabbath (1) +3836+4879
some time ago (1) +608+792
that was the time (1) +1697+1877+3836
the next day (1) +1651+3552
the next morning (1) +1181
them^s (1) +3836
this day (1) +3836+4958
three in the afternoon (1)
+1888+3836+6052
today (1) +1877+3836+4958
week (1) +2231
when (1) +1877
while (1)
untranslated (6)

2466 ἡμέτερος *hēmeteros* (7)
our (4)
our own (1)
ours (1)
us (1)

2467 ἡμιθανής *hēmithanēs* (1)
half dead (1)

2468 ἥμισυς *hēmisys* (5)
half (5)

2469 ἡμιώριον *hēmiōrion* (1)
half an hour (1)

2470 ἡμίωρος *hēmiōros*
Variant; not used

2471 ἡνίκα *hēnika* (2)
when (1) +323
whenever (1) +1569

2472 ἤπερ *ēper* (1)
than (1)

2473 ἤπιος *ēpios* (2)
gentle (1)
kind (1)

2474 Ἤρ *Ēr* (1)
Er (1)

2475 ἤρεμος *ēremos* (1)
peaceful (1)

2476 Ἡρῴδης *Hērōdēs* (43)
　　Herod (38)
　　Herod's (5)

2477 Ἡρῳδιανοί *Hērōdianoi* (3)
　　Herodians (3)

2478 Ἡρῳδιάς *Hērōdias* (6)
　　Herodias (6)

2479 Ἡρῳδίων *Hērōdiōn* (1)
　　Herodion (1)

2480 Ἡσαΐας *Ēsaias* (22)
　　Isaiah (22)

2481 Ἡσαῦ *Ēsau* (3)
　　Esau (3)

2482 ἥσσων *hēssōn* (2)
　　harm (1)
　　less (1)

2483 ἡσυχάζω *hēsychazō* (5)
　　gave up (1)
　　lead a quiet life (1)
　　no objections (1)
　　rested (1)
　　silent (1)

2484 ἡσυχία *hēsychia* (4)
　　quiet (1)
　　quietness (1)
　　settle down (1) +3552
　　silent (1)

2485 ἡσύχιος *hēsychios* (2)
　　quiet (2)

2486 ἤτοι *ētoi* (1)
　　whether (1)

2487 ἡττάομαι *hēttaomai* (2)
　　mastered (1)
　　overcome (1)

2488 ἥττημα *hēttēma* (2)
　　defeated (1)
　　loss (1)

2489 ἥττων *hēttōn*
　　Variant; not used

2490 ἠχέω *ēcheō* (1)
　　resounding (1)

2491 ἦχος1 *ēchos1* (3)
　　blast (1)
　　news (1)
　　sound (1)

2492 ἦχος2 *ēchos2* (1)
　　roaring (1)

2493 ἠχώ *ēchō*
　　Variant; not used

2494 θ *th*
　　Variant; not used

2495 θά *tha*
　　Variant; not used

2496 θάβιτα *thabita*
　　Variant; not used

2497 Θαδδαῖος *Thaddaios* (2)
　　Thaddaeus (2)

2498 θάλασσα *thalassa* (91)
　　sea (56)
　　lake (23)
　　waves (4)
　　water (2)
　　coast (1)
　　seashore (1)
　　seashore (1) +3836+5927
　　water's edge (1)
　　waters (1)
　　untranslated (1)

2499 θάλπω *thalpō* (2)
　　cares for (1)

caring for (1)

2500 Θαμάρ *Thamar* (1)
　　Tamar (1)

2501 θαμβέω *thambeō* (3)
　　amazed (2)
　　astonished (1)

2502 θάμβος *thambos* (3)
　　amazed (1)
　　astonished (1) +4321
　　wonder (1)

2503 θανάσιμος *thanasimos* (1)
　　deadly poison (1) +5516

2504 θανατηφόρος *thanatēphoros* (1)
　　deadly (1)

2505 θάνατος *thanatos* (120)
　　death (104)
　　fatal (3)
　　died (2)
　　put to death (2) +5462
　　deadly (1)
　　death sentence (1)
　　die (1) +3972
　　died (1) +1181
　　exposed to death (1)
　　grounds for the death penalty (1) +165
　　plague (1)
　　untranslated (2)

2506 θανατόω *thanatoō* (11)
　　put to death (8)
　　died (1)
　　face death (1)
　　killed (1)

2507 θάπτω *thaptō* (11)
　　buried (7)
　　bury (4)

2508 Θάρα *Thara* (1)
　　Terah (1)

2509 θαρρέω *tharreō* (6)
　　bold (2)
　　confident (2)
　　confidence (1)
　　with confidence (1)

2510 θαρσέω *tharseō* (7)
　　take courage (3)
　　take heart (3)
　　cheer up (1)

2511 θάρσος *tharsos* (1)
　　was encouraged (1) +3284

2512 θαῦμα *thauma* (2)
　　astonished (1) +2513
　　wonder (1)

2513 θαυμάζω *thaumazō* (43)
　　amazed (11)
　　astonished (8)
　　surprised (5)
　　amazement (4)
　　amazed at (3)
　　astonished (1) +2512
　　astonishment (1)
　　flatter (1) +4725
　　marveled (1) +1639
　　marveled at (1)
　　marveling (1)
　　surprise (1)
　　utterly amazed (1) +2014
　　was amazed (1)
　　wonder (1)
　　wondering (1)
　　wondering why (1)

2514 θαυμάσιος *thaumasios* (1)
　　wonderful (1)

2515 θαυμαστός *thaumastos* (6)
　　marvelous (4)

remarkable (1)
wonderful (1)

2516 θεά *thea* (1)
　　goddess (1)

2517 θεάομαι *theaomai* (22)
　　seen (8)
　　saw (7)
　　see (4)
　　look at (1)
　　looked at (1)
　　visit (1)

2518 θεατρίζω *theatrizō* (1)
　　publicly exposed (1)

2519 θέατρον *theatron* (3)
　　theater (2)
　　spectacle (1)

2520 θεῖον *theion* (7)
　　sulfur (7)

2521 θεῖος *theios* (3)
　　divine (2)
　　divine being (1)

2522 θειότης *theiotēs* (1)
　　divine nature (1)

2523 θειώδης *theiōdēs* (1)
　　yellow as sulfur (1)

2524 Θέκλα *Thekla*
　　Variant; not used

2525 θέλημα *thelēma* (62)
　　will (53)
　　decision (1)
　　desires (1)
　　please (1)
　　unwilling (1) +4024
　　want (1)
　　wanted (1)
　　wants (1)
　　willing (1)
　　untranslated (1)

2526 θέλησις *thelēsis* (1)
　　will (1)

2527 θέλω *thelō* (207)
　　want (74)
　　wants (19)
　　wanted (17)
　　willing (15)
　　desire (7)
　　like (7)
　　will (7)
　　would (7)
　　refused (6) +4024
　　wish (6)
　　wanting (3)
　　chosen (2)
　　longed (2)
　　mean (2) +1639
　　trying (2)
　　wished (2)
　　wishes (2)
　　choose (1)
　　chooses (1)
　　choosing (1)
　　chose (1)
　　decided (1)
　　deliberately (1)
　　delights (1)
　　determined (1)
　　have desire (1)
　　make a defense (1) +664
　　pleased (1)
　　pleases (1)
　　prefer (1)
　　purposely (1)
　　refuse (1) +4024
　　refusing (1) +4024
　　request (1)

tries (1)
unwilling (1) +4024
want to (1)
wants to (1)
was (1)
willingness (1)
wish that (1)
wishing (1)
would rather (1)
untranslated (1)

2528 θεμέλιον *themelion* (1)
foundations (1)

2529 θεμέλιος *themelios* (15)
foundation (12)
foundations (3)

2530 θεμελιόω *themelioō* (5)
established (2)
foundation (1)
laid the foundations of (1)
steadfast (1)

2531 θεοδίδακτος *theodidaktos* (1)
taught by God (1)

2532 θεολόγος *theologos*
Variant; not used

2533 θεομαχέω *theomacheō*
Variant; not used

2534 θεομάχος *theomachos* (1)
fighting against God (1)

2535 θεόπνευστος *theopneustos* (1)
God-breathed (1)

2536 θεός *theos* (1316)
God (1149)
God's (123)
gods (8)
him[s] (7) +3836
god (5)
he[s] (5) +3836
his[s] (4) +3836
divine (2)
God-fearing (2) +3836+5828
godly (2) +2848
God-fearing gentiles (1) +3836+5828
goddess (1)
godly (1)
in God's sight (1) +3836+4123
in God's sight (1) +4123
of God (1)
untranslated (3)

2537 θεοσέβεια *theosebeia* (1)
worship God (1)

2538 θεοσεβής *theosebēs* (1)
godly man (1)

2539 θεοστυγής *theostygēs* (1)
God-haters (1)

2540 θεότης *theotēs* (1)
Deity (1)

2541 Θεόφιλος *Theophilos* (2)
Theophilus (2)

2542 θεραπεία *therapeia* (3)
healing (2)
servants (1)

2543 θεραπεύω *therapeuō* (43)
healed (22)
heal (12)
cured (3)
healing (3)
cure (1)
cured (1) +1639
served (1)

2544 θεράπων *therapōn* (1)
servant (1)

2545 θερίζω *therizō* (21)

reap (10)
reaper (2)
reaps (2)
harvest (1)
harvested (1)
harvesters (1)
harvesting (1)
reap a harvest (1)
reap harvest (1)
reaping (1)

2546 θερισμός *therismos* (13)
harvest (10)
harvest field (2)
that[s] (1) +3836

2547 θεριστής *theristēs* (2)
harvesters (2)

2548 θερμαίνω *thermainō* (6)
warming (3)
keep warm (1)
warm (1)
warmed (1)

2549 θέρμη *thermē* (1)
heat (1)

2550 θέρος *theros* (3)
summer (3)

2551 Θεσσαλία *Thessalia*
Variant; not used

2552 Θεσσαλονικεύς *Thessalonikeus* (4)
from Thessalonica (2)
Thessalonians (2)

2553 Θεσσαλονίκη *Thessalonikē* (5)
Thessalonica (4)
Thessalonians (1) +1877

2554 Θευδᾶς *Theudas* (1)
Theudas (1)

2555 θεωρέω *theōreō* (58)
see (22)
saw (18)
sees (5)
watching (3)
can see (1)
look at (1)
looked on (1)
looks (1)
looks at (1)
see here (1) +4047
seeing (1)
seen (1)
think (1)
watched (1)

2556 θεωρία *theōria* (1)
sight (1)

2557 θήκη *thēkē* (1)
away[s] (1) +1650+3836

2558 θηλάζω *thēlazō* (5)
nursing mothers (3)
infants (1)
nursed (1)

2559 θῆλυς *thēlys* (5)
female (3)
women (2)

2560 θήρα *thēra* (1)
trap (1)

2561 θηρεύω *thēreuō* (1)
catch (1)

2562 θηριομαχέω *thēriomacheō* (1)
fought wild beasts (1)

2563 θηρίον *thērion* (45)
beast (35)
snake (2)
wild beasts (2)
animal (1)

animals (1)
brutes (1)
it[s] (1) +1635+3836+3836
wild animals (1)
untranslated (1)

2564 θησαυρίζω *thēsaurizō* (8)
store up (2)
hoarded wealth (1)
reserved (1)
save up (1)
stores up (1)
storing up (1)
sum of money (1)

2565 θησαυρός *thēsauros* (18)
treasure (8)
treasures (5)
stored up (4)
storeroom (1)

2566 θιγγάνω *thinganō* (3)
touch (2)
touches (1)

2567 θλίβω *thlibō* (10)
persecuted (2)
crowding (1)
distressed (1)
harassed (1)
hard pressed (1)
narrow (1)
those in trouble (1)
trouble (1)
troubled (1)

2568 θλῖψις *thlipsis* (45)
trouble (8)
troubles (7)
distress (6)
suffering (4)
hardships (3)
persecution (3)
afflictions (2)
sufferings (2)
trials (2)
affliction (1)
anguish (1)
hard pressed (1)
persecuted (1)
severe trial (1) +1509
suffer (1)
suffer persecution (1) +2400
tribulation (1)

2569 θνῄσκω *thnēskō* (9)
dead (9)

2570 θνητός *thnētos* (6)
mortal (6)

2571 θορυβάζω *thorybazō* (1)
upset (1)

2572 θορυβέω *thorybeō* (4)
alarmed (1)
commotion (1)
noisy (1)
riot (1)

2573 θόρυβος *thorybos* (7)
uproar (3)
commotion (1)
disturbance (1)
riot (1)
riot (1) +1639

2574 θραυματίζω *thraumatizō*
Variant; not used

2575 θραύω *thrauō* (1)
oppressed (1)

2576 θρέμμα *thremma* (1)
flocks and herds (1)

2577 θρηνέω *thrēneō* (4)
sang a dirge (2)

mourn (1)
wailed for (1)

2578 θρῆνος *thrēnos*
Variant; not used

2579 θρησκεία *thrēskeia* (4)
religion (3)
worship (1)

2580 θρῆσκος *thrēskos* (1)
religious (1)

2581 θριαμβεύω *thriambeuō* (2)
leads in triumphal procession (1)
triumphing over (1)

2582 θρίξ *thrix* (15)
hair (11)
hairs (2)
their hair (1) +2400
untranslated (1)

2583 θροέω *throeō* (3)
alarmed (3)

2584 θρόμβος *thrombos* (1)
drops (1)

2585 θρόνος *thronos* (62)
throne (52)
thrones (7)
it^s (1) +3836
them^s (1) +3836
untranslated (1)

2586 θρύπτω *thryptō*
Variant; not used

2587 Θυάτειρα *Thyateira* (4)
Thyatira (4)

2588 θυγάτηρ *thygatēr* (28)
daughter (23)
daughters (4)
descendant (1) +1666+3836

2589 θυγάτριον *thygatrion* (2)
little daughter (2)

2590 θύελλα *thyella* (1)
storm (1)

2591 θύϊνος *thyinos* (1)
citron (1)

2592 θυμίαμα *thymiama* (6)
incense (5)
burning of incense (1)

2593 θυμιατήριον *thymiatērion* (1)
altar of incense (1)

2594 θυμιάω *thymiaō* (1)
burn incense (1)

2595 θυμομαχέω *thymomacheō* (1)
quarreling (1)

2596 θυμός *thymos* (18)
wrath (4)
fury (3)
anger (2)
maddening (2)
rage (2)
fits of rage (1)
furious (1) +4398
furious (1) +4441
fury (1) +3489
outbursts of anger (1)

2597 θυμόω *thymoō* (1)
furious (1) +3336

2598 θύρα *thyra* (39)
door (21)
doors (6)
gate (5)
entrance (4)
doorway (1)
gates (1)
outer entrance (1) +4784

2599 θυρεός *thyreos* (1)
shield (1)

2600 θυρίς *thyris* (2)
window (2)

2601 θυρωρός *thyrōros* (4)
door (1)
girl on duty (1)
one at the door (1)
watchman (1)

2602 θυσία *thysia* (28)
sacrifices (16)
sacrifice (11)
offering (1)

2603 θυσιαστήριον *thysiastērion* (23)
altar (22)
altars (1)

2604 θύω *thyō* (14)
kill (5)
sacrificed (2)
butchered (1)
killed (1)
offer sacrifices (1)
sacrifice (1)
sacrifices offered (1)
sacrificing (1)
untranslated (1)

2605 Θωμᾶς *Thōmas* (11)
Thomas (11)

2606 θώραξ *thōrax* (5)
breastplate (2)
breastplates (2)
their breastplates were (1) +2400

2607 ι *i*
Variant; not used

2608 Ἰάϊρος *Iairos* (2)
Jairus (2)

2609 Ἰακώβ *Iakōb* (27)
Jacob (26)
Jacob's (1)

2610 Ἰάκωβος *Iakōbos* (42)
James (41)
his^s (1) +3836

2611 ἴαμα *iama* (3)
healing (3)

2612 Ἰαμβρῆς *Iambrēs* (1)
Jambres (1)

2613 Ἰανναί *Iannai* (1)
Jannai (1)

2614 Ἰάννης *Iannēs* (1)
Jannes (1)

2615 ἰάομαι *iaomai* (26)
healed (15)
heal (6)
healing (2)
freed (1)
heals (1)
you may be healed (1)

2616 Ἰάρετ *Iaret* (1)
Jared (1)

2617 ἴασις *iasis* (3)
heal (1)
heal people (1) +699
healed (1)

2618 ἴασπις *iaspis* (4)
jasper (3)
jasper (1) +3345

2619 Ἰάσων *Iasōn* (5)
Jason (4)
Jason's (1)

2620 ἰατρός *iatros* (6)
doctor (4)

doctors (1)
physician (1)

2621 Ἰαχίν *Iachin*
Variant; not used

2622 ιβ´ *ib*
Variant; not used

2623 ἴδε *ide*
Variant; not used

2624 ἰδέα *idea*
Variant; not used

2625 ἴδιος *idios* (112)
his own (37)
their own (11)
his (10)
privately (6) +2848
aside (3) +2848
its own (3)
own (3)
their (3)
themselves (3)
your (3)
himself (2)
our own (2)
your own (2)
all had (1) +3836
alone (1)
alone (1) +2848
belongs (1)
friends (1)
her (1)
her own (1)
him (1)
his home (1) +3836
his native language (1) +1666+3836
his own home (1) +3836
his relatives (1)
home (1) +3836
its (1)
its proper (1)
owns (1) +1639
private (1)
proper (1)
whose (1)
your own (1) +3836
yourselves (1)
untranslated (3)

2626 ἰδιώτης *idiōtēs* (5)
not trained (1)
ordinary (1)
some who do not understand (1)
someone who does not understand (1)
those who do not understand (1)

2627 ἰδού *idou* (200)
look (14)
here (11)
see (10)
now (9)
there before (9)
behold (4)
suddenly (4)
here is (2)
I tell you (2)
there (2)
as can see (1)
as know (1)
but (1)
consider (1)
here's (1)
I assure you (1)
indeed (1) +2779
just then (1)
just then (1) +2779
listen (1)
on one occasion (1) +2779
see how (1)
so (1)
suddenly (1) +2779
surely (1)

without warning (1)
yes (1) +1609
yet (1)
untranslated (115)

2628 Ἰδουμαία Idoumaia (1)
Idumea (1)

2629 ἱδρώς hidrōs (1)
sweat (1)

2630 Ἰεζάβελ Iezabel (1)
Jezebel (1)

2631 Ἱεράπολις Hierapolis (1)
Hierapolis (1)

2632 ἱερατεία hierateia (2)
priesthood (1)
priests (1)

2633 ἱεράτευμα hierateuma (2)
priesthood (2)

2634 ἱερατεύω hierateuō (1)
serving as priest (1)

2635 Ἰερεμίας Ieremias (3)
Jeremiah (3)

2636 ἱερεύς hiereus (31)
priest (16)
priests (15)

2637 Ἰεριχώ Ierichō (7)
Jericho (6)
untranslated (1)

2638 ἱερόθυτος hierothytos (1)
offered in sacrifice (1)

2639 ἱερόν hieron (71)
temple (32)
temple courts (23)
temple area (10)
its⁵ (1) +3836
temple grounds (1)
temple guard (1)
there⁵ (1) +1877+3836
untranslated (2)

2640 ἱεροπρεπής hieroprepēs (1)
reverent (1)

2641 ἱερός hieros (2)
holy (1)
temple (1)

2642 Ἱεροσόλυμα Hierosolyma
Variant; not used

2643 Ἱεροσολυμίτης Hierosolymitēs (2)
people of Jerusalem (2)

2644 ἱεροσυλέω hierosyleō (1)
rob temples (1)

2645 ἱερόσυλος hierosylos (1)
robbed temples (1)

2646 ἱερουργέω hierourgeō (1)
priestly duty (1)

2647 Ἰερουσαλήμ Ierousalēm (139)
Jerusalem (136)
city of Jerusalem (2)
untranslated (1)

2648 ἱερωσύνη hierōsynē (3)
priesthood (3)

2649 Ἰεσσαί Iessai (5)
Jesse (5)

2650 Ἰεφθάε Iephthae (1)
Jephthah (1)

2651 Ἰεχονίας Iechonias (2)
Jeconiah (2)

2652 Ἰησοῦς Iēsous (916)
Jesus (882)
Jesus' (14)
he⁵ (7) +3836

him⁵ (6) +3836
Joshua (3)
he⁵ (1)
his⁵ (1) +3836
Jesus (1) +899
untranslated (1)

2653 ἱκανός hikanos (39)
many (5)
long (4)
large (3)
deserve (2) +1639
number (2)
some (2)
worthy (2)
bright (1)
competent (1)
considerable (1)
deserve (1)
enough (1)
equal (1)
fit (1)
great (1)
great number (1)
large number (1)
large numbers (1)
large sum (1)
much (1)
post bond (1)
qualified (1)
satisfy (1) +4472
sufficient (1)
wept (1) +1181+3088
untranslated (1)

2654 ἱκανότης hikanotēs (1)
competence (1)

2655 ἱκανόω hikanoō (2)
made competent (1)
qualified (1)

2656 ἱκετηρία hiketēria (1)
petitions (1)

2657 ἱκμάς ikmas (1)
moisture (1)

2658 Ἰκόνιον Ikonion (6)
Iconium (6)

2659 ἱλαρός hilaros (1)
cheerful (1)

2660 ἱλαρότης hilarotēs (1)
cheerfully (1) +1877

2661 ἱλάσκομαι hilaskomai (2)
make atonement for (1)
mercy on (1)

2662 ἱλασμός hilasmos (2)
atoning sacrifice (2)

2663 ἱλαστήριον hilastērion (2)
atonement cover (1)
sacrifice of atonement (1)

2664 ἵλεως hileōs (2)
forgive (1) +1639
never (1)

2665 Ἰλλυρικόν Illyrikon (1)
Illyricum (1)

2666 ἱμάς himas (4)
thongs (3)
flog (1)

2667 ἱματίζω himatizō (2)
dressed (2)

2668 ἱμάτιον himation (61)
clothes (23)
cloak (13)
cloaks (7)
garment (6)
robe (4)
garments (2)

clothing (1)
dressed (1) +4314
one⁵ (1)
outer clothing (1)
stripped (1) +3836+4351
untranslated (1)

2669 ἱματισμός himatismos (5)
clothes (3)
clothing (2)

2670 ἱμείρομαι himeiromai
Variant; not used

2671 ἵνα hina (663)
so that (195)
to (165)
that (117)
in order that (16)
so (12)
for (11)
in order to (10)
or (7) +3590
to let (6)
want (5)
then (4)
so as to (3)
and (2)
let (2)
meant to be (2)
reason to (2)
therefore (2)
when (2)
aim is to (1)
as (1)
as to (1)
at (1)
because (1)
before (1) +3590
bent on (1)
by (1)
expecting to (1)
for fear that (1) +3590
for if (1) +3607
from (1) +3590
hoped (1)
if (1)
in the hope that (1)
intent that (1)
is to (1)
it was intended that (1)
lest (1) +3590
only (1)
purpose that (1)
purpose to (1)
rather than (1) +3590
this happened that (1)
to keep from (1) +3590
wants (1)
were looking for (1) +2351
which (1)
untranslated (72)

2672 ἵνατί hinati (6)
why (6)

2673 Ἰόππη Ioppē (10)
Joppa (10)

2674 Ἰορδάνης Iordanēs (15)
Jordan (15)

2675 ἰός ios (3)
poison (2)
corrosion (1)

2676 Ἰουδά Iouda
Variant; not used

2677 Ἰουδαία Ioudaia (44)
Judea (43)
Judean (1)

2678 ἰουδαΐζω ioudaizō (1)
follow Jewish customs (1)

2679 Ἰουδαϊκός Ioudaikos (1)
Jewish (1)

2680 Ἰουδαϊκῶς *Ioudaikōs* (1)
like a Jew (1)

2681 Ἰουδαῖος *Ioudaios* (194)
Jews (149)
Jew (18)
Jewish (18)
Jew (2) +467
Jewess (2)
Judean (2)
Jew (1) +476
Jewish community (1) +4436
Jews (1) +467

2682 Ἰουδαϊσμός *Ioudaismos* (2)
Judaism (2)

2683 Ἰούδας *Ioudas* (44)
Judas (32)
Judah (10)
Jude (1)
Judea (1)

2684 Ἰουλία *Ioulia* (1)
Julia (1)

2685 Ἰούλιος *Ioulios* (2)
Julius (2)

2686 Ἰουνία *Iounia*
Variant; not used

2687 Ἰουνιᾶς *Iounias* (1)
Junias (1)

2688 Ἰοῦστος *Ioustos* (3)
Justus (3)

2689 ἱππεύς *hippeus* (2)
cavalry (1)
horsemen (1)

2690 ἱππικός *hippikos* (1)
mounted (1)

2691 ἵππος *hippos* (17)
horses (9)
horse (7)
horses' (1)

2692 ἶρις *iris* (2)
rainbow (2)

2693 Ἰσαάκ *Isaak* (20)
Isaac (20)

2694 ἰσάγγελος *isangelos* (1)
like angels (1)

2695 Ἰσαχάρ *Isachar*
Variant; not used

2696 Ἰσκαριώθ *Iskariōth*
Variant; not used

2697 Ἰσκαριώτης *Iskariōtēs* (11)
Iscariot (11)

2698 ἴσος *isos* (8)
agree (2)
equal (2)
as (1)
equality (1) +1639+3836
in full (1) +3836
same (1)

2699 ἰσότης *isotēs* (3)
equality (2)
fair (1)

2700 ἰσότιμος *isotimos* (1)
as precious as (1)

2701 ἰσόψυχος *isopsychos* (1)
like (1)

2702 Ἰσραήλ *Israēl* (68)
Israel (53)
Israelites (6) +5626
Israel (3) +3875
Israel (3) +5626
Israel's (1)

Israelites (1) +3836+5626
people Israel (1) +5626

2703 Ἰσραηλίτης *Israēlitēs* (9)
of Israel (6)
Israelite (2)
Israelites (1)

2704 Ἰσσαχάρ *Issachar* (1)
Issachar (1)

2705 ἵστημι *histēmi* (163)
standing (40)
stand (33)
stood (29)
stand firm (8)
stood up (5)
stopped (5)
stands (3)
appear (2)
establish (2)
established (2)
got up (2)
standing firm (2)
there (2)
brought (1)
counted out (1)
feet (1)
had to wait (1)
hold (1)
holding (1)
is (1)
made stand (1)
make stand (1)
on trial (1) +3212
present (1)
presented (1)
produced (1)
proposed (1)
put (1)
set (1)
settled the matter (1) +1612
stand fast (1)
standing (1) +1639
stands firm (1)
stayed (1)
stood (1) +1639
stop (1)
take stand (1)
taken stand (1)
uphold (1)
waits (1)
was there (1)

2706 ἱστίον *histion*
Variant; not used

2707 ἱστορέω *historeō* (1)
get acquainted with (1)

2708 ἰσχυρός *ischyros* (28)
strong (8)
mighty (7)
loud (2)
more powerful than (2)
stronger (2)
forceful (1)
greatly (1)
more powerful (1)
power (1)
powerful (1)
severe (1)
stronger than (1)

2709 ἰσχύς *ischys* (10)
strength (6)
mighty (2)
power (1)
stronger (1)

2710 ἰσχύω *ischyō* (28)
could (8)
able (5)
strong (3)
healthy (2)

can do (1)
gave beating (1)
good (1)
grew (1)
had (1)
powerful (1)
takes effect (1)
unable (1) +4024
unable (1) +4033
value (1)

2711 ἴσως *isōs* (1)
perhaps (1)

2712 Ἰταλία *Italia* (4)
Italy (4)

2713 Ἰταλικός *Italikos* (1)
Italian (1)

2714 Ἰτουραῖος *Itouraios* (1)
Iturea (1)

2715 ἰχθύδιον *ichthydion* (2)
small fish (2)

2716 ἰχθύς *ichthys* (20)
fish (19)
untranslated (1)

2717 ἴχνος *ichnos* (3)
follow the same course (1)
footsteps (1)
steps (1)

2718 Ἰωαθάμ *Iōatham* (2)
Jotham (2)

2719 Ἰωακίμ *Iōakim*
Variant; not used

2720 Ἰωανάν *Iōanan* (1)
Joanan (1)

2721 Ἰωάννα *Iōanna* (2)
Joanna (2)

2722 Ἰωάννης *Iōannēs* (135)
John (119)
John's (14)
John's (1) +899
untranslated (1)

2723 Ἰωάς *Iōas*
Variant; not used

2724 Ἰώβ *Iōb* (1)
Job's (1)

2725 Ἰωβήδ *Iōbēd* (3)
Obed (3)

2726 Ἰωδά *Iōda* (1)
Joda (1)

2727 Ἰωήλ *Iōēl* (1)
Joel (1)

2728 Ἰωνάθας *Iōnathas*
Variant; not used

2729 Ἰωνάμ *Iōnam* (1)
Jonam (1)

2730 Ἰωνάν *Iōnan*
Variant; not used

2731 Ἰωνᾶς *Iōnas* (9)
Jonah (9)

2732 Ἰωράμ *Iōram* (2)
Jehoram (2)

2733 Ἰωρίμ *Iōrim* (1)
Jorim (1)

2734 Ἰωσαφάτ *Iōsaphat* (2)
Jehoshaphat (2)

2735 Ἰωσή *Iōsē*
Variant; not used

2736 Ἰωσῆς *Iōsēs* (4)
Joses (3)

Joseph (1)

2737 Ἰωσήφ *Iōsēph* (34)
Joseph (31)
Joseph's (3)

2738 Ἰωσήχ *Iōsēch* (1)
Josech (1)

2739 Ἰωσίας *Iōsias* (2)
Josiah (2)

2740 ἰῶτα *iōta* (1)
the smallest letter (1)

2741 κ *k*
Variant; not used

2742 κάβος *kabos*
Variant; not used

2743 κἀγώ *kagō*
Variant; not used

2744 κάδος *kados*
Variant; not used

2745 καθά *katha* (1)
as (1)

2746 καθαίρεσις *kathairesis* (3)
demolish (1)
pulling down (1)
tearing down (1)

2747 καθαιρέω *kathaireō* (9)
took down (3)
brought down (1)
demolish (1)
overthrew (1)
robbed (1)
take down (1)
tear down (1)

2748 καθαίρω *kathairō* (1)
prunes (1)

2749 καθάπερ *kathaper* (13)
just as (5)
like (2)
as (1)
for (1)
matched (1) +2779+4048
the same thing (1) +2779
untranslated (2)

2750 καθάπτω *kathaptō* (1)
fastened (1)

2751 καθαρίζω *katharizō* (31)
clean (7)
cleansed (5)
cured (4)
make clean (3)
purify (3)
cleanse (2)
made clean (2)
purified (2)
cleansing (1)
purifies (1)
wash (1)

2752 καθαρισμός *katharismos* (7)
ceremonial washing (2)
cleansing (2)
purification (2)
cleansed (1)

2753 κάθαρμα *katharma*
Variant; not used

2754 καθαρός *katharos* (26)
clean (11)
pure (11)
clear (3)
innocent (1)

2755 καθαρότης *katharotēs* (1)
clean (1)

2756 καθέδρα *kathedra* (3)

benches (2)
seat (1)

2757 καθέζομαι *kathezomai* (7)
seated (2)
sitting (2)
sat (1)
sat down (1)
stayed (1)

2758 καθείς *katheis*
Variant; not used

2759 καθεξῆς *kathexēs* (5)
after this (1) +1877+3836
as it had happened (1)
from place to place (1)
on (1) +2779+3836
orderly (1)

2760 καθερίζω *katherizō*
Variant; not used

2761 καθεύδω *katheudō* (22)
sleeping (10)
asleep (6)
sleep (2)
fell asleep (1)
sleeper (1)
sleeping (1) +1877
sleeps (1)

2762 καθηγητής *kathēgētēs* (2)
teacher (2)

2763 καθήκω *kathēkō* (2)
fit (1)
ought to be done (1)

2764 κάθημαι *kathēmai* (91)
sitting (28)
seated (12)
sit (12)
sits (10)
sat (8)
rider (4) +3836
sat down (4)
live (2)
living (2)
rider (2)
sitting down (2)
rider (1) +899+2093
riders (1) +899+2093
riders (1) +2093+3836
seat (1)
untranslated (1)

2765 καθημέραν *kathēmeran*
Variant; not used

2766 καθημερινός *kathēmerinos* (1)
daily (1)

2767 καθίζω *kathizō* (46)
sat down (15)
sit (10)
sat (4)
sit down (3)
ridden (2)
seated (2)
appoint as judges (1)
came to rest (1)
convened (1)
convened the court (1) +1037+2093+3836
place (1)
sets up (1)
sits (1)
sitting down (1)
stay (1)
stayed (1)

2768 καθίημι *kathiēmi* (4)
let down (2)
lowered (1)
lowered (1) +5899

2769 καθιστάνω *kathistanō*
Variant; not used

2770 καθίστημι *kathistēmi* (21)
made (5)
put in charge (5)
appointed (3)
appoint (1)
appoints (1)
becomes (1)
escorted (1)
keep (1)
puts in charge (1)
turn over to (1)
untranslated (1)

2771 καθό *katho*
Variant; not used

2772 καθολικός *katholikos*
Variant; not used

2773 καθόλου *katholou* (1)
at all (1)

2774 καθοπλίζω *kathoplizō* (1)
fully armed (1)

2775 καθοράω *kathoraō* (1)
clearly seen (1)

2776 καθότι *kathoti* (6)
because (3)
as (1)
as (1) +323
for (1)

2777 καθώς *kathōs* (182)
as (82)
just as (47)
even as (5)
like (3)
since (3)
because (2)
for (2)
in accordance with (2)
what (2)
according to (1)
and (1)
any more than (1) +4024
as much as (1)
as well as (1)
but (1) +4024
equal with us (1) +1609+2779
how (1)
just (1)
just as (1) +2779
just as (1) +4048
just what (1)
that (1)
that way (1)
the same (1) +3931
this agrees with (1)
this is why (1)
which agrees with (1)
untranslated (16)

2778 καθώσπερ *kathōsper* (1)
just as (1)

2779 καί *kai* (9139)
and (4847)
also (244)
then (230)
but (173)
even (104)
so (93)
or (58)
too (36)
yet (36)
and then (23)
with (23)
now (15)
when (15)
both (14)
and so (12)
and also (10)
as (10)
and yet (9)

as well (8)
still (7)
where (7)
while (7)
as well as (6)
in fact (6)
so that (6)
there (6)
and even (5)
nor (5)
what do want with (5) +5515
including (4)
though (4)
though (4) +1623
whether (4)
again (3)
along with (3)
and too (3)
even though (3)
if (3)
in turn (3)
nor (3) +4024
afterward (2)
because (2)
but even (2)
he (2)
in fact (2) +1142
in the same way (2) +4048
later (2)
man (2) +135+4922
meanwhile (2)
rather than (2) +4024
therefore (2)
thus (2)
until (2)
with that (2)
430 (1) +5484+5558
450 (1) +4299+5484
accompanied by (1) +2262
and (1) +1181
and (1) +5538
and alike (1) +5445
and as (1) +4099
and as well (1)
and both (1)
and even more (1) +4707+5148
and indeed (1)
and others (1)
and still (1)
and though (1)
and up (1)
and what is more (1)
　　　　　+247+1145+4047+4246+5250
as for (1)
as it is (1) +1142
at (1)
at least (1) +1569
at that (1)
at this (1)
both (1) +4047
both of you (1) +899+5148
but (1) +1623
but also (1)
but still (1)
by (1)
eighteen (1) +1274+3893
equal with us (1) +1609+2777
even (1) +1569
for (1)
forty-six (1) +1971+5477
fully convinced (1) +3857+4275
furthermore (1)
greatly increased (1) +889+4437
if so (1)
in addition (1) +247
in fact (1) +1254
in this same way (1) +4048
indeed (1)
indeed (1) +247
indeed (1) +1254
indeed (1) +2627

instead of (1) +4049
it is the same (1) +4048
it is with (1)
just (1) +1569
just as (1) +2777
just as though (1) +899+1651+3836
just then (1) +2627
likewise (1) +1142
likewise (1) +4048
matched (1) +2749+4048
more than that (1)
moved about freely (1) +1660+1744
neither (1) +4024
nor (1) +3590
now (1) +1181
on (1) +2759+3836
on both sides (1) +2277+3957
on each side (1) +1696+1949
on one occasion (1)
on one occasion (1) +2627
once (1)
once (1) +1181
once more (1) +4099
one day (1) +1181
one on each side (1) +1949+1949
or (1) +4024
or even (1)
rather than (1) +3590
same as (1) +4005
searched intently and with the greatest care
　　　　　　　　(1) +1699+2001
so it is with (1) +4048
so too (1)
some (1)
soon (1)
suddenly (1) +2627
than that (1) +3590
the same as (1) +6055
the same thing (1) +2749
the same way (1) +6055
the two of you (1) +899+5148
their (1)
then (1) +4099
they$ (1) +899+899+3412+3836
thirty-eight (1) +3893+5558
though (1) +1145
to this (1)
together with (1)
what is more (1) +247+1254+3667+4024
why do involve (1) +5515
without (1) +3590
without (1) +4024
yet even (1)
untranslated (2958)

2780 Καϊάφας *Kaiaphas* (9)
Caiaphas (9)

2781 καίγε *kaige*
Variant; not used

2782 Κάϊν *Kain* (3)
Cain (3)

2783 Καϊνάμ *Kainam* (2)
Cainan (1)
Kenan (1)

2784 Καϊνάν *Kainan*
Variant; not used

2785 καινός *kainos* (42)
new (39)
anew (2)
latest (1)

2786 καινότης *kainotēs* (2)
new (1)
new way (1)

2787 καινοφωνία *kainophōnia*
Variant; not used

2788 καίπερ *kaiper* (5)
even though (2)
though (2)

although (1)

2789 καιρός *kairos* (85)
time (50)
times (8)
opportunity (3)
age (2)
dates (2)
right time (2)
the proper time (2)
a while (1)
always (1) +1877+4246
appointed season (1)
at just the right time (1) +2848
due time (1)
find convenient (1) +3561
in seasons (1)
make the most of opportunity (1)
+1973+3836
occasions (1)
opportune time (1)
present (1) +3814+3836
present time (1)
proper time (1)
season (1)
seasons (1)
untranslated (1)

2790 Καῖσαρ *Kaisar* (29)
Caesar (20)
Caesar's (9)

2791 Καισάρεια *Kaisareia* (17)
Caesarea (17)

2792 καίτοι *kaitoi* (2)
and yet (1)
yet (1)

2793 καίτοιγε *kaitoige* (1)
although in fact (1)

2794 καίω *kaiō* (12)
burning (5)
blazing (2)
burned (2)
all ablaze (1) +4786
flames (1)
light (1)

2795 κἀκεῖ *kakei*
Variant; not used

2796 κἀκεῖθεν *kakeithen*
Variant; not used

2797 κἀκεῖνος *kakeinos*
Variant; not used

2798 κακία *kakia* (11)
malice (5)
evil (3)
depravity (1)
trouble (1)
wickedness (1)

2799 κακοήθεια *kakoētheia* (1)
malice (1)

2800 κακολογέω *kakologeō* (4)
curses (2)
maligned (1)
say bad about (1)

2801 κακοπάθεια *kakopatheia* (1)
suffering (1)

2802 κακοπαθέω *kakopatheō* (3)
endure hardship (1)
suffering (1)
trouble (1)

2803 κακοποιέω *kakopoieō* (4)
do evil (2)
does what is evil (1)
doing evil (1)

2804 κακοποιός *kakopoios* (3)
criminal (1)

doing wrong (1)
do wrong (1)

2805 κακός *kakos* (50)
evil (25)
wrong (8)
crime (3)
harm (3)
bad (2)
wicked (2)
criminal (1) +4472
harm (1) +4556
ill effects (1)
ugly (1)
wretches (1)
wrongdoer (1) +4556
wrongs (1)

2806 κακοῦργος *kakourgos* (4)
criminals (3)
criminal (1)

2807 κακουχέω *kakoucheō* (2)
mistreated (2)

2808 κακόω *kakoō* (6)
harm (2)
mistreated (1)
oppressed (1)
persecute (1)
poisoned (1)

2809 κακῶς *kakōs* (16)
sick (7) +2400
wrong (2)
diseases (1) +3798
evil (1)
greatly (1)
terribly (1)
was sick (1) +2400
were ill (1) +2400
wretched (1)

2810 κάκωσις *kakōsis* (1)
oppression (1)

2811 καλάμη *kalamē* (1)
straw (1)

2812 κάλαμος *kalamos* (12)
reed (4)
staff (3)
rod (2)
stick (2)
pen (1)

2813 καλέω *kaleō* (148)
called (85)
call (12)
invited (11)
calls (8)
give (3)
host (2)
invite (2)
invites (2)
known as (2)
reckoned (2)
call (1) +3836+3950
calling received (1) +3104
consecrated (1) +41
gave (1)
given (1)
guests (1)
has (1)
host who invited (1)
name (1)
name (1) +3836+3950
named (1)
named (1) +3950
said to be (1)
tell (1)
was known as (1)
untranslated (4)

2814 καλλιέλαιος *kallielaios* (1)
cultivated olive tree (1)

2815 καλοδιδάσκαλος *kalodidaskalos* (1)
teach what is good (1)

2816 Καλοὶ λιμένες *Kaloi limenes* (1)
fair Havens (1)

2817 καλοκαγαθία *kalokagathia*
Variant; not used

2818 καλοποιέω *kalopoieō* (1)
doing what is right (1)

2819 καλός *kalos* (100)
good (65)
better (9)
right (5)
beautiful (3)
noble (3)
excellent (2)
fine (2)
best (1)
choice (1)
clear (1)
faithfully (1) +6055
firm (1)
goodness (1)
great (1)
itˢ (1) +3836
theseˢ (1) +2240
untranslated (2)

2820 κάλυμμα *kalymma* (4)
veil (4)

2821 καλύπτω *kalyptō* (8)
veiled (2)
concealed (1)
cover (1)
cover over (1)
covers over (1)
hides (1)
swept over (1)

2822 καλῶς *kalos* (37)
well (12)
good (8)
right (6)
the truth (2)
easily (1)
fine way (1)
good (1) +4472
granted (1)
honorably (1)
rightly (1)
the right thing (1)
very well (1)
well said (1)

2823 κάμηλος *kamēlos* (6)
camel (4)
camel's (2)

2824 κάμιλος *kamilos*
Variant; not used

2825 κάμινος *kaminos* (4)
furnace (4)

2826 καμμύω *kammyō* (2)
closed (2)

2827 κάμνω *kamnō* (2)
grow weary (1)
sick (1)

2828 κάμπτω *kamptō* (4)
bow (1)
bowed (1)
kneel (1) +1205+3836
should bow (1)

2829 κἄν *kan*
Variant; not used

2830 Κανά *Kana* (4)
Cana (4)

2831 Καναναῖος *Kananaios* (2)
Zealot (2)

2832 Κανανίτης *Kananitēs*
Variant; not used

2833 Κανδάκη *Kandakē* (1)
Candace (1)

2834 κανών *kanōn* (4)
area of activity (1)
field (1) +3586+3836
rule (1)
territory (1)

2835 Καπερναούμ *Kapernaoum*
Variant; not used

2836 καπηλεύω *kapēleuō* (1)
peddle for profit (1)

2837 καπνός *kapnos* (13)
smoke (13)

2838 Καππαδοκία *Kappadokia* (2)
Cappadocia (2)

2839 καραδοκία *karadokia*
Variant; not used

2840 καρδία *kardia* (157)
hearts (69)
heart (60)
mind (3)
minds (2)
to himself (2) +899+1877+3836
decided (1) +326+2093+3836
experts (1) +1214
heart's (1)
himself (1) +899
inmost (1)
made think (1) +1877+3836+5502
make up mind (1) +1877+3836+5502
prompted (1) +965+1650+3836
self (1) +476+3836
stand firm (1) +3836+5114
themselves (1) +899+3836
thought (1)
wholeheartedly (1) +1666
wondered about (1) +1877+3836+5502
untranslated (7)

2841 καρδιογνώστης *kardiognōstēs* (2)
know heart (1)
knows heart (1)

2842 Κάρπος *Karpos* (1)
Carpus (1)

2843 καρπός *karpos* (66)
fruit (41)
crop (6)
harvest (4)
crops (3)
benefit (2)
grain (2)
child bear (1) +3120+3836
descendants (1) +3836+4019
fruitful (1)
fruitful (1) +5770
grapes (1)
heads (1)
seeds (1)
untranslated (1)

2844 καρποφορέω *karpophoreō* (8)
bearing fruit (2)
produce a crop (2)
bear fruit (1)
bore fruit (1)
produces a crop (1)
produces grain (1)

2845 καρποφόρος *karpophoros* (1)
crops (1)

2846 καρτερέω *kartereō* (1)
persevered (1)

2847 κάρφος *karphos* (6)
speck (4)
speck of sawdust (2)

2848 κατά *kata* (477)
against (47)
according to (46)
in (40)
by (34)
as (17)
every (10)
about (6)
for (6)
in accordance with (6)
privately (6) +2625
to (6)
at (5)
because of (5)
daily (5) +2465
like (5)
on (4)
over (4)
with (4)
along (3)
aside (3) +2625
based on (3)
down (3)
in every (3)
in keeping with (3)
in various (3)
just as (3)
of (3)
through (3)
as for (2)
case (2) +3836
contrary to (2)
day after day (2) +2465
earthly (2) +4922
every (2) +4246
every day (2) +2465
from house to house (2) +3875
from one to another (2)
godly (2) +2536
in obedience to (2)
in the ordinary way (2) +4922
is concerned (2)
just as (2) +4012
natural (2) +5882
off (2)
on the basis of (2)
out of (2)
required (2)
that is how (2) +899+3836
throughout (2)
throughout (2) +3910
your own (2) +5148
a follower of (1)
actions deserve (1) +2240
after (1)
agrees with (1)
all over (1) +3910
alone (1) +2625
alone (1) +3668
among (1)
annual (1) +1929
anywhere else in (1)
as does (1)
as intended (1)
as much as were able (1) +1539
as on (1)
as to (1)
as usual (1) +899+3836
as usual (1) +1621+3836
as was (1)
at just the right time (1) +2789
before (1)
before (1) +4725
by means of (1)
by standards (1)
by the standards of (1)
carrying out (1)
commanding (1) +2198+3306
conforms to (1)
considerate (1) +1194
covered (1) +2400

daily (1) +1667+2465
day by day (1) +2465+4246
deny truth (1) +237+6017
depends on (1)
down from (1)
during (1)
each (1)
each (1) +1651+1651
everyone (1) +4246
extreme (1) +958
faced (1) +4725
followed (1)
forced (1) +340
found in (1)
from a worldly point of view (1) +4922
from after town (1)
from everyday life (1) +476
from house to house (1) +3836+3875
from human point of view (1) +476
from one synagogue to another (1)
                                    +4246+5252
from village to village (1) +3267+3836
great (1) +5651
happened (1) +5175
how (1) +3836
how (1) +5515
human (1) +476
in any way (1) +3594+5573
in conformity with (1)
in each (1)
in regard to (1)
in response to (1)
in the way does (1)
in their homes (1) +3875
in this way⁵ (1) +4922
in turn (1) +1651
in whole (1)
indicating that (1) +4005
intensely (1) +5651
just as (1) +4005+4048+5573
just as (1) +4005+5573
just like this (1) +899+3836
leads to (1)
member (1) +3517+3836
most excellent (1) +5651
near (1)
observer of law (1) +3795
one at a time (1) +1651+1651
opposed to (1)
opposite (1)
orderly way (1) +5423
out of favoritism (1) +4680
over against (1)
prescribed by (1)
reasonable (1) +3364
required by (1)
requires (1)
something man made up (1) +476
spontaneous (1) +1730
surface (1) +4725
that (1) +4005
that far outweighs them all (1)
                        +983+1650+5651+5651
that meets in (1)
this is (1) +3836
thoroughly (1) +205
to my shame (1) +871
to suit (1)
toward (1)
what has happened to (1) +3836
when (1)
when face to face (1) +4725
where (1)
with regard to (1)
year after year (1) +1929
your (1) +5148
untranslated (42)

2849 καταβαίνω *katabainō* (81)
come down (14)
went down (13)

came down (12)
coming down (9)
go down (6)
descended (3)
descending (3)
comes down (2)
down (2)
goes down (2)
going down (2)
arrived (1)
came (1)
come (1)
comes (1)
descend (1)
falling (1)
fell (1)
go downstairs (1)
gone down (1)
got down (1)
on the way (1)
went (1)
untranslated (1)

2850 καταβάλλω *kataballō* (2)
laying (1)
struck down (1)

2851 καταβαρέω *katabareō* (1)
burden to (1)

2852 καταβαρύνω *katabarynō* (1)
heavy (1)

2853 κατάβασις *katabasis* (1)
place where the road goes down (1)

2854 καταβιβάζω *katabibazo*
Variant; not used

2855 καταβοάω *kataboaō*
Variant; not used

2856 καταβολή *katabolē* (11)
creation (9)
become a father (1) +3284+5065
beginning (1)

2857 καταβραβεύω *katabrabeuō* (1)
disqualify for the prize (1)

2858 καταγγελεύς *katangeleus* (1)
advocating (1)

2859 καταγγέλλω *katangellō* (18)
proclaim (4)
proclaimed (3)
preach (2)
preached (2)
proclaiming (2)
advocating (1)
foretold (1)
preaching (1)
reported (1)
telling (1)

2860 καταγελάω *katagelaō* (3)
laughed at (3)

2861 καταγινώσκω *kataginōskō* (3)
condemn (2)
clearly in the wrong (1)

2862 κατάγνυμι *katagnymi* (4)
break (2)
broke (1)
broken (1)

2863 καταγράφω *katagraphō* (1)
write (1)

2864 κατάγω *katagō* (9)
bring (2)
brought (2)
bring down (1)
landed (1)
pulled up (1)
put in (1)
took down (1)

2865 καταγωνίζομαι *katagōnizomai* (1)
conquered (1)

2866 καταδέω *katadeō* (1)
bandaged (1)

2867 κατάδηλος *katadēlos* (1)
clear (1)

2868 καταδικάζω *katadikazō* (5)
condemned (4)
condemn (1)

2869 καταδίκη *katadikē* (1)
be condemned (1)

2870 καταδιώκω *katadiōkō* (1)
to look for (1)

2871 καταδουλόω *katadouloō* (2)
enslaves (1)
make slaves (1)

2872 καταδυναστεύω *katadynasteuō* (2)
exploiting (1)
under the power (1)

2873 κατάθεμα *katathema* (1)
curse (1)

2874 καταθεματίζω *katathematizō* (1)
call down curses (1)

2875 καταισχύνω *kataischynō* (13)
put to shame (3)
dishonors (2)
shame (2)
ashamed (1)
ashamed of (1)
disappoint (1)
embarrassed (1)
humiliate (1)
humiliated (1)

2876 κατακαίω *katakaiō* (12)
burned (4)
burned up (4)
burn (1)
burn up (1)
burning up (1)
consumed (1)

2877 κατακαλύπτω *katakalyptō* (3)
cover (3)

2878 κατακαυχάομαι *katakauchaomai* (4)
boast (1)
boast over (1)
triumphs over (1)
untranslated (1)

2879 κατάκειμαι *katakeimai* (12)
eating (3)
lying (2)
bedridden (1) +2093+3187
dinner (1)
in bed (1)
lie (1)
lying on (1)
reclining at the table (1)
sick in bed (1)

2880 κατακλάω *kataklaō* (2)
broke (2)

2881 κατακλείω *katakleiō* (2)
locked (1)
put (1)

2882 κατακληροδοτέω *kataklērodoteō*
Variant; not used

2883 κατακληρονομέω *kataklēronomeō* (1)
gave to as inheritance (1)

2884 κατακλίνω *kataklinō* (5)
at the table (1)
reclined at the table (1)
sat down (1)
sit down (1)
take (1) +1650

2885 κατακλύζω *kataklyzō* (1)
deluged (1) +5623

2886 κατακλυσμός *kataklysmos* (4)
flood (4)

2887 κατακολουθέω *katakoloutheō* (2)
followed (2)

2888 κατακόπτω *katakoptō* (1)
cut (1)

2889 κατακρημνίζω *katakrēmnizō* (1)
throw down the cliff (1)

2890 κατάκριμα *katakrima* (3)
condemnation (3)

2891 κατακρίνω *katakrinō* (18)
condemned (9)
condemn (7)
condemning (1)
condemns (1)

2892 κατάκρισις *katakrisis* (2)
condemn (1)
condemns (1)

2893 κατακύπτω *katakyptō* (1)
stooped down (1)

2894 κατακυριεύω *katakyrieuō* (4)
lord it over (2)
lording it over (1)
overpowered (1)

2895 καταλαλέω *katalaleō* (5)
slander (2)
speaks against (2)
accuse (1)

2896 καταλαλιά *katalalia* (2)
slander (2)

2897 κατάλαλος *katalalos* (1)
slanderers (1)

2898 καταλαμβάνω *katalambanō* (15)
caught (1)
caught in the act (1) +900+2093
found (1)
get the prize (1)
grasp (1)
obtained (1)
overtakes (1)
realize (1)
realized (1)
seizes (1)
surprise (1)
take hold (1)
taken hold of (1)
took hold of (1)
understood (1)

2899 καταλέγω *katalegō* (1)
put on the list (1)

2900 κατάλειμμα *kataleimma*
Variant; not used

2901 καταλείπω *kataleipō* (24)
left (11)
leave (4)
leaving (3)
leaves (1)
leaving behind (1)
neglect (1)
passing (1)
reserved (1)
stands (1)

2902 καταλιθάζω *katalithazō* (1)
stone (1)

2903 καταλλαγή *katallagē* (4)
reconciliation (4)

2904 καταλλάσσω *katallassō* (6)
reconciled (5)
reconciling (1)

2905 κατάλοιπος *kataloipos* (1)
remnant (1)

2906 κατάλυμα *katalyma* (3)
guest room (2)
inn (1)

2907 καταλύω *katalyō* (17)
destroy (6)
thrown down (3)
abolish (2)
destroyed (2)
fail (1)
guest (1)
lodging (1)
stop (1)

2908 καταμανθάνω *katamanthanō* (1)
see (1)

2909 καταμαρτυρέω *katamartyreō* (3)
testimony bringing against (3)

2910 καταμένω *katamenō* (1)
staying (1)

2911 καταμόνας *katamonas*
Variant; not used

2912 κατανάθεμα *katanathema*
Variant; not used

2913 καταναθεματίζω *katanathematizō*
Variant; not used

2914 καταναλίσκω *katanaliskō* (1)
consuming (1)

2915 καταναρκάω *katanarkaō* (3)
burden (2)
burden to (1)

2916 κατανεύω *kataneuō* (1)
signaled (1)

2917 κατανοέω *katanoeō* (14)
consider (3)
pay attention to (2)
faced the fact (1)
fix thoughts on (1)
look (1)
look more closely (1)
looked (1) +867
looking at (1)
looks at (1)
saw (1)
saw through (1)

2918 καταντάω *katantaō* (13)
arrived (4)
reach (2)
attain (1)
came (1)
came to (1)
come (1)
landed (1)
reached (1)
see fulfilled (1)

2919 κατάνυξις *katanyxis* (1)
stupor (1)

2920 κατανύσσομαι *katanyssomai* (1)
cut to (1)

2921 καταξιόω *kataxioō* (3)
counted worthy (2)
considered worthy of (1)

2922 καταπατέω *katapateō* (5)
trample (1)
trampled (1)
trampled on (1)
trampled under foot (1)
trampling on (1)

2923 κατάπαυσις *katapausis* (9)
rest (8)
resting (1)

2924 καταπαύω *katapauō* (4)
given rest (1)
keeping (1)
rested (1)
rests (1)

2925 καταπέτασμα *katapetasma* (6)
curtain (6)

2926 καταπίμπρημι *katapimprēmi*
Variant; not used

2927 καταπίνω *katapinō* (7)
swallowed up (2)
devour (1)
drowned (1)
overwhelmed (1)
swallow (1)
swallowing (1)

2928 καταπίπτω *katapiptō* (3)
fell (2)
fall (1)

2929 καταπλέω *katapleō* (1)
sailed (1)

2930 καταπονέω *kataponeō* (2)
distressed (1)
him[s] (1) +3836

2931 καταποντίζω *katapontizō* (2)
drowned (1)
sink (1)

2932 κατάρα *katara* (6)
curse (3)
accursed (1)
being cursed (1)
cursing (1)

2933 καταράομαι *kataraomai* (5)
curse (3)
cursed (2)

2934 καταργέω *katargeō* (27)
destroy (3)
destroyed (3)
nullify (3)
fading away (2)
released (2)
abolished (1)
abolishing (1)
alienated (1)
cease (1)
coming to nothing (1)
disappears (1)
do away with (1)
done away with (1)
fading (1)
pass away (1)
put behind (1)
taken away (1)
use up (1)
worthless (1)

2935 καταριθμέω *katarithmeō* (1)
number (1)

2936 καταρτίζω *katartizō* (13)
prepared (2)
preparing (2)
restore (2)
aim for perfection (1)
equip (1)
formed (1)
fully trained (1)
ordained (1)
perfectly united (1) +899+3836
supply (1)

2937 κατάρτισις *katartisis* (1)
perfection (1)

2938 καταρτισμός *katartismos* (1)
prepare (1)

2939 κατασείω *kataseiō* (4)
motioned (3)

motioned (1) +3836+5931

2940 κατασκάπτω *kataskaptō* (2)
ruins (1)
torn down (1)

2941 κατασκευάζω *kataskeuazō* (11)
built (3)
prepare (3)
builder of (2)
arranged (1)
prepared (1)
set up (1)

2942 κατασκηνόω *kataskēnoō* (4)
perch (2)
live (1)
perched (1)

2943 κατασκήνωσις *kataskēnōsis* (2)
nests (2)

2944 κατασκιάζω *kataskiazō* (1)
overshadowing (1)

2945 κατασκοπέω *kataskopeō* (1)
spy on (1)

2946 κατάσκοπος *kataskopos* (1)
spies (1)

2947 κατασοφίζομαι *katasophizomai* (1)
dealt treacherously with (1)

2948 καταστέλλω *katastellō* (2)
quiet (1)
quieted (1)

2949 κατάστημα *katastēma* (1)
way live (1)

2950 καταστολή *katastolē* (1)
modestly (1) +3177

2951 καταστρέφω *katastrephō* (2)
overturned (2)

2952 καταστρηνιάω *katastrēniaō* (1)
sensual desires overcome their
dedication to (1)

2953 καταστροφή *katastrophē* (1)
ruins (1)

2954 καταστρώννυμι *katastrōnnymi* (1)
scattered (1)

2955 κατασύρω *katasyrō* (1)
drag off (1)

2956 κατασφάζω *katasphazō* (1)
kill (1)

2957 κατασφάττω *katasphattō*
Variant; not used .

2958 κατασφραγίζω *katasphragizō* (1)
sealed (1)

2959 κατάσχεσις *kataschesis* (2)
possess (1)
took (1)

2960 κατατίθημι *katatithēmi* (2)
do (1)
grant (1)

2961 κατατομή *katatomē* (1)
mutilators (1)

2962 κατατοξεύω *katatoxeuō*
Variant; not used

2963 κατατρέχω *katatrechō* (1)
ran down (1)

2964 καταυγάζω *kataugazō*
Variant; not used

2965 καταφέρω *katapherō* (4)
bringing against (1)
cast against (1)
sinking (1)
sound asleep (1) +608+3836+5678

2966 καταφεύγω *katapheugō* (2)
fled (2)

2967 καταφθείρω *kataphtheirō* (1)
depraved (1)

2968 καταφιλέω *kataphileō* (6)
kissed (5)
kissing (1)

2969 καταφρονέω *kataphroneō* (9)
despise (4)
look down on (2)
scorning (1)
show contempt for (1)
show less respect (1)

2970 καταφρονητής *kataphronētēs* (1)
scoffers (1)

2971 καταφωνέω *kataphōneō*
Variant; not used

2972 καταχέω *katacheō* (2)
poured (1)
poured on (1)

2973 καταχθόνιος *katachthonios* (1)
under the earth (1)

2974 καταχράομαι *katachraomai* (2)
engrossed in (1)
make use of (1)

2975 καταψηφίζομαι *katapsēphizomai*
Variant; not used

2976 καταψύχω *katapsychō* (1)
cool (1)

2977 κατείδωλος *kateidōlos* (1)
full of idols (1)

2978 κατέναντι *katenanti* (8)
ahead (3)
in the sight (2)
opposite (2)
before (1)

2979 κατενώπιον *katenōpion* (3)
in sight (2)
before (1)

2980 κατεξουσιάζω *katexousiazō* (2)
exercise authority over (2)

2981 κατεργάζομαι *katergazomai* (22)
do (3)
produced (3)
brings (2)
done (2)
accomplished (1)
achieving (1)
carry out (1)
committed (1)
develops (1)
did (1)
does (1)
doing (1)
made (1)
produces (1)
result in (1)
work out (1)

2982 κατέρχομαι *katerchomai* (16)
came down (4)
went down (4)
landed (3)
went (2)
arrived (1)
came (1)
come down (1)

2983 κατεσθίω *katesthiō* (14)
ate up (3)
devour (3)
ate (1)
consume (1)
devoured (1)
devouring (1)

devours (1)
eat (1)
exploits (1)
squandered (1)

2984 κατέσθω *katesthō*
Variant; not used

2985 κατευθύνω *kateuthynō* (3)
clear (1)
direct (1)
guide (1)

2986 κατευλογέω *kateulogeō* (1)
blessed (1)

2987 κατεφίσταμαι *katephistamai* (1)
made a attack on (1)

2988 κατέχω *katechō* (17)
hold on to (2)
keep (2)
bound (1)
hold (1)
hold firmly (1)
hold to (1)
holding back (1)
holding to (1)
holds back (1)
made (1)
possessing (1)
retain (1)
suppress (1)
take (1)
theirs to keep (1)

2989 κατηγορέω *katēgoreō* (23)
accuse (5)
accusing (3)
accused (2)
accused of (1)
accuser (1)
accuses (1)
accusing of (1)
bring charges (1)
charge to bring against (1)
charges (1)
charges bringing against (1)
charges brought against (1)
charges making against (1)
he[s] (1) +3836
presented case (1)
press charges against (1)

2990 κατηγορία *katēgoria* (3)
accusation (1)
charge (1)
charges (1)

2991 κατήγορος *katēgoros* (4)
accusers (3)
accusers (1) +2400

2992 κατήγωρ *katēgōr* (1)
accuser (1)

2993 κατήφεια *katēpheia* (1)
gloom (1)

2994 κατηχέω *katecheō* (8)
informed (1)
instruct (1)
instructed (1)
instructed in (1)
instructor (1)
receives instruction in (1)
reports (1)
taught (1)

2995 κατιόω *katioō* (1)
corroded (1)

2996 κατισχύω *katischyō* (3)
be able (1)
overcome (1)
prevailed (1)

2997 κατοικέω *katoikeō* (44)

inhabitants (7)
live (7)
living (5)
lived (4)
dwell (3)
in (2)
lived in (2)
lives (2)
living in (2)
dwells in (1)
home (1)
inhabit (1)
inhabitants of (1)
live in (1)
residents of (1)
settled (1)
staying (1)
them[s] (1) +1178+2093+3836+3836
untranslated (1)

2998 κατοίκησις *katoikēsis* (1)
lived (1) +2400+3836

2999 κατοικητήριον *katoikētērion* (2)
dwelling (1)
home (1)

3000 κατοικία *katoikia* (1)
live (1)

3001 κατοικίζω *katoikizō* (1)
live (1)

3002 κατοπτρίζω *katoptrizō* (1)
reflect (1)

3003 κατόρθωμα *katorthōma*
Variant; not used

3004 κάτω *katō* (9)
below (3)
down (3)
bottom (2)
to the ground (1)

3005 κατώτερος *katōteros* (1)
lower (1)

3006 κατωτέρω *katōterō* (1)
under (1)

3007 Καῦδα *Kauda* (1)
Cauda (1)

3008 καῦμα *kauma* (2)
heat (1)
scorching heat (1)

3009 καυματίζω *kaumatizō* (4)
scorched (2)
scorch (1)
seared (1)

3010 καυματόω *kaumatoō*
Variant; not used

3011 καῦσις *kausis* (1)
burned (1)

3012 καυσόω *kausoō* (2)
fire (1)
heat (1)

3013 καυστηριάζω *kaustēriazō* (1)
seared as with a hot iron (1)

3014 καύσων *kausōn* (3)
heat of the day (1)
hot (1)
scorching heat (1)

3015 καυτηριάζω *kautēriazō*
Variant; not used

3016 καυχάομαι *kauchaomai* (36)
boast (16)
boasting (4)
rejoice (3)
boast about (2)
boasts (2)
take pride (2)

boast of (1)
boasted (1)
boasting about (1)
boasting of (1)
brag (1)
brag about (1)
glory (1)

3017 καύχημα *kauchēma* (11)
boast (4)
boasting (2)
pride (2)
boast (1) +1639
joy (1)
something to boast about (1)

3018 καύχησις *kauchēsis* (11)
boasting (4)
pride (2)
boast (1)
boasting about (1)
glory (1)
glory in (1) +2400
glory over (1) +2400

3019 Καφαρναούμ *Kapharnaoum* (16)
Capernaum (16)

3020 Κεγχρεαί *Kenchreai* (2)
Cenchrea (2)

3021 κέδρος *kedros*
Variant; not used

3022 Κεδρών *Kedrōn* (1)
Kidron (1)

3023 κεῖμαι *keimai* (24)
lying (4)
destined (2)
is (2)
laid (2)
there (2)
been (1)
by itself (1) +1650+1651+5536+6006
covers (1) +2093
laid out (1)
laid up (1)
lay (1)
made (1)
put here (1)
stood (1) +1639
under the control (1)
was (1)
untranslated (1)

3024 κειρία *keiria* (1)
strips of linen (1)

3025 κείρω *keirō* (4)
cut off (2)
hair cut (1)
shearer (1)

3026 κέλευσμα *keleusma* (1)
loud command (1)

3027 κελεύω *keleuō* (25)
ordered (18)
gave orders (2)
command (1)
commanding (1)
directed (1)
give order (1)
tell (1)

3028 κενεμβατεύω *kenembateuō*
Variant; not used

3029 κενοδοξία *kenodoxia* (1)
vain conceit (1)

3030 κενόδοξος *kenodoxos* (1)
conceited (1)

3031 κενός *kenos* (18)
empty-handed (3)
empty (2)
in vain (2)

useless (2)
vain (2)
failure (1)
foolish (1)
hollow (1)
nothing (1)
so[s] (1)
without effect (1)
untranslated (1)

3032 κενοφωνία *kenophōnia* (2)
chatter (2)

3033 κενόω *kenoō* (5)
deprive (1)
emptied (1)
made nothing (1)
no value (1)
prove hollow (1)

3034 κέντρον *kentron* (4)
sting (2)
goads (1)
stings (1)

3035 κεντυρίων *kentyriōn* (3)
centurion (3)

3036 κενῶς *kenōs* (1)
without reason (1)

3037 κεραία *keraia* (2)
least stroke of a pen (2)

3038 κεραμεύς *kerameus* (3)
potter's (2)
potter (1)

3039 κεραμικός *keramikos* (1)
pottery (1) +5007

3040 κεράμιον *keramion* (2)
jar (2)

3041 κέραμος *keramos* (1)
tiles (1)

3042 κεράννυμι *kerannymi* (3)
mix (1)
poured (1)
untranslated (1)

3043 κέρας *keras* (11)
horns (10)
horn (1)

3044 κεράτιον *keration* (1)
pods (1)

3045 κερδαίνω *kerdainō* (17)
win (5)
gained (4)
gain (3)
won over (2)
gains (1)
make money (1)
spared (1)

3046 κέρδος *kerdos* (3)
gain (2)
profit (1)

3047 κέρμα *kerma* (1)
coins (1)

3048 κερματιστής *kermatistēs* (1)
exchanging money (1)

3049 κεφάλαιον *kephalaion* (2)
price (1)
the point is this (1)

3050 κεφαλαιόω *kephalaioō*
Variant; not used

3051 κεφαλή *kephalē* (75)
head (50)
heads (18)
capstone (5) +1224
hair (1)
untranslated (1)

3052 κεφαλιόω *kephalioō* (1)
struck on the head (1)

3053 κεφαλίς *kephalis* (1)
untranslated (1)

3054 κηδεύω *kēdeuō*
Variant; not used

3055 κημόω *kēmoō* (1)
muzzle (1)

3056 κῆνσος *kēnsos* (4)
taxes (3)
tax (1)

3057 κῆπος *kēpos* (5)
garden (3)
grove (2)

3058 κηπουρός *kēpouros* (1)
gardener (1)

3059 κηρίον *kērion*
Variant; not used

3060 κήρυγμα *kērygma* (8)
preaching (5)
message (1)
proclamation (1)
what was preached (1)

3061 κῆρυξ *kēryx* (3)
herald (2)
preacher (1)

3062 κηρύσσω *kēryssō* (61)
preach (16)
preached (16)
preaching (10)
proclaim (3)
proclaimed (3)
proclaiming (3)
preaches (2)
message (1)
preach (1) +3306
preached (1) +2400
talk (1)
talking about (1)
tell (1)
told (1)
untranslated (1)

3063 κῆτος *kētos* (1)
huge fish (1)

3064 Κηφᾶς *Kēphas* (9)
Peter (5)
Cephas (4)

3065 κιβώριον *kibōrion*
Variant; not used

3066 κιβωτός *kibōtos* (6)
ark (6)

3067 κιθάρα *kithara* (4)
harp (2)
harps (2)

3068 κιθαρίζω *kitharizō* (2)
playing (1)
untranslated (1)

3069 κιθαρῳδός *kitharōdos* (2)
harpists (2)

3070 Κιλικία *Kilikia* (8)
Cilicia (7)
provinces of Cilicia (1)

3071 Κίλιξ *Kilix*
Variant; not used

3072 κινάμωμον *kinamōmon*
Variant; not used

3073 κινδυνεύω *kindyneuō* (4)
danger (2)
danger that (1)
endanger (1)

3074 κίνδυνος *kindynos* (9)
danger (9)

3075 κινέω *kineō* (8)
move (2)
shaking (2)
aroused (1)
remove (1)
removed (1)
stirring up (1)

3076 κίνησις *kinēsis*
Variant; not used

3077 κιννάμωμον *kinnamōmon* (1)
cinnamon (1)

3078 Κίς *Kis* (1)
Kish (1)

3079 κίχρημι *kichrēmi* (1)
lend (1)

3080 κλάδος *klados* (11)
branches (9)
twigs (2)

3081 κλαίω *klaiō* (40)
weep (10)
crying (5)
weeping (5)
wept (5)
mourn (4)
wailing (3)
cry (2)
wail (1)
weeping (1) +4472
weeping for (1)
wept and wept (1) +4498
with tears (1)
untranslated (1)

3082 κλάσις *klasis* (2)
breaking (1)
broke (1)

3083 κλάσμα *klasma* (9)
broken pieces (5)
pieces (4)

3084 Κλαῦδα *Klauda*
Variant; not used

3085 Κλαύδη *Klaudē*
Variant; not used

3086 Κλαυδία *Klaudia* (1)
Claudia (1)

3087 Κλαύδιος *Klaudios* (3)
Claudius (3)

3088 κλαυθμός *klauthmos* (9)
weeping (7)
weeping (1) +3836
wept (1) +1181+2653

3089 κλάω *klaō* (14)
broke (12)
break (2)

3090 κλείς *kleis* (6)
key (4)
keys (2)

3091 κλείω *kleiō* (16)
shut (8)
locked (5)
close (1)
has no pity (1) +3836+5073
shuts (1)

3092 κλέμμα *klemma* (1)
thefts (1)

3093 Κλεοπᾶς *Kleopas* (1)
Cleopas (1)

3094 κλέος *kleos* (1)
credit (1)

3095 κλέπτης *kleptēs* (16)
thief (12)

thieves (4)

3096 κλέπτω *kleptō* (13)
steal (10)
stealing (2)
stole (1)

3097 κλῆμα *klēma* (4)
branch (3)
branches (1)

3098 Κλήμης *Klēmēs* (1)
Clement (1)

3099 κληρονομέω *klēronomeō* (18)
inherit (15)
inherited (1)
share in the inheritance (1)
take inheritance (1)

3100 κληρονομία *klēronomia* (14)
inheritance (14)

3101 κληρονόμος *klēronomos* (15)
heir (8)
heirs (6)
inherit (1)

3102 κλῆρος *klēros* (11)
lots (5)
inheritance (1)
lot (1)
place (1)
share (1)
shared (1) +3275+3836
untranslated (1)

3103 κληρόω *klēroō* (1)
chosen (1)

3104 κλῆσις *klēsis* (11)
called (4)
calling (3)
call (1)
calling received (1) +2813
life (1)
situation (1)

3105 κλητός *klētos* (10)
called (9)
invited (1)

3106 κλίβανος *klibanos* (2)
fire (2)

3107 κλίμα *klima* (3)
regions (2)
untranslated (1)

3108 κλινάριον *klinarion* (1)
beds (1)

3109 κλίνη *klinē* (8)
bed (4)
mat (3)
bed of suffering (1)

3110 κλινίδιον *klinidion* (2)
mat (2)

3111 κλίνω *klinō* (7)
lay (2)
almost over (1)
bowed (1)
bowed down (1)
late in afternoon (1) +806+2465
routed (1)

3112 κλισία *klisia* (1)
groups (1)

3113 κλοπή *klopē* (2)
theft (2)

3114 κλύδων *klydōn* (2)
raging (1)
wave (1)

3115 κλυδωνίζομαι *klydōnizomai* (1)
tossed back and forth by the waves (1)

3116 Κλωπᾶς *Klōpas* (1)

Clopas (1)

3117 κνήθω *knēthō* (1)
itching (1)

3118 Κνίδος *Knidos* (1)
Cnidus (1)

3119 κοδράντης *kodrantēs* (2)
a fraction of a penny (1)
penny (1)

3120 κοιλία *koilia* (23)
stomach (8)
birth (4) +3613
womb (3)
appetites (1)
belly (1)
child bear (1) +2843+3836
conceived (1) +1877+3836+5197
mother (1)
within (1)
wombs (1)
untranslated (1)

3121 κοιμάω *koimaō* (18)
fallen asleep (7)
asleep (2)
died (2)
fell asleep (2)
dies (1)
fall asleep (1)
sleep (1)
sleeping (1)
sleeps (1)

3122 κοίμησις *koimēsis* (1)
natural sleep (1) +3836+3836+5678

3123 κοινός *koinos* (16)
unclean (5)
impure (4)
call impure (2)
common (1)
in common (1)
share (1)
shared (1)
unholy (1)

3124 κοινόω *koinoō* (12)
make unclean (7)
makes unclean (2)
ceremonially unclean (1)
defiled (1)
what makes unclean (1)

3125 κοινωνέω *koinōneō* (8)
share (2)
have (1)
participate (1)
share with (1)
shared (1)
shared in (1)
shares in (1)

3126 κοινωνία *koinōnia* (19)
fellowship (10)
sharing (3)
participation (2)
contribution (1)
fellowship of sharing (1)
partnership (1)
share (1)

3127 κοινωνικός *koinōnikos* (1)
share (1)

3128 κοινωνός *koinōnos* (10)
partner (2)
participants (1)
participate (1) +1639
participate in (1) +1181
partners (1)
share (1)
share (1) +1639
side by side (1)
taken part (1) +1639

3129 κοινῶς *koinōs* (1)
Variant; not used

3130 κοίτη *koitē* (4)
bed (1)
marriage bed (1)
sexual immorality (1)
untranslated (1)

3131 κοιτών *koitōn* (1)
trusted personal servant (1) +2093+3836

3132 κόκκινος *kokkinos* (6)
scarlet (6)

3133 κόκκος *kokkos* (7)
seed (6)
kernel (1)

3134 κολάζω *kolazō* (2)
punish (1)
punishment (1)

3135 κολακεία *kolakeia* (1)
flattery (1)

3136 κόλασις *kolasis* (2)
punishment (2)

3137 Κολασσαεύς *Kolassaeus*
Variant; not used

3138 Κολασσαί *Kolassai*
Variant; not used

3139 κολαφίζω *kolaphizō* (5)
struck with fists (2)
brutally treated (1)
receive a beating (1)
torment (1)

3140 κολλάω *kollaō* (12)
join (2)
unites (2)
associate with (1)
became followers of (1)
cling (1)
hired out to (1)
piled up (1)
stay near (1)
sticks (1)
united to (1)

3141 κολλούριον *kollourion* (1)
salve (1)

3142 κολλυβιστής *kollybistēs* (3)
money changers (3)

3143 κολοβόω *koloboō* (4)
cut short (2)
shortened (2)

3144 Κολοσσαεύς *Kolossaeus*
Variant; not used

3145 Κολοσσαί *Kolossai* (1)
Colosse (1)

3146 κόλπος *kolpos* (6)
side (3)
bay (1)
lap (1)
untranslated (1)

3147 κολυμβάω *kolymbaō* (1)
swim (1)

3148 κολυμβήθρα *kolymbēthra* (3)
pool (3)

3149 κολωνία *kolōnia* (1)
Roman colony (1)

3150 κομάω *komaō* (2)
has long hair (2)

3151 κόμη *komē* (1)
long hair (1)

3152 κομίζω *komizō* (10)
receive (3)
brought (1)

receive back (1)
received (1)
received back (1)
receiving (1)
repaid (1)
reward (1)

3153 κομψότερον *kompsoteron* (1)
better (1)

3154 κονιάω *koniaō* (2)
whitewashed (2)

3155 κονιορτός *koniortos* (5)
dust (5)

3156 κοπάζω *kopazō* (3)
died down (3)

3157 κοπετός *kopetos* (1)
mourned deeply (1) +3489+4472

3158 κοπή *kopē* (1)
defeat (1)

3159 κοπιάω *kopiaō* (23)
labor (5)
hard work (2)
work (2)
work hard (2)
worked (2)
worked hard (2)
efforts (1)
grown weary (1)
hardworking (1)
labors (1)
tired (1)
weary (1)
work hard (1) +2237
worked for (1)

3160 κόπος *kopos* (18)
labor (5)
bothering (3) +4218
hard work (2)
bother (1) +4218
efforts (1)
labored (1)
laboring (1)
toil (1)
trouble (1)
work (1)
worked (1)

3161 κοπρία *kopria* (1)
manure pile (1)

3162 κόπριον *koprion* (1)
fertilize (1) +965

3163 κόπρος *kopros*
Variant; not used

3164 κόπτω *koptō* (8)
mourn (4)
cut (2)
mourned (1)
mourning (1)

3165 κόραξ *korax* (1)
ravens (1)

3166 κοράσιον *korasion* (8)
girl (6)
little girl (1)
she^s (1) +3836

3167 κορβᾶν *korban* (1)
Corban (1)

3168 κορβανᾶς *korbanas* (1)
treasury (1)

3169 Κόρε *Kore* (1)
Korah's (1)

3170 κορέννυμι *korennymi* (2)
eaten as much as wanted (1)
have all you want (1) +1639

3171 Κορίνθιος *Korinthios* (2)

Corinthians (2)

3172 Κόρινθος *Korinthos* (6)
Corinth (6)

3173 Κορνήλιος *Kornēlios* (8)
Cornelius (8)

3174 κόρος *koros* (1)
thousand bushels (1) +1669

3175 κοσμέω *kosmeō* (10)
put in order (2)
adorned (1)
beautifully dressed (1)
decorate (1)
decorated (1)
dress (1)
make attractive (1)
make beautiful (1)
trimmed (1)

3176 κοσμικός *kosmikos* (2)
earthly (1)
worldly (1)

3177 κόσμιος *kosmios* (2)
modestly (1) +2950
respectable (1)

3178 κοσμίως *kosmiōs*
Variant; not used

3179 κοσμοκράτωρ *kosmokratōr* (1)
powers of world (1)

3180 κόσμος *kosmos* (186)
world (173)
it^s (3) +3836
universe (2)
adornment (1)
earth (1)
it^s (1)
material (1)
people (1)
world's (1)
worldly (1) +3836
untranslated (1)

3181 Κούαρτος *Kouartos* (1)
Quartus (1)

3182 κοῦμ *koum* (1)
koum (1)

3183 κούμι *koumi*
Variant; not used

3184 κουστωδία *koustōdia* (3)
guard (2)
guards (1)

3185 κουφίζω *kouphizō* (1)
lightened (1)

3186 κόφινος *kophinos* (6)
basketfuls (2)
basketfuls (2) +4441
basketfuls (1) +4445
baskets (1)

3187 κράβαττος *krabattos* (11)
mat (8)
mats (2)
bedridden (1) +2093+2879

3188 κράββατος *krabbatos*
Variant; not used

3189 κράζω *krazō* (56)
shouted (13)
cried out (7)
shouting (7)
called out (3)
cry out (3)
cries out (2)
cry (2)
crying out (2)
a loud voice (1)
called (1)

calling out (1)
calls out (1)
cried (1)
cried out (1) +3306
cried out (1) +3489+5889
crying out (1) +3306
exclaim (1)
exclaimed (1)
gave a shout (1) +5889
screams (1)
shout (1)
shouted (1) +1181
shouted all the more (1) +3437+4498
shrieked (1)
yelling (1)

3190 κραιπάλη *kraipalē* (1)
dissipation (1)

3191 κρανίον *kranion* (4)
skull (4)

3192 κράσπεδον *kraspedon* (5)
edge (4)
tassels (1)

3193 κραταιός *krataios* (1)
mighty (1)

3194 κραταιόω *krataioō* (4)
strong (2)
became strong (1)
strengthen (1) +1443

3195 κρατέω *krateō* (47)
arrest (8)
arrested (5)
took (5)
seized (4)
hold to (3)
hold on to (2)
clasped (1)
grabbed (1)
held on to (1)
hold firmly to (1)
hold on (1)
holding back (1)
holding on to (1)
holding to (1)
holds (1)
kept (1)
kept from (1)
lost connection with (1) +4024
not forgive (1)
not forgiven (1)
observe (1)
obtained (1)
remain true to (1)
take charge of (1)
take hold (1)
take hold of (1)

3196 κράτιστος *kratistos* (4)
most excellent (3)
excellency (1)

3197 κράτος *kratos* (12)
power (8)
might (2)
mighty deeds (1)
strength (1)

3198 κραυγάζω *kraugazō* (9)
shouting (4)
shouted (3)
called (1)
cry out (1)

3199 κραυγή *kraugē* (6)
brawling (1)
cries (1)
cry (1)
crying (1)
uproar (1)
voice (1)

3200 κρέας *kreas* (2)
meat (2)

3201 κρείσσων *kreissōn*
Variant; not used

3202 κρείττων *kreittōn* (19)
better (14)
superior to (2)
better (1) +3437
good (1)
greater (1)

3203 κρεμάννυμι *kremannymi* (7)
hanging (3)
hung (3)
hang (1)

3204 κρημνός *krēmnos* (3)
steep bank (3)

3205 Κρής *Krēs* (2)
Cretans (2)

3206 Κρήσκης *Krēskēs* (1)
Crescens (1)

3207 Κρήτη *Krētē* (5)
Crete (5)

3208 κριθή *krithē* (1)
barley (1)

3209 κρίθινος *krithinos* (2)
barley (1)
small barley (1)

3210 κρίμα *krima* (27)
judgment (12)
condemnation (3)
be punished (2) +3284
be judged (1) +3284
judge (1)
judgments (1)
lawsuits (1)
penalty (1)
punishment (1)
sentence (1)
sentenced (1)
the same way[s] (1)
way treated[s] (1)

3211 κρίνον *krinon* (2)
lilies (2)

3212 κρίνω *krinō* (114)
judge (37)
judged (14)
judges (7)
condemn (6)
condemned (6)
decided (4)
judging (4)
consider (3)
pass judgment on (3)
considers (2)
stand trial (2)
come under judgment (1)
condemning (1)
convinced (1)
decided that (1)
decision that (1)
decisions (1)
goes to law (1)
judgment (1)
judgment that (1)
made up (1)
made up mind (1)
make judgment (1) +3213
make up mind (1)
on trial (1)
on trial (1) +2705
pass judgment (1)
passed judgment on (1)
passing judgment on (1)
punish (1)
resolved (1)

stand on trial (1)
sue (1)
take judgment (1)
there is a judge (1) +2400+3836
tried (1)
until judge (1) +4024

3213 κρίσις *krisis* (47)
judgment (28)
justice (5)
condemned (2)
judge (2) +4472
judgments (2)
accusation (1)
accusations (1)
be condemned (1) +4406+5679
condemned (1) +1650+2262
decisions (1)
doom (1)
make judgment (1) +3212
verdict (1)

3214 Κρίσπος *Krispos* (2)
Crispus (2)

3215 κριτήριον *kritērion* (3)
court (1)
disputes (1)
judge cases (1)

3216 κριτής *kritēs* (19)
judge (14)
judges (4)
sitting in judgment (1)

3217 κριτικός *kritikos* (1)
judges (1)

3218 κρούω *krouō* (9)
knock (3)
knocks (3)
knocking (2)
knocked at (1)

3219 κρύπτη *kryptē* (1)
place hidden (1)

3220 κρυπτός *kryptos* (17)
secret (7)
hidden (4)
secrets (2)
inner (1)
inwardly (1) +1877+3836
is hidden (1)
unseen (1) +1877+3836

3221 κρύπτω *kryptō* (18)
hidden (9)
hid (7)
hide (1)
secretly (1)

3222 κρυσταλλίζω *krystallizō* (1)
clear as crystal (1)

3223 κρύσταλλος *krystallos* (2)
crystal (2)

3224 κρυφαῖος *kryphaios* (2)
secret (1)
unseen (1) +1877+3836

3225 κρυφῇ *kryphē* (1)
secret (1)

3226 κρύφιος *kryphios*
Variant; not used

3227 κτάομαι *ktaomai* (7)
bought (1)
buy (1)
control (1)
gain (1)
get (1)
pay for (1)
take along (1)

3228 κτῆμα *ktēma* (4)
wealth (2)

piece of property (1)
possessions (1)

3229 κτῆνος *ktēnos* (4)
animals (1)
cattle (1)
donkey (1)
mounts (1)

3230 κτήτωρ *ktētōr* (1)
owned (1) +5639

3231 κτίζω *ktizō* (15)
created (11)
creator (3)
create (1)

3232 κτίσις *ktisis* (19)
creation (15)
authority (1)
created things (1)
creature (1)
world (1)

3233 κτίσμα *ktisma* (4)
created (2)
creature (1)
creatures (1)

3234 κτίστης *ktistēs* (1)
creator (1)

3235 κυβεία *kybeia* (1)
cunning (1)

3236 κυβέρνησις *kybernēsis* (1)
those with gifts of administration (1)

3237 κυβερνήτης *kybernētēs* (2)
pilot (1)
sea captain (1)

3238 κυκλεύω *kykleuō* (1)
surrounded (1)

3239 κυκλόθεν *kyklothen* (3)
all around (1)
encircled (1)
surrounding (1)

3240 κυκλόω *kykloō* (4)
gathered around (2)
marched around (1)
surrounded (1)

3241 κύκλῳ *kyklō* (8)
around (3)
surrounding (2)
encircled (1)
from village to village (1) +3267
in a circle (1)

3242 κύλισμα *kylisma*
Variant; not used

3243 κυλισμός *kylismos* (1)
wallowing (1)

3244 κυλίω *kyliō* (1)
rolled around (1)

3245 κυλλός *kyllos* (4)
crippled (2)
maimed (2)

3246 κῦμα *kyma* (5)
waves (4)
surf (1)

3247 κύμβαλον *kymbalon* (1)
cymbal (1)

3248 κύμινον *kyminon* (1)
cummin (1)

3249 κυνάριον *kynarion* (4)
dogs (4)

3250 Κύπριος *Kyprios* (3)
from Cyprus (3)

3251 Κύπρος *Kypros* (5)
Cyprus (5)

3252 κύπτω *kyptō* (2)
bent (1)
stoop down (1)

3253 Κυρεῖνος *Kyreinos*
Variant; not used

3254 Κυρηναῖος *Kyrēnaios* (6)
from Cyrene (3)
of Cyrene (2)
Cyrene (1)

3255 Κυρήνη *Kyrēnē* (1)
Cyrene (1)

3256 Κυρήνιος *Kyrēnios* (1)
Quirinius (1)

3257 κυρία *kyria* (2)
dear lady (1)
lady (1)

3258 κυριακός *kyriakos* (2)
Lord's (2)

3259 κυριεύω *kyrieuō* (7)
lord it over (2)
authority over (1)
has mastery over (1)
Lord (1)
lords (1)
master (1)

3260 Κυρίνιος *Kyrinios*
Variant; not used

3261 κύριος *kyrios* (720)
Lord (600)
master (35)
Lord's (32)
sir (23)
master's (6)
masters (6)
owner (6)
lords (3)
owners (3)
belong to Lord (1) +1639
he^s (1) +3836
his majesty (1)
masters' (1)
owns (1) +1639
sirs (1)

3262 κυριότης *kyriotēs* (4)
authority (2)
dominion (1)
powers (1)

3263 κυρόω *kyroō* (2)
duly established (1)
reaffirm (1)

3264 κύων *kyōn* (5)
dogs (4)
dog (1)

3265 κῶλον *kōlon* (1)
bodies (1)

3266 κωλύω *kōlyō* (23)
hinder (3)
stop (3)
forbid (2)
keep from (2)
kept from (2)
prevented from (2)
hindered (1)
oppose (1)
opposes (1)
permit (1) +3594
restrained (1)
shouldn't (1)
stop from taking (1)
stops (1)
told to stop (1)

3267 κώμη *kōmē* (27)
village (16)
villages (8)

from village to village (1) +2848+3836
from village to village (1) +3241
town (1)

3268 κωμόπολις *kōmopolis* (1)
villages (1)

3269 κῶμος *kōmos* (3)
orgies (3)

3270 κώνωψ *kōnōps* (1)
gnat (1)

3271 Κῶς *Kōs* (1)
Cos (1)

3272 Κωσάμ *Kōsam* (1)
Cosam (1)

3273 κωφός *kōphos* (14)
deaf (5)
mute (4)
man who had been mute (2)
could not talk (1)
he^s (1) +3836
unable to speak (1)

3274 λ *l*
Variant; not used

3275 λαγχάνω *lanchanō* (4)
chosen by lot (1)
decide by lot (1)
received (1)
shared (1) +3102+3836

3276 Λάζαρος *Lazaros* (15)
Lazarus (15)

3277 λάθρᾳ *lathra* (4)
quietly (2)
aside (1)
secretly (1)

3278 λαῖλαψ *lailaps* (3)
squall (2) +449
storm (1)

3279 λακάω *lakaō* (1)
burst (1)

3280 λακτίζω *laktizō* (1)
kick (1)

3281 λαλέω *laleō* (296)
speak (62)
speaking (38)
spoke (33)
said (25)
speaks (18)
spoken (17)
say (16)
told (16)
saying (6)
talk (6)
tell (5)
talked (4)
talking (4)
telling (3)
preached (2)
proclaimed (2)
says (2)
teach (2)
address (1)
announced (1)
boast (1) +5665
bring (1)
bring a message (1) +4839
claiming (1)
declaring (1)
distort the truth (1) +1406
he^s (1) +3836
help speaking about (1) +3590
insisted (1)
lies (1) +3836+6022
may declare (1)
message (1)
preaching (1)

presenting (1)
proclaim (1)
promised (1)
said (1) +3306
say about (1)
speak about (1)
speaker (1)
speech (1)
spoke about (1)
talking about (1)
tells (1)
use language (1)
utter (1)
utters (1)
whispered (1)
untranslated (5)

3282 λαλιά *lalia* (3)
accent (1)
language (1)
said (1)

3283 λαμά *lama*
Variant; not used

3284 λαμβάνω *lambanō* (257)
receive (38)
took (38)
received (37)
take (24)
accept (9)
taking (9)
receives (7)
accepts (5)
taken (4)
bring (3)
collect (3)
receiving (3)
seized (3)
accepted (2)
be punished (2) +3210
caught (2)
gathered (2)
get (2)
married (2)
marry (2)
seizing (2)
take up (2)
amazed (1) +1749
appointed (1)
be edified (1) +3868
be judged (1) +3210
be rewarded (1) +3635
become (1)
become a father (1) +2856+5065
circumcised (1) +4362
circumcised (1) +4364
collected (1)
collectors of tax (1)
collects (1)
commanded (1) +1953
decided to (1) +5206
devised a plan (1) +5206
draw (1)
draws (1)
faced (1) +4278
filled with awe (1) +5832
forgotten that (1) +3330
gets (1)
given (1)
got (1)
guiding (1)
had (1)
have (1)
judge by external appearance (1) +476+4725
laid plans (1) +5206
made (1)
made king (1) +993+3836
married (1) +1222
married a woman (1) +1222
money (1) +1797
obtained (1)
on authority (1) +2026

picked up (1)
plotted (1) +5206
put on (1)
reminded (1) +5704
repayment (1)
seizes (1)
selected (1)
show partiality (1) +4725
succeeded (1) +1345
take over (1)
takes (1)
takes advantage of (1)
to the decision (1) +5206
took up (1)
tried to do (1) +4278
was encouraged (1) +2511
with instructions (1) +1953
untranslated (4)

3285 Λάμεχ *Lamech* (1)
Lamech (1)

3286 λαμπάς *lampas* (9)
lamps (7)
lanterns (1)
torch (1)

3287 λαμπρός *lampros* (9)
bright (2)
fine (2)
shining (2)
clear (1)
elegant (1)
splendor (1)

3288 λαμπρότης *lamprotēs* (1)
brighter than (1) +5642

3289 λαμπρῶς *lamprōs* (1)
in luxury (1)

3290 λάμπω *lampō* (7)
shine (2)
shone (2)
gives light (1)
lights up (1)
made shine (1)

3291 λανθάνω *lanthanō* (6)
forget (2)
escaped notice (1)
go unnoticed (1)
keep secret (1)
without knowing (1)

3292 λαξευτός *laxeutos* (1)
cut in the rock (1)

3293 Λαοδίκεια *Laodikeia* (6)
Laodicea (6)

3294 Λαοδικεύς *Laodikeus* (1)
Laodiceans (1)

3295 λαός *laos* (142)
people (127)
peoples (4)
people's (3)
crowd (2)
assembled worshipers (1) +3836+4436
crowd (1) +3836+4436
in public (1) +1883+3836
public (1)
them^s (1) +3836
those^s (1) +3836

3296 λάρυγξ *larynx* (1)
throats (1)

3297 Λασαία *Lasaia* (1)
Lasea (1)

3298 Λασέα *Lasea*
Variant; not used

3299 λάσκω *laskō*
Variant; not used

3300 λατομέω *latomeō* (2)

cut (1) +1639
cut out (1)

3301 λατρεία *latreia* (5)
act of worship (1)
ministry (1)
service (1)
temple worship (1)
worship (1)

3302 λατρεύω *latreuō* (21)
serve (10)
worship (5)
minister (1)
serve at a sanctuary (1)
served (1)
worshiped (1)
worshiper, (1)
worshipers (1)

3303 λάχανον *lachanon* (4)
garden plants (2)
garden herbs (1)
vegetables (1)

3304 Λεββαῖος *Lebbaios*
Variant; not used

3305 λεγιών *legiōn* (4)
legion (3)
legions (1)

3306 λέγω *legō* (2355)
said (784)
tell (216)
say (186)
asked (153)
replied (92)
told (92)
says (83)
saying (77)
answered (52)
called (31)
spoken (16)
ask (15)
speak (12)
spoke (10)
telling (10)
call (9)
claim (9)
declared (8)
talking (7)
talking about (7)
speaking (6)
words of (5)
claiming (4)
claims (4)
continued (4)
declares (4)
exclaimed (4)
asking (3)
asks (3)
calls (3)
claimed (3)
demanded (3)
is (3)
mean (3)
mention (3)
ordered (3)
speaks (3)
spoken of (3)
tells (3)
added (2)
answer (2)
calling (2)
challenged (2)
known as (2)
means (2)
meant (2)
meant (2) +4309
name (2)
objected (2)
protested (2)
replied (2) +899

say about (2)
shouted (2)
shouting (2)
speak of (2)
stated (2)
told (2) +4192
words (2)
accuse (1)
addressed (1)
addressed (1) +4639
adds (1)
admit (1)
advise (1)
agree (1) +899+3836
announced (1)
are words of (1)
as has just been said (1) +1877+3836
asks for (1)
assure (1) +237+2093
at this (1) +4047
began to speak (1) +487+3836+5125
begged (1)
begged (1) +4151
boasted (1)
boasts (1)
by (1) +4005
by saying (1) +4005
call out (1)
called out (1)
called out (1) +3489+5889
charged (1)
claimed (1)
commanded (1)
commanding (1) +2198+2848
cried (1)
cried out (1)
cried out (1) +3189
cry (1)
cry out (1)
crying out (1) +3189
directed (1)
discuss (1)
explain (1)
grant (1)
I put this in human terms (1) +474
inquired (1)
insisted (1)
made statement (1) +4839
means (1) +1639
named (1)
not saying a word (1) +4029
one might even say (1) +2229+6055
order (1)
pleading (1)
prayed (1)
praying (1)
preach (1)
preach (1) +3062
present (1)
promised (1)
prophesied (1) +4736
question (1)
quote (1)
referring (1)
remarking (1)
repeat (1) +4099
replied (1) +646+4022
reply (1)
respond (1)
said (1) +3281
sang (1)
sent for (1) +5888
shouting at the top of voice (1)
                     +3489+5889
singing (1)
so-called (1)
so-called (1) +6055
speak about (1)
speaks of (1)
spoke about (1)
spoke up (1)

spoken (1) +3306
state (1)
take an example (1)
talk (1)
telling about (1)
testified (1)
thought (1)
turned (1)
urged (1)
used (1)
using argument (1)
warned (1)
welcome (1) +5897
welcomes (1) +5897
went on (1)
what[s] (1) +3836
with that (1) +4047
with the news (1)
with the plea (1)
with the words (1)
with this (1) +4047
word (1)
untranslated (286)

3307 λεῖμμα *leimma* (1)
remnant (1)

3308 λεῖος *leios* (1)
smooth (1)

3309 λείπω *leipō* (6)
have everything need (1) +3594
lack (1)
lacking (1)
lacks (1)
left (1)
untranslated (1)

3310 λειτουργέω *leitourgeō* (3)
performs religious duties (1)
share (1)
worshiping (1)

3311 λειτουργία *leitourgia* (6)
service (2)
ceremonies (1)
help (1)
ministry (1)
service that perform (1) +1355+3836+4047

3312 λειτουργικός *leitourgikos* (1)
ministering (1)

3313 λειτουργός *leitourgos* (5)
servants (2)
minister (1)
serves (1)
take care (1)

3314 λείχω *leichō*
Variant; not used

3315 Λέκτρα *Lektra*
Variant; not used

3316 λεμά *lema* (2)
lama (2)

3317 λέντιον *lention* (2)
towel (2)

3318 λεπίς *lepis* (1)
scales (1)

3319 λέπρα *lepra* (4)
leprosy (4)

3320 λεπρός *lepros* (9)
have leprosy (3)
leper (2)
man with leprosy (2)
had leprosy (1)
with leprosy (1)

3321 λεπτός *leptos* (3)
small copper coins (2)
penny (1)

3322 Λευί *Leui* (8)
Levi (8)

3323 Λευίς *Leuis*
Variant; not used

3324 Λευίτης *Leuitēs* (3)
Levite (2)
Levites (1)

3325 Λευιτικός *Leuitikos* (1)
Levitical (1)

3326 λευκαίνω *leukainō* (2)
bleach (1)
made white (1)

3327 λευκοβύσσινος *leukobyssinos*
Variant; not used

3328 λευκός *leukos* (25)
white (22)
bright (1)
ripe (1)
white (1) +3336

3329 λέων *leōn* (9)
lion (5)
lions (2)
lion's (1)
lions' (1)

3330 λήθη *lēthē* (1)
forgotten that (1) +3284

3331 λῆμψις *lēmpsis* (1)
receiving (1)

3332 ληνός *lēnos* (5)
winepress (3)
press (1)
winepress (1) +3836+3885

3333 λῆρος *lēros* (1)
nonsense (1)

3334 λῃστής *lēstēs* (15)
robbers (9)
leading a rebellion (3)
bandits (1)
had taken part in a rebellion (1) +1639
robber (1)

3335 λῆψις *lēpsis*
Variant; not used

3336 λίαν *lian* (12)
great (3)
very (3)
completely (1) +1666+4356
furious (1) +2597
greatly (1)
strongly (1)
violent (1) +5901
white (1) +3328

3337 λίβανος *libanos* (2)
frankincense (1)
incense (1)

3338 λιβανωτός *libanōtos* (2)
censer (2)

3339 Λιβερτῖνος *Libertinos* (1)
freedmen (1)

3340 Λιβύη *Libyē* (1)
Libya (1)

3341 Λιβυστῖνος *Libystinos*
Variant; not used

3342 λιθάζω *lithazō* (9)
stone (5)
stoned (3)
stoning (1)

3343 λίθινος *lithinos* (3)
stone (2)
of stone (1)

3344 λιθοβολέω *lithoboleō* (7)
stone (4)
stoned (2)
stoning (1)

3345 λίθος *lithos* (59)
stone (35)
stones (14)
another[s] (4)
boulder (1)
jasper (1) +2618
jewel (1)
millstone (1) +3683
stone's (1)
untranslated (1)

3346 λιθόστρωτος *lithostrōtos* (1)
stone Pavement (1)

3347 λικμάω *likmaō* (2)
crushed (2)

3348 λιμήν *limēn* (2)
harbor (2)

3349 λίμνη *limnē* (11)
lake (10)
water's (1)

3350 λιμός *limos* (12)
famine (7)
famines (3)
hunger (1)
starving to death (1) +660

3351 λίνον *linon* (2)
linen (1)
wick (1)

3352 Λίνος *Linos* (1)
Linus (1)

3353 λιπαρός *liparos* (1)
riches (1)

3354 λίτρα *litra* (2)
about a pint (1)
seventy-five pounds (1) +1669

3355 λίψ *lips* (1)
southwest (1)

3356 λογεία *logeia* (2)
collection (1)
collections (1)

3357 λογίζομαι *logizomai* (40)
credited (10)
consider (3)
think (3)
count (2)
realize (2)
reasoned (2)
regard (2)
regarded (2)
claim (1)
considered (1)
counting (1)
credit (1)
credits (1)
discredited (1) +1650+4029
expect (1)
held (1)
maintain (1)
numbered (1)
record of (1)
regards (1)
think about (1)
think that (1)

3358 λογικός *logikos* (2)
spiritual (2)

3359 λόγιον *logion* (3)
words (3)

3360 λόγιος *logios* (1)
learned (1)

3361 λογισμός *logismos* (2)
arguments (1)
thoughts (1)

3362 λογομαχέω *logomacheō* (1)
quarreling about words (1)

3363 λογομαχία *logomachia* (1)
    quarrels about words (1)

3364 λόγος *logos* (331)
    word (126)
    words (53)
    message (29)
    saying (10)
    teaching (9)
    account (6)
    speech (5)
    this^s (5) +3836
    news (4)
    question (4)
    said (3)
    command (2)
    instruction (2)
    matter (2)
    report (2)
    speaker (2)
    speaking (2)
    talk (2)
    talking (2)
    thing (2)
    this^s (2) +3836+4047
    account (1) +625
    accounts (1)
    am about to tell (1) +3836+4047
    appearance (1)
    book (1)
    conversation (1)
    eloquence (1)
    further word spoken (1) +4707
    grievance (1)
    heard (1)
    it^s (1) +3836
    maliciously (1) +4505
    ministry (1)
    nothing (1) +4029
    preaching (1) +1877
    preaching (1) +3836
    proposal (1)
    questions (1)
    reason (1)
    reasonable (1) +2848
    reply (1)
    rule (1)
    rumor (1)
    say (1)
    sentence (1)
    settled accounts (1) +5256
    something he said (1)
    speak (1)
    stated (1)
    statement (1)
    stories (1)
    story (1)
    teachings (1)
    things (1)
    this^s (1) +1609+3836+4047
    took at word (1) +4409
    truths (1)
    what said (1)
    what says (1)
    what^s (1) +3836
    why (1) +5515
    word of mouth (1)
    untranslated (15)

3365 λόγχη *lonchē* (1)
    spear (1)

3366 λοιδορέω *loidoreō* (4)
    hurled insults at (2)
    cursed (1)
    insult (1)

3367 λοιδορία *loidoria* (3)
    insult (2)
    slander (1)

3368 λοίδορος *loidoros* (2)
    slanderer (1)
    slanderers (1)

3369 λοιμός *loimos* (2)
    pestilences (1)
    troublemaker (1)

3370 λοιπός *loipos* (55)
    rest (15)
    other (9)
    others (9)
    finally (5) +3836
    else (3)
    finally (3)
    now (2)
    still (2) +3836
    beyond that (1)
    everybody else (1)
    from now on (1) +3836
    further (1)
    remains (1)
    since that time (1) +3836
    survivors (1)

3371 Λουκᾶς *Loukas* (3)
    Luke (3)

3372 Λούκιος *Loukios* (2)
    Lucius (2)

3373 λουτρόν *loutron* (2)
    washing (2)

3374 λούω *louō* (5)
    washed (4)
    had a bath (1)

3375 Λύδδα *Lydda* (3)
    Lydda (3)

3376 Λυδία *Lydia* (2)
    Lydia (1)
    Lydia's (1)

3377 Λυκαονία *Lykaonia* (1)
    Lycaonian (1)

3378 Λυκαονιστί *Lykaonisti* (1)
    the Lycaonian language (1)

3379 Λυκία *Lykia* (1)
    Lycia (1)

3380 λύκος *lykos* (6)
    wolves (4)
    wolf (2)

3381 λυμαίνω *lymainō* (1)
    began destroy (1)

3382 λυπέω *lypeō* (26)
    grieve (5)
    distressed (3)
    sad (3)
    sorrowful (3)
    grieved (2)
    hurt (2)
    sorrow (2)
    caused grief (1)
    caused sorrow (1)
    filled with grief (1) +5379
    made sorry (1)
    saddened (1)
    suffer grief (1)

3383 λύπη *lypē* (16)
    sorrow (7)
    grief (2)
    pain (2)
    distressed (1) +2400
    is time of grief (1) +2400
    painful (1)
    painful (1) +1877
    reluctantly (1) +1666

3384 Λυσανίας *Lysanias* (1)
    Lysanias (1)

3385 Λυσίας *Lysias* (2)
    Lysias (2)

3386 λύσις *lysis* (1)
    divorce (1)

3387 λυσιτελέω *lysiteleō* (1)
    better (1)

3388 Λύστρα *Lystra* (6)
    Lystra (6)

3389 λύτρον *lytron* (2)
    ransom (2)

3390 λυτρόω *lytroō* (3)
    redeem (2)
    redeemed (1)

3391 λύτρωσις *lytrōsis* (3)
    redemption (2)
    redeemed (1) +4472

3392 λυτρωτής *lytrōtēs* (1)
    deliverer (1)

3393 λυχνία *lychnia* (12)
    lampstands (6)
    stand (4)
    lampstand (2)

3394 λύχνος *lychnos* (14)
    lamp (12)
    lamps (1)
    light (1)

3395 λύω *lyō* (42)
    untie (8)
    untying (3)
    destroyed (3)
    released (3)
    broken (2)
    destroy (2)
    loose (2)
    loosed (2)
    set free (2)
    take off (2)
    break (1)
    breaking (1)
    breaks (1)
    broken to pieces (1)
    destruction (1)
    dismissed (1)
    freed (1)
    freeing (1)
    loosened (1)
    release (1)
    unmarried (1) +608+1222
    untied (1)

3396 Λωΐς *Lōis* (1)
    Lois (1)

3397 Λώτ *Lōt* (4)
    Lot (3)
    Lot's (1)

3398 μ *m*
    Variant; not used

3399 Μάαθ *Maath* (1)
    Maath (1)

3400 Μαγαδάν *Magadan* (1)
    Magadan (1)

3401 Μαγδαλά *Magdala*
    Variant; not used

3402 Μαγδαληνή *Magdalēnē* (12)
    Magdalene (12)

3403 Μαγεδών *Magedōn*
    Variant; not used

3404 μαγεία *mageia* (1)
    magic (1)

3405 μαγεύω *mageuō* (1)
    practiced sorcery (1)

3406 μαγία *magia*
    Variant; not used

3407 μάγος *magos* (6)
    Magi (4)
    sorcerer (2)

3408 Μαγώγ *Magōg* (1)
Magog (1)

3409 Μαδιάμ *Madiam* (1)
Midian (1) +1178

3410 μαζός *mazos*
Variant; not used

3411 μαθητεύω *mathēteuō* (4)
become a disciple (1)
instructed (1)
make disciples (1)
won disciples (1)

3412 μαθητής *mathētēs* (261)
disciples (222)
disciple (24)
student (3)
them^s (3) +899+3836
they^s (2) +3836
all disciples (1) +3836+4436
disciples' (1)
followers (1)
them^s (1) +3836
they^s (1) +899+3836
they^s (1) +899+899+2779+3836
untranslated (1)

3413 μαθήτρια *mathētria* (1)
disciple (1)

3414 Μαθθαῖος *Maththaios* (5)
Matthew (5)

3415 Μαθθάτ *Maththat* (2)
Matthat (2)

3416 Μαθθίας *Maththias* (2)
Matthias (2)

3417 Μαθουσαλά *Mathousala* (1)
Methuselah (1)

3418 Μαϊνάν *Mainan*
Variant; not used

3419 μαίνομαι *mainomai* (5)
out of mind (3)
insane (1)
raving mad (1)

3420 μακαρίζω *makarizō* (2)
call blessed (1)
consider blessed (1)

3421 μακάριος *makarios* (50)
blessed (44)
good (4)
fortunate (1)
happier (1)

3422 μακαρισμός *makarismos* (3)
blessedness (2)
joy (1)

3423 Μακεδονία *Makedonia* (22)
Macedonia (21)
Macedonian (1)

3424 Μακεδών *Makedōn* (5)
Macedonians (2)
from Macedonia (1)
Macedonian (1)
of Macedonia (1)

3425 μάκελλον *makellon* (1)
meat market (1)

3426 μακράν *makran* (10)
far (4)
far away (3)
far off (1) +1650
long way off (1)
some distance (1)

3427 μακρόθεν *makrothen* (14)
distance (6)
far off (3) +608
at a distance (2)
a distance (1)

far away (1) +608
long distance (1)

3428 μακροθυμέω *makrothymeō* (10)
patient (8)
putting off (1)
waiting patiently (1)

3429 μακροθυμία *makrothymia* (14)
patience (11)
great patience (1) +4246
patient (1)
patiently (1)

3430 μακροθύμως *makrothymōs* (1)
patiently (1)

3431 μακρός *makros* (4)
distant (2)
lengthy (2)

3432 μακροχρόνιος *makrochronios* (1)
enjoy long life (1) +1639

3433 μαλακία *malakia* (3)
sickness (3)

3434 μαλακός *malakos* (4)
fine clothes (2)
fine (1)
male prostitutes (1)

3435 Μαλελεήλ *Maleleēl* (1)
Mahalalel (1)

3436 μάλιστα *malista* (12)
especially (9)
especially so (1)
most (1)
very (1)

3437 μᾶλλον *mallon* (81)
more (22)
rather (15)
all the more (4)
instead (3)
especially (2)
instead of (2) +2445
more than (2)
all the harder (1)
all the more (1) +4498
all the more (1) +5537
better (1) +3202
do so (1) +5968
do so more and more (1) +4355
do this more and more (1) +4355
greater (1)
greater than ever (1)
happier (1) +5897
how greater (1)
instead (1) +247
instead (1) +1883+3836
instead of (1)
less (1)
more (1) +4358
more and more (1)
more than that (1)
much (1)
on the contrary (1) +247+4498
prefer (1) +2305
rather (1) +1254
really (1)
shouted all the more (1) +3189+4498
than (1) +2445
then (1)
very (1)
untranslated (4)

3438 Μάλχος *Malchos* (1)
Malchus (1)

3439 μάμμη *mammē* (1)
grandmother (1)

3440 μαμωνᾶς *mamōnas* (4)
money (2)
wealth (2)

3441 Μαναήν *Manaēn* (1)
Manaen (1)

3442 Μανασσῆς *Manassēs* (3)
Manasseh (3)

3443 μανθάνω *manthanō* (25)
learn (10)
learned (8)
get into the habit of being (1)
inquire about (1)
instructed (1)
know (1)
learning (1)
learns (1)
studied (1)

3444 μανία *mania* (1)
insane (1)

3445 μάννα *manna* (5)
manna (5)

3446 μαντεύομαι *manteuomai* (1)
fortune-telling (1)

3447 μαραίνω *marainō* (1)
fade away (1)

3448 μαράνα θά *marana tha* (1)
come Lord (1)

3449 μαργαρίτης *margaritēs* (9)
pearls (7)
pearl (1)
untranslated (1)

3450 Μάρθα *Martha* (13)
Martha (13)

3451 Μαρία *Maria* (54)
Mary (51)
Mary's (2)
she^s (1) +3836

3452 Μαριάμ *Mariam*
Variant; not used

3453 Μᾶρκος *Markos* (8)
mark (8)

3454 μάρμαρος *marmaros* (1)
marble (1)

3455 μαρτυρέω *martyreō* (77)
testify (21)
testifies (6)
testified (5)
commended (4)
testifies to (3)
declared (2)
given^s (2)
respected (2)
spoke well of (2)
testified about (2)
testify about (2)
testify to (2)
testimony (2)
witness (2)
appearing witness (1)
confirmed (1)
gave testimony (1)
give testimony (1)
given testimony (1)
known (1)
pointed out (1)
showed (1)
speak (1)
speak well of (1)
spoke well (1)
spread the word (1)
tell about (1)
testifying (1)
testimony (1) +3456+4005
told about (1)
vouch (1)
warn (1)
well known (1)

well spoken of (1)

3456 μαρτυρία *martyria* (37)
testimony (31)
certified (1) +3836+5381
evidence (1)
reputation (1)
statements (1)
testimony (1) +3455+4005
witness (1)

3457 μαρτύριον *martyrion* (20)
testimony (12)
witnesses (3)
testifies (1)
testify (1)
testify (1) +1639
testify to (1) +625
testifying (1) +1650

3458 μαρτύρομαι *martyromai* (4)
declare (2)
insist on it (1)
urging (1)

3459 μάρτυς *martys* (35)
witnesses (20)
witness (10)
bore testimony (1)
martyr (1)
testify (1)
testify (1) +1639
testimony (1)

3460 μασάομαι *masaomai* (1)
gnawed (1)

3461 μασθός *masthos*
Variant; not used

3462 μασσάομαι *massaomai*
Variant; not used

3463 μαστιγόω *mastigoō* (7)
flog (4)
flogged (2)
punishes (1)

3464 μαστίζω *mastizō* (1)
flog (1)

3465 μάστιξ *mastix* (6)
suffering (2)
diseases (1)
flogged (1)
flogging (1)
sicknesses (1)

3466 μαστός *mastos* (3)
breasts (1)
chest (1)
untranslated (1)

3467 ματαιολογία *mataiologia* (1)
meaningless talk (1)

3468 ματαιολόγος *mataiologos* (1)
mere talkers (1)

3469 μάταιος *mataios* (6)
futile (2)
worthless (2)
empty (1)
useless (1)

3470 ματαιότης *mataiotēs* (3)
empty (1)
frustration (1)
futility (1)

3471 ματαιόω *mataioō* (1)
futile (1)

3472 μάτην *matēn* (2)
in vain (2)

3473 Ματθαῖος *Matthaios*
Variant; not used

3474 Ματθάν *Matthan* (2)
Matthan (2)

3475 Ματθάτ *Matthat*
Variant; not used

3476 Ματθίας *Matthias*
Variant; not used

3477 Ματταθά *Mattatha* (1)
Mattatha (1)

3478 Ματταθίας *Mattathias* (2)
Mattathias (1)
of Mattathias (1)

3479 μάχαιρα *machaira* (29)
sword (20)
swords (7)
edge sword (1) +5125
sword (1) +5125

3480 μάχη *machē* (4)
quarrels (3)
conflicts (1)

3481 μάχομαι *machomai* (4)
quarrel (2)
argue sharply (1)
fighting (1)

3482 μεγαλαυχέω *megalaucheō*
Variant; not used

3483 μεγαλεῖος *megaleios* (1)
wonders (1)

3484 μεγαλειότης *megaleiotēs* (3)
divine majesty (1)
greatness (1)
majesty (1)

3485 μεγαλοπρεπής *megaloprepēs* (1)
majestic (1)

3486 μεγαλύνω *megalynō* (8)
exalted (1)
expand (1)
glorifies (1)
held in high honor (1)
highly regarded (1)
long (1)
praising (1)
shown great (1)

3487 μεγάλως *megalōs* (1)
greatly (1)

3488 μεγαλωσύνη *megalōsynē* (3)
majesty (3)

3489 μέγας *megas* (194)
great (89)
loud (31)
large (10)
greatest (5)
severe (4)
completely (3)
big (2)
furious (2)
high (2)
high officials (2)
huge (2)
much (2)
strong (2)
terrified (2) +5828+5832
violent (2)
at the top of (1)
at the top of voice (1) +5889
at the top of voices (1) +5889
called out (1) +3306+5889
complete (1)
cried out (1) +3189+5889
enormous (1)
fear (1) +5832
filled with joy (1) +5915
fury (1) +2596
gigantic (1)
greatly (1)
grown up (1) +1181
intense (1)

intensely (1)
long (1)
mourned deeply (1) +3157+4472
overjoyed (1) +5379+5897+5915
profound (1)
proud (1)
richly (1)
roar (1) +5889
shouted (1) +3836+5774+5889
shouted (1) +5888+5889
shouting at the top of voice (1)
+3306+5889
shriek (1) +5888+5889
shrieks (1) +1066+5889
special (1)
surprising (1)
terrible (1)
terror (1) +5832
tremendous (1) +5496
very (1)
with a great crash (1)
+899+1639+3836+4774

3490 μέγεθος *megethos* (1)
great (1)

3491 μεγιστάν *megistan* (3)
great (1)
high officials (1)
princes (1)

3492 μέγιστος *megistos* (1)
very great (1)

3493 μεθερμηνεύω *methermēneuō* (8)
means (5) +1639
means (2)
is (1) +1639

3494 μέθη *methē* (3)
drunkenness (3)

3495 μεθιστάνω *methistanō*
Variant; not used

3496 μεθίστημι *methistēmi* (5)
brought (1)
led astray (1)
lose (1) +1666
move (1)
removing (1)

3497 μεθοδεία *methodeia* (2)
schemes (1)
scheming (1)

3498 μεθόριον *methorion*
Variant; not used

3499 μεθύσκω *methyskō* (5)
get drunk (3)
had too much to drink (1)
intoxicated (1)

3500 μέθυσος *methysos* (2)
drunkard (1)
drunkards (1)

3501 μεθύω *methyō* (5)
drunk (2)
drunkards (1)
get drunk (1)
gets drunk (1)

3502 μείγνυμι *meignymi* (4)
mixed (4)

3503 μειγνύω *meignyō*
Variant; not used

3504 μειζότερος *meizoteros* (1)
greater than (1)

3505 μείζων *meizōn* (47)
greater than (18)
greater (10)
greatest (8)
more (3)
largest (2)

all the louder (1)
bigger (1)
greater than (1) +3836
older (1)
one greater than (1)
weightier than (1)

3506 μέλας *melas* (6)
black (3)
ink (3)

3507 Μελεά *Melea* (1)
Melea (1)

3508 μέλει *melei* (10)
care (2)
cares (2)
swayed (2)
cared (1)
concerned (1)
showed concern (1)
trouble (1)

3509 μελετάω *meletaō* (2)
give yourself wholly to (1)
plot (1)

3510 μέλι *meli* (4)
honey (4)

3511 μελισσεῖον *melisseion*
Variant; not used

3512 μελισσίον *melission*
Variant; not used

3513 μελίσσιος *melissios*
Variant; not used

3514 Μελίτη *Melitē* (1)
Malta (1)

3515 Μελιτήνη *Melitēnē*
Variant; not used

3516 μέλλω *mellō* (109)
about to (21)
going to (18)
will (17)
would (8)
to come (7)
coming (4)
later (4)
intend (3)
intended (2)
the future (2)
to be (2)
wanting (2)
about (1)
as (1)
close (1)
come (1)
dawn (1) +1181+2465
future (1)
going (1)
going to happen to (1)
nearly (1)
never (1) +3600
next (1) +1650+3836
should (1)
that are coming (1)
to (1)
to come (1) +2262
waiting for (1)
was (1)
was coming (1) +1451
untranslated (1)

3517 μέλος *melos* (34)
members (7)
part (6)
parts (6)
parts of body (3)
part of body (2)
bodies (1)
each one[s] (1)
member (1) +2848+3836

members of body (1)
nature (1)
part of the body (1)
parts of the body (1)
them[s] (1) +3836+5148
unite (1) +4472
within (1) +1877+3836

3518 Μελχί *Melchi* (2)
Melki (2)

3519 Μελχισέδεκ *Melchisedek* (8)
Melchizedek (8)

3520 μέλω *melō*
Variant; not used

3521 μεμβράνα *membrana* (1)
parchments (1)

3522 μέμφομαι *memphomai* (2)
blame (1)
found fault with (1)

3523 μεμψίμοιρος *mempsimoiros* (1)
faultfinders (1)

3524 μέμψις *mempsis*
Variant; not used

3525 μέν *men* (178)
some (6) +4005
some (5) +3836
indeed (2)
one (2) +4005
some (2)
though (2)
as far as (1)
certainly (1)
even though (1) +1142
he (1) +3836
his son[s] (1) +3836
however (1) +4036
if (1) +1623
in the one case (1) +6045
inasmuch as (1) +2093+4012+4036
latter (1)
now (1)
one (1) +3836
others (1) +3836
our fathers[s] (1) +3836
Paul[s] (1) +3836
Peter and John[s] (1) +3836
sometimes (1) +4047
the apostles[s] (1) +3836
the men[s] (1) +3836
then (1)
they (1) +3836
those who (1) +4005
to be sure (1)
to the one (1) +4005
untranslated (135)

3526 Μενάμ *Menam*
Variant; not used

3527 Μεννά *Menna* (1)
Menna (1)

3528 μενοῦν *menoun* (1)
rather (1)

3529 μενοῦνγε *menounge* (3)
but (1)
of course (1)
what is more (1) +247

3530 μέντοι *mentoi* (8)
but (4)
nevertheless (1)
really (1)
very (1)
yet (1)

3531 μένω *menō* (118)
remain (24)
stay (14)
lives (12)

remains (11)
stayed (11)
continue (4)
live (4)
endures (2)
enduring (2)
living (2)
remained (2)
staying (2)
be (1)
belong (1)
belongs (1)
continues (1)
does[s] (1) +1877+5148
dwell (1) +2400
facing (1)
hold (1)
keep on (1)
last (1)
lasting (1)
lasts (1)
left (1)
lived (1)
permanent place (1)
spend time (1) +2093+5989
spent (1)
stand (1)
stands (1)
stayed (1) +1695
stays (1)
still (1)
survives (1)
waited for (1)
would not move (1) +810
untranslated (3)

3532 μερίζω *merizō* (14)
divided (9)
assigned (2)
divide (1)
gave (1)
given (1)

3533 μέριμνα *merimna* (6)
worries (3)
anxieties (1)
anxiety (1)
concern (1)

3534 μεριμνάω *merimnaō* (19)
worry about (5)
concerned about (4)
worry (4)
worrying (2)
anxious about (1)
have concern (1)
takes interest (1)
worried (1)

3535 μερίς *meris* (5)
district (1)
in common (1)
part (1)
share (1)
what[s] (1)

3536 μερισμός *merismos* (2)
dividing (1)
gifts distributed (1)

3537 μεριστής *meristēs* (1)
arbiter (1)

3538 μέρος *meros* (42)
part (8)
place (3)
region (3)
in part (2) +608
parts (2)
area (1)
comparison with (1)
detail (1)
district (1)
dividing into shares (1) +4472
extent (1)

imperfect (1) +1666
interior (1) +541
matter (1)
on some points (1) +608
one at a time (1) +324
one^s (1)
piece (1)
regions (1)
share (1)
share (1) +2095
side (1)
some (1) +1651+3836
to some extent (1) +247+608
trade (1)
while (1)
with regard to (1) +1877
untranslated (2)

3539 μεσάζω *mesazō*
Variant; not used

3540 μεσημβρία *mesēmbria* (2)
noon (1)
south (1)

3541 μεσιτεύω *mesiteuō* (1)
confirmed (1)

3542 μεσίτης *mesitēs* (6)
mediator (5)
mediator between (1)

3543 μεσονύκτιον *mesonyktion* (4)
midnight (3)
at midnight (1)

3544 Μεσοποταμία *Mesopotamia* (2)
Mesopotamia (2)

3545 μέσος *mesos* (58)
among (14) +1877
middle (5)
center (3)
among (2) +1650+3836
front of everyone (2) +3836
in (2) +1877
among (1)
among (1) +324
before (1) +1650+3836
before (1) +1877
before (1) +1877+3836
before the group (1) +1877
before them (1) +1650
between (1)
between (1) +324
fellowship (1)
for (1) +1877+3836
from (1)
in (1)
in two (1)
into (1) +324
midnight (1) +3816
midnight (1) +3816+3836
noon (1) +2465
open (1)
presence (1)
there (1) +1877
way (1)
with (1)
with (1) +1877
untranslated (6)

3546 μεσότοιχον *mesotoichon* (1)
dividing wall (1)

3547 μεσουράνημα *mesouranēma* (3)
midair (3)

3548 μεσόω *mesoō* (1)
halfway through (1)

3549 Μεσσίας *Messias* (2)
Messiah (2)

3550 μεστός *mestos* (9)
full (6)
full of (1)

soaked (1)
untranslated (1)

3551 μεστόω *mestoō* (1)
had too much (1) +1639

3552 μετά *meta* (468)
with (263)
after (66)
to (11)
along with (9)
against (8)
later (7)
among (6)
later (6) +4047
companions (5) +3836
between (3)
in (3)
after (2) +3836
afterward (2) +4047
away (2)
by (2)
companions (2) +1639+3836
joyfully (2) +5915
on (2)
through (2)
when (2)
a week later (1) +2465+3893
afraid (1) +5832
afterward (1)
along (1)
and (1)
and to (1)
before very long (1) +4024+4498
behind (1)
boldly (1) +4244
bringing (1) +1571+2400
close (1)
companions (1)
confidently (1) +4244
disastrous (1) +5615
finally (1) +4047
first (1) +3836
followed (1) +4344
following (1)
humiliated (1) +158
hurried (1) +1656+5082
hurried (1) +4513+5082
in presence (1) +3836+4725
involved in (1)
is one of us (1) +199+1609
separate from (1) +4024
settle down (1) +2484
some time after (1)
some time later (1) +4047
that would follow (1) +4047
the next day (1) +1651+2465
together with (1)
under (1)
urgently (1) +4155+4498
use force (1) +1040
welcomed (1) +1312+1645
when (1) +3836
when later (1)
wholeheartedly (1) +2334
yet (1) +4047
untranslated (24)

3553 μεταβαίνω *metabainō* (12)
leave (3)
move (2)
crossed over (1)
going on (1)
left (1)
left there (1) +1696
move around (1)
passed (1)
went on (1)

3554 μεταβάλλω *metaballō* (1)
changed minds (1)

3555 μετάγω *metagō* (2)
steered (1)

turn (1)

3556 μεταδίδωμι *metadidōmi* (5)
share with (2)
contributing (1)
impart (1)
share (1)

3557 μετάθεσις *metathesis* (3)
change (1)
removing (1)
taken (1)

3558 μεταίρω *metairō* (2)
left (1)
moved on (1)

3559 μετακαλέω *metakaleō* (4)
for (1)
send for (1)
sent for (1) +690
untranslated (1)

3560 μετακινέω *metakineō* (1)
moved (1)

3561 μεταλαμβάνω *metalambanō* (7)
eat (1) +5575
find convenient (1) +2789
receive a share (1)
receives (1)
share in (1)
take (1)
together (1)

3562 μετάλημψις *metalēmpsis* (1)
be received with (1)

3563 μεταλλάσσω *metallassō* (2)
exchanged (2)

3564 μεταμέλομαι *metamelomai* (6)
regret (2)
change mind (1)
changed mind (1)
repent (1)
seized with remorse (1)

3565 μεταμορφόω *metamorphoō* (4)
transfigured (2)
transformed (1)
transformed into (1)

3566 μετανοέω *metanoeō* (34)
repent (23)
repented (5)
refused to repent (2) +4024
who repents (2)
repents (1)
untranslated (1)

3567 μετάνοια *metanoia* (22)
repentance (19)
change of mind (1)
repent (1)
turn in repentance (1)

3568 μεταξύ *metaxy* (9)
between (6)
meanwhile (1) +1877+3836
next (1)
untranslated (1)

3569 μεταπέμπω *metapempō* (9)
sent for (5)
bring back (1)
come (1)
for (1)
have transferred (1)

3570 μεταστρέφω *metastrephō* (2)
pervert (1)
turned (1)

3571 μετασχηματίζω *metaschēmatizō* (5)
applied (1)
masquerade (1)
masquerades (1)
masquerading (1)

transform (1)

3572 μετατίθημι *metatithēmi* (6)
change (2)
brought back (1)
deserting (1) +608
taken away (1)
taken from (1)

3573 μετατρέπω *metatrepō* (1)
change (1)

3574 μεταφυτεύω *metaphyteuō*
Variant; not used

3575 μετέπειτα *metepeita* (1)
afterward (1)

3576 μετέχω *metechō* (8)
belonged to (1)
have (1)
have a part (1)
lives on (1)
partake (1)
shared in (1)
sharing in (1)
take part (1)

3577 μετεωρίζομαι *meteōrizomai* (1)
worry about (1)

3578 μετοικεσία *metoikesia* (4)
exile (4)

3579 μετοικίζω *metoikizō* (2)
send into exile (1)
sent (1)

3580 μετοχή *metochē* (1)
in common (1)

3581 μέτοχος *metochos* (6)
companions (1)
partners (1)
share in (1)
shared in (1) +1181
undergoes (1) +1181
who share in (1)

3582 μετρέω *metreō* (11)
measure (4)
measured (4)
use^s (3)

3583 μετρητής *metrētēs* (1)
twenty to thirty gallons (1)
　　　　　　　　+1545+2445+5552

3584 μετριοπαθέω *metriopatheō* (1)
deal gently (1)

3585 μετρίως *metriōs* (1)
greatly (1) +4024

3586 μέτρον *metron* (14)
measure (7)
apportioned (1)
field (1)
field (1) +2834+3836
limit (1)
measurement (1)
measuring (1)
untranslated (1)

3587 μέτωπον *metōpon* (8)
foreheads (5)
forehead (3)

3588 μέχρι *mechri* (17)
until (5)
to (4)
until (2) +4005
all the way to (1)
at (1)
even to the point of (1)
till (1)
to the point of (1)
untranslated (1)

3589 μέχρις *mechris*

Variant; not used

3590 μή *mē* (1039)
not (524)
no (58)
except (36) +1623
never (34) +4024
not (31) +4024
unless (31) +1569
don't (24)
but (10) +1623
only (10) +1623
without (8)
certainly not (7) +4024
or (7) +2671
nothing (6)
stop (6)
never (5)
only (5) +1623+4024
without (5) +2400
by no means (4) +1181
from (4)
neither (4)
never (4) +172+1650+3836+4024
not at all (4) +1181
or (4)
avoid (3)
cannot (3)
cannot (3) +1538
do^s (3) +1145
don't (3) +4024
none (3)
that (3)
won't (3)
absolutely not (2) +1181
against (2)
blind (2) +1063
but only (2) +1623
certainly not (2) +1181
does^s (2) +1145
doesn't (2)
fearing that (2) +5828
how (2)
if he does (2) +1254+1623
keep from (2)
no (2) +4024
not are you (2)
not at all (2) +4024
not only (2)
nothing (2) +5516
that (2) +4803
unless (2) +1623
unless (2) +1623+1760
unseen (1) +1063
abstains (1) +2266
at once (1) +3890
be unable to see (1) +1063
before (1) +2671
bound to come (1) +450+2262
but (1) +1569
cover (1) +5746
didn't (1)
die (1) +2441
displease (1) +743
ever (1)
ever no (1) +4024
evidently (1) +1623
except (1)
except for (1) +1623
fail (1) +1569
fail (1) +4049
for (1) +1142
for (1) +4803
for fear that (1) +2671
for fear that (1) +4803
free from fear of (1) +5828
from (1) +2671
haven't (1) +2400
help speaking about (1) +3281
how (1) +1142
how dare you (1)
if (1)

isn't at all (1) +4024
kept from (1)
lest (1) +2671
may never (1) +1181
may this never (1)
never (1) +173+1650+3836+4024
never (1) +1181
never (1) +4024+4033
never (1) +4024+4537
never (1) +4024+4799
never again (1) +172+1650+3836+4024
never again (1) +4024
nevertheless (1) +1623
no longer (1) +4024
nobody (1) +5516
none (1) +5516
nor (1) +2779
not (1) +4029
not anything (1) +3594
not one (1) +4024
nothing (1) +4024+4029
nothing (1) +5515
nothing ever (1)
only (1) +1569
only (1) +1623+3668
only to (1) +1623+4029
or at least (1) +1254+1623
otherwise (1) +1254+1623
otherwise (1) +1623+1760
prevent (1)
prevent from blowing (1) +4463
rather than (1) +2671
rather than (1) +2779
refused to worship (1) +4686
shallow (1) +958
shallow (1) +958+2400
shouldn't (1)
sincere (1) +1474
spare (1) +2400
than that (1) +2779
to keep from (1) +2671
to keep from (1) +3836+4639
to prevent (1)
together (1) +6006
unable (1) +1538
unashamed (1) +159
until (1) +1569+4754
until (1) +1623+4020
without (1) +1569
without (1) +1650
without (1) +2779
without light (1) +5743
untranslated (64)

3591 μήγε *mēge* (1)
not (1)

3592 μηδαμῶς *mēdamōs* (2)
surely not (2)

3593 μηδέ *mēde* (57)
or (25)
not (11)
and not (5)
nor (5)
not even (4)
and (1)
and don't (1)
don't (1)
go running off after (1) +599+1503
or anything (1) +3836
untranslated (2)

3594 μηδείς *mēdeis* (90)
not anyone (13)
nothing (11)
no (10)
no one (9)
not (8)
don't anyone (5)
not anything (5)
don't (3)
without (3)

anyone (2)
not any (2)
any (1)
any way (1)
anyone's (1)
don't anything (1)
don't this (1)
have everything need (1) +3309
haven't anything (1)
in any way (1) +2848+5573
nobody (1)
not any way (1)
not anybody (1)
not anything (1) +3590
not in the least (1)
permit (1) +3266
without anything (1)
untranslated (4)

3595 μηδέποτε *mēdepote* (1)
never (1)

3596 μηδέπω *mēdepō* (1)
not yet (1)

3597 Μῆδος *Mēdos* (1)
Medes (1)

3598 μηθαμῶς *mēthamōs*
Variant; not used

3599 μηθείς *mētheis*
Variant; not used

3600 μηκέτι *mēketi* (22)
no longer (9)
stop (3)
again (1)
any longer (1)
don't any more (1)
leave your life of sin (1) +279
never (1)
never (1) +3516
never again (1)
no (1)
no more (1)
not (1)

3601 μῆκος *mēkos* (3)
long (3)

3602 μηκύνω *mēkynō* (1)
grows (1)

3603 μηλωτή *mēlōtē* (1)
sheepskins (1)

3604 μήν1 *mēn1* (18)
months (11)
month (4)
half (2) +1971
a half (1) +1971

3605 μήν2 *mēn2* (1)
surely (1) +1623

3606 μηνύω *mēnyō* (4)
informed (1)
report (1)
showed (1)
told (1)

3607 μήποτε *mēpote* (25)
or (5)
otherwise (4)
so that not (3)
if you do (2)
that none (2) +5516
because (1)
for (1)
for if (1) +2671
if (1)
in the hope that (1)
never (1)
no (1)
only (1)
untranslated (1)

3608 μήπου *mēpou*
Variant; not used

3609 μήπω *mēpō* (2)
not yet (1)
yet before (1)

3610 μήπως *mēpōs*
Variant; not used

3611 μηρός *mēros* (1)
thigh (1)

3612 μήτε *mēte* (34)
or (13)
no (5)
nor (4)
not (4)
neither (3)
either (1)
without (1)
untranslated (3)

3613 μήτηρ *mētēr* (83)
mother (73)
birth (4) +3120
mother's (3)
mothers (2)
untranslated (1)

3614 μήτι *mēti* (17)
not (2)
surely not (2)
unless (2) +1623
except (1) +323+1623
untranslated (10)

3615 μήτιγε *mētige* (1)
how much more (1)

3616 μήτρα *mētra* (2)
firstborn (1) +1380
womb (1)

3617 μητραλῴας *mētralōas*
Variant; not used

3618 μητρολῴας *mētrolōas* (1)
mothers (1)

3619 μητρόπολις *mētropolis*
Variant; not used

3620 μιαίνω *miainō* (5)
corrupted (2)
ceremonial uncleanness (1)
defile (1)
pollute (1)

3621 μίασμα *miasma* (1)
corruption (1)

3622 μιασμός *miasmos* (1)
corrupt (1)

3623 μίγμα *migma* (1)
mixture (1)

3624 μίγνυμι *mignymi*
Variant; not used

3625 μικρός *mikros* (46)
little (20)
a little while (7)
small (7)
least (4)
short (2)
smallest (2)
before long (1) +2285
low (1)
short (1) +2461+3836
younger (1)

3626 Μίλητος *Milētos* (3)
Miletus (3)

3627 μίλιον *milion* (1)
mile (1)

3628 μιμέομαι *mimeomai* (4)
imitate (2)

follow (1)
follow example (1)

3629 μιμητής *mimētēs* (6)
imitators (3)
follow example (1) +1181
imitate (1)
imitate (1) +1181

3630 μιμνήσκομαι *mimnēskomai* (23)
remember (10)
remembered (6)
remembering (2)
are mindful (1)
realize (1)
recall (1)
recalled (1)
recalling (1)

3631 μισέω *miseō* (40)
hate (13)
hates (12)
hated (9)
hate (3) +1639
hating (2)
detestable (1)

3632 μισθαποδοσία *misthapodosia* (3)
punishment (1)
reward (1)
rewarded (1)

3633 μισθαποδότης *misthapodotēs* (1)
rewards (1) +1181

3634 μίσθιος *misthios* (2)
hired men (2)

3635 μισθός *misthos* (29)
reward (17)
wages (7)
be rewarded (1) +3284
paid (1)
profit (1)
rewarded (1) +655
rewarding (1) +1443+3836

3636 μισθόω *misthoō* (2)
hire (1)
hired (1)

3637 μίσθωμα *misthōma* (1)
rented house (1)

3638 μισθωτός *misthōtos* (3)
hired hand (2)
hired men (1)

3639 Μιτυλήνη *Mitylēnē* (1)
Mitylene (1)

3640 Μιχαήλ *Michaēl* (2)
Michael (2)

3641 μνᾶ *mna* (9)
mina (4)
minas (2)
more[s] (1)
untranslated (2)

3642 μνάομαι *mnaomai*
Variant; not used

3643 Μνάσων *Mnasōn* (1)
Mnason (1)

3644 μνεία *mneia* (7)
remember (2) +4472
memories (1)
mentioning (1) +4472
remember (1)
remember (1) +2400
remembering (1) +4472

3645 μνῆμα *mnēma* (8)
tomb (4)
tombs (3)
burial (1) +1650+5502

3646 μνημεῖον *mnēmeion* (40)
tomb (31)

tombs (5)
graves (3)
untranslated (1)

3647 μνήμη *mnēmē* (1)
remember (1) +4472

3648 μνημονεύω *mnēmoneuō* (21)
remember (16)
forgets (1) +4033
remembered (1)
remembering (1)
spoke (1)
thinking (1)

3649 μνημόσυνον *mnēmosynon* (3)
memory (2)
memorial offering (1)

3650 μνηστεύω *mnēsteuō* (3)
pledged to be married (3)

3651 μογγιλάλος *mongilalos*
Variant; not used

3652 μογιλάλος *mogilalos* (1)
could hardly talk (1)

3653 μόγις *mogis* (1)
scarcely ever (1)

3654 μόδιος *modios* (3)
bowl (3)

3655 μοιχαλίς *moichalis* (7)
adulterous (4)
adulteress (2)
adultery (1)

3656 μοιχάω *moichaō* (4)
commits adultery (4)

3657 μοιχεία *moicheia* (3)
adultery (3)

3658 μοιχεύω *moicheuō* (15)
commit adultery (10)
commits adultery (2)
adultery (1)
become an adulteress (1)
committed adultery with (1)

3659 μοιχός *moichos* (3)
adulterers (2)
adulterer (1)

3660 μόλις *molis* (6)
difficulty (2)
hard (1)
hardly (1)
very rarely (1)
with difficulty (1)

3661 Μολόχ *Moloch* (1)
Molech (1)

3662 μολύνω *molynō* (3)
defile (1)
defiled (1)
soiled (1)

3663 μολυσμός *molysmos* (1)
that contaminates (1)

3664 μομφή *momphē* (1)
grievances (1)

3665 μονή *monē* (2)
home (1)
rooms (1)

3666 μονογενής *monogenēs* (9)
one and only (5)
only (2)
one and only son (1)
only (1) +1639

3667 μόνον *monon* (40)
only (24)
alone (3)
but (3)
just (3)

all alone (1)
all they asked was (1)
merely (1)
what is more (1) +247+1254+2779+4024
untranslated (3)

3668 μόνος *monos* (74)
only (38)
alone (12)
just (4)
simply (2)
all (1)
alone (1) +2848
by himself (1) +899
by myself (1)
by ourselves (1)
by themselves (1)
even (1)
just one (1) +4047
only (1) +1623+3590
only a single (1)
private (1)
whatever happens (1)
untranslated (6)

3669 μονόφθαλμος *monophthalmos* (2)
one eye (2)

3670 μονόω *monoō* (1)
left all alone (1)

3671 μορφή *morphē* (3)
nature (2)
form (1)

3672 μορφόω *morphoō* (1)
formed (1)

3673 μόρφωσις *morphōsis* (2)
embodiment (1)
form (1)

3674 μοσχοποιέω *moschopoieō* (1)
made in the form of a calf (1)

3675 μόσχος *moschos* (6)
calf (3)
calves (2)
ox (1)

3676 μουσικός *mousikos* (1)
musicians (1)

3677 μόχθος *mochthos* (3)
hardship (1)
toiled (1)
toiling (1)

3678 μυελός *myelos* (1)
marrow (1)

3679 μυέω *myeō* (1)
learned the secret (1)

3680 μῦθος *mythos* (5)
myths (4)
stories (1)

3681 μυκάομαι *mykaomai* (1)
roar (1)

3682 μυκτηρίζω *myktērizō* (1)
mocked (1)

3683 μυλικός *mylikos* (1)
millstone (1) +3345

3684 μύλινος *mylinos* (1)
millstone (1)

3685 μύλος *mylos* (4)
millstone (2)
hand mill (1)
large millstone (1) +3948

3686 μυλών *mylōn*
Variant; not used

3687 μυλωνικός *mylōnikos*
Variant; not used

3688 Μύρα *Myra* (1)
Myra (1)

3689 μυριάς *myrias* (8)
ten thousand (2)
thousands upon thousands (2)
fifty thousand (1) +4297
many thousands (1)
thousands (1)
two hundred million (1) +1490

3690 μυρίζω *myrizō* (1)
poured perfume on to prepare (1)

3691 μύριοι *myrioi* (1)
ten thousand (1)

3692 μυρίος *myrios* (2)
ten thousand (2)

3693 μύρον *myron* (15)
perfume (12)
it^s (1) +3836
myrrh (1)
perfumes (1)

3694 Μύρρα *Myrra*
Variant; not used

3695 Μυσία *Mysia* (2)
Mysia (2)

3696 μυστήριον *mystērion* (27)
mystery (18)
secret (3)
mysteries (2)
secrets (2)
deep truths (1)
secret (1) +1877

3697 μυωπάζω *myōpazō* (1)
nearsighted (1)

3698 μώλωψ *mōlōps* (1)
wounds (1)

3699 μωμάομαι *mōmaomai* (2)
criticism (1)
discredited (1)

3700 μῶμος *mōmos* (1)
blemishes (1)

3701 μωραίνω *mōrainō* (4)
fools (1)
loses (1)
loses its saltiness (1)
made foolish (1)

3702 μωρία *mōria* (5)
foolishness (5)

3703 μωρολογία *mōrologia* (1)
foolish talk (1)

3704 μωρός *mōros* (12)
foolish (7)
fool (2)
fools (2)
foolishness (1)

3705 Μωσεύς *Mōseus*
Variant; not used

3706 Μωσῆς *Mōsēs*
Variant; not used

3707 Μωϋσῆς *Mōysēs* (80)
Moses (77)
Moses' (2)
he^s (1) +3836

3708 ν *n*
Variant; not used

3709 Ναασσών *Naassōn* (3)
Nahshon (3)

3710 Ναγγαί *Nangai* (1)
Naggai (1)

3711 Ναζαρά *Nazara*
Variant; not used

3712 Ναζαράθ *Nazarath*
Variant; not used

3713 Ναζαράτ *Nazarat*
Variant; not used

3714 Ναζαρέθ *Nazareth* (12)
Nazareth (12)

3715 Ναζαρέτ *Nazaret*
Variant; not used

3716 Ναζαρηνός *Nazarēnos* (6)
of Nazareth (4)
Nazarene (2)

3717 Ναζωραῖος *Nazōraios* (13)
of Nazareth (11)
Nazarene (2)

3718 Ναθάμ *Natham* (1)
Nathan (1)

3719 Ναθάν *Nathan*
Variant; not used

3720 Ναθαναήλ *Nathanaēl* (6)
Nathanael (6)

3721 ναί *nai* (34)
yes (32)
so (1)
untranslated (1)

3722 Ναιμάν *Naiman* (1)
Naaman (1)

3723 Ναΐν *Nain* (1)
Nain (1)

3724 ναός *naos* (45)
temple (42)
shrines (1)
temples (1)
untranslated (1)

3725 Ναούμ *Naoum* (1)
Nahum (1)

3726 νάρδος *nardos* (2)
nard (2)

3727 Νάρκισσος *Narkissos* (1)
Narcissus (1)

3728 ναυαγέω *nauageō* (2)
shipwrecked (2)

3729 ναύκληρος *nauklēros* (1)
owner of the ship (1)

3730 ναῦς *naus* (1)
ship (1)

3731 ναύτης *nautēs* (3)
sailors (3)

3732 Ναχώρ *Nachōr* (1)
Nahor (1)

3733 νεανίας *neanias* (3)
young man (3)

3734 νεανίσκος *neaniskos* (11)
young man (7)
young men (4)

3735 Νεά πολις *Nea polis* (1)
Neapolis (1)

3736 Νεάπολις *Neapolis*
Variant; not used

3737 Νεεμάν *Neeman*
Variant; not used

3738 νεκρός *nekros* (129)
dead (123)
death (3)
corpse (1)
died (1) +1181
died (1) +2093

3739 νεκρόω *nekroō* (3)
as good as dead (1) +2453
dead (1)
put to death (1)

3740 νέκρωσις *nekrōsis* (2)
dead (1)
death (1)

3741 νεομηνία *neomēnia* (1)
new Moon celebration (1)

3742 νέος *neos* (23)
new (11)
younger (8)
young (3)
youngest (1)

3743 νεοσσός *neossos*
Variant; not used

3744 νεότης *neotēs* (4)
boy (2)
child (1)
young (1)

3745 νεόφυτος *neophytos* (1)
recent convert (1)

3746 Νέρων *Nerōn*
Variant; not used

3747 Νεύης *Neuēs*
Variant; not used

3748 νεύω *neuō* (2)
motioned (2)

3749 νεφέλη *nephelē* (25)
cloud (18)
clouds (7)

3750 Νεφθαλίμ *Nephthalim* (3)
Naphtali (3)

3751 νέφος *nephos* (1)
cloud (1)

3752 νεφρός *nephros* (1)
minds (1)

3753 νεωκόρος *neōkoros* (1)
guardian of the temple (1)

3754 νεωτερικός *neōterikos* (1)
of youth (1)

3755 νή *nē* (1)
I mean that just as surely (1)

3756 νήθω *nēthō* (2)
spin (2)

3757 νηπιάζω *nēpiazō* (1)
infants (1)

3758 νήπιος *nēpios* (14)
child (5)
infants (3)
children (2)
little children (2)
childish (1) +3836
infant (1)

3759 Νηρεύς *Nēreus* (1)
Nereus (1)

3760 Νηρί *Nēri* (1)
Neri (1)

3761 νησίον *nēsion* (1)
small island (1)

3762 νῆσος *nēsos* (9)
island (9)

3763 νηστεία *nēsteia* (5)
fasting (2)
fast (1)
gone without food (1)
hunger (1)

3764 νηστεύω *nēsteuō* (20)
fast (11)
fasting (6)
fasted (1)
untranslated (2)

3765 νῆστις *nēstis* (2)
hungry (2)

3766 νηφαλέος *nēphaleos*
Variant; not used

3767 νηφάλιος *nēphalios* (3)
temperate (3)

3768 νήφω *nēphō* (6)
self-controlled (5)
keep head (1)

3769 Νίγερ *Niger* (1)
Niger (1)

3770 Νικάνωρ *Nikanōr* (1)
Nicanor (1)

3771 νικάω *nikaō* (28)
overcomes (10)
overcome (8)
overcame (2)
conquer (1)
conqueror (1)
conquest (1)
overpower (1)
overpowers (1)
prevail (1)
triumphed (1)
victorious (1)

3772 νίκη *nikē* (1)
victory (1)

3773 Νικόδημος *Nikodēmos* (5)
Nicodemus (5)

3774 Νικολαΐτης *Nikolaitēs* (2)
Nicolaitans (2)

3775 Νικόλαος *Nikolaos* (1)
Nicolas (1)

3776 Νικόπολις *Nikopolis* (1)
Nicopolis (1)

3777 νῖκος *nikos* (4)
victory (4)

3778 Νινευή *Nineuē*
Variant; not used

3779 Νινευί *Nineui*
Variant; not used

3780 Νινευίτης *Nineuitēs* (3)
Nineveh (1)
Ninevites (1)

3781 νιπτήρ *niptēr* (1)
basin (1)

3782 νίπτω *niptō* (17)
wash (10)
washed (4)
washing (3)

3783 νοέω *noeō* (14)
understand (7)
see (3)
imagine (1)
know (1)
reflect on (1)
understood (1)

3784 νόημα *noēma* (6)
minds (4)
schemes (1)
thought (1)

3785 νόθος *nothos* (1)
illegitimate children (1)

3786 νομή *nomē* (2)
pasture (1)
spread (1) +2400

3787 νομίζω *nomizō* (15)
thought (3)
expected (2)
think (2)
think that (2)
thinking (2)
assumed (1)

suppose (1)
thinks (1)
thought that (1)

3788　νομικός nomikos (9)
experts in the law (5)
expert in the law (2)
about law (1)
lawyer (1)

3789　νομίμως nomimōs (2)
according to the rules (1)
properly (1)

3790　νόμισμα nomisma (1)
coin (1)

3791　νομοδιδάσκαλος nomodidaskalos (3)
teachers of the law (2)
teacher of the law (1)

3792　νομοθεσία nomothesia (1)
receiving of the law (1)

3793　νομοθετέω nomotheteō (2)
founded (1)
law was given (1)

3794　νομοθέτης nomothetēs (1)
lawgiver (1)

3795　νόμος nomos (194)
law (181)
it^s (2)
lawbreaker (2) +4127
laws (2)
it^s (1) +1650
law's (1)
legalistic (1) +1877
observer of law (1) +2848
principle (1)
regulation (1)
that^s (1)

3796　νοσέω noseō (1)
unhealthy (1)

3797　νόσημα nosēma
Variant; not used

3798　νόσος nosos (11)
diseases (5)
disease (3)
diseases (1) +2809
illnesses (1)
sickness (1) +820

3799　νοσσιά nossia (1)
chicks (1)

3800　νοσσίον nossion (1)
chicks (1)

3801　νοσσός nossos (1)
young (1)

3802　νοσφίζω nosphizō (3)
kept (1)
kept back (1)
steal (1)

3803　νότος notos (7)
south (5)
south wind (2)

3804　νουθεσία nouthesia (3)
instruction (1)
warn (1)
warnings (1)

3805　νουθετέω noutheteō (8)
warn (3)
admonish (2)
admonishing (1)
instruct (1)
warning (1)

3806　νουμηνία noumēnia
Variant; not used

3807　νουνεχῶς nounechōs (1)
wisely (1)

3808　νοῦς nous (24)
mind (15)
minds (4)
insight (1)
intelligible (1) +1609+3836
thinking (1)
understanding (1)
untranslated (1)

3809　Νύμφαν Nymphan (1)
Nympha (1)

3810　Νυμφᾶς Nymphas
Variant; not used

3811　νύμφη nymphē (8)
bride (5)
daughter-in-law (3)

3812　νυμφίος nymphios (16)
bridegroom (11)
he^s (3) +3836
bridegroom's (1)
him^s (1)

3813　νυμφών nymphōn (3)
bridegroom (3)

3814　νῦν nyn (147)
now (110)
present (9)
now on (4) +3836
now (3) +3836
as it is (2)
as it is (2) +1254
now on (2)
a short while ago (1)
again (1) +608+3836
at present (1)
for now (1) +2400+3836
in present (1)
instead (1) +1254
just (1)
now (1) +608+3836
now then (1)
present (1) +2789+3836
present time (1)
still (1) +2285
untranslated (3)

3815　νυνί nyni (20)
now (16)
as it is (1)
in fact (1)
indeed (1)
untranslated (1)

3816　νύξ nyx (61)
night (51)
nights (3)
each evening (1) +3836
last night (1) +3836+4047
midnight (1) +3545
midnight (1) +3545+3836
night (1) +1328+4246
tonight (1)
tonight (1) +3836+4047

3817　νύσσω nyssō (1)
pierced (1)

3818　νυστάζω nystazō (2)
became drowsy (1)
sleeping (1)

3819　νυχθήμερον nychthēmeron (1)
a night and a day (1)

3820　Νῶε Nōe (8)
noah (8)

3821　νωθρός nōthros (2)
lazy (1)
slow (1)

3822　νῶτος nōtos (1)
backs (1)

3823　ξ x
Variant; not used

3824　ξαίνω xainō
Variant; not used

3825　ξενία xenia (2)
guest room (1)
place where staying (1)

3826　ξενίζω xenizō (10)
entertained (2)
staying (2)
a guest (1)
be guests (1)
stay (1)
strange (1)
surprised (1)
think it strange (1)

3827　ξενοδοχέω xenodocheō (1)
showing hospitality (1)

3828　ξένος xenos (14)
foreigners (4)
stranger (4)
strange (2)
aliens (1)
foreign (1)
hospitality (1)
strangers (1)

3829　ξέστης xestēs (1)
pitchers (1)

3830　ξηραίνω xērainō (15)
withered (6)
withers (3)
becomes rigid (1)
dried up (1)
ripe (1)
shriveled (1)
stopped (1)
wither (1)

3831　ξηρός xēros (8)
shriveled (4)
dry (2)
land (1)
paralyzed (1)

3832　ξύλινος xylinos (2)
of wood (1)
wood (1)

3833　ξύλον xylon (20)
tree (11)
clubs (5)
wood (3)
stocks (1)

3834　ξυράω xyraō (3)
shaved (2)
shaved off (1)

3835　ο o
Variant; not used

3836　ὁ ho (19856)
the (7395)
who (381)
those who (271)
his (199)
a (164)
what (160)
the who (153)
that (143)
he who (108)
their (92)
your (77)
this (76)
the son (74)
him who (73)
he (70) +1254
those (70)
our (52)
they (49) +1254
my (41)
he (35)
whoever (35)

which (28)
anyone who (27)
her (26)
Jesus[s] (25) +1254
forever (23) +172+1650
they (22)
its (21)
an (15)
to (15) +1650
so that (14) +1650
you who (14)
one (12)
one who (12)
whom (12)
because (10) +1328
these (10)
things (10)
all things (9) +4246
son (9)
everything (8) +4246
she (8) +1254
the that (8)
when (8) +1877
he[s] (7) +2652
him[s] (7) +2536
O (7)
that (7) +1650
him[s] (6) +2652
so that (6)
companions (5) +3552
finally (5) +3370
he[s] (5) +2536
some (5)
some (5) +3525
this[s] (5) +3364
we (5)
back (4) +1650+3958
him[s] (4) +476
his[s] (4) +2536
Jesus[s] (4)
never (4) +172+1650+3590+4024
now on (4) +3814
rider (4) +2764
someone (4)
the man[s] (4) +1254
whose (4)
you (4)
a man[s] (3)
and so (3) +1650
anyone (3)
God[s] (3)
he[s] (3) +3812
in order that (3) +1650
it (3)
it[s] (3) +3180
looked up (3) +2048+4057
mother (3)
now (3) +3814
others (3)
others (3) +1254
people who (3)
that (3) +899
that which (3)
the man[s] (3)
them[s] (3) +899+3412
to (3)
together (3) +899+2093
while (3) +1877
affairs (2)
after (2) +3552
among (2) +1650+3545
anything (2)
as (2) +1877
associates (2) +5250
beyond limits (2) +296+1650
case (2) +2848
companions (2) +1639+3552
companions (2) +1639+5250
companions (2) +5250
each (2)
forever (2) +1457+1650

front of everyone (2) +3545
God-fearing (2) +2536+5828
have (2) +2400
him[s] (2) +81+899
home (2) +899+3875
household (2)
I have (2) +1847
in (2)
interests (2)
it[s] (2) +1046
it[s] (2) +4450
landed (2) +1178+2093+2262
men (2) +476+3836+5626
never (2) +172+1650+4024
outsiders (2) +2032
people (2)
possessions (2) +5639
rich (2) +2400+5975
seized (2) +2093+2095+5931
seized (2) +2095+5931
she who (2)
some time ago (2) +2465+4047+4574
still (2) +3370
such (2)
that is how (2) +899+2848
the disciples[s] (2) +1254
the men[s] (2) +1254
the one (2)
the son[s] (2)
them (2)
they[s] (2) +476
they[s] (2) +3412
this[s] (2) +2465+4047
this[s] (2) +3364+4047
those (2) +1254
those that (2)
those who are[s] (2) +5626
those whose (2)
to himself (2) +899+1877+2840
tomorrow (2) +892
what is (2)
what was promised (2) +2039
which[s] (2) +180
whoever (2) +4246
you (2) +4725+5148
according to means (1) +1666+2400
across (1) +1650+4305
after this (1) +1877+2759
again (1) +172+1650
again (1) +608+3814
agree (1) +899+3306
all (1)
all along (1) +794
all disciples (1) +3412+4436
all had (1) +2625
all who (1)
altogether (1) +4246
always (1) +2465+4246
am about to tell (1) +3364+4047
and thus (1) +1650
another (1) +1254
another (1) +2283
any (1)
any way (1) +5515
anyone[s] (1)
anyone[s] (1) +476
arrest (1) +2093+2095+5931
arrested (1) +2093+2095+5931
arrested (1) +2095+5931
arrived (1) +4242
as a result (1) +1650
as follows (1) +2400+4047+5596
as has just been said (1) +1877+3306
as to (1)
as usual (1) +899+2848
as usual (1) +1621+2848
ashore (1) +1178+1650
assembled worshipers (1) +3295+4436
at all (1) +1650+4117
at once (1) +899+6052
at the meal (1) +367

away[s] (1) +1650+2557
baptized (1) +966
be proud (1) +5734+5858
before (1) +1650+3545
before (1) +1877+3545
beg (1) +160+1797
began to speak (1) +487+3306+5125
begging (1) +1797+4639
being like-minded (1) +899+5858
believers (1) +2400+4411
believers (1) +4411
besides everything else (1) +4211+6006
betray (1) +1639+4140
bleeding (1) +135+4380
blemish[s] (1) +5525
blindfolded (1) +4328+4725
both[s] (1) +1545
brag (1) +224+1877
but (1) +1254+1883
call (1) +2813+3950
called (1) +3950+4005
certified (1) +3456+5381
child bear (1) +2843+3120
childish (1) +3758
circumstances (1)
come together (1) +899+1639+2093
comes together (1) +899+2093+5302
coming (1) +2262
companions (1) +4309
completely (1) +1650+4117
conceived (1) +1877+3120+5197
convened the court (1) +1037+2093+2767
Cornelius[s] (1) +1254
crowd (1) +3295+4436
decided (1) +326+2093+2840
demon-possessed (1)
    +2400+3836+4460+4505
descendant (1) +1666+2588
descendants (1) +2843+4019
did (1) +2240
dressed ready for service (1) +4019+4322
each day (1) +2465
each evening (1) +3816
each one (1) +324
each other (1) +1651+1651
elementary truths (1) +794+5122
embraced (1) +2093+2158+5549
enabling (1) +1328+1443+5931
endlessly (1) +1457+1650
envious (1) +1639+4057+4505
equal (1) +899
equality (1) +1639+2698
ever (1) +172+1650
ever (1) +172+1666
ever-increasing wickedness (1)
    +490+490+1650
everyone (1) +4246
everyone who (1)
evildoers (1) +490+2237
extraordinary (1) +4024+5593
family (1)
family (1) +3875
family (1) +4123
field (1) +2834+3586
finally (1) +5465
first (1) +3552
footstool (1) +4546+5711
for (1) +1328
for (1) +1650
for (1) +1877+3545
for (1) +4639
for all time (1) +1457+1650
for now (1) +2400+3814
forevermore (1) +172+1650+4246
from bad to worse (1) +2093+5937
from house to house (1) +2848+3875
from house to house (1) +3864
from now on (1) +3370
from town to town (1) +4484
from village to village (1) +2848+3267
give (1) +1443

give in (1) +1634+5717
God who^s (1)
God's^s (1)
God-fearing gentiles (1) +2536+5828
gods^s (1)
grasp the meaning (1) +1539+3857
greater than (1) +3505
grew (1) +1650+2262
guard carefully (1) +1428
had been converted (1) +2189
had^s (1) +4123
has (1) +5639
has no pity (1) +3091+5073
he (1) +899+1328+5931
he (1) +3525
he that (1)
he^s (1) +235
he^s (1) +467
he^s (1) +476
he^s (1) +476+1697
he^s (1) +508
he^s (1) +804
he^s (1) +899+899+1877+4460
he^s (1) +995
he^s (1) +1333
he^s (1) +2989
he^s (1) +3261
he^s (1) +3273
he^s (1) +3281
he^s (1) +3707
healed (1) +5392
heavenly bodies (1) +1539+4041
heavenly things (1) +1877+4041
her own (1)
her who (1)
her^s (1) +4086
highly valued (1) +5734
him (1)
him whose (1)
him^s (1) +81+1609
him^s (1) +467
him^s (1) +476+1877+4047
him^s (1) +2930
him^s (1) +4263
him^s (1) +4737
him^s (1) +5108
him^s (1) +5986
himself^s (1) +899+3950
his fellow (1) +899+5250
his fellowman^s (1) +2283
his home (1) +2625
his native language (1) +1666+2625
his own (1)
his own home (1) +2625
his son^s (1)
his son^s (1) +3525
his^s (1) +2610
his^s (1) +2652
his^s (1) +4511
home (1) +899+1650+3875
home (1) +1650+3875
home (1) +1650+3875+5148
home (1) +2625
house (1)
how (1) +2848
how (1) +4309
human standards (1) +4922
I (1) +1609+6034
illness (1) +819+4922
immediately (1) +899+1877+6052
in agreement (1) +1650+1651
in full (1) +2698
in God's sight (1) +2536+4123
in number (1) +750+4005
in one place (1) +899+2093
in order to (1)
in person (1) +3836+4242+5393
in presence (1) +3552+4725
in public (1) +1883+3295
indoors (1) +1650+3864
instead (1) +1883+3437

intelligible (1) +1609+3808
inwardly (1) +1877+3220
inwardly (1) +2276
Israelites (1) +2702+5626
it depends on you (1) +1666+5148
it that (1)
it^s (1) +27
it^s (1) +69
it^s (1) +229
it^s (1) +993+1847+3836
it^s (1) +1155+4047
it^s (1) +1561
it^s (1) +1609+5013
it^s (1) +1631
it^s (1) +1635+2563+3836
it^s (1) +1847
it^s (1) +2240+5516
it^s (1) +2295
it^s (1) +2585
it^s (1) +2819
it^s (1) +3364
it^s (1) +3693
it^s (1) +3954
it^s (1) +4047+4839
it^s (1) +4384
it^s (1) +4784
it^s (1) +5853
it^s (1) +5890
it^s (1) +6029
it^s (1) +6052
its^s (1) +899+4725
its^s (1) +1178
its^s (1) +2639
its^s (1) +4922
its^s (1) +5393
Jesus' followers^s (1) +1254
Jesus'^{s} (1)
Jews (1) +1169+1609+1877
just after sunrise (1) +422+2463
just as though (1) +899+1651+2779
just like this (1) +899+2848
keep in suspense (1) +149+6034
kill (1) +660
kneel (1) +1205+2828
knelt (1) +1205+5502
knelt down (1) +1205+5502
landed (1) +609+1178+1650
last night (1) +3816+4047
lies (1) +3281+6022
listen carefully (1)
              +1650+4044+5148+5148+5502
live in harmony (1) +899+5858
lived (1) +2400+2998
living (1) +2400+6034
look up (1) +2048+4057
looked (1) +149+4057
looked (1) +2048+4057
looking (1) +2048+4057
lustfully (1) +2121+4639
made king (1) +993+3284
made think (1) +1877+2840+5502
make the most of opportunity (1)
                            +1973+2789
make up mind (1) +1877+2840+5502
man whose^s (1)
man's^s (1)
Mary'^{s} (1) +1254
matters (1)
me (1) +1609+3950
me (1) +1609+6034
meanwhile (1) +1877+3568
member (1) +2848+3517
men who^s (1)
men^s (1)
met personally (1) +1877+3972+4725+4922
midnight (1) +3545+3816
might say (1) +1666+5125
money (1)
most (1) +4498
motioned (1) +2939+5931
my (1) +1831+4309

name (1) +2813+3950
natural sleep (1) +3122+3836+5678
nearby (1) +899
nearby (1) +4309+5536
never (1) +173+1650+3590+4024
never again (1) +172+1650+3590+4024
next (1) +1650+3516
nine in the morning (1) +2465+5569+6052
now (1) +608+3814
of you (1) +1639+1877+5148
on (1) +2759+2779
on board (1) +1877+4450
one (1) +899
one (1) +1651
one (1) +3525
one Sabbath (1) +1877+4879
or anything (1) +3593
others (1) +3525
our companions (1) +1609+5250
our fathers^s (1) +3525
outward (1) +1877+5745
outwardly (1) +476+2032
outwardly (1) +1877+5745
own (1)
Paul^s (1) +3525
people (1) +5626
people live scattered among (1) +1402
perfectly united (1) +899+2936
person who (1)
Peter and John^s (1) +3525
Peter^s (1)
Pilate^s (1) +1254
pointing (1) +899+1753+5931
possess (1) +5639
possessions (1)
preaching (1) +3364
prepare for action (1) +350+4019
present (1) +2789+3814
prompted (1) +965+1650+2840
property (1) +5639
publicly (1) +1967+4436
reached for (1) +1753+5931
reaching more and more (1)
                       +1328+4429+4498
resolutely (1) +4725+5114
result (1) +1650
return (1) +1650+2262+4099
returned (1) +1877+2059
rewarding (1) +1443+3635
riders (1) +2093+2764
Sabbath (1) +2465+4879
seashore (1) +2498+5927
seed (1) +5078
self (1) +476+2840
self-seeking (1) +1571+2426
service that perform (1) +1355+3311+4047
shared (1) +3102+3275
she^s (1) +1222
she^s (1) +3166
she^s (1) +3451
short (1) +2461+3625
shouted (1) +2048+5889
shouted (1) +3489+5774+5889
sighed deeply (1) +417+4460
since (1) +1328
since that time (1) +3370
sins (1) +281+4472
so (1)
so (1) +1650
so as (1) +1650
so he (1) +1254
so that (1) +4639
so then (1) +1650
so they (1) +1254
some (1) +1651+3538
some way (1) +4802
some who (1)
something (1)
soon afterward (1) +1877+2009
sound asleep (1) +608+2965+5678
speak (1) +487+5125

spirit of unity (1) +899+5858
spoken freely (1) +487+5125
stand firm (1) +2840+5114
still others (1) +1254
stripped (1) +2668+4351
such a (1)
such things[s] (1) +4998
terms (1)
terrorists (1) +467+4974
that had touched (1) +608+5999
that is (1)
that same (1)
that was the time (1) +1697+1877+2465
that[s] (1) +2434
that[s] (1) +2546
the affairs (1)
the affairs[s] (1)
the apostles[s] (1) +3525
the expert in the law[s] (1) +1254
the father[s] (1) +1254
the interests (1)
the man (1)
the man's[s] (1) +1254
the manager[s] (1) +1254
the men[s] (1) +3525
the parts[s] (1) +4047+5393
the people (1)
the people[s] (1) +1254
the rioters[s] (1) +1254
the soldiers[s] (1)
the things (1)
the whom (1)
the wife (1)
their (1) +899
them[s] (1) +476
them[s] (1) +899+4546
them[s] (1) +899+5284
them[s] (1) +1177
them[s] (1) +1178+2093+2997+3836
them[s] (1) +1609+4252
them[s] (1) +2239
them[s] (1) +2465
them[s] (1) +2585
them[s] (1) +3295
them[s] (1) +3412
them[s] (1) +3517+5148
them[s] (1) +3836+4556+5525
them[s] (1) +4063
themselves (1) +899+2840
themselves (1) +899+6034
then will be able (1) +1650
there (1) +1877+5536
there is a judge (1) +2400+3212
there[s] (1) +1650+2038
there[s] (1) +1877+2639
there[s] (1) +1877+4047+4484
they (1) +213+899
they (1) +899+4057
they (1) +3525
they who (1)
they[s] (1) +899+1204
they[s] (1) +899+3412
they[s] (1) +899+6001
they[s] (1) +899+899+2779+3412
they[s] (1) +1322
they[s] (1) +4998
they[s] (1) +5861
things that (1)
thinking (1) +1181+5856
this day (1) +2465+4958
this is (1) +2848
this man[s] (1)
this or that (1) +3840
this way (1)
this[s] (1) +899+4246
this[s] (1) +1609+3364+4047
this[s] (1) +4047+4839
those who (1) +1254
those who marry[s] (1) +5525
those who who who (1)
those[s] (1) +3295

three in the afternoon (1)
                    +1888+2465+6052
threw his arms around (1)
                    +2093+2158+5549
to keep from (1) +3590+4639
to show that (1) +4639
to their number (1) +899+2093
today (1) +1877+2465+4958
tonight (1) +3816+4047
trusted personal servant (1) +2093+3131
trying to kill (1) +2426+6034
turned around (1) +1650+3958+5138
turned back (1) +599+1650+3958
under (1) +4123+4546
unnatural ones (1) +4123+5882
unseen (1) +1877+3220
unseen (1) +1877+3224
us who (1)
we who (1)
weapons fight with (1) +3960+5127
weeping (1) +3088
what had been promised (1) +2039
what had happened to (1)
what has been promised (1) +2039
what has happened to (1) +2848
what we are writing[s] (1) +899
what will happen (1) +4471
what you ought to do (1) +465
what[s] (1) +2240
what[s] (1) +2240+5516
what[s] (1) +3306
what[s] (1) +3364
whatever (1) +4246
whatever give (1)
when (1) +3552
when are tempted (1) +4280+5250
where[s] (1) +1650+5596
while (1) +1639+1877
who[s] (1) +476
whoever (1) +323
wife (1)
winepress (1) +3332+3885
with (1) +1650
with a great crash (1)
                    +899+1639+3489+4774
with great fervor (1) +2417+4460
within (1) +1877+3517
wondered about (1) +1877+2840+5502
worldly (1) +3180
wounded (1) +2400+4435
you (1) +3950+5148
you (1) +4364+5148
you have (1) +5050
your family (1) +5050
your own (1) +5050
your own (1) +2625
yours (1) +5050
untranslated (9007)

3837 ὀγδοήκοντα *ogdoēkonta* (2)
eight hundred (1)
eighty-four (1) +2291+5475

3838 ὄγδοος *ogdoos* (5)
eighth (3)
eight (1)
untranslated (1)

3839 ὄγκος *onkos* (1)
hinders (1)

3840 ὅδε *hode* (10)
these (7)
she (1)
this or that (1) +3836
untranslated (1)

3841 ὁδεύω *hodeuō* (1)
traveled (1)

3842 ὁδηγέω *hodēgeō* (5)
lead (2)
explains to (1)
guide (1)

leads (1)

3843 ὁδηγός *hodēgos* (5)
guides (3)
guide (2)

3844 ὁδοιπορέω *hodoiporeō* (1)
on their journey (1)

3845 ὁδοιπορία *hodoiporia* (2)
journey (1)
on the move (1)

3846 ὁδοποιέω *hodopoieō*
Variant; not used

3847 ὁδός *hodos* (100)
way (50)
road (17)
path (7)
ways (5)
journey (4)
roadside (3)
paths (2)
direction (1)
on a journey (1)
roads (1)
route (1)
Sabbath day's walk from (1)
                    +1584+2400+4879
street (1)
streets (1)
walked along (1) +4472
way of life (1)
untranslated (3)

3848 ὀδούς *odous* (12)
teeth (10)
tooth (2)

3849 ὀδυνάω *odynaō* (4)
in agony (2)
anxiously (1)
grieved (1)

3850 ὀδύνη *odynē* (2)
anguish (1)
griefs (1)

3851 ὀδυρμός *odyrmos* (2)
deep sorrow (1)
mourning (1)

3852 Ὀζίας *Ozias* (2)
Uzziah (2)

3853 ὄζω *ozō* (1)
a bad odor (1)

3854 ὅθεν *hothen* (15)
where (3)
therefore (2)
and so (1)
for this reason (1)
from death[s] (1)
from there (1)
left (1) +2002
so then (1)
that (1)
this is how (1)
this is why (1)
untranslated (1)

3855 ὀθόνη *othonē* (2)
sheet (2)

3856 ὀθόνιον *othonion* (5)
strips of linen (4)
linen (1)

3857 οἶδα *oida* (319)
know (225)
knew (19)
knows (13)
knowing (12)
realize (8)
known (7)
understand (5)

idea (2)
acquainted with (1)
aware (1)
be sure (1) +1182
can see (1)
fathom (1)
fully convinced (1) +2779+4275
get learning (1) +1207
grasp the meaning (1) +1539+3836
had idea (1)
in mind (1)
knew about (1)
knew who was (1)
knows how (1)
knows thoughts (1)
learn (1)
recognize (1)
regard (1)
remember (1)
respect (1)
sure (1)
take note of (1)
tell (1)
though know (1)
understanding (1)
who knows (1)
untranslated (3)

3858 οἰκεῖος *oikeios* (3)
belong to family (1)
immediate family (1)
members of household (1)

3859 οἰκετεία *oiketeia* (1)
servants in household (1)

3860 οἰκέτης *oiketēs* (4)
servant (2)
servants (1)
slaves (1)

3861 οἰκέω *oikeō* (9)
lives (3)
living (3)
live (2)
lives in (1)

3862 οἴκημα *oikēma* (1)
cell (1)

3863 οἰκητήριον *oikētērion* (2)
dwelling (1)
home (1)

3864 οἰκία *oikia* (93)
house (66)
home (11)
household (4)
houses (4)
homes (3)
family (1)
from house to house (1) +3836
indoors (1) +1650+3836
live in (1)
untranslated (1)

3865 οἰκιακός *oikiakos* (2)
members of household (2)

3866 οἰκοδεσποτέω *oikodespoteō* (1)
manage homes (1)

3867 οἰκοδεσπότης *oikodespotēs* (12)
owner of the house (5)
landowner (2) +476
head of the house (1)
landowner (1)
owner (1)
owner of a house (1) +476
owner's (1)

3868 οἰκοδομέω *oikodomeō* (40)
build (12)
built (10)
builders (4)
building (3)
build up (2)

edifies (2)
be edified (1) +3284
builds up (1)
constructive (1)
emboldened (1)
rebuild (1)
rebuild (1) +4099
strengthened (1)

3869 οἰκοδομή *oikodomē* (18)
building (3)
building up (3)
buildings (3)
strengthening (3)
build up (2)
builds up (1)
built up (1)
edification (1)
be edified (1) +3284

3870 οἰκοδομία *oikodomia*
Variant; not used

3871 οἰκοδόμος *oikodomos* (1)
builders (1)

3872 οἰκονομέω *oikonomeō* (1)
be manager (1)

3873 οἰκονομία *oikonomia* (9)
administration (2)
job (2)
commission (1)
management (1)
put into effect (1)
trust (1)
work (1)

3874 οἰκονόμος *oikonomos* (10)
manager (4)
administering (1)
director of public works (1)
entrusted with work (1)
have been given a trust (1)
those entrusted with (1)
trustees (1)

3875 οἶκος *oikos* (114)
house (59)
home (14)
household (8)
family (7)
Israel (3) +2702
from house to house (2) +2848
home (2) +899+1650
home (2) +899+3836
descendant (1) +1666
family (1) +3836
from house to house (1) +2848+3836
home (1) +899+1650+3836
home (1) +1650+3836
home (1) +1650+3836+5148
home (1) +5148
households (1)
houses (1)
in their homes (1) +2848
indoors (1) +1650
itself⁵ (1)
market (1) +1866
members of household (1)
palace (1)
palaces (1)
sanctuary (1)

3876 οἰκουμένη *oikoumenē* (15)
world (13)
Roman world (2)

3877 οἰκουργός *oikourgos* (1)
busy at home (1)

3878 οἰκουρός *oikouros*
Variant; not used

3879 οἰκτείρω *oikteirō*
Variant; not used

3880 οἰκτιρμός *oiktirmos* (5)
compassion (3)
mercy (2)

3881 οἰκτίρμων *oiktirmōn* (3)
merciful (2)
mercy (1)

3882 οἰκτίρω *oiktirō* (2)
compassion (2)

3883 οἶμαι *oimai*
Variant; not used

3884 οἰνοπότης *oinopotēs* (2)
drunkard (2)

3885 οἶνος *oinos* (34)
wine (32)
winepress (1) +3332+3836
untranslated (1)

3886 οἰνοφλυγία *oinophlygia* (1)
drunkenness (1)

3887 οἴομαι *oiomai* (3)
suppose (1)
supposing (1)
think (1)

3888 οἶος *hoios* (14)
as (5)
how (1)
like (1)
the (1)
unequaled (1) +1181+4024
unequaled (1) +1181+4024+5525
what (1)
what kinds of (1)
untranslated (2)

3889 οἱοσδηποτοῦν *hoiosdēpotoun*
Variant; not used

3890 ὀκνέω *okneō* (1)
at once (1) +3590

3891 ὀκνηρός *oknēros* (3)
lacking (1)
lazy (1)
trouble (1)

3892 ὀκταήμερος *oktaēmeros* (1)
eighth day (1)

3893 ὀκτώ *oktō* (8)
eight (4)
a week later (1) +2465+3552
eighteen (1) +1274+2779
eighth (1)
thirty-eight (1) +2779+5558

3894 ὀλεθρευτής *olethreutēs*
Variant; not used

3895 ὀλεθρεύω *olethreuō*
Variant; not used

3896 ὀλέθριος *olethrios*
Variant; not used

3897 ὄλεθρος *olethros* (4)
destruction (2)
destroyed (1)
ruin (1)

3898 ὀλιγοπιστία *oligopistia* (1)
little faith (1)

3899 ὀλιγόπιστος *oligopistos* (5)
of little faith (5)

3900 ὀλίγος *oligos* (40)
few (15)
little (8)
little while (3)
some (2)
a little (1)
a long time (1) +4024+5989
a short time (1)
briefly (1) +1328

briefly (1) +*1877*
continued raging (1) +*2130+4024*
great disturbance (1) +*4024+5431*
many (1) +*4024*
sharp (1) +*4024*
short (1) +*2400*
short time (1) +*1877*
small (1)

3901 ὀλιγόψυχος *oligopsychos* (1)
timid (1)

3902 ὀλιγωρέω *oligōreō* (1)
make light of (1)

3903 ὀλίγως *oligōs* (1)
just (1)

3904 ὀλοθρευτής *olothreutēs* (1)
destroying (1)

3905 ὀλοθρεύω *olothreuō* (1)
destroyer (1)

3906 ὁλοκαύτωμα *holokautōma* (3)
burnt offerings (3)

3907 ὁλοκληρία *holoklēria* (1)
complete healing (1)

3908 ὁλόκληρος *holoklēros* (2)
complete (1)
whole (1)

3909 ὀλολύζω *ololyzō* (1)
wail (1)

3910 ὅλος *holos* (108)
whole (52)
all (34)
throughout (6) +*1877*
entire (2)
throughout (2) +*1650*
throughout (2) +*2848*
all (1) +*4012*
all long (1)
all over (1)
all over (1) +*1650*
all over (1) +*2848*
completely (1)
steeped (1)
throughout (1)
to bottom (1) +*1328*
whole (1) +*4116*

3911 ὁλοτελής *holotelēs* (1)
through and through (1)

3912 Ὀλυμπᾶς *Olympas* (1)
Olympas (1)

3913 ὄλυνθος *olynthos* (1)
late (1)

3914 ὅλως *holōs* (4)
at all (2)
actually (1)
completely (1)

3915 ὄμβρος *ombros* (1)
going to rain (1) +*2262*

3916 ὁμείρομαι *homeiromai* (1)
loved (1)

3917 ὁμιλέω *homileō* (4)
talked (2)
talking (2)

3918 ὁμιλία *homilia* (1)
company (1)

3919 ὅμιλος *homilos*
Variant; not used

3920 ὁμίχλη *homichlē* (1)
mists (1)

3921 ὄμμα *omma* (2)
eyes (2)

3922 ὄμνυμι *omnymi*
Variant; not used

3923 ὀμνύω *omnyō* (26)
swears (10)
swore (5)
swear (4)
declared on oath (2)
swear by (2)
promised (1)
promised with an oath (1)
sworn (1)

3924 ὁμοθυμαδόν *homothymadon* (11)
together (4)
all (2)
agreed (1) +*1181*
as one man (1)
heart (1)
joined together (1)
united (1)

3925 ὁμοιάζω *homoiazō*
Variant; not used

3926 ὁμοιοπαθής *homoiopathēs* (2)
human like (1)
just like (1)

3927 ὅμοιος *homoios* (45)
like (36)
as (2)
like (1) +*4047*
looked like (1) +*3930*
looks like (1) +*1639*
of (1)
resembled (1) +*1639*
resembling (1) +*3970*
similar (1)

3928 ὁμοιότης *homoiotēs* (2)
like (1)
untranslated (1)

3929 ὁμοιόω *homoioō* (15)
like (8)
compare (4)
form (1)
made like (1)
say is like (1)

3930 ὁμοίωμα *homoiōma* (6)
likeness (2)
as (1)
like (1)
look like (1)
looked like (1) +*3927*

3931 ὁμοίως *homoiōs* (31)
in the same way (10)
likewise (3)
the same (3)
also (2)
like (1)
same (1)
similarly (1)
so (1)
so do (1)
the same (1) +*2777*
the same thing (1)
too (1)
untranslated (5)

3932 ὁμοίωσις *homoiōsis* (1)
likeness (1)

3933 ὁμολογέω *homologeō* (26)
acknowledge (6)
confess (6)
acknowledges (4)
acknowledged that (1)
acknowledges that (1)
admit (1)
admitted (1)
claim (1)
confessed (1)
made confession (1) +*3934*
promised (1)
tell plainly (1)

untranslated (1)

3934 ὁμολογία *homologia* (6)
profess (2)
confess (1)
confession (1)
made confession (1)
made confession (1) +*3933*

3935 ὁμολογουμένως *homologoumenōs* (1)
beyond all question (1)

3936 ὁμόσε *homose*
Variant; not used

3937 ὁμότεχνος *homotechnos* (1)
as (1)

3938 ὁμοῦ *homou* (4)
together (3)
untranslated (1)

3939 ὁμόφρων *homophrōn* (1)
live in harmony with (1)

3940 ὅμως *homōs* (3)
at the same time (1)
even in the case of (1)
just as (1)

3941 ὄναρ *onar* (6)
dream (6)

3942 ὀνάριον *onarion* (1)
young donkey (1)

3943 ὀνειδίζω *oneidizō* (9)
insult (3)
heaped insults on (2)
denounce (1)
finding fault (1)
insulted (1)
rebuked (1)

3944 ὀνειδισμός *oneidismos* (5)
disgrace (3)
insult (1)
insults (1)

3945 ὄνειδος *oneidos* (1)
disgrace (1)

3946 Ὀνήσιμος *Onēsimos* (2)
Onesimus (2)

3947 Ὀνησίφορος *Onēsiphoros* (2)
Onesiphorus (2)

3948 ὀνικός *onikos* (2)
large (1)
large millstone (1) +*3685*

3949 ὀνίνημι *oninēmi* (1)
benefit (1)

3950 ὄνομα *onoma* (231)
name (156)
named (31)
names (9)
named (2) +*899*
call (1) +*2813+3836*
called (1)
called (1) +*3836+4005*
called (1) +*4005*
himself[s] (1) +*899+3836*
invoke the name (1) +*3951*
me (1) +*1609+3836*
name (1) +*2813+3836*
name's (1)
named (1) +*2813*
people (1)
reputation (1)
title (1)
title given (1) +*3951*
you (1) +*3836+5148*
untranslated (18)

3951 ὀνομάζω *onomazō* (10)
a hint of (1)
confesses (1)

derives name (1)
designated (1)
designating (1)
invoke the name (1) +3950
known (1)
named (1)
title given (1) +3950
calls (1)

3952 ὄνος *onos* (5)
donkey (4)
donkey's (1)

3953 ὄντως *ontōs* (10)
really (5)
certainly (1)
indeed (1)
it is true (1)
surely (1)
truly (1)

3954 ὄξος *oxos* (6)
wine vinegar (4)
it[s] (1) +3836
untranslated (1)

3955 ὀξύς *oxys* (8)
sharp (7)
swift (1)

3956 ὀπή *opē* (2)
holes (1)
spring (1)

3957 ὄπισθεν *opisthen* (7)
behind (4)
after (1)
in back (1)
on both sides (1) +2277+2779

3958 ὀπίσω *opisō* (36)
after (11)
behind (5)
back (4) +1650+3836
follow (3)
follow (2) +4513
back (1)
follow (1) +199
follow (1) +2262
followed (1)
followed (1) +599
from (1)
overtake (1)
perversion (1) +599+2283+4922
turned around (1) +1650+3836+5138
turned back (1) +599+1650+3836
untranslated (1)

3959 ὁπλίζω *hoplizō* (1)
arm (1)

3960 ὅπλον *hoplon* (6)
instruments (2)
weapons (2)
armor (1)
weapons fight with (1) +3836+5127

3961 ὁποῖος *hopoios* (5)
the quality (1)
what (1)
what (1) +5525
what kind of (1)
whatever (1)

3962 ὁπότε *hopote*
Variant; not used

3963 ὅπου *hopou* (82)
where (58)
wherever (5) +1569
wherever (3)
here (2)
whenever (2) +1569
wherever (2) +323
above (1)
in the case of (1)
on the other side[s] (1)

since (1)
the place where (1)
together (1)
yet even (1)
untranslated (3)

3964 ὀπτάνομαι *optanomai* (1)
appeared (1)

3965 ὀπτασία *optasia* (4)
vision (3)
visions (1)

3966 ὀπτός *optos* (1)
broiled (1)

3967 ὀπώρα *opōra* (1)
fruit (1)

3968 ὅπως *hopōs* (53)
so that (16)
to (15)
that (10)
so (3)
how (2)
in order to (1)
so that (1) +323
then (1)
untranslated (4)

3969 ὅραμα *horama* (12)
vision (8)
had a vision (1) +3972
sight (1)
vision (1) +3972
seen (1)

3970 ὅρασις *horasis* (4)
appearance (1)
resembling (1) +3927
vision (1)
visions (1)

3971 ὁρατός *horatos* (1)
visible (1)

3972 ὁράω *horaō* (481)
saw (182)
see (122)
seen (62)
appeared (17)
look (14)
looked (9)
seeing (7)
here (4)
realized (4)
perceiving (3)
see that (3)
watched (3)
careful (2)
do it[s] (2)
here is (2)
look at (2)
looked at (2)
noticed (2)
noticing (2)
see to it (2)
sees (2)
appear (1)
body decayed (1) +1426
came upon (1)
consider (1)
consider (1) +4309
die (1) +2505
experience (1)
find (1)
found (1)
had a vision (1) +3969
indeed seen (1) +3972
listen (1)
make sure that (1)
mark my words (1)
met personally (1) +1877+3836+4725+4922
met with (1)
mourn (1) +4292
saw that (1)

seen of (1)
settle the matter (1)
show (1)
surely (1)
that's your responsibility (1) +5148
the sight of (1)
vision (1) +3969
visit (1)
watch out (1)
watching (1)
well (1)
your responsibility (1) +5148
untranslated (3)

3973 ὀργή *orgē* (36)
wrath (27)
anger (7)
angry (1)
punishment (1)

3974 ὀργίζω *orgizō* (8)
angry (4)
anger (2)
enraged (2)

3975 ὀργίλος *orgilos* (1)
quick-tempered (1)

3976 ὀργυιά *orgyia* (2)
a hundred and twenty feet deep (1) +1633
ninety feet deep (1) +1278

3977 ὀρέγω *oregō* (3)
eager for (1)
longing for (1)
sets heart on being (1)

3978 ὀρεινός *oreinos* (2)
hill country (2)

3979 ὄρεξις *orexis* (1)
lust (1)

3980 ὀρθοποδέω *orthopodeō* (1)
acting in line (1)

3981 ὀρθός *orthos* (2)
level (1)
stand up (1) +482

3982 ὀρθοτομέω *orthotomeō* (1)
correctly handles (1)

3983 ὀρθρίζω *orthrizō* (1)
came early in the morning (1)

3984 ὀρθρινός *orthrinos* (1)
early morning (1)

3985 ὄρθριος *orthrios*
Variant; not used

3986 ὄρθρος *orthros* (3)
dawn (1)
daybreak (1)
very early in the morning (1) +960

3987 ὀρθῶς *orthōs* (4)
correctly (2)
plainly (1)
what is right (1)

3988 ὁρίζω *horizō* (8)
appointed (2)
set (2)
decided (1)
declared (1)
decreed (1)
determined (1)

3989 ὄρινξ *orinx*
Variant; not used

3990 ὅριον *horion* (12)
region (6)
vicinity (5)
area (1)

3991 ὁρκίζω *horkizō* (2)
command to come out (1)
swear (1)

3992 ὅρκος *horkos* (10)
oath (6)
oaths (3)
untranslated (1)

3993 ὁρκωμοσία *horkōmosia* (4)
oath (4)

3994 ὁρμάω *hormaō* (5)
rushed (5)

3995 ὁρμή *hormē* (2)
pilot (1)
plot afoot (1)

3996 ὅρμημα *hormēma* (1)
violence (1)

3997 ὄρνεον *orneon* (3)
birds (2)
bird (1)

3998 ὄρνις *ornis* (2)
hen (2)

3999 ὁροθεσία *horothesia* (1)
exact places (1)

4000 ὅρος *horos*
Variant; not used

4001 ὄρος *oros* (65)
mountain (22)
mount (15)
mountains (9)
mountainside (8)
hill (5)
hills (3)
hillside (2)
place (1)

4002 ὀρύσσω *oryssō* (3)
dug (2)
dug a hole (1)

4003 ὀρφανός *orphanos* (2)
orphans (2)

4004 ὀρχέομαι *orcheomai* (4)
dance (2)
danced (2)

4005 ὅς *hos* (1409)
what (137)
who (123)
whom (113)
which (112)
that (82)
him (58)
he (43)
them (23)
whose (21)
whoever (19) +323
anyone (17)
one (16)
these (14)
this (14)
they (13)
until (13) +2401
it (12)
whatever (11) +1569
the (10)
the one (9)
those (8)
their (7)
whatever (7)
when (7)
his (6)
some (6) +3525
when (6) +1877
whoever (6) +1569
those who (5)
until (5) +948
whoever (5)
another (4) +1254
because (4) +505
where (4) +1877
whom (4) +323
anyone who (3) +323

as (3) +5573
her (3)
the life[s] (3)
this gospel[s] (3)
what (3) +1569
where (3) +1650
while (3) +1877
and some (2) +1254
anything (2) +1569
as (2)
because (2) +2093
ever since (2) +608
its (2)
one (2) +3525
others (2) +1254
since (2) +608
that which (2)
the man[s] (2)
the men[s] (2)
the one whom (2)
theirs (2)
things (2)
until (2) +3588
whatever (2) +323+1650
whatever (2) +323+5516
when (2) +323
while (2) +2401
who (2) +1328
why (2) +162+1328
a man[s] (1)
about (1) +4309
Abraham[s] (1)
ago (1) +608
all the world (1) +476+1639+5515
also (1)
another (1)
another man (1) +1254
any (1) +323+5516
anyone (1) +1569
anyone who (1)
anyone who (1) +1569
anything (1) +1569+4246+4547
anything that (1)
as long as (1) +948
be (1)
because (1) +1641
because (1) +1877
before (1) +2401
both of them (1) +1877
by (1) +3306
by saying (1) +3306
called (1) +3836+3950
called (1) +3950
children[s] (1)
Christ[s] (1)
discipline[s] (1)
duty (1) +4053+4472
faith[s] (1)
for work (1) +1256+1877+2237
from the time (1) +608
God[s] (1)
he who (1)
him (1) +4123
his faith[s] (1)
holiness[s] (1)
I (1)
if any (1) +323
in keeping with income (1)
             +1569+2338+5516
in number (1) +750+3836
in that case (1) +4309
in the same way (1) +5573
in these (1)
including (1) +1639
indicating that (1) +2848
it[s] (1) +201+608+794
just as (1) +2848+4048+5573
just as (1) +2848+5573
just as (1) +5573
just before (1) +948
matters (1)

means (1) +1639
native (1) +1164+1877
now (1) +608
of them (1)
on (1)
once (1) +323+608
one of these journeys[s] (1)
or (1) +1254
others (1)
owner of (1) +467
Paul[s] (1)
peace[s] (1)
same as (1) +2779
she (1)
so (1)
so (1) +162+1328
so (1) +1328
someone (1)
something (1)
such a man (1)
such a man's[s] (1)
testimony (1) +3455+3456
that (1) +2848
that day[s] (1)
that is why (1) +162+1328
that tribe[s] (1)
the authority[s] (1)
the death[s] (1)
the fact[s] (1)
the glory[s] (1)
the gospel[s] (1)
the Jesus[s] (1)
the lawless one[s] (1)
the man whose (1)
the matters (1)
the name[s] (1)
the one (1) +323
the other (1) +1254
the promise[s] (1)
the situation (1)
the son[s] (1)
the tabernacle[s] (1)
the whom (1)
then (1) +948
there (1)
therefore (1) +162+1328
therefore (1) +5920
these men[s] (1)
these waters[s] (1)
this ark[s] (1)
this hope[s] (1)
this inscription (1) +2108
this man[s] (1)
those for whom (1)
those who (1) +3525
those whom (1)
those whom (1) +1569
to the one (1) +3525
to the other (1) +1254
to this end (1) +1650
until (1) +323+948
until (1) +1877
what (1) +2093
what (1) +5515
what (1) +5516
whatever (1) +323
whatever (1) +1569+5516
when (1) +1650+2401
where (1) +1877+5536
where (1) +2093
where (1) +4123
whom (1) +1569
whose (1) +899
whose (1) +2400
with (1) +2400
you (1)
your (1)
untranslated (269)

4006 ὁσάκις *hosakis* (3)
whenever (2) +1569

as often as (1)

4007 ὅσγε *hosge*
Variant; not used

4008 ὅσιος *hosios* (8)
holy (7)
holy blessings promised (1)

4009 ὁσιότης *hosiotēs* (2)
holiness (2)

4010 ὁσίως *hosiōs* (1)
holy (1)

4011 ὀσμή *osmē* (6)
fragrance (3)
fragrant (2) +2380
smell (1)

4012 ὅσος *hosos* (109)
all who (11)
whatever (8)
what (6)
everything (5)
how much (5)
as (4)
everything (4) +4246
that (4)
who (4)
all (3)
all (3) +4246
those who (3)
all that (2)
as long as (2) +2093+5989
as much as (2)
how many (2)
just as (2) +2848
whatever (2) +1569
whatever (2) +2093
whatever (2) +4246
all (1) +3910
all of (1)
all who (1) +323
all who (1) +1569
all whom (1) +323
anyone (1) +1569
as as (1)
as long as (1) +2093
as many as (1)
ever (1)
everything (1) +323+4246
everything (1) +1569+4246
everything that (1)
inasmuch as (1) +2093+3525+4036
more (1)
only as long as (1) +2093+5989
other (1)
people (1)
so long as (1) +5989
those (1)
those whom (1)
very while (1) +2285+4012
what (1) +1569
whatever (1) +323
while (1) +2093
who ever (1)
untranslated (7)

4013 ὅσπερ *hosper*
Variant; not used

4014 ὀστέον *osteon* (4)
bones (4)

4015 ὅστις *hostis* (144)
who (33)
they (23)
which (15)
whoever (6)
that (5)
this (5)
it (4)
them (3)
these (3)
until (3) +2401

others (2)
she (2)
some (2)
someone (2)
whoever (2) +323
you (2)
a (1)
another who (1)
anyone who (1)
Barabbasˢ (1)
he (1)
hear (1) +201
her (1)
such regulationsˢ (1)
that templeˢ (1)
the cavalryˢ (1)
the one (1)
the peopleˢ (1)
those (1)
those who (1)
we (1)
whatever (1)
while (1) +2401
whoever (1) +1569
whoever (1) +4246
you who (1)
your generosityˢ (1)
untranslated (11)

4016 ὀστοῦν *ostoun*
Variant; not used

4017 ὀστράκινος *ostrakinos* (2)
clay (2)

4018 ὄσφρησις *osphrēsis* (1)
sense of smell (1)

4019 ὀσφῦς *osphys* (8)
waist (2)
belt (1)
body (1)
descendants (1) +2843+3836
descended from (1) +2002
dressed ready for service (1) +3836+4322
prepare for action (1) +350+3836

4020 ὅταν *hotan* (123)
when (95)
whenever (5)
after (4)
as soon as (2)
as soon as (2) +2317
while (2)
any time (1)
as soon as (1) +2453
at once (1) +2317
before (1)
once (1)
the moment (1)
until (1) +1623+3590
untranslated (6)

4021 ὅτε *hote* (102)
when (83)
after (6)
as (4)
once (2)
while (2)
after (1) +5538
as soon as (1)
before (1)
untranslated (2)

4022 ὅτι *hoti* (1298)
that (492)
because (205)
for (145)
how (6)
since (5)
this (3)
as (2)
by (2)
of (2)
about (1)

although (1)
as it is (1) +1254
but (1) +1254
here (1)
how (1) +5515
if (1)
in this (1)
is that why (1)
replied (1) +646+3306
the fact that (1)
this message (1)
though (1)
though actually (1)
to be (1)
what (1)
which (1)
why (1)
why (1) +5515
untranslated (417)

4023 οὗ *hou* (24)
where (19)
one in which (1)
the place where (1)
there (1)
to which (1)
wherever (1) +1569

4024 οὐ *ou* (1621)
not (1032)
no (142)
don't (55)
cannot (40) +1538
never (34) +3590
not (31) +3590
never (15)
nothing (15)
didn't (8)
certainly not (7) +3590
cannot (6)
refused (6) +2527
can't (5) +1538
doesn't (5)
isn't (5) +1639
neither (5)
nothing (5) +4029
only (5) +1623+3590
aren't (4)
haven't (4)
never (4) +172+1650+3590+3836
no one (4) +4246
unlawful (4) +2003
without (4)
don't (3) +3590
fail (3)
no (3) +4246
no more (3)
no one (3) +4029
none (3)
noneˢ (3) +4956
nor (3)
nor (3) +2779
aren't (2) +1639
cannot (2) +1639
cease to be (2) +1639
couldn't (2) +1538
few (2) +4498
never (2) +172+1650+3836
no (2) +3590
no (2) +4029
no at all (2)
not at all (2) +3590
nothing (2) +5515
nothing (2) +5516
rather than (2) +2779
refused to repent (2) +3566
a long time (1) +3900+5989
against (1)
any more than (1) +2777
before very long (1) +3552+4498
blinded (1) +1838
but (1) +2777

cannot (1) +2400
cannot do (1) +1538
continued raging (1) +2130+3900
declined (1) +2153
does so[s] (1) +2266
ever no (1) +3590
extraordinary (1) +3836+5593
from (1)
getting nowhere (1) +4029+6067
great disturbance (1) +3900+5431
greatly (1) +3585
impossible (1) +1543
is it possible that (1)
isn't (1)
isn't at all (1) +3590
lack (1)
lawful for (1) +2003
lost connection with (1) +3195
many (1) +3900
neither (1) +2779
never (1) +173+1650+3590+3836
never (1) +3590+4033
never (1) +3590+4537
never (1) +3590+4799
never (1) +4537
never again (1) +172+1650+3590+3836
never again (1) +2285
never again (1) +3590
no longer (1) +3590
no place (1) +4544
nobody (1)
nobody (1) +5516
none (1) +570
none (1) +4029
none (1) +4246
not clear (1) +1182
not even (1) +4028
not one (1) +3590
nothing (1) +3590+4029
nothing (1) +4246
nothing (1) +4246+4839
nothing at all (1) +4029
nothing false (1) +94
one (1) +257+1651
only (1) +2445+4498
or (1) +2779
out of place (1) +465
refuse (1)
refuse (1) +918
refuse (1) +2527
refused (1) +1312
refused (1) +4657
refusing (1) +2527
separate from (1) +3552
sharp (1) +3900
shouldn't (1)
shouldn't (1) +1256
staying away from (1) +1877+4344
the law forbids (1) +2003
unable (1) +1538
unable (1) +2710
unaware (1) +1182
unequaled (1) +1181+3888
unequaled (1) +1181+3888+5525
unless (1) +1623
unlike (1) +6055
until judge (1) +3212
unusual (1) +5593
unwilling (1) +2525
unwilling (1) +2527
wasn't (1)
what is more (1) +247+1254+2779+3667
without (1) +1666
without (1) +2779
without sin (1) +281
yet (1) +4037
untranslated (39)

4025 οὐά *oua* (1)
so (1)

4026 οὐαί *ouai* (46)
woe (42)

how dreadful (3)
woes (1)

4027 οὐδαμῶς *oudamōs* (1)
by no means (1)

4028 οὐδέ *oude* (143)
or (35)
nor (28)
not (18)
not even (15)
neither (8)
no (7)
and (5)
and no (3)
don't (2)
even not (2)
not either (2)
and cannot (1) +1538
and not (1)
and nothing (1)
and nothing (1) +5516
but not (1)
cannot do (1) +1538
haven't (1)
never (1)
never again (1) +2285
no (1) +4246
not even (1) +4024
nothing (1) +1651
only (1) +1651
untranslated (5)

4029 οὐδείς *oudeis* (234)
no one (89)
nothing (37)
no (21)
anyone (7)
none (7)
not any (6)
not one (6)
nothing (5) +4024
any (3)
anything (3)
no one (3) +4024
not anything (3)
no (2) +4024
no one who (2)
not (2)
not anyone (2)
at all (1)
conscience is clear (1) +5323
discredited (1) +1650+3357
getting nowhere (1) +4024+6067
haven't anything (1)
men (1)
men[s] (1)
never (1)
no anything (1)
no at all (1)
no one (1) +476
no truth (1)
no way (1)
no whatever (1)
nobody (1)
none (1) +4024
nor anyone (1) +1254
not (1) +3590
not a thing (1)
not anyone's (1)
not in the least (1)
not saying a word (1) +3306
nothing (1) +3364
nothing (1) +3590+4024
nothing at all (1) +4024
one (1)
only to (1) +1623+3590
was getting nowhere (1) +6067
without (1)
untranslated (7)

4030 οὐδέποτε *oudepote* (16)
never (13)

nothing ever (2)
no one ever (1)

4031 οὐδέπω *oudepō* (4)
not yet (2)
ever (1)
still not (1)

4032 οὐθείς *outheis*
Variant; not used

4033 οὐκέτι *ouketi* (47)
no longer (27)
any more (3)
again (2)
no more (2)
cannot again (1)
ever again (1)
forgets (1) +3648
from then on (1)
never (1) +3590+4024
never again (1)
no (1)
no any more (1)
not (1)
not anymore (1)
not longer (1)
still no (1)
unable (1) +2710

4034 οὐκοῦν *oukoun* (1)
then (1)

4035 Οὐλαμμαούς *Oulammaous*
Variant; not used

4036 οὖν *oun* (497)
then (110)
therefore (71)
so (62)
now (12)
but (5)
therefore (5) +726
at this (4)
and (3)
finally (3)
when (3)
consequently (2) +726
meanwhile (2)
now then (2)
so then (2)
thus (2)
after all (1)
again (1)
as (1)
at that point (1)
because of (1)
conclude then (1)
finally (1) +5538
however (1) +3525
inasmuch as (1) +2093+3525+4012
still (1)
that (1)
this made (1)
too (1)
well then (1)
what (1) +5515
what shall we do (1) +1639+5515
yet (1)
untranslated (192)

4037 οὔπω *oupō* (27)
not yet (16)
still not (3)
still to come (2)
before (1)
ever (1)
still no (1)
up to that time not (1)
yet (1) +4024
yet not (1)

4038 οὐρά *oura* (5)
tails (4)
tail (1)

4039 οὐράνιος *ouranios* (8)
heavenly (7)
in heaven (1)

4040 οὐρανόθεν *ouranothen* (2)
from heaven (2)

4041 οὐρανός *ouranos* (274)
heaven (220)
sky (21)
heavens (15)
air (9)
heavenly (3)
skies (2)
heavenly (1) +1666
heavenly bodies (1) +1539+3836
heavenly things (1) +1877+3836
untranslated (1)

4042 Οὐρβανός *Ourbanos* (1)
Urbanus (1)

4043 Οὐρίας *Ourias* (1)
Uriah's (1)

4044 οὖς *ous* (36)
ears (21)
ear (13)
hearing (1)
listen carefully (1)
         +1650+3836+5148+5148+5502

4045 οὐσία *ousia* (2)
estate (1)
wealth (1)

4046 οὔτε *oute* (87)
nor (30)
neither (19)
or (14)
not (7)
and (1)
and no (1)
and none (1) +5516
cannot (1) +1538
don't (1)
either (1)
never (1) +4537
never (1) +4799
no (1)
not any (1)
nothing (1)
nothing (1) +5516
or even (1)
refuses to (1)
untranslated (3)

4047 οὗτος *houtos* (1382)
this (620)
these (207)
he (41)
that (39)
him (25)
therefore (23) +1328
they (21)
such (15)
them (15)
it (12)
for this reason (9) +1328
she (9)
those (7)
later (6) +3552
this is how (6) +1877
that is why (5) +1328
the reason (5) +1328
what (5)
who (5)
Jesus[s] (4)
so (4) +1328
this is why (4) +1328
this very (4)
because (3) +1328
the latter[s] (3)
afterward (2) +3552
for that reason (2) +4123

for this reason (2) +5920
here (2) +1877
his (2)
so (2)
so then (2) +1328
some time ago (2) +2465+3836+4574
that was why (2) +1328
this one (2)
this[s] (2) +2465+3836
this[s] (2) +3364+3836
above all (1) +4754
am about to tell (1) +3364+3836
and what is more (1)
         +247+1145+2779+4246+5250
Andrew[s] (1)
any such person (1)
appointed (1)
as (1)
as follows (1) +2400+3836+5596
as I did (1) +899
at other times (1) +1254
at this (1) +3306
at this point (1) +1254
both (1) +2779
by all this (1) +1328
come out of (1) +2002
everything (1)
finally (1) +3552
first of all (1) +4754
following (1)
for that very reason (1) +1328
for the express purpose (1) +899+1650
for this reason (1) +505
for this reason (1) +1650
for this very reason (1) +899
for this very reason (1) +1328
from then on (1) +1666
governing[s] (1) +899
happening[s] (1)
he's (1)
hear (1) +201+1639
here (1)
him[s] (1) +476+1877+3836
his master[s] (1)
how far will they go (1) +1639+5515
in other words (1) +1639
in the following (1)
it[s] (1) +1155+3836
it[s] (1) +3836+4839
John's disciples[s] (1)
Judas[s] (1)
just one (1) +3668
just then (1) +2093
last night (1) +3816+3836
like (1) +3927
men[s] (1)
of this (1) +2401
others (1)
pray[s] (1) +4472
present (1)
remember this (1) +1254
see here (1) +2555
service that perform (1) +1355+3311+3836
so doing[s] (1)
some (1)
some time later (1) +3552
sometimes (1) +3525
such sins[s] (1)
that is why (1) +1650
that is why (1) +2093
that would follow (1) +3552
the Bereans[s] (1)
the parts[s] (1) +3836+5393
the passage above (1)
the reason (1) +1142+1650
the reason (1) +1650
the reason (1) +5920
the same (1)
the very thing (1) +899
the women[s] (1)
their (1)

their work[s] (1)
there[s] (1) +1877+3836+4484
they the kind (1) +1666
this is how (1) +1666
this is the reason (1) +1650
this makes (1) +1877
this same (1)
this very reason (1) +1650
this way (1)
this[s] (1) +1609+3364+3836
this[s] (1) +3836+4839
thus (1) +1877
to (1) +1650
tonight (1) +3816+3836
what going on (1) +323+5515
what I meant (1) +4309
what Paul said[s] (1)
which (1)
who are here (1)
with that (1) +3306
with this (1) +3306
yet (1) +3552
untranslated (169)

4048 οὕτως *houtōs* (208)
so (63)
in the same way (11)
in this way (8)
like this (8)
this (8)
this is how (8)
this is what (6)
that is how (5)
like (3)
then (3)
true (3)
in the same way (2) +2779
in these words (2)
like that (2)
likewise (2)
that (2)
that way (2)
this way (2)
according to (1)
and (1)
as (1)
as is[s] (1)
as it has (1)
as you are (1)
at that (1)
by this kind (1)
does[s] (1) +1181
exactly (1)
how (1)
in such a way (1)
in this same way (1) +2779
in way (1)
it is the same (1) +2779
it was so (1) +2400
just as (1) +2777
just as (1) +2848+4005+5573
just as if (1)
likewise (1) +2779
matched (1) +2749+2779
so it is with (1) +2779
so much (1)
so then (1)
such things (1)
that is why (1)
the same (1)
the way (1)
this is (1)
this is the way (1)
this the way (1)
to (1)
to marry[s] (1) +1181
with such (1)
untranslated (34)

4049 οὐχί *ouchi* (54)
not (37)
no (7)

didn't (3)
aren't (2) +1639
fail (1) +3590
instead of (1) +2779
isn't (1) +1639
shouldn't (1)
won't (1)

4050 ὀφειλέτης *opheiletēs* (7)
obligated (2)
debtors (1)
guilty (1)
have an obligation (1) +1639
owe (1) +1639
owed (1)

4051 ὀφειλή *opheilē* (3)
debt (1)
duty (1)
owe (1)

4052 ὀφείλημα *opheilēma* (2)
debts (1)
obligation (1)

4053 ὀφείλω *opheilō* (35)
ought (13)
owe (4)
owed (3)
bound by his oath (2)
must (2)
should (2)
debt (1)
debt remain outstanding (1)
duty (1) +4005+4472
had (1)
has to (1)
have (1)
owes (1)
should have (1)
sins (1)

4054 ὄφελον *ophelon* (4)
I wish (2)
how I wish that (1)
I hope (1)

4055 ὄφελος *ophelos* (3)
good (2)
gained (1)

4056 ὀφθαλμοδουλία *ophthalmodoulia* (2)
eye is on (2)

4057 ὀφθαλμός *ophthalmos* (100)
eyes (59)
eye (25)
looked up (3) +2048+3836
sight (3)
envious (1) +1639+3836+4505
envy (1) +4505
eyes (1) +2400
look up (1) +2048+3836
looked (1) +149+3836
looked (1) +2048+3836
looking (1) +2048+3836
open eyes (1) +2048
they (1) +899+3836
untranslated (1)

4058 ὄφις *ophis* (14)
snakes (6)
serpent (3)
snake (3)
serpent's (1)
serpent's (1) +899

4059 ὀφρῦς *ophrys* (1)
brow (1)

4060 ὀχετός *ochetos*
Variant; not used

4061 ὀχλέω *ochleō* (1)
tormented (1)

4062 ὀχλοποιέω *ochlopoieō* (1)
formed a mob (1)

4063 ὄχλος *ochlos* (174)
crowd (106)
people (30)
crowds (25)
multitude (3)
mob (2)
crowd of people (1)
crowds of people (1)
group (1)
many people (1)
multitudes (1)
number (1)
numbers of people (1)
themˢ (1) +3836

4064 Ὀχοζίας *Ochozias*
Variant; not used

4065 ὀχύρωμα *ochyrōma* (1)
strongholds (1)

4066 ὀψάριον *opsarion* (5)
fish (4)
small fish (1)

4067 ὀψέ *opse* (3)
after the Sabbath (1) +4879
evening (1)
in the evening (1)

4068 ὀψία *opsia*
Variant; not used

4069 ὄψιμος *opsimos* (1)
spring (1)

4070 ὄψιος *opsios* (15)
evening (12)
late (1)
on the evening (1) +1639
that evening (1) +1181

4071 ὄψις *opsis* (3)
face (2)
appearances (1)

4072 ὀψώνιον *opsōnion* (4)
expense (1)
pay (1)
support (1)
wages (1)

4073 π *p*
Variant; not used

4074 παγιδεύω *pagideuō* (1)
trap (1)

4075 παγίς *pagis* (5)
trap (4)
snare (1)

4076 πάγος *pagos*
Variant; not used

4077 πάθημα *pathēma* (16)
sufferings (10)
passions (2)
suffering (2)
suffered (1)
what was suffered (1)

4078 παθητός *pathētos* (1)
suffer (1)

4079 πάθος *pathos* (3)
lust (2)
lusts (1)

4080 παιδαγωγός *paidagōgos* (3)
guardians (1)
put in charge to lead (1)
supervision (1)

4081 παιδάριον *paidarion* (1)
boy (1)

4082 παιδεία *paideia* (6)
discipline (3)
training (2)
disciplined (1)

4083 παιδευτής *paideutēs* (2)
disciplined (1)
instructor (1)

4084 παιδεύω *paideuō* (13)
disciplined (3)
beaten (1)
discipline (1)
disciplines (1)
educated (1)
instruct (1)
punish (1)
punished (1)
taught (1)
teaches (1)
trained (1)

4085 παιδιόθεν *paidiothen* (1)
childhood (1)

4086 παιδίον *paidion* (52)
child (21)
children (7)
little child (7)
little children (7)
child's (2)
dear children (2)
baby (1)
boy's (1)
children's (1)
friends (1)
herˢ (1) +3836
children (1)

4087 παιδίσκη *paidiskē* (13)
servant girl (4)
slave woman (4)
girl (1)
maidservants (1)
servant girls (1)
slave girl (1)
slave woman's (1)

4088 παιδόθεν *paidothen*
Variant; not used

4089 παίζω *paizō* (1)
indulge in pagan revelry (1)

4090 παῖς *pais* (24)
servant (12)
boy (4)
attendants (1)
boys (1)
child (1)
child's (1)
children (1)
menservants (1)
servants (1)
young man (1)

4091 παίω *paiō* (5)
hit (2)
struck (2)
strikes (1)

4092 Πακατιανός *Pakatianos*
Variant; not used

4093 πάλαι *palai* (7)
long ago (3)
all along (1)
already (1)
in the past (1)
past (1)

4094 παλαιός *palaios* (19)
old (19)

4095 παλαιότης *palaiotēs* (1)
old way (1)

4096 παλαιόω *palaioō* (4)
wear out (2)
made obsolete (1)
obsolete (1)

4097 πάλη *palē* (1)
struggle (1)

4098 παλιγγενεσία *palingenesia* (2)
  rebirth (1)
  renewal (1)

4099 πάλιν *palin* (141)
  again (84)
  back (9)
  once more (7)
  then after (3)
  another (2)
  second time (2) +1311+1666
  then (2)
  yet (2)
  again (1) +1309
  all over again (1) +540
  also (1)
  and as (1) +2779
  another time (1)
  elsewhere (1)
  later (1)
  now (1)
  once again (1)
  once more (1) +1663
  once more (1) +2779
  rebuild (1) +3868
  repeat (1) +3306
  return (1) +1650+2262+3836
  returned to place (1) +404
  second (1) +1311
  then (1) +2779
  untranslated (13)

4100 παλινγενεσία *palingenesia*
  Variant; not used

4101 παμπληθεί *pamplēthei* (1)
  with one voice (1)

4102 πάμπολυς *pampolys*
  Variant; not used

4103 Παμφυλία *Pamphylia* (5)
  Pamphylia (5)

4104 πανδοκεῖον *pandokeion*
  Variant; not used

4105 πανδοκεύς *pandokeus*
  Variant; not used

4106 πανδοχεῖον *pandocheion* (1)
  inn (1)

4107 πανδοχεύς *pandocheus* (1)
  innkeeper (1)

4108 πανήγυρις *panēgyris* (1)
  joyful assembly (1)

4109 πανοικεί *panoikei* (1)
  whole family (1)

4110 πανοπλία *panoplia* (3)
  full armor (2)
  armor (1)

4111 πανουργία *panourgia* (5)
  craftiness (2)
  cunning (1)
  duplicity (1)
  use deception (1) +1877+4344

4112 πανοῦργος *panourgos* (1)
  crafty (1)

4113 πανπληθεί *panplēthei*
  Variant; not used

4114 πανταχῇ *pantachē* (1)
  everywhere (1)

4115 πανταχόθεν *pantachothen*
  Variant; not used

4116 πανταχοῦ *pantachou* (7)
  everywhere (6)
  whole (1) +3910

4117 παντελής *pantelēs* (2)
  at all (1) +1650+3836
  completely (1) +1650+3836

4118 πάντη *pantē* (1)
  every (1)

4119 πάντοθεν *pantothen* (3)
  from everywhere (1)
  gold-covered (1) +4328+5992
  on every side (1)

4120 παντοκράτωρ *pantokratōr* (10)
  Almighty (10)

4121 πάντοτε *pantote* (41)
  always (35)
  at all times (2)
  any (1)
  constantly (1)
  forever (1)
  from now on (1)

4122 πάντως *pantōs* (8)
  at all (2)
  surely (2)
  by all possible means (1)
  certainly (1)
  must (1)
  quite (1)

4123 παρά *para* (194)
  from (47)
  with (26)
  by (11)
  at (9)
  than (9)
  along (7)
  beside (4)
  contrary to (3)
  to (3)
  among (2)
  before (2)
  for that reason (2) +4047
  more than (2)
  of (2)
  other than (2)
  rather than (2)
  above (1)
  against (1)
  any more (1) +4498
  beyond (1)
  conceited (1) +4932+5861
  family (1) +3836
  had ˢ (1) +3836
  him (1) +4005
  in (1)
  in God's sight (1) +2536
  in God's sight (1) +2536+3836
  in presence (1)
  in the presence (1)
  me say (1) +1609
  minus (1)
  near (1)
  on (1)
  out (1)
  past (1)
  presence (1)
  they (1) +899
  under (1) +3836+4546
  unnatural ones (1) +3836+5882
  where (1) +4005
  you have (1) +5148
  untranslated (36)

4124 παραβαίνω *parabainō* (3)
  break (2)
  left (1)

4125 παραβάλλω *paraballō* (1)
  crossed over (1)

4126 παράβασις *parabasis* (7)
  breaking (1)
  breaking a command (1)
  sinner (1)
  sins (1)
  transgression (1)
  transgressions (1)

  violation (1)

4127 παραβάτης *parabatēs* (5)
  lawbreaker (2) +3795
  break (1) +1639
  lawbreaker (1)
  lawbreakers (1)

4128 παραβιάζομαι *parabiazomai* (2)
  persuaded (1)
  urged strongly (1)

4129 παραβολεύομαι *paraboleuomai* (1)
  risking (1)

4130 παραβολή *parabolē* (50)
  parable (30)
  parables (15)
  lesson (2)
  figuratively speaking (1) +1877
  illustration (1)
  proverb (1)

4131 παραβουλεύομαι *parabouleuomai*
  Variant; not used

4132 παραγγελία *parangelia* (5)
  command (1)
  gave strict orders (1) +4133
  instruction (1)
  instructions (1)
  orders (1)

4133 παραγγέλλω *parangellō* (31)
  command (7)
  commanded (4)
  ordered (4)
  told (3)
  instructions (2)
  cautioned (1)
  charge (1)
  commands (1)
  directives (1)
  gave command (1)
  gave rule (1)
  gave strict orders (1) +4132
  give instructions (1)
  give this command (1)
  required (1)
  strictly warned (1) +2203

4134 παραγίνομαι *paraginomai* (37)
  came (14)
  arrived (4)
  arriving (4)
  appeared (3)
  come (3)
  arrive (1)
  came back (1)
  came to support (1)
  come from (1)
  coming (1)
  get here (1)
  present (1)
  went on (1) +1451
  untranslated (1)

4135 παράγω *paragō* (10)
  went on (2)
  going by (1)
  pass away (1)
  passing (1)
  passing away (1)
  passing by (1)
  walked along (1)
  walked beside (1)
  went along (1)

4136 παραδειγματίζω *paradeigmatizō* (1)
  subjecting to public disgrace (1)

4137 παράδεισος *paradeisos* (3)
  paradise (3)

4138 παραδέχομαι *paradechomai* (6)
  accept (3)
  accepts (1)

entertain (1)
welcomed (1)

4139 παραδιατριβή *paradiatribē*
Variant; not used

4140 παραδίδωμι *paradidōmi* (119)
handed over (19)
betray (16)
betrayed (14)
hand over (9)
entrusted (6)
betrayer (4)
gave over (4)
passed on (4)
betrays (3)
committed (3)
gave up (3)
handed down (3)
arrest (2)
delivered (2)
gave (2)
given over (2)
put in prison (2)
turn over (2)
arrested (1)
betray (1) +1639+3836
betraying (1)
commended (1)
deliver (1)
delivered over (1)
given (1)
hand over to (1) +1650+5931
handing over (1)
hands over (1)
put (1)
putting into (1)
ripe (1)
risked (1)
surrender (1)
surrendered (1)
throwing (1)
traitor (1)
turned over (1)

4141 παράδοξος *paradoxos* (1)
remarkable (1)

4142 παράδοσις *paradosis* (13)
tradition (7)
traditions (3)
passed on (1)
teaching (1)
teachings (1)

4143 παραζηλόω *parazēloō* (4)
make envious (2)
arouse jealousy (1)
arouse to envy (1)

4144 παραθαλάσσιος *parathalassios* (1)
by the lake (1)

4145 παραθεωρέω *paratheōreō* (1)
overlooked (1)

4146 παραθήκη *parathēkē* (3)
deposit entrusted to (1)
have entrusted to (1)
what has been entrusted to care (1)

4147 παραινέω *paraineō* (2)
urge (1)
warned (1)

4148 παραιτέομαι *paraiteomai* (12)
excuse (2) +2400
nothing to do with (2)
refuse (2)
begged (1)
don't have anything to do with (1)
make excuses (1)
not put on such a list (1)
refused (1)
requested (1)

4149 παρακαθέζομαι *parakathezomai* (1)
sat (1)

4150 παρακαθίζω *parakathizō*
Variant; not used

4151 παρακαλέω *parakaleō* (109)
urge (20)
encourage (13)
begged (12)
pleaded with (7)
comforted (6)
encouraged (6)
urged (6)
encouraging (5)
appeal to (4)
invited (4)
plead with (3)
begging (2)
comfort (2)
comforts (2)
answer kindly (1)
appeal (1)
appease (1)
asked (1)
asking for help (1)
begged (1) +3306
call on (1)
exhort (1)
exhorted (1)
given (1)
listen to appeal (1)
making appeal (1)
pleading with (1)
received (1)
request that (1)
speaking encouragement to (1)
urgently requested (1) +160

4152 παρακαλύπτω *parakalyptō* (1)
hidden (1)

4153 παρακαταθήκη *parakatathēkē*
Variant; not used

4154 παράκειμαι *parakeimai* (2)
have (1)
right there (1)

4155 παράκλησις *paraklēsis* (29)
encouragement (10)
comfort (8)
appeal (2)
be encouraged (1) +2400
consolation (1)
encourage (1)
encouraged (1)
encouraging message (1)
exhortation (1)
greatly encouraged (1) +4444
preaching (1)
urgently (1) +3552+4498

4156 παράκλητος *paraklētos* (5)
counselor (4)
one who speaks in defense (1)

4157 παρακοή *parakoē* (3)
disobedience (2)
act of disobedience (1)

4158 παρακολουθέω *parakoloutheō* (4)
accompany (1)
followed (1)
investigated (1)
know all about (1)

4159 παρακούω *parakouō* (3)
refuses to listen (2)
ignoring (1)

4160 παρακύπτω *parakyptō* (5)
bending over (1)
bent over (1)
bent over to look (1)
look (1)
looks intently (1)

4161 παραλαμβάνω *paralambanō* (49)
took (15)

received (7)
take (6)
taken (4)
receive (2)
takes (2)
took along (2)
took aside (2)
took with (2)
accepted (1)
instructed (1)
received from (1)
receiving (1)
took (1) +72
took charge of (1)
traditions (1)

4162 παραλέγομαι *paralegomai* (2)
moved along (1)
sailed (1)

4163 παράλιος *paralios* (1)
coast (1)

4164 παραλλαγή *parallagē* (1)
change (1) +1913

4165 παραλογίζομαι *paralogizomai* (2)
deceive (2)

4166 παραλυτικός *paralytikos* (10)
paralytic (7)
paralyzed (3)

4167 παράλυτος *paralytos*
Variant; not used

4168 παραλύω *paralyō* (5)
paralytic (2)
paralytics (1)
paralyzed (1)
weak (1)

4169 παραμένω *paramenō* (4)
continue with (1)
continues (1)
continuing (1)
stay awhile (1)

4170 παραμυθέομαι *paramytheomai* (4)
comforting (2)
comfort (1)
encourage (1)

4171 παραμυθία *paramythia* (1)
comfort (1)

4172 παραμύθιον *paramythion* (1)
comfort (1)

4173 παράνοια *paranoia*
Variant; not used

4174 παρανομέω *paranomeō* (1)
violate the law (1)

4175 παρανομία *paranomia* (1)
wrongdoing (1)

4176 παραπικραίνω *parapikrainō* (1)
rebelled (1)

4177 παραπικρασμός *parapikrasmos* (2)
rebellion (2)

4178 παραπίπτω *parapiptō* (1)
fall away (1)

4179 παραπλέω *parapleō* (1)
sail past (1)

4180 παραπλήσιος *paraplēsios* (1)
almost (1)

4181 παραπλησίως *paraplēsiōs* (1)
too (1)

4182 παραπορεύομαι *paraporeuomai* (5)
passed by (2)
going (1)
passed (1)
went along (1)

4183 παράπτωμα *paraptōma* (20)
sins (8)
trespass (5)
transgression (2)
transgressions (2)
sin (1)
sin against (1)
trespasses (1)

4184 παραρρέω *pararreō* (1)
drift away (1)

4185 παράσημος *parasēmos* (1)
figurehead (1)

4186 παρασκευάζω *paraskeuazō* (4)
ready (2)
get ready (1)
prepared (1)

4187 παρασκευή *paraskeuē* (6)
day of preparation (3)
preparation day (2)
preparation (1)

4188 παραστάτις *parastatis*
Variant; not used

4189 παρατείνω *parateinō* (1)
kept on (1)

4190 παρατηρέω *paratēreō* (6)
watched closely (2)
carefully watched (1)
keeping a close watch (1)
kept close watch on (1)
observing (1)

4191 παρατήρησις *paratērēsis* (1)
careful observation (1)

4192 παρατίθημι *paratithēmi* (19)
set before (5)
commit (3)
told (2) +3306
committed (1)
did so[s] (1)
distribute (1)
entrust (1)
entrusted with (1)
give (1)
proving (1)
put before (1)
set a meal before (1) +5544

4193 παρατυγχάνω *paratynchanō* (1)
happened to be there (1)

4194 παραυτίκα *parautika* (1)
momentary (1)

4195 παραφέρω *parapherō* (4)
take (2)
blown along (1)
carried away (1)

4196 παραφρονέω *paraphroneō* (1)
out of mind (1)

4197 παραφρονία *paraphronia* (1)
madness (1)

4198 παραφροσύνη *paraphrosynē*
Variant; not used

4199 παραχειμάζω *paracheimazō* (4)
winter (2)
spend the winter (1)
wintered (1)

4200 παραχειμασία *paracheimasia* (1)
winter in (1)

4201 παραχράομαι *parachraomai*
Variant; not used

4202 παραχρήμα *parachrēma* (18)
immediately (9)
at once (4)
instantly (2)

at that moment (1)
just (1)
so quickly (1)

4203 πάρδαλις *pardalis* (1)
leopard (1)

4204 παρεδρεύω *paredreuō* (1)
serve at (1)

4205 πάρειμι *pareimi* (25)
come (7)
have (2)
am (1)
am with (1)
are here (1)
are present (1)
be (1)
came for (1)
here (1)
is here (1)
leaving undone (1)
now have (1)
present (1)
sought an audience (1)
time (1)
was (1)
was with (1)
were present (1)

4206 παρεισάγω *pareisagō* (1)
secretly introduce (1)

4207 παρείσακτος *pareisaktos* (1)
infiltrated ranks (1) +4209

4208 παρεισδύω *pareisdyō* (1)
secretly slipped in (1)

4209 παρεισέρχομαι *pareiserchomai* (2)
added (1)
infiltrated ranks (1) +4207

4210 παρεισφέρω *pareispherō* (1)
make (1)

4211 παρεκτός *parektos* (3)
except for (2)
besides everything else (1) +3836+6006

4212 παρεμβάλλω *paremballō* (1)
build (1)

4213 παρεμβολή *parembolē* (10)
barracks (6)
camp (3)
armies (1)

4214 παρενοχλέω *parenochleō* (1)
make it difficult for (1)

4215 παρεπίδημος *parepidēmos* (3)
strangers (3)

4216 παρέρχομαι *parerchomai* (29)
pass away (10)
disappear (4)
pass (2)
after (1)
be taken (1)
be taken away (1)
come (1)
come along (1)
disobeyed (1)
getting (1)
gone (1)
neglect (1)
pass by (1)
passed by (1)
passing by (1)
past (1)

4217 πάρεσις *paresis* (1)
left unpunished (1)

4218 παρέχω *parechō* (16)
bothering (3) +3160
became (1)
bother (1) +3160

brought in (1)
cause (1)
do (1)
earned (1)
given proof (1) +4411
promote (1)
provide with (1)
provides with (1)
set (1)
showed (1)
turn (1)

4219 παρηγορία *parēgoria* (1)
comfort (1)

4220 παρθενία *parthenia* (1)
untranslated (1)

4221 παρθένος *parthenos* (15)
virgin (8)
virgins (3)
pure (1)
unmarried (1)
virgin's (1)
untranslated (1)

4222 Πάρθοι *Parthoi* (1)
Parthians (1)

4223 παρίημι *pariēmi* (1)
feeble (1)

4224 παριστάνω *paristanō*
Variant; not used

4225 παρίστημι *paristēmi* (41)
present (7)
offer (6)
standing near (5)
stood beside (2)
bring near (1)
come (1)
give (1)
handed over (1)
nearby (1)
presented (1)
prove (1)
provide (1)
put at disposal (1)
showed (1)
stand (1)
stand before (1)
stand trial before (1)
standing around (1)
standing by (1)
standing nearby (1)
stands (1)
stood around (1)
stood at side (1)
stood there (1)
take stand (1)

4226 Παρμενᾶς *Parmenas* (1)
Parmenas (1)

4227 πάροδος *parodos* (1)
passing (1)

4228 παροικέω *paroikeō* (2)
made home (1)
visitor to (1)

4229 παροικία *paroikia* (2)
stay (1)
strangers (1)

4230 πάροικος *paroikos* (4)
aliens (2)
settled as foreigner (1)
strangers (1)

4231 παροιμία *paroimia* (5)
figuratively (1) +1877
figure of speech (1)
figures of speech (1)
proverbs (1)
this kind of[s] (1) +1877

4232 πάροινος *paroinos* (2)

4233 παροίχομαι *paroichomai* (1)
past (1) +1155

4234 παρομοιάζω *paromoiazō* (1)
like (1)

4235 παρόμοιος *paromoios* (1)
like (1)

4236 παροξύνω *paroxynō* (2)
easily angered (1)
greatly distressed (1)

4237 παροξυσμός *paroxysmos* (2)
sharp disagreement (1)
spur on (1) +1650

4238 παροράω *paroraō*
Variant; not used

4239 παροργίζω *parorgizō* (2)
exasperate (1)
make angry (1)

4240 παροργισμός *parorgismos* (1)
angry (1)

4241 παροτρύνω *parotrynō* (1)
incited (1)

4242 παρουσία *parousia* (24)
coming (17)
comes (1)
arrived (1) +3836
being (1)
in person (1) +3836+3836+5393
presence (1)

4243 παροψίς *paropsis* (2)
dish (2)

4244 παρρησία *parrēsia* (31)
confidence (7)
plainly (4)
courage (3)
publicly (3)
a public figure (1) +1877
assurance (1)
be bold (1) +2400+4498
bold (1) +5968
boldly (1)
boldly (1) +3552
boldness (1)
clearly (1) +1877
confident (1) +2400
confidently (1) +3552
fearlessly (1)
freedom (1)
openly (1)
public (1)

4245 παρρησιάζομαι *parrēsiazomai* (9)
speaking boldly (2)
boldly (1)
dared (1)
fearlessly (1)
freely (1)
preached fearlessly (1)
speak boldly (1)
spoke boldly (1)

4246 πᾶς *pas* (1240)
all (666)
every (127)
everything (108)
everyone (92)
whole (24)
any (17)
anyone (15)
all things (9) +3836
everything (8) +3836
full (8)
everyone (6) +476
always (5)
anything (4)
everybody (4)
everything (4) +4012

great (4)
no one (4) +4024
one (4) +4922
all (3) +4012
always (3) +1328
everywhere (3) +1877+5536
no (3) +4024
all over (2)
continually (2) +1328
entire (2)
every (2) +2848
everybody (2) +476
everyone (2) +6034
everyone's (2)
publicly (2) +1967
regularly (2) +1328
very (2)
whatever (2)
whatever (2) +4012
whoever (2) +3836
absolute (1)
all (1) +476
altogether (1) +3836
always (1) +1877+2789
always (1) +2465+3836
and what is more (1)
              +247+1145+2779+4047+5250
any and every (1)
anyone (1) +1569+6034
anything (1) +1569+4005+4547
complete (1)
complete (1) +1877
complete (1) +4444
completely (1)
day after day (1) +2465
day by day (1) +2465+2848
depth (1)
everybody's (1)
everyone (1) +323
everyone (1) +1667
everyone (1) +2848
everyone (1) +3836
everything (1) +323+4012
everything (1) +1569+4012
everywhere (1) +5536
finally (1) +5731
forever (1) +1328
forevermore (1) +172+1650+3836
free and belong to no man (1) +1666+1801
from one synagogue to another (1)
              +2848+5252
fully (1)
great endurance (1) +5705
great humility (1) +5425
great patience (1) +3429
in all (1)
in everything (1)
night (1) +1328+3816
no (1) +4028
none (1)
none (1) +4024
nothing (1) +4024
nothing (1) +4024+4839
one (1)
perfectly (1) +1877
profound (1)
proper (1)
pure (1)
securely (1) +854+1877
strict (1)
sufficient (1)
the whole (1)
the world[s] (1)
this[s] (1) +899+3836
throughout (1) +1650
throughout (1) +2093
traveled about the country (1) +1328+1451
whatever (1) +3836
whoever (1) +4015
whole universe (1)
whole world (1)

without (1) +6006
untranslated (33)

4247 πάσχα *pascha* (29)
Passover (26)
Passover lamb (3)

4248 πάσχω *paschō* (41)
suffer (21)
suffered (14)
suffering (5)
suffers (1)

4249 Πάταρα *Patara* (1)
Patara (1)

4250 πατάσσω *patassō* (10)
strike (4)
struck (3)
killing (1)
strike down (1)
struck down (1)

4251 πατέω *pateō* (5)
trample (1)
trample on (1)
trampled (1)
trampled on (1)
treads (1)

4252 πατήρ *patēr* (413)
father (335)
fathers (35)
father's (21)
forefathers (13)
patriarchs (4)
ancestor (2)
father who (1)
parents (1)
them[s] (1) +1609+3836

4253 Πάτμος *Patmos* (1)
Patmos (1)

4254 πατραλῴας *patralōas*
Variant; not used

4255 πατριά *patria* (3)
family (1)
line (1)
peoples (1)

4256 πατριάρχης *patriarchēs* (4)
patriarch (2)
patriarchs (2)

4257 πατρικός *patrikos* (1)
fathers (1)

4258 πατρίς *patris* (8)
hometown (6)
country (1)
country of their own (1)

4259 Πατροβᾶς *Patrobas* (1)
Patrobas (1)

4260 πατρολῴας *patrolōas* (1)
kill their fathers (1)

4261 πατροπαράδοτος *patroparadotos* (1)
handed down from forefathers (1)

4262 πατρῷος *patrōos* (3)
fathers (2)
ancestors (1)

4263 Παῦλος *Paulos* (158)
Paul (150)
Paul's (6)
him[s] (1) +3836
Paulus (1)

4264 παύω *pauō* (15)
stopped (6)
finished (2)
done with (1)
ended (1)
keep (1)
stilled (1)

stop (1)
stops (1)
subsided (1)

4265 Πάφος *Paphos* (2)
Paphos (2)

4266 παχύνω *pachynō* (2)
calloused (2)

4267 πέδη *pedē* (3)
foot (2)
irons on feet (1)

4268 πεδινός *pedinos* (1)
level (1)

4269 πεζεύω *pezeuō* (1)
on foot (1)

4270 πεζῇ *pezē* (2)
on foot (2)

4271 πεζός *pezos*
Variant; not used

4272 πειθαρχέω *peitharcheō* (4)
obey (2)
obedient (1)
taken advice (1)

4273 πειθός *peithos* (1)
persuasive (1)

4274 πειθώ *peithō*
Variant; not used

4275 πείθω *peithō* (52)
convinced (7)
confident (5)
persuaded (5)
confidence (2)
confident of (2)
followers (2)
persuade (2)
put confidence (2)
convince (1)
convinced of (1)
convinced that (1)
dissuaded (1)
encouraged (1)
follow (1)
fully convinced (1) +2779+3857
give in (1)
listening to (1)
make obey (1)
obey (1)
obeying (1)
persuasively (1)
put trust (1) +1639
rely (1) +1639
satisfy (1)
secured the support (1)
set at rest (1)
sure (1)
trusted (1)
trusts (1)
trying to persuade (1)
trying to win the approval of (1)
urged (1)
won over (1)

4276 Πειλᾶτος *Peilatos*
Variant; not used

4277 πεινάω *peinaō* (23)
hungry (17)
go hungry (3)
hunger (3)

4278 πεῖρα *peira* (2)
faced (1) +3284
tried to do (1) +3284

4279 πειράζω *peirazō* (39)
tempted (11)
tested (8)
test (7)
tried (3)

tempt (2)
tempter (2)
trying to trap (2)
did[s] (1)
examine (1)
tempting (1)
trap (1)

4280 πειρασμός *peirasmos* (20)
temptation (8)
trial (4)
trials (4)
testing (2)
tempting (1)
when are tempted (1) +3836+5250

4281 πειράω *peiraō* (1)
tried (1)

4282 πεισμονή *peismonē* (1)
persuasion (1)

4283 πέλαγος *pelagos* (2)
depths (1)
open sea (1)

4284 πελεκίζω *pelekizō* (1)
beheaded (1)

4285 πεμπταῖος *pemptaios*
Variant; not used

4286 πέμπτος *pemptos* (4)
fifth (4)

4287 πέμπω *pempō* (79)
sent (44)
send (20)
sending (7)
sent (2) +4707
take (2)
provide (1)
send for (1)
sends (1)
untranslated (1)

4288 πένης *penēs* (1)
poor (1)

4289 πενθερά *penthera* (6)
mother-in-law (6)

4290 πενθερός *pentheros* (1)
father-in-law (1)

4291 πενθέω *pentheō* (10)
mourn (6)
mourning (2)
filled with grief (1)
grieved over (1)

4292 πένθος *penthos* (5)
mourning (3)
grief (1)
mourn (1) +3972

4293 πενιχρός *penichros* (1)
poor (1)

4294 πεντάκις *pentakis* (1)
five times (1)

4295 πεντακισχίλιοι *pentakischilioi* (6)
five thousand (6)

4296 πεντακόσιοι *pentakosioi* (2)
five hundred (2)

4297 πέντε *pente* (38)
five (35)
fifty thousand (1) +3689
seventy-five (1) +1573
three or three and a half miles (1)
　　　　+1633+2445+5084+5558

4298 πεντεκαιδέκατος *pentekaidekatos* (1)
fifteenth (1)

4299 πεντήκοντα *pentēkonta* (7)
fifty (3)
153 (1) +1669+5552

450 (1) +2779+5484
fifties (1)
four hundred (1)

4300 πεντηκοστή *pentēkostē* (3)
Pentecost (3)

4301 πεποίθησις *pepoithēsis* (6)
confidence (4)
confident of (1)
untranslated (1)

4302 περ *per*
Variant; not used

4303 Πέραια *Peraia*
Variant; not used

4304 περαιτέρω *peraiterō* (1)
further (1)

4305 πέραν *peran* (22)
other side (7)
across (5)
on the other side (3)
across (1) +1650+3836
along (1)
crossed (1)
on the opposite shore (1)
regions across (1)
to the far shore (1)
to other side (1)

4306 πέρας *peras* (4)
ends (3)
end (1)

4307 Πέργαμος *Pergamos* (2)
Pergamum (2)

4308 Πέργη *Pergē* (3)
Perga (3)

4309 περί *peri* (332)
about (132)
for (52)
of (17)
around (11)
concerning (11)
in regard to (5)
on (5)
because (4)
in (4)
by (3)
to (3)
with (3)
against (2)
as (2)
from (2)
meant (2) +3306
on behalf (2)
sin offerings (2) +281
about (1) +4005
about (1) +6059
as for (1)
as to (1)
at (1)
besiege with questions (1) +694+4498
companions (1) +3836
concerned (1)
consider (1) +3972
go with (1)
how (1) +3836
in case (1)
in favor (1)
in that case (1) +4005
interest in (1)
my (1) +1831+3836
nearby (1) +3836+5536
over (1)
over the matter of (1)
regarding (1)
see about (1)
surrounding (1) +899
to do with (1)
to help (1)

what I meant (1) +4047
untranslated (45)

4310 περιάγω *periagō* (6)
groped about (1)
take along (1)
travel over (1)
went (1)
went around (1)
went through (1)

4311 περιαιρέω *periaireō* (5)
cutting loose (1)
gave up (1)
set sail (1)
take away (1)
taken away (1)

4312 περιάπτω *periaptō* (1)
kindled (1)

4313 περιαστράπτω *periastraptō* (2)
flashed around (2)

4314 περιβάλλω *periballō* (23)
dressed in (4)
wear (3)
clothed (2)
clothed in (2)
dressed (2)
clothe (2)
dressed (2) +2668
dressing in (1)
in (1)
robed in (1)
wearing (1)
wearing nothing (1) +1218+2093
wrap around (1)

4315 περιβλέπω *periblepō* (7)
looked around at (3)
looked around (2)
looked at (1)
looking around (1)

4316 περιβόλαιον *peribolaion* (2)
covering (1)
robe (1)

4317 περιδέω *perideō* (1)
around (1)

4318 περιεργάζομαι *periergazomai* (1)
busybodies (1)

4319 περίεργος *periergos* (2)
busybodies (1)
sorcery (1)

4320 περιέρχομαι *perierchomai* (3)
going about (1)
went about (1)
went around (1)

4321 περιέχω *periechō* (2)
astonished (1) +2502
says (1)

4322 περιζώννυμι *perizōnnymi* (6)
buckled around waist (1)
dress to serve (1)
dressed ready for service (1) +3836+4019
get ready (1)
wore (1)
untranslated (1)

4323 περιζωννύω *perizōnnyō*
Variant; not used

4324 περίθεσις *perithesis* (1)
wearing (1)

4325 περιΐστημι *periistēmi* (4)
avoid (2)
standing here (1)
stood around (1)

4326 περικάθαρμα *perikatharma* (1)
scum (1)

4327 περικαθίζω *perikathizō*
Variant; not used

4328 περικαλύπτω *perikalyptō* (3)
blindfolded (1)
blindfolded (1) +3836+4725
gold-covered (1) +4119+5992

4329 περίκειμαι *perikeimai* (5)
tied around (2)
bound (1)
subject to (1)
surrounded (1)

4330 περικεφαλαία *perikephalaia* (2)
helmet (2)

4331 περικρατής *perikratēs* (1)
secure (1)

4332 περικρύβω *perikrybō* (1)
in seclusion (1)

4333 περικυκλόω *perikykloō* (1)
encircle (1)

4334 περιλάμπω *perilampō* (2)
blazing around (1)
shone around (1)

4335 περιλείπομαι *perileipomai* (2)
left (2)

4336 περιλείχω *perileichō*
Variant; not used

4337 περίλυπος *perilypos* (4)
overwhelmed with sorrow (2)
greatly distressed (1)
very sad (1)

4338 περιμένω *perimenō* (1)
wait for (1)

4339 πέριξ *perix* (1)
around (1)

4340 περιοικέω *perioikeō* (1)
neighbors (1)

4341 περίοικος *perioikos* (1)
neighbors (1)

4342 περιούσιος *periousios* (1)
his very own (1)

4343 περιοχή *periochē* (1)
passage (1)

4344 περιπατέω *peripateō* (95)
walk (25)
live (17)
walking (14)
walked (4)
walks (4)
live a life (3)
act (2)
acting (2)
walk around (2)
behave (1)
daily life (1)
did^s (1)
do (1)
eat (1)
followed (1) +3552
go (1)
idle (1) +865
live lives (1)
living (1)
moved about (1)
passing by (1)
prowls around (1)
retain the place in life (1)
staying away from (1) +1877+4024
use deception (1) +1877+4111
walk along (1)
walking around (1)
walks around (1)
went (1)
went around (1)

untranslated (1)

4345 περιπείρω *peripeirō* (1)
pierced (1)

4346 περιπίπτω *peripiptō* (3)
face (1)
fell into the hands of (1)
struck (1)

4347 περιποιέω *peripoieō* (3)
bought (1)
gain (1)
keep (1)

4348 περιποίησις *peripoiēsis* (5)
belonging (1) +1650
possession (1)
receive (1)
saved (1) +1650+6034
share (1)

4349 περιραίνω *perirainō*
Variant; not used

4350 περιραντίζω *perirantizō*
Variant; not used

4351 περιρήγνυμι *perirēgnymi* (1)
stripped (1) +2668+3836

4352 περισπάω *perispaō* (1)
distracted (1)

4353 περισσεία *perisseia* (4)
abundant provision (1)
greatly (1) +1650
overflowing (1)
prevalent (1)

4354 περίσσευμα *perisseuma* (5)
overflow (2)
plenty (2)
left over (1)

4355 περισσεύω *perisseuō* (39)
left over (5)
overflow (5)
excel (3)
abound (2)
have an abundance (2)
overflowing (2)
wealth (2)
abundance (1)
better (1)
do so more and more (1) +3437
do this more and more (1) +3437
enhances (1)
flow over (1)
give fully (1)
grew (1)
have to spare (1)
is (1)
lavished (1)
living in plenty (1)
make abound (1)
more (1)
overflows (1)
plenty (1)
surpasses (1) +4498
welled up (1)

4356 περισσός *perissos* (6)
advantage (1)
beyond (1)
completely (1) +1666+3336
more (1)
no need (1)
to the full (1)

4357 περισσότερον *perissoteron*
Variant; not used

4358 περισσότερος *perissoteros* (16)
more (2)
more than (2)
most severely (2)
special (1)

excessive (1)
freely (1)
greater (1)
harder than (1)
more (1) +3437
more important than (1)
much more (1)
very (1)

4359 περισσοτέρως *perissoterōs* (12)
more (2)
delighted (1) +5897
depth (1)
especially (1)
every (1)
extremely (1)
greater (1)
more careful (1)
more frequently (1)
much harder (1)
particularly (1)

4360 περισσῶς *perissōs* (4)
all the louder (2)
even more (1)
obsession (1) +1841

4361 περιστερά *peristera* (10)
doves (5)
dove (4)
pigeons (1)

4362 περιτέμνω *peritemnō* (17)
circumcised (12)
circumcise (4)
circumcised (1) +3284

4363 περιτίθημι *peritithēmi* (8)
put on (4)
put around (2)
set on (1)
treat with (1)

4364 περιτομή *peritomē* (36)
circumcision (18)
circumcised (6)
Jews (4)
circumcised (3) +1666
after he was circumcised (1) +1639+1877
circumcised (1) +3284
Jews (1) +1666
you (1) +3836+5148
untranslated (1)

4365 περιτρέπω *peritrepō* (1)
driving (1)

4366 περιτρέχω *peritrechō* (1)
ran throughout (1)

4367 περιφέρω *peripherō* (3)
blown here and there (1)
carried (1)
carry around (1)

4368 περιφρονέω *periphroneō* (1)
despise (1)

4369 περίχωρος *perichōros* (9)
region (3)
surrounding country (3)
country around (1)
countryside (1)
surrounding (1)

4370 περίψημα *peripsēma* (1)
refuse (1)

4371 περπερεύομαι *perpereuomai* (1)
boast (1)

4372 Περσίς *Persis* (1)
Persis (1)

4373 πέρυσι *perysi* (2)
last year (2)

4374 πετεινόν *peteinon* (14)
birds (14)

4375 πέτομαι *petomai* (5)
flying (4)
fly (1)

4376 πέτρα *petra* (15)
rock (12)
rocks (3)

4377 Πέτρος *Petros* (155)
Peter (150)
Peter's (5)

4378 πετρώδης *petrōdēs* (4)
rocky places (4)

4379 πήγανον *pēganon* (1)
rue (1)

4380 πηγή *pēgē* (11)
springs (5)
spring (2)
well (2)
bleeding (1) +135+3836
untranslated (1)

4381 πήγνυμι *pēgnymi* (1)
set up (1)

4382 πηδάλιον *pēdalion* (2)
rudder (1)
rudders (1)

4383 πηλίκος *pēlikos* (2)
how great (1)
what large (1)

4384 πηλός *pēlos* (6)
mud (4)
it⁵ (1) +3836
untranslated (1)

4385 πήρα *pēra* (6)
bag (6)

4386 πηρόω *pēroō*
Variant; not used

4387 πήρωσις *pērōsis*
Variant; not used

4388 πῆχυς *pēchys* (4)
hour (2)
cubits (1)
hundred yards (1) +1357

4389 πιάζω *piazō* (12)
arrest (3)
seize (3)
caught (2)
arresting (1)
captured (1)
seized (1)
taking (1)

4390 πιέζω *piezō* (1)
pressed down (1)

4391 πιθανολογία *pithanologia* (1)
fine-sounding arguments (1)

4392 πιθός *pithos*
Variant; not used

4393 πικραίνω *pikrainō* (4)
be harsh (1)
bitter (1)
turn sour (1)
turned sour (1)

4394 πικρία *pikria* (4)
bitterness (2)
bitter (1)
bitterness (1) +5958

4395 πικρός *pikros* (2)
bitter (1)
salt water (1)

4396 πικρῶς *pikrōs* (2)
bitterly (2)

4397 Πιλᾶτος *Pilatos* (55)
Pilate (54)

Pilate's (1)

4398 πίμπλημι *pimplēmi* (24)
filled (15)
completed (2)
came (1)
fulfillment (1)
furious (1) +486
furious (1) +2596
time (1)
uproar (1) +5180
untranslated (1)

4399 πίμπρημι *pimprēmi* (1)
swell up (1)

4400 πινακίδιον *pinakidion* (1)
writing tablet (1)

4401 πινακίς *pinakis*
Variant; not used

4402 πίναξ *pinax* (5)
platter (4)
dish (1)

4403 πίνω *pinō* (72)
drink (46)
drinking (10)
drinks (8)
drank (5)
drink from (1)
drinks in (1)
take (1)

4404 πιότης *piotēs* (1)
nourishing (1)

4405 πιπράσκω *pipraskō* (9)
sold (7)
sales (1)
selling (1)

4406 πίπτω *piptō* (90)
fell (38)
fall (13)
fallen (8)
falls (8)
fell down (7)
collapsed (2)
fall down (2)
be condemned (1) +3213+5679
beat (1)
bow down (1)
bowed down (1)
came (1)
died (1)
drop out (1)
fails (1)
fall (1) +1639
fell to the ground (1)
threw himself (1) +2093+4725
untranslated (1)

4407 Πισιδία *Pisidia* (1)
Pisidia (1)

4408 Πισίδιος *Pisidios* (1)
Pisidian (1)

4409 πιστεύω *pisteuō* (241)
believe (114)
believed (57)
believes (23)
believers (7)
put faith (5)
trusts (5)
trust (4)
entrusted with (3)
faith (3)
believing (2)
entrusted (2)
put trust (2)
became believers (1)
believe (1) +1877
believe in (1)
believed in (1)

believed on (1)
come to believe (1)
committed (1)
did[s] (1)
do[s] (1)
entrust (1)
putting faith (1)
rely on (1)
took at word (1) +3364
trusted (1)

4410 πιστικός *pistikos* (2)
pure (2)

4411 πίστις *pistis* (242)
faith (221)
believe (4)
faithfulness (4)
have faith (2) +1666
belief (1)
believe (1) +1666
believe (1) +2400
believers (1) +2400+3836
believers (1) +3836
believing (1)
faith from first to last (1) +1650+4411
faithful (1)
given proof (1) +4218
pledge (1)
trusted (1)

4412 πιστός *pistos* (67)
faithful (36)
trustworthy (13)
believe (5)
believer (3)
believers (3)
can be trusted (2)
believer (1) +1639
believing (1)
faith (1)
reliable (1)
sure (1)

4413 πιστόω *pistoō* (1)
convinced (1)

4414 πλανάω *planaō* (39)
deceived (8)
deceive (6)
deceives (3)
going astray (3)
deceiving (2)
in error (2)
lead astray (2)
wandered off (2)
be deceived (1)
deluded (1)
leads astray (1)
led astray (1)
misleads (1)
misled (1)
mistaken (1)
wander (1)
wander off (1)
wandered (1)
wanders away (1)

4415 πλάνη *planē* (10)
error (5)
deceitful (1)
deception (1)
delusion (1)
falsehood (1)
perversion (1)

4416 πλάνης *planēs*
Variant; not used

4417 πλανήτης *planētēs* (1)
wandering (1)

4418 πλάνος *planos* (5)
deceiver (2)
deceivers (1)
deceiving (1)

impostors (1)

4419 πλάξ *plax* (3)
tablets (2)
stone tablets (1)

4420 πλάσμα *plasma* (1)
is formed (1)

4421 πλάσσω *plassō* (2)
formed (2)

4422 πλαστός *plastos* (1)
made up (1)

4423 πλατεῖα *plateia* (9)
streets (5)
great street (2)
street (2)

4424 πλάτος *platos* (4)
wide (3)
breadth (1)

4425 πλατύνω *platynō* (3)
make wide (1)
open wide (1)
opened wide (1)

4426 πλατύς *platys* (1)
wide (1)

4427 πλέγμα *plegma* (1)
braided hair (1)

4428 πλέκω *plekō* (3)
twisted together (3)

4429 πλεονάζω *pleonazō* (9)
increase (2)
increasing (2)
credited (1)
have too much (1)
increased (1)
make increase (1)
reaching more and more (1)
+1328+3836+4498

4430 πλεονεκτέω *pleonekteō* (5)
exploit (2)
exploited (1)
outwit (1)
take advantage of (1)

4431 πλεονέκτης *pleonektēs* (4)
greedy (3)
greedy person (1)

4432 πλεονεξία *pleonexia* (10)
greed (8)
lust (1)
one grudgingly given (1)

4433 πλευρά *pleura* (5)
side (5)

4434 πλέω *pleō* (6)
sail (2)
sailed (2)
sailing (1)
travel by ship (1)

4435 πληγή *plēgē* (22)
plagues (10)
plague (3)
wound (2)
beat (1) +2202
beatings (1)
flogged (1)
flogged (1) +2202
punishment (1)
wounded (1) +2400+3836
wounds (1)

4436 πλῆθος *plēthos* (31)
number (6)
assembly (3)
crowd (3)
people (3)
all (2)

multitude (2)
assembled worshipers (1) +3295+3836
church (1)
crowd (1) +3295+3836
crowds (1)
great company (1)
great number (1)
group (1)
Jewish community (1) +2681
large number (1)
numerous (1)
pile (1)
publicly (1) +1967+3836

4437 πληθύνω *plēthynō* (11)
abundance (3)
increase (2)
give many descendants (1) +4437
greatly increased (1) +889+2779
grew in numbers (1)
increased (1)
increasing (1)
spread (1)

4438 πλήκτης *plēktēs* (2)
violent (2)

4439 πλήμμυρα *plēmmyra* (1)
flood (1)

4440 πλήν *plēn* (31)
but (14)
however (4)
only (4)
yet (4)
beyond (1)
except (1)
important thing (1)
in any case (1)
untranslated (1)

4441 πλήρης *plērēs* (16)
full (9)
basketfuls (2) +3186
always (1)
basketfuls (1) +5083
covered (1)
fully (1)
furious (1) +2596

4442 πληροφορέω *plērophoreō* (6)
discharge all (1)
fulfilled (1)
fully (1)
fully assured (1)
fully convinced (1)
fully persuaded (1)

4443 πληροφορία *plērophoria* (4)
complete (1)
conviction (1)
full assurance (1)
sure (1)

4444 πληρόω *plēroō* (86)
fulfilled (21)
fulfill (11)
filled (10)
complete (7)
fill (3)
come (2)
completed (2)
filled with (2)
finished (2)
full (2)
after had passed (1)
amply supplied (1)
bring to fulfillment (1)
come true (1)
complete (1) +4246
completing (1)
fill up (1)
fill with (1)
filled in (1)
fills (1)

finds fulfillment (1)
fully (1)
fully met (1)
given fullness (1) +1639
gone by (1)
greatly encouraged (1) +4155
happened (1)
make complete (1)
make complete (1) +1639
meet (1)
passed (1)
present in its fullness (1)
summed up (1)
untranslated (1)

4445 πλήρωμα *plērōma* (17)
fullness (7)
fulfillment (2)
basketfuls (1) +3186
basketfuls (1) +5083
everything (1)
full measure (1)
full number (1)
fully (1)
untranslated (2)

4446 πλησίον *plēsion* (17)
neighbor (15)
near (1)
other (1)

4447 πλησμονή *plēsmonē* (1)
indulgence (1)

4448 πλήσσω *plēssō* (1)
struck (1)

4449 πλοιάριον *ploiarion* (5)
boat (2)
boats (2)
small boat (1)

4450 πλοῖον *ploion* (68)
boat (39)
ship (17)
boats (5)
ships (3)
it's (2) +3836
on board (1) +1877+3836
ship's (1)

4451 πλοκή *plokē*
Variant; not used

4452 πλόος *ploos* (3)
voyage (2)
sailing (1)

4453 πλοῦς *plous*
Variant; not used

4454 πλούσιος *plousios* (28)
rich (26)
wealth (1)
wealthy (1)

4455 πλουσίως *plousiōs* (4)
richly (2)
generously (1)
rich (1)

4456 πλουτέω *plouteō* (12)
rich (7)
acquired wealth (1)
gained wealth (1)
get rich (1)
grew rich (1)
richly (1)

4457 πλουτίζω *ploutizō* (3)
enriched (1)
made rich (1)
making rich (1)

4458 πλοῦτος *ploutos* (22)
riches (14)
wealth (6)
rich (1)

value (1)

4459 πλύνω *plynō* (3)
wash (1)
washed (1)
washing (1)

4460 πνεῦμα *pneuma* (379)
spirit (325)
spirits (32)
breath (3)
ghost (2)
spirit's (2)
spiritual (2)
attitude (1)
demon-possessed (1)
                    +2400+3836+3836+4505
gently (1) +1877+4559
he's +899+899+1877+3836
heart (1)
mind (1)
prophecy (1)
sighed deeply (1) +417+3836
spirit which predicted the future (1) +4780
wind (1)
winds (1)
with great fervor (1) +2417+3836
untranslated (1)

4461 πνευματικός *pneumatikos* (26)
spiritual (25)
spiritually (1)

4462 πνευματικῶς *pneumatikōs* (2)
figuratively (1)
spiritually (1)

4463 πνέω *pneō* (7)
blew (2)
blowing (1)
blows (1)
prevent from blowing (1) +3590
wind (1)
wind blows (1)

4464 πνίγω *pnigō* (3)
choke (1)
choked (1)
drowned (1)

4465 πνικτός *pniktos* (3)
meat of strangled animals (3)

4466 πνοή *pnoē* (2)
breath (1)
wind (1)

4467 ποδαπός *podapos*
Variant; not used

4468 ποδήρης *podērēs* (1)
a robe reaching down to feet (1)

4469 ποδονιπτήρ *podoniptēr*
Variant; not used

4470 πόθεν *pothen* (29)
where from (16)
where (7)
from which (1)
how (1)
how can (1)
what causes (1)
why (1)
untranslated (1)

4471 ποία *poia*
Variant; not used

4472 ποιέω *poieō* (568)
do (157)
doing (43)
did (38)
done (37)
made (35)
make (26)
does (24)
performed (7)

produce (6)
bear (5)
committed (5)
give (4)
making (4)
treated (4)
appointed (3)
bears (3)
do with (3)
put into practice (3)
put up (3)
was (3)
acted (2)
be (2)
bring (2)
carry out (2)
cause (2)
formed (2)
give to the needy (2) +1797
given (2)
judge (2) +3213
kept (2)
makes (2)
perform (2)
performing (2)
practice (2)
practiced (2)
practices (2)
pray (2) +1255
preparing (2)
provide (2)
puts into practice (2)
remember (2) +3644
sin (2) +281
sins (2) +281+3836
spending (2)
tell (2) +5745
treat (2)
work (2)
accomplish (1)
accomplished (1)
accomplishing (1)
act (1)
acts (1)
agreeing (1) +1191+1651
are (1)
attack (1) +4483
avenged (1) +1689
bearing (1)
bears (1) +1639
been (1)
began (1)
breaks law (1) +490
bring about (1)
business (1) +5515
carrying out (1)
causes (1)
causing (1)
celebrate (1)
claim (1) +4932
claimed to be (1) +1571
claims to be (1) +1571
commits (1)
consider (1)
created things (1)
criminal (1) +2805
delay (1) +332
dividing into shares (1) +3538
done (1) +1639
duty (1) +4005+4053
earned (1)
exercise (1)
exercised (1)
following (1)
forced (1)
forcing (1)
gain (1)
gaining (1)
gave (1)
gave to in need (1) +1797
get (1)

gives away (1) +*1316*
good (1) +*2822*
grows (1) +*890*
had (1)
have (1)
have do (1)
he sacrificed[s] (1)
healing (1) +*5618*
held (1)
help (1) +*2292*
helping the poor (1) +*1797*
involved in (1)
keep (1)
keeps (1)
kept up (1)
live by (1)
lives by (1)
made out to be (1)
make out to be (1)
mentioning (1) +*3644*
mourned deeply (1) +*3157+3489*
obey (1)
peacemakers (1) +*1645*
pray[s] (1) +*4047*
prepared (1)
provided (1)
put (1)
put out of the synagogue (1) +*697*
reached (1)
redeemed (1) +*3391*
remember (1) +*3647*
remembering (1) +*3644*
satisfy (1) +*2653*
see (1)
set up (1)
show (1)
sinned (1) +*281+1639*
spend (1)
spent (1)
stayed (1)
stirring up (1) +*2180*
sweep away with the torrent (1) +*4533*
think about (1) +*4630*
those who do (1)
treat (1) +*1650*
turn into (1)
turned into (1)
unite (1) +*3517*
walked along (1) +*3847*
weeping (1) +*3081*
who do you think you are (1) +*4932+5515*
win (1)
worked (1)
wrote (1)
yielded (1)
yielding (1)
untranslated (3)

4473 ποίημα *poiēma* (2)
made (1)
workmanship (1)

4474 ποίησις *poiēsis* (1)
does (1)

4475 ποιητής *poiētēs* (6)
do (1)
do (1) +*1181*
doing (1)
keeping (1)
obey (1)
poets (1)

4476 ποικίλος *poikilos* (10)
all kinds of (4)
various (4)
many kinds (1)
various kinds (1)

4477 ποιμαίνω *poimainō* (11)
rule (3)
be shepherds of (2)
be shepherd (1)
be shepherd of (1)

looking after sheep (1)
shepherds (1)
take care of (1)
tends (1)

4478 ποιμήν *poimēn* (18)
shepherd (13)
shepherds (4)
pastors (1)

4479 ποίμνη *poimnē* (5)
flock (3)
flocks (1)
untranslated (1)

4480 ποίμνιον *poimnion* (5)
flock (5)

4481 ποῖος *poios* (33)
what (20)
which (4)
kind of (3)
what kind of (2)
a way (1)
how is it (1)
the (1)
what will happen (1) +*3836*

4482 πολεμέω *polemeō* (7)
fight (2)
fought (2)
make war (2)
makes war (1)

4483 πόλεμος *polemos* (18)
battle (6)
wars (5)
war (4)
attack (1) +*4472*
fights (1)
go war (1) +*5202*

4484 πόλις *polis* (162)
city (86)
town (51)
towns (12)
cities (8)
city's (1)
from town to town (1) +*3836*
there[s] (1) +*1877+3836+4047*
village (1)
untranslated (1)

4485 πολιτάρχης *politarchēs* (2)
city officials (2)

4486 πολιτεία *politeia* (2)
citizenship (2)

4487 πολίτευμα *politeuma* (1)
citizenship (1)

4488 πολιτεύομαι *politeuomai* (2)
conduct yourselves (1)
fulfilled duty (1)

4489 πολίτης *politēs* (4)
citizen (2)
neighbor (1)
subjects (1)

4490 πολλάκις *pollakis* (18)
often (10)
again and again (3)
many times (2)
constantly (1)
many a time (1)
untranslated (1)

4491 πολλαπλασίων *pollaplasiōn* (1)
many times as much (1)

4492 πολυεύσπλαγχνος *polyeusplanchnos*
Variant; not used

4493 πολύλαλος *polylalos*
Variant; not used

4494 πολυλογία *polylogia* (1)
many words (1)

4495 πολυμερῶς *polymerōs* (1)
at many times (1)

4496 πολυπλήθεια *polyplētheia*
Variant; not used

4497 πολυποίκιλος *polypoikilos* (1)
manifold (1)

4498 πολύς *polys* (413)
many (193)
great (35)
much (31)
large (30)
more (16)
most (8)
greater (6)
how much (4)
more than (3)
rushing (3)
very (3)
a great deal of (2)
all (2)
few (2) +*4024*
long (2)
majority (2)
number (2)
plentiful (2)
plenty (2)
strict (2)
a great deal (1)
a long time (1) +*2093*
again and again (1)
all silent (1) +*4968*
all the more (1) +*3437*
any further (1) +*2093*
any more (1) +*4123*
badly (1)
be bold (1) +*2400+4244*
before very long (1) +*3552+4024*
besiege with questions (1) +*694+4309*
better (1)
big (1)
bigger (1)
by far (1)
considerable (1)
deep (1)
earnestly (1)
even more so[s] (1) +*5080*
freely (1)
further (1)
generously (1)
get very far (1) +*2093+4621*
great deal (1)
greatly (1)
hard (1) +*2400*
high (1)
intense (1)
larger (1)
late in the day (1) +*6052*
long (1) +*2465*
long period (1)
long time (1)
loudly (1)
more and more (1) +*2093*
most (1) +*3836*
often (1)
on and on (1) +*2093*
on the contrary (1) +*247+3437*
only (1) +*2445+4024*
over (1)
plenty of (1)
reaching more and more (1)
                   +*1328+3836+4429*
several (1)
severe (1)
severely (1)
shouted all the more (1) +*3189+3437*
so many (1)
strong (1)
strongly (1)
surpasses (1) +*4355*
urgently (1) +*3552+4155*

very hard (1)
very late (1) +6052
violent (1)
violently (1)
warmly (1)
wept and wept (1) +3081
widespread (1)
untranslated (4)

4499 πολύσπλαγχνος *polysplanchnos* (1)
full of compassion (1)

4500 πολυτελής *polytelēs* (3)
expensive (1)
great worth (1)
very expensive (1)

4501 πολύτιμος *polytimos* (3)
expensive (1)
great value (1)
greater worth (1)

4502 πολυτρόπως *polytropōs* (1)
in various ways (1)

4503 πόμα *poma* (2)
drink (2)

4504 πονηρία *ponēria* (7)
evil (3)
wickedness (2)
malice (1)
wicked ways (1)

4505 πονηρός *ponēros* (78)
evil (47)
wicked (11)
bad (7)
more wicked than (2)
crimes (1)
demon-possessed (1)
+2400+3836+3836+4460
envious (1) +1639+3836+4057
envy (1) +4057
evil one (1)
evils (1)
guilty conscience (1) +5287
maliciously (1) +3364
painful (1)
serious (1)
sinful (1)

4506 πόνος *ponos* (4)
agony (1)
pain (1)
pains (1)
working (1)

4507 Ποντικός *Pontikos* (1)
of Pontus (1)

4508 Πόντιος *Pontios* (3)
Pontius (3)

4509 Πόντος *pontos* (2)
Pontus (2)

4510 Πόντος *Pontos*
Variant; not used

4511 Πόπλιος *Poplios* (2)
his[s] (1) +3836
Publius (1)

4512 πορεία *poreia* (2)
goes about his business (1)
way (1)

4513 πορεύομαι *poreuomai* (153)
go (61)
went (22)
going (13)
goes (7)
on way (4)
follow (2)
follow (2) +3958
gone (2)
left (2)
living (2)

went on way (2)
went out (2)
about (1)
accompany (1) +5250
came (1)
companions (1) +5250
continued on way (1)
depart (1)
departed (1)
enter (1) +1650
following (1)
go back (1)
go on way (1)
heading (1)
hurried (1) +3552+5082
leave (1)
leaving (1)
leaving (1) +608
observing (1) +1877
on journey (1) +1877
set out (1)
started out (1)
taken (1)
traveled (1)
walking (1)
walking away (1)
way (1)
went along (1)
went into (1) +1656
went out (1) +2002
untranslated (4)

4514 πορθέω *portheō* (3)
destroy (1)
raised havoc (1)
tried destroy (1)

4515 πορία *poria*
Variant; not used

4516 πορισμός *porismos* (2)
gain (1)
means to financial gain (1)

4517 Πόρκιος *Porkios* (1)
Porcius (1)

4518 πορνεία *porneia* (25)
sexual immorality (13)
adulteries (5)
immorality (2)
marital unfaithfulness (2)
illegitimate children (1) +1164+1666
sexual sin (1)
untranslated (1)

4519 πορνεύω *porneuō* (8)
committed adultery (3)
commit sexual immorality (1)
committing sexual immorality (1)
did[s] (1)
sexual immorality (1)
sins sexually (1)

4520 πόρνη *pornē* (12)
prostitute (8)
prostitutes (4)

4521 πόρνος *pornos* (10)
sexually immoral (7)
immoral (2)
adulterers (1)

4522 πόρρω *porrō* (4)
far (2)
farther (1)
long way off (1)

4523 πόρρωθεν *porrōthen* (2)
at a distance (1)
from a distance (1)

4524 πορρωτέρω *porrōterō*
Variant; not used

4525 πορφύρα *porphyra* (4)
purple (2)

purple robe (2)

4526 πορφύρεος *porphyreos* (4)
purple (4)

4527 πορφυρόπωλις *porphyropōlis* (1)
dealer in purple cloth (1)

4528 πορφυροῦς *porphyrous*
Variant; not used

4529 ποσάκις *posakis* (3)
how often (2)
how many times (1)

4530 πόσις *posis* (3)
drink (2)
drinking (1)

4531 πόσος *posos* (27)
how much (11)
how many (10)
how (1)
how great (1)
how much more (1)
what (1)
untranslated (2)

4532 ποταμός *potamos* (17)
river (9)
rivers (3)
streams (3)
torrent (2)

4533 ποταμοφόρητος *potamophorētos* (1)
sweep away with the torrent (1) +4472

4534 ποταπός *potapos* (7)
what kind of (4)
how great (1)
what magnificent (1)
what massive (1)

4535 ποταπῶς *potapōs*
Variant; not used

4536 πότε *pote* (19)
when (11)
how long (4) +2401
long (3)
to return (1) +386

4537 ποτέ *pote* (29)
once (6)
at one time (3)
ever (3)
formerly (3)
used to (2)
ago (1)
at last (1) +2453
had been (1)
never (1) +3590+4024
never (1) +4024
never (1) +4046
now at last (1) +2453
of the past (1)
previous (1)
were (1) +1639
when (1)
untranslated (1)

4538 πότερον *poteron* (1)
whether (1)

4539 ποτήριον *potērion* (31)
cup (29)
cups (1)
gives a cup (1) +4540

4540 ποτίζω *potizō* (16)
gave to drink (2)
give to drink (2)
offered to drink (2)
waters (2)
drunk (1)
gave (1)
give water (1)
given to drink (1)
gives a cup (1) +4539

gives water to (1)
made drink (1)
watered (1)

4541 Ποτίολοι *Potioloi* (1)
Puteoli (1)

4542 πότος *potos* (1)
carousing (1)

4543 πού *pou* (4)
a place where (1)
about (1)
somewhere (1)
untranslated (1)

4544 ποῦ *pou* (48)
where (43)
place (2)
what (2)
no place (1) +4024

4545 Πούδης *Poudēs* (1)
Pudens (1)

4546 πούς *pous* (93)
feet (76)
foot (8)
foot of ground (1) +1037
footstool (1) +3836+5711
legs (1)
themˢ (1) +899+3836
under (1) +3836+4123
untranslated (4)

4547 πρᾶγμα *pragma* (11)
matter (2)
anything (1) +1569+4005+4246
dispute (1)
practice (1)
thing (1)
things (1)
things that (1)
what (1)
untranslated (2)

4548 πραγματεία *pragmateia* (1)
civilian affairs (1) +1050

4549 πραγματεύομαι *pragmateuomai* (1)
put to work (1)

4550 πραιτώριον *praitōrion* (8)
palace (4)
Praetorium (2)
palace guard (1)
palace of the governor (1)

4551 πράκτωρ *praktōr* (2)
officer (2)

4552 πρᾶξις *praxis* (6)
action (1)
deeds (1)
function (1)
has done (1)
misdeeds (1)
practices (1)

4553 πρᾶος *praos*
Variant; not used

4554 πραότης *praotēs*
Variant; not used

4555 πρασιά *prasia* (1)
groups (1) +4555

4556 πράσσω *prassō* (39)
do (9)
done (6)
doing (4)
acted (1)
collect (1)
collected (1)
deeds (1)
defying (1) +595
did (1)
does (1)

done (1) +1639
harm (1) +2805
indulged (1)
live (1)
mind business (1)
observe (1)
practice (1)
practiced (1)
preachˢ (1)
put into practice (1)
themˢ (1) +3836+3836+5525
wrongdoer (1) +2805
untranslated (1)

4557 πραϋπαθία *praupathia* (1)
gentleness (1)

4558 πραΰς *praus* (4)
gentle (3)
meek (1)

4559 πραΰτης *prautēs* (11)
gentleness (3)
gentle (2)
gently (1) +1877
gently (1) +1877+4460
humbly (1) +1877
humility (1)
meekness (1)
true humility (1)

4560 πρέπω *prepō* (7)
proper (2)
appropriate (1)
fitting (1)
in accord (1)
meets need (1)
untranslated (1)

4561 πρεσβεία *presbeia* (2)
delegation (2)

4562 πρεσβευτής *presbeutēs*
Variant; not used

4563 πρεσβεύω *presbeuō* (2)
ambassador (1)
ambassadors (1)

4564 πρεσβυτέριον *presbyterion* (3)
body of elders (1)
council (1)
council of elders (1)

4565 πρεσβύτερος *presbyteros* (66)
elders (56)
elder (3)
older (3)
ancients (1)
old (1)
older man (1)
those who are older (1)

4566 πρεσβύτης *presbytēs* (3)
old man (2)
older (1)

4567 πρεσβῦτις *presbytis* (1)
older (1)

4568 πρηνής *prēnēs* (1)
fell headlong (1) +1181

4569 πρίζω *prizō* (1)
sawed in two (1)

4570 πρίν *prin* (13)
before (9)
before (3) +2445
before (1) +323+2445

4571 Πρίσκα *Priska* (6)
Priscilla (6)

4572 Πρίσκιλλα *Priskilla*
Variant; not used

4573 πρίω *priō*
Variant; not used

4574 πρό *pro* (47)
before (30)
ahead (4) +4725
at (3)
above (2)
some time ago (2) +2465+3836+4047
ago (1)
ahead (1)
before (1) +4725
just outside (1)
on ahead (1) +4725
untranslated (1)

4575 προάγω *proagō* (20)
go ahead of (2)
go on ahead of (2)
going ahead of (2)
went ahead of (2)
bring (1)
bring out (1)
brought (1)
brought before (1)
entering ahead of (1)
former (1)
leading (1)
led the way (1)
once made (1)
reaching ahead of (1)
runs ahead (1)
went ahead (1)

4576 προαιρέω *proaireō* (1)
decided (1)

4577 προαιτιάομαι *proaitiaomai* (1)
already made the charge (1)

4578 προακούω *proakouō* (1)
already heard about (1)

4579 προαμαρτάνω *proamartanō* (2)
sinned earlier (2)

4580 προαύλιον *proaulion* (1)
entryway (1)

4581 προβαίνω *probainō* (5)
well along (2)
going on (1)
gone farther (1)
old (1) +1877+2465

4582 προβάλλω *proballō* (2)
pushed to the front (1)
sprout leaves (1)

4583 προβατικός *probatikos* (1)
sheep Gate (1)

4584 προβάτιον *probation*
Variant; not used

4585 πρόβατον *probaton* (39)
sheep (38)
sheep's (1)

4586 προβιβάζω *probibazō* (1)
prompted (1)

4587 προβλέπω *problepō* (1)
planned (1)

4588 προγίνομαι *proginomai* (1)
committed beforehand (1)

4589 προγινώσκω *proginōskō* (5)
foreknew (2)
already know (1)
chosen before (1)
known (1)

4590 πρόγνωσις *prognōsis* (2)
foreknowledge (2)

4591 πρόγονος *progonos* (2)
my forefathers (1)
parents and grandparents (1)

4592 προγράφω *prographō* (4)
already written (1)

portrayed (1)
was written about (1)
written in the past (1)

4593 πρόδηλος *prodēlos* (3)
obvious (2)
clear (1)

4594 προδίδωμι *prodidōmi* (1)
given (1)

4595 προδότης *prodotēs* (3)
betrayed (1) +1181
traitor (1)
treacherous (1)

4596 πρόδρομος *prodromos* (1)
went before (1)

4597 προεῖπον *proeipon*
Variant; not used

4598 προελπίζω *proelpizō* (1)
first to hope (1)

4599 προενάρχομαι *proenarchomai* (2)
earlier made a beginning (1)
the first (1)

4600 προεπαγγέλλω *proepangellō* (2)
promised (1)
promised beforehand (1)

4601 προέρχομαι *proerchomai* (9)
going farther (2)
went on ahead (2)
go on (1)
got there ahead of (1)
leading (1)
visit in advance (1) +1650
walked (1)

4602 προετοιμάζω *proetoimazō* (2)
prepared in advance (2)

4603 προευαγγελίζομαι *proeuangelizomai* (1)
announced the gospel in advance (1)

4604 προέχω *proechō* (1)
better (1)

4605 προηγέομαι *proēgeomai* (1)
above (1)

4606 πρόθεσις *prothesis* (12)
purpose (5)
consecrated (3)
consecrated bread (1) +788
plan (1)
true (1)
wanted (1)

4607 προθεσμία *prothesmia* (1)
time set (1)

4608 προθυμία *prothymia* (5)
eagerness (3)
eager (1)
willingness (1)

4609 πρόθυμος *prothymos* (3)
willing (2)
eager (1)

4610 προθύμως *prothymōs* (1)
eager (1)

4611 πρόϊμος *proimos* (1)
autumn rains (1)

4612 πρόϊνός *proinos*
Variant; not used

4613 προΐστημι *proistēmi* (8)
manage (2)
devote (1)
devote to (1)
direct (1)
leadership (1)
manage and see that (1)
over (1)

4614 προκαλέω *prokaleō* (1)
provoking (1)

4615 προκαταγγέλλω *prokatangellō* (2)
foretold (1)
predicted (1)

4616 προκαταρτίζω *prokatartizō* (1)
finish the arrangements for (1)

4617 προκατέχω *prokatechō*
Variant; not used

4618 πρόκειμαι *prokeimai* (5)
marked out (1)
offered (1)
serve as (1)
set before (1)
there (1)

4619 προκηρύσσω *prokēryssō* (1)
preached (1)

4620 προκοπή *prokopē* (3)
progress (2)
advance (1)

4621 προκόπτω *prokoptō* (6)
advancing (1)
get very far (1) +2093+4498
go (1)
grew (1)
indulge (1)
nearly over (1)

4622 πρόκριμα *prokrima* (1)
partiality (1)

4623 προκυρόω *prokyroō* (1)
previously established (1)

4624 προλαμβάνω *prolambanō* (3)
beforehand (1)
caught (1)
goes ahead (1)

4625 προλέγω *prolegō* (15)
said before (2)
told ahead of time (2)
already gave warning (1)
already said (1)
already told (1)
did before^s (1)
foretold (1)
repeat (1)
said previously (1)
spoke long ago (1)
spoken in the past (1)
telling (1)
warn (1)

4626 προμαρτύρομαι *promartyromai* (1)
predicted (1)

4627 προμελετάω *promeletaō* (1)
worry beforehand (1)

4628 προμεριμνάω *promerimnaō* (1)
worry beforehand about (1)

4629 προνοέω *pronoeō* (3)
careful (1)
provide for (1)
taking pains (1)

4630 πρόνοια *pronoia* (2)
foresight (1)
think about (1) +4472

4631 πρόοιδα *prooida*
Variant; not used

4632 προοράω *prooraō* (4)
foresaw (1)
previously seen (1) +1639
saw (1)
seeing what was ahead (1)

4633 προορίζω *proorizō* (6)
predestined (4)
decided beforehand (1)

destined (1)

4634 προπάσχω *propaschō* (1)
previously suffered (1)

4635 προπάτωρ *propatōr* (1)
forefather (1)

4636 προπέμπω *propempō* (9)
accompanied (2)
send on way (2)
assist on journey (1)
help on journey (1)
help on way (1)
send on their way (1)
sent on way (1)

4637 προπετής *propetēs* (2)
rash (2)

4638 προπορεύομαι *proporeuomai* (2)
go before (1)
go on (1)

4639 πρός *pros* (698)
to (379)
with (47)
for (24)
at (21)
against (17)
toward (8)
before (7)
in (7)
among (6)
around (6)
of (4)
in order to (3)
lead to (3)
them (3) +899
about (2)
as (2)
because (2)
into (2)
joined (2) +2262
so that (2)
addressed (1) +3306
approaching (1) +2262
begging (1) +1797+3836
beside (1)
comparing with (1)
concerning (1)
end (1) +1639
for (1) +3836
for a little while (1) +6052
gave (1) +2400
him (1) +899
in approaching (1)
in restraining (1)
in to (1)
join (1) +2262
leads to (1)
lustfully (1) +2121+3836
nearly (1)
on (1)
one another (1) +257+257
outside (1)
see (1) +2262
so as to (1)
so that (1) +3836
talked the matter over (1) +253+1368
they (1) +899
to keep from (1) +3590+3836
to see (1)
to show that (1) +3836
together (1) +253
told him (1) +899+1181
up to (1)
vicinity of (1)
visited (1) +2262
untranslated (117)

4640 προσάββατον *prosabbaton* (1)
day before the Sabbath (1)

4641 προσαγορεύω *prosagoreuō* (1)
designated to be (1)

4642 προσάγω *prosagō* (4)
bring (2)
approaching (1)
brought before (1)

4643 προσαγωγή *prosagōgē* (3)
access (2)
approach (1) +2400

4644 προσαιτέω *prosaiteō* (2)
beg (1)
begging (1)

4645 προσαίτης *prosaitēs* (1)
begging (1)

4646 προσαναβαίνω *prosanabainō* (1)
move (1)

4647 προσαναλαμβάνω *prosanalambanō*
Variant; not used

4648 προσαναλίσκω *prosanaliskō*
Variant; not used

4649 προσαναλόω *prosanaloō*
Variant; not used

4650 προσαναπληρόω *prosanaplēroō* (2)
supplied (1)
supplying (1)

4651 προσανατίθημι *prosanatithēmi* (1)
consult (1)

4652 προσανέχω *prosanechō*
Variant; not used

4653 προσαπειλέω *prosapeileō* (1)
further threats (1)

4654 προσαχέω *prosacheō*
Variant; not used

4655 προσδαπανάω *prosdapanaō* (1)
extra expense (1)

4656 προσδέομαι *prosdeomai* (1)
needed (1)

4657 προσδέχομαι *prosdechomai* (14)
waiting for (5)
wait for (2)
accepted (1)
looking forward to (1)
receive (1)
refused (1) +4024
welcome (1)
welcomes (1)
untranslated (1)

4658 προσδίδωμι *prosdidōmi*
Variant; not used

4659 προσδοκάω *prosdokaō* (16)
expect (5)
expecting (3)
looking forward to (2)
expected (1)
look forward to (1)
suspense (1)
waiting (1)
waiting expectantly (1)
waiting for (1)

4660 προσδοκία *prosdokia* (2)
anticipating (1)
apprehensive (1)

4661 προσεάω *proseaō* (1)
allow to hold course (1)

4662 προσεγγίζω *prosengizō*
Variant; not used

4663 προσεδρεύω *prosedreuō*
Variant; not used

4664 προσεργάζομαι *prosergazomai* (1)
earned more (1)

4665 προσέρχομαι *proserchomai* (86)
came to (34)
came (10)
went to (8)
come to (4)
going to (4)
came up (3)
went (3)
came forward (2)
came up to (2)
draw near (2)
agree to (1)
approach (1)
approached (1)
came before (1)
comes (1)
coming (1)
go to (1)
stepped forward (1)
visit (1)
went over (1)
went up (1)
went up to (1)
untranslated (2)

4666 προσευχή *proseuchē* (36)
prayer (16)
prayers (12)
place of prayer (2)
praying (2)
ask God (1)
pray (1)
prayed earnestly (1) +4667
praying (1) +1181

4667 προσεύχομαι *proseuchomai* (85)
pray (42)
prayed (17)
praying (12)
prayer (5)
prays (3)
make prayers (2)
pray for (2)
prayed earnestly (1) +4666
praying to (1)

4668 προσέχω *prosechō* (24)
on guard (4)
careful (2)
devote (2)
pay attention (2)
attention (1)
beware (1)
consider carefully (1)
follow (1)
followed (1)
guard (1)
indulging (1)
keep watch over (1)
paid close attention to (1)
pay attention to (1)
respond to (1)
served at (1)
watch (1)
watch out (1)

4669 προσηλόω *prosēloō* (1)
nailing (1)

4670 προσήλυτος *prosēlytos* (4)
converts to Judaism (2)
convert (1)
convert to Judaism (1)

4671 πρόσθεσις *prosthesis*
Variant; not used

4672 πρόσκαιρος *proskairos* (4)
only a short time (2)
a short time (1)
temporary (1)

4673 προσκαλέω *proskaleō* (29)
called (8)
called to (7)
called in (3)
call (2)

called together (2)
calling to (2)
sent for (2)
calling (1)
gathered together (1)
summoning (1)

4674 προσκαρτερέω *proskartereō* (10)
attendants (1)
continued (1)
devote (1)
devoted to (1) +1639
faithful (1)
followed everywhere (1)
give attention (1)
give full time (1)
joined constantly (1)
ready (1)

4675 προσκαρτέρησις *proskarterēsis* (1)
keep on (1)

4676 προσκεφάλαιον *proskephalaion* (1)
cushion (1)

4677 προσκληρόω *prosklēroō* (1)
joined (1)

4678 πρόσκλησις *prosklēsis*
Variant; not used

4679 προσκλίνω *prosklinō* (1)
rallied (1)

4680 πρόσκλισις *prosklisis* (1)
out of favoritism (1) +2848

4681 προσκολλάω *proskollaō* (2)
united to (2)

4682 πρόσκομμα *proskomma* (6)
causes men to stumble (2)
stumbling block (2)
stumble (1)
stumbling (1)

4683 προσκοπή *proskopē* (1)
stumbling block (1)

4684 προσκόπτω *proskoptō* (8)
strike (2)
stumble (2)
beat against (1)
cause fall (1)
stumbled over (1)
stumbles (1)

4685 προσκυλίω *proskyliō* (2)
rolled (1)
rolled in front of (1)

4686 προσκυνέω *proskyneō* (60)
worship (28)
worshiped (17)
knelt before (3)
worshipers (3)
fall down (1)
fell on knees in front of (1)
kneeling down (1)
on knees before (1)
paid homage (1)
refused to worship (1) +3590
reverence (1)
worshiping (1)
worships (1)

4687 προσκυνητής *proskynētēs* (1)
worshipers (1)

4688 προσλαλέω *proslaleō* (2)
talk with (1)
talked with (1)

4689 προσλαμβάνω *proslambanō* (12)
accept (2)
accepted (2)
took aside (2)
ate (1)
eaten (1)

invited to home (1)
rounded up (1)
welcome (1)
welcomed (1)

4690 προσλέγω *proslegō*
Variant; not used

4691 πρόσλημψις *proslēmpsis* (1)
acceptance (1)

4692 πρόσληψις *proslēpsis*
Variant; not used

4693 προσμένω *prosmenō* (7)
with (2)
continue in (1)
continues (1)
remain (1)
stay (1)
stayed (1)

4694 προσορμίζω *prosormizō* (1)
anchored (1)

4695 προσοφείλω *prosopheilō* (1)
owe (1)

4696 προσοχθίζω *prosochthizō* (2)
angry (2)

4697 προσπαίω *prospaiō*
Variant; not used

4698 πρόσπεινος *prospeinos* (1)
hungry (1)

4699 προσπήγνυμι *prospēgnymi* (1)
nailing to cross (1)

4700 προσπίπτω *prospiptō* (8)
fell at feet (3)
beat against (1)
fell (1)
fell at (1)
fell before (1)
fell down before (1)

4701 προσποιέω *prospoieō* (1)
acted as if (1)

4702 προσπορεύομαι *prosporeuomai* (1)
came to (1)

4703 προσρήγνυμι *prosrēgnymi* (2)
struck (2)

4704 προσρήσσω *prosrēssō*
Variant; not used

4705 προστάσσω *prostassō* (7)
commanded (5)
ordered (1)
set (1)

4706 προστάτις *prostatis* (1)
help (1)

4707 προστίθημι *prostithēmi* (19)
added (5)
add (2)
given (2)
sent (2) +4287
added to (1)
and even more (1) +2779+5148
brought (1)
buried (1)
further word spoken (1) +3364
increase (1)
proceeded (1)
went on (1)

4708 προστρέχω *prostrechō* (4)
ran up to (2)
outran (1) +5441
ran (1)

4709 προσφάγιον *prosphagion* (1)
fish (1)

4710 πρόσφατος *prosphatos* (1)
new (1)

4711 προσφάτως *prosphatōs* (1)
recently (1)

4712 προσφέρω *prospherō* (47)
brought (12)
offered (8)
offer (7)
offer sacrifices (3)
bringing (2)
offering (2)
bring (1)
get (1)
lifted (1)
made[s] (1)
offered as a sacrifice (1)
offered up (1)
offering made (1) +4714
offers (1)
presented with (1)
repeated[s] (1)
sacrifice (1)
sacrificed (1)
treating (1)

4713 προσφιλής *prosphilēs* (1)
lovely (1)

4714 προσφορά *prosphora* (9)
offering (3)
sacrifice (3)
offerings (2)
offering made (1) +4712

4715 προσφωνέω *prosphōneō* (7)
calling out (2)
appealed (1)
called forward (1)
called to (1)
said (1)
speak (1)

4716 προσχαίρω *proschairō*
Variant; not used

4717 πρόσχυσις *proschysis* (1)
sprinkling (1)

4718 προσψαύω *prospsauō* (1)
lift (1)

4719 προσωπολημπτέω *prosōpolēmpteō* (1)
show favoritism (1)

4720 προσωπολήμπτης *prosōpolēmptēs* (1)
show favoritism (1) +1639

4721 προσωπολημψία *prosōpolēmpsia* (4)
favoritism (2)
show favoritism (1) +1639
show favoritism (1) +1877

4722 προσωπολημπτέω *prosōpolēpteō*
Variant; not used

4723 προσωπολήπτης *prosōpolēptēs*
Variant; not used

4724 προσωπολημψία *prosōpolēpsia*
Variant; not used

4725 πρόσωπον *prosōpon* (76)
face (24)
faces (7)
ahead (4) +4574
presence (3)
appearance (2)
pay attention who they are (2) +476+1063
sight (2)
you (2) +3836+5148
before (1) +608
before (1) +2848
before (1) +4574
blindfolded (1) +3836+4328
can see it[s] (1) +1711
faced (1) +2848
facedown (1) +2093
flatter (1) +2513
in person (1)

in presence (1) +3552+3836
its[s] (1) +899+3836
judge by external appearance (1) +476+3284
met personally (1) +1877+3836+3972+4922
on ahead (1) +4574
personally (1)
resolutely (1) +3836+5114
seen (1)
show partiality (1) +3284
surface (1) +2848
threw himself (1) +2093+4406
when face to face (1) +2848
untranslated (9)

4726 προτάσσω *protassō*
Variant; not used

4727 προτείνω *proteinō* (1)
stretched out (1)

4728 πρότερος *proteros* (11)
first (3)
earlier (2)
formerly (2)
before (1)
former (1)
once (1)
when (1)

4729 προτίθημι *protithēmi* (3)
planned (1)
presented (1)
purposed (1)

4730 προτρέπω *protrepō* (1)
encouraged (1)

4731 προτρέχω *protrechō* (1)
ran (1)

4732 προϋπάρχω *prouparchō* (2)
before this been (1) +1639
for some time (1)

4733 πρόφασις *prophasis* (6)
show (2)
excuse (1)
false motives (1)
pretending (1)
put on a mask to cover up (1)

4734 προφέρω *propherō* (2)
brings (2)

4735 προφητεία *prophēteia* (19)
prophecy (12)
prophecies (3)
prophesying (2)
gift of prophecy (1)
prophetic message (1)

4736 προφητεύω *prophēteuō* (28)
prophesy (12)
prophesied (7)
prophesies (5)
prophecy (1)
prophesied (1) +3306
prophesying (1)
spoke (1)

4737 προφήτης *prophētēs* (144)
prophets (80)
prophet (60)
prophet's (2)
him[s] (1) +3836
prophet (1) +467

4738 προφητικός *prophētikos* (2)
of prophets (1)
prophetic (1)

4739 προφῆτις *prophētis* (2)
prophetess (2)

4740 προφθάνω *prophthanō* (1)
first (1)

4741 προχειρίζω *procheirizō* (3)
appoint (1)

appointed (1)
chosen (1)

4742 προχειροτονέω *procheirotoneō* (1)
already chosen (1)

4743 Πρόχορος *Prochoros* (1)
Procorus (1)

4744 πρύμνα *prymna* (3)
stern (3)

4745 πρωΐ *prōi* (12)
early (3)
early in the morning (2)
in the morning (2)
at dawn (1)
early in the morning (1) +275
early morning (1)
morning (1)
very early in the morning (1) +2317

4746 πρωΐα *prōia* (2)
early in the morning (1)
early in the morning (1) +1181

4747 πρώϊμος *prōimos*
Variant; not used

4748 πρωϊνός *prōinos* (2)
morning (2)

4749 πρῷρα *prōra* (2)
bow (2)

4750 πρωτεύω *prōteuō* (1)
supremacy (1)

4751 πρωτοκαθεδρία *prōtokathedria* (4)
most important seats (4)

4752 πρωτοκλισία *prōtoklisia* (5)
place of honor (2)
places of honor (2)
places of honor at the table (1)

4753 πρωτόμαρτυς *prōtomartys*
Variant; not used

4754 πρῶτον *prōton* (58)
first (45)
first of all (4)
above all (1) +4047
after (1)
at first (1)
begins (1)
earlier (1)
first of all (1) +4047
in early days (1)
in the first place (1)
until (1) +1569+3590

4755 πρῶτος *prōtos* (97)
first (77)
leading (3)
before (2)
leaders (2)
most important (2)
worst (2)
as of first importance (1) +1877
beginning (1)
best (1)
chief official (1)
former (1)
leaders (1) +1639
old (1)
outer (1)
prominent (1)

4756 πρωτοστάτης *prōtostatēs* (1)
ringleader (1)

4757 πρωτοτόκια *prōtotokia* (1)
inheritance rights as the oldest son (1)

4758 πρωτότοκος *prōtotokos* (8)
firstborn (8)

4759 πρώτως *prōtōs* (1)
first (1)

4760 πταίω *ptaiō* (5)
at fault (1)
fall (1)
stumble (1)
stumble in (1)
stumbles (1)

4761 πτέρνα *pterna* (1)
heel (1)

4762 πτερύγιον *pterygion* (2)
highest point (2)

4763 πτέρυξ *pteryx* (5)
wings (5)

4764 πτηνός *ptēnos* (1)
birds (1)

4765 πτοέω *ptoeō* (2)
frightened (1)
startled (1)

4766 πτόησις *ptoēsis* (1)
give way (1)

4767 Πτολεμαΐς *Ptolemais* (1)
Ptolemais (1)

4768 πτύον *ptyon* (2)
winnowing fork (2)

4769 πτύρω *ptyrō* (1)
frightened (1)

4770 πτύσμα *ptysma* (1)
saliva (1)

4771 πτύσσω *ptyssō* (1)
rolled up (1)

4772 πτύω *ptyō* (3)
spit (3)

4773 πτῶμα *ptōma* (7)
body (3)
bodies (2)
carcass (1)
untranslated (1)

4774 πτῶσις *ptōsis* (2)
falling (1)
with a great crash (1)
         +899+1639+3489+3836

4775 πτωχεία *ptōcheia* (3)
poverty (3)

4776 πτωχεύω *ptōcheuō* (1)
poor (1)

4777 πτωχός *ptōchos* (34)
poor (31)
beggar (2)
miserable (1)

4778 πυγμή *pygmē* (1)
ceremonial (1)

4779 Πύθιος *Pythios*
Variant; not used

4780 πύθων *pythōn* (1)
spirit which predicted the future (1) +4460

4781 πυκνός *pyknos* (3)
frequent (1)
frequently (1)
often (1)

4782 πυκτεύω *pykteuō* (1)
fight (1)

4783 πύλη *pylē* (10)
gate (6)
city gate (2)
city gates (1)
gates (1)

4784 πυλών *pylōn* (18)
gates (8)
gate (3)
door (1)

gateway (1)
it[s] (1) +3836
outer entrance (1) +2598
untranslated (3)

4785 πυνθάνομαι *pynthanomai* (12)
asked (5)
ask (2)
asking (1)
information (1)
inquired (1)
learning (1)
question (1)

4786 πῦρ *pyr* (71)
fire (57)
fiery (5)
burning (4)
flames (2)
all ablaze (1) +2794
spark (1)
untranslated (1)

4787 πυρά *pyra* (2)
fire (2)

4788 πύργος *pyrgos* (4)
tower (2)
watchtower (2)

4789 πυρέσσω *pyressō* (2)
with a fever (2)

4790 πυρετός *pyretos* (6)
fever (6)

4791 πύρινος *pyrinos* (1)
fiery red (1)

4792 πυρόω *pyroō* (6)
burn with passion (1)
fire (1)
flaming (1)
glowing (1)
inwardly burn (1)
refined (1)

4793 πυρράζω *pyrrazō* (2)
red (2)

4794 πυρρός *pyrros* (2)
fiery red (1)
red (1)

4795 Πύρρος *Pyrros* (1)
Pyrrhus (1)

4796 πύρωσις *pyrōsis* (3)
burning (2)
painful (1)

4797 πωλέω *pōleō* (22)
sold (8)
sell (7)
selling (5)
buying (2)

4798 πῶλος *pōlos* (12)
colt (12)

4799 πώποτε *pōpote* (6)
ever (3)
never (1)
never (1) +3590+4024
never (1) +4046

4800 πωρόω *pōroō* (5)
hardened (2)
deadened (1)
hardened (1) +2400
made dull (1)

4801 πώρωσις *pōrōsis* (3)
hardening (2)
stubborn (1)

4802 πῶς *pōs* (102)
how (77)
how is it (8)
how can (5)

what (3)
even (1)
some way (1)
some way (1) +3836
under what circumstances (1)
way (1)
why (1)
untranslated (3)

4803 πώς *pōs* (14)
so that (2)
somehow (2)
that (2) +3590
for (1) +3590
for fear that (1) +3590
hoping (1) +1623
in some way (1)
somehow (1) +1623
that (1)
that (1) +1623
untranslated (1)

4804 ρ *r*
Variant; not used

4805 Ῥαάβ *Rhaab* (2)
Rahab (2)

4806 ῥαββί *rhabbi* (15)
Rabbi (15)

4807 ῥαββονί *rhabboni*
Variant; not used

4808 ῥαββουνί *rhabbouni* (2)
Rabbi (1)
Rabboni (1)

4809 ῥαββωνί *rhabbōni*
Variant; not used

4810 ῥαβδίζω *rhabdizō* (2)
beaten (1)
beaten with rods (1)

4811 ῥάβδος *rhabdos* (12)
staff (5)
scepter (4)
measuring rod (1)
whip (1)
untranslated (1)

4812 ῥαβδοῦχος *rhabdouchos* (2)
officers (2)

4813 ῥαβιθά *rhabitha*
Variant; not used

4814 Ῥαγαύ *Rhagau* (1)
Reu (1)

4815 ῥαδιούργημα *rhadiourgēma* (1)
crime (1)

4816 ῥαδιουργία *rhadiourgia* (1)
trickery (1)

4817 ῥαίνω *rhainō*
Variant; not used

4818 Ῥαιφάν *Rhaiphan* (1)
Rephan (1)

4819 ῥακά *rhaka* (1)
Raca (1)

4820 ῥάκος *rhakos* (2)
cloth (2)

4821 Ῥαμά *Rhama* (1)
Ramah (1)

4822 ῥαντίζω *rhantizō* (4)
sprinkled (2)
sprinkled on (1)
sprinkled to cleanse (1)

4823 ῥαντισμός *rhantismos* (2)
sprinkled (1)
sprinkling (1)

4824 ῥαπίζω *rhapizō* (2)

slapped (1)
strikes (1)

4825 ῥάπισμα *rhapisma* (3)
struck in the face (2) +1443
beat (1)

4826 ῥάσσω *rhassō*
Variant; not used

4827 ῥαφίς *rhaphis* (2)
needle (2)

4828 ῥαχά *rhacha*
Variant; not used

4829 Ῥαχάβ *Rhachab* (1)
Rahab (1)

4830 Ῥαχήλ *Rhachēl* (1)
Rachel (1)

4831 Ῥεβέκκα *Rhebekka* (1)
Rebekah's (1)

4832 ῥέδη *rhedē* (1)
carriages (1)

4833 Ῥεμφάν *Rhemphan*
Variant; not used

4834 Ῥεφάν *Rhephan*
Variant; not used

4835 ῥέω *rheō* (1)
flow (1)

4836 Ῥήγιον *Rhēgion* (1)
Rhegium (1)

4837 ῥῆγμα *rhēgma* (1)
destruction (1)

4838 ῥήγνυμι *rhēgnymi* (7)
burst (3)
break forth (1)
tear to pieces (1)
threw to the ground (1)
throws to the ground (1)

4839 ῥῆμα *rhēma* (68)
word (16)
words (16)
things (6)
say (4)
matter (2)
bring a message (1) +3281
charge (1)
command (1)
itˢ (1) +3836+4047
made statement (1) +3306
meaning (1)
meant (1)
message (1)
nothing (1) +4024+4246
promised (1)
said (1)
saying (1)
sayings (1)
says (1)
thing (1)
thisˢ (1) +3836+4047
what said (1)
untranslated (7)

4840 Ῥησά *Rhēsa* (1)
Rhesa (1)

4841 ῥήσσω *rhēssō*
Variant; not used

4842 ῥήτωρ *rhētōr* (1)
lawyer (1)

4843 ῥητῶς *rhētōs* (1)
clearly (1)

4844 ῥίζα *rhiza* (17)
root (16)
roots (1)

4845 ῥιζόω *rhizoō* (2)

rooted (2)

4846 ῥιπή *rhipē* (1)
twinkling (1)

4847 ῥιπίζω *rhipizō* (1)
tossed (1)

4848 ῥιπτέω *rhipteō*
Variant; not used

4849 ῥίπτω *rhiptō* (8)
dropped (1)
helpless (1)
laid (1)
threw (1)
threw down (1)
threw overboard (1)
throwing off (1)
thrown (1)

4850 Ῥοβοάμ *Rhoboam* (2)
Rehoboam (2)

4851 Ῥόδη *Rhodē* (1)
Rhoda (1)

4852 Ῥόδος *Rhodos* (1)
Rhodes (1)

4853 ῥοιζηδόν *rhoizēdon* (1)
with a roar (1)

4854 Ῥομφά *Rhompha*
Variant; not used

4855 ῥομφαία *rhomphaia* (7)
sword (7)

4856 ῥοπή *rhopē*
Variant; not used

4857 Ῥουβήν *Rhoubēn* (1)
Reuben (1)

4858 Ῥούθ *Rhouth* (1)
Ruth (1)

4859 Ῥοῦφος *Rhouphos* (2)
Rufus (2)

4860 ῥύμη *rhymē* (4)
street (2)
alleys (1)
streets (1)

4861 ῥύομαι *rhyomai* (17)
rescue (5)
rescued (4)
deliver (3)
delivered (3)
deliverer (1)
rescues (1)

4862 ῥυπαίνω *rhypainō* (1)
vile (1)

4863 ῥυπαρεύω *rhypareuō*
Variant; not used

4864 ῥυπαρία *rhyparia* (1)
moral filth (1)

4865 ῥυπαρός *rhyparos* (2)
shabby (1)
vile (1)

4866 ῥύπος *rhypos* (1)
dirt (1)

4867 ῥυπόω *rhypoō*
Variant; not used

4868 ῥύσις *rhysis* (3)
subject to bleeding (2) +135+1877
bleeding (1) +135+3836+3836

4869 ῥυτίς *rhytis* (1)
wrinkle (1)

4870 Ῥωμαϊκός *Rhōmaikos*
Variant; not used

4871 Ῥωμαῖος *Rhōmaios* (12)
Roman citizen (4)

Romans (2)
Roman (1)
Roman citizen (1) +476
Roman citizens (1)
Roman citizens (1) +476
Romans (1) +1639
Rome (1)

4872 Ῥωμαϊστί *Rhōmaisti* (1)
Latin (1)

4873 Ῥώμη *Rhōmē* (8)
Rome (8)

4874 ῥώννυμι *rhōnnymi* (1)
farewell (1)

4875 σ *s*
Variant; not used

4876 σαβαχθάνι *sabachthani* (2)
sabachthani (2)

4877 Σαβαώθ *Sabaōth* (2)
Almighty (2)

4878 σαββατισμός *sabbatismos* (1)
Sabbath-rest (1)

4879 σάββατον *sabbaton* (68)
Sabbath (51)
week (8)
after the Sabbath (1) +4067
day of the week (1)
one Sabbath (1) +1877
one Sabbath (1) +1877+3836
Sabbath (1) +2465+3836
Sabbath day (1)
Sabbath day's walk from (1)
+1584+2400+3847
Sabbath days (1)
untranslated (1)

4880 σαγήνη *sagēnē* (1)
net (1)

4881 Σαδδουκαῖος *Saddoukaios* (14)
Sadducees (14)

4882 Σαδώκ *Sadōk* (2)
Zadok (2)

4883 σαίνω *sainō* (1)
unsettled (1)

4884 σάκκος *sakkos* (4)
sackcloth (4)

4885 Σαλά *Sala* (2)
Salmon (1)
Shelah (1)

4886 Σαλαθιήλ *Salathiēl* (3)
Shealtiel (3)

4887 Σαλαμίς *Salamis* (1)
Salamis (1)

4888 σαλεύω *saleuō* (15)
shaken (8)
swayed (2)
agitating (1)
shake (1)
shaken together (1)
shook (1)
unsettled (1)

4889 Σαλήμ *Salēm* (2)
Salem (2)

4890 Σαλίμ *Salim* (1)
Salim (1)

4891 Σαλμών *Salmōn* (2)
Salmon (2)

4892 Σαλμώνη *Salmōnē* (1)
Salmone (1)

4893 σάλος *salos* (1)
tossing (1)

4894 σάλπιγξ *salpinx* (11)
trumpet (7)

trumpet call (2)
trumpets (2)

4895 σαλπίζω *salpizō* (12)
sounded trumpet (7)
announce with trumpets (1)
sound (1)
sound trumpet (1)
sounded (1)
trumpet sound (1)

4896 σαλπιστής *salpistēs* (1)
trumpeters (1)

4897 Σαλώμη *Salōmē* (2)
Salome (2)

4898 Σαλωμών *Salōmōn*
Variant; not used

4899 Σαμάρεια *Samareia* (11)
Samaria (10)
Samaritan (1)

4900 Σαμαρία *Samaria*
Variant; not used

4901 Σαμαρίτης *Samaritēs* (9)
Samaritan (5)
Samaritans (4)

4902 Σαμαρῖτις *Samaritis* (2)
Samaritan (2)

4903 Σαμοθρᾴκη *Samothrakē* (1)
Samothrace (1)

4904 Σάμος *Samos* (1)
Samos (1)

4905 Σαμουήλ *Samouēl* (3)
Samuel (3)

4906 Σαμφουρειν *Samphourein*
Variant; not used

4907 Σαμψών *Sampsōn* (1)
Samson (1)

4908 σανδάλιον *sandalion* (2)
sandals (1)
sandals (1) +5686

4909 σανίς *sanis* (1)
planks (1)

4910 Σαούλ *Saoul* (7)
Saul (7)

4911 σαπρός *sapros* (8)
bad (7)
unwholesome (1)

4912 Σάπφιρα *Sapphira* (1)
Sapphira (1)

4913 σάπφιρος *sapphiros* (1)
sapphire (1)

4914 σαργάνη *sarganē* (1)
basket (1)

4915 Σάρδεις *Sardeis* (3)
Sardis (3)

4916 σάρδινος *sardinos*
Variant; not used

4917 σάρδιον *sardion* (2)
carnelian (2)

4918 σαρδόνυξ *sardonyx* (1)
sardonyx (1)

4919 Σάρεπτα *Sarepta* (1)
Zarephath (1)

4920 σαρκικός *sarkikos* (7)
worldly (3)
material (2)
of the world (1)
sinful (1)

4921 σάρκινος *sarkinos* (4)
ancestry (1)

of human (1)
unspiritual (1)
worldly (1)

4922 σάρξ *sarx* (147)
flesh (33)
sinful nature (23)
body (20)
one (4) +4246
human (3)
people (3)
sinful man (3)
earthly (2) +2848
in the ordinary way (2) +2848
man (2) +135+2779
nature (2)
physical (2)
the world (2)
as a man (1) +1877
birth (1)
bodies (1)
corrupted flesh (1)
earthly (1)
external (1)
from a worldly point of view (1) +2848
human ancestry (1)
human effort (1)
human nature (1)
human standards (1) +3836
illness (1) +819+3836
in this way[s] (1) +2848
it[s] (1)
its[s] (1) +3836
life (1)
life on earth (1)
man (1)
mankind (1)
men (1)
met personally (1) +1877+3836+3972+4725
natural (1)
natural selves (1)
outwardly (1)
outwardly (1) +1877
perversion (1) +599+2283+3958
sensual (1)
sinful (1)
sinful human nature (1)
this world (1)
unspiritual (1)
world (1)
worldly manner (1)
untranslated (13)

4923 Σαρούχ *Sarouch*
Variant; not used

4924 σαρόω *saroō* (3)
swept clean (2)
sweep (1)

4925 Σάρρα *Sarra* (4)
Sarah (3)
Sarah's (1)

4926 Σαρών *Sarōn* (1)
Sharon (1)

4927 Σατάν *Satan*
Variant; not used

4928 Σατανᾶς *Satanas* (36)
Satan (35)
Satan's (1)

4929 σάτον *saton* (2)
amount (1)
large amount of flour (1) +236+5552

4930 Σαῦλος *Saulos* (17)
Saul (17)

4931 σβέννυμι *sbennymi* (6)
quenched (2)
extinguish (1)
going out (1)
put out (1)

snuff out (1)

4932 σεαυτοῦ *seautou* (96)
yourself (32)
yourselves (27)
you (9)
your own (4)
each other (3)
one another (3)
your (3)
claim (1) +4472
conceited (1) +4123+5861
take care of mat (1) +5143
take revenge (1) +1688
watch out (1) +1063
who do you think you are (1) +4472+5515
your life (1)
your very self (1)
untranslated (7)

4933 σεβάζομαι *sebazomai* (1)
worshiped (1)

4934 σέβασμα *sebasma* (2)
objects of worship (1)
worshiped (1)

4935 σεβαστός *sebastos* (3)
Emperor (1)
Emperor's (1)
imperial (1)

4936 σέβω *sebō* (10)
worship (3)
God-fearing (2)
worshiper of (2)
devout (1)
God-fearing Greeks (1)
worshiped (1)

4937 σειρά *seira*
Variant; not used

4938 σειρός *seiros*
Variant; not used

4939 σεισμός *seismos* (14)
earthquake (9)
earthquakes (3)
quake (1)
storm (1)

4940 σείω *seiō* (5)
shook (2)
shake (1)
shaken (1)
stirred (1)

4941 Σεκοῦνδος *Sekoundos* (1)
Secundus (1)

4942 Σελεύκεια *Seleukeia* (1)
Seleucia (1)

4943 σελήνη *selēnē* (9)
moon (9)

4944 σεληνιάζομαι *selēniazomai* (2)
seizures (2)

4945 Σεμεΐ *Semei*
Variant; not used

4946 Σεμεΐν *Semein* (1)
Semein (1)

4947 σεμίδαλις *semidalis* (1)
fine flour (1)

4948 σεμνός *semnos* (4)
worthy of respect (3)
noble (1)

4949 σεμνότης *semnotēs* (3)
holiness (1)
respect (1)
seriousness (1)

4950 Σέργιος *Sergios* (1)
Sergius (1)

4951 Σερούκ *Serouk*
Variant; not used

4952 Σερούχ *Serouch* (1)
Serug (1)

4953 Σήθ *Sēth* (1)
Seth (1)

4954 Σήμ *Sēm* (1)
Shem (1)

4955 σημαίνω *sēmainō* (6)
indicate (1)
indicating (1)
made known (1)
predicted (1)
show (1)
specifying (1)

4956 σημεῖον *sēmeion* (77)
miraculous signs (23)
sign (18)
signs (15)
miraculous sign (11)
none[s] (3) +4024
miracle (2)
mark (1)
miraculously (1)
signal (1)
the distinguishing mark (1)
wondrous sign (1)

4957 σημειόω *sēmeioō* (1)
take special note (1)

4958 σήμερον *sēmeron* (41)
today (32)
day (2)
very day (2) +2465
days (1)
this day (1)
this day (1) +2465+3836
today (1) +1877+2465+3836
today's (1)

4959 σημικίνθιον *sēmikinthion*
Variant; not used

4960 σήπω *sēpō* (1)
rotted (1)

4961 σηρικός *sērikos*
Variant; not used

4962 σής *sēs* (3)
moth (3)

4963 σητόβρωτος *sētobrōtos* (1)
moths have eaten (1) +1181

4964 σθενόω *sthenoō* (1)
firm (1)

4965 σιαγών *siagōn* (2)
cheek (2)

4966 σιαίνομαι *siainomai*
Variant; not used

4967 σιγάω *sigaō* (10)
quiet (3)
silent (3)
finished (1)
hidden (1)
kept this to themselves (1)
stop (1)

4968 σιγή *sigē* (2)
all silent (1) +4498
silence (1)

4969 σιδήρεος *sidēreos* (5)
iron (4)
of iron (1)

4970 σίδηρος *sidēros* (1)
iron (1)

4971 σιδηροῦς *sidērous*
Variant; not used

4972 Σιδών *Sidōn* (10)
Sidon (10)

4973 Σιδώνιος *Sidōnios* (1)
Sidon (1)

4974 σικάριος *sikarios* (1)
terrorists (1) +467+3836

4975 σίκερα *sikera* (1)
fermented drink (1)

4976 Σίλας *Silas* (12)
Silas (12)

4977 Σιλουανός *Silouanos* (4)
Silas (4)

4978 Σιλωάμ *Silōam* (3)
Siloam (3)

4979 Σιμαίας *Simaias*
Variant; not used

4980 σιμικίνθιον *simikinthion* (1)
aprons (1)

4981 Σίμων *Simōn* (75)
Simon (69)
Simon's (4)
belonging to Simon (1) +1639
his[s] (1)

4982 Σινά *Sina* (4)
Sinai (4)

4983 σίναπι *sinapi* (5)
mustard (5)

4984 σινδών *sindōn* (6)
linen cloth (3)
garment (1)
linen (1)
linen garment (1)

4985 σινιάζω *siniazō* (1)
sift (1)

4986 σιρικός *sirikos* (1)
silk (1)

4987 σιρός *siros* (1)
dungeons (1)

4988 σιτευτός *siteutos* (3)
fattened (3)

4989 σιτίον *sition* (1)
grain (1)

4990 σιτιστός *sitistos* (1)
fattened cattle (1)

4991 σιτομέτριον *sitometrion* (1)
food allowance (1)

4992 σῖτος *sitos* (14)
wheat (11)
grain (2)
kernel (1)

4993 Σιχάρ *Sichar*
Variant; not used

4994 Σιών *Siōn* (7)
Zion (7)

4995 σιωπάω *siōpaō* (10)
quiet (5)
silent (5)

4996 σιωπῇ *siōpē*
Variant; not used

4997 σκανδαλίζω *skandalizō* (29)
causes to sin (8)
fall away (7)
offend (2)
took offense (2)
cause to fall (1)
cause to sin (1)
causes fall into sin (1)
causes sin (1)
falls away (1)

go astray (1)
led into sin (1)
offended (1)
turn away (1)
untranslated (1)

4998 σκάνδαλον *skandalon* (15)
stumbling block (3)
makes fall (2)
cause people to sin (1)
causes sin (1)
entice (1) +965+1967
obstacle (1)
obstacles (1)
offense (1)
stumble (1)
such things[s] (1) +3836
they[s] (1) +3836
things that cause to sin (1)

4999 σκάπτω *skaptō* (3)
dig (2)
dug (1)

5000 Σκαριώθ *Skariōth*
Variant; not used

5001 Σκαριώτης *Skariōtēs*
Variant; not used

5002 σκάφη *skaphē* (3)
lifeboat (3)

5003 σκέλος *skelos* (3)
legs (3)

5004 σκέπασμα *skepasma* (1)
clothing (1)

5005 Σκευᾶς *Skeuas* (1)
Sceva (1)

5006 σκευή *skeuē* (1)
tackle (1)

5007 σκεῦος *skeuos* (23)
instrument (2)
jar (2)
objects (2)
possessions (2)
articles (1)
body (1)
goods (1)
jars (1)
kind (1)
merchandise (1)
partner (1)
pottery (1)
pottery (1) +3039
sea anchor (1)
sheet (1)
untranslated (4)

5008 σκηνή *skēnē* (21)
tabernacle (9)
shelters (3)
room (2)
tent (2)
dwelling (1)
dwelling place (1)
dwellings (1)
shrine (1)
tents (1)

5009 σκηνοπηγία *skēnopēgia* (1)
tabernacles (1)

5010 σκηνοποιός *skēnopoios* (1)
tentmaker (1)

5011 σκῆνος *skēnos* (1)
tent (1)

5012 σκηνόω *skēnoō* (5)
live (2)
dwell (1)
made his dwelling (1)
spread tent (1)

5013 σκήνωμα *skēnōma* (3)
dwelling place (1)
it[s] (1) +1609+3836
tent (1)

5014 σκιά *skia* (7)
shadow (6)
shade (1)

5015 σκιρτάω *skirtaō* (3)
leaped (2)
leap for joy (1)

5016 σκληροκαρδία *sklērokardia* (3)
hearts hard (2)
stubborn refusal (1)

5017 σκληρός *sklēros* (5)
hard (3)
harsh (1)
strong (1)

5018 σκληρότης *sklērotēs* (1)
stubbornness (1)

5019 σκληροτράχηλος *sklērotrachēlos* (1)
stiff-necked (1)

5020 σκληρύνω *sklērynō* (6)
harden (3)
hardened (1)
hardens (1)
obstinate (1)

5021 σκολιός *skolios* (4)
crooked (2)
corrupt (1)
harsh (1)

5022 σκόλοψ *skolops* (1)
thorn (1)

5023 σκοπέω *skopeō* (6)
fix eyes on (1)
look to (1)
see to it (1)
take note of (1)
watch (1)
watch out for (1)

5024 σκοπός *skopos* (1)
goal (1)

5025 σκορπίζω *skorpizō* (5)
scatters (3)
scattered (1)
scattered abroad (1)

5026 σκορπίος *skorpios* (5)
scorpions (3)
scorpion (2)

5027 σκοτεινός *skoteinos* (3)
full of darkness (2)
dark (1)

5028 σκοτία *skotia* (16)
darkness (11)
dark (5)

5029 σκοτίζομαι *skotizomai* (6)
darkened (5)
turned dark (1)

5030 σκότος *skotos* (31)
darkness (29)
dark (2)

5031 σκοτόω *skotoō* (2)
darkened (1)
darkness (1)

5032 σκύβαλον *skybalon* (1)
rubbish (1)

5033 Σκύθης *Skythēs* (1)
Scythian (1)

5034 σκυθρωπός *skythrōpos* (2)
downcast (1)
look somber (1) +1181

5035 σκύλλω *skyllō* (4)
bother (2)

harassed (1)
trouble (1)

5036 σκῦλον *skylon* (1)
spoils (1)

5037 σκωληκόβρωτος *skōlēkobrōtos* (1)
eaten by worms (1)

5038 σκώληξ *skōlēx* (1)
worm (1)

5039 σμαράγδινος *smaragdinos* (1)
emerald (1)

5040 σμάραγδος *smaragdos* (1)
emerald (1)

5041 σμῆγμα *smēgma*
Variant; not used

5042 σμίγμα *smigma*
Variant; not used

5043 σμύρνα1 *smyrna1* (2)
myrrh (2)

5044 Σμύρνα2 *Smyrna2* (2)
Smyrna (2)

5045 Σμυρναῖος *Smyrnaios*
Variant; not used

5046 σμυρνίζω *smyrnizō* (1)
mixed with myrrh (1)

5047 Σόδομα *Sodoma* (9)
Sodom (7)
Sodom (2) +1178

5048 Σολομών *Solomōn* (12)
Solomon (7)
Solomon's (5)

5049 σορός *soros* (1)
coffin (1)

5050 σός *sos* (26)
your (12)
yours (5)
belongs to you (1)
belongs to you (1) +2400
you (1)
you have (1) +3836
your family (1) +3836
your own (1)
yours (1) +3836
untranslated (2)

5051 σουδάριον *soudarion* (4)
burial cloth (1)
cloth (1)
handkerchiefs (1)
piece of cloth (1)

5052 Σουσάννα *Sousanna* (1)
Susanna (1)

5053 σοφία *sophia* (51)
wisdom (48)
wise (2)
superior wisdom (1) +5667

5054 σοφίζω *sophizō* (2)
cleverly invented (1)
make wise (1)

5055 σοφός *sophos* (20)
wise (18)
expert (1)
wiser (1)

5056 Σπανία *Spania* (2)
Spain (2)

5057 σπαράσσω *sparassō* (3)
convulsed (1)
shook violently (1)
throws into convulsions (1)

5058 σπαργανόω *sparganoō* (2)
wrapped in cloths (2)

5059 σπαταλάω *spatalaō* (2)
lives for pleasure (1)
self-indulgence (1)

5060 σπάω *spaō* (2)
drew (2)

5061 σπεῖρα *speira* (7)
company of soldiers (2)
detachment of soldiers (2)
regiment (2)
Roman troops (1)

5062 σπείρω *speirō* (52)
sow (9)
sown (9)
sows (8)
farmer (4)
seed sown (4)
received seed that fell (3)
sower (3)
plant (2)
planted (2)
scattering the seed (2)
sow seed (2)
sowed (2)
scattering seed (1)
sown seed (1)

5063 σπεκουλάτωρ *spekoulatōr* (1)
executioner (1)

5064 σπένδω *spendō* (2)
poured out like a drink offering (2)

5065 σπέρμα *sperma* (43)
seed (11)
descendants (10)
offspring (8)
children (3)
descendant (2)
have children (2) +1985
seeds (2)
become a father (1) +2856+3284
child (1)
descended from (1) +1666
family (1)
have children (1) +482

5066 σπερμολόγος *spermologos* (1)
babbler (1)

5067 σπεύδω *speudō* (6)
at once (1)
hurried off (1) +2262
immediately (1)
in a hurry (1)
quick (1)
speed (1)

5068 σπήλαιον *spēlaion* (6)
den (3)
caves (2)
cave (1)

5069 σπιλάς *spilas* (1)
blemishes (1)

5070 σπίλος *spilos* (2)
blots (1)
stain (1)

5071 σπιλόω *spiloō* (2)
corrupts (1)
stained (1)

5072 σπλαγχνίζομαι *splanchnizomai* (12)
had compassion (4)
have compassion (2)
took pity (2)
filled with compassion (1)
filled with compassion for (1)
heart went out (1)
take pity (1)

5073 σπλάγχνον *splanchnon* (11)
affection (3)
dearly (1)

has no pity (1) +3091+3836
heart (1)
hearts (1)
intestines (1)
tender mercy (1) +1799
tenderness (1)
very heart (1)

5074 σπόγγος *spongos* (3)
sponge (3)

5075 σποδός *spodos* (3)
ashes (3)

5076 σπορά *spora* (1)
seed (1)

5077 σπόριμος *sporimos* (3)
grainfields (3)

5078 σπόρος *sporos* (6)
seed (5)
seed (1) +3836

5079 σπουδάζω *spoudazo* (11)
do best (4)
make every effort (4)
eager (2)
made effort (1)

5080 σπουδαῖος *spoudaios* (3)
enthusiasm (1)
even more so[s] (1) +4498
zealous (1)

5081 σπουδαίως *spoudaiōs* (4)
all the more eager (1)
earnestly (1)
everything you can (1)
hard (1)

5082 σπουδή *spoudē* (12)
earnestness (3)
concern (1)
devoted (1)
diligence (1)
diligently (1) +1877
eager (1)
effort (1)
hurried (1) +1656+3552
hurried (1) +3552+4513
zeal (1)

5083 σπυρίς *spyris* (5)
basketfuls (2)
basket (1)
basketfuls (1) +4441
basketfuls (1) +4445

5084 στάδιον *stadion* (7)
stadia (2)
distance (1)
race (1)
seven miles (1) +2008
three or three and a half miles (1)
                 +1633+2445+4297+5558
two miles (1) +1278

5085 στάμνος *stamnos* (1)
jar (1)

5086 στασιαστής *stasiastēs* (1)
insurrectionists (1)

5087 στάσις *stasis* (9)
dispute (3)
insurrection (2)
rioting (1)
riots (1)
standing (1)
uprising (1)

5088 στατήρ *statēr* (1)
four-drachma coin (1)

5089 σταυρός *stauros* (27)
cross (26)
crosses (1)

5090 σταυρόω *stauroō* (46)
crucified (31)

crucify (15)

5091 σταφυλή *staphylē* (3)
grapes (3)

5092 στάχυς1 *stachys1* (5)
heads of grain (3)
head (2)

5093 Στάχυς2 *Stachys2* (1)
Stachys (1)

5094 στέγη *stegē* (3)
roof (3)

5095 στέγω *stegō* (4)
stand (2)
protects (1)
put up with (1)

5096 στεῖρα *steira* (5)
barren (3)
barren woman (1)
barren women (1)

5097 στέλλω *stellō* (2)
avoid (1)
keep away (1)

5098 στέμμα *stemma* (1)
wreaths (1)

5099 στεναγμός *stenagmos* (2)
groaning (1)
groans (1)

5100 στενάζω *stenazō* (6)
groan (3)
burden (1)
grumble (1)
with a deep sigh (1)

5101 στενός *stenos* (3)
narrow (2)
small (1)

5102 στενοχωρέω *stenochōreō* (3)
withholding (2)
crushed (1)

5103 στενοχωρία *stenochōria* (4)
difficulties (1)
distress (1)
distresses (1)
hardship (1)

5104 στερεός *stereos* (4)
solid (3)
standing firm (1)

5105 στερεόω *stereoō* (3)
strong (2)
strengthened (1)

5106 στερέωμα *stereōma* (1)
firm (1)

5107 Στεφανᾶς *Stephanas* (3)
Stephanas (3)

5108 Στέφανος1 *Stephanos1* (7)
Stephen (6)
him[s] (1) +3836

5109 στέφανος2 *stephanos2* (18)
crown (15)
crowns (3)

5110 στεφανόω *stephanoō* (3)
crowned (2)
receive the victor's crown (1)

5111 στῆθος *stēthos* (5)
breast (1)
breasts (1)
chests (1)
untranslated (1)

5112 στήκω *stēkō*
Variant; not used

5113 στηριγμός *stērigmos* (1)
secure position (1)

5114 στηρίζω *stērizō* (13)
strengthen (6)
make strong (2)
establish (1)
firmly established (1)
fixed (1)
resolutely (1) +3836+4725
stand firm (1) +2840+3836

5115 στιβάς *stibas* (1)
branches (1)

5116 στίγμα *stigma* (1)
marks (1)

5117 στιγμή *stigmē* (1)
instant (1) +5989

5118 στίλβω *stilbō* (1)
dazzling (1)

5119 στοά *stoa* (4)
Colonnade (3)
covered colonnades (1)

5120 στοιβάς *stoibas*
Variant; not used

5121 Στοϊκός *Stoikos* (1)
stoic (1)

5122 στοιχεῖον *stoicheion* (7)
basic principles (3)
elements (2)
elementary truths (1) +794+3836
principles (1)

5123 στοιχέω *stoicheō* (5)
follow (1)
keep in step (1)
live up (1)
living (1)
walk (1)

5124 στολή *stolē* (9)
robes (4)
robe (3)
flowing robes (2)

5125 στόμα *stoma* (78)
mouth (42)
mouths (9)
lips (6)
face (4)
testimony (2)
words (2)
began to speak (1) +487+3306+3836
edge sword (1) +3479
might say (1) +1666+3836
speak (1) +487+3836
spoken freely (1) +487+3836
sword (1) +3479
that⁵ (1)
untranslated (6)

5126 στόμαχος *stomachos* (1)
stomach (1)

5127 στρατεία *strateia* (2)
fight (1)
weapons fight with (1) +3836+3960

5128 στράτευμα *strateuma* (8)
troops (3)
armies (2)
army (2)
soldiers (1)

5129 στρατεύομαι *strateuomai* (7)
battle (1)
fight (1)
serves as a soldier (1)
serving as a soldier (1)
soldiers (1)
wage war (1)
war (1)

5130 στρατηγός *stratēgos* (10)
magistrates (5)

captain (3)
officers of guard (1)
officers of the temple guard (1)

5131 στρατιά *stratia* (2)
bodies (1)
host (1)

5132 στρατιώτης *stratiōtēs* (26)
soldiers (22)
soldier (3)
them⁵ (1)

5133 στρατολογέω *stratologeō* (1)
commanding officer (1)

5134 στρατοπεδάρχης *stratopedarchēs*
Variant; not used

5135 στρατοπέδαρχος *stratopedarchos*
Variant; not used

5136 στρατόπεδον *stratopedon* (1)
armies (1)

5137 στρεβλόω *streblóō* (1)
distort (1)

5138 στρέφω *strephō* (21)
turned (7)
turn (5)
turning (2)
change (1)
returned (1)
turned around (1) +1650+3836+3958
turned away (1)
turned back (1)
turned toward (1)
turning around (1)

5139 στρηνιάω *strēniaō* (2)
luxury (1)
shared luxury (1)

5140 στρῆνος *strēnos* (1)
luxuries (1)

5141 στρουθίον *strouthion* (4)
sparrows (4)

5142 στρώννυμι *strōnnymi*
Variant; not used

5143 στρωννύω *strōnnyō* (6)
spread (3)
furnished (2)
take care of mat (1) +4932

5144 στυγητός *stygētos* (1)
hated (1)

5145 στυγνάζω *stygnazō* (2)
face fell (1)
overcast (1)

5146 στῦλος *stylos* (4)
pillar (2)
pillars (2)

5147 Στωϊκός *Stōikos*
Variant; not used

5148 σύ *sy* (2898)
you (1991)
your (700)
yours (15)
yourselves (11)
your own (8)
please (2) +1289
please (2) +2263
you (2) +3836+4725
you (2) +6034
you yourselves (2)
your own (2) +2848
and even more (1) +2779+4707
both of you (1) +899+2779
does⁵ (1) +1877+3531
home (1) +1650+3836+3875
home (1) +3875
it depends on you (1) +1666+3836

listen carefully (1)
+1650+3836+4044+5148+5502
of you (1) +1639+1877+3836
that's your responsibility (1) +3972
the two of you (1) +899+2779
them⁵ (1) +3517+3836
us (1)
you (1) +2093
you (1) +3836+3950
you (1) +3836+4364
you can see (1) +595
you have (1) +1877
you have (1) +4123
you yourself (1)
you're (1)
your (1) +1869
your (1) +1877
your (1) +2848
your responsibility (1) +3972
yourself (1)
yourselves (1) +6034
untranslated (135)

5149 συγγένεια *syngeneia* (3)
family (1)
people (1)
relatives (1)

5150 συγγενής *syngenēs* (11)
relatives (8)
relative (2)
race (1)

5151 συγγενίς *syngenis* (1)
relative (1)

5152 συγγνώμη *syngnōmē* (1)
concession (1)

5153 συγκάθημαι *synkathēmai* (2)
sat (1) +1639
sitting with (1)

5154 συγκαθίζω *synkathizō* (2)
sat down together (1)
seated with (1)

5155 συγκακοπαθέω *synkakopatheō* (2)
endure with (1)
join in suffering (1)

5156 συγκακουχέομαι *synkakoucheomai* (1)
mistreated along with (1)

5157 συγκαλέω *synkaleō* (8)
called together (6)
calls together (2)

5158 συγκαλύπτω *synkalyptō* (1)
concealed (1)

5159 συγκάμπτω *synkamptō* (1)
bent (1)

5160 συγκαταβαίνω *synkatabainō* (1)
come with (1)

5161 συγκατάθεσις *synkatathesis* (1)
agreement (1)

5162 συγκατανεύω *synkataneuō*
Variant; not used

5163 συγκατατίθημι *synkatatithēmi* (1)
consented (1)

5164 συγκαταψηφίζομαι
synkatapsēphizomai (1)
added (1)

5165 σύγκειμαι *synkeimai*
Variant; not used

5166 συγκεράννυμι *synkerannymi* (2)
combine with (1)
combined (1)

5167 συγκινέω *synkineō* (1)
stirred up (1)

5168 συγκλείω *synkleiō* (4)
bound over (1)

caught (1)
locked up (1)
prisoner (1)

5169 συγκληρονόμος *synklēronomos* (4)
heirs with (2)
co-heirs with (1)
heirs together with (1)

5170 συγκοινωνέω *synkoinōneō* (3)
share (2)
to do with (1)

5171 συγκοινωνός *synkoinōnos* (4)
share (2) +1181
companion (1)
share with (1) +1639

5172 συγκομίζω *synkomizō* (1)
buried (1)

5173 συγκρίνω *synkrinō* (3)
compare (2)
expressing (1)

5174 συγκύπτω *synkyptō* (1)
bent over (1)

5175 συγκυρία *synkyria* (1)
happened (1) +2848

5176 συγχαίρω *synchairō* (7)
rejoice with (4)
rejoices with (2)
shared joy (1)

5177 συγχέω *syncheō* (5)
baffled (1)
bewilderment (1)
confusion (1)
in an uproar (1)
stirred up (1)

5178 συγχράομαι *synchraomai* (1)
associate with (1)

5179 συγχύνω *synchynō*
Variant; not used

5180 σύγχυσις *synchysis* (1)
uproar (1) +4398

5181 συγχωρέω *synchōreō*
Variant; not used

5182 συζάω *syzaō* (3)
live with (2)
live (1)

5183 συζεύγνυμι *syzeugnymi* (2)
joined together (2)

5184 συζητέω *syzēteō* (10)
question (2)
argue with (1)
arguing (1)
arguing about (1)
asked (1)
debated (1)
debating (1)
discussed (1)
discussing (1)

5185 συζήτησις *syzētēsis*
Variant; not used

5186 συζητητής *syzētētēs* (1)
philosopher (1)

5187 σύζυγος *syzygos* (1)
yokefellow (1)

5188 συζωοποιέω *syzōopoieō* (2)
made alive with (2)

5189 συκάμινος *sykaminos* (1)
mulberry tree (1)

5190 συκῆ *sykē* (16)
fig tree (14)
figs (1)
tree (1)

5191 συκομορέα *sykomorea* (1)
sycamore-fig tree (1)

5192 σῦκον *sykon* (4)
figs (4)

5193 συκοφαντέω *sykophanteō* (2)
accuse falsely (1)
cheated out of (1)

5194 συλαγωγέω *sylagōgeō* (1)
takes captive (1) +1639

5195 συλάω *sylaō* (1)
robbed (1)

5196 συλλαλέω *syllaleō* (6)
talking with (3)
conferred with (1)
discussed with (1)
said (1)

5197 συλλαμβάνω *syllambanō* (16)
arrested (2)
capture (2)
help (2)
seized (2)
conceived (1)
conceived (1) +1877+3120+3836
have (1)
pregnant (1)
seize (1)
seizing (1)
taken (1)
with child (1) +1143+1877

5198 συλλέγω *syllegō* (8)
pick (2)
collect (1)
collected (1)
pull up (1)
pulled up (1)
pulling (1)
weed (1)

5199 συλλογίζομαι *syllogizomai* (1)
discussed (1)

5200 συλλυπέω *syllypeō* (1)
deeply distressed (1)

5201 συμβαίνω *symbainō* (8)
happened (3)
had to be (1)
happen (1)
happening (1)
of them (1) +899
untranslated (1)

5202 συμβάλλω *symballō* (6)
a help (1)
conferred (1)
dispute with (1)
go war (1) +4483
met (1)
pondered (1)

5203 συμβασιλεύω *symbasileuō* (2)
kings with (1)
reign with (1)

5204 συμβιβάζω *symbibazō* (7)
held together (2)
concluding (1)
instruct (1)
instructions to (1)
proving (1)
united (1)

5205 συμβουλεύω *symbouleuō* (4)
advised (1)
conspired (1)
counsel (1)
plotted (1)

5206 συμβούλιον *symboulion* (8)
council (1)
decided to (1) +3284
decision (1)

devised a plan (1) +3284
laid plans (1) +3284
plot (1) +1443
plotted (1) +3284
to the decision (1) +3284

5207 σύμβουλος *symboulos* (1)
counselor (1)

5208 Συμεών *Symeōn* (7)
Simeon (5)
Simon (2)

5209 συμμαθητής *symmathētēs* (1)
rest of the disciples (1)

5210 συμμαρτυρέω *symmartyreō* (3)
bearing witness (1)
confirms (1)
testifies with (1)

5211 συμμερίζομαι *symmerizomai* (1)
share (1)

5212 συμμέτοχος *symmetochos* (2)
partners with (1)
sharers together in (1)

5213 συμμιμητής *symmimētēs* (1)
join with others following example (1)
+1181

5214 συμμορφίζω *symmorphizō* (1)
becoming like (1)

5215 σύμμορφος *symmorphos* (2)
conformed (1)
like (1)

5216 συμμορφόω *symmorphoō*
Variant; not used

5217 συμπαθέω *sympatheō* (2)
sympathize with (1)
sympathized with (1)

5218 συμπαθής *sympathēs* (1)
sympathetic (1)

5219 συμπαραγίνομαι *symparaginomai* (1)
gathered (1)

5220 συμπαρακαλέω *symparakaleō* (1)
mutually encouraged (1)

5221 συμπαραλαμβάνω *symparalambanō* (4)
take (1)
take with (1)
taking with (1)
took along (1)

5222 συμπαραμένω *symparamenō*
Variant; not used

5223 συμπάρειμι *sympareimi* (1)
present with (1)

5224 συμπάσχω *sympaschō* (2)
share in sufferings (1)
suffers with (1)

5225 συμπέμπω *sympempō* (2)
sending (1)
sending with (1)

5226 συμπεριέχω *symperiechō*
Variant; not used

5227 συμπεριλαμβάνω *symperilambanō* (1)
put arms around (1)

5228 συμπίνω *sympinō* (1)
drank (1)

5229 συμπίπτω *sympiptō* (1)
collapsed (1)

5230 συμπληρόω *symplēroō* (3)
approached (1)
came (1)
swamped (1)

5231 συμπνίγω *sympnigō* (5)
choke (2)

choked (2)
crushed (1)

5232 συμπολίτης *sympolitēs* (1)
fellow citizens with (1)

5233 συμπορεύομαι *symporeuomai* (4)
came (1)
traveling with (1)
walked along with (1)
went along with (1)

5234 συμποσία *symposia*
Variant; not used

5235 συμπόσιον *symposion* (1)
groups (1) +5235

5236 συμπρεσβύτερος *sympresbyteros* (1)
fellow elder (1)

5237 συμφέρω *sympherō* (15)
better (5)
good (3)
beneficial (1)
best (1)
brought together (1)
for good (1)
gained (1)
helpful (1)
is beneficial (1)

5238 σύμφημι *symphēmi* (1)
agree (1)

5239 σύμφορος *symphoros* (2)
good (2)

5240 συμφορτίζω *symphortizō*
Variant; not used

5241 συμφυλέτης *symphyletēs* (1)
countrymen (1)

5242 σύμφυτος *symphytos* (1)
united (1)

5243 συμφύω *symphyō* (1)
grew up with (1)

5244 συμφωνέω *symphōneō* (6)
agree (3)
agreed (1)
in agreement with (1)
match (1)

5245 συμφώνησις *symphōnēsis* (1)
harmony (1)

5246 συμφωνία *symphōnia* (1)
music (1)

5247 σύμφωνος *symphōnos* (1)
mutual consent (1)

5248 συμψηφίζω *sympsēphizō* (1)
calculated (1)

5249 σύμψυχος *sympsychos* (1)
spirit (1)

5250 σύν *syn* (128)
with (75)
and (11)
together with (7)
along with (6)
associates (2) +3836
companions (2) +1639+3836
companions (2) +3836
accompanied (1) +5302
accompanied by (1)
accompany (1) +4513
along (1) +899
and what is more (1)
    +247+1145+2779+4047+4246
as (1)
attendant of (1)
companions (1) +4513
his fellow (1) +899+3836
join in (1)
on (1)

our companions (1) +1609+3836
sided with (1) +1639
through (1)
when are tempted (1) +3836+4280
untranslated (8)

5251 συνάγω *synagō* (59)
gathered (12)
gather (10)
gathered together (5)
met (5)
assembled (3)
gathering (2)
got together (2)
invite in (2)
meeting (2)
met together (2)
store (2)
bring together (1)
called meeting (1)
called together (1)
came together (1)
caught (1)
come together (1) +1639
gather together (1)
harvests (1)
invited in (1)
picked up (1)
store away (1)
went (1)

5252 συναγωγή *synagōgē* (57)
synagogue (30)
synagogues (23)
congregation (1)
from one synagogue to another (1)
            +2848+4246
meeting (1)
untranslated (1)

5253 συναγωνίζομαι *synagōnizomai* (1)
join in struggle (1)

5254 συναθλέω *synathleō* (2)
contended at side (1)
contending as (1)

5255 συναθροίζω *synathroizō* (2)
called together (1)
gathered (1)

5256 συναίρω *synairō* (3)
settle (1)
settled accounts (1) +3364
settlement (1)

5257 συναιχμάλωτος *synaichmalōtos* (3)
fellow prisoner (2)
in prison with (1)

5258 συνακολουθέω *synakoloutheō* (3)
follow (1)
followed (1)
following (1)

5259 συναλίζω *synalizō* (1)
eating (1)

5260 συναλίσκομαι *synaliskomai*
Variant; not used

5261 συναλλάσσω *synallassō* (1)
reconcile (1) +1645+1650

5262 συναναβαίνω *synanabainō* (2)
come up with (1)
traveled with (1)

5263 συνανάκειμαι *synanakeimai* (7)
dinner guests (2)
at the table with (1)
ate with (1)
eating with (1)
fellow guests (1)
guests (1)

5264 συναναμείγνυμι *synanameignymi* (3)
associate with (3)

5265 συναναπαύομαι *synanapauomai* (1)
together refreshed (1)

5266 συναναστρέφομαι *synanastrephomai*
Variant; not used

5267 συναντάω *synantaō* (6)
met (4)
happen (1)
meet (1)

5268 συνάντησις *synantēsis*
Variant; not used

5269 συναντιλαμβάνομαι *synantilambanomai*
(2)
help (1)
helps (1)

5270 συναπάγω *synapagō* (3)
carried away (1)
led astray (1)
willing to associate (1)

5271 συναποθνήσκω *synapothnēskō* (3)
die with (2)
died with (1)

5272 συναπόλλυμι *synapollymi* (1)
killed with (1)

5273 συναποστέλλω *synapostellō* (1)
sent with (1)

5274 συναρμολογέω *synarmologeō* (2)
joined (1)
joined together (1)

5275 συναρπάζω *synarpazō* (4)
seized (3)
caught (1)

5276 συναυλίζομαι *synaulizomai*
Variant; not used

5277 συναυξάνω *synauxanō* (1)
grow together (1)

5278 σύνδεσμος *syndesmos* (4)
binds together (1) +1639
bond (1)
captive (1)
sinews (1)

5279 συνδέω *syndeō* (1)
fellow prisoners (1)

5280 συνδοξάζω *syndoxazō* (1)
share in glory (1)

5281 σύνδουλος *syndoulos* (10)
fellow servant (4)
fellow servants (3)
fellow servant with with (2)
servants (1)

5282 συνδρομή *syndromē* (1)
running (1)

5283 συνεγείρω *synegeirō* (3)
raised (1)
raised up with (1)
raised with (1)

5284 συνέδριον *synedrion* (22)
Sanhedrin (19)
councils (1)
local councils (1)
them[s] (1) +899+3836

5285 συνέδριος *synedrios*
Variant; not used

5286 σύνεδρος *synedros*
Variant; not used

5287 συνείδησις *syneidēsis* (30)
conscience (23)
consciences (4)
conscious (1)
felt guilty (1)
guilty conscience (1) +4505

5288 συνείδω *syneidō*
Variant; not used

5289 σύνειμι1 *syneimi1* (2)
companions (1)
were with (1)

5290 σύνειμι2 *syneimi2* (1)
gathering (1)

5291 συνεισέρχομαι *syneiserchomai* (2)
entered (1)
went with into (1)

5292 συνέκδημος *synekdēmos* (2)
accompany (1)
traveling companions (1)

5293 συνεκλεκτός *syneklektos* (1)
chosen together with (1)

5294 συνεκπορεύομαι *synekporeuomai*
Variant; not used

5295 συνελαύνω *synelaunō*
Variant; not used

5296 συνεπιμαρτυρέω *synepimartyreō* (1)
also testified (1)

5297 συνεπίσκοπος *synepiskopos*
Variant; not used

5298 συνεπιτίθημι *synepitithēmi* (1)
joined in the accusation (1)

5299 συνέπομαι *synepomai* (1)
accompanied by (1)

5300 συνεργέω *synergeō* (5)
fellow workers (1)
joins in the work (1)
worked with (1)
working together (1)
works (1)

5301 συνεργός *synergos* (13)
fellow worker (6)
fellow workers (5)
work together (1) +1181
work with (1) +1639

5302 συνέρχομαι *synerchomai* (30)
come together (5)
came together (3)
gathered (3)
come with (2)
accompanied (1) +5250
assemble (1)
assembled (1)
came (1)
came with (1)
come along with (1)
comes together (1) +899+2093+3836
continued with (1)
gathering (1)
going with (1)
meet together (1)
meetings (1)
met together (1)
there (1)
went along (1)
went with (1)
with (1)

5303 συνεσθίω *synesthiō* (5)
ate with (2)
eat (1)
eats with (1)
with eat (1)

5304 σύνεσις *synesis* (7)
understanding (4)
insight (2)
intelligence (1)

5305 συνετός *synetos* (4)
intelligent (2)
learned (2)

5306 συνευδοκέω *syneudokeō* (6)
approve of (2)
giving approval (2)
willing (2)

5307 συνευωχέομαι *syneuōcheomai* (2)
eating with (1)
feast with (1)

5308 συνεφίστημι *synephistēmi* (1)
joined in the attack (1)

5309 συνέχω *synechō* (12)
suffering (2)
compels (1)
covered (1)
crowding against (1)
devoted (1)
distressed (1)
guarding (1)
hem in (1)
overcome (1)
suffering from (1)
torn (1)

5310 συνήδομαι *synēdomai* (1)
delight (1)

5311 συνήθεια *synētheia* (3)
accustomed to (1)
custom (1)
practice (1)

5312 συνηλικιώτης *synēlikiōtēs* (1)
of own age (1)

5313 συνθάπτω *synthaptō* (2)
buried with (2)

5314 συνθλάω *synthlaō* (2)
broken to pieces (2)

5315 συνθλίβω *synthlibō* (2)
crowding against (1)
pressed around (1)

5316 συνθρύπτω *synthryptō* (1)
breaking (1)

5317 συνίημι *syniēmi* (26)
understand (14)
understood (4)
understanding (3)
understands (2)
did[s] (1)
realize (1)
wise (1)

5318 συνιστάω *synistaō*
Variant; not used

5319 συνίστημι *synistēmi* (17)
commend (6)
commends (2)
brings out more clearly (1)
commended (1)
demonstrates (1)
formed (1)
hold together (1)
prove that (1)
proved (1)
short (1)
standing with (1)

5320 συνίω *syniō*
Variant; not used

5321 συνοδεύω *synodeuō* (1)
traveling with (1)

5322 συνοδία *synodia* (1)
company (1)

5323 σύνοιδα *synoida* (2)
conscience is clear (1) +4029
full knowledge (1)

5324 συνοικέω *synoikeō* (1)
live with (1)

5325 συνοικοδομέω *synoikodomeō* (1)

built together (1)

5326 συνομιλέω *synomileō* (1)
talking with (1)

5327 συνομορέω *synomoreō* (1)
next door (1)

5328 συνοράω *synoraō* (2)
dawned on (1)
found out about (1)

5329 συνορία *synoria*
Variant; not used

5330 συνοχή *synochē* (2)
anguish (2)

5331 συνταράσσω *syntarassō*
Variant; not used

5332 συντάσσω *syntassō* (3)
commanded (1)
directed (1)
instructed (1)

5333 συντέλεια *synteleia* (6)
end (5)
very end (1)

5334 συντελέω *synteleō* (6)
end (1)
finality (1)
finished (1)
fulfilled (1)
make (1)
over (1)

5335 συντέμνω *syntemnō* (1)
speed (1)

5336 συντεχνίτης *syntechnitēs*
Variant; not used

5337 συντηρέω *syntēreō* (3)
preserved (1)
protected (1)
treasured up (1)

5338 συντίθημι *syntithēmi* (3)
agreed (2)
decided (1)

5339 συντόμως *syntomōs* (1)
briefly (1)

5340 συντρέχω *syntrechō* (3)
came running (1)
plunge with (1)
ran (1)

5341 συντρίβω *syntribō* (7)
broke (2)
broken (1)
bruised (1)
crush (1)
dash to pieces (1)
destroying (1)

5342 σύντριμμα *syntrimma* (1)
ruin (1)

5343 σύντροφος *syntrophos* (1)
brought up with (1)

5344 συντυγχάνω *syntynchanō* (1)
get near (1)

5345 Συντύχη *Syntychē* (1)
Syntyche (1)

5346 συντυχία *syntychia*
Variant; not used

5347 συνυποκρίνομαι *synypokrinomai* (1)
joined in hypocrisy (1)

5348 συνυπουργέω *synypourgeō* (1)
help (1)

5349 συνωδίνω *synōdinō* (1)
in the pains of childbirth (1)

5350 συνωμοσία *synōmosia* (1)
plot (1)

5351 Σύρα *Syra*
Variant; not used

5352 Συράκουσαι *Syrakousai* (1)
Syracuse (1)

5353 Συρία *Syria* (8)
Syria (8)

5354 Σύρος *Syros* (1)
Syrian (1)

5355 Συροφοινίκισσα *Syrophoinikissa* (1)
Syrian Phoenicia (1)

5356 Συροφοίνισσα *Syrophoinissa*
Variant; not used

5357 συρρήγνυμι *syrrēgnymi*
Variant; not used

5358 Σύρτις *Syrtis* (1)
sandbars of Syrtis (1)

5359 σύρω *syrō* (5)
dragged (2)
dragged off (1)
swept (1)
towing (1)

5360 συσπαράσσω *sysparassō* (2)
in a convulsion (1)
threw into a convulsion (1)

5361 σύσσημον *syssēmon* (1)
signal (1)

5362 σύσσωμος *syssōmos* (1)
members together of one body (1)

5363 συστασιαστής *systasiastēs*
Variant; not used

5364 συστατικός *systatikos* (1)
recommendation (1)

5365 συσταυρόω *systauroō* (5)
crucified with (5)

5366 συστέλλω *systellō* (1)
wrapped up (1)

5367 συστενάζω *systenazō* (1)
groaning (1)

5368 συστοιχέω *systoicheō* (1)
corresponds (1)

5369 συστρατιώτης *systratiōtēs* (2)
fellow soldier (2)

5370 συστρέφω *systrephō* (2)
came together (1)
gathered (1)

5371 συστροφή *systrophē* (2)
commotion (1)
conspiracy (1)

5372 συσχηματίζω *syschēmatizō* (2)
conform (1)
conform to the pattern of (1)

5373 Συχάρ *Sychar* (1)
Sychar (1)

5374 Συχέμ *Sychem* (2)
Shechem (2)

5375 σφαγή *sphagē* (3)
slaughter (2)
slaughtered (1)

5376 σφάγιον *sphagion* (1)
offerings (1)

5377 σφάζω *sphazō* (10)
slain (5)
had wound (1)
killed (1)
murder (1)
murdered (1)
slay (1)

5378 σφάλλω *sphallō*
Variant; not used

5379 σφόδρα *sphodra* (11)
greatly (2)
terrified (2) +5828
very (2)
filled with grief (1) +3382
great (1)
overjoyed (1) +3489+5897+5915
rapidly (1)
so (1)

5380 σφοδρῶς *sphodrōs* (1)
such violent (1)

5381 σφραγίζω *sphragizō* (15)
sealed (4)
seal up (2)
certified (1) +3456+3836
made sure that (1)
marked with a seal (1)
on placed seal (1)
put a seal (1)
putting a seal on (1)
set seal of ownership on (1)
untranslated (2)

5382 σφραγίς *sphragis* (16)
seal (10)
seals (5)
sealed with (1) +2400

5383 σφυδρόν *sphydron* (1)
ankles (1)

5384 σφυρόν *sphyron*
Variant; not used

5385 σχεδόν *schedon* (3)
almost (1)
nearly (1)
practically (1)

5386 σχῆμα *schēma* (2)
form (1)
in appearance (1)

5387 σχίζω *schizō* (11)
torn (5)
divided (2)
split (1)
tear (1)
tears (1)
torn open (1)

5388 σχίσμα *schisma* (8)
divided (3)
divisions (2)
tear (2)
division (1)

5389 σχοινίον *schoinion* (2)
cords (1)
ropes (1)

5390 σχολάζω *scholazō* (2)
devote (1)
unoccupied (1)

5391 σχολή *scholē* (1)
lecture hall (1)

5392 σῴζω *sōzō* (106)
saved (45)
save (37)
healed (12)
saved (2) +1639
bring safely (1)
cured (1)
delivered (1)
get better (1)
healed (1) +3836
made well (1)
make well (1)
saves (1)
survive (1)
survive (1) +323

5393 σῶμα *sōma* (142)
body (115)

bodies (14)
dead (1)
dead body (1)
in person (1) +3836+3836+4242
its[s] (1) +3836
person (1)
physical (1)
physically (1)
reality (1)
the parts[s] (1) +3836+4047
untranslated (4)

5394 σωματικός *sōmatikos* (2)
bodily (1)
physical (1)

5395 σωματικῶς *sōmatikōs* (1)
in bodily form (1)

5396 Σώπατρος *Sōpatros* (1)
Sopater (1)

5397 σωρεύω *sōreuō* (2)
heap (1)
loaded down (1)

5398 Σωσθένης *Sōsthenēs* (2)
Sosthenes (2)

5399 Σωσίπατρος *Sōsipatros* (1)
Sosipater (1)

5400 σωτήρ *sōtēr* (24)
savior (24)

5401 σωτηρία *sōtēria* (45)
salvation (36)
be saved (2)
are saved (1) +1650
be saved (1) +1650
deliverance (1)
rescue (1) +1443
save (1)
saved (1)
survive (1)

5402 σωτήριον *sōtērion*
Variant; not used

5403 σωτήριος *sōtērios* (5)
salvation (5)

5404 σωφρονέω *sōphroneō* (6)
in right mind (3)
clear minded (1)
self-controlled (1)
sober judgment (1)

5405 σωφρονίζω *sōphronizō* (1)
train (1)

5406 σωφρονισμός *sōphronismos* (1)
self-discipline (1)

5407 σωφρόνως *sōphronōs* (1)
self-controlled (1)

5408 σωφροσύνη *sōphrosynē* (3)
propriety (2)
reasonable (1)

5409 σώφρων *sōphrōn* (4)
self-controlled (3)
who is self-controlled (1)

5410 τ *t*
Variant; not used

5411 ταβέρναι *tabernai*
Variant; not used

5412 Ταβιθά *Tabitha* (2)
Tabitha (2)

5413 τάγμα *tagma* (1)
turn (1)

5414 τακτός *taktos* (1)
appointed (1)

5415 ταλαιπωρέω *talaipōreō* (1)
grieve (1)

5416 ταλαιπωρία *talaipōria* (2)
  misery (2)

5417 ταλαίπωρος *talaipōros* (2)
  wretched (2)

5418 ταλαντιαῖος *talantiaios* (1)
  hundred pounds (1)

5419 τάλαντον *talanton* (14)
  talents (7)
  talent (3)
  talents of money (1)
  untranslated (3)

5420 ταλιθά *talitha* (1)
  Talitha (1)

5421 ταμεῖον *tameion* (4)
  inner rooms (2)
  room (1)
  storeroom (1)

5422 τανῦν *tanyn*
  Variant; not used

5423 τάξις *taxis* (9)
  order (6)
  orderly (1)
  orderly way (1) +2848
  untranslated (1)

5424 ταπεινός *tapeinos* (8)
  humble (4)
  downcast (1)
  in humble circumstances (1)
  of low position (1)
  timid (1)

5425 ταπεινοφροσύνη *tapeinophrosynē* (7)
  humility (5)
  great humility (1) +4246
  humble (1)

5426 ταπεινόφρων *tapeinophrōn* (1)
  humble (1)

5427 ταπεινόω *tapeinoō* (14)
  humbled (4)
  humbles (4)
  humble (3)
  lower (1)
  made low (1)
  need (1)

5428 ταπείνωσις *tapeinōsis* (4)
  humble state (1)
  humiliation (1)
  low position (1)
  lowly (1)

5429 ταράσσω *tarassō* (17)
  troubled (6)
  disturbed (2)
  terrified (2)
  throwing into confusion (2)
  frightened (1)
  startled (1)
  stirred (1)
  stirring up (1)
  thrown into turmoil (1)

5430 ταραχή *tarachē*
  Variant; not used

5431 τάραχος *tarachos* (2)
  commotion (1)
  great disturbance (1) +3900+4024

5432 Ταρσεύς *Tarseus* (2)
  from Tarsus (1)
  man from Tarsus (1)

5433 Ταρσός *Tarsos* (3)
  Tarsus (3)

5434 ταρταρόω *tartaroō* (1)
  sent to hell (1)

5435 τάσσω *tassō* (8)
  appointed (2)

  arranged (1)
  assigned (1)
  devoted (1)
  established (1)
  told (1)
  untranslated (1)

5436 ταῦρος *tauros* (4)
  bulls (3)
  oxen (1)

5437 ταὐτά *tauta*
  Variant; not used

5438 ταφή *taphē* (1)
  burial place (1)

5439 τάφος *taphos* (7)
  tomb (4)
  tombs (2)
  graves (1)

5440 τάχα *tacha* (2)
  perhaps (1)
  possibly (1)

5441 ταχέως *tacheōs* (15)
  quickly (6)
  soon (5)
  easily (1)
  hasty (1)
  outran (1) +4708
  very soon (1)

5442 ταχινός *tachinos* (2)
  soon (1)
  swift (1)

5443 τάχος *tachos* (8)
  soon (5) +1877
  immediately (1) +1877
  quick (1) +1877
  quickly (1) +1877

5444 ταχύς *tachys* (13)
  soon (6)
  quickly (3)
  quick (2)
  hurried away from (1) +599
  in the next moment (1)

5445 τέ *te* (215)
  and (42)
  both (13)
  but (4)
  then (4)
  so (3)
  and also (2)
  even (2)
  and alike (1) +2779
  as (1)
  between (1)
  or (1)
  that is (1)
  whether (1)
  yes (1) +2285
  untranslated (138)

5446 τεῖχος *teichos* (9)
  wall (6)
  walls (3)

5447 τεκμήριον *tekmērion* (1)
  convincing proofs (1)

5448 τεκνίον *teknion* (8)
  dear children (7)
  children (1)

5449 τεκνογονέω *teknogoneō* (1)
  have children (1)

5450 τεκνογονία *teknogonia* (1)
  childbearing (1)

5451 τέκνον *teknon* (99)
  children (73)
  son (14)
  child (5)

  children's (2)
  brood (1)
  daughters (1)
  dear children (1)
  objects (1)
  sons (1)

5452 τεκνοτροφέω *teknotropheō* (1)
  bringing up children (1)

5453 τεκνόω *teknoō*
  Variant; not used

5454 τέκτων *tektōn* (2)
  carpenter (1)
  carpenter's (1)

5455 τέλειος *teleios* (19)
  perfect (10)
  mature (5)
  adults (1)
  finish (1) +2400
  mature (1) +467
  perfection (1)

5456 τελειότης *teleiotēs* (2)
  maturity (1)
  perfect (1)

5457 τελειόω *teleioō* (22)
  made perfect (8)
  made complete (4)
  finish (3)
  make perfect (2)
  clear (1)
  complete (1)
  completing (1)
  over (1)
  reach goal (1)

5458 τελείως *teleiōs* (1)
  fully (1)

5459 τελείωσις *teleiōsis* (2)
  accomplished (1)
  perfection (1)

5460 τελειωτής *teleiōtēs* (1)
  perfecter (1)

5461 τελεσφορέω *telesphoreō* (1)
  mature (1)

5462 τελευτάω *teleutaō* (11)
  died (5)
  die (2)
  put to death (2) +2505
  dead (1)
  end was near (1)

5463 τελευτή *teleutē* (1)
  death (1)

5464 τελέω *teleō* (29)
  finished (8)
  completed (4)
  fulfilled (4)
  ended (2)
  pay (2)
  accomplished (1)
  carried out (1)
  done (1)
  finish (1)
  gratify (1)
  keep (1)
  made perfect (1)
  obeys (1)
  over (1)

5465 τέλος *telos* (40)
  end (20)
  fulfillment (2)
  goal (2)
  outcome (2)
  result (2)
  revenue (2)
  destiny (1)
  duty (1)

end (1) +2400
eventually (1) +1650
finally (1)
finally (1) +3836
fully (1) +2401
last (1)
the full extent of (1) +1650
untranslated (1)

5466 τελωνεῖον *telōneion*
Variant; not used

5467 τελώνης *telōnēs* (21)
tax collectors (15)
tax collector (6)

5468 τελώνιον *telōnion* (3)
tax collector's booth (2)
tax booth (1)

5469 τέρας *teras* (16)
wonders (13)
miracles (3)

5470 Τέρτιος *Tertios* (1)
Tertius (1)

5471 Τέρτουλλος *Tertoullos*
Variant; not used

5472 Τέρτυλλος *Tertyllos* (2)
Tertullus (2)

5473 τεσσαράκοντα *tessarakonta*
Variant; not used

5474 τεσσαρακονταετής *tessarakontaetēs*
Variant; not used

5475 τέσσαρες *tessares* (40)
four (29)
twenty-four (6) +1633
144,000 (3) +1669+5477+5942
144 (1) +1669+5477
eighty-four (1) +2291+3837

5476 τεσσαρεσκαιδέκατος
         tessareskaidekatos (2)
fourteen (1)
fourteenth (1)

5477 τεσσεράκοντα *tesserakonta* (22)
forty (15)
144,000 (3) +1669+5475+5942
144 (1) +1669+5475
42 (1) +1545
forty-six (1) +1971+2779
forty-two (1) +1545

5478 τεσσερακονταετής *tesserakontaetēs* (2)
forty years (2)

5479 τεταρταῖος *tetartaios* (1)
four days (1)

5480 τέταρτος *tetartos* (10)
fourth (9)
four (1)

5481 τετράγωνος *tetragōnos* (1)
square (1)

5482 τετράδιον *tetradion* (1)
four squads (1)

5483 τετρακισχίλιοι *tetrakischilioi* (5)
four thousand (5)

5484 τετρακόσιοι *tetrakosioi* (4)
four hundred (2)
430 (1) +2779+5558
450 (1) +2779+4299

5485 τετράμηνος *tetramēnos* (1)
four months (1)

5486 τετραπλόος *tetraploos* (1)
four times (1)

5487 τετραπλοῦς *tetraplous*
Variant; not used

5488 τετράπους *tetrapous* (3)

four-footed animals (2)
animals (1)

5489 τετραρχέω *tetrarcheō* (3)
tetrarch (3)

5490 τετράρχης *tetrarchēs* (4)
tetrarch (4)

5491 τεφρόω *tephroō* (1)
burning to ashes (1)

5492 τέχνη *technē* (3)
skill (1)
trade (1)
untranslated (1)

5493 τεχνίτης *technitēs* (4)
craftsmen (2)
architect (1)
workman (1)

5494 τήκομαι *tēkomai* (1)
melt (1)

5495 τηλαυγῶς *tēlaugōs* (1)
clearly (1)

5496 τηλικοῦτος *tēlikoutos* (4)
so large (1)
such (1)
such great (1)
tremendous (1) +3489

5497 τηνικαῦτα *tēnikauta*
Variant; not used

5498 τηρέω *tēreō* (71)
obey (16)
keep (10)
kept (10)
keeps (5)
held (3)
obeyed (3)
obeys (2)
protect (2)
reserved (2)
do (1)
do so⁵ (1)
does (1)
guard (1)
guarding (1)
guards (1)
held over (1)
hold (1)
keep under guard (1)
keeps safe (1)
kept watch over (1)
not marry (1)
observe (1)
protected (1)
save (1)
saved (1)
stood (1)
take to heart (1)

5499 τήρησις *tērēsis* (3)
jail (2)
keeping (1)

5500 Τιβεριάς *Tiberias* (3)
Tiberias (3)

5501 Τιβέριος *Tiberios* (1)
Tiberius (1)

5502 τίθημι *tithēmi* (100)
put (21)
laid (10)
lay down (8)
placed (7)
appointed (5)
made (5)
lay (4)
make (3)
puts (3)
assign (2)
put in (2)

appoint (1)
appointing (1)
arranged (1)
brings out (1)
burial (1) +1650+3645
committed (1)
decided (1)
decided that (1) +1087
destined (1)
falling on (1)
fastened (1)
fell on (1)
got down (1)
knelt (1) +1205+3836
knelt down (1) +1205
knelt down (1) +1205+3836
laid down (1)
laid in (1)
lays (1)
lays down (1)
listen carefully (1)
         +1650+3836+4044+5148+5148
made think (1) +1877+2840+3836
make up mind (1) +1877+2840+3836
offer (1)
planted (1)
set (1)
set aside (1)
took off (1)
use (1)
wondered about (1) +1877+2840+3836

5503 τίκτω *tiktō* (18)
gave birth to (3)
give birth to (3)
born (2)
baby to be born (1)
bears children (1)
born to (1)
give birth (1)
give birth (1) +6048
given birth to (1)
gives birth to (1)
giving birth to a child (1)
have baby (1)
produces (1)

5504 τίλλω *tillō* (3)
pick (3)

5505 Τίμαιος *Timaios* (1)
Timaeus (1)

5506 τιμάω *timaō* (21)
honor (16)
give recognition to (1)
honored (1) +5507
price set on (1) +5507
show proper respect to (1)
untranslated (1)

5507 τιμή *timē* (42)
honor (23)
money (3)
noble purposes (2)
price (2)
respect (2)
value (2)
blood money (1) +135
honorable (1)
honored (1) +5506
noble (1)
precious (1)
price set on (1) +5506
special treatment (1)
sum (1)

5508 τίμιος *timios* (13)
precious (6)
costly (1)
honored (2)
valuable (1)
very precious (1)
worth (1)

5509 τιμιότης *timiotēs* (1)
wealth (1)

5510 Τιμόθεος *Timotheos* (24)
Timothy (24)

5511 Τίμων *Timōn* (1)
Timon (1)

5512 τιμωρέω *timōreō* (2)
punished (2)

5513 τιμωρία *timōria* (1)
punished (1)

5514 τίνω *tinō* (1)
punished (1) +1472

5515 τίς *tis* (553)
what (220)
who (122)
why (73)
why (23) +1328
which (20)
whom (9)
whose (7)
how (6)
what do want with (5) +2779
how (4) +1877
why (4) +1650
how is it that (3) +1328
suppose one (3)
any (2)
nothing (2) +4024
one (2)
something (2)
was there ever (2)
all the world (1) +476+1639+4005
any way (1) +3836
anyone's (1)
business (1) +4472
each (1)
how (1) +2848
how (1) +4022
how far will they go (1) +1639+4047
my supper (1) +1268
nothing (1) +3590
suppose a (1)
suppose a (1) +1569
suppose one (1) +476
those (1)
what (1) +1650
what (1) +1877
what (1) +4005
what (1) +4036
what business is it of mine (1) +1609
what does it matter (1) +1142
what going on (1) +323+4047
what shall we do (1) +1639+4036
what the meaning of (1)
what's (1)
where (1)
which (1) +323
who do you think you are (1) +4472+4932
why (1) +1915
why (1) +3364
why (1) +4022
why (1) +5920
why do involve (1) +2779
untranslated (12)

5516 τις *tis* (534)
some (106)
a (85)
anyone (75)
one (35)
anything (31)
any (25)
someone (22)
something (18)
a certain (8)
he (7)
anybody (5)
an (4)
anyone who (4)

certain (4)
one (3) +1651
others (3)
several (3)
whatever (3) +1569
any one (2)
nothing (2) +3590
nothing (2) +4024
that none (2) +3607
the (2)
whatever (2) +323+4005
whatever (2) +1623
who (2)
whoever (2) +1569
a few (1)
a kind of (1)
and none (1) +4046
and nothing (1) +4028
another (1) +257
any (1) +323+4005
any other (1)
anyone (1) +1569
anyone who (1) +1569
anyone's (1)
anything (1) +1569
deadly poison (1) +2503
he who (1)
ideasˢ (1)
important (1)
in keeping with income (1)
    +1569+2338+4005
itˢ (1) +2240+3836
man'sˢ (1)
membersˢ (1)
named (1)
nobody (1) +3590
nobody (1) +4024
none (1) +3590
nothing (1) +4046
person who (1)
persons (1)
pieces (1)
some point (1)
somebody (1)
somewhat (1)
them (1)
thing (1)
what (1)
what (1) +323
what (1) +1623
what (1) +4005
what'sˢ (1) +2240+3836
whatever (1)
whatever (1) +323
whatever (1) +1569+4005
who (1) +1569
untranslated (34)

5517 Τίτιος *Titios* (1)
Titius (1)

5518 τίτλος *titlos* (2)
had a notice prepared (1) +1211
sign (1)

5519 Τίτος *Titos* (13)
Titus (13)

5520 τοί *toi*
Variant; not used

5521 τοιγαροῦν *toigaroun* (2)
therefore (2)

5522 τοίγε *toige*
Variant; not used

5523 τοίνυν *toinyn* (3)
then (2)
therefore (1)

5524 τοιόσδε *toiosde* (1)
untranslated (1)

5525 τοιοῦτος *toioutos* (57)
such (22)

such as these (4)
him (3)
like this (2)
so (2)
such a man (2)
this (2)
blemishˢ (1) +3836
he (1)
man like that (1)
men like him (1)
of a kind (1)
related tradesˢ (1)
similar (1)
such a (1)
that (1)
themˢ (1) +3836+3836+4556
these (1)
they are the kind (1)
those who marryˢ (1) +3836
unequaled (1) +1181+3888+4024
what (1) +3961
untranslated (5)

5526 τοῖχος *toichos* (1)
wall (1)

5527 τόκος *tokos* (2)
interest (2)

5528 τολμάω *tolmaō* (16)
dare (6)
dared (5)
boldly (1)
courageously (1)
dares (1)
venture (1)
untranslated (1)

5529 τολμηρός *tolmēros* (1)
quite boldly (1)

5530 τολμηρότερον *tolmēroteron*
Variant; not used

5531 τολμηροτέρως *tolmēroterōs*
Variant; not used

5532 τολμητής *tolmētēs* (1)
bold (1)

5533 τομός *tomos* (1)
sharper (1)

5534 τόξον *toxon* (1)
bow (1)

5535 τοπάζιον *topazion* (1)
topaz (1)

5536 τόπος *topos* (94)
place (63)
places (6)
everywhere (3) +1877+4246
room (3)
area (2)
among (1)
by itself (1) +1650+1651+3023+6006
everywhere (1) +4246
foothold (1)
nearby (1) +3836+4309
opportunity (1)
rocks (1) +5550
sandbar (1) +1458
seat (1)
spot (1)
there (1) +1877+3836
where (1) +1650
where (1) +1877+4005
untranslated (4)

5537 τοσοῦτος *tosoutos* (20)
such great (4)
as much (2)
so many (2)
such (2)
this (2)
all (1)

all the more (1) +3437
all these (1)
enough (1)
long (1)
so much (1)
that (1)
these (1)

5538 τότε *tote* (160)
then (105)
at that time (11)
so (4)
that time (2)
that time on (2)
when (2)
after (1) +4021
and (1)
and (1) +2779
as soon as (1)
at that (1)
finally (1)
finally (1) +4036
formerly (1)
of that time (1)
once (1)
then on (1)
untranslated (23)

5539 τοὐναντίον *tounantion*
Variant; not used

5540 τοὔνομα *tounoma*
Variant; not used

5541 τοὐπίσω *toupisō*
Variant; not used

5542 τουτέστιν *toutestin*
Variant; not used

5543 τράγος *tragos* (3)
goats (3)

5544 τράπεζα *trapeza* (15)
table (9)
tables (4)
deposit (1)
set a meal before (1) +4192

5545 τραπεζίτης *trapezitēs* (1)
bankers (1)

5546 τραῦμα *trauma* (1)
wounds (1)

5547 τραυματίζω *traumatizō* (2)
bleeding (1)
wounded (1)

5548 τραχηλίζω *trachēlizō* (1)
laid bare (1)

5549 τράχηλος *trachēlos* (7)
neck (3)
embraced (1) +2093+2158+3836
necks (1)
risked lives (1) +5719
threw his arms around (1)
                      +2093+2158+3836

5550 τραχύς *trachys* (2)
rocks (1) +5536
rough (1)

5551 Τραχωνῖτις *Trachōnitis* (1)
Traconitis (1)

5552 τρεῖς *treis* (68)
three (63)
153 (1) +1669+4299
large (1)
large amount of flour (1) +236+4929
twenty to thirty gallons (1)
                      +1545+2445+3583
twenty-three (1) +1633

5553 Τρεῖς ταβέρναι *Treis tabernai* (1)
three Taverns (1)

5554 τρέμω *tremō* (3)

trembling (2)
afraid (1)

5555 τρέφω *trephō* (9)
feeds (2)
taken care of (2)
brought up (1)
fattened (1)
feed (1)
food supply (1)
nursed (1)

5556 τρέχω *trechō* (20)
ran (6)
run (5)
running (3)
effort (1)
run race (1)
runners (1)
running a race (1)
rushing (1)
spread rapidly (1)

5557 τρῆμα *trēma* (1)
eye (1)

5558 τριάκοντα *triakonta* (11)
thirty (8)
430 (1) +2779+5484
thirty-eight (1) +2779+3893
three or three and a half miles (1)
                      +1633+2445+4297+5084

5559 τριακόσιοι *triakosioi* (2)
the money worth a year's wages (1) +1324
untranslated (1)

5560 τρίβολος *tribolos* (2)
thistles (2)

5561 τρίβος *tribos* (3)
paths (3)

5562 τριετία *trietia* (1)
three years (1)

5563 τρίζω *trizō* (1)
gnashes (1)

5564 τρίμηνος *trimēnos* (1)
three months (1)

5565 τρίς *tris* (12)
three times (12)

5566 τρίστεγον *tristegon* (1)
third story (1)

5567 τρισχίλιοι *trischilioi* (1)
three thousand (1)

5568 τρίτον *triton* (8)
third time (6)
third (2)

5569 τρίτος *tritos* (48)
third (45)
nine (1) +6052
nine in the morning (1) +2465+3836+6052
third time (1) +1666

5570 τρίχινος *trichinos* (1)
made of hair (1)

5571 τρόμος *tromos* (5)
trembling (3)
fear (1)
Trembling (1) +899+2400

5572 τροπή *tropē* (1)
shadows (1)

5573 τρόπος *tropos* (13)
way (4)
as (3) +4005
in any way (1) +2848+3594
in the same way (1) +4005
just as (1) +2848+4005
just as (1) +2848+4005+4048
just as (1) +4005
lives (1)

5574 τροποφορέω *tropophoreō* (1)
endured (1)

5575 τροφή *trophē* (16)
food (12)
ate (1)
eat (1) +3561
keep (1)
untranslated (1)

5576 Τρόφιμος *Trophimos* (3)
Trophimus (3)

5577 τροφός *trophos* (1)
mother (1)

5578 τροφοφορέω *trophophoreō*
Variant; not used

5579 τροχιά *trochia* (1)
paths (1)

5580 τροχός *trochos* (1)
course (1)

5581 τρύβλιον *tryblion* (2)
bowl (2)

5582 τρυγάω *trygaō* (3)
gather (1)
gathered (1)
untranslated (1)

5583 τρυγών *trygōn* (1)
doves (1)

5584 τρυμαλιά *trymalia* (1)
eye (1)

5585 τρύπημα *trypēma* (1)
eye (1)

5586 Τρύφαινα *Tryphaina* (1)
Tryphena (1)

5587 τρυφάω *tryphaō* (1)
lived in luxury (1)

5588 τρυφή *tryphē* (2)
carouse (1)
luxury (1)

5589 Τρυφῶσα *Tryphōsa* (1)
Tryphosa (1)

5590 Τρῳάς *Trōas* (6)
Troas (6)

5591 Τρωγύλλιον *Trōgyllion*
Variant; not used

5592 τρώγω *trōgō* (6)
eats (2)
feeds on (2)
eating (1)
shares (1)

5593 τυγχάνω *tynchanō* (12)
enjoyed (1)
extraordinary (1) +3836+4024
gain (1)
had (1)
obtain (1)
perhaps (1)
perhaps (1) +1623
provide (1)
received (1)
taking part (1)
undoubtedly (1) +1623
unusual (1) +4024

5594 τυμπανίζω *tympanizō* (1)
tortured (1)

5595 τυπικῶς *typikōs* (1)
examples (1)

5596 τύπος *typos* (15)
pattern (4)
example (2)
examples (2)
model (2)

as follows (1) *+2400+3836+4047*
form (1)
idols (1)
marks (1)
where[s] (1) *+1650+3836*

5597 τύπτω *typtō* (13)
beat (5)
strike (2)
struck on (2)
beating (1)
strikes (1)
struck (1)
wound (1)

5598 Τύραννος1 *Tyrannos1* (1)
Tyrannus (1)

5599 τύραννος2 *tyrannos2*
Variant; not used

5600 τυρβάζω *tyrbazō*
Variant; not used

5601 Τύριος *Tyrios* (1)
people of Tyre (1)

5602 Τύρος *Tyros* (11)
Tyre (11)

5603 τυφλός *typhlos* (49)
blind (49)

5604 τυφλόω *typhloō* (3)
blinded (3)

5605 τυφόομαι *typhoomai* (3)
conceited (2)
become conceited (1)

5606 τύφω *typhō* (1)
smoldering (1)

5607 τυφωνικός *typhōnikos* (1)
of hurricane force (1)

5608 Τυχικός *Tychikos* (5)
Tychicus (5)

5609 υ *y*
Variant; not used

5610 ὑακίνθινος *hyakinthinos* (1)
dark blue (1)

5611 ὑάκινθος *hyakinthos* (1)
jacinth (1)

5612 ὑάλινος *hyalinos* (3)
of glass (2)
untranslated (1)

5613 ὕαλος *hyalos* (2)
glass (2)

5614 ὑβρίζω *hybrizō* (5)
insult (2)
insulted (1)
mistreat (1)
mistreated (1)

5615 ὕβρις *hybris* (3)
damage (1)
disastrous (1) *+3552*
insults (1)

5616 ὑβριστής *hybristēs* (2)
insolent (1)
violent man (1)

5617 ὑγιαίνω *hygiainō* (12)
sound (8)
enjoy good health (1)
healthy (1)
safe and sound (1)
well (1)

5618 ὑγιής *hygiēs* (11)
well (4)
cured (1)
freed (1)
healed (1)

healing (1) *+4472*
made well (1)
sound (1)
soundness (1)

5619 ὑγρός *hygros* (1)
green (1)

5620 ὑδρία *hydria* (3)
jars (1)
water jar (1)
water jars (1)

5621 ὑδροποτέω *hydropoteō* (1)
drinking only water (1)

5622 ὑδρωπικός *hydrōpikos* (1)
suffering from dropsy (1)

5623 ὕδωρ *hydōr* (76)
water (65)
waters (10)
deluged (1) *+2885*

5624 ὑετός *hyetos* (5)
rain (3)
it[s] (1)
raining (1)

5625 υἱοθεσία *huiothesia* (5)
adoption as sons (2)
adopted as sons (1)
full rights of sons (1)
sonship (1)

5626 υἱός *huios* (376)
son (299)
sons (36)
Israelites (6) *+2702*
people (6)
children (3)
guests (3)
Israel (3) *+2702*
child (2)
descendants (2)
man (2)
men (2) *+476+3836+3836*
those who are[s] (2) *+3836*
children (1) *+1169*
foal (1)
followers (1)
heirs (1)
Israelites (1) *+2702+3836*
one[s] (1)
people (1) *+3836*
people Israel (1) *+2702*
subjects (1)
whose[s] (1)

5627 ὕλη *hylē* (1)
forest (1)

5628 Ὑμέναιος *Hymenaios* (2)
Hymenaeus (2)

5629 ὑμέτερος *hymeteros* (11)
you (5)
your (2)
your own (2)
yours (2)

5630 ὑμνέω *hymneō* (4)
sung a hymn (2)
sing praises (1)
singing hymns (1)

5631 ὕμνος *hymnos* (2)
hymns (2)

5632 ὑπάγω *hypagō* (79)
go (44)
going (18)
get (2)
going away (2)
went (2)
away (1)
go I wish you well (1) *+1645+1877*
goes (1)

going back (1)
going out (1)
going over (1)
heading (1)
leave (1)
leaving (1)
on way (1)
returning (1)

5633 ὑπακοή *hypakoē* (15)
obedience (8)
obedient (3)
obey (3)
obeying (1)

5634 ὑπακούω *hypakouō* (21)
obey (14)
obeyed (4)
accepted (1)
answer (1)
obedient (1)

5635 ὕπανδρος *hypandros* (1)
married (1)

5636 ὑπαντάω *hypantaō* (10)
met (6)
went out to meet (2)
meet (1)
oppose (1)

5637 ὑπάντησις *hypantēsis* (3)
meet (3)

5638 ὕπαρξις *hyparxis* (2)
goods (1)
possessions (1)

5639 ὑπάρχω *hyparchō* (60)
was (9)
are (8)
is (7)
possessions (7)
be (3)
possessions (2) *+3836*
baptized (1) *+966*
being (1)
contained (1) *+1877*
gone (1)
has (1) *+3836*
have (1)
indulge (1)
loved money (1) *+5795*
means (1)
owned (1)
owned (1) *+3230*
possess (1)
possess (1) *+3836*
property (1)
property (1) *+3836*
that am (1)
was that belonged (1)
wasn't (1)
untranslated (6)

5640 ὑπείκω *hypeikō* (1)
submit (1)

5641 ὑπεναντίος *hypenantios* (2)
enemies (1)
stood opposed (1) *+1639*

5642 ὑπέρ *hyper* (150)
for (92)
about (7)
in (6)
more than (5)
above (4)
beyond (4)
for the sake of (4)
on behalf (4)
concerning (2)
for sake (2)
on behalf of (2)
over (2)
to (2)

according to (1)
as for (1) +1664
because of (1)
better than (1)
brighter than (1) +3288
Christ's (1) +5986
more (1)
shrewd (1) +5861
take place (1)
than (1)
to help (1)
untranslated (3)

5643 ὑπεραίρομαι *hyperairomai* (3)
conceited (1)
exalt himself (1)
untranslated (1)

5644 ὑπέρακμος *hyperakmos* (1)
getting along in years (1)

5645 ὑπεράνω *hyperanō* (3)
above (1)
far above (1)
higher (1)

5646 ὑπερασπίζω *hyperaspizō*
Variant; not used

5647 ὑπεραυξάνω *hyperauxanō* (1)
growing more and more (1)

5648 ὑπερβαίνω *hyperbainō* (1)
wrong (1)

5649 ὑπερβαλλόντως *hyperballontōs* (1)
more severely (1)

5650 ὑπερβάλλω *hyperballō* (5)
surpassing (2)
incomparable (1)
incomparably (1)
surpasses (1)

5651 ὑπερβολή *hyperbolē* (7)
all-surpassing (1)
great (1) +2848
intensely (1) +2848
most excellent (1) +2848
surpassingly great (1)
that far outweighs them all (1)
+983+1650+2848+5651
utterly (1)

5652 ὑπερεγώ *hyperegō*
Variant; not used

5653 ὑπερείδω *hypereidō*
Variant; not used

5654 ὑπερέκεινα *hyperekeina* (1)
beyond (1)

5655 ὑπερεκπερισσοῦ *hyperekperissou* (3)
highest regard (1)
immeasurably (1)
most earnestly (1)

5656 ὑπερεκπερισσῶς *hyperekperissōs*
Variant; not used

5657 ὑπερεκτείνω *hyperekteinō* (1)
going too far (1)

5658 ὑπερεκχύννω *hyperekchynnō* (1)
running over (1)

5659 ὑπερεντυγχάνω *hyperentynchanō* (1)
intercedes for (1)

5660 ὑπερέχω *hyperechō* (5)
better than (1)
governing (1)
supreme authority (1)
surpassing greatness (1)
transcends (1)

5661 ὑπερηφανία *hyperēphania* (1)
arrogance (1)

5662 ὑπερήφανος *hyperēphanos* (5)
proud (4)

arrogant (1)

5663 ὑπερλίαν *hyperlian* (2)
super-apostles (2) +693

5664 ὑπερνικάω *hypernikaō* (1)
more than conquerors (1)

5665 ὑπέρογκος *hyperonkos* (2)
boast (1) +3281
boastful (1)

5666 ὑπεροράω *hyperoraō* (1)
overlooked (1)

5667 ὑπεροχή *hyperochē* (2)
authority (1)
superior wisdom (1) +5053

5668 ὑπερπερισσεύω *hyperperisseuō* (2)
increased all the more (1)
knows no bounds (1)

5669 ὑπερπερισσῶς *hyperperissos* (1)
overwhelmed with amazement (1) +1742

5670 ὑπερπλεονάζω *hyperpleonazō* (1)
poured out abundantly (1)

5671 ὑπερυψόω *hyperypsoō* (1)
exalted to the highest place (1)

5672 ὑπερφρονέω *hyperphroneō* (1)
think highly (1)

5673 ὑπερῷον *hyperōon* (4)
upstairs room (3)
room (1)

5674 ὑπέχω *hypechō* (1)
suffer (1)

5675 ὑπήκοος *hypēkoos* (3)
obedient (2)
obey (1) +1181

5676 ὑπηρετέω *hypēreteō* (3)
served (1)
supplied (1)
take care of needs (1)

5677 ὑπηρέτης *hypēretēs* (20)
officials (5)
guards (4)
servants (3)
officers (2)
temple guards (2)
attendant (1)
helper (1)
officer (1)
servant (1)

5678 ὕπνος *hypnos* (6)
natural sleep (1) +3122+3836+3836
sleep (1)
slumber (1)
sound asleep (1) +608+2965+3836
very sleepy (1) +976
untranslated (1)

5679 ὑπό *hypo* (220)
by (96)
under (37)
from (7)
of (3)
in (2)
subject to (2)
at (1)
at their hands (1) +899
be condemned (1) +3213+4406
established (1)
for (1)
he (1) +899
him (1) +899
on (1)
reached by (1)
result of (1)
she (1) +899
they (1) +899
untranslated (61)

5680 ὑποβάλλω *hypoballō* (1)
secretly persuaded (1)

5681 ὑπογραμμός *hypogrammos* (1)
example (1)

5682 ὑπόδειγμα *hypodeigma* (6)
example (4)
copies (1)
copy (1)

5683 ὑποδείκνυμι *hypodeiknymi* (6)
show (3)
warned (2)
showed (1)

5684 ὑποδεικνύω *hypodeiknyō*
Variant; not used

5685 ὑποδέχομαι *hypodechomai* (4)
gave lodging to (1)
opened home to (1)
welcomed (1)
welcomed into house (1)

5686 ὑποδέω *hypodeō* (3)
fitted (1)
sandals (1) +4908
wear (1)

5687 ὑπόδημα *hypodēma* (10)
sandals (10)

5688 ὑπόδικος *hypodikos* (1)
held accountable (1) +1181

5689 ὑποζύγιον *hypozygion* (2)
donkey (1)
donkey beast (1)

5690 ὑποζώννυμι *hypozōnnymi* (1)
passed under to hold together (1)

5691 ὑποκάτω *hypokatō* (11)
under (9)
untranslated (2)

5692 ὑπόκειμαι *hypokeimai*
Variant; not used

5693 ὑποκρίνομαι *hypokrinomai* (1)
pretended (1)

5694 ὑπόκρισις *hypokrisis* (6)
hypocrisy (5)
hypocritical (1)

5695 ὑποκριτής *hypokritēs* (17)
hypocrites (14)
hypocrite (2)
Hypocrites (1)

5696 ὑπολαμβάνω *hypolambanō* (5)
suppose (2)
hid (1)
reply (1)
show hospitality to (1)

5697 ὑπολαμπάς *hypolampas*
Variant; not used

5698 ὑπόλειμμα *hypoleimma* (1)
remnant (1)

5699 ὑπολείπω *hypoleipō* (1)
left (1)

5700 ὑπολήνιον *hypolēnion* (1)
pit for the winepress (1)

5701 ὑπολιμπάνω *hypolimpanō* (1)
leaving (1)

5702 ὑπομένω *hypomenō* (18)
endure (5)
stands firm (3)
endured (2)
perseveres (2)
patient (1)
persevered (1)
persevered (1) +2400
stayed (1)

stayed behind (1)
stood ground (1)

5703 ὑπομιμνήσκω *hypomimnēskō* (7)
remind (3)
call attention to (1)
remembered (1)
remind of (1)
reminding of (1)

5704 ὑπόμνησις *hypomnēsis* (3)
memory (1)
reminded (1) +3284
reminders (1)

5705 ὑπομονή *hypomonē* (31)
perseverance (13)
endurance (7)
patient endurance (4)
great endurance (1) +4246
patiently (1) +1328
persevering (1)
persistence (1)
standing firm (1)
to endure patiently (1)
to persevere (1)

5706 ὑπονοέω *hyponoeō* (3)
expected (1)
sensed (1)
think (1)

5707 ὑπόνοια *hyponoia* (1)
suspicions (1)

5708 ὑποπιάζω *hypopiazō*
Variant; not used

5709 ὑποπλέω *hypopleō* (2)
passed to the lee of (1)
sailed to the lee of (1)

5710 ὑποπνέω *hypopneō* (1)
gentle blow (1)

5711 ὑποπόδιον *hypopodion* (7)
footstool (5)
feet (1)
footstool (1) +3836+4546

5712 ὑπόστασις *hypostasis* (5)
being (1)
confidence (1)
confident (1) +1877
self-confident (1)
sure (1)

5713 ὑποστέλλω *hypostellō* (4)
hesitated (2)
draw back (1)
shrinks back (1)

5714 ὑποστολή *hypostolē* (1)
shrink back (1)

5715 ὑποστρέφω *hypostrephō* (35)
returned (18)
return (4)
came back (2)
returning (2)
decay (1) +1426+1650
go back (1)
home (1)
left (1)
on way home (1)
return (1) +1650
turn their backs (1)
went away (1)
went back (1)

5716 ὑποστρωννύω *hypostrōnnyō* (1)
spread (1)

5717 ὑποταγή *hypotagē* (4)
give in (1) +1634+3836
obedience (1)
obey (1) +2400
submission (1)

5718 ὑποτάσσω *hypotassō* (38)
submit (13)
put under (5)
subject (5)
subjected (3)
submissive (3)
in submission (2)
bring under control (1)
doneˢ (1)
obedient (1)
placed under (1)
putting under (1)
subject to the control (1)
submits (1)

5719 ὑποτίθημι *hypotithēmi* (2)
point out (1)
risked lives (1) +5549

5720 ὑποτρέχω *hypotrechō* (1)
passed to the lee of (1)

5721 ὑποτύπωσις *hypotypōsis* (2)
example (1)
pattern (1)

5722 ὑποφέρω *hypopherō* (3)
bears up under (1)
endured (1)
stand up under (1)

5723 ὑποχωρέω *hypochōreō* (2)
withdrew (1)
withdrew (1) +1639

5724 ὑπωπιάζω *hypōpiazō* (2)
beat (1)
wear out (1)

5725 ὗς *hys* (1)
sow (1)

5726 ὑσσός *hyssos*
Variant; not used

5727 ὕσσωπος *hyssōpos* (2)
branches of hyssop (1)
hyssop plant (1)

5728 ὑστερέω *hystereō* (16)
lack (4)
inferior to (2)
destitute (1)
fall short (1)
fallen short (1)
gone (1)
in want (1)
lacked (1)
misses (1)
need (1)
needed (1)
worse (1)

5729 ὑστέρημα *hysterēma* (9)
lacking (2)
need (2)
could not give (1)
needed (1)
needs (1)
poverty (1)
what is lacking (1)

5730 ὑστέρησις *hysterēsis* (2)
need (1)
poverty (1)

5731 ὕστερος *hysteros* (13)
later (5)
finally (2)
finally (1) +4246
last of all (1)
later on (1)
then (1)
untranslated (2)

5732 ὑφαίνω *hyphainō*
Variant; not used

5733 ὑφαντός *hyphantos* (1)

woven (1)

5734 ὑψηλός *hypsēlos* (12)
high (6)
arrogant (1) +5858
be proud (1) +3836+5858
exalted above (1)
heaven (1)
highly valued (1) +3836
mighty (1)

5735 ὑψηλοφρονέω *hypsēlophroneō* (1)
be arrogant (1)

5736 ὕψιστος *hypsistos* (13)
most High (9)
highest (4)

5737 ὕψος *hypsos* (6)
high (3)
heaven (1)
high position (1)
on high (1)

5738 ὑψόω *hypsoō* (20)
lifted up (8)
exalted (5)
exalts (3)
lift up (2)
elevate (1)
made prosper (1)

5739 ὕψωμα *hypsōma* (2)
height (1)
pretension (1)

5740 φ *ph*
Variant; not used

5741 φάγος *phagos* (2)
glutton (2)

5742 φαιλόνης *phailonēs* (1)
cloak (1)

5743 φαίνω *phainō* (31)
appeared (7)
shine (3)
shining (3)
visible (2)
appear (1)
appear as (1)
appears (1)
be seen (1)
become (1)
gave light (1)
look (1)
obvious (1)
recognized (1)
see (1)
seemed (1)
seen (1)
shines (1)
show (1)
think (1)
without light (1) +3590

5744 Φάλεκ *Phalek* (1)
Peleg (1)

5745 φανερός *phaneros* (18)
open (2)
tell (2) +4472
clear (1)
disclosed (1)
know (1) +1639
knows (1)
laid bare (1)
learned about (1) +1181
obvious (1)
outward (1) +1877+3836
outwardly (1) +1877+3836
plain (1)
see (1)
show (1) +1181
shown (1)
well known (1)

5746 φανερόω *phaneroō* (49)
appeared (9)
revealed (9)
appears (4)
disclosed (3)
appear (2)
made known (2)
plain (2)
show (2)
showed (2)
appeared (1) +1571
brought to light (1)
cover (1) +3590
displayed (1)
expose (1)
made clear (1)
made plain (1)
makes visible (1)
proclaim clearly (1)
see (1)
seen plainly (1)
spreads (1)
visible (1)
untranslated (1)

5747 φανερῶς *phaneros* (3)
distinctly (1)
openly (1)
publicly (1)

5748 φανέρωσις *phanerōsis* (2)
manifestation (1)
setting forth plainly (1)

5749 φανός *phanos* (1)
torches (1)

5750 Φανουήλ *Phanouēl* (1)
Phanuel (1)

5751 φαντάζω *phantazō* (1)
sight (1)

5752 φαντασία *phantasia* (1)
pomp (1)

5753 φάντασμα *phantasma* (2)
ghost (2)

5754 φάραγξ *pharanx* (1)
valley (1)

5755 Φαραώ *Pharaō* (5)
Pharaoh (3)
Pharaoh's (2)

5756 Φαρές *Phares* (3)
Perez (3)

5757 Φαρισαῖος *Pharisaios* (98)
Pharisees (84)
Pharisee (12)
Pharisee's (2)

5758 φαρμακεία *pharmakeia* (2)
magic spell (1)
witchcraft (1)

5759 φαρμακεύς *pharmakeus*
Variant; not used

5760 φάρμακον *pharmakon* (1)
magic arts (1)

5761 φάρμακος *pharmakos* (2)
practice magic arts (1)
those who practice magic arts (1)

5762 φάσις *phasis* (1)
news (1)

5763 φάσκω *phaskō* (3)
claimed (2)
asserting that (1)

5764 φάτνη *phatnē* (4)
manger (3)
stall (1)

5765 φαῦλος *phaulos* (6)
bad (3)

evil (3)

5766 φέγγος *phengos* (2)
light (2)

5767 φείδομαι *pheidomai* (10)
spare (9)
refrain (1)

5768 φειδομένως *pheidomenōs* (2)
sparingly (2)

5769 φελόνης *phelonēs*
Variant; not used

5770 φέρω *pherō* (66)
brought (17)
bring (12)
bear (6)
bringing (3)
came (2)
carried (2)
bearing (1)
bears (1)
blowing (1)
bore (1)
carry (1)
carrying (1)
charge (1) +162
did so[s]
driven along (1)
fruitful (1) +2843
given (1)
go on (1)
lead (1)
leading (1)
let driven along (1)
multiplying (1)
origin (1)
produces (1)
prove (1)
put (1)
reach out (1)
sustaining (1)
take (1)
took (1)

5771 φεύγω *pheugō* (29)
flee (9)
fled (7)
escape (3)
ran off (3)
flee from (2)
elude (1) +608
escaped (1)
fled away (1)
run away (1)
runs away (1)

5772 Φῆλιξ *Phēlix* (9)
Felix (9)

5773 φήμη *phēmē* (2)
news (2)

5774 φημί *phēmi* (66)
said (25)
replied (17)
answered (7)
asked (3)
declared (2)
mean (2)
say (2)
claim (1)
declare (1)
replied (1) +646
shouted (1) +3489+3836+5889
untranslated (4)

5775 φημίζω *phēmizō*
Variant; not used

5776 Φῆστος *Phēstos* (13)
Festus (13)

5777 φθάνω *phthanō* (7)
come (3)

attained (2)
get (1)
precede (1)

5778 φθαρτός *phthartos* (6)
perishable (4)
mortal (1)
not last (1)

5779 φθέγγομαι *phthengomai* (3)
mouth words (1)
speak (1)
spoke (1)

5780 φθείρω *phtheirō* (9)
corrupted (3)
destroy (2)
corrupts (1)
destroys (1)
led astray (1)
perish (1) +5785

5781 φθινοπωρινός *phthinopōrinos* (1)
autumn (1)

5782 φθόγγος *phthongos* (2)
notes (1)
voice (1)

5783 φθονέω *phthoneō* (1)
envying (1)

5784 φθόνος *phthonos* (9)
envy (8)
envies (1)

5785 φθορά *phthora* (9)
corruption (1)
decay (1)
depravity (1)
destroyed (1)
destruction (1)
perish (1)
perish (1) +5780
perishable (1)
perishable (1) +1877

5786 φιάλη *phialē* (12)
bowl (7)
bowls (5)

5787 φιλάγαθος *philagathos* (1)
one who loves what is good (1)

5788 Φιλαδέλφεια *Philadelpheia* (2)
Philadelphia (2)

5789 φιλαδελφία *philadelphia* (6)
brotherly kindness (2)
brotherly love (2)
love for brothers (1)
loving each other as brothers (1)

5790 φιλάδελφος *philadelphos* (1)
love as brothers (1)

5791 φίλανδρος *philandros* (1)
love their husbands (1)

5792 φιλανθρωπία *philanthrōpia* (2)
kindness (1)
love (1)

5793 φιλανθρώπως *philanthrōpōs* (1)
in kindness (1) +5968

5794 φιλαργυρία *philargyria* (1)
love of money (1)

5795 φιλάργυρος *philargyros* (2)
loved money (1) +5639
lovers of money (1)

5796 φίλαυτος *philautos* (1)
lovers of themselves (1)

5797 φιλέω *phileō* (25)
love (13)
loves (6)
kiss (3)
loved (3)

5798 φιλήδονος *philēdonos* (1)
lovers of pleasure (1)

5799 φίλημα *philēma* (7)
kiss (7)

5800 Φιλήμων *Philēmōn* (1)
Philemon (1)

5801 Φίλητος *Philētos* (1)
Philetus (1)

5802 φιλία *philia* (1)
friendship (1)

5803 Φιλιππήσιος *Philippēsios* (1)
Philippians (1)

5804 Φίλιπποι *Philippoi* (4)
Philippi (4)

5805 Φίλιππος *Philippos* (36)
Philip (32)
Philip's (2)
Philippi (2)

5806 φιλόθεος *philotheos* (1)
lovers of God (1)

5807 Φιλόλογος *Philologos* (1)
Philologus (1)

5808 φιλονεικία *philoneikia* (1)
dispute (1)

5809 φιλόνεικος *philoneikos* (1)
contentious (1)

5810 φιλοξενία *philoxenia* (2)
entertain strangers (1)
hospitality (1)

5811 φιλόξενος *philoxenos* (3)
hospitable (2)
hospitality (1)

5812 φιλοπρωτεύω *philoprōteuō* (1)
loves to be first (1)

5813 φίλος *philos* (29)
friends (17)
friend (12)

5814 φιλοσοφία *philosophia* (1)
philosophy (1)

5815 φιλόσοφος *philosophos* (1)
philosophers (1)

5816 φιλόστοργος *philostorgos* (1)
devoted (1)

5817 φιλότεκνος *philoteknos* (1)
children (1)

5818 φιλοτιμέομαι *philotimeomai* (3)
ambition (1)
make it ambition (1)
make it goal (1)

5819 φιλοφρόνως *philophronōs* (1)
hospitably (1)

5820 φιλόφρων *philophrōn*
Variant; not used

5821 φιμόω *phimoō* (7)
quiet (2)
muzzle (1)
silence talk (1)
silenced (1)
speechless (1)
still (1)

5822 φλαγελλόω *phlagelloō*
Variant; not used

5823 Φλέγων *Phlegōn* (1)
Phlegon (1)

5824 φλογίζω *phlogizō* (2)
set on fire (1)
sets on fire (1)

5825 φλόξ *phlox* (7)
blazing (4)
flames (2)
fire (1)

5826 φλυαρέω *phlyareō* (1)
gossiping about (1)

5827 φλύαρος *phlyaros* (1)
gossips (1)

5828 φοβέομαι *phobeomai* (95)
afraid (41)
fear (14)
afraid of (12)
feared (4)
alarmed (2)
fearing that (2) +3590
God-fearing (2) +2536+3836
terrified (2) +3489+5832
terrified (2) +5379
be careful (1)
fear for (1)
fearing (1)
fears (1)
filled with awe (1)
free from fear of (1) +3590
God-fearing gentiles (1) +2536+3836
in fear (1)
respect (1)
reverence (1)
reverence for (1)
terrified (1)
who feared (1)
worship (1)

5829 φοβερός *phoberos* (3)
dreadful (1)
fearful (1)
terrifying (1)

5830 φοβέω *phobeō*
Variant; not used

5831 φόβητρον *phobētron* (1)
fearful events (1)

5832 φόβος *phobos* (47)
fear (18)
respect (5)
awe (3)
reverence (3)
terrified (2) +3489+5828
afraid (1)
afraid (1) +3552
alarm (1)
fear (1) +3489
feared (1)
fears (1)
filled with awe (1) +3284
gripped with fear (1) +2158
hold terror (1) +1639
reverent fear (1)
seized with fear (1) +2158
terrified (1)
terrified (1) +1328
terror (1)
terror (1) +3489
warning (1)

5833 Φοίβη *Phoibē* (1)
Phoebe (1)

5834 Φοινίκη *Phoinikē* (3)
Phoenicia (3)

5835 Φοινίκισσα *Phoinikissa*
Variant; not used

5836 φοῖνιξ1 *phoinix1* (2)
palm (1)
palm branches (1)

5837 Φοῖνιξ2 *Phoinix2* (1)
Phoenix (1)

5838 φονεύς *phoneus* (7)
murderers (3)
murderer (2)
murdered (1)
murderer (1) +467

5839 φονεύω *phoneuō* (12)
murder (6)
murdered (3)
commit murder (1)
kill (1)
murders (1)

5840 φόνος *phonos* (9)
murder (6)
murderous (1)
murders (1)
put to death (1) +633+1877

5841 φορέω *phoreō* (6)
bear (2)
wearing (2)
borne (1)
wear (1)

5842 φόρον *phoron* (1)
Forum (1)

5843 φόρος *phoros* (5)
taxes (5)

5844 φορτίζω *phortizō* (2)
burdened (1)
load down (1)

5845 φορτίον *phortion* (6)
burden (1)
burdens (1)
cargo (1)
help (1)
load (1)
loads (1)

5846 φόρτος *phortos*
Variant; not used

5847 Φορτουνᾶτος *Phortounatos* (1)
Fortunatus (1)

5848 φραγέλλιον *phragellion* (1)
whip (1)

5849 φραγελλόω *phragelloō* (2)
had flogged (2)

5850 φραγμός *phragmos* (4)
wall (2)
barrier (1)
country lanes (1)

5851 φράζω *phrazō* (1)
explain (1)

5852 φράσσω *phrassō* (3)
shut (1)
silenced (1)
stop (1)

5853 φρέαρ *phrear* (7)
well (3)
Abyss (1)
it^s (1) +3836
shaft (1)
untranslated (1)

5854 φρεναπατάω *phrenapataō* (1)
deceives (1)

5855 φρεναπάτης *phrenapatēs* (1)
deceivers (1)

5856 φρήν *phrēn* (2)
thinking (1)
thinking (1) +1181+3836

5857 φρίσσω *phrissō* (1)
shudder (1)

5858 φρονέω *phroneō* (26)
have in mind (2)
mind (2)
agree with (1)
arrogant (1) +5734
attitude (1)

be proud (1) +3836+5734
being like-minded (1) +899+3836
concern (1)
concerned (1)
does so[s] (1)
feel (1)
live in harmony (1) +899+3836
minds set on (1)
on think (1)
purpose (1)
regards (1)
set minds on (1)
spirit of unity (1) +899+3836
take such a view of things (1)
take view (1)
think (1)
thought (1)
views are (1)
untranslated (1)

5859 φρόνημα *phronēma* (4)
mind (4)

5860 φρόνησις *phronēsis* (2)
understanding (1)
wisdom (1)

5861 φρόνιμος *phronimos* (14)
wise (8)
conceited (1)
conceited (1) +4123+4932
sensible (1)
shrewd (1)
shrewd (1) +5642
they[s] (1) +3836

5862 φρονίμως *phronimōs* (1)
shrewdly (1)

5863 φροντίζω *phrontizō* (1)
careful (1)

5864 φρουρέω *phroureō* (4)
guard (1)
guarded (1)
held prisoners (1)
shielded (1)

5865 φρυάσσω *phryassō* (1)
rage (1)

5866 φρύγανον *phryganon* (1)
brushwood (1)

5867 Φρυγία *Phrygia* (3)
Phrygia (3)

5868 φυγαδεύω *phygadeuō*
Variant; not used

5869 Φύγελος *Phygelos* (1)
Phygelus (1)

5870 φυγή *phygē* (1)
flight (1)

5871 φυλακή *phylakē* (46)
prison (31)
jail (3)
haunt (2)
watch (2)
cell (1)
guard (1)
guards (1)
imprisonments (1)
keeping watch (1) +5875
prisons (1)
time of night (1)
watch of the night (1)

5872 φυλακίζω *phylakizō* (1)
imprison (1)

5873 φυλακτήριον *phylaktērion* (1)
phylacteries (1)

5874 φύλαξ *phylax* (3)
guards (2)
sentries (1)

5875 φυλάσσω *phylassō* (31)
keep (5)
guard (4)
kept (3)
obey (3)
kept under guard (2)
on guard (2)
abstain from (1)
guarded (1)
guarding (1)
guards (1)
in obedience to (1)
keep from (1)
keeping watch (1) +5871
kept safe (1)
obeyed (1)
on guard against (1)
protect (1)
protected (1)

5876 φυλή *phylē* (31)
tribe (24)
tribes (5)
nations (1)
peoples (1)

5877 φύλλον *phyllon* (6)
leaves (5)
in leaf (1) +2400

5878 φύραμα *phyrama* (5)
batch (2)
batch of dough (2)
lump of clay (1)

5879 φυσικός *physikos* (3)
natural (2)
creatures of instinct (1)

5880 φυσικῶς *physikōs* (1)
instinct (1)

5881 φυσιόω *physioō* (7)
arrogant (2)
proud (2)
puffs up (2)
take pride (1)

5882 φύσις *physis* (14)
nature (7)
natural (2) +2848
birth (1)
kinds (1)
physically (1) +1666
unnatural ones (1) +3836+4123
untranslated (1)

5883 φυσίωσις *physiōsis* (1)
arrogance (1)

5884 φυτεία *phyteia* (1)
plant (1)

5885 φυτεύω *phyteuō* (11)
planted (7)
plants (3)
planting (1)

5886 φύω *phyō* (3)
came up (2)
grows (1)

5887 φωλεός *phōleos* (2)
holes (2)

5888 φωνέω *phōneō* (42)
called (9)
crows (7)
call (3)
called out (3)
calling (3)
crowed (3)
called to (2)
summoned (2)
asking for (1)
called in (1)
calls (1)
crow (1)

invite (1)
said (1)
sent for (1)
sent for (1) +3306
shouted (1) +3489+5889
shriek (1) +3489+5889

5889 φωνή *phōnē* (139)
voice (85)
sound (8)
voices (5)
rumblings (4)
roar (2)
shouts (2)
words (2)
at the top of voice (1) +3489
at the top of voices (1) +3489
blasts (1)
call (1)
called out (1) +2048
called out (1) +3306+3489
called out in a loud voice (1) +149
cried out (1) +3189+3489
cry (1)
gave a shout (1) +3189
heard sound (1) +1181
languages (1)
music (1)
peals (1)
roar (1) +3489
shouted (1) +2048+3836
shouted (1) +3489+3836+5774
shouted (1) +3489+5888
shouting at the top of voice (1)
                +3306+3489
shriek (1) +3489+5888
shrieks (1) +1066+3489
someone is saying (1)
sounded (1)
sounds (1)
thundering (1)
tone (1)
untranslated (5)

5890 φῶς *phōs* (73)
light (66)
daylight (2)
lights (2)
fire (1)
firelight (1)
it[s] (1) +3836

5891 φωστήρ *phōstēr* (2)
brilliance (1)
stars (1)

5892 φωσφόρος *phōsphoros* (1)
morning star (1)

5893 φωτεινός *phōteinos* (5)
full of light (3)
bright (1)
lighted (1)

5894 φωτίζω *phōtizō* (11)
enlightened (2)
bring to light (1)
brought to light (1)
give light (1)
gives light (1)
gives light to (1)
illuminated (1)
make plain to (1)
received light (1)
shines on (1)

5895 φωτισμός *phōtismos* (2)
light (2)

5896 χ *ch*
Variant; not used

5897 χαίρω *chairō* (74)
rejoice (17)
glad (13)
greetings (6)

delighted (3)
hail (3)
joy (3)
rejoicing (3)
delight (2)
happy (2)
joyful (2)
joyfully (2)
be glad (1)
delighted (1) +4359
full of joy (1)
full of joy (1) +5915
gladly (1)
gloat (1)
good-by (1)
happier (1) +3437
joy have (1) +5915
make rejoice (1)
overjoyed (1)
overjoyed (1) +22
overjoyed (1) +3489+5379+5915
pleased (1)
rejoices (1)
welcome (1) +3306
welcomes (1) +3306
untranslated (1)

5898 χάλαζα *chalaza* (4)
hail (2)
hailstones (1)
hailstorm (1)

5899 χαλάω *chalaō* (7)
let down (3)
lowered (3)
lowered (1) +2768

5900 Χαλδαῖος *Chaldaios* (1)
Chaldeans (1)

5901 χαλεπός *chalepos* (2)
terrible (1)
violent (1) +3336

5902 χαλιναγωγέω *chalinagōgeō* (2)
keep a tight rein on (1)
keep in check (1)

5903 χαλινός *chalinos* (2)
bits (1)
bridles (1)

5904 χαλινόω *chalinoō*
Variant; not used

5905 χάλκεος *chalkeos* (1)
bronze (1)

5906 χαλκεύς *chalkeus* (1)
metalworker (1)

5907 χαλκηδών *chalkēdōn* (1)
chalcedony (1)

5908 χαλκίον *chalkion* (1)
kettles (1)

5909 χαλκολίβανον *chalkolibanon* (2)
bronze (1)
burnished bronze (1)

5910 χαλκός *chalkos* (5)
money (2)
bronze (1)
copper (1)
gong (1)

5911 χαλκοῦς *chalkous*
Variant; not used

5912 χαμαί *chamai* (2)
on the ground (1)
to the ground (1)

5913 Χανάαν *Chanaan* (2)
Canaan (1)
Canaan (1) +1178

5914 Χαναναῖος *Chananaios* (1)
Canaanite (1)

5915 χαρά *chara* (59)
joy (44)
happiness (2)
joyfully (2) +3552
rejoicing (2)
filled with joy (1) +22
filled with joy (1) +3489
full of joy (1) +5897
glad (1)
happy (1)
joy have (1) +5897
overjoyed (1)
overjoyed (1) +3489+5379+5897
pleasant (1)

5916 χάραγμα *charagma* (8)
mark (7)
image (1)

5917 χαρακτήρ *charaktēr* (1)
exact representation (1)

5918 χάραξ *charax* (1)
embankment (1)

5919 χαρίζομαι *charizomai* (23)
forgive (5)
forgave (3)
canceled (2)
gave (2)
hand over (2)
forgiven (1)
forgiving (1)
freely given (1)
graciously give (1)
graciously given (1)
granted (1)
in grace gave (1)
released (1)
restored (1)

5920 χάριν *charin* (9)
for (2)
for this reason (2) +4047
because of (1)
for the sake of (1)
the reason (1) +4047
therefore (1) +4005
why (1) +5515

5921 χάρις *charis* (155)
grace (119)
favor (6)
thanks (5)
credit (3)
thank (3) +2400
commendable (2)
gift (2)
act of grace (1)
another[s] (1)
benefit (1) +1443
benefit (1) +2400
blessing (1)
enjoying favor (1) +2400
goodwill (1)
gracious (1)
gracious gift (1)
gratitude (1)
offering (1)
privilege (1)
thank (1)
thankful (1) +2400
thankfulness (1)

5922 χάρισμα *charisma* (17)
gift (8)
gifts (7)
gracious favor granted (1)
spiritual gift (1)

5923 χαριτόω *charitoō* (2)
freely given (1)
highly favored (1)

5924 Χαρράν *Charran* (2)
Haran (2)

5925 χάρτης *chartēs* (1)
paper (1)

5926 χάσμα *chasma* (1)
chasm (1)

5927 χεῖλος *cheilos* (7)
lips (6)
seashore (1) +2498+3836

5928 χειμάζω *cheimazō* (1)
took a battering from the storm (1)

5929 χείμαρρος *cheimarros* (1)
valley (1)

5930 χειμών *cheimōn* (6)
winter (4)
storm (1)
stormy (1)

5931 χείρ *cheir* (177)
hand (75)
hands (70)
seized (2) +2093+2095+3836
seized (2) +2095+3836
arms (1)
arrest (1) +2093+2095+3836
arrested (1) +2093+2095+3836
arrested (1) +2095+3836
by (1) +1877
clutches (1)
enabling (1) +1328+1443+3836
finger (1)
grasp (1)
hand over to (1) +1650+4140
he (1) +899+1328+3836
help (1)
man-made (1) +1181+1328
motioned (1) +2939+3836
pointing (1) +899+1753+3836
power (1)
reached for (1) +1753+3836
through (1) +5250
under power (1) +1650
using (1) +1328
with (1) +1328
wrists (1)
untranslated (6)

5932 χειραγωγέω *cheiragōgeō* (2)
by the hand (1)
led by the hand (1)

5933 χειραγωγός *cheiragōgos* (1)
someone to lead by the hand (1)

5934 χειρόγραφον *cheirographon* (1)
written code (1)

5935 χειροποίητος *cheiropoiētos* (6)
man-made (3)
built by hands (1)
done by the hands (1)
made by men (1)

5936 χειροτονέω *cheirotoneō* (2)
appointed (1)
chosen (1)

5937 χείρων *cheirōn* (11)
worse (4)
worse than (4)
from bad to worse (1) +2093+3836
more severely (1)
worse off than (1)

5938 Χερούβ *Cheroub* (1)
cherubim (1)

5939 χήρα *chēra* (26)
widow (12)
widows (10)
widows' (2)
widow (1) +1222
untranslated (1)

5940 χθές *chthes*
Variant; not used

5941 χιλίαρχος *chiliarchos* (21)
commander (17)
generals (2)
high ranking officers (1)
military commanders (1)

5942 χιλιάς *chilias* (23)
12,000 (13) +1557
thousand (5)
144,000 (3) +1669+5475+5477
thousands (2)

5943 χίλιοι *chilioi* (11)
thousand (8)
1,260 (2) +1357+2008
1,600 (1) +1980

5944 Χίος *Chios* (1)
Kios (1)

5945 χιτών *chitōn* (11)
tunic (5)
clothes (1)
clothing (1)
garment (1)
robes (1)
tunics (1)
undergarment (1)

5946 χιών *chiōn* (2)
snow (2)

5947 χις᾽ *chis'*
Variant; not used

5948 χλαμύς *chlamys* (2)
robe (2)

5949 χλευάζω *chleuazō* (1)
sneered (1)

5950 χλιαρός *chliaros* (1)
lukewarm (1)

5951 Χλόη *Chloē* (1)
Chloe's (1)

5952 χλωρός *chlōros* (4)
green (2)
pale (1)
plant (1)

5953 χξς᾽ *chxs'*
Variant; not used

5954 χοϊκός *choikos* (4)
earthly (2)
dust (1)
earth (1)

5955 χοῖνιξ *choinix* (2)
quart (1)
quarts (1)

5956 χοῖρος *choiros* (12)
pigs (12)

5957 χολάω *cholaō* (1)
angry (1)

5958 χολή *cholē* (2)
bitterness (1) +4394
gall (1)

5959 χόος *choos*
Variant; not used

5960 Χοραζίν *Chorazin* (2)
Korazin (2)

5961 χορηγέω *chorēgeō* (2)
provides (1)
supply (1)

5962 χορός *choros* (1)
dancing (1)

5963 χορτάζω *chortazō* (15)
satisfied (6)
feed (2)
well fed (2)
eat (1)

eat all they want (1)
fill (1)
filled (1)
gorged (1)

5964 χόρτασμα *chortasma* (1)
food (1)

5965 χόρτος *chortos* (15)
grass (9)
field (1)
hay (1)
plant (1)
stalk (1)
wheat (1)
wild (1)

5966 Χουζᾶς *Chouzas* (1)
Cuza (1)

5967 χοῦς *chous* (2)
dust (2)

5968 χράομαι *chraomai* (11)
use (4)
bold (1) +4244
do (1)
do so (1) +3437
in kindness (1) +5793
used (1)
uses (1)
untranslated (1)

5969 χράω *chraō*
Variant; not used

5970 χρεία *chreia* (49)
need (26) +2400
need (5)
needs (5) +2400
needs (4)
needed (2)
needed (2) +2400
be dependent on (1) +2400
daily necessities (1) +338
need (1) +1181+2400
responsibility (1)
who need (1) +2400

5971 χρεοφειλέτης *chreopheiletēs* (2)
debtors (1)
owed money to (1) +1639

5972 χρεωφειλέτης *chreōpheiletēs*
Variant; not used

5973 χρή *chrē* (1)
should (1)

5974 χρῄζω *chrēzō* (5)
need (4)
needs (1)

5975 χρῆμα *chrēma* (6)
money (3)
rich (2) +2400+3836
bribe (1)

5976 χρηματίζω *chrēmatizō* (9)
warned (5)
called (2)
revealed (1)
told (1)

5977 χρηματισμός *chrēmatismos* (1)
God's (1)

5978 χρήσιμος *chrēsimos* (1)
value (1)

5979 χρῆσις *chrēsis* (2)
relations (2)

5980 χρηστεύομαι *chrēsteuomai* (1)
kind (1)

5981 χρηστολογία *chrēstologia* (1)
smooth talk (1)

5982 χρηστός *chrēstos* (7)
good (2)

kind (2)
better (1)
easy (1)
kindness (1)

5983 χρηστότης *chrēstotēs* (10)
kindness (9)
good (1)

5984 χρῖσμα *chrisma* (3)
anointing (3)

5985 Χριστιανός *Christianos* (3)
Christian (2)
Christians (1)

5986 Χριστός *Christos* (528)
Christ (515)
Christ's (9)
anointed one (1)
belongs to Christ (1) +1639
Christ's (1) +5642
him[s] (1) +3836

5987 χρίω *chriō* (5)
anointed (4)
anointing (1)

5988 χρονίζω *chronizō* (5)
a long time in coming (1)
delay (1)
stayed so long (1)
staying away a long time (1)
taking a long time (1)

5989 χρόνος *chronos* (54)
time (27)
times (5)
as long as (2) +2093+4012
beginning of time (2) +173
long (2)
a long time (1) +3900+4024
delay (1)
instant (1) +5117
life (1)
lives (1)
longer (1) +2285
old (1)
only as long as (1) +2093+4012
past (1)
so long as (1) +4012
some time (1)
spend time (1) +2093+3531
spend time (1) +2152
stayed a little longer (1) +2091
while (1)
untranslated (1)

5990 χρονοτριβέω *chronotribeō* (1)
spending time (1) +1181

5991 χρύσεος *chryseos* (18)
golden (12)
of gold (5)
gold (1)

5992 χρυσίον *chrysion* (12)
gold (10)
gold jewelry (1)
gold-covered (1) +4119+4328

5993 χρυσοδακτύλιος *chrysodaktylios* (1)
wearing a gold ring (1)

5994 χρυσόλιθος *chrysolithos* (1)
chrysolite (1)

5995 χρυσόπρασος *chrysoprasos* (1)
chrysoprase (1)

5996 χρυσός *chrysos* (10)
gold (10)

5997 χρυσοῦς *chrysous*
Variant; not used

5998 χρυσόω *chrysoō* (2)
glittering (2)

5999 χρώς *chrōs* (1)
that had touched (1) +608+3836

6000 χωλός *chōlos* (14)
lame (10)
crippled (3)
cripples (1)

6001 χώρα *chōra* (28)
country (8)
region (8)
fields (3)
land (2)
area (1)
countryside (1)
ground (1)
they^s (1) +899+3836
untranslated (3)

6002 Χωραζίν *Chōrazin*
Variant; not used

6003 χωρέω *chōreō* (10)
accept (3)
room for (2)
come (1)
goes (1)
holding (1)
make room for (1)
room (1)

6004 χωρίζω *chōrizō* (13)
separate (5)
leave (2)
do so^s (1)
does^s (1)
leaves (1)
left (1)
separated from (1)
set apart (1)

6005 χωρίον *chōrion* (10)
field (3)
land (2)
place (2)
estate (1)
lands (1)
plot of ground (1)

6006 χωρίς *chōris* (41)
without (23)
apart from (7)
besides (2)
not (2)
besides everything else (1) +3836+4211
by itself (1) +1650+1651+3023+5536
independent of (1)
separate from (1)
together (1) +3590
without (1) +4246
untranslated (1)

6007 χωρισμός *chōrismos*
Variant; not used

6008 χῶρος *chōros* (1)
northwest (1)

6009 ψ *ps*
Variant; not used

6010 ψάλλω *psallō* (5)
sing (2)
make music (1)
sing hymns (1)
sing songs of praise (1)

6011 ψαλμός *psalmos* (7)
Psalms (3)
psalms (2)
hymn (1)
Psalm (1)

6012 ψευδάδελφος *pseudadelphos* (2)
false brothers (2)

6013 ψευδαπόστολος *pseudapostolos* (1)
false apostles (1)

6014 ψευδής *pseudēs* (3)
false (2)
liars (1)

6015 ψευδοδιδάσκαλος *pseudodidaskalos* (1)
false teachers (1)

6016 ψευδολόγος *pseudologos* (1)
liars (1)

6017 ψεύδομαι *pseudomai* (12)
lie (4)
lying (3)
deny truth (1) +237+2848
falsely (1)
liars (1)
lied (1)
lied to (1)

6018 ψευδομαρτυρέω *pseudomartyreō* (5)
give false testimony (3)
gave false testimony (1)
testified falsely (1)

6019 ψευδομαρτυρία *pseudomartyria* (3)
false evidence (1)
false testimony (1)
false witnesses (1)

6020 ψευδόμαρτυς *pseudomartys* (1)
false witnesses (1)

6021 ψευδοπροφήτης *pseudoprophētēs* (11)
false prophets (7)
false prophet (4)

6022 ψεῦδος *pseudos* (10)
lie (4)
counterfeit (2)
falsehood (2)
deceitful (1)
lies (1) +3281+3836

6023 ψευδόχριστος *pseudochristos* (2)
false Christs (2)

6024 ψευδώνυμος *pseudōnymos* (1)
falsely called (1)

6025 ψεῦσμα *pseusma* (1)
falsehood (1)

6026 ψεύστης *pseustēs* (10)
liar (8)
liars (2)

6027 ψηλαφάω *psēlaphaō* (4)
touched (2)
reach out for (1)
touch (1)

6028 ψηφίζω *psēphizō* (2)
calculate (1)
estimate (1)

6029 ψῆφος *psēphos* (3)
it^s (1) +3836
stone (1)
vote (1)

6030 ψιθυρισμός *psithyrismos* (1)
gossip (1)

6031 ψιθυριστής *psithyristēs* (1)
gossips (1)

6032 ψίξ *psix*
Variant; not used

6033 ψιχίον *psichion* (2)
crumbs (2)

6034 ψυχή *psychē* (102)
life (32)
soul (19)
souls (6)
lives (5)
heart (4)
everyone (2) +4246
minds (2)
you (2) +5148

all (1)
anyone (1) +1569+4246
being (1)
he's (1) +899+1639
I (1) +1609
I (1) +1609+3836
keep in suspense (1) +149+3836
living (1) +2400+3836
man (1)
me (1) +1609
me (1) +1609+3836
mind (1)
myself (1) +1609
people (1)
saved (1) +1650+4348
themselves (1) +899+3836
thing (1)
trying to kill (1) +2426+3836
unstable (1) +844
us^s (1)
you^s (1)
yourselves (1) +5148
untranslated (8)

6035 ψυχικός *psychikos* (6)
natural (3)
follow mere natural instincts (1)
unspiritual (1)
without the spirit (1)

6036 ψῦχος *psychos* (3)
cold (3)

6037 ψυχρός *psychros* (4)
cold (3)
one^s (1)

6038 ψύχω *psychō* (1)
grow cold (1)

6039 ψωμίζω *psōmizō* (2)
feed (1)
give to the poor (1)

6040 ψωμίον *psōmion* (4)
bread (2)
piece of bread (2)

6041 ψώχω *psōchō* (1)
rub (1)

6042 Ὦ1 *Ō1* (3)
Omega (3)

6043 ὦ2 *ō2* (17)
O (4)
you (3)
how foolish you are (1) +485
oh (1)
untranslated (8)

6044 Ὠβήδ *Ōbēd*
Variant; not used

6045 ὧδε *hōde* (61)
here (50)
this (1)
here's (1)
in the one case (1) +3525
there (1)
this calls for (1)
untranslated (3)

6046 ᾠδή *ōdē* (7)
song (5)
songs (2)

6047 ὠδίν *ōdin* (4)
birth pains (2)
agony (1)
labor pains (1)

6048 ὠδίνω *ōdinō* (3)
give birth (1) +5503
have labor pains (1)
in the pains of childbirth (1)

6049 ὦμος *ōmos* (2)
shoulders (2)

6050 ὠνέομαι ōneomai (1)
bought (1)

6051 ᾠόν ōon (1)
egg (1)

6052 ὥρα hōra (106)
hour (52)
time (31)
moment (6)
hours (3)
at hour (1) +1181
at once (1) +899+3836
for a little while (1) +4639
immediately (1) +899+1877+3836
it^s (1) +3836
late (1)
late in the day (1) +4498
little while (1)
nine (1) +5569
nine in the morning (1) +2465+3836+5569
noon (1) +1761
short (1)
three in the afternoon (1)
+1888+2465+3836
very late (1) +4498

6053 ὡραῖος hōraios (4)
beautiful (4)

6054 ὠρύομαι ōryomai (1)
roaring (1)

6055 ὡς hōs (502)
as (152)
like (124)
when (33)
about (18)
just as (17)
as if (16)
how (11)
as though (5)
that (5)
while (5)
after (4)
and (3)
so (3)
like that of (2)
meaning (2)
of (2)
on (2)
on the pretext of (2)
regarded as (2)
resembled (2)
when (2) +323
according to (1)
and to which (1)
are (1)
as soon as (1)

as soon as (1) +323
at (1)
blood red (1) +135
considered (1) +2400
faithfully (1) +2819
for (1)
hardship like (1)
if only (1)
in accordance with (1)
is (1)
just (1)
just like (1)
like (1) +1569
looked like (1)
one might even say (1) +2229+3306
seem (1)
seemed (1)
since (1)
so-called (1) +3306
somehow or other (1) +323
something (1)
supposed (1)
that is (1)
the same as (1) +2779
the same way (1) +2779
the size of (1)
to (1)
unlike (1) +4024
what (1)
what sounded like (1)
when (1) +1254
untranslated (55)

6056 ὡσάν hōsan
Variant; not used

6057 ὡσαννά hōsanna (6)
Hosanna (6)

6058 ὡσαύτως hōsautōs (17)
in the same way (6)
likewise (2)
the same (2)
the same thing (2)
also (1)
similarly (1)
so also (1)
the same way (1)
too (1)

6059 ὡσεί hōsei (21)
about (10)
like (6)
about (1) +4309
as (1)
looked so much like (1) +1181
numbering about (1)
what seemed to be (1)

6060 Ὡσηέ Hōsēe (1)
Hosea (1)

6061 ὥσπερ hōsper (36)
as (15)
just as (10)
like (6)
as indeed (1)
the way (1)
unlike (1)
what (1)
untranslated (1)

6062 ὡσπερεί hōsperei (1)
as (1)

6063 ὥστε hōste (83)
so that (20)
so (19)
therefore (13)
that (9)
to (4)
as a result (3)
so then (3)
and (1)
consequently (1)
in order to (1)
now (1)
such that (1)
then (1)
untranslated (6)

6064 ὠτάριον ōtarion (2)
ear (2)

6065 ὠτίον ōtion (3)
ear (3)

6066 ὠφέλεια ōpheleia (2)
advantage (1)
value (1)

6067 ὠφελέω ōpheleō (15)
value (4)
good (2)
counts for (1)
devoted (1)
gain (1)
getting better (1)
getting nowhere (1) +4024+4029
good for (1)
good to (1)
help received (1)
was getting nowhere (1) +4029

6068 ὠφέλιμος ōphelimos (4)
value (2)
profitable (1)
useful (1)

NUMBERING SYSTEM
INDEXES

FEATURES OF THE INDEX OF STRONG → GOODRICK/KOHLENBERGER NUMBERS

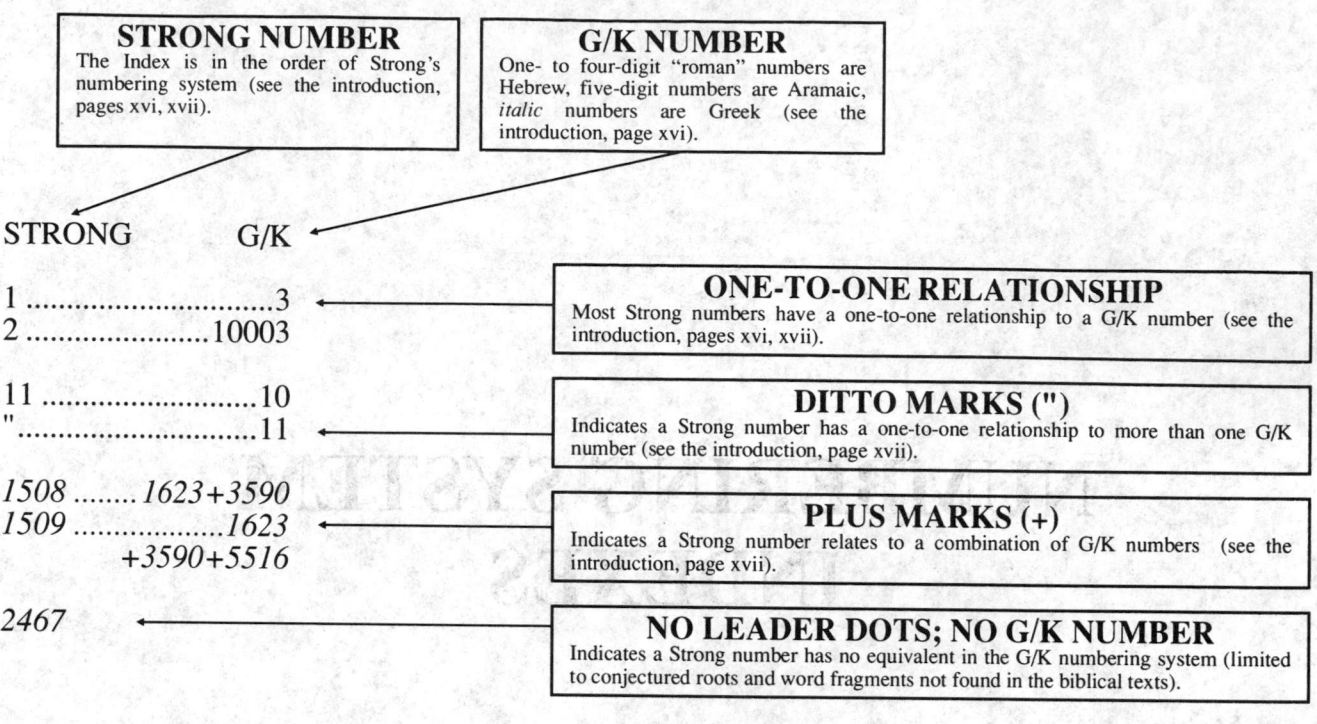

STRONG NUMBER
The Index is in the order of Strong's numbering system (see the introduction, pages xvi, xvii).

G/K NUMBER
One- to four-digit "roman" numbers are Hebrew, five-digit numbers are Aramaic, *italic* numbers are Greek (see the introduction, page xvi).

STRONG   G/K

1 3
2 10003

ONE-TO-ONE RELATIONSHIP
Most Strong numbers have a one-to-one relationship to a G/K number (see the introduction, pages xvi, xvii).

11 10
" 11

DITTO MARKS (")
Indicates a Strong number has a one-to-one relationship to more than one G/K number (see the introduction, page xvii).

1508 ....1623+3590
1509 1623
         +3590+5516

PLUS MARKS (+)
Indicates a Strong number relates to a combination of G/K numbers (see the introduction, page xvii).

2467

NO LEADER DOTS; NO G/K NUMBER
Indicates a Strong number has no equivalent in the G/K numbering system (limited to conjectured roots and word fragments not found in the biblical texts).

FEATURES OF THE INDEX OF GOODRICK/ KOHLENBERGER → STRONG NUMBERS

G/K NUMBER
One- to four-digit "roman" numbers are Hebrew, five-digit numbers are Aramaic, *italic* numbers are Greek (see the introduction, page xvi).

STRONG NUMBER
"Roman" numbers are Hebrew or Aramaic; *italic* numbers are Greek (see the introduction, page xvii).

G/K   STRONG

3 1
4 3

ONE-TO-ONE RELATIONSHIP
Most G/K numbers have a one-to-one relationship to a Strong number (see the introduction, page xvii).

10513 5559
" 5267

DITTO MARKS (")
Indicates a G/K number has a one-to-one relationship to more than one Strong number (see the introduction, page xvii).

1276 ....1176+1803
1277 1176
         +2532+3638

PLUS MARKS (+)
Indicates a G/K number relates to a combination of Strong numbers (see the introduction, pages xiii-xv).

1432
1433

NO LEADER DOTS; NO STRONG NUMBER
Indicates a G/K number has no equivalent in the Strong numbering system (see the introduction, page xvii).

INDEX OF STRONG →
GOODRICK/KOHLENBERGER NUMBERS

HEBREW / ARAMAIC OLD TESTAMENT	
STRONG	G/K
1	3
2	10003
3	4
4	10004
5	5
6	6
7	10005
8	7
9	8
10	9
11	10
"	11
12	12
13	13
14	14
15	20
"	1066
16	15
17	16
18	17
19	18
20	19
21	23
22	24
23	25
24	26
25	3+1500
26	28
27	29
28	30
29	31
"	32
30	33
31	34
32	35
"	38
33	49
34	36
35	37
36	39
37	40
38	41
39	42
40	43
41	44
42	45
43	47
44	48
45	50
"	6588
46	51
47	52
48	53
49	54
50	55
51	56
52	57
"	93
53	58
"	94
54	59
55	60
56	61
"	62
57	63
58	64
59	63

STRONG	G/K
"	64
60	65
61	66
62	68
63	69
"	2243
64	70
65	71
"	4552
66	72
67	73
68	74
69	10006
70	78
71	76
72	75
"	2193
73	77
74	46
"	79
75	80
76	81
77	82
78	83
79	84
80	85
81	86
82	87
83	88
84	89
85	90
86	91
87	92
88	95
89	96
90	97
91	98
92	99
93	100
94	101
95	102
96	103
97	104
98	106
"	107
99	108
100	109
101	110
102	111
103	112
104	10007
105	113
106	114
107	115
108	116
109	117
110	118
111	119
112	120
113	123
114	124
115	126
116	10008
117	129
118	130
119	131
120	132
"	133
"	135
121	134
"	136
122	137
123	121

STRONG	G/K
"	139
124	138
125	140
126	144
127	141
"	143
128	142
129+5346	146
130	122
131	147
132	145
133	148
134	149
135	150
136	151
137	152
138	125
"	153
"	154
139	155
140	156
141	157
142	158
143	160
144	10009
145	159
146	161
"	162
147	10010
148	10011
149	10012
150	163
151	127
"	164
152	165
"	166
153	10013
154	167
155	168
156	169
157	170
158	172
159	171
160	173
"	174
161	176
162	177
163	178
164	179
165	180
166	183
167	182
168	185
169	186
170	188
171	190
172	191
173	192
174	184
"	189
"	193
175	195
176	196
"	197
177	198
178	199
"	200
179	201
180	67
181	202
182	128
183	203
184	204

STRONG	G/K
185	205
186	206
187	207
188	208
189	209
190	210
191	211
192	213
193	212
"	214
"	215
194	218
195	217
196	216
197	221
198	220
199	219
200	222
201	223
202	226
203	227
204	228
205	224
"	230
206	225
207	229
208	231
209	232
210	233
211	234
"	235
212	236
213	237
214	238
215	239
216	240
217	241
218	243
"	244
219	245
"	246
220	774
221	247
"	788
222	248
223	249
"	250
224	242
"	251
"	797
225	252
226	253
227	255
228	10015
229	256
230	10014
231	257
232	258
233	259
234	260
235	261
236	10016
237	262
238	263
239	264
240	266
241	265
242	267
243	268
244	269
"	270
245	271
246	272

STRONG	G/K
247	273
248	274
249	275
250	276
251	278
252	10017
253	277
254	279
255	280
256	281
"	282
257	283
258	284
259	285
260	286
261	287
262	289
263	10018
264	288
265	291
266	292
267	293
268	294
269	295
270	290
"	296
"	297
271	298
272	299
273	300
274	301
"	302
275	303
276	304
277	306
278	305
279	307
280	10019
281	308
"	309
282	310
283	311
284	312
285	313
286	314
287	315
288	316
289	317
290	318
291	319
292	320
293	321
294	322
295	323
296	324
297	325
298	326
299	327
300	328
301	329
302	330
303	331
304	333
305	332
306	334
307	10020
308	335
309	336
310	339
"	343
311	10021
312	337
313	338

STRONG	G/K
314	340
315	341
316	342
"	4406
317	10023
318	10024
319	344
320	10022
321	10025
322	345
323	346
324	10026
325	347
"	348
326	349
"	2028
327	350
"	854
328	351
"	356
329	353
"	354
330	355
331	357
332	358
333	359
334	360
335	361
336	364
337	365
"	388
338	363
339	362
340	366
341	367
342	368
343	369
344	370
345	371
346	372
347	373
348	374
349	375
"	377
"	379
350	376
351	378
352	380
"	381
"	382
"	383
"	442
"	443
"	444
"	444
353	384
354	385
355	387
356	390
"	391
"	472
357	389
358	392
"	1104
359	393
"	397
360	394
361	395
362	396
363	10027
364	386
365	387
366	398
367	399
"	568

STRONG	G/K
368	400
369	401
"	4406
370	402
371	403
372	404
373	405
374	406
375	407
376	408
"	409
377	899
378	410
379	412
380	413
381	408+2657
382	411
383	10029
384	417
385	418
386	419
387	420
388	923
389	421
390	422
391	423
392	424
393	425
394	426
395	427
396	428
397	429
398	430
399	10030
400	431
401	432
402	433
403	434
"	435
404	436
405	437
406	438
407	439
408	440
409	10031
410	445
"	446
411	447
412	10032
413	448
414	452
415	449
416	450
417	453
418	454
419	455
"	485
420	456
421	458
422	457
423	460
424	461
425	462
"	463
426	10033
427	464
428	187
"	459
"	465
429	10034
430	466
431	10035

STRONG	G/K
432	467
433	468
434	470
435	469
436	471
437	473
438	474
439	475
"	1139
440	533
441	476
"	477
442	478
443	479
444	480
445	481
446	482
447	483
448	484
"	517
449	485
450	486
451	487
452	488
"	489
453	490
"	491
454	492
"	493
455	494
456	495
457	496
458	497
459	10036
460	498
461	499
462	501
463	500
464	502
465	503
466	504
467	505
"	550
468	506
469	507
"	553
470	508
471	509
472	510
473	511
474	512
475	513
476	514
477	515
478	516
479	10037
480	518
481	519
"	520
482	521
483	522
484	523
485	524
486	525
487	526
488	527
"	528
489	529
490	530
491	531
492	532
493	534
494	535

STRONG	G/K
495	536
496	537
497	538
498	539
499	540
500	541
"	542
501	543
502	544
503	545
504	546
505	547
"	548
506	10038
507	549
"	2030
508	551
509	552
510	554
511	555
512	556
513	557
514	558
"	559
515	560
516	8845
517	562
518	561
519	563
520	564
"	567
521	10039
522	565
523	569
524	10040
525	570
526	571
527	572
528	572
529	573
"	574
530	575
531	576
532	577
533	579
534	580
535	581
"	582
536	583
537	584
538	585
539	586
"	587
540	10041
541	587
542	588
543	589
544	590
545	594
546	593
547	595
548	591
549	592
550	578
"	596
551	597
552	598
553	599
554	600
555	601
556	602
557	603
558	604
"	605
559	606
"	607
560	10042
561	609
"	610
"	611
562	608
563	10043
564	612
"	613
565	614
"	615
566	617
567	616
568	618
"	619
569	620
570	621
571	622
572	623
573	624
574	10028
575	625
576	10044
577	626
"	629
578	627
579	628
580	630
581	10045
582	632

STRONG	G/K
"	10046
583	633
584	634
585	635
586	10047
587	636
588	637
589	638
590	639
591	641
592	640
593	642
594	643
595	644
596	645
597	646
598	10048
599	647
600	10049
601	649
602	650
603	651
604	652
605	631
"	653
606	10050
607	10051
"	10052
608	10053
609	654
610	655
611	656
612	657
613	10054
614	658
615	659
616	660
617	661
618	662
619	663
620	10055
621	664
622	665
"	4417
623	666
624	667
625	668
626	669
627	670
628	671
629	10056
630	672
631	673
632	674
633	10057
634	675
635	676
636	10058
637	677
638	10059
639	678
"	690
640	679
641	681
642	682
643	683
644	684
"	685
645	686
646	680
647	688
648	689
"	10069
649	691
650	692
"	693
651	695
652	694
653	696
654	697
655	698
656	699
657	700
"	701
658	702
"	1956
659	703
660	704
661	705
"	803
662	706
663	707
664	708
665	709
666	710
667	711
668	712
669	713
670	10060
671	10061
"	10062
672	714
"	715
"	716
"	717
673	718
674	10063

STRONG	G/K
675	719
676	720
677	10064
678	721
"	722
679	723
680	724
681	725
682	727
"	728
683	729
684	730
685	731
686	732
687	733
688	734
689	735
690	736
691	737
692	739
"	740
693	741
694	742
695	743
696	744
697	746
698	747
699	748
700	749
701	750
702	752
703	10065
704	753
705	754
706	752
707	755
708	756
709	758
"	759
710	760
711	10066
712	761
713	763
714	764
715	765
716	766
717	768
718	10067
719	770
720	769
721	773
722	771
"	772
723	774
"	795
724	776
725	777
726	145
727	778
728	779
"	819
729	775
730	780
731	781
732	782
733	783
734	784
735	10068
736	785
737	786
738	787
"	10069
739	738
740	790
"	791
741	789
742	767
743	792
744	793
745	794
746	796
"	10070
747	798
748	799
"	837
749	10071
750	800
"	803
751	804
752	801
753	802
754	10073
755	10072
756	10074
757	805
758	806
759	810
760	809
761	812
"	8246
762	811
763	808
"	5645
764	813
765	814

STRONG	G/K
766	815
767	816
768	817
769	818
770	820
771	821
772	10075
773	10076
774	822
775	823
776	824
777	825
778	10077
779	826
780	827
781	829
782	830
783	831
"	10078
784	836
785	10080
786	838
787	10079
788	839
789	840
790	841
791	842
792	843
793	845
794	844
795	846
796	847
797	848
798	849
799	850
800	836
801	852
802	851
803	853
"	859
804	855
805	856
"	857
806	858
807	860
808	861
809	862
810	863
811	864
812	865
"	866
813	867
814	868
815	869
816	870
817	871
818	872
819	873
820	875
821	874
822	876
823	877
824	878
825	879
826	10081
827	880
828	881
829	882
830	883
831	884
832	885
833	886
"	887
834	889
"	948
"	3876
"	4424
835	890
"	897
836	888
837	891
838	892
"	893
"	894
839	9309
840	832
841	833
842	895
843	896
"	898
844	835
845	834
846	10082
847	900
848	901
849	10083
850	902
851	903
"	904
852	10084
853	254
"	906
854	907
"	4425
855	908

STRONG	G/K
856	909
857	910
858	10085
859	905
"	911
"	914
"	917
"	920
860	912
861	10086
862	913
"	916
863	416
"	915
864	918
865	919
866	921
867	922
868	925
869	924
870	10087
"	10092
871	926
872	929
873	10090
874	930
875	931
876	932
877	934
878	938
879	935
880	939
881	940
882	941
883	936
"	4307
"	8022
884	933
"	937
"	8682
885	942
886	943
887	944
888	10091
889	945
890	947
891	946
892	949
893	950
894	951
895	10093
896	10094
897	952
898	953
899	954
"	955
900	956
901	957
902	958
903	960
904	961
"	962
905	963
"	964
"	4224
906	965
907	966
"	967
908	968
909	969
910	970
911	971
912	973
913	974
"	975
914	976
915	977
916	978
"	1428
917	979
918	980
919	981
920	982
921	10095
922	983
923	985
924	10096
925	986
926	987
927	10218
"	10097
928	988
929	989
930	990
931	984
"	991
932	992
933	993
934	994
935	995
"	4215
936	996
937	997
938	998
939	999
940	1000

STRONG	G/K
941	1001
942	1002
943	1003
944	1005
"	1006
945	1004
946	1007
947	1008
948	1009
949	1010
950	1011
951	1012
952	1013
953	1014
"	1071
954	1017
"	1018
955	1019
956	10102
957	1020
958	1021
959	1022
960	1022
961	1023
962	1024
963	1025
964	1026
965	1027
966	1028
967	1029
968	1030
969	1031
970	1033
"	1037
971	1032
"	1039
972	1040
973	1041
"	1042
974	1043
975	1044
976	1046
977	1034
"	1047
"	1048
978	1049
979	1035
980	1036
"	1038
981	1051
982	1052
"	1053
"	1054
983	1055
984	1056
985	1057
986	1059
987	1058
988	1060
989	10098
990	1061
991	1062
992	1063
993	1064
994	1065
995	1067
996	1068
"	1075
997	10099
998	1069
999	10100
1000	1070
1001	10101
1002	1072
1003	1073
1004	1074
1005	10103
1006	1076
1007	1077
1008	1078
1009	745
"	1079
1010	1081
"	1110
1011	1082
"	1348
1012	1083
1013	1084
1014	1085
1015	1086
"	1814
1016	1087
1017	1088
"	2029
1018	726
"	4442
"	1089
"	2032
1019	1090
1020	1093
"	2127
"	3811
1021	1094
"	2130

STRONG	G/K
1022	1095
"	2140
1023	1092
1024	1096
"	1112
"	2175
1025	1097
"	2195
1026	1098
"	2196
1027	1099
"	2234
1028	1100
1029	1101
"	2242
1030	1128
"	9090
1031	1102
1032	1103
"	2582
1033	1105
"	4122
1034	1106
1035	1107
1036	1108
"	4364
"	6765
1037	1109
1038	1111
1039	1113
1040	1114
1041	1115
1042	1116
"	6712
1043	1117
1044	1118
"	6820
1045	1119
1046	1120
1047	1121
1048	1122
"	7208
1049	1123
"	7449
1050	1124
1051	1125
1052	1126
"	8632
"	9093
1053	1127
1054	1130
1055	1131
1056	1133
1057	1132
1058	1134
1059	1135
1060	1147
1061	1137
1062	1148
1063	1136
1064	1138
1065	1140
1066	1141
1067	1142
1068	1143
1069	1144
1070	1145
1071	1146
1072	1149
1073	1136
1074	1150
1075	1152
1076	1151
1077	1153
1078	1154
"	1155
1079	10104
1080	10106
1081	1156
1082	1158
1083	1159
1084	1160
1085	1161
1086	1162
1087	1165
1088	1163
1089	1164
1090	1167
"	1168
1091	1166
1092	1169
1093	10107
1094	1170
1095	1171
1096	10108
1097	1172
"	4442
1098	1173
1099	1174
1100	1175
1101	1176
"	1177
1102	1178
1103	1179
1104	1180

STRONG	G/K
"	1181
"	1182
1105	1183
"	1184
1106	1185
"	1186
1107	1187
1108	1188
1109	1189
"	1190
1110	1191
"	4444
1111	1192
1112	1157
1113	10105
1114	1193
1115	1194
1116	1195
1117	1196
1118	1197
1119	1198
1120	1199
"	1200
1121	1201
"	1217
"	4240
1122	1202
1123	10110
1124	10111
1125	1203
1126	1204
1127	1205
1128	1206
1129	1215
1130	1207
1131	1218
1132	1209
1133	1210
1134	1211
1135	1212
1136	1213
1137	1220
1138	1221
1139	1222
"	1400
1140	1224
1141	1225
"	1226
1142	1223
1143	1227
1144	1228
1145	1229
1146	1230
1147	10112
1148	1231
1149	10113
1150	1232
1151	1214
1152	1233
1153	1234
1154	1235
1155	1235
1156	10114
1157	1237
"	1238
1158	1239
"	1240
1159	10115
1160	1242
1161	1243
1162	1244
"	1245
1163	1246
1164	1247
1165	1248
1166	1241
"	1249
1167	1250
"	1251
1168	1252
1169	10116
1170	1253
1171	1254
1172	1266
1173	1267
1174	1255
1175	1268
"	6599
1176	1256
1177	1257
1178	1258
1179	1259
1180	1266
1181	1252+1195
1182	1269
1183	1270
1184	1270
1185	1271
1186	1260
1187	1261
1188	1262
1189	1263
1190	1264
1191	1272

STRONG	G/K	STRONG	G/K	STRONG	G/K	STRONG	G/K	STRONG	G/K	STRONG	G/K	STRONG	G/K	STRONG	G/K
1192	1273	"	1357	1367	1474	1462	1479	1552	1666	1646	1766	1735	1845	"	1946
1193	1265	1275	1373	1368	1475	"	1571	1553	1667	1647	1768	1736	1859	1818	1947
1194	1274	1276	1379	1369	1476	1463	1573	1554	1668	1648	1767	"	1863	1819	1948
1195	1275	1277	1374	1370	10130	1464	1574	1555	1669	1649	1769	1737	1862	1820	1949
1196	1276	1278	1375	1371	1477	1465	1576	1556	1670	1650	1770	1738	1864	"	1950
1197	1277	1279	1376	1372	1478	1466	1576	"	1671	1651	1771	1739	1865	1821	10179
"	1278	1280	1378	1373	1480	1467	1575	1557	1672	1652	1772	1740	1866	1822	1951
"	1279	1281	1371	1374	1481	"	10136	1558	1673	1653	1773	1741	1867	1823	1952
1198	1280	1282	1377	1375	1483	1468	1577	1559	959	1654	1774	1742	1868	1824	1953
1199	1281	1283	1380	1376	1484	1469	1578	"	1674	"	1776	1743	1870	"	1954
1200	1282	1284	1381	1377	1485	1470	1579	1560	10146	1655	10151	1744	1871	1825	1955
1201	1284	1285	1382	1378	1486	1471	1580	1561	1645	1656	1775	1745	1872	1826	1957
1202	1283	1286	451	1379	1487	"	1582	1562	1675	1657	1777	1746	1873	"	1958
1203	1285	1287	1383	1380	1488	1472	1581	1563	1676	1658	1778	"	1874	"	1959
1204	1286	1288	1384	1381	1489	1473	1583	1564	1677	1659	1779	1747	1875	1827	1960
1205	1287	"	1385	1382	1490	1474	1584	1565	1678	1660	1780	1748	1876	1828	1961
1206	1288	1289	10121	1383	1491	1475	1585	1566	1679	1661	1781	1749	1880	1829	1962
1207	1289	"	10122	1384	1492	1476	1586	1567	1681	1662	1783	1750	1881	1830	1963
1208	1290	1290	1386	1385	1482	1477	1587	1568	1680	1663	1785	1751	1882	1831	1964
1209	1291	1291	10123	1386	1493	1478	1588	1569	1682	1664	1786	1752	1883	1832	1965
1210	1292	1292	1387	1387	1494	1479	1589	1570	1683	1665	1787	"	1884	1833	1967
"	1293	1293	1388	1388	1495	1480	1590	1571	1685	1666	1788	1753	10163	1834	1877
1211	1294	1294	1389	1389	1496	1481	1591	1572	1686	1667	1784	1754	1885	"	1966
1212	1295	"	1390	1390	1497	"	1592	1573	1687	1668	10154	"	3903	"	2008
1213	1296	1295	1391	1391	1500	"	1593	1574	1688	1669	1790	1755	1886	1835	1968
"	1297	1296	1392	1392	1499	1482	1594	1575	1689	1670	1791	"	1887	"	1969
1214	1298	"	1393	1393	1498	1483	1595	1576	1691	1671	1792	1756	1799	1836	10180
1215	1299	1297	10124	1394	1501	1484	1596	1577	1690	1672	1793	"	1888	1837	1972
1216	1301	1298	1396	"	1502	1485	1597	1578	1692	1673	1795	1757	10164	1838	1973
1217	1302	1299	1397	1395	1503	1486	1598	1579	1693	"	1869	1758	1889	1839	1974
1218	1304	1300	1398	1396	1504	1487	1599	1580	1694	1674	1796	1759	10165	1840	1971
1219	1305	1301	1399	1397	1505	"	1641	1581	1695	1675	1797	1760	1890	"	1975
"	1306	1302	1401	1398	1506	1488	1600	1582	1696	1676	1798	"	1891	1841	10181
"	1307	1303	1402	1399	1504	1489	1601	1583	1697	1677	1800	1761	10166	1842	1970
1220	1309	1304	1403	1400	10131	1490	10139	1584	1698	1678	10155	1762	1892	1843	1976
1221	1310	"	1404	1401	10132	1491	1602	1585	10147	1679	1801	1763	10167	1844	1978
"	1311	1305	1359	1402	1507	1492	1603	1586	1699	1680	1803	1764	1893	1845	1979
1222	1309	"	1405	1403	1508	1493	1604	"	1700	1681	1804	1765	1894	1846	1980
1223	1312	"	1406	1404	1509	1494	1605	1587	1701	1682	1805	1766	1895	1847	1981
1224	1313	1306	1407	1405	1510	1495	1606	"	1702	1683	1806	1767	972	"	1982
"	7652	1307	1409	1406	1511	1496	1607	1588	1703	1684	10156	"	1896	"	1983
1225	1315	1308	1410	1407	1512	1497	1608	"	2056	1685	10157	"	3904	1848	1984
"	7394	1309	1415	1408	1513	1498	1610	1589	1704	1686	1807	"	4514	1849	1985
1226	1314	1310	1418	1409	1513	1499	1609	1590	1705	1687	1808	1768	10168	1850	1986
"	1316	1311	1419	1410	1514	1500	1611	1591	1706	1688	1809	1769	1897	1851	1987
1227	1317	1312	1420	1411	10133	1501	1612	1592	1707	"	1810	1770	1899	1852	1988
1228	1318	1313	1411	1412	1516	1502	1613	1593	1708	1689	1812	1771	1900	1853	1989
1229	1319	1314	1411	1413	1517	1503	1614	1594	1708	1690	1811	1772	1901	1854	1990
1230	1320	1315	1412	"	1518	1504	1615	1595	1709	1691	1813	1773	1902	1855	10182
1231	1321	1316	1421	1414	10134	"	1616	"	1710	1692	1815	1774	1903	1856	1991
1232	1322	"	1422	1415	1519	1505	10140	1596	10148	1693	10158	1775	1904	1857	1992
1233	1323	1317	1423	1416	1522	1506	1617	1597	1711	1694	1817	1776	1905	1858	1993
1234	1324	1318	1424	1417	1521	1507	1618	1598	1713	1695	1816	1777	1878	1859	10183
1235	1325	1319	1413	1418	1523	1508	1619	1599	1714	1696	1818	"	1879	1860	1994
1236	10117	1320	1414	1419	1472	1509	1620	"	1715	"	1819	"	1906	1861	1995
1237	1326	1321	10125	"	1524	1510	10141	1600	1716	1697	1821	1778	10169	"	1996
1238	1327	1322	1425	"	2045	1511	1621	1601	1717	1698	1822	1779	1907	1862	1997
"	1328	1323	1426	1420	1525	"	1747	1602	1718	"	1823	"	8723	1863	1998
1239	1329	1324	1427	1421	1526	1512	1623	1603	1720	1699	1824	"	8726	1864	1999
1240	10118	1325	10126	"	1528	1513	1624	1604	1719	1699'	1825	1780	10170	1865	2001
1241	1330	1326	1429	1422	1527	"	1625	1605	1721	1700	1826	1781	1908	"	2002
1242	1331	1327	1431	1423	1531	1514	1626	1606	1722	1701	10159	1782	10171	1866	2000
"	1332	1328	1432	1424	1533	1515	1627	1607	1723	1702	1827	1783	1909	1867	2003
1243	1333	"	1433	1425	1532	1516	1628	1608	1724	1703	1830	1784	10172	1868	10184
1244	1334	1329	1434	1426	1534	1517	1630	1609	1725	1704	1828	1785	1911	1869	2005
1245	1335	1330	1435	1427	1535	1518	1622	1610	1726	1705	1829	1786	1912	1870	2006
1246	1336	1331	1436	1428	1536	"	1631	"	1727	1706	1831	1787	1914	1871	2007
1247	10120	1332	1437	1429	1537	1519	10137	1611	10149	1707	1832	1788	1913	1872	10185
1248	1337	1333	1438	1430	1538	1520	1632	1612	1728	1708	1833	1789	1915	1873	2009
1249	1338	1334	1439	"	1539	1521	1633	1613	1729	1709	1794	1790	1916	1874	2010
1250	1339	1335	1440	1431	1540	1522	1634	1614	1730	"	1834	1791	10173	1875	2004
"	1340	1336	1441	1432	1541	1523	1635	1615	1732	1710	1836	1792	1917	"	2011
1251	10119	1337	1442	1433	1542	1524	1636	1616	1731	1711	1835	1793	1918	1876	2012
1252	1341	1338	1443	1434	1544	"	1637	1617	1733	1712	1837	"	1919	1877	2013
1253	1342	1339	1444	1435	1543	1525	1638	1618	1734	1713	1838	1794	1920	1878	2014
1254	1343	1340	1445	1436	1545	1526	1639	1619	1735	"	1839	1795	1921	1879	2015
"	1344	1341	1447	"	1546	1527	1640	"	1736	1714	1840	1796	1922	1880	2016
"	1345	1342	1448	1437	1547	1528	10142	1620	1737	1715	1841	1797	10174	1881	2017
1255	1347	1343	1450	1438	1548	1529	1642	1621	1738	1716	1842	1798	10175	1882	10186
1256	1349	1344	1449	1439	1549	1530	1643	1622	1739	1717	1843	1799	10176	1883	10187
1257	1350	1345	1451	1440	1550	"	1644	1623	1740	1718	1844	"	10177	1884	10188
1258	1351	1346	1452	1441	1551	1531	1646	1624	1741	1719	1847	1800	1924	1885	2018
1259	1352	1347	1454	1442	1552	1532	1647	1625	1742	1720	1848	1801	1925	1886	2019
1260	1354	1348	1455	1443	1553	1533	1648	1626	1743	1721	1849	1802	1926	1887	2026
"	1355	1349	1456	1444	1555	1534	1649	1627	1744	"	8102	"	1927	1888	10194
1261	1353	1350	1453	1445	1554	"	1650	1629	1746	"	8114	1803	1929	"	10195
1262	1346	"	1457	1446	1529	1535	10143	1630	1748	1722	10160	"	1930	1889	2027
"	1356	1351	1458	"	1530	1536	1651	1631	1749	1723	10161	1804	1931	1890	2037
"	1357	1352	1459	1447	1555	1537	1652	1632	1754	"	10162	1805	1932	1891	2038
1263	1358	1353	1460	1448	1556	"	2055	1633	1750	1724	1850	1806	1933	1892	2039
1264	1394	1354	1461	"	2055	1538	1653	"	1751	1725	1851	"	1934	1893	2040
1265	1360	"	1462	1449	1557	1539	1654	1634	1752	1726	1852	1807	1935	1894	2041
1266	1361	1355	10128	1450	1558	1540	1655	1635	10150	1727	1853	1808	1936	1895	2042
1267	1362	1356	1463	1451	1559	1541	10144	1636	1753	1728	1854	1809	1937	1896	2043
1268	1363	"	1464	1452	1561	1542	1656	1637	1755	1729	1855	"	1938	"	2051
"	1408	1357	1466	1453	1562	1543	1657	1638	1756	1730	1856	1810	1939	1897	2047
1269	1364	1358	10129	1454	1563	"	1684	1639	1757	1731	1857	1811	1940	1898	2048
"	1365	1359	1570	1455	1564	1544	1658	"	1758	1732	1858	"	1941	1899	2049
1270	1366	1360	1465	1456	1565	1545	1659	1640	1759	1733	1846	1812	1942	1900	2050
1271	1367	1361	1467	1457	1566	1546	1661	1641	1760	1734	1846	1813	1943	1901	2052
1272	1368	1362	1468	1458	1567	1547	10145	1642	1761	"	1861	1814	1944	1902	2053
"	1369	1363	1470	1459	10135	1548	1662	1643	1762			1815	10178	1903	2054
"	1370	1364	1469	1460	1568	1549	1663	1644	1763			1816	1945	1904	2057
1273	1372	1365	1471	"	1569	1550	1664	"	1764			1817	1923	1905	2058
1274	1356	1366	1473	1461	1572	1551	1665	1645	1765			"	1928	1906	2059

STRONG	G/K	STRONG	G/K	STRONG	G/K	STRONG	G/K	STRONG	G/K	STRONG	G/K	STRONG	G/K	STRONG	G/K
1907	10196	1996	2163	2088	2296	2175	2383	2259	2480	2350	2574	2436	2576	2523	2766
1908	2060	1997	2164	2089	8445	2176	2384	2260	2479	2351	2575	"	2668	2524	2767
1909	2061	1998	2166	2090	2297	2177	2385	2261	2483	2352	2987	2437	2669	2525	2768
1910	2062	1999	2167	2091	2298	2178	10235	2262	2484	2353	2580	2438	2670	2526	2769
1911	2063	2000	2169	2092	2299	2179	2386	2263	2485	2354	2581	"	2671	2527	2770
1912	2064	"	2170	2093	2300	2180	2387	2264	2486	2355	2583	2439	2590	2528	10270
1913	2066	2001	2172	2094	2301	2181	2388	2265	2487	2356	2986	2440	2673	2529	2772
"	2067	2002	10211	"	2302	"	2389	2266	2248	2357	2578	2441	2674	2530	2773
1914	2068	"	10212	2095	10224	"	2390	"	2488	2358	10254	2442	2675	"	2776
1915	2070	2003	2173	2096	2303	2182	2391	"	2489	2359	2585	2443	2676	2531	2774
1916	2071	2004	2177	2097	2305	"	2392	2267	2490	2360	2584	2444	2677	2532	2775
1917	10197	2005	2176	2098	2306	2183	2393	2268	2491	2361	2586	2445	10265	2533	2777
1918	2072	2006	10213	2099	2304	2184	2394	2269	10245	2362	2588	2446	2678	2534	2771
1919	2073	2007	2179	2100	2307	2185	2390	2270	2492	2363	2590	2447	2679	"	2778
1920	2074	2008	2178	2101	2308	2186	2395	2271	2493	"	2591	2448	2680	"	2779
1921	2065	2009	2180	2102	2326	"	2396	2272	2494	2364	2592	2449	2681	2535	2780
"	2075	2010	2182	2103	10225	2187	2397	2273	10246	2365	2593	2450	2682	2536	2781
1922	10198	2011	1208	2104	2309	2188	2399	2274	2495	2366	2594	2451	2683	2537	2782
1923	10199	"	2183	2105	2311	2189	2400	2275	2496	"	3123	2452	10266	"	2795
1924	2076	2012	2184	2106	2312	2190	2401	"	2497	"	3131	2453	2685	2538	2783
1925	2078	2013	2187	2107	2313	2191	2402	"	6306	2367	2595	2454	2684	2539	2784
1926	2077	"	2188	2108	2314	2192	10236	2276	2498	2368	2597	2455	2687	2540	2785
1927	2079	2014	2198	2109	2315	2193	2403	2277	2499	2369	2598	2456	2688	2541	2787
1928	2080	2015	2200	"	3469	2194	2404	2278	2500	2370	10255	2457	2689	2542	2788
1929	2081	2016	2201	2110	10226	2195	2405	2279	2501	2371	2599	2458	2690	2543	2789
1930	2082	2017	2201	2111	2316	2196	2406	2280	2502	2372	2604	2459	2693	"	2790
1931	2085	2018	2202	"	2398	"	2407	2281	2503	2373	2601	2460	2694	2544	2791
"	2115	2019	2203	2112	10227	2197	2408	2282	2504	2374	2602	2461	2692	2545	2792
1932	10200	2020	2208	2113	2317	2198	2409	2283	2505	"	2603	2462	2695	2546	2793
"	10205	2021	2210	2114	2319	2199	2410	2284	2506	2375	2605	2463	2696	2547	2794
1933	2092	2022	2215	"	2320	2200	10237	2285	2507	2376	10256	2464	2697	2548	2796
"	2093	2023	2216	2115	2318	2201	2411	2286	2508	2377	2606	2465	2698	2549	2797
1934	10201	2024	2217	2116	2318	2202	2412	"	2509	2378	2608	2466	2699	2550	2798
1935	2086	2025	2219	2117	2321	2203	2413	2287	2510	2379	10257	2467	2700	"	2800
1936	2087	2026	2222	2118	2310	2204	2416	2288	2511	2380	2607	2468	2701	2551	2799
1937	2088	2027	2223	2119	2323	2205	2418	2289	2513	2381	2609	2469	2702	2552	2801
1938	2089	2028	2224	"	2324	2206	2417	2290	2512	2382	2610	2470	2703	2553	2802
1939	2069	2029	2105	2120	2325	2207	2419	"	2514	2383	2611	"	2704	2554	2803
"	2090	"	2225	2121	2327	2208	2421	2291	2515	2384	2612	2471	2705	"	2804
1940	2091	2030	2226	2122	10228	2209	2420	2292	2516	2385	2613	2472	2706	2555	2805
1941	2091	"	2230	2123	2328	2210	2422	"	10247	2386	2614	2473	2708	2556	2786
1942	2094	2031	10217	"	2329	2211	10238	2293	2517	2387	2615	2474	2707	"	2806
"	2095	2032	2228	2124	2330	2212	2423	2294	2518	2388	2616	"	2709	"	2807
1943	2096	"	2231	2125	2331	2213	2425	2295	2519	2389	2617	2475	2710	"	2808
1944	2097	2033	2229	2126	2332	2214	2424	2296	2520	2390	2618	2476	2711	2557	2809
1945	2098	2034	2232	2127	2333	"	2426	2297	2522	2391	2619	2477	2712	"	4721
1946	10202	2035	2233	2128	2334	2215	2427	2298	10248	2392	2620	2478	2713	2558	2810
1947	2099	2036	2235	"	2335	2216	2428	2299	2521	2393	2621	2479	2714	2559	2811
1948	2100	2037	2227	2129	2336	2217	10239	2300	2523	2394	2622	2480	2715	2560	2812
1949	2101	2038	2236	2130	2337	2218	2429	"	2527	2395	2623	2481	2717	"	2813
1950	2102	2039	2237	2131	2338	2219	2430	2301	2524	2396	2624	2482	2718	"	2814
1951	2103	2040	2238	"	2414	"	2431	2302	2525	"	2625	2483	2716	2561	2815
1952	2104	2041	2239	"	2415	"	4664	"	2526	2397	2626	2484	2719	2562	10271
1953	2106	2042	2215	2132	2339	"	4668	2303	2529	2398	2627	2485	2720	2563	2816
1954	2107	2043	828	2133	2340	2220	2432	2304	2530	"	2630	2486	2721	"	2817
1955	2108	"	2034	2134	2341	2221	2433	2305	10250	"	3148	2487	2722	"	2818
1956	2110	"	2240	2135	2342	2222	2434	2306	10249	2399	2628	2488	2723	2564	2819
1957	2111	2044	2244	2136	10229	"	2449	2307	2531	2400	2629	2489	2724	2565	2798
1958	2113	2045	2245	2137	2343	2223	2435	2308	2532	2401	2631	"	3875	2566	2820
1959	2116	2046	2247	2138	2344	2224	2436	"	2533	2402	10258	2490	2725	2567	2821
1960	2117	2047	2251	2139	2346	2225	2437	2309	2535	2403	2632	"	2726	2568	2822
1961	181	2048	2252	2140	2347	2226	2438	2310	2534	"	2633	"	2727	2569	2823
"	2118	"	9438	2141	2348	2227	2439	2311	2536	2404	2634	2491	2728	2570	2824
1962	2119	2049	2253	2142	2349	2228	2440	2312	2537	2405	2635	"	2729	2571	2821
1963	2120	2050	2109	"	2350	2229	2441	2313	2538	2406	2636	2492	2730	2572	2825
1964	2121	"	2254	"	4654	"	2442	2314	2539	2407	2637	"	2731	"	2826
1965	10206	2051	2258	2143	2352	2230	2443	2315	2540	2408	10259	2493	10267	2573	2827
1966	2122	2052	2259	"	2354	2231	2444	2316	2540	2409	10260	2494	2732	2574	2828
1967	2123	2053	2260	2144	2353	2232	2445	2317	2541	2410	2638	2495	2733	"	4217
1968	2124	2054	2261	2145	2351	2233	2446	2318	2542	2411	2639	2496	2734	2575	2829
1969	2125	2055	2262	2146	2355	2234	10240	2319	2543	2412	2640	2497	2735	"	2830
1970	2128	2056	2263	2147	2356	2235	2447	2320	2544	2413	2641	2498	2736	2576	2831
"	2686	2057	2264	2148	2357	"	2448	2321	2545	2414	2642	"	2737	2577	2833
1971	2129	2058	2265	"	2358	2236	2450	2322	2546	2415	2643	2499	10268	2578	2832
1972	2133	2059	2266	"	10230	"	2451	2323	10251	2416	2644	2500	2739	2579	2828+8041
1973	2131	2060	2267	2149	2359	2237	2452	2324	10252	"	2645	2501	2738	2580	2834
"	2134	2061	2269	2150	2360	"	2453	2325	2549	"	2646	2502	2740	2581	2835
1974	2136	2062	2270	2151	2361	2238	2454	2326	2550	"	2651	"	2741	2582	2836
1975	2137	2063	2271	"	2362	2239	2455	2327	2551	"	2652	2503	2742	2583	2837
"	4208	2064	2272	2152	2363	2240	2456	2328	2552	"	2653	2504	2743	2584	2839
1976	2138	2065	2273	2153	2364	2241	2457	2329	2553	2417	10261	2505	2744	2585	2840
1977	2139	2066	2274	2154	2365	2242	2458	2330	2554	2418	10262	"	2745	"	2841
1978	2141	2067	2275	2155	2366	2243	2460	2331	2555	2419	2647	"	2746	2586	2842
1979	2142	2068	2276	2156	2367	2244	2461	"	2556	2420	2648	2506	2749	2587	2843
1980	2143	2069	2277	2157	2368	2245	2462	2332	2558	2421	2649	"	2750	2588	2844
1981	10207	"	2278	2158	2369	2246	2463	2333	2557	2422	2649	2507	2751	2589	2838
1982	2144	2070	2279	2159	2370	2247	2464	2334	2596	2423	10263	2508	10269	2590	2845
1983	10208	2071	2280	2160	2371	2248	10242	2335	2559	2424	2654	2509	2747	"	2846
1984	2145	2072	2281	2161	2372	2249	2466	2336	2560	2425	2649	2510	2748	"	2847
"	2146	2073	2291	2162	2373	2250	2467	2337	2561	2426	2658	2511	2747	2591	10272
"	2147	"	2292	2163	2374	2251	2468	2338	10253	2427	2659	2512	2752	2592	2848
1985	2148	2074	2282	2164	10231	2252	2469	2339	2562	"	2660	2513	2753	2593	2849
1986	2150	2075	2283	2165	2375	2253	2470	2340	2563	2428	2657	"	2754	2594	2850
1987	2152	2076	2284	2166	10232	2254	2471	2341	2564	"	2662	2514	2756	2595	2851
1988	2151	2077	2285	2167	2376	"	2472	2342	2565	2429	10264	2515	2755	2596	2852
1989	2153	2078	2286	2168	2377	"	2473	"	2655	2430	2658	2516	2757	2597	10273
1990	2154	2079	2287	2169	2378	2255	10243	2343	2566	2431	2663	2517	2758	2598	2853
1991	2155	2080	2288	2170	10233	2256	2474	2344	2567	"	2691	2518	2759	2599	2854
1992	2156	2081	2289	2171	10234	"	2475	"	2568	2432	2661	"	2760	2600	2855
"	2160	2082	2290	2172	2379	"	2476	2345	2569	"	2664	2519	2761	2601	2856
"	2161	2083	2291	2173	2380	"	2477	2346	2570	2433	2665	2520	2762	2602	2857
1993	2159	2084	10223	2174	2381	"	2482	2347	2571	2434	2666	2521	2211	2603	2858
1994	10210	2085	2293	"	2382	2257	10244	2348	2572	2435	2667	"	2763	"	2859
1995	2162	2086	2294			2258	2478	2349	2573			2522	2764	2604	10274
"	2171	2087	2295			"	2481					"	2765	2605	2860

STRONG	G/K
2606	2861
2607	2862
2608	2863
"	2864
"	10275
2609	2865
2610	2866
2611	2867
"	2868
2612	2869
2613	2870
2614	2871
2615	2872
2616	2873
"	2874
2617	2875
"	2876
2618	2877
2619	2878
2620	2879
2621	2880
"	2881
2622	2882
2623	2883
2624	2884
2625	2885
2626	2886
2627	10276
2628	2887
2629	2888
2630	2889
2631	10277
2632	10278
2633	2890
2634	2891
2635	10279
2636	2892
2637	2893
2638	2894
2639	2895
2640	2896
2641	2897
2642	2898
2643	2899
2644	2901
2645	2902
2646	2903
2647	2904
2648	2905
2649	2906
2650	2907
2651	2908
2652	2909
2653	2910
2654	2911
"	2912
2655	2913
2656	2914
2657	2915
2658	2916
2659	2917
2660	2918
"	2919
2661	7249
2662	2920
2663	2921
2664	2924
2665	2925
2666	2926
2667	2927
2668	2928
2669	2929
"	2931
2670	2930
2671	2932
2672	2933
"	2934
"	2935
2673	2936
2674	2937
"	2938
2675	2548
"	2939
2676	2940
2677	2942
"	2944
2678	2943
2679	4971
2680	4971
2681	2948
2682	2945
"	2946
"	2947
2683	2949
2684	2950
2685	10280
2686	2951
"	2952
2687	2953
2688	2954
2689	2956
2690	2955
"	2957
2691	2958
"	2973
2692	2960
2693	1520
"	2961
2694	2250
"	2959
"	2962
2695	2968
"	2974
2696	2969
"	2970
2697	2971
2698	2972
2699	2958
2700	2975
2701	2963
2702	2964
"	6065
2703	2965
"	6541
2704	2966
2705	2967
2706	2976
2707	2977
2708	2978
2709	2979
2710	2980
2711	2981
2712	2577
"	2982
2713	2983
2714	2984
2715	2985
2716	2989
2717	2990
"	2991
2718	10281
2719	2995
2720	2992
2721	2996
"	2997
2722	2998
2723	2999
2724	3000
2725	3001
2726	3002
"	3003
2727	3004
2728	3005
2729	3006
2730	3007
2731	3010
2732	3011
2733	3009
"	3012
2734	3013
2735	1515
"	2044
"	2988
2736	3015
"	3029
2737	3016
2738	3017
2739	3018
2740	3019
2741	3020
"	3042
2742	3021
"	3022
"	3023
"	3025
"	3026
2743	3027
2744	3028
2745	3030
2746	3031
2747	3032
2748	3033
2749	10282
2750	3034
2751	3035
2752	3036
2753	3037
2754	3038
2755	3039
2756	3040
2757	3043
"	3044
2758	3045
2759	3046
2760	3047
2761	10283
2762	3048
2763	3049
"	3050
2764	3051
"	3052
2765	3054
2766	3053
2767	3055
2768	3056
2769	3057
2770	3058
2771	3059
"	3060
2772	3061
2773	2589
2774	3062
2775	3063
"	3064
"	3066
2776	3065
2777	3067
"	3068
2778	3069
"	3070
"	3071
"	3072
2779	3074
2780	3073
2781	3075
2782	3024
"	3076
"	3077
2783	10284
2784	3078
2785	3079
2786	3080
2787	2579
"	3014
"	3081
"	3082
2788	3083
2789	3084
2790	3086
"	3087
2791	3089
2792	3090
2793	3091
"	3092
2794	3086
2795	3094
2796	3088
"	3093
2797	3095
2798	1629
"	3096
2799	3098
2800+1471	2046
2800+1471	3099
2801	3100
2802	3101
2803	3108
"	3110
2804	10285
2805	3109
2806	3111
2807	3112
2808	3113
2809	3114
2810	3115
2811	3116
"	3117
2812	3118
2813	3119
2814	3120
2815	3121
2816	10286
2817	3102
2818	10287
"	10288
2819	10289
2820	3104
2821	3124
"	3127
2822	3125
2823	3126
2824	3128
2825	3128
2826	3129
2827	10290
2828	3130
2829	3132
2830	3133
2831	3134
2832	3135
2833	3136
2834	3103
"	3106
"	3107
2835	3105
2836	3137
"	3138
2837	3139
2838	3122
2839	3140
2840	3141
2841	3142
2842	3143
2843	3144
2844	3145
"	3146
2845	3147
2846	3149
2847	3150
2848	3151
2849	3152
2850	3153
2851	3154
2852	3155
2853	3156
2854	3157
2855	3158
2856	3159
2857	10291
2858	3160
2859	3161
"	3162
"	3165
2860	3163
2861	3164
2862	3166
2863	3167
2864	3168
2865	3169
2866	3170
2867	3171
2868	10293
2869	10294
2870	3174
"	3175
2871	3178
2872	3179
2873	3180
2874	3181
"	3183
2875	3182
2876	3184
2877	10295
2878	3186
2879	3185
2880	3187
2881	3188
2882	3189
2883	3190
2884	3191
2885	3192
2886	3193
2887	3194
2888	3195
2889	3196
2890	3196
2891	3197
2892	3198
"	3199
"	4756
2893	3200
2894	3173
2895	3512
2896	3176
"	3177
"	3201
"	3202
"	3205
"	3208
2897	3203
"	3204
2898	3206
2899	3207
2900	3209
"	3210
2901	3211
"	3684
2902	3212
"	3220
2903	3213
2904	3214
2905	3215
2906	10296
2907	3216
2908	10297
2909	3217
2910	3219
2911	3218
2912	3221
"	3223
2913	3222
2914	3224
2915	3225
2916	3226
2917	10298
2918	3227
2919	3228
2920	10299
2921	3229
2922	3231
2923	3230
2924	3231
2925	3232
2926	3233
2927	10300
2928	3234
"	3235
2929	3236
2930	3237
"	3239
2931	3238
2932	3240
2933	3241
"	3242
2934	3243
2935	3244
2936	3245
2937	3246
2938	3247
2939	10301
2940	3248
2941	10301
2942	10302
2943	3250
2944	3249
2945	3251
"	3252
2946	3253
"	3254
2947	3255
"	3257
"	3258
2948	3256
2949	3259
2950	3260
2951	3261
2952	3262
2953	10303
2954	3263
2955	3264
2956	3265
2957	10304
2958	3266
2959	3267
2960	3268
2961	3269
2962	3270
2963	3271
2964	3272
2965	3273
2966	3274
2967	10305
2968	3277
2969	3278
2970	3280
2971	3281
2972	3285
2973	3282
2974	3283
2975	3284
2976	3286
2977	3287
"	3288
2978	415
"	3289
2979	3290
2980	3291
2981	3292
2982	3293
2983	3294
2984	3295
2985	3296
2986	3297
2987	10308
2988	3298
2989	3299
2990	3301
2991	3300
2992	3302
2993	3303
2994	3304
2995	3305
2996	3306
2997	3307
2998	3308
2999	3309
3000	3310
3001	3312
3002	3313
3003	3314
"	3315
"	3316
3004	3317
3005	3311
3006	3318
3007	10309
3008	3319
3009	3320
3010	3321
3011	3322
3012	3323
3013	3324
"	5652
3014	3325
3015	3326
3016	3328
3017	3327
3018	3330
3019	3329
3020	3332
3021	3333
3022	3334
3023	3335
3024	3331
3025	3336
3026	3337
"	8447
"	10310
"	10679
3027	3338
3028	10311
3029	10312
3030	3339
3031	3340
3032	3341
3033	3342
3034	3343
"	3344
3035	3345
"	3346
"	3350
3036	3347
3037	3348
3038	3349
"	3353
"	3357
3039	3351
3040	3352
3041	3354
3042	3355
3043	3356
3044	3358
3045	1977
"	3359
3046	10313
3047	3360
3048	3361
3049	3362
3050	3363
"	3364
3051	2035
"	3364
3052	10314
3053	3365
3054	3366
3055	3372
3056	3367
3057	3368
3058	3369
3059	3370
3060	3371
3061	10315
3062	10316
3063	3373
3064	3374
3065	3375
3066	3376
3067	3376
"	3377
3068	3378
3069	3378
3070	3378+8011
3071	3378+5812
3072	3378+7404
3073	3378+8934
3074	3378+9004
3075	3379
3076	3380
3077	3381
3078	3382
3079	3383
"	3451
3080	3384
3081	3385
3082	3386
3083	3387
3084	3388
3085	3389
3086	3390
"	3391
3087	3392
3088	3393
"	3454
3089	3394
3090	3395
3091	3397
3092	3398
"	3399
3093	3400
3094	3401
3095	3402
3096	3403
"	3404
3097	3405
3098	3406
3099	3407
3100	3408
3101	3409
3102	3410
3103	3411
"	3412
3104	3413
3105	3414
3106	3415
3107	3416
3108	3417
3109	3418
3110	3419
3111	3421
3112	3422
3113	3423
3114	3424
3115	3425
3116	3426
3117	3427
"	3428
3118	10317
3119	3429
3120	3430
3121	3431
3122	3432
3123	3433
3124	3434
3125	3436
3126	3437
3127	3438
3128	3439
3129	3440
3130	3441
3131	3442
3132	3443
3133	3444
3134	3445
3135	3447
3136	3449
"	10318
3137	3451
3138	3453
3139	3454
3140	3455
3141	3456
3142	3457
3143	3458
3144	3459
3145	3460
3146	3461
3147	3462
3148	3463
3149	3464
"	3465
3150	3466
3151	3467
3152	3468
3153	3470
"	3471
3154	3472
3155	3473
3156	3474
3157	3475
"	3476
3158	3477
3159	3477
3160	2465
"	3478
3161	3479
3162	3480
"	3481
3163	3482
3164	3484
3165	3485
3166	3487
3167	3488
3168	3489
3169	3490
"	3491
3170	3492
3171	3486
"	3493
3172	3494
3173	3495
3174	3496
3175	3497
3176	3498
3177	3499
3178	3500
3179	3501
3180	3502
3181	3503
3182	3504
3183	3505
3184	3506
3185	3507
3186	3508
3187	3509
3188	2249
"	3510
3189	3511
3190	3512
3191	10320
3192	3513
3193	3514
3194	3420
3195	3515
3196	3516
3197	3517
3198	3519
3199	3520
"	3521
3200	3522
3201	3523
3202	10321
3203	3524
"	3525
3204	3518
"	3526
"	3527
3205	3528
"	6805
3206	3529
3207	3530
3208	3531
3209	3533
3210	3534
3211	3535
3212	2143
3213	3536
3214	3537
3215	3538
3216	4363
3217	3539
3218	3540
3219	3541
3220	3542
3221	10322
3222	3553
3223	3543
3224	3544
3225	3545
3226	3546
3227	3549
3228	3547
3229	3550
"	3551
3230	3552
3231	3554
3232	3555
3233	3548
"	3556
3234	3557
3235	3558
3236	3559
3237	3560
3238	3435
"	3561
3239	3562
"	3563
3240	4965
3241	3564
"	3565
3242	3566
3243	3567
"	4787
"	5682
3244	3568
3245	3569
"	3570
3246	3571
3247	3572
3248	3573
3249	6073
3250	3574
3251	3575
3252	3576
3253	3577
3254	3578
"	6231
3255	10323
3256	3579
"	3580
"	3581
3257	3582
3258	3583
"	3584
3259	3585
3260	3587
"	3588
3261	3589
3262	3590
3263	3591
3264	3623
3265	3592
"	3600
3266	3593
3267	3594
3268	3595
3269	3596
3270	3597
3271	3598
3272	10324
"	10325
3273	3599
3274	3601
3275	3602
3276	3603
3277	3604
3278	3605
3279	3606
"	3608
3280	3607
3281	3609
3282	3610
3283	3612
"	6720
3284	3613
3285	3614
3286	3615
3287	3617
3288	3616
"	3618
3289	3446
"	3619
3290	3620
3291	3621
3292	3622
3293	3623
"	3624
"	3625
3294	3586
"	3628

STRONG	G/K
3295	3626
"	3627
3296	762
"	3629
3297	3630
3298	3631
3299	3632
"	3633
3300	3634
3301	3635
3302	3636
3303	3637
3304	3638
"	3645
3305	3639
3306	3640
3307	3641
3308	3642
3309	3643
"	3644
3310	3646
3311	3647
3312	3648
3313	3649
3314	3650
3315	3651
3316	3652
"	3653
3317	3654
3318	3448
"	3655
"	7361
3319	10707
3320	3656
"	7388
3321	10326
3322	3657
3323	3658
3324	3659
3325	3660
3326	3661
"	3662
"	3666
3327	3663
3328	3664
3329	3665
3330	10327
3331	3667
3332	3668
3333	3669
3334	7674
3335	3450
"	3670
3336	3671
3337	3672
3338	3674
3339	3673
3340	3672
3341	3675
3342	3676
3343	3677
3344	3678
"	3683
3345	10328
3346	10329
3347	3680
3348	3681
3349	3682
3350	3679
3351	3685
3352	3686
3353	3687
3354	3688
3355	3690
3356	3691
3357	3692
3358	10330
3359	3693
3360	3694
3361	3695
3362	3696
3363	3697
3364	3699
3365	3700
3366	3702
3367	10331
3368	3698
"	3701
"	3703
"	7941
3369	3704
3370	3705
3371	3706
3372	3707
"	3708
3373	3710
3374	3711
3375	3712
3376	3713
3377	3714
3378	3715
3379	3716
3380	3717
3381	3718
3382	3719

STRONG	G/K
3383	3720
3384	3452
"	3709
"	3721
"	3722
"	3723
3385	3725
3386	3726
3387	3728
3388	3729
"	3730
3389	3731
3390	10332
3391	3732
3392	3733
3393	10333
3394	3734
3395	3736
3396	3737
3397	3738
3398	3739
3399	3740
"	8184
3400	3741
3401	3742
3402	3743
3403	3744
3404	3745
"	3746
3405	3735
"	3747
3406	3748
"	3755
"	3756
3407	3749
3408	3750
3409	3751
3410	10334
3411	3752
3412	3754
3413	3757
3414	3758
"	3759
3415	3760
3416	3761
3417	3762
3418	3764
3419	3763
3420	3766
3421	3767
3422	3768
3423	3769
3424	3771
3425	3772
3426	3780
3427	3782
"	3794
3428	3784
3429	3783
3430	3785
"	3787
3431	3786
3432	3795
3433	3788
3434	3790
3435	3791
3436	3792
3437	3793
"	3806
3438	3796
3439	3797
3440	3798
3441	3799
3442	3800
"	3801
3443	10336
3444	3802
3445	3803
3446	3773
3447	3804
"	3805
3448	414
3449	3807
"	3808
3450	3774
3451	3809
"	3812
3452	3810
3453	3813
3454	3814
3455	3775
3456	3815
3457	3816
3458	3817
3459	3818
3460	3819
"	3820
3461	3821
3462	3822
"	3823
3463	3825
3464	3826
3465	3824
3466	3827
3467	3828

STRONG	G/K
"	3830
"	4635
3468	3829
3469	3831
3470	3832
"	3833
3471	3835
3472	3834
3473	3836
3474	3837
"	9223
3475	3840
3476	3841
3477	3838
"	3839
3478	3776
3479	10335
3480	3777
3481	3778
3482	3778
3483	3842
3484	3843
3485	3779
3486	3844
3487	10337
3488	10338
3489	3845
3490	3846
3491	3847
3492	3848
3493	10339
3494	3849
3495	3850
3496	3853
3497	3854
3498	3855
3499	3856
"	3857
3500	3858
3501	3859
3502	3860
3503	3861
3504	3862
3505	3863
3506	3864
3507	3865
3508	3866
3509	3867
3510	3872
3511	3873
3512	3874
3513	3877
3514	3880
3515	3878
3516	3879
3517	3881
3518	3882
3519	3883
3520	3884
"	3885
3521	3886
3522	3887
3523	3889
3524	3888
3525	3890
3526	3891
3527	3892
3528	3893
3529	3894
3530	3896
3531	3895
3532	3897
3533	3899
3534	3900
3535	3898
3536	3901
3537	3902
3538	10343
3539	3905
3540	3906
3541	3907
3542	10345
3543	3908
"	3909
3544	3910
3545	3911
3546	10346
3547	3912
3548	3913
3549	10347
3550	3914
3551	10348
3552	3915
3553	3916
3554	3917
3555	3918
3556	3919
3557	3920
3558	3921
3559	3922
"	5787
"	5788
3560	3923
3561	3924
3562	3925

STRONG	G/K
3563	3926
"	3927
3564	3929
3565	3930
3566	3931
3567	10350
3568	3932
"	3933
3569	3934
3570	3935
3571	3934
3572	3936
3573	3937
"	8403
3574	3938
3575	3939
"	3940
3576	3941
3577	3942
3578	3943
3579	3944
3580	3945
3581	3946
"	3947
3582	3948
3583	3949
3584	3950
3585	3951
3586	3952
3587	3953
3588	3954
3589	3957
3590	3958
3591	3959
3592	3961
3593	3960
3594	3962
3595	3963
3596	3964
3597	3965
3598	3966
3599	3967
3600	3968
3601	3969
3602	3970
3603	3971
3604	10352
3605	3972
3606	10353
3607	3973
"	3974
"	3984
3608	3975
3609	3976
3610	3977
3611	3978
3612	3979
"	3981
3613	3980
3614	3982
3615	3983
3616	3985
3617	3986
3618	3987
3619	3990
3620	3991
3621	3992
3622	3988
"	3993
3623	3994
3624	3995
3625	3996
3626	3997
3627	3998
3628	3989
"	3999
3629	4000
3630	4002
3631	4001
3632	4003
3633	4004
3634	4005
3635	10354
3636	4006
3637	4007
3638	4008
3639	4009
3640	4010
3641	4011
"	4012
3642	4014
3643	4016
"	4018
3644	4017
3645	4019
3646	4021
3647	4022
3648	4023
3649	4024
3650	4025
3651	4026
"	4027
"	4028
"	4338

STRONG	G/K
3652	10357
3653	4029
"	4030
3654	4031
"	4038
3655	4033
3656	4034
3657	4035
3658	4036
3659	4037
3660	10358
3661	
3662	4039
3663	4040
"	4041
"	4042
3664	4043
3665	4044
3666	4045
3667	4046
"	4047
3668	4049
3669	4048
"	4050
"	4051
3670	4052
3671	4053
3672	4054
"	4055
3673	10359
3674	4056
3675	10360
3676	4058
3677	4057
"	4060
3678	4058
"	4061
3679	10361
3680	4059
3681	4062
3682	4064
3683	4065
3684	4067
3685	4068
3686	4069
3687	4070
3688	4071
3689	4072
"	4073
3690	4074
3691	4075
3692	4077
3693	4076
3694	4063
3695	4078
3696	4079
3697	4080
3698	4081
3699	4082
3700	4083
3701	4084
3702	10362
3703	4085
3704	4086
3705	10363
3706	10364
"	10365
"	10563
3707	4087
3708	4088
"	4089
3709	4090
3710	4091
3711	4092
3712	4093
3713	4094
"	4095
3714	4096
3715	4097
"	4099
3716	4098
3717	4100
3718	4101
3719	4102
3720	4103
3721	4104
3722	4105
"	4106
3723	4107
3724	4108
"	4109
"	4110
"	4111
3725	4113
3726	2194
"	4112
"	6671
3727	4114
3728	4115
3729	10366
3730	4117
3731	4116
3732	4118
3733	4119
"	4120

STRONG	G/K
"	4121
3734	4123
"	10367
3735	10369
3736	4124
3737	10368
3738	3928
"	4125
"	4127
"	4128
3739	4126
3740	4130
3741	4129
3742	4131
3743	4132
3744	10370
3745	10371
3746	4133
3747	4134
3748	4135
3749	4136
3750	4137
3751	4138
3752	4139
3753	4140
3754	4142
"	4148
3755	4141
"	4144
3756	4145
3757	4146
3758	4147
3759	4149
"	4152
3760	4150
"	4151
3761	4153
3762	4153
3763	4154
3764	10372
3765	4155
3766	4156
3767	4157
3768	4158
3769	4159
3770	4160
3771	4161
3772	4162
3773	4164
3774	4165
3775	4166
3776	4167
3777	4168
3778	4169
3779	10373
3780	4170
3781	4172
3782	4173
3783	4174
3784	4175
3785	4176
3786	4177
3787	4178
3788	4179
3789	4180
3790	10374
3791	4181
3792	10375
3793	4182
3794	4183
3795	4184
3796	4185
3797	10376
3798	4186
3799	4187
3800	4188
3801	4189
3802	4190
3803	4192
"	4193
"	4194
3804	4195
3805	4196
3806	4197
3807	4198
3808	2132
"	4202
"	4257
3809	10379
"	10384
3810	4203
"	4274
3811	4206
3812	4207
3813	4209
3814	4319
3815	4210
3816	4211
3817	4212
3818	4204
3819	4205
"	6652
"	8170
3820	4213
3821	10380

STRONG	G/K
3822	4219
3823	4220
"	4221
3824	4222
3825	10381
3826	4226
3827	4225
3828	4227
"	4247
3829	4228
3830	4229
3831	10382
3832	4231
3833	4216
"	4218
"	4232
"	4233
"	4234
3834	4223
3835	4235
"	4236
3836	4237
3837	4238
"	4239
3838	4241
"	4245
3839	4242
3840	4246
3841	4243
3842	4244
3843	4246
3844	4248
3845	4249
3846	4250
3847	4252
3848	10383
3849	4253
3850	4254
3851	4258
3852	4259
3853	4260
3854	4261
3855	4262
3856	3532
"	4263
"	4264
"	4271
3857	4265
"	4266
3858	4267
"	4268
3859	4269
3860	2176
3861	10385
"	10386
3862	4272
3863	4273
3864	4275
3865	4276
3866	4276
3867	4277
"	4278
3868	4279
3869	4280
3870	4281
3871	4283
3872	4284
"	4304
3873	2135
3874	4286
3875	4287
3876	4288
3877	4289
3878	4290
"	4291
3879	10387
3880	4292
3881	4291
3882	4293
3883	4294
3884	4295
3885	4296
"	4328
"	4349
3886	4362
3887	4329
"	4370
3888	4297
3889	4298
3890	10388
3891	4299
3892	4300
3893	4301
3894	4302
"	4303
3895	4305
3896	4306
3897	4308
3898	4309
"	4310
3899	4312
3900	10389

STRONG	G/K
3901	4311
3902	4313
3903	4314
3904	10390
3905	4315
3906	4316
3907	4317
3908	4318
3909	4319
3910	4320
3911	4321
3912	4322
3913	4323
3914	4324
3915	4325
"	4326
3916	10391
3917	4327
3918	4330
3919	4298
"	4331
"	4332
"	4333
3920	4334
3921	4335
3922	4336
3923	4337
3924	4339
3925	4340
3926	4344
3927	4345
3928	4341
3929	4347
3930	4350
3931	4351
3932	4352
3933	4353
3934	4354
3935	4355
3936	4356
3937	4357
3938	4358
3939	4360
3940	4365
3941	4366
3942	7156
3943	4369
3944	4371
3945	4372
3946	4373
3947	3689
"	4374
"	7774
3948	4375
3949	4376
3950	4377
3951	4378
3952	4379
3953	4380
3954	4381
3955	4382
3956	4383
3957	4384
3958	4385
3959	4386
3960	4387
3961	10392
3962	4388
3963	4390
3964	10394
3965	4393
3966	4394
3967	4395
"	4405
3968	4396
3969	10395
3970	4397
3971	4398
"	4583
3972	4399
3973	4400
3974	4401
3975	4402
3976	4404
3977	10396
3978	4407
3979	4408
3980	4409
3981	4410
3982	4411
3983	10397
3984	10398
3985	4412
3986	4413
3987	4414
3988	4415
"	4416
"	5806
3989	4418
3990	4419
3991	4420
3992	4421
3993	4422
3994	4423
3995	4426

STRONG	G/K
3996	4427
3997	4427
3998	4428
3999	4429
4000	4430
4001	4431
4002	4432
4003	4433
4004	4435
4005	4436
4006	4437
4007	4438
4008	4439
4009	4440
4010	4443
4011	4445
4012	4446
4013	4448
"	4450
4014	4449
4015	4451
4016	4434
4017	4452
4018	4453
4019	4455
4020	4456
4021	4457
4022	4458
4023	4459
"	4461
4024	4460
"	4465
4025	4462
4026	4463
4027	4466
"	4464+446
4028	4467
4029	4468
4030	4469
"	4458
4031	4470
4032	4471
4033	4472
"	4473
4034	4475
4035	4476
4036	4474
"	4992
4037	4477
4038	4478
4039	4479
4040	10399
4041	4480
4042	4481
4043	4482
"	4483
"	4484
4044	4485
4045	4486
4046	4487
4047	4488
4048	4489
4049	10400
4050	4490
4051	4491
4052	4492
4053	4493
4054	4494
"	4495
4055	4496
4056	10401
4057	4497
"	4498
4058	4499
4059	4499
4060	4500
"	4501
"	4515
4061	10402
"	10429
4062	4502
"	5290
4063	4503
4064	4504
4065	4505
4066	4506
4067	4517
"	4528
4068	4507
4069	4508
4070	10403
4071	4509
4072	4510
4073	4511
4074	4512
4075	4513
4076	10404
4077	10404
4078	4537+1896
4079	4506
4080	4518
4081	4516
4082	4519
4083	10406
4084	4520
4085	4521
4086	4522
4087	4523
4088	4524
4089	4525
"	4526
4090	4506
4091	4527
4092	4520
4093	4529
4094	4532
4095	4533
4096	4534
4097	4535
4098	4536
4099	2158
4100	4342
"	4537
"	4768
"	8975
4101	10408
4102	4538
4103	4539
4104	4540
4105	4541
4106	4542
4107	4543
4108	4544
4109	4544
4110	4545
4111	4546
4112	4547
4113	4549
4114	4550
4115	4551
4116	4554
4117	4555
"	4556
4118	4557
4119	4558
4120	4559
4121	4560
4122	4561
4123	4562
4124	4565
"	4566
4125	4567
4126	4569
4127	4570
4128	4571
4129	4530
4130	4531
4131	4572
4132	4573
4133	4574
4134	4575
4135	4576
"	4577
4136	4346
"	4568
"	4578
4137	4579
4138	4580
4139	4581
4140	4582
4141	6015
4142	6015
4143	4586
4144	4587
4145	4588
4146	4589
4147	4591
"	4593
4148	4592
4149	4594
"	5035
4150	4595
4151	4596
4152	4597
4153	4598
4154	5048
4155	4599
4156	4600
4157	4601
4158	4602
"	4789
4159	4603
4160	5160
4161	4604
4162	4605
4163	4606
4164	4607
4165	4608
4166	4609
4167	4610
4168	4611
4169	4612
4170	4613
4171	4614
"	4615
4172	4616
4173	4617
4174	4618
4175	4619
"	4620
"	4621
4176	4622
4177	4623
4178	5307
4179	5317
4180	4625
"	4626
4181	4627
4182	4628
4183	4629
4184	4630
4185	4631
4186	4632
4187	4633
4188	4634
4189	5436
4190	4636
4191	4637
4192	4637
4193	10409
4194	4638
4195	4639
4196	4640
4197	4641
4198	4642
4199	4645
4200	4646
4201	4647
4202	4648
4203	10410
4204	4650
4205	4649
4206	4651
"	4652
"	4653
4207	4656
"	4657
"	4658
4208	4655
4209	4659
4210	4660
4211	4661
4212	4662
4213	4663
4214	4665
4215	4668
4216	4666
4217	4667
4218	4669
4219	4670
4220	4671
4221	4672
4222	4673
4223	10411
4224	4675
"	4676
4225	4678
4226	4677
4227	4679
4228	4680
4229	4674
"	4681
"	4682
"	4683
4230	4684
4231	4685
4232	4686
"	4696
4233	4687
4234	4688
4235	4689
4236	4690
4237	4691
4238	4692
4239	4693
4240	4694
4241	4695
4242	4697
4243	4698
4244	4702
4245	4700
"	4701
4246	4703
4247	4704
4248	4705
4249	4706
4250	4707
4251	4708
4252	4709
4253	4710
4254	4711
4255	10412
4256	4713
4257	4714
4258	4715
4259	4716
4260	4717
4261	4718
4262	4719
4263	4720
4264	4722
4265	4723
4266	4724
4267	4725
4268	4726
4269	4727
4270	4728
4271	4729
4272	4730
4273	4731
4274	4732
4275	4733
4276	4734
4277	4735
4278	4736
4279	4737
4280	4738
4281	4739
4282	4739
4283	4740
4284	4742
4285	4743
4286	4741
4287	4744
4288	4745
4289	4746
4290	4747
4291	10413
4292	4748
4293	4749
4294	4751
4295	4752
4296	4753
4297	4754
4298	4755
4299	4757
4300	4758
4301	4759
4302	4760
4303	4761
4304	4762
4305	4763
4306	4764
4307	4766
4308	4765
4309	4767
4310	4769
4311	4772
4312	4773
4313	2126
"	3765
"	4770
4314	4771
4315	4774
4316	4775
4317	4776
4318	4777
4319	4778
4320	4779
4321	4781
4322	4780
4323	4782
4324	4783
4325	4784
4326	4785
4327	4786
4328	4588
4329	4590
"	4788
4330	4790
4331	4791
4332	4792
4333	10414
4334	4793
4335	4794
4336	10415
4337	4796
4338	4795
4339	4797
4340	4798
4341	4799
4342	3892
4343	4800
4344	4801
4345	4803
4346	4802
4347	4804
4348	4805
4349	4806
4350	4807
4351	4808
4352	4809
4353	4810
4354	4811
4355	4812
4356	4813
4357	4816
4358	4814
4359	4817
4360	4815
4361	4818
4362	4819
4363	4820
"	4825
4364	4821
4365	4822
"	4823
4366	4826
4367	4827
4368	4828
4369	4807
4370	4829
4371	4830
4372	4832
4373	4831
4374	4833
4375	4834
4376	4835
4377	4836
4378	4837
4379	4838
4380	4839
4381	4840
4382	4841
4383	4842
4384	4843
4385	4844
4386	4845
4387	4846
4388	4847
4389	4847
4390	4848
"	4862
4391	10416
4392	4849
4393	4850
4394	4854
4395	4852
4396	4853
4397	4855
4398	10417
4399	4856
4400	4857
4401	4858
4402	4859
4403	4860
4404	4861
"	4905
4405	4863
4406	10418
4407	4851
"	4864
4408	4865
4409	4866
"	4868
"	4883
4410	4867
4411	4869
4412	4870
4413	4871
4414	4872
"	4873
4415	10419
4416	4420
4417	4875
4418	4874
4419	4876
4420	4877
4421	4878
4422	4880
"	4881
4423	4879
4424	4882
4425	4884
4426	4886
4427	4887
4428	4889
"	4890
4429	4889
4430	10421
4431	10422
4432	4891
4433	10423
4434	4892
4435	4894
4436	4893
4437	10424
4438	4895
4439	4896
4440	4897
4441	4898
"	4899
4442	4900
4443	4901
4444	4902
4445	4903
"	4904
4446	4906
4447	2168
"	4907
4448	4910
"	4911
4449	10425
4450	4912
4451	4913
4452	4914
4453	4915
4454	4916
4455	4917
"	4918
4456	4919
4457	4920
4458	4921
4459	4922
4460	4923
4461	4924
4462	4584
"	4925
4463	4926
4464	4927
4465	4928
4466	4929
4467	4930
4468	4931
4469	4932
4470	4933
4471	4934
"	4935
4472	4936
4473	4937
4474	4938
4475	4939
4476	4940
4477	4941
4478	4942
"	4943
4479	10426
4480	4946
"	4974
4481	10427
4482	4944
"	4945
4483	10431
4484	10428
4485	4947
4486	10430
4487	4948
4488	4949
4489	4951
4490	4950
4491	4952
4492	4953
4493	4954
4494	4955
4495	4956
4496	4957
"	4967
4497	4959
4498	4960
4499	4961
4500	4962
4501	4963
4502	4964
4503	4966
4504	10432
4505	4968
4506	4969
"	4970
4507	4972
4508	4973
4509	4975
4510	10433
4511	4976
"	4977
4512	4978
4513	4979
4514	4980
4515	4981
4516	4982
4517	4983
4518	4984
4519	4985
4520	4986
4521	4987
4522	4989
4523	4988
4524	4990
"	4991
4525	4993
"	4994
4526	4995
4527	4996
4528	4997
4529	4998
4530	5002
4531	4999
4532	5001
4533	5003
4534	5004
4535	5005
4536	5006
4537	5007
4538	5008
4539	5009
4540	5010
4541	5011
"	5012
"	5013
4542	5014
4543	5016
4544	5017
4545	5018
4546	5019
4547	5020
4548	5021
4549	5022
4550	5023
4551	5024
"	5025
4552	5026
4553	5027
4554	5028
4555	5029
4556	5030
4557	5031
4558	5032
4559	5033
4560	5034
4561	5036
4562	5037
4563	5039
4564	5040
4565	5041
4566	5042
4567	10434
4568	5043
4569	5044
"	5045
4570	5046
"	5047
4571	5048
4572	5049
4573	5050
4574	5052
4575	5051
4576	5053
4577	10435
4578	5055
4579	5054
4580	5056
4581	5057
"	5058
4582	5059
4583	5060
"	5061
"	5079
4584	5062
"	5063
4585	5104
4586	5064
4587	5065
4588	5066
4589	5067
4590	5068
"	5069
4591	5070
4592	5071
4593	6487
4594	5073
4595	5074
4596	5075
4597	5076
4598	5077
4599	5078
4600	5080
4601	5081
"	5082
"	5083
4602	5084
4603	5085
4604	5086
4605	5087
"	5093
4606	10436
4607	5089
4608	5090
4609	5091
"	5092
4610	5090+6832
4611	5094
"	5095
4612	5096
4613	5097
4614	5098
4615	5099
4616	4348
4617	5101
"	5102
4618	5103
"	5105
4619	5106
4620	5107
4621	5108
4622	5109
4623	5110
4624	5111
4625	5112
4626	5113
4627	5114
4628	5115
4629	5116
4630	5120
4631	5117
4632	5118
"	6869
4633	5119
4634	5120
4635	5121
4636	5122
4637	5124
4638	5125
4639	5126
4640	5127
4641	5128
"	5129
4642	5131
4643	5130
4644	5132
4645	5133
4646	5134
4647	5135
4648	5136
4649	5137
4650	5138
4651	5139
4652	5140
4653	5141
4654	5142
"	5143
4655	5144
4656	5145
4657	5146
4658	5147
4659	5148
"	5149
4660	5150
4661	5151
4662	5152
4663	5152
4664	5153
4665	5154
4666	5155
4667	5156
4668	5158
4669	5157
4670	5159
4671	5161
4672	5162
4673	5163
4674	5164
4675	5165
"	5166
4676	5167
4677	5168
4678	5169
"	5170
4679	5171
4680	5172
4681	5173
4682	5174
4683	5175
4684	5177
4685	5178
"	5179
4686	5180
"	5181
"	5192
4687	5184
4688	5185
"	5198
4689	5186
4690	5187
4691	5188
4692	5189
4693	5191
4694	5193
"	5211
4695	5194
"	5195
4696	5196
4697	5196
4698	5197
4699	5185
4700	5199
4701	5200
4702	5201
4703	5202
4704	7582
4705	5203
4706	5204
4707	5205
4708	5206
4709	5207
4710	5208
4711	5209
4712	5210
4713	5212
4714	5213
4715	5214
4716	5215
4717	5216
4718	5216
"	5217
4719	5218
4720	5219
4721	5220
4722	5221
4723	5223
"	5224
"	7745
"	7750
4724	5225
4725	5226

STRONG	G/K
4726	5227
4727	5228
4728	5229
4729	5230
4730	5233
4731	5234
4732	5235
4733	5236
4734	5237
4735	5238
4736	5239
4737	5240
4738	5241
4739	5242
4740	5243
4741	5244
4742	7910
4743	5245
4744	5246
4745	5247
4746	5248
4747	5249
4748	5250
4749	5251
4750	5252
4751	5253
"	5287
4752	5254
4753	5255
4754	5256
"	5257
4755	5259
4756	10437
4757	5282
4758	5260
4759	5261
"	5262
4760	5263
4761	5265
4762	5358
"	5359
4763	5265
"	8039
4764	5266
4765	5267
4766	5269
4767	5268
4768	5270
4769	5271
4770	5272
4771	5273
4772	5274
4773	5275
4774	5276
4775	5277
4776	10438
4777	5278
4778	5279
4779	10439
4780	5280
4781	5281
4782	5283
4783	5284
4784	5286
4785	5288
4786	5289
4787	5285
4788	5291
4789	5292
4790	5293
4791	5294
4792	5295
4793	5296
4794	5297
4795	5299
4796	5300
4797	5301
4798	5301
4799	5302
4800	5303
4801	5305
4802	5306
4803	5307
4804	10440
4805	5308
4806	5258
"	5309
4807	5311
"	5314
4808	5312
4809	5313
4810	5311
4811	5316
4812	5318
4813	5319
4814	5320
4815	5321
4816	5322
4817	5323
4818	5324
4819	5326
4820	5327
4821	5328
4822	5329
4823	5330
4824	5331
4825	5332
4826	5333
4827	5334
4828	5335
4829	5337
4830	5338
4831	5339
4832	5340
"	5341
"	5342
4833	5343
4834	5344
4835	5298
4836	5345
4837	5346
4838	5347
4839	5348
4840	5349
4841	5350
4842	5351
4843	5352
4844	5353
4845	5354
4846	5355
4847	5356
4848	5357
4849	5360
4850	5361
4851	5390
4852	5392
4853	5362
"	5363
4854	5364
4855	5391
4856	5365
4857	5393
4858	5366
4859	5394
4860	5396
4861	5398
4862	5399
4863	5400
4864	5367
"	5368
4865	5401
4866	5402
4867	5403
4868	5404
4869	5369
"	5370
4870'	5405
4871	5406
4872	5407
4873	10441
4874	5408
4875	5409
4876	5397
"	5410
4877	5411
4878	5412
4879	5413
4880	5414
"	5415
4881	5372
4882	5416
4883	5373
4884	5374
4885	5375
"	5376
4886	5417
4887	10442
4888	5418
"	5419
"	5420
"	5421
4889	5422
4890	5377
4891	5423
4892	5424
4893	5425
"	5426
4894	5427
4895	5378
4896	5428
4897	5429
4898	5430
4899	5431
4900	5432
4901	5433
4902	5434
4903	10444
4904	5435
4905	5380
4906	5381
4907	10445
4908	5438
4909	5382
4910	5440
4911	5439
"	5441
4912	5442
4913	5443
4914	5446
4915	5444
"	5445
4916	5447
"	5448
4917	5449
4918	5450
4919	5451
4920	5452
"	5453
4921	5454
4922	5455
4923	5457
4924	5458
"	5460
"	9044
4925	5459
4926	5461
4927	5462
4928	5463
4929	5464
"	5465
4930	5383
4931	5466
4932	5467
4933	5468
4934	5469
4935	5470
4936	5471
4937	5472
"	5473
4938	5474
"	5475
4939	5384
4940	5476
4941	5477
4942	5478
4943	5479
4944	5480
4945	5482
"	5483
4946	5484
4947	5485
4948	5486
4949	5487
4950	5488
4951	5385
4952	5489
4953	10446
4954	5490
4955	5386
4956	5387
4957	5388
4958	5389
4959	5491
4960	5492
4961	10447
4962	5493
"	5494
4963	5495
4964	5496
4965	566
"	2031
"	5497
4966	5498
4967	5499
4968	5500
4969	5501
4970	5503
4971	5504
4972	5505
4973	5506
4974	5507
4975	5516
4976	5508
4977	5509
4978	10448
4979	5510
4980	5511
4981	5512
4982	5513
4983	5514
"	5515
4984	5951
4985	5517
4986	5518
4987	5519
4988	5517
4989	5520
4990	5521
4991	5522
4992	5523
4993	5524
"	5525
4994	5528
4995	5529
4996	5530
4997	5532
4998	5533
4999	5661
5000	5534
5001	5535
5002	5536
5003	5537
5004	5539
5005	5538
5006	5540
5007	5541
"	5542
5008	5543
5009	5544
5010	5545
5011	5546
5012	5547
5013	10451
5014	5548
"	5554
5015	5549
"	5550
"	5551
5016	5553
5017	10452
5018	5555
5019	5556
"	5557
5020	10453
5021	5558
5022	5559
5023	10454
5024	5560
5025	5561
"	5562
5026	5563
5027	5564
5028	5565
5029	10455
5030	5566
5031	5567
5032	5568
5033	5569
5034	5570
"	5571
5035	5574
"	5575
5036	5572
5037	5573
5038	5577
5039	5576
5040	5578
5041	5579
5042	5580
5043	10456
5044	5581
5045	5582
5046	5583
5047	10457
5048	5584
5049	10458
5050	5585
5051	5586
5052	5587
5053	10459
5054	5588
5055	5590
5056	5591
5057	5592
5058	5593
5059	5594
5060	5595
5061	5596
5062	5597
5063	5598
5064	5599
"	5600
5065	5601
5066	5602
5067	5603
5068	5605
5069	10461
"	10219
5070	5606
5071	5607
5072	5608
5073	10462
5074	5610
5075	10463
5076	5611
5077	5604
"	5612
5078	5613
5079	5614
5080	5615
"	5616
5081	5618
5082	5619
5083	5621
5084	5620
5085	10464
5086	5622
5087	5623
5088	5624
5089	5625
5090	5627
"	5628
5091	5629
"	5630
5092	5631
5093	5632
5094	10466
"	10467
"	10465
5095	5633
5096	5634
"	5636
5097	5635
5098	5637
5099	5638
5100	5639
5101	5640
5102	5641
"	5642
5103	10468
5104	5643
5105	5644
5106	5648
5107	5649
5108	5650
"	5762
5109	5651
"	5763
5110	5653
5111	10469
5112	5617
"	5654
5113	5655
5114	5656
5115	5657
"	5658
5116	5659
"	5660
5117	5663
"	5664
"	5698
5118	5665
5119	5666
5120	5667
5121	5662
"	5668
"	5766
5122	10470
5123	5670
5124	5671
5125	5672
"	5768
5126	5673
5127	5674
5128	5675
5129	5676
5130	2185
"	5677
"	5678
5131	5679
5132	5680
5133	5681
"	5901
"	5902
5134	3567
5135	10471
5136	5683
5137	5684
"	5685
5138	5686
5139	5687
5140	5688
"	5689
5141	5690
5142	10472
5143	5691
5144	5692
"	5693
5145	5694
5146	5695
5147	5696
5148	5697
5149	5700
"	5719
5150	5699
5151	5699
5152	5701
5153	5702
5154	5703
5155	5704
5156	5705
5157	5706
5158	5707
"	5708
"	5711
5159	5709
5160	5712
5161	5713
5162	5714
5163	5715
5164	5716
5165	5717
5166	5718
5167	5720
5168	5721
5169	5722
5170	5724
"	5725
5171	5726
5172	5727
5173	5728
5174	10473
5175	5729
5176	5731
5177	5732
5178	5733
"	5734
5179	5735
5180	5736
5181	5737
5182	10474
5183	5738
"	5739
5184	5740
5185	5741
5186	5742
5187	5744
5188	5755
5189	5746
5190	5747
5191	10475
5192	5748
5193	5749
5194	5750
5195	5745
5196	5751
5197	5752
5198	5753
"	5754
5199	5756
5200	5743
5201	5757
"	5758
5202	10476
5203	5759
5204	5760
5205	5764
5206	5765
5207	5767
5208	10478
5209	5769
5210	5770
5211	5771
5212	5772
5213	5773
5214	5774
5215	5776
5216	5775
"	5944
5217	5777
5218	5778
"	5779
5219	5780
5220	5781
5221	5782
5222	5784
5223	5783
5224	5786
"	5785
5225	5789
5226	5790
5227	5790
5228	5791
5229	5791
5230	5792
5231	5793
5232	10479
5233	5794
5234	5795
"	5796
5235	5798
5236	5797
5237	5799
5238	5800
5239	5801
5240	1022
5241	5803
5242	5804
5243	4908
"	4909
5244	5805
5245	10480
5246	5807
5247	5809
5248	5808
5249	5810
5250	5811
5251	5812
5252	5813
5253	8450
5254	5814
5255	5815
5256	10481
5257	5816
"	5817
5258	5818
5259	5819
5260	10482
5261	10483
5262	5821
"	5822
5263	5823
5264	5824
5265	5825
5266	5826
5267	10513
5268	5827
5269	5828
5270	5829
5271	5830
"	5831
5272	5832
5273	5833
"	5834
5274	5835
"	5836
5275	5837
5276	5838
5277	5839
5278	5840
5279	5841
"	5842
5280	5844
5281	5843
5282	5846
5283	5845
5284	5847
5285	5848
5286	5849
5287	5850
"	5851
5288	5853
5289	5852
5290	5854
5291	5855
5292	5856
"	5857
5293	5858
5294	5859
5295	5860
5296	5861
5297	5862
5298	5863
5299	5864
"	5865
5300	5866
"	5867
"	5875
5301	5870
5302	5871
5303	5872
5304	5873
5305	5874
5306	5876
5307	5877
5308	10484
5309	5878
5310	5879
"	5880
5311	5881
5312	10485
5313	10486
5314	5882
5315	5883
5316	5868
"	5884
5317	5885
5318	5886
5319	5887
5320	5888
5321	5889
5322	5890
"	5891
5323	5892
5324	2205
"	5893
"	5894
"	5895
5325	5896
5326	10487
5327	5897
"	5898
5328	5900
5329	5904
5330	10488
5331	5905
5332	5906
5333	5907
5334	5908
5335	5909
5336	5910
5337	5911
5338	10489
5339	5912
5340	5913
5341	5903
"	5915
"	5917
5342	5916
5343	10490
5344	5918
"	5919
5345	5920
"	5921
5346	2186
5347	5922
5348	5923
5349	5924
5350	5926
5351	5925
5352	5927
5353	5928
5354	7752
5355	5929
"	5930
5356	5931
"	7734
5357	5932
5358	5933
5359	5934
5360	5935
5361	5936
5362	5937
"	5938
5363	5939
5364	5940
5365	5941
5366	5942
5367	5943
5368	10491
5369	5945
5370	5946
5371	5947
5372	8087
5373	5948
5374	5949
"	5950
5375	5951
5376	10492
5377	5958
5378	5957
"	5961
5379	5951
5380	5959
5381	5371
"	5952
5382	5960
5383	5957
5384	5962
5385	5953
5386	5963
5387	5954
"	5955
5388	5964
5389	10493
5390	5965
5391	5966
"	5967
5392	5968
5393	5969
5394	5970
5395	5971
5396	10494
5397	5972
5398	5973
5399	5974
5400	5956
5401	5975
"	5976
5402	5977
"	5978
5403	10495
5404	5979
5405	5980
5406	5981
5407	10496
5408	5983
5409	5984
5410	5985
"	5986
5411	5982
"	5987
5412	10497
5413	5988
5414	3851
"	3852
"	5989
5415	10498
5416	5990
5417	5991
5418	5992
"	5993
5419	5994
5420	5995
5421	5996
5422	5997
5423	5998
5424	5999
5425	6000
"	6001
"	6002
5426	10499
5427	6003
5428	6004
5429	6006
5430	6007
5431	6008
5432	6009
5433	6010
"	6012
5434	6013
5435	6011
5436	6014
5437	6015
5438	6016
5439	4585
"	6017
5440	6018
5441	6020

STRONG	G/K
5442	6019
5443	10501
"	10676
5444	6021
5445	6022
5446	10502
5447	6023
5448	6024
5449	6025
5450	6026
5451	6027
5452	10503
5453	6028
5454	6029
"	6030
5455	6031
5456	6032
5457	10504
5458	6033
5459	6035
5460	10505
5461	6036
5462	6034
"	6037
"	6038
5463	10506
5464	6039
5465	6040
5466	6041
5467	6042
5468	6043
5469	6044
5470	6045
5471	6046
5472	6047
5473	6048
5474	6050
5475	6051
5476	6052
5477	6053
5478	6054
5479	6055
5480	6057
5481	10507
5482	6059
5483	6061
"	6062
"	6101
5484	6063
5485	6064
5486	6066
5487	10508
5488	6068
5489	6069
5490	6067
5491	10509
5492	6070
"	6071
5493	6073
"	6233
"	8462
5494	6074
"	6076
5495	6075
5496	6077
5497	6078
5498	6079
5499	6080
5500	6081
5501	6082
5502	2900
"	6085
5503	6086
5504	6087
5505	6086
5506	6088
5507	6089
5508	6090
5509	6049
"	6092
"	6213
5510	6094
5511	6095
5512	6096
"	6097
5513	6098
5514	6099
5515	6060
"	6100
5516	6102
5517	6103
"	6104
5518	6105
"	6106
5519	6107
5520	6108
5521	6109
5522	6110
5523	6111
5524	6112
5525	6113
5526	6056
"	6058
"	6114
"	6115
"	6116
"	8503
5527	6117
5528	6118
5529	6120
5530	6119
5531	6121
"	8508
5532	6122
"	6125
5533	5015
"	6123
"	6124
5534	6126
"	6127
5535	6129
5536	6130
5537	6131
5538	6133
5539	6134
5540	6135
5541	6136
"	6137
5542	6138
5543	6132
"	6139
"	6140
"	6144
5544	6141
5545	6142
5546	6143
5547	6145
5548	6146
5549	6147
"	6148
5550	6149
5551	6150
5552	6151
5553	6152
5554	6153
5555	2165
"	4712
"	6154
5556	6155
5557	6156
5558	6157
5559	10513
5560	6159
5561	6160
5562	5552
"	6161
"	6162
5563	6163
5564	6164
5565	6165
5566	6166
5567	6168
5568	6169
5569	6170
5570	2189
"	2190
"	6171
5571	6172
5572	6174
5573	6175
5574	6176
5575	6177
5576	6178
5577	6180
5578	6179
5579	6181
5580	6182
5581	6183
5582	6184
5583	10514
5584	6185
5585	6186
"	6187
5586	6188
5587	6191
"	8546
5588	6189
5589	6190
5590	6192
5591	6193
"	6194
5592	6195
"	6196
"	6197
5593	6198
5594	6199
5595	6200
5596	6202
"	6203
"	8558
5597	6204
5598	6205
5599	6206
"	6207
5600	6208
5601	6209
5602	6210
5603	6201
"	6211
5604	6212
5605	6214
5606	6215
"	6216
5607	6217
"	8565
5608	6218
"	6221
5609	10515
5610	6222
5611	6223
5612	6219
"	6220
"	6225
5613	10516
5614	6224
5615	6228
5616	6227
5617	6226
5618	2191
"	6072
"	6230
5619	6232
5620	6234
5621	6235
5622	10517
5623	6236
5624	6237
5625	6238
5626	6241
5627	6239
"	6240
5628	6242
"	6243
"	6244
5629	6245
5630	6246
5631	6247
5632	10518
5633	6248
"	6249
5634	6250
5635	6251
5636	6252
5637	6253
5638	6255
"	6257
5639	6256
5640	6258
"	8608
5641	6259
5642	10519
"	10520
5643	6260
"	6261
5644	6262
5645	6265
"	6266
"	6267
5646	6264
5647	6268
5648	10522
5649	10523
5650	6269
5651	6270
5652	6271
5653	6272
5654	6273
5655	6274
5656	6275
5657	6276
5658	6277
"	6278
5659	6285
5660	6279
5661	6280
5662	6281
"	6282
5663	6283
5664	5589
"	6284
5665	10524
5666	6286
5667	6287
5668	6288
5669	6289
5670	6292
"	6293
5671	6294
5672	6295
5673	10525
5674	6296
"	6297
5675	10526
5676	6298
5677	6299
5678	6301
5679	6302
5680	6303
5681	6304
5682	6305
5683	2496
5684	6307
5685	6308
5686	6309
5687	6290
5688	6291
"	6310
5689	6311
5690	6313
5691	6312
5692	6314
5693	6315
5694	6316
5695	6319
5696	6318
5697	6320
5698	6321
5699	6317
"	6322
5700	6323
"	6324
5701	6327
5702	6328
5703	6329
5704	6330
5705	10527
5706	6331
5707	6332
5708	6340
5709	10528
5710	6334
"	6335
5711	6336
5712	6337
5713	6338
5714	6333
"	6341
"	6342
"	6345
"	10529
5715	6343
5716	6344
5717	6346
5718	6347
"	6348
5719	6349
5720	6350
5721	6351
5722	6352
5723	6353
5724	6354
5725	6355
5726	6356
5727	6357
5728	6362
"	6364
5729	6361
5730	6358
"	6366
5731	6359
"	6360
5732	10530
5733	6363
5734	6365
"	6367
5735	6368
"	6900
5736	6369
5737	6370
"	6371
"	6372
5738	6376
5739	6373
5740	6374
"	6375
5741	6377
5742	6378
5743	6380
5744	6381
5745	6382
5746	6383
5747	6384
5748	6385
5749	6386
"	6387
5750	6388
5751	10531
5752	6389
5753	6390
"	6391
5754	6392
5755	6379
"	6393
"	6394
5756	6395
5757	6398
5758	10532
5759	6396
5760	6397
5761	6398
"	6399
5762	6400
"	6511
5763	6402
5764	6403
5765	6401
5766	6404
"	6406
"	6593
"	6637
5767	6405
5768	6407
"	6408
5769	6409
5770	6523
5771	6411
5772	6703
5773	6413
5774	6414
"	6415
"	6545
"	6758
"	9507
5775	6416
5776	10533
5777	6769
5778	6417
"	6550
5779	6418
5780	6419
"	6420
5781	6421
5782	6424
"	6749
5783	6423
5784	10534
5785	6425
5786	6422
5787	6426
5788	6427
"	6428
5789	6429
5790	6431
5791	6430
5792	6432
5793	6433
5794	6434
"	6435
5795	6436
5796	10535
5797	6437
5798	6438
"	6446
5799	6439
5800	6440
"	6441
5801	6442
5802	6443
5803	6444
5804	6445
5805	6447
5806	6448
5807	6449
5808	6450
5809	6473
5810	6451
5811	6452
5812	6453
5813	6454
5814	6455
5815	6456
5816	6457
5817	6458
5818	6459
"	6460
5819	6461
5820	6462
"	6463
5821	6464
5822	6465
5823	6466
5824	10536
5825	6467
5826	6468
5827	6470
5828	6469
5829	6470
"	6472
5830	6474
5831	10537
5832	6475
5833	6476
5834	6477
5835	6478
5836	6479
5837	6480
5838	6481
"	6482
5839	10538
5840	6483
5841	6484
5842	6485
5843	10539
5844	6486
"	6487
5845	6489
5846	6490
5847	6491
5848	6488
"	6493
"	6494
5849	6496
"	6497
5850	6498
5851	6499
5852	6500
5853	6501
5854	6502
5855	6503
"	8794
5856	6505
5857	6504
"	6509
"	6569
5858	6506
"	6507
"	6508
5859	6510
5860	6512
"	6513
5861	6514
5862	6515
5863	2192
"	6300
"	6516
5864	6517
5865	6518
5866	6519
5867	6520
"	6521
5868	6522
5869	6412
"	6524
5870	10540
5871	6526
5872	6527
5872 to 5887	6525
5873	1712
5874	6529
5875	2213
"	6530
5876	6532
5877	6533
5878	3008
"	6534
5879	6542
"	6543
5880	6535
5881	6544
5882	6325
"	6536
5883	6537
"	8080
5884	6538
5885	6539
5886	5624+9478
5887	6540
5888	6545
5889	6546
5890	6547
5891	6548
"	6549
5892	6551
"	6552
5893	6553
5894	10541
5895	6554
"	6555
5896	6562
5897	6563
5898	6558
5899	6559
5900	6564
5901	6565
5902	6566
5903	6567
5904	5730
"	6560
5905	6561
5906	6568
5907	6570
5908	6571
5909	6572
5910	6573
5911	6574
5912	6575
5913	6576
5914	6577
5915	6578
5916	6579
5917	6580
5918	6581
5919	6582
5920	6583
5921	6584
5922	10542
5923	6585
5924	10543
5925	6587
5926	6589
5927	6158
"	6590
5928	10545
5929	6591
5930	6592
5931	10544
5932	6594
5933	6595
"	6607
5934	6596
5935	6597
"	6615
5936	6598
5937	6600
5938	6601
5939	6602
5940	6605
5941	6603
5942	6604
"	6606
5943	10546
5944	6608
5945	6609
"	6610
5946	10548
5947	6611
5948	6612
5949	6613
5950	6614
5951	6617
5952	10547
5953	6618
"	6619
"	6620
"	6621
5954	10549
5955	6622
5956	6623
5957	10550
5958	6624
5959	6625
5960	6626
5961	6628
5962	10551
5963	6627
5964	6630
5965	6631
5966	6632
5967	10552
5968	6634
5969	6635
5970	6636
5971	6638
"	6639
5972	10553
5973	6640
5974	10554
5975	6641
5976	5048
5977	6642
5978	6643
5979	6644
5980	6645
5981	6646
5982	6647
5983	6648
5984	6649
5985	6649
5986	6650
5987	6651
5988	6653
5989	6654
5990	6655
5991	6656
5992	6657
5993	5816+6639
5994	10555
5995	6658
5996	6659
5997	6660
5998	6661
5999	6662
6000	6663
6001	6664
"	6665
6002	6667
6003	6668
6004	6669
"	6670
6005	6672
6006	6673
6007	6674
6008	6675
6009	6676
6010	6677
6011	6679
6012	6680
6013	6678
6014	6682
"	6683
6015	10556
6016	6684
"	6685
6017	6686
6018	6687
6019	6688
6020	6689
6021	6690
6022	6691
6023	6692
6024	6693
6025	6694
6026	6695
6027	6696
6028	6697
6029	6698
6030	4361
"	6410
"	6699
"	6702
6031	6700
"	6701
6032	10558
6033	10559
6034	6704
6035	6705
6036	6718
6037	6709
6038	6708
6039	6713
6040	6715
6041	6714
6042	6706
"	6716
6043	6717
6044	6719
6045	6721
6046	6722
6047	6723
6048	6724
6049	6725
"	6726
6050	10560
6051	6727
6052	6728
6053	6729
6054	6730
6055	6731
6056	10561
6057	6733
6058	6734
6059	6735
6060	6736
6061	6710
6062	6737
6063	6738
"	6739
6064	6711
"	6740
6065	10562
6066	6741
6067	6742
6068	6743
"	6744
6069	6745
6070	6746
6071	6747
6072	6748
6073	6751
6074	10564
6075	6752
"	6753
6076	6754
6077	6755
6078	6756
6079	6757
6080	6759
6081	6761
6082	6762
6083	6760
6084	6763
"	6764
6085	6766
"	6767
6086	6770
6087	6771
"	6772
6088	10565
6089	6775
6090	6777
"	6776
6091	6773
6092	6774
6093	6779
6094	6780
6095	6781
6096	6782
6097	6785
6098	6783
"	6784
6099	6786
6100	6787
6101	6788
6102	6789
6103	6790
6104	6791
6105	6793
"	6794
6106	6795
6107	6796
"	6799
6108	6797
"	6798

STRONG	G/K	STRONG	G/K	STRONG	G/K	STRONG	G/K	STRONG	G/K	STRONG	G/K	STRONG	G/K	STRONG	G/K
6109	6800	6203	6902	6293	7003	6379	7096	6468	7190	6558	7291	6647	10607	6733	7491
6110	6802	6204	6905	6294	7004	6380	2207	6469	7191	6559	7292	6648	7389	6734	7492
6111	6801	6205	6906	6295	7005	"	7097	6470	7192	6560	7290	6649	7390	6735	7493
6112	6804	6206	5123	6296	7006	6381	7098	6471	7193	6561	7293	6650	7391	"	7494
6113	6806	"	6907	6297	7007	6382	7099	6472	7194	6562	10596	6651	7392	"	7495
6114	6807	6207	6908	6298	7008	6383	7100	6473	7196	6563	7294	6652	7393	"	7496
6115	6808	6208	6909	6299	7009	6384	7101	6474	7197	6564	7295	6653	7395	6736	7497
6116	6809	6209	6910	6300	7010	6385	7103	6475	7198	6565	7296	6654	7396	6737	7493
6117	6810	6210	6911	6301	7011	6386	10583	6476	7199	"	7297	"	7397	"	7494
6118	6813	6211	6931	6302	7012	6387	10584	"	7200	6566	7298	6655	10608	"	7495
6119	6811	"	6932	6303	7013	6388	7104	6477	7201	6567	7300	6656	10609	"	7496
6120	6812	"	6933	6304	7014	6389	7105	6478	7202	"	7301	6657	7398	6738	7498
6121	6814	6211'	10572	"	7151	6390	7106	6479	7203	6568	10597	6658	7399	6739	10612
"	6815	6212	6912	6305	7015	6391	7107	6480	7204	6569	7302	"	7400	6740	7499
6122	6817	6213	6913	"	7016	6392	10585	6481	7205	6570	7303	6659	7401	6741	7500
6123	6818	"	6914	6306	7017	6393	7110	6482	7206	6571	7304	6660	7402	6742	7501
6124	6819	6214	6915	"	7018	6394	7109	6483	2204	"	7305	6661	7403	"	7508
6125	6821	6215	6916	6307	7019	6395	7111	"	7209	6572	7306	6662	7404	6743	7502
6126	6822	6216	6934	"	7020	6396	7112	6484	7210	"	7358	6663	7405	"	7503
6127	6823	6217	6935	6308	7021	6397	7113	6485	7212	6573	10598	6664	7406	6744	10613
6128	6824	6218	6917	6309	7022	6398	7114	"	7217	6574	7307	6665	10610	6745	7505
6129	6825	6219	6936	6310	7023	6399	10586	"	7227	6575	7308	6666	7407	6746	7504
6130	6826	6220	6937	6311	7024	6400	7115	6486	7213	6576	7299	6667	7408	6747	7505
6131	6827	6221	6918	6312	7025	6401	7116	6487	7214	6577	7309	"	7409	"	7506
"	6828	6222	6919	"	7026	6402	10587	6488	7215	6578	7310	6668	5176	6748	7507
6132	10566	6223	6938	"	7030	6403	7117	6489	7216	6579	7312	6669	7411	6749	7510
6133	6830	6224	6920	6313	7028	6404	7118	6490	7218	6580	7317	6670	7412	6750	7509
6134	6831	6225	6939	6314	7029	6405	7119	6491	7219	6581	7313	"	7413	6751	7511
6135	6829	6226	6942	6315	7031	6406	7120	6492	7220	6582	7318	6671	7414	6752	7498
6136	10567	6227	6940	"	7032	6407	7121	6493	7221	6583	7319	6672	7415	6753	2209
6137	6832	6228	6941	6316	7033	6408	7122	6494	7222	6584	7320	"	7416	6754	7512
6138	6833	6229	6921	6317	7034	6409	7123	6495	7223	6585	7314	6673	7417	"	7513
6139	6834	6230	6922	6318	7035	6410	7124	"	7751	6586	7321	6674	7364	6755	10614
6140	6835	6231	6943	6319	7036	"	7125	6496	7224	6587	7315	6675	7363	6756	7514
6141	6836	6232	6944	"	7280	6411	7102	6497	7225	6588	7322	6676	10611	"	7515
6142	6837	6233	6945	6320	7037	"	7126	6498	7226	6589	7316	6677	7418	6757	7516
6143	6838	6234	6946	6321	7038	6412	7127	6499	7228	6590	10599	"	7454	6758	7517
6144	6840	6235	6924	6322	7039	"	7128	6500	7229	6591	10600	6678	7419	6759	7518
6145	6839	"	6927	"	7040	6413	7129	6501	7230	6592	7323	"	7420	6760	7519
6146	10568	6236	10573	6323	687	6414	7130	"	7241	6593	7324	6679	7421	6761	7520
6147	6841	6237	6923	"	7041	6415	7131	6502	7231	6594	7325	"	7472	6762	7522
6148	6842	6238	6947	6324	7027	6416	7132	6503	7232	6595	7326	6680	7422	6763	7521
"	6843	6239	6948	"	7043	6417	7133	"	7247	"	7336	6681	7423	6764	7523
6149	6844	6240	6925	6325	7044	6418	7134	6504	7233	6596	7327	6682	7424	6765	7524
6150	6845	"	6926	6326	7045	"	7135	6505	7234	6597	7328	6683	7425	6766	7525
6151	10569	"	6930	6327	7046	6419	7136	6506	7235	6598	7329	6684	7426	6767	7526
6152	6846	6241	6928	"	7047	"	7137	6507	7237	6599	7330	6685	7427	"	7527
"	6851	6242	6929	"	7207	6420	7138	6508	7236	6600	10601	6686	7428	"	7528
"	6852	6243	10574	6328	7048	6421	7139	6509	7238	6601	7331	6687	7429	"	7529
6153	6847	6244	6949	6329	7048	6422	7140	"	7311	"	7332	6688	7430	6768	7530
6154	6848	6245	6950	"	7049	6423	7141	6510	7239	6602	7333	6689	7431	6769	7531
"	6849	"	6951	6330	7050	6424	7142	6511	7240	6603	7334	"	7433	6770	7532
"	6850	6246	10575	6331	7051	"	7143	6512	7051	6604	7335	"	7434	6771	7534
6155	6857	6247	6952	6332	7052	6425	7144	6513	7242	6605	7337	"	7487	6772	7533
6156	6853	6248	6953	6333	7053	6426	7145	6514	7243	"	7338	6690	7432	6773	7535
6157	6856	6249	6954	6334	7054	6427	7146	"	7263	6606	10602	6691	7436	6774	7536
6158	6854	6250	6955	6335	7055	6428	7147	6515	7245	6607	7339	6692	7437	6775	7537
6159	6855	6251	6957	"	7056	6429	7148	6516	7246	6608	7340	"	7438	6776	7538
6160	6858	6252	6958	6336	7057	6430	7149	6517	7248	6609	7347	6693	7439	6777	7539
6161	6859	6253	6956	6337	7058	6431	7150	6518	7250	6610	7341	6694	7440	6778	7540
6162	6860	6254	6960	6338	7059	6432	7152	6519	7244	6611	7342	6695	7441	6779	7541
6163	6861	6255	6959	6339	7060	6433	10588	"	7252	6612	7343	"	7442	6780	7542
"	6862	6256	6961	6340	7061	6434	7157	6520	7251	"	7344	6696	7443	6781	7543
6164	6863	6257	6963	6341	7062	6435	7153	6521	7253	6613	10603	"	7444	"	7544
6165	6864	6258	6964	"	7063	6436	7154	6522	7254	6614	7345	6697	7445	6782	7545
6166	6865	6259	6965	6342	7064	6437	7042	6523	10591	6615	7346	"	7446	6783	7552
"	6866	6260	6966	6343	7065	"	7155	6524	7255	6616	7348	"	7447	6784	7546
6167	10570	6261	6967	6344	7066	6438	7157	"	7256	6617	7349	6698	7448	6785	7547
6168	6867	6262	6968	6345	7067	6439	7158	"	7257	"	9520	6699	7451	6786	7548
6169	6868	6263	10577	6346	7068	"	7159	6525	7258	6618	7350	6700	7452	6787	7549
6170	6870	6264	6969	6347	10580	"	7160	6526	7259	6619	7351	6701	7453	6788	7550
6171	6871	6265	6970	6348	7069	"	7161	6527	7260	6620	7352	6702	7455	6789	7551
6172	6872	6266	6971	6349	7070	6440	4367	6528	7261	6621	7353	6703	7456	6790	7554
6173	10571	6267	6972	6350	7071	"	4368	6529	7262	6622	7354	6704	7457	6791	7553
6174	6873	6268	10578	6351	7072	"	7156	6530	7264	6623	7355	6705	7458	6792	7555
6175	6874	6269	6973	6352	7073	6441	7163	"	7265	6624	7356	6706	7460	"	7556
6176	6875	6270	6974	6353	10581	6442	7164	6531	7266	6625	7357	6707	7461	6793	7557
"	6898	6271	6975	6354	7074	6443	7162	6532	7267	6626	7359	6708	7459	"	7558
6177	6876	"	6976	6355	7075	"	7165	6533	7268	6627	7362	6709	7462	"	7559
6178	6877	6272	6977	6356	7076	6444	7166	6534	7269	6628	7365	6710	7463	6794	7562
6179	6878	6273	6978	6357	7077	6445	7167	6535	7270	6629	7366	6711	7464	6795	7563
6180	6879	6274	6979	6358	7080	6446	7168	6536	7271	6630	7367	6712	7465	6796	7564
6181	6880	6275	6980	6359	7078	6447	10589	6537	10592	6631	7368	6713	7466	6797	7561
6182	6881	6276	6982	6360	7079	6448	7170	"	10593	6632	7369	6714	7468	"	7565
6183	6882	6277	6981	6361	10582	6449	7171	6538	7272	"	7370	6715	7467	"	7566
6184	6883	6278	6962	6362	7080	6450	7169	6539	7273	6633	7371	6716	7469	6798	7567
6185	6884	6279	6983	6363	7081	6451	7172	6540	10594	6634	10605	6717	7471	6799	7569
6186	6885	6280	6984	"	7082	6452	7173	6541	7274	6635	7372	6718	7473	6800	7560
6187	6886	6281	6987	6364	7083	"	7174	6542	7275	"	7378	"	7474	"	7570
6188	6887	6282	6985	6365	7085	6453	7175	6543	10595	6636	7375	6719	7475	6801	7571
6189	6888	"	6986	6366	7023	6454	7176	6544	7276	"	7387	6720	7476	6802	7572
6190	2197	6283	6988	6367	2112	6455	7177	"	7277	6637	2206	6721	7477	6803	7573
"	6889	6284	6990	"	2672	6456	7178	6545	7279	"	7376	6722	7479	6804	7574
6191	6891	6285	6991	"	7084	6457	7179	6546	7278	6638	7377	6723	7480	6805	7575
6192	6890	"	6992	6368	7086	6458	7180	6547	7281	6639	7379	6724	7481	6806	7576
6193	6892	"	6993	6369	7087	6459	7181	6548	2922	6640	10606	6725	7483	6807	7577
6194	6894	6286	6994	6370	7108	6460	10590	6549	7281+5785	6641	7380	6726	7482	"	7578
6195	6893	"	6995	6371	7089	6461	7182	6550	7282	6642	7381	6727	7484	6808	7579
6196	6895	6287	6996	6372	7090	6462	7183	6551	7283	6643	7373	6728	7470	6809	7581
6197	6896	6288	6997	6373	7091	6463	7184	6552	7284	"	7374	6729	7485	6810	7582
6198	6897	"	6998	6374	7092	6464	7185	6553	7285	"	7382	6730	7486	6811	7583
6199	6899	6289	6999	6375	7211	"	7187	6554	7286	"	7383	6731	7488	6812	7584
6200	6901	6290	7000	6376	7093	6465	7186	6555	7287	6644	7384	6732	7489	6813	7585
6201	6903	6291	7001	6377	7094	6466	7188	6556	7288	6645	7385			6814	7586
6202	6904	6292	7002	6378	7095	6467	7189	6557	7289	6646	7386				

STRONG	G/K	STRONG	G/K	STRONG	G/K	STRONG	G/K	STRONG	G/K	STRONG	G/K	STRONG	G/K	STRONG	G/K
6815	1300	6896	7687	6981	7927	7072	7868	7159	7965	7248	4454	7336	8142	7424	8247
"	7587	6897	7687	6982	7771	7073	7869	7160	7966	"	8059	7337	8143	7425	8248
"	7588	6898	7688	6983	7772	7074	7870	7161	7967	7249	8060	7338	8144	7426	8250
6816	7589	6899	7689	6984	7773	7075	7871	"	7969	"	8042+6247	7339	8148	7427	8129
6817	7590	6900	7690	6985	7775	7076	7872	7162	10641	7250	8061	7340	8149	7428	8236
6818	7591	6901	7691	6986	7776	7077	7873	7163	2199	7251	8062	"	8150	7429	8252
6819	7592	6902	10618	6987	7776	7078	7874	"	7968	7252	8061	7341	8145	7430	8253
6820	7580	6903	10619	6988	7777	7079	7875	7164	7970	7253	8063	7342	8146	7431	8254
"	7593	6904	7692	6989	7778	7080	7876	7165	7971	7254	8061	7343	8147	7432	8255
6821	7594	6905	7692	6990	3684	7081	7877	7166	7972	"	8064	7344	8151	7433	8240
6822	7595	6906	7693	6991	7779	7082	7878	7167	7973	7255	8065	7345	8152	7434	2174
6823	7596	6907	7694	6992	10625	7083	7879	7168	7974	"	8066	"	8153	"	8256
6824	7597	6908	7695	6993	7780	7084	7881	7169	7975	7256	8067	7346	8154	7435	8258
6825	7598	6909	7696	6994	7781	7085	7882	7170	10642	7257	8069	7347	8160	7436	7435
"	7609	6910	7697	6995	7782	7086	7883	7171	7976	7258	8070	7348	8156	7437	8257
6826	7599	6911	7698	6996	7783	7087	7884	7172	7977	7259	8071	"	10662	7438	8260
6827	7602	6912	7699	"	7785	"	7885	7173	7978	7260	10647	7349	8157	7439	8261
6828	7600	6913	7700	6997	2214	7088	7886	7174	7980	7261	10652	7350	8158	7440	8262
6829	7601	6914	2246	"	7784	7089	7888	7175	7983	7262	8072	7351	8112	7441	8263
6830	7603	"	7701	6998	7786	7090	7887	7176	7984	7263	8073	"	8159	7442	8130
6831	7604	6915	7702	6999	5231	7091	7889	7177	7985	7264	8074	7352	10663	7443	8264
"	7612	6916	7703	"	5232	7092	7890	7178	7986	7265	10653	7353	8161	7444	8264
6832	7605	6917	7704	"	7787	7093	7891	7179	7990	7266	10654	7354	8162	7445	8265
"	7616	6918	7705	7000	7788	7094	7892	7180	7991	7267	8075	7355	8163	7446	8267
6833	7606	6919	7706	7001	10626	7095	7893	7181	7992	7268	8076	7356	8166	7447	8268
6834	7607	6920	7707	7002	7789	7096	7894	7182	7993	7269	8077	"	8171	"	8269
6835	7608	6921	7708	7003	7790	7097	7895	7183	7994	7270	8078	7357	8165	7448	8270
6836	7610	6922	10620	7004	7792	"	7897	"	7995	7271	10655	7358	8167	7449	8271
6837	7611	6923	7709	7005	7793	7098	7896	7184	7987	7272	8079	7359	10664	7450	8272
6838	7613	6924	7710	7006	7794	"	7901	7185	7996	7273	8081	7360	8164	7451	8273
6839	7614	"	7711	7007	10627	7099	7898	7186	7997	7274	8082	"	8168	"	8274
6840	7615	"	7714	7008	7798	7100	7902	7187	10643	7275	8083	7361	8169	7452	8275
6841	10615	6925	10621	7009	7799	7101	7903	7188	7998	7276	8084	7362	8172	7453	8276
6842	7618	6926	7713	7010	10628	7102	7904	7189	7999	7277	8086	7363	8173	7454	8277
6843	7619	6927	7712	7011	10629	7103	7905	"	8000	7278	8085	"	8174	7455	8278
6844	7620	6928	10622	7012	7800	7104	6681	7190	8001	7279	8087	7364	8175	7456	8279
6845	7621	6929	7715	7013	7802	"	7906	7191	8002	7280	8088	7365	10665	"	8281
"	7636	6930	7716	7014	7803	7105	7907	7192	7988	"	8089	7366	8176	7457	8280
6846	7622	6931	7719	"	7804	"	7908	7193	7989	7281	8092	7367	8177	7458	8280
"	7623	6932	7717	"	7805	7106	7909	7194	8003	7282	8091	7368	8178	7459	8282
6847	7195	6933	10623	7015	7806	"	7910	7195	8004	7283	8093	7369	8179	7460	8283
"	7624	6934	7718	7016	7807	7107	7911	7196	8005	7284	10656	7370	8180	7461	8284
6848	7625	6935	7720	7017	7808	7108	10633	7197	8006	7285	8094	7371	8181	"	8285
"	7626	6936	7721	7018	7809	7109	10634	"	8007	"	8095	7372	8182	7462	8287
6849	7617	6937	7722	7019	7811	7110	7912	7198	8008	7286	8096	7373	8183	"	8289
6850	7627	6938	7723	7020	7812	"	7913	7199	8009	7287	8097	7374	8185	7463	8291
6851	7628	6939	7724	7021	7813	7111	7914	7200	8011	"	8098	7375	8186	7464	8292
6852	7629	6940	7725	7022	7814	7112	7899	"	8013	7288	8099	7376	8187	"	8300
6853	10616	6941	7726	7023	7815	"	7915	"	8021	7289	8100	7377	8188	7465	8288
6854	7630	6942	7727	7024	7816	7113	10635	7201	8012	7290	8101	7378	8189	7466	8293
6855	7631	6943	7730	"	7817	7114	7900	7202	8011	7291	8103	7379	8190	7467	8294
6856	7632	6944	7731	7025	3085	"	7917	7203	8014	7292	8104	"	8191	7468	8295
6857	7634	6945	7728	"	3097	7115	7918	"	8015	7293	8105	7380	8192	7469	8296
6858	7633	6946	7729	"	7818	"	7919	7204	2218	7294	8105	7381	8194	7470	10668
6859	7635	6947	1395	"	7819	7116	7920	7205	8017	7295	8107	7382	10666	7471	8297
6860	7637	"	7732	7026	7820	7117	7921	7206	8018	7296	8106	7383	8195	7472	8298
6861	7638	6948	7728	7027	7821	7118	10636	7207	8019	7297	3724	7384	1910	7473	8286
6862	7639	6949	7733	7028	7822	7119	7922	7208	8020	"	8109	"	8196	7474	8299
"	7640	6950	7735	7029	7823	7120	7923	7209	8023	7298	8110	7385	8198	7475	8301
"	7641	6951	7736	7030	10644	7121	7924	7210	8024	"	8111	7386	8199	7476	10669
6863	7643	6952	7737	"	10630	7122	7925	7211	8016	7299	10657	7387	8200	7477	8302
6864	7644	6953	7738	7031	7824	7123	10637	"	8025	7300	8113	7388	8202	7478	8303
6865	7450	6954	7739	7032	10631	7124	7926	7212	8026	7301	8115	7389	8203	7479	8304
"	7645	6955	7740	7033	7828	7125	7925	7213	8027	7302	8116	7390	8205	7480	8305
6866	7646	6956	7741	7034	7829	7126	7928	7214	8028	7303	8108	7391	8204	7481	8306
6867	7647	6957	7742	7035	7827	7127	10638	7215	8029	"	8117	7392	8206	"	8307
"	7648	"	7743	7036	7830	7128	7930	7216	8030	7304	8118	7393	8207	7482	8308
6868	7649	"	7744	7037	7831	7129	10639	7217	10646	7305	8119	7394	8209	7483	8309
6869	7650	6958	7794	7038	7832	7130	7931	7218	8031	7306	8193	"	8211	"	8310
"	7651	"	7796	7039	7833	7131	7929	"	8034	7307	8120	7395	8208	7484	8311
"	7659	6959	7746	7040	7834	7132	7932	7219	8032	7308	10658	7396	8210	"	8312
"	7676	6960	7747	7041	7835	7133	7933	7220	8033	7309	8121	7397	8212	7485	8313
6870	7653	"	7748	7042	7836	"	7934	"	8396	7310	8122	7398	8213	7486	8314
6871	7654	6961	7749	7043	7837	7134	7935	7221	8035	7311	3727	7399	8214	7487	10670
6872	7655	6962	7752	7044	7838	7135	7938	7222	8036	"	3753	7400	8215	7488	8315
"	7656	"	7753	7045	7839	7136	7936	7223	8037	"	8123	7401	8216	7489	5336
"	7657	"	7754	7046	7840	"	7939	7224	8038	"	8225	7402	8217	"	8316
6873	7658	6963	7825	7047	7841	7137	7937	7225	8040	"	8249	7403	8218	"	8317
6874	7662	"	7826	7048	7842	7138	7940	7226	8031	7312	8124	7404	8219	"	8318
6875	7661	6964	7755	7049	7843	7139	7942	7227	8041	7313	10659	7405	8220	7490	10671
6876	7660	6965	7756	"	7844	7140	7943	"	8042	7314	10660	7406	8221	7491	8319
6877	7663	"	7856	7050	7845	7141	7946	7228	8043	7315	8125	7407	8222	7492	8320
6878	7664	"	9539	"	7846	7142	7944	7229	10647	7316	8126	7408	8223	7493	8321
6879	7665	6966	10624	7051	7847	7143	7945	7230	8044	7317	8127	7409	8224	7494	8323
6880	7667	6967	7757	7052	7848	7144	7942	7231	8045	7318	8128	7410	8226	7495	8324
6881	7666	6968	7758	7053	7849	7145	7948	7232	8046	7319	8129	7411	8227	7496	8327
6882	7668	6969	7759	7054	7850	7146	7947	7233	8047	7320	6471	"	8228	7497	8328
"	7670	"	7801	7055	7851	"	7949	7234	8048	"	8251	7412	10667	7498	8325
6883	7669	6970	7760	7056	7852	7147	7950	7235	2220	7321	8131	7413	8229	"	8334
6884	7671	6971	7761	7057	7853	7148	7951	"	2221	7322	8344	7414	8230	7499	8337
6885	7672	6972	7763	7058	7854	7149	10640	"	8049	7323	8132	"	8259	7500	8326
6886	7673	6973	7762	7059	7855	7150	7952	"	8050	"	8350	7415	8231	7501	8330
6887	7674	6974	7763	7060	7857	7151	7953	7236	10648	7324	8197	7416	8232	7502	8331
"	7675	"	7810	7061	7858	"	7956	7237	8051	7325	8201	7417	8233	7503	8332
"	7677	6975	7764	7062	7859	7152	7954	7238	10650	7326	8133	"	8234	7504	8333
6888	7678	"	7765	7063	7853	7153	7957	7239	8052	7327	8134	"	8235	7505	8336
6889	7679	6976	2212	7064	7860	"	7959	7240	10649	7328	10661	"	8237	7506	8338
6890	2241	"	7766	7065	7861	7154	7958	7241	8053	7329	8135	7418	8238	7507	8339
"	7680	6977	7767	7066	10632	7155	2941	7242	8054	7330	8136	"	8241	7508	8340
6891	7681	6978	7743+7743	7067	7862	"	7960	7243	8055	7331	8139	7419	8239	7509	8341
6892	7683	6979	7769	7068	7863	7156	7964	"	8068	7332	8137	7420	8242	7510	8335
"	7795	"	7979	7069	7864	7157	7961	7244	10651	7333	8138	7421	811	"	8342
6893	7684	"	7981	"	7865	7158	6173	7245	8056	7334	8140	7422	8243		
6894	7685	"	7982	7070	7866	"	7962	7246	8057	7335	8141	7423	8244		
6895	7686	6980	7770	7071	7867	"	7963	7247	8058			"	8245		

STRONG	G/K	STRONG	G/K	STRONG	G/K	STRONG	G/K	STRONG	G/K	STRONG	G/K	STRONG	G/K	STRONG	G/K
7511	8346	7605	8637	7693	8711	7782	8795	7879	8490	7967	8935	8061	9026	"	9112
7512	10672	7606	10692	7694	8712	7783	8796	7880	8489	7968	8937	8062	9027	8151	9113
7513	8343	7607	8638	7695	10699	7784	8798	7881	8491	7969	5456	8063	8526	8152	9114
7514	8345	7608	8640	7696	8713	7785	8797	7882	8864	"	8993	8064	9028	8153	3822
7515	8346	7609	8641	7697	8714	7786	8606	7883	8865	7970	9001	8065	10723	8154	9115
7516	8347	7610	8639	7698	8715	7787	8492	7884	4251	7971	8938	8066	9029	8155	9116
7517	8348	7611	8642	7699	8716	7788	8801	"	8866	7972	10714	8067	9030	8156	9117
7518	8349	7612	8643	"	8718	7789	8800	7885	8868	7973	8939	8068	9031	8157	9118
7519	8351	7613	8420	7700	8717	7790	8803	7886	8869	"	8945	"	9032	8158	9119
7520	8353	"	8421	7701	8719	7791	8805	"	8926	7974	8941	8069	9033	8159	9120
7521	8352	7614	8644	7702	8440	7792	10703	"	8931	7975	8940	"	9034	8160	10734
"	8354	7615	8645	7703	8720	7793	8804	7887	8870	"	8942	8070	9035	8161	9121
"	8355	7616	8646	7704	8441	7794	8802	7888	8872	7976	8943	"	9082	8162	9122
7522	8356	7617	8647	"	8442	7795	8463	7889	8873	7977	8944	8071	8529	8163	8537
7523	8357	7618	8648	7705	8721	7796	8604	7890	8875	7978	8946	8072	8528	"	8538
7524	8358	7619	8649	7706	8724	7797	8464	7891	8876	7979	8947	8073	8530	"	8539
7525	8359	"	8742	7707	8725	7798	8807	7892	8877	7980	8948	"	8978	8164	8540
7526	8360	7620	8651	7708	8443	7799	8808	"	8878	7981	10715	"	9036	8165	8541
7527	8361	"	8652	7709	8727	7800	8809	7893	8880	7982	8949	8074	9037	"	8542
7528	8362	7621	8678	7710	8728	7801	10704	7894	8881	7983	8950	8075	10724	8166	8544
7529	8363	7622	8654	7711	8729	7802	8808+6343	7895	8810	7984	10716	8076	9038	8167	8545
7530	8364	"	8669	"	8730	7803	8811	"	8882	7985	10717	8077	9039	8168	9123
7531	8365	7623	8655	7712	10700	7804	10706	7896	8883	7986	8951	"	9040	8169	9124
"	8367	"	8656	7713	8444	7805	8812	7897	8884	7987	8952	8078	9041	"	9125
7532	8366	7624	10693	7714	8731	7806	8813	7898	8885	7988	8953	8079	8532	8170	9126
7533	8368	7625	10694	7715	10701	7807	8814	7899	8493	7989	8954	8080	9042	8171	9127
7534	8369	7626	8657	7716	8445	7808	8465	7900	8494	7990	10718	8081	9043	8172	9128
7535	8370	7627	8658	7717	8446	7809	8815	7901	8886	7991	8955	8082	9045	8173	9129
7536	8371	7628	8660	7718	8732	7810	8816	7902	8887	"	8956	8083	9046	"	9130
7537	8372	"	8665	7719	8733	7811	8466	7903	8888	"	8957	8084	9047	8174	9131
7538	8373	7629	8661	7720	8448	7812	8817	7904	8889	"	8998	8085	9048	8175	8547
"	8374	7630	8662	7721	5951	7813	8467	7905	8496	7992	8958	"	9049	"	8548
7539	8375	7631	10695	7722	8738	7814	8468	7906	8497	"	8999	8086	10725	"	8549
7540	8376	7632	8663	"	8739	7815	8818	7907	8498	7993	8959	8087	9050	8176	9132
7541	8377	7633	8664	7723	8736	7816	8819	7908	8890	7994	8960	8088	9051	8177	10687
7542	8378	7634	8499	7724	8737	7817	8820	7909	8891	7995	8961	8089	9053	8178	8550
7543	8379	7635	8666	7725	8740	"	8863	"	8892	7996	8962	8090	9054	"	8551
7544	8380	7636	8667	7726	8743	7818	8469	7910	8893	7997	8963	8091	9052	8179	9133
7545	8381	7637	8668	7727	8744	7819	8821	7911	4171	"	8964	8092	9055	8180	9134
7546	8382	7638	8422	7728	8745	"	8822	"	8894	7998	8965	8093	9056	8181	8552
7547	8383	7639	8422	7729	8746	"	8823	7912	10708	7999	8966	8094	9057	8182	9135
7548	8384	7640	8670	7730	8449	7820	8822	7913	8895	8000	10719	8095	9058	8183	8554
7549	8385	7641	8672	7731	8747	7821	8824	7914	8500	8001	10720	8096	9059	8184	8555
7550	8386	"	8673	7732	8748	7822	8825	7915	8501	8002	8968	8097	9060	8185	8553
7551	8387	7642	8671	7733	8749	7823	6084	7916	8502	8003	8969	8098	9061	8186	9136
7552	8388	7643	8423	7734	6047	"	8826	7917	8502	8004	8970	"	9062	8187	9137
"	8389	"	8424	7735	8451	7824	8470	7918	8896	8005	8972	8099	9063	"	9138
"	8390	7644	8674	7736	8720	7825	8827	7919	8505	8006	8973	8100	9064	8188	8556
7553	8391	"	8675	7737	8750	7826	8828	"	8506	8007	8514	8101	9065	8189	9139
7554	8392	7645	8676	"	8751	7827	8829	7920	10683	8008	8515	8102	9066	8190	9140
7555	8393	"	8677	7738	9589	7828	8830	7921	5437	8009	8516	8103	9067	8191	9141
7556	8394	7646	8425	7739	10702	7829	8831	"	8897	8010	8976	8104	9068	8192	9142
7557	8395	7647	8426	7740	8753	7830	8832	7922	8507	8011	8974	8105	9069	8193	8557
7558	8397	7648	8427	7741	8754	7831	8833	7923	8898	8012	8517	8106	9070	8194	9147
7559	8398	7649	8428	7742	8452	"	8834	7924	10684	8013	8977	"	9013	8195	9143
7560	10673	7650	8678	7743	8755	7832	8471	7925	8899	8014	8518	8107	9081	"	9156
7561	8399	7651	8679	7744	8756	7833	8835	7926	8900	8015	8979	8108	9072	8196	9144
7562	8400	7652	8680	7745	8757	7834	8836	7927	8901	8016	8980	8109	9073	8197	8792
7563	8401	"	8681	7746	8758	7835	8837	"	8902	8017	8981	8110	9074	"	9145
7564	8402	7653	8430	7747	8760	7836	8838	7928	8903	8018	8982	"	9075	"	9146
7565	8404	7654	8429	7748	8761	7837	8840	7929	8900	"	8983	8111	9076	8198	9148
7566	8405	7655	10696	7749	8762	7838	8839	7930	8904	8019	8984	8112	5264	8199	9149
7567	8406	7656	8683	7750	6091	7839	8841	7931	8905	"	8985	"	9077	8200	10735
7568	8407	7657	8684	"	8454	7840	8842	7932	10709	8020	8986	8113	9078	8201	9150
7569	8408	7658	8685	7751	8763	7841	8843	7933	8905	8021	8988	8114	9079	8202	9151
7570	8409	7659	8686	7752	8765	7842	8844	7934	8907	8022	8987	"	9080	8203	9152
7571	8410	7660	8687	"	8766	7843	8845	7935	8908	8023	8989	8115	10726	"	9153
7572	8411	7661	8688	"	8867	7844	10705	"	8909	8024	8989	8116	9083	8204	9154
7573	8412	7662	10697	7753	8455	7845	8846	7936	6128	8025	8990	8117	9084	8205	9155
7574	8413	7663	8431	7754	8456	7846	8473	7937	8509	8026	8991	8118	9085	8206	9157
7575	8414	"	8432	"	8457	7847	8474	"	8910	8027	8992	8119	9086	"	9158
7576	8415	7664	8433	7755	8458	7848	8847	"	8912	8028	8994	8120	10727	8207	9159
7577	8416	7665	8653	"	8459	7849	8848	7938	8512	8029	9000	8121	9087	8208	9160
7578	8417	"	8689	7756	8460	7850	8849	7939	8510	8030	8996	8122	10728	8209	10736
7579	8612	7666	8690	7757	8767	7851	8850	7940	8511	8031	8995	8123	9088	8210	8564
7580	8613	7667	8691	7758	8768	7852	8475	7941	8911	8032	8997	8124	10729	"	9161
7581	8614	"	8694	"	8871	7853	8476	7942	8914	8033	9004	8125	9091	8211	9162
7582	8615	7668	8692	7759	8769	7854	8477	7943	8913	8034	9005	8126	9092	8212	9163
"	8616	7669	8693	7760	8461	7855	8478	7944	8915	8035	9006	8127	9094	8213	9164
7583	8617	7670	8695	"	8492	7856	8479	7945	8611	8036	10721	8128	10730	8214	10737
7584	8618	7671	8696	7761	10682	7857	8851	7946	8916	8037	9007	8129	9095	8215	10738
7585	8619	7672	10698	7762	8770	7858	8852	7947	8917	8038	9008	8130	8533	8216	9165
7586	8620	7673	8697	7763	9071	7859	10680	7948	8918	8039	9009	8131	10686	8217	9166
7587	8621	"	8698	7764	8771	7860	8853	7949	8919	8040	8520	8132	9096	8218	9168
7588	8622	7674	8700	7765	8772	7861	8855	7950	8920	8041	8520	"	9101	8219	9169
"	8623	7675	8699	7766	8773	"	9231	"	8921	"	8521	8133	10731	8220	9170
7589	8624	7676	8701	"	9231	7862	8856	7951	8922	8042	8522	8134	9098	8221	9172
7590	8764	7677	8702	7767	8774	7863	8480	7952	8923	8043	9010	8135	8534	8222	8559
7591	8625	7678	8703	7768	8775	7864	8857	7953	8923	8044	9011	8136	9099	8223	9171
7592	8626	7679	8434	7769	8780	7865	8481	7954	10710	8045	9012	8137	9100	8224	8560
"	8628	7680	10677	"	8782	7866	8858	7955	10685	8046	10722	8138	9101	8225	9175
7593	10689	7681	8707	7770	8781	7867	8482	"	10711	8047	9014	8139	10733	8226	8561
7594	8627	7682	8435	7771	8777	7868	10681	7956	8924	8048	9015	8140	10732	8227	9176
7595	10690	7683	1417	7772	8778	"	10675	"	8925	8049	9016	8141	9102	"	9177
7596	8629	"	8704	"	8779	7869	8483	7957	8927	8050	9017	8142	9097	8228	9179
7597	8630	7684	8705	7773	8776	7870	8860	"	8928	8051	9018	"	9104	8229	9180
"	9003	7685	8436	7774	8783	7871	8859	7958	8513	8052	9019	8143	2036	8230	9181
7598	10691	7686	8706	7775	8784	7872	8484	7959	8930	8053	9020	"	9105	8231	9182
7599	8631	7687	8437	7776	8785	7873	8485	7960	10712	8054	9021	8144	9106	8232	10739
7600	8633	"	8439	7777	8786	7874	8486	7961	8929	8055	8523	8145	9108	8233	9183
7601		7688	8708	"	8787	7875	6093	7962	8932	8056	8524	8146	8535	8234	9184
7602	8634	7689	8438	7778	8788	"	8487	7963	10713	8057	8525	8147	9109	8235	9185
"	8635	7690	10678	7779	8789	7876	8861	7964	8933	8058	9023	8148	9110	8236	9186
7603	8419	7691	8709	"	8790	7877	8862	7965	8934	8059	9024	8149	8536	8237	9187
7604	8636	7692	8710	7780	8791	7878	8488	7966	8936	8060	9025	8150	9111		
				7781	8793										

STRONG	G/K
"	9188
8238	10740
8239	9189
8240	9190
"	9191
8241	9192
8242	8566
8243	10741
8244	8567
8245	9193
"	9194
"	9195
8246	5481
8247	9196
8248	9197
8249	9198
8250	9198
8251	9199
8252	9200
8253	9201
8254	9202
8255	9203
8256	9204
8257	9205
8258	9206
8259	9207
8260	9208
8261	9209
8262	9210
8263	9211
8264	8799
"	9212
8265	8568
8266	9213
8267	9214
8268	9216
8269	6254
"	8569
8270	9218
"	9219
8271	10742
8272	8570
8273	9220
8274	9221
8275	9222
8276	8571
8277	8572
8278	8573
8279	8574
8280	8575
8281	9223
"	9224
8282	8576
8283	8577
8284	9224
8285	9217
"	9225
8286	8578
8287	9226
8288	8579
8289	4389
"	9227
8290	9228
8291	8602
"	8604
8292	9229
"	9241
8293	9230
8294	8580
8295	8581
8296	8582
"	8583
8297	8584
8298	9232
8299	8585
8300	8586
8301	8587
8302	9233
"	9234
8303	8590
8304	8588
"	8589
8305	8591
8306	9235
8307	9244
8308	8592
8309	9173
"	9236
8310	8593
8311	8594
8312	8595
8313	8596
8314	8597
8315	8598
8316	8599
8317	9237
8318	9238
8319	9239
8320	8601
8321	8603
8322	8605
"	9240
8323	8606
8324	8806
8325	9242

STRONG	G/K
"	9243
8326	9247
8327	9245
8328	9247
8329	9246
8330	10743
8331	9249
8332	10744
"	10745
8333	9248
"	9249
8334	9250
8335	9251
8336	9253
"	9254
8337	9252
8338	9255
8339	9256
8340	10746
8341	9257
8342	8607
8343	9258
8344	9259
8345	9261
8346	9262
8347	9263
8348	9264
8349	9265
8350	9266
8351	9268
8352	9269
8353	10747
8354	9272
8355	10748
8356	9271
8357	9268
8358	9275
8359	9274
8360	9276
8361	10749
8362	9278
8363	9277
8364	9279
8365	9280
"	8874
8366	9281
"	9282
8367	9284
8368	8609
8369	9285
8370	10750
8371	9286
8372	9288
8373	9289
8374	9290
8375	9291
8376	9292
8377	9293
8378	9294
8379	9295
8380	9296
"	9339
8381	9297
8382	9298
8383	9303
8384	9300
8385	9299
"	9301
8386	9302
8387	9304
8388	9305
"	9306
8389	9307
8390	9308
8391	9309
8392	9310
8393	9311
8394	9312
"	9341
8395	9313
8396	9314
8397	9316
8398	9315
8399	9318
8400	9319
8401	9320
8402	9321
8403	9322
8404	9323
8405	9324
8406	10752
8407	9325
"	9433
8408	9326
8409	9327
8410	9329
8411	10753
8412	9330
8413	9331
8414	9332
8415	9333
8416	9335
8417	9334
8418	9336
8419	9337

STRONG	G/K
8420	9338
8421	10754
8422	9317
8423	9340
8424	9342
8425	9328
8426	9343
8427	9344
8428	9345
8429	10755
8430	9346
8431	9347
8432	9348
8433	9349
"	9350
8434	9351
8435	9352
8436	9353
"	9400
8437	9354
8438	9355
"	9357
8439	9356
8440	9358
8441	9359
8442	9360
8443	9361
8444	9362
8445	9363
8446	9365
8447	9366
8448	9366
8449	9367
8450	10756
8451	9368
8452	9368
8453	9369
8454	9370
8455	9371
8456	9372
8457	9373
8458	9374
8459	9375
8460	10757
8461	9376
8462	9378
8463	9377
8464	9379
8465	9380
8466	9381
"	9385
"	9386
8467	9382
8468	9383
8469	9384
8470	9385
8471	9387
8472	9388
8473	9389
8474	3013
8475	9390
8476	9391
8477	9392
8478	5502
"	9393
8479	10757
8480	9394
"	9395
8481	9396
8482	9397
8483	2547
"	9398
8484	9399
8485	9401
8486	9402
8487	9403
8488	9405
8489	9404
8490	9406
8491	9407
8492	3770
8493	9409
8494	9410
8495	9411
8496	9412
8497	9413
8498	9414
8499	9414
8500	9415
8501	9412
8502	9416
8503	9417
8504	9418
8505	9419
8506	9420
8507	9421
8508	9422
8509	9423
8510	9424
8511	9428
8512	9425
8513	9430
8514	9429
8515	9431

STRONG	G/K
"	9445
8516	9432
8517	10758
8518	9434
8519	9442
8520	9436
8521	9426
8522	9437
8523	10759
8524	9435
8525	9439
8526	9440
8527	9441
8528	9427
8529	9443
8530	9444
8531	10760
8532	10761
8533	10762
8534	9446
8535	9447
8536	10764
8537	9448
8538	9450
8539	9449
8540	10763
8541	9451
8542	9452
8543	9453
8544	9454
8545	9455
8546	9456
8547	9457
8548	9458
8549	9459
8550	9460
8551	9461
8552	9462
8553	9463
8554	9464
8555	9465
8556	9466
"	9467
8557	9468
8558	9469
8559	9470
"	9471
8560	9472
"	9473
8561	9474
8562	9475
8563	9476
8564	9477
8565	9478
8566	9479
8567	9480
8568	9478
8569	9481
8570	9482
8571	9483
8572	9484
8573	9485
8574	9486
8575	9487
"	9488
8576	9489
8577	9490
8578	10765
8579	10766
8580	9491
"	9492
8581	9493
8582	9494
8583	9495
"	9497
8584	9496
8585	9498
"	9499
8586	9500
8587	9502
8588	9503
8589	9504
8590	9505
8591	9506
8592	9508
8593	9509
8594	9510
8595	9511
8596	4191
"	9512
"	9513
8597	9514
8598	9515
8599	9516
"	9517
8600	9518
8601	9519
8602	9521
"	9522
8603	9523
8604	9524
8605	9525
8606	9526
8607	9527
8608	9528

STRONG	G/K
8609	9529
8610	9530
8611	9531
8612	9532
8613	9533
8614	10767
8615	9535
"	9536
8616	9534
"	9537
8617	9538
8618	9539
8619	9540
8620	9541
8621	9542
8622	9543
8623	9544
8624	10768
8625	10769
"	10770
8626	9545
8627	10771
8628	9364
"	9546
8629	9547
8630	9548
8631	10772
8632	10773
"	10774
8633	9549
8634	9550
8635	9551
8636	9552
8637	8078
8638	9553
8639	9554
8640	9555
8641	9556
8642	9557
8643	9558
8644	9559
8645	9560
8646	9561
"	9562
8647	9563
8648	10775
"	10778
8649	9564
"	9566
8650	9568
8651	10776
8652	10777
8653	9570
8654	9571
8655	9572
8656	9573
"	9574
8657	9575
8658	9577
8659	9576
"	9578
8660	9579
8661	9580
8662	9581
8663	9583
8664	9585
8665	9587
8666	9588
8667	9582
8668	9591
8669	9592
8670	9593
8671	9595
8672	9596
8673	9597
8674	10779

GREEK NEW TESTAMENT

STRONG	G/K
1	1
"	270
2	2
3	3
4	4
5	5
6	6
7	7
8	8
9	9
10	10
11	11
12	12
13	13
14	14
15	16
16	17
17	18
18	19

STRONG	G/K
19	20
20	21
21	22
22	23
23	24
24	25
25	26
26	27
27	28
28	29
29	30
30	31
"	35
31	32
32	34
33	72
34	36
35	37
36	38
37	39
"	420
38	40
39	41
40	41
41	42
42	43
43	44
44	45
45	46
46	47
47	48
48	49
49	50
50	51
51	52
52	53
53	54
54	55
55	56
56	57
57	58
58	59
59	60
60	61
61	62
62	63
63	64
64	65
65	66
66	67
67	68
68	69
69	70
70	71
71	72
72	73
73	74
74	75
75	76
76	77
77	78
78	79
79	80
80	81
81	82
82	83
83	84
84	85
85	194
"	86
86	87
87	88
88	89
89	90
90	91
"	916
"	917
91	92
92	93
93	94
94	96
95	97
96	99
97	100
98	101
99	102
100	103
101	104
102	105
103	106
104	107
105	108
106	109
107	110
108	111
109	113
110	114
111	116
112	117
113	118
114	119
115	120
116	121
117	122
118	123

STRONG	G/K
119	124
120	126
121	127
122	128
123	129
124	130
125	131
126	132
127	133
"	1290
128	134
129	135
130	136
131	137
132	138
133	139
134	140
135	141
136	142
137	143
138	145
139	146
140	147
141	148
142	149
143	150
144	151
145	152
146	153
147	154
148	155
149	156
150	156
151	157
152	158
153	159
154	160
155	161
156	162
157	163
"	166
158	165
159	165
160	167
161	168
162	169
163	170
164	171
165	172
166	173
167	174
168	175
169	176
170	177
171	178
172	179
173	180
174	181
175	182
176	183
177	184
178	185
179	186
180	187
"	188
181	189
182	190
183	191
184	192
185	193
186	195
187	196
188	197
189	198
190	199
191	200
"	201
192	202
193	203
194	204
195	205
196	206
197	209
198	208
199	209
200	210
201	211
202	212
203	213
204	214
205	215
206	216
207	217
208	218
209	219
210	220
211	222
"	223
212	224
213	225
214	226
215	227
216	228
217	221
"	229

STRONG	G/K
218	230
219	231
220	232
221	233
222	234
223	235
224	236
225	237
226	238
227	239
228	240
229	241
230	242
231	243
232	244
233	245
234	246
235	247
236	248
237	249
238	251
239	252
240	253
241	254
242	256
"	380
243	257
244	258
245	259
246	260
247	261
248	262
249	263
250	264
251	265
252	266
253	267
254	268
255	269
256	271
257	272
258	273
259	274
260	275
261	276
262	277
263	278
264	279
265	280
266	281
267	282
268	283
269	285
270	286
271	287
272	288
273	289
274	290
275	291
276	292
277	293
278	294
279	295
280	296
281	297
282	298
283	299
284	300
285	302
286	303
287	304
288	306
289	307
290	308
291	309
292	310
293	312
294	313
"	314
295	315
296	316
297	317
298	318
299	320
300	321
301	322
302	323
303	324
304	325
305	326
306	327
307	328
308	329
309	330
310	331
311	332
312	334
313	335
314	336
315	337
316	338
317	339
318	340
319	341
320	342

STRONG	G/K
321	343
322	344
323	345
324	346
325	347
326	348
327	349
328	350
329	351
330	352
331	353
332	354
333	355
"	1461
334	356
335	357
336	358
337	359
338	360
339	361
340	362
341	363
342	364
343	365
344	366
345	367
346	368
347	369
348	370
349	371
350	373
351	374
352	376
353	377
354	378
355	379
"	384
356	381
357	382
358	383
359	385
360	386
361	387
362	388
363	389
364	390
365	391
366	392
367	393
368	394
369	395
370	396
371	397
372	398
373	399
374	400
375	402
376	401
377	404
378	405
379	406
380	408
381	409
382	410
383	411
384	412
385	413
386	414
387	415
388	416
389	417
390	418
391	419
392	421
393	422
394	423
395	424
396	426
397	427
398	428
399	429
400	430
401	431
402	432
403	433
404	434
405	435
406	436
407	437
408	438
409	439
410	441
411	442
412	443
413	444
414	445
415	446
416	448
417	449
418	450
419	451
420	452
421	453
422	454
423	455
424	456
425	457
426	458
427	459
428	460
429	461
430	462
431	463
432	464
433	465
434	466
435	467
436	468
437	469
438	470
439	471
440	472
441	473
442	474
443	475
444	476
445	477
446	478
447	479
448	447
"	480
449	481
450	403
"	482
451	483
452	484
453	485
"	493
454	486
455	487
"	1986
456	488
457	489
458	490
459	491
460	492
461	494
462	495
463	496
464	497
465	498
466	499
467	500
468	501
469	502
470	503
471	515
472	504
473	505
474	506
475	507
476	508
477	509
478	510
479	511
480	512
481	513
482	514
483	515
484	516
485	517
486	518
487	519
"	520
488	520
489	521
490	522
491	523
492	524
493	525
494	526
495	527
496	528
497	529
498	530
499	531
500	532
501	533
502	534
"	535
503	535
504	536
505	537
506	538
507	539
508	333
509	540
510	425
"	541
511	542
512	543
513	544
514	545
515	546
516	547
517	548
518	33
"	550
519	551
520	552
521	553
522	554
523	555
524	556
525	557
526	558
527	559
528	560
529	561
530	562
531	563
532	564
533	565
534	567
535	568
536	569
537	570
538	572
539	573
540	574
541	575
542	927
543	577
544	578
545	579
546	580
547	581
548	582
549	583
550	584
"	2171
551	585
552	586
553	587
554	588
555	589
556	590
557	591
"	1852
558	592
559	593
560	594
561	584
"	595
562	596
563	597
564	598
565	599
566	600
567	600
568	600
569	601
570	602
"	3898
571	603
572	605
573	604
"	606
574	607
575	608
576	609
577	610
578	611
579	612
580	613
581	614
582	615
583	616
584	617
585	618
586	619
"	620
587	621
588	622
589	623
590	624
591	625
592	626
593	627
594	628
595	629
596	630
597	631
598	632
599	633
600	634
"	635
601	636
602	637
603	638
"	2839
604	639
605	640
"	4076
606	641
607	642
608	643
609	644
610	645
611	646
612	647
613	648
614	649
615	650
"	651
616	652
617	375
"	653
618	655
619	656
620	657
621	658
"	2143
"	3314
"	4336
622	660
623	661
624	662
625	663
626	664
627	665
628	666
629	667
630	668
631	669
632	671
633	672
634	674
635	675
636	676
637	677
638	678
639	679
640	680
641	681
642	682
643	683
"	2171
644	684
645	685
646	686
647	687
648	689
649	690
"	1852
650	691
"	935
651	692
652	693
653	694
654	695
655	696
656	697
657	698
658	699
659	700
660	701
661	702
662	703
663	704
664	705
665	706
666	707
667	708
668	709
669	710
670	711
671	712
672	713
673	714
674	715
675	716
676	717
677	718
678	719
679	720
680	721
681	721
"	4312
682	722
683	723
684	724
685	725
686	726
687	727
688	728
689	98
"	730
"	763
690	732
691	733
692	734
693	735
"	739
694	736
695	737
696	738
697	740
"	4076
698	741
699	742
700	743
701	744
702	745
703	746
704	748
705	749
706	750
707	751
708	752
709	753
710	754
"	2360
711	755
712	756
713	757
714	758
715	759
"	760
716	761
717	762
"	3403
718	764
719	765
720	766
721	768
722	769
723	770
724	771
725	772
726	773
727	774
728	775
729	731
730	776
"	781
731	777
732	778
"	779
733	780
734	782
735	783
736	784
737	785
738	786
739	787
740	788
741	789
742	790
743	791
744	792
745	793
746	794
747	795
748	796
749	797
750	799
751	800
752	801
753	802
754	803
755	804
756	806
757	806
758	807
759	808
760	809
"	811
761	810
762	812
763	813
764	814
765	815
766	816
767	817
768	818
769	819
770	820
771	821
772	822
773	823
774	824
775	825
776	826
777	827
778	828
779	829
780	830
781	831
782	571
"	832
783	833
784	834
"	305
"	5646
785	835
786	836
787	837
788	839
789	840
790	841
791	842
792	843
793	844
794	845
795	846
796	847
797	848
798	849
799	850
800	851
801	852
802	853
803	854
804	855
805	856
806	857
807	858
"	2360
808	859
809	860
810	861
811	862
812	863
813	864
814	865
815	866
816	867
817	868
818	869
"	870
819	871
820	872
821	873
822	874
823	875
824	876
825	877
826	878
"	2964
827	879
828	880
829	881
830	882
831	883
832	884
833	885
834	886
835	887
836	888
837	889
"	891
838	890
839	892
840	893
841	894
842	895
843	896
844	897
845	898
846	899
847	898
848	898
849	901
"	2742
850	903
"	2744
851	904
852	905
853	906
854	907
855	908
"	4060
856	909
857	910
858	911
859	912
860	913
861	914
862	915
863	918
"	1889
864	919
865	920
866	921
867	922
868	923
869	924
870	925
871	926
872	927
873	928
874	929
875	930
876	931
877	932
878	933
879	934
880	936
881	937
882	938
883	939
884	940
885	943
886	942
887	944
888	945
889	946
890	947
891	948
892	949
893	950
894	951
"	952
895	953
896	955
897	956
898	957
899	958
900	959
901	960
902	961
903	962
904	963
905	964
906	965
907	966
908	967
909	968
910	969
911	970
"	4817
912	972
913	973
914	974
915	975
916	976
917	977
918	978
919	979
920	971
"	980
"	981
921	982
922	983
923	984
924	985
925	986
"	2852
926	987
927	988
928	989
929	990
930	991
931	992
932	993
933	994
934	994
935	995
936	996
937	997
"	998
938	999
939	1000
940	1001
941	1002
942	1003
943	1004
"	2742
944	1005
945	1006
946	1007
947	1008
948	1009
949	1010
950	1011
951	1012
952	1013
953	1014
954	1015
955	1016
956	1018
957	1019
958	1020
"	1021
959	1022
960	1023
961	1024
962	1028
"	1030
963	1029
964	1031
965	1033
966	1034
"	1035
967	1036
968	1037
969	1039
970	1040
971	1041
972	1042
973	1043
974	1044
"	1045
975	1046
976	1047
977	1048
978	1049
979	1050
980	1051
981	1052
982	1053
983	1054
984	1055
985	1056
"	1057
986	1058
987	1059
"	1555
988	1060
989	1061
990	1062
991	1063
992	1064
993	1065
994	1066
995	1068
996	1069
997	1070
998	1071
999	1072
1000	1074
1001	1075
1002	1076
1003	1067
"	1077
"	1078
1004	1079
1005	1080
1006	1081
1007	1026
"	1027
"	1082
1008	1083
1009	1084
1010	1085
1011	1086
1012	1087
1013	1088
1014	1089
1015	1090
1016	1091
1017	1092
1018	1093
1019	1094
1020	1095
1021	1096
1022	1097
1023	1098
1024	1099
1025	1100
1026	1101
1027	1103
1028	1104
1029	1105
1030	1106
1031	1107
1032	1108
1033	1109
1034	1110
1035	1111
1036	1112
1037	1113
1038	1114
1039	1115
"	3327
1040	1116
1041	1117
1042	1119
1043	1120
1044	1121
1045	1122
1046	1123
1047	1125
1048	1124
1049	1126
1050	1127
1051	1128
1052	1129
1053	1130
"	1135
1054	1131
1055	1132
1056	1133
1057	1134
1058	1136
1059	1137
1060	1138
1061	1139
"	1140
1062	1141
1063	1142
1064	1143
1065	1145
1066	1146
1067	1147
1068	1148
"	1149
1069	1150
1070	1151
1071	1152
1072	1153
1073	1154
1074	1155
1075	1156
1076	1157
1077	1158
"	1159
"	1160
1078	1161
1079	1162
1080	1164
1081	1163
"	1165
1082	1166
1083	1167
1084	1168
1085	1169
1086	1170
"	1171
1087	1172
1088	1173
1089	1174

STRONG	G/K	STRONG	G/K	STRONG	G/K	STRONG	G/K	STRONG	G/K	STRONG	G/K	STRONG	G/K	STRONG	G/K
1090	1175	1186	1285	"	1396	"	1508	1483	1619	1581	1716	"	1826	1768	1916
1091	1176	1187	1286	1285	1397	1382	1509	1484	1620	1582	1717	1679	1827	1769	1917
1092	1177	"	1287	1286	1398	1383	1510	1485	1621	1583	1718	1680	1828	"	1934
1093	1178	1188	1288	1287	1399	1384	1511	1486	1622	1584	1719	1681	1829	1770	1935
1094	1179	1189	1289	1288	1400	1385	1512	"	1665	1585	1720	"	2287	1771	1936
1095	1180	1190	1291	1289	1401	1386	1513	1487	1623	1586	1721	1682	1830	1772	1937
1096	1181	"	1523	1290	1402	1387	1514	1488	1639	1587	1722	1683	1831	1773	1939
1097	1182	1191	1292	1291	1403	1388	1515	1489	1623+1145	1588	1723	1684	1832	1774	1940
1098	1183	1192	1293	1292	1404	1389	1516	1490	1623+1254 +3590+1145	1589	1724	1685	1833	1775	1942
1099	1184	1193	1294	1293	1405	1390	1517	1491	1626	1590	1725	1686	1834	1776	1943
1100	1185	1194	1296	1294	1406	1391	1518	1492	3857	1591	1726	"	1835	1777	1944
1101	1186	1195	1297	1295	1407	1392	1519	1493	1627	1592	1727	1687	1836	1778	1945
1102	1187	1196	1298	1296	1408	1393	1520	1494	1628	1593	1728	1688	1837	1779	1946
1103	1188	1197	1299	1297	1409	1394	1521	"	2638	1594	1729	1689	1838	1780	1947
1104	1189	1198	1300	1298	1410	1395	1522	1495	1630	1595	1730	1690	1102	1781	1353
1105	1190	1199	1301	1299	1411	1396	1524	1496	1629	1596	1731	"	1839	"	1948
1106	1191	1200	1302	1300	1412	1397	1525	1497	1631	1597	1732	1691	1609	1782	1925
1107	1192	1201	1303	1301	1413	1398	1526	1498	1639	1598	1733	1692	1840	"	1949
1108	1194	1202	1304	1302	1414	1399	1527	1499	1623+2779	1599	1734	1693	1841	1783	1950
1109	1195	1203	1305	1303	1415	1400	1528	1500	1632	1600	1736	1694	1842	1784	1952
1110	1193	1204	1306	"	1416	1401	1528	1501	1633	1601	1738	1695	1843	1785	1953
"	1196	1205	1307	1304	1417	"	1529	1502	1634	1602	1739	"	4035	1786	1954
1111	1197	1206	1308	1305	1418	1402	1530	1503	2036	1603	1740	1696	1844	1787	1955
1112	1198	1207	1310	1306	1419	1403	1531	1504	1635	1604	1741	1697	1846	1788	1956
1113	1199	1208	1309	1307	1420	1404	1532	1505	1636	1605	1742	1698	1609	1789	1957
1114	1200	"	1311	"	1421	1405	1533	1506	1637	1606	1743	1699	1847	1790	1764
1115	1201	1209	1312	1308	1422	1406	1534	1507	1813	1607	1744	1700	1609	"	1958
1116	1202	1210	1313	1309	1423	1407	1535	1508	1623+3590	1608	1745	1701	1849	1791	1959
1117	1203	1211	1314	1310	1424	1408	1536	1509	1623 +3590+5516	1609	1746	1702	1850	1792	1960
1118	1204	1212	1316	"	5775	1409	1537	1510	1639	1610	1748	1703	1851	1793	1961
1119	1205	1213	1317	1311	1425	1410	1538	1511	1639	1611	1749	1704	1853	1794	1962
1120	1206	1214	1318	1312	1426	1411	1539	1512	1642	1612	1750	1705	1854	1795	1963
1121	1207	1215	1319	1313	1427	1412	1540	1513	1643	1613	1752	"	1855	1796	1964
1122	1208	1216	1320	1314	1428	1413	1541	1514	1644	1614	1753	"	1857	1797	1965
1123	1209	1217	1321	1315	1429	1414	1542	1515	1645	1615	1754	"	1858	1798	1966
1124	1210	1218	1322	1316	1431	1415	1543	1516	1646	1616	1755	1706	1860	1799	1967
1125	1211	1219	1323	1317	1434	1416	1544	1517	1647	1617	1757	1707	1861	1800	1968
"	2863	1220	1324	1318	1435	1417	1545	1518	1648	1618	1756	1708	1862	1801	1969
1126	1212	1221	1325	1319	1436	1418		1519	1650	1619	1757	"	4451	1802	1970
1127	1213	1222	1327	1320	1437	1419	1546	1520	1651	1620	1758	1709	1863	1803	1971
1128	1214	1223	1328	1321	1438	1420	1547	1521	1652	1621	1759	1710	1864	1804	1972
1129	1215	1224	1329	1322	1439	"	1548	1522	1653	1622	1760	1711	1865	1805	1973
1130	1216	1225	1330	1323	1440	1421	1549	1523	1654	1623	1761	1712	1866	1806	1974
"	1217	1226	1331	1324	1441	1422	1551	1524	1655	1624	1762	1713	1867	1807	1975
1131	1218	1227	1332	1325	1442	1423	1552	1525	1656	1625	1763	1714	1856	1808	1976
1132	1219	1228	1333	"	1443	1424	1553	1526	1639	1626	1765	"	1859	1809	1977
1133	1220	1229	1334	1326	1444	1425	1554	1527	1651+2848	1627	1766	1715	1869	1810	1978
1134	1221	1230	1335	1327	1447	1426	1556	1528	1657	1628	1767	1716	1870	"	2005
1135	1222	1231	1336	1328	1449	1427	1557	1529	1658	1629	1768	1717	1871	1811	1979
1136	1223	1232	1337	"	2256	1428	1558	1530	1659	1630	1769	1718	1872	1812	1980
1137	1224	1233	1338	1329	1450	1429	1559	"	1737	1631	1770	1719	1873	1813	1981
1138	1226	1234	1339	1330	1451	1430	1560	1531	1660	1632	1772	1720	1874	1814	1982
"	1253	1235	1340	1331	1452	1431	1561	1532	1661	"	1773	1721	1875	1815	1983
1139	1227	1236	1341	1332	1453	1432	1562	1533	1662	1633	1774	"	1877	1816	1677
1140	1228	1237	1342	1333	1454	1433	1563	1534	1663	1634	1775	1722	1877	"	1984
1141	1229	1238	1343	1334	1455	1434	1564	1535	1664	1635	1776	1723	1878	1817	1985
1142	1230	1239	1344	1335	1456	1435	1565	1536	1623+5516	1636	1777	1724	1879	1818	1987
1143	1231	1240	1345	1336	1457	1436	1568	1537	1666	1637	1778	1725	1882	1819	1988
1144	1232	1241	1346	1337	1458	1437	1569	1538	1667	1638	1779	1726	1883	1820	1989
1145	1233	1242	1347	1338	1459	1438	1571	1539	1668	1639	1780	1727	1885	1821	1990
1146	1234	1243	1348	1339	1460	1439	1572	1540	1669	1640	1781	1728	1887	1822	1992
1147	1235	1244	1349	1340	1462	1440	1573	1541	1670	"	1784	1729	1890	1823	1993
1148	1236	1245	1350	1341	1464	1441	1574	1542	1671	1641	1782	1730	1891	1824	1994
1149	1237	"	1351	1342	1465	1442	1575	1543	1672	1642	1783	1731	1892	1825	1995
1150	1238	1246	1352	1343	1466	1443	1576	"	1673	1643	1785	1732	1893	1826	1996
1151	1239	1247	1354	1344	1467	1444	1577	1544	1675	1644	1786	1733	1894	1827	1998
1152	1240	1248	1355	1345	1468	1445	1578	1545	1676	1645	1787	1734	1895	1828	1999
1153	1241	"	1566	1346	1469	1446	1579	1546	1678	1646	1788	1735	1896	1829	2000
1154	1242	1249	1356	1347	1470	1447	1580	1547	1679	1647	1788	1736	1897	1830	2001
1155	1244	1250	1357	1348	1471	1448	1581	1548	1680	1648	1789	1737	1898	1831	2002
"	1247	1251	1358	1349	1472	1449	1582	1549	1681	1649	1792	1738	1899	"	1446
1156	1245	1252	1359	1350	1473	1450	1583	1550	1682	1650	1791	1739	1900	"	1674
"	1249	"	2869	1351	1474	1451	1584	1551	1683	"	1793	"	1908	1832	1997
1157	1246	1253	1360	1352	1475	1452	1585	1552	1684	1651	1794	1740	1901	"	2003
"	1250	1254	1361	1353	1476	1453	1586	1553	1685	1652	1795	1741	1902	1833	2004
1158	1248	1255	1362	1354	1477	1454	1587	1554	1686	1653	1790	1742	1903	1834	2007
1159	1251	1256	1363	1355	1478	1455	1588	1555	1687	"	1796	1743	1904	1835	2008
1160	1252	1257	1364	1356	1479	1456	1589	1556	1688	1654	1797	1744	1905	1836	2009
1161	1254	1258	1365	1357	1481	1457	1590	1557	1689	1655	1798	1745	1906	1837	2010
1162	1255	1259	1367	1358	1482	1458	1592	1558	1690	1656	1799	1746	1907	1838	2011
1163	1256	1260	1368	1359	1483	1459	1593	1559	1691	1657	1800	1747	1909	1839	2012
1164	1257	1261	1369	1360	1484	1460	1594	1560	1692	1658	1801	1748	1910	"	2013
1165	1258	1262	1370	1361	1485	1461	1596	1561	1693	1659	1802	1749	1911	"	2014
1166	1259	1263	1371	1362	1486	1462	1598	1562	1694	1660	1803	1750	1912	1840	2015
"	1260	1264	1372	"	1487	1463	1599	1563	1695	1661	1804	1751	1913	1841	2016
1167	1261	1265	1373	1363	1488	1464	1600	1564	1696	1662	1805	1752	1641	1842	2017
1168	1262	1266	1374	1364	1489	"	1715	1565	1697	"	1806	"	1914	1843	2018
1169	1264	1267	1375	1365	1491	1465	1601	1566	1698	1663	1808	"	1915	1844	2019
1170	1265	1268	1376	1366	1492	1466	1602	1567	1699	1664	1809	1753	1918	1845	2020
1171	1267	1269	1377	1367	1493	1467	1603	1568	1701	1665	1810	1754	1919	1846	2021
1172	1268	1270	1378	1368	1494	1468	1604	1569	1702	1666	1811	1755	1920	1847	2022
1173	1271	1271	1379	1369	1495	1469	1605	1570	1704	1667	1813	1756	1886	"	2023
1174	1273	1272	1380	1370	1496	1470	1606	1571	1705	1668	1814	"	1921	1848	2024
1175	1272	1273	1381	1371	1497	1471	1607	1572	1706	1669	1815	1757	1922	"	2025
1176	1274	1274	1382	1372	1498	1472	1608	1573	1591	1670	1816	1758	1923	1849	2026
1177	1275	1275	1383	1373	1499	1473	1609	"	1707	1671	1817	1759	1924	1850	2027
1178	1278	1276	1385	1374	1500	1474	1610	1574	1708	1672	1818	1760	1445	1851	2029
1179	1279	1277	1386	1375	1501	1475	1611	1575	1709	1673	1819	"	1926	1852	2030
1180	1280	1278	1387	1376	1502	1476	1612	1576	1710	1674	1820	1761	1927	1853	2031
1181	1281	1279	1388	1377	1503	1477	1613	1577	1711	1675	1821	1762	1928	1854	2032
1182	1281	1280	1389	1378	1504	1478	1614	1578	1712	1676	1822	1763	1929	1855	2033
1183	1282	1281	1390	1379	1505	1479	1615	1579	1713	1677	1823	1764	1931	1856	2034
1184	1283	1282	1391	1380	1506	1480	1616	1580	1714	"	1824	1765	1932	1857	2035
1185	1284	1283	1395	1381	1507	1481	1617			1678	1825	1766	1888	1858	2037
		1284	1392			1482	1618					1767	1933	1859	2038
		"	1393												

STRONG	G/K	STRONG	G/K	STRONG	G/K	STRONG	G/K	STRONG	G/K	STRONG	G/K	STRONG	G/K	STRONG	G/K
1860	2039	1958	2149	"	2253	2150	2354	2250	2465	2346	2567	2446	2674	2535	2782
1861	2040	1959	2150	2057	2254	2151	2355	2251	2466	2347	2568	2447	2675	2536	2783
1862	2041	1960	2151	2058	1448	2152	2356	2252	1639	2348	2569	2448	2676	"	2784
1863	2042	1961	2152	"	2255	2153	2357	2253	2467	2349	2570	2449	2677	2537	2785
1864	2043	1962	2153	2059	2257	2154	2358	2254	1609	2350	2572	2450	2678	2538	2786
1865	2044	1963	2154	2060	2258	2155	2359	2255	2468	2351	2573	2451	2679	2539	2788
1866	2045	1964	2155	2061	2259	2156	2361	2256	2469	2352	2574	2452	2680	2540	2789
1867	2046	1965	2156	2062	2260	2157	2362	"	2470	"	2575	2453	2681	2541	2790
1868	2047	1966	2079	2063	2261	2158	2363	2257	1609	2353	2576	2454	2682	2542	2791
1869	2048	1967	2157	2064	2262	2159	2364	2258	1639	2354	2577	2455	2623	2543	2792
1870	2049	1968	2158	2065	2263	2160	2365	2259	2471	2355	2578	"	2726	2544	2793
1871	2050	1969	2159	2066	2264	2161	2366	2260	2472	2356	2579	2456	549	2545	2794
1872	2051	1970		2067	2265	2162	2367	2261	2473	2357	2580	"	2684	2546	2795
1873	2052	1971	2160	2068	2266	2163	2368	2262	2474	2358	2581	"	2686	2547	2796
1874	2053	1972	2161	"	2267	2164	2369	2263	2475	2359	1295	2457	2685	2548	2797
1875	2054	1973	2162	2069	2268	2165	2370	2264	2476	"	2582	2458	2687	2549	2798
1876	2055	1974	2163	2070	1639	2166	2371	2265	2477	2360	2583	2459	2688	2550	2799
1877	2056	1975	2164	2071	1639	2167	2372	2266	2478	2361	2584	"	5517	2551	2800
1878	2057	1976	2165	2072	2269	2168	2373	2267	2479	2362	2585	2460	2689	2552	2801
1879	2058	"	2193	2073	2270	2169	2374	2268	2480	2363	2587	2461	2690	"	2817
1880	2059	1977	2166	2074	2272	2170	2375	2269	2481	2364	2588	2462	2691	2553	2802
1881	2060	1978	2168	2075	1639	2171	2376	2270	2483	2365	2589	2463	2692	2554	2803
1882	2061	1979	2169	2076	1639	2172	2377	2271	2484	2366	2590	2464	2693	2555	2804
1883	2062	1980	2170	2077	1639	2173	2378	2272	2485	2367	2591	2465	2694	2556	2805
1884	2064	1981	2172	2078	2274	2174	2379	2273	2486	2368	2592	2466	2695	2557	2806
1885	2065	1982	2173	2079	2275	2175	2380	2274	2273	2369	2593	"	2704	2558	2807
"	2066	1983	2174	2080	2276	2176	2381	"	2487	2370	2594	2467		2559	2808
1886	2068	1984	2175	2081	2277	2177	1880	2275	2488	2371	2595	2468	1639	2560	2809
1887	2069	1985	2176	2082	2278	"	2383	2276	2482	2372	2596	2469	2696	2561	2810
1888	900	1986	2177	2083	2279	2178	2384	"	2489	2373	2597	"	2697	2562	2811
"	2070	1987	2179	2084	2280	2179	2385	2277	1639	2374	2598	"	5000	2563	2812
1889	2071	1988	2181	2085	2281	2180	2386	2278	2490	2375	2599	"	5001	2564	2813
1890	576	1989	2182	2086	2282	2181	2387	2279	2491	2376	2600	2470	2698	2565	2814
"	2072	1990	2184	2087	255	2182	2388	"	2492	2377	2601	2471	2699	2566	2819
1891	2073	1991	2185	"	2283	2183	2389	2280	2497	2378	2602	2472	2700	2567	2815
1892	2074	1992	2186	2088	2284	2184	2390	2281	2498	2379	2603	2473	2701	2568	2816
1893	2075	1993	2187	2089	2285	2185	2391	2282	2499	2380	2124	2474	2702	2569	2818
1894	2076	1994	2188	2090	2286	2186	2392	2283	2500	"	2604	2475	2703	2570	2819
1895	2077	1995	2189	2091	2288	2187	2394	2284	2501	2381	2605	2476	2705	2571	2820
1896	2078	1996	2190	2092	2289	2188	2395	2285	2502	2382	2606	2477	2707	2572	2821
"	2393	1997	2191	2093	2290	2189	2397	2286	2503	2383	2608	2478	2708	2573	2822
1897	2080	1998	2192	2094	2291	2190	2398	2287	2504	2384	2609	2479	2709	2574	2823
1898	2081	1999	2180	2095	2292	2191	2399	2288	2505	2385	2610	2480	2710	"	2824
1899	2083	"	2194	"	2301	2192	2400	2289	2506	2386	2611	2481	2711	2575	2825
1900	2084	2000	2195	2096	2293	2193	2401	2290	2507	2387	2612	2482	2712	2576	2826
1901	2085	2001	2196	2097	2294	2194	2404	2291	2508	2388	2613	2483	2713	2577	2827
1902	2086	2002	2197	2098	2295	2195	2405	2292	2509	2389	2614	2484	2714	2578	2828
1903	2087	2003	2198	2099	2296	2196	2406	2293	2510	2390	2615	2485	2715	2579	2829
1904	2082	2004	2199	2100	2297	2197	2408	2294	2511	2391	2616	2486	2716	2580	2830
"	2088	2005	2200	2101	2298	2198	2409	2295	2512	2392	2617	2487	2717	2581	2831
1905	2089	2006	2201	2102	2299	2199	2411	2296	1703	2393	2618	2488	2718	"	2832
1906	2090	2007	2202	2103	2300	2200	2412	"	2513	2394	2619	2489	2720	2582	2833
1907	2091	2008	2203	2104	2302	2201	2414	2297	2514	2395	2620	"	2721	2583	2834
1908	2092	2009	2204	2105	2304	2202	2415	2298	2515	2396	2623	2490	2722	2584	2835
1909	2093	2010	2205	2106	2305	2203	2416	2299	2516	2397	1624	2491	2722	"	3019
1910	2094	"	5181	2107	2306	2204	2417	2300	2517	"	2624	"	2728	2585	2836
1911	2095	2011	2207	2108	2307	2205	2419	2301	2518	2398	2625	2492	2724	2586	2837
1912	2096	2012	2208	2109	2308	2206	2418	2302	2519	2399	2626	2493	2727	2587	2838
1913	2097	2013	2209	2110	2309	"	2420	2303	2520	2400	2627	2494	2729	2588	2840
1914	2098	2014	2210	2111	2310	2207	2421	2304	2521	2401	2628	"	2730	2589	2841
1915	2099	2015	2211	2112	2311	2208	2421	2305	2522	2402	2629	2495	2731	2590	2843
1916	2100	2016	2212	2113	2312	2209	2422	2306	2523	2403	2630	2496	2732	2591	2842
1917	2101	2017	2213	2114	2313	2210	2423	2307	2525	2404	2631	2497	2733	2592	2844
1918	2102	"	2223	2115	2314	2211	2424	2308	2526	2405	2632	2498	2734	2593	2845
1919	2103	2018	2214	"	2315	2212	2426	2309	2527	2406	2633	2499	2735	2594	2846
1920	2104	2019	2215	2116	2316	2213	2427	2310	2528	2407	2634	2500	2736	2595	2847
1921	2105	"	2971	2117	2317	2214	1700	"	2529	2408	2635	2501	2737	2596	2848
1922	2106	2020	2216	"	2318	"	2428	2311	2530	2409	2636	"	2738	2597	2849
1923	2107	2021	2217	2118	2319	2215	2429	2312	2531	2410	2637	2502	2739	2598	2850
1924	2108	2022	2219	2119	2320	2216	2431	2312'	2532	2411	2639	2503	2740	2599	2851
1925	2109	2023	2220	2120	2321	2217	2432	2313	2533	2412	2640	2504	2743	2600	2853
1926	2110	2024	2221	2121	2322	2218	2433	2314	2534	2413	2641	2505	2745	2601	2854
1927	2111	2025	2222	2122	2323	2219	2434	2315	2535	2414	2642	2506	2746	2602	2856
1928	2112	2026	2224	2123	2324	2220	2435	2316	2536	2415	2643	2507	2747	2603	2857
1929	2113	2027	2131	2124	2325	2221	2436	2317	2537	2416	2644	2508	2748	2604	2858
"	4658	"	2225	2125	2326	2222	2437	2318	2538	2417	2645	2509	2749	2605	2859
1930	2114	2028	2226	2126	2327	2223	2438	2319	2539	2418	2646	"	2778	2606	2860
1931	2115	2029	2227	2127	2328	2224	2439	2320	2540	2419	2647	2510	2750	2607	2861
1932	2116	2030	2228	"	2986	"	2440	2321	2541	2420	2648	2511	2751	2608	2862
1933	2117	2031	2229	2128	2329	2225	2441	2322	2542	2421	2649	"	2760	2609	2864
1934	2118	2032	2230	2129	2303	2226	2442	"	3859	2422	2650	2512	2752	2610	2865
1935	2119	2033	2231	"	2330	2227	2443	2323	2543	2423	2651	2513	2754	2611	2866
1936	2120	2034	2232	2130	2331	2228	2445	2324	2544	2424	2652	2514	2755	2612	2867
1937	2121	2035	2233	2131	2332	2229	2446	2325	2545	2425	2653	2515	2756	2613	1463
1938	2122	2036	3306	2132	2333	2230	2448	2326	2546	2426	2654	2516	2757	"	2868
1939	2123	2037	2235	2133	2334	2231	2449	2327	2547	2427	2655	2517	2759	2614	2870
1940	2125	2038	2237	2134	2335	2232	2450	2328	2548	2428	2656	2518	2761	2615	2871
1941	2126	2039	2238	2135	2336	2233	2206	2329	2549	2429	2657	2519	2762	2616	2872
1942	2127	2040	2239	2136	2337	"	2451	2330	2550	2430	2658	2520	2763	2617	2875
1943	2128	2041	2240	2137	2338	2234	2452	2331	2552	2431	2659	2521	2764	2618	2876
1944	2063	2042	2241	2138	2340	2235	2453	2332	2553	2432	2660	2522	2766	2619	2877
"	2129	2043	2242	2139	2341	2236	2452	2333	2554	2433	2661	2523	2767	2620	1595
1945	2130	2044	2243	"	2342	2237	2454	2334	2555	2434	2662	2524	2768	"	2878
1946	2134	2045	2236	2140	2343	2238	2455	2335	2556	2435	2663	2525	2769	2621	2879
1947	2135	2046	3306	2141	2344	2239	2456	2336	2557	2436	2664	"	2770	2622	2880
1948	2137	2047	2244	2142	2345	2240	2457	2337	2558	2437	2665	2526	2771	2623	1597
1949	2138	2048	2245	2143	2346	2241	2458	2338	2559	2438	2666	2526'	2772	"	2881
1950	2140	2049	2246	2144	2347	2242	2459	2339	2560	2439	2667	2527	2773	2624	2882
1951	2141	2050	2247	2145	2339	2243	2460	2340	2561	2440	2668	2528	2774	"	2883
1952	2142	2051	2248	"	2348	2244	2461	2341	2562	2441	2669	2529	2775	2625	2884
1953	2144	2052	2249	2146	2349	2245	2462	2342	2563	2442	2670	2530	2776	2626	2885
1954	2145	2053	2250	2147	2351	2246	2463	2343	2564	"	3916	2531	2777	2627	2886
1955	2146	2054	2251	2148	2350	2247	2464	2344	2565	2443	2671	2532	2779	2628	2887
1956	2147	2055	2252	"	2352	2248	1609	2345	2566	2444	2672	2533	2780	2629	2888
1957	2148	2056	144	2149	2353	2249	1609			2445	2673	2534	2781	2630	2889

STRONG	G/K
2631	2890
2632	2891
2633	2892
2634	2894
2635	2895
2636	2896
2637	2897
2638	2898
2639	2899
2640	2900
"	5698
2641	2901
2642	2902
2643	2903
2644	2904
2645	2905
2646	2906
2647	2907
2648	2908
2649	2909
2650	2910
2651	2911
2652	2873
"	2912
2653	2874
"	2913
2654	2914
2655	2915
2656	2916
2657	2917
2658	2918
2659	2919
2660	2920
2661	2921
2662	2922
2663	2923
2664	2924
2665	2925
2666	2927
2667	2928
2668	2929
2669	2930
2670	2931
2671	2932
2672	2933
2673	2934
2674	2935
2675	2936
2676	2937
2677	2938
2678	2939
2679	2940
2680	2941
2681	2942
2682	2943
2683	2944
2684	2945
2685	2946
2686	2947
2687	2948
2688	2949
2689	2950
2690	2951
2691	2952
2692	2953
2693	2954
2694	2955
2695	2956
"	2957
2696	2958
2697	2959
2698	2960
2699	2961
2700	2962
2701	2963
2702	2965
2703	2966
2704	2967
2705	2968
2706	2969
2707	2970
2708	2972
2709	2973
2710	2974
"	4201
2711	2976
2712	2977
2713	2978
2714	2979
2715	2980
2716	2981
[2717 Omitted by Strong]	
2718	2982
2719	2983
"	2984
2720	2985
2721	2987
2722	2988
2723	2989
2724	2990
2725	2991
"	2992
2726	2993
2727	2994

STRONG	G/K
2728	2995
2729	2996
2730	2997
"	3001
2731	2998
2732	2999
2733	3000
2734	3002
2735	1480
"	3003
2736	3004
"	3006
2737	3005
2738	3008
2739	3009
"	3010
2740	3011
2741	3012
2742	3014
2743	3013
"	3015
2744	3016
2745	3017
2746	3018
2747	3020
2748	3021
"	3022
2749	3023
2750	3024
2751	3025
2752	3026
2753	3027
2754	3029
2755	3030
2756	3031
2757	2787
"	3032
2758	3033
2759	3034
2760	3035
2761	3036
2762	3037
2763	3038
2764	3039
2765	3040
2766	3041
2767	3042
2768	3043
2769	3044
2770	2132
"	3045
2771	3046
2772	3047
2773	3048
2774	3049
2775	3050
"	3052
2776	3051
2777	3053
2778	2133
"	3056
2779	3057
2780	3058
2781	3059
2782	3060
2783	3061
2784	3062
2785	3063
2786	3064
2787	3066
2788	3067
2789	3068
2790	3069
2791	3070
"	3071
2792	3072
"	3077
2793	3073
2794	3074
2795	3075
2796	3076
2797	3078
2798	3080
2799	3081
2800	3082
2801	3083
2802	1144
"	3007
"	3084
"	3085
2803	3086
2804	3087
2805	3088
2806	3089
2807	3090
2808	3091
2809	3092
2810	3093
2811	3094
2812	3095
2813	3096
2814	3097
2815	3098
2816	3099
2817	3100

STRONG	G/K
2818	3101
2819	3102
2820	3103
2821	3104
2822	3105
2823	3106
2824	3107
2825	3108
"	3109
2826	3110
2827	3111
2828	3112
2829	3113
2830	3114
2831	3115
2832	3116
2833	3117
2834	3118
2835	3119
2836	3120
2837	3121
2838	3122
2839	3123
2840	3124
2841	3125
2842	3126
2843	3127
2844	3128
2845	3130
2846	3131
2847	3132
2848	3133
2849	3134
2850	3135
2851	3136
2852	3139
2853	3140
2854	3141
2855	3142
2856	3143
2857	3138
"	3145
2858	3137
"	3144
2859	3146
2860	3147
2861	3148
2862	3149
2863	3150
2864	3151
2865	3152
2866	3153
2867	3154
2868	3155
2869	3156
2870	3157
2871	3158
2872	3159
2873	3160
2874	3161
"	3162
"	3163
2875	3164
2876	3165
2877	3166
2878	3167
"	3168
2879	3169
2880	3170
2881	3171
2882	3172
2883	3173
2884	3174
2885	3175
2886	3176
2887	3177
"	3178
2888	3179
2889	3180
2890	3181
2891	3182
"	3183
2892	3184
2893	3185
2894	3186
2895	3187
"	3188
2896	3189
2897	3190
2898	3191
2899	3192
2900	3193
2901	3194
2902	3195
2903	3196
2904	3197
2905	3198
2906	3199
2907	3200
2908	3201
2909	3202
2910	3203
2911	3204
2912	3205
2913	3206

STRONG	G/K
2914	3207
2915	3208
2916	3209
2917	3210
2918	3211
2919	3212
2920	3213
2921	3214
2922	3215
2923	3216
2924	3217
2925	3218
2926	3219
2927	3220
"	3224
"	3226
2928	3221
2929	3222
2930	3223
2931	3225
2932	3227
2933	3228
2934	3229
2935	3230
2936	3231
2937	3232
2938	3233
2939	3234
2940	3235
2941	3236
2942	3237
2943	3239
2944	3238
"	3240
2945	3241
2946	3242
"	3243
2947	3244
2948	3245
2949	3246
2950	3247
2951	3248
2952	3249
2953	3250
2954	3251
2955	3252
2956	3253
"	3254
2957	3255
2958	3256
"	3260
2959	3257
2960	3258
2961	3259
2962	3261
2963	3262
2964	3263
2965	3264
2966	3265
2967	3266
2968	3267
2969	3268
2970	3269
2971	3270
2972	3271
2973	3272
2974	3273
2975	3275
2976	3276
2977	3277
"	4996
2978	3278
2979	3280
2980	654
"	3281
2981	3282
2982	3283
"	3316
2983	3284
2984	3285
2985	3286
"	5697
2986	3287
2987	3288
2988	3289
2989	2139
"	3290
2990	3291
2991	3292
2992	3295
2993	3293
2994	3294
2995	3296
2996	3297
"	3298
2997	3279
"	3299
2998	3300
2999	3301
3000	3302
3001	3303
3002	3304
3003	3305
3004	1649
"	3306

STRONG	G/K
3005	3307
3006	3308
3007	3309
3008	3310
3009	3311
3010	3312
3011	3313
3012	3317
3013	3318
3014	3319
3015	3320
3016	3321
3017	3322
3018	3323
3019	3324
3020	3325
3021	3326
3022	3328
3023	3329
3024	3330
3025	3332
3026	3333
3027	798
"	3334
3028	3331
"	3335
3029	3336
3030	3337
3031	3338
3032	3339
"	3341
3033	3340
3034	3342
3035	3343
3036	3344
3037	3345
3038	3346
3039	3347
3040	3348
3041	3349
3042	3350
3043	3351
3044	3352
3045	3353
3046	3354
3047	3355
3048	3356
3049	3357
3050	3358
3051	3359
3052	3360
3053	3361
3054	3362
3055	3363
3056	3364
3057	3365
3058	3366
3059	3367
3060	3368
3061	3369
3062	3370
3063	3370
3064	3370
3065	3371
3066	3372
3067	3373
3068	3374
3069	3375
3070	3376
3071	3377
3072	3378
3073	3379
3074	3380
3075	3381
3076	3382
3077	3383
3078	3384
3079	3385
3080	3386
3081	3387
3082	3388
3083	3389
3084	3390
3085	3391
3086	3392
3087	3393
3088	3394
3089	3395
3090	3396
3091	3397
3092	3399
3093	3400
"	3401
3094	3402
3095	3404
"	3406
3096	3405
3097	3407
3098	3408
3099	3409
3100	3411
3101	3412
3102	3413
3103	3417
3104	3418

STRONG	G/K
"	3526
3105	3419
3106	3420
3107	3421
3108	3422
3109	3423
3110	3424
3111	3425
3112	3426
3113	3427
3114	3428
3115	3429
3116	3430
3117	3431
3118	3432
3119	3433
3120	3434
3121	3435
3122	3436
3123	3437
3124	3438
3125	3439
3126	3440
3127	3441
3128	3442
3129	3443
3130	3444
3131	3445
3132	3446
3133	3447
3134	2495
"	3448
3135	3449
3136	3450
3137	3451
"	3452
3138	3453
3139	3454
3140	3455
3141	3456
3142	3457
3143	3458
3144	3459
"	4753
3145	3460
"	3462
3146	3463
3147	3464
3148	3465
3149	3461
"	3461
"	3466
3150	3467
3151	3468
3152	3469
3153	3470
3154	3471
3155	3472
3156	3414
"	3473
3157	3474
3158	3415
"	3475
3159	3416
"	3476
3160	3477
3161	3478
3162	3479
3163	3480
3164	3481
3165	1609
3166	902
"	3482
3167	3483
3168	3484
3169	3485
3170	3486
3171	3487
3172	3488
3173	3489
3174	3490
3175	3491
3176	3492
3177	3493
3178	3494
3179	3495
"	3496
3180	3497
3181	3498
3182	3499
3183	3500
3184	3501
3185	3505
3186	3504
3187	3505
3188	3506
3189	3506
3190	3507
3191	3509
3192	3510
3193	3511
"	3512
"	3513
3194	3514
"	3515

STRONG	G/K
3195	3516
3196	3517
3197	3518
3198	3519
3199	3508
"	3520
3200	3521
3201	3522
3202	3523
[3202 to 3304 Omitted by Strong]	
3303	3525
3304	3528
"	3529
3305	3530
3306	3531
3307	3532
3308	3533
3309	3534
3310	3535
3311	3536
3312	3537
3313	3538
3314	3540
3315	3541
3316	3542
3317	3543
3318	3544
3319	3545
3320	3546
3321	3547
3322	3539
"	3548
3323	3549
3324	3550
3325	3551
3326	3552
3327	3553
3328	3554
3329	3555
3330	3556
3331	3557
3332	3558
3333	3559
3334	3560
3335	3561
3336	3562
3337	3563
3338	3564
3339	3565
3340	3566
3341	3567
3342	3568
3343	3569
3344	3570
"	3573
3345	3571
3346	3572
3347	3575
3348	3576
3349	3577
3350	3578
3351	3579
3352	3580
3353	3581
3354	3582
3355	3583
3356	3584
3357	3585
3358	3586
3359	3587
3360	3588
"	3589
3361	3590
3362	1569+3590
3363	2671+3590
3364	4024+3590
3365	3592
"	3598
3366	3593
3367	3594
"	3599
3368	3595
3369	3596
3370	3597
3371	3600
"	3601
3372	3601
3373	3602
3374	3603
3375	3604
3376	3605
3377	3606
3378	3590+4024
3379	3607
3380	3609
3381	3610
3382	3611
3383	3612
3384	3613
3385	3614
3386	3615
3387	3614
3388	3616
3389	3617
"	3618

STRONG	G/K
3390	3619
3391	1651
3392	3620
3393	3621
3394	3622
3395	1807
"	3623
"	5041
"	5042
3396	3502
"	3503
"	3624
3397	3625
3398	3625
3399	3626
3400	3627
3401	3628
3402	3629
3403	3630
3404	3631
3405	3632
3406	3633
3407	3634
3408	3635
3409	3636
3410	3637
3411	3638
3412	3639
3413	3640
3414	3641
3415	3642
3416	3643
3417	3644
3418	3645
3419	3646
3420	3647
3421	3648
3422	3649
3423	3650
3424	3651
"	3652
3425	3653
3426	3654
3427	1609
3428	3655
3429	3656
3430	3657
3431	3658
3432	3659
3433	3660
3434	3661
3435	3662
3436	3663
3437	3524
3438	3664
3439	3665
3440	3666
3441	3667
3442	3668
3443	3669
3444	3671
3445	3672
3446	3673
3447	3674
3448	3675
3449	3677
3450	1609
3451	3676
3452	3678
3453	3679
3454	3680
3455	3681
3456	3682
3457	3683
3458	3684
3459	3685
3460	3686
3461	3689
3462	3690
3463	3691
3464	3693
3465	3695
3466	3696
3467	3697
3468	3698
3469	3699
3470	3700
3471	3701
3472	3702
3473	3703
3474	3704
3475	3705
"	3706
3476	3709
3477	3710
3478	3711
"	3712
"	3713
"	3714
"	3715

STRONG	G/K	STRONG	G/K	STRONG	G/K	STRONG	G/K	STRONG	G/K	STRONG	G/K	STRONG	G/K	STRONG	G/K
3479	3716	3575	3820	3672	3935	3770	4039	3864	4144	3963	4253	4060	4363	4159	4470
3480	3717	3576	3821	3673	3937	3771	4040	3865	4145	3964	4254	4061	4364	4160	4472
3481	3718	3577	3822	3674	3938	3772	4041	3866	4146	"	4260	4062	4365	4161	4473
"	3719	3578	3825	3675	3939	3773	4042	3867	4147	3965	4255	4063	4366	4162	4474
3482	3720	3579	3826	3676	3940	3774	4043	3868	4148	3966	4256	4064	4367	4163	4475
3483	3721	3580	3827	3677	3941	3775	4044	3869	4149	3967	4257	4065	4368	4164	4476
3484	3723	3581	3828	3678	3942	3776	4045	"	4150	3968	4258	4066	4369	4165	4477
3485	3724	3582	3829	3679	3943	3777	4046	3870	4151	3969	4259	4067	4370	4166	4478
3486	3725	3583	3830	3680	3944	3778	4047	3871	4152	3970	4261	4068	4371	4167	4479
3487	3726	3584	3831	3681	3945	3779	4048	3872	4153	3971	4262	4069	4372	4168	4480
3488	3727	3585	3832	3682	3946	3780	4049	3873	4154	3972	4263	4070	4373	4169	4471
3489	3728	3586	3833	3683	3947	3781	4050	3874	4155	3973	4264	4071	4374	"	4481
3490	3729	3587	3834	3684	3948	3782	4051	3875	4156	3974	4265	4072	4375	4170	4482
3491	3730	3588	3836	3685	3949	3783	4052	3876	4157	3975	4266	4073	4376	4171	4483
3492	3731	3589	3837	3686	3950	3784	4053	3877	4158	3976	4267	4074	4377	4172	4484
3493	3732	3590	3838	3687	3951	3785	4054	3878	4159	3977	4268	4075	4378	4173	4485
3494	3733	3591	3839	3688	3952	3786	4055	3879	4160	3978	4269	4076	4379	4174	4486
3495	3734	3592	3840	3689	3903	3787	4056	3880	4161	3979	4270	4077	4380	4175	4487
3496	3735	3593	3841	"	3953	3788	4057	3881	4162	"	4271	4078	4381	4176	4488
"	3736	3594	3842	3690	3954	3789	4058	3882	4163	3980	4272	4079	4382	4177	4489
3497	3722	3595	3843	3691	3955	3790	4059	3883	4164	3981	4273	4080	4383	4178	4490
"	3737	3596	3844	3692	3956	3791	4061	3884	4165	"	4274	4081	4384	"	1930
3498	3738	3597	3845	3693	3957	3792	4062	3885	4166	3982	2167	4082	4385	4179	2234
3499	3739	3598	3847	3694	3958	3793	4063	"	4167	"	4275	4083	4388	"	4491
3500	3740	3599	3848	"	5541	3794	4065	3886	4168	3983	4277	4084	4389	4180	4494
3501	3742	3600	3849	3695	3959	3795	4066	3887	4169	3984	4278	4085	4390	4181	4495
3502	3743	3601	3850	3696	3960	3796	4067	3888	4170	3985	4279	4086	4391	4182	4497
"	3801	3602	3851	3697	3961	3797	4069	3889	4171	3986	4280	4087	4393	4183	4498
3503	3744	3603	4005+1639	3698	3962	3798	4068	3890	4172	3987	4281	4088	4394	4184	4492
3504	3745	3604	3852	3699	3963	"	4070	3891	4174	3988	4282	4089	4395	"	4499
3505	3746	3605	3853	3700	3964	3799	4071	3892	4175	3989	4283	4090	4396	4185	4500
3506	3748	3606	3854	3701	3965	3800	4072	3893	4176	3990	4284	4091	4276	4186	4501
3507	3749	3607	3855	3702	3966	3801	3836+1639 +2779+2262	3894	4177	3991	4286	"	4397	4187	4502
3508	3750	3608	3856	3703	3967	3802	4074	3895	4178	3992	4287	4092	4399	4188	4503
3509	3751	3609	3858	3704	3968	3803	4075	3896	4179	3993	4288	4093	4400	4189	4504
3510	3752	3610	3860	3705	3969	3804	4077	3897	4180	3994	4289	"	4401	4190	4505
3511	3753	3611	3861	3706	3970	3805	4078	3898	4181	3995	4290	4094	4402	4191	4505
3512	3754	3612	3862	3707	3971	3806	4079	3899	4182	3996	4291	4095	4403	4192	4506
3513	3755	3613	3863	3708	1625	3807	4080	3900	4183	3997	4292	4096	4404	4193	4507
3514	3756	3614	3864	"	3972	3808	4081	3901	4184	3998	4293	4097	4405	4194	4508
3515	3757	3615	3865	3709	3973	3809	4082	3902	4185	3999	4294	4098	4406	4195	4510
3516	3758	3616	3866	3710	3974	3810	4083	3903	4186	"	5229	4099	4407	4196	4511
3517	3759	3617	3867	3711	3975	3811	4084	3904	4187	4000	4295	"	4408	"	4515
3518	3760	3618	3868	3712	3976	3812	4085	3905	4189	4001	4296	4100	4409	4197	4512
3519	3761	"	3871	3713	3977	"	4088	3906	4190	4002	4297	4101	4410	"	4515
3520	3762	3619	3869	3714	3978	3813	4086	3907	4191	4003	4298	4102	4411	4198	4513
3521	3763	3620	3870	3715	3979	3814	4087	3908	4192	4004	4299	4103	4412	4199	4514
3522	3764	3621	3872	3716	3980	3815	4089	3909	4193	4005	4300	4104	4413	4200	4516
3523	3765	3622	3873	3717	3981	3816	4090	3910	4194	4006	4301	4105	4414	4201	4517
3524	3766	3623	3874	3718	3982	3817	4091	3911	4195	4007	4302	4106	4415	4202	4518
"	3767	3624	3875	3719	3983	3818	4092	3912	4196	4008	4305	4107	4416	4203	4519
3525	3768	3625	3876	3720	3984	3819	4093	3913	4173	4009	4306	"	4417	4204	4520
3526	3769	3626	3877	3721	3985	3820	4094	"	4197	4010	4307	4108	4418	4205	4521
3527	3770	"	3878	3722	3986	3821	4095	3914	4199	4011	4308	4109	4419	4206	4522
3528	3771	3627	3879	3723	3987	3822	4096	3915	4200	4012	4309	4110	4420	4207	4523
3529	3772	"	3882	3724	3988	3823	4097	3916	4202	4013	4310	4111	4421	4208	4524
3530	3773	3628	3880	3725	3990	3824	4098	3917	4203	4014	4311	4112	4422	4209	4525
3531	3774	3629	3881	3726	1941	"	4100	3918	4205	4015	4313	4113	4423	4210	4526
3532	3775	3630	3884	3727	3992	3825	4099	3919	4206	4016	4212	4114	4424	"	4528
3533	3776	3631	3885	3728	3993	3826	4101	3920	4207	"	4314	4115	4425	4211	4527
3534	3777	3632	3886	3729	3994	"	4113	3921	4208	4017	4315	4116	4426	4212	4529
3535	3778	3633	3883	3730	3995	3827	4102	3922	4209	4018	4316	4117	4427	4213	4530
"	3779	"	3887	3731	3996	3828	4103	3923	4210	4019	4317	4118	4498	4214	4531
3536	3780	3634	3888	3732	3997	3829	4104	3924	4211	4020	4318	4119	4498	4215	4532
3537	3781	3635	3890	3733	3989	"	4106	3925	4213	4021	4319	4120	4428	4216	4533
"	4469	3636	3891	"	3998	3830	4105	3926	4214	4022	4320	4121	4429	4217	4467
3538	3782	3637	3892	3734	3999	"	4107	3927	4215	4023	4321	4122	4430	"	4534
3539	3783	3638	3893	3735	4001	3831	4108	3928	4216	4024	4322	4123	4431	4218	4537
3540	3784	3639	3896	3736	4002	3832	4109	3929	4217	"	4323	4124	4432	4219	4536
3541	3785	"	3897	3737	4003	3833	4110	3930	4218	4025	4324	4125	4433	4220	4538
3542	3786	3640	3899	3738	4004	3834	4111	3931	4219	4026	4325	4126	4434	4221	4539
3543	3787	3641	3900	3739	4005	3835	4112	3932	4220	4027	2753	4127	4435	4222	4540
3544	3788	3642	3901	3740	4006	3836	4115	3933	4221	"	4326	4128	4436	4223	4541
3545	3789	3643	3902	3741	4008	3837	4114	3934	4222	4028	4328	4129	4437	4224	4542
3546	3790	3644	3894	3742	4009	"	4116	3935	4223	4029	4329	4130	4398	4225	4543
3547	3791	"	3904	3743	4010	3838	4117	3936	4224	4030	4330	4131	4438	4226	4544
3548	3792	3645	3895	3744	4011	3839	4118	"	4225	4031	4331	4132	4439	4227	4545
3549	3793	"	3905	3745	4012	3840	4119	3937	4226	4032	4332	4133	4440	4228	4546
3550	3794	3646	3906	3746	4013	3841	4120	3938	4227	4033	4333	4134	4441	4229	4547
3551	3795	3647	3907	3747	4014	3842	4121	3939	4228	4034	4334	4135	4442	4230	4548
3552	3796	3648	3908	"	4016	3843	4122	3940	4229	4035	4335	4136	4443	4231	4549
3553	3797	3649	3909	3748	4015	3844	4123	3941	4230	4036	4337	4137	4444	4232	4550
3554	3798	3650	3910	3749	4017	3845	4124	3942	4231	4037	4338	4138	4445	4233	4551
3555	3799	3651	3911	3750	4018	3846	4125	3943	4232	4038	4339	4139	4446	4234	4552
3556	3800	3652	3912	3751	4019	3847	4126	3944	4233	4039	4340	4140	4447	4235	4553
3557	3802	3653	3913	3752	4020	3848	688	3945	4234	4040	4341	4141	4448	4236	4554
3558	3803	3654	3914	3753	4021	"	4127	3946	4235	4041	4342	4142	4449	"	4557
3559	3804	3655	3915	3754	4022	3849	4128	3947	4236	4042	4343	4143	4450	4237	4555
3560	3805	3656	3917	3755	4015	3850	4130	3948	4237	4043	4344	4144	4452	4238	407
3561	3741	3657	3918	3756	4024	3851	4129	3949	4239	4044	4345	"	4453	"	4556
"	3806	3658	3919	3757	4023	"	4131	3950	4240	4045	4346	4145	4454	4239	4558
3562	3807	3659	3921	3758	4025	3852	4132	3951	4241	4046	4347	4146	4455	4240	4559
3563	3808	3660	3922	3759	4026	3853	4133	3952	4242	4047	4348	4147	4456	4241	4560
3564	3809	"	3923	3760	4027	3854	4134	3953	4243	4048	4351	4148	4457	4242	4561
"	3810	3661	3924	3761	4028	3855	4135	3954	4244	4049	4352	4149	4458	4243	4563
3565	3811	3662	3925	3762	4029	3856	4136	3955	4245	4050	4353	4150	4459	4244	4564
3566	3812	3663	3926	"	4032	3857	4137	3956	4246	4051	4354	4151	4460	4245	4565
3567	3813	3664	3927	3763	4030	3858	4138	3957	4247	4052	4355	4152	4461	4246	4562
3568	3814	3665	3928	3764	4031	3859	1384	3958	4248	4053	4356	4153	4462	"	4566
3569	5422	3666	3929	3765	4033	"	4139	3959	4249	4054	4357	4154	4463	4247	4567
3570	3815	3667	3930	3766	4034	3860	4140	3960	4250	4055	4358	4155	4464	4248	4568
3571	3816	3668	3931	3767	4036	3861	4141	3961	4251	4056	4359	4156	4465	4249	4569
3572	3817	3669	3932	3768	4037	3862	4142	3962	4635	4057	4360	4157	4466	"	4573
3573	3818	3670	3933	3769	4038	3863	4143			4058	4361	4158	4468	4250	4570
3574	3819	3671	3934							4059	4362			4251	4571
														4252	4572

STRONG	G/K	STRONG	G/K	STRONG	G/K	STRONG	G/K	STRONG	G/K	STRONG	G/K	STRONG	G/K	STRONG	G/K
4253	4574	4345	4677	4437	4781	"	4966	4619	4990	4720	5093	4815	5197	4909	5306
4254	4575	4346	4678	4438	4782	4526	4884	4620	4991	4721	5094	4816	5198	4910	5307
4255	4576	"	4680	4439	4783	4527	4885	4621	4989	4722	5095	4817	5199	4911	5308
4256	164	4347	4681	4440	4784	4528	4886	"	4992	4723	5096	4818	5200	4912	5309
"	4577	"	4679	4441	4785	4529	4887	4622	4994	4724	5097	4819	5201	4913	5310
4257	4578	4348	4682	4442	4786	4530	4890	4623	4995	4725	5098	4820	5202	4914	5311
4258	4579	4349	4683	4443	4787	4531	4888	4624	4997	4726	5099	4821	5203	4915	5312
4259	4580	4350	4684	4444	4788	4532	4889	4625	4998	4727	5100	4822	5204	4916	5313
4260	4581	4351	4685	4445	4789	4533	4891	4626	4999	4728	5101	4823	5205	4917	5314
4261	4582	4352	4686	4446	4790	4534	4892	4627	5002	4729	5102	4824	5206	4918	5315
4262	4583	4353	4687	4447	4791	4535	4893	4628	5003	4730	5103	4825	5207	4919	5316
4263	4584	4354	4688	4448	4792	4536	4894	4629	5004	4731	5104	4826	5208	4920	5317
"	4585	4355	4647	4449	4793	4537	4895	4630	5005	4732	5105	4827	5209	"	5320
4264	4586	"	4689	4450	4794	4538	4896	4631	5006	4733	5106	4828	5210	4921	5318
4265	4587	4356	4691	4451	4796	4539	4897	4632	5007	4734	5107	4829	5211	"	5319
4266	4588	"	4692	4452	4803	4540	4899	4633	5008	4735	5109	4830	5212	4922	5321
4267	4589	4357	4693	4453	4797	"	4900	4634	5009	4736	5108	4831	5213	4923	5322
4268	4590	4358	4694	4454	4798	4541	4901	4635	5010	4737	5110	4832	5215	4924	5324
4269	4591	4359	4695	4455	4799	4542	4902	4636	5011	4738	5111	4833	5214	4925	5325
4270	4592	4360	4696	4456	4386	4543	4903	4637	5012	4739	5112	"	5216	4926	5326
4271	4593	4361	4698	"	4800	4544	4904	4638	5013	4740	5113	"	5240	4927	5327
4272	4594	4362	4699	4457	4387	4545	4905	4639	5014	4741	5114	4834	5217	4928	5330
4273	4595	4363	4700	4458	4535	4546	4907	4640	5015	4742	5116	4835	5218	4929	5332
4274	4596	4364	4701	"	4803	4547	4908	4641	5016	4743	5117	4836	5219	4930	5333
4275	4632	4365	4702	4459	4802	4548	4909	4642	5017	4744	5118	4837	5220	4931	5334
4276	4598	4366	4703	4460	4805	4549	4910	4643	5018	4745	5119	4838	5221	4932	5335
4277	4625	"	4704	4461	4806	4550	4911	4644	5019	4746	5115	4839	5222	4933	5337
"	4597	4367	4705	4462	4807	4551	4912	4645	5020	"	5120	4840	5223	4934	5298
4278	4599	4368	4188	"	4808	4552	4913	4646	5021	4747	5122	4841	5224	"	5338
4279	4600	"	4706	"	4809	4553	4914	4647	5022	4748	5123	4842	5225	4935	5339
4280	4625	4369	4707	4463	4810	4554	4915	4648	5023	4749	5124	4843	5227	4936	5340
"	4597	4370	4708	4464	4811	4555	4916	4649	5024	4750	5125	4844	5228	4937	5341
4281	4601	"	4716	4465	4812	4556	4917	4650	5025	4751	5126	4845	5230	4938	5342
4282	4602	4371	4709	4466	4814	4557	4918	4651	5026	4752	5127	4846	5231	4939	5343
4283	4603	4372	4710	4467	4815	4558	4919	4652	5027	4753	5128	4847	5232	4940	5344
4284	4604	4373	4711	4468	4816	4559	4920	4653	5028	4754	5129	4848	5233	4941	5345
"	4617	4374	4712	4469	4819	4560	4921	4654	5029	4755	5130	4849	5234	4942	5347
4285	4605	4375	4713	"	4828	4561	4922	4655	5030	4756	5131	"	5235	4943	5348
4286	4606	4376	4714	4470	4820	4562	4923	4656	5031	4757	5132	4850	5236	4944	5349
"	4671	4377	4715	4471	4821	"	4951	4657	5032	4758	5133	4851	5237	4945	5350
4287	4607	4378	4717	4472	4822	"	4952	4658	5033	4759	5134	"	5239	4946	5352
4288	4608	4379	4718	4473	4823	4563	4924	4659	5034	"	5135	4852	5238	4947	5353
4289	4609	4380	4719	4474	4824	4564	4925	4660	5035	4760	5136	4853	5241	4948	5354
4290	4610	"	4722	4475	4825	4565	838	4661	5036	4761	5137	4854	5242	4949	5351
4291	4613	4381	4720	4476	1017	"	4926	4662	5037	4762	5138	4855	5243	"	5355
4292	4614	"	4723	"	4827	4566	4927	4663	5038	4763	5139	4856	5244	"	5356
4293	4615	4382	4721	4477	4829	4567	4928	4664	5039	4764	5140	4857	5245	"	5835
4294	4616	"	4724	4478	4830	4568	4929	4665	5040	4765	5141	4858	5246	4950	5358
4295	4618	4383	4725	4479	4831	4569	4930	4666	5043	4766	5142	4859	5247	4951	5359
4296	4619	4384	4726	4480	4832	4570	2410	4667	2430	"	5143	4860	5248	4952	5331
4297	4620	4385	4727	4481	4818	"	4931	"	5044	4767	5144	4861	5249	"	5360
4298	4621	4386	4728	"	4833	4571	5148	4668	5045	4768	5145	4862	5250	4953	5361
4299	4622	4387	4728	"	4834	4572	4932	4669	5046	4769	5146	4863	5251	4954	5362
4300	4623	4388	4729	"	4854	4573	4933	4670	5047	4770	5121	4864	5252	4955	5086
4301	4624	4389	4730	4482	4835	4574	4934	4671	5148	"	5147	4865	5253	"	5363
4302	4625	4390	4731	4483	3306	4575	4935	4672	4898	4771	5148	4866	5254	4956	5364
"	4597	4391	4732	4484	4836	4576	4936	"	5048	4772	5149	4867	125	4957	5365
4303	4626	4392	4733	4485	4837	4577	4937	4673	5049	4773	5150	"	5255	4958	5366
4304	4627	4393	4734	4486	4826	"	4938	4674	5050	"	5151	4868	5256	4959	5367
4305	4628	4394	4735	"	4838	"	4987	4675	5148	4774	5152	4869	5257	4960	5368
4306	4629	4395	4736	"	4841	4578	4939	4676	5051	4775	5153	4870	5258	4961	5369
4307	4630	4396	4737	4487	4839	4579	4940	4677	5052	4776	4327	4871	5259	4962	5370
4308	4631	4397	4738	4488	4840	4580	4941	4678	5053	"	5154	"	5260	4963	5371
"	4632	4398	4739	4489	4842	4581	4942	4679	5054	4777	5155	"	5276	4964	5372
4309	4633	4399	4740	4490	4843	4582	4943	4680	5055	4778	5156	4872	5262	4965	4993
4310	4634	4400	4741	4491	4844	4583	4944	4681	5056	4779	5157	4873	5263	"	5373
4311	4636	4401	4742	4492	4845	4584	4945	4682	5057	4780	5158	"	5165	4966	5374
4312	4637	4402	4743	4493	4846	"	4946	4683	5058	4781	5159	4874	5264	4967	5375
4313	4638	4403	4744	"	4856	4585	4947	4684	5059	4782	5160	4875	5265	4968	5376
4314	4639	4404	4745	4494	4847	4586	4948	4685	5060	4783	5161	4876	5267	4969	5377
4315	4640	4405	4746	4495	4848	4587	4949	4686	5061	4784	5163	4877	5268	4970	5379
4316	4641	4406	4611	4496	4849	4588	4950	4687	2178	4785	2975	4878	5269	4971	5380
4317	4642	"	4747	4497	4850	4589	4953	"	5062	"	5164	4879	5270	4972	5381
"	4652	4407	4612	4498	4851	4590	4954	4688	5063	4786	5166	4880	5271	4973	5382
"	4654	"	4748	4499	4852	4591	4955	4689	5064	4787	5167	4881	5272	4974	5383
4318	4643	4408	4749	4500	4853	4592	4956	4690	5065	4788	5168	4882	5273	"	5384
4319	4644	4409	4750	4501	4855	4593	4957	4691	5066	4789	5169	4883	5274	4975	5385
"	4645	4410	4751	4502	4857	4594	4958	4692	5067	4790	5170	4884	5275	4976	5386
4320	4646	4411	4752	4503	4858	4595	4960	4693	5068	4791	5171	4885	5277	4977	5387
4321	4648	4412	4754	4504	4859	4596	4961	4694	5069	4792	5172	4886	5278	4978	5388
"	4649	"	4759	4505	4860	"	4986	4695	5071	4793	5173	4887	5279	4979	5389
4322	4650	4413	4755	4506	4861	4597	4962	4696	5070	4794	5174	4888	5280	4980	5390
4323	4651	4414	4756	4507	4864	4598	4963	4697	5072	4795	5175	4889	5281	4981	5391
4324	4653	4415	4757	4508	4865	4599	4964	4698	5073	"	5346	4890	5282	4982	1751
4325	4655	4416	4758	4509	4866	4600	4965	4699	5074	4796	5176	4891	5283	"	5392
4326	4656	4417	4760	4510	4862	4601	4967	4700	5075	4797	5177	4892	5284	4983	5393
4327	4657	4418	4761	"	4863	4602	4968	4701	5076	"	5179	4893	5287	4984	5394
4328	4659	4419	4762	"	4867	4603	4969	4702	5077	4798	5178	4894	5288	4985	5395
4329	4660	4420	4763	4511	4868	"	4971	4703	5078	4799	5180	"	5323	4986	5396
4330	4661	4421	4764	4512	4869	4604	4970	4704	5079	4800	5182	"	5328	4987	5397
4331	4662	4422	4765	4513	4870	4605	4972	4705	5080	4801	2413	4895	5289	4988	5398
4332	4204	4423	4766	4514	4871	4606	4973	4706	5080	"	5183	4896	5290	4989	5399
"	4663	4424	4767	4515	4872	4607	4974	4707	5080	4802	5184	4897	5291	4990	5400
4333	4664	4425	4768	4516	4873	4608	4975	4708	5081	4803	5185	4898	5292	4991	5401
4334	4665	4426	4769	4517	4874	4609	4976	4709	5081	4804	5186	4899	5293	4992	5402
4335	4666	4427	4770	4518	2407	4610	4977	4710	5082	4805	5187	4900	5261	"	5403
4336	4667	4428	4771	"	4876	4611	4978	4711	5083	4806	5188	"	5295	4993	5404
4337	4668	4429	4772	4519	4877	4612	4959	4712	5084	4807	5189	4901	5296	4994	5405
4338	4669	4430	4773	4520	4878	"	4980	4713	5085	4808	5190	4902	5299	4995	5406
4339	4670	4431	4774	4521	4879	4613	4981	4714	5087	4809	5191	4903	5300	4996	5407
4340	4672	4432	4775	4522	4880	4614	4982	4715	5088	4810	5192	4904	5301	4997	5408
4341	4673	4433	4776	4523	4881	4615	4983	4716	5089	4811	5193	4905	5302	4998	5409
4342	4674	4434	4777	4524	4882	4616	4984	4717	5090	4812	5194	4906	5303	4999	5411
4343	4675	4435	4778	4525	4883	4617	4985	4718	5091	4813	5195	4907	5304	5000	5412
4344	4676	4436	4780			4618	4988	4719	5092	4814	5196	4908	5305	5001	5413

STRONG	G/K	STRONG	G/K	STRONG	G/K	STRONG	G/K	STRONG	G/K	STRONG	G/K	STRONG	G/K	STRONG	G/K
5002	5414	5081	1315	5159	5574	"	5666	5314	5741	5394	5824	5473	5908	5550	5989
5003	5415	"	5495	"	5578	5238	5654	5315	2266	5395	5825	5474	5909	5551	5990
5004	5416	5082	5496	5160	5575	5239	5657	5316	5743	5396	5826	5475	5910	5552	5991
5005	5417	5083	5498	5161	5576	5240	5655	5317	5744	5397	5827	5476	5912	"	5997
5006	5418	5084	5499	5162	5577	"	5656	5318	5745	5398	5829	5477	5913	5553	5992
5007	5419	5085	5500	5163	5579	"	5658	5319	5746	5399	5828	5478	5914	5554	5993
5008	2496	5086	5501	5164	5580	5241	5659	5320	5747	"	5830	5479	5915	5555	5994
"	5420	5087	5502	5165	5581	5242	5660	5321	5748	5400	5831	5480	5916	5556	5995
5009	5421	5088	5503	5166	5582	5243	5661	5322	5749	5401	5832	5481	5917	5557	5996
5010	5423	5089	5504	5167	5583	5244	5662	5323	5750	5402	5833	5482	5918	5558	5998
5011	5424	5090	5505	5168	5584	"	5663	5324	5751	5403	5834	5483	5919	5559	5999
5012	5425	5091	5506	5169	5557	5245	5664	5325	5752	5404	5836	5484	5920	5560	6000
5013	5427	5092	5507	"	5585	5246	5665	5326	5753	5405	5837	5485	5921	5561	6001
5014	5428	5093	5508	5170	5586	5247	5667	5327	5754	5406	5838	5486	5922	5562	6003
5015	5429	5094	5509	5171	5587	5248	5668	5328	5755	5407	5839	5487	5923	5563	6004
5016	5430	5095	5510	5172	5588	5249	5669	5329	5756	5408	5840	5488	5924	5564	6005
5017	5431	5096	5511	5173	5589	5250	5670	5330	5757	5409	5841	5489	5925	5565	6006
5018	5432	5097	5512	5174	5590	5251	5671	5331	5758	5410	5842	5490	5926	5566	6008
5019	5433	5098	5513	5175	5591	5252	5672	"	5760	5411	5843	5491	5927	5567	6010
5020	5434	5099	5514	5176	5592	5253	5673	5332	5759	5412	5844	5492	5928	5568	6011
5021	5435	5100	5516	5177	5593	5254	5674	5333	5761	5413	5845	5493	5929	5569	6012
5022	5436	5101	5515	5178	5594	5255	5675	5334	5762	5414	5846	5494	5930	5570	6013
5023	4047	5102	5518	5179	5595	5256	5676	5335	5763	5415	5847	5495	5931	5571	6014
5024	5437	5103	5519	"	5596	5257	5677	5336	5764	5416	5848	5496	5932	5572	6015
5025	4047	5104	5520	5180	5597	5258	5678	5337	5765	5417	5849	5497	5933	5573	6016
5026	4047	5105	5521	5181	5598	5259	5679	5338	5766	"	5822	5498	5934	5574	6017
5027	5438	"	5522	5182	2571	5260	5680	5339	5767	5418	5850	5499	5935	5575	6018
5028	5439	5106	5523	"	5600	5261	5681	5340	5768	5419	5851	5500	5936	5576	6018
5029	5440	5107	5524	5183	5601	5262	5682	5341	5742	5420	5852	5501	5937	5577	6019
5030	5441	5108	5525	5184	5602	5263	5683	"	5769	5421	5853	5502	5938	5578	6021
5031	5442	5109	5526	5185	5603	"	5684	5342	5770	5422	5854	5503	5939	5579	6022
5032	5441	5110	5527	5186	5604	5264	5685	5343	5771	5423	5855	5504	2396	5580	6023
5033	5441	5111	5528	5187	5605	5265	5686	5344	5772	5424	5856	"	5940	5581	6024
5034	5443	5112	5529	5188	5606	5266	5687	5345	5773	5425	5857	5505	5942	5582	6025
5035	5444	"	5530	5189	5607	5267	5688	5346	5774	5426	5858	5506	5941	5583	6026
5036	5444	"	5531	5190	5608	5268	5689	5347	5776	5427	5859	5507	5943	5584	6027
5037	5445	5113	5532	5191	5610	5269	5690	5348	5777	5428	5860	5508	5944	5585	6028
5038	5446	5114	5533	5192	5611	5270	5691	5349	5778	5429	5861	5509	5945	5586	6029
5039	5447	5115	5534	5193	5612	5271	5693	5350	5779	5430	5862	5510	5946	5587	6030
5040	5448	5116	5535	5194	5613	5272	5694	5351	5780	5431	5863	5511	5948	5588	6031
5041	5449	5117	5536	5195	5614	5273	5695	5352	5781	5432	5864	5512	1430	5589	6032
5042	5450	"	4509	5196	5615	5274	5696	5353	5782	5433	5865	"	5949	"	6033
"	4509	5118	5537	5197	5616	5275	5699	5354	5783	5434	5866	5513	5950	5590	6034
5043	5451	5119	5538	5198	5617	5276	5700	5355	5784	5435	5867	5514	5951	5591	6035
5044	5452	5120	3836	5199	5618	5277	659	5356	5785	5436	5869	5515	5952	5592	6036
5045	5454	5121	5539	5200	5619	"	5701	5357	5786	5437	5870	5516	5947	5593	6037
5046	5455	5122	5540	5201	5620	5278	670	5358	5787	5438	5871	"	5953	5594	6038
5047	5456	5123	5542	5202	5621	"	5702	5359	5788	5439	5872	5517	5954	5595	6039
5048	5457	5124	4047	5203	5622	5279	5703	5360	5789	5440	5873	5518	5955	5596	6040
5049	5458	5125	4047	5204	5623	5280	5704	5361	5790	5441	5874	5519	5956	5597	6041
5050	5459	5126	4047	5205	5624	5281	5705	5362	5791	5442	5875	5520	5957	5598	6042
5051	5460	5127	4047	5206	5625	5282	5706	5363	5792	5443	5876	5521	5958	5599	6043
5052	5461	5128	4047	5207	5626	5283	5707	5364	5793	5444	5877	5522	5967	5600	1639
5053	5462	5129	4047	5208	5627	5284	5709	5365	5794	5445	5878	"	5959	5601	2725
5054	5463	5130	4047	5209	5148	5285	5710	5366	5795	5446	5879	5523	5960	"	6044
5055	5464	5131	5543	5210	5148	5286	5711	5367	5796	5447	5880	"	6002	5602	6045
5056	5465	5132	5544	5211	5628	5287	5712	5368	5797	5448	5881	5524	5961	5603	6046
5057	5467	5133	5545	5212	5629	5288	5713	5369	5798	5449	5882	5525	5962	5604	6047
5058	5466	5134	5546	5213	5148	5289	5714	5370	5799	5450	5883	5526	5963	5605	6048
"	5468	5135	5547	5214	5630	5290	5715	5371	5800	5451	5884	5527	5964	5606	6049
5059	5469	5136	5548	5215	5631	5291	5716	5372	5801	5452	5885	5528	5965	5607	1639
5060	5470	5137	5549	5216	5148	5292	5717	5373	5802	5453	5886	5529	5966	5608	6050
5061	5472	5138	5550	5217	5632	5293	5718	5374	5803	5454	5887	5530	5968	5609	6051
5062	5473	5139	5551	5218	5633	5294	5719	5375	5804	5455	1876	5531	3079	5610	6052
"	5477	5140	5552	5219	5634	5295	5720	5376	5805	"	5888	"	5969	5611	6053
5063	5474	5141	5554	5220	5635	5296	5721	5377	5806	5456	5889	5532	5970	5612	6054
"	5478	5142	5555	5221	5636	5297	5722	5378	5807	5457	5890	5533	5971	5613	6055
5064	5475	5143	5556	5222	5637	5298	5723	5379	5808	5458	5891	"	5972	5614	6057
5065	5476	5144	5558	5223	5638	5299	5708	5380	5809	5459	5892	5534	5973	5615	6058
5066	5479	5145	5559	5224	5639	"	5724	5381	5810	5460	5893	5535	5974	5616	6059
5067	5480	5146	5560	5225	5639	5300	5725	5382	5811	5461	5894	5536	5975	5617	6060
5068	5481	5147	5561	5226	5640	5301	5727	5383	5812	5462	5895	5537	5976	5618	6061
5069	5482	5148	5562	5227	5641	5302	5728	5384	5813	5463	5897	5538	5977	5619	6062
5070	5483	5149	5563	5228	5642	5303	5729	5385	5814	5464	5898	5539	5978	5620	6063
5071	5484	5150	5564	5229	5643	5304	5730	5386	5815	5465	5899	5540	5979	5621	6064
5072	5485	5151	5565	5230	5644	5305	5731	5387	5816	5466	5900	5541	5980	"	6065
5073	5486	5152	5566	5231	5645	5306	5731	5388	5817	5467	5901	5542	5981	5622	6066
"	5487	5153	5567	5232	5647	5307	5733	5389	5818	5468	5902	5543	5982	5623	6067
5074	5488	5154	5568	5233	5648	5308	5734	5390	5819	"	5904	5544	5983	5624	6068
5075	5489	"	5569	5234	5649	5309	5735	5391	5426	5469	5903	5545	5984		
5076	5490	5155	5570	5235	5650	5310	5736	"	5820	5470	5905	5546	5985		
5077	5491	5156	5571	5236	5651	5311	5737	5392	3055	"	5911	5547	5986		
5078	5492	5157	5572	5237	4238	5312	5738	"	5821	5471	5906	5548	5987		
5079	5493	5158	5573	"	5653	5313	5739	5393	5823	5472	5907	5549	5988		
5080	5494														

INDEX OF GOODRICK/KOHLENBERGER → STRONG NUMBERS

HEBREW OLD TESTAMENT (first column group)

G/K	STRONG	G/K	STRONG	G/K	STRONG	G/K	STRONG	G/K	STRONG	G/K	STRONG	G/K	STRONG	G/K	STRONG
		67	180	140	125	212	193	285	259	358	332	430	398	502	464
		68	62	141	127	213	192	286	260	359	333	431	400	503	465
		69	63	142	128	214	193	287	261	360	334	432	401	504	466
		70	64	143	127	215	193	288	264	361	335	433	402	505	467
		71	65	144	126	216	196	289	262	362	339	434	403	506	468
1		72	66	145	132	217	195	290	270	363	338	435	403	507	469
2		73	67	"	726	218	194	291	265	364	336	436	404	508	470
3	1	74	68	146	129+5346	219	199	292	266	365	337	437	405	509	471
4	3	75	72	147	131	220	198	293	267	366	340	438	406	510	472
5	5	76	71	148	133	221	197	294	268	367	341	439	407	511	473
6	6	77	73	149	134	222	200	295	269	368	342	440	408	512	474
7	8	78	70	150	135	223	201	296	270	369	343	441		513	475
8	9	79	74	151	136	224	205	297	270	370	344	442	352	514	476
9	10	80	75	152	137	225	206	298	271	371	345	443	352	515	477
10	11	81	76	153	138	226	202	299	272	372	346	444	352	516	478
11	11	82	77	154	138	227	203	300	273	373	347	445	410	517	448
12	12	83	78	155	139	228	204	301	274	374	348	446	410	518	480
13	13	84	79	156	140	229	207	302	274	375	349	447	411	519	481
14	14	85	80	157	141	230	205	303	275	376	350	448	413	520	481
15	16	86	81	158	142	231	208	304	276	377	349	449	415	521	482
16	17	87	82	159	145	232	209	305	278	378	351	450	416	522	483
17	18	88	83	160	143	233	210	306	277	379	349	451	1286	523	484
18	19	89	84	161	146	234	211	307	279	380	352	452	414	524	485
19	20	90	85	162	146	235	211	308	281	381	352	453	417	525	486
20	15	91	86	163	150	236	212	309	281	382	352	454	418	526	487
21		92	87	164	151	237	213	310	282	383	352	455	419	527	488
22		93	52	165	152	238	214	311	283	384	353	456	420	528	488
23	21	94	53	166	152	239	215	312	284	385	354	457	422	529	489
24	22	95	88	167	154	240	216	313	285	386	364	458	421	530	490
25	23	96	89	168	155	241	217	314	286	387	355	459	428	531	491
26	24	97	90	169	156	242	224	315	287	"	365	460	423	532	492
27		98	91	170	157	243	218	316	288	388	337	461	424	533	440
28	26	99	92	171	159	244	218	317	289	389	357	462	425	534	493
29	27	100	93	172	158	245	219	318	290	390	356	463	425	535	494
30	28	101	94	173	160	246	219	319	291	391	356	464	427	536	495
31	29	102	95	174	160	247	221	320	292	392	358	465	428	537	496
32	29	103	96	175		248	222	321	293	393	359	466	430	538	497
33	30	104	97	176	161	249	223	322	294	394	360	467	432	539	498
34	31	105		177	162	250	223	323	295	395	361	468	433	540	499
35	32	106	98	178	163	251	224	324	296	396	362	469	435	541	500
36	34	107	98	179	164	252	225	325	297	397	359	470	434	542	500
37	35	108	99	180	165	253	226	326	298	398	366	471	436	543	501
38	32	109	100	181	1961	254	853	327	299	399	367	472	356	544	502
39	36	110	101	182	167	255	227	328	300	400	368	473	437	545	503
40	37	111	102	183	166	256	229	329	301	401	369	474	438	546	504
41	38	112	103	184	174	257	231	330	302	402	370	475	439	547	505
42	39	113	105	185	168	258	232	331	303	403	371	476	441	548	505
43	40	114	106	186	169	259	233	332	305	404	372	477	441	549	507
44	41	115	107	187	428	260	234	333	304	405	373	478	442	550	467
45	42	116	108	188	170	261	235	334	306	406	374	479	443	551	508
46	74	117	109	189	174	262	237	335	308	407	375	480	444	552	509
47	43	118	110	190	171	263	238	336	309	408	376	481	445	553	469
48	44	119	111	191	172	264	239	337	312	409	376	482	446	554	510
49	33	120	112	192	173	265	241	338	313	410	378	483	447	555	511
50	45	121	123	193	174	266	240	339	310	411	382	484	448	556	512
51	46	122	130	194		267	242	340	314	412	379	485	419	557	513
52	47	123	113	195	175	268	243	341	315	413	380	"	449	558	514
53	48	124	114	196	176	269	244	342	316	414	3448	486	450	559	514
54	49	125	138	197	176	270	244	343	310	415	2978	487	451	560	515
55	50	126	115	198	177	271	245	344	319	416	863	488	452	561	518
56	51	127	151	199	178	272	246	345	322	417	384	489	452	562	517
57	52	128	182	200	178	273	247	346	323	418	385	490	453	563	519
58	53	129	117	201	179	274	248	347	325	419	386	491	453	564	520
59	54	130	118	202	181	275	249	348	325	420	387	492	454	565	522
60	55	131	119	203	183	276	250	349	326	421	389	493	454	566	4965
61	56	132	120	204	184	277	253	350	327	422	390	494	455	567	520
62	56	133	120	205	185	278	251	351	328	423	391	495	456	568	367
63	57	134	121	206	186	279	254	352		424	392	496	457	569	523
"	59	135	120	207	187	280	255	353	329	425	393	497	458	570	525
64	58	136	121	208	188	281	256	354	329	426	394	498	460	"	527
"	59	137	122	209	189	282	256	355	330	427	395	499	461	"	539
65	60	138	124	210	190	283	257	356	328	428	396	500	463	571	526
66	61	139	123	211	191	284	258	357	331	429	397	501	462	572	527

G/K	STRONG	G/K	STRONG	G/K	STRONG	G/K	STRONG	G/K	STRONG	G/K	STRONG	G/K	STRONG	G/K	STRONG
1397	1299	1500	1391	1601	1489	1706	1591	1809	1688	1913	1788	2017	1881	2121	1964
1398	1300	1501	1394	1602	1491	1707	1592	1810	1688	1914	1787	2018	1885	2122	1966
1399	1301	1502	1394	1603	1492	1708	1593	1811	1690	1915	1789	2019	1886	2123	1967
1400	1139	1503	1395	1604	1493	"	1594	1812	1689	1916	1790	2020		2124	1968
1401	1302	1504	1396	1605	1494	1709	1595	1813	1691	1917	1792	2021		2125	1969
1402	1303	"	1399	1606	1495	1710	1595	1814	1015	1918	1793	2022		2126	4313
1403	1304	1505	1397	1607	1496	1711	1597	1815	1692	1919	1793	2023		2127	1020
1404	1304	1506	1398	1608	1497	1712	5873	1816	1695	1920	1794	2024		2128	1970
1405	1305	1507	1402	1609	1499	1713	1598	1817	1694	1921	1795	2025		2129	1971
1406	1305	1508	1403	1610	1498	1714	1599	1818	1696	1922	1796	2026	1887	2130	1021
1407	1306	1509	1404	1611	1500	1715	1599	1819	1696	1923	1817	2027	1889	2131	1973
1408	1268	1510	1405	1612	1501	1716	1600	1820	1696	1924	1800	2028	326	2132	3808
1409	1307	1511	1406	1613	1502	1717	1601	1821	1697	1925	1801	2029	1017	2133	1972
1410	1308	1512	1407	1614	1503	1718	1602	1822	1698	1926	1802	2030	507	2134	1973
1411	1313	1513	1408	1615	1504	1719	1604	1823	1698	1927	1802	2031	4965	2135	3873
"	1314	"	1409	1616	1504	1720	1603	1824	1699	1928	1817	2032	1018	2136	1974
1412	1315	1514	1410	1617	1506	1721	1605	1825	1699'	1929	1803	2033	7151+704	2137	1975
1413	1319	1515	2735	1618	1507	1722	1606	1826	1700	1930	1803	2034	2043	2138	1976
1414	1320	1516	1412	1619	1508	1723	1607	1827	1702	1931	1804	2035	3051	2139	1977
1415	1309	1517	1413	1620	1509	1724	1608	1828	1704	1932	1805	2036	8143	2140	1022
1416		1518	1413	1621	1511	1725	1609	1829	1705	1933	1806	2037	1890	2141	1978
1417	7683	1519	1415	1622	1518	1726	1610	1830	1703	1934	1806	2038	1891	2142	1979
1418	1310	1520	2693	1623	1512	1727	1610	1831	1706	1935	1807	2039	1892	2143	1980
1419	1311	1521	1417	1624	1513	1728	1612	1832	1707	1936	1808	2040	1893	"	3212
1420	1312	1522	1416	1625	1513	1729	1613	1833	1708	1937	1809	2041	1894	2144	1982
1421	1316	1523	1418	1626	1514	1730	1614	1834	1709	1938	1809	2042	1895	2145	1984
1422	1316	1524	1419	1627	1515	1731	1616	1835	1711	1939	1810	2043	1896	2146	1984
1423	1317	1525	1420	1628	1516	1732	1615	1836	1710	1940	1811	2044	2735	2147	1984
1424	1318	1526	1421	1629	2798	1733	1617	1837	1712	1941	1811	2045	1419	2148	1985
1425	1322	1527	1422	1630	1517	1734	1618	1838	1713	1942	1812	2046	2800+1471	2149	1984+3050
1426	1323	1528	1421	1631	1518	1735	1619	1839	1713	1943	1813	2047	1897	2150	1986
1427	1324	1529	1446	1632	1520	1736	1619	1840	1714	1944	1814	2048	1898	2151	1988
1428	1004	1530	1446	1633	1521	1737	1620	1841	1715	1945	1816	2049	1899	2152	1987
1429	1326	1531	1423	1634	1522	1738	1621	1842	1716	1946	1817	2050	1900	2153	1989
1430		1532	1425	1635	1523	1739	1622	1843	1717	1947	1818	2051	1896	2154	1990
1431	1327	1533	1424	1636	1524	1740	1623	1844	1718	1948	1819	2052	1901	2155	1991
1432	1328	1534	1426	1637	1524	1741	1624	1845	1735	1949	1820	2053	1902	2156	1992
1433	1328	1535	1427	1638	1525	1742	1625	1846	1734	1950	1820	2054	1903	2157	
1434	1329	1536	1428	1639	1526	1743	1626	1847	1719	1951	1822	2055	1537	2158	4099
1435	1330	1537	1429	1640	1527	1744	1627	1848	1719	1952	1823	2056	1588	2159	1993
1436	1331	1538	1430	1641	1487	1745	1628+3643	"	1720	1953	1824	2057	1904	2160	1992
1437	1332	1539	1430	1642	1529	1746	1629	1849	1721	1954	1824	2058	1905	2161	1992
1438	1333	1540	1431	1643	1530	1747	1511	1850	1724	1955	1825	2059	1906	2162	1995
1439	1334	1541	1432	1644	1530	1748	1630	1851	1725	1956	658	2060	1908	2163	1996
1440	1335	1542	1433	1645	1561	1749	1631	1852	1726	"	6450	2061	1909	2164	1997
1441	1336	1543	1435	1646	1531	1750	1633	"	6450	1957	1826	2062	1910	2165	5555
1442	1337	1544	1434	1647	1532	1751	1633	1853	1727	1958	1826	2063	1911	2166	1998
1443	1338	1545	1436	1648	1533	1752	1634	1854	1728	1959	1826	2064	1912	2167	1999
1444	1339	1546	1436	1649	1534	1753	1636	1855	1729	1960	1827	2065	1921	2168	4447
1445	1340	1547	1437	1650	1534	1754	1632	1856	1730	1961	1828	2066	1913	2169	2000
1446		1548	1438	1651	1536	1755	1637	1857	1731	1962	1829	2067	1913	2170	2000
1447	1341	1549	1439	1652	1537	1756	1638	1858	1732	1963	1830	2068	1914	2171	1995
1448	1342	1550	1440	1653	1538	1757	1639	1859	1736	1964	1831	2069	1939	2172	2001
1449	1344	1551	1441	1654	1539	1758	1639	1860	1733	1965	1832	2070	1915	2173	2003
1450	1343	1552	1442	1655	1540	1759	1640	1861	1734	1966	1834	2071	1916	2174	7434
1451	1345	1553	1443	1656	1542	1760	1641	1862	1737	1967	1833	2072	1918	2175	1024
1452	1346	1554	1445	1657	1543	1761	1642	1863	1736	1968	1835	2073	1919	2176	2005
1453	1350	1555	1444	1658	1544	1762	1643	1864	1738	1969	1835	2074	1920	"	3860
1454	1347	"	1447	1659	1545	1763	1644	1865	1739	1970	1842	2075	1921	2177	2004
1455	1348	1556	1448	1660		1764	1644	1866	1740	1971	1840	2076	1924	2178	2008
1456	1349	1557	1449	1661	1546	1765	1645	1867	1741	1972	1837	2077	1926	2179	2007
1457	1350	1558	1450	1662	1548	1766	1646	1868	1742	1973	1838	2078	1925	2180	2009
1458	1351	1559	1451	1663	1549	1767	1648	1869	1673	1974	1839	2079	1927	2181	
1459	1352	1560	1448	1664	1550	1768	1647	1870	1743	1975	1840	2080	1928	2182	2010
1460	1353	1561	1452	1665	1551	1769	1649	1871	1744	1976	1843	2081	1929	2183	2011
1461	1354	1562	1453	1666	1552	1770	1650	1872	1745	1977	3045	2082	1930	2184	2012
1462	1354	1563	1454	1667	1553	1771	1651	1873	1746	1978	1844	2083		2185	5130
1463	1356	1564	1455	1668	1554	1772	1652	1874	1746	1979	1845	2084		2186	5346
1464	1356	1565	1456	1669	1555	1773	1653	1875	1747	1980	1846	2085	1931	2187	2013
1465	1360	1566	1457	1670	1556	1774	1654	1876	1748	1981	1847	2086	1935	2188	2013
1466	1357	1567	1458	1671	1556	1775	1656	1877	1834	1982	1847	2087	1936	2189	5570
1467	1361	1568	1460	1672	1557	1776	1654	1878	1777	1983	1847	2088	1937	2190	5570
1468	1362	1569	1460	1673	1558	1777	1657	1879	1777	1984	1848	2089	1938	2191	5618
"	1364	1570	1459	1674	1559	1778	1658	1880	1749	1985	1849	2090	1939	2192	5863
1469	1364	1571	1462	1675	1562	1779	1659	1881	1750	1986	1850	2091	1940	2193	72
1470	1363	1572	1461	1676	1563	1780	1660	1882	1751	1987	1851	"	1941	2194	3726
1471	1365	1573	1463	1677	1564	1781	1661	1883	1752	"	1941	2092	1933	2195	1025
1472	1419	1574	1464	1678	1565	1782	1662	1884	1752	1988	1852	2093	1933	2196	1026
1473	1366	1575	1467	1679	1566	"	1667	1885	1754	1989	1853	2094	1942	2197	6190
1474	1367	1576	1465	1680	1568	1783	1662	1886	1755	1990	1854	2095	1942	2198	2014
1475	1368	"	1466	1681	1567	1784	1667	1887	1755	1991	1856	2096	1943	2199	7163
1476	1369	1577	1468	1682	1569	1785	1663	1888	1756	1992	1857	2097	1944	2200	2015
1477	1371	1578	1469	1683	1570	1786	1664	1889	1758	1993	1858	2098	1945	2201	2016
1478	1372	1579	1470	1684	1543	1787	1665	1890	1760	1994	1860	2099	1947	"	2017
1479	1462	1580	1471	1685	1571	1788	1666	1891	1760	1995	1861	2100	1948	2202	2018
1480	1373	1581	1472	1686	1572	1789		1892	1762	1996	1861	2101	1949	2203	2019
1481	1374	1582	1471	1687	1573	1790	1669	1893	1764	1997	1862	2102	1950	2204	6483
1482	1385	1583	1473	1688	1574	1791	1670	1894	1765	1998	1863	2103	1951	2205	5324
1483	1375	1584	1474	1689	1575	1792	1671	1895	1766	1999	1864	2104	1952	2206	6637
1484	1376	1585	1475	1690	1577	1793	1672	1896	1767	2000	1866	2105	2029	2207	6380
1485	1377	1586	1476	1691	1576	1794	1709	1897	1769	2001	1865	2106	1953	2208	2020
1486	1378	1587	1477	1692	1578	1795	1673	1898	1769+1410	2002	1865	2107	1954	2209	6753
1487	1379	1588	1478	1693	1579	1796	1674	1899	1770	2003	1867	2108	1955	2210	2021
1488	1380	1589	1479	1694	1580	1797	1675	1900	1771	2004	1875	2109	2050	2211	2521
1489	1381	1590	1480	1695	1581	1798	1676	1901	1772	2005	1869	2110	1956	2212	6976
1490	1382	1591	1481	1696	1582	1799	1756	1902	1773	2006	1870	2111	1957	2213	5875
1491	1383	1592	1481	1697	1583	1800	1677	1903	1774	2007	1871	2112	6367	2214	6997
1492	1384	1593	1481	1698	1584	1801	1679	1904	1775	2008	1834	2113	1958	2215	2022
1493	1386	1594	1482	1699	1586	1802		1905	1776	2009	1873	2114		"	2042
1494	1387	1595	1483	1700	1586	1803	1680	1906	1777	2010	1874	2115	1931	2216	2023
1495	1388	1596	1484	1701	1587	1804	1681	1907	1779	2011	1875	2116	1959	2217	2024
1496	1389	1597	1485	1702	1587	1805	1682	1908	1781	2012	1876	2117	1960	2218	7204
1497	1390	1598	1486	1703	1588	1806	1683	1909	1783	2013	1877	2118	1961	2219	2025
1498	1393	1599	1487	1704	1589	1807	1686	1910	7384	2014	1878	2119	1962	2220	7235
1499	1392	1600	1488	1705	1590	1808	1687	1911	1785	2015	1879	2120	1963	2221	7235
								1912	1786	2016	1880				

G/K	STRONG	G/K	STRONG	G/K	STRONG	G/K	STRONG	G/K	STRONG	G/K	STRONG	G/K	STRONG	G/K	STRONG
3049	2763	3152	2849	3255	2947	3360	3047	3462	3147	3565	3241	3668	3332	3771	3424
3050	2763	3153	2850	3256	2948	3361	3048	3463	3148	3566	3242	3669	3333	3772	3425
3051	2764	3154	2851	3257	2947	3362	3049	3464	3149	3567	3243	3670	3335	3773	3446
3052	2764	3155	2852	3258	2947	3363	3050	3465	3149	"	5134	3671	3336	3774	3450
3053	2766	3156	2853	3259	2949	3364	3051	3466	3150	3568	3244	3672	3337	3775	3455
3054	2765	3157	2854	3260	2950	3365	3053	3467	3151	3569	3245	"	3340	3776	3478
3055	2767	3158	2855	3261	2951	3366	3054	3468	3152	3570	3245	3673	3339	3777	3480
3056	2768	3159	2856	3262	2952	3367	3056	3469	2109	3571	3246	3674	3338	3778	3481
3057	2769	3160	2858	3263	2954	3368	3057	3470	3153	3572	3247	3675	3341	"	3482
3058	2770	3161	2859	3264	2955	3369	3058	3471	3153	3573	3248	3676	3342	3779	3485
3059	2771	3162	2859	3265	2956	3370	3059	3472	3154	3574	3250	3677	3343	3780	3426
3060	2771	3163	2860	3266	2958	3371	3060	3473	3155	3575	3251	3678	3344	3781	
3061	2772	3164	2861	3267	2959	3372	3055	3474	3156	3576	3252	3679	3350	3782	3427
3062	2774	3165	2859	3268	2960	3373	3063	3475	3157	3577	3253	3680	3347	3783	3429
3063	2775	3166	2862	3269	2961	3374	3064	3476	3157	3578	3254	3681	3348	3784	3428
3064	2775	3167	2863	3270	2962	3375	3065	3477	3158	3579	3256	3682	3349	3785	3430
3065	2776	3168	2864	3271	2963	3376	3066	"	3159	3580	3256	3683	3344	3786	3431
3066	2775	3169	2865	3272	2964	3377	3067	3478	3160	3581	3256	3684	2901	3787	3430
3067	2777	3170	2866	3273	2965	3378	3068	3479	3161	3582	3257	"	6990	3788	3433
3068	2777	3171	2867	3274	2966	"	3069	3480	3162	3583	3258	3685	3351	3789	
3069	2778	3172		3275		3379	3075	3481	3162	3584	3258	3686	3352	3790	3434
3070	2778	3173	2894	3276		3380	3076	3482	3163	3585	3259	3687	3353	3791	3435
3071	2778	3174	2870	3277	2968	3381	3077	3483		3586	3294	3688	3354	3792	3436
3072	2778	3175	2870	3278	2969	3382	3078	3484	3164	3587	3260	3689	3947	3793	3437
3073	2780	3176	2896	3279	2970	3383	3079	3485	3165	3588	3260	3690	3355	3794	3427
3074	2779	3177	2896	3280	2970	3384	3080	3486	3171	3589	3261	3691	3356	3795	3432
3075	2781	3178	2871	3281	2971	3385	3081	3487	3166	3590	3262	3692	3357	3796	3438
3076	2782	3179	2872	3282	2973	3386	3082	3488	3167	3591	3263	3693	3359	3797	3439
3077	2782	3180	2873	3283	2974	3387	3083	3489	3168	3592	3265	3694	3360	3798	3440
3078	2784	3181	2874	3284	2975	3388	3084	3490	3169	3593	3266	3695	3361	3799	3441
3079	2785	3182	2875	3285	2972	3389	3085	3491	3169	3594	3267	3696	3362	3800	3442
3080	2786	3183	2874	3286	2976	3390	3086	3492	3170	3595	3268	3697	3363	3801	3442
3081	2787	3184	2876	3287	2977	3391	3086	3493	3171	3596	3269	3698	3368	3802	3444
3082	2787	3185	2879	3288	2977	3392	3087	3494	3172	3597	3270	3699	3364	3803	3445
3083	2788	3186	2878	3289	2978	3393	3088	3495	3173	3598	3271	3700	3365	3804	3447
3084	2789	3187	2880	3290	2979	3394	3089	3496	3174	3599	3273	3701	3368	3805	3448
3085	7025	3188	2881	3291	2980	3395	3090	3497	3175	3600	3274	3702	3366	3806	3437
3086	2790	3189	2882	3292	2981	3396		3498	3176	3601	3275	3703	3368	3807	3449
"	2794	3190	2883	3293	2982	3397	3091	3499	3177	3602	3275	3704	3369	3808	3449
3087	2790	3191	2884	3294	2983	3398	3092	3500	3178	3603	3276	3705	3370	3809	3451
3088	2796	3192	2885	3295	2984	3399	3092	3501	3179	3604	3277	3706	3371	3810	3452
3089	2791	3193	2886	3296	2985	3400	3093	3502	3180	3605	3278	3707	3372	3811	1020
3090	2792	3194	2887	3297	2986	3401	3094	3503	3181	3606	3279	3708	3372	3812	3451
3091	2793	3195	2888	3298	2988	3402	3095	3504	3182	3607	3280	3709	3384	3813	3453
3092	2793	3196	2889	3299	2989	3403	3096	3505	3183	3608	3279	3710	3373	3814	3454
3093	2796	"	2890	3300	2991	3404	3096	3506	3184	3609	3281	3711	3374	3815	3456
3094	2795	3197	2891	3301	2990	3405	3097	3507	3185	3610	3282	3712	3375	3816	3457
3095	2797	3198	2892	3302	2992	3406	3098	3508	3186	3611		3713	3376	3817	3458
3096	2798	3199	2892	3303	2993	3407	3099	3509	3187	3612	3283	3714	3377	3818	3459
3097	7025	3200	2893	3304	2994	3408	3100	3510	3188	3613	3284	3715	3378	3819	3460
3098	2799	3201	2896	3305	2995	3409	3101	3511	3189	3614	3285	3716	3379	3820	3460
3099	2800+1471	3202	2896	3306	2996	3410	3102	3512	2895	3615	3286	3717	3380	3821	3461
3100	2801	3203	2897	3307	2997	3411	3103	"	3190	3616	3288	3718	3381	3822	3462
3101	2802	3204	2897	3308	2998	3412	3103	3513	3192	3617	3287	3719	3382	"	8153
3102	2817	3205	2896	3309	2999	3413	3104	3514	3193	3618	3288	3720	3383	3823	3462
3103	2834	3206	2898	3310	3000	3414	3105	3515	3195	3619	3289	3721	3384	3824	3465
3104	2820	3207	2899	3311	3005	3415	3106	3516	3196	3620	3290	3722	3384	3825	3463
3105	2835	3208	2896	3312	3001	3416	3107	3517	3197	3621	3291	3723	3384	3826	3464
3106	2834	3209	2900	3313	3002	3417	3108	3518	3204	3622	3292	3724	7297	3827	3466
3107	2834	3210	2900	3314	3003	3418	3109	3519	3198	3623	3264	3725	3385	3828	3467
3108	2803	3211	2901	3315	3003	3419	3110	3520	3199	"	3293	3726	3386	3829	3468
3109	2805	3212	2902	3316	3003	3420	3194	3521	3199	3624	3293	3727	7311	3830	3467
3110	2803	3213	2903	3317	3004	3421	3111	3522	3200	3625	3293	3728	3387	3831	3469
3111	2806	3214	2904	3318	3006	3422	3112	3523	3201	3626	3295	3729	3388	3832	3470
3112	2807	3215	2905	3319	3008	3423	3113	3524	3203	3627	3295	3730	3388	3833	3470
3113	2808	3216	2907	3320	3009	3424	3114	3525	3203	3628	3294	3731	3389	3834	3472
3114	2809	3217	2909	3321	3010	3425	3115	3526	3204	3629	3296	3732	3391	3835	3471
3115	2810	3218	2911	3322	3011	3426	3116	3527	3204	3630	3297	3733	3392	3836	3473
3116	2811	3219	2910	3323	3012	3427	3117	3528	3205	3631	3298	3734	3394	3837	3474
3117	2811	3220	2902	3324	3013	3428	3117	3529	3206	3632	3299	3735	3405	3838	3477
3118	2812	3221	2912	3325	3014	3429	3119	3530	3207	3633	3299	3736	3395	3839	3477
3119	2813	3222	2913	3326	3015	3430	3120	3531	3208	3634	3300	3737	3396	3840	3475
3120	2814	3223	2912	3327	3017	3431	3121	3532	3856	3635	3301	3738	3397	3841	3476
3121	2815	3224	2914	3328	3016	3432	3122	3533	3209	3636	3302	3739	3398	3842	3483
3122	2838	3225	2915	3329	3019	3433	3123	3534	3210	3637	3303	3740	3399	3843	3484
3123	2366	3226	2916	3330	3018	3434	3124	3535	3211	3638	3304	3741	3400	3844	3486
3124	2821	3227	2918	3331	3024	3435	3238	3536	3213	3639	3305	3742	3401	3845	3489
3125	2822	3228	2919	3332	3020	3436	3125	3537	3214	3640	3306	3743	3402	3846	3490
3126	2823	3229	2921	3333	3021	3437	3126	3538	3215	3641	3307	3744	3403	3847	3491
3127	2821	3230	2923	3334	3022	3438	3127	3539	3217	3642	3308	3745	3404	3848	3492
3128	2824	3231	2922	3335	3023	3439	3128	3540	3218	3643	3309	3746	3404	3849	3494
"	2825	"	2924	3336	3025	3440	3129	3541	3219	3644	3309	3747	3405	3850	3495
3129	2826	3232	2925	3337	3026	3441	3130	3542	3220	3645	3304	3748	3406	3851	5414
3130	2828	3233	2926	3338	3027	3442	3131	3543	3223	3646	3310	3749	3407	3852	5414
3131	2366	3234	2928	3339	3030	3443	3132	3544	3224	3647	3311	3750	3408	3853	3496
3132	2829	3235	2928	3340	3031	3444	3133	3545	3225	3648	3312	3751	3409	3854	3497
3133	2830	3236	2929	3341	3032	3445	3134	3546	3226	3649	3313	3752	3411	3855	3498
3134	2831	3237	2930	3342	3033	3446	3289	3547	3228	3650	3314	3753	7311	3856	3499
3135	2832	3238	2931	3343	3034	3447	3135	3548	3233	3651	3315	3754	3412	3857	3499
3136	2833	3239	2930	3344	3034	3448	3318	3549	3227	3652	3316	3755	3406	3858	3500
3137	2836	3240	2932	3345	3035	3449	3136	3550	3229	3653	3316	3756	3406	3859	3501
3138	2836	3241	2933	3346	3035	3450	3335	3551	3229	3654	3317	3757	3413	3860	3502
3139	2837	3242	2933	3347	3036	3451	3079	3552	3230	3655	3318	3758	3414	3861	3503
3140	2839	3243	2934	3348	3037	"	3137	3553	3222	3656	3320	3759	3414	3862	3504
3141	2840	3244	2935	3349	3038	3452	3384	3554	3231	3657	3322	3760	3415	3863	3505
3142	2841	3245	2936	3350	3035	3453	3138	3555	3232	3658	3323	3761	3416	3864	3506
3143	2842	3246	2937	3351	3039	3454	3088	3556	3233	3659	3324	3762	3417	3865	3507
3144	2843	3247	2938	3352	3040	"	3139	3557	3234	3660	3325	3763	3419	3866	3508
3145	2844	3248	2940	3353	3038	3455	3140	3558	3235	3661	3326	3764	3418	3867	3509
3146	2844	3249	2944	3354	3041	3456	3141	3559	3236	3662	3326	3765	4313	3868	
3147	2845	3250	2943	3355	3042	3457	3142	3560	3237	3663	3327	3766	3420	3869	
3148	2398	3251	2945	3356	3043	3458	3143	3561	3238	3664	3328	3767	3421	3870	
3149	2846	3252	2945	3357	3038	3459	3144	3562	3239	3665	3329	3768	3422	3871	
3150	2847	3253	2946	3358	3044	3460	3145	3563	3239	3666	3326	3769	3423	3872	3510
3151	2848	3254	2946	3359	3045	3461	3146	3564	3241	3667	3331	3770	8492	3873	3511

G/K	STRONG	G/K	STRONG	G/K	STRONG	G/K	STRONG	G/K	STRONG	G/K	STRONG	G/K	STRONG	G/K	STRONG
3874	3512	3976	3609	4080	3697	4184	3795	4287	3875	4389	8289	4491	4051	4590	4329
3875	2489	3977	3610	4081	3698	4185	3796	4288	3876	4390	3963	4492	4052	4591	4147
3876	834	3978	3611	4082	3699	4186	3798	4289	3877	4391		4493	4053	4592	4148
3877	3513	3979	3612	4083	3700	4187	3799	4290	3878	4392		4494	4054	4593	4147
3878	3515	3980	3613	4084	3701	4188	3800	4291	3878	4393	3965	4495	4054	4594	4149
3879	3516	3981	3612	4085	3703	4189	3801	"	3881	4394	3966	4496	4055	4595	4150
3880	3514	3982	3614	4086	3704	4190	3802	4292	3880	4395	3967	4497	4057	4596	4151
3881	3517	3983	3615	4087	3707	4191	8596	4293	3882	4396	3968	4498	4057	4597	4152
3882	3518	3984	3607	4088	3708	4192	3803	4294	3883	4397	3970	4499	4058	4598	4153
3883	3519	3985	3616	4089	3708	4193	3803	4295	3884	4398	3971	"	4059	4599	4155
3884	3520	3986	3617	4090	3709	4194	3803	4296	3885	4399	3972	4500	4060	4600	4156
3885	3520	3987	3618	4091	3710	4195	3804	4297	3888	4400	3973	4501	4060	4601	4157
3886	3521	3988	3622	4092	3711	4196	3805	4298	3889	4401	3974	4502	4062	4602	4158
3887	3522	3989	3628	4093	3712	4197	3806	"	3919	4402	3975	4503	4063	4603	4159
3888	3524	3990	3619	4094	3713	4198	3807	4299	3891	4403		4504	4064	4604	4161
3889	3523	3991	3620	4095	3713	4199		4300	3892	4404	3976	4505	4065	4605	4162
3890	3525	3992	3621	4096	3714	4200		4301	3893	4405	3967	4506	4066	4606	4163
3891	3526	3993	3622	4097	3715	4201		4302	3894	4406	369	"	4079	4607	4164
3892	3527	3994	3623	4098	3716	4202	3808	4303	3894	4407	3978	"	4090	4608	4165
"	4342	3995	3624	4099	3715	4203	3810	4304	3872	4408	3979	4507	4068	4609	4166
3893	3528	3996	3625	4100	3717	4204	3818	4305	3895	4409	3980	4508	4069	4610	4167
3894	3529	3997	3626	4101	3718	4205	3819	4306	3896	4410	3981	4509	4071	4611	4168
3895	3531	3998	3627	4102	3719	4206	3811	4307	883	4411	3982	4510	4072	4612	4169
3896	3530	3999	3628	4103	3720	4207	3812	4308	3897	4412	3985	4511	4073	4613	4170
3897	3532	4000	3629	4104	3721	4208	1975	4309	3898	4413	3986	4512	4074	4614	4171
3898	3535	4001	3631	4105	3722	4209	3813	4310	3898	4414	3987	4513	4075	4615	4171
3899	3533	4002	3630	4106	3722	4210	3815	4311	3901	4415	3988	4514	1767	4616	4172
3900	3534	4003	3632	4107	3723	4211	3816	4312	3899	4416	3988	4515	4060	4617	4173
3901	3536	4004	3633	4108	3724	4212	3817	4313	3902	4417	622	4516	4081	4618	4174
3902	3537	4005	3634	4109	3724	4213	3820	4314	3903	4418	3989	4517	4067	4619	4175
3903	1754	4006	3636	4110	3724	4214	3820+6965	4315	3905	4419	3990	4518	4080	4620	4175
3904	1767	4007	3637	4111	3724	4215	935	4316	3906	4420	3991	4519	4082	4621	4175
3905	3539	4008	3638	4112	3726	4216	3833	4317	3907	4421	3992	4520	4084	4622	4176
3906	3540	4009	3639	4113	3725	4217	2574	4318	3908	4422	3993	"	4092	4623	4177
3907	3541	4010	3640	4114	3727	4218	3833	4319	3814	4423	3994	4521	4085	4624	4172
3908	3543	4011	3641	4115	3728	4219	3822	"	3909	4424	834	4522	4086	4625	4180
3909	3543	4012	3641	4116	3731	4220	3823	4320	3910	4425	854	4523	4087	4626	4180
3910	3544	4013		4117	3730	4221	3823	4321	3911	4426	3995	4524	4088	4627	4181
3911	3545	4014	3642	4118	3732	4222	3824	4322	3912	4427	3996	4525	4089	4628	4182
3912	3547	4015	3588+4100	4119	3733	4223	3834	4323	3913	"	3997	4526	4089	4629	4183
3913	3548	4016	3643	4120	3733	4224	905	4324	3914	4428	3998	4527	4091	4630	4184
3914	3550	4017	3644	4121	3733	4225	3827	4325	3915	4429	3999	4528	4067	4631	4185
3915	3552	4018	3643	4122	1033	4226	3826	4326	3915	4430	4000	4529	4093	4632	4186
3916	3553	4019	3645	4123	3734	4227	3828	4327	3917	4431	4001	4530	4129	4633	4187
3917	3554	4020	3645	4124	3736	4228	3829	4328	3885	4432	4002	4531	4130	4634	4188
3918	3555	4021	3646	4125	3738	4229	3830	4329	3887	4433	4003	4532	4094	4635	3467
3919	3556	4022	3647	4126	3739	4230	3830	4330	3918	4434	4016	4533	4095	4636	4190
3920	3557	4023	3648	4127	3738	4231	3832	4331	3919	4435	4004	4534	4096	4637	4191
3921	3558	4024	3649	4128	3738	4232	3833	4332	3919	4436	4005	4535	4097	"	4192
3922	3559	4025	3650	4129	3741	4233	3833	4333	3919	4437	4006	4536	4098	4638	4194
3923	3560	4026	3651	4130	3740	4234	3833	4334	3920	4438	4007	4537	4100	4639	4195
3924	3561	4027	3651	4131	3742	4235	3835	4335	3921	4439	4008	4538	4102	4640	4196
3925	3562	4028	3651	4132	3743	4236	3835	4336	3922	4440	4009	4539	4103	4641	4197
3926	3563	4029	3653	4133	3746	4237	3836	4337	3923	4441		4540	4104	4642	4198
3927	3563	4030	3653	4134	3747	4238	3837	4338	3651	4442	1097	4541	4105	4643	4100+2088
3928	3738	4031	3654	4135	3748	4239	3837	4339	3924	4443	4010	4542	4106	4644	4100+2088
3929	3564	4032		4136	3749	4240	1121	4340	3925	4444	1110	4543	4107	4645	4199
3930	3565	4033	3655	4137	3750	4241	3838	4341	3928	4445	4011	4544	4108	4646	4200
3931	3566	4034	3656	4138	3751	4242	3839	4342	4100	4446	4012	"	4109	4647	4201
3932	3568	4035	3657	4139	3752	4243	3841	4343		4447		4545	4110	4648	4202
3933	3568	4036	3658	4140	3753	4244	3842	4344	3926	4448	4013	4546	4111	4649	4205
3934	3569	4037	3659	4141	3755	4245	3838	4345	3927	4449	4014	4547	4112	4650	4204
"	3571	4038	3654	4142	3754	4246	3840	4346	4136	4450	4013	4548		4651	4206
3935	3570	4039	3662	4143		"	3843	4347	3929	4451	4015	4549	4113	4652	4206
3936	3572	4040	3663	4144	3755	4247	3828	4348	4616	4452	4017	4550	4114	4653	4206
3937	3573	4041	3663	4145	3756	4248	3844	4349	3885	4453	4018	4551	4115	4654	2142
3938	3574	4042	3663	4146	3757	4249	3845	4350	3930	4454	7248	4552	65	4655	4208
3939	3575	4043	3664	4147	3758	4250	3846	4351	3931	4455	4019	4553		4656	4207
3940	3575	4044	3665	4148	3754	4251	7884	4352	3932	4456	4020	4554	4116	4657	4207
3941	3576	4045	3666	4149	3759	4252	3847	4353	3933	4457	4021	4555	4117	4658	4207
3942	3577	4046	3667	4150	3760	4253	3849	4354	3934	4458	4022	4556	4117	4659	4209
3943	3578	4047	3667	4151	3760	4254	3850	4355	3935	"	4030	4557	4118	4660	4210
3944	3579	4048	3669	4152	3759	4255	1688	4356	3936	4459	4023	4558	4119	4661	4211
3945	3580	4049	3668	4153	3761	4256	3205	4357	3937	4460	4024	4559	4120	4662	4212
3946	3581	4050	3669	"	3762	4257	3808	4358	3938	4461	4023	4560	4121	4663	4213
3947	3581	4051	3669	4154	3763	4258	3851	4359		4462	4025	4561	4122	4664	2219
3948	3582	4052	3670	4155	3765	4259	3852	4360	3939	4463	4026	4562	4123	4665	4214
3949	3583	4053	3671	4156	3766	4260	3853	4361	6030	4464	4027	4563		4666	4216
3950	3584	4054	3672	4157	3767	4261	3854	4362	3886	"	4028	4564		4667	4217
3951	3585	4055	3672	4158	3768	4262	3855	4363	3216	4465	4024	4565	4124	4668	2219
3952	3586	4056	3674	4159	3769	4263	3856	4364	1036	4466	4027	4566	4124	"	4215
3953	3587	4057	3677	4160	3770	4264	3856	4365	3940	4467	4028	4567	4125	4669	4218
3954	3588	4058	3676	4161	3771	4265	3857	4366	3941	4468	4029	4568	4136	4670	4219
3955	3588+518	"	3678	4162	3772	4266	3857	4367	6440	4469	4030	4569	4126	4671	4220
3956	3588 +408+3651	4059	3680	4163		4267	3858	4368	6440	4470	4031	4570	4127	4672	4221
3957	3589	4060	3677	4164	3773	4268	3858	4369	3943	4471	4032	4571	4128	4673	4222
3958	3590	4061	3678	4165	3774	4269	3859	4370	3887	4472	4033	4572	4131	4674	4229
3959	3591	4062	3681	4166	3775	4270		4371	3944	4473	4033	4573	4132	4675	4224
3960	3593	4063	3694	4167	3776	4271	3856	4372	3945	4474	4036	4574	4133	4676	4224
3961	3592	4064	3682	4168	3777	4272	3862	4373	3946	4475	4034	4575	4134	4677	4226
3962	3594	4065	3683	4169	3778	4273	3863	4374	3947	4476	4035	4576	4135	4678	4225
3963	3595	4066	3678+3050	4170	3780	4274	3810	4375	3948	4477	4037	4577	4135	4679	4227
3964	3596	4067	3684	4171	7911	4275	3864	4376	3949	4478	4038	4578	4136	4680	4228
3965	3597	4068	3685	4172	3781	4276	3865	4377	3950	4479	4039	4579	4137	4681	4229
3966	3598	4069	3686	4173	3782	"	3866	4378	3951	4480	4041	4580	4138	4682	4229
3967	3599	4070	3687	4174	3783	4277	3867	4379	3952	4481	4042	4581	4139	4683	4229
3968	3600	4071	3688	4175	3784	4278	3867	4380	3953	4482	4043	4582	4140	4684	4230
3969	3601	4072	3689	4176	3785	4279	3868	4381	3954	4483	4043	4583	3971	4685	4231
3970	3602	4073	3689	4177	3786	4280	3869	4382	3955	4484	4043	4584	4462	4686	4232
3971	3603	4074	3690	4178	3787	4281	3870	4383	3956	4485	4044	4585	5439	4687	4233
3972	3605	4075	3691	4179	3788	4282		4384	3957	4486	4045	4586	4143	4688	4234
3973	3607	4076	3693	4180	3789	4283	3871	4385	3958	4487	4046	4587	4144	4689	4235
3974	3607	4077	3692	4181	3791	4284	3872	4386	3959	4488	4047	4588	4145	4690	4236
3975	3608	4078	3695	4182	3793	4285	3873	4387	3960	4489	4048	"	4328	"	4328
		4079	3696	4183	3794	4286	3874	4388	3962	4490	4050	4589	4146	4691	4237
														4692	4238

G/K	STRONG	G/K	STRONG	G/K	STRONG	G/K	STRONG	G/K	STRONG	G/K	STRONG	G/K	STRONG	G/K	STRONG
4693	4239	4797	4339	4898	4441	5001	4532	5104	4585	5206	4708	"	4803	5410	4876
4694	4240	4798	4340	4899	4441	5002	4530	5105	4618	5207	4709	5308	4805	5411	4877
4695	4241	4799	4341	4900	4442	5003	4533	5106	4619	5208	4710	5309	4806	5412	4878
4696	4232	4800	4343	4901	4443	5004	4534	5107	4620	5209	4711	5310	4807	5413	4879
4697	4242	4801	4344	4902	4444	5005	4535	5108	4621	5210	4712	"	4810	5414	4880
4698	4243	4802	4346	4903	4445	5006	4536	5109	4622	5211	4694	5311	4807	5415	4880
4699	2256+392	4803	4345	4904	4445	5007	4537	5110	4623	5212	4713	"	4810	5416	4882
4700	4245	4804	4347	4905	4404	5008	4538	5111	4624	5213	4714	5312	4808	5417	4886
4701	4245	4805	4348	4906	4446	5009	4539	5112	4625	5214	4715	5313	4809	5418	4888
4702	4244	4806	4349	4907	4447	5010	4540	5113	4626	5215	4716	5314	4810	5419	4888
4703	4246	4807	4350	4908	5243	5011	4541	5114	4627	5216	4717	5315	4809+6946	5420	4888
4704	4247	"	4369	4909	5243	5012	4541	5115	4628	"	4718	5316	4811	5421	4888
4705	4248	4808	4351	4910	4448	5013	4541	5116	4629	5217	4718	5317	4179	5422	4889
4706	4249	4809	4352	4911	4448	5014	4542	5117	4631	5218	4719	5318	4812	5423	4891
4707	4250	4810	4353	4912	4450	5015	5533	5118	4632	5219	4720	5319	4813	5424	4892
4708	4251	4811	4354	4913	4451	5016	4543	5119	4633	5220	4721	5320	4814	5425	4893
4709	4252	4812	4355	4914	4452	5017	4544	5120	4630	5221	4722	5321	4815	5426	4893
4710	4253	4813	4356	4915	4453	5018	4545	"	4634	5222		5322	4816	5427	4894
4711	4254	4814	4358	4916	4454	5019	4546	5121	4635	5223	4723	5323	4817	5428	4896
4712	5555	4815	4360	4917	4455	5020	4547	5122	4636	5224	4723	5324	4818	5429	4897
4713	4256	4816	4357	4918	4455	5021	4548	5123	6206	5225	4724	5325		5430	4898
4714	4257	4817	4359	4919	4456	5022	4549	5124	4637	5226	4725	5326	4819	5431	4899
4715	4258	4818	4361	4920	4457	5023	4550	5125	4638	5227	4726	5327	4820	5432	4900
4716	4259	4819	4362	4921	4458	5024	4551	5126	4639	5228	4727	5328	4821	5433	4901
4717	4260	4820	4363	4922	4459	5025	4551	5127	4640	5229	4728	5329	4822	5434	4902
4718	4261	4821	4364	4923	4460	5026	4552	5128	4641	5230	4729	5330	4823	5435	4904
4719	4262	4822	4365	4924	4461	5027	4553	5129	4641	5231	6999	5331	4824	5436	4189
4720	4263	4823	4365	4925	4462	5028	4554	5130	4643	5232	6999	5332	4825	5437	7921
4721	2557	4824	4365	4926	4463	5029	4555	5131	4642	5233	4730	5333	4826	5438	4908
4722	4264	4825	4363	4927	4464	5030	4556	5132	4644	5234	4731	5334	4827	5439	4911
4723	4265	4826	4366	4928	4465	5031	4557	5133	4645	5235	4732	5335	4828	5440	4910
4724	4266	4827	4367	4929	4466	5032	4558	5134	4646	5236	4733	5336	7489	5441	4911
4725	4267	4828	4368	4930	4467	5033	4559	5135	4647	5237	4734	5337	4829	5442	4912
4726	4268	4829	4370	4931	4468	5034	4560	5136	4648	5238	4735	5338	4830	5443	4913
4727	4269	4830	4371	4932	4469	5035	4149	5137	4649	5239	4736	5339	4831	5444	4915
4728	4270	4831	4373	4933	4470	5036	4561	5138	4650	5240	4737	5340	4832	5445	4915
4729	4271	4832	4372	4934	4471	5037	4562	5139	4651	5241	4738	5341	4832	5446	4914
4730	4272	4833	4374	4935	4471	5038		5140	4652	5242	4739	5342	4832	5447	4916
4731	4273	4834	4375	4936	4472	5039	4563	5141	4653	5243	4740	5343	4833	5448	4916
4732	4274	4835	4376	4937	4473	5040	4564	5142	4654	5244	4741	5344	4834	5449	4917
4733	4275	4836	4377	4938	4474	5041	4565	5143	4654	5245	4743	5345	4836	5450	4918
4734	4276	4837	4378	4939	4475	5042	4566	5144	4655	5246	4744	5346	4837	5451	4919
4735	4277	4838	4379	4940	4476	5043	4568	5145	4656	5247	4745	5347	4838	5452	4920
4736	4278	4839	4380	4941	4477	5044	4569	5146	4657	5248	4746	5348	4839	5453	4920
4737	4279	4840	4381	4942	4478	5045	4569	5147	4658	5249	4747	5349	4840	5454	4921
4738	4280	4841	4382	4943	4478	5046	4570	5148	4659	5250	4748	5350	4841	5455	4922
4739	4281	4842	4383	4944	4482	5047	4570	5149	4659	5251	4749	5351	4842	5456	7969
"	4282	4843	4384	4945	4482	5048	4154	5150	4660	5252	4750	5352	4843	5457	4923
4740	4283	4844	4385	4946	4480	"	4571	5151	4661	5253	4751	5353	4844	5458	4924
4741	4286	4845	4386	4947	4485	"	5976	5152	4662	5254	4752	5354	4845	5459	4925
4742	4284	4846	4387	4948	4487	5049	4572	"	4663	5255	4753	5355	4846	5460	4924
4743	4285	4847	4388	4949	4488	5050	4573	5153	4664	5256	4754	5356	4847	5461	4926
4744	4287	"	4389	4950	4490	5051	4575	5154	4665	5257	4754	5357	4848	5462	4927
4745	4288	4848	4390	4951	4489	5052	4574	5155	4666	5258	4806	5358	4762	5463	4928
4746	4289	4849	4392	4952	4491	5053	4576	5156	4667	5259	4755	5359	4762	5464	4929
4747	4290	4850	4393	4953	4492	5054	4579	5157	4669	5260	4758	5360	4849	5465	4929
4748	4292	4851	4407	4954	4493	5055	4578	5158	4668	5261	4759	5361	4850	5466	4931
4749	4293	4852	4395	4955	4494	5056	4580	5159	4670	5262	4759	5362	4853	5467	4932
4750		4853	4396	4956	4495	5057	4581	5160	4160	5263	4760	5363	4853	5468	4933
4751	4294	4854	4394	4957	4496	5058	4581	5161	4671	5264	8112	5364	4854	5469	4934
4752	4295	4855	4397	4958	5186+4512	5059	4582	5162	4672	5265	4761	5365	4856	5470	4935
4753	4296	4856	4399	4959	4497	5060	4583	5163	4673	"	4763	5366	4858	5471	4936
4754	4297	4857	4400	4960	4498	5061	4583	5164	4674	5266	4764	5367	4864	5472	4937
4755	4298	4858	4401	4961	4499	5062	4584	5165	4675	5267	4765	5368	4864	5473	4937
4756	2892	4859	4402	4962	4500	5063	4584	5166	4675	5268	4767	5369	4869	5474	4938
4757	4299	4860	4403	4963	4501	5064	4586	5167	4676	5269	4766	5370	4869	5475	4938
4758	4300	4861	4404	4964	4502	5065	4587	5168	4677	5270	4768	5371	5381	5476	4940
4759	4301	4862	4390	4965	3240	5066	4588	5169	4678	5271	4769	5372	4881	5477	4941
4760	4302	4863	4405	"	5117	5067	4589	5170	4678	5272	4770	5373	4883	5478	4942
4761	4303	4864	4407	4966	4503	5068	4590	5171	4679	5273	4771	5374	4884	5479	4943
4762	4304	4865	4408	4967	4496	5069	4590	5172	4680	5274	4772	5375	4885	5480	4944
4763	4305	4866	4409	4968	4505	5070	4591	5173	4681	5275	4773	5376	4885	5481	8246
4764	4306	4867	4410	4969	4506	5071	4592	5174	4682	5276	4774	5377	4890	5482	4945
4765	4308	4868	4409	4970	4506	5072		5175	4683	5277	4775	5378	4895	5483	4945
4766	4307	4869	4411	4971	2679	5073	4594	5176	6668	5278	4777	5379	4881	5484	4946
4767	4309	4870	4412	"	2680	5074	4595	5177	4684	5279	4778	5380	4905	5485	4947
4768	4100	4871	4413	4972	4507	5075	4596	5178	4685	5280	4780	5381	4906	5486	4948
4769	4310	4872	4414	4973	4508	5076	4597	5179	4685	5281	4781	5382	4909	5487	4949
4770	4313	4873	4414	4974	4480	5077	4598	5180	4686	5282	4757	5383	4930	5488	4950
4771	4314	4874	4418	4975	4509	5078	4599	5181	4686	5283	4782	5384	4939	5489	4952
4772	4311	4875	4417	4976	4511	5079	4583	5182	4685	5284	4783	5385	4951	5490	4954
4773	4312	4876	4419	4977	4511	5080	4600	5183	4685	5285	4787	5386	4955	5491	4959
4774	4315	4877	4420	4978	4512	5081	4601	5184	4687	5286	4784	5387	4956	5492	4960
4775	4316	4878	4421	4979	4513	5082	4601	5185	4688	5287	4751	5388	4957	5493	4962
4776	4317	4879	4423	4980	4514	5083	4601	"	4699	5288	4785	5389	4958	5494	4962
4777	4318	4880	4422	4981	4515	5084	4602	5186	4689	5289	4786	5390	4851	5495	4963
4778	4319	4881	4422	4982	4516	5085	4603	5187	4690	5290	4062	5391	4855	5496	4964
4779	4320	4882	4424	4983	4517	5086	4604	5188	4691	5291	4788	5392	4852	5497	4965
4780	4322	4883	4409	4984	4518	5087	4605	5189	4692	5292	4789	5393	4857	5498	4966
4781	4321	4884	4425	4985	4519	5088	4480+5921	5190	4692	5293	4790	5394	4859	5499	4967
4782	4323	4885	3887	4986	4520	5089	4607	5191	4693	5294	4791	5395		5500	4968
4783	4324	"	3945	4987	4521	5090	4608	5192	4686	5295	4792	5396	4860	5501	4969
4784	4325	4886	4426	4988	4523	5091	4609	5193	4694	5296	4793	5397	4876	5502	8478
4785	4326	4887	4427	4989	4522	5092	4609	5194	4695	5297	4794	5398	4861	5503	4970
4786	4327	4888	4427	4990	4524	5093	4605	5195	4696	5298	4835	5399	4862	5504	4971
4787	3243	4889	4428	4991	4524	5094	4611	5196	4697	5299	4795	5400	4863	5505	4972
4788	4329	"	4429	4992	4036	5095	4611	5197	4698	5300	4796	5401	4865	5506	4973
4789	4158	4890	4428	4993	4525	5096	4612	5198	4688	5301	4797	5402	4866	5507	4974
4790	4330	4891	4432	4994	4525	5097	4613	5199	4700	"	4798	5403	4867	5508	4976
4791	4331	4892	4434	4995	4526	5098	4614	5200	4701	5302	4799	5404	4868	5509	4977
4792	4332	4893	4436	4996	4527	5099	4615	5201	4702	5303	3800	5405	4870'	5510	4979
4793	4334	4894	4435	4997	4528	5100	4616	5202	4703	5304	4800+3050	5406	4871	5511	4980
4794	4335	4895	4438	4998	4529	5101	4617	5203	4705	5305	4801	5407	4872	5512	4981
4795	4338	4896	4439	4999	4531	5102	4617	5204	4706	5306	4802	5408	4874	5513	4982
4796	4337	4897	4440	5000	4531	5103	4618	5205	4707	5307	4178	5409	4875	5514	4983

G/K	STRONG	G/K	STRONG	G/K	STRONG	G/K	STRONG	G/K	STRONG	G/K	STRONG	G/K	STRONG	G/K	STRONG
5515	4983	5619	5082	"	2787	5825	5265	5929	5355	6028	5453	6130	5536	6235	5621
5516	4975	5620	5084	5724	5170	5826	5266	5930	5355	6029	5454	6131	5537	6236	5623
5517	4985	5621	5083	5725	5170	5827	5268	5931	5356	6030	5454	6132	5543	6237	5624
"	4988	5622	5086	5726	5171	5828	5269	5932	5357	6031	5455	6133	5538	6238	5625
5518	4986	5623	5087	5727	5172	5829	5270	5933	5358	6032	5456	6134	5539	6239	5627
5519	4987	5624	5088	5728	5173	5830	5271	5934	5359	6033	5458	6135	5540	6240	5627
5520	4989	5625	5089	5729	5175	5831	5271	5935	5360	6034	5462	6136	5541	6241	5626
5521	4990	5626		5730	5904	5832	5272	5936	5361	6035	5459	6137	5541	6242	5628
5522	4991	5627	5090	5731	5176	5833	5273	5937	5362	6036	5461	6138	5542	6243	5628
5523	4992	5628	5090	5732	5177	5834	5273	5938	5362	6037	5462	6139	5543	6244	5628
5524	4993	5629	5091	5733	5178	5835	5274	5939	5363	6038	5462	6140	5543	6245	5629
5525	4993	5630	5091	5734	5178	5836	5274	5940	5364	6039	5464	6141	5544	6246	5630
5526		5631	5092	5735	5179	5837	5275	5941	5365	6040	5465	6142	5545	6247	5631
5527		5632	5093	5736	5180	5838	5276	5942	5366	6041	5466	6143	5546	6248	5633
5528	4994	5633	5095	5737	5181	5839	5277	5943	5367	6042	5467	6144	5543	6249	5633
5529	4995	5634	5096	5738	5183	5840	5278	5944	5216	6043	5468	6145	5547	6250	5634
5530	4996	5635	5097	5739	5183	5841	5279	5945	5369	6044	5469	6146	5548	6251	5635
5531	527+4996	5636	5096	5740	5184	5842	5279	5946	5370	6045	5470	6147	5549	6252	5636
5532	4997	5637	5098	5741	5185	5843	5281	5947	5371	6046	5471	6148	5549	6253	5637
5533	4998	5638	5099	5742	5186	5844	5280	5948	5373	6047	5472	6149	5550	6254	8269
5534	5000	5639	5100	5743	5200	5845	5283	5949	5374	"	7734	6150	5551	6255	5638
5535	5001	5640	5101	5744	5187	5846	5282	5950	5374	6048	5473	6151	5552	6256	5639
5536	5002	5641	5102	5745	5195	5847	5284	5951	4984	6049	5509	6152	5553	6257	5638
5537	5003	5642	5102	5746	5189	5848	5285	"	5375	6050	5474	6153	5554	6258	5640
5538	5005	5643	5104	5747	5190	5849	5286	"	5379	6051	5475	6154	5555	6259	5641
5539	5004	5644	5105	5748	5192	5850	5287	"	7721	6052	5476	6155	5556	6260	5643
5540	5006	5645	763	5749	5193	5851	5287	5952	5381	6053	5477	6156	5557	6261	5643
5541	5007	5646		5750	5194	5852	5289	5953	5385	6054	5478	6157	5558	6262	5644
5542	5007	5647		5751	5196	5853	5288	5954	5387	6055	5479	6158	5927	6263	
5543	5008	5648	5106	5752	5197	5854	5290	5955	5387	6056	5526	6159	5560	6264	5646
5544	5009	5649	5107	5753	5198	5855	5291	5956	5400	6057	5480	6160	5561	6265	5645
5545	5010	5650	5108	5754	5198	5856	5292	5957	5378	6058	5526	6161	5562	6266	5645
5546	5011	5651	5109	5755	5188	5857	5292	"	5383	6059	5482	6162	5562	6267	5645
5547	5012	5652	3013	5756	5199	5858	5293	5958	5377	6060	5515	6163	5563	6268	5647
5548	5014	5653	5110	5757	5201	5859	5294	5959	5380	6061	5483	6164	5564	6269	5650
5549	5015	5654	5112	5758	5201	5860	5295	5960	5382	6062	5483	6165	5565	6270	5651
5550	5015	5655	5113	5759	5203	5861	5296	5961	5378	6063	5484	6166	5566	6271	5652
5551	5015	5656	5114	5760	5204	5862	5297	5962	5384	6064	5485	6167		6272	5653
5552	5562	5657	5115	5761		5863	5298	5963	5386	6065	2702	6168	5567	6273	5654
5553	5016	5658	5115	5762	5108	5864	5299	5964	5388	6066	5486	6169	5568	6274	5655
5554	5014	5659	5116	5763	5109	5865	5299	5965	5390	6067	5490	6170	5569	6275	5656
5555	5018	5660	5116	5764	5205	5866	5300	5966	5391	6068	5488	6171	5570	6276	5657
5556	5019	5661	4999	5765	5206	5867	5300	5967	5391	6069	5489	6172	5571	6277	5658
5557	5019	5662	5121	5766	5121	5868	5316	5968	5392	6070	5492	6173	7158	6278	5658
5558	5021	5663	5117	5767	5207	5869	5299+1756	5969	5393	6071	5492	6174	5572	6279	5660
5559	5022	5664	5117	5768	5125	5870	5301	5970	5394	6072	5618	6175	5573	6280	5661
5560	5024	5665	5118	5769	5209	5871	5302	5971	5395	6073	3249	6176	5574	6281	5662
5561	5025	5666	5119	5770	5210	5872	5303	5972	5397	"	5493	6177	5575	6282	5662
5562	5025	5667	5120	5771	5211	5873	5304	5973	5398	6074	5494	6178	5576	6283	5663
5563	5026	5668	5121	5772	5212	5874	5305	5974	5399	6075	5495	6179	5578	6284	5664
5564	5027	5669		5773	5213	5875	5300	5975	5401	6076	5494	6180	5577	6285	5659
5565	5028	5670	5123	5774	5214	5876	5306	5976	5401	6077	5496	6181	5579	6286	5666
5566	5030	5671	5124	5775	5216	5877	5307	5977	5402	6078	5497	6182	5580	6287	5667
5567	5031	5672	5125	5776	5215	5878	5309	5978	5402	6079	5498	6183	5581	6288	5668
5568	5032	5673	5126	5777	5217	5879	5310	5979	5404	6080	5499	6184	5582	6289	5669
5569	5033	5674	5127	5778	5218	5880	5310	5980	5405	6081	5500	6185	5584	6290	5687
5570	5034	5675	5128	5779	5218	5881	5311	5981	5406	6082	5501	6186	5585	6291	5688
5571	5034	5676	5129	5780	5219	5882	5314	5982	5411	6083		6187	5585	6292	5670
5572	5036	5677	5130	5781	5220	5883	5315	5983	5408	6084	7823	6188	5586	6293	5670
5573	5037	5678	5130	5782	5221	5884	5316	5984	5409	6085	5502	6189	5588	6294	5671
5574	5035	5679	5131	5783	5223	5885	5317	5985	5410	6086	5503	6190	5589	6295	5672
5575	5035	5680	5132	5784	5222	5886	5318	5986	5410	"	5505	6191	5587	6296	5674
5576	5039	5681	5133	5785	5224	5887	5319	5987	5411	6087	5504	6192	5590	6297	5674
5577	5038	5682	3243	"	6549	5888	5320	5988	5413	6088	5506	6193	5591	6298	5676
5578	5040	5683	5136	5786	5224	5889	5321	5989	5414	6089	5507	6194	5591	6299	5677
5579	5041	5684	5137	5787	3559	5890	5322	5990	5416	6090	5508	6195	5592	6300	5863
5580	5042	5685	5137	5788	3559	5891	5322	5991	5417	6091	7750	6196	5592	6301	5678
5581	5044	5686	5138	5789	5225	5892	5323	5992	5418	6092	5509	6197	5592	6302	5679
5582	5045	5687	5139	5790	5226	5893	5324	5993	5418	6093	7875	6198	5593	6303	5680
5583	5046	5688	5140	"	5227	5894	5324	5994	5419	6094	5510	6199	5594	6304	5681
5584	5048	5689	5140	5791	5228	5895	5324	5995	5420	6095	5511	6200	5595	6305	5682
5585	5050	5690	5141	"	5229	5896	5325	5996	5421	6096	5512	6201	5603	6306	2275
5586	5051	5691	5143	5792	5230	5897	5327	5997	5422	6097	5512	6202	5596	6307	5684
5587	5052	5692	5144	5793	5231	5898	5327	5998	5423	6098	5513	6203	5596	6308	5685
5588	5054	5693	5144	5794	5233	5899		5999	5424	6099	5514	6204	5597	6309	5686
5589	5664	5694	5145	5795	5234	5900	5328	6000	5425	6100	5515	6205	5598	6310	5688
5590	5055	5695	5146	5796	5234	5901	5133	6001	5425	6101	5483	6206	5599	6311	5689
5591	5056	5696	5147	5797	5236	5902	5133	6002	5425	6102	5516	6207	5599	6312	5691
5592	5057	5697	5148	5798	5235	5903	5341	6003	5427	6103	5517	6208	5600	6313	5690
5593	5058	5698	5117	5799	5237	5904	5329	6004	5428	6104	5517	6209	5601	6314	5692
5594	5059	5699	5151	5800	5238	5905	5331	6005		6105	5518	6210	5602	6315	5693
5595	5060	5700	5149	5801	5239	5906	5332	6006	5429	6106	5518	6211	5603	6316	5694
5596	5061	5701	5152	5802	959	5907	5333	6007	5430	6107	5519	6212	5604	6317	5699
5597	5062	5702	5153	5803	5241	5908	5334	6008	5431	6108	5520	6213	5509	6318	5696
5598	5063	5703	5154	5804	5242	5909	5335	6009	5432	6109	5521	6214	5605	6319	5695
5599	5064	5704	5155	5805	5244	5910	5336	6010	5433	6110	5522	6215	5606	6320	5697
5600	5064	5705	5156	5806	3988	5911	5337	6011	5435	6111	5523	6216	5606	6321	5698
5601	5065	5706	5157	5807	5246	5912	5339	6012	5433	6112	5524	6217	5607	6322	5699
5602	5066	5707	5158	5808	5248	5913	5340	6013	5434	6113	5525	6218	5608	6323	5700
5603	5067	5708	5158	5809	5247	5914	5006	6014	5436	6114	5526	6219	5612	6324	5700
5604	5077	5709	5159	5810	5249	"	5132	6015	4141	6115	5526	6220	5612	6325	5882
5605	5068	5710		5811	5250	5915	5341	"	4142	6116	5526	6221	5608	6326	5697+7992
5606	5070	5711	5158	5812	5251	5916	5342	"	5437	6117	5527	6222	5610	6327	5701
5607	5071	5712	5160	5813	5252	5917	5341	6016	5438	6118	5528	6223	5611	6328	5702
5608	5072	5713	5161	5814	5254	5918	5344	6017	5439	6119	5530	6224	5614	6329	5703
5609	1713	5714	5162	5815	5255	5919	5344	6018	5440	6120	5529	6225	5612	6330	5704
5610	5074	5715	5163	5816	5257	5920	5345	6019	5442	6121	5531	6226	5617	6331	5706
5611	5076	5716	5164	5817	5257	5921	5346	6020	5441	6122	5532	6227	5616	6332	5707
5612	5077	5717	5165	5818	5258	5922	5347	6021	5444	6123	5533	6228	5615	6333	5714
5613	5078	5718	5166	5819	5259	5923	5348	6022	5445	6124	5533	6229		6334	5710
5614	5079	5719	5150	5820	5258	5924	5349	6023	5447	6125	5532	6230	5618	6335	5710
5615	5080	5720	5167	5821	5262	5925	5351	6024	5448	6126	5534	6231	3254	6336	5711
5616	5080	5721	5168	5822	5262	5926	5350	6025	5449	6127	5534	6232	5619	6337	5712
5617	5112	5722	5169	5823	5263	5927	5352	6026	5450	6128	7936	6233	5493	6338	5713
5618	5081	5723	2734	5824	5264	5928	5353	6027	5451	6129	5535	6234	5620		

G/K	STRONG	G/K	STRONG	G/K	STRONG	G/K	STRONG	G/K	STRONG	G/K	STRONG	G/K	STRONG	G/K	STRONG
7989	7193	8088	7280	8191	7379	8294	7467	8398	7559	8500	7914	8603	8321	8706	7686
7990	7179	8089	7280	8192	7380	8295	7468	8399	7561	8501	7915	8604	7796	8707	7681
7991	7180	8090	7280	8193	7306	8296	7469	8400	7562	8502	7916	"	8291	8708	7688
7992	7181	8091	7282	8194	7381	8297	7471	8401	7563	"	7917	8605	8322	8709	7691
7993	7182	8092	7281	8195	7383	8298	7472	8402	7564	8503	5526	8606	7786	8710	7692
7994	7183	8093	7283	8196	7384	8299	7474	8403	3573	8504		"	8323	8711	7693
7995	7183	8094	7285	8197	7324	8300	7464	8404	7565	8505	7919	8607	8342	8712	7694
7996	7185	8095	7285	8198	7385	8301	7475	8405	7566	8506	7919	8608	5640	8713	7696
7997	7186	8096	7286	8199	7386	8302	7477	8406	7567	8507	7922	8609	8368	8714	7697
7998	7188	8097	7287	8200	7387	8303	7478	8407	7568	8508	5531	8610		8715	7698
7999	7189	8098	7287	8201	7325	8304	7479	8408	7569	8509	7937	8611	7945	8716	7699
8000	7189	8099	7288	8202	7388	8305	7480	8409	7570	8510	7939	8612	7579	8717	7700
8001	7190	8100	7289	8203	7389	8306	7481	8410	7571	8511	7940	8613	7580	8718	7699
8002	7191	8101	7290	8204	7391	8307	7481	8411	7572	8512	7938	8614	7581	8719	7701
8003	7194	8102	1721	8205	7390	8308	7482	8412	7573	8513	7958	8615	7582	8720	7703
8004	7195	8103	7291	8206	7392	8309	7483	8413	7574	8514	8007	8616	7582	"	7736
8005	7196	8104	7292	8207	7393	8310	7483	8414	7575	8515	8008	8617	7583	8721	7705
8006	7197	8105	7293	8208	7395	8311	7484	8415	7576	8516	8009	8618	7584	8722	
8007	7197	"	7294	8209	7394	8312	7484	8416	7577	8517	8012	8619	7585	8723	1779
8008	7198	8106	7296	8210	7396	8313	7485	8417	7578	8518	8014	8620	7586	8724	7706
8009	7199	8107	7295	8211	7394	8314	7486	8418		8519		8621	7587	8725	7707
8010		8108	7303	8212	7397	8315	7488	8419	7603	8520	8040	8622	7588	8726	1779
8011	7200	8109	7297	8213	7398	8316	7488	8420	7613	"	8041	8623	7588	8727	7709
"	7202	8110	7298	8214	7399	8317	7489	8421	7613	8521	8041	8624	7589	8728	7710
8012	7201	8111	7298	8215	7400	8318	7489	8422	7638	8522	8042	8625	7591	8729	7711
8013	7200	8112	7351	8216	7401	8319	7491	"	7639	8523	8055	8626	7592	8730	7711
8014	7203	8113	7300	8217	7402	8320	7492	8423	7643	8524	8056	8627	7594	8731	7714
8015	7203	8114	1721	8218	7403	8321	7493	8424	7643	8525	8057	8628	7592	8732	7718
8016	7211	8115	7301	8219	7404	8322	7493	8425	7646	8526	8063	8629	7596	8733	7719
8017	7205	8116	7302	8220	7405	8323	7494	8426	7647	8527		8630	7597	8734	
8018	7206	8117	7303	8221	7406	8324	7495	8427	7648	8528	8072	8631	7599	8735	
8019	7207	8118	7304	8222	7407	8325	7498	8428	7649	8529	8071	8632	1052	8736	7723
8020	7208	8119	7305	8223	7408	8326	7500	8429	7654	8530	8073	8633	7600	8737	7724
8021	7200	8120	7307	8224	7409	8327	7496	8430	7653	8531		8634	7602	8738	7722
8022	883	8121	7309	8225	7311	8328	7497	8431	7663	8532	8079	8635	7602	8739	7722
8023	7209	8122	7310	8226	7410	8329	7497	8432	7663	8533	8130	8636	7604	8740	7725
8024	7210	8123	7311	8227	7411	8330	7501	8433	7664	8534	8135	8637	7605	8741	
8025	7211	8124	7312	8228	7411	8331	7502	8434	7679	8535	8146	8638	7607	8742	7619
8026	7212	8125	7315	8229	7413	8332	7503	8435	7682	8536	8149	8639	7610	8743	7726
8027	7213	8126	7316	8230	7414	8333	7504	8436	7685	8537	8163	8640	7608	8744	7727
8028	7214	8127	7317	8231	7415	8334	7498	8437	7687	8538	8163	8641	7609	8745	7728
8029	7215	8128	7318	8232	7416	8335	7510	8438	7689	8539	8163	8642	7611	8746	7729
8030	7216	8129	7319	8233	7417	8336	7505	8439	7687	8540	8164	8643	7612	8747	7731
8031	7218	"	7427	8234	7417	8337	7499	8440	7702	8541	8165	8644	7614	8748	7732
"	7226	8130	7442	8235	7417	8338	7506	8441	7704	8542	8165	8645	7615	8749	7733
8032	7219	8131	7321	8236	7428	8339	7507	8442	7704	8543	8165	8646	7616	8750	7737
8033	7220	8132	7323	8237	7417	8340	7508	8443	7708	8544	8166	8647	7617	8751	7737
8034	7218	8133	7326	8238	7418	8341	7509	8444	7713	8545	8167	8648	7618	8752	
8035	7221	8134	7327	8239	7419	8342	7510	8445	2089	8546	5587	8649	7619	8753	7740
8036	7222	8135	7329	8240	7433	8343	7513	"	7716	8547	8175	8650		8754	7741
8037	7223	8136	7330	8241	7418	8344	7322	8446	7717	8548	8175	8651	7620	8755	7743
8038	7224	8137	7332	8242	7420	8345	7514	8447	3026	8549	8175	8652	7621	8756	7744
8039	4763	8138	7333	8243	7422	8346	7511	8448	7720	8550	8178	8653	7665	8757	7745
8040	7225	8139	7331	8244	7423	"	7515	8449	7730	8551	8178	8654	7622	8758	7746
8041	7227	8140	7334	8245	7423	8347	7516	8450	5253	8552	8181	8655	7623	8759	
8042	7227	8141	7335	8246	761	8348	7517	8451	7735	8553	8185	8656	7623	8760	7747
8043	7228	8142	7336	8247	7424	8349	7518	8452	7742	8554	8183	8657	7626	8761	7748
8044	7230	8143	7337	8248	7425	8350	7323	8453		8555	8184	8658	7627	8762	7749
8045	7231	8144	7338	8249	7311	8351	7519	8454	7750	8556	8188	8659		8763	7751
8046	7232	8145	7341	8250	7426	8352	7521	8455	7753	8557	8193	8660	7628	8764	7590
8047	7233	8146	7342	8251	7320	8353	7520	8456	7754	8558	5596	8661	7629	8765	7752
8048	7234	8147	7343	8252	7429	8354	7521	8457	7754	8559	8222	8662	7630	8766	7752
8049	7235	8148	7339	8253	7430	8355	7521	8458	7755	8560	8224	8663	7632	8767	7757
8050	7235	8149	7340	8254	7431	8356	7522	8459	7755	8561	8226	8664	7633	8768	7758
8051	7237	8150	7340	8255	7432	8357	7523	8460	7756	8562	5606	8665	7628	8769	7759
8052	7239	8151	7344	8256	7434	8358	7524	8461	7760	8563	5606	8666	7635	8770	7762
8053	7241	8152	7345	8257	7437	8359	7525	8462	5493	8564	8210	8667	7636	8771	7764
8054	7242	8153	7345	8258	7435	8360	7526	8463	7795	8565	5607	8668	7637	8772	7765
8055	7243	8154	7346	8259	7414	8361	7527	8464	7797	8566	8242	8669	7622	8773	7766
8056	7245	8155	7344+5892	8260	7438	8362	7528	8465	7808	8567	8244	8670	7640	8774	7767
8057	7246	8156	7348	8261	7439	8363	7529	8466	7811	8568	8265	8671	7642	8775	7768
8058	7247	8157	7349	8262	7440	8364	7530	8467	7813	8569	8269	8672	7641	8776	7773
8059	7248	8158	7350	8263	7441	8365	7531	8468	7814	8570	8272	8673	7641	8777	7771
8060	7249	8159	7351	8264	7442	8366	7532	8469	7818	8571	8276	8674	7644	8778	7772
8061	7250	8160	7347	"	7444	8367	7531	8470	7824	8572	8277	8675	7644	8779	7772
"	7252	8161	7353	8265	7445	8368	7533	8471	7832	8573	8278	8676	7645	8780	7769
"	7254	8162	7354	8266	7443	8369	7534	8472		8574	8279	8677	7645	8781	7770
8062	7251	8163	7355	8267	7446	8370	7535	8473	7846	8575	8280	8678	7650	8782	7769
8063	7253	8164	7360	8268	7447	8371	7536	8474	7847	8576	8282	8679	7651	8783	7774
8064	7254	8165	7357	8269	7447	8372	7537	8475	7852	8577	8283	8680	7652	8784	7775
8065	7255	8166	7356	8270	7448	8373	7538	8476	7853	8578	8286	8681	7652	8785	7776
8066	7255	8167	7358	8271	7449	8374	7538	8477	7854	8579	8288	8682	884	8786	7777
8067	7256	8168	7360	8272	7450	8375	7539	8478	7855	8580	8294	8683	7656	8787	7777
8068	7243	8169	7361	8273	7451	8376	7540	8479	7856	8581	8295	8684	7657	8788	7778
8069	7257	8170	3819	8274	7451	8377	7541	8480	7863	8582	8296	8685	7658	8789	7779
8070	7258	8171	7356	8275	7452	8378	7542	8481	7865	8583	8296	8686	7659	8790	7779
8071	7259	8172	7362	8276	7453	8379	7543	8482	7867	8584	8297	8687	7660	8791	7780
8072	7262	8173	7363	8277	7454	8380	7544	8483	7869	8585	8299	8688	7661	8792	8197
8073	7263	8174	7363	8278	7455	8381	7545	8484	7872	8586	8300	8689	7665	8793	7781
8074	7264	8175	7364	8279	7456	8382	7546	8485	7873	8587	8301	8690	7666	8794	5855
8075	7267	8176	7366	8280	7457	8383	7547	8486	7874	8588	8304	8691	7667	8795	7782
8076	7268	8177	7367	"	7458	8384	7548	8487	7875	8589	8304	8692	7668	8796	7783
8077	7269	8178	7368	8281	7456	8385	7549	8488	7878	8590	8303	8693	7669	8797	7785
8078	7270	8179	7369	8282	7459	8386	7550	8489	7880	8591	8305	8694	7667	8798	7784
"	8637	8180	7370	8283	7460	8387	7551	8490	7879	8592	8308	8695	7670	8799	8264
8079	7272	8181	7371	8284	7461	8388	7552	8491	7881	8593	8310	8696	7671	8800	7789
8080	5883	8182	7372	8285	7461	8389	7552	8492	7760	8594	8311	8697	7673	8801	7788
8081	7273	8183	7373	8286	7473	8390	7552	"	7787	8595	8312	8698	7673	8802	7794
8082	7274	8184	3399	8287	7462	8391	7553	8493	7899	8596	8313	8699	7675	8803	7790
8083	7275	8185	7374	8288	7465	8392	7554	8494	7900	8597	8314	8700	7674	8804	7793
8084	7276	8186	7375	8289	7462	8393	7555	8495		8598	8315	8701	7676	8805	7791
8085	7278	8187	7376	8290		8394	7556	8496	7905	8599	8316	8702	7677	8806	8324
8086	7277	8188	7377	8291	7463	8395	7561	8497	7906	8600		8703	7679	8807	7798
8087	5372	8189	7378	8292	7464	8396	7220	8498	7907	8601	8320	8704	7683	8808	7799
"	7279	8190	7379	8293	7466	8397	7558	8499	7634	8602	8291	8705	7684	8809	7800

G/K	STRONG	G/K	STRONG	G/K	STRONG	G/K	STRONG	G/K	STRONG	G/K	STRONG	G/K	STRONG	G/K	STRONG
8810	7895	8911	7941	9014	8047	9118	8157	9222	8275	9321	8402	9421	8507	9525	8605
8811	7803	8912	7937	9015	8048	9119	8158	9223	3474	9322	8403	9422	8508	9526	8606
8812	7805	8913	7943	9016	8049	9120	8159	"	8281	9323	8404	9423	8509	9527	8607
8813	7806	8914	7942	9017	8050	9121	8161	9224	8281	9324	8405	9424	8510	9528	8608
8814	7807	8915	7944	9018	8051	9122	8162	"	8284	9325	8407	9425	8512	9529	8609
8815	7809	8916	7946	9019	8052	9123	8168	9225	8285	9326	8408	9426	8521	9530	8610
8816	7810	8917	7947	9020	8053	9124	8169	9226	8287	9327	8409	9427	8528	9531	8611
8817	7812	8918	7948	9021	8054	9125	8169	9227	8289	9328	8425	9428	8511	9532	8612
8818	7815	8919	7949	9022		9126	8170	9228	8290	9329	8410	9429	8514	9533	8613
8819	7816	8920	7950	9023	8058	9127	8171	9229	8292	9330	8412	9430	8513	9534	8616
8820	7817	8921	7950	9024	8059	9128	8172	9230	8293	9331	8413	9431	8515	9535	8615
8821	7819	8922	7951	9025	8060	9129	8173	9231	7861	9332	8414	9432	8516	9536	8615
8822	7819	8923	7952	9026	8061	9130	8173	9232	8298	9333	8415	9433	8407	9537	8616
"	7820	"	7953	9027	8062	9131	8174	9233	8302	9334	8417	9434	8518	9538	8617
8823	7819	8924	7956	9028	8064	9132	8176	9234	8302	9335	8416	9435	8524	9539	6965
8824	7821	8925	7956	9029	8066	9133	8179	9235	8306	9336	8418	9436	8520	"	8618
8825	7822	8926	7887	9030	8067	9134	8180	9236	8309	9337	8419	9437	8522	9540	8619
8826	7823	8927	7957	9031	8068	9135	8182	9237	8317	9338	8420	9438	2048	9541	8620
8827	7825	8928	7957	9032	8068	9136	8186	9238	8318	9339	8380	9439	8525	9542	8621
8828	7826	8929	7961	9033	8069	9137	8187	9239	8319	9340	8423	9440	8526	9543	8622
8829	7827	8930	7959	9034	8069	9138	8187	9240	8322	9341	8394	9441	8527	9544	8623
8830	7828	8931	7887	9035	8070	9139	8189	9241	8292	9342	8424	9442	8519	9545	8626
8831	7829	8932	7962	9036	8073	9140	8190	9242	8325	9343	8426	9443	8529	9546	8628
8832	7830	8933	7964	9037	8074	9141	8191	9243	8325	9344	8427	9444	8530	9547	8629
8833	7831	8934	7965	9038	8076	9142	8192	9244	8307	9345	8428	9445	8515	9548	8630
8834	7831	8935	7967	9039	8077	9143	8195	9245	8327	9346	8430	9446	8534	9549	8633
8835	7833	8936	7966	9040	8077	9144	8196	9246	8329	9347	8431	9447	8535	9550	8634
8836	7834	8937	7968	9041	8078	9145	8197	9247	8326	9348	8432	9448	8537	9551	8635
8837	7835	8938	7971	9042	8080	9146	8197	"	8328	9349	8433	9449	8539	9552	8636
8838	7836	8939	7973	9043	8081	9147	8194	9248	8333	9350	8433	9450	8538	9553	8638
8839	7838	8940	7975	9044	4924	9148	8198	9249	8333	9351	8434	9451	8541	9554	8639
8840	7837	8941	7974	9045	8082	9149	8199	9250	8334	9352	8435	9452	8542	9555	8640
8841	7839	8942	7975	9046	8083	9150	8201	9251	8335	9353	8436	9453	8543	9556	8641
8842	7840	8943	7976	9047	8084	9151	8202	9252	8337	9354	8437	9454	8544	9557	8642
8843	7841	8944	7977	9048	8085	9152	8203	9253	8336	9355	8438	9455	8545	9558	8643
8844	7842	8945	7973	9049	8085	9153	8203	9254	8336	9356	8439	9456	8546	9559	8644
8845	516	8946	7978	9050	8087	9154	8204	9255	8338	9357	8438	9457	8547	9560	8645
"	7843	8947	7979	9051	8088	9155	8205	9256	8339	9358	8440	9458	8548	9561	8646
8846	7845	8948	7980	9052	8091	9156	8195	9257	8341	9359	8441	9459	8549	9562	8646
8847	7848	8949	7982	9053	8089	9157	8206	9258	8343	9360	8442	9460	8550	9563	8647
8848	7849	8950	7983	9054	8090	9158	8206	9259	8344	9361	8443	9461	8551	9564	8649
8849	7850	8951	7986	9055	8092	9159	8207	9260		9362	8444	9462	8552	9565	
8850	7851	8952	7987	9056	8093	9160	8208	9261	8345	9363	8445	9463	8553	9566	8649
8851	7857	8953	7988	9057	8094	9161	8210	9262	8346	9364	8628	9464	8554	9567	8649
8852	7858	8954	7989	9058	8095	9162	8211	9263	8347	9365	8446	9465	8555	9568	8650
8853	7860	8955	7991	9059	8096	9163	8212	9264	8348	9366	8447	9466	8556	9569	8649
8854		8956	7991	9060	8097	9164	8213	9265	8349	9367	8449	9467	8556	9570	8653
8855	7861	8957	7991	9061	8098	9165	8216	9266	8350	9368	8451	9468	8557	9571	8654
8856	7862	8958	7992	9062	8098	9166	8217	9267		"	8452	9469	8558	9572	8655
8857	7864	8959	7993	9063	8099	9167		/9268	8351	9369	8453	9470	8559	9573	8656
8858	7866	8960	7994	9064	8100	9168	8218	"	8352	9370	8454	9471	8559	9574	8656
8859	7871	8961	7995	9065	8101	9169	8219	"	8357	9371	8455	9472	8560	9575	8657
8860	7870	8962	7996	9066	8102	9170	8220	9269	8352	9372	8456	9473	8560	9576	8659
8861	7876	8963	7997	9067	8103	9171	8223	9270		9373	8457	9474	8561	9577	8658
8862	7877	8964	7997	9068	8104	9172	8221	9271	8356	9374	8458	9475	8562	9578	8659
8863	7817	8965	7998	9069	8105	9173	8309	9272	8354	9375	8459	9476	8563	9579	8660
8864	8366	8966	7999	9070	8106	9174		9273		9376	8461	9477	8564	9580	8661
8865	7883	8967		9071	7763	9175	8225	9274	8359	9377	8463	9478	8565	9581	8662
8866	7884	8968	8002	9072	8108	9176	8227	9275	8358	9378	8462	"	8568	9582	8667
8867	7752	8969	8003	9073	8109	9177	8227	9276	8360	9379	8464	9479	8566	9583	8663
8868	7885	8970	8004	9074	8110	9178		9277	8363	9380	8465	9480	8567	9584	
8869	7886	8971		9075	8110	9179	8228	9278	8362	9381	8466	9481	8569	9585	8664
8870	7887	8972	8005	9076	8111	9180	8229	9279	8364	9382	8467	9482	8570	9586	8664
8871	7758	8973	8006	9077	8112	9181	8230	9280	8365	9383	8468	9483	8571	9587	8665
8872	7888	8974	8011	9078	8113	9182	8231	9281	8365	9384	8469	9484	8572	9588	8666
8873	7889	8975	4100	9079	8114	9183	8233	9282	8366	9385	8466	9485	8573	9589	7738
8874	8366	8976	8010	9080	8114	9184	8234	9283		9386	8466	9486	8574	"	8663
8875	7890	8977	8013	9081	8107	9185	8235	9284	8367	9387	8471	9487	8575	9590	
8876	7891	8978	8073	9082	8070	9186	8236	9285	8369	9388	8472	9488	8575	9591	8668
8877	7892	8979	8015	9083	8116	9187	8237	9286	8371	9389	8473	9489	8576	9592	8669
8878	7892	8980	8016	9084	8117	9188	8237	9287		9390	8475	9490	8577	9593	8670
8879		8981	8017	9085	8118	9189	8239	9288	8372	9391	8476	9491	8580	9594	
8880	7893	8982	8018	9086	8119	9190	8240	9289	8373	9392	8477	9492	8580	9595	8671
8881	7894	8983	8018	9087	8121	9191	8240	9290	8374	9393	8478	9493	8581	9596	8672
8882	7895	8984	8019	9088	8123	9192	8241	9291	8375	9394	8480	9494	8582	9597	8673
8883	7896	8985	8019	9089	8124	9193	8245	9292	8376	9395	8480	9495	8583		
8884	7897	8986	8020	9090	1030	9194	8245	9293	8377	9396	8481	9496	8584		
8885	7898	8987	8022	9091	8125	9195	8245	9294	8378	9397	8482	9497	8583	**ARAMAIC**	
8886	7901	8988	8021	9092	8126	9196	8247	9295	8379	9398	8483	9498	8585	**OLD**	
8887	7902	8989	8023	9093	1052	9197	8248	9296	8380	9399	8484	9499	8585	**TESTAMENT**	
8888	7903	"	8024	9094	8127	9198	8249	9297	8381	9400	8436	9500	8586		
8889	7904	8990	8025	9095	8129	"	8250	9298	8382	9401	8485	9501		10001	
8890	7908	8991	8026	9096	8132	9199	8251	9299	8385	9402	8486	9502	8587	10002	
8891	7909	8992	8027	9097	8142	9200	8252	9300	8384	9403	8487	9503	8588	10003	2
8892	7909	8993	7969	9098	8134	9201	8253	9301	8385	9404	8489	9504	8589	10004	4
8893	7910	8994	8028	9099	8136	9202	8254	9302	8386	9405	8488	9505	8590	10005	7
8894	7911	8995	8031	9100	8137	9203	8255	9303	8383	9406	8490	9506	8591	10006	69
8895	7913	8996	8030	9101	8132	9204	8256	9304	8387	9407	8491	9507	5774	10007	104
8896	7918	8997	8032	"	8138	9205	8257	9305	8388	9408	8492	9508	8592	10008	116
8897	7921	8998	7991	9102	8141	9206	8258	9306	8388	9409	8493	9509	8593	10009	144
8898	7923	8999	7992	9103		9207	8259	9307	8389	9410	8494	9510	8594	10010	147
8899	7925	9000	8029	9104	8142	9208	8260	9308	8390	9411	8495	9511	8595	10011	148
8900	7926	9001	7970	9105	8143	9209	8261	9309	839	9412	8496	9512	8596	10012	149
"	7929	9002		9106	8144	9210	8262	"	8391	"	8501	9513	8596	10013	153
8901	7927	9003	7597	9107		9211	8263	9310	8392	9413	8497	9514	8597	10014	230
8902	7927	9004	8033	9108	8145	9212	8264	9311	8393	9414	8498	9515	8598	10015	228
8903	7928	9005	8034	9109	8147	9213	8266	9312	8394	"	8499	9516	8599	10016	236
8904	7930	9006	8035	9110	8148	9214	8267	9313	8395	9415	8500	9517	8599	10017	252
8905	7931	9007	8037	9111	8150	9215		9314	8396	9416	8502	9518		10018	263
"	7933	9008	8038	9112	8150	9216	8268	9315	8398	9417	8503	9519	8601	10019	280
8906		9009	8039	9113	8151	9217	8285	9316	8397	9418	8504	9520	6617	10020	307
8907	7934	9010	8043	9114	8152	9218	8270	9317	8422	9419	8505	9521	8602	10021	311
8908	7935	9011	8044	9115	8154	9219	8270	9318	8399	9420	8506	9522	8602	10022	320
8909	7935	9012	8045	9116	8155	9220	8273	9319	8400			9523	8603	10023	317
8910	7937	9013	8106	9117	8156	9221	8274	9320	8401			9524	8604		

G/K	STRONG	G/K	STRONG	G/K	STRONG	G/K	STRONG	G/K	STRONG	G/K	STRONG	G/K	STRONG
10024	318	10129	1358	10234	2171	10339	3493	10442	4887	10546	5943	10650	7238
10025	321	10130	1370	10235	2178	10340		10443	4887	10547	5952	10651	7244
10026	324	10131	1400	10236	2192	10341		10444	4903	10548	5946	10652	7261
10027	363	10132	1401	10237	2200	10342		10445	4907	10549	5954	10653	7265
10028	574	10133	1411	10238	2211	10343	3538	10446	4953	10550	5957	10654	7266
10029	383	10134	1414	10239	2217	10344		10447	4961	10551	5962	10655	7271
10030	399	10135	1459	10240	2234	10345	3542	10448	4978	10552	5967	10656	7284
10031	409	10136	1467	10241		10346	3546	10449		10553	5972	10657	7299
10032	412	10137	1519	10242	2248	10347	3549	10450		10554	5974	10658	7308
10033	426	10138		10243	2255	10348	3551	10451	5013	10555	5994	10659	7313
10034	429	10139	1490	10244	2257	10349		10452	5017	10556	6015	10660	7314
10035	431	10140	1505	10245	2269	10350	3567	10453	5020	10557	3705	10661	7328
10036	459	10141	1510	10246	2273	10351		10454	5023	10558	6032	10662	7348
10037	479	10142	1528	10247	2292	10352	3604	10455	5029	10559	6033	10663	7352
10038	506	10143	1535	10248	2298	10353	3606	10456	5043	10560	6050	10664	7359
10039	521	10144	1541	10249	2306	10354	3635	10457	5047	10561	6056	10665	7365
10040	524	10145	1547	10250	2305	10355		10458	5049	10562	6065	10666	7382
10041	540	10146	1560	10251	2323	10356	4101	10459	5053	10563	3706	10667	7412
10042	560	10147	1585	10252	2324	10357	3652	10460	5665	10564	6074	10668	7470
10043	563	10148	1596	10253	2338	10358	3660	10461	5069	10565	6088	10669	7476
10044	576	10149	1611	10254	2358	10359	3673	10462	5073	10566	6132	10670	7487
10045	581	10150	1635	10255	2370	10360	3675	10463	5075	10567	6136	10671	7490
10046	582	10151	1655	10256	2376	10361	3679	10464	5085	10568	6146	10672	7512
10047	586	10152		10257	2379	10362	3702	10465	5094	10569	6151	10673	7560
10048	598	10153		10258	2402	10363	3705	10466	5094	10570	6167	10674	
10049	600	10154	1668	10259	2408	10364	3706	10467	5094	10571	6173	10675	7868
10050	606	10155	1678	10260	2409	10365	3706	10468	5103	10572	6211	10676	5443
10051	607	10156	1684	10261	2417	10366	3729	10469	5111	10573	6236	10677	7680
10052	607	10157	1685	10262	2418	10367	3734	10470	5122	10574	6243	10678	7690
10053	608	10158	1693	10263	2423	10368	3737	10471	5135	10575	6246	10679	3026
10054	613	10159	1701	10264	2429	10369	3735	10472	5142	10576	3706	10680	7859
10055	620	10160	1722	10265	2445	10370	3744	10473	5174	10577	6263	10681	7868
10056	629	10161	1723	10266	2452	10371	3745	10474	5182	10578	6268	10682	7761
10057	633	10162	1723	10267	2493	10372	3764	10475	5191	10579		10683	7920
10058	636	10163	1753	10268	2499	10373	3779	10476	5202	10580	6347	10684	7924
10059	638	10164	1757	10269	2508	10374	3790	10477		10581	6353	10685	7955
10060	670	10165	1759	10270	2528	10375	3792	10478	5208	10582	6361	10686	8131
10061	671	10166	1761	10271	2562	10376	3797	10479	5232	10583	6386	10687	8177
10062	671	10167	1763	10272	2591	10377		10480	5245	10584	6387	10688	
10063	674	10168	1768	10273	2597	10378		10481	5256	10585	6392	10689	7593
10064	677	10169	1778	10274	2604	10379	3809	10482	5260	10586	6399	10690	7595
10065	703	10170	1780	10275	2608	10380	3821	10483	5261	10587	6402	10691	7598
10066	711	10171	1782	10276	2627	10381	3825	10484	5308	10588	6433	10692	7606
10067	718	10172	1784	10277	2631	10382	3831	10485	5312	10589	6447	10693	7624
10068	735	10173	1791	10278	2632	10383	3848	10486	5313	10590	6460	10694	7625
10069	738	10174	1797	10279	2635	10384	3809	10487	5326	10591	6523	10695	7631
10070	746	10175	1798	10280	2685	10385	3861	10488	5330	10592	6537	10696	7655
10071	749	10176	1799	10281	2718	10386	3861	10489	5338	10593	6537	10697	7662
10072	755	10177	1799	10282	2749	10387	3879	10490	5343	10594	6540	10698	7672
10073	754	10178	1815	10283	2761	10388	3890	10491	5368	10595	6543	10699	7695
10074	756	10179	1821	10284	2783	10389	3900	10492	5376	10596	6562	10700	7712
10075	772	10180	1836	10285	2804	10390	3904	10493	5389	10597	6568	10701	7715
10076	773	10181	1841	10286	2816	10391	3916	10494	5396	10598	6573	10702	7739
10077	778	10182	1855	10287	2818	10392	3961	10495	5403	10599	6590	10703	7792
10078	783	10183	1859	10288	2818	10393		10496	5407	10600	6591	10704	7801
10079	787	10184	1868	10289	2819	10394	3964	10497	5412	10601	6600	10705	7844
10080	785	10185	1872	10290	2827	10395	3969	10498	5415	10602	6606	10706	7804
10081	826	10186	1882	10291	2857	10396	3977	10499	5426	10603	6613	10707	3319
10082	846	10187	1883	10292		10397	3983	10500		10604		10708	7912
10083	849	10188	1884	10293	2868	10398	3984	10501	5443	10605	6634	10709	7932
10084	852	10189		10294	2869	10399	4040	10502	5446	10606	6640	10710	7954
10085	858	10190		10295	2877	10400	4049	10503	5452	10607	6647	10711	7955
10086	861	10191		10296	2906	10401	4056	10504	5457	10608	6655	10712	7960
10087	870	10192		10297	2908	10402	4061	10505	5460	10609	6656	10713	7963
10088		10193		10298	2917	10403	4070	10506	5463	10610	6665	10714	7972
10089		10194	1888	10299	2920	10404	4076	10507	5481	10611	6676	10715	7981
10090	873	10195	1888	10300	2927	"	4077	10508	5487	10612	6739	10716	7984
10091	888	10196	1907	10301	2939	10405	4076	10509	5491	10613	6744	10717	7985
10092	870	10197	1917	10302	2942	"	4077	10510	5481	10614	6755	10718	7990
10093	895	10198	1922	10303	2953	10406	4083	10511	7859	10615	6841	10719	8000
10094	896	10199	1923	10304	2957	10407	4070	10512	5481	10616	6853	10720	8001
10095	921	10200	1932	10305	2967	10408	4101	10513	5559	10617		10721	8036
10096	924	10201	1934	10306		10409	4193	"	5267	10618	6902	10722	8046
10097	927	10202	1946	10307		10410	4203	10514	5583	10619	6903	10723	8065
10098	989	10203		10308	2987	10411	4223	10515	5609	10620	6922	10724	8075
10099	997	10204		10309	3007	10412	4255	10516	5613	10621	6925	10725	8086
10100	999	10205	1932	10310	3026	10413	4291	10517	5622	10622	6928	10726	8115
10101	1001	10206	1965	10311	3028	10414	4333	10518	5632	10623	6933	10727	8120
10102	956	10207	1981	10312	3029	10415	4336	10519	5642	10624	6966	10728	8122
10103	1005	10208	1983	10313	3046	10416	4391	10520	5642	10625	6992	10729	8124
10104	1079	10209		10314	3052	10417	4398	10521		10626	7001	10730	8128
10105	1113	10210	1994	10315	3061	10418	4406	10522	5648	10627	7007	10731	8133
10106	1080	10211	2002	10316	3062	10419	4415	10523	5649	10628	7010	10732	8140
10107	1093	10212	2002	10317	3118	10420	4416	10524	5665	10629	7011	10733	8139
10108	1096	10213	2006	10318	3136	10421	4430	10525	5673	10630	7030	10734	8160
10109	1113	10214		10319		10422	4431	10526	5675	10631	7032	10735	8200
10110	1123	10215		10320	3191	10423	4433	10527	5705	10632	7066	10736	8209
10111	1124	10216		10321	3202	10424	4437	10528	5709	10633	7108	10737	8214
10112	1147	10217	2031	10322	3221	10425	4449	10529	5714	10634	7109	10738	8215
10113	1149	10218	927	10323	3255	10426	4479	10530	5732	10635	7113	10739	8232
10114	1156	10219	5069	10324	3272	10427	4481	10531	5751	10636	7118	10740	8238
10115	1159	10220		10325	3272	10428	4484	10532	5758	10637	7123	10741	8243
10116	1169	10221		10326	3321	10429	4061	10533	5776	10638	7127	10742	8271
10117	1236	10222		10327	3330	10430	4486	10534	5784	10639	7129	10743	8330
10118	1240	10223	2084	10328	3345	10431	4483	10535	5796	10640	7149	10744	8332
10119	1251	10224	2095	10329	3346	10432	4504	10536	5824	10641	7162	10745	8332
10120	1247	10225	2103	10330	3358	10433	4510	10537	5831	10642	7170	10746	8340
10121	1289	10226	2110	10331	3367	10434	4567	10538	5839	10643	7187	10747	8353
10122	1289	10227	2112	10332	3390	10435	4577	10539	5843	10644	7030	10748	8355
10123	1291	10228	2122	10333	3393	10436	4606	10540	5870	10645		10749	8361
10124	1297	10229	2136	10334	3410	10437	4756	10541	5894	10646	7217	10750	8370
10125	1321	10230	2148	10335	3479	10438	4776	10542	5922	10647	7229	10751	
10126	1325	10231	2164	10336	3443	10439	4779	10543	5924	"	7260	10752	8406
10127		10232	2166	10337	3487	10440	4804	10544	5931	10648	7236	10753	8411
10128	1355	10233	2170	10338	3488	10441	4873	10545	5928	10649	7240	10754	8421

G/K	STRONG
10755	8429
10756	8450
10757	8460
"	8479
10758	8517
10759	8523
10760	8531
10761	8532
10762	8533
10763	8540
10764	8536
10765	8578
10766	8579
10767	8614
10768	8624
10769	8625
10770	8625
10771	8627
10772	8631
10773	8632
10774	8632
10775	8648
10776	8651
10777	8652
10778	8648
10779	8674

GREEK NEW TESTAMENT

G/K	STRONG
1	1
2	2
3	3
4	4
5	5
6	6
7	7
8	8
9	9
10	10
11	11
12	12
13	13
14	14
15	18+2041
16	15
17	16
18	17
19	18
20	19
21	20
22	21
23	22
24	23
25	24
26	25
27	26
28	27
29	28
30	29
31	30
32	31
33	518
34	32
35	30
36	34
37	35
38	36
39	37
40	38
41	39
"	40
42	41
43	42
44	43
45	44
46	45
47	46
48	47
49	48
50	49
51	50
52	51
53	52
54	53
55	54
56	55
57	56
58	57
59	58
60	59
61	60
62	61
63	62
64	63
65	64
66	65
67	66
68	67
69	68
70	69
71	70
72	33

G/K	STRONG	G/K	STRONG	G/K	STRONG	G/K	STRONG	G/K	STRONG	G/K	STRONG	G/K	STRONG	G/K	STRONG
"	71	175	168	279	264	384	355	489	457	592	558	695	654	799	750
73	72	176	169	280	265	385	359	490	458	593	559	696	655	800	751
74	73	177	170	281	266	386	360	491	459	594	560	697	656	801	752
75	74	178	171	282	267	387	361	492	460	595	561	698	657	802	753
76	75	179	172	283	268	388	362	493	453	596	562	699	658	803	754
77	76	180	173	284		389	363	494	461	597	563	700	659	804	755
78	77	181	174	285	269	390	364	495	462	598	564	701	660	805	
79	78	182	175	286	270	391	365	496	463	599	565	702	661	806	756
80	79	183	176	287	271	392	366	497	464	600	566	703	662	"	757
81	80	184	177	288	272	393	367	498	465	"	567	704	663	807	758
82	81	185	178	289	273	394	368	499	466	"	568	705	664	808	759
83	82	186	179	290	274	395	369	500	467	601	569	706	665	809	760
84	83	187	180	291	275	396	370	501	468	602	570	707	666	810	761
85	84	188	180	292	276	397	371	502	469	603	571	708	667	811	760
86	85	189	181	293	277	398	372	503	470	604	573	709	668	812	762
87	86	190	182	294	278	399	373	504	472	605	572	710	669	813	763
88	87	191	183	295	279	400	374	505	473	606	573	711	670	814	764
89	88	192	184	296	280	401	376	506	474	607	574	712	671	815	765
90	89	193	185	297	281	402	375	507	475	608	575	713	672	816	766
91	90	194	85	298	282	403	450	508	476	609	576	714	673	817	767
92	91	195	186	299	283	404	377	509	477	610	577	715	674	818	768
93	92	196	187	300	284	405	378	510	478	611	578	716	675	819	769
94	93	197	188	301		406	379	511	479	612	579	717	676	820	770
95	94+2923	198	189	302	285	407	4238	512	480	613	580	718	677	821	771
96	94	199	190	303	286	408	380	513	481	614	581	719	678	822	772
97	95	200	191	304	287	409	381	514	482	615	582	720	679	823	773
98	689	201	191	305	880	410	382	515	471	616	583	721	680	824	774
99	96	202	192	306	288	411	383	"	483	617	584	"	681	825	775
100	97	203	193	307	289	412	384	516	484	618	585	722	682	826	776
101	98	204	194	308	290	413	385	517	485	619	586	723	683	827	777
102	99	205	195	309	291	414	386	518	486	620	586	724	684	828	778
103	100	206	196	310	292	415	387	519	487	621	587	725	685	829	779
104	101	207		311	906+293	416	388	520	488	622	588	726	686	830	780
105	102	208	198	312	293	417	389	521	489	623	589	727	687	831	781
106	103	209	199	313	294	418	390	522	490	624	590	728	688	832	782
107	104	"	197	314	294	419	391	523	491	625	591	729		833	783
108	105	210	200	315	295	420	37	524	492	626	592	730	689	834	784
109	106	211	201	316	296	421	392	525	493	627	593	731	729	835	785
110	107	212	202	317	297	422	393	526	494	628	594	732	690	836	786
111	108	213	203	318	298	423	394	527	495	629	595	733	691	837	787
112		214	204	319		424	395	528	496	630	596	734	692	838	4565
113	109	215	205	320	299	425	510	529	497	631	597	735	693	839	788
114	110	216	206	321	300	426	396	530	498	632	598	736	694	840	789
115	2288+1	217	207	322	301	427	397	531	499	633	599	737	695	841	790
116	111	218	208	323	302	428	398	532	500	634	600	738	696	842	791
117	112	219	209	324	303	429	399	533	501	635	600	739	693	843	792
118	113	220	210	325	304	430	400	534	502	636	601	740	697	844	793
119	114	221	217	326	305	431	401	535	503	637	602	741	698	845	794
120	115	222	211	327	306	432	402	536	504	638	603	742	699	846	795
121	116	223	211	328	307	433	403	537	505	639	604	743	700	847	796
122	117	224	212	329	308	434	404	538	506	640	605	744	701	848	797
123	118	225	213	330	309	435	405	539	507	641	606	745	702	849	798
124	119	226	214	331	310	436	406	540	509	642	607	746	703	850	799
125	4867	227	215	332	311	437	407	541	510	643	608	747		851	800
126	120	228	216	333	508	438	408	542	511	644	609	748	704	852	801
127	121	229	217	334	312	439	409	543	512	645	610	749	705	853	802
128	122	230	218	335	313	440	507+2821	544	513	646	611	750	706	854	803
129	123	231	219	336	314	441	410	545	514	647	612	751	707	855	804
130	124	232	220	337	315	442	411	546	515	648	613	752	708	856	805
131	125	233	221	338	316	443	412	547	516	649	614	753	709	857	806
132	126	234	222	339	317	444	413	548	517	650	615	754	710	858	807
133	127	235	223	340	318	445	414	549	2456	651	615	755	711	859	808
134	128	236	224	341	319	446	415	550	518	652	616	756	712	860	809
135	129	237	225	342	320	447	448	551	519	653	617	757	713	861	810
136	130	238	226	343	321	448	416	552	520	654	2980	758	714	862	811
137	131	239	227	344	322	449	417	553	521	655	618	759	715	863	812
138	132	240	228	345	323	450	418	554	522	656	619	760	715	864	813
139	133	241	229	346	324	451	419	555	523	657	620	761	716	865	814
140	134	242	230	347	325	452	420	556	524	658	621	762	717	866	815
141	135	243	231	348	326	453	421	557	525	659	5277	763	689	867	816
142	136	244	232	349	327	454	422	558	526	660	622	764	718	868	817
143	137	245	233	350	328	455	423	559	527	661	623	765	719	869	818
144	2056	246	234	351	329	456	424	560	528	662	624	766	720	870	818
145	138	247	235	352	330	457	425	561	529	663	625	767		871	819
146	139	248	236	353	331	458	426	562	530	664	626	768	721	872	820
147	140	249	237	354	332	459	427	563	531	665	627	769	722	873	821
148	141	250		355	333	460	428	564	532	666	628	770	723	874	822
149	142	251	238	356	334	461	429	565	533	667	629	771	724	875	823
150	143	252	239	357	335	462	430	566	575+737	668	630	772	725	876	824
151	144	253	240	358	336	463	431	567	534	669	631	773	726	877	825
152	145	254	241	359	337	464	432	568	535	670	5278	774	727	878	826
153	146	255	2087	360	338	465	433	569	536	671	632	775	728	879	827
154	147	256	242	361	339	466	434	570	537	672	633	776	730	880	828
155	148	257	243	362	340	467	435	571	782	673	575+3992	777	731	881	829
156	149	258	244	363	341	468	436	572	538	674	634	778	732	882	830
"	150	259	245	364	342	469	437	573	539	675	635	779	732	883	831
157	151	260	246	365	343	470	438	574	540	676	636	780	733	884	832
158	152	261	247	366	344	471	439	575	541	677	637	781	730	885	833
159	153	262	248	367	345	472	440	576	1890	678	638	782	734	886	834
160	154	263	249	368	346	473	441	577	543	679	639	783	735	887	835
161	155	264	250	369	347	474	442	578	544	680	640	784	736	888	836
162	156	265	251	370	348	475	443	579	545	681	641	785	737	889	837
163	157	266	252	371	349	476	444	580	546	682	642	786	738	890	838
164	4256	267	253	372		477	445	581	547	683	643	787	739	891	837
165	158	268	254	373	350	478	446	582	548	684	644	788	740	892	839
"	159	269	255	374	351	479	447	583	549	685	645	789	741	893	840
166	157	270	1	375	617	480	448	584	550	686	646	790	742	894	841
167	160	271	256	376	352	481	449	"	561	687	647	791	743	895	842
168	161	272	257	377	353	482	450	585	551	688	3848	792	744	896	843
169	162	273	258	378	354	483	451	586	552	689	648	793	745	897	844
170	163	274	259	379	355	484	452	587	553	690	649	794	746	898	845
171	164	275	260	380	242	485	453	588	554	691	650	795	747	899	846
172	165	276	261	381	356	486	454	589	555	692	651	796	748	"	847
173	166	277	262	382	357	487	455	590	556	693	652	797	748	"	848
174	167	278	263	383	358	488	456	591	557	694	653	798	3027	900	1888

G/K	STRONG	G/K	STRONG	G/K	STRONG	G/K	STRONG	G/K	STRONG	G/K	STRONG	G/K	STRONG	G/K	STRONG
901	849	1004	943	1109	1033	1214	1128	1317	1213	1422	1308	1527	1399	1621	1485
902	3166	1005	944	1110	1034	1215	1129	1318	1214	1423	1309	1528	1400	1622	1486
903	850	1006	945	1111	1035	1216	1130	1319	1215	1424	1310	"	1401	1623	1487
904	851	1007	946	1112	1036	1217	1130	1320	1216	1425	1311	1529	1401	1624	2397
905	852	1008	947	1113	1037	1218	1131	1321	1217	1426	1312	1530	1402	1625	3708
906	853	1009	948	1114	1038	1219	1132	1322	1218	1427	1313	1531	1403	1626	1491
907	854	1010	949	1115	1039	1220	1133	1323	1219	1428	1314	1532	1404	1627	1493
908	855	1011	950	1116	1040	1221	1134	1324	1220	1429	1315	1533	1405	1628	1494
909	856	1012	951	1117	1041	1222	1135	1325	1221	1430	5512	1534	1406	1629	1496
910	857	1013	952	1118		1223	1136	1326		1431	1316	1535	1407	1630	1495
911	858	1014	953	1119	1042	1224	1137	1327	1222	1432		1536	1408	1631	1497
912	859	1015	954	1120	1043	1225		1328	1223	1433		1537	1409	1632	1500
913	860	1016	955	1121	1044	1226	1138	1329	1224	1434	1317	1538	1410	1633	1501
914	861	1017	4476	1122	1045	1227	1139	1330	1225	1435	1318	1539	1411	1634	1502
915	862	1018	956	1123	1046	1228	1140	1331	1226	1436	1319	1540	1412	1635	1504
916	90	1019	957	1124	1048	1229	1141	1332	1227	1437	1320	1541	1413	1636	1505
917	90	1020	958	1125	1047	1230	1142	1333	1228	1438	1321	1542	1414	1637	1506
918	863	1021	958	1126	1049	1231	1143	1334	1229	1439	1322	1543	1415	1638	2229+3375
919	864	1022	959	1127	1050	1232	1144	1335	1230	1440	1323	1544	1416	1639	1488
920	865	1023	960	1128	1051	1233	1145	1336	1231	1441	1324	1545	1417	"	1498
921	866	1024	961	1129	1052	1234	1146	1337	1232	1442	1325	1546	1419	"	1510
922	867	1025		1130	1053	1235	1147	1338	1233	1443	1325	1547	1420	"	1511
923	868	1026	1007	1131	1054	1236	1148	1339	1234	1444	1326	1548	1420	"	1526
924	869	1027	1007	1132	1055	1237	1149	1340	1235	1445	1760	1549	1421	"	2070
925	870	1028	962	1133	1056	1238	1150	1341	1236	1446	1831	1550		"	2071
926	871	1029	963	1134	1057	1239	1151	1342	1237	1447	1327	1551	1422	"	2252
927	542	1030	962	1135	1053	1240	1152	1343	1238	1448	2058	1552	1423	"	2258
"	872	1031	964	1136	1058	1241	1153	1344	1239	1449	1328	1553	1424	"	2277
928	873	1032	964	1137	1059	1242	1154	1345	1240	1450	1329	1554	1425	"	2468
929	874	1033	965	1138	1060	1243		1346	1241	1451	1330	1555	987	"	5600
930	875	1034	966	1139	1061	1244	1155	1347	1242	1452	1331	1556	1426	"	5607
931	876	1035	966	1140	1061	1245	1156	1348	1243	1453	1332	1557	1427	1640	
932	877	1036	967	1141	1062	1246	1157	1349	1244	1454	1333	1558	1428	1641	1752
933	878	1037	968	1142	1063	1247	1155	1350	1245	1455	1334	1559	1429	1642	1512
934	879	1038		1143	1064	1248	1158	1351	1245	1456	1335	1560	1430	1643	1513
935	650	1039	969	1144	2802	1249	1156	1352	1246	1457	1336	1561	1431	1644	1514
936	880	1040	970	1145	1065	1250	1157	1353	1781	1458	1337	1562	1432	1645	1515
937	881	1041	971	1146	1066	1251	1159	1354	1247	1459	1338	1563	1433	1646	1516
938	882	1042	972	1147	1067	1252	1160	1355	1248	1460	1339	1564	1434	1647	1517
939	883	1043	973	1148	1068	1253	1138	1356	1249	1461	333	1565	1435	1648	1518
940	884	1044	974	1149	1068	1254	1161	1357	1250	1462	1340	1566	1248	1649	3004
941	881	1045	974	1150	1069	1255	1162	1358	1251	1463	2613	1567		1650	1519
942	886	1046	975	1151	1070	1256	1163	1359	1252	1464	1341	1568	1436	1651	1520
943	885	1047	976	1152	1071	1257	1164	1360	1253	1465	1342	1569	1437	"	3391
944	887	1048	977	1153	1072	1258	1165	1361	1254	1466	1343	1570	1437+4007	1652	1521
945	888	1049	978	1154	1073	1259	1166	1362	1255	1467	1344	1571	1438	1653	1522
946	889	1050	979	1155	1074	1260	1166	1363	1256	1468	1345	1572	1439	1654	1523
947	890	1051	980	1156	1075	1261	1167	1364	1257	1469	1346	1573	1440	1655	1524
948	891	1052	981	1157	1076	1262	1168	1365	1258	1470	1347	1574	1441	1656	1525
949	892	1053	982	1158	1077	1263		1366		1471	1348	1575	1442	1657	1528
950	893	1054	983	1159	1077	1264	1169	1367	1259	1472	1349	1576	1443	1658	1529
951	894	1055	984	1160	1077	1265	1170	1368	1260	1473	1350	1577	1444	1659	1530
952	894	1056	985	1161	1078	1266		1369	1261	1474	1351	1578	1445	1660	1531
953	895	1057	985	1162	1079	1267	1171	1370	1262	1475	1352	1579	1446	1661	1532
954		1058	986	1163	1081	1268	1172	1371	1263	1476	1353	1580	1447	1662	1533
955	896	1059	987	1164	1080	1269		1372	1264	1477	1354	1581	1448	1663	1534
956	897	1060	988	1165	1081	1270	1173	1373	1265	1478	1355	1582	1449	1664	1535
957	898	1061	989	1166	1082	1271	1173	1374	1266	1479	1356	1583	1450	1665	1486
958	899	1062	990	1167	1083	1272	1175	1375	1267	1480	2735	1584	1451	1666	1537
959	900	1063	991	1168	1084	1273	1174	1376	1268	1481	1357	1585	1452	1667	1538
960	901	1064	992	1169	1085	1274	1176	1377	1269	1482	1358	1586	1453	1668	1539
961	902	1065	993	1170	1086	1275	1177	1378	1270	1483	1359	1587	1454	1669	1540
962	903	1066	994	1171	1086	1276	1176+1803	1379	1271	1484	1360	1588	1455	1670	1541
963	904	1067	1003	1172	1087	1277	1176 +2532+3638	1380	1272	1485	1361	1589	1456	1671	1542
964	905	1068	995	1173	1088	1278	1178	1381	1273	1486	1362	1590	1457	1672	1543
965	906	1069	996	1174	1089	1279	1179	1382	1274	1487	1362	1591	1573	1673	1543
966	907	1070	997	1175	1090	1280	1180	1383	1275	1488	1363	1592	1458	1674	1831
967	908	1071	998	1176	1091	1281	1181	1384	3859	1489	1364	1593	1459	1675	1544
968	909	1072	999	1177	1092	"	1182	1385	1276	1490	1417+3461	1594	1460	1676	1545
969	910	1073	999	1178	1093	1282	1183	1386	1277	1491	1365	1595	2620	1677	1816
970	911	1074	1000	1179	1094	1283	1184	1387	1278	1492	1366	1596	1461	1678	1546
971	920	1075	1001	1180	1095	1284	1185	1388	1279	1493	1367	1597	2623	1679	1547
972	912	1076	1002	1181	1096	1285	1186	1389	1280	1494	1368	1598	1462	1680	1548
973	913	1077	1003	1182	1097	1286	1187	1390	1281	1495	1369	1599	1463	1681	1549
974	914	1078	1003	1183	1098	1287	1187	1391	1282	1496	1370	1600	1464	1682	1550
975	915	1079	1004	1184	1099	1288	1188	1392	1284	1497	1371	1601	1465	1683	1551
976	916	1080	1005	1185	1100	1289	1189	1393	1284	1498	1372	1602	1466	1684	1552
977	917	1081	1006	1186	1101	1290	127	1394		1499	1373	1603	1467	1685	1553
978	918	1082	1007	1187	1102	1291	1190	1395	1283	1500	1374	1604	1468	1686	1554
979	919	1083	1008	1188	1103	1292	1191	1396	1284	1501	1375	1605	1469	1687	1555
980	920	1084	1009	1189	1104	1293	1192	1397	1285	1502	1376	1606	1470	1688	1556
981	920	1085	1010	1190	1105	1294	1193	1398	1286	1503	1377	1607	1471	1689	1557
982	921	1086	1011	1191	1106	1295	2359	1399	1287	1504	1378	1608	1472	1690	1558
983	922	1087	1012	1192	1107	1296	1194	1400	1288	1505	1379	1609	1473	1691	1559
984	923	1088	1013	1193	1110	1297	1195	1401	1289	1506	1380	"	1691	1692	1560
985	924	1089	1014	1194	1108	1298	1196	1402	1290	1507	1381	"	1698	1693	1561
986	925	1090	1015	1195	1109	1299	1197	1403	1291	1508	1381	"	1700	1694	1562
987	926	1091	1016	1196	1110	1300	1198	1404	1292	1509	1382	"	2248	1695	1563
988	927	1092	1017	1197	1111	1301	1199	1405	1293	1510	1383	"	2249	1696	1564
989	928	1093	1018	1198	1112	1302	1200	1406	1294	1511	1384	"	2254	1697	1565
990	929	1094	1019	1199	1113	1303	1201	1407	1295	1512	1385	"	2257	1698	1566
991	930	1095	1020	1200	1114	1304	1202	1408	1296	1513	1386	"	3165	1699	1567
992	931	1096	1021	1201	1115	1305	1203	1409	1297	1514	1387	"	3427	1700	2214
993	932	1097	1022	1202	1116	1306	1204	1410	1298	1515	1388	"	3450	1701	1568
994	933	1098	1023	1203	1117	1307	1205	1411	1299	1516	1389	1610	1474	1702	1569
"	934	1099	1024	1204	1118	1308	1206	1412	1300	1517	1390	1611	1475	1703	2296
995	935	1100	1025	1205	1119	1309	1208	1413	1301	1518	1391	1612	1476	1704	1570
996	936	1101	1026	1206	1120	1310	1207	1414	1302	1519	1392	1613	1477	1705	1571
997	937	1102	1690	1207	1121	1311	1208	1415	1303	1520	1393	1614	1478	1706	1572
998	937	1103	1027	1208	1122	1312	1209	1416	1303	1521	1394	1615	1479	1707	1573
999	938	1104	1028	1209	1123	1313	1210	1417	1304	1522	1395	1616	1480	1708	1574
1000	939	1105	1029	1210	1124	1314	1211	1418	1305	1523	1190	1617	1481	1709	1575
1001	940	1106	1030	1211	1125	1315	5081	1419	1306	1524	1396	1618	1482	1710	1576
1002	941	1107	1031	1212	1126	1316	1212	1420	1307	1525	1397	1619	1483	1711	1577
1003	942	1108	1032	1213	1127			1421	1307	1526	1398	1620	1484	1712	1578

G/K	STRONG	G/K	STRONG	G/K	STRONG	G/K	STRONG	G/K	STRONG	G/K	STRONG	G/K	STRONG	G/K	STRONG
1713	1579	1815	1669	1920	1755	2025	1848	2130	1945	2235	2037	2339	2145	2443	2227
1714	1580	1816	1670	1921	1756	2026	1849	2131	2027	2236	2045	2340	2138	2444	
1715	1464	1817	1671	1922	1757	2027	1850	2132	2770	2237	2038	2341	2139	2445	2228
1716	1581	1818	1672	1923	1758	2028		2133	2778	2238	2039	2342	2139	2446	2229
1717	1582	1819	1673	1924	1759	2029	1851	2134	1946	2239	2040	2343	2140	2447	2229+3375
1718	1583	1820	1674	1925	1782	2030	1852	2135	1947	2240	2041	2344	2141	2448	2230
1719	1584	1821	1675	1926	1760	2031	1853	2136		2241	2042	2345	2142	2449	2231
1720	1585	1822	1676	1927	1761	2032	1854	2137	1948	2242	2043	2346	2143	2450	2232
1721	1586	1823	1677	1928	1762	2033	1855	2138	1949	2243	2044	2347	2144	2451	2233
1722	1587	1824	1677	1929	1763	2034	1856	2139	2989	2244	2047	2348	2145	2452	2234
1723	1588	1825	1678	1930	4178	2035	1857	2140	1950	2245	2048	2349	2146	"	2236
1724	1589	1826	1678	1931	1764	2036	1503	2141	1951	2246	2049	2350	2148	2453	2235
1725	1590	1827	1679	1932	1765	2037	1858	2142	1952	2247	2050	2351	2147	2454	2237
1726	1591	1828	1680	1933	1767	2038	1859	2143	621	2248	2051	2352	2148	2455	2238
1727	1592	1829	1681	1934	1769	2039	1860	2144	1953	2249	2052	2353	2149	2456	2239
1728	1593	1830	1682	1935	1770	2040	1861	2145	1954	2250	2053	2354	2150	2457	2240
1729	1594	1831	1683	1936	1771	2041	1862	2146	1955	2251	2054	2355	2151	2458	2241
1730	1595	1832	1684	1937	1772	2042	1863	2147	1956	2252	2055	2356	2152	2459	2242
1731	1596	1833	1685	1938	1722+3551	2043	1864	2148	1957	2253	2056	2357	2153	2460	2243
1732	1597	1834	1686	1939	1773	2044	1865	2149	1958	2254	2057	2358	2154	2461	2244
1733	1598	1835	1686	1940	1774	2045	1866	2150	1959	2255	2058	2359	2155	2462	2245
1734	1599	1836	1687	1941	3726	2046	1867	2151	1960	2256	1328	2360	807	2463	2246
1735	1537+4053	1837	1688	1942	1775	2047	1868	2152	1961	2257	2059	2361	2156	2464	2247
1736	1600	1838	1689	1943	1776	2048	1869	2153	1962	2258	2060	2362	2157	2465	2250
1737	1530	1839	1690	1944	1777	2049	1870	2154	1963	2259	2061	2363	2158	2466	2251
1738	1601	1840	1692	1945	1778	2050	1871	2155	1964	2260	2062	2364	2159	2467	2253
1739	1602	1841	1693	1946	1779	2051	1872	2156	1965	2261	2063	2365	2160	2468	2255
1740	1603	1842	1694	1947	1780	2052	1873	2157	1967	2262	2064	2366	2161	2469	2256
1741	1604	1843	1695	1948	1781	2053	1874	2158	1968	2263	2065	2367	2162	2470	2256
1742	1605	1844	1696	1949	1782	2054	1875	2159	1969	2264	2066	2368	2163	2471	2259
1743	1606	1845	1722+3319	1950	1783	2055	1876	2160	1971	2265	2067	2369	2164	2472	2260
1744	1607	1846	1697	1951		2056	1877	2161	1972	2266	2068	2370	2165	2473	2261
1745	1608	1847	1699	1952	1784	2057	1878	2162	1973	"	5315	2371	2166	2474	2262
1746	1609	1848		1953	1785	2058	1879	2163	1974	2267	2068	2372	2167	2475	2263
1747		1849	1701	1954	1786	2059	1880	2164	1975	2268	2069	2373	2168	2476	2264
1748	1610	1850	1702	1955	1787	2060	1881	2165	1976	2269	2072	2374	2169	2477	2265
1749	1611	1851	1703	1956	1788	2061	1882	2166	1977	2270	2073	2375	2170	2478	2266
1750	1612	1852	649	1957	1789	2062	1883	2167	3982	2271		2376	2171	2479	2267
1751	4982	1853	1704	1958	1790	2063	1944	2168	1978	2272	2074	2377	2172	2480	2268
1752	1613	1854	1705	1959	1791	2064	1884	2169	1979	2273	2274	2378	2173	2481	2269
1753	1614	1855	1705	1960	1792	2065	1885	2170	1980	2274	2078	2379	2174	2482	2276
1754	1615	1856	1714	1961	1793	2066	1885	2171	643	2275	2079	2380	2175	2483	2270
1755	1616	1857	1705	1962	1794	2067		2172	1981	2276	2080	2381	2176	2484	2271
1756	1618	1858	1705	1963	1795	2068	1886	2173	1982	2277	2081	2382		2485	2272
1757	1617	1859	1714	1964	1796	2069	1887	2174	1983	2278	2082	2383	2177	2486	2273
"	1619	1860	1706	1965	1797	2070	1888	2175	1984	2279	2083	2384	2178	2487	2274
1758	1620	1861	1707	1966	1798	2071	1889	2176	1985	2280	2084	2385	2179	2488	2275
1759	1621	1862	1708	1967	1799	2072	1890	2177	1986	2281	2085	2386	2180	2489	2276
1760	1622	1863	1709	1968	1800	2073	1891	2178	4687	2282	2086	2387	2181	2490	2278
1761	1623	1864	1710	1969	1801	2074	1892	2179	1987	2283	2087	2388	2182	2491	2279
1762	1624	1865	1711	1970	1802	2075	1893	2180	1999	2284	2088	2389	2183	2492	2279
1763	1625	1866	1712	1971	1803	2076	1894	2181	1988	2285	2089	2390	2184	2493	2279
1764	1790	1867	1713	1972	1804	2077	1895	2182	1989	2286	2090	2391	2185	2494	
1765	1626	1868	1714	1973	1805	2078	1896	2183		2287	1681	2392	2186	2495	3134
1766	1627	1869	1715	1974	1806	2079	1966	2184	1990	2288	2091	2393	1896	2496	5008
1767	1628	1870	1716	1975	1807	2080	1897	2185	1991	2289	2092	2394	2187	2497	2280
1768	1629	1871	1717	1976	1808	2081	1898	2186	1992	2290	2093	2395	2188	2498	2281
1769	1630	1872	1718	1977	1809	2082	1904	2187	1993	2291	2094	2396	5504	2499	2282
1770	1631	1873	1719	1978	1810	2083	1899	2188	1994	2292	2095	2397	2189	2500	2283
1771	1537+5455	1874	1720	1979	1811	2084	1900	2189	1995	2293	2096	2398	2190	2501	2284
1772	1632	1875	1721	1980	1812	2085	1901	2190	1996	2294	2097	2399	2191	2502	2285
1773	1632	1876	5455	1981	1813	2086	1902	2191	1997	2295	2098	2400	2192	2503	2286
1774	1633	1877	1722	1982	1814	2087	1903	2192	1998	2296	2099	2401	2193	2504	2287
1775	1634	1878	1723	1983	1815	2088	1904	2193	1976	2297	2100	2402		2505	2288
1776	1635	1879	1724	1984	1816	2089	1905	2194	1999	2298	2101	2403		2506	2289
1777	1636	1880	2177	1985	1817	2090	1906	2195	2000	2299	2102	2404	2194	2507	2290
1778	1637	1881		1986	455	2091	1907	2196	2001	2300	2103	2405	2195	2508	2291
1779	1638	1882	1725	1987	1818	2092	1908	2197	2002	2301	2095	2406	2196	2509	2292
1780	1639	1883	1726	1988	1819	2093	1909	2198	2003	2302	2104	2407	4518	2510	2293
1781	1640	1884		1989	1820	2094	1910	2199	2004	2303	2129	2408	2197	2511	2294
1782	1641	1885	1727	1990	1821	2095	1911	2200	2005	2304	2105	2409	2198	2512	2295
1783	1642	1886	1756	1991		2096	1912	2201	2006	2305	2106	2410	4570	2513	2296
1784	1640	1887	1728	1992	1822	2097	1913	2202	2007	2306	2107	2411	2199	2514	2297
1785	1643	1888	1766	1993	1823	2098	1914	2203	2008	2307	2108	2412	2200	2515	2298
1786	1644	1889	863	1994	1824	2099	1915	2204	2009	2308	2109	2413	4801	2516	2299
1787	1645	1890	1729	1995	1825	2100	1916	2205	2010	2309	2110	2414	2201	2517	2300
1788	1646	1891	1730	1996	1826	2101	1917	2206	2233	2310	2111	2415	2202	2518	2301
"	1647	1892	1731	1997	1832	2102	1918	2207	2011	2311	2112	2416	2203	2519	2302
1789	1648	1893	1732	1998	1827	2103	1919	2208	2012	2312	2113	2417	2204	2520	2303
1790	1653	1894	1733	1999	1828	2104	1920	2209	2013	2313	2114	2418	2206	2521	2304
1791	1650	1895	1734	2000	1829	2105	1921	2210	2014	2314	2115	2419	2205	2522	2305
1792	1649	1896	1735	2001	1830	2106	1922	2211	2015	2315	2115	2420	2206	2523	2306
1793	1650	1897	1736	2002	1831	2107	1923	2212	2016	2316	2116	2421	2207	2524	
1794	1651	1898	1737	2003	1832	2108	1924	2213	2017	2317	2117	"	2208	2525	2307
1795	1652	1899	1738	2004	1833	2109	1925	2214	2018	2318	2117	2422	2209	2526	2308
1796	1653	1900	1739	2005	1810	2110	1926	2215	2019	2319	2118	2423	2210	2527	2309
1797	1654	1901	1740	2006		2111	1927	2216	2020	2320	2119	2424	2211	2528	2310
1798	1655	1902	1741	2007	1834	2112	1928	2217	2021	2321	2120	2425		2529	2310
1799	1656	1903	1742	2008	1835	2113	1929	2218		2322	2121	2426	2212	2530	2311
1800	1657	1904	1743	2009	1836	2114	1930	2219	2022	2323	2122	2427	2213	2531	2312
1801	1658	1905	1744	2010	1837	2115	1931	2220	2023	2324	2123	2428	2214	2532	2312'
1802	1659	1906	1745	2011	1838	2116	1932	2221	2024	2325	2124	2429	2215	2533	2313
1803	1660	1907	1746	2012	1839	2117	1933	2222	2025	2326	2125	2430	4667	2534	2314
1804	1661	1908	1739	2013	1839	2118	1934	2223	2017	2327	2126	2431	2216	2535	2315
1805	1662	1909	1747	2014	1839	2119	1935	2224	2026	2328	2127	2432	2217	2536	2316
1806	1662	1910	1748	2015	1840	2120	1936	2225	2027	2329	2128	2433	2218	2537	2317
1807	3395	1911	1749	2016	1841	2121	1937	2226	2028	2330	2129	2434	2219	2538	2318
1808	1663	1912	1750	2017	1842	2122	1938	2227	2029	2331	2130	2435	2220	2539	2319
1809	1664	1913	1751	2018	1843	2123	1939	2228	2030	2332	2131	2436	2221	2540	2320
1810	1665	1914	1752	2019	1844	2124	2380	2229	2031	2333	2132	2437	2222	2541	2321
1811	1666	1915	1752	2020	1845	2125	1940	2230	2032	2334	2133	2438	2223	2542	2322
1812	1666	1916	1768	2021	1846	2126	1941	2231	2033	2335	2134	2439	2224	2543	2323
1813	1507	1917	1769	2022	1847	2127	1942	2232	2034	2336	2135	2440	2225	2544	2324
"	1667	1918	1753	2023	1847	2128	1943	2233	2035	2337	2136	2441	2225	2545	2325
1814	1668	1919	1754	2024	1848	2129	1944	2234	4179	2338	2137	2442	2226	2546	2326

G/K	STRONG	G/K	STRONG	G/K	STRONG	G/K	STRONG	G/K	STRONG	G/K	STRONG	G/K	STRONG	G/K	STRONG
2547	2327	2652	2424	2756	2515	2860	2606	2965	2702	3070	2791	3175	2885	3279	2997
2548	2328	2653	2425	2757	2516	2861	2607	2966	2703	3071	2791	3176	2886	3280	2979
2549	2329	2654	2426	2758	2596+1520	2862	2608	2967	2704	3072	2792	3177	2887	3281	2980
2550	2330	2655	2427	2759	2517	2863	1125	2968	2705	3073	2793	3178	2887	3282	2981
2551		2656	2428	2760	2511	2864	2609	2969	2706	3074	2794	3179	2888	3283	2982
2552	2331	2657	2429	2761	2518	2865	2610	2970	2707	3075	2795	3180	2889	3284	2983
2553	2332	2658	2430	2762	2519	2866	2611	2971	2019	3076	2796	3181	2890	3285	2984
2554	2333	2659	2431	2763	2520	2867	2612	2972	2708	3077	2792	3182	2891	3286	2985
2555	2334	2660	2432	2764	2521	2868	2613	2973	2709	3078	2797	3183	2891	3287	2986
2556	2335	2661	2433	2765	2596+2250	2869	1349	2974	2710	3079	5531	3184	2892	3288	2987
2557	2336	2662	2434	2766	2522	2870	2614	2975	4785	3080	2798	3185	2893	3289	2988
2558	2337	2663	2435	2767	2523	2871	2615	2976	2711	3081	2799	3186	2894	3290	2989
2559	2338	2664	2436	2768	2524	2872	2616	2977	2712	3082	2800	3187	2895	3291	2990
2560	2339	2665	2437	2769	2525	2873	2652	2978	2713	3083	2801	3188	2895	3292	2991
2561	2340	2666	2438	2770	2525	2874	2653	2979	2714	3084	2802	3189	2896	3293	2993
2562	2341	2667	2439	2771	2526	2875	2617	2980	2715	3085	2802	3190	2897	3294	2994
2563	2342	2668	2440	2772	2526'	2876	2618	2981	2716	3086	2803	3191	2898	3295	2992
2564	2343	2669	2441	2773	2527	2877	2619	2982	2718	3087	2804	3192	2899	3296	2995
2565	2344	2670	2442	2774	2528	2878	2620	2983	2719	3088	2805	3193	2900	3297	2996
2566	2345	2671	2443	2775	2529	2879	2621	2984	2719	3089	2806	3194	2901	3298	2996
2567	2346	2672	2444	2776	2530	2880	2622	2985	2720	3090	2807	3195	2902	3299	2997
2568	2347	2673	2445	2777	2531	2881	2623	2986	2127	3091	2808	3196	2903	3300	2998
2569	2348	2674	2446	2778	2509	2882	2624	2987	2721	3092	2809	3197	2904	3301	2999
2570	2349	2675	2447	2779	2532	2883	2624	2988	2722	3093	2810	3198	2905	3302	3000
2571	5182	2676	2448	2780	2533	2884	2625	2989	2723	3094	2811	3199	2906	3303	3001
2572	2350	2677	2449	2781	2534	2885	2626	2990	2724	3095	2812	3200	2907	3304	3002
2573	2351	2678	2450	2782	2535	2886	2627	2991	2725	3096	2813	3201	2908	3305	3003
2574	2352	2679	2451	2783	2536	2887	2628	2992	2725	3097	2814	3202	2908	3306	2036
2575	2352	2680	2452	2784	2536	2888	2629	2993	2726	3098	2815	"	2909	"	2046
2576	2353	2681	2453	2785	2537	2889	2630	2994	2727	3099	2816	3203	2910	"	3004
2577	2354	2682	2454	2786	2538	2890	2631	2995	2728	3100	2817	3204	2911	"	4483
2578	2355	2683	2455	2787	2757	2891	2632	2996	2729	3101	2818	3205	2912	3307	3005
2579	2356	2684	2456	2788	2539	2892	2633	2997	2730	3102	2819	3206	2913	3308	3006
2580	2357	2685	2457	2789	2540	2893	2596+2955	2998	2731	3103	2820	3207	2914	3309	3007
2581	2358	2686	2456	2790	2541	2894	2634	2999	2732	3104	2821	3208	2915	3310	3008
2582	2359	2687	2458	2791	2542	2895	2635	3000	2733	3105	2822	3209	2916	3311	3009
2583	2360	2688	2459	2792	2543	2896	2636	3001	2730	3106	2823	3210	2917	3312	3010
2584	2361	2689	2460	2793	2544	2897	2637	3002	2734	3107	2824	3211	2918	3313	3011
2585	2362	2690	2461	2794	2545	2898	2638	3003	2735	3108	2825	3212	2919	3314	621
2586		2691	2462	2795	2546	2899	2639	3004	2736	3109	2825	3213	2920	3315	
2587	2363	2692	2463	2796	2547	2900	2640	3005	2737	3110	2826	3214	2921	3316	2982
2588	2364	2693	2464	2797	2548	2901	2641	3006	2736	3111	2827	3215	2922	3317	3012
2589	2365	2694	2465	2798	2549	2902	2642	3007	2802	3112	2828	3216	2923	3318	3013
2590	2366	2695	2466	2799	2550	2903	2643	3008	2738	3113	2829	3217	2924	3319	3014
2591	2367	2696	2469	2800	2551	2904	2644	3009	2739	3114	2830	3218	2925	3320	3015
2592	2368	2697	2469	2801	2552	2905	2645	3010	2739	3115	2831	3219	2926	3321	3016
2593	2369	2698	2470	2802	2553	2906	2646	3011	2740	3116	2832	3220	2927	3322	3017
2594	2370	2699	2471	2803	2554	2907	2647	3012	2741	3117	2833	3221	2928	3323	3018
2595	2371	2700	2472	2804	2555	2908	2648	3013	2743	3118	2834	3222	2929	3324	3019
2596	2372	2701	2473	2805	2556	2909	2649	3014	2742	3119	2835	3223	2930	3325	3020
2597	2373	2702	2474	2806	2557	2910	2650	3015	2743	3120	2836	3224	2927	3326	3021
2598	2374	2703	2475	2807	2558	2911	2651	3016	2744	3121	2837	3225	2931	3327	1039
2599	2375	2704	2466	2808	2559	2912	2652	3017	2745	3122	2838	3226	2927	3328	3022
2600	2376	2705	2476	2809	2560	2913	2653	3018	2746	3123	2839	3227	2932	3329	3023
2601	2377	2706		2810	2561	2914	2654	3019	2584	3124	2840	3228	2933	3330	3024
2602	2378	2707	2477	2811	2562	2915	2655	3020	2747	3125	2841	3229	2934	3331	3028
2603	2379	2708	2478	2812	2563	2916	2656	3021	2748	3126	2842	3230	2935	3332	3025
2604	2380	2709	2479	2813	2564	2917	2657	3022	2748	3127	2843	3231	2936	3333	3026
2605	2381	2710	2480	2814	2565	2918	2658	3023	2749	3128	2844	3232	2937	3334	3027
2606	2382	2711	2481	2815	2567	2919	2659	3024	2750	3129		3233	2938	3335	3028
2607		2712	2482	2816	2568	2920	2660	3025	2751	3130	2845	3234	2939	3336	3029
2608	2383	2713	2483	2817	2552	2921	2661	3026	2752	3131	2846	3235	2940	3337	3030
2609	2384	2714	2484	2818	2569	2922	2662	3027	2753	3132	2847	3236	2941	3338	3031
2610	2385	2715	2485	2819	2566	2923	2663	3028		3133	2848	3237	2942	3339	3032
2611	2386	2716	2486	"	2570	2924	2664	3029	2754	3134	2849	3238	2944	3340	3033
2612	2387	2717	2487	2820	2571	2925	2665	3030	2755	3135	2850	3239	2943	3341	3032
2613	2388	2718	2488	2821	2572	2926		3031	2756	3136	2851	3240	2944	3342	3034
2614	2389	2719		2822	2573	2927	2666	3032	2757	3137	2858	3241	2945	3343	3035
2615	2390	2720	2489	2823	2574	2928	2667	3033	2758	3138	2857	3242	2946	3344	3036
2616	2391	2721	2489	2824	2574	2929	2668	3034	2759	3139	2852	3243	2946	3345	3037
2617	2392	"	2490	2825	2575	2930	2669	3035	2760	3140	2853	3244	2947	3346	3038
2618	2393	2722	2491	2826	2576	2931	2670	3036	2761	3141	2854	3245	2948	3347	3039
2619	2394	2723		2827	2577	2932	2671	3037	2762	3142	2855	3246	2949	3348	3040
2620	2395	2724	2492	2828	2578	2933	2672	3038	2763	3143	2856	3247	2950	3349	3041
2621		2725	5601	2829	2579	2934	2673	3039	2764	3144	2858	3248	2951	3350	3042
2622		2726	2455	2830	2580	2935	2674	3040	2765	3145	2857	3249	2952	3351	3043
2623	2396	2727	2493	2831	2581	2936	2675	3041	2766	3146	2859	3250	2953	3352	3044
2624	2397	2728	2491	2832	2581	2937	2676	3042	2767	3147	2860	3251	2954	3353	3045
2625	2398	2729	2494	2833	2582	2938	2677	3043	2768	3148	2861	3252	2955	3354	3046
2626	2399	2730	2494	2834	2583	2939	2678	3044	2769	3149	2862	3253	2956	3355	3047
2627	2400	2731	2495	2835	2584	2940	2679	3045	2770	3150	2863	3254	2956	3356	3048
2628	2401	2732	2496	2836	2585	2941	2680	3046	2771	3151	2864	3255	2957	3357	3049
2629	2402	2733	2497	2837	2586	2942	2681	3047	2772	3152	2865	3256	2958	3358	3050
2630	2403	2734	2498	2838	2587	2943	2682	3048	2773	3153	2866	3257	2959	3359	3051
2631	2404	2735	2499	2839	603	2944	2683	3049	2774	3154	2867	3258	2960	3360	3052
2632	2405	2736	2500	2840	2588	2945	2684	3050	2775	3155	2868	3259	2961	3361	3053
2633	2406	2737	2501	2841	2589	2946	2685	3051	2776	3156	2869	3260	2958	3362	3054
2634	2407	2738	2501	2842	2591	2947	2686	3052	2775	3157	2870	3261	2962	3363	3055
2635	2408	2739	2502	2843	2590	2948	2687	3053	2777	3158	2871	3262	2963	3364	3056
2636	2409	2740	2503	2844	2592	2949	2688	3054		3159	2872	3263	2964	3365	3057
2637	2410	2741		2845	2593	2950	2689	3055	5392	3160	2873	3264	2965	3366	3058
2638	1494	2742	943	2846	2594	2951	2690	3056	2778	3161	2874	3265	2966	3367	3059
2639	2411	2743	2504	2847	2595	2952	2691	3057	2779	3162	2874	3266	2967	3368	3060
2640	2412	2744	943	2848	2596	2953	2692	3058	2780	3163	2874	3267	2968	3369	3061
2641	2413	2745	2505	2849	2597	2954	2693	3059	2781	3164	2875	3268	2969	3370	3062
2642	2414	2746	2506	2850	2598	2955	2694	3060	2782	3165	2876	3269	2970	"	3063
2643	2415	2747	2507	2851	2599	2956	2695	3061	2783	3166	2877	3270	2971	"	3064
2644	2416	2748	2508	2852	925	2957	2695	3062	2784	3167	2878	3271	2972	3371	3065
2645	2417	2749	2509	2853	2600	2958	2696	3063	2785	3168	2878	3272	2973	3372	3066
2646	2418	2750	2510	2854	2601	2959	2697	3064	2786	3169	2879	3273	2974	3373	3067
2647	2419	2751	2511	2855		2960	2698	3065		3170	2880	3274		3374	3068
2648	2420	2752	2512	2856	2602	2961	2699	3066	2787	3171	2881	3275	2975	3375	3069
2649	2421	2753	4027	2857	2603	2962	2700	3067	2788	3172	2882	3276	2976	3376	3070
2650	2422	2754	2513	2858	2604	2963	2701	3068	2789	3173	2883	3277	2977	3377	3071
2651	2423	2755	2514	2859	2605	2964	826	3069	2790	3174	2884	3278	2978	3378	3072

G/K	STRONG	G/K	STRONG	G/K	STRONG	G/K	STRONG	G/K	STRONG	G/K	STRONG	G/K	STRONG	G/K	STRONG
3379	3073	3484	3168	3587	3359	3690	3462	3795	3551	3899	3640	4004	3738	4097	3823
3380	3074	3485	3169	3588	3360	3691	3463	3796	3552	3900	3641	4005	3739	4098	3824
3381	3075	3486	3170	3589	3360	3692	3463	3797	3553	3901	3642	4006	3740	4099	3825
3382	3076	3487	3171	3590	3361	3693	3464	3798	3554	3902	3643	4007	3739+1065	4100	3824
3383	3077	3488	3172	3591	3361+1065	3694	3460	3799	3555	3903	3689	4008	3741	4101	3826
3384	3078	3489	3173	3592	3365	3695	3465	3800	3556	3904	3644	4009	3742	4102	3827
3385	3079	3490	3174	3593	3366	3696	3466	3801	3502	3905	3645	4010	3743	4103	3828
3386	3080	3491	3175	3594	3367	3697	3467	3802	3557	3906	3646	4011	3744	4104	3829
3387	3081	3492	3176	3595	3368	3698	3468	3803	3558	3907	3647	4012	3745	4105	3830
3388	3082	3493	3177	3596	3369	3699	3469	3804	3559	3908	3648	4013	3746	4106	3829
3389	3083	3494	3178	3597	3370	3700	3470	3805	3560	3909	3649	4014	3747	4107	3830
3390	3084	3495	3179	3598	3365	3701	3471	3806	3561	3910	3650	4015	3748	4108	3831
3391	3085	3496	3179	3599	3367	3702	3472	3807	3562	3911	3651	"	3755	4109	3832
3392	3086	3497	3180	3600	3371	3703	3473	3808	3563	3912	3652	4016	3747	4110	3833
3393	3087	3498	3181	3601	3372	3704	3474	3809	3564	3913	3653	4017	3749	4111	3834
3394	3088	3499	3182	3602	3373	3705	3475	3810	3564	3914	3654	4018	3750	4112	3835
3395	3089	3500	3183	3603	3374	3706	3475	3811	3565	3915	3655	4019	3751	4113	3826
3396	3090	3501	3184	3604	3375	3707	3475	3812	3566	3916	2442	4020	3752	4114	3837
3397	3091	3502	3396	3605	3376	3708		3813	3567	3917	3656	4021	3753	4115	3836
3398		3503	3396	3606	3377	3709	3476	3814	3568	3918	3657	4022	3754	4116	3837
3399	3092	3504	3186	3607	3379	3710	3477	3815	3570	3919	3658	4023	3757	4117	3838
3400	3093	3505	3185	3608	3361+4225	3711	3478	3816	3571	3920		4024	3756	4118	3839
3401	3093	"	3187	3609	3380	3712	3478	3817	3572	3921	3659	4025	3758	4119	3840
3402	3094	3506	3188	3610	3381	3713	3478	3818	3573	3922	3660	4026	3759	4120	3841
3403	717	"	3189	3611	3382	3714	3478	3819	3574	3923	3660	4027	3760	4121	3842
3404	3095	3507	3190	3612	3383	3715	3478	3820	3575	3924	3661	4028	3761	4122	3843
3405	3096	3508	3199	3613	3384	3716	3479	3821	3576	3925	3662	4029	3762	4123	3844
3406	3095	3509	3191	3614	3385	3717	3480	3822	3577	3926	3663	4030	3763	4124	3845
3407	3097	3510	3192	"	3387	3718	3481	3823		3927	3664	4031	3764	4125	3846
3408	3098	3511	3193	3615	3386	3719	3481	3824	837	3928	3665	4032	3762	4126	3847
3409	3099	3512	3193	3616	3388	3720	3482	3825	3578	3929	3666	4033	3765	4127	3848
3410	3149	3513	3193	3617	3389	3721	3483	3826	3579	3930	3667	4034	3766	4128	3849
3411	3100	3514	3194	3618	3389	3722	3497	3827	3580	3931	3668	4035	1695	4129	3851
3412	3101	3515	3194	3619	3390	3723	3484	3828	3581	3932	3669	4036	3767	4130	3850
3413	3102	3516	3195	3620	3392	3724	3485	3829	3582	3933	3670	4037	3768	4131	3851
3414	3156	3517	3196	3621	3393	3725	3486	3830	3583	3934	3671	4038	3769	4132	3852
3415	3158	3518	3197	3622	3394	3726	3487	3831	3584	3935	3672	4039	3770	4133	3853
3416	3159	3519	3198	3623	3395	3727	3488	3832	3585	3936		4040	3771	4134	3854
3417	3103	3520	3199	3624	3396	3728	3489	3833	3586	3937	3673	4041	3772	4135	3855
3418	3104	3521	3200	3625	3397	3729	3490	3834	3587	3938	3674	4042	3773	4136	3856
3419	3105	3522	3201	"	3398	3730	3491	3835		3939	3675	4043	3774	4137	3857
3420	3106	3523	3202	3626	3399	3731	3492	3836	3588	3940	3676	4044	3775	4138	3858
3421	3107	3524	3437	3627	3400	3732	3493	"	5120	3941	3677	4045	3776	4139	3859
3422	3108	3525	3303	3628	3401	3733	3494	3837	3589	3942	3678	4046	3777	4140	3860
3423	3109	3526	3104	3629	3402	3734	3495	3838	3590	3943	3679	4047	3778	4141	3861
3424	3110	3527		3630	3403	3735	3496	3839	3591	3944	3680	"	5023	4142	3862
3425	3111	3528	3304	3631	3404	3736	3496	3840	3592	3945	3681	"	5025	4143	3863
3426	3112	3529	3304	3632	3405	3737	3497	3841	3593	3946	3682	"	5026	4144	3864
3427	3113	3530	3305	3633	3406	3738	3498	3842	3594	3947	3683	"	5123	4145	3865
3428	3114	3531	3306	3634	3407	3739	3499	3843	3595	3948	3684	"	5124	4146	3866
3429	3115	3532	3307	3635	3408	3740	3500	3844	3596	3949	3685	"	5125	4147	3867
3430	3116	3533	3308	3636	3409	3741	3561	3845	3597	3950	3686	"	5127	4148	3868
3431	3117	3534	3309	3637	3410	3742	3501	3846	3598+4160	3951	3687	"	5128	4149	3869
3432	3118	3535	3310	3638	3411	3743	3502	3847	3598	3952	3688	"	5129	4150	3869
3433	3119	3536	3311	3639	3412	3744	3503	3848	3599	3953	3689	"	5130	4151	3870
3434	3120	3537	3312	3640	3413	3745	3504	3849	3600	3954	3690	4048	3779	4152	3871
3435	3121	3538	3313	3641	3414	3746	3505	3850	3601	3955	3691	4049	3780	4153	3872
3436	3122	3539	3322	3642	3415	3747		3851	3602	3956	3692	4050	3781	4154	3873
3437	3123	3540	3314	3643	3416	3748	3506	3852	3604	3957	3693	4051	3782	4155	3874
3438	3124	3541	3315	3644	3417	3749	3507	3853	3605	3958	3694	4052	3783	4156	3875
3439	3125	3542	3316	3645	3418	3750	3508	3854	3606	3959	3695	4053	3784	4157	3876
3440	3126	3543	3317	3646	3419	3751	3509	3855	3607	3960	3696	4054	3785	4158	3877
3441	3127	3544	3318	3647	3420	3752	3510	3856	3608	3961	3697	4055	3786	4159	3878
3442	3128	3545	3319	3648	3421	3753	3511	3857	1492	3962	3698	4056	3787	4160	3879
3443	3129	3546	3320	3649	3422	3754	3512	3858	3609	3963	3699	4057	3788	4161	3880
3444	3130	3547	3321	3650	3423	3755	3513	3859	2322	3964	3700	4058	3789	4162	3881
3445	3131	3548	3322	3651	3424	3756	3514	3860	3610	3965	3701	4059	3790	4163	3882
3446	3132	3549	3323	3652	3424	3757	3515	3861	3611	3966	3702	4060	856	4164	3883
3447	3133	3550	3324	3653	3425	3758	3516	3862	3612	3967	3703	4061	3791	4165	3884
3448	3134	3551	3325	3654	3426	3759	3517	3863	3613	3968	3704	4062	3792	4166	3885
3449	3135	3552	3326	3655	3428	3760	3518	3864	3614	3969	3705	4063	3793	4167	3885
3450	3136	3553	3327	3656	3429	3761	3519	3865	3615	3970	3706	4064		4168	3886
3451	3137	3554	3328	3657	3430	3762	3520	3866	3616	3971	3707	4065	3794	4169	3887
3452	3137	3555	3329	3658	3431	3763	3521	3867	3617	3972	3708	4066	3795	4170	3888
3453	3138	3556	3330	3659	3432	3764	3522	3868	3618	3973	3709	4067	3796	4171	3889
3454	3139	3557	3331	3660	3433	3765	3523	3869	3619	3974	3710	4068	3798	4172	3890
3455	3140	3558	3332	3661	3434	3766	3524	3870	3620	3975	3711	4069	3797	4173	3913
3456	3141	3559	3333	3662	3435	3767	3524	3871	3618	3976	3712	4070	3798	4174	3891
3457	3142	3560	3334	3663	3436	3768	3525	3872	3621	3977	3713	4071	3799	4175	3892
3458	3143	3561	3335	3664	3437	3769	3526	3873	3622	3978	3714	4072	3800	4176	3893
3459	3144	3562	3336	3665	3438	3770	3527	3874	3623	3979	3715	4073		4177	3894
3460	3145	3563	3337	3666	3439	3771	3528	3875	3624	3980	3716	4074	3802	4178	3895
3461	3149	3564	3338	3667	3440	3772	3529	3876	3625	3981	3717	4075	3803	4179	3896
3462	3145	3565	3339	3668	3441	3773	3530	3877	3626	3982	3718	4076	697	4180	3897
3463	3146	3566	3340	3669	3442	3774	3531	3878	3626	3983	3719	4077	3804	4181	3898
3464	3147	3567	3341	3670	3443	3775	3532	3879	3627	3984	3720	4078	3805	4182	3899
3465	3148	3568	3342	3671	3444	3776	3533	3880	3628	3985	3721	4079	3806	4183	3900
3466	3149	3569	3343	3672	3445	3777	3534	3881	3629	3986	3722	4080	3807	4184	3901
3467	3150	3570	3344	3673	3446	3778	3535	3882	3627	3987	3723	4081	3808	4185	3902
3468	3151	3571	3345	3674	3447	3779	3535	3883	3633	3988	3724	4082	3809	4186	3903
3469	3152	3572	3346	3675	3448	3780	3536	3884	3630	3989	3733	4083	3810	4187	3904
3470	3153	3573	3344	3676	3451	3781	3537	3885	3631	3990	3725	4084	3811	4188	4368
3471	3154	3574		3677	3449	3782	3538	3886	3632	3991	3726	4085	3812	4189	3905
3472	3155	3575	3347	3678	3452	3783	3539	3887	3633	3992	3727	4086	3813	4190	3906
3473	3156	3576	3348	3679	3453	3784	3540	3888	3634	3993	3728	4087	3814	4191	3907
3474	3157	3577	3349	3680	3454	3785	3541	3889		3994	3729	4088	3812	4192	3908
3475	3158	3578	3350	3681	3455	3786	3542	3890	3635	3995	3730	4089	3815	4193	3909
3476	3159	3579	3351	3682	3456	3787	3543	3891	3636	3996	3731	4090	3816	4194	3910
3477	3160	3580	3352	3683	3457	3788	3544	3892	3637	3997	3732	4091	3817	4195	3911
3478	3161	3581	3353	3684	3458	3789	3545	3893	3638	3998	3733	4092	3818	4196	3912
3479	3162	3582	3354	3685	3458	3790	3546	3894	3644	3999	3734	4093	3819	4197	3913
3480	3163	3583	3355	3686	3459	3791	3547	3895	3645	4000		4094	3820	4198	3913
3481	3164	3584	3356	3687		3792	3548	3896	3639	4001	3735	4095	3821	4199	3914
3482	3166	3585	3357	3688	3460	3793	3549	3897	3639	4002	3736	4096	3822	4200	3915
3483	3167	3586	3358	3689	3461	3794	3550	3898	570	4003	3737			4201	2710

G/K	STRONG	G/K	STRONG	G/K	STRONG	G/K	STRONG	G/K	STRONG	G/K	STRONG	G/K	STRONG	G/K	STRONG
5034	4659	5136	4760	5234	4849	5339	4935	5442	5031	5546	5134	5650	5235	5754	5327
5035	4660	5137	4761	5235	4849	5340	4936	5443	5034	5547	5135	5651	5236	5755	5328
5036	4661	5138	4762	5236	4850	5341	4937	5444	5035	5548	5136	5652	5228+1473	5756	5329
5037	4662	5139	4763	5237	4851	5342	4938	"	5036	5549	5137	5653	5237	5757	5330
5038	4663	5140	4764	5238	4852	5343	4939	5445	5037	5550	5138	5654	5238	5758	5331
5039	4664	5141	4765	5239	4851	5344	4940	5446	5038	5551	5139	5655	5240	5759	5332
5040	4665	5142	4766	5240	4833	5345	4941	5447	5039	5552	5140	5656	5240	5760	5331
5041	3395	5143	4766	5241	4853	5346	4795	5448	5040	5553	5140+4999	5657	5239	5761	5333
5042	3395	5144	4767	5242	4854	5347	4942	5449	5041	5554	5141	5658	5240	5762	5334
5043	4666	5145	4768	5243	4855	5348	4943	5450	5042	5555	5142	5659	5241	5763	5335
5044	4667	5146	4769	5244	4856	5349	4944	5451	5043	5556	5143	5660	5242	5764	5336
5045	4668	5147	4770	5245	4857	5350	4945	5452	5044	5557	5169	5661	5243	5765	5337
5046	4669	5148	4571	5246	4858	5351	4949	5453		5558	5144	5662	5244	5766	5338
5047	4670	"	4671	5247	4859	5352	4946	5454	5045	5559	5145	5663	5244	5767	5339
5048	4672	"	4675	5248	4860	5353	4947	5455	5046	5560	5146	5664	5245	5768	5340
5049	4673	"	4771	5249	4861	5354	4948	5456	5047	5561	5147	5665	5246	5769	5341
5050	4674	"	5209	5250	4862	5355	4949	5457	5048	5562	5148	5666	5237	5770	5342
5051	4676	"	5210	5251	4863	5356	4949	5458	5049	5563	5149	5667	5247	5771	5343
5052	4677	"	5213	5252	4864	5357		5459	5050	5564	5150	5668	5248	5772	5344
5053	4678	"	5216	5253	4865	5358	4950	5460	5051	5565	5151	5669	5249	5773	5345
5054	4679	5149	4772	5254	4866	5359	4951	5461	5052	5566	5152	5670	5250	5774	5346
5055	4680	5150	4773	5255	4867	5360	4952	5462	5053	5567	5153	5671	5251	5775	1310
5056	4681	5151	4773	5256	4868	5361	4953	5463	5054	5568	5154	5672	5252	5776	5347
5057	4682	5152	4774	5257	4869	5362	4954	5464	5055	5569	5154	5673	5253	5777	5348
5058	4683	5153	4775	5258	4870	5363	4955	5465	5056	5570	5155	5674	5254	5778	5349
5059	4684	5154	4776	5259	4871	5364	4956	5466	5058	5571	5156	5675	5255	5779	5350
5060	4685	5155	4777	5260	4871	5365	4957	5467	5057	5572	5157	5676	5256	5780	5351
5061	4686	5156	4778	5261	4900	5366	4958	5468	5058	5573	5158	5677	5257	5781	5352
5062	4687	5157	4779	5262	4872	5367	4959	5469	5059	5574	5159	5678	5258	5782	5353
5063	4688	5158	4780	5263	4873	5368	4960	5470	5060	5575	5160	5679	5259	5783	5354
5064	4689	5159	4781	5264	4874	5369	4961	5471		5576	5161	5680	5260	5784	5355
5065	4690	5160	4782	5265	4875	5370	4962	5472	5061	5577	5162	5681	5261	5785	5356
5066	4691	5161	4783	5266		5371	4963	5473	5062	5578	5159	5682	5262	5786	5357
5067	4692	5162		5267	4876	5372	4964	5474	5063	5579	5163	5683	5263	5787	5358
5068	4693	5163	4784	5268	4877	5373	4965	5475	5064	5580	5164	5684	5263	5788	5359
5069	4694	5164	4785	5269	4878	5374	4966	5476	5065	5581	5165	5685	5264	5789	5360
5070	4696	5165	4873	5270	4879	5375	4967	5477	5062	5582	5166	5686	5265	5790	5361
5071	4695	5166	4786	5271	4880	5376	4968	5478	5063	5583	5167	5687	5266	5791	5362
5072	4697	5167	4787	5272	4881	5377	4969	5479	5066	5584	5168	5688	5267	5792	5363
5073	4698	5168	4788	5273	4882	5378		5480	5067	5585	5169	5689	5268	5793	5364
5074	4699	5169	4789	5274	4883	5379	4970	5481	5068	5586	5170	5690	5269	5794	5365
5075	4700	5170	4790	5275	4884	5380	4971	5482	5069	5587	5171	5691	5270	5795	5366
5076	4701	5171	4791	5276	4871	5381	4972	5483	5070	5588	5172	5692		5796	5367
5077	4702	5172	4792	5277	4885	5382	4973	5484	5071	5589	5173	5693	5271	5797	5368
5078	4703	5173	4793	5278	4886	5383	4974	5485	5072	5590	5174	5694	5272	5798	5369
5079	4704	5174	4794	5279	4887	5384	4974	5486	5073	5591	5175	5695	5273	5799	5370
5080	4705	5175	4795	5280	4888	5385	4975	5487	5073	5592	5176	5696	5274	5800	5371
"	4706	5176	4796	5281	4889	5386	4976	5488	5074	5593	5177	5697	2985	5801	5372
"	4707	5177	4797	5282	4890	5387	4977	5489	5075	5594	5178	5698	2640	5802	5373
5081	4708	5178	4798	5283	4891	5388	4978	5490	5076	5595	5179	5699	5275	5803	5374
"	4709	5179	4797	5284	4892	5389	4979	5491	5077	5596	5179	5700	5276	5804	5375
5082	4710	5180	4799	5285		5390	4980	5492	5078	5597	5180	5701	5277	5805	5376
5083	4711	5181	2010	5286		5391	4981	5493	5079	5598	5181	5702	5278	5806	5377
5084	4712	5182	4800	5287	4893	5392	4982	5494	5080	5599		5703	5279	5807	5378
5085	4713	5183	4801	5288	4894	5393	4983	5495	5081	5600	5182	5704	5280	5808	5379
5086	4955	5184	4802	5289	4895	5394	4984	5496	5082	5601	5183	5705	5281	5809	5380
5087	4714	5185	4803	5290	4896	5395	4985	5497		5602	5184	5706	5282	5810	5381
5088	4715	5186	4804	5291	4897	5396	4986	5498	5083	5603	5185	5707	5283	5811	5382
5089	4716	5187	4805	5292	4898	5397	4987	5499	5084	5604	5186	5708	5299	5812	5383
5090	4717	5188	4806	5293	4899	5398	4988	5500	5085	5605	5187	5709	5284	5813	5384
5091	4718	5189	4807	5294		5399	4989	5501	5086	5606	5188	5710	5285	5814	5385
5092	4719	5190	4808	5295	4900	5400	4990	5502	5087	5607	5189	5711	5286	5815	5386
5093	4720	5191	4809	5296	4901	5401	4991	5503	5088	5608	5190	5712	5287	5816	5387
5094	4721	5192	4810	5297	4862+1985	5402	4992	5504	5089	5609		5713	5288	5817	5388
5095	4722	5193	4811	5298	4934	5403	4992	5505	5090	5610	5191	5714	5289	5818	5389
5096	4723	5194	4812	5299	4902	5404	4993	5506	5091	5611	5192	5715	5290	5819	5390
5097	4724	5195	4813	5300	4903	5405	4994	5507	5092	5612	5193	5716	5291	5820	5391
5098	4725	5196	4814	5301	4904	5406	4995	5508	5093	5613	5194	5717	5292	5821	5392
5099	4726	5197	4815	5302	4905	5407	4996	5509	5094	5614	5195	5718	5293	5822	5417
5100	4727	5198	4816	5303	4906	5408	4997	5510	5095	5615	5196	5719	5294	5823	5393
5101	4728	5199	4817	5304	4907	5409	4998	5511	5096	5616	5197	5720	5295	5824	5394
5102	4729	5200	4818	5305	4908	5410		5512	5097	5617	5198	5721	5296	5825	5395
5103	4730	5201	4819	5306	4909	5411	4999	5513	5098	5618	5199	5722	5297	5826	5396
5104	4731	5202	4820	5307	4910	5412	5000	5514	5099	5619	5200	5723	5298	5827	5397
5105	4732	5203	4821	5308	4911	5413	5001	5515	5101	5620	5201	5724	5299	5828	5399
5106	4733	5204	4822	5309	4912	5414	5002	5516	5100	5621	5202	5725	5300	5829	5398
5107	4734	5205	4823	5310	4913	5415	5003	5517	2459	5622	5203	5726		5830	5399
5108	4736	5206	4824	5311	4914	5416	5004	5518	5102	5623	5204	5727	5301	5831	5400
5109	4735	5207	4825	5312	4915	5417	5005	5519	5103	5624	5205	5728	5302	5832	5401
5110	4737	5208	4826	5313	4916	5418	5006	5520	5104	5625	5206	5729	5303	5833	5402
5111	4738	5209	4827	5314	4917	5419	5007	5521	5105	5626	5207	5730	5304	5834	5403
5112	4739	5210	4828	5315	4918	5420	5008	5522	5105	5627	5208	5731	5305	5835	4949
5113	4740	5211	4829	5316	4919	5421	5009	5523	5106	5628	5211	"	5306	5836	5404
5114	4741	5212	4830	5317	4920	5422	3569	5524	5107	5629	5212	5732		5837	5405
5115	4746	5213	4831	5318	4921	5423	5010	5525	5108	5630	5214	5733	5307	5838	5406
5116	4742	5214	4833	5319	4921	5424	5011	5526	5109	5631	5215	5734	5308	5839	5407
5117	4743	5215	4832	5320	4920	5425	5012	5527	5110	5632	5217	5735	5309	5840	5408
5118	4744	5216	4833	5321	4922	5426	5391	5528	5111	5633	5218	5736	5310	5841	5409
5119	4745	5217	4834	5322	4923	5427	5013	5529	5112	5634	5219	5737	5311	5842	5410
5120	4746	5218	4835	5323	4894	5428	5014	5530	5112	5635	5220	5738	5312	5843	5411
5121	4770	5219	4836	5324	4924	5429	5015	5531	5112	5636	5221	5739	5313	5844	5412
5122	4747	5220	4837	5325	4925	5430	5016	5532	5113	5637	5222	5740		5845	5413
5123	4748	5221	4838	5326	4926	5431	5017	5533	5114	5638	5223	5741	5314	5846	5414
5124	4749	5222	4839	5327	4927	5432	5018	5534	5115	5639	5224	5742	5341	5847	5415
5125	4750	5223	4840	5328	4894	5433	5019	5535	5116	"	5225	5743	5316	5848	5416
5126	4751	5224	4841	5329		5434	5020	5536	5117	5640	5226	5744	5317	5849	5417
5127	4752	5225	4842	5330	4928	5435	5021	5537	5118	5641	5227	5745	5318	5850	5418
5128	4753	5226		5331	4952	5436	5022	5538	5121	5642	5228	5746	5319	5851	5419
5129	4754	5227	4843	5332	4929	5437	5024	5539	5121	5643	5229	5747	5320	5852	5420
5130	4755	5228	4844	5333	4930	5438	5027	5540	5122	5644	5230	5748	5321	5853	5421
5131	4756	5229	4098	5334	4931	5439	5028	5541	3694	5645	5231	5749	5322	5854	5422
5132	4757	5230	4845	5335	4932	5440	5029	5542	5123	5646	784	5750	5323	5855	5423
5133	4758	5231	4846	5336		5441	5030	5543	5131	5647	5232	5751	5324	5856	5424
5134	4759	5232	4847	5337	4933	"	5032	5544	5132	5648	5233	5752	5325	5857	5425
5135	4759	5233	4848	5338	4934	"	5033	5545	5133	5649	5234	5753	5326	5858	5426

G/K	STRONG	G/K	STRONG	G/K	STRONG	G/K	STRONG	G/K	STRONG	G/K	STRONG	G/K	STRONG	G/K	STRONG
5859	5427	5886	5453	5913	5477	5940	5504	5967	5522	5994	5555	6021	5578	6048	5605
5860	5428	5887	5454	5914	5478	5941	5506	5968	5530	5995	5556	6022	5579	6049	5606
5861	5429	5888	5455	5915	5479	5942	5505	5969	5531	5996	5557	6023	5580	6050	5608
5862	5430	5889	5456	5916	5480	5943	5507	5970	5532	5997	5552	6024	5581	6051	5609
5863	5431	5890	5457	5917	5481	5944	5508	5971	5533	5998	5558	6025	5582	6052	5610
5864	5432	5891	5458	5918	5482	5945	5509	5972	5533	5999	5559	6026	5583	6053	5611
5865	5433	5892	5459	5919	5483	5946	5510	5973	5534	6000	5560	6027	5584	6054	5612
5866	5434	5893	5460	5920	5484	5947	5516	5974	5535	6001	5561	6028	5585	6055	5613
5867	5435	5894	5461	5921	5485	5948	5511	5975	5536	6002	5523	6029	5586	6056	5613+302
5868		5895	5462	5922	5486	5949	5512	5976	5537	6003	5562	6030	5587	6057	5614
5869	5436	5896		5923	5487	5950	5513	5977	5538	6004	5563	6031	5588	6058	5615
5870	5437	5897	5463	5924	5488	5951	5514	5978	5539	6005	5564	6032	5589	6059	5616
5871	5438	5898	5464	5925	5489	5952	5515	5979	5540	6006	5565	6033	5589	6060	5617
5872	5439	5899	5465	5926	5490	5953	5516	5980	5541	6007		6034	5590	6061	5618
5873	5440	5900	5466	5927	5491	5954	5517	5981	5542	6008	5566	6035	5591	6062	5619
5874	5441	5901	5467	5928	5492	5955	5518	5982	5543	6009		6036	5592	6063	5620
5875	5442	5902	5468	5929	5493	5956	5519	5983	5544	6010	5567	6037	5593	6064	5621
5876	5443	5903	5469	5930	5494	5957	5520	5984	5545	6011	5568	6038	5594	6065	5621
5877	5444	5904	5468	5931	5495	5958	5521	5985	5546	6012	5569	6039	5595	6066	5622
5878	5445	5905	5470	5932	5496	5959	5522	5986	5547	6013	5570	6040	5596	6067	5623
5879	5446	5906	5471	5933	5497	5960	5523	5987	5548	6014	5571	6041	5597	6068	5624
5880	5447	5907	5472	5934	5498	5961	5524	5988	5549	6015	5572	6042	5598		
5881	5448	5908	5473	5935	5499	5962	5525	5989	5550	6016	5573	6043	5599		
5882	5449	5909	5474	5936	5500	5963	5526	5990	5551	6017	5574	6044	5601		
5883	5450	5910	5475	5937	5501	5964	5527	5991	5552	6018	5576	6045	5602		
5884	5451	5911	5470	5938	5502	5965	5528	5992	5553	6019	5577	6046	5603		
5885	5452	5912	5476	5939	5503	5966	5529	5993	5554	6020	5575	6047	5604		

COLOPHON

The Portland Index database from which
The NIV Exhaustive Concordance was extracted was produced by
John R. Kohlenberger III and Edward W. Goodrick, using original
software designed by Dennis Thomas and Barbara Perz for the Wang
2200 computer linked to a Control Data Plato terminal.

The database was edited and managed on
AST Premium/286 and Premium/386 computers.

The Main Concordance was produced from the Portland Index
with original software created by Dennis Thomas for the
AT&T UnixPC. The Main Concordance was typeset by
John R. Kohlenberger III, using Xerox Ventura Publisher 2.0 with
the Professional Extension.

The Index of Articles Etc. was generated with
WordCruncher 4.3 from the Electronic Text Corporation and was
typeset by John R. Kohlenberger III, using WordPerfect 5.0
from the WordPerfect Corporation.

The Biblical-Language Index-Lexicons were produced from the
Portland Index with original software created by Dennis Thomas for
the AT&T UnixPC. These indexes were typeset by John R.
Kohlenberger III, using WordPerfect 5.0. The Hebrew, Greek, and
Aramaic fonts were generated with Scripture Fonts, a product of
Zondervan Electronic Publishing.

Final camera-ready pages were produced on a Linotype Linotronic
P200 at the facilities of Multnomah Graphics in Portland, Oregon.

The NIV Exhaustive Concordance was designed and edited by
John R. Kohlenberger III, Ed M. van der Maas,
Stanley N. Gundry, and Donald L. Potts.